The Westminster Study Bible

New Revised Standard Version Updated Edition

The Westminster Study Bible

New Revised Standard Version Updated Edition

with the Deuterocanonical/Apocryphal Books

General Editors
Emerson B. Powery
Stacy Davis
Mary F. Foskett
Brent A. Strawn

Associate Editors
J. Todd Hibbard
Jennifer L. Koosed
Davina C. Lopez
Henry W. Morisada Rietz
Claudia Setzer

WJK WESTMINSTER
JOHN KNOX PRESS
LOUISVILLE · KENTUCKY

First edition
Published by Westminster John Knox Press
Louisville, Kentucky

24 25 26 27 28 29 30 31 32 33—10 9 8 7 6 5 4 3 2 1

Book design by Allison Taylor and Scribe Inc.
Cover design by Kevin van der Leek

Library of Congress Cataloging-in-Publication Data

Names: Powery, Emerson B., editor.
Title: The Westminster study Bible : new revised standard version updated edition with the Deuterocanonical/Apocryphal books / general editors, Emerson B. Powery, Stacy Davis, Mary F. Foskett, Brent A. Strawn ; associate editors, J. Todd Hibbard, Jennifer L. Koosed, Davina C. Lopez, Henry W. Morisada Rietz, Claudia Setzer.
Other titles: Bible. English. New revised standard version updated edition. 2024.
Description: First edition. | Louisville : Westminster John Knox Press, [2024] | Includes index. | Summary: "Provides up-to-date scholarly insights into the biblical texts and their ancient contexts while fostering critical thought about the important role the Bible has played throughout history and in our contemporary cultural contexts"—Provided by publisher.
Identifiers: LCCN 2024016323 (print) | LCCN 2024016324 (ebook) | ISBN 9780664266974 | ISBN 9781646982899 (ebook)
Classification: LCC BS191.5. A1 2024 L (Louisville) 2024 (print) | LCC BS191.5. (ebook) | DDC 220.5/20434—dc23/eng/20240522
LC record available at https://lccn.loc.gov/2024016323
LC ebook record available at https://lccn.loc.gov/2024016324

The New Testament

Essays

Contents

The Hebrew Bible (Old Testament / Tanakh)

The Deuterocanonical/Apocryphal Books Variously Included in Roman Catholic, Greek, and Slavonic Bibles

Color Maps

Editors

General Editors

Emerson B. Powery
Dean of the School of Arts, Culture, and Society and Professor of Biblical Studies
Messiah University
Lead Editor; Deuterocanonical/Apocryphal Books; Hebrews, the General Epistles, and Revelation

Stacy Davis
Professor Emerita of Religious Studies and Theology
Saint Mary's College
Former Prophets / Historical Books; Latter Prophets / Prophetic Books

Mary F. Foskett
Wake Forest Kahle Professor of Religious Studies and John Thomas Albritton Fellow
Wake Forest University
Gospels and Acts; Hebrews, the General Epistles, and Revelation

Brent A. Strawn
D. Moody Smith Distinguished Professor of Old Testament and Professor of Law
Duke University
Torah/Pentateuch; The Writings

Associate Editors

J. Todd Hibbard
Professor of Religious Studies
University of Detroit Mercy
Latter Prophets / Prophetic Books

Henry W. Morisada Rietz
George A. Drake Professor of Religious Studies
Grinnell College
Deuterocanonical/Apocryphal Books

Jennifer L. Koosed
Professor of Religious Studies
Albright College
Torah/Pentateuch; The Writings

Claudia Setzer
Professor of Religious Studies
Manhattan College
Gospels and Acts

Davina C. Lopez
Professor of Religious Studies
Eckerd College
Pauline Letters

Contributors

John Ahn, Associate Professor of Hebrew Bible, Howard University; *1 Maccabees*

Margaret Aymer, Vice President for Academic Affairs and Academic Dean, and The First Presbyterian Church, Shreveport, D. Thomason Professor of New Testament Studies, Austin Presbyterian Theological Seminary; *James, Jude*

Debra Scoggins Ballentine, Associate Professor of Religion, Rutgers University; *Micah*

W. H. Bellinger, Jr., Professor of Religion Emeritus, Baylor University; *Psalms*

Bryan Bibb, Professor of Religion, Furman University; *Leviticus*

Shelley L. Birdsong, Associate Professor of Religious Studies, North Central College; *1 Samuel*

Fiona C. Black, Walter B. Cowan Professor of Religious Studies, Mount Allison University; *Song of Songs*

Alejandro F. Botta, Associate Professor of Hebrew Bible, Boston University School of Theology; *Joshua*

Brennan Breed, Associate Professor of Old Testament, Columbia Theological Seminary; *Daniel*

Corrine L. Carvalho, Professor of Theology, University of St. Thomas; *Ezekiel*

Jeremiah W. Cataldo, Professor of History, Grand Valley State University; *Hosea*

Christy Cobb, Associate Professor of Christianity, University of Denver; *The Acts of the Apostles*

J. Blake Couey, Professor of Religion, Gustavus Adolphus College; *Isaiah*

Andrew R. Davis, Professor Ordinarius, Boston College Clough School of Theology and Ministry; *Amos, Obadiah*

Stacy Davis, Professor Emerita of Religious Studies and Theology, Saint Mary's College; *Joel, Baruch, The Letter of Jeremiah*

Deirdre A. Dempsey, Associate Professor, Department of Theology, Marquette University; *2 Samuel*

David A. deSilva, Trustees' Distinguished Professor of New Testament and Greek, Ashland Theological Seminary; *Esther (The Greek Version Containing the Additional Chapters), 1 Peter*

Liane M. Feldman, Assistant Professor of Religion and Program in Judaic Studies, Princeton University; *Ecclesiasticus, or the Wisdom of Jesus Son of Sirach*

Judy Fentress-Williams, Dodge Professor of Biblical Interpretation, Virginia Theological Seminary; *Exodus*

Robert L. Foster, Senior Lecturer in Religion and New Testament, University of Georgia; *Haggai*

Arminta M. Fox, Assistant Professor of Religion, Philosophy, and Classics, Augustana University; *2 Corinthians*

Wil Gafney, The Right Rev. Sam B. Hulsey Professor of Hebrew Bible, Brite Divinity School; *Nahum, Habakkuk, Zephaniah*

Jennifer A. Glancy, The Rev. Kevin G. O'Connell, S.J., Distinguished Teaching Professor in the Humanities, Le Moyne College; *The Gospel according to Luke*

Rhiannon Graybill, Marcus M. and Carole M. Weinstein and Gilbert M. and Fannie S. Rosenthal Chair of Jewish Studies, University of Richmond; *Jonah*

Rebecca L. Harris, Assistant Professor of Biblical and Religious Studies, Messiah University; *2 Maccabees, 4 Maccabees*

Kerry Hasler-Brooks, Associate Professor of English and Chair of the Language, Literature, and Writing Department, Messiah University; *The Bible in Literature*

Jimmy Hoke, Adjunct Professor of Queer and Trans Studies and Biblical Studies, United Theological Seminary of the Twin Cities; *Romans*

T. Christopher Hoklotubbe, Assistant Professor of Classics, Cornell College; Director of Graduate Studies of NAIITS: An Indigenous Learning Community; *1–2 Timothy*, *Titus*

Cameron B. R. Howard, Associate Professor of Old Testament, Luther Seminary; *1 Chronicles*

Lynn R. Huber, Maude Sharpe Powell Professor of Religious Studies, Elon University; *Revelation*

Sara Raup Johnson, Associate Professor of Classics and Ancient Mediterranean Studies, University of Connecticut; *3 Maccabees*

John Kaltner, Virginia Ballou McGehee Professor of Muslim-Christian Relations, Rhodes College; *Jonah*

Sylvia C. Keesmaat, Founder and Lead Instructor, Bible Remixed; *Colossians*

HyeRan Kim-Cragg, Principal and Professor of Preaching, Emmanuel College of Victoria University, University of Toronto; *2 Thessalonians*

Jennifer L. Koosed, Professor of Religious Studies, Albright College; *Ecclesiastes*

Joseph Lam, Associate Professor of Religious Studies, University of North Carolina at Chapel Hill; *Malachi*

Eunny P. Lee, Professor of Biblical and Religious Studies, Azusa Pacific University; *Ruth*

Won W. Lee, Professor of Old Testament, Calvin University; *Numbers*

Ingrid E. Lilly, Associate Professor of Religious Studies, Wofford College; *Job*

Francisco Lozada, Jr., Vice President for Faculty Affairs and Dean of the Faculty, and Professor of New Testament Studies, Christian Theological Seminary; *The Gospel according to John*; *1, 2, 3 John*

Matthew J. Lynch, Associate Professor of Old Testament, Regent College; *2 Chronicles*

J. L. Manzo, Associate Professor of Scripture, Mexican American Catholic College; *Tobit*

Herbert Robinson Marbury, Associate Professor of the Hebrew Bible and Black Religious Studies, Vanderbilt Divinity School; *Ezra–Nehemiah*

Joseph A. Marchal, Professor of Religious Studies and Women's and Gender Studies Affiliated Faculty, Ball State University; *Philippians*

Madipoane Masenya (Ngwan'a Mphahlele), Professor of Old Testament Studies, Department of Biblical and Ancient Studies, University of South Africa; *Proverbs*

Steven L. McKenzie, Professor of Religious Studies and Spence L. Wilson Senior Research Fellow, Rhodes College; *Jonah*

Anna C. Miller, Associate Professor of New Testament and Early Christianity, Xavier University; *1 Corinthians*

Judith H. Newman, Professor of Hebrew Bible / Old Testament and Early Judaism, Emmanuel College of Victoria University, University of Toronto; *Judith*

Richard W. Newton, Jr., Associate Professor of Religious Studies and Undergraduate Director, University of Alabama; *Philemon*

Hugh R. Page, Jr., Vice President for Institutional Transformation and Advisor to the President, and Professor of Theology and Africana Studies, University of Notre Dame; *Wisdom of Solomon*

Song-Mi Suzie Park, Associate Professor of Hebrew Bible, Austin Presbyterian Theological Seminary; *2 Kings*

Wongi Park, Assistant Professor of Religion, Belmont University; *The Gospel according to Matthew*

Donald C. Polaski, Associate Professor of Religious Studies, Randolph-Macon College; *Zechariah*

Emerson B. Powery, Dean of the School of Arts, Culture, and Society and Professor of Biblical Studies, Messiah University; *2 Maccabees*

Brian Rainey, Lecturer in Biblical Studies, Princeton Theological Seminary; *1 Kings*

Annette Yoshiko Reed, Krister Stendahl Professor of Divinity and Professor of New Testament and Early Christianity, Harvard Divinity School; *Ecclesiasticus, or the Wisdom of Jesus Son of Sirach*

Justin Michael Reed, Assistant Professor of Old Testament / Hebrew Bible, Louisville Seminary; *Judges*

Caryn A. Reeder, Professor of New Testament and Coordinator of Gender Studies, Westmont College; *Ephesians*

Stephen Breck Reid, Professor of Christian Scriptures and Vice Provost for Faculty Diversity and Belonging, George W. Truett Theological Seminary, Baylor University; *Psalms*

Henry W. Morisada Rietz, George A. Drake Professor of Religious Studies, Grinnell College; *Prayer of Manasseh, Psalm 151*

Sarah E. Rollens, R. A. Webb Associate Professor of Religious Studies, Rhodes College; *1 Thessalonians*

Tyler M. Schwaller, Student Equity Officer (Title IX Coordinator), Portland Public Schools; *Galatians*

Shayna Sheinfeld, Assistant Professor of Religion and Philosophy, Augsburg University; *2 Esdras*

Abraham Smith, Professor of New Testament, Perkins School of Theology / Southern Methodist University; *The Gospel according to Mark*

Brian Albert Smith, Professor of Hebrew Bible, Messiah University; *Esther*

Shively T. J. Smith, Associate Professor of New Testament, Boston University School of Theology; *2 Peter*

Daniel L. Smith-Christopher, Professor of Theological Studies (Old Testament), Loyola Marymount University; *1 Esdras*

Elsie R. Stern, Professor of Bible, Reconstructionist Rabbinical College; *Lamentations*

Adam Oliver Stokes, Adjunct Professor of Hebrew Bible and Theology, Saint Joseph's University; *The Additions to Daniel (The Prayer of Azariah and the Song of the Three Jews, Susanna, Bel and the Dragon)*

C. A. Strine, Senior Lecturer in Ancient Near Eastern History and Literature, University of Sheffield; *Genesis*

Paavo N. Tucker, Adjunct Professor of Hebrew and Old Testament, Lipscomb University Hazelip School of Theology; *Deuteronomy*

Jaime L. Waters, Associate Professor of Old Testament, Boston College Clough School of Theology and Ministry; *Jeremiah*

Bryan J. Whitfield, Professor of Religion, Mercer University; *Hebrews*

Preface to *The Westminster Study Bible*

The Westminster Study Bible (WSB) acknowledges that reading the Bible today is not as simple as discovering what it meant in its own time in order to determine what it means for all time. Despite the Bible's antiquity, both those who have contributed to the WSB and those who will use it are contemporary readers who bring their own perspectives to the reading of the Bible. In other words, the themes or ideas we notice in the Bible and that strike us as important tend to be those that resonate with us and our present situations in some way. Through study notes, excursuses, and accompanying essays, the WSB recognizes this fact by delving into the ancient contexts of the biblical text and its continually evolving present interpretations, thereby exploring both the biblical world and its contemporary reading and reception.

This approach makes the WSB an ideal textbook for a range of biblical studies courses as well as courses in religion, philosophy, and the general humanities, whether introductory or advanced. In addition to its particular attention to classroom use, the WSB is a resource written for teachers and by teachers. Among its many features, it pays close attention to the interdisciplinary connections that contemporary students and teachers will find both useful and relevant. We expect this emphasis will also make it helpful in many different learning contexts, including religious congregations and organizations.

Contributors to the WSB teach in a variety of educational settings. The configuration of these scholars and the places they work is representative of the array of spaces in which the Bible is studied in today's world. WSB contributors use the Bible in undergraduate liberal arts and seminary classrooms, religious services, academic conferences, and a host of other locations and thus understand what it means to think about the Bible in and for vastly different contexts. These teacher-scholars also know what it means to interpret from a particular place and time, as they are situated and embodied readers of texts that also come from very different places and times. The contributors to the WSB have been carefully selected: each is an expert in the ancient contexts of the Bible, but each is also sensitive to how the biblical texts have been received and how readers might hear them now in multiple contemporary contexts. The Bible is, after all, a classic of world literature that has been taken up and utilized in various art forms and expressions for millennia. Consequently, the features of the WSB attend to the cultural impact of the Bible in its original setting as well as its impact on later readers and communities, up to and including present-day readers. The classroom is in many ways the ideal place for these multiple "worlds" of text and interpretation to come together in a larger conversation that invites all sorts of readers—experts, novices, and those in between—to listen and learn from all parties involved.

We encourage users of the WSB to read the biblical text itself first before turning to the other features that have been included here. The most extensive of these features are the *study notes*, commentaries on the biblical text that provide invaluable information that is not easily available or widely known to the average reader. Among other things, the study notes include cultural insights from the ancient world—its religious ideas, practices, and settings—as well as information about ancient languages, locations, and artifacts. These notes also often discuss examples of how the biblical texts have moved beyond their ancient contexts into subsequent worlds of possible meaning. They are designed to be helpful aids to readers, who may then return to the biblical texts with additional windows onto their meanings. On the one hand, these notes are crafted to help readers hear something of what ancient audiences would have heard; on the other hand, they also guide students to grasp how certain texts may have functioned in much later periods and far different settings. Together, these two points of access—*back then* and *since then*—allow contemporary readers to have a richer, fuller discussion about the meanings of the Bible, whether inside or outside the classroom.

The *excursuses* embedded throughout the WSB supplement the study notes by offering new or more expansive discussions of important items relating to the biblical text. Each one deals with aspects of the Bible and its interpretation that augment and enrich further reading and research. Four types of excursuses are found in the WSB:

- "Reading through Time" excursuses provide a glimpse into how the interpretation of a particular text has changed through the years and across different communities of readers.
- "Making Connections" excursuses show how the biblical text may be related to events or circumstances outside and beyond the immediate passage at hand.
- "Focus On" excursuses offer a more detailed consideration of a theme, concept, figure, or place that appears in a passage or across many passages.
- "Going Deeper" excursuses afford a more thorough exploration of a topic than can be offered in the briefer study notes.

Whichever type, these additional aids will expand readers' understanding of the Bible's meaning, impact, and relevance both *back then* and *since then*.

The *essays* gathered at the back of the WSB provide longer discussions of various topics that are crucial for biblical interpretation. Included here are more general, wide-ranging treatments of the different ways the Bible may be read and interpreted, the aspects of the Bible's history and its ancient contexts, the various themes in biblical literature as they relate to contemporary concerns and issues, and how the Bible has been received and interpreted in culture and science over many centuries and across communities and locations. These essays situate the Bible and its study in a much larger history and realm of discourse and demonstrate how its interpretation and the academic discipline of biblical studies are deeply related to a host of other fields of human inquiry.

The Bible offers readers a front-row seat not only to the culture and religious ideas of the past but to those of the present. The lives and ideas of the Israelites in the ancient Near East and the first followers of Jesus in the Roman Empire continue to influence the ethical and religious practices of billions of religious (and nonreligious) people today. The Bible remains foundational, for example, in Jewish life—shaping traditions from clothing to food to holidays. In Christianity, it is a primary resource for religious faith and practice. Islam, too, recognizes in it a repository of revelations given to earlier prophets, though Islam does not consider the Bible itself sacred. The Bible has also played an important role in political and cultural debates, where it often figures prominently in a range of hot-button issues: from justifying slavery to motivating its abolition, from mandating the death penalty to calling for its abolishment, from debates over marriage and sexuality to discussions regarding civil rights and care for the environment. In these ways, the Bible continues to be profoundly important even for people who are not religious in any way or who are otherwise uninterested in it. It is a kind of catalyst for a large number of conversations in the contemporary world and a literary repository that has generated a wide variety of cultural products in literature, art, music, and more. Knowing the Bible, therefore—its historical contexts as well as its past and present interpretations—casts significant light on the many and diverse ways scholars, politicians, activists, artists, and everyday people have used and sometimes misused it to support particular agendas and objectives. To study the Bible, therefore, is in a very real way to study the world and to study humanity in the world. It is our profound hope that the WSB aids in that pursuit.

The Editors
In memory of Daniel Tran Foskett Hudgins

To the Reader

From the National Council of the Churches of Christ in the USA

[The following essay is part of the *New Revised Standard Version Updated Edition* (NRSVue) text and is included here according to agreement with the NRSVue copyright holder, the National Council of the Churches of Christ in the USA.]

Motivated by love and respect for Scripture, the National Council of the Churches of Christ in the USA (NCC) hopes that you will find this *New Revised Standard Version Updated Edition* (*NRSVue*) suitable to inspire, inform, and guide daily living. The goal of the *NRSVue* is to offer a readable and accurate version of the Holy Bible to the global English-speaking community for public worship and personal study, for scholarship and study in classrooms, and for informing faith and action in response to God.

Together with religious leaders from diverse communities of faith, we join in the conviction that the Scriptures offer good news of God's love—wisdom to guide, hope to sustain, truth to empower, forgiveness to change, and peace to bless all of creation.

The *NRSVue* extends the *New Revised Standard Version's* (*NRSV*) purpose to deliver an accurate, readable, up-to-date, and inclusive version of the Bible. It also continues the work of offering a version as free as possible from the gender bias inherent in the English language, which can obscure earlier oral and written renditions. The *NRSVue*, like the *NRSV*, follows "in the tradition of the *King James Bible*, [introducing] such changes as are warranted on the basis of accuracy, clarity, euphony, and current English usage, . . . as literal as possible, as free as necessary" (*NRSV's* preface "To the Reader"). As also stated in the *NRSV* preface, the Bible's message "must not be disguised in phrases that are no longer clear or hidden under words that have changed or lost their meaning; it must be presented in language that is direct and plain and meaningful to people today."

Why an Update?

The *NRSV* has been called the most accurate of English-language translations, based on the available manuscript evidence, textual analysis, and philological understanding. In the more than thirty years since its first publication, hundreds of ancient manuscripts have been studied in exacting detail. The *NRSVue* is informed by the results of this research. Laboring through this material has deepened scholarly insight into Jewish and Christian sacred texts and advanced understanding of ancient languages. With new textual evidence, historical insights, and philological understandings (which include exploring the meanings of ancient texts in light of the cultures that produced them), the *NRSVue* brings greater precision in interpreting Scripture today. The goal of these practices has been to translate the ancient texts as accurately as possible while reflecting the cultural differences across time and conditions. Such a translation approach permitted the Editorial Committee to present the text as literally as possible and as freely as necessary.

The Update Process

The current updating process involves scores of scholars and leaders from multiple faith communities, inclusive of gender and ethnic identities, with the unwavering goal to render an accurate version of original source texts into the most current understandings of contemporary language and culture.

It is for this reason, too, that the NCC commissioned the Society of Biblical Literature (SBL), the leading international association of biblical scholars, to review and update the *NRSV*. The SBL's mandate and process were single-mindedly intended to ensure the currency and integrity of the *NRSVue* as the most up-to-date and reliable Bible for use and study in English-language religious communities and educational institutions.

A Final Word

Since its beginnings in the early 1950s, the NCC has supported the work of scholars who dedicate their lives to the study of the Hebrew and Christian Scriptures. Likewise, the NCC's steadfast aim has been to encourage readers to study the Scriptures so they will be inspired and informed in their faithful action to love God with their hearts, souls, minds, and strength and to love each other as God loves.

The communions of the National Council of the Churches of Christ in the USA have undertaken this work as a sacred trust.

Preface to the *NRSV Updated Edition*

From the Society of Biblical Literature

[The following essay is part of the *New Revised Standard Version Updated Edition*
(NRSVue) text and is included here according to agreement with the NRSVue copyright
holder, the National Council of the Churches of Christ in the USA.]

Purpose of the Revision

First published in 1611, the *King James Version* slowly but steadily attained a well-deserved stature as the English language's "Authorized Version" of the Scriptures. At the same time, the scholarly foundation that produced the *King James Version* shifted as new manuscripts came to light and philological understandings improved. As a result of these scholarly advances, the *Revised Standard Version* was authorized to improve the translation, based on more evidence of the original texts and early translations of the Bible, the meanings of its original languages (Hebrew, Aramaic, and Greek, as well as ancient translations into Arabic, Armenian, Coptic, Ethiopic, Georgian Greek, Syriac, and Latin), and changes to the English language itself. The forty years between the *Revised Standard Version* and the *New Revised Standard Version* likewise witnessed many developments in biblical scholarship, textual criticism, linguistics, and philology. The same has occurred over the last thirty years, including the publication of all the biblical texts discovered near the Dead Sea, and these developments warrant this update. As with its predecessors, the *NRSVue* can claim a well-known line from the 1611 preface to the *King James Version*: "We never thought from the beginning that we should need to make a new translation . . . but to make a good one better."

The National Council of Churches, which holds the copyright of the *New Revised Standard Version*, commissioned the Society of Biblical Literature to direct the *NRSVue* revision project thirty years after its original publication. The editors of this edition encourage readers to read the excellent prefaces to both the *Revised Standard Version* (1952) and the *New Revised Standard Version* (1989); some elements of the latter have been incorporated herein. This preface also outlines the process of the update and the mandate under which it was conducted.

Process of the Revision

The review managed by the Society of Biblical Literature included seven general editors and fifty-six book editors, with several general editors serving also as book editors. The general editors were divided into three teams: Old Testament (also known as the Hebrew Scriptures), Apocrypha (also known as the Deuterocanon), and the New Testament. In addition to the seven general editors, the National Council of Churches appointed two members of its Bible Translation and Utilization Advisory Committee to serve as liaisons to the committee of general editors appointed by the Society of Biblical Literature. Three members of the Society's staff participated in and managed the project.

Beginning in 2017, each book of the Bible was assigned to one or more book editors. Over the course of two years (2018–2019), the book editors submitted their proposed updates to the general editors. Each of the three teams of general editors met at least once a month for two years (2019–2020) to review and discuss the proposed updates submitted by the book editors. The accepted updates were submitted to the National Council of Churches in 2021 for its final review and approval of what is now the *NRSVue*.

The *NRSVue* presents approximately 12,000 substantive edits and 20,000 total changes, which include alterations in grammar and punctuation.

Like its predecessors, this *NRSVue* has relied on the best results of modern discovery and scholarship. The mandate primarily focused on two types of revisions: text-critical and philological. The *New Revised Standard Version Updated Edition* (*NRSVue*) is not a new translation. While some stylistic improvements have been made, these were reserved for instances where the translation was awkward, unclear, or inaccurate. Other changes involve matters of consistency, grammar and punctuation, and general improvements that render the translation and notes more consistent and uniform.

Text-Critical Revisions

The role of text criticism in Bible translation is to establish a base text from which to translate, a text reconstructed from the earliest versions in the original languages (Hebrew, Aramaic, and Greek), as well as in ancient translations of the books of the Old Testament, Apocrypha, and New Testament. Translators rely on scholarly critical editions of the Bible for their work. A typical text-critical resource establishes a text based on scholarly judgment of the preferred reading among the readings available, with important alternative readings provided in a detailed apparatus. Scholars follow well-established rules in their effort to determine one preferred or superior reading from among others, though this remains both art and science. The challenge of establishing the Hebrew and Aramaic text of the Old Testament is different from the corresponding challenge in the New Testament. For the New Testament, a large number of Greek manuscripts exist, preserving many variant forms of the text. Some of them were copied only two or three centuries later than the original composition of the books. While the Dead Sea Scrolls dramatically improved the resources for Old Testament textual criticism, most translations, including the *NRSVue*, still rely especially on a standardized form of the text established many centuries after the books were written.

The goal of the text-critical review was to evaluate whether or not to modify the textual basis for the revision. To this end, the text underlying the *New Revised Standard Version* was examined in the light of all available evidence, making use of new data, perspectives, and scholarly resources. The review occasionally resulted in a change to the translation itself or to the textual notes that have been an integral feature of the *New Revised Standard Version*.

For the Old Testament, the team made use of the *Biblia Hebraica Quinta* (2004–) for those books published to date and the *Biblia Hebraica Stuttgartensia* (1977; ed. sec. emendata, 1983) for the remaining books. Both are editions of the Hebrew and Aramaic text as current early in the Christian era and fixed by Jewish scholars (the Masoretes) of the sixth to the ninth centuries. The vowel signs, which were added by the Masoretes, are accepted in the main, but where a more probable and convincing reading can be obtained by assuming different vowels, we adopted that reading. No notes are given in such cases because the vowel points are more recent and less reliably original than the consonants.

Departures from the consonantal text of the best manuscripts have been made only where it seems clear that errors in copying were introduced before the Masoretes standardized the Hebrew text. Most of the corrections adopted in the *NRSVue* are based on other ancient Hebrew manuscripts or on the ancient versions (translations into Greek, Aramaic, Syriac, and Latin), which were made prior to the time of the work of the Masoretes and which therefore may reflect earlier forms of the Hebrew text. In such instances a note specifies the manuscript, version, or versions attesting the correction and also gives a translation of the Masoretic Text.

Since the Dead Sea Scrolls and the Septuagint translation predate the Christian era, they present for certain books an earlier and more original version in the development of the texts. Each of the versions was considered authoritative by a community. This advance in textual scholarship is recent, however, so the *NRSVue* retains for its translation the version presented by the Masoretic Text, whether it attests the earlier, parallel, or later version. The differences between these major versions are larger than can be added to the notes.

The *NRSVue* uses double brackets in the Old Testament in the same way the *New Revised Standard Version* did in the New Testament: to enclose passages that are now regarded to be later additions to the text but that have been retained because of their evident antiquity and their importance in the textual tradition. In short, the text-critical basis for the Old Testament is an improved Masoretic Text, which was the goal of the *New Revised Standard Version*. The Masoretic Text has been given preference where there is no scholarly consensus in favor of another reading or where the arguments are equivocal.

The *Revised Standard Version of the Bible* containing both the Old and New Testaments was published in 1952; a translation of the Apocrypha in the Old Testament followed in 1957. In 1977, this collection was issued in an expanded edition containing three additional texts considered canonical by Eastern Orthodox communions (3 and 4 Maccabees and Psalm 151). Thereafter the *Revised Standard Version* gained the distinction of being officially authorized for use by all major Christian churches: Protestant, Anglican, Roman Catholic, and Eastern Orthodox. The translation of the Apocrypha, therefore, is not peripheral but of equal import as the translation of the Old Testament and

the New Testament. Indeed, some of the deuterocanonical books were originally written in Hebrew or Aramaic and were considered sacred texts by the early Jewish communities who first transmitted them and the later Christians who preserved them.

The *NRSVue* includes a considerable number of changes to the Apocrypha. Because there is no single critical edition for the books in this collection, the team made use of a number of texts. For most books the basic Greek text used was the edition of the Septuagint prepared by Alfred Rahlfs (Stuttgart, 1935). For several books the more recent volumes of the Göttingen Septuagint project were utilized. *A New English Translation of the Septuagint* (Oxford, 2009) also served as a resource to compare translations and evaluate critical texts for individual books.

For the book of Tobit, the *New Revised Standard Version* relied on the shorter Greek manuscript tradition; the *NRSVue* translated the longer Greek tradition (preserved in Codex Sinaiticus), while taking the Qumran manuscripts and other ancient witnesses into account. For the three Additions to Daniel, the Committee continued to use the Greek version attributed to Theodotion. Ecclesiasticus has an especially challenging textual history. The team generally followed the Greek text of Joseph Ziegler (and the versification in the Prologue), while giving particular consideration to the earliest Hebrew manuscripts from the Dead Sea region, with occasional recourse to the Syriac. The versification of 1 Esdras now follows Robert Hanhart's edition (Göttingen, 1974), which also brings the book into conformity with its usage in the Eastern Orthodox tradition. The basic text adopted in rendering 2 Esdras is the Latin version given in Robert Weber's *Biblia Sacra* (Stuttgart, 1971), with consultation of the Latin texts of R. L. Bensly (1895) and Bruno Violet (1910), as well as by taking into account the Syriac, Ethiopic, Arabic, Armenian, and Georgian versions. Since the Additions to the Book of Esther are disjointed and unintelligible as they stand in most editions of the Apocrypha, we provide them with their original context by translating the entirety of Greek Esther from Hanhart's edition (Göttingen, 1983). The versification of the Letter of Jeremiah now conforms to Ziegler's edition (Göttingen, 1957, 1976). The Septuagint's Psalm 151 is an abbreviated version of the Hebrew composition found in the 11QPsalms[a] scroll. While the Greek remains the basis for the translation, the team also consulted that scroll.

For the New Testament, the team based its work on three recent editions of the Greek New Testament: (1) *The Greek New Testament*, 5th revised edition (United Bible Societies, 2014); (2) *The Greek New Testament: SBL Edition* (Society of Biblical Literature and Logos Bible Software, 2010); and, (3) for Acts and the Catholic Letters, *Novum Testamentum Graecum: Editio Critica Maior* (Deutsche Bibelgesellschaft, 2013, 2017). Occasionally these editions differ in regard to text or punctuation; in such cases the team followed the reading best supported by a combination of both traditional and more recent approaches and considerations. As in the original *NRSV*, double brackets are used to enclose a few passages that are generally regarded to be later additions to the text but that have been retained because of their antiquity and importance in the textual tradition. Here and there in the notes the phrase "Other ancient authorities read" identifies alternative readings preserved by Greek manuscripts and early versions. In both Testaments, other possible translations of the text are indicated by the word "Or."

Textual criticism continues to evolve. Not only have additional manuscripts become available, but some of the goals and methodology have changed over the last several decades. This is more the case for reconstructing the books of the Old Testament and Apocrypha, but it is generally true for the entire enterprise. In the *NRSVue*, care was taken not to push too far ahead of the existing critical editions or to turn the translation itself and its notes into a critical edition. Nevertheless, a careful reader will notice in general a more generous use of the notes for alternative readings. The editors hope that this work will serve translators in the future.

Philological Revisions

Deciphering the meanings of the Bible's ancient languages involves a host of efforts: the study of the languages themselves, the comparative study of cognate languages from the ancient Near East and the Greco-Roman world, the disciplines of philology and linguistics, and the historical study of the social, cultural, and economic contexts in which the Bible was written. The *NRSVue* took special care not to use terms in ways that are historically or theologically anachronistic, though, as in every translation, anachronism is unavoidable.

The *NRSVue* continues and improves the effort to eliminate masculine-oriented language when it can be done without altering passages that reflect the historical situation of ancient patriarchal

culture. This goal is to provide a historically accurate and acceptable rendering without using contrived English. Only occasionally has the pronoun "he" or "him" or other gendered language been retained in passages where the reference may have been to a woman as well as to a man, for example, in several legal texts in Leviticus and Deuteronomy. In such instances of formal, legal language, the options of either putting the passage in the plural or of introducing additional nouns to avoid masculine pronouns in English could easily obscure the historical background to and literary character of the original. In the vast majority of cases, however, inclusiveness has been attained by simple rephrasing or by introducing plural forms when this does not distort meaning.

The *NRSVue* also continues the well-established practice of using in the Old Testament the word LORD (or, in certain cases, GOD). This represents the traditional way that English versions render the Divine Name, the "Tetragrammaton" (see the notes on Exodus 3.14, 15), following the precedent of the ancient Greek and Latin translators and the long-established practice in the reading of the Hebrew Scriptures in the synagogue.

The Future of Revisions and a Virtue of This Translation

The *NRSVue* represents a base text that was produced from a variety of textual witnesses, a text that was not used by any one community but combines readings from several of them. This, however, may well be a model and a reminder to us today: it results in a text that can be used across both Jewish and Christian traditions and in all their diverse communities. Indeed, this model stretches back to 1611, the origin of this edition. The translators of the *King James Version* took into account all of the preceding English versions and owed something to each of them. In 1977 the *Revised Standard Version* incorporated books that permitted it to become officially authorized by all the major Christian churches, and the use of the Masoretic Text of the Hebrew Scriptures reflects the use of that text in synagogues. Beginning with the Revised Standard Version Bible Committee, the translation teams became both ecumenical and interfaith. The process that produced this translation of the Bible represents an ideal and a virtue. It is a Bible produced by consensus that can be used among and across pluralistic communities in contexts both academic and religious.

In the future, new text-critical resources will become available, the methodology and goals of textual criticism may change, translation theory may evolve, and the need to reflect contemporary language will be constant. In short, efforts to update the translation of the Bible will continue. As they do, it is the hope of the Society of Biblical Literature that this translation will continue to be produced by a diverse team and for diverse readers.

Alphabetical List of the Books of the Bible

Acts of the Apostles	1886	Lamentations	1115
Amos	1254	Letter of Jeremiah	1514
Baruch	1506	Leviticus	143
Bel and the Dragon	1528	Luke	1800
1 Chronicles	541	1 Maccabees	1532
2 Chronicles	582	2 Maccabees	1571
Colossians	2019	3 Maccabees	1628
1 Corinthians	1955	4 Maccabees	1682
2 Corinthians	1977	Malachi	1326
Daniel	1200	Mark	1769
Deuteronomy	245	Matthew	1719
Ecclesiastes	904	Micah	1277
Ephesians	2003	Nahum	1287
1 Esdras	1601	Nehemiah	651
2 Esdras	1644	Numbers	187
Esther	670	Obadiah	1268
Esther (The Greek Version Containing		1 Peter	2085
the Additional Chapters)	1382	2 Peter	2094
Exodus	82	Philemon	2056
Ezekiel	1126	Philippians	2012
Ezra	634	Prayer of Azariah and	
Galatians	1993	the Song of the Three Jews	1518
Genesis	13	Prayer of Manasseh	1623
Habakkuk	1292	Proverbs	860
Haggai	1305	Psalm 151	1626
Hebrews	2060	Psalms	738
Hosea	1226	Revelation	2114
Isaiah	932	Romans	1932
James	2078	Ruth	371
Jeremiah	1031	1 Samuel	379
Job	684	2 Samuel	422
Joel	1247	Sirach (Ecclesiasticus)	1429
John	1847	Song of Songs	920
1 John	2099	Susanna	1523
2 John	2107	1 Thessalonians	2027
3 John	2108	2 Thessalonians	2033
Jonah	1271	1 Timothy	2037
Joshua	297	2 Timothy	2045
Jude	2110	Titus	2051
Judges	334	Tobit	1336
Judith	1358	Wisdom of Solomon	1399
1 Kings	460	Zechariah	1309
2 Kings	500	Zephaniah	1298

Canonical Orders of the Books of the Bible

The Jewish Canon

The Jewish Bible consists of three sections: the Torah (the "Law" or "Teaching"), the Nevi'im (the "Prophets"), and the Ketuvim (the "Writings"). The first letters of these three parts form an acronym—Tanakh—which is the designation for this collection in Judaism.

The sections may reflect the canonization process. The first five books (Torah or Pentateuch) were deemed authoritative early and may have been read publicly after the Babylonian exile. The Prophets contains a historical survey that runs from the entrance into the land to the Babylonian destruction (Joshua through 2 Kings) and prophetic books that speak to the historical circumstances of Israel from the Assyrian threats of the seventh century BCE through the restoration during the Persian period in the fifth century BCE. This collection probably took its current form during the late Persian period. The Writings contain many genres, including short stories, hymns, love poetry, philosophical reflection, and historical account. Some books may fit more logically in the Prophets, but their presence in the third and final section suggests a later date of either composition or authoritative status, after the Nevi'im stabilized. There was discussion concerning exactly what to include in this final section into the first century CE. There is some variation in the ordering of the books of the Writings, but the collection always ends with 2 Chronicles, the final passage a hopeful note about returning to and rebuilding Jerusalem.

Torah	Nevi'im (Prophets)	Ketuvim (Writings)
Genesis	Joshua	Psalms
Exodus	Judges	Proverbs
Leviticus	1 and 2 Samuel	Job
Numbers	1 and 2 Kings	Song of Songs
Deuteronomy	Isaiah	Ruth
	Jeremiah	Lamentations
	Ezekiel	Ecclesiastes
	The Twelve	Esther
	Hosea	Daniel
	Joel	Ezra–Nehemiah
	Amos	1 and 2 Chronicles
	Obadiah	
	Jonah	
	Micah	
	Nahum	
	Habakkuk	
	Zephaniah	
	Haggai	
	Zechariah	
	Malachi	

The Protestant Canon

In the Christian canons, the most common designation for the books that predate the origins of Christianity is called the Old Testament (OT). The categorization presumes a New Testament (NT) to follow. In the Protestant Christian canon, the OT consists of four parts: the (commonly called) Pentateuch (Genesis–Deuteronomy); the Historical Books (Joshua–Esther); the Poetic, or Wisdom, Books (Job–Song of Songs); and the Prophetic Books (Isaiah–Malachi). The NT consists of four parts as well in all the Christian canons, specifically the Gospels (Matthew–John), History (Acts), Letters—designated for specific churches and individuals (Pauline Letters) and more general or universal letters (Hebrews–Jude)—and an Apocalypse (Revelation). The ordering of the NT is consistent across the Christian canons.

In the Protestant Bible, the last section of the OT (Prophetic Books) leads "naturally" to the story of the Gospels—that is, the arrival of Jesus Christ. In some ways, the four-part structure of the NT mimics the OT's own sequence in the Protestant Bible, and much has been made of the corresponding parallels. In any case, there is a basic thematic sequence within the NT's order, again true in all Christian canons. The religious movement commences with Jesus Christ's life, mission, death, and resurrection (Gospels). The growth of the movement is explored (Acts). Newly formed assemblies in various quarters of the Roman Empire are impacted, and communications among the groups point to developing networks throughout the Mediterranean world (Letters). With its creative, apocalyptic images, the final book of the collection conceives of the end of world history and the place of Christ followers within it (Revelation).

Old Testament

(Pentateuch)
Genesis
Exodus
Leviticus
Numbers
Deuteronomy

(Historical Books)
Joshua
Judges
Ruth
1 Samuel
2 Samuel
1 Kings
2 Kings
1 Chronicles
2 Chronicles
Ezra
Nehemiah
Esther

(Poetic, or Wisdom, Books)
Job
Psalms

Proverbs
Ecclesiastes
Song of Songs

(Prophetic Books)
Isaiah
Jeremiah
Lamentations
Ezekiel
Daniel
Hosea
Joel
Amos
Obadiah
Jonah
Micah
Nahum
Habakkuk
Zephaniah
Haggai
Zechariah
Malachi

New Testament

Matthew	1 Timothy
Mark	2 Timothy
Luke	Titus
John	Philemon
Acts	Hebrews
Romans	James
1 Corinthians	1 Peter
2 Corinthians	2 Peter
Galatians	1 John
Ephesians	2 John
Philippians	3 John
Colossians	Jude
1 Thessalonians	Revelation
2 Thessalonians	

The Roman Catholic Canon

The Roman Catholic Church's Bible consists of forty-six books in the Old Testament (OT) and, as with all the Christian canons, twenty-seven books in the New Testament (NT). This canon following the Latin Vulgate was affirmed by the Council of Trent in 1546 in response to the tendency of Protestant Christians to exclude the deuterocanonical books (Tobit, Judith, 1 Maccabees, 2 Maccabees, Wisdom of Solomon, Sirach, and Baruch, including the Letter of Jeremiah). The council recognized as authoritative these books "with all their parts" and so also canonized Esther, including the additions found in the Greek version, and Daniel, including the Prayer of Azariah and the Song of the Three Jews, Susanna, and Bel and the Dragon. In the Roman Catholic Church, the deuterocanonical books are as equally authoritative as other books.

There is some variation in the order and titles of books in the Catholic Old Testament. The order below is used in most contemporary Catholic Bibles. Some Catholic Bibles omit the divisions, while others provide different titles to the divisions. Some Catholic Bibles designate Tobit, Judith, Esther, 1 Maccabees, and 2 Maccabees as "Biblical Novellas." Other Catholic Bibles place 1–2 Maccabees after Malachi. Some copies of the Latin Vulgate (and English translations) also include as an appendix 1–2 Esdras (called 3–4 Esdras in the Vulgate) and the Prayer of Manasseh, books that were not canonized by the Council of Trent.

Old Testament

(Pentateuch)
Genesis
Exodus
Leviticus
Numbers
Deuteronomy

(Historical Books)
Joshua
Judges
Ruth
1 Samuel (or 1 Kings)
2 Samuel (or 2 Kings)
1 Kings (or 3 Kings)
2 Kings (or 4 Kings)
1 Chronicles (or 1 Paralipomenon)
2 Chronicles (or 2 Paralipomenon)
Ezra (or 1 Esdras)
Nehemiah (or 2 Esdras)
Tobit
Judith
Esther (the longer Greek Esther)
1 Maccabees
2 Maccabees

(Wisdom Books)
Job
Psalms

Proverbs
Ecclesiastes
Song of Songs
Wisdom of Solomon
Sirach (or Ecclesiasticus)

(Prophetic Books)
Isaiah
Jeremiah
Lamentations
Baruch (chap. 6 = Letter of Jeremiah)
Ezekiel
Daniel (including the Prayer of Azariah and
	the Song of the Three Jews, Susanna,
	and Bel and the Dragon)
Hosea
Joel
Amos
Obadiah
Jonah
Micah
Nahum
Habakkuk
Zephaniah
Haggai
Zechariah
Malachi

The Orthodox Canons

The Greek Bible of the Greek Orthodox Church and the Slavonic Bible of the Russian Orthodox Church contain forty-nine books in the Old Testament (OT) and, as with all the Christian canons, twenty-seven books in the New Testament (NT).

Orthodox Bibles use different titles for some of the same books in other canons. Here 1–2 Samuel and 1–2 Kings are called 1–4 Kingdoms, and 1–2 Chronicles are also called 1 Paralipomenon and 2 Paralipomenon. In the Greek Bible, 2 Esdras is the name given to the book known as Ezra in other canons. In some Orthodox Bibles, 2 Esdras also includes Nehemiah. The book of 1 Esdras in Greek Bibles is called 2 Esdras in Slavonic Bibles. Orthodox Bibles number the Psalms differently after Psalm 8 and also include Psalm 151. In both Greek and Slavonic Bibles, Esther is the longer version (Greek Esther), and Daniel includes the Prayer of Azariah and the Song of the Three Jews, Susanna, and Bel and the Dragon. The Prayer of Manasseh may be included in 2 Chronicles or in an appendix alongside 4 Maccabees. Slavonic Bibles also include in this appendix "3 Esdras," which is 2 Esdras in the Deuterocanon/Apocrypha.

Old Testament

(Historical Books)
Genesis
Exodus
Leviticus
Numbers
Deuteronomy
Joshua
Judges
Ruth
1 Kingdoms (or 1 Samuel)
2 Kingdoms (or 2 Samuel)
3 Kingdoms (or 1 Kings)
4 Kingdoms (or 2 Kings)
1 Chronicles (or 1 Paralipomenon)
2 Chronicles (or 2 Paralipomenon)
1 Esdras (called 2 Esdras in Slavonic Bibles)
2 Esdras (Ezra; not the 2 Esdras in the
        Apocrypha)
Nehemiah
Tobit
Judith
Esther (the longer Greek Esther)
1 Maccabees
2 Maccabees
3 Maccabees

(Poetic and Didactic Books)
Psalms (with Psalm 151)
Job

Proverbs
Ecclesiastes
Song of Songs (or Asma)
Wisdom of Solomon
Wisdom of Sirach

(Prophetic Books)
Hosea
Amos
Micah
Joel
Obadiah
Jonah
Nahum
Habakkuk
Zephaniah
Haggai
Zechariah
Malachi
Isaiah
Jeremiah
Baruch
Lamentations of Jeremiah
Letter of Jeremiah
Ezekiel
Daniel (including the Prayer of Azariah and
        the Song of the Three Jews, Susanna,
        Bel and the Dragon)

(Appendices in Greek Orthodox Bibles include 4 Maccabees and the Prayer of Manasseh. In addition to these, Slavonic Bibles also include Apocrypha 2 Esdras—titled as 3 Esdras—as an appendix.)

List of Excursuses

"Reading through Time" excursuses provide a glimpse into how the interpretation of a particular text has changed through the years and across different communities of readers.

"Making Connections" excursuses show how the biblical text may be related to events or circumstances outside and beyond the immediate passage at hand.

"Focus On" excursuses offer a more detailed consideration of a theme, concept, figure, or place that appears in a passage or across many passages.

"Going Deeper" excursuses afford a more thorough exploration of a topic than can be offered in the briefer study notes.

Additional Excursuses Contributors

Stephanie Buckhanon Crowder, Professor of New Testament and Culture,
    Chicago Theological Seminary

Michael E. Fuller, Professor of Early Jewish and New Testament Studies, Lee University

Todd Penner, Visiting Professor of Religious Studies, Eckerd College

List of Abbreviations

Biblical book abbreviations:

Hebrew Bible

Gen. / Genesis
Exod. / Exodus
Lev. / Leviticus
Num. / Numbers
Deut. / Deuteronomy
Josh. / Joshua
Judg. / Judges
Ruth / Ruth
1 Sam. / 1 Samuel
2 Sam. / 2 Samuel
1 Kgs. / 1 Kings
2 Kgs. / 2 Kings
1 Chr. / 1 Chronicles
2 Chr. / 2 Chronicles
Ezra / Ezra
Neh. / Nehemiah
Esth. / Esther
Job / Job
Ps. or Pss. / Psalms
Prov. / Proverbs

Eccl. / Ecclesiastes
Song / Song of Songs
Isa. / Isaiah
Jer. / Jeremiah
Lam. / Lamentations
Ezek. / Ezekiel
Dan. / Daniel
Hos. / Hosea
Joel / Joel
Amos / Amos
Obad. / Obadiah
Jonah / Jonah
Mic. / Micah
Nah. / Nahum
Hab. / Habakkuk
Zeph. / Zephaniah
Hag. / Haggai
Zech. / Zechariah
Mal. / Malachi

Deuterocanonical/Apocryphal Books

Tob. / Tobit
Jdt. / Judith
Gk. Esth. / Esther (The Greek Version
    Containing the Additional Chapters)
Wis. / Wisdom of Solomon
Sir. / Sirach (Ecclesiasticus)
Bar. / Baruch
Ep. Jer. / Letter (Epistle) of Jeremiah
Add. Dan. / Additions to Daniel
Pr. Azar. / Prayer of Azariah
Sg. Three / Song of the Three Jews

Sus. / Susanna
Bel / Bel and the Dragon
1 Macc. / 1 Maccabees
2 Macc. / 2 Maccabees
1 Esd. / 1 Esdras
Pr. Man. / Prayer of Manasseh
Ps. 151 / Psalm 151
3 Macc. / 3 Maccabees
2 Esd. / 2 Esdras
4 Macc. / 4 Maccabees

New Testament

Matt. / Matthew
Mark / Mark
Luke / Luke
John / John
Acts / Acts
Rom. / Romans
1 Cor. / 1 Corinthians
2 Cor. / 2 Corinthians
Gal. / Galatians
Eph. / Ephesians
Phil. / Philippians
Col. / Colossians
1 Thess. / 1 Thessalonians
2 Thess. / 2 Thessalonians

1 Tim. / 1 Timothy
2 Tim. / 2 Timothy
Titus / Titus
Phlm. / Philemon
Heb. / Hebrews
Jas. / James
1 Pet. / 1 Peter
2 Pet. / 2 Peter
1 John / 1 John
2 John / 2 John
3 John / 3 John
Jude / Jude
Rev. / Revelation

The following abbreviations are used in the text notes to the books of the Bible:

Aquila	Aquila's Greek Old Testament	ms(s)	manuscript(s)
Arab	Arabic	MT	vocalized Masoretic Text
Aram	Aramaic	OL	Old Latin
Arm	Armenian	Q	Qumran
Cn	Correction; provides the most probable reconstruction of the original text where the text has suffered in transmission and the versions provide no satisfactory restoration	S	Codex Sinaiticus
		Sam	Samaritan Hebrew text of the Old Testament
		Symmachus	Symmachus's Greek Old Testament
		Syr	Syriac Version of the Old Testament
Ethiop	Ethiopic		
Georg	Georgian	Syr H	Syriac Version of Origen's Hexapla
Gk	Greek		
Heb	Hebrew	Theodotion	Theodotion's Greek Old Testament
Jerome	Jerome's Latin translation of Psalms based on the Hebrew		
		Tg	Targum
Lat	Latin	Vg	Vulgate

Abbreviations used in the study notes, essays, and excursuses:
(In a few places references are made to specific Dead Sea Scrolls. Those references include, but are not limited to, 4Q365, 1QS, 4Q186, 4Q561, 4Q525, 4Q184, 11QPsª, 11Q18, etc. Q refers to Qumran, the location of the early Jewish community that stored the Dead Sea Scrolls in caves above the northwestern shore of the Dead Sea. The initial number denotes the cave number. The second number or letter(s) identifies the specific manuscript found in that cave. Readers who take a special interest in the naming conventions of the Dead Sea Scrolls are encouraged to consult *The SBL Handbook of Style*.)

//	parallel	BASOR	*Bulletin of the American Schools of Oriental Research*
Aeth.	*Aethiopica* (Heliodorus)		
Ag. Ap.	*Against Apion* (Josephus)	BCE	before the Common Era
Akk.	Akkadian	*Bib. hist.*	*Bibliotheca historica* (Diodorus Siculus)
Alleg. Interp.	*Allegorical Interpretation* (Philo)		
		c.	century
Am.	*Amores* (Ovid)	ca.	circa
ANE	ancient Near Eastern	CD	Cairo Genizah copy of the *Damascus Document*
Ant.	*Jewish Antiquities* (Josephus)		
Apoc. Ab.	Apocalypse of Abraham	CE	Common Era
Apoc. Pet.	Apocalypse of Peter	CEB	Common English Bible
Ar.	Aramaic	cf.	compare
b.	Babylonian Talmud	chap./chaps.	chapter/chapters
b.	born	1 Clem.	1 Clement
b. Ber.	Babylonian Berakhot	*Cyr.*	*Cyropaedia* (Xenophon)
b. Hag.	Babylonian Hagigah	d.	died
b. Ned.	Babylonian Nedarim	DH	Deuteronomistic History
b. Sanh.	Babylonian Sanhedrin	DSS	Dead Sea Scrolls
b. Yebam.	Babylonian Yevamot	e.g.	*exempli gratia*, for example
2 Bar.	2 Baruch	1 En.	1 Enoch
		2 En.	2 Enoch

3 En.	3 Enoch	m. Suk.	Mishnah Sukkah
Ench.	*Enchiridion* (Epictetus)	m. Taʿan	Mishnah Ta'anit
Eng.	English	*Mart.*	*Exhortation to Martyrdom* (Origen)
Ep.	*Epistulae morales* (Seneca)		
ESV	English Standard Version	*Mart. Pal.*	*The Martyrs of Palestine* (Eusebius)
et al.	*et alii*, and others		
Eth. nic.	*Nicomachean Ethics* (Aristotle)	*Mor.*	*Moralia* (Plutarch)
		MOTB	Museum of the Bible
Eunuch.	*The Eunuch* (Lucian)	MT	Masoretic Text
Flacc.	*In Flaccum* (Philo)	n	note
Geogr.	*Geography* (Strabo)	NASB	New American Standard Bible
Gk.	Greek	*Nat. Hist.*	*Natural History* (Pliny)
Gos. Pet.	Gospel of Peter	NIV	New International Version
Gos. Thom.	Gospel of Thomas	NRSV	New Revised Standard Version
Haer.	*Heresies* (Hippolytus)	NRSVue	New Revised Standard Version Updated Edition
HB	Hebrew Bible		
Heb.	Hebrew	NT	New Testament
Heb. Esth.	Hebrew Esther	*Od.*	*Odyssey* (Homer)
Herc. fur.	*Hercules furens* (Seneca)	*Oed. tyr.*	*Oedipus tyrannus* (Sophocles)
Herm. Mand.	Shepherd of Hermas, Mandate	*Off.*	*De officiis* (Cicero)
Herm. Sim.	Shepherd of Hermas, Similitude	*Opif.*	*De opificio mundi* (Philo)
		OT	Old Testament
Hist.	*Historiae* (Tacitus)	P	papyrus
Hist.	*Histories* (Herodotus)	p./pp.	page/pages
Hist.	*Histories* (Polybius)	Pesiq. Rab.	Pesiqta Rabbati
Hist. rom.	*Roman History* (Appian)	*Phaed.*	*Phaedo* (Plato)
Ign. *Pol.*	Ignatius, *To Polycarp*	pl.	plural
Il.	*Iliad* (Homer)	[*Plac. philos.*]	*De placita philosophorum* (Plutarch)
ISV	International Standard Version		
J.W.	*Jewish War* (Josephus)	*Poet.*	*Poetics* (Aristotle)
Jos. Asen.	Joseph and Aseneth	*Pol.*	*Politics* (Aristotle)
Jub.	Jubilees	Pol. *Phil.*	Polycarp, *To the Philippians*
KJV	King James Version	PrNab	Prayer of Nabonidus
km	kilometers	Pss. Sol.	Psalms of Solomon
LAB	*Liber antiquitatum biblicarum* (Pseudo–Philo)	*QG*	*Questions and Answers on Genesis* (Philo)
Lat.	Latin	r.	reigned
Leg.	*Legum allegoriae* (Philo)	*Resp.*	*Republic* (Plato)
LXX	Septuagint	sg.	singular
m. Avot	Mishnah Avot	St.	Saint
m. B. Qam.	Mishnah Bava Qamma	*Strom.*	*Miscellanies* (Clement of Alexandria)
m. Ber.	Mishnah Berakhot		
m. Bik.	Mishnah Bikkurim	*Syr.*	*Syrian Wars* (Appian)
m. Hag.	Mishnah Hagigah	T. Job	Testament of Job
m. Meg.	Mishnah Me'ilah	T. Jos.	Testament of Joseph
m. Mo'ed Qaṭ.	Mishnah Mo'ed Qatan	T. Levi	Testament of Levi
m. Roš Haš.	Mishnah Rosh Hashanah	T. Mos.	Testament of Moses

t. Yad.	Tosefta Yadayim		v./vv.	verse/verses
Tg. Isa.	Targum Isaiah		*Virt. mor.*	*De virtute morali* (Plutarch)
Tro.	*Daughters of Troy* (Euripides)		*Vita*	*Vita* (Josephus)
Tyr.	*The Tyrannicide* (Lucian)		vs.	versus (in other uses)
v.	versus (in legal cases)		y.	Jerusalem Talmud
			y. Sanh.	Jerusalem Sanhedrin

YHWH: A Note

Like other gods in the ancient world, the deity venerated by Israel and Judah in the biblical text was known by a proper name, not simply as God. Because the earliest biblical texts were written without vowels, there is some uncertainty about the name's pronunciation. Furthermore, out of reverence, the divine name eventually became unspoken. Consequently, the name is often written in the Hebrew Bible using only its four consonants: in English, YHWH (called the Tetragrammaton). However, in the NRSVue, the name is translated as "the Lord" using small capitals (which should be distinguished from "the Lord," usually a title). Authors of annotations and excurses have been given the freedom to refer to God in these cases in the way each author prefers. As such, readers should be aware that God might be referred to in the nonbiblical texts in *The Westminster Study Bible* as YHWH, Lord, or God.

The Hebrew Bible:

Also Called the Old Testament and Tanakh

New Revised Standard Version Updated Edition

Introduction to the Hebrew Bible: Also Called the Old Testament and Tanakh

The Bible is an anthology of ancient texts read and valued by different religious communities that view it as sacred. The number and order of the books composing the Bible vary in different traditions (see **"The Bible as a Collection," pp. 2145–47**). The first part of the collection is known as the Hebrew Bible, or simply the Bible in Judaism, but is traditionally called the Old Testament in Christianity. In the Jewish tradition, the books are grouped in a different order than in most English Bibles and are arranged into three categories known by the acronym TNK, commonly pronounced as *Tanakh* (see **"The Jewish Canon," p. xxi**):

- *T* stands for *Torah*, the first five books of the Bible.
- *N* stands for *Nevi'im* (Prophets). This second division has two subdivisions: Former Prophets and Latter Prophets.
- *K* stands for *Ketuvim* (Writings).

Early Christians read these books most often in an early Greek translation of the Hebrew Bible known as the Septuagint, which also contained additional books (see **"Introduction to the Deuterocanonical/ Apocryphal Books," p. 1333**; these books do not appear in editions of the Hebrew Bible today). The typical order of the books in the Greek tradition was different from Hebrew editions in some respects, and this fact, along with the influence of another alternative ordering found in the Latin translation of the Bible known as the Vulgate, impacted the ordering of the Christian canon. The arrangement of books used in *The Westminster Study Bible* follows the Protestant Christian tradition, which uses four categories derived from the earlier Greek and Latin orderings instead of the three categories of the Tanakh (see **"The Protestant Canon," p. xxii**):

- The Law, or Pentateuch
- The Historical Books
- The Poetic and Wisdom Books
- The Prophetic Books

The following essay introduces the contents of the Hebrew Bible, or Old Testament, using a modified order of the categories used in Judaism, each of which is followed by the corresponding canonical category in Protestant Christianity (wherever possible): Torah / Pentateuch, Former Prophets / Historical Books, Writings, and Latter Prophets / Prophetic Books. Since the Writings do not correspond as directly to the Poetic and Wisdom Books in Christianity, only the Jewish terminology is used (see **"Introduction to the Writings," pp. 6–9**). The decision to privilege the canonical categories used in Judaism in the introductory essay highlights the fact that these texts and subdivisions belonged first to the Jewish religious tradition.

Since *The Westminster Study Bible* follows the canonical order used in the Protestant tradition, a few of the biblical books are introduced in Jewish categories that differ from their placement in the Protestant ordering of the text (see **"Canonical Orders of the Books of the Bible," p. xxi**). For example, Daniel and Lamentations appear among the Prophets in the Christian tradition, but in the Jewish tradition, both of these compositions are placed in the Writings. In the essay that follows, these books are introduced as part of the Writings (see **"Introduction to the Writings," pp. 6–9**, and **"Introduction to the Latter Prophets / Prophetic Books," pp. 9–12**). Additionally, Ruth, 1 and 2 Chronicles, Ezra, Nehemiah, and Esther also occur in the Writings and so are introduced there; in the Christian tradition, these books occur in the Historical Books (see **"Introduction to the Writings," pp. 6–9**, and **"Introduction to the Former Prophets / Historical Books," pp. 4–6**). Beyond this introductory essay, more information on each biblical book can be found in its own introduction.

Readers should also take into account that the varying orders found in the Jewish and Christian traditions can impact the reading process differently. Putting the Prophets at the end of the Old Testament allows Christians to see them as pointing toward what comes to pass later, in the New Testament. It is

a small step, it seems, from Malachi's promise of Elijah's return (Mal. 4:5–6) to Gospel texts where John the Baptist is identified with Elijah (Matt. 11:14; 17:10–13; Mark 9:11–13; Luke 1:17) and where that same prophet appears with Jesus in the transfiguration (Matt. 17:3; Mark 9:4; Luke 9:30). The ending of the Hebrew Bible with the Writings, and specifically with 2 Chr. 36, creates a very different effect. The final words of the Hebrew Bible recount the edict of the Persian king Cyrus that allowed the Judean exiles to return home to Israel and rebuild the temple (2 Chr. 36:22–23). Rather than pointing forward to John the Baptist, this ending returns readers back to the heart of the Hebrew Bible and to the concepts of God's promised land, temple, and people.

By presenting the books of the Hebrew Bible in the four-part order commonly found in most English Bibles, while keying the introductions that follow to the tripartite Tanakh structure, *The Westminster Study Bible* hopes to help readers experience the richness of the Bible via two of its major traditional arrangements.

Introduction to the Torah/Pentateuch

The first five books of the Bible are frequently called the *Pentateuch*, a Greek term for a five-book collection (*pentateuchos*). The Hebrew name used for this same collection is *Torah*, a word that can mean "law" but also "instruction" or "teaching." Both terms, *Pentateuch* and *Torah*, aptly describe these five books, which contain legal material and also much that is not law but instructive nevertheless.

Origins of the Torah/Pentateuch
In many ways, modern academic study of the Bible begins with the Torah and a number of thorny interpretive problems that its five books present. Several of these problems concern the compositional history of the Pentateuch as a whole and also of its constituent books. Early tradition—beginning already in the Bible itself—associated this material with Moses. This makes good sense for a number of reasons. After God, Moses is the most important character in the Torah. He is born in Exod. 2 and dominates Pentateuchal narrative from that point forward until his death in Deut. 34. Despite his importance, premodern readers occasionally indicated that a single author for the entire Torah was unlikely. Parts of the Torah are written in very different styles than other parts, for example, with each one apparently reflecting different time periods and circumstances. As a result of such differences, modern scholars began to construct theories about the origin and authorship of the five books of the Torah.

Moses's importance cannot be overestimated, however, and plays a large role in the traditional association of the Torah with him. He is said to be God's servant, for example, which is a rare and exalted epithet (Exod. 14:31; Num. 12:8; Deut. 34:5; cf. Josh. 1:1–2, 13). It is also reported that the Lord spoke to Moses "face to face, as one speaks to a friend" (Exod. 33:11). Moses had unique access to God (Exod. 33:7–11) and was granted a rare vision of God (Exod. 33:12–34:7). Unsurprisingly, the Torah concludes with a remarkable commendation of him and his work: "Never since has there arisen a prophet in Israel like Moses, whom the Lord knew face to face. He was unequaled for all the signs and wonders that the Lord sent him to perform in the land of Egypt, against Pharaoh and all his servants and his entire land, and for all the mighty deeds and all the terrifying displays of power that Moses performed in the sight of all Israel" (Deut. 34:10–12). A few Pentateuchal texts also identify Moses as a literate individual, which was truly exceptional in the ancient world outside of specially trained scribes. The things Moses is said to have written down include divine laws (see Exod. 24:4; 34:27–28), narratives (see Exod. 17:14; Num. 33:2), some combination of those two things (see Deut. 31:9, 24), and even a song (Deut. 31:19, 22).

Texts like these, along with Moses's prominence in the Pentateuch, explain why early tradition ascribed the Torah to him. Outside the Pentateuch—indeed, already in Joshua (see Josh. 8:31–32; 23:6)—we encounter references to "the law of Moses" (see, e.g., 1 Kgs. 2:3; 2 Kgs. 14:6; 23:25; 2 Chr. 23:18; 30:16; Ezra 3:2; 7:6; Neh. 8:1; Dan. 9:11, 13) and "the book of Moses" (2 Chr. 25:4; cf. Mark 12:26). Even in the New Testament, texts from the Pentateuch can be referred to as "the law of Moses" (Luke 2:22; 24:44; John 7:23; Acts 13:39; 15:5; 28:23; 1 Cor. 9:9; Heb. 10:28). The New Testament also makes mention of Moses writing or giving the law (John 1:45; 7:19; Rom. 10:5). Indeed, the New Testament occasionally refers to the Torah's directives as simply "of Moses" or by stating that this or that matter was what Moses said,

taught, or commanded (Matt. 8:4; 19:7–8; 22:24; Mark 1:44; 7:10; 10:3–5; 12:19; Luke 5:14; 16:29, 31; 20:28; John 1:17; 5:46; 7:22; 8:5; Acts 3:22; 15:1; 26:22; Rom. 10:19). Given this biblical precedent, it is common even today to hear the Torah called the "Five Books of Moses" (cf. Mark 12:26; 2 Chr. 25:4). And yet, as already n oted, even in antiquity readers suspected that some of the passages found in the "Books of Moses" simply could not have been written by him. These would include the passage that praises him for his great humility (Num. 12:3) and the account of his death and burial (Deut. 34:5–6). Insights like these—coupled with different writing styles, distinctive vocabulary, duplicate narratives, and so forth—eventually led modern biblical scholars to posit not one but many authors for the Pentateuch as it now stands. Some interpreters would still attribute portions of the Torah to Moses or at least trace parts of it back to his time, but many would not, seeing the final form of the five books and the collection as a whole as the achievement of a much later period, the product of many hands, and the end result of a complex set of processes.

The first comprehensive theory about the composition of the Torah, set forth in the nineteenth century, is called the Documentary Hypothesis. For many years, this theory held sway; it posits that the Pentateuch is composed of four, originally discrete documents—each from a different time and author. This theory no longer commands the consensus it once did. While some scholars still hold to a version of it, others believe the Pentateuch is better understood as a kind of pastiche of large units of tradition that were only secondarily edited together. These units, like the four hypothetical strands of the Documentary Hypothesis, likely stem from diverse points of origin. Given the speculative nature of these types of analyses, still other interpreters choose to forgo inquiry into the compositional history of the Pentateuch altogether, focusing instead on the literary qualities of the books of the Torah in their current form. The questions surrounding the origin and development of the Pentateuch are deeply contested ones despite several hundred years of research, with scholars continuing to debate them to this day.

Narrative

Readers will encounter different kinds of literature in the Torah. The first to be encountered is *narrative*. The Torah opens with not one but two narratives about God's creation of the world (Gen. 1:1–2:4a; 2:4b–25). The existence of two different accounts of creation supports the idea that multiple hands lie behind the present text of Genesis. But these two stories also illustrate different narrative styles, quite apart from questions of composition. The first story is on the high end of the prose spectrum; some have called it Israel's poem of creation. The eloquence of Gen. 1 does not manifest many of the techniques that mark formal Hebrew poetry, however. Indeed, the brief poetic insert in Gen. 1:27 is instructive in revealing that the surrounding material is not poetry, in fact, but prose. The second creation story is less formal and more folksy, although it too contains a poetic insert in 2:23.

Most of Genesis is prose narrative, and the same holds true for the first half of Exodus. Beginning in earnest in Exod. 20, the Torah shifts to a different genre—that of *law*—but even then narrative continues to be found, peppered in throughout what follows, providing connective tissue and an overall narrative arc (e.g., Exod. 24:1–18; 32:1–35; 40:16–38). Leviticus follows Exodus and is dominated by law, but it too contains a narrative section regarding the ordination of Aaron and his sons to the priesthood (Lev. 8:1–10:19), which provides a link back and conclusion to Exod. 29:1–35. The book of Numbers contains a great deal of narrative material alongside some law, before Deuteronomy closes the Torah with a recapitulation of much of the narrative and law that has come before it. Deuteronomy contains the last words of Moses before Israel crosses into the land promised to the ancestors back in Genesis. In this way, from Genesis to Deuteronomy, the Torah presents a large narrative sweep from the creation of the world to the borders of Canaan.

Law

The Pentateuch's narrative arc is dominated by Israel's stay at Mount Sinai, the mountain of God. Israel remains at this mountain for most of the Pentateuch (Exod. 19:1–Num. 10:11), and it is here where Israel receives God's *law*—a second major genre that readers will encounter in the Torah.

While narrative provides the overarching framework of the Pentateuch, divine law is at its heart, and the heart of the law is the covenant at Sinai, beginning with the Ten Commandments (Exod. 20:1–17; repeated also in Deut. 5:6–21). Divine law begins earlier still, however: already in the opening creation accounts, God speaks in the imperative mood, issuing commandments—in other words, giving law (see

Gen. 1:22, 28; 2:16–17). In fact, in the Jewish tradition, Gen. 1:22 is considered the first commandment, with the total number of laws in the Torah coming in at 613.

Pentateuchal law is diverse, extensive, and complex. Scholars have identified no fewer than four distinct legal corpora in the Torah. In their presumed chronological order, these four bodies of law are the book of the covenant in Exod. 20:22–23:19, the central legal collection in Deuteronomy (chaps. 12–28), the Priestly legislation (found throughout Leviticus and Numbers), and the Holiness Code (Lev. 17–26). Various subtypes of law have also been identified. Some laws, like the Ten Commandments themselves, are absolute or apodictic: "You shall not steal" (Lev. 19:11). Other formulations are called casuistic or case law because they entertain different scenarios with different outcomes (e.g., Num. 35:16–28). Adding to the Torah's complexity, the legal materials exist in something of a symbiotic relationship with the surrounding and intervening narratives. The narratives help explain why Israel owes its allegiance and obedience to God—namely, because of God's love for the ancestors and God's deliverance of Israel from Egyptian slavery (see Deut. 4:37; 7:8). Motivations and explanations for law are unheard of in modern legislation but are prominent in the Bible—and not just in the narrative portions of the Torah, even within the laws themselves. An instructive example is Exod. 23:9: "You shall not oppress a resident alien; you know the heart of an alien, for you were aliens in the land of Egypt" (cf. Exod. 22:21; Lev. 19:34). Another instance is the way the Ten Commandments begin: "I am the Lord your God, who brought you out of the land of Egypt, out of the house of slavery" (Exod. 20:2).

Poetry

A final genre that appears in the Torah, but more sporadically, is poetry. As noted earlier, a few interpreters understand Gen. 1 as more poetry than prose, but the Torah contains a number of texts that indubitably qualify as instances of Hebrew poetry. Identifying a text as poetry depends on the presence of certain characteristics. These characteristics can appear in prose, too, but appear with particular density in poetic texts. In addition to Gen. 1:27 and 2:23, the NRSVue identifies the following texts of Genesis as poetry: 3:14–19; 4:23–24; 9:6, 25–27; 14:19–20; 16:11–12; 24:60; 25:23; 27:27–29, 39–40; 48:15–16, 20; 49:2–27. All these texts except for Gen. 49 are short poetic insets within larger narrative blocks. Genesis 49 is also an inset poem but is a very long one comprising Jacob's blessing of his sons, the twelve tribes of Israel. In addition to Gen. 49, the Torah has several other extended poems: Exod. 15 (the Song of the Sea), portions of Num. 23–24 (Balaam's oracles), Deut. 32 (the Song of Moses), and Deut. 33 (the Blessing of Moses). These longer compositions seem to be placed at key junctures in the narrative and at climactic points in their respective books and contain important information, whether of celebration, warning, or blessing. It is possible that these poems antedate the prose that currently surrounds them and that they once existed independently; whatever the case, the poems in the Pentateuch show that many genres are needed to adequately recount the long and complicated relationship of God and Israel as found in the Torah, with its fascinating weave of narrative, law, and poetry.

Brent A. Strawn

Introduction to the Former Prophets / Historical Books

The books of Joshua, Judges, 1–2 Samuel, and 1–2 Kings are known as the Former Prophets in the Jewish canon and as the Historical Books in the Christian canon. The Christian canon also includes Ruth, 1–2 Chronicles, Ezra, Nehemiah, and Esther as Historical Books; the Catholic Bible includes, in addition, Tobit, Judith, and 1–2 Maccabees. These books are considered historical in the Christian tradition because they describe events during the periods of the judges, the united and then divided monarchy (Israel and Judah), the exiles to Assyria and Babylon, and postexilic life during the Persian and Greek periods. The ancient view of history, however, is not the modern one, which engages with factual names, dates, and times in order to attempt to gain a better sense of what happened and why. Instead, events need not be factual to be historical in the ancient understanding, and a theological or social view of what happened can be considered a historical analysis of events.

Determining why the same books have different canonical titles in the Jewish and the Christian

traditions leads to the basic questions of who, what, when, where, and why regarding these books' writing and categorization. These questions will shape this introduction.

Who: The author (or authors) of the books is unknown. Samuel and Kings were originally one book respectively but were later divided into two. Whatever person or group put the books together used multiple sources, especially for 1–2 Kings, including the book of the Acts of Solomon (1 Kgs. 11:41), the book of the Annals of the Kings of Israel (1 Kgs. 14:19; 15:31; 16:5, 14, 20, 27; 22:39; 2 Kgs. 1:18; 10:34; 13:8, 12; 14:15, 28; 15:11, 15, 21, 26, 31), and the book of the Annals of the Kings of Judah (1 Kgs. 14:29; 15:23; 22:45; 2 Kgs. 8:23; 12:19; 14:18; 15:6; 16:19; 20:20; 21:17, 25; 23:28; 24:5). Other sources were used to recount stories about the prophets Elijah (1 Kgs. 17–21; 2 Kgs. 1–2), Elisha (2 Kgs. 2–9, 13), and Isaiah (2 Kgs. 18:1–20:19; see also Isa. 36:1–39:8). Additionally, the Former Prophets / Historical Books include songs (Judg. 5; 1 Sam. 2; 2 Sam. 22).

What: Joshua, Judges, 1–2 Samuel, and 1–2 Kings describe events from the conquest of Canaan to the fall of Judah in 587/586 BCE. They are often called the Deuteronomistic History because of their emphasis on Deuteronomy's theory of divine retribution, which argues that God always rewards obedience and punishes disobedience. Additionally, it is thought that the discovery of "the book of the law in the house of the LORD" (2 Kgs. 22:8) might have been an early version of Deuteronomy. The book of Ruth comes between Judges and 1 Samuel in the Christian canon; while Ruth gives the genealogy of David, the primary character from 1 Sam. 16 to 1 Kgs. 2, it does not have the same emphasis or style as the Deuteronomistic History. In the Jewish canon, it is part of the Writings and not the Former Prophets (see **"Introduction to the Writings," pp. 6–9**, for more on the book of Ruth).

In the book of Joshua, the people obey God's command to conquer the land and leave behind no idolaters; by the time of Judges, however, the people have become disobedient, indicative in their worship of other gods. This leads to a multigenerational cycle of enslavement, repentance for idolatry, deliverance from slavery by a judge, and peace. Perhaps giving the reader a clue to what will happen next, the book of Judges concludes any description of appalling behavior—including the gang rape and murder of a woman and the near extermination of the tribe of the rapists' origin—with the following phrase: "In those days there was no king in Israel; all the people did what was right in their own eyes" (Judg. 21:25; see also 17:6; 18:1; 19:1). The books of 1–2 Samuel describe the establishment of the monarchy through Saul and his ally (but later enemy) David as well as the establishment of Jerusalem as the kingdom's capital. At the beginning of 1 Kings, David's son Solomon inherits the throne and builds the First Temple. Due to his disobedience, however, the kingdom is divided between the north (Israel) under Jeroboam and the south (Judah) under Solomon's son Rehoboam. At that point, the narrative alternates between the political intrigues and theological failures of the north and south, with almost all kings classified as evil. According to these accounts, evil kings lead to the fall of Israel to Assyria in 722 BCE and the fall of Judah to Babylon in 587/586 BCE. The book of 2 Kings ends with the release of Judah's king Jehoiachin from a prison in Babylon, having been captured and exiled in 597 BCE as a consequence of an earlier rebellion.

In the Christian tradition, Joshua–2 Kings are considered Historical Books because of their emphasis on names, dates, and events. In the Jewish tradition, the books are part of the prophetic canon because of the appearance of prophets and the consistent warning that disobedience will lead to punishment. Notably, 1–2 Chronicles rewrites many of the stories found in the books of Samuel and Kings but with greater attention to the temple and no mention of King David's domestic troubles in 2 Sam. 11–20. The books of 1–2 Chronicles immediately follow 1–2 Kings in the Christian canon as Historical Books, along with Ezra, Nehemiah, and Esther in the Protestant canon, but none of these are considered prophetic in the Jewish canon. Instead, they are part of the Writings (see **"Introduction to the Writings," pp. 6–9**, for more on these books).

When: Based on their descriptions of exilic events (after 587/586 BCE), the books most likely took their final forms after the Babylonian exile ended in 539 BCE, even though they describe events from approximately the twelfth to the sixth century BCE. While the books are considered historical, the events described in Joshua–2 Samuel cannot be independently verified in other sources from the ancient Near East. Scholars debate, for example, whether there was a military conquest of Canaan

by Israelites or whether the Israelite tribes were already in the land. As a result, only 1–2 Kings can be considered historical in the modern sense of retelling events that took place, such as the building of the First Temple, the division of the land into Israel and Judah, and the conflicts between both kingdoms and neighboring countries like Aram. However, even events thought to be historical are described with theological language, which complicates assessing their historicity.

Where: All the events described take place in what is now the state of Israel, the West Bank, and Gaza, along with parts of Jordan, Lebanon, and Syria. According to the book of Joshua, parts of the tribes of Asher, Naphtali, and Dan settled in what is now Lebanon and Syria, while parts of Manasseh, Reuben, and Gad settled east of the Jordan River in what is now Jordan. After the kingdom divided, the only tribes in the south were Judah and Benjamin. When the north fell to Assyria in 722 BCE, many of the people were deported inland to other parts of the Assyrian Empire. When the south fell to Babylon in 587/586 BCE, many of its leading inhabitants were deported to Babylon, while mostly poor people remained in Judah according to the biblical text.

Why: The story of the settlement, rise, and fall of Israel is told primarily from a theological, not a political, perspective. From that perspective, both exiles happened because the people disobeyed God and worshiped other gods, committing idolatry (2 Kgs. 17, 21, 25), encouraged to do so by their kings, particularly Manasseh (2 Kgs. 21). The exceptions were Hezekiah and Josiah of Judah (2 Kgs. 18, 23). Politically, however, Israel and Judah were always vulnerable to stronger countries and empires. By the time Israel fell in 722 BCE, both Israel and Judah were Assyrian vassals, whose job was to provide financial tribute and obedience in exchange for political protection and limited independence. When Israel rebelled, Assyria responded by destroying it. The Assyrian Empire fell to Babylon in the late seventh century BCE, and soon thereafter Judah became a Babylonian vassal. Like Israel, Judah rebelled twice against Babylon, who responded with an initial exile of King Jehoiachin and other political and religious leaders in 597 BCE. A siege of Jerusalem and the destruction of the First Temple followed in 587/586 BCE. All these events are described through the Deuteronomic principle of divine retribution—if the people had obeyed God and listened to the prophets, God's messengers, disaster could have been avoided. Consequently, the books are both historical (a description of events from a particular perspective) and prophetic (the inclusion of the words of prophets that the exile was God's punishment).

In addition to the theme of divine retribution, readers should be alert to the violence in the texts, particularly against non-Israelites in Joshua, against worshipers of other deities in 1 Kings, and against women in Judges, 2 Samuel, and 2 Kings. In many cases, the violence against women leads to more violence. The texts are written from the perspective of men, and so the rape of Bathsheba, for example, is often miscategorized as adultery. Modern ideas of multiculturalism, religious tolerance, and gender equity are not ancient ones. The texts, however, are unsparing in their criticism of people's disobedience and yet end with the hope that even in exile, life could improve. They serve as a reminder of what happened and a reminder of what can happen if readers learn from the people's past mistakes.

Stacy Davis

Introduction to the Writings

The Writings (Heb. Ketuvim) is the third and final division of the Hebrew Bible as it is structured in Judaism. In Christian classification, the books that compose this section include Historical, Poetic, Wisdom, and Prophetic texts. It is a vast and variegated collection following no single coherent organizing principle. The three-part division of the Hebrew Bible and the variability of this third section may reflect how the canon was formed. The first five books (Heb. Torah) were held to be authoritative first, perhaps enshrined as canon as early as the Persian period (533–333 BCE)—hence the relative stability of the Pentateuch, the name for these five books in the Christian tradition. Next, the collection called the Prophets (Heb. Nevi'im), consisting of the Former Prophets

(Joshua, Judges, 1 and 2 Samuel, and 1 and 2 Kings) along with the Latter Prophets (Jeremiah, Isaiah, Ezekiel, and the Book of the Twelve), would have come together. Finally, other books were gathered in the Ketuvim, though what, exactly, constituted this section remained in flux until after the destruction of the Second Temple in 70 CE. This canonical trajectory was neither singular nor linear, however, and different communities not infrequently had different canons in terms of what books were included and also in terms of how those books were ordered. Some of these differences are reflected in the dissimilarities among the Jewish Bible, the Protestant Bible, and the Catholic Bible today.

For various reasons, some traditional and some the result of biblical scholarship, the books belonging to the Writings can be grouped in different ways. One is the large-scale division between poetry and prose. More specifically, at least three of the books are typically classified as Wisdom literature. Others are treated as Historical Books; Daniel is among the Prophets in Christian classification but labeled an apocalypse by biblical scholarship. In the Jewish canon, five books (Ruth, Song of Songs, Lamentations, Ecclesiastes, and Esther) that are read in their entirety on certain Jewish holidays are placed together and called the Megillot. Whatever the case, it is clear that, in many ways, the Writings is something of a "catchall" category into which everything that did not belong to the Torah or the Prophets found a home. Although some of the material contained in the Ketuvim may span hundreds of years of traditions (especially some of the psalms and proverbs), it is believed that most of the Ketuvim arose, or took final shape, in the Persian and Hellenistic periods (533–165 BCE).

In Jewish Bibles today, the ordering of the Ketuvim is as follows: Psalms, Proverbs, Job, the Megillot, Daniel, Ezra, Nehemiah, and 1–2 Chronicles. *The Westminster Study Bible* follows the Protestant ordering of the biblical books. Consequently, a reader will encounter the book of Ruth first, situated between Judges and 1 Samuel. After the Historical Books of Samuel and Kings (see **"Introduction to the Former Prophets / Historical Books," pp. 4–6**), a second collection of Historical Books (1 and 2 Chronicles, Ezra, Nehemiah, and Esther) recounts the history of Israel from Adam through the Persian period. Next, the reader will find the Poetic Books (Job, Psalms, Proverbs, Ecclesiastes, and Song of Songs), three of which (Job, Proverbs, and Ecclesiastes) are also classified as Wisdom literature. The Latter Prophets then begins (see **"Introduction to the Latter Prophets / Prophetic Books," pp. 9–12**), interrupted twice by books of the Ketuvim: Lamentations follows Jeremiah, and Daniel follows Ezekiel.

Prose Narratives: Story and History

In contrast to modern English prose, Hebrew prose is characterized by its terseness as well as its penchant for repetition, especially in vocabulary. Biblical characters are sketched succinctly and are rarely given backstories or internal lives. Plots are quick moving, and narrators are often tight lipped on matters of causation or on morals to be drawn from the stories. Description is only in service to advancing the plots; it is not to fill out readers' imaginations. Prose is well represented in the Writings. The framing narrative of Job is a prose short story; Ruth and Esther, too, are examples of this genre. The first six chapters of Daniel may be similarly classified but may also be seen as a collection of court tales, with the same true of Esther. These texts, like the story of Joseph in Gen. 37–50, recount the adventures of Israelite heroes in foreign courts.

Many of the prose narratives in the Ketuvim have historical themes or recount historical events. Whereas the book of Ruth is a fictional short story that belongs to the Megillot in the Hebrew canon, it also addresses the time of the judges and connects that period with the monarchy through a genealogy that runs from Ruth to King David. It is no doubt for these reasons that Ruth is placed between Judges and Samuel in the Greek Septuagint (a version of the Hebrew Bible translated for Greek-speaking Jews during the Hellenistic period), which governs the order reflected in Christian versions of the Old Testament. The books of Chronicles (divided into two parts, like the books of Samuel and Kings) retell the history of Israel from Adam to the end of the Babylonian exile, with a focus on the southern kingdom of Judah and its Davidic monarchy. Although not a work of pure fiction, Chronicles does creatively retell and reinterpret the history found in Samuel and Kings according to its own theological perspective. Ezra and Nehemiah pick up where Chronicles leaves off: with those who have returned from exile and who face new challenges as they try to rebuild Jerusalem. Esther, much like Ruth—and another one of the

Megillot—appears to be a piece of historical fiction set within a particular time period, addressing concerns of that time period if not also others.

Included with the prophetic corpus in the Christian ordering of the Old Testament, Daniel also reflects historical themes and is found in the Writings in the Hebrew Bible. The first section of Daniel, a collection of court tales, is situated in Babylon and addresses the real concerns and challenges of Jews living in diaspora even in much later periods. The book ends with an apocalypse that addresses, covertly, the period of Antiochus IV Epiphanes, a Hellenistic king (ca. 215–164 BCE). Because of the references to this much later, Hellenistic period, Daniel is typically dated to the middle of the second century BCE, during the time of the Maccabean Revolt. As such, it is the latest-written book in the Hebrew Bible canon.

Although these "Historical" books could be arranged in chronological order beginning with Ruth and ending with Daniel, they are instead grouped together and arranged according to other principles in both the Hebrew and the Greek Septuagint canons. Of particular note is the placement of the books of Chronicles. In the Greek ordering (ultimately adopted by Christians), 1 and 2 Chronicles immediately follow the books of Kings. However, in the Hebrew ordering (used in today's Jewish canon), not only does Chronicles conclude the Writings; it also ends the entire Jewish Bible. The final chapter, 2 Chr. 36, recounts the edict from King Cyrus of Persia by which he ends the Babylonian exile, allowing the Judean exiles to return home. The last verse is full of hopeful expectations for a rebuilt temple and a rebuilt Jerusalem. In words that have proven to reverberate throughout Jewish history, Cyrus's proclamation calls the exiled people of God back to Jerusalem. The final word of Cyrus's edict and thus the Hebrew Bible is "let them go up" (2 Chr. 36:23 CEB).

Poetry: Hymns and Songs

The bulk of the poetic material in the Hebrew Bible is found in the Writings. The book of Psalms is an anthology of sacred songs, often considered the hymnbook of the Second Temple period. Job combines poetry within a prose framework: it is a short story pulled apart into separate bookends by a significant portion of poetry within. Proverbs, Ecclesiastes, Lamentations, and Song of Songs are all poetic collections but of different kinds. Proverbs and Ecclesiastes reflect on the meaning of life and how to live it well; the poetry of Lamentations mourns the destruction of the First Temple; Song of Songs is a collection of love poetry.

Biblical poetry shares many of the features found in other poetries, including metaphor and symbolism, assonance and consonance. Producing phrases that are multivalent, evocative, and beautiful sounding is the goal of poets the world over. Unlike poetry in some other languages, however, biblical poetry does not rhyme, nor are there established patterns of rhythm and meter (except, perhaps, in a few cases). Instead, what scholars have called *parallelism* is the distinguishing characteristic of Hebrew poetry (see **"Hebrew Poetry," p. 741**).

Wisdom Literature

Proverbs, Job, and Ecclesiastes are typically grouped together as Wisdom literature, an academic classification that recognizes that these three books (along with the Wisdom of Solomon and the Wisdom of Ben Sira, also called Sirach or Ecclesiasticus, in the deuterocanonical/apocryphal literature) align in form and content with other writings from across the ancient Near East. This type of literature contains maxims about how to live and conduct oneself in the world, including ethics and social mores. It also reflects on the deeper meaning of life, drawing on observation and experience in coming to its conclusions and making its claims. Unlike other biblical books, Wisdom does not address central components of Israelite religion—there is little to no reference to other biblical figures (save Solomon in some cases), to the temple, or to temple worship, priests, or law. In this way, Wisdom materials give the impression of being more universal and international in scope as well as more "this-worldly." Although reflection on the nature of God and theological worldviews are present in Wisdom texts, they can sometimes fit oddly with or challenge other theological statements found in the Hebrew Bible.

Despite their similarities, there are some sharp distinctions among the three Wisdom Books that appear in the Hebrew Bible. Proverbs is not a single, coherent work but an anthology of sayings grounded in folk wisdom, based on the instruction parents give children. Some proverbs reflect a royal context, perhaps indicating an originating context and final audience of a professional class of

sages working in the palace. The theology of the book, regardless, is generally positive: if someone observes the order and structure of the universe and comports oneself accordingly, then they will prosper—defined as having wealth and a long life.

Job and Ecclesiastes also offer sayings based on the speaker's observations of the world, but both books reflect a mood that seems at profound odds with Proverbs' more optimistic tenor. In Job, the righteousness of the main character is initially rewarded. Job's unparalleled righteousness also leads to his suffering, however, because he becomes the focus of a supernatural wager between God and a heavenly adversary (called "the *satan*" in Hebrew). Job ends up expressing the view that any too-neat theology of retribution—that the good always prosper and the wicked always suffer— does not invariably hold true. Ecclesiastes has a similar perspective, also based on the teacher's experience of the world. In Job, God becomes an active partner in the dialogue (at least at the end); in Ecclesiastes, God remains distant and inscrutable.

Although the utility of "Wisdom literature" as a schema for classifying and understanding these three books has been called into question, it remains true that reading them together reveals important insights about the complexities of human life, even as these books also raise profound questions about suffering and evil in the world and the role of God therein.

Megillot
Each of the five Megillot plays an important role in Jewish liturgical practice, with each traditionally read in its entirety on a particular Jewish festival: Song of Songs is read on Passover, Ruth is read on Shavuot (the Feast of Weeks), Lamentations is read on Tisha B'Av (the ninth of the month of Av), Ecclesiastes is read on Sukkot (the Feast of Booths), and Esther is read on Purim. In some cases, the connection between the book and the holiday is obvious. Purim celebrates Esther's saving of the Jewish people in Persia after they were subjected to a genocidal decree. Tisha B'Av commemorates the date of the destruction of the First and Second Temples, with Lamentations describing and lamenting the destruction of the First. The links between the other three books and their holidays are less clear, however, and the lack of obvious connections opens up interpretive possibilities.

For example, Ecclesiastes is read during Sukkot, when Jews construct temporary outdoor struc- tures in which to dwell (Lev. 23:33–36; Deut. 16:13–15). In contemporary practice, these booths become gathering places for welcoming guests and eating meals. They provide spaces for reflecting on people's connections to and reliance on the natural world, the fragility and contingency of life. Read in this context, Ecclesiastes then underscores life's mysteries, the inevitability of death, and the idea that despite any homes we might have, people are spiritually just wandering in the wilderness in search of the promised land. Perhaps Ecclesiastes serves as a sober call to reflection amid the fes- tival, therefore. Alternatively, in its calls to enjoy life, especially in the moment, perhaps Ecclesiastes functions to underscore the joy, even if only temporary, of life, especially during celebrations. After all, Sukkot is also called "the season of our joy." Whatever the case, it seems that there is no one single way to connect this book to the holiday but several lively interpretive options.

Jennifer L. Koosed

Introduction to the Latter Prophets / Prophetic Books

The Phenomenon of Prophecy
The phenomenon of prophecy was widely attested in the ancient world. Early testimonies of proph- ecy in ancient West Asia come from as early as the third millennium BCE. At its most basic level, prophecy represented a type of intermediation in which the prophet acted as a messenger of a god or gods, communicating something from the divine realm to human beings, especially to kings. Broadly speaking, it was one form of ancient divination, which designated various methods, modes, and techniques of communication between the divine and human worlds. Some forms of divination required learning technical skills like reading animal entrails or bird flight patterns to discern divine intention, but prophecy relied on the idea of direct communication with gods and goddesses. Fur- thermore, because of their audiences, prophets were often associated with temples or the royal court.

Prophets and prophecy in the biblical tradition should be understood within this larger context. More than two dozen prophets appear in the Hebrew Bible, though there were presumably more than this in ancient Israel and Judah—the two kingdoms devoted to YHWH, divided after the reign of Solomon. The biblical text identifies prophets using a variety of terms, including *nabi'* and *nabi'ah* (one called), *ro'eh* (seer), *hozeh* (visionary, seer), and *'ish ha-elohim* (man of God). These designations all point to some element of the prophetic role as understood in the biblical period. The majority of prophets mentioned in the Hebrew Bible are men, but women also appear as important prophetic figures (e.g., Deborah, Huldah, Miriam). These men and women are presented as speaking on behalf of Israel's god, YHWH, to advise kings, priests, and others in matters political, social, economic, legal, and religious. Their messages could take the form of comfort or critique, though the latter far outweighs the former in the biblical prophets.

Prophecy was both an oral and a written phenomenon. Prophets delivered their oral messages in private or public settings, including the royal court, the temple, and homes. Some prophetic oracles were subsequently written, perhaps by the prophets themselves or, more likely, by their supporters (e.g., Isa. 8; Jer. 36). Preserving oral prophecies through the medium of writing represented a secondary stage in the transmission of prophecy. However, some prophetic material undoubtedly originated as written compositions. In the biblical tradition, the textualization of prophecy led to a unique feature of the genre as it is found in the Bible: the composition of books associated with fifteen named prophetic figures in the Jewish canon of the Bible (Isaiah, Jeremiah, Ezekiel, and the Book of the Twelve; the Christian Bible also includes Daniel and Lamentations—see **"Prophets in the Canon"** in this essay and **"Introduction to the Writings," pp. 6–9**, for more on these two books). These prophetic books contain edited collections of oracles, but they are much more than simply prophetic anthologies. Several of them also contain prose narratives featuring the prophets after whom they are named. Finally, many include textual additions added over an extended period that were intended to make the books meaningful to later audiences. As such, not everything in them should be understood as originating with the prophets whose names stand at the heads of the books. Later additions could be quite small (e.g., Amos 9:11–15) or entail the inclusion of large sections (e.g., Isa. 40–66). The precise compositional history of a given book can be difficult to determine, however. Thus, a process that likely began with the preservation of relatively brief prophetic oracles eventually became the written prophetic tradition found in the Bible today. This literature has a complex literary history that has given rise to composite literary creations shaped by particular theological interests.

Written prophecy as found in the Bible began to appear in the mid- to late eighth century BCE, though prophets were certainly part of ancient Israel's and Judah's religious and cultural lives before then. Though written prophecy is associated exclusively with male prophets, this should not be interpreted as implying the absence of female prophets. Later scribes have added superscriptions at the beginning of several prophetic books (e.g., Isa. 1:1; Hos. 1:1; Amos 1:1; etc.) linking them with 1–2 Kings, an attempt to situate these prophets in the theological histories of Israel and Judah. Amos, Hosea, Micah, and Isaiah were each active in the second half of the eighth century BCE, though each book contains material added in later periods. These decades witnessed the expansion of the Assyrian Empire into Southwest Asia, and the material from these prophets often reflects political, religious, social, and economic issues confronting Israel and Judah because of this imperial expansion. Amos and Hosea directed their words to the kingdom of Israel, while Isaiah and Micah concerned themselves largely with Judah. All four of these prophets simultaneously both assert that YHWH controls the Assyrians and argue for Israel's and Judah's culpability in the crises created by Assyria's expansion because of the two kingdoms' own sins.

The momentous events ushering in Babylonian domination in the late seventh and sixth centuries BCE prompted shorter prophetic books like Nahum, Zephaniah, Habakkuk, and Obadiah as well as the lengthier scrolls of Jeremiah and Ezekiel. The forced exile of elements of Judean society and Jerusalem's destruction, which included the temple of YHWH, prompted enormous political, social, and theological upheaval. Jeremiah argued that this crisis was the result of Judah having broken its covenant with YHWH. He also counseled Judean kings to capitulate to the Babylonians to preserve the state, but to no avail. Ezekiel was himself exiled to Babylon. His oracles emphasized that the destruction of Jerusalem and the temple was necessary because illicit actions had rendered them ritually (and morally) impure. A few decades later, the anonymous prophet of the exile whose words are found in Isa. 40–55 understood the rise of the Persian Empire and its defeat of the Babylonians

as taking place under YHWH's direction. The late sixth century and subsequent decades brought prophetic books such as Haggai, Zechariah, and Malachi as well as the last section of Isaiah (chaps. 56–66). These prophetic collections reveal early hope for the success of the restoration of Jerusalem and the rebuilding of the temple followed by deep disappointment over the restoration's failure to realize those early hopes. Finally, the lack of historical specificity in books like Joel and Jonah makes them difficult to situate historically, though many scholars date them to the postmonarchic period.

Interpreting Prophecy and Prophetic Books
Form
The Prophetic Books of the Hebrew Bible and Old Testament contain various types of literature. This includes prophetic oracles (often written as poetry), narratives, psalms, proverbs, and other literary forms. The most common of these are prophetic oracles, which often begin with "Thus says the Lord." Broadly speaking, two kinds of prophetic oracles appear: those of judgment and those of hope or salvation. The former announce condemnation for Israel, Judah, or others and assert they will be punished because of their sins. These oracles generally follow a similar pattern, which includes the reason for the judgment and a statement of condemnation (e.g., Amos 2:4–5; Ezek. 7:2–4). Several variations on this basic form exist, including "woe oracles," which begin with "Woe" or "Ah" in the NRSVue (e.g., Isa. 5:8–10), and covenant lawsuits, in which the prophet argues that the people have broken the covenant with YHWH (e.g., Jer. 2). "Oracles against the nations" deliver judgments against foreign nations (e.g., Isa. 13–23; Jer. 46–51; Ezek. 25–32; Amos 1:2–2:3). Oracles of hope or salvation express YHWH's comfort and consolation for the people, usually after calamity or crisis. These oracles are often thought to have followed words of judgment to express YHWH's continued commitment to Israel and Judah.

The Prophetic Books also contain narratives depicting the prophets interacting with kings and other leaders, facing persecution, and undertaking symbolic actions (e.g., Isa. 36–39; Jer. 26–45; Amos 7:10–17). The latter are communicated through symbolic action reports, which feature the prophets behaving in unusual ways to express God's judgment (e.g., Isa. 20:1–6; Hos. 1; 3). Vision reports feature the prophets receiving visual messages of some sort, generally followed by questions inquiring as to their meaning (e.g., Isa. 6; Zech. 1–6). Finally, nearly the entirety of the book of Jonah is a narrative depicting the prophet in conflict with God.

Style
Prophetic literature is written predominantly as poetry, printed in the NRSVue as verse, though in some prophetic books the line between poetry and prose is difficult to discern (e.g., Ezekiel). Structurally, classical Hebrew poetry was organized around parallelism, the repetition of similar or related words or lines (e.g., Isa. 1:10). The relationship between parallel words or lines varies but includes cases where they express similar ideas (e.g., Isa. 5:11) or opposite ideas (e.g., Isa. 54:7) or where the second line continues to develop the first (e.g., Isa. 5:2). Parallel lines could be organized into larger units called stanzas. In its use of poetry, prophecy shares literary qualities present in nonprophetic biblical books like Psalms, Job, and Proverbs.

Because they are poetry, prophetic oracles also rely on numerous literary devices, including repetition, wordplay, simile, metaphor, alliteration, hyperbole, and irony. Poetic imagery is especially important in extended metaphors, which were often drawn from Israel's social and political reality. For example, several prophets describe YHWH using masculine images like warrior, king, and father. Isaiah describes YHWH as a giant enthroned king whose robe fills the temple (Isa. 6:1) and who uses the earth as his footstool (Isa. 66:1), visually reinforcing notions of divine superiority. On the other hand, Jerusalem is described using feminine imagery frequently, including as a mother (e.g., Isa. 49:22–23; 54:1–4; 62:1–5). Prophets also assign symbolic names, including to children (e.g., Isa. 7:1–8:4; Hos. 1) and Jerusalem (e.g., Isa. 62:4, 12).

Prophets in the Canon
Both the Jewish and Christian Bibles include a section devoted to prophetic literature. In the Jewish canon of the Bible, the section known as the Prophets (Nevi'im) is the second of three divisions, following the Torah and preceding the Writings (Ketuvim). It is divided into two parts, the Former Prophets (Joshua, Judges, 1–2 Samuel, and 1–2 Kings) and the Latter Prophets (Isaiah, Jeremiah,

Ezekiel, and the Book of the Twelve). (For more on the Former Prophets, see **"Introduction to the Former Prophets / Historical Books," pp. 4–6**.) The Book of the Twelve was considered to be a single book, but it is actually composed of twelve smaller prophetic books that ancient scribes copied onto a single scroll: Hosea, Joel, Amos, Obadiah, Jonah, Micah, Nahum, Habakkuk, Zephaniah, Haggai, Zechariah, and Malachi. Editorial additions were inserted by scribes that linked these twelve books thematically and theologically.

In the Christian tradition, this section is known simply as the Prophetic Books and comes last in the organization of the canon of the Old Testament. Further, it is divided into two parts, the Major Prophets and the Minor Prophets. This division is based on the size of the books and does not refer to their relative importance. The Major Prophets includes Isaiah, Jeremiah, and Ezekiel, and the Minor Prophets identifies the same contents as the Book of the Twelve. Finally, the Christian tradition includes two books—Daniel and Lamentations—located in the Writings in the Jewish organization of the canon (see **"Introduction to the Writings," pp. 6–9**, for more on Daniel and Lamentations). The Roman Catholic Bible includes an additional book, Baruch, after Jeremiah. The Orthodox Christian Bible adds both Baruch and the Letter of Jeremiah. These two books are found in the Apocrypha in this edition of the Bible (see **"Introduction to the Deuterocanonical/Apocryphal Books," p. 1333**, for more on Baruch and the Letter of Jeremiah).

The order of the fifteen prophetic books named after prophets in the Jewish Bible (which excludes Daniel, Lamentations, Baruch, and the Letter of Jeremiah) has become standardized based on the medieval Hebrew Masoretic Text (MT). However, various sources reveal that the order of these books in the collection varied over time. In a rabbinic-era composition, Baba Batra 14b, Isaiah is placed after Ezekiel and before the Book of the Twelve. In the Greek translation known as the Septuagint, the Book of the Twelve appears to have been intentionally rearranged to place these books in their "correct" historical order. Nevertheless, the order found in the MT has been standard for centuries and follows its own historical logic organized around three "eras"—before the exile, during the exile, and after the exile. Isaiah and the Book of the Twelve focus on the first and third of these, since they contain materials dealing with preexilic and postexilic Israel and Judah. Jeremiah and Ezekiel are more narrowly focused on events related to Jerusalem's destruction and the early exilic period—that is, the second era—and so are placed between Isaiah and the Twelve. The inclusion of the book of Daniel after Ezekiel in the Christian Old Testament is based on the Greek order, which was influenced by the narrative portrayal of Daniel as one of the Jewish exiles in Babylon. Finally, the insertion of Lamentations after Jeremiah derived from the fact that it was thought to have been written by Jeremiah.

J. Todd Hibbard

GENESIS

Literary History and Growth

Two of the basic facts modern readers want to know about a text are when and where it was written. Indeed, in the contemporary world, it is hard to imagine a text lacking a precise time-date stamp with atomic-clock precision and location of origin verified by GPS. Not so in the ancient world. This feature is important to bear in mind when reading Genesis.

One thing it upends is our idea that Genesis is a book. That term comes with so many presuppositions that do not fit this text. It can be more helpful to think of it as a compilation or an anthology of stories woven together into a loose narrative chronology for audience convenience. Genesis is more a repository of things ancient people believed worth preserving over many generations than a single story conceived by a single mind, or even than a unified story envisioned by a group of minds working in conscious collaboration with one another.

The oldest stories in Genesis may have an oral history going back before 1000 BCE, and some of those stories may have first been committed into writing not long thereafter. It is impossible to know on the basis of the information available to us. Nevertheless, scholars continue to work carefully to identify what can be said about the times and places from which the stories originated. For instance, the similarity between the flood account in Gen. 6–9 and Mesopotamian stories has convinced scholars this material drew on Assyrian and Babylonian culture. That might have been possible across many centuries, however, meaning that any conclusion on their origin must remain tentative.

Where scholars are more confident is in placing a date by which the text we know as Genesis reached the form represented here. It is widely accepted this occurred by sometime in the fifth century BCE, a period when the Persian Empire controlled Israel, and a new temple in Jerusalem dedicated to YHWH stood in place of the first one.

Whereas the primeval history (Gen. 1–11) and the Abraham narrative (Gen. 12–25) appear to be collections of many shorter stories knit together over centuries, the Jacob and Joseph narratives (Gen. 26–50) exhibit a coherence and shape that suggest each was created as a piece of literature with a purposeful narrative arc. What remains under debate among scholars is how these three major sections of the book called Genesis found their way into the shape known to us. The broader import of such arguments is that this text is the product of protracted development (some signs of which are still visible) that underscores the significant and sustained efforts of generations of priests, scribes, and others willing to preserve them. Whatever one makes of these stories, one cannot deny they were greatly valued by generations of people in antiquity.

Furthermore, the book called Genesis was also integrated into the larger tradition known as the Torah or Pentateuch, the first five books of the Hebrew Bible or Old Testament. In this way, it became the opening act in an account of the origin and history of Israel prior to its establishment as a political entity in the Levant, itself a product of people collecting stories over centuries.

Authorship

While identifying a precise author for any of the texts in Genesis is impossible, this does not make it unique in the ancient world. Anonymous authorship was ubiquitous and hardly seemed to cause any issue in antiquity. And yet, there are some features of the unnamed authors of parts of Genesis one can specify.

A substantial number of stories in the book exhibit knowledge of and interest in the priestly world. Avoiding any role for sacrifice (preserved for the temple in Jerusalem), the use of the divine name YHWH (only revealed later to Moses; see **"God's Name," p. 89**), and a penchant for genealogy characterize these texts. Many theories have prevailed at one time or another about the other material in Genesis, but none has won the day. While it is clear these stories exhibit different interests and sensibilities than the Priestly ones, their origin remains elusive. One result of this feature is the prevalence of repetition in Genesis, which most often occurs when a Priestly version of a story and a non-Priestly version are both preserved. Frequently these stories occur one after another, creating a disorienting duplication for contemporary readers unaccustomed to this strategy.

History and Historicity

It is unavoidable to wonder whether anything that Genesis says reflects actual historical events. To answer that question one must, above all, note that the sort of modern historical documentation this question has in mind does not appear to have been a primary interest of any of the authors of this text. Rather, their desire was to preserve important ideas and to express theological views, something that seems to have been more significant to them than the contemporary wish they would have recorded events in the ancient equivalent of a newspaper account. Even so, place and personal names, the duration of lives and events, and attention to details of obvious historical import do figure regularly in these texts. While it is true that these stories bear a certain historical veracity in depicting life in ways that would have been familiar and believable to audiences in the first millennium BCE, it is equally true that attempts to use Genesis to confidently reconstruct historical events of the Bronze and Iron Ages misunderstand its nature. Genesis does not provide us with enough detail to make such reconstructions fully compelling.

Reading Guide

Despite its long and winding development, the form of Genesis has an easily identifiable two-part structure. It first provides a primeval history, then offers a narrative of the ancestors of Israel.

The primeval history comprises chaps. 1–11. Beginning with a dual account of the creation of the world (chaps. 1–3), it traces the growth of humanity with its accompanying increase of sin (chaps. 4–5), leading to God's decision to deal with this creeping iniquity through a catastrophic flood (chaps. 6–9). The result of the flood is a covenant between God and Noah never to allow such a catastrophe to ever again destroy humanity, which will now proceed from Noah's line. Humanity does not reform itself, however, epitomized in the Tower of Babel story. There, humanity's desire to seize divine prerogatives results in the confusion of their language by God, making such large-scale cooperation impossible ever again. A helpful way to remember the shape of this section is the schema of creation (chaps. 1–3), uncreation (chaps. 6–7), and re-creation (chaps. 8–11).

In the closing verses of chap. 11, the primeval history narrows its focus onto a single family from southern Mesopotamia. This family produces the ancestors of Israel, and so this account of its patriarchs and matriarchs is widely known as the ancestral narrative (chaps. 12–50). Most often, it is further divided into three parts, identified by the three patriarchs that dominate them: Abraham (chaps. 12–25), Jacob (chaps. 26–36), and Joseph (chaps. 37–50). Among the numerous themes that link these parts, two stand out: migration and the subversion of birth order (primogeniture). The centrality of migration to Genesis is often overlooked. Every major figure in the ancestral narrative not only migrates during their life but migrates involuntarily at least once. Their experiences of and responses to migration merit the reader's attention. Likewise, the repeated pattern, subverting custom, whereby the firstborn son does not become the primary heir of his father provides the central narrative tension of each story and can orient one throughout chaps. 12–50.

C. A. Strine

1 When God began to create[a] the heavens and the earth, [2]the earth was complete chaos, and darkness covered the face of the deep, while a wind from God[b] swept over the face of the waters. [3]Then God said, "Let there be light," and there was light. [4]And God saw that the light was good, and God separated the light from the darkness. [5]God called the light Day, and the darkness he called Night. And there was evening and there was morning, the first day.

[6] And God said, "Let there be a dome in the midst of the waters, and let it separate the waters from the waters." [7]So God made the dome and separated the waters that were under the dome from the waters that were above the dome. And it was so. [8]God called the dome Sky. And there was evening and there was morning, the second day.

[9] And God said, "Let the waters under the sky be gathered together into one place, and let the dry land appear." And it was so. [10]God called the dry land Earth, and the waters that were gathered together he called Seas. And God saw that it was good. [11]Then God said, "Let the earth put forth vegetation: plants yielding seed and fruit trees of every kind on earth that bear fruit with the seed in it." And it was so. [12]The earth brought forth vegetation: plants yielding seed of every kind and trees of every kind bearing fruit with the seed in it. And God saw that it was good. [13]And there was evening and there was morning, the third day.

[14] And God said, "Let there be lights in the dome of the sky to separate the day from the night, and let them be for signs and for seasons and for days and years, [15]and let them be lights in the dome of the sky to give light upon the earth." And it was so. [16]God made the two great lights—the greater light to rule the day and the lesser light to rule the night—and the stars. [17]God set them in the dome of the sky to give light upon the earth, [18]to rule over the day and over the night, and to separate the light from the darkness. And God saw that it was good. [19]And there was evening and there was morning, the fourth day.

[20] And God said, "Let the waters bring forth swarms of living creatures, and let birds fly above the earth across the dome of the sky." [21]So God created the great sea

a 1.1 Or *In the beginning God created*   b 1.2 Or *while the spirit of God* or *while a mighty wind*

1:1–2:4 This section recounts God creating in seven days. It is the first of two accounts of creation that open this book. **1:1** In some translations, the first verse of the Bible is read as a complete sentence that introduces the seven-day creation story to follow. The syntax seems modeled on other ancient Near Eastern creation stories, however, that also open with a temporal clause using "when." **1:2** The preexisting state of things when God begins to create is chaos. The totality is expressed here with the adjective *complete*; the intent of the text is to present a diametrically opposed state to what will exist at the end of this account of divinely ordered creation. A neutral emptiness, formless and void, is a state of disorder that carries aspects of danger and inhospitableness. A divine presence lurks within this chaotic sea. Whether it is a physical manifestation (wind) or a nonphysical one (spirit) remains a debate that goes far beyond how one translates the Hebrew word in question. The point of the statement is to specify that God was neither absent nor unaware of the state of things in this precreation stage. **1:3–5** God creates light but not the sun or moon, which come on day four. This light is of a different character and quality that is not described. The light is separable from the darkness nonetheless, and God produces this distinction to establish day and night. Theologically speaking, this establishes a new form of chronology: time, or at least a new way of reckoning with and speaking of it. **1:6–7** Now a *dome* is placed within the chaos to separate the tumultuous waters. The word translated as *dome* denotes a piece of metal, a sort of roof made from such metal being formed into a thin sheet. It causes the waters to divide into those above, which fall as rain, and those below, which rise as springs. **1:9–12** Day three focuses on what happens below the "dome" (1:7). Its waters gather, revealing dry land that generates plants and trees. At the end of this day, halfway through the process of creation, God has organized all visible space. It stands empty, so to speak, waiting for God to fill it with living creatures. That process occurs on days four to six, which parallel days one to three. **1:14–16** God creates the greater light and lesser light on the fourth day. The delay from the first day and the avoidance of the terms *sun* and *moon* likely reflect an avoidance of interpreting the sun and moon as divine beings to be worshiped. Common in the ancient Near East, sun and moon worship is condemned by various texts in the Hebrew Bible / Old Testament (e.g., Deut. 4:19). **1:20–22** In parallel with the creation of space on day two, the waters below the *dome* now fill up with creatures, and winged beings inhabit the open space above the waters. In other ancient

Going Deeper: Creation (Genesis 1)

The Bible begins with not one but two accounts of creation: Gen. 1:1–2:4a and 2:4b–25 (or 2:4b–3:24). Biblical scholars have long viewed these two divergent accounts as a problem to be solved in terms of the composition history of the Pentateuch (see **"Introduction to the Torah/Pentateuch," pp. 2–4**). According to some interpreters, the two accounts reflect two different authors or schools of thought separated by many years, perhaps even centuries. Others attempt to read the two accounts together: not by simple harmonization but by hearing them "in stereo," with both revealing different aspects of Israel's understanding of creation.

The Genesis stories are famous—perhaps because they come first—but other biblical texts also address the creation of the world, offering additional and different details. For example, unlike the peaceful creation by divine speech in Gen. 1, Ps. 74 presents God's creation as a combat with and divine victory over sea dragons. Psalm 104, by contrast, is more idyllic, with all creatures coming from God and awaiting divine sustenance. Proverbs 8:22–36 offers yet another perspective: it states that the first of God's creations was Wisdom (personified here as female) and that she was beside God "like a master worker" (v. 30; see NRSVue text note and **"Woman Wisdom (Proverbs)," p. 872**). The New Testament adds further to this roundtable discussion. John 1 asserts that it was the Word (*logos*), not Wisdom, that was present at creation, and that "all things came into being through him" (v. 3). For John, the Word is none other than Jesus Christ, the very Son of God (vv. 14–18). Colossians 1 mirrors both Proverbs and John by declaring that Christ is "the firstborn of all creation" in whom "all things in heaven and on earth were created" (vv. 15–16).

The details found in these accounts seem hopelessly contradictory in some ways, particularly on the method of creation: Did God create by speaking (Gen. 1) or by shaping (Gen. 2) or by fighting (Ps. 74)? Was Wisdom there to help (Prov. 8) or was it instead the Word (John 1)? While certain details regarding *how* God created vary, the biblical creation texts are altogether united in that God founded and established the world (Ps. 24:1–2). For Israel, it is *God and God alone* who creates, although exactly *how* that happened remains open to different understandings—a perspective shared by early Christian communities too (see **"The Bible, Science, and the Environment," pp. 2180–81**).

Brent A. Strawn

monsters and every living creature that moves, of every kind, with which the waters swarm and every winged bird of every kind. And God saw that it was good. [22]God blessed them, saying, "Be fruitful and multiply and fill the waters in the seas, and let birds multiply on the earth." [23]And there was evening and there was morning, the fifth day.

[24]And God said, "Let the earth bring forth living creatures of every kind: cattle and creeping things and wild animals of the earth of every kind." And it was so. [25]God made the wild animals of the earth of every kind and the cattle of every kind and everything that creeps upon the ground of every kind. And God saw that it was good.

[26]Then God said, "Let us make humans[c] in our image, according to our likeness, and let them have dominion over the fish of the sea and over the birds of the air and over the cattle and over all the wild animals of the earth[d] and over every creeping thing that creeps upon the earth."

[27] So God created humans[e] in his image,
    in the image of God he created them;[f]
    male and female he created them.

c 1.26 Heb *adam*   d 1.26 Syr: Heb *and over all the earth*
e 1.27 Heb *adam*   f 1.27 Heb *him*

creation stories, the deity must defeat a sea monster that symbolizes chaos, but not here. Rather, any such being is created by the deity, not a viable opponent to them (see **"Creation," p. 16**). These animals should *be fruitful and multiply* to ensure the world has its designated residents in perpetuity. **1:24** Population of the dry land from day three begins with land animals, who now accompany the vegetation from 1:11–12. **1:26–27** The clearly anticipated culmination arrives: humanity completes the installation of living beings on the dry land. The plural subject (*let us*) suggests God is speaking with the divine council, a concept well known in the ancient world. Verse 27 is clear that God alone retains the choice and power to create humans. Humans are made *in the image of God* (often referred to as the *imago Dei*, its Latin form). Very often, kings were described in this manner as a way of communicating their close relationship with the deity and their authority to act for the deity on earth. Applying that concept to humanity in general

²⁸God blessed them, and God said to them, "Be fruitful and multiply and fill the earth and subdue it and have dominion over the fish of the sea and over the birds of the air and over every living thing that moves upon the earth." ²⁹God said, "See, I have given you every plant yielding seed that is upon the face of all the earth and every tree with seed in its fruit; you shall have them for food. ³⁰And to every beast of the earth and to every bird of the air and to everything that creeps on the earth, everything that has the breath of life, I have given every green plant for food." And it was so. ³¹God saw everything that he had made, and indeed, it was very good. And there was evening and there was morning, the sixth day.

2 Thus the heavens and the earth were finished and all their multitude. ²On the sixthᵍ day God finished the work that he had done, and he rested on the seventh day from all the work that he had done. ³So God blessed the seventh day and hallowed it,

because on it God rested from all the work that he had done in creation.

4 These are the generations of the heavens and the earth when they were created.

In the day that the LORDᵇ God made the earth and the heavens, ⁵when no plant of the field was yet in the earth and no vegetation of the field had yet sprung up—for the LORD God had not caused it to rain upon the earth, and there was no one to till the ground, ⁶but a stream would rise from the earth and water the whole face of the ground—⁷then the LORD God formed man from the dust of the groundⁱ and breathed into his nostrils the breath of life, and the man became a living being. ⁸And the LORD God planted a garden in Eden, in the east, and there he put the man whom he had formed. ⁹Out of the ground the LORD God made to grow every tree that is pleasant to the sight and good for food, the tree of life also in the

g 2.2 Sam Gk Syr: MT *seventh*   h 2.4 Heb *YHWH*, as in other places where "LORD" is spelled with capital letters (see also Ex 3.14–15 with notes)   i 2.7 In Heb the word for *ground* resembles the word for *man*

is democratizing, perhaps reflecting discomfort with royal prerogative or abuse of power. **1:28–29** Like the other creatures, humanity is to perpetuate itself and even increase in number. Unlike other creatures, they are given authority. First, they are to subdue the earth; this task parallels God's work to organize chaos described in this account. It is not warrant for environmental carelessness—indeed, most now see this mandate requiring the exact opposite by making humanity responsible for the care of creation (see **"The Bible, Science, and the Environment," pp. 2180–81**). Second, humans receive dominion, but this authority is restricted to the other created beings that populate the world. It is now often noted that such dominion is balanced with a command for humans to eat only seed and fruit, leaving the plants for other animals. Genesis will later revise this command (see 9:1–5), so the primary message seems to be one of harmony between humans and animals that provides for their mutual flourishing. **2:2–3** The activity of creating ends on the sixth day, but the absence of work on the seventh day is no less crucial to this account. Rather, God's rest confers blessing on the day (*hallowed it*) and communicates its perfect consummation. The divine act of rest becomes the model for human rest, which Judaism enshrined in Shabbat (the Sabbath). Indeed, 2:1–3 begins the Jewish liturgy for Shabbat, and that may have already been true in antiquity. **2:4a** This formula recurs throughout Genesis. These refrains, introduced with the Hebrew "toledot" (*generations*), reflect one way ancient communities divided this lengthy text into sections long before chapter and verse divisions were added to the biblical text in the medieval period.

2:4b–25 This second account of creation depicts God making humans from the dust of the earth and placing them in the garden of Eden. It should be read as a companion to the first creation account, exhibiting some areas of agreement with it and some areas of divergence. **2:5–6** The second creation account immediately reveals a different understanding of events. Rather than dry land with vegetation emerging as soon as possible, as in the first creation story, in this second account, the land stood without such growth for some time. The different order of events becomes all the more clear in v. 7, when humanity is created before all other living things. **2:7** Whereas the prior creation account concludes with God creating humanity via simple verbal order, here God creates a single person first and does so in a gritty, hands-on, personal manner from the dust of the uncovered ground. The first account is often said to reflect God's transcendence and omnipotence; this one, divine immanence and desire for relationship with human beings. **2:8–9** Eden comes from a word having to do with fertility, thus its suitability for a garden's name. Readers often overlook that Eden is only a part of creation, and it seems a small part based on the description. Amid the garden are two trees: one offering life (a common

midst of the garden, and the tree of the knowledge of good and evil.

10 A river flows out of Eden to water the garden, and from there it divides and becomes four branches. ¹¹The name of the first is Pishon; it is the one that flows around the whole land of Havilah, where there is gold, ¹²and the gold of that land is good; bdellium and onyx stone are there. ¹³The name of the second river is Gihon; it is the one that flows around the whole land of Cush. ¹⁴The name of the third river is Tigris, which flows east of Assyria. And the fourth river is the Euphrates.

15 The LORD God took the man and put him in the garden of Eden to till it and keep it. ¹⁶And the LORD God commanded the man, "You may freely eat of every tree of the garden, ¹⁷but of the tree of the knowledge of good and evil you shall not eat, for in the day that you eat of it you shall die."

18 Then the LORD God said, "It is not good that the man should be alone; I will make him a helper as his partner." ¹⁹So out of the ground the LORD God formed every animal of the field and every bird of the air and brought them to the man to see what he would call them, and whatever the man called every living creature, that was its name. ²⁰The man gave names to all cattle and to the birds of the air and to every animal of the field, but for the man^j there was not found a helper as his partner. ²¹So the LORD God caused a deep sleep to fall upon the man, and he slept; then he took one of his ribs and closed up its place with flesh. ²²And the rib that the LORD God had taken from the man he made into a woman and brought her to the man. ²³Then the man said,

"This at last is bone of my bones
    and flesh of my flesh;
this one shall be called Woman,
    for out of Man this one was taken."

²⁴Therefore a man leaves his father and his mother and clings to his wife, and they become one flesh. ²⁵And the man and his wife were both naked and were not ashamed.

3 Now the serpent was more crafty than any other wild animal that the LORD God had made. He said to the woman, "Did God say, 'You shall not eat from any tree in the garden'?" ²The woman said to the serpent, "We may eat of the fruit of the trees in the garden, ³but God said, 'You shall not eat of the fruit of the tree that is in the middle of the garden, nor shall you touch it, or you shall die.'" ⁴But the serpent said to the woman, "You will not die, ⁵for God knows that when you eat of it your eyes will be opened, and you will be like God,^k knowing

j 2.20 Or for Adam   k 3.5 Or gods

image in the ancient Near East) and one offering moral knowledge (uncommon by comparison). **2:10–14** The location of the garden is cryptic at best. The Pishon is unknown; the Gihon, a modest spring in Jerusalem. The Tigris and Euphrates are major rivers in Mesopotamia, a great distance from Jerusalem. If a real, physical location was ever in view, it is impossible to reconstruct it from this description. The point seems to be to portray a land with all the resources needed for life. **2:15–17** God assigns the first person—not yet differentiated in terms of sex, despite the translation (see v. 23)—the role of farmer. This individual is to care for the garden, perhaps in lieu of the deity doing it. There are other ancient creation accounts where humans provide this sort of labor for a deity. In order to sustain this work, the first human is allowed to eat the garden's produce but not from the tree of the knowledge of good and evil. **2:20** God determines that the first person requires a partner; it is not good to be alone. God creates every living creature in an effort to find that helper, but to no avail. What sounds like a failure according to the first creation account is clearly believed to reveal diligence and power in the second one. **2:21–23** God determines that an acceptable partner must be of the same species. Rather than working with dust, this time God creates with a human bone. From this skeletal plank, God fashions a second person. Here in vv. 22–23, a clear distinction between the sexes appears: the first person will be called *man* ("ish"), with the person made from the man's rib called *woman* ("ishah").

2:25–3:1 The humans are naked (Heb. "arummmim") without any concern. This likely connotes both moral innocence and a sense of ignorance. The serpent is crafty or shrewd (Heb. "arum").

3:2–6 The serpent questions God's intentions regarding the prohibition of eating from the special tree. The woman's answer adds to the divine command because there is no prior mention of touching the tree. (Though according to chap. 2, the woman was not yet created when God gave the mandate to the first human.) The serpent then accuses God of dishonesty over the consequences. The serpent's argument, combining falsehood and truth, persuades the woman. She eats the fruit, and she gives some to the man, who was apparently there the entire time. He, too, eats of it—evidently willingly.

good and evil." ⁶So when the woman saw that the tree was good for food and that it was a delight to the eyes and that the tree was to be desired to make one wise, she took of its fruit and ate, and she also gave some to her husband, who was with her, and he ate. ⁷Then the eyes of both were opened, and they knew that they were naked, and they sewed fig leaves together and made loincloths for themselves.

8 They heard the sound of the Lord God walking in the garden at the time of the evening breeze, and the man and his wife hid themselves from the presence of the Lord God among the trees of the garden. ⁹But the Lord God called to the man and said to him, "Where are you?" ¹⁰He said, "I heard the sound of you in the garden, and I was afraid, because I was naked, and I hid myself." ¹¹He said, "Who told you that you were naked? Have you eaten from the tree of which I commanded you not to eat?" ¹²The man said, "The woman whom you gave to be with me, she gave me fruit from the tree, and I ate." ¹³Then the Lord God said to the woman, "What is this that you have done?" The woman said, "The serpent tricked me, and I ate." ¹⁴The Lord God said to the serpent,

"Because you have done this,
    cursed are you among all animals
    and among all wild creatures;
upon your belly you shall go,
    and dust you shall eat
    all the days of your life.
¹⁵ I will put enmity between you and the
        woman
    and between your offspring and
        hers;

he will strike your head,
    and you will strike his heel."
¹⁶To the woman he said,
"I will make your pangs in childbirth
        exceedingly great;
    in pain you shall bring forth children,
yet your desire shall be for your
        husband,
    and he shall rule over you."
¹⁷And to the man¹ he said,
"Because you have listened to the voice
        of your wife
    and have eaten of the tree
about which I commanded you,
    'You shall not eat of it,'
cursed is the ground because of you;
    in toil you shall eat of it all the days of
        your life;
¹⁸thorns and thistles it shall bring forth for
        you;
    and you shall eat the plants of the
        field.
¹⁹By the sweat of your face
    you shall eat bread
until you return to the ground,
    for out of it you were taken;
you are dust,
    and to dust you shall return."

20 The man named his wife Eveᵐ because she was the mother of all living. ²¹And the Lord God made garments of skins for the manⁿ and for his wife and clothed them.

22 Then the Lord God said, "See, the humans have become like one of us, knowing

l 3.17 Or *to Adam*   *m* 3.20 In Heb *Eve* resembles the word for *living*   *n* 3.21 Or *for Adam*

3:14–15 The first consequence (or curse) of the humans' disobedience to God's command falls upon the serpent. Although the text makes no association with the serpent and a supernatural, demonic being, the conflict announced here informs later ideas about Satan (the devil).

3:16 The second consequence falls upon the woman. The text explains a familiar phenomenon (etiology) related to one of humanity's assigned roles: to be fruitful and multiply. The curse is gendered, but it is also one that makes all human relationships harder.

3:17–18 The third consequence is directed toward the man. His work to till and to keep the land (2:15) shall now be complicated because God will make the ground less hospitable for the task. Again, the curse is directed toward the man but confounds an aim given to all humanity.

3:19 Finally, God declares that all humans shall die. In comparable ancient creation accounts, human disobedience thwarts the offer of immortality set before them by a deity. This theme may be taken over from such accounts, then adapted to the particular context of this story.

3:21 In some interpretations, God's act of clothing the now self-conscious and ashamed humans is taken as a model for ethical behavior. Others have associated this with the origin of animal sacrifices to God, believing the life of an animal would be required to make such *skins*. The text nowhere indicates that an animal was killed, however. Quite to the contrary, God is able to create at will.

3:22–24 Banishing the humans so they might not achieve immortality gives further weight to the notion that this widely known ancient idea influenced the shape of this story (see v. 19). The placement

good and evil, and now they might reach out their hands and take also from the tree of life and eat and live forever"—[23]therefore the Lord God sent them forth from the garden of Eden, to till the ground from which they were taken. [24]He drove out the humans, and at the east of the garden of Eden he placed the cherubim and a sword flaming and turning to guard the way to the tree of life.

[4] Now the man knew his wife Eve, and she conceived and bore Cain,[o] saying, "I have produced a man with the help of the Lord." [2]Next she bore his brother Abel. Now Abel was a keeper of sheep, and Cain a tiller of the ground. [3]In the course of time Cain brought to the Lord an offering of the fruit of the ground, [4]and Abel for his part brought of the firstlings of his flock, their fat portions. And the Lord had regard for Abel and his offering, [5]but for Cain and his offering he had no regard. So Cain was very angry, and his countenance fell. [6]The Lord said to Cain, "Why are you angry, and why has your countenance fallen? [7]If you do well, will you not be accepted? And if you do not do well, sin is lurking at the door; its desire is for you, but you must master it."

8 Cain said to his brother Abel, "Let us go out to the field."[p] And when they were in the field, Cain rose up against his brother Abel and killed him. [9]Then the Lord said to Cain, "Where is your brother Abel?" He said, "I do not know; am I my brother's keeper?" [10]And the Lord said, "What have you done? Listen, your brother's blood is crying out to me from the ground! [11]And now you are cursed from the ground, which has opened its mouth to receive your brother's blood from your hand. [12]When you till the ground, it will no longer yield to you its strength; you will be a fugitive and a wanderer on the earth." [13]Cain said to the Lord, "My punishment is greater than I can bear! [14]Today you have driven me away from the soil, and I shall be hidden from your face; I shall be a fugitive and a wanderer on the earth, and anyone who meets me may kill me." [15]Then the Lord said to him, "Not so![q] Whoever kills Cain will suffer a seven-fold vengeance." And the Lord put a mark on Cain, so that no one who came upon him would kill him. [16]Then Cain went away from the presence of the Lord and settled in the land of Nod,[r] east of Eden.

17 Cain knew his wife, and she conceived and bore Enoch, and he built a city and named it Enoch after his son Enoch. [18]To Enoch was born Irad, and Irad was the father of Mehujael, and Mehujael the father of Methushael, and Methushael the father of Lamech. [19]Lamech took two wives; the name of the one was Adah, and the name of the other Zillah. [20]Adah bore Jabal; he was the ancestor of those who live in tents and have livestock. [21]His brother's name was Jubal; he was the ancestor of all those who play the lyre and pipe. [22]Zillah bore Tubal-cain, who made all kinds of bronze and iron tools. The sister of Tubal-cain was Naamah.

o 4.1 In Heb *Cain* resembles the word for *produced*
p 4.8 Sam Gk Syr Vg: MT lacks *Let us go out to the field*
q 4.15 Gk Syr Vg: Heb *Therefore*   r 4.16 That is, *wandering*

---

of cherubim—supernatural beings that protect sacred items and places—makes the garden a prohibited place and implies this is because of a special divine presence there.

4:1–16 This is the famous story of Cain and Abel and how their enmity results in the first murder. **4:3–5** It is unclear why God accepts Abel's offering and not Cain's. Perhaps the narrative sees a difference between the value in the *fat portions* Abel brings and the *fruit of the ground* Cain dedicates. **4:7** The Hebrew of this verse is notoriously difficult, and scholars disagree over its precise meaning. The main point is not actually in contention: either Cain resolves himself to divine choice—whether it makes sense to him or not—or the temptation of disobedience to God, with its negative consequences, lies in wait. To that extent, the verse echoes the story of Eve and Adam in the garden. **4:9** This verse has produced one of the most familiar ideas in English speech on ethics and community cohesion. It is another echo of the garden, resembling Adam's dissembling response to God's inquiry about eating the fruit of the tree. In point of fact, humans do not "keep" other persons as a regular practice, but God does (Ps. 121:3–5). Cain's technically correct comment urges God to care for Abel. **4:11–15** Throughout the ancient Near East and elsewhere in the Old Testament, murder elicits capital punishment. Here, God spares Cain's life and protects it from others who might kill him (vv. 14–15), opting for a punishment that evokes the curse placed on Adam in Gen. 3.

4:17–22 The point of this genealogy is to explain the origins of urban life versus those of rural life. Such explanations are known across the ancient world, and this likely draws on such larger ideas.

23 Lamech said to his wives:
"Adah and Zillah, hear my voice;
    you wives of Lamech, listen to what
        I say:
I have killed a man for wounding me,
    a young man for striking me.
24If Cain is avenged sevenfold,
    truly Lamech seventy-sevenfold."

25 Adam knew his wife again, and she bore a son and named him Seth,ˢ for she said, "God has appointed for me another child instead of Abel, because Cain killed him." 26To Seth also a son was born, and he named him Enosh. At that time people began to invoke the name of the Lord.

5 This is the list of the descendants of Adam. When God created humans,ᵗ he made themᵘ in the likeness of God. 2Male and female he created them, and he blessed them and called them humansᵛ when they were created.

3 When Adam had lived one hundred thirty years, he became the father of a son in his likeness, according to his image, and named him Seth. 4The days of Adam after he became the father of Seth were eight hundred years, and he had other sons and daughters. 5Thus all the days that Adam lived were nine hundred thirty years, and he died.

6 When Seth had lived one hundred five years, he became the father of Enosh. 7Seth lived after the birth of Enosh eight hundred seven years and had other sons and daughters.

8Thus all the days of Seth were nine hundred twelve years, and he died.

9 When Enosh had lived ninety years, he became the father of Kenan. 10Enosh lived after the birth of Kenan eight hundred fifteen years and had other sons and daughters. 11Thus all the days of Enosh were nine hundred five years, and he died.

12 When Kenan had lived seventy years, he became the father of Mahalalel. 13Kenan lived after the birth of Mahalalel eight hundred and forty years and had other sons and daughters. 14Thus all the days of Kenan were nine hundred and ten years, and he died.

15 When Mahalalel had lived sixty-five years, he became the father of Jared. 16Mahalalel lived after the birth of Jared eight hundred thirty years and had other sons and daughters. 17Thus all the days of Mahalalel were eight hundred ninety-five years, and he died.

18 When Jared had lived one hundred sixty-two years he became the father of Enoch. 19Jared lived after the birth of Enoch eight hundred years and had other sons and daughters. 20Thus all the days of Jared were nine hundred sixty-two years, and he died.

21 When Enoch had lived sixty-five years, he became the father of Methuselah. 22Enoch walked with God after the birth of Methuselah three hundred years and had other sons and daughters. 23Thus all the days of Enoch

s 4.25 In Heb *Seth* resembles the word for *appointed*
t 5.1 Heb *adam*   u 5.1 Heb *him*   v 5.2 Heb *adam*

4:23–24 Lamech's poem depicts a growing role of violence in the line of Cain and even a sort of revelry in it. This sentiment likely anticipates the indictment of human behavior that features in the flood narrative of chaps. 6–9.

4:26 This verse specifies the purported time when people began to seek YHWH, the patron deity of the people of Israel and Judah. The divine name is never spoken in contemporary Judaism but, when found in the text, is replaced by "Adonai," Hebrew for "Lord." Thus, in English translation, YHWH is represented by the special form Lord (see **"God's Name," p. 89**).

5:1–2 This account of Adam's descendants starts with the generation formula (Heb. "toledot"), marking the beginning of a new section in the story (see note at 2:4a). The language employs the imagery of Gen. 1, speaking of humans as made in God's likeness. This marks a break from Gen. 4, which connects with the second creation account rather than the first. The combined evidence of repeated material with different language has convinced many that Gen. 5 belongs with the first creation story (see **"Introduction to the Torah/Pentateuch," pp. 2–4**).

5:3–8 This genealogy implicitly shows a preference for the line of Seth, the child who replaces Abel. It is through Seth, not Cain, that God will continue God's work in creation.

5:9–20 These long lifetimes are probably predicated on an ancient idea that one thousand years symbolized immortality. As the patriarchs' lives shorten and draw further away from one thousand years, the sense is of growing distance from that ideal.

5:21–24 Enoch is the seventh of ten generations, occupying a special place in the genealogy. His 365 years may be associated with a solar cycle. The meaning of *walked with God* is unspecified, but it

were three hundred sixty-five years. [24]Enoch walked with God; then he was no more, because God took him.

25 When Methuselah had lived one hundred eighty-seven years, he became the father of Lamech. [26]Methuselah lived after the birth of Lamech seven hundred eighty-two years and had other sons and daughters. [27]Thus all the days of Methuselah were nine hundred sixty-nine years, and he died.

28 When Lamech had lived one hundred eighty-two years, he became the father of a son; [29]he named him Noah, saying, "Out of the ground that the LORD has cursed this one shall bring us relief from our work and from the toil of our hands." [30]Lamech lived after the birth of Noah five hundred ninety-five years and had other sons and daughters. [31]Thus all the days of Lamech were seven hundred seventy-seven years, and he died.

32 After Noah was five hundred years old, Noah became the father of Shem, Ham, and Japheth.

6 When people began to multiply on the face of the ground, and daughters were born to them, [2]the sons of God saw that they were fair, and they took wives for themselves of all that they chose. [3]Then the LORD said, "My spirit shall not abide[w] in mortals forever, for they are flesh; their days shall be one hundred twenty years." [4]The Nephilim were on the earth in those days—and also afterward—when the sons of God went in to the daughters of humans, who bore children to them. These were the heroes that were of old, warriors of renown.

5 The LORD saw that the wickedness of humans was great in the earth and that every inclination of the thoughts of their hearts was only evil continually. [6]And the LORD was sorry that he had made humans on the earth, and it grieved him to his heart. [7]So the LORD said, "I will blot out from the earth the humans I have created—people together with animals and creeping things and birds of the air—for I am sorry that I have made them." [8]But Noah found favor in the sight of the LORD.

9 These are the descendants of Noah. Noah was a righteous man, blameless in his generation; Noah walked with God. [10]And Noah had three sons: Shem, Ham, and Japheth.

11 Now the earth was corrupt in God's sight, and the earth was filled with violence. [12]And God saw that the earth was corrupt, for all flesh had corrupted its ways upon the earth. [13]And God said to Noah, "I have determined to make an end of all flesh, for the earth is filled with violence because of them; now I am going to destroy them along with the earth. [14]Make yourself an ark of cypress[x] wood; make rooms in the ark, and cover it inside and out with pitch. [15]This is how you are to make it: the length of the ark three hundred cubits, its width fifty cubits, and its height thirty cubits. [16]Make a roof[y] for the ark, and finish it to a cubit above, and put the door of

w 6.3 Meaning of Heb uncertain   x 6.14 Meaning of Heb uncertain   y 6.16 Or *window*

suggests a level of obedience and intimacy beyond normal. The strong sense of v. 24 is that Enoch does not die—similar to Elijah (cf. 2 Kgs. 2:11–12).

5:29 Noah's special role is specified by explaining his name with an etiology. The explanation recalls both the creation of the first human (2:7) and the curse on Adam (3:17–19). The story frames him as a redeemer from his first appearance.

6:1–9:17 In these three chapters, one finds the well-known flood story in which Noah is selected by God to continue the human race after a catastrophic flood designed to cleanse the world of increasing disobedience to God. The text as it stands is a product of two originally independent flood stories that have been interwoven with each other. This can make it difficult to follow.

6:1–4 This unit speaks of supernatural figures in the form of the children of God, or Nephilim (cf. Num. 13:31–33), mating with human women to produce renowned warriors.

6:5–8 In Gen. 1, God "saw" creation and called it good; now God sees what creation has become and feels remorse. The result is God's resolution to eradicate humanity, save Noah.

6:9 Noah's righteousness contrasts with humanity's wickedness. Like Enoch before (5:21–23), Noah walks with God. This verse also repeats the generation formula, indicating that ancient scribes saw this as the beginning of a new section.

6:14–16 The word for ark appears only here and in the story of Moses's mother setting him out on the Nile (Exod. 2:3). This ark has similarities to boats used to transit the rivers of Mesopotamia but is described as a massive, windowless box.

Focus On: Covenant (Genesis 6)

Covenant is the word used to describe the formal relationship between God and a number of uniquely selected individuals or groups in the Bible. There are at least five distinct covenants in the Bible: the Noachic, the Abrahamic, the Davidic, the Sinaitic, and the New Covenant.

The first covenant is with Noah and his family to save them on the ark (Gen. 6:18). After the flood, this covenant is extended when God promises to never again flood the earth, a promise symbolized by the rainbow (Gen. 9:8–17). Because Noah is the ancestor of all postflood peoples, the Noachic covenant is with everyone everywhere. The Abrahamic covenant, by way of contrast, is focused on one couple and their offspring who become the nation of Israel. God calls Abram (later renamed Abraham) in Gen. 12:1–4 and promises him progeny and posterity; these promises include the gift of land in Gen. 15, formalized with a sacrifice. In Gen. 17, the Abrahamic covenant is further solemnized by the rite of circumcision, the "sign of the covenant" (17:11). The Davidic covenant concerns the Israelite monarchy and is recounted in 2 Sam. 7. There, instead of David building a house (temple) for the Lord, God promises to build David a house—that is, a dynasty—that "shall be established forever" (2 Sam. 7:16).

The preceding covenants are unconditional, though the Davidic covenant mentions divine punishment in the case of wrongdoing (2 Sam. 7:14), and it is revised—made more conditional—after David's adultery with Bathsheba and the murder of Uriah (2 Sam. 12:7–14). Also conditional is the Sinaitic covenant, which is introduced in Exod. 19:1–6 with an *if-then* construction: *If* Israel will obey the Torah (law or instruction; see **"Law/Decalogue," p. 112**), *then* it will be God's "treasured possession" (v. 5). God can also fail to uphold the covenant: Ps. 89, for example, complains of God's "renouncing" the Davidic covenant (see vv. 19–45).

The title "New Testament" comes from the Latin translation of "New Covenant." At the last supper, in language likely influenced by Jer. 31:31–34, Jesus speaks of "the new covenant in my blood" (Luke 22:20; cf. 1 Cor. 11:25). The New Testament devotes considerable attention to this new covenant and what it means vis-à-vis the first covenant (or "Old Testament"), especially once the Gentiles are included among God's covenant partners (see, e.g., Rom. 9–11; 2 Cor. 3:6; Heb. 8:8–9:28; 12:24)—a situation that recalls the Noachic covenant (cf. Isa. 2:2–4; 19:23–25; Ps. 87).

Brent A. Strawn

the ark in its side; make it with lower, second, and third decks. [17]For my part, I am going to bring a flood of waters on the earth, to destroy from under heaven all flesh in which is the breath of life; everything that is on the earth shall die. [18]But I will establish my covenant with you, and you shall come into the ark, you, your sons, your wife, and your sons' wives with you. [19]And of every living thing, of all flesh, you shall bring two of every kind into the ark, to keep them alive with you; they shall be male and female. [20]Of the birds according to their kinds and of the animals according to their kinds, of every creeping thing of the ground according to its kind, two of every kind shall come in to you, to keep them alive. [21]Also take with you every kind of food that is eaten, and store it up, and it shall serve as food for you and for them." [22]Noah did this; he did all that God commanded him.

7 Then the LORD said to Noah, "Go into the ark, you and all your household, for I have seen that you alone are righteous before me in this generation. [2]Take with you seven pairs of all clean animals, the male and its

6:17 Stories of catastrophic floods are known the world over. In Mesopotamia, such legends predate Genesis by hundreds of years. Particularly close is the *Gilgamesh Epic* tablet 11—so much so that this is often taken as the most obvious case of biblical dependence on cuneiform literature.

6:18 This is the first mention of the key concept of covenant between God and humanity in Genesis (see **"Covenant (Genesis 6)," p. 23**). God will establish covenants with Noah and Abraham. The covenant with Noah is centered on the commitment by God never to annihilate humans and animals in this way again.

6:19–20 The underlying logic of pairs for future repopulation is clear. It contrasts with 7:2, which distinguishes between clean and unclean animals, requiring seven pairs of the clean animals. The seven pairs allow Noah to sacrifice some of the clean animals but still ultimately preserve their existence. Since sacrifice is a feature of the Priestly texts, the divergent details suggest two separate stories have been woven together. (See **"The Bible and Methods," p. 2148**.)

mate; and a pair of the animals that are not clean, the male and its mate; [3]and seven pairs of the birds of the air also, male and female, to keep their kind alive on the face of all the earth. [4]For in seven days I will send rain on the earth for forty days and forty nights, and every living thing that I have made I will blot out from the face of the ground." [5]And Noah did all that the Lord had commanded him.

6 Noah was six hundred years old when the flood of waters came on the earth. [7]And Noah with his sons and his wife and his sons' wives went into the ark to escape the waters of the flood. [8]Of clean animals and of animals that are not clean and of birds and of everything that creeps on the ground, [9]two and two, male and female, went into the ark with Noah, as God had commanded Noah. [10]And after seven days the waters of the flood came on the earth.

11 In the six hundredth year of Noah's life, in the second month, on the seventeenth day of the month, on that day all the fountains of the great deep burst forth, and the windows of the heavens were opened. [12]The rain fell on the earth forty days and forty nights. [13]On the very same day Noah with his sons, Shem and Ham and Japheth, and Noah's wife and the three wives of his sons entered the ark, [14]they and every wild animal of every kind and all domestic animals of every kind and every creeping thing that creeps on the earth and every bird of every kind.[z] [15]They went into the ark with Noah, two and two of all flesh in which there was the breath of life. [16]And those that entered, male and female of all flesh, went in as God had commanded him, and the Lord shut him in.

17 The flood continued forty days on the earth, and the waters increased and bore up the ark, and it rose high above the earth. [18]The waters swelled and increased greatly

on the earth, and the ark floated on the face of the waters. [19]The waters swelled so mightily on the earth that all the high mountains under the whole heaven were covered; [20]the waters swelled above the mountains, covering them fifteen cubits deep. [21]And all flesh died that moved on the earth, birds, domestic animals, wild animals, all swarming creatures that swarm on the earth, and all human beings; [22]everything on dry land in whose nostrils was the breath of life died. [23]He blotted out every living thing that was on the face of the ground, human beings and animals and creeping things and birds of the air; they were blotted out from the earth. Only Noah was left and those with him in the ark. [24]And the waters swelled on the earth for one hundred fifty days.

8 But God remembered Noah and all the wild animals and all the domestic animals that were with him in the ark. And God made a wind blow over the earth, and the waters subsided; [2]the fountains of the deep and the windows of the heavens were closed, the rain from the heavens was restrained, [3]and the waters gradually receded from the earth. At the end of one hundred fifty days the waters had abated, [4]and in the seventh month, on the seventeenth day of the month, the ark came to rest on the mountains of Ararat. [5]The waters continued to abate until the tenth month; in the tenth month, on the first day of the month, the tops of the mountains appeared.

6 At the end of forty days Noah opened the window of the ark that he had made [7]and sent out the raven, and it went to and fro until the waters were dried up from the earth. [8]Then he

z 7.14 Gk: Heb adds *every bird, every winged creature*

7:4–5 The numbers seven and forty draw on their symbolic values of perfection (seven) and fullness or completeness (forty). In the perfect amount of time, God will allow it to rain until the waters completely flood the earth.

7:11 When God created the world in chap. 1, chaotic waters were split into those above and below. When the flood undoes that creation, the waters rush forth from above and below, allowing the chaos back into existence, albeit for a confined period of time. The situation is reversed in 8:2.

7:24 In another sign that two originally separate, parallel stories coexist, the 150 days of flood in this verse contrast with the forty days and nights of v. 17.

8:4 The mountains of Ararat are an area in ancient Urartu known for its hilly terrain, not a single peak. Contrary to attempts to "find the ark," this biblical detail does not offer sufficient information to identify a precise location; rather, it reflects the general idea that the ark would come to rest on a high point of land as the waters receded.

8:6–12 The technique of testing for dry land with flying creatures occurs in the older, Mesopotamian

sent out the dove from him to see if the waters had subsided from the face of the ground, [9]but the dove found no place to set its foot, and it returned to him to the ark, for the waters were still on the face of the whole earth. So he put out his hand and took it and brought it into the ark with him. [10]He waited another seven days, and again he sent out the dove from the ark, [11]and the dove came back to him in the evening, and there in its beak was a freshly plucked olive leaf; so Noah knew that the waters had subsided from the earth. [12]Then he waited another seven days and sent out the dove, and it did not return to him any more.

[13] In the six hundred first year, in the first month, on the first day of the month, the waters were dried up from the earth, and Noah removed the covering of the ark and looked and saw that the face of the ground was drying. [14]In the second month, on the twenty-seventh day of the month, the earth was dry. [15]Then God said to Noah, [16]"Go out of the ark, you and your wife and your sons and your sons' wives with you. [17]Bring out with you every living thing that is with you of all flesh—birds and animals and every creeping thing that creeps on the earth—so that they may abound on the earth and be fruitful and multiply on the earth." [18]So Noah went out with his sons and his wife and his sons' wives. [19]And every animal, every creeping thing, and every bird, everything that moves on the earth, went out of the ark by families.

[20] Then Noah built an altar to the LORD and took of every clean animal and of every clean bird and offered burnt offerings on the altar. [21]And when the LORD smelled the pleasing odor, the LORD said in his heart, "I will never again curse the ground because of humans, for the inclination of the human heart is evil from youth; nor will I ever again destroy every living creature as I have done. [22]As long as the earth endures,

> seedtime and harvest, cold and heat,
> summer and winter, day and night
> shall not cease."

9 God blessed Noah and his sons and said to them, "Be fruitful and multiply and fill the earth. [2]The fear and dread of you shall rest on every animal of the earth and on every bird of the air, on everything that creeps on the ground and on all the fish of the sea; into your hand they are delivered. [3]Every moving thing that lives shall be food for you, and just as I gave you the green plants, I give you everything. [4]Only, you shall not eat flesh with its life, that is, its blood. [5]For your own lifeblood I will surely require a reckoning: from every animal I will require it and from human beings, each one for the blood of another, I will require a reckoning for human life.
[6]Whoever sheds the blood of a human,

> by a human shall that person's blood
> be shed,
> for in his own image
> God made humans.

[7]"And you, be fruitful and multiply, abound on the earth and have dominion over[a] it."

[8] Then God said to Noah and to his sons with him, [9]"As for me, I am establishing my

a 9.7 Gk mss: Heb *multiply in*

versions of the flood. The association of a dove with an olive branch of peace may have connections to this feature.

8:13 Although the Jewish tradition now places the beginning of its year in the autumn (known as Rosh Hashanah), at some time in antiquity Israel celebrated a spring new year (two weeks before Passover begins). The flood account works with this latter understanding.

8:20–22 Across the ancient world, it was customary to offer a sacrifice in thanks to divine protection as Noah does here. Likewise, the image of a deity smelling a pleasing odor and responding with further blessing occurs across the ancient Near East. The Lord responds with a promise about the enduring stability of the natural world and ecosystem.

9:1 The commission to humans in 1:28 is reiterated here. The divine project of 1:1–2:4a begins anew.

9:2–3 Whereas humans are originally given only seeds and fruit to eat (1:29), now all animals and plants are designated as food for them.

9:4–6 Now God specifies the punishment for murder: a life for a human life.

9:8–17 The covenant promised in 6:18 is now established between God and Noah. Noah represents all humanity (v. 9) and all living creatures (v. 10). God commits never to allow another annihilating flood. God selects a sign of the covenant: the rainbow, associated with the end of a great rainstorm, will hark back to this commitment. The sign may be for God's remembrance as much as humanity's.

Reading through Time: The Curse of Canaan (Genesis 9)

Genesis 9:18–27 describes Noah's intoxication and the response of his three sons. Ham reports to his brothers, Shem and Japheth, that Noah is drunk and has passed out naked. These brothers cover their father without looking at him and, when Noah awakes, he blesses them. In sharp contrast, Ham's son Canaan is cursed to be his uncles' slave. This strange passage appears intended to explain animosity between Israelites and Canaanites, but Canaan plays no role in the story and is not mentioned at all until Noah's curse.

In the history of Christian interpretation, the curse of Canaan came to be applied to anyone seen as an enemy worthy of enslavement and condemnation. This was facilitated in part by the multiple senses of Scripture, in which interpreters could read a text in its "plain sense" (the literal sense) but also in other ways that permitted the substitution of different characters for the original ones (the figural sense). In the figural interpretation of St. Augustine (354–430 CE), the Canaanites were identified with the Jewish people, who were condemned to slavery because they had not accepted Jesus. This reading waned in the Middle Ages, when Christians reemphasized the plain sense and engaged with Jewish interpretations that resisted equating the Jewish people with slavery. In the sixteenth century, anti-Jewish readings of the text shifted to anti-African readings. This shift was facilitated by an argument that the curse should apply to Ham, not Canaan, and therefore also to Africans, since, according to the genealogy of Gen. 10, Ham is the father of the African peoples. By the nineteenth century, the use of "the curse of Ham" as divine justification for African slavery was the most common interpretation of the passage in the United States, with its supporters arguing that it was both obvious and correct. Abolitionists disagreed strongly, though theirs was the minority position. (See **"The Bible, Race, and Ethnicity," pp. 2163–64.**)

The use of this text in anti-Jewish and anti-African ways demonstrates, historically, that those in power may interpret a text in ways that denigrate other people and consider them to be inferior. There is a warning here: interpretation is always a product of texts *and* their interpreters (and these interpreters' environments). Racist readings of the curse of Canaan would not have occurred without preexisting cultural biases that were incorporated into these interpretations, often without question or textual warrant.

Stacy Davis

covenant with you and your descendants after you [10]and with every living creature that is with you, the birds, the domestic animals, and every animal of the earth with you, as many as came out of the ark.[b] [11]I establish my covenant with you, that never again shall all flesh be cut off by the waters of a flood, and never again shall there be a flood to destroy the earth." [12]God said, "This is the sign of the covenant that I make between me and you and every living creature that is with you, for all future generations: [13]I have set my bow in the clouds, and it shall be a sign of the covenant between me and the earth. [14]When I bring clouds over the earth and the bow is seen in the clouds, [15]I will remember my covenant that is between me and you and every living creature of all flesh, and the waters shall never again become a flood to destroy all flesh. [16]When the bow is in the clouds, I will see it and remember the everlasting covenant between God and every living creature

of all flesh that is on the earth." [17]God said to Noah, "This is the sign of the covenant that I have established between me and all flesh that is on the earth."

18 The sons of Noah who went out of the ark were Shem, Ham, and Japheth. Ham was the father of Canaan. [19]These three were the sons of Noah, and from these the whole earth was peopled.

20 Noah, a man of the soil, was the first to plant a vineyard. [21]He drank some of the wine and became drunk, and he lay uncovered in his tent. [22]And Ham, the father of Canaan, saw the nakedness of his father and told his two brothers outside. [23]Then Shem and Japheth took a garment, laid it on both their shoulders, and walked backward and covered the nakedness of their father; their faces were turned away, and they did not see their father's nakedness. [24]When Noah awoke

[b] 9.10 Gk: Heb adds *every animal of the earth*

9:20–23 This short story reads like a cautionary tale. Noah unwisely consumes too much wine, and Ham unwisely gazes at his father. This story gives some indication of the cultural norms of the time but is far from clear.

from his wine and knew what his youngest son had done to him, [25]he said,

> "Cursed be Canaan;
>   lowest of slaves shall he be to his
>   brothers."

[26]He also said,

> "Blessed by the LORD my God be Shem,
>   and let Canaan be his slave.
> [27] May God make space for Japheth,[c]
>   and let him live in the tents of Shem,
>   and let Canaan be his slave."

[28] After the flood Noah lived three hundred fifty years. [29]All the days of Noah were nine hundred fifty years, and he died.

10 These are the descendants of Noah's sons, Shem, Ham, and Japheth; children were born to them after the flood.

[2] The descendants of Japheth: Gomer, Magog, Madai, Javan, Tubal, Meshech, and Tiras. [3]The descendants of Gomer: Ashkenaz, Riphath, and Togarmah. [4]The descendants of Javan: Elishah, Tarshish, Kittim, and Rodanim.[d] [5]From these the coastland peoples spread. These are the descendants of Japheth[e] in their lands, with their own language, by their families, in their nations.

[6] The descendants of Ham: Cush, Egypt, Put, and Canaan. [7]The descendants of Cush: Seba, Havilah, Sabtah, Raamah, and Sabteca. The descendants of Raamah: Sheba and Dedan. [8]Cush became the father of Nimrod; he was the first on earth to become a mighty warrior. [9]He was a mighty hunter before the LORD; therefore it is said, "Like Nimrod a mighty hunter before the LORD." [10]The beginning of his kingdom was Babel, Erech, Akkad, and Calneh in the land of Shinar. [11]From that land he went into Assyria and built Nineveh, Rehoboth-ir, Calah, and [12]Resen between Nineveh and Calah; that is the great city. [13]Egypt became the father of Ludim, Anamim, Lehabim, Naphtuhim, [14]Pathrusim, Casluhim, from whom the Philistines come, and Caphtorim.

[15] Canaan became the father of Sidon, his firstborn, and Heth [16]and the Jebusites, the Amorites, the Girgashites, [17]the Hivites, the Arkites, the Sinites, [18]the Arvadites, the Zemarites, and the Hamathites. Afterward the families of the Canaanites spread abroad. [19]And the territory of the Canaanites extended from Sidon in the direction of Gerar as far as Gaza and in the direction of Sodom, Gomorrah, Admah, and Zeboiim as far as Lasha. [20]These are the descendants of Ham, by their families, their languages, their lands, and their nations.

[21] To Shem also, the father of all the children of Eber, the elder brother of Japheth, children were born. [22]The descendants of Shem: Elam, Asshur, Arpachshad, Lud, and Aram. [23]The descendants of Aram: Uz, Hul, Gether, and Mash. [24]Arpachshad became the father of Shelah, and Shelah became the father of Eber. [25]To Eber were born two sons: the name of the one was Peleg,[f] for in his days the earth was divided, and his brother's name was Joktan. [26]Joktan became the father of Almodad, Sheleph, Hazarmaveth, Jerah, [27]Hadoram, Uzal, Diklah, [28]Obal, Abimael, Sheba, [29]Ophir, Havilah, and Jobab; all these were the descendants of Joktan. [30]The territory in which they lived extended from Mesha

c 9.27 In Heb *Japheth* resembles the verb for *make space*
d 10.4 Heb mss Sam Gk: MT *Dodanim*   e 10.5 Heb lacks
These are the descendants of Japheth   f 10.25 That is, *division*

9:25–27 The tale allows the author a chance to justify a contemporary phenomenon: enslavement of Canaanites. The Canaanites—an ethnic group similar to but distinguished from the Israelites, who lived in the same area—were viewed as subservient on the basis of this misdeed by their eponymous ancestor (see **"Curse of Canaan," p. 26**).

10:2–5 These descendants of Japheth occupy the areas known as Anatolia (perhaps leading up into the Balkans) and the northern reaches of Mesopotamia.

10:6–20 The descendants of Ham reside in north Africa, appearing to be connected with the reaches of Egyptian power in the late Bronze and early Iron Ages. Among them is Canaan, whose descendants reside in the area associated with Israel and Judah throughout the Old Testament. The overlap between the names of ancestors and later states reflects a tendency in Genesis to link those two things. Political connections are often imagined to be the result of the "family" connections between such states—though it is also true that some fierce rivalries between states are found within these "family" relationships.

10:21 The descendants of Shem live on the Arabian peninsula and the southern regions of Mesopotamia. It is from this line that Abraham, and thus Israel, will eventually emerge (11:10–30). Note how this embeds the need for a migration from southern Mesopotamia to the Levant for their ancestors to arrive in the audience's homeland long before Abraham's actual journey appears in the story (12:1–9).

in the direction of Sephar, the hill country of the east. [31]These are the descendants of Shem, by their families, their languages, their lands, and their nations.

32 These are the families of Noah's sons, according to their genealogies, in their nations, and from these the nations spread abroad on the earth after the flood.

11 Now the whole earth had one language and the same words. [2]And as they migrated from the east,[g] they came upon a plain in the land of Shinar and settled there. [3]And they said to one another, "Come, let us make bricks and fire them thoroughly." And they had brick for stone and bitumen for mortar. [4]Then they said, "Come, let us build ourselves a city and a tower with its top in the heavens, and let us make a name for ourselves; otherwise we shall be scattered abroad upon the face of the whole earth." [5]The LORD came down to see the city and the tower, which mortals had built. [6]And the LORD said, "Look, they are one people, and they have all one language, and this is only the beginning of what they will do; nothing that they propose to do will now be impossible for them. [7]Come, let us go down and confuse their language there, so that they will not understand one another's speech." [8]So the LORD scattered them abroad from there over the face of all the earth, and they left off building the city. [9]Therefore it was called Babel,[b] because there the LORD confused the language of all the earth, and from there the LORD scattered them abroad over the face of all the earth.

10 These are the descendants of Shem. When Shem was one hundred years old, he became the father of Arpachshad two years after the flood, [11]and Shem lived after the birth of Arpachshad five hundred years and had other sons and daughters.

12 When Arpachshad had lived thirty-five years, he became the father of Shelah, [13]and Arpachshad lived after the birth of Shelah four hundred three years and had other sons and daughters.

14 When Shelah had lived thirty years, he became the father of Eber, [15]and Shelah lived after the birth of Eber four hundred three years and had other sons and daughters.

16 When Eber had lived thirty-four years, he became the father of Peleg, [17]and Eber lived after the birth of Peleg four hundred thirty years and had other sons and daughters.

18 When Peleg had lived thirty years, he became the father of Reu, [19]and Peleg lived after the birth of Reu two hundred nine years and had other sons and daughters.

20 When Reu had lived thirty-two years, he became the father of Serug, [21]and Reu lived after the birth of Serug two hundred seven years and had other sons and daughters.

22 When Serug had lived thirty years, he became the father of Nahor, [23]and Serug lived after the birth of Nahor two hundred years and had other sons and daughters.

24 When Nahor had lived twenty-nine years, he became the father of Terah, [25]and Nahor lived after the birth of Terah one

g 11.2 Or *migrated eastward*   b 11.9 In Heb *Babel* is a play on the verb meaning *to confuse*

10:32 The genealogy reflects Noah's success in accomplishing the mandate to be fruitful and multiply. It describes the known world of the audience as fully populated.
11:1–9 The Tower of Babel story is one of the most well known in the whole Old Testament. Its brevity leaves many details unclear. As a result, many details have been introduced by later interpreters of the story. An example is the famous painting of the story by Pieter Bruegel the Elder (1563). **11:2** The people migrate from the east because they are coming from the garden in Eden, which is located "in the east" (2:8). **11:4** The desire of the people to *make a name* for themselves introduces the central issue of the story. The people seem to want to acquire high status similar to kings, who represent the deity on earth. Some interpreters thus see the core issue to be whether humans can become godlike. Others disagree, since the humans also seem to express a fear of being scattered. **11:5** A subtle but cutting indictment of the humans: they build the highest tower they can, and yet the Lord must still come down to see it. **11:6–7** Similar to the episode in the garden of Eden, the potential for human wrongdoing prompts God to act. The plural in v. 7 suggests the divine council, just as in 1:26.
11:10–28 A ten-generation genealogy from Shem to Abram provides a quick narrative transition from the primeval story to the ancestral narrative that will focus on the patriarchs and matriarchs of Israel. The ten generations of this genealogy recall the same span of generations as Gen. 5. Both depict a substantial passage of time that indicates a move from one era of history to another.

hundred nineteen years and had other sons and daughters.

26 When Terah had lived seventy years, he became the father of Abram, Nahor, and Haran.

27 Now these are the descendants of Terah. Terah was the father of Abram, Nahor, and Haran, and Haran was the father of Lot. [28]Haran died before his father Terah in the land of his birth, in Ur of the Chaldeans. [29]Abram and Nahor took wives; the name of Abram's wife was Sarai, and the name of Nahor's wife was Milcah. She was the daughter of Haran the father of Milcah and Iscah. [30]Now Sarai was barren; she had no child.

31 Terah took his son Abram and his grandson Lot son of Haran and his daughter-in-law Sarai, his son Abram's wife, and they went out together from Ur of the Chaldeans to go into the land of Canaan, but when they came to Haran, they settled there. [32]The days of Terah were two hundred five years, and Terah died in Haran.

12 Now the LORD said to Abram, "Go from your country and your kindred and your father's house to the land that I will show you. [2]I will make of you a great nation, and I will bless you and make your name great, so that you will be a blessing. [3]I will bless those who bless you, and the one who curses you I will curse, and in you all the families of the earth shall be blessed."[i]

4 So Abram went, as the LORD had told him, and Lot went with him. Abram was seventy-five years old when he departed from Haran. [5]Abram took his wife Sarai and his brother's son Lot and all the possessions that they had gathered and the persons whom they had acquired in Haran, and they set forth to go to the land of Canaan. When they had come to the land of Canaan, [6]Abram passed through the land to the place at Shechem, to the oak[j] of Moreh. At that time the Canaanites were in the land. [7]Then the LORD appeared to Abram and said, "To your offspring I will give this land." So he built there an altar to the LORD, who had appeared to him. [8]From there he moved on to the hill country on the east of Bethel and pitched his tent, with Bethel on the west and Ai on the east, and there he built an altar to the LORD and invoked the name of the LORD. [9]And Abram journeyed on by stages toward the Negeb.

10 Now there was a famine in the land. So Abram went down to Egypt to reside there as an alien, for the famine was severe in the land.

i 12.3 Or *by you all the families of the earth shall bless themselves*
j 12.6 Or *terebinth*

11:29–30 Abram and his brother Nahor both marry, so readers are now introduced to Sarai. Whereas Nahor's wife, Milcah, is given a family history, Sarai is not. Rather, Sarai is only said to be infertile, emphasizing the importance of this detail by omitting any other information about her.
11:31 From Ur, in the southern part of Mesopotamia near the Persian Gulf, Terah takes his family, save Nahor, to Haran. The text connects that location with Terah's deceased son, but it probably originates from an Akkadian word meaning "main road." The sense is thus of a town on a major travel route from Mesopotamia to the west. This supports views locating the place in southern Anatolia along the busiest roads connecting Egypt with Mesopotamia.
12:1–9 Often known as the Call of Abraham, this text depicts God's command for Abram to migrate and to make his way to a heretofore unknown place in which he should settle. This is the first indication of how crucial migration will be to Abram and Sarai's story. **12:2** Contrary to the human desire to make a name for itself with the Tower of Babel, here God decides to make a human's name great. The inverse parallel sets the tenor for the account, which is God—not human—directed. **12:6** Canaan, and its inhabitants the Canaanites, will feature repeatedly from this point on in Genesis. The boundaries of it as a territory are never specified, but the way in which the text uses the term indicates they are roughly coterminous with those of Israel and Judah: the land between the Mediterranean Sea and the Jordan River, north of the Arabian Desert and south of the land controlled by Damascus. **12:7** The Lord appears and promises Abram that he will possess the land of Canaan. This promise will shape the rest of not only Genesis but much of the Old Testament, as these texts reflect on its fulfillment, loss, and potential restoration over the first millennium before the Common Era. **12:9** From Shechem in the northern portion of Canaan, Abram moves southward in stages toward the Arabian Desert. This prepares him for the journey to Egypt in the next scene.
12:10–13:1 This is the first of three endangered ancestress stories that explore how the ancestors respond to involuntary migration that places them among an unknown, foreign host culture. **12:10** Famine was a perennial feature of life in the Levant, where rainfall levels often barely exceeded the amount

Focus On: Land (Genesis 12:1–7)

The first verse of the Bible mentions land, since the Hebrew word translated as "earth" (*'erets*) more frequently means "land." God is the creator of land, and so, not surprisingly, God claims sole proprietary rights to the land (Exod. 19:5; Lev. 25:23). Everyone else is transient; as a result, no one can own any particular plot of land forever, nor are people allowed to farm, buy, or sell only according to their own preferences. Since God possesses the land in perpetuity, God may do with it as God pleases, including gifting it or taking it away. Not only is this true for the people of Israel, the primary focus of the biblical text—God also gives other people their land (see Deut. 2:5, 9–12, 19–23; Amos 9:7).

God's land ownership lies behind the promise to the ancestors to give them the land of Canaan. This promise is hinted at in Gen. 12:1–4 but is further clarified later to both Abram (see, e.g., 13:14–17; 15:12–16; 17:8) and his descendants (see, e.g., 35:12). The repeated description of Canaan as a "land flowing with milk and honey" (see, e.g., Exod. 3:8, Ezek. 20:15) underscores its beauty and bounty. The problem is that other people inhabit the land (Gen. 12:6). How the land transfer will occur is therefore complicated and includes military combat, which raises ethical questions for many readers (see **"Conquest," p. 317**, and **"Genocide," p. 305**). The Bible carefully, though sometimes subtly, establishes both God's owner-ship of the land and how it is ceded to Israel: mostly by divine fiat but also at times by purchase (Gen. 23:1–20; 33:19–20) and at other times as judgment against prior inhabitants (Gen. 15:16). In the case of the latter, the land wants nothing to do with wickedness. Leviticus personifies the land, saying it vom-ited out its prior inhabitants—a strong and visceral image (Lev. 18:27–28). This becomes a cautionary tale: Israel, too, could get vomited out (20:22).

Indeed, as the land is invaded by enemies and Israel dispersed and exiled, the loss of land is some-times understood as divine punishment (see, e.g., 2 Kgs. 17:1–23). Israel's story is thus one of a people on the move from landedness to land*less*ness and back again. The land looms large in both Israel's history and imagination (see **"Exile (2 Kings)," p. 539**, and **"Exile and Restoration Metanarratives," p. 637**). Land *really matters*, therefore, even as Israel's writings show that it does not matter *ultimately*.

Brent A. Strawn

[11]When he was about to enter Egypt, he said to his wife Sarai, "I know well that you are a woman beautiful in appearance, [12]and when the Egyptians see you, they will say, 'This is his wife'; then they will kill me, but they will let you live. [13]Say you are my sister, so that it may go well with me because of you and that my life may be spared on your account." [14]When Abram entered Egypt the Egyptians saw that the woman was very beautiful. [15]When the officials of Pharaoh saw her, they praised her to Pharaoh. And the woman was taken into Pharaoh's house. [16]And for her sake he dealt well with Abram, and he had sheep, oxen, male donkeys, male and female slaves, female donkeys, and camels.

[17] But the LORD afflicted Pharaoh and his house with great plagues because of Sarai, Abram's wife. [18]So Pharaoh called Abram and said, "What is this you have done to me? Why did you not tell me that she was your wife? [19]Why did you say, 'She is my sister,' so that I took her for my wife? Now then, here is your wife, take her, and be gone." [20]And Pharaoh gave his men orders concerning him, and they set him on the way with his wife and all that he had.

13 So Abram went up from Egypt, he and his wife and all that he had and Lot with him, into the Negeb.

2 Now Abram was very rich in livestock, in silver, and in gold. [3]He journeyed on by stages

required for subsistence farming. It is the cause of numerous migrations in Genesis, including this one. *Alien* translates the Hebrew term "ger," meaning "temporary resident." It specifies someone who is recog-nizably foreign. **12:15–16** The precise meaning of Pharaoh taking Sarai into his house is unclear. Some interpret it as a euphemism for Sarai entering a harem and thus having a sexual encounter with the Pharaoh. Others see it as symbolic of enslavement, foreshadowing Exodus's depiction of Israel in bond-age. The former fits better with the gifts to Abram (a sort of dowry) and Pharaoh's anger that Sarai's marriage to Abram has not been disclosed (v. 19). **12:20** The end result of the ancestors' scheme is to survive the famine and enrich themselves too. This narrative structure recurs in chaps. 20 and 26. It sug-gests a story embraced by people experiencing oppression by foreign powers to celebrate their ability to outsmart those imperial agents to survive, and even at times to thrive.

13:2–18 This scene recounts Abram and Lot departing from each other, with Abram serendipitously

Making Connections: Election (Genesis 12)

Election is the term used to refer to God's choice of certain individuals, like Abram (see Gen. 12:1–4a; 18:19), or entire groups, like Israel in the Hebrew Bible (see Deut. 7:6–8; 10:15; 14:2) or the church in the New Testament (see Rom. 11:28; 2 Tim. 2:10; Titus 1:1; 2 Pet. 1:10). In the Bible, God makes such choices, though the reasons for these divine "elections" often go unexpressed. God's call to Abram, for example, is not explained. We are not told *why* God called Abram, only *that* God did so; the same holds true for Mary (Luke 1:26–38) or the calling of the twelve disciples (Matt. 10:1–4) in the New Testament. Later texts sometimes add further details, which could be used to understand or explain God's choices after the fact. For example, the New Testament speaks of Abraham's faith when he was called (Heb. 11:8). But texts can also be quite explicit that there are no external—or internal!—reasons for God's election of individuals or communities (see Deut. 7:7–8; 9:4).

The concept of election implies a close relationship between God and God's chosen partner. This relationship can be expressed in terms of special feelings like love (Deut. 4:37) or being treasured (Exod. 19:5; Deut. 7:6; 14:2; 26:18b), but it can also be expressed in terms of special service (Exod. 19:6; Deut. 26:18a) or even special punishment in the face of wrongdoing (Amos 3:1–2). It is common, therefore, for election to involve a formal relationship called a covenant. Covenants involve two parties and can be different in substance (see **"Covenant (Genesis 6)," p. 23**). As part of his election, Abraham entered into a covenant (see Gen. 15 and 17), as did David (2 Sam. 7:1–17) and the people of Israel as a whole (Exod. 19:1–Num. 10:11).

Election of certain individuals or groups implies the *non*election of others. In the biblical tradition, nonelect people are not necessarily evil; nor are the chosen allowed to mistreat or harm the nonelect (see Deut. 2:1–25), except perhaps in certain apocalyptic texts, which can manifest violent and dualist worldviews. In fact, the Bible contains texts where nonelect peoples are shown care and concern by God (e.g., Isa. 19:19–25; Ps. 87); maybe this implies their own kind of election that is not further explicated (see Amos 9:7). The Bible also contains accounts where the elect misbehave and so become nonelect (Josh. 7:1–25; Acts 5:1–11). Conversely, the nonelect can become elect, particularly through faith and right action (Josh. 2:1–14; Ruth; 2 Kgs. 5:1–19; Jonah).

Brent A. Strawn

from the Negeb as far as Bethel, to the place where his tent had been at the beginning, between Bethel and Ai, ⁴to the place where he had made an altar at the first, and there Abram called on the name of the LORD. ⁵Now Lot, who went with Abram, also had flocks and herds and tents, ⁶and the land could not support both of them living together because their possessions were so great that they could not live together. ⁷Thus strife arose between the herders of Abram's livestock and the herders of Lot's livestock. At that time the Canaanites and the Perizzites lived in the land.

8 Then Abram said to Lot, "Let there be no strife between you and me and between your herders and my herders, for we are kindred. ⁹Is not the whole land before you? Separate yourself from me. If you take the left hand, then I will go to the right, or if you take the right hand, then I will go to the left." ¹⁰Lot looked about him and saw that the plain of the Jordan was well watered everywhere like the garden of the LORD, like the land of Egypt, in the direction of Zoar; this was before the LORD destroyed Sodom and Gomorrah. ¹¹So Lot chose for himself all the plain of the Jordan, and Lot journeyed eastward, and they separated from each other. ¹²Abram settled in the land of Canaan, while Lot settled among the cities of the plain and moved his tent as far as Sodom. ¹³Now the people of Sodom were wicked, great sinners against the LORD.

gaining access to the land God had earlier promised to him. **13:5–7** Lot, who has not featured since his introduction in 11:27, now appears in the care of his uncle. Even so, Lot has substantial possessions in his own right, so is not dependent on Abram. What follows has the feel of a wisdom tale, contrasting the wisdom of the experienced elder (Abram) with the ambition of the younger (Lot). **13:10–11** The plain of the Jordan suggests those areas watered by seasonal flooding of the Jordan or small-scale irrigation drawing from it. **13:12–13** There is a sense of contrast between rural life (Abram) and urban life (Lot) reflected here. This may be a vestige of a tradition that advocated for the rural, pastoral life that characterizes Abraham and Jacob, the two dominant characters in Gen. 12–50. What is totally clear

14 The Lord said to Abram, after Lot had separated from him, "Raise your eyes now, and look from the place where you are, northward and southward and eastward and westward, [15]for all the land that you see I will give to you and to your offspring forever. [16]I will make your offspring like the dust of the earth, so that if one can count the dust of the earth, your offspring also can be counted. [17]Rise up, walk through the length and the breadth of the land, for I will give it to you." [18]So Abram moved his tent and came and settled by the oaks[k] of Mamre, which are at Hebron, and there he built an altar to the Lord.

14 In the days of King Amraphel of Shinar, King Arioch of Ellasar, King Chedorlaomer of Elam, and King Tidal of Goiim, [2]these kings made war with King Bera of Sodom, King Birsha of Gomorrah, King Shinab of Admah, King Shemeber of Zeboiim, and the king of Bela, that is, Zoar. [3]All these joined forces in the Valley of Siddim, that is, the Dead Sea.[l] [4]Twelve years they had served Chedorlaomer, but in the thirteenth year they rebelled. [5]In the fourteenth year Chedorlaomer and the kings who were with him came and subdued the Rephaim in Ashteroth-karnaim, the Zuzim in Ham, the Emim in Shaveh-kiriathaim, [6]and the Horites in the hill country of Seir as far as El-paran on the edge of the wilderness; [7]then they turned back and came to En-mishpat, that is, Kadesh, and subdued all the country of the Amalekites and also the Amorites who lived in Hazazon-tamar. [8]Then the king of Sodom, the king of Gomorrah, the king of Admah, the king of Zeboiim, and the king of Bela, that is, Zoar, went out, and they joined battle in the Valley of Siddim [9]with King Chedorlaomer of Elam, King Tidal of Goiim, King Amraphel of Shinar, and King Arioch of Ellasar, four kings against five. [10]Now the Valley of Siddim was full of bitumen pits, and as the kings of Sodom and Gomorrah fled, some fell into them, and the rest fled to the hill country. [11]So the enemy took all the goods of Sodom and Gomorrah and all their provisions and went their way; [12]they also took Lot, the son of Abram's brother, who lived in Sodom, and his goods and departed.

[13] Then one who had escaped came and told Abram the Hebrew, who was living by the oaks[m] of Mamre the Amorite, brother of Eshcol and of Aner; these were allies of Abram. [14]When Abram heard that his nephew had been taken captive, he led forth his trained men, born in his house, three hundred eighteen of them, and went in pursuit as far as Dan. [15]He divided his forces against them by night, he and his servants, and routed them and pursued them to Hobah, north of Damascus. [16]Then he brought

k 13.18 Or *terebinths*   l 14.3 Heb *Salt Sea*   m 14.13 Or *terebinths*

is that Sodom should be avoided. **13:14–15** In reiterating the promise that Abram will possess the land, this description lacks any sense that people already inhabit it. Along with the simplistic division of it between Abram and Lot, it suggests a tradition in which the ancestors migrate from Mesopotamia to an empty land, which has been incorporated into a different tradition in which Abram and his descendants must compete with others for possession of the land. **13:16** God now introduces the second promise to Abram: he will have innumerable descendants. The audience would have immediately recalled 11:30—where Sarai is described as not just childless but barren—so that the narrative tension ratchets up quickly. Chapter 15 will engage directly with the tension that is left implicit here.

14:1–16 This section presents Abram saving Lot from peril for the first, but not the last, time. **14:1–9** The identities of the various kings and states here have generated much debate about the historical accuracy of these places and events. While many of the places can be identified, the individuals cannot. In the case of Sodom and Gomorrah—the focal point because of Lot's presence there—the names are probably symbolic: *Bera* means "in evil" and *Birsha* "in wickedness." This implies a figurative and literary design rather than historiographical intent. **14:11–12** Despite all the detail given to this point, the key bit of information is that these conquering kings take Lot, with his possessions, when they defeat Sodom and Gomorrah. **14:13–15** The portrayal of Abram in military action departs from his behavior in the rest of the ancestral narrative. Nevertheless, presented with the information of Lot's capture, he does not hesitate. The ability to muster 318 trained men presents Abram as a man of substantial wealth and considerable power, another aspect of this story that deviates from the rest of Genesis. Abram's pursuit goes to Dan, associated with the far northern border of Canaan, and then even past Damascus. This lengthy quest underscores the lengths to which Abram goes in this rescue operation.

Making Connections: Blessing (Genesis 14)

Blessing is a concept that feels familiar but is hard to define. There are at least two ways blessing is understood and presented in the Bible.

Blessing is, first, a way to honor something or someone. In Genesis, Melchizedek blesses Abraham (Gen. 14) and Jacob blesses Pharaoh (Gen. 47:7, 10) and also his twelve sons (Gen. 49). Such passages often reflect a person's esteem or reverence for another—the bestowal of material goods is not involved. This first sense of blessing is also found in the New Testament. For instance, the repeated refrain "blessed are" in some of the Beatitudes evokes this sense of blessing as reverence for a person or group of people (Matt. 5:1–12). It is the peacemakers who will be called children of God (Matt. 5:9): a statement of respect, not about material goods per se.

Other Beatitudes do seem to reflect concrete gifts, however, which leads to the second way blessing is presented in the Bible. This second way is likely more familiar—it is simply that a person who has experienced blessing is someone who is successful, which is most often measured by possessing some sort of material good. This second understanding occurs in Genesis as, for example, in how God makes Abram's name great or in the ways the ancestors receive wealth and possessions during their various travels and exploits. This more material understanding of blessing is also found in the blessings associated with the divine covenant (see, e.g., Deut. 30). The same holds true for Ps. 1, which contrasts the blessed (or happy) person who is exceedingly fruitful and prosperous with the wicked who are blown away like dust, unable to stand up at the time of judgment. Once again, this second understanding is also found in the Beatitudes, which assert that the meek are blessed because they will inherit the earth (Matt. 5:5).

This second understanding of blessing, with its connections to success and material possessions, dominates much contemporary talk of blessing. This understanding prompts celebrities to refer to themselves as "blessed" due to their popularity, wealth, and so forth. There is a strong connection between this understanding of blessing and what has been called the "prosperity gospel"—the notion that obedience to God brings material blessing. But the Bible knows the opposite is also true and thinks the gift of children is as much a blessing as anything else (Ps. 127:3–5).

C. A. Strine

back all the goods and also brought back his nephew Lot with his goods and the women and the people.

17 After his return from the defeat of Chedorlaomer and the kings who were with him, the king of Sodom went out to meet him at the Valley of Shaveh, that is, the King's Valley. ¹⁸And King Melchizedek of Salem brought out bread and wine; he was priest of God Most High.ⁿ ¹⁹He blessed him and said,

> "Blessed be Abram by God Most
> High,^o
> maker of heaven and earth,
> ²⁰ and blessed be God Most High,^p
> who has delivered your enemies into
> your hand!"

And Abram gave him one-tenth of everything. ²¹Then the king of Sodom said to Abram, "Give me the persons, but take the goods for yourself." ²²But Abram said to the king of Sodom, "I have sworn to God^q Most High,^r maker of heaven and earth, ²³that I would not take a thread or a sandal strap or anything that is yours, so that you might not say, 'I have made Abram rich.' ²⁴I will take nothing but what the young men have eaten and the share of the men who went with me: Aner, Eshcol, and Mamre. Let them take their share."

n 14.18 Heb *El Elyon*   *o* 14.19 Heb *El Elyon*   *p* 14.20 Heb *El Elyon*   *q* 14.22 Gk Syr: MT *the* Lord *God*   *r* 14.22 Heb *El Elyon*

14:18–20 Melchizedek is one of the most enigmatic figures in the Old Testament. He appears both as a king and a priest (cf. Ps. 110). Although Salem is provided no context here, its role elsewhere suggests it refers to the place later known as Jerusalem (see Ps. 76:2). Melchizedek employs the title God Most High, known from earlier Ugaritic sources as a reference to the Canaanite god El, whom YHWH resembles in various ways. Abram responds to Melchizedek's recognition of his divinely favored status by offering him a gift from the spoils: a tithe of 10 percent.

14:23 The sentiment of Abram's response is to ensure he is in the debt of no one who lives around him. Taken alongside the narrative of Abram as a foreigner living among potentially hostile outsiders, this reflects a migrant seeking recognition as a legitimate resident dependent on no other for their living.

15 After these things the word of the Lord came to Abram in a vision, "Do not be afraid, Abram, I am your shield; your reward shall be very great." ²But Abram said, "O Lord God, what will you give me, for I continue childless, and the heir of my house is Eliezer of Damascus?"ˢ ³And Abram said, "You have given me no offspring, so a slave born in my house is to be my heir." ⁴But the word of the Lord came to him, "This man shall not be your heir; no one but your very own issue shall be your heir." ⁵He brought him outside and said, "Look toward heaven and count the stars, if you are able to count them." Then he said to him, "So shall your descendants be." ⁶And he believed the Lord, and the Lordᵗ reckoned it to him as righteousness.

7 Then he said to him, "I am the Lord who brought you from Ur of the Chaldeans, to give you this land to possess." ⁸But he said, "O Lord God, how am I to know that I shall possess it?" ⁹He said to him, "Bring me a heifer three years old, a female goat three years old, a ram three years old, a turtledove, and a young pigeon." ¹⁰He brought him all these and cut them in two, laying each half over against the other, but he did not cut the birds in two. ¹¹And when birds of prey came down on the carcasses, Abram drove them away.

12 As the sun was going down, a deep sleep fell upon Abram, and a deep and terrifying darkness descended upon him. ¹³Then the Lordᵘ said to Abram, "Know this for certain, that your offspring shall be aliens in a land that is not theirs and shall be slaves there, and they shall be oppressed for four hundred years, ¹⁴but I will bring judgment on the nation that they serve, and afterward they shall come out with great possessions. ¹⁵As for yourself, you shall go to your ancestors in peace; you shall be buried in a good old age. ¹⁶And they shall come back here in the fourth generation, for the iniquity of the Amorites is not yet complete."

17 When the sun had gone down and it was dark, a smoking fire pot and a flaming torch passed between these pieces. ¹⁸On that day the Lord made a covenant with Abram, saying, "To your descendants I give this land, from the river of Egypt to the great river, the River Euphrates, ¹⁹the land of the Kenites, the Kenizzites, the Kadmonites, ²⁰the Hittites, the Perizzites, the Rephaim, ²¹the Amorites, the Canaanites, the Girgashites, and the Jebusites."

16 Now Sarai, Abram's wife, bore him no children. She had an Egyptian slave whose name was Hagar, ²and Sarai said to Abram, "You see that the Lord has prevented me from bearing children; go in to my slave; it may be that I shall obtain children by her."

s 15.2 Meaning of Heb uncertain t 15.6 Heb *he*
u 15.13 Heb *he*

15:1–21 God now establishes a covenant with Abram that reaffirms God's promise to bless him with land in this new country to which he has migrated and offspring to inherit that land from him. 15:2–3 The main point of these verses is to voice Abram's concern that God's promise cannot be fulfilled because he has no children of his own. They suggest, simultaneously, that Abram has adopted Eliezer of Damascus—a person outside his family and with no connection to his ancestral home or line. All this reminds the audience of Sarai's status as barren (11:30). 15:6 God reassures Abram by simply restating the promise. The subsequent statement of Abram's trust in God provides a model of faith throughout the Old Testament, and in the New Testament too (see Gal. 3). 15:7 This verse is very close to the prelude to the Ten Commandments (Exod. 20:2; Deut. 5:6) and serves as the first of many ways this passage points toward the exodus narrative. 15:9–11 God and Abram now perform a ritual act, familiar from Mesopotamia. The symbolism of the severed animals, and then the procession through them (v. 17), is a self-curse that the fate of the animal should befall anyone who is not true to the promise they are about to make. 15:13–16 God refers proleptically to the four-hundred-year oppression of Israel's enslavement in Egypt and its exodus out of that bondage, described in Exodus. 15:17 The smoke and flame suggest God's manifestation in the exodus as a pillar of fire and a cloud of smoke leading the people of Israel through the wilderness for forty years. 15:18 The extent of the land stated here far exceeds anything Israel and Judah ever controlled. This indicates control of the entire ancient Near East from the heart of Mesopotamia (the Euphrates) to the Nile (the river of Egypt). Rarely did even the most powerful empires of the ancient world control such a swath of land, and neither Israel nor Judah ever rose to anything like that prominence. This description suggests an ideal envisioned by those with great hopes for Israel.

16:2 Sarai, still childless, offers her slave Hagar to Abram as a possible surrogate. Such a practice was not unknown in the ancient world, so Sarai appears to be acting according to a sort of accepted custom.

And Abram listened to the voice of Sarai. ³So, after Abram had lived ten years in the land of Canaan, Sarai, Abram's wife, took Hagar the Egyptian, her slave, and gave her to her husband Abram as a wife. ⁴He went in to Hagar, and she conceived, and when she saw that she had conceived, she looked with contempt on her mistress. ⁵Then Sarai said to Abram, "May the wrong done to me be on you! I gave my slave to your embrace, and when she saw that she had conceived, she looked on me with contempt. May the Lord judge between you and me!" ⁶But Abram said to Sarai, "Your slave is in your power; do to her as you please." Then Sarai dealt harshly with her, and she ran away from her.

7 The angel of the Lord found her by a spring of water in the wilderness, the spring on the way to Shur. ⁸And he said, "Hagar, slave of Sarai, where have you come from and where are you going?" She said, "I am running away from my mistress Sarai." ⁹The angel of the Lord said to her, "Return to your mistress, and submit to her." ¹⁰The angel of the Lord also said to her, "I will so greatly multiply your offspring that they cannot be counted for multitude." ¹¹And the angel of the Lord said to her,

"Now you have conceived and shall bear
    a son;
  you shall call him Ishmael,ᵛ
  for the Lord has given heed to your
    affliction.
¹² He shall be a wild ass of a man,
  with his hand against everyone,
    and everyone's hand against him,
  and he shall live at odds with all his kin."

¹³So she named the Lord who spoke to her, "You are El-roi,"ʷ for she said, "Have I really seen God and remained alive after seeing him?"ˣ ¹⁴Therefore the well was called Beer-lahai-roi;ʸ it lies between Kadesh and Bered.

15 Hagar bore Abram a son, and Abram named his son, whom Hagar bore, Ishmael. ¹⁶Abram was eighty-six years old when Hagar bore himᶻ Ishmael.

17 When Abram was ninety-nine years old, the Lord appeared to Abram and said to him, "I am God Almighty;ᵃ walk before me, and be blameless. ²And I will make my covenant between me and you and will make you exceedingly numerous." ³Then Abram fell on his face, and God said to him, ⁴"As for me, this is my covenant with you: You shall be the ancestor of a multitude of nations. ⁵No longer shall your name be Abram,ᵇ but your name shall be Abraham,ᶜ for I have made you the ancestor of a multitude of nations. ⁶I will make you exceedingly fruitful, and I will make nations of you, and kings shall come from you. ⁷I will establish my covenant between me and you and your offspring after you throughout their generations, for an everlasting covenant, to be God to you and to your offspring after you. ⁸And I will give to you and to your offspring after you the land where you are now an alien, all

v 16.11 That is, *God hears*   w 16.13 Perhaps *God of seeing* or *God who sees*   x 16.13 Meaning of Heb uncertain   y 16.14 That is, *well of the living one who sees me*   z 16.16 Heb *Abram*   a 17.1 Traditional rendering of Heb *El Shaddai*   b 17.5 That is, *exalted ancestor*   c 17.5 That is, *ancestor of a multitude*

16:4–5 Sarai's plan works, but she immediately abhors its success because she believes Hagar now loathes her. When Sarai demands Abram deal with the issue as the patriarchal head of house, he places responsibility back in Sarai's control.

16:7 Hagar's flight into the wilderness anticipates the exodus, but in reverse: it is an Israelite that enslaves an Egyptian and sees them flee from it. Encounters at water sources (here a spring, often at a well) play an important role in the narrative of Genesis. In this case, God makes a promise to Hagar and her offspring that closely resembles that made to Abram and his offspring (v. 10).

16:13 Hagar's amazement reflects a belief that is often found in the Old Testament—namely, if someone sees God they will die. Hagar avoids that end and reflects on God's willingness to look on her in the name she uses of God. Notably, Hagar is the only figure in Genesis to give a name to God. Her prerogative to do so infers that she is favored by God (see **"Hagar," p. 42**).

17:1–27 This chapter forms the final scene in the triptych of chaps. 15–17. Instead of resolving the tension of whether Abram will have an heir born of Sarai, it ratchets the tension up higher. The divine promise of a child by Sarai calls into question Ishmael's role and how this problem might find resolution. The chapter also introduces one of the most important features of Israelite ritual practice: male circumcision. **17:1** Hebrew "El Shaddai," translated as *God Almighty*, may have originated in connection with deities residing on mountains. Their geographic height is also reflected in the title God Most High. **17:5** Names were far more than identifiers in the ancient world, often describing an attribute in the person they

the land of Canaan, for a perpetual holding, and I will be their God."

9 God said to Abraham, "As for you, you shall keep my covenant, you and your offspring after you throughout their generations. [10]This is my covenant, which you shall keep, between me and you and your offspring after you: Every male among you shall be circumcised. [11]You shall circumcise the flesh of your foreskins, and it shall be a sign of the covenant between me and you. [12]Throughout your generations every male among you shall be circumcised when he is eight days old, including the slave born in your house and the one bought with your money from any foreigner who is not of your offspring. [13]Both the slave born in your house and the one bought with your money must be circumcised. So shall my covenant be in your flesh an everlasting covenant. [14]Any uncircumcised male who is not circumcised in the flesh of his foreskin shall be cut off from his people; he has broken my covenant."

15 God said to Abraham, "As for Sarai your wife, you shall not call her Sarai, but Sarah shall be her name. [16]I will bless her and also give you a son by her. I will bless her, and she shall give rise to nations; kings of peoples shall come from her." [17]Then Abraham fell on his face and laughed and said to himself, "Can a child be born to a man who is a hundred years old? Can Sarah, who is ninety years old, bear a child?" [18]And Abraham said to God, "O that Ishmael might live in your sight!" [19]God said, "No, but your wife Sarah shall bear you a son, and you shall name him Isaac.[d] I will establish my covenant with him as an everlasting covenant for his offspring after him. [20]As for Ishmael, I have heard you; I will bless him and make him fruitful and exceedingly numerous; he shall be the father of twelve princes, and I will make him a great nation. [21]But my covenant I will establish with Isaac, whom Sarah shall bear to you at this season next year." [22]And when he had finished talking with him, God went up from Abraham.

23 Then Abraham took his son Ishmael and all the slaves born in his house or bought with his money, every male among the men of Abraham's house, and he circumcised the flesh of their foreskins that very day, as God had said to him. [24]Abraham was ninety-nine years old when he was circumcised in the flesh of his foreskin. [25]And his son Ishmael was thirteen years old when he was circumcised in the flesh of his foreskin. [26]That very day Abraham and his son Ishmael were circumcised, [27]and all the men of his house, slaves born in the house and those bought with money from a foreigner, were circumcised with him.

18

The LORD appeared to Abraham[e] by the oaks[f] of Mamre, as he sat at the

d 17.19 That is, he laughs e 18.1 Heb him f 18.1 Or terebinths

marked. To change a name was to say something indelible about the person changed. Abram's change of name represents a transition, though in his case it is a reaffirmation of what God has ascribed to him all along. **17:10–14** The sign of circumcision will from here on represent the covenant between God and Abraham just as the rainbow symbolized the Noachic covenant (see **"Covenant (Genesis 6)," p. 23**). Circumcision was known in the ancient world but more often performed at the transition from childhood to adulthood (ca. thirteen years old). To prescribe the rite on the eighth day of a boy's life stands out from the wider practice. Throughout the Old Testament, the importance of circumcision as a marker of identity and communal belonging obtains great importance, such that Israel's enemies can often be framed as the "uncircumcised" (see 1 Sam. 17:26). **17:15–16** God now changes Sarai's name to Sarah. While both are forms of the Hebrew word for princess, this is an important moment of transition for the matriarch. For the first time, God promises that Sarah will have a son—no imagined alternative to this will be the resolution to God's pledge. **17:18–21** In addition to his incredulity that Sarah will bear a child, Abraham is concerned for the future of his son Ishmael, whom he already has. God insists the covenant promise will fall to Isaac, but Ishmael will also be the father of a great nation. This indicates that the distinction between them concerns which son will inherit the land God has promised to Abraham. **17:25** Ishmael, like all the males of any origin in Abraham's household, is circumcised. It is at the notable age of thirteen that Ishmael undergoes the ritual, which raises the prospect that at some point Israel's practice may have followed the more common ancient Near Eastern pattern of marking the transition to adulthood.

18:1–19:38 The narrative of Sodom's downfall spans these two chapters. Many argue the story follows a chiastic structure: the first section (18:1–15) announcing Sarah will conceive Isaac matches the final section (19:30–38) covering the births of Moab and Ben-ammi. In between, judgment is announced on

entrance of his tent in the heat of the day. [2]He looked up and saw three men standing near him. When he saw them, he ran from the tent entrance to meet them and bowed down to the ground. [3]He said, "My lord, if I find favor with you, do not pass by your servant. [4]Let a little water be brought, and wash your feet, and rest yourselves under the tree. [5]Let me bring a little bread, that you may refresh yourselves, and after that you may pass on—since you have come to your servant." So they said, "Do as you have said." [6]And Abraham hastened into the tent to Sarah and said, "Make ready quickly three measures[g] of choice flour, knead it, and make cakes." [7]Abraham ran to the herd and took a calf, tender and good, and gave it to the servant, who hastened to prepare it. [8]Then he took curds and milk and the calf that he had prepared and set it before them, and he stood by them under the tree while they ate.

[9]They said to him, "Where is your wife Sarah?" And he said, "There, in the tent." [10]Then one said, "I will surely return to you in due season, and your wife Sarah shall have a son." And Sarah was listening at the tent entrance behind him. [11]Now Abraham and Sarah were old, advanced in age; it had ceased to be with Sarah after the manner of women. [12]So Sarah laughed to herself, saying, "After I have grown old, and my husband is old, shall I be fruitful?" [13]The Lord said to Abraham, "Why did Sarah laugh and say, 'Shall I indeed bear a child, now that I am old?' [14]Is anything too wonderful for the Lord? At the set time I will return to you, in due season, and Sarah shall have a son." [15]But Sarah denied, saying, "I did not laugh," for she was afraid. He said, "Yes, you did laugh."

[16] Then the men set out from there, and they looked toward Sodom, and Abraham went with them to set them on their way.

[17]The Lord said, "Shall I hide from Abraham what I am about to do, [18]seeing that Abraham shall become a great and mighty nation, and all the nations of the earth shall be blessed in him?[b] [19]No, for I have chosen[i] him, that he may charge his children and his household after him to keep the way of the Lord by doing righteousness and justice, so that the Lord may bring about for Abraham what he has promised him." [20]Then the Lord said, "How great is the outcry against Sodom and Gomorrah and how very grave their sin! [21]I must go down and see whether they have done altogether according to the outcry that has come to me, and if not, I will know."

[22] So the men turned from there and went toward Sodom, while Abraham remained standing before the Lord.[j] [23]Then Abraham came near and said, "Will you indeed sweep away the righteous with the wicked? [24]Suppose there are fifty righteous within the city; will you then sweep away the place and not forgive it for the fifty righteous who are in it? [25]Far be it from you to do such a thing, to slay the righteous with the wicked, so that the righteous fare as the wicked! Far be that from you! Shall not the Judge of all the earth do what is just?" [26]And the Lord said, "If I find at Sodom fifty righteous in the city, I will forgive the whole place for their sake." [27]Abraham answered, "Let me take it upon myself to speak to my lord, I who am but dust and ashes. [28]Suppose five of the fifty righteous are lacking? Will you destroy the whole city for lack of five?" And he said, "I will not destroy it if I find forty-five there." [29]Again he spoke to him, "Suppose forty are found there." He answered, "For the sake of forty I will not

g 18.6 Heb seahs   h 18.18 Or and all the nations of the earth shall bless themselves by him   i 18.19 Heb known   j 18.22 Or while the Lord remained standing before Abraham

Sodom (18:16–33) and that destruction comes to pass (19:1–29). Such a pattern (also called an envelope structure) was a common device for organizing material in the ancient world. **18:2** The identity of the three men is much debated, as the story later depicts the Lord as one of the visitors (18:16–33). It may be that the Lord is one of the three, with two other divine attendants accompanying him, a scenario known in ancient Near Eastern iconography. **18:11–12** This is a euphemistic way of describing Sarah as postmenopausal and thus incapable of conceiving a child. Sarah laughs at the prediction in a similar fashion to Abraham in 17:17. **18:17–19** Now the Lord wonders aloud how much Abraham should know about what is to come. This frames Abraham as a prophet, who will momentarily be in dialogue with the Lord over the justice of God's actions. **18:23–33** This discourse between God and Abraham borrows aspects of legal thinking and prophetic rhetoric from the ancient world. On one hand, Abraham sounds like a legal advocate, working out the limits of God's judgment and seeking to understand if it is proportional to the crime. On the other hand, Abraham acts like a prophet that intercedes on behalf of a group of people to seek divine mercy in the face of potential judgment (cf. Moses in Exod. 32 and Samuel in

do it." [30]Then he said, "Oh, do not let my lord be angry if I speak. Suppose thirty are found there." He answered, "I will not do it, if I find thirty there." [31]He said, "Let me take it upon myself to speak to my lord. Suppose twenty are found there." He answered, "For the sake of twenty I will not destroy it." [32]Then he said, "Oh, do not let my lord be angry if I speak just once more. Suppose ten are found there." He answered, "For the sake of ten I will not destroy it." [33]And the LORD went his way, when he had finished speaking to Abraham, and Abraham returned to his place.

19 The two angels came to Sodom in the evening, and Lot was sitting in the gateway of Sodom. When Lot saw them, he rose to meet them and bowed down with his face to the ground. [2]He said, "Please, my lords, turn aside to your servant's house and spend the night and wash your feet; then you can rise early and go on your way." They said, "No; we will spend the night in the square." [3]But he urged them strongly, so they turned aside to him and entered his house, and he made them a feast and baked unleavened bread, and they ate. [4]But before they lay down, the men of the city, the men of Sodom, both young and old, all the people to the last man, surrounded the house, [5]and they called to Lot, "Where are the men who came to you tonight? Bring them out to us, so that we may know them." [6]Lot went out of the door to the men, shut the door after him, [7]and said, "I beg you, my brothers, do not act so wickedly. [8]Look, I have two daughters who have not known a man; let me bring them out to you, and do to them as you please; only do nothing to these men, for they have come under the shelter of my roof." [9]But they replied, "Stand back!" And they said, "This fellow came here as an alien, and he would play the judge! Now we will deal worse with you than with them." Then they pressed hard against the man Lot

and came near the door to break it down. [10]But the men inside reached out their hands and brought Lot into the house with them and shut the door. [11]And they struck with blindness the men who were at the door of the house, both small and great, so that they were unable to find the door.

12 Then the men said to Lot, "Have you anyone else here? Sons-in-law, sons, daughters, or anyone you have in the city—bring them out of the place. [13]For we are about to destroy this place, because the outcry against its people has become great before the LORD, and the LORD has sent us to destroy it." [14]So Lot went out and said to his sons-in-law, who were to marry his daughters, "Up, get out of this place, for the LORD is about to destroy the city." But he seemed to his sons-in-law to be jesting.

15 When morning dawned, the angels urged Lot, saying, "Get up, take your wife and your two daughters who are here, or else you will be consumed in the punishment of the city." [16]But he lingered, so the men seized him and his wife and his two daughters by the hand, the LORD being merciful to him, and they brought him out and left him outside the city. [17]When they had brought them outside, they[k] said, "Flee for your life; do not look back or stop anywhere in the plain; flee to the hills, or else you will be consumed." [18]And Lot said to them, "Oh, no, my lords; [19]your servant has found favor with you, and you have shown me great kindness in saving my life, but I cannot flee to the hills, for fear the disaster will overtake me and I die. [20]Look, that city is near enough to flee to, and it is a little one. Let me escape there—is it not a little one?—and my life will be saved!" [21]He said to him, "Very well, I grant you this favor too and will not overthrow the city of which you have spoken. [22]Hurry, escape there, for I can do nothing until you arrive there." Therefore the city was

k 19.17 Gk Syr Vg: Heb *he*

1 Sam. 12:19–25). All this frames Abraham as clever, merciful, and attentive to God—a stark contrast to Lot's behavior in all that follows. **19:5** In another euphemism, the men of Sodom ask to *know* the visitors. The phrase "to know" (a person) is sometimes used of sexual intercourse, which is the sense here. **19:8–9** Lot's lack of wisdom and mercy manifests most acutely in his astonishing and reprehensible offer of his virgin daughters to these men as sexual partners in lieu of the two male visitors. The offer makes no difference to the mob outside Lot's house, and they disparage him as a foreigner in their rejection of his offer. **19:10–11** The visitors take matters into their own hands, removing Lot from the imminent danger and revealing their supernatural ability in stunning the mob with blindness. **19:14–16** Whereas God took Abraham's concerns seriously, Lot's sons-in-law take him for a fool and not a messenger of impending danger. This underscores how the two characters reflect opposite character traits. Indeed, Lot does not

called Zoar.*l* ²³The sun had risen on the earth when Lot came to Zoar.

24 Then the Lord rained on Sodom and Gomorrah sulfur and fire from the Lord out of heaven, ²⁵and he overthrew those cities and all the plain and all the inhabitants of the cities and what grew on the ground. ²⁶But Lot's wife, behind him, looked back, and she became a pillar of salt.

27 Abraham went early in the morning to the place where he had stood before the Lord, ²⁸and he looked down toward Sodom and Gomorrah and toward all the land of the plain and saw the smoke of the land going up like the smoke of a furnace.

29 So it was that, when God destroyed the cities of the plain, God remembered Abraham and sent Lot out of the midst of the overthrow, when he overthrew the cities in which Lot had settled.

30 Now Lot went up out of Zoar and settled in the hills with his two daughters, for he was afraid to stay in Zoar, so he lived in a cave with his two daughters. ³¹And the firstborn said to the younger, "Our father is old, and there is not a man on earth to come in to us after the manner of all the world. ³²Come, let us make our father drink wine, and we will lie with him, so that we may preserve offspring through our father." ³³So they made their father drink wine that night, and the firstborn went in and lay with her father; he did not know when she lay down or when she rose. ³⁴On the next day, the firstborn said to the younger, "Look, I lay last night with my father; let us make him drink wine tonight also; then you go in and lie with him, so that we may preserve offspring through our father." ³⁵So they

made their father drink wine that night also, and the younger rose and lay with him, and he did not know when she lay down or when she rose. ³⁶Thus both the daughters of Lot became pregnant by their father. ³⁷The firstborn bore a son and named him Moab;*m* he is the ancestor of the Moabites to this day. ³⁸The younger also bore a son and named him Ben-ammi;*n* he is the ancestor of the Ammonites to this day.

20 From there Abraham journeyed toward the region of the Negeb and settled between Kadesh and Shur. While residing in Gerar as an alien, ²Abraham said of his wife Sarah, "She is my sister." And King Abimelech of Gerar sent and took Sarah. ³But God came to Abimelech in a dream by night and said to him, "You are about to die because of the woman whom you have taken, for she is a married woman." ⁴Now Abimelech had not approached her, so he said, "Lord, will you destroy an innocent people? ⁵Did he not himself say to me, 'She is my sister'? And she herself said, 'He is my brother.' I did this in the integrity of my heart and the innocence of my hands." ⁶Then God said to him in the dream, "Yes, I know that you did this in the integrity of your heart; furthermore, it was I who kept you from sinning against me. Therefore I did not let you touch her. ⁷Now then, return the man's wife, for he is a prophet, and he will pray for you, and you shall live. But if you do not restore her, know that you shall surely die, you and all that are yours."

8 So Abimelech rose early in the morning

l 19.22 That is, *little*   *m* 19.37 That is, *from the father*
n 19.38 That is, *son of my kinsman*

even take the message from these two supernatural messengers seriously enough to flee the city when they tell him to go. It is only their mercy for Lot and supernatural powers that spare him. **19:31** The statement suggests hyperbole, for the story has already spoken of people living in many places beyond Sodom. However, in a culture where marriage was often restricted to those within a relatively close kinship group, the idea that acceptable men to marry might not exist may have seemed plausible to the audience. **19:33** The story resembles Ham's treatment of Noah after the flood (see 9:20–27), and it seems likely the audience was to make that connection. This depicts the daughters' actions as morally questionable. **19:37–38** The two sons produced by the daughters' actions become the ancestors of the states of Moab and Ammon, with whom Israel and Judah are often in conflict.

20:1–18 This account of Abraham and Sarah resembles the one from 12:10–13:1 and thus is grouped with it and 26:1–33 as one of the endangered ancestress stories. It is important to note that the resolution of this story comes in 21:22–34, from which it is separated by the story of Isaac's birth and Ishmael's expulsion. **20:3–6** Sarah is once again taken into the house of a foreign leader because Abraham has presented her as his sister. Unlike the encounter with Pharaoh (see 12:10–20), which leaves the nature of his relationship with Sarah unclear, this story makes plain that Abimelech does not have a sexual relationship with Sarah. There is a heightened sensitivity to this matter now, as the audience knows

and called all his servants and told them all these things, and the men were very much afraid. ⁹Then Abimelech called Abraham and said to him, "What have you done to us? How have I sinned against you, that you have brought such great guilt on me and my kingdom? You have done things to me that ought not to be done." ¹⁰And Abimelech said to Abraham, "What were you thinking, that you did this thing?" ¹¹Abraham said, "I did it because I thought, Surely there is no fear of God in this place, and they will kill me because of my wife. ¹²Besides, she is indeed my sister, the daughter of my father but not the daughter of my mother, and she became my wife. ¹³And when God caused me to wander from my father's house, I said to her, 'This is the kindness you must do me: at every place to which we come, say of me, He is my brother.'" ¹⁴Then Abimelech took sheep and oxen and male and female slaves and gave them to Abraham and restored his wife Sarah to him. ¹⁵Abimelech said, "My land is before you; settle where it pleases you." ¹⁶To Sarah he said, "Look, I have given your brother a thousand pieces of silver; it is your exoneration before all who are with you; you are completely vindicated." ¹⁷Then Abraham prayed to God, and God healed Abimelech and also healed his wife and female slaves so that they bore children. ¹⁸For the LORD had closed fast all the wombs of the house of Abimelech because of Sarah, Abraham's wife.

21 The LORD dealt with Sarah as he had said, and the LORD did for Sarah as he had promised. ²Sarah conceived and bore Abraham a son in his old age, at the time of which God had spoken to him. ³Abraham gave the name Isaac to his son whom Sarah bore him. ⁴And Abraham circumcised his son Isaac when he was eight days old, as God had commanded him. ⁵Abraham was a hundred years old when his son Isaac was born to him. ⁶Now Sarah said, "God has brought laughter for me; everyone who hears will laugh with me." ⁷And she said, "Who would ever have said to Abraham that Sarah would nurse children? Yet I have borne him a son in his old age."

8 The child grew and was weaned, and Abraham made a great feast on the day that Isaac was weaned. ⁹But Sarah saw the son of Hagar the Egyptian, whom she had borne to Abraham, playing with her son Isaac.ᵒ ¹⁰So she said to Abraham, "Cast out this slave woman with her son, for the son of this slave woman shall not inherit along with my son Isaac." ¹¹The matter was very distressing to Abraham on account of his son. ¹²But God said to Abraham, "Do not be distressed because of the boy and because of your slave woman; whatever Sarah says to you, do as she tells you, for it is through Isaac that offspring shall be named

o 21.9 Gk Vg: Heb lacks *with her son Isaac*

Sarah will become pregnant (18:14): Will this encounter risk that son's father being someone other than Abraham? **20:11–12** Abraham is called to account for his actions. He justifies them in two ways. First, he identifies the people of Gerar as godless. Somewhat surprisingly, this does not appear to upset them in any way. Second, he identifies a loophole in which his statement is not specifically false: Sarah is his half sibling and thus his sister in a manner of speaking (cf. 12:13). One senses the narrator wants to preserve Abraham's moral rectitude that has been so carefully established in chaps. 18–19, even if it requires some tortured logic. **20:14–16** Just as in their encounter with Pharaoh, Abraham and Sarah emerge from this situation wealthier than they entered. Indeed, Abimelech even offers them a sort of protected resident status (v. 15) so they can continue to live in Gerar without fear of retribution. The conclusion of the story in 21:22–34 will reveal the flaw in this arrangement. **20:17–18** Abraham once again behaves like a prophet interceding for those in trouble. Not only does this entrench the idea that Abraham has a prophetic role; it goes some way further in rehabilitating his moral character by suggesting he sympathizes with the Gerarites' present barrenness.

21:1–7 This brief account of Isaac's birth, naming, and circumcision brings one aspect of the narrative tension in view since Gen. 12 to resolution. And yet, this will soon be thrown back into question in Gen. 22. In this section, however, Abraham and Sarah are presented as obedient to all the instructions God has given them for the naming and ritual inclusion of this child into the covenant (see **"Covenant (Genesis 6)," p. 23**).

21:11 When Sarah's jealous request for Hagar and Ishmael to leave forces Abraham into a decision, he is said to be distressed because of his son. Is that Ishmael? In the context, this seems likely. Yet it could also be Isaac. Or, read another way, it could be both of his sons in turn. The ambiguity in the text reflects something of the lack of clarity Abraham has in the situation.

for you. [13]As for the son of the slave woman, I will make a nation of him also, because he is your offspring." [14]So Abraham rose early in the morning and took bread and a skin of water and gave it to Hagar, putting it on her shoulder, along with the child, and sent her away. And she departed and wandered about in the wilderness of Beer-sheba.

[15] When the water in the skin was gone, she cast the child under one of the bushes. [16]Then she went and sat down opposite him a good way off, about the distance of a bowshot, for she said, "Do not let me look on the death of the child." And as she sat opposite him, she lifted up her voice and wept. [17]And God heard the voice of the boy, and the angel of God called to Hagar from heaven and said to her, "What troubles you, Hagar? Do not be afraid, for God has heard the voice of the boy where he is. [18]Come, lift up the boy and hold him fast with your hand, for I will make a great nation of him." [19]Then God opened her eyes, and she saw a well of water. She went and filled the skin with water and gave the boy a drink.

[20] God was with the boy, and he grew up; he lived in the wilderness and became an expert with the bow. [21]He lived in the wilderness of Paran, and his mother got a wife for him from the land of Egypt.

[22] At that time Abimelech, with Phicol the commander of his army, said to Abraham, "God is with you in all that you do; [23]now therefore swear to me here by God that you will not deal falsely with me or with my offspring or with my posterity, but as I have dealt loyally with you, you will deal with me and with the land where you have resided as an alien." [24]And Abraham said, "I swear it."

[25] When Abraham complained to Abimelech about a well of water that Abimelech's servants had seized, [26]Abimelech said, "I do not know who has done this; you did not tell me, and I have not heard of it until today." [27]So Abraham took sheep and oxen and gave them to Abimelech, and the two men made a covenant. [28]Abraham set apart seven ewe lambs of the flock. [29]And Abimelech said to Abraham, "What is the meaning of these seven ewe lambs that you have set apart?" [30]He said, "These seven ewe lambs you shall accept from my hand in order that you may be a witness for me that I dug this well." [31]Therefore that place was called Beer-sheba,*p* because there both of them swore an oath. [32]When they had made a covenant at Beer-sheba, Abimelech, with Phicol the commander of his army, left and returned to the land of the Philistines. [33]Abraham*q* planted a tamarisk tree in Beer-sheba and there called on the name of the LORD, the Everlasting God.*r* [34]And Abraham resided as an alien many days in the land of the Philistines.

p 21.31 That is, *well of seven* or *well of the oath*   *q* 21.33 Heb *He*   *r* 21.33 Or *the* LORD, *El Olam*

21:13 This promise for Ishmael, though hardly consolation for the rejection in the circumstance, reaffirms what was said in 17:20. Ishmael will not inherit the promises of the covenant with God but will have a substantial legacy nonetheless.

21:15 The image is of a mother who cannot bear to watch their small child suffer and likely die. This is problematic in the context: Ishmael is already thirteen when Isaac is conceived (17:25); the weaning process would have been completed at about age three; the narrative suggests he is a young man of sixteen, not a small child. Many scholars explain the discrepancy by reference to critical arguments that suggest one source provides the content of this story and another source provides a chronology from a different version of Abraham's life.

21:17–19 Just as in Gen. 16, God is alert to Hagar and Ishmael's struggles and responds quickly. In this case, God provides the water they need. Much like Gen. 16 presents the Egyptian Hagar experiencing the provision God would provide for the Israelites in the exodus, here too Hagar and Ishmael receive similar provision—namely, water to sustain them during their wandering in the wilderness (see **"Hagar," p. 42**).

21:22–34 The story returns to Abraham and Sarah's life in Gerar now without any transition. This concluding passage returns to the theme of migrants and their reception, in this case reflecting how differently people within a place might respond to immigrants. **21:25–26** Abraham's identity as a foreigner means that Abimelech's servants feel empowered to seize a well the patriarch has opened. It reflects a different attitude among the wider population toward this immigrant than that of Abimelech. **21:31** The name *Beer-sheba* means "well of the oath" or "well of seven" in Hebrew. This explanation of Beer-sheba's origin draws on that first meaning. **21:34** Reflecting the importance of migration in the story, this concluding comment makes it plain that Abraham was known, indeed celebrated, for being a migrant among the communities that preserved these stories.

Reading through Time: Hagar (Genesis 21)

Hagar has been interpreted in a wide variety of ways across the millennia, largely because so many of the details readers would like to know about her remain unexpressed in Genesis. In the New Testament, Hagar features in the theology of the apostle Paul as articulated in Galatians. In Islam, Hagar is also important—even more so than in Christianity or Judaism—because she is the mother of Ishmael, from whom the prophet Muhammad descends and many Muslim communities trace descent. During the annual pilgrimage to Mecca, known as the Hajj, people run between two hills (Al-Safa and Al-Marwah) in a ritualized reenactment of Hagar's search for water to keep Ishmael alive (Gen. 21) until God provided the needed water (in Muslim tradition, from the Zamzam well).

In the more recent past, Hagar has been interpreted as bearing various racial and ethnic identities. During the nineteenth century, for example, interpreters tended to focus on Hagar's Egyptian identity (Gen. 16:1). In the latter portion of the twentieth century, Hagar's status as an Egyptian has been interpreted as her being African and a character that reflects much of the African American experience. Indeed, Hagar has become an important figure in womanist approaches to the Bible: readings from an African American perspective that show how the experiences and concerns of Black women can shape the interpretations of texts and the theology done with them. Womanist interpreters have recognized that Hagar's identity is shaped not only by her ethnicity but also by her status within Abram and Sarai's house, which is related to both her gender and her class. Hagar is called the "slave" or "servant" (*shiphah*) of Sarai (16:1), who gives her to Abram as a second "wife" (16:3). The purpose of this arrangement is progeny for Sarai (16:2). Womanist readings have noted the intersectional nature of Hagar's subjugation as both an enslaved women and a forced surrogate mother, therefore, in addition to other considerations.

C. A. Strine

22 After these things God tested Abraham. He said to him, "Abraham!" And he said, "Here I am." ²He said, "Take your son, your only son Isaac, whom you love, and go to the land of Moriah and offer him there as a burnt offering on one of the mountains that I shall show you." ³So Abraham rose early in the morning, saddled his donkey, and took two of his young men with him and his son Isaac; he cut the wood for the burnt offering and set out and went to the place in the distance that God had shown him. ⁴On the third day Abraham looked up and saw the place far away. ⁵Then Abraham said to his young men, "Stay here with the donkey; the boy and I will go over there; we will worship, and then we will come back to you." ⁶Abraham took the wood of the burnt offering and laid it on his son Isaac, and he himself carried the fire and the knife. And the two of them walked on together. ⁷Isaac said to his father Abraham, "Father!" And he said, "Here I am, my son." He said, "The fire and the wood are here, but where is the lamb for a burnt offering?" ⁸Abraham said, "God himself will provide the lamb for a burnt offering, my son." And the two of them walked on together.

9 When they came to the place that God had shown him, Abraham built an altar there and laid the wood in order. He bound his son Isaac and laid him on the altar on top of the wood. ¹⁰Then Abraham reached out his hand and took the knife to kill⁵ his son. ¹¹But the angel of the Lord called to him from heaven

⁵ 22.10 Or *to slaughter*

22:1–19 This story is one of the most famous in the Bible, not just for its theological import but also for the literary skill with which it is told. Known in Judaism as the "Akedah" (Heb. for "binding"), perhaps no other story has received as much discussion in Jewish commentary. More often called the "sacrifice of Isaac" among Christians, it has equally generated much discussion. **22:2** The multiple references to Isaac create even more tension in their wooden rendering: *your son, your only son Isaac, whom you love*. Only with the final word does Abraham find out what God is asking of him. The son who was the fulfillment of the central promise of God to Abraham now becomes the central feature of God's test for Abraham. **22:3–4** As Hagar and Ishmael had left before, so now Abraham and Isaac go. The journey is not a short one. Indeed, this detail increases the narrative tension by elongating the events depicted. **22:6** The image of Isaac carrying the means of his own death is a powerful one. Many Christian theologians see it as an anticipation of the passion narrative, in which Jesus of Nazareth carries the cross on which he will be crucified. **22:7–8** The narrative does not make it clear how old Isaac is, and so this question can be read either as innocent inquiry or as knowing trepidation. **22:11** Abraham's response,

and said, "Abraham, Abraham!" And he said, "Here I am." [12]He said, "Do not lay your hand on the boy or do anything to him, for now I know that you fear God, since you have not withheld your son, your only son, from me." [13]And Abraham looked up and saw a ram, caught in a thicket by its horns. Abraham went and took the ram and offered it up as a burnt offering instead of his son. [14]So Abraham called that place "The LORD will provide,"[t] as it is said to this day, "On the mount of the LORD it shall be provided."[u]

15 The angel of the LORD called to Abraham a second time from heaven [16]and said, "By myself I have sworn, says the LORD: Because you have done this, and have not withheld your son, your only son, [17]I will indeed bless you, and I will make your offspring as numerous as the stars of heaven and as the sand that is on the seashore. And your offspring shall possess the gate of their enemies, [18]and by your offspring shall all the nations of the earth gain blessing for themselves, because you have obeyed my voice." [19]So Abraham returned to his young men, and they arose and went together to Beer-sheba, and Abraham lived at Beer-sheba.

20 Now after these things it was told Abraham, "Milcah also has borne children to your brother Nahor: [21]Uz the firstborn, Buz his brother, Kemuel the father of Aram, [22]Chesed, Hazo, Pildash, Jidlaph, and Bethuel." [23]Bethuel became the father of Rebekah. These eight Milcah bore to Nahor, Abraham's brother. [24]Moreover, his concubine, whose name was Reumah, bore Tebah, Gaham, Tahash, and Maacah.

23

Sarah lived one hundred twenty-seven years; this was the length of Sarah's life. [2]And Sarah died at Kiriath-arba, that is, Hebron, in the land of Canaan, and Abraham went in to mourn for Sarah and to weep for her. [3]Abraham rose up from beside his dead and said to the Hittites, [4]"I am a stranger and an alien residing among you; give me property among you for a burying place, so that I may bury my dead out of my sight." [5]The Hittites answered Abraham, [6]"Hear us, my lord; you are a mighty prince among us. Bury your dead in the choicest of our burial places; none of us will withhold from you any burial ground for burying your dead." [7]Abraham rose and bowed to the Hittites, the people of the land. [8]He said to them, "If you are willing that I should bury my dead out of my sight, hear me and entreat for me Ephron son of Zohar, [9]so that he may give me the cave of Machpelah, which he owns; it is at the end of his field. For the full price let him give it to me in your presence as a possession for a burying place." [10]Now Ephron was sitting among the Hittites, and Ephron the Hittite answered Abraham in the hearing

t 22.14 Or *will see*; Heb traditionally transliterated *Jehovah Jireh*   u 22.14 Or *he shall be seen*

Here I am, translates a Hebrew exclamation (also in 22:1, 7) that expresses not just presence but a sense of readiness to respond. In this case, one might even read it as a relieved exclamation—a father ready, waiting, and hoping for any sign that he may cease this dastardly act. **22:14** Abraham follows custom to name this place according to what happens there. The meaning of the LORD will provide is then linked with the height of the place to make the place the mount of the LORD. In Jewish tradition, this place (Mount Moriah) is identified as the Temple Mount, where both of the temples in Jerusalem stood. Today, this is the location of the Dome of the Rock, one of Islam's holiest sites.

22:20–24 In a sign that the narrative is now winding toward conclusion, these verses flash back to Nahor and Milcah, introduced in 11:29. The births of these children parallel the birth—now survival too—of Isaac to Abraham and Sarah and draw the main plot to a close.

23:2 *Hebron*—about twenty miles south-southwest of Jerusalem—plays a role throughout the narrative of Abraham and Sarah, but Sarah's death and burial here enshrine it as part of Israel and Judah's history. Since it is also where David finds his original power base, it remains important throughout the story of these two states.

23:4–9 Abraham self-identifies as an immigrant and emphasizes this by stating that he owns no land where he can bury his partner. The *Hittites* offer Abraham the burial place of his choosing, expressing their solidarity with him. Though the language used is of the native residents *giv[ing]* a place, Abraham is emphatic that he will pay for it. Much like Gen. 14, where the patriarch refuses to keep any material good that might put him in another's debt, here he makes plain that he wants to purchase the plot so that he remains fully independent. This reflects the desires of many migrants, who want to establish their residence and independence in a new place as a sign of equal standing with those there before them.

of the Hittites, of all who went in at the gate of his city, [11]"No, my lord, hear me; I give you the field, and I give you the cave that is in it; in the presence of my people I give it to you; bury your dead." [12]Then Abraham bowed down before the people of the land. [13]He said to Ephron in the hearing of the people of the land, "If you only will listen to me! I will give the price of the field; accept it from me, so that I may bury my dead there." [14]Ephron answered Abraham, [15]"My lord, listen to me; a piece of land worth four hundred shekels of silver—what is that between you and me? Bury your dead." [16]Abraham agreed with Ephron, and Abraham weighed out for Ephron the silver that he had named in the hearing of the Hittites, four hundred shekels of silver, according to the weights current among the merchants.

17 So the field of Ephron in Machpelah, which was to the east of Mamre, the field with the cave that was in it and all the trees that were in the field, throughout its whole area, passed [18]to Abraham as a possession in the presence of the Hittites, in the presence of all who went in at the gate of his city. [19]After this, Abraham buried Sarah his wife in the cave of the field of Machpelah facing Mamre, that is, Hebron, in the land of Canaan. [20]The field and the cave that is in it passed from the Hittites into Abraham's possession as a burying place.

24 Now Abraham was old, advanced in years, and the Lord had blessed Abraham in all things. [2]Abraham said to his servant, the oldest of his house, who had charge of all that he had, "Put your hand under my thigh, [3]and I will make you swear by the Lord, the God of heaven and earth, that you will not get a wife for my son from the daughters of the Canaanites, among whom I live, [4]but will go to my country and to my kindred and get a wife for my son Isaac." [5]The servant said to him, "Perhaps the woman may not be willing to follow me to this land; must I then take your son back to the land from which you came?" [6]Abraham said to him, "See to it that you do not take my son back there. [7]The Lord, the God of heaven, who took me from my father's house and from the land of my birth and who spoke to me and swore to me, 'To your offspring I will give this land,' he will send his angel before you, and you shall take a wife for my son from there. [8]But if the woman is not willing to follow you, then you will be free from this oath of mine; only you must not take my son back there." [9]So the servant put his hand under the thigh of Abraham his master and swore to him concerning this matter.

10 Then the servant took ten of his master's camels and departed, taking all kinds of choice gifts from his master, and he set out and went to Aram-naharaim, to the city of Nahor. [11]He made the camels kneel down outside the city by the well of water; it was toward evening, the time when women go out to draw water. [12]And he said, "O Lord, God of my master Abraham, please grant me success today and show steadfast love to my master Abraham. [13]I am standing here by the spring

23:18–20 The language of *possession* in these verses represents an initial fulfillment of the promise God has made for Abraham to possess this land and for subsequent generations to inherit it. Indeed, the term used in v. 20 has a legal connotation in the way it is used here and often in other texts associated with the Priestly literature that gives sustained attention to those matters. (See **"The Bible and Methods," p. 2148**.) **24:1–67** This story, the longest chapter in Genesis, trains its focus for the first time on the generation that will follow Abraham. Despite all the concern for Isaac's conception and birth, even his near-death experience, the generation that will inherit God's promise to Abraham has remained entirely theoretical, something of an abstraction. This story changes all that—though it is not Isaac who changes that situation. Rather, it is Rebekah, who will become Isaac's wife, that gives color and vibrancy to the continuation of the ancestral line. **24:2** Placing the hand under the thigh appears to be a well-known custom for swearing an oath. **24:3–4** Abraham's insistence that Isaac does not marry among the Canaanites underscores his immigrant status. Indeed, the desire for the next generation to marry within their own community is common among migrant communities. **24:6** At the same time Abraham insists on an endogamous marriage for Isaac, he also will not consider his departure from the land now in his possession in Canaan. The conflicting desires illustrate the challenge of Abraham's status as a migrant who is acutely aware he is among communities that might not welcome his continued presence. **24:11** The role of the well is not incidental. Throughout Genesis, important events occur adjacent to water sources. Earlier it was God's conversation with Hagar (Gen. 21). Later it will be Joseph and his brothers (Gen. 37). This

of water, and the daughters of the townspeople are coming out to draw water. [14]Let the young woman to whom I shall say, 'Please offer your jar that I may drink,' and who shall say, 'Drink, and I will water your camels'—let her be the one whom you have appointed for your servant Isaac. By this I shall know that you have shown steadfast love to my master."

15 Before he had finished speaking, there was Rebekah, who was born to Bethuel son of Milcah, the wife of Nahor, Abraham's brother, coming out with her water jar on her shoulder. [16]The young woman was very fair to look upon, a virgin, whom no man had known. She went down to the spring, filled her jar, and came up. [17]Then the servant ran to meet her and said, "Please let me sip a little water from your jar." [18]"Drink, my lord," she said and quickly lowered her jar upon her hand and gave him a drink. [19]When she had finished giving him a drink, she said, "I will draw for your camels also, until they have finished drinking." [20]So she quickly emptied her jar into the trough and ran again to the well to draw, and she drew for all his camels. [21]The man gazed at her in silence to learn whether or not the LORD had made his journey successful.

22 When the camels had finished drinking, the man took a gold nose ring weighing a half shekel and two bracelets for her arms weighing ten gold shekels [23]and said, "Tell me whose daughter you are. Is there room in your father's house for us to spend the night?" [24]She said to him, "I am the daughter of Bethuel son of Milcah, whom she bore to Nahor." [25]She added, "We have plenty of straw and fodder and a place to spend the night." [26]The man bowed his head and worshiped the LORD [27]and said, "Blessed be the LORD, the God of my master Abraham, who has not forsaken his steadfast love and his faithfulness toward my master. As for me, the LORD has led me on the way to the house of my master's kin."

28 Then the young woman ran and told her mother's household about these things. [29]Rebekah had a brother whose name was Laban, and Laban ran out to the man, to the spring. [30]As soon as he had seen the nose ring and the bracelets on his sister's arms and when he heard the words of his sister Rebekah, "Thus the man spoke to me," he went to the man, and there he was, standing by the camels at the spring. [31]He said, "Come in, O blessed of the LORD. Why do you stand outside when I have prepared the house and a place for the camels?" [32]So the man came into the house, and Laban unloaded the camels and gave him straw and fodder for the camels and water to wash his feet and the feet of the men who were with him. [33]Then food was set before him to eat, but he said, "I will not eat until I have told my errand." He said, "Speak on."

34 So he said, "I am Abraham's servant. [35]The LORD has greatly blessed my master, and he has become wealthy; he has given him flocks and herds, silver and gold, male and female slaves, camels and donkeys. [36]And Sarah my master's wife bore a son to my master when she was old, and he has given him all that he has. [37]My master made me swear, saying, 'You shall not take a wife for my son from the daughters of the Canaanites in whose land I live, [38]but you shall go to my father's house, to my kindred, and get a wife for my son.' [39]I said to my master, 'Perhaps the woman will not follow me.' [40]But he said to me, 'The LORD, before whom I walk, will send his angel with you and make your way successful. You shall get a wife for my son from my kindred, from my father's house. [41]Then you will be free from my oath, when you come to my kindred; even if they will not give her to you, you will be free from my oath.'

42 "I came today to the spring and said, 'O LORD, God of my master Abraham, if now you will only make successful the way I am going! [43]I am standing here by the spring of water; let the young woman who comes out to draw, to whom I shall say, "Please give me a little water from your jar to drink," [44]and who will say to me, "Drink, and I will draw for your camels also"—let her be the woman whom the LORD has appointed for my master's son.'

45 "Before I had finished speaking in my heart, there was Rebekah coming out with her water jar on her shoulder, and she went down

pattern recurs in the New Testament, where Jesus has a significant encounter with a woman at a well (John 4). **24:24** While Rebekah's immediate generosity provides some insight as to her character, the most important element of her identity is articulated here: as the granddaughter of Nahor, Abraham's brother, she is from an acceptable family for marriage to Isaac. **24:29** *Laban* plays an important role in facilitating the arrangement for Rebekah to marry Isaac, but this is just a prelude to the central part he has in the narrative about Jacob, one of Rebekah and Isaac's two sons. He will reappear in Gen. 29, but

to the spring and drew. I said to her, 'Please let me drink.' ⁴⁶She quickly let down her jar from her shoulder and said, 'Drink, and I will also water your camels.' So I drank, and she also watered the camels. ⁴⁷Then I asked her, 'Whose daughter are you?' She said, 'The daughter of Bethuel, Nahor's son, whom Milcah bore to him.' So I put the ring on her nose and the bracelets on her arms. ⁴⁸Then I bowed my head and worshiped the LORD and blessed the LORD, the God of my master Abraham, who had led me by the right way to obtain the daughter of my master's kinsman for his son. ⁴⁹Now then, if you will deal loyally and truly with my master, tell me; and if not, tell me, so that I may turn either to the right hand or to the left."

50 Then Laban and Bethuel answered, "The thing comes from the LORD; we cannot speak to you anything bad or good. ⁵¹Look, Rebekah is before you, take her and go, and let her be the wife of your master's son, as the LORD has spoken."

52 When Abraham's servant heard their words, he bowed himself to the ground before the LORD. ⁵³And the servant brought out jewelry of silver and of gold and garments and gave them to Rebekah; he also gave to her brother and to her mother costly ornaments. ⁵⁴Then he and the men who were with him ate and drank, and they spent the night there. When they rose in the morning, he said, "Send me back to my master." ⁵⁵Her brother and her mother said, "Let the young woman remain with us a while, at least ten days; after that she may go." ⁵⁶But he said to them, "Do not delay me, since the LORD has made my journey successful; let me go that I may go to my master." ⁵⁷They said, "We will call the young woman and ask her." ⁵⁸And they called Rebekah and said to her, "Will you go with this man?" She said, "I will." ⁵⁹So they sent away

their sister Rebekah and her nurse along with Abraham's servant and his men. ⁶⁰And they blessed Rebekah and said to her,

"May you, our sister, become
    thousands of myriads;
may your offspring gain possession
    of the gates of their foes."

⁶¹Then Rebekah and her maids rose up, mounted the camels, and followed the man, and the servant took Rebekah and went his way.

62 Now Isaac had come from* Beer-lahai-roi and was settled in the Negeb. ⁶³Isaac went out in the evening to walk* in the field, and, looking up, he saw camels coming. ⁶⁴And Rebekah looked up, and when she saw Isaac, she slipped quickly from the camel ⁶⁵and said to the servant, "Who is the man over there, walking in the field to meet us?" The servant said, "It is my master." So she took her veil and covered herself. ⁶⁶And the servant told Isaac all the things that he had done. ⁶⁷Then Isaac brought her into his mother Sarah's tent. He took Rebekah, and she became his wife, and he loved her. So Isaac was comforted after his mother's death.

25 Abraham took another wife, whose name was Keturah. ²She bore him Zimran, Jokshan, Medan, Midian, Ishbak, and Shuah. ³Jokshan was the father of Sheba and Dedan. The sons of Dedan were Asshurim, Letushim, and Leummim. ⁴The sons of Midian were Ephah, Epher, Hanoch, Abida, and Eldaah. All these were the children of Keturah. ⁵Abraham gave all he had to Isaac. ⁶But to the sons of his concubines Abraham gave gifts, while he was still living, and he sent them away from his son Isaac, eastward to the east country.

v 24.62 Syr Tg: Heb *from coming to*   w 24.63 Meaning of Heb uncertain

this glimpse of him in Gen. 24 provides important context to that story. **24:57–58** Following ancient Near Eastern custom, the marriage between Isaac and Rebekah is agreed upon by her father and, in this case, her brother too. Lest one read the story as somehow more progressive than it is, the option for Rebekah's consent here appears to be the ten-day delay in her departure, not whether she will depart or not. Nevertheless, Rebekah signals some modicum of willingness in agreeing to go immediately. **24:60** This blessing has a number of connections to the promises made to Abraham, and passed on to Isaac, by God (see **"Blessing," p. 33**). It also anticipates some of the conflict between Rebekah's two sons, Esau and Jacob, that will follow later in the book.

25:1–18 It is surprising that there is no great account to draw Abraham's narrative to a close, but his story culminates with two genealogies and a prosaic account of his death. **25:1–5** Without any context, the story recounts the name and children of Abraham's second wife. The practice of polygamy appears very common in the ancient Near East, so there is a sense of commonality about it. The short account serves primarily to reaffirm how Abraham handles his estate: everything of significance passes to Isaac

7 This is the length of Abraham's life, one hundred seventy-five years. [8]Abraham breathed his last and died in a good old age, old and full of years, and was gathered to his people. [9]His sons Isaac and Ishmael buried him in the cave of Machpelah, in the field of Ephron son of Zohar the Hittite, east of Mamre, [10]the field that Abraham purchased from the Hittites. There Abraham was buried with his wife Sarah. [11]After the death of Abraham, God blessed his son Isaac. And Isaac settled at Beer-lahai-roi.

12 These are the descendants of Ishmael, Abraham's son, whom Hagar the Egyptian, Sarah's slave, bore to Abraham. [13]These are the names of the sons of Ishmael, named in the order of their birth: Nebaioth, the first-born of Ishmael; and Kedar, Adbeel, Mibsam, [14]Mishma, Dumah, Massa, [15]Hadad, Tema, Jetur, Naphish, and Kedemah. [16]These are the sons of Ishmael, and these are their names, by their villages and by their encampments, twelve princes according to their tribes. [17](This is the length of the life of Ishmael, one hundred thirty-seven years; he breathed his last and died and was gathered to his people.) [18]They settled from Havilah to Shur, which is opposite Egypt in the direction of Assyria; he settled down[x] alongside[y] all his people.

19 These are the descendants of Isaac, Abraham's son: Abraham was the father of Isaac, [20]and Isaac was forty years old when he married Rebekah, daughter of Bethuel the Aramean of Paddan-aram, sister of Laban the Aramean. [21]Isaac prayed to the LORD for his wife because she was barren, and the LORD granted his prayer, and his wife Rebekah conceived. [22]The children struggled together within her, and she said, "If it is to be this way, why do I live?"[z] So she went to inquire of the LORD. [23]And the LORD said to her,

"Two nations are in your womb,
    and two peoples born of you shall be
        divided;
the one shall be stronger than the other;
    the elder shall serve the younger."

[24]When her time to give birth was at hand, there were twins in her womb. [25]The first came out red, all his body like a hairy mantle, so they named him Esau. [26]Afterward his brother came out, with his hand gripping Esau's heel, so he was named Jacob.[a] Isaac was sixty years old when she bore them.

27 When the boys grew up, Esau was a skillful hunter, a man of the field, while Jacob was a quiet man, living in tents. [28]Isaac loved Esau because he was fond of game, but Rebekah loved Jacob.

29 Once when Jacob was cooking a stew, Esau came in from the field, and he was famished. [30]Esau said to Jacob, "Let me eat some of that red stuff, for I am famished!" (Therefore he was called Edom.[b]) [31]Jacob said, "First sell me your birthright." [32]Esau said, "I am about to die; of what use is a birthright to me?" [33]Jacob said, "Swear to me first." So he swore to him and sold his birthright to Jacob. [34]Then Jacob gave Esau bread and lentil stew,

x 25.18 Heb he fell   y 25.18 Or down in opposition to
z 25.22 Syr: Meaning of Heb uncertain   a 25.26 That is, he
takes by the heel or he supplants   b 25.30 That is, red

(v. 5), but the other children receive some material support. **25:9** This is the first time since Gen. 21 that Ishmael and Isaac appear together. Together, they bury their father in *Machpelah*, the field and cave to which Abraham gave so much importance in chap. 23.

25:19 The presence of another generation formula (Heb. "toledot") indicates the beginning of a new section here (see note at 2:4). Attention turns to Isaac—but as will become evident quickly, it is not him, but his wife Rebekah and his sons Esau and Jacob who are actually the focus of the story.

25:25 Esau's name is a play on word and sound in Hebrew. The word for hairy sounds like Seir, a designation for him and his descendants that would have been known to the audience. He is also described as reddish, which sounds close to Edom, another designation for Esau's ancestors.

25:26 Likewise, Jacob's name is a description of his birth and his character in later life. The Hebrew means "to take by the heel" or "to supplant." This provides an early indication, and a reminder every time his name occurs, that he and not his older brother will inherit the covenant promises through Isaac.

25:30 Here is yet another wordplay in a story filled with them: the reddish Esau cries out for the red-colored dish Jacob is cooking. Some interpreters have seen this as a means of making Esau out to be controlled by carnal desires, not higher thinking. One might equally see Esau as legitimately starving from an extended hunt to provide for the family. The text leaves the question open, likely because it wanted the audience to start pondering the character of these two figures.

25:31–34 The birthright refers to a common inheritance practice in the ancient Near East and the Old

and he ate and drank and rose and went his way. Thus Esau despised his birthright.

26 Now there was a famine in the land, besides the former famine that had occurred in the days of Abraham. And Isaac went to Gerar, to King Abimelech of the Philistines. ²The LORD appeared to Isaac[c] and said, "Do not go down to Egypt; settle in the land that I shall show you. ³Reside in this land as an alien, and I will be with you and will bless you, for to you and to your descendants I will give all these lands, and I will fulfill the oath that I swore to your father Abraham. ⁴I will make your offspring as numerous as the stars of heaven and will give to your offspring all these lands, and all the nations of the earth shall gain blessing for themselves through your offspring, ⁵because Abraham obeyed my voice and kept my charge, my commandments, my statutes, and my laws."

6 So Isaac settled in Gerar. ⁷When the men of the place asked him about his wife, he said, "She is my sister," for he was afraid to say "my wife," thinking, "or else the men of the place might kill me for the sake of Rebekah, because she is attractive in appearance." ⁸When Isaac had been there a long time, King Abimelech of the Philistines looked out of a window and saw him fondling his wife Rebekah. ⁹So Abimelech called for Isaac and said, "So she is your wife! Why, then, did you say, 'She is my sister'?" Isaac said to him, "Because I thought I might die because of her." ¹⁰Abimelech said, "What is this you have done to us? One of the people might easily have lain with your wife, and you would have brought guilt upon us." ¹¹So Abimelech warned all the people, saying, "Whoever touches this man or his wife shall be put to death."

12 Isaac sowed seed in that land and in the same year reaped a hundredfold. The LORD blessed him, ¹³and the man became rich; he prospered more and more until he became very wealthy. ¹⁴He had possessions of flocks and herds and a great household, so that the Philistines envied him. ¹⁵(Now the Philistines had stopped up and filled with earth all the wells that his father's servants had dug in the days of his father Abraham.) ¹⁶And Abimelech said to Isaac, "Go away from us; you have become too powerful for us."

17 So Isaac departed from there and camped in the Wadi Gerar and settled there. ¹⁸Isaac dug again the wells of water that had been dug in the days of his father Abraham, for the Philistines had stopped them up after the death of Abraham, and he gave them the names that his father had given them. ¹⁹But when Isaac's servants dug in the valley and found there a well of spring water, ²⁰the herders of Gerar quarreled with Isaac's herders, saying, "The water is ours." So he called the well Esek,[d] because they contended with him. ²¹Then they dug another well, and they

c 26.2 Heb *him*   d 26.20 That is, *contention*

Testament wherein the oldest son receives a double portion of the family wealth when all other sons receive a single portion.

26:1–35 For the sole time in Genesis, Isaac functions as the active protagonist in the narrative. This chapter is the third and final of the endangered ancestress stories, resembling 12:10–13:1 and 20:1–18 but expanding upon both of them in noteworthy ways. **26:1–2** Just as in chap. 12, the proximate cause for the ancestors to be living among foreigners is a famine. Isaac and Rebekah choose Gerar—the same place Abraham and Sarah go in chap. 20—where Abimelech remains the king. The prohibition to go to Egypt provides a contrast with the companion story in chap. 12 but also suggests hesitance to leave the land that God had promised to Abraham and now to Isaac (see **"Land," p. 30**). **26:8–11** Although the premise of this story is unchanged from chaps. 12 and 20, some of the details vary. Abimelech never takes Rebekah into his house but instead observes Isaac and Rebekah in an intimate encounter. The result is no different: the king expresses frustration at the patriarch's dishonesty but mercifully offers protection to them. **26:12–14** The result of Abimelech's pledge of security for Isaac is his enrichment. This maps directly onto the outcome of the similar schemes in chaps. 12 and 20. The Philistines are far from pleased with this outcome—an understandable response and the same one they had to Abraham's presence in 21:22–34, the conclusion to the time Abraham and Sarah spent in Gerar. **26:17–25** What occurs now is low-grade conflict between Isaac and the people of Gerar. When Isaac establishes the physical infrastructure needed for his continued residence (the opening of wells) it prompts the Philistines to seize those resources and compel him to move onward. This occurs three times, until Isaac opens the well at Beer-sheba. The location is no accident: in 21:22–34, it is the place where Abimelech

quarreled over that one also, so he called it Sitnah.*[e] [22]He moved from there and dug another well, and they did not quarrel over it, so he called it Rehoboth,[f] saying, "Now the Lord has made room for us, and we shall be fruitful in the land."

23 From there he went up to Beer-sheba. [24]And that very night the Lord appeared to him and said, "I am the God of your father Abraham; do not be afraid, for I am with you and will bless you and make your offspring numerous for my servant Abraham's sake." [25]So he built an altar there, called on the name of the Lord, and pitched his tent there. And there Isaac's servants dug a well.

26 Then Abimelech went to him from Gerar, with Ahuzzath his adviser and Phicol the commander of his army. [27]Isaac said to them, "Why have you come to me, seeing that you hate me and have sent me away from you?" [28]They said, "We see plainly that the Lord has been with you, so we say, let there be an oath between you and us, and let us make a covenant with you [29]so that you will do us no harm, just as we have not touched you and have done to you nothing but good and have sent you away in peace. You are now the blessed of the Lord." [30]So he made them a feast, and they ate and drank. [31]In the morning they rose early and exchanged oaths, and Isaac set them on their way, and they departed from him in peace. [32]That same day Isaac's servants came and told him about the well that they had dug and said to him, "We have found water!" [33]He called it Shibah;[g] therefore the name of the city is Beer-sheba[h] to this day.

34 When Esau was forty years old, he married Judith daughter of Beeri the Hittite and Basemath daughter of Elon the Hittite, [35]and they made life bitter for Isaac and Rebekah.

27 When Isaac was old and his eyes were dim so that he could not see, he called his elder son Esau and said to him, "My son," and he answered, "Here I am." [2]He said, "See, I am old; I do not know the day of my death. [3]Now then, take your weapons, your quiver and your bow, and go out to the field, and hunt game for me. [4]Then prepare for me savory food, such as I like, and bring it to me to eat, so that I may bless you before I die."

5 Now Rebekah was listening when Isaac spoke to his son Esau. So when Esau went to the field to hunt for game for his father,[i] [6]Rebekah said to her son Jacob, "I heard your father say to your brother Esau, [7]'Bring me game, and prepare for me savory food to eat, that I may bless you before the Lord before I die.' [8]Now therefore, my son, obey my word as I command you. [9]Go to the flock, and get me two choice kids, so that I may prepare from them savory food for your father, such as he likes, [10]and you shall take it to your father to eat, so that he may bless you before he dies." [11]But Jacob said to his mother Rebekah, "Look, my brother Esau is a hairy man, and I am a man of smooth skin. [12]Perhaps my father will feel me, and I shall seem to be mocking him and bring a curse on myself and not a

e 26.21 That is, *enmity* f 26.22 That is, *broad places* or *room* g 26.33 In Heb *Shibah* resembles the word for *oath* h 26.33 That is, *well of the oath* or *well of seven* i 27.5 Gk: Heb *to bring*

and Abraham reach a nonaggression pact so that the ancestors can live there. **26:26–31** In almost identical fashion to 21:22–34, Isaac negotiates a settlement with Abimelech that ends the hostilities with the Philistines and allows the ancestors to settle in Beer-sheba. **26:32–33** This etiology for the name of *Beer-sheba* uses the same play on the word for "oath." But since the account attributes the name to a different set of events, it suggests there were different traditions about which ancestor established the town. **26:34–35** This addendum to the chapter prepares for the following material. Esau's marriage to someone outside his ethnic group furnishes an explanation for tension in the family, which the subsequent stories will explore in great detail.

27:1–45 While Gen. 26 briefly attended to Isaac, attention now turns to Esau and Jacob. By the end of this story, the focus will narrow further to Jacob—on whom it will remain for the rest of the book. This story manifests the full implications of Esau's willingness to sell his birthright in chap. 25. **27:1–4** The premise for the story relies on the earlier statement that Isaac prefers Esau because he is a hunter (25:27–28). This story plays on that fact and the idea that this may be one of Isaac's final meals. **27:5–11** Whereas Isaac appears as a docile figure, Rebekah is active, influential, and unafraid. She instigates the trick that will obtain Isaac's blessing of Jacob, and later she will ensure that Jacob does not lose his life for it. Like Sarah before her, she uses her position of knowledge and influence in order to obtain the covenantal blessing for a younger son, upending what would have been the usually

blessing." [13]His mother said to him, "Let your curse be on me, my son; only obey my word, and go, get them for me." [14]So he went and got them and brought them to his mother, and his mother prepared savory food, such as his father loved. [15]Then Rebekah took the best garments of her elder son Esau, which were with her in the house, and put them on her younger son Jacob, [16]and she put the skins of the kids on his hands and on the smooth part of his neck. [17]Then she handed the savory food and the bread that she had prepared to her son Jacob.

[18] So he went in to his father and said, "My father," and he said, "Here I am; who are you, my son?" [19]Jacob said to his father, "I am Esau your firstborn. I have done as you told me; now sit up and eat of my game, so that you may bless me." [20]But Isaac said to his son, "How is it that you have found it so quickly, my son?" He answered, "Because the LORD your God granted me success." [21]Then Isaac said to Jacob, "Come near, that I may feel you, my son, to know whether you are really my son Esau or not." [22]So Jacob went up to his father Isaac, who felt him and said, "The voice is Jacob's voice, but the hands are the hands of Esau." [23]He did not recognize him because his hands were hairy like his brother Esau's hands, so he blessed him. [24]He said, "Are you really my son Esau?" He answered, "I am." [25]Then he said, "Bring it to me, that I may eat of my son's game and bless you." So he brought it to him, and he ate, and he brought him wine, and he drank. [26]Then his father Isaac said to him, "Come near and kiss me, my son." [27]So he came near and kissed him, and he smelled the smell of his garments and blessed him and said,

"Ah, the smell of my son
   is like the smell of a field that the
      LORD has blessed.
[28] May God give you of the dew of heaven
      and of the fatness of the earth
      and plenty of grain and wine.

[29] Let peoples serve you
      and nations bow down to you.
   Be lord over your brothers,
      and may your mother's sons bow
         down to you.
   Cursed be everyone who curses you,
      and blessed be everyone who blesses
         you!"

[30] As soon as Isaac had finished blessing Jacob, when Jacob had scarcely gone out from the presence of his father Isaac, his brother Esau came in from his hunting. [31]He also prepared savory food and brought it to his father. And he said to his father, "Let my father sit up and eat of his son's game, so that you may bless me." [32]His father Isaac said to him, "Who are you?" He answered, "I am your firstborn son, Esau." [33]Then Isaac trembled violently and said, "Who was it then that hunted game and brought it to me, and I ate it all before you came, and I have blessed him?—yes, and blessed he shall be!" [34]When Esau heard his father's words, he cried out with an exceedingly great and bitter cry and said to his father, "Bless me, me also, father!" [35]But he said, "Your brother came deceitfully, and he has taken away your blessing." [36]Esau said, "Is he not rightly named Jacob?[j] For he has supplanted me these two times. He took away my birthright, and look, now he has taken away my blessing." Then he said, "Have you not reserved a blessing for me?" [37]Isaac answered Esau, "I have already made him your lord, and I have given him all his brothers as servants, and with grain and wine I have sustained him. What then can I do for you, my son?" [38]Esau said to his father, "Have you only one blessing, father? Bless me, me also, father!" And Esau lifted up his voice and wept.

[39] Then his father Isaac answered him:
"See, away from the fatness of the earth
      shall your home be
   and away from the dew of heaven on
      high.

[j] 27.36 That is, *he supplants* or *he takes by the heel*

---

anticipated outcome. **27:21-27** Blind Isaac depends on his other senses in this episode. Some have argued that it emphasizes that his appetite overrides his logic. Certainly he has to be persuaded to disbelieve his ears (27:22). There is also a sense of comedy in the idea that Esau's hands can be mistaken for goat hair. Equally likely is that this is the narrator's way of showing how Rebekah and Jacob are skilled tricksters. **27:33-35** The emotion in Isaac and Esau's reactions is palpable. Even if one might have suspected this outcome from the exchange of birthright in chap. 25, the full realization of Jacob usurping his brother is no less excruciating for father or eldest son. **27:39-40** Like Ishmael, Esau does receive a notable blessing, albeit not the inheritance of the covenant blessings from God. Since Esau represents the Edomites, this may also be a way of implicitly admitting the Edomites' strength relative

[40] By your sword you shall live,
    and you shall serve your brother,
but when you break loose,[k]
    you shall break his yoke from your
        neck."

41 Now Esau hated Jacob because of the blessing with which his father had blessed him, and Esau said to himself, "The days of mourning for my father are approaching; then I will kill my brother Jacob." [42]But the words of her elder son Esau were told to Rebekah, so she sent and called her younger son Jacob and said to him, "Your brother Esau is consoling himself by planning to kill you. [43]Now therefore, my son, obey my voice; flee at once to my brother Laban in Haran, [44]and stay with him a while, until your brother's fury turns away—[45]until your brother's anger against you turns away, and he forgets what you have done to him; then I will send and bring you back from there. Why should I lose both of you in one day?"

46 Then Rebekah said to Isaac, "I am weary of my life because of the Hittite women. If Jacob marries one of the Hittite women such as these, one of the women of the land, what good will my life be to me?"

28 Then Isaac called Jacob and blessed him and charged him, "You shall not marry one of the Canaanite women. [2]Go at once to Paddan-aram to the house of Bethuel, your mother's father, and take as wife from there one of the daughters of Laban, your mother's brother. [3]May God Almighty[l] bless you and make you fruitful and numerous, that you may become a company of peoples.

[4]May he give to you the blessing of Abraham, to you and to your offspring with you, so that you may take possession of the land where you now live as an alien, land that God gave to Abraham." [5]Thus Isaac sent Jacob away, and he went to Paddan-aram, to Laban son of Bethuel the Aramean, the brother of Rebekah, Jacob's and Esau's mother.

6 Now Esau saw that Isaac had blessed Jacob and sent him away to Paddan-aram to take a wife from there and that as he blessed him he charged him, "You shall not marry one of the Canaanite women," [7]and that Jacob had obeyed his father and his mother and gone to Paddan-aram. [8]So when Esau saw that the Canaanite women did not please his father Isaac, [9]Esau went to Ishmael and took Mahalath daughter of Abraham's son Ishmael and sister of Nebaioth to be his wife in addition to the wives he had.

10 Jacob left Beer-sheba and went toward Haran. [11]He came to a certain place and stayed there for the night, because the sun had set. Taking one of the stones of the place, he put it under his head and lay down in that place. [12]And he dreamed that there was a stairway[m] set up on the earth, the top of it reaching to heaven, and the angels of God were ascending and descending on it. [13]And the LORD stood beside him[n] and said, "I am the LORD, the God of Abraham your father and the God of Isaac; the land on which you lie I will give to you and to your offspring, [14]and your offspring shall be like the dust of the earth, and you

k 27.40 Meaning of Heb uncertain   l 28.3 Traditional rendering of Heb El Shaddai   m 28.12 Or ramp   n 28.13 Or stood above it

to Israel and Judah in later times. **27:41–45** When Esau declares his intention to kill Jacob upon Isaac's passing—presumably not far into the future—Rebekah once again acts. She sends Jacob to seek protection with her brother, Laban, in Haran. She makes her son into something like an asylum seeker, compelling him to migrate to find protection from a legitimate threat on his life. This dynamic will feature prominently during Jacob's time under Laban's protection in chaps. 29–31.

27:46–28:9 Many scholars argue that since this section offers a different reason for Jacob's departure, it comes from a different source than 27:1–45. That may be the case, but there is another possible interpretation. Rebekah knows from her own history with Isaac that an exogamous marriage for his son is unthinkable. She uses this knowledge and her position of influence to establish an undeniable reason for Jacob's departure. Like people seeking asylum who benefit from the intervention of a lawyer or governmental advocate, Jacob benefits from the mediation of an influential person on his behalf.

28:10–22 This passage recounts Jacob's dream at Bethel. It is far better known as "Jacob's ladder," a reference to the ascending and descending of the angels in his vision. **28:12–13** The ladder reaches from the ground into the heavens. The image likely evokes the ramps or stairways on Mesopotamian ziggurats thought to allow one to ascend to the place where the deity might appear. Since Jacob is headed toward Haran, a place with strong connections to Mesopotamia, it seems that this architectural background informed the story. **28:14–15** Scholars note how this passage affirms that Jacob will inherit the covenant

shall spread abroad to the west and to the east and to the north and to the south, and all the families of the earth shall be blessed[o] in you and in your offspring. [15]Know that I am with you and will keep you wherever you go and will bring you back to this land, for I will not leave you until I have done what I have promised you." [16]Then Jacob woke from his sleep and said, "Surely the Lord is in this place—and I did not know it!" [17]And he was afraid and said, "How awesome is this place! This is none other than the house of God, and this is the gate of heaven."

18 So Jacob rose early in the morning, and he took the stone that he had put under his head and set it up for a pillar and poured oil on the top of it. [19]He called that place Bethel,[p] but the name of the city was Luz at the first. [20]Then Jacob made a vow, saying, "If God will be with me and will keep me in this way that I go and will give me bread to eat and clothing to wear, [21]so that I come again to my father's house in peace, then the Lord shall be my God, [22]and this stone, which I have set up for a pillar, shall be God's house, and of all that you give me I will surely give one-tenth to you."

29 Then Jacob went on his journey and came to the land of the people of the east. [2]As he looked, he saw a well in the field and three flocks of sheep lying there beside it, for out of that well the flocks were watered. The stone on the well's mouth was large, [3]and when all the flocks were gathered there, the shepherds would roll the stone from the mouth of the well and water the

sheep and put the stone back in its place on the mouth of the well.

4 Jacob said to them, "My brothers, where do you come from?" They said, "We are from Haran." [5]He said to them, "Do you know Laban son of Nahor?" They said, "We do." [6]He said to them, "Is it well with him?" "Yes," they replied, "and here is his daughter Rachel, coming with the sheep." [7]He said, "Look, it is still broad daylight; it is not time for the animals to be gathered together. Water the sheep, and go, pasture them." [8]But they said, "We cannot until all the flocks are gathered together, and the stone is rolled from the mouth of the well; then we water the sheep."

9 While he was still speaking with them, Rachel came with her father's sheep, for she kept them. [10]Now when Jacob saw Rachel, the daughter of his mother's brother Laban, and the sheep of his mother's brother Laban, Jacob went up and rolled the stone from the well's mouth and watered the flock of his mother's brother Laban. [11]Then Jacob kissed Rachel and wept aloud. [12]And Jacob told Rachel that he was her father's kinsman and that he was Rebekah's son, and she ran and told her father.

13 When Laban heard the news about his sister's son Jacob, he ran to meet him; he embraced him and kissed him and brought him to his house. Jacob[q] told Laban all these things, [14]and Laban said to him, "Surely you are my bone and my flesh!" And he stayed with him a month.

o 28.14 Or *shall bless themselves*   p 28.19 That is, *house of God*
q 29.13 Heb *He*

blessings previously promised to Abraham and Isaac (see **"Covenant," p. 23**). That is true, but v. 15 underscores that the Lord will oversee Jacob's experience as a migrant. This deity will accompany Jacob as he seeks protection in a foreign land and return him again. Jacob takes note of this, and it informs his response in vv. 20–22. **28:17** The name Bethel—which means "house of God" in Hebrew—plays on Jacob's realization when he awakes that God is in that place. **28:18** The practice of pouring oil over the erected stone pillar is a form of sacrifice, a recognition that Bethel is a sacred place where one may encounter the Lord. **28:20–22** The content of Jacob's vow is directly related to his migratory experience. He does not make reference to the covenant promises of land or descendants, only to God's promise to protect him and return him to Canaan. If God is faithful in that, then Jacob promises a tithe in response. The content of Jacob's vow underscores how central the experience of migration is for this narrative.

29:1–30 This chapter tells two interconnected stories. First, Jacob arrives in Haran seeking asylum, which his uncle Laban grants. Second, Jacob marries two of Laban's daughters, the result of an underhanded scheme by Laban that reveals the imbalanced nature of their relationship with each other. **29:2–6** As noted in chap. 24, a well often provides the background for important events in the ancestral narrative. In this case, it is Jacob's search for protection from Esau that will take place at the well. **29:9–11** The implication of v. 8 is that the stone to be rolled away is very large and only a group of men can move it. Thus, when Jacob undertakes this upon Rachel's arrival, the narrator attributes immense strength to him. **29:12–14** When Rebekah becomes aware of Jacob's identity, she immediately alerts her father.

15 Then Laban said to Jacob, "Because you are my kinsman, should you therefore serve me for nothing? Tell me, what shall your wages be?" ¹⁶Now Laban had two daughters; the name of the elder was Leah, and the name of the younger was Rachel. ¹⁷Leah's eyes were weak,ʳ but Rachel was graceful and beautiful. ¹⁸Jacob loved Rachel, so he said, "I will serve you seven years for your younger daughter Rachel." ¹⁹Laban said, "It is better that I give her to you than that I should give her to any other man; stay with me." ²⁰So Jacob served seven years for Rachel, and they seemed to him but a few days because of his love for her.

21 Then Jacob said to Laban, "Give me my wife that I may go in to her, for my time is completed." ²²So Laban gathered together all the people of the place and made a feast. ²³But in the evening he took his daughter Leah and brought her to Jacob, and he went in to her. ²⁴(Laban gave his maid Zilpah to his daughter Leah to be her maid.) ²⁵When morning came, it was Leah! And Jacob said to Laban, "What is this you have done to me? Did I not serve with you for Rachel? Why then have you deceived me?" ²⁶Laban said, "This is not done in our country—giving the younger before the firstborn. ²⁷Complete the week of this one, and we will give you the other also in return for serving me another seven years." ²⁸Jacob did so and completed her week; then Laban gave him his daughter Rachel as a wife.

²⁹(Laban gave his maid Bilhah to his daughter Rachel to be her maid.) ³⁰So Jacob went in to Rachel also, and he loved Rachel more than Leah. He served Labanˢ for another seven years.

31 When the LORD saw that Leah was unloved, he opened her womb, but Rachel was barren. ³²Leah conceived and bore a son, and she named him Reuben,ᵗ for she said, "Because the LORD has looked on my affliction, surely now my husband will love me." ³³She conceived again and bore a son and said, "Because the LORD has heard that I am hated, he has given me this son also," and she named him Simeon.ᵘ ³⁴Again she conceived and bore a son and said, "Now this time my husband will be joined to me, because I have borne him three sons"; therefore he was named Levi.ᵛ ³⁵She conceived again and bore a son and said, "This time I will praise the LORD," therefore she named him Judah;ʷ then she ceased bearing.

30

When Rachel saw that she bore Jacob no children, she envied her sister, and she said to Jacob, "Give me children, or I shall die!" ²Jacob became very angry with

r 29.17 Gk: Meaning of Heb uncertain   s 29.30 Heb him   t 29.32 That is, see, a son   u 29.33 In Heb Simeon resembles the verb for has heard   v 29.34 In Heb Levi resembles the verb for will be joined   w 29.35 In Heb Judah resembles the verb for I will praise

The brief, easily missed point at the end of v. 13 that Jacob recounts *these things*—an oblique reference to his conflict with Esau—calls forth Laban's declaration that Jacob is family and can remain in his home and under his protection. This is a form of ancient asylum, and it makes Jacob into a sort of refugee. **29:18–20** The offer to serve Laban without compensation for seven years in order to marry Rachel is an extraordinarily large offer. While it no doubt indicates Jacob's deep desire for Rachel, it also has a logic related to his migratory status. By agreeing to this term of service, Jacob obtains an assurance that he can live safe from Esau's threat for a long time. One can see that this offer has a number of things that make it attractive to Jacob. **29:25–26** The morning after the wedding, Jacob discovers what Laban has done. He exclaims his displeasure with the father's dishonesty. Laban's response is revealing: by saying that Jacob's request to marry the younger daughter is not something done *in our country*, he makes clear that Jacob remains a foreigner, even if he has been allowed to live in Haran. Laban feels empowered to treat Jacob dishonestly at least in part because he believes a migrant like Jacob may be handled thus. **29:28** Despite his anger and Laban's manipulation, Jacob agrees to another seven-year term for Rachel. Not only does this underscore even further his love for her; it extends the time he may remain safe from Esau. This is not unlike contemporary asylum seekers, who often accept arrangements they deem unfair or unpalatable (such as living in a refugee camp) because they have no other good options available to them. **29:31–35** The now familiar pattern of the ancestral narrative occurs again: one unfavored woman bears children for the patriarch while another looks on dismayed by this situation. Here, Leah bears Jacob four sons—God's recompense to her, since she is unloved by Jacob. **30:1–24** This section depicts the birth of seven more sons and one daughter to Jacob. These sons will become the patriarchs of the tribes of Israel. While the birth of the children takes center stage, the conflict between Leah and Rachel continues to simmer in the background. **30:1** A clearer statement

Rachel and said, "Am I in the place of God, who has withheld from you the fruit of the womb?" [3]Then she said, "Here is my maid Bilhah; go in to her, that she may bear upon my knees and that I too may have children through her." [4]So she gave him her maid Bilhah as a wife, and Jacob went in to her. [5]And Bilhah conceived and bore Jacob a son. [6]Then Rachel said, "God has judged me and has also heard my voice and given me a son"; therefore she named him Dan.[x] [7]Rachel's maid Bilhah conceived again and bore Jacob a second son. [8]Then Rachel said, "With mighty wrestlings I have wrestled with my sister and have prevailed," so she named him Naphtali.[y]

9 When Leah saw that she had ceased bearing children, she took her maid Zilpah and gave her to Jacob as a wife. [10]Then Leah's maid Zilpah bore Jacob a son. [11]And Leah said, "Good fortune!" So she named him Gad.[z] [12]Leah's maid Zilpah bore Jacob a second son. [13]And Leah said, "Happy am I! For the women will call me happy," so she named him Asher.[a]

14 In the days of wheat harvest Reuben went and found mandrakes in the field and brought them to his mother Leah. Then Rachel said to Leah, "Please give me some of your son's mandrakes." [15]But she said to her, "Is it a small matter that you have taken away my husband? Would you take away my son's mandrakes also?" Rachel said, "Then he may lie with you tonight for your son's mandrakes." [16]When Jacob came from the field in the evening, Leah went out to meet him and said, "You must come in to me, for I have hired you with my son's mandrakes." So he lay with her that night. [17]And God heeded Leah, and she conceived and bore Jacob a fifth son. [18]Leah said, "God has given me my hire because I gave my maid to my husband," so she named him Issachar.[b] [19]And Leah conceived again, and she bore Jacob a sixth son. [20]Then Leah said, "God has endowed me with a good gift; now my husband will honor me, because I have borne him six sons," so she named him Zebulun.[c] [21]Afterwards she bore a daughter and named her Dinah.

22 Then God remembered Rachel, and God heeded her and opened her womb. [23]She conceived and bore a son and said, "God has taken away my reproach," [24]and she named him Joseph,[d] saying, "May the LORD add to me another son!"

25 When Rachel had borne Joseph, Jacob said to Laban, "Send me away, that I may go to my own home and country. [26]Give me my wives and my children for whom I have served you, and let me go, for you know very well the service I have given you." [27]But

---

x 30.6 That is, *he judged*   y 30.8 In Heb *Naphtali* resembles the verb for *I have wrestled*   z 30.11 That is, *fortune*   a 30.13 That is, *happy*   b 30.18 In Heb *Issachar* resembles the word for *my hire*   c 30.20 In Heb *Zebulun* resembles the verb for *honor*   d 30.24 That is, *he adds*

---

of the tension between Leah and Rachel is hard to imagine. By opening this account with such a fierce demand from Rachel, the narrator makes clear that the contest between the two sister-wives will not fade away. **30:3-8** Just as Sarah first attempted to address her childlessness through the surrogacy of her maidservant (see 16:1–4), so too does Rachel. Bilhah, her servant, bears two boys. The names of the boys reflect Rachel's interpretation of events: *Dan*, meaning "he judged," and *Naphtali*, representing "I have wrestled," articulate Rachel's sense of vindication. **30:9-13** Turnabout being fair play, Leah now has her maidservant Zilpah bear children with Jacob. The result is two more sons, *Gad* and *Asher*, each given a name that reflects Leah's sense of vindication. **30:14-18** This vignette relies on the idea that the mandrake functioned as an aphrodisiac (see Song. 7:13). Leah's sense of rejection punctures the surface in v. 15, but in keeping with the theme of the ancestral narrative, she uses the situation to her advantage too. The resulting son is called *Issachar*, connected in v. 18 to *my hire*. **30:21** The birth of *Dinah*, Jacob's only named daughter, is an aside here. She will feature again in chap. 34. **30:22-24** One expects the mandrakes to play some role in Rachel's fertility, but they remain unmentioned. Perhaps that is intended to further emphasize that it is YHWH that opens her womb and provides her a son. The boy, named *Joseph* (from "he adds"), will become the final main character of Genesis in chaps. 37-50.

30:25-43 This narrative returns to Jacob's role as a trickster, using deception to his benefit. In this case, it closely parallels the endangered ancestress stories in chaps. 12, 20, and 26, where the migrant in a foreign land employs deception toward their host and emerges wealthier from the encounter. **30:25-30** The premise for the story is Jacob's fulfillment of his contract with Laban and his desire to choose where he shall live. Laban, however, refuses to recognize Jacob's good faith, and attempts to compel him to stay longer in an arrangement he knows has benefited him far more than Jacob. **30:31-36** Jacob

Laban said to him, "If you will allow me to say so, I have learned by divination that the LORD has blessed me because of you; ²⁸name your wages, and I will give it." ²⁹Jacob said to him, "You yourself know how I have served you and how your livestock have fared with me. ³⁰For you had little before I came, and it has increased abundantly, and the LORD has blessed you wherever I turned. But now when shall I provide for my own household also?" ³¹He said, "What shall I give you?" Jacob said, "You shall not give me anything; if you will do this for me, I will again feed your flock and keep it: ³²let me pass through all your flock today, removing from it every speckled and spotted sheep and every black lamb and the spotted and speckled among the goats, and such shall be my wages. ³³So my honesty will answer for me later, when you come to look into my wages with you. Every one that is not speckled and spotted among the goats and black among the lambs, if found with me, shall be counted stolen." ³⁴Laban said, "Good! Let it be as you have said." ³⁵But that day Laban removed the male goats that were striped and spotted, and all the female goats that were speckled and spotted, every one that had white on it, and every lamb that was black and put them in charge of his sons, ³⁶and he set a distance of three days' journey between himself and Jacob, while Jacob was pasturing the rest of Laban's flock.

37 Then Jacob took fresh rods of poplar and almond and plane and peeled white streaks in them, exposing the white of the rods. ³⁸He set the rods that he had peeled in front of the flocks in the troughs, that is, the watering places, where the flocks came to drink. And since they bred when they came to drink, ³⁹the flocks bred in front of the rods, and so the flocks produced young that were striped, speckled, and spotted. ⁴⁰Jacob separated the lambs and set the faces of the flocks toward the striped and the completely black animals in the flock of Laban, and he put his own droves apart and did not put them with Laban's flock. ⁴¹Whenever the stronger of the flock were breeding, Jacob laid the rods in the troughs before the eyes of the flock, that they might breed among the rods, ⁴²but for the feebler of the flock he did not lay them there, so the feebler were Laban's and the stronger Jacob's. ⁴³Thus the man grew exceedingly rich and had large flocks and male and female slaves and camels and donkeys.

31 Now Jacob heard that the sons of Laban were saying, "Jacob has taken all that was our father's; he has gained all this wealth from what belonged to our father." ²And Jacob saw that Laban did not regard him as favorably as he did before. ³Then the LORD said to Jacob, "Return to the land of your ancestors and to your kindred, and I will be with you." ⁴So Jacob sent and called Rachel and Leah into the field where his flock was ⁵and said to them, "I see that your father does not regard me as favorably as he did before. But the God of my father has been with me. ⁶You know that I have served your father with all my strength, ⁷yet your father has cheated me and changed my wages ten times, but God did not permit him to harm me. ⁸If he said, 'The speckled shall be your wages,' then all the flock bore speckled, and if he said, 'The striped shall be your wages,' then all the flock bore striped. ⁹Thus God has taken away the livestock of your father and given them to me.

10 "During the mating of the flock I once had a dream in which I looked up and saw that the male goats that leaped upon the flock were striped, speckled, and mottled. ¹¹Then the angel of God said to me in the dream, 'Jacob,' and I said, 'Here I am!' ¹²And he said, 'Look up and see that all the goats that leap on the flock are striped, speckled, and mottled, for I have seen all that Laban is doing to you.

---

proposes a division of the livestock to which Laban agrees—but then immediately undermines. If there were any doubt left of Laban's duplicitous character after his conduct in chap. 29, there can be none now. **30:37–43** This account of how Jacob defeats Laban's scheme depends on the ancient belief that the offspring of animals were determined in part by what they saw while mating. Such "magical" understandings appear in many ancient contexts, and legendary stories like this one preserve them for future generations. The particular irony of this story is that the word for white in v. 37 uses the same letters as Laban's name. The turn of phrase would have not been lost on ancient audiences.

31:1–54 Jacob, with the help of his wives Leah and Rachel, now wins his freedom from Laban. Once again, this is only possible through deception, though in this instance it is Rachel, not Jacob, who does the

[13]I am the God of Bethel, where you anointed a pillar and made a vow to me. Now leave this land at once and return to the land of your birth.'" [14]Then Rachel and Leah answered him, "Is there any portion or inheritance left to us in our father's house? [15]Are we not regarded by him as foreigners? For he has sold us, and he has been using up the money given for us. [16]All the property that God has taken away from our father belongs to us and to our children; now then, do whatever God has said to you."

17 So Jacob arose and set his children and his wives on camels, [18]and he drove away all his livestock, all the property that he had gained, the livestock in his possession that he had acquired in Paddan-aram, to go to his father Isaac in the land of Canaan.

19 Now Laban had gone to shear his sheep, and Rachel stole her father's household gods. [20]And Jacob deceived Laban the Aramean, in that he did not tell him that he intended to flee. [21]So he fled with all that he had; starting out he crossed the Euphrates[e] and set his face toward the hill country of Gilead.

22 On the third day Laban was told that Jacob had fled. [23]So he took his kinsfolk with him and pursued him for seven days until he caught up with him in the hill country of Gilead. [24]But God came to Laban the Aramean in a dream by night and said to him, "Take heed that you say not a word to Jacob, either good or bad."

25 Laban overtook Jacob. Now Jacob had pitched his tent in the hill country, and Laban with his kinsfolk camped in the hill country of Gilead. [26]Laban said to Jacob, "What have you done? You have deceived me and carried away my daughters like captives of the sword. [27]Why did you flee secretly and deceive me and not tell me? I would have sent you away with mirth and songs, with tambourine and lyre. [28]And why did you not permit me to kiss my sons and my daughters farewell? What you have done is foolish. [29]It is in my power to do you harm, but the God of your father spoke to me last night, saying, 'Take heed that you speak to Jacob neither good nor bad.' [30]Even though you had to go because you longed greatly for your father's house, why did you steal my gods?" [31]Jacob answered Laban, "Because I was afraid, for I thought that you would take your daughters from me by force. [32]But anyone with whom you find your gods shall not live. In the presence of our kinsfolk, point out what I have that is yours, and take it." Now Jacob did not know that Rachel had stolen the gods.[f]

33 So Laban went into Jacob's tent and into Leah's tent and into the tent of the two maids, but he did not find them. And he went out of Leah's tent and entered Rachel's. [34]Now Rachel had taken the household gods and put them in the camel's saddle and sat on them. Laban felt all about in the tent but did not find them. [35]And she said to her father, "Let not my lord be angry that I cannot rise before you, for the way of women is upon me." So he searched but did not find the household gods.

36 Then Jacob became angry and upbraided Laban. Jacob said to Laban, "What is my

e 31.21 Heb *the river* f 31.32 Heb *them*

deceiving. **31:13** This dream provides a companion to the one Jacob had in chap. 28. There, his encounter with YHWH elicited a promise to serve YHWH if the deity protected him and returned him to Canaan. This dream expresses YHWH's willingness to fulfill that request. **31:14–16** Laban's schemes have not only been intended to defraud Jacob but also plundered the dowries for Leah and Rachel. Both women recognize their hope for future protection and care lies with Jacob and their children. They now side with Jacob against their father, partially out of resentment and partially out of self-preservation. **31:19–21** The precise nature of the household gods is unclear, but they were a common feature in ancient homes (see 1 Sam. 19:13). Rachel's intent in taking the statues is unclear, but its main function in the story is to create irony in Jacob's honest declaration that he has not taken them despite them being in his traveling party. Moreover, Rachel's act underscores that she has committed her future to Jacob at the expense of her relationship with her father. **31:29–31** Laban finally admits his power over Jacob. He also allows that it has taken a dream from God to convince him to refrain from harming Jacob (v. 29). For his part, Jacob states his behavior has all been motivated by fear too. The exchange highlights how the migrant Jacob, disempowered by his reliance on Laban for protection, has felt compelled to act in certain ways because of the imbalance in power between the two. **31:32** Jacob makes this promise without knowing what Rachel has done. Many interpreters see her early death during childbirth in chap. 35 as the unintended fulfillment of this statement. **31:35** Rachel claims she cannot stand because of her menstrual period. The cunning excuse not only protects Rachel from being found out; it takes the audience's mind back to the centrality of fertility in the whole story. **31:36–42** Jacob berates Laban for his treatment of him. Unlike the man who willingly offered to serve the excessively long

offense? What is my sin, that you have hotly pursued me? [37]Although you have felt about through all my goods, what have you found of all your household goods? Set it here before my kinsfolk and your kinsfolk, so that they may decide between us two. [38]These twenty years I have been with you; your ewes and your female goats have not miscarried, and I have not eaten the rams of your flocks. [39]That which was torn by wild beasts I did not bring to you; I bore the loss of it myself; of my hand you required it, whether stolen by day or stolen by night. [40]It was like this with me: by day the heat consumed me and the cold by night, and my sleep fled from my eyes. [41]These twenty years I have been in your house; I served you fourteen years for your two daughters and six years for your flock, and you have changed my wages ten times. [42]If the God of my father, the God of Abraham and the Fear[g] of Isaac, had not been on my side, surely now you would have sent me away empty-handed. God saw my affliction and the labor of my hands and rebuked you last night."

43 Then Laban answered and said to Jacob, "The daughters are my daughters, the children are my children, the flocks are my flocks, and all that you see is mine. But what can I do today about these daughters of mine or about their children whom they have borne? [44]Come now, let us make a covenant, you and I, and let it be a witness between you and me." [45]So Jacob took a stone and set it up as a pillar. [46]And Jacob said to his kinsfolk, "Gather stones," and they took stones and made a heap, and they ate there by the heap. [47]Laban called it Jegar-sahadutha,[b] but Jacob called it Galeed.[i] [48]Laban said, "This heap is a witness between you and me today." Therefore he called it Galeed [49]and the pillar[j] Mizpah, for he said, "The LORD watch between you and me, when we are absent one from the other. [50]If you ill-treat my daughters or if you take wives in addition to my daughters,

though no one else is with us, remember that God is witness between you and me."

51 Then Laban said to Jacob, "See this heap and see the pillar, which I have set between you and me. [52]This heap is a witness, and the pillar is a witness, that I will not pass beyond this heap to you, and you will not pass beyond this heap and this pillar to me, for harm. [53]May the God of Abraham and the God of Nahor[k] judge between us." So Jacob swore by the Fear of his father Isaac, [54]and Jacob offered a sacrifice on the height and called his kinsfolk to eat bread, and they ate bread and tarried all night in the hill country.

55 [l]Early in the morning Laban rose up and kissed his grandchildren and his daughters and blessed them; then he departed and returned home.

32 Jacob went on his way, and the angels of God met him; [2]when Jacob saw them he said, "This is God's camp!" So he called that place Mahanaim.[m]

3 Jacob sent messengers before him to his brother Esau in the land of Seir, the country of Edom, [4]instructing them, "Thus you shall say to my lord Esau: Thus says your servant Jacob, 'I have lived with Laban as an alien and stayed until now, [5]and I have oxen, donkeys, flocks, male and female slaves, and I have sent to tell my lord, in order that I may find favor in your sight.' "

6 The messengers returned to Jacob, saying, "We came to your brother Esau, and he is coming to meet you, and four hundred men are with him." [7]Then Jacob was greatly afraid and distressed, and he divided the people who were with him and the flocks and herds and camels into two companies, [8]thinking, "If

g 31.42 Meaning of Heb uncertain   h 31.47 In Aramaic, *heap of witness*   i 31.47 In Hebrew, *heap of witness*   j 31.49 Cn: MT lacks *pillar*   k 31.53 Heb mss Gk: MT adds *the God of their father*   l 31.55 32.1 in Heb   m 32.2 That is, *two camps*

terms for both of Laban's daughters because of his fear, now Jacob speaks with confidence and conviction. Freed from Laban's immense power over him, Jacob is empowered to act in his own interest.
32:1–32 Jacob's attention immediately turns toward what will face him as he enters Canaan: the threat upon his life from Esau. This chapter is a prelude to their encounter in chap. 33 and prepares the audience for it. **32:1–2** Jacob once again sees the angels of God (see 28:12). Concluding he is in God's presence he names the place *God's camp*. The name, however, uses a Hebrew form called the dual, meaning there are two of a thing. Calling the place "two camps" anticipates the strategy he will use to appease Esau. **32:3–8** Jacob moves proactively to reconcile with Esau by sending an envoy bearing gifts. When his envoys return and report Esau is traveling with four hundred men, Jacob concludes they are an army, not a welcoming convoy. He decides to divide his group into two, with the hope of

Esau comes to the one company and destroys it, then the company that is left will escape."

9 And Jacob said, "O God of my father Abraham and God of my father Isaac, O LORD who said to me, 'Return to your country and to your kindred, and I will do you good,' ¹⁰I am not worthy of the least of all the steadfast love and all the faithfulness that you have shown to your servant, for with only my staff I crossed this Jordan, and now I have become two companies. ¹¹Deliver me, please, from the hand of my brother, from the hand of Esau, for I am afraid of him; he may come and kill us all, the mothers with the children. ¹²Yet you have said, 'I will surely do you good and make your offspring as the sand of the sea, which cannot be counted because of their number.'"

13 So he spent that night there, and from what he had with him he took a present for his brother Esau, ¹⁴two hundred female goats and twenty male goats, two hundred ewes and twenty rams, ¹⁵thirty milch camels and their colts, forty cows and ten bulls, twenty female donkeys and ten male donkeys. ¹⁶These he delivered into the hand of his servants, every drove by itself, and said to his servants, "Pass on ahead of me, and put a space between drove and drove." ¹⁷He instructed the one in the lead, "When Esau my brother meets you and asks you, 'To whom do you belong? Where are you going? And whose are these ahead of you?' ¹⁸then you shall say, 'They belong to your servant Jacob; they are a present sent to my lord Esau, and moreover he is behind us.'" ¹⁹He likewise instructed the second and the third and all who followed the droves, "You shall say the same thing to Esau when you meet him, ²⁰and you shall say, 'Moreover your servant Jacob is behind us.'" For he thought, "I may appease him with the present that goes ahead of me, and afterwards I shall see his face; perhaps he will accept me." ²¹So the present passed

on ahead of him, and he himself spent that night in the camp.

22 The same night he got up and took his two wives, his two maids, and his eleven children and crossed the ford of the Jabbok. ²³He took them and sent them across the stream, and likewise everything that he had. ²⁴Jacob was left alone, and a man wrestled with him until daybreak. ²⁵When the man saw that he did not prevail against Jacob, he struck him on the hip socket, and Jacob's hip was put out of joint as he wrestled with him. ²⁶Then he said, "Let me go, for the day is breaking." But Jacob said, "I will not let you go, unless you bless me." ²⁷So he said to him, "What is your name?" And he said, "Jacob." ²⁸Then the man" said, "You shall no longer be called Jacob, but Israel,° for you have striven with God and with humans^p and have prevailed." ²⁹Then Jacob asked him, "Please tell me your name." But he said, "Why is it that you ask my name?" And there he blessed him. ³⁰So Jacob called the place Peniel,^q saying, "For I have seen God face to face, yet my life is preserved." ³¹The sun rose upon him as he passed Penuel, limping because of his hip. ³²Therefore to this day the Israelites do not eat the thigh muscle that is on the hip socket, because he struck Jacob on the hip socket at the thigh muscle.

33 Now Jacob looked up and saw Esau coming, and four hundred men with him. So he divided the children among Leah and Rachel and the two maids. ²He put the maids with their children in front, then Leah with her children, and Rachel and Joseph last of all. ³He himself went on ahead of them, bowing himself to the ground seven times, until he came near his brother.

4 But Esau ran to meet him and embraced him and fell on his neck and kissed him, and

n 32.28 Heb *he*   o 32.28 That is, *the one who strives with God* or *God strives*   p 32.28 Or *with divine and human beings*   q 32.30 That is, *the face of God*

saving some even if others are captured. **32:24–28** The identity of *the man* that wrestles Jacob remains unclear. The audience might believe him to be human at first, though the remainder of the scene will dispel that idea. To defeat Jacob, the figure dislocates Jacob's hip (v. 25). Jacob still will not release his opponent, demanding a blessing before doing so (see **"Blessing," p. 33**). The figure offers him a new name, not a blessing per se: Jacob shall now be known as Israel, meaning the one who strives with God. **32:29–32** Names are key to the passage. Jacob demands his opponent's name, but he is rebuffed. Finally, Jacob receives his blessing, though its contents remain unstated. Nevertheless, Jacob knows he has encountered God, so he names this place *Peniel*, "the face of God."

33:1–20 This chapter presents the climax of the story that began in chap. 25 with the conflict between Esau and Jacob. While Jacob fears he will encounter a bitter and aggrieved brother, time has changed

they wept. [5]When Esau looked up and saw the women and children, he said, "Who are these with you?" Jacob said, "The children whom God has graciously given your servant." [6]Then the maids drew near, they and their children, and bowed down; [7]Leah likewise and her children drew near and bowed down; and finally Joseph and Rachel drew near, and they bowed down. [8]Esau said, "What do you mean by all this company that I met?" Jacob answered, "To find favor with my lord." [9]But Esau said, "I have enough, my brother; keep what you have for yourself." [10]Jacob said, "No, please; if I find favor with you, then accept my present from my hand, for truly to see your face is like seeing the face of God, since you have received me with such favor. [11]Please accept my gift that is brought to you, because God has dealt graciously with me and because I have everything I want." So he urged him, and he took it.

[12] Then Esau said, "Let us journey on our way, and I will go alongside you." [13]But Jacob said to him, "My lord knows that the children are frail and that the flocks and herds, which are nursing, are a care to me, and if they are overdriven for one day, all the flocks will die. [14]Let my lord pass on ahead of his servant, and I will lead on slowly, according to the pace of the cattle that are before me and according to the pace of the children, until I come to my lord in Seir."

[15] So Esau said, "Let me leave with you some of the people who are with me." But he said, "Why should my lord be so kind to me?" [16]So Esau returned that day on his way to Seir. [17]But Jacob journeyed to Succoth[r] and built himself a house and made booths for his cattle; therefore the place is called Succoth.

[18] Jacob came safely to the city of Shechem, which is in the land of Canaan, on his way from Paddan-aram, and he camped before the city. [19]And from the sons of Hamor, Shechem's father, he bought for one hundred pieces of money[s] the plot of land on which he had pitched his tent. [20]There he erected an altar and called it El-Elohe-Israel.[t]

34 Now Dinah the daughter of Leah, whom she had borne to Jacob, went out to visit the daughters of the region. [2]When Shechem son of Hamor the Hivite, prince of the region, saw her, he seized her and lay with her by force. [3]And his soul was drawn to Dinah daughter of Jacob; he loved the young woman and spoke tenderly to her. [4]So Shechem spoke to his father Hamor, saying, "Get me this girl to be my wife."

[5] Now Jacob heard that Shechem[u] had defiled his daughter Dinah, but his sons were with his cattle in the field, so Jacob held his peace until they came. [6]And Hamor the father of Shechem went out to Jacob to speak with him, [7]just as the sons of Jacob came in from

r 33.17 That is, *booths*   s 33.19 Heb *one hundred qesitah*
t 33.20 That is, *God, the God of Israel*   u 34.5 Heb *he*

Esau. Rather than kill his brother, Esau seeks reconciliation. **33:8–9** The depth of Esau's transformation emerges here. The figure who once trembled with anger and voiced death threats because of his lost inheritance now proclaims that his own wealth is more than sufficient. **33:10** Jacob now makes a direct comparison between seeing Esau face-to-face and encountering God in the same fashion the night before. The prevailing view was that anyone who saw a deity directly would die (see Exod. 33:19–20). Jacob was spared this fate when wrestling God at the Jabbok, and he is equally amazed to be spared death when he stands before Esau. **33:12–17** Now comes the test of Jacob's transformation. Esau has extended the offer of peace and reconciliation, reflected by his invitation for Jacob to join him in Seir. Though Jacob states his intention to do so, this is yet another lie. Rather, Jacob remains dishonest, heading instead to Succoth. Some interpret this as Jacob's refusal to integrate with outsiders as Esau has done (recall his marriage in 28:6–9). Others see a man whose character remains questionable, deploying yet another falsehood. The latter interpretation seems most likely but perhaps understandable: Jacob has been a migrant who was oppressed by Laban, who appeared welcoming to him but used his authority in unfair ways. **33:18–20** Reminiscent of Abraham's purchase of Machpelah in chap. 23, Jacob obtains a plot of land to represent his presence in Canaan. He builds a place of worship there and names it to show his allegiance to the deity who has returned him safely to Canaan.

34:1–31 This grisly story of rape and murder contains a great deal of uncomfortable material. Its aim is to reinforce Jacob's identity as a migrant among other communities, unsure of his status and safety living in close proximity to them. **34:2–4** *Dinah*, Jacob's only named daughter, is sexually assaulted and raped. *Shechem*, a prince from the Hivites, one of the other communities dwelling in the area, is the assailant. The horror of the act is not mitigated by his adoption of the common ancient practice

the field. When they heard of it, the men were indignant and very angry, because he had committed an outrage in Israel by lying with Jacob's daughter, for such a thing ought not to be done.

8 But Hamor spoke with them, saying, "The heart of my son Shechem longs for your daughter; please give her to him in marriage. ⁹Make marriages with us; give your daughters to us, and take our daughters for yourselves. ¹⁰You shall live with us, and the land shall be open to you; live and trade in it and get property in it." ¹¹Shechem also said to her father and to her brothers, "Let me find favor with you, and whatever you say to me I will give. ¹²Put the marriage present and gift as high as you like, and I will give whatever you ask me; only give me the young woman to be my wife."

13 The sons of Jacob answered Shechem and his father Hamor deceitfully because he had defiled their sister Dinah. ¹⁴They said to them, "We cannot do this thing, to give our sister to one who is uncircumcised, for that would be a disgrace to us. ¹⁵Only on this condition will we consent to you: that you will become as we are and every male among you be circumcised. ¹⁶Then we will give our daughters to you, and we will take your daughters for ourselves, and we will live among you and become one people. ¹⁷But if you will not listen to us and be circumcised, then we will take our daughter and be gone."

18 Their words pleased Hamor and Hamor's son Shechem. ¹⁹And the young man did not delay to do the thing because he was delighted with Jacob's daughter. Now he was the most honored of all his family. ²⁰So Hamor and his son Shechem came to the gate of their city and spoke to the men of their city, saying, ²¹"These people are friendly with us; let them live in the land and trade in it, for the land is large enough for them; let us take their daughters in marriage, and let us give them our daughters. ²²Only on this condition will they agree to live among us, to become one people: that every male among us be circumcised as they are circumcised. ²³Will not their livestock, their property, and all their animals be ours? Only let us agree with them, and they will live among us." ²⁴And all who went out of the city gate heeded Hamor and his son Shechem, and every male was circumcised, all who went out of the gate of his city.

25 On the third day, when they were still in pain, two of the sons of Jacob, Simeon and Levi, Dinah's brothers, took their swords and came against the city unawares and killed all the males. ²⁶They killed Hamor and his son Shechem with the sword and took Dinah out of Shechem's house and went away. ²⁷And the other sons of Jacob came upon the slain and plundered the city because their sister had been defiled. ²⁸They took their flocks and their herds, their donkeys, and whatever was in the city and in the field. ²⁹All their wealth, all their little ones and their wives, all that was in the houses, they captured and made their prey. ³⁰Then Jacob said to Simeon and Levi, "You have brought trouble on me by making me odious to the inhabitants of the land, the Canaanites and the Perizzites; my numbers are few, and if they gather themselves against me and attack me, I shall be destroyed, both I and my household." ³¹But they said, "Should our sister be treated like a prostitute?"

whereby a man might lay claim to marrying a woman he has raped. **34:8–12** *Hamor* spares no lengths in seeking to persuade Jacob to marry Dinah to Shechem. He offers a sort of permanent resident status (v. 10) and offers to pay a bride price set as high as Jacob likes. **34:13–15** Jacob's sons seize on the idea that no expense will be spared for Dinah. Rather than ask for wealth, they instead demand action: the Hivites must circumcise themselves for Shechem to marry Dinah and for a wider partnership to form. Like father, like sons: the offer is a deceptive scheme cut from the same cloth as those Jacob has performed against Esau and Laban. **34:25–29** Now the intent of the demand for circumcision becomes clear. Jacob's sons have neutered the Hivites' strength, allowing a successful attack. Indeed, their retribution goes far beyond just the rape of one woman, increasing the depravity on display in this story. **34:30** Jacob has been silent to this point. When he finally speaks up, it is as an anxious migrant unsure of his position. Jacob condemns his sons' actions—not for their heinous nature but because they may make him a target for outside groups who have lived in the land longer. Despite all that has occurred in his life, Jacob continues to behave as a migrant in a perilous situation who must always be alert to how his hosts might treat him. **34:31** The final statement of the passage hardly resolves its problematic nature. Rather, the sons' rejoinder frames a crucial question for the audience: Where is the line at which one sets aside worries over acceptance by outsiders and instead defends one's own community? The

35 God said to Jacob, "Arise, go up to Bethel, and settle there. Make an altar there to the God who appeared to you when you fled from your brother Esau." ²So Jacob said to his household and to all who were with him, "Put away the foreign gods that are among you, and purify yourselves, and change your clothes; ³then come, let us go up to Bethel, that I may make an altar there to the God who answered me in the day of my distress and has been with me wherever I have gone." ⁴So they gave to Jacob all the foreign gods that they had and the rings that were in their ears, and Jacob hid them under the oak that was near Shechem.

5 As they journeyed, a terror from God fell upon the cities all around them, so that no one pursued them. ⁶Jacob came to Luz, that is, Bethel, which is in the land of Canaan, he and all the people who were with him, ⁷and there he built an altar and called the place El-bethel,ᵛ because it was there that God had revealed himself to him when he fled from his brother. ⁸And Deborah, Rebekah's nurse, died, and she was buried under an oak below Bethel. So it was called Allon-bacuth.ʷ

9 God appeared to Jacob again when he came from Paddan-aram, and he blessed him. ¹⁰God said to him, "Your name is Jacob; no longer shall you be called Jacob, but Israel shall be your name." So he was called Israel. ¹¹God said to him, "I am God Almighty:ˣ be fruitful and multiply; a nation and a company of nations shall come from you, and kings shall spring from you. ¹²The land that I gave to Abraham and Isaac I will give to you, and I will give the land to your offspring after you." ¹³Then God went up from him at the place where he had spoken with him. ¹⁴Jacob set up a pillar in the place where he had spoken with him, a pillar of stone, and he poured out a drink offering on it and poured oil on it. ¹⁵So Jacob called the place where God had spoken with him Bethel.

16 Then they journeyed from Bethel, and when they were still some distance from Ephrath, Rachel was in childbirth, and she had hard labor. ¹⁷When she was in her hard labor, the midwife said to her, "Do not be afraid, for now you have another son." ¹⁸As her soul was departing, for she was dying, she named him Ben-oni,ʸ but his father called him Benjamin.ᶻ ¹⁹And Rachel died, and she was buried on the way to Ephrath, that is, Bethlehem, ²⁰and Jacob set up a pillar at her grave; it is the pillar of Rachel's tomb, which is there to this day. ²¹Israel journeyed on and pitched his tent beyond the tower of Eder.

22 While Israel lived in that land, Reuben went and lay with Bilhah his father's concubine, and Israel heard of it.

Now the sons of Jacob were twelve. ²³The sons of Leah: Reuben (Jacob's firstborn), Simeon, Levi, Judah, Issachar, and Zebulun. ²⁴The sons of Rachel: Joseph and Benjamin. ²⁵The sons of Bilhah, Rachel's maid: Dan and Naphtali. ²⁶The sons of Zilpah, Leah's maid: Gad and Asher. These were the sons of Jacob who were born to him in Paddan-aram.

27 Jacob came to his father Isaac at Mamre, or Kiriath-arba, that is, Hebron, where Abraham and Isaac had resided as aliens. ²⁸Now the days of Isaac were one hundred eighty years. ²⁹And Isaac breathed his last; he died and was gathered to his people, old and full of days, and his sons Esau and Jacob buried him.

ᵛ 35.7 That is, *God of Bethel* ʷ 35.8 That is, *oak of weeping* ˣ 35.11 Traditional rendering of Heb *El Shaddai* ʸ 35.18 That is, *son of my sorrow* ᶻ 35.18 That is, *son of the right hand* or *son of the south*

conclusion problematizes any attempt to draw a straightforward moral principle from the story and encourages one to see it as a foundation for debate rather than as an object lesson.

35:1–28 This chapter recounts Jacob's return to where his emigration from Canaan had begun. The narrative culminates with his return to Bethel, the birth of his twelfth and final son, and the death of Rachel. **35:6–8** *Bethel* is an important cult site in the history of Israel and Judah. Standing on the border between the northern and southern kingdoms, it was often a place of conflict. Perhaps this is because it was a revered site, reflected in the attention given to its legendary origin and names. **35:18** At some point, Rachel has conceived again. The birth of her final child is not smooth, and sensing she will die, she names the child "son of my sorrow." Jacob overrules his wife, naming the boy *Benjamin*—"son of the right hand," connoting power or prominence. In either case, the next stage of the ancestral narrative will make clear that Jacob's youngest children are his favorites.

35:27–29 Almost as an afterthought, Isaac reappears only to die and be buried. This brief interlude serves to connect Jacob to Abraham and Isaac once more and also to signal that this stage of the narrative is reaching its end.

36

These are the descendants of Esau, that is, Edom. [2]Esau took his wives from the Canaanites: Adah daughter of Elon the Hittite, Oholibamah daughter of Anah son[a] of Zibeon the Hivite, [3]and Basemath, Ishmael's daughter, sister of Nebaioth. [4]Adah bore Eliphaz to Esau; Basemath bore Reuel; [5]and Oholibamah bore Jeush, Jalam, and Korah. These are the sons of Esau who were born to him in the land of Canaan.

6 Then Esau took his wives, his sons, his daughters, and all the members of his household, his cattle, all his livestock, and all the property he had acquired in the land of Canaan, and he moved to a land some distance from his brother Jacob. [7]For their possessions were too great for them to live together; the land where they were staying could not support them because of their livestock. [8]So Esau settled in the hill country of Seir; Esau is Edom.

9 These are the descendants of Esau, ancestor of the Edomites, in the hill country of Seir. [10]These are the names of Esau's sons: Eliphaz, the son of Adah the wife of Esau; Reuel, the son of Esau's wife Basemath. [11]The sons of Eliphaz were Teman, Omar, Zepho, Gatam, and Kenaz. [12]Timna was a concubine of Eliphaz, Esau's son; she bore Amalek to Eliphaz. These were the sons of Adah, Esau's wife. [13]These were the sons of Reuel: Nahath, Zerah, Shammah, and Mizzah. These were the sons of Basemath, Esau's wife. [14]These were the sons of Esau's wife Oholibamah, daughter of Anah son[b] of Zibeon; she bore to Esau Jeush, Jalam, and Korah.

15 These are the clans[c] of the sons of Esau. The sons of Eliphaz the firstborn of Esau: the clans[d] Teman, Omar, Zepho, Kenaz, [16]Korah, Gatam, and Amalek; these are the clans[e] of Eliphaz in the land of Edom; they are the sons of Adah. [17]These are the sons of Esau's son Reuel: the clans[f] Nahath, Zerah, Shammah, and Mizzah; these are the clans[g] of Reuel in the land of Edom; they are the sons of Esau's wife Basemath. [18]These are the sons of Esau's wife Oholibamah: the clans[h] Jeush, Jalam, and Korah; these are the clans[i] born of Esau's wife Oholibamah, the daughter of Anah. [19]These are the sons of Esau, that is, Edom, and these are their clans.[j]

20 These are the sons of Seir the Horite, the inhabitants of the land: Lotan, Shobal, Zibeon, Anah, [21]Dishon, Ezer, and Dishan; these are the clans[k] of the Horites, the sons of Seir in the land of Edom. [22]The sons of Lotan were Hori and Heman, and Lotan's sister was Timna. [23]These are the sons of Shobal: Alvan, Manahath, Ebal, Shepho, and Onam. [24]These are the sons of Zibeon: Aiah and Anah; he is the Anah who found the springs[l] in the wilderness as he pastured the donkeys of his father Zibeon. [25]These are the children of Anah: Dishon and Oholibamah daughter of Anah. [26]These are the sons of Dishon: Hemdan, Eshban, Ithran, and Cheran. [27]These are the sons of Ezer: Bilhan, Zaavan, and Akan. [28]These are the sons of Dishan: Uz and Aran. [29]These are the clans[m] of the Horites: the clans[n] Lotan, Shobal, Zibeon, Anah, [30]Dishon, Ezer, and Dishan; these are the clans[o] of the Horites, clan by clan[p] in the land of Seir.

31 These are the kings who reigned in the land of Edom before any king reigned over the Israelites. [32]Bela son of Beor reigned in Edom, the name of his city being Dinhabah. [33]Bela died, and Jobab son of Zerah of Bozrah succeeded him as king. [34]Jobab died, and Husham of the land of the Temanites succeeded him as king. [35]Husham died, and Hadad son of Bedad, who defeated Midian in the country of Moab, succeeded him as king, the name of his city being Avith. [36]Hadad died, and Samlah of Masrekah succeeded him as king. [37]Samlah died, and Shaul of Rehoboth on the Euphrates succeeded him as king. [38]Shaul died, and Baalhanan son of Achbor succeeded him as king. [39]Baal-hanan son of Achbor died, and Hadar succeeded him as king, the name of his city being Pau; his wife's name was Mehetabel, the daughter of Matred, daughter of Me-zahab.

40 These are the names of the clans[q] of Esau, according to their families and their localities by their names: the clans[r] Timna,

a 36.2 Sam Gk Syr: Heb *daughter*   b 36.14 Gk Syr: Heb
daughter   c 36.15 Or *chiefs*   d 36.15 Or *chiefs*   e 36.16 Or
chiefs   f 36.17 Or *chiefs*   g 36.17 Or *chiefs*   h 36.18 Or
chiefs   i 36.18 Or *chiefs*   j 36.19 Or *chiefs*   k 36.21 Or *chiefs*
l 36.24 Meaning of Heb uncertain   m 36.29 Or *chiefs*
n 36.29 Or *chiefs*   o 36.30 Or *chiefs*   p 36.30 Or *chief by chief*
q 36.40 Or *chiefs*   r 36.40 Or *chiefs*

36:1–43 This chapter recounts the descendants of Esau, known as the Edomites. **36:6–8** This account of Esau's departure from Canaan recalls the separation of Abraham and Lot in chap. 13. Edom, a land to the east of the Jordan River and a rival to Israel and Judah for regional power prior to the conquest of those states by Assyria and Babylonia in turn, would have been well known, and probably disliked, by the audience.

Alvah, Jetheth, [41]Oholibamah, Elah, Pinon, [42]Kenaz, Teman, Mibzar, [43]Magdiel, and Iram; these are the clans[s] of Edom, that is, Esau, the father of Edom, according to their settlements in the land that they held.

37 Jacob settled in the land where his father had lived as an alien, the land of Canaan. [2]These are the descendants of Jacob.

Joseph, being seventeen years old, was shepherding the flock with his brothers; he was a helper to the sons of Bilhah and Zilpah, his father's wives, and Joseph brought a bad report of them to their father. [3]Now Israel loved Joseph more than any other of his children because he was the son of his old age, and he made him an ornamented robe.[t] [4]But when his brothers saw that their father loved him more than all his brothers, they hated him and could not speak peaceably to him.

5 Once Joseph had a dream, and when he told it to his brothers, they hated him even more. [6]He said to them, "Listen to this dream that I dreamed. [7]There we were, binding sheaves in the field. Suddenly my sheaf rose and stood upright; then your sheaves gathered around it and bowed down to my sheaf." [8]His brothers said to him, "Are you indeed to reign over us? Are you indeed to have dominion over us?" So they hated him even more because of his dreams and his words.

9 He had another dream and told it to his brothers, saying, "Look, I have had another dream: the sun, the moon, and eleven stars were bowing down to me." [10]But when he told it to his father and to his brothers, his father rebuked him and said to him, "What kind of dream is this that you have had? Shall we indeed come, I and your mother and your brothers, and bow to the ground before you?" [11]So his brothers were jealous of him, but his father kept the matter in mind.

12 Now his brothers went to pasture their father's flock near Shechem. [13]And Israel said to Joseph, "Are not your brothers pasturing the flock at Shechem? Come, I will send you to them." He answered, "Here I am." [14]So he said to him, "Go now, see if it is well with your brothers and with the flock, and bring word back to me." So he sent him from the valley of Hebron.

He came to Shechem, [15]and a man found him wandering in the fields; the man asked him, "What are you seeking?" [16]"I am seeking my brothers," he said; "tell me, please, where they are pasturing the flock." [17]The man said, "They have gone away, for I heard them say, 'Let us go to Dothan.' " So Joseph went after his brothers and found them at Dothan. [18]They saw him from a distance, and before he came near to them they conspired to kill him. [19]They said to one another, "Here comes this dreamer. [20]Come now, let us kill him and throw him into one of the pits; then we shall say that a wild animal has devoured him, and we shall see what will become of his dreams." [21]But when Reuben heard it, he delivered him out of their hands, saying, "Let us not take his life." [22]Reuben said to them, "Shed no blood; throw him into this pit here in the wilderness, but lay no hand on him"—that he might rescue him out of their hand and restore him to his father. [23]So when Joseph came to his brothers, they stripped him of his robe, the ornamented robe[u] that he wore, [24]and they

---

[s] 36.43 Or *chiefs*   [t] 37.3 Or (compare Gk): *a coat of many colors*; meaning of Heb uncertain   [u] 37.23 Or (compare Gk): *a coat of many colors*; meaning of Heb uncertain

---

37:1–36 Here opens the last major section of Genesis. The focus now turns from Jacob to Joseph, though Jacob will not disappear entirely from view. Chapter 37 establishes the family dynamic between Jacob and his sons and among those sons, which provides essential context for the remainder of the narrative. **37:2** The generation formula (Heb. "toledot") is used again here, this time of Jacob and his family. Here is another major section break within the larger narrative (see note at 2:4). **37:3** Translators have variously understood Joseph's coat. Traditionally, it has been seen as a coat of many colors or, as here, as an ornamented robe. Whatever the case, the point is that Jacob clothes Joseph in a costly garment that visibly and undeniably expresses that he is Jacob's favorite. **37:5–8** Joseph exhibits a lack of maturity in the way he treats his brothers. Literally, the dream of the sheaves foretells the central plot later in the story: a famine, or lack of wheat, will force Joseph and his brothers to reconcile with one another. **37:14** Two things stand out in the command for Joseph to go to *Shechem*. First, it is a great distance from Hebron, so a significant journey. Second, the audience will recall that Shechem was the location for Dinah's rape and the gruesome encounter with the Hivites (see 34:1–31). It does not bode well for Joseph and his brothers to be there. **37:21–22** *Reuben*, the oldest of Jacob's sons, develops a scheme by which he can appease his brothers' anger but also keep his youngest brother safe. He shares it with

took him and threw him into a pit. The pit was empty; there was no water in it.

25 Then they sat down to eat, and looking up they saw a caravan of Ishmaelites coming from Gilead, with their camels carrying gum, balm, and resin, on their way to carry it down to Egypt. 26Then Judah said to his brothers, "What profit is it if we kill our brother and conceal his blood? 27Come, let us sell him to the Ishmaelites and not lay our hands on him, for he is our brother, our own flesh." And his brothers agreed. 28When some Midianite traders passed by, they drew Joseph up, lifting him out of the pit, and sold him to the Ishmaelites for twenty pieces of silver. And they took Joseph to Egypt.

29 When Reuben returned to the pit and saw that Joseph was not in the pit, he tore his clothes. 30He returned to his brothers and said, "The boy is gone, and I, where can I turn?" 31Then they took Joseph's robe, slaughtered a goat, and dipped the robe in the blood. 32They had the ornamented robe' taken to their father, and they said, "This we have found; see now whether it is your son's robe or not." 33He recognized it and said, "It is my son's robe! A wild animal has devoured him; Joseph has surely been torn to pieces." 34Then Jacob tore his garments and put sackcloth on his loins and mourned for his son many days. 35All his sons and all his daughters sought to comfort him, but he refused to be comforted and said, "No, I shall go down to Sheol to my son, mourning." Thus his father bewailed him.

36Meanwhile the Midianites had sold him in Egypt to Potiphar, one of Pharaoh's officials, the captain of the guard.

38 It happened at that time that Judah went down from his brothers and settled near a certain Adullamite whose name was Hirah. 2There Judah saw the daughter of a certain Canaanite whose name was Shua; he married her and went in to her. 3She conceived and bore a son, and he named him Er. 4Again she conceived and bore a son whom she named Onan. 5Yet again she bore a son, and she named him Shelah. She' was in Chezib when she bore him. 6Judah took a wife for Er his firstborn; her name was Tamar. 7But Er, Judah's firstborn, was wicked in the sight of the LORD, and the LORD put him to death. 8Then Judah said to Onan, "Go in to your brother's wife and perform the duty of a brother-in-law to her; raise up offspring for your brother." 9But since Onan knew that the offspring would not be his, he spilled his semen on the ground whenever he went in to his brother's wife, so that he would not give offspring to his brother. 10What he did was displeasing in the sight of the LORD, and he put him to death also. 11Then Judah said to his daughter-in-law Tamar, "Remain a widow in your father's house until my son Shelah grows up," for he feared that he too

v 37.32 Or (compare Gk): *a coat of many colors*; meaning of Heb uncertain w 38.5 Gk: Heb *He*

no one—and soon it will be thwarted by another plan. **37:26–27** *Judah*, the fourth oldest son, comes forward with a plan for dealing with Joseph. His proposal is accepted by the others, and it suggests both the sway he holds among the group and the brothers' desire to profit from Joseph's demise. **37:28** This verse introduces a problem. The *Midianites* appear here out of the blue. Though some argue this is another way to refer to the Ishmaelites, that would be unprecedented. Many modern scholars think that two separate stories of Joseph's sale have been interwoven here: one where Reuben wants to save Joseph but the Midianites take him without his knowledge; another where Judah plans to sell Joseph and the Ishmaelite caravan presents the perfect opportunity for trafficking the boy. **37:31–34** The irony that Jacob is deceived by the use of a goat's blood when he himself deceived Isaac using a goat's hair would not be lost on the ancient audience. **37:36** The final verse of the chapter reminds the audience that despite all the broken family relationships and duplicitous dealing among them, this is a story about a trafficked person: Joseph is sold against his will into slavery in Egypt. Like Abraham, Isaac, and Jacob before him, his life will now be indelibly marked by the experience of being an involuntary migrant.

38:1–30 This chapter is an interlude to the larger story about Joseph, focusing on Judah. The time spent on him indicates his importance in the family: his line will produce the kings of Judah enthroned in Jerusalem, who would have been in power when these stories gained their status as the sacred origin stories of the nation. **38:8–10** The story revolves around the practice of levirate marriage, something known across the ancient Near East. Levirate marriage expects the brother of a deceased man to take his brother's widow as a wife and, if possible, to father a child with her. This son could then care for her financially (cf. Deut. 25:5–6). This practice sounds odd to contemporary readers but was a feature of

would die, like his brothers. So Tamar went to live in her father's house.

12 In course of time the wife of Judah, Shua's daughter, died; when Judah's time of mourning was over,ˣ he went up to Timnah to his sheepshearers, he and his friend Hirah the Adullamite. ¹³When Tamar was told, "Your father-in-law is going up to Timnah to shear his sheep," ¹⁴she put off her widow's garments, put on a veil, wrapped herself up, and sat down at the entrance to Enaim, which is on the road to Timnah. She saw that Shelah was grown up, yet she had not been given to him in marriage. ¹⁵When Judah saw her, he thought her to be a prostitute, for she had covered her face. ¹⁶He went over to her at the roadside and said, "Come, let me come in to you," for he did not know that she was his daughter-in-law. She said, "What will you give me, that you may come in to me?" ¹⁷He answered, "I will send you a kid from the flock." And she said, "Only if you give me a pledge until you send it." ¹⁸He said, "What pledge shall I give you?" She replied, "Your signet and your cord and the staff that is in your hand." So he gave them to her and went in to her, and she conceived by him. ¹⁹Then she got up and went away, and taking off her veil she put on the garments of her widowhood.

20 When Judah sent the kid by his friend the Adullamite to recover the pledge from the woman, he could not find her. ²¹He asked the townspeople, "Where is the prostitute who was at Enaim by the wayside?" But they said, "No prostitute has been here." ²²So he returned to Judah and said, "I have not found her; moreover, the townspeople said, 'No prostitute has been here.' " ²³Judah replied, "Let her keep the things as her own, otherwise we will be laughed at; you see, I sent this kid, and you could not find her."

24 About three months later Judah was told, "Your daughter-in-law Tamar has prostituted herself; moreover, she is pregnant as a result of prostitution." And Judah said, "Bring her out, and let her be burned." ²⁵As she was being brought out, she sent word to her father-in-law, "It was the owner of these who made me pregnant." And she said, "Take note, please, whose these are, the signet and the cord and the staff." ²⁶Then Judah acknowledged them and said, "She is more in the right than I, since I did not give her to my son Shelah." And he did not lie with her again.

27 When the time of her delivery came, there were twins in her womb. ²⁸While she was in labor, one put out a hand, and the midwife took and bound on his hand a crimson thread, saying, "This one came out first." ²⁹But just then he drew back his hand and out came his brother, and she said, "What a breach you have made for yourself!" Therefore he was named Perez.ʸ ³⁰Afterward his brother came out with the crimson thread on his hand, and he was named Zerah.ᶻ

39 Now Joseph was taken down to Egypt, and Potiphar, an officer of Pharaoh, the captain of the guard, an Egyptian, bought him from the Ishmaelites who had brought him down there. ²The LORD was with Joseph, and he became a successful man; he was in the house of his Egyptian master. ³His master saw that the LORD was with him and that the LORD caused all that he did to prosper in

x 38.12 Heb *when Judah was comforted* y 38.29 That is, *a breach* z 38.30 That is, *brightness*, perhaps alluding to the crimson thread

ancient patriarchal societies. In this case, Onan attempts to show fidelity to his duty on the surface but, by actively denying Tamar another child, refuses it in practice. **38:14** When Tamar ascertains that Judah will not be faithful to his promise of giving her to Shelah as a wife in order to bear a child, she takes matters into her own hands. **38:24** When Judah finds out that Tamar is pregnant, he presumes that she is guilty of adultery. Punishable by death, Tamar's adultery would offer Judah the ideal resolution to his problem by eliminating Tamar and her claims on his family while making him appear rigorously moral. **38:25–26** Tamar's scheme now comes to fruition. She has applied a sophisticated knowledge of ancient law in order to arrange this result. Knowing that her pregnancy would produce a charge of adultery, prosecuted by her father-in-law, she engineers the circumstances in which her evidence will convict him. When Judah recognizes that she is *more in the right than I*, this has moral weight; it also has juridical sense, connoting a legal victory. **38:27–30** Tamar has twins. Their struggle recalls that of Esau and Jacob. Since *Perez*, the younger of the two twins, will be the ancestor of King David and his line (cf. Ruth 4:12, 18–22), it seems this story fits the larger pattern of younger sons being privileged over older ones.

39:1–23 The narrative now refocuses on Joseph. This story, where Joseph rebuffs the advances of his master's wife, shows some similarities to the Egyptian "Story of Two Brothers." This gives the impression

his hands. ⁴So Joseph found favor in his sight and attended him; he made him overseer of his house and put him in charge of all that he had. ⁵From the time that he made him overseer in his house and over all that he had, the LORD blessed the Egyptian's house for Joseph's sake; the blessing of the LORD was on all that he had, in house and field. ⁶So he left all that he had in Joseph's charge, and with him there he had no concern for anything but the food that he ate.

Now Joseph was handsome and good-looking. ⁷And after a time his master's wife cast her eyes on Joseph and said, "Lie with me." ⁸But he refused and said to his master's wife, "Look, with me here, my master has no concern about anything in the house, and he has put everything that he has in my hand. ⁹He is not greater in this house than I am, nor has he kept back anything from me except yourself, because you are his wife. How then could I do this great wickedness and sin against God?" ¹⁰And although she spoke to Joseph day after day, he would not consent to lie beside her or to be with her. ¹¹One day, however, when he went into the house to do his work, and while no one else was in the house, ¹²she caught hold of his garment, saying, "Lie with me!" But he left his garment in her hand and fled and ran outside. ¹³When she saw that he had left his garment in her hand and had fled outside, ¹⁴she called out to the members of her household and said to them, "See, my husband*a* has brought among us a Hebrew to insult us! He came in to me to lie with me, and I cried out with a loud voice, ¹⁵and when he heard me raise my voice and cry out, he left his garment beside me and fled outside." ¹⁶Then she kept his garment by her until his master came home, ¹⁷and she told him the same story, saying, "The Hebrew servant, whom you have brought among us, came in to me to insult me, ¹⁸but as soon as I raised my voice and cried out, he left his garment beside me and fled outside."

19 When his master heard the words that his wife spoke to him, saying, "This is the way your servant treated me," he became enraged. ²⁰And Joseph's master took him and put him into the prison, the place where the king's prisoners were confined; he remained there in prison. ²¹But the LORD was with Joseph and showed him steadfast love; he gave him favor in the sight of the chief jailer. ²²The chief jailer committed to Joseph's care all the prisoners who were in the prison, and whatever was done there, he was the one who did it. ²³The chief jailer paid no heed to anything that was in Joseph's care because the LORD was with him, and whatever he did, the LORD made it prosper.

40 Some time after this, the cupbearer of the king of Egypt and his baker offended their lord the king of Egypt. ²Pharaoh was angry with his two officers, the chief cupbearer and the chief baker, ³and he put them in custody in the house of the captain of the guard, in the prison where Joseph was confined. ⁴The captain of the guard charged Joseph with them, and he waited on them, and they continued for some time in custody. ⁵One night they both dreamed—the cupbearer and the baker of the king of Egypt who were confined in the prison—each his own dream and each

a 39.14 Heb *he*

of an Egyptian origin for it, though that remains a point of scholarly debate. **39:4–6** This will become a leading theme for Joseph's life in Egypt: when others place him in a position of responsibility, he is very successful. Throughout the story, this success is attributed to God, even by Joseph. **39:7** When Potiphar's wife seeks to initiate a sexual relationship with Joseph, he resists. Among the dynamics one must bear in mind here is Joseph's status as a trafficked person. Without rights or access to anyone to defend him, his already precarious position is made even more uncertain. **39:11–15** Potiphar's wife, never named in the story, takes advantage of Joseph's precarious position as a foreign slave to accuse him of an unwanted sexual advance. The story plays on a standard rape myth but is intriguing for the way it inverts and undermines its prevalent assumptions about male behavior. **39:21–23** As this chapter ends, Joseph has seen his position worsened. For the second time in his life, he is imprisoned. Nevertheless, his jailer recognizes his skill and entrusts him with significant responsibilities. Joseph is again exceedingly successful.

40:1–41:57 The next scene in Joseph's life attends to four dreams that need interpretation. The story recalls Joseph's own dreams in chap. 37, playing on his ability to interpret such enigmatic messages with clarity. Whereas Joseph's interpretation of those earlier dreams led to his brothers selling him into

dream with its own meaning. [6]When Joseph came to them in the morning, he saw that they were troubled. [7]So he asked Pharaoh's officers, who were with him in custody in his master's house, "Why are your faces downcast today?" [8]They said to him, "We have had dreams, and there is no one to interpret them." And Joseph said to them, "Do not interpretations belong to God? Please tell them to me."

[9] So the chief cupbearer told his dream to Joseph and said to him, "In my dream there was a vine before me, [10]and on the vine there were three branches. As soon as it budded, its blossoms came out, and the clusters ripened into grapes. [11]Pharaoh's cup was in my hand, and I took the grapes and pressed them into Pharaoh's cup and placed the cup in Pharaoh's hand." [12]Then Joseph said to him, "This is its interpretation: the three branches are three days; [13]within three days Pharaoh will lift up your head and restore you to your office, and you shall place Pharaoh's cup in his hand, just as you used to do when you were his cupbearer. [14]But remember me when it is well with you; please do me the kindness to make mention of me to Pharaoh, and so get me out of this place. [15]For in fact I was stolen out of the land of the Hebrews, and here also I have done nothing that they should have put me into the dungeon."

[16] When the chief baker saw that the interpretation was favorable, he said to Joseph, "I also had a dream: there were three cake baskets on my head, [17]and in the uppermost basket there were all sorts of baked food for Pharaoh, but the birds were eating it out of the basket on my head." [18]And Joseph answered, "This is its interpretation: the three baskets are three days; [19]within three days Pharaoh will lift up your head—from you!—and hang you on a pole, and the birds will eat the flesh from you."

[20] On the third day, which was Pharaoh's birthday, he made a feast for all his servants and lifted up the head of the chief cupbearer and the head of the chief baker among his servants. [21]He restored the chief cupbearer to his cupbearing, and he placed the cup in Pharaoh's hand, [22]but the chief baker he hanged, just as Joseph had interpreted to them. [23]Yet the chief cupbearer did not remember Joseph but forgot him.

41 After two whole years, Pharaoh dreamed that he was standing by the Nile, [2]and there came up out of the Nile seven sleek and fat cows, and they grazed in the reed grass. [3]Then seven other cows, ugly and thin, came up out of the Nile after them and stood by the other cows on the bank of the Nile. [4]The ugly and thin cows ate up the seven sleek and fat cows. And Pharaoh awoke. [5]Then he fell asleep and dreamed a second time; seven ears of grain, plump and good, were growing on one stalk. [6]Then seven ears, thin and blighted by the east wind, sprouted after them. [7]The thin ears swallowed up the seven plump and full ears. Pharaoh awoke, and it was a dream. [8]In the morning his spirit was troubled, so he sent and called for all the magicians of Egypt and all its wise men. Pharaoh told them his dreams, but there was no one who could interpret them to Pharaoh.

slavery and later imprisonment, his explanation of these visions will free him from prison. **40:8** Before even hearing the dreams of Pharaoh's deposed cupbearer and baker, Joseph attributes the interpretation of them to God. This contributes to the repeated message advanced in this story that Joseph is specially favored by God and chosen for a special role on the world stage. **40:12–14** The cupbearer's role was a critical one in the ancient world. Chief among his responsibilities was to ensure no one could assassinate the ruler by poisoning his wine. The cupbearer was a form of bodyguard, or royal security detail, who required the king's complete trust. When Joseph seeks the favor of the cupbearer who will be restored, he solicits the sponsorship of a strategically placed government official who might quickly change his situation. Pleading innocence to the cupbearer is not an irrational proclamation of innocence but a shrewd strategy utilized with careful intent. **40:15** The English translation conceals that Joseph now connects his treatment by his brothers and his treatment in Egypt. In chap. 37, Joseph's brothers throw him in a pit (Heb. "bor") to hold him for sale; now, Joseph calls his Egyptian cell a dungeon using the same Hebrew word. This same term appears widely in the Hebrew Bible, where it is sometimes a synonym for Sheol, the place where the dead reside (e.g., Isa. 14:15; Ezek. 31:14; Pss. 28:1; 30:3; 88:4). Joseph's statement subtly compares his situation to death. Since his father and brothers think him dead, the sentiment may be without irony. **41:1** The aside that two years have passed can be missed, but it plays a role in making Joseph's plight all the more hopeless at this stage. **41:8** Along with Joseph's

9 Then the chief cupbearer said to Pharaoh, "I remember my faults today. [10]Once Pharaoh was angry with his servants and put me and the chief baker in custody in the house of the captain of the guard. [11]We dreamed on the same night, he and I, each having a dream with its own meaning. [12]A young Hebrew was there with us, a servant of the captain of the guard. When we told him, he interpreted our dreams to us, giving an interpretation to each according to his dream. [13]As he interpreted to us, so it turned out; I was restored to my office, and the baker was hanged."

14 Then Pharaoh sent for Joseph, and he was hurriedly brought out of the dungeon. When he had shaved himself and changed his clothes, he came in before Pharaoh. [15]And Pharaoh said to Joseph, "I had a dream, and there is no one who can interpret it. I have heard it said of you that when you hear a dream you can interpret it." [16]Joseph answered Pharaoh, "It is not I; God will give Pharaoh a favorable answer." [17]Then Pharaoh said to Joseph, "In my dream I was standing on the banks of the Nile, [18]and seven cows, fat and sleek, came up out of the Nile and fed in the reed grass. [19]Then seven other cows came up after them, poor, very ugly, and thin. Never had I seen such ugly ones in all the land of Egypt. [20]The thin and ugly cows ate up the first seven fat cows, [21]but when they had eaten them no one would have known that they had done so, for they were still as ugly as before. Then I awoke. [22]I fell asleep a second time,[b] and I saw in my dream seven ears of grain, full and good, growing on one stalk, [23]and seven ears, withered, thin, and blighted by the east wind, sprouting after them, [24]and the thin ears swallowed up the seven good ears. But when I told it to the magicians, there was no one who could explain it to me."

25 Then Joseph said to Pharaoh, "Pharaoh's dreams are one and the same; God has revealed to Pharaoh what he is about to do. [26]The seven good cows are seven years, and the seven good ears are seven years; the dreams are one. [27]The seven lean and ugly cows that came up after them are seven years, as are the seven empty ears blighted by the east wind. They are seven years of famine. [28]It is as I told Pharaoh; God has shown to Pharaoh what he is about to do. [29]There will come seven years of great plenty throughout all the land of Egypt. [30]After them there will arise seven years of famine, and all the plenty will be forgotten in the land of Egypt; the famine will consume the land. [31]The plenty will no longer be known in the land because of the famine that will follow, for it will be very grievous. [32]And the doubling of Pharaoh's dream means that the thing is fixed by God, and God will shortly bring it about. [33]Now therefore let Pharaoh select a man who is discerning and wise and set him over the land of Egypt. [34]Let Pharaoh proceed to appoint overseers over the land and take one-fifth of the produce of the land of Egypt during the seven plenteous years. [35]Let them gather all the food of these good years that are coming and lay up grain under the authority of Pharaoh for food in the cities, and let them keep it. [36]That food shall be a reserve for the land against the seven years of famine that are to befall the land of Egypt, so that the land may not perish through the famine."

37 The proposal pleased Pharaoh and all his servants. [38]Pharaoh said to his servants, "Can we find anyone else like this, one in whom is the spirit of God?" [39]So Pharaoh said to Joseph, "Since God has shown you all this, there is no one so discerning and wise as you. [40]You shall be over my house, and all my people shall order themselves as you command; only with regard to the throne will I be greater than you." [41]And Pharaoh said to Joseph, "See, I have set you over all the land

b 41.22 Gk Syr Vg: Heb lacks *I fell asleep a second time*

earlier proclamation that God gives interpretations for such dreams (40:8), this may be an implicit criticism of the divination practices used by priests and prophets across the ancient world (see further 41:15). **41:22–23** Pharaoh's second dream features a grain harvest, just as Joseph's second dream referred to a grain harvest. This creates yet another connection between those two scenes. **41:33–36** Joseph now goes beyond interpreting the meaning of Pharaoh's dreams to offering a strategy for how to handle the oncoming crisis. One can interpret this as taking Pharaoh's assigned task of interpretation to its logical conclusion; however, one could equally see this as Joseph overstepping his bounds with the result of angering Pharaoh and undoing all the goodwill he has just accrued. **41:38–40** Any tension quickly dissipates as Pharaoh embraces not only Joseph's strategy but Joseph as the proper person to implement it. Just as in Potiphar's house and the Egyptian prison, Joseph will now be given immense

of Egypt." [42]Removing his signet ring from his hand, Pharaoh put it on Joseph's hand; he arrayed him in garments of fine linen and put a gold chain around his neck. [43]He had him ride in the chariot of his second-in-command, and they cried out in front of him, "Bow the knee!"[c] Thus he set him over all the land of Egypt. [44]Moreover, Pharaoh said to Joseph, "I am Pharaoh, and without your consent no one shall lift up hand or foot in all the land of Egypt." [45]Pharaoh gave Joseph the name Zaphenath-paneah, and he gave him Asenath daughter of Potiphera, priest of On, as his wife. Thus Joseph gained authority over the land of Egypt.

46 Joseph was thirty years old when he entered the service of Pharaoh king of Egypt. And Joseph went out from the presence of Pharaoh and went through all the land of Egypt. [47]During the seven plenteous years the earth produced abundantly. [48]He gathered up all the food of the seven years when there was plenty[d] in the land of Egypt and stored up food in the cities; he stored up in every city the food from the fields around it. [49]So Joseph stored up grain in such abundance—like the sand of the sea—that he stopped measuring it; it was beyond measure.

50 Before the years of famine came, Joseph had two sons, whom Asenath daughter of Potiphera, priest of On, bore to him. [51]Joseph named the firstborn Manasseh,[e] "For," he said, "God has made me forget all my hardship and all my father's house." [52]The second he named Ephraim,[f] "For God has made me fruitful in the land of my misfortunes."

53 The seven years of plenty that prevailed in the land of Egypt came to an end, [54]and the seven years of famine began to come, just as Joseph had said. There was famine in every country, but throughout the land of Egypt there was bread. [55]When all the land of Egypt was famished, the people cried to Pharaoh for bread. Pharaoh said to all the Egyptians, "Go to Joseph; what he says to you, do." [56]And since the famine had spread over all the land, Joseph opened all the storehouses[g] and sold to the Egyptians, for the famine was severe in the land of Egypt. [57]Moreover, all the world came to Joseph in Egypt to buy grain, because the famine became severe throughout the world.

42 When Jacob learned that there was grain in Egypt, he said to his sons, "Why do you keep looking at one another? [2]I have heard," he said, "that there is grain in Egypt; go down and buy grain for us there, that we may live and not die." [3]So ten of Joseph's brothers went down to buy grain in Egypt. [4]But Jacob did not send Joseph's brother Benjamin with his brothers, for he feared that harm might come to him. [5]Thus the sons of Israel were among the people who came to buy grain, for the famine had reached the land of Canaan.

6 Now Joseph was governor over the land; it was he who sold to all the people of the

c 41.43 Meaning of Heb uncertain   d 41.48 Sam Gk: MT lacks *plenty*   e 41.51 That is, *making to forget*   f 41.52 In Heb *Ephraim* is related to the word for *fruitful*   g 41.56 Gk Vg Compare Syr: Heb *opened all that was in* (or, *among*) *them*

responsibility. **41:42** Just as in chap. 37, a garment signifies Joseph's favored status. Here, it is Pharaoh's ring and fine Egyptian robes that denote his significance. **41:45** Joseph now begins to integrate into Egyptian culture. He takes on an Egyptian name and an Egyptian wife. This is a marked break from Abraham, Isaac, and Jacob, all of whom resist integration with other cultures and refuse to marry across ethnic lines. **41:50–52** To further emphasize the degree to which Joseph adopts an Egyptian identity, the names of his two boys reflect a rejection of Jacob and his ancestors in the Levant. His firstborn *Manasseh*'s name (meaning "making to forget") symbolizes an effort to forget his earlier hardship; his second son, *Ephraim* (relating to the word "fruitful"), symbolizes his success in Egypt. **41:56–57** Joseph is sometimes styled as a generous servant of the poor who saves them from famine in his wise plan. While there is some truth there—Joseph's strategy does mean food is available for all—neither he nor Pharaoh appears entirely selfless in their conduct. Note that Joseph sells, rather than gives, this grain to the Egyptians and the foreigners. Later in the story (47:13–26), Pharaoh and Joseph remain so committed to their profit motives that they bankrupt many of the Egyptian people.

42:1–38 Now the famine reaches Jacob and his sons still in Canaan. As a result, Joseph's brothers come to Egypt and encounter him. Their roles are reversed from chap. 37, just as Joseph's dreams had predicted. **42:1–2** Through some form of international knowledge network, Jacob becomes aware that there is grain for sale in Egypt. He determines his sons should go to purchase some to ensure his household is not caught helpless by the famine. **42:4** Jacob's preference for Rachel's sons appears

land. And Joseph's brothers came and bowed themselves before him with their faces to the ground. [7]When Joseph saw his brothers, he recognized them, but he treated them like strangers and spoke harshly to them. "Where do you come from?" he said. They said, "From the land of Canaan to buy food." [8]Although Joseph had recognized his brothers, they did not recognize him. [9]Joseph also remembered the dreams that he had dreamed about them. He said to them, "You are spies; you have come to see the nakedness of the land!" [10]They said to him, "No, my lord; your servants have come to buy food. [11]We are all sons of one man; we are honest men; your servants have never been spies." [12]But he said to them, "No, you have come to see the nakedness of the land!" [13]They said, "We, your servants, are twelve brothers, the sons of a certain man in the land of Canaan; the youngest, however, is now with our father, and one is no more." [14]But Joseph said to them, "It is just as I have said to you; you are spies! [15]Here is how you shall be tested: as Pharaoh lives, you shall not leave this place unless your youngest brother comes here! [16]Let one of you go and bring your brother, while the rest of you remain in prison, in order that your words may be tested, whether there is truth in you, or else, as Pharaoh lives, surely you are spies." [17]And he put them all together in prison for three days.

[18] On the third day Joseph said to them, "Do this and you will live, for I fear God: [19]if you are honest men, let one of your brothers stay here where you are imprisoned. The rest of you shall go and carry grain for the famine of your households [20]and bring your youngest brother to me. Thus your words will be verified, and you shall not die." And they agreed to do so. [21]They said to one another, "Alas, we are paying the penalty for what we did to our brother; we saw his anguish when he pleaded with us, but we would not listen. That is why this anguish has come upon us." [22]Then Reuben answered them, "Did I not tell you not to

wrong the boy? But you would not listen. So now there comes a reckoning for his blood." [23]They did not know that Joseph understood them, since he spoke with them through an interpreter. [24]He turned away from them and wept; then he returned and spoke to them. And he picked out Simeon and had him bound before their eyes. [25]Joseph then gave orders to fill their bags with grain, to return every man's money to his sack, and to give them provisions for their journey. This was done for them.

[26] They loaded their donkeys with their grain and departed. [27]When one of them opened his sack to give his donkey fodder at the lodging place, he saw his money at the top of the sack. [28]He said to his brothers, "My money has been put back; here it is in my sack!" At this they lost heart and turned trembling to one another, saying, "What is this that God has done to us?"

[29] When they came to their father Jacob in the land of Canaan, they told him all that had happened to them, saying, [30]"The man, the lord of the land, spoke harshly to us and charged us with spying on the land. [31]But we said to him, 'We are honest men; we are not spies. [32]We are twelve brothers, sons of our father; one is no more, and the youngest is now with our father in the land of Canaan.' [33]Then the man, the lord of the land, said to us, 'By this I shall know that you are honest men: leave one of your brothers with me, take grain for the famine of your households, and go your way. [34]Bring your youngest brother to me, and I shall know that you are not spies but honest men. Then I will release your brother to you, and you may trade in the land.'"

[35] As they were emptying their sacks, there in each one's sack was his bag of money. When they and their father saw their bundles of money, they were dismayed. [36]And their father Jacob said to them, "I am the one you have bereaved of children: Joseph is no more, and Simeon is no more, and now you would take Benjamin. All this has happened to me!"

again. Earlier it was Joseph; now it is Benjamin. **42:13** Joseph, unrecognized and unrecognizable to his brothers, accuses them of being spies. Whereas they had been able to convince their father, Jacob, of a lie, now they struggle to persuade Joseph of what is true. It is symbolic of how everyone's position in the story has changed. **42:22–24** Reuben now recalls his own desire to save Joseph. He interprets that failure as requiring a just punishment, now imminent in his mind. Joseph selects Simeon as the deposit for their return to Canaan. There is a symbolic feature here: Simeon, second son of Leah, is required as collateral until Benjamin, second son of Rachel, is produced. **42:36–38** Jacob expresses understandable anger and sadness at the situation. Yet, just as in chap. 34 with Dinah's rape and his sons' revenge, Jacob remains focused on himself. He exclaims that this has happened *to me!* When Reuben offers the

[37]Then Reuben said to his father, "You may kill my two sons if I do not bring him back to you. Put him in my hands, and I will bring him back to you." [38]But he said, "My son shall not go down with you, for his brother is dead, and he alone is left. If harm should come to him on the journey that you are to make, you would bring down my gray hairs with sorrow to Sheol."

43 Now the famine was severe in the land. [2]And when they had eaten up the grain that they had brought from Egypt, their father said to them, "Go again; buy us a little more food." [3]But Judah said to him, "The man solemnly warned us, saying, 'You shall not see my face unless your brother is with you.' [4]If you will send our brother with us, we will go down and buy you food, [5]but if you will not send him, we will not go down, for the man said to us, 'You shall not see my face, unless your brother is with you.'" [6]Israel said, "Why did you treat me so badly as to tell the man that you had another brother?" [7]They replied, "The man questioned us carefully about ourselves and our kindred, saying, 'Is your father still alive? Have you another brother?' What we told him was in answer to these questions. Could we in any way know that he would say, 'Bring your brother down'?" [8]Then Judah said to his father Israel, "Send the boy with me, and let us be on our way, so that we may live and not die—you and we and also our little ones. [9]I myself will be surety for him; you can hold me accountable for him. If I do not bring him back to you and set him before you, then let me bear the blame forever. [10]If we had not delayed, we would now have returned twice."

11 Then their father Israel said to them, "If it must be so, then do this: take some of the choice fruits of the land in your bags, and carry them down as a present to the man: a little balm and a little honey, gum, resin, pistachio nuts, and almonds. [12]Take double the money with you. Carry back with you the money that was returned in the top of your sacks; perhaps it was an oversight. [13]Take your brother also, and be on your way again to the man; [14]may God Almighty[b] grant you mercy before the man, so that he may send back your other brother and Benjamin. As for me, if I am bereaved of my children, I am bereaved." [15]So the men took the present, and they took double the money with them, as well as Benjamin. Then they went on their way down to Egypt and stood before Joseph.

16 When Joseph saw Benjamin with them, he said to the steward of his house, "Bring the men into the house, and slaughter an animal and make ready, for the men are to dine with me at noon." [17]The man did as Joseph said and brought the men to Joseph's house. [18]Now the men were afraid because they were brought to Joseph's house, and they said, "It is because of the money, replaced in our sacks the first time, that we have been brought in, so that he may have an opportunity to fall upon us, to make slaves of us and take our donkeys." [19]So they went up to the steward of Joseph's house and spoke with him at the entrance to the house. [20]They said, "Oh, my lord, we came down the first time to buy food, [21]and when we came to the lodging place we opened our sacks, and there was each one's money in the top of his sack, our money in full weight. So we have brought it back with us. [22]Moreover, we have brought down with us additional money to buy food. We do not know who put our money in our sacks." [23]He replied, "Rest assured; do not be afraid; your God and the

b 43.14 Traditional rendering of Heb *El Shaddai*

lives of his own two sons as assurance that he will escort Benjamin safely, not even this satisfies Jacob. The chapter ends with the family at an impasse.

43:1–34 This chapter sees the family move past the impasse regarding Benjamin. Progress on the matter comes not from Jacob's change of view but because the famine becomes so severe that recalcitrance becomes too dangerous. **43:7** Jacob's sons set this story in motion when their anger led them to traffic their brother and lie about it to their father. Here again it seems they cannot tell the truth to their father. They volunteer the information about their family in 42:9–13. Even if their intention now is to save others rather than to eliminate another, they cannot tell the truth to do so. **43:11–15** Although the severity of the famine prods the story line onward, it seems that Jacob's accumulated wealth has not yet been totally exhausted. He can, therefore, send his sons with great wealth, including fruits and nuts from Canaan. This detail is a reminder that the wealthiest are impacted by environmental factors like famine less severely and more slowly than those with few resources. **43:23** The Egyptian who oversees Joseph's home attributes the good fortune of the brothers to favor from their god. This view was

God of your father must have put treasure in your sacks for you; I received your money." Then he brought Simeon out to them. ²⁴When the steward[i] had brought the men into Joseph's house and given them water, and they had washed their feet, and when he had given their donkeys fodder, ²⁵they made the present ready for Joseph's coming at noon, for they had heard that they would dine there.

26 When Joseph came home, they brought him the present that they had carried into the house and bowed to the ground before him. ²⁷He inquired about their welfare and said, "Is your father well, the old man of whom you spoke? Is he still alive?" ²⁸They said, "Your servant our father is well; he is still alive." And they bowed their heads and did obeisance. ²⁹Then he looked up and saw his brother Benjamin, his mother's son, and said, "Is this your youngest brother, of whom you spoke to me? God be gracious to you, my son!" ³⁰With that, Joseph hurried out, because he was overcome with affection for his brother, and he was about to weep. So he went into a private room and wept there. ³¹Then he washed his face and came out, and controlling himself he said, "Serve the meal." ³²They served him by himself and them by themselves, and the Egyptians who ate with him by themselves, because the Egyptians could not eat with the Hebrews, for that is an abomination to the Egyptians. ³³When they were seated before him, the firstborn according to his birthright and the youngest according to his youth, the men looked at one another in amazement. ³⁴Portions were taken to them from Joseph's table, but Benjamin's portion was five times as much as any of theirs. So they drank and were merry with him.

44 Then he commanded the steward of his house, "Fill the men's sacks with food, as much as they can carry, and put each man's money in the top of his sack. ²Put my cup, the silver cup, in the top of the sack of the youngest, with his money for the grain." And he did as Joseph told him. ³As soon as the morning was light, the men were sent away with their donkeys. ⁴When they had gone only a short distance from the city, Joseph said to his steward, "Go, follow after the men, and when you overtake them, say to them, 'Why have you returned evil for good? Why have you stolen my silver cup?[j] ⁵Is it not from this that my lord drinks? Does he not indeed use it for divination? You have done wrong in doing this.'"

6 When he overtook them, he repeated these words to them. ⁷They said to him, "Why does my lord speak such words as these? Far be it from your servants that they should do such a thing! ⁸Look, the money that we found at the top of our sacks, we brought back to you from the land of Canaan; why then would we steal silver or gold from your lord's house? ⁹Should it be found with any one of your servants, let him die; moreover, the rest of us will become my lord's slaves." ¹⁰He said, "Even so; in accordance with your words, let it be: he with whom it is found shall become my slave, but the rest of you shall go free." ¹¹Then each one quickly lowered his sack to the ground, and each opened his sack. ¹²He searched, beginning with the eldest and ending with the youngest, and the cup was found in Benjamin's sack. ¹³At this they tore their clothes. Then each one loaded his donkey, and they returned to the city.

14 Judah and his brothers came to Joseph's house while he was still there, and they fell to

---

i 43.24 Heb *the man*   j 44.4 Gk Compare Vg: Heb lacks *Why have you stolen my silver cup?*

---

common across the ancient Near East, where such favorable outcomes would have been interpreted as divine blessings (see **"Blessing," p. 33**). **43:32** The precise reason for the Egyptians refusing to eat with the Hebrews is unstated. Perhaps it relates to the later statement that they refuse to associate with shepherds (46:34; Exod. 8:22). Regardless, the sharp division between the two groups serves to remind the audience what a significant boundary Joseph has crossed in adopting Egyptian identity, wife, and names for his children. **44:1–34** Before the tension in the narrative resolves, it rises to yet one higher level: Joseph frames his brother Benjamin. From the narrator's omniscient perspective, this appears to be Joseph's test of his brothers: Will they allow Benjamin to take the blame and consequences of this situation alone, or will they protect him in a way that they never did for Joseph? **44:6–13** This encounter recalls the one between Laban and Jacob, when Laban claims (correctly) that his household gods have been stolen by someone in Jacob's party. Like Jacob's confident (but incorrect) assertion of innocence, so too do Jacob's sons proclaim their innocence. **44:14** Here, in a peculiar way, Joseph's dream is fulfilled: his brothers bow

the ground before him. [15]Joseph said to them, "What deed is this that you have done? Do you not know that one such as I can practice divination?" [16]And Judah said, "What can we say to my lord? What can we speak? How can we clear ourselves? God has found out the guilt of your servants; here we are then, my lord's slaves, both we and also the one in whose possession the cup has been found." [17]But he said, "Far be it from me that I should do so! Only the one in whose possession the cup was found shall be my slave, but as for you, go up in peace to your father."

18 Then Judah stepped up to him and said, "O my lord, let your servant please speak a word in my lord's ears, and do not be angry with your servant, for you are like Pharaoh himself. [19]My lord asked his servants, saying, 'Have you a father or a brother?' [20]And we said to my lord, 'We have a father, an old man, and a young brother, the child of his old age. His brother is dead; he alone is left of his mother's children, and his father loves him.' [21]Then you said to your servants, 'Bring him down to me, so that I may set my eyes on him.' [22]We said to my lord, 'The boy cannot leave his father, for if he should leave his father, his father would die.' [23]Then you said to your servants, 'Unless your youngest brother comes down with you, you shall see my face no more.' [24]When we went back to your servant my father we told him the words of my lord. [25]And when our father said, 'Go again; buy us a little food,' [26]we said, 'We cannot go down. Only if our youngest brother goes with us will we go down, for we cannot see the man's face unless our youngest brother is with us.' [27]Then your

servant my father said to us, 'You know that my wife bore me two sons; [28]one left me, and I said, Surely he has been torn to pieces, and I have never seen him since. [29]If you take this one also from me and harm comes to him, you will bring down my gray hairs in sorrow to Sheol.' [30]Now therefore, when I come to your servant my father and the boy is not with us, then, as his life is bound up in the boy's life, [31]when he sees that the boy is not with us, he will die, and your servants will bring down the gray hairs of your servant our father with sorrow to Sheol. [32]For your servant became surety for the boy to my father, saying, 'If I do not bring him back to you, then I will bear the blame in the sight of my father all my life.' [33]Now therefore, please let your servant remain as a slave to my lord in place of the boy, and let the boy go back with his brothers. [34]For how can I go back to my father if the boy is not with me? I fear to see the suffering that would come upon my father."

45 Then Joseph could no longer control himself before all those who stood by him, and he cried out, "Send everyone away from me." So no one stayed with him when Joseph made himself known to his brothers. [2]And he wept so loudly that the Egyptians heard it, and the household of Pharaoh heard it. [3]Joseph said to his brothers, "I am Joseph. Is my father still alive?" But his brothers could not answer him, so dismayed were they at his presence.

4 Then Joseph said to his brothers, "Come closer to me." And they came closer. He said, "I am your brother, Joseph, whom you sold

down before him as his dream of the sheaves of wheat foreshadowed (37:5–8). **44:16** Judah takes the lead among the brothers. This will continue throughout the rest of this chapter. The prominence given to Judah in the denouement of events in the story has encouraged some scholars to see this as one way in which the Davidic kings, claiming descent from Judah, made the case for their monarchy. **44:27–31** Judah reports to Joseph the details of Jacob's response to his falsely reported death and his unwillingness to allow Benjamin to depart on account of it. This is the first time in the narrative that Joseph hears these details. Judah, however, continues on and goes so far as to make the claim that Joseph's decisions will cause Jacob's death. **44:33** Judah now makes the offer that will prove to be the critical turning point in the story. Knowing how much Jacob would be distressed about Benjamin's imprisonment and absence, Judah offers to be enslaved in his younger brother's place.

45:1–28 The primary plot point in the story resolves itself in this chapter. Joseph reveals his true identity to his brothers, reconciles with them, and then puts in motion his reunion with his father. While the narrative will continue on for a few chapters, the rest has the feel of an epilogue to the main events recounted in this chapter. **45:4–8** Joseph now explains his entire Egyptian ordeal as ordained by God for the preservation of life. The role of divine direction fits within the larger theme found particularly in the dream narratives in which God directs and reveals all things. The question as to which lives Joseph has been sent to Egypt to save remains. Verse 7 suggests it is the lives of his family and their future

into Egypt. [5]And now do not be distressed or angry with yourselves because you sold me here, for God sent me before you to preserve life. [6]For the famine has been in the land these two years, and there are five more years in which there will be neither plowing nor harvest. [7]God sent me before you to preserve for you a remnant on earth and to keep alive for you many survivors. [8]So it was not you who sent me here but God; he has made me a father to Pharaoh and lord of all his house and ruler over all the land of Egypt. [9]Hurry and go up to my father and say to him, 'Thus says your son Joseph, God has made me lord of all Egypt; come down to me; do not delay. [10]You shall settle in the land of Goshen, and you shall be near me, you and your children and your children's children, as well as your flocks, your herds, and all that you have. [11]I will provide for you there, since there are five more years of famine to come, so that you and your household and all that you have will not come to poverty.' [12]And now your eyes and the eyes of my brother Benjamin see that it is my own mouth that speaks to you. [13]You must tell my father how greatly I am honored in Egypt and all that you have seen. Hurry and bring my father down here." [14]Then he fell upon his brother Benjamin's neck and wept, while Benjamin wept upon his neck. [15]And he kissed all his brothers and wept upon them, and after that his brothers talked with him.

16 When the report was heard in Pharaoh's house, "Joseph's brothers have come," Pharaoh and his servants were pleased. [17]Pharaoh said to Joseph, "Say to your brothers, 'Do this: load your animals and go back to the land of Canaan. [18]Take your father and your households and come to me, so that I may give you the best of the land of Egypt, and you may enjoy the fat of the land.' [19]You are further charged to say, 'Do this: take wagons from the land of Egypt for your little ones and for your wives, and bring your father, and come. [20]Give no thought to your possessions, for the best of all the land of Egypt is yours.'"

21 The sons of Israel did so. Joseph gave them wagons according to the instruction of Pharaoh, and he gave them provisions for the journey. [22]To each one of them he gave a set of garments, but to Benjamin he gave three hundred pieces of silver and five sets of garments. [23]To his father he sent the following: ten donkeys loaded with the good things of Egypt and ten female donkeys loaded with grain, bread, and provision for his father on the journey. [24]Then he sent his brothers on their way, and as they were leaving he said to them, "Do not quarrel[k] along the way."

25 So they went up out of Egypt and came to their father Jacob in the land of Canaan. [26]And they told him, "Joseph is still alive! He is even ruler over all the land of Egypt." He was stunned; he could not believe them. [27]But when they told him all the words of Joseph that he had said to them, and when he saw the wagons that Joseph had sent to carry him, the spirit of their father Jacob revived. [28]Israel said, "Enough! My son Joseph is still alive. I must go and see him before I die."

46

When Israel set out on his journey with all that he had and came to Beersheba, he offered sacrifices to the God of his

k 45.24 Or *be agitated*

descendants, not a wider group that might include the Egyptians he is ostensibly meant to protect as Pharaoh's vizier. This raises the question of who Joseph feels allegiance to: Is it his family and their descendants, or is it the Egyptians, whose culture and wealth he has adopted without reservation? See also 50:20. **45:9–13** Joseph now explains to his brothers the immensity of the famine, which will last for another five years. His instruction for Jacob to come to Egypt and live in Goshen is generous, but one should not miss that it is yet another case in which the ancestral family must survive a migration. In direct contrast to God's command to Isaac not to migrate to Egypt to survive a famine (26:2), now God is at work through Joseph to persuade Jacob to emigrate there in order to survive. **45:25–28** One might expect skepticism from Jacob upon hearing the report that Joseph is alive. His sons have not behaved in a way that inspires confidence in their truthfulness. Jacob seems to need persuading (v. 26), but it does not take long to overcome his doubt. To enhance the sense of urgency, Jacob declares that he may not have long to live (v. 28).

46:1–27 Jacob journeys to Egypt at Joseph's request, but in the shadow of an ever-worsening famine. This migration is neither wholly involuntary nor voluntary. This story, however, reflects a wider concern that will become more prevalent in the final chapters of Genesis: preparing a link to the larger exodus narrative that follows it in the Torah. **46:1–4** Beer-sheba is a symbolic location for several

father Isaac. [2]God spoke to Israel in visions of the night and said, "Jacob, Jacob." And he said, "Here I am." [3]Then he said, "I am God,[l] the God of your father; do not be afraid to go down to Egypt, for I will make of you a great nation there. [4]I myself will go down with you to Egypt, and I will also bring you up again, and Joseph's own hand shall close your eyes."

5 Then Jacob set out from Beer-sheba, and the sons of Israel carried their father Jacob, their little ones, and their wives in the wagons that Pharaoh had sent to carry him. [6]They also took their livestock and the goods that they had acquired in the land of Canaan, and they came into Egypt, Jacob and all his offspring with him, [7]his sons, and his sons' sons with him, his daughters, and his sons' daughters; all his offspring he brought with him into Egypt.

8 Now these are the names of the Israelites, Jacob and his offspring, who came to Egypt. Reuben, Jacob's firstborn, [9]and the children of Reuben: Hanoch, Pallu, Hezron, and Carmi. [10]The children of Simeon: Jemuel, Jamin, Ohad, Jachin, Zohar, and Shaul, the son of a Canaanite woman. [11]The children of Levi: Gershon, Kohath, and Merari. [12]The children of Judah: Er, Onan, Shelah, Perez, and Zerah (but Er and Onan died in the land of Canaan), and the children of Perez were Hezron and Hamul. [13]The children of Issachar: Tola, Puvah, Jashub,[m] and Shimron. [14]The children of Zebulun: Sered, Elon, and Jahleel. [15]These are the sons of Leah whom she bore to Jacob in Paddan-aram, together with his daughter Dinah; in all, his sons and his daughters numbered thirty-three. [16]The children of Gad: Ziphion, Haggi, Shuni, Ezbon, Eri, Arodi, and Areli. [17]The children of Asher: Imnah, Ishvah, Ishvi, Beriah, and their sister Serah.

The children of Beriah: Heber and Malchiel. [18]These are the children of Zilpah, whom Laban gave to his daughter Leah, and these she bore to Jacob—sixteen persons. [19]The children of Jacob's wife Rachel: Joseph and Benjamin. [20]To Joseph in the land of Egypt were born Manasseh and Ephraim, whom Asenath daughter of Potiphera, priest of On, bore to him. [21]The children of Benjamin: Bela, Becher, Ashbel, Gera, Naaman, Ehi, Rosh, Muppim, Huppim, and Ard. [22]These are the children of Rachel who were born to Jacob—fourteen persons in all. [23]The children of Dan: Hashum.[n] [24]The children of Naphtali: Jahzeel, Guni, Jezer, and Shillem. [25]These are the children of Bilhah, whom Laban gave to his daughter Rachel, and these she bore to Jacob—seven persons in all. [26]All the persons belonging to Jacob who came into Egypt who were his own offspring, not including the wives of his sons, were sixty-six persons in all. [27]The children of Joseph who were born to him in Egypt were two; all the persons of the house of Jacob who came into Egypt were seventy.

28 Israel[o] sent Judah ahead to Joseph to lead the way before him into Goshen. When they came to the land of Goshen, [29]Joseph made ready his chariot and went up to meet his father Israel in Goshen. He presented himself to him, fell on his neck, and wept on his neck a good while. [30]Israel said to Joseph, "I can die now, having seen for myself that you are still alive." [31]Joseph said to his brothers and to his father's household, "I will go up and tell Pharaoh and will say to him, 'My brothers and my father's household, who

l 46.3 Heb *the God*   m 46.13 Compare Sam Gk: MT *Iob*
n 46.23 Gk: Heb *Hushim*   o 46.28 Heb *He*

reasons. First, it recalls the place where Abraham and Sarah (chap. 20) and then Isaac and Rebekah (chap. 26) survived similar famines. Second, it stands as a sort of southern border town, past which one leaves the boundaries of the land God has promised to the patriarchs. It represents the point where Jacob will leave the covenantal inheritance. To add further symbolic weight, the message from God strongly resembles Jacob's dream at Bethel in chap. 28, where he first connects his allegiance to YHWH to the contingency that the deity protect him during his migration and return him to Canaan.
46:8-27 This is the sort of genealogy that has represented the end of other narratives in Genesis. It is not the final word on Jacob but does signal the story is reaching its conclusion. For all the details of the genealogy, the key theme comes in its concluding summary: seventy—a multiple of seven, the number representing wholeness or perfection—connotes that Jacob's family is the ideal size.
46:28 *Goshen* is an area in the northernmost part of Egypt, on the eastern side of the Nile delta. It was a fertile region, thus it fits Pharaoh's instruction to dwell in the best parts of the land (47:6). At the same time, it appears to be at some distance from the centers of Egyptian life, thus satisfying the Egyptians' desire to be separate from shepherds—as suggested in chap. 43 and made explicit here.

were in the land of Canaan, have come to me. ³²The men are shepherds, for they have been keepers of livestock, and they have brought their flocks and their herds and all that they have.' ³³When Pharaoh calls you and says, 'What is your occupation?' ³⁴you shall say, 'Your servants have been keepers of livestock from our youth even until now, both we and our ancestors,' in order that you may settle in the land of Goshen, because all shepherds are abhorrent to the Egyptians."

47 So Joseph went and told Pharaoh, "My father and my brothers, with their flocks and herds and all that they possess, have come from the land of Canaan; they are now in the land of Goshen." ²From among his brothers he took five men and presented them to Pharaoh. ³Pharaoh said to his brothers, "What is your occupation?" And they said to Pharaoh, "Your servants are shepherds, as our ancestors were." ⁴They said to Pharaoh, "We have come to reside as aliens in the land, for there is no pasture for your servants' flocks because the famine is severe in the land of Canaan. Now, we ask you, let your servants settle in the land of Goshen." ⁵Then Pharaoh said to Joseph, "Your father and your brothers have come to you. ⁶The land of Egypt is before you; settle your father and your brothers in the best part of the land; let them live in the land of Goshen; and if you know that there are capable men among them, put them in charge of my livestock."

7 Then Joseph brought in his father Jacob and presented him before Pharaoh, and Jacob blessed Pharaoh. ⁸Pharaoh said to Jacob, "How many are the years of your life?" ⁹Jacob said to Pharaoh, "The years of my earthly sojourn are one hundred thirty; few and hard have been the years of my life. They do not compare with the years of the life of my ancestors during their long sojourn." ¹⁰Then Jacob blessed Pharaoh and went out from the presence of Pharaoh. ¹¹Joseph settled his father and his brothers and granted them a holding in the land of Egypt, in the best part of the land, in the land of Rameses, as Pharaoh had instructed. ¹²And Joseph provided his father, his brothers, and all his father's household with food, according to the number of their dependents.

13 Now there was no food in all the land, for the famine was very severe. The land of Egypt and the land of Canaan languished because of the famine. ¹⁴Joseph collected all the money to be found in the land of Egypt and in the land of Canaan in exchange for the grain that they bought, and Joseph brought the money into Pharaoh's house. ¹⁵When the money from the land of Egypt and from the land of Canaan was spent, all the Egyptians came to Joseph and said, "Give us food! Why should we die before your eyes? For our money is gone." ¹⁶And Joseph answered, "Give me your livestock, and I will give you food in exchange for your livestock, if your money is gone." ¹⁷So they brought their livestock to Joseph, and Joseph gave them food in exchange for the horses, the flocks, the herds, and the donkeys. That year he supplied them with food in exchange for all their livestock. ¹⁸When that year was ended, they came to him the following year and said to him, "We cannot hide from my lord that our money is all spent, and the herds of cattle are my lord's. There is nothing left in the sight of my lord but our bodies

47:1–12 In this brief vignette, Jacob meets Pharaoh. In a fashion similar to the endangered ancestress stories (chaps. 12, 20, and 26), this encounter makes clear that Jacob will benefit financially from a migration that is compelled by famine. The closest comparison is Abraham's interaction with Abimelech (20:17–18), in which he prays for and blesses Abimelech. 47:11 This verse names the area of Goshen as *the land of Rameses*. While some have used this detail as a key to determining the precise date of the events depicted in the story—perhaps even to argue they are historically accurate—caution is in order. Rameses, a name meaning "son of Ra," the Egyptian sun god, was used by many Pharaohs during the nineteenth and especially the twentieth dynasties. This means the reference here might allude to a period of at least a century, perhaps longer.

47:13–26 Attention finally returns to the fate of the Egyptians who were nominally identified as the beneficiaries of Joseph's strategy adopted by Pharaoh in chap. 41. One discovers here that Joseph's plan has preserved many Egyptian lives but also effects an immense transfer of wealth from the people to Pharaoh. 47:14–17 Once Joseph has extracted all the cash of the people of Egypt in exchange for the food the state has stockpiled, he begins to claim their capital assets. This begins with the livestock, which as both the means that made farming possible and a source of food, resembles making a contemporary

and our lands. ¹⁹Shall we die before your eyes, both we and our land? Buy us and our land in exchange for food. We with our land will become slaves to Pharaoh; just give us seed, so that we may live and not die and that the land may not become desolate."

20 So Joseph bought all the land of Egypt for Pharaoh. All the Egyptians sold their fields, because the famine was severe upon them, and the land became Pharaoh's. ²¹As for the people, he made slaves of them*ᵖ* from one end of Egypt to the other. ²²Only the land of the priests he did not buy, for the priests had a fixed allowance from Pharaoh and lived on the allowance that Pharaoh gave them; therefore they did not sell their land. ²³Then Joseph said to the people, "Now that I have this day bought you and your land for Pharaoh, here is seed for you; sow the land. ²⁴And at the harvests you shall give one-fifth to Pharaoh, and four-fifths shall be your own, as seed for the field and as food for yourselves and your households and as food for your little ones." ²⁵They said, "You have saved our lives; may it please my lord, we will be slaves to Pharaoh." ²⁶So Joseph made it a statute concerning the land of Egypt, and it stands to this day, that Pharaoh should have the fifth. The land of the priests alone did not become Pharaoh's.

27 Thus Israel settled in the land of Egypt, in the region of Goshen, and they gained possessions in it and were fruitful and multiplied exceedingly. ²⁸Jacob lived in the land of Egypt seventeen years, so the days of Jacob, the years of his life, were one hundred forty-seven years.

29 When the time of Israel's death drew near, he called his son Joseph and said to him, "If I have found favor with you, put your hand under my thigh and promise to deal loyally and truly with me. Do not bury me in Egypt. ³⁰When I lie down with my ancestors, carry me out of Egypt and bury me in their burial place." He answered, "I will do as you have said." ³¹And he said, "Swear to me," and he swore to him. Then Israel bowed himself on the head of his bed.

48 After this Joseph was told, "Your father is ill." So he took with him his two sons, Manasseh and Ephraim. ²When Jacob was told, "Your son Joseph has come to you," heᵍ summoned his strength and sat up in bed. ³And Jacob said to Joseph, "God Almightyʳ appeared to me at Luz in the land of Canaan, and he blessed me ⁴and said to me, 'I am going to make you fruitful and increase your numbers; I will make of you a company of peoples and will give this land to your offspring after you for a perpetual holding.' ⁵Therefore your two sons, who were born to you in the land of

p 47.21 Sam Gk Compare Vg: MT *He removed them to the cities* *q* 48.2 Heb *Israel* *r* 48.3 Traditional rendering of Heb *El Shaddai*

family sell their cars and valuables in order to purchase basic necessities. **47:19–22** The following year, the people do not hide that they have nothing left to use as payment for food. They offer their land and their own selves in exchange for food. Joseph accepts their offer and obtains for Pharaoh all their land and persons. The only exception is the priestly class, who have an existing arrangement for payment as a result of their elite status and role as divine intermediaries. **47:23–26** Joseph's concession, if one can call it that, is to tax the people at 20 percent of their income going forward. The story envisions an entire society of tenant farmers, fully indebted to the state, who increase the tax revenue of the state and Pharaoh's wealth as they increase their agricultural output. Whether or not this arrangement has any basis in an actual economic structure is highly debatable, but it shows that sophisticated economic thinking (and planning) was not beyond ancient societies.

47:27–28 This final note on Jacob shows a chasm between the experience of the Egyptians, from whom Joseph extracts great wealth, and his family, who emerge from this environmental disaster even wealthier than they entered.

47:29–31 Just as Abraham insisted on burying Sarah in Canaan, and being buried there himself, so too does Jacob require Joseph to promise he will not be laid to rest in Egypt. Jacob's refusal to integrate into Egyptian life, to the point of refusing a burial there, contrasts with Joseph taking on an Egyptian name and family.

48:1–22 The next two chapters recount Jacob's last words, presented as coming from his deathbed. The first half of this testament focuses on Joseph and particularly his two sons, Manasseh and Ephraim. Jacob will institute in the next generation the same pattern his mother and he established in his: the younger child will inherit what typically falls to the firstborn. **48:3–4** *Luz* is better known as Bethel throughout Genesis. Here, it appears as the older name for the place featured in this story. **48:5–7** Jacob

Egypt before I came to you in Egypt, are now mine; Ephraim and Manasseh shall be mine, just as Reuben and Simeon are. ⁶As for the offspring born to you after them, they shall be yours. They shall be recorded under the names of their brothers with regard to their inheritance. ⁷For when I came from Paddan, Rachel, alas, died in the land of Canaan on the way, while there was still some distance to go to Ephrath, and I buried her there on the way to Ephrath, that is, Bethlehem."

8 When Israel saw Joseph's sons, he said, "Who are these?" ⁹Joseph said to his father, "They are my sons, whom God has given me here." And he said, "Bring them to me, please, that I may bless them." ¹⁰Now the eyes of Israel were dim with age, and he could not see well. So Joseph brought them near him, and he kissed them and embraced them. ¹¹Israel said to Joseph, "I did not expect to see your face, and here God has let me see your children also." ¹²Then Joseph removed them from his father's knees,ˢ and he bowed himself with his face to the earth. ¹³Joseph took them both, Ephraim in his right hand toward Israel's left and Manasseh in his left hand toward Israel's right, and brought them near him. ¹⁴But Israel stretched out his right hand and laid it on the head of Ephraim, who was the younger, and his left hand on the head of Manasseh, crossing his hands, for Manasseh was the firstborn. ¹⁵He blessed Joseph and said,

"The God before whom my ancestors
    Abraham and Isaac walked,
the God who has been my shepherd all
    my life to this day,

¹⁶ the angel who has redeemed me from all
    harm, bless the boys,
and in them let my name be perpetuated
    and the name of my ancestors
    Abraham and Isaac,
and let them grow into a multitude on
    the earth."

17 When Joseph saw that his father laid his right hand on the head of Ephraim, it displeased him, so he took his father's hand, to remove it from Ephraim's head to Manasseh's head. ¹⁸Joseph said to his father, "Not so, my father! Since this one is the firstborn, put your right hand on his head." ¹⁹But his father refused and said, "I know, my son, I know; he also shall become a people, and he also shall be great. Nevertheless his younger brother shall be greater than he, and his offspring shall become a multitude of nations." ²⁰So he blessed them that day, saying,

"By you Israel will invoke blessings,
    saying,
'God make you like Ephraim and like
    Manasseh.'"

So he put Ephraim ahead of Manasseh. ²¹Then Israel said to Joseph, "I am about to die, but God will be with you and will bring you again to the land of your ancestors. ²²I now give to you one portionᵗ more than to your brothers, the portionᵘ that I took from the hand of the Amorites with my sword and with my bow."

s 48.12 Heb *from his knees*   t 48.22 Or *mountain slope*
u 48.22 Or *mountain slope*

informs Joseph that he will adopt his two sons, *Ephraim and Manasseh*, because of his affection for Rachel, their grandmother. In doing so, Jacob promotes these two grandsons to the status of tribal patriarchs like his other sons. Jacob specifies that any further children born to Joseph would be made "sons" of these two boys (v. 6). Though complicated and confusing, this is not unusual. Throughout the Hebrew Bible, listings of the twelve tribes sometimes include Joseph and Levi—with the latter representing the priestly clan of the community. Elsewhere, Levi is absent and Ephraim and Manasseh appear to make the number of tribes twelve. The evidence indicates that in antiquity there was either flexibility in the list of tribes or open disagreement about which formulation of twelve was the correct one. **48:8–11** Some scholars argue that v. 8 continues v. 2, with the interceding verses from a different source (the Priestly one; see **"The Bible and Methods," p. 2148**). Alternatively, one can read this statement as recalling Isaac's own lack of cognition when Jacob enters his room to receive his father's blessing. **48:17–20** The surprising reassignment of the eldest child's blessing to his younger brother that plays out more slowly and with greater tension in chap. 27 occurs with clear intent and great speed here. Joseph expresses his discomfort with Jacob's "confusion," which his father explains is not confusion at all. The explanation for Jacob placing Ephraim above Manasseh resembles the language of Isaac in chap. 27. One may interpret Jacob's actions here as taking divine precedent from his own experience or, perhaps less charitably, as an attempt to set a precedent that absolves him of any guilt for his earlier deception of Isaac.

49

Then Jacob called his sons and said, "Gather around, that I may tell you what will happen to you in days to come.

² Assemble and hear, O sons of Jacob;
>   listen to Israel your father.

³ Reuben, you are my firstborn,
>   my might and the first fruits of my
>   vigor,
>   excelling in rank and excelling in
>   power.
⁴ Unstable as water, you shall no longer
>   excel
>   because you went up onto your
>   father's bed;
>   then you defiled it—you' went up
>   onto my couch!

⁵ Simeon and Levi are brothers;
>   weapons of violence are their
>   swords.
⁶ May I never come into their council;
>   may I not be joined to their company,
>   for in their anger they killed men,
>   and at their whim they hamstrung
>   oxen.
⁷ Cursed be their anger, for it is fierce,
>   and their wrath, for it is cruel!
>   I will divide them in Jacob
>   and scatter them in Israel.

⁸ Judah, your brothers shall praise you;
>   your hand shall be on the neck of
>   your enemies;
>   your father's sons shall bow down
>   before you.

⁹ Judah is a lion's whelp;
>   from the prey, my son, you have
>   gone up.
>   He crouches down, he stretches out like
>   a lion,
>   like a lioness—who dares rouse
>   him up?
¹⁰ The scepter shall not depart from Judah,
>   nor the ruler's staff from between his
>   feet,
>   until tribute comes to him,ʷ
>   and the obedience of the peoples is his.
¹¹ Binding his foal to the vine
>   and his donkey's colt to the choice vine,
>   he washes his garments in wine
>   and his robe in the blood of grapes;
¹² his eyes are darker than wine
>   and his teeth whiter than milk.

¹³ Zebulun shall settle at the shore of the
>   sea;
>   he shall be a haven for ships,
>   and his border shall be at Sidon.

¹⁴ Issachar is a strong donkey,
>   lying down between the sheepfolds;
¹⁵ he saw that a resting place was good
>   and that the land was pleasant,
>   so he bowed his shoulder to the burden
>   and became a slave at forced labor.

¹⁶ Dan shall judge his people
>   as one of the tribes of Israel.

v 49.4 Gk Syr Tg: Heb *he* w 49.10 Or *until Shiloh comes* or *until he comes to Shiloh* or (with Syr) *until he comes to whom it belongs*

49:1–28 Now Jacob proceeds to bless all twelve of his sons. The order of appearance is hard to decipher. The sons appear ordered by mother: Leah, then Zilpah (her maid), followed by Bilhah (Rachel's maid), then Rachel. Within that, however, they do not always occur in birth order. Somewhat clearer is the attention given to various tribes: Judah and Joseph get the lengthiest parts, reflecting their direct association with the monarchies of the northern and southern kingdoms. The blessings employ a number of wordplays, archaic forms of words, and other subtle connections that are very difficult to reflect in translation. **49:4** The condemnation of Reuben refers to the aside about his relationship with Bilhah noted in 35:22. Despite being the firstborn of all Jacob's children, the tribe of Reuben does not feature prominently in the stories about Israel and Judah in the Hebrew Bible. In view of how Genesis treats firstborn sons, perhaps that is no surprise. **49:5** Simeon and Levi operate together in chap. 34, and that may be why they are linked here. **49:7** The division and scattering mentioned in this verse may refer to Levi's role as the priestly tribe, with members living among every other tribe but simultaneously losing the land rights ascribed to those other groups. **49:8–12** This stanza begins with the assertion that Judah will rule over his brothers, a statement pointing toward the royal lineage of this tribe. Verse 10 contains a hard-to-interpret phrase, sometimes seen as a reference to the tabernacle's time in Shiloh. Many ancient interpreters viewed this as a messianic promise, and that view is adopted in the New Testament, where Jesus of Nazareth's descent from the tribe of Judah plays an important role in the presentation of him as a messianic figure. **49:16** The statement that *Dan shall judge*, or govern, his people is a wordplay

¹⁷ Dan shall be a snake by the roadside,
    a viper along the path,
that bites the horse's heels
    so that its rider falls backward.

¹⁸ I wait for your salvation, O LORD.

¹⁹ Gad shall be raided by raiders,
    but he shall raid at their heels.

²⁰ Asher's*ˣ* food shall be rich,
    and he shall provide royal delicacies.

²¹ Naphtali is a doe let loose
    that bears lovely fawns.*ʸ*

²² Joseph is a fruitful bough,*ᶻ*
    a fruitful bough by a spring;
    his branches run over the wall.*ᵃ*
²³ The archers fiercely attacked him;
    they shot at him and pressed him
    hard.
²⁴ Yet his bow remained taut,
    and his arms*ᵇ* were made agile
by the hands of the Mighty One of Jacob,
    by the name of the Shepherd, the
    Rock of Israel,
²⁵ by the God of your father, who will help
    you,
    by the Almighty*ᶜ* who will bless you
    with blessings of heaven above,
blessings of the deep that lies
    beneath,
    blessings of the breasts and of the
    womb.
²⁶ The blessings of your father
    are stronger than the blessings of the
    eternal mountains,
    the bounties*ᵈ* of the everlasting hills;
may they be on the head of Joseph,
    on the brow of him who was set apart
    from his brothers.

²⁷ Benjamin is a ravenous wolf,
    in the morning devouring the prey
    and at evening dividing the spoil."

28 All these are the twelve tribes of Israel, and this is what their father said to them when he blessed them, blessing each one of them with a suitable blessing.
29 Then he charged them, saying to them, "I am about to be gathered to my people. Bury me with my ancestors in the cave in the field of Ephron the Hittite, ³⁰in the cave in the field at Machpelah, near Mamre, in the land of Canaan, in the field that Abraham bought from Ephron the Hittite as a burial site. ³¹There Abraham and his wife Sarah were buried; there Isaac and his wife Rebekah were buried; and there I buried Leah. ³²The field and the cave that is in it were purchased from the Hittites." ³³When Jacob ended his charge to his sons, he drew up his feet into the bed, breathed his last, and was gathered to his people.

50 Then Joseph threw himself on his father's face and wept over him and kissed him. ²Joseph commanded the physicians in his service to embalm his father. So the physicians embalmed Israel; ³they spent forty days doing this, for that is the time required for embalming. And the Egyptians wept for him seventy days.
4 When the days of weeping for him were past, Joseph addressed the household of Pharaoh, "If now I have found favor with you, please speak to Pharaoh as follows: ⁵My father made me swear an oath; he said, 'I am about to die. In the tomb that I hewed out

x 49.20 Gk Vg Syr: Heb *From Asher* y 49.21 Or *that gives beautiful words* z 49.22 Meaning of Heb uncertain a 49.22 Meaning of Heb uncertain b 49.24 Heb *the arms of his hands* c 49.25 Traditional rendering of Heb *Shaddai* d 49.26 Cn Compare Gk: Heb *of my progenitors to the boundaries*

since the verb form used (Heb. "yadin") puns on the name Dan (see 30:6). **49:22** The lengthy blessing of Joseph begins here with an image that connotes fertility and great abundance. **49:23–25** The imagery is of one under attack who is protected by a patron deity. The references to heaven above and the deep beneath recall the forces of nature subdued in chap. 1; the references to breast and womb concern fertility, implying a large group of descendants capable of fighting.
  49:29–50:26 With his blessings bestowed on his children, Jacob's life now ends. Joseph mourns his father and fulfills his wish of burying him in Canaan. All that remains is for Joseph's own life to reach its end. Notably, Joseph is not returned to Canaan; his dead body is embalmed according to Egyptian practice and remains there. This variation in burial practice presents the final moment of divergence between the father, Jacob, who will not integrate with any outsider and insists on burial in Canaan, and Joseph, who willingly assimilates into Egyptian culture. **50:2–3** Joseph commands his servants to embalm Jacob according to Egyptian practice. The Egyptians mourn Jacob, indicating that he was highly respected, even if

for myself in the land of Canaan, there you shall bury me.' Now therefore let me go up, so that I may bury my father; then I will return." ⁶Pharaoh answered, "Go up and bury your father, as he made you swear to do."

7 So Joseph went up to bury his father. With him went up all the servants of Pharaoh, the elders of his household, and all the elders of the land of Egypt, ⁸as well as all the household of Joseph, his brothers, and his father's household. Only their children, their flocks, and their herds were left in the land of Goshen. ⁹Both chariots and charioteers went up with him. It was a very great company. ¹⁰When they came to the threshing floor of Atad, which is beyond the Jordan, they held there a very great and sorrowful lamentation, and he observed a time of mourning for his father seven days. ¹¹When the Canaanite inhabitants of the land saw the mourning on the threshing floor of Atad, they said, "This is a grievous mourning on the part of the Egyptians." Therefore the place was named Abel-mizraim;ᵉ it is beyond the Jordan. ¹²Thus his sons did for him as he had instructed them. ¹³They carried him to the land of Canaan and buried him in the cave of the field at Machpelah, the field near Mamre, which Abraham bought as a burial site from Ephron the Hittite. ¹⁴After he had buried his father, Joseph returned to Egypt with his brothers and all who had gone up with him to bury his father.

15 Realizing that their father was dead, Joseph's brothers said, "What if Joseph still bears a grudge against us and pays us back in full for all the wrong that we did to him?"

¹⁶So they approachedᶠ Joseph, saying, "Your father gave this instruction before he died, ¹⁷'Say to Joseph: I beg you, forgive the crime of your brothers and the wrong they did in harming you.' Now therefore please forgive the crime of the servants of the God of your father." Joseph wept when they spoke to him. ¹⁸Then his brothers also wept,ᵍ fell down before him, and said, "We are here as your slaves." ¹⁹But Joseph said to them, "Do not be afraid! Am I in the place of God? ²⁰Even though you intended to do harm to me, God intended it for good, in order to preserve a numerous people, as he is doing today. ²¹So have no fear; I myself will provide for you and your little ones." In this way he reassured them, speaking kindly to them.

22 So Joseph remained in Egypt, he and his father's household, and Joseph lived one hundred ten years. ²³Joseph saw Ephraim's children of the third generation; the children of Machir son of Manasseh were also born on Joseph's knees.

24 Then Joseph said to his brothers, "I am about to die, but God will surely come to you and bring you up out of this land to the land that he swore to Abraham, to Isaac, and to Jacob." ²⁵So Joseph made the Israelites swear, saying, "When God comes to you, you shall carry up my bones from here." ²⁶And Joseph died, being one hundred ten years old; he was embalmed and placed in a coffin in Egypt.

e 50.11 That is, *mourning of Egypt* f 50.16 Gk Syr: Heb *they commanded* g 50.18 Cn: Heb *also came*

---

only for his association with Joseph. **50:7–9** Joseph leads a massive procession of both Jacob's family and Pharaoh's household for the burial in Canaan. The state procession adds to the sense that the deceased is a figure of great importance—something made explicit in v. 11. **50:10** The procession does not go directly up to Canaan but through the desert and across the Jordan River. There is no reason given, but the route resembles the one that Israel will take in the exodus later in the Torah, and it may be meant to foreshadow that. **50:19–21** When Joseph's brothers express their concern that he will now seek vengeance on them, he responds by returning to one of the themes of the narrative: the ultimate authority of God over all things. Just as the deity gives Joseph the ability to interpret dreams for a larger purpose, now Joseph indicates that the divine plan remains the same. This statement ensures the audience does not miss the importance of the theme of divine control that has featured throughout the story. **50:24–26** Everything in this final scene reflects Joseph's connection to Egypt until vv. 24–25. There is no doubt vv. 24–25 point forward to the exodus narrative that follows, especially in suggesting that Joseph's body be returned to Canaan. Many scholars argue that these two verses were placed here to establish a connection between the narrative about Joseph and the book of Exodus that did not originally exist. Indeed, the way that v. 26 returns to the prevalent connection between Joseph and Egypt feels out of character with vv. 24–25. Without v. 25, one would have no reason to believe Joseph would want anything other than a proper burial in Egypt. One can take away from this tension that the broader Torah brings together a number of origin stories connected to Israel and Judah that have been, over many generations, formed into a compilation that is meant to work together. Even so, such a process has not fully erased every trace of how these sources were once discrete.

EXODUS

Name of the Book

Exodus is the origin story—the birth narrative—of the nation of Israel. The Greek name *Exodus*, which means "way out," refers to the story of the Israelites' liberation from Egyptian slavery. A passage from Deuteronomy aptly summarizes the plot of Exodus: "When the Egyptians treated us harshly and afflicted us, by imposing hard labor on us, we cried to the LORD, the God of our ancestors; the LORD heard our voice and saw our affliction, our toil, and our oppression. The LORD brought us out of Egypt with a mighty hand and an outstretched arm, with a terrifying display of power, and with signs and wonders" (Deut. 26:6–8). The Hebrew title for the book of Exodus is Shemot, or "names," and stems from the first verse and the book's opening genealogy of Jacob's descendants, God's chosen people. Whereas the first part of the book is an account of God leading the people out of bondage in Egypt (chaps. 1–15), the remainder of the book is a record of events in the wilderness and at Sinai (chaps. 16–40). It is here that Israel enters into a covenant relationship with God and lives into that relationship through trial and error. It is in Exodus that the identity of the people is established: first through rescue from slavery, then through the receiving of covenant regulations and by building the tabernacle.

Story and Truth

Resisting a simple one-to-one correspondence to modern rationalistic understandings, the book of Exodus is more than history: it is best understood as a true story. The historical elements in the book are in service to the larger story of Israel's redemption and formation as a people. In this sense, each episode, from Moses's birth to the completion of the tabernacle, functions as a testimony to God's power, provision, and presence.

As Israel's origin story, the exodus provides the root metaphor for this people's identity. On numerous occasions in the Torah, God tells the people, "I am the LORD your God, who brought you out of the land of Egypt, out of the house of slavery" (Exod. 20:2; see also 29:46; Lev. 11:45; 19:36; 25:38; 26:13; Num. 15:41; Deut. 5:6). The exodus is God's signature act. Israel repeatedly refers to God's redemptive act "with a mighty hand and an outstretched arm" (Deut. 5:15; see also Exod. 6:6; Deut. 4:34; 7:19; 9:29; 11:2; 26:8; Ps. 136:12), acknowledging the centrality of the exodus to their very existence. Israel is redeemed by and belongs to God.

Moses, the main human character in Exodus, is cast as an unlikely hero who escapes Pharaoh's genocide as a baby only to find himself exiled as a murderer in Midian. It is from this place of exile that Moses encounters God on Mount Horeb. God calls Moses to confront Pharaoh—a commission that would be daunting for any person, including the most eloquent, which Moses is not. Arguably the most important part of Moses's call is the revelation of the divine name. The God of Israel is "I AM WHO I AM" (3:14) and also YHWH ("The LORD"; see **"God's Name," p. 89**). God's name is presented as the key answer to Moses's objections to his calling. God's call is not unique to Moses, however, given the number of female characters who delivered this famous Israelite deliverer. The midwives Shiphrah and Puah; Moses's birth mother, Jochebed; his adoptive mother, Pharaoh's daughter; his sister, Miriam; and his wife, Zipporah, are all used at crucial moments in the story to save Moses. These women are the embodiment of God's redemptive work, prefiguring not just what God will do but also how it will happen in unexpected ways with unlikely people.

Covenant

The account of the exodus from Egypt takes up less than half of the book (chaps. 1–15). The remaining twenty-five chapters occur in the wilderness, where the people struggle to realize they have been freed from Pharaoh to serve another master, the Lord. The giving of the law is the second part of establishing Israel as a nation. On Mount Sinai, God makes a covenant with the people in the form of the Ten Commandments (or Decalogue) and additional legislation known as the covenant code (see **"Law/Decalogue," p. 112**). The covenant is the contractual agreement by which God and the people enter into and maintain their relationship (see **"Covenant (Genesis 6)," p. 23**). The covenant establishes God as Israel's Lord, leader, or ruler. The structure of the book of Exodus makes clear

that the purpose of the exodus event is to enter into a covenant relationship with God, which has ramifications for all members of the community.

With the covenant ratified, the Lord accompanies the people as they sojourn in the wilderness in the book of Numbers. It is in the inhospitable terrain of the desert that the covenant is tested and enacted. In this liminal space, God teaches the people what is most essential for being the Lord's treasured possession. The murmuring and complaining episodes that are present in Exodus before the arrival at Mount Sinai anticipate those in Numbers; in both cases, they are a part of the process for a people who struggle to trust and depend on the Lord (see Exod. 15:22–27; 16:1–20; 17:1–7; cf. Num. 11:1–15; 14:1–12). Underlying each crisis is the question of God's presence. In Exodus, the question of God's ongoing presence with the people is answered in the construction of the tabernacle, which facilitates the worship of God in the wilderness. The amount of attention devoted to the tabernacle, its plans, and its execution signals the centrality of the sanctuary for a wandering people longing for a homeland. This mobile tabernacle is evidence that God is not limited to just one space; it is proof that God is bound to this people, especially in worship.

Reading Guide

Exodus is a text containing multiple voices. The book is the result of a variety of oral sources that, over time, were collected, curated, and eventually written down. Scholarly consensus tells us the final editing stages occurred centuries after the exodus, when Israel was in Babylonian exile (if not even later). This stretch of time means that the story of God's initial deliverance and redemption from Egypt has also been shaped by subsequent experiences of displacement. How might the circumstances of exile contribute to the way Israel tells the story of a God who is mightier than the mightiest empire? How might this influence the ways the exiles described the covenantal relationship and the consequences of keeping or not keeping the law? How does the wilderness function symbolically in later times, and what should we make of all the details about the tabernacle in light of the fact that the temple had been destroyed when these texts were being shaped into the book of Exodus as it now stands?

The book of Exodus has numerous functions. It is a theological, political, historiographic, and liturgical text that informs the core identity of God's people. The story of God delivering the oppressed has resonated with many communities who, like the enslaved Hebrews, have put their faith in this God who delivers. Notably, many African captives in the United States responded to the exodus story by identifying with the Hebrew slaves and claiming the God of the exodus for their own. Latin American liberation theology has also used the exodus story to support its claim that God is on the side of the oppressed and has a preference for the poor.

Judy Fentress-Williams

1 These are the names of the sons of Israel who came to Egypt with Jacob, each with his household: ²Reuben, Simeon, Levi, and Judah, ³Issachar, Zebulun, and Benjamin, ⁴Dan and Naphtali, Gad and Asher. ⁵The total number of people born to Jacob was seventy. (Joseph was already in Egypt.) ⁶Then Joseph died, and all his brothers, and that whole generation. ⁷But the Israelites were fruitful and prolific; they multiplied and grew exceedingly strong, so that the land was filled with them.

1:1 The book of Exodus opens with a genealogy that resumes the story of Jacob/Israel and Joseph from the end of Genesis. This list of Jacob's (Israel's) sons is the basis for the book's Hebrew name, "Shemot" ("names"). The sons of Jacob's wives, Leah and Rachel, are listed before the sons of his concubines, Bilhah and Zilpah. Because this list only mentions sons, Jacob's daughter, Dinah, does not appear.

1:5 *Seventy.* Consistent with Gen. 46:27, the number seventy is likely stylized, representing completeness.

1:7 A fulfillment of God's promise to Abraham in Gen. 12 that his descendants would be many.

8 Now a new king arose over Egypt who did not know Joseph. ⁹He said to his people, "Look, the Israelite people are more numerous and more powerful than we. ¹⁰Come, let us deal shrewdly with them, or they will increase and, in the event of war, join our enemies and fight against us and escape from the land." ¹¹Therefore they set taskmasters over them to oppress them with forced labor. They built supply cities, Pithom and Rameses, for Pharaoh. ¹²But the more they were oppressed, the more they multiplied and spread, so that the Egyptians came to dread the Israelites. ¹³The Egyptians subjected the Israelites to hard servitude ¹⁴and made their lives bitter with hard servitude in mortar and bricks and in every kind of field labor. They were ruthless in all the tasks that they imposed on them.

15 The king of Egypt said to the Hebrew midwives, one of whom was named Shiphrah and the other Puah, ¹⁶"When you act as midwives to the Hebrew women and see them on the birthstool, if it is a son, kill him, but if it is a daughter,

she shall live." ¹⁷But the midwives feared God; they did not do as the king of Egypt commanded them, but they let the boys live. ¹⁸So the king of Egypt summoned the midwives and said to them, "Why have you done this and allowed the boys to live?" ¹⁹The midwives said to Pharaoh, "Because the Hebrew women are not like the Egyptian women, for they are vigorous and give birth before the midwife comes to them." ²⁰So God dealt well with the midwives, and the people multiplied and became very strong. ²¹And because the midwives feared God, he gave them families. ²²Then Pharaoh commanded all his people, "Every son that is born to the Hebrews*a* you shall throw into the Nile, but you shall let every daughter live."

2 Now a man from the house of Levi went and married a Levite woman. ²The woman conceived and bore a son, and when she saw that he was a fine baby, she hid him

a 1.22 Sam Gk Tg: Heb lacks to the Hebrews

1:8–14 The *new king* of Egypt is unnamed and described as one *who did not know Joseph*. With these words, the story turns. Without a relationship, the numerous Israelites are now a threat. Although Joseph was instrumental in saving Egypt and the surrounding areas in Genesis, lack of knowledge about him pits Egypt against the family of a man who once was second in command of Egypt (see Gen. 41:37–49). Pharaoh's response to his perceived threat is oppression. **1:11** The practice of enslaving foreigners is not unique to this story or to Egypt. In fact, one of the words used of the people, *Hebrew* (see 1:15), may be related to a term that means mixed multitude (cf. 12:38) and/or designate a people without land, who are, as such, members of the population vulnerable to exploitation. Without the relationship established by Joseph in Genesis, the descendants of Abraham are "other" to the Egyptians. In 1:11, the Israelites are tasked with building two supply cities for Pharaoh named Pithom and Rameses. The name of the former suggests it likely included a temple ("the House of Atum") for the Egyptian creator god; the latter may have been a residence for the Pharaoh (cf. note at 36:8–37). **1:12** In spite of Pharaoh's harsh treatment, the narrative describes the people's growth in diametric opposition to their oppression—yet another sign of the power of God's promise.

1:15–22 The midwives' story is the continuation of the trickster motif present in the Jacob cycle in the book of Genesis. In the ancestral narratives, Jacob is known for his deception and trickery (Gen. 25:29–34; 27:1–29; 30:25–40), which often accompany or facilitate his blessing. Pharaoh commands two midwives, Shiphrah and Puah, to kill Israelite boys. The midwives defy this directive out of their "fear" of or respect for God. When questioned by Pharaoh, they lie, claiming the Hebrew women are *vigorous* and deliver the children before they arrive, likely playing into presumed stereotypes of the Hebrews as more animal-like than the refined Egyptians. The text does not condemn the midwives for their deception; rather, God blesses them. In fact, Shiphrah and Puah are the first deliverers in Exodus's story of deliverance. Their exact ethnicity is unclear. They may be Hebrew midwives or (Egyptian?) midwives to the Hebrews. If the latter, proper fear of God is not limited to Israel alone (cf. Exod. 9:20).

2:1–2 The account of Moses's birth takes the form of the endangered infant narrative. Like the earlier legend of Sargon, the infant is placed in a waterproofed reed basket and sent down the river to be rescued and adopted. The story includes Moses's pedigree—both of his parents are from the priestly tribe of Levi—and provides the etymology for his name. **2:2** The phrase *fine baby* is the exact same language used in Gen. 1 to describe God's creation as "good." Readers are reminded that this baby is a part of God's creation and, for that reason, "good."

Making Connections: Pharaoh (Exodus 1)

Exodus begins with the genealogy of Jacob (Israel), followed quickly by the mention of Pharaoh. If we read the genealogy as the fulfillment of God's promise to the ancestors, then Pharaoh is a threat to that promise. The new Pharaoh is described as one who did not know Joseph (Exod. 1:8), suggesting that the king's lack of relationship with the ancestors has led to the highly fraught situation that now faces Israel.

Although Pharaoh goes unnamed, scholars who place the exodus in the thirteenth century BCE have deduced that the king mentioned in Exod. 1:8 might be Rameses, especially given the supply city of the same name (1:11). The absence of personal names for the Pharaohs of Exodus complicates historical reconstruction; this lack also creates an expansive literary effect. Precisely because he goes unnamed, "Pharaoh" is less a specific individual than a ubiquitous symbol of oppression and empire.

In contrast to Pharaoh, the midwives who defy his command to kill the Israelite boys *are* named: Shiphrah and Puah (1:15). In this light, Pharaoh's lack of name emphasizes his unimportance and inability to outmaneuver the wily midwives who fear God and whose names are remembered for posterity (1:17).

In the plague narrative, Pharaoh is characterized by his refusal to free the Israelites, regardless of the consequences. Pharaoh is said to harden his own heart, but the text also asserts that his heart is hardened by his opponent, the Lord God of Israel, who may do so to move the events to the final, climactic plague. The theological and ethical dilemmas raised by the divine hardening of Pharaoh's heart are complicated. If Pharaoh was understood as a god, then YHWH is manipulating and overpowering another deity in the plagues. Pharaoh's hard heart reflects a position that is formidable and resolute, but in the end, even the greatest ruler is no match for God.

If Pharaoh was understood as a god (or demigod), he is, again, something more than a single human individual, representing Egyptian empire, oppression, and religion. But he is outsmarted by two midwives, manipulated by YHWH, and becomes, finally, nothing more than an unnamed pawn in the Lord's plan to rescue Israel from bondage. For oppressed people everywhere, therefore, Pharaoh is the symbol par excellence of oppression. As one reads the book of Exodus, one sees that Pharaoh—in whatever instantiation—is always defeated.

Judy Fentress-Williams

three months. ³When she could hide him no longer she got a papyrus basket for him and plastered it with bitumen and pitch; she put the child in it and placed it among the reeds on the bank of the river. ⁴His sister stood at a distance, to see what would happen to him.

5 The daughter of Pharaoh came down to bathe at the river, while her attendants walked beside the river. She saw the basket among the reeds and sent her maid to bring it. ⁶When she opened it, she saw the child. He was crying, and she took pity on him. "This must be one of the Hebrews' children," she said. ⁷Then his sister said to Pharaoh's daughter, "Shall I go and get you a nurse from the Hebrew women to nurse the child for you?" ⁸Pharaoh's daughter said to her, "Yes." So the girl went and called the child's mother. ⁹Pharaoh's daughter said to her, "Take this child and nurse it for me, and I will give you your wages." So the woman took the child and nursed it. ¹⁰When the child grew up, she brought him to Pharaoh's

2:3 Moses's placement in the Nile is an ironic fulfillment of Pharaoh's order that all the male children be thrown into the Nile (1:22). The Hebrew term for *basket* is the same word used to describe Noah's ark in Gen. 6. Both arks preserve life and both function symbolically as wombs: places of new life. Water is yet another symbol of birth and life. Here, baby Moses is transported from one mother to another on the river, while his sister, later identified as Miriam, watches over the entire process. The Nile was considered divine in Egyptian religion, so from an Egyptian perspective, the Nile goddess delivers the child to Pharaoh's daughter.

2:6 Note the verbs associated with Pharaoh's daughter, who *saw* the child, heard him while *he was crying*, and *took pity on him*. Her three actions prefigure God's response to Israel's suffering in Exod. 2:24–25 and 3:7, 9, where God sees the people, hears their cry, and is compassionate. This intertextual connection invites us to think of God as a mother rescuing her child, and it forces us to see Pharaoh's daughter as something more than the enemy. Moses's survival depends on a number of women, not all of them Israelites.

2:9 In the trickster tradition, Moses's birth mother ends up being paid to nurse him.

2:10 The name *Moses* can be understood via Egyptian and Hebrew etymologies. In Egyptian, the

daughter, and he became her son. She named him Moses,[b] "because," she said, "I drew him out of the water."

11 One day after Moses had grown up, he went out to his people and saw their forced labor. He saw an Egyptian beating a Hebrew, one of his own people. [12]He looked this way and that, and seeing no one he killed the Egyptian and hid him in the sand. [13]When he went out the next day, he saw two Hebrews fighting, and he said to the one who was in the wrong, "Why do you strike your fellow Hebrew?" [14]He answered, "Who made you a ruler and judge over us? Do you mean to kill me as you killed the Egyptian?" Then Moses was afraid and thought, "Surely the thing is known." [15]When Pharaoh heard of it, he sought to kill Moses. So Moses fled from Pharaoh. He settled in the land of Midian and sat down by a well. [16]The priest of Midian had seven daughters. They came to draw water and filled the troughs to water their father's flock. [17]But some shepherds came and drove them away. Moses got up and came to their defense and watered their flock. [18]When they returned to their father Reuel, he said, "How is it that you have come back so soon today?" [19]They said, "An Egyptian helped us against the shepherds; he even drew water for us and watered the flock." [20]He said to his daughters, "Where is he? Why did you leave the man? Invite him to share a meal." [21]Moses agreed to stay with the man, and he gave Moses his daughter Zipporah in marriage. [22]She bore a son, and he named him Gershom,[c] for he said, "I have been an alien residing in a foreign land."

23 After a long time the king of Egypt died. The Israelites groaned under their slavery and cried out. Their cry for help rose up to God from their slavery. [24]God heard their groaning, and God remembered his covenant with Abraham, Isaac, and Jacob. [25]God looked upon the Israelites, and God took notice of them.

3 Moses was keeping the flock of his father-in-law Jethro, the priest of Midian;

b 2.10 In Heb *Moses* resembles the word for *drew*   c 2.22 In Heb *Gershom* resembles the word for *alien*

name means "son" as in "Thutmose," "son of the god Thoth." In Hebrew, Moses's name is related to the verbal root "m-sh-h," "to take out" or "save." Pharaoh's daughter makes this connection, saying she *drew him out of the water*. But the name can be understood as active: "one who takes out" or "one who saves," prefiguring Moses's role as a liberator.

2:11–15 Moses is a child of two houses, two religions, two cultures, and two competing identities. The tension between these two worlds comes to a head in v. 11. According to Joseph Campbell's understanding of the hero's journey, the episode recounted in 2:11–15 is the first part of the hero's "call to adventure." After Moses kills an Egyptian overseer, he must flee from his familiar world as a wanted murderer. **2:15** The language used here, *Pharaoh . . . sought to kill Moses*, evokes the king's earlier attempt to take Moses's life as an infant (1:15–16). Midian is located in Arabia. The Midianites are claimed as descendants from Abraham and Keturah (Gen. 25:1). Sometimes the term Midianite is interchanged with Ishmaelite.

2:18 Reuel means "friend of God," though Moses's father-in-law is called Jethro in other passages (3:1; 18:1). Elsewhere in the Torah he is named Hobab (Num. 10:29).

2:21 Zipporah means "bird." She plays a critical role in saving Moses in 4:24–26.

2:22 The boy's name speaks to Moses's status (cf. 18:3): one-time prince of Egypt and would-be deliverer, he has now become an immigrant ("ger") there ("sham") in Midian. The word *alien* is best understood, in contemporary parlance, as referring to immigrant status.

2:23–25 The turning point in the exodus account. In addition to hearing and seeing, God is said to remember the covenant with the ancestors of old. God also *took notice* of the Israelites. All these verbs signal God's impending action.

3:1–4:17 The call narrative of Moses is set on Mount Horeb, which is also known as Mount Sinai, the mountain of God. Mountains were often considered holy places, in part because of their proximity to the heavens, where most of the gods were thought to reside. In the case of Israel, Mount Horeb/Sinai has tremendous significance because it is the location for profound moments of encounter with the Lord. Moses resists God's commission with a series of questions and protestations but to no avail. God responds to each one with an answer and a solution. The prophet Jeremiah is considered to be a prophet in the Mosaic tradition in part because his call narrative has the same elements of call and resistance (see Jer. 1:4–19). **3:1** Moses is tending sheep when God calls him, perhaps signaling his future role as shepherd of the people.

he led his flock beyond the wilderness and came to Mount Horeb,*d* the mountain of God. ²There the angel of the Lord appeared to him in a flame of fire out of a bush; he looked, and the bush was blazing, yet it was not consumed. ³Then Moses said, "I must turn aside and look at this great sight and see why the bush is not burned up." ⁴When the Lord saw that he had turned aside to see, God called to him out of the bush, "Moses, Moses!" And he said, "Here I am." ⁵Then he said, "Come no closer! Remove the sandals from your feet, for the place on which you are standing is holy ground." ⁶He said further, "I am the God of your father, the God of Abraham, the God of Isaac, and the God of Jacob." And Moses hid his face, for he was afraid to look at God.

7 Then the Lord said, "I have observed the misery of my people who are in Egypt; I have heard their cry on account of their taskmasters. Indeed, I know their sufferings, ⁸and I have come down to deliver them from the Egyptians and to bring them up out of that land to a good and spacious land, to a land flowing with milk and honey, to the country of the Canaanites, the Hittites, the Amorites, the Perizzites, the Hivites, and the Jebusites. ⁹The cry of the Israelites has now come to me; I have also seen how the Egyptians oppress them. ¹⁰Now go, I am sending you to Pharaoh to bring my people, the Israelites, out of Egypt." ¹¹But Moses said to God, "Who

am I that I should go to Pharaoh and bring the Israelites out of Egypt?" ¹²He said, "I will be with you, and this shall be the sign for you that it is I who sent you: when you have brought the people out of Egypt, you shall serve God on this mountain."

13 But Moses said to God, "If I come to the Israelites and say to them, 'The God of your ancestors has sent me to you,' and they ask me, 'What is his name?' what shall I say to them?" ¹⁴God said to Moses, "I AM WHO I AM."*e* He said further, "Thus you shall say to the Israelites, 'I AM has sent me to you.' " ¹⁵God also said to Moses, "Thus you shall say to the Israelites, 'The Lord,*f* the God of your ancestors, the God of Abraham, the God of Isaac, and the God of Jacob, has sent me to you':

This is my name forever,
    and this my title for all generations.
¹⁶"Go and assemble the elders of Israel and say to them, 'The Lord, the God of your ancestors, the God of Abraham, Isaac, and Jacob, has appeared to me, saying: I have given heed to you and to what has been done to you in Egypt. ¹⁷I declare that I will bring you up out of the misery of Egypt, to the land of the Canaanites, the Hittites, the Amorites,

---

d 3.1 Gk: Heb reads *to the mountain of God, to Horeb*
e 3.14 Or *I AM WHAT I AM* or *I WILL BE WHAT I WILL BE*
f 3.15 The word "Lord" when spelled with capital letters stands for the divine name, *YHWH*, which is here connected with the verb *hayah*, "to be"

The name Horeb is associated with certain traditions in the Pentateuch (Elohist and Deuteronomistic), while the name Sinai is associated with others (Yahwist and Priestly sources). See **"Introduction to the Torah/Pentateuch," pp. 2–4. 3:2** The burning bush and/or the angel's presence in the bush get Moses's attention so that God can issue the call. **3:4** Moses's name is repeated for emphasis. **3:5** Maintaining proper distance and removing sandals are signs of humility and an acknowledgment of the presence of the holy. This is the first time the adjective *holy* is used in the Bible (see **"Holiness (Exodus 3:5)," p. 88**). **3:8** The promise of deliverance is tied to the Abrahamic promise of land. This *good and spacious land* is presently territory inhabited by others. **3:12** The promised sign comes after the hard work of deliverance; it is to return and worship God on the mountain of God. **3:13–15** The special divine name of God is revealed here for the first time. A divine name connotes a deity's essence and conveys power. According to this text, the Lord was previously known as *the God of your ancestors, the God of Abraham, . . . Isaac, and . . . Jacob*. But after the exchange with Moses, God is now known as *I AM WHO I AM* (or "I AM WHAT I AM" or "I WILL BE WHAT I WILL BE"; see the text notes to the NRSVue). The verbal root used in the Lord's name appears to be the verb "to be" ("hyh"). God uses the verb in the first person ("I am"), but others use it in the third person singular *about* God, so it becomes YHWH ("he is"). Both forms employ the verb in a way that suggests ongoing or incomplete action. This is a God who is still active, which suggests that more will be revealed as the book continues. God and God's name take on increased specificity in the exodus event. At some point in early Judaism, the divine name YHWH was deemed too holy to pronounce. This gave rise to the practices of saying *Adonai* ("my lord") instead of the divine name and of representing the divine name with "the Lord" in English translations. For more on these matters, see **"God's**

Going Deeper: Holiness (Exodus 3:5)

The concept of holiness is an important one in the Bible, especially in the Pentateuch's Priestly writings. The first time a verb relating to the Hebrew root for *holiness* (*q-d-sh*) appears is in Gen. 2:3, which states that God "hallowed" (*q-d-sh*) the seventh day of creation, the day the Lord rested. This creation account is typically ascribed to the Priestly source. The next time the Hebrew root appears is as a noun in Exod. 3:5, where Moses is instructed to take off his sandals when encountering God. These two references already cast important light on holiness in the Bible: it is associated with God—whether God's actions or God's location—and it can be communicated from and attributed by God, specifically to times or places.

Leviticus, the biblical book most concerned with holiness, speaks of holy times and holy places but also of holy things like sacrifices and offerings (see, e.g., Lev. 2:3; 6:17–18; 7:1; 10:17). (See **"Holiness and Purity (Leviticus 10)," p. 158.**) Leviticus also knows of holy people. The latter includes, unsurprisingly, the priests, who are "consecrated" (e.g., Lev. 8:30). Holiness also marks—or is *supposed* to mark—the entire people of God. The manifestation of divine holiness can be dangerous, as demonstrated in the story of Nadab and Abihu's disobedience (Lev. 10:3). More positively, Israel's holiness is meant somehow to reflect God's own or God's purposes in the world (see Lev. 11:44; 19:2; also Exod. 19:6).

But the question of what holiness is remains. To be holy is to be set apart. Holiness is an essential characteristic of God, and God's holiness can be communicated to others and even shared by God's people. In some crucial (if not entirely clear) way, God's holy otherness is manifest in the holy otherness of Israel, even in its daily practices of commerce, social interaction, and diet (see, e.g., Lev. 19). By various means, therefore, the holiness of God's people serves to make the Lord known and serves as—for example, in fifteen instances in Lev. 19 alone—motivation or justification for Leviticus's holy hodgepodge of law: "I am the Lord" (see 19:3, 4, 10, 12, 14, 16, 18, 25, 28, 30, 31, 32, 34, 36, and 37). Israel's participation in one of the main divine attributes helps explain a later text: Heb. 12, which says that God disciplines people "in order that [they] may share his holiness" (v. 10). As a result, individuals should "pursue peace with everyone and the holiness without which no one will see the Lord" (v. 14).

Brent A. Strawn

the Perizzites, the Hivites, and the Jebusites, a land flowing with milk and honey.' ¹⁸They will listen to your voice, and you and the elders of Israel shall go to the king of Egypt and say to him, 'The Lord, the God of the Hebrews, has met with us; let us now go a three days' journey into the wilderness, so that we may sacrifice to the Lord our God.' ¹⁹I know, however, that the king of Egypt will not let you go except by a mighty hand. ²⁰So I will stretch out my hand and strike Egypt with all my wonders that I will perform in it; after that he will let you go. ²¹I will bring this people into such favor with the Egyptians that, when you go, you will not go empty-handed; ²²each woman shall ask her neighbor and any woman living in the neighbor's house for jewelry of silver and of gold and clothing, and you shall put them on your sons and on your daughters; so you shall plunder the Egyptians."

4 Then Moses answered, "But look, they may not believe me or listen to me but say, 'The Lord did not appear to you.'" ²The Lord said to him, "What is that in your hand?" He said, "A staff." ³And he said, "Throw it on the ground." So he threw the staff on the ground, and it became a snake, and Moses drew back from it. ⁴Then the Lord said to Moses, "Reach out your hand and seize it by the tail"—so he reached out

Name," p. 89. 3:18 Three days is a literary convention that can indicate a long time. **3:20** God's might is often described anthropomorphically using God's hand or arm. **4:1–17** Moses's call includes signs, evidence of God's power. God shows Moses two signs and describes a third that he is to perform for the elders as proof that God sent him. His rod becomes a snake and is returned to its original state. His hand becomes leprous and returns to its original state. He is instructed to take water from the Nile, and when he pours it out, it will become blood. In addition to performing these signs for the elders (4:29–30), the first sign is used when Moses and Aaron confront Pharaoh (7:8–10), and the third sign is on display also in the first plague (7:14–25). While there may be natural explanations for some of the signs described in Exodus, the text

Going Deeper: God's Name (Exodus 3:14–15)

God is called by many different names or titles in the Bible. Two texts from Exodus are noteworthy because they present God's self-revelation of the divine name YHWH. In Hebrew, the word is written without vowels and is therefore unpronounceable. It is commonly rendered in English translations as "the Lord." In Exod. 3, in response to Moses's question regarding who is sending him to deliver the Israelites from Egypt, God offers an evasive answer ("I am who I am. . . . I am has sent me to you"; v. 14, see the text note) but in the very next verse clarifies: "'The Lord [YHWH] . . . has sent me to you': This is my name forever" (v. 15). In Hebrew, "I am" and YHWH are related to the same verbal root "to be." In Exod. 6, God curiously states that the name YHWH was not known to Abraham, Isaac, or Jacob. However, "Lord" occurs more than 140 times in Genesis and is uttered by the ancestors themselves (see, e.g., Gen. 13:22; 26:22; 28:16). Indeed, Gen. 4:26 reports that "people began to invoke the name of the Lord" some seventeen generations before Abraham (see Gen. 5:1–32; 10:1–32; 11:10–26; 1 Chr. 1:1–24). While Gen. 1 uses a more generic name for God (Heb. *Elohim*), the divine name YHWH is found already in Gen. 2:4 (and then used throughout the second creation story) in combination with *Elohim*: "the Lord God." Such varying details have raised questions about the composition history of the Pentateuch (see **"Introduction to the Torah/Pentateuch," pp. 2–4**). However those details are explained, God does have a personal name. That name is given but remains elusive in some fashion, unpronounceable and lacking precise translation. It is found more than six thousand times in the Hebrew Bible; thus, the commandment about not taking the Lord's name "in vain" (KJV; Exod. 20:7; Deut. 5:11; NRSVue: "wrongful use") is likely about using God's name in trivial matters rather than an injunction never to use it. Israelites even swear oaths using the divine name. In the Septuagint, the Greek translation of the Hebrew Bible, YHWH is translated as *kyrios*, "Lord," which is then a common term for God and Jesus in the (Greek) New Testament. The divine name may be in mind in Phil. 2:9, where God gives Christ Jesus "the name that is above every other name."

Brent A. Strawn

his hand and grasped it, and it became a staff in his hand—⁵"so that they may believe that the Lord, the God of their ancestors, the God of Abraham, the God of Isaac, and the God of Jacob, has appeared to you."

6 Again, the Lord said to him, "Put your hand inside your cloak." He put his hand into his cloak, and when he took it out, his hand was diseased, as white as snow. ⁷Then God said, "Put your hand back into your cloak"— so he put his hand back into his cloak, and when he took it out, it was restored like the rest of his body—⁸"If they will not believe you or heed the first sign, they may believe the second sign. ⁹If they will not believe even these two signs or listen to you, you shall take some water from the Nile and pour it on the dry ground, and the water that you shall take from the Nile will become blood on the dry ground."

10 But Moses said to the Lord, "O my Lord, I have never been eloquent, neither in the past nor even now that you have spoken to your servant, but I am slow of speech and slow of tongue." ¹¹Then the Lord said to him, "Who gives speech to mortals? Who makes them mute or deaf, seeing or blind? Is it not I, the Lord? ¹²Now go, and I will be with your mouth and teach you what you are to speak." ¹³But he said, "O my Lord, please send someone else." ¹⁴Then the anger of the Lord was kindled against Moses, and he said, "What of your brother Aaron, the Levite? I know that he can speak well; even now he is coming out to meet you, and when he sees you his heart will be glad. ¹⁵You shall speak to him and put the words in his mouth, and I will be with your mouth and with his mouth and will teach you what you shall do. ¹⁶He indeed shall speak for you to the people; he shall serve as a mouth for you, and you shall serve as God for him. ¹⁷Take in your hand this staff, with which you shall perform the signs."

presents them as supernatural manifestations of God's power over the created realm. **4:10** *Slow of speech and slow of tongue* may refer to ineloquence, limited facility in other dialects, or a speech impediment. **4:10–17** These signs do not reassure Moses, who protests again, this time citing his lack of eloquence. God responds, but Moses pleads that someone else be sent. Aaron is introduced as the spokesperson for Moses.

18 Moses went back to his father-in-law Jethro and said to him, "Please let me go back to my own people in Egypt and see whether they are still living." And Jethro said to Moses, "Go in peace." [19]The LORD said to Moses in Midian, "Go back to Egypt, for all those who were seeking your life are dead." [20]So Moses took his wife and his sons, put them on a donkey, and went back to the land of Egypt, and Moses carried the staff of God in his hand.

21 And the LORD said to Moses, "When you go back to Egypt, see that you perform before Pharaoh all the wonders that I have put in your power, but I will harden his heart, so that he will not let the people go. [22]Then you shall say to Pharaoh, 'Thus says the LORD: Israel is my firstborn son. [23]I said to you, "Let my son go that he may serve me." But you refused to let him go; now I will kill your firstborn son.'"

24 On the way, at a place where they spent the night, the LORD met him and tried to kill him. [25]But Zipporah took a flint and cut off her son's foreskin, touched his feet with it, and said, "Truly you are a bridegroom of blood to me!" [26]So he let him alone. It was then that she said "a bridegroom of blood," because of the circumcision.

27 The LORD said to Aaron, "Go into the wilderness to meet Moses." So he went, and he met him at the mountain of God and kissed him. [28]Moses told Aaron all the words of the LORD with which he had sent him and all the signs with which he had charged him. [29]Then Moses and Aaron went and assembled all the elders of the Israelites. [30]Aaron spoke all the words that the LORD had spoken to Moses and performed the signs in the sight of the people. [31]The people believed, and when they heard that the LORD had given heed to the Israelites and that he had seen their misery, they bowed down and worshiped.

5 Afterward Moses and Aaron went to Pharaoh and said, "Thus says the LORD, the God of Israel: Let my people go, so that they may celebrate a festival to me in the wilderness." [2]But Pharaoh said, "Who is the LORD, that I should listen to him and let Israel go? I do not know the LORD, and I will not let

4:18–23 Moses prepares to leave for Egypt but asks permission from his father-in-law first. After this, God informs Moses that the *wonders* he will perform will not be successful. The exodus will not happen quickly. Pharaoh will resist, and God's message in response is *I will kill your firstborn son* (v. 23). God uses parental language here to describe the relationship to Israel. This recalls the birth imagery from chaps. 1 and 2, but here the reference serves also to prefigure the final plague. **4:21** Here is the first of many references to the hardening of Pharaoh's heart. Three different verbs are used for this hardening, and they mean "to make heavy" (Heb. "kabed"), "to strengthen" (Heb. "hazaq"), and "to harden" (Heb. "qasah"). In the first five plagues, Pharaoh is the subject of the sentence (7:13, 14, 22; 8:15, 19, 32; 9:7, 34, 35). Later in the narrative, God hardens Pharaoh's heart (9:12; 10:1, 20, 27; 11:10; 14:4, 8, 17), perhaps in fulfillment of the statements like the one here (see also 7:3). This hardening is not presented as a permanent state. God hardens the hearts of Pharaoh's officials in 10:1, but in 10:7 they urge Pharaoh to let the Israelites go.

4:24–26 God's promise to kill Egypt's firstborn son leads directly to a strange story of God's attempt to kill *him*. The subject of this pronoun is unclear: it could be either Moses or his son, and much of this short story is confusing. Zipporah saves Moses or Gershom with an "emergency" circumcision of her son. She then touches *his feet*—which could be a euphemism for the genitalia—with the foreskin. The act signifies sacrifice and bloodshed, both of which are key elements in the exodus narrative generally and in the account of the final plague and Passover specifically. The fact that this encounter happens somewhere between Midian and Egypt heightens the reader's awareness of Moses's transition from one world to another.

4:27–31 Aaron, acting as Moses's spokesperson, speaks the words and performs the signs successfully. The people believe. Their response to the message is worship, a reminder that worship is the end goal of the exodus (3:12; 5:1).

5:1 God's demand, in Moses's first encounter with Pharaoh, is specific: the people are to be sent out so they can worship their God in the wilderness.

5:2 Pharaoh's response is to question the identity of this God. The request that Moses and Aaron make of Pharaoh is an affront to the king's authority and power. Readers should be mindful of the audacity of the request, which comes from an unknown God of slaves to the head of state of the world's greatest superpower.

Israel go." ³Then they said, "The God of the Hebrews has revealed himself to us; let us go a three days' journey into the wilderness to sacrifice to the Lord our God, or he will fall upon us with pestilence or sword." ⁴But the king of Egypt said to them, "Moses and Aaron, why are you taking the people away from their work? Get to your labors!" ⁵Pharaoh continued, "Now they are more numerous than the people of the land*g* and yet you want them to stop laboring!" ⁶That same day Pharaoh commanded the taskmasters of the people, as well as their supervisors, ⁷"You shall no longer give the people straw to make bricks, as before; let them go and gather straw for themselves. ⁸But you shall require of them the same quantity of bricks as they have made previously; do not diminish it, for they are lazy; that is why they cry, 'Let us go and sacrifice to our God.' ⁹Let heavier work be laid on them; then they will pay attention to*b* it and not to deceptive words."

10 So the taskmasters and the supervisors of the people went out and said to the people, "Thus says Pharaoh: I will not give you straw. ¹¹Go and get straw yourselves, wherever you can find it, but your work will not be lessened in the least." ¹²So the people scattered throughout the land of Egypt to gather stubble for straw. ¹³The taskmasters urged them on, saying, "Complete your work, the same daily assignment as when you were given straw."*i* ¹⁴And the Israelite supervisors whom Pharaoh's taskmasters had set over them were beaten and were asked, "Why did you not finish the required quantity of bricks yesterday and today, as you did before?"

15 Then the Israelite supervisors came to Pharaoh and cried, "Why do you treat your servants like this? ¹⁶No straw is given to your servants, yet they say to us, 'Make bricks!' Look how your servants are beaten! But the fault is with you."*j* ¹⁷He said, "You are lazy, lazy; that is why you say, 'Let us go and sacrifice to the Lord.' ¹⁸Go now and work, for no straw shall be given you, but you shall still deliver the same number of bricks." ¹⁹The Israelite supervisors saw that they were in trouble when they were told, "You shall not lessen your daily number of bricks." ²⁰As they left Pharaoh, they came upon Moses and Aaron, who were waiting to meet them. ²¹They said to them, "The Lord look upon you and judge! You have brought us into bad odor with Pharaoh and his officials and have put a sword in their hand to kill us."

22 Then Moses turned to the Lord and said, "O my Lord, why have you mistreated this people? Why did you ever send me? ²³Since I first came to Pharaoh to speak in your name, he has mistreated this people, and you have done nothing at all to deliver your people."

6 Then the Lord said to Moses, "Now you shall see what I will do to Pharaoh: indeed, by a mighty hand he will let them go; by a mighty hand he will drive them out of his land."

2 God also spoke to Moses and said to him, "I am the Lord. ³I appeared to Abraham,

g 5.5 Sam: MT *The people of the land are now many*   *h* 5.9 Sam Gk Syr: MT *they will do*   *i* 5.13 Sam Gk Vg: MT *as when there was straw*   *j* 5.16 Cn: MT *but the fault of your people*

5:3 Three days is often a literary convention that means an extended time (see, e.g., Jonah 3:3) The request thus involves enslaved Israelites being far away from their masters. If they went to worship, would they ever return? This time, the request for departure comes with a threat of reprisal if Pharaoh refuses.

5:5 Pharaoh again makes reference to the size of the Hebrew population, a point of obvious concern for him. He describes the words of Aaron and Moses as "deceptive" (v. 9).

5:7–8 Pharaoh's requirement to have the Hebrews gather their own straw adds to their oppression, and they in turn complain to Moses (5:20–21), who complains to God (5:22–23), establishing a pattern that will recur throughout the wilderness period (see, e.g., 16:7; Num. 14:27, 36). The phrase *bricks without straw*, derived from this story, has become a figure of speech connoting a task or assignment that outweighs resources.

5:9 Pharaoh employs a strategy of increased oppression to eliminate or distract from a call for freedom.

6:1–13 God assures Moses, reiterating some of the promises made earlier. Vv. 2–13 rehearse some of the material found in chaps. 3–4, suggesting that chap. 6 is another version of Moses's call from another source. In the present form of Exodus, this second call serves as a reaffirmation after Pharaoh's refusal and brutal command to make bricks without straw. **6:2** *El Shaddai* is a name for God

Isaac, and Jacob as God Almighty,*k* but by my name 'The LORD'*l* I did not make myself known to them. 4I also established my covenant with them, to give them the land of Canaan, the land in which they resided as aliens. 5I have also heard the groaning of the Israelites whom the Egyptians have enslaved, and I have remembered my covenant. 6Say therefore to the Israelites: I am the LORD, and I will free you from the burdens of the Egyptians and deliver you from slavery to them. I will redeem you with an outstretched arm and with great acts of judgment. 7I will take you as my people, and I will be your God. You shall know that I am the LORD your God, who has freed you from the burdens of the Egyptians. 8I will bring you into the land that I swore to give to Abraham, Isaac, and Jacob; I will give it to you for a possession. I am the LORD." 9Moses told this to the Israelites, but they would not listen to Moses, because of their broken spirit and their cruel slavery.

10 Then the LORD spoke to Moses, 11"Go and tell Pharaoh king of Egypt to let the Israelites go out of his land." 12But Moses spoke to the LORD, "The Israelites have not listened to me; why should Pharaoh listen to me, poor speaker that I am?"*m* 13Thus the LORD spoke to Moses and Aaron and gave them orders regarding the Israelites and Pharaoh king of Egypt, to free the Israelites from the land of Egypt.

14 The following are the heads of their ancestral houses: the sons of Reuben, the firstborn of Israel: Hanoch, Pallu, Hezron, and Carmi; these are the families of Reuben. 15The sons of Simeon: Jemuel, Jamin, Ohad, Jachin, Zohar, and Shaul, the son of a Canaanite woman; these are the families of Simeon. 16The following are the names of the sons of Levi according to their genealogies: Gershon,

Kohath, and Merari, and the length of Levi's life was one hundred thirty-seven years. 17The sons of Gershon: Libni and Shimei, by their families. 18The sons of Kohath: Amram, Izhar, Hebron, and Uzziel, and the length of Kohath's life was one hundred thirty-three years. 19The sons of Merari: Mahli and Mushi. These are the families of the Levites according to their genealogies. 20Amram married Jochebed his aunt, and she bore him Aaron and Moses, and the length of Amram's life was one hundred thirty-seven years. 21The sons of Izhar: Korah, Nepheg, and Zichri. 22The sons of Uzziel: Mishael, Elzaphan, and Sithri. 23Aaron married Elisheba, daughter of Amminadab and sister of Nahshon, and she bore him Nadab, Abihu, Eleazar, and Ithamar. 24The sons of Korah: Assir, Elkanah, and Abiasaph; these are the families of the Korahites. 25Aaron's son Eleazar married one of the daughters of Putiel, and she bore him Phinehas. These are the heads of the ancestral houses of the Levites by their families.

26 It was this same Aaron and Moses to whom the LORD said, "Bring the Israelites out of the land of Egypt, company by company." 27It was they who spoke to Pharaoh king of Egypt to bring the Israelites out of Egypt, the same Moses and Aaron.

28 On the day when the LORD spoke to Moses in the land of Egypt, 29the LORD said to Moses, "I am the LORD; tell Pharaoh king of Egypt all that I am speaking to you." 30But Moses said to the LORD, "Since I am a poor speaker,*n* why should Pharaoh listen to me?"

7 The LORD said to Moses, "See, I have made you like God to Pharaoh, and your brother Aaron shall be your prophet.

k 6.3 Traditional rendering of Heb El Shaddai l 6.3 Heb YHWH; see note at 3.15 m 6.12 Heb me? I am uncircumcised of lips n 6.30 Heb am uncircumcised of lips

traditionally translated as "God Almighty." It can also mean God of the mountain or God of the breast.

6:14–30 This genealogy begins with the sons of Jacob in birth order—Reuben, Simeon—and then follows Levi's line all the way to Moses. The other sons are not mentioned. Biblical genealogies serve various purposes, and this one is to confirm Moses's lineage in the tribe of Levi, the line of priests, to identify his parents (Amram and Jochebed); his brother, Aaron; and Aaron's descendants. Only occasionally are women—wives, mothers, and daughters—mentioned in biblical genealogies. In addition to Jochebed, this genealogy mentions several: the Canaanite mother of Shaul, Elisheba, and a daughter of Putiel. Notably, Aaron and Moses's sister, Miriam, does not appear in this list (see 2:4; 15:20; and Num. 26:59).

7:1–7 These verses are similar in content to God's message to Moses in the call narrative in chaps. 3–4. Before the first plague event is God's description of what will happen. The shift from God's

²You shall speak all that I command you, and your brother Aaron shall tell Pharaoh to let the Israelites go out of his land. ³But I will harden Pharaoh's heart, and I will multiply my signs and wonders in the land of Egypt. ⁴When Pharaoh does not listen to you, I will lay my hand upon Egypt and bring my people the Israelites, company by company, out of the land of Egypt by great acts of judgment. ⁵The Egyptians shall know that I am the LORD when I stretch out my hand against Egypt and bring the Israelites out from among them." ⁶Moses and Aaron did so; they did just as the LORD commanded them. ⁷Moses was eighty years old and Aaron eighty-three when they spoke to Pharaoh.

8 The LORD said to Moses and Aaron, ⁹"When Pharaoh says to you, 'Perform a wonder,' then you shall say to Aaron, 'Take your staff and throw it down before Pharaoh, and it will become a snake.'" ¹⁰So Moses and Aaron went to Pharaoh and did as the LORD had commanded; Aaron threw down his staff before Pharaoh and his officials, and it became a snake. ¹¹Then Pharaoh summoned the wise men and the sorcerers, and they also, the magicians of Egypt, did the same by their secret arts. ¹²Each one threw down his staff, and they became snakes, but Aaron's staff swallowed up theirs. ¹³However, Pharaoh's heart was hardened, and he would not listen to them, as the LORD had said.

14 Then the LORD said to Moses, "Pharaoh's heart is hardened; he refuses to let the people go. ¹⁵Go to Pharaoh in the morning, as he is going out to the water; stand by at the bank of the Nile to meet him, and take in your hand the staff that was turned into a snake. ¹⁶Say to him, 'The LORD, the God of the Hebrews, sent me to you to say, "Let my people go, so that they may serve me in the wilderness." But until now you have not listened.' ¹⁷Thus says the LORD, "By this you shall know that I am the LORD." See, with the staff that is in my hand I will strike the water that is in the Nile, and it shall be turned to blood. ¹⁸The fish in the river shall die, the river itself shall stink, and the Egyptians shall be unable to drink water from the Nile.'" ¹⁹The LORD said to Moses, "Say to Aaron: Take your staff and stretch out your hand over the waters of Egypt—over its rivers, its canals, and its ponds, and all its pools of water—so that they may become blood, and there shall be blood throughout the whole land of Egypt, even in vessels of wood and in vessels of stone."

20 Moses and Aaron did just as the LORD commanded. In the sight of Pharaoh and of his officials he lifted up the staff and struck the water in the Nile; all the water in the river was turned into blood, ²¹and the fish

description of what will happen to what actually happens is almost imperceptible, perhaps implying the power of God's word: that it is as real as or the same as the event itself.

7:8–13 The miracle of Aaron's rod turning into a serpent is initially matched by the magicians of Pharaoh, who perform the same sign except that Aaron's serpent eats those of the Egyptian sorcerers. This small episode serves as a preview of the ensuing narrative. The freedom of the Hebrews will emerge only after a prolonged struggle. **7:13** The motif of the hard heart is an essential and complex element of the exodus narrative. See note at 4:21. In some instances, Pharaoh hardens his own heart; in others, the Lord hardens the monarch's heart. Pharaoh's *hardened* heart serves as a response to the signs from Aaron and Moses. The resistance of his hard heart escalates the action and moves to the first plague.

7:14 The first plague of turning the Nile to blood occurs because Pharaoh did not respond appropriately to the earlier sign, which was initially replicated by his magicians. Pharaoh has no need to concede to an unknown deity at this point, and his reluctance to acknowledge God will invite more plagues. The plague account is part of the contest between Moses and Pharaoh. The combined Pentateuchal sources give ten plagues, and the text presents them in three sets of three, with the tenth plague as a climactic conclusion. Each set of three begins with an exchange between Pharaoh and Moses. Some of the plagues can be understood as some type of naturally occurring event. The Nile could be made red as a result of red sediment that came into the water and disrupted the water's ecosystem, for example. From the perspective of the narrative, however, whether the plagues can be explained naturalistically or not, they are signs of God's supernatural power as Lord of creation. A plague on the water source threatens the source of life. The plagues can also be read with religious overtones. The Nile represented the Egyptian god Hapi, and so manipulation of the river could be seen as a direct attack on that god.

in the river died. The river stank so that the Egyptians could not drink its water, and there was blood throughout the whole land of Egypt. ²²But the magicians of Egypt did the same by their secret arts; so Pharaoh's heart remained hardened, and he would not listen to them, as the LORD had said. ²³Pharaoh turned and went into his house, and he did not take even this to heart. ²⁴And all the Egyptians had to dig along the Nile for water to drink, for they could not drink the water of the river.

25 Seven days passed after the LORD had struck the Nile.

8 ᵒThen the LORD said to Moses, "Go to Pharaoh and say to him, 'Thus says the LORD: Let my people go, so that they may serve me. ²If you refuse to let them go, I will plague your whole country with frogs. ³The Nile shall swarm with frogs; they shall come up into your palace, into your bedchamber and your bed, into the houses of your officials and of your people,ᵖ and into your ovens and your kneading bowls. ⁴The frogs shall come up on you and on your people and on all your officials.'" ⁵ᵠAnd the LORD said to Moses, "Say to Aaron, 'Stretch out your hand with your staff over the rivers, the canals, and the pools, and make frogs come up on the land of Egypt.'" ⁶So Aaron stretched out his hand over the waters of Egypt, and the frogs came up and covered the land of Egypt. ⁷But the magicians did the same by their secret arts and brought frogs up on the land of Egypt.

8 Then Pharaoh called Moses and Aaron and said, "Pray to the LORD to take away the frogs from me and my people, and I will let the people go to sacrifice to the LORD." ⁹Moses said to Pharaoh, "Kindly tell me when I am to pray for you and for your officials and for your people, that the frogs may be removed from you and your houses and be left only in the Nile." ¹⁰And he said, "Tomorrow." Moses said, "As you say! So that you may know that there is no one like the LORD our God, ¹¹the frogs shall leave you and your houses and your officials and your people; they shall be left only in the Nile." ¹²Then Moses and Aaron went out from Pharaoh, and Moses cried out to the LORD concerning the frogs that he had brought upon Pharaoh. ¹³And the LORD did as Moses requested: the frogs died in the houses, the courtyards, and the fields. ¹⁴And they gathered them together in heaps, and the land stank. ¹⁵But when Pharaoh saw that there was a respite, he hardened his heart and would not listen to them, just as the LORD had said.

16 Then the LORD said to Moses, "Say to Aaron, 'Stretch out your staff and strike the dust of the earth, so that it may become gnats throughout the whole land of Egypt.'" ¹⁷And they did so; Aaron stretched out his hand with his staff and struck the dust of the earth, and gnats came on humans and animals alike; all the dust of the earth turned into gnats throughout the whole land of Egypt. ¹⁸The magicians tried to produce gnats by their

o 8.1 7.26 in Heb   p 8.3 Gk: Heb *upon your people*   q 8.5 8.1 in Heb

7:22 The magicians are again able to replicate the plague.
8:1–15 The second plague: frogs. The rotting fish resulting from the first plague might have contributed to frogs coming onto the land as they do in this story. But again, the plague tradition is not presented as a series of natural phenomena. These things happened in the way they did and at the time they did as a demonstration of God's power over the created order and perhaps also the Egyptian religious order (the Egyptian god Heqt had a frog's head). **8:3** The Hebrew verb used here, "sharats" (meaning *swarm* or "teem"), is the same term used to describe the proliferation of the Hebrews in 1:7. **8:7** Again the magicians are able to perform the same sign, but apparently, they cannot make the frogs go away. Although Pharaoh agreed to let the people go if the Lord removed the frogs, he hardened his heart once relief came. This same motif is seen in 8:8, 28; 9:28; 10:8, 24; and 12:31. **8:14** The land stank from the dead frogs. In 7:21, the rivers stank from rotting fish. The odors from the plagues recall the Hebrews' fear that they would be "smelly" to the Egyptians (see 5:21). **8:15** The plague sequence includes several motifs: the Lord's announcement of the plague; the plague event itself; Pharaoh's response, often including a promise to let the Israelites go; the abatement of the plague; and then the hardening of Pharaoh's heart, which leads to the next plague.
8:16–19 The third plague: gnats (some small insect). There is an intensification at this point in the plague cycle. The first two plagues are replicated by Pharaoh's magicians, but after that, Pharaoh's

secret arts, but they could not. There were gnats on both humans and animals. [19]And the magicians said to Pharaoh, "This is the finger of God!" But Pharaoh's heart was hardened, and he would not listen to them, just as the LORD had said.

20 Then the LORD said to Moses, "Rise early in the morning and present yourself before Pharaoh, as he goes out to the water, and say to him, 'Thus says the LORD: Let my people go, so that they may serve me, [21]because if you will not let my people go, I will send swarms of flies on you, your officials, and your people, and into your houses. The houses of the Egyptians shall be filled with swarms of flies, as will the land where they live. [22]But on that day I will set apart the land of Goshen, where my people live, so that no swarms of flies shall be there, that you may know that I the LORD am in this land. [23]Thus I will make a distinction[r] between my people and your people. This sign shall appear tomorrow.' " [24]The LORD did so, and great swarms of flies came into the house of Pharaoh and into his officials' houses; in all of Egypt the land was ruined because of the flies.

25 Then Pharaoh summoned Moses and Aaron and said, "Go, sacrifice to your God within the land." [26]But Moses said, "It would not be right to do so, for the sacrifices that we offer to the LORD our God are offensive to the Egyptians. If we offer in the sight of the Egyptians sacrifices that are offensive to them, will they not stone us? [27]We must go a three days' journey into the wilderness and sacrifice to the LORD our God as he commands us." [28]So Pharaoh said, "I will let you go to sacrifice to the LORD your God in the wilderness, provided you do not go very far away. Pray for me." [29]Then Moses said, "As soon as I leave you, I will pray to the LORD that the swarms of flies may depart tomorrow from Pharaoh, from his officials, and from his people; only do not let Pharaoh again deal falsely by not letting the people go to sacrifice to the LORD."

30 So Moses went out from Pharaoh and prayed to the LORD. [31]And the LORD did as Moses asked: he removed the swarms of flies from Pharaoh, from his officials, and from his people; not one remained. [32]But Pharaoh hardened his heart this time also and would not let the people go.

9 Then the LORD said to Moses, "Go to Pharaoh and say to him, 'Thus says the LORD, the God of the Hebrews: Let my people go, so that they may serve me. [2]For if you refuse to let them go and still hold them, [3]the hand of the LORD will strike with a deadly pestilence your livestock in the field: the horses, the donkeys, the camels, the herds, and the flocks. [4]But the LORD will make a distinction between the livestock of Israel and the livestock of Egypt, so that nothing shall die of all that belongs to the Israelites.' " [5]The LORD set a time, saying, "Tomorrow the LORD will do this thing in the land." [6]And on the next day the LORD did so; all of the Egyptians' livestock died, but none of the Israelites' livestock died. [7]Pharaoh inquired and found that not even one of the Israelites' livestock had died. But the heart of Pharaoh was hardened, and he would not let the people go.

8 Then the LORD said to Moses and Aaron, "Take handfuls of soot from the kiln, and let Moses throw it in the air in the sight of Pharaoh. [9]It shall become dust all over the land of Egypt and shall cause festering boils on humans and animals throughout the whole land of Egypt." [10]So they took soot from the kiln and stood before Pharaoh, and Moses threw it in the air, and it caused festering boils on humans and animals. [11]The magicians could not stand before Moses because of the boils, for the boils afflicted the magicians as well as all the Egyptians. [12]But the LORD hardened the heart of Pharaoh, and he

r 8.23 Gk Syr Vg: Heb *will set redemption*

magicians can no longer compete. There is also a progression in the plagues as they move from water, to earth, and then to the sky. **8:19** The magicians acknowledge *this is the finger of God*.

8:20–30 The fourth plague: flies. The plague is preceded by Moses bringing a word from God to Pharaoh announcing the plague. This time only the Egyptians are affected. **8:28** Pharaoh seems willing to allow the sacrifice in the wilderness, but not *very far away*.

9:1–7 Like the previous plague, the fifth plague, pestilence, affects only Egyptian livestock. This distinction prefigures the major distinction between Egypt and Israel in the final plague.

9:8–12 The sixth plague: boils. This plague, like the third, comes with no announcement. This time, the magicians themselves are afflicted with boils.

would not listen to them, just as the LORD had spoken to Moses.

13 Then the LORD said to Moses, "Rise up early in the morning and present yourself before Pharaoh and say to him, 'Thus says the LORD, the God of the Hebrews: Let my people go, so that they may serve me. ¹⁴For this time I will send all my plagues upon you yourself, your officials, and your people, so that you may know that there is no one like me in all the earth. ¹⁵Indeed, by now I could have stretched out my hand and struck you and your people with pestilence, and you would have been cut off from the earth. ¹⁶But this is why I have let you live: to show you my power and to make my name resound through all the earth. ¹⁷You are still exalting yourself against my people by not letting them go. ¹⁸Tomorrow at this time I will cause the heaviest hail to fall that has ever fallen in Egypt from the day it was founded until now. ¹⁹Send, therefore, and have your livestock and everything that you have in the open field brought to a secure place; every human or animal that is in the open field and is not brought under shelter will die when the hail comes down upon them.' " ²⁰Those officials of Pharaoh who feared the word of the LORD hurried their slaves and livestock off to a secure place, ²¹but those who did not regard the word of the LORD left their slaves and livestock in the open field.

22 The LORD said to Moses, "Stretch out your hand toward heaven so that hail may fall on the whole land of Egypt, on humans and animals and all the plants of the field in the land of Egypt." ²³Then Moses stretched out his staff toward heaven, and the LORD sent thunder and hail, and fire came down on the earth. And the LORD rained hail on the land of Egypt; ²⁴there was hail with fire flashing continually in the midst of it, such heavy hail as had never fallen in all the land of Egypt since it became a nation. ²⁵The

hail struck down everything that was in the open field throughout all the land of Egypt, both human and animal; the hail also struck down all the plants of the field and shattered every tree in the field. ²⁶Only in the land of Goshen, where the Israelites were, was there no hail.

27 Then Pharaoh summoned Moses and Aaron and said to them, "This time I have sinned; the LORD is in the right, and I and my people are in the wrong. ²⁸Pray to the LORD! Enough of God's thunder and hail! I will let you go; you need stay no longer." ²⁹Moses said to him, "As soon as I have gone out of the city, I will stretch out my hands to the LORD; the thunder will cease, and there will be no more hail, so that you may know that the earth is the LORD's. ³⁰But as for you and your officials, I know that you do not yet fear the LORD God." ³¹(Now the flax and the barley were ruined, for the barley was in the ear and the flax was in bud. ³²But the wheat and the spelt were not ruined, for they are late in coming up.) ³³So Moses left Pharaoh, went out of the city, and stretched out his hands to the LORD; then the thunder and the hail ceased, and the rain no longer poured down on the earth. ³⁴But when Pharaoh saw that the rain and the hail and the thunder had ceased, he sinned once more and hardened his heart, he and his officials. ³⁵So the heart of Pharaoh was hardened, and he would not let the Israelites go, just as the LORD had spoken through Moses.

10 Then the LORD said to Moses, "Go to Pharaoh, for I have hardened his heart and the heart of his officials, in order that I may show these signs of mine among them ²and that you may tell your children and grandchildren how I have made fools of the Egyptians and what signs I have done among them—so that you may know that I am the LORD."

9:13–35 The seventh plague: heavy hail. Here we learn the previous plagues did not directly affect Pharaoh. 9:16 This verse clarifies the Lord's end game in the plagues: *to make my name resound through all the earth*. 9:20–21 As in the final plague, those Egyptians who listen to God's word will be able to protect their slaves and livestock. Goshen, the area where the Israelite slaves live, is spared this plague. 9:34 Pharaoh and his officials hardened their hearts. See note at 4:21.

10:1 The eighth plague: locusts. At this point, the hard-heart motif shifts. Now it is the Lord alone who makes the hearts of Pharaoh and his officers hard *in order that I may show these signs of mine among them*. The reader is again reminded that God's agenda is to establish the name (i.e., reputation) of the Lord for Egypt and for the Israelites. Pharaoh, his courtiers, and their hearts are subject to this agenda.

3 So Moses and Aaron went to Pharaoh and said to him, "Thus says the Lord, the God of the Hebrews: How long will you refuse to humble yourself before me? Let my people go, so that they may serve me. ⁴For if you refuse to let my people go, tomorrow I will bring locusts into your country. ⁵They shall cover the surface of the land, so that no one will be able to see the land. They shall devour the last remnant left you after the hail, and they shall devour every tree of yours that grows in the field. ⁶They shall fill your houses and the houses of all your officials and of all the Egyptians—something that neither your parents nor your grandparents have seen, from the day they came on earth to this day." Then he turned and went out from Pharaoh.

7 Pharaoh's officials said to him, "How long shall this fellow be a snare to us? Send the people away, so that they may serve the Lord their God. Do you not yet understand that Egypt is ruined?" ⁸So Moses and Aaron were brought back to Pharaoh, and he said to them, "Go, serve the Lord your God! But which ones are to go?" ⁹Moses said, "We will go with our young and our old; we will go with our sons and daughters and with our flocks and herds, because we have the Lord's festival to celebrate." ¹⁰He said to them, "The Lord indeed will be with you, if ever I let your little ones go with you! Plainly, you have some evil purpose in mind. ¹¹No, never! Your men may go and serve the Lord, for that is what you are asking." And they were driven out from Pharaoh's presence.

12 Then the Lord said to Moses, "Stretch out your hand over the land of Egypt, so that the locusts may come upon it and eat every plant in the land, all that the hail has left." ¹³So Moses stretched out his staff over the land of Egypt, and the Lord brought an east wind upon the land all that day and all that night. When morning came, the east wind had brought the locusts. ¹⁴The locusts came

upon all the land of Egypt and settled on the whole country of Egypt, such a dense swarm of locusts as had never been before nor ever shall be again. ¹⁵They covered the surface of the whole land, so that the land was black, and they ate all the plants in the land and all the fruit of the trees that the hail had left. Nothing green was left on the trees or on the plants in the fields, in all the land of Egypt. ¹⁶Pharaoh hurriedly summoned Moses and Aaron and said, "I have sinned against the Lord your God and against you. ¹⁷Do forgive my sin this once, and pray to the Lord your God that at the least he remove this deadly thing from me." ¹⁸So he went out from Pharaoh and prayed to the Lord. ¹⁹The Lord changed the wind into a very strong west wind, which lifted the locusts and drove them into the Red Sea;ˢ not a single locust was left in all the country of Egypt. ²⁰But the Lord hardened Pharaoh's heart, and he would not let the Israelites go.

21 Then the Lord said to Moses, "Stretch out your hand toward heaven so that there may be darkness over the land of Egypt, a darkness that can be felt." ²²So Moses stretched out his hand toward heaven, and there was dense darkness in all the land of Egypt for three days. ²³People could not see one another, and for three days they could not move from where they were, but all the Israelites had light where they lived. ²⁴Then Pharaoh summoned Moses and said, "Go, serve the Lord. Only your flocks and your herds shall remain behind. Even your little ones may go with you." ²⁵But Moses said, "You must also let us have sacrifices and burnt offerings to sacrifice to the Lord our God. ²⁶Our livestock also must go with us; not a hoof shall be left behind, for we must choose some of them to serve the Lord our God, and we will not know what to use to serve the Lord until we arrive there." ²⁷But the Lord hardened Pharaoh's

s 10.19 Or *Sea of Reeds*

10:7 This time, Pharaoh's officials urge him to free the Hebrews.

10:8 Again, Pharaoh negotiates with the Lord over who will be sent out to worship in the wilderness. Readers familiar with Exodus know that Pharaoh is right to suspect that something else is behind the request to depart for a festival to God in the desert.

10:19 A wind drives the locusts into the Red Sea, perhaps prefiguring the route of Israel's escape.

10:21 The ninth plague: darkness for three days for the Egyptians, but not for the Israelites. Like the third and sixth plagues, there is no announcement of this plague.

10:24 Once again Pharaoh attempts negotiation, this time offering that everyone may go except the livestock.

heart, and he was unwilling to let them go. [28]Then Pharaoh said to him, "Get away from me! Take care that you do not see my face again, for on the day you see my face you shall die." [29]Moses said, "Just as you say! I will never see your face again."

11 The Lord said to Moses, "I will bring one more plague upon Pharaoh and upon Egypt; afterward he will let you go from here; indeed, when he lets you go, he will drive you away. [2]Tell the people that every man is to ask his neighbor and every woman is to ask her neighbor for objects of silver and gold." [3]The Lord gave the people favor in the sight of the Egyptians. Moreover, Moses himself was a man of great importance in the land of Egypt, in the sight of Pharaoh's officials and in the sight of the people.

[4] Moses said, "Thus says the Lord, 'About midnight I will go out through Egypt. [5]Every firstborn in the land of Egypt shall die, from the firstborn of Pharaoh who sits on his throne to the firstborn of the female slave who is behind the handmill and all the firstborn of the livestock. [6]Then there will be a loud cry throughout the whole land of Egypt, such as has never been or will ever be again. [7]But not a dog shall growl at any of the Israelites—not at people, not at animals—so that you may know that the Lord makes a distinction between Egypt and Israel.' [8]Then all these officials of yours shall come down to me and bow low to me, saying, 'Leave us, you and all the people who follow you.' After that I will leave." And in hot anger he left Pharaoh.

[9] The Lord said to Moses, "Pharaoh will not listen to you, in order that my wonders may be multiplied in the land of Egypt." [10]Moses and Aaron performed all these wonders before Pharaoh, but the Lord hardened Pharaoh's heart, and he would not let the Israelites go out of his land.

12 The Lord said to Moses and Aaron in the land of Egypt, [2]"This month shall mark for you the beginning of months; it shall be the first month of the year for you. [3]Tell the whole congregation of Israel that on the tenth of this month they are to take a lamb for each family, a lamb for each household. [4]If a household is too small for a whole lamb, it shall join its closest neighbor in obtaining one; the lamb shall be divided in proportion to the number of people who

10:28 Pharaoh's final threat to Moses as he sends him away proves to be an empty one.

11:1–10 The description of the final plague. Chap. 11 is the transition between the plague narrative and God's final act: the exodus. It summarizes what has happened and prepares the reader for what is to come. The book of Exodus pauses here before the final plague as if recognizing the gravity of what is to come. What seems awkward chronologically—how is Moses before Pharaoh again after saying that he will never see Pharaoh's face again in 10:29?—works literarily in this perspective.

11:1 The word for *plague* comes from the root "naga," meaning "to touch, reach, strike," suggesting God's power is such that a single "touch" can result in catastrophic events.

Exod. 12 This chapter describes the Passover and the Feast of Unleavened Bread (vv. 1–28), which is followed by the account of the final plague (vv. 29–32), the exodus (vv. 33–42), and additional directions for the Passover observance (vv. 43–51). In the current form of Exodus, therefore, the remembrance of God's redemptive act precedes the act itself. The Passover is an element of the final plague. God spares or "passes over" those who follow the instructions in these verses. The Passover is also the ongoing observance of God's mighty deeds. The structure of the chapter suggests the keeping of the Passover is as important as, if not more important than, the event itself. The focus is liturgical: the prelude to the departure (exodus) from Egypt is directed to how Israel will commemorate and remember what God has done. The term *perpetual ordinance* appears throughout the chapter (vv. 14, 17, 24), along with the command to *keep this observance* (v. 25) and to teach it to the children.

12:2 The calendar is reorganized so as to begin with the month of the exodus. Time is now measured in reference to the moment of redemption. The New Year begins with the exodus liturgy. The remembrance of what God has done is central to the identity of the Israelites.

12:3 The tenth day of the seventh month is the Day of Atonement according to Lev. 23:27.

12:5 *Without blemish, a year-old male.* The female animals were set aside for milk production and breeding.

12:3–11 Details for the observance of Passover. The people will observe the celebration in anticipation of what God will do.

Making Connections: Passover (Exodus 12)

In Exodus, the institution of Passover *precedes* the actual exodus from Egypt. This ordering suggests that the commemoration of God's redemption of Israel is tantamount to the event itself and that the historical event cannot be separated from its reality as a liturgical event. Remembrance is essential to Israelite identity.

The Passover liturgy both shapes and transcends time. Its celebration in the first month means that every year begins with the redemptive story of Exodus. The Passover celebration thus functions as an orienting experience that is at once liturgical, theological, and formational—among other things, remembering God's deliverance evokes gratitude and a sense of obligation. In the process, every generation also enters into the experience of the Hebrew slaves. When contemporary individuals celebrate the Passover using the liturgy known as the Passover Seder, they not only tell and remember the exodus; they also become part of it, participating in and inhabiting it. In this way, the Seder recognizes that God's work in the world is not finished but continues, even to the present day.

The Passover is thus something of a composite, building on preexisting celebrations while (re)activating what already exists here and now. This judgment holds true even for the first Passover. Exodus 12 describes the Passover, with Exod. 13 detailing a seven-day feast of unleavened bread. These two festivals were likely rooted in preexisting springtime agricultural rituals that were combined and reframed in Exodus by Israel's redemption in the exodus. Passover is thus inherently open to new iterations. Centuries later, early Christians articulated their understanding of Jesus's death and resurrection through the biblical accounts they knew, including Passover and the exodus. In this iteration of Passover, Jesus becomes the unblemished, sacrificial lamb who atones for the sins of all humanity.

The Passover is highly mobile. The first Passover is celebrated in Egypt, the house of slavery, making it a proleptic celebration of God's redemption and, simultaneously, an act of defiance against Pharaoh's oppressive regime. In this way, Passover transforms Israel's reality *before* they are freed. Much later, Passovers celebrated in Jewish ghettos or in concentration camps during World War II similarly represented hope in God's redemptive power despite the presence of unspeakable oppression. In these moments—indeed, in *every* moment it is celebrated—the Passover continues to proclaim the power of a liberating God over Pharaoh and all his ilk.

Judy Fentress-Williams

eat of it. ⁵Your lamb shall be without blemish, a year-old male; you may take it from the sheep or from the goats. ⁶You shall keep it until the fourteenth day of this month; then the whole assembled congregation of Israel shall slaughter it at twilight. ⁷They shall take some of the blood and put it on the two doorposts and the lintel of the houses in which they eat it. ⁸They shall eat the lamb that same night; they shall eat it roasted over the fire with unleavened bread and bitter herbs. ⁹Do not eat any of it raw or boiled in water but roasted over the fire, with its head, legs, and inner organs. ¹⁰You shall let none of it remain until the morning; anything that remains until the morning you shall burn with fire. ¹¹This is how you shall eat it: your loins girded, your sandals on your feet, and your staff in your hand, and you shall eat it hurriedly. It is the Passover of the Lord. ¹²I will pass through the land of Egypt that night, and I will strike down every firstborn in the land of Egypt, from human to animal, and on all the gods of Egypt I will execute judgments: I am the Lord. ¹³The blood shall be a sign for you on the houses where you live: when I see the blood, I will pass over you, and no plague shall destroy you when I strike the land of Egypt.

14 "This day shall be a day of remembrance for you. You shall celebrate it as a festival to the Lord; throughout your generations you

12:11–12 The name of the Passover festival derives from a verb meaning "to pass/spring over." The festival commemorates both God's salvation of the Israelites and the destruction of the enemy. The ritual is symbolically fraught: the origin and birth of Israel as a nation are connected to blood, sacrifice, and the killing of a lamb.

12:14–20 The Feast of Unleavened Bread is a week-long festival that is combined with the Passover. For seven days, leaven (yeast) is forbidden. The people are also instructed to refrain from work except for food preparation. Both the Passover and Feast of Unleavened Bread commemorate the salvific acts of the exodus on behalf of a particular people. God takes sides in the exodus story.

shall observe it as a perpetual ordinance. [15]Seven days you shall eat unleavened bread; on the first day you shall remove leaven from your houses, for whoever eats leavened bread from the first day until the seventh day shall be cut off from Israel. [16]On the first day you shall hold a solemn assembly and on the seventh day a solemn assembly; no work shall be done on those days; only what everyone must eat, that alone may be prepared by you. [17]You shall observe the Festival of Unleavened Bread, for on this very day I brought your companies out of the land of Egypt: you shall observe this day throughout your generations as a perpetual ordinance. [18]In the first month, from the evening of the fourteenth day until the evening of the twenty-first day, you shall eat unleavened bread. [19]For seven days no leaven shall be found in your houses, for whoever eats what is leavened shall be cut off from the congregation of Israel, whether an alien or a native of the land. [20]You shall eat nothing leavened; in all your settlements you shall eat unleavened bread."

21 Then Moses called all the elders of Israel and said to them, "Go, select lambs for your families, and slaughter the Passover lamb. [22]Take a bunch of hyssop, dip it in the blood that is in the basin, and touch the lintel and the two doorposts with the blood in the basin. None of you shall go outside the door of your house until morning. [23]For the Lord will pass through to strike down the Egyptians; when he sees the blood on the lintel and on the two doorposts, the Lord will pass over that door and will not allow the destroyer to enter your houses to strike you down. [24]You shall observe this as a perpetual ordinance for you and your children. [25]When you come to the land that the Lord will give you, as he has promised,

you shall keep this observance. [26]And when your children ask you, 'What does this observance mean to you?' [27]you shall say, 'It is the Passover sacrifice to the Lord, for he passed over the houses of the Israelites in Egypt when he struck down the Egyptians but spared our houses.' " And the people bowed down and worshiped.

28 The Israelites went and did just as the Lord had commanded Moses and Aaron; so they did.

29 At midnight the Lord struck down all the firstborn in the land of Egypt, from the firstborn of Pharaoh who sat on his throne to the firstborn of the prisoner who was in the dungeon and all the firstborn of the livestock. [30]Pharaoh arose in the night, he and all his officials and all the Egyptians, and there was a loud cry in Egypt, for there was not a house without someone dead. [31]Then he summoned Moses and Aaron in the night and said, "Rise up, go away from my people, both you and the Israelites! Go, serve the Lord, as you said. [32]Take your flocks and your herds, as you said, and be gone. And ask a blessing for me, too!"

33 The Egyptians urged the people to hasten their departure from the land, for they said, "We shall all be dead." [34]So the people took their dough before it was leavened, with their kneading bowls wrapped up in their cloaks on their shoulders. [35]The Israelites had acted according to the word of Moses; they had asked the Egyptians for jewelry of silver and gold and for clothing, [36]and the Lord had given the people favor in the sight of the Egyptians, so that they let them have what they asked. And so they plundered the Egyptians.

37 The Israelites journeyed from Rameses to Succoth, about six hundred thousand men on foot, besides little ones. [38]A mixed crowd

12:21–28 Instructions for placing blood on the lintel and doorposts—the top and sides of the doorframe—are an outward sign of obedience to God's command. **12:26–27** The explanation to the children is also a reminder to the parents of God's work.

12:29–32 The final plague comes in the middle of the night and in the midst of instructions for the Passover observance. It is the fulfillment of what God told Moses in 4:22–23.

12:35 The Israelites plunder the Egyptians. This is anticipated already in chap. 3. The enslaved Israelites do not leave empty-handed. They receive reparations of a sort by plundering the Egyptians. In Deut. 15:13, the Israelites will be forbidden to send out their own enslaved males "empty-handed."

12:37–38 The route of the exodus. Rameses to Succoth was approximately one day's journey. *Six hundred thousand men* (alone) would mean there were over two million Israelites, including women and children. The Hebrew word translated here as *thousand* could be more nondescript: "clan." **12:38** People other than the Israelites also left Egypt in the exodus. Some scholars connect this mixed multitude with the riffraff in Num. 11:4.

also went up with them and livestock in great numbers, both flocks and herds. [39]They baked unleavened cakes of the dough that they had brought out of Egypt; it was not leavened, because they were driven out of Egypt and could not wait, nor had they prepared any provisions for themselves.

40 The time that the Israelites had lived in Egypt was four hundred thirty years. [41]At the end of four hundred thirty years, on that very day, all the companies of the Lord went out from the land of Egypt. [42]That was for the Lord a night of vigil, to bring them out of the land of Egypt. That same night is a vigil to be kept for the Lord by all the Israelites throughout their generations.

43 The Lord said to Moses and Aaron, "This is the ordinance for the Passover: no foreigner shall eat of it, [44]but any slave who has been purchased may eat of it after he has been circumcised; [45]no bound or hired servant may eat of it. [46]It shall be eaten in one house; you shall not take any of the animal outside the house, and you shall not break any of its bones. [47]The whole congregation of Israel shall do this. [48]If an alien who resides with you wants to celebrate the Passover to the Lord, all his males shall be circumcised; then he may draw near to celebrate it; he shall be regarded as a native of the land. But no uncircumcised person shall eat of it; [49]there shall be one law for the native-born and for the alien who resides among you."

50 All the Israelites did just as the Lord had commanded Moses and Aaron. [51]That very day the Lord brought the Israelites out of the land of Egypt, company by company.

13 The Lord said to Moses, [2]"Consecrate to me all the firstborn; whatever is the first to open the womb among the Israelites, of human beings and animals, is mine."

3 Moses said to the people, "Remember this day on which you came out of Egypt, out of the house of slavery, because the Lord brought you out from there by strength of hand; no leavened bread shall be eaten. [4]Today, in the month of Abib, you are going out. [5]When the Lord brings you into the land of the Canaanites, the Hittites, the Amorites, the Hivites, and the Jebusites, which he swore to your ancestors to give you, a land flowing with milk and honey, you shall keep this observance in this month. [6]Seven days you shall eat unleavened bread, and on the seventh day there shall be a festival to the Lord. [7]Unleavened bread shall be eaten for seven days; no leavened bread shall be seen in your possession, and no leaven shall be seen among you in all your territory. [8]You shall tell your child on that day, 'It is because of what the Lord did for me when I came out of Egypt.' [9]It shall serve for you as a sign on your hand and as a reminder on your forehead, so that the teaching of the Lord may be on your lips, for with a strong hand the Lord brought you out of Egypt. [10]You shall keep this ordinance at its proper time from year to year.

11 "When the Lord has brought you into the land of the Canaanites, as he swore to you and your ancestors, and has given it to you, [12]you shall set apart to the Lord all that first opens the womb. All the firstborn offspring of your livestock that are males shall be the Lord's. [13]But every firstborn donkey you shall redeem with a sheep; if you do not redeem it, you must break its neck. Every firstborn male among your children you shall redeem. [14]When in the future your child asks you, 'What does this mean?' you shall answer, 'By strength of hand the Lord brought us out of Egypt, from the house of slavery. [15]When Pharaoh stubbornly refused to let us go, the Lord killed all the firstborn

---

12:40 Cf. Gen. 15:13.

12:43–51 The final directions for Passover address those who may participate in the festival. Circumcised servants and immigrants may do so.

13:1–10 The earlier instructions for the Feast of Unleavened Bread emphasize the first and seventh days. In this passage, the emphasis is on the latter and the consecration (setting apart) of the firstborn. **13:9** The sign on the hand and forehead occurs also in Deut. 6:8.

13:11–16 Consecration of the firstborn males involves either sacrifice or redemption. While the animals are sacrificed, male children, like the Israelites themselves in the exodus, are *redeem[ed]*, a term that means they are purchased or bought back. One animal, the donkey, may also be "redeemed" with a sheep: the sheep is sacrificed in the place of the donkey. The method of redemption for firstborn male children is not detailed here, but see Num. 18:16.

in the land of Egypt, from human firstborn to the firstborn of animals. Therefore I sacrifice to the Lord every male that first opens the womb, but every firstborn of my sons I redeem.' ¹⁶It shall serve as a sign on your hand and as an emblem*f* on your forehead that by strength of hand the Lord brought us out of Egypt."

17 When Pharaoh let the people go, God did not lead them by way of the land of the Philistines, although that was nearer, for God thought, "If the people face war, they may change their minds and return to Egypt." ¹⁸So God led the people by the roundabout way of the wilderness bordering the Red Sea.*u* The Israelites went up out of the land of Egypt prepared for battle. ¹⁹And Moses took with him the bones of Joseph, who had required a solemn oath of the Israelites, saying, "God will surely come to you, and then you must carry my bones with you from here." ²⁰They set out from Succoth and camped at Etham, on the edge of the wilderness. ²¹The Lord went in front of them in a pillar of cloud by day, to lead them along the way, and in a pillar of fire by night, to give them light, so that they might travel by day and by night. ²²Neither the pillar of cloud by day nor the pillar of fire by night left its place in front of the people.

14 Then the Lord said to Moses, ²"Tell the Israelites to turn back and camp in front of Pi-hahiroth, between Migdol and

the sea, in front of Baal-zephon; you shall camp opposite it, by the sea. ³Pharaoh will say of the Israelites, 'They are wandering aimlessly in the land; the wilderness has closed in on them.' ⁴I will harden Pharaoh's heart, and he will pursue them, so that I will gain glory for myself over Pharaoh and all his army, and the Egyptians shall know that I am the Lord." And they did so.

5 When the king of Egypt was told that the people had fled, the minds of Pharaoh and his officials were changed toward the people, and they said, "What have we done, letting Israel leave our service?" ⁶So he had his chariot made ready and took his army with him; ⁷he took six hundred elite chariots and all the other chariots of Egypt with officers over all of them. ⁸The Lord hardened the heart of Pharaoh king of Egypt, and he pursued the Israelites, who were going out boldly. ⁹The Egyptians pursued them, all Pharaoh's horses and chariots, his chariot drivers and his army; they overtook them camped by the sea, by Pi-hahiroth, in front of Baal-zephon.

10 As Pharaoh drew near, the Israelites looked back, and there were the Egyptians advancing on them. In great fear the Israelites cried out to the Lord. ¹¹They said to Moses, "Was it because there were no graves in Egypt that you have taken us away to die in the

t 13.16 Or *as a frontlet*; meaning of Heb uncertain
u 13.18 Or *Sea of Reeds*

13:17–22 God's presence with the people is ongoing and obvious. The Israelites are led supernaturally, by the angel of God (see 14:19) in the form of a *pillar of cloud* and *pillar of fire* by day and by night, respectively. **13:18** The route of the exodus taken here, a *roundabout* way, has the purpose of protecting the people. The body of water the Israelites cross, traditionally known as the Red Sea, can also be translated as "Sea of Reeds." Today, the Red Sea is the Gulf of Suez; the "Reed Sea" could be another body of water. The exact body of water remains a matter of debate. **13:19** On Joseph's bones, see Gen. 50:25. Burial practices dictate burial with one's ancestors. See Gen. 23:19; 25:9; 35:29; and 49:29–32. Taking Joseph's bones out of Egypt is thus returning Joseph home.

14:1–31 The prose account of the crossing of the Red Sea is the final act of the exodus. Once again, God repeats the goal *the Egyptians shall know that I am the Lord*. This statement of God's triumph precedes the event. The miraculous crossing of the sea incorporates birth and creation imagery. The miracle takes place overnight, evoking the pattern of evening and morning in the creation account. The water the Israelites pass through, evocative of the birth process, becomes instead the water of chaos for the Egyptians, destroying them. The references to defeated horses, chariots, and chariot officers substantiate the power of the Lord God of Israel. **14:2** Pi-hahiroth may be the name of a temple site, which along with the other two locations is on the north Syrian coast. Migdol in Hebrew means "tower." Baal-zephon incorporates the name of the Canaanite storm god (Baal) and his traditional abode (Zaphon). **14:8** This is the last time God hardens Pharaoh's heart. **14:11–12** The complaint of the Israelites is dramatic, detailed, and sardonic, more in line with the murmuring that occurs after the people have been in the wilderness. It reflects uncertainty about God's presence and power. The complaint suggests that it is very difficult for the Israelites to shift from

wilderness? What have you done to us, bringing us out of Egypt? [12]Is this not the very thing we told you in Egypt, 'Let us alone so that we can serve the Egyptians'? For it would have been better for us to serve the Egyptians than to die in the wilderness." [13]But Moses said to the people, "Do not be afraid, stand firm, and see the deliverance that the LORD will accomplish for you today, for the Egyptians whom you see today you shall never see again. [14]The LORD will fight for you, and you have only to keep still."

15 Then the LORD said to Moses, "Why do you cry out to me? Tell the Israelites to go forward. [16]But you lift up your staff and stretch out your hand over the sea and divide it, that the Israelites may go into the sea on dry ground. [17]Then I will harden the hearts of the Egyptians so that they will go in after them, and so I will gain glory for myself over Pharaoh and all his army, his chariots, and his chariot drivers. [18]Then the Egyptians shall know that I am the LORD, when I have gained glory for myself over Pharaoh, his chariots, and his chariot drivers."

19 The angel of God who was going before the Israelite army moved and went behind them, and the pillar of cloud moved from in front of them and took its place behind them. [20]It came between the army of Egypt and the army of Israel. And so the cloud was there with the darkness, and it lit up the night; one did not come near the other all night.

21 Then Moses stretched out his hand over the sea. The LORD drove the sea back by a strong east wind all night and turned the sea into dry land, and the waters were divided. [22]The Israelites went into the sea on dry ground, the waters forming a wall for them on their right and on their left. [23]The Egyptians pursued and went into the sea after them, all of Pharaoh's horses, chariots, and chariot drivers. [24]At the morning watch the LORD, in the pillar of fire and cloud, looked down on the Egyptian army and threw the Egyptian army into a panic. [25]He clogged' their chariot wheels so that they turned with difficulty. The Egyptians said, "Let us flee from the Israelites, for the LORD is fighting for them against Egypt."

26 Then the LORD said to Moses, "Stretch out your hand over the sea, so that the water may come back upon the Egyptians, upon their chariots and chariot drivers." [27]So Moses stretched out his hand over the sea, and at dawn the sea returned to its normal depth. As the Egyptians fled before it, the LORD tossed the Egyptians into the sea. [28]The waters returned and covered the chariots and the chariot drivers, the entire army of Pharaoh that had followed them into the sea; not one of them remained. [29]But the Israelites walked on dry ground through the sea, the waters forming a wall for them on their right and on their left.

30 Thus the LORD saved Israel that day from the Egyptians, and Israel saw the Egyptians dead on the seashore. [31]Israel saw the great work that the LORD did against the Egyptians. So the people feared the LORD and believed in the LORD and in his servant Moses.

15 Then Moses and the Israelites sang this song to the LORD:

v 14.25 Sam Gk Syr: MT *removed*

the predictable experience of slavery to the unpredictability of following God. See Exod. 5:20–21. **14:14** Moses's words of reassurance are in line with the theme of God's presence and power. **14:15– 18** God's response will require Moses to do something (stretch out his hand), and it also reveals God's agenda to gain glory over Pharaoh and recognition by the Egyptians. See 5:2. **14:21** The miracle of the sea becoming dry land is the result of a *strong east wind* that blows all night. The word for wind here is the same one used in Gen. 1, thereby evoking the innovative power in creation. God is the creator and ruler of all. **14:22** The text emphasizes that the people crossed on dry ground and designates the event as miraculous. See also Josh. 3:17. **14:26** The drowning of the Egyptian army fulfills God's earlier words in 14:13, 17–18. God is not only Israel's divine emancipator; God is also their divine warrior. **14:31** Israel's response is fear of God (a posture of reverence and worship) and belief in both God and Moses.

15:1–19 The narrative of the Israelites crossing the sea is followed by Moses's song. This is one of a few places in Scripture where a poetic account appears in a narrative (see Gen. 49) or a poetic account follows a narrative account (see Judg. 5). The poem in Exod. 15 (see **"Hebrew Poetry," p. 741**), also known as the Song of the Sea, celebrates the Lord's triumph as divine warrior over Egypt. The language of the song includes archaic elements and may be one of the oldest texts in the Bible. **15:1** Moses leads the Israelites in song using the first-person singular pronoun.

"I will sing to the Lord, for he has
    triumphed gloriously;
  horse and rider he has thrown into
    the sea.
[2] The Lord is my strength and my
    might,"[w]
  and he has become my salvation;
this is my God, and I will praise him;
  my father's God, and I will exalt him.
[3] The Lord is a warrior;
  the Lord is his name.

[4] Pharaoh's chariots and his army he cast
    into the sea;
  his elite officers were sunk in the Red
    Sea.[x]
[5] The floods covered them;
  they went down into the depths like
    a stone.
[6] Your right hand, O Lord, glorious in
    power—
  your right hand, O Lord, shattered the
    enemy.
[7] In the greatness of your majesty you
    overthrew your adversaries;
  you sent out your fury; it consumed
    them like stubble.
[8] At the blast of your nostrils the waters
    piled up;
  the floods stood up in a heap;
  the deeps congealed in the heart of
    the sea.
[9] The enemy said, 'I will pursue; I will
    overtake;
  I will divide the spoil; my desire shall
    have its fill of them.
  I will draw my sword; my hand shall
    destroy them.'

[10] You blew with your wind; the sea
    covered them;
  they sank like lead in the mighty
    waters.
[11] Who is like you, O Lord, among the
    gods?
  Who is like you, majestic in holiness,
    awesome in splendor, doing wonders?
[12] You stretched out your right hand;
  the earth swallowed them.

[13] In your steadfast love you led the people
    whom you redeemed;
  you guided them by your strength to
    your holy abode.
[14] The peoples heard; they trembled;
  pangs seized the inhabitants of
    Philistia.
[15] Then the chiefs of Edom were
    dismayed;
  trembling seized the leaders of
    Moab;
  all the inhabitants of Canaan melted
    away.
[16] Terror and dread fell upon them;
  by the might of your arm, they
    became still as a stone
until your people, O Lord, passed by,
  until the people whom you acquired
    passed by.
[17] You brought them in and planted them
    on the mountain of your own
    possession,
  the place, O Lord, that you made your
    abode,

w 15.2 Or *song*   x 15.4 Or *Sea of Reeds*

15:3 God is presented as a divine warrior, going to battle and defeating the enemies of Israel, matching the power and force of Pharaoh's military might. For more on the *name* of God, see note at 3:13–15. **15:5** The Hebrew term used for the *floods* here evokes the primordial chaos that God subdued to establish order in creation (cf. Gen. 1:2). **15:6** The right hand is the one used for holding weapons in ancient Near Eastern mythology. **15:8** The mighty wind is depicted as a blast of the Divine Warrior's nostrils. The anthropomorphic imagery portrays God as so much bigger than human scale. **15:11** In a polytheistic world, the song asserts God's superiority. This may not yet be fully developed monotheism but is a predication of the Lord's supremacy. **15:12** See note at 15:6. **15:13–16** God's power and might are on display in destructive and creative acts. What is experienced by Israel as a show of God's steadfast love incites fear and trembling in the surrounding nations. The defeat of the enemy is interpreted as a demonstration of God's love and fidelity to God's people. **15:17** The song does more than celebrate the crossing of the sea: it ends with the people "planted" on God's mountain. This could be a reference to Sinai/Horeb, showing that the point of the exodus is to deliver the people into the covenantal relationship with God. If the poem stems from a later time, the mountain could be an allusion to Zion/Jerusalem. The *sanctuary* may be an allusion to what comes later (see 25:8). See **"Horab/Sinai," p. 248.**

Reading through Time: The Exodus Event (Exodus 15)

The exodus event is the primary lens that informs Israel's identity and a key motif that shapes its imagination. The exodus is, as a result, not limited to the book of Exodus. The exodus motif is found also in the Psalms, the Prophets, and numerous narratives throughout the Bible. Every year the Passover Seder invites participants to inhabit the exodus story. The New Testament authors used the Passover event to frame their understanding of Jesus's death as redemptive.

The exodus story has been received in the Americas in a number of ways. Many African captives read themselves into the exodus story of redemption, identifying with the Israelites who were rescued from slavery by God's outstretched hand and mighty arm, as attested in Black spirituals and enslaved preachers' sermons. The liberation theology birthed in Latin America interpreted the exodus as attesting to the divine warrior who will act on behalf of the oppressed and support God's preference for the poor.

Cecil B. DeMille's iconic movie *The Ten Commandments* (1956) is another instance of the reception and use of the exodus. With the Cold War as the political context of his day, DeMille, in an unprecedented move, addressed the audience directly to declare that the exodus is about "freedom" and the choice to be made between freedom and tyrannical despots. The biblical story is used in this case to support American democratic ideals.

Other readings of Exodus showcase the important role played by cultural context in interpretation. In his work on the heroic monomyth, Joseph Campbell argued that Moses's story exemplified the hero's separation, initiation, and return, thus highlighting and emphasizing Moses's character and literary presentation. Later interpretations offered other nuances, noting Moses's occasionally *anti*heroic characteristics and recognizing "minor" characters as liberators alongside the great Israelite leader (see **"Pharaoh," p. 85**). By remembering the pivotal roles played by the midwives (Shiphrah and Puah), Moses's birth and adoptive mothers, his Midianite wife (Zipporah), and his sister (Miriam), these interpretations emphasize God's work of liberation in and through a larger community. It took a village, one might say, to raise Moses.

The consistent element in all the retellings and interpretations of the exodus is a mighty God who overturns the institutional oppression of a superpower to redeem God's people and enter into a covenant relationship with them forever.

Judy Fentress-Williams

the sanctuary, O Lord, that your
hands have established.
¹⁸ The Lord will reign forever and
ever."
19 When the horses of Pharaoh with his chariots and his chariot drivers went into the sea, the Lord brought back the waters of the sea upon them, but the Israelites walked through the sea on dry ground.

20 Then the prophet Miriam, Aaron's sister, took a tambourine in her hand, and all the women went out after her with tambourines and with dancing. ²¹And Miriam sang to them:

"Sing to the Lord, for he has triumphed
gloriously;
horse and rider he has thrown into the
sea."

15:20–21 This unit is often called the Song of Miriam. It seems that it was not uncommon for women to lead victory celebrations (see Judg. 5; 1 Sam. 18:6–7). Moses's song begins with a first-person future verb, "I will sing" (v. 1). Miriam's song begins with a plural imperative, a command to all: "Sing!" According to some interpreters, Miriam's song may have been the original version, with her "Sing!" leading to Moses's song that begins (as a kind of reply) "I will sing." It is also possible that Miriam led the women in song and Moses led the men, though v. 1 seems inclusive of all the children of Israel. In the present form of the chapter, Miriam's song is a response to Moses's song. **15:20** Miriam is identified by name for the first time in the narrative. She is also identified as Aaron's sister and as a prophet. Miriam is the most frequently mentioned woman in the Old Testament (15:20–21; Num. 12:1, 4–5, 10, 15; 20:1; 26:59; Deut. 24:9; 1 Chr. 6:3; Mic. 6:4). She is also the first woman in the Bible to receive the title of prophet. The others are Deborah (Judg. 4:4), Huldah (2 Kgs. 22:14; 2 Chr. 34:22), and Noadiah (Neh. 6:14). Rabbinic tradition adds Hannah, Abigail, and Esther to bring the total to seven.

22 Then Moses ordered Israel to set out from the Red Sea,[y] and they went into the wilderness of Shur. They went three days in the wilderness and found no water. [23]When they came to Marah, they could not drink the water of Marah because it was bitter. That is why it was called Marah.[z] [24]And the people complained against Moses, saying, "What shall we drink?" [25]He cried out to the Lord, and the Lord showed him a piece of wood; he threw it into the water, and the water became sweet.

There the Lord[a] made for them a statute and an ordinance, and there he put them to the test. [26]He said, "If you will listen carefully to the voice of the Lord your God, and do what is right in his sight, and give heed to his commandments and keep all his statutes, I will not bring upon you any of the diseases that I brought upon the Egyptians, for I am the Lord who heals you."

27 Then they came to Elim, where there were twelve springs of water and seventy palm trees, and they camped there by the water.

16 The whole congregation of the Israelites set out from Elim and came to the wilderness of Sin, which is between Elim and Sinai, on the fifteenth day of the second month after they had departed from the land of Egypt. [2]The whole congregation of the Israelites complained against Moses and Aaron in the wilderness. [3]The Israelites said to them, "If only we had died by the hand of the Lord in the land of Egypt, when we sat by the pots of meat and ate our fill of bread, for you have brought us out into this wilderness to kill this whole assembly with hunger."

4 Then the Lord said to Moses, "I am going to rain bread from heaven for you, and each day the people shall go out and gather enough for that day. In that way I will test them, whether they will follow my instruction or not. [5]On the sixth day, when they prepare what they bring in, it will be twice as much as they gather on other days." [6]So Moses and Aaron said to all the Israelites,

y 15.22 Or *Sea of Reeds*   z 15.23 That is, *bitterness*
a 15.25 Heb *he*

15:22–27 The event at Marah is Israel's first taste of freedom, but freedom from Egypt's oppression is also freedom from Egypt's provision. God uses the water crisis at Marah as a platform to give rules, statutes, and ordinances to the people. This story is a transition to the wilderness tradition, where the people must depend on God for everything. **15:22** Three days can be used to designate a long time (see the notes at 3:18; 5:3). The wilderness of Shur is between Egypt and the Negeb. **15:23** Marah means "bitterness," which refers perhaps to both the water and the experience of Israel at that place. **15:24** The episode at Marah is the first in a series of stories highlighting Israel's complaints (e.g., 16:3, 8; 17:2–3). The need in this case is quite legitimate: both the people and their livestock require water. **15:24–25** The people complain to Moses, who in turn cries out to God. God resolves the crisis. In contrast to other complaint stories, there is no punishment for Israel's grumbling here. **15:25** In 7:19, God instructs Moses to have Aaron hold his rod over the water to turn it to blood. In chap. 14, God instructs Moses to hold his staff over the water to divide it. Here God instructs Moses to throw a piece of wood into the water to cure it. The notion of a *test* will return later: God will test the people (see 16:4; 20:20), and the people in turn will test God (see 17:2, 7). **15:26** The diseases in this verse may refer not to the ten plagues but to other kinds of sickness in the land of Egypt (see Deut. 7:15; 28:27, 60). **15:27** The narrative ends in the oasis of Elim (see Num. 33:9), an ideal location with twelve springs and seventy palm trees, both of which are ideal numbers.

16:1 The episode at Marah is followed immediately by stories about manna and quail, thereby addressing the basic human need of water and food. God provides food and drink but also forms the people by giving them ordinances and instructions along with these gifts. By pairing them, the narrative suggests that obedience to God's rules is as essential as food and water.

16:2 The people complain again; see 15:24. For *Aaron*'s role, see 16:9 and note at 4:27–31.

16:3 The people's complaint includes memories of Egypt that are centered around food, to the neglect of any other detail about their time in Egypt.

16:4 God tells Moses what will happen before it occurs. In addition to receiving the gifts of bread and meat, the people must follow God's instructions for the use of the gifts. The verb for rain here is the same one used to describe the hail in 9:18.

16:5 The portion of food on the sixth day anticipates the seventh. See 16:22.

"In the evening you shall know that it was the LORD who brought you out of the land of Egypt, [7]and in the morning you shall see the glory of the LORD, because he has heard your complaining against the LORD. For what are we, that you complain against us?" [8]And Moses said, "When the LORD gives you meat to eat in the evening and your fill of bread in the morning, because the LORD has heard the complaining that you utter against him—what are we? Your complaining is not against us but against the LORD."

[9] Then Moses said to Aaron, "Say to the whole congregation of the Israelites: 'Draw near to the LORD, for he has heard your complaining.'" [10]And as Aaron spoke to the whole congregation of the Israelites, they looked toward the wilderness, and the glory of the LORD appeared in the cloud. [11]The LORD spoke to Moses, [12]"I have heard the complaining of the Israelites; say to them, 'At twilight you shall eat meat, and in the morning you shall have your fill of bread; then you shall know that I am the LORD your God.'"

[13] In the evening quails came up and covered the camp, and in the morning there was a layer of dew around the camp. [14]When the layer of dew lifted, there on the surface of the wilderness was a fine flaky substance, as fine as frost on the ground. [15]When the Israelites saw it, they said to one another, "What is it?"[b] For they did not know what it was. Moses said to them, "It is the bread that the LORD has given you to eat. [16]This is what the LORD has commanded: Gather as much of it as each of you needs, an omer per person according to the number of persons, all providing for those in their own tents." [17]The Israelites did so, some gathering more, some less. [18]But when they measured it with an omer, those who gathered much had nothing over, and those who gathered little had no shortage; they gathered as much as each of them needed. [19]And Moses said to them, "Let no one leave any of it over until morning." [20]But they did not listen to Moses; some left part of it until morning, and it became wormy and rotten. And Moses was angry with them. [21]Morning by morning they gathered it, as much as each needed, but when the sun grew hot, it melted.

[22] On the sixth day they gathered twice as much food, two omers apiece. When all the leaders of the congregation came and told Moses, [23]he said to them, "This is what the LORD has commanded: Tomorrow is a day of solemn rest, a holy Sabbath to the LORD; bake what you want to bake and boil what you want to boil, and all that is left over put aside to be kept until morning." [24]So they put it aside until morning, just as Moses commanded them, and it did not rot, and there were no maggots in it. [25]Moses said, "Eat it today, for today is a Sabbath to the LORD; today you will not find it in the field. [26]Six days you shall gather it, but on the seventh day, which is a Sabbath, there will be none."

[27] On the seventh day some of the people went out to gather, and they found none. [28]The LORD said to Moses, "How long will you refuse to keep my commandments and instructions? [29]See! The LORD has given you the Sabbath; therefore on the sixth day he gives you food for two days; each of you stay where you are; do not leave your place on the seventh day." [30]So the people rested on the seventh day.

[31] The Israelites called it manna; it was like white coriander seed, and the taste of it was like wafers made with honey. [32]Moses said, "This is what the LORD has commanded: Let an omer of it be kept throughout your generations in order that they may see the food with which I fed you in the wilderness when I brought you out of the land of Egypt." [33]And Moses said to Aaron, "Take a jar, and put an

b 16.15 Or *"It is manna"*

16:7 The *glory of the* LORD appears to be a visible presence leading the Israelites (see 16:10; 24:17).

16:11–12 Bread and quail occur together here. In the similar story in Num. 11, the quail is given after the people complain about only having manna.

16:15 Manna is from a Hebrew phrase that means "What is it?" or "It is manna."

16:15–21 God's provision comes with instruction.

16:22 Sabbath observance is incorporated into the manna account. The double portion of manna collected on the sixth day is miraculously preserved so no gathering is required on the seventh day, the Sabbath, when work like cooking is prohibited. On the *leaders of the congregation*, see 22:28; 34:31; 35:27.

16:33–34 A jar of manna is placed *before the* LORD and *before the covenant*. The latter presumably

omer of manna in it, and place it before the LORD, to be kept throughout your generations." [34]Just as the LORD commanded Moses, so Aaron placed it before the covenant, for safekeeping. [35]The Israelites ate manna forty years, until they came to a habitable land; they ate manna, until they came to the border of the land of Canaan. [36](An omer is a tenth of an ephah.)

17 From the wilderness of Sin the whole congregation of the Israelites journeyed by stages, as the LORD commanded. They camped at Rephidim, but there was no water for the people to drink. [2]The people quarreled with Moses and said, "Give us water to drink." Moses said to them, "Why do you quarrel with me? Why do you test the LORD?" [3]But the people thirsted there for water, and the people complained against Moses and said, "Why did you bring us out of Egypt, to kill us and our children and livestock with thirst?" [4]So Moses cried out to the LORD, "What shall I do for this people? They are almost ready to stone me." [5]The LORD said to Moses, "Go on ahead of the people and take some of the elders of Israel with you; take in your hand the staff with which you struck the Nile and go. [6]I will be standing there in front of you on the rock at Horeb. Strike the rock, and water will come out of it, so that the people may drink." Moses did so, in the sight of the elders of Israel. [7]He called the place Massah[c] and Meribah,[d] because the Israelites quarreled and tested the LORD, saying, "Is the LORD among us or not?"

[8] Then Amalek came and fought with Israel at Rephidim. [9]Moses said to Joshua, "Choose some men for us and go out; fight with Amalek. Tomorrow I will stand on the top of the hill with the staff of God in my hand." [10]So Joshua did as Moses told him and fought with Amalek, while Moses, Aaron, and Hur went up to the top of the hill. [11]Whenever Moses held up his hand, Israel prevailed, and whenever he lowered his hand, Amalek prevailed. [12]But Moses's hands grew heavy, so they took a stone and put it under him, and he sat on it. Aaron and Hur held up his hands, one on

c 17.7 That is, *test* *d* 17.7 That is, *quarrel*

means inside the ark of the covenant; the jar of manna is joined later by the tablets containing the Ten Commandments (see 25:16) and Aaron's rod (see Num. 17:1–10).

16:35 The Israelites eat manna until they are in the land of Canaan, where it is no longer required and so, suddenly, stops (see Josh. 5:11–12). The details here are anachronistic, betraying an authorial hand writing at a later date.

16:36 An "omer" is a unit of measurement equivalent to one person's daily portion.

17:1–7 The event at Massah, meaning "test," and Meribah, which means "argument," is also recounted in Num. 20:2–13. Here in Exodus, Moses is instructed to strike the rock, which he does (17:6). In the Numbers account, Moses is instructed to command the rock to yield water, but in anger strikes the rock twice. This is deemed an act of disobedience and the reason Moses will not enter the promised land (Num. 20:12). As was the case in the Marah story (cf. Exod. 15:22–27), the presenting crisis concerns water but is ultimately about trust in God, a point underscored by the questions in v. 7: *Is the LORD among us or not?* **17:2** The previous complaint stories in Exod. 15 and 16 used the word "complain." Chap. 17 adds a new verb, *quarrel*, which is stronger and comes from a legal context. This type of complaint assumes, therefore, a legal or covenantal relationship. The quarrel constitutes a test of the Lord, and this provides the explanation for the place name, since Massah means "test." **17:5** Moses is instructed to use the staff used previously to part the Red Sea (Exod. 14) and to turn the Nile into blood (Exod. 7). The *elders of Israel*—a group distinct from the "leaders of the congregation"—occasionally receive special privileges (see 18:12; 19:7; 24:1, 14). **17:6** God's presence is emphasized, described in anthropomorphic terms. **17:7** Explanation of the names Massah ("test") and Meribah ("quarrel").

17:8–16 The battle with Amalek (see also Deut. 25:17–19). This short narrative of a miraculous victory in battle includes a unique name for God—"YHWH-nissi," *The LORD is my banner*—and also explains the perpetual conflict with Amalek: *The LORD will have war with Amalek from generation to generation.* **17:9** Joshua appears in the role of military leader, but his prominence will increase as the book continues (cf. 24:13; 32:17; 33:11). **17:10** Aaron is mentioned here along with Hur as Moses's helpers. Hur is the grandfather of Bezalel, the artisan mentioned later in 31:2, and belongs to the tribe of Judah. **17:11** Moses's uplifted hands are a sign of strength and victory. The lifting up

either side, so his hands were steady until the sun set. [13]And Joshua defeated Amalek and his people with the sword.

14 Then the LORD said to Moses, "Write this as a remembrance in a book and recite it in the hearing of Joshua: I will utterly blot out the memory of Amalek from under heaven." [15]And Moses built an altar and called it, The LORD is my banner. [16]He said, "A hand upon the banner of the LORD![e] The LORD will have war with Amalek from generation to generation."

18 Jethro, the priest of Midian, Moses's father-in-law, heard of all that God had done for Moses and for his people Israel, how the LORD had brought Israel out of Egypt. [2]After Moses had sent away his wife Zipporah, his father-in-law Jethro took her back, [3]along with her two sons. The name of the one was Gershom[f] (for he had said, "I have been an alien in a foreign land"), [4]and the name of the other was Eliezer[g] (for he had said, "The God of my father was my help and delivered me from the sword of Pharaoh"). [5]Jethro, Moses's father-in-law, along with Moses's sons and wife, came into the wilderness where Moses was encamped at the mountain of God. [6]He sent word to Moses, "I, your father-in-law Jethro, am coming to you, with your wife and her two sons." [7]So Moses went out to meet his father-in-law; he bowed down and kissed him; each asked after the other's welfare, and they went into the tent. [8]Then Moses told his father-in-law all that the LORD had done to Pharaoh and to the Egyptians for Israel's sake, all the hardship that had found them on the way, and how the LORD had delivered them. [9]Jethro rejoiced for all the good that the LORD had done to Israel, in delivering them from the Egyptians.

10 Jethro said, "Blessed be the LORD, who has delivered you from the Egyptians and from Pharaoh. [11]Now I know that the LORD is greater than all gods, because he delivered the people from the Egyptians,[b] when they dealt arrogantly with them." [12]And Jethro, Moses's father-in-law, brought a burnt offering and sacrifices to God, and Aaron came with all the elders of Israel to eat bread with Moses's father-in-law in the presence of God.

13 The next day Moses sat as judge for the

e 17.16 Cn: Meaning of Heb uncertain   f 18.3 In Heb *Gershom* resembles the word for *alien*   g 18.4 That is, *my God helps*   h 18.11 The clause *because . . . Egyptians* has been transposed from verse 10

of the staff is a show of the power of God (see Exod. 14). **17:14** Amalek is specifically designated to be remembered as an enemy of Israel. Later, God will command Saul to attack Amalek because of "what they did in opposing the Israelites when they came up out of Egypt" (1 Sam. 15:2–3). **17:15** An altar is built to bear witness to the battle and to thank God. The name of the altar is also a name for the Lord: *The LORD is my banner.* The name suggests Moses held up his staff, a military banner, with his lifted arms. **17:16** The Amalekites are presented here as God's enemies, introducing the possibility that this battle might be seen as an instance of holy war (though the Bible never uses the phrase "holy war" and never calls war "holy"). The Amalekites reappear later as the enemy in other narratives (see, e.g., Num. 14:44–45; 1 Sam. 15; 1 Chr. 4:43). *From generation to generation* is a formulaic phrase that often means "eternity" or "forever." The Amalekites are portrayed as an enduring enemy of Israel, and the narrative justifies and sustains the rationale for treating Amalek as an enemy. Much later, in the book of Esther, the enemy of the Jews known as Haman in that story is identified as an Amalekite.

18:1 Moses's father-in-law, Jethro, is known in some traditions by the name Reuel (cf. 2:16–22). In another tradition, there is confusion between the names Reuel and Hobab (see Num. 10:29; Judg. 4:11).

18:1–3 With Jethro's visit to Moses, the reader learns that Zipporah and the children, who accompanied Moses to Egypt, had at some point been sent back to Midian. **18:3** See 2:22.

18:4 Moses's second son is named here (see 4:20). Eliezer means "my God is my help."

18:5 Moses and the people are now at Sinai, the *mountain of God* (see 3:1).

18:10–12 Jethro, the priest of Midian, brings a blessing, an acknowledgment of the God of Israel, an offering, and a sacrifice. Part of this sacrifice is offered up to the deity, and the rest is part of a festival meal; it may indicate some type of treaty or agreement. See the later feast in chap. 24. **18:12** *In the presence of God:* at the base of the mountain.

18:13 This passage shows Moses adjudicating or judging between and for the people before they receive the divine legislation at Sinai.

people, while the people stood around him from morning until evening. ¹⁴When Moses's father-in-law saw all that he was doing for the people, he said, "What is this that you are doing for the people? Why do you sit alone, while all the people stand around you from morning until evening?" ¹⁵Moses said to his father-in-law, "Because the people come to me to inquire of God. ¹⁶When they have a dispute, they come to me, and I decide between one person and another, and I make known to them the statutes and instructions of God." ¹⁷Moses's father-in-law said to him, "What you are doing is not good. ¹⁸You will surely wear yourself out, both you and these people with you, for the task is too heavy for you; you cannot do it alone. ¹⁹Now listen to me. I will give you counsel, and God be with you! You should represent the people before God and bring their cases to God. ²⁰Teach them the statutes and instructions and make known to them the way they are to go and the things they are to do. ²¹You should also look for able men among all the people, men who fear God, are trustworthy, and hate dishonest gain; set them as officers over thousands, hundreds, fifties, and tens. ²²Let them sit as judges for the people at all times; let them bring every important case to you but decide every minor case themselves. So it will be easier for you, and they will bear the burden with you. ²³If you do this and God so commands you, then you will be able to endure, and all these people will go to their homes in peace."

24 So Moses listened to his father-in-law and did all that he had said. ²⁵Moses chose able men from all Israel and appointed them as heads over the people, as officers over thousands, hundreds, fifties, and tens. ²⁶And they judged the people at all times; hard cases they brought to Moses, but any minor case they decided themselves. ²⁷Then Moses let his father-in-law depart, and he went off to his own country.

19 On the third new moon after the Israelites had gone out of the land of Egypt, on that very day, they came into the wilderness of Sinai. ²They journeyed from Rephidim, entered the wilderness of Sinai, and camped in the wilderness; Israel camped there in front of the mountain. ³Then Moses went up to God; the LORD called to him from the mountain, "Thus you shall say to the house of Jacob and tell the Israelites: ⁴'You have seen what I did to the Egyptians and how I bore you on eagles' wings and brought you to myself. ⁵Now, therefore, if you obey my voice and keep my covenant, you shall be my treasured possession out of all the peoples. Indeed, the whole earth is mine, ⁶but you shall be for me a priestly kingdom and a holy nation.' These are the words that you shall speak to the Israelites."

7 So Moses went, summoned the elders of the people, and set before them all these words that the LORD had commanded him. ⁸The people all answered as one, "Everything that the LORD has spoken we will do." Moses reported the words of the people to the LORD. ⁹Then the LORD said to Moses, "I am going to come to you in a dense cloud, in order that the people may hear when I speak with you and so trust you ever after."

When Moses had told the words of the people to the LORD, ¹⁰the LORD said to Moses,

18:24 In Deut. 1:9–18, Moses takes credit for establishing the model for settling disputes.

18:27 The implication is that Zipporah and her two sons remained with Moses (cf. 18:1–3).

19:1–2 The people arrive at Sinai (cf. 18:5), the mountain of God, which fulfills the announcement of God's promised sign in 3:12.

19:3–6 God's declaration and invitation to the people is similar to the prologue of the Decalogue in the following chapter. By reminding the people that they have been redeemed (v. 4), God sets the terms for what is to come, which expects covenantal fidelity and obedience. **19:4** *On eagles' wings* is an image of God's redemptive work (see also Deut. 32:11). The eagle has an impressive wingspan and is capable of flying at great heights. The wings evoke God saving with an outstretched arm in other places (e.g., 6:6).

19:7 On *elders*, see note at 17:5.

19:8 The people's response is characterized as unified and affirmative.

19:9 A possible variation of the pillar of cloud from 13:21.

19:10 A set of physical and ritual practices indicate that the people are about to engage in a sacred encounter. This includes separation from the mountain. One of the possible meanings of

"Go to the people and consecrate them today and tomorrow. Have them wash their clothes [11]and prepare for the third day, because on the third day the Lord will come down upon Mount Sinai in the sight of all the people. [12]You shall set limits for the people all around, saying, 'Be careful not to go up the mountain or to touch the edge of it. Any who touch the mountain shall be put to death. [13]No hand shall touch them, but they shall be stoned or shot with arrows;[i] whether animal or human being, they shall not live.' When the trumpet sounds a long blast, they may go up on the mountain." [14]So Moses went down from the mountain to the people. He consecrated the people, and they washed their clothes. [15]And he said to the people, "Prepare for the third day; do not go near a woman."

16 On the morning of the third day there was thunder and lightning, as well as a thick cloud on the mountain and a blast of a trumpet so loud that all the people who were in the camp trembled. [17]Moses brought the people out of the camp to meet God. They took their stand at the foot of the mountain. [18]Now all of Mount Sinai was wrapped in smoke, because the Lord had descended upon it in fire; the smoke went up like the smoke of a kiln, while the whole mountain shook violently. [19]As the blast of the trumpet grew louder and louder, Moses would speak and God would answer him in thunder. [20]When the Lord descended upon Mount Sinai, to the top of the mountain, the Lord summoned Moses to the top of the mountain, and Moses went up. [21]Then the Lord said to Moses, "Go down and warn the people not to break through to see the Lord; otherwise many of them will perish. [22]Even the priests who approach the Lord must consecrate themselves, or the Lord will break out against them." [23]Moses said to the Lord, "The people are not permitted to come up to Mount Sinai, for you yourself warned us, saying, 'Set limits around the mountain and keep it holy.'" [24]The Lord said to him, "Go down, then come back up and bring Aaron with you, but do not let either the priests or the people break through to come up to the Lord; otherwise he will break out against them." [25]So Moses went down to the people and told them.

20 Then God spoke all these words, 2 "I am the Lord your God, who brought you out of the land of Egypt, out of

i 19.13 Heb lacks *with arrows*

"holy" or "holiness" is "set apart" (see **"Holiness (Exodus 3:5)," p. 88**). Certain things are removed from daily life and everyday access due to their specialness or significance. The purification ritual here signals the importance of what is to come.

19:15 The prohibition *do not go near a woman* is clearly directed to a male audience and likely refers to sexual relations, which were thought to result in ritual impurity.

19:16, 18–19 The Lord is described in the terms of a storm god. Smoke, thunder, and lightning accompany God's presence on the mountain.

19:23 The people's separation from the mountain is an indication of God's holiness and the caution that it warrants. Moses, as leader and intermediary, moves up and down the mountain as God directs.

19:24 Aaron is singled out from the other priests (v. 22) and will accompany Moses up the mountain.

20:1–21 The Ten Commandments or Decalogue ("ten words") are placed first in the legal collection of Exodus (see **"Law/Decalogue," p. 112**). They are not only placed first but also said to be given directly by God to the people (20:1). God spoke these words and also wrote them on the original tablets. The Decalogue is thus given pride of place in the covenant at Sinai and in the entire collection of legal material that follows in Exodus and beyond. As the first obligations of the covenant, the Ten Commandments are the terms of Israel's freedom. The Ten Commandments are repeated with slight variations in Deut. 5:6–21 (see also the presence of some of the commandments in Lev. 19:3–4, 11–13, 15–16, 30, 32). Most of the Ten Commandments are prohibitions, listing behaviors that must be avoided. Only two are expressed affirmatively. The Sabbath command is often seen as the last to be primarily concerned with Israel's relationship to God, with the parent command subsequently seen as the first that speaks to Israel's interpersonal relationships. This distinction can be challenged, but it is clear that the Decalogue begins with the relationship with God and ends with the relationships to the neighbor. **20:1** *I am the Lord your God*. The first part of the Decalogue is often deemed a prologue or analogy with ancient Near Eastern suzerainty treaty forms. In such texts, the suzerain (more powerful monarch) begins with a word of self-identification

Making Connections: Law/Decalogue (Exodus 20)

Legal material in the Bible is concentrated in the Pentateuch and especially in the covenant that takes place at Mount Sinai, where Israel is located for the majority of the Torah (Exod. 19:1–Num. 10:11). Divine commands appear much earlier than Sinai, however, whenever God utters imperatives—as in Gen. 1:22, 28, where God orders humans and animals to be fruitful and multiply. The Torah, a Hebrew word meaning "law" or "instruction," contains much more than just law. From Genesis through Deuteronomy, the Torah contains a long narrative arc and includes poetry peppered throughout (see **"Introduction to the Torah/Pentateuch," pp. 2–4**). Torah is something of a macrocategory, Israel's "law" containing story and poetry alongside legal pre- and proscriptions.

A microcosm of this situation is found in the legal collection called the Ten Commandments or Decalogue (Exod. 20:2–17 and repeated in Deut. 5:6–21). The title comes from the Hebrew phrase "the ten words" found elsewhere in the Bible (see Exod. 34:28; Deut. 10:4). Interpreters have disagreed on how exactly to number these ten. The Decalogue begins with a statement concerning what God did for Israel in bringing them "out of the land of Egypt, out of the house of slavery" (Exod. 20:2 // Deut. 5:6). This verse is the first commandment in the Jewish tradition but is considered a narrative prelude to the commandments in the Christian tradition. Differences in how to divide and count the verses continue among Jewish, Protestant, Orthodox, and Catholic communities as well as with other interpreters. However divided, the Ten Commandments include negative commands like "You shall not murder" (Exod. 20:13) but also positive injunctions like "Honor your father and your mother" (v. 12). In some cases, the commands include reasons motivating their adherence (see Exod. 20:11 and Deut. 5:15; Exod. 20:12b and Deut. 5:16b). In all cases, the Ten Commandments are absolute law as opposed to case law, which describes various legal circumstances.

The importance of the Decalogue is underscored by its standing in first position in the legal corpus and its coming directly from God to all Israel. In contrast, the law that follows the Decalogue is mediated through Moses (see Exod. 20:18–21). The Decalogue's significance is also felt through repetition in other texts like Lev. 19 or Jesus's Sermon on the Mount in Matt. 5–7. Though Christians have typically not observed many of the laws of the Torah (see Acts 15:1–35), they have traditionally upheld the Decalogue as universally valid, though they differ on how to interpret and apply it.

Brent A. Strawn

the house of slavery; ³you shall have no other gods before^j me.

4 "You shall not make for yourself an idol, whether in the form of anything that is in heaven above or that is on the earth beneath or that is in the water under the earth. ⁵You shall not bow down to them or serve them, for I the LORD your God am a jealous God, punishing children for the iniquity of parents to the third and the fourth generation of those who reject me ⁶but showing steadfast love to the thousandth generation^k of those who love me and keep my commandments.

j 20.3 Or *besides* k 20.6 Or *to thousands*

and a recounting of benevolent activity. The prologue to the Decalogue does the same, identifying the God who delivers by personal name (YHWH) and recalling the mighty acts of the exodus. This justifies the law that follows. In Judaism, this "prologue" is considered the first of the Ten Commandments: it is to remember what God has done. **20:3** *You shall have no other gods before me.* This commandment does not deny the existence of other gods; rather, it demands Israel's sole fidelity to this one God alone. Even so, some see in this commandment the beginning stages of what will eventually become full-blown exclusive and theoretical monotheism (cf. Deut. 5:7). **20:4** The prohibition of images speaks to God's transcendence of any one image. Depictions of gods in artistic form (idols) often emphasize a specific attribute of the deity. God resists such identification in this prohibition—a resistance that seems already at work in the name, "I AM WHAT I AM." God's essence is elusive and on the move. Images seem to be attempts to limit divine freedom (cf. Deut. 5:8–9). **20:5** *Jealous God.* The God of Israel is passionate about the people's faithfulness. The use of strong emotional language speaks to the depth of God's investment in this relationship and evokes the marriage covenant, where fidelity is expected. In contrast, infidelity carries the expectation of harsh punishment (cf. Lev. 20:10; Deut. 22:22). **20:5–6** Israel's adherence to the covenant, or lack of adherence, has serious implications for the community in space and time. Individual behavior has an impact on the entire community, even on future generations. The difference between generational

7 "You shall not make wrongful use of the name of the LORD your God, for the LORD will not acquit anyone who misuses his name.

8 "Remember the Sabbath day and keep it holy. ⁹Six days you shall labor and do all your work. ¹⁰But the seventh day is a Sabbath to the LORD your God; you shall not do any work—you, your son or your daughter, your male or female slave, your livestock, or the alien resident in your towns. ¹¹For in six days the LORD made heaven and earth, the sea, and all that is in them, but rested the seventh day; therefore the LORD blessed the Sabbath day and consecrated it.

12 "Honor your father and your mother, so that your days may be long in the land that the LORD your God is giving you.

13 "You shall not murder.ᶦ

14 "You shall not commit adultery.

15 "You shall not steal.

16 "You shall not bear false witness against your neighbor.

17 "You shall not covet your neighbor's house; you shall not covet your neighbor's wife, male or female slave, ox, donkey, or anything that belongs to your neighbor."

18 When all the people witnessed the

l 20.13 Or *kill*

punishment (third and fourth generations) and generational benevolence (thousandth generation) is incomparable: God's steadfast love exponentially surpasses divine punishment. **20:7** *Wrongful use* likely refers to false oaths that use God's name, including invoking God's name for nothing (in vain), which would constitute frivolous use of the divine name (cf. Deut. 5:11). See **"God's Name," p. 89**. This commandment differs from the one on false witness against a neighbor, likely in a court setting. **20:8–11** The verbal form of the *Sabbath* means "to cease, desist, or rest." The noun, in its simplest form, refers to a cessation. In Exodus, the rationale for the commandment is the divine rest after the six days of creation (see Gen. 1:1–2:4), applying God's action (and inaction) to the covenantal community in its entirety. To remember the Sabbath is to observe or practice it. The rationale for the commandment in Deuteronomy differs (see Deut. 5:12–15). **20:10** On *alien*, see note at 2:22. **20:12** Something that is honored is given weight or its due. The commandment thus mandates respect, honor, and reverence for one's parents; "obedience" is not explicitly stated. It is particularly noteworthy that this commandment cuts across gender lines and applies to mothers and fathers, daughters and sons. It is also a commandment with an extensive motivation (or promise; cf. Eph. 6:2). **20:13** This commandment is the first of a series of three that consist of just two words: the negative article and a verb prohibiting, respectively, killing, adultery, and theft. The verb used in v. 13 is somewhat unclear as evidenced by the textual note. The verb can refer to murder but also unintentional homicide (see Deut. 4:41–42). It can also refer to executing a convicted killer (Num. 35:30). Scholars are divided over the proper interpretation and translation of the word. **20:14** The high esteem ascribed to the family unit is reflected in this commandment. The prohibition against adultery uses a verb that applies to women and men. In the ancient Near Eastern environment, where polygamy was sometimes practiced but where its counterpart (polyandry) did not exist, a man committed adultery when he slept with a woman married to someone else (see Lev. 18:20); a married woman committed adultery by any extramarital sexual activity. Other texts specify that the punishment for adultery was death (Lev. 20:10; Deut. 22:22). The Decalogue does not specify punishment for this or any of the commandments. **20:15** The prohibition of theft consists of a verb that is fairly broad, and some scholars have argued it may have once originally referred to kidnaping on the basis of texts like Exod. 21:16 and Deut. 24:7. **20:16** The commandment forbidding false witness envisions deceitful testimony and spurious charges in a legal setting. In later reception, this commandment was thought to include lying more generally. **20:17** Coveting the possessions of one's neighbor includes both items and people. The verb used conveys a sense of inordinate desire that tends toward idolatry. It is the motivation behind adultery, stealing, bearing false witness. The coveting command honors the full humanity of every member of the community. No one is expendable for the sake of another's gain. The inclusion of *your neighbor's wife* in this list suggests a male-gendered audience for this discourse. The formulation in Deut. 5:21, while still presented in terms of the husband's perspective, is seen by some as an improvement over the Exodus version. **20:18–21** God's presence is made manifest in a display of sight and sound. Thunder, lightning, smoke, and the trumpet overwhelm the people. Israel's response to their proximity to God is one of fear. In spite of Moses's reassurance, they insist that Moses serve as intermediary for all the subsequent proceedings. **20:18** God's manifestation is inherently and intentionally awe-inspiring and memorable.

thunder and lightning, the sound of the trumpet, and the mountain smoking, they were afraid[m] and trembled and stood at a distance ¹⁹and said to Moses, "You speak to us, and we will listen, but do not let God speak to us, lest we die." ²⁰Moses said to the people, "Do not be afraid, for God has come only to test you and to put the fear of him upon you so that you do not sin." ²¹Then the people stood at a distance, while Moses drew near to the thick darkness where God was.

22 The LORD said to Moses, "Thus you shall say to the Israelites: You have seen for yourselves how I spoke with you from heaven. ²³You shall not make gods of silver alongside me, nor shall you make for yourselves gods of gold. ²⁴You need make for me only an altar of earth and sacrifice on it your burnt offerings and your offerings of well-being, your sheep and your oxen; in every place where I cause my name to be remembered I will come to you and bless you. ²⁵But if you make for me an altar of stone, do not build it of hewn stones, for if you use a chisel upon it you profane it. ²⁶You shall not go up by steps

to my altar, so that your nakedness may not be exposed on it.

21 "These are the ordinances that you shall set before them:

2 "When you buy a male Hebrew slave, he shall serve six years, but in the seventh he shall go out a free person, without debt. ³If he comes in single, he shall go out single; if he comes in married, then his wife shall go out with him. ⁴If his master gives him a wife and she bears him sons or daughters, the wife and her children shall be her master's, and he shall go out alone. ⁵But if the slave declares, 'I love my master, my wife, and my children; I will not go out a free person,' ⁶then his master shall bring him before God. He shall be brought to the door or the doorpost, and his master shall pierce his ear with an awl, and he shall serve him for life.

7 "When a man sells his daughter as a slave, she shall not go out as the male slaves do. ⁸If she does not please her master, who

m 20.18 Sam Gk Syr Vg: MT *they saw*

20:22–26 These verses begin what is often called the covenant code or book of the covenant (20:22–23:33). This legal collection includes absolute or universal law, like that found in the Decalogue, but the majority of what is found here is case law, where the law depends on the circumstances. The collection offers insight into the life and practices of ancient Israel but, in context, also reflects the desire to shape a newly freed community into a covenant people. The archaic language found here, as well as parallels with Mesopotamian law, has led some scholars to believe that the book of the covenant contains some of Israel's oldest legal material. **20:26** This prohibition guards against unseemly nudity. Some ancient religions practiced ritual nudity, and a man's clothing did not always include undergarments. Exodus will later include regulations for priestly attire, including linen undergarments (28:42). Such prescriptions function to set Israelite religion apart from its counterparts. **21:1** The law is *set before* the people, suggesting that these rules are for everyone. **21:2** Regulations regarding the enslaved seem inapt for a people who have been just freed from slavery themselves. The slavery spoken of here, however, is not chattel slavery but debt slavery of one Israelite to another—a service limited to a period of six years, with the provision that the slave may go free thereafter with no further obligation. Deuteronomy 15:12–15 goes even further, indicating that slaveholders must not set debt servants free "empty-handed" but must provide liberally for them. **21:2–6** The practice described here refers to sons. Daughters sold into slavery are discussed in 21:7–11. The legal status of the children is determined by the mother; they become the property of the enslaver (v. 4). See **"Human Bondage in Ancient Israel (the Law)," p. 115**. **21:5–6** A debt slave could opt into permanent servitude. Such a decision reflects the harsh economic realities that led people into debt slavery. Such realities are the likely result of the difficulties facing an agrarian, subsistence-based economy. The decision for permanent servitude requires bodily marking in a religious ceremony carried out in the presence of the deity (*before God*). **21:7–11** Daughters sold into slavery have a different status than sons. The sale of daughters was often as wives or concubines. A differentiation exists between women and men, even in the context of debt slavery. **21:7** This verse applies to a woman sold as a wife or concubine. The rules for a woman sold solely for domestic work are found in Deut. 15:12–18. If a girl or woman is sold as a wife or concubine, she is due the protection and rights of a wife, even if her husband takes another wife. **21:8** The woman is protected from being sold to foreigners (where her slavery would likely

Focus On: Human Bondage in Ancient Israel (The Law) (Exodus 21)

Israel maintained the widespread, common practice of human bondage, despite its own tradition of enslavement when the Israelites "were Pharaoh's slaves in Egypt" (Deut. 6:21). While some individuals might have sold themselves into slavery because of their impoverished conditions (Deut. 15:12), more people were enslaved through war than debt bondage. Little evidence exists of the practice of trading in humans until Hellenistic times (cf. 1 Macc. 3:38–41). Israelite law provides some insight into the troubling aspects surrounding the human bondage condition.

Exodus 21 regulates the common practice of debt slavery for wealthy landowners. After a six-year period of service, the enslaver must allow the enslaved male to depart. However, a master could exploit the enslaved person's procreative abilities. If the man was granted "a wife and she bears him sons or daughters," his family belonged to the enslaver (21:4). Nearing the time of his release, the man may choose to stay because of "love" (21:5). To enter into chattel (permanent) slavery requires a religious act ("before God") and a physical marking on his body (21:6). The law stipulates variations when females—sold by their fathers into slavery—were involved. These Israelite enslaved women should not be sold to non-Israelites (21:8), partly because of the complicated procreative abilities of these women, who function as "wives" to their enslavers or the sons of their enslavers (21:8–10).

Later laws slightly revise these earlier regulations. Deuteronomy 15:12–18 reiterates the law of Exodus with the addition of fair payment for the six years of service (15:14), recalling the tradition of Israel's own bondage in Egypt (15:15). The Deuteronomic law is also more inclusive, as enslaved females should be treated in the same manner as their male counterparts (15:17). Leviticus permits the enslavement of non-Israelites with impunity (Lev. 25:44–46), but bars enslaving fellow Israelites. Those who sell themselves into these conditions become "bound laborers" not "slaves" (25:39–40). Leviticus also advocates for a "Jubilee" decree every fiftieth year in which all should be freed from bondage (25:10–11), but there is no evidence that this ever transpired in Israel's history. In fact, there is literary evidence of the complications of such attempts (see Jer. 34:8–22).

Other laws curb inhumane treatment of the enslaved. Apparently, individual escapees—presumably due to poor (violent?) conditions—should be granted permission to live elsewhere (cf. Deut. 23:15–16). Israel's Sabbath provision required rest even for the enslaved (Exod. 20:10). Whether the enslaved among Israel were treated more humanely than among other people groups remains debated.

Emerson B. Powery

designated her for himself, then he shall let her be redeemed; he shall have no right to sell her to a foreign people, since he has dealt unfairly with her. ⁹If he designates her for his son, he shall deal with her as with a daughter. ¹⁰If he takes another wife to himself, he shall not diminish the food, clothing, or marital rights of the first wife.ⁿ ¹¹And if he does not do these three things for her, she shall go out without debt, without payment of money.

12 "Whoever strikes a person mortally

shall be put to death. ¹³If it was not premeditated but came about by an act of God, then I will appoint for you a place to which the killer may flee. ¹⁴But if someone willfully attacks and kills another by treachery, you shall take the killer from my altar for execution.

15 "Whoever strikes father or mother shall be put to death.

16 "Whoever kidnaps a person, whether

n 21.10 Heb *of her*

be permanent) if she does not *please* her master. She can be redeemed—which is to say, bought back—by her family.

21:12–13 The homicide legislation recognizes both premeditated murder and unintentional homicide. The Decalogue forbids murder but lacks any discussion of what happens when the law is violated. The book of the covenant specifies here that premeditated murder is punishable by death. A person who commits unintentional homicide, by contrast, is provided asylum. Other legislation calls for the creation of cities of asylum, where unintentional killers may flee (see, e.g., Num. 35:6–15; Josh. 20:7–9).

21:15–17 Physical and verbal abuse of parents is especially heinous, punishable by death. Such legislation rounds out the more laconic injunction to honor one's father and mother in the Decalogue. **21:16** See 20:15.

that person has been sold or is still held in possession, shall be put to death.

17 "Whoever curses father or mother shall be put to death.

18 "When individuals quarrel and one strikes the other with a stone or fist so that the injured party, though not dead, is confined to bed ¹⁹but recovers and walks around outside with the help of a staff, then the assailant shall be free of liability, except to pay for the loss of time and to arrange for full recovery.

20 "When a slaveowner strikes a male or female slave with a rod and the slave dies immediately, the owner shall be punished. ²¹But if the slave survives a day or two, there is no punishment, for the slave is the owner's property.

22 "When people who are fighting injure a pregnant woman so that there is a miscarriage and yet no further harm follows, the one responsible shall be fined what the woman's husband demands, paying as much as the judges determine. ²³If any harm follows, then you shall give life for life, ²⁴eye for eye, tooth for tooth, hand for hand, foot for foot, ²⁵burn for burn, wound for wound, stripe for stripe.

26 "When a slaveowner strikes the eye of a male or female slave, destroying it, the owner shall let the slave go, a free person, to compensate for the eye. ²⁷If the owner knocks out a tooth of a male or female slave, the slave shall be let go, a free person, to compensate for the tooth.

28 "When an ox gores a man or a woman to death, the ox shall be stoned, and its flesh shall not be eaten, but the owner of the ox shall not be liable. ²⁹If the ox has been accustomed to gore in the past and its owner has been warned but did not restrain it, and it kills a man or a woman, the ox shall be stoned, and its owner also shall be put to death. ³⁰If a ransom is imposed on the owner, then the owner shall pay whatever is imposed for the redemption of the victim's life. ³¹If it gores a boy or a girl, the owner shall be dealt with according to this same rule. ³²If the ox gores a male or female slave, the owner shall pay to the slaveowner thirty shekels of silver, and the ox shall be stoned.

33 "If someone leaves a pit open or digs a pit and does not cover it, and an ox or a donkey falls into it, ³⁴the owner of the pit shall make restitution, giving money to its owner but keeping the dead animal.

35 "If someone's ox hurts the ox of another, so that it dies, then they shall sell the live ox and divide the price of it, and the dead animal they shall also divide. ³⁶But if it was known that the ox was accustomed to gore in the past and its owner did not restrain it, the owner shall restore ox for ox but keep the dead animal.

22 ᵒ"When someone steals an ox or a sheep and slaughters it or sells it, the

o 22.1 21.37 in Heb

21:18–21 The specificity of these laws reflects the nature of case law, arising out of real-life experiences. The language used here—*shall be punished* (v. 20) but not put to death—suggests the lesser value of enslaved persons' lives because they are seen as *the owner's property* (v. 21).

21:22 This law is consistent with ancient Near Eastern legal collections that also require compensation for the loss of the fetus.

21:23 *If any harm follows* most likely refers to additional harm to, or the death of, the mother.

21:24 *Eye for eye, tooth for tooth* is an example of the law of retaliation, "lex talionis," where the punishment must fit the crime: no more, no less. In addition to making sure punishment is just, not cruel or unusual, this type of law prohibits the wealthy from simply buying their way out of punishment. No monetary price can be put on human life.

21:26–27 *Eye . . . tooth*, and presumably other body parts as well. Compensatory damage for a debt slave's eye or tooth is freedom, a reminder of the servant's inherent value apart from the debt owed the master. The biblical legislation makes no room for justifiable injury of a debt slave—a situation that has no counterpart in ancient Near Eastern legal collections.

21:28–32 The goring ox legislation is a striking example of the specificity of case law. Three scenarios are given: an animal who injures for the first time, an animal that has harmed before and its owner is aware of the same, and an animal that harms a debt slave. **21:29** Owners are expected to be responsible for repeated aggressive animal behavior. See also 21:36.

22:1–4 Restitution for one who *steals* recalls the commandment from the Decalogue that in an ideal world, there would be no theft (see 20:15). The legislation for a thief caught in the act considers

thief shall pay five oxen for an ox and four sheep for a sheep. ²ᵖ(If the thief is found breaking in and is struck dead, no bloodguilt is incurred; ³but if it happens after sunrise, bloodguilt is incurred.) The thief shall make full restitution or, if unable to do so, shall be sold for the theft. ⁴When the animal, whether ox or donkey or sheep, is found alive in the thief's possession, the thief shall pay double.

5 "When someone causes a field or vineyard to be grazed over or lets livestock loose to graze in someone else's field, restitution shall be made from the best in the owner's field or vineyard.

6 "When fire breaks out and catches in thorns so that the stacked grain or the standing grain or the field is consumed, the one who started the fire shall make full restitution.

7 "When someone delivers to a neighbor money or goods for safekeeping and they are stolen from the neighbor's house, then the thief, if caught, shall pay double. ⁸If the thief is not caught, the owner of the house shall be brought before God, to determine whether or not the owner had laid hands on the neighbor's goods.

9 "In any case of disputed ownership involving ox, donkey, sheep, clothing, or any other loss, of which one party says, 'This is mine,' the case of both parties shall come before God; the one whom God condemns shall pay double to the other.

10 "When someone delivers to another a donkey, ox, sheep, or any other animal for safekeeping and it dies or is injured or is carried off without anyone seeing it, ¹¹an oath before the Lord shall decide between the two of them that the one has not laid hands on the property of the other; the owner shall accept the oath, and no restitution shall be made. ¹²But if it was stolen, restitution shall be made to its owner. ¹³If it was mangled by beasts, let it be brought as evidence; restitution shall not be made for the mangled remains.

14 "When someone borrows an animal from another and it is injured or dies, the owner not being present, full restitution shall be made. ¹⁵If the owner was present, there shall be no restitution; if it was hired, only the hiring fee is due.

16 "When a man seduces a virgin who is not engaged to be married and lies with her, he shall give the bride-price for her and make her his wife. ¹⁷But if her father refuses to give her to him, he shall pay an amount equal to the bride-price for virgins.

18 "You shall not permit a female sorcerer to live.

19 "Whoever has intercourse with an animal shall be put to death.

20 "Whoever sacrifices to any god other than the Lord alone shall be devoted to destruction.

p 22.2 22.1 in Heb

the time of the theft and the possible consequences, including restitution for the owner as well as the owner's culpability if the thief is killed. *Bloodguilt* here means unjustified homicide.

22:7–11 Both cases require that an individual or party come *before God*, which suggests swearing under oath (cf. 18:22–25) and/or an expectation of some type of divine oracle, as in v. 9.

22:16–17 This legislation about a young woman being seduced follows rules about compensation for lost property. *Seduces* means deceive or entice. This law offers a way for a man who takes a woman sexually and then marries her to make restitution via a bride-price to the woman's father. Comparable legislation in Deut. 22:28–29 addresses a case of a man who "seizes" a young woman who is unengaged, which implies rape, as opposed to one who *seduces* a young woman who is not engaged. The law in Exodus is disturbing, regardless, because the woman in question is likely young and with little or no power. Indeed, the law, which places a price on a woman's virginity, reflects a significantly different (and lower) legal status for unmarried women who are still a part of their father's household.

22:18 The specificity of the diviner's gender here may be another example of a law that results from a particular case, or it may reflect an intentional emphasis on women's association with certain forms of divination (cf. Deut. 18:10–14, which appears more gender inclusive).

22:19 This prohibition appears in the Holiness Code of Leviticus as well (see Lev. 18:23; 20:15–16).

22:20 This can be seen as an elaboration of 20:5, the prohibition of having other gods. The language of *devoted to destruction* is somewhat unclear, though in some cases where this verb is found elsewhere, the action appears to involve capital punishment.

21 "You shall not wrong or oppress a resident alien, for you were aliens in the land of Egypt. [22]You shall not abuse any widow or orphan. [23]If you do abuse them, when they cry out to me, I will surely heed their cry; [24]my wrath will burn, and I will kill you with the sword, and your wives shall become widows and your children orphans.

25 "If you lend money to my people, to the poor among you, you shall not deal with them as a creditor; you shall not exact interest from them. [26]If you take your neighbor's cloak as guarantee, you shall restore it before the sun goes down, [27]for it may be your neighbor's only clothing to use as a cover. In what else shall that person sleep? And when your neighbor cries out to me, I will listen, for I am compassionate.

28 "You shall not revile God or curse a leader of your people.

29 "You shall not delay to make offerings from the fullness of your harvest and from the outflow of your presses.[q]

"The firstborn of your sons you shall give to me. [30]You shall do the same with your oxen and with your sheep: seven days it shall remain with its mother; on the eighth day you shall give it to me.

31 "You shall be people consecrated to me, so you shall not eat any meat that is mangled by beasts in the field; you shall throw it to the dogs.

23 "You shall not spread a false report. You shall not join hands with the wicked to act as a malicious witness. [2]You shall not follow a majority in wrongdoing; when you bear witness in a lawsuit, you shall not side with the majority so as to pervert justice,[r] [3]nor shall you be partial to the poor in a lawsuit.

4 "When you come upon your enemy's ox or donkey going astray, you shall bring it back.

5 "When you see the donkey of one who hates you struggling under its burden and you would hold back from setting it free, you must help to set it free.

6 "You shall not pervert the justice due to your poor in their lawsuits. [7]Keep far from a false charge, and do not kill the innocent and those in the right, for I will not acquit the guilty. [8]You shall take no bribe, for a bribe blinds officials and subverts the cause of those who are in the right.

9 "You shall not oppress a resident alien; you know the heart of an alien, for you were aliens in the land of Egypt.

10 "Six years you shall sow your land and gather in its yield, [11]but the seventh year you shall let it rest and lie fallow so that the poor of your people may eat, and what they leave

q 22.29 Meaning of Heb uncertain   r 23.2 Gk: Heb lacks justice

22:21–27 In these regulations, there is protection for those with less agency and power. Care for the triad of *aliens* (immigrants), widows, and orphans is a recurrent trope in biblical law that has been foundational to its message of social justice. 22:21 On the language of *alien*, see note at 2:22. The Israelites' treatment of aliens (immigrants) is rooted in their own experience of being immigrants in Egypt. The commandment thus depends on and invites Israel into empathy. 22:22–27 God promises to hear the cry of the oppressed and act on their behalf against their oppressors, even within Israel itself. Israel's special status as a covenant partner with God does not make Israel exempt from punishment if and whenever they oppress others, especially widows, orphans, and immigrants (see 22:21, 23; cf. 2:22). Although *interest* could be expected of some (v. 25), it should not be expected of economically poorer Israelites.

22:29–30 The first fruits, animate and inanimate, belong to God in principle. In this passage, the required action is to *give* them to God (cf. 13:11–16, which uses the verb "set apart"). Some interpreters understand 22:29 to support the practice of designating the firstborn son to priestly service.

22:31 Consecration to God includes dietary laws.

23:1–3 Justice in legal settings may relate to the earlier prohibition in the Decalogue against bearing false witness against a neighbor in a legal setting (cf. 20:16).

23:4–7 Justice is to be extended even to one's enemies. The formation of Israel as God's covenant people includes the imperative that justice is also for enemies and the poor.

23:9 Justice extends to outsiders and *aliens* (see note at 2:22). The command to give proper treatment to immigrants often comes with a reminder that Israel itself was once *aliens*. In this way, the law warns the community against forgetting its past.

23:10–12 The concept of rest and cessation of work that is symbolized by and enacted on the Sabbath is for the entire creation. The law includes provisions for the land's own rest: fallow ground

the wild animals may eat. You shall do the same with your vineyard and with your olive orchard.

12 "Six days you shall do your work, but on the seventh day you shall rest so that your ox and your donkey may have relief and your homeborn slave and the resident alien may be refreshed. [13]Be attentive to all that I have said to you. Do not invoke the names of other gods; do not let them be heard on your lips.

14 "Three times in the year you shall hold a festival for me. [15]You shall observe the Festival of Unleavened Bread; as I commanded you, you shall eat unleavened bread for seven days at the appointed time in the month of Abib, for in it you came out of Egypt.

"No one shall appear before me empty-handed.

16 "You shall observe the Festival of Harvest, of the first fruits of your labor, of what you sow in the field. You shall observe the Festival of Ingathering at the end of the year, when you gather in from the field the fruit of your labor. [17]Three times in the year all your males shall appear before the Lord GOD.

18 "You shall not offer the blood of my sacrifice with anything leavened or let the fat of my festival remain until the morning.

19 "The choicest of the first fruits of your ground you shall bring into the house of the LORD your God.

"You shall not boil a kid in its mother's milk.

20 "I am going to send an angel in front of you, to guard you on the way and to bring you to the place that I have prepared. [21]Be attentive to him and listen to his voice; do not rebel against him, for he will not pardon your transgression, for my name is in him.

22 "But if you listen attentively to his voice and do all that I say, then I will be an enemy to your enemies and a foe to your foes.

23 "When my angel goes in front of you and brings you to the Amorites, the Hittites, the Perizzites, the Canaanites, the Hivites, and the Jebusites, and I blot them out, [24]you shall not bow down to their gods or serve them or follow their practices, but you shall utterly demolish them and break their pillars in pieces. [25]You shall serve the LORD your God, and I[s] will bless your bread and your water, and I will take sickness away from among you. [26]No one shall miscarry or be barren in your land; I will fulfill the number of your days. [27]I will send my terror in front of you and will throw into confusion all the people against whom you shall come, and I will make all your enemies turn their backs to you. [28]And I will send swarms of hornets[t] in front of you, which shall drive out the Hivites, the Canaanites, and the Hittites from before you. [29]I will not drive them out from

s 23.25 Gk Vg: Heb *he*   *t* 23.28 Meaning of Heb uncertain

allows the soil to recover and be replenished. Moreover, Sabbath legislation for the land assumes that not all that is planted is solely for the landowner or farmer. Finally, when the land lies fallow, the poor may harvest. In this way, there is provision for all. On "Sabbath," see note at 20:8–11. *Homeborn slave* is a rare formulation (cf. Jer. 2:14) and may simply clarify that all members of the household, including debt servants of whatever generation, are included in the Sabbath rest.

23:15 The Festival of Unleavened Bread precedes the spring grain harvest and is the first of three major festivals. The month *Abib* (ca. March–April) was renamed Nisan in the postbiblical period.

23:16 The second festival, the Festival of Harvest, is also known as the Feast of Weeks because it takes place seven weeks after the spring harvest begins. Later Greek-speaking Jews called this festival Pentecost, since the holiday happens on the day after the seventh week (forty-nine days). The third festival, the Festival of Ingathering, takes place after the fall harvest. It is also known as the Festival of Booths (or Tabernacles). According to Lev. 23:42–43, the booths recall the way Israel lived in huts when they came out of Egypt.

23:17 *All your males* indicates the male-centered orientation of this legislation (cf. 20:17).

23:20–33 The final unit in the book of the covenant looks forward to the entry to the land of Canaan, forging a connection between obedience to the law and God's actions on Israel's behalf. The language that describes the Israelites' entry to the land is militaristic, with the inhabitants described as enemies (v. 27). **23:20** The presence of *an angel* is listed here as one who will protect and guide the people and communicate with them (cf. 23:23; 32:34; 33:2). **23:21** *My name is in him* indicates the authority of this messenger. **23:24** The admonition to *not bow down to their gods* recalls the Decalogue's commandment that in an ideal world, this would not occur (20:3–4).

before you in one year, lest the land become desolate and the wild animals multiply against you. ³⁰Little by little I will drive them out from before you, until you have increased and possess the land. ³¹I will set your borders from the Red Sea" to the sea of the Philistines and from the wilderness to the Euphrates, for I will hand over to you the inhabitants of the land, and you shall drive them out before you. ³²You shall make no covenant with them and their gods. ³³They shall not live in your land, lest they make you sin against me, for if you serve their gods, it will surely be a snare to you."

24 Then he said to Moses, "Come up to the LORD, you and Aaron, Nadab and Abihu, and seventy of the elders of Israel, and worship at a distance. ²Moses alone shall come near the LORD, but the others shall not come near, and the people shall not come up with him."

3 Moses went and told the people all the words of the LORD and all the ordinances, and all the people answered with one voice and said, "All the words that the LORD has spoken we will do." ⁴And Moses wrote down all the words of the LORD. He rose early in the morning, built an altar at the foot of the mountain, and set up twelve pillars, corresponding to the twelve tribes of Israel. ⁵He sent young men of the Israelites, who offered burnt offerings and sacrificed oxen as offerings of well-being to the LORD. ⁶Moses took half of the blood and put it in basins, and half of the blood he dashed against the altar. ⁷Then he took the book of the covenant and read it in the hearing of the

people, and they said, "All that the LORD has spoken we will do, and we will be obedient." ⁸Moses took the blood and dashed it on the people, and said, "Here is the blood of the covenant that the LORD has made with you in accordance with all these words."

9 Then Moses and Aaron, Nadab and Abihu, and seventy of the elders of Israel went up, ¹⁰and they saw the God of Israel. Under his feet there was something like a pavement of sapphire stone, like the very heaven for clearness. ¹¹God ᵛ did not lay his hand on the chief men of the Israelites; they beheld God, and they ate and drank.

12 The LORD said to Moses, "Come up to me on the mountain and wait there; I will give you the tablets of stone, with the law and the commandment, which I have written for their instruction." ¹³So Moses set out with his assistant Joshua, and Moses went up onto the mountain of God. ¹⁴To the elders he had said, "Wait here for us, until we come back to you. Look, Aaron and Hur are with you; whoever has a dispute may go to them."

15 Then Moses went up on the mountain, and the cloud covered the mountain. ¹⁶The glory of the LORD settled on Mount Sinai, and the cloud covered it for six days; on the seventh day he called to Moses out of the cloud. ¹⁷Now the appearance of the glory of the LORD was like a devouring fire on the top of the mountain in the sight of the Israelites. ¹⁸Moses entered the cloud and went up on the mountain. Moses was on the mountain for forty days and forty nights.

u 23.31 Or *Sea of Reeds*   v 24.11 Heb *He*

24:1–8 The covenant or treaty (see **"Covenant (Genesis 6)," p. 23**) that has been given is ratified in this ritual. 24:1 Nadab and Abihu are Aaron's eldest sons (6:23). The number seventy is symbolic and conveys completion. The complement of elders and Aaron's sons approach the mountain but remain at a distance. 24:2 Moses ascends alone, emphasizing his special role as sole mediator of the covenant. 24:3 The people verbally agree to the covenant (see also v. 7). 24:4 The writing or recording of the covenant is a part of the ratification process. 24:5–8 The covenant agreement is sealed with sacrificial blood.

24:9–18 The covenant is celebrated as Moses and the elders have a meal with God on the mountain. Close encounters with God are dangerous (see 19:21; 20:19), so it is remarkable that in this passage, the leaders not only *saw* but also *beheld* the God of Israel (vv. 10–11). This may suggest a deeper kind of prolonged visionary experience. 24:10 Sapphire stone is also mentioned in Ezekiel's vision of God (Ezek. 1:26). 24:13–14 *Joshua*, not Aaron, is the only one to join Moses farther up the mountain. On his role, see note at 17:9. 24:17 *The appearance of the glory of the LORD.* The language attempts to describe a supernatural appearance in natural terms, including that of a consuming fire, which likely conveys power and purity. 24:18 *Forty days and forty nights.* A common symbolic number that indicates a significant period of time.

25 The Lord said to Moses, [2]"Tell the Israelites to take for me an offering; from all whose hearts prompt them to give you shall receive the offering for me. [3]This is the offering that you shall receive from them: gold, silver, and bronze, [4]blue, purple, and crimson yarns and fine linen, goats' hair, [5]tanned rams' skins, fine leather,[w] acacia wood, [6]oil for the lamps, spices for the anointing oil and for the fragrant incense, [7]onyx stones and gems to be set in the ephod and for the breastpiece. [8]And they shall make me a sanctuary so that I may dwell among them. [9]In accordance with all that I show you concerning the pattern of the tabernacle and of all its furniture, so you shall make it.

10 "They shall make an ark of acacia wood; it shall be two and a half cubits long, a cubit and a half wide, and a cubit and a half high. [11]You shall overlay it with pure gold, inside and outside you shall overlay it, and you shall make a molding of gold upon it all around. [12]You shall cast four rings of gold for it and put them on its four feet, two rings on one side of it and two rings on the other side. [13]You shall make poles of acacia wood and overlay them with gold. [14]And you shall put the poles into the rings on the sides of the ark, for carrying the ark. [15]The poles shall remain in the rings of the ark; they shall not be removed. [16]You shall put the covenant that I am giving you into the ark.

17 "Then you shall make a cover of pure gold; two cubits and a half shall be its length and a cubit and a half its width. [18]You shall make two cherubim of gold; you shall make them of hammered work at the two ends of the cover. [19]Make one cherub at one end and one cherub at the other; of one piece with the cover you shall make the cherubim at its two ends. [20]The cherubim shall spread out their wings above, overshadowing the cover with their wings. They shall face one to another; the faces of the cherubim shall be turned

w 25.5 Meaning of Heb uncertain

25:1–31:18 The final fifteen chapters of Exodus may be subdivided into three large units: instructions for the tabernacle (25:1–31:18), the golden calf incident (32:1–34:35), and the construction of the tabernacle (35:1–40:38). The final third of Exodus is thus about worship and God's presence (see 5:3).

25:1 The formula of divine address occurs six times in the instructions for the tabernacle (25:1; 30:11, 17, 22, 34; 31:1), a kind of structural allusion to the six days of creation in Gen. 1, which emphasizes God's creative power in the wilderness. Chap. 25 is the first in a larger unit containing instructions for building the tabernacle. The unit begins with the ark of the covenant, the table, the lampstand, and various items inside the holy place and the most holy place. The materials for making the tabernacle and its implements come from the donations by the people. The sheer quantity and rich quality of the materials provided for the tabernacle stand in strongest contrast to the harsh realities of the wilderness. The tabernacle is an alternative universe.

25:3 Precious metals are listed here in descending order of value. The materials for the tabernacle structure include metals, yarn, fabric, leather, wood, oil, spices, and precious stones.

25:5 The Hebrew term for skins here is unusual and uncertain. It could refer to the skin of an animal or to a yellow or orange color.

25:8 The purpose of the tabernacle is to permit God's dwelling among the people. The topic of God's presence runs throughout the final sections of Exodus.

25:9 The instructions for the tabernacle in all their specific detail come directly from God. Similarly, 1 Chr. 28:11–19 indicates that David received the instructions for the (later) temple from God. These buildings are sacred from their initial conception and design.

25:10–22 Instructions for the ark of the covenant. The ark of the covenant is a chest that, once constructed, will reside in the most holy place within the tabernacle. The ark houses the two tablets containing the Ten Commandments. Two other sacred items—a container of manna (16:32) and Aaron's rod (Num. 17:1–10)—were also associated with the ark. In some traditions, these items are placed in the ark along with the Decalogue. **25:10** The word for cubit comes from the word for forearm; a cubit is around eighteen inches, or forty-five centimeters. *Two and a half cubits long, a cubit and a half wide, and a cubit and a half high* is approximately 3¾ feet long by 2¼ feet wide and 2¼ feet high. **25:17** The word describing the cover of the ark is related to a verb that means to reconcile or atone. Inherent in this cover is thus some sense of reconciliation and atonement. **25:18** A range of creatures in the ancient Near East seem to qualify as what the Bible describes as cherubim. Some

toward the cover. ²¹You shall put the cover on the top of the ark, and in the ark you shall put the covenant that I am giving you. ²²There I will meet with you, and from above the cover, from between the two cherubim that are on the ark of the covenant, I will tell you all that I am commanding you for the Israelites.

23 "You shall make a table of acacia wood, two cubits long, one cubit wide, and a cubit and a half high. ²⁴You shall overlay it with pure gold and make a molding of gold around it. ²⁵You shall make around it a rim a handbreadth wide and a molding of gold around the rim. ²⁶You shall make for it four rings of gold and fasten the rings to the four corners at its four legs. ²⁷The rings that hold the poles used for carrying the table shall be close to the rim. ²⁸You shall make the poles of acacia wood and overlay them with gold, and the table shall be carried with these. ²⁹You shall make its plates and dishes and its flagons and bowls with which to pour drink offerings; you shall make them of pure gold. ³⁰And you shall set the bread of the Presence on the table before me continually.

31 "You shall make a lampstand of pure gold. The base and the shaft of the lampstand shall be made of hammered work; its cups, its calyxes, and its petals shall be of one piece with it; ³²and there shall be six branches going out of its sides: three branches of the lampstand out of one side of it and three branches of the lampstand out of the other side of it; ³³three cups shaped like almond blossoms, each with calyx and petals, on one branch, and three cups shaped like almond blossoms, each with calyx and petals, on the other branch—so for the six branches going out of the lampstand. ³⁴On the lampstand itself there shall be four cups shaped like almond blossoms, each with its calyxes and petals. ³⁵There shall be a calyx of one piece with it under the first pair of branches, a calyx of one piece with it under the next pair of branches, and a calyx of one piece with it under the last pair of branches—so for the six branches that go out of the lampstand. ³⁶Their calyxes and their branches shall be of one piece with it, the whole of it one hammered piece of pure gold. ³⁷You shall make seven lamps for it, and the lamps shall be set up so as to give light on the space in front of it. ³⁸Its snuffers and trays shall be of pure gold. ³⁹It and all these utensils shall be made from a talent of pure gold. ⁴⁰And see that you make them according to the pattern for them, which is being shown you on the mountain.

26 "The tabernacle itself you shall make with ten curtains of fine twisted

have multiple faces, others are part human and part animal, and all are winged. The cherubim that are stationed on the two ends of the cover of the ark of the covenant extend their wings over the cover and meet, forming a seat or throne for God's glory. Psalms 80:1 and 99:1 refer to God as sitting or being enthroned "upon the cherubim."

25:30 The bread of the presence refers to twelve loaves of bread (perhaps one per tribe) placed on a table in the tabernacle as a token offering. Every Sabbath, the priest lays out the bread as a sign of the people's covenant with God. According to Lev. 24:5–9, this bread was consumed by the priests as a holy portion of food for them. David and his soldiers are reported to have eaten this bread when they were at Nob (see 1 Sam. 21:2–7).

25:31 The lampstand has a center column with three offshoots on each side for a total of seven lights. The word for these offshoots comes from the word for cane, reed, or stalk; the shape of the lampstand and its language thus evoke a tree.

25:32 Seven is a number of completion and perfection.

25:33 The almond tree is an early-blossoming tree in Israel, and almonds are "choice" products of Canaan (see Gen. 43:11).

26:1–14 The plans for the tabernacle are exceedingly detailed, with extensive discussion of both materials and measurements. The frame of the tabernacle space is covered with four layers. The details lend themselves to models and floorplans of this sacred space. 26:1 The Hebrew word for tabernacle means "dwelling place"; the structure is the physical manifestation and reminder of God's presence. The fact that this sacred space is mobile means that the people can access God beyond and far from the designated holy mountain of God, Sinai. For later audiences in exile and without a temple, the tabernacle is a reminder that God is not limited to the temple. *Twisted linen* refers to a weaving technique that is repeated at 26:36. The embroidered curtain within the tabernacle is the threshold between the holy place and the most holy place, where the ark resides.

linen and blue, purple, and crimson yarns; you shall make them with cherubim skillfully worked into them. [2]The length of each curtain shall be twenty-eight cubits and the width of each curtain four cubits; all the curtains shall be of the same size. [3]Five curtains shall be joined to one another, and the other five curtains shall be joined to one another. [4]You shall make loops of blue on the edge of the outermost curtain in the first set, and likewise you shall make loops on the edge of the outermost curtain in the second set. [5]You shall make fifty loops on the one curtain, and you shall make fifty loops on the edge of the curtain that is in the second set; the loops shall be opposite one another. [6]You shall make fifty clasps of gold and join the curtains to one another with the clasps, so that the tabernacle may be one whole.

7 "You shall also make curtains of goats' hair for a tent over the tabernacle; you shall make eleven curtains. [8]The length of each curtain shall be thirty cubits and the width of each curtain four cubits; the eleven curtains shall be of the same size. [9]You shall join five curtains by themselves and six curtains by themselves, and the sixth curtain you shall double over at the front of the tent. [10]You shall make fifty loops on the edge of the curtain that is outermost in one set and fifty loops on the edge of the curtain that is outermost in the second set.

11 "You shall make fifty clasps of bronze and put the clasps into the loops and join the tent together, so that it may be one whole. [12]The part that remains of the curtains of the tent, the half curtain that remains, shall hang over the back of the tabernacle. [13]The cubit on one side and the cubit on the other side of what remains in the length of the curtains of the tent shall hang over the sides of the tabernacle, on this side and that side, to cover it. [14]You shall make for the tent a covering of tanned rams' skins and an outer covering of fine leather.[x]

15 "You shall make upright frames of acacia wood for the tabernacle. [16]Ten cubits shall be the length of a frame and a cubit and a half the width of each frame. [17]There shall be two pegs in each frame to fit the frames together; you shall make these for all the frames of the tabernacle. [18]You shall make the frames for the tabernacle: twenty frames for the south side; [19]and you shall make forty bases of silver under the twenty frames: two bases under the first frame for its two pegs and two bases under the next frame for its two pegs; [20]and for the second side of the tabernacle, on the north side twenty frames, [21]and their forty bases of silver: two bases under the first frame and two bases under the next frame; [22]and for the rear of the tabernacle westward you shall make six frames. [23]You shall make two frames for corners of the tabernacle in the rear; [24]they shall be separate beneath but joined at the top at the first ring; it shall be the same with both of them; they shall form the two corners. [25]And so there shall be eight frames, with their bases of silver, sixteen bases: two bases under the first frame and two bases under the next frame.

26 "You shall make bars of acacia wood: five for the frames of one side of the tabernacle, [27]and five bars for the frames of the other side of the tabernacle, and five bars for the frames of the side of the tabernacle at the rear westward. [28]The middle bar, halfway up the frames, shall pass through from end to end. [29]You shall overlay the frames with gold and shall make their rings of gold to hold the bars, and you shall overlay the bars with gold. [30]Then you shall erect the tabernacle according to the plan for it that you were shown on the mountain.

31 "You shall make a curtain of blue, purple, and crimson yarns and of fine twisted linen; it shall be made with cherubim skillfully worked into it. [32]You shall hang it on four

x 26.14 Meaning of Heb uncertain

26:2 On *cubits*, see note at 25:10. 26:4 The term for loops is used only in connection with the tabernacle. 26:6 The term for clasps is also unique to the tabernacle narrative. 26:7–9 Curtain panels make for ease of transport.

26:15 The frames for the tabernacle are made of acacia wood with gold overlay. Of the many varieties of acacia tree, only a few types would be suitable for making the frames described here.

26:23 Frames at each end of the western wall cover the open space in the rear.

26:30 This verse recalls that the plans for the tabernacle were given at Sinai (see 25:40). The tabernacle measured 30 × 30 × 10 cubits or approximately 45 feet × 45 feet × 15 feet.

pillars of acacia overlaid with gold, which have hooks of gold and rest on four bases of silver. [33]You shall hang the curtain under the clasps and bring the ark of the covenant in there, within the curtain, and the curtain shall separate for you the holy place from the most holy place. [34]You shall put the cover on the ark of the covenant in the most holy place. [35]You shall set the table outside the curtain and the lampstand on the south side of the tabernacle opposite the table, and you shall put the table on the north side.

36 "You shall make a screen for the entrance of the tent, of blue, purple, and crimson yarns and of fine twisted linen, embroidered with needlework. [37]You shall make for the screen five pillars of acacia and overlay them with gold; their hooks shall be of gold, and you shall cast five bases of bronze for them.

27 "You shall make the altar of acacia wood, five cubits long and five cubits wide; the altar shall be square, and it shall be three cubits high. [2]You shall make horns for it on its four corners; its horns shall be of one piece with it, and you shall overlay it with bronze. [3]You shall make pots for its ashes and shovels and basins and forks and firepans; you shall make all its utensils of bronze. [4]You shall also make for it a grating, a network of bronze, and on the net you shall make four bronze rings at its four corners. [5]You shall set it under the ledge of the altar so that the net shall extend halfway down the altar. [6]You shall make poles for the altar, poles of acacia

wood, and overlay them with bronze; [7]the poles shall be put through the rings, so that the poles shall be on the two sides of the altar when it is carried. [8]You shall make it hollow, with boards. They shall be made just as you were shown on the mountain.

9 "You shall make the court of the tabernacle. On the south side the court shall have hangings of fine twisted linen one hundred cubits long for that side; [10]its twenty pillars and their twenty bases shall be of bronze, but the hooks of the pillars and their bands shall be of silver. [11]Likewise for its length on the north side there shall be hangings one hundred cubits long, their pillars twenty and their bases twenty, of bronze, but the hooks of the pillars and their bands shall be of silver. [12]For the width of the court on the west side there shall be fifty cubits of hangings, with ten pillars and ten bases. [13]The width of the court on the front to the east shall be fifty cubits. [14]There shall be fifteen cubits of hangings on one side, with three pillars and three bases. [15]There shall be fifteen cubits of[y] hangings on the other side, with three pillars and three bases. [16]For the gate of the court there shall be a screen twenty cubits long, of blue, purple, and crimson yarns and of fine twisted linen, embroidered with needlework; it shall have four pillars and with them four bases. [17]All the pillars around the court shall be banded with silver; their hooks shall be of silver and their bases of bronze. [18]The length of the court shall be one hundred cubits, the width fifty,

y 27.15 Gk Sam: MT lacks *cubits of*

26:33 The tabernacle has three sections or areas: the courtyard for all the people, the holy place, and the most holy place. These sections may correspond to the three zones at Mount Sinai. The people gathered at the bottom of the mountain, where the altar was, like the courtyard of the tabernacle with its altar. The mountain itself was accessible only by the priests and elders, similar to the tabernacle's holy place. Finally, only Moses went to the top of the mountain; only the high priest was permitted to enter the most holy place and then only once a year.

27:1 A sacrificial altar covered in bronze is to be positioned across from the entrance to the tabernacle. Like the ark of the covenant, the altar will have rings for poles so that it can be easily carried.

27:2 The horns on the four corners of the altar were splattered with the blood of sacrificed animals. For the crime of unintentional homicide (manslaughter), an individual could seek asylum at the altar, grab onto its horns, and seek clemency. See Exod. 21:12–14; 1 Kgs. 1:50; 2:28–32. Altars with horns have been uncovered in archaeological excavations.

27:8 The recurring refrain that the instructions for the tabernacle came from Mount Sinai speaks to the holiness and otherworldliness of this building. Other ancient Near Eastern cultures also credit the gods with plans for holy places.

27:9 The courtyard, or uncovered outer court, measures 50 × 100 cubits or approximately 75 feet × 100 feet with the short sides facing east and west. It surrounds the tabernacle structure on the west side and the altar on the east side. The entrance to the tabernacle is on the east side.

and the height five cubits, with hangings of fine twisted linen and bases of bronze. ¹⁹All the utensils of the tabernacle for every use, and all its pegs and all the pegs of the court, shall be of bronze.

20 "You shall further command the Israelites to bring you pure oil of beaten olives for the light, so that a lamp may be set up to burn continually. ²¹In the tent of meeting, outside the curtain that is before the covenant, Aaron and his sons shall tend it from evening to morning before the LORD. It shall be a perpetual ordinance to be observed throughout their generations by the Israelites.

28 "Then bring near to you your brother Aaron and his sons with him, from among the Israelites, to serve me as priests—Aaron and Aaron's sons: Nadab and Abihu, Eleazar and Ithamar. ²You shall make sacred vestments for the glorious adornment of your brother Aaron. ³And you shall speak to all who are skillful, whom I have endowed with skill, so that they make Aaron's vestments to consecrate him for my priesthood. ⁴These are the vestments that they shall make: a breastpiece, an ephod, a robe, a checkered tunic, a turban, and a sash. When they make these sacred vestments for your brother Aaron and his sons to serve me as priests, ⁵they shall use gold, blue, purple, and crimson yarns and fine linen.

6 "They shall make the ephod of gold, of blue, purple, and crimson yarns, and of fine twisted linen, skillfully worked. ⁷It shall have two shoulder pieces attached to its two edges,

so that it may be joined together. ⁸The decorated band on it shall be of the same workmanship and materials, of gold, of blue, purple, and crimson yarns, and of fine twisted linen. ⁹You shall take two onyx stones and engrave on them the names of the sons of Israel, ¹⁰six of their names on the one stone and the names of the remaining six on the other stone, in the order of their birth. ¹¹As a gem cutter engraves signets, so you shall engrave the two stones with the names of the sons of Israel; you shall mount them in settings of gold filigree. ¹²You shall set the two stones on the shoulder pieces of the ephod, as stones of remembrance for the sons of Israel, and Aaron shall bear their names before the LORD on his two shoulders for remembrance. ¹³You shall make settings of gold filigree ¹⁴and two chains of pure gold, twisted like cords, and you shall attach the corded chains to the settings.

15 "You shall make a breastpiece of judgment, in skilled work; you shall make it in the style of the ephod; of gold, of blue, purple, and crimson yarns, and of fine twisted linen you shall make it. ¹⁶It shall be square and doubled, a span in length and a span in width. ¹⁷You shall set in it four rows of stones. A row of carnelian, chrysolite, and emerald shall be the first row; ¹⁸and the second row a turquoise, a sapphire,ᶻ and a moonstone; ¹⁹and the third row a jacinth, an agate, and an amethyst; ²⁰and the fourth row a beryl, an onyx, and a jasper; they shall be set in gold

z 28.18 Or *lapis lazuli*

27:20–21 The lamp is to burn from evening to morning every night and is maintained by the priests (cf. 1 Sam. 3:3). *Aaron and his sons* are the key priestly figures responsible for the upkeep of the sacred spaces (cf. 6:23; 28:1–5). **27:21** *Tent of meeting* is another term used for the tabernacle.

28:1–5 The detailed description of the priestly vestments, like the materials used for the tabernacle, underscores the sacred nature of the priestly task and the holiness of the cult. Additional items are mentioned later in this chapter (see 28:36–38, 42–43). **28:1** *To you* implies that YHWH addresses Moses (only) and not the people here so that he would prepare Aaron and his sons as priests (see v. 41). *Nadab and Abihu* (cf. 24:1) and *Eleazar and Ithamar* are Aaron's sons (6:23). **28:4** *Checkered* here means fringed.

28:6 Several biblical texts refer to the ephod, which suggests that they existed in more than one type. Goliath's sword was kept behind an ephod at Nob (1 Sam. 21:9). An ephod could be used in divination; in Judges, Gideon's ephod led to the people's apostasy (Judg. 8:27). The ephod described in Exodus is most likely a long vest that fastened at the top and connected to the breastpiece.

28:6–12 The breastpiece lies on top of the ephod. It is a square with four rows, each containing three precious stones, which, all together, represent the twelve tribes. Whenever Aaron enters the holy place, he carries the names of the tribes of Israel "before the LORD" (v. 29).

28:15 The breastpiece of judgment holds the Urim and Thummim, items used for divination. See note at 28:30.

filigree. ²¹There shall be twelve stones with names corresponding to the names of the sons of Israel; they shall be like signets, each engraved with its name, for the twelve tribes. ²²You shall make for the breastpiece chains of pure gold, twisted like cords, ²³and you shall make for the breastpiece two rings of gold and put the two rings on the two edges of the breastpiece. ²⁴You shall put the two cords of gold in the two rings at the edges of the breastpiece; ²⁵the two ends of the two cords you shall attach to the two settings and so attach it in front to the shoulder pieces of the ephod. ²⁶You shall make two rings of gold and put them at the two ends of the breastpiece, on its inside edge next to the ephod.[a] ²⁷You shall make two rings of gold and attach them in front to the lower part of the two shoulder pieces of the ephod, at its joining above the decorated band of the ephod. ²⁸The breastpiece shall be bound by its rings to the rings of the ephod with a blue cord, so that it may lie on the decorated band of the ephod and so that the breastpiece shall not come loose from the ephod. ²⁹So Aaron shall bear the names of the sons of Israel in the breastpiece of judgment on his heart when he goes into the holy place, for a continual remembrance before the LORD. ³⁰In the breastpiece of judgment you shall put the Urim and the Thummim, and they shall be on Aaron's heart when he goes in before the LORD; thus Aaron shall bear the judgment of the Israelites on his heart before the LORD continually.

31 "You shall make the robe of the ephod all of blue. ³²It shall have an opening for the head in the middle of it, with a woven binding around its edge, like the opening in a garment,[b] so that it may not be torn. ³³On its lower hem you shall make pomegranates of blue, purple, and crimson yarns, all around the lower hem, with bells of gold between them all around— ³⁴a golden bell and a pomegranate alternating all around the lower hem of the robe. ³⁵Aaron shall wear it when he

ministers, and its sound shall be heard when he goes into the holy place before the LORD and when he comes out, so that he may not die.

36 "You shall make a rosette of pure gold and engrave on it, like the engraving of a signet, 'Holy to the LORD.' ³⁷You shall fasten it on the turban with a blue cord; it shall be on the front of the turban. ³⁸It shall be on Aaron's forehead, and Aaron shall take on himself any guilt incurred in the holy offerings that the Israelites consecrate as their sacred donations; it shall always be on his forehead, in order that they may find favor before the LORD.

39 "You shall make the checkered tunic of fine linen, and you shall make a turban of fine linen, and you shall make a sash embroidered with needlework.

40 "For Aaron's sons you shall make tunics and sashes and headdresses; you shall make them for their glorious adornment. ⁴¹You shall put them on your brother Aaron and on his sons with him and shall anoint them and ordain them and consecrate them, so that they may serve me as priests. ⁴²You shall make for them linen undergarments to cover their naked flesh; they shall reach from the hips to the thighs. ⁴³They shall be worn by Aaron and his sons when they go into the tent of meeting or when they come near the altar to minister in the holy place, so that they do not bring guilt on themselves and die. This shall be a perpetual ordinance for him and for his descendants after him.

29 "Now this is what you shall do to them to consecrate them to serve me as priests. Take one young bull and two rams without blemish, ²and unleavened bread, unleavened cakes mixed with oil, and unleavened wafers spread with oil. You shall make them of choice wheat flour. ³You shall

a 28.26 Meaning of Heb uncertain   b 28.32 Meaning of Heb uncertain

---

28:30 The Urim and Thummim are a kind of sacred dice or stones, which are cast for the purpose of divination. See 1 Sam. 14:41, when Saul seeks an answer from God by means of this practice. Note also Lev. 8:8; Num. 27:1; Deut. 33:8; 1 Sam. 28:6; Ezra 2:63; Neh. 7:65.

28:36–38 The rosette, a gold plate worn over the turban, is inscribed with the words *Holy to the* LORD. The phrase applies to the priest but perhaps also the people represented by the priest.

28:40–43 Attire for Aaron's sons: tunics, sashes, and headdresses. **28:42** The term for undergarments appears only with reference to priestly attire in the Bible. On nakedness, see also 20:26.

29:1 The act of consecration sets the priests apart from all others. The ordination process consists of ritual sacrifice, baptism, anointing, and dressing.

put them in one basket and bring them in the basket and bring the bull and the two rams. ⁴You shall bring Aaron and his sons to the entrance of the tent of meeting and wash them with water. ⁵Then you shall take the vestments and put on Aaron the tunic and the robe of the ephod and the ephod and the breastpiece and gird him with the decorated band of the ephod, ⁶and you shall set the turban on his head and put the holy diadem on the turban. ⁷You shall take the anointing oil and pour it on his head and anoint him. ⁸Then you shall bring his sons and put tunics on them, ⁹and you shall gird them, Aaron and his sons, with sashes and tie headdresses on them, and the priesthood shall be theirs by a perpetual ordinance. You shall then ordain Aaron and his sons.

10 "You shall bring the bull in front of the tent of meeting. Aaron and his sons shall lay their hands on the head of the bull, ¹¹and you shall slaughter the bull before the Lord, at the entrance of the tent of meeting, ¹²and shall take some of the blood of the bull and put it on the horns of the altar with your finger, and all the rest of the blood you shall pour out at the base of the altar. ¹³You shall take all the fat that covers the entrails and the appendage of the liver and the two kidneys with the fat that is on them and turn them into smoke on the altar. ¹⁴But the flesh of the bull and its skin and its dung you shall burn with fire outside the camp. It is a purification offering.

15 "Then you shall take one of the rams, and Aaron and his sons shall lay their hands on the head of the ram, ¹⁶and you shall slaughter the ram and shall take its blood and dash it against all sides of the altar. ¹⁷Then you shall cut the ram into its parts and wash its entrails and its legs and put them with its parts and its head ¹⁸and turn the rest of the ram into smoke on the altar. It is a burnt offering to the Lord; it is a pleasing odor, an offering by fire*c* to the Lord.

19 "You shall take the other ram, and Aaron and his sons shall lay their hands on the head of the ram, ²⁰and you shall slaughter the ram and take some of its blood and put it on the lobe of Aaron's right ear and on the lobes of the right ears of his sons and on the thumbs of their right hands and on the big toes of their right feet and dash the rest of the blood against all sides of the altar. ²¹Then you shall take some of the blood that is on the altar and some of the anointing oil and sprinkle it on Aaron and his vestments and on his sons and his sons' vestments with him; then he and his vestments shall be holy, as well as his sons and his sons' vestments with him.

22 "You shall also take the fat of the ram, the fatty tail, the fat that covers the entrails, the appendage of the liver, the two kidneys with the fat that is on them, and the right thigh (for it is a ram of ordination), ²³and one loaf of bread, one cake of bread made with oil, and one wafer, out of the basket of unleavened bread that is before the Lord, ²⁴and you shall place all these on the palms of Aaron and on the palms of his sons and raise them as an elevation offering before the Lord. ²⁵Then you shall take them from their hands and turn them into smoke on the altar on top of the burnt offering for a pleasing odor before the Lord. It is an offering by fire*d* to the Lord.

26 "You shall take the breast of the ram of Aaron's ordination and raise it as an elevation offering before the Lord, and it shall be your portion. ²⁷You shall consecrate the breast that was raised as an elevation offering and the thigh that was lifted up as an offering from the ram of ordination, from that which belonged to Aaron and his sons. ²⁸These things shall be a perpetual ordinance for Aaron and his sons from the Israelites, for this is an offering, and it shall be an offering by the Israelites from their sacrifice of offerings of well-being, their offering to the Lord.

29 "The sacred vestments of Aaron shall be passed on to his sons after him; they shall be anointed in them and ordained in them. ³⁰The son who is priest in his place shall wear them

c 29.18 Or *a gift*   d 29.25 Or *a gift*

29:10 The practice of laying hands on an animal may signal a transfer of guilt (Lev. 16:21–22).

29:15 See note for 29:10.

29:19 See note for 29:10.

29:20 Blood is placed on the ear, hand, and foot in the priestly purification rite. The hands and feet are extremities, perhaps signaling action, with the ear signifying hearing. If so, the priest's ability to correctly listen and then correctly do God's work is captured by the rite.

29:29 The priesthood is established as passing on through Aaron's family line.

29:30 Seven days signals wholeness and completeness.

seven days when he comes into the tent of meeting to minister in the holy place.

31 "You shall take the ram of ordination and boil its flesh in a holy place, ³²and Aaron and his sons shall eat the flesh of the ram and the bread that is in the basket at the entrance of the tent of meeting. ³³They shall eat the food by which atonement is made, to ordain and consecrate them, but no one else shall eat of it, because it is holy. ³⁴If any of the flesh for the ordination or of the bread remains until the morning, then you shall burn the remainder with fire; it shall not be eaten, because it is holy.

35 "Thus you shall do to Aaron and to his sons, just as I have commanded you; through seven days you shall ordain them. ³⁶Also every day you shall offer a bull as a purification offering for atonement. Also you shall offer a sin offering for the altar, when you make atonement for it, and shall anoint it, to consecrate it. ³⁷Seven days you shall make atonement for the altar and consecrate it, and the altar shall be most holy; whatever touches the altar shall become holy.

38 "Now this is what you shall offer on the altar: two lambs a year old regularly each day. ³⁹One lamb you shall offer in the morning, and the other lamb you shall offer in the evening, ⁴⁰and with the first lamb one-tenth of a measure of choice flour mixed with one-fourth of a hin of beaten oil, and one-fourth of a hin of wine for a drink offering. ⁴¹And the other lamb you shall offer in the evening and shall offer with it a grain offering and its drink offering, as in the morning, for a pleasing odor, an offering by fire* to the Lord. ⁴²It shall be a regular burnt offering throughout your generations at the entrance of the tent of meeting before the Lord, where I will meet with you, to speak to you there. ⁴³I will meet with the Israelites there, and it shall be sanctified by my glory; ⁴⁴I will consecrate the tent of meeting and the altar; Aaron also and his sons I will consecrate to serve me as priests. ⁴⁵I will dwell among the Israelites, and I will be their God. ⁴⁶And they shall know that I am the Lord their God, who brought them out of the land of Egypt that I might dwell among them; I am the Lord their God.

30

"You shall make an altar on which to offer incense; you shall make it of acacia wood. ²It shall be one cubit long and one cubit wide; it shall be square and shall be two cubits high; its horns shall be of one piece with it. ³You shall overlay it with pure gold, its top and its sides all around and its horns, and you shall make for it a molding of gold all around. ⁴And you shall make two golden rings for it; under its molding on two opposite sides of it you shall make them, and they shall hold the poles for carrying it. ⁵You shall make the poles of acacia wood and overlay them with gold. ⁶You shall place it in front of the curtain that is above the ark of the covenant, in front of the cover that is over the covenant, where I will meet with you. ⁷Aaron shall offer fragrant incense on it; every morning when he dresses the lamps he shall offer it, ⁸and when Aaron sets up the lamps in the evening, he shall offer it, a regular incense offering before the Lord throughout your generations. ⁹You shall not offer unholy incense on it or a burnt offering or a grain offering, and you shall not pour a drink offering on it. ¹⁰Once a year Aaron shall perform the rite of atonement on its horns. Throughout your generations he shall perform the atonement for it once a year with the blood of the atoning purification offering. It is most holy to the Lord."

11 The Lord spoke to Moses, ¹²"When you take a census of the Israelites to register them, at registration all of them shall give a ransom for their lives to the Lord, so that no plague may come upon them for being registered. ¹³This is what each one who is registered shall give: half a shekel according to the shekel of the sanctuary (the shekel is twenty gerahs),

e 29.41 Or *a gift*

29:37 The consecration of the altar is another seven-day ritual connoting wholeness and completeness.

29:45–46 God's presence is the ultimate goal of this process.

30:1 The incense altar is inside the tabernacle, in front of the curtain that leads to the holy place. Here an annual atonement rite takes place, possibly the Day of Atonement spoken of in Lev. 16.

30:9 For *unholy incense*, compare with Lev. 10:1–2.

30:11–12 The census applies to men over the age of twenty. The ransom is a form of protection against plague and war believed to be brought on by the census; see 2 Sam. 24.

half a shekel as an offering to the LORD. [14]Each one who is registered, from twenty years old and up, shall give the LORD's offering. [15]The rich shall not give more and the poor shall not give less than the half shekel, when you bring this offering to the LORD to make atonement for your lives. [16]You shall take the atonement money from the Israelites and shall designate it for the service of the tent of meeting; before the LORD it will be a reminder to the Israelites of the ransom given for your lives."

[17] The LORD spoke to Moses, [18]"You shall make a bronze basin with a bronze stand for washing. You shall put it between the tent of meeting and the altar, and you shall put water in it; [19]with the water[f] Aaron and his sons shall wash their hands and their feet. [20]When they go into the tent of meeting or when they come near the altar to minister to make an offering by fire[g] to the LORD, they shall wash with water, so that they may not die. [21]They shall wash their hands and their feet, so that they may not die: it shall be a perpetual ordinance for them, for him and for his descendants throughout their generations."

[22] The LORD spoke to Moses, [23]"Take the finest spices: of liquid myrrh five hundred shekels, and of sweet-smelling cinnamon half as much, that is, two hundred fifty, and two hundred fifty of aromatic cane, [24]and five hundred of cassia—measured by the sanctuary shekel—and a hin of olive oil, [25]and you shall make of these a sacred anointing oil blended as by the perfumer; it shall be a holy anointing oil. [26]With it you shall anoint the tent of meeting and the ark of the covenant [27]and the table and all its utensils and the lampstand and its utensils and the altar of incense [28]and the altar of burnt offering with all its utensils and the basin with its stand; [29]you shall consecrate them, so that they

may be most holy; whatever touches them will become holy. [30]You shall anoint Aaron and his sons and consecrate them to serve me as priests. [31]You shall say to the Israelites: This shall be my holy anointing oil throughout your generations. [32]It shall not be used in any ordinary anointing of the body, and you shall make no other like it in composition; it is holy, and it shall be holy to you. [33]Whoever blends any like it or whoever puts any of it on an unqualified person shall be cut off from the people."

[34] The LORD said to Moses, "Take sweet spices, stacte, and onycha, and galbanum, sweet spices with pure frankincense (an equal part of each), [35]and make an incense blended as by the perfumer, seasoned with salt, pure and holy, [36]and you shall beat some of it into powder and put part of it before the covenant in the tent of meeting, where I shall meet with you; it shall be most holy for you. [37]When you make incense according to this composition, you shall not make it for yourselves; it shall be regarded by you as holy to the LORD. [38]Whoever makes any like it to use as perfume shall be cut off from the people."

31

The LORD spoke to Moses, [2]"See, I have called by name Bezalel son of Uri son of Hur, of the tribe of Judah, [3]and I have filled him with a divine spirit,[b] with ability, intelligence, and knowledge, and every kind of skill, [4]to devise artistic designs, to work in gold, silver, and bronze, [5]in cutting stones for setting, and in carving wood, to work in every kind of craft. [6]Moreover, I have appointed with him Oholiab son of Ahisamach, of the tribe of Dan, and I have given skill to all the skillful, so that they may make all that I

f 30.19 Heb it   g 30.20 Or a gift   h 31.3 Or with the spirit of God

30:15 All lives, regardless of social status, have equal value when it comes to atonement.

30:16 The half shekel of atonement money goes to the tabernacle.

30:18–19 The bronze basin and bronze stand are situated between the altar and the entrance to the tent of meeting, signifying the necessity of cleanliness (see 30:21).

30:22–25 The ingredients for the anointing oil are listed along with a prohibition of its use for any other purpose (e.g., perfume) because it is set apart as *holy*.

30:34–38 The incense is to be prepared according to a specific formula; it is to be used only for sacred purposes.

31:2 Bezalel's name means "in the shade of God." For *Hur*, his grandfather, see 17:10–14.

31:6 Oholiab's name means "my tent is the father [God]." Metalwork, stonework, carving, and weaving for the tabernacle all fall under the purview of Bezalel the Judahite and Oholiab from the tribe of Dan. Their gifts as artisans come from God's spirit. Their names and tribes lend support to their significance in the narrative.

have commanded you: [7]the tent of meeting, and the ark of the covenant, and the cover that is on it, and all the furnishings of the tent, [8]the table and its utensils, and the pure lampstand with all its utensils, and the altar of incense, [9]and the altar of burnt offering with all its utensils, and the basin with its stand, [10]and the finely worked vestments, the holy vestments for the priest Aaron and the vestments of his sons, for their service as priests, [11]and the anointing oil and the fragrant incense for the holy place. They shall do just as I have commanded you."

[12] The LORD said to Moses, [13]"You yourself are to speak to the Israelites, 'You shall surely keep my Sabbaths, for this is a sign between me and you throughout your generations, given in order that you may know that I, the LORD, sanctify you. [14]You shall keep the Sabbath, because it is holy for you; everyone who profanes it shall be put to death; whoever does any work on it shall be cut off from among the people. [15]Six days shall work be done, but the seventh day is a Sabbath of solemn rest, holy to the LORD; whoever does any work on the Sabbath day shall be put to death. [16]Therefore the Israelites shall keep the Sabbath, observing the Sabbath throughout their generations, as a perpetual covenant. [17]It is a sign forever between me and the Israelites that in six days the LORD made heaven and earth, and on the seventh day he rested and was refreshed.'"

[18] When God[i] finished speaking with Moses on Mount Sinai, he gave him the two tablets of the covenant, tablets of stone, written with the finger of God.

32 When the people saw that Moses delayed to come down from the mountain, the people gathered around Aaron and said to him, "Come, make gods for us, who shall go before us; as for this Moses, the man who brought us up out of the land of Egypt, we do not know what has become of him." [2]Aaron said to them, "Take off the gold rings that are on the ears of your wives, your sons, and your daughters and bring them to me." [3]So all the people took off the gold rings from their ears and brought them to Aaron. [4]He took these from them, formed them in a mold,[j] and cast an image of a calf, and they said, "These are your gods, O Israel, who brought you up out of the land of Egypt!"

i 31.18 Heb *he*   *j* 32.4 Or *fashioned it with an engraving tool*; meaning of Heb uncertain

31:10 For the appointment of *Aaron* and *his sons* as priests, see 28:1–3.

31:13 The instructions for the tabernacle conclude with regulation for the observance of the Sabbath. The idea of the tabernacle as a sacred space is tied to the concept of Sabbath as sacred time. Keeping the Sabbath, too, is a kind of sanctification in which the observant are set apart as belonging to God. On *Sabbath*, see note at 20:8–11.

31:15 *Shall be put to death:* such a practice may have been infrequent, but other texts preserve instances of it (e.g., Num. 15:32–36).

31:17 The creation is invoked as a rationale for the Sabbath, as it is in the Decalogue in Exod. 20 (the version in Deut. 5:12 differs).

31:18 The Sabbath regulation is the last part of God's instruction before the tablets are given to Moses. God is said to have written the two tablets directly and to have given them to Moses. Although references to God's hand and arm appear with some regularity in the exodus story, this verse refers to God's finger. Deuteronomy 9:10 also describes the tablets as inscribed by the finger of God. The Egyptian magicians described the third plague as the "finger of God" (Exod. 8:19), while Ps. 8 describes the stars as the work of God's fingers.

32:1–35 The golden calf episode is positioned between the instructions for the tabernacle and its construction. The location of this episode raises serious questions about covenantal fidelity— both Israel's and God's. The transgression of the commandments, especially those concerned with other gods and the making of images, interrupts the narrative and threatens the future of Israel. By the end of chaps. 32–34, one sees that while there are dire consequences for disobedience, God does not abandon Israel in the wilderness. The tabernacle's construction can move forward after forgiveness and reconciliation have taken place. **32:1** According to the narrative, Moses has been on the mountain for forty days and forty nights (cf. 24:18). This symbolic number connotes a substantial elapse of time. The people experience this delay as a crisis of God's presence and provoke Aaron to act. **32:4** The text describes the construction of a single calf, yet the people refer to plural gods. Compare 1 Kgs. 12:28 and Jeroboam's construction of two calves for people in the northern

5When Aaron saw this, he built an altar before it, and Aaron made a proclamation and said, "Tomorrow shall be a festival to the LORD." 6They rose early the next day and offered burnt offerings and brought sacrifices of well-being, and the people sat down to eat and drink and rose up to revel.

7 The LORD said to Moses, "Go down at once! Your people, whom you brought up out of the land of Egypt, have acted perversely; 8they have been quick to turn aside from the way that I commanded them; they have cast for themselves an image of a calf and have worshiped it and sacrificed to it and said, 'These are your gods, O Israel, who brought you up out of the land of Egypt!'" 9The LORD said to Moses, "I have seen this people, how stiff-necked they are. 10Now let me alone so that my wrath may burn hot against them and I may consume them, and of you I will make a great nation."

11 But Moses implored the LORD his God and said, "O LORD, why does your wrath burn hot against your people, whom you brought out of the land of Egypt with great power and with a mighty hand? 12Why should the Egyptians say, 'It was with evil intent that he brought them out to kill them in the mountains and to consume them from the face of the earth'? Turn from your fierce wrath; change your mind and do not bring disaster on your people. 13Remember Abraham, Isaac, and Israel, your servants, how you swore to them by your own self, saying to them, 'I will multiply your descendants like the stars of heaven, and all this land that I have promised I will give to your descendants, and they shall inherit it forever.'" 14And the LORD changed his mind about the disaster that he planned to bring on his people.

15 Then Moses turned and went down from the mountain, carrying the two tablets of the covenant in his hands, tablets that were written on both sides, written on the front and on the back. 16The tablets were the work of God, and the writing was the writing of God, engraved upon the tablets. 17When Joshua heard the noise of the people as they shouted, he said to Moses, "There is a noise of war in the camp." 18But he said,

"It is not the sound made by victors
  or the sound made by losers;
  it is the sound of singing that I hear."

19As soon as he came near the camp and

kingdom to worship. According to many scholars, these texts are linked, which connects Jeroboam's sin directly to the offense at Mount Sinai. Nehemiah 9:18, which also refers to the golden calf, uses singular forms. Whatever the case, the golden calf might be seen as less a replacement for God than a representation of the Lord, reflecting the people's need and desire for God's presence. Even so, the plural forms in Exod. 32:4 do seem to suggest apostasy. **32:5** Aaron associates the image of the calf with the Lord, not with multiple gods. By building an altar, Aaron sets the stage for sacrifice and worship. A common symbol for the Canaanite deities like Baal, the calf or bull is also a generic symbol of strength and fertility. The bull was commonly seen as a god's pedestal or mount. The calf in Exod. 32 might have been similarly intended: as the base of God's throne or the animal upon which the Lord rode. **32:6** Sacrificing is followed by feasting (cf. 24:9–11). The verb *to revel* could refer to dancing (see v. 19). In some contexts, the verb may carry sexual connotations, but this is not certain (see Gen. 26:8; 39:14, 17). **32:7** Moses is commanded to descend from the mountain. The timing is highly ironic, especially considering the contrast between the immediacy of this verse and the delay mentioned in 32:1. **32:8** God describes the people as Moses's own—as "*your* people" (v. 7, emphasis added; see v. 12)—and details their transgression, which is a clear violation of the Decalogue (see 20:4–5). **32:9** *Stiff-necked* is a term used to describe people as if they were stubborn farm animals. **32:10** God threatens to have his *wrath . . . burn hot* and destroy the people and make a *great nation* from Moses instead. This sentiment harkens back to God's promise to Abraham (see Gen. 12:2–3), with Moses poised to be the new Abraham. **32:11–14** Moses intercedes with the Lord. What God threatens to do is untenable precisely because of the earlier promises to the ancestors. Even though something unimaginable has happened, God cannot utterly forsake the people because God is bound by the divine promises. Even so, Moses is unable to withhold his own violent response (see v. 28). **32:14** God changes the divine plan after Moses's shrewd intercession, which includes a subtle but important change in v. 13, altering the usual formulation of "Abraham, Isaac, and Jacob" (2:24; 6:3) to "Abraham, Isaac, and Israel." While Israel is the (later) name of Jacob, it is also the name for the people and thus brings the people as a whole to God's attention. **32:16** The description of the tablets stresses their origin. They are God's work and God's writing. **32:17** *Joshua* was the only leader who went with Moses up onto the mountain (cf. 24:13). **32:19** Now Moses's *anger burned hot*

saw the calf and the dancing, Moses's anger burned hot, and he threw the tablets from his hands and broke them at the foot of the mountain. ²⁰He took the calf that they had made, burned it with fire, ground it to powder, scattered it on the water, and made the Israelites drink it.

21 Moses said to Aaron, "What did this people do to you that you have brought so great a sin upon them?" ²²And Aaron said, "Do not let the anger of my lord burn hot; you know the people, that they are wicked. ²³They said to me, 'Make gods for us, who shall go before us; as for this Moses, the man who brought us up out of the land of Egypt, we do not know what has become of him.' ²⁴So I said to them, 'Whoever has gold, take it off'; so they gave it to me, and I threw it into the fire, and out came this calf!"

25 When Moses saw that the people were out of control (for Aaron had lost control of them, prompting derision among their enemies), ²⁶then Moses stood in the gate of the camp and said, "Who is on the LORD's side? Come to me!" And all the sons of Levi gathered around him. ²⁷He said to them, "Thus says the LORD, the God of Israel: Put your sword on your side, each of you! Go back and forth from gate to gate throughout the camp, and each of you kill your brother, your friend, and your neighbor." ²⁸The sons of Levi did as Moses commanded, and about three thousand of the people fell on that day. ²⁹Moses said, "Today you have been ordained for the service of the LORD, each one at the cost of a son or a brother, and so have brought a blessing on yourselves this day."

30 On the next day Moses said to the people, "You have sinned a great sin. But now I will go up to the LORD; perhaps I can make atonement for your sin." ³¹So Moses returned to the LORD and said, "Alas, this people has sinned a great sin; they have made for themselves gods of gold. ³²But now, if you will only forgive their sin—but if not, please blot me out of the book that you have written." ³³But the LORD said to Moses, "Whoever has sinned against me I will blot out of my book. ³⁴But now go, lead the people to the place about which I have spoken to you; see, my angel shall go in front of you. Nevertheless, when the day for punishment comes, I will punish them for their sin."

35 Then the LORD sent a plague on the people, because they made the calf—the one that Aaron had made.

33 The LORD said to Moses, "Go, leave this place, you and the people whom you have brought up out of the land of Egypt, and go to the land of which I swore to Abraham, Isaac, and Jacob, saying, 'To your descendants I will give it.' ²I will send an angel before you, and I will drive out the Canaanites, the Amorites, the Hittites, the Perizzites, the Hivites, and the Jebusites. ³Go up^k to a land flowing with milk and honey, but I will not go up among you, or I would consume you on the way, for you are a stiff-necked people."

4 When the people heard these harsh words, they mourned, and no one put on ornaments.

k 33.3 Heb lacks *Go up*

(cf. God's anger in v. 10). In breaking the tablets, Moses renders the covenant invalid, a symbolic act that reflects Israel's violation of the covenant. **32:20** The punishment for the sin of idolatry here is similar to the punishment of an unfaithful wife (see Num. 5:12–31). The similarities suggest that Israel is an unfaithful spouse—an image that is also found in the prophetic tradition, which occasionally describes Israel's apostasy using the metaphor of an unfaithful wife. **32:21–24** Aaron's explanation of what happened does not align with the narrative description of the same event earlier in the chapter. **32:25** This verse condemns Aaron's lack of leadership. **32:26** Moses's tribe, the Levites, is depicted as the group that upholds the covenant. This is the tribe designated for service in the Lord's sanctuary (see 32:29; Deut. 10:8). **32:27–28** Part of the punishment for the sin of worshiping the calf comes in the Levites' killing of those responsible. **32:31–34** Moses puts himself on the line in advocating for the people's forgiveness. God's response, however, is to postpone, not revoke, divine punishment. On the *angel*, see note at 23:20. **32:35** The plague referred to here may be not an additional punishment but connected to the ordeal in v. 20.

33:1–3 In the wake of the golden calf debacle, God commands Israel to go to Canaan—not entirely unlike the command given to Abram in Gen. 12, but this time Israel will go with God's direct accompaniment. On the *angel*, see note at 23:20.

33:4–6 The gap between God's holiness and the people's inability to remain obedient is made evident.

⁵For the LORD had said to Moses, "Say to the Israelites, 'You are a stiff-necked people; if for a single moment I should go up among you, I would consume you. So now take off your ornaments, and I will decide what to do to you.'" ⁶Therefore the Israelites stripped themselves of their ornaments, from Mount Horeb onward.

7 Now Moses used to take the tent and pitch it outside the camp, far off from the camp; he called it the tent of meeting. And everyone who sought the LORD would go out to the tent of meeting, which was outside the camp. ⁸Whenever Moses went out to the tent, all the people would rise and stand, each of them, at the entrance of their tents and watch Moses until he had gone into the tent. ⁹When Moses entered the tent, the pillar of cloud would descend and stand at the entrance of the tent, and the LORD*l* would speak with Moses. ¹⁰When all the people saw the pillar of cloud standing at the entrance of the tent, all the people would rise and bow down, all of them, at the entrance of their tent. ¹¹Thus the LORD used to speak to Moses face to face, as one speaks to a friend. Then he would return to the camp, but his young assistant, Joshua son of Nun, would not leave the tent.

12 Moses said to the LORD, "See, you have said to me, 'Bring up this people,' but you have not let me know whom you will send with me. Yet you have said, 'I know you by name, and you have also found favor in my sight.' ¹³Now if I have found favor in your sight, please show me your ways, so that I may know you and find favor in your sight. Consider, too, that this nation is your people." ¹⁴He said, "My presence will go with you, and I will give you rest." ¹⁵And he said to him, "If your presence will not go, do not bring us up from here. ¹⁶For how shall it be known that I have found favor in your sight, I and your people, unless you go with us? In this way, we shall be distinct, I and your people, from every people on the face of the earth."

17 The LORD said to Moses, "I will also do this thing that you have asked, for you have found favor in my sight, and I know you by name." ¹⁸Moses*m* said, "Please show me your glory." ¹⁹And he said, "I will make all my goodness pass before you and will proclaim before you the name, 'The LORD,'*n* and I will be gracious to whom I will be gracious and will show mercy on whom I will show mercy. ²⁰But," he said, "you cannot see my face, for

l 33.9 Heb *he*   *m* 33.18 Heb *he*   *n* 33.19 Heb *YHWH*; see note at 3.15

God's holiness would *consume* the people. **33:5** God's command in v. 5 and the people's compliance in v. 6 are anticipated already in v. 4. This is perhaps a sign that the people are capable of obedience.

33:7–11 God's presence at the tent of meeting (an alternate name for the tabernacle) and Moses's role as intermediary are outlined in this passage. The pillar of cloud—which represents God's presence—has accompanied the people from Egypt. **33:11** *Face to face* is a figure of speech indicating the unique and intimate relationship God has with Moses. This expression appears in Deut. 34:10. This verse also highlights the special role of Joshua, Moses's assistant (see note at Exod. 17:9).

33:12–23 The exchange between Moses and God reflects the same dynamic between Israel and God. Moses, like the people, is unwilling to go without God's accompaniment. Chap. 33, no less than chap. 32, centers on the question of God's holy presence amid an unfaithful people. In the wake of Israel's breach of covenant, especially at the very start of the covenant, the question of God's ongoing presence is a live one, with God's absence the greatest punishment imaginable. **33:12–16** Moses intercedes for the people and makes a request for himself. Both requests seek assurance that God will be present. In this exchange comes the realization that the covenant will require Israel's obedience and God's mercy. **33:12** To find favor with God is a special status afforded to Moses and Noah (Gen. 6:8). **33:13** *Know you* suggests intimacy with God. **33:17** God grants Moses's request because Moses has a special relationship with God (see 33:12) and because God knows him by name. **33:18** The word for glory has to do with weight and significance. God's glory is thus weighty in some way, a perceivable proof of God's presence (see note at 16:7). Moses requests an encounter with the Lord that he can actually feel, something that will strengthen him for the task before him. **33:19** *Goodness* is a common term but one that also appears in treaties. God's words and actions might be seen as a matter of covenant renewal after the golden calf episode. This verse depicts a God who is both powerful and merciful. God's special name, *The Lord*, is offered as another sign of divine favor (see note at 3:13–15). God reveals his nature to Moses because God chooses to do so. **33:20** Closeness to God also involves real danger, and looking into the face of the deity is said to be impossible—a statement that is at odds with 24:10–11. Even if God's essence cannot be seen, God's

no one shall see me and live." ²¹And the Lord continued, "See, there is a place by me where you shall stand on the rock, ²²and while my glory passes by I will put you in a cleft of the rock, and I will cover you with my hand until I have passed by; ²³then I will take away my hand, and you shall see my back, but my face shall not be seen."

34 The Lord said to Moses, "Cut two tablets of stone like the former ones, and I will write on the tablets the words that were on the former tablets, which you broke. ²Be ready in the morning and come up in the morning to Mount Sinai and present yourself there to me on the top of the mountain. ³No one shall come up with you, and do not let anyone be seen throughout all the mountain, and do not let flocks or herds graze in front of that mountain." ⁴So Moses cut two tablets of stone like the former ones, and he rose early in the morning and went up on Mount Sinai, as the Lord had commanded him, and took in his hand the two tablets of stone. ⁵The Lord descended in the cloud and stood with him there and proclaimed the name, "The Lord."ᵒ ⁶The Lord passed before him and proclaimed,

"The Lord, the Lord,
a God merciful and gracious,
slow to anger,
and abounding in steadfast love and
    faithfulness,
⁷ keeping steadfast love for the
    thousandth generation,ᵖ
forgiving iniquity and transgression and
    sin,
yet by no means clearing the guilty,
but visiting the iniquity of the parents
    upon the children
and the children's children
to the third and the fourth generation."

⁸And Moses quickly bowed down to the ground and worshiped. ⁹He said, "If now I have found favor in your sight, my Lord, I pray, let my Lord go with us. Although this is a stiff-necked people, pardon our iniquity and our sin, and take us for your inheritance."

10 He said, "I hereby make a covenant. Before all your people I will perform marvels, such as have not been doneᵠ in all the earth or in any nation, and all the people among whom you live shall see the work of the Lord, for it is an awesome thing that I will do with you.

o 34.5 Heb *YHWH*; see note at 3.15   p 34.7 Or *for thousands*
q 34.10 Heb *created*

attributes—God's glory, for example, or God's goodness—may be experienced. **33:22** God blesses Moses with a vision and experience of God's presence and simultaneously protects Moses from the danger involved. In terms of the larger narrative, this moment is a promising move forward: God can and will protect, and God can and will be present despite the real dangers posed by this deity. **33:23** God's back may be understood as residual glory, the afterglow of God's presence.

34:1-2 After the golden calf incident, Moses must first reaffirm his relationship with God in chap. 33 before the covenant is renewed between God and the people in chap. 34. New tablets are required, since the old ones were broken. The tablets are a piece of Sinai that goes forth with Israel; they are literal and figurative fragments of the sacred ground on which they received (and broke) the covenant.

34:3 Not even Aaron or Joshua will accompany Moses this time (see 19:24; 24:13-14; 32:17).

34:5-7 Here God self-identifies using a description that occurs in the same or nearly the same form in a number of other texts (see, e.g., Exod. 20:5-7; Num. 14:18; Neh. 9:17; Jer. 32:18; Joel 2:13; Jonah 4:2; Nah. 1:3; Pss. 86:15; 103:8; 145:8; cf. note at Exod. 33:19). It may be the closest thing ancient Israel ever got to a creedal statement. This unit is referred to in Jewish tradition as the thirteen attributes of God. The unit portrays God as both merciful and punitive, though the balance of the poetry says the former far outweighs the latter (e.g., a thousand generations to three or four). That said, both aspects of the divine nature are important to recognize given Israel's great disobedience with the golden calf and the divine punishment that followed. God's punitive side explains that punishment, even as God's inordinate, almost infinite mercy is what explains God's continued presence with Israel thereafter. **34:6** God's personal name is invoked twice, perhaps for emphasis (see note at 33:19). See **"God's Name," p. 89.**

34:9 In the role of intermediary, Moses asks for the forgiveness of the people.

34:10 The tablets, a physical reminder of the holy mountain, are to be housed in the tabernacle, the movable sanctuary, signaling that Israel's God will not be restricted to a single location, though the fundamental nature of that location remains pertinent and present.

34:10-27 This section contains a mixture of elements from the preceding legal material found in

11 "Observe what I command you today. See, I will drive out before you the Amorites, the Canaanites, the Hittites, the Perizzites, the Hivites, and the Jebusites. ¹²Take care not to make a covenant with the inhabitants of the land to which you are going, or it will become a snare among you. ¹³Rather, you shall tear down their altars, break their pillars, and cut down their sacred poles,ʳ ¹⁴for you shall worship no other god, because the LORD, whose name is Jealous, is a jealous God. ¹⁵You shall not make a covenant with the inhabitants of the land, for when they prostitute themselves to their gods and sacrifice to their gods, someone among them will invite you, and you will eat of the sacrifice, ¹⁶and you will take wives from among their daughters for your sons, and their daughters who prostitute themselves to their gods will make your sons also prostitute themselves to their gods.

17 "You shall not make cast idols.

18 "You shall keep the Festival of Unleavened Bread. Seven days you shall eat unleavened bread, as I commanded you, at the time appointed in the month of Abib, for in the month of Abib you came out from Egypt.

19 "All that first opens the womb is mine, all your maleˢ livestock, the firstborn of cow and sheep. ²⁰The firstborn of a donkey you shall redeem with a lamb, or if you will not redeem it you shall break its neck. All the firstborn of your sons you shall redeem.

"No one shall appear before me empty-handed.

21 "Six days you shall work, but on the seventh day you shall rest; even in plowing time and in harvest time you shall rest. ²²You shall observe the Festival of Weeks, the first fruits of wheat harvest, and the Festival of Ingathering at the turn of the year. ²³Three times in the year all your males shall appear before

the LORD God, the God of Israel. ²⁴For I will cast out nations before you and enlarge your borders; no one shall covet your land when you go up to appear before the LORD your God three times in the year.

25 "You shall not offer the blood of my sacrifice with leaven, and the sacrifice of the festival of the Passover shall not be left until the morning.

26 "The best of the first fruits of your ground you shall bring to the house of the LORD your God.

"You shall not boil a kid in its mother's milk."

27 The LORD said to Moses, "Write these words, for in accordance with these words I have made a covenant with you and with Israel." ²⁸He was there with the LORD forty days and forty nights; he neither ate bread nor drank water. And he wrote on the tablets the words of the covenant, the ten commandments.ᵗ

29 Moses came down from Mount Sinai. As he came down from the mountain with the two tablets of the covenant in his hand, Moses did not know that the skin of his face shone because he had been talking with God. ³⁰When Aaron and all the Israelites saw Moses, the skin of his face was shining, and they were afraid to come near him. ³¹But Moses called to them, and Aaron and all the leaders of the congregation returned to him, and Moses spoke with them. ³²Afterward all the Israelites came near, and he gave them in commandment all that the LORD had spoken with him on Mount Sinai. ³³When Moses had finished speaking with them, he put a veil on his face, ³⁴but whenever Moses went in before the LORD to speak with him, he would take the

r 34.13 Or *Asherahs* s 34.19 Gk Theodotion Vg Tg: Meaning of Heb uncertain t 34.28 Heb *the ten words*

the Ten Commandments and the book of the covenant. It includes the prohibition against worshiping other gods and casting idols, bringing to mind the transgression in the previous chapter. Indeed, this passage is sometimes called "the ritual Decalogue," since it focuses on worship, the precise way Israel broke the covenant with the golden calf.

34:28 Once again, the period of time is said to be forty days and forty nights (see 24:18).

34:29 Moses comes down from Sinai (cf. 32:15) but this time with a shining face—further proof of the power of God's glory, even if only residually. The word for Moses's radiant face, or rays, is similar to the word for horn, which led to later artists' depictions of Moses with horns, most notably Michelangelo's statue of Moses.

34:33 The veil over Moses's face, like the veil separating the holy of holies from the rest of the tabernacle, identifies the holy place or thing as sacred and set apart. Moses is marked as just such a holy thing; his shining face is the proof of that, with the veil enabling access to Moses while still serving as a reminder of his holiness, which depends on God's.

veil off until he came out, and when he came out and told the Israelites what he had been commanded, ³⁵the Israelites would see the face of Moses, that the skin of his face was shining, and Moses would put the veil on his face again until he went in to speak with him.

35 Moses assembled all the congregation of the Israelites and said to them, "These are the things that the LORD has commanded you to do:

2 "Six days shall work be done, but on the seventh day you shall have a holy Sabbath of solemn rest to the LORD; whoever does any work on it shall be put to death. ³You shall kindle no fire in all your dwellings on the Sabbath day."

4 Moses said to all the congregation of the Israelites, "This is the thing that the LORD has commanded: ⁵Take from among you an offering to the LORD; let whoever is of a generous heart bring the LORD's offering: gold, silver, and bronze; ⁶blue, purple, and crimson yarns and fine linen; goats' hair, ⁷tanned rams' skins, and fine leather;ᵘ acacia wood, ⁸oil for the light, spices for the anointing oil and for the fragrant incense, ⁹and onyx stones and gems to be set in the ephod and the breastpiece.

10 "All who are skillful among you shall come and make all that the LORD has commanded: ¹¹the tabernacle, its tent and its covering, its clasps and its frames, its bars, its pillars, and its bases; ¹²the ark with its poles, the cover, and the curtain for the screen; ¹³the table with its poles and all its utensils and the bread of the Presence; ¹⁴and the lampstand for the light, with its utensils and its lamps and the oil for the light; ¹⁵and the altar of incense, with its poles, and the anointing oil and the fragrant incense, and the screen for the entrance, the entrance of the tabernacle; ¹⁶the altar of burnt offering, with its grating of bronze, its poles, and all its utensils, the basin with its stand; ¹⁷the hangings of the court, its pillars and its bases, and the screen for the gate of the court; ¹⁸the pegs of the tabernacle and the pegs of the court and their cords; ¹⁹the finely worked vestments for ministering in the holy place, the holy vestments for the priest Aaron, and the vestments of his sons, for their service as priests."

20 Then all the congregation of the Israelites withdrew from the presence of Moses. ²¹And they came, everyone whose heart was stirred and everyone whose spirit was willing, and brought the LORD's offering to be used for the tent of meeting and for all its service and for the sacred vestments. ²²So they came, both men and women; all who were of a willing heart brought brooches and earrings and signet rings and pendants, all sorts of gold objects, everyone bringing an offering of gold to the LORD. ²³And everyone who possessed blue or purple or crimson yarn or fine linen or goats' hair or tanned rams' skins or fine leatherᵛ brought them. ²⁴Everyone who could make an offering of silver or bronze brought it as the LORD's offering, and everyone who possessed acacia wood of any use in the work brought it. ²⁵All the skillful women spun with their hands and brought what they had spun in blue and purple and crimson yarns and fine linen; ²⁶all the women whose hearts moved them to use their skill spun the goats' hair.

u 35.7 Meaning of Heb uncertain   *v* 35.23 Meaning of Heb uncertain

35:1 *All the congregation of the Israelites*, inclusive of men and women.

35:2–3 See 31:15. These instructions for the Sabbath observance continue the material found at the end of chap. 31, before the golden calf incident. This brings Israel and the narrative back on course and to the building of the tabernacle. Once again, the mention of Sabbath in connection with the tabernacle indicates that the construction of sacred space is tied to sacred time. On *Sabbath*, see note at 20:8–11.

35:4–9 Compare 25:1–9. The gathering of materials is the necessary step that precedes construction. The level of detail both inspires imagination and satisfies curiosity. The *ephod* and *breastpiece* (v. 9) are what Aaron (as high priest) will wear. **35:4** See note at 35:1.

35:10 Once again, the phrasing is inclusive of men and women. See also 35:22, 29.

35:20 Once again, *all the congregation* includes both women and men. In a patriarchal culture, the text of Exodus seems intentional about inclusivity here and in subsequent verses where it explicitly mentions "men and women" (vv. 22, 29) and skillful women (vv. 25–26).

35:20–29 The description of these offerings may be profitably compared to the offerings for the golden calf found in 32:2–3. **35:25–26** The two references to women are noteworthy: they not only include but emphasize the contribution of women to the tabernacle construction.

²⁷And the leaders brought onyx stones and gems to be set in the ephod and the breastpiece ²⁸and spices and oil for the light and for the anointing oil and for the fragrant incense. ²⁹All the Israelite men and women whose hearts made them willing to bring anything for the work that the LORD had commanded by Moses to be done brought it as a freewill offering to the LORD.

30 Then Moses said to the Israelites, "See, the LORD has called by name Bezalel son of Uri son of Hur, of the tribe of Judah; ³¹he has filled him with a divine spirit,ʷ with ability, intelligence, and knowledge, and with every kind of skill, ³²to devise artistic designs, to work in gold, silver, and bronze, ³³in cutting stones for setting, and in carving wood, in every kind of artistic craft. ³⁴And he has inspired him to teach, both him and Oholiab son of Ahisamach, of the tribe of Dan. ³⁵He has filled them with skill to do every kind of work done by an artisan or by a designer or by an embroiderer in blue, purple, and crimson yarns and in fine linen or by a weaver—by any sort of skilled worker or designer.

36 "Bezalel and Oholiab and every skilled person to whom the LORD has given skill and understanding to know how to do any work in the construction of the sanctuary shall work in accordance with all that the LORD has commanded."

2 Moses then called Bezalel and Oholiab and every skilled person to whom the LORD had given skill, everyone whose heart was stirred to come to do the work, ³and they received from Moses all the offerings that the Israelites had brought for the work of constructing the sanctuary. They still kept bringing him freewill offerings every morning, ⁴so that all the skilled workers who were doing every sort of task on the sanctuary came, each from the task being performed, ⁵and said to Moses, "The people are bringing much more than enough for doing the work that the LORD has commanded us to do." ⁶So Moses gave command, and word was proclaimed throughout the camp: "No man or woman is to make anything else as an offering for the sanctuary." So the people were restrained from bringing, ⁷for what they had already brought was more than enough to do all the work.

8 All those with skill among the workers made the tabernacle with ten curtains; they were made of fine twisted linen and blue, purple, and crimson yarns, with cherubim skillfully worked into them. ⁹The length of each curtain was twenty-eight cubits and the width of each curtain four cubits; all the curtains were of the same size.

10 He joined five curtains to one another, and the other five curtains he joined to one another. ¹¹He made loops of blue on the edge of the outermost curtain of the first set; likewise he made them on the edge of the outermost curtain of the second set; ¹²he made fifty loops on the one curtain, and he made fifty loops on the edge of the curtain that was in the second set; the loops were opposite one another. ¹³And he made fifty clasps of gold and joined the curtains one to the other with clasps; so the tabernacle was one whole.

14 He also made curtains of goats' hair for a tent over the tabernacle; he made eleven

w 35.31 Or *the spirit of God*

35:30–36:7 For *Bezalel* and *Oholiab* (v. 34), see note at 31:6. **36:3–7** The offering of materials exceeds the need. In the context of the barren wilderness where this takes place, the abundance of freewill offerings is a stark contrast. As with God's gift of the manna, Israel's gifts to the tabernacle are more than enough.

36:8–38 The execution of the plans is consistent with the detail in the earlier chapters, with all the parts carefully made: coverings (vv. 8–19), frames (vv. 20–34), and the partitions (vv. 35–38). The recurring refrain that the work takes place in accordance with God's instructions means that the tabernacle is an earthly manifestation of a heavenly design and that Israel is indeed capable of full obedience to the God of the covenant. The level of detail in the tabernacle material is a visual feast. For later communities like the exilic one, the tabernacle's description is not only a reminder that God's presence is mobile; it also invites their imaginations to enter into sacred space where so much can be imagined on the basis of the literary details. For formerly enslaved people, the creation of their own buildings, institutions, traditions, rituals, and the like is both proof and the fruit of emancipation. Unlike their forced labor for Pharaoh's cities (see note at 1:11), Israel now willingly brings goods and offers skilled labor to create a sanctuary for the Lord, who brought them out of slavery. On *cubits* (v. 9), see note at 25:10.

curtains. ¹⁵The length of each curtain was thirty cubits and the width of each curtain four cubits; the eleven curtains were of the same size. ¹⁶He joined five curtains by themselves and six curtains by themselves. ¹⁷He made fifty loops on the edge of the outermost curtain of the one set and fifty loops on the edge of the other connecting curtain. ¹⁸He made fifty clasps of bronze to join the tent together so that it might be one whole. ¹⁹And he made for the tent a covering of tanned rams' skins and an outer covering of fine leather.ˣ

20 Then he made the upright frames for the tabernacle of acacia wood. ²¹Ten cubits was the length of a frame and a cubit and a half the width of each frame. ²²Each frame had two pegs for fitting together; he did this for all the frames of the tabernacle. ²³The frames for the tabernacle he made in this way: twenty frames for the south side, ²⁴and he made forty bases of silver under the twenty frames, two bases under the first frame for its two pegs and two bases under the next frame for its two pegs. ²⁵For the second side of the tabernacle, on the north side, he made twenty frames ²⁶and their forty bases of silver, two bases under the first frame and two bases under the next frame. ²⁷For the rear of the tabernacle westward he made six frames. ²⁸He made two frames for the corners of the tabernacle in the rear. ²⁹They were separate beneath but joined at the top at the first ring; he made two of them in this way for the two corners. ³⁰There were eight frames with their bases of silver: sixteen bases, under every frame two bases.

31 He made bars of acacia wood: five for the frames of the one side of the tabernacle, ³²and five bars for the frames of the other side of the tabernacle, and five bars for the frames of the tabernacle at the rear westward. ³³He made the middle bar to pass through from end to end halfway up the frames. ³⁴And he overlaid the frames with gold and made rings of gold for them to hold the bars and overlaid the bars with gold.

35 He made the curtain of blue, purple, and crimson yarns and fine twisted linen, with cherubim skillfully worked into it. ³⁶He made for it four pillars of acacia and overlaid them with gold; their hooks were of gold, and he cast for them four bases of silver. ³⁷He also made a screen for the entrance to the tent, of blue, purple, and crimson yarns and fine twisted linen, embroidered with needlework, ³⁸and its five pillars with their hooks. He overlaid their capitals and their bases with gold, but their five bases were of bronze.

37 Bezalel made the ark of acacia wood; it was two and a half cubits long, a cubit and a half wide, and a cubit and a half high. ²He overlaid it with pure gold inside and outside and made a molding of gold around it. ³He cast for it four rings of gold for its four feet, two rings on its one side and two rings on its other side. ⁴He made poles of acacia wood and overlaid them with gold ⁵and put the poles into the rings on the sides of the ark, to carry the ark. ⁶He made a cover of pure gold; two cubits and a half was its length and a cubit and a half its width. ⁷He made two cherubim of hammered gold; at the two ends of the cover he made them, ⁸one cherub at one end and one cherub at the other end; of one piece with the cover he made the cherubim at its two ends. ⁹The cherubim spread out their wings above, overshadowing the cover with their wings. They faced one another; the faces of the cherubim were turned toward the cover.

10 He also made the table of acacia wood, two cubits long, one cubit wide, and a cubit and a half high. ¹¹He overlaid it with pure gold and made a molding of gold around it. ¹²He also made around it a rim a handbreadth wide, and he made a molding of gold around the rim. ¹³He cast for it four rings of gold and fastened the rings to the four corners at its four legs. ¹⁴The rings that held the poles used for carrying the table were close to the rim. ¹⁵He made the poles of acacia wood to carry the table and overlaid them with gold. ¹⁶And

x 36.19 Meaning of Heb uncertain

37:1 The order of construction in this chapter begins with the ark, then moves outward from the most holy place. The work is done in accordance with the plans detailed in 25:10–14. The extensive repetition here, as elsewhere, emphasizes that the ark (and the tabernacle as a whole) was made in obedience to the divine plans God gave to Moses. On *Bezalel*, see note at 31:2, 6. On *cubits*, see note at 25:10.

37:10–16 The table for the bread of the presence is made per the instructions in 25:23–29. The items to be placed on the table are listed: plates and dishes for incense and bowls for drink offerings.

he made the vessels of pure gold that were to be on the table, its plates and dishes for incense and its bowls and flagons with which to pour drink offerings.

17 He also made the lampstand of pure gold. The base and the shaft of the lampstand were made of hammered work; its cups, its calyxes, and its petals were of one piece with it. [18]There were six branches going out of its sides, three branches of the lampstand out of one side of it and three branches of the lampstand out of the other side of it; [19]three cups shaped like almond blossoms, each with calyx and petals, on one branch, and three cups shaped like almond blossoms, each with calyx and petals, on the other branch—so for the six branches going out of the lampstand. [20]On the lampstand itself there were four cups shaped like almond blossoms, each with its calyxes and petals. [21]There was a calyx of one piece with it under the first pair of branches, a calyx of one piece with it under the next pair of branches, and a calyx of one piece with it under the last pair of branches—so for the six branches going out of it. [22]Their calyxes and their branches were of one piece with it, the whole of it one hammered piece of pure gold. [23]He made its seven lamps and its snuffers and its trays of pure gold. [24]He made it and all its utensils of a talent of pure gold.

25 He made the altar of incense of acacia wood, one cubit long and one cubit wide; it was square and was two cubits high; its horns were of one piece with it. [26]He overlaid it with pure gold, its top and its sides all around and its horns, and he made a molding of gold around it [27]and two golden rings for it under its molding, on two opposite sides of it, to hold the poles with which to carry it. [28]And he made the poles of acacia wood and overlaid them with gold.

29 He made the holy anointing oil also and the pure fragrant incense, blended as by the perfumer.

38

He made the altar of burnt offering of acacia wood; it was five cubits long and five cubits wide; it was square and was three cubits high. [2]He made horns for it on its four corners; its horns were of one piece with it, and he overlaid it with bronze. [3]He made all the utensils of the altar: the pots, the shovels, the basins, the forks, and the firepans; all its utensils he made of bronze. [4]He made for the altar a grating, a network of bronze, under its ledge, extending halfway down. [5]He cast four rings on the four corners of the bronze grating to hold the poles; [6]he made the poles of acacia wood and overlaid them with bronze. [7]And he put the poles through the rings on the sides of the altar, to carry it with them; he made it hollow, with boards.

8 He made the basin of bronze with its stand of bronze, from the mirrors of the women who served at the entrance to the tent of meeting.

9 He made the court; for the south side the hangings of the court were of fine twisted linen, one hundred cubits long; [10]its twenty pillars and their twenty bases were of bronze, but the hooks of the pillars and their bands were of silver. [11]For the north side there were hangings[y] one hundred cubits long; its twenty pillars and their twenty bases were of bronze, but the hooks of the pillars and their bands were of silver. [12]For the west side there were hangings fifty cubits long, with ten pillars and ten bases; the hooks of the pillars and their bands were of silver. [13]And for the front to the east, fifty cubits. [14]The hangings for one side of the gate were fifteen cubits, with three pillars and three bases. [15]And likewise for the other side: on each side of the gate of the court were hangings of fifteen cubits, with three pillars and three bases. [16]All the hangings around the court were of fine twisted linen. [17]The bases for the pillars were of bronze, but the hooks of the pillars and

y 38.11 Heb lacks *there were hangings*

37:17–24 For the lampstand, see 25:31–39.

37:25–28 For the incense altar, see 30:1–5. On *cubits*, see note at 25:10.

38:1–8 See 27:1–8. The text is careful to point out that Bezalel made all the items for the altar for burnt offerings. According to Num. 16:38–39, Eleazar made the coverings for the altar. **38:8** The term used to describe the women and their service is used to refer to the temple service of the Gershonites in Num. 4:23 and the Levites in Num. 8:24. First Samuel 2:22 also makes reference to these women who served at the tent of meeting. See the specific inclusion of women elsewhere (cf. Exod. 35:22, 25, 26, 29).

38:9–20 The construction of the court; see 27:9–19. On *cubits* (vv. 9, 11–15, 18), see note at 25:10.

their bands were of silver; the overlaying of their capitals was also of silver, and all the pillars of the court were banded with silver. [18]The screen for the entrance to the court was embroidered with needlework in blue, purple, and crimson yarns and fine twisted linen. It was twenty cubits long and, along the width of it, five cubits high, corresponding to the hangings of the court. [19]There were four pillars; their four bases were of bronze, their hooks of silver, and the overlaying of their capitals and their bands of silver. [20]All the pegs for the tabernacle and for the court all around were of bronze.

21 These are the records of the tabernacle, the tabernacle of the covenant, which were drawn up at the commandment of Moses, the work of the Levites being under the direction of Ithamar son of the priest Aaron. [22]Bezalel son of Uri son of Hur, of the tribe of Judah, made all that the LORD commanded Moses, [23]and with him was Oholiab son of Ahisamach, of the tribe of Dan, engraver, designer, and embroiderer in blue, purple, and crimson yarns and in fine linen.

24 All the gold that was used for the work, in all the construction of the sanctuary, the gold from the offering, was twenty-nine talents and seven hundred thirty shekels, measured by the sanctuary shekel. [25]The silver from those of the congregation who were counted was one hundred talents and one thousand seven hundred seventy-five shekels, measured by the sanctuary shekel, [26]a beka a head (that is, half a shekel, measured by the sanctuary shekel) for everyone who was counted in the census, from twenty years old and up, for six hundred three thousand, five hundred fifty men. [27]The hundred talents of silver were for casting the bases of the sanctuary and the bases of the curtain, one hundred bases for the hundred talents, one talent per base. [28]Of the thousand seven hundred seventy-five shekels he made hooks for the pillars and overlaid their capitals and made bands for them. [29]The bronze offering was seventy talents and two thousand four hundred shekels; [30]with it he made the bases for the entrance of the tent of meeting, the bronze altar and the bronze grating for it

and all the utensils of the altar, [31]the bases all around the court, and the bases of the gate of the court, all the pegs of the tabernacle, and all the pegs around the court.

39 Of the blue, purple, and crimson yarns they made finely worked vestments, for ministering in the holy place; they made the sacred vestments for Aaron, as the LORD had commanded Moses.

2 He made the ephod of gold, of blue, purple, and crimson yarns, and of fine twisted linen. [3]Gold leaf was hammered out and cut into threads to work into the blue, purple, and crimson yarns and into the fine twisted linen, in skilled design. [4]They made for the ephod shoulder pieces, joined to it at its two edges. [5]The decorated band on it was of the same materials and workmanship, of gold, of blue, purple, and crimson yarns, and of fine twisted linen, as the LORD had commanded Moses.

6 The onyx stones were prepared, enclosed in settings of gold filigree and engraved like the engravings of a signet, according to the names of the sons of Israel. [7]He set them on the shoulder pieces of the ephod, to be stones of remembrance for the sons of Israel, as the LORD had commanded Moses.

8 He made the breastpiece, in skilled work, like the work of the ephod, of gold, of blue, purple, and crimson yarns, and of fine twisted linen. [9]It was square; the breastpiece was made double, a span in length and a span in width when doubled. [10]They set in it four rows of stones. A row of carnelian,*z* chrysolite, and emerald was the first row; [11]and the second row, a turquoise, a sapphire,*a* and a moonstone; [12]and the third row, a jacinth, an agate, and an amethyst; [13]and the fourth row, a beryl, an onyx, and a jasper; they were enclosed in settings of gold filigree. [14]There were twelve stones with names corresponding to the names of the sons of Israel; they were engraved like signets, each with its name, for the twelve tribes. [15]They made on the breastpiece chains of pure gold, twisted like cords, [16]and they made two settings of gold filigree and two gold rings and put the two rings on

z 39.10 The identification of several of these stones is uncertain   a 39.11 Or *lapis lazuli*

38:21–30 Records of the material used; see 30:12–16. For *Bezalel* and *Oholiab* (vv. 22–23), see note at 31:6. For the *census* (v. 26), see note at 30:11–12.

39:1–31 The priestly garments are made according to the instructions in chap. 28. **39:1** The phrase *as the LORD had commanded [Moses]* occurs ten times in this chapter (see vv. 5, 7, 21, 26, 29, 31, 32,

the two edges of the breastpiece, [17]and they put the two cords of gold in the two rings at the edges of the breastpiece. [18]Two ends of the two cords they had attached to the two settings of filigree; in this way they attached it in front to the shoulder pieces of the ephod. [19]Then they made two rings of gold and put them at the two ends of the breastpiece, on its inside edge next to the ephod. [20]They made two rings of gold and attached them in front to the lower part of the two shoulder pieces of the ephod, at its joining above the decorated band of the ephod. [21]They bound the breastpiece by its rings to the rings of the ephod with a blue cord, so that it should lie on the decorated band of the ephod and that the breastpiece should not come loose from the ephod, as the LORD had commanded Moses.

22 He also made the robe of the ephod woven all of blue yarn, [23]and the opening of the robe in the middle of it was like the opening in a garment,[b] with a binding around its edge, so that it might not be torn. [24]On the lower hem of the robe they made pomegranates of blue, purple, and crimson yarns and of fine twisted linen.[c] [25]They also made bells of pure gold and put the bells between the pomegranates on the lower hem of the robe all around, between the pomegranates, [26]a bell and a pomegranate, a bell and a pomegranate all around on the lower hem of the robe for ministering, as the LORD had commanded Moses.

27 They also made the tunics, woven of fine linen, for Aaron and his sons, [28]and the turban of fine linen, and the headdresses of fine linen, and the linen undergarments of fine twisted linen, [29]and the sash of fine twisted linen, and of blue, purple, and crimson yarns, embroidered with needlework, as the LORD had commanded Moses.

30 They made the rosette of the holy diadem of pure gold and wrote on it an inscription, like the engraving of a signet, "Holy to the LORD." [31]They tied to it a blue cord, to fasten it on the turban above, as the LORD had commanded Moses.

32 Thus all the work of the tabernacle of the tent of meeting was finished; the Israelites had done everything just as the LORD had commanded Moses. [33]Then they brought the tabernacle to Moses, the tent and all its utensils, its clasps, its frames, its bars, its pillars, and its bases; [34]the covering of tanned rams' skins and the covering of fine leather[d] and the curtain for the screen; [35]the ark of the covenant with its poles and the cover; [36]the table with all its utensils and the bread of the Presence; [37]the pure lampstand with its lamps set on it and all its utensils and the oil for the light; [38]the golden altar, the anointing oil and the fragrant incense, and the screen for the entrance of the tent; [39]the bronze altar and its grating of bronze, its poles, and all its utensils; the basin with its stand; [40]the hangings of the court, its pillars, and its bases, and the screen for the gate of the court, its cords, and its pegs; and all the utensils for the service of the tabernacle, for the tent of meeting; [41]the finely worked vestments for ministering in the holy place, the sacred vestments for the priest Aaron, and the vestments of his sons to serve as priests. [42]The Israelites had done all of the work as the LORD had commanded Moses. [43]When Moses saw that they had done all the work as the LORD had commanded, he blessed them.

40 The LORD spoke to Moses, [2]"On the first day of the first month you shall set up the tabernacle of the tent of meeting. [3]You shall put in it the ark of the covenant, and you shall screen the ark with the curtain. [4]You shall bring in the table and arrange its setting, and you shall bring in the lampstand and set up its lamps. [5]You shall put the golden altar for incense before the ark of the covenant and set up the screen for the entrance of the tabernacle. [6]You shall set the altar of burnt offering before the entrance of the tabernacle of the tent of meeting [7]and place the basin between the tent of meeting and the

b 39.23 Meaning of Heb uncertain   *c* 39.24 Sam Gk Syr Vg: MT lacks *fine linen*   *d* 39.34 Meaning of Heb uncertain

42, 43). It underscores the careful and precise nature of Israel's obedience even as it underscores Moses's import as mediator. **39:30** For the function of the inscription *Holy to the* LORD, see 28:36–38.

39:32 The building is completed in obedience to God's instructions to Moses (see note at 39:1). The verb used to describe the tabernacle being *finished* is the same used in Gen. 2:1–2.

39:42–43 In Genesis, God blesses creation upon its completion. Here in Exodus, analogically, Moses blesses the people who have fulfilled the Lord's commandments.

40:1–15 Consistent with prior patterns in the book, God first instructs, and the commands are executed (vv. 16–33). **40:2** The erection of the temple takes place at the beginning of the year and,

altar and put water in it. [8]You shall set up the court all around and hang up the screen for the gate of the court. [9]Then you shall take the anointing oil and anoint the tabernacle and all that is in it and consecrate it and all its furniture, so that it shall become holy. [10]You shall also anoint the altar of burnt offering and all its utensils and consecrate the altar, so that the altar shall be most holy. [11]You shall also anoint the basin with its stand and consecrate it. [12]Then you shall bring Aaron and his sons to the entrance of the tent of meeting and wash them with water [13]and put on Aaron the sacred vestments, and you shall anoint him and consecrate him, so that he may serve me as priest. [14]You shall bring his sons also and put tunics on them [15]and anoint them, as you anointed their father, that they may serve me as priests; their anointing shall admit them to a perpetual priesthood throughout all their generations."

16 Moses did everything just as the Lord had commanded him. [17]In the first month in the second year, on the first day of the month, the tabernacle was set up. [18]Moses set up the tabernacle; he laid its bases and set up its frames and put in its poles and raised up its pillars, [19]and he spread the tent over the tabernacle and put the covering of the tent over it as the Lord had commanded Moses. [20]He took the covenant and put it into the ark and put the poles on the ark and set the cover above the ark, [21]and he brought the ark into the tabernacle and set up the curtain for screening and screened the ark of the covenant as the Lord had commanded Moses. [22]He put the table in the tent of meeting, on the north side of the tabernacle, outside the curtain, [23]and set the bread in order on it before the Lord as

the Lord had commanded Moses. [24]He put the lampstand in the tent of meeting, opposite the table on the south side of the tabernacle, [25]and set up the lamps before the Lord as the Lord had commanded Moses. [26]He put the golden altar in the tent of meeting before the curtain [27]and offered fragrant incense on it as the Lord had commanded Moses. [28]He also put in place the screen for the entrance of the tabernacle. [29]He set the altar of burnt offering at the entrance of the tabernacle of the tent of meeting and offered on it the burnt offering and the grain offering as the Lord had commanded Moses. [30]He set the basin between the tent of meeting and the altar and put water in it for washing, [31]with which Moses and Aaron and his sons washed their hands and their feet. [32]When they went into the tent of meeting and when they approached the altar, they washed as the Lord had commanded Moses. [33]He set up the court around the tabernacle and the altar and put up the screen at the gate of the court. So Moses finished the work.

34 Then the cloud covered the tent of meeting, and the glory of the Lord filled the tabernacle. [35]Moses was not able to enter the tent of meeting because the cloud settled upon it, and the glory of the Lord filled the tabernacle. [36]Whenever the cloud was taken up from the tabernacle, the Israelites would set out on each stage of their journey, [37]but if the cloud was not taken up, then they did not set out until the day that it was taken up. [38]For the cloud of the Lord was on the tabernacle by day, and fire was in the cloud[e] by night, before the eyes of all the house of Israel at each stage of their journey.

e 40.38 Heb it

like the Passover, orients the people liturgically. **40:9** Anointing with oil is a method of consecration. This verse in Exodus may evoke the consecration of the Sabbath in Gen. 2:3.

40:15 The priesthood of Aaron and his sons is meant to be perpetual.

40:16–23 Once again, the refrain *as the Lord had commanded [Moses]* recurs frequently (vv. 16, 19, 21, 23, 25, 27, 29, 32), reinforcing Moses's role as leader extraordinaire and certifying that this sanctuary is indeed God's design.

40:31 Even *Moses* has to wash before entrance, an addition to the earlier instruction (cf. 30:18–20).

40:33 Moses *finished* the work, with the verb again echoing God's completion of creation in Gen. 2:2 (see note at Exod. 39:32).

40:34–38 Once everything is in place, God's glory comes to dwell in the tabernacle in the form of the cloud and the pillar of fire that had been with the people since they came out of Egypt. At the end of Exodus, the traditions of the cloud and pillar of fire, the covenant at Sinai (present via the tablets in the ark), and the tabernacle structure itself all come together. **40:36** The language indicates God's presence is ongoing and visible. The people follow obediently. **40:38** The book closes with a note on God's accompanying presence with Israel *at each stage of their journey*.

LEVITICUS

In the Torah, there is a collection of texts that detail the legal and ritual laws at the heart of Israel's covenant with God, particularly as it pertains to the temple and the priesthood (see **"Priests (Leviticus)," p. 176**). From a narrative point of view, most of this Priestly material is divine speech at Mount Sinai, delivered by God to Moses in the presence of the people after Israel's escape from Egyptian bondage. This Sinai scene runs from Exod. 19 through Num. 10:10, at which time Israel forms into ranks and marches into the wilderness. In the center of this collection of Priestly texts is the book of Leviticus.

Leviticus has many textual links with both Exodus and Numbers, but it does stand alone as a separate book. The first half, sometimes called "the Priestly Torah," forms its own coherent unit:

Chaps. 1–3: The three main forms of sacrifice
Chaps. 4–5: Purification and guilt offerings
Chaps. 6–7: Instructions for priests regarding sacrificial rituals
Chaps. 8–10: The consecration and initiation of Aaron and his sons
Chaps. 11–15: Purity regulations
Chap. 16: The Day of Atonement

The second half of Leviticus includes the Holiness Code (chaps. 17–26), called such because of the repeated use of the word "holy." The "code" ends with covenantal "blessings and curses," followed by an appendix of supplementary laws concerning votive offerings (chap. 27). The Holiness Code may be divided into these sections:

Chaps. 17–20: Ritual and ethical laws
Chaps. 21–22: Further instructions for priests
Chaps. 23–25: The holy festival calendar
Chap. 26: Covenant blessings and curses
Chap. 27: Appendix

Date, Authorship, and Literary History

The authorship and date of Leviticus are a matter of debate. Some scholars have argued for a preexilic origin for some or all of this material, and others would date it to the period of the Babylonian exile (586–533 BCE) or even later. Complicating this question is the matter of the two halves of the book: whether they are from different traditions and which one came first. Even though the book contains at least two sections of ritual legislation, they have been integrated by the final editors into the Sinai narrative. In this way, ritual laws about how priests should perform sacrifices, which animals are considered clean, and the like are placed in the words of God spoken to Moses on the mountain and repeated by Moses to the people. This editorial placement functions to locate the foundations of Priestly law firmly in the mythic past, giving the Priestly legislation both cultural significance and rhetorical power.

One common view is that Lev. 1–16 originated in the preexilic First Temple period, while Lev. 17–26 is the product of the so-called Holiness School during the exile (see **"Exile (2 Kings)," p. 539**). The latter (and later) writers would have edited the first part of the book lightly (see Lev. 11:44–45) and added a second set of ritual and ethical laws that redefine the most important concept in the Priestly worldview—namely, holiness (see **"Holiness (Exodus)," p. 88**, and **"Holiness and Purity," p. 158**). Whereas the Priestly Torah of chaps. 1–16 restricts holiness to the physical space around the deity—largely because humanity's normal state is "common" (that is, *not* holy; Lev. 10:10)—the Holiness Code commands all of Israel to "be holy" (Lev. 19:2). This expansion of the concept of holiness changes the relationship between God and the people and creates a more dynamic link between the domains of ritual and morality: to disobey God's moral law is to violate the demands of holiness, to perform illegitimate or incorrect rituals is to sin against God (see **"Sin," p. 150**), and the way in which Israel becomes holy is not by approaching the sanctuary but through careful obedience to God's covenantal commands. This expansion of holiness beyond the realm of the

sanctuary or (later) temple makes good sense within the historical context and social experience of the Israelites in exile, where they lived far from Jerusalem after the First Temple was destroyed.

Reading Guide

In Leviticus, God delivers through Moses the instructions that the people must follow to manage the spread of ritual impurity and to facilitate the relationship between God and Israel and among the Israelites themselves. Textual refrains reveal the movement of the text through different topics, particularly variations on "The LORD spoke to Moses, saying," "Speak to the Israelites, saying," and the like (see, e.g., Lev. 1:1; 4:1–2; 8:1; and 11:1). In the first few chapters (Lev. 1–7), God describes the three main types of offerings (the burnt offering, the grain offering, and the sacrifice of well-being), including how the burnt offering is to be used in both purification and guilt rituals (see **"Offerings and Sacrifices," p. 146**). Repetition plays an important role in these chapters, indicating the importance of precision in both teaching the law and following it. In chaps. 11–15, the same precision attends rules about impurity deriving from unclean animals, childbirth, skin diseases, and other maladies. When Aaron and his sons (the priests) perform the rituals for the first time in chaps. 8–10, everything seems to go well until disaster strikes. In chap. 10, Aaron's sons are consumed by divine fire for making an important (but not entirely clear) mistake. This leads to dismay from Aaron and a renewed flurry of law giving from Moses, culminating in Aaron's initial performance of the solemn and dangerous Day of Atonement ritual in chap. 16. Similar ambiguity followed by caution can be seen in the final narrative in the book, the story of the blasphemer (chap. 24). In sum, the ritual and narrative sections function together to emphasize the need for precision in following ritual instructions and also reflect the inherent unknowns that come from dwelling with a holy God who is sometimes inscrutable and always uncontrollable.

The second half of Leviticus turns mostly to moral and ethical topics and emphasizes the need for integrity among priests and worshipers alike. Passages about illicit sex in chaps. 18 and 20 are some of the more quoted parts of the book in many contemporary circles, though they require greater care in interpretation than they sometimes receive. The laws about the Sabbath, the agricultural Sabbath year, and the yearly festivals found in this part of Leviticus (see chaps. 23, 25) are important in the history and contemporary practice of Judaism. The overall covenantal structure of the Priestly writings is evident in the blessings and curses that are found in chap. 26 (cf. Deut. 28). The laws in Leviticus may seem at times weighty and difficult to follow. However, if the people are careful to observe the laws, God promises to provide abundance, security, and peace. Most significant of all, God will "place my dwelling in your midst. . . . I will be your God, and you shall be my people" (Lev. 26:11–12). The care and precision that the priests embody in the performance of rituals enable the people to live within the boundaries of the covenant for the well-being and flourishing of Israel.

Bryan Bibb

1 The LORD summoned Moses and spoke to him from the tent of meeting, saying, ²"Speak to the Israelites and say to them: When any of you bring an offering of livestock to the LORD, you shall bring your offering from the herd or from the flock.

3 "If the offering is a burnt offering from the herd, you shall offer a male without blemish;

1:1–2 Leviticus continues the story of the revelation of God to Moses at Mount Sinai after Israel's escape from Egypt. The book is almost entirely quoted speech. God addresses Moses from inside the Holy of Holies in the tent of meeting, with Moses listening outside the screened entrance (Exod. 26:36). Moses is told to *speak to the Israelites* what God has spoken to him. It is central to Priestly theology that the people know what the law requires and that the priests perform the majority of their service in full view of the congregation. These instructions are for *any of you* who brings an offering, which includes both men and women, all Israelites, and sometimes even "aliens residing in Israel" (Lev. 22:18).

1:3 The first of the three main types of sacrificial rites outlined in Leviticus is the *burnt offering*

you shall bring it to the entrance of the tent of meeting, for acceptance on your behalf before the Lord. ⁴You shall lay your hand on the head of the burnt offering, and it shall be acceptable on your behalf as atonement for you. ⁵The bull shall be slaughtered before the Lord, and Aaron's sons the priests shall offer the blood, dashing the blood against all sides of the altar that is at the entrance of the tent of meeting. ⁶The burnt offering shall be flayed and cut up into its parts. ⁷The sons of the priest Aaron shall put fire on the altar and arrange wood on the fire. ⁸Aaron's sons the priests shall arrange the parts, with the head and the suet, on the wood that is on the fire on the altar, ⁹but its entrails and its legs shall be washed with water. Then the priest shall turn the rest into smoke on the altar as a burnt offering, an offering by fire*ᵃ* of pleasing odor to the Lord.

10 "If your gift for a burnt offering is from the flock, from the sheep or goats, your offering shall be a male without blemish. ¹¹It shall be slaughtered on the north side of the altar before the Lord, and Aaron's sons the priests shall dash its blood against all sides of the altar. ¹²It shall be cut up into its parts, with its head and its suet, and the priest shall arrange them on the wood that is on the fire on the altar, ¹³but the entrails and the legs shall be washed with water. Then the priest shall offer the rest and turn it into smoke on the altar; it is a burnt offering, an offering by fire*ᵇ* of pleasing odor to the Lord.

14 "If your offering to the Lord is a burnt offering of birds, you shall choose your offering from turtledoves or pigeons. ¹⁵The priest shall bring it to the altar and wring off its head and turn it into smoke on the altar, and its blood shall be drained out against the side of the altar. ¹⁶He shall remove its entrails close to its tail feathers and throw it at the east side of the altar, in the place for ashes. ¹⁷He shall tear it open by its wings without severing it. Then the priest shall turn it into smoke on the altar, on the wood that is on the fire; it is a burnt offering, an offering by fire*ᶜ* of pleasing odor to the Lord.

2 "When anyone presents a grain offering to the Lord, the offering shall be of

a 1.9 Or *a gift*   *b* 1.13 Or *a gift*   *c* 1.17 Or *a gift*

("olah"), in which the offering is turned entirely into smoke. The offered object varies depending on the occasion and the economic means of the person bringing the sacrifice. The first set of instructions concerns a bull, which must be *without blemish*. Priests bear responsibility for ensuring that sacrificial animals meet the ritual requirements.

1:4 *As atonement for you.* The English word *atonement* was used first in William Tyndale's 1526 New Testament, as a way to describe the reconciliation between God and humans brought by Jesus. Tyndale then applied this term to the Hebrew concept "kipper" in Leviticus, the removal of ritual impurities often through the detergent properties of blood, and subsequent translators have followed him in using *atonement* here. This creates some confusion because "kipper" carries a narrowly ritual meaning in Leviticus, not the broader theological meaning that Tyndale brought into the text. However, in other parts of the Hebrew Bible, "kipper" does have a broader moral application to the cleansing of sin in general (Isa. 6:7; Jer. 18:23; Ps. 65:3). The same words can have different meanings in different parts of the Bible.

1:4-5 The sacrifice begins with the Israelite laying a hand on the animal to establish the ritual connection between them, "acceptance on your behalf before the Lord" (v. 3). After the animal is killed, the priests *dash* its blood on the sides of the altar for the cleansing of impurities. Blood is central to the Priestly system; in other texts it is sprinkled around the sanctuary (4:5-7; 16:14), put on the horns of the altar (4:25), and dabbed on the priests' ears and clothing (8:23-30) and on worshipers and their dwellings (14:25, 48-51). No one is allowed to eat any food with blood in it because "the life of every creature—its blood is its life" (17:14).

1:9 In other ancient contexts, sacrifice was often considered the food of the gods, and gods depended on priestly offerings for daily sustenance. The Bible rejects the notion that God needs the sacrificial offering. However, a small vestige of that idea remains in the notion that the burnt offering is *an offering by fire of pleasing odor to the Lord.* The priestly system invests sacrifice with deeply emotional significance for both worshipers and God.

1:10-17 Instructions continue for *sheep, goats, turtledoves,* and *pigeons.* The major difference is that birds are torn apart rather than cut into pieces, and their *entrails* are discarded rather than washed of dung (vv. 13, 16).

2:1 The second major form of sacrifice in Leviticus is the *grain offering* ("minha"), which can take

LEVITICUS 2

Focus On: Offerings and Sacrifices (Leviticus 1)

Ritual sacrifice was a common form of worship across the ancient Near East and Mediterranean. As a highly symbolic practice, sacrifice can be understood in multiple ways. Essentially, it is a gift to God, which can function as a form of thanksgiving. It can build community, establishing order within society as well as relationship between the people and God. It is also a way of procuring meat to eat, a way that acknowledges the profundity of taking life, even animal life. The Priestly system of offerings and sacrifices is laid out neatly in the first seven chapters of Leviticus. There are three main forms of offering: the burnt offering (*olah*), the grain offering (*minha*), and the offering of well-being (*shelamim*). The burnt offering (in which the whole animal is consumed by fire, given completely up to God; see Lev. 1) is the most important. It is used for the daily offerings (Exod. 29:38–42), in the inauguration of the priests (Lev. 9:12–14), as part of the purification process (Lev. 12:6), and throughout the yearly festivals (Lev. 23). But most importantly, it functions for the purposes of both purification and expiation of guilt. The purification offering (4:1–5:13), along with the application of blood to the altar and to the sanctuary furnishings, serves to cleanse the holy areas of impurity so that they do not come into contact with God's holiness (see **"Holiness and Purity," p. 158**). The guilt offering (Lev. 5:14–6:7) serves a similar purpose but specifically relates to actions in which a person has failed to fulfill their religious or social obligations (see **"Sin," p. 150**). The other two forms of sacrifice—the grain offering (Lev. 2) and the offering of well-being (Lev. 3)—require only a token portion of the offering to be burned as a gift to God, and the remainder becomes food either for the priests or for the people in communal celebration. In all these cases there is an accommodation for people who cannot afford an expensive offering. Individuals contribute as they are able for the health of the community, while the corporate worship of the community ensures the well-being of each individual, whether rich or poor. In this way, the sacrificial system is integral to Israel's practice of justice and righteousness.

Bryan Bibb

choice flour; the worshiper shall pour oil on it and put frankincense on it ²and bring it to Aaron's sons the priests. After taking from it a handful of the choice flour and oil, with all its frankincense, the priest shall turn this token portion into smoke on the altar, an offering by fire*d* of pleasing odor to the LORD. ³And what is left of the grain offering shall be for Aaron and his sons, a most holy part of the offerings by fire*e* to the LORD.

4 "When you present a grain offering baked in the oven, it shall be of choice flour: unleavened cakes mixed with oil or unleavened wafers spread with oil. ⁵If your offering is grain prepared on a griddle, it shall be of choice flour mixed with oil, unleavened; ⁶break it in pieces and pour oil on it; it is a grain offering. ⁷If your offering is grain prepared in a pan, it shall be made of choice flour in oil. ⁸You shall bring to the LORD the grain offering that is prepared in any of these ways, and when it is presented to the priest, he shall take it to the altar. ⁹The priest shall remove from the grain offering its token portion and

d 2.2 Or *a gift*   *e* 2.3 Or *the gifts*

a number of forms but functions primarily to provide food for the priests. This first option is "choice flour and oil, with all its frankincense" (v. 2), but it may also consist of an unleavened wafer or cake prepared in an oven, griddle, or pan (vv. 4–7) or harvested grain, crushed and roasted (v. 14).

2:2 The priest is to burn a *token portion* of the grain offering on the altar, which serves to honor and please God in the *offering by fire of pleasing odor*, similar to the burnt offering (1:13). This portion functions as a reminder that all resources come from and belong to God and that this small part offered to God stands in for the whole. The handful that the priest scoops out presumably includes the frankincense spice that is placed on top of the flour for aromatic incense offerings (Exod. 30:7–8).

2:3 The grain that goes to the priests is *most holy*, a term that separates the offerings that are partially eaten from those that are burned up completely (see also 6:10, 18; 7:6).

2:4 The cooked versions of the grain offerings do not include the frankincense spice. In the same way that the other main types of offerings allow variants for poor worshipers, this mode of grain offering may represent a cheaper option for those who cannot afford frankincense.

2:9–10 After the *token portion* is burned on the altar, the remainder is *for Aaron and his sons*.

turn this into smoke on the altar, an offering by fire[f] of pleasing odor to the Lord. [10]And what is left of the grain offering shall be for Aaron and his sons; it is a most holy part of the offerings by fire[g] to the Lord.

[11] "No grain offering that you bring to the Lord shall be made with leaven, for you must not turn any leaven or honey into smoke as an offering by fire[h] to the Lord. [12]You may bring them to the Lord as an offering of choice products, but they shall not be offered on the altar for a pleasing odor. [13]All your grain offerings you shall season with salt; you shall not omit from your grain offerings the salt of the covenant with your God; with all your offerings you shall offer salt.

[14] "If you bring a grain offering of first fruits to the Lord, you shall bring as the grain offering of your first fruits crushed new grain from fresh ears, roasted in fire. [15]You shall add oil to it and lay frankincense on it; it is a grain offering. [16]And the priest shall turn a token portion of it into smoke—some of the crushed grain and oil with all its frankincense; it is an offering by fire[i] to the Lord.

3 "If the offering is a sacrifice of well-being, if you offer an animal from the herd, whether male or female, you shall offer one without blemish before the Lord. [2]You shall lay your hand on the head of the offering and slaughter it at the entrance of the tent of meeting, and Aaron's sons the priests shall dash the blood against all sides of the altar. [3]You shall offer from the sacrifice of well-being, as an offering by fire[j] to the Lord, the fat that covers the entrails and all the fat

that is around the entrails, [4]the two kidneys with the fat that is on them at the loins, and the appendage of the liver, which he shall remove with the kidneys. [5]Then Aaron's sons shall turn these into smoke on the altar, with the burnt offering that is on the wood on the fire, as an offering by fire[k] of pleasing odor to the Lord.

[6] "If your offering for a sacrifice of well-being to the Lord is from the flock, male or female, you shall offer one without blemish. [7]If you present a sheep as your offering, you shall bring it before the Lord [8]and lay your hand on the head of the offering. It shall be slaughtered before the tent of meeting, and Aaron's sons shall dash its blood against all sides of the altar. [9]You shall present its fat from the sacrifice of well-being, as an offering by fire[l] to the Lord: the whole fatty tail, which shall be removed close to the backbone, the fat that covers the entrails and all the fat that is around the entrails, [10]the two kidneys with the fat that is on them at the loins, and the appendage of the liver, which you shall remove with the kidneys. [11]Then the priest shall turn these into smoke on the altar as a food offering by fire[m] to the Lord.

[12] "If your offering is a goat, you shall bring it before the Lord [13]and lay your hand on its head; it shall be slaughtered before the tent of meeting, and the sons of Aaron shall dash its blood against all sides of the altar. [14]You shall present as your offering from it, as an offering by fire[n] to the Lord, the fat that covers

f 2.9 Or *a gift* g 2.10 Or *the gifts* h 2.11 Or *a gift* i 2.16 Or *a gift* j 3.3 Or *a gift* k 3.5 Or *a gift* l 3.9 Or *a gift* m 3.11 Or *a food gift* n 3.14 Or *a gift*

As in 1:7–8, the sons of Aaron function as priests and are presented in the Priestly literature as the founders of an Aaronic priestly line (Exod. 28:1). Priesthood is a hereditary profession, and since the priests have no other work or means of support, they obtain their food through the grain offering.

2:14 The option to offer *crushed* and *roasted* grain may be a reference to barley, while the "choice flour" of v. 1 would refer to wheat flour. As part of the *first fruits* offering, this form of the grain offering would be mandatory rather than optional (Num. 28:26).

3:1 *Sacrifice of well-being* ("shelamim"), sometimes translated as "peace offering" or "fellowship offering," refers to a form of animal sacrifice that is not burned up completely but instead becomes the basis of communal eating and celebration. It has a variety of different uses, most notably the "thank offering," the "votive offering," and the "freewill offering" (7:11–18).

3:3–5 In this case the *offering by fire of pleasing odor to the* Lord consists only of the suet, the thick fat layer that covers the organs, along with the kidneys and the *appendage of the liver*, the caudate lobe. After he pours out the blood, the priest burns these parts in remembrance and honor of God.

3:6 Similar to the burnt offering, if the worshiper cannot afford a bull, they may bring a sheep or a goat (v. 12) to be processed and offered in the same manner as the bull.

the entrails and all the fat that is around the entrails, [15]the two kidneys with the fat that is on them at the loins, and the appendage of the liver, which you shall remove with the kidneys. [16]Then the priest shall turn these into smoke on the altar as a food offering by fire[o] for a pleasing odor.

"All fat is the LORD's. [17]It shall be a perpetual statute throughout your generations, in all your settlements: you must not eat any fat or any blood."

4 The LORD spoke to Moses, saying, [2]"Speak to the Israelites, saying: When anyone sins unintentionally in any of the LORD's commandments about things not to be done and does any one of them:

[3] "If it is the anointed priest who sins, thus bringing guilt on the people, he shall offer for the sin that he has committed a bull of the herd as a purification offering to the LORD. [4]He shall bring the bull to the entrance of the tent of meeting before the LORD and lay his hand on the head of the bull; the bull shall be slaughtered before the LORD. [5]The anointed priest shall take some of the blood of the bull and bring it into the tent of meeting.

[6]The priest shall dip his finger in the blood and sprinkle some of the blood seven times before the LORD in front of the curtain of the sanctuary. [7]The priest shall put some of the blood on the horns of the altar of fragrant incense that is in the tent of meeting before the LORD, and the rest of the blood of the bull he shall pour out at the base of the altar of burnt offering, which is at the entrance of the tent of meeting. [8]He shall remove all the fat from the bull of purification offering: the fat that covers the entrails and all the fat that is around the entrails, [9]the two kidneys with the fat that is on them at the loins, and the lobe of the liver, which he shall remove with the kidneys, [10]just as these are removed from the ox of the sacrifice of well-being. The priest shall turn them into smoke upon the altar of burnt offering. [11]But the skin of the bull and all its flesh, as well as its head, its legs, its entrails, and its dung—[12]all the rest of the bull—he shall carry out to a clean place outside the camp, to the ash heap, and shall burn it on a wood fire; at the ash heap it shall be burned.

o 3.16 Or *a food gift*

3:16 It is unclear why *all fat is the LORD's*. However, note that this requirement means that all meat intended for the table must originate in a sacrificial rite. Leviticus assumes that altars are present around the country for this purpose. In Deuteronomy, which requires all sacrifices to take place in Jerusalem, provision is made for profane slaughter, the processing of animals in the field for consumption (contrast 17:3–7 and Deut. 12:15–16).

4:1–2 This begins the section that addresses the situation *when anyone sins unintentionally* by doing something that God has commanded *not to be done* (chaps. 4–5). These two sacrifices, purification and guilt offerings, almost entirely address violations through negligence or ignorance. The Priestly sacrificial system is designed to deal with impurities generated in everyday life, including inadvertent violations, not intentional and willful disobedience to God's commands. Those who commit intentional sins are punished by exclusion from the sanctuary and a variety of other penalties, including death, and they rely entirely on the mercy of God, not the performance of a ritual to restore them. The only possible exceptions in the Priestly material in which we see deliberate sins addressed through sacrifice are 5:1–4; 16:21; 26:40; and Num. 5:6–7.

4:3 The *anointed priest* must perform the highest level of burnt offering, *a bull of the herd* for his *purification offering* ("hattat"). The translation of the phrase has traditionally been "sin offering," based on the use of the Hebrew term for "sin" in other contexts (see **"Sin," p. 150**).

4:5–6 The blood ritual in which the priest shall *sprinkle some of the blood seven times* inside the tent of meeting reflects the fact that the priests' negligence generates impurities that invade the holy areas of the sanctuary. He also puts blood on the two altars (v. 18). This blood ritual cleanses impurity in the sacred space so that the holy God will not be forced to abandon the sanctuary.

4:8–12 This ritual begins the same way as the sacrifice of well-being, but instead of becoming a meal, the rest of the bull is burned in *a clean place outside the camp*. This version of the offering for unintentional violation by the anointed priest or by the community as a whole (vv. 13–21) requires a higher-than-normal level of precaution: blood is sprinkled inside the tent and on the incense altar, and the remaining flesh is burned outside the camp rather than eaten (cf. 5:13; 6:26, 30).

13 "If the whole congregation of Israel errs unintentionally, and the matter escapes the notice of the assembly, and they do any one of the things that by the LORD's commandments ought not to be done and incur guilt, [14]when the sin that they have committed becomes known, the assembly shall offer a bull of the herd for a purification offering and bring it before the tent of meeting. [15]The elders of the congregation shall lay their hands on the head of the bull before the LORD, and the bull shall be slaughtered before the LORD. [16]The anointed priest shall bring some of the blood of the bull into the tent of meeting, [17]and the priest shall dip his finger in the blood and sprinkle it seven times before the LORD, in front of the curtain. [18]He shall put some of the blood on the horns of the altar that is before the LORD in the tent of meeting, and the rest of the blood he shall pour out at the base of the altar of burnt offering that is at the entrance of the tent of meeting. [19]He shall remove all its fat and turn it into smoke on the altar. [20]He shall do with the bull just as is done with the bull of purification offering; he shall do the same with this. The priest shall make atonement for them, and they shall be forgiven. [21]He shall carry the bull outside the camp and burn it as he burned the first bull; it is the purification offering for the assembly.

22 "When a ruler sins, doing unintentionally any one of all the things that by the commandments of the LORD his God ought not to be done and incurs guilt, [23]once the sin that he has committed is made known to him, he shall bring as his offering a male goat without blemish. [24]He shall lay his hand on the head of the goat; it shall be slaughtered at the spot where the burnt offering is slaughtered before the LORD; it is a purification offering. [25]The priest shall take some of the blood of the purification offering with his finger and put it on the horns of the altar of burnt offering and pour out the rest of its blood at the base of the altar of burnt offering. [26]All its fat he shall turn into smoke on the altar, like the fat of the sacrifice of well-being. Thus the priest shall make atonement on his behalf for his sin, and he shall be forgiven.

27 "If anyone of the ordinary people among you sins unintentionally in doing any one of the things that by the LORD's commandments ought not to be done and incurs guilt, [28]when the sin that you have committed is made known to you, you shall bring a female goat without blemish as your offering, for the sin that you have committed. [29]You shall lay your hand on the head of the purification offering; the purification offering shall be slaughtered at the place of the burnt offering. [30]The priest shall take some of its blood with his finger and put it on the horns of the altar of burnt offering, and he shall pour out the rest of its blood at the base of the altar. [31]He shall remove all its fat, as the fat is removed from the sacrifice of well-being, and the priest shall turn it into smoke on the altar for a pleasing odor to the LORD. Thus the priest shall make atonement on your behalf, and you shall be forgiven.

32 "If the offering you bring as a purification offering is a sheep, you shall bring a female without blemish. [33]You shall lay your hand on the head of the purification offering; it shall be slaughtered as a purification offering at the spot where the burnt offering is slaughtered. [34]The priest shall take some of the blood of the purification offering with his finger and put it on the horns of the altar of burnt offering and pour out the rest of its blood at the base of the altar. [35]You shall remove all its fat, as the fat of the sheep is removed from the sacrifice of well-being, and the priest shall turn it into smoke on the altar, with the offerings by fire[p] to the LORD. Thus

p 4.35 Or *the gifts*

4:13 This version of the purification ritual concerns the unintentional sin of the *whole congregation of Israel.*

4:15 Note that the priest lays his hand on the bull in v. 4, and here that act of identification is performed by *the elders of the congregation.*

4:20 The priest is the agent of the *atonement* (see note on 1:4), but God is the agent through whom *they shall be forgiven.* (See **"Atonement (Reconciliation),"** p. 168.)

4:22–23 The purification offering for a ruler requires blood to be poured only on the main altar, and the meat left after the burning of the fat belongs to the priest. The same process applies to the purification offering of "ordinary people" (v. 27). The ruler is to bring *a male goat* while other people may bring either a "female goat" (v. 28) or a female sheep (v. 32).

Focus On: Sin (Leviticus 4)

Broadly, "sin" refers to any transgression of God's commandments through either the commission of an act or the neglect of an obligation. The list of specific sins in Leviticus is long, encompassing violations of a ritual (5:3; 19:7; 22:1–30), sexual (18:6–23; 20:10–21), social (6:1–5; 19:9–17), and theological nature (18:24–30; 20:1–9). The Hebrew term *hattat* is used both for sin *and* for the sacrifice that cleanses the impurity generated by sin (Lev. 4). This "purification offering" is often called in English the "sin offering," a translation that leads to the mistaken conclusion that Israel's priests performed animal sacrifices to bring about forgiveness through the shedding of blood. Sacrifice in Leviticus is more narrowly focused: the purification offering and the blood rituals that go with it serve the purpose of cleansing the impurities that are generated by sinful actions (see **"Holiness and Purity," p. 158**). In addition, the Priestly writers emphasize the role of intention in the commission of sin. The purification offering and guilt offering (see **"Offerings and Sacrifices," p. 146**) almost exclusively apply to cases of *unintentional* sin. Even in the few cases in which a sacrifice accompanies an *intentional* sin, the sacrifice itself does not generate forgiveness. Only God can forgive sin. Therefore, the person who has sinned must confess to God and rely on God's mercy for forgiveness (note the role of confession in Lev. 5:1–6; 16:21; 26:40). Purification offerings thus do not generate forgiveness of sin, and they are not required for forgiveness. Much of the Priestly text was written or collected during the Babylonian exile, when the people had no temple or altar; they were acutely aware of their reliance on the mercy of God. Another common misconception is that sin is unavoidable or inevitable. While the Torah certainly recognizes the pervasive nature of sin and the people's constant need of mercy, the legal system itself is based on the affirmation that people are in fact able to obey the law. The law itself is a gracious revelation of God's vision for the human community, and if the people obey it, they will see their lives and world flourish (see Deut. 6:20–25). Sin is therefore a choice that leads to the rupture of the relationship between God and the people and to the degradation of justice and righteousness in the community.

Bryan Bibb

the priest shall make atonement on your behalf for the sin that you have committed, and you shall be forgiven.

5 "When any of you sin in that you have heard a public adjuration to testify and, although able to testify as one who has seen or learned of the matter, do not speak up, you are subject to punishment. ²Or when any of you touch any unclean thing, whether the carcass of an unclean beast or the carcass of unclean livestock or the carcass of an unclean swarming thing, and are unaware of it, you have become unclean and are guilty. ³Or when you touch human uncleanness—any uncleanness by which one can become unclean—and are unaware of it, when you come to know it, you shall be guilty. ⁴Or when any of you utter aloud a rash oath for a bad or a good purpose, whatever people utter in an oath and are unaware of it, when you come to know it, you shall in any of these be guilty. ⁵When you realize your guilt in any of these, you shall confess the sin that you have committed, ⁶and you shall bring to the Lord, as your penalty for the sin that you have committed, a female from the flock, a sheep or a goat, as a purification offering, and the priest shall make atonement on your behalf for your sin.

7 "But if you cannot afford a sheep, you shall bring to the Lord, as your penalty for the sin that you have committed, two turtledoves or two pigeons, one for a purification offering and the other for a burnt offering. ⁸You shall bring them to the priest, who shall offer first the one for the purification offering, wringing its head at the nape without severing it.

5:1–4 The list of circumstances that require a purification offering continues with failing to *testify* (v. 1), touching an unclean thing and being *unaware of it* (i.e., inadvertently; vv. 2–3), or uttering a *rash oath* (v. 4).

5:5 *Confess the sin that you have committed.* The act of confession is mentioned only elsewhere in 16:21 and 26:40, which seem to address situations in which a person has sinned deliberately. The confession in this case refers to the verbal declaration of guilt, not merely an internal feeling of contrition. Confession perhaps transfers intentional sin into the ritual category of unintentional sin, which can then be addressed through a purification ritual (see **"Sin," p. 150**).

[9]He shall sprinkle some of the blood of the purification offering on the side of the altar, while the rest of the blood shall be drained out at the base of the altar; it is a purification offering. [10]And the second he shall offer for a burnt offering according to the regulation. Thus the priest shall make atonement on your behalf for the sin that you have committed, and you shall be forgiven.

[11] "But if you cannot afford two turtledoves or two pigeons, you shall bring as your offering for the sin that you have committed one-tenth of an ephah of choice flour for a purification offering; you shall not put oil on it or lay frankincense on it, for it is a purification offering. [12]You shall bring it to the priest, and the priest shall scoop up a handful of it as its memorial portion and turn this into smoke on the altar, with the offerings by fire[q] to the LORD; it is a purification offering. [13]Thus the priest shall make atonement on your behalf for whichever of these sins you have committed, and you shall be forgiven. As with the grain offering, the rest shall be for the priest."

[14] The LORD spoke to Moses, saying, [15]"When any of you commit a trespass and sin unintentionally against any of the holy things of the LORD, you shall bring, as your guilt offering to the LORD, a ram without blemish from the flock, convertible into silver by the sanctuary shekel; it is a guilt offering. [16]And you shall make restitution for the holy thing in which you were remiss and shall add one-fifth to it and give it to the priest. The priest shall make atonement on your behalf with the ram of the guilt offering, and you shall be forgiven.

[17] "If any of you sin without knowing it, doing any of the things that by the LORD's commandments ought not to be done, you have incurred guilt and are subject to punishment. [18]You shall bring to the priest a ram without blemish from the flock, or the equivalent, as a guilt offering, and the priest shall make atonement on your behalf for the error that you committed unintentionally, and you shall be forgiven. [19]It is a guilt offering; you have incurred guilt before the LORD."

6 [1]The LORD spoke to Moses, saying, [2]"When any of you sin and commit a trespass against the LORD by deceiving a neighbor in a matter of a deposit or a pledge or by robbery or if you have defrauded a neighbor [3]or have found something lost and lied about it—if you swear falsely regarding any of the various things that one may do and sin—[4]when you have sinned and recognize your guilt and would restore what you took by robbery or by fraud or the deposit that was committed to you or the lost thing that you found [5]or anything else about which you have sworn falsely, you shall repay the principal amount and add one-fifth to it. You shall pay it to its owner when you recognize your guilt. [6]And you shall bring to the priest, as your guilt offering to the LORD, a ram without blemish from the flock, or its equivalent, for a guilt

q 5.12 Or the gifts   r 6.1 5.20 in Heb

5:11 If a person cannot afford a sheep or even two birds (v. 7), they can bring as their purification offering a measure of *choice flour* equaling around 2.3 liters, traditionally understood as one day's worth of bread flour for one person. A token portion is burned and the rest is given to the priest, as in the grain offering (chap. 2).

5:15 *Guilt offering* ("asham"), the second primary function of the burnt offering, is used when *any of you . . . sin unintentionally against any of the holy things of the* LORD and with respect to breaking sacred oaths (6:1–7). Notably, this is the only sacrificial requirement that is *convertible into silver*. A better term for *guilt offering* might be "reparation offering," since its purpose is to provide restitution for negligent or inadvertent breaches of holy obligations.

5:16 The sum of the silver payment amounts to the value of the *holy thing in which you were remiss* plus 20 percent. The *restitution* achieved in this payment accompanies the *atonement* accomplished by the *guilt offering*, resulting in the person being *forgiven*. The concepts of guilt, restitution, atonement, and forgiveness are closely related but have distinct meanings and roles in the technical Priestly system.

6:2–3 Cases of guilt offerings having to do with the violation of sacred oaths and matters of deposit, pledge, robbery, fraud, or lost property. In each of these cases, the offenders then *swear falsely* and thus commit a violation of their sacred duty to God.

6:4–6 Forgiveness for such acts requires full restitution plus a 20 percent penalty to the person who was defrauded and the offering of a ram for a guilt offering, which can be paid in silver instead.

offering. [7]The priest shall make atonement on your behalf before the Lord, and you shall be forgiven for any of the things that one may do and incur guilt thereby."

8 [8]The Lord spoke to Moses, saying, [9]"Command Aaron and his sons: This is the rule of the burnt offering. The burnt offering itself shall remain on the hearth upon the altar all night until the morning, while the fire on the altar shall be kept burning. [10]The priest shall put on his linen vestments after putting on his linen undergarments next to his body, and he shall take up the ashes to which the fire has reduced the burnt offering on the altar and place them beside the altar. [11]Then he shall take off his vestments and put on other garments and carry the ashes out to a clean place outside the camp. [12]The fire on the altar shall be kept burning; it shall not go out. Every morning the priest shall add wood to it, lay out the burnt offering on it, and turn into smoke the fat pieces of the offerings of well-being. [13]A perpetual fire shall be kept burning on the altar; it shall not go out.

14 "This is the rule of the grain offering: The sons of Aaron shall offer it before the Lord, in front of the altar. [15]They shall take from it a handful of the choice flour and oil of the grain offering, with all the frankincense that is on the offering, and they shall turn its memorial portion into smoke on the altar as a pleasing odor to the Lord. [16]Aaron and his sons shall eat what is left of it; it shall be eaten as unleavened cakes in a holy place; in the court of the tent of meeting they shall eat it. [17]It shall not be baked with leaven. I have given it as their portion of my offerings by fire;[t] it is most holy, like the purification offering and the guilt offering. [18]Every male among the descendants of Aaron shall eat of it, as their perpetual due throughout your generations, from the Lord's offerings by fire;[u] anything that touches them shall become holy."

19 The Lord spoke to Moses, saying, [20]"This is the offering that Aaron and his sons shall offer to the Lord on the day when he is anointed: one-tenth of an ephah of choice flour as a regular grain offering, half of it in the morning and half in the evening. [21]It shall be made with oil on a griddle; you shall bring it well soaked, as a grain offering of baked[v] pieces, and you shall present it as a pleasing odor to the Lord. [22]And so the priest, anointed from among Aaron's descendants as a successor, shall prepare it; it is the Lord's—a perpetual due—to be turned entirely into smoke. [23]Every grain offering of a priest shall be wholly burned; it shall not be eaten."

24 The Lord spoke to Moses, saying, [25]"Speak to Aaron and his sons, saying: This is the rule of the purification offering. The purification offering shall be slaughtered before the Lord at the spot where the burnt offering is slaughtered; it is most holy. [26]The priest who offers it as a purification offering shall eat of it; it shall be eaten in a holy place, in the court of the tent of meeting. [27]Whatever touches its flesh shall become holy, and when any of its blood is spattered on a garment, you shall wash the bespattered part in a holy place. [28]A clay vessel in which it was boiled shall be broken, but if it is boiled in a bronze vessel, that shall be scoured and rinsed in water. [29]Every male among the priests shall eat of it; it is most holy. [30]But no purification offering shall be eaten from which any blood is brought into the tent of

s 6.8 6.1 in Heb   *t* 6.17 Or *my gifts*   *u* 6.18 Or *the Lord's gifts*
v 6.21 Meaning of Heb uncertain

6:8–7:38 Instructions that supplement the laws found in chaps. 1–5, marked by the phrases *the Lord spoke to Moses* and *this is the rule of*. **6:8** V. 6:1 in the Hebrew text. **6:10–11** The priest wears special garments while in the holy areas serving as priest (see 8:6–10). He must never wear these items outside the holy area, and so here he changes into *other garments* for the disposal of ashes outside the camp in order to avoid the mixing of the holy and the impure in the camp (see **"Holiness and Purity," p. 158**). **6:16–18** This description of the grain offering (chap. 2) clarifies that the food generated can be eaten by any of the priests *as their perpetual due*. They are to eat of it in a *holy place*— that is, their dining area in the courtyard beside the altar. **6:19–22** In contrast to the grain offering by the laity in chap. 2, this refers to the *regular grain offering* offered by Aaron (i.e., the high priest) daily and like the burnt offering *turned entirely into smoke*. The grain offering given by the laity provides food for the priests, but Aaron's grain offering is the *perpetual due* of God. **6:26** *The priest who offers it* might suggest that *only* this priest eats of the meat. However, v. 29 clarifies that all the priests may eat of it, so evidently the offering priest must eat some of the meat, and then it is available for all the priests in the holy area. **6:27–29** The *most holy* status of the purification offering means that extra

meeting for atonement in the holy place; it shall be burned with fire.

7 "This is the rule of the guilt offering; it is most holy. [2]At the spot where the burnt offering is slaughtered, they shall slaughter the guilt offering, and its blood shall be dashed against all sides of the altar. [3]All its fat shall be offered: the fatty tail, the fat that covers the entrails, [4]the two kidneys with the fat that is on them at the loins, and the appendage of the liver, which shall be removed with the kidneys. [5]The priest shall turn them into smoke on the altar as an offering by fire[w] to the LORD; it is a guilt offering. [6]Every male among the priests shall eat of it; it shall be eaten in a holy place; it is most holy.

7 "The guilt offering is like the purification offering; the same rule applies to them: the priest who makes atonement with it shall have it. [8]So, too, the priest who offers a burnt offering for anyone shall keep the skin of the burnt offering that he has offered. [9]And every grain offering baked in the oven and all that is prepared in a pan or on a griddle shall belong to the priest who offers it. [10]But every other grain offering, mixed with oil or dry, shall belong to all the sons of Aaron equally.

11 "This is the rule of the sacrifice of well-being that one may offer to the LORD. [12]If you offer it for thanksgiving, you shall offer with the thank offering unleavened cakes mixed with oil, unleavened wafers spread with oil, and cakes of choice flour well soaked in oil. [13]With your thanksgiving sacrifice of well-being you shall bring your offering with cakes of leavened bread. [14]From this you shall offer one cake from each offering, as a gift to the LORD; it shall belong to the priest who dashes the blood of the offering of well-being. [15]And the flesh of your thanksgiving sacrifice of well-being shall be eaten on the day it is offered; you shall not leave any of it until morning. [16]But if the sacrifice you offer is a votive offering or a freewill offering, it shall be eaten on the day that you offer your sacrifice, and what is left of it shall be eaten the next day, [17]but what is left of the flesh of the sacrifice shall be burned up on the third day. [18]If any of the flesh of your sacrifice of well-being is eaten on the third day, it shall not be acceptable, nor shall it be credited to the one who offers it; it shall be an abomination, and the one who eats of it shall incur guilt.

19 "Flesh that touches any unclean thing shall not be eaten; it shall be burned up. As for other flesh, all who are clean may eat such flesh. [20]But those who eat flesh from the LORD's sacrifice of well-being while in a state of uncleanness shall be cut off from their people. [21]When any one of you touches any unclean thing—human uncleanness or an unclean animal or any unclean creature—and then eats flesh from the LORD's sacrifice of well-being, you shall be cut off from your people."

22 The LORD spoke to Moses, saying, [23]"Speak to the Israelites: You shall eat no fat of ox or sheep or goat. [24]The fat of an animal

w 7.5 Or *a gift*

care must be taken to ensure that the holiness that is transferred to the objects used in the sacrifice does not later come into contact with impurity. **7:1–6** This passage describes the ritual process for the reparation offering (see 5:14–19; 6:1–7). It is possible that the earlier text, which was addressed to the laity, omitted the ritual itself because those who offer sacrifice are generally expected to convert their offering to silver. However, these instructions addressed to the priests cover how to do the ritual in case it is not converted to its monetary equivalent. **7:2–3** The procedure is the same as that of the well-being offering in chap. 3. **7:11–36** Three types of *sacrifice of well-being*, an expansion of the rules found in chap. 3: the *thank offering* (or thanksgiving offering), the *votive offering*, and the *freewill offering*. After the priestly portion, the food generated by these offerings is served to the family of the person making the offering or the community as part of their shared celebration and gratitude to God. The food-related instructions in this chapter are addressed to the laity. Special oversight is needed by the priests because this is the only meat offering that is consumed by the laity, and one of the breads associated with the thanksgiving offering is leavened (v. 13) and must not contaminate anything going to the altar, where leaven is forbidden (see chap. 2). **7:15–18** The meat of the thanksgiving offering must be eaten on the day of its sacrifice, while the votive and freewill offering meat can last one day more. Eating from that meat on the third day invalidates the offering and brings guilt on the layperson who does so. These rules presumably also apply to the bread that goes along with the meat sacrifice. The penalty is being "cut off from your people" (v. 21). **7:21** A person must be in a clean state to participate in the offering of well-being,

that died or was torn by wild animals may be put to any other use, but you must not eat it. [25]If any one of you eats the fat from an animal of which an offering by fire[x] may be made to the LORD, you who eat it shall be cut off from your people. [26]You must not eat any blood whatever, either of bird or of animal, in any of your settlements. [27]Any one of you who eats any blood shall be cut off from your people."

28 The LORD spoke to Moses, saying, [29]"Speak to the Israelites: Any one of you who would offer to the LORD your sacrifice of well-being must yourself bring to the LORD your offering from your sacrifice of well-being. [30]Your own hands shall bring the LORD's offering by fire;[y] you shall bring the fat with the breast, so that the breast may be raised as an elevation offering before the LORD. [31]The priest shall turn the fat into smoke on the altar, but the breast shall belong to Aaron and his sons. [32]And the right thigh from your sacrifices of well-being you shall give to the priest as an offering; [33]the one among the sons of Aaron who offers the blood and fat of the offering of well-being shall have the right thigh for a portion. [34]For I have taken the breast of the elevation offering and the thigh that is offered from the Israelites, from their sacrifices of well-being, and have given them to Aaron the priest and to his sons, as a perpetual due from the Israelites. [35]This is the portion allotted to Aaron and to his sons from the offerings made by fire[z] to the LORD, once they have been brought forward to serve the LORD as priests; [36]these the LORD commanded to be given them, when he anointed them, as a perpetual due from the Israelites throughout their generations."

37 This is the rule of the burnt offering, the grain offering, the purification offering, the guilt offering, the offering of ordination, and the sacrifice of well-being, [38]which the LORD commanded Moses on Mount Sinai, when he commanded the Israelites to bring their offerings to the LORD, in the wilderness of Sinai.

8 The LORD spoke to Moses, saying, [2]"Take Aaron and his sons with him, the vestments, the anointing oil, the bull for the purification offering, the two rams, and the basket of unleavened bread; [3]and assemble the whole congregation at the entrance of the tent of meeting." [4]And Moses did as the LORD had commanded him. When the congregation was assembled at the entrance of the tent of meeting, [5]Moses said to the congregation, "This is what the LORD has commanded to be done."

6 Then Moses brought Aaron and his sons forward and washed them with water. [7]He put the tunic on him, fastened the sash around him, clothed him with the robe, and put the ephod on him. He then put the decorated band of the ephod around him, tying the ephod to him with it. [8]He placed the breastpiece on him, and in the breastpiece he put the Urim and the Thummim. [9]And he set the turban on his head, and on the turban, in front, he set the golden ornament, the holy diadem, as the LORD had commanded Moses.

10 Then Moses took the anointing oil and anointed the tabernacle and all that was in

x 7.25 Or *a gift*   y 7.30 Or *the LORD's gift*   z 7.35 Or *the gifts*

even as the recipient of food. A person who happens to be unclean is not prohibited from eating in general, of course, but impurity must not go near anything that is holy or otherwise dedicated to God. **7:22–27** Two further violations that lead to being *cut off* are the eating of fat from a sacrificial animal (i.e., the layer of suet that is to be burned on the altar; v. 25) or *any blood whatever* (v. 26). **7:30** The breast of the animal is *raised as an elevation offering before the LORD*. The breast belongs to the priests as their choice portion, and the right thigh of the animal goes to the officiating priest (v. 32). See the note at 8:27. **7:37–38** A concluding statement summarizing the particular ritual topics covered in the supplemental laws of chaps. 6–7. However, the *offering of ordination* is found in chap. 8. Its inclusion in this list may mean that chap. 8 was originally earlier in the text and moved for its thematic connection to chap. 9.

8:1–36 God tells Moses to assemble the resources necessary to ordain Aaron and his sons as priests, repeating the instructions from Exod. 29. **8:4** *And Moses did as the LORD had commanded him* reflects the absolute centrality of command and fulfillment in the Priestly worldview. Following God's ritual and ethical commands is the path to well-being and success in the cult and in the community as a whole, while disobeying God leads to possible catastrophic failure. **8:6** *Then Moses brought Aaron* begins the first narrative portion of Leviticus (chaps. 8–10), picking up where Exod. 40 leaves off. The alternation of legal and narrative sections gives structure to the book. **8:8** The list

it and consecrated them. ¹¹He sprinkled some of it on the altar seven times and anointed the altar and all its utensils and the basin and its base, to consecrate them. ¹²He poured some of the anointing oil on Aaron's head and anointed him, to consecrate him. ¹³And Moses brought forward Aaron's sons and clothed them with tunics and fastened sashes around them and tied headdresses on them, as the LORD had commanded Moses.

14 He led forward the bull of purification offering, and Aaron and his sons laid their hands upon the head of the bull for the purification offering, ¹⁵and it was slaughtered. Moses took the blood and with his finger put some on each of the horns of the altar, purifying the altar; then he poured out the blood at the base of the altar. Thus he consecrated it, to make atonement for it. ¹⁶Moses took all the fat that was around the entrails and the appendage of the liver and the two kidneys with their fat and turned them into smoke on the altar. ¹⁷But the bull itself, its skin and flesh and its dung, he burned with fire outside the camp, as the LORD had commanded Moses.

18 Then he brought forward the ram of burnt offering. Aaron and his sons laid their hands on the head of the ram, ¹⁹and it was slaughtered. Moses dashed the blood against all sides of the altar. ²⁰The ram was cut into its parts, and Moses turned into smoke the head and the parts and the suet. ²¹And after the entrails and the legs were washed with water, Moses turned into smoke the rest of the ram on the altar; it was a burnt offering for a pleasing odor, an offering by fire[a] to the LORD, as the LORD had commanded Moses.

22 Then he brought forward the second ram, the ram of ordination. Aaron and his sons laid their hands on the head of the ram, ²³and it was slaughtered. Moses took some of

its blood and put it on the lobe of Aaron's right ear and on the thumb of his right hand and on the big toe of his right foot. ²⁴After Aaron's sons were brought forward, Moses put some of the blood on the lobes of their right ears and on the thumbs of their right hands and on the big toes of their right feet, and Moses dashed the rest of the blood against all sides of the altar. ²⁵He took the fat—the fatty tail, all the fat that was around the entrails, the appendage of the liver, and the two kidneys with their fat—and the right thigh. ²⁶From the basket of unleavened bread that was before the LORD, he took one cake of unleavened bread, one cake of bread with oil, and one wafer and placed them on the fat and on the right thigh. ²⁷He placed all these on the palms of Aaron and on the palms of his sons and raised them as an elevation offering before the LORD. ²⁸Then Moses took them from their hands and turned them into smoke on the altar with the burnt offering. This was an ordination offering for a pleasing odor, an offering by fire[b] to the LORD. ²⁹Moses took the breast and raised it as an elevation offering before the LORD; it was Moses's portion of the ram of ordination, as the LORD had commanded Moses.

30 Then Moses took some of the anointing oil and some of the blood that was on the altar and sprinkled them on Aaron and his vestments and also on his sons and their vestments. Thus he consecrated Aaron and his vestments and also his sons and their vestments.

31 And Moses said to Aaron and his sons, "Boil the flesh at the entrance of the tent of meeting, and eat it there with the bread that is in the basket of ordination offerings, as I was commanded, 'Aaron and his sons shall eat it,' ³²and what remains of the flesh and the

a 8.21 Or a gift   b 8.28 Or a gift

of priestly garments worn by Aaron includes *the Urim and the Thummim*. Called "the breastpiece of judgment" in Exod. 28:30, these items are used for casting lots, a form of divination through which the priests render divine decisions. See also Num. 27:21 and 1 Sam. 14:41. **8:14–30** The three sacrifices as part of the ordination ritual are *the bull of purification offering* (v. 14), *the ram of burnt offering* (v. 18), and *the ram of ordination* (v. 22). These are preceded and followed by ritual sprinklings of oil (v. 10) and oil mixed with blood (v. 30). **8:22–24** *The ram of ordination* leads to the special rite of dabbing sacrificial blood on the ears, thumbs, and big toes of Aaron and his sons. These body parts may represent the priestly responsibilities of hearing God's commands and following them with hands and feet. Also compare the similar ritual for the cleansing of the person with defiling skin disease in 14:14. **8:27–28** *Elevation offering* appears in a number of contexts in which the portion of a sacrifice is lifted up by the priest before it is burned in fire (see 7:30; 9:21; 14:12; 23:17). In this special case, Moses assists by placing the elements on the priests' hands and lifting them to

bread you shall burn with fire. [33]You shall not go outside the entrance of the tent of meeting for seven days, until the day when your period of ordination is completed. For it will take seven days to ordain you; [34]as has been done today, the LORD has commanded to be done to make atonement for you. [35]You shall remain at the entrance of the tent of meeting day and night for seven days, keeping the LORD's charge so that you do not die, for so have I been commanded." [36]Aaron and his sons did all the things that the LORD had commanded through Moses.

9 On the eighth day Moses summoned Aaron and his sons and the elders of Israel. [2]He said to Aaron, "Take a bull calf for a purification offering and a ram for a burnt offering, without blemish, and offer them before the LORD. [3]And say to the Israelites, 'Take a male goat for a purification offering; a calf and a lamb, yearlings without blemish, for a burnt offering; [4]and an ox and a ram for an offering of well-being to sacrifice before the LORD; and a grain offering mixed with oil. For today the LORD will appear to you.' " [5]They brought what Moses commanded to the front of the tent of meeting, and the whole congregation drew near and stood before the LORD. [6]And Moses said, "This is the thing that the LORD commanded you to do, so that the glory of the LORD may appear to you." [7]Then Moses said to Aaron, "Draw near to the altar and sacrifice your purification offering and your burnt offering and make atonement for yourself and for the people, and sacrifice the offering of the people and make atonement for them, as the LORD has commanded."

[8] Aaron drew near to the altar and slaughtered the calf of the purification offering, which was for himself. [9]The sons of Aaron presented the blood to him, and he dipped his finger in the blood and put it on the horns of the altar, and the rest of the blood he poured out at the base of the altar. [10]But the fat, the kidneys, and the appendage of the liver from the purification offering he turned into smoke on the altar, as the LORD had commanded Moses, [11]and the flesh and the skin he burned with fire outside the camp.

[12] Then he slaughtered the burnt offering. Aaron's sons brought him the blood, and he dashed it against all sides of the altar. [13]And they brought him the burnt offering piece by piece and the head, which he turned into smoke on the altar. [14]He washed the entrails and the legs and, with the burnt offering, turned them into smoke on the altar.

[15] Next he presented the people's offering. He took the goat of the purification offering that was for the people and slaughtered it and presented it as a purification offering like the first one. [16]He presented the burnt offering and sacrificed it according to regulation. [17]He presented the grain offering, and, taking a handful of it, he turned it into smoke on the altar, in addition to the burnt offering of the morning.

[18] He slaughtered the ox and the ram as a sacrifice of well-being for the people. Aaron's sons brought him the blood, which he dashed against all sides of the altar, [19]and the fat of the ox and of the ram: the fatty tail, the fat that covers the entrails, the two kidneys and the fat on them,[c] and the appendage of the liver. [20]They first laid the fat on the breasts, and the fat was turned into

c 9.19 Gk: Heb *the fatty tail, and that which covers, and the kidneys*

God, by which both the offering and the person making the offering are dedicated to God's service. **8:33** The priests remain in the tent of meeting for seven full days. The ritual term for this interval of time is liminality. In many societies, rituals of ordination, coming of age, and repentance involve a transitional period of "in-betweenness" in which the subject has moved out of one category but has not yet rejoined the world in their new identity.

9:1–7 Now that Aaron and his sons have been ordained as priests, Moses instructs them to perform each of the various types of sacrifices for the first time, *on the eighth day.* **9:5** The people of the community have been gathered outside the tent of meeting overhearing and observing, and now they stand *before the LORD*, drawing near to the holiness of God in the same way as the priests but kept safe by the priests' intermediation.

9:8–21 What is commanded is now fulfilled. The ritual performance mirrors closely the respective instructions that have been given earlier in the book. Aaron sacrifices a calf for a *purification offering* (v. 8) and a ram as a *burnt offering* (v. 12) for himself and then the *people's offering* of purification (v. 15), grain (v. 17), and well-being (v. 18).

smoke on the altar, [21]and the breasts and the right thigh Aaron raised as an elevation offering before the LORD, as Moses had commanded.

22 Aaron lifted his hands toward the people and blessed them, and he came down after sacrificing the purification offering, the burnt offering, and the offering of well-being. [23]Moses and Aaron entered the tent of meeting and then came out and blessed the people, and the glory of the LORD appeared to all the people. [24]Fire came out from the LORD and consumed the burnt offering and the fat on the altar, and when all the people saw it, they shouted and fell on their faces.

10 Now Aaron's sons Nadab and Abihu each took his censer, put fire in it, and laid incense on it, and they offered unholy fire before the LORD, such as he had not commanded them. [2]And fire came out from the presence of the LORD and consumed them, and they died before the LORD. [3]Then Moses said to Aaron, "This is what the LORD meant when he said,

'Through those who are near me
    I will show myself holy,
and before all the people
    I will be glorified.'"
And Aaron was silent.

4 Moses summoned Mishael and Elzaphan, sons of Uzziel the uncle of Aaron, and said to them, "Come forward and carry your kinsmen away from the front of the sanctuary to a place outside the camp." [5]They came forward and carried them by their tunics out of the camp, as Moses had ordered. [6]And Moses said to Aaron and to his sons Eleazar and Ithamar, "Do not dishevel your hair and do not tear your vestments, or you will die, and wrath will strike all the congregation; but your kindred, the whole house of Israel, may mourn

9:22–24 Benediction and celebration are the dramatic climax of Leviticus—and arguably the whole Torah. Instructions for essential rites have been given and followed, the priests are ordained and functioning successfully in their new roles, and now *the glory of the* LORD appears to the people. Thus, fulfilled is the promise of God's glorious appearance ("theophany") in v. 6. The *glory of the* LORD is described as a cloud settled in the tent of meeting (Exod. 40:34), and it appears in several other Priestly passages during moments of God's judgment (Num. 14:10; 16:19; 20:6). The cloud has a fiery luminescence that can be seen at night (Exod. 24:17; 40:38). **9:24** *Fire came out from the* LORD *and consumed the burnt offering*, leading understandably to a response of awe and submission from the people (see Judg. 13:15–20; 1 Kgs. 18:22–39; 1 Chr. 21:26; and 2 Chr. 7:1–3 for similar occurrences). Note that the fire had already been lit on the altar and the sacrifices were burning at the normal slow rate (*turned . . . into smoke* in vv. 13, 14, and 17). This act communicates divine acceptance of the priests and of the offerings they perform and reinforces the reality that all their ritual actions are being performed before the Lord on God's direct command. The sobering nature of this reality will become immediately evident in Lev. 10.

10:1 Two of Aaron's sons prepare to offer an incense offering inside the tent of meeting, but they make the mistake of bringing *unholy fire*, or "unauthorized coals." The meaning of this term is obscure, but it might be related to a mistake in the coals' origin or incense composition as laid out in Exod. 30:34–38. Possibly, they offered the incense in an unclean state, at the wrong time, or with the wrong attitude. Interpreters through the centuries have speculated on the nature of Nadab and Abihu's violation. Also compare the role of incense in God's judgment and healing of the people in the story of Korah's rebellion in Num. 16.

10:2 The penalty for their ritual violation is immediate and severe, as *fire came out from the presence of the* LORD *and consumed them*, which implies that they died at the entrance to the tent. Note the parallel between this incident and the fire that consumes the initial burnt offering in 9:24. The requirements for those who bring offerings before the holy God must be followed with precision and completely. The consequences of ritual failure are dire. In five other instances God's fire consumes people (Num. 11:1; 16:35; Job 1:16; 2 Kgs. 1:10, 12).

10:3 Moses, while not particularly compassionate in the moment, explains the consuming fire as a manifestation of God's holiness and glory. The awe that resulted from the fire in 9:24 turns toward fear in light of this ritual tragedy.

10:4–7 The dead bodies of Nadab and Abihu are now a major ritual problem. They must be removed and disposed of properly, and their brothers are forbidden to begin mourning rituals while they are still on priestly duty and *the anointing oil of the* LORD (v. 7) is on them.

Going Deeper: Holiness and Purity (Leviticus 10)

In Lev. 10:10, Moses declares that the priests are to "distinguish between the holy and the common and between the unclean and the clean." These concepts are central to the Priestly worldview, which imagines an environment filled with numinous and powerful substances. God is the source of all *holiness*, and the holiness of God radiates from the place where God's presence dwells—that is, in the inner sanctum of the tent of meeting (see **"Holiness (Exodus)," p. 88**). Anyone who approaches God enters a space filled with holiness and therefore becomes "holy." In this way, "holy" means a state of being that is specially set apart for service to God, and it can apply to people, objects, and places. In the Priestly system, the default state is the opposite of holy, that is to say, "common." Rituals enable the transfer between holy and common, as seen in the consecration and ordination of the priests in Lev. 8. In addition to holiness, the other numinous and powerful substance in this environment is *impurity*. The normal state of a person, object, or place is "clean" or "pure," though that state can change to "unclean" or "impure." Impurity is generated in the process of everyday life. Some of the things that generate impurity are dead bodies, contact with certain animals, sexual intercourse, skin diseases, and sin (see **"Sin," p. 150**). Impurity is itself not sin; nor is it sinful. In fact, many activities that are commanded—burying the dead, procreating—render people impure. Rather, it is a ritual problem that must be managed because as impurity is generated and spreads, it can infect the holy areas, including the altar and tent of meeting. Rituals enable the transfer from an impure to a pure state by means of cleansing or "purification." Some impurities are cleansed by water and the passage of time. Purification offerings feature prominently in special cases (such as purification after childbirth, Lev. 12) and on holy days (most notably on the Day of Atonement in Lev. 16). The detergent that is able to cleanse impurity is blood, which is used in a variety of ways in sacrificial offerings, and commonly it is applied directly to the altar (Lev. 4:7) and sprinkled around the sanctuary (Lev. 16:15–16). The ritual concept of purity elsewhere becomes a metaphor for spiritual uprightness (see Pss. 24:4; 51:10; Isa. 1:16).

Bryan Bibb

the burning that the LORD has sent. [7]You shall not go outside the entrance of the tent of meeting, lest you die, for the anointing oil of the LORD is on you." And they did as Moses had ordered.

8 And the LORD spoke to Aaron, [9]"Drink no wine or strong drink, neither you nor your sons, when you enter the tent of meeting, that you may not die; it is a statute forever throughout your generations. [10]You are to distinguish between the holy and the common and between the unclean and the clean, [11]and you are to teach the Israelites all the statutes that the LORD has spoken to them through Moses."

12 Moses spoke to Aaron and to his remaining sons, Eleazar and Ithamar, "Take the grain offering that is left from the LORD's offerings by fire,[d] and eat it unleavened beside the altar, for it is most holy; [13]you shall eat it in a holy place, because it is your due and your sons' due, from the offerings by fire[e] to the LORD, for

so I am commanded. [14]But the breast that is elevated and the thigh that is raised, you and your sons and daughters as well may eat in any clean place, for they have been assigned to you and your children from the sacrifices of well-being of the Israelites. [15]The thigh that is raised and the breast that is elevated they shall bring, together with the offerings by fire[f] of the fat, to raise for an elevation offering before the LORD; they are to be your due and that of your children forever, as the LORD has commanded."

16 Then Moses made inquiry about the goat of the purification offering, and it had already been burned! He was angry with Eleazar and Ithamar, Aaron's remaining sons, and said, [17]"Why did you not eat the purification offering in the sacred area? For it is most holy, and God[g] has given it to you that

d 10.12 Or *the LORD's gifts* e 10.13 Or *the gifts* f 10.15 Or *the gifts* g 10.17 Heb *he*

10:8–15 Priests must be diligent in performing their duties. They are to avoid alcohol while serving (v. 8), to teach carefully about ritual categories and their associated regulations (vv. 10–11), and to be sure to eat the correct parts of the animal sacrifices in the right place and at the right time (vv. 12–15). **10:10** The responsibility *to distinguish between the holy and the common and between the unclean and the clean* is central to the Priestly calling (see **"Holiness and Purity," p. 158**).

10:16–18 Another ritual violation is revealed in the priests' failure to eat the purification offering (v. 17) and perform the proper blood ritual (v. 18). Why God did not punish Eleazar and Ithamar

you may remove the guilt of the congregation, to make atonement on their behalf before the LORD. [18]Its blood was not brought into the inner part of the sanctuary. You should certainly have eaten it in the sanctuary, as I commanded." [19]And Aaron spoke to Moses, "See, today they offered their purification offering and their burnt offering before the LORD, and yet such things as these have befallen me! If I had eaten the purification offering today, would it have been agreeable to the LORD?" [20]And when Moses heard that, he agreed.

11 The LORD spoke to Moses and Aaron, saying to them, [2]"Speak to the Israelites: "From among all the land animals, these are the creatures that you may eat. [3]Any animal that has divided hoofs and is cleft-footed and chews the cud—such you may eat. [4]But among those that chew the cud or have divided hoofs, you shall not eat the following: the camel, for even though it chews the cud, it does not have divided hoofs; it is unclean for you. [5]The rock badger, for even though it chews the cud, it does not have divided hoofs;

it is unclean for you. [6]The hare, for even though it chews the cud, it does not have divided hoofs; it is unclean for you. [7]The pig, for even though it has divided hoofs and is cleft-footed, it does not chew the cud; it is unclean for you. [8]Of their flesh you shall not eat, and their carcasses you shall not touch; they are unclean for you.

9 "These you may eat, of all that are in the waters. Everything in the waters that has fins and scales, whether in the seas or in the streams—such you may eat. [10]But anything in the seas or the streams that does not have fins and scales, of the swarming creatures in the waters and among all the other living creatures that are in the waters—they are detestable to you, [11]and detestable they shall remain. Of their flesh you shall not eat, and their carcasses you shall regard as detestable. [12]Everything in the waters that does not have fins and scales is detestable to you.

13 "These you shall regard as detestable among the birds. They shall not be eaten; they are an abomination: the eagle, the vulture, the osprey, [14]the buzzard, the kite of any kind; [15]every raven of any kind; [16]the ostrich,

when the earlier event resulted in death is unclear; maybe Nadab and Abihu performed some willful act rather than an inadvertent mistake.

10:19–20 Aaron seems frustrated that Moses is pointing out their mistakes on today of all days, when his sons have been killed by God. This conversation is ambiguous, but their disagreement seems to rest on a small ritual issue, whether this purification offering should have been eaten or burned. Moses comes to agree with Aaron.

11:2 *These are the creatures that you may eat*, the foundation of the Israelite and Jewish system of kosher laws related to food consumption. The general categories are land animals, birds, fish, and insects, and each category has its own internal logic.

11:3–4 Clean quadrupeds must have *divided hoofs* and *chew the cud*. Animals that have only one of the characteristics and are therefore unclean include camels, rock badgers, hares, and (most famously) pigs. Creatures are only considered "clean" when they correspond fully to their category. The categorical requirements themselves may be arbitrary, but they are followed as an exercise in obedience to God.

11:7 The origin of the prohibition against pigs is a matter of debate. A health-related reason has sometimes been offered—that is, that the ancients were intuitively aware of the dangers of the pork-related malady trichinosis. Such concerns are not found in the text, and many other food prohibitions have no such basis. It is more likely that pigs are forbidden because of their use in non-Israelite religious contexts, as Leviticus is much concerned with avoiding foreign practices (see 20:22–26, which associates unclean animals with foreign abominations).

11:8 These unclean animals cannot be eaten or touched, which also suggests that the prohibition is not related to health concerns. There is no penalty for violating this rule, per se, but there are serious consequences if the resulting impurity is not addressed before a person enters the sacred precincts (see vv. 24–28).

11:9 Clean animals in water have *fins and scales*, which is the basis for the kosher prohibition of shellfish and shrimp.

11:13 Prohibited birds are those that come into contact with meat either as hunters (eagles, ospreys) or carrion eaters (buzzards, vultures).

the nighthawk, the sea gull, the hawk of any kind; [17]the little owl, the cormorant, the great owl, [18]the water hen, the desert owl,[b] the carrion vulture, [19]the stork, the heron of any kind, the hoopoe, and the bat.[i]

20 "All winged insects that walk upon all fours are detestable to you. [21]But among the winged insects that walk on all fours you may eat those that have jointed legs above their feet, with which to leap on the ground. [22]Of them you may eat: locusts of every kind, bald locusts of every kind, crickets of every kind, and grasshoppers of every kind. [23]But all other winged insects that have four feet are detestable to you.

24 "By these you shall become unclean; whoever touches the carcass of any of them shall be unclean until the evening, [25]and whoever carries any part of the carcass of any of them shall wash his clothes and be unclean until the evening. [26]Every animal that has divided hoofs but is not cleft-footed or does not chew the cud is unclean for you; everyone who touches one of them shall be unclean. [27]All that walk on their paws, among the animals that walk on all fours, are unclean for you; whoever touches the carcass of any of them shall be unclean until the evening, [28]and the one who carries the carcass shall wash his clothes and be unclean until the evening; they are unclean for you.

29 "These are unclean for you among the creatures that swarm upon the earth: the weasel, the mouse, lizards of every kind, [30]the gecko, the land crocodile, the lizard, the sand lizard, and the chameleon. [31]These are unclean for you among all that swarm; whoever touches one of them when they are dead shall be unclean until the evening. [32]And anything upon which any of them falls when they are dead shall be unclean, whether an article of wood or cloth or leather or sackcloth, any article that is used for any purpose; it shall be dipped in water, and it shall be unclean

until the evening, and then it shall be clean. [33]And if any of them falls into any clay vessel, all that is in it shall be unclean, and you shall break the vessel. [34]Any food that could be eaten shall be unclean if water from any such vessel comes upon it, and any liquid that could be drunk shall be unclean if it was in any such vessel. [35]Everything on which any part of the carcass falls shall be unclean; whether an oven or stove, it shall be broken in pieces; they are unclean and shall remain unclean for you. [36]But a spring or a cistern holding water shall be clean, while whatever touches the carcass in it shall be unclean. [37]If any part of their carcass falls upon any seed set aside for sowing, it is clean, [38]but if water is put on the seed and any part of their carcass falls on it, it is unclean for you.

39 "If an animal of which you may eat dies, anyone who touches its carcass shall be unclean until the evening. [40]Those who eat of its carcass shall wash their clothes and be unclean until the evening, and those who carry the carcass shall wash their clothes and be unclean until the evening.

41 "All creatures that swarm upon the earth are detestable; they shall not be eaten. [42]Whatever moves on its belly and whatever moves on all fours or whatever has many feet, all the creatures that swarm upon the earth you shall not eat, for they are detestable. [43]You shall not make yourselves detestable with any creature that swarms; you shall not defile yourselves with them and so become unclean. [44]For I am the LORD your God; sanctify yourselves, therefore, and be holy, for I am holy. You shall not defile yourselves with any swarming creature that moves on the earth. [45]For I am the LORD who brought you up from the land of Egypt, to be your God; you shall be holy, for I am holy.

46 "This is the law pertaining to land

11:20 Winged insects are forbidden except those with jointed legs that leap—that is, locusts, crickets, and grasshoppers. All other insects (defined as creatures with four legs and wings) are forbidden.

11:24–28 Touching an unclean thing is not a moral failing or a sin. It generates ritual impurity that must be cleansed through washing and a period of waiting *until the evening*.

11:29 *Creatures that swarm upon the earth* are distinguished from quadrupeds and those that swarm in the air or water. The extra rules about contaminated clothing, vessels, cisterns, and other objects reflect the insidious nature of small-animal infestation.

11:44–45 This is an editorial insertion by a later editor associated with the Holiness School. See the note on 17:1.

animal and bird and every living creature that moves through the waters and every creature that swarms upon the earth, ⁴⁷to make a distinction between the unclean and the clean and between the living creature that may be eaten and the living creature that may not be eaten."

12 The Lᴏʀᴅ spoke to Moses, saying, ²"Speak to the Israelites, saying:

"If a woman conceives and bears a male child, she shall be unclean seven days; as at the time of her menstruation, she shall be unclean. ³On the eighth day the flesh of his foreskin shall be circumcised. ⁴Her time of blood purification shall be thirty-three days; she shall not touch any holy thing or come into the sanctuary until the days of her purification are completed. ⁵If she bears a female child, she shall be unclean two weeks, as in her menstruation; her time of blood purification shall be sixty-six days.

6 "When the days of her purification are completed, whether for a son or for a daughter, she shall bring to the priest at the entrance of the tent of meeting a lamb in its first year for a burnt offering and a pigeon or a turtledove for a purification offering. ⁷He shall offer it before the Lᴏʀᴅ and make atonement on her

behalf; then she shall be clean from her flow of blood. This is the law for her who bears a child, male or female. ⁸If she cannot afford a sheep, she shall take two turtledoves or two pigeons, one for a burnt offering and the other for a purification offering, and the priest shall make atonement on her behalf, and she shall be clean."

13 The Lᴏʀᴅ spoke to Moses and Aaron, saying:

2 "When a person has on the skin of his body a swelling^j or an eruption or a spot and it turns into a defiling disease on the skin of his body, he shall be brought to Aaron the priest or to one of his sons the priests. ³The priest shall examine the disease on the skin of his body, and if the hair in the diseased area has turned white and the disease appears to be deeper than the skin of his body, it is a defiling disease; after the priest has examined him he shall pronounce him unclean. ⁴But if the spot is white in the skin of his body and appears no deeper than the skin and the hair in it has not turned white, the priest shall confine the diseased person for seven days. ⁵The priest shall examine him on the seventh

j 13.2 Meaning of Heb uncertain

12:2–5 The purity regulations for a woman giving birth involve two intervals: her time of being _unclean_ (vv. 2 and 5) and her time of _blood purification_ (vv. 4 and 5). For a boy, the woman observes seven days of uncleanliness and thirty-three days of blood purification. Both of these periods are doubled for female children—that is, two weeks and sixty-six days. No reason for this difference is given. Possibly it is related to the general discomfort with women's bodies in patriarchal culture, so the presence of two female bodies doubles the time of impurity. It is notable, however, that the child is not unclean and not defiling; the mother's impurity is the result of the flow of blood _as at the time of her menstruation_. This places childbirth in the conversation about the complex ritual significance of blood.

12:3 The editorial insertion here concerns the unique timing of the Israelite circumcision rite for boys: in infancy and precisely on the eighth day. Other ancient cultures that practiced circumcision applied the rite at puberty or marriage. In Israel, circumcision is an expression of the covenantal link between all of Israel and God, seen more clearly in the Priestly account of the Abrahamic covenant (Gen. 17:9–14). The phrase _flesh of his foreskin_ is more accurately rendered "the foreskin of his penis" (Heb. "basar," translated as "member" in Lev. 15:2).

12:6–8 The ritual of purification for a new mother includes both a lamb for a burnt offering and a bird for the purification offering. A woman who cannot afford a lamb may bring two birds instead.

13:1–14:57 Several different maladies of the skin and hair and signs of disease in clothing are addressed with their associated diagnoses and ritual treatments. **13:2** _Defiling disease_ ("tsaraat") is an improved translation over the traditional "leprous disease." In fact, the skin disease described is not what came to be known in the medieval period as leprosy, a condition caused by _Mycobacterium leprae_. Rather, it is a broad term for a variety of scabrous and inflamed skin conditions. The Septuagint (LXX) uses the term "lepra," which at that time was similarly broad, and it is only through a misapplication of the medieval medical term that "leprosy" came into English translation. The other technical terms in the chapter—rendered here as _swelling, eruption,_ and _spot_—are similarly uncertain. **13:4** Even if the spot appears to be of no concern, still _the priest shall confine the diseased_

day, and if he sees that the disease is checked and the disease has not spread in the skin, then the priest shall confine him seven days more. [6]The priest shall examine him again on the seventh day, and if the disease has abated and the disease has not spread in the skin, the priest shall pronounce him clean; it is only an eruption, and he shall wash his clothes and be clean. [7]But if the eruption spreads in the skin after he has shown himself to the priest for his cleansing, he shall appear again before the priest. [8]The priest shall make an examination, and if the eruption has spread in the skin, the priest shall pronounce him unclean; it is defiling.

9 "When a person contracts a defiling skin disease, he shall be brought to the priest. [10]The priest shall make an examination, and if there is a white swelling[k] in the skin that has turned the hair white and there is a patch of raw flesh in the swelling,[l] [11]it is a chronic defiling disease in the skin of his body. The priest shall pronounce him unclean; he shall not confine him, for he is unclean. [12]But if the defiling disease breaks out in the skin so that it covers all the skin of the diseased person from head to foot, so far as the priest can see, [13]then the priest shall make an examination, and if the defiling disease has covered all his body, he shall pronounce him clean of the disease; since it has all turned white, he is clean. [14]But if raw flesh ever appears on him, he shall be unclean; [15]the priest shall examine the raw flesh and pronounce him unclean. Raw flesh is unclean; it is defiling. [16]But if the raw flesh again turns white, he shall come to the priest; [17]the priest shall examine him, and if the disease has turned white, the priest shall pronounce the diseased person clean. He is clean.

18 "When there is on the skin of one's body a boil that has healed, [19]and in the place of the boil there appears a white swelling[m] or a reddish-white spot, it shall be shown to the priest. [20]The priest shall make an examination, and if it appears deeper than the skin and its hair has turned white, the priest shall pronounce him unclean; this is a defiling disease, broken out in the boil. [21]But if the priest examines it and the hair on it is not white nor is it deeper than the skin but has abated, the priest shall confine him seven days. [22]If it spreads in the skin, the priest shall pronounce him unclean; it is diseased. [23]But if the spot remains in one place and does not spread, it is the scar of the boil; the priest shall pronounce him clean.

24 "Or when the body has a burn on the skin and the patch of the burn becomes a spot, reddish-white or white, [25]the priest shall examine it. If the hair in the spot has turned white and appears deeper than the skin, it is defiling; it has broken out in the burn, and the priest shall pronounce him unclean. This is a defiling disease. [26]But if the priest examines it and the hair in the spot is not white and it is no deeper than the skin but has abated, the priest shall confine him seven days. [27]The priest shall examine him the seventh day; if it is spreading in the skin, the priest shall pronounce him unclean. This is a defiling disease. [28]But if the spot remains in one place and does not spread in the skin but has abated, it is a swelling[n] from the burn, and the priest shall pronounce him clean, for it is the scar of the burn.

29 "When a man or a woman has a disease on the head or in the beard, [30]the priest shall examine the disease. If it appears deeper than the skin and the hair in it is yellow and thin, the priest shall pronounce him unclean; it is an itch, a defiling disease of the head or the beard. [31]If the priest examines the itching disease, and it appears no deeper than the skin and there is no black hair in it, the priest shall confine the person with the itching disease for seven days. [32]On the seventh day the

k 13.10 Meaning of Heb uncertain   l 13.10 Meaning of Heb uncertain   m 13.19 Meaning of Heb uncertain   n 13.28 Meaning of Heb uncertain

person for seven days. As with any kind of infectious testing, some time is needed to observe any problematic changes that might occur. Even those only suspected of being diseased are ritually impure. **13:8** *It is defiling.* These examinations and quarantine periods culminate in the unfortunate person being certified *unclean.* The purpose of the preceding quarantine periods is to see if the infection is of shorter duration. The condition could last for years and might never heal, leading to the separation of the individual from the community (see vv. 45–46). **13:12-13** A person who has a case of defiling disease that *covers all the skin* of the person is pronounced—surprisingly—clean. Does this mean that the concern is primarily with blotchy mixtures of colors on the skin? Or does the all-white condition mean that the person is medically cured in some way? Perhaps the consistent coloration indicates that the sores are gone and the underlying skin bears the scars of a disease

priest shall examine the itch; if the itch has not spread and there is no yellow hair in it and the itch appears to be no deeper than the skin, [33]he shall shave, but the itch he shall not shave. The priest shall confine the person with the itch for seven days more. [34]On the seventh day the priest shall examine the itch; if the itch has not spread in the skin and it appears to be no deeper than the skin, the priest shall pronounce him clean. He shall wash his clothes and be clean. [35]But if the itch spreads in the skin after he was pronounced clean, [36]the priest shall examine him. If the itch has spread in the skin, the priest need not seek for the yellow hair; he is unclean. [37]But if in his eyes the itch is checked and black hair has grown in it, the itch is healed; he is clean, and the priest shall pronounce him clean.

[38] "When a man or a woman has spots on the skin of the body, white spots, [39]the priest shall make an examination, and if the spots on the skin of the body are of a dull white, it is a rash that has broken out on the skin; he is clean.

[40] "If anyone loses the hair from his head, he is bald, but he is clean. [41]If he loses the hair from his forehead and temples, he has baldness of the forehead, but he is clean. [42]But if there is on the bald head or the bald forehead a reddish-white diseased spot, it is a defiling disease breaking out on his bald head or his bald forehead. [43]The priest shall examine him; if the diseased swelling[o] is reddish-white on his bald head or on his bald forehead, which resembles a defiling disease in the skin of the body, [44]he is defiled; he is unclean. The priest shall pronounce him unclean; the disease is on his head.

[45] "The person who has the defiling disease shall wear torn clothes and let the hair of his head be disheveled, and he shall cover his upper lip and cry out, 'Unclean, unclean.' [46]He shall remain unclean as long as he has the disease; he is unclean. He shall live alone; his dwelling shall be outside the camp.

[47] "Concerning clothing: when a defiling disease appears in it, in woolen or linen cloth, [48]in warp or woof of linen or wool or in a skin or in anything made of skin, [49]if the disease shows greenish or reddish in the garment, whether in warp or woof or in skin or in anything made of skin, it is a defiling disease and shall be shown to the priest. [50]The priest shall examine the disease and put the diseased article aside for seven days. [51]He shall examine the disease on the seventh day. If the disease has spread in the cloth, in warp or woof, or in the skin, whatever be the use of the skin, this is a spreading defiling disease; it is unclean. [52]He shall burn the clothing, whether diseased in warp or woof, woolen or linen, or anything of skin, for it is a spreading defiling disease; it shall be burned in fire.

[53] "If the priest makes an examination and the disease has not spread in the clothing, in warp or woof, or in anything of skin, [54]the priest shall command that the diseased article be washed, and he shall put it aside seven days more. [55]The priest shall examine the diseased article after it has been washed. If the diseased spot has not changed color, though the disease has not spread, it is unclean; you shall burn it in fire, whether the worn[p] spot is on the inside or on the outside.

[56] "If the priest makes an examination, and the disease has abated after it is washed, he shall tear the spot out of the cloth, in warp or woof, or out of skin. [57]If it appears again in the garment, in warp or woof, or in anything of skin, it is spreading; you shall burn with fire that in which the disease appears. [58]But the cloth, warp or woof, or anything of skin from which the disease disappears when you have washed it shall then be washed a second time, and it shall be clean.

[59] "This is the rule for a defiling disease in a cloth of wool or linen, either in warp or woof, or in anything of skin, to decide whether it is clean or unclean."

14 The Lord spoke to Moses, saying, [2]"This shall be the rule for the person with a defiling skin disease at the time of his cleansing:

o 13.43 Meaning of Heb uncertain   p 13.55 Meaning of Heb uncertain

healed? There is no clear way to explain this particular variation. **13:45–46** The person with *defiling disease* is to *live alone* and announce their condition lest anyone come into inadvertent contact with the impurity. On first glance this may seem like a cruel fate. However, these precautions protect the whole community because unchecked impurity would have disastrous consequences. Also, the person is not exiled or cut off from the community; though physically separated, they are still part of the community and will have their needs met. The ritual system provides for their well-being

"He shall be brought to the priest; [3]the priest shall go out of the camp, and the priest shall make an examination. If the disease is healed in the defiled person, [4]the priest shall command that two living clean birds and cedarwood and crimson yarn and hyssop be brought for the one who is to be cleansed. [5]The priest shall command that one of the birds be slaughtered over fresh water in a clay vessel. [6]He shall take the living bird with the cedarwood and the crimson yarn and the hyssop and dip them and the living bird in the blood of the bird that was slaughtered over the fresh water. [7]He shall sprinkle it seven times upon the one who is to be cleansed of the defiling disease; then he shall pronounce him clean, and he shall let the living bird go into the open field. [8]The one who is to be cleansed shall wash his clothes and shave off all his hair and bathe himself in water, and he shall be clean. After that he shall come into the camp but shall live outside his tent seven days. [9]On the seventh day he shall shave all his hair: of head, beard, eyebrows; he shall shave all his hair. Then he shall wash his clothes and bathe his body in water, and he shall be clean.

10 "On the eighth day he shall take two male lambs without blemish and one ewe lamb in its first year without blemish and a grain offering of three-tenths of an ephah of choice flour mixed with oil and one log[q] of oil. [11]The priest who cleanses shall set the person to be cleansed, along with these things, before the LORD, at the entrance of the tent of meeting. [12]The priest shall take one of the lambs and offer it as a guilt offering, along with the log[r] of oil, and raise them as an elevation offering before the LORD. [13]He shall slaughter the lamb in the place where the purification offering and the burnt offering are slaughtered in the holy place, for the guilt offering, like the purification offering, belongs to the priest; it is most holy. [14]The priest shall take some of the blood of the guilt offering and put it on the lobe of the right ear of the one to be cleansed and on the thumb of the right hand and on the big toe of the right foot. [15]The priest shall take some of the log[s] of oil and pour it into the palm of his own left hand [16]and dip his right finger in the oil that is in his left hand and sprinkle some oil with his finger seven times before the LORD. [17]Some of the oil that remains in his hand the priest shall put on the lobe of the right ear of the one to be cleansed and on the thumb of the right hand and on the big toe of the right foot, on top of the blood of the guilt offering. [18]The rest of the oil that is in the priest's hand he shall put on the head of the one to be cleansed. Then the priest shall make atonement on his behalf before the LORD: [19]the priest shall offer the purification offering, to make atonement for the one to be cleansed from his uncleanness. Afterward he shall slaughter the burnt offering, [20]and the priest shall offer the burnt offering and the grain offering on the altar. Thus the priest shall make atonement on his behalf, and he shall be clean.

21 "But if he is poor and cannot afford so much, he shall take one male lamb for a guilt offering to be elevated, to make atonement on his behalf, and one-tenth of an ephah of choice flour mixed with oil for a grain offering and a log[t] of oil, [22]also two turtledoves or two pigeons, such as he can afford, one for a purification offering and the other for a burnt

q 14.10 A liquid measure   r 14.12 A liquid measure
s 14.15 A liquid measure   t 14.21 A liquid measure

in the midst of serious illness and their reintegration upon their healing (chap. 14). **14:2** After the person with a *defiling skin disease* has been healed, they are brought back into the community by means of a set of purification rituals. **14:3–9** The first step is ritual examination by the priest *out of the camp*, where the person has been living. If they are now pronounced clean, there is a peculiar blood ritual in which a bird is dipped in the blood of another bird along with *cedarwood, crimson yarn*, and *hyssop* (v. 4). The blood is sprinkled seven times on the individual, and then the living bird is released into the wild, carrying the person's impurity with it. This ritual resonates with the blood ritual of the purification rite (4:6) and the freeing of the goat into the wilderness on the Day of Atonement (16:21–22). After shaving and washing, the person performs seven days of liminality, followed by another round of washing and shaving, *and he shall be clean* (v. 9). **14:10–18** The sacrificial ritual for the healed person takes three animals, three times the normal amount of flour for a grain offering, and a measure of oil (v. 10). A lamb along with the oil becomes a guilt offering (see chap. 5), though this animal cannot be converted to silver because its blood is needed for the ceremony (vv. 14–17). **14:19–20** The ewe becomes a *purification offering*, the second lamb serves as a *burnt offering*, and the grain is for a *grain offering*. Thus, the healed person is purified, atoned for,

offering. ²³On the eighth day he shall bring them for his cleansing to the priest, to the entrance of the tent of meeting, before the LORD, ²⁴and the priest shall take the lamb of the guilt offering and the log" of oil, and the priest shall raise them as an elevation offering before the LORD. ²⁵The priest shall slaughter the lamb of the guilt offering and shall take some of the blood of the guilt offering and put it on the lobe of the right ear of the one to be cleansed and on the thumb of the right hand and on the big toe of the right foot. ²⁶The priest shall pour some of the oil into the palm of his own left hand ²⁷and shall sprinkle with his right finger some of the oil that is in his left hand seven times before the LORD. ²⁸The priest shall put some of the oil that is in his hand on the lobe of the right ear of the one to be cleansed and on the thumb of the right hand and the big toe of the right foot, where the blood of the guilt offering was placed. ²⁹The rest of the oil that is in the priest's hand he shall put on the head of the one to be cleansed, to make atonement on his behalf before the LORD. ³⁰And he shall offer, of the turtledoves or pigeons, such as he can afford, ³¹one" for a purification offering and the other for a burnt offering, along with a grain offering, and the priest shall make atonement before the LORD on behalf of the one being cleansed. ³²This is the rule for the one who has a defiling disease who cannot afford the offerings for his cleansing."

33 The LORD spoke to Moses and Aaron, saying:

34 "When you come into the land of Canaan, which I give you for a possession, and I put a defiling disease in a house in the land of your possession, ³⁵the owner of the house shall come and tell the priest, saying, 'There seems to me to be some sort of disease in my house.' ³⁶The priest shall command that they empty the house before the priest goes to examine the disease, or all that is in the house will become unclean, and afterward the priest shall go in to inspect the house. ³⁷He shall examine the disease; if the disease is in the walls of the house with greenish or reddish spots, and if it appears to be deeper than the surface, ³⁸the priest shall go outside to the door of the house and shut up the house seven days. ³⁹The priest shall come again on the seventh day and make an inspection; if the disease has spread in the walls of the house, ⁴⁰the priest shall command that the stones in which the disease appears be taken out and thrown into an unclean place outside the city. ⁴¹He shall have the inside of the house scraped thoroughly, and the plaster that is scraped off shall be dumped in an unclean place outside the city. ⁴²They shall take other stones and put them in the place of those stones and take other plaster and plaster the house.

43 "If the disease breaks out again in the house, after he has taken out the stones and scraped the house and plastered it, ⁴⁴the priest shall go and make inspection; if the disease has spread in the house, it is a spreading defiling disease in the house; it is unclean. ⁴⁵He shall have the house torn down, its stones and timber and all the plaster of the house, and taken outside the city to an unclean place. ⁴⁶All who enter the house while it is shut up shall be unclean until the evening, ⁴⁷and all who sleep in the house shall wash their clothes, and all who eat in the house shall wash their clothes.

48 "If the priest comes and makes an inspection and the disease has not spread in the house after the house was plastered, the priest shall pronounce the house clean; the disease is healed. ⁴⁹For the cleansing of the house he shall take two birds, with cedarwood and crimson yarn and hyssop, ⁵⁰and shall slaughter one of the birds over fresh water in a clay vessel ⁵¹and shall take the cedarwood and the hyssop and the crimson yarn, along with the living bird, and dip them in the blood of the slaughtered bird and the fresh water and sprinkle the house seven times. ⁵²Thus he shall cleanse the house with the blood of the bird, and with the fresh water, and with the living bird, and with the cedarwood and hyssop and

u 14.24 A liquid measure   *v* 14.31 Gk Syr: Heb *afford, ³¹such as he can afford, one*

and *clean.* **14:30** In the case of economic need, two *turtledoves or pigeons* may be substituted for one lamb and the ewe. **14:34** Even though God has *put a defiling disease in a house,* this is merely an acknowledgment that God is responsible for all that happens. The situation is not a punishment for sin. **14:44** *A spreading defiling disease* in the house is declared after multiple examinations and failed repairs; it is dismantled and removed for disposal *outside the city* in an *unclean place.* **14:48** If he pronounces the house *clean,* the priest performs a version of the bird ritual in vv. 3–9, with the addition of an amount of "fresh water" (v. 52) so that the blood can be sprinkled all around

crimson yarn, [53]and he shall let the living bird go out of the city into the open field; so he shall make atonement for the house, and it shall be clean.

54 "This is the rule for any defiling disease: for an itch, [55]for defiling diseases in clothing and houses, [56]and for a swelling[w] or an eruption or a spot, [57]to determine when it is unclean and when it is clean. This is the rule for defiling diseases."

15

The LORD spoke to Moses and Aaron, saying, [2]"Speak to the Israelites and say to them:

"When any man has a discharge from his member,[x] his discharge makes him unclean. [3]The uncleanness of his discharge is this: whether his member[y] flows with its discharge or is stopped from discharging, he is unclean during the entire period his member[z] flows or is stopped from discharging; this is his uncleanness.[a] [4]Every bed on which the one with the discharge lies shall be unclean, and everything on which he sits shall be unclean. [5]Anyone who touches his bed shall wash his clothes and bathe in water and be unclean until the evening. [6]All who sit on anything on which the one with the discharge has sat shall wash their clothes and bathe in water and be unclean until the evening. [7]All who touch the body of the one with the discharge shall wash their clothes and bathe in water and be unclean until the evening. [8]If the one with the discharge spits on persons who are clean, then they shall wash their clothes and bathe in water and be unclean until the evening. [9]Any saddle on which the one with the discharge rides shall be unclean. [10]All who touch anything that was under him shall be unclean until the evening, and all who carry such a thing shall wash their clothes and bathe in water and be unclean until the evening. [11]All those whom the one with the discharge touches without his having rinsed his hands in water shall wash their clothes and bathe in water and be unclean until the evening. [12]Any clay vessel that the one with the discharge touches shall be broken, and every vessel of wood shall be rinsed in water.

13 "When the one with a discharge is cleansed of his discharge, he shall count seven days for his cleansing; he shall wash his clothes and bathe his body in fresh water, and he shall be clean. [14]On the eighth day he shall take two turtledoves or two pigeons and come before the LORD to the entrance of the tent of meeting and give them to the priest. [15]The priest shall offer them, one for a purification offering and the other for a burnt offering, and the priest shall make atonement on his behalf before the LORD for his discharge.

16 "If a man has an emission of semen, he shall bathe his whole body in water and be unclean until the evening. [17]Everything made of cloth or of leather on which the semen falls shall be washed with water and be unclean until the evening. [18]If a man lies with a woman and has an emission of semen, both of them shall bathe in water and be unclean until the evening.

19 "When a woman has a discharge of blood that is a menstrual discharge from her body, she shall be in her impurity for seven days, and whoever touches her shall be unclean until the evening. [20]Everything upon

w 14.56 Meaning of Heb uncertain x 15.2 Heb *flesh* y 15.3 Heb *flesh* z 15.3 Heb *flesh* a 15.3 Q ms Gk Sam: MT lacks *during . . . uncleanness*

the house. **14:53** The ritual accomplishes *atonement for the house*, confirming the argument that atonement is a narrow ritual issue of purity in the Priestly writing, not a matter of moral sin and forgiveness (see **"Holiness and Purity," p. 158**).

15:1–33 Procedures for handling the impurity generated by various forms of bodily discharges from both men and women. **15:2** An abnormal *discharge* from a man's penis, perhaps a venereal disease, *makes him unclean*. **15:4–12** Anything that the person lies on (v. 4), sits on (v. 6), or rides (v. 9) is unclean, and anyone who subsequently touches that object will be unclean until the evening (vv. 5, 6, 7, 10). Further, if the suffering person spits on someone (v. 8) or touches someone *without his having rinsed his hands in water* (v. 11), they must wash their clothes and be unclean until the evening. The focus is not on the one suffering the condition but on the effects on objects and other people. **15:16–18** Unlike the discharge in vv. 2–15, the emission of semen is normal and only a minor source of impurity. The man who has ejaculated will wash his body and anything that has come into contact with the semen and be unclean until evening. In the case of sex, the woman must also bathe and be unclean until evening. **15:19–24** The case of a menstruating woman is similar to the case of semen emission (vv. 16–18), except that the impurity lasts for seven days. In that period, anything or

which she lies during her impurity shall be unclean; everything also upon which she sits shall be unclean. ²¹Whoever touches her bed shall wash his clothes and bathe in water and be unclean until the evening. ²²Whoever touches anything upon which she sits shall wash his clothes and bathe in water and be unclean until the evening; ²³whether it is the bed or anything upon which she sits, when he touches it he shall be unclean until the evening. ²⁴If any man lies with her and her impurity falls on him, he shall be unclean seven days, and every bed on which he lies shall be unclean.

25 "If a woman has a discharge of blood for many days, not at the time of her menstrual impurity, or if she has a discharge beyond the time of her menstrual impurity, all the days of the discharge she shall continue in uncleanness; as in the days of her impurity, she shall be unclean. ²⁶Every bed on which she lies during all the days of her discharge shall be treated as the bed of her impurity, and everything on which she sits shall be unclean, as in the uncleanness of her impurity. ²⁷Whoever touches these things shall be unclean and shall wash his clothes and bathe in water and be unclean until the evening. ²⁸If she is cleansed of her discharge, she shall count seven days, and after that she shall be clean. ²⁹On the eighth day she shall take two turtledoves or two pigeons and bring them to the priest at the entrance of the tent of meeting. ³⁰The priest shall offer one for a purification offering and the other for a burnt offering, and the priest shall make atonement on her behalf before the Lord for her unclean discharge.

31 "Thus you shall keep the Israelites separate from their uncleanness, so that they do not die in their uncleanness by defiling my tabernacle that is in their midst.

32 "This is the rule for those who have a discharge: for him who has an emission of semen, becoming unclean thereby; ³³for her who is in the infirmity of her menstrual period; for anyone, male or female, who has a discharge; and for the man who lies with a woman who is unclean."

16 The Lord spoke to Moses after the death of the two sons of Aaron, when they drew near before the Lord and died. ²The Lord said to Moses:

"Tell your brother Aaron not to come just at any time into the sanctuary inside the curtain before the cover that is upon the ark, or he will die, for I appear in the cloud upon the cover. ³Thus shall Aaron come into the holy place: with a young bull for a purification offering and a ram for a burnt offering. ⁴He shall put on the holy linen tunic and shall have the linen undergarments next to his body, fasten the linen sash, and wear the linen turban; these are the holy vestments. He shall bathe his body in water and then put them on. ⁵He shall take from the

anyone that comes into contact with the woman will be unclean until the evening. If a man has sex with a woman during her menstrual cycle, he too becomes unclean for seven days and can pass that impurity to other surfaces. Notably, nothing in this chapter treats sex or the body as dirty or sinful. *Unclean* is a narrow ritual concept and has nothing to do with sin. Even having sex during a woman's period is not forbidden; it merely generates impurity that must be handled carefully. Contrast the menstrual sex prohibition—and penalty for both man and woman—in 20:18. **15:25** The final case has to do with an abnormal flow of blood, which is treated in exactly the same way as the man with a discharge from his penis (vv. 2–12). **15:31** Left unchecked, the impurities generated by everyday life will build up and then defile the sanctuary, causing them to *die in their uncleanness*. God's holiness is incompatible with impurity, and the careful application of the Priestly system—both the sacrifices in chaps. 1–7 and the purity regulations in chaps. 11–15—will ensure that God may continue to dwell in the midst of the people.

16:1 The narrative picks up after the deaths of Nadab and Abihu (chap. 10) to describe Aaron's first performance of the Day of Atonement ("yom kippur").

16:2 *The sanctuary*, or tent of meeting, is a literary space—since the laws are recorded during Israel's exile (see 26:34)—based on the design of the Jerusalem temple. Outside the tent is the courtyard with the main altar and wash basin, and any ritually pure worshiper may enter this area. Inside the tent, the main room contains the incense altar, and the priests enter here daily to light incense. In the rear of the tent is *the sanctuary inside the curtain*, the holiest place, where resides the ark of the covenant (containing the Ten Commandments) and God's very presence. No person is allowed to enter this holy place except the high priest, once per year.

Making Connections: Atonement (Reconciliation) (Leviticus 16)

The word *atonement*—first used in an English Bible translation by Tyndale in 1526 CE—usually refers to the repair or renewal of the relationship between God and God's people. The word means to be unified and in agreement: "at one." The word has become an umbrella term for a number of ritual and theological concepts found in the Bible and in the history of Jewish and Christian thought. One of these is found in the Torah's Priestly traditions, where the verb *kipper* refers to the ritual cleansing of the altar, the sanctuary, and the people around it. In the Priestly understanding, God is holy, and those who approach God's dwelling place must also take on holiness; nothing "unclean" may come into contact with the "holy." Priests thus must perform various rituals and offerings to cleanse the impurities generated by everyday life and unintentional sins (see Lev. 4:20; 5:18; 14:30; 17:11). The "Day of Atonement" in Lev. 16 and 23:26–32 serves a special purpose in this regard.

While atonement is primarily a ritual concern and not a matter of intentional transgression and forgiveness in the Priestly material, other biblical texts extend the notion of atonement more broadly. Psalm 51, for instance, calls for God to "cleanse" the sin of the worshiper (Ps. 51:2), and Sirach says that righteous living "is an atonement" (Sir. 35:5; cf. Prov. 16:6). New Testament authors describe the death of Jesus as a "sacrifice of atonement" (Rom. 3:25; Heb. 2:17; 1 John 2:2; cf. 4 Macc. 17:22) and frequently refer to Christ's blood as a means of cleansing or forgiveness (Matt. 26:28; Rom. 5:9; Col. 1:20; Heb. 9:12–14).

In the absence of a sacrificial cult, rabbinic Judaism considered acts of religious devotion (e.g., repentance and prayer) to be means of atonement. In Christian theology, atonement figures importantly in the doctrine of salvation (soteriology), especially with regard to how Jesus's death accomplished reconciliation (atonement) between God and the world. St. Anselm's notion of "substitutionary atonement" drew on various ritual concepts to understand Jesus's death as a sacrifice demanded by God as "satisfaction" (payment) for sin. Other Christian understandings of atonement focus on the life and teachings of Jesus, view Jesus's ministry as a reversal of the sinful course begun by Adam and Eve, focus on Jesus's resurrection as a victory over sin and death, or emphasize that Jesus suffered not only "for" but also "with" humanity in solidarity with suffering, particularly as a result of injustice.

Bryan Bibb

congregation of the Israelites two male goats for a purification offering and one ram for a burnt offering.

6 "Aaron shall offer the bull as a purification offering for himself and shall make atonement for himself and for his house. ⁷He shall take the two goats and set them before the LORD at the entrance of the tent of meeting, ⁸and Aaron shall cast lots on the two goats, one lot for the LORD and the other lot for Azazel. ⁹Aaron shall present the goat on which the lot fell for the LORD and offer it as a purification offering, ¹⁰but the goat on which the lot fell for Azazel shall be presented alive before the LORD to make atonement over it, that it may be sent away into the wilderness to Azazel.

11 "Aaron shall present the bull as a purification offering for himself and shall make atonement for himself and for his house; he shall slaughter the bull as a purification offering for himself. ¹²He shall take a censer full of coals of fire from the altar before the LORD and two handfuls of crushed sweet incense, and he shall bring it inside the curtain ¹³and put the incense on the fire before the LORD,

16:6–10 The day's sacrifices require four animals: a bull for the *purification offering*; a ram for the "burnt offering" (v. 3); and two goats, one *for the* LORD and one *for Azazel*. The goat ritual is unusual and its origin obscure, though it bears some similarity to the release of the second bird in 14:3–9. After casting lots, Aaron offers one goat as a purification offering, and the second is *sent away into the wilderness to Azazel*. This may reflect a vestigial cultural memory of a desert demon named Azazel, but in the theology of the Priestly writer its function is clear: the sins of the people are transferred to the goat and sent out into the void (vv. 21–22). This ritual is the origin of the term "scapegoat."

16:12–13 Aaron next fills the inner space with a heavy cloud of incense by burning altar coals, and then he sprinkles blood from the purification offering on the ark's solid gold *cover* (traditionally "mercy seat"). The cloud shields Aaron from the presence of God, thus sparing his life. This is the day of greatest danger in the worship calendar and thus the most crucial to perform correctly.

that the cloud of the incense may shroud the cover that is upon the covenant, or he will die. [14]He shall take some of the blood of the bull and sprinkle it with his finger on the front of the cover, and before the cover he shall sprinkle the blood with his finger seven times.

15 "He shall slaughter the goat of the purification offering that is for the people and bring its blood inside the curtain and do with its blood as he did with the blood of the bull, sprinkling it upon the cover and before the cover. [16]Thus he shall make atonement for the sanctuary, because of the uncleannesses of the Israelites and because of their transgressions, all their sins, and so he shall do for the tent of meeting, which remains with them in the midst of their uncleanness. [17]No one shall be in the tent of meeting from the time he enters to make atonement in the sanctuary until he comes out and has made atonement for himself and for his house and for all the assembly of Israel. [18]Then he shall go out to the altar that is before the LORD and make atonement on its behalf and shall take some of the blood of the bull and of the blood of the goat and put it on each of the horns of the altar. [19]He shall sprinkle some of the blood on it with his finger seven times and cleanse it and sanctify it from the uncleannesses of the Israelites.

20 "When he has finished atoning for the holy place and the tent of meeting and the altar, he shall present the live goat. [21]Then Aaron shall lay both his hands on the head of the live goat and confess over it all the iniquities of the Israelites, and all their transgressions, all their sins, putting them on the head of the goat and sending it away into the wilderness by means of someone designated for the task.[b] [22]The goat shall bear on itself all their iniquities to a barren region, and the goat shall be set free in the wilderness.

23 "Then Aaron shall enter the tent of meeting and shall take off the linen vestments that he put on when he went into the holy place and shall leave them there. [24]He shall bathe his body in water in a holy place and put on his vestments; then he shall come out and offer his burnt offering and the burnt offering of the people, making atonement for himself and for the people. [25]The fat of the purification offering he shall turn into smoke on the altar. [26]The one who sets the goat free for Azazel shall wash his clothes and bathe his body in water and afterward may come into the camp. [27]The bull of the purification offering and the goat of the purification offering, whose blood was brought in to make atonement in the holy place, shall be taken outside the camp; their skin and their flesh and their dung shall be consumed in fire. [28]The one who burns them shall wash his clothes and bathe his body in water and afterward may come into the camp.

29 "This shall be a statute to you forever: In the seventh month, on the tenth day of the month, you shall humble yourselves[c] and shall do no work, neither the native-born nor the alien who resides among you. [30]For on this day atonement shall be made for you, to cleanse you; from all your sins you shall be clean before the LORD. [31]It is a Sabbath of complete rest to you, and you shall humble yourselves;[d] it is a statute forever. [32]The priest who is anointed and consecrated as priest in his father's place shall make atonement, wearing the linen vestments, the holy vestments. [33]He shall make atonement for the sanctuary, and

b 16.21 Meaning of Heb uncertain   c 16.29 Or shall fast
d 16.31 Or shall fast

16:15 The bull is a purification offering for Aaron, and the goat is *for the people*. Its blood is also sprinkled *inside the curtain*, Aaron's third entrance into that holy space.

16:18–19 Aaron daubs blood on the *horns of the altar* (hornlike projections at each of the four corners) in the main courtyard and sprinkles blood on the whole altar *seven times*. These actions *cleanse* the altar from any lingering impurities that may have become attached to it (see the note on 1:4) and *sanctify* it for its holy purpose.

16:29–31 Yom Kippur continues as the holiest day in the Jewish calendar, set aside for rest, fasting, repentance, and prayer. **16:29** *The alien ["ger"] who resides among you*, the non-Israelite who resides in the Israelite camp, sometimes translated as "foreigner," "stranger," "immigrant," or "resident alien." The term can refer to anyone living outside of their own land or away from their people. Abraham and Moses each refer to themselves as "ger" when not in Israel (Gen. 23:4 and Exod. 2:22, respectively). Because Israelites were once "ger," they are enjoined to treat foreigners in their communities well (see Deut. 23:7 and Exod. 23:9). The "ger" also has ethical and ritual obligations, like refraining from work on the Day of Atonement.

he shall make atonement for the tent of meeting and for the altar, and he shall make atonement for the priests and for all the people of the assembly. ³⁴This shall be an everlasting statute for you, to make atonement for the Israelites once in the year for all their sins." And Moses did as the LORD had commanded him.

17 The LORD spoke to Moses: ²"Speak to Aaron and his sons and to all the Israelites and say to them: This is what the LORD has commanded. ³If anyone of the house of Israel slaughters an ox or a lamb or a goat in the camp or slaughters it outside the camp ⁴and does not bring it to the entrance of the tent of meeting, to present it as an offering to the LORD before the tabernacle of the LORD, he shall be held guilty of bloodshed; he has shed blood, and he shall be cut off from the people. ⁵This is in order that the Israelites may bring their sacrifices that they offer in the open field, that they may bring them to the LORD, to the priest at the entrance of the tent of meeting, and offer them as sacrifices of well-being to the LORD. ⁶The priest shall dash the blood against the altar of the LORD at the entrance of the tent of meeting and turn the fat into smoke as a pleasing odor to the LORD, ⁷so that they may no longer offer their sacrifices for goat-demons, to whom they prostitute themselves. This shall be a statute forever to them throughout their generations.

⁸"And say to them further: Anyone of the house of Israel or of the aliens who reside among them who offers a burnt offering or sacrifice ⁹and does not bring it to the entrance of the tent of meeting, to sacrifice it to the LORD, shall be cut off from the people.

¹⁰"If anyone of the house of Israel or of the aliens who reside among them eats any blood, I will set my face against that person who eats blood and will cut that person off from the people. ¹¹For the life of the flesh is in the blood, and I have given it to you for making atonement for your lives on the altar, for, as life, it is the blood that makes atonement. ¹²Therefore I have said to the Israelites, 'No person among you shall eat blood, nor shall any alien who resides among you eat blood.'

¹³"And anyone of the Israelites or of the aliens who reside among them who hunts down an animal or bird that may be eaten shall pour out its blood and cover it with earth. ¹⁴For the life of every creature—its blood is its life; therefore I have said to the Israelites, 'You shall not eat the blood of any creature, for the life of every creature is its blood; whoever eats it shall be cut off.' ¹⁵All persons, native-born or alien, who eat what dies of itself or what has been torn by wild animals shall wash their clothes and bathe themselves in water and be unclean until the evening; then they shall be clean. ¹⁶But if they do not wash themselves

17:1–26:46 The Holiness Code. Often identified as a stand-alone set of laws, it is better to think of these chapters, along with certain editorial insertions in the first half of Leviticus, as part of a priestly "Holiness School" that has embraced, yet recontextualized, the Priestly Torah found in chaps. 1–16. The primary theological difference is that in the first half of Leviticus, "holiness" is a narrow ritual term that applies only to the sacred precincts, and in this latter half, all of Israel is declared to be holy as God is holy (19:2; and see the editorial insertion at 11:44–45). Whereas in the Priestly Torah one's normal ritual state is "common" (i.e., unclean), the Holiness School reinterprets holiness as a moral category that applies widely to Israel.

17:3–4 All killing of sacrificial animals is sacred (ox, lamb, or goat), including for the consumption of meat. A person must not kill an animal *in the camp* or *outside the camp* but must present it at the altar *as an offering to the LORD*. This rule assumes that there are convenient altars spread throughout the land (see note on 3:16 and cf. Deut. 12:15–18).

17:9 The penalty for performing a sacrifice elsewhere is to be *cut off from the people*. The meaning of *cut off* ("karet") is debated, but it could refer to early death, exile, the termination of one's family line in Israel, or (per rabbinic Judaism) spiritual exclusion from the afterlife.

17:10–11 The five laws in this chapter survey the text's primary concern: the blood released in the killing of an animal. Blood must be manipulated properly at the altar (v. 6), covered with earth in the field when allowed (v. 13), and cleansed when it has contaminated a person or clothing (v. 15). And most centrally, it must not be consumed. Anyone who *eats blood* will be "cut off," receiving the same penalty as in v. 9. Blood occupies its own ritual category because in the blood is *the life of the flesh*, and its detergent properties are necessary for *atonement*.

or bathe their body, they shall bear their guilt."

18 The Lord spoke to Moses, saying: 2 "Speak to the Israelites and say to them: I am the Lord your God. ³You shall not do as they do in the land of Egypt, where you lived, and you shall not do as they do in the land of Canaan, to which I am bringing you. You shall not follow their statutes. ⁴My ordinances you shall observe, and my statutes you shall keep, following them: I am the Lord your God. ⁵You shall keep my statutes and my ordinances; by doing so one shall live: I am the Lord.

6 "None of you shall approach anyone near of kin to uncover nakedness: I am the Lord. ⁷You shall not uncover the nakedness of your father, which is the nakedness of your mother; she is your mother; you shall not uncover her nakedness. ⁸You shall not uncover the nakedness of your father's wife; it is the nakedness of your father. ⁹You shall not uncover the nakedness of your sister, your father's daughter or your mother's daughter, whether born at home or born abroad. ¹⁰You shall not uncover the nakedness of your son's daughter or of your daughter's daughter, for their nakedness is your own nakedness. ¹¹You shall not uncover the nakedness of your father's wife's daughter, born in your father's house, since she is your sister. ¹²You shall not uncover the nakedness of your father's sister; she is your father's flesh. ¹³You shall not uncover the nakedness of your mother's sister, for she is your mother's flesh. ¹⁴You shall not uncover the nakedness of your father's brother; that is, you shall not approach his wife; she is your aunt. ¹⁵You shall not uncover the nakedness of your daughter-in-law: she is your son's wife; you shall not uncover her nakedness. ¹⁶You shall not uncover the nakedness of your brother's wife; it is your brother's nakedness. ¹⁷You shall not uncover the nakedness of a woman and her daughter, and you shall not take*ᵉ* her son's daughter or her daughter's daughter to uncover her nakedness; they are your*ᶠ* flesh; it is depravity. ¹⁸And you shall not take*ᵍ* a woman as a rival to her sister, uncovering her nakedness while her sister is still alive.

19 "You shall not approach a woman to uncover her nakedness while she is in her menstrual uncleanness. ²⁰You shall not have sexual relations with your neighbor's wife

e 18.17 Or *marry* *f* 18.17 Gk: Heb lacks *your* *g* 18.18 Or *marry*

18:3 The variety of sexual prohibitions in chap. 18 are associated with foreign practices, *as they do in the land of Egypt* and *as they do in the land of Canaan* (see also chap. 20). Our direct knowledge of the religious practices of Israel's neighbors is limited, though it is certainly possible that they practiced some of the various "abomination[s]" (vv. 22, 26, 29) ascribed to them here. Each law also connects to the internal logic of the Priestly system.

18:5 *I am the* Lord appears some forty-five times between this verse and the end of Leviticus, usually as a motivational statement for why Israel should follow a particular command. This significant statement is related to the central command of chaps. 17–26: "You shall be holy, for I the Lord your God am holy" (19:2). God is holy, and by proximity and covenantal agreement the people of God are also to be holy. Therefore, the fact that God makes a certain command is the most important reason it must be followed.

18:6-18 *You shall not uncover the nakedness* of certain family members establishes the rules concerning endogamy—that is, forbidding marriage to close relatives. There are social, psychological, and evolutionary reasons for this fairly universal type of regulation. However, these rules are also designed to protect the normal functioning of the patriarchal family. The regulations are framed around women and the men who have control over their sexuality in a patriarchal system—that is, their fathers and husbands. These rules ensure that procreation supports the patriarchy in an orderly and controlled way.

18:19-24 This section prohibits a number of practices that are in some way associated with *the nations I am casting out before you*. In addition to having sex with a menstruating woman and bestiality, it includes the infamous rule, *you shall not lie with a male as with a woman* (v. 22; see also 20:13). Rather than being universal moral law, these rules are concerned with the rejection of particular cultural practices and motivated by the needs of the patriarchy mentioned in the note for 18:6–18. Each of these cases will either result in no child, the death of a child, or (in the case of adultery) an illegitimate child that undermines the patriarchal rights of the neighbor. All law in Leviticus is

and defile yourself with her. [21]You shall not give any of your offspring to sacrifice them[b] to Molech and so profane the name of your God: I am the LORD. [22]You shall not lie with a male as with a woman; it is an abomination. [23]You shall not have sexual relations with any animal and defile yourself with it, nor shall any woman give herself to an animal to have sexual relations with it; it is perversion.

[24]"Do not defile yourselves in any of these ways, for by all these practices the nations I am casting out before you have defiled themselves. [25]Thus the land became defiled, and I punished it for its iniquity, and the land vomited out its inhabitants. [26]But you shall keep my statutes and my ordinances and commit none of these abominations, either the native-born or the alien who resides among you [27](for the inhabitants of the land, who were before you, committed all of these abominations, and the land became defiled); [28]otherwise the land will vomit you out for defiling it, as it vomited out the nation that was before you. [29]For whoever commits any of these abominations shall be cut off from their people. [30]So keep my charge not to commit any of these abominations that were done before you and not to defile yourselves by them: I am the LORD your God."

19 The LORD spoke to Moses, saying: [2]"Speak to all the congregation of the Israelites and say to them: You shall be holy, for I the LORD your God am holy. [3]You shall each revere your mother and father, and you shall keep my Sabbaths: I am the LORD your God. [4]Do not turn to idols or make cast images for yourselves: I am the LORD your God.

[5]"When you offer a sacrifice of well-being to the LORD, offer it in such a way that it is acceptable on your behalf. [6]It shall be eaten on the same day you offer it or on the next day, and anything left over until the third day shall be consumed in fire. [7]If any of it is eaten on the third day, it is an abomination; it will not be acceptable. [8]All who eat it shall be subject to punishment, because they have profaned what is holy to the LORD, and any such person shall be cut off from the people.

[9]"When you reap the harvest of your land, you shall not reap to the very edges of your field or gather the gleanings of your harvest. [10]You shall not strip your vineyard bare or gather the fallen grapes of your vineyard; you shall leave them for the poor and the alien: I am the LORD your God.

[11]"You shall not steal; you shall not deal falsely; and you shall not lie to one another. [12]And you shall not swear falsely by my name, profaning the name of your God: I am the LORD.

[13]"You shall not defraud your neighbor; you shall not steal; and you shall not keep for yourself the wages of a laborer until morning. [14]You shall not revile the deaf or put a stumbling block before the blind; you shall fear your God: I am the LORD.

[15]"You shall not render an unjust judgment; you shall not be partial to the poor or defer to the great: with justice you shall judge your neighbor. [16]You shall not go around as a

b 18.21 Heb to pass them over

essentially religious in that it is rooted in theology and strongly connected to the worship life of the people; this is not civil or secular law. **18:21** On the practice of child sacrifice, see the note on 20:2.

19:1–37 *Be holy.* The series of community-oriented regulations in this following section ground the people's social obligations in the holiness of God and the holiness of God's people. Note the combination of different types of regulation: laws about integrity in dealing with others (vv. 9–18, 32–36), ritual concerns (vv. 5–8, 19, 26–28, 30–31), and the mixture of these two in the context of sex with a slave (vv. 20–22). The law of holiness makes no distinction between the way that people honor God through ritual and the way they honor God through acts of justice and compassion for the vulnerable. **19:2** *Be holy, for I the LORD your God am holy* is the most important single statement in chaps. 17–26 and the ground on which all other commands must be understood (see note on 18:5). **19:9–10** See also Deut. 24:19–22, the story in Ruth 2, and the note on Lev. 19:15. **19:15** It is sometimes thought that the Torah contains rigid and "legalistic" rules, while the Israelite prophets reject the law in favor of true justice and righteousness. Aside from the fact that the prophets quote the Torah and draw heavily on Israel's legal traditions (see, for instance, the reference to the Decalogue in Jer. 7:9), the ritual system itself includes a comprehensive commitment to justice and integrity. When Amos denounces Israel for perverting the judicial system and oppressing the poor (see Amos 5:10–11), he expresses the same moral imperative found here (see also the comparison between the

slanderer among your people, and you shall not stand idly by when the blood[i] of your neighbor is at stake: I am the LORD.

17 "You shall not hate in your heart anyone of your kin; you shall reprove your neighbor, or you will incur guilt yourself. 18You shall not take vengeance or bear a grudge against any of your people, but you shall love your neighbor as yourself: I am the LORD.

19 "You shall keep my statutes. You shall not let your animals breed with a different kind; you shall not sow your field with two kinds of seed; nor shall you put on a garment made of two different materials.

20 "If a man has sexual relations with a woman who is a slave, designated for another man but not ransomed or given her freedom, an inquiry shall be held. They shall not be put to death, since she has not been freed, 21but he shall bring a guilt offering for himself to the LORD, at the entrance of the tent of meeting, a ram as guilt offering. 22And the priest shall make atonement for him with the ram of guilt offering before the LORD for his sin that he committed, and the sin he committed shall be forgiven him.

23 "When you come into the land and plant all kinds of trees for food, then you shall regard their fruit as forbidden;[j] three years it shall be forbidden[k] to you; it must not be eaten. 24In the fourth year all their fruit shall be set apart for rejoicing in the LORD. 25But in the fifth year you may eat of their fruit, that their yield may be increased for you: I am the LORD your God.

26 "You shall not eat anything with its blood. You shall not practice augury or witchcraft. 27You shall not round off the hair on your temples or mar the edges of your beard. 28You shall not make any gashes in your flesh for the dead or tattoo any marks upon you: I am the LORD.

29 "Do not profane your daughter by making her a prostitute, that the land not become prostituted and full of depravity. 30You shall keep my Sabbaths and revere my sanctuary: I am the LORD.

31 "Do not turn to mediums and spiritualists; do not seek them out, to be defiled by them: I am the LORD your God.

32 "You shall rise before the aged and defer to the old, and you shall fear your God: I am the LORD.

33 "When an alien resides with you in your land, you shall not oppress the alien. 34The alien who resides with you shall be to you as the native-born among you; you shall love the alien as yourself, for you were aliens in the land of Egypt: I am the LORD your God.

35 "You shall not cheat in measuring length, weight, or quantity. 36You shall have honest balances, honest weights, an honest ephah, and an honest hin: I am the LORD your God who brought you out of the land of Egypt. 37You shall keep all my statutes and all my ordinances and observe them: I am the LORD."

20 The LORD spoke to Moses, saying, 2"Say further to the Israelites:

"Any of the Israelites or of the aliens who reside in Israel who give any of their offspring to Molech shall be put to death; the people of the land shall stone them to death. 3I myself will set my face against them and will cut

i 19.16 Heb *stand against the blood*   j 19.23 Heb *as their uncircumcision*   k 19.23 Heb *uncircumcision*

honest weights of Lev. 19:36 and Amos 8:5). **19:18** *Love your neighbor as yourself* is identified by Jesus as one of the two greatest commandments (Mark 12:28–31), along with Deut. 6:4–5. **19:23–25** Priestly theology pays close attention to creation and to the needs of the environment. This law gives fruit trees time to mature before they are harvested for food. See also the laws of Sabbath for fields (25:1–7). **19:29** *Profane*, the opposite state of being holy. In the first half of Leviticus, *profane* is better translated as "common," as it is the normal state for those people, places, and objects not particularly dedicated to altar service. However, here *profane* means to degrade, to denigrate, or to reduce something in social value. Rather than being the common state, it is a state of *depravity*. A person can not only profane themselves among society (21:4) but also profane another person, in this case one's daughter by selling her into sex slavery.

20:2 There are several references to child sacrifice in the Bible, including the specious claim that Israelites sacrifice their children to Molech in the "valley of Hinnom" just outside Jerusalem (Jer. 32:35). First Kings 11:7 suggests that Solomon built such an altar, which was dismantled by Josiah in his Deuteronomistic reforms (2 Kgs. 23:10). There is no archaeological evidence to suggest that Israel engaged in child sacrifice. This rule in Leviticus probably reflects a cultural memory of such practices in ancient Canaan and/or an exaggerated polemic against the worship of Molech in general.

them off from the people, because they have given of their offspring to Molech, defiling my sanctuary and profaning my holy name. ⁴And if the people of the land should ever close their eyes to them, when they give of their offspring to Molech, and do not put them to death, ⁵I myself will set my face against them and against their family and will cut them off from among their people, them and all who follow them in prostituting themselves to Molech.

6 "If any turn to mediums or spiritualists, prostituting themselves to them, I will set my face against them and will cut them off from the people. ⁷Consecrate yourselves, therefore, and be holy, for I am the Lord your God. ⁸Keep my statutes and observe them: I am the Lord; I sanctify you. ⁹All who curse father or mother shall be put to death; having cursed father or mother, their bloodguilt is upon them.

10 "If a man commits adultery with the wife of[l] his neighbor, both the adulterer and the adulteress shall be put to death. ¹¹The man who lies with his father's wife has uncovered his father's nakedness; both of them shall be put to death; their bloodguilt is upon them. ¹²If a man lies with his daughter-in-law, both of them shall be put to death; they have committed perversion; their bloodguilt is upon them. ¹³If a man lies with a male as with a woman, both of them have committed an abomination; they shall be put to death; their bloodguilt is upon them. ¹⁴If a man takes a wife and her mother also, it is depravity; they shall be burned to death, both he and they, that there may be no depravity among you. ¹⁵If a man has sexual relations with an animal, he shall be put to death, and you shall kill the animal. ¹⁶If a woman approaches any animal and has sexual relations with it, you shall kill the woman and the animal; they shall be put to death; their bloodguilt is upon them.

17 "If a man takes his sister, a daughter of his father or a daughter of his mother, and sees her nakedness, and she sees his nakedness, it is a disgrace, and they shall be cut off in the sight of their people; he has uncovered his sister's nakedness; he shall be subject to punishment. ¹⁸If a man lies with a woman during her period and uncovers her nakedness, he has laid bare her flow, and she has laid bare her flow of blood; both of them shall be cut off from their people. ¹⁹You shall not uncover the nakedness of your mother's sister or of your father's sister, for that is to lay bare one's own flesh; they shall be subject to punishment. ²⁰If a man lies with his uncle's wife, he has uncovered his uncle's nakedness; they shall be subject to punishment; they shall die childless. ²¹If a man takes his brother's wife, it is impurity; he has uncovered his brother's nakedness; they shall be childless.

22 "You shall keep all my statutes and all my ordinances and observe them, so that the land to which I bring you to settle in may not vomit you out. ²³You shall not follow the practices of the nation that I am driving out before you. Because they did all these things, I abhorred them. ²⁴But I have said to you, 'You shall inherit their land, and I will give it to you to possess, a land flowing with milk and honey. I am the Lord your God; I have separated you from the peoples.' ²⁵You shall therefore make a distinction between the clean animal and the unclean and between the unclean bird and the clean; you shall not bring abomination on yourselves by animal or by bird or by anything with which the ground teems, which I have set apart for you to hold unclean. ²⁶You shall be holy to me, for I the Lord am holy, and I have separated you from the other peoples to be mine.

27 "A man or a woman who is a medium or a spiritualist shall be put to death; they shall be stoned to death; their bloodguilt is upon them.'"

_l_ 20.10 Heb repeats _if a man commits adultery with the wife of_

20:6–21 There are many instances of repetition in this section, including the rule about _mediums_ and _spiritualists_ (vv. 6, 27; see also 19:31), adultery (v. 10; see also 18:20), incest (vv. 11–12, 14, 17, 19–21; see also chap. 18), sexual relations between men (v. 13; see also 18:22), bestiality (vv. 15–16; see also 18:23), and sexual relations with a menstruating woman (v. 18; see also 18:19). The legal sections and particular regulations in the holiness material (chaps. 17–26) are less organized than those in the Priestly Torah of chaps. 1–16.

20:27 Practices of divination, sorcery, and necromancy are strictly forbidden throughout the Torah and a focus of condemnation in the prophets (Mic. 5:12; Isa. 47:12–13; Ezek. 13:23). Note that Saul consults a medium to communicate with the deceased Samuel (1 Sam. 28).

21 The LORD said to Moses, "Speak to the priests, the sons of Aaron, and say to them:

"No one shall defile himself for a dead person among his relatives, [2]except for his nearest kin: his mother, his father, his son, his daughter, his brother; [3]likewise, for a virgin sister close to him because she has had no husband, he may defile himself for her. [4]But he shall not defile himself for those related to him by marriage and so profane himself. [5]They shall not make bald spots upon their heads or shave off the edges of their beards or make any gashes in their flesh. [6]They shall be holy to their God and not profane the name of their God, for they offer the LORD's offerings by fire,[m] the food of their God; therefore they shall be holy. [7]They shall not marry a prostitute or a woman who has been defiled; neither shall they marry a woman divorced from her husband. For they are holy to their God, [8]and you shall treat them as holy, since they offer the food of your God; they shall be holy to you, for I the LORD, I who sanctify you, am holy. [9]When the daughter of a priest profanes herself through prostitution, she profanes her father; she shall be burned to death.

10 "The priest who is exalted above his brothers, on whose head the anointing oil has been poured and who has been consecrated to wear the vestments, shall not dishevel his hair nor tear his vestments. [11]He shall not go where there is a dead body; he shall not defile himself even for his father or mother. [12]He shall not go outside the sanctuary and thus profane the sanctuary of his God, for the consecration of the anointing oil of his God is upon him: I am the LORD. [13]He shall marry only a woman who is a virgin. [14]A widow or a divorced woman or a woman who has been defiled, a prostitute—these he shall not marry. He shall marry a virgin of his own people, [15]that he may not profane his offspring among his people, for I am the LORD; I sanctify him."

16 The LORD spoke to Moses, saying, [17]"Speak to Aaron and say: No one of your offspring throughout their generations who has a blemish may approach to offer the food of his God. [18]Indeed, no one who has a blemish shall draw near, one who is blind or lame, or one who is mutilated or deformed,[n] [19]or one who has a broken foot or a broken hand, [20]or a hunchback, or a dwarf, or a man with a defect in his eyes or an itching disease or scabs or crushed testicles. [21]No descendant of Aaron the priest who has a blemish shall come near to offer the LORD's offerings by fire;[o] since he has a blemish, he shall not come near to offer the food of his God. [22]He may eat the food of his God, of the most holy as well as of the holy. [23]But he shall not come near the curtain or approach the altar because he has

m 21.6 Or the LORD's gifts   n 21.18 Meaning of Heb uncertain   o 21.21 Or the LORD's gifts

21:1–3 This strict separation of burial from the sacrificial system is unusual in the ancient world, where elaborate funeral rituals were the norm. Israelite priests have no part in easing a soul's passage to the afterlife, appeasing the gods on behalf of the departed, or praying to ancestors for their protection or prophecy, to name a few specific ritual functions of ancient Near Eastern priests. Israelite priests may not even participate in funeral rites except for *nearest kin* (see **"Priests (Leviticus),"** p. 176).

21:4 *Defile himself . . . profane himself.* Even though the concept of holiness is expanded to all of Israel in the second half of Leviticus, the ritual system is still designed to manage and cleanse impurities and priests are subject to greater restrictions; ritual and moral considerations come together in the rules for the priest and the high priest, especially around issues of marriage and death. See **"Holiness and Purity,"** p. 158.

21:5 Mourning rituals forbidden to the priests.

21:9 Even daughters of priests are subject to greater restrictions, and penalties for violating the restrictions are severe.

21:10 Mourning rituals forbidden to the priests.

21:16–20 The rules for who may serve as priest exclude anyone with a malformation or physical disability, either congenital or acquired, and match those for the selection of a sacrificial animal (22:21–25).

21:21–23 While these rules are based in theological reasoning—focused on concepts of wholeness, integrity, and purity—they also reflect common societal prejudice against those with disabilities. However, since the priesthood is a hereditary line, these individuals have priestly status and the societal honor that goes with that identity. They are entitled to the priestly prerogatives and

Reading through Time: Priests (Leviticus 21)

Priests in the Hebrew Bible serve a number of functions, but the most important are teaching the law and mediating between God and the people through ritual. In the Priestly worldview, God dwells in the midst of the people, and God's holiness must never be threatened by encroaching impurity (see **"Holiness and Purity," p. 158**). Therefore, the priests' role is to master the ritual and ethical requirements that God has placed on Israel and to manage the sacrificial system in a way that ensures Israel's well-being and ongoing relationship with God. Priests sometimes became important political figures, such as Zadok (2 Sam. 15; 1 Kgs. 1), Hilkiah (2 Kgs. 22), Ezra, and the Hasmoneans (1 Macc.). Later prophets give a role to the high priest in scenes of messianic hope (Hag. 2; Zech. 3), and the Dead Sea Scrolls community seems to have expected both a political "Messiah of Israel" and a priestly "Messiah of Aaron." In Judaism, the teaching role of the priest was taken up by rabbis, as study of the Torah and acts of *hesed* (see **"Hesed," p. 375**) came to replace rituals of sacrifice after the temple was destroyed. Unlike the priesthood, however, the rabbinate is not hereditary, nor are rabbis needed to mediate between the people and God. In the trajectory of Christian tradition, the NT book of Hebrews identifies Jesus as the "high priest" appointed by God to offer a sacrifice of atonement for the people (Heb. 2:17) not each day but once through the decisive offering of himself (Heb. 7:26–27). During the Last Supper, Jesus assumes a priestly role in the offering of his body and blood at the Passover (Luke 22). This scene establishes the importance of Christian priests in their administration of the Eucharist and other sacraments. In traditional Catholic theology, the priest serves a similar mediating function to the Israelite priest, being ordained to perform rites on behalf of the people. And as with the priestly portion of the offerings, Catholic priests must either consume or properly dispose of unused consecrated Eucharist elements. The Protestant tradition has emphasized the priesthood of the believer, the idea that all baptized Christians are priests before God (1 Pet. 2:9). Protestant clergy are still ordained for particular roles (teaching, offering the sacraments), but each Christian may approach God themselves for forgiveness and salvation, mediated by Christ.

Bryan Bibb

a blemish, that he may not profane my sanctuaries, for I am the Lᴏʀᴅ; I sanctify them." ²⁴Thus Moses spoke to Aaron and to his sons and to all the Israelites.

22 The Lᴏʀᴅ spoke to Moses, saying: ²ᵃ"Direct Aaron and his sons to deal carefully with the sacred donations of the Israelites, which they dedicate to me, so that they may not profane my holy name: I am the Lᴏʀᴅ. ³Say to them, 'If anyone among all your offspring throughout your generations comes near the sacred donations, which the Israelites dedicate to the Lᴏʀᴅ, while he is in a state of uncleanness, that person shall be cut off from my presence: I am the Lᴏʀᴅ.' ⁴No one of Aaron's offspring who has a defiling skin disease or suffers a discharge may eat of the sacred donations until he is clean. Whoever touches anything made unclean by a corpse or a man who has had an emission of semen, ⁵and whoever touches any swarming thing by which he may be made unclean or any human being by whom he may be made

economic support, to *eat the food of his God*, although they may not approach the altar or tent of meeting in ritual service.

21:24 In giving these laws to the priests *and to all the Israelites*, Moses shows that Priestly regulations are a matter of public concern to which everyone should carefully attend.

22:2–3 *So that they may not profane my holy name.* Actions that *profane* God's name include sacrificing a child to Molech (18:21), priests participating in funeral rites (21:6), and priests officiating while in a state of uncleanness (v. 3). See the summary admonition in vv. 31–33.

22:4–9 Miscellaneous purity rules for priests who are serving at the altar or eating *the sacred donations*, the priestly portion of offerings in the sanctuary. Several of the topics are covered earlier in chaps. 11–16: defiling skin disease (v. 4; see chap. 13), genital discharge and semen emission (v. 4; see chap. 15), touching an unclean *swarming* animal or eating an animal carcass (vv. 5–8; see chap. 11). The earlier texts apply to all the people, but these verses clarify that a priest who finds himself in an unclean state may not officiate at the altar. For instance, a layperson who eats from an animal carcass simply must wash and be impure until evening (17:15), but if a priest performs his sacred duties after eating such food, he is subject to *die because of it* (vv. 8–9).

unclean—whatever his uncleanness may be—[6]the person who touches any such shall be unclean until evening and shall not eat of the sacred donations unless he has washed his body in water. [7]When the sun sets he shall be clean, and afterward he may eat of the sacred donations, for they are his food. [8]That which died or was torn by wild animals he shall not eat, becoming unclean by it: I am the LORD. [9]They shall keep my charge, so that they may not incur guilt and die because of it for having profaned them: I am the LORD; I sanctify them.

10 "No layperson shall eat of the sacred donations. No bound or hired servant of the priest shall eat of the sacred donations, [11]but if a priest acquires anyone by purchase, the person may eat of them, and those who are born in his house may eat of his food. [12]If a priest's daughter marries a layman, she shall not eat of the offering of the sacred donations, [13]but if a priest's daughter is widowed or divorced, without offspring, and returns to her father's house, as in her youth, she may eat of her father's food. No layperson shall eat of it. [14]If a man eats of the sacred donation unintentionally, he shall add one-fifth of its value to it and give the sacred donation to the priest. [15]No one shall profane the sacred donations of the Israelites, which they offer to the LORD, [16]causing them to bear guilt requiring a guilt offering, by eating their sacred donations, for I am the LORD; I sanctify them."

17 The LORD spoke to Moses, saying, [18]"Speak to Aaron and his sons and all the Israelites and say to them: When anyone of the house of Israel or of the aliens residing in Israel presents an offering, whether in payment of a vow or as a freewill offering that is offered to the LORD as a burnt offering, [19]to be acceptable on your behalf it shall be a male without blemish, of the cattle or the sheep or the goats. [20]You shall not offer anything that has a blemish, for it will not be acceptable on your behalf.

21 "When anyone offers a sacrifice of well-being to the LORD, in fulfillment of a vow or as a freewill offering, from the herd or from the flock, to be acceptable it must be perfect; there shall be no blemish in it. [22]Anything blind or injured or maimed or having a discharge or an itch or scabs—these you shall not offer to the LORD or put any of them on the altar as offerings by fire[p] to the LORD. [23]An ox or a lamb that is deformed or stunted you may present for a freewill offering, but it will not be accepted for a vow. [24]Any animal that has its testicles bruised or crushed or torn or cut, you shall not offer to the LORD; such you shall not do within your land, [25]nor shall you accept any such animals from a foreigner to offer as food to your God; since they are mutilated, with a blemish in them, they shall not be accepted on your behalf."

26 The LORD spoke to Moses, saying, [27]"When an ox or a sheep or a goat is born, it shall remain seven days with its mother, and from the eighth day on it shall be acceptable as the LORD's offering by fire.[q] [28]But you shall not slaughter, from the herd or the flock, an animal with its young on the same day. [29]When you sacrifice a thanksgiving offering to the LORD, you shall sacrifice it so that it may be acceptable on your behalf. [30]It shall be eaten on the same day; you shall not leave any of it until morning: I am the LORD.

31 "Thus you shall keep my commandments and observe them: I am the LORD. [32]You shall not profane my holy name, that I may be sanctified among the Israelites: I am the LORD;

p 22.22 Or *as gifts*   *q* 22.27 Or *the LORD's gift*

22:10–13 The *sacred donations* include the priestly portions of both animal and grain offerings, and they may only be eaten by priests. As exceptions to this rule, a person enslaved by a priest may eat the food (v. 11), as can the priest's widowed or divorced (and childless) daughter, if she *returns to her father's house.*

22:18–20 The passage turns from blemished and impure priests to the question of blemished animals for sacrifice. In speaking to the priests *and all the Israelites*, Moses makes both the priest and the person bringing the offering responsible for ensuring that a sacrificial animal is *acceptable.*

22:31–33 This exhortation expresses the moral weight of the preceding chapters of purity and ritual commandments. A series of motivational statements indicate why the Israelites should obey these regulations: God's name is holy; God is the Lord (see note on 18:5); God sanctifies the people; God brought the people out of Egypt. This passage, therefore, is a descriptive reformulation of the central command in the Holiness Code: *You shall be holy, for I the LORD your God am holy* (19:2). See **"God's Name," p. 89**.

I sanctify you, [33]I who brought you out of the land of Egypt to be your God: I am the LORD."

23 The LORD spoke to Moses, saying, [2]"Speak to the Israelites and say to them: These are the appointed festivals of the LORD that you shall proclaim as holy convocations, my appointed festivals.

3 "Six days shall work be done, but the seventh day is a Sabbath of complete rest, a holy convocation; you shall do no work: it is a Sabbath to the LORD throughout your settlements. 4 "These are the appointed festivals of the LORD, the holy convocations, that you shall celebrate at the time appointed for them. [5]In the first month, on the fourteenth day of the month, at twilight,[r] there shall be a Passover offering to the LORD, [6]and on the fifteenth day of the same month is the Festival of Unleavened Bread to the LORD; seven days you shall eat unleavened bread. [7]On the first day you shall have a holy convocation; you shall not work at your occupations. [8]For seven days you shall present the LORD's offerings by fire;[s] on the seventh day there shall be a holy convocation: you shall not work at your occupations."

9 The LORD spoke to Moses, [10]"Speak to the Israelites and say to them: When you enter the land that I am giving you and you reap its harvest, you shall bring the sheaf of the first fruits of your harvest to the priest. [11]He shall raise the sheaf before the LORD, that you may find acceptance; on the day after the Sabbath the priest shall raise it. [12]On the day when you raise the sheaf, you shall offer a lamb a year old, without blemish, as a burnt offering to the LORD. [13]And the grain offering with it shall be two-tenths of an ephah of choice flour mixed with oil, an offering by fire[t] of pleasing odor to the LORD, and the drink offering with it shall be of wine, one-fourth of a hin. [14]You shall eat no bread or parched grain or fresh ears until that very day, until you have brought the offering of your God. This is a statute forever throughout your generations in all your settlements.

15 "And from the day after the Sabbath, from the day on which you bring the sheaf of the elevation offering, you shall count seven full weeks. [16]You shall count until the day after the seventh Sabbath, fifty days; then you shall present an offering of new grain to the LORD. [17]You shall bring from your settlements two loaves of bread as an elevation offering, each made of two-tenths of an ephah; they shall be of choice flour, baked with leaven, as first fruits to the LORD. [18]You shall present with the bread seven lambs a year old without blemish, one bull of the herd, and two rams; they shall be a burnt offering to the LORD, along with their grain offering and their drink offerings, an offering by fire[u] of pleasing odor to the LORD. [19]You shall also offer one male goat for a purification offering and two lambs a year old as a sacrifice of well-being. [20]The priest shall raise them with the bread of the first fruits as an elevation offering before

r 23.5 Heb *between the two evenings*   s 23.8 Or the LORD's gifts
t 23.13 Or *a gift*   u 23.18 Or *a gift*

23:2 *The appointed festivals* are the regular celebrations that form the structure of the Israelite calendar. See also Num. 28–29.

23:3 The Sabbath regulation to *do no work* is presented as an absolute, though questions arise as to what constitutes *work*—specifically, which activities are forbidden and which activities are allowed. Different Jewish groups have understood the prohibition on work differently, and debates continue in Jewish communities today.

23:5–8 *Passover offering.* In Exod. 12, the assumption is that the meal would take place at home, but Deut. 16 sets Passover in Jerusalem because Deuteronomy centralizes worship in the temple, and that is the only place where one may offer an animal sacrifice. On the *Festival of Unleavened Bread*, see also Num. 28:16–25. *Work* is prohibited, like with the Sabbath (v. 3), on the first and seventh days.

23:9–14 The offering of *first fruits* is a harvest festival focused on presenting God's token portion of the barley crop (the earliest grain to ripen) along with the *burnt offering, grain offering*, and *drink offering*. This is the only reference to a *drink offering* in Leviticus, though it is mentioned numerous times in Num. 15 and 28–29.

23:15–18 The Festival of Weeks (as named in Exod. 34:22 and Deut. 16:10) takes place seven weeks after the barley harvest and the offering of first fruits, on the fiftieth day. Most likely timed to the wheat harvest, it includes an *elevation offering* of bread presented to the priests and a large number of animal sacrifices, along with a day of Sabbath rest.

the Lord, together with the two lambs; they shall be holy to the Lord for the priest. [21]On that same day you shall make proclamation; you shall hold a holy convocation; you shall not work at your occupations. This is a statute forever in all your settlements throughout your generations.

22 "When you reap the harvest of your land, you shall not reap to the very edges of your field or gather the gleanings of your harvest; you shall leave them for the poor and for the alien: I am the Lord your God."

23 The Lord spoke to Moses, saying, [24]"Speak to the Israelites, saying: In the seventh month, on the first day of the month, you shall observe a day of complete rest, a holy convocation commemorated with trumpet blasts. [25]You shall not work at your occupations, and you shall present the Lord's offering by fire."[v]

26 The Lord spoke to Moses, saying, [27]"Now, the tenth day of this seventh month is the Day of Atonement; it shall be a holy convocation for you: you shall humble yourselves[w] and present the Lord's offering by fire,[x] [28]and you shall do no work during that entire day, for it is a Day of Atonement, to make atonement on your behalf before the Lord your God. [29]For those who do not humble themselves[y] during that entire day shall be cut off from the people. [30]And anyone who does any work during that entire day, such a one I will destroy from the midst of the people. [31]You shall do no work. This is a statute forever throughout your generations in all your settlements. [32]It shall be to you a Sabbath of complete rest, and you shall humble yourselves;[z] on the ninth day of the month at evening, from evening to evening you shall keep your Sabbath."

33 The Lord spoke to Moses, saying, [34]"Speak to the Israelites, saying: On the fifteenth day of this seventh month and lasting seven days, there shall be the Festival of Booths[a] to the Lord. [35]The first day shall be a holy convocation; you shall not work at your occupations. [36]Seven days you shall present the Lord's offerings by fire;[b] on the eighth day you shall observe a holy convocation and present the Lord's offerings by fire;[c] it is a solemn assembly; you shall not work at your occupations.

37 "These are the appointed festivals of the Lord that you shall celebrate as times of holy convocation, for presenting to the Lord offerings by fire[d]—burnt offerings and grain offerings, sacrifices and drink offerings, each on its proper day—[38]apart from the Sabbaths of the Lord and apart from your gifts and apart from all your votive offerings and apart from all your freewill offerings that you give to the Lord.

39 "Now, the fifteenth day of the seventh month, when you have gathered in the produce of the land, you shall keep the festival of the Lord, lasting seven days, a complete rest on the first day and a complete rest on the eighth day. [40]On the first day you shall take the fruit of majestic[e] trees, branches of palm trees, boughs of leafy trees, and willows of the brook, and you shall rejoice before the Lord your God for seven days. [41]You shall keep it as a festival to the Lord lasting seven days in the year; you shall keep it in the seventh month as a statute forever throughout your generations. [42]You shall live in booths for seven days; all who are native-born in Israel shall live in booths, [43]so that your generations may

v 23.25 Or the Lord's gift w 23.27 Or shall fast x 23.27 Or the Lord's gift y 23.29 Or do not fast z 23.32 Or shall fast a 23.34 Or Tabernacles b 23.36 Or the Lord's gifts c 23.36 Or the Lord's gifts d 23.37 Or gifts e 23.40 Meaning of Heb uncertain

23:22 On compassion for the poor, see the notes on 19:9–10 and 19:15.

23:23–25 The Festival of Trumpets begins three observances in the seventh month. Work is prohibited; the sacrifices included in this offering by fire are enumerated in Num. 29:1–6. Although not noted as such in the Bible, this festival will come to mark the beginning of the Jewish year.

23:26–32 The Day of Atonement ritual is detailed in chap. 16, which focuses on the role of the high priest in the ceremony. This passage concerns the responsibilities of the people, who are to do no work and to humble themselves (sometimes translated as "deny yourselves" and understood to command fasting) on the most solemn and ritually vital day of the year.

23:33–43 The Festival of Booths is a singularly joyous celebration. Similar to Passover, work is forbidden on the first and the last days of the festival (vv. 35–36). Offerings by fire are required (v. 36). It includes a day on which the people rejoice before the Lord while waving branches and tree boughs (v. 40) and a week in which they live in booths. The Festival of Booths is a harvest festival (v. 39) and a commemoration of Israel's generation-long wilderness wandering after the exodus (v. 43).

know that I made the Israelites live in booths when I brought them out of the land of Egypt: I am the Lord your God."

44 Thus Moses declared to the Israelites the appointed festivals of the Lord.

24 The Lord spoke to Moses, saying, [2]"Command the Israelites to bring you pure oil of beaten olives for the lamp, that a light may be kept burning regularly. [3]Aaron shall set it up in the tent of meeting, outside the curtain of the covenant, to burn from evening to morning before the Lord regularly; it shall be a statute forever throughout your generations. [4]He shall set up the lamps on the lampstand of pure gold[f] before the Lord regularly.

5 "You shall take choice flour and bake twelve loaves of it; two-tenths of an ephah shall be in each loaf. [6]You shall place them in two rows, six in a row, on the table of pure gold before the Lord.[g] [7]You shall put pure frankincense with each row, to be a token offering for the bread, as an offering by fire[h] to the Lord. [8]Every Sabbath day Aaron shall set them in order before the Lord regularly as a commitment of the Israelites, as a covenant forever. [9]They shall be for Aaron and his descendants, who shall eat them in a holy place, for they are most holy portions for him from the offerings by fire[i] to the Lord, a perpetual due."

10 A man whose mother was an Israelite and whose father was an Egyptian came out among the Israelites, and the Israelite woman's son and a certain Israelite began fighting in the camp. [11]The Israelite woman's son blasphemed the Name in a curse. And they brought him to Moses—now his mother's name was Shelomith daughter of Dibri, of the tribe of Dan—[12]and they put him in custody, until the decision of the Lord should be made clear to them.

13 The Lord spoke to Moses, saying, [14]"Take the blasphemer outside the camp, and let all who were within hearing lay their hands on his head, and let the whole congregation stone him. [15]And speak to the Israelites, saying: Anyone who curses God shall incur guilt. [16]One who blasphemes the name of the Lord shall be put to death; the whole congregation shall stone the blasphemer. Aliens as well as the native-born, when they blaspheme the Name, shall be put to death. [17]Anyone who kills a human being shall be put to death. [18]Anyone who kills an animal shall make restitution for it, life for life. [19]Anyone who maims another shall suffer the same injury in return: [20]fracture for fracture, eye for eye, tooth for tooth; the injury inflicted is the injury to be suffered. [21]One who kills an

---

f 24.4 Heb *pure lampstand*   *g* 24.6 Heb *pure table*   *h* 24.7 Or *a gift*   *i* 24.9 Or *the gifts*

24:2–9 This chapter begins with two details related to fixtures in the tent of meeting and priestly duties associated with them. First, the high priest is responsible for burning oil lamps on a golden lampstand, which is set up before the inner curtain that separates the most holy chamber where God's presence dwells (vv. 2–4). Second, he should place on the table in the tent of meeting each Sabbath twelve loaves of bread, which the priests will eat *in a holy place*—that is, in the priestly area of the sanctuary courtyard (vv. 5–9).

24:10–23 *The blasphemer.* This narrative is only the third in Leviticus, the first two being the story of the priests' consecration and installation (chaps. 8–10) and Aaron's initial performance of the yearly atonement ritual (chap. 16). As in the book of Numbers, Leviticus is structured around alternating ritual and narrative sections, each commenting on the other. In this case, the story of the blasphemer leads to the revelation of seven new laws of "talion"—that is, retributive justice in which the penalty matches the crime. See also Exod. 21:23 and Deut. 19:21. **24:10** The blasphemer's case is ambiguous because his *father was an Egyptian.* The question at hand is whether non-Israelites dwelling with the people are required to follow the rules respecting the holiness of God. One purpose of this text is to demonstrate the mediating role of the priest in receiving and interpreting the commands of God for the people. The law as it stands does not clearly address every possible situation, and so priests (and in the judicial context, judges) are empowered to interpret and apply the law fairly and with wisdom (see Num. 9:1–14; 15:32–36; and 27:1–11 for similar stories of legal judgment). **24:14** The judgment is to *let the whole congregation stone him.* In death penalty cases in the Torah, execution is always performed by the people. **24:16** *Aliens as well as the native-born* are equally punished for the crime of blasphemy, thus resolving the question posed in v. 10. **24:17–22** Other crimes for which the law is the same for foreigners and Israelites alike.

animal shall make restitution for it, but one who kills a human being shall be put to death. [22]You shall have one law for the alien and for the native-born, for I am the LORD your God." [23]Moses spoke thus to the Israelites, and they took the blasphemer outside the camp and stoned him to death. The Israelites did as the LORD had commanded Moses.

25 The LORD spoke to Moses on Mount Sinai, saying, [2]"Speak to the Israelites and say to them: When you enter the land that I am giving you, the land shall observe a Sabbath for the LORD. [3]Six years you shall sow your field, and six years you shall prune your vineyard and gather in their yield, [4]but in the seventh year there shall be a Sabbath of complete rest for the land, a Sabbath for the LORD: you shall not sow your field or prune your vineyard. [5]You shall not reap the aftergrowth of your harvest or gather the grapes of your unpruned vine: it shall be a year of complete rest for the land. [6]You may eat what the land yields during its Sabbath—you, your male and female slaves, your hired and your bound laborers who live with you, [7]for your livestock also, and for the wild animals in your land all its yield shall be for food.

8 "You shall count off seven weeks[j] of years, seven times seven years, so that the period of seven weeks of years gives forty-nine years. [9]Then you shall have the trumpet sounded loud; on the tenth day of the seventh month—on the Day of Atonement—you shall

have the trumpet sounded throughout all your land. [10]And you shall hallow the fiftieth year, and you shall proclaim liberty throughout the land to all its inhabitants. It shall be a Jubilee for you: you shall return, every one of you, to your property and every one of you to your family. [11]That fiftieth year shall be a Jubilee for you: you shall not sow or reap the aftergrowth or harvest the unpruned vines. [12]For it is a Jubilee; it shall be holy to you: you shall eat only what the field itself produces.

13 "In this year of Jubilee you shall return, every one of you, to your property. [14]When you make a sale to your neighbor or buy from your neighbor, you shall not cheat one another. [15]When you buy from your neighbor, you shall pay only for the number of years until the Jubilee; the seller shall charge you only for the remaining crop years. [16]If the years are more, you shall increase the price, and if the years are fewer, you shall diminish the price, for it is a certain number of harvests that are being sold to you. [17]You shall not cheat one another, but you shall fear your God, for I am the LORD your God.

18 "You shall observe my statutes and faithfully keep my ordinances, so that you may live on the land securely. [19]The land will yield its fruit, and you will eat your fill and live on it securely. [20]Should you ask, 'What shall we eat in the seventh year, if we may not sow or gather in our crop?' [21]I will order my blessing for you in the sixth year, so that it will yield

j 25.8 Or *Sabbaths*

24:23 The report that Moses spoke and the Israelites *did as the LORD had commanded Moses* shows the absolute importance of command and fulfillment in the Priestly worldview. The ritual and legal system requires precision in teaching and close attention to detail in the application of God's commands.

25:2-7 *The land shall observe a Sabbath.* Priestly cosmology includes attention to sacred space and sacred time. In the Priestly creation story, God rests on the seventh day, thus establishing Sabbath as a pillar of creation itself (Gen. 2:2–3). Here, the Sabbath is extended to the land every seventh year. People may eat of the land's natural bounty (v. 6; see Exod. 23:10–11) but may not cultivate or harvest.

25:8-12 The year of *Jubilee* is a special time of rest and restoration for the people and also for the land. The calendar relationship between the seventh Sabbath year (i.e., year 49) and the Jubilee (year 50) has been a matter of great debate, but clearly the text considers them to overlap; *seven times seven years* (v. 8) is the same period as *the fiftieth year* (v. 10). A more important question is whether this event was ever actually implemented. Since Jubilee is mentioned nowhere outside Leviticus and Numbers and also is not found in any extrabiblical evidence, it is best to see this passage as an expression of theological hope rather than a description of historical practice.

25:13 In the Jubilee year, any ancestral land that has been sold outside the family is returned. The number of years remaining before the Jubilee must be considered in the sale price. All the land belongs to God, and the people are merely residing in it on God's terms (v. 23).

a crop for three years. [22]When you sow in the eighth year, you will be eating from the old crop; until the ninth year, when its produce comes in, you shall eat the old. [23]The land shall not be sold in perpetuity, for the land is mine; with me you are but aliens and tenants. [24]Throughout the land that you hold, you shall provide for the redemption of the land.

25 "If anyone of your kin falls into difficulty and sells a piece of property, then the next of kin shall come and redeem what the relative has sold. [26]If the person has no one to redeem it but then prospers and finds sufficient means to do so, [27]the years since its sale shall be computed and the difference refunded to the person to whom it was sold, and the property shall be returned. [28]But if there are not sufficient means to recover it, what was sold shall remain with the purchaser until the year of Jubilee; in the Jubilee it shall be released, and the property shall be returned.

29 "If anyone sells a dwelling house in a walled city, it may be redeemed until a year has elapsed since its sale; the right of redemption shall be one year. [30]If it is not redeemed before a full year has elapsed, a house that is in a walled city shall pass in perpetuity to the purchaser, throughout the generations; it shall not be released in the Jubilee. [31]But houses in villages that have no walls around them shall be classed as open country; they may be redeemed, and they shall be released in the Jubilee. [32]As for the cities of the Levites, the Levites shall forever have the right of redemption of the houses in the cities belonging to them. [33]Whatever property of the Levites that may be redeemed, that is, houses sold in a city belonging to them, shall be released in the Jubilee, for the houses in the cities of the Levites are their possession among the Israelites. [34]But the pasturelands around their cities may not be sold, for that is their possession for all time.

35 "If any of your kin fall into difficulty and become dependent on you,[k] you shall support them; they shall live with you as though resident aliens. [36]Do not take interest in advance or otherwise make a profit from them, but fear your God; let them live with you. [37]You shall not lend them your money at interest taken in advance or provide them food at a profit. [38]I am the LORD your God who brought you out of the land of Egypt, to give you the land of Canaan, to be your God.

39 "If any who are dependent on you become so impoverished that they sell themselves to you, you shall not make them serve as slaves. [40]They shall remain with you as hired or bound laborers. They shall serve with you until the year of the Jubilee. [41]Then they and their children with them shall go out from your authority; they shall go back to their own family and return to their ancestral property. [42]For they are my servants whom I brought out of the land of Egypt; they shall not be sold as slaves are sold. [43]You shall not rule over them with harshness but shall fear your God. [44]As for the male and female slaves whom you may have, it is from the nations around you that you may acquire male and female slaves. [45]You may also acquire them from among the aliens residing with you and

k 25.35 Meaning of Heb uncertain

25:25 Property that is sold outside the family can be repurchased by another family member even before the Jubilee year.

25:29–34 These details reflect the complexity of property law. The Jubilee year primarily concerns land; houses in a city are not redeemed in the fiftieth year, though houses in the country are redeemed, presumably because they are supported by the land around them. Special rules apply as well to the Levites, who do not have ancestral holdings (Num. 18:23–24). Their homes in the Levitical cities may be redeemed, and the pasture around their cities may never be sold. For the establishment of Levite cities and pastureland, see Num. 35:1–7 and Josh. 21:20–41.

25:35–43 Obligations of family when a family member has fallen into economic crisis, and the difference between bonded service and slavery. An Israelite may sell themselves into bonded servitude until the Jubilee year; neither they nor their children become slaves (v. 42). Notice the difference in Exod. 21:3–6, in which children born to a bond servant during his six years of service belong to the master. Amos denounces the rich for their abuse of this system of debt slavery in oppressing the poor (Amos 2:6). See **"Human Bondage," p. 115**.

25:44–46 Unlike Israelites, foreigners may be enslaved and are treated as property (see Exod. 21:20–21). They can be passed down as part of an inheritance (v. 46) and, unlike Israelite servants, may be treated with harshness.

from their families who are with you who have been born in your land; they may be your property. ⁴⁶You may keep them as a possession for your children after you, for them to inherit as property. These you may treat as slaves, but as for your fellow Israelites, no one shall rule over the other with harshness.

47 "If resident aliens among you prosper, and if any of your kin fall into difficulty with one of them and sell themselves to an alien or to a branch of the alien's family, ⁴⁸even after they have sold themselves they shall have the right of redemption; one of their brothers may redeem them, ⁴⁹or their uncle or their uncle's son may redeem them, or anyone of their family who is of their own flesh may redeem them, or if they prosper they may redeem themselves. ⁵⁰They shall compute with the purchaser the total from the year when they sold themselves to the alien until the Jubilee year; the price of the sale shall be applied to the number of years: the time they were with the owner shall be rated as the time of a hired laborer. ⁵¹If many years remain, they shall pay for their redemption in proportion to the purchase price, ⁵²and if few years remain until the Jubilee year, they shall compute thus: according to the years involved they shall make payment for their redemption. ⁵³As a laborer hired by the year they shall be under the alien's authority, who shall not, however, rule with harshness over them in your sight. ⁵⁴And if they have not been redeemed in any of these ways, they and their children with them shall go out in the Jubilee year. ⁵⁵For to me the Israelites are servants; they are my servants whom I brought out from the land of Egypt: I am the Lord your God.

26 "You shall make for yourselves no idols and erect no carved images or pillars, and you shall not place figured stones in your land, to worship at them, for I am the Lord your God. ²You shall keep my Sabbaths and revere my sanctuary: I am the Lord.

3 "If you follow my statutes and keep my commandments and observe them faithfully, ⁴I will give you your rains in their season, and the land shall yield its produce, and the trees of the field shall yield their fruit. ⁵Your threshing shall overlap the vintage, and the vintage shall overlap the sowing; you shall eat your bread to the full and live securely in your land. ⁶And I will grant peace in the land, and you shall lie down, and no one shall make you afraid; I will remove dangerous animals from the land, and no sword shall go through your land. ⁷You shall give chase to your enemies, and they shall fall before you by the sword. ⁸Five of you shall give chase to a hundred, and a hundred of you shall give chase to ten thousand; your enemies shall fall before you by the sword. ⁹I will look with favor upon you and make you fruitful and multiply you, and I will maintain my covenant with you. ¹⁰You shall eat old grain long stored, and you shall have to clear out the old to make way for the new. ¹¹I will place my dwelling in your midst, and I shall not abhor you. ¹²Iˡ will be your God, and you shall be my people. ¹³I am the Lord your God who brought you out of the land of Egypt, to be their slaves no more; I have broken the bars of your yoke and made you walk erect.

14 "But if you will not obey me and do not observe all these commandments, ¹⁵if you spurn my statutes and abhor my ordinances,

l 26.12 Q ms: MT adds *I will walk among you, and I*

26:1 The items mentioned here—*idols, images, pillars,* and *figured stones*—appear in many texts throughout the Hebrew Bible along with a number of other technical terms for cultic objects. This type of stone or carved image is forbidden in the commandments (Deut. 5:8), destroyed by reforming kings in Judah (2 Kgs. 23:14), and identified as a worthless object by the prophets (Isa. 44:10). **26:3–45** Traditionally, law codes conclude with a section of blessings and curses. See also Deut. 28 and Exod. 23:25–33. **26:5–6** The promise of bounty and security in this passage resonates with the postexilic addition to the book of Amos (9:13–15), which promises that the harvest will not even be finished before it is time to plant again and that the people will no longer be subject to attack and exile. **26:11–13** This concluding summary statement includes three of the most important motifs in Priestly theology: (1) God literally dwells in the midst of the community, (2) God and Israel are bound together in covenant, and (3) the revelation of the law is rooted in God's prior gracious act of rescuing the people from Egypt. **26:14–33** As in Deut. 28, the description of punishments is more specific and brutal than the idealistic and somewhat vague description of blessings. Rhetorically, there are similarities between the curses and prophetic condemnations in Amos or Jeremiah. As in the prophets, God employs natural elements, animals, and foreign armies as agents in carrying out

so that you will not observe all my commandments and you break my covenant, [16]I in turn will do this to you: I will bring terror on you, consumption and fever that waste the eyes and cause life to pine away. You shall sow your seed in vain, for your enemies shall eat it. [17]I will set my face against you, and you shall be struck down by your enemies; your foes shall rule over you, and you shall flee though no one pursues you. [18]And if in spite of this you will not obey me, I will continue to punish you sevenfold for your sins. [19]I will break your proud glory, and I will make your sky like iron and your earth like copper. [20]Your strength shall be spent to no purpose: your land shall not yield its produce, and the trees of the land shall not yield their fruit.

[21] "If you continue hostile to me and will not obey me, I will continue to plague you sevenfold for your sins. [22]I will let loose wild animals against you, and they shall bereave you of your children and destroy your livestock; they shall make you few in number, and your roads shall be deserted.

[23] "If in spite of these punishments you have not turned back to me but continue hostile to me, [24]then I, too, will continue hostile to you: I myself will strike you sevenfold for your sins. [25]I will bring the sword against you, executing vengeance for the covenant, and if you withdraw into your cities, I will send pestilence among you, and you shall be delivered into enemy hands. [26]When I cut off your supply of bread,[m] ten women shall bake your bread in a single oven, and they shall dole out your bread by weight, and though you eat, you shall not be satisfied.

[27] "But if, despite this, you disobey me and continue hostile to me, [28]I will continue hostile to you in fury; I in turn will punish you myself sevenfold for your sins. [29]You shall eat the flesh of your sons, and you shall eat the flesh of your daughters. [30]I will destroy your high places and cut down your incense altars; I will heap your carcasses on the carcasses of your idols. I will abhor you. [31]I will lay your cities waste, will make your sanctuaries desolate, and I will not smell your pleasing odors. [32]I will devastate the land, so that your enemies who come to settle in it shall be appalled at it. [33]And you I will scatter among the nations, and I will unsheathe the sword against you; your land shall be a desolation and your cities a waste.

[34] "Then the land shall enjoy[n] its Sabbath years as long as it lies desolate, while you are in the land of your enemies; then the land shall rest and enjoy[o] its Sabbath years. [35]As long as it lies desolate, it shall have the rest it did not have on your Sabbaths when you were living on it. [36]And as for those of you who survive, I will send faintness into their hearts in the lands of their enemies; the sound of a driven leaf shall put them to flight, and they shall flee as one flees from the sword, and they shall fall though no one pursues. [37]They shall stumble over one another, as if to escape a sword, though no one pursues, and you shall have no power to stand against your enemies. [38]You shall perish among the nations, and the land of your enemies shall devour you. [39]And those of you who survive shall languish in the land of your enemies because of their iniquities; they shall also languish because of the iniquities of their ancestors.

[40] "But if they confess their iniquity and the iniquity of their ancestors—their treachery against me and also their continued hostility to me, [41]so that I in turn was hostile to them and brought them into the land of their enemies—if, then, their uncircumcised heart is humbled and they make amends for their iniquity, [42]then will I remember my covenant with Jacob; I will remember also my covenant with Isaac and also my covenant with Abraham, and I will remember the land. [43]For the land shall be deserted by them and enjoy[p] its Sabbath years by lying desolate without them, while they shall make amends for

m 26.26 Heb *staff of bread*   n 26.34 Or *make up for*
o 26.34 Or *make up for*   p 26.43 Or *make up for*

divine wrath. **26:34** *In the land of your enemies* supports the supposition that the Holiness material in Leviticus (17–26) dates to the period of the Babylonian exile. As in the description of exile in Deut. 28:64–65, the text is not specific, but the historical reference is clear. **26:40–41** The possibility that Israel in exile can *confess their iniquity* to God and be forgiven and restored is found also in Deut. 30. Whereas the theology of that latter passage turns on the people's obedience and God's compassion, in Leviticus the focus is on the people's confession and God's remembrance of their covenantal relationship. The covenant of old is being remembered by God and brought back into fulfillment because the people have made *amends for their iniquity*.

their iniquity, because they dared to spurn my ordinances, and they abhorred my statutes. ⁴⁴Yet for all that, when they are in the land of their enemies, I will not spurn them or abhor them so as to destroy them utterly and break my covenant with them, for I am the Lord their God, ⁴⁵but I will remember in their favor the covenant with their ancestors whom I brought out of the land of Egypt in the sight of the nations, to be their God: I am the Lord."

46 These are the statutes and ordinances and laws that the Lord established between himself and the Israelites on Mount Sinai through Moses.

27 The Lord spoke to Moses, saying, ²"Speak to the Israelites and say to them: When a person makes an explicit vow to the Lord concerning the equivalent for a human being, ³the equivalent for a male shall be: from twenty to sixty years of age the equivalent shall be fifty shekels of silver by the sanctuary shekel. ⁴If the person is a female, the equivalent is thirty shekels. ⁵If the age is from five to twenty years of age, the equivalent is twenty shekels for a male and ten shekels for a female. ⁶If the age is from one month to five years, the equivalent for a male is five shekels of silver, and for a female the equivalent is three shekels of silver. ⁷And if the person is sixty years old or over, then the equivalent for a male is fifteen shekels and for a female ten shekels. ⁸If any cannot afford the equivalent, they shall be brought before the priest and the priest shall assess them; the priest shall assess them according to what each one making a vow can afford.

9 "If the vow concerns an animal that may be brought as an offering to the Lord, any such animal that may be given to the Lord shall be holy. ¹⁰Another shall not be exchanged or substituted for it, either good for bad or bad for good, and if one animal is substituted for another, both that one and its substitute shall be holy. ¹¹If the vow concerns any unclean animal that may not be brought as an offering to the Lord, the animal shall be presented before the priest. ¹²The priest shall assess it: whether good or bad, according to the assessment of the priest, so it shall be. ¹³But if it is to be redeemed, one-fifth must be added to the assessment.

14 "If a person consecrates a house to the Lord, the priest shall assess it: whether good or bad, as the priest assesses it, so it shall stand. ¹⁵And if the one who consecrates the house wishes to redeem it, one-fifth shall be added to its assessed value, and it shall revert to the original owner.

16 "If a person consecrates to the Lord any inherited landholding, its assessment shall be in accordance with its seed requirements: fifty shekels of silver to a homer of barley seed. ¹⁷If the person consecrates the field as of the year of Jubilee, that assessment shall stand, ¹⁸but if the field is consecrated after the Jubilee, the priest shall compute the price for it according to the years that remain until the year of Jubilee, and the assessment shall be reduced. ¹⁹And if the one who consecrates the field wishes to redeem it, then one-fifth shall be added to its assessed value, and it shall revert to the original owner, ²⁰but if the field is not redeemed or if it has been sold to someone else, it shall no longer be redeemable. ²¹But when the field is released in the Jubilee, it shall be holy to the Lord as a devoted field; it becomes the priest's holding. ²²If someone consecrates to the Lord a field that has been purchased that is not a part of the inherited landholding, ²³the priest shall compute for it the proportionate assessment up to the year of Jubilee, and the assessment shall be paid as of that day, a sacred donation to the Lord.

27:1–34 Given the summary statement at the end of chap. 26, most interpreters consider chap. 27 to be a later addition to the book. These laws concern financial technicalities related to a person's *vow to the Lord* (v. 2). 27:2–8 *Vow . . . concerning the equivalent for a human being* applies when a person makes a vow in which they are or another person is pledged to God's service. This promise can be fulfilled by the payment of a fixed amount based on gender and age. Compare with the story of Hannah (1 Sam. 1:11), where the child Samuel serves Eli in the sanctuary (1 Sam. 3). Women can make vows (in addition to 1 Sam. 1, see the law of the Nazirite in Num. 6:2–4 and the rules for vows made by women in Num. 30); however, the worth of their service is less. Note as well the rules for redeeming the firstborn of both humans and animals, which belong to God (Num. 18:14–18). 27:9–33 In addition to the value placed on humans, vows could relate to animals, houses, landholdings, and resources due as tithes. The priest is responsible for calculating the amount based on the value

24In the year of Jubilee the field shall return to the one from whom it was bought, whose holding the land is. 25All assessments shall be by the sanctuary shekel: twenty gerahs shall make a shekel.

26 "A firstling of animals, however, which as a firstling belongs to the Lord, cannot be consecrated by anyone; whether ox or sheep, it is the Lord's. 27If it is an unclean animal, it shall be ransomed at its assessment, with one-fifth added; if it is not redeemed, it shall be sold at its assessment.

28 "Nothing that a person owns that has been devoted to destruction for the Lord, be it human or animal or inherited landholding, may be sold or redeemed; every devoted thing is most holy to the Lord. 29No human beings who have been devoted to destruction can be ransomed; they shall be put to death.

30 "All tithes from the land, whether the seed from the ground or the fruit from the tree, are the Lord's; they are holy to the Lord. 31If persons wish to redeem any of their tithes, they must add one-fifth to them. 32All tithes of herd and flock, every tenth one that passes under the shepherd's staff, shall be holy to the Lord. 33Let no one inquire whether it is good or bad or make substitution for it; if one makes substitution for it, then both it and the substitute shall be holy and cannot be redeemed."

34 These are the commandments that the Lord gave to Moses for the Israelites on Mount Sinai.

and condition of the item. **27:28–29** *Devoted to destruction* ("herem") generally refers to the killing of all humans and animals through sanctioned acts of violence against the enemy during war. Property might be devoted to destruction (Deut. 13:16–17) or given to the sanctuary treasury (Josh. 6:16–19). In other cases, animals or virgin girls might be kept as the spoils of war (Num. 31:17–18; Judg. 21:11–12). This special notice in the midst of mundane financial accounting is startling. The moral implications of this practice are troubling to modern readers.

NUMBERS

Title

The English title "Numbers," derived from the Greek Septuagint (*Arithmoi*) and the Latin Vulgate (*Numeri*) translations, alludes to the instructions for taking a census of the people in chaps. 1–4 and 26. The Hebrew title *Bemidbar* ("In the Wilderness"), taken from the fifth word in the first chapter, refers to the wilderness setting of the content of the book.

Literary Characters, Authorship, and Composition

The book contains a wide range of dramatic stories: a wife suspected of adultery suffers a repulsive ordeal to satisfy her jealous husband; a man is stoned to death for gathering sticks on the Sabbath; the earth swallows up rebellious Levites; a foreign diviner is scolded by his talking donkey, and more. It also contains different types of literature: lists, case laws, ritual instructions, rebellion stories, battle reports, itineraries, poetic oracles, popular songs, and a cultic calendar. Such disparate material seems poorly organized without an identifiable intention. No apparent overarching structure that accounts for all the details of the book is readily discernible.

This complex narrative raises the validity of the Mosaic authorship of the Pentateuch. Attributing the Pentateuchal material to Moses would give it divine sanction, since Moses is regarded as God's representative. Its status as the revelation of YHWH to Moses helps constitute Israel's identity throughout their history, especially after their return from the Babylonian exile. Despite the theological significance of the Mosaic authorship, Numbers reflects a complicated history of becoming a book within the Pentateuch over an extended time, from the era of the monarchs to the postexilic period. Three distinct materials underlying the book can be identified—Priestly laws and instructions, the non-Priestly narrative about the wilderness journey, and independent poems and records—and most of the Priestly material provides a unified plot and cohesive progression of the wilderness journey from Sinai toward the promised land. As this material reflects the need to reconstitute Israel as a religious community during the Second Temple period (after 515 BCE), the composition history of Numbers offers insights into how the later generations continually reuse memories of the wilderness journey for their identity.

Reading Guide

The two titles associated with the book provide guidance for discerning theological themes connecting its diverse materials. The title "Numbers" accentuates the two accounts of the census of the Israelites in chaps. 1 and 26, which divide the book into two parts. The first twenty-five chapters recount the fate of the exodus generation, who die in the wilderness because of their repeated rebellions, while the following eleven chapters focus on a potential future of the new generation, who had not been in Egypt, ready to enter Canaan. This outline highlights God's faithfulness in keeping the ancestral land promise. When the exodus generation refuses to take the land (Num. 13–14), they are condemned to death in the wilderness and excluded from entering the promised land. Nevertheless, God carries God's promise out by raising another generation in the wilderness.

The other title, "In the Wilderness," connects the book to the grand story of the Israelites' journey from Egypt to the promised land and focuses on their preparations for departure from Sinai to their journey to the plains of Moab, opposite the promised land. After organizing themselves as a sanctuary-centered military camp at Sinai (1:1–10:10), they journey through the wilderness, accompanied by cultic instructions, rebellion stories, battle reports, and itinerary statements (10:11–21:35). Finally, they arrive at the plains of Moab (22:1) and stay there until they attempt to cross the Jordan (Deut. 1:1; Josh. 3:1). The book ends with a situation in which they have not entered the land, the goal of their journey. This progression underscores God's guidance of Israel through the wilderness. God prepares and leads the exodus generation's military march toward the land, endures their rebellions along the journey, and prepares the new generation for the eventual entering of the land. Undoubtedly, these themes are present in other books of the Pentateuch, but they take a distinctive accent in Numbers, where readers see God's visual, active, and intimate presence in Israel's midst.

In the larger narrative context of the Pentateuch, Numbers presents a turning point in Israel's ultimate objective: entering the promised land. In the spy story (Num. 13–14) they are located at

the edge of Canaan and have the opportunity to conquer its land for the first time since their liberation from Egypt, but they forfeit that chance by not trusting YHWH and are condemned to death in the wilderness. However, they are still assured that the land promise will be fulfilled by a new generation. Thus, this story divides the book into two parts and suggests an understanding of "the wilderness" as a place of God's punishment and forgiveness. Up to Num. 13–14, Israel is systematically organized and murmurs against God repeatedly, murmurs that are met by God's severe punishments. The following events in 15:1–20:29 offer a justification for the inclusion of the human leaders (the Levites, Aaron, and Moses) in the doomed fate of the exodus generation. At the same time, several instructions—introduced with the YHWH speech formula and connected to a theme of "land" (15:1–16, 17–31, 37–41; 17:12–18:32; 19:1–22)—function to show the validity of the land promise and the leadership roles of Moses, Aaron, the priests, and the Levites. Their leadership is still divinely ordained and effective in the land despite their fatal destiny in the wilderness.

The rest of Numbers demonstrates YHWH's forgiveness for Israel's failure by affirming that YHWH's land promise remains unbroken and will be carried out by the new generation. Numbers 21:1–3 heralds the entrance of the second generation, as it recounts Israel's first military victory against the Canaanites, the inhabitants of the promised land. After the death of Miriam and Aaron, the sin of Moses and Aaron, and Moses's failure to go through the Edomite territory in chap. 20, the Israelites are acting as a single, unified political entity, assisted by YHWH, who permits Israel's vow of holy war. This successful campaign is done without Moses at the end of the fortieth year of the wilderness journey. Numbers 21:4–25:18 characterizes the second generation as possessing incomparable confidence to carry out God's land promise, evident in their continual victories over the Transjordanian enemies, and as having a rebellious attitude similar to the chronic pattern of the exodus generation (21:4–9; 25:1–18). Yet they receive God's blessings from a foreign diviner, Balaam, without their knowledge. Numbers 26–36 focuses on the issue of land. Beginning with a census of the new generation for the appropriation of land (26:1–65), the rest of the book reports various instructions around the theme of the land, including the allotment of Canaan to the Israelite tribes (32:1–35:34), enveloped by God's favorable ruling of female inheritance in chap. 27 and its subsequent modification by restricting their marriage options in chap. 36.

Implied in the Hebrew title of the book, Numbers offers a theological meaning of "the wilderness." In contrast to the tendency to characterize the wilderness either as a place of trial, indicating God's testing of Israel's qualifications to enter the promised land, or as a place of inhospitality symbolized by its barren and desolate conditions, or as a place of "birth" of Israel's nationhood, the book of Numbers redefines the wilderness as the place of God's punishment as well as God's forgiveness of Israel's rebellions.

Won W. Lee

1 The LORD spoke to Moses in the wilderness of Sinai, in the tent of meeting, on the first day of the second month, in the second year after they had come out of the land of Egypt, saying, ²"Take a census of the whole congregation of Israelites, in their clans, by ancestral houses, according to the number of names, every male individually, ³from twenty years old and up, everyone in Israel able to go to war. You and Aaron shall enroll

1:1–2:34 The conscription and mobilization of the twelve tribes. YHWH commanded Moses to take a census of Israelites eligible for military duty, excluding the Levites. Moses executed God's command with the help of the leaders of the twelve tribes. Consequently, Israel is organized as a military camp with a huge militia in preparing for the journey from Sinai to the wilderness. **1:1** *The LORD spoke to Moses*, a divine speech formula, characterizes what follows as the will and plan of God; thus, it is authoritative and compulsory. *The wilderness of Sinai* connects the census to the larger context of the Israelites' arrival at this place (Exod. 19:1) and their departure (Num. 10:11–12). *The tent of meeting*, used thirty-two times in the description of building the sanctuary (Exod. 25–40), is interchangeable and synonymous with "the tabernacle" (Num. 3:38). *The first day of the second month, in the second year after they had come out of the land of Egypt* indicates one month after the erection of the tabernacle (Exod. 40:17) and eleven months staying in the Sinai desert (Exod. 19:1). **1:2–3** Not all Israelites are counted. Only males twenty years and older are eligible for military service. They are counted in ever-narrowing units: tribe, clan, paternal house, and individual. **1:4–16** Twelve men, one from each

them, company by company. ⁴A man from each tribe shall be with you, each man the head of his ancestral house. ⁵These are the names of the men who shall assist you:

From Reuben, Elizur son of Shedeur.
⁶ From Simeon, Shelumiel son of Zurishaddai.
⁷ From Judah, Nahshon son of Amminadab.
⁸ From Issachar, Nethanel son of Zuar.
⁹ From Zebulun, Eliab son of Helon.
¹⁰ From the sons of Joseph:
from Ephraim, Elishama son of Ammihud;
from Manasseh, Gamaliel son of Pedahzur.
¹¹ From Benjamin, Abidan son of Gideoni.
¹² From Dan, Ahiezer son of Ammishaddai.
¹³ From Asher, Pagiel son of Ochran.
¹⁴ From Gad, Eliasaph son of Deuel.
¹⁵ From Naphtali, Ahira son of Enan."

¹⁶These were the ones chosen from the congregation, the leaders of their ancestral tribes, the heads of the divisions of Israel.

17 Moses and Aaron took these men who had been designated by name, ¹⁸and on the first day of the second month they assembled the whole congregation together. They registered themselves in their clans, by their ancestral houses, according to the number of names from twenty years old and up, individually, ¹⁹as the LORD had commanded Moses. So he enrolled them in the wilderness of Sinai.

20 The descendants of Reuben, Israel's firstborn, their lineage, in their clans, by their ancestral houses, according to the number of names, individually, every male from twenty years old and up, everyone able to go to war: ²¹those enrolled of the tribe of Reuben were forty-six thousand five hundred.

22 The descendants of Simeon, their lineage, in their clans, by their ancestral houses, those of them who were numbered, according to the number of names, individually, every male from twenty years old and up, everyone able to go to war: ²³those enrolled of the tribe of Simeon were fifty-nine thousand three hundred.

24 The descendants of Gad, their lineage, in their clans, by their ancestral houses, according to the number of names, from twenty years old and up, everyone able to go to war: ²⁵those enrolled of the tribe of Gad were forty-five thousand six hundred fifty.

26 The descendants of Judah, their lineage, in their clans, by their ancestral houses, according to the number of names, from twenty years old and up, everyone able to go to war: ²⁷those enrolled of the tribe of Judah were seventy-four thousand six hundred.

28 The descendants of Issachar, their lineage, in their clans, by their ancestral houses, according to the number of names, from twenty years old and up, everyone able to go to war: ²⁹those enrolled of the tribe of Issachar were fifty-four thousand four hundred.

30 The descendants of Zebulun, their lineage, in their clans, by their ancestral houses, according to the number of names, from twenty years old and up, everyone able to go to war: ³¹those enrolled of the tribe of Zebulun were fifty-seven thousand four hundred.

32 The descendants of Joseph: the descendants of Ephraim, their lineage, in their clans, by their ancestral houses, according to the number of names, from twenty years old and up, everyone able to go to war: ³³those enrolled of the tribe of Ephraim were forty thousand five hundred; ³⁴the descendants of Manasseh, their lineage, in their clans, by their ancestral houses, according to the number of names, from twenty years old and up, everyone able to go to war: ³⁵those enrolled of the tribe of Manasseh were thirty-two thousand two hundred.

36 The descendants of Benjamin, their lineage, in their clans, by their ancestral houses, according to the number of names, from twenty years old and up, everyone able to go to war: ³⁷those enrolled of the tribe of

---

tribe, are appointed to assist Moses and Aaron with counting. They are described as *chosen, leaders*, and *heads* (v. 16) and play both military (2:3–31; 10:14–27) and economic roles (7:1–88). Listed according to their origins from the twelve sons of Jacob (Gen. 29:31–30:24; 35:22–26)—the sons of Leah (Reuben, Simeon, [no Levi], Judah, Issachar, Zebulun), the sons of Rachel (Joseph [divided into Ephraim and Manasseh], Benjamin), and the sons of Zilpah and Bilhah, handmaidens of Leah and Rachel (Dan, Asher, Gad, Naphtali)—the twelvefold structure of the tribal league is reflected. **1:20–43** Each tribe's report follows a formula: the tribe's name, the criteria and categories of the enlisted, and the total number of soldiers. The pattern indicates equal treatment of all twelve tribes, regardless of the number of soldiers in each tribe. The different numbers of soldiers among tribes

Benjamin were thirty-five thousand four hundred.

38 The descendants of Dan, their lineage, in their clans, by their ancestral houses, according to the number of names, from twenty years old and up, everyone able to go to war: [39]those enrolled of the tribe of Dan were sixty-two thousand seven hundred.

40 The descendants of Asher, their lineage, in their clans, by their ancestral houses, according to the number of names, from twenty years old and up, everyone able to go to war: [41]those enrolled of the tribe of Asher were forty-one thousand five hundred.

42 The descendants of Naphtali, their lineage, in their clans, by their ancestral houses, according to the number of names, from twenty years old and up, everyone able to go to war: [43]those enrolled of the tribe of Naphtali were fifty-three thousand four hundred.

44 These are those who were enrolled, whom Moses and Aaron enrolled with the help of the leaders of Israel, twelve men, each representing his ancestral house. [45]So all those enrolled of the Israelites, by their ancestral houses, from twenty years old and up, everyone able to go to war in Israel—[46]all those enrolled were six hundred three thousand five hundred fifty. [47]The Levites, however, were not numbered by their ancestral tribe along with them.

48 The LORD spoke to Moses, saying, [49]"Only the tribe of Levi you shall not enroll, and you shall not take a census of them with the other Israelites. [50]Rather, you shall appoint the Levites over the tabernacle of the covenant and over all its equipment and over all that belongs to it; they are to carry the tabernacle and all its equipment, and they shall tend it and shall camp around the tabernacle. [51]When the tabernacle is to set out, the Levites shall take it down, and when the tabernacle is to be pitched, the Levites shall set it up. And any outsider who comes near shall be put to death. [52]The other Israelites shall camp in their respective regimental camps, by companies, [53]but the Levites shall camp around the tabernacle of the covenant, that there may be no wrath on the congregation of the Israelites, and the Levites shall perform the duties of the tabernacle of the covenant." [54]The Israelites did so; they did just as the LORD commanded Moses.

2 The LORD spoke to Moses and Aaron, saying, [2]"The Israelites shall camp each in their respective regiments, under ensigns by their ancestral houses; they shall camp

distinguish their relative military strength. **1:46** The total number, *six hundred three thousand five hundred fifty*, is in the same range as the number of people who came out from Egypt (six hundred thousand men, besides children; Exod. 12:37) and the number of soldiers counted after forty years in the wilderness (Num. 26:51). This unrealistically high number has numerous explanations, such as translating "thousand" to "unit" in each case (e.g., the tribe of Reuben consists of forty-six units with five hundred soldiers; so, if applied to all twelve tribes, the total is reduced to 5,550), or as a testament to God's fulfillment of the fertility blessing promised to Abram (Gen. 15:5). Regardless, the number may well reveal Israel's military strength before launching a campaign. **1:48–54** The Levites' exemption from military conscription is mandatory and just as important as the census. God's speech begins with the twofold prohibition stating the exemption itself, followed by three commands related to the tabernacle (the tasks of the Levites, warning of non-Levites' encroachment, and designated campsites for all Israelites, including the Levites), and ending with an inclusive statement of complete compliance. **1:51** The tabernacle is transportable, indicating God's mobility. **1:53** Besides caring for the *tabernacle* and its vessels and performing ceremonies, the Levites must guard it from unlawful approach, thereby protecting the camp from the wrath of God. This performance underscores the military nature of their task, illustrated by their execution of idol worshipers in the golden bull incident (Exod. 32:25–29). **1:54** The whole of Israel has complied with God's command completely. God commands, Moses and Aaron supervise, tribal leaders execute, individual recruits comply, and the Levites and other people obey—all according to God's instructions.

2:1–34 Encampment and marching order. The conscripted militia are divided into four divisions with three tribes each. The middle of the three is assigned a leadership role under whose banner all three are united. The banner tribes are Judah (with Issachar on one side and Zebulun on the other), Reuben (Simeon, Gad), Ephraim (Manasseh, Benjamin), and Dan (Asher, Naphtali). Each division is positioned around the tent of meeting (v. 17) clockwise starting from the east. East is the primary

facing the tent of meeting on every side. [3]Those to camp on the east side toward the sunrise shall be of the regimental encampment of Judah by companies. The leader of the people of Judah shall be Nahshon son of Amminadab, [4]with a company as enrolled of seventy-four thousand six hundred. [5]Those to camp next to him shall be the tribe of Issachar. The leader of the Issacharites shall be Nethanel son of Zuar, [6]with a company as enrolled of fifty-four thousand four hundred. [7]Then the tribe of Zebulun. The leader of the Zebulunites shall be Eliab son of Helon, [8]with a company as enrolled of fifty-seven thousand four hundred. [9]The total enrollment of the camp of Judah, by companies, is one hundred eighty-six thousand four hundred. They shall set out first.

[10] "On the south side shall be the regimental encampment of Reuben by companies. The leader of the Reubenites shall be Elizur son of Shedeur, [11]with a company as enrolled of forty-six thousand five hundred. [12]And those to camp next to him shall be the tribe of Simeon. The leader of the Simeonites shall be Shelumiel son of Zurishaddai, [13]with a company as enrolled of fifty-nine thousand three hundred. [14]Then the tribe of Gad. The leader of the Gadites shall be Eliasaph son of Deuel,[a] [15]with a company as enrolled of forty-five thousand six hundred fifty. [16]The total enrollment of the camp of Reuben, by companies, is one hundred fifty-one thousand four hundred fifty. They shall set out second.

[17] "The tent of meeting, with the camp of the Levites, shall set out in the center of the camps; they shall set out just as they camp, each in position, by their regiments.

[18] "On the west side shall be the regimental encampment of Ephraim by companies. The leader of the people of Ephraim shall be Elishama son of Ammihud, [19]with a company as enrolled of forty thousand five hundred. [20]Next to him shall be the tribe of Manasseh. The leader of the people of Manasseh shall be Gamaliel son of Pedahzur, [21]with a company as enrolled of thirty-two thousand two hundred. [22]Then the tribe of Benjamin. The leader of the Benjaminites shall be Abidan son of Gideoni, [23]with a company as enrolled of thirty-five thousand four hundred. [24]The total enrollment of the camp of Ephraim, by companies, is one hundred eight thousand one hundred. They shall set out third.

[25] "On the north side shall be the regimental encampment of Dan by companies. The leader of the Danites shall be Ahiezer son of Ammishaddai, [26]with a company as enrolled of sixty-two thousand seven hundred. [27]Those to camp next to him shall be the tribe of Asher. The leader of the Asherites shall be Pagiel son of Ochran, [28]with a company as enrolled of forty-one thousand five hundred. [29]Then the tribe of Naphtali. The leader of the Naphtalites shall be Ahira son of Enan, [30]with a company as enrolled of fifty-three thousand four hundred. [31]The total enrollment of the camp of Dan is one hundred fifty-seven thousand six hundred. They shall set out last, by their regiments."

[32] This was the enrollment of the Israelites by their ancestral houses; the total enrollment in the camps by their companies was six hundred three thousand five hundred fifty. [33]Just as the LORD had commanded Moses, the Levites were not enrolled among the other Israelites.

[34] The Israelites did just as the LORD had commanded Moses: they camped by regiments, and they set out the same way, everyone by clans, according to ancestral houses.

a 2.14 Heb mss Sam Vg: MT *Reuel*

side due to the direction of the rising sun (v. 3) and the opening of the tabernacle. Putting Judah to the east and mentioning Judah first (deviating from the conscription account that begins with Reuben, the firstborn son of Jacob, 1:5, 20) underscores its prominence among the tribes (Gen. 49:8–12). Judah is assigned to protect the most important side of the camp, since it has the largest number of soldiers (74,600) and its division has the largest number of troops (186,400). The encampment order of the tribes sets the order for the march, placing the Levites with the tabernacle in the middle (Num. 10:14–28): Judah, Reuben, Levites (tabernacle), Ephraim, then Dan. This marching order is clearly offensive in nature, ready to respond promptly to anticipated hostility by concentrating military strength (337,850) up front while also protecting the rear of the camp with substantial power (265,700). Together with the events of chap. 1, Israel is mobilized for the impending campaign from Sinai. **2:3–9** The literary pattern for describing the formation of the east side of the camp is also used for the south (vv. 10–16), west (vv. 18–24), and north (vv. 25–31) sides of the camp.

3 This is the lineage of Aaron and Moses at the time when the LORD spoke with Moses on Mount Sinai. ²These are the names of the sons of Aaron: Nadab the firstborn and Abihu, Eleazar, and Ithamar; ³these are the names of the sons of Aaron, the anointed priests, whom he ordained to serve as priests. ⁴Nadab and Abihu died before the LORD when they offered unholy fire before the LORD in the wilderness of Sinai, and they had no children. Eleazar and Ithamar served as priests in the lifetime of their father Aaron.

5 Then the LORD spoke to Moses, saying, ⁶"Bring the tribe of Levi near and set them before Aaron the priest, so that they may assist him. ⁷They shall perform duties for him and for the whole congregation in front of the tent of meeting, doing service at the tabernacle; ⁸they shall be in charge of all the furnishings of the tent of meeting and attend to the duties for the Israelites as they do service at the tabernacle. ⁹You shall give the Levites to Aaron and his descendants; they are unreservedly given to him from among the Israelites. ¹⁰But you shall enroll Aaron and his descendants; it is they who shall attend to the priesthood, and any outsider who comes near shall be put to death."

11 Then the LORD spoke to Moses, saying, ¹²"I hereby take the Levites from among the Israelites as substitutes for all the firstborn that open the womb among the Israelites. The Levites shall be mine, ¹³for all the firstborn are mine; when I killed all the firstborn in the land of Egypt, I consecrated for my own all the firstborn in Israel, both human and animal; they shall be mine. I am the LORD."

14 Then the LORD spoke to Moses in the wilderness of Sinai, saying, ¹⁵"Enroll the Levites by ancestral houses and by clans. You shall enroll every male from a month old and up." ¹⁶So Moses enrolled them according to the word of the LORD, as he was commanded. ¹⁷These were the sons of Levi, by their names: Gershon, Kohath, and Merari. ¹⁸These were the names of the sons of Gershon by their clans: Libni and Shimei. ¹⁹The sons of Kohath by their clans: Amram, Izhar, Hebron, and Uzziel. ²⁰The sons of Merari by their clans: Mahli and Mushi. These were the clans of the Levites, by their ancestral houses.

21 To Gershon belonged the clan of the Libnites and the clan of the Shimeites; these were the clans of the Gershonites. ²²Their enrollment, counting all the males from a month old and up, was seven thousand five hundred. ²³The clans of the Gershonites were to camp behind the tabernacle on the west, ²⁴with Eliasaph son of Lael as head of the ancestral house of the Gershonites. ²⁵The responsibility of the sons of Gershon in the tent of meeting was the tabernacle, the tent with its covering, the screen for the entrance of the tent of meeting, ²⁶the hangings of the court, the screen for the entrance of the court that is around the tabernacle and the altar, and its cords—all the service pertaining to these.

27 To Kohath belonged the clan of the Amramites, the clan of the Izharites, the clan

---

3:1–4 A genealogy of Aaron. The Aaronites were set apart from the Levites for the priesthood. The consecration of priests is commanded in Exod. 29 and performed in Lev. 8. Among the named four sons of Aaron, Nadab and Abihu forfeited their priesthood by offering unauthorized sacrifices (Lev. 10:1–5; 16:1–2), while Eleazar and Ithamar continued to serve as priests (Num. 4:16, 28, 33). *This is the lineage of*, the genealogical formula, appears often at the beginning of narratives (Gen. 2:4; 5:1; 6:9; 10:1; 11:10; 25:12; 36:1; 37:2; Exod. 6:16) highlighting the transmission of God's blessings from creation through the chosen Israelite ancestors to the sons of Levi and the Aaronide priesthood.

3:5–4:49 The conscription and mobilization of the Levites. 3:5–10 The Levites are *unreservedly given to* Aaron (v. 9), indicating their subordinate nature to the Aaronide priests. Besides assisting them in front of the tent of meeting, the Levites also guard its holiness from the unlawful encroachment of non-Levites. **3:11–13** The Levites serve as substitutions for the Israelite firstborn (8:16–18). It is based on God's claim on all the firstborns of human beings, the Israelites, and animals (Exod. 13:2, 11–16; 22:29–30; 34:19–20) and expressed not as God's command but God's declaration: *I hereby take. . . . I am the LORD.* **3:14–39** For the role of substitution, the Levites are to be numbered. Moses executed God's command to enroll all male Levites one month old and older according to their genealogical affiliation (vv. 14–15) by specifying numbers and duties of the three Levitical houses (vv. 16–39). **3:21–37** A fixed sequence is used for describing each of the three Levitical houses—Gershon (vv. 21–26), Kohath (vv. 27–32), and Merari (vv. 33–37): (1) the house and its clans, (2) the total number of males older than one month, (3) the camp's location relative to the tabernacle, (4) the

of the Hebronites, and the clan of the Uzz-ielites; these were the clans of the Kohathites. [28]Counting all the males, from a month old and up, there were eight thousand six hundred performing the duties of the sanctuary. [29]The clans of the Kohathites were to camp on the south side of the tabernacle, [30]with Elizaphan son of Uzziel as head of the ancestral house of the clans of the Kohathites. [31]Their responsibility was the ark, the table, the lampstand, the altars, the vessels of the sanctuary with which the priests minister, and the screen—all the service pertaining to these. [32]Eleazar son of Aaron the priest was to be chief over the leaders of the Levites and to have oversight of those who performed the duties of the sanctuary.

33 To Merari belonged the clan of the Mahlites and the clan of the Mushites; these were the clans of Merari. [34]Their enrollment, counting all the males from a month old and up, was six thousand two hundred. [35]The head of the ancestral house of the clans of Merari was Zuriel son of Abihail; they were to camp on the north side of the tabernacle. [36]The responsibility assigned to the sons of Merari was the frames of the tabernacle, the bars, the pillars, the bases, and all their accessories—all the service pertaining to these, [37]also the pillars of the court all around, with their bases and pegs and cords.

38 Those who were to camp in front of the tabernacle on the east—in front of the tent of meeting toward the sunrise—were Moses and Aaron and Aaron's sons, who were to perform the duties of the sanctuary, whatever had to be done for the Israelites, and any outsider who came near was to be put to death. [39]The total enrollment of the Levites whom Moses and Aaron enrolled at the commandment of the LORD, by their clans, all the males from a month old and up, was twenty-two thousand.

40 Then the LORD said to Moses, "Enroll all the firstborn males of the Israelites, from a month old and up, and count their names. [41]But you shall take the Levites for me—I am the LORD—as substitutes for all the firstborn among the Israelites and the livestock of the Levites as substitutes for all the firstborn among the livestock of the Israelites." [42]So Moses enrolled all the firstborn among the Israelites, as the LORD commanded him. [43]The total enrollment, all the firstborn males from a month old and up, counting the number of names, was twenty-two thousand two hundred seventy-three.

44 Then the LORD spoke to Moses, saying, [45]"Take the Levites as substitutes for all the firstborn among the Israelites and the livestock of the Levites as substitutes for their livestock, and the Levites shall be mine. I am the LORD. [46]As the price of redemption of the two hundred seventy-three of the firstborn of the Israelites, over and above the number of the Levites, [47]you shall take five shekels apiece, reckoning by the shekel of the sanctuary, a shekel of twenty gerahs. [48]Give to Aaron and his sons the money by which the excess number of them is redeemed." [49]So Moses took the redemption money from those who were over and above those redeemed by the Levites; [50]from the firstborn of the Israelites he took the money, one thousand three hundred sixty-five shekels, reckoned by the shekel of the sanctuary, [51]and Moses gave the redemption money to Aaron and his sons, according to the word of the LORD, as the LORD had commanded Moses.

4 The LORD spoke to Moses and Aaron, saying, [2]"Take a census of the Kohathites

chieftain's name, and (5) the objects it is responsible for guarding. **3:38–39** While the Gershonites, Kohathites, and Merarites encamp to the west, south, and north of the tabernacle respectively, the Aaronide priests occupy the most preeminent position, the east, facing its entrance. **3:40–51** The total number of Levitical firstborn males one month and older (twenty-two thousand) is 273 fewer than the Israelites. In the substitution of person for person, the deficit calls for a solution, the paying of *the price of redemption* for the excess firstborns of the Israelites. The ransom money for each person amounts to five shekels, the currency of the sanctuary. The total of 1,365 (273 × 5) shekels is given to the Aaronide priests, just as the Levites are considered a gift to them from the Israelites. **4:1–49** Levites aged thirty to fifty years and qualified to work at the sanctuary are numbered. Except for vv. 17–20, the same literary pattern for each of the three Levitical houses is used: taking the census (vv. 1–3, 21–23, 29–30), detailing duties (vv. 4–15, 24–28a, 31–33a), and indicating supervision by the Aaronide priests (vv. 16, 28b, 33b). The total number is 8,580. **4:1–20** The Kohathites are mentioned first, deviating from the order in chap. 3, and they receive more elaborate instructions compared to

separate from the other Levites, by their clans and their ancestral houses, ³from thirty years old up to fifty years old, all who qualify to do work relating to the tent of meeting. ⁴The service of the Kohathites relating to the tent of meeting concerns the most holy things.

5 "When the camp is to set out, Aaron and his sons shall go in and take down the screening curtain and cover the ark of the covenant with it; ⁶then they shall put on it a covering of fine leather*b* and spread over that a cloth all of blue and put its poles in place. ⁷Over the table of the Presence they shall spread a blue cloth and put on it the plates, the dishes for incense, the bowls, and the flagons for the drink offering; the regular bread also shall be on it; ⁸then they shall spread over them a crimson cloth and cover it with a covering of fine leather*c* and put its poles in place. ⁹They shall take a blue cloth and cover the lampstand for the light, with its lamps, its snuffers, its trays, and all the vessels for oil with which it is supplied, ¹⁰and they shall put it with all its utensils in a covering of fine leather*d* and put it on the carrying frame. ¹¹Over the golden altar they shall spread a blue cloth and cover it with a covering of fine leather*e* and put its poles in place, ¹²and they shall take all the utensils of the service that are used in the sanctuary and put them in a blue cloth and cover them with a covering of fine leather*f* and put them on the carrying frame. ¹³They shall take away the ashes from the altar and spread a purple cloth over it, ¹⁴and they shall

put on it all the utensils of the altar, which are used for the service there, the firepans, the forks, the shovels, and the basins, all the utensils of the altar, and they shall spread on it a covering of fine leather*g* and put its poles in place. ¹⁵When Aaron and his sons have finished covering the sanctuary and all the furnishings of the sanctuary, as the camp sets out, after that the Kohathites shall come to carry these, but they must not touch the holy things, or they will die. These are the things of the tent of meeting that the Kohathites are to carry.

16 "Eleazar son of Aaron the priest shall have charge of the oil for the light, the fragrant incense, the regular grain offering, and the anointing oil, the oversight of all the tabernacle and all that is in it, in the sanctuary and in its utensils."

17 Then the LORD spoke to Moses and Aaron, saying, ¹⁸"You must not let the tribe of the clans of the Kohathites be destroyed from among the Levites. ¹⁹This is how you shall deal with them in order that they may live and not die when they come near the most holy things: Aaron and his sons shall go in and assign each to a particular task or burden. ²⁰But the Kohathites*h* must not go in to look on the holy things even for a moment, or they will die."

21 Then the LORD spoke to Moses, saying, ²²"Take a census of the Gershonites also, by

b 4.6 Meaning of Heb uncertain   *c* 4.8 Meaning of Heb uncertain   *d* 4.10 Meaning of Heb uncertain   *e* 4.11 Meaning of Heb uncertain   *f* 4.12 Meaning of Heb uncertain   *g* 4.14 Meaning of Heb uncertain   *h* 4.20 Heb *they*

the two other Levitical houses. This is because they are assigned to carry the most holy vessels, only after Aaron and his sons have finished covering them (vv. 5–15). They are not even allowed to see them *or they will die* (v. 20). Their work is completely dependent on the tasks of Aaron and his sons, indicating a gradation of holiness. **4:5–15** Only the Aaronide priests may touch the holiest things to wrap them. This is done in the order of holiness associated with the furnishings and vessels, beginning with the ark (located in the holiest place) and moving outward to the utensils of the burnt offerings altar (in the courtyard outside the dwelling). They are to cover them carefully and prepare them for transport by inserting poles or placing them on carrying frames. Only after this meticulous process could the Kohathites enter the sanctuary to carry them out. **4:5** *When the camp is to set out*. The tasks for the Levitical houses are to be understood as preparation for departure from Sinai. *Screening curtain* (see Exod. 26:31; 35:12; 39:34; 40:21; Lev. 4:6; 24:3). *The ark of the covenant* (see Exod. 25:10–22). **4:7–8** *The table of the Presence*, located in the north side of the tabernacle (Exod. 25:23–30). Upon it, a loaf of bread is displayed (Exod. 25:30; Lev. 24:5–9). **4:9–10** *The lampstand* (see Exod. 25:31–40). **4:11–14** *The golden altar*, located in front of the screen outside the most holy place and called the incense altar (Exod. 30:1–10). *The altar*, located in the courtyard outside the dwelling and called the altar of burnt offerings (Exod. 27:1–8). **4:16** *The oil for the light* (see Exod. 27:20–21); *the fragrant incense* (see Exod. 30:34–38); *the regular grain offering* (see Lev. 2:1–16; 6:14–18); and *the anointing oil* (see Exod. 30:22–33). **4:21–33** Under the supervision of Ithamar, the Gershonites and the Merarites work together to carry the sanctuary itself—the former, its curtains and

their ancestral houses and by their clans; [23]from thirty years old up to fifty years old you shall enroll them, all who qualify to do work in the tent of meeting. [24]This is the service of the clans of the Gershonites, in serving and bearing burdens: [25]They shall carry the curtains of the tabernacle, and the tent of meeting with its covering, and the outer covering of fine leather[i] that is on top of it, and the screen for the entrance of the tent of meeting, [26]and the hangings of the court, and the screen for the entrance of the gate of the court that is around the tabernacle and the altar, and their cords, and all the equipment for their service, and they shall do all that needs to be done with regard to them. [27]All the service of the Gershonites shall be at the command of Aaron and his sons, in all that they are to carry and in all that they have to do, and you shall assign to them as duties all that they are to carry. [28]This is the service of the clans of the Gershonites relating to the tent of meeting, and their duties are to be under the oversight of Ithamar son of Aaron the priest.

[29] "As for the Merarites, you shall enroll them by their clans and their ancestral houses; [30]from thirty years old up to fifty years old you shall enroll them, everyone who qualifies to do the work of the tent of meeting. [31]This is their duty to carry, as the whole of their service in the tent of meeting: the frames of the tabernacle, with its bars, pillars, and bases, [32]and the pillars of the court all around with their bases, pegs, and cords, with all their equipment and all their related service, and you shall assign by name the objects that they are required to carry. [33]This is the service of the clans of the Merarites, the whole of their service relating to the tent of meeting, under the hand of Ithamar son of Aaron the priest."

[34] So Moses and Aaron and the leaders of the congregation enrolled the Kohathites, by their clans and their ancestral houses, [35]from thirty years old up to fifty years old, everyone who qualified for work relating to the tent of meeting, [36]and their enrollment by clans was two thousand seven hundred fifty. [37]This was the enrollment of the clans of the Kohathites, all who served at the tent of meeting, whom Moses and Aaron enrolled according to the commandment of the LORD by Moses.

[38] The enrollment of the Gershonites, by their clans and their ancestral houses, [39]from thirty years old up to fifty years old, everyone who qualified for work relating to the tent of meeting—[40]their enrollment by their clans and their ancestral houses was two thousand six hundred thirty. [41]This was the enrollment of the clans of the Gershonites, all who served at the tent of meeting, whom Moses and Aaron enrolled according to the commandment of the LORD.

[42] The enrollment of the clans of the Merarites, by their clans and their ancestral houses, [43]from thirty years old up to fifty years old, everyone who qualified for work relating to the tent of meeting, [44]and their enrollment by their clans was three thousand two hundred. [45]This is the enrollment of the clans of the Merarites, whom Moses and Aaron enrolled according to the commandment of the LORD by Moses.

[46] All those who were enrolled of the Levites, whom Moses and Aaron and the leaders of Israel enrolled, by their clans and their ancestral houses, [47]from thirty years old up to fifty years old, all who qualified to do the work of service and the work of bearing burdens relating to the tent of meeting, [48]and their enrollment was eight thousand five hundred eighty. [49]According to the commandment of the LORD through Moses, they were appointed to their several tasks of serving or carrying; thus they were enrolled by him, as the LORD commanded Moses.

5 The LORD spoke to Moses, saying, [2]"Command the Israelites to put out of the camp everyone who has a defiling skin disease or a discharge and everyone who is unclean through contact with a corpse; [3]you shall put out both male and female, putting them outside the camp; they must not defile

i 4.25 Meaning of Heb uncertain

covers (3:25–26); the latter, its structure (3:36–37). **4:34–49** Summary of the execution of God's commands, emphasizing the complete obedience of Moses and Aaron.
   5:1–6:27 Matters concerning the purity of the camp. This section focuses on the priests' handling of various affairs to maintain ritual purity and high moral standing among the Israelites, without which the holy God cannot dwell in the camp. **5:1–4** A person's impurity is contagious, defiling the entire camp. The unclean persons must be *[put] outside the camp* (not expelled permanently) to

their camp, where I dwell among them." ⁴The Israelites did so, putting them outside the camp; as the Lᴏʀᴅ had spoken to Moses, so the Israelites did.

5 The Lᴏʀᴅ spoke to Moses, saying, ⁶"Speak to the Israelites: When a man or a woman wrongs another, breaking faith with the Lᴏʀᴅ, that person incurs guilt ⁷and shall confess the sin that has been committed. The person shall make full restitution for the wrong, adding one-fifth to it and giving it to the one who was wronged. ⁸If the injured party has no next of kin to whom restitution may be made for the wrong, the restitution for wrong shall go to the Lᴏʀᴅ for the priest, in addition to the ram of atonement with which atonement is made for the guilty party. ⁹Among all the sacred donations of the Israelites, every gift that they bring to the priest shall be his. ¹⁰The sacred donations of all are their own; whatever anyone gives to the priest shall be his."

11 The Lᴏʀᴅ spoke to Moses, saying, ¹²"Speak to the Israelites and say to them: If any man's wife goes astray and is unfaithful to him, ¹³if a man has had intercourse with her but it is hidden from her husband, so that she is undetected though she has defiled herself, and there is no witness against her since she was not caught in the act; ¹⁴if a spirit of jealousy comes on him and he is jealous of his wife who has defiled herself, or if a spirit of jealousy comes on him and he is jealous of his wife, though she has not defiled herself, ¹⁵then the man shall bring his wife to the priest. And he shall bring the offering required for her, one-tenth of an ephah of barley flour. He shall pour no oil on it and put no frankincense on it, for it is a grain offering of jealousy, a grain offering of remembrance, bringing iniquity to remembrance.

16 "Then the priest shall bring her near and set her before the Lᴏʀᴅ; ¹⁷the priest shall take holy water in an earthen vessel and take some of the dust that is on the floor of the tabernacle and put it into the water. ¹⁸The priest shall set the woman before the Lᴏʀᴅ, dishevel the woman's hair, and place in her hands the grain offering of remembrance, which is the grain offering of jealousy. In his own hand the priest shall have the water of bitterness that brings the curse. ¹⁹Then the priest shall make her take an oath, saying, 'If no man has lain with you, if you have not turned aside to uncleanness while under your husband's authority, be immune to this water of bitterness that brings the curse. ²⁰But if you have gone astray while under your husband's authority, if you have defiled yourself and some man other than your husband has had intercourse with you,' ²¹—let the priest make the woman take the oath of the curse and say to the woman—'the Lᴏʀᴅ make you an execration and an oath among your people, when the Lᴏʀᴅ makes your uterus drop, your womb discharge;ʲ ²²now may this water that brings the curse enter your bowels and make your womb discharge, your uterus drop!'ᵏ And the woman shall say, 'Amen. Amen.'

23 "Then the priest shall put these curses in writing and wash them off into the water of bitterness. ²⁴He shall make the woman drink the water of bitterness that brings the curse, and the water that brings the curse shall enter her and cause bitter pain. ²⁵The priest shall take the grain offering of jealousy out of the woman's hand and shall elevate the grain offering before the Lᴏʀᴅ and bring it to the altar,

j 5.21 Heb *makes your thigh fall and your belly distend*
k 5.22 Heb *make the belly distend and the thigh fall*

maintain the presence of the holy God in its midst. *A defiling skin disease* (see Lev. 13:45–46); *a discharge* (see Lev. 15:31–33); *contact with a corpse* (see Lev. 21:1–3, 11; Num. 6:6–12; 19:11–22). **5:5–10** Supplementing Lev. 6:1–7, this case law adds a sacred dimension to the act (Num. 5:6b), requiring a confession from the guilty party (v. 7a), and designating the priests for the requisite payment when no next of kin of the injured party is available to receive it (v. 8a). It offers the culprit the opportunity to reconcile with the one wronged and with God, thus becoming part of the community again. **5:11–31** This case law deals with a husband's suspicion of his wife's possible adultery. She is presumed guilty; *she is undetected though she has defiled herself . . . though she has not defiled herself* (vv. 13–14). In contrast, her husband's reactions are presumptive, dominated by *a spirit of jealousy*. His jealousy, however, proves nothing about her guilt or innocence; it provides the legal ground for a trial. To discern the divine will, an elaborate ritual-judicial procedure is prescribed and carried out by the priests in seven stages (vv. 16, 17, 18, 19–22, 23–24, 25, 26). However intrusive these stages for determining innocence may be, they must be followed judiciously to protect her from her husband's impulsive revenge. However, the husband is free from guilt regardless of the outcome, even if he may have unjustly accused his wife and forced her to go through the ordeal (v. 31). The husband's jealousy

²⁶and the priest shall take a handful of the grain offering as its memorial portion and turn it into smoke on the altar and afterward shall make the woman drink the water. ²⁷When he has made her drink the water, then, if she has defiled herself and has been unfaithful to her husband, the water that brings the curse shall enter into her and cause bitter pain, and her womb shall discharge, her uterus drop,ᴵ and the woman shall become an execration among her people. ²⁸But if the woman has not defiled herself and is clean, then she shall be immune and be able to conceive children.

29 "This is the law in cases of jealousy, when a wife, while under her husband's authority, goes astray and defiles herself, ³⁰or when a spirit of jealousy comes on a man and he is jealous of his wife, then he shall set the woman before the LORD, and the priest shall apply this entire law to her. ³¹The man shall be free from iniquity, but the woman shall bear her iniquity."

6 The LORD spoke to Moses, saying, ²"Speak to the Israelites and say to them: When either men or women make a special vow, the vow of a nazirite, to separate themselves to the LORD, ³they shall separate themselves from wine and strong drink; they shall drink no wine vinegar or other vinegar and shall not drink any grape juice or eat grapes, fresh or dried. ⁴All their days as nazirites they shall eat nothing that is produced by the grapevine, not even the seeds or the skins.

5 "All the days of their nazirite vow no razor shall come upon the head; until the time is completed for which they separate themselves to the LORD, they shall be holy; they shall let the locks of the head grow long.

6 "All the days that they separate themselves to the LORD they shall not go near a corpse. ⁷Even if their father or mother, brother or sister, should die, they may not defile themselves, because their consecration to God is upon the head. ⁸All their days as nazirites they are holy to the LORD.

9 "If someone suddenly dies nearby, defiling the head of the nazirite, then they shall shave the head on the day of their cleansing; on the seventh day they shall shave it. ¹⁰On the eighth day they shall bring two turtledoves or two young pigeons to the priest at the entrance of the tent of meeting, ¹¹and the priest shall offer one as a purification offering and the other as a burnt offering and make atonement for them, because they incurred guilt by reason of the corpse. They shall sanctify the head that same day ¹²and separate themselves to the LORD for their days as nazirites and bring a male lamb a year old as a guilt offering. The former time shall be void because the nazirite was defiled.

13 "This is the law for the nazirites when the time of their consecration has been completed: they shall be brought to the entrance

l 5.27 Heb make her belly distend and her thigh fall

is dangerous to the well-being and purity of the community; thus, it must be eliminated through a ritual-judicial process under the priest's control. **6:1–21** The term *nazirite* connotes "restriction or abstinence." Traditionally, the nazirites were individuals distinguished by YHWH for a specific task for their whole lives (e.g., Samson [Judg. 13–16], Samuel [1 Sam. 1:21–28]), and they were to restrict themselves from drinking alcohol, cutting their hair, and touching the dead, which would make them ritually unclean and unable to perform their duty. This text, however, focuses on the specific case of someone taking an initiative to become a nazirite for a limited time. For the voluntary and temporary nature of being a nazirite, it stipulates greater restrictions compared to other nazirites. It also prescribes ritual procedures for an accidental defilement and the termination of their vows, performed and supervised by the priests. **6:3–8** The first prohibition is total abstinence from everything from the grapevine, expressed in descending order: from drinking *wine and strong drink, wine vinegar*, or unfermented grape juice to eating grapes themselves. The second is to allow their hair to grow loose and untouched. It is much stricter than the instruction for the priests (Lev. 21:5). The third is to avoid any contact with the dead, even including immediate family members (cf. Lev. 21:1–4). **6:9–12** An accidental contamination by a corpse requires purification rituals similar to those for people who have become unclean from physical disorders (Lev. 12–15). A *purification offering* (see Lev. 4:1–5:13; Num. 15:22–31) is given for cleansing the polluted sanctuary caused by the contaminated nazirite. A *burnt offering* is given to God alone, as all sacrificial animals are completely incinerated (Lev. 1:3–17; 6:8–13). The *guilt offering* could be better understood as "reparation" (see Lev. 7:1–6) for God's loss, as the defiled nazirite could not perform their duties for God. **6:13–20** To end the temporary nazirite state, five offerings are given. The sequence of these offerings is understandable, beginning with

Focus On: The Priestly Blessing (Numbers 6:22–27)

After the introductory speech formula (v. 22), which established Moses as the mediator of compliance with God's command, the YHWH speech covers the rest of the unit, instructing the Aaronide priest to bless Israel (vv. 23–27). The blessing itself (vv. 24–26) is concisely and systematically formulated with twelve Hebrew words, not including the name of God, divided into three sentences of three, five, and seven words respectively, suggesting a rhythmical ascension for an oral performance. Each of the three sentences begins with God's name to affirm the divine agency of all pronounced blessings and is followed by two verbal clauses, expressing the divine actions encompassing the life of Israel comprehensively: *bless*, indicating any good thing that Israel could wish for, including progeny and prosperity; *keep*, connoting guard or watch over from all forms of evil, particularly for safety on a dangerous journey or security for living in the land; *make his face to shine*, referring to a positive and benevolent presence of God; *be gracious*, pointing to a kind action of a superior to an inferior, regardless of whether the inferior deserves such action; *lift up his countenance*, showing favor, as a judge treats the guilty favorably by turning his face toward him; and *give [you] peace*, providing well-being in all areas of life, including physical and relational spheres. These six verbs may underscore six separate acts of God or three divine actions with three concrete manifestations (as the second verb in each sentence indicates the result of the first). V. 27 completes the unit by ensuring that the blessings are rendered effective because of the invoking of God's name, not the enunciation by the priests, and that they will materialize in the future, as the Israelites live out their lives with God's name in their hearts. The future orientation distinguishes the priestly blessing from the well-known Beatitudes (Ps. 1; Matt. 5:3–12), which are focused on present reality.

The priestly blessing had a considerable impact on the liturgical life of ancient Israel, evidenced by its language and imagery found elsewhere in Scripture, especially the Psalter (Pss. 4, 67). It could be pronounced at the conclusion of the worship service, as shown in Aaron's blessing on the people following his performance of a series of offerings (Lev. 9:22–24). In this case, the worshipers receive God's blessings, without which they could not sustain their covenantal life, as they head out to the world.

Won W. Lee

of the tent of meeting, [14]and they shall offer their gift to the Lord, one male lamb a year old without blemish as a burnt offering, one ewe lamb a year old without blemish as a purification offering, one ram without blemish as an offering of well-being, [15]and a basket of unleavened bread, cakes of choice flour mixed with oil, and unleavened wafers spread with oil, with their grain offering and their drink offerings. [16]The priest shall present them before the Lord and offer their purification offering and burnt offering [17]and offer the ram as a sacrifice of well-being to the Lord, with the basket of unleavened bread; the priest also shall make the accompanying grain offering and drink offering. [18]Then the nazirites shall shave the consecrated head at the entrance of the tent of meeting and shall take the hair from the consecrated head and put it on the fire under the sacrifice of well-being. [19]The priest shall take the shoulder of the ram, when it is boiled, and one unleavened cake out of the basket and one unleavened wafer and shall put them in the palms of the nazirites, after they have shaved the consecrated head. [20]Then the priest shall elevate them as an elevation offering before the Lord; they are a holy portion for the priest, together with the breast that is elevated and the thigh that is offered. After that the nazirites may drink wine.

21 "This is the law for the nazirites who take a vow. Their offering to the Lord must be in accordance with the nazirite vow, apart from what else they can afford. In accordance with whatever vow they take, so they shall do, following the law for their consecration."

22 The Lord spoke to Moses, saying, [23]"Speak to Aaron and his sons, saying: Thus

the burnt offering (invoking God's presence), followed by the purification offering (purifying any possible contamination of the sanctuary), the well-being offering (sharing the offering together with the priests in the presence of God, Lev. 3:1–17; 7:11–36) together with the grain offering (Lev. 2:1–16; 6:7–11) and the drink offering (Num. 15:1–21), and ending with the elevation offering (Lev. 7:30–34), marking the completion of the transition from the holy state of the nazirites to their normal state.
6:22–27 The Aaronide priests are instructed to recite God's blessings for Israel. Expressed in six acts of God—*bless, keep, make his face shine, be gracious, lift up his countenance, give*—the benediction covers the life of Israel comprehensively. See **"The Priestly Blessing," p. 198.**

you shall bless the Israelites: You shall say to them:

[24] The LORD bless you and keep you;
[25] the LORD make his face to shine upon you
and be gracious to you;
[26] the LORD lift up his countenance upon
you and give you peace.

27 "So they shall put my name on the Israelites, and I will bless them."

7 On the day when Moses had finished setting up the tabernacle and had anointed and consecrated it with all its furnishings and had anointed and consecrated the altar with all its utensils, [2]the leaders of Israel, heads of their ancestral houses, the leaders of the tribes, who were over those who were enrolled, made offerings. [3]They brought their offerings before the LORD, six covered wagons and twelve oxen, a wagon for every two of the leaders and for each one an ox; they presented them before the tabernacle. [4]Then the LORD said to Moses, [5]"Accept these from them, that they may be used in doing the service of the tent of meeting, and give them to the Levites, to each according to his service." [6]So Moses took the wagons and the oxen and gave them to the Levites. [7]Two wagons and four oxen he gave to the Gershonites, according to their service, [8]and four wagons and eight oxen he gave to the Merarites, according to their service, under the direction of Ithamar son of Aaron the priest. [9]But to the Kohathites he gave none, because they were charged with the care of the holy things that had to be carried on the shoulders.

10 The leaders also presented offerings for the dedication of the altar at the time when it was anointed; the leaders presented their offering before the altar. [11]The LORD said to Moses, "They shall present their offerings, one leader each day, for the dedication of the altar."

12 The one who presented his offering the first day was Nahshon son of Amminadab, of the tribe of Judah; [13]his offering was one silver plate weighing one hundred thirty shekels, one silver basin weighing seventy shekels, according to the shekel of the sanctuary, both of them full of choice flour mixed with oil for a grain offering; [14]one golden dish weighing ten shekels, full of incense; [15]one young bull, one ram, one male lamb a year old, for a burnt offering; [16]one male goat for a purification offering; [17]and for the sacrifice of well-being, two oxen, five rams, five male goats, and five male lambs a year old. This was the offering of Nahshon son of Amminadab.

18 On the second day Nethanel son of Zuar, the leader of Issachar, presented an offering; [19]he presented for his offering one silver plate weighing one hundred thirty shekels, one silver basin weighing seventy shekels, according to the shekel of the sanctuary, both of them full of choice flour mixed with oil for a grain offering; [20]one golden dish weighing ten shekels, full of incense; [21]one young bull, one ram, one male lamb a year old, as a burnt offering; [22]one male goat as a purification offering; [23]and for the sacrifice of well-being, two oxen, five rams, five male goats, and five male lambs a year old. This was the offering of Nethanel son of Zuar.

24 On the third day Eliab son of Helon, the leader of the Zebulunites: [25]his offering was one silver plate weighing one hundred thirty shekels, one silver basin weighing seventy shekels, according to the shekel of the sanctuary, both of them full of choice flour mixed with oil for a grain offering; [26]one golden dish weighing ten shekels, full of incense; [27]one young bull, one ram, one male lamb a year old, for a burnt offering; [28]one male goat for a purification offering; [29]and for the sacrifice of well-being, two oxen, five rams, five male goats, and five male lambs a year old. This was the offering of Eliab son of Helon.

7:1–10:10 Matters concerning the inner camp. This section focuses on the priests' handling of matters that specifically relate to the tabernacle and range from its maintenance to its role in the camp's march from Sinai.

7:1–89 The priests and Levites do not own any supply mechanisms for carrying out their cultic duties. They are solely dependent on the initiative of the people, represented through their leaders. Each tribal leader brings the same number of gifts voluntarily for the tabernacle and the altar. **7:1** *On the day when* refers to Exod. 40:17, and *anointed and consecrated* confirms Moses's compliance with Exod. 40:9–10. **7:2–9** Each tribal leader contributes an equal share, regardless of the different sizes of the tribes. Their offerings are given to the Levitical houses for transport to the tabernacle. **7:10–88** The twelve leaders individually bring gifts for the service of the altar on twelve consecutive days. Their names and the order of the tribes are the same as in the census (1:5–15) and

30 On the fourth day Elizur son of Shedeur, the leader of the Reubenites: [31]his offering was one silver plate weighing one hundred thirty shekels, one silver basin weighing seventy shekels, according to the shekel of the sanctuary, both of them full of choice flour mixed with oil for a grain offering; [32]one golden dish weighing ten shekels, full of incense; [33]one young bull, one ram, one male lamb a year old, for a burnt offering; [34]one male goat for a purification offering; [35]and for the sacrifice of well-being, two oxen, five rams, five male goats, and five male lambs a year old. This was the offering of Elizur son of Shedeur.

36 On the fifth day Shelumiel son of Zurishaddai, the leader of the Simeonites: [37]his offering was one silver plate weighing one hundred thirty shekels, one silver basin weighing seventy shekels, according to the shekel of the sanctuary, both of them full of choice flour mixed with oil for a grain offering; [38]one golden dish weighing ten shekels, full of incense; [39]one young bull, one ram, one male lamb a year old, for a burnt offering; [40]one male goat for a purification offering; [41]and for the sacrifice of well-being, two oxen, five rams, five male goats, and five male lambs a year old. This was the offering of Shelumiel son of Zurishaddai.

42 On the sixth day Eliasaph son of Deuel, the leader of the Gadites: [43]his offering was one silver plate weighing one hundred thirty shekels, one silver basin weighing seventy shekels, according to the shekel of the sanctuary, both of them full of choice flour mixed with oil for a grain offering; [44]one golden dish weighing ten shekels, full of incense; [45]one young bull, one ram, one male lamb a year old, for a burnt offering; [46]one male goat for a purification offering; [47]and for the sacrifice of well-being, two oxen, five rams, five male goats, and five male lambs a year old. This was the offering of Eliasaph son of Deuel.

48 On the seventh day Elishama son of Ammihud, the leader of the Ephraimites: [49]his offering was one silver plate weighing one hundred thirty shekels, one silver basin weighing seventy shekels, according to the shekel of the sanctuary, both of them full of choice flour mixed with oil for a grain offering; [50]one golden dish weighing ten shekels, full of incense; [51]one young bull, one ram, one male lamb a year old, for a burnt offering; [52]one male goat for a purification offering; [53]and for the sacrifice of well-being, two oxen, five rams, five male goats, and five male lambs a year old. This was the offering of Elishama son of Ammihud.

54 On the eighth day Gamaliel son of Pedahzur, the leader of the Manassites: [55]his offering was one silver plate weighing one hundred thirty shekels, one silver basin weighing seventy shekels, according to the shekel of the sanctuary, both of them full of choice flour mixed with oil for a grain offering; [56]one golden dish weighing ten shekels, full of incense; [57]one young bull, one ram, one male lamb a year old, for a burnt offering; [58]one male goat for a purification offering; [59]and for the sacrifice of well-being, two oxen, five rams, five male goats, and five male lambs a year old. This was the offering of Gamaliel son of Pedahzur.

60 On the ninth day Abidan son of Gideoni, the leader of the Benjaminites: [61]his offering was one silver plate weighing one hundred thirty shekels, one silver basin weighing seventy shekels, according to the shekel of the sanctuary, both of them full of choice flour mixed with oil for a grain offering; [62]one golden dish weighing ten shekels, full of incense; [63]one young bull, one ram, one male lamb a year old, for a burnt offering; [64]one male goat for a purification offering; [65]and for the sacrifice of well-being, two oxen, five rams, five male goats, and five male lambs a year old. This was the offering of Abidan son of Gideoni.

66 On the tenth day Ahiezer son of Ammishaddai, the leader of the Danites: [67]his offering was one silver plate weighing one hundred thirty shekels, one silver basin weighing seventy shekels, according to the shekel of the sanctuary, both of them full of choice flour mixed with oil for a grain offering; [68]one golden dish weighing ten shekels, full of incense; [69]one young bull, one ram, one male lamb a year old, for a burnt offering; [70]one male goat for a purification offering; [71]and for the sacrifice of well-being, two oxen, five rams, five male goats, and five male lambs a year old. This was the offering of Ahiezer son of Ammishaddai.

the description of the camp (2:3–31). The description of each leader's gift is identical and repeated for each of the twelve tribes: the day and name of the leader followed by a record of gifts related to four types of offerings (grain, burnt, purification, and well-being). Similarly to their tabernacle

72 On the eleventh day Pagiel son of Ochran, the leader of the Asherites: [73]his offering was one silver plate weighing one hundred thirty shekels, one silver basin weighing seventy shekels, according to the shekel of the sanctuary, both of them full of choice flour mixed with oil for a grain offering; [74]one golden dish weighing ten shekels, full of incense; [75]one young bull, one ram, one male lamb a year old, for a burnt offering; [76]one male goat for a purification offering; [77]and for the sacrifice of well-being, two oxen, five rams, five male goats, and five male lambs a year old. This was the offering of Pagiel son of Ochran.

78 On the twelfth day Ahira son of Enan, the leader of the Naphtalites: [79]his offering was one silver plate weighing one hundred thirty shekels, one silver basin weighing seventy shekels, according to the shekel of the sanctuary, both of them full of choice flour mixed with oil for a grain offering; [80]one golden dish weighing ten shekels, full of incense; [81]one young bull, one ram, one male lamb a year old, for a burnt offering; [82]one male goat for a purification offering; [83]and for the sacrifice of well-being, two oxen, five rams, five male goats, and five male lambs a year old. This was the offering of Ahira son of Enan.

84 This was the dedication offering for the altar, at the time when it was anointed, from the leaders of Israel: twelve silver plates, twelve silver basins, twelve golden dishes, [85]each silver plate weighing one hundred thirty shekels and each basin seventy, all the silver of the vessels two thousand four hundred shekels according to the shekel of the sanctuary, [86]the twelve golden dishes, full

of incense, weighing ten shekels apiece according to the shekel of the sanctuary, all the gold of the dishes being one hundred twenty shekels; [87]all the livestock for the burnt offering twelve bulls, twelve rams, twelve male lambs a year old, with their grain offering; and twelve male goats for a purification offering; [88]and all the livestock for the sacrifice of well-being twenty-four bulls, sixty rams, sixty male goats, and sixty male lambs a year old. This was the dedication offering for the altar, after it was anointed.

89 When Moses went into the tent of meeting to speak with the LORD,[m] he would hear the voice speaking to him from above the cover that was on the ark of the covenant from between the two cherubim; thus it spoke to him.[n]

8 The LORD spoke to Moses, saying, [2]"Speak to Aaron and say to him: When you set up the lamps, the seven lamps shall give light in front of the lampstand." [3]Aaron did so; he set up its lamps in front of the lampstand, as the LORD had commanded Moses. [4]Now this was how the lampstand was made, out of hammered work of gold. From its base to its flowers, it was hammered work; according to the pattern that the LORD had shown Moses, so he made the lampstand.

5 The LORD spoke to Moses, saying, [6]"Take the Levites from among the Israelites and cleanse them. [7]Thus you shall do to them, to cleanse them: sprinkle the water of purification on them; have them shave their whole

m 7.89 Heb him   n 7.89 Or and he would speak to him

gifts, each leader brings the same types and number of gifts, and the total amount is enormous (vv. 84–88). Offerings are given at the leaders' own initiative rather than in response to a priestly demand or God's command. As they support the cultic practices in front of the altar, they are presented as equal in the eyes of God and thus enjoy equal status before God. **7:89** After anointing and consecrating the tabernacle, Moses finally communes directly with God, which he was not able to do before (Exod. 40:34–35). The leaders' voluntary offerings culminate in the dedication of the tabernacle and enable the fulfillment of God's promise of fellowship with the Israelites (Exod. 25:22).

8:1–4 This clarifies ambiguities related to the lampstand in earlier materials. First, only Aaron, not his sons, is assigned to lift the seven lamps, although his sons are responsible to take care of them (Exod. 27:20–21; Lev. 24:2–4). Second, the lamps are lifted such that the lights shine specifically toward the front of the lampstand (Exod. 25:37; for how the lampstand was made, see Exod. 25:31–40; 37:17–24). The lampstand's flowery design may symbolize the tree of life (Gen. 3:22, 24).

8:5–22 The Levites' installation of the work at the tent of meeting involves four agents with specific roles. Moses separates the Levites from the Israelites, cleanses them with the water of purification, brings a bull for their purification, and brings them before the meeting tent. Then he gathers all the Israelites and presents the Levites to Aaron and his sons. Aaron dedicates the Levites to God for their service and offers purification and burnt offerings on their behalf. The Levites

body with a razor and wash their clothes and so cleanse themselves. ⁸Then let them take a young bull and its grain offering of choice flour mixed with oil, and you shall take another young bull for a purification offering. ⁹You shall bring the Levites before the tent of meeting and assemble the whole congregation of the Israelites. ¹⁰When you bring the Levites before the LORD, the Israelites shall lay their hands on the Levites, ¹¹and Aaron shall present the Levites before the LORD as an elevation offering from the Israelites, that they may do the service of the LORD. ¹²The Levites shall lay their hands on the heads of the bulls, and he shall offer the one for a purification offering and the other for a burnt offering to the LORD, to make atonement for the Levites. ¹³Then you shall have the Levites stand before Aaron and his sons, and you shall present them as an elevation offering to the LORD.

14 "Thus you shall separate the Levites from among the other Israelites, and the Levites shall be mine. ¹⁵Thereafter the Levites may go in to do service at the tent of meeting, once you have cleansed them and presented them as an elevation offering. ¹⁶For they are unreservedly given to me from among the Israelites; I have taken them for myself, in place of all that open the womb, the firstborn of all the Israelites. ¹⁷For all the firstborn among the Israelites are mine, both human and animal. On the day that I struck down all the firstborn in the land of Egypt I consecrated them

for myself, ¹⁸but I have taken the Levites in place of all the firstborn among the Israelites. ¹⁹Moreover, I have given the Levites as a gift to Aaron and his sons from among the Israelites, to do the service for the Israelites at the tent of meeting and to make atonement for the Israelites, in order that there may be no plague among the Israelites for coming too close to the sanctuary."

20 Moses and Aaron and the whole congregation of the Israelites did with the Levites accordingly; the Israelites did with the Levites just as the LORD had commanded Moses concerning them. ²¹The Levites purified themselves from sin and washed their clothes; then Aaron presented them as an elevation offering before the LORD, and Aaron made atonement for them to cleanse them. ²²Thereafter the Levites went in to do their service in the tent of meeting in attendance on Aaron and his sons. As the LORD had commanded Moses concerning the Levites, so they did with them.

23 The LORD spoke to Moses, saying, ²⁴"This applies to the Levites: from twenty-five years old and up they shall begin to do duty in the service of the tent of meeting; ²⁵and from the age of fifty years they shall retire from the duty of the service and serve no more. ²⁶They may assist their brothers in the tent of meeting in carrying out their duties, but they shall perform no service. Thus you shall do with the Levites in assigning their duties."

cleanse themselves (including shaving their bodies and washing their clothes), bring a bull with a grain offering, and lay hands on their and Moses's bulls. The Israelites lay hands on the Levites. This comprehensive participation is confirmed (v. 20). The Levites are purified for their work so they do not defile the sanctuary, which would endanger the entire community from God's wrath. They are also an offering presented to God as a ransom for the Israelites' firstborns (vv. 14–22). They are not consecrated like the priests (Lev. 8), but they are presented to Aaron and dedicated to YHWH, indicating their position within the sanctuary's hierarchical order. **8:8–13** After a water ceremony (v. 7), the main sacrificial ceremony is described. As laying hands symbolizes identification or substitution, *the Israelites shall lay their hands on the Levites. . . . The Levites shall lay their hands on the heads of the bulls* implies that the impurity of the Israelites is transferred to the bulls via the Levites. As the bulls are slaughtered, the Levites are offered to God on behalf of the Israelites.

8:23–26 This text changes the age limitations for the Levites from chap. 4 (4:3, 23, 30, 35, 39, 43, 47). First, it lowers the age of entry from thirty to twenty-five years old, which might address an insufficient Levitical workforce or a need for additional physical strength in dismantling, carrying, and reassembling the sanctuary structures. Second, it adds *and up*, suggesting that the Levites can enter service at any time after twenty-five. It qualifies the two numbers (thirty and fifty) in 4:3 and sets only the limit for entering service. Third, it describes what the Levites can do *from the age of fifty years*, retiring from the workforce and assisting fellow Levites serving at the tent of meeting. As a result, the text adjusts the total working period for the Levites downward and clarifies the participation of the older Levites according to their physical strength.

9 The Lord spoke to Moses in the wilderness of Sinai, in the first month of the second year after they had come out of the land of Egypt, saying, ²"Let the Israelites keep the Passover at its appointed time. ³On the fourteenth day of this month, at twilight,ᵒ you shall keep it at its appointed time; according to all its statutes and all its regulations you shall keep it." ⁴So Moses told the Israelites that they should keep the Passover. ⁵They kept the Passover in the first month, on the fourteenth day of the month, at twilight,ᵖ in the wilderness of Sinai. Just as the Lord had commanded Moses, so the Israelites did. ⁶Now there were certain people who were unclean through touching a corpse, so that they could not keep the Passover on that day. They came before Moses and Aaron on that day ⁷and said to him, "Although we are unclean through touching a corpse, why must we be kept from presenting the Lord's offering at its appointed time among the Israelites?" ⁸Moses said to them, "Wait, so that I may hear what the Lord will command concerning you."

9 The Lord spoke to Moses, saying, ¹⁰"Speak to the Israelites, saying: Anyone of you or your descendants who is unclean through touching a corpse or is away on a journey shall still keep the Passover to the Lord. ¹¹In the second month on the fourteenth day, at twilight,ᵠ they shall keep it; they shall eat it with unleavened bread and bitter herbs. ¹²They shall leave none of it until morning nor break a bone of it; according to all the statute for the Passover they shall keep it. ¹³But anyone who is clean and is not on a journey and yet refrains from keeping the Passover shall be cut off from the people for not presenting the Lord's offering at its appointed time; such a one shall bear the consequences for the sin. ¹⁴Any alien residing among you who wishes to keep the Passover to the Lord shall do so according to the statute of the Passover and according to its regulation; you shall have one statute for both the resident alien and the native of the land."

15 On the day the tabernacle was set up, the cloud covered the tabernacle, the tent of the covenant, and from evening until morning it was over the tabernacle, having the appearance of fire. ¹⁶It was always so: the cloud covered it by dayʳ and the appearance of fire by night. ¹⁷Whenever the cloud lifted from over the tent, then the Israelites would set out, and in the place where the cloud settled down, there the Israelites would camp. ¹⁸At

o 9.3 Heb *between the two evenings* p 9.5 Heb *between the two evenings* q 9.11 Heb *between the two evenings* r 9.16 Gk Syr Vg: Heb lacks *by day*

9:1–14 Supplementing the Passover regulations in Exod. 12, this text explains what to do for ceremonially unclean and traveling persons who are unable to keep the Passover in the appointed time. The unclean persons should have known that they must be separated from the camp so as not to defile the rest of the community (Num. 5:1–4; 6:6–12; 19:1–22). Yet they ask Moses and Aaron in v. 7, which presupposes that the Passover at Sinai is kept beyond family boundaries (Exod. 12:21–28) and celebrated at the sanctuary with fellow Israelites. The divine instruction affirms the communal nature of the Passover by allowing the unclean and the travelers, both separated from the community, to observe, albeit at the second month. All Israelites, including foreign immigrants, must keep the Passover at the appointed time with the entire community and in a legitimate place (sanctuary or temple; Lev. 23:4–8; Deut. 16:1–8; Josh. 5:10–12; 2 Kgs. 23:21–23; 2 Chr. 30:1–27; 35:1–19; Ezra 6:19–22). **9:1–5** *In the first month of the second year* refers to when Moses erected the tabernacle (Exod. 40:17) and continues the flashback begun at Num. 7:1. Mentioning this month, although a month earlier than the date in 1:1, highlights that Israel kept the Passover at Sinai *at its appointed time* (see Exod. 12:2). **9:14** *Any alien residing among you* is distinguished from the foreigner, temporary resident, and day laborer (in Exodus), all of whom are forbidden to eat the lamb (Exod. 12:43, 45). In Exodus, furthermore, "resident aliens," meaning foreign immigrants, must be circumcised to observe Passover (Exod. 12:48).

9:15–23 Reminiscent of Exod. 40:34–38, this text summarizes divine guidance for Israel's march (vv. 15–17) and their exact obedience (vv. 18–23). Whenever the fire-cloud, symbolizing God's presence, descends over the tabernacle, the people make camp; whenever it rises, they break camp and continue their march. No matter how long it remains over the tabernacle, whether it is only *from evening until morning* or *two days or a month or a longer time*, as soon as it lifts, Israel departs. God's total control of the schedule for Israel's march is confirmed by seven occurrences of *[at / according to] the command of the Lord* (vv. 18 [twice], 20 [twice], 23 [three times]); thus, Israel's march toward the promised land is transformed into God's own march.

the command of the LORD the Israelites would set out, and at the command of the LORD they would camp. As long as the cloud rested over the tabernacle, they would remain in camp. [19]Even when the cloud continued over the tabernacle many days, the Israelites would keep the charge of the LORD and would not set out. [20]Sometimes the cloud would remain a few days over the tabernacle, and according to the command of the LORD they would remain in camp; then according to the command of the LORD they would set out. [21]Sometimes the cloud would remain from evening until morning, and when the cloud lifted in the morning, they would set out, or if it continued for a day and a night, when the cloud lifted they would set out. [22]Whether it was two days or a month or a longer time that the cloud continued over the tabernacle, resting upon it, the Israelites would remain in camp and would not set out, but when it lifted they would set out. [23]At the command of the LORD they would camp, and at the command of the LORD they would set out. They kept the charge of the LORD, at the command of the LORD by Moses.

10 The LORD spoke to Moses, saying, [2]"Make two silver trumpets; you shall make them of hammered work, and you shall use them for summoning the congregation and for breaking camp. [3]When both are blown, the whole congregation shall assemble before you at the entrance of the tent of meeting. [4]But if only one is blown, then the leaders, the heads of the tribes of Israel, shall assemble before you. [5]When you blow an alarm, the camps on the east side shall set out; [6]when you blow a second alarm, the camps on the south side shall set out. An alarm is to be blown whenever they are to set out. [7]But when the assembly is to be gathered, you shall blow, but you shall not sound an alarm. [8]The sons of Aaron, the priests, shall blow the trumpets; this shall be a perpetual institution for you throughout your generations. [9]When you go to war in your land against the adversary who oppresses you, you shall sound an alarm with the trumpets, so that you may be remembered before the LORD your God and be saved from your enemies. [10]Also on your days of rejoicing, at your appointed festivals, and at the beginnings of your months, you shall blow the trumpets over your burnt offerings and over your sacrifices of well-being; they shall serve as a reminder on your behalf before the LORD your God: I am the LORD your God."

11 In the second year, in the second month, on the twentieth day of the month, the cloud lifted from over the tabernacle of the covenant. [12]Then the Israelites set out by stages from the wilderness of Sinai, and the cloud settled down in the wilderness of Paran. [13]They set out for the first time at the command of the LORD by Moses. [14]The standard of the camp of Judah set out first, company by company, and over the whole company was

10:1–10 In Sinai, the two trumpets are used for summoning the congregation and signaling march (vv. 2–8). In the settled land, they are used for signaling occasional warfare and regular worship at the sanctuary (vv. 9–10). These two sections are connected with two different sounds: *blow* (a long blast) summons the entire community, gathers the leaders to Moses at the entrance of the tent of meeting (vv. 3–4), and calls for the sacrifices at appointed communal celebrations (v. 10), whereas *blow/sound an alarm* (a series of short blasts) signals breaking camp (vv. 5–6) and serves as a military alarm (v. 9). For Israel, God will be present in their land as God was present in Sinai. In war, God will deliver them from enemies just as God led their campaign from Sinai. In sacrifices, God will be honored as God was honored when the trumpets summoned the entire community to the tent of meeting. By blowing the trumpets, the Aaronide priests actualize this relationship perpetually. While 9:15–23 focuses primarily on God's presence and guidance, this text emphasizes the priests' role in maintaining God's ongoing relationship with Israel.

10:11–36 Programmatic departure. As a liberated (Exod. 1–18), covenantal (Exod. 19–40), holy (Leviticus), and military (Num. 1:1–10:10) community, Israel set out from Sinai toward the promised land. The text underscores the ideal beginning of Israel's march, a sharp contrast in their behaviors from 11:1–3 on. **10:11–28** The date is related to the Exodus event (Exod. 12), eleven months after the arrival at Sinai (Exod. 19:1), and nineteen days after the census of Israel's militia (Num. 1:1). The marching camp uses the same list of tribes (2:3–31; 7:10–83) with the same leaders (1:5b–15). The marching order of the four-by-three tribal regiments and Levitical responsibilities follow the instructions in chaps. 2–3. Although the camp's quadrangular formation is made linear, maximum

Nahshon son of Amminadab. [15]Over the company of the tribe of Issachar was Nethanel son of Zuar, [16]and over the company of the tribe of Zebulun was Eliab son of Helon.

17 Then the tabernacle was taken down, and the Gershonites and the Merarites, who carried the tabernacle, set out. [18]Next the standard of the camp of Reuben set out, company by company, and over the whole company was Elizur son of Shedeur. [19]Over the company of the tribe of Simeon was Shelumiel son of Zurishaddai, [20]and over the company of the tribe of Gad was Eliasaph son of Deuel.

21 Then the Kohathites, who carried the holy things, set out, and the tabernacle was set up before their arrival. [22]Next the standard of the camp of Ephraim set out, company by company, and over the whole company was Elishama son of Ammihud. [23]Over the company of the tribe of Manasseh was Gamaliel son of Pedahzur, [24]and over the company of the tribe of Benjamin was Abidan son of Gideoni.

25 Then the standard of the camp of Dan, acting as the rear guard of all the camps, set out, company by company, and over the whole company was Ahiezer son of Ammishaddai. [26]Over the company of the tribe of Asher was Pagiel son of Ochran, [27]and over the company of the tribe of Naphtali was Ahira son of Enan. [28]This was the order of march of the Israelites, company by company, when they set out.

29 Moses said to Hobab son of Reuel the Midianite, Moses's father-in-law, "We are setting out for the place of which the LORD said, 'I will give it to you'; come with us, and we will treat you well, for the LORD has promised good to Israel." [30]But he said to him, "I will not go, but I will go back to my own land and to my kindred." [31]He said, "Do not leave us, for you know where we should camp in the wilderness, and you will serve as eyes for us. [32]Moreover, if you go with us, whatever good the LORD does for us, the same we will do for you."

33 So they set out from the mount of the LORD three days' journey with the ark of the covenant of the LORD going before them three days' journey, to seek out a resting place for them, [34]the cloud of the LORD being over them by day when they set out from the camp.

35 Whenever the ark set out, Moses would say,

"Arise, O LORD, let your enemies be
    scattered
  and your foes flee before you."
[36]And whenever it came to rest, he would say,
  "Return, O LORD, to the ten thousand
    thousands of Israel."*s*

11 Now when the people complained in the hearing of the LORD about their misfortunes, the LORD heard it, and his anger was kindled. Then the fire of the LORD burned against them and consumed some outlying parts of the camp. [2]But the people cried out to Moses, and Moses prayed to the LORD, and the fire abated. [3]So that place was called Taberah,*t* because the fire of the LORD burned against them.

4 The camp followers with them had a strong craving, and the Israelites also wept

s 10.36 Meaning of Heb uncertain   *t* 11.3 That is, *burning*

protection of the tabernacle is still achieved. **10:29–34** Compared to vv. 11–28, several differences are notable: (1) Moses asks Hobab the Midianite twice for help navigating the desert, as if the guidance of the cloud were not sufficient. (2) Moses initiates this assistance, not God. (3) The ark of the covenant marches ahead of Israel, not in the middle of the march. (4) The cloud is simply present over Israel during their march, not actively guiding them from the tabernacle. **10:35–36** The Song to the Ark reflects the tradition of viewing the ark as a throne from which the divine warrior executes a well-prepared campaign (1 Sam. 4–6; 2 Sam. 6; 1 Kgs. 8:1–21; Ps. 24:7–10). No human agents, including Moses and especially Hobab, are ultimately in charge of Israel's march in the desert. Instead, Israel's God will lead the battle on their behalf and keep fighting until the promised land is conquered.

11:1–14:45 Failure of the exodus generation.

11:1–3 Patterned after the murmuring stories in the wilderness (complaining, punishment, plea for help, intercession, and deliverance), this first rebellion story in Numbers highlights the stark contrast from previous sections (the perfect preparation and ideal departure from Sinai) and marks the beginning of Israel's constant complaints. *Taberah*, a wordplay on "burning," corresponds with what happened there.

11:4–34 This second rebellion story is far more complex. The Israelites' complaint over meat led Moses to complain about bearing responsibility for them. In response, God provides seventy elders

again and said, "If only we had meat to eat! [5]We remember the fish we used to eat in Egypt for nothing, the cucumbers, the melons, the leeks, the onions, and the garlic, [6]but now our strength is dried up, and there is nothing at all but this manna to look at."

[7] Now the manna was like coriander seed, and its color was like the color of gum resin. [8]The people went around and gathered it, ground it in mills or beat it in mortars, then boiled it in pots and made cakes of it, and the taste of it was like the taste of cakes baked with oil. [9]When the dew fell on the camp in the night, the manna would fall with it.

[10] Moses heard the people weeping throughout their families, all at the entrances of their tents. Then the Lord became very angry, and Moses was displeased. [11]So Moses said to the Lord, "Why have you treated your servant so badly? Why have I not found favor in your sight, that you lay the burden of all this people on me? [12]Did I conceive all this people? Did I give birth to them, that you should say to me, 'Carry them in your bosom as a wet nurse carries a nursing child, to the land that you promised on oath to their ancestors'? [13]Where am I to get meat to give to all this people? For they come weeping to me, saying, 'Give us meat to eat!' [14]I am not able to carry all this people alone, for they are too heavy for me. [15]If this is the way you are going to treat me, put me to death at once—if I have found favor in your sight—and do not let me see my misery."

[16] So the Lord said to Moses, "Gather for me seventy of the elders of Israel, whom you know to be the elders of the people and officers over them; bring them to the tent of meeting and have them take their place there with you. [17]I will come down and speak with you there, and I will take some of the spirit that is on you and put it on them, and they shall bear the burden of the people along with you so that you will not bear it all by yourself. [18]And say to the people, 'Consecrate yourselves for tomorrow, and you shall eat meat, for you have wailed in the hearing of the Lord, saying, "If only we had meat to eat! Surely it was better for us in Egypt." Therefore the Lord will give you meat, and you shall eat. [19]You shall eat not only one day, or two days, or five days, or ten days, or twenty days, [20]but for a whole month, until it comes out of your nostrils and becomes loathsome to you—because you have rejected the Lord who is among you and have wailed before him, saying, "Why did we ever leave Egypt?"'" [21]But Moses said, "The people I am with number six hundred thousand on foot, and you say, 'I will give them meat, that they may eat for a whole month'! [22]Are there enough flocks and herds to slaughter for them? Are there enough fish in the sea to catch for them?" [23]The Lord said to Moses, "Is the Lord's power limited?[u] Now you shall see whether my word will come true for you or not."

[24] So Moses went out and told the people the words of the Lord, and he gathered seventy of the elders of the people and placed them all around the tent. [25]Then the Lord came down in the cloud and spoke to him and took some of the spirit that was on him and put it on the seventy elders, and when the spirit rested upon them, they prophesied. But they did not do so again.

u 11.23 Heb Lord's hand too short?

to share Moses's responsibility as well as the meat that the people crave, along with a plague as punishment for their rebellion. **11:4–9** *The camp followers with them* may refer to non-Israelites who went along with the Israelites from Egypt (Exod. 12:38). Against their claim of the insufficiency of manna, Exod. 16:14–21 describes it as tasty, substantial, and daily provision. **11:10–15** Moses's charge portrays God as having conceived and given birth to the Israelites but neglected to nurse these suckling children (cf. Deut. 32:18; Isa. 40:11) by handing them over to Moses. Moses's complaint is not about the responsibility itself but about having to carry it out alone. **11:16–34** Seventy elders share leadership responsibility with Moses. They are subordinate to Moses, as they witness God's intimate relation to him at the tent of meeting, receive the spirit given to him, and can prophesy (v. 25). Moses's superior status is maintained even in the case of the two men remaining in the camp (vv. 26–29) because it is God who gives the spirit. God's spirit is subsequently given to various people (24:2; 27:18; 1 Sam. 10:5–10) and is transferable (2 Kgs. 2:9). Just as the spirit of God resolves the leadership problem, the wind (same as the Hebrew word for spirit) of God solves the food problem by bringing a vast flock of quail (Exod. 16:13; Ps. 78:26–31). But before they finish eating, God strikes them with a deadly plague (Exod. 3:20; 9:15), showing God's provision turned into judgment and providing an etiology of *Kibroth-hattaavah* (graves of craving).

26 Two men remained in the camp, one named Eldad and the other named Medad, and the spirit rested on them; they were among those registered, but they had not gone out to the tent, so they prophesied in the camp. ²⁷And a young man ran and told Moses, "Eldad and Medad are prophesying in the camp." ²⁸And Joshua son of Nun, the assistant of Moses, one of his chosen men,ᵛ said, "My lord Moses, stop them!" ²⁹But Moses said to him, "Are you jealous for my sake? Would that all the LORD's people were prophets and that the LORD would put his spirit on them!" ³⁰And Moses and the elders of Israel returned to the camp.

31 Then a wind went out from the LORD, and it brought quails from the sea and let them fall beside the camp, about a day's journey on this side and a day's journey on the other side, all around the camp, about two cubits deep on the ground. ³²So the people worked all that day and night and all the next day gathering the quails; the least anyone gathered was ten homers, and they spread them out for themselves all around the camp. ³³But while the meat was still between their teeth, before it was consumed, the anger of the LORD was kindled against the people, and the LORD struck the people with a very great plague. ³⁴So that place was called Kibroth-hattaavah,ʷ because there they buried the people who had the craving. ³⁵From Kibroth-hattaavah the people journeyed to Hazeroth.

12 While they were at Hazeroth, Miriam and Aaron spoke against Moses because of the Cushite woman whom he had married (for he had indeed married a Cushite woman), ²and they said, "Has the LORD spoken only through Moses? Has he not spoken through us also?" And the LORD heard it. ³Now the man Moses was very humble, more so than anyone else on the face of the earth. ⁴Suddenly the LORD said to Moses, Aaron, and Miriam, "Come out, you three, to the tent of meeting." So the three of them came out. ⁵Then the LORD came down in a pillar of cloud and stood at the entrance of the tent and called Aaron and Miriam, and they both came forward. ⁶And he said, "Hear my words:

When there are prophets among you,
    I the LORD make myself known to
        them in visions;
    I speak to them in dreams.
⁷ Not so with my servant Moses;
    he is faithful in all my house.
⁸ With him I speak face to face—clearly,
        not in riddles,
    and he beholds the form of the LORD.

"Why then were you not afraid to speak against my servant Moses?" ⁹And the anger of the LORD was kindled against them, and he departed.

10 When the cloud went away from over the tent, Miriam's skin had become diseased, as white as snow. And Aaron turned toward Miriam and saw that she was diseased. ¹¹Then Aaron said to Moses, "Oh, my lord, do not punish usˣ for a sin that we have so foolishly committed. ¹²Do not let her be like one stillborn, whose flesh is half consumed when it comes out of its mother's womb." ¹³And Moses cried to the LORD, saying, "O God, please heal her." ¹⁴But the LORD said to Moses, "If her father had but spit in her face, would she not bear her shame for seven days? Let her be shut out of the camp for seven days, and after

v 11.28 Or *of Moses from his youth* w 11.34 That is, *graves of craving* x 12.11 Heb *do not lay sin upon us*

11:35–12:16 This third rebellion story affirms Moses's prophetic authority over all of Israel, despite Miriam and Aaron's reasonable complaint. **12:1–2a** *The Cushite woman* might be Zipporah (Exod. 2:15–22), as Cush appears in tandem with Midian (Hab. 3:7), or another woman from Ethiopia. Miriam and Aaron murmur against Moses's marrying her, which in turn leads to complaints about Moses's role as the sole spokesman of God's word. Their challenge is understandable, since Miriam is called a "prophet" (Exod. 15:20), Aaron is a spokesman for God (Exod. 4:15), and others have received God's spirit (Num. 11:4–35). **12:2b–14** God's response to their charge begins with a parenthetical description of Moses's character: *humble*, denoting an unassuming integrity to conduct one's duty. God calls him *my servant*, acknowledges his faithfulness, speaks to him directly and intimately ("face to face": Exod. 33:7–11; Deut. 34:10), and allows him to see God's form (Exod. 24:9–11)—all illustrate Moses's incomparable nature. In addition, God punishes Miriam with a skin disease *as white as snow* (perhaps leprosy). Aaron, exempted from God's physical punishment, pleads with Moses (not God), with whom he wanted to be equal, for Miriam's restoration. God's answer to Moses's intercession for Miriam reaffirms the intention of this text, Moses's unique relationship with God, and his authority over all

that she may be brought in again." [15]So Miriam was shut out of the camp for seven days, and the people did not set out on the march until Miriam had been brought in again. [16]After that the people set out from Hazeroth and camped in the wilderness of Paran.

13 The LORD spoke to Moses, saying, [2]"Send men to spy out the land of Canaan, which I am giving to the Israelites; from each of their ancestral tribes you shall send a man, every one a leader among them." [3]So Moses sent them from the wilderness of Paran, according to the command of the LORD, all of them leading men among the Israelites. [4]These were their names: from the tribe of Reuben, Shammua son of Zaccur; [5]from the tribe of Simeon, Shaphat son of Hori; [6]from the tribe of Judah, Caleb son of Jephunneh; [7]from the tribe of Issachar, Igal son of Joseph; [8]from the tribe of Ephraim, Hoshea son of Nun; [9]from the tribe of Benjamin, Palti son of Raphu; [10]from the tribe of Zebulun, Gaddiel son of Sodi; [11]from the tribe of Joseph (that is, from the tribe of Manasseh), Gaddi son of Susi; [12]from the tribe of Dan, Ammiel son of Gemalli; [13]from the tribe of Asher, Sethur son of Michael; [14]from the tribe of Naphtali, Nahbi son of Vophsi; [15]from the tribe of Gad, Geuel son of Machi. [16]These were the names of the men whom Moses sent to spy out the land. And Moses changed the name of Hoshea son of Nun to Joshua.

[17]Moses sent them to spy out the land of Canaan and said to them, "Go up there into the Negeb, and go up into the hill country, [18]and see what the land is like and whether the people who live in it are strong or weak, whether they are few or many, [19]and whether the land they live in is good or bad, and whether the towns that they live in are unwalled or fortified, [20]and whether the land is rich or poor, and whether there are trees in it or not. Be bold, and bring some of the fruit of the land." Now it was the season of the first ripe grapes.

[21]So they went up and spied out the land from the wilderness of Zin to Rehob, near Lebo-hamath. [22]They went up into the Negeb and came to Hebron, and Ahiman, Sheshai, and Talmai, the Anakites, were there. (Hebron was built seven years before Zoan in Egypt.) [23]And they came to the Wadi Eshcol and cut down from there a branch with a single cluster of grapes, and they carried it on a pole between two of them. They also brought some pomegranates and figs. [24]That place was called the Wadi Eshcol[y] because of the cluster that the Israelites cut down from there.

[25]At the end of forty days they returned from spying out the land. [26]And they came to Moses and Aaron and to all the congregation of the Israelites in the wilderness of Paran, at Kadesh; they brought back word to them and to all the congregation and showed them the fruit of the land. [27]And they reported to him and said, "We came to the land to which you sent us; it flows with milk and honey, and this is its fruit. [28]Yet the people who live in the land are strong, and the towns are fortified and very large, and besides, we saw the

y 13.24 That is, *cluster*

God's people. **12:15–16** Miriam and Aaron's complaint against Moses ultimately prevents Israel from marching forward. Miriam's restoration into the community must precede the journey's continuation.
13:1–14:45 This fourth rebellion story reports Israel's initial and disastrous attempt to enter the promised land from the south. In response, God punishes those who experienced the exodus to die in the wilderness during forty years of wandering, except Caleb and Joshua. God's promise to Israel's ancestors is instead fulfilled by a new generation. See **"Murmuring Motif," p. 209. 13:1–2** *The LORD spoke* differs from the parallel account in Deut. 1:19–46, where the people approach Moses and request that he send out the spies. *Which I am giving to the Israelites* recalls God's promise to Israel's ancestors (Lev. 14:34; 18:3; 25:38; Num. 32:30). **13:3–17a** The tribal order begins with Reuben as in chap. 1. The chosen spies are not the same as in 1:5–15 and are never mentioned in the Bible again, except for Hoshea and Caleb. Joshua, renamed from Hoshea, is the representative of Ephraim, the northern Israelite territory, while Caleb is the representative of Judah, in the south. **13:17b–33** After scouting the land *from the wilderness of Zin to Rehob, near Lebo-hamath,* which is the full extent of the land of Canaan from the south to the north (cf. 34:7–9; Josh. 15:1–3; Ezek. 48:1), the spies discovered its fertility ("flowing with milk and honey," Exod. 3:8; 13:5; Deut. 6:3; 31:20) and the formidability of the towns and people, including *Anakites* (legendary warriors of great size related to the Nephilim; Gen. 6:1–4). In contrast to Caleb's exhortation on Israel's ability and readiness to fight, other scouts denigrate the land as one that *devours its inhabitants* and themselves as *grasshoppers.*

Going Deeper: Murmuring Motif (Numbers 13:1–14:35; 16:1–50)

In the Pentateuch, the phrase "to murmur against" appears in only five episodes: three in Exodus (15:22–27; 16:1–35; 17:1–7), reporting the people's murmurings about bread and water, which are not condemned but met by God's provisions; and two in Numbers (13:1–14:35; 16:1–50), narrating their challenge of the authority of Moses (and Aaron), which results in a heavy punishment. These stories are not simple complaints, muttering of disaffected people about the conditions of their life in the wilderness, but open rebellions to reject God's representatives for bringing them into the promised land. Thus, the murmuring motif must be considered in a broader context of rebellion stories.

From a literary perspective, God's responses to Israel's murmurings become progressively more negative from Exodus to Numbers. Before Sinai, they were sharply reprimanded by YHWH, but no one died. While in Sinai, Moses ordered the Levites to kill the people for making the golden calf (Exod. 32), and only Nadab and Abihu were killed because of their unholy fire (Lev. 10:10–17). However, after Sinai, all rebellion stories in Numbers conclude with divine punishment, manifesting as death (11:4–34; 21:4–9; 25:1–8), the march's delay (11:35–12:16), or the termination of the prophetic leadership of Moses and Aaron (20:1–13). As such, the heavy concentration of the phrase "to murmur against" in Num. 13–14 could be pointing to the whole congregation's rebellion against entering the promised land as the climax of all the murmurings.

From a traditional-historical perspective, the murmuring motif is not an original part of the wilderness traditions, which highlight God's gracious provision for Israel's needs without punishment. Rather, it is attached secondarily to the various complaint narratives, including the people's desire to reverse the exodus. This inversion occurred in Jerusalem in the early period of the divided monarchy to show that northern Israel's rights to election (grounded in the exodus) were forfeited when their ancestors rebelled and wanted to return to Egypt, but southern Judah's election was confirmed by God's covenant with David (Ps. 78:67–72; George W. Coats, *Rebellion in the Wilderness*). After the destruction of northern Israel, the murmuring motif is broadened into a test, exposing Israel's faithlessness in the wilderness (Deuteronomy) and ultimately explaining the exile (Ezek. 20). This historical reconstruction opens up many other explanations on how and why later generations of Israelites reused the murmuring motif to understand their ancestors' wilderness experience.

Won W. Lee

descendants of Anak there. ²⁹The Amalekites live in the land of the Negeb; the Hittites, the Jebusites, and the Amorites live in the hill country, and the Canaanites live by the sea and along the Jordan."

30 But Caleb quieted the people before Moses and said, "Let us go up at once and occupy it, for we are well able to overcome it." ³¹Then the men who had gone up with him said, "We are not able to go up against this people, for they are stronger than we." ³²So they brought to the Israelites an unfavorable report of the land that they had spied out, saying, "The land that we have gone through as spies is a land that devours its inhabitants, and all the people that we saw in it are of great size. ³³There we saw the Nephilim (the Anakites come from the Nephilim), and to

ourselves we seemed like grasshoppers, and so we seemed to them."

14 Then all the congregation raised a loud cry, and the people wept that night. ²And all the Israelites complained against Moses and Aaron; the whole congregation said to them, "Would that we had died in the land of Egypt! Or would that we had died in this wilderness! ³Why is the LORD bringing us into this land to fall by the sword? Our wives and our little ones will become plunder; would it not be better for us to go back to Egypt?" ⁴So they said to one another, "Let us choose a captain and go back to Egypt."

5 Then Moses and Aaron fell on their faces before all the assembly of the congregation of the Israelites. ⁶And Joshua son of Nun and

In their eyes, they are small, and the land is not worth fighting for. **14:1–4** *All the congregation* is involved in this radical rebellion. The intensity of their emotions increases from raising a loud voice, to weeping, to complaining. More than simply fearing military threat, they question God's motive for bringing them out of Egypt in the first place, construe the promised land as worse than Egypt or the wilderness, and express their desire to return to Egypt. They plot to replace Moses with a new leader and reverse the exodus altogether. **14:5–10a** Moses and Aaron's initial response is *[falling]*

Caleb son of Jephunneh, who were among those who had spied out the land, tore their clothes [7]and said to all the congregation of the Israelites, "The land that we went through as spies is an exceedingly good land. [8]If the LORD is pleased with us, he will bring us into this land and give it to us, a land that flows with milk and honey. [9]Only, do not rebel against the LORD, and do not fear the people of the land, for they are no more than bread for us; their protection is removed from them, and the LORD is with us; do not fear them." [10]But the whole congregation threatened to stone them.

Then the glory of the LORD appeared at the tent of meeting to all the Israelites. [11]And the LORD said to Moses, "How long will this people despise me? And how long will they refuse to believe in me, in spite of all the signs that I have done among them? [12]I will strike them with pestilence and disinherit them, and I will make of you a nation greater and mightier than they."

13 But Moses said to the LORD, "Then the Egyptians will hear of it, for in your might you brought up this people from among them, [14]and they will tell the inhabitants of this land. They have heard that you, O LORD, are in the midst of this people, for you, O LORD, are seen face to face, and your cloud stands over them and you go in front of them, in a pillar of cloud by day and in a pillar of fire by night. [15]Now if you kill this people as one, then the nations who have heard about you will say, [16]'It is because the LORD was not able to bring this people into the land he swore to give them that he has slaughtered them in the wilderness.' [17]And now, therefore, let the power of the LORD be great in the way that you promised when you spoke, saying,

[18] 'The LORD is slow to anger
and abounding in steadfast love,
    forgiving iniquity and transgression,

but by no means clearing the guilty,
visiting the iniquity of the parents
    upon the children
to the third and the fourth generation.'
[19]"Forgive the iniquity of this people according to the greatness of your steadfast love, just as you have pardoned this people, from Egypt even until now."

20 Then the LORD said, "I do forgive, just as you have asked; [21]nevertheless, as I live and as all the earth shall be filled with the glory of the LORD, [22]none of the people who have seen my glory and the signs that I did in Egypt and in the wilderness and yet have tested me these ten times and have not obeyed my voice [23]shall see the land that I swore to give to their ancestors; none of those who despised me shall see it. [24]But my servant Caleb, because he has a different spirit and has followed me wholeheartedly, I will bring into the land into which he went, and his descendants shall possess it. [25]Now, since the Amalekites and the Canaanites live in the valleys, turn tomorrow and set out for the wilderness by the way to the Red Sea."[z]

26 And the LORD spoke to Moses and to Aaron, saying, [27]"How long shall this wicked congregation complain against me? I have heard the complaints of the Israelites, which they complain against me. [28]Say to them, 'As I live,' says the LORD, 'I will do to you the very things I heard you say: [29]your dead bodies shall fall in this very wilderness, and of all your number included in the census from twenty years old and up who have complained against me, [30]not one of you shall come into the land in which I swore to settle you, except Caleb son of Jephunneh and Joshua son of Nun. [31]But your little ones, who you said would become plunder, I will bring in, and they shall know the land that you have

z 14.25 Or Sea of Reeds

on their faces before (showing deference to a superior) the assembled Israelite community. In a larger context, it may suggest their preparation for God's imminent appearance (v. 10b). Joshua and Caleb [tear] their clothes (a mark of distress), restate the land's fertility, and reconstitute Israel as victors who will devour the spoils. **14:10b-35** God's first response (vv. 10b-12) highlights Israel's actions (despise, refuse to believe) while stating God's punishments comprehensively. Moses's intercession on behalf of Israel (vv. 13-19) is based on the reputation of God's power in the world, unique relationship with Israel, special character (Exod. 34:6-7), and legacy of forgiveness. Persuaded by Moses, God modifies the initial punishment. Essentially, God punishes Israel with what they asked for: granting their desire for death in the wilderness (vv. 2 // 32-33) and actualizing their false perception of God's intention (vv. 3a, 29), their claim about the fate of their children (vv. 3b, 33), and their rejection of going into the promised land (vv. 3c, 22-23). Yet God does not abandon them completely. They will remain as God's own inheritance, and their children whom they thought

despised. ³²But as for you, your dead bodies shall fall in this wilderness. ³³And your children shall be shepherds in the wilderness for forty years and shall suffer for your faithlessness, until the last of your dead bodies lies in the wilderness. ³⁴According to the number of the days in which you spied out the land, forty days, for every day a year, you shall bear your iniquity, forty years, and you shall know my displeasure.' ³⁵I the LORD have spoken; surely I will do thus to all this wicked congregation gathered together against me: in this wilderness they shall come to a full end, and there they shall die."

36 And the men whom Moses sent to spy out the land who returned and made all the congregation complain against him by bringing a bad report about the land, ³⁷the men who brought an unfavorable report about the land died by a plague before the LORD. ³⁸But Joshua son of Nun and Caleb son of Jephunneh alone remained alive, of those men who went to spy out the land.

39 When Moses told these words to all the Israelites, the people mourned greatly. ⁴⁰They rose early in the morning and went up to the heights of the hill country, saying, "Here we are. We will go up to the place that the LORD has promised, for we have sinned." ⁴¹But Moses said, "Why do you continue to transgress the command of the LORD? That will not succeed. ⁴²Do not go up, for the LORD is not with you; do not let yourselves be struck down before your enemies. ⁴³For the Amalekites and the Canaanites will confront

you there, and you shall fall by the sword; because you have turned back from following the LORD, the LORD will not be with you." ⁴⁴But they presumed to go up to the heights of the hill country, even though the ark of the covenant of the LORD and Moses had not left the camp. ⁴⁵Then the Amalekites and the Canaanites who lived in that hill country came down and defeated them, pursuing them as far as Hormah.

15 The LORD spoke to Moses, saying, ²"Speak to the Israelites and say to them: When you come into the land you are to inhabit, which I am giving you, ³and you make an offering by fire*a* to the LORD from the herd or from the flock—whether a burnt offering or a sacrifice, to fulfill a vow or as a freewill offering or at your appointed festivals—to make a pleasing odor for the LORD, ⁴then whoever presents such an offering to the LORD shall present also a grain offering, one-tenth of an ephah of choice flour, mixed with one-fourth of a hin of oil. ⁵Moreover, you shall offer one-fourth of a hin of wine as a drink offering with the burnt offering or the sacrifice, for each lamb. ⁶For a ram, you shall offer a grain offering, two-tenths of an ephah of choice flour mixed with one-third of a hin of oil, ⁷and as a drink offering you shall offer one-third of a hin of wine, a pleasing odor to the LORD. ⁸When you offer a bull as a burnt offering or a sacrifice,

a 15.3 Or *a gift*

would become *plunder* will enter the land that they *despised* (v. 31). **14:36–45** God's punishment for the chosen scouts is realized immediately. Others attempt to conquer the land from the south (vv. 44–45), disobeying God's direct command, *set[ting] out for the wilderness by the way to the Red Sea* (v. 25b). They recklessly march against the Amalekites and the Canaanites without Moses and the ark, ignoring the prescribed campaign order (2:3–34; 10:33–35). The result is their complete defeat all the way to Hormah (meaning "utter destruction"). The city reappears in 21:1–3, where the new generation utterly destroys the Canaanites.

15:1–19:22 Cultic regulations and Aaron's priestly leadership. Five regulations, related to Israel's life in the promised land, function to reaffirm the validity of God's land promise even if Israel forfeited it by their failure to enter from the south. The Levites and leaders' rebellion, located in the middle of these regulations, serves to illustrate their shared fate with the entire exodus generation. By affirming the special status of the Aaronide priests, God desires to protect the people from the danger incurred by polluting God's holiness. God's continual presence in the camp and the land is imperative for Israel's well-being.

15:1–16 As part of their future life, the Israelites are to accompany the grain and drink offerings with animal sacrifices (Lev. 1–2). The quantity of these offerings increases with the size of the animal (from lamb, to ram, to bull). An *ephah* is approximately twenty-two liters and a *hin* about 3.6 liters. Unlike the Passover (Exod. 12:48), both *native Israelite* and *resident alien* will perform these offerings, suggesting that the latter is given equal status before God.

to fulfill a vow or as an offering of well-being to the LORD, [9]then you shall present with the bull a grain offering, three-tenths of an ephah of choice flour, mixed with half a hin of oil, [10]and you shall present as a drink offering half a hin of wine, as an offering by fire,[b] a pleasing odor to the LORD.

[11]"Thus it shall be done for each ox or ram or for each of the male lambs or the kids. [12]According to the number that you offer, so you shall do with each and every one. [13]Every native Israelite shall do these things in this way, in presenting an offering by fire,[c] a pleasing odor to the LORD. [14]An alien who lives with you or who takes up permanent residence among you and wishes to offer an offering by fire,[d] a pleasing odor to the LORD, shall do as you do. [15]As for the assembly, there shall be for both you and the resident alien a single statute, a perpetual statute throughout your generations; you and the alien shall be alike before the LORD. [16]You and the alien who resides with you shall have the same law and the same ordinance."

[17] The LORD spoke to Moses, saying, [18]"Speak to the Israelites and say to them: After you come into the land to which I am bringing you, [19]whenever you eat of the bread of the land you shall present a donation to the LORD. [20]From your first batch of dough you shall present a loaf as a donation; you shall present it just as you present a donation from the threshing floor. [21]Throughout your generations you shall give to the LORD a donation from the first of your batch of dough.

[22]"But if you unintentionally fail to observe all these commandments that the LORD has spoken to Moses—[23]everything that the LORD has commanded you by Moses, from the day the LORD gave commandment and thereafter, throughout your generations—[24]then if it was done unintentionally without the knowledge[e] of the congregation, the whole congregation shall offer one young bull for a burnt offering, a pleasing odor to the LORD, together with its grain offering and its drink offering, according to the ordinance, and one male goat for a purification offering. [25]The priest shall make atonement for all the congregation of the Israelites, and they shall be forgiven; it was unintentional, and they have brought their offering, an offering by fire[f] to the LORD, and their purification offering before the LORD, for their error. [26]All the congregation of the Israelites shall be forgiven, as well as the aliens residing among you, because the whole people was involved in the error.

[27]"An individual who sins unintentionally shall present a female goat a year old for a purification offering. [28]And the priest shall make atonement before the LORD for the one who commits an error, when it is unintentional, to make atonement for the person, who then shall be forgiven. [29]For both the native among the Israelites and the alien residing among you, you shall have the same law for anyone who acts in error. [30]But whoever acts high-handedly, whether native-born or an alien, affronts the LORD and shall be cut off from among the people. [31]Because of having despised the word of the LORD and broken his commandment, such a person shall be utterly cut off and bear the guilt."

[32] When the Israelites were in the wilderness, they found a man gathering sticks on the Sabbath day. [33]Those who found him gathering sticks brought him to Moses, Aaron, and

b 15.10 Or a gift c 15.13 Or a gift d 15.14 Or a gift
e 15.24 Heb far from the eyes f 15.25 Or a gift

15:17–31 This regulation combines two seemingly distinct issues together: a donation of the first bread and purification offerings (Lev. 4–5). *From your first batch of dough:* the "first" refers to the best quality as well as the first in the sequence of baking (cf. Lev. 23:9–14). Different from Lev. 4–5, the regulations of purification offerings speak of sins of omission (a failure to perform God's commandments), include resident immigrants, mention the grain and drink offerings accompanying animal offerings, and firmly condemn those who sin intentionally against God. In Lev. 5:1–6, even intentional sins can be forgiven with a public confession. But here, anyone, native or resident immigrant, shall be cut off from the community if they sin intentionally.

15:32–36 This is an example of intentionally committed sin. Regardless of the purpose for the wood, the text stresses his intentional action on the Sabbath day, which amounts to breaking the Sabbath (Exod. 31:14–15; 35:2) and is punishable by death. The procedure moves quickly from defining the case, to arresting and detaining the offender, to the community's execution of God's verdict. It underscores the severity of the case and the punishment for intentionally violating the Sabbath or any other cultic ordinance (cf. Lev. 24:10–16).

NUMBERS 16

the whole congregation. ³⁴They put him in custody because it was not clear what should be done to him. ³⁵Then the LORD said to Moses, "The man shall be put to death; all the congregation shall stone him outside the camp." ³⁶The whole congregation brought him outside the camp and stoned him to death, just as the LORD had commanded Moses.

37 The LORD said to Moses, ³⁸"Speak to the Israelites, and tell them to make fringes on the corners of their garments throughout their generations and to put a blue cord on the fringe at each corner. ³⁹You have the fringe so that, when you see it, you will remember all the commandments of the LORD and do them and not follow the lust of your own heart and your own eyes. ⁴⁰So you shall remember and do all my commandments, and you shall be holy to your God. ⁴¹I am the LORD your God who brought you out of the land of Egypt to be your God: I am the LORD your God."

16 Now Korah son of Izhar son of Kohath son of Levi, along with Dathan and Abiram sons of Eliab, and On son of Peleth son^g of Reuben, took ²two hundred fifty Israelite men, leaders of the congregation, chosen from the assembly, well-known men, and they confronted Moses. ³They assembled against Moses and against Aaron and said to them, "You have gone too far! All the congregation are holy, every one of them, and the LORD is among them. So why then do you exalt yourselves above the assembly of the LORD?" ⁴When Moses heard it, he fell

on his face. ⁵Then he spoke to Korah and all his congregation, saying, "In the morning the LORD will make known who is his and who is holy and who will be allowed to approach him; the one whom he will choose he will allow to approach him. ⁶Do this: take censers, Korah and all your^b congregation, ⁷and tomorrow put fire in them, and lay incense on them before the LORD, and the man whom the LORD chooses shall be the holy one. You Levites have gone too far!" ⁸Then Moses said to Korah, "Hear now, you Levites! ⁹Is it too little for you that the God of Israel has separated you from the congregation of Israel to allow you to approach him in order to perform the duties of the LORD's tabernacle and to stand before the congregation and serve them? ¹⁰He has allowed you to approach him, and all your brother Levites with you, yet you seek the priesthood as well! ¹¹Therefore you and all your congregation have gathered together against the LORD. What is Aaron that you rail against him?"

12 Moses sent for Dathan and Abiram sons of Eliab, but they said, "We will not come! ¹³Is it too little that you have brought us up out of a land flowing with milk and honey to kill us in the wilderness, that you must also lord it over us? ¹⁴It is clear you have not brought us into a land flowing with milk and honey or given us an inheritance of fields and vineyards. Would you put out the eyes of these men? We will not come!"

g 16.1 Heb mss Sam Q ms Gk: Heb *descendants*   h 16.6 Heb *his*

15:37–41 By affixing blue cords onto their clothing fringes, the Israelites remember and keep God's commandments (Deut. 22:12) and identify themselves as being holy to God. Holiness is an intrinsic quality of God, demonstrated by liberating Israel from Egyptian bondage. As God is holy, Israel is called to be holy (Exod. 19:6; Lev. 19:2) and show their holiness by observing all God's commandments.
16:1–50 Five rebellion stories—Korah and the Levites vs. Aaron (vv. 8–11); Dathan and Abiram vs. Moses (vv. 12–15, 24–34); Korah and the leaders vs. Aaron (vv. 16–18); Korah and the whole congregation vs. Moses and Aaron (vv. 16–23); the whole congregation vs. Moses and Aaron (vv. 41–50)—are combined with the dominant figure, Korah. They deal with Moses's authority to lead the people and the legitimacy of the Aaronide priesthood. 16:1–3 This summarizes the essence of all five rebellions. *Korah* belonged to the Kohathites, a group of Levites responsible for the most holy things (4:4); *Dathan, Abiram,* and *On* are members of the tribe of Reuben, prominent among the twelve tribes as the first son of Jacob; *two hundred fifty men* have been chosen by the community to provide advice or counsel. These three groups argue that Moses and Aaron have no special privileges for the priesthood and no prerogatives for leadership in everyday affairs, since the Israelites, collectively as well as individually, are holy (15:40; Exod. 19:6). 16:4–19a This reports Moses's inadequate response. Rather than waiting for God's instructions (*fell on his face,* v. 4; see also vv. 22, 45b), Moses proposes a test, offering incense before God, based on the argument that God's separation of the Levites ensures an honorable vocation of serving the tabernacle but does not entail privilege. Asking for

HEBREW BIBLE | 213

15 Moses was very angry and said to the LORD, "Pay no attention to their offering. I have not taken one donkey from them, and I have not harmed any one of them." 16And Moses said to Korah, "As for you and all your congregation, be present tomorrow before the LORD, you and they and Aaron, 17and let each one of you take his censer and put incense on it and each one of you present his censer before the LORD, two hundred fifty censers, you also, and Aaron, each his censer." 18So each man took his censer, and they put fire in the censers and laid incense on them, and they stood at the entrance of the tent of meeting with Moses and Aaron. 19Then Korah assembled the whole congregation against them at the entrance of the tent of meeting. And the glory of the LORD appeared to the whole congregation.

20 Then the LORD spoke to Moses and to Aaron, saying, 21"Separate yourselves from this congregation, so that I may consume them in a moment." 22They fell on their faces and said, "O God, the God of the spirits of all flesh, shall one person sin and you become angry with the whole congregation?"

23 And the LORD spoke to Moses: 24"Speak to the congregation, saying: Get away from the dwellings of Korah, Dathan, and Abiram." 25So Moses got up and went to Dathan and Abiram; the elders of Israel followed him. 26He spoke to the congregation, saying, "Turn away from the tents of these wicked men and touch nothing of theirs, or you will be swept away for all their sins." 27So they got away from the dwellings of Korah, Dathan, and Abiram, and Dathan and Abiram came out and stood at the entrances of their tents,

together with their wives, their children, and their little ones. 28And Moses said, "This is how you shall know that the LORD has sent me to do all these works; it has not been of my own accord: 29If these people die a natural death or if a natural fate comes on them, then the LORD has not sent me. 30But if the LORD creates something new and the ground opens its mouth and swallows them up, with all that belongs to them, and they go down alive into Sheol, then you shall know that these men have despised the LORD."

31 As soon as he finished speaking all these words, the ground under them was split apart. 32The earth opened its mouth and swallowed them up, along with their households—everyone who belonged to Korah and all their goods. 33So they with all that belonged to them went down alive into Sheol; the earth closed over them, and they perished from the midst of the assembly. 34All Israel around them fled at their outcry, for they said, "The earth will swallow us, too!" 35And fire came out from the LORD and consumed the two hundred fifty men offering the incense.

36 ⁱThen the LORD spoke to Moses, saying, 37"Tell Eleazar son of Aaron the priest to take the censers out of the blaze, then scatter the fire far and wide. 38For the censers of these sinners have become holy at the cost of their lives. Make them into hammered plates as a covering for the altar, for they presented them before the LORD and they became holy. Thus they shall be a sign to the Israelites." 39So Eleazar the priest took the bronze censers

i 16.36 17.1 in Heb

more power and prestige is considered rebellion against the one who called (v. 11). But Dathan, Abiram, and On insist on Moses's misappropriation of authority for the entire journey (vv. 12–14) by claiming that Moses has deceived the people by making false promises, creating a hierarchical structure, leading them into the hostile wilderness, and abusing his power. To this attack, Moses reacts with anger (unlike in v. 4) and pleads for God's vindication (*I have not taken one donkey from them*; see 1 Sam. 8:16; 12:3). Moses repeats his proposal to Korah with significant changes, adding Aaron and 250 leaders and specifying the site of the test, the entrance of the meeting tent (vv. 16–19a). This addition indicates the interrelatedness of the sacred and secular aspects of their rebellion. The two are inseparable and need to be resolved by the holy God, not by humans. **16:19b–50** This reports God's responses. God's initial punishment is deadly and immediate, corresponding to their intentional rebellions. With Moses's intercession that such annihilation does not suit the creator of all life, who does not punish the righteous along with the wicked (Gen. 18:23–25; Ezek. 18:4), God modifies the intended punishment to apply only to the households of Korah, Dathan, and Abiram. The punishment creates two problems. The first is about the *censers* (metal trays on which incense is burned) used by the 250 leaders. Once they are offered to God, they become holy (vv. 36–40). The solution is to make them into a covering for the altar; in turn, they serve as a reminder that only

that had been presented by those who were burned, and they were hammered out as a covering for the altar—⁴⁰a reminder to the Israelites that no outsider, who is not of the descendants of Aaron, shall approach to offer incense before the LORD, so as not to become like Korah and his congregation, just as the LORD had said to him through Moses.

41 On the next day, however, the whole congregation of the Israelites rebelled against Moses and against Aaron, saying, "You have killed the people of the LORD." ⁴²And when the congregation had assembled against them, Moses and Aaron turned toward the tent of meeting; the cloud had covered it, and the glory of the LORD appeared. ⁴³Then Moses and Aaron came to the front of the tent of meeting, ⁴⁴and the LORD spoke to Moses, saying, ⁴⁵"Get away from this congregation, so that I may consume them in a moment." And they fell on their faces. ⁴⁶Moses said to Aaron, "Take your censer, put fire on it from the altar and lay incense on it and carry it quickly to the congregation and make atonement for them. For wrath has gone out from the LORD; the plague has begun." ⁴⁷So Aaron took it as Moses had ordered and ran into the middle of the assembly, where the plague had already begun among the people. He put on the incense and made atonement for the people. ⁴⁸He stood between the dead and the living, and the plague was stopped. ⁴⁹Those who died by the plague were fourteen thousand seven hundred, besides those who died in the affair of Korah. ⁵⁰When the plague was stopped, Aaron returned to Moses at the entrance of the tent of meeting.

17 ʲThe LORD spoke to Moses, saying, ²"Speak to the Israelites, and get twelve staffs from them, one for each ancestral house, from all the leaders of their ancestral houses. Write each man's name on his staff, ³and write Aaron's name on the staff of Levi. For there shall be one staff for the head of each ancestral house. ⁴Place them in the tent of meeting before the covenant, where I meet with you. ⁵And the staff of the man whom I choose shall sprout; thus I will put a stop to the complaints of the Israelites that they continually make against you." ⁶Moses spoke to the Israelites, and all their leaders gave him staffs, one for each leader, according to their ancestral houses, twelve staffs; and the staff of Aaron was among theirs. ⁷So Moses placed the staffs before the LORD in the tent of the covenant.

8 When Moses went into the tent of the covenant on the next day, the staff of Aaron for the house of Levi had sprouted. It put forth buds, produced blossoms, and bore ripe almonds. ⁹Then Moses brought out all the staffs from before the LORD to all the Israelites, and they looked, and each man took his staff. ¹⁰And the LORD said to Moses, "Put back the staff of Aaron before the covenant, to be kept as a warning to rebels, so that you may make an end of their complaints against me, or else they will die." ¹¹Moses did so; just as the LORD commanded him, so he did.

12 The Israelites said to Moses, "We are perishing; we are lost; all of us are lost! ¹³Everyone who approaches the tabernacle of the LORD will die. Are we all to perish?"

ʲ 17.1 17.16 in Heb

Aaronide priests are allowed to approach God to burn incense (v. 40). The unqualified incense is transformed to solidify the unique prerogative of the priests. The second is how to deal with the fear of the whole congregation (vv. 34, 41–50). The solution is through Aaron's intercessory role. After hearing God's same reaction (vv. 21, 45), Moses delegates his intercessory role to Aaron, whose incense offering is ultimately successful in stopping the plague, but only after the deaths of 14,700 people. The Aaronide priests play a special role as they stand *between the dead and the living* (v. 48) to seek reconciliation for the people.

17:1–13 Aaron's budding staff answers the questions prompted by God's acceptance of the 250 leaders' censers as holy in the previous story (16:38)—the Levites are set apart from the people. Neither Aaron's priestly prerogative nor his distinction from the Levites is mentioned. Instead, Aaron's name is *on the staff of Levi* and his staff is *for the house of Levi*. His staff is put to the same test along with the twelve staffs (representing the twelve tribes). Only Aaron's rod has grown overnight, blossomed, and produced almonds, revealing the Levites' life-enhancing role amid the people. The deposit of the budding staff *before the LORD in the tent of the covenant* signifies the privilege of the Levites vis-à-vis other tribes; stops the Israelites from continually complaining against Moses, Aaron, and God (vv. 5, 10); and warns of God's punishment of rebellious people.

18 The Lord said to Aaron, "You and your sons and your ancestral house with you shall bear responsibility for offenses connected with the sanctuary, while you and your sons alone shall bear responsibility for offenses connected with the priesthood. ²So bring with you also your brothers of the tribe of Levi, your ancestral tribe, in order that they may be joined to you and serve you while you and your sons with you are in front of the tent of the covenant. ³They shall perform duties for you and for the whole tent. But they must not approach either the utensils of the sanctuary or the altar, or else both they and you will die. ⁴They are attached to you in order to perform the duties of the tent of meeting, for all the service of the tent; no outsider shall approach you. ⁵You yourselves shall perform the duties of the sanctuary and the duties of the altar, so that wrath may never again come upon the Israelites. ⁶It is I who now take your brother Levites from among the Israelites; they are now yours as a gift, dedicated to the Lord, to perform the service of the tent of meeting. ⁷But you and your sons with you shall diligently perform your priestly duties in all that concerns the altar and the area behind the curtain. I give your priesthood as a gift;ᵏ any outsider who approaches shall be put to death."

8 The Lord spoke to Aaron, "I have given you charge of the offerings made to me, all the holy gifts of the Israelites; I have given them to you and your sons as a priestly portion due you in perpetuity. ⁹This shall be yours from the most holy things, reserved from the fire: every offering of theirs that they render to me as a most holy thing, whether grain offering, purification offering, or guilt offering, shall belong to you and your sons. ¹⁰As a most holy thing you shall eat it; every male may eat it; it shall be holy to you. ¹¹This also is yours: I have given to you, together with your sons and daughters, as a perpetual due, whatever is set aside from the gifts of all the elevation offerings of the Israelites; everyone who is clean in your house may eat them. ¹²All the best of the oil and all the best of the wine and of the grain, the choice produce that they give to the Lord, I have given to you. ¹³The first fruits of all that is in their land that they bring to the Lord shall be yours; everyone who is clean in your house may eat of it. ¹⁴Every devoted thing in Israel shall be yours. ¹⁵The first issue of the womb of all creatures, human and animal, that is offered to the Lord shall be yours, but the firstborn of human beings you shall redeem, and the firstborn of unclean animals you shall redeem. ¹⁶Their redemption price, reckoned from one month of age, you shall fix at five shekels of silver, according to the shekel of the sanctuary (that is, twenty gerahs). ¹⁷But the firstborn of a cow or the firstborn of a sheep or the firstborn of a goat you shall not redeem; they are holy. You shall dash their blood on the altar and turn their fat into smoke as an offering by fireˡ for a pleasing odor to the Lord, ¹⁸but their flesh shall be yours, just as the breast that is elevated and as the right thigh are yours. ¹⁹All the holy offerings that the Israelites present to the Lord I have given to you, together with your sons and daughters, as a perpetual due; it is a covenant of salt forever before the Lord for you and your descendants as well." ²⁰Then the Lord said to Aaron, "You shall have no

k 18.7 Heb *as a service of gift*   l 18.17 Or *a gift*

18:1–32 In response to the people's cry (17:12-13), the Aaronide priests and other Levites must guard the sanctuary and take the blame for any encroachment on it. The result is that the people may continue to worship God without risking their lives. In return, the people compensate priests and Levites for their service. The priests have higher status and a potentially more fatal responsibility in protecting the sanctuary than the Levites; thus, their rewards are greater. 18:1–24 The three divine speeches to Aaron alone are rare occurrences (Lev. 10:8). The first (Num. 18:1-7) is to define the priests' duties as bearing the consequences (divine punishment of death) for defiling the sanctuary. The priests receive the Levites as a gift who serve them before the tent of covenant, perform all the physical labor related to the tent, and guard the sanctuary from trespassing (1:50-53; 3:5-10; 4:1-33; 8:14-19). The second (vv. 8-19) is to determine the priests' compensations: from the most holy offerings ("grain," Lev. 2; "purification," Lev. 4; "guilt offering," Lev. 5-6; only eaten by "every male"), the holy offerings (eaten by ritually clean members of the priests' families), and the ransom price for firstborns unfit for sacrifice and the meat of firstborn animals fit for sacrifice. The third (vv. 20-24) extends their compensation in terms of inheritance. Instead of their own territory, they receive YHWH as an inheritance. The Levites receive a tithe from the people and forty-eight cities to

allotment in their land, nor shall you have any share among them; I am your share and your possession among the Israelites.

21 "To the Levites I have given every tithe in Israel for a possession in return for the service that they perform, the service in the tent of meeting. ²²From now on the Israelites shall no longer approach the tent of meeting, or else they will incur guilt and die. ²³But the Levites shall perform the service of the tent of meeting, and they shall bear responsibility for their own offenses; it shall be a perpetual statute throughout your generations. But among the Israelites they shall have no allotment, ²⁴because I have given to the Levites as their portion the tithe of the Israelites, which they set apart as an offering to the LORD. Therefore I have said of them that they shall have no allotment among the Israelites."

25 The LORD spoke to Moses, saying, ²⁶"You shall say to the Levites: When you receive from the Israelites the tithe that I have given you from them for your portion, you shall set apart an offering from it to the LORD, a tithe of the tithe. ²⁷It shall be reckoned to you as your gift, the same as the grain of the threshing floor and the fullness of the winepress. ²⁸Thus you also shall set apart an offering to the LORD from all the tithes that you receive from the Israelites, and from them you shall give the LORD's offering to the priest Aaron. ²⁹Out of all the gifts to you, you shall set apart every offering due to the LORD; the best of all of them is the part to be consecrated. ³⁰Say also to them: When you have set apart the best of it, then the rest shall be reckoned to the Levites as produce of the threshing floor and as produce of the winepress. ³¹You may eat it in any place, you and your households,

for it is your payment for your service in the tent of meeting. ³²You shall incur no guilt by reason of it, when you have offered the best of it. But you shall not profane the holy gifts of the Israelites, on pain of death."

19

The LORD spoke to Moses and Aaron, saying, ²"This is a statute of the law that the LORD has commanded: Tell the Israelites to bring you a red heifer without defect, in which there is no blemish and on which no yoke has been laid. ³You shall give it to the priest Eleazar, and it shall be taken outside the camp and slaughtered in his presence. ⁴The priest Eleazar shall take some of its blood with his finger and sprinkle it seven times toward the front of the tent of meeting. ⁵Then the heifer shall be burned in his sight; its skin, its flesh, and its blood, with its entrails,ᵐ shall be burned. ⁶The priest shall take cedarwood, hyssop, and crimson material and throw them into the fire in which the heifer is burning. ⁷Then the priest shall wash his clothes and bathe his body in water, and afterward he may come into the camp, but the priest shall remain unclean until evening. ⁸The one who burns the heiferⁿ shall wash his clothes in water and bathe his body in water; he shall remain unclean until evening. ⁹Then someone who is clean shall gather up the ashes of the heifer and deposit them outside the camp in a clean place, and they shall be kept for the congregation of the Israelites for the water for cleansing. It is a purification offering. ¹⁰The one who gathers the ashes of the heifer shall wash his clothes and be unclean until evening.

m 19.5 Or *dung*   n 19.8 Heb *it*

live in for their service (35:1–8). *Tithe* is a form of taxation to support the king (1 Sam. 8:15–17) and the temple (Lev. 27:30–33; Deut. 12:6–18; 14:22–29; 26:12–15). **18:25–32** The Levites are obligated to bring a tenth of what they receive to God as a gift offering (*a tithe of the tithe*) and give it to the priests. It must be *the best of all of them*, as the Israelites' tithes were to be the best, and it is *to be consecrated*, since it is dedicated to the priests. The rest shall no longer be holy but become ordinary, like the produce of the land, and be considered wages for their work. This they can consume anywhere and will not be punished for doing so outside the sacred precincts.

19:1–22 The ideas—contact with a corpse makes a person ritually unclean, contagious to others in the camp, and ultimately dangerous to the sanctuary—are well established (Lev. 5:2; 11:8, 24–25; 21:1-4, 11; Num. 5:2; 6:6–12; 9:6–7, 10–11). This chapter provides instructions for cleansing those contaminated by touching the corpse through *the water for cleansing*. **19:1–10** This subsection details how to make the water. *The priest Eleazar*, Aaron's son, is chosen for the procedure either to prevent the high priest from dealing with a dead body (Lev. 21:11) or to underscore the regulation's perpetuity (Num. 19:10, 21). A *red* (symbolic of blood; hence ensuring the efficacy of the rite) heifer *on which no yoke has been laid* (never been used for physical work, Deut. 21:3) is slaughtered

"This shall be a perpetual statute for the Israelites and for the alien residing among them. ¹¹Those who touch the dead body of any human being shall be unclean seven days. ¹²They shall purify themselves with the water on the third day and on the seventh day and so be clean, but if they do not purify themselves on the third day and on the seventh day, they will not become clean. ¹³All who touch a corpse, the body of a human being who has died, and do not purify themselves defile the tabernacle of the LORD; such persons shall be cut off from Israel. Since water for cleansing was not dashed on them, they remain unclean; their uncleanness is still on them.

14 "This is the law when someone dies in a tent: everyone who comes into the tent and everyone who is in the tent shall be unclean seven days. ¹⁵And every open vessel with no cover fastened on it is unclean. ¹⁶Whoever in the open field touches one who has been killed by a sword or who has died naturally,° or a human bone, or a grave shall be unclean seven days. ¹⁷For the unclean they shall take some ashes of the burnt purification offering, and running water shall be added in a vessel; ¹⁸then a clean person shall take hyssop, dip it in the water, and sprinkle it on the tent, on all the furnishings, on the persons who were there, and on whoever touched

the bone, the slain, the corpse, or the grave. ¹⁹The clean person shall sprinkle the unclean ones on the third day and on the seventh day, thus purifying them on the seventh day. Then they shall wash their clothes and bathe themselves in water, and at evening they shall be clean. ²⁰Any who are unclean but do not purify themselves, those persons shall be cut off from the assembly, for they have defiled the sanctuary of the LORD. Since the water for cleansing has not been dashed on them, they are unclean.

21 "It shall be a perpetual statute for them. The one who sprinkles the water for cleansing shall wash his clothes, and whoever touches the water for cleansing shall be unclean until evening. ²²Whatever the unclean person touches shall be unclean, and anyone who touches it shall be unclean until evening."

20 The Israelites, the whole congregation, came into the wilderness of Zin in the first month, and the people stayed in Kadesh. Miriam died there and was buried there.

2 Now there was no water for the congregation, so they gathered together against Moses and against Aaron. ³The people quarreled with Moses and said, "Would that we

o 19.16 Heb lacks *naturally*

outside the camp (due to the danger of contamination by the uncleanness transferred to the heifer). *[Sprinkling the blood] seven times toward the front of the tent of meeting* is like the practice of the purification offering (Lev. 4:6, 17; 16:14–15; 17:6; Num. 8:7) but with a different location (not before the veil). *Blood* is the primary agent for purification, and burning it achieves the continuation of its cleansing power in the ashes. All participants (the priest, the one burning the heifer, and the one gathering the ashes) become impure in carrying out the preparation; thus, they need to be purified before entering the camp. **19:11–22** This subsection consists of two parts. The first (vv. 11–16) is to illustrate the circumstances calling for the use of *the water for cleansing* including persons coming into contact with a corpse, whether by actual touch or related objects, and any objects in a closed space. Their uncleanness has the fatal consequence of defiling the sanctuary. The second (vv. 17–22) is to provide practical steps for purifying the contaminated persons or objects. Instead of the priest that was heavily involved in the preparation of the water, *a clean person* administers it twice, on the third and seventh days. That the person who touches the water *will be unclean until evening* seems paradoxical, since the water of purification cleanses the unclean person. Perhaps, this is intended to avoid bestowing magical power on the water itself. Even if the water is prepared flawlessly (everything is burned by fire under the supervision of a priest) and handled by a clean person, it does not have inherent purifying power. Only God cleanses the unclean. The frequent occurrence of "law" (vv. 2a, 14a) and "perpetual statute" (vv. 10b, 21a), along with the warning of defiling God's sanctuary (vv. 13, 20), stresses this point.

20:1–29 Three events, occurring at the fortieth year of Israel's journey in the wilderness, accentuate the end of the exodus generation. **20:1–13** God denies Moses's and Aaron's leadership for their unfaithful reaction to Israel's complaint about the lack of water. **20:1–8** Miriam died and was buried at *Kadesh* (the same place where the spies returned, 13:26) *in the first month* of the fortieth

had died when our kindred died before the LORD! ⁴Why have you brought the assembly of the LORD into this wilderness for us and our livestock to die here? ⁵Why have you brought us up out of Egypt to bring us to this wretched place? It is no place for grain or figs or vines or pomegranates, and there is no water to drink." ⁶Then Moses and Aaron went away from the assembly to the entrance of the tent of meeting; they fell on their faces, and the glory of the LORD appeared to them. ⁷The LORD spoke to Moses, saying, ⁸"Take the staff, and assemble the congregation, you and your brother Aaron, and command the rock before their eyes to yield its water. Thus you shall bring water out of the rock for them; thus you shall provide drink for the congregation and their livestock."

9 So Moses took the staff from before the LORD, as he had commanded him. ¹⁰Moses and Aaron gathered the assembly together before the rock, and he said to them, "Listen, you rebels; shall we bring water for you out of this rock?" ¹¹Then Moses lifted up his hand and struck the rock twice with his staff; water came out abundantly, and the congregation and their livestock drank. ¹²But the LORD said to Moses and Aaron, "Because you did not trust in me, to show my holiness before the eyes of the Israelites, therefore you shall not bring this assembly into the land that I have

given them." ¹³These are the waters of Meri-bah,ᵖ where the Israelites quarreled with the LORD and through which he showed himself to be holy.

14 Moses sent messengers from Kadesh to the king of Edom, "Thus says your brother Israel: You know all the adversity that has befallen us, ¹⁵how our ancestors went down to Egypt, and we lived in Egypt a long time, and the Egyptians oppressed us and our ancestors, ¹⁶and when we cried to the LORD, he heard our voice and sent an angel and brought us out of Egypt, and here we are in Kadesh, a town on the edge of your territory. ¹⁷Now let us pass through your land. We will not pass through field or vineyard or drink water from any well; we will go along the King's Highway, not turning aside to the right hand or to the left until we have passed through your territory."

18 But Edom said to him, "You shall not pass through, or we will come out with the sword against you." ¹⁹The Israelites said to him, "We will stay on the highway, and if we drink of your water, we and our livestock, then we will pay for it. It is only a small matter; just let us pass through on foot." ²⁰But he said, "You shall not pass through." And Edom came out against them with a large force, heavily armed. ²¹Thus Edom refused to give

ᵖ 20.13 That is, *quarrel*

year of their journey (33:38). The Israelites' complaint about the lack of water is understandable (cf. Exod. 17:1–7). *There was no water* bookends their quarrel. To address this, God appears to Moses and Aaron and provides step-by-step instructions for water: *take the staff* (Aaron's budding staff placed in the tabernacle to calm the rebels, Num. 17:10), *assemble the congregation . . . command the rock* to produce water. No evidence of God's anger is reported, in contrast to the previous rebellion stories (11:1, 20, 33; 12:9; 14:11–12; 16:46). **20:9–11** Moses speaks not to the rock but to the people, calling them *rebels* (cf. 20:24; 27:14; God uses the same word to denote Moses's and Aaron's transgression). He strikes the rock twice with his own rod (v. 11a). *Shall we bring water for you out of this rock?* sounds distrustful (Why on earth is God asking us to produce water for people who do not deserve it?) rather than discrediting of God for producing water, since God says "you shall bring water" (v. 8). Inexact obedience is the same as disobedience. Despite their negative responses, God provides water for the congregation and their animals. **20:12** God charges Moses and Aaron with *not [trusting]* in God (the same as God's charge against the people in the spy story, 14:11) *to show [God's] holiness* (denoting their misrepresenting God's intention to provide). They commit the same sin as the exodus generation in chaps. 13–14. Now they share their same fate of not entering the promised land. **20:14–21** After Israel's failure to enter Canaan from the south (14:39–45), Moses attempts to pass through Edom, the best route from the east. His initial request is based on family relationships, beliefs, and customary practice: *your brother*, referring to Edom's relationship to Jacob (Gen. 25:24–26); *how our ancestors*, stressing the shared history of bondage, freedom, and divine guidance (cf. Deut. 26:5–8); *the King's Highway*, an ancient north-south roadway on the east side of the Jordan River, implying a well-tread, wide, and guarded road that any larger group could travel without difficulty. In response to Edom's refusal, Moses modifies his request with economic (*if we drink of your water . . . we will pay for it*) and nonmilitary (*just let us pass through on foot*)

Israel passage through their territory, so Israel turned away from them.

22 They set out from Kadesh, and the Israelites, the whole congregation, came to Mount Hor. ²³Then the LORD said to Moses and Aaron at Mount Hor, on the border of the land of Edom, ²⁴"Let Aaron be gathered to his people. For he shall not enter the land that I have given to the Israelites, because you rebelled against my command at the waters of Meribah. ²⁵Take Aaron and his son Eleazar, and bring them up Mount Hor; ²⁶strip Aaron of his vestments, and put them on his son Eleazar. But Aaron shall be gathered to his people^q and shall die there." ²⁷Moses did as the LORD had commanded; they went up Mount Hor in the sight of the whole congregation. ²⁸Moses stripped Aaron of his vestments and put them on his son Eleazar, and Aaron died there on the top of the mountain. Moses and Eleazar came down from the mountain. ²⁹When all the congregation saw that Aaron had died, all the house of Israel mourned for Aaron thirty days.

21 When the Canaanite, the king of Arad, who lived in the Negeb, heard that Israel was coming by the way of Atharim, he fought against Israel and took some of them captive. ²Then Israel made a vow to the LORD and said, "If you will indeed give this people into our hands, then we will utterly destroy their towns." ³The LORD listened to the voice of Israel and handed over the Canaanites, and they utterly destroyed them and their towns; so the place was called Hormah.^r

4 From Mount Hor they set out by the way to the Red Sea,^s to go around the land of Edom, but the people became discouraged on the way. ⁵The people spoke against God and against Moses, "Why have you brought us up out of Egypt to die in the wilderness? For there is no food and no water, and we detest this miserable food." ⁶Then the LORD sent poisonous^t serpents among the people, and they bit the people, so that many Israelites died. ⁷The people came to Moses and said, "We have sinned by speaking

q 20.26 Heb lacks *to his people*   r 21.3 That is, *destruction*
s 21.4 Or *Sea of Reeds*   t 21.6 Or *fiery*

considerations. Moses's requests were met twice with not only a short, direct, firm statement of refusal but also a show of force (Num. 20:20), fulfilling Edom's threat (v. 18). Israel is forced to turn away from Edom and find another route to Canaan. Moses's failure exemplifies God's denial of his leadership (v. 12), as Moses does not follow God's instruction, as he "set out for the wilderness by the way to the Red Sea" (14:25). **20:22–29** Aaron died at *Mount Hor* (location unknown, 33:38; Deut. 32:50; cf. Moserah in Deut. 10:6) because he *rebelled* against God's command *at the waters of Meribah* (Num. 20:9–11). *Gathered to his people* is a figure of speech referring to death (Abraham [Gen. 25:8], Isaac [Gen. 35:29], Jacob [Gen. 49:33], and Moses [Num. 27:13; Deut. 32:50]). *Thirty days* for mourning exceeds the customary seven days (Gen. 50:10; 1 Sam. 31:13), reflecting Aaron's status. Putting Aaron's vestments (Exod. 28; Lev. 8:7–8) on his son Eleazar indicates the transfer of the priestly office (Exod. 29:29–30). Aaron's death, together with Miriam's death (Num. 20:1) and the deaths of Korah (Levites) and the 250 leaders (16:31–50), hints at the end of the generation who left Egypt (14:26–35).

21:1–25:18 The beginning of the new generation. With God's approval, Israel utterly destroys the Canaanites, signaling a turning point for the new generation. After this initial victory, they are portrayed ambivalently. Unlike the exodus generation, they confidently carry out God's plan for the land promise (21:21–35); yet they behave like the exodus generation by complaining of hardships (21:4–9) and worshiping other gods (25:1–18). But God uses Balaam, the foreign diviner, to bless them unknowingly (22:1–24:25). God intends to fulfill the land promise not because of the obedience/disobedience of the new/old generation but because of God's own faithfulness to the promise.

21:1–3 After initial defeat by the Canaanite king of *Arad* (south of Hebron), Israel makes a vow to *destroy* the enemy *utterly* (a technical term for sacred warfare, totally destroying the enemy and dedicating their lives and spoils to God, Deut. 7:1–2; Josh. 6:17). God approves their vow, and they utterly destroy the Canaanites. See **"The Divine Mandate to Exterminate the Canaanites," p. 313**. *Hormah*, derived from the Hebrew word for "complete destruction," is the same place where the exodus generation were defeated completely at their campaign's beginning (Num. 14:45). As God gives the Canaanites to Israel, this victory signals an appropriate beginning of the new generation.

21:4–9 The story depicts the new generation's rebellious attitude. They begin the journey by obeying God's command, *set[ting] out . . . by the way to the Red Sea* (14:25b). But shortly, they behave like the old generation by accusing *God* and Moses of the exodus and hardships in the wilderness, common elements in earlier rebellion stories (Exod. 17:2–3; Num. 11:4–35; 16:13–14; 20:4–5).

Making Connections: The Bronze Serpent (Numbers 21:4–9)

The snake-entwined staff, known as the "rod of Asclepius" (the ancient Greek god of healing in the fourth century BCE), is widely recognized today as a symbol of the health-care community and is notably featured on the flag of the United Nations World Health Organization. Different theories have been proposed for its common use, including the snake's ability to shed its skin as a symbol of regeneration and its association with poison and death as a parallel to the properties of medicine. This staff is strikingly similar to the bronze serpent on a pole that Moses made. This connection raises the question, Is there a role of the serpent in healing?

One explanation of the use of snakes to symbolize healing is that they possess antivenom against their own poison, which can be used to cure a snakebite victim. Or, as snakes are potent symbols of life and death in ancient Near Eastern culture, the serpent in Numbers may be a symbol for YHWH, who holds the power to determine life and death. Another possibility is that the story may reflect the Egyptian practices of "sympathetic magic," creating a symbolic model of an object to remove or destroy the effects of the real object. All these explanations revolve around the bronze serpent becoming a miraculous antidote, one that is progressively venerated in Jerusalem until destroyed by King Hezekiah (2 Kgs. 18:4).

However, the term *serpent* in the Old Testament never carries a positive connotation, nor does it symbolize YHWH or YHWH's power. It leads us to reconsider the whole of YHWH's instructions to Moses—making the serpent, setting it on a pole, and healing the bitten—as simply a sign for the people, lacking in itself any magical power to heal. Ancient Jewish traditions attest to this interpretation: beholding the bronze serpent causes the people to behold God (Philo, *Alleg. Interp.* 2.81) as "a sign of salvation to remind them of the commandments of [God's] law" (Wis. 16:6); a sign of admitting their sin and repentance that results in forgiveness (m. Rosh Hashanah 3:8); and a sign of their faith *in* YHWH, who commanded Moses to make it (Mekilta 2:144). Furthermore, these Jewish midrashic traditions influence the Gospel of John's christocentric use of the image of the elevated serpent as a figure for Jesus's own elevation (John 3:14; cf. 8:28; 12:32).

Won W. Lee

against the LORD and against you; pray to the LORD to take away the serpents from us." So Moses prayed for the people. [8]And the LORD said to Moses, "Make a poisonous*u* serpent, and set it on a pole, and everyone who is bitten shall look at it and live." [9]So Moses made a serpent of bronze and put it upon a pole, and whenever a serpent bit someone, that person would look at the serpent of bronze and live.

[10] The Israelites set out and camped in Oboth. [11]They set out from Oboth and camped at Iye-abarim, in the wilderness bordering Moab toward the sunrise. [12]From there they set out and camped in the Wadi Zered. [13]From there they set out and camped on the other side of the Arnon, in*v* the wilderness that extends from the boundary of the Amorites, for the Arnon is the boundary of Moab, between Moab and the Amorites. [14]Wherefore it is said in the Book of the Wars of the LORD,

"Waheb in Suphah and the wadis.
The Arnon [15]and the slopes of the wadis
that extend to the seat of Ar
and lie along the border of Moab."*w*

u 21.8 Or *fiery*   *v* 21.13 Gk: Heb *which is in*   *w* 21.15 Meaning of Heb uncertain

There is no mention of Moses's initial response, God's appearance, or the provision of water and food. Instead, YHWH punishes them immediately with *poisonous* (or winged burning) *serpents*. Their plea, *take away the serpents from us*, implies that the biting continues even after repentance; the effects of sin linger until God's concrete act of forgiveness is in place. Responding to Moses's intercession, YHWH provides a conditional remedy. *A serpent of bronze* serves only as a symbol to affirm God's healing power. This healing depends on obedience to God's command to *look at the serpent of bronze*. See **"The Bronze Serpent," p. 221**.

21:10–20 Israel journeys from Mount Hor to the top of Pisgah in Moab through nine stations, taking them around Edom and Moab and skirting Amorite territory. The exact locations of these stations are uncertain, and their sequence does not correspond with the itinerary in 33:41–49. *The Book of the Wars of the LORD* may refer to a collection of poems about Israel's warfare (similar to the book of Jashar in Josh. 10:13; 2 Sam. 1:18). The Song of the Well (Num. 21:17–18a) describes what workers would sing while digging a well, highlighting God's provision of water during the wilderness journey.

16 From there they continued to Beer;[x] that is the well of which the Lord said to Moses, "Gather the people together, and I will give them water." [17]Then Israel sang this song:

"Spring up, O well!—Sing to it!—
[18] the well that the leaders sank,
　that the nobles of the people dug,
　with the scepter, with the staff."

From the wilderness to Mattanah, [19]from Mattanah to Nahaliel, from Nahaliel to Ba-moth, [20]and from Bamoth to the valley lying in the region of Moab by the top of Pisgah that overlooks the wasteland.[y]

21 Then Israel sent messengers to King Sihon of the Amorites, saying, [22]"Let me pass through your land; we will not turn aside into field or vineyard; we will not drink the water of any well; we will go by the King's Highway until we have passed through your territory." [23]But Sihon would not allow Israel to pass through his territory. Sihon gathered all his people together and went out against Israel to the wilderness; he came to Jahaz and fought against Israel. [24]Israel put him to the sword and took possession of his land from the Arnon to the Jabbok, as far as to the Ammonites, for the boundary of the Ammonites was strong. [25]Israel took all these towns, and Israel settled in all the towns of the Amorites, in Heshbon, and in all its villages. [26]For Heshbon was the city of King Sihon of the Amorites, who had fought against the former king of Moab and captured all his land as far as the Arnon. [27]Therefore the singers say,

"Come to Heshbon; let it be built;
　let the city of Sihon be established.
[28] For fire came out from Heshbon,
　flame from the city of Sihon.

It devoured Ar of Moab
　and swallowed up[z] the heights of the
　Arnon.
[29] Woe to you, O Moab!
　You are undone, O people of Chemosh!
He has made his sons fugitives
　and his daughters captives
　to an Amorite king, Sihon.
[30] So their posterity perished
　from Heshbon[a] to Dibon,
　and we laid waste until fire spread to
　Medeba."[b]

31 Thus Israel settled in the land of the Amorites. [32]Moses sent to spy out Jazer, and they captured its villages and dispossessed the Amorites who were there.

33 Then they turned and went up the road to Bashan, and King Og of Bashan came out against them, he and all his people, to battle at Edrei. [34]But the Lord said to Moses, "Do not be afraid of him, for I have given him into your hand, with all his people and his land. You shall do to him as you did to King Sihon of the Amorites, who lived in Heshbon." [35]So they killed him, his sons, and all his people, until there was no survivor left, and they took possession of his land.

22 The Israelites set out and camped in the plains of Moab across the Jordan from Jericho. [2]Now Balak son of Zippor saw all that Israel had done to the Amorites. [3]Moab was in great dread of the people, because they were so numerous; Moab was overcome with fear of the Israelites. [4]And

x 21.16 That is, *well*　y 21.20 Or *Jeshimon*　z 21.28 Gk: Heb *and the lords of*　a 21.30 Gk: Heb *we have shot at them; Heshbon has perished*　b 21.30 Compare Sam Gk: Meaning of MT uncertain

21:21–31 Like the encounter with Edom, Israel requests a peaceful passage through Amorite territory, which was refused by *King Sihon of the Amorites* (sometimes "of Heshbon," Deut. 2:26; Josh. 12:5). This time, Israel defeats the Amorite force at *Jahaz* (later given to the Levites, 1 Chr. 6:78) and takes possession of their entire land, including their capital, *Heshbon* (located about forty-seven miles east of Jerusalem and later given to the Levites, Josh. 21:39), *as far as to the Ammonites* (cf. Deut. 2:19). The song praising Sihon's victory at Heshbon (Num. 21:27–30) provides a rationale for Israel's occupation of his territory. Sihon the Amorite displaced the Moabites from the city; now, the Israelites displace Sihon.

21:32–35 This text opens with Israel's victory over *Jazer*, located on the Ammonite border. Here, Israel issues no request for passage such as with Edom and the Amorites. Thus, this victory serves as a prelude to the following battle initiated by King Og of Bashan. As the victory over Sihon illustrates, Israel should utterly defeat Og (cf. 21:1–3; Deut. 3:1–3). These consecutive victories underscore Israel's formidable military strength.

22:1–24:25 The Balaam story narrates Balak's failed plan to curse Israel without Israel's involvement. God works behind the scenes to turn a dangerous situation into a marvelous blessing

Moab said to the elders of Midian, "This horde will now lick up all that is around us, as an ox licks up the grass of the field." Now Balak son of Zippor was king of Moab at that time. [5]He sent messengers to Balaam son of Beor at Pethor, which is on the Euphrates,[c] in the land of Amaw,[d] to summon him, saying, "A people has come out of Egypt; they have spread over the face of the earth, and they have settled next to me. [6]Come now, curse this people for me, since they are stronger than I; perhaps I shall be able to defeat them and drive them from the land, for I know that whomever you bless is blessed, and whomever you curse is cursed."

7 So the elders of Moab and the elders of Midian departed with the fees for divination in their hand, and they came to Balaam and gave him Balak's message. [8]He said to them, "Stay here tonight, and I will bring back word to you, just as the LORD speaks to me"; so the officials of Moab stayed with Balaam. [9]God came to Balaam and said, "Who are these men with you?" [10]Balaam said to God, "King Balak son of Zippor of Moab has sent me this message: [11]'Look, a people has come[e] out of Egypt and has spread over the face of the earth; now come, curse them for me; perhaps I shall be able to fight against them and drive them out.'" [12]God said to Balaam, "You shall not go with them; you shall not curse the people, for they are blessed." [13]So Balaam rose in the morning and said to the officials of Balak, "Go to your own land, for the LORD has refused to let me go with you." [14]So the officials of Moab rose and went to Balak and said, "Balaam refuses to come with us."

15 Once again Balak sent officials, more numerous and more distinguished than these. [16]They came to Balaam and said to him, "Thus says Balak son of Zippor: Do not let anything hinder you from coming to me, [17]for I will surely do you great honor, and whatever you say to me I will do; come, curse this people for me." [18]But Balaam replied to the servants of Balak, "Although Balak were to give me his house full of silver and gold, I could not go beyond the command of the LORD my God, to do less or more. [19]You also stay here overnight, so that I may learn what more the LORD may say to me." [20]That night God came to Balaam and said to him, "If the men have come to summon you, get up and go with them, but do only what I tell you to do." [21]So Balaam got up in the morning, saddled his donkey, and went with the officials of Moab.

22 God's anger was kindled because he was going, and the angel of the LORD took his stand in the road as his adversary. Now he was riding on the donkey, and his two servants were with him. [23]The donkey saw the angel of the LORD standing in the road, with a drawn sword in his hand, so the donkey turned off the road and went into the field, and Balaam struck the donkey, to turn it back onto the road. [24]Then the angel of the LORD stood in a narrow path between the vineyards, with a wall on either side. [25]When the donkey saw the angel of the LORD, it scraped against the wall and scraped Balaam's foot against the wall, so he struck it again. [26]Then the angel of the LORD went ahead and stood

c 22.5 Heb *the river* d 22.5 Or *land of his kinsfolk* e 22.11 Heb ms Sam Q ms Gk: MT *The people that is coming*

without their knowledge. See **"Balaam," p. 226**. **22:1–6** The Israelites camp in *the plains of Moab* (northeast of the Dead Sea; 26:3; Deut. 34:1; Josh. 13:32). With *the elders of Midian* (anticipating Num. 25:6–18), he hires Balaam, son of Beor *at Pethor* (370 miles from Moab) and a diviner with an international reputation for his power. **22:7–20** Balaam's virtue is highlighted. He is a professional whose service could render power for the right price; yet, he stresses his utter dependency on the word of YHWH (22:8, 18, 35, 38; 23:3, 5, 8, 12, 16, 20, 26; 24:13). He has no commitment to either Israel or Moab but only to YHWH, as he obeys YHWH's command to not curse Israel. Balak, however, assumes Balaam's refusal to be a negotiation tactic for a higher fee suitable to his reputation; hence, Balak sends officials of higher rank with greater incentives. Balaam's initial response matches the seriousness of the proposal, as he uses an exaggerated hypothetical condition of reward and unshakable conviction of his ability to do nothing without the command of *the LORD my God*. Balaam proves Balak's assumption for his first rejection to be false. Unlike the first encounter, God permits Balaam to accept the invitation with a stern admonition of performing only what God commands him to do. As an obedient servant, Balaam goes with the officials of Moab. **22:21–40** The fable of Balaam and his speaking donkey (vv. 22–35) disrupts the flow of the story and portrays him negatively. The esteemed professional seer could not see YHWH's messenger, whereas his donkey could see him clearly. He behaves like a beast in beating her, and while she argues persuasively, he is not

in a narrow place, where there was no way to turn either to the right or to the left. ²⁷When the donkey saw the angel of the Lord, it lay down under Balaam, and Balaam's anger was kindled, and he struck the donkey with his staff. ²⁸Then the Lord opened the mouth of the donkey, and it said to Balaam, "What have I done to you, that you have struck me these three times?" ²⁹Balaam said to the donkey, "Because you have made a fool of me! I wish I had a sword in my hand! I would kill you right now!" ³⁰But the donkey said to Balaam, "Am I not your donkey, which you have ridden all your life to this day? Have I been in the habit of treating you this way?" And he said, "No."

31 Then the Lord opened the eyes of Balaam, and he saw the angel of the Lord standing in the road, with his drawn sword in his hand, and he bowed down, falling on his face. ³²The angel of the Lord said to him, "Why have you struck your donkey these three times? I have come out as an adversary because your way is perverse*ᶠ* before me. ³³The donkey saw me and turned away from me these three times. If it had not turned away from me, surely just now I would have killed you and let it live." ³⁴Then Balaam said to the angel of the Lord, "I have sinned, for I did not know that you were standing in the road to oppose me. Now therefore, if it is displeasing to you, I will return home." ³⁵The angel of the Lord said to Balaam, "Go with the men, but speak only what I tell you to speak." So Balaam went on with the officials of Balak.

36 When Balak heard that Balaam had come, he went out to meet him at Ir-moab, on the boundary formed by the Arnon, at the farthest point of the boundary. ³⁷Balak said to Balaam, "Did I not send to summon you? Why did you not come to me? Am I not able to honor you?" ³⁸Balaam said to Balak, "I have come to you now, but do I have power to say just anything? The word God puts in my mouth,

that is what I must say." ³⁹Then Balaam went with Balak, and they came to Kiriath-huzoth. ⁴⁰Balak sacrificed oxen and sheep and sent them to Balaam and to the officials who were with him.

41 On the next day Balak took Balaam and brought him up to Bamoth-baal, and from there he could see part of the people of Israel.*ᵍ*

23

¹Then Balaam said to Balak, "Build me seven altars here, and prepare seven bulls and seven rams for me." ²Balak did as Balaam had said and offered*ʰ* a bull and a ram on each altar. ³Then Balaam said to Balak, "Stay here beside your burnt offerings while I go aside. Perhaps the Lord will come to meet me. Whatever he shows me I will tell you." And he went to a bare height.

4 Then God met Balaam, and Balaam*ⁱ* said to him, "I have arranged the seven altars and have offered a bull and a ram on each altar." ⁵The Lord put a word in Balaam's mouth and said, "Return to Balak, and this is what you must say." ⁶So he returned to Balak,*ʲ* who was standing beside his burnt offerings with all the officials of Moab. ⁷Then Balaam*ᵏ* uttered his oracle, saying,

"Balak has brought me from Aram,
    the king of Moab from the eastern
        mountains:
'Come, curse Jacob for me.
    Come, denounce Israel!'
⁸ How can I curse whom God has not
        cursed?
    How can I denounce those whom the
        Lord has not denounced?
⁹ For from the top of the crags I see him;
    from the hills I behold him.
Here is a people living alone
    and not reckoning itself among the
        nations!

---

f 22.32 Meaning of Heb uncertain   *g* 22.41 Heb lacks *of Israel*   *h* 23.2 Heb mss Gk: MT reads *Balak and Balaam offered*   *i* 23.4 Heb *he*   *j* 23.6 Heb *him*   *k* 23.7 Heb *he*

---

able to challenge her and only agrees with her arguments. **22:41–24:24** Balak's three attempts to curse Israel (22:41–23:12; 23:13–26; 23:27–24:24) follow the same pattern: preparation (preparatory sacrifice and moving to another location), oracle (divine revelation, Balaam's return, oracle proper), and response. A progressive movement from Balaam's vantage point is noticeable from seeing the entire people of Israel (22:41), to part of them (23:13), to only wasteland (23:28). Correspondingly, Balak's plan goes in a downward spiral as Israel gets increasingly blessed while his own country is predicted to be utterly destroyed in the near future. Under God's protection, Israel will be secure; under God's provision, Israel will prosper. **23:7–10** This first oracle teaches Balaam about Israel. Until this, no specific description of Israel is given to Balaam. Now he learns that Israel is an elected nation: *Jacob* (revealing its long history), *living alone* (or dwelling apart, indicating Israel's special status of being singled-out or among the nations), and *the dust of Jacob* (numerous, cf. Gen. 22:17).

¹⁰ Who can count the dust of Jacob
    or number the dust cloud^l of Israel?
Let me die the death of the upright,
    and let my end be like his!"

11 Then Balak said to Balaam, "What have you done to me? I brought you to curse my enemies, but now you have done nothing but bless them." ¹²He answered, "Must I not take care to say what the LORD puts into my mouth?"

13 So Balak said to him, "Come with me to another place from which you may see them; you shall see only part of them and shall not see them all; then curse them for me from there." ¹⁴So he took him to the field of Zophim, to the top of Pisgah. He built seven altars and offered a bull and a ram on each altar. ¹⁵Balaam^m said to Balak, "Stand here beside your burnt offerings, while I meet the LORD over there." ¹⁶The LORD met Balaam, put a word into his mouth, and said, "Return to Balak, and this is what you shall say." ¹⁷When he came to him, he was standing beside his burnt offerings with the officials of Moab. Balak said to him, "What has the LORD said?" ¹⁸Then Balaam^n uttered his oracle, saying,

    "Rise, Balak, and hear;
        listen to me, O son of Zippor:
¹⁹ God is not a human being, that he should lie,
        or a mortal, that he should change his mind.
    Has he promised, and will he not do it?
        Has he spoken, and will he not fulfill it?
²⁰ See, I received a command to bless;
        he has blessed, and I cannot revoke it.
²¹ He has not beheld misfortune in Jacob,
        nor has he seen trouble in Israel.
    The LORD their God is with them,
        acclaimed as a king among them.

²² God, who brings them out of Egypt,
        is like the horns of a wild ox for them.
²³ Surely there is no enchantment against Jacob,
    no divination against Israel;
    now it shall be said of Jacob and Israel,
        'See what God has done!'
²⁴ Look, a people rising up like a lioness
        and rousing itself like a lion!
    It does not lie down until it has eaten the prey
        and drunk the blood of the slain."

25 Then Balak said to Balaam, "Do not curse them at all, and do not bless them at all." ²⁶But Balaam answered Balak, "Did I not speak to you, saying, 'Whatever the LORD says, that is what I must do'?"

27 So Balak said to Balaam, "Come now, I will take you to another place; perhaps it will please God that you may curse them for me from there." ²⁸So Balak took Balaam to the top of Peor, which overlooks the wasteland.^{o} ²⁹Balaam said to Balak, "Build me seven altars here, and prepare seven bulls and seven rams for me." ³⁰So Balak did as Balaam had said and offered a bull and a ram on each altar.

24 Now Balaam saw that it pleased the LORD to bless Israel, so he did not go, as at other times, to look for omens but set his face toward the wilderness. ²Balaam looked up and saw Israel camping tribe by tribe. Then the spirit of God came upon him, ³and he uttered his oracle, saying,

    "The oracle of Balaam son of Beor,
        the oracle of the man whose eye is clear,^{p}
⁴ the oracle of one who hears the words of God,

l 23.10 Or *fourth part* m 23.15 Heb *he* n 23.18 Heb *he*
o 23.28 Or *overlooks Jeshimon* p 24.3 Or *closed* or *open*

Thus, Balaam desires to be like Israel. **23:18–24** The second oracle teaches Balak about God and Israel. Balak, who wants to change the future through sorcery, must learn that God is reliable, trustworthy, and faithful in fulfilling his promises. Balak, the king of Moab, should recognize that God is the king of Israel, who protected them from all trouble and liberated them from Egypt. Balak should acknowledge that Israel's future is so secure that no omen or divination would be able to work any harm against them. Instead, he underestimates the threat of Israel, *a lion* (Gen. 49:9; Deut. 33:20; Jer. 2:30; 12:8; Mic. 5:8). **24:3–9** The third oracle portrays Balaam as an exceptional seer (in contrast to the story of the talking/seeing donkey) and focuses on the fate of Israel. It underscores Israel's prosperity in the land, illustrated by the fertility imagery and coupled with the promise of Israel's continued existence in the land. Its political and military strength in the future (defeating Agag the Amalekite king, 1 Sam. 15:8) grows out of God's power demonstrated in the past—specifically, the exodus event. Its security and prosperity will be normative in interactions with other nations, whose fate (whether in blessing or curse) will depend on how they treat Israel (Gen. 12:3a, 27:29).

Reading through Time: Balaam (Numbers 22–24)

In Num. 22–24, Balaam, a pagan seer from Pethor in northern Mesopotamia, is described as a genuine prophet of God. He neither accepts nor rejects Balak's invitation on his own initiative. He does not negotiate over a price for his service. Instead, he does nothing but speak the word YHWH puts into his mouth, regardless of the consequences. The fable of the speaking donkey (22:22–35) ultimately has little effect on his reputation, as it focuses on the power of God over that of Balaam, who sees only what God permits.

However, the rest of the Bible, except Mic. 6:5, does not share this positive image of Balaam. Linked with Israel's apostasy at Baal Peor, he bears the guilt for seducing the Midianite women to cause the devastating plague (Num. 31:16; Rev. 2:14); thus, he must be executed along with the Midianite kings (Num. 31:8; Josh. 13:22). He actually plans to curse Israel (or has already done so), but at the last moment YHWH turns his curse into a blessing; thus, he is a false prophet, cursing against God's people and practicing divination (Deut. 23:5; Josh. 24:9; Neh. 13:2). He exemplifies someone who uses his power and knowledge for monetary gain (2 Pet. 2:15–16; Jude 11).

The ambivalent portrayal of Balaam continues in postbiblical presentations of Judaism and Christianity. He is a typical pagan soothsayer (Philo) who wanted to curse Israel (Josephus) and whose ability of prophecy has been gradually diminished (Pseudo-Philo). In rabbinic traditions, he is utterly wicked, corrupting and swallowing a people; immoral, committing bestiality with his donkey and practicing magic, and greedy for wrong reasons. At the same time, he is a prophet whose power is equal to Moses's, sent by God to teach Balak about the Jewish people and their special relationship to God and predict the ultimate redemption for Israel (Num. 24:17). His word in Num. 24:5 was chosen to begin the daily liturgy and has become a popular contemporary song. Similarly, in Christian traditions, Balaam is a magician and diviner who uses unworthy ways to achieve his ends. Yet he is the prophet of the Gentiles. Though a non-Israelite, he is faithful to the word of YHWH, teaches the three magi in Matthew pointing to the star, and receives prophecy by God to prophesy (in Christian tradition) the coming of Jesus Christ (Num. 24:17). Balaam becomes an important figure for the later church's self-understanding as one that embraces the Gentiles.

Won W. Lee

who sees the vision of the Almighty,*q*
who falls down but with eyes
uncovered:
⁵ How fair are your tents, O Jacob,
your encampments, O Israel!
⁶ Like palm groves that stretch far away,
like gardens beside a river,
like aloes that the Lᴏʀᴅ has planted,
like cedar trees beside the waters.
⁷ Water shall flow from his buckets,
and his seed shall have abundant water;
his king shall be higher than Agag,
and his kingdom shall be exalted.
⁸ God, who brings him out of Egypt,
is like the horns of a wild ox for him;
he shall devour the nations that are his
foes
and break their bones.
He shall strike with his arrows.*r*
⁹ He crouched; he lay down like a lion
and like a lioness; who will rouse him
up?

Blessed is everyone who blesses you,
and cursed is everyone who curses
you."
10 Then Balak's anger was kindled against Balaam, and he struck his hands together. Balak said to Balaam, "I summoned you to curse my enemies, but instead you have blessed them these three times. ¹¹Now be off with you! Go home! I said, 'I will reward you richly,' but the Lᴏʀᴅ has denied you any reward." ¹²And Balaam said to Balak, "Did I not speak to your messengers whom you sent to me, saying, ¹³'If Balak should give me his house full of silver and gold, I would not be able to go beyond the word of the Lᴏʀᴅ, to do either good or bad of my own will; what the Lᴏʀᴅ says, that is what I will say'? ¹⁴So now, I am going to my people; let me advise you what this people will do to your people in days to come."

q 24.4 Traditional rendering of Heb *Shaddai*   *r* 24.8 Meaning of Heb uncertain

24:10–14 Balak's disappointment is intensified in three attempts, moving from total denial to partial denial to, finally, full recognition of God's control. Balaam's reply to Balak is essentially the same as the one given when he began (22:18), yet he adds free advice for the future of Moab and three

15 So he uttered his oracle, saying,
"The oracle of Balaam son of Beor,
    the oracle of the man whose eye is
      clear,[s]
[16] the oracle of one who hears the words of
      God
    and knows the knowledge of the Most
      High,[t]
who sees the vision of the Almighty,[u]
    who falls down but with eyes
      uncovered:
[17] I see him but not now;
    I behold him but not near—
a star shall come out of Jacob,
    and a scepter shall rise out of Israel;
it shall crush the foreheads[v] of Moab
    and the heads[w] of all the Shethites.
[18] Edom will become a possession,
    Seir a possession of its enemies,
      while Israel does valiantly.
[19] One out of Jacob shall rule
    and destroy the survivors of Ir."

20 Then he looked on Amalek and uttered his oracle, saying,
"First among the nations was Amalek,
    but its end is to perish forever."

21 Then he looked on the Kenite and uttered his oracle, saying,
"Enduring is your dwelling place,
    and your nest is set in the rock,
[22] yet Kain is destined for burning.

How long shall Asshur take you away
    captive?"
23 Again he uttered his oracle, saying,
"Alas, who shall live when God does
    this?[x]
[24]   But ships shall come from Kittim
and shall afflict Asshur and Eber,
    and he also shall perish forever."
25 Then Balaam got up and went back to his place, and Balak also went his way.

25 While Israel was staying at Shittim, the people began to have sexual relations with the women of Moab. [2]These invited the people to the sacrifices of their gods, and the people ate and bowed down to their gods. [3]Thus Israel yoked itself to the Baal of Peor, and the Lord's anger was kindled against Israel. [4]The Lord said to Moses, "Take all the chiefs of the people and impale them in the sun before the Lord, in order that the fierce anger of the Lord may turn away from Israel." [5]And Moses said to the judges of Israel, "Each of you shall kill any of your people who have yoked themselves to the Baal of Peor."

6 Just then one of the Israelites came and brought a Midianite woman into his family,

s 24.15 Or *closed* or *open*   t 24.16 Or *of Elyon*   u 24.16 Traditional rendering of Heb *Shaddai*   v 24.17 Or *borderlands*   w 24.17 Or *territory*   x 24.23 Meaning of Heb uncertain

other nations in relation to Israel. **24:15–19** Israel will destroy Moab and Edom. **24:17** Balaam's oracle uses an image of *a star*, referring to a victorious king (cf. the Babylonian king in Isa. 14:12 and the risen Jesus in Rev. 22:16 are each called a morning star); a *scepter*, a distinguishing mark of a royal office (Amos 1:5, 8; Ps. 45:6); and *the heads of all the Shethites*, leaders of the descendants of Seth (Gen. 4:25–26). This prophecy may be related to David's victory over the Moabites (2 Sam. 8:2). **24:18–19** *Edom* refers to the people, while *Seir* refers to its land and *Ir* refers to its capital city. This prophecy may be related to David's victory over Edom (2 Sam. 8:13–14; 1 Kgs. 11:15–16). **24:20–24** Balaam predicts the fates of *Amalek*—a powerful adversary against Israel (Exod. 17:8–16; Num. 14:25), later defeated by Saul (1 Sam. 15:1–3) and David (1 Sam. 30:1–31)—and *the Kenite[s]*, descendants from Cain (Gen. 4:1–15) and associated with the Amalekites, though they enjoyed a friendly relationship with Israel (Judg. 1:16; 1 Sam. 15:4–9). *Kittim* refers to a force based in Cyprus that will defeat *Asshur* (Assyria, a superpower in the ancient Near Eastern world) and *Eber* to the land west of the Euphrates, possibly Babylonia; but they too will be defeated eventually. The God of Israel controls the fates of these nations.

25:1–18 In sharp contrast to God's blessings in the Balaam story, Israel commits an apostasy (see "Apostasy," p. 1238) at Baal Peor before entering the promised land. The execution of the transgressors stops God's punishment, which in turn restores God's holiness in the camp. Fierce loyalty to God is essential for inheriting the land. **25:1–5** *Shittim:* the last place of Israel's march (33:49; Josh. 2:1; 3:1; 4:18). Israel's sexual relations with Moabite women lead to worship of and sacrifice to their gods: *Israel yoked itself* (see Ps. 106:28) *to the Baal of Peor* (the Canaanite storm god of fertility worshiped at Peor, Num. 23:28). *Impale them in the sun:* a public execution (cf. the death of Saul's seven sons, 2 Sam. 21:6). **25:6–13** As a continuation of the story, this part provides a specific case of the apostasy at Baal Peor. Amid communal mourning for the plague victims, an individual

in the sight of Moses and in the sight of the whole congregation of the Israelites, while they were weeping at the entrance of the tent of meeting. [7]When Phinehas son of Eleazar, son of Aaron the priest, saw it, he got up and left the congregation. Taking a spear in his hand, [8]he went after the Israelite man into the tent and pierced the two of them, the Israelite and the woman, through the belly. So the plague was stopped among the Israelites. [9]Nevertheless those who died by the plague were twenty-four thousand.

10 The LORD spoke to Moses, saying, [11]"Phinehas son of Eleazar, son of Aaron the priest, has turned back my wrath from the Israelites by manifesting such zeal among them on my behalf that in my jealousy I did not consume the Israelites. [12]Therefore say, 'I hereby grant him my covenant of peace. [13]It shall be for him and for his descendants after him a covenant of perpetual priesthood, because he was zealous for his God and made atonement for the Israelites.'"

14 The name of the slain Israelite man who was killed with the Midianite woman was Zimri son of Salu, head of an ancestral house belonging to the Simeonites. [15]The name of the Midianite woman who was killed was Cozbi daughter of Zur, who was the head of a clan, an ancestral house in Midian.

16 The LORD spoke to Moses, saying, [17]"Harass the Midianites, and defeat them, [18]for they have harassed you by the trickery with which they deceived you in the affair of Peor, and in the affair of Cozbi, the daughter of a leader of Midian, their sister; she was killed on the day of the plague that resulted from Peor."

26 After the plague the LORD said to Moses and to Eleazar[y] the priest, [2]"Take a census of the whole congregation of the Israelites, from twenty years old and up, by their ancestral houses, everyone in Israel able to go to war." [3]Moses and Eleazar the priest spoke with them in the plains of Moab by the Jordan opposite Jericho, saying, [4]"Take a census of the people,[z] from twenty years old and up," as the LORD commanded Moses.

The Israelites who came out of the land of Egypt were:

y 26.1 Gk OL: Heb *Eleazar son of Aaron*   z 26.4 Heb lacks *take a census of the people*

Israelite engages in another sexual activity publicly, which is the cause of the deadly plague in the first place. *Phinehas*, the grandson of Aaron through the line of Eleazar (Exod. 6:25) executes the guilty parties, which appeases the divine wrath. *So the plague was stopped:* his action sanctifies the community, recalling Aaron's previous action (16:46–48). Phinehas was jealous with *[God's] jealousy* (expressing God's desire for an exclusive relationship) in Israel's midst. Phinehas's action represents his fierce loyalty to God and effects the well-being of the entire community, which suffers for a violation of that loyalty. *Covenant of peace* may indicate God's protection of Phinehas from bloodguilt and revenge by Zimri's clan. *Covenant of perpetual priesthood:* Phinehas's action is understood as cultic. By killing the guilty, he mediates between God and Israel, averts God's wrath, secures God's atonement, and ultimately restores the broken relationship. Recalling the ordination of the Levites in the golden calf story (Exod. 32:25–29), Phinehas's action legitimizes the Aaronide priesthood permanently. **25:14–18** *Cozbi* means "deceitful," connecting the *trickery* or deception in the affair of Peor. This divine command to Moses anticipates the Midianite war (chap. 31) and lays a foundation for the perpetual hostility between Israel and Midian.

26:1–36:13 Instructions for inheritance of the land. This section opens with the census of the second generation for the apportionment of Canaan. The remainder is bookended by the case of the daughters of Zelophehad (heiresses' right to inherit the land) with various units grouped together to highlight the life in Canaan.

26:1–65 This census shares a basic literary pattern with the first census in Num. 1. However, it differs slightly; it is for the second generation taken by Moses and Eleazar (not Aaron) at the edge of the promised land (not the Sinai desert), includes previous events (Korah's rebellion, the death of Er and Onan, and the deaths of Nadab and Abihu), and focuses on providing a basis for the division of the land. **26:1–4a** *After the plague* recalls the event in 25:1–18. *In the plains of Moab by the Jordan opposite Jericho* is the same location as 22:1. **26:4b–51** For the list of clan names, see Gen. 46:8–26. Recording the five tribes (Simeon, Gad, Issachar, Zebulun, and Naphtali) follows the pattern of (a) the tribe's name and counting method, (b) a list of clan names, and (c) confirmation that the clans belong to the tribe and the total number. The other seven tribal entries depart from the pattern

5 Reuben, the firstborn of Israel. The descendants of Reuben: of Hanoch, the clan of the Hanochites; of Pallu, the clan of the Palluites; [6]of Hezron, the clan of the Hezronites; of Carmi, the clan of the Carmites. [7]These are the clans of the Reubenites; the number of those enrolled was forty-three thousand seven hundred thirty. [8]And the descendants of Pallu: Eliab. [9]The descendants of Eliab: Nemuel, Dathan, and Abiram. These are the same Dathan and Abiram, chosen from the congregation, who rebelled against Moses and Aaron in the congregation of Korah, when they rebelled against the LORD, [10]and the earth opened its mouth and swallowed them up along with Korah, when that congregation died, when the fire devoured two hundred fifty men, and they became a warning. [11]Notwithstanding, the sons of Korah did not die.

12 The descendants of Simeon by their clans: of Nemuel, the clan of the Nemuelites; of Jamin, the clan of the Jaminites; of Jachin, the clan of the Jachinites; [13]of Zerah, the clan of the Zerahites; of Shaul, the clan of the Shaulites.[a] [14]These are the clans of the Simeonites: twenty-two thousand two hundred.

15 The descendants of Gad by their clans: of Zephon, the clan of the Zephonites; of Haggi, the clan of the Haggites; of Shuni, the clan of the Shunites; [16]of Ozni, the clan of the Oznites; of Eri, the clan of the Erites; [17]of Arod, the clan of the Arodites; of Areli, the clan of the Arelites. [18]These are the clans of the descendants of Gad by the number of those enrolled: forty thousand five hundred.

19 The sons of Judah: Er and Onan; Er and Onan died in the land of Canaan. [20]The descendants of Judah by their clans were: of Shelah, the clan of the Shelanites; of Perez, the clan of the Perezites; of Zerah, the clan of the Zerahites. [21]The descendants of Perez were: of Hezron, the clan of the Hezronites; of Hamul, the clan of the Hamulites. [22]These are the clans of Judah by the number of those enrolled: seventy-six thousand five hundred.

23 The descendants of Issachar by their clans: of Tola, the clan of the Tolaites; of Puvah, the clan of the Punites; [24]of Jashub, the clan of the Jashubites; of Shimron, the clan of the Shimronites. [25]These are the clans of Issachar by the number of those enrolled: sixty-four thousand three hundred.

26 The descendants of Zebulun by their clans: of Sered, the clan of the Seredites; of Elon, the clan of the Elonites; of Jahleel, the clan of the Jahleelites. [27]These are the clans of the Zebulunites by the number of those enrolled: sixty thousand five hundred.

28 The sons of Joseph by their clans: Manasseh and Ephraim. [29]The descendants of Manasseh: of Machir, the clan of the Machirites; and Machir was the father of Gilead; of Gilead, the clan of the Gileadites. [30]These are the descendants of Gilead: of Iezer, the clan of the Iezerites; of Helek, the clan of the Helekites; [31]and of Asriel, the clan of the Asrielites; and of Shechem, the clan of the Shechemites; [32]and of Shemida, the clan of the Shemidaites; and of Hepher, the clan of the Hepherites. [33]Now Zelophehad son of Hepher had no sons, only daughters, and the names of the daughters of Zelophehad were Mahlah, Noah, Hoglah, Milcah, and Tirzah. [34]These are the clans of Manasseh; the number of those enrolled was fifty-two thousand seven hundred.

35 These are the descendants of Ephraim according to their clans: of Shuthelah, the clan of the Shuthelahites; of Becher, the clan of the Becherites; of Tahan, the clan of the Tahanites. [36]And these are the descendants

a 26.13 Or Saul... Saulites

by supplementing materials germane to each respective tribe. **26:5–11** The rebellion of Korah, Dathan, and Abiram (16:1–50) may be related to Reuben's (Gen. 46:9; cf. Exod. 6:14) decreased population. Yet Korah's clans continue, as seen in later descriptions of the sons of Korah as temple singers (Pss. 42, 44–49, 84–85, 87) and temple guards (1 Chr. 9:19). **26:12–14** Simeon's (Gen. 46:10) decreased population might be related to Num. 25:1–18. **26:15–18** *Gad* (Gen. 46:16). **26:19–22** *Judah* (Gen. 46:12). The death of Er and Onan (Gen. 38:1–10) and extension of generations through the line of Perez (cf. Ruth 4:18–22) recall the story of Judah and Tamar (Gen. 38). **26:23–25** *Issachar* (Gen. 46:13). **26:26–27** *Zebulun* (Gen. 46:14). **26:28** Dividing the tribe of Joseph into two compensates for the exclusion of the Levites from the twelve-tribe system. **26:29–34** *Manasseh* (cf. Josh. 17:1–3). The tribal entry extends to the third generation (Manasseh-Machir-Gilead) anticipating the possession of the Transjordan area by half of the tribe (Num. 32:39–42). It also elaborates on the descendants of Gilead, including the names of Zelophehad's daughters, who petition to inherit their father's portion of the land (27:1–11; 36:1–13). **26:35–37** *Ephraim* (cf. 1 Chr. 7:20–27).

of Shuthelah: of Eran, the clan of the Eranites. [37]These are the clans of the Ephraimites by the number of those enrolled: thirty-two thousand five hundred. These are the descendants of Joseph by their clans.

38 The descendants of Benjamin by their clans: of Bela, the clan of the Belaites; of Ashbel, the clan of the Ashbelites; of Ahiram, the clan of the Ahiramites; [39]of Shephupham, the clan of the Shuphamites; of Hupham, the clan of the Huphamites. [40]And the sons of Bela were Ard and Naaman: of Ard, the clan of the Ardites; of Naaman, the clan of the Naamites. [41]These are the descendants of Benjamin by their clans; the number of those enrolled was forty-five thousand six hundred.

42 These are the descendants of Dan by their clans: of Shuham, the clan of the Shuhamites. These are the clans of Dan by their clans. [43]All the clans of the Shuhamites by the number of those enrolled: sixty-four thousand four hundred.

44 The descendants of Asher by their clans: of Imnah, the clan of the Imnites; of Ishvi, the clan of the Ishvites; of Beriah, the clan of the Beriites. [45]Of the descendants of Beriah: of Heber, the clan of the Heberites; of Malchiel, the clan of the Malchielites. [46]And the name of the daughter of Asher was Serah. [47]These are the clans of the descendants of Asher by the number of those enrolled: fifty-three thousand four hundred.

48 The descendants of Naphtali by their clans: of Jahzeel, the clan of the Jahzeelites; of Guni, the clan of the Gunites; [49]of Jezer, the clan of the Jezerites; of Shillem, the clan of the Shillemites. [50]These are the clans of Naphtali by their clans; the number of those enrolled was forty-five thousand four hundred.

51 This was the number of the Israelites enrolled: six hundred and one thousand seven hundred thirty.

52 The LORD spoke to Moses, saying, [53]"To these the land shall be apportioned for inheritance according to the number of names. [54]To a large tribe you shall give a large inheritance, and to a small tribe you shall give a small inheritance; every tribe shall be given its inheritance according to its enrollment. [55]But the land shall be apportioned by lot; according to the names of their ancestral tribes they shall inherit. [56]Their inheritance shall be apportioned according to lot between the larger and the smaller."

57 This is the enrollment of the Levites by their clans: of Gershon, the clan of the Gershonites; of Kohath, the clan of the Kohathites; of Merari, the clan of the Merarites. [58]These are the clans of Levi: the clan of the Libnites, the clan of the Hebronites, the clan of the Mahlites, the clan of the Mushites, the clan of the Korahites. Now Kohath was the father of Amram. [59]The name of Amram's wife was Jochebed daughter of Levi, who was born to Levi in Egypt, and she bore to Amram: Aaron, Moses, and their sister Miriam. [60]To Aaron were born Nadab, Abihu, Eleazar, and Ithamar. [61]But Nadab and Abihu died when they offered unholy fire before the LORD. [62]The number of those enrolled was twenty-three thousand, every male one month old and up, for they were not enrolled among the Israelites because there was no allotment given to them among the Israelites.

63 These were those enrolled by Moses and Eleazar the priest, who enrolled the Israelites in the plains of Moab by the Jordan at Jericho. [64]Among these there was not one of those enrolled by Moses and Aaron the priest, who had enrolled the Israelites in the wilderness of Sinai. [65]For the LORD had said of them, "They shall die in the wilderness." Not one of them was left, except Caleb son of Jephunneh and Joshua son of Nun.

26:38–41 *Benjamin* (Gen. 46:21; cf. 1 Chr. 7:6–12; 8:1–40). **26:42–43** *Dan* (Gen. 46:23). **26:44–47** *Asher* (Gen. 46:17). Mentioning Asher's daughter might be related to the right of inheritance for daughters, like the case of Zelophehad's daughters. **26:48–50** *Naphtali* (Gen. 46:24). **26:52–56** The division of the land is determined *according to the number of names* (by the size of the tribe) and *by lot* (by the divine will, cf. Josh. 14–17). **26:57–62** The male Levites are counted from one month of age and older due to their unique duties (3:15). Instead of receiving a portion of the land, they are assigned Levitical towns (35:1–8). The clan of Kohath—from which Moses, Aaron, and Miriam came—receives elaboration (vv. 58–61). Listing Aaron's descendants (neither Moses's nor Miriam's) and recalling the death of two of his sons (Lev. 10:1–7) may underscore the exclusive right for his priesthood. **26:63–65** A possible confusion from v. 4b (*The Israelites who came out of the land of Egypt were*) is clarified by recalling God's solemn oath in response to the exodus generation's radical rebellion (chaps. 13–14).

27 Then the daughters of Zelophehad came forward. Zelophehad was son of Hepher son of Gilead son of Machir son of Manasseh, of the clans of Manasseh, son of Joseph. The names of his daughters were Mahlah, Noah, Hoglah, Milcah, and Tirzah. [2]They stood before Moses, Eleazar the priest, the leaders, and all the congregation, at the entrance of the tent of meeting, saying, [3]"Our father died in the wilderness; he was not among the congregation of those who gathered themselves together against the LORD in the congregation of Korah but died for his own sin, and he had no sons. [4]Why should the name of our father be taken away from his clan because he had no son? Give to us a possession among our father's brothers."

5 Moses brought their case before the LORD. [6]And the LORD spoke to Moses, saying, [7]"The daughters of Zelophehad are right in what they are saying; you shall indeed let them possess an inheritance among their father's brothers and pass the inheritance of their father on to them. [8]You shall also speak to the Israelites, saying: If a man dies and has no son, then you shall pass his inheritance on to his daughter. [9]If he has no daughter, then you shall give his inheritance to his brothers. [10]If he has no brothers, then you shall give his inheritance to his father's brothers. [11]And if his father has no brothers, then you shall give his inheritance to the nearest kinsman of his clan, and he shall possess it. It shall be for the Israelites a statute and ordinance, as the LORD commanded Moses."

12 The LORD said to Moses, "Go up this mountain of the Abarim range, and see the land that I have given to the Israelites. [13]When you have seen it, you also shall be gathered to your people, as your brother Aaron was, [14]because you rebelled against my word in the wilderness of Zin when the congregation quarreled with me.[b] You did not show my holiness before their eyes at the waters." (These are the waters of Meribath-kadesh in the wilderness of Zin.) [15]Moses spoke to the LORD, saying, [16]"Let the LORD, the God of the spirits of all flesh, appoint someone over the congregation [17]who shall go out before them and come in before them, who shall lead them out and bring them in, so that the congregation of the LORD may not be like sheep without a shepherd." [18]So the LORD said to Moses, "Take Joshua son of Nun, a man in whom is the spirit, and lay your hand upon him; [19]have him stand before Eleazar the priest and all the congregation and commission him in their sight. [20]You shall give him some of your authority, so that all the congregation of the Israelites may obey. [21]But he shall stand before Eleazar the priest, who shall inquire for him by the decision of the Urim before the LORD; at his word they shall go out, and at his word they shall come in, both he and all the

b 27.14 Heb lacks *with me*

27:1–11 Land is divinely granted in perpetuity and cannot be permanently sold or taken away from its family of origin. Land inheritance follows the line of succession of male heirs (Lev. 25; Num. 26:52–54; 1 Kgs. 21:1–4). This, however, creates a legal problem when no male heir is alive to inherit the family property, just as in the case brought by the *daughters of Zelophehad*. Their case deals with a civil issue, as it is brought to the entire public, but it needs to be resolved by God (Lev. 24:10–23; Num. 9:6–14; 15:32–36). God grants them the privilege to possess their father's inheritance, which is carried out later (Josh. 17:3–6). God's favorable ruling leads them to redefine the line of succession, applicable to all Israel, to be that if the deceased man has no daughters, then the line runs entirely through the male relatives of the patriarch. See **"Zelophehad's Daughters," p. 232**.

27:12–23 Commissioning Joshua as Moses's successor follows a pattern similar to the death report of Aaron (20:22–29): specific places (Mount Hor / Abarim), God's prediction of and reason for the death (20:1–13), appointment of a successor (Eleazar/Joshua), and Moses's execution of God's command. However, Moses's actual death and the people's mourning (Deut. 34:4–8) are not mentioned, and the request for a successor originates from Moses, not from God. Moreover, the commissioning procedure is greatly expanded, stressing Joshua's subordination to the priest. **27:12–14** *Abarim* (see 33:47–48; Deut. 32:49); *shall be gathered to your people:* the idiomatic expression of one's death (20:24; Judg. 2:10); *because you rebelled against my word* (Num. 20:1–13). **27:15–17** *Go out . . . come in . . . lead them out and bring them in* expresses military activity (Deut. 31:2–3; Josh. 14:11). Moses's leadership in military campaigns is not hereditary, unlike Aaron's priesthood. **27:18–21** *Joshua son of Nun* (Exod. 17:8–16; Num. 13–14; 32:28). *A man in whom is the spirit* recalls the sharing of Moses's spirit with the seventy elders (11:16–27), although Joshua is not mentioned

Focus On: Zelophehad's Daughters (Numbers 27:1-11; 36:1-12)

The story of the daughters of Zelophehad has received much attention in recent scholarly works. Focusing on the literary structure of 27:1-11 (which is similar to other cases: Lev. 24:10-23; Num. 9:6-14; 15:32-36)—(a) a case brought to authority figures, (b) asking God for a solution because the law is unknown, (c) God's verdict expressed in case-by-case style, and (d) enacting the law with a compliance formula—some scholars explain the growth and development of legal formulations from ordinary life events. The daughters' case is unique in that the ruling in favor of female inheritance (27:8) was modified later in 36:1-12 to uphold the principle of ancestral inheritance: it remains within the clan of the tribe through the male family line. This reformulation is achieved with remarkable linguistic consistency and structural arrangement between the two passages.

Why, then, are the two passages separated in Numbers? Of many explanations, the following could be instructive. Chapter 27 is tied closely with chapter 26, where Zelophehad's situation of having no sons, listing his five daughters' names, and distributing the land through the names of the tribes are stated. Together, these two conclude the book of Numbers by mentioning Moses's imminent death and commissioning Joshua as his successor (27:12-23). Deuteronomy, Moses's final speeches to the people poised to cross the Jordan in which he exhorts their faithfulness as the condition for the successful conquest and continual living in the land, is separated from the Deuteronomistic History (historical account of Israel from Deuteronomy to Kings) to form the present Pentateuch, which ends with the story of Moses's death. In this redactional process, chapters 27 and 36 form an inclusio for various instructions around the theme of the land, including the apportionment of Canaan to the Israelite tribes (32:1-35:34); thus, chapter 36 presents an appropriate conclusion to Numbers, not simply a thoughtless appendix.

Others have looked to the daughters of Zelophehad as protofeminists, challenging the judicial powers regarding female inheritance rights. Their names appear three times (26:33; 27:1; 36:11), their behavior is audacious, and their request is well-crafted to compel God to change the law. In the Hebrew Bible, the land is constitutive of the integrity of the Israelites' existence; thus, its possession means to participate in society as an equal. Despite the marriage restriction (36:6), they emerge as symbols of the powerless to achieve a measure of justice.

Won W. Lee

Israelites with him, the whole congregation." [22]So Moses did as the LORD commanded him. He took Joshua and had him stand before Eleazar the priest and the whole congregation; [23]he laid his hands on him and commissioned him, as the LORD had directed through Moses.

28 The LORD spoke to Moses, saying, [2]"Command the Israelites, and say to them: My offering, the food for my offerings by fire,[c] my pleasing odor, you shall take care to offer to me at its appointed time. [3]And you shall say to them: This is the offering by fire[d] that you shall offer to the LORD: two male lambs a year old without blemish, daily, as a regular offering. [4]One lamb you shall offer in the morning, and the other lamb you shall offer at twilight;[e] [5]also one-tenth of an ephah of choice flour for a grain offering, mixed with one-fourth of a hin of beaten oil. [6]It is a regular burnt offering, ordained at Mount Sinai for a pleasing odor, an offering by fire[f] to the LORD. [7]Its drink offering shall

c 28.2 Or *my gifts*   d 28.3 Or *the gift*   e 28.4 Heb *between the two evenings*   f 28.6 Or *a gift*

as one of them (cf. Deut. 34:9). *Lay your hand upon him* reflects contact with sacrificial ritual (8:10). *Give him some of your authority* hints at Joshua's inferior status compared to Moses. *Stand before Eleazar the priest . . . the decision of the Urim* suggests Joshua's dependence on the high priest's mediation for God's will. His leadership must be authenticated by the high priest, who uses the Urim and the Thummim (small stone objects with impressed symbols indicating affirmative and negative answers) to discern God's will (1 Sam. 14:41; Ezra 2:63; Neh. 7:65).

28:1-29:40 This ritual calendar provides instructions for the daily, Sabbath, monthly, and yearly festival offerings the Israelites ought to publicly perform in the sanctuary. It is more detailed regarding the times and quantities for each occasion than other ritual calendars (Exod. 23:10-19; 34:18-26; Lev. 23:1-44; Deut. 16:1-17; Ezek. 45:23-46:15). **28:1-2** *The food for my offerings by fire, my pleasing odor* (Lev. 21:6; Num. 15:3-13). *At its appointed time* refers to sacred times/seasons that structured Israel's worship life (Lev. 23:2, 4). **28:3-8** The daily offering (cf. Exod. 29:38-46) is a regular offering

be one-fourth of a hin for each lamb; in the sanctuary you shall pour out a drink offering of strong drink to the LORD. [8]The other lamb you shall offer at twilight[g] with a grain offering and a drink offering like the one in the morning; you shall offer it as an offering by fire,[h] a pleasing odor to the LORD.

9 "On the Sabbath day: two male lambs a year old without blemish and two-tenths of an ephah of choice flour for a grain offering, mixed with oil, and its drink offering—[10]this is the burnt offering for every Sabbath, in addition to the regular burnt offering and its drink offering.

11 "At the beginnings of your months you shall offer a burnt offering to the LORD: two young bulls, one ram, seven male lambs a year old without blemish; [12]also three-tenths of an ephah of choice flour for a grain offering, mixed with oil, for each bull; and two-tenths of choice flour for a grain offering, mixed with oil, for the one ram; [13]and one-tenth of choice flour mixed with oil as a grain offering for each lamb—a burnt offering of pleasing odor, an offering by fire[i] to the LORD. [14]Their drink offerings shall be half a hin of wine for a bull, one-third of a hin for a ram, and one-fourth of a hin for a lamb. This is the burnt offering of every month throughout the months of the year. [15]And there shall be one male goat for a purification offering to the LORD; it shall be offered in addition to the regular burnt offering and its drink offering.

16 "On the fourteenth day of the first month there shall be a Passover offering to the LORD. [17]And on the fifteenth day of this month is a festival; seven days shall unleavened bread be eaten. [18]On the first day there shall be a holy convocation. You shall not work at your occupations. [19]You shall offer an offering by fire,[j] a burnt offering to the LORD: two young bulls, one ram, and seven male lambs a year old; see that they are without blemish. [20]Their grain offering shall be of choice flour mixed with oil: three-tenths of an ephah shall you offer for a bull and two-tenths for a ram; [21]one-tenth shall you offer for each of the seven lambs; [22]also one male goat for a purification offering, to make atonement for you. [23]You shall offer these in addition to the burnt offering of the morning, which belongs to the regular burnt offering. [24]In the same way you shall offer daily, for seven days, the food of an offering by fire,[k] a pleasing odor to the LORD; it shall be offered in addition to the regular burnt offering and its drink offering. [25]And on the seventh day you shall have a holy convocation; you shall not work at your occupations.

26 "On the day of the first fruits, when you offer a grain offering of new grain to the LORD at your Festival of Weeks, you shall have a holy convocation; you shall not work at your occupations. [27]You shall offer a burnt offering, a pleasing odor to the LORD: two young bulls, one ram, seven male lambs a year old. [28]Their grain offering shall be of choice flour mixed with oil: three-tenths of an ephah for each bull, two-tenths for the one ram, [29]one-tenth

g 28.8 Heb *between the two evenings*   h 28.8 Or *a gift*
i 28.13 Or *a gift*   j 28.19 Or *a gift*   k 28.24 Or *a gift*

of the entire animal consumed by the altar fire (Lev. 1:3–17; 6:8–13). This offering is foundational for the rest of the offerings, which are offered *in addition to* (28:10, 15, 24, 31; 29:6, 11, 16, 19, 22, 25, 28, 31, 34, 38). **28:9–10** The Sabbath offering is given in addition to the daily offering. Unlike in Lev. 23:3, the Sabbath labor prohibition is not mentioned. **28:11–15** The monthly offering occurs on the first day of the month or the new moon and requires the same sacrificial animals as each of the seven days of the celebration of the Unleavened Bread (28:19) and on the day of the Festival of Weeks (28:27). **28:16–29:38** Yearly sacrificial festivals are concentrated in the first and seventh months (except for the Festivals of Weeks / First Fruits), reflecting a close connection to annual harvest times (spring and fall) as well as to the history of Israel (exodus, receiving the law from Mount Sinai, and the wilderness journey). **28:16** The Passover offering (Lev. 23:5; Num. 9:1–14) takes place on the fourteenth day of the first month, the beginning of the barley harvest in the spring. It is a family-oriented celebration to remember God's saving of Israel in Egypt (Exod. 12:3–14). **28:17–25** The Feast of Unleavened Bread (Exod. 12:15–20; Lev. 23:6–8) begins on the fifteenth day of the first month and lasts for seven days. The number of offerings for each day is the same as for the monthly offerings (without the drink offering). *A holy convocation:* this may be related to Israel's pilgrimage to the sanctuary on the fifteenth and twenty-first days of the first month of every year to celebrate God's mighty act of the exodus. **28:26–31** *Festival of Weeks* (Exod. 34:22; Deut. 16:10) is also called the Festival of the Harvest (Exod. 23:16) or Pentecost (Acts 2). It marks the wheat harvest, although no specific date is stated here. However, it could be offered fifty days from the day on

for each of the seven lambs, [30]with one male goat, to make atonement for you. [31]In addition to the regular burnt offering with its grain offering, you shall offer them and their drink offering. They shall be without blemish.

29

[1]"On the first day of the seventh month you shall have a holy convocation; you shall not work at your occupations. It is a day for you to blow the trumpets, [2]and you shall offer a burnt offering, a pleasing odor to the LORD: one young bull, one ram, seven male lambs a year old without blemish. [3]Their grain offering shall be of choice flour mixed with oil: three-tenths of an ephah for a bull, two-tenths for a ram, [4]and one-tenth for each of the seven lambs, [5]with one male goat for a purification offering, to make atonement for you. [6]These are in addition to the burnt offering of the new moon and its grain offering, and the regular burnt offering and its grain offering, and their drink offerings, according to the ordinance for them, a pleasing odor, an offering by fire[l] to the LORD.

[7]"On the tenth day of this seventh month you shall have a holy convocation and humble yourselves;[m] you shall do no work. [8]You shall offer a burnt offering to the LORD, a pleasing odor: one young bull, one ram, seven male lambs a year old. They shall be without blemish. [9]Their grain offering shall be of choice flour mixed with oil, three-tenths of an ephah for the bull, two-tenths for the one ram, [10]one-tenth for each of the seven lambs,

[11]with one male goat for a purification offering, in addition to the purification offering of atonement, and the regular burnt offering and its grain offering, and their drink offerings.

[12]"On the fifteenth day of the seventh month you shall have a holy convocation; you shall not work at your occupations. You shall celebrate a festival to the LORD seven days. [13]You shall offer a burnt offering, an offering by fire,[n] a pleasing odor to the LORD: thirteen young bulls, two rams, fourteen male lambs a year old. They shall be without blemish. [14]Their grain offering shall be of choice flour mixed with oil, three-tenths of an ephah for each of the thirteen bulls, two-tenths for each of the two rams, [15]and one-tenth for each of the fourteen lambs; [16]also one male goat for a purification offering, in addition to the regular burnt offering, its grain offering, and its drink offering.

[17]"On the second day: twelve young bulls, two rams, fourteen male lambs a year old without blemish, [18]with the grain offering and the drink offerings for the bulls, for the rams, and for the lambs, as prescribed in accordance with their number; [19]also one male goat for a purification offering, in addition to the regular burnt offering and its grain offering and their drink offerings.

[20]"On the third day: eleven bulls, two rams, fourteen male lambs a year old without blemish, [21]with the grain offering and the

_l_ 29.6 Or _a gift_   _m_ 29.7 Or _fast_   _n_ 29.13 Or _a gift_

which the new crop of wheat is presented to God for the priests' use (Lev. 23:9–22; Num. 18:12–13). **29:1–6** The _first day of the seventh month_ indicates the beginning of the agricultural year (cf. Exod. 23:16). The blowing of _the trumpets_ (differing from the metal trumpets in Num. 10:2–10) announces this beginning (Lev. 23:23–25). Jewish tradition adopts this day as the first day of the New Year, called Rosh Hashanah. **29:7–11** Derived from Lev. 23:26–32, these public offerings on the tenth day of the seventh month are called offerings on the Day of Atonement (Yom Kippur) to cleanse the defiled sanctuary. The offerings are similar to those of the New Year's Day celebration, with two significant departures: _humble yourselves_ (literally "torment your bodies" [Lev. 16:31; 23:27], which could refer to fasting [Ps. 35:13; Isa. 58:3]), and _a purification offering, in addition to the purification offering of atonement_ (referring to one for the high priest and his household [Lev. 16:6; a bull, not a male goat] and another on behalf of the people [Lev. 16:7–9]). **29:12–38** No name is given for this festival here, but it is called elsewhere the Festival of Booths (Lev. 23:33–43; Deut. 16:13–15) or the Festival of Ingathering (Exod. 23:16; 34:22). Far more animals are required for this festival than any other, reflecting the abundant productivity of the land, from which the Israelites can express their gratitude to God. This festival concludes with an eighth-day celebration (Num. 29:35–38), which is different from the instruction of the seven days celebration (v. 12). The eighth day is called _a solemn assembly_ (not _a holy convocation_), offering only one bull, one ram, and seven yearling male lambs for a burnt offering. This celebration, however, includes the prohibition of labor with the same additional grain and drink offerings. Perhaps it is later integrated into the Festival of Booths, despite its distinct origin (1 Kgs. 8:2, 65–66).

drink offerings for the bulls, for the rams, and for the lambs, as prescribed in accordance with their number; ²²also one male goat for a purification offering, in addition to the regular burnt offering and its grain offering and its drink offering.

23 "On the fourth day: ten bulls, two rams, fourteen male lambs a year old without blemish, ²⁴with the grain offering and the drink offerings for the bulls, for the rams, and for the lambs, as prescribed in accordance with their number; ²⁵also one male goat for a purification offering, in addition to the regular burnt offering, its grain offering, and its drink offering.

26 "On the fifth day: nine bulls, two rams, fourteen male lambs a year old without blemish, ²⁷with the grain offering and the drink offerings for the bulls, for the rams, and for the lambs, as prescribed in accordance with their number; ²⁸also one male goat for a purification offering, in addition to the regular burnt offering and its grain offering and its drink offering.

29 "On the sixth day: eight bulls, two rams, fourteen male lambs a year old without blemish, ³⁰with the grain offering and the drink offerings for the bulls, for the rams, and for the lambs, as prescribed in accordance with their number; ³¹also one male goat for a purification offering, in addition to the regular burnt offering, its grain offering, and its drink offerings.

32 "On the seventh day: seven bulls, two rams, fourteen male lambs a year old without blemish, ³³with the grain offering and the drink offerings for the bulls, for the rams, and for the lambs, as prescribed in accordance with their number; ³⁴also one male goat for a purification offering, besides the regular burnt offering, its grain offering, and its drink offering.

35 "On the eighth day you shall have a solemn assembly; you shall not work at your occupations. ³⁶You shall offer a burnt offering, an offering by fire,ᵒ a pleasing odor to the LORD: one bull, one ram, seven male lambs a year old without blemish, ³⁷and the grain offering and the drink offerings for the bull, for the ram, and for the lambs, as prescribed in accordance with their number; ³⁸also one male goat for a purification offering, in addition to the regular burnt offering and its grain offering and its drink offering.

39 "These you shall offer to the LORD at your appointed festivals, in addition to your votive offerings and your freewill offerings, as your burnt offerings, your grain offerings, your drink offerings, and your offerings of well-being."

40 ᵖSo Moses told the Israelites everything just as the LORD had commanded Moses.

30 Then Moses spoke to the heads of the tribes of the Israelites, saying, "This is what the LORD has commanded. ²When a man makes a vow to the LORD or swears an oath to bind himself by a pledge, he shall not break his word; he shall do according to all that proceeds out of his mouth.

3 "When a woman makes a vow to the LORD or binds herself by a pledge while within her father's house, in her youth, ⁴and her father hears of her vow or her pledge by which she has bound herself and says nothing to her, then all her vows shall stand, and any pledge by which she has bound herself shall stand. ⁵But if her father overrules her at the time that he hears of it, no vow of hers and no pledge by which she has bound herself shall stand, and the LORD will forgive her because her father overruled her.

6 "If she marries, while obligated by her vows or any thoughtless utterance of her lips by which she has bound herself, ⁷and her husband hears of it and says nothing to her at the time that he hears, then her vows

o 29.36 Or *a gift* p 29.40 30.1 in Heb

30:1–16 A vow, once made, must be kept. This legislation stipulates male responsibility for the validity of vows. It places special focus on the vows made by women in the father's house, married women, widows, and divorced women, emphasizing the power of male authority to determine the legal responsibility facing these women. **30:2** *Makes a vow:* committing to do something for God in exchange for divine support; swearing *an oath to bind himself by a pledge*: a commitment that involves one's life tied up in the agreement. **30:3–15** The circumstances where fathers (vv. 3–5) and husbands (vv. 6–15) can nullify vows made by their daughters and wives are outlined. If the father or husband says *nothing to her* (assuming legal responsibility for fulfillment) on the day he hears of her vow or pledge, they shall *stand* (remain binding). However, if he *overrules* her upon first hearing her vow, that vow will be annulled without bearing guilt. Both the cancellation of her vow and the divine forgiveness for her potentially not fulfilling the vow depend only on the father's or husband's action. This hierarchical pattern indicates that a man is legally autonomous, while a woman remains under

shall stand, and her pledges by which she has bound herself shall stand. ⁸But if, at the time that her husband hears of it, he overrules her, then he shall nullify the vow by which she was obligated or the thoughtless utterance of her lips by which she bound herself, and the LORD will forgive her. ⁹(But every vow of a widow or of a divorced woman, by which she has bound herself, shall be binding upon her.) ¹⁰And if she made a vow in her husband's house or bound herself by a pledge with an oath ¹¹and her husband heard it and said nothing to her and did not overrule her, then all her vows shall stand, and any pledge by which she bound herself shall stand. ¹²But if her husband nullifies them at the time that he hears them, then whatever proceeds out of her lips concerning her vows or concerning her pledge shall not stand. Her husband has nullified them, and the LORD will forgive her. ¹³Any vow or any binding oath to humble herself,ᵠ her husband may allow to stand or her husband may nullify. ¹⁴But if her husband says nothing to her from day to day,ʳ then he validates all her vows or all her pledges by which she is obligated; he has validated them because he said nothing to her at the time that he heard of them. ¹⁵But if he nullifies them some time after he has heard of them, then he shall bear her guilt."

16 These are the statutes that the LORD commanded Moses concerning a husband and his wife and a father and his daughter while she is still young and in her father's house.

31 The LORD spoke to Moses, saying, ²"Avenge the Israelites on the Midianites;

afterward you shall be gathered to your people." ³So Moses spoke to the people, saying, "Arm some of your number for the war, so that they may go against Midian, to execute the LORD's vengeance on Midian. ⁴You shall send a thousand from each of the tribes of Israel to the war." ⁵So out of the thousands of Israel, a thousand from each tribe were conscripted, twelve thousand armed for battle. ⁶Moses sent them to the war, a thousand from each tribe, along with Phinehas son of Eleazar the priest,ˢ with the vessels of the sanctuary and the trumpets for sounding the alarm in his hand. ⁷They did battle against Midian, as the LORD had commanded Moses, and killed every male. ⁸They killed the kings of Midian: Evi, Rekem, Zur, Hur, and Reba, the five kings of Midian, in addition to others who were slain by them, and they also killed Balaam son of Beor with the sword. ⁹The Israelites took the women of Midian and their little ones captive, and they plundered all their cattle, their flocks, and all their goods. ¹⁰All their towns where they had settled, and all their encampments, they burned, ¹¹but they took all the spoil and all the plunder, both people and animals. ¹²Then they brought the captives and the plunder and the spoil to Moses, to Eleazar the priest, and to the congregation of the Israelites, at the camp on the plains of Moab by the Jordan opposite Jericho.

13 Moses, Eleazar the priest, and all the leaders of the congregation went to meet them outside the camp. ¹⁴Moses became angry with the officers of the army, the commanders of

q 30.13 Or *to fast*   r 30.14 Or *from that day to the next*
s 31.6 Gk: Heb adds *to the war*

the legal guardianship of her father or husband. **30:9** Widows or divorced women are obligated to keep their vows, as are men. A widow still remains under the authority of her husband's house (cf. Gen. 38) unless she returns to her father's house (cf. Ruth 1:8) or lives with her son. It is the same for a divorced woman unless there is a concrete action taken for her rejection (divorce papers or sending her out of the husband's house; see Deut. 24:1–4).

31:1–54 The battle report highlights Israel's fulfillment of God's command at Midian (25:16–18). It uses incidents and regulations from many other passages and characterizes the battle as a holy endeavor, a total sacrificial extermination of the enemy. **31:1–2** *Avenge:* vindicating the honor of God and Israel after the incident at Baal Peor (25:6–9). *Afterward* recalls Moses's imminent death (27:13). **31:3–4** *The LORD's vengeance* implies a sacred warfare. **31:5–12** *Phinehas,* the priest (not Moses or Joshua) who showed zeal for God by killing the Midianite woman and the Israelite man for their sin of intermarriage (25:6–15), accompanied by the sanctuary equipment and blowing trumpets (10:2–10), leads a small number of soldiers (one thousand from each tribe) to *[kill] every male* of the Midianites (total extermination), including the five slain Midianite kings and *Balaam son of Beor* (Josh. 13:21–22), and to burn all the towns and plunder all the spoils (Deut. 20:1–18). See **"The Divine Mandate to Exterminate the Canaanites,"** p. 313. **31:13–20** The commanders' and officers' actions match the rules of war given in Deut. 20:10–14, killing all males but taking the women, children, and animals as

thousands and the commanders of hundreds, who had come from service in the war. [15]Moses said to them, "Have you allowed all the women to live? [16]These women here, on Balaam's advice, made the Israelites act treacherously against the LORD in the affair of Peor, so that the plague came among the congregation of the LORD. [17]Now therefore, kill every male among the little ones, and kill every woman who has known a man by sleeping with him. [18]But all the young girls who have not known a man by sleeping with him, keep alive for yourselves. [19]Camp outside the camp seven days, whoever of you has killed any person or touched a corpse; purify yourselves, you and your captives, on the third and on the seventh day. [20]You shall purify every garment, every article of skin, everything made of goats' hair, and every article of wood."

21 Eleazar the priest said to the troops who had gone to battle, "This is the statute of the law that the LORD has commanded Moses: [22]gold, silver, bronze, iron, tin, and lead—[23]everything that can withstand fire, you shall pass through fire, and it shall be clean. Nevertheless, it shall also be purified with the water for purification, and whatever cannot withstand fire, you shall pass through the water. [24]You must wash your clothes on the seventh day, and you shall be clean; afterward you may come into the camp."

25 The LORD spoke to Moses, saying, [26]"You and Eleazar the priest and the heads of the ancestral houses of the congregation make an inventory of the plunder captured, both human and animal. [27]Divide the plunder into two parts, between the warriors who went out to battle and all the congregation. [28]From the share of the warriors who went out to battle, set aside as tribute for the LORD one item out of every five hundred, whether persons, oxen, donkeys, or sheep. [29]Take it from their half and give it to Eleazar the priest as an offering to the LORD. [30]But from the Israelites' half you shall take one out of every fifty, whether persons, oxen, donkeys, or sheep—all the animals—and give them to the Levites, who perform the duties of the tabernacle of the LORD."

31 Then Moses and Eleazar the priest did as the LORD had commanded Moses.

32 The plunder remaining from the spoils that the troops had taken totaled six hundred seventy-five thousand sheep, [33]seventy-two thousand oxen, [34]sixty-one thousand donkeys, [35]and thirty-two thousand persons in all, women who had not known a man by sleeping with him.

36 The half-share, the portion of those who had gone out to war, was in number three hundred thirty-seven thousand five hundred sheep, [37]and the LORD's tribute of sheep was six hundred seventy-five. [38]The oxen were thirty-six thousand, of which the LORD's tribute was seventy-two. [39]The donkeys were thirty thousand five hundred, of which the LORD's tribute was sixty-one. [40]The persons were sixteen thousand, of which the LORD's tribute was thirty-two persons. [41]Moses gave the tribute, the offering for the LORD, to Eleazar the priest, as the LORD had commanded Moses.

42 As for the Israelites' half, which Moses separated from that of the troops, [43]the congregation's half was three hundred thirty-seven thousand five hundred sheep, [44]thirty-six thousand oxen, [45]thirty thousand five hundred donkeys, [46]and sixteen thousand persons. [47]From the Israelites' half Moses took one of every fifty, both of persons and of animals, and gave them to the Levites, who perform the duties of the tabernacle of the LORD, as the LORD had commanded Moses.

48 Then the officers who were over the thousands of the army, the commanders of

plunder. Yet Moses becomes angry at the Israelites for sparing the Midianite women and commands them to kill all the male children and women who are not virgins because he recalls the role the Midianite women played in the Baal Peor affair, luring the Israelites to idolatrous rebellion. *On Balaam's advice* portrays Balaam negatively, even though he was not present in that incident. The virgins are spared *for yourselves*—that is, for marriage or enslavement. The army leaders must undergo a purification after contact with the dead (19:11–19). **31:21–24** Eleazar orders the troops to purify the spoils made of metal, which requires a combination of fire and the water of purification (19:1–10). War inevitably defiles all participants, including the nonhuman spoils. Just as they need to be in a holy state to engage in war (1 Sam. 21:4–5), they must be purified after war. **31:25–47** The human (virgins) and animal spoils are to be distributed equally between the warriors and all other Israelites (Josh. 22:8; 1 Sam. 30:23–25). Each warrior takes 1/500th (0.2 percent) from his portion to support the priests, whereas each remaining Israelite takes 1/50th (2 percent) to support the Levites. The

thousands and the commanders of hundreds, approached Moses [49]and said to Moses, "Your servants have counted the warriors who are under our command, and not one of us is missing. [50]And we have brought the LORD's offering, what each of us found, articles of gold, armlets and bracelets, signet rings, earrings, and pendants, to make atonement for ourselves before the LORD." [51]Moses and Eleazar the priest received the gold from them, all in the form of crafted articles. [52]And all the gold of the offering that they offered to the LORD, from the commanders of thousands and the commanders of hundreds, was sixteen thousand seven hundred fifty shekels. [53](The troops had all taken plunder for themselves.) [54]So Moses and Eleazar the priest received the gold from the commanders of thousands and of hundreds and brought it into the tent of meeting as a memorial for the Israelites before the LORD.

32 Now the Reubenites and the Gadites owned a very great number of cattle. When they saw that the land of Jazer and the land of Gilead was a good place for cattle, [2]the Gadites and the Reubenites came and spoke to Moses, to Eleazar the priest, and to the leaders of the congregation, saying, [3]"Ataroth, Dibon, Jazer, Nimrah, Heshbon, Elealeh, Sebam, Nebo, and Beon—[4]the land that the LORD subdued before the congregation of Israel—is a land for cattle, and your servants have cattle." [5]They continued, "If we have found favor in your sight, let this land be given to your servants for a possession; do not make us cross the Jordan."

[6] But Moses said to the Gadites and to the Reubenites, "Shall your brothers go to war while you sit here? [7]Why will you discourage the hearts of the Israelites from going over into the land that the LORD has given them? [8]Your fathers did this, when I sent them from Kadesh-barnea to see the land. [9]When they went up to the Wadi Eshcol and saw the land, they discouraged the hearts of the Israelites from going into the land that the LORD had given them. [10]The LORD's anger was kindled on that day, and he swore, saying, [11]'Surely none of the people who came up out of Egypt, from twenty years old and up, shall see the land that I swore to give to Abraham, to Isaac, and to Jacob, because they have not unreservedly followed me—[12]none except Caleb son of Jephunneh the Kenizzite and Joshua son of Nun, for they have unreservedly followed the LORD.' [13]And the LORD's anger was kindled against Israel, and he made them wander in the wilderness for forty years, until all the generation that had done evil in the sight of the LORD had disappeared. [14]And now you, a brood of sinners, have risen in place of your fathers, to increase the LORD's fierce anger against Israel! [15]If you turn away from following him, he will again abandon them in the wilderness, and you will destroy all this people."

[16] Then they came up to him and said, "We will build sheepfolds here for our flocks and towns for our little ones, [17]but we will take up arms as a vanguard[t] before the Israelites, until we have brought them to their place. Meanwhile our little ones will stay in the fortified towns because of the inhabitants of the land.

t 32.17 Gk: Heb *hurrying*

total plunder is exceptionally large. **31:48–54** The commanders and officers of the army voluntarily offer gold articles to God for making *atonement for* themselves *before the LORD*. The gift could be to acknowledge God's miraculous care (no single Israelite soldier was killed), to express their gratitude for God's sparing of their lives in war, or to serve as a ransom to God in order to avoid God's wrath for taking a census (*Your servants have counted the warriors who are under our command*) without God's command (cf. Exod. 30:11–16; David's census in 2 Sam. 24).

32:1–42 The negotiation between the tribes of Reuben and Gad and Moses results in their settlement in the Transjordan, conditional only on their active participation in the conquest of the land west of the Jordan (Deut. 3:12–20; cf. Josh. 22). The half-tribe of Manasseh also receives an inheritance of land in Transjordan, even though they are not involved in the negotiation. **32:1–5** The tribes of Reuben and Gad publicly request to settle in the Transjordan. *Jazer.* An Amorite city that Israel conquered (21:32). *The land of Gilead.* The southern region between the Arnon River and the Jabbok River. **32:6–15** Moses's objection presupposes that only the land of Canaan across the Jordan is considered the promised land (Exod. 16:35; Deut. 32:49; Josh. 22:9–11; Judg. 21:12); thus, he accuses the two tribes of committing the same crime as the old generation (Num. 13–14) and of instigating disunity. He adds a severe warning that they would intensify God's anger against Israel and incur an even more disastrous consequence: the destruction of the entire people. **32:16–27** The two tribes negotiate with Moses in private with a revised proposal. It consists of participating fully in the sacred war, vowing not to return to their homes until the conquest is complete

¹⁸We will not return to our homes until all the Israelites have obtained their inheritance. ¹⁹We will not inherit with them on the other side of the Jordan and beyond, because our inheritance has come to us on this side of the Jordan to the east."

20 So Moses said to them, "If you do this—if you take up arms to go before the LORD for the war ²¹and all those of you who bear arms cross the Jordan before the LORD, until he has driven out his enemies from before him ²²and the land is subdued before the LORD—then after that you may return and be free of obligation to the LORD and to Israel, and this land shall be your possession before the LORD. ²³But if you do not do this, you have sinned against the LORD, and be sure your sin will find you out. ²⁴Build towns for your little ones and folds for your flocks, but do what you have promised."

25 Then the Gadites and the Reubenites said to Moses, "Your servants will do as my lord commands. ²⁶Our little ones, our wives, our flocks, and all our livestock shall remain there in the towns of Gilead, ²⁷but your servants will cross over, everyone armed for war, to do battle for the LORD, just as my lord orders."

28 So Moses gave command concerning them to Eleazar the priest, to Joshua son of Nun, and to the heads of the ancestral houses of the Israelite tribes. ²⁹And Moses said to them, "If the Gadites and the Reubenites, everyone armed for battle before the LORD, will cross over the Jordan with you and the land shall be subdued before you, then you shall give them the land of Gilead for a possession,

³⁰but if they will not cross over with you armed, they shall have possessions among you in the land of Canaan." ³¹The Gadites and the Reubenites answered, saying, "As the LORD has spoken to your servants, so we will do. ³²We will cross over armed before the LORD into the land of Canaan, but the possession of our inheritance shall remain with us on this side of𝘶 the Jordan."

33 Moses gave to them—to the Gadites and to the Reubenites and to the half-tribe of Manasseh son of Joseph—the kingdom of King Sihon of the Amorites and the kingdom of King Og of Bashan, the land and its towns, with the territories of the surrounding towns. ³⁴And the Gadites rebuilt Dibon, Ataroth, Aroer, ³⁵Atroth-shophan, Jazer, Jogbehah, ³⁶Beth-nimrah, and Beth-haran, fortified cities, and folds for sheep. ³⁷And the Reubenites rebuilt Heshbon, Elealeh, Kiriathaim, ³⁸Nebo, and Baal-meon (some names being changed), and Sibmah, and they gave names to the towns that they rebuilt. ³⁹The descendants of Machir son of Manasseh went to Gilead, captured it, and dispossessed the Amorites who were there, ⁴⁰so Moses gave Gilead to Machir son of Manasseh, and he settled there. ⁴¹Jair son of Manasseh went and captured their villages and renamed them Havvoth-jair.𝘷 ⁴²And Nobah went and captured Kenath and its villages and renamed it Nobah after himself.

33 These are the stages by which the Israelites went out of the land of Egypt in military formation under the leadership of

𝘶 32.32 Heb *beyond*   𝘷 32.41 That is, *the villages of Jair*

---

and all the Israelites receive their *inheritance*, and not receiving land west of the Jordan. Moses reformulates their proposal with the language of sacred warfare: all their activities must be done *before the* LORD. God is in charge of fulfilling the land promise, and participation in God's war is not optional. Moses frames the deal in a covenantal law: *If you do this. . . . But if you do not do this.* The two tribes accept the terms of the contract and pledge to send their soldiers *before the* LORD for participating in the sacred war. See **"Genocide," p. 305. 32:28–32** The negotiated contract is ratified publicly before Eleazar, Joshua, and the leaders of the tribes, who serve as witnesses to the deal. **32:33–42** The two tribes receive the land with its cities that have already been conquered (21:21–35). However, the half-tribe of Manasseh is mentioned for the first time as an additional beneficiary (Deut. 3:13–15; Josh. 13:29–31). Its way of settlement, *Machir . . . went . . . captured . . . Jair . . . went and captured . . . Nobah went and captured*, contradicts the standards of sacred war, which requires full participation from all of Israel's tribes. These clans of Manasseh act independently to conquer their respective villages, which were previously unconquered.

33:1–49 The itinerary of Israel's journey from Rameses to the plains of Moab contains forty-two campsites, of which many cannot be identified with any certainty. It includes seventeen sites not mentioned elsewhere in the Old Testament and omits a few places mentioned in Exodus and Numbers: the wilderness of Shur (Exod. 15:22), Taberah (Num. 11:3), Hormah (14:45; 21:3), the valley of Zered (21:12), Beer (21:16), Mattanah (21:18–19), Nahaliel (21:19), and Bamoth (21:19–20). Compared to similar ancient Near Eastern texts, it resembles a record of military campaigns or presents the route for a pilgrimage. **33:1–2** Israel engages in a military campaign led by Moses and Aaron,

Moses and Aaron. [2]Moses wrote down their starting points, stage by stage, by command of the LORD, and these are their stages according to their starting places. [3]They set out from Rameses in the first month, on the fifteenth day of the first month; on the day after the Passover the Israelites went out boldly in the sight of all the Egyptians, [4]while the Egyptians were burying all their firstborn, whom the LORD had struck down among them. The LORD executed judgments even against their gods.

5 So the Israelites set out from Rameses and camped at Succoth. [6]They set out from Succoth and camped at Etham, which is on the edge of the wilderness. [7]They set out from Etham and turned back to Pi-hahiroth, which faces Baal-zephon, and they camped before Migdol. [8]They set out from Pi-hahiroth,[w] passed through the sea into the wilderness, went a three days' journey in the wilderness of Etham, and camped at Marah. [9]They set out from Marah and came to Elim; at Elim there were twelve springs of water and seventy palm trees, and they camped there. [10]They set out from Elim and camped by the Red Sea.[x] [11]They set out from the Red Sea[y] and camped in the wilderness of Sin. [12]They set out from the wilderness of Sin and camped at Dophkah. [13]They set out from Dophkah and camped at Alush. [14]They set out from Alush and camped at Rephidim, where there was no water for the people to drink. [15]They set out from Rephidim and camped in the wilderness of Sinai. [16]They set out from the wilderness of Sinai and camped at Kibroth-hattaavah. [17]They set out from Kibroth-hattaavah and camped at Hazeroth. [18]They set out from Hazeroth and camped at Rithmah. [19]They set out from Rithmah and camped at Rimmon-perez. [20]They set out from Rimmon-perez and camped at Libnah. [21]They set out from Libnah and camped at Rissah. [22]They set out from Rissah and camped at Kehelathah. [23]They set out from Kehelathah and camped at Mount Shepher. [24]They set out from Mount Shepher and camped at Haradah. [25]They set out from Haradah and camped at Makheloth. [26]They set out from Makheloth and camped at Tahath. [27]They set out from Tahath and camped at Terah. [28]They set out from Terah and camped at Mithkah. [29]They set out from Mithkah and camped at Hashmonah. [30]They set out from Hashmonah and camped at Moseroth. [31]They set out from Moseroth and camped at Bene-jaakan. [32]They set out from Bene-jaakan and camped at Hor-haggidgad. [33]They set out from Hor-haggidgad and camped at Jotbathah. [34]They set out from Jotbathah and camped at Abronah. [35]They set out from Abronah and camped at Ezion-geber. [36]They set out from Ezion-geber and camped in the wilderness of Zin (that is, Kadesh). [37]They set out from Kadesh and camped at Mount Hor, on the edge of the land of Edom.

38 Aaron the priest went up Mount Hor at the command of the LORD and died there in the fortieth year after the Israelites had come out of the land of Egypt, on the first day of the fifth month. [39]Aaron was one hundred twenty-three years old when he died on Mount Hor.

40 The Canaanite, the king of Arad, who lived in the Negeb in the land of Canaan, heard of the coming of the Israelites.

41 They set out from Mount Hor and camped at Zalmonah. [42]They set out from Zalmonah

w 33.8 Heb mss Sam Syr OL Vg: MT *from before Habiroth*
x 33.10 Or *Sea of Reeds*   y 33.11 Or *Sea of Reeds*

---

anticipated in the characterization of Israel's camp (1:1–10:10). *Moses wrote down* is a rare expression of Moses's writing activity (cf. Exod. 24:4). **33:3–5** "They *set out from* A and *camped at* B" is a typical literary pattern for describing the journey, except in two places: Rameses, the beginning of the journey (Exod. 12:37), and Mount Hor, the end of their march (Num. 33:37–40; 20:22–29; 21:1–3). **33:5–11** Journey to the wilderness of Sin: *Succoth* (see Exod. 12:37), *Etham* (see Exod. 13:20), *Pi-hahiroth* (see Exod. 14:2, 9), *Marah* (see Exod. 15:23), *Elim* (see Exod. 15:27), *camped by the Red Sea* (cf. Exod. 16:1). In Exodus, the event at the Red Sea (Exod. 14:21–29) occurs before entering the desert, stressing God's saving act, whereas in Numbers it happens in the desert away from Egypt, underscoring God's continual guidance through the wilderness. **33:12–15** Journey to the wilderness of Sinai, the location for making the covenant, building the sanctuary, and organizing the camp (Exod. 19:1–Num. 10:10). *Dophkah* and *Alush* are unidentified campsites. *Rephidim* (see Exod. 17:1–7). **33:16–36** Journey to the wilderness of Zin (20:1): *Kibroth-hattaavah* (see 11:4–35); *Hazeroth* (see 11:35; 12:16); *Moseroth, Bene-jaakan, Hor-haggidgad, Jotbathah* (see Deut. 10:6–9); *Ezion-geber* (see Deut. 2:8). **33:37–40** This recalls the death of Aaron (20:22–29) and adds the date and his age when he died. *The Canaanite, the king of Arad* alludes to the first military victory of the Israelites (21:1–3), the beginning of the new generation. **33:41–49** Journey to the plains of Moab (see chap. 21).

and camped at Punon. ⁴³They set out from Punon and camped at Oboth. ⁴⁴They set out from Oboth and camped at Iye-abarim, in the territory of Moab. ⁴⁵They set out from Iyim and camped at Dibon-gad. ⁴⁶They set out from Dibon-gad and camped at Almon-diblathaim. ⁴⁷They set out from Almon-diblathaim and camped in the mountains of Abarim, before Nebo. ⁴⁸They set out from the mountains of Abarim and camped in the plains of Moab by the Jordan opposite Jericho; ⁴⁹they camped by the Jordan from Beth-jeshimoth as far as Abel-shittim in the plains of Moab.

50 In the plains of Moab by the Jordan opposite Jericho, the LORD spoke to Moses, saying, ⁵¹"Speak to the Israelites, and say to them: When you cross over the Jordan into the land of Canaan, ⁵²you shall drive out all the inhabitants of the land from before you, destroy all their figured stones, destroy all their cast images, and demolish all their high places. ⁵³You shall take possession of the land and settle in it, for I have given you the land to possess. ⁵⁴You shall apportion the land by lot according to your clans; to a large one you shall give a large inheritance, and to a small one you shall give a small inheritance; the inheritance shall belong to the person on whom the lot falls; according to your ancestral tribes you shall apportion it. ⁵⁵But if you do not drive out the inhabitants of the land from before you, then those whom you let remain shall be as barbs in your eyes and thorns in your sides; they shall trouble you in the land where you are settling. ⁵⁶And I will do to you as I thought to do to them."

34 The LORD spoke to Moses, saying, ²"Command the Israelites, and say to them: When you enter the land of Canaan (this is the land that shall fall to you for an inheritance, the land of Canaan, defined by its boundaries), ³your south sector shall extend from the wilderness of Zin along the side of Edom. Your southern boundary shall begin from the end of the Dead Sea[z] on the east; ⁴your boundary shall turn south of the ascent of Akrabbim and cross to Zin, and its outer limit shall be south of Kadesh-barnea; then it shall go on to Hazar-addar and cross to Azmon; ⁵the boundary shall turn from Azmon to the Wadi of Egypt, and its termination shall be at the Sea.

6 "For the western boundary, you shall have the Great Sea and its[a] coast; this shall be your western boundary.

7 "This shall be your northern boundary: from the Great Sea you shall mark out your line to Mount Hor; ⁸from Mount Hor you shall mark it out to Lebo-hamath, and the outer limit of the boundary shall be at Zedad; ⁹then the boundary shall extend to Ziphron, and its end shall be at Hazar-enan; this shall be your northern boundary.

10 "You shall mark out your eastern boundary from Hazar-enan to Shepham, ¹¹and the boundary shall continue down from Shepham to Riblah on the east side of Ain, and the boundary shall go down and reach the eastern slope of the sea of Chinnereth, ¹²and the boundary shall go down to the Jordan, and

z 34.3 Heb *Salt Sea*   a 34.6 Syr: Heb lacks *its*

33:50–56 The conquest is authorized by God (v. 53b) and aims to drive the Canaanites out of their land, destroy their cultic furnishings (Deut. 12:2–3), and possess their land. After repeating the principles of dividing the land (Num. 26:52–56), the instructions end with a warning, promoting the exact execution in the future. God will dispossess Israel if Israel does not dispossess the Canaanites from the land. See **"The Divine Mandate to Exterminate the Canaanites," p. 313**.

34:1–12 The boundaries of the promised land are defined starting clockwise from the south to the east and excluding the Transjordan territory. They are wider than a common designation of the land, "from Dan to Beer-sheba" (1 Sam. 3:20; 2 Sam. 3:10; 17:11; 24:2; 1 Kgs. 4:25), as the southern border (Kadesh-barnea) is farther south than Beer-sheba and the northern border (Lebo-hamath) is farther north than Dan. These expanded borders recall the spy story (Num. 13–14) and correspond to the land of Canaan known from Near Eastern (fifteenth century BCE) and Egyptian (thirteenth century BCE) texts. It reflects the conviction of Canaan as God's gift for Israel's inheritance. **34:3–5** The southern border (cf. Josh. 15:1–4; Ezek. 47:19). **34:6** The western border is marked by a single landmark, *the Great Sea* (the Mediterranean Sea), without mentioning the Judahites (Josh. 15:12) or the link to Lebo-hamath (Ezek. 47:20). **34:7–9** The northern border (Ezek. 47:15–17) differs from Josh. 15:5b–11, which marks the northern tip of the Dead Sea as the beginning of the border and includes many more locations. **34:10–12** The eastern border (Josh. 15:5a; Ezek. 47:18) clearly distinguishes heritable land in Canaan from the land in the Transjordan.

its end shall be at the Dead Sea.[b] This shall be your land with its boundaries all around."

13 Moses commanded the Israelites, saying, "This is the land that you shall apportion by lot, which the LORD has commanded to give to the nine tribes and to the half-tribe, [14]for the tribe of the Reubenites by their ancestral houses and the tribe of the Gadites by their ancestral houses have taken their inheritance and also the half-tribe of Manasseh; [15]the two tribes and the half-tribe have taken their inheritance beyond the Jordan at Jericho eastward, toward the sunrise."

16 The LORD spoke to Moses, saying, [17]"These are the names of the men who shall apportion the land to you for inheritance: the priest Eleazar and Joshua son of Nun. [18]You shall take one leader of every tribe to apportion the land for inheritance. [19]These are the names of the men: Of the tribe of Judah, Caleb son of Jephunneh. [20]Of the tribe of the Simeonites, Shemuel son of Ammihud. [21]Of the tribe of Benjamin, Elidad son of Chislon. [22]Of the tribe of the Danites a leader, Bukki son of Jogli. [23]Of the Josephites: of the tribe of the Manassites a leader, Hanniel son of Ephod, [24]and of the tribe of the Ephraimites a leader, Kemuel son of Shiphtan. [25]Of the tribe of the Zebulunites a leader, Eli-zaphan son of Parnach. [26]Of the tribe of the Issacharites a leader, Paltiel son of Azzan. [27]And of the tribe of the Asherites a leader, Ahihud son of Shelomi. [28]Of the tribe of the Naphtalites a leader, Pedahel son of Ammihud. [29]These were the

ones whom the LORD commanded to apportion the inheritance for the Israelites in the land of Canaan."

35 In the plains of Moab by the Jordan opposite Jericho, the LORD spoke to Moses, saying, [2]"Command the Israelites to give, from the inheritance that they possess, towns for the Levites to live in; you shall also give to the Levites pasturelands surrounding the towns. [3]The towns shall be theirs to live in, and their pasturelands shall be for their cattle, for their livestock, and for all their animals. [4]The pasturelands of the towns, which you shall give to the Levites, shall reach from the wall of the town outward a thousand cubits all around. [5]You shall measure, outside the town, for the east side two thousand cubits, for the south side two thousand cubits, for the west side two thousand cubits, and for the north side two thousand cubits, with the town in the middle; this shall belong to them as pastureland for their towns.

6 "The towns that you give to the Levites shall include the six cities of refuge, where you shall permit a slayer to flee, and in addition to them you shall give forty-two towns. [7]The towns that you give to the Levites shall total forty-eight, with their pasturelands. [8]And as for the towns that you shall give from the possession of the Israelites, from the

b 34.12 Heb *Salt Sea*

34:13–15 This reaffirms the principle of distribution of the land (26:52–56) as well as the decision made for the tribes of Reuben, Gad, and half of Manasseh (32:1–32).

34:16–29 The ten tribal leaders are named to assist Eleazar and Joshua in distributing the land for the nine and a half tribes. Aside from Caleb (13:6; 14:24), all the other names are new in Numbers and appear rarely in other texts. The order of the tribes is also new and reflects Israel's settlement from the south (Judah, Simeon, Benjamin, and Dan) to the central region (half of Manasseh and Ephraim), and to the north (Zebulun, Issachar, Asher, and Naphtali). The tribe of Judah is prominent, placed first (2:3–9; 7:12–17; 10:14).

35:1–8 The Levites are separated from the other tribes in the wilderness camp: they are counted separately (1:48–53), are given special tasks in caring for the tabernacle (3:5–4:49), and belong to God as a substitution for Israel's firstborn (8:5–26). For this service, they receive a tithe from the Israelites instead of inheriting land (18:21–24). Their special status must be maintained in the promised land: they live in forty-eight towns with associated pastures (including six designated cities of refuge) throughout the land, given by each tribe proportional to its land inheritance. **35:4–5** V. 4 describes the size of the pasturelands, while v. 5 describes the size of the town; the total area would then be three thousand cubits squared (1 cubit = 1.5 feet). Perhaps v. 4 describes the size of the pastureland from one direction, whereas v. 5 describes the combination of both sides (east and west; south and north); the total area then would be the size of the town (whatever that might be) plus two thousand cubits of the pastureland surrounding the town. **35:6–7** *Total forty-eight* indicates four cities from each of nine tribes, eight from Judah, one from Simeon, and three from Naphtali (Josh. 21:1–40).

larger tribes you shall take many, and from the smaller tribes you shall take few; each, in proportion to the inheritance that it obtains, shall give of its towns to the Levites."

9 The LORD spoke to Moses, saying, ¹⁰"Speak to the Israelites and say to them: When you cross the Jordan into the land of Canaan, ¹¹then you shall select cities to be cities of refuge for you, so that a slayer who kills a person without intent may flee there. ¹²The cities shall be for you a refuge from the avenger, so that the slayer may not die until there is a trial before the congregation.

13 "The cities that you designate shall be six cities of refuge for you: ¹⁴you shall designate three cities beyond the Jordan, and three cities in the land of Canaan, to be cities of refuge. ¹⁵These six cities shall serve as refuge for the Israelites, for the resident or transient alien among them, so that anyone who kills a person without intent may flee there.

16 "But anyone who strikes another with an iron object, and death ensues, is a murderer; the murderer shall be put to death. ¹⁷Or anyone who strikes another with a stone in hand that could cause death, and death ensues, is a murderer; the murderer shall be put to death. ¹⁸Or anyone who strikes another with a weapon of wood in hand that could cause death, and death ensues, is a murderer; the murderer shall be put to death. ¹⁹The avenger of blood is the one who shall put the murderer to death; when they meet, the avenger of blood shall execute the sentence. ²⁰Likewise, if someone pushes another from hatred or hurls something at another, lying in wait, and death ensues, ²¹or in enmity strikes another with the hand, and death ensues, then the one who struck the blow shall be put to death; that person is a murderer; the avenger of blood shall put the murderer to death when they meet.

22 "But if someone pushes another suddenly without enmity or hurls any object without lying in wait, ²³or, while handling any stone that could cause death, unintentionally^c drops it on another and death ensues, though they were not enemies and no harm was intended, ²⁴then the congregation shall judge between the slayer and the avenger of blood, in accordance with these ordinances, ²⁵and the congregation shall rescue the slayer from the avenger of blood. Then the congregation shall send the slayer back to the original city of refuge. The slayer shall live in it until the death of the high priest who was anointed with the holy oil. ²⁶But if the slayer shall at any time go outside the bounds of the original city of refuge ²⁷and is found by the avenger of blood outside the bounds of the city of refuge and is killed by the avenger, no blood-guilt shall be incurred. ²⁸For the slayer must remain in the city of refuge until the death of the high priest, but after the death of the high priest the slayer may return to his property.

29 "These things shall be a statute and ordinance for you throughout your generations wherever you live.

30 "If anyone kills another, the murderer shall be put to death on the evidence of witnesses, but no one shall be put to death on the testimony of a single witness. ³¹Moreover you shall accept no ransom for the life of a murderer who is subject to the death penalty; a murderer must be put to death. ³²Nor shall you accept ransom for one who has fled to a city of refuge, enabling the fugitive to return to live in the land before the death of the high priest. ³³You shall not pollute the land in which you

c 35.23 Heb *without seeing*

35:9–34 Instructions for protecting the killer from the traditional death by an avenger of the blood (cf. Deut. 19:1–13; Josh. 20:1–9). 35:10–15 *Cities of refuge:* places of asylum for involuntary homicide. Six cities are allocated (Deut. 4:41–43; Josh. 21): three inside of Canaan—Kedesh in the north (Naphtali), Shechem in the center (Ephraim), Hebron in the south (Judah); three in Transjordan—Bezer in the south (Reuben), Ramoth-gilead in the center (Gad), and Golan in the north (Manasseh). 35:16–21 The object used (iron, stone, or wood) and motive (hatred or hostility) determine the killer's intention. The *murderer* must be executed because intentionally committed sin will not be forgiven through sacrifices (15:30–31). 35:22–28 For unintentional homicide, the community, not the relative of the dead, adjudicates the case. The slayer is confined in a designated refuge city, away from the avenger of blood and the rest of the community, until the death of the high priest. If the slayer goes outside the boundaries of the refuge city before the death of the high priest, he is subject to the just action of the avenger. 35:30–32 Additional legislations underscore the importance of the life of a killer (by following due process) and the life of the victim (by closing loopholes). 35:33–34 The rationale for the legislation regarding homicide is that taking human life pollutes the land, which, in

live, for blood pollutes the land, and no expiation can be made for the land for the blood that is shed in it, except by the blood of the one who shed it. [34]You shall not defile the land in which you live, in which I also dwell, for I the LORD dwell among the Israelites."

36 The heads of the ancestral houses of the clans of the descendants of Gilead son of Machir son of Manasseh, of the Josephite clans, came forward and spoke in the presence of Moses and the leaders, the heads of the ancestral houses of the Israelites; [2]they said, "The LORD commanded my lord to give the land for inheritance by lot to the Israelites, and my lord was commanded by the LORD to give the inheritance of our brother Zelophehad to his daughters. [3]But if they are married into another Israelite tribe, then their inheritance will be taken from the inheritance of our ancestors and added to the inheritance of the tribe into which they marry, so it will be taken away from the allotted portion of our inheritance. [4]And when the Jubilee of the Israelites comes, then their inheritance will be added to the inheritance of the tribe into which they have married, and their inheritance will be taken from the inheritance of our ancestral tribe."

5 Then Moses commanded the Israelites according to the word of the LORD, saying, "The descendants of the tribe of Joseph are right in what they are saying. [6]This is what the LORD commands concerning the daughters of Zelophehad, saying: Let them marry whom they think best; only it must be into a clan of their father's tribe that they are married, [7]so that no inheritance of the Israelites shall be transferred from one tribe to another, for all Israelites shall retain the inheritance of their ancestral tribes. [8]Every daughter who possesses an inheritance in any tribe of the Israelites shall marry one from the clan of her father's tribe, so that all Israelites may continue to possess their ancestral inheritance. [9]No inheritance shall be transferred from one tribe to another, for each of the tribes of the Israelites shall retain its own inheritance."

10 The daughters of Zelophehad did as the LORD had commanded Moses. [11]Mahlah, Tirzah, Hoglah, Milcah, and Noah, the daughters of Zelophehad, married sons of their father's brothers. [12]They were married into the clans of the descendants of Manasseh son of Joseph, and their inheritance remained in the tribe of their father's clan.

13 These are the commandments and the ordinances that the LORD commanded through Moses to the Israelites in the plains of Moab by the Jordan opposite Jericho.

---

turn, makes the people living in the land unclean. God's holiness cannot tolerate impurity, as either God will abandon the defiled land or the land will vomit out its inhabitants (Lev. 18:24–25).

36:1–12 The previous ruling for the daughters of Zelophehad (27:1–11) is modified by stipulating that they must marry into a clan of their father's tribe to hold heritable property within the tribe. This marriage provision is applied to all heiresses so that no inheritance is transferred from one tribe to another. The inheritance given to each tribe is inalienable (26:55; 33:54). **36:1** *Came forward* connotes a step in the judicial procedure of challenging a case in court (27:1). **36:2–4** *When the Jubilee . . . comes:* on this occasion, the purchased property (land and slaves), not inherited land, returns to the original owners (Lev. 25:14–55). Ancestral land transferred to another tribe through heiresses marrying outside their tribe would not be recoverable even at the time of the Jubilee.

36:13 This concluding statement on God's laws covers all the materials from 22:1—in particular, 26:1–36:12 on the issue of land, the goal of the new generation's campaign.

DEUTERONOMY

Date, Authorship, and Literary History

Deuteronomy recounts the last speech of Moses, in which he gives instructions to Israel on the eve of their entrance into the land of Canaan. The book itself is anonymous, though it—along with the other books of the Pentateuch—has been traditionally ascribed to Moses. Various theories have been advanced by modern scholars about how the traditions *about* Moses developed into the current form of Deuteronomy, which is presented as a representation of the authoritative voice of Moses to later generations. Many scholars propose that the original core of the book consisted of the laws of Deut. 12–26 surrounded by a frame of speeches—often considered to be at least chaps. 5–11 and 27–28—which were later supplemented at different points by material in chaps. 1–4 and 29–34 so as to address new circumstances in the Assyrian, Babylonian, and Persian periods. Deuteronomy's distinctive literary style and scholarly theories about its origin(s) and development have earned it an important place in discussions of the composition history of the Pentateuch (see **"Introduction to the Torah/Pentateuch," pp. 2–4**).

Deuteronomy in Jewish and Christian Tradition

Deuteronomy has occupied a central position in Jewish and Christian traditions. The influence of Deuteronomy is seen throughout the Hebrew Bible, where it especially impacted the preaching of the prophets and the reforms of Josiah (2 Kgs. 22–23) and the period of Ezra-Nehemiah. In Judaism, Deuteronomy was one of the primary sources for legal reflection in rabbinic literature and the Dead Sea Scrolls. The recitation of the *Shema* (Deut. 6:4–9), the observance of food laws of Deut. 14, and the celebration of the festivals of Deut. 16 remain central features in Judaism. In the New Testament, dozens of references to Deuteronomy are used to articulate key theological themes (cf. Matt. 4:4 / Deut. 8:3; Matt. 22:37 / Deut. 6:4–5; Rom. 10:6–8 / Deut. 30:12–14), thus ensuring the importance of the book within Christianity. Deuteronomy has also had an inestimable impact on conceptions of justice, human rights, and politics in Western civilization.

Reading Guide

The title of Deuteronomy, which comes from the Greek translation of the phrase "copy of this law" (Deut. 17:18; *deutero-nomium* = "second law"), identifies the book as a repetitive exposition of the laws of Exodus, Leviticus, and Numbers. Jewish tradition takes the Hebrew name of the book, "The Words" (*debarim*), from its initial phrase (1:1). The hermeneutical key to reading Deuteronomy is recognizing that the book—as the culmination of the Pentateuch and transition to the Historical Books that follow—is an exposition of the theological, ethical, and religious traditions that were revealed to the first generation of Israelites at Horeb and to a new generation of Israelites who are poised to enter the land of Canaan.

The book is structured into four speeches: the first speech (1:6–4:43) recounts Israel's deliverance from Egypt and sojourn in the wilderness as an exhortation to obedience. The second speech (4:44–26:19) contains the main body of teachings, beginning with the Decalogue (Deut. 5:1–21), followed by theological sermons (chaps. 6–11) and "statutes and ordinances" (chaps. 12–26). The third speech consists of a list of covenant blessings and curses (27:1–29:1), and the fourth (29:2–30:20) is a culminating exhortation for Israel to obey the covenant. The book concludes with Moses's plans for transferring leadership after his death (31:1–34:12), including instructions for installing Joshua as a successor and for the regular public reading of the book (chap. 31), and two poems—a song and a blessing—that describe Israel's identity and relationship to the Lord (chaps. 32–33).

The entire book of Deuteronomy—though a mix of genres such as biography, narrative, historiography, law, poetry, and ritual—is defined as *torah*, "law" (1:5; or "instruction"). This torah-instruction outlines a comprehensive way of life that is characterized by love and devotion to the Lord with all of Israel's "heart," "soul," and "might" (6:5). Reading Deuteronomy well requires paying attention to the ways that the various genres—building on genres known from ancient Near Eastern literature—are integrated to apply Israel's theological and ethical traditions to new circumstances and motivate Israel's obedience. The structure of the book is often characterized as a law collection (chaps. 12–26) surrounded by narratives (chaps. 1–11, 27–34), which frame the book according to

ancient Near Eastern treaty conventions. In this regard, Deuteronomy is profitably compared with Hittite, Aramean, and Assyrian treaty texts that define relationships between dominating kings and their subjugated vassals. These treaties usually consist of a preamble and prologue, stipulations, instructions for a covenant ceremony, blessings and curses, and an invocation of witnesses. The occurrence of these elements in Deuteronomy places obedience to the instructions of Moses within a relational context of submission to God as the sovereign Lord of Israel: the preamble and prologue (Deut. 1–11) describe the historical relationship that grounds the expectation of obedience to the covenant stipulations (12–26), while the instructions for the covenant ceremony, with a recital of blessings and curses (27–31), establish guidelines for solemnizing and perpetuating the covenant. The biographical elements of the book as a testimonial speech from what appears to be the last day of Moses's life (1:1–5; 34:1–12) frame the book according to the features of ancient Near Eastern testimonial or instructional literature, wherein a parental sage passes on wisdom to the next generation to attain a flourishing life (cf. 6:1–25). The "statutes and ordinances" (12:1–26:19), which bear many resemblances to ancient Near Eastern laws such as those found in the Code of Hammurabi, interpret the laws of Exodus, Leviticus, and Numbers for Israel's new circumstances in the land of Canaan. Deuteronomy's establishment of Israel's collective identity as a chosen and holy people subverts traditional ancient political conceptions of monarchy and tribal patriarchy by defining Israel as a fraternal and egalitarian citizenry. Cultic centralization (Deut. 12), in particular, had a wide-ranging impact on Israel's religion, economics, and judicial system, as reflected in many of the changes seen in the laws of Deuteronomy in comparison to earlier traditions. Scholars continue to debate whether Deuteronomy was intended to subvert, replace, or supplement those earlier laws.

The various features described above make Deuteronomy a hermeneutical key that enables Israel to properly evaluate its past, discern how to faithfully apply its traditions to changing circumstances, and set forth a vision of a flourishing society as a constitutional framework that Israel is called to live up to. The historiographical perspective of the Deuteronomistic History (Joshua–2 Kings; see **"Deuteronomistic History," p. 337**) and the preaching of the Hebrew Prophets appeal to and perpetuate the vision of Deuteronomy as the theological and ethical standard to which the people of Israel are held.

Paavo N. Tucker

1 These are the words that Moses spoke to all Israel beyond the Jordan—in the wilderness, on the plain opposite Suph, between Paran and Tophel, Laban, Hazeroth, and Dizahab. [2](By the way of Mount Seir it takes eleven days to reach Kadesh-barnea from Horeb.) [3]In the fortieth year, on the first day of the eleventh month, Moses spoke to the Israelites just as the LORD had commanded him to speak to them. [4]This was after he had defeated King Sihon of the Amorites, who reigned in Heshbon, and King Og of Bashan, who reigned in Ashtaroth in Edrei. [5]Beyond the Jordan in the land of Moab, Moses undertook to expound this law as follows:

[6] "The LORD our God spoke to us at Horeb, saying, 'You have stayed long enough at this mountain. [7]Resume your journey, and go into the hill country of the Amorites as well as into the neighboring regions—the Arabah, the hill country, the Shephelah, the Negeb,[a]

a 1.7 Q ms Sam Vg: MT *and the Negeb*

1:1–8 Preamble. Deuteronomy begins with a preamble that introduces the book as the words of Moses that were spoken to Israel *beyond the Jordan*, in the land of Moab. Thus, the perspective of the narrator is from within the promised land and, hence, temporally subsequent to the conquest that is forecast as a future event in the book. **1:2–4** The preamble recounts Israel's journey from *Horeb*, where Israel camped in the book of Exodus (cf. Exod. 19, where the mountain is called Sinai; see **"Horeb/Sinai," p. 248**). The journey should have taken *eleven days*, but due to Israel's disobedience in the wilderness—as described in the book of Numbers—the journey lasted forty years. On the defeats of *Sihon* and *Og*, see Num. 21:1–35; Deut. 2:26–37; 3:1–7. **1:5** On the verge of entering the promised land, Moses *undertook to expound this law*—that is, to interpret and apply the meaning of the instructions that the Lord had given Israel in Exodus–Numbers, which also includes promulgating additional teachings. The meaning of the Hebrew for law ("torah") encompasses any kind of instruction, whether in legal or narrative form.

Making Connections: Moses (Deuteronomy 1:1-5)

No character in the Hebrew Bible has received as much attention in reception history of the text as Moses. Born a Hebrew but raised in the courts of Egypt, he spent his early adult life in exile in Midian after he stood up for his enslaved fellow Hebrews and killed an Egyptian taskmaster (Exod. 1-2). Having married the daughter of a mysterious Midianite priest, Moses returned to Egypt after receiving a commission from the Lord to rescue Israel out of slavery and lead them to the promised land. In the process, Moses attained a quasi-divine status as a miracle worker and mediator of the voice of God (Exod. 3-24). Due to Israel's rebellions in the wilderness, Moses was not allowed to enter the promised land (Num. 27:12-23; cf. Deut. 3:23-29). Moses had a massive influence on Israelite religion as the founder of its worship, judicial tradition, and the prophetic office. His partial apotheosis (Exod. 4:16; 7:1; 34:29-35) and enigmatic death (Deut. 34:1-8) ensured that he has enjoyed a vibrant afterlife in Jewish and Christian tradition, giving rise to theories in Jewish apocalyptic literature that he ascended to heaven and took on angelic qualities (Testament of Moses, Assumption of Moses; cf. Jude 9). In Greco-Roman Judaism, Moses was cast as a philosopher-king or divine man who brought the wisdom of the divine realm to humanity (Philo, Josephus). In the New Testament, Moses is remembered as a lawgiver and prophet who is a foundational type for understanding the significance of the revelation of God in Christ: Jesus delivers the authoritative interpretation of the law of God from a mountain like Moses (Matt. 5-7) and is the ultimate fulfillment of the prophetic office like Moses (Acts 3:22-26). Moses even makes an appearance on the Mount of Transfiguration to encourage Jesus in his role as leader of an "exodus" (Luke 9:28-36; cf. v. 31). In Islamic tradition, Moses (Musa) has a prominent role in bringing Israel out of Egypt and receiving revelation from Allah and also, in his postmortem state, offering guidance to the prophet Muhammad. In Western culture, Moses has been a frequent subject of literature, music, and art. As the champion of monotheism and originator of the first democratic political system, Moses is often seen as a foundational figure not only for the Abrahamic religions but for all of Western civilization.

Paavo N. Tucker

and the seacoast—the land of the Canaanites and the Lebanon, as far as the great river, the River Euphrates. [8]See, I have set the land before you; go in and take possession of the land that the Lord swore to your ancestors, to Abraham, to Isaac, and to Jacob, to give to them and to their descendants after them.'

9 "At that time I said to you, 'I am unable by myself to bear you. [10]The Lord your God has multiplied you, so that today you are as numerous as the stars of heaven. [11]May the Lord, the God of your ancestors, increase you a thousand times more and bless you, as he has promised you! [12]But how can I bear the heavy burden of your disputes all by myself? [13]Choose for each of your tribes individuals who are wise, discerning, and reputable, and I will make them your leaders.' [14]You answered me, 'The plan you have proposed is a good one.' [15]So I took the leaders of your tribes, wise and reputable individuals, and installed them as leaders over you, commanders of thousands, commanders of hundreds, commanders of fifties, commanders of tens, and officials, throughout your tribes. [16]I charged your judges at that time: 'Give the members of your community a fair hearing and judge rightly between one person and another, whether kin or resident alien. [17]You must not be partial in judging: hear out the small and the great alike; you shall not be intimidated by anyone, for the judgment is God's. Any case that is too hard for you, bring to me, and I will hear it.' [18]So I charged you at that time with all the things that you should do.

19 "Then, just as the Lord our God had ordered us, we set out from Horeb and went through all that great and terrible wilderness that you saw, on the way to the hill country of the Amorites, until we reached Kadesh-barnea. [20]I said to you, 'You have reached the hill country of the Amorites, which the Lord

1:9-18 Appointing judges. *Leaders* and *judges* are installed to implement justice with wisdom and impartiality. This justice is to be extended to the *kin and resident alien*—that is, to foreigners who live among the people of Israel who are given legal protection and rights. Compare Exod. 18:13-27 for a parallel account.

1:19-45 Rebellion in the wilderness. Deuteronomy bears similarities here to ancient Near Eastern treaty texts, where treaty stipulations are preceded by a historical prologue that defines the relational context within which the treaty is established. The recollections of Deut. 1-3 emphasize the

Going Deeper: Horeb/Sinai (Deuteronomy 1:6)

In Deuteronomy, Horeb is named nine times as the mountain where the Lord gives the commandments to Israel (e.g., 1:2, 6, 19; 4:10, 15; 5:2), while it is called Sinai only once (33:2). The reference in Deut. 33:2 reflects a tradition of Sinai as the mountain home of the Lord, who emerges from there as a Divine Warrior to battle for Israel (cf. Judg. 5:5; Ps. 68:8, 17). In Exodus-Leviticus-Numbers, the location for giving the law is called Sinai thirty times (see, e.g., Exod. 19:1–2; 24:16) and Horeb only three times (Exod. 3:1; 17:6; 33:6). According to some scholars, these differences are due to distinct sources that use different names for the mountain. Alternatively, the terms *Horeb* and *Sinai* could refer to a mountain range versus a particular peak; hence, one of the terms could be a designation for a geographical area and the other a specific location. The meaning of Horeb indicates dryness or wilderness, while Sinai may be a wordplay on the Hebrew for "bush" (*seneh*; cf. Exod. 3:2). Outside the Pentateuch, there is surprisingly little interest in the mountain; it features prominently only in 1 Kgs. 19:8, where a despondent Elijah travels there to hear the voice of God. The identification of the location of Horeb—which depends on theories about the route of the exodus—is widely thought to be in the southern Sinai Peninsula, though other proposals suggest a location farther north, or in Midian, due to the association of the site with Jethro the Midianite, father-in-law of Moses (Exod. 3:1). Since the fourth century CE, the location has often been thought to have been Mount Musa in the southern part of Sinai, where St. Catherine's monastery was built in the fifth century CE to commemorate the site.

Paavo N. Tucker

our God is giving us. ²¹See, the Lord your God has given the land to you; go up, take possession, as the Lord, the God of your ancestors, has promised you; do not fear or be dismayed.'

22 "All of you came to me and said, 'Let us send men ahead of us to explore the land for us and bring back a report to us regarding the route by which we should go up and the cities we will come to.' ²³The plan seemed good to me, and I selected twelve of you, one from each tribe. ²⁴They set out and went up into the hill country, and when they reached the Wadi Eshcol they spied it out ²⁵and gathered some of the land's produce, which they brought down to us. They brought back a report to us and said, 'It is a good land that the Lord our God is giving us.'

26 "But you were unwilling to go up. You rebelled against the command of the Lord your God; ²⁷you grumbled in your tents and said, 'It is because the Lord hates us that he has brought us out of the land of Egypt, to hand us over to the Amorites to destroy us. ²⁸Where are we headed? Our kindred have made our hearts melt by reporting, "The people are stronger and taller than we; the cities are large and fortified up to heaven! We actually saw there the offspring of the Anakim!"'

²⁹I said to you, 'Have no dread or fear of them. ³⁰The Lord your God, who goes before you, is the one who will fight for you, just as he did for you in Egypt before your very eyes ³¹and in the wilderness, where you saw how the Lord your God carried you, just as one carries a child, all the way that you traveled until you reached this place. ³²But in spite of this, you have no trust in the Lord your God, ³³who goes before you on the way to seek out a place for you to camp, in fire by night, and in the cloud by day, to show you the route you should take.'

34 "When the Lord heard your words, he was wrathful and swore, ³⁵'Not one of these—not one of this evil generation—shall see the good land that I swore to give to your ancestors, ³⁶except Caleb son of Jephunneh. He shall see it, and to him and to his descendants I will give the land on which he set foot, because of his complete fidelity to the Lord.' ³⁷Even with me the Lord was angry on your account, saying, 'You also shall not enter there. ³⁸Joshua son of Nun, your assistant, shall enter there; encourage him, for he is the one who will secure Israel's possession of it. ³⁹And as for your little ones who you thought would become plunder, your children who today do not yet know right from wrong, they

faithfulness of the suzerain (overlord)—God, in this case, which is contrasted with the disobedience of the vassal, Israel. **1:30–37** The people refused to enter the land or trust the Lord. In response, the Lord swears that the disobedient generation—Moses included—may not enter the land (cf. 3:24–28; Num. 13–14; see **"Murmuring," p. 209**). **1:39** The second generation of Israelites, along with Caleb and Joshua, are the audience of Deuteronomy who are poised on the edge of the promised land and who must choose to obey where the previous generations failed. The phrase *do not yet know right*

shall enter there; to them I will give it, and they shall take possession of it. ⁴⁰But as for you, journey back into the wilderness, in the direction of the Red Sea.'ᵇ

41 "You answered me, 'We have sinned against the LORD! We are ready to go up and fight, just as the LORD our God command-ed us.' So all of you strapped on your battle gear and thought it easy to go up into the hill country. ⁴²The LORD said to me, 'Say to them: "Do not go up, and do not fight, for I am not in the midst of you; otherwise you will be defeated by your enemies." ' ⁴³Al-though I told you, you would not listen. You rebelled against the command of the LORD and presumptuously went up into the hill country. ⁴⁴The Amorites who lived in that hill country then came out against you and chased you as bees do. They beat you down in Seir as far as Hormah. ⁴⁵When you re-turned and wept before the LORD, the LORD would neither heed your voice nor pay you any attention.

46 "After you had stayed at Kadesh as many days as you did, ¹we journeyed back into the wilderness, in the direction of the Red Sea,ᶜ as the LORD had told me, and skirted Mount Seir for many days. ²Then the LORD said to me, ³'You have been skirting this hill country long enough. Head north, ⁴and charge the people as follows: "You are about to pass through the territory of your kindred, the descendants of Esau, who live in Seir. They will be afraid of you, so be very careful ⁵not to engage in battle with them, for I will not give you even so much as a foot's length of their land, since I have giv-en Mount Seir to Esau as a possession. ⁶You shall purchase food from them for money,

so that you may eat, and you shall also buy water from them for money, so that you may drink. ⁷Surely the LORD your God has blessed you in all your undertakings; he knows your going through this great wilderness. These forty years the LORD your God has been with you; you have lacked nothing." ' ⁸So we passed by our kin, the descendants of Esau who live in Seir, leaving behind the route of the Arabah and leaving behind Elath and Ezion-geber.

"When we had headed out along the route of the wilderness of Moab, ⁹the LORD said to me, 'Do not harass Moab or engage them in battle, for I will not give you any of its land as a posses-sion, since I have given Ar as a possession to the descendants of Lot.' ¹⁰(The Emim—a large and numerous people, as tall as the Anakim—had formerly inhabited it. ¹¹Like the Anakim, they are usually reckoned as Rephaim, though the Moabites call them Emim. ¹²Moreover, the Horim had formerly inhabited Seir, but the de-scendants of Esau dispossessed them, destroy-ing them and settling in their place, as Israel has done in the land that the LORD gave them as a possession.) ¹³Now then, proceed to cross over the Wadi Zered.'

"So we crossed over the Wadi Zered. ¹⁴And the length of time we had traveled from Kadesh-barnea until we crossed the Wadi Zered was thirty-eight years, until the en-tire generation of warriors had perished from the camp, as the LORD had sworn con-cerning them. ¹⁵Indeed, the LORD's own hand was against them, to root them out from the camp, until all had perished.

16 "Just as soon as all the warriors had died

b 1.40 Or Sea of Reeds   c 2.1 Or Sea of Reeds

from wrong ("good and evil" in the Hebrew) recalls the moral innocence that the primordial couple shared in the garden prior to eating of the tree of knowledge of "good and evil" (cf. Gen. 2:9; 3:5) and echoes the responsibility that Israel now has to obey the voice of the Lord in order to enter the garden-like promised land. **1:46–2:23 Edom, Moab, giants, and Ammon. 2:2–5** *Seir* is the land of the Edomites, who were descendants of Esau, the twin brother of Jacob the Israelite patriarch (Gen. 25–36). Because of this kinship, Israel is not to engage in conflict with Edom. **2:8–9** *Moab* is related to Israel through Lot, the nephew of Abraham (Gen. 11:27–31; 19:37), and hence Israel is not to *harass* them. **2:10–12** The *Emim, Anakim* (descendants of the Nephilim, cf. Gen. 6:1–4 and Num. 13:32–33), and *Rephaim* were inhab-itants of Canaan who were giants or supernatural beings with ties to the underworld (cf. Ps. 88:10; Isa. 14:9). Egyptian papyri warn of sizable warriors who lived in the land of Canaan, and in Ugaritic texts, the *Rephaim* were deceased warrior-kings who lived in the realm of the dead and straddled the divine and human realms. On the *Horim* (or Hurrians) who were inhabitants of Seir, see Gen. 14:6; 36:20–30. **2:14** The wandering in the wilderness continued *until the entire generation of warriors had perished*, and the second generation of Israelites, who had not disobeyed the Lord, was left to

off from among the people, [17]the LORD spoke to me, saying, [18]'Today you are going to cross the boundary of Moab at Ar. [19]When you approach the frontier of the Ammonites, do not harass them or engage them in battle, for I will not give the land of the Ammonites to you as a possession, because I have given it to the descendants of Lot.' [20](It also is usually reckoned as a land of Rephaim. Rephaim formerly inhabited it, though the Ammonites call them Zamzummim, [21]a strong and numerous people, as tall as the Anakim. But the LORD destroyed them from before the Ammonites[d] so that they could dispossess them and settle in their place. [22]He did the same for the descendants of Esau, who live in Seir, by destroying the Horites before them so that they could dispossess them and settle in their place even to this day. [23]As for the Avvim, who had lived in settlements in the vicinity of Gaza, the Caphtorim, who came from Caphtor, destroyed them and settled in their place.) [24]'Proceed on your journey and cross the Wadi Arnon. See, I have handed over to you King Sihon the Amorite of Heshbon, and his land. Begin to take possession by engaging him in battle. [25]This day I will begin to put the dread and fear of you upon the peoples everywhere under heaven; when they hear report of you, they will tremble and be in anguish because of you.'

26 "So I sent messengers from the wilderness of Kedemoth to King Sihon of Heshbon with the following terms of peace: [27]'If you let me pass through your land, I will travel only along the road; I will turn aside neither to the right nor to the left. [28]You shall sell me food for money, so that I may eat, and supply me water for money, so that I may drink. Only allow me to pass through on foot—[29]just as the descendants of Esau who live in Seir have done for me and likewise the Moabites who live in Ar—until I cross the Jordan into the land that the LORD our God is giving us.' [30]But King Sihon of Heshbon was not willing to let us pass through, for the LORD your God had hardened his spirit and made his heart defiant in order to hand him over to you, as he has now done.

31 "The LORD said to me, 'See, I have begun to give Sihon and his land over to you. Begin now to take possession of his land.' [32]So when Sihon came out against us, he and all his people for battle at Jahaz, [33]the LORD our God gave him over to us, and we struck him down, along with his offspring and all his people. [34]At that time we captured all his towns, and in each town we utterly destroyed men, women, and children. We left not a single survivor. [35]Only the livestock we kept as spoil for ourselves, as well as the plunder of the towns that we had captured. [36]From Aroer on the edge of the Wadi Arnon (including the town that is in the wadi itself) as far as Gilead, there was no citadel too high for us. The LORD our God gave everything to us. [37]You did not encroach, however, on the land of the Ammonites, avoiding the whole upper region of the Wadi Jabbok as well as the towns of the hill country, just as[e] the LORD our God had charged.

d 2.21 Heb *before them*   *e* 2.37 Gk Tg: Heb *and all*

enter the land. **2:19** The *Ammonites* were descendants of *Lot*, and thus kin to Israel. **2:23** The *Avvim* (cf. Josh. 13:3) lived on the Mediterranean coast before they were displaced by the *Caphtorim*, who were sea peoples who migrated from Crete.

2:24–37 Sihon king of the Amorites. 2:24 Having bypassed the lands of their kinsmen, Israel is to take possession of the land of *Sihon*, whom the Lord gives into their hands. See Num. 21:21–34. **2:30** Israel approaches Sihon with terms of peace, but these are rejected, as the Lord *hardened* the heart of Sihon to resist Israel. **2:34** Israel responds by *utterly destroy[ing]* the population. The meaning of the term *utterly destroy* that occurs here and in 3:6 to describe the battles with Sihon and Og, as well as in 7:1–5 in the instructions for the future Israelite conquest, is debated. The term likely does not imply complete annihilation but rather a religiously sanctioned destruction of an object or person as a means of devoting it to God (often translated as "devoted to destruction," cf. ESV). See the fuller discussion at 7:1–5. See **"Genocide," p. 305**. The land of the *Amorites* is then apportioned to the tribes of Israel that settled on the Transjordan side of the promised land (Deut. 3:8–17). Theologically, the narrative models faithful obedience in conquest and exemplifies the complex interplay between divine sovereignty and human responsibility: though the Lord hardens Sihon's heart and gives him into the hands of Israel, Sihon is responsible for resisting the offer of peace, and Israel must do its part in the victory that the Lord is giving them.

3 "When we headed up the road to Bashan, King Og of Bashan came out against us, he and all his people, for battle at Edrei. [2]The LORD said to me, 'Do not fear him, for I have handed him over to you, along with his people and his land. Do to him as you did to King Sihon of the Amorites, who reigned in Heshbon.' [3]So the LORD our God also handed over to us King Og of Bashan and all his people. We struck him down until not a single survivor was left. [4]At that time we captured all his towns; there was no citadel that we did not take from them: sixty towns, the whole region of Argob, the kingdom of Og in Bashan. [5]All these were fortress towns with high walls, double gates, and bars, besides a great many villages. [6]And we utterly destroyed them, as we had done to King Sihon of Heshbon, in each city utterly destroying men, women, and children. [7]But all the livestock and the plunder of the towns we kept as spoil for ourselves.

8 "So at that time we took from the two kings of the Amorites the land beyond the Jordan, from the Wadi Arnon to Mount Hermon [9](the Sidonians call Hermon Sirion, while the Amorites call it Senir), [10]all the towns of the tableland, the whole of Gilead, and all of Bashan, as far as Salecah and Edrei, towns of Og's kingdom in Bashan. [11](Now only King Og of Bashan was left of the remnant of the Rephaim. In fact, his bed, an iron bed, can still be seen in Rabbah of the Ammonites. By the common cubit it is nine cubits long and four cubits wide.) [12]As for the land that we took possession of at that time, I gave to the Reubenites and Gadites the territory north of Aroer[f] that is on the edge of the Wadi Arnon, as well as half the hill country of Gilead with its towns, [13]and I gave to the half-tribe of Manasseh the rest of Gilead and all of Bashan,

Og's kingdom. (The whole region of Argob: all that portion of Bashan used to be called a land of Rephaim; [14]Jair the Manassite acquired the whole region of Argob as far as the border of the Geshurites and the Maacathites, and he named them—that is, Bashan—after himself, Havvoth-jair,[g] as it is to this day.) [15]To Machir I gave Gilead. [16]And to the Reubenites and the Gadites I gave the territory from Gilead as far as the Wadi Arnon, with the middle of the wadi as a boundary, and up to the Jabbok, the wadi being boundary of the Ammonites; [17]the Arabah also, with the Jordan and its banks, from Chinnereth down to the sea of the Arabah, the Dead Sea,[h] with the lower slopes of Pisgah on the east.

18 "At that time, I charged you as follows: 'Although the LORD your God has given you this land to occupy, all your troops shall cross over armed as the vanguard of your Israelite kin. [19]Only your wives, your children, and your livestock—I know that you have much livestock—shall stay behind in the towns that I have given to you. [20]When the LORD gives rest to your kindred, as to you, and they also have occupied the land that the LORD your God is giving them beyond the Jordan, then each of you may return to the property that I have given to you.' [21]And I charged Joshua as well at that time, saying: 'Your own eyes have seen everything that the LORD your God has done to these two kings; so the LORD will do to all the kingdoms into which you are about to cross. [22]Do not fear them, for it is the LORD your God who fights for you.'

23 "At that time, too, I entreated the LORD, saying, [24]"O Lord GOD, you have only begun to show your servant your greatness and your might. What god in heaven or on earth can

f 3.12 Heb *territory from Aroer*   g 3.14 That is, *settlement of Jair*   h 3.17 Heb *Salt Sea*

3:1–7 Og king of Bashan. *Og* and his kingdom are *utterly destroyed* (cf. 2:34; 7:1–7). Bashan was a fertile agricultural area in the northern part of the Transjordan region. See Num. 21:33–35.
3:8–22 The Transjordan conquest. The Transjordan region, which reaches from the *Wadi Arnon* to *Mount Hermon* in the north—including *Gilead* and *Bashan*—is divided among the *Reubenites, Gadites,* and the *half-tribe of Manasseh* as well as *Machir* and *Jair,* the sons of Manasseh (Gen. 50:23; Num. 32:41). These tribes are nevertheless required to join the conquest of the promised land with the other tribes. See Num. 32 for a parallel account. **3:21–22** Joshua has *seen everything that the LORD . . . has done* to Sihon and Og and therefore can take confidence that the Lord will do the same *to all the kingdoms* that will oppose Israel if Joshua is obedient to the Lord.
3:23–29 Moses denied access to the land. According to Num. 27:12–23, Moses is not permitted to enter the promised land due to his rebellion. The Deuteronomic account here exonerates Moses and places the blame on the people of Israel, as the Lord is angry with Moses on account of the people. Thus, Moses is characterized as a leader who vicariously suffers on behalf of the people and

perform deeds and mighty acts like yours? ²⁵Let me cross over to see the good land beyond the Jordan, that good hill country and the Lebanon.' ²⁶But the LORD was angry with me on your account and would not heed me. The LORD said to me, 'Enough from you! Never speak to me of this matter again! ²⁷Go up to the top of Pisgah and look around you to the west, to the north, to the south, and to the east. Look well, for you shall not cross over this Jordan. ²⁸But charge Joshua and encourage and strengthen him, because it is he who shall cross over at the head of this people and who shall secure their possession of the land that you will see.' ²⁹So we remained in the valley opposite Beth-peor.

4 "So now, Israel, give heed to the statutes and ordinances that I am teaching you to observe, so that you may live to enter and occupy the land that the LORD, the God of your ancestors, is giving you. ²You must neither add anything to what I command you nor take away anything from it, but keep the commandments of the LORD your God with which I am charging you. ³You have seen for yourselves what the LORD did with regard to the Baal of Peor, how the LORD your God destroyed from among you everyone who followed the Baal of Peor, ⁴while those of you who held fast to the LORD your God are all alive today.

5 "See, just as the LORD my God has charged me, I now teach you statutes and ordinances for you to observe in the land that you are about to enter and occupy. ⁶You must observe them and perform them, for this will show your wisdom and discernment to the peoples, who, when they hear all these statutes, will say, 'Surely this great nation is a wise and discerning people!' ⁷For what other great nation has a god so near to it as the LORD our God is whenever we call to him? ⁸And what other great nation has statutes and ordinances as just as this entire law that I am setting before you today?

9 "But take care and watch yourselves closely, so as neither to forget the things that your eyes have seen nor to let them slip from your mind all the days of your life; make them known to your children and your children's children—¹⁰how you once stood before the LORD your God at Horeb, when the LORD said to me, 'Assemble the people for me, and I will let them hear my words, so that they may learn to fear me as long as they live on the earth and may teach their children so'; ¹¹you approached and stood at the foot of the mountain while the mountain was blazing up to the very heavens, shrouded in dark clouds. ¹²Then the LORD spoke to you out of the fire. You heard the sound of words but saw no form; there was only a voice. ¹³He declared to you his covenant, which he charged you to observe, that is, the ten commandments,ⁱ and he wrote them on two stone tablets. ¹⁴And the LORD charged me at that time to teach you statutes and ordinances for you to observe in

i 4.13 Heb the ten words

as an individual connected to the collective guilt of his generation, whereas the second generation is allowed to enter where he himself could not. See **"Moses," p. 247**.

4:1–40 Israel at Horeb. The first speech of Moses concludes with reflections on Israel's experience at Horeb (Exod. 19–24). **4:1–2** Israel is called to *give heed*—that is, to "hear" and obey Moses's *teaching*. Moses takes the role of a teacher who not only conveys the content of the *statutes and ordinances* but also explains the rationales behind the commandments and persuades Israel to obey them for their good. **4:3–4** *Baal of Peor* recalls the events from Num. 25, where many Israelites worshiped the Canaanite deity Baal and were judged. This incident is mentioned as a warning to preface the teaching on idolatry in Deut. 4. **4:5–7** Israel's obedience to the instruction will result in the nations recognizing its *wisdom and discernment*. These nations will acknowledge that Israel is a *great nation*, with a deity who is *near* and responsive—that is, who is personally involved in revealing law and administering justice. **4:8** The nations will also recognize the justice of the *entire law*. This section counters popular ancient Near Eastern conceptions of law—seen, for example, in the laws of Hammurabi—where a wise king promulgates just laws. In Deuteronomy, the laws originate from Israel's covenant deity, and obedience to the laws reveals the entire nation to be wise and the laws to be just. **4:9–11** Moses reminds the new generation of Israelites of their ancestors' experience at Horeb in detail, making this history vividly present as a foundation for Israel's covenant relationship with the Lord. See **"Horeb/Sinai," p. 248**. **4:12–19** The events of Horeb presuppose a theology of aniconism: Israel heard the words of the Lord, but they did not see a visual representation of God.

the land that you are about to cross into and occupy.

15 "Since you saw no form when the LORD spoke to you at Horeb out of the fire, watch yourselves closely, [16]so that you do not act corruptly by making an idol for yourselves in the form of any figure: the likeness of male or female, [17]the likeness of any animal that is on the earth, the likeness of any winged bird that flies in the air, [18]the likeness of anything that creeps on the ground, the likeness of any fish that is in the water under the earth. [19]And when you look up to the heavens and see the sun, the moon, and the stars, all the host of heaven, do not be led astray and bow down to them and serve them, things that the LORD your God has allotted to all the peoples everywhere under heaven. [20]But the LORD has taken you and brought you out of the iron smelter, out of Egypt, to become a people of his very own possession, as you are now.

21 "The LORD was angry with me because of you, and he vowed that I should not cross the Jordan and that I should not enter the good land that the LORD your God is giving for your possession. [22]For I am going to die in this land without crossing over the Jordan, but you are going to cross over to take possession of that good land. [23]So be careful, lest you forget the covenant that the LORD your God made with you and make for yourselves an idol in the form of anything that the LORD your God has forbidden you. [24]For the LORD your God is a devouring fire, a jealous God.

25 "When you have had children and children's children and become complacent in the land, if you act corruptly by making an idol in the form of anything, thus doing what is evil in the sight of the LORD your God and provoking him to anger, [26]I call heaven and earth to witness against you today that you will soon utterly perish from the land that you are crossing the Jordan to occupy; you will not live long on it but will be utterly destroyed. [27]The LORD will scatter you among the peoples; only a few of you will be left among the nations where the LORD will lead you. [28]There you will serve gods made by human hands, objects of wood and stone that neither see, nor hear, nor eat, nor smell. [29]From there you will seek the LORD your God, and you will find him if you search after him with all your heart and soul. [30]In your distress, when all these things have happened to you in time to come, you will return to the LORD your God and heed him. [31]Because the LORD your God is a merciful God, he will neither abandon you nor destroy you; he will not forget the covenant with your ancestors that he swore to them.

32 "For ask now about former ages, long before your own, ever since the day that God created human beings on the earth; ask from one end of heaven to the other: Has anything so great as this ever happened, or has its like ever been heard of? [33]Has any people ever heard the voice of a god speaking out of a fire, as you have heard, and lived? [34]Or has any god ever attempted to go and take a nation for himself from the midst of another nation, by trials, by signs and wonders, by war, by a mighty hand and an outstretched arm, and by terrifying displays of power, as the LORD your God did for you in Egypt before your very eyes? [35]To you it was shown so that you would acknowledge that the LORD is God; there is no other besides him. [36]From heaven he made you hear his voice to discipline you. On earth he showed you his great fire, while you heard his words coming out of the fire. [37]And because he loved your ancestors, he chose their descendants after them. He brought you out of Egypt with his own presence, by his great power, [38]driving out before you nations greater and mightier than yourselves, to bring you in, giving you their land for a possession, as it is still today. [39]So acknowledge today and take to heart that the LORD is God in heaven above and on the earth beneath; there is no other. [40]Keep his statutes and his commandments, which I am commanding you today for your own well-being and that of your descendants after you, so that you may long remain in the land that the LORD your God is giving you for all time."

Therefore, Israel is not to make idols of created things or representations of the deity as the nations do. The Decalogue (v. 13; cf. the "Ten Words" in 5:1–21) is described as a *covenant*, defining the relationship between the Lord and Israel in the wilderness period. **4:20** The Lord brought Israel out of Egypt, and took Israel as his *possession* (cf. Deut. 32:8–9). **4:27–31** Moses anticipates that Israel will succumb to the temptation of idolatry and face the punishment of exile; nevertheless, the Lord will respond with mercy. **4:32–39** The unique actions of the Lord on behalf of Israel move Israel toward monotheism, defining the Lord as Israel's exclusive deity beside whom *there is no other* (see Deut. 32:8).

41 Then Moses set apart on the east side of the Jordan three cities [42]to which a homicide could flee, someone who unintentionally kills another person, the two not having been at enmity before; the homicide could flee to one of these cities and live: [43]Bezer in the wilderness on the tableland belonging to the Reubenites, Ramoth in Gilead belonging to the Gadites, and Golan in Bashan belonging to the Manassites.

44 This is the law that Moses set before the Israelites. [45]These are the decrees and the statutes and ordinances that Moses spoke to the Israelites when they had come out of Egypt, [46]beyond the Jordan in the valley opposite Beth-peor, in the land of King Sihon of the Amorites, who reigned at Heshbon, whom Moses and the Israelites defeated when they came out of Egypt. [47]They occupied his land and the land of King Og of Bashan, the two kings of the Amorites on the eastern side of the Jordan: [48]from Aroer, which is on the edge of the Wadi Arnon, as far as Mount Sirion[j] (that is, Hermon), [49]together with all the Arabah on the east side of the Jordan as far as the Sea of the Arabah, under the slopes of Pisgah.

5 Moses convened all Israel and said to them:

"Hear, O Israel, the statutes and ordinances that I am addressing to you today; you shall learn them and observe them diligently. [2]The Lord our God made a covenant with us at Horeb. [3]Not with our ancestors did the Lord make this covenant but with us, who are all of us here alive today. [4]The Lord spoke with you face to face at the mountain, out of the fire. [5](At that time I was standing between the Lord and you to declare to you the word of the Lord, for you were afraid because of the fire and did not go up the mountain.) And he said:

6 " 'I am the Lord your God, who brought you out of the land of Egypt, out of the house of slavery; [7]you shall have no other gods before[k] me.

8 " 'You shall not make for yourself an idol, whether in the form of anything that is in heaven above or that is on the earth beneath or that is in the water under the earth. [9]You shall not bow down to them or serve them, for I the Lord your God am a jealous God, punishing children for the iniquity of parents to the third and fourth generation of those who reject me [10]but showing steadfast love to the thousandth generation[l] of those who love me and keep my commandments.

j 4.48 Syr: Heb *Sion*   k 5.7 Or *besides*   l 5.10 Or *to thousands*

4:41–43 Cities of refuge. See note at Deut. 19:1–13; cf. Num. 35:9–15.

4:44–49 Introduction to second speech. The second speech of Moses encompasses Deut. 4:44–26:19. The speech begins with a series of sermons in 5:1–11:32 that persuade Israel to obey the instruction.

5:1–21 The Decalogue. See "Law/Decalogue," p. 112. **5:1–4** The Horeb covenant (Exod. 19–24) that the Lord made with the first generation of Israelites who had come out of Egypt is actualized now for the second generation, as Moses places the second generation at Mount Horeb as if they were original participants in that covenant at that time by declaring that *the Lord our God made a covenant with us*. In Jewish tradition, all Israelites—past, present, and future, including converts—are to understand themselves as having stood before the Lord at Horeb and should think of the commandments as given directly to them (*b. Shevuot* 39a). **5:6–21** The Decalogue (cf. Exod. 20:1–17) means "Ten Words," which is what this unit is called in Hebrew (Deut. 4:13). These words are not just commandments but distillations of theology that articulate the principles that underlie the instructions that follow in Deut. 6–26. The ethical principles of the commandments have had an inestimable impact on Jewish and Christian moral discourse and, through that, on Western civilization writ large, and the commandments can still be found posted in many public spaces in the United States. **5:6–10** In Jewish tradition, the first "word" (commandment) is v. 6, *I am the Lord your God, who brought you out of the land of Egypt*, and the second "word" is the prohibition of idolatry encompassing vv. 7–10, whereas in Christian tradition, vv. 6–7 are considered the first commandment. The Jewish enumeration highlights the relational context of v. 6 as the foundational "word" within which the other words find their meaning. The first set of commandments focuses on the divine-human relationship (vv. 6–15), while the second set guides relationships within the community (vv. 16–21). Nevertheless, interpersonal and religious behavior are inextricably intertwined here and throughout the ensuing laws of Deut. 12–26 that explicate the principles of the Decalogue. To have no other gods *before* the Lord (v. 7) in the Hebrew is "upon the face" of the Lord, which likely

11 "'You shall not make wrongful use of the name of the LORD your God, for the LORD will not acquit anyone who misuses his name.

12 "'Observe the Sabbath day and keep it holy, as the LORD your God commanded you. [13]Six days you shall labor and do all your work. [14]But the seventh day is a Sabbath to the LORD your God; you shall not do any work—you, or your son or your daughter, or your male or female slave, or your ox or your donkey, or any of your livestock, or the resident alien in your towns, so that your male and female slave may rest as well as you. [15]Remember that you were a slave in the land of Egypt, and the LORD your God brought you out from there with a mighty hand and an outstretched arm; therefore the LORD your God commanded you to keep the Sabbath day.

16 "'Honor your father and your mother, as the LORD your God commanded you, so that your days may be long and that it may go well with you in the land that the LORD your God is giving you.

17 "'You shall not murder.'[m]

18 "'Neither shall you commit adultery.

19 "'Neither shall you steal.

20 "'Neither shall you bear false witness against your neighbor.

21 "'Neither shall you covet your neighbor's wife.

"'Neither shall you desire your neighbor's house, or field, or male or female slave, or ox, or donkey, or anything that belongs to your neighbor.'

22 "These words the LORD spoke with a loud voice to your whole assembly at the mountain, out of the fire, the cloud, and the thick darkness, and he added no more. He wrote them on two stone tablets and gave them to me. [23]When you heard the voice out of the darkness, while the mountain was burning with fire, you approached me, all the heads of your tribes and your elders, [24]and you said, 'Look, the LORD our God has shown us his glory and greatness, and we have heard his voice out of the fire. We have seen this day that God may speak to someone and the person may still live. [25]But now why should we die? For this great fire will consume us; if we hear the voice of the LORD our God any longer, we shall die. [26]For who is there of all flesh that has heard the voice of the living God speaking out of the fire, as we have, and lived? [27]Go near, you yourself, and hear all that the LORD our God will say. Then tell us everything that the LORD our God tells you, and we will listen and do it.'

28 "The LORD heard your words when you spoke to me, and the LORD said to me, 'I have heard the words of this people, which they have spoken to you; they are right in all that they have spoken. [29]If only they had such a mind as this, to fear me and to keep all my commandments always, so that it might go well with them and with their children forever! [30]Go say to them, "Return to your tents." [31]But you, stand here by me, and I will tell you all the commandments, the statutes and the ordinances, that you shall teach them, so that they may do them in the land that I am giving them to possess.' [32]You must therefore be careful to do as the LORD your God has commanded you; you shall not turn to the right or to the left. [33]You must follow exactly the path that the LORD your God has commanded you, so that you may live and that it may go well with you and that you may live long in the land that you are to possess.

6 "Now this is the commandment—the statutes and the ordinances—that the

m 5.17 Or kill

intends for Israelites to not accept other "gods" in the presence of the Lord—that is, in his divine council (see Deut. 32:8). **5:11** Making *wrongful use of the name* of the Lord means to misrepresent the character of the Lord in word or deed. See **"God's Name," p. 89.** The Hebrew phrase elsewhere describes the priests "bearing the names" of the tribes of Israel before the Lord as representatives of the people (Exod. 28:12, 29). **5:12–15** The law of the Sabbath motivates observance through the remembrance of the exodus and the humanitarian concern that the experience of liberation from Egypt should press upon all Israel. **5:16–21** The command to honor parents and the prohibition of coveting indicate that the words are concerned not only with prescribing actions but with cultivating interior attitudes and desires.

5:22–33 Moses as mediator. Moses is established as a mediator between the Lord and Israel, thus legitimizing his role as the teacher of Israel. See **"Moses," p. 247.**

6:1–9 The "Shema." Moses teaches the transgenerational transmission of the *commandment* as a total way of life that is rooted in the love and fear of the Lord. The singular commandment is likely

LORD your God charged me to teach you to observe in the land that you are about to cross into and occupy, [2]so that you and your children and your children's children may fear the LORD your God all the days of your life and keep all his decrees and his commandments that I am commanding you, so that your days may be long. [3]Hear therefore, O Israel, and observe them diligently, so that it may go well with you and so that you may multiply greatly in a land flowing with milk and honey, as the LORD, the God of your ancestors, has promised you.

[4]"Hear, O Israel: The LORD is our God, the LORD alone."[n] [5]You shall love the LORD your God with all your heart and with all your soul and with all your might. [6]Keep these words that I am commanding you today in your heart. [7]Recite them to your children and talk about them when you are at home and when you are away, when you lie down and when you rise. [8]Bind them as a sign on your hand, fix them as an emblem[o] on your forehead, [9]and write them on the doorposts of your house and on your gates.

[10]"When the LORD your God has brought you into the land that he swore to your ancestors, to Abraham, to Isaac, and to Jacob, to give you—a land with fine, large cities that you did not build, [11]houses filled with all sorts of goods that you did not fill, hewn cisterns that you did not hew, vineyards and olive groves that you did not plant—and when you have eaten your fill, [12]take care that you do not forget the LORD, who brought you out of the land of Egypt, out of the house of slavery. [13]The LORD your God you shall fear, him you shall serve, and by his name alone you shall swear. [14]Do not follow other gods, any of the gods of the peoples who are all around you, [15]because the LORD your God, who is present with you, is a jealous God. The anger of the LORD your God would be kindled against you and he would destroy you from the face of the earth.

16 "Do not put the LORD your God to the test, as you tested him at Massah. [17]You must diligently keep the commandments of the LORD your God and his decrees and his statutes that he has commanded you. [18]Do what is right and good in the sight of the LORD, so that it may go well with you and so that you may go in and occupy the good land that the LORD swore to your ancestors, [19]thrusting out all your enemies from before you, as the LORD has promised.

20 "When your children ask you in time to come, 'What is the meaning of the decrees and the statutes and the ordinances that the LORD our God has commanded you?' [21]then you shall say to your children, 'We were Pharaoh's slaves in Egypt, but the LORD brought us out of Egypt with a mighty hand. [22]The LORD displayed before our eyes great and awesome signs and wonders against Egypt, against Pharaoh and all his household. [23]He brought us out from there in order to bring us in, to give us the land that he promised on oath to our ancestors. [24]Then the LORD commanded us to observe all these statutes, to fear the LORD our God, for our lasting good, so as to keep us alive, as is now the case. [25]If we diligently observe this entire commandment before the

n 6.4 Or *The LORD our God is one LORD*, or *The LORD our God, the LORD is one*, or *The LORD is our God, the LORD is one*
o 6.8 Or *as a frontlet*

understood to encompass the multitude of "statutes and ordinances" in chapters 12–26 as a distillation of what is involved in showing devotion to the Lord. **6:4–5** *Hear, O Israel.* These verses outline the context of covenant relationship between the Lord and Israel with a creedal proclamation known as the "Shema" ("hear"), which defines the unique relationship between the Lord and Israel. See **"The *Shema*," p. 257**. **6:6–9** *Recite . . . bind . . . fix . . . write* establish a habitus by which the commandment is to be transmitted through an embodied pedagogy that encompasses everyday life. Israel as a whole is enjoined to engrave the tradition on their hearts, thus becoming a nation of educators. This was a unique privilege for Israel, as education was reserved for the literary elite in the ancient Near East. Fixing the teachings on the forehead ("totafot") and doorposts ("mezuzot") as reminders of the commandment—and to provide blessing and protection—continues to be practiced in Jewish communities today.

6:10–25 Warnings upon entering the land. Moses warns Israel to not become complacent once they have attained the blessings of the Lord; rather, they are to regularly remember the covenant and gratefully express their allegiance to the Lord. **6:20–24** Coming generations are to be taught the *meaning of the decrees and the statutes and the ordinances* so that they may be motivated to observe them *for [their] lasting good.*

Focus On: The Shema (Deuteronomy 6:4–5)

The creedal proclamation of the *Shema* (Deut. 6:4–5) is one of the most familiar texts in the Hebrew Bible. The grammar of the sentence, "The LORD is our God, the LORD alone," is ambiguous in the Hebrew. The primary interpretive options are to read it as an affirmation of either the "oneness/unity" of the Lord or the uniqueness of the Lord. Ancient Near Eastern religions were characterized by theologies wherein gods were thought to have fluid and multiple manifestations in different locations, and hence a deity could patronize multiple religious sites. Within this context, the *Shema*—combined with the theology of centralization that limits worship to one site (Deut. 12)—can be read as an affirmation of the oneness or unity of the Lord that is a denial of the fluid and fragmented conceptions of the gods that were common in the ancient world. On the other hand, grammatical parallels to Song 6:9 ("my dove, my perfect one, is the only one") suggest that the meaning of the *Shema* is to be understood in the context of singular devotion to the Lord as the one and only or unique deity worthy of Israel's unreserved love. Loving the Lord with the *heart*, *soul*, and *might* expresses an all-encompassing devotion that leads to fearing the Lord in reverent obedience (v. 2), thus bringing together love and fear as the foundational dynamics of devotion to YHWH. The language of loving obedience may also reflect rhetoric seen in Assyrian vassal treaties, wherein the kings of Assyria required their vassals to show "love" by committed obedience to the treaty. Elements of the treaty genre have been combined in Deut. 6:4–9 with the instruction genre, wherein a parental sage (Moses) passes on traditional wisdom to future generations so that they can flourish. The *Shema* is still recited as a central aspect of Jewish synagogue liturgy, and the text of the *Shema* is often written within a *mezuzah* box that is affixed to the doorpost of Jewish homes in obedience to the pedagogical instructions to display, recite, and transmit the text in Deut. 6:6–9. Reciting the *Shema*, as a distillation of Israelite theology, renews commitment to take up the "yoke of the kingdom of Heaven" (m. Berakhot 2:2).

Paavo N. Tucker

LORD our God, as he has commanded us, we will be in the right.'

7 "When the LORD your God brings you into the land that you are about to enter and occupy and he clears away many nations before you—the Hittites, the Girgashites, the Amorites, the Canaanites, the Perizzites, the Hivites, and the Jebusites, seven nations more numerous and mightier than you—²and when the LORD your God gives them over to you and you defeat them, then you must utterly destroy them. Make no covenant with them and show them no mercy. ³Do not intermarry with them, giving your daughters to their sons or taking their daughters for

7:1–26 Israel as chosen people. 7:1 The Lord promises to *clear away* seven nations from the promised land: *the Hittites, Girgashites, Amorites, Canaanites, Perizzites, Hivites*, and *Jebusites*. The Hittites, who originated in Anatolia (modern Turkey), are reported to have lived in the land already in the time of Abraham (Gen. 15:20). The Jebusites controlled the area of Jerusalem until David conquered the city (2 Sam. 5). **7:2** Israel is to *utterly destroy* these nations because Israel—as a *holy* and *chosen* people that is the Lord's *treasured possession* (v. 6; cf. Exod. 19:3–5)—is to be set apart from the nations. The meaning of the Hebrew phrase translated as "to utterly destroy" the population is heavily debated, however, and the biblical textual evidence does not bear out a consistent sense of utter destruction. Ancient Near Eastern military records speak of completely annihilating enemies in statements juxtaposed with accounts according to which the destruction was not thorough, which suggests that the language of utter destruction is to some degree hyperbolic speech used in military contexts. These accounts utilized such rhetoric to communicate the urgency of religious and political ideology, and the context of Deut. 7 suggests the same function for the commandments here (see **"Genocide," p. 305; "The Divine Mandate to Exterminate the Canaanites," p. 313; "Conquest," p. 317**). The prohibitions of making covenants and intermarriage with the foreign population (vv. 2–3) would only be necessary if it is assumed that non-Israelite peoples will remain in the land despite the command to utterly destroy them. Likewise, the ensuing narrative accounts of the conquest—wherein natives like Rahab (Josh. 2) could sojourn among Israel, intermarry, and be integrated into the people of Israel through covenant ceremonies (Josh. 8:30–35)—undermine straightforward readings of the command as requiring complete annihilation. See also the presence

your sons, [4]for that would turn away your children from following me, to serve other gods. Then the anger of the LORD would be kindled against you, and he would destroy you quickly. [5]But this is how you must deal with them: break down their altars, smash their pillars, cut down their sacred poles,[p] and burn their idols with fire. [6]For you are a people holy to the LORD your God; the LORD your God has chosen you out of all the peoples on earth to be his people, his treasured possession.

7 "It was not because you were more numerous than any other people that the LORD set his heart on you and chose you, for you were the fewest of all peoples. [8]It was because the LORD loved you and kept the oath that he swore to your ancestors that the LORD has brought you out with a mighty hand and redeemed you from the house of slavery, from the hand of Pharaoh king of Egypt. [9]Know, therefore, that the LORD your God is God, the faithful God who maintains covenant loyalty with those who love him and keep his commandments, to a thousand generations, [10]and who repays in their own person those who reject him. He does not delay but repays in their own person those who reject him. [11]Therefore, observe diligently the commandment—the statutes and the ordinances—that I am commanding you today.

12 "If you heed these ordinances by diligently observing them, the LORD your God will maintain with you the covenant loyalty that he swore to your ancestors; [13]he will love you, bless you, and multiply you; he will bless the fruit of your womb and the fruit of your ground, your grain and your wine and your oil, the increase of your cattle and the issue of your flock, in the land that he swore to your ancestors to give you. [14]You shall be the most blessed of peoples, with neither sterility nor barrenness among you or your livestock. [15]The LORD will turn away from you every illness; all the dread diseases of Egypt that you experienced, he will not inflict on you, but he will lay them on all who hate you. [16]You shall devour all the peoples that the LORD your God is giving over to you, showing them no pity; you shall not serve their gods, for that would be a snare to you.

17 "If you say to yourself, 'These nations are more numerous than I; how can I dispossess them?' [18]do not be afraid of them. Just remember what the LORD your God did to Pharaoh and to all Egypt, [19]the great trials that your eyes saw, the signs and wonders, the mighty hand and the outstretched arm by which the LORD your God brought you out. The LORD your God will do the same to all the peoples of whom you are afraid. [20]Moreover, the LORD your God will send swarms of hornets[q] against them until even the survivors and the fugitives are destroyed. [21]Have no dread of them, for the LORD your God, who is present with you, is a great and awesome God. [22]The LORD your God will clear away these nations before you little by little; you will not be able to make a quick end of them, otherwise the wild animals would become too numerous for you. [23]But the LORD your God will give them over to you and throw them into great panic until they are destroyed. [24]He will hand their kings over to you, and you shall blot out their name from under heaven; no one will be able to stand against you until you have

p 7.5 Or *Asherahs* *q* 7.20 Meaning of Heb uncertain

of foreigners living among the Israelites that is assumed in various laws of Deut. 12–26 (e.g., 23:1–8), which indicates that Deuteronomy does not offer unreserved approval of the command to destroy non-Israelites. **7:4–5** The concern of these commandments to utterly destroy the inhabitants is so that Israel would not *turn away . . . from following [the LORD], to serve other gods* (cf. v. 16). Hence Israel was to destroy the local population and their religious infrastructure—including *pillars* and *sacred poles*, which were artifacts used in religious rites for securing prosperity and fertility. Texts like this advocating for the destruction of Israel's enemies must be read with caution, as such texts have been used to justify violence against opponents of communities of faith in the history of Christianity. Whatever "utter destruction" means, it appears to limit the use of violence to a particular time and place and for a particular purpose of curtailing idolatry and safeguarding Israelite identity, and it can be seen as hyperbolic rhetoric articulating the importance of complete devotion to the Lord. This devotion is to be expressed by destroying Canaanite religious artifacts and refusing to intermarry or make covenants (vv. 2–3) with the non-Israelite natives of the land who may influence Israel to turn away from the Lord, and even, if necessary, by eliminating those that would entice Israel to idolatry.

destroyed them. [25]The images of their gods you shall burn with fire. Do not covet the silver or the gold that is on them and take it for yourself, because you could be ensnared by it, for it is abhorrent to the LORD your God. [26]Do not bring an abhorrent thing into your house, or you will be set apart for destruction like it. You must utterly detest and abhor it, for it is set apart for destruction.

8 [1]"The entire commandment that I command you today you must diligently observe, so that you may live and increase and go in and occupy the land that the LORD promised on oath to your ancestors. [2]Remember the long way that the LORD your God has led you these forty years in the wilderness, in order to humble you, testing you to know what was in your heart, whether or not you would keep his commandments. [3]He humbled you by letting you hunger, then by feeding you with manna, with which neither you nor your ancestors were acquainted, in order to make you understand that one does not live by bread alone but by every word that comes from the mouth of the LORD. [4]The clothes on your back did not wear out, and your feet did not swell these forty years. [5]Know, then, in your heart that, as a parent disciplines a child, so the LORD your God disciplines you. [6]Therefore keep the commandments of the LORD your God by walking in his ways and by fearing him. [7]For the LORD your God is bringing you into a good land, a land with flowing streams, with springs and underground waters welling up in valleys and hills, [8]a land of wheat and barley, of vines and fig trees and pomegranates, a land of olive oil and honey, [9]a land where you may eat bread without scarcity, where you will lack nothing, a land whose stones are iron and from whose hills you may mine copper. [10]You

shall eat your fill and bless the LORD your God for the good land that he has given you.

[11]"Take care that you do not forget the LORD your God by failing to keep his commandments, his ordinances, and his statutes that I am commanding you today. [12]When you have eaten your fill and have built fine houses and live in them [13]and when your herds and flocks have multiplied and your silver and gold is multiplied and all that you have is multiplied, [14]then do not exalt yourself, forgetting the LORD your God, who brought you out of the land of Egypt, out of the house of slavery, [15]who led you through the great and terrible wilderness, an arid wasteland with poisonous[r] snakes and scorpions. He made water flow for you from flint rock. [16]He fed you in the wilderness with manna that your ancestors did not know, to humble you and to test you and in the end to do you good. [17]Do not say to yourself, 'My power and the might of my own hand have gotten me this wealth.' [18]But remember the LORD your God, for it is he who gives you power to get wealth, so that he may confirm his covenant that he swore to your ancestors, as he is doing today. [19]If you do forget the LORD your God and follow other gods to serve and worship them, I solemnly warn you today that you shall surely perish. [20]Like the nations that the LORD is destroying before you, so shall you perish, because you would not obey the voice of the LORD your God.

9 [1]"Hear, O Israel! You are about to cross the Jordan today, to go in and dispossess nations larger and mightier than you, great cities, fortified to the heavens, [2]a strong and tall people, the offspring of the Anakim, whom you know. You have heard it said,

r 8.15 Or *fiery*

8:1–20 Lessons of the wilderness. Moses recounts Israel's wilderness wandering (Num. 11–36) to warn of the dangers of arrogance and highlight the importance of humility. Israel's wandering was a pedagogical experience of learning to obey the Lord that serves as a case study showing how obedience leads to life. **8:3** The provision of *manna* and water exemplifies the care of the Lord (cf. Num. 11:7–8; 20:2–13). Remembering the wilderness experience will teach Israel to live *by every word that comes from the mouth of the LORD* (cf. Matt. 4:4). **8:5** The Lord is revealed as a parent who provides for all the needs of the children of Israel, but also *disciplines* Israel as a loving parent would.

9:1–29 Warning against rebellion. Continuing the theme of anticipating the future conquest of the land and the challenges that will ensue from it (chaps. 7–8), here Moses exhorts Israel regarding the dangers of self-reliance and rebellion against God. The sermon recalls God's oath to the patriarchs and Israel's ensuing history of rebellion against God as a warning to Israel to not be tempted to self-righteousness and self-sufficiency in presuming that it is their strength that removes the

'Who can stand up to the Anakim?' [3]Know, then, today that the LORD your God is the one who crosses over before you as a devouring fire; he will defeat them and subdue them before you, so that you may dispossess and destroy them quickly, as the LORD has promised you.

4 "When the LORD your God thrusts them out before you, do not say to yourself, 'It is because of my righteousness that the LORD has brought me in to occupy this land'; it is rather because of the wickedness of these nations that the LORD is dispossessing them before you. [5]It is not because of your righteousness or the uprightness of your heart that you are going in to occupy their land, but because of the wickedness of these nations the LORD your God is dispossessing them before you, in order to fulfill the promise that the LORD made on oath to your ancestors, to Abraham, to Isaac, and to Jacob.

6 "Know, then, that the LORD your God is not giving you this good land to occupy because of your righteousness, for you are a stubborn people. [7]Remember; do not forget how you provoked the LORD your God to wrath in the wilderness; you have been rebellious against the LORD from the day you came out of the land of Egypt until you came to this place.

8 "Even at Horeb you provoked the LORD to wrath, and the LORD was so angry with you that he was ready to destroy you. [9]When I went up the mountain to receive the stone tablets, the tablets of the covenant that the LORD made with you, I remained on the mountain forty days and forty nights; I neither ate bread nor drank water. [10]And the LORD gave me the two stone tablets written with the finger of God; on them were all the words that the LORD had spoken to you at the mountain out of the fire on the day of the assembly. [11]At the end of forty days and forty nights the LORD gave me the two stone tablets, the tablets of the covenant. [12]Then the LORD said to me, 'Get up; go down quickly from here, for your people whom you have brought from Egypt have acted corruptly. They have been quick to turn from the way that I commanded them; they have cast an image for themselves.' [13]Furthermore, the LORD said to me, 'I have seen that this people is indeed a stubborn people. [14]Let me alone that I may destroy them and blot out their name from under heaven, and I will make of you a nation mightier and more numerous than they.'

15 "So I turned and went down from the mountain, while the mountain was ablaze; the two tablets of the covenant were in my two hands. [16]Then I saw that you had indeed sinned against the LORD your God, by casting for yourselves an image;[s] you had been quick to turn from the way that the LORD had commanded you. [17]So I took hold of the two tablets and flung them from my two hands, smashing them before your eyes. [18]Then I lay prostrate before the LORD as before, forty days and forty nights; I neither ate bread nor drank water because of all the sin you had committed, provoking the LORD by doing what was evil in his sight. [19]For I was afraid that the anger that the LORD bore against you was so fierce that he would destroy you. But the LORD listened to me that time also. [20]The LORD was so angry with Aaron that he was ready to destroy him, but I interceded also on behalf of Aaron at that same time. [21]Then I took the sinful thing you had made, the calf, and burned it with fire and crushed it, grinding it thoroughly, until it was reduced to dust, and I threw the dust into the stream that runs down the mountain.

22 "At Taberah also, and at Massah, and at Kibroth-hattaavah, you provoked the LORD to wrath. [23]And when the LORD sent you from Kadesh-barnea, saying, 'Go up and occupy the land that I have given you,' you rebelled against the command of the LORD your God, neither trusting him nor obeying him. [24]You have been rebellious against the LORD as long as he has[t] known you.

s 9.16 Gk: Heb *image of a calf*   t 9.24 Sam Gk: MT *I have*

Anakim (see note at 2:10–12). **9:4–5** Nor has the righteousness of Israel earned them the Lord's blessing. Rather, the Lord removes the Anakim because of their wickedness and in order to *fulfill the promise* that the Lord made to Abraham, Isaac, and Jacob. **9:6–7** Moses highlights the mercy of the Lord, who persistently bears with Israel despite their having been *stubborn* and *rebellious* since the beginning of their relationship with the Lord. **9:8–21** The golden calf incident that took place at Horeb (Exod. 32–34) reminds the people of their stubbornness and of Moses's role as mediator and intercessor on behalf of the people. **9:22–23** *Taberah* (Num. 11:1–3), *Massah* (Exod. 17:1–7), *Kibroth-hattaavah* (Num. 11:31–34), and *Kadesh-barnea* (Num. 13–14) likewise recall episodes of disobedience

25 "Throughout the forty days and forty nights that I lay prostrate before the Lord when the Lord intended to destroy you, ²⁶I prayed to the Lord and said, 'Lord God, do not destroy your people, your very own possession, whom you redeemed in your greatness, whom you brought out of Egypt with a mighty hand. ²⁷Remember your servants, Abraham, Isaac, and Jacob; pay no attention to the stubbornness of this people, their wickedness and their sin, ²⁸lest the land from which you have brought us say, "Because the Lord was not able to bring them into the land that he promised them and because he hated them, he has brought them out to let them die in the wilderness." ²⁹For they are your people, your very own possession, whom you brought out by your great power and by your outstretched arm.'

10 "At that time the Lord said to me, 'Carve out two tablets of stone like the former ones, and come up to me on the mountain, and make an ark of wood. ²I will write on the tablets the words that were on the former tablets, which you smashed, and you shall put them in the ark.' ³So I made an ark of acacia wood, cut two tablets of stone like the former ones, and went up the mountain with the two tablets in my hand. ⁴Then he wrote on the tablets the same words as before, the ten commandments[u] that the

Lord had spoken to you on the mountain out of the fire on the day of the assembly, and the Lord gave them to me. ⁵So I turned and came down from the mountain and put the tablets in the ark that I had made, and there they are, as the Lord commanded me."

6 (The Israelites journeyed from Beeroth-bene-jaakan[v] to Moserah. There Aaron died, and there he was buried; his son Eleazar succeeded him as priest. ⁷From there they journeyed to Gudgodah, and from Gudgodah to Jotbathah, a land with flowing streams. ⁸At that time the Lord set apart the tribe of Levi to carry the ark of the covenant of the Lord, to stand before the Lord to minister to him and to bless in his name, to this day. ⁹Therefore Levi has no allotment or inheritance with his kindred; the Lord is his inheritance, as the Lord your God promised him.)

10 "I stayed on the mountain forty days and forty nights, as I had done the first time. And once again the Lord listened to me. The Lord was unwilling to destroy you. ¹¹The Lord said to me, 'Get up, go on your journey at the head of the people, that they may go in and occupy the land that I swore to their ancestors to give them.'

12 "So now, O Israel, what does the Lord your God require of you? Only to fear the

u 10.4 Heb *the ten words* v 10.6 Or *the wells of the Bene-jaakan*

and rebellion. **9:26–29** Moses petitions the Lord to have mercy on the people—including on Aaron, the high priest and brother of Moses who had made the calf—with a range of reasons given to persuade the Lord. The successful intercession of Moses in this gravest of situations gives hope that also in future failures of the people there is a possibility of grace and restoration (cf. Deut. 29–30). **10:1–11 At Horeb. 10:1–5** Moses returns up the mountain to receive the second *tablets of stone* after he had broken the first tablets (Exod. 34). In Exodus, the ark, made by the craftsman Bezalel (Exod. 37:1), contains the covenant that the Lord made with Israel. It is covered by a gold mercy seat and cherubim as the throne of the Lord from which the Lord speaks to Israel (Exod. 25:21–22). Deuteronomy, on the other hand, focuses on the role of Moses in making the ark and mediating the voice of the Lord to the people. The function of the ark is as a reminder of the covenant, but the ark itself is empty—the book of the law is placed beside the ark as a "witness" (Deut. 31:25–26). These perspectives on the ark reflect different theological emphases regarding the function of religious artifacts and the nature of the presence of God in Israel. **10:6–9** *Aaron dies* (Num. 33:38–39), and *the tribe of Levi* is given the responsibility to fulfill the priestly duties: carrying the ark, ministering to the Lord, and blessing in the name of the Lord (see **"Priests (Leviticus)," p. 176; "Priestly Blessing (Numbers)," p. 198**). The Levites do not receive an allotment of land; rather, they are to be cared for from donations by the people. This arrangement was established in the aftermath of the golden calf episode when the Levites rose up to prosecute the judgment of God on those who worshiped the calf (Exod. 32:26–28). **10:10–11** Following the incident of the golden calf, Moses intercedes for the people, and the Lord allows the people to proceed to the promised land. However, that generation of Israelites continued to rebel against the Lord, and they were not allowed to enter the land.

10:12–22 Fear and love God. *So now.* Culminating the history of rebellion, Moses draws conclusions for the present generation of Israelites. Their history has shown that they need a fundamental

LORD your God, to walk in all his ways, to love him, to serve the LORD your God with all your heart and with all your soul, [13]and to keep the commandments of the LORD and his decrees that I am commanding you today, for your own well-being. [14]Although heaven and the heaven of heavens belong to the LORD your God, the earth with all that is in it, [15]yet the LORD set his heart in love on your ancestors alone and chose you, their descendants after them, out of all the peoples, as it is today. [16]Circumcise, then, the foreskin of your heart, and do not be stubborn any longer. [17]For the LORD your God is God of gods and Lord of lords, the great God, mighty and awesome, who is not partial and takes no bribe, [18]who executes justice for the orphan and the widow, and who loves the strangers, providing them food and clothing. [19]You shall also love the stranger, for you were strangers in the land of Egypt. [20]You shall fear the LORD your God; him you shall serve; to him you shall hold fast; and by his name you shall swear. [21]He is your praise; he is your God who has done for you these great and awesome things that your own eyes have seen. [22]Your ancestors went down to Egypt seventy persons, and now the LORD your God has made you as numerous as the stars in heaven.

11 "You shall love the LORD your God, therefore, and keep his charge, his decrees, his ordinances, and his commandments always. [2]Remember today that it was not your children (who have not known or seen the discipline of the LORD your God), but it is you who must acknowledge his greatness, his mighty hand, and his outstretched arm, [3]his signs and his deeds that he did in Egypt to Pharaoh, the king of Egypt, and to all his land; [4]what he did to the Egyptian army, to their horses and chariots, how he made the water of the Red Sea[w] flow over them as they

pursued you, so that the LORD has destroyed them to this day; [5]what he did to you in the wilderness until you came to this place; [6]and what he did to Dathan and Abiram, sons of Eliab son of Reuben, how in the midst of all Israel the earth opened its mouth and swallowed them up, along with their households, their tents, and every living being in their company; [7]for it is your own eyes that have seen every great deed that the LORD did.

8 "Keep, then, the entire commandment that I am commanding you today, so that you may have strength to go in and occupy the land that you are crossing over to occupy [9]and so that you may live long in the land that the LORD swore to your ancestors to give them and to their descendants, a land flowing with milk and honey. [10]For the land that you are about to enter to occupy is not like the land of Egypt, from which you have come, where you sow your seed and irrigate by foot like a vegetable garden. [11]But the land that you are crossing over to occupy is a land of hills and valleys watered by rain from the sky, [12]a land that the LORD your God looks after. The eyes of the LORD your God are always on it, from the beginning of the year to the end of the year.

13 "If you will only heed his every commandment[x] that I am commanding you today—loving the LORD your God and serving him with all your heart and with all your soul—[14]then he[y] will give the rain for your land in its season, the early rain and the later rain, and you will gather in your grain, your wine, and your oil, [15]and he[z] will give grass in your field for your livestock, and you will eat your fill. [16]Take care, or you will be seduced into turning away, serving other gods and worshiping them, [17]for then the anger of the LORD will be kindled against you, and he will

w 11.4 Or *Sea of Reeds*   x 11.13 Compare Gk: Heb *my commandments*   y 11.14 Sam Gk Vg: MT *I*   z 11.15 Sam Gk Vg: MT *I*

change of heart in order to obey the Lord. **10:15–18** Moses expounds a theology of the gratuitous love of God for Israel as the foundational reason for Israel to fear, serve, and love the Lord with all their *heart* (v. 12). This heart—as the seat of moral discernment and decision-making—was hardened by Israel's rebellion, and they needed to symbolically *circumcise* it as a sign of sensitive obedience. **10:19** The character of the Lord as impartial, just, and loving is set forth as a paradigm for Israel's ethics of familial care, which is to include foreigners living among them.
11:1–31 Blessings for obedience. The chapter concludes the sermons of Deut. 6–11 by recalling the "Shema" (cf. especially vv. 18–21; Deut. 6:4–5) to remind Israel of the responsibility to love and obey the Lord as a prerequisite for dwelling in the promised land. **11:9–17** Moses describes the promised land as a *land flowing with milk and honey*, which is cared for by the Lord. This affirmation contrasts with the Canaanite religion of the local populations, whereby it was presumed that the storm god

shut up the heavens, so that there will be no rain, and the land will not yield its produce; then you will perish quickly off the good land that the LORD is giving you.

18 "You shall put these words of mine in your heart and soul, and you shall bind them as a sign on your hand and fix them as an emblem on your forehead. [19]Teach them to your children, talking about them when you are at home and when you are away, when you lie down and when you rise up. [20]Write them on the doorposts of your house and on your gates, [21]so that your days and the days of your children may be multiplied in the land that the LORD swore to your ancestors to give them, as long as the heavens are above the earth.

22 "If you will diligently observe this entire commandment that I am commanding you, loving the LORD your God, walking in all his ways, and holding fast to him, [23]then the LORD will drive out all these nations before you, and you will dispossess nations larger and mightier than you. [24]Every place on which you set foot shall be yours; your territory shall extend from the wilderness to the Lebanon and from the River, the River Euphrates, to the Western Sea. [25]No one will be able to stand against you; the LORD your God will put the fear and dread of you on all the land on which you set foot, as he promised you.

26 "See, I am setting before you today a blessing and a curse: [27]the blessing, if you obey the commandments of the LORD your God that I am commanding you today; [28]and the curse, if you do not obey the commandments of the LORD your God but turn from the way that I am commanding you today, to follow other gods that you have not known.

29 "When the LORD your God has brought you into the land that you are entering to occupy, you shall set the blessing on Mount Gerizim and the curse on Mount Ebal. [30]As you know, they are beyond the Jordan, some distance to the west, in the land of the Canaanites who live in the Arabah, opposite Gilgal, beside the oak[a] of Moreh.

31 "When you cross the Jordan to go in to occupy the land that the LORD your God is giving you and when you occupy it and live in it, [32]you must diligently observe all the statutes and ordinances that I am setting before you today.

12 "These are the statutes and ordinances that you must diligently observe in the land that the LORD, the God of your ancestors, has given you to occupy all the days that you live on the earth.

a 11.30 Gk Syr: Heb *oaks* or *terebinths*

Baal provides the fertility of the land. **11:26** Moses sets before Israel *a blessing and a curse*, calling for Israel to consider the consequences of obedience (blessing) and disobedience (curse) in order to form their moral imagination and motivate them to obey YHWH (cf. Deut. 30:15–20). **11:29** At the culmination of the legal stipulations of Deut. 12–26, Israel will have a covenant ceremony in which blessings and curses will be declared to the people (Deut. 27:12–13).

12:1 Statutes and ordinances. *These are the statutes and ordinances.* Deuteronomy uses a range of terms to characterize the legislation that is found in Deut. 12–26; see **"Law/Decalogue," p. 112.** Scholars have divided biblical laws into two kinds: apodictic laws (often called *statutes*) are commands or prohibitions that express legal principles, and casuistic or case laws (*ordinances* or judgments) are applications of the principles of apodictic laws to specific circumstances. Case laws are expressed in a conditional format, with the protasis outlining the circumstance, "if," and the apodosis prescribing a verdict, "then." The legislation of Deut. 12–26 follows a pattern of beginning a section with statutes or principles, which are then elaborated with cases illustrating how the principle applies in various circumstances. The instructions revise and supplement the laws of Exodus, Leviticus, and Numbers to address new situations. Particularly, the centralization of the cult had a wide-ranging impact on the laws, as did humanitarian concerns to advance the rights of women, the poor, and foreigners. The laws are filled with theological statements, exhortations, warnings, explanations, and motivations to teach and persuade Israel of the importance of obedience. They combine a range of legal principles and examples of applied law, which Israelite scribes, priests, and judges could study and teach in preparation for a career in administration and leadership as part of a scribal curriculum for theological, moral, and leadership formation. The pervasive concern in the laws of Deuteronomy to pursue "justice, and only justice" (16:20)—especially in the advances that Deuteronomy makes in the area of human rights—has left an indelible mark on the trajectory of ethics, judicial systems, and politics in Western civilization.

Going Deeper: Cult Centralization (Deuteronomy 12)

Centralization of the cult is key to understanding the legal hermeneutics of Deut. 12–26. Whereas Exod. 20:24 envisions multiple locations where the Lord will appear to bless Israel, Deuteronomy identifies a single, exclusive place where the presence of the Lord is to be known. The motivation for centralization is not made explicit, though contextually it is associated with curtailing idolatry. Centralization also had significant political and economic consequences, resulting in more concentrated power and wealth at the one chosen site. The "centralization formula" referring to this site occurs primarily in the laws of Deut. 12–18 (12:5, 11, 14, 18, 21, 26; 14:23–25; 15:20; 16:2, 6, 7, 11, 15, 16; 17:8, 10; 18:6; 26:2), where the impact of centralization results in the revision of numerous laws, such as those governing sacrifices, animal slaughter, tithes, festivals, judicial systems, leadership, and economic legislation. The identity of the chosen place is unspecified in Deuteronomy, leaving it open for a sequence of possible identifications of the site with Gerizim, Shiloh (Josh. 18:1; 21:2; 1 Sam. 1–3), and Jerusalem (1 Kgs. 6–8). The prescriptions for a covenant ceremony on Mount Ebal and Gerizim in Samaria (Deut. 27) have resulted in the Samaritan community viewing Gerizim as the chosen place to this day.

Centralization is tied to Israel's attainment of "rest" (Deut. 12:8–10); notably, the Jerusalem temple is built by Solomon after the Lord provides rest in 1 Kgs. 8:56. However, with Jeroboam I's revolt and decentralizing actions (1 Kgs. 11), a period of unrest ensues. Following the division of the kingdom, the state of decentralization remained until the time of Hezekiah (2 Kgs. 18–20), during whose reign centralization was forced by the Assyrian campaign that decimated the Judean countryside. Following the apostasies of Manasseh, the reforms of Josiah exhibit significant overlap with the Deuteronomic program of centralization as part of an anti-idolatry program of cleansing the land and also of reversing the decentralizing moves of Jeroboam I (2 Kgs. 22–23).

Paavo N. Tucker

2 "You must demolish completely all the places where the nations whom you are about to dispossess served their gods, on the mountain heights, on the hills, and under every leafy tree. ³Break down their altars, smash their pillars, burn their sacred poles[b] with fire, and cut down the idols of their gods, and thus blot out their name from their places. ⁴You shall not serve the Lord your God in such ways. ⁵But you shall seek the place that the Lord your God will choose out of all your tribes as his habitation to put his name there. You shall go there, ⁶bringing there your burnt offerings and your sacrifices, your tithes and your donations, your votive gifts, your freewill offerings, and the firstlings of your herds and flocks. ⁷And you shall eat there in the presence of the Lord your God, you and your households together, rejoicing in all the undertakings in which the Lord your God has blessed you.

8 "You shall not act as we are acting here today, all of us according to our own desires, ⁹for you have not yet come into the rest and the possession that the Lord your God is giving you. ¹⁰When you cross over the Jordan and live in the land that the Lord your God is allotting to you, and when he gives you rest from your enemies all around so that you live in safety, ¹¹then you shall bring everything that I command you to the place that the Lord your God will choose as a dwelling for his name: your burnt offerings and your sacrifices, your tithes and your donations, and all your choice votive gifts that you vow to the Lord. ¹²And you shall rejoice before the Lord your God, you together with your sons and your daughters, your male and female slaves, and the Levites who reside in your towns

b 12.3 Or Asherahs

12:2–28 Centralization. Centralizing worship and sacrifice to one location—that is, to the *place* that the Lord chooses—revolutionizes Israelite religion (cf. 12:5, 11, 12, 13, 14, 18, 21, 26); see **"Cult Centralization," p. 264. 12:2–3** Centralization counters the threat of idolatry; it is accompanied by commands to destroy the *places* where the nations worshiped their gods and to *blot out [the] name* of these other gods. **12:5** The Lord inhabits the chosen place—that is, puts *his name there*, which is a collocation based on an Akkadian phrase for divine habitation. See **"God's Name," p. 89.** The phrase builds on the formulation of Exod. 20:24, which allowed for multiple locations of worship, by specifying that only one place is acceptable for worship. **12:10–11** The Lord is to give Israel *rest* as a prerequisite for establishing the chosen place. This is fulfilled in 1 Kgs. 8:56, when Solomon builds the temple in Jerusalem. In the Samaritan Pentateuch, the chosen place is considered to be Mount

(since they have no allotment or inheritance with you).

13 "Take care that you do not offer your burnt offerings at any place you happen to see. 14But only at the place that the Lord will choose in one of your tribes—there you shall offer your burnt offerings, and there you shall do everything I command you.

15 "Yet whenever you desire you may slaughter and eat meat within any of your towns, according to the blessing that the Lord your God has given you; the unclean and the clean may eat of it, as they would of gazelle or deer. 16The blood, however, you must not eat; you shall pour it out on the ground like water. 17Nor may you eat within your towns the tithe of your grain, your wine, and your oil, the firstlings of your herds and your flocks, any of your votive gifts that you vow, your freewill offerings, or your donations; 18these you shall eat in the presence of the Lord your God at the place that the Lord your God will choose, you together with your son and your daughter, your male and female slaves, and the Levites resident in your towns, rejoicing in the presence of the Lord your God in all your undertakings. 19Take care that you do not neglect the Levite as long as you live in your land.

20 "When the Lord your God enlarges your territory, as he has promised you, and you say, 'I am going to eat some meat,' because you wish to eat meat, you may eat meat whenever you have the desire. 21If the place where the Lord your God will choose to put his name is too far from you, and you slaughter as I have commanded you any of your herd or flock that the Lord has given you, then you may eat within your towns whenever you desire. 22Indeed, just as gazelle or deer is eaten, so you may eat it; the unclean

and the clean alike may eat it. 23Only be sure that you do not eat the blood, for the blood is the life, and you shall not eat the life with the meat. 24Do not eat it; you shall pour it out on the ground like water. 25Do not eat it, so that it may go well with you and your children after you, because you do what is right in the sight of the Lord. 26But the sacred donations that are due from you and your votive gifts you shall bring to the place that the Lord will choose. 27You shall present your burnt offerings, both the meat and the blood, on the altar of the Lord your God; the blood of your other sacrifices shall be poured out beside^c the altar of the Lord your God, but the meat you may eat.

28 "Be careful to obey all these words that I command you, so that it may go well with you and with your children after you forever, because you will be doing what is good and right in the sight of the Lord your God.

29 "When the Lord your God has cut off before you the nations whom you are about to enter to dispossess them, when you have dispossessed them and live in their land, 30take care that you are not snared into imitating them, after they have been destroyed before you; do not inquire concerning their gods, saying, 'How did these nations serve their gods? I also want to do the same.' 31You must not do the same for the Lord your God, because every abhorrent thing that the Lord hates they have done for their gods. They would even burn their sons and their daughters in the fire to their gods. 32dYou must diligently observe everything that I command you; do not add to it or take anything from it.

c 12.27 Or *on*   d 12.32 13.1 in Heb

Gerizim in Samaria, where a temple was built in the fifth century BCE (cf. Deut. 27:3–13; Josh. 8:30; John 4:20). **12:15** *You may slaughter and eat meat within any of your towns.* Limiting worship to the singular chosen place creates a problem of whether animals can be slaughtered and eaten elsewhere (cf. Lev. 17:2–9, where Israel may only consume meat that is slaughtered as part of a sacrificial ritual at the tent of meeting). Deuteronomy 12 solves this problem by allowing profane slaughter away from the chosen place, as long as the blood—which was considered a life-sustaining power given by the Lord—was properly disposed of. **12:18** *Rejoicing in the presence of the* Lord expresses the essence of Deuteronomic religion: Israel was to bring their offerings and tithes to the chosen place for a communal meal that is enjoyed before the Lord.

12:29–13:18 Warnings against apostasy. Upon entering the land, Israel is to resist enticements to idolatry, the dangers of which are outlined in three scenarios (13:1–5, 6–11, 12–18). **12:32** Using language common in ancient Near Eastern treaties, Israel is prohibited to *add to* or *take* from the teachings of Moses. With the ensuing section warning of false prophets (13:1–5), Deuteronomy is especially concerned here with limiting prophetic revelation from supplanting the teachings of

13

¹"If prophets or those who divine by dreams appear among you and show you omens or portents, ²and the omens or the portents declared by them take place, and they say, 'Let us follow other gods' (whom you have not known) 'and let us serve them,' ³you must not heed the words of those prophets or those who divine by dreams, for the LORD your God is testing you, to know whether you indeed love the LORD your God with all your heart and soul. ⁴The LORD your God you shall follow, him alone you shall fear, his commandments you shall keep, his voice you shall obey, him you shall serve, and to him you shall hold fast. ⁵But those prophets or those who divine by dreams shall be put to death for having spoken treason against the LORD your God who brought you out of the land of Egypt and redeemed you from the house of slavery, to turn you from the way in which the LORD your God commanded you to walk. So you shall purge the evil from your midst.

6 "If anyone secretly entices you—even if it is your brother, your father's son or^f your mother's son, or your own son or daughter, or the wife you embrace, or your most intimate friend—saying, 'Let us go serve other gods,' whom neither you nor your ancestors have known, ⁷any of the gods of the peoples who are around you, whether near you or far away from you, from one end of the earth to the other, ⁸you must not yield to or heed any such persons. Show them no pity or compassion, and do not shield them. ⁹But you shall surely kill them; your own hand shall be first against them to execute them and afterward the hand of all the people. ¹⁰Stone them to death for trying to turn you away from the LORD your God, who brought you out of the

land of Egypt, out of the house of slavery. ¹¹Then all Israel shall hear and be afraid and never again do any such wickedness.

12 "If you hear it said about one of the towns that the LORD your God is giving you to live in, ¹³that scoundrels from among you have gone out and led the inhabitants of the town astray, saying, 'Let us go and serve other gods,' whom you have not known, ¹⁴then you shall inquire and make a thorough investigation. If the charge is established that such an abhorrent thing has been done among you, ¹⁵you shall put the inhabitants of that town to the sword, utterly destroying it and everything in it, even putting its livestock to the sword. ¹⁶All of its spoil you shall gather into its public square, then burn the town and all its spoil with fire as a whole burnt offering to the LORD your God. It shall remain a perpetual ruin, never to be rebuilt. ¹⁷Do not let anything devoted to destruction stick to your hand, so that the LORD may turn from his fierce anger and show you compassion, and in his compassion multiply you, as he swore to your ancestors, ¹⁸if you obey the voice of the LORD your God by keeping all his commandments that I am commanding you today, doing what is right in the sight of the LORD your God.

14

"You are children of the LORD your God. You must not lacerate yourselves or shave your forelocks for the dead. ²For you are a people holy to the LORD your God; it is you the LORD has chosen out of all the peoples on earth to be his people, his treasured possession.

3 "You shall not eat any abhorrent thing. ⁴These are the animals you may eat: the ox,

e 13.1 13.2 in Heb *f* 13.6 Sam Gk Compare Tg: MT lacks *your father's son or*

Moses (see also 18:15–22). **13:1–11** Enticements to idolatry can come from religious authorities such as false *prophets* or diviners, from family and friends, or from entire communities that have gone astray. The standard for evaluating prophetic revelation is not the charismatic authority or power of the prophet but submission to the law of Moses (cf. Deut. 18:18). Enticement to idolatry is an existential threat, and Israel as a community has the responsibility to eliminate such threats.

14:1–21 Holy children. 14:1–2 Moses articulates the chosen identity of Israel as the *children of the LORD* who are a *people holy to the LORD* and his *treasured possession*. This identity establishes the character of the people from which their behavior is intended to flow. Because of their particular identity, Israelites are not to *lacerate* themselves or *shave* their *forelocks for the dead*. These practices were done in ancestral cults in the ancient Near East. They are prohibited for priests in Lev. 19:27–28, and Deuteronomy extends this prohibition to the entire nation of Israel. **14:3–20** The identity of Israel as a holy people is to be reflected in their diet. The list of animals is divided into land animals (vv. 4–8), aquatic animals (vv. 9–10), and flying creatures (vv. 11–20). The list, building on Lev. 11:2–23, is based on systematic categories rooted in the creation order that define species

the sheep, the goat, [5]the deer, the gazelle, the roebuck, the wild goat, the ibex, the antelope, and the mountain sheep. [6]Any animal that divides the hoof and has the hoof cleft in two and chews the cud, among the animals, you may eat. [7]Yet of those that chew the cud or have the hoof cleft you shall not eat these: the camel, the hare, and the rock badger because they chew the cud but do not divide the hoof; they are unclean for you. [8]And the pig, because it divides the hoof but does not chew the cud, is unclean for you. You shall not eat their meat, and you shall not touch their carcasses.

9 "Of all that live in water you may eat these: whatever has fins and scales you may eat. [10]And whatever does not have fins and scales you shall not eat; it is unclean for you.

11 "You may eat any clean birds. [12]But these are the ones that you shall not eat: the eagle, the vulture, the osprey, [13]the buzzard, the kite of any kind; [14]every raven of any kind; [15]the ostrich, the nighthawk, the sea gull, the hawk of any kind; [16]the little owl and the great owl, the water hen [17]and the desert owl,[g] the carrion vulture and the cormorant, [18]the stork, the heron of any kind, the hoopoe, and the bat.[b] [19]And all winged insects are unclean for you; they shall not be eaten. [20]You may eat any clean winged creature.

21 "You shall not eat anything that dies of itself; you may give it to aliens residing in your towns for them to eat, or you may sell it to a foreigner. For you are a people holy to the LORD your God.

"You shall not boil a kid in its mother's milk.

22 "Set apart a tithe of all the yield of your seed that is brought in yearly from the field. [23]In the presence of the LORD your God, in the place that he will choose as a dwelling for his name, you shall eat the tithe of your grain, your wine, and your oil, as well as the firstlings of your herd and flock, so that you may learn to fear the LORD your God always. [24]But if, when the LORD your God has blessed you, the distance is so great that you are unable to transport it, because the place where the LORD your God will choose to set his name is too far away from you, [25]then you may turn it into money. With the money secure in hand, go to the place that the LORD your God will choose; [26]spend the money for whatever you wish: oxen, sheep, wine, strong drink, or whatever you desire. And you shall eat there in the presence of the LORD your God, you and your household rejoicing together. [27]As for the Levites resident in your towns, do not neglect them, because they have no allotment or inheritance with you.

28 "Every third year you shall bring out the full tithe of your produce for that year and store it within your towns; [29]the Levites, because they have no allotment or inheritance with you, as well as the resident aliens, the orphans, and the widows in your towns, may come and eat their fill so that the LORD your

g 14.17 Or *pelican* h 14.18 Identification of several of the birds in 14.12–18 is uncertain

according to features that are viewed as normative for the species. Species that do not fit the categories are considered *unclean*—that is, ritually impure. The identification of many of the animals is uncertain; see **"Diet," p. 268; "Holiness and Purity," p. 158. 14:21** *Aliens* are non-Israelites dwelling among the Israelites in the promised land—in other words, immigrants. These immigrants were granted many privileges in the Israelite community and also were expected to live according to some Israelite customs. Here, they are allowed to eat meat from a carcass, which Israelites are not allowed to do. The prohibition to *not boil a kid in its mother's milk* is often understood to mean that the young goat (kid) cannot be boiled in milk. Grammatically it can also be a prohibition of boiling a kid that is still "at" its mother's milk—that is, at the age of nursing. This prohibition is the basis for not mixing meat and dairy products in Jewish laws of "kashrut" (see **"Diet," p. 268**). As part of Deuteronomic creation theology, the command pertains to a larger consideration of animal rights; see also Deut. 22:6–7.

14:22–29 Tithes. Offering a percentage of produce to a ruler was common in the ancient world. Deuteronomy's tithe laws for offering a tenth of produce to the Lord reveal central characteristics of Deuteronomy: the tithe, which is a blessing of abundance from the Lord, is enjoyed in a communal celebration in *the presence of the LORD* at the chosen place. In contrast to practices that legislate tithes for rulers and priests, the Deuteronomic tithe—supplementing the laws of Exod. 22:28–30—becomes a social program for supporting the disadvantaged in society, as it is to be enjoyed by those who produced the tithe as well as by the *resident aliens, orphans, widows*, and Levitical priests who do not own land (vv. 27, 29).

Going Deeper: Diet (Deuteronomy 14:3–20)

Diet was an important part of religion in the ancient world, as it is today, and often defined key aspects of the relationship between humanity, creation, and the deity. Limiting human desires, including appetites, is a frequent theme throughout the Pentateuch, beginning with the prohibition of the fruit of the tree of knowledge in the garden of Eden (Gen. 2:16–17) and the limitations on eating blood in the postflood world of Gen. 9:3–4. Within the context of Deut. 14:1–2, 21, which emphasizes Israel's holiness, the laws of clean and unclean animals in Deut. 14:3–20 contribute to defining the identity of Israel as the chosen people of the Lord (see also the similar list in Lev. 11, which Deuteronomy elaborates on). The rationale for the allowance or prohibition of the animals listed is not explicit, and various theories have not garnered consensus, though it is likely that the laws have little to do with hygiene and are best understood as anti-Canaanite identity-defining measures. Particularly, the exclusion of the pig from the diet would have set Israel apart from its neighbors. The association with holiness, based on conceptions of cleanness/uncleanness, connects the restrictions to the maintenance of creational order. The notion that something could cause pollution was common in the ancient world, and here, animals that do not fit what is regarded as categorically normative are considered unclean and thus viewed as causing pollution. Obedience to the commandments establishes a daily discipline in which Israelites must curtail their appetites in service of maintaining the order of creation in submission to the Lord. The laws of Deut. 14 and Lev. 11 became the foundation for the Jewish dietary laws of *kashrut* (keeping "kosher"), one of the central characteristics of Jewish religious practice to this day. In early Christianity, following the teachings of Jesus (Mark 7:18–23) and the vision of Peter in Acts 10:10–16, the dietary laws were not considered necessary for Gentile Christians (Acts 15:19–21).

Paavo N. Tucker

God may bless you in all the work that you undertake.

15 "Every seventh year you shall grant a remission of debts. [2]And this is the manner of the remission: every creditor shall remit the claim that is held against a neighbor, not exacting it,[i] because the Lord's remission has been proclaimed. [3]Of a foreigner you may exact it, but you must remit your claim on whatever any member of your community owes you. [4]There will, however, be no one in need among you, because the Lord is sure to bless you in the land that the Lord your God is giving you as a possession to occupy, [5]if only you will obey the Lord your God by diligently observing this entire commandment that I command you today. [6]When the Lord your God has blessed you, as he promised you, you will lend to many nations, but you will not borrow; you will rule over many nations, but they will not rule over you.

7 "If there is among you anyone in need, a member of your community in any of your towns within the land that the Lord your God is giving you, do not be hard-hearted or tight-fisted toward your needy neighbor. [8]You should rather open your hand, willingly

i 15.2 Q ms: MT adds *of a neighbor who is a member of the community*

15:1–18 Release of debts. In the ancient world, debt was used to maintain power in the hands of the ruling elite. It ensured cheap labor and reinforced distinctions in social class that engrained generational patterns of wealth and poverty, especially through the control of land. **15:1** Deuteronomy 15:1–18 undermines the systemic power of debt by legislating a *remission of debts* every seven years as an economic safety net to protect the most vulnerable in society and preserve their access to the land that the Lord had given. Such debt-release measures were also occasionally practiced in the ancient Near East, often as a propagandistic means of generating popularity when new rulers came into power. **15:3** The basis of the legislation is the "familial" nature of all Israel (vv. 3, 7, 12, translated as "member of your community")—including debtors, enslaved persons, and women within the general kinship designation of siblings—whose rights to economic self-sufficiency must be protected. **15:4** Because of the abundance that the Lord will provide and the "remission" that YHWH has granted Israel in bringing Israel out of Egypt, the Israelites must also be gracious toward the disadvantaged in their community. Ideally, this should result in eliminating poverty in the community (cf. Acts 2:42–45; 4:34–35 for an implementation of this social vision in early Christianity). If someone has taken a loan—usually due to hardship or failure of an agricultural endeavor—the community must ensure that the debtor does not get caught in a cycle of debt leading to debt slavery.

lending enough to meet the need, whatever it may be. [9]Be careful that you do not entertain a mean thought, thinking, 'The seventh year, the year of remission, is near,' and therefore view your needy neighbor with hostility and give nothing; your neighbor[j] might cry to the LORD against you, and you would incur guilt. [10]Give liberally and be ungrudging when you do so, for on this account the LORD your God will bless you in all your work and in all that you undertake. [11]Since there will never cease to be some in need on the earth, I therefore command you, 'Open your hand to the poor and needy neighbor in your land.'

[12] "If a member of your community, whether a Hebrew man or a Hebrew woman, is sold[k] to you and works for you six years, in the seventh year you shall set that person free. [13]And when you send a male slave[l] out from you a free person, you shall not send him out empty-handed. [14]Provide for him liberally out of your flock, your threshing floor, and your winepress, thus giving to him some of the bounty with which the LORD your God has blessed you. [15]Remember that you were a slave in the land of Egypt, and the LORD your God redeemed you; for this reason I lay this command upon you today. [16]But if he says to you, 'I will not go out from you,' because he loves you and your household, since he is well off with you, [17]then you shall take an awl and thrust it through his earlobe into the door, and he shall be your slave forever.

"You shall do the same with regard to your female slave.

[18] "Do not consider it a hardship when you send them out from you free persons, because for six years they have given you services worth the wages of hired laborers, and the LORD your God will bless you in all that you do.

[19] "Every firstling male born of your herd and flock you shall consecrate to the LORD your God; you shall not do work with your firstling ox nor shear the firstling of your flock. [20]You shall eat it, you together with your household, in the presence of the LORD your God year by year at the place that the LORD will choose. [21]But if it has any defect—any serious defect, such as lameness or blindness—you shall not sacrifice it to the LORD your God; [22]within your towns you may eat it, the unclean and the clean alike, as you would a gazelle or deer. [23]Its blood, however, you must not eat; you shall pour it out on the ground like water.

16 "Observe the month[m] of Abib by keeping the Passover to the LORD your God, for in the month of Abib the LORD your God

j 15.9 Heb *he*   k 15.12 Or *sells himself or herself*   l 15.13 Heb *him*   m 16.1 Or *new moon*

15:12–17 Deuteronomy combines the laws of slavery and remission of land from Exod. 21:2–6 and 23:10–11 by extending the law of remission to apply to the release of both male and female Hebrews who have been sold into slavery and by legislating for securing provisions for a released enslaved person. The enslaved person is to be treated well, and their needs are to be cared for, including providing them a foundation for sustaining their economic freedom once their servitude is released (cf. Jer. 34:6–22 for an implementation of the release laws). Slavery, which usually resulted from a person falling into unpayable debt or military captivity, was relatively common in Israel and the ancient world. The laws on slavery in Deuteronomy presume the economic reality of the establishment while protecting some of the rights of enslaved persons and providing them a path to being restored to self-sufficiency (cf. Deut. 23:15–17). Tragically, many of the Pentateuchal laws regulating slavery were selectively used to justify chattel slavery by Christian slave-owners in the eighteenth and nineteenth centuries. See **"Human Bondage," p. 115**.

15:19–23 Firstborn. As an act of faith in the provision of the Lord, Israel is to consecrate the firstborn of their flock to the Lord (cf. Exod. 13). Nevertheless, the people are to eat this offering themselves. If it is unblemished, it is to be eaten before the Lord at the chosen place; if it is defective, it may be eaten at home.

16:1–17 Festivals. Three festivals articulate central aspects of Deuteronomy's liturgical and sacramental theology: Passover / Unleavened Bread (vv. 1–8; see **"Passover," p. 99**), Feast of Weeks (vv. 9–12), and Feast of Booths (vv. 13–15). Centralization transforms these occasions from domestic celebrations into pilgrimage festivals at the central sanctuary (v. 16; cf. Exod. 12–13; 23:14–17; 34:18–25; Lev. 23; Num. 28–29 for other festival legislation). See **"Cult Centralization," p. 264**. Each of the festivals is tied to the agricultural calendar, with Passover at the beginning of the harvest, while Weeks occurs during the harvest of firstfruits, seven weeks later. The Feast of Booths, during which

brought you out of Egypt by night. [2]You shall offer the Passover sacrifice to the LORD your God from the flock and the herd, at the place that the LORD will choose as a dwelling for his name. [3]You must not eat with it anything leavened. For seven days you shall eat unleavened bread with it—the bread of affliction—because you came out of the land of Egypt in great haste, so that all the days of your life you may remember the day of your departure from the land of Egypt. [4]No leaven shall be seen with you in all your territory for seven days, and none of the meat of what you slaughter on the evening of the first day shall remain until morning. [5]You are not permitted to offer the Passover sacrifice within any of your towns that the LORD your God is giving you. [6]But at the place that the LORD your God will choose as a dwelling for his name, only there shall you offer the Passover sacrifice, in the evening at sunset, the time of day when you departed from Egypt. [7]You shall cook it and eat it at the place that the LORD your God will choose; the next morning you may go back to your tents. [8]For six days you shall continue to eat unleavened bread, and on the seventh day there shall be a solemn assembly for the LORD your God, when you shall do no work.

9 "You shall count seven weeks; begin to count the seven weeks from the time the sickle is first put to the standing grain. [10]Then you shall keep the Festival of Weeks to the LORD your God, contributing a freewill offering in proportion to the blessing that you have received from the LORD your God. [11]Rejoice before the LORD your God—you and your sons and your daughters, your male and female slaves, the Levites resident in your towns, as well as the strangers, the orphans, and the widows who are among you—at the place that the LORD your God will choose as a dwelling for his name. [12]Remember that you were a slave in Egypt, and diligently observe these statutes.

13 "You shall keep the Festival of Booths" for seven days, when you have gathered in the produce from your threshing floor and your winepress. [14]Rejoice during your festival, you and your sons and your daughters, your male and female slaves, as well as the Levites, the strangers, the orphans, and the widows resident in your towns. [15]Seven days you shall keep the festival to the LORD your God at the place that the LORD will choose, for the LORD your God will bless you in all your produce and in all your undertakings, and you shall surely celebrate.

16 "Three times a year all your males shall appear before the LORD your God at the place that he will choose: at the Festival of Unleavened Bread, at the Festival of Weeks, and at the Festival of Booths.[o] They shall not appear before the LORD empty-handed; [17]all shall give as they are able, according to the blessing of the LORD your God that he has given you.

18 "You shall appoint judges and officials throughout your tribes, in all your towns that the LORD your God is giving you, and

n 16.13 Or *Tabernacles*   o 16.16 Or *Tabernacles*

Israelites are to camp in the fields during the harvest, occurs as a celebration at the end of the harvest. The agricultural festivals have been infused with theological significance as celebrations of the historical deliverances of Israel (cf. Deut. 16:6, 12; and Lev. 23:43, where the camping in booths is a reminder of Israel's exodus and sojourn in the wilderness). The Passover is blended with the Feast of Unleavened Bread, and the original prescription to slaughter a lamb and place its blood on the doorposts of Israelite houses in Egypt (Exod. 12:1–13) has been transformed into a sacrifice at the chosen place (Deut. 16:2). Passover remains the central festival of Judaism to this day, the Feast of Weeks has become associated with the giving of the law at Sinai, and the completion of the annual Torah-reading cycle is celebrated at the Feast of Booths. In Christianity, with the passion of Jesus described in the Gospels as taking place during Passover, the festival provides a context of meaning for the death and resurrection of Jesus as a redemptive sacrifice (cf. 1 Cor. 5:7).

16:18–17:13 Justice. A section on laws for public leadership extends from 16:18 to 18:22. Establishing justice (*just decisions*, 16:18) is the primary concern in casting a vision for societal governance and power structures, a unique vision in the ancient Near East. Addressing the roles of the judicial system (16:18–17:13), the monarchy (17:14–20), priests (18:1–8), and prophets (18:9–22), among whom power is distributed equally, the model of societal administration subordinates each leadership role to the authority of the Mosaic instruction. Each leader is responsible for pursuing Deuteronomy's standard of justice that is promised to result in a prosperous life for Israel (16:20). **16:18–19** *Judges and officials* are to be appointed throughout the land in order to administer justice on a local level

they shall render just decisions for the people. [19]You must not distort justice; you must not show partiality; and you must not accept a bribe, for a bribe blinds the eyes of the wise and subverts the cause of those who are in the right. [20]Justice, and only justice, you shall pursue, so that you may live and occupy the land that the LORD your God is giving you.

21 "You shall not plant any tree as a sacred pole[p] beside the altar that you make for the LORD your God, [22]nor shall you set up a stone pillar—things that the LORD your God hates.

17 "You must not sacrifice to the LORD your God an ox or a sheep that has a defect, anything seriously wrong, for that is abhorrent to the LORD your God.

2 "If there is found among you, in one of your towns that the LORD your God is giving you, a man or woman who does what is evil in the sight of the LORD your God and transgresses his covenant [3]by going to serve other gods and worshiping them—whether the sun or the moon or any of the host of heaven, which I have forbidden—[4]and if it is reported to you or you hear of it, and you make a thorough inquiry, and the charge is proved true that such an abhorrent thing has occurred in Israel, [5]then you shall bring out to your gates that man or that woman who has committed this crime, and you shall stone the man or woman to death. [6]On the evidence of two or three witnesses the death sentence shall be executed; a person must not be put to death on the evidence of only one witness. [7]The hands of the witnesses shall be the first raised against the person to execute the death penalty and afterward the hands of all the people. So you shall purge the evil from your midst.

8 "If a judicial decision is too difficult for you to make between one kind of bloodshed and another, one kind of legal right and another, or one kind of assault and another—any such matters of dispute in your towns—then you shall immediately go up to the place that the LORD your God will choose, [9]where you shall consult with the Levitical priests and the judge who is in office in those days; they shall announce to you the decision in the case. [10]Carry out exactly the decision that they announce to you from the place that the LORD will choose, diligently observing everything they instruct you. [11]You must carry out the law that they interpret for you or the ruling that they announce to you; do not turn aside from the decision that they announce to you, either to the right or to the left. [12]As for anyone who presumes to disobey the priest appointed to minister there to the LORD your God or the judge, that person shall die. So you shall purge the evil from Israel. [13]All the people will hear and be afraid and will not act presumptuously again.

14 "When you have come into the land that the LORD your God is giving you and have taken possession of it and settled in it, and you say, 'I will set a king over me, like all the nations that are around me,' [15]you may indeed set over you a king whom the LORD your God will choose. One of your own community you may set as king over you; you are not permitted to put a foreigner over you, who is not of

p 16.21 Or *Asherah*

(cf. Deut. 1:13–17). The inclusion of Israel as a whole in the process of appointing judges limits the possibility of perpetuating corruption in structures of power in the judicial system. **16:21–17:1** The *sacred pole* and *stone pillar* were worshiped in Canaanite religion (16:21–22; 17:2–3). Along with offering defective sacrifices (17:1), these are practices that would distort Israel's sense of justice. Here Deuteronomy highlights the connection between cultic practice and social justice that is seen throughout the book. **17:2–7** Israel is responsible for prosecuting and punishing idolatry, which is an existential threat that has to be purged, lest it contaminate others. The charge should be investigated with a *thorough inquiry* and corroborated by the evidence of at least two witnesses. If the charge is proven, the offender is to be executed by stoning at the *gates* of the city, which was the locus for the communal administration of justice (vv. 4, 6). **17:8–13** Cases that are *too difficult* to decide in local towns are to be referred to the Levitical priests at the chosen *place*.

17:14–20 Kingship. Moses anticipates that Israel will ask to be ruled by a king *like all the nations* (cf. 1 Sam. 8:5; see **"Kingship/Monarchy," p. 390**). The political vision of Deuteronomy contrasts with ancient Near Eastern conceptions of kingship, where monarchs, as divine-like figures, had unlimited authority—including in the administration of justice and the cult. Deuteronomy places strict conditions for the monarchy: the king, who is chosen from among the Israelites, must not acquire many horses (as a symbol of military prowess), have multiple wives (in making international marriage

your own community. [16]Even so, he must not acquire many horses for himself or return the people to Egypt in order to acquire more horses, since the LORD has said to you, 'You must never return that way again.' [17]And he must not acquire many wives for himself or else his heart will turn away; also silver and gold he must not acquire in great quantity for himself. [18]When he has taken the throne of his kingdom, he shall write for himself a copy of this law on a scroll in the presence of the Levitical priests. [19]It shall remain with him, and he shall read in it all the days of his life, so that he may learn to fear the LORD his God, diligently observing all the words of this law and these statutes, [20]neither exalting himself above other members of the community nor turning aside from the commandment, either to the right or to the left, so that he and his descendants may reign long over his kingdom in Israel.

18

"The Levitical priests, the whole tribe of Levi, shall have no allotment or inheritance within Israel. They may eat the offerings by fire[q] that are the LORD's portion,[r] [2]but they shall have no inheritance among the other members of the community; the LORD is their inheritance, as he promised them.

[3] "This shall be the priests' due from the people, from those offering a sacrifice, whether an ox or a sheep: they shall give to the priest the shoulder, the two jowls, and the stomach. [4]The first fruits of your grain, your wine, and your oil, as well as the first of the fleece of your sheep, you shall give him. [5]For the LORD your God has chosen Levi[s] out of all your tribes to stand and minister in the name of the LORD, him and his sons for all time.

[6] "If a Levite leaves any of your towns, from wherever he has been residing in Israel, and comes to the place that the LORD will choose (and he may come whenever he wishes), [7]then he may minister in the name of the LORD his God, like all his fellow-Levites who stand to minister there before the LORD. [8]They shall have equal portions to eat, even though they have income from the sale of family possessions.[t]

[9] "When you come into the land that the LORD your God is giving you, you must not learn to imitate the abhorrent practices of those nations. [10]No one shall be found among you who makes a son or daughter pass through fire, or who practices divination, or is a soothsayer, or an augur, or a sorcerer, [11]or one who casts spells, or who consults ghosts or spirits, or who seeks oracles from the dead. [12]For whoever does these things is abhorrent to the LORD; it is because of such abhorrent practices that the LORD your God is driving them out before you. [13]You must remain completely loyal to the LORD your God. [14]Although these nations that you are about to dispossess do give heed to soothsayers and diviners, as for you, the LORD your God does not permit you to do so.

[15] "The LORD your God will raise up for you a prophet like me from among your own people; you shall heed such a prophet.[u] [16]This is what you requested of the LORD your God

q 18.1 Or *the gifts*   r 18.1 Meaning of Heb uncertain
s 18.5 Heb *him*   t 18.8 Meaning of Heb uncertain
u 18.15 Heb *him*

---

alliances), or amass excessive wealth. These pursuits are prohibited, as they can take the king's focus away from the Lord (cf. the downfall of Solomon in 1 Kgs. 10–11). **17:19–20** The primary role of the king is to be an exemplary scribe who studies, transmits, and obeys the teachings of Moses.

18:1–8 Levites. The privileges and responsibilities of *Levitical priests* are described, with an emphasis on the status of the *whole tribe of Levi* (see **"Priests (Leviticus)," p. 176**). This specification contrasts with the focus on the roles of the Aaronic priests from within the tribe of Levi that is seen in Leviticus and Numbers (cf. Num. 18). Because the Levites do not receive an allotment of land to support themselves with, the rest of the community is to provide for their needs with a portion of their produce. **18:6** Levites who live away from the chosen place may come to the central sanctuary and minister as priests, thus equalizing any potential geographical rivalry among the priesthood that may emerge due to centralization.

18:9–22 Revelation from the spiritual realm. 18:9–14 The section on prophets (18:15–22) is preceded by prohibitions of illegitimate practices of seeking power or revelation from the spiritual realm. **18:15–22** For Israel, the legitimate means of revelation is the *prophet like* Moses, whom the Lord will raise up and who will speak only the words of the Lord. Their primary role is to call Israel to fidelity to the covenant and pursuit of justice, though they may also predict future circumstances (cf. Deut. 32:1–43). These predictions would nevertheless be conditionally dependent on Israel's

at Horeb on the day of the assembly when you said, 'Let me not hear again the voice of the Lord my God or see this great fire any more, lest I die.' [17]Then the Lord replied to me, 'They are right in what they have said. [18]I will raise up for them a prophet like you from among their own people; I will put my words in the mouth of the prophet,[v] who shall speak to them everything that I command. [19]Anyone who does not heed the words that the prophet[w] shall speak in my name, I myself will hold accountable. [20]But any prophet who presumes to speak in my name a word that I have not commanded the prophet to speak or who speaks in the name of other gods, that prophet shall die.' [21]You may say to yourself, 'How can we recognize a word that the Lord has not spoken?' [22]If a prophet speaks in the name of the Lord but the thing does not take place or prove true, it is a word that the Lord has not spoken. The prophet has spoken it presumptuously; do not be frightened by it.

19 "When the Lord your God has cut off the nations whose land the Lord your God is giving you and you have dispossessed them and settled in their towns and in their houses, [2]you shall set apart three cities in the land that the Lord your God is giving you to possess. [3]You shall calculate the distances[x] and divide into three regions the land that the Lord your God gives you as a possession, so that any homicide can flee to one of them.

4 "Now this is the case of a homicide who might flee there and live, that is, someone who has killed another person unintentionally when the two had not been at enmity before. [5]Suppose someone goes into the forest with another to cut wood, and when one of them swings the ax to cut down a tree, the head slips from the handle and strikes the other person, who then dies; the killer may flee to one of these cities and live. [6]But if the distance is too great, the avenger of blood in hot anger might pursue and overtake and put the killer to death, although a death sentence was not deserved, since the two had not been at enmity before. [7]Therefore I command you: You shall set apart three cities.

8 "If the Lord your God enlarges your territory, as he swore to your ancestors—and he will give you all the land that he promised your ancestors to give you, [9]provided you diligently observe this entire commandment that I command you today, by loving the Lord your God and walking always in his ways—then you shall add three more cities to these three, [10]so that the blood of an innocent person may not be shed in the land that the Lord your God is giving you as an inheritance, thereby bringing bloodguilt upon you.

11 "But if someone at enmity with another lies in wait and attacks and takes the life of that person and flees into one of these cities, [12]then the elders of the killer's city shall send to have the culprit taken from there and handed over to the avenger of blood to be put to death. [13]Show no pity; you shall purge the guilt of innocent blood from Israel, so that it may go well with you.

14 "You must not move your neighbor's boundary marker, set up by former generations, on the property that will be allotted to you in the land that the Lord your God is giving you to possess.

15 "A single witness shall not suffice to

v 18.18 Heb *in his mouth*   *w* 18.19 Heb *he*   *x* 19.3 Or *prepare roads to them*

response to the word of the Lord—predictions of judgment would thus not come true if the prophet was successful in persuading the people to repent and change course. **18:20–22** False prophets are those who speak falsely in the name of the Lord or in the name of other deities. See **"God's Name," p. 89**. Their words can be evaluated based on whether they conform to the teachings of Moses, but their predictions can only be judged after the fact. The performance of signs and wonders cannot be taken as evidence of true prophecy (Deut. 13:1–5).

19:1–13 Cities of refuge. An older tradition of receiving asylum at an altar of the Lord is updated by the arrangement of cities of refuge, which are spread out at accessible intervals throughout the land (Exod. 21:12–14; Deut. 4:41–43). These cities are established as asylums to secure evidence-based justice that protects the accused from biases and hasty vigilante vengeance.

19:14 Boundaries. The promised land was parceled out to the tribes and families of Israel as an inalienable inheritance from the Lord. Hence moving boundary markers is prohibited.

19:15–21 Evidence and witnesses. This section sets out criteria for evaluating evidence and witnesses. **19:15–20** Multiple witnesses are required to confirm a charge, and warnings are given against potentially *malicious* or *false* witnesses. To establish the truth of a charge, *judges*

convict a person of any crime or wrongdoing in connection with any offense that may be committed. Only on the evidence of two or three witnesses shall a charge be sustained. [16]If a malicious witness comes forward to accuse someone of wrongdoing, [17]then both parties to the dispute shall appear before the Lord, before the priests and the judges who are in office in those days, [18]and the judges shall make a thorough inquiry. If the witness is a false witness, having testified falsely against another, [19]then you shall do to the false witness just as the false witness had meant to do to the other. So you shall purge the evil from your midst. [20]The rest shall hear and be afraid, and a crime such as this shall never again be committed among you. [21]Show no pity: life for life, eye for eye, tooth for tooth, hand for hand, foot for foot.

20 "When you go out to war against your enemies and see horses and chariots, an army larger than your own, do not fear them, for the Lord your God is with you, who brought you up from the land of Egypt. [2]Before you engage in battle, the priest shall come forward and speak to the troops [3]and shall say to them, 'Hear, O Israel! Today you are drawing near to do battle against your enemies. Do not lose heart or be afraid or panic or be in dread of them, [4]for it is the Lord your God who goes with you, to fight for you against your enemies, to give you victory.' [5]Then the officers shall address the troops, saying, 'Has anyone built a new house but not dedicated it? He should go back to his house, lest he die in the battle and another dedicate it. [6]Has anyone planted a vineyard but not yet enjoyed its fruit? He should go back to his house, lest he die in the battle and another be first to enjoy its fruit. [7]Has anyone become engaged to a woman but not yet married her? He should go back to his house, lest he die in the battle and another marry her.' [8]The officers shall continue to address the troops, saying, 'Is anyone afraid or disheartened? He should go back to his house, or he might cause the heart of his comrades to melt like his own.' [9]When the officers have finished addressing the troops, then the commanders shall take charge of them.

10 "When you draw near to a town to fight against it, offer it terms of peace. [11]If it accepts your terms of peace and surrenders to you, then all the people in it shall serve you at forced labor. [12]But if it does not accept your terms of peace and makes war against you, then you shall besiege it, [13]and when the Lord your God gives it into your hand, you shall put all its males to the sword. [14]You may, however, take as your plunder the women, the children, livestock, and everything else in the town, all its spoil. You may enjoy the spoil of your enemies, which the Lord your God has given you. [15]Thus you shall treat all the towns that are very far from you, which are not towns of these nations here. [16]But as for the towns of these peoples that the Lord your God is giving you as an inheritance, you must not let anything that breathes remain alive. [17]Indeed, you shall annihilate them—the Hittites and the Amorites, the Canaanites and the Perizzites, the Hivites and the Jebusites—just as the Lord your God has commanded, [18]so that they may not teach you

---

shall make a thorough inquiry that includes an evaluation of the trustworthiness of witnesses. **19:21** The law of talion—*life for life, eye for eye*—establishes an unbiased foundation for justice that would apply equally to all social classes and curtail escalations of vengeance.

20:1–20 Warfare. **20:1–4** In all areas of life, including warfare, Israel is to put its trust in the Lord. The instructions bear out the harsh realities of war that Israel would encounter. **20:5–9** Nevertheless, the allowances for avoiding conscription cover building, farming, and marriage as well as being *afraid or disheartened*, leaving open a wide range of possibilities for the avoidance of warfare and undermining militaristic ideology. **20:10–14** When fighting cities that are outside the promised land, Israel is to offer terms of peace. If the terms are accepted, the people of the town are to submit to Israel as *forced labor*; if the terms are rejected, then Israel shall kill all the males and take the women, children, and livestock as plunder. It is possible that the general principle of initially offering peace to cities that are attacked from v. 10 was originally intended to govern also the procedure of approaching towns within the promised land as well (so Maimonides), though **20:15–18** specify that the Israelites are to *annihilate* towns that are within the promised land (see **"Genocide," p. 305**, and **"The Divine Mandate to Exterminate the Canaanites," p. 313**). The motive of the instruction is due to the urgency to mitigate the threat of the idolatrous influence of the native population and

to do all the abhorrent things that they do for their gods and you thus sin against the LORD your God.

19 "If you besiege a town for a long time, making war against it in order to take it, you must not destroy its trees by wielding an ax against them. Although you may take food from them, you must not cut them down. Are trees in the field human beings that they should come under siege from you? 20You may destroy only the trees that you know do not produce food; you may cut them down for use in building siegeworks against the town that makes war with you, until it falls.

21 "If, in the land that the LORD your God is giving you to possess, a body is found lying in open country, and it is not known who struck the person down, 2then your elders and your judges shall come out to measure the distances to the towns that are near the body. 3The elders of the town nearest the body shall take a heifer that has never been worked, one that has not pulled in the yoke; 4the elders of that town shall bring the heifer down to a wadi with running water, which is neither plowed nor sown, and shall break the heifer's neck there in the wadi. 5Then the priests, the sons of Levi, shall come forward, for the LORD your God has chosen them to minister to him and to pronounce blessings in the name of the LORD, and by their decision all cases of dispute and assault shall be settled. 6All the elders of that town nearest the body shall wash their hands over the heifer whose neck was broken in the wadi, 7and they shall declare, 'Our hands did not shed this blood, nor were we witnesses to it. 8Absolve, O LORD, your people Israel, whom you redeemed; do not let the guilt of innocent blood remain in the midst of your people Israel.' Then they will be absolved of bloodguilt. 9So you shall purge the guilt of innocent blood from your midst, because you must do what is right in the sight of the LORD.

10 "When you go out to war against your enemies and the LORD your God hands them over to you and you take them captive, 11suppose you see among the captives a beautiful woman whom you desire and want to marry, 12and so you bring her home to your house: she shall shave her head, pare her nails, 13discard her captive's garb, and remain in your house a full month mourning for her father and mother; after that you may go in to her and be her husband, and she shall be your wife. 14But if you are not satisfied with her, you shall let her go free and certainly not sell her for money. You must not treat her as a slave, since you have dishonored her.

15 "If a man has two wives, one of them loved and the other disliked, and if both the loved and the disliked have borne him sons, the firstborn being the son of the one who is

exhort Israel to singular devotion to the Lord (cf. Deut. 7:1–5). **20:19–20** Destroying trees was part of scorched-earth military policies practiced by Egypt and Assyria. Fruit and olive trees were valuable commodities and essential for thriving agriculture, and it would take decades for them to be regrown if destroyed.

21:1–9 Unresolved homicide. *A body is found . . . and it is not known who struck the person.* The law indicates how to bring closure in a case of homicide where the culprit cannot be determined. **21:9** Murder brings guilt upon the land, and the leaders of the town closest to the corpse are required to absolve that guilt through a ritual killing of a heifer and declaring an exculpating oath that purges *the guilt of innocent blood*.

21:10–25:19 Family and civic laws. This section contains laws largely pertaining to family and civic relationships. Many of the laws reflect assumptions that were shared across ancient Near Eastern family customs, warfare practices, and economic systems that modern readers would view as problematic. Israel's applications of these laws serve as windows into an ancient culture that grappled with the process of extending the implications of Israel's revelation of the Lord's covenantal will and demand for Israel to pursue justice (16:18) in every area of life. The scenarios seen in these laws—often recounting extreme circumstances—served as material for ethical and theological reflection. Several of the sections focus on the rights of women, offering women protections that mitigated the worst-case scenarios of male abuse of women in a patriarchal society (cf. 21:10–14, 15–17, 18–20; 22:13–19, 25–29; 24:1–4; 25:5–10). The family laws in Deuteronomy subvert the absolute powers of tribal patriarchy and advocate for a more collective administration of justice.

21:10–14 Captive woman. The laws of 21:10–21 on the captive woman, inheritance, and rebellious son each limit the absolute power of the male head of a household ("pater familias"), distributing

disliked, [16]then on the day when he wills his possessions to his sons, he is not permitted to treat the son of the loved as the firstborn in preference to the son of the disliked, who is the firstborn. [17]He must acknowledge as first-born the son of the one who is disliked, giving him a double portion[y] of all that he has; since he is the first issue of his virility, the right of the firstborn is his.

[18] "If someone has a stubborn and rebellious son who will not obey his father and mother, who does not heed them when they discipline him, [19]then his father and his mother shall take hold of him and bring him out to the elders of his town at the gate of that place. [20]They shall say to the elders of his town, 'This son of ours is stubborn and rebellious. He will not obey us. He is a glutton and a drunkard.' [21]Then all the men of the town shall stone him to death. So you shall purge the evil from your midst, and all Israel will hear and be afraid.

[22] "When someone is convicted of a crime punishable by death and is executed and you hang him on a tree, [23]his corpse must not remain all night upon the tree; you must bury him that same day, for anyone hung on a tree is under God's curse. You must not defile the land that the LORD your God is giving you for possession.

22 "You shall not watch your neighbor's ox or sheep straying away and ignore them; you shall take them back to their owner. [2]If the owner does not reside near you or you do not know who the owner is, you shall bring it to your own house, and it shall remain with you until the owner claims it; then you shall return it. [3]You shall do the same with a neighbor's donkey; you shall do the same with a neighbor's garment; and you shall do the same with anything else that

y 21.17 Heb two-thirds

authority to the courts, family, and elders. An Israelite who sees a *beautiful woman* whom he desires to marry from among the captives of a conquered people may do so under certain conditions: he is to grant her a time of mourning and thereafter take her as a lawful wife and thus not treat her as an enslaved person. According to rabbinical tradition, though this law is morally challenging, it presupposes the brokenness of humanity and the realities of warfare and as such is intended to mitigate worst-case scenarios. Across the ancient Near East, it was assumed that captives became the possession of their captors, and the most likely scenario would be for a captured woman to be raped by an invading soldier and then be forced into slavery. Within this context, the Deuteronomic law presumably protects the personhood of the woman by requiring the man to grant the woman rights of mourning and the rights of citizenship and inheritance that would follow from official marriage.

21:15–17 Inheritance. In ancient Near Eastern custom, firstborn sons were given priority in inheritance laws, though other arrangements are also attested. Within this context, Deut. 21:15–17 affirms the rights of the firstborn son and protects the family from the potential negative impact of the favoritism that a patriarch might be tempted to exert by instead securing a nonprejudiced allotment of the inheritance in polygamous situations (cf. Gen. 25–27).

21:18–21 Rebellious child. 21:19–20 The disciplining of a *stubborn and rebellious* son—an adult or late adolescent who persistently engages in rebellious activity that threatens the viability of the family—is unique in its ancient context in the requirement that the mother is included in bringing the charge against the son. The participation of *the elders of his town* in the procedure also limits the absolute authority of a patriarch (cf. Gen. 38:24, where Judah orders the execution of his daughter-in-law without a trial). Respect toward parents was considered the foundation of order in tribal societies; hence, persistent rebellion was viewed as an existential threat to communal stability that warranted strong rhetoric to dissuade such rebellion and punishments deterring such unrepentant rebellion (cf. Deut. 5:16; see Jer. 5:20–29 for an application of the law to Israel as the "rebellious son" of the Lord).

21:22–23 Corpses. Leaving an impaled corpse hanging would degrade the criminal by denying them a burial as well as serve as a deterrent (cf. Gen. 40:19; Josh. 8:29; 10:27). In the ancient Near Eastern worldview, improper burial could result in evil spirits attaching to the body—hence the urgent concern for proper burial. In Deuteronomy, leaving the corpse to hang causes ritual defilement to the land (cf. Ezek. 39:11–16). See Gal. 3:13 for the application of this text to understanding the significance of the death of Jesus on the cross.

22:1–4 Responsibility for property. The laws advance a proactive ethos of caring for a neighbor's property.

your neighbor loses and you find. You may not withhold your help.

4 "You shall not see your neighbor's donkey or ox fallen on the road and ignore it; you shall help to lift it up.

5 "A woman shall not wear a man's apparel, nor shall a man put on a woman's garment, for whoever does such things is abhorrent to the LORD your God.

6 "If you come on a bird's nest, in any tree or on the ground, with fledglings or eggs, with the mother sitting on the fledglings or on the eggs, you shall not take the mother with the young. ⁷Let the mother go, taking only the young for yourself, in order that it may go well with you and you may live long.

8 "When you build a new house, you shall make a parapet for your roof; otherwise you might have bloodguilt on your house, if anyone should fall from it.

9 "You shall not sow your vineyard with two kinds of seed, or the whole yield will be forbidden, both the crop that you have sown and the yield of the vineyard itself.

10 "You shall not plow with an ox and a donkey yoked together.

11 "You shall not wear clothes made of wool and linen woven together.

12 "You shall make tassels on the four corners of the cloak with which you cover yourself.

13 "Suppose a man marries a woman but after going in to her dislikes her ¹⁴and makes up charges against her, slandering her by saying, 'I married this woman, but when I lay with her, I did not find evidence of her virginity.' ¹⁵The father of the young woman and her mother shall then submit the evidence of the young woman's virginity to the elders of the city at the gate. ¹⁶The father of the young

22:5 *A woman shall not wear a man's apparel.* In the ancient Near East, religious rituals sometimes involved dressing practices that differed from gender norms of the time, and soldiers could humiliate male prisoners of war by forcing them to wear clothing commonly worn by females. The prohibition was likely intended to preclude associations with ancient Near Eastern religious practices and to maintain creational boundaries between gender categories (cf. also the laws defining categories in 22:9–11).

22:6–7 Creation care. Taking both a mother bird and its young at the same time is prohibited, as this would be a disruption of the created order. Compare Lev. 22:28, which also prohibits the contemporaneous elimination of two generations of the same animal.

22:8 Proactive responsibility. Justice demands that dangerous construction sites are to be safeguarded proactively.

22:9–11 Prohibited mixtures. Prohibiting sowing *two kinds of seed*, plowing with an *ox and a donkey*, and wearing *clothes made of wool and linen* could simply be advice on not diluting agricultural produce and choice fabrics and for how to get the most out of working animals. The rationale of the laws could also be to prohibit unwarranted mixtures that violate category boundaries established at creation.

22:12 Tassels. Tassels were worn as signs of royalty or religious status in the ancient world. Wearing tassels elevates the dignity of all Israel as a priestly nation (cf. Num. 15:37–41, where tassels are prescribed for all).

22:13–30 Marriage relationships. A series of case laws regulate sexual relationships that transgress the customs of marriage, which is here primarily viewed as an economic arrangement between the husband and the father of the bride (see **"The Bible, Gender, and Sexuality," p. 2160**). Violating the norms of marriage was seen as an existential threat to the community. These laws reflect a traditional ancient Near Eastern male-centric perspective on family systems. Nevertheless, various details of the laws also protect the rights of women in a context where male honor was a driving force for justice in cases of sexual misconduct. This male-centric perspective seen in ancient Near Eastern customs was focused on preserving the honor of the household, which resulted in legislation that could demand a victim of rape to marry the offender or laws for exacting revenge for rape by raping a member of the offender's family. In Deuteronomy, the focus of the laws is not on (male) honor and shame but on the preservation of the integrity of the covenantal community. The voice of females is valued in the courts of law, the absolute power of patriarchy is curtailed by involving the mother and the community in adjudication, consent is taken into consideration, and judgments are made based on evidence. **22:13–21** The charge of unchastity is made by the suitor who wants to get out of the marriage while preserving the bride-price. The *evidence of her virginity* could be bloodied

woman shall say to the elders: 'I gave my daughter in marriage to this man, but he dislikes her, [17]and now he has made up charges against her, saying, "I did not find evidence of your daughter's virginity." But here is the evidence of my daughter's virginity.' Then they shall spread out the cloth before the elders of the town. [18]The elders of that town shall take the man and punish him; [19]they shall fine him one hundred shekels of silver (which they shall give to the young woman's father) because he has slandered a virgin of Israel. She shall remain his wife; he shall not be permitted to divorce her as long as he lives.

20 "If, however, this charge is true, that evidence of the young woman's virginity was not found, [21]then they shall bring the young woman out to the entrance of her father's house, and the men of her town shall stone her to death, because she committed a disgraceful act in Israel by prostituting herself in her father's house. So you shall purge the evil from your midst.

22 "If a man is discovered lying with the wife of another man, both of them shall die, the man who lay with the woman as well as the woman. So you shall purge the evil from Israel.

23 "If there is a young woman, a virgin already engaged to be married, and a man meets her in the town and lies with her, [24]you shall bring both of them to the gate of that town and stone them to death, the young woman because she did not cry for help in the town and the man because he violated his neighbor's wife. So you shall purge the evil from your midst.

25 "But if the man meets the engaged woman in the open country and the man seizes her and lies with her, then only the man who lay with her shall die. [26]You shall do nothing to the young woman; the young woman has not committed an offense punishable by death, because this case is like that of someone who attacks and murders a neighbor. [27]Since he found her in the open country, the engaged woman may have cried for help, but there was no one to rescue her.

28 "If a man meets a virgin who is not engaged and seizes her and lies with her, and they are discovered, [29]the man who lay with her shall give fifty shekels of silver to the young woman's father, and she shall become his wife. Because he violated her, he shall not be permitted to divorce her as long as he lives.

30 [z]"A man shall not marry his father's wife, thereby violating his father's rights.[a]

23 "No one whose testicles are crushed or whose penis is cut off shall come into the assembly of the LORD.

2 "Those born of an illicit union shall not come into the assembly of the LORD. Even to the tenth generation, none of their

z 22.30 23.1 in Heb   a 22.30 Heb *uncovering his father's skirt*

bedsheets that prove her hymen had broken or undergarments from her previous menstrual cycle that show she was not pregnant prior to the marriage. The law enables the parents—including the mother in the process—to protect the daughter from the absolute power of the husband and to require the man to commit to taking responsibility for the wife. **22:23-27** Accountability is to be established based on circumstances: If a man lies with an engaged virgin within the city limits where cries for help could be heard, the woman is held responsible because she could have called—and presumably would have unless the act was consensual—for help and been heard. If it happens in the open country, the woman is not responsible; in this scenario, the assumption is that the woman would have cried out for help—and presumably did—but her cries were not heard. The victim of rape is assumed to be innocent in this latter scenario and is expected to report the violation to the community so that it can be prosecuted. **22:28-29** A man who has *violated* an unbetrothed virgin is required to pay the bride-price to her father and marry her, thus protecting the woman from being discarded and remaining unmarried for the rest of her life. The Hebrew for violate (inah) means to lower the social status of the woman, which is what takes place in the premarital sexual activity; it does not always imply a rape, unless there is additional, clarifying language that indicates such. Throughout the section, violations of marriage are seen as not only individual wrongdoings but transgressions against Israel's covenant relationship with the Lord. The language of *purge the evil* from Israel's midst (vv. 21, 22, 24) warns of the impact of sexual sin spreading to degrade the entire community.

23:1-8 Assembly of the Lord. The *assembly of the LORD* is the governing body responsible for community administration. Becoming a member of the assembly would be tantamount to being

descendants shall come into the assembly of the Lord.

3 "No Ammonite or Moabite shall come into the assembly of the Lord even to the tenth generation. None of their descendants shall come into the assembly of the Lord forever, [4]because they did not meet you with food and water on your journey out of Egypt and because they hired against you Balaam son of Beor, from Pethor of Mesopotamia, to curse you. [5](Yet the Lord your God refused to heed Balaam; the Lord your God turned the curse into a blessing for you, because the Lord your God loved you.) [6]You shall never promote their welfare or their prosperity as long as you live.

7 "You shall not abhor any of the Edomites, for they are your kin. You shall not abhor any of the Egyptians, because you were an alien residing in their land. [8]The children of the third generation that are born to them may come into the assembly of the Lord.

9 "When you are encamped against your enemies, you shall guard against every evil thing.

10 "If one of you becomes unclean because of a nocturnal emission, then he shall go outside the camp; he must not come within the camp. [11]When evening comes, he shall wash himself with water, and when the sun has set, he may come back into the camp.

12 "You shall have a designated area outside the camp to which you shall go. [13]With your tools you shall have a trowel; when you relieve yourself outside, you shall dig a hole with it and then cover up your excrement. [14]Because the Lord your God travels along with your camp, to save you and to hand over your enemies to you, therefore your camp must be holy, so that he may not see anything indecent among you and turn away from you.

15 "You shall not return to their owners slaves who have escaped to you from their owners. [16]They shall reside with you, in your midst, in any place they choose in any one of your towns, wherever they please; you shall not oppress them.

17 "None of the daughters of Israel shall serve in an illicit shrine; none of the sons of Israel shall serve in an illicit shrine. [18]You shall not bring the fee of a prostitute or the wages of a dog into the house of the Lord your God in payment for any vow, for both of these are abhorrent to the Lord your God.

19 "You shall not charge interest on loans to another Israelite,[b] interest on money, interest on provisions, interest on anything that is lent. [20]On loans to a foreigner you may charge interest, but on loans to another Israelite[c] you may not charge interest, so that the Lord your God may bless you in all your undertakings in the land that you are about to enter and possess.

21 "If you make a vow to the Lord your God, do not postpone fulfilling it, for the Lord your God will surely require it of you, and you would incur guilt. [22]But if you refrain from

b 23.19 Heb *to your brother*   c 23.20 Heb *to your brother*

a full citizen of the Israelite community. Those with damage to their genitalia—a criterion that also barred men from the priesthood (Lev. 21:17–23)—are excluded from the assembly, as are those *born of an illicit union*. Eunuchs may be excluded due to their associations with foreign religions. But see Isa. 56:1–8 for an alternative vision of the place of foreigners and eunuchs in Israel's worship. **23:3–8** Ammonites and Moabites are excluded because of their hostility to Israel (cf. Num. 22–23; Neh. 13:1), while Edomites and Egyptians are granted the possibility to enter the assembly. These groups were also afforded rights as foreign immigrants living among Israel, which evidences a more inclusive and open perspective on Israelite identity that contrasts with other absolute statements apparently advocating for the destruction of non-Israelites (see note at Deut. 7:1–5). **23:9–25 Sanitary, ritual, and humanitarian instructions. 23:9–14** The laws for guarding against uncleanness in military encampments suppose that the *camp must be holy* because the Lord *travels along with your camp*. **23:15–16** Requiring asylum for escaped enslaved persons contrasts with the laws of Hammurabi, where escapees had to be returned to their masters. The law implies that there are strong incentives for owners to treat enslaved persons with kindness, since they would be freed if they ran away. **23:17–18** Israelites are not to participate in prostitution or make offerings to the Lord using income from prostitution. **23:19–20** The system of loans and debts was a primary way in which individuals fell into poverty and slavery in the ancient world; taking interest in loans from fellow Israelites is prohibited, which is a further way Deuteronomy works to end indebtedness and its correlate, debt slavery. **23:21–23** With its concern for vows, sharing produce with the disadvantaged, and protecting the divorced woman, Deut. 23:21–24:4 establishes principles to support the

vowing, you will not incur guilt. ²³Whatever your lips utter you must diligently perform, just as you have freely vowed to the Lᴏʀᴅ your God with your own mouth.

24 "If you go into your neighbor's vineyard, you may eat your fill of grapes, as many as you wish, but you shall not put any in a container.

25 "If you go into your neighbor's standing grain, you may pluck the ears with your hand, but you shall not put a sickle to your neighbor's standing grain.

24 "Suppose a man enters into marriage with a woman but she does not please him because he finds something objectionable about her, so he writes her a certificate of divorce, puts it in her hand, and sends her out of his house; ²she then leaves his house and goes off to become another man's wife. ³Then suppose the second man dislikes her, writes her a certificate of divorce, puts it in her hand, and sends her out of his house (or the second man who married her dies): ⁴her first husband, who sent her away, is not permitted to take her again to be his wife after she has been defiled, for that would be abhorrent to the Lᴏʀᴅ, and you shall not bring guilt on the land that the Lᴏʀᴅ your God is giving you as a possession.

5 "When a man is newly married, he shall not go out with the army or be charged with any related duty. He shall be free at home one year, to be happy with the wife whom he has married.

6 "No one shall take a mill or an upper millstone in pledge, for that would be taking a life in pledge.

7 "If someone is caught kidnaping another Israelite, enslaving or selling the Israelite, then that kidnaper shall die. So you shall purge the evil from your midst.

8 "Guard against an outbreak of a defiling skin disease by being very careful; you shall carefully observe whatever the Levitical priests instruct you, just as I have commanded them. ⁹Remember what the Lᴏʀᴅ your God did to Miriam on your journey out of Egypt.

10 "When you make your neighbor a loan of any kind, you shall not go into the house to take the pledge. ¹¹You shall wait outside while the person to whom you are making the loan brings the pledge out to you. ¹²If the person is poor, you shall not sleep in the garment given you as*ᵈ* the pledge. ¹³You shall give the pledge back by sunset, so that your neighbor may sleep in the cloak and bless you, and it will be to your credit before the Lᴏʀᴅ your God.

14 "You shall not withhold the wages of poor and needy laborers, whether other Israelites or aliens who reside in your land in one of your towns. ¹⁵You shall pay them their wages daily before sunset, because they are

d 24.12 Heb lacks *the garment given you as*

---

poor and women in society. Vows were a verbal declaration of intention to act on behalf of the deity in response to or in exchange for the deity granting a request. **23:24–25** Laws on eating produce from a neighbor's field legislate the provision for those who are in urgent need.

24:1–4 Divorce. If a man finds something *objectionable* about his wife, he may give her a *certificate of divorce* and release her from the marriage. It is unclear what the objectionable grounds for the divorce may be. According to Exod. 21:10–11, a husband was expected to provide "food, clothing, and marital rights" to a wife, who otherwise would be allowed to leave the marriage. Something similar could be surmised for what the husband might expect of the wife. The certificate allows the woman to start a new life and seek economic security by marrying again. The focus of the law is on prohibiting a man from remarrying a woman whom he had already divorced and thus humiliated. According to Jer. 3:1–5, however, the Lord circumvents this very law by "remarrying" an idolatrous Israel whom he had divorced earlier.

24:5–25:3 Miscellaneous laws. 24:5 Newly married husbands are exempt from military duty for one year in order to honor the marriage covenant and safeguard ideal conditions for producing offspring. **24:6** The *mill* and *millstone* were essential for the economic viability of life, hence taking one as a pledge from a neighbor is considered *taking a life*. **24:7** Kidnaping is treated as a capital offense, as it removes an Israelite from the covenant community and cuts them off from the possibility of life. **24:8–9** *Skin disease* is listed in detail in Lev. 13–14 (see **"Holiness and Purity," p. 158**). In Deuteronomy, Israelites must listen to the instructions of the *Levitical priests* to manage the diagnosis and treatment of these diseases that rendered Israelites unclean from cultic participation. The reference to Miriam—who is afflicted by a skin disease in Num. 12:10–15—is a warning that reminds Israel of the urgency of obedience in matters of skin diseases. **24:10–15** These laws advocate for

poor and their livelihood depends on them; otherwise they might cry to the Lord against you, and you would incur guilt.

16 "Parents shall not be put to death for their children, nor shall children be put to death for their parents; only for their own crimes may persons be put to death.

17 "You shall not deprive a resident alien or an orphan of justice; you shall not take a widow's garment in pledge. [18]Remember that you were a slave in Egypt and the Lord your God redeemed you from there; therefore I command you to do this.

19 "When you reap your harvest in your field and forget a sheaf in the field, you shall not go back to get it; it shall be left for the alien, the orphan, and the widow, so that the Lord your God may bless you in all your undertakings. [20]When you beat your olive trees, do not strip what is left; it shall be for the alien, the orphan, and the widow.

21 "When you gather the grapes of your vineyard, do not glean what is left; it shall be for the alien, the orphan, and the widow. [22]Remember that you were a slave in the land of Egypt; therefore I am commanding you to do this.

25 "Suppose two persons have a dispute and enter into litigation, and the judges decide between them, declaring one to be in the right and the other to be in the wrong. [2]If the one in the wrong deserves to be flogged, the judge shall make that person lie down and be beaten in his presence with the number of lashes proportionate to the offense. [3]Forty lashes may be given but not more; if more lashes than these are given, your neighbor will be degraded in your sight.

4 "You shall not muzzle an ox while it is treading out the grain.

5 "When brothers reside together and one of them dies and has no son, the wife of the deceased shall not be married outside the family to a stranger. Her husband's brother shall go in to her, taking her in marriage and performing the duty of a husband's brother to her, [6]and the firstborn whom she bears shall succeed to the name of the deceased brother, so that his name may not be blotted out of Israel. [7]But if the man has no desire to marry his brother's widow, then his brother's widow shall go up to the elders at the gate and say, 'My husband's brother refuses to perpetuate his brother's name in Israel; he will not perform the duty of a husband's brother to me.' [8]Then the elders of his town shall summon him and speak to him. If he persists, saying, 'I have no desire to marry her,' [9]then his brother's wife shall go up to him in the presence of the elders, pull his sandal off his foot, spit in his face, and declare, 'This is what is done to the man who does not build up his brother's house.' [10]Throughout Israel his family shall be known as 'the house of him whose sandal was pulled off.'

11 "If men get into a fight with one another

the rights of the poor in matters of pledges and wages. **24:16** Individuals are responsible for their *own crimes* in matters of human jurisdiction. This law breaks with the ancient Near Eastern custom of collective and transgenerational punishment for offenses. According to Deut. 5:9, however, the Lord's prerogative is to extend transgenerational judgment in matters of religious violations; see also the collective responsibility in 13:12–17 and 21:1–9. **24:17–22** Moses reminds Israel of their own experience and redemption from Egypt as the motivation to advocate for the justice of the *resident alien, orphan*, and *widow*. Fields, olive groves, and vineyards are to be left with gleanings for those who are less fortunate. **25:1–3** The law prescribes corporal punishment within controlled boundaries, limited proportionate to the offense. The motivation clause, so that *your neighbor* (v. 3; "brother" in Hebrew) is not *degraded in your sight*, indicates that the punishment is intended to be restorative, defining offenders as siblings whose dignity is to be respected so that they may return to the community once the penalty has been suffered.

25:4–12 Sustainability of life. Just treatment of animals is part of Deuteronomy's creation theology. This law—along with the law of Levirate marriage and protecting genitalia in 25:5–12—pertains to the principle of the sustainability of life. As interpreted in 1 Tim. 5:18, the principle implies that all laborers deserve their wages. **25:5–10** According to the law of Levirate marriage, a brother is required to marry the widow of a deceased brother in order to provide for the family and have offspring to preserve the *name* and family line of the deceased brother. Refusing this essential responsibility would require the brother to undergo a shameful act of renouncing the right (cf. Ruth 4:3–12 for a similar rite). The removal of the sandal symbolizes relinquishing the claim to the land of the deceased brother. **25:11–12** Damaging genitalia endangers the potential to perpetuate life, hence the harsh punishment.

and the wife of one intervenes to rescue her husband from the grip of his opponent by reaching out and seizing his genitals, [12]you shall cut off her hand; show no pity.

13 "You shall not have in your bag two kinds of weights, large and small. [14]You shall not have in your house two kinds of measures, large and small. [15]You shall have only a full and honest weight; you shall have only a full and honest measure, so that your days may be long in the land that the LORD your God is giving you. [16]For all who do such things, all who act dishonestly, are abhorrent to the LORD your God.

17 "Remember what Amalek did to you on your journey out of Egypt, [18]how he attacked you on the way, when you were faint and weary, and struck down all who lagged behind you; he did not fear God. [19]Therefore when the LORD your God has given you rest from all your enemies on every hand, in the land that the LORD your God is giving you as an inheritance to possess, you shall blot out the remembrance of Amalek from under heaven; do not forget.

26 "When you have come into the land that the LORD your God is giving you as an inheritance to possess and you possess it and settle in it, [2]you shall take some of the first of all the fruit of the ground, which you harvest from the land that the LORD your God is giving you, and you shall put it in a basket and go to the place that the LORD your God will choose as a dwelling for his name. [3]You shall go to the priest who is in office at that time and say to him, 'Today I declare to the LORD your God that I have come into the land

that the LORD swore to our ancestors to give us.' [4]When the priest takes the basket from your hand and sets it down before the altar of the LORD your God, [5]you shall make this response before the LORD your God: 'A wandering Aramean was my ancestor; he went down into Egypt and lived there as an alien, few in number, and there he became a great nation, mighty and populous. [6]When the Egyptians treated us harshly and afflicted us, by imposing hard labor on us, [7]we cried to the LORD, the God of our ancestors; the LORD heard our voice and saw our affliction, our toil, and our oppression. [8]The LORD brought us out of Egypt with a mighty hand and an outstretched arm, with a terrifying display of power, and with signs and wonders; [9]and he brought us into this place and gave us this land, a land flowing with milk and honey. [10]So now I bring the first of the fruit of the ground that you, O LORD, have given me.' You shall set it down before the LORD your God and bow down before the LORD your God. [11]Then you, together with the Levites and the aliens who reside among you, shall celebrate with all the bounty that the LORD your God has given to you and to your house.

12 "When you have finished paying all the tithe of your produce in the third year (which is the year of the tithe), giving it to the Levites, the aliens, the orphans, and the widows, so that they may eat their fill within your towns, [13]then you shall say before the LORD your God, 'I have removed the sacred portion from the house, and I have given it to the Levites, the resident aliens, the orphans, and the widows, in accordance with your entire commandment that you commanded me; I have neither

25:13–26:15 Obligations. The section is concerned with obligations, financial transactions, Israel's responsibility toward Amalek, and Israel's obligations toward YHWH. See "The Divine Mandate to Exterminate the Canaanites," p. 313. 25:13–16 Honesty in economic transactions was a foundational pillar of communal order and justice. 25:17–19 Israel is reminded to destroy the Amalekites, who had attacked them in the wilderness (Exod. 17:8–16). 26:1–15 The section on statutes and ordinances (chaps. 12–26) concludes with instructions for Israelites to bring the firstfruits of their first harvest to the chosen place when they have entered the land (vv. 1–11) and for bringing their tri-annual tithes to be shared with the Levites, the aliens, the orphans, and the widows (vv. 12–15). The commands encapsulate Deuteronomic theology, describing a communal celebration of the blessings of the Lord at the chosen place (see note at 27:1–10). 26:5–9 The one who brings the offering declares a succinct creed of Israelite faith, which recounts Israel's journey with the Lord, beginning with an unnamed ancestor as a wandering Aramean and concluding with the Lord delivering Israel from Egypt and bringing them into the promised land. On the association of the ancestors of Israel with Aram, see Gen. 24:48; 25:20; cf. "Election," p. 31; "Exodus," p. 105. 26:11 After the recital, the worshiper, the priests, and the entire community celebrate before the Lord. The tithe—as an expression of faith in the Lord's provision—is offered with a confession of faith and declaration of compliance with the commandment.

transgressed nor forgotten any of your commandments: [14]I have not eaten of it while in mourning; I have not removed any of it while I was unclean; and I have not offered any of it to the dead. I have obeyed the LORD my God, doing just as you commanded me. [15]Look down from your holy habitation, from heaven, and bless your people Israel and the ground that you have given us, as you swore to our ancestors, a land flowing with milk and honey.'

16 "This very day the LORD your God is commanding you to observe these statutes and ordinances, so observe them diligently with all your heart and with all your soul. [17]Today you have obtained the LORD's agreement: to be your God; and for you to walk in his ways, to keep his statutes, his commandments, and his ordinances, and to obey him. [18]Today the LORD has obtained your agreement: to be his treasured people, as he promised you, and to keep all his commandments; [19]for him to set you high above all nations that he has made, in praise and in fame and in honor; and for you to be a people holy to the LORD your God, as he promised."

27 Then Moses and the elders of Israel charged all the people as follows: "Keep the entire commandment that I am commanding you today. [2]On the day that you cross over the Jordan into the land that the LORD your God is giving you, you shall set up large stones and cover them with plaster. [3]You shall write on them all the words of this law when you have crossed over, to enter the land that the LORD your God is giving you, a land flowing with milk and honey, as the LORD, the God of your ancestors, promised you. [4]So when you have crossed over the Jordan, you shall set up these stones about which I am commanding you today on Mount Ebal, and you shall cover them with plaster. [5]And you shall build an altar there to the LORD your God, an altar of stones on which you have not used an iron tool. [6]You must build the altar of the LORD your God of unhewn[e] stones. Then offer up burnt offerings on it to the LORD your God; [7]make sacrifices of well-being, and eat them there, rejoicing before the LORD your God. [8]You shall write on the stones all the words of this law very clearly."

9 Then Moses and the Levitical priests spoke to all Israel, saying, "Keep silence and hear, O Israel! This very day you have become the people of the LORD your God. [10]Therefore obey the LORD your God, observing his commandments and his statutes that I am commanding you today."

11 The same day Moses charged the people as follows: [12]"When you have crossed over the Jordan, these shall stand on Mount Gerizim

e 27.6 Heb *whole*

26:14–15 The tithe is to be presented with a disavowal, affirming that it has not been offered *while in mourning*, nor has any of it been offered *to the dead*. These declarations attest that the tithe has not been associated with Canaanite religious practices that were connected to ancestral cults or the deity Baal, who was seen as the lord of the fertility of creation.
    26:16–19 Concluding exhortation. As a precursor to the covenant ceremony at Shechem in Deut. 27:1–10 and the ratification of the covenant of Moab in Deut. 29–30, Israel is exhorted to *observe these statutes and ordinances*, which are the basis for maintaining the covenant relationship between Israel and the Lord. **26:17–19** Mutual declarations of oaths, like the one here binding the Lord and Israel into relationship with each other, were common in ancient Near Eastern treaties.
    27:1–10 Inscribed stones on Mount Ebal. In addition to the covenants at Horeb and Moab, Moses prescribes a covenant ceremony to be performed on Mount Ebal (vv. 4, 13) and Mount Gerizim (v. 12) once Israel enters the land. The archaeological site of El-Burnat on Mount Ebal, near modern Shechem, has yielded an Iron-Age cultic site that is often considered to be the one described in Deut. 27, though the interpretation of the site is debated. The liturgy recalls the covenant ceremony of Horeb/Sinai in Exod. 24:1–11, where the laws of God were transcribed on stone tablets, and an altar of stones was built for offerings. The ceremony resulted in Gerizim being viewed as the chosen place (Deut. 12) in Samaritan tradition. See Josh. 8:30–35 for an implementation of the instructions. See **"Cult Centralization," p. 264**. **27:3** Inscribing the *words of this law* on plastered stones recalls the ancient Near Eastern practice of carving treaties on large rock monuments (stelae), and the ensuing blessings and curses that describe the consequences of obedience and disobedience likewise were a common feature of ancient Near Eastern treaties.
    27:11–26 Twelve curses. Six tribes are to stand on Mount Gerizim to *bless the people* (see 28:1–14), while the other six tribes are to stand on the other side of the valley of Shechem on Mount Ebal

to bless the people: Simeon, Levi, Judah, Issachar, Joseph, and Benjamin. [13]And these shall stand on Mount Ebal for the curse: Reuben, Gad, Asher, Zebulun, Dan, and Naphtali. [14]Then the Levites shall declare in a loud voice to all the Israelites,

15 "'Cursed be anyone who makes an idol or casts an image, anything abhorrent to the LORD, the work of an artisan, and sets it up in secret.' All the people shall respond, saying, 'Amen!'

16 "'Cursed be anyone who dishonors father or mother.' All the people shall say, 'Amen!'

17 "'Cursed be anyone who moves a neighbor's boundary marker.' All the people shall say, 'Amen!'

18 " 'Cursed be anyone who misleads a blind person on the road.' All the people shall say, 'Amen!'

19 " 'Cursed be anyone who deprives an alien, an orphan, or a widow of justice.' All the people shall say, 'Amen!'

20 " 'Cursed be anyone who lies with his father's wife, because he has violated his father's rights.'[f] All the people shall say, 'Amen!'

21 " 'Cursed be anyone who lies with any animal.' All the people shall say, 'Amen!'

22 " 'Cursed be anyone who lies with his sister, whether the daughter of his father or the daughter of his mother.' All the people shall say, 'Amen!'

23 " 'Cursed be anyone who lies with his mother-in-law.' All the people shall say, 'Amen!'

24 " 'Cursed be anyone who strikes down a neighbor in secret.' All the people shall say, 'Amen!'

25 " 'Cursed be anyone who takes a bribe to shed innocent blood.' All the people shall say, 'Amen!'

26 " 'Cursed be anyone who does not uphold the words of this law by observing them.' All the people shall say, 'Amen!'

28 "If you will only obey the LORD your God, by diligently observing all his commandments that I am commanding you today, the LORD your God will set you high above all the nations of the earth; [2]all these blessings shall come upon you and overtake you, if you obey the LORD your God:

3 "Blessed shall you be in the city, and blessed shall you be in the field.

4 "Blessed shall be the fruit of your womb, the fruit of your ground, and the fruit of your livestock, both the increase of your cattle and the issue of your flock.

5 "Blessed shall be your basket and your kneading bowl.

6 "Blessed shall you be when you come in, and blessed shall you be when you go out.

7 "The LORD will cause your enemies who rise against you to be defeated before you; they shall come out against you one way and flee before you seven ways. [8]The LORD will command the blessing upon you in your barns and in all that you undertake; he will bless you in the land that the LORD your God is giving you. [9]The LORD will establish you as his holy people, as he has sworn to you, if you keep the commandments of the LORD your God and walk in his ways. [10]All the peoples of the earth shall see that you are called by the name of the LORD, and they shall be afraid of you. [11]The LORD will make you abound in prosperity, in the fruit of your womb, in the fruit of your livestock, and in the fruit of your ground in the land that the LORD swore to your ancestors to give you. [12]The LORD will open for you his rich storehouse, the heavens, to give the rain of your land in its season and to bless all your undertakings. You will lend to many nations, but you will not borrow. [13]The LORD will make you the head and not the tail; you shall be only at the top and not at

f 27.20 Heb *uncovered his father's skirt*

to recite the curses (see 28:15–68). The Levites announce curses that will come upon those who violate the covenant, after which the people declare their agreement—amen!—to take the curses upon themselves if they disobey. The detailed offenses cover many of the topics from Deuteronomy, while the final curse comes upon those who do not *uphold the words of this law*—that is, all the instructions of Deuteronomy.

28:1–14 Blessings for obedience. Vv. 1–2 declare the conditions by which the blessings of vv. 3–14 are attained. Many of the themes are found in ancient Near Eastern treaties, as the blessings correspond to expectations of financial, agricultural, and military prosperity that ancient Near Eastern deities promised their devotees. **28:13–14** Israel's attainment of the blessings depends on obeying the commandments of the Lord. The promises of blessing and warnings of curses express the sovereignty of the Lord over creation and humanity. The threat of judgment and potential of restoration afterward

the bottom—if you obey the commandments of the LORD your God that I am commanding you today by diligently observing them, [14] and if you do not turn aside from any of the words that I am commanding you today, either to the right or to the left, following other gods to serve them.

15 "But if you will not obey the LORD your God by diligently observing all his commandments and decrees that I am commanding you today, then all these curses shall come upon you and overtake you:

16 "Cursed shall you be in the city, and cursed shall you be in the field.

17 "Cursed shall be your basket and your kneading bowl.

18 "Cursed shall be the fruit of your womb, the fruit of your ground, the increase of your cattle and the issue of your flock.

19 "Cursed shall you be when you come in, and cursed shall you be when you go out.

20 "The LORD will send upon you disaster, panic, and frustration in everything you attempt to do, until you are destroyed and perish quickly, on account of the evil of your deeds with which you have forsaken me. [21] The LORD will make the pestilence cling to you until it has consumed you off the land that you are entering to possess. [22] The LORD will afflict you with consumption, fever, inflammation, with fiery heat and drought,[g] and with blight and mildew; they shall pursue you until you perish. [23] The sky over your head shall be bronze and the earth under you iron. [24] The LORD will change the rain of your land into powder, and only dust shall come down upon you from the sky until you are destroyed.

25 "The LORD will cause you to be defeated before your enemies; you shall go out against them one way and flee before them seven ways. You shall become an object of horror to all the kingdoms of the earth. [26] Your corpses shall be food for every bird of the air and animal of the earth, and there shall be no one to frighten them away. [27] The LORD will afflict you with the boils of Egypt, with tumors, scurvy, and itch, of which you cannot be healed. [28] The LORD will afflict you with madness, blindness, and confusion of mind; [29] you shall grope about at noon as blind people grope in darkness, but you shall be unable to find your way, and you shall be continually abused and robbed, without anyone to help. [30] You shall become engaged to a woman, but another man shall lie with her. You shall build a house but not live in it. You shall plant a vineyard but not enjoy its fruit. [31] Your ox shall be butchered before your eyes, but you shall not eat of it. Your donkey shall be stolen in front of you and shall not be restored to you. Your sheep shall be given to your enemies without anyone to help you. [32] Your sons and daughters shall be given to another people while you look on; you will strain your eyes looking for them all day but be powerless to do anything. [33] A people whom you do not know shall eat up the fruit of your ground and of all your labors; you shall be continually abused and crushed [34] and driven mad by the sight that your eyes shall see. [35] The LORD will strike you on the knees and on the legs with grievous boils of which you cannot be healed, from the sole of your foot to the crown of your head. [36] The LORD will bring you and the king whom you set over you to a nation that neither you nor your ancestors have known, where you shall serve other gods, of wood and stone. [37] You shall become an object of horror, a proverb, and a byword among all the peoples where the LORD will lead you.

g 28.22 Gk Syr Tg: MT *the sword*

communicate the moral character of the Lord as a God who is just as well as merciful (cf. Exod. 34:6–7). The successful role of Moses in interceding for Israel and the repentance of the people in the golden calf incident (Deut. 9) offer hope for the possibility of restoration. See **"Moses," p. 247**.

28:15–68 Warnings against disobedience. The ultimate threat of the curses is that Israel would be removed from relationship with the Lord at the chosen place and the promised land by forced deportation (vv. 36, 41, 48, 63–68). This threat of exile is realized for the kingdom of Israel at the hands of the Assyrians in 722 BCE (2 Kgs. 17) and the kingdom of Judah in 597–585 BCE at the hands of the Babylonians (2 Kgs. 25). The books of 1–2 Kings evaluate the history of Israel and Judah from the perspective of Deuteronomy to explain that the judgment on the people has resulted from disobedience to the teachings of Moses (see **"Deuteronomistic History," p. 337**). Many biblical traditions resist such a conclusion (cf. Job, Ecclesiastes). The same resistance is evident, to some degree, in the Moab covenant in Deut. 29–31. The curses in Deut. 28 reverse the blessings of vv. 1–14, with vv. 15–46 defining the destruction of agricultural blessings and vv. 47–68 outlining an enemy

38 "You shall carry much seed into the field but shall gather little in, for the locust shall consume it. ³⁹You shall plant vineyards and dress them, but you shall neither drink the wine nor gather the grapes, for the worm shall eat them. ⁴⁰You shall have olive trees throughout all your territory, but you shall not anoint yourself with the oil, for your olives shall drop off. ⁴¹You shall have sons and daughters, but they shall not remain yours, for they shall go into captivity. ⁴²All your trees and the fruit of your ground the cicada shall take over. ⁴³Aliens residing among you shall ascend above you higher and higher, while you shall descend lower and lower. ⁴⁴They shall lend to you, but you shall not lend to them; they shall be the head, and you shall be the tail.

45 "All these curses shall come upon you, pursuing and overtaking you until you are destroyed, because you did not obey the Lord your God by observing the commandments and the decrees that he commanded you. ⁴⁶They shall be among you and your descendants as a sign and a portent forever.

47 "Because you did not serve the Lord your God joyfully and with gladness of heart for the abundance of everything, ⁴⁸therefore you shall serve your enemies whom the Lord will send against you, in hunger and thirst, in nakedness and lack of everything. He will put an iron yoke on your neck until he has destroyed you. ⁴⁹The Lord will bring a nation from far away, from the end of the earth, to swoop down on you like an eagle, a nation whose language you do not understand, ⁵⁰a grim-faced nation showing no respect to the old or favor to the young. ⁵¹It shall consume the fruit of your livestock and the fruit of your ground until you are destroyed, leaving you neither grain, wine, and oil nor the increase of your cattle and the issue of your flock, until it has made you perish. ⁵²It shall besiege you in all your towns until your high and fortified walls, in which you trusted, come down throughout your land; it shall besiege you in all your towns throughout the land that the Lord your God has given you.

⁵³In the desperate straits to which the enemy siege reduces you, you will eat the fruit of your womb, the flesh of your own sons and daughters whom the Lord your God has given you. ⁵⁴Even the most refined and gentle of men among you will begrudge food to his own brother, to the wife whom he embraces, and to the last of his remaining children, ⁵⁵giving to none of them any of the flesh of his children whom he is eating, because nothing else remains to him, in the desperate straits to which the enemy siege will reduce you in all your towns. ⁵⁶She who is the most refined and gentle among you, so gentle and refined that she does not venture to set the sole of her foot on the ground, will begrudge food to the husband whom she embraces, to her own son, and to her own daughter, ⁵⁷begrudging even the afterbirth that comes out from between her thighs and the children that she bears, because she is eating them in secret for lack of anything else, in the desperate straits to which the enemy siege will reduce you in your towns.

58 "If you do not diligently observe all the words of this law that are written in this book, fearing this glorious and awesome name, the Lord your God, ⁵⁹then the Lord will overwhelm both you and your offspring with severe and lasting afflictions and grievous and lasting maladies. ⁶⁰He will bring back upon you all the diseases of Egypt, of which you were in dread, and they shall cling to you. ⁶¹Every other malady and affliction, even though not recorded in the book of this law, the Lord will inflict on you until you are destroyed. ⁶²Although once you were as numerous as the stars in heaven, you shall be left few in number because you did not obey the Lord your God. ⁶³And just as the Lord took delight in making you prosperous and numerous, so the Lord will take delight in bringing you to ruin and destruction; you shall be plucked off the land that you are entering to possess. ⁶⁴The Lord will scatter you among all peoples, from one end of the earth to the other, and there you shall serve other gods, of wood and stone, which neither you

invasion and its consequences. **28:45** *Curses shall come upon you, pursuing and overtaking you.* There is a sense that the curses are triggered automatically by disobedience but also that there is divine agency in prosecuting the curses (vv. 20, 21, 22, 24, 25, 27, 28, 35, 36, 37, 48, 49). **28:47** The cardinal sin is not serving the Lord *joyfully and with gladness of heart for the abundance of everything* that the Lord has given. Thus, a failure to participate in Deuteronomy's joyful liturgies that keep Israel's perspective on dependence and gratitude to the Lord is viewed as leading to idolatry.

nor your ancestors have known. [65]Among those nations you shall find no ease, no resting place for the sole of your foot. There the LORD will give you a trembling heart, failing eyes, and a languishing spirit. [66]Your life shall hang in doubt before you; night and day you shall be in dread, with no assurance of your life. [67]In the morning you shall say, 'If only it were evening!' and at evening you shall say, 'If only it were morning!'—because of the dread that your heart shall feel and the sights that your eyes shall see. [68]The LORD will bring you back in ships to Egypt, by a route that I promised you would never see again, and there you shall offer yourselves for sale to your enemies as male and female slaves, but there will be no buyer."

29 [b]These are the words of the covenant that the LORD commanded Moses to make with the Israelites in the land of Moab, in addition to the covenant that he had made with them at Horeb.

2 [i]Moses summoned all Israel and said to them, "You have seen all that the LORD did before your eyes in the land of Egypt, to Pharaoh and to all his servants and to all his land, [3]the great trials that your eyes saw, the signs, and those great wonders. [4]But to this day the LORD has not given you a mind to understand or eyes to see or ears to hear. [5]I have led you forty years in the wilderness. The clothes on your back have not worn out, and the sandals on your feet have not worn out; [6]you have not eaten bread, and you have not drunk wine or strong drink—so that you may know that I am the LORD your God. [7]When you came to this place, King Sihon of Heshbon and King Og of Bashan came out against us for battle, but we defeated them. [8]We took their land and gave it as an inheritance to the Reubenites, the Gadites, and the half-tribe of Manasseh. [9]Therefore observe the words of this covenant and perform them, in order that you may succeed[j] in everything that you do.

10 "You stand assembled today, all of you, before the LORD your God—the leaders of your tribes,[k] your elders, and your officials, all the men of Israel, [11]your children, your women, and the aliens who are in your camp, both those who cut your wood and those who draw your water—[12]to enter into the covenant of the LORD your God, sworn by an oath, which the LORD your God is making with you today, [13]in order that he may establish you today as his people and that he may be your God, as he promised you and as he swore to your ancestors, to Abraham, to Isaac, and to Jacob. [14]I am making this covenant, sworn by an oath, not only with you [15]who stand here with us today before the LORD our God but also with those who are not here with us today. [16]You know how we lived in the land of Egypt and how we came through the midst of the nations through which you passed. [17]You have seen their detestable things, the filthy idols of wood and stone, of silver and gold, that were among them. [18]It may be that there is among you a man or woman or a family or tribe whose heart is already turning away from the LORD our God to serve the gods of those nations. It may be that there is among

h 29.1 28.69 in Heb   *i* 29.2 29.1 in Heb   *j* 29.9 Or *deal wisely*   *k* 29.10 Gk Syr: Heb *your leaders, your tribes*

28:68 The sequence of curses culminates in Israel being returned to Egypt in an undoing of Israel's history of salvation.

   29:1–29 Covenant at Moab. 29:1 The verse is sometimes read as a subscript to the preceding chapter, thus concluding the section of 4:44–28:68, but is better seen as a superscript to the following, as with the other superscriptions in Deuteronomy introducing subsequent material (e.g., 1:1; 4:44). The verse transitions into the fourth speech of Moses, which encompasses 29:1–30:20 and focuses on a call to obedience. The superscript identifies the following as *the words of the covenant* that the Lord made with Israel in Moab, thus identifying the ensuing content as a covenant *in addition to the covenant* that the Lord made with Israel at Horeb that is recapitulated in Deut. 1–28. **29:2** *You have seen all that the LORD did before your eyes.* Moses places the second generation of Israelites in the position of having imaginatively experienced the Lord's salvation in Egypt. This rhetoric also invites future generations of Israelites to see themselves as beneficiaries of the salvation of the Lord (cf. Deut. 5:2–3). **29:4** Moses addresses the question of religious epistemology, arguing that it requires direct action from the Lord for Israel to have a *mind* (Heb. "heart") *to understand or eyes to see or ears to hear* the will of God. **29:6** Israel is to discern the work and provision of the Lord that they *may know that . . . the LORD* is their God and thus be motivated to obedience. **29:10–15** The covenant includes all Israelites—male and female, native and foreigners, wealthy and poor, present

you a root sprouting poisonous and bitter growth. [19]All who hear the words of this oath and bless themselves, thinking in their hearts, 'We are safe even though we go our own stubborn ways' (thus sweeping away the moist with the dry)[l]—[20]the Lord will be unwilling to pardon them, for then the Lord's anger and passion will smoke against them. All the curses written in this book will descend on them, and the Lord will blot out their names from under heaven. [21]The Lord will single them out from all the tribes of Israel for calamity, in accordance with all the curses of the covenant written in this book of the law. [22]The next generation, your children who rise up after you, as well as the foreigner who comes from a distant country, will see the devastation of that land and the afflictions with which the Lord has afflicted it—[23]all its soil burned out by sulfur and salt, nothing planted, nothing sprouting, unable to support any vegetation, like the destruction of Sodom and Gomorrah, Admah and Zeboiim, which the Lord destroyed in his fierce anger—[24]they and indeed all the nations will wonder, 'Why has the Lord done thus to this land? What caused this great display of anger?' [25]They will conclude, 'It is because they abandoned the covenant of the Lord, the God of their ancestors, which he made with them when he brought them out of the land of Egypt. [26]They turned and served other gods, worshiping them, gods whom they had not known and whom he had not allotted to them; [27]so the anger of the Lord was kindled against that land, bringing on it every curse written in this book. [28]The Lord uprooted them from their land in anger, fury, and great wrath and cast them into another land, as is now the case.' [29]The secret things belong to the Lord our God, but the revealed things belong to us and to our children forever, to observe all the words of this law.

30 "When all these things have happened to you, the blessings and the curses that I have set before you, if you call them to mind among all the nations where the Lord your God has driven you [2]and return to the Lord your God, and you and your children obey him with all your heart and with all your soul, just as I am commanding you today, [3]then the Lord your God will return you from your captivity and have compassion on you, gathering you again from all the peoples among whom the Lord your God has scattered you. [4]Even if you are exiled to the ends of the world,[m] from there the Lord your God will gather you, and from there he will take you back. [5]The Lord your God will bring you into the land that your ancestors possessed, and you will possess it; he will make you more prosperous and numerous than your ancestors.

6 "Moreover, the Lord your God will circumcise your heart and the heart of your descendants, so that you will love the Lord your God with all your heart and with all your soul, in order that you may live. [7]The Lord your God

l 29.19 Meaning of Heb uncertain   m 30.4 Heb *of heaven*

and future generations—who all stand as equals in the covenant before the Lord. **29:23** References to the destruction of *Sodom and Gomorrah, Admah and Zeboiim* (cf. Gen. 19:24–25) remind them of the consequences of disobedience. **29:29** Contextually, the *secret things* may refer to sins that are committed in secret (cf. 29:19), which the Lord would take responsibility to judge, leaving the *revealed things* as known sins that Israel is responsible for judging. Alternatively, the *secret things* may refer to the future, which Israel is to entrust to the Lord, or to unknown rationales behind the laws, which Israel is not always privy to, but they are still responsible for obeying the laws (cf. 30:1–4).

30:1–10 Promises of restoration. Whereas Deut. 29 warned of the exile of a disobedient Israel, these verses use the Hebrew word for "return" five times to affirm the possibility of Israel's restoration. The possibility of forgiveness and restoration that the Deuteronomic covenant envisions— paradigmatically modeled in the aftermath of the golden calf incident recounted in Deut. 9—was unique in ancient Near Eastern covenants. **30:1–5** Moses asserts that if the Israelites *call . . . to mind* (Heb. "returns to heart") the words of the Lord and *return to the Lord* and *obey him with all [their] heart and with all [their] soul*, then *the Lord . . . will return [them] from [their] captivity and have compassion on [them]*, returning them to the land and restoring their fortunes. **30:6** This return will involve God circumcising the hearts of Israel *so that [they] will love the Lord . . . with all [their] heart*. As seen throughout Deuteronomy, the heart is the locus of moral discernment and decision-making (e.g., Deut. 6:5–6; 8:2; 11:13; 29:18). Whereas in Deut. 10:16 Israel was exhorted to circumcise their own hearts, Deut. 30:6 follows the anticipated judgment of exile, and so this procedure will

will put all these curses on your enemies and on the adversaries who took advantage of you. [8]Then you shall again obey the LORD, observing all his commandments that I am commanding you today, [9]and the LORD your God will make you abundantly prosperous in all your undertakings, in the fruit of your body, in the fruit of your livestock, and in the fruit of your soil. For the LORD will again take delight in prospering you, just as he delighted in prospering your ancestors, [10]when you obey the LORD your God by observing his commandments and decrees that are written in this book of the law, because you turn to the LORD your God with all your heart and with all your soul.

[11] "Surely, this commandment that I am commanding you today is not too hard for you, nor is it too far away. [12]It is not in heaven, that you should say, 'Who will go up to heaven for us and get it for us so that we may hear it and observe it?' [13]Neither is it beyond the sea, that you should say, 'Who will cross to the other side of the sea for us and get it for us so that we may hear it and observe it?' [14]No, the word is very near to you; it is in your mouth and in your heart for you to observe.

[15] "See, I have set before you today life and prosperity, death and adversity. [16]If you obey the commandments of the LORD your God[n] that I am commanding you today, by loving the LORD your God, walking in his ways, and observing his commandments, decrees, and ordinances, then you shall live and become numerous, and the LORD your God will bless you in the land that you are entering to possess. [17]But if your heart turns away and you do not hear but are led astray to bow down to other gods and serve them, [18]I declare to you today that you shall certainly perish; you shall not live long in the land that you are crossing the Jordan to enter and possess. [19]I call heaven and earth to witness against you today that I have set before you life and death, blessings and curses. Choose life so that you and your descendants may live, [20]loving the LORD your God, obeying him, and holding fast to him, for that means life to you and length of days, so that you may live in the land that the LORD swore to give to your ancestors, to Abraham, to Isaac, and to Jacob."

31 When Moses had finished speaking all[o] these words to all Israel, [2]he said to them, "I am now one hundred twenty years

n 30.16 Gk: Heb lacks *If you obey the commandments of the LORD your God*   o 31.1 Q ms Gk: MT *Moses went and spoke*

now be the result of direct divine action. As is affirmed in 29:4, Israel needs divine grace to have a heart that understands and obeys the commandments of the Lord. **30:8–9** Once transformed, Israel will *again* (return to) *obey*, and YHWH will *again* (return to) *take delight* in the people.

30:11–20 The possibility of choice. 30:11–12 *[It] is not too hard for you, nor is it too far away. It is not in heaven.* Ancient Near Eastern wisdom denied that it was possible for humanity to reach the heavens to discern the will of the gods or find the way of life. In contrast, Deuteronomy affirms that the words of God are *very near to you . . . in your mouth and in your heart for you to observe.* Moses's rhetorical efforts have given Israel a chance at understanding, loving, and obeying the Lord with their entire hearts (Deut. 6:4–5) while recognizing the difficulty of this task and the need for divine grace due to the stubbornness of human hearts (30:6). The tension in the difficulty of keeping the commandments of God by imperfect human hearts is reflected in the Hebrew prophets, who spoke of a time when the Lord would create a new heart and write the covenant directly in the hearts of Israel, thus enabling them to keep the Torah (Ezek. 11:19; 36:26; Jer. 31:31–33). This theme is elaborated on in later Christian circles, where Paul (in Rom. 10:5–10) quotes Deut. 30:11–14 to make the point that Jesus Christ makes the word of God accessible and enables obedience to the commandments of God. **30:15–20** Moses concludes that Israel is to *see* that he has *set before* them *life and prosperity, death and adversity*, with the call to "see" being an invitation to insight. Moses has cast a vision of obedience to the instruction that leads to life and of disobedience that leads to death, thus cultivating Israel's moral imagination to enable them to be a people that make wise decisions once they enter the promised land.

31:1–34:12 Transference of leadership. Moses prepares Israel for his impending absence. The section contains many parallels with ancient Near Eastern instructional and testament literature in which a revered sage or parental figure passes on traditional knowledge to the next generation in order for them to live a successful life. See **"Moses," p. 247**. The transference of authority involves establishing three *witness[es]* to Israel: the Song of Moses (31:19), the book of the law (31:26), and heaven and earth (31:28).

31:1–23 Joshua as successor and the reciting of the law. Moses transfers the leadership to his

old. I am no longer able to get about, and the LORD has told me, 'You shall not cross over this Jordan.' [3]The LORD your God himself will cross over before you. He will destroy these nations before you, and you shall dispossess them. Joshua also will cross over before you, as the LORD promised. [4]The LORD will do to them as he did to Sihon and Og, the kings of the Amorites, and to their land, when he destroyed them. [5]The LORD will give them over to you, and you shall deal with them in full accord with the command that I have given to you. [6]Be strong and bold; have no fear or dread of them, because it is the LORD your God who goes with you; he will not fail you or forsake you."

7 Then Moses summoned Joshua and said to him in the sight of all Israel, "Be strong and bold, for you are the one who will go with this people into the land that the LORD has sworn to their ancestors to give them, and you will put them in possession of it. [8]It is the LORD who goes before you. He will be with you; he will not fail you or forsake you. Do not fear or be dismayed."

9 Then Moses wrote down this law and gave it to the priests, the sons of Levi, who carried the ark of the covenant of the LORD, and to all the elders of Israel. [10]Moses commanded them, "Every seventh year, in the scheduled year of remission, during the Festival of Booths,[p] [11]when all Israel comes to appear before the LORD your God at the place that he will choose, you shall read this law before all Israel in their hearing. [12]Assemble the people—men, women, and children, as well as the aliens residing in your towns—so that they may hear and learn to fear the LORD your God and to observe diligently all the words of this law [13]and so that their children,

who have not known it, may hear and learn to fear the LORD your God, as long as you live in the land that you are crossing over the Jordan to possess."

14 The LORD said to Moses, "Your time to die is near; call Joshua and present yourselves in the tent of meeting, so that I may commission him." So Moses and Joshua went and presented themselves in the tent of meeting, [15]and the LORD appeared at the tent in a pillar of cloud; the pillar of cloud stood at the entrance to the tent.

16 The LORD said to Moses, "Soon you will lie down with your ancestors. Then this people will begin to prostitute themselves to the foreign gods in their midst, the gods of the land into which they are going; they will forsake me, breaking my covenant that I have made with them. [17]My anger will be kindled against them on that day. I will forsake them and hide my face from them; they will become easy prey, and many terrible troubles will come upon them. On that day they will say, 'Have not these troubles come upon us because our God is not in our midst?' [18]On that day I will surely hide my face on account of all the evil they have done by turning to other gods. [19]Now, therefore, write this song, and teach it to the Israelites; put it in their mouths, in order that this song may be a witness for me against the Israelites. [20]For when I have brought them into the land flowing with milk and honey, which I promised on oath to their ancestors, and they have eaten their fill and grown fat, they will turn to other gods and serve them, despising me and breaking my covenant. [21]And when many terrible troubles come upon them, this song will confront

p 31.10 Or *Tabernacles*

successor, Joshua, while reminding Israel of the limits of human leadership. Ultimately, it is the Lord himself who leads the people into the land. **31:9–13** In the absence of Moses, the instruction is written down and given to the Levitical priests and elders, who are responsible for assembling Israel at the chosen place every seven years—in the year of remission during the Feast of Booths (Deut. 15:1–11; 16:13–15)—to read the law to the people. The periodic public reading of covenants was a common way to solidify political and religious commitments in the ancient world. Moses's instructions prescribe a way to disseminate the teachings of Deuteronomy across Israelite society—including to women, foreigners, and the children of future generations (cf. 2 Kgs. 23:2; Neh. 8:1–18; 9:3; 13:1). **31:14–15** The Lord calls Moses and Joshua to the tent of meeting—where the Lord appeared in a pillar of cloud to speak with Moses in Exod. 33:7–11—so as to commission Joshua. **31:16–19** In anticipation of the people rebelling in Moses's absence, the Lord instructs Moses to write down and teach Israel a song that is to be *a witness for* the Lord *against the Israelites*. **31:21** The song that follows in Deut. 32:1–43 is a witness in the sense of proving the faithfulness of the Lord to Israel in anticipation of the disobedience of the people.

them as a witness because it will not be lost from the mouths of their descendants. For I know what they are inclined to do even now, before I have brought them into the land that I promised them on oath." ²²That very day Moses wrote this song and taught it to the Israelites.

23 Then the Lord*q* commissioned Joshua son of Nun and said, "Be strong and bold, for you shall bring the Israelites into the land that I promised them; I will be with you."

24 When Moses had finished writing down in a book the words of this law to the very end, ²⁵Moses commanded the Levites who carried the ark of the covenant of the Lord, saying, ²⁶"Take this book of the law and put it beside the ark of the covenant of the Lord your God; let it remain there as a witness against you. ²⁷For I know well how rebellious and stubborn you are. If you already have been so rebellious toward the Lord while I am still alive among you, how much more after my death! ²⁸Assemble to me all the elders of your tribes and your officials, so that I may recite these words in their hearing and call heaven and earth to witness against them. ²⁹For I know that after my death you will surely act corruptly, turning aside from the way that I have commanded you. In time to come trouble will befall you, because you will do what is evil in the sight of the Lord, provoking him to anger through the work of your hands."

30 Then Moses recited the words of this song, to the very end, in the hearing of the whole assembly of Israel:

32

"Give ear, O heavens, and I will speak;
  let the earth hear the words of my mouth.
² May my teaching drop like the rain,
  my speech condense like the dew,
like gentle rain on grass,
  like showers on new growth.
³ For I will proclaim the name of the Lord,
  ascribe greatness to our God!

⁴ The Rock, his work is perfect,
  and all his ways are just.
A faithful God, without deceit,
  just and upright is he;
⁵ yet his degenerate children have dealt falsely with him,*r*
  a perverse and crooked generation.

q 31.23 Heb *he*   *r* 32.5 Meaning of Heb uncertain

31:24–29 Depositing the book. Once Moses writes *in a book the words of this law,* he deposits it with the Levites beside the *ark of the covenant,* where it will remain *as a witness* against Israel. *Heaven and earth*—signifying the entirety of creation—are also called to *witness* against the people. The teaching will serve as a witness in the sense of being a reminder of Israel's commitment to the covenant, which is ratified here before all creation. In ancient Near Eastern treaties, the deities of the nations involved in the treaty would be summoned as witnesses to safeguard the observance of the covenant and enact consequences for disobedience. In Deuteronomy, the role of oversight is assigned to heaven and earth—the created order—which is responsible for prosecuting covenant violations. This ties the moral order of covenant obedience to the order of creation, as attested also in the rhetoric of the prophets, where violations of the covenant are understood to result in the dissolution of creation (cf. Jer. 4:23; Hos. 4:1–3). After depositing the tablets, Moses summons the elders and officials of the tribes to recite the words of the law to them. Babylonian tradition held that tablets containing the destinies of humanity were decreed by the gods and deposited before the gods in the temple; in contrast to this notion, the destiny of Israel is to be determined by their obedience to the covenant contained on the tablets.

32:1–43 The Song of Moses. The poetic Song of Moses—often referred to as "Ha'azinu" ("give ear!") by its first Hebrew word—is a warning and a help that anticipates Israel's rebellion and restoration. The characteristic feature of Hebrew poetry is parallelism, whereby juxtaposed lines of a poem are used to develop or contrast the ideas of the first line in subsequent lines (see **"Hebrew Poetry," p. 741**). Here parallelism is used to *proclaim the name of the Lord* (v. 3)—that is, to describe the character of God using various metaphors: a rock that is *just and upright* (vv. 4–5, 15, 18, 30–31), a father who created and cared for Israel (v. 6), a mother who gave birth to Israel (v. 18), and an eagle who protectively hovered over Israel (v. 11). The metaphors mix images that were common in ancient Near Eastern iconography to draw a wide-ranging portrait of the character and work of the Lord, which Israel is called to remember and respond to (vv. 7, 18). **32:4–7** The Lord is set forth as a paradigm for justice and righteousness that Israel is to follow. In contrast to the faithfulness of

⁶ Do you thus repay the LORD,
    O foolish and senseless people?
Is not he your father who created you,
    who made you and established you?
⁷ Remember the days of old;
    consider the years long past;
ask your father, and he will inform you,
    your elders, and they will tell you.
⁸ When the Most High⁵ apportioned the
        nations,
    when he divided humankind,
he fixed the boundaries of the peoples
    according to the number of the gods;ᵗ
⁹ the LORD's own portion was his people,
    Jacob his allotted share.

¹⁰ He sustainedᵘ him in a desert land,
    in a howling wilderness waste;
he shielded him, cared for him,
    guarded him as the apple of his eye.
¹¹ As an eagle stirs up its nest
    and hovers over its young,
as it spreads its wings, takes them up,
    and bears them aloft on its pinions,
¹² the LORD alone guided him;
    no foreign god was with him.
¹³ He set him atop the heights of the land
    and fed him withᵛ produce of the
        field;
he nursed him with honey from the
        crags,
    with oil from flinty rock,
¹⁴ curds from the herd, and milk from the
        flock,
    with fat of lambs and rams,
Bashan bulls and goats,
    together with the choicest wheat—
    you drank fine wine from the blood
        of grapes.

¹⁵ Jacob ate his fill;ʷ
    Jeshurun grew fat and kicked.
    You grew fat, bloated, and gorged!
He abandoned God who made him
    and scoffed at the Rock of his
        salvation.
¹⁶ They made him jealous with strange gods;
    with abhorrent things they provoked
        him.
¹⁷ They sacrificed to demons, not God,
    to deities they had never known,
to new ones recently arrived,
    whom your ancestors had not feared.
¹⁸ You were unmindful of the Rock that
        bore you;ˣ
    you forgot the God who gave you birth.

¹⁹ The LORD saw it and was jealous;ʸ
    he spurnedᶻ his sons and daughters.
²⁰ He said, 'I will hide my face from them;
    I will see what their end will be,
for they are a perverse generation,
    children in whom there is no
        faithfulness.
²¹ They made me jealous with what is no god,
    provoked me with their idols.
So I will make them jealous with what is
        no people,
    provoke them with a foolish nation.
²² For a fire is kindled by my anger
    and burns to the depths of Sheol;
it devours the earth and its increase
    and sets on fire the foundations of the
        mountains.

s 32.8 Traditional rendering of Heb *Elyon*   t 32.8 Q
ms Compare Gk Tg: MT *the Israelites*   u 32.10 Sam Gk
Compare Tg: MT *found*   v 32.13 Sam Gk Syr Tg: MT *he ate*
w 32.15 Q mss Sam Gk: MT lacks *Jacob ate his fill*   x 32.18 Or
that fathered you   y 32.19 Q mss Gk: MT lacks *was jealous*
z 32.19 Cn: Heb *he spurned because of provocation*

the Lord, Israel—the children of the Lord—is *degenerate, crooked, foolish and senseless* and deals *falsely with [the LORD]*, their covenant suzerain. **32:8–9** The tradition communicates the sovereignty of the Lord and election of Israel using language familiar from Canaanite religion wherein a Most High god rules over smaller deities or spiritual beings in a divine council. Here this language shows that the Lord God of Israel is the Most High deity who chose Israel as his special portion and divided up oversight of the other nations in the divine council according to the *number of the gods*. The underlying Hebrew from the Masoretic Text for the phrase that is translated as *the gods* reads "the Israelites," while the Dead Sea Scrolls attest the reading "children of God," and the Septuagint has "angels of God" (see text note in NRSVue). It is likely that the Dead Sea Scrolls preserve a more original reading that the Masoretic tradition modified, perhaps to avoid polytheistic implications of the phrase "children of God." The term can simply mean a spiritual being ("angel"; cf. the Septuagint reading) in the heavenly council who is subordinate to the Lord (cf. Job 1:6). **32:17–21** The song charges Israel with the idolatry of worshiping demons and other deities, lesser spiritual beings in the divine council who have led Israel astray (cf. Gen. 6:1–4 for a glimpse into the activities of the "sons of God" to entice humanity). The Lord responds with the jealousy of a spurned lover.

²³ I will heap disasters upon them,
 spend my arrows against them:
²⁴ wasting hunger,
 burning consumption,
 bitter pestilence.
The teeth of beasts I will send against
 them,
 with venom of things crawling in the
 dust.
²⁵ In the street the sword shall bereave,
 and in the chambers terror
for young man and woman alike,
 nursing child and old gray head.
²⁶ I said, "I will make an end of them*a*
 and blot out the memory of them
 from humankind,"
²⁷ but I feared provocation by the enemy,
 for their adversaries might
 misunderstand
and say, "Our hand is triumphant;
 it was not the LORD who did all this."'

²⁸ They are a nation void of sense;
 there is no understanding in them.
²⁹ If they were wise, they would understand
 this;
 they would discern what their end
 would be.
³⁰ How could one have routed a thousand
 and two put a myriad to flight,
unless their Rock had sold them,
 the LORD had given them up?
³¹ Indeed, their rock is not like our Rock;
 our enemies are fools.*b*
³² Their vine comes from the vinestock of
 Sodom,
 from the vineyards of Gomorrah;
 their grapes are grapes of poison;
 their clusters are bitter;
³³ their wine is the poison of serpents,
 the cruel venom of asps.

³⁴ Is not this laid up in store with me,
 sealed up in my treasuries,
³⁵ for the day of vengeance*c* and
 recompense,
 for the time when their foot shall slip?

Because the day of their calamity is at
 hand;
 their doom comes swiftly.

³⁶ Indeed, the LORD will vindicate his people,
 have compassion on his servants,
when he sees that their power is gone,
 neither bond nor free remaining.
³⁷ Then he will say, 'Where are their gods,
 the rock in which they took refuge,
³⁸ who ate the fat of their sacrifices
 and drank the wine of their libations?
Let them rise up and help you;
 let them be your protection!

³⁹ See now that I, even I, am he;
 there is no god besides me.
I kill, and I make alive;
 I wound, and I heal;
 and no one can deliver from my hand.
⁴⁰ For I lift up my hand to heaven
 and swear, As I live forever,
⁴¹ when I whet my flashing sword
 and my hand takes hold on judgment,
I will take vengeance on my adversaries
 and will repay those who hate me.
⁴² I will make my arrows drunk with blood,
 and my sword shall devour flesh—
with the blood of the slain and the
 captives,
 from the long-haired enemy.'

⁴³ Praise, O heavens,*d* his people;
 worship him, all you gods!*e*
For he will avenge the blood of his
 children*f*
 and take vengeance on his adversaries;
he will repay those who hate him*g*
 and cleanse the land for his people."*h*

44 Moses came and recited all the words
of this song in the hearing of the people, he
and Joshua*i* son of Nun. ⁴⁵When Moses had

a 32.26 Gk: Meaning of Heb uncertain *b* 32.31 Gk: Heb
judges *c* 32.35 Sam Gk: MT *vengeance is mine* *d* 32.43 Q
ms Gk: MT *nations* *e* 32.43 Q ms Gk: MT lacks this line
f 32.43 Q ms Gk: MT *his servants* *g* 32.43 Q ms Gk: MT lacks
this line *h* 32.43 Q ms Sam Gk Vg: MT *his land his people*
i 32.44 Sam Gk Syr Vg: MT *Hoshea*

32:36–38 Ultimately, the Lord turns to compassion to *vindicate his people*. Because of the Lord's persistent provision for Israel, they will finally recognize that their worship of idols is futile and that the gods that these idols represent are not real deities. **32:39** *There is no god besides me*. Though the song allows for a divine council of heavenly beings, Israel is prohibited from worshiping these other beings alongside YHWH.

　32:44–52 Ascending Nebo. Following the recitation of the song (vv. 44–47), the Lord tells Moses to ascend Mount Nebo in Moab, where he is to view the land of Canaan before his death.

finished reciting all these words to all Israel, [46]he said to them, "Take to heart all the words that I am giving in witness against you today; give them as a command to your children, so that they may diligently observe all the words of this law. [47]This is no trifling matter for you but rather your very life; through it you may live long in the land that you are crossing over the Jordan to possess."

48 On that very day the LORD addressed Moses as follows: [49]"Ascend this mountain of the Abarim, Mount Nebo, which is in the land of Moab across from Jericho, and view the land of Canaan, which I am giving to the Israelites for a possession; [50]you shall die there on the mountain that you ascend and shall be gathered to your kin, as your brother Aaron died on Mount Hor and was gathered to his kin, [51]because both of you broke faith with me among the Israelites at the waters of Meribath-kadesh in the wilderness of Zin, by failing to maintain my holiness among the Israelites. [52]Although you may view the land from a distance, you shall not enter it, the land that I am giving to the Israelites."

33

This is the blessing with which Moses, the man of God, blessed the Israelites before his death. [2]He said,

"The LORD came from Sinai
    and dawned from Seir upon us;[j]
    he shone forth from Mount Paran.
With him were myriads of holy ones,[k]
    at his right, a host of his own.[l]
[3] Indeed, O favorite among[m] peoples,
    all his holy ones were in your charge;
they marched at your heels,
    accepted direction from you.

[4] Moses charged us with the law
    as a possession for the assembly of
        Jacob.
[5] There arose a king in Jeshurun
    when the leaders of the people
        assembled,
    the united tribes of Israel.

[6] May Reuben live and not die out,
    even though his numbers are few."

[7]And this he said of Judah,
    "O LORD, give heed to Judah,
        and bring him to his people;
    strengthen his hands for him,"
        and be a help against his
            adversaries."

[8]And of Levi he said,
    "Give to Levi[o] your Thummim
        and your Urim to your loyal one,
    whom you tested at Massah,
        with whom you contended at the
            waters of Meribah,
[9] who said of his father and mother,
        'I regard them not';
    he ignored his kin
        and did not acknowledge his children.
    For they observed your word
        and kept your covenant.
[10] They teach Jacob your ordinances
        and Israel your law;
    they place incense before you

j 33.2 Gk Syr Vg Compare Tg: Heb *upon them*   k 33.2 Cn Compare Gk Sam Syr Vg: MT *He came from Ribeboth-kodesh*,   l 33.2 Cn Compare Gk: Meaning of Heb uncertain   m 33.3 Or *O lover of the*   n 33.7 Cn: Meaning of Heb uncertain   o 33.8 Q ms Gk: MT lacks *Give to Levi*

32:50 Being *gathered to your kin* reflects the notion of the reunion of the spirit of a person with deceased family in Sheol, the realm of the dead.

33:1–29 The blessing of Moses. At his death, Moses is portrayed as a patriarch of Israel bestowing a paternal blessing on the people (cf. Gen. 49:1–28). Beginning and ending with an invocation to Israel as a whole (vv. 1–5, 26–29), Moses addresses each tribe with a personalized prophetic blessing. The poem opens with language reflecting a divine theophany. Traditions recalling the giving of the law at Horeb—called Sinai here, which is the name used for Horeb in Exod. 19–24 (see **"Horeb/Sinai," p. 248**)—are blended with traditions of the Lord as a Divine Warrior. **33:2–5** The Lord, accompanied by a divine council (*holy ones . . . host*), comes from the mountains of Edom (Seir/Paran, cf. Hab. 3:3; Judg. 5:4) to rescue the people, give them the law, and reign as king over *Jeshurun* (a poetic name for Israel, vv. 5, 26). Alternatively, some scholars read the language of kingship as applying to Moses's role as the leader of Israel. In comparison to the blessing of Jacob in Gen. 49, where Judah is given the most focus, the tribes that receive the most attention in Deut. 33 are the tribes of Levi and Joseph—the rest of the tribes have only one or two verses devoted to them. **33:7** Moses entreats the Lord to deliver Judah, whose status is precarious. **33:8–11** Levi's role is teaching the law and discerning the will of God with the *Thummim* and *Urim*, stones used by the high priest to determine the

and whole burnt offerings on your
    altar.
11 Bless, O Lord, his substance,
    and accept the work of his hands;
    crush the loins of his adversaries,
    of those who hate him, so that they do
        not rise again."

12 Of Benjamin he said,
    "The beloved of the Lord rests in safety—
    the Most High[p] surrounds him all day
        long—
    and he rests between his shoulders."

13 And of Joseph he said,
    "Blessed by the Lord be his land,
    with the choice gifts of heaven above
    and of the deep that lies beneath,
14 with the choice fruits of the sun
    and the rich yield of the months,
15 with the finest produce of the ancient
        mountains
    and the abundance of the everlasting
        hills,
16 with the choice gifts of the earth and its
        fullness
    and the favor of the one who dwells
        on Sinai.[q]
    Let these come on the head of Joseph,
    on the brow of the prince among his
        brothers.
17 A firstborn[r] bull—majesty is his!
    His horns are the horns of a wild ox;
    with them he gores the peoples
    all together to the ends of the earth;
    such are the myriads of Ephraim,
    such the thousands of Manasseh."

18 And of Zebulun he said,
    "Rejoice, Zebulun, in your going out,

and Issachar, in your tents.
19 They call peoples to the mountain;
    there they offer the right sacrifices,
    for they suck the affluence of the seas
    and the hidden treasures of the sand."

20 And of Gad he said,
    "Blessed be the enlargement of Gad!
    Like a lion he lives;
    he tears at arm and scalp.
21 He chose the best for himself,
    for there a commander's allotment
        was reserved;
    he came at the head of the people;
    he executed the justice of the Lord
    and his ordinances with Israel."

22 And of Dan he said,
    "Dan is a lion's whelp
    that leaps forth from Bashan."

23 And of Naphtali he said,
    "O Naphtali, sated with favor,
    full of the blessing of the Lord,
    possess the west and the south."

24 And of Asher he said,
    "Most blessed of sons be Asher;
    may he be the favorite of his brothers,
    and may he dip his foot in oil.
25 Your bars are iron and bronze,
    and as your days, so is your strength.[s]

26 There is none like God, O Jeshurun,
    who rides through the heavens to
        your help,
    majestic through the clouds.

p 33.12 Cn: Heb *above him*   q 33.16 Cn: Heb *in the bush*
r 33.17 Q ms Gk Syr Vg: MT *His firstborn*   s 33.25 Gk:
Meaning of Heb uncertain

will of God (Exod. 28:30). **33:13–17** Joseph receives the most substantial blessing, which emphasizes agricultural abundance and prosperity. These focal points in the tribal listing hint at the social
location of Deuteronomy: the influence of Judah is minimal, the Levites are given prominence as
teachers, and the extensive blessing of Joseph may suggest a northern Israelite provenance of the
author and audience (see also the prominence of Shechem in Deut. 27). A comparison with Gen. 49
indicates that the identity and numbering of the tribes were often in flux. The list in Gen. 49 contains Simeon (mentioned in combination with Levi; Gen. 49:5), but Simeon is absent from Deut. 33
(but see Deut. 27:12), while the sons of Joseph—Ephraim and Manasseh—are not on the list of Gen.
49 but are present in Deut. 33. **33:26–29** The poem concludes with a return to the Divine Warrior
motif to celebrate the Lord's deliverance of Israel. Using language common in Canaanite mythology
to describe Baal as a storm god, Moses asserts that just as the Lord is incomparable as a deity who
rides through the heavens and *subdues the ancient gods* to destroy Israel's enemies (vv. 26–27), so
also Israel as a nation is an incomparably *happy* (or blessed) people who are saved by the Lord and
dwell safely in a prosperous land (v. 29).

27 He subdues the ancient gods,[t]
    shatters[u] the forces of old;[v]
he drove out the enemy before you
    and said, 'Destroy!'
28 So Israel lives in safety,
    untroubled is Jacob's abode[w]
in a land of grain and wine,
    where the heavens drop down dew.
29 Happy are you, O Israel! Who is like you,
    a people saved by the LORD,
the shield of your help
    and the sword of your triumph!
Your enemies shall come fawning to you,
    but you shall tread on their backs."

34 Then Moses went up from the plains of Moab to Mount Nebo, to the top of Pisgah, which is opposite Jericho, and the LORD showed him the whole land: Gilead as far as Dan, 2all Naphtali, the land of Ephraim and Manasseh, all the land of Judah as far as the Western Sea, 3the Negeb, and the Plain—that is, the valley of Jericho, the city of palm trees—as far as Zoar. 4The LORD said to him, "This is the land of which I swore to Abraham, to Isaac, and to Jacob, saying, 'I will give it to your descendants.' I have let you see it with your eyes, but you shall not cross over there." 5Then Moses, the servant of the LORD, died there in the land of Moab, at the LORD's command. 6He buried him in a valley in the land of Moab, opposite Beth-peor, but no one knows his burial place to this day. 7Moses was one hundred twenty years old when he died; his sight was unimpaired, and his vigor had not abated. 8The Israelites wept for Moses in the plains of Moab thirty days; then the period of mourning for Moses was ended.

9 Joshua son of Nun was full of the spirit of wisdom because Moses had laid his hands on him, and the Israelites obeyed him, doing as the LORD had commanded Moses.

10 Never since has there arisen a prophet in Israel like Moses, whom the LORD knew face to face. 11He was unequaled for all the signs and wonders that the LORD sent him to perform in the land of Egypt, against Pharaoh and all his servants and his entire land, 12and for all the mighty deeds and all the terrifying displays of power that Moses performed in the sight of all Israel.

t 33.27 Cn: Heb *The eternal God is a dwelling place* u 33.27 Cn: Heb *from underneath* v 33.27 Or *the everlasting arms* w 33.28 Or *fountain*

34:1–12 The death of Moses. 34:1–8 Deuteronomy, and concomitantly the Pentateuch or Torah, concludes with the death of Moses, which also culminates the narrative arc of the life of Moses that began in Exod. 2. The theme of the land that the Lord had promised to Abraham in Gen. 12 that has carried the plot of the Pentateuch is reiterated but is ultimately left unresolved, as Moses is granted a glimpse of the land but is not allowed to enter. **34:5** Moses is remembered as *the servant of the LORD*—that is, as a model vassal who shows Israel the way of humble obedience to the suzerain Lord. In the ancient Near East, a servant was considered a high-standing official or trustworthy representative of the government, thus the title identifies Moses as a representative of the Lord whom Israel is to listen to. **34:6** The Lord (*He*) buries Moses in an unknown location, potentially to stave off the temptation for Israel to venerate the figure of Moses who has attained quasi-divine status. The ambiguity of the details surrounding Moses's death gave rise to theories that Moses was taken to heaven (cf. Jude 9; see **"Moses," p. 247**). **34:9** The laying on of hands is a way to transfer spiritual authority or power. Moses imparts *the spirit of wisdom* to Joshua that transfers Moses's authority of leadership and wisdom in Torah interpretation to Joshua. The authority of Joshua is recognized, and the people succeed in doing *as the LORD had commanded Moses*. **34:10–12** Moses is praised as an unparalleled prophet in Israel, *whom the LORD knew face to face* in an immediate relationship and who humbly worked *signs and wonders* as a servant of the Lord to free Israel from Egypt. As with other descriptions of prophecy in Deuteronomy (13:1–6; 18:15–22), the concern of the concluding statement is to ensure that future prophetic revelation does not supplant the authority of the teachings of Moses, who was the prophet par excellence.

JOSHUA

The book of Joshua is part of the Historical Books in the Christian tradition and of the Former Prophets in the Jewish tradition. A rabbinical text reveals at least one perspective on the central figure of this book: "Moses' sons did not inherit his position, only Joshua. 'He who safeguards his master will be honored' (Prov. 27:18)—this refers to Joshua who served Moses day and night. Because he served his master, he earned the holy spirit, he earned prophecy" (Bemidbar Rabbah 12:9).

As in most of the books of the Hebrew Bible, scholars struggle with the complexities of Joshua's redactional history (how the text was assembled and revised over time), its historicity, and its relationship with other sections of the Bible. Some scholars read Joshua as the sixth book of a Hexateuch (Genesis–Joshua), finding in Joshua the same source traditions that are found in the Pentateuch (the Yahwist, the Elohist, and the Priestly traditions), along with the Deuteronomist tradition (see **"The Bible and Methods," pp. 2148–49**); others argue for a Tetrateuch (Genesis–Numbers), placing Deuteronomy as the first book of the Deuteronomistic History (DH), including Joshua through 2 Kings. See **"The Deuteronomistic History," p. 337**.

It is not necessary to choose between these two alternatives to see a clear Deuteronomistic theological framework in the book of Joshua, which emphasizes divine retribution. Joshua 1 and 23 proclaim the Deuteronomistic understanding that when Israel is faithful to the covenant, God acts favorably and blesses the people. And on the contrary, when the people follow other gods or do not fulfill God's commandments (Josh. 7–8), God punishes them. The Deuteronomist writer connects the mission of Joshua with Moses (1:1–18; 8:30–35; 12:1–6; 21:43–22:6; 23:1–16) and conveys the message that the whole set of events is a matter of faithfulness to God and the commandments. In addition to the dominant Deuteronomistic perspective, redactional touches reflecting the Priestly source tradition can also be found in the final form of Joshua (especially Josh. 5:10; 13–21, etc.).

Redactional History

The book's oldest core traditions were local folktales, sometimes connected to one of the sanctuaries like Gilgal, in use before the establishment of Jerusalem as the primary place of worship (Josh. 4). These folktales were most likely transmitted orally and plausibly collected in Jerusalem during the united monarchy (Israel and Judah; see **"Introduction to the Former Prophets / Historical Books," pp. 4–6**). The "conquest saga," most likely composed in Jerusalem in Hezekiah's court in the southern kingdom of Judah shortly after the fall of the northern kingdom of Samaria (Israel; 722 BCE), added a narrative framework raising awareness of the heterogeneous elements in Israel (Josh. 9). It is in this period of textual additions when Joshua is presented as a charismatic warrior and leader. During Josiah's reign (640–609 BCE) the compilation of the text was enriched according to Judah's territorial ambitions (additions of Josh. 10; 11:1–11; 12:7–24). This is also the time when some administrative documents were added to the conquest narrative (the parts of Canaan still to be possessed, Josh. 13–19). A first Deuteronomic redaction reinterprets previous materials in Joshua by rereading the history from the theological perspective of the exile of Judah to Babylon. That perspective argues that the people lost the land due to disobedience to God. So the redaction unequivocally asserts that only being faithful to the Torah will allow the people to remain in the promised land. The story becomes a holy war against non-Yahwistic practices (hence the *herem*, a term that denotes in this context what is consecrated to God, on the one hand, and what is under ban and is devoted to destruction; *herem* is the noun form, *haram* the verb form in Hebrew). The speech of Josh. 23 constitutes the conclusion of a second Deuteronomic redaction after the exile, which talks less about the importance of holy war. Finally, some Priestly touches (fourth century BCE)—noticeable by a very particular vocabulary and theological foci—accentuate the liturgical aspect of some stories in Joshua and adapt the whole to a new, more communitarian social reality, leading to the additions of Josh. 20–22 and 24.

Archaeology has challenged the historicity of the sequence of conquests narrated in the book of Joshua, and recent scholarship has also questioned the tradition that most of ancient Israel was enslaved in Egypt and foreign to Canaan. It is likely that only the Levites came out of Egypt and that the core of the population of ancient Israel originated in the hill country of southern Canaan. What

we have in this collection of folk traditions, legendary materials, and stories is a theological and literary work that conveys the beliefs and political persuasions of later editors and redactors. An alternative tradition in 1 Chr. 7:20–28 presents Ephraim and Joshua as local to Canaan, already established in the land, completely ignoring their time in Egypt and omitting the conquest narratives.

Reading Guide

Set after the people of Israel have been liberated from forced labor in Egypt and received the commandments at Sinai/Horeb, the book's main character, Joshua (Heb. Yehoshua = "YHWH is salvation"), is introduced as the successor of Moses and the person who will lead God's people to the possession of the promised land—the main focus of the book. The book brings to fulfillment (from the literary point of view) God's promises to the patriarchs, the liberation from Egypt, and the promises to Moses; all God's promises are fulfilled (Josh. 21:43–45; 23:14). Even though it is Joshua who leads the people, it is the God of Israel who is in charge, the one who gifted the land to the people of Israel (Josh. 21:43), the one who "gave them rest on every side" (Josh. 21:44). The book of Sirach or Ecclesiasticus describes quite accurately the general motif of the book: "Joshua son of Nun was mighty in war and was the successor of Moses in the prophetic office. He became, as his name implies, a great savior of God's elect, to take vengeance on the enemies who rose against them, so that he might give Israel its inheritance" (Sir. 46:1).

The theological/political message of the book highlights the essential connection between the promised land and the unity of the people of Israel ("all Israel," Josh. 3:7; 4:14; 7:25; 8:24), which is also a fundamental theological concept in Deuteronomy (Deut. 1:1; 5:1; 11:6; 27:9; 29:2; 31:1, 7, 11; 32:45; 34:12). Another fundamental belief reflected in Joshua is that the land of Canaan is the land that God promised to the patriarchs of Israel (Josh. 2:9, 24; 3:10; 5:12; 10:40–42; 11:16–17, 23; 12:7–8; 14:15b; 21:43–45; 23:4–5; 24:13, 28) and, therefore, that its occupation is a sacred duty where total obedience is required (Josh. 1:7–8, 13; 4:10; 8:30–35; 9:24; 10:40; 11:12, 15, 20; 13:6; 14:2, 5; 17:4; 21:2, 8; 22:2, 5).

Alejandro F. Botta

1 After the death of Moses the servant of the LORD, the LORD spoke to Joshua son of Nun, Moses's assistant, saying, ²"My servant Moses is dead. Now proceed to cross the Jordan, you and all this people, into the land that I am giving to them, to the Israelites. ³Every place that the sole of your foot will tread upon I have given to you, as I promised to Moses. ⁴From the wilderness and the Lebanon as far as the great river, the River Euphrates, all the land of the Hittites, to the Great Sea in the west shall be your territory. ⁵No one shall be able to stand against you all the days of your life. As I was with Moses, so I will be with you; I will not fail you or

1:1–18 Deuteronomistic language and theology are evident in the theological significance of Joshua's commission, the conquest, and the connection with Moses. See **"Conquest," p. 317. 1:1** *After the death of Moses.* A literary device to connect the book of Joshua with the book of Deuteronomy (Deut. 34:5–6). *Servant of the LORD.* A title used for Moses (see Deut. 34:5; Josh. 1:13, 15; 8:31, 33; 11:12; 12:6; 13:8; 14:7; 18:7; 22:2, 4–5; 2 Kgs. 18:12; 2 Chr. 1:3; 24:6) and later for Joshua (Josh. 24:29; Judg. 2:8), King David (Pss. 18, 36), Zerubbabel (1 Esd. 6:26), and Mary in the New Testament (Luke 1:38). *Moses's assistant.* Heb. "mesharet" (also used for Joshua in Num. 11:28) can also be translated as "adjutant," a military officer or "minister" of Moses. The role of Joshua in the exodus and the conquest saga goes beyond being the mere "helper" or "assistant" of Moses but displays a higher degree of responsibility and leadership. **1:4** *From the wilderness and the Lebanon as far as the great river, the River Euphrates.* The Bible offers two boundaries for the promised land: "from Dan to Beer-sheba" (2 Sam. 24:2–8, 15; 1 Kgs. 4:25), which is roughly the land that ancient Israel controlled at some point, and another ideal described here and in other passages (Gen. 15:18; Deut. 1:7; 11:24, etc.) and said to be fulfilled during the reign of Solomon (1 Kgs. 4:21). *The land of the Hittites.* Not a reference to the Hittite empire but to northern Canaan, where neo-Hittite states flourished between

forsake you. [6]Be strong and courageous, for you shall lead this people to possess the land that I swore to their ancestors to give them. [7]Only be strong and very courageous, being careful to act in accordance with all the law that my servant Moses commanded you; do not turn from it to the right hand or to the left, so that you may be successful wherever you go. [8]This book of the law shall not depart out of your mouth; you shall meditate on it day and night, so that you may be careful to act in accordance with all that is written in it. For then you shall make your way prosperous, and then you shall be successful. [9]I hereby command you: Be strong and courageous; do not be frightened or dismayed, for the LORD your God is with you wherever you go."

10 Then Joshua commanded the officers of the people, [11]"Pass through the camp and command the people, 'Prepare your provisions, for in three days you are to cross over this Jordan, to go in to take possession of the land that the LORD your God gives you to possess.'"

12 But to the Reubenites, the Gadites, and the half-tribe of Manasseh Joshua said, [13]"Remember the word that Moses the servant of the LORD commanded you, saying, 'The LORD your God is providing you a place of rest and will give you this land.' [14]Your wives, your little ones, and your livestock shall remain in the land that Moses gave you beyond the Jordan. But all the warriors among you shall cross over armed before your kindred and shall help them, [15]until the LORD gives rest to your kindred as well as to you, and they also take possession of the land that the LORD your God is giving them. Then you shall return to your own land and take possession of it, the land that Moses the servant of the LORD gave you beyond the Jordan to the east."

16 They answered Joshua, "All that you have commanded us we will do, and wherever you send us we will go. [17]Just as we obeyed Moses in all things, so we will obey you. Only may the LORD your God be with you, as he was with Moses! [18]Whoever rebels against your orders and disobeys your words, whatever you command, shall be put to death. Only be strong and courageous."

2 Then Joshua son of Nun sent two men secretly from Shittim as spies, saying, "Go, view the land, especially Jericho." So they went and entered the house of a prostitute whose name was Rahab and spent the night there. [2]The king of Jericho was told, "Some Israelites have come here tonight to search out the land." [3]Then the king of Jericho sent orders to Rahab, "Bring out the men who have come to you, who entered your house, for they have come to search out the whole land." [4]But the woman took the two men and hid them.[a] Then

a 2.4 Gk: Heb him

the tenth and seventh centuries BCE. **1:6** _Be strong and courageous._ An expression of reassurance in the face of danger (Josh. 1:9, 18; 10:25; Dan. 10:19). **1:7** _To act in accordance with all the law that my servant Moses commanded you._ Literally "to observe and do," an expression typical of Deuteronomy followed by "all his commandments" (Deut. 28:1, 15) or "all the words of this law" (Deut. 32:46). **1:8** _This book of the law._ Referring to the book of Deuteronomy, at least chaps. 12–26. Second Kings 22:8–11 reports the finding of the book in the temple. Compare Deut. 28:61; 29:21; 30:10; 31:26. **1:10** _Officers of the people._ Muster officers, in charge of assembling (troops), especially for inspection or in preparation for battle. **1:16–18** In the case of a military campaign, disobedience equals desertion and treason.

Josh. 2–11 These stories do not reflect Deuteronomistic theological foci, because of their emphasis on military battles with little reference to the theological implications of those battles, and have a pre–Deuteronomistic History (DH) origin, probably oral traditions associated with events and places. See **"The Deuteronomistic History," p. 337**.

Josh. 2 Following Moses's example (Num. 13:1–33), Joshua also sends scouts secretly to assess the best way to enter the land and the strength of what could be the main obstacle, the city of Jericho. Sending spies to collect strategical information, or to allow themselves to be captured and provide false information to the enemy, was a practice attested in the Egyptian Annals of Rameses II in his conflict against the Hittites in Kadesh (1274 BCE). **2:1** _Shittim_ ("acacia wood") is an area in the hills of Moab (Num. 25:1; 33:49; Mic. 6:5) northeast of the Dead Sea. Its precise location is debated. _Jericho_, modern-day Tell es-Sultan (five miles west of the Jordan River) and one of the earliest

she said, "True, the men came to me, but I did not know where they came from. [5]And when it was time to close the gate at dark, the men went out. Where the men went I do not know. Pursue them quickly, for you can overtake them." [6]She had, however, brought them up to the roof and hidden them with the stalks of flax that she had laid out on the roof. [7]So the men pursued them on the way to the Jordan as far as the fords. As soon as the pursuers had gone out, the gate was shut.

8 Before they went to sleep, she came up to them on the roof [9]and said to the men, "I know that the LORD has given you the land and that dread of you has fallen on us and that all the inhabitants of the land melt in fear before you. [10]For we have heard how the LORD dried up the water of the Red Sea[b] before you when you came out of Egypt and what you did to the two kings of the Amorites who were beyond the Jordan, to Sihon and Og, whom you utterly destroyed. [11]As soon as we heard it, our hearts melted, and there was no courage left in any of us because of you. The LORD your God is indeed God in heaven above and on earth below. [12]Now then, since I have dealt kindly with you, swear to me by the LORD that you in turn will deal kindly with my family. Give me a sign of good faith [13]that you will spare my father and mother, my brothers and sisters, and all who belong to them and deliver our lives from death." [14]The men said to her, "Our life for yours! If you do not tell this business of ours, then we will deal kindly and faithfully with you when the LORD gives us the land."

15 Then she let them down by a rope through the window, for her house was on the outer side of the city wall and she resided within the wall itself. [16]She said to them, "Go toward the hill country, so that the pursuers may not come upon you. Hide yourselves there three days, until the pursuers have returned; then afterward you may go your way." [17]The men said to her, "We will be released from this oath that you have made us swear to you [18]if we invade the land and you do not tie this crimson cord in the window through which you let us down and you do not gather into your house your father and mother, your brothers, and all your family. [19]If any of you go out of the doors of your house into the street, they shall be responsible for their own death, and we shall be innocent, but if a hand is laid upon any who are with you in the house, we shall bear the responsibility for their death. [20]But if you tell this business of ours, then we shall be released from this oath that you made us swear to you." [21]She said, "According to your words, so be it." She sent them away, and they departed. Then she tied the crimson cord in the window.

22 They departed and went into the hill country and stayed there three days, until the pursuers returned. The pursuers had searched all along the way and found nothing. [23]Then the two men came down again from the hill country. They crossed over,

b 2.10 Or Sea of Reeds

communities in the land, had been settled (with some gaps) since the ninth millennium BCE. It was heavily fortified during the Middle Bronze Age but destroyed at the end of this period. No walled fortification has been found from the Late Bronze Age (Joshua's period). It flourished again around the eleventh century BCE during the Iron Age. **2:5** *Time to close the gate at dark.* Strong walls and a city gate were the common fortifications of city-states in ancient Canaan and Israel. **2:6** *Stalks of flax that she had laid out on the roof* suggest the story is set in the seventh month, the time of the flax harvest according to the Gezer calendar (March–April). **2:10** *Whom you utterly destroyed*, Heb. "haram," means "to devote to destruction, dedicate to God" as promised by the Israelites in Num. 21:2. The practice is also attested in the Moabite Mesha Stele (ninth century BCE), where a whole population is consecrated to the Moabite god Chemosh. The Deuteronomistic religious rationale for this practice is explained in Deut. 7:4–6; 20:16–18. It is highly unlikely that such utter destruction / extermination ever occurred. See **"Genocide," p. 305**. **2:11** *God in heaven.* Rahab's statement suggests a Persian-period reformulation of Deuteronomistic theology (Deut. 4:39; 1 Kgs. 8.23). The expression is widely attested in postexilic biblical texts (Ezra 1:2; Jonah 1:9; Neh. 1:4–5) and in the Jewish texts from the island of Elephantine. Compare the positive reception of Rahab in the New Testament: Matt. 1:5; Heb. 11:31; and Jas. 2:25. **2:19** *Shall be responsible for their own death.* Literally "his blood will be on his own head," denoting legal responsibility (1 Sam. 25:39; 1 Kgs. 2:32; Esth. 9:25; Ps. 7:16; Ezek. 17:19; 18:13). Also in legal documents from the ancient Near East.

came to Joshua son of Nun, and told him all that had happened to them. ²⁴They said to Joshua, "Truly the Lord has given all the land into our hands; moreover, all the inhabitants of the land melt in fear before us."

3 Early in the morning Joshua rose and set out from Shittim with all the Israelites, and they came to the Jordan. They camped there before crossing over. ²At the end of three days, the officers went through the camp ³and commanded the people, "When you see the ark of the covenant of the Lord your God being carried by the Levitical priests, then you shall set out from your place. Follow it, ⁴so that you may know the way you should go, for you have not passed this way before. Yet there shall be a space between you and it, a distance of about two thousand cubits; do not come any nearer to it." ⁵Then Joshua said to the people, "Sanctify yourselves, for tomorrow the Lord will do wonders among you." ⁶To the priests Joshua said, "Take up the ark of the covenant, and pass on in front of the people." So they took up the ark of the covenant and went in front of the people.

7 The Lord said to Joshua, "This day I will begin to exalt you in the sight of all Israel, so that they may know that I will be with you as I was with Moses. ⁸You are the one who shall command the priests who bear the ark of the covenant, 'When you come to the edge of the waters of the Jordan, you shall stand still in the Jordan.'" ⁹Joshua then said to the Israelites, "Draw near and hear the words of the Lord your God." ¹⁰Joshua said, "By this you shall know that among you is the living God who without fail will drive out from before you the Canaanites, Hittites, Hivites, Perizzites, Girgashites, Amorites, and Jebusites: ¹¹the ark of the covenant of the Lord of all the earth is going to pass before you into the Jordan. ¹²So now select twelve men from the tribes of Israel, one from each tribe. ¹³When the soles of the feet of the priests who bear the ark of the Lord, the Lord of all the earth, come to rest in the waters of the Jordan, the waters of the Jordan flowing from above shall be cut off; they shall stand in a single heap."

14 When the people set out from their tents to cross over the Jordan, the priests bearing the ark of the covenant were in front of the people. ¹⁵Now the Jordan overflows all its banks throughout the time of harvest. So when those who bore the ark had come to the Jordan and the feet of the priests bearing the ark were dipped in the edge of the water, ¹⁶the waters flowing from above stood still, rising up in a single heap far off at Adam, the city that is beside Zarethan, while those flowing toward the sea of

3:1–4:24 This section brings to a successful end the journey that took Israel out of Egypt and through the wilderness. The references to the exodus (3:7; 4:14, 23) highlight the continuity of the divine plan. **3:1** *Early in the morning Joshua rose.* The expression used here is used elsewhere to highlight eagerness and an action that triggers the significant events that follow (Gen. 19:27; 21:14; 22:3; 28:18; Exod. 24:4). **3:3** *The ark of the covenant of the Lord your God* (or ark of the testimony) will lead the way as it did before (Num. 10:33–36). It contained the tablets of the covenant (Deut. 10:1–5) and it represented God's presence among God's people. *Levitical priests.* Deuteronomy 18:1 described the whole tribe of Levi as priests, a view not shared by the Priestly tradition that established that only the descendants of Aaron were to serve as priests (Num. 18). **3:4** *Two thousand cubits.* Roughly 0.57 miles (cf. Num. 35:5). **3:5** *Sanctify yourselves.* Resembling the encounter with God as a prelude to the giving of the Ten Commandments (Exod. 19:9–25), the form of the Hebrew verb used here ("hitpael") usually denotes preparation or consecration for a divinely sanctioned event (Josh. 7:13; 1 Sam. 16:5). **3:10** *Canaanites, Hittites, Hivites, Perizzites, Girgashites, Amorites, and Jebusites*, the standard Deuteronomistic list of seven nations. The list of the inhabitants of ancient Canaan, however, varies in the Bible. Canaan is presented as the father of Sidon, Heth, and the Jebusites, Amorites, Girgashites, Hivites, Arkites, Sinites, Arvadites, Zemarites, and Hamathites in Gen. 10:15–18. Exodus 3:7 and 23:23 omit the Girgashites, and 13:5 omits the Perizzites and Girgashites; Exod. 23:28 only mentions the Hivites, the Canaanites, and the Hittites. **3:13, 16** *[They shall stand] in a single heap* as in Exod. 15:8; Pss. 78:13; 114:3, 5; Sir. 39:17. **3:15** *The Jordan overflows.* It is only during the harvest season in the spring (March–April) that the melting snow from Mount Hermon overflows the lower Jordan River. The flow of the river has been occasionally blocked by mudslides. **3:16** *Adam* is modern-day Tell ed-Damiyeh, a city located at the meeting of

the Arabah, the Dead Sea,[c] were wholly cut off. Then the people crossed over opposite Jericho. [17]While all Israel were crossing over on dry ground, the priests who bore the ark of the covenant of the LORD stood firmly on dry ground in the middle of the Jordan, until the entire nation finished crossing over the Jordan.

4 When the entire nation had finished crossing over the Jordan, the LORD said to Joshua, [2]"Select twelve men from the people, one from each tribe, [3]and command them, 'Take twelve stones from here out of the middle of the Jordan, from the place where the priests' feet stood, carry them over with you, and lay them down in the place where you camp tonight.'" [4]Then Joshua summoned the twelve men whom he had appointed from the Israelites, one from each tribe. [5]Joshua said to them, "Pass on before the ark of the LORD your God into the middle of the Jordan, and each of you take up a stone on his shoulder, according to the number of the tribes of the Israelites, [6]so that this may be a sign among you. When your children ask in time to come, 'What do those stones mean to you?' [7]then you shall tell them that the waters of the Jordan were cut off in front of the ark of the covenant of the LORD. When it crossed over the Jordan, the waters of the Jordan were cut off. So these stones shall be to the Israelites a memorial forever."

8 The Israelites did as Joshua command- ed. They took up twelve stones out of the middle of the Jordan, according to the number of the tribes of the Israelites, as the LORD had told Joshua, carried them over with them to the place where they camped, and laid them down there. [9](Joshua set up twelve stones in the middle of the Jordan, in the place where the feet of the priests bear- ing the ark of the covenant had stood, and they are there to this day.)

10 The priests who bore the ark remained standing in the middle of the Jordan until everything was finished that the LORD had commanded Joshua to tell the people, ac- cording to all that Moses had commanded Joshua. The people crossed over in haste. [11]As soon as all the people had finished crossing over, the ark of the LORD and the priests crossed over to the front of the peo- ple. [12]The Reubenites, the Gadites, and the half-tribe of Manasseh crossed over armed before the Israelites, as Moses had ordered them. [13]About forty thousand armed for war crossed over before the LORD to the plains of Jericho for battle.

14 On that day the LORD exalted Joshua in the sight of all Israel, and they stood in awe of him, as they had stood in awe of Moses all the days of his life.

15 The LORD said to Joshua, [16]"Command the priests who bear the ark of the covenant to come up out of the Jordan." [17]Joshua therefore commanded the priests, "Come up out of the Jordan." [18]When the priests bearing the ark of the covenant of the LORD came up from the middle of the Jordan and the soles of the priests' feet touched dry

c 3.16 Heb *Salt Sea*

the Jordan River and Wadi Far'ah, seventeen miles north of Jericho. **4:1–8** Explains the presence of the twelve stones in the sanctuary of Gilgal. Joshua follows the example of Moses in Exod. 24:4 (cf. Deut. 27:2–3). This is the first of two different traditions about the stones brought together by the editor. **4:1** The conquest that follows is to be understood as commanded and directed by God from the beginning and the transition from the promise of the land to its fulfillment. **4:2** *Twelve men from the people, one from each tribe*, representing the entire nation of Israel (Deut. 1:23). **4:6–7** This high- lights the importance of preserving the memory of God's salvific acts for the education of future generations (cf. Exod. 12:26–27; 13:8–9; Deut. 6:20–25), one of the emphases of the Deuteronomist (see Deut. 6:8; 11:18; 28:46). *When your children ask.* Compare Deut. 6:20. **4:8** *The Israelites did as Joshua commanded* points to an effective leader and an obedient generation.

4:9–13 The second tradition about the stones; this time they are set up in the Jordan River. **4:9** *To this day.* A formula frequently used to connect a known custom, tradition, name, or geographical feature with its origins (cf. Gen. 26:33; 32:32; 35:20; 47:26; Deut. 3:14; Josh. 5:9; 7:26; 8:28; 13:13). **4:12** *Crossed over armed.* Compare 1:14. All the tribes are united in the conquest (Deut. 3:18–20). **4:13** *Thousand*, Heb. "lep," can also mean unit or regiment—that is, "forty units." **4:14** The exaltation of Joshua fulfills 3:7. The comparison with Moses highlights the continuity of God's presence with the new leader.

ground, the waters of the Jordan returned to their place and overflowed all its banks, as before.

19 The people came up out of the Jordan on the tenth day of the first month, and they camped in Gilgal on the east border of Jericho. ²⁰Those twelve stones that they had taken out of the Jordan, Joshua set up in Gilgal, ²¹saying to the Israelites, "When your children ask their parents in time to come, 'What do these stones mean?' ²²then you shall let your children know, 'Israel crossed over the Jordan here on dry ground.' ²³For the Lord your God dried up the waters of the Jordan for you until you crossed over, as the Lord your God did to the Red Sea,ᵈ which he dried up for us until we crossed over, ²⁴so that all the peoples of the earth may know that the hand of the Lord is mighty and so that you may fear the Lord your God forever."

5 ᵉWhen all the kings of the Amorites beyond the Jordan to the west and all the kings of the Canaanites by the sea heard that the Lord had dried up the waters of the Jordan for the Israelites until they had crossed over, their hearts melted, and there was no longer any spirit in them because of the Israelites.

2 At that time the Lord said to Joshua, "Make flint knives and circumcise the Israelites a second time." ³So Joshua made flint knives and circumcised the Israelites at Gibeath-haaraloth.ᶠ ⁴This is the reason why Joshua circumcised them: all the males of the people who came out of Egypt, all the warriors, had died during the journey through the wilderness after they had come out of Egypt. ⁵Although all the people who came out had been circumcised, yet all the people born on the journey through the wilderness after they had come out of Egypt had not been circumcised. ⁶For the Israelites traveled forty years in the wilderness, until all the nation, the warriors who came out of Egypt, perished, not having listened to the voice of the Lord. To them the Lord swore that he would not let them see the land that he had sworn to their ancestors to give us, a land flowing with milk and honey. ⁷So it was their children, whom he raised up in their place, that Joshua circumcised, for they were uncircumcised because they had not been circumcised on the way.

8 When the circumcising of all the nation was done, they remained in their places in the camp until they were healed. ⁹The Lord said to Joshua, "Today I have rolled away from you the disgrace of Egypt." And so that place is called Gilgalᵍ to this day.

10 While the Israelites were camped in Gilgal, they kept the Passover in the

ᵈ 4.23 Or *Sea of Reeds* ᵉ 5.1 Q ms places 8.30–35 before 5.1 ᶠ 5.3 That is, *the hill of the foreskins* ᵍ 5.9 In Heb *Gilgal* is related to the verb *rolled*

4:19 *The first month* of the ancient Hebrew calendar, Abib, March–April of the Julian calendar (Exod. 13:4; 23:15; 34:18; Deut. 16:1). After the exile, it was named Nisan (Neh. 2:1; Esth. 3:7; 1 Esd. 5:6).
4:19–20 *Gilgal*, "circle of stone," a national shrine during the early Israelite period (cf. 1 Sam. 7:16; 10:8; 11:14, 15; 13:4, 7, 8, 12, 15; 15:12, 21, 33) and place of later infidelities by the people (Hos. 4:15; 9:15; 12:11; Amos 4:4; 5:5). It was also the name of other locations (Deut. 11:30; 2 Kgs. 2:1).
4:24 *All the peoples of the earth* expands the worship of the God of Israel beyond the national tribal boundaries to include every nation (1 Kgs. 8:42, 60; 2 Kgs. 19:19).
5:1 *Their hearts melted.* Compare the same language in 2:10–11 and Exod. 15:13–17.
5:2 *Flint knives.* Evidence that the practice began before metal was widely used (cf. Exod. 4:25). Circumcision has been traced to the third millennium and is graphically depicted in the Egyptian necropolis at Saqqara (ca. 2400 BCE). Compare Gen. 17:10–14; Exod. 4:24–26; 12:48; Lev. 12:3. It was a requirement to celebrate the Passover (Exod. 12:43–49).
5:3 *Gibeath-haaraloth.* Mentioned only here.
5:6 *A land flowing with milk and honey.* This expression, emphasizing the richness and fertility of the promised land, appears only here in Joshua but several times in the Pentateuch (Exod. 3:8, 17; 13:5; 33:3; Lev. 20:24; Num. 16:13–14; Deut. 6:3; 11:9; 26:9, 15; 27:3) and later prophetic texts (Jer. 11:5; 32:22; Ezek. 20:6, 15).
5:8 *Until they were healed.* Usually seven to ten days.
5:9 *The disgrace of Egypt.* Probably the oppression of slavery under the Egyptians. *Gilgal.* Compare 4:19–20.
5:10–12 *The Passover* (Exod. 12:1–27) was celebrated on the fourteenth of Nisan (cf. Num. 9:1–14;

evening on the fourteenth day of the month in the plains of Jericho. [11]On the day after the Passover, on that very day, they ate the produce of the land, unleavened cakes and roasted grain. [12]The manna ceased on the day they ate the produce of the land, and the Israelites no longer had manna; they ate the crops of the land of Canaan that year.

13 Once when Joshua was by Jericho, he looked up and saw a man standing before him with a drawn sword in his hand. Joshua went to him and said to him, "Are you one of us or one of our adversaries?" [14]He replied, "Neither, but as commander of the army of the Lord I have now come." And Joshua fell on his face to the earth and worshiped, and he said to him, "What do you command your servant, my lord?" [15]The commander of the army of the Lord said to Joshua, "Remove the sandals from your feet, for the place where you stand is holy." And Joshua did so.

6 Now Jericho was shut up inside and out because of the Israelites; no one came out, and no one went in. [2]The Lord said to Joshua, "See, I have handed Jericho over to you, along with its king and soldiers. [3]You shall march around the city, all the warriors circling the city once. Thus you shall do for six days, [4]with seven priests bearing seven trumpets of rams' horns before the ark. On the seventh day you shall march around the city seven times, the priests blowing the trumpets. [5]When they make a long blast with the ram's horn, as soon as you hear the sound of the trumpet, then all the people shall shout with a great shout, and the wall of the city will fall down flat, and all the people shall charge straight ahead." [6]So Joshua son of Nun summoned the priests and said to them, "Take up the ark of the covenant and have seven priests carry seven trumpets of rams' horns in front of the ark of the Lord." [7]To the people he said, "Go forward and march around the city; have the armed men pass on before the ark of the Lord."

8 As Joshua had commanded the people, the seven priests carrying the seven trumpets of rams' horns before the Lord went forward, blowing the trumpets, with the ark of the covenant of the Lord following them. [9]And the armed men went before the priests who blew the trumpets; the rear guard came after the ark, while the trumpets blew continually. [10]To the people Joshua gave this command: "You shall not shout or let your voice be heard, nor shall you utter a word until the day I tell you to shout. Then you shall shout." [11]So the ark of the Lord went around the city, circling it once, and they came into the camp and spent the night in the camp.

2 Kgs. 23:21–23). Israel can now enjoy the produce of the land. **5:12** The manna tradition. Compare Exod. 16:13–35.

5:13–14 An encounter with a supernatural warrior who represents God's presence in the divinely sanctioned conquest. It has been interpreted as a theophany, a visible manifestation of God or a divine/supernatural creature (as in Dan. 8:13), or as a divine messenger (Judg. 6:11; Exod. 3:2; 14:19).

5:15 *Remove the sandals from your feet.* A clear reference to Exod. 3:5, where Moses faced the divine presence.

6:1 *Jericho,* see 2:1. During Joshua's period, Jericho was most likely an insignificant village with no fortification but later, during the time of the writing of the DH, was a very important and influential city. See **"Deuteronomistic History," p. 337**.

6:2 *The Lord said to Joshua.* A change of divine speaker; instead of the "commander of the army of the Lord" as in 5:13–15, now it is the Lord who addresses Joshua. *To you* (sg.). Literally "given into your hand"; God gave Jericho to Joshua. This is a common Semitic expression denoting a god-enacted victory over enemies. God has promised that Joshua would conquer Jericho (Num. 21:34; Deut. 2:24; 3:2).

6:3 *You shall march around.* "You" (pl.) commands Joshua and the people to surround the city (cf. 2 Kgs. 6:15; Eccl. 9:14; 2 Kgs. 3:25).

6:4 *On the seventh day.* A ceremonial procession lasting seven days before military action is also attested in Ugarit, an ancient Canaanite community. See also 1 Kgs. 20:29. *The priests blowing the trumpets.* The usual way to begin and end military actions (Judg. 3:27; 6:34; 2 Sam. 2:28; 18:16; 20:22).

6:6 *The ark of the covenant.* See note to 3:3. *Trumpets of rams' horns.* Used in religious ceremonies and to announce the jubilee (cf. 1 Chr. 15:28; 2 Chr. 15:14; Ps. 98:6; Dan. 3:5, 7, 10, 15; Hos. 5:8).

Making Connections: Genocide (Joshua 6)

The Jewish lawyer Raphael Lemkin (June 24, 1900–August 28, 1959) conceived the term *genocide* in 1944 to describe the European anti-Semitic policies that led to the Shoah (the Holocaust).

The text of Joshua includes passages that give the appearance of the commission of genocide (*haram*) against the Canaanite population. The command is very clearly stated in Deut. 20:16–17: "But as for the towns of these peoples that the Lᴏʀᴅ your God is giving you as an inheritance, you must not let anything that breathes remain alive. Indeed, you shall annihilate them—the Hittites and the Amorites, the Canaanites and the Perizzites, the Hivites and the Jebusites—just as the Lᴏʀᴅ your God has commanded" (see also Deut. 7:2, 26; 13:17–18). The command seems to be implemented in Josh. 6–11.

Ancient Near Eastern texts offer examples of such a genre: the stela of the Pharaoh Merneptah (1213–1203 BCE) proclaims that at least two groups of people, Yano'am ("is made nonexistent") and Israel ("is wasted, its seed is not"), suffered such annihilation during his campaign in Canaan. But it is also clear that the seed of Israel remained. The Inscription of King Mesha of Moab (835 BCE) is another relevant example of the use of *haram*, as he declares, "(I) killed all the people [from] the city (Ataroth) as a sacrifice(?) for Kemosh and for Moab," and a few lines later states, "and I killed [its] whole population, seven thousand male citizens(?) and aliens(?), and female citizens(?) and aliens(?), 15 and servant girls; for I had put it to the ban for Ashtar Kemosh" ("The Inscription of King Mesha," in *Monumental Inscriptions from the Biblical World*). It is very unlikely that any of these "genocides" ever occurred.

It is also evident from the book of Joshua itself that such genocide never happened (Josh. 15:63; 16:10; 17:13) and that the populations that were supposed to be annihilated were still around during the time of the Judges (Judg. 1) and the times of David and Solomon, who "conscripted [the populations] for slave labor" (1 Kgs. 9:20–21). Those populations remained in the land even after the return from the exile (Ezra 9:1; cf. 1 Esd. 8:66). The use of such a horrific expression, even in the case of war, should be understood in its ancient Near Eastern contexts and the Deuteronomic program of exclusive Yahwism that saw any contact with non-Yahwist populations as a potential threat to Israel's traditional beliefs.

Alejandro F. Botta

12 Then Joshua rose early in the morning, and the priests took up the ark of the Lᴏʀᴅ. ¹³The seven priests carrying the seven trumpets of rams' horns before the ark of the Lᴏʀᴅ passed on, blowing the trumpets continually. The armed men went before them, and the rear guard came after the ark of the Lᴏʀᴅ, while the trumpets blew continually. ¹⁴On the second day they marched around the city once and then returned to the camp. They did this for six days.

15 On the seventh day they rose early, at dawn, and marched around the city in the same manner seven times. It was only on that day that they marched around the city seven times. ¹⁶And at the seventh time, when the priests had blown the trumpets, Joshua said to the people, "Shout! For the Lᴏʀᴅ has given you the city. ¹⁷The city and all that is in it shall be devoted to the Lᴏʀᴅ for destruction. Only Rahab the prostitute and all who are with her in her house shall live because she hid the messengers we sent. ¹⁸As for you,

keep away from the things devoted to destruction, so as not to covet*ᵇ* and take any of the devoted things and make the camp of Israel an object for destruction, bringing trouble upon it. ¹⁹But all silver and gold and vessels of bronze and iron are sacred to the Lᴏʀᴅ; they shall go into the treasury of the Lᴏʀᴅ." ²⁰So the people shouted, and the trumpets were blown. As soon as the people heard the sound of the trumpets, they raised a great shout, and the wall fell down flat, so the people charged straight ahead into the city and captured it. ²¹Then they devoted to destruction by the edge of the sword all in the city, both men and women, young and old, oxen, sheep, and donkeys.

22 But to the two men who had spied out the land, Joshua said, "Go into the prostitute's house, and bring the woman out of it and all who belong to her, as you swore to her." ²³So the young men who had been spies went in and brought Rahab out, along

b 6.18 Gk: Heb *devote to destruction*

6:21 *By the edge of the sword.* Literally "by the mouth of the sword," an expression also found in 8:24; 10:28, 30, 32, 35, 37, 39; 11:12, 14. Sirach wisely advises, "Many have fallen by the edge of the sword, but not as many as have fallen because of the tongue" (Sir. 28:18).
6:23 *Set them outside the camp of Israel.* For reasons of ritual purity (cf. Deut. 23:10–14).

with her father, her mother, her brothers, and all who belonged to her—they brought all her kindred out—and set them outside the camp of Israel. ²⁴They burned down the city and everything in it; only the silver and gold and the vessels of bronze and iron they put into the treasury of the house of the LORD. ²⁵But Rahab the prostitute, with her family and all who belonged to her, Joshua spared. Her family[i] has lived in Israel ever since. For she hid the messengers whom Joshua sent to spy out Jericho.

26 Joshua then pronounced this oath, saying,

"Cursed before the LORD be anyone
    who tries
to build this city, Jericho!
At the cost of his firstborn he shall lay
    its foundation,
and at the cost of his youngest he
    shall set up its gates!"

27 So the LORD was with Joshua, and his fame was in all the land.

7 But the Israelites broke faith in regard to the devoted things: Achan son of Carmi son of Zabdi son of Zerah, of the tribe of Judah, took some of the devoted things, and the anger of the LORD burned against the Israelites.

2 Joshua sent men from Jericho to Ai, which is near Beth-aven, east of Bethel, and said to them, "Go up and spy out the land." And the men went up and spied out Ai. ³Then they returned to Joshua and said to him, "Not all the people need go up; about two or three thousand men should go up and attack Ai. Since they are so few, do not make the whole people toil up there." ⁴So about three thousand of the people went up there, and they fled before the men of Ai. ⁵The men of Ai killed about thirty-six of them, chasing them from outside the gate as far as Shebarim and killing them on the slope. The hearts of the people melted and turned to water.

6 Then Joshua tore his clothes and fell to the ground on his face before the ark of the LORD until the evening, he and the elders of Israel, and they put dust on their heads. ⁷Joshua said, "Ah, Lord GOD! Why have you brought this people across the Jordan at all,

i 6.25 Heb She

6:24 *Put into the treasury of the house of the LORD.* An anachronism, since the temple has not yet been built (cf. 1 Chr. 9:26; 26:20, 22, 24; 29:8; 2 Chr. 5:1; 16:2; 36:18). LXX: "the treasury of the Lord" is preferable, emphasizing that the booty belongs to God / the priests and not the political/military leaders or the people.

6:26 *Cursed before the LORD.* Compare 1 Kgs. 16:34. A similar curse is also attested in early Hittite documents from the seventeenth century BCE.

6:27 Fulfilling God's promise (cf. 1:5, 9, 17; 3:7). *His fame.* Only said of Moses (Deut. 2:25), Solomon (1 Kgs. 10:1 // 2 Chr. 9:1), and Mordecai (Esth. 9:4).

7:1 This episode seems to belong to an independent tradition not related to the conquests of the cities of Jericho and Ai. *Broke faith* Heb. "act unfaithfully, treacherously." *Took some of the devoted things.* Deuteronomy 13:17 and Lev. 27:28 make clear the prohibition of taking for oneself what has been consecrated to God. Compare Josh. 22:16, 20, 22.

7:2 *Ai* is identified with the archaeological site of Khirbet et-Tell (Gen. 12:8; 13:3; Josh. 7–8; Ezra 2:28; Neh. 7:32; Jer. 49:3), located near modern-day Beitin (biblical Bethel). *Bethel* appears prominently in the patriarchal narratives. Its name is attributed to Jacob, who changed it from Luz to Bethel (Gen. 28:18–19, Jacob's dream in Bethel; 35:15); in Gen. 31:13, God identifies himself as the "God of Bethel." Bethel became a sanctuary where the ancient Israelites went to consult God (Judg. 20:18, 26; 21:2; 1 Sam. 10:3). After the division of the kingdom, Jeroboam made sacrifices in Bethel and established it as a national sanctuary for the northern kingdom (1 Kgs. 12:32–33). The prophets condemned this practice (Jer. 48:13; Amos 3:14; 4:4; 5:6; Hos. 10:15). The sanctuary was later destroyed during the reforms of King Josiah (2 Kgs. 23:15, 19).

7:6–9 The defeat at Ai elicits Joshua's intercessory prayer including contrition (v. 6), grievance (v. 7), and intercession. 7:6 *Tore his clothes . . . they put dust on their heads.* Mourning and contrition rituals, as in Gen. 37:34; Num. 14:6; Jonah 3:6; Dan. 9:3; Job 42:6. The elders are representing the people in their penitence (see Num. 11 and Deut. 1). *Elders of Israel.* Tribal and political leaders (cf. Judg. 8:14, 16; 11:5–11; Ruth 4:1–12; 1 Sam. 11:3; 16:4; 2 Sam. 3:17; 5:3; 17:4; 19:12–13). 7:7 Similar to Moses's prayers in Exod. 32:11; Num. 14:13–16; Deut. 9:18–19. Tasking God to act to safeguard his

to hand us over to the Amorites so as to destroy us? Would that we had been content to settle beyond the Jordan! [8]O Lord, what can I say, now that Israel has turned their backs to their enemies! [9]The Canaanites and all the inhabitants of the land will hear of it and surround us and cut off our name from the earth. Then what will you do for your great name?"

10 The Lord said to Joshua, "Stand up! Why have you fallen on your face? [11]Israel has sinned; they have transgressed my covenant that I imposed on them. They have taken some of the devoted things; they have stolen, they have acted deceitfully, and they have put them among their own belongings. [12]Therefore the Israelites are unable to stand before their enemies; they turn their backs to their enemies because they have become a thing devoted for destruction themselves. I will be with you no more unless you destroy the devoted things from among you. [13]Proceed to sanctify the people and say, 'Sanctify yourselves for tomorrow, for thus says the Lord, the God of Israel: There are devoted things among you, O Israel; you will be unable to stand before your enemies until you take away the devoted things from among you. [14]In the morning, therefore, you shall come forward tribe by tribe. The tribe that the Lord takes shall come near by clans, the clan that the Lord takes shall come near by households, and the household that the Lord takes shall come near one by one. [15]And the one who is taken as having the devoted things shall be burned with fire, together with all that he has, for having transgressed the covenant of the Lord and for having done an outrageous thing in Israel.'"

16 So Joshua rose early in the morning and brought Israel near tribe by tribe, and the tribe of Judah was taken. [17]He brought near the clans of Judah, and the clan of the Zerahites was taken, and he brought near the clan of the Zerahites by households,[j] and Zabdi was taken. [18]And he brought near his household one by one, and Achan son of Carmi son of Zabdi son of Zerah, of the tribe of Judah, was taken. [19]Then Joshua said to Achan, "My son, give glory to the Lord God of Israel and make confession to him. Tell me now what you have done; do not hide it from me." [20]And Achan answered Joshua, "It is true; I am the one who sinned against the Lord God of Israel. This is what I did: [21]when I saw among the spoil a beautiful mantle from Shinar and two hundred shekels of silver and a bar of gold weighing fifty shekels, then I coveted them and took them. They now lie hidden in the ground inside my tent, with the silver underneath."

22 So Joshua sent messengers, and they ran to the tent, and there it was, hidden in his tent with the silver underneath. [23]They took them out of the tent and brought them to Joshua and all the Israelites, and they spread them out before the Lord. [24]Then Joshua and all Israel with him took Achan son of Zerah, with the silver, the mantle, and the bar of gold, with his sons and daughters, with his oxen, donkeys, and sheep, and his tent and all that he had, and they brought them up to the Valley of Achor. [25]Joshua said, "Why did you bring trouble on us? The Lord is bringing trouble on you today." And all Israel stoned him to death; they burned them with fire, cast stones on them, [26]and raised over him a great heap of stones that remains to this day. Then the Lord turned

j 7.17 Heb mss Syr: MT *one by one*

honor is very common in the Psalms (23:3; 25:11; 31:3; 54:3; 79:9; 106:8; 109:21; 143:11). *Ah, Lord God!* A common expression of sorrow in the late prophetic corpus (Jer. 1:6; 4:10; 14:13; 32:17; Ezek. 4:14; 9:8; 11:13; 20:49).

7:11 *Israel has sinned.* The actions of Achan (corporate responsibility) bring consequences for the whole people (cf. 2 Sam. 21:1–10).

7:13 *Thus says the Lord.* The messenger formula used in letters to highlight the exact words of the sender is frequently used by Moses (Exod. 4:22; 5:1; 7:17; 8:1, 20; 9:1, 13; 10:3; 11:4; 32:27) and the prophets of Israel.

7:21 *Shinar.* Sumer in ancient Mesopotamia.

7:24 *Valley of Achor*, Heb. "Devastation Valley" (Josh. 15:7), an isolated and barren plain west of Qumran.

7:25 *All Israel stoned him to death.* The community acts collectively, taking responsibility for the death sentence.

from his burning anger. Therefore that place to this day is called the Valley of Achor.[k]

8 Then the LORD said to Joshua, "Do not fear or be dismayed; take all the fighting men with you, and go up to Ai. See, I have handed over to you the king of Ai with his people, his city, and his land. ²You shall do to Ai and its king as you did to Jericho and its king, except that you may take its spoil and plunder its livestock for yourselves. Set an ambush against the city, behind it."

3 So Joshua and all the fighting men set out to go up against Ai. Joshua chose thirty thousand warriors and sent them out by night ⁴with the command, "You shall lie in ambush against the city, behind it; do not go very far from the city, but all of you stay alert. ⁵I and all the people who are with me will approach the city. When they come out against us, as before, we will flee from them. ⁶They will come out after us until we have drawn them away from the city, for they will say, 'They are fleeing from us as before.' While we flee from them, ⁷you shall rise up from the ambush and seize the city, for the LORD your God will give it into your hand. ⁸And when you have taken the city, you shall set the city on fire, doing as the LORD has ordered; see, I have commanded you." ⁹So Joshua sent them out, and they went to the place of ambush and lay between Bethel and Ai, to the west of Ai, but Joshua spent that night with the people.[l]

10 In the morning Joshua rose early and mustered the people and went up, with the elders of Israel, before the people to Ai. ¹¹All the fighting men who were with him went up and drew near before the city and camped on the north side of Ai, with a ravine between them and Ai. ¹²Taking about five thousand men, he set them in ambush between Bethel and Ai, to the west of the city. ¹³So they stationed the forces, the main encampment that was north of the city and its rear guard west of the city, and Joshua went that night into the valley. ¹⁴When the king of Ai saw this, he and all his people, the inhabitants of the city, hurried out early in the morning to the meeting place facing the Arabah to meet Israel in battle, but he did not know that there was an ambush against him behind the city. ¹⁵And Joshua and all Israel made a pretense of being beaten before them and fled in the direction of the wilderness. ¹⁶So all the people who were in the city were called together to pursue them, and as they pursued Joshua they were drawn away from the city. ¹⁷There was not a man left in Ai[m] who did not go out after Israel; they left the city open and pursued Israel.

18 Then the LORD said to Joshua, "Stretch out the sword that is in your hand toward Ai, for I will give it into your hand." And Joshua stretched out the sword that was in his hand toward the city. ¹⁹As soon as he stretched out his hand, the troops in ambush rose quickly out of their place and rushed forward. They entered the city, took it, and at once set the city on fire. ²⁰So when the men of Ai looked back, the smoke of the city was rising to the sky. They had no power to flee this way or that, for the people who fled to the wilderness turned back against the pursuers. ²¹When Joshua and all Israel saw that the ambush had taken the city and that the smoke of the city was rising, then they turned back and struck down the men of Ai. ²²And the other Israelites came out from the city against them, so they were surrounded by Israelites, some on one side and some on the other, and Israel struck them down until no one was left who survived or escaped. ²³But the king of Ai was taken alive and brought to Joshua.

k 7.26 That is, *trouble* l 8.9 Heb *among the people*
m 8.17 Gk: Heb adds *or Bethel*

Josh. 8 Despite agreeing on the central components of the story, the MT and the LXX differ in length and in the sequences of events in this chapter. Joshua 8:4 and most of 8:12–13, 20, 26 are not present in the LXX. **8:1** *Do not fear or be dismayed.* A typical Deuteronomic expression of encouragement in the face of battle (Deut. 1:21; 31:8; cf. 2 Chr. 20:15, 17). **8:2** Unlike in Jericho (6:15–19) we have here a modified version of the "herem" allowing the people to take booty for themselves (cf. 1 Sam. 15:9–10). See note on Josh. 2:10. **8:3–6** These verses present challenges to the understanding of the right order of events. *Thirty thousand warriors.* An unlikely high number of warriors. A similar problem is attested in other battle-like situations in the MT (Judg. 20:2, 15, 17, 25, 34, 35, 44, 45, 46). **8:4** *Behind it.* Opposite the main gate. **8:12** *Five thousand men.* Or "five contingents." **8:14** *The Arabah.* Plain of the Jordan River's valley. **8:15** *In the direction of the wilderness.* The surroundings of

24 When Israel had finished killing all the inhabitants of Ai in the open wilderness where they pursued them, and when all of them to the very last had fallen by the edge of the sword, all Israel returned to Ai and attacked it with the edge of the sword. 25The total of those who fell that day, both men and women, was twelve thousand—all the people of Ai. 26For Joshua did not draw back his hand with which he stretched out the sword until he had utterly destroyed all the inhabitants of Ai. 27Only the livestock and the spoil of that city Israel plundered for themselves, according to the word of the LORD that he had issued to Joshua. 28So Joshua burned Ai and made it forever a heap of ruins, as it is to this day. 29And he hanged the king of Ai on a tree until evening, and at sunset Joshua commanded, and they took his body down from the tree, threw it down at the entrance of the gate of the city, and raised over it a great heap of stones, which stands there to this day.

30 "Then Joshua built on Mount Ebal an altar to the LORD, the God of Israel, 31just as Moses the servant of the LORD had commanded the Israelites, as it is written in the book of the law of Moses, "an altar of unhewn° stones, on which no iron tool has been used," and they offered on it burnt offerings to the LORD and sacrificed offerings of well-being. 32And there, in the presence of the Israelites, Joshua𝑝 wrote on the stones a copy of the law of Moses that he had written. 33All Israel, alien as well as native-born, with their elders and officers and their judges, stood on opposite sides of the ark

in front of the Levitical priests who carried the ark of the covenant of the LORD, half of them in front of Mount Gerizim and half of them in front of Mount Ebal, as Moses the servant of the LORD had commanded earlier, that they should bless the people of Israel. 34And afterward he read all the words of the law, blessings and curses, according to all that is written in the book of the law. 35There was not a word of all that Moses commanded that Joshua did not read before all the assembly of Israel, and the women, and the little ones, and the aliens who resided among them.

9 Now when all the kings who were beyond the Jordan in the hill country and in the lowland all along the coast of the Great Sea toward Lebanon—the Hittites, the Amorites, the Canaanites, the Perizzites, the Hivites, and the Jebusites—heard of this, 2they gathered together with one accord to fight Joshua and Israel.

3 But when the inhabitants of Gibeon heard what Joshua had done to Jericho and to Ai, 4they on their part acted with cunning: they went and prepared provisions𝑞 and took worn-out sacks for their donkeys and wineskins, worn out and torn and mended, 5with worn-out, patched sandals on their feet and worn-out clothes, and all their provisions were dry and moldy. 6They went to Joshua in the camp at Gilgal and said to him and to the Israelites, "We have

n 8.30 Q ms places 8.30–35 before 5.1   o 8.31 Heb *whole*
p 8.32 Heb *he*   q 9.4 Heb mss Gk Syr: Meaning of MT uncertain

the Jordan River's valley. **8:24** *By the edge of the sword.* See note on 6:21. This fulfills the command of Deut. 13:15 and 20:13. It appears for the first time in Gen. 34:26 and it is used in Exod. 17:13 when Joshua defeats Amalek. **8:28** *As it is to this day.* Ai will remain in ruins as it happened to Jericho. **8:29** Compare Deut. 21:22–23; the body should be removed before sunset. *Heap of stones.* Similarly in Josh. 10:26–27. Compare 1 Sam. 31:10. **8:30–35** Deuteronomistic language and theology are evident in the theological significance of the covenant, reading of the Torah, and connection with Moses. **8:31–32** *The law of Moses.* A recurrent expression in the DH (Josh. 23:6; 1 Kgs. 2:3; 2 Kgs. 14:6; 23:25) and postexilic texts (2 Chr. 23:18; 30:16; Ezra 3:2; 7:6; Neh. 8:1; Dan. 9:11, 13; Tob. 1:8; 7:13; Bar. 2:2; Sus. 3, 62; 1 Esd. 8:3; 9:39). See **"The Deuteronomistic History," p. 337. 8:35** Compare Exod. 24:7.

9:1 *Now when.* An expression introducing a new stage in the conquest of the promised land. *The lowland.* The Shephelah was a lowland from the perspective of the hill country of Judah. Its hills range from three hundred to one thousand feet high, less than half the height of the Judean highlands. *Coast of the Great Sea.* The coast of the Mediterranean Sea.

9:3 *Gibeon.* A city situated on a hill five and a half miles northwest of Jerusalem in a strategic location on the road connecting Jerusalem with the Mediterranean. It is identified with modern-day al-Jib.

9:6 *We have come from a far country.* Exodus 23:32–33 and Deut. 7:1–6 required that the nations of the land promised to Israel be "utterly destroyed." Deut. 20:10 mandates establishing peaceful

come from a far country, so now make a treaty with us." [7]But the Israelites said to the Hivites, "Perhaps you live among us; then how can we make a treaty with you?" [8]They said to Joshua, "We are your servants." And Joshua said to them, "Who are you? And where do you come from?" [9]They said to him, "Your servants have come from a very far country because of the name of the LORD your God, for we have heard a report of him, of all that he did in Egypt [10]and of all that he did to the two kings of the Amorites who were beyond the Jordan, King Sihon of Heshbon and King Og of Bashan who lived in Ashtaroth. [11]So our elders and all the inhabitants of our country said to us, 'Take provisions in your hand for the journey; go to meet them, and say to them, "We are your servants; come now, make a treaty with us."' [12]Here is our bread; it was still warm when we took it from our houses as our food for the journey, on the day we set out to come to you, but now, see, it is dry and moldy; [13]these wineskins were new when we filled them, and see, they are burst, and these garments and sandals of ours are worn out from the very long journey." [14]So the leaders[r] partook of their provisions and did not ask direction from the LORD. [15]And Joshua made peace with them, guaranteeing their lives by a treaty, and the leaders of the congregation swore an oath to them.

16 But when three days had passed after they had made a treaty with them, they heard that they were their neighbors and were living among them. [17]So the Israelites set out and reached their cities on the third day. Now their cities were Gibeon, Chephirah, Beeroth, and Kiriath-jearim. [18]But the Israelites did not attack them because the leaders of the congregation had sworn to them by the LORD, the God of Israel. Then all the congregation murmured against the leaders. [19]But all the leaders said to all the congregation, "We have sworn to them by the LORD, the God of Israel, and now we must not touch them. [20]This is what we will do to them: we will let them live, so that wrath may not come upon us, because of the oath that we swore to them." [21]The leaders said to them, "Let them live." So they became woodcutters and drawers of water for all the congregation, as the leaders had decided concerning them.

22 Joshua summoned them and said to them, "Why did you deceive us, saying, 'We are very far from you,' while in fact you are living among us? [23]Now, therefore, you are cursed, and some of you shall always be slaves, woodcutters and drawers of water for the house of my God." [24]They answered Joshua, "Because it was told to your servants for a certainty that the LORD your God had commanded his servant Moses to give you all the land and to destroy all the inhabitants of the land before you, so we were in great fear for our lives because of you and did this thing. [25]And now we are in your hand: do as it seems good and right in your sight to do to us." [26]This is what he did for them: he saved them from the Israelites, and they did not kill them. [27]But on that day Joshua made them woodcutters and drawers of water for the congregation and for the altar of the LORD, to continue to this day, in the place that he should choose.

r 9.14 Gk: Heb *men*

relationships with faraway nations. The Gibeonites were able to avoid extermination by making Joshua believe that they were coming from afar.

9:7 The Hivites were not exterminated but made peace with Israel (cf. Exod. 23:23, 28; 34:11; Deut. 7:1; 20:17) where they were supposed to fall under the haram (see note on Josh. 2:10).

9:10 *Heshbon.* A city situated in Transjordan (the area east of the Jordan River), seven and a half miles from modern-day Madaba (Josh. 2:9; Deut. 1:4; 2:34). *Bashan* refers to the northern Transjordanian region, from Gilead in the south to Mount Hermon in the north. *Ashtaroth* is identified with modern-day Tell Ashtara, about twenty-two miles east of the Lake of Gennesaret (Deut. 1:4; Josh. 12:4; 13:12). It was another strategic enclave situated on the "King's Highway" (Num. 20:17; 21:22) that connected Damascus with Elath and Midian.

9:14 *Did not ask direction from the LORD.* Numbers 27:21 established the way to do that through the Urim and Thummim.

9:17 Compare Josh. 15:9, 60; 18:14-15, 24-28.

9:23 Compare 2 Sam. 21:2-14; 1 Kgs. 9:20.

10 When King Adoni-zedek of Jerusalem heard how Joshua had taken Ai and had utterly destroyed it, doing to Ai and its king as he had done to Jericho and its king, and how the inhabitants of Gibeon had made peace with Israel and were among them, ²he⁵ became greatly frightened, because Gibeon was a large city, like one of the royal cities, and was larger than Ai, and all its men were warriors. ³So King Adoni-zedek of Jerusalem sent a message to King Hoham of Hebron, to King Piram of Jarmuth, to King Japhia of Lachish, and to King Debir of Eglon, saying, ⁴"Come up and help me, and let us attack Gibeon, for it has made peace with Joshua and with the Israelites." ⁵Then the five kings of the Amorites— the king of Jerusalem, the king of Hebron, the king of Jarmuth, the king of Lachish, and the king of Eglon—gathered their forces and went up with all their armies and camped against Gibeon and made war against it.

6 And the Gibeonites sent to Joshua at the camp in Gilgal, saying, "Do not abandon your servants; come up to us quickly and save us and help us, for all the kings of the Amorites who live in the hill country are gathered against us." ⁷So Joshua went up from Gilgal, he and all the fighting force with him, all the mighty warriors. ⁸The Lord said to Joshua, "Do not fear them, for I have handed them over to you; not one of them shall stand before you." ⁹So Joshua came upon them suddenly, having marched up all night from Gilgal. ¹⁰And the Lord threw them into a panic before Israel, who inflicted a crushing blow on them at Gibeon, chased them by the way of the ascent of Beth-horon, and struck them down as far as Azekah and Makkedah. ¹¹As they fled before Israel, while they were going down the slope of Beth-horon, the Lord threw down huge stones from heaven on them as far as Azekah, and they died; there were more who died because of the hailstones than the Israelites killed with the sword.

12 On the day when the Lord gave the Amorites over to the Israelites, Joshua spoke to the Lord, and he said in the sight of Israel,

"Sun, stand still at Gibeon,
    and Moon, in the valley of Aijalon."
¹³ And the sun stood still, and the moon
    stopped
    until the nation took vengeance on
        their enemies.

Is this not written in the Book of Jashar? The sun stopped in midheaven and did not hurry to set for about a whole day. ¹⁴There has been no day like it before or since, when the Lord heeded a human voice, for the Lord fought for Israel.

15 Then Joshua returned, and all Israel with him, to the camp at Gilgal.

16 Meanwhile, these five kings fled and hid themselves in the cave at Makkedah. ¹⁷And it was told Joshua, "The five kings have been found, hidden in the cave at Makkedah." ¹⁸Joshua said, "Roll large stones against the mouth of the cave, and set men by it to guard them, ¹⁹but do not stay there yourselves; pursue your enemies and attack them from the rear. Do not let them enter their towns, for the Lord your God has given them into your hand." ²⁰When Joshua and the Israelites had finished inflicting a very great blow on them, until they were wiped out, and when the survivors had entered into the fortified towns, ²¹all the people returned safe to Joshua in the camp at Makkedah; no one dared to speakᵗ against any of the Israelites.

---

s 10.2 Heb ms Syr ms Vg: MT *they* | *t* 10.21 Heb *moved his tongue*

Josh. 10 This chapter describes the defeat of the southern coalition that opposed Joshua and Israel. **10:1** *Jerusalem.* The first mention of Jerusalem in the Bible. It means "the god Salem is its founder." It was mentioned already in Egyptian texts from the nineteenth century BCE and conquered by David (2 Sam. 5:7) when it was still occupied by the Jebusites. **10:2** *Greatly frightened.* The peace with Gibeon opened the Ayalon Valley road to Joshua's army. **10:3** *Hebron* is located twenty miles south of Jerusalem, a significant place in the patriarchal narratives (Gen. 13:18; 23:2; 35:27) and David's story (2 Sam. 2:3, 11; 3:2–5). *Jarmuth.* A city identified as Khirbet el-Yarmûk (= Tel Yarmut), showing occupation as early as the Early Bronze Age (2650–2350 BCE). It is located sixteen miles southwest of Jerusalem. *Lachish.* A fortified city in the Shephelah Tell ed-Duweir (= Tel Lachish). It was conquered in 701 BCE during Sennacherib's campaign (2 Kgs. 18:13–17; 19:8; 2 Chr. 32:9; Isa. 36:2–3; 37:8), fell again to Babylon (Jer. 34:7), and was resettled during the restoration period (Neh. 11:30). *Eglon.* A city on the Shephelah identified by some scholars as modern-day Tell 'Aitun. **10:13** *Book of Jashar.* Probably an older text, also mentioned in 2 Sam. 1:18. **10:14** Compare

22 Then Joshua said, "Open the mouth of the cave and bring those five kings out to me from the cave." [23]They did so and brought the five kings out to him from the cave, the king of Jerusalem, the king of Hebron, the king of Jarmuth, the king of Lachish, and the king of Eglon. [24]When they brought the kings out to Joshua, Joshua summoned all the Israelites and said to the chiefs of the warriors who had gone with him, "Come near, put your feet on the necks of these kings." Then they came near and put their feet on their necks. [25]And Joshua said to them, "Do not be afraid or dismayed; be strong and courageous, for thus the Lord will do to all the enemies against whom you fight." [26]Afterward Joshua struck them down and put them to death, and he hung them on five trees. And they hung on the trees until evening. [27]At sunset Joshua commanded, and they took them down from the trees and threw them into the cave where they had hidden themselves; they set large stones against the mouth of the cave that remain to this very day.

28 Joshua took Makkedah on that day and struck it and its king with the edge of the sword; he utterly destroyed every person in it; he left no one remaining. And he did to the king of Makkedah as he had done to the king of Jericho.

29 Then Joshua passed on from Makkedah, and all Israel with him, to Libnah and fought against Libnah. [30]The Lord gave it also and its king into the hand of Israel, and he struck it with the edge of the sword, and every person in it; he left no one remaining in it, and he did to its king as he had done to the king of Jericho.

31 Next Joshua passed on from Libnah, and all Israel with him, to Lachish and laid siege to it and assaulted it. [32]The Lord gave Lachish into the hand of Israel, and he took it on the second day and struck it with the edge of the sword, and every person in it, as he had done to Libnah.

33 Then King Horam of Gezer came up to help Lachish, and Joshua struck him and his people, leaving him no survivors.

34 From Lachish Joshua passed on with all Israel to Eglon, and they laid siege to it and assaulted it, [35]and they took it that day and struck it with the edge of the sword, and every person in it he utterly destroyed that day, as he had done to Lachish.

36 Then Joshua went up with all Israel from Eglon to Hebron; they assaulted it [37]and took it and struck it with the edge of the sword, and its king and its towns and every person in it; he left no one remaining, just as he had done to Eglon, and utterly destroyed it with every person in it.

38 Then Joshua, with all Israel, turned back to Debir and assaulted it, [39]and he took it with its king and all its towns; they struck them with the edge of the sword and utterly destroyed every person in it; he left no one remaining; just as he had done to Hebron and as he had done to Libnah and its king, so he did to Debir and its king.

40 So Joshua defeated the whole land, the hill country and the Negeb and the lowland and the slopes and all their kings; he left no one remaining but utterly destroyed all that breathed, as the Lord God of Israel had commanded. [41]And Joshua defeated them from Kadesh-barnea to Gaza and all the country of Goshen, as far as Gibeon. [42]Joshua took all these kings and their land at one time because the Lord God of Israel fought for Israel. [43]Then Joshua returned, and all Israel with him, to the camp at Gilgal.

10:42; 23:3–10; Exod. 14:4–25; Deut. 1:30. **10:28–39** These literary depictions of the destruction of the cities of Makkedah (v. 28), Libnah (vv. 29–30), Lachish (vv. 31–32), Gezer (v. 33), Eglon (vv. 34–35), Hebron (vv. 36–37), and Debir (v. 38) share a common pattern. Every city is "struck [with the edge of the sword]" (see note to 8:24) and utterly destroyed. Other passages seem to be more historically plausible (14:6–15; 15:13–17; Judg. 1:9–15). See **"The Divine Mandate to Exterminate the Canaanites," p. 313**. **10:33** *Gezer.* Identified as Tell Jezer (Tell el-Jazari), it was a strategic city later occupied by the Philistines (2 Sam. 5:22–25). **10:40–42** *The whole land.* The geographical description corresponds to the later kingdom of Judah. **10:40** *He left no one remaining but utterly destroyed all that breathed.* This is one of the "herem" passages (see note on Josh. 2:10) that is contradicted by other statements that state that certain groups, like the Jebusites (Josh. 15:63), remained in the land. Despite the fact that 2 Sam. 5:6–9 relates the capture of Jebus by David, there is no evidence that they were exterminated (cf. 2 Sam. 24:18–24, where David buys land from a Jebusite). See also Josh. 11:18–19.

Reading through Time: The Divine Mandate to Exterminate the Canaanites (Joshua 10:29–11:23)
In the Hebrew Bible, God promises to grant the land of Canaan to the chosen people, but the acquisition of that promised land includes God's command to exterminate every native inhabitant (Deut. 7:1–6; 20:16–18). This divine command—and narrator's commendation (Josh. 10:29–11:23)—for genocidal conquest has been a long-standing ethical concern for Bible readers. Since ancient times, critics have challenged that either the God of the Bible is not good or the Bible is untrue.

One early and enduring response has been to avoid these problematic passages. In the second century, Marcion saw the violent God of the Hebrew Bible as incompatible with the teachings of Jesus. Thus, his Bible only included selections of the New Testament and none of these genocidal passages. In a less extreme example of selectiveness, many religious communities today avoid reading the most unsettling parts of God's promise of land.

Another strategy has been to discount the historicity of these accounts by contextualizing the biblical genocide as part of an ancient hyperbolic genre or contrasting biblical texts with archaeological evidence (see **"Genocide," p. 305**). Long before modern archaeology, Christians sidestepped the historicity of these passages by spiritualizing their message: God's command is to completely eradicate sin from the believer's life, not to wipe out literal people.

An opposite approach has been the insistence that the genocidal conquest is historical but not atrocious. From the composition of Second Temple Jewish literature until today, interpreters have tranquilized their conscience by insisting that the native people's depravity merited genocide, that these Canaanites could have converted but declined, or that God was merciful in not destroying them earlier (see, e.g., how Wis. 12:3–11 and Jub. 10:27–34 build upon biblical texts like Gen. 15:16 and Lev. 18:27–28). Lacking an explanation, others assert that God's justice is beyond human comprehension.

Reading these texts has real consequences. Interpreters have justified horrific violence, including genocide and conquest, as God's will during the Christian crusades, the Reconquista, settler colonialism in the Americas, and more. Concerning Israel and Palestine, some Christian and Jewish religious Zionists continue to use these texts to interpret Jewish occupation as rightful resettlement or justifiable conquest in the face of resistant Palestinians. By contrast, interpreters sensitive to this historical weaponization insist that the most ethical readings must center the perspective of the Canaanites in the text and communities today who endure similar circumstances. When resisting the image of YHWH as conqueror, these interpreters sometimes point to other texts—like 1 Kgs. 21, where God condemns the violent theft of a native person's land.

Justin Michael Reed

11 When King Jabin of Hazor heard of this, he sent to King Jobab of Madon, to the king of Shimron, to the king of Achshaph, [2]and to the kings who were in the northern hill country, and in the Arabah south of Chinneroth, and in the lowland, and in Naphoth-dor on the west, [3]to the Canaanites in the east and the west, the Amorites, the Hittites, the Perizzites, and the Jebusites in the hill country, and the Hivites under Hermon in the land of Mizpah. [4]They came out, with all their troops, a great army, in number

Josh. 11 This chapter describes the military campaign against northern kings following a similar pattern to the previous campaign: a king "hears" about Joshua's victories (v. 1), a group of Canaanite kings forms a coalition to oppose Israel (vv. 1–5), the Lord promises Joshua that he will be victorious (v. 6), and the attack and the defeat of the enemy coalition (vv. 7–9). **11:1** *Hazor.* Located at Tell el-Qedah, it was a prominent fortified city and commercial enclave located nine miles north of the Sea of Galilee. It was reinforced by Solomon (1 Kgs. 9:15) and fell during the Assyrian conquest in 722 BCE (2 Kgs. 15:29). *Madon.* Probably a variant of Merom, which is mentioned in Egyptian texts from the sixteenth century BCE and also Assyrian texts from the eighth century BCE. *Achshaph.* Its precise location is debated. It was later assigned to the tribe of Asher (Josh. 19:25). *Arabah.* One of the main geographical regions of ancient Canaan south of the Dead Sea basin. *Chinneroth.* Kinneret: an important Canaanite city (now modern-day Tel Kinrot) that gives the name (in Hebrew) to the Sea of Galilee (Num. 34:11; Deut. 3:17). *Naphoth-dor.* "Dune of Dor," between Mount Carmel and Caesarea, refers to the coastal city of Dor. **11:3** *Hermon.* Associated with the root "haram" meaning "consecrate, sacred" (Josh. 11:17; 12:1, 5; 13:5, 11) and also called Baal-Hermon (Judg. 3:3; 1 Chr. 5:23). It marks the northern limit of Joshua's conquest. See **"The Divine Mandate to Exterminate the Canaanites," p. 313.**

like the sand on the seashore, with very many horses and chariots. ⁵All these kings joined their forces and came and camped together at the waters of Merom, to fight with Israel.

6 And the LORD said to Joshua, "Do not be afraid of them, for tomorrow at this time I will hand over all of them, slain, to Israel; you shall hamstring their horses and burn their chariots with fire." ⁷So Joshua came suddenly upon them with all his fighting force, by the waters of Merom, and fell upon them. ⁸And the LORD handed them over to Israel, who attacked them and chased them as far as Great Sidon and Misrephoth-maim and eastward as far as the valley of Mizpeh. They struck them down until they had left no one remaining. ⁹And Joshua did to them as the LORD had commanded him; he hamstrung their horses and burned their chariots with fire.

10 Joshua turned back at that time and took Hazor and struck its king down with the sword. Before that time Hazor was the head of all those kingdoms. ¹¹And they put to the sword all who were in it, utterly destroying them; there was no one left who breathed, and he burned Hazor with fire. ¹²And all the towns of those kings and all their kings, Joshua took and struck them with the edge of the sword, utterly destroying them, as Moses the servant of the LORD had commanded. ¹³But Israel burned none of the towns that stood on mounds except Hazor, which Joshua did burn. ¹⁴All the spoil of these towns and the livestock the Israelites plundered for themselves, but all the people they struck down with the edge of the sword, until they had destroyed them, and they did not leave any who breathed. ¹⁵As the LORD had commanded his servant Moses, so Moses commanded Joshua, and so Joshua did; he left nothing undone of all that the LORD had commanded Moses.

16 So Joshua took all that land: the hill country and all the Negeb and all the land of Goshen and the lowland and the Arabah and the hill country of Israel and its lowland, ¹⁷from Mount Halak, which rises toward Seir, as far as Baal-gad in the valley of Lebanon below Mount Hermon. He took all their kings, struck them down, and put them to death. ¹⁸Joshua made war a long time with all those kings. ¹⁹There was not a town that made peace with the Israelites except the Hivites, the inhabitants of Gibeon; all were taken in battle. ²⁰For it was the LORD's doing to harden their hearts so that they would come against Israel in battle, in order that they might be utterly destroyed and might receive no mercy but be exterminated, just as the LORD had commanded Moses.

21 At that time Joshua came and wiped out the Anakim from the hill country, from Hebron, from Debir, from Anab, and from all the hill country of Judah, and from all the hill country of Israel; Joshua utterly destroyed them with their towns. ²²None of the Anakim was left in the land of the Israelites; some remained only in Gaza, in Gath, and in Ashdod. ²³So Joshua took the whole land, according to all that the LORD had spoken to Moses, and Joshua gave it for an inheritance to Israel according to their tribal allotments. And the land had rest from war.

12 Now these are the kings of the land whom the Israelites defeated, whose land they occupied beyond the Jordan toward

---

11:8 *Great Sidon.* "Fishing town." The most important Phoenician city, twenty-five miles south of modern-day Beirut. It is often associated with Tyre (Jer. 47:4; Joel 3:4; Zech. 9:2), and it was inhabited since prehistoric times. Sidon was "the firstborn of Canaan" (Gen. 10:15). Sidon was also used to refer to Phoenicia in general (Judg. 10:12; 18:7; 1 Kgs. 5:6; 11:1, 5; 16:31; 2 Kgs. 23:13; Ezek. 32:30). **11:15** Shows the direct connection between obedience to God's command and the successful conquest and possession of the land. **11:16–23** Another haram passage that shows the complexities of the conquest, where there were groups that made peace with the Israelites (the Hivites; cf. 9:7) contrary to what is promised in Exod. 23:23, 28; 34:11; Deut. 7:1; 20:17. See **"Genocide," p. 305**. See also note on Josh. 2:10. **11:16–17** Compare similar summaries in 10:40–42; 12:7–8. **11:23** *And the land had rest from war.* The promise of the land as a place of rest and peace is fulfilled (cf. 14:15; 21:44; Judg. 3:11, 30; 5:31; 8:28).

Josh. 12 This chapter offers a summary of the conquest on both sides of the Jordan River and serves as a transition between the narrative of the first half of the book and the list of land allocations (Josh. 13–21). **12:1–6** The conquest of Transjordan, where Deuteronomistic language and theology are evident in the theological significance of the conquest, the unity of Israel, and the connection with Moses (cf. Num. 21:21–35; Deut. 2:26–3:11). For Transjordan, see note on Josh. 9:10. **12:1** *Wadi Arnon to Mount Hermon.* That is, Transjordan (cf. Deut. 3:8).

the east, from the Wadi Arnon to Mount Hermon, with all the Arabah eastward: ²King Sihon of the Amorites who lived at Heshbon and ruled from Aroer, which is on the edge of the Wadi Arnon, and from the middle of the valley as far as the Wadi Jabbok, the boundary of the Ammonites, that is, half of Gilead, ³and the Arabah to the Sea of Chinneroth eastward, and in the direction of Beth-jeshimoth, to the sea of the Arabah, the Dead Sea,ᵘ southward to the foot of the slopes of Pisgah; ⁴and King Ogᵛ of Bashan, one of the last of the Rephaim, who lived at Ashtaroth and at Edrei ⁵and ruled over Mount Hermon and Salecah and all Bashan to the boundary of the Geshurites and the Maacathites, and over half of Gilead to the boundary of King Sihon of Heshbon. ⁶Moses, the servant of the Lord, and the Israelites defeated them, and Moses the servant of the Lord gave their land for a possession to the Reubenites and the Gadites and the half-tribe of Manasseh.

7 The following are the kings of the land whom Joshua and the Israelites defeated on the west side of the Jordan, from Baal-gad in the valley of Lebanon to Mount Halak, which rises toward Seir (and Joshua gave their land to the tribes of Israel as a possession according to their allotments, ⁸in the hill country, in the lowland, in the Arabah, in the slopes, in the wilderness, and in the Negeb, the land of the Hittites, Amorites, Canaanites, Perizzites, Hivites, and Jebusites):

⁹ the king of Jericho .... one
  the king of Ai, which is next to
    Bethel..one

¹⁰ the king of Jerusalem ....one
   the king of Hebron.................................one
¹¹ the king of Jarmuth ....one
   the king of Lachish................................one
¹² the king of Eglon ....one
   the king of Gezer....................................one
¹³ the king of Debir ....one
   the king of Geder ....one
¹⁴ the king of Hormah ....one
   the king of Arad ....one
¹⁵ the king of Libnah ....one
   the king of Adullam ....one
¹⁶ the king of Makkedah............................one
   the king of Bethel ....one
¹⁷ the king of Tappuah ....one
   the king of Hepher ....one
¹⁸ the king of Aphek ....one
   the king of Lasharon ....one
¹⁹ the king of Madon ....one
   the king of Hazor ....one
²⁰ the king of Shimron-meron ....one
   the king of Achshaph.............................one
²¹ the king of Taanach ....one
   the king of Megiddo ....one
²² the king of Kedesh ....one
   the king of Jokneam in Carmel ....one
²³ the king of Dor in Naphath-dor........one
   the king of Goiim in Galileeʷ.............one
²⁴ the king of Tirzah ....one
thirty-one kings in all.

13 Now Joshua was old and advanced in years, and the Lord said to him, "You are old and advanced in years, and

u 12.3 Heb *Salt Sea*   v 12.4 Gk: Heb *the boundary of King Og*
w 12.23 Gk: Heb *Gilgal*

12:3 *Sea of Chinneroth.* Sea of Galilee. *Beth-jeshimoth.* City east of the Jordan River (Num. 33:49; Josh. 13:20; Ezek. 25:9). *Slopes of Pisgah.* Mount Nebo. Compare Deut. 3:27; 4:49; 34:1. **12:4** *Bashan.* Modern-day Golan Heights. *The last of the Rephaim.* Legendary people from ancient Canaan famous for their unusual height. Deuteronomy 3:11 describes one of their beds as being nine cubits long and four cubits wide (13½ feet × 6 feet; cf. Gen. 14:5; 15:20; Deut. 2:11, 20–21; 3:11; Josh. 15:13–14). **12:5** *Geshurites . . . Maacathites.* Peoples east of the Jordan River and the Sea of Galilee (Deut. 3:14). **12:7** *Allotments.* Compare 11:23. **12:7–8** The enumeration follows 11:16–17. **12:9–24** An independent source used by the DH. **12:13** *Geder.* "Wall of stones" or "a walled place." Localization uncertain ("Gader" in the LXX). **12:14** *Hormah . . . Arad.* Cities of the Negev mentioned in Num. 21:1–3 as conquered by Israel before entering Canaan. Hormah's precise location is unknown. It is mentioned also in Josh. 15:30 (belonging to Judah) and 19:4 (belonging to Simeon). Arad, "hard ground," has been identified with Tell 'Arad, six miles west of modern-day Arad. **12:16** *Bethel.* "House of god," absent in the LXX. Joshua 1–11 does not mention the conquest of Bethel and Judg. 1:22–26 attributes its conquest to the house of Joseph. **12:19–20** *Madon, Hazor, Shimron-meron,* and *Achshaph* are the kings who fought Joshua in the battle of the waters of Merom (Josh. 11).

Josh. 13–19 The second part of the book of Joshua narrates the division of the land among the Israelite tribes.

13:1 *Old and advanced in years.* An expression also used in Gen. 24:1; Josh. 23:1; 1 Sam. 17:12; and

very much of the land still remains to be possessed. ²This is the land that still remains: all the regions of the Philistines, and all those of the Geshurites ³(from the Shihor, which is near Egypt, northward to the boundary of Ekron, it is reckoned as Canaanite; there are five rulers of the Philistines, those of Gaza, Ashdod, Ashkelon, Gath, and Ekron), and those of the Avvim ⁴in the south; all the land of the Canaanites, and Mearah that belongs to the Sidonians, to Aphek, to the boundary of the Amorites, ⁵and the land of the Gebalites, and all Lebanon, toward the east, from Baal-gad below Mount Hermon to Lebo-hamath, ⁶all the inhabitants of the hill country from Lebanon to Misrephoth-maim, even all the Sidonians. I will myself drive them out from before the Israelites; only allot the land to Israel for an inheritance, as I have commanded you. ⁷Now, therefore, divide this land for an inheritance to the nine tribes and the half-tribe of Manasseh."

8 With the other half-tribe of Manasseh^x the Reubenites and the Gadites received their inheritance, which Moses gave them, beyond the Jordan eastward, as Moses the servant of the Lord gave them: ⁹from Aroer, which is on the edge of the Wadi Arnon, and the town that is in the middle of the valley, and all the tableland from^y Medeba as far as Dibon; ¹⁰and all the cities of King Sihon of the Amorites, who reigned in Heshbon, as far as the boundary of the Ammonites; ¹¹and Gilead, and the region of the Geshurites and Maacathites, and all Mount Hermon, and all Bashan to Salecah; ¹²all the kingdom of Og in Bashan, who reigned in Ashtaroth and in Edrei (he alone was left of the survivors of the Rephaim); these Moses had defeated and driven out. ¹³Yet the Israelites did not drive out the Geshurites or the Maacathites, but Geshur and Maacath live within Israel to this day.

14 To the tribe of Levi alone Moses gave no inheritance; the offerings by fire^z to the Lord God of Israel are their inheritance, as he said to them.

15 Moses gave an inheritance to the tribe of the Reubenites according to their families. ¹⁶Their territory was from Aroer, which

x 13.8 Cn Compare Gk: Heb *With it*   y 13.9 Compare Gk: Heb lacks *from*   z 13.14 Or *the gifts*

1 Kgs. 1:1 signaling physical decay. *Very much of the land still remains to be possessed.* A strong contrast between the image of a swift conquest and possession and historical reality. A parallel tradition of the people that the ancient Israelites could not conquer is also found in Judg. 3:3. See **"Conquest," p. 317**.

13:2 The *Philistines* appear in Canaan in the early twelfth century BCE by land (causing the fall of the Hittites, Ugarit, and Amurru) and by sea. They also try to settle in Egypt but are defeated by the Egyptian pharaoh Rameses III around 1178 BCE.

13:3 *Shihor.* Egyptian word meaning "waters of Horus" (cf. Isa. 23:3; Jer. 2:18; 1 Chr. 13:5). It has been identified with the Pelusian branch of the Nile (cf. 1 Chr. 13:5). *Five rulers of the Philistines.* The five cities are mentioned also in 1 Sam. 6:17. Other texts mention four (Jer. 25:20; Amos 1:7–8). *Gaza.* Located 2.5 miles from the Mediterranean, it was a strategic enclave for its control of trading routes. It had been under Egyptian control at least since the fifteenth century BCE until the Philistine invasion. It was later conquered by David (2 Sam. 8:1), becoming the southern border of the territory controlled by Solomon (1 Kgs. 4:24). *Ashdod.* Modern-day Tel Asdod, nine miles north of Ashkelon and about two and a half miles from the Mediterranean. It was the first place where the Philistines took the ark of the covenant after defeating the Israelites in the battle of Ebenezer (1 Sam. 5:1–7). *Ashkelon.* Identified as the contemporary Ashkelon in Israel, located twelve miles north of Gaza and thirty miles south of Tel Aviv. It appears prominently in the Samson saga (Judg. 14:10–19) and another place where the Philistines took the ark of the covenant (1 Sam. 6:17). *Gath.* Situated in the Shephelah, the Judean foothills, it was the closest Philistine city to the Judean territory (1 Sam. 17:52). It was the second place where the ark of the covenant was brought by the Philistines, which brought them pestilence as God's punishment (1 Sam. 5:9). It was David's refuge while fleeing from Saul (1 Sam. 21:10–15), and he later served its king (1 Sam. 27:1–12). *Ekron.* Identified as Tel Miqneh, twenty-two miles west of Jerusalem, Ekron was the largest fortified city found in the region. *The Avvim.* Only mentioned here and in Deut. 2:23. Identified as the Hivites in the LXX.

13:4 *All the land of the Canaanites* includes land from Arah to Aphek to the border of the Amorites.

Going Deeper: Conquest (Joshua 13)

At first sight, the book presents Joshua as the leader of a unified conquest in fulfillment of God's promise to Israel's ancestors (Josh. 10:40–42). The text, however, shows that the conquest was not completed, and several areas remained under Canaanite control (11:22; 13:1–5; 15:63; 16:10; 17:11–12), which fits with the picture of territories/populations not controlled by the Israelite tribes in the book of Judges. The attempts to harmonize the biblical narrative, taken at face value, with the archaeological record have led scholars to propose either the end of the fifteenth century BCE or the thirteenth century BCE as the date for the events narrated in Joshua. However, today's consensus among biblical scholars and archaeologists studying the emergence of ancient Israel rejects the conquest narrative as historically accurate, at the same time recognizing that the traditions about conflicts among the several groups that inhabited Canaan and Israel reflect a situation that extended for several centuries. We have also two alternative biblical traditions to the conquest narrative of the emergence of Israel. The book of Judges presents the origins of Israel as a long process of tribal conflicts instead of a unified conquest, and the book of Chronicles, which lists ancestors of Joshua (1 Chr. 7:25–27), presents Joshua as already established on the land instead of coming out of Egypt, crossing the Jordan, and leading the conquest of Canaan. The "conquest narrative," in its context of Josiah's reform and within the Deuteronomistic History, is better understood as a proclamation of the faithfulness and power of the God of Israel and the belief that if the people remained faithful to the Mosaic covenant, they would be able to enjoy the benefits of God's protection and blessing.

Alejandro F. Botta

is on the edge of the Wadi Arnon, and the town that is in the middle of the valley, and all the tableland by Medeba; [17]with Heshbon, and all its towns that are in the tableland; Dibon, and Bamoth-baal, and Beth-baal-meon, [18]and Jahaz, and Kedemoth, and Mephaath, [19]and Kiriathaim, and Sibmah, and Zereth-shahar on the hill of the valley, [20]and Beth-peor, and the slopes of Pisgah, and Beth-jeshimoth, [21]that is, all the towns of the tableland, and all the kingdom of King Sihon of the Amorites, who reigned in Heshbon, whom Moses defeated with the leaders of Midian, Evi and Rekem and Zur and Hur and Reba, as princes of Sihon, who lived in the land. [22]Along with the rest of those they put to death, the Israelites also put to the sword Balaam son of Beor, who practiced divination. [23]And the border of the Reubenites was the Jordan and its banks. This was the inheritance of the Reubenites according to their families, with their towns and villages.

24 Moses gave an inheritance also to the tribe of the Gadites, according to their families. [25]Their territory was Jazer, and all the towns of Gilead, and half the land of the Ammonites, to Aroer, which is near Rabbah, [26]and from Heshbon to Ramath-mizpeh and Betonim, and from Mahanaim to the territory of Debir,[a] [27]and in the valley Beth-haram, Beth-nimrah, Succoth, and Zaphon, the rest of the kingdom of King Sihon of Heshbon, the Jordan and its banks, as far as the lower end of the Sea of Chinnereth, eastward beyond the Jordan. [28]This is the inheritance of the Gadites according to their families, with their towns and villages.

29 Moses gave an inheritance to the half-tribe of Manasseh; it was allotted to the half-tribe of the Manassites according to their families. [30]Their territory extended from Mahanaim, through all Bashan,

a 13.26 Gk Syr Vg: Heb Lidebir

13:15–23 Reuben ("see, a son") was the first son of Jacob and Leah (Gen. 29:32). Its territory was located east of the Jordan River, and its borders were Gad to the north, the Ammonites to the east, the Moabites to the south, and the Dead Sea to the west. The census in Num. 1:20–21 lists 46,500 men twenty and older. Compare Moses's blessing in Deut. 33:6.

13:21b–22 Compare Num. 31:8.

13:24–28 Gad ("fortune") was Jacob's seventh son and the second with Leah's maiden, Zilpah (Gen. 30:11). Its territory was located east of the Jordan, limiting to the east with the Ammonites, to the north with Manasseh, to the south with Reuben, and to the west with the Jordan River. The roster in 1:24–25 lists 45,650 men able to go to war. Compare Moses's blessing in Deut. 33:20.

13:29–31 Manasseh ("God has made me forget all my hardship and all my father's house") was born in Egypt as the first son of Joseph and the Egyptian Asenath (Gen. 41:51–52). Manasseh's

the whole kingdom of King Og of Bashan, and all the settlements of Jair, which are in Bashan, sixty towns, [31]and half of Gilead, and Ashtaroth, and Edrei, the towns of the kingdom of Og in Bashan; these were allotted to the people of Machir son of Manasseh according to their families, for half the Machirites.

32 These are the inheritances that Moses distributed in the plains of Moab, beyond the Jordan east of Jericho. [33]But to the tribe of Levi Moses gave no inheritance; the LORD God of Israel is their inheritance, as he said to them.

14 These are the inheritances that the Israelites received in the land of Canaan, which the priest Eleazar, and Joshua son of Nun, and the heads of the families of the tribes of the Israelites distributed to them. [2]Their inheritance was by lot, as the LORD had commanded Moses for the nine and one-half tribes. [3]For Moses had given an inheritance to the two and one-half tribes beyond the Jordan, but to the Levites he gave no inheritance among them. [4]For the people of Joseph were two tribes, Manasseh and Ephraim, and no portion was given to the Levites in the land but only towns to live in, with their pasturelands for their flocks and herds. [5]The Israelites did as the LORD had commanded Moses; they allotted the land.

6 Then the people of Judah came to Joshua at Gilgal, and Caleb son of Jephunneh the Kenizzite said to him, "You know what the LORD said to Moses the man of God in Kadesh-barnea concerning you and me. [7]I was forty years old when Moses the servant of the LORD sent me from Kadesh-barnea to spy out the land, and I brought him an honest report. [8]But my companions who went up with me made the heart of the people melt, yet I wholeheartedly followed the LORD my God. [9]And Moses swore on that day, saying, 'Surely the land on which your foot has trodden shall be an inheritance for you and your children forever, because you have wholeheartedly followed the LORD my God.' [10]And now, as you see, the LORD has kept me alive, as he said, these forty-five years since the time that the LORD spoke this word to Moses, while Israel was journeying through the wilderness, and here I am today, eighty-five years old. [11]I am still as strong today as I was on the day that Moses sent me; my strength now is as my strength was then, for war and for going and coming.

territory occupied sections on both sides of the Jordan River (see Josh. 17:1–13 for the western half of the tribe). The census in Num. 1:34–35 lists 32,200 men over twenty and able to go to battle. Both sons of Joseph, Ephraim and Manasseh, were adopted by Jacob (Gen. 48:13–14). Compare Moses's blessing of Ephraim and Manasseh in Deut. 33:17.

14:1–2 The presence of the priest Eleazar, one of Aaron's four children (Exod. 6:25; Num. 3:2; 26:60) and chief of the Levites (Num. 3:32), side by side with Joshua possibly reflects a Priestly redaction (see also Josh. 19:51 and 21:1–2). *The land of Canaan.* A typical Priestly expression (see Gen. 11:31; 12:5; 13:12; 16:3) used also in the DH (Deut. 32:49; Josh. 5:12; 14:1; 21:2, etc.). For Priestly, see **"The Bible and Methods," p. 2148.** For DH, see **"The Deuteronomistic History," p. 337.** *Heads of the families of the tribes.* Their names and tribes are found in Num. 34:16–29. **14:2** Fulfilling Num. 33:54; 34:13. The land is distributed among the nine and a half tribes that had not received their portion yet. Reuben, Gad, and Manasseh had received their allotments in Transjordan, and the tribe of Levi did not receive a territory but cities and pasturelands (cf. Josh. 21). *Their inheritance was by lot.* Compare Num. 26:55–56; 33:54; 34:13. The use of lots was understood as an impartial method and a revelation of God's will. They were used to identify a guilty party (Josh. 7:14; 1 Sam. 14:42; Jonah 1:7) or to select sacrifices (Lev. 16:7–10). **14:5** *As the LORD had commanded Moses.* A typical Priestly formula (see note on 14:1–2) used extensively in Exodus (7:6, 10, 20; 12:28, 50; 16:34; 34:4; 39:1, 5, 7, 21, 26, 29, 31, 43; 40:19, 21, 23, 25, 27, 29, 32) and Leviticus (8:4, 9, 13, 17, 21, 29; 9:7, 10; 10:15; 16:34; 24:23). **14:6–15** Post-DH addition. For DH, see **"The Deuteronomistic History," p. 337.** Caleb belongs to the tribe of Judah (Num. 13:6; 34:19) and is rewarded for his faithfulness (Num. 13–14; Deut. 1:22–28) fulfilling Moses's promise (Deut. 1:36). **14:6b** *Moses the man of God.* A title attributed to Moses also in Deut. 33:1; 1 Chr. 23:14; 2 Chr. 30:16; Ps. 90; and also used for Samuel, David, and anonymous prophets (1 Sam. 2:27). Later it became an honorific title, as in the cases of David and Moses. **14:11** *For war and for going and coming.* LXX "for going

¹²So now give me this hill country of which the LORD spoke on that day, for you heard on that day how the Anakim were there, with great fortified cities; it may be that the LORD will be with me, and I will drive them out, as the LORD said."

13 Then Joshua blessed him and gave Hebron to Caleb son of Jephunneh for an inheritance. ¹⁴So Hebron became the inheritance of Caleb son of Jephunneh the Kenizzite to this day, because he wholeheartedly followed the LORD, the God of Israel. ¹⁵Now the name of Hebron formerly was Kiriath-arba; Arba was*b* the greatest man among the Anakim. And the land had rest from war.

15 The lot for the tribe of the people of Judah according to their families reached southward to the boundary of Edom, to the wilderness of Zin at the farthest south. ²And their south boundary ran from the end of the Dead Sea,*c* from the bay that faces southward; ³it goes out southward of the ascent of Akrabbim, passes along to Zin, and goes up south of Kadesh-barnea, along by Hezron, up to Addar, makes a turn to Karka, ⁴passes

along to Azmon, goes out by the Wadi of Egypt, and comes to its end at the sea. This shall be your south boundary. ⁵And the east boundary is the Dead Sea,*d* to the mouth of the Jordan. And the boundary on the north side runs from the bay of the sea at the mouth of the Jordan; ⁶and the boundary goes up to Beth-hoglah and passes along north of Beth-arabah; and the boundary goes up to the Stone of Bohan, Reuben's son; ⁷and the boundary goes up to Debir from the Valley of Achor, and so northward, turning toward Gilgal, which is opposite the ascent of Adummim, which is on the south side of the valley; and the boundary passes along to the waters of En-shemesh, and ends at En-rogel; ⁸then the boundary goes up by the valley of the son of Hinnom at the southern slope of the Jebusites (that is, Jerusalem); and the boundary goes up to the top of the mountain that lies over against the valley of Hinnom, on the west, at the northern end of the valley of Rephaim; ⁹then the boundary extends from the top of the mountain to

b 14.15 Heb lacks *Arba was*   *c* 15.2 Heb *Salt Sea*   *d* 15.5 Heb *Salt Sea*

forth and returning from the battle." **14:15** *Hebron formerly was Kiriath-arba.* Compare Gen. 23:2; 35:27.

15:1–12 *Judah,* "praise" (Gen. 29:35), was the fourth son of Jacob with Leah (Gen. 35:23). Its territory's borders were Benjamin to the north, Dan to the northwest, and the Dead Sea to the east. It included the hill country, the fertile coastal region of the Shephelah, the Negev, and the arid wilderness. The census in Num. 1:26 counts 74,600 men able to go to war. Compare Moses's blessing in Deut. 33:7. **15:1** *Lot.* Heb. "haggorol." Also used in 16:1 and 17:1 and is understood by the LXX as "hagevul," meaning "border, territory" (cf. Josh. 18:16). *Wilderness of Zin.* Compare Num. 13:21 and 20:1. **15:2** *The bay that faces southward.* Literally "the turning tongue," denoting the shape of the bay or peninsula. *The Dead Sea.* Literally "Sea of salt." **15:2–4** Southern border (cf. Num. 34:3–5). **15:3** *The ascent of Akrabbim.* Literally "the Scorpion's Pass," identified as Naqb es-Safa, about twenty-one miles southwest of the Dead Sea. *Kadesh-barnea.* Identified as tel-Ain el-Qudeirat. *Hezron.* Meaning "enclosure," identified as modern-day Ain Qedeis. *Karka.* Meaning "floor," possibly Ain el Qoseimeh. **15:4** *Wadi of Egypt.* Likely Wadi el-Arish, a seasonal stream flowing into the Mediterranean Sea south of Gaza (Josh. 15:47; 1 Kgs. 8:65; Isa. 27:12; 2 Chr. 7:8). *The sea.* The Mediterranean Sea, usually called the Great Sea (Num. 34:6; Josh. 1:4; 9:1; Ezek. 47:10, 15, 19–20; 48:28). **15:6** *Beth-arabah.* Modern-day Ain el-Gharabeh, three miles southeast of Jericho. *Stone of Bohan.* Meaning "thumb," probably a topographical feature whose exact location is unknown. It served as the border between Judah and Benjamin (cf. Josh. 18:17). **15:7** *Achor.* A valley northwest of the Dead Sea (Josh. 7:14–26; Isa. 65:10; Hos. 2:15). *Debir.* Not the southern hill city near Hebron mentioned in Josh. 10:38–39; 11:21; 12:13; and 15:49. Perhaps related to the modern-day Wadi ed Dabr. *Gilgal.* A city in the hill country of Ephraim, not to be confused with the Gilgal mentioned in 4:19–20; 5:9–10. *Ascent of Adummim.* Modern-day Ma'ale Adumim, six miles southwest of Jericho. *Waters of En-shemesh.* Meaning "spring of the sun." Identified as modern-day Ain el-Hod, two miles east of Jerusalem. *En-rogel.* "Spring of the fuller (or the explorer)" in modern-day Bir Ayyub; "Job's well" in Wadi Qidron, one of Jerusalem's sources of water, southeast of the city in the confluence of the valleys of Qidron and Ben Hinnom (18:16; 2 Sam. 17:17; 1 Kgs. 1:9).

the spring of the Waters of Nephtoah, and from there to the towns of Mount Ephron; then the boundary bends around to Baalah (that is, Kiriath-jearim); [10]and the boundary circles west of Baalah to Mount Seir, passes along to the northern slope of Mount Jearim (that is, Chesalon), and goes down to Beth-shemesh, and passes along by Timnah; [11]the boundary goes out to the slope of the hill north of Ekron, then the boundary bends around to Shikkeron, and passes along to Mount Baalah, and goes out to Jabneel; then the boundary comes to an end at the sea. [12]And the west boundary is the Mediterranean with its coast. This is the boundary surrounding the people of Judah according to their families.

13 But to Caleb son of Jephunneh, Joshua[e] gave a portion among the people of Judah according to the commandment of the LORD to Joshua, Kiriath-arba, that is, Hebron (Arba was the father of Anak). [14]And Caleb drove out from there the three sons of Anak: Sheshai, Ahiman, and Talmai, the descendants of Anak. [15]From there he went up against the inhabitants of Debir; now the name of Debir formerly was Kiriath-sepher. [16]And Caleb said, "Whoever attacks Kiriath-sepher and takes it, to him I will give my daughter Achsah as wife." [17]Othniel son of Kenaz, the brother of Caleb, took it, and he gave him his daughter Achsah as wife. [18]When she came to him, she urged him to ask her father for a field. As she dismounted from her donkey, Caleb said to her, "What do you wish?" [19]She said to him, "Give me a present; since you have set me in the land of the Negeb, give me springs of water as well." So Caleb gave her the upper springs and the lower springs.

20 This is the inheritance of the tribe of the people of Judah according to their families. [21]The towns belonging to the tribe of the people of Judah in the extreme south, toward the boundary of Edom, were Kabzeel, Eder, Jagur, [22]Kinah, Dimonah, Adadah, [23]Kedesh, Hazor, Ithnan, [24]Ziph, Telem, Bealoth, [25]Hazor-hadattah, Kerioth-hezron (that is, Hazor), [26]Amam, Shema, Moladah, [27]Hazar-gaddah, Heshmon, Beth-pelet, [28]Hazar-shual, Beersheba, Biziothiah, [29]Baalah, Iim, Ezem, [30]Eltolad, Chesil, Hormah, [31]Ziklag, Madmannah, Sansannah, [32]Lebaoth, Shilhim, Ain, and Rimmon: in all, twenty-nine towns, with their villages.

33 And in the lowland, Eshtaol, Zorah, Ashnah, [34]Zanoah, En-gannim, Tappuah, Enam, [35]Jarmuth, Adullam, Socoh, Azekah, [36]Shaaraim, Adithaim, Gederah, Gederothaim: fourteen towns with their villages.

37 Zenan, Hadashah, Migdal-gad, [38]Dilan, Mizpeh, Jokthe-el, [39]Lachish, Bozkath, Eglon, [40]Cabbon, Lahmam, Chitlish, [41]Gederoth, Beth-dagon, Naamah, and Makkedah: sixteen towns with their villages.

42 Libnah, Ether, Ashan, [43]Iphtah, Ashnah, Nezib, [44]Keilah, Achzib, and Mareshah: nine towns with their villages.

45 Ekron, with its towns and its villages; [46]from Ekron to the sea, all that were near Ashdod, with their villages.

47 Ashdod, its towns and its villages; Gaza, its towns and its villages; to the Wadi of Egypt, and the Great Sea with its coast.

48 And in the hill country, Shamir, Jattir, Socoh, [49]Dannah, Kiriath-sannah (that is,

e 15.13 Heb *he*

15:13–19 Post-DH addition. See **"The Deuteronomistic History," p. 337**.

15:23 *Kedesh.* Here, a city on the southern border of Judah; called Kishion in 21:28. Different from the fortified city of Naphtali in Josh. 19:37 assigned as a city of refuge in Josh. 20:7.

15:28 *Hazar-shual.* Listed under Judah here and in Neh. 11:27; under Simeon in Josh. 19:3 and 1 Chr. 4:28. Its location is unknown. *Beer-sheba.* "Well of seven" or "well of the oath," also listed under Simeon in 19:2. Located near the modern-day city of Be'er-Sheva, it is a prominent city in the patriarchal narratives and in the patriarchs' relationship with God (Gen. 21:14; 21:30–33; 26:23–25). "From Dan to Beer-sheba" is a common expression to denote the whole land of Israel (Judg. 20:1; 1 Sam. 3:20; 2 Sam. 3:10).

15:21–63 Twelve administrative districts in the following order, listed earlier in the chapter: south (vv. 2–4); east (v. 5a); north (vv. 5b–11); west (v. 12). (i) southern Negev (vv. 21b–32a); (ii) cities and villages of the foothills (vv. 33b–36a); (iii) Lachish and its surroundings (vv. 37–41a); (iv) Maresha and its surroundings (vv. 42–44a); (v) Ekron district (v. 45); (vi) the hill-country district (vv. 48b–51a); (vii) Hebron district (vv. 52–54a); (viii) (vv. 55–57a); (ix) Beth-Zur district (vv. 58–59a); (x) according to the LXX, Bethlelem-Ephrathah district (v. 59); (xi) Jerusalem district (v. 60a); (xii) Judah

Debir), ⁵⁰Anab, Eshtemoh, Anim, ⁵¹Goshen, Holon, and Giloh: eleven towns with their villages.

52 Arab, Dumah, Eshan, ⁵³Janim, Beth-tappuah, Aphekah, ⁵⁴Humtah, Kiriath-arba (that is, Hebron), and Zior: nine towns with their villages.

55 Maon, Carmel, Ziph, Juttah, ⁵⁶Jezreel, Jokdeam, Zanoah, ⁵⁷Kain, Gibeah, and Timnah: ten towns with their villages.

58 Halhul, Beth-zur, Gedor, ⁵⁹Maarath, Beth-anoth, and Eltekon: six towns with their villages.

60 Kiriath-baal (that is, Kiriath-jearim) and Rabbah: two towns with their villages.

61 In the wilderness, Beth-arabah, Middin, Secacah, ⁶²Nibshan, the City of Salt, and En-gedi: six towns with their villages.

63 But the people of Judah could not drive out the Jebusites, the inhabitants of Jerusalem, so the Jebusites live with the people of Judah in Jerusalem to this day.

16 The allotment of the Josephites went from the Jordan by Jericho, east of the waters of Jericho, into the wilderness, going up from Jericho into the hill country to Bethel; ²then going from Bethel to Luz, it passes along to Ataroth, the territory of the Archites; ³then it goes down westward to the territory of the Japhletites, as far as the territory of Lower Beth-horon, then to Gezer, and it ends at the sea.

4 The Josephites—Manasseh and Ephraim—received their inheritance.

5 The territory of the Ephraimites by their families was as follows: the boundary of their inheritance on the east was Ataroth-addar as far as Upper Beth-horon, ⁶and the boundary goes from there to the sea; on the north is Michmethath; then on the east the boundary makes a turn toward Taanath-shiloh and passes along beyond it on the east to Janoah, ⁷then it goes down from Janoah to Ataroth and to Naarah and touches Jericho, ending at the Jordan. ⁸From Tappuah the boundary goes westward to the Wadi Kanah and ends at the sea. Such is the inheritance of the tribe of the Ephraimites by their families, ⁹together with the towns that were set apart for the Ephraimites within the inheritance of the Manassites, all those towns with their villages. ¹⁰They did not, however, drive out the Canaanites who lived in Gezer, so the Canaanites have lived within Ephraim to this day but have been made to do forced labor.

wilderness district (vv. 61b–62a). **15:31** *Sansannah.* Khir-bet esh-Shamsaniyat, three miles northwest of Beer-sheba. **15:63** *Jebusites.* Mentioned often in the list of Canaanites to be conquered (Exod. 3:8, 17; 23:23; 33:2; 34:11; Deut. 20:17; Josh. 9:1; 11:3; 12:8; Judg. 3:5; Neh. 9:8). Their presence here is in harmony with Judg. 1:21 but in tension with Josh. 15:8; 18:16, 28, where they belong to the territory of Benjamin. See 2 Sam. 5:6–9.
   16:1–10 *Ephraim*, "to be fruitful," was the second son of Joseph and the Egyptian Asenath (Gen. 41:52). Its borders were Manasseh to the north, Dan to the west and southwest, Benjamin to the south, and Manasseh to the east. The census of Ephraim in Num. 2:24 lists 108,100. Joshua belonged to this tribe (Num. 13:8). **16:1** *The allotment* to the "sons of Joseph" (*Josephites*). Five ways of referring to the distribution of the promised land are found in Joshua: "the lot" in the case of the tribe of Judah (15:1); "the allotment . . . went" in the cases of the sons of Joseph (16:1); "the lot came out" in the cases of Simeon (19:1), Issachar (19:17), Asher (19:24), Naphtali (19:32), and Dan (19:40); and "the lot . . . came up" in the case of the tribe of Benjamin (18:11); and "the third lot came up" in the case of Zebulun (19:10). *Waters of Jericho.* Ain el-Sultan; Elisha's Spring (see 2 Kgs. 2:19–22). **16:2** *From Bethel to Luz.* The text distinguishes between Bethel and Luz (in tension with Gen. 28:19; 35:6; Josh. 18:13; Judg. 1:23). The text only highlights the southern border of the Josephites, which is marked by Jericho, Bethel, Luz, Ataroth, Lower Beth-horon, Gezer, and the Mediterranean Sea. The borders are similar to the northern border of Benjamin (Josh. 18:12–14). **16:5** The southern border of Ephraim meets with the northern border of Judah. **16:9** The allocation of cities belonging to Ephraim within the tribe of Manasseh makes drawing precise borders difficult. **16:10** *Gezer.* Compare Josh. 10:33; 12:12; Judg. 1:29. Identified as Tell el-Jezer near Ramleh, it is another example of the partial possession of the land. Second Samuel 5:25 suggests that it was occupied by the Philistines. Gezer was later conquered by the Egyptians, who gave it to Solomon as a wedding present, according to 1 Kgs. 9:16. It was destroyed by the Assyrians in 734/733 BCE and again by the Neo-Babylonian army in 587/586 BCE. *Forced labor.* Compare Gen. 49:15; 1 Kgs. 9:21.

17 Then allotment was made to the tribe of Manasseh, for he was the firstborn of Joseph. To Machir the firstborn of Manasseh, the father of Gilead, were allotted Gilead and Bashan, because he was a warrior. [2]And allotments were made to the rest of the tribe of Manasseh by their families, Abiezer, Helek, Asriel, Shechem, Hepher, and Shemida; these were the male descendants of Manasseh son of Joseph by their families.

3 Now Zelophehad son of Hepher son of Gilead son of Machir son of Manasseh had no sons but only daughters, and these are the names of his daughters: Mahlah, Noah, Hoglah, Milcah, and Tirzah. [4]They came before the priest Eleazar and Joshua son of Nun and the leaders and said, "The LORD commanded Moses to give us an inheritance along with our male kin." So according to the commandment of the LORD he gave them an inheritance among the kinsmen of their father. [5]Thus there fell to Manasseh ten portions, besides the land of Gilead and Bashan, which is on the other side of the Jordan, [6]because the daughters of Manasseh received an inheritance along with his sons. The land of Gilead was allotted to the rest of the Manassites.

7 The territory of Manasseh reached from Asher to Michmethath, which is east of Shechem; then the boundary goes along southward to the inhabitants of En-tappuah. [8]The land of Tappuah belonged to Manasseh, but the town of Tappuah on the boundary of Manasseh belonged to the Ephraimites. [9]Then the boundary went down to the Wadi Kanah. The towns here, to the south of the wadi, among the towns of Manasseh, belong to Ephraim. Then the boundary of Manasseh goes along the north side of the wadi and ends at the sea. [10]The land to the south is Ephraim's and that to the north is Manasseh's, with the sea forming its boundary; on the north Asher is reached and on the east Issachar. [11]Within Issachar and Asher, Manasseh had Beth-shean and its villages, Ibleam and its villages, the inhabitants of Dor and its villages, the inhabitants of En-dor and its villages, the inhabitants of Taanach and its villages, and the inhabitants of Megiddo and its villages (the third is Naphath).[f] [12]Yet the Manassites could not take possession of those towns, but the Canaanites continued to live in that land. [13]But when the Israelites grew strong, they put the Canaanites to forced labor but did not utterly drive them out.

14 The tribe of Joseph spoke to Joshua, saying, "Why have you given me but one lot and one portion as an inheritance, since we are a numerous people, whom all along the LORD has blessed?" [15]And Joshua said to them, "If you are a numerous people, go up to the forest and clear ground there for yourselves in the land of the Perizzites

f 17.11 Meaning of Heb uncertain

17:1–13 *Manasseh.* See note to 13:29–31. The relationships between Gilead, Machir, and Manasseh are obscure. Compare Num. 26:28–34 and 1 Chr. 7:14–19, where Manasseh's clans descended from Gilgal, son of Machir. Judges 5:14 mentions Machir instead of Manasseh. **17:2–6** Compare Num. 26:29–33; 27:1–11. Post-DH addition. See **"The Deuteronomistic History," p. 337. 17:7** *Shechem.* Identified as Tell Balatah, forty miles north of Jerusalem. It was strategically located in the center of the country and later served as an important administrative and political center for the Israelite tribes (cf. 1 Kgs. 12:1–2). It was destroyed during the Assyrian invasion (734–721 BCE) and lost its influence after that. **17:12–13** Another example of a group under the haram that was not utterly destroyed. See note on Josh. 2:10. Compare Judg. 1:27–28. It was not until the time of David that these territories were controlled by Israel (cf. 2 Sam. 24; 1 Kgs. 4).

17:14–18 Post-DH addition (see **"The Deuteronomistic History," p. 337**). This text is composed of the doublets 17:14–15 and 17:16–18 (the oldest account), both considering the house of Joseph one tribe instead of two. **17:14** *Numerous people.* Literally "great people" (cf. Num. 21:6; Josh. 11:4; 2 Sam. 13:34). Numbers 26:54; 33:54a required a larger portion for larger groups. **17:15** *Land of the Perizzites and the Rephaim.* According to Gen. 13:7 and Judg. 1:4, 9, Perizzites are found in the south of Canaan; in Deut. 2:10–11, 20–21, they seem to occupy Transjordan. For Transjordan, see note on Josh. 9:10. The land of the Rephaim is described as the region of Argob, part of Bashan (Deut. 3:13). King Og of Bashan is described as "one of the last of the Rephaim" (Josh. 12:4). *Hill country of Ephraim.* The mountain chain that runs from north to south is divided into three areas in Josh. 20:7: the hill country of Naphtali, the hill country of Ephraim, and the hill

and the Rephaim, since the hill country of Ephraim is too narrow for you." ¹⁶The tribe of Joseph said, "The hill country is not enough for us, yet all the Canaanites who live in the plain have chariots of iron, both those in Beth-shean and its villages and those in the Valley of Jezreel." ¹⁷Then Joshua said to the house of Joseph, to Ephraim and Manasseh, "You are indeed a numerous people and have great power; you shall not have one lot only, ¹⁸but the hill country shall be yours, for though it is a forest, you shall clear it and possess it to its farthest borders, for you shall drive out the Canaanites, though they have chariots of iron and though they are strong."

18 Then the whole congregation of the Israelites assembled at Shiloh and set up the tent of meeting there. The land lay subdued before them.

2 There remained among the Israelites seven tribes whose inheritance had not yet been apportioned. ³So Joshua said to the Israelites, "How long will you be slack about going in and taking possession of the land that the LORD, the God of your ancestors, has given you? ⁴Provide three men from each tribe, and I will send them out that they may begin to go throughout the land, writing a description of it with a view to their inheritances. Then come back to me. ⁵They shall divide it into seven portions, Judah continuing in its territory on the south and the house of Joseph in their territory on the north. ⁶You shall write a description

of the land in seven divisions and bring the description here to me, and I will cast lots for you here before the LORD our God. ⁷The Levites have no portion among you, for the priesthood of the LORD is their heritage, and Gad and Reuben and the half-tribe of Manasseh have received their inheritance beyond the Jordan eastward, which Moses the servant of the LORD gave them."

8 So the men started on their way, and Joshua charged those who went to write the description of the land, saying, "Go throughout the land and write a description of it and come back to me, and I will cast lots for you here before the LORD in Shiloh." ⁹So the men went and traversed the land and set down in a book a description of it by towns in seven divisions; then they came back to Joshua in the camp at Shiloh, ¹⁰and Joshua cast lots for them in Shiloh before the LORD, and there Joshua apportioned the land to the Israelites, to each a portion.

11 The lot of the tribe of Benjamin according to its families came up, and the territory allotted to it fell between the tribe of Judah and the tribe of Joseph. ¹²On the north side their boundary began at the Jordan; then the boundary goes up to the slope of Jericho on the north, then up through the hill country westward; and it ends at the wilderness of Beth-aven. ¹³From there the boundary passes along southward in the direction of Luz, to the slope of Luz (that is, Bethel), then the boundary goes down to Ataroth-addar, on the mountain that lies south of

country of Judah. **17:16** *Chariots of iron.* Chariots fully made of iron began to be used around 700 BCE, after the time of the events being described; more likely, the text refers to chariots reinforced with it. **17:17** *House of Joseph.* Compare Judg. 1:22–26. **17:18** The LXX reads "when you shall have utterly destroyed the Canaanites . . . because you are stronger than them."

18:1–28 Administrative districts. **18:1** *Shiloh.* Identified with Khirbet Seilun, located about nineteen miles north of Jerusalem. It is not attributed to any of the tribes; it served as a pan-Israelite sanctuary during the time of the Judges (Judg. 18:31; 1 Sam. 4:4, 12) and is remembered as an important sanctuary (Jer. 7:14; 26:6). It is a key gathering point here and in 22:12. *Tent of meeting.* The tabernacle was the place where God spoke with Moses (Exod. 33:11; Num. 12:8) and where Moses served as an intermediary between God and the people (Exod. 33:7). The Priestly tradition describes it in detail in Exod. 26; 36:8–38. For Priestly, see note on Josh. 14:1–2. **18:3–10** After the allotment of land to Gad, Reuben, Judah, and the house of Joseph, territory needs to be taken and distributed to the remaining tribes. Joshua gives a motivational speech (cf. Exod. 16:28; Num. 14:11; Ps. 13:2–3). **18:3** *The God of your ancestors, has given you.* Compare 1:2, 6; 11:23. **18:11–28** *Benjamin.* Called Ben-oni, "son of my affliction," by Rachel on her deathbed but renamed Benjamin (etymology uncertain) by Jacob. Benjamin was Jacob's twelfth son and his second son with Rachel (Gen. 46:19). Its territory is limited with Manasseh in the north and east, Dan in the west, and Judah in the south. The census in Num. 26:41 lists their numbers as 45,600. Compare Moses's blessing of

Lower Beth-horon. ¹⁴Then the boundary goes in another direction, turning on the western side southward from the mountain that lies to the south, opposite Beth-horon, and it ends at Kiriath-baal (that is, Kiriath-jearim), a town belonging to the tribe of Judah. This forms the western side. ¹⁵The southern side begins at the outskirts of Kiriath-jearim on the west,ᵍ and the boundary comes out at the spring of the Waters of Nephtoah; ¹⁶then the boundary goes down to the border of the mountain that overlooks the valley of the son of Hinnom, which is at the north end of the valley of Rephaim; and it then goes down the valley of Hinnom, south of the slope of the Jebusites, and downward to En-rogel; ¹⁷then it bends in a northerly direction going on to En-shemesh, and from there goes to Geliloth, which is opposite the ascent of Adummim; then it goes down to the Stone of Bohan, Reuben's son; ¹⁸and passing on to the north of the slope of Beth-arabahᵇ it goes down to the Arabah; ¹⁹then the boundary passes on to the north of the slope of Beth-hoglah; and the boundary ends at the northern bay of the Dead Sea,ⁱ at the south end of the Jordan: this is the southern border. ²⁰The Jordan forms its boundary on the eastern side. This is the inheritance of the tribe of Benjamin, according to its families, boundary by boundary all around.

21 Now the towns of the tribe of Benjamin according to their families were Jericho, Beth-hoglah, Emek-keziz, ²²Beth-arabah, Zemaraim, Bethel, ²³Avvim, Parah, Ophrah, ²⁴Chephar-ammoni, Ophni, and

Geba—twelve towns with their villages; ²⁵Gibeon, Ramah, Beeroth, ²⁶Mizpeh, Chephirah, Mozah, ²⁷Rekem, Irpeel, Taralah, ²⁸Zela, Haeleph, Jebusʲ (that is, Jerusalem), Gibeah,ᵏ and Kiriath-jearimˡ—fourteen towns with their villages. This is the inheritance of the tribe of Benjamin according to its families.

19 The second lot came out for Simeon, for the tribe of Simeon, according to its families; its inheritance lay within the inheritance of the tribe of Judah. ²It had for its inheritance Beer-sheba, Sheba, Moladah, ³Hazar-shual, Balah, Ezem, ⁴Eltolad, Bethul, Hormah, ⁵Ziklag, Beth-marcaboth, Hazar-susah, ⁶Beth-lebaoth, and Sharuhen—thirteen towns with their villages; ⁷Ain, Rimmon, Ether, and Ashan—four towns with their villages; ⁸together with all the villages all around these towns as far as Baalath-beer, Ramah of the Negeb. This was the inheritance of the tribe of Simeon according to its families. ⁹The inheritance of the tribe of Simeon formed part of the territory of Judah; because the portion of the tribe of Judah was too large for them, the tribe of Simeon obtained an inheritance within their inheritance.

10 The third lot came up for the tribe of Zebulun, according to its families. The boundary of its inheritance reached as far as Sarid; ¹¹then its boundary goes up

g 18.15 Meaning of Heb uncertain   h 18.18 Gk: Heb *to the slope over against the Arabah*   i 18.19 Heb *Salt Sea*   j 18.28 Gk Syr Vg: Heb *the Jebusite*   k 18.28 Heb *Gibeath*   l 18.28 Gk: Heb *Kiriath*

Benjamin in Deut. 33:12. **18:14** *Kiriath-jearim.* "City of the woods," identified as Tell el-Achar, nine miles north of Jerusalem.

19:1–9 *Simeon,* "because the Lᴏʀᴅ has heard" (Gen. 29:33) was Jacob's second son with Leah (Gen. 35:23). No borders for Simeon are mentioned (cf. Gen. 49:7), but a list of cities is given within the territory of Judah in Josh. 15. Genesis 49:7 tells us that Simeon and Levi were going to be divided and scattered in Israel without having a territory like their brothers. Judges 1:17 recounts an old tradition where Simeon and Judah conquered Hormah together (cf. Josh. 19:9). **19:4–5** The cities Ziklag, Beth-marcaboth, Hazar-susah, and Beth-lebaoth appear in Judah's list as Ziklag, Madmannah, Sansannah, and Lebaoth (Josh. 15:31–32). *Beth-marcaboth.* "House of chariots," not mentioned in Josh. 15 (cf. 2 Chr. 9:25, "the chariot cities"). *Hazar-susah.* "Village of the horse." Possibly the same as "Sansannah" in Josh. 15:31. **19:6** *Sharuhen.* Shilhim in Josh. 15:32. **19:7** *Ain, Rimmon,* agreeing with 1 Chr. 4:32. The LXX reads instead both nouns as one city, En-rimmon. **19:8** *Baalath-beer.* "Lady of the Well." Identified as Bir Rakhmeh nineteen miles southeast of Beer-sheba.

19:10–16 *Zebulun* (see Gen. 30:20, etymology uncertain) was Jacob's tenth son and his sixth with Leah (Gen. 35:23). The territory of Zebulun presents several textual difficulties; the tribe is mentioned in Gen. 49:13 and Deut. 33:18–19. Its territory was in lower Galilee between Naphtali (19:32–39) and Asher (19:24–31). Compare Moses's blessing to Zebulun and Issachar in Deut. 33:18–19.

westward, and on to Maralah, and touches Dabbesheth, then the wadi that is near Jokneam; [12]from Sarid it goes in the other direction eastward toward the sunrise to the boundary of Chisloth-tabor; from there it goes to Daberath, then up to Japhia; [13]from there it passes along on the east toward the sunrise to Gath-hepher, to Eth-kazin, and going on to Rimmon it bends toward Neah; [14]then on the north the boundary makes a turn to Hannathon, and it ends at the valley of Iphtah-el; [15]and Kattath, Nahalal, Shimron, Idalah, and Bethlehem—twelve towns with their villages. [16]This is the inheritance of the tribe of Zebulun, according to its families, these towns with their villages.

17 The fourth lot came out for Issachar, for the tribe of Issachar, according to its families. [18]Its territory included Jezreel, Chesulloth, Shunem, [19]Hapharaim, Shion, Anaharath, [20]Rabbith, Kishion, Ebez, [21]Remeth, En-gannim, En-haddah, Bethpazzez; [22]the boundary also touches Tabor, Shahazumah, and Beth-shemesh, and its boundary ends at the Jordan—sixteen towns with their villages. [23]This is the inheritance of the tribe of Issachar, according to its families, the towns with their villages.

24 The fifth lot came out for the tribe of Asher according to its families. [25]Its boundary included Helkath, Hali, Beten, Achshaph, [26]Allammelech, Amad, and Mishal; on the west it touches Carmel and Shihor-libnath, [27]then it turns eastward, goes to Beth-dagon, and touches Zebulun and the valley of Iphtah-el northward to Beth-emek and Neiel; then it continues in the north to Cabul, [28]Ebron, Rehob, Hammon, Kanah, as far as Great Sidon; [29]then the boundary turns to Ramah, reaching to the fortified city of Tyre; then the boundary turns to Hosah, and it ends at the sea; Mahaleb,[m] Achzib, [30]Ummah, Aphek, and Rehob—twenty-two towns with their villages. [31]This is the inheritance of the tribe of Asher according to its families, these towns with their villages.

32 The sixth lot came out for the tribe of Naphtali, for the tribe of Naphtali according to its families. [33]And its boundary ran from Heleph, from the oak in Zaanannim, and Adami-nekeb, and Jabneel, as far as Lakkum; and it ended at the Jordan; [34]then the boundary turns westward to Aznoth-tabor and goes from there to Hukkok, touching Zebulun at the south, and Asher on the west, and Judah on the east at the Jordan. [35]The fortified towns are Ziddim, Zer, Hammath, Rakkath, Chinnereth, [36]Adamah, Ramah, Hazor, [37]Kedesh, Edrei, En-hazor, [38]Iron, Migdal-el, Horem, Beth-anath, and Beth-shemesh—nineteen towns with their villages. [39]This is the inheritance of the tribe of Naphtali according to its families, the towns with their villages.

m 19.29 Cn Compare Gk: Heb *Mehebel*

19:12 *Chisloth-tabor.* Called Chesulloth in 19:18, identified as modern-day Iksal, four miles south of Nazareth. *Daberath.* Listed as a Levitical town in 21:28. **19:15** *Bethlehem.* A Galilean city, different from Bethlehem in Judah mentioned in 1 Sam. 16:4; 17:12; and the New Testament.

19:17–23 *Issachar,* "God has given me my hire" (Gen. 30:18, etymology uncertain), was Jacob's ninth son and his fifth son with Leah (Gen. 35:23; cf. Gen. 49:14–15; Deut. 33:18–19). Its territory is located south of the Sea of Galilee, west of the Jordan River, bordered on the north with Naphtali, on the west with Zebulun, and on the south with Manasseh. Their census in Num. 1:28–29 counts 54,400 over twenty and able to go to war. Compare Moses's blessing to Zebulun and Issachar in Deut. 33:18–19. **19:18** *Jezreel.* Modern-day Zer'in located at the base of Mount Gilboa. *Chesulloth.* Chisloth-tabor in 19:12. **19:22** *Beth-shemesh.* "House of the Sun (god)." There are two other cities with the same name, one assigned to Judah (15:10) and another to Naphtali (19:38). *Tabor.* Compare Judg. 4:6, 12, 14. Mount Tabor, 1,850 feet high.

19:24–31 *Asher,* "happy" (Gen. 30:13), was Jacob's eighth son and his second with Leah's maid Zilpah (Gen. 35:26). Its territory covered eastern Galilee bordered by Phoenicia in the north, Naphtali and Zebulun in the east, Manasseh in the south, and the Mediterranean in the west. Their census in Num. 1:41 counts 41,500 men over twenty and able to go to war. Compare Moses's blessing in Deut. 33:24–25. **19:26** *Carmel.* Coastal mountain range, twenty miles long, 1,791 feet at its highest, stretching east from the Mediterranean. It relates to the Elijah stories (1 Kgs. 18:19–40; 2 Kgs. 2:25; 4:25).

19:32–39 *Naphtali,* "my struggle" (Gen. 30:8), was Jacob's sixth son and his second with Rachel's maid, Bilhah (Gen. 35:25). The tribe's territory is located in the heartland of Galilee, west of the Sea

40 The seventh lot came out for the tribe of Dan according to its families. **41**The territory of its inheritance included Zorah, Eshtaol, Ir-shemesh, **42**Shaalabbin, Aijalon, Ithlah, **43**Elon, Timnah, Ekron, **44**Eltekeh, Gibbethon, Baalath, **45**Jehud, Bene-berak, Gath-rimmon, **46**Me-jarkon, and Rakkon at the border opposite Joppa. **47**When the territory of the Danites was lost to them, the Danites went up and fought against Leshem, and after capturing it and putting it to the sword, they took possession of it and settled in it, calling Leshem Dan, after their ancestor Dan. **48**This is the inheritance of the tribe of Dan, according to their families, these towns with their villages.

49 When they had finished distributing the several territories of the land as inheritances, the Israelites gave an inheritance among them to Joshua son of Nun. **50**By command of the LORD they gave him the town that he asked for, Timnath-serah in the hill country of Ephraim; he rebuilt the town and settled in it.

51 These are the inheritances that the priest Eleazar and Joshua son of Nun and the heads of the families of the tribes of the Israelites distributed by lot at Shiloh before the LORD, at the entrance of the tent of meeting. So they finished dividing the land.

20 Then the LORD spoke to Joshua, saying, **2**"Say to the Israelites: Appoint the cities of refuge, of which I spoke to you through Moses, **3**so that anyone who kills a person without intent or by mistake may flee there; they shall be for you a refuge from the avenger of blood. **4**The slayer shall flee to one of these cities and shall stand at the entrance of the gate of the city and explain the case to the elders of that city; then the fugitive shall be taken into the city and given a place and shall remain with them. **5**And if the avenger of blood is in pursuit, they shall not give up the slayer because the neighbor was killed by mistake, there having been no enmity between them before. **6**The slayer shall remain in that city until there is a trial before the congregation, until the death of the one who is high priest at the time; then the slayer may return home, to the town in which the deed was done."

7 So they set apart Kedesh in Galilee in the hill country of Naphtali, and Shechem in the hill country of Ephraim, and Kiriath-arba

of Galilee. Its borders were Dan in the north, the Jordan River in the east, Zebulun in the south, and Asher in the west. Their census in Num. 1:43 counts 53,400 men over twenty and ready to go to war. Compare Moses's blessing in Deut. 33:23.

19:40–48 Dan, "judgment," was the fifth son of Jacob and his first son with Rachel's maid, Bilhah (Gen. 30:6). The tribe's territory is located here just north of Philistia. Its borders were Ephraim and Benjamin in the west and Judah in the south. Dan later migrated to the north (Judg. 18). Their census in Num. 1:39 counts 62,700 men over twenty and ready to go to war. Compare Moses's blessing in Deut. 33:22.

Josh. 20 and 21 were added to Joshua at a later date and follow the theology and motifs of Deuteronomy.

20:1 *Then the LORD spoke to* is a common Priestly expression in the Bible but occurs only here in Joshua (Exod. 6:10; Num. 3:5, 11, 14, 44; 4:17, 21; 16:20, 36; 18:25; Deut. 4:12). For Priestly, see note on Josh. 14:1–2.

20:2 *Cities of refuge.* Already mentioned in Num. 35:6, 9–34; Deut. 4:41–43; 19:1–13 (cf. also Exod. 21:12–21). In Deuteronomy, Moses assigned three cities of refuge in Transjordan (Deut. 4:41–43) and another three in a tripartite division of the country (Deut. 19:1–3) with the possibility of adding more cities if Israel conquered more territory (19:7–9). Compare Num. 35. The right of sanctuary was an accepted practice in the ancient world, but the system described here is unique to Israel. It is possible though that these cities were chosen because of the presence of sanctuaries there (cf. 1 Kgs. 2:28–35).

20:3 *Avenger of blood.* Exodus 21:13 established a place where the perpetrator of involuntary homicide could find refuge; premeditated murder, however, was not granted any kind of sanctuary (Exod. 21:14; cf. Num. 35:12, 19–29; 2 Sam. 3:27).

20:4 *Entrance of the gate of the city,* where judicial processes and public business were sometimes carried out by the leaders of the city.

20:6 *Until the death of the one who is high priest at the time.* The reason for this amnesty is not explained, but it sets a limit for the confinement. Compare Num. 35:25–28.

20:7 *Kedesh.* See note to 15:23. *Shechem.* See note to 17:7. *Kiriath-arba (that is, Hebron).* See note to 10:3.

(that is, Hebron) in the hill country of Judah. [8]And beyond the Jordan east of Jericho, they appointed Bezer in the wilderness on the tableland, from the tribe of Reuben, and Ramoth in Gilead, from the tribe of Gad, and Golan in Bashan, from the tribe of Manasseh. [9]These were the cities designated for all the Israelites and for the aliens residing among them, that anyone who killed a person without intent could flee there, so as not to die by the hand of the avenger of blood, until there was a trial before the congregation.

21 Then the heads of the families of the Levites came to the priest Eleazar and to Joshua son of Nun and to the heads of the families of the tribes of the Israelites; [2]they said to them at Shiloh in the land of Canaan, "The LORD commanded through Moses that we be given towns to live in, along with their pasturelands for our livestock." [3]So by command of the LORD the Israelites gave to the Levites the following towns and pasturelands out of their inheritance.

[4] The lot came out for the families of the Kohathites. So those Levites who were descendants of Aaron the priest received by lot thirteen towns from the tribes of Judah, Simeon, and Benjamin.

[5] The rest of the Kohathites received by lot ten towns from the families of the tribe of Ephraim, from the tribe of Dan, and from the half-tribe of Manasseh.

[6] The Gershonites received by lot thirteen towns from the families of the tribe of Issachar, from the tribe of Asher, from the tribe of Naphtali, and from the half-tribe of Manasseh in Bashan.

[7] The Merarites according to their families received twelve towns from the tribe of Reuben, the tribe of Gad, and the tribe of Zebulun.

[8] These towns and their pasturelands the Israelites gave by lot to the Levites, as the LORD had commanded through Moses.

[9] Out of the tribe of Judah and the tribe of Simeon they gave the following towns mentioned by name, [10]which went to the descendants of Aaron, one of the families of the Kohathites who belonged to the Levites, since the lot fell to them first. [11]They gave them Kiriath-arba (Arba being the father of Anak), that is, Hebron, in the hill country of Judah, along with the pasturelands around it. [12]But the fields of the town and its villages had been given to Caleb son of Jephunneh as his holding.

[13] To the descendants of Aaron the priest they gave Hebron, the city of refuge for the slayer, with its pasturelands, Libnah with its pasturelands, [14]Jattir with its pasturelands, Eshtemoa with its pasturelands, [15]Holon with its pasturelands, Debir with its pasturelands, [16]Ain with its pasturelands, Juttah with its pasturelands, and Bethshemesh with its pasturelands—nine towns out of these two tribes. [17]Out of the tribe of Benjamin: Gibeon with its pasturelands, Geba with its pasturelands, [18]Anathoth with its pasturelands, and Almon with its pasturelands—four towns. [19]The towns of the descendants of Aaron, the priests, were thirteen in all, with their pasturelands.

[20] As to the rest of the Kohathites belonging to the Kohathite families of the Levites, the towns allotted to them were out of the tribe of Ephraim. [21]To them were given Shechem, the city of refuge for the slayer, with its pasturelands in the hill country of Ephraim, Gezer with its pasturelands, [22]Kibzaim with its pasturelands, and Bethhoron with its pasturelands—four towns.

21:1–3 Post-DH, Priestly addition. For DH, see **"The Deuteronomistic History," p. 337**; for Priestly, see note on Josh. 14:1–2. Compare Num. 32:28. **21:1** *Heads of the families of the Levites.* Only mentioned here and in Exod. 6:25. *Eleazar.* Compare 14:1; 17:4; 19:51. **21:2** *The LORD commanded through Moses.* The Levites were left without territory (Num. 18:20–24); this situation is addressed in Num. 35:1–8, where they are given "towns . . . to live in." After the division of the kingdom, Jeroboam took away their rights (1 Kgs. 12:31). Another list of Levitical cities is found in 1 Chr. 6:54–81.

21:4–7 Four subdivisions of the Levites following the sons of Levi, Gershon, Kohath, and Merari (Gen. 46:11) are listed: Kohathites (v. 4); Gershonites (v. 6); Merarites (v. 7); and a fourth part to the "descendants of Aaron" (v. 10) who were part of the Kohathites.

21:9 There is a clear connection with the list of cities of refuge (Josh. 20). The first city mentioned in each of the regions happens to be a city of refuge (21:13, Hebron; 21:21, Shechem; 21:27, Golan; 21:32, Kedesh; and 21:36, Bezer).

²³Out of the tribe of Dan: Elteke with its pasturelands, Gibbethon with its pasturelands, ²⁴Aijalon with its pasturelands, Gath-rimmon with its pasturelands—four towns. ²⁵Out of the half-tribe of Manasseh: Taanach with its pasturelands, and Gath-rimmon with its pasturelands—two towns. ²⁶The towns of the families of the rest of the Kohathites were ten in all, with their pasturelands.

27 To the Gershonites, one of the families of the Levites, were given out of the half-tribe of Manasseh, Golan in Bashan with its pasturelands, the city of refuge for the slayer, and Beeshterah with its pasturelands—two towns. ²⁸Out of the tribe of Issachar: Kishion with its pasturelands, Daberath with its pasturelands, ²⁹Jarmuth with its pasturelands, En-gannim with its pasturelands—four towns. ³⁰Out of the tribe of Asher: Mishal with its pasturelands, Abdon with its pasturelands, ³¹Helkath with its pasturelands, and Rehob with its pasturelands—four towns. ³²Out of the tribe of Naphtali: Kedesh in Galilee with its pasturelands, the city of refuge for the slayer, Hammoth-dor with its pasturelands, and Kartan with its pasturelands—three towns. ³³The towns of the several families of the Gershonites were in all thirteen, with their pasturelands.

34 To the rest of the Levites—the Merarite families—were given out of the tribe of Zebulun: Jokneam with its pasturelands, Kartah with its pasturelands, ³⁵Dimnah with its pasturelands, Nahalal with its pasturelands—four towns. ³⁶Out of the tribe of Reuben: Bezer with its pasturelands, Jahzah with its pasturelands, ³⁷Kedemoth with its pasturelands, and Mephaath with its pasturelands—four towns. ³⁸Out of the tribe of Gad: Ramoth in Gilead with its pasturelands, the city of refuge for the slayer, Mahanaim with its pasturelands, ³⁹Heshbon with its pasturelands, Jazer with its pasturelands—four towns in all. ⁴⁰As for the towns of the several Merarite families, that is, the remainder of the families of the Levites, those allotted to them were twelve in all.

41 The towns of the Levites within the holdings of the Israelites were in all forty-eight towns with their pasturelands. ⁴²Each of these towns had its pasturelands around it; so it was with all these towns.

43 Thus the Lord gave to Israel all the land that he swore to their ancestors that he would give them, and having taken possession of it, they settled there. ⁴⁴And the Lord gave them rest on every side, just as he had sworn to their ancestors; not one of all their enemies had withstood them, for the Lord had given all their enemies into their hands. ⁴⁵Not one of all the good promises that the Lord had made to the house of Israel had failed; all came to pass.

22 Then Joshua summoned the Reubenites, the Gadites, and the half-tribe of Manasseh ²and said to them, "You have observed all that Moses the servant of the Lord commanded you and have obeyed me in all that I have commanded you; ³you have not forsaken your kindred these

---

21:25 *Gath-rimmon.* First Chronicles 6:70 lists Bileam instead.

21:43 *Gave to Israel all the land.* The gift of the land is a typical Deuteronomic motif. *Ancestors* could mean the patriarchs but also the desert generation.

21:44 *And the Lord gave them rest.* The concept of rest (in most cases from enemies) is important in Deuteronomy (Deut. 3:20; 12:10; 25:19) and Joshua (1:13, 15; 22:4). *Given all their enemies into their hand.* Compare Deut. 12:10 and 25:19. The author reinterprets Moses's promise as God's promise.

21:45 *All came to pass.* A reaffirmation of God's faithfulness. None of God's promises failed. Compare Josh. 1:6; 23:14.

22:1–6 At the very beginning of the conquest, Joshua asked the Reubenites, the Gadites, and the half-tribe of Manasseh (1:12–18) to join the rest of the tribes in crossing the Jordan and taking possession of the land. Now that the conquest was completed, Joshua blesses them to return to their territories in Transjordan. **22:5** *Love the Lord.* "To love" in the ancient Near East and in the Bible means, in most cases, putting someone in a place of primacy or choosing someone over others (Gen. 35:3). On the other hand, "to hate" means "rejection, separation." To "love the Lord" is also a typical Deuteronomic expression (Deut. 6:5; 11:1; 13:3; 30:6). *All your heart and with all your soul.* A typical Deuteronomic expression, part of the Shema (Deut. 6:4–9). See **"The *Shema*," p. 257.** Compare Deut. 4:29; 6:5; 10:12; 11:13, 18; 13:3; 26:16; 30:2, 6, 10.

many days, down to this day, but have been careful to keep the charge of the Lord your God. ⁴And now the Lord your God has given rest to your kindred, as he promised them; therefore turn and go to your tents in the land where your possession lies, which Moses the servant of the Lord gave you on the other side of the Jordan. ⁵Take good care to observe the commandment and instruction that Moses the servant of the Lord commanded you, to love the Lord your God, to walk in all his ways, to keep his commandments, and to hold fast to him, and to serve him with all your heart and with all your soul." ⁶So Joshua blessed them and sent them away, and they went to their tents.

7 Now to the one half of the tribe of Manasseh Moses had given a possession in Bashan, but to the other half Joshua had given a possession beside their fellow Israelites in the land west of the Jordan. And when Joshua sent them away to their tents and blessed them, ⁸he said to them, "Go back to your tents with much wealth and with very much livestock, with silver, gold, bronze, and iron, and with a great quantity of clothing; divide the spoil of your enemies with your kindred." ⁹So the Reubenites and the Gadites and the half-tribe of Manasseh returned home, parting from the Israelites at Shiloh, which is in the land of Canaan, to go to the land of Gilead, their own land of which they had taken possession by command of the Lord through Moses.

10 When they came to the region" near the Jordan that lies in the land of Canaan, the Reubenites and the Gadites and the half-tribe of Manasseh built there an altar by the Jordan, an altar of great size. ¹¹The Israelites heard that the Reubenites and the Gadites and the half-tribe of Manasseh had built an altar opposite the land of Canaan, in the region⁰ near the Jordan, across from the Israelites. ¹²And when the people of Israel heard of it, the whole assembly of the Israelites gathered at Shiloh to make war against them.

13 Then the Israelites sent the priest Phinehas son of Eleazar to the Reubenites and the Gadites and the half-tribe of Manasseh, in the land of Gilead, ¹⁴and with him ten chiefs, one from each of the tribal families of Israel, every one of them the head of a family among the clans of Israel. ¹⁵They came to the Reubenites, the Gadites, and the half-tribe of Manasseh, in the land of Gilead, and they said to them, ¹⁶"Thus says the whole congregation of the Lord: What is this treachery that you have committed against the God of Israel in turning away today from following the Lord, by building yourselves an altar today in rebellion against the Lord? ¹⁷Have we not had enough of the sin at Peor, from which even yet we have not cleansed ourselves and for which a plague came upon the congregation of the Lord, ¹⁸that you must turn away today from following the Lord? If you rebel against the Lord today, he will be angry with the whole congregation of Israel tomorrow. ¹⁹But now, if your land is unclean, cross over into the Lord's land, where the Lord's tabernacle now stands, and take for yourselves a possession among us; only do not rebel against the Lord or rebel against us° by building

n 22.10 Or to Geliloth   o 22.11 Or at Geliloth   p 22.19 Or make rebels of us

---

22:8 Collecting the spoil of the enemies was one of the incentives to go to war and a standard practice in the ancient Near East and the Bible (1 Sam. 30:21–25).

22:9–34 Priestly expressions appear in vv. 9, 19, 22, and 29. For Priestly, see note on Josh. 14:1–2.
22:10 The Bible mentions several individuals who built altars before the time of Joshua: the patriarchs, Abraham (Gen. 12:7–8; 13:18; 22:9), Isaac (Gen. 26:25), and Jacob (Gen. 33:20; 35:1, 3, 7); but also Moses (Exod. 17:15; 24:4). It was allowed "in every place where I cause my name to be remembered," said the Lord in Exod. 20:24. But there were certain limitations regarding altars of stone (Exod. 20:24–25). Deuteronomy 12, however, allowed sacrifices only in one place. **22:12** *The whole assembly.* In 18:1, the same Hebrew expression is translated as "whole congregation." Both events are placed in Shiloh but in 18:1 it is a gathering to fight together and here to fight against each other. **22:16** *Turning away today from following the Lord.* Compare Num. 14:43. First Kings 9:6 denotes abandonment (see 2 Sam. 11:15). The prophets used the same verb to call the people to return to the Lord (Isa. 19:22; Jer. 3:12, 22; 4:1; 24:7; Hos. 5:4; 7:10; 11:5; 12:6; 14:2). *In rebellion.* The Hebrew term (also used in 22:18, 19, 22, 29) is mostly used to denote political rebellion (2 Kgs. 18:7, 20; Isa. 36:5; 2 Kgs. 24:20; Jer. 52:3; Neh. 2:19; 6:6). **22:17** *The sin at Peor* refers to Israel's intercourse with Moabite

yourselves an altar other than the altar of
the LORD our God. [20]Did not Achan son of
Zerah break faith in the matter of the devoted things, and wrath fell upon all the congregation of Israel? And he did not perish
alone for his iniquity!"

21 Then the Reubenites, the Gadites, and
the half-tribe of Manasseh said in answer
to the heads of the families of Israel, [22]"The
LORD, God of gods! The LORD, God of gods!
He knows, and let Israel itself know! If it
was in rebellion or in breach of faith toward the LORD, do not spare us today [23]for
building an altar to turn away from following the LORD, or if we did so to offer burnt
offerings or grain offerings or offerings of
well-being on it, may the LORD himself take
vengeance. [24]No! We did it from fear that
in time to come your children might say to
our children, 'What have you to do with
the LORD, the God of Israel? [25]For the LORD
has made the Jordan a boundary between
us and you, you Reubenites and Gadites;
you have no portion in the LORD.' So your
children might make our children cease to
worship the LORD. [26]Therefore we said, 'Let
us now build an altar, not for burnt offering nor for sacrifice, [27]but to be a witness
between us and you and between the generations after us, that we do perform the
service of the LORD in his presence with
our burnt offerings and sacrifices and offerings of well-being, so that your children
may never say to our children in time to
come, "You have no portion in the LORD."'
[28]And we thought, 'If this should be said to
us or to our descendants in time to come,
we could say, "Look at this copy of the altar of the LORD that our ancestors made, not
for burnt offerings nor for sacrifice, but to
be a witness between us and you." [29]Far be
it from us that we should rebel against the
LORD and turn away this day from following the LORD by building an altar for burnt
offering, grain offering, or sacrifice other
than the altar of the LORD our God that
stands before his tabernacle!'"

30 When the priest Phinehas and the
chiefs of the congregation, the heads of the
families of Israel who were with him, heard
the words that the Reubenites and the Gadites and the Manassites spoke, they were
satisfied. [31]The priest Phinehas son of Eleazar said to the Reubenites and the Gadites
and the Manassites, "Today we know that
the LORD is among us, because you have not
committed this treachery against the LORD;
now you have saved the Israelites from the
hand of the LORD."

32 Then the priest Phinehas son of Eleazar and the chiefs returned from the Reubenites and the Gadites in the land of Gilead
to the land of Canaan, to the Israelites, and
brought back word to them. [33]The report
pleased the Israelites, and the Israelites
blessed God and spoke no more of making
war against them, to destroy the land where
the Reubenites and the Gadites were settled.
[34]The Reubenites and the Gadites called the
altar Witness,[q] "for," they said, "it is a witness between us that the LORD is God."

23 A long time afterward, when the
LORD had given rest to Israel from
all their enemies all around and Joshua was
old and well advanced in years, [2]Joshua

q 22.34 Heb mss Syr: MT lacks *Witness*

women and their worship of Baal (Num. 25:1–3). **22:21–28** The accused tribes reject the accusation, make a declaration of innocence, and reaffirm their loyalty to God (cf. 1 Kgs. 18:39). They explain that the altar was not meant to compete with the central sanctuary but as a witness (cf. Gen. 31:43–54) between the eastern and western tribes to the service performed by the Reubenites, the Gadites, and the half-tribe of Manasseh in the conquest of the land.

23:1–16 The farewell speech of Joshua parallels that of Moses in Deut. 31. Deuteronomistic language and theology are evident in the theological significance of the conquest and the connection with Moses, as Joshua insists that continued possession of the land depends on the people obeying God and God's commandments. This chapter is a key component of the biblical story and theology, foretelling the tragic end of the kingdoms of Israel and Judah, which occurs due to idolatry, according to 2 Kings. The chapter interpolates statements about the past (vv. 3–5 and 9–10, victories over local populations; v. 14, fulfillment of God's promises) and the future (vv. 6–8, observance of Moses's law; vv. 11–13, love the Lord and avoid local populations; vv. 15–16, the fulfillment of the threats/curses because of unfaithfulness). **23:1** *The LORD had given rest to Israel.* See note to 21:44. **23:2** *Elders.* A technical term referring to leader of a community (Gen. 50:7; Exod. 3:16), they sometimes appear as

summoned all Israel, their elders and heads, their judges and officers, and said to them, "I am now old and well advanced in years, [3]and you have seen all that the LORD your God has done to all these nations for your sake, for it is the LORD your God who has fought for you. [4]I have allotted to you as an inheritance for your tribes those nations that remain, along with all the nations that I have already cut off, from the Jordan to the Great Sea in the west. [5]The LORD your God will push them back before you and drive them out of your sight, and you shall possess their land, as the LORD your God promised you. [6]Therefore be very steadfast to observe and do all that is written in the book of the law of Moses, turning aside from it neither to the right nor to the left, [7]so that you may not be mixed with these nations left here among you, or make mention of the names of their gods, or swear by them, or serve them, or bow yourselves down to them, [8]but hold fast to the LORD your God, as you have done to this day. [9]For the LORD has driven out before you great and strong nations, and as for you, no one has been able to withstand you to this day. [10]One of you puts to flight a thousand, since it is the LORD your God who fights for you, as he promised you. [11]Be very careful, therefore, to love the LORD your God. [12]For if you turn back and join the survivors of these nations left here among you and intermarry with them, so that you marry their women and they yours, [13]know assuredly that the LORD your God will not continue to drive out these nations before you, but they shall be a snare and a trap for you, a scourge on your sides, and thorns in your eyes, until you perish from this good land that the LORD your God has given you.

14 "And now I am about to go the way of all the earth, and you know in your hearts and souls, all of you, that not one thing has failed of all the good things that the LORD your God promised concerning you; all have come to pass for you; not one of them has failed. [15]But just as all the good things that the LORD your God promised concerning you have been fulfilled for you, so the LORD will bring upon you all the bad things until he has destroyed you from this good land that the LORD your God has given you. [16]If you transgress the covenant of the LORD your God, which he enjoined on you, and go and serve other gods and bow down to them, then the anger of the LORD will be kindled against you, and you shall perish quickly from the good land that he has given to you."

24 Then Joshua gathered all the tribes of Israel to Shechem and summoned the elders, the heads, the judges, and the officers of Israel, and they presented themselves before God. [2]And Joshua said to all

the only group side by side with Joshua (in 7:6; 8:10; 24:31). Their political influence is more evident during the monarchy (1 Sam. 8:4–5; 2 Sam. 5:3; 1 Kgs. 8:1–3). *Heads.* Another term for leaders: heads of families (Exod. 6:14, 25; Num. 7:2) or tribes (Num. 1:16; 32:28; Deut. 1:15; 1 Kgs. 8:1). *Judges.* The word connotes a different kind of leadership in the Bible, in some cases implying a proper judicial activity (Exod. 18:22, 26; Deut. 1:16; 16:18) but in others meaning "to rule, to lead" (Judg. 10:2, 3; 12:7, 8–9, 11, 13–14; 15:20; 16:31). *Officers.* Officials and administrators sometimes in charge of mustering troops (Deut. 20:5) **23:3** *All that the LORD your God has done.* Compare Deut. 3:21. *God who has fought for you.* Compare Deut. 3:22. **23:5** *Push them back before you.* Compare Deut. 6:19; 9:4. *Drive them out.* Compare Deut. 4:38; 11:23; 1 Kgs. 14:24; 21:26; 2 Kgs. 16:3; 17:8; 21:2; Ps. 44:3. *You shall possess.* Compare Deut. 11:23–31; 19:1; 31:3; Josh. 1:5. **23:4–5, 12–13** The language of haram is replaced by expulsion and prohibition of intermarriage. See note on Josh. 2:10. **23:15–16** The promise is fulfilled in 2 Kgs. 17 when the capital of the northern kingdom of Israel is destroyed and their population carried captive to Assyria and in 2 Kgs. 24 and 25 when Judah is conquered by the Babylonians and its leadership is exiled. **23:16** *Transgress the covenant.* Compare Deut. 17:2; Josh. 7:15. Expressed also as "forget the covenant" (Deut. 4:23) or "abandoned the covenant" (Deut. 29:25; Jer. 22:9). *The anger of the LORD.* Compare Josh. 7:1; Deut. 7:4; 11:17. *You shall perish quickly.* Compare Deut. 11:17.

24:1–28 Possibly a later Deuteronomistic addition, this is the renewal of the covenant previously affirmed in Exod. 24:1–11; 34:27–28 (cf. Josh. 8:30–35). **24:1** *Shechem* was considered a sacred place (cf. Gen. 12:6–7; 33:18–20) where remains of a temple dating to the twelfth century BCE were found. *Presented themselves before God.* Possibly implying the presence of a sanctuary where the presence of the gods was experienced in the ancient Near East. Compare Josh. 8:30–35, where Joshua

the people, "Thus says the LORD, the God of Israel: Long ago your ancestors—Terah and his sons Abraham and Nahor—lived beyond the Euphrates and served other gods. ³Then I took your father Abraham from beyond the River and led him through all the land of Canaan and made his offspring many. I gave him Isaac, ⁴and to Isaac I gave Jacob and Esau. I gave Esau the hill country of Seir to possess, but Jacob and his children went down to Egypt. ⁵Then I sent Moses and Aaron, and I plagued Egypt with what I did in its midst, and afterward I brought you out. ⁶When I brought your ancestors out of Egypt, you came to the sea, and the Egyptians pursued your ancestors with chariots and horsemen to the Red Sea.ʳ ⁷When they cried out to the LORD, he put darkness between you and the Egyptians and made the sea come upon them and cover them, and your eyes saw what I did to Egypt. Afterward you lived in the wilderness a long time. ⁸Then I brought you to the land of the Amorites, who lived on the other side of the Jordan; they fought with you, and I handed them over to you, and you took possession of their land, and I destroyed them before you. ⁹Then King Balak son of Zippor of Moab set out to fight against Israel. He sent and invited Balaam son of Beor to curse you, ¹⁰but I would not listen to Balaam; therefore he blessed you, so I rescued you out of his hand. ¹¹When you went over the Jordan and came to Jericho, the citizens of Jericho fought against you, as well as the Amorites, the Perizzites, the Canaanites, the Hittites, the Girgashites, the Hivites, and the Jebusites, and I handed them over to you. ¹²I sent swarms of hornetsˢ ahead of you that drove out before you the two kings of the Amorites; it was not by your sword or by your bow. ¹³I gave you a land on which you had not labored and towns that you had not built, and you live in them; you eat the fruit of vineyards and oliveyards that you did not plant.

14 "Now, therefore, revere the LORD and serve him in sincerity and in faithfulness; put away the gods that your ancestors served beyond the River and in Egypt and serve the LORD. ¹⁵Now if you are unwilling to serve the LORD, choose this day whom you will serve, whether the gods your ancestors served in the region beyond the River or the gods of the Amorites in whose land you are living, but as for me and my household, we will serve the LORD."

16 Then the people answered, "Far be it from us that we should forsake the LORD to serve other gods, ¹⁷for it is the LORD our God who brought us and our ancestors up from the land of Egypt, out of the house of slavery, and who did those great signs in our sight. He protected us along all the way that we went and among all the peoples through whom we passed, ¹⁸and the LORD drove out before us all the peoples, the Amorites who lived in the land. Therefore we also will serve the LORD, for he is our God."

19 But Joshua said to the people, "You cannot serve the LORD, for he is a holy God. He is a jealous God; he will not forgive your transgressions or your sins. ²⁰If you forsake the LORD and serve foreign gods, then he will turn and do you harm and consume you, after having done you good." ²¹And the people said to Joshua, "No, we will serve the LORD!" ²²Then Joshua said to the people, "You are witnesses against yourselves that you have chosen the LORD, to serve him." And they said, "We are witnesses." ²³He said, "Then put away the foreign gods that are among you, and incline your hearts to the LORD, the God of Israel." ²⁴The people said to Joshua, "The LORD our God we will serve, and him we will obey." ²⁵So Joshua made a covenant with the people that day and made statutes and ordinances for them

r 24.6 Or *Sea of Reeds*   s 24.12 Meaning of Heb uncertain

built an altar on Mount Ebal and performed a covenant ceremony there. **24:2–13** A summary of the interactions between God and Israel and their ancestors. Similarly, see Exod. 6:2–8; Deut. 6:21–24; Ezek. 20:5–26; Pss. 78; 105; Acts 7:2–50. **24:2** *Thus says the LORD.* See note to 7:13. *The Euphrates.* Literally "the river." Compare Gen. 31:21; 36:37; Exod. 23:31; Num. 22:5. **24:4** *The hill country of Seir.* Seir has been identified as Shoresh Beth-Meir, nine miles west of Jerusalem (cf. Deut. 1:44; Josh. 15:10). **24:12** *Hornets.* Possible meanings also "terror," "dejection, discouragement," and "pestilence" (Exod. 23:28; Deut. 7:20). **24:19** *A jealous God.* Demanding exclusive service or punishing God's enemies (Exod. 20:5; 34:14; Deut. 4:24; 5:9; 6:15). **24:23** *Incline your hearts.* The heart is the

at Shechem. [26]Joshua wrote these words in the book of the law of God, and he took a large stone and set it up there under the oak in the sanctuary of the LORD. [27]Joshua said to all the people, "See, this stone shall be a witness against us, for it has heard all the words of the LORD that he spoke to us; therefore it shall be a witness against you if you deal falsely with your God." [28]So Joshua sent the people away to their inheritances.

[29] After these things Joshua son of Nun, the servant of the LORD, died, being one hundred ten years old. [30]They buried him in his own inheritance at Timnath-serah, which is in the hill country of Ephraim, north of Mount Gaash.

[31] Israel served the LORD all the days of Joshua and all the days of the elders who outlived Joshua and had known all the work that the LORD did for Israel.

[32] The bones of Joseph, which the Israelites had brought up from Egypt, were buried at Shechem, in the portion of ground that Jacob had bought from the children of Hamor, the father of Shechem, for one hundred pieces of money;[t] it became an inheritance of the descendants of Joseph.

[33] Eleazar son of Aaron died, and they buried him at Gibeah, the town of his son Phinehas, which had been given him in the hill country of Ephraim.

t 24.32 Heb *one hundred qesitah*

base of thought, mind, and will—not of feelings—in the Bible (cf. Gen. 6:5). **24:26** *The oak in the sanctuary.* Oak trees played a significant role in divine encounters in the Bible (Gen. 13:18; Judg. 6:11) and places of pagan worship (Hos. 4:13; Isa. 57:5; Ezek. 6:13; cf. Gen. 35:4; Judg. 9:6).

24:28–31 Deuteronomistic language and theology are evident in the theological significance of the conquest and the connection with Moses, as Joshua reminds the people again that their continued success depends on their loyalty to God.

24:32 *Bones of Joseph.* Compare Gen. 50:24–25; Exod. 13:19. *Pieces of money.* An amount of unknown value (Gen. 33:19; Job 42:11).

JUDGES

Historical Context and Authorship

The book of Judges is set in Canaan during Iron Age I (ca. 1200–1000 BCE), the era when archaeologists can first identify the historical people who eventually would become Israel. Although some contingent of ancient Israel may derive from foreign origins, archaeological excavations suggest that the majority of these proto-Israelites originally lived within Canaanite society before gradually migrating to the central highlands west of the Jordan River. As they grew and expanded their territory, they came into military conflict with the people in the same land (Canaanites and Philistines) as well as neighboring territories (Moabites, Ammonites, etc.). While the book of Judges does not describe Israelite origins as largely indigenous to Canaan, these stories of tribes battling without a monarchy, centralized religion, or organized army do have a flavor of historicity authentic to Iron Age I. However, it is also clear that the book as a whole was composed much later than the date when these events supposedly occurred. Various earlier sources—including etiologies (stories asserting the origin for some contemporary name or practice), poems, and folk legends about local heroes—were edited to fit into the larger theological framework of the **Deuteronomistic History** (see **p. 337**).

Reading Guide

The Deuteronomistic Historians supplemented the earlier material that they received and organized the book of Judges in a way that neatly fits into three main sections: a pair of introductions present the overarching theme of the book (1:1–2:5 and 2:6–3:6); several stories of progressively worse judges/deliverers show God's dynamic relationship with Israel (3:7–16:31); and in concluding tales, self-destructive chaos hints at the need for a king (17:1–21:25).

The first introductory section narrates victories led by the tribe of Judah, but neither Judah nor any of the other tribes can completely drive out their enemies. Since YHWH is the ultimate power behind Israelite military success, a messenger of YHWH explains that their failures are God's punishment for covenant disloyalty (2:2–3).

The second introduction continues with this theme but also places it into a larger structure. The Israelites do "evil in the eyes of YHWH" (Judg. 2:11, literal translation) by serving other gods, which provokes YHWH to hand them over to be oppressed by their enemies. Fortunately, YHWH also has compassion on the suffering people and "raised up judges who delivered them out of the power of those who plundered them" (2:16). However, "whenever the judge died, they would relapse and behave worse than their ancestors" (2:19). Therefore, the cycle of doing "evil in the eyes of YHWH" repeats. In the core of the book, the Deuteronomistic Historian fits six of the stories of judges into this cycle (3:7–11, 12–30; 4:1–5:31; 6:1–8:32; 10:6–12:7; 13:1–16:31). Interspersed between these longer narratives are notices of Shamgar, Tola, Jair, Ibzan, Elon, and Abdon (3:31; 10:1–5; 12:8–15)—characters conventionally labeled minor judges because of the brevity of their mention.

Although the term *judges* occurs in the introduction, the word *judge* does not seamlessly translate across cultures. The Hebrew root *sh-p-t* can mean "judge" in the sense of an authority figure deciding a dispute (Deut. 25:1), but that definition only describes the activity of Deborah and God in Judges (4:4–5; 11:27). Otherwise, the frequent note that a certain person "judged Israel" (3:10; 4:4; 10:2, etc.) seems to connote their authority as a leader (cf. 2 Kgs. 15:5), and that authority is most often tied to their martial ability to deliver the people.

The tales of these bellicose heroes start with the prosaic account of Othniel mechanically fitting into the pattern of the judges (3:7–11). However, the next story, about Ehud, is much more dramatic with wordplay, irony, suspense, and even (possibly) bathroom humor (3:12–30). A reader might wonder the degree to which these stories were originally meant to entertain; or, from another perspective, one might be interested to learn how faith communities across centuries have interpreted the literary qualities of accounts like this.

The next protagonist is Deborah the prophet. In a prose and poetic account, she leads multiple tribes against a technologically advanced and imposing Canaanite army at a time when an Israelite military leader, Barak, and other tribes hesitate to enter the fray. In the end, another woman (in fact, a non-Israelite woman), Jael, earns high praise for killing the Canaanite commander (5:24–27).

Stories of unlikely leaders continue with Gideon, the weakest member of the smallest clan in his tribe (6:15). He destroys his father's altar devoted to Baal (6:25–32), and he delivers the people from Midianite oppression while diplomatically defusing intratribal aggression (6:33–8:3). In spite of these good qualities, the narrator critiques Gideon for creating an illicit sacred object that the Israelites worshiped (8:27). His legacy is further stained by a son, Abimelech, who murders seventy of his brothers in a vie for rulership (9:5) before God orchestrates his downfall at the hands of a woman (9:53–56).

In each of the previous four episodes, God raised up and worked through a deliverer when the people cried out for help, but God eventually tires of the perpetual disloyalty. "Go and cry to the gods whom you have chosen," YHWH says; "let them deliver you in the time of your distress" (10:14). In response, the Israelites admit their sin for the first and only time in the book. So God uses Jephthah—an outcast from his family and community—to defeat Ammonite oppressors. Like Gideon, Jephthah's legacy is tainted. In his case, he makes a rash vow, sacrifices his daughter (11:30–39), and kills thousands of fellow Israelites (12:6).

By the time of the final judge, Samson, the people and the judges have reached new lows. The Israelites never cry out to God (13:1), and they even turn Samson over to their oppressors rather than fight (15:12). In their defense, Samson is an unhelpful deliverer. Instead of using the superhuman strength that God grants him to fight for the people, he only follows what is "right in [his] eyes" (literal translation of 14:3, 7). This leads him to two pivotal women: he marries a Philistine, which starts his violent conflicts with her people and leads to them killing her; then he falls in love with Delilah, whom the Philistines pay handsomely when she uncovers the secret to Samson's strength so that they bind and blind him as a captive. In the end, God gives Samson strength to get revenge for his blinded eyes in a suicidal mass killing.

The concluding section builds on the theme of Samson's worst trait as a flaw of all the people and a reason to look forward to the monarchy. We find the repeated refrain "in those days there was no king in Israel" (17:6; 18:1; 19:1; 21:25), and twice—including in the final verse of the book—we read the consequence, "all the people did what was right in their own eyes" (17:6; 21:25). From the perspective of the narrator, the major events of this section—establishing a sanctuary at Dan, the rape of the Levite's concubine, civil war, near genocide, kidnaping wives at Shiloh—are all expressions of chaos without a king. Thus, the end of Judges naturally foreshadows the following books in the Deuteronomistic History (1 and 2 Samuel), in which the Israelite monarchy might make things better.

Justin Michael Reed

1 After the death of Joshua, the Israelites inquired of the Lord, "Who shall go up first for us against the Canaanites, to fight against them?" ²The Lord said, "Judah shall go up. I hereby give the land into his hand." ³Judah said to his brother Simeon, "Come up with me into the territory allotted to me, that we may fight against the Canaanites; then I, too, will go with you into the territory allotted to you." So Simeon went

1:1–36 Judges 1 and 2 present different introductions to the book of Judges. In the first introduction, the narrator focuses on the need for leadership in the aftermath of Joshua's death. YHWH gives more military success to the tribe of Judah (partnered with Simeon) than the other (northern) tribes. Each tribe is personified in this chapter. **1:1–2** God brought the Israelites out of slavery in Egypt to forcibly take possession of a land inhabited by Canaanites (Exod. 3:8; 23:20–33; Deut. 7; 20:16–18). According to Josh. 10–12, the Israelites successfully destroyed all the inhabitants of the land, but the book of Judges (and Josh. 13:1–7) describes ongoing conflict with the native inhabitants. **1:1** *Inquired of the Lord* indicates an ancient southwest Asian and northeast African practice of receiving divine guidance by oracles or casting lots. Numbers 34:1–12 indicates borders for the land of Canaan. Although its inhabitants did not consider themselves to be a political or cultural unit, ancient sources and modern scholars refer to this region as Canaan and the inhabitants as *Canaanites* on account of their shared culture. In the Hebrew Bible, the term is typically singular ("the Canaanite"), including in this verse. **1:2** YHWH selects Judah to lead here and in 20:18. This suggests that a Judean author framed earlier traditions (mostly about northern judges) with the addition of chaps. 1 and 20–21. **1:3** The territory for the tribe of Simeon is within the territory of the tribe of Judah (Josh. 19:9). **1:4** A precise meaning of

with him. [4]Then Judah went up, and the LORD gave the Canaanites and the Perizzites into their hand, and they defeated ten thousand of them at Bezek. [5]They came upon Adoni-bezek at Bezek and fought against him and defeated the Canaanites and the Perizzites. [6]Adoni-bezek fled, but they pursued him and caught him and cut off his thumbs and big toes. [7]Adoni-bezek said, "Seventy kings with their thumbs and big toes cut off used to pick up scraps under my table; as I have done, so God has paid me back." They brought him to Jerusalem, and he died there.

8 Then the people of Judah fought against Jerusalem and took it. They put it to the sword and set the city on fire. [9]Afterward the people of Judah went down to fight against the Canaanites who lived in the hill country, in the Negeb, and in the lowland. [10]Judah went against the Canaanites who lived in Hebron (the name of Hebron was formerly Kiriath-arba), and they defeated Sheshai and Ahiman and Talmai.

11 From there they went against the inhabitants of Debir (the name of Debir was formerly Kiriath-sepher). [12]Then Caleb said, "Whoever attacks Kiriath-sepher and takes it, I will give him my daughter Achsah as wife." [13]And Othniel son of Kenaz, Caleb's younger brother, took it, and he gave him his daughter Achsah as wife. [14]When she came to him, she urged him to ask her father for a field. As she dismounted from her donkey, Caleb said to her, "What do you wish?" [15]She said to him, "Give me a blessing; since you have set me in the land of the Negeb, give me also Gulloth-mayim."[a] So Caleb gave her Upper Gulloth and Lower Gulloth.

16 The descendants of Hobab[b] the Kenite, Moses's father-in-law, went up with the people of Judah from the city of palms into the wilderness of Judah, which lies in the Negeb near Arad. Then they went and settled with the Amalekites.[c] [17]Judah went with his brother Simeon, and they defeated the Canaanites who inhabited Zephath and devoted it to destruction. So the city was called Hormah. [18]Judah took Gaza with its territory, Ashkelon with its territory, and Ekron with its territory. [19]The LORD was with Judah, and he took possession

a 1.15 That is, *basins of water*   b 1.16 Gk: Heb lacks *Hobab*
c 1.16 OL: Heb *people*

the Perizzites is uncertain. It may refer to native inhabitants of Canaan living outside of fortified towns. **1:7** The mutilation of captured enemies is a past and present practice in warfare with physical, social, and psychological consequences. **1:8** According to 2 Sam. 5:5–10, Jerusalem was not conquered until the reign of David. **1:10** *Kiriath-arba* literally means "the city of Arba" in Hebrew. According to Josh. 14:15 "Arba" is the name of a native Anakite who lived there. The Anakites (including *Sheshai and Ahiman and Talmai*) were a race of giants (Num. 13:26–33). Biblical legends about Anakites and other giants formerly living in the land of Canaan may have derived from the presence of dolmens (giant stone arrangements from the Intermediate Bronze Age) that the Israelites imagined as the ancient furniture remains of giants (e.g., Deut. 3:11). **1:11–15** Compare this to the nearly identical narrative in Josh. 15:13–19. **1:12** *Caleb* (meaning "Dog" in Hebrew), as the lone survivor from the first generation of the exodus (Num. 14:21–24), would have had great prominence and property (Josh. 14:13–14). He says *I will give him my daughter Achsah*, which fits with ancient practices of rulers bartering marriage to their daughters. **1:13** *Othniel* (perhaps meaning "my strength is God" in Hebrew) is a close relative of Caleb. Many biblical texts show a priority for marriage with close kin, especially to retain land within a family clan (Num. 36:7–9). **1:15** Achsah's requests fit with the custom of a father giving a dowry to his daughter and son-in-law. She requests *Gulloth-mayim* ("basins of water") because the *Negeb* (in southern Canaan) is a dry desert. **1:16** The Kenites were a nomadic group associated with the Israelites. The NRSVue follows the Old Latin translation of the Bible in stating that *they . . . settled with the Amalekites* (cf. Num. 24:20–22; 1 Sam. 15:6), but the Hebrew literally says "people," which might refer to Israelites (cf. 4:17; 5:24). *The Amalekites* were located in the Negeb and an eternal enemy of YHWH and the Israelites (Exod. 17:8–16; Deut. 25:19). **1:17** *Devoted it to destruction* translates the Hebrew root "kh-r-m." It means that all, or the majority, of potential spoils of war (including people and animals) are destroyed. Biblical (Deut. 20:16–17) and non-Israelite (the Mesha Stele) sources depict "kh-r-m" as desired by ancient deities. The name of the city *Hormah* comes from the same root word. See **"Genocide," p. 305. 1:18** *Gaza . . . Ashkelon . . . and Ekron*, along with Ashdod and Gath, make up the five major Philistine cities. In contrast to this verse, 3:3 suggests Judah did not take the major Philistine cities. **1:19** *Chariots of iron* are protected by metal siding. Elsewhere Israel and YHWH can defeat

Going Deeper: The Deuteronomistic History (Judges 1)

Joshua, Judges, 1–2 Samuel, and 1–2 Kings are known as the Former Prophets in Jewish tradition. These books narrate the Israelite conquest of Canaanites, the emergence of the monarchy with the famous kings of David and Solomon, the split of that monarchy into separate kingdoms of Israel and Judah, and the eventual exile of Israel (722 BCE) and Judah (587/586 BCE). Over the course of this long story, the Former Prophets share a certain style, key terms, major themes, and an overall theological perspective that is strikingly similar to Deuteronomy but distinct from what one finds in the Yahwist, Elohistic, and Priestly sources that make up Genesis to Numbers (see **"The Bible and Methods," pp. 2148–49**). Consequently, biblical scholars call these books the Deuteronomistic History.

Although the Deuteronomistic History tells a largely unified story, it is clear that its authors (the Deuteronomistic Historians) were drawing on diverse, earlier sources. In fact, they cite some sources by name such as "the Book of Jashar" (Josh. 10:13; 2 Sam. 1:18), "the Book of the Acts of Solomon" (1 Kgs. 11:41), "the Book of the Annals of the Kings of Israel" (1 Kgs. 14:19, etc.), and "the Book of the Annals of the Kings of Judah" (1 Kgs. 14:29, etc.). In spite of diverse perspectives in older traditions, the Deuteronomistic Historians shaped the received material into a larger story that promotes exclusive loyalty to YHWH, religious devotion at one sanctuary (eventually in Jerusalem), and praise for a Davidic dynasty (even while kingship itself is viewed ambivalently).

Most scholars believe that the Deuteronomistic History was written in two or three main stages. The final major stage was written in the sixth century BCE by an exilic author who interprets the Assyrian exile of Israel and the Babylonian exile of Judah as divine retribution for apostasy. Traces of this idea are found throughout the Deuteronomistic History. However, some passages give the impression that editions possibly existed before the Babylonian exile. Texts that shower praise on Hezekiah (2 Kgs. 18:5–7) or Josiah (1 Kgs. 13:2; 2 Kgs. 23:25) lead some scholars to assert that an earlier stage in the Deuteronomistic History might have been completed during one, or each, of their reigns while reflecting positively on Jerusalem's survival in the face of the Assyrian Empire, which crushed their northern neighbor Israel and its capital city of Samaria.

Justin Michael Reed

of the hill country but could not drive out the inhabitants of the plain, because they had chariots of iron. [20]Hebron was given to Caleb, as Moses had said, and he drove out from it the three sons of Anak. [21]But the Benjaminites did not drive out the Jebusites who lived in Jerusalem; so the Jebusites have lived in Jerusalem among the Benjaminites to this day.

22 The house of Joseph also went up against Bethel, and the LORD was with them. [23]The house of Joseph sent out spies to Bethel (the name of the city was formerly Luz). [24]When the spies saw a man coming out of the city, they said to him, "Show us the way into the city, and we will deal kindly with you." [25]So he showed them the way into the city, and they put the city to the sword, but they let the man and all his family go. [26]So the man went to the land of the Hittites

and built a city and named it Luz; that is its name to this day.

27 Manasseh did not drive out the inhabitants of[d] Beth-shean and its villages, or Taanach and its villages, or the inhabitants of Dor and its villages, or the inhabitants of Ibleam and its villages, or the inhabitants of Megiddo and its villages, but the Canaanites continued to live in that land. [28]When Israel grew strong, they put the Canaanites to forced labor but did not in fact drive them out.

29 And Ephraim did not drive out the Canaanites who lived in Gezer, but the Canaanites lived among them in Gezer.

30 Zebulun did not drive out the inhabitants of Kitron or the inhabitants of Nahalol, but the Canaanites lived among them and became subject to forced labor.

31 Asher did not drive out the inhabitants

d 1.27 Heb lacks *the inhabitants of*

chariots of iron (4:13–16). **1:21** The description of Jebusites residing in Jerusalem *to this day* shows the etiological function of this and other stories (1:26; 6:24; 10:4; 15:19; 18:12). **1:28** *Forced labor*, debt slavery (Deut. 15:12; 2 Kgs. 4:1), and chattel slavery (Lev. 25:44–46) are the three main types of slavery described in the Hebrew Bible. "Forced labor" denotes people unwillingly conscripted to serve the ruler.

of Acco or the inhabitants of Sidon, or of Mahalab,[e] or of Achzib, or of Helbah, or of Aphik, or of Rehob, [32]but the Asherites lived among the Canaanites, the inhabitants of the land, for they did not drive them out.

33 Naphtali did not drive out the inhabitants of Beth-shemesh or the inhabitants of Beth-anath but lived among the Canaanites, the inhabitants of the land; nevertheless, the inhabitants of Beth-shemesh and of Beth-anath became subject to forced labor for them.

34 The Amorites pressed the Danites back into the hill country; they did not allow them to come down to the plain. [35]The Amorites continued to live in Har-heres, in Aijalon, and in Shaalbim, but the hand of the house of Joseph rested heavily on them, and they became subject to forced labor. [36]The border of the Amorites ran from the ascent of Akrabbim, from Sela and upward.

2 Now the angel of the Lord went up from Gilgal to Bochim and said, "I brought you up from Egypt and brought you into the land that I had promised to your ancestors. I said, 'I will never break my covenant with you. [2]For your part, do not make a covenant with the inhabitants of this land; tear down their altars.' But you have not obeyed my command. See what you have done! [3]So now I say, I will not drive them out before you, but they shall become adversaries[f] to you, and their gods shall be a snare to you." [4]When the angel of the Lord spoke these words to all the Israelites, the people lifted up their voices and wept. [5]So they named that place Bochim,[g] and there they sacrificed to the Lord.

6 When Joshua dismissed the people, the Israelites all went to their own inheritances to take possession of the land. [7]The people served the Lord all the days of Joshua and all the days of the elders who outlived Joshua, who had seen all the great work that the Lord had done for Israel. [8]Joshua son of Nun, the servant of the Lord, died at the age of one hundred ten years. [9]So they buried him within the bounds of his inheritance in Timnath-heres, in the hill country of Ephraim, north of Mount Gaash. [10]Moreover, that whole generation was gathered to their ancestors, and another generation grew up after them who did not know the Lord or the work that he had done for Israel.

11 Then the Israelites did what was evil in the sight of the Lord and served the Baals, [12]and they abandoned the Lord, the God of their ancestors, who had brought them out of the land of Egypt; they followed other gods, from among the gods of the peoples who were all around them, and bowed down to them, and they provoked the Lord to anger. [13]They abandoned the Lord and served Baal and the Astartes. [14]So the anger of the Lord was kindled against Israel, and he gave them over to plunderers who plundered them, and he sold them into the power of their enemies all around, so that they could no longer withstand their enemies. [15]Whenever

e 1.31 Cn: Heb *Ahlab* f 2.3 Gk OL Vg: Heb *sides* g 2.5 That is, *weepers*

2:1–5 The Israelites' failure to avoid a *covenant* with the Canaanites and *tear down their altars* results in YHWH refusing to assist Israelite conquest. Instead, the Canaanites will be a constant threat and temptation. This message fits with the theology of the **Deuteronomistic History** (see **p. 337**). See also **"Divine Retribution," p. 339**. **2:4–5** *Bochim* means "weepers" in Hebrew. This etiology explains a strange place name to the author's contemporaries.

2:6–10 *When Joshua dismissed the people* naturally parallels "So Joshua sent the people away" (Josh. 24:28). Judges 2:6–10 repeats the same information that concludes the life of Joshua and his generation (Josh. 24:29–33) and then introduces the contrasting new generation *who did not know the Lord* (2:10). Thus, these verses seem like a continuation from the end of Joshua before Judg. 1:1–2:5 was inserted as a frame for the book of Judges (see note on 1:2).

2:11–23 These verses introduce a pattern that recurs six times in Judges (3:7–11, 12–30; 4:1–5:31; 6:1–8:32; 10:6–12:7; 13:1–16:31) with important variations: (a) Israelites do *evil in the sight of the Lord*, (b) YHWH delivers them to enemies, (c) they experience *great distress* and (not mentioned here) they cry out, (d) YHWH raises up *judges who delivered them out of the power of those who plundered them*, and (e) (not mentioned here) the land has rest. **2:11** Baal literally means "lord" or "master" in Hebrew. In Ugaritic texts, it was the standard title of Hadad, the ruling storm god and source of fertility. Here, Israelite authors use *Baals*, in the plural, to refer indiscriminately to Canaanite deities. See **"Baal," p. 489**. **2:13** Astarte was a Sidonian goddess of fertility and war. As with 2:11,

Focus On: Divine Retribution (Judges 2)

Divine retribution, the idea that God punishes in response to wrongdoing, is a major theme throughout the Hebrew Bible. In some texts, divine retribution benefits the Israelites. For example, many passages describe the Israelite exodus from slavery in Egypt as divine retribution against their oppressors (Gen. 15:13–14; Exod. 4:21–23), and their acquisition of Canaan is divine retribution against its original inhabitants (Lev. 18:24–28). Furthermore, the psalmists often hope for divine retribution against their enemies (Pss. 3:7; 5:6, 10; 9:19–20; 10:15, etc.). In other texts, divine retribution threatens Israelite well-being, like when the people of God invoke curses on themselves for covenant disloyalty (Lev. 26:14–39; Deut. 27:9–26; 28:15–68) and in narratives of God causing Israelite oppression (Josh. 7:11–12; Judg. 2:11–15; 2 Kgs. 17:7–23).

Most often, divine retribution impacts people beyond any individual wrongdoer. Although Ezek. 18 prophesies a future when divine retribution will only affect the wrongdoer (Ezek. 18:20), the norm is that God can direct punishment for a man's sins at children (Exod. 20:5), wives (Deut. 28:30), or a whole community (Gen. 12:17).

Given the prevalence of divine retribution across the Hebrew Bible, the book of Job stands out for the vigorous debate between Job and his friends over whether divine retribution explains Job's suffering. Job adamantly rejects a theology of "blaming the victim" for their own suffering, and readers are privy to the accuracy of Job's argument: the prologue shows he suffers for being righteous, not for sinning (Job 1:8–12).

The book of Job notwithstanding, most biblical authors wholeheartedly incorporated the theme of divine retribution, and some scholars offer a historical and psychological rationale for why that is the case. The idea that God causes suffering because of human wrongdoing can function to give a sense of order and control to a community in the aftermath of devastating trauma. Instead of reasoning that the life-shattering experiences of two major exiles (in 722 and 587/586 BCE) were merely the result of the tyrannical forces of the Assyrian and Babylonian Empires, biblical authors asserted God was really in control. If God allowed (or caused) these catastrophes as retribution for Israelite wrongdoing, then there is a logic behind their suffering, and the people can feel a sense of control to change their behavior and regain God's favor. Over the centuries, many religious communities have read the Bible and their experiences through this same lens.

Justin Michael Reed

they marched out, the hand of the Lord was against them to bring misfortune, as the Lord had warned them and sworn to them, and they were in great distress.

16 Then the Lord raised up judges who delivered them out of the power of those who plundered them. [17]Yet they did not listen even to their judges, for they lusted after other gods and bowed down to them. They soon turned aside from the way in which their ancestors had walked, who had obeyed the commandments of the Lord; they did not follow their example. [18]Whenever the Lord raised up judges for them, the Lord was with the judge, and he delivered them from the hand of their enemies all the days of the judge, for the Lord would be moved to pity by their groaning because of those who persecuted and oppressed them. [19]But whenever the judge died, they would relapse and behave worse than their ancestors, following other gods, serving them and bowing down to them. They would not drop any of their practices or their stubborn ways. [20]So the anger of the Lord was kindled against Israel, and he said, "Because this nation has transgressed my covenant that I commanded their ancestors and have not obeyed my voice, [21]I will no longer drive out before them any of the nations that Joshua left when he died." [22]In order to test Israel, whether or not they would take care to walk in the way of the Lord as their ancestors did, [23]the Lord had left those nations, not driving them out at once, and had not handed them over to Joshua.

the plural usage, *Astartes*, refers indiscriminately to Canaanite goddesses. **2:17** The description of persistent unfaithfulness intensifies from asserting that Israelites "followed other gods" (v. 12) to stating that they *lusted after other gods* in this verse. The metaphorical description of covenant infidelity as sexual unfaithfulness is common in the Hebrew Bible. (See Hos. 2 and Jer. 2–3.)

2:20–3:4 Three reasons are offered for YHWH's decision to leave Canaanites in the land: as punishment because they *transgressed my covenant* (2:20–21); *to test Israel* regarding potential fidelity

3 Now these are the nations that the LORD left to test all those in Israel who had no experience of war in Canaan ²(it was only for successive generations of Israelites, to teach war to those who had no experience of it): ³the five lords of the Philistines, and all the Canaanites, and the Sidonians, and the Hivites who lived on Mount Lebanon, from Mount Baal-hermon as far as Lebo-hamath. ⁴They were for the testing of Israel, to know whether Israel would obey the commandments of the LORD that he commanded their ancestors by Moses. ⁵So the Israelites lived among the Canaanites, the Hittites, the Amorites, the Perizzites, the Hivites, and the Jebusites, ⁶and they took their daughters as wives for themselves, and their own daughters they gave to their sons, and they served their gods.

7 The Israelites did what was evil in the sight of the LORD, forgetting the LORD their God and serving the Baals and the Asherahs. ⁸Therefore the anger of the LORD was kindled against Israel, and he sold them into the hand of King Cushan-rishathaim of Aram-naharaim, and the Israelites served Cushan-rishathaim eight years. ⁹But when the Israelites cried out to the LORD, the LORD raised up a deliverer for the Israelites who delivered them, Othniel son of Kenaz, Caleb's younger brother. ¹⁰The spirit of the LORD came upon him, and he judged Israel; he went out to war, and the LORD gave King Cushan-rishathaim of Aram into his hand, and his hand prevailed over Cushan-rishathaim. ¹¹So the land had rest forty years. Then Othniel son of Kenaz died.

12 The Israelites again did what was evil in the sight of the LORD, and the LORD strengthened King Eglon of Moab against Israel, because they had done what was evil in the sight of the LORD. ¹³In alliance with the Ammonites and the Amalekites, he went and defeated Israel, and they took possession of the city of palms. ¹⁴So the Israelites served King Eglon of Moab eighteen years.

15 But when the Israelites cried out to the LORD, the LORD raised up for them a

to the covenant (2:22–23; 3:4); or *to teach war to* a generation without experience (3:1–2). **3:3** *The five lords of the Philistines* correspond to the five major Philistine cities (see note on 1:18). *The Philistines* were "sea peoples" who came to southwestern Canaan around the twelfth century BCE. On *the Canaanites*, see note on 1:1. *The Sidonians* were Phoenicians in the northern city-state of Sidon. There are no ancient records about *the Hivites*.

3:5 The Hebrew Bible describes *the Amorites* as native inhabitants of Canaan, distinct from the Canaanites and notable for their stature (Amos 2:9).

3:6 The Deuteronomistic History displays a major concern against intermarriage with Canaanites (Deut. 7:3–4).

3:7–11 On *Othniel*, see 1:11–15 and Josh. 15:13–19. Othniel's story neatly fits the judges pattern (see note on Judg. 2:11–23). **3:7–8** On *the Baals and the Asherahs* as plural forms, see notes on 2:11 and 13. Asherah was the mother goddess and consort of the Canaanite father of the pantheon, El. The difference between Astartes (2:13) and *Asherahs* in this verse likely derives from a biblical author that did not care to accurately distinguish rival goddesses. *Cushan-rishathaim* means "Cushan–doubly wicked" in Hebrew. The first half of the name derives from Cush, a people group south of Egypt (possibly on both sides of the Red Sea) or the Kassites in Mesopotamia; the latter half seems to be a pun intentionally corrupting a name. *Aram-naharaim* refers to a region in northern Mesopotamia, while "Aram" (3:10) typically denotes an area closer to Israel around Damascus. **3:10** *The spirit of the LORD* (in Hebrew, a grammatically feminine description of God's activity) comes on Othniel, Gideon (6:34), Jephthah (11:29), and Samson (13:25; 14:6, 19; 15:14) to enable them to lead and win in battle. Her spontaneity matches the spontaneous development of leaders in the book of Judges.

3:12–30 Since wordplay, exaggeration, and potential incongruity can be discerned in Ehud's story, many scholars read this narrative as humorous. **3:12** YHWH's control over events is described as strengthening the power of a foreign king as opposed to simply giving (2:14) or selling (3:8) Israelites into the power of their oppressor. The name *Eglon* seems to derive from the Hebrew word for a "fattened calf." *Moab* was east of the Dead Sea, north of Edom. In the Hebrew Bible, Moabites are frequently enemies of Israel (Num. 22–24), but the book of Ruth depicts Ruth and her descendant King David as Moabite and part-Moabite, respectively, which might suggest a tradition of Moabite inclusion contrary to the standard aversion (see Deut. 23:3–4). **3:13** For *Amalekites*, see note on 1:16. *The Ammonites* are from Ammon, east of the Dead Sea and north of Moab. **3:15** *Ehud* is literally "hindered in

deliverer, Ehud son of Gera, a Benjaminite, a left-handed man. The Israelites sent tribute by him to King Eglon of Moab. [16]Ehud made for himself a sword with two edges, a cubit in length, and he fastened it on his right thigh under his clothes. [17]Then he presented the tribute to King Eglon of Moab. Now Eglon was a very fat man. [18]When Ehud had finished presenting the tribute, he sent the people who carried the tribute on their way. [19]But he himself turned back at the sculptured stones near Gilgal and said, "I have a secret message for you, O king." So the king said,[b] "Silence!" and all his attendants went out from his presence. [20]Ehud came to him, while he was sitting alone in his cool roof chamber, and said, "I have a message from God for you." So he rose from his seat. [21]Then Ehud reached with his left hand, took the sword from his right thigh, and thrust it into Eglon's[i] belly; [22]the hilt also went in after the blade, and the fat closed over the blade, for he did not draw the sword out of his belly, and the dirt[j] came out. [23]Then Ehud went out into the vestibule[k] and closed the doors of the roof chamber on him and locked them.

24 After he had gone, the servants came. When they saw that the doors of the roof chamber were locked, they thought, "He must be relieving himself[l] in the cool chamber." [25]So they waited until they were embarrassed. When he still did not open the doors of the roof chamber, they took the key and opened them. There was their lord lying dead on the floor.

26 Ehud escaped while they delayed and passed beyond the sculptured stones and escaped to Seirah. [27]When he arrived, he sounded the trumpet in the hill country of Ephraim, and the Israelites went down with him from the hill country, having him at their head. [28]He said to them, "Follow after me, for the Lord has given your enemies the Moabites into your hand." So they went down after him and seized the fords of the Jordan against the Moabites and allowed no one to cross over. [29]At that time they killed about ten thousand of the Moabites, all strong, able-bodied men; no one escaped. [30]So Moab was subdued that day under the hand of Israel. And the land had rest eighty years.

31 After him came Shamgar son of Anath, who killed six hundred of the Philistines with an oxgoad. He, too, delivered Israel.

4 The Israelites again did what was evil in the sight of the Lord, after Ehud died. [2]So the Lord sold them into the hand of King Jabin of Canaan, who reigned in Hazor; the commander of his army was Sisera, who lived in Harosheth-ha-goiim. [3]Then the Israelites cried out to the Lord for help, for he had nine hundred chariots of iron and had oppressed the Israelites cruelly twenty years.

4 At that time Deborah, a prophet, wife of Lappidoth, was judging Israel. [5]She used to sit under the palm of Deborah between Ramah and Bethel in the hill country of

b 3.19 Heb *he said*   i 3.21 Heb *his*   j 3.22 Compare Tg Vg: Meaning of Heb uncertain   k 3.23 Meaning of Heb uncertain   l 3.24 Heb *covering his feet*

his right hand." Often this is translated as *left-handed*, although the literal meaning might indicate the ability of certain elite warriors to skillfully use their left hand when the right one is incapacitated (Judg. 20:16; 1 Chr. 12:1–2). Either understanding is ironic, since he is from the tribe of Benjamin, which literally means "son of the right [hand]" (see text note on Gen. 35:18). **3:16** Ehud's *sword* must have been short enough to hide *on his right thigh under his clothes*. The unit of measurement translated as *cubit* only occurs in this verse. **3:17** The description of Eglon as *a very fat man* in this verse and the over-the-top description of fat enveloping the blade that kills him in v. 22 might indicate that his name is a satirical moniker (see note on 3:12). **3:19** The word *message* here and in 3:20 translates from the Hebrew "dabar," which can mean "a word" or "a thing." Eglon's reaction suggests that he expects a word; what he gets is "a whole different thing," so to speak. **3:29** The note that *no one escaped* in spite of the Moabites' stature and number shows the magnitude of this success and of the forthcoming fall in 4:1.

3:31 Scholars debate whether to count *Shamgar* as a judge or a nonjudicial deliverer like Jael. *Anath* is the name of a Canaanite goddess.

4:2 *King Jabin of Canaan* is an unlikely title, since Canaanite city-states had many rulers (see note on 1:1). *Hazor* is in the eastern Galilee region.

4:4–5 *Deborah* means "Bee" in Hebrew. She is one of several women prophets in the Hebrew Bible (Exod. 15:20; Isa. 8:3; Neh. 6:14; 2 Kgs. 22:14). *Wife of Lappidoth* could also be translated as

Reading through Time: The Judges (Judges 4)
Over the centuries, people in various contexts have found creative ways of fashioning meaning from the stories of the judges in conversation with contemporary issues. The following is a small taste of the diverse meanings and uses of a few of the judges.

Many people have appealed to the story of Deborah (Judg. 4–5) in debates about women: how women should behave; the appropriateness of an unwed woman monarch; women's rights to preach, vote, and hold office; and a woman's role as a mother, wife, and professional. For some, Deborah's story speaks powerfully as a precedent and divine approval of expanding women's place in synagogues, churches, and society, but opponents see her story fitting with their contemporary patriarchal worldview.

The story of Gideon (Judg. 6–8) has informed and been informed by cultural and historical understandings of what it means to be a man. Some interpreters have seen Gideon's hesitancy and testing God (Judg. 6:11–40) as unmanly, while others have praised these same events as modeling ideal manhood. Perhaps most famously, the Gideons International (an organization of "men and their wives" famous for distributing "Gideon Bibles") picked their name in 1899 out of aspirations to be men like Gideon and the few brave and obedient men God used in Judg. 7.

Wrestling meaning from the story of Jephthah's vow and sacrifice of his daughter (Judg. 11) has been no mean feat. Opposite reactions include praise for Jephthah's faithfulness or condemnation of his tragically rash behavior. The interpretative afterlife of his daughter also includes diametrically opposed responses: depicting her as a relatable martyr (even a precursor to Jesus for Christians) or arguing that she was never really sacrificed. In communities as far apart as the Eastern Stars (in North America) and iBandla lamaNazaretha (in South Africa), Jephthah's daughter serves as a profound symbol for women who engage in community binding (and building) ceremonies that rehearse passages and paraphrases from Judg. 11.

Finally, the most famous judge, Samson (Judg. 13–16), has a wealth of interpretive traditions attached to his name. One particular tradition, Black Americans fighting for liberation throughout the nineteenth and twentieth centuries, has appropriated him in diverse and contradictory ways—from a rebel to a staunch patriot, from a loyal slave to an abolitionist, from an exemplar of prudent resistance to a lesson on suicidal shortsightedness, from a dangerous warrior to a pitiful captive, and more.

Justin Michael Reed

Ephraim, and the Israelites came up to her for judgment. ⁶She sent and summoned Barak son of Abinoam from Kedesh in Naphtali and said to him, "The Lord, the God of Israel, commands you, 'Position yourself at Mount Tabor, taking ten thousand from the tribe of Naphtali and the tribe of Zebulun. ⁷I will draw out Sisera, the general of Jabin's army, to meet you by the Wadi Kishon with his chariots and his troops, and I will give him into your hand.'" ⁸Barak said to her, "If you will go with me, I will go, but if you will not go with me, I will not go." ⁹And she said, "I will surely go with you; nevertheless, the road on which you are going will not lead to your glory, for the Lord will sell Sisera into the hand of a woman." Then Deborah got up and went with Barak to Kedesh. ¹⁰Barak summoned Zebulun and Naphtali to Kedesh, and ten thousand warriors went up behind him, and Deborah went up with him.

11 Now Heber the Kenite had separated from the other Kenites,ᵐ that is, the descendants of Hobab the father-in-law of Moses, and had encamped as far away as Elon-bezaanannim, which is near Kedesh.

m 4.11 Heb *from the Kain*

"woman of torches." Such a designation would describe Deborah according to an ancient practice of interpreting divine messages through "reading" flames. Among the so-called judges, only Deborah has people coming *up to her for judgment*.

4:6 *Barak* means "Lightning" in Hebrew.

4:7–9 Deborah proclaims YHWH's unqualified confidence in victory. Barak's less-than-eager response solicits Deborah's prophecy that the military commander will be outshined: *the Lord will sell Sisera into the hand of a woman*. Barak may have assumed Deborah is the woman. It is unclear if Deborah thought of herself or someone else.

4:11 On *the Kenite*, see note on 1:16.

12 When Sisera was told that Barak son of Abinoam had gone up to Mount Tabor, ¹³Sisera called out all his chariots, nine hundred chariots of iron, and all the troops who were with him, from Harosheth-ha-goiim to the Wadi Kishon. ¹⁴Then Deborah said to Barak, "Up! For this is the day on which the Lᴏʀᴅ has given Sisera into your hand. Has not the Lᴏʀᴅ gone out before you?" So Barak went down from Mount Tabor with ten thousand warriors following him. ¹⁵And the Lᴏʀᴅ threw Sisera and all his chariots and all his army into a panic" before Barak; Sisera got down from his chariot and fled away on foot, ¹⁶while Barak pursued the chariots and the army to Harosheth-ha-goiim. All the army of Sisera fell by the sword; not one was left.

17 Now Sisera had fled away on foot to the tent of Jael wife of Heber the Kenite, for there was peace between King Jabin of Hazor and the clan of Heber the Kenite. ¹⁸Jael came out to meet Sisera and said to him, "Turn aside, my lord, turn aside to me; have no fear." So he turned aside to her into the tent, and she covered him with a rug. ¹⁹Then he said to her, "Please give me a little water to drink, for I am thirsty." So she opened a skin of milk and gave him a drink and covered him. ²⁰He said to her, "Stand at the entrance of the tent, and if anybody comes and asks you, 'Is anyone here?' say, 'No.'" ²¹But Jael wife of Heber took a tent peg and took a hammer in her hand and went softly to him and drove the peg into his temple, until it went down into the ground—he was lying fast asleep

from weariness—and he died. ²²Then, as Barak came in pursuit of Sisera, Jael went out to meet him and said to him, "Come, and I will show you the man whom you are seeking." So he went into her tent, and there was Sisera lying dead, with the tent peg in his temple.

23 So on that day God subdued King Jabin of Canaan before the Israelites. ²⁴Then the hand of the Israelites bore harder and harder on King Jabin of Canaan, until they destroyed King Jabin of Canaan.

5 Then Deborah and Barak son of Abinoam sang on that day,
² "When locks are long in Israel,
    when the people offer themselves
        willingly°—
    bless the Lᴏʀᴅ!

³ Hear, O kings; give ear, O princes;
    to the Lᴏʀᴅ I will sing;
    I will make melody to the Lᴏʀᴅ, the
        God of Israel.

⁴ Lᴏʀᴅ, when you went out from Seir,
    when you marched from the region
        of Edom,
the earth trembled,
    and the heavens poured;
    the clouds indeed poured water.
⁵ The mountains quaked before the Lᴏʀᴅ,
    the One of Sinai,
    before the Lᴏʀᴅ, the God of Israel.

n 4.15 Heb adds *to the sword*   o 5.2 Meaning of Heb uncertain

4:15 YHWH functions as a divine warrior (Exod. 15:3) who throws enemies *into a panic* (similarly, see Josh. 10:10; Exod. 14:24).

4:17 *Jael* means "mountain goat" in Hebrew. She, like other nomadic women in the Hebrew Bible, has her own tent dwelling apart from her husband (cf. Gen. 31:33).

4:18 Milk was normally converted into other products for adults to consume in ancient southwest Asia and northeast Africa. Thus, it seems strange for Jael to offer milk (not wine) and (perhaps childlike) for Sisera to drink it.

5:1–31 Most scholars believe the Song of Deborah is one of the oldest passages in the Hebrew Bible and that chap. 4 is a narrative retelling based on this poem. Only northern tribes are mentioned here (Judah, Simeon, and Levi are absent). The poem has an opening that invokes listeners (vv. 2–3), a closing that celebrates allegiance with YHWH (v. 31a), and three central sections: YHWH's power in contrast to Israel's oppression (vv. 4–11c), a (cosmic) conflict against the Canaanites (vv. 11d–23), and Jael's defeat of Sisera in contrast to the imagination of Sisera's mother (vv. 24–30). **5:1** The Hebrew verb translated as *sang* is feminine and singular, which prioritizes Deborah as the primary singer. **5:2** The translation *when locks are long* is unclear in Hebrew. This phrase might evoke images of Nazirites growing their hair in devotion to God (Num. 6:5). A very different translation is "when the leaders took the lead." **5:4** This is one of many depictions in the Hebrew Bible of a theophany, an event in which God shows up, causing a jarring reaction from the natural world. *Edom* is to the

⁶ In the days of Shamgar son of Anath,
   in the days of Jael, caravans ceased,
   and travelers kept to the byways.
⁷ The peasantry prospered in Israel;
   they grew fat on plunder,
because*ᵖ* you arose, Deborah,
   arose as a mother in Israel.
⁸ When new gods were chosen,
   then war was in the gates.
Was shield or spear to be seen
   among forty thousand in Israel?
⁹ My heart goes out to the commanders
   of Israel
who offered themselves willingly
   among the people.
   Bless the Lord.

¹⁰ Sing of it, you who ride on white
   donkeys,
you who sit on rich carpets,*q*
   and you who walk by the way.
¹¹ To the sound of musicians*r* at the
   watering places,
there they repeat the triumphs of
   the Lord,
the triumphs of his peasantry in
   Israel.

Then down to the gates marched the
   people of the Lord.
¹² Awake, awake, Deborah!
   Awake, awake, utter a song!
Arise, Barak, lead away your captives,
   O son of Abinoam.
¹³ Then down marched the remnant of
   the nobles;
the people of the Lord marched
   down for him*s* against the mighty.
¹⁴ From Ephraim they set out*t* into the
   valley,*u*

following you, Benjamin, with your
   kin;
from Machir marched down the
   commanders,
   and from Zebulun those who bear
   the marshal's staff;
¹⁵ the chiefs of Issachar came with
   Deborah,
and Issachar faithful to Barak;
   into the valley they rushed out at his
   heels.
Among the clans of Reuben
   there were great searchings of
   heart.
¹⁶ Why did you tarry among the
   sheepfolds,
   to hear the piping for the flocks?
Among the clans of Reuben
   there were great searchings of
   heart.
¹⁷ Gilead stayed beyond the Jordan,
   and Dan, why did he abide with the
   ships?
Asher sat still at the coast of the sea,
   settling down by his landings.
¹⁸ Zebulun is a people that scorned death;
   Naphtali, too, on the heights of the
   field.

¹⁹ The kings came; they fought;
   then fought the kings of Canaan,
at Taanach, by the waters of Megiddo;
   they got no spoils of silver.
²⁰ The stars fought from heaven;
   from their courses they fought
   against Sisera.

p 5.7 Or *ceased in Israel, ceased until*   *q* 5.10 Meaning of Heb uncertain *r* 5.11 Meaning of Heb uncertain *s* 5.13 Gk mss: Heb *me* *t* 5.14 Cn: Heb *From Ephraim their root* *u* 5.14 Gk: Heb *in Amalek*

south of Moab, and *Seir* is an important mountain there. This southern locale is treated as the direction from which YHWH marches (similarly, see Deut. 33:2; Hab. 3:3). A southern origin for YHWH may reflect the direction from which storms arise (with the depiction of YHWH as a storm god) or a historical memory of the geographical region from which worship of YHWH was introduced to Israelites. **5:6** On *Shamgar*, see note on 3:31. **5:7** On *Deborah*, see note on 4:4–5. Here the title *a mother in Israel* supplements her other titles (see note on 2 Sam. 20:19). Deborah's actions as *a mother* contrast "the mother of Sisera" (Judg. 5:28–30). **5:8** Worshiping *new gods* is the problem here like "other gods" in 2:12. **5:11** *Watering places* and *the gates* (of the city) are important places of meeting (Gen. 24:11; Deut. 21:18–19). **5:14–18** Six tribes heed the call to battle: *Ephraim, Benjamin, Machir* (a son of Manasseh in Josh. 17:1), *Zebulun, Issachar,* and *Naphtali*. Four tribes receive reproach for their unwillingness to join: *Reuben, Gilead* (a descendant of Manasseh in Josh. 17:3, but many scholars see them as representing Gad because of Josh. 13:24–25), *Dan,* and *Asher*. These are all northern tribes. The southern tribes of Judah and Simeon along with (landless) Levi are missing. **5:20–22** The earthly battle joins a cosmic contest as *the stars fought from heaven . . . against Sisera*.

²¹ The torrent Kishon swept them
    away,
  the onrushing torrent, the torrent
    Kishon.
  March on, my soul, with might!

²² Then loud beat the horses' hoofs
  with the galloping, galloping of his
    steeds.

²³ Curse Meroz, says the angel of the
    Lord;
  curse bitterly its inhabitants,
because they did not come to the help
    of the Lord,
  to the help of the Lord against the
    mighty.

²⁴ Most blessed of women be Jael,
  the wife of Heber the Kenite,
  of tent-dwelling women most
    blessed.
²⁵ Water he asked, milk she gave;
  she brought him curds in a lordly
    bowl.
²⁶ She put her hand to the tent peg
  and her right hand to the workers'
    mallet;
she struck Sisera a blow;
  she crushed his head;
  she shattered and pierced his
    temple.
²⁷ Between her feet he sank, he fell,
  he lay still;
between her feet he sank, he fell;
  where he sank, there he fell dead.

²⁸ Out of the window she peered;
  the mother of Sisera gazedᵛ through
    the lattice:
'Why is his chariot so long in coming?
  Why tarry the hoofbeats of his
    chariots?'

²⁹ Her wisest ladies make answer;
  indeed, she answers the question
    herself:
³⁰ 'Are they not finding and dividing the
    spoil?
  A woman or two for every man;
spoil of dyed stuffs for Sisera,
  spoil of dyed stuffs embroidered,
  two pieces of dyed work
    embroidered for my neck as
    spoil?'

³¹ So perish all your enemies, O Lord!
  But may your friends be like the sun
    as it rises in its might."

And the land had rest forty years.

6 The Israelites did what was evil in the sight of the Lord, and the Lord gave them into the hand of Midian seven years. ²The hand of Midian prevailed over Israel, and because of Midian the Israelites provided for themselves hiding places in the mountains, caves and strongholds. ³For whenever the Israelites put in seed, the Midianites and the Amalekites and the people of the east would come up against them. ⁴They would encamp against them and destroy the produce of the land, as far as the neighborhood of Gaza, and leave no sustenance in Israel, nor any sheep or ox or donkey. ⁵For they and their livestock would come up, and they would even bring their tents, as thick as locusts; neither they nor their camels could be counted, so they wasted the land as they came in. ⁶Thus Israel was greatly impoverished because of Midian, and the Israelites cried out to the Lord for help.

v 5.28 Gk Compare Tg: Heb *exclaimed*

The *onrushing torrent* seems to imply that the stars contributed stormy rainfall against the Canaanites. **5:23** The identity of *Meroz* is uncertain. **5:24–27** This poetry parallels 4:18–22 and emphasizes praise on Jael. **5:28–30** These verses present an ironic contrast between what happened in a tent (death of Sisera at the hands of a woman) and what Sisera's mother imagines peering *out of the window* of a house (Sisera capturing women as spoils of war).

    6:1 The pattern of judges introduced in 2:11–23 recurs for the fourth time.

    6:2–6 For the first time in the judges pattern, oppression is specific, not generic. *Midianites* are descendants of Abraham (Gen. 25:2), sometimes depicted as friends (Exod. 2:15–22; 18:1–27) and other times as foes of Israel (Num. 31:1–12). See note on 1:16 for *Amalekites*. Both groups, and *people of the east*, are depicted as nomads who intentionally ruin Israelite harvests, an example of environmental degradation as a military strategy (similarly, see 15:5).

[[7 When the Israelites cried to the Lord on account of the Midianites, [8]the Lord sent a prophet to the Israelites, and he said to them, "Thus says the Lord, the God of Israel: I led you up from Egypt and brought you out of the house of slavery, [9]and I delivered you from the hand of the Egyptians and from the hand of all who oppressed you and drove them out before you and gave you their land, [10]and I said to you, 'I am the Lord your God; you shall not pay reverence to the gods of the Amorites in whose land you live.' But you have not given heed to my voice."[w]]]

11 Now the angel of the Lord came and sat under the oak at Ophrah, which belonged to Joash the Abiezrite, as his son Gideon was beating out wheat in the winepress, to hide it from the Midianites. [12]The angel of the Lord appeared to him and said to him, "The Lord is with you, you mighty warrior." [13]Gideon answered him, "But sir, if the Lord is with us, why then has all this happened to us? And where are all his wonderful deeds that our ancestors recounted to us, saying, 'Did not the Lord bring us up from Egypt?' But now the Lord has cast us off and given us into the hand of Midian." [14]Then the Lord turned to him and said, "Go in this might of yours and deliver Israel from the hand of Midian; I hereby commission you." [15]He responded, "But sir, how can I deliver Israel? My clan is the weakest in Manasseh, and I am the least in my family." [16]The Lord said to him, "But I will be with you, and you shall strike down the Midianites, every one of them." [17]Then he said to him, "If now I have found favor with you, then show me a sign that it is you who speak with me. [18]Do not depart from here until I come to you and bring out my present and set it before you." And he said, "I will stay until you return."

19 So Gideon went into his house and prepared a kid and unleavened cakes from an ephah of flour; the meat he put in a basket, and the broth he put in a pot and brought them to him under the oak and presented them. [20]The angel of God said to him, "Take the meat and the unleavened cakes and put them on this rock and pour out the broth." And he did so. [21]Then the angel of the Lord reached out the tip of the staff that was in his hand and touched the meat and the unleavened cakes, and fire sprang up from the rock and consumed the meat and the unleavened cakes, and the angel of the Lord vanished from his sight. [22]Then Gideon perceived that it was the angel of the Lord, and Gideon said, "Help me, Lord God! For I have seen the angel of the Lord face to face." [23]But the Lord said to him, "Peace be to you; do not fear; you shall not die." [24]Then Gideon built an altar there to the Lord and called it, "The Lord is peace." To this day it still stands at Ophrah, which belongs to the Abiezrites.

25 That night the Lord said to him, "Take your father's bull, the second bull seven years old, and pull down the altar of Baal that belongs to your father and cut down the sacred pole[x] that is beside it [26]and build an altar to the Lord your God on the top of the stronghold here, in proper order;[y] then take the second bull and offer it as a burnt offering with the wood of the sacred pole[z] that you cut down." [27]So Gideon took ten of his servants and did as the Lord had told him, but because he was too afraid of his

w 6.10 Q ms lacks 6.7–10   x 6.25 Or *Asherah*
y 6.26 Meaning of Heb uncertain   z 6.26 Or *Asherah*

6:7–10 These verses (missing from 4QJudgᵃ, a Dead Sea Scroll manuscript) have the Israelites cry out to YHWH, who then scolds them. They do not include an Israelite reaction to divine scolding.
6:11–27 YHWH calls Gideon to destroy an altar to Baal (see notes on 2:1–5 and 2:11). Gideon exhibits suspicion, leading him to test the divine messenger thrice. **6:11** The *angel* [or "messenger"] *of the Lord* appears here, and elsewhere in the Bible, in ways in which the angel's identity is not always clear. The narrator or a character sometimes equates the messenger with God (Exod. 3:2–4; Gen. 16:11–13) or confuses them for a human (Josh. 5:13–14). *Under the oak* alludes to an ancient practice of revering trees as sacred sites (Gen. 18:1). *Gideon* means "hewer" or "cutter" in Hebrew; God commands him to cut down an idol in Judg. 6:25. An *Abiezrite* is a descendant of the clan of Abiezer, a son of Manasseh (Josh. 17:2). **6:16** In response to Gideon's fear of powerlessness, (the messenger of) YHWH responds, *I will be with you* (cf. Exod. 3:11–12). But Gideon does not yet know with whom he is speaking. **6:22** Gideon's fear upon realizing the speaker's identity matches a prevalent fear throughout the Hebrew Bible that looking upon a divine being can be deadly (13:22). **6:24** On *to this day*, see note on 1:21. **6:25** A *sacred pole* is an object for worshiping Asherah (see note on 3:7–8).

family and the townspeople to do it by day, he did it by night.

28 When the townspeople rose early in the morning, the altar of Baal was broken down, and the sacred pole[a] beside it was cut down, and the second bull was offered on the altar that had been built. [29]So they said to one another, "Who has done this?" After searching and inquiring, they were told, "Gideon son of Joash did it." [30]Then the townspeople said to Joash, "Bring out your son so that he may die, for he has pulled down the altar of Baal and cut down the sacred pole[b] beside it." [31]But Joash said to all who were arrayed against him, "Will you contend for Baal? Or will you defend his cause? Whoever contends for him shall be put to death by morning. If he is a god, let him contend for himself, because his altar has been pulled down." [32]Therefore on that day Gideon[c] was called Jerubbaal, that is to say, "Let Baal contend against him," because he pulled down his altar.

33 Then all the Midianites and the Amalekites and the people of the east came together, and they crossed over and encamped in the Valley of Jezreel. [34]But the spirit of the LORD took possession of Gideon, and he sounded the trumpet, and the Abiezrites were called out to follow him. [35]He sent messengers throughout all Manasseh, and they, too, were called out to follow him. He also sent messengers to Asher, Zebulun, and Naphtali, and they went up to meet them.

36 Then Gideon said to God, "In order to see whether you will deliver Israel by my hand, as you have said, [37]I am going to lay a fleece of wool on the threshing floor; if there is dew on the fleece alone, and it is dry on all the ground, then I shall know that you will deliver Israel by my hand, as you have said." [38]And it was so. When he rose early next morning and squeezed the fleece, he wrung enough dew from the fleece to fill a bowl with water. [39]Then Gideon said to God, "Do not let your anger burn against me, but let me speak one more time; let me, please, make trial with the fleece just once more; let it be dry only on the fleece, and on all the ground let there be dew." [40]And God did so that night. It was dry on the fleece only, and on all the ground there was dew.

7 Then Jerubbaal (that is, Gideon) and all the troops who were with him rose early and encamped beside the spring of Harod, and the camp of Midian was north of them, below[d] the hill of Moreh, in the valley.

2 The LORD said to Gideon, "The troops with you are too many for me to give the Midianites into their hand. Israel would only take the credit away from me, saying, 'My own hand has delivered me.' [3]Now, therefore, proclaim this in the hearing of the troops, 'Whoever is fearful and trembling, let him return home.'" Thus Gideon sifted them out;[e] twenty-two thousand returned, and ten thousand remained.

4 Then the LORD said to Gideon, "The troops are still too many; take them down to the water, and I will sift them out for you there. When I say, 'This one shall go with you,' he shall go with you, and when I say, 'This one shall not go with you,' he shall not go." [5]So he brought the troops down to the water, and the LORD said to Gideon, "All those who lap the water with their tongues, as a dog laps, you shall put to one side; all those who kneel down to drink, putting their hands to their mouths,[f] you shall put to the other side." [6]The number of those

a 6.28 Or Asherah   b 6.30 Or Asherah   c 6.32 Heb he
d 7.1 Heb from   e 7.3 Cn: Heb home, and depart from Mount Gilead'"   f 7.5 Heb places putting their hands to their mouths after lapped in 7.6

6:32 Gideon earns the name Jerubbaal for contending against Baal. Since it is abnormal for a person's name to denigrate a deity, this story likely covers up the original meaning of Jerubbaal, "Baal contends [for me]."
7:1–8 After Gideon has tested YHWH three times (6:17–21, 36–40), YHWH brings about tests meant to show the divine source of victory. 7:2 God makes the goal of the following tests clear: to create a competitive disadvantage such that Israel will not say My own hand has delivered me. 7:4–7 Distinguishing the selected from the dismissed group is more confusing in Hebrew than in this translation. God instructs Gideon to separate people who (a) lap . . . as a dog laps from those who (b1) kneel down to drink (b2) putting their hands to their mouths. The selected group of three hundred (a) lapped (b2) putting their hand to their mouths. Regardless of confusion, the main goal of selecting fewer people is accomplished.

who lapped was three hundred, but all the rest of the troops knelt down to drink water. [7]Then the LORD said to Gideon, "With the three hundred who lapped I will deliver you and give the Midianites into your hand. Let all the others go to their homes." [8]So the people took provisions in their hands and their trumpets, and he sent all the rest of Israel back to their own tents but retained the three hundred. The camp of Midian was below him in the valley.

[9] That same night the LORD said to him, "Get up; attack the camp, for I have given it into your hand. [10]But if you fear to attack, go down to the camp with your servant Purah, [11]and you shall hear what they say, and afterward your hands shall be strengthened to attack the camp." Then he went down with his servant Purah to the outposts of the armed men who were in the camp. [12]The Midianites and the Amalekites and all the people of the east lay along the valley as thick as locusts, and their camels were without number, countless as the sand on the seashore. [13]When Gideon arrived, there was a man telling a dream to his comrade, and he said, "I had a dream, and in it a cake of barley bread tumbled into the camp of Midian and came to the tent and struck it so that it fell; it turned upside down, and the tent collapsed." [14]And his comrade answered, "This is no other than the sword of Gideon son of Joash, a man of Israel; into his hand God has given Midian and all the army."

[15] When Gideon heard the telling of the dream and its interpretation, he worshiped, and he returned to the camp of Israel and said, "Get up, for the LORD has given the army of Midian into your hand." [16]After he divided the three hundred men into three companies and put trumpets into the hands of all of them and empty jars, with torches inside the jars, [17]he said to them, "Look at me, and do the same; when I come to the outskirts of the camp, do as I do. [18]When I blow the trumpet, I and all who are with me, then you also blow the trumpets around the whole camp and shout, 'For the LORD and for Gideon!'"

[19] So Gideon and the hundred who were with him came to the outskirts of the camp at the beginning of the middle watch, when they had just set the watch, and they blew the trumpets and smashed the jars that were in their hands. [20]So the three companies blew the trumpets and broke the jars, holding in their left hands the torches and in their right hands the trumpets to blow, and they cried, "A sword for the LORD and for Gideon!" [21]Every man stood in his place all around the camp, and all the men in camp ran; they cried out and fled. [22]When they blew the three hundred trumpets, the LORD set every man's sword against his fellow and against all the army, and the army fled as far as Beth-shittah toward Zererah,[g] as far as the border of Abel-meholah, by Tabbath. [23]And the men of Israel were called out from Naphtali and from Asher and from all Manasseh, and they pursued after the Midianites.

[24] Then Gideon sent messengers throughout all the hill country of Ephraim, saying, "Come down against the Midianites and seize the waters against them, as far as Beth-barah and the Jordan." So all the men of Ephraim were called out, and they seized the waters as far as Beth-barah and the Jordan. [25]They captured the two captains of Midian, Oreb and Zeeb; they killed Oreb at the rock of Oreb, and Zeeb they killed at the winepress of Zeeb, as they pursued the Midianites. They brought the heads of Oreb and Zeeb to Gideon beyond the Jordan.

8 Then the Ephraimites said to him, "What have you done to us, not to call us when you went to fight against the

g 7.22 Another reading is *Zeredah*

7:12 *The Amalekites and all the people of the east* are mentioned alongside the Midianites in this verse (like in 6:3). However, the Amalekites and people of the east drop from the story after this point.

7:13 Dreams are often represented as divine messages in the ancient world (Gen. 40:8–22). In the dream symbolism of this verse, *barley bread* represents Israelite farmers, and the fallen *tent* represents Midianite nomads.

7:25 *Oreb* means "raven"; *Zeeb* means "wolf" in Hebrew. Both locations are uncertain.

8:1–3 Although Gideon called Ephraimites to join the battle (7:24), they were not among the first people he summoned (6:35; 7:23). The Ephraimites' offense might come from a desire for better

Midianites?" And they upbraided him violently. ²So he said to them, "What have
I done now in comparison with you? Is
not the gleaning of the grapes of Ephraim
better than the vintage of Abiezer? ³God
has given into your hands the captains
of Midian, Oreb and Zeeb; what have I
been able to do in comparison with you?"
When he said this, their anger against him
subsided.

4 Then Gideon came to the Jordan and
crossed over, he and the three hundred who
were with him, exhausted but still pursuing.
⁵So he said to the people of Succoth, "Please
give some loaves of bread to my followers,
for they are exhausted, and I am pursuing
Zebah and Zalmunna, the kings of Midian."
⁶But the officials of Succoth said, "Do you
already have in your possession the hands
of Zebah and Zalmunna, that we should
give bread to your army?" ⁷Gideon replied,
"Well then, when the Lord has given Zebah
and Zalmunna into my hand, I will trample
your flesh on the thorns of the wilderness
and on briers." ⁸From there he went up to
Penuel and made the same request of them,
and the people of Penuel answered him as
the people of Succoth had answered. ⁹So
he said to the people of Penuel, "When I
come back victorious, I will break down
this tower."

10 Now Zebah and Zalmunna were in
Karkor with their army, about fifteen thousand men, all who were left of all the army
of the people of the east, for one hundred
twenty thousand men bearing arms had
fallen. ¹¹So Gideon went up by the caravan
route east of Nobah and Jogbehah and attacked the army, for the army was off its

guard. ¹²Zebah and Zalmunna fled, and he
pursued them and took the two kings of
Midian, Zebah and Zalmunna, and threw
all the army into a panic.

13 When Gideon son of Joash returned
from the battle by the ascent of Heres, ¹⁴he
caught a young man, one of the people of
Succoth, and questioned him, and he listed
for him the officials and elders of Succoth,
seventy-seven people. ¹⁵Then he came to the
people of Succoth and said, "Here are Zebah and Zalmunna, about whom you taunted me, saying, 'Do you already have in your
possession the hands of Zebah and Zalmunna, that we should give bread to your
troops who are exhausted?' " ¹⁶So he took
the elders of the city, and he took thorns of
the wilderness and briers, and with them he
trampled[b] the people of Succoth. ¹⁷He also
broke down the tower of Penuel and killed
the men of the city.

18 Then he said to Zebah and Zalmunna, "What about the men whom you killed
at Tabor?" They answered, "As you are, so
were they, every one of them; they resembled the sons of a king." ¹⁹And he replied,
"They were my brothers, the sons of my
mother; as the Lord lives, if you had saved
them alive, I would not kill you." ²⁰So he said
to Jether his firstborn, "Go kill them!" But
the boy did not draw his sword, for he was
afraid, because he was still a boy. ²¹Then Zebah and Zalmunna said, "You come and kill
us, for as the man is, so is his strength." So
Gideon went and killed Zebah and Zalmunna, and he took the crescents that were on
the necks of their camels.

b 8.16 Compare Gk: Heb *he taught*

plunder. **8:2** *Gleaning*, which occurs at the end of a harvest, is like Ephraim joining at the end of the
battle. *The vintage* is selection of the choicest harvest. For *Abiezer*, see note on 6:11. Gideon appears
to be creating or adjusting a known Israelite saying in order to assert that the Ephraimites fared well
in their plunder by joining the battle later.

8:4–21 While Gideon pursues Midianite leaders in Transjordan, the Israelite cities of Succoth and
Penuel refuse to offer assistance. Gideon punishes them severely. **8:5** *Succoth* means "booths" or
"tents" in Hebrew. **8:6** *The hands* (or another body part) of an enemy are sometimes cut off as
evidence of fatalities (1 Sam. 18:25–27). The question from the leaders of Succoth implies that they
would rather only help Gideon's crew if they were already successful; otherwise, they might suffer
retaliation from Midianites if Gideon fails. **8:8** *Penuel* means "the face of God" in Hebrew (see Gen.
32:23–31). **8:18–19** This is the first mention of an incident at *Tabor*. In a family structure with multiple wives, *sons of my mother* indicates closeness even beyond *my brothers*. Apparently, Zebah and
Zalmunna had killed Gideon's literal siblings or people he describes with the intimate language of
family. **8:20** *Jether* means "Remainder" in Hebrew. **8:21** By taunting Gideon, Zebah and Zalmunna
are able to avoid the disgrace of death by a child.

22 Then the Israelites said to Gideon, "Rule over us, you and your son and your grandson also, for you have delivered us out of the hand of Midian." ²³Gideon said to them, "I will not rule over you, and my son will not rule over you; the Lord will rule over you." ²⁴Then Gideon said to them, "Let me make a request of you; each of you give me an earring he has taken as spoil." (For the enemy*ⁱ* had golden earrings because they were Ishmaelites.) ²⁵"We will willingly give them," they answered. So they spread a garment, and each threw into it an earring he had taken as spoil. ²⁶The weight of the golden earrings that he requested was one thousand seven hundred shekels of gold (apart from the crescents and the pendants and the purple garments worn by the kings of Midian and the collars that were on the necks of their camels). ²⁷Gideon made an ephod of it and put it in his town, in Ophrah, and all Israel prostituted themselves to it there, and it became a snare to Gideon and to his family. ²⁸So Midian was subdued before the Israelites, and they lifted up their heads no more. So the land had rest forty years in the days of Gideon.

29 Jerubbaal son of Joash went to live in his own house. ³⁰Now Gideon had seventy sons, his own offspring, for he had many wives. ³¹His concubine who was in Shechem also bore him a son, and he named him Abimelech. ³²Then Gideon son of Joash died at a good old age and was buried in the tomb of his father Joash at Ophrah of the Abiezrites.

33 As soon as Gideon died, the Israelites relapsed and prostituted themselves with the Baals, making Baal-berith their god. ³⁴The Israelites did not remember the Lord their God, who had rescued them from the hand of all their enemies on every side, ³⁵and they did not exhibit loyalty to the house of Jerubbaal (that is, Gideon) in return for all the good that he had done to Israel.

9 Now Abimelech son of Jerubbaal went to Shechem to his mother's kinsfolk and said to them and to the whole clan of his mother's family, ²"Say in the hearing of all the lords of Shechem, 'Which is better for you, that all seventy of the sons of Jerubbaal rule over you or that one rule over you?' Remember also that I am your bone and your flesh." ³So his mother's kinsfolk spoke all these words on his behalf in the hearing of all the lords of Shechem, and their hearts inclined to follow Abimelech, for they said, "He is our brother." ⁴They gave him seventy pieces of silver out of the temple of Baal-berith with which Abimelech hired worthless and reckless fellows who followed him. ⁵He went to his father's house at Ophrah and killed his brothers

i 8.24 Heb *they*

8:22–23 Technically, the people do not ask Gideon to be "king," but the reference to rule passed down to *your son and your grandson* resembles kingship. Gideon's response, *the Lord will rule over you*, fits with the idea that God alone is king. However, Gideon's words may belie the fact that he actually acts as king (see note on 8:31).

8:24–27 An *ephod* is sometimes a priestly garment (1 Sam. 2:18), elsewhere a cultic object that can be stationed (1 Sam. 21:9). The joint participation of Gideon and the people in creating an ephod that they worship is reminiscent of Aaron and the people in Exod. 32:2–4.

8:28 This is the final time that *the land had rest* in the judges pattern (see note on 2:11–23).

8:31 *Concubine* is not the best translation for the complex Hebrew word "pilegesh," which sometimes implies the youth (cf. 19:1 with 19:4), lifetime bondage (cf. Gen. 29:29 with 35:22), or lower status of this woman relative to another of the husband's/master's women (Gen. 25:5–6; 1 Kgs. 11:3). *Abimelech* means "my father is king" in Hebrew. This is an ironic contrast with Gideon's refusal of kingship in 8:23.

8:32 Gideon being *buried in the tomb of his father* reflects the common Iron Age practice of family tombs in caves where newly deceased members would consistently be added over generations.

8:33 *Baal-berith* means "lord of covenant" in Hebrew. It is likely the same as "El-berith" in 9:46.

9:1–6 Abimelech deceitfully appeals to kinship as a reason he should be king even while he also kills his closest kin. 9:1 *Shechem* is an important religious and political site in ancient Israel (Gen. 12:6; 33:18–20; Josh. 24:1). 9:4 The Hebrew phrase translated as *worthless* (men) might better indicate their poverty/unemployment. The word translated as *reckless* indicates their existence beyond state control. 9:5 *Jotham* means "YHWH perfects" in Hebrew. His survival is similar to Joash's survival in 2 Kgs. 11:1–2.

the sons of Jerubbaal, seventy men, on one stone, but Jotham, the youngest son of Jerubbaal, survived, for he hid himself. ⁶Then all the lords of Shechem and all Beth-millo came together, and they went and made Abimelech king, by the oak of the pillar^j at Shechem.

7 When it was told to Jotham, he went and stood on the top of Mount Gerizim and cried aloud and said to them, "Listen to me, you lords of Shechem, so that God may listen to you.

⁸ The trees once went out
to anoint a king over themselves.
So they said to the olive tree,
'Reign over us.'
⁹ The olive tree answered them,
'Shall I stop producing my rich oil
by which gods and mortals are
honored
and go to sway over the trees?'
¹⁰ Then the trees said to the fig tree,
'You come and reign over us.'
¹¹ But the fig tree answered them,
'Shall I stop producing my
sweetness
and my delicious fruit
and go to sway over the trees?'
¹² Then the trees said to the vine,
'You come and reign over us.'
¹³ But the vine said to them,
'Shall I stop producing my wine
that cheers gods and mortals
and go to sway over the trees?'
¹⁴ So all the trees said to the bramble,
'You come and reign over us.'
¹⁵ And the bramble said to the trees,
'If in good faith you are anointing
me king over you,
then come and take refuge in my
shade,

but if not, let fire come out of the
bramble
and devour the cedars of Lebanon.'
16 "Now therefore, if you acted in good faith and honor when you made Abimelech king, and if you have dealt well with Jerubbaal and his house and have done to him as his actions deserved—¹⁷for my father fought for you and risked his life and rescued you from the hand of Midian, ¹⁸but you have risen up against my father's house this day and have killed his sons, seventy men on one stone, and have made Abimelech, the son of his slave woman, king over the lords of Shechem, because he is your kinsman—¹⁹if, I say, you have acted in good faith and honor with Jerubbaal and with his house this day, then rejoice in Abimelech, and let him also rejoice in you, ²⁰but if not, let fire come out from Abimelech and devour the lords of Shechem and Beth-millo, and let fire come out from the lords of Shechem and from Beth-millo and devour Abimelech." ²¹Then Jotham ran away and fled, going to Beer, where he remained for fear of his brother Abimelech.

22 Abimelech ruled over Israel three years. ²³But God sent an evil spirit between Abimelech and the lords of Shechem, and the lords of Shechem dealt treacherously with Abimelech. ²⁴This happened so that the violence done to the seventy sons of Jerubbaal might be avenged^k and their blood be laid on their brother Abimelech, who killed them, and on the lords of Shechem, who strengthened his hands to kill his brothers. ²⁵So the lords of Shechem set ambushes against him on the mountaintops. They robbed all who passed by them along that way, and it was reported to Abimelech.

j 9.6 Cn: Meaning of Heb uncertain   k 9.24 Heb *might come*

9:7–15 In Jotham's fable, talking plants decline the opportunity to reign because it is incompatible with their productive qualities. Only the useless bramble accepts kingship and warns of horrible repercussions. This plot loosely matches 8:22–23 and 9:1–6. Most likely an independent antimonarchical fable was annexed to this narrative as a critique of Abimelech's reign.

9:16–21 Jotham's curse is contingent on the sincerity and righteousness of the lords of Shechem in their interactions with Gideon/Jerubbaal and Abimelech. His curse draws on the destructive language of fire from the fable and proclaims its scourge against the lords of Shechem and Abimelech. **9:21** *Beer* means "well" in Hebrew.

9:22 The Hebrew verb for *ruled* is different from the word used for "rule" in 8:22–24 and 9:2.

9:23–24 The narrator explains vengeance against Abimelech and the lords of Shechem for the blood of Gideon's sons (9:5–6) as the reason *God sent an evil spirit*. Jotham's curse (9:16–21) mentions this massacre.

26 When Gaal son of Ebed moved into
Shechem with his kinsfolk, the lords of
Shechem put confidence in him. 27They
went out into the field and gathered the
grapes from their vineyards, trod them, and
celebrated. Then they went into the temple
of their god, ate and drank, and ridiculed
Abimelech. 28Gaal son of Ebed said, "Who
is Abimelech, and who are we of Shechem,
that we should serve him? Did not the son
of Jerubbaal and Zebul his officer serve the
men of Hamor father of Shechem? Why
then should we serve him? 29If only this
people were under my command! Then I
would remove Abimelech; I would say[l] to
him, 'Increase your army and come out.'"

30 When Zebul the ruler of the city heard
the words of Gaal son of Ebed, his anger
was kindled. 31He sent messengers to Abimelech at Arumah,[m] saying, "Look, Gaal
son of Ebed and his kinsfolk have come to
Shechem, and they are stirring up[n] the city
against you. 32Now therefore, go by night,
you and the troops who are with you, and
lie in wait in the fields. 33Then early in the
morning, as soon as the sun rises, get up and
rush on the city, and when he and the troops
who are with him come out against you,
you may deal with them as best you can."

34 So Abimelech and all the troops with
him got up by night and lay in wait against
Shechem in four companies. 35When Gaal
son of Ebed went out and stood in the entrance of the gate of the city, Abimelech
and the troops with him rose from the ambush. 36And when Gaal saw them, he said
to Zebul, "Look, people are coming down
from the mountaintops!" And Zebul said to
him, "The shadows on the mountains look
like people to you." 37Gaal spoke again and
said, "Look, people are coming down from
Tabbur-erez, and one company is coming
from the direction of Elon-meonenim."[o]
38Then Zebul said to him, "Where is your
boast[p] now, you who said, 'Who is Abimelech, that we should serve him?' Are not
these the troops you made light of? Go out
now and fight with them." 39So Gaal went
out at the head of the lords of Shechem
and fought with Abimelech. 40Abimelech
chased him, and he fled before him. Many
fell wounded, up to the entrance of the gate.
41So Abimelech resided at Arumah, and Zebul drove out Gaal and his kinsfolk, so that
they could not live on at Shechem.

42 On the following day the people went
out into the fields. When Abimelech was
told, 43he took his troops and divided them
into three companies and lay in wait in the
fields. When he looked and saw the people
coming out of the city, he rose against them
and killed them. 44Abimelech and the company that was[q] with him rushed forward
and stood at the entrance of the gate of the
city, while the two companies rushed on
all who were in the fields and killed them.
45Abimelech fought against the city all that
day; he took the city and killed the people
who were in it, and he razed the city and
sowed it with salt.

46 When all the lords of the Tower of
Shechem heard of it, they entered the
stronghold of the temple of El-berith. 47Abi-
melech was told that all the lords of the
Tower of Shechem were gathered together.
48So Abimelech went up to Mount Zalmon,
he and all the troops who were with him.
Abimelech took an ax in his hand, cut down
a bundle of brushwood, and took it up and
laid it on his shoulder. Then he said to the
troops with him, "What you have seen me
do, do quickly, as I have done." 49So every

l 9.29 Gk: Heb *and he said* *m* 9.31 Cn: Heb *Tormah*
n 9.31 Cn: Heb *are besieging* *o* 9.37 That is, *diviners' oak*
p 9.38 Heb *mouth* *q* 9.44 Gk Syr Vg Tg: Heb *companies that were*

9:26 *Gaal* means "he redeemed" in Hebrew. *Ebed* means "servant/slave" in Hebrew. The English translation could be "Gaal, son of a slave."

9:28 Once Gaal has been incorporated into the community of Shechem (9:26), he harkens back to their early history (Gen. 34) and includes himself as an insider (*we of Shechem*) ridiculing Abimelech as an outsider. Gaal's rhetoric suggests the possibility of ethnic assimilation among ancient Israel's tribes.

9:37 *Tabbur-erez*, "the navel of the earth" in Hebrew, is an idiom.

9:42 *The people went out into the fields* because they mistakenly believe that there is no more threat, since Gaal fled from Abimelech.

9:45 Along with physical destruction, Abimelech *sowed it with salt* as a symbolic action. Shechem is not inhabited again until Jeroboam's reign (1 Kgs. 12:1, 25).

one of the troops cut down a bundle and following Abimelech put it against the stronghold, and they set the stronghold on fire over them, so that all the people of the Tower of Shechem also died, about a thousand men and women.

50 Then Abimelech went to Thebez and encamped against Thebez and took it. ⁵¹But there was a strong tower within the city, and all the men and women and all the lords of the city fled to it and shut themselves in, and they went to the roof of the tower. ⁵²Abimelech came to the tower and fought against it and came near to the entrance of the tower to burn it with fire. ⁵³But a certain woman threw an upper millstone on Abimelech's head and crushed his skull. ⁵⁴Immediately he called to the young man who carried his armor and said to him, "Draw your sword and kill me, so people will not say about me, 'A woman killed him.' " So the young man thrust him through, and he died. ⁵⁵When the Israelites saw that Abimelech was dead, they all went home. ⁵⁶Thus God repaid Abimelech for the crime he committed against his father in killing his seventy brothers; ⁵⁷and God also made all the wickedness of the people of Shechem fall back on their heads, and on them came the curse of Jotham son of Jerubbaal.

10 After Abimelech, Tola son of Puah son of Dodo, a man of Issachar, who lived at Shamir in the hill country of Ephraim, rose to deliver Israel. ²He judged Israel twenty-three years. Then he died and was buried at Shamir.

3 After him came Jair the Gileadite, who judged Israel twenty-two years. ⁴He had thirty sons who rode on thirty donkeys, and they had thirty towns, which are in the land of Gilead and are called Havvoth-jair to this day. ⁵Jair died and was buried in Kamon.

6 The Israelites again did what was evil in the sight of the LORD, serving the Baals and the Astartes, the gods of Aram, the gods of Sidon, the gods of Moab, the gods of the Ammonites, and the gods of the Philistines. Thus they abandoned the LORD and did not worship him. ⁷So the anger of the LORD was kindled against Israel, and he sold them into the hand of the Philistines and into the hand of the Ammonites, ⁸and they crushed and oppressed the Israelites that year. For eighteen years they oppressed all the Israelites who were beyond the Jordan in the land of the Amorites, which is in Gilead. ⁹The Ammonites also crossed the Jordan to fight against Judah and against Benjamin and against the house of Ephraim, so that Israel was greatly distressed.

10 So the Israelites cried to the LORD, saying, "We have sinned against you, because we have abandoned our God and have served the Baals." ¹¹And the LORD said to the Israelites, "Did I not deliver you*r* from the Egyptians and from the Amorites, from the Ammonites and from the Philistines? ¹²The Sidonians also, and the Amalekites, and the Maonites

r 10.11 Heb lacks *Did I not deliver you*

9:54 Abimelech's bias about women's inferiority (militarily and perhaps otherwise) leads him to plead for a more honorable death; this sexism also undergirds the narrator's assumptions in 4:8–9 and 5:24–27.

9:56–57 Although God is not mentioned in the core story, the narrator introduces God's control and the fulfillment of Jotham's curse as a frame to the story of Abimelech's demise starting in 9:23 and resuming with *thus God repaid Abimelech*.

10:1–5 The narrator introduces two consecutive judges without the characteristic pattern established in 2:11–23. The brief mention of these two judges (and three more in 12:8–14) with details about their lives but no story of deliverance has led scholars to label them as "minor judges." 10:1 In Hebrew, *Tola* refers to kermes, an insect from which crimson dye was extracted, and *Puah* is a madder plant, also used for red dye. *Son of Dodo* could be translated as "son of his [Abimelech's] uncle." If *Dodo* is a name, it could mean "his beloved" (Heb.), or it might derive from an Arabic word for "worm." In Jewish midrash, a *Shamir* is a mythical worm Solomon used while constructing the temple. 10:3 *Jair* means "he will illuminate" in Hebrew. 10:4 See note on 1:21 for *to this day*.

10:6–18 The judges pattern resumes (see note on 2:11–23). 10:6 On *Baals* and *Astartes*, see note on 2:11 and 2:13. On *Aram*, see note on 3:7–8. On *Moab*, see note on 3:12. On *Ammonites*, see note on 3:13. On *Sidon* and *Philistines*, see note on 3:3. 10:11–14 YHWH breaks from the pattern of sending a deliverer by pointing out how past efforts to raise up a deliverer did not prevent continual apostasy.

oppressed you, and you cried to me, and I delivered you out of their hand. ¹³Yet you have abandoned me and served other gods; therefore I will deliver you no more. ¹⁴Go and cry to the gods whom you have chosen; let them deliver you in the time of your distress." ¹⁵And the Israelites said to the Lᴏʀᴅ, "We have sinned; do to us whatever seems good to you, but deliver us this day!" ¹⁶So they put away the foreign gods from among them and served the Lᴏʀᴅ, and he could no longer bear to see Israel suffer.

17 Then the Ammonites were called to arms, and they encamped in Gilead, and the Israelites came together, and they encamped at Mizpah. ¹⁸The commanders of the people of Gilead said to one another, "Who will begin the fight against the Ammonites? He shall be head over all the inhabitants of Gilead."

11 Now Jephthah the Gileadite, the son of a prostitute, was a mighty warrior. Gilead was the father of Jephthah. ²Gilead's wife also bore him sons, and when his wife's sons grew up, they drove Jephthah away, saying to him, "You shall not inherit anything in our father's house, for you are the son of another woman." ³Then Jephthah fled from his brothers and lived in the land of Tob. Outlaws gathered around Jephthah and went raiding with him.

4 After a time the Ammonites made war against Israel. ⁵And when the Ammonites made war against Israel, the elders of Gilead

went to bring Jephthah from the land of Tob. ⁶They said to Jephthah, "Come and be our commander, so that we may fight with the Ammonites." ⁷But Jephthah said to the elders of Gilead, "Are you not the very ones who rejected me and drove me out of my father's house? So why do you come to me now when you are in trouble?" ⁸The elders of Gilead said to Jephthah, "Nevertheless, we have now turned back to you, so that you may go with us and fight with the Ammonites and become head over us, over all the inhabitants of Gilead." ⁹Jephthah said to the elders of Gilead, "If you bring me home again to fight with the Ammonites and the Lᴏʀᴅ gives them over to me, I will be your head." ¹⁰And the elders of Gilead said to Jephthah, "The Lᴏʀᴅ will be witness between us; we will surely do as you say." ¹¹So Jephthah went with the elders of Gilead, and the people made him head and commander over them, and Jephthah spoke all his words before the Lᴏʀᴅ at Mizpah.

12 Then Jephthah sent messengers to the king of the Ammonites and said, "What is there between you and me, that you have come to me to fight against my land?" ¹³The king of the Ammonites answered the messengers of Jephthah, "Because Israel, on coming from Egypt, took away my land from the Arnon to the Jabbok and to the Jordan; now, therefore, restore it peaceably." ¹⁴Once again Jephthah sent messengers to the king of the Ammonites ¹⁵and said to him, "Thus says Jephthah: Israel did not take away the

YHWH aims to show the falsity of other gods by goading the Israelites, *Go and cry to the gods whom you have chosen.* **10:15–16** In Judges, admitting *we have sinned* and putting *away the foreign gods* only occurs here. Since YHWH *could no longer bear to see Israel suffer*, God sends a deliverer; in previous instances, it was because the people "cried out" (3:9, 15; 4:3; 6:6–7). **10:17–18** After YHWH's reticence to help (10:11–14), the people of Gilead do not ask YHWH to select a leader like in 1:1–2. Instead, they pledge loyalty to whoever has courage to begin the fight against the Ammonites.

11:1 In Hebrew, *Jephthah* means "he [God] opens [the womb]" (cf. Gen. 29:31; 30:22). *Prostitute* can refer to a sex worker, promiscuous person, or adulterer. The Hebrew phrase translated as *mighty warrior* can also indicate clout for nonmilitary men (Ruth 2:1).

11:2 The brothers selfishly *drove Jephthah away* because a son can inherit from his father regardless of his mother's status (Deut. 21:15–17).

11:3 *Tob* means "good" in Hebrew. The Hebrew for *outlaws* matches the note on "worthless" from 9:4.

11:6–8 *The elders of Gilead* first offer for Jephthah to be a military *commander* but elevate the offer to *become head over us* (like 10:17–18). Their change of strategy comes because Jephthah accuses them of being complicit or primarily responsible when his brothers "drove Jephthah away" (11:2).

11:12–28 The king of the Ammonites requests a peaceful return of an Ammonite territory that the Israelites are occupying. Jephthah's response builds on details previously narrated in Num. 20:14–21:35 and Deut. 2. According to Jephthah, the disputed land belonged to Amorites until their king,

land of Moab or the land of the Ammonites, [16]but when they came up from Egypt, Israel went through the wilderness to the Red Sea[s] and came to Kadesh. [17]Israel then sent messengers to the king of Edom, saying, 'Let us pass through your land,' but the king of Edom would not listen. They also sent to the king of Moab, but he would not consent. So Israel remained at Kadesh. [18]Then they journeyed through the wilderness, went around the land of Edom and the land of Moab, arrived on the east side of the land of Moab, and camped on the other side of the Arnon. They did not enter the territory of Moab, for the Arnon was the boundary of Moab. [19]Israel then sent messengers to King Sihon of the Amorites, king of Heshbon, and Israel said to him, 'Let us pass through your land to our country.' [20]But Sihon did not trust Israel to pass through his territory, so Sihon gathered all his people together and encamped at Jahaz and fought with Israel. [21]Then the LORD, the God of Israel, gave Sihon and all his people into the hand of Israel, and they defeated them, so Israel occupied all the land of the Amorites, who inhabited that country. [22]They occupied all the territory of the Amorites from the Arnon to the Jabbok and from the wilderness to the Jordan. [23]So now the LORD, the God of Israel, has conquered the Amorites for the benefit of his people Israel. Do you intend to take their place? [24]Should you not possess what your god Chemosh gives you to possess? And should we not be the ones to possess everything that the LORD our God has conquered for our benefit? [25]Now are you any better than King Balak son of Zippor of Moab? Did he ever enter into conflict with Israel, or did he ever go to war with them? [26]While Israel lived in Heshbon and its villages, and in Aroer and its villages, and in all the towns that are along the Arnon, three hundred years, why did you not recover them within that time? [27]It is not I who have sinned against you, but you are the one who does me wrong by making war on me. Let the LORD, who is judge, decide today for the Israelites or for the Ammonites." [28]But the king of the Ammonites did not heed the message that Jephthah sent him.

29 Then the spirit of the LORD came upon Jephthah, and he passed through Gilead and Manasseh. He passed on to Mizpah of Gilead, and from Mizpah of Gilead he passed on to the Ammonites. [30]And Jephthah made a vow to the LORD and said, "If you will give the Ammonites into my hand, [31]then whatever[t] comes out of the doors of my house to meet me, when I return victorious from the Ammonites, shall be the LORD's, to be offered up by me as a burnt offering." [32]So Jephthah crossed over to the Ammonites to fight against them, and the LORD gave them into his hand. [33]He inflicted a massive defeat on them from Aroer to the neighborhood of Minnith, twenty towns, and as far as Abel-keramim. So the Ammonites were subdued before the Israelites.

34 Then Jephthah came to his home at Mizpah, and there was his daughter coming out to meet him with timbrels and with dancing. She was his only child; he had no son or daughter except her. [35]When he saw her, he tore his clothes and said, "Alas, my daughter! You have brought me very low; you have become the cause of great trouble to me. For I have opened my mouth to the LORD, and I cannot take back my vow." [36]She said to him, "My father, if you have

s 11.16 Or Sea of Reeds   t 11.31 Or whoever

Sihon, fought against Israel. YHWH gave Israel victory and the land. Since the gods are ultimately in control, Jephthah is asserting that the land will remain Israelite unless the gods decide otherwise. **11:24** Here, *your god Chemosh* refers to an Ammonite deity, but Chemosh was the god of Moab, while Molech/Milcom was the Ammonite god (1 Kgs. 11:5, 7, 33; 2 Kgs. 23:13).

11:29 On *the spirit of the* LORD, see note on 3:10.

11:31 Jephthah may have expected *whatever comes out of the doors of my house* to be an animal, since ancient Israelites shared their living space with livestock.

11:34 Jephthah's daughter greets her father *with timbrels* (likely a hand drum without jingles) *and with dancing* in keeping with a custom of women celebrating military victory (Exod. 15:20-21; 1 Sam. 18:6). The Hebrew for *his only child* could also indicate love and favoritism.

11:35-36 Jephthah's and his daughter's acquiescence to human sacrifice fits with other biblical texts about ancient Israelites sacrificing children (Gen. 22; Exod. 22:29-30; Jer. 7:30-31; 19:5-6; Ezek. 20:25-26; Mic. 6:7).

opened your mouth to the LORD, do to me according to what has gone out of your mouth, now that the LORD has given you vengeance against your enemies, the Ammonites." [37]And she said to her father, "Let this thing be done for me: grant me two months, so that I may go and wander" on the mountains and bewail my virginity, my companions and I." [38]"Go," he said, and he sent her away for two months. So she departed, she and her companions, and bewailed her virginity on the mountains. [39]At the end of two months, she returned to her father, who did with her according to the vow he had made. She had never slept with a man. So there arose an Israelite custom that [40]for four days every year the daughters of Israel would go out to lament the daughter of Jephthah the Gileadite.

12 The men of Ephraim were called to arms, and they crossed to Zaphon and said to Jephthah, "Why did you cross over to fight against the Ammonites and did not call us to go with you? We will burn your house down over you!" [2]Jephthah said to them, "My people and I were engaged in conflict with the Ammonites who oppressed us[v] severely. But when I called you, you did not deliver me from their hand. [3]When I saw that you would not deliver me, I took my life in my hand and crossed over against the Ammonites, and the LORD gave them into my hand. Why then have you come up to me this day, to fight against me?" [4]Then Jephthah gathered all the men of Gilead and fought with Ephraim, and the men of Gilead defeated Ephraim, because they said, "You are fugitives from Ephraim, you Gileadites, in the heart of Ephraim and Manasseh."[w] [5]Then the Gileadites took the fords of the Jordan against the Ephraimites. Whenever one of the fugitives of Ephraim said, "Let me go over," the men of Gilead would say to him, "Are you an Ephraimite?" When he said, "No," [6]they said to him, "Then say Shibboleth," and he said, "Sibboleth," for he could not pronounce it right. Then they seized him and killed him at the fords of the Jordan. Forty-two thousand of the Ephraimites fell at that time.

7 Jephthah judged Israel six years. Then Jephthah the Gileadite died and was buried in his town in Gilead.[x]

8 After him Ibzan of Bethlehem judged Israel. [9]He had thirty sons. He gave his thirty daughters in marriage outside his clan and brought in thirty young women from outside for his sons. He judged Israel seven years. [10]Then Ibzan died and was buried at Bethlehem.

11 After him Elon the Zebulunite judged Israel, and he judged Israel ten years. [12]Then Elon the Zebulunite died and was buried at Aijalon in the land of Zebulun.

13 After him Abdon son of Hillel the Pirathonite judged Israel. [14]He had forty sons and thirty grandsons who rode on seventy donkeys; he judged Israel eight years.

u 11.37 Cn: Heb *go down*   v 12.2 Gk OL Syr H: Heb lacks *who oppressed us*   w 12.4 Meaning of Heb uncertain: Gk omits *because... Manasseh*   x 12.7 Gk: Heb *in the towns of Gilead*

11:37–40 *Her virginity* may refer to her youth or lack of sexual experience. Although most interpreters believe Jephthah killed his daughter, some have argued that *did with her according to the vow he had made* involves some sort of dedication of the rest of her life to YHWH. This story explains a periodic ritual by *the daughters of Israel* that carries on into the author's time.

12:1 *Zaphon* is a mountain to the north and the mythical home of the Canaanite god El. Often it indicates a northern direction. Compare the Ephraimites' reaction here to 8:1.

12:2–3 With repeated emphasis on *I* and *me*, Jephthah asserts that the contention with Ammonites was personal. Furthermore, he claims *when I called you, you did not deliver me*. However, there is no evidence he summoned Ephraim in the previous chapter.

12:4–6 The modern noun "shibboleth" comes from this story. A shibboleth is something that distinguishes a particular group of people. Here, one's pronunciation of the word *Shibboleth/Sibboleth* distinguishes Ephraimites from Gileadites. It suggests the tribes had different accents. *Killed him* literally is "slaughtered him" in Hebrew.

12:8–13 See note on 10:1–5. **12:8** *Ibzan* might mean a person from Ebez, a town in Issachar (Josh. 19:20). **12:9** Compare Ibzan to Jair in 10:3. His daughters' marriages to other clans show political savvy. **12:11** *Elon* means "oak" in Hebrew. **12:13** *Abdon* is a name derived from the Hebrew word for "servant or slave." *Hillel* means "praise" in Hebrew.

[15]Then Abdon son of Hillel the Pirathonite died and was buried at Pirathon in the land of Ephraim, in the hill country of the Amalekites.

13 The Israelites again did what was evil in the sight of the Lord, and the Lord gave them into the hand of the Philistines forty years.

2 There was a certain man of Zorah, of the tribe of the Danites, whose name was Manoah. His wife was barren, having borne no children. [3]And the angel of the Lord appeared to the woman and said to her, "Although you are barren, having borne no children, you shall conceive and bear a son. [4]Now be careful not to drink wine or strong drink or to eat anything unclean, [5]for you shall conceive and bear a son. No razor is to come on his head, for the boy shall be a nazirite to God from birth. It is he who shall begin to deliver Israel from the hand of the Philistines." [6]Then the woman came and told her husband, "A man of God came to me, and his appearance was like that of an angel[y] of God, most awe-inspiring; I did not ask him where he came from, and he did not tell me his name, [7]but he said to me, 'You shall conceive and bear a son. So then, drink no wine or strong drink and eat nothing unclean, for the boy shall be a nazirite to God from birth to the day of his death.'"

8 Then Manoah entreated the Lord and said, "O my Lord, I pray, let the man of God whom you sent come to us again and teach us what we are to do concerning the boy who will be born." [9]God listened to Manoah, and the angel of God came again to the woman as she sat in the field, but her husband Manoah was not with her. [10]So the woman ran quickly and told her husband, "The man who came to me the other day has appeared to me." [11]Manoah got up and followed his wife and came to the man and said to him, "Are you the man who spoke to this woman?" And he said, "I am." [12]Then Manoah said, "Now when your words come true, what is to be the boy's rule of life; what is he to do?" [13]The angel of the Lord said to Manoah, "Let the woman give heed to all that I said to her. [14]She may not eat of anything that comes from the vine. She is not to drink wine or strong drink or eat any unclean thing. She is to observe everything that I commanded her."

15 Manoah said to the angel of the Lord, "Allow us to detain you and prepare a kid for you." [16]The angel of the Lord said to Manoah, "If you detain me, I will not eat your food, but if you want to prepare a burnt offering, then offer it to the Lord." (For Manoah did not know that he was the angel of the Lord.) [17]Then Manoah said to the angel of the Lord, "What is your name, so

y 13.6 Or *the angel*

12:15 On *the Amalekites*, see the note on 1:16.

13:1 This is the sixth and final episode in the judges pattern (see note on 2:11–23). For the first time the Israelites do not cry out during their oppression. On *the Philistines*, see the note on 3:3.

13:2 *Zorah* is a city in the Shephelah, the foothills between Dan and Judah bordering Philistine territory. *Manoah* means "rest" in Hebrew. A Jewish tradition names Manoah's wife Hazzelelponi (1 Chr. 4:3).

13:3 On *the angel of the Lord*, see the note on 6:11. God allowing barren women to conceive is a theme in many stories (Gen. 11:30; 17:16; 25:21; 29:31; 30:22).

13:4–5 According to Num. 6:1–21, a *nazirite* is a man or woman who makes a vow to separate themselves in dedication to YHWH for a period of time. They cannot drink alcohol or consume anything from the grapevine, cut their hair, or go near a dead body. In this case, Manoah's wife must follow specific rules before she births a son whose nazirite separation will endure for his entire lifetime. The only rule mentioned for the son is about hair.

13:7 Manoah's wife adds *to the day of his death*.

13:8–14 Originally, the angel appeared to Manoah's wife when no one had cried out for help. When Manoah prays, the angel again goes to his wife, who must lead Manoah to the angel. In response to Manoah's question about *the boy's rule of life*, the angel reemphasizes instructions already given to Manoah's wife. In this chapter, she is the main focus for bringing about God's plan.

13:15 Compare 6:19.

13:16 Although Manoah's wife told him that this visitor was probably an angel (13:6), Manoah *did not know*.

that we may honor you when your words come true?" [18]But the angel of the LORD said to him, "Why do you ask my name? It is too wonderful."

19 So Manoah took the kid with the grain offering and offered it on the rock to the LORD, to him who works[z] wonders.[a] [20]When the flame went up toward heaven from the altar, the angel of the LORD ascended in the flame of the altar while Manoah and his wife looked on, and they fell on their faces to the ground. [21]The angel of the LORD did not appear again to Manoah and his wife. Then Manoah realized that it was the angel of the LORD. [22]And Manoah said to his wife, "We shall surely die, for we have seen God." [23]But his wife said to him, "If the LORD had meant to kill us, he would not have accepted a burnt offering and a grain offering at our hands or shown us all these things or[b] announced to us such things as these."

24 The woman bore a son and named him Samson. The boy grew, and the LORD blessed him. [25]The spirit of the LORD began to stir him in Mahaneh-dan, between Zorah and Eshtaol.

14 Once Samson went down to Timnah, and at Timnah he saw a Philistine woman. [2]Then he came up and told his father and mother, "I saw a Philistine woman at Timnah; now get her for me as my wife." [3]But his father and mother said to him, "Is there not a woman among your kin or among all our[c] people, that you must go to take a wife from the uncircumcised Philistines?" But Samson said to his father, "Get her for me, because she pleases me." [4]His father and mother did not know that this was from the LORD, for he was seeking a pretext to act against the Philistines. At that time the Philistines had dominion over Israel.

5 Then Samson went down with his father and mother to Timnah. When he came to the vineyards of Timnah, suddenly a young lion roared at him. [6]The spirit of the LORD rushed on him, and he tore the lion apart barehanded as one might tear apart a kid. But he did not tell his father or his mother what he had done. [7]Then he went down and talked with the woman, and she pleased Samson. [8]After a while he returned to marry her, and he turned aside to see the carcass of the lion, and there was a swarm of bees in the body of the lion and honey. [9]He scraped it out into his hands and went on, eating as he went. When he came to his father and mother, he gave some to them, and they ate it. But he did not tell them that he had taken the honey from the carcass of the lion.

10 His father went down to the woman, and Samson made a feast there, as the

z 13.19 Gk Vg: Heb *and working* a 13.19 Heb *wonders, while Manoah and his wife looked on* b 13.23 Gk OL Vg: Heb adds *now* c 14.3 Cn: Heb *my*

13:19–22 Compare 6:21–22.

13:23 With three explanations, Manoah's wife demonstrates that she is much more rational and trusting in God than her husband. Perhaps this explains the angel's focus on her (see note on 13:8–14).

13:24–25 *Samson* might mean "little sun" in Hebrew. *Mahaneh-dan* means "the camp of Dan" in Hebrew.

14:1 *Timnah* means "allotted portion" in Hebrew. On *Philistine*, see the note on 3:3.

14:2–3 The response of Samson's parents fits with polemics in Deuteronomy against exogamy (marrying outside one's own social group; Deut. 7:3–4; 23:3), even though there is no specific censure against marrying Philistines. The Philistines are often derided as *uncircumcised* (Judg. 15:18; 1 Sam. 14:6; 17:26, 36; 31:4). After his parents refuse, Samson repeats the request *to his father* only. *Pleases me* literally translates "upright in my eyes" (and in 14:7), and the same idiom recurs in 17:6 and 21:25 to denote the chaos of this era without a king. Contrast a focus on what is "evil in the sight [literally 'eyes'] of the LORD" (see note on 2:11–23).

14:4 With this verse, the Deuteronomistic Historian fits the Samson story into the divine plan for deliverance found in all the previous judges' stories (see **"Deuteronomistic History," p. 337**).

14:6 On *the spirit of the LORD*, see note on 3:10. Here, the spirit uniquely grants supernatural strength and keeps Samson alive against unlikely odds.

14:8–9 Samson's physical contact with a lion carcass would violate a typical nazirite vow (see note on 13:4–5).

14:10 Samson's mother is conspicuously absent from the wedding although she made the trip

young men were accustomed to do. [11]When the people saw him, they brought thirty companions to be with him. [12]Samson said to them, "Let me now put a riddle to you. If you can explain it to me within the seven days of the feast and find it out, then I will give you thirty linen garments and thirty festal garments. [13]But if you cannot explain it to me, then you shall give me thirty linen garments and thirty festal garments." So they said to him, "Ask your riddle; let us hear it." [14]He said to them,

"Out of the eater came something to
    eat.
Out of the strong came something
    sweet."

But for three days they could not explain the riddle.

15 On the fourth[d] day they said to Samson's wife, "Coax your husband to explain the riddle to us, or we will burn you and your father's house with fire. Have you invited us here to impoverish us?" [16]So Samson's wife wept before him, saying, "You hate me; you do not really love me. You have asked a riddle of my people, but you have not explained it to me." He said to her, "Look, I have not told my father or my mother. Why should I tell you?" [17]She wept before him the seven days that their feast lasted, and because she nagged him, on the seventh day he told her. Then she explained

the riddle to her people. [18]The men of the town said to him on the seventh day before the sun went down,

"What is sweeter than honey?
What is stronger than a lion?"

And he said to them,

"If you had not plowed with my heifer,
you would not have found out my
    riddle."

[19]Then the spirit of the LORD rushed on him, and he went down to Ashkelon. He killed thirty men of the town, took their spoil, and gave the festal garments to those who had explained the riddle. In hot anger he went back to his father's house. [20]And Samson's wife was given to his companion, who had been his best man.

15 After a while, at the time of the wheat harvest, Samson went to visit his wife, bringing along a kid. He said, "I want to go into my wife's room." But her father would not allow him to go in. [2]Her father said, "I was sure that you had rejected her, so I gave her to your companion. Is not her younger sister prettier than she? Why not take her instead?" [3]Samson said to them, "This time, when I do mischief to the Philistines, I will be without blame." [4]So Samson went and caught three

d 14.15 Gk Syr: Heb *seventh*

---

before (14:5) and is still alive (14:16). *Feast* comes from a Hebrew root word that indicates drinking. It might imply Samson consumes alcohol in violation of a typical nazirite vow (see note on 13:4–5).

14:11–14 Samson's riddle collapses the distinctions between opposites (eater-food, strong-sweet) like this marriage feast collapses antagonistic ethnic distinctions. The answer to the riddle may be a less profound literal statement of what Samson saw (a lion carcass with honey in it) or did (Samson shared honey with his parents). Some scholars propose that a bridegroom and vomit (from drinking too much sweet wine) would be a more plausible answer at a wedding feast.

14:15–17 *Nagged* is better translated as "pressed." Perhaps she does not know that Samson has the strength and temperament to kill thirty men who threaten his wife, or she may know and not want a violent outcome at all.

14:18 The Philistines respond with a question that answers the riddle and poses another. While their response could evoke what Samson literally saw or did, it is also true that love and knowledge are two major themes in the Samson story (see 16:15) that are *sweeter than honey* and *stronger than a lion*.

14:19 Since *Ashkelon* is a Philistine city, Samson kills Philistines to pay Philistines.

14:20 *His best man* seems to be a different person from the "thirty companions" mentioned in 14:11 (see 15:6).

15:1 Spring, around May, is *the time of the wheat harvest*.

15:2 *You had rejected her* (literally, "you hated her") is the disposition of a husband divorcing a wife (Deut. 24:3). Since marriages can have social, political, and economic benefits to families involved, the father offering *her younger sister* would have benefits similar to the original marriage. However, he notes her attractiveness because that is what Samson cares about (14:3).

hundred foxes and took some torches, and he turned the foxes' tail to tail and put a torch between each pair of tails. ⁵When he had set fire to the torches, he let the foxes go into the standing grain of the Philistines and burned up the shocks and the standing grain, as well as the vineyards and' olive groves. ⁶Then the Philistines asked, "Who has done this?" And they said, "Samson, the son-in-law of the Timnite, because he has taken Samson's wife and given her to his companion." So the Philistines came up and burned her and her father. ⁷Samson said to them, "If this is what you do, I swear I will not stop until I have taken revenge on you." ⁸He struck them down hip and thigh with a massive defeat, and he went down and stayed in the cleft of the rock of Etam.

9 Then the Philistines came up and encamped in Judah and made a raid on Lehi. ¹⁰The men of Judah said, "Why have you come up against us?" They said, "We have come up to bind Samson, to do to him as he did to us." ¹¹Then three thousand men of Judah went down to the cleft of the rock of Etam, and they said to Samson, "Do you not know that the Philistines are rulers over us? What then have you done to us?" He replied, "As they did to me, so I have done to them." ¹²They said to him, "We have come down to bind you, so that we may give you into the hands of the Philistines." Samson answered them, "Swear to me that you yourselves will not attack me." ¹³They said to him, "No, we will only bind you and give you into their hands; we will not kill you." So they bound him with two new ropes and brought him up from the rock.

14 When he came to Lehi, the Philistines came shouting to meet him, and the spirit of the LORD rushed on him, and the ropes that were on his arms became like flax that has caught fire, and his bonds melted off his hands. ¹⁵Then he found a fresh jawbone of a donkey, reached down and took it, and with it he killed a thousand men. ¹⁶And Samson said,

"With the jawbone of a donkey,
    heaps upon heaps,
with the jawbone of a donkey
    I have slain a thousand men."

¹⁷When he had finished speaking, he threw away the jawbone, and that place was called Ramath-lehi.ᵍ

18 By then he was very thirsty, and he called on the LORD, saying, "You have granted this great victory by the hand of your servant. Am I now to die of thirst and fall into the hands of the uncircumcised?" ¹⁹So God split open the hollow place that is at Lehi, and water came from it. When he drank, his spirit returned, and he revived. Therefore it was named En-hakkore,ʰ which is at Lehi to this day. ²⁰And he judged Israel in the days of the Philistines twenty years.

e 15.4 Heb lacks *the foxes* f 15.5 Gk Tg Vg: Heb lacks *and* g 15.17 That is, *hill of the jawbone* h 15.19 That is, *spring of the one who called*

15:6 The Philistines commit the exact fatal violence they threatened in 14:15.

15:7–8 Prior to this point, neither Samson nor the Philistines have targeted their violence against the specific person/people that they are contending with. *Hip and thigh* is an idiom that the narrator clarifies by adding *a massive defeat* (literally, "a massive strike"). *Etam* means "place of birds of prey" in Hebrew.

15:9 *Lehi* means "jawbone" in Hebrew (see 15:14–17).

15:11 *Rulers over us* can also be translated with a homonym as "speakers of proverbs over us." Perhaps the wordplay is a reminder that links Philistine dominance with the contest of riddles from chap. 14.

15:12–13 The scene of Israelites delivering their (eventual) judge into the hands of the enemy is the exact opposite of previous judges leading Israelites in battle.

15:14 On *the spirit of the LORD*, see note on 14:6.

15:15 The *jawbone of a donkey* likely describes an ancient sickle in which an animal's jawbone was fitted with flint teeth. Use of this tool violates typical nazirite rules (see note on 13:4–5). In European art, there is a strong tradition of interpreting this tool as Cain's weapon in Gen. 4:8.

15:16 *Donkey* and *heaps* are homonyms in Hebrew. With this poetic victory song, Samson has the last word in the contest of wordplay that he began in 14:12.

15:18 On *uncircumcised*, see note on 14:2–3.

15:19 On *to this day*, see note on 1:21.

15:20 *He judged Israel . . . twenty years* is repeated at the end of chap. 16. This phrase normally

16 Once Samson went to Gaza, where he saw a prostitute and went in to her. ²The Gazites were told,ⁱ "Samson has come here." So they circled around and lay in wait for him all night at the city gate. They kept quiet all night, thinking, "Let us waitʲ until the light of the morning; then we will kill him." ³But Samson lay only until midnight. Then at midnight he rose up, took hold of the doors of the city gate and the two posts, pulled them up, bar and all, put them on his shoulders, and carried them to the top of the hill that is in front of Hebron.

4 After this he fell in love with a woman in the valley of Sorek whose name was Delilah. ⁵The lords of the Philistines came to her and said to her, "Coax him, and find out what makes his strength so great and how we may overpower him, so that we may bind him in order to subdue him, and we will each give you eleven hundred pieces of silver." ⁶So Delilah said to Samson, "Please tell me what makes your strength so great and how you could be bound, so that one could subdue you." ⁷Samson said to her, "If they bind me with seven fresh bowstrings that are not dried out, then I shall become weak and be like anyone else." ⁸Then the lords of the Philistines brought her seven fresh bowstrings that had not dried out, and she bound him with them. ⁹While men were lying in wait in an inner chamber, she said to him, "The Philistines are upon you, Samson!" But he snapped the bowstrings as a strand of fiber

snaps when it touches the fire. So the secret of his strength was not known.

10 Then Delilah said to Samson, "You have mocked me and told me lies; please tell me how you could be bound." ¹¹He said to her, "If they bind me with new ropes that have not been used, then I shall become weak and be like anyone else." ¹²So Delilah took new ropes and bound him with them and said to him, "The Philistines are upon you, Samson!" (The men lying in wait were in an inner chamber.) But he snapped the ropes off his arms like a thread.

13 Then Delilah said to Samson, "Until now you have mocked me and told me lies; tell me how you could be bound." He said to her, "If you weave the seven locks of my head with the web and make it tight with the pin, then I shall become weak and be like anyone else." ¹⁴So while he slept, Delilah took the seven locks of his head and wove them into the webᵏ and made them tight with the pin. Then she said to him, "The Philistines are upon you, Samson!" But he awoke from his sleep and pulled away the pin, the loom, and the web.

15 Then she said to him, "How can you say, 'I love you,' when your heart is not with me? You have mocked me three times now and have not told me what makes your strength so great." ¹⁶Finally, after she had nagged him with her words day after day

i 16.2 Gk: Heb lacks *were told*   *j* 16.2 Heb lacks *Let us wait*
k 16.14 Compare Gk: Heb lacks *and make it tight . . . into the web*

coincides with the narrator ending the story of a judge (3:10; 10:2; 12:7, 9, 11, 14). Perhaps an earlier version of Samson's story ended here.

16:1 On *Gaza*, see note on 1:18. On *prostitute*, see note on 11:1.

16:3 Contemporary city gates were massive (at least two stories high), and *Hebron* is about thirty-five miles from Gaza.

16:4 *The valley of Sorek* is a border region between Israelites and Philistines. The meaning of *Delilah* is uncertain. It may relate to loose hair, small stature, or flirtation. The previous episode includes the very similar-sounding Hebrew word for "the night" ("hallayla") repeated four times in just two verses. Perhaps the wordplay forebodes Delilah's ability to rival Samson, whose name is related to the Hebrew word for "sun."

16:5 The five *lords of the Philistines* (see note on 1:18) offer Delilah a combined 5,500 *pieces of silver*, which is an incredible amount. Contrast the "ten pieces of silver a year" for a Levite priest in 17:10.

16:6 The word translated *subdue* here (used previously in 16:5; Heb. "anah") sometimes denotes a sexual violation (Gen. 34:2; Deut. 22:24; Judg. 19:24; 2 Sam. 13:12, 14, 22, 32). Perhaps Samson acquiesces to being *bound, so that one could subdue* him as part of sadomasochistic play with Delilah.

16:13 Unlike Samson's previous lies about "fresh bowstrings" and "new ropes," the reference to *seven locks of my head* is a partial truth insofar as it refers to his hair.

16:16 *Nagged* is better translated as "pressed." Samson's exhaustion *to death* uses the same idiom as Elijah (1 Kgs. 19:4) and Jonah (Jonah 4:8).

and pestered him, he was tired to death. [17]So he told her his whole secret and said to her, "A razor has never come upon my head, for I have been a nazirite to God from my mother's womb. If my head were shaved, then my strength would leave me; I would become weak and be like anyone else."

18 When Delilah realized that he had told her his whole secret, she sent and called the lords of the Philistines, saying, "This time come up, for he has told his whole secret to me." Then the lords of the Philistines came up to her and brought the money in their hands. [19]She let him fall asleep on her lap, and she called a man and had him shave off the seven locks of his head. He began to weaken,[l] and his strength left him. [20]Then she said, "The Philistines are upon you, Samson!" When he awoke from his sleep, he thought, "I will go out as at other times and shake myself free." But he did not know that the Lord had left him. [21]So the Philistines seized him and gouged out his eyes. They brought him down to Gaza and bound him with bronze shackles, and he ground at the mill in the prison. [22]But the hair of his head began to grow again after it had been shaved.

23 Now the lords of the Philistines gathered to offer a great sacrifice to their god Dagon and to rejoice, for they said, "Our god has given Samson our enemy into our hand." [24]When the people saw him, they praised their god, for they said, "Our god has given our enemy into our hand, the ravager of our country, who has killed many of us." [25]And when their hearts were merry, they said, "Call Samson, and let him entertain us." So they called Samson out of the prison, and he performed for them. They made him stand between the pillars, [26]and Samson said to the attendant who held him by the hand, "Let me feel the pillars on which the house rests, so that I may lean against them." [27]Now the house was full of men and women; all the lords of the Philistines were there, and on the roof there were about three thousand men and women who looked on while Samson performed.

28 Then Samson called to the Lord and said, "Lord God, remember me and strengthen me only this once, O God, so that with this one act of revenge I may pay back the Philistines for my two eyes."[m] [29]And Samson grasped the two middle pillars on which the house rested, and he leaned his weight against them, his right hand on the one and his left hand on the other. [30]Then Samson said, "Let me die with the Philistines." He strained with all his might, and the house fell on the lords and all the people who were in it. So those he killed at his death were more than those he had killed during his life. [31]Then his kindred and all his family came down and took him and brought him up and buried him between Zorah and Eshtaol in the tomb of his father Manoah. He had judged Israel twenty years.

17 There was a man in the hill country of Ephraim whose name was Micah. [2]He said to his mother, "The eleven hundred pieces of silver that were taken from you,

l 16.19 Gk: Heb *She began to torment him*   *m* 16.28 Or *so that I may be avenged upon the Philistines for one of my two eyes*

16:17 On *nazirite*, see note on 13:4–5.

16:19 Scholars debate whether the Hebrew indicates that Delilah cut Samson's hair or she *had him* (the man she called) *shave off the seven locks of his head*.

16:20 Since Samson thought *I will go out as at other times and shake myself free*, he might not have believed that the secret he revealed (16:17) would take away his strength.

16:21 Samson's (now gouged-out) *eyes* started this whole mess (see note on 14:2–3).

16:23–24 *Dagon* (meaning "grain" in Hebrew) was a Canaanite god who the Philistines adopted as their own. Unlike the Israelites, who—other than Deborah (Judg. 5)—do not praise YHWH for repeatedly delivering them, the Philistines praise their god for deliverance. Ironically, delivering Samson alive *into our hand* will lead to their downfall.

16:25 Ironically, the Hebrew verb for *entertain*, "s-kh-q," rhymes with "sh-kh-q," meaning to "crush/beat" something down to dust (2 Sam. 22:43; Ps. 18:42).

16:28 Samson's final ambition is an *act of revenge*, not Israelite deliverance like previous judges.

16:31 On *the tomb of his father*, see the note on 8:32. On *he had judged*, see note on 15:20.

17:1 *Micah* means "Who is like YHWH?" in Hebrew.

17:2 *May my son be blessed by the Lord!* functions to counteract her previous *curse*. Compare the people who proclaim an oath to save Jonathan from a previously uttered curse in 1 Sam. 14:24, 43–45.

about which you uttered a curse and even spoke it in my hearing—that silver is in my possession; I took it, but now I will return it to you."[n] And his mother said, "May my son be blessed by the LORD!" ³Then he returned the eleven hundred pieces of silver to his mother, and his mother said, "I consecrate the silver to the LORD from my hand for my son, to make an idol of cast metal." ⁴So when he returned the money to his mother, his mother took two hundred pieces of silver and gave it to the silversmith, who made it into an idol of cast metal, and it was in the house of Micah. ⁵This man Micah had a shrine, and he made an ephod and teraphim and installed one of his sons, who became his priest. ⁶In those days there was no king in Israel; all the people did what was right in their own eyes.

7 Now there was a young man of Bethlehem in Judah, of the clan of Judah. He was a Levite residing there. ⁸This man left the town of Bethlehem in Judah to live wherever he could find a place. He came to the house of Micah in the hill country of Ephraim to carry on his work.[o] ⁹Micah said to him, "From where do you come?" He replied, "I am a Levite of Bethlehem in Judah, and I am going to live wherever I can find a place." ¹⁰Then Micah said to him, "Stay with me, and be to me a father and a priest, and I will give you ten pieces of silver a year, a set of clothes, and your living."[p] ¹¹The Levite agreed to stay with the man, and the young man became to him like one of his sons. ¹²So Micah installed the Levite, and the young man became his priest and was in the house of Micah. ¹³Then Micah said, "Now I know that the LORD will prosper me because the Levite has become my priest."

18 In those days there was no king in Israel. And in those days the tribe of the Danites was seeking for itself a territory to live in, for until then no territory among the tribes of Israel had been allotted to them. ²So the Danites sent five valiant men from the whole number of their clan, from Zorah and from Eshtaol, to spy out the land and to explore it, and they said to them, "Go, explore the land." When they came to the hill country of Ephraim, to the house of Micah, they stayed there. ³While they were at Micah's house, they recognized the voice of the young Levite, so they went over and asked him, "Who brought you here? What are you doing in this place? What is your business here?" ⁴He said to them, "Micah did such and such for me, and he hired me, and I have become his priest." ⁵Then they said to him,

n 17.2 The words *but now I will return it to you* are transposed from the end of 17.3 in Heb   o 17.8 Or *Ephraim, continuing his journey*   p 17.10 Heb *living, and the Levite went*

17:3 *An idol of cast metal* is prohibited according to Exod. 20:4–6 and Deut. 5:8–10.

17:4 Giving only *two hundred pieces of silver* for the idol does not match her vow from the previous verse.

17:5 On *ephod*, see note on 8:24–27. *Teraphim* are sacred statues or figurines that Israelites used in representing household gods (Gen. 31:19). Some biblical texts speak against their usage (1 Sam. 15:23; 2 Kgs. 23:24), but other texts treat them as a normal part of worship (Hos. 3:4).

17:6 The first half of this verse repeats in 18:1 and 19:1. The entire verse is repeated as the last verse of judges (21:25). This repeated refrain in the last chapters of the book—where there are no more judges mentioned—conveys a longing for the benefits of a monarchy as a corrective to the wanton behavior going on. See note on "pleases me" in 14:2–3.

17:7 The *Levite* is a resident alien living in the territory of Judah, since Levites had no tribal allotment of land (Deut. 18:1–2).

17:10 Referring to the Levite as *father* is a sign of respect and honor like referring to Deborah as "a mother in Israel" (5:7).

17:13 Micah reasons that his shrine will become an effective cultic site because Levites are legitimate priests (Deut. 18:1–8).

18:1 On *in those days there was no king in Israel*, see note on 17:6. Although this verse says *no territory among the tribes of Israel had been allotted to* the Danites, Josh. 19:40–48 describes their allotment (including Zorah and Eshtaol, mentioned in 13:2, 25; and 18:2, 8), and the Danites struggle to attain "Leshem," a city with a similar name to "Laish" (18:7).

18:3 On *they recognized the voice*, see note on 12:4–6.

18:5 On *inquire of God*, see note on 1:1.

"Inquire of God that we may know whether the mission we are undertaking will succeed." [6]The priest replied, "Go in peace. The mission you are on is under the eye of the LORD."

7 The five men went on, and when they came to Laish, they observed the people who were there living securely, after the manner of the Sidonians, quiet and unsuspecting, lacking[q] nothing on earth, and possessing wealth.[r] Furthermore, they were far from the Sidonians and had no dealings with Aram.[s] [8]When they came to their kinsfolk at Zorah and Eshtaol, they said to them, "What do you report?" [9]They said, "Come, let us go up against them, for we have seen the land, and it is very good. Will you do nothing? Do not be slow to go, but enter in and possess the land. [10]When you go, you will come to an unsuspecting people. The land is broad—God has indeed given it into your hands—a place where there is no lack of anything on earth."

11 Six hundred men of the Danite clan, armed with weapons of war, set out from Zorah and Eshtaol [12]and went up and encamped at Kiriath-jearim in Judah. On this account that place is called Mahaneh-dan[t] to this day; it is west of Kiriath-jearim. [13]From there they passed on to the hill country of Ephraim and came to the house of Micah.

14 Then the five men who had gone to spy out the land (that is, Laish) said to their comrades, "Do you know that in these buildings there are an ephod, teraphim, and an idol of cast metal? Now, therefore, consider what you will do." [15]So they turned in that direction and came to the house of the young Levite at the home of Micah and greeted him. [16]While the six hundred men of the Danites, armed with their weapons of war, stood by the entrance of the gate, [17]the five men who had gone to spy out the land proceeded to enter and take the idol of cast metal, the ephod, and the teraphim.[u] The priest was standing by the entrance of the gate with the six hundred men armed with weapons of war. [18]When the men went into Micah's house and took the idol of cast metal, the ephod, and the teraphim, the priest said to them, "What are you doing?" [19]They said to him, "Keep quiet! Put your hand over your mouth, and come with us, and be to us a father and a priest. Is it better for you to be priest to the house of one person or to be priest to a tribe and clan in Israel?" [20]Then the priest accepted the offer. He took the ephod, the teraphim, and the idol and went along with the people.

21 So they resumed their journey, putting the little ones, the livestock, and the goods in front of them. [22]When they were some distance from the home of Micah, the men who were in the houses near Micah's house were called out, and they overtook the Danites. [23]They shouted to the Danites, who turned around and said to Micah, "What is the matter that you come with such a company?" [24]He replied, "You take my gods that I made and the priest and go away, and what have I left? How then can you ask me, 'What is the matter?' " [25]And the Danites said to him, "You had better not let your voice be heard among us, or else hot-tempered fellows will attack you, and you will lose your life and the lives of your household." [26]Then the Danites went their way. When Micah saw that they were too strong for him, he turned and went back to his home.

27 The Danites, having taken what Micah had made and the priest who belonged to him, came to Laish, to a people quiet and unsuspecting, put them to the sword, and

q 18.7 Cn: Meaning of Heb uncertain   r 18.7 Meaning of Heb uncertain   s 18.7 Gk: Heb *with anyone*
t 18.12 That is, *camp of Dan*   u 18.17 Gk: Heb *teraphim and the cast metal*

18:7 *Laish* is a northern city whose name means "lion" in Hebrew. On *Sidonians*, see note on 3:3. On *Aram*, see note on 3:7–8.

18:12 On *to this day*, see note on 1:21. *Kiriath-jearim* means "city of forests."

18:14 On the *ephod* and *teraphim*, see note on 17:5.

18:19 On *a father and a priest*, see notes on 17:10 and 17:13. According to Num. 26:42–43, Dan was a single *tribe and clan in Israel*.

18:22 Since Micah's shrine, ephod, teraphim, and priest attracted people seeking cultic practices (like the Danites in 18:5), this theft also robs *the men who were in the houses near Micah's house*.

18:25 Other passages attest to the Danites' violent temperament (Gen. 49:17; Deut. 33:22).

burned down the city. ²⁸There was no deliverer because it was far from Sidon, and they had no dealings with Aram.ʸ It was in the valley that belongs to Beth-rehob. They rebuilt the city and lived in it. ²⁹They named the city Dan after their ancestor Dan, who was born to Israel, but the name of the city was formerly Laish. ³⁰Then the Danites set up the idol for themselves. Jonathan son of Gershom son of Mosesʷ and his sons were priests to the tribe of the Danites until the time the land went into captivity. ³¹So they maintained as their own Micah's idol that he had made, as long as the house of God was at Shiloh.

19 In those days, when there was no king in Israel, a certain Levite residing in the remote parts of the hill country of Ephraim took to himself a concubine from Bethlehem in Judah. ²But his concubine became angry withˣ him, and she went away from him to her father's house at Bethlehem in Judah and was there some four months. ³Then her husband set out after her, to speak tenderly to her and bring her back. He had with him his servant and a couple of donkeys. When he reachedʸ her father's house, the young woman's father saw him and came with joy to meet him. ⁴His father-in-law, the young woman's father,

made him stay, and he remained with him three days; so they ate and drank, and heᶻ stayed there. ⁵On the fourth day they got up early in the morning, and he prepared to go, but the young woman's father said to his son-in-law, "Fortify yourself with a bit of food, and after that you may go." ⁶So the two men sat and ate and drank together, and the young woman's father said to the man, "Why not spend the night and enjoy yourself?" ⁷When the man got up to go, his father-in-law kept urging him until he spent the night there again. ⁸On the fifth day he got up early in the morning to leave, and the young woman's father said, "Fortify yourself and linger until the day declines." So the two of them ate. ⁹When the man with his concubine and his servant got up to leave, his father-in-law, the young woman's father, said to him, "Look, the day has worn on until it is almost evening. Spend the night. See, the day has drawn to a close. Spend the night here and enjoy yourself. Tomorrow you can get up early in the morning for your journey and go home."

10 But the man would not spend the

v 18.28 Cn: Heb *with anyone* w 18.30 Another reading is *son of Manasseh* x 19.2 Gk OL: Heb *prostituted herself against* y 19.3 Gk: Heb *she brought him to* z 19.4 Compare Gk: Heb *they*

18:28 Ironically, Dan acts like the oppressors who, until this point, have been the reason that Israel needs God or a judge as their *deliverer* or savior (2:18; 3:9, 15, 31; 6:9, 14; 8:34; 10:1, 12; 13:5). *Beth-rehob* means "house of the open square" in Hebrew.

18:30 The Hebrew text has one small letter inserted (as if as a superscript) so the passage reads "son of Manasseh" (see text note w). Most likely *Moses* (who has a son named Gershom in Exod. 2:22) is the original reading, and a scribe added this letter to distance Moses's name from Dan's suspect priesthood. *Captivity* is the Assyrian conquest of the northern kingdom of Israel in 722 BCE.

18:31 The narrator disregards Dan's sanctuary—and subsequent worship that would happen there (1 Kgs. 12:29–30)—by asserting God's presence at *Shiloh*.

19:1 On *in those days, when there was no king in Israel*, see note on 17:6. On *concubine*, see note on 8:31.

19:2 The Hebrew literally says that she "prostituted herself against him," but the Hebrew Bible often uses the language of prostitution metaphorically (see note on 2:17). Since the Levite seeks reconciliation as if he were in the wrong (19:3–9), some scholars argue that this verse treats "prostituting herself against him" as an idiom equivalent to her leaving the Levite's house. The translation *became angry with him* derives from this reasoning.

19:3–9 *Speak tenderly* is literally "speak to her heart" in Hebrew, but the narrator only describes the husband interacting with his father-in-law. In ancient Israel, marriage was largely understood as an agreement between a husband and the father (or parents) of the bride (Exod. 22:16–17; Deut. 22:13–19, 28–29). The Levite's concubine is described as *the young woman* in six of her seven mentions in these verses to emphasize her youth and dependency on her father.

19:10–11 *Jerusalem* remains *Jebus*, the city of *Jebusites*, until David conquers it and establishes it as his capital (2 Sam. 5:6–9).

19:10–30 Compare with Gen. 19:1–17. **19:12** *Gibeah* is a town that Levites would presumably

night; he got up and departed and arrived opposite Jebus (that is, Jerusalem). He had with him a couple of saddled donkeys, and his concubine was with him. ¹¹When they were near Jebus, the day was far spent, and the servant said to his master, "Come now, let us turn aside to this city of the Jebusites and spend the night in it." ¹²But his master said to him, "We will not turn aside into a city of foreigners, who do not belong to the people of Israel, but we will continue on to Gibeah." ¹³Then he said to his servant, "Come, let us try to reach one of these places and spend the night at Gibeah or at Ramah." ¹⁴So they passed on and went their way, and the sun went down on them near Gibeah, which belongs to Benjamin. ¹⁵They turned aside there, to go in and spend the night at Gibeah. He went in and sat down in the open square of the city, but no one took them in to spend the night.

16 Then at evening there was an old man coming from his work in the field. The man was from the hill country of Ephraim, and he was residing in Gibeah. (The people of the place were Benjaminites.) ¹⁷When the old man looked up and saw the wayfarer in the open square of the city, he said, "Where are you going, and where do you come from?" ¹⁸He answered him, "We are passing from Bethlehem in Judah to the remote parts of the hill country of Ephraim, from which I come. I went to Bethlehem in Judah, and I am going to my home.ᵃ Nobody has offered to take me in. ¹⁹We have straw and fodder for our donkeys, with bread and wine for me and the woman and the young man along

with us. Your servants need nothing more." ²⁰The old man said, "Peace be to you. I will care for all your wants; only do not spend the night in the square." ²¹So he brought him into his house and fed the donkeys; they washed their feet and ate and drank.

22 While they were enjoying themselves, the men of the city, a perverse lot, surrounded the house and started pounding on the door. They said to the old man, the master of the house, "Bring out the man who came into your house, so that we may have intercourse with him." ²³And the man, the master of the house, went out to them and said to them, "No, my brothers, do not act so wickedly. Since this man is my guest, do not do this vile thing. ²⁴Here are my virgin daughter and his concubine; let me bring them out now. Ravish them and do whatever you want to them, but against this man do not do such a vile thing." ²⁵But the men would not listen to him. So the man seized his concubine and put her out to them. They wantonly raped her and abused her all through the night until the morning. And as the dawn began to break, they let her go. ²⁶As morning appeared, the woman came and fell down at the door of the man's house where her master was, until it was light.

27 In the morning her master got up, opened the doors of the house, and when he went out to go on his way, there was the woman, his concubine, lying at the door of the house, with her hands on the threshold. ²⁸"Get up," he said to her, "we are going."

---

a 19.18 Gk: Heb *to the house of the* LORD

---

esteem because it was the home of Phinehas and burial place of Eleazar, priestly sons of Aaron (Josh. 24:33). **19:15–21** Hospitality toward strangers (ignored by the people of Gibeah but honored by *an old man. . . . from the hill country of Ephraim*) was a high virtue for the ancient Israelites (Gen. 18:2–8) and is even framed as an obligation based on their past foreign status in Egypt (Lev. 19:34). **19:22** *A perverse lot* literally translates "sons of Belial," a phrase that likely derives from underworld mythology and leads to common derogatory uses of "Belial" in metaphors for people as "scoundrel/s" (Deut. 13:13; 1 Sam. 2:12; 2 Sam. 16:7) or "worthless" (1 Sam. 1:16; 10:27), things as "base" (Ps. 101:3), and circumstances as tortuously deadly ("torrents of perdition"; Ps. 18:4). **19:23** *Vile thing* refers to an illicit sexual violation in the majority of its occurrences in the Hebrew Bible (Gen. 34:7; Deut. 22:21; Judg. 19:24; 20:6, 10; 2 Sam. 13:12; Jer. 29:23). *The master of the house* values hospitality to his male guests (the Levite and his servant) over the protection of his female guest ("his concubine"; Judg. 19:24) and even his own "virgin daughter" (v. 24). **19:25** It is unclear which *man seized his concubine*. **19:26–27** Up to this point, the Levite is referred to as "master" in relation to his servant (vv. 11–12) but "man/husband" in relation to the concubine (vv. 3, 6, 7, 9, 10). After this act of cowardly exercising his dominance over her, the narrator calls him *her master*. **19:28–30** After being brutally raped, the concubine may have provided *no answer* to the Levite's callous command because she was exhausted or dead; the narrator does not indicate whether the

But there was no answer. Then he put her on the donkey, and the man set out for his home. [29]When he had entered his house, he took a knife, and grasping his concubine he cut her into twelve pieces, limb by limb, and sent her throughout all the territory of Israel. [30]Then he commanded the men whom he sent, saying, "Thus shall you say to all the Israelites: Has such a thing ever happened[b] since the day that the Israelites came up from the land of Egypt until this day? Consider it, take counsel, and speak out."

20 Then all the Israelites came out, from Dan to Beer-sheba, including the land of Gilead, and the congregation assembled in one body before the LORD at Mizpah. [2]The chiefs of all the people, of all the tribes of Israel, presented themselves in the assembly of the people of God, four hundred thousand foot soldiers bearing arms. [3](Now the Benjaminites heard that the Israelites had gone up to Mizpah.) And the Israelites said, "Tell us, how did this criminal act come about?" [4]The Levite, the husband of the woman who was murdered, answered, "I came to Gibeah that belongs to Benjamin, I and my concubine, to spend the night. [5]The lords of Gibeah rose up against me and surrounded the house at night. They intended to kill me, and they raped my concubine until she died. [6]Then I took my concubine and cut her into pieces and sent her throughout the whole extent of Israel's territory, for they have committed a vile outrage in Israel. [7]So now, you Israelites, all of you, give your advice and counsel here."

8 All the people got up as one, saying, "We will not any of us go to our tents, nor will any of us return to our houses. [9]But now this is what we will do to Gibeah: we will go up[c] against it by lot. [10]We will take ten men of a hundred throughout all the tribes of Israel, and a hundred of a thousand, and a thousand of ten thousand, to bring provisions for the troops who will go to repay[d] Gibeah of Benjamin for all the disgrace that they have done in Israel." [11]So all the men of Israel gathered against the city, united as one.

12 The tribes of Israel sent men through all the tribe of Benjamin, saying, "What crime is this that has been committed among you? [13]Now then, hand over those scoundrels in Gibeah so that we may put them to death and purge the evil from Israel." But the Benjaminites would not listen to their kinsfolk, the Israelites. [14]The Benjaminites came together out of the towns to Gibeah, to go out to battle against the Israelites. [15]On that day the Benjaminites mustered twenty-six thousand armed men from their towns, besides the inhabitants of Gibeah, who mustered seven hundred picked men. [16]Of all this force, there were seven hundred picked men who were left-handed; every one could sling

b 19.30 Compare Gk: Heb *[30]And all who saw it said, "Such a thing has not happened or been seen* c 20.9 Gk: Heb lacks *we will go up* d 20.10 Compare Gk: Meaning of Heb uncertain

latter is true before the Levite dismembers her. Cutting *her into twelve pieces* to send as a battle call for *all the territory of Israel* forms a grotesque caricature of the future king Saul, a Benjaminite from Gibeah (1 Sam. 10:20–21, 26), summoning troops by dismembering two oxen (1 Sam. 11:7).

20:1 *Dan to Beer-sheba* denotes northern and southern extremes of Israel.

20:5 The Levite says *they intended to kill me*, but in 19:22 the people intended to rape him. The Levite adds that *they raped my concubine until she died* without noting that he (or the "master of the house") "seized" her and "put her out to them" (19:25). This dishonesty heaps all blame for her death on the people of Gibeah, but it also undermines the Levite's credibility for readers who know the whole truth. Is he lying about her being dead before he dismembers her?

20:6 On *vile outrage*, see note on "vile thing" in 19:23.

20:9 *By lot* refers to the practice of casting lots: the interpretation of seemingly random arrangements of objects (like modern dice or drawing straws) for decision-making.

20:11 *All the men of Israel gathered* together *united as one* to fight an enemy for the first time in Judges. Otherwise, they are only described as united like this in apostasy (2:4; 8:27).

20:13 *Purge the evil* literally translates "burn the evil," an idiom used often in Deuteronomy to call for corporate responsibility to eradicate (often with capital punishment) perpetrators of wrongdoing (Deut. 13:5; 17:7, 12; 19:19; 21:21; 22:21, 22, 24; 24:7). *Scoundrels* literally translates "sons of Belial" in Hebrew (see note on 19:22).

20:16 On *left-handed*, see note on 3:15.

a stone at a hair and not miss. [17]And the Israelites, apart from Benjamin, mustered four hundred thousand armed men, all of them warriors.

18 The Israelites proceeded to go up to Bethel, where they inquired of God, "Which of us shall go up first to battle against the Benjaminites?" And the LORD answered, "Judah shall go up first."

19 Then the Israelites got up in the morning and encamped against Gibeah. [20]The Israelites went out to battle against Benjamin, and the Israelites drew up the battle line against them at Gibeah. [21]The Benjaminites came out of Gibeah and struck down on that day twenty-two thousand of the Israelites. [23e]The Israelites went up and wept before the LORD until the evening, and they inquired of the LORD, "Shall we again draw near to battle against our kinsfolk the Benjaminites?" And the LORD said, "Go up against them." [22]The Israelites strengthened themselves and again formed the battle line in the same place where they had formed it on the first day.

24 So the Israelites advanced against the Benjaminites the second day. [25]Benjamin moved out against them from Gibeah the second day and struck down eighteen thousand of the Israelites, all of them armed men. [26]Then all the Israelites, the whole army, went back to Bethel and wept, sitting there before the LORD; they fasted that day until evening. Then they offered burnt offerings and sacrifices of well-being before the LORD. [27]And the Israelites inquired of the LORD (for the ark of the covenant of God was there in those days, [28]and Phinehas son of Eleazar, son of Aaron, ministered before it in those days), saying, "Shall we go out once more to battle against our kinsfolk the Benjaminites, or shall we desist?" The LORD answered, "Go up, for tomorrow I will give them into your hand."

29 So Israel stationed men in ambush around Gibeah. [30]Then the Israelites went up against the Benjaminites on the third day and set themselves in array against Gibeah as before. [31]When the Benjaminites went out against the army, they were drawn away from the city. As before, they began to inflict casualties on the troops along the main roads, one of which goes up to Bethel and the other to Gibeah, as well as in the open country, killing about thirty men of Israel. [32]The Benjaminites thought, "They are being routed before us, as previously." But the Israelites said, "Let us retreat and draw them away from the city toward the roads." [33]The main body of the Israelites drew back its battle line to Baal-tamar, while those Israelites who were in ambush rushed out of their place west[f] of Geba. [34]There came against Gibeah ten thousand picked men out of all Israel, and the battle was fierce. But the Benjaminites did not realize that disaster was close upon them.

35 The LORD defeated Benjamin before Israel, and the Israelites struck down twenty-five thousand one hundred men of Benjamin that day, all of them armed.

36 Then the Benjaminites saw that they were defeated.

The Israelites gave ground to Benjamin because they relied on the troops in ambush that they had stationed against Gibeah. [37]The troops in ambush rushed quickly upon Gibeah. Then they put the whole city to the sword. [38]Now the agreement between the main body of Israel and the men in ambush was that when they sent up a cloud of smoke out of the city [39]the main body of Israel should turn in battle. But Benjamin had begun to inflict casualties on the Israelites, killing about thirty of them, so they thought, "Surely they are defeated before us, as in the first battle." [40]But when the cloud, a column of smoke, began to rise out of the city, the Benjaminites looked

e 20.23 Verses 22 and 23 are transposed   f 20.33 Gk Vg: Heb *in the plain*

20:18 As v. 27 reveals, "the ark of the covenant of God" was in *Bethel* at that time. The importance of Bethel as a sanctuary goes back to the time of Jacob (Gen. 28:10–22; 35:1–7) and continues after the monarchy divides (1 Kgs. 12:28–29). On *inquired of God*, see the note on "inquired of the LORD" on Judg. 1:1. Also see note on 1:2. Unfortunately, the situation has devolved from God's guidance against the inhabitants of Canaan to a civil war.

20:28 *Phinehas* is an Egyptian name meaning "the Nubian." *Eleazar* means "God helped" in Hebrew. The meaning of the name *Aaron* is debated, but it is likely Egyptian. Their Levitical priestly pedigree lends legitimacy to the sanctuary at Bethel.

behind them—and there was the whole city going up in smoke toward the sky! [41]Then the main body of Israel turned, and the Benjaminites were dismayed, for they saw that disaster was close upon them. [42]Therefore they turned away from the Israelites in the direction of the wilderness, but the battle overtook them, and those who came out of the city[g] were striking them down in between.[b] [43]Surrounding the Benjaminites, they pursued them from Nohah[i] and trod them down as far as a place east of Gibeah. [44]Eighteen thousand Benjaminites fell, all of them courageous fighters. [45]When they turned and fled toward the wilderness to the rock of Rimmon, five thousand of them were cut down on the main roads, and they were pursued as far as Gidom, and two thousand of them were slain. [46]So all who fell that day of Benjamin were twenty-five thousand arms-bearing men, all of them courageous fighters. [47]But six hundred turned and fled toward the wilderness to the rock of Rimmon and remained at the rock of Rimmon for four months. [48]Meanwhile, the Israelites turned back against the Benjaminites and put them to the sword—the city, the people, the animals, and all that remained. Also the remaining towns they set on fire.

21 Now the Israelites had sworn at Mizpah, "No one of us shall give his daughter in marriage to Benjamin." [2]And the people came to Bethel and sat there until evening before God, and they lifted up their voices and wept bitterly. [3]They said, "O Lord, the God of Israel, why has it come to pass that today there should be one tribe lacking in Israel?" [4]On the next day, the people got up early and built an altar there and offered burnt offerings and sacrifices of well-being. [5]Then the Israelites said, "Who out of all the tribes of Israel did not come up in the assembly to the Lord?" For a solemn oath had been taken concerning whoever did not come up to the Lord to Mizpah, saying, "That one shall be put to death." [6]But the Israelites had compassion for Benjamin their kin and said, "One tribe is cut off from Israel this day. [7]What shall we do for wives for those who are left, since we have sworn by the Lord that we will not give them any of our daughters as wives?"

8 Then they said, "Is there anyone from the tribes of Israel who did not come up to the Lord to Mizpah?" It turned out that no one from Jabesh-gilead had come to the camp, to the assembly. [9]For when the roll was called among the people, not one of the inhabitants of Jabesh-gilead was there. [10]So the congregation sent twelve thousand soldiers there and commanded them, "Go, put the inhabitants of Jabesh-gilead to the sword, including the women and the little ones. [11]This is what you shall do; every male and every woman who has lain with a male you shall devote to destruction." [12]And they found among the inhabitants of Jabesh-gilead four hundred young virgins who had

g 20.42 Compare Vg and Gk mss: Heb *cities*   h 20.42 Compare Syr: Meaning of Heb uncertain   i 20.43 Gk mss: Heb *pursued them at their resting place*

20:47–48 This nearly complete extermination of Benjaminites is attributed to YHWH (20:35) and matches Judah's God-given success in 1:2–20 contrasted against the other tribes' failure to exterminate all inhabitants in 1:21–36.

21:1 Although the Israelites did gather at *Mizpah* in 20:1, there is no previous mention of this oath (repeated in 21:7) forbidding giving one's *daughter in marriage to Benjamin*.

21:4 The Israelites' constructing *an altar* after YHWH gave them victory is the inverse of Gideon building an altar before preparing for battle (6:25–27; 7:1–25).

21:5 There is no previous mention of this oath promising to *put to death* whoever *did not come up in the assembly to the Lord*.

21:8 Elsewhere in the Hebrew Bible, *Jabesh-Gilead* is associated with the Benjaminite Saul: he saves the city from destruction (1 Sam. 13), and they care for his remains after he dies in battle (1 Sam. 31:11–13; 2 Sam. 2:4–7).

21:11 For *devote to destruction*, see note on 1:17. See **"The Divine Mandate to Exterminate the Canaanites," p. 313**.

21:12–14 Kidnaping girls and women into forced marriage is a practice (and sometimes the goal) in warfare in ancient and modern times. Deuteronomy 21:10–14 regulates how Israelites were to take girls. See **"Genocide," p. 305**.

never slept with a man and brought them to the camp at Shiloh, which is in the land of Canaan.

13 Then the whole congregation sent word to the Benjaminites who were at the rock of Rimmon and proclaimed peace to them. [14]Benjamin returned at that time, and they gave them the women whom they had saved alive of the women of Jabesh-gilead, but they did not suffice for them.

15 The people had compassion on Benjamin because the LORD had made a breach in the tribes of Israel. [16]So the elders of the congregation said, "What shall we do for wives for those who are left, since there are no women left in Benjamin?" [17]And they said, "There must be heirs for the survivors of Benjamin, in order that a tribe may not be blotted out from Israel. [18]Yet we cannot give any of our daughters to them as wives." For the Israelites had sworn, "Cursed be anyone who gives a wife to Benjamin." [19]So they said, "Look, the yearly festival of the LORD is taking place at Shiloh, which is north of Bethel, on the east of the highway that goes up from Bethel to Shechem and south of Lebonah." [20]And they instructed the Benjaminites, saying, "Go and lie in wait in the vineyards [21]and watch; when the young women of Shiloh come out to dance in the dances, then come out of the vineyards and each of you carry off a wife for himself from the young women of Shiloh and go to the land of Benjamin. [22]Then if their fathers or their brothers come to complain to us, we will say to them, 'Be generous and allow us to have them, because we did not capture in battle a wife for each man. But neither did you incur guilt by giving your daughters to them.'" [23]The Benjaminites did so; they took wives for each of them from the dancers whom they abducted. Then they went and returned to their territory and rebuilt the towns and lived in them. [24]So the Israelites departed from there at that time by tribes and families, and they went out from there to their own territories.

25 In those days there was no king in Israel; all the people did what was right in their own eyes.

21:19 According to Exod. 34:23, the Israelites were obliged to appear before God thrice annually. Judges 18:31 indicates that "the house of God was at Shiloh."

21:20–21 Some scholars think this description of kidnaping for marriage reflects an actual Israelite custom of simulating capture of wives at Shiloh.

21:25 On this verse, see note on 17:6. As the conclusion to the book of Judges, this negative evaluation of the era (especially the illegitimate shrine, bellicose Danites, inhospitality, rape and murder, civil war, genocide, and kidnaping crunched into chaps. 17–20) highlight the need for a king to emerge in 1 Samuel.

RUTH

The book of Ruth begins with famine, migration, and a family on the brink of extinction and ends with redemption, marriage, and the birth of a family destined for royalty. The focus is on the tragic losses of a woman named Naomi and her eventual restoration. However, this transformation is made possible by the remarkable faithfulness of Ruth, her Moabite daughter-in-law, and their Israelite kinsman Boaz. Their acts of good faith are all the more memorable because they transcend self-interests and cultural boundaries. Indeed, this exquisitely crafted story not only delights but also provokes serious reflection on matters of ethnicity, gender, sexuality, and the possibility of kinship with those who are other (see **"The Bible, Race, and Ethnicity," pp. 2163–64**, and **"The Bible, Gender, and Sexuality," pp. 2160–62**).

Cultural Setting

The story is set in the time of the "judges," before the rise of the monarchy in Israel (ca. 1200–1020 BCE; see **"The Judges," p. 342**). The book of Judges depicts this period as one of lawlessness and increasing violence, especially violence against women (Judg. 19–21). In striking contrast, Ruth offers a vision of a caring community. This sense is reinforced by its peaceful agrarian setting with its bountiful harvests, where men and women work together to produce the grain that feeds their families. Yet the idyllic tone does not obscure the risks confronting Naomi and Ruth. In this patriarchal society, widows suffered the loss of not just their husbands but the social structure that ensured their basic economic well-being. Additionally, Ruth's "immigrant" status would have made her situation all the more precarious (2:9, 15, 22).

Biblical law thus included provisions to mitigate the vulnerability of widows, families in distress, and other marginalized peoples. To support herself and Naomi, Ruth relies on a custom that permitted foreigners, widows, and the poor to glean leftover grain during harvest (Lev. 19:9–10; 23:22; Deut. 24:19–22). Pivotal to the story is Boaz's role as "redeemer," a relative within their kinship circle, with the responsibility to protect the property and honor of the family (hence the alternative translation "next-of-kin"; Lev. 25:25; Jer. 32:6–15). There are allusions to levirate marriage, a custom designed to preserve a dead man's estate and protect the welfare of his widow (Gen. 38; Deut. 25:5–10), when Boaz finally marries Ruth and secures the women's future.

Date, Purpose, and Religious Function

There is no scholarly consensus about the date of composition. Given the Davidic genealogy that concludes the book, some argue that it was written during the monarchy to celebrate David's ancestry and defend his dynasty. Others suggest that the book emerged in the postexilic era, as a polemic against the exclusionary policies of Ezra and Nehemiah (Ezra 9–10; Neh. 13; see **"Intermarriage," p. 649**). Yet the story does not have either a propagandistic or polemical tone, and the themes of kindness, family loyalty, and openness to outsiders are timeless.

The Hebrew Bible places Ruth in the Writings (the third part of the Jewish canon), among the five festal scrolls. Ruth is read publicly in synagogues during the Feast of Weeks (Shavuot), which celebrates the harvest season. The feast also commemorates the giving of Torah to Moses, a theme that is related to the rabbinic interpretation of Ruth as the ideal convert, who models obedience to Torah (see **"Gentile Conversion," p. 1530**). The story thus functions as a regular prompt to (re)imagine faithfulness to Torah. In Christian Bibles, Ruth is located between Judges and 1 Samuel (following the sequence of the Septuagint and Vulgate) as a transition between the period of the judges and the establishment of the Davidic monarchy. This canonical placement highlights the significance of Naomi's family history for Israel's larger metanarrative. Moreover, for Christian readers, Ruth's place in that story is further valorized by her inclusion in the Matthean genealogy (Matt. 1:5), where she is joined by Tamar, Rahab, and "the wife of Uriah"—all non-Israelite women of questionable repute who prepare the way for Jesus's scandalous birth and the gospel's inclusion of all peoples (see **"Race and Ethnicities in Biblical Genealogies," p. 1723**).

Reading Guide

The story is elegantly structured in four symmetrical chapters that highlight the movement from loss to restoration. Chapter 1 consists of three scenes: a family history of loss (1:1–5), negotiation of kinship ties among women (1:6–18), and Naomi's lament before the women of Bethlehem (1:19–22). These scenes are rounded out by the three scenes of the final chapter: kinship negotiations among men (4:1–12), the women's celebration over Naomi's restoration (4:13–17), and a family history of abundant life (4:18–22). Similarly, the two middle chapters parallel each other, as Ruth moves back and forth between Naomi and Boaz to restore family ties and bring "seeds of hope" to Naomi. The steady movement from emptiness to fullness is further underscored by wordplays and images that are deftly woven throughout the story.

Many readers, past and present, have highlighted the book's depiction of *hesed* (kindness or covenant faithfulness) as its central theme (see **"Hesed," p. 375**). The principal characters embody this quality in their generous care for one another (1:8; 2:20; 3:10). Related to this motif is God's covenant faithfulness. The theological framework of the book affirms that fertile grounds and fertile marriages are ultimately divine gifts (1:6; 4:13); however, elsewhere in the story, God does not intervene directly, perhaps indicating that divine providence is at work via human agents. Indeed, human kindness and divine kindness work together to transform Naomi's sorrow to joy (1:8; 2:20). Finally, Ruth's Moabite background—emphasized repeatedly in the book (1:22; 2:2, 6, 21; 4:5, 10)—raises questions about how kinship ties may be forged across notions of otherness. The story's widespread use of dialogue invites its characters and readers alike to continue the conversation.

Eunny P. Lee

1 In the days when the judges ruled, there was a famine in the land, and a certain man of Bethlehem in Judah went to live in the country of Moab, he and his wife and two sons. ²The name of the man was Elimelech and the name of his wife Naomi, and the names of his two sons were Mahlon[a] and Chilion;[b] they were Ephrathites from Bethlehem in Judah. They went into the country of Moab and remained there. ³But Elimelech, the husband of Naomi, died, and she was left with her two sons. ⁴These took Moabite wives; the name of the one was Orpah and the name of the other Ruth. When they had lived there about ten years, ⁵both Mahlon and Chilion also died, so that the woman was left without her two sons and her husband.

6 Then she started to return with her daughters-in-law from the country of Moab, for she had heard in the country of Moab that the LORD had considered his people and given them food. ⁷So she set out from the place where she had been living, she and her two daughters-in-law, and they went on their way to go back to the land of Judah. ⁸But Naomi said to her two daughters-in-law, "Go back each of you

a 1.2 That is, *sickly* b 1.2 That is, *frail*

1:1–5 Migration to Moab. 1:1 *Judges*, military chieftains who ruled the tribes of Israel before the monarchy. The precise phrase *there was a famine in the land* occurs also in Gen. 12:10 and 26:1, where famine forces Israel's ancestors to forsake their homeland. In both cases, migrating into foreign territory endangers the matriarch and the future of the family. *Bethlehem*, five miles south of Jerusalem, was the home of David's family (1 Sam. 16:1–5). The conclusion of the story reveals that the future of the Davidic monarchy is at stake in the future of this family. *Moab* is located east of the Dead Sea in Transjordan. Biblical narratives acknowledge a distant kinship between Israel and Moab (Gen. 19:37; Deut. 2:9). But the relationship is often depicted negatively (see especially Num. 25:1–3; Deut. 23:3–6; Isa. 15; Ezra 9–10; Neh. 13). Here, Bethlehem (literally "house of bread") is ironically depleted by famine, and Moab offers sustenance. **1:2** *Ephrathites*, people of Ephrathah, another name for the region of Bethlehem (cf. 4:11; 1 Sam. 17:12).

1:6–18 The journey home. With the death of the men, the women take center stage; each must decide where home is. **1:6** The narrator reports divine activity twice, here and in 4:13. *Return*. The Hebrew verb ("shuv," translated also as "turn/go back") is used twelve times in this chapter. **1:8** The expression *mother's house* rather than the usual "father's house" occurs in narratives that highlight

Reading through Time: Ruth and Naomi (Ruth 1)

The relationship between Ruth and Naomi is at the heart of the book of Ruth, but this relationship has been understood in more than one way. As in-laws, their relationship is both familial and legal, but it moves beyond normal expectations. Among other features, this relationship is characterized by love and *hesed* (see **"Hesed," p. 375**). The term *hesed* describes Ruth's loyalty to and care of Naomi, which serve as an example of ethical behavior and even mirror God's own relationship with God's people.

Because the relationship between Ruth and Naomi is one of the only extended and positively portrayed bonds between women in the Bible—and because it connects two women of different ages, ethnicities, and religions—many interpreters have lauded it as a model for female solidarity and sisterhood. Some readers have even wondered if Ruth and Naomi might be romantically involved. Such an interpretation derives from Ruth's passionate declaration of undying devotion (1:16–17); the note that she "clung" to Naomi (1:14), a verb that is sometimes used to characterize the marital bond (Gen. 2:24); and the community's acknowledgment of Ruth's love and Naomi's parenthood of Obed (Ruth 4:15–17). Although none of these details point unequivocally to a romantic relationship, the amorous aspects of Ruth 1:16–17 may be tacitly acknowledged in how these verses are often read at weddings to this day. An understanding of Naomi and Ruth's relationship as romantic in some fashion has played a role in the reception of the book, as in Fannie Flagg's *Fried Green Tomatoes at the Whistle Stop Cafe* (1987; made into the movie *Fried Green Tomatoes* in 1991), Jeanette Winterson's *Oranges Are Not the Only Fruit* (1985), and Amos Gitai's film *Golem, the Spirit of the Exile* (1992).

If the nature of Ruth's love for Naomi—platonic, familial, merely dutiful, or romantic—remains an open question, the same is true for Naomi's feelings for Ruth. Indeed, her actions toward Ruth may be interpreted negatively. Naomi does not reciprocate Ruth's passionate declaration in chapter 1; she proclaims herself empty when she returns to Bethlehem even though Ruth is at her side (1:20–21); she arranges for Ruth's encounter with Boaz (3:1–4), perhaps using her daughter-in-law's sexuality to procure her own economic security. Beautifully crafted but sparse, the text contains gaps and indeterminate language, thus rendering Ruth and Naomi's relationship indeterminate as well.

Jennifer L. Koosed

to your mother's house. May the LORD deal kindly with you, as you have dealt with the dead and with me. ⁹The LORD grant that you may find security, each of you in the house of your husband." Then she kissed them, and they wept aloud. ¹⁰They said to her, "No, we will return with you to your people." ¹¹But Naomi said, "Turn back, my daughters. Why will you go with me? Do I still have sons in my womb that they may become your husbands? ¹²Turn back, my daughters, go your way, for I am too old to have a husband. Even if I thought there was hope for me, even if I should have a husband tonight and bear sons, ¹³would you then wait until they were grown? Would you then refrain from marrying? No, my daughters, it has been far more bitter for me than for you, because the hand of the LORD has turned against me." ¹⁴Then they wept aloud again. Orpah kissed her mother-in-law goodbye, but Ruth clung to her.

15 So she said, "Look, your sister-in-law has gone back to her people and to her gods; return after your sister-in-law." ¹⁶But Ruth said,

"Do not press me to leave you,
  to turn back from following you!
Where you go, I will go;
  where you lodge, I will lodge;
your people shall be my people
  and your God my God.

women's agency, especially when marriage may be in view (Gen. 24:28; Song 3:4; 8:2). *Deal kindly*, see **"Hesed," p. 375**. **1:9** In patriarchal societies, women find social and economic *security* in marriage. **1:11** In Israelite law, when a married man died childless, his brother was to marry the widow to bear a child for the dead man's family line and provide for the widow (Deut. 25:5–10). Naomi alludes to this practice but points to its impossibility in her case. **1:14** Some readers herald Orpah's departure as an independent decision to honor her own roots. *Clung to her* indicates deep commitment, as in marriage (cf. Gen. 2:24). **1:16–17** These words are often invoked in marriage ceremonies; here, a woman commits herself to her mother-in-law (see **"Ruth and Naomi," p. 373**). *May the LORD do thus*, a solemn oath formula.

[17] Where you die, I will die,
  and there will I be buried.
May the Lord do thus to me,
  and more as well,
if even death parts me from you!"
[18] When Naomi saw that she was deter-mined to go with her, she said no more to her.

19 So the two of them went on until they came to Bethlehem. When they came to Bethlehem, the whole town was stirred be-cause of them, and the women said, "Is this Naomi?" [20] She said to them,

"Call me no longer Naomi;[c]
  call me Mara,[d]
  for the Almighty[e] has dealt bitterly
    with me.
[21] I went away full,
  but the Lord has brought me back
    empty;
why call me Naomi
  when the Lord has dealt harshly
    with[f] me
  and the Almighty[g] has brought
    calamity upon me?"

22 So Naomi returned together with Ruth the Moabite, her daughter-in-law, who came back with her from the country of Moab. They came to Bethlehem at the be-ginning of the barley harvest.

2 Now Naomi had a kinsman on her husband's side, a prominent rich man of the family of Elimelech whose name was Boaz. [2] And Ruth the Moabite said to Naomi, "Let me go to the field and glean among the ears of grain behind someone in whose sight I may find favor." She said to her, "Go, my daughter." [3] So she went. She came and gleaned in the field behind the reapers. As it happened, she came to the part of the field belonging to Boaz, who was of the family of Elimelech. [4] Just then Boaz came from Bethlehem. He said to the reapers, "The Lord be with you." They an-swered, "The Lord bless you." [5] Then Boaz said to his young man who was in charge of the reapers, "To whom does this young woman belong?" [6] The young man who was in charge of the reapers answered, "She is the young Moabite woman who came back with Naomi from the country of Moab. [7] She said, 'Please, let me glean and gath-er among the sheaves behind the reapers.' So she came, and she has been on her feet from early this morning until now without resting even for a moment."[b]

8 Then Boaz said to Ruth, "Now listen, my daughter, do not go to glean in anoth-er field or leave this one, but keep close to my young women. [9] Keep your eyes on the field that is being reaped and follow be-hind them. I have ordered the young men not to bother you. If you get thirsty, go to the vessels and drink from what the young men have drawn." [10] Then she fell prostrate, with her face to the ground, and said to him, "Why have I found favor in your sight, that you should take notice of me, when I am a foreigner?" [11] But Boaz answered her, "All

c 1.20 That is, *pleasant* d 1.20 That is, *bitter* e 1.20 Tra-ditional rendering of Heb *Shaddai* f 1.21 Or *has testified against* g 1.21 Traditional rendering of Heb *Shaddai* h 2.7 Compare Gk Vg: Meaning of Heb uncertain

1:19–22 Naomi's homecoming. The women of Bethlehem prompt Naomi to give fuller expression to her despair (cf. 4:17, where they celebrate her restoration). **1:20–21** Naomi's lament evokes Job's indictment of God (Job 27:2). *Almighty* (Hebrew "Shaddai"). This epithet for God is used frequently in Job and also in the ancestral narratives, where it is associated with the God of fecundity. Naomi's usage is poignant in its irony.

2:1–3 Ruth's strategy for survival. 2:1 *Prominent rich man.* The Hebrew expression connotes a man of great worth, in every sense of the word (cf. 3:11). **2:2** *Glean,* gathering leftover grain. Israelite law required landowners to extend this form of charity to widows, orphans, and foreign immigrants—those without land of their own (Lev. 19:9–10; 23:22; Deut. 24:19–22). Artist Jean-Francois Millet depicts the backbreaking nature of this work (*The Gleaners*, 1857). In the illustrations of Jewish artist David Wander, Ruth forages for recyclable cans (*Ruth*, 2011).

2:4–17 Boaz's public hospitality. In kinship-based societies, women were important economic producers; here, they work alongside men in the fields of rural Bethlehem. **2:4** A character's first words are telling, and Boaz appears on the scene pronouncing blessing. **2:5** He expresses interest in Ruth, probing the stranger's connections to his community. **2:8–9** Boaz's instructions point to Ruth's vulnerability and signal that he will act as protector. **2:10** *Take notice* ("nakar") and *for-eigner* ("nokkriyah") come from the same Hebrew root. The verb may mean "recognize" or "treat

Focus On: Hesed (Ruth 2)

The Hebrew word *hesed*—variously rendered as "kindness," "loyalty," "steadfast love," and the like—conveys an essential element in the theological vision of the book of Ruth. Elsewhere in the Bible, the word is used most often to describe God's benevolent, faithful care of God's people. This care is demonstrated in God's deliverance of Israel from Egyptian servitude (Exod. 15:13) and is included among the divine attributes that are foundational for the covenant with Israel (Exod. 20:6; Deut. 5:10). Although a covenant relationship is often presupposed (Deut. 7:9, 12; 2 Sam. 7:15; 1 Kgs. 8:23), God's abundant goodness extends to all creatures (Ps. 136:23–25; Jonah 4:2). Hence biblical poetry repeatedly celebrates God's *hesed* or appeals to it in prayers for help in times of trouble (e.g., Pss. 6:4; 86:13; Job 10:12). *Hesed* is also associated with divine justice (Pss. 33:5; 62:12; Mic. 6:8; Hos. 12:6). At the same time, it entails forgiveness, mercy, and faithfulness that endures for "a thousand generations" (Exod. 34:6–7; Deut. 7:9; Jer. 32:18).

There is a strong ethical dimension to *hesed*. Those who are beneficiaries of God's benevolence are called to imitate it in their relationships (Mic. 6:8; Hos. 6:6; Prov. 3:3–4). Indeed, *hesed* is what creates the bonds of friendship (1 Sam. 20:8) and loyalty among relatives and allies (Gen. 21:23; 24:49; 47:29). The word frequently occurs in the expression "to do *hesed*," suggesting that concrete actions are in view. Often these are acts that preserve life and promote the welfare of someone in need; they are done out of goodwill, not obligation (Gen. 40:14; 1 Kgs. 20:31). Those who practice this virtue go beyond legal requirements and cultural expectations to care for another, sometimes at a cost to oneself. However, because *hesed* takes place in a relationship of mutuality, one act of good faith may elicit another in response (Josh. 2:12–14; 1 Sam. 20:8; 2 Sam. 9:1; 1 Kgs. 2:7).

The book of Ruth offers a narrative enactment of *hesed*. Ruth embodies this quality when she relinquishes ties to her own people to stand in solidarity with her mother-in-law. Her resilient care for Naomi inspires Boaz's extraordinary generosity to Ruth (2:8–12), which in turn moves Naomi to consider Ruth's welfare (3:1). Moreover, the word occurs in a series of blessings that suggest that human kindness and divine kindness are at work together to transform a story of loss to one of new life (1:8; 2:20; 3:10).

Eunny P. Lee

that you have done for your mother-in-law since the death of your husband has been fully told me, how you left your father and mother and your native land and came to a people that you did not know before. [12]May the Lord reward you for your deeds, and may you have a full reward from the Lord, the God of Israel, under whose wings you have come for refuge!" [13]Then she said, "May I continue to find favor in your sight, my lord, for you have comforted me and spoken kindly to your servant, even though I am not one of your servants."

14 At mealtime Boaz said to her, "Come here and eat some of this bread and dip your morsel in the sour wine." So she sat beside the reapers, and he heaped up for her some parched grain. She ate until she was satisfied, and she had some left over. [15]When she got up to glean, Boaz instructed his young men, "Let her glean even among the standing sheaves, and do not reproach her. [16]You must also pull out some handfuls for her from the bundles and leave them for her to glean, and do not rebuke her."

17 So she gleaned in the field until evening. Then she beat out what she had gleaned, and it was about an ephah of barley. [18]She picked it up and came into the town, and her mother-in-law saw how much she had gleaned. Then she took out and gave her what was left over after she herself had been satisfied. [19]Her mother-in-law said to her, "Where did you glean today? And where have you worked? Blessed be the man who took notice of you." So

as a stranger," depending on the conjugation. Ruth's wordplay expresses gratitude for Boaz's unexpected hospitality but also subtly presses him to recognize her place in the community. **2:12** The imagery of protective *wings* is picked up in 3:9, when Ruth asks Boaz to spread his "cloak" (literally "wing") over her. **2:13** *You have . . . spoken kindly* (literally "spoken to the heart") connotes reassuring speech but is also used of a man wooing a woman (Gen. 34:3; Judg. 19:3; Hos. 2:14). **2:14** Boaz includes Ruth in a communal meal and serves her a substantial meal. **2:15-16** He extends her gleaning privileges beyond the norm.

2:17-23 Seeds of hope. 2:17 An *ephah of barley* would weigh at least thirty pounds, a staggering

she told her mother-in-law with whom she had worked, saying, "The name of the man with whom I worked today is Boaz." [20]Then Naomi said to her daughter-in-law, "Blessed be he by the LORD, whose kindness has not forsaken the living or the dead!" Naomi also said to her, "The man is a relative of ours, one of our nearest kin."[i] [21]Then Ruth the Moabite said, "He even said to me, 'Stay close by my young men until they have finished all my harvest.' " [22]Naomi said to Ruth, her daughter-in-law, "It is better, my daughter, that you go out with his young women, otherwise someone might bother you in another field." [23]So she stayed close to the young women of Boaz, gleaning until the end of the barley and wheat harvests, and she lived with her mother-in-law.

3 Naomi her mother-in-law said to her, "My daughter, I need to seek some security for you, so that it may be well with you. [2]Now here is our kinsman Boaz, with whose young women you have been working. See, he is winnowing barley tonight at the threshing floor. [3]Now wash and anoint yourself, and put on your best clothes and go down to the threshing floor, but do not make yourself known to the man until he has finished eating and drinking. [4]When he lies down, observe the place where he lies; then go and uncover his feet and lie down, and he will tell you what to do." [5]She said to her, "All that you say I will do."

6 So she went down to the threshing floor and did just as her mother-in-law had instructed her. [7]When Boaz had eaten and drunk and was in a contented mood, he went to lie down at the end of the heap of grain. Then she came stealthily and uncovered his feet and lay down. [8]At midnight the man was startled and turned over, and there, lying at his feet, was a woman! [9]He said, "Who are you?" And she answered, "I am Ruth, your servant; spread your cloak over your servant, for you are next-of-kin."[j] [10]He said, "May you be blessed by the LORD, my daughter; this last instance of your loyalty is better than the first; you have not gone after young men, whether poor or rich. [11]And now, my daughter, do not be afraid, I will do for you all that you ask, for all the assembly of my people know that you are a worthy woman. [12]But now, though

i 2.20 Or *one with the right to redeem*   *j* 3.9 Or *one with the right to redeem*

amount for one day's gleanings. **2:20** Naomi recognizes the *kindness* ("hesed") of God toward her, expressed through the generous provisions of a *nearest kin*—that is, a relative with the responsibility of "redeeming" or "reclaiming" what was lost to the family (Lev. 25; Num. 5:5–8; Jer. 32:6–25). **2:23** *The barley and wheat harvests* occur in succession. The end of the harvest season signals the end to Ruth's gleanings.

3:1–5 Naomi's strategy for survival. As unattached women, Naomi and Ruth face subsistence-level poverty and need a strategy for long-term survival. **3:1** As in 1:9, *security* implies marriage. **3:2** *Threshing floor*, a communal space where kernels of grain were separated from the husks. *Winnowing* was often done in the evening, when strong winds would blow away the chaff. Hos. 9:1 associates the place with sexual laxity. **3:3–4** Naomi's instructions are highly suggestive and risky for Ruth. **3:4** The Hebrew word for *feet* may be a euphemism for genitals. The sexual overtones are reinforced by the repeated use of the verbs *uncover* and *lie down* throughout the chapter. The scenario is reminiscent of Hebrew Bible narratives in which women use trickery and sexuality to force a man to do right by them (Gen. 19:30–38; 29:21–30; 38:6–26). Rather than condemning such tactics, these narratives memorialize the struggles of women who risk everything just to survive.

3:6–15 Boaz's private promise. The atmosphere is marked by secrecy, ambiguity, and danger. **3:8** Identities are kept hidden; the narrative speaks of *the man* and *a woman*. But the night becomes a moment of "uncovering" on multiple levels. **3:9** Ruth identifies herself by name—the only character to do so in the book. Rather than waiting for Boaz to tell her what to do (3:4), she tells him what to do. *Spread your cloak* (literally "wing"), a request that Boaz fulfill his prayer in 2:12 and provide her the protection of marriage (cf. Ezek. 16:8). She grounds the request in Boaz's identity as *next-of-kin* (see note on 2:20). Nowhere in the Bible is there a connection between redemption laws and levirate marriage (see note on 1:11), and Ruth is not a candidate for levirate marriage in any case. Ruth thus asks Boaz to go beyond the requirements of the law. **3:10** Boaz recognizes Ruth's "proposal" as an act of *loyalty* ("hesed") to Naomi's family. Ruth may marry anyone; only marriage to Boaz extends the protection to Naomi. **3:11** *Worthy woman*. The Hebrew word for "worth" may also

it is true that I am a near kinsman, there is another kinsman more closely related than I. [13]Remain this night, and in the morning, if he will act as next-of-kin[k] for you, good; let him do it. But if he is not willing to act as next-of-kin[l] for you, then, as the LORD lives, I will act as next-of-kin[m] for you. Lie down until the morning."

14 So she lay at his feet until morning but got up before one person could recognize another, for he said, "It must not be known that the woman came to the threshing floor." [15]Then he said, "Bring the cloak you are wearing and hold it out." So she held it, and he measured out six measures of barley and put it on her back; then he went into the town. [16]She came to her mother-in-law, who said, "How did things go with you,[n] my daughter?" Then she told her all that the man had done for her, [17]saying, "He gave me these six measures of barley, for he said, 'Do not go back to your mother-in-law empty-handed.'" [18]She replied, "Wait, my daughter, until you learn how the matter turns out, for the man will not rest but will settle the matter today."

4 No sooner had Boaz gone up to the gate and sat down there than the next-of-kin[o] of whom Boaz had spoken came passing by. So Boaz said, "Come over;[p] sit down here." And he went over and sat down. [2]Then Boaz took ten men of the elders of the town and said, "Sit down here," so they sat down. [3]He then said to the next-of-kin,[q] "Naomi, who has come back from the country of Moab, is selling the parcel of land that belonged to our kinsman Elimelech. [4]So I thought I would tell you of it and say: Buy it in the presence of those sitting here and in the presence of the elders of my people. If you will redeem it, redeem it; but if you[r] will not, tell me, so that I may know; for there is no one prior to you to redeem it, and I come after you." So he said, "I will redeem it." [5]Then Boaz said, "The day you acquire the field from the hand of Naomi, you are also acquiring Ruth[s] the Moabite, the widow of the dead man, to maintain the dead man's name on his inheritance." [6]At this, the next-of-kin[t] said, "I cannot redeem it for myself without damaging my own inheritance. Take my right of redemption yourself, for I cannot redeem it."

7 Now this was the custom in former times in Israel concerning redeeming and exchanging to confirm a transaction: the one took off a sandal and gave it to the other; this was the manner of attesting in Israel. [8]So when the next-of-kin[u] said to Boaz, "Acquire it for yourself," he took off his sandal. [9]Then Boaz said to the elders and all the people, "You are witnesses today that I have acquired from the hand of Naomi all that belonged to Elimelech and

---

k 3.13 Or *one with the right to redeem   l* 3.13 Or *one with the right to redeem   m* 3.13 Or *one with the right to redeem   n* 3.16 Or *"Who are you,   o* 4.1 Or *one with the right to redeem   p* 4.1 Heb *Come over, so and so   q* 4.3 Or *one with the right to redeem   r* 4.4 Heb mss Gk Syr Vg: MT *if he   s* 4.5 OL Vg: Heb *from the hand of Naomi and from Ruth   t* 4.6 Or *one with the right to redeem   u* 4.8 Or *one with the right to redeem*

---

indicate "strength," "valor," or "wealth" and is used to describe Boaz as a "prominent rich man" (2:1). Boaz thus acknowledges Ruth as a fitting partner (cf. Prov. 31:10; see **"Woman of Worth," p. 903**).

3:16–18 Further seeds of hope. 3:17 *Empty-handed* explicitly overturns Naomi's emptiness in 1:21.

4:1–12 Redemption at the gate. The *gate* represents the town's legal assembly, where important cases were adjudicated. It was a locus of male power but also where social justice was to be upheld (Amos 5:12, 15). **4:1** *Next-of-kin.* In Hebrew, Boaz addresses his relative as "peloni 'almoni," an expression used when a name is being deliberately avoided (as in "so-and-so" or "Joe Schmoe"). The narrative suppresses the name of the nearer kinsman and memorializes Boaz's name (4:11, 21). **4:4** In Hebrew, Boaz omits the object pronoun ("If you will redeem, redeem") and creates ambiguity about what is at stake. **4:5** Boaz switches the terms of the agreement and adds the further responsibility of marrying Ruth and producing an heir for Mahlon (see note on 3:9). An alternative Hebrew scribal tradition has Boaz declaring that *he* will marry Ruth. According to biblical law, neither man is obligated to do so. Taking his cue from Ruth (3:9), Boaz successfully builds his negotiations on the premise that a redeemer ought also to marry the widow. **4:6** The kinsman would expend capital for property that would eventually be claimed by Ruth's future child for the line of Elimelech. **4:7–8** The *sandal* ritual has resonances with levirate law (Deut. 25:9–10), but the circumstances described here suggest that it symbolizes the kinsman's relinquishment of his obligation and right.

all that belonged to Chilion and Mahlon. ¹⁰I have also acquired Ruth the Moabite, the wife of Mahlon, to be my wife, to maintain the dead man's name on his inheritance, in order that the name of the dead may not be cut off from his kindred and from the gate of his native place; today you are witnesses." ¹¹Then all the people who were at the gate, along with the elders, said, "We are witnesses. May the Lord make the woman who is coming into your house like Rachel and Leah, who together built up the house of Israel. May you produce children*ᵛ* in Ephrathah and bestow a name in Bethlehem; ¹²and, through the children that the Lord will give you by this young woman, may your house be like the house of Perez, whom Tamar bore to Judah."

13 So Boaz took Ruth, and she became his wife. When they came together, the Lord made her conceive, and she bore a son.

¹⁴Then the women said to Naomi, "Blessed be the Lord, who has not left you this day without next-of-kin,"ʷ and may his name be renowned in Israel! ¹⁵He shall be to you a restorer of life and a nourisher of your old age, for your daughter-in-law who loves you, who is more to you than seven sons, has borne him." ¹⁶Then Naomi took the child and laid him in her bosom and became his nurse. ¹⁷The women of the neighborhood gave him a name, saying, "A son has been born to Naomi." They named him Obed; he became the father of Jesse, the father of David.

18 Now these are the descendants of Perez: Perez became the father of Hezron, ¹⁹Hezron of Ram, Ram of Amminadab, ²⁰Amminadab of Nahshon, Nahshon of Salmon,ˣ ²¹Salmon of Boaz, Boaz of Obed, ²²Obed of Jesse, and Jesse of David.

v 4.11 Or *wealth*   *w* 4.14 Or *one with the right to redeem*   *x* 4.20 Gk: Heb *Salmah*

4:10 The language of "acquiring" a wife was used when the marriage was legally bound up with a commercial transaction. **4:11–12** The blessing compares Ruth to *Rachel and Leah*, Israel's founding mothers. *Tamar*, like Ruth, used scandalous means to secure her future and establish the *name* of her husband's family (Gen. 38). *Perez*, one of the twins born to Tamar and Judah, and Boaz's ancestor (4:18). The references to *Ephrathah*, *Bethlehem*, and *Judah* (David's ancestor) point forward to the royal dynasty that will emerge from this union (see note on 1:2).

4:13–17 Naomi's restoration. 4:13 God's role in Ruth's conception is emphasized (see note on 1:6). **4:15** *Restorer of life* (derived from the verb "to return") rounds out the story of Naomi's return (see note on 1:6). **4:16** Naomi becomes the child's caregiver. In 1:5, she was "left without her two sons" (literally "boys"); now she cradles another "boy" in her arms. **4:17** The unusual birth announcement focuses on Naomi and her reintegration into the community. Neither parent is mentioned; the women of the town surround Naomi and name the child.

4:18–22 Genealogy. A family history of fecundity concludes the story that began with barrenness and loss. Boaz occupies the symbolic seventh place in the genealogy, and David the tenth.

1 SAMUEL

1 Samuel in the Canon

First and Second Samuel are two parts to one book focusing on the formation and cessation of the monarchy in ancient Israel and Judah. The books take their name from a prophet, priest, and judge named Samuel, whose life marks the transition from the period of the judges to the era of kings. In the Jewish canon, 1 Samuel lies between Judges and 2 Samuel in the section of the Tanakh called the Prophets. In Christian canons, 1 Samuel is slotted between Ruth and 2 Samuel in the Historical Books.

1 Samuel as Literary, Theological, and Political Document

Though 1 Samuel has been deemed a "historical" book, it is more appropriately understood as a piece of ancient literature. It has a narrative trajectory with well-developed characters, episodic dilemmas, and literary depth. The major conflicts include whether or not the people of Israel should have a king, and if so, whom should it be—Saul or David? As the story moves forward, Saul is consumed by uncontrollable jealousy as all his family and followers abandon him, transferring their loyalties to David, a young handsome warrior with military prowess and Machiavellian strategy. Ultimately, David becomes the victorious ruler, and Saul dies a tragic death on the battlefield, his body desecrated by his enemies.

Interwoven with the social and military drama are strong theological judgments. David is portrayed as above reproach, a man after God's own heart. He repeatedly asks God what to do and obediently follows divine commands. In contrast, Saul is disparaged as a divine reject who fails God and falls into mental and moral disorder. These biased overtones point to the fact that 1 Samuel is a religious and political document. The aim is not simply to report the events of the early monarchy but, instead, to exalt David as the true and right king and lift him as an exemplar of religious obedience and its rewards (however, see 2 Samuel, where David's seemingly perfect image tarnishes). These religious and political themes correspond with those found throughout the Deuteronomistic History (see **"Introduction to the Former Prophets / Historical Books," pp. 4–6;** and **"The Deuteronomistic History," p. 337**).

Whether or not one subscribes to the theory of the Deuteronomistic History and its editorial hypotheses, an astute reader of 1 Samuel should consider the so-called textual problems in the book. These include repetitions, contradictions, and interruptions. For instance, Saul is chosen as king three times (1 Sam. 9:1–10:6; 10:17–27; 11:1–15) and divinely rejected twice (13:13–14; 15:10–26); David is introduced three times (16:1–13; 16:14–23; 17:1–58); Jonathan makes a covenant with David three times (18:3; 20:8; 23:18); and David spares Saul's life twice (24:1–22; 26:1–25). In 1 Sam. 17:49–50, David kills Goliath with a sling and a stone, but in 17:51, he kills him with a sword. In 1 Sam. 1:1, Elkanah is from Ephraim, but in 1:19, he is from Benjamin. A long speech from Samuel (12:1–25) interrupts Saul's military exploits; several episodes (10:9–13:7) interrupt Saul waiting for Samuel at Gilgal; and the parable of the foolish Nabal and the wise Abigail (25:2–44) interrupts David's evasions of Saul. Such phenomena have led scholars to propose several explanations, all of which may be at play to some degree. These hypotheses include several separate stories being woven together into one, shorter earlier traditions growing and being added to over time, or simply literary custom or device (for more information about these scholarly propositions, see **"Introduction to the Former Prophets / Historical Books," pp. 4–6**). Regardless of one's conclusions, 1 Samuel is a rich text full of interpretive possibilities.

1 Samuel as Historical Document

Since so much internal evidence suggests that 1 Samuel is more of a literary, religious, and political document, historians are hesitant to accept it as a historical report. Those who believe there is some historical base underneath the layers of literary flair and religious bias recognize that they must expertly peel back those layers to get at what is often called the "kernel of truth." Historians in the late nineteenth and early twentieth centuries were confident they could excavate fact from fiction; however, their conclusions are myriad and divergent, which suggests it is not so simple. Contemporary scholars continue to debate what, if anything, is historically accurate in 1 Samuel, recognizing that the likelihood of consensus is doubtful.

Another issue is the lack of corroborating evidence. There is no textual evidence, outside the Bible, that the events in 1 Samuel happened. Moreover, the archaeological evidence indicates a slower and later centralization of government and culture than the speedy unification presented in the Bible. All this makes it difficult for historians to come to any solid conclusions about the veracity of 1 Samuel.

Reading Guide

First Samuel has three main sections, following the main characters—Samuel (chaps. 1–8), Saul (chaps. 9–15), and David (chaps. 16–31). Samuel, the book's namesake, is a prophet and priest who also serves as the final regional and premonarchic leader, or judge, among the tribes of Israel. His main role is as a prophet who intercedes between God and the people. As such, he warns the people against choosing a king, since God is supposed to be the direct ruler of Israel (chap. 8). However, the people refuse to listen, a Deuteronomistic theme, and demand their hearts' desire. God ultimately heeds their request and calls Samuel to anoint Saul king (chap. 9). Though Saul is tall and protects the land against foreign adversaries, he does not follow prophetic commands meticulously—a shortcoming that results in the retraction of his divine appointment (chaps. 10–15). God chooses to replace Saul with David, the youngest of his family but a brave shepherd and warrior who can outwit any predator—beast, giant, or king (chaps. 16–17). The portrayal of David as a young boy of humble beginnings who slays an evil villain and rises to the height of power is the stereotypical underdog story, which has inspired countless retellings, especially in American popular culture. But in order to win the day, David must evade repeated assassination attempts by Saul, who, despite becoming David's father-in-law, hunts him down like a "flea" (chaps. 18–26). David eludes the king and his servants several times by trickery and with help from his trusted allies, defectors from Saul's inner circle. The themes of deception and (dis)loyalty run throughout 1 Samuel and elicit ethical questions for interpreters to unpack. The issue of moral responsibility for taking life also arises, as multiple characters kill others for religious, military, or personal reasons. Indeed, the story ends with Saul's sons being killed by David's allies and Saul falling on his own sword (chap. 31). After their bodies are fastened to the city walls by their enemies, mourners come and take them down, burn them, and bury them. David will grieve their deaths in 2 Samuel, but he will also supplant their dynasty.

Shelley L. Birdsong

1 There was a certain man of Ramathaim, a Zuphite[a] from the hill country of Ephraim, whose name was Elkanah son of Jeroham son of Elihu son of Tohu son of Zuph, an Ephraimite. ²He had two wives; the name of one was Hannah, and the name of the other Peninnah. Peninnah had children, but Hannah had no children.

3 Now this man used to go up year by year from his town to worship and to sacrifice to the LORD of hosts at Shiloh, where the two sons of Eli, Hophni and Phinehas,

a 1.1 Compare Gk: Heb *Ramathaim-zophim*

1:1–28 Hannah bears and dedicates Samuel. 1:1 *There was a certain man* is a typical introduction to a parable or story with a moral (for similar introductions, see Judg. 13:2; 17:1; 19:1b; 1 Sam. 9:1). In v. 1, Elkanah is *of Ramathaim* in *Ephraim*. However, in v. 19, he and his family return to their home in "Ramah," which is known to be in the tribal land of Benjamin. Discrepancies, like this one, appear throughout 1 Samuel and may be the result of multiple, divergent traditions being edited together (see also 1 Chr. 6:26, where Elkanah is associated with the Levitical tribe of Kohath). *Ephraim* is an area later associated with the northern kingdom of Israel. Ephraim means "doubly fruitful," and *Elkanah* means "God creates"; both names have relevance for the unfolding story. **1:2** *He had two wives. . . . Peninnah had children, but Hannah had no children*. The narrative conflict between two wives over fertility matters appears elsewhere in the Bible (see Gen. 16, 21, and 29–30). *Hannah* means "favor," which God will show her (vv. 18–20). **1:3** *The LORD of hosts*. The term *hosts* ("tsevaot") can also be translated as "armies," which would be appropriate for the context of 1 Samuel, where God is often called upon in times of hand-to-hand combat against the enemies of Israel. *Shiloh* is a local place of sacrifice and worship, housing the ark of the covenant—a gilded chest, which carried

were priests of the LORD. ⁴On the day when Elkanah sacrificed, he would give portions to his wife Peninnah and to all her sons and daughters, ⁵but to Hannah he gave a double portionᵇ because he loved her, though the LORD had closed her womb. ⁶Her rival used to provoke her severely, to irritate her, because the LORD had closed her womb. ⁷So it went on year by year; as often as she went up to the house of the LORD, she used to provoke her. Therefore Hannah wept and would not eat. ⁸Her husband Elkanah said to her, "Hannah, why do you weep? Why do you not eat? Why is your heart sad? Am I not more to you than ten sons?"

9 After they had eaten and drunk at Shiloh, Hannah rose and presented herself before the LORD.ᶜ Now Eli the priest was sitting on the seat beside the doorpost of the temple of the LORD. ¹⁰She was deeply distressed and prayed to the LORD and wept bitterly. ¹¹She made this vow: "O LORD of hosts, if only you will look on the misery of your servant and remember me and not forget your servant but will give to your servant a male child, then I will set him before you as a nazirite until the day of his death. He shall drink neither wine nor intoxicants,ᵈ and no razor shall touch his head."

12 As she continued praying before the LORD, Eli observed her mouth. ¹³Hannah was praying silently; only her lips moved, but her voice was not heard; therefore Eli thought she was drunk. ¹⁴So Eli said to her, "How long will you make a drunken spectacle of yourself? Put away your wine." ¹⁵But Hannah answered, "No, my lord, I am a woman deeply troubled; I have drunk neither wine nor strong drink, but I have been pouring out

my soul before the LORD. ¹⁶Do not regard your servant as a worthless woman, for I have been speaking out of my great anxiety and vexation all this time." ¹⁷Then Eli answered, "Go in peace; the God of Israel grant the petition you have made to him." ¹⁸And she said, "Let your servant find favor in your sight." Then the woman went her way and ate and drank with her husband,ᵉ and her countenance was sad no longer.ᶠ

19 They rose early in the morning and worshiped before the LORD; then they went back to their house at Ramah. Elkanah knew his wife Hannah, and the LORD remembered her. ²⁰In due time Hannah conceived and bore a son. She named him Samuel, for she said, "I have asked him of the LORD."

21 The man Elkanah and all his household went up to offer to the LORD the yearly sacrifice and to pay his vow. ²²But Hannah did not go up, for she said to her husband, "As soon as the child is weaned, I will bring him, that he may appear in the presence of the LORD and remain there forever; I will offer him as a nazirite for all time."ᵍ ²³Her husband Elkanah said to her, "Do what seems best to you; wait until you have weaned him; only, may the LORD establish yourᵇ word." So the woman remained and nursed her son until she weaned him. ²⁴When she had weaned him, she took him up with her, along with a three-year-old bull,ⁱ an ephah of flour, and a skin of wine. She brought him to the house of

b 1.5 Syr: Meaning of Heb uncertain   c 1.9 Gk: Heb lacks *and presented herself before the* LORD   d 1.11 Cn Compare Gk Q ms: MT *child, then I will give him to the* LORD *all the days of his life*   e 1.18 Gk: Heb lacks *and drank with her husband*   f 1.18 Gk: Meaning of Heb uncertain   g 1.22 Cn Compare Q ms: MT lacks *I will offer him as a nazirite for all time*   h 1.23 Q ms Gk Syr: MT *his*   i 1.24 Q ms Gk Syr: MT *three bulls*

sacred objects and served as the throne (also called the mercy seat) of God (4:4). **1:5–6** *The* LORD *had closed her womb*. In the ancient Near East, fertility was understood as a gift given (or withheld) by the gods (see note on 1:2). **1:7–18** Hannah's distress, refusal to eat, and desperate supplication mirror those of Saul at the end of 1 Samuel (chap. 28). In both stories, they are finally convinced to eat after hearing God's decision from a spiritual intermediary, and then they meet their fate—Hannah will give life, and Saul will lose it (chap. 31). **1:11** *She made this vow*. Israelite women were allowed to make vows, but they could be voided by a father or husband under certain circumstances (Num. 30:3–16). An individual who set themselves apart *as a nazirite* for God was prohibited from going near a corpse, cutting their hair, or consuming anything from a grapevine (Num. 6). **1:18** *Let your servant find favor*. See note on 1:2. **1:20** *She named him Samuel, for she said, "I have asked him of the* LORD.*"* Samuel's name means "God hears," which comes from the Hebrew root "shama." Hannah emphasizes asking ("shaal"), which is connected to Saul's name, not Samuel's. There are other uses of the root "shaal" in vv. 17 and 27, referring to Hannah's petition. These linguistic connections have led some scholars to believe this was originally Saul's birth narrative, not Samuel's. Others simply think it is a foreshadowing device connecting Samuel to Saul, whom he will anoint as king (10:1).

the Lord at Shiloh, and the child was young. [25]Then they slaughtered the bull and brought the child to Eli. [26]And she said, "Oh, my lord! As you live, my lord, I am the woman who was standing here in your presence praying to the Lord. [27]For this child I prayed, and the Lord has granted me the petition that I made to him. [28]Therefore I have lent him to the Lord; as long as he lives, he is given to the Lord." And they worshiped the Lord there.

2 Hannah prayed and said,
    "My heart exults in the Lord;
       my strength is exalted in my God.[j]
    My mouth derides my enemies
       because I rejoice in your victory.

[2] There is no Holy One like the Lord,
    no one besides you;
    there is no Rock like our God.
[3] Talk no more so very proudly;
    let not arrogance come from your
       mouth,
for the Lord is a God of knowledge,
    and by him actions are weighed.
[4] The bows of the mighty are broken,
    but the feeble gird on strength.
[5] Those who were full have hired
       themselves out for bread,
    but those who were hungry are fat
       with spoil.
The barren has borne seven,
    but she who has many children is
       forlorn.
[6] The Lord kills and brings to life;
    he brings down to Sheol and raises up.
[7] The Lord makes poor and makes rich;
    he brings low; he also exalts.
[8] He raises up the poor from the dust;
    he lifts the needy from the ash heap
to make them sit with princes
    and inherit a seat of honor.
For the pillars of the earth are the
    Lord's,
    and on them he has set the world.

[9] He will guard the feet of his faithful
    ones,
    but the wicked will perish in
       darkness,
    for not by might does one prevail.
[10] The Lord! His adversaries will be
       shattered;
    the Most High[k] will thunder in
       heaven.
The Lord will judge the ends of the
       earth;
    he will give strength to his king
    and exalt the power of his anointed."

[11] Then they left him there before the Lord and went[l] home to Ramah, while the boy remained to minister to the Lord in the presence of the priest Eli.

[12] Now the sons of Eli were scoundrels; they had no regard for the Lord [13]or for the duties of the priests to the people. When anyone offered sacrifice, the priest's servant would come, while the meat was boiling, with a three-pronged fork in his hand, [14]and he would thrust it into the pan, kettle, caldron, or pot; all that the fork brought up the priest would take for himself.[m] This is what they did at Shiloh to all the Israelites who came there. [15]Moreover, before the fat was burned, the priest's servant would come and say to the one who was sacrificing, "Give meat for the priest to roast, for

j 2.1 Gk: Heb *the* Lord   k 2.10 Cn: Heb *against him he*
l 2.11 Gk: Heb *Then Elkanah went*   m 2.14 Gk Syr Vg: Heb
with it

2:1–10 Hannah's thanksgiving prayer. Poems, such as Hannah's prayer, included in prose narratives were likely separate traditions inserted into the story later (see also Exod. 15; Judg. 5; Jonah 2). **2:5** *The barren has borne seven, but she who has many children is forlorn*. A detail in the poem that may have led to its inclusion in Hannah's story. **2:6** *Sheol* is the underworld and residence of the dead. See **"Sheol," p. 695**. **2:10** *He will give strength to his king and exalt the power of his anointed*. The mention of a king and his anointed suggests that this poem dates to the time of the monarchy, not the time period of the judges. Anointing someone with oil sanctified them for a special role, such as being a priest or king. The ritual involved pouring oil over the head of the initiate, accompanied by a prayer or prophetic word by the anointer. The term *anointed one* is "meshiakh" or messiah. See **"The Judges," p. 342**.
    2:11–4:1a The fall of the house of Eli and the rise of Samuel. 2:11, 18 The statement that the boy, Samuel, ministered to the Lord encloses the story of Eli's selfish and unrighteous sons, creating a strong literary and moral contrast. A similar refrain is repeated in 2:26 and 3:1. **2:12–17** It was customary for priests to receive a portion of the sacrifice, while leaving the fat and other prescribed

he will not accept boiled meat from you but only raw." [16]And if the man said to him, "Let them burn the fat first and then take whatever you wish," he would say, "No, you must give it now; if not, I will take it by force." [17]Thus the sin of the young men was very great in the sight of the LORD, for they treated the offerings of the LORD with contempt.

18 Samuel was ministering before the LORD, a boy wearing a linen ephod. [19]His mother used to make for him a little robe and take it to him each year when she went up with her husband to offer the yearly sacrifice. [20]Then Eli would bless Elkanah and his wife and say, "May the LORD repay[n] you with children by this woman for the loan that she made to[o] the LORD," and then they would return to their home.

21 And[p] the LORD took note of Hannah; she conceived and bore three sons and two daughters. And the boy Samuel grew up in the presence of the LORD.

22 Now Eli was very old. He heard all that his sons were doing to all Israel and how they lay with the women who served at the entrance to the tent of meeting. [23]He said to them, "Why do you do such things? For I hear of your evil dealings from all these people. [24]No, my sons; it is not a good report that I hear the people of the LORD spreading abroad. [25]If one person sins against another, someone can intercede for the sinner with the LORD,[q] but if someone sins against the LORD, who can make intercession?" But they would not listen to the voice of their father, for it was the will of the LORD to kill them.

26 Now the boy Samuel continued to grow both in stature and in favor with the LORD and with the people.

27 A man of God came to Eli and said to him, "Thus the LORD has said: I revealed[r] myself to the family of your ancestor in Egypt when they were slaves[s] to the house of Pharaoh. [28]I chose him out of all the tribes of Israel to be my priest, to go up to my altar, to offer incense, to wear an ephod before me, and I gave to the family of your ancestor all my offerings by fire[t] from the Israelites. [29]Why then look[u] with greedy eye at my sacrifices and my offerings[v] and honor your sons more than me by fattening yourselves on the choicest parts of every offering of my people Israel? [30]Therefore the LORD the God of Israel declares: I promised that your family and the family of your ancestor should go in and out before me forever, but now the LORD declares: Far be it from me, for those who honor me I will honor, and those who despise me shall be treated with contempt. [31]See, a time is coming when I will cut off your strength and the strength of your ancestor's family.[w] [32]No one in your family shall ever live to old age. [33]The only one of you whom I shall not cut off from my altar shall be spared to weep out his[x] eyes and grieve his[y] heart; all the members of your household shall die by the sword.[z] [34]The fate of your two sons, Hophni and Phinehas, shall be the sign to you: both of them shall die on the same

n 2.20 Q ms Gk: MT *give*   o 2.20 Q ms Gk: MT *for the request that she asked of*   p 2.21 Q ms Gk: MT *When* q 2.25 Gk Q ms: MT *another, God will intercede for him* r 2.27 Gk Tg Syr: Heb *Did I reveal*   s 2.27 Q ms Gk: MT lacks *slaves*   t 2.28 Or *my gifts*   u 2.29 Q ms Gk: MT *then kick*   v 2.29 Q ms Gk: MT adds *that I commanded at this dwelling*   w 2.31–32 Q ms Gk: MT adds *so that no one in your family will live to old age. ³²Then in a distressed place you will look upon all the prosperity of Israel. No one*   x 2.33 Q ms Gk: MT *your*   y 2.33 Q ms Gk: MT *your*   z 2.33 Q ms Gk: MT *die like mortals*

portions for God. However, Eli's sons defy the rules even by threat. **2:18** *Ephod.* A sacred apron-like garment. **2:21** Bearing many children was seen as a blessing of God (see note on 1:5–6). **2:22** *They lay with the women* is a euphemism for sexual intercourse. *Served at the entrance to the tent of meeting.* The service the women rendered is not known and open to interpretation. **2:25** *Sins against the LORD.* Like the misappropriation of the sacrifices in vv. 12–17, lying with the women who served the Lord is a sin against the divine. **2:27–36** Eli's failures and the sin of his sons bring on an oracle of doom, which repeals an earlier promise to Eli's ancestor (v. 30) and replaces it. God will similarly repeal and replace the divine promise to Saul (13:13–14). **2:27–28** *The family of your ancestor.* Most likely Aaron (a Levite). **2:31–35** This prophecy is later associated with the priests Abiathar and Zadok in 1 Kgs. 2:26–35. Abiathar is the only survivor of the massacre of the priests at Nob (1 Sam. 22:20), and Solomon alludes to the word of the Lord against the house of Eli when he banishes Abiathar from his post in Jerusalem (1 Kgs. 2:26–27). Consequently, Zadok, whom Solomon appoints in Abiathar's place, becomes the *faithful priest* for whom God will build a strong house—a promise also given to King David in 2 Sam. 7. **2:34** *The sign to you.* Prophetic oracles sometimes included

day. [35]I will raise up for myself a faithful priest who shall do according to what is in my heart and in my mind. I will build him a sure house, and he shall go in and out before my anointed one forever. [36]Everyone who is left in your family shall come and prostrate himself before him for a piece of silver or a loaf of bread and shall say, 'Please put me in one of the priest's places, that I may eat a morsel of bread.'"

3 Now the boy Samuel was ministering to the LORD under Eli. The word of the LORD was rare in those days; visions were not widespread.

[2] At that time Eli, whose eyesight had begun to grow dim so that he could not see, was lying down in his room; [3]the lamp of God had not yet gone out, and Samuel was lying down in the temple of the LORD, where the ark of God was. [4]Then the LORD called, "Samuel! Samuel!"[a] and he said, "Here I am!" [5]and ran to Eli and said, "Here I am, for you called me." But he said, "I did not call; lie down again." So he went and lay down. [6]The LORD called again, "Samuel!" Samuel got up and went to Eli and said, "Here I am, for you called me." But he said, "I did not call, my son; lie down again." [7]Now Samuel did not yet know the LORD, and the word of the LORD had not yet been revealed to him. [8]The LORD called Samuel again, a third time. And he got up and went to Eli and said, "Here I am, for you called me." Then Eli perceived that the LORD was calling the boy. [9]Therefore Eli said to Samuel, "Go, lie down, and if he calls you, you shall say, 'Speak, LORD, for your servant is listening.'" So Samuel went and lay down in his place.

[10] Now the LORD came and stood there, calling as before, "Samuel! Samuel!" And Samuel said, "Speak, for your servant is listening." [11]Then the LORD said to Samuel, "See, I am about to do something in Israel that will make both ears of anyone who hears of it tingle. [12]On that day I will fulfill against Eli all that I have spoken concerning his house, from beginning to end. [13]For I have told him that I am about to punish his house forever for the iniquity that he knew, because his sons were blaspheming God,[b] and he did not restrain them. [14]Therefore I swear to the house of Eli that the iniquity of Eli's house shall not be expiated by sacrifice or offering forever."

[15] Samuel lay there until morning; then he opened the doors of the house of the LORD. Samuel was afraid to tell the vision to Eli. [16]But Eli called Samuel and said, "Samuel, my son." He said, "Here I am." [17]Eli said, "What was it that he told you? Do not hide it from me. May God do so to you and more also, if you hide anything from me of all that he told you." [18]So Samuel told him everything and hid nothing from him. Then he said, "It is the LORD; let him do what seems good to him."

[19] As Samuel grew up, the LORD was with him and let none of his words fall to the ground. [20]And all Israel from Dan to Beersheba knew that Samuel was a trustworthy prophet of the LORD. [21]The LORD continued to appear at Shiloh, for the LORD revealed himself to Samuel at Shiloh by the word of

a 3.4 Q ms Gk: MT *called to Samuel*   b 3.13 Gk: Heb *cursing for themselves*

a sign, which confirmed the authenticity of the prophecy. See **"Prophecy," p. 484**. **2:35** *Anointed one*. See note on 2:10. **3:1** *The word of the LORD was rare in those days; visions were not widespread*. Hearing a divine word and seeing a vision were the primary tasks of prophets. The acknowledgment adds gravity to the words of God that do come against Eli in 2:2–36 and 3:4–14. **3:3** *Samuel was lying down in the temple of the LORD, where the ark of God was*. Samuel maintains physical closeness to spaces and objects associated with God's presence. **3:8** Eli's slow comprehension of God's call to Samuel affirms that his time as Israel's spiritual intercessor is over. Samuel will replace him. **3:11–14** Though the primary culprits of the offense are Hophni and Phinehas, it is Eli's whole house that will bear the punishment. Communal guilt is a prominent theological theme throughout the Hebrew Bible, although the concept is not accepted unanimously (cf. Deut. 24:16; Jer. 31:30; Ezek. 18:20). **3:19** It is repeated three times that Samuel grows in the presence or favor of the Lord (see also 2:21 and 2:26) and that he ministers to the Lord (see 2:11, 18; 3:1). These phrases tie Samuel's origin stories together. *None of his words fall to the ground*. An expression meaning that everything Samuel said came to pass. **3:20** *From Dan to Beer-sheba* is a common designation to refer to all Israel (from north to south). **3:20–21** The repetition of Samuel's trustworthiness and revelatory experiences reinforce Samuel's exalted status in "all Israel" over and against the house of Eli.

4 the LORD. [1]And the word of Samuel came to all Israel.

In those days the Philistines mustered for war against Israel,[c] and Israel went out to battle against them;[d] they encamped at Ebenezer, and the Philistines encamped at Aphek. [2]The Philistines drew up in line against Israel, and when the battle was joined,[e] Israel was defeated by the Philistines, who killed about four thousand men on the field of battle. [3]When the troops came to the camp, the elders of Israel said, "Why has the LORD put us to rout today before the Philistines? Let us bring the ark of the covenant of the LORD here from Shiloh, so that he may come among us and save us from the power of our enemies." [4]So the people sent to Shiloh and brought from there the ark of the covenant of the LORD of hosts, who is enthroned on the cherubim. The two sons of Eli, Hophni and Phinehas, were there with the ark of the covenant of God.

[5] When the ark of the covenant of the LORD came into the camp, all Israel gave a mighty shout, so that the earth resounded. [6]When the Philistines heard the noise of the shouting, they said, "What does this great shouting in the camp of the Hebrews mean?" When they learned that the ark of the LORD had come to the camp, [7]the Philistines were afraid, for they said, "Gods have[f] come into the camp." They also said, "Woe to us! For nothing like this has happened before. [8]Woe to us! Who can deliver us from the power of these mighty gods? These are the gods who struck the Egyptians with every sort of plague in the wilderness. [9]Take courage, and be men, O Philistines, in order not to become slaves to the Hebrews as they have been to you; be men and fight."

[10] So the Philistines fought; Israel was defeated, and they fled, everyone to his home. There was a very great slaughter, for there fell of Israel thirty thousand foot soldiers. [11]The ark of God was captured, and the two sons of Eli, Hophni and Phinehas, died.

[12] A man of Benjamin ran from the battle line and came to Shiloh the same day, with his clothes torn and with earth upon his head. [13]When he arrived, Eli was sitting upon his seat by the road watching, for his heart trembled for the ark of God. When the man came into the city and told the news, all the city cried out. [14]When Eli heard the sound of the outcry, he said, "What is this uproar?" Then the man came quickly and told Eli. [15]Now Eli was ninety-eight years old, and his eyes were set, so that he could not see. [16]The man said to Eli, "I have just come from the battle; I fled from the battle today." He said, "How did it go, my son?" [17]The messenger replied,

c 4.1 Gk: Heb lacks *In those days the Philistines mustered for war against Israel* d 4.1 Gk: Heb *against the Philistines* e 4.2 Meaning of Heb uncertain f 4.7 Or *A god has*

4:1b–7:1 Ark Narrative. This section, entitled the Ark Narrative by scholars, is often considered a separate story (along with 2 Sam. 6) that was added into or combined with the Samuel narrative. It interrupts the story of Samuel and focuses on the ark of the covenant instead. **4:1** *The Philistines* lived on the coast of Canaan along the Mediterranean Sea. They are depicted as one of Israel's greatest military foes in Judges and Samuel. **4:3** As the throne of God, the ark's proximity implies the nearness of God's presence and the divine power to defeat armies, which the Philistines clearly fear in vv. 7–9. However, the ark does not provide the victory the Israelites were hoping for (vv. 10–11). **4:4** *The cherubim* were mythical composite creatures, which were associated with power and might and therefore often depicted on ancient Near Eastern thrones. The presence of Eli's sons, *Hophni and Phinehas*, forebodes impending doom (2:27–36; 3:11–14). **4:7–8** *Gods have come . . . these mighty gods.* The Philistines refer to the divine as "elohim," which is a plural noun. It has been translated primarily in two ways in English Bibles (though there are others; see 1 Sam. 28:13). The first translation is "gods" (plural), as it is here. However, it is more often translated as the singular "God," which serves as a title for YHWH, the god of Israel. The translational choice is affected by contextual variables. Here, the Philistines refer to "elohim" as "these," leading translators to choose "gods" over "God." There is an implication that the Israelites were not known to be monotheists. See **"God's Name," p. 89**. **4:8** The Philistines have heard the famous stories of God thwarting the Egyptians; here, the Philistines appear to conflate the plagues of Egypt and the plagues against the Israelites in the wilderness (Exod.–Num.). **4:10–11** Despite the Israelites' and Philistines' belief that the ark would bring defeat to the Philistines, the reverse happens, and the ark is captured. Unsurprisingly, Hophni and Phinehas die, fulfilling the words of God in 2:27–36 and

"Israel has fled before the Philistines, and there has also been a great slaughter[g] among the troops; your two sons also, Hophni and Phinehas, are dead, and the ark of God has been captured." [18]When he mentioned the ark of God, Eli[b] fell over backward from his seat by the side of the gate, and his neck was broken, and he died, for he was an old man and heavy. He had judged Israel forty years.

19 Now his daughter-in-law, the wife of Phinehas, was pregnant, about to give birth. When she heard the news that the ark of God was captured and that her father-in-law and her husband were dead, she bowed and gave birth, for her labor pains overwhelmed her. [20]As she was about to die, the women attending her said to her, "Do not be afraid, for you have borne a son." But she did not answer or give heed. [21]She named the child Ichabod, meaning, "The glory has departed from Israel," because the ark of God had been captured and because of her father-in-law and her husband. [22]She said, "The glory has departed from Israel, for the ark of God has been captured."

5 When the Philistines captured the ark of God, they brought it from Ebenezer to Ashdod; [2]then the Philistines took the ark of God and brought it into the house of Dagon and placed it beside Dagon. [3]When the people of Ashdod rose early the next day, there was Dagon, fallen on his face to the ground before the ark of the LORD. So they took Dagon and put him back in his place. [4]But when they rose early on the next morning, Dagon had fallen on his face to the ground before the ark of the LORD, and the head of Dagon and both his hands were lying cut off upon the threshold; only the trunk of[i] Dagon was left to him. [5]This is why the priests of Dagon and all who enter the house of Dagon do not step on the threshold of Dagon in Ashdod to this day.

6 The hand of the LORD was heavy upon the people of Ashdod, and he terrified and struck them with tumors, both in Ashdod and in its territory. [7]And when the inhabitants of Ashdod saw how things were, they said, "The ark of the God of Israel must not remain with us, for his hand is heavy on us and on our god Dagon." [8]So they sent and gathered together all the lords of the Philistines and said, "What shall we do with the ark of the God of Israel?" The inhabitants of Gath replied, "Let the ark of God be moved on to us."[j] So they moved the ark of the God of Israel to Gath.[k] [9]But after they had brought it to Gath,[l] the hand of the LORD was against the city, causing a very great panic; he struck the inhabitants of the city, both young and old, so that tumors broke out on them. [10]So they sent the ark of the God of Israel[m] to Ekron. But when the ark of God came to Ekron, the people of Ekron cried out, "Why[n] have they brought around to us[o] the ark of the God of Israel to kill us and our[p] people?" [11]They sent therefore and

g 4.17 Heb *plague*   h 4.18 Heb *he*   i 5.4 Gk Syr Tg Vg: Heb lacks *the trunk of*   j 5.8 Gk Compare Q ms: MT *They replied, "Let the ark of the God of Israel be brought around to Gath."*   k 5.8 Gk: Heb lacks *to Gath*   l 5.9 Q ms: MT lacks *to Gath*   m 5.10 Q ms Gk mss: MT lacks *of Israel*   n 5.10 Q ms Gk: MT lacks *Why*   o 5.10 Heb *me*   p 5.10 Heb *me and my*

3:11–14. **4:18** Eli's death also fulfills the words of the Lord in 2:27–36 and 3:11–14. Eli's period of judgment, listed at forty years, signifies the end of an era. Yet Eli receives no fanfare, just a narratorial description as old and heavy (Hebrew "kaved"). The author is making a pun here with the Hebrew root "kavad," which means "weighty" and can imply "fat" or "of great value." **4:19–22** Ichabod's name, literally "there is no glory," is also based on the Hebrew root "kavad" (see note on 4:18). Chapter 4 ends with a quick, cyclical succession of death (Eli and sons), life (Ichabod), and death (Ichabod's mother). **5:2** *House of Dagon*, or temple of Dagon. **5:3–4** *Fallen on his face*. A sign of inferiority and submission. **5:4–5** *The threshold*. Thresholds are liminal spaces. Here and in Judg. 19:27, lying at the threshold signifies helplessness and death, including severed body parts. *This is why . . . to this day* signals an etiology—a story that explains a cultural custom, geographical marker, or natural occurrence. **5:6** *The hand of the LORD was heavy*. The motifs of "hands" (v. 4) and "heaviness/glory" (4:18–22) continue (see also 5:7, 9, 11; 6:3, 5, 9). Unlike the hands of Dagon that are cut off, God's heavy/glorious hand strikes against the Philistines. *Tumors*, or boils or hemorrhoids, are reminiscent of the plagues brought upon the Egyptians in Exod. 7–12, especially the boils (Exod. 9:8–12). **5:8** *Moved the ark of the God of Israel to Gath*. Everywhere the ark (presence of God) goes, trouble follows, from Ashdod (5:1) to Gath and Ekron (5:10). These cities are part of a pentapolis (a grouping of five major cities) in Philistia. **5:9, 12** *Tumors*. See note on 5:6.

gathered together all the lords of the Philistines and said, "Send away the ark of the God of Israel, and let it return to its own place, that it may not kill us and our*q* people." For there was a deathly panic throughout the whole city. The hand of God was very heavy there; ¹²those who did not die were stricken with tumors, and the cry of the city went up to heaven.

6 The ark of the Lord was in the country of the Philistines seven months. ²Then the Philistines called for the priests and the diviners and said, "What shall we do with the ark of the Lord? Tell us what we should send with it to its place." ³They said, "If you send away the ark of the God of Israel, do not send it empty, but by all means return it with a guilt offering. Then you will be healed and forgiven;*r* will not his hand then turn from you?" ⁴And they said, "What is the guilt offering that we shall send to him?" They answered, "Five gold tumors and five gold mice, according to the number of the lords of the Philistines, for the same plague was upon all of you and upon your lords. ⁵So you must make images of your tumors and images of your mice that ravage the land and give glory to the God of Israel; perhaps he will lighten his hand on you and your gods and your land. ⁶Why should you harden your hearts as the Egyptians and Pharaoh hardened their hearts? After he had made fools of them, did they not let the people go, and they departed? ⁷Now then, get ready a new cart and two milch cows that have never borne a yoke, and yoke the cows to the cart, but take their calves home, away from them. ⁸Take the ark of the Lord and place it on the cart, and put in a box at its side the figures of gold that you are sending to him as a guilt offering. Then send it off, and let it go its way. ⁹And watch: if it goes up on the way to its own land, to Beth-shemesh, then it is he who has done us this great harm; but if not, then we shall know that it is not his hand that struck us; it happened to us by chance."

10 The men did so; they took two milch cows and yoked them to the cart and shut up their calves at home. ¹¹They put the ark of the Lord on the cart and the box with the gold mice and the images of their tumors. ¹²The cows went straight in the direction of Beth-shemesh along one highway, lowing as they went; they turned neither to the right nor to the left, and the lords of the Philistines went after them as far as the border of Beth-shemesh.

13 Now the people of Beth-shemesh were reaping their wheat harvest in the valley. When they looked up and saw the ark, they went with rejoicing to meet it.*s* ¹⁴The cart came into the field of Joshua of Beth-shemesh and stopped there. A large stone was there; so they split up the wood of the cart and offered the cows as a burnt offering to the Lord. ¹⁵The Levites took down the ark of the Lord and the box beside it in which were the gold objects and set them on the large stone. Then the people of Beth-shemesh offered burnt offerings and presented sacrifices on that day to the Lord. ¹⁶When the five lords of the Philistines saw it, they returned that day to Ekron.

17 These are the gold tumors that the Philistines returned as a guilt offering to the Lord: one for Ashdod, one for Gaza, one for Ashkelon, one for Gath, one for Ekron; ¹⁸also the gold mice, according to the number of all the cities of the Philistines belonging to the five lords, both fortified cities and unwalled villages. The great stone, beside which they set down the ark of the Lord, is a witness to this day in the field of Joshua of Beth-shemesh.

q 5.11 Heb *me and my* *r* 6.3 Q ms Gk: MT *and it will be known to you* *s* 6.13 Gk: Heb *rejoiced to see it*

6:2 *Called for the priests and the diviners.* In chap. 5, the "people" of Ekron tell the lords of the Philistines to send away the ark. In chap. 6, the Philistines ask *the priests and the diviners* for an answer. They give detailed ritualistic instructions regarding a guilt offering, and when the ark returns to the Israelites, they offer sacrifices to the Lord. This may suggest two alternate traditions or sources regarding the ark in Philistia. **6:6** *Why should you harden your hearts as the Egyptians and Pharaoh hardened their hearts?* An explicit connection of this plague with the ones from Exodus; see note on 4:8. **6:7–12** Letting the cows go free served as an act of divination—the direction they went revealed the truth of whether or not the God of Israel has brought about the plague. Watching for such signs is a theme in 1 Samuel. **6:13** *Rejoicing.* King David will also rejoice before the ark when it is brought into Jerusalem on a new cart (2 Sam. 6).

19 The descendants of Jeconiah did not rejoice with the people of Beth-shemesh when they greeted* the ark of the Lord, and he killed seventy men of them.* The people mourned because the Lord had made a great slaughter among the people. ²⁰Then the people of Beth-shemesh said, "Who is able to stand before the Lord, this holy God? To whom shall he go so that we may be rid of him?" ²¹So they sent messengers to the inhabitants of Kiriath-jearim, saying, "The Philistines have returned the ark of the Lord. Come down and take it up to you." ¹And the people of Kiriath-jearim came and took up the ark of the Lord and brought it to the house of Abinadab on the hill. They consecrated his son, Eleazar, to have charge of the ark of the Lord.

2 From the day that the ark was lodged at Kiriath-jearim, a long time passed, some twenty years, and all the house of Israel lamented* after the Lord.

3 Then Samuel said to all the house of Israel, "If you are returning to the Lord with all your heart, then put away the foreign gods and the Astartes from among you. Direct your heart to the Lord and serve him only, and he will deliver you out of the hand of the Philistines." ⁴So Israel put away the Baals and the Astartes, and they served the Lord only.

5 Then Samuel said, "Gather all Israel at Mizpah, and I will pray to the Lord for you." ⁶So they gathered at Mizpah and drew water and poured it out before the Lord. They fasted that day and said, "We have sinned against the Lord." And Samuel judged the Israelites at Mizpah.

7 When the Philistines heard that the Israelites had gathered at Mizpah, the lords of the Philistines went up against Israel. And when the Israelites heard of it, they were afraid of the Philistines. ⁸The Israelites said to Samuel, "Do not cease to cry out to the Lord our God for us, and pray that he may save us from the hand of the Philistines." ⁹So Samuel took a sucking lamb and offered it as a whole burnt offering to the Lord; Samuel cried out to the Lord for Israel, and the Lord answered him. ¹⁰As Samuel was offering up the burnt offering, the Philistines drew near to attack Israel, but the Lord thundered with a mighty voice that day against the Philistines and threw them into confusion, and they were routed before Israel. ¹¹And the men of Israel went out of Mizpah and pursued the Philistines and struck them down as far as beyond Beth-car.

12 Then Samuel took a stone and set it up between Mizpah and Jeshanah* and named it Ebenezer,* for he said, "Thus far the Lord has helped us." ¹³So the Philistines were subdued and did not again enter the territory of Israel; the hand of the Lord was against the Philistines all the days of Samuel. ¹⁴The towns that the Philistines had taken from Israel were restored to Israel, from Ekron to Gath, and Israel recovered their territory from the hand of the Philistines. There was peace also between Israel and the Amorites.

15 Samuel judged Israel all the days of his life. ¹⁶He went on a circuit year by year to Bethel, Gilgal, and Mizpah, and he judged Israel in all these places. ¹⁷Then he would come back to Ramah, for his home was there; he administered justice there to Israel and built there an altar to the Lord.

t 6.19 Gk: Heb *¹⁹And he killed some of the people of Beth-shemesh, because they looked into*   *u* 6.19 Cn: Heb *killed seventy men, fifty thousand men*   *v* 7.2 Meaning of Heb uncertain   *w* 7.12 Gk Syr: Heb *Shen*   *x* 7.12 That is, *stone of help*

7:2–17 Samuel judges Israel. 7:2–14 Now that the ark is back in Israel with a consecrated attendant, and the people and priest act in accordance with God's will (vv. 3–9), Israel triumphs over the Philistines (vv. 10–14). The episode is a direct contrast with the story in 4:1–18. **7:3** *Then Samuel* returns the reader back to the story of Samuel that ended in 4:1. **7:3–5** *Baals . . . Astartes.* Common Canaanite gods. **7:6** *And Samuel judged.* Samuel and his sons (8:1–2) are the last judges of the people before Israel becomes a nation with a king. See **"The Judges," p. 342**. **7:8** Samuel returns to the role of priest and intercessor; he sacrifices and calls out to the Lord on behalf of the people. **7:10** *The Lord thundered with a mighty voice.* Thunder and lightning were associated with warrior gods in the ancient Near East; cf. 1 Sam. 5 where it was God's "hand" that brought chaos. **7:12** A short etiology for the marker, Ebenezer (see note on 5:5). It was common to set a stone upright as a marker of an important site or event. **7:13–14** The first conclusion to Samuel's leadership, which focuses on restoration and peace in the land. **7:15–17** A second conclusion to Samuel's leadership, which focuses on justice and the sacred site of Ramah.

8 When Samuel became old, he made his sons judges over Israel. [2]The name of his firstborn son was Joel, and the name of his second was Abijah; they were judges in Beer-sheba. [3]Yet his sons did not follow in his ways but turned aside after gain; they took bribes and perverted justice.

4 Then all the elders of Israel gathered together and came to Samuel at Ramah [5]and said to him, "You are old, and your sons do not follow in your ways; appoint for us, then, a king to govern us, like other nations." [6]But the thing displeased Samuel when they said, "Give us a king to govern us." Samuel prayed to the LORD, [7]and the LORD said to Samuel, "Listen to the voice of the people in all that they say to you, for they have not rejected you, but they have rejected me from being king over them. [8]Just as they have done to me[y] from the day I brought them up out of Egypt to this day, forsaking me and serving other gods, so also they are doing to you. [9]Now then, listen to their voice; only, you shall solemnly warn them and show them the ways of the king who shall reign over them."

10 So Samuel reported all the words of the LORD to the people who were asking him for a king. [11]He said, "These will be the ways of the king who will reign over you: he will take your sons and appoint them to his chariots and to be his horsemen, and to run before his chariots, [12]and he will appoint for himself commanders of thousands and commanders of fifties and some to plow his ground and to reap his harvest and to make his implements of war and the equipment of his chariots. [13]He will take your daughters to be perfumers and cooks and bakers. [14]He will take the best of your fields and vineyards and olive orchards and give them to his courtiers. [15]He will take one-tenth of your grain and of your vineyards and give it to his officers and his courtiers. [16]He will take your male and female slaves and the best of your cattle[z] and donkeys and put them to his work. [17]He will take one-tenth of your flocks, and you shall be his slaves. [18]And on that day you will cry out because of your king, whom you have chosen for yourselves, but the LORD will not answer you on that day."

19 But the people refused to listen to the voice of Samuel; they said, "No! We are determined to have a king over us, [20]so that we also may be like other nations and that our king may govern us and go out before us and fight our battles." [21]When Samuel heard all the words of the people, he repeated them in the ears of the LORD. [22]The LORD said to Samuel, "Listen to their voice and set a king over them." Samuel then said to the Israelites, "Each of you return home."

y 8.8 Gk: Heb lacks *to me*   z 8.16 Gk: Heb *young men*

8:1–22 The request for a king. 8:1 *When Samuel became old* ties the following story of Samuel's elder years with the stories of his growth (2:21, 26; 3:19) and ministry (2:11, 18; 3:1) as well as the failure of Eli's sons in his old age (2:22–36). Verses 1–3 set up the question of who will lead Israel after Samuel's death, which leads to the possibility of a king (v. 4). **8:4–22** Israel asks Samuel to appoint a king over the people, but he warns them of the cost. The portrayal of the people as desperate, even for a tyrannical king, alludes to Judg. 9, where Abimelech becomes king by fratricide. His brother, Jotham, who escapes, tells a foreboding fable to the people about their cursed future for installing a treacherous king. Thus, the allusion and the present text foreshadow an ominous fate if the people should appoint a king. **8:5** *Like other nations.* Throughout most of the Prophetic Books (which include Samuel in the Jewish tradition—see **"The Bible as a Collection," pp. 2145–47**), the Israelites are to be distinct (i.e., holy) from other nations. Here, asking for a king so that they can be like other nations is synonymous with idolatry (v. 8) and a rejection of God (v. 7). **8:11–17a** *He will take.* Like most governments, the new king of Israel will tax the people and require government service. **8:17b–18** *You shall be his slaves. And on that day you will cry out . . . but the LORD will not answer you on that day.* From the time of the exodus and throughout the time of the judges, when foreign overlords oppressed the Israelites, God would hear the people cry out, and God would save them as their king and god. But God will not save them from their own choice to be oppressed by an Israelite king. **8:20** *Like other nations.* See note on 8:5. **8:22** *Listen to their voice.* God tells Samuel to listen to the voice of the people three times (vv. 7, 9, 22), although they refused to listen to Samuel (v. 19). *Set a king over them.* God allows Samuel to anoint a king despite the foreseen consequences.

Focus On: Kingship/Monarchy (1 Samuel 8)

Between the tenth and fourth centuries BCE, when the Hebrew Bible was written, empires in the ancient Near East had a centralized and hierarchical government system, ruled by a monarch who was believed to reflect divine authority on earth. Oftentimes, smaller vassal nations or city-states within the empire were allowed to maintain their own semiautonomous monarchies as long as they abided by the treaty, or covenant, enforced by the dominant state. If they failed to adhere to the terms, they suffered the consequences, which ranged from more taxes to decimation. The kingdoms of Israel and Judah developed in the shadows of such empires and lasted about four hundred years.

According to the biblical texts, David was the first king to unify the twelve tribes of Israel, but he was largely a military leader (1 Sam. 16–1 Kgs. 2). His son, Solomon, codified the bureaucracy and built the temple-palace complex that symbolized monarchical rule (1 Kgs. 1–11). Thereafter, the short-lived "united monarchy" split into two smaller kingdoms—Israel in the north and Judah in the south. Though these nations had seasons of independence, they were often scrimmaging with neighboring states for territory and ultimately served as vassals to larger empires. Numerous Israelite and Judahite monarchs reneged on their covenantal obligations and were consequently destroyed by the empire—Israel by Assyria in 722 BCE and Judah by Babylon in 586 BCE.

The biblical authors present the fall of Israel and Judah as divine punishment. The kings were viewed as vassals to the God of Israel, "the king of the earth." God made covenants with their ancestors, containing laws the kings were expected to abide (e.g., Deut. 17:14–20; 1 Sam. 12:13–15). Throughout 1–2 Samuel, 1–2 Kings, and 1–2 Chronicles, the kings are largely judged as failures who did "evil in the sight of the LORD." Similarly, in the Prophetic Books, the kings are warned repeatedly to turn back from their wicked ways and to realign their agendas with God's. Few heed the call, and those who do not are blamed for the final eradication of the kingdoms.

Postdestruction, contingents of Israelites and Judahites are forced into exile in the east, where they lament the end of the supposedly eternal Davidic dynasty (2 Sam. 7; cf. 1 Kgs. 2:1–4). In exile and when they return home two generations later, they pine for the restoration of the monarchy ruled by a perfect and righteous king—a messiah—who will serve God, act justly, and lead the people into a new era of independence.

Shelley L. Birdsong

9 There was a man of Benjamin whose name was Kish son of Abiel son of Zeror son of Becorath son of Aphiah, a Benjaminite, a man of wealth. ²He had a son whose name was Saul, a handsome young man. There was not a man among the Israelites more handsome than he; he stood head and shoulders above everyone else.

3 Now the donkeys of Kish, Saul's father, had strayed. So Kish said to his son Saul, "Take one of the young men with you; go and look for the donkeys." ⁴He passed through the hill country of Ephraim and passed through the land of Shalishah, but they did not find them. And they passed through the land of Shaalim, but they were not there. Then he passed through the land of Benjamin, but they did not find them.

5 When they came to the land of Zuph, Saul said to the young man who was with him, "Let us turn back, or my father will stop worrying about the donkeys and worry about us." ⁶But he said to him, "There is a man of God in this town; he is a man held in honor. Whatever he says always comes true. Let us go there now; perhaps he will tell us about the journey on which we have set out." ⁷Then Saul replied to the young man, "But if we go, what can we bring the man? For the bread in our sacks is gone, and there is no present to bring to the man of God. What have we?" ⁸The young man answered Saul again, "Here, I have with me a quarter

9:1–11:16 Saul becomes king and prophet. 9:1 *There was a man.* A repetition of the first words of the book, both of which introduce the father of a prominent character (Samuel and Saul respectively) and their geographical/tribal identification (Ephraim, Benjamin). **9:2** Biblical characters are seldom described physically unless it is crucial to the plot and signifies status. Saul is described as a tall, *handsome young man.* On the surface, he looks like a good leader. **9:3–5** Saul's journey to find the donkeys causes him to pass through Ephraim and Benjamin (see note on 9:1) to Zuph (v. 5), bringing him back to where 1 Samuel began, with Samuel's father, Elkanah (1:1).

shekel of silver; I will give it to the man of God, to tell us our way." [9](Formerly in Israel, anyone who went to inquire of God would say, "Come, let us go to the seer," for the one who is now called a prophet was formerly called a seer.) [10]Saul said to the young man, "Good; come, let us go." So they went to the town where the man of God was.

11 As they went up the hill to the town, they met some young women coming out to draw water and said to them, "Is the seer here?" [12]They answered, "Yes, there he is just ahead of you. Hurry; he has come just now to the town because the people have a sacrifice today at the shrine. [13]As soon as you enter the town, you will meet him before he goes up to the shrine to eat. For the people will not eat until he comes, since he must bless the sacrifice; afterward those eat who are invited. Now go up, for you will meet him immediately." [14]So they went up to the town. As they were entering the town, they saw Samuel coming out toward them on his way up to the shrine.

15 Now the day before Saul came, the LORD had revealed to Samuel: [16]"Tomorrow about this time I will send to you a man from the land of Benjamin, and you shall anoint him to be ruler over my people Israel. He shall save my people from the hand of the Philistines, for I have seen the suffering of[a] my people, because their outcry has come to me." [17]When Samuel saw Saul, the LORD told him, "Here is the man of whom I spoke to you. He it is who shall rule over my people." [18]Then Saul approached Samuel inside the gate and said, "Tell me, please, where is the house of the seer?" [19]Samuel answered Saul, "I am the seer; go up before me to the shrine, for today you shall eat with me, and in the morning I will let you go and will tell you all that is on your mind. [20]As for your donkeys that were lost three days ago, give no further thought to them, for they have been found. And on whom is all Israel's desire fixed, if not on you and on all your ancestral house?" [21]Saul answered, "I am only a Benjaminite, from the least of the tribes of Israel, and my family is the humblest of all the families of the tribe of Benjamin. Why then have you spoken to me in this way?"

22 Then Samuel took Saul and the young man and brought them into the hall and gave them a place at the head of those who had been invited, of whom there were about thirty. [23]And Samuel said to the cook, "Bring the portion I gave you, the one I asked you to put aside." [24]The cook took up the upper thigh[b] and set it before Saul. Samuel said, "See, what was reserved is set before you. Eat, for it was kept for you for this appointed time, so that you might eat with the guests."[c]

So Saul ate with Samuel that day. [25]When they came down from the shrine into the town, a bed was spread for Saul[d] on the roof, and he lay down to sleep.[e] [26]Then at the break of dawn[f] Samuel called to Saul upon the roof, "Get up, so that I may send you on your way." Saul got up, and both he and Samuel went out into the street.

27 As they were going down to the outskirts of the town, Samuel said to Saul, "Tell the young man to go on before us, and when

a 9.16 Gk: Heb lacks *the suffering of*   b 9.24 Meaning of Heb uncertain   c 9.24 Cn: Heb *time, saying, I have invited the people*   d 9.25 Gk: Heb *and he spoke with Saul*   e 9.25 Gk: Heb lacks *and he lay down to sleep*   f 9.26 Gk: Heb *and they arose early and at break of dawn*

9:9 An editorial aside that indicates that the story was written down at a much later date than when the story is set. **9:13** *The people will not eat until he comes, since he must bless the sacrifice* is an ironic foreshadow because Saul will fail to wait for Samuel in order to sacrifice (13:8–15), which will cost him his kingship. **9:16** *Anoint him.* See note on 2:10. *He shall save my people . . . their outcry has come to me.* Though God initially chooses not to save the people from their own Israelite king in 1 Sam. 8:17b–18, God is still willing to heed their cry for help against foreign oppressors. **9:17** *Rule over.* The more common verb for *rule* ("mashal") is not used here. Instead, God uses the less common verb "atsar," which carries the connotation of restraining or enslaving (see 1 Sam. 8:17b). **9:18** *Inside the gate.* The city gate was a lively place where judicial and business matters were conducted. Samuel was likely there to serve in his capacity as judge. **9:21** *Only a Benjaminite, from the least of the tribes.* Benjamin was the last child of Jacob, whom Rachel bore the least (Gen. 35:16–20). The fact that Saul is a Benjaminite has severe implications when read alongside Judges (chaps. 17–21), where the Benjaminites are portrayed as lawless evildoers. **9:23–24** Just as Saul will be sanctified or set apart when anointed, so too this special meal and piece of meat (the thigh, reserved for the gods and their priests) has been set aside for him, since he is chosen

he has passed on, stop here yourself for a while, that I may make known to you the word of God." [1]Samuel took a vial of oil and poured it on his head and kissed him; he said, "The LORD has anointed you ruler over his people Israel. You shall reign over the people of the LORD, and you will save them from the hand of their enemies all around. Now this shall be the sign to you that the LORD has anointed you ruler[g] over his heritage: [2]When you depart from me today you will meet two men by Rachel's tomb in the territory of Benjamin at Zelzah; they will say to you, 'The donkeys that you went to seek are found, and now your father has stopped worrying about them and is worrying about you, saying: "What shall I do about my son?"' [3]Then you shall go on from there further and come to the oak of Tabor; three men going up to God at Bethel will meet you there: one carrying three kids, another carrying three loaves of bread, and another carrying a skin of wine. [4]They will greet you and give you two loaves of bread, which you shall accept from them. [5]After that you shall come to Gibeath-elohim,[b] at the place where the Philistine garrison is; there, as you come to the town, you will meet a band of prophets coming down from the shrine with harp, tambourine, flute, and lyre playing in front of them; they will be in a prophetic frenzy. [6]Then the spirit of the LORD will possess you, and you will be in a prophetic frenzy along with them and be turned into a different person. [7]Now when these signs meet you,

do whatever you see fit to do, for God is with you. [8]And you shall go down to Gilgal ahead of me; then I will come down to you to present burnt offerings and offer sacrifices of well-being. Seven days you shall wait, until I come to you and show you what you shall do."

9 As he turned away to leave Samuel, God gave him another heart, and all these signs were fulfilled that day. [10]When they were going from there to Gibeah,[i] a band of prophets met him, and the spirit of God possessed him, and he fell into a prophetic frenzy along with them. [11]When all who knew him before saw how he prophesied with the prophets, the people said to one another, "What has come over the son of Kish? Is Saul also among the prophets?" [12]A man of the place answered, "And who is their father?" Therefore it became a proverb, "Is Saul also among the prophets?" [13]When his prophetic frenzy had ended, he went home.[j]

14 Saul's uncle said to him and to the young man, "Where did you go?" And he replied, "To seek the donkeys, and when we saw they were not to be found, we went to Samuel." [15]Saul's uncle said, "Tell me what Samuel said to you." [16]Saul said to his uncle, "He told us that the donkeys had been found." But about the matter of the kingship, of which Samuel had spoken, he did not tell him anything.

17 Samuel summoned the people to the

g 10.1 Gk: Heb lacks *over his people Israel. You shall . . . anointed you ruler* h 10.5 Or *the hill of God* i 10.10 Or *the hill* j 10.13 Cn: Heb *went to the shrine*

to rule the people. **10:1** The appointed anointing (see 9:16) finally takes place. Oil is poured over the head of the designated person, and various rituals ensue. Here, Samuel kisses Saul and gives him his charge as ruler or chieftain ("nagid"), not king. He is enlisted to save the people from their enemies, which is reminiscent of the judges. *The sign.* See note on 2:34. **10:2–3** The first two signs refer to Jacob (via Bethel; Gen. 28:10–22; 35:9–15) and Rachel, the ancestors of the Benjaminites, the tribe from which Saul descends. *Rachel's tomb . . . at Zelzah.* Zelzah's exact location is unknown, and the location of Rachel's tomb varies (cf. Gen. 35:19; 48:7; Jer. 31:15). **10:5** *Band of prophets.* Ancient prophets were not always lone figures; individual prophets often worked with a mentor/mentee or group. The translation *prophetic frenzy* has a negative connotation that is not necessarily present in the original language. The verb form (Hebrew "mitnabim") is intensive or reflexive grammatically and should be translated as "fervently prophesying" or "prophesying among themselves." **10:6, 10** The spirit of God possesses leaders among the Israelites, including Saul and Samson (Judg. 14–15). What the spirit causes the individual to do can be unexpected or unusual. **10:8** *Seven days you shall wait.* See note on 9:13. **10:11–13** A story that explains the origin of the proverb. It is unclear whether the townspeople are shocked, suspicious, or proud (cf. 19:19–24 and Luke 4:14–30). **10:16** *He did not tell.* Also reminiscent of Samson (Judg. 14:6; see note on 10:6, 10). Withholding information is a motif in 1 Samuel (see also 14:1; 25:19, 36), which dovetails with

LORD at Mizpah ¹⁸and said to the Israelites, "Thus says the LORD, the God of Israel, 'I brought up Israel out of Egypt, and I rescued you from the hand of the Egyptians and from the hand of all the kingdoms that were oppressing you.' ¹⁹But today you have rejected your God, who saves you from all your calamities and your distresses, and you have said, 'No, but set a king over us.' Now, therefore, present yourselves before the LORD by your tribes and by your clans."

20 Then Samuel brought all the tribes of Israel near, and the tribe of Benjamin was taken by lot. ²¹He brought the tribe of Benjamin near by its families, and the family of the Matrites was taken by lot. Finally he brought the family of the Matrites near man by man,ᵏ and Saul the son of Kish was taken by lot. But when they sought him, he could not be found. ²²So they inquired again of the LORD, "Did the man come here?"ˡ And the LORD said, "See, he has hidden himself among the baggage." ²³Then they ran and brought him from there. When he took his stand among the people, he was head and shoulders taller than any of them. ²⁴Samuel said to all the people, "Do you see the one whom the LORD has chosen? There is no one like him among all the people." And all the people shouted, "Long live the king!"

25 Samuel told the people the rights and duties of the kingship, and he wrote them in a book and laid it up before the LORD. Then Samuel sent all the people back to their homes. ²⁶Saul also went to his home at Gibeah, and with him went warriors whose hearts God had touched. ²⁷But some worthless fellows said, "How can this man save us?" They despised him and brought him no present. But he held his peace.

Now Nahash, king of the Ammonites, had been grievously oppressing the Gadites and the Reubenites. He would gouge out the right eye of each of them and would not grant Israel a deliverer. No one was left of the Israelites across the Jordan whose right eye Nahash, king of the Ammonites, had not gouged out. But there were seven thousand men who had escaped from the Ammonites and had entered Jabesh-gilead."

11 About a month later," Nahash the Ammonite went up and besieged Jabesh-gilead, and all the men of Jabesh said to Nahash, "Make a treaty with us, and we will serve you." ²But Nahash the Ammonite said to them, "On this condition I will make a treaty with you, namely, that I gouge out everyone's right eye and thus put disgrace upon all Israel." ³The elders of Jabesh said to him, "Give us seven days' respite that we may send messengers through all the territory of Israel. Then, if there is no one to save us, we will give ourselves up to you." ⁴When the messengers came to Gibeah of Saul, they reported the matter in the hearing of the people, and all the people wept aloud.

k 10.21 Gk: Heb lacks *Finally ... man by man*   l 10.22 Gk: Heb *is there yet a man here?*   m 10.27 Q ms: MT lacks *Now Nahash ... entered Jabesh-gilead.*   n 11.1 Q ms Gk: MT lacks *About a month later*

the theme of deception more prominent in chaps. 19–22. **10:19** *You have rejected your God.* See 8:7. **10:20–21** *Taken by lot.* The casting of lots was a practice by which an item, person, or course of action was singled out from a group (cf. Josh. 7:14; 1 Sam. 14:41; Jonah 1:7). Here, the method of discernment is not identified (see 14:41–42 for the use of Urim and Thummim). **10:22** *Inquired.* The word for "inquire" in Hebrew has the same root as Saul's name, making this a pun (see note on 1:20). **10:23** See note on 9:2. **10:25** *Wrote them in a book.* Writing was most often the task of scribes (e.g., Jer. 36:32), but prophets—such as Moses (Exod. 24:4; 34:28) and Jeremiah (Jer. 51:60)—were also known to write down information of import. **10:26** The first clear reference to *Gibeah* as Saul's hometown. Gibeah features prominently in Judg. 19–20, which casts a dark shadow on Gibeah and its inhabitants, who are described as worthless scoundrels (Judg. 19:22; 20:13) just like the men in v. 27. **10:26–27a** A contrast is set up between those who follow Saul—warriors whose hearts have been touched by God—and those who do not—worthless fellows. The dichotomy foreshadows the divide that has already begun as a result of the monarchy. **10:27b** The Ammonites were a neighboring people who were often in territorial disputes with the Israelites, particularly the tribes of Gad and Reuben, who lived to the east of the Jordan. Jabesh-gilead is north of the disputed territory. *Gouge out the right eye,* a wound of humiliation (see also Judg. 16:21; 2 Kgs. 25:7; Jer. 39:7; 52:11). **11:1** Nahash likely besieged Jabesh-gilead because of the Gadites and Reubenites who had fled there (10:27b), yet it is the men of Jabesh who attempt to make the treaty with Nahash. **11:2** *Gouge*

5 Now Saul was coming from the field behind the oxen, and Saul said, "What is the matter with the people, that they are weeping?" So they told him the message from the inhabitants of Jabesh. 6And the spirit of God came upon Saul in power when he heard these words, and his anger was greatly kindled. 7He took a yoke of oxen and cut them in pieces and sent them throughout all the territory of Israel by the messengers, saying, "Whoever does not come out after Saul and Samuel, so shall it be done to his oxen!" Then the dread of the LORD fell upon the people, and they came out as one. 8When he mustered them at Bezek, those from Israel were three hundred thousand, and those from Judah seventy[o] thousand. 9They said to the messengers who had come, "Thus shall you say to the inhabitants of Jabesh-gilead: Tomorrow, by the time the sun is hot, you shall have deliverance." When the messengers came and told the inhabitants of Jabesh, they rejoiced. 10So the inhabitants of Jabesh said, "Tomorrow we will give ourselves up to you, and you may do to us whatever seems good to you." 11The next day Saul put the people in three companies. At the morning watch they came into the camp and cut down the Ammonites until the heat of the day, and those who survived were scattered, so that no two of them were left together.

12 The people said to Samuel, "Who is it that said, 'Shall Saul reign over us?' Give them to us so that we may put them to death." 13But Saul said, "No one shall be put to death this day, for today the LORD has brought deliverance to Israel." 14 Samuel said to the people, "Come, let us go to Gilgal and there renew the kingship." 15So all the people went to Gilgal, and there they made Saul king before the LORD in Gilgal. There they sacrificed offerings of well-being before the LORD, and there Saul and all the Israelites rejoiced greatly.

12 Samuel said to all Israel, "I have listened to you in all that you have said to me and have set a king over you. 2See, it is the king who leads you now; I am old and gray, but my sons are with you. I have led you from my youth until this day. 3Here I am; testify against me before the LORD and before his anointed. Whose ox have I taken? Or whose donkey have I taken? Or whom have I defrauded? Whom have I oppressed? Or from whose hand have I taken a bribe to blind my eyes with it? Testify against me,[p] and I will restore it to you." 4They said, "You have not defrauded us or oppressed us or taken anything from the hand of anyone." 5He said to them, "The LORD is witness against you, and his anointed is witness this day, that you have not found anything in my hand." And they said, "He is witness."

6 Samuel said to the people, "The LORD is witness, who[q] appointed Moses and Aaron and brought your ancestors up out of the land of Egypt. 7Now, therefore, take your stand so that I may enter into judgment with you before the LORD, and I will declare to[r] you all the righteous acts of the LORD that he performed for you and for your ancestors. 8When Jacob went into Egypt and the

---

out. See note on 10:27b. **11:5** *Behind the oxen.* Saul was plowing a field to prepare for planting. **11:6** *Spirit of God.* See note on 10:6, 10. **11:7** The act of cutting up an animal was symbolic; here, it serves as a threat to kill the livestock of those who do not answer the call to arms (see also Judg. 19). Saul mentions Samuel, but he is otherwise absent from the episode thus far and only appears again after the battle (vv. 12-15). **11:11** *Morning watch* refers to the few hours before sunrise. They begin their attack when it is still dark and fight throughout the day in order to defeat the Ammonites. *Cut down.* To attack, to kill. **11:12** The rescued want to kill those who doubted Saul's leadership. **11:13** Saul shows himself a worthy and righteous king by calling for peace among the Israelites and giving credit to God for their military victory. **11:14** *Renew the kingship.* See chap. 10.

12:1-25 Samuel's speech. Chapter 12 is a retirement speech—inserted into the larger narrative concerning Saul and his military skirmishes—that recalls the mighty deeds of the Lord and calls for servitude to the divine. It is similar to the final speeches of Moses in Deuteronomy and is considered a Deuteronomistic addition by many scholars. See **"The Deuteronomistic History," p. 337.** **12:3, 5** *His anointed* refers to Saul, who was anointed by Samuel in chap. 10. See note on 2:10 on the ritual of anointing. **12:6-13** A recounting of the history of Israel from the exodus to the present.

Egyptians oppressed them,[s] then your ancestors cried to the LORD, and the LORD sent Moses and Aaron, who brought forth your ancestors out of Egypt and settled them in this place. [9]But they forgot the LORD their God, and he sold them into the hand of Sisera, commander of the army of King Jabin of[t] Hazor, and into the hand of the Philistines, and into the hand of the king of Moab, and they fought against them. [10]Then they cried to the LORD and said, 'We have sinned, for we have forsaken the LORD and have served the Baals and the Astartes, but now rescue us out of the hand of our enemies, and we will serve you.' [11]And the LORD sent Jerubbaal and Barak,[u] and Jephthah, and Samson[v] and rescued you out of the hand of your enemies on every side, and you lived in safety. [12]But when you saw that King Nahash of the Ammonites came against you, you said to me, 'No, but a king shall reign over us,' though the LORD your God was your king. [13]See, here is the king whom you have chosen, for whom you have asked; see, the LORD has set a king over you. [14]If you will fear the LORD and serve him and heed his voice and not rebel against the commandment of the LORD, and if both you and the king who reigns over you will follow the LORD your God, it will be well; [15]but if you will not heed the voice of the LORD but rebel against the commandment of the LORD, then the hand of the LORD will be against you and your king.[w] [16]Now, therefore, take your stand and see this great thing that the LORD will do before your eyes. [17]Is it not the wheat harvest today? I will call upon the LORD, that he may send thunder and rain, and you shall know and see that the wickedness that you have done in the sight of the LORD is great in demanding a king for yourselves." [18]So

Samuel called upon the LORD, and the LORD sent thunder and rain that day, and all the people greatly feared the LORD and Samuel.

19 All the people said to Samuel, "Pray to the LORD your God for your servants, so that we may not die, for we have added to all our sins the evil of demanding a king for ourselves." [20]And Samuel said to the people, "Do not be afraid; you have done all this evil, yet do not turn aside from following the LORD, but serve the LORD with all your heart, [21]and do not turn aside after useless things that cannot profit or save, for they are useless. [22]For the LORD will not cast away his people, for his great name's sake, because it has pleased the LORD to make you a people for himself. [23]Moreover as for me, far be it from me that I should sin against the LORD by ceasing to pray for you, and I will instruct you in the good and the right way. [24]Only fear the LORD and serve him faithfully with all your heart, for consider what great things he has done for you. [25]But if you still do wickedly, you shall be swept away, both you and your king."

13 Saul was . . .[x] years old when he began to reign, and he reigned . . . and two[y] years over Israel.

2 Saul chose three thousand out of Israel; two thousand were with Saul in Michmash and the hill country of Bethel, and a thousand were with Jonathan in Gibeah of Benjamin; the rest of the people he sent home to their tents. [3]Jonathan defeated the garrison

s 12.8 Gk: Heb lacks *and the Egyptians oppressed them* t 12.9 Gk: Heb lacks *King Jabin of* u 12.11 Gk Syr: Heb *Bedan* v 12.11 Gk: Heb *Samuel* w 12.15 Gk: Heb *and your ancestors* x 13.1 The number is lacking in the Heb text (13.1 is lacking in Gk mss). y 13.1 *Two* is not the entire number; something has dropped out.

Samuel focuses on the people's rejection of God. **12:14–15** Standard blessings and curses like the ones in Deuteronomy. **12:17–18** Elijah will also call on God for rain (and fire) as a symbol of divine power (1 Kgs. 18). **12:20–25** A reiteration of the Deuteronomistic blessings and curses for obedience to God or lack thereof. **12:21** *Useless things.* Presumably other gods. **12:25** *Both you and your king.* The concept of communal guilt and punishment was prevalent, although not unanimously accepted (see note on 3:11–14).
13:1–7 Introduction to Saul's battle with the Philistines. 13:1 Saul's age and length of reign are not accurately preserved in the Hebrew manuscript tradition and are absent from the Greek. **13:2** An abrupt entry into a battle narrative in another time and geographical location. Verse 2 also introduces Jonathan, Saul's son, without acknowledging the familial relation or his backstory. **13:2–3** Michmash, Gibeah, and Geba are all located in Benjamin. Michmash and the other two cities are connected to one another via a narrow pass (v. 23) in the hill country. **13:3** *The Hebrews.*

of the Philistines that was at Geba, and the Philistines heard of it. And Saul blew the trumpet throughout all the land, saying, "Let the Hebrews hear!" ⁴When all Israel heard that Saul had defeated the garrison of the Philistines and also that Israel had become odious to the Philistines, the people were called out to join Saul at Gilgal.

5 The Philistines mustered to fight with Israel: thirty thousand chariots, and six thousand horsemen, and troops like the sand on the seashore in multitude; they came up and encamped at Michmash, to the east of Beth-aven. ⁶When the Israelites saw that they were in distress (for the troops were hard pressed), the people hid themselves in caves and in holes and in rocks and in tombs and in cisterns. ⁷Some Hebrews crossed the Jordan to the land of Gad and Gilead. Saul was still at Gilgal, and all the people followed him trembling.

8 He waited seven days, the time appointed by Samuel, but Samuel did not come to Gilgal, and the people began to slip away from Saul.ᶻ ⁹So Saul said, "Bring the burnt offering here to me and the offerings of well-being." And he offered the burnt offering. ¹⁰As soon as he had finished offering the burnt offering, Samuel arrived, and Saul went out to meet him and salute him. ¹¹Samuel said, "What have you done?" Saul replied, "When I saw that the people were slipping away from me and that you did not come within the days appointed and that the Philistines were mustering at Michmash, ¹²I said, 'Now the Philistines will come down upon me at Gilgal, and I have not entreated the favor of the Lord,' so I forced myself and offered the burnt offering." ¹³Samuel said to Saul, "You have done foolishly; you have not kept the commandment of the Lord your God, which he commanded you. The Lord would have established your kingdom over Israel forever, ¹⁴but now your kingdom will not continue; the Lord has sought out a man after his own heart, and the Lord has appointed him to be ruler over his people because you have not kept what the Lord commanded you." ¹⁵And Samuel left and went on his way from Gilgal.ᵃ The rest of the people followed Saul to join the army; they went up from Gilgal toward Gibeah of Benjamin.ᵇ

Saul counted the people who were present with him, about six hundred men. ¹⁶Saul, his son Jonathan, and the people who were present with them stayed in Geba of Benjamin, but the Philistines encamped at Michmash. ¹⁷And raiders came out of the camp of the Philistines in three companies; one company turned toward Ophrah to the land of Shual, ¹⁸another company turned toward Beth-horon, and another company turned toward the mountainᶜ that looks down upon the valley of Zeboim toward the wilderness.

19 Now there was no smith to be found throughout all the land of Israel, for the Philistines said, "The Hebrews must not make swords or spears for themselves," ²⁰so all the Israelites went down to the Philistines to sharpen their plowshares,

z 13.8 Heb *him* a 13.15 Gk: Heb *went up from Gilgal to Gibeah of Benjamin* b 13.15 Gk: Heb lacks *The rest . . . of Benjamin* c 13.18 Cn: Heb *border road*

Another, earlier, name for the Israelites, which is ethnic rather than national. **13:4** *Become odious* is an expression of distaste. **13:5** The Philistine army is massive and well-equipped—a theme throughout 1 Samuel. **13:8** *Waited seven days, the time appointed by Samuel.* The seven days of waiting at Gilgal for Samuel likely refers back to 10:8 (see also note on 9:13).

13:8–14 Saul's first divine rejection. 13:8–12 The exchange between Saul and Samuel loosely reflects that of Aaron and Moses in Exod. 32. Saul and Aaron each offer sacrifices due to the absence of the prophet and anxiety regarding the people. Both are reprimanded by the prophet for their choice. **13:13–14** According to Samuel, Saul loses his dynasty for not keeping God's command. Which command Saul failed to keep is not explicitly noted, although context suggests that it was not waiting for Samuel and/or performing Samuel's duties as priest. Interpreters have long wondered why Saul's actions earned such a harsh punishment. *A man after his own heart.* A foreshadowing of the anointing and reign of David.

13:15–23 Jonathan and Saul's victory over the Philistines. Here, the narrative about the conflict with the Philistines in the hill country from vv. 2–7 continues. The Philistines have the upper hand with more troops and a monopoly on metallurgy—the perfect setup for an underdog story. The metal implements listed in vv. 20–21 are agrarian equipment rather than weapons. The pre- and early monarchic Israelites were not primarily warriors but farmers and shepherds.

mattocks, axes, or sickles.*d 21*The charge was two-thirds of a shekel*e* for the plowshares and for the mattocks and one-third of a shekel for sharpening the axes and for setting the goads.*f 22*So on the day of the battle neither sword nor spear was to be found in the possession of any of the people with Saul and Jonathan, but Saul and his son Jonathan had them.

23 Now a garrison of the Philistines had gone out to the pass of Michmash.

14 ¹One day Jonathan son of Saul said to the young man who carried his armor, "Come, let us go over to the Philistine garrison on the other side." But he did not tell his father. ²Saul was staying in the outskirts of Gibeah under the pomegranate tree that is at Migron; the troops who were with him were about six hundred men, ³along with Ahijah son of Ahitub, Ichabod's brother, son of Phinehas son of Eli, the priest of the LORD in Shiloh, carrying an ephod. Now the people did not know that Jonathan had gone. ⁴In the pass*g* by which Jonathan tried to go over to the Philistine garrison there was a rocky crag on one side and a rocky crag on the other; the name of the one was Bozez, and the name of the other was Seneh. ⁵One crag rose on the north in front of Michmash and the other on the south in front of Geba.

6 Jonathan said to the young man who carried his armor, "Come, let us go over to the garrison of these uncircumcised; it may be that the LORD will act for us, for nothing can hinder the LORD from saving by many or by few." ⁷His armor-bearer said to him, "Do all that your mind inclines to.*h* I am with you; as your mind is, so is mine."*i* ⁸Then Jonathan said, "Now we will cross over to those men and will show ourselves to them. ⁹If they say

to us, 'Wait until we come to you,' then we will stand still in our place, and we will not go up to them. ¹⁰But if they say, 'Come up to us,' then we will go up, for the LORD has given them into our hand. That will be the sign for us." ¹¹So both of them showed themselves to the garrison of the Philistines, and the Philistines said, "Look, Hebrews are coming out of the holes where they have hidden themselves." ¹²The men of the garrison hailed Jonathan and his armor-bearer, saying, "Come up to us, and we will show you something." Jonathan said to his armor-bearer, "Come up after me, for the LORD has given them into the hand of Israel." ¹³Then Jonathan climbed up on his hands and feet, with his armor-bearer following after him. The Philistines*j* fell before Jonathan, and his armor-bearer coming after him killed them. ¹⁴In that first attack Jonathan and his armor-bearer killed about twenty men within an area about half a furrow long in an acre*k* of land. ¹⁵There was a panic in the camp, in the field, and among all the people; the garrison and even the raiders trembled; the earth quaked; and it became a very great panic.

16 Saul's lookouts in Gibeah of Benjamin were watching as the multitude was surging back and forth.*l* ¹⁷Then Saul said to the troops who were with him, "Call the roll and see who has gone from us." When they called the roll, Jonathan and his armor-bearer were not there. ¹⁸Saul said to Ahijah, "Bring the ark of God here." For at that time the ark of God went with the Israelites. ¹⁹While Saul was talking to the priest,

d 13.20 Gk: Heb *plowshare*   *e* 13.21 Heb *was a pim*
f 13.21 Cn: Meaning of Heb uncertain   *g* 14.4 Heb
Between the passes   *h* 14.7 Gk: Heb *Do all that is in your mind.*
Turn   *i* 14.7 Gk: Heb lacks *so is mine*   *j* 14.13 Heb *They*
k 14.14 Heb *yoke*   *l* 14.16 Gk: Heb *they went and there*

14:1–46 *Saul's curse and Jonathan's redemption.* **14:1** *But he did not tell his father.* Keeping secrets creates narrative tension (see note on 10:16). **14:3** *Ahijah* is a priest of the line of Eli, who mentored Samuel (chaps. 1–4). *Ephod.* A sacred apron-like garment that has power to assist in contacting the divine (see vv. 18–19). **14:6–23** Jonathan's ruse is reminiscent of Gideon's secret attack on the Midianites (Judg. 7). **14:6** *Uncircumcised.* A common Israelite slur denoting the perceived inferiority of the Philistines. For Israelites, circumcision was a sign of their special covenant with the God of Israel (Gen. 17). **14:14** *Half a furrow long in an acre of land* is an ancient measurement. A yoke or acre refers to the amount of land that could be plowed by a yoke of oxen (see textual note k). It is a relatively small area to contain twenty corpses. **14:17** Jonathan is pinpointed via roll call just as Saul was pinpointed as king in chap. 10. **14:18** The Hebrew reads "ark," but the Greek has "ephod," which is contextually the better reading (see v. 3). Saul calls for the priest and the ark/ephod to inquire of the Lord about the tumult. **14:19** *Withdraw your hand.* Some scholars suggest that Ahijah had his hands lifted in inquiry to God, and Saul grew impatient (13:8–9). It may also be that Ahijah

the tumult in the camp of the Philistines increased more and more, and Saul said to the priest, "Withdraw your hand." [20]Then Saul and all the people who were with him rallied and went into the battle, and every sword was against the other, so that there was very great confusion. [21]Now the Hebrews who previously had been with the Philistines and had gone up with them into the camp turned and joined the Israelites who were with Saul and Jonathan. [22]Likewise, when all the Israelites who had gone into hiding in the hill country of Ephraim heard that the Philistines were fleeing, they also followed closely after them in the battle. [23]So the LORD gave Israel the victory that day.

The battle passed beyond Beth-aven, and the troops with Saul numbered altogether about ten thousand men.[m] The battle spread out over the hill country of Ephraim.

24 Now Saul committed a very rash act on that day.[n] He had laid an oath on the troops, saying, "Cursed be anyone who eats food before it is evening and I have been avenged on my enemies." So none of the troops tasted food. [25]All the troops[o] came upon a honeycomb, and there was honey on the ground. [26]When the troops came upon the honeycomb, the honey was dripping out, but they did not put their hands to their mouths, for they feared the oath. [27]But Jonathan had not heard his father charge the troops with the oath, so he extended the staff that was in his hand and dipped the tip of it in the honeycomb and put his hand to his mouth, and his eyes brightened. [28]Then one of the soldiers said, "Your father strictly charged the troops with an oath, saying, 'Cursed be anyone who eats food this day.' And so the troops are faint." [29]Then Jonathan said, "My father has troubled the land;

see how my eyes have brightened because I tasted a little of this honey. [30]How much better if today the troops had eaten freely of the spoil taken from their enemies, for now the defeat of the Philistines has not been great."

31 After they had struck down the Philistines that day from Michmash to Aijalon, the troops were very faint, [32]so the troops flew upon the spoil and took sheep and oxen and calves and slaughtered them on the ground, and the troops ate them with the blood. [33]Then it was reported to Saul, "Look, the troops are sinning against the LORD by eating with the blood." And he said, "You have dealt treacherously; roll a large stone before me here."[p] [34]Saul said, "Disperse yourselves among the troops and say to them: Let all bring their oxen or their sheep, and slaughter them here and eat, and do not sin against the LORD by eating with the blood." So all of the troops brought their oxen with them that night and slaughtered them there. [35]And Saul built an altar to the LORD; it was the first altar that he built to the LORD.

36 Then Saul said, "Let us go down after the Philistines by night and despoil them until the morning light; let us not leave one of them." They said, "Do whatever seems good to you." But the priest said, "Let us draw near to God here." [37]So Saul inquired of God, "Shall I go down after the Philistines? Will you give them into the hand of Israel?" But he did not answer him that day. [38]Saul said, "Come here, all you leaders of the people, and let us find out how this sin has arisen today. [39]For as the LORD lives who saves Israel, even if it is in

m 14.23 Gk OL: Heb lacks and the troops . . . Ephraim
n 14.24 Gk: Heb The Israelites were distressed that day
o 14.25 Heb land   p 14.33 Gk: Heb me this day

had his hand on the ephod in order to affect the current predicament and protect Jonathan (cf. Exod. 17:8–16). However, when Saul hears the tumult, he thinks it is not working, so he orders the priest to stop. **14:21** *Hebrews*. See note on 13:3. Israelites (including David) *who previously had been with the Philistines* were mercenaries (chaps. 27–29). **14:23** Saul's troop numbers go from six hundred to ten thousand, which amplifies the miraculous change in circumstances. **14:24** The curse is the oath. **14:27** *Eyes brightened* is an expression of improved health and delight as compared to the faintness of the troops (v. 28). **14:32–34** To slaughter animals on the ground and eat them with their blood was an offense against Levitical law (Lev. 19:26; Deut. 12:16). Hence Saul's outcry against the sin and his call for a stone to be brought near. Slaughtering on a raised surface allowed the blood to flow out of the animal before it was consumed. **14:37–38** Saul understands that God has not answered because of a sin among the people. See 4:18 and 7:2–14 regarding the ark and its functionality in relationship to sin. **14:39** *As the LORD lives* is another expression of swearing, like the

my son Jonathan, he shall surely die!" But there was no one among all the people who answered him. [40]He said to all Israel, "You shall be on one side, and I and my son Jonathan will be on the other side." The people said to Saul, "Do what seems good to you." [41]Then Saul said, "O LORD God of Israel, why have you not answered your servant today? If this guilt is in me or in my son Jonathan, O LORD God of Israel, give Urim, but if this guilt is in your people Israel,[q] give Thummim." And Jonathan and Saul were indicated by the lot, but the people were cleared. [42]Then Saul said, "Cast the lot between me and my son Jonathan." And Jonathan was taken.

43 Then Saul said to Jonathan, "Tell me what you have done." Jonathan told him, "I tasted a little honey with the tip of the staff that was in my hand; here I am; I will die." [44]Saul said, "God do so to me and more also; you shall surely die, Jonathan!" [45]Then the people said to Saul, "Shall Jonathan die, who has accomplished this great victory in Israel? Far from it! As the LORD lives, not one hair of his head shall fall to the ground, for he has worked with God today." So the people ransomed Jonathan, and he did not die. [46]Then Saul withdrew from pursuing the Philistines, and the Philistines went to their own place.

47 When Saul had taken the kingship over Israel, he fought against all his enemies on every side: against Moab, against the Ammonites, against Edom, against the kings of Zobah, and against the Philistines; wherever he turned he routed them. [48]He did valiantly and struck down the Amalekites and rescued Israel out of the hands of those who plundered them.

49 Now the sons of Saul were Jonathan, Ishvi, and Malchishua, and the names of his two daughters were these: the name of the firstborn was Merab, and the name of the younger was Michal. [50]The name of Saul's wife was Ahinoam daughter of Ahimaaz. And the name of the commander of his army was Abner son of Ner, Saul's uncle; [51]Kish was the father of Saul, and Ner the father of Abner was the son of Abiel.

52 There was hard fighting against the Philistines all the days of Saul, and when Saul saw any strong or valiant warrior, he took him into his service.

15 Samuel said to Saul, "The LORD sent me to anoint you king over his people Israel; now therefore listen to the words of the LORD. [2]Thus says the LORD of hosts: I will punish the Amalekites for what they did in opposing the Israelites when they came up out of Egypt. [3]Now go and attack Amalek and utterly destroy all that they have; do not spare them, but kill both man and woman, child and infant, ox and sheep, camel and donkey."

4 So Saul summoned the people and numbered them in Telaim, two hundred thousand foot soldiers and ten thousand soldiers of Judah. [5]Saul came to the city of the Amalekites and lay in wait in the valley. [6]Saul said to the Kenites, "Go! Leave! Withdraw from among the Amalekites, or I will destroy you with them, for you showed kindness to all the Israelites when they came up out of Egypt." So the Kenites withdrew from the Amalekites. [7]Saul defeated the Amalekites, from Havilah as far as

q 14.41 Gk OL: Heb *q Saul said to the* LORD, *the God of Israel*

oath in v. 24 (see also v. 45). **14:41–42** On the casting of lots, see note on 10:20–21. Here, the text explicitly identifies that the guilty and innocent will be determined by Urim and Thummim—sacred objects utilized to perceive God's will (Exod. 28:30; Lev. 8:8; Deut. 33:8; 1 Sam. 28:6; Ezra 2:63; Neh. 7:65). Some manuscripts do not include Saul's question or the Urim (see textual notes). Nevertheless, Jonathan is still the one identified (literally "taken") by God and stands as the accused party. **14:45** *As the* LORD *lives*. See note on 14:39. The concept of ransoming has a narrow meaning, in which one literally gives a monetary or animal substitute for the one ransomed, or a broad meaning, in which someone is simply rescued.

14:47–52 Narratorial summary of Saul's career and progeny. A genealogy buttressed by two editorial summaries (vv. 47–48, 52) of Saul's deeds as king. These verses were likely at the end of one version of Saul's story but now sit among a collection of traditions about Saul.

15:1–35 Saul's second divine rejection. 15:1 *To anoint you king*. See note on 2:10. **15:2** LORD *of hosts*. See note on 1:3. **15:6** *The Kenites* are traditionally understood as the descendants of Cain (Gen. 4). Throughout the Hebrew Bible, the Kenites show kindness or loyalty to the Israelites (see

Shur, which is east of Egypt. [8]He took King Agag of the Amalekites alive but utterly destroyed all the people with the edge of the sword. [9]Saul and the people spared Agag and the best of the sheep and of the cattle and of the fatted calves,[r] and the lambs, and all that was valuable and would not utterly destroy them; all that was despised and worthless they utterly destroyed.

[10] The word of the LORD came to Samuel: [11]"I regret that I made Saul king, for he has turned back from following me and has not carried out my commands." Samuel was angry, and he cried out to the LORD all night. [12]Samuel rose early in the morning to meet Saul, and Samuel was told, "Saul went to Carmel, where he set up a monument for himself, and on returning he passed on down to Gilgal." [13]When Samuel came to Saul, Saul said to him, "May you be blessed by the LORD; I have carried out the command of the LORD." [14]But Samuel said, "What then is this bleating of sheep in my ears and the lowing of cattle that I hear?" [15]Saul said, "They have brought them from the Amalekites, for the people spared the best of the sheep and the cattle to sacrifice to the LORD your God, but the rest we have utterly destroyed." [16]Then Samuel said to Saul, "Stop! I will tell you what the LORD said to me last night." He replied, "Speak."

[17] Samuel said, "Though you are little in your own eyes, are you not the head of the tribes of Israel? The LORD anointed you king over Israel. [18]And the LORD sent you on a mission and said, 'Go, utterly destroy the sinners, the Amalekites, and fight against them until they are consumed.' [19]Why then did you not obey the voice of the LORD? Why did you swoop down on the spoil and do what was evil in the sight of the LORD?" [20]Saul said to Samuel, "I have obeyed the voice of the LORD. I have gone on the mission on which the LORD sent me. I have brought Agag the king of Amalek, and I have utterly destroyed the Amalekites. [21]But from the spoil the people took sheep and cattle, the best of the things devoted to destruction, to sacrifice to the LORD your God in Gilgal." [22]And Samuel said,

"Has the LORD as great delight in burnt
        offerings and sacrifices
    as in obedience to the voice of the
        LORD?
Surely, to obey is better than sacrifice
    and to heed than the fat of rams.
[23] For rebellion is no less a sin than
        divination,
    and stubbornness is like iniquity and
        idolatry.
Because you have rejected the word of
        the LORD,
    he has also rejected you from being
        king."

[24] Saul said to Samuel, "I have sinned, for I have transgressed the commandment of the LORD and your words because I feared the people and obeyed their voice. [25]Now therefore, I pray, pardon my sin, and return with me, so that I may worship the LORD." [26]Samuel said to Saul, "I will not return with you, for you have rejected the word of the

r 15.9 Cn: Heb *the second ones*

also Judg. 5). Here, Saul is repaying the debt. **15:8–26** Much time has been spent judging Saul for his actions in vv. 8–25. How one judges Saul depends on whose words are given more credence. If the reader sides with Samuel and God, Saul has gravely sinned and disobeyed a direct command with knowledge and indignation (vv. 3, 8, 10, 19, 23). He deserves rejection. If the reader sides with Saul, he dutifully destroyed the Amalekites as instructed and even let the people keep an offering to present to God, which would be an appropriate act of thanks (vv. 7, 13, 15, 18, 20–21). It does not appear that he knows he has committed a sin until v. 24, after Samuel alerts him to his error. Throughout the millennia, various interpreters have condemned Saul and his actions throughout his kingship, while others have had a more sympathetic view of him as a tragic and imperfect hero who is outshone by David. **15:11** *I regret*. Contemporary readers can find the emotional response of God surprising. However, it was typical to give human qualities to the gods in the ancient world. God "regrets" or "changes [God's] mind" several times in the Hebrew Bible (see, e.g., Gen. 6:6–7; Exod. 32:14; 1 Sam. 15:35; 2 Sam. 24:16; Jer. 26:19; cf. 1 Sam. 15:29). **15:22–23 Obedience versus sacrifice.** Samuel's poetic response to the king is typical of the prophets. The theme of obedience is also central to the Hebrew Bible, especially the books scholars include in the Deuteronomistic History. See **"The Deuteronomistic History," p. 337. 15:24–25** *I have sinned . . . pardon my sin*. Saul immediately accepts his indictment by Samuel and asks for forgiveness. God is not consistently portrayed when

LORD, and the LORD has rejected you from being king over Israel." [27]As Samuel turned to go away, Saul caught hold of the hem of his robe, and it tore. [28]And Samuel said to him, "The LORD has torn the kingdom of Israel from you this very day and has given it to a neighbor of yours who is better than you. [29]Moreover, the Glory of Israel will not deceive or change his mind, for he is not a mortal, that he should change his mind." [30]Then Saul[s] said, "I have sinned; yet honor me now before the elders of my people and before Israel, and return with me, so that I may worship the LORD your God." [31]So Samuel turned back after Saul, and Saul worshiped the LORD.

[32] Then Samuel said, "Bring Agag king of the Amalekites here to me." And Agag came to him haltingly.[t] Agag said, "Surely death is bitter."[u] [33]Samuel said,

> "As your sword has made women
> childless,
> so your mother shall be childless
> among women."

And Samuel hewed Agag in pieces before the LORD in Gilgal.

[34] Then Samuel went to Ramah, and Saul went up to his house in Gibeah of Saul. [35]Samuel did not see Saul again until the day of his death, but Samuel grieved over Saul. And the LORD was sorry that he had made Saul king over Israel.

16 The LORD said to Samuel, "How long will you grieve over Saul? I have rejected him from being king over Israel. Fill your horn with oil and set out; I will send you to Jesse the Bethlehemite, for I have provided for myself a king among his sons." [2]Samuel said, "How can I go? If Saul hears of it, he will kill me." And the LORD said, "Take a heifer with you and say, 'I have come to sacrifice to the LORD.' [3]Invite Jesse to the sacrifice, and I will show you what you shall do, and you shall anoint for me the one whom I name to you." [4]Samuel did what the LORD commanded and came to Bethlehem. The elders of the city came to meet him trembling and said, "Do you come peaceably?" [5]He said, "Peaceably. I have come to sacrifice to the LORD; sanctify yourselves and come with me to the sacrifice." And he sanctified Jesse and his sons and invited them to the sacrifice.

[6] When they came, he looked on Eliab and thought, "Surely his anointed is now before the LORD." [7]But the LORD said to Samuel, "Do not look on his appearance or on the height of his stature, because I have rejected him, for the LORD does not see as mortals see; they look on the outward appearance, but the LORD looks on the heart." [8]Then Jesse called Abinadab and made him pass before Samuel. He said, "Neither has the LORD chosen this one." [9]Then Jesse made Shammah pass by. And he said, "Neither has the LORD chosen this one." [10]Jesse made seven of his sons pass before Samuel, and Samuel said to Jesse, "The LORD has not chosen any of these." [11]Samuel said to Jesse, "Are all your sons here?" And he said, "There remains yet the youngest, but he is keeping the sheep." And Samuel said to Jesse, "Send and bring him, for we will not sit down until he comes here." [12]He sent and brought him in. Now he was ruddy and had beautiful eyes and was handsome. The LORD said, "Rise and anoint him, for this is the one." [13]Then Samuel took the horn of oil and anointed him in the

s 15.30 Heb *he*   t 15.32 Cn Compare Gk: Meaning of Heb uncertain   u 15.32 Gk Syr OL: Heb *Surely the bitterness of death is past*

it comes to forgiveness; some people receive it, others do not. Saul does not. This is one of the many ways his story will be contrasted with that of King David, who will commit a laundry list of sins but be forgiven and never rejected by God (see 2 Sam. 10–11 for the most famous errors of David). See **"Davidic Covenant," p. 433**. **15:27–28** The act of tearing a robe, and its symbolism of a kingdom ripped from someone and given to another, also features in the story of Jeroboam, the first king of northern Israel (1 Kgs. 11:26–40). **15:29** *Change his mind*. See note on 15:11. **15:33** *Samuel hewed Agag in pieces*. It was not out of the ordinary for prophets to kill others. For example, see the stories of Elijah (1 Kgs. 18:39–40), Elisha (2 Kgs. 2:23–25), and Saul, who was counted among the prophets (1 Sam. 9–31).

16:1–13 The selection and anointing of David. The first introduction to David sets him up as an underdog. The underdog motif is common in both biblical and American literature. David starts as the youngest and smallest of the sons of Jesse, but he is chosen to be king of Israel. **16:13** *Anointed him*. See note on 2:10.

presence of his brothers, and the spirit of the LORD came mightily upon David from that day forward. Samuel then set out and went to Ramah.

14 Now the spirit of the LORD departed from Saul, and an evil spirit from the LORD tormented him. ¹⁵And Saul's servants said to him, "See now, an evil spirit from God is tormenting you. ¹⁶Let our lord now command the servants who attend you to look for someone who is skillful in playing the lyre, and when the evil spirit from God is upon you, he will play it, and you will feel better." ¹⁷So Saul said to his servants, "Provide for me someone who can play well, and bring him to me." ¹⁸One of the young men answered, "I have seen a son of Jesse the Bethlehemite who is skillful in playing, a man of valor, a warrior, prudent in speech, and a man of good presence, and the LORD is with him." ¹⁹So Saul sent messengers to Jesse and said, "Send me your son David, who is with the sheep." ²⁰Jesse took a donkey loaded with bread, a skin of wine, and a kid and sent them by his son David to Saul. ²¹And David came to Saul and entered his service. Saul[ᵛ] loved him greatly, and he became his armor-bearer. ²²Saul sent to Jesse, saying, "Let David remain in my service, for he has found favor in my sight." ²³And whenever the evil spirit from God came upon Saul, David took the lyre and played it with his hand, and Saul would be relieved and feel better, and the evil spirit would depart from him.

17 Now the Philistines gathered their armies for battle; they were gathered at Socoh, which belongs to Judah, and encamped between Socoh and Azekah, in Ephes-dammim. ²Saul and the Israelites gathered and encamped in the valley of Elah and formed ranks against the Philistines. ³The Philistines stood on the mountain on the one side, and Israel stood on the mountain on the other side, with a valley between them. ⁴And there came out from the camp of the Philistines a champion named Goliath, of Gath, whose height was four[ʷ] cubits and a span. ⁵He had a helmet of bronze on his head, and he was armed with a coat of mail; the weight of the coat was five thousand shekels of bronze. ⁶He had greaves of bronze on his legs and a javelin of bronze slung between his shoulders. ⁷The shaft of his spear was like a weaver's beam, and his spear's head weighed six hundred shekels of iron, and his shield-bearer went before him. ⁸He stood and shouted to the ranks of Israel, "Why have you come out to draw up for battle? Am I not a Philistine, and are you not servants of Saul? Choose[ˣ] a man for yourselves, and let him come down to me. ⁹If he is able to

v 16.21 Heb *He*   w 17.4 Q ms Gk: MT *six*   x 17.8 Gk: Meaning of Heb uncertain

16:14–23 David plays the lyre for Saul. The second introduction to David, which contrasts him with Saul. **16:14** *The spirit of the LORD* is an important theological and narrative device in the Deuteronomistic History. See **"The Deuteronomistic History," p. 337.** *The spirit* comes to rest on important characters and sometimes departs from them, as it has from Saul. The movement of the spirit signals divine favor (or lack thereof) and comes with divine gifts or abilities. Like the spirit of the Lord, *an evil spirit* can be sent by God, affect humans, and function as a theological and narrative device. An evil spirit torments Saul throughout the rest of his life and kingship, signifying his spiritual and political rejection by God. Some scholars have explored the possibility that those who are identified as spiritually tormented in the Bible may have been suffering from mental illness. For example, some postulate that Saul had depression or paranoid schizophrenia. While contemporary psychologists would identify his symptoms (throughout 1 Sam., he will exhibit paranoia, mood swings, and violent outbursts) with chemical imbalance or psychological distress, the ancients concluded that he was being attacked by an evil spirit. **16:16** Despite the varying contextual diagnoses, humans have long recognized that music is a therapeutic treatment for such illnesses. Saul's servants call for someone to play the lyre so that he *will feel better.*

17:1–51 David and Goliath. The third and final introduction to David, which strategically elevates him above Saul as a warrior and leader of Israel. The biblical text and its manuscript tradition provide evidence for the fact that there were several traditions concerning the defeat of giant Philistines (see 2 Sam. 21:15–22, esp. v. 19; 1 Chr. 20:4–8) and at least two different versions of David slaying Goliath (the Greek version does not include vv. 12–31, 50, 55–58). **17:4–7** Goliath receives a lengthy description, with special attention to his body and armor, heightening the narrative drama and

fight with me and kill me, then we will be your servants, but if I prevail against him and kill him, then you shall be our servants and serve us." [10]And the Philistine said, "Today I defy the ranks of Israel! Give me a man, that we may fight together." [11]When Saul and all Israel heard these words of the Philistine, they were dismayed and greatly afraid.

12 Now David was the son of an Ephrathite of Bethlehem in Judah named Jesse, who had eight sons. In the days of Saul the man was already old and advanced in years.[y] [13]The three eldest sons of Jesse had followed Saul to the battle; the names of his three sons who went to the battle were Eliab the firstborn, and next to him Abinadab, and the third Shammah. [14]David was the youngest; the three eldest followed Saul, [15]but David went back and forth from Saul to feed his father's sheep at Bethlehem. [16]For forty days the Philistine came forward and took his stand, morning and evening.

17 Jesse said to his son David, "Take for your brothers an ephah of this parched grain and these ten loaves, and carry them quickly to the camp to your brothers; [18]also take these ten cheeses to the commander of their thousand. See how your brothers fare, and bring some token from them."

19 Now Saul, and they, and all the men of Israel were in the valley of Elah fighting with the Philistines. [20]David rose early in the morning, left the sheep with a keeper, took the provisions, and went as Jesse had commanded him. He came to the encampment as the army was going forth to the battle line, shouting the war cry. [21]Israel and the Philistines drew up for battle, army against army. [22]David left the things in charge of the keeper of the baggage, ran to the ranks, and went and greeted his brothers. [23]As he talked with them, the champion, the Philistine of Gath, Goliath by name, came up out of the ranks of the Philistines

and spoke the same words as before. And David heard him.

24 All the Israelites, when they saw the man, fled from him and were very much afraid. [25]The Israelites said, "Have you seen this man who has come up? Surely he has come up to defy Israel. The king will greatly enrich the man who kills him and will give him his daughter and make his family free in Israel." [26]David said to the men who stood by him, "What shall be done for the man who kills this Philistine and takes away the reproach from Israel? For who is this uncircumcised Philistine that he should defy the armies of the living God?" [27]The people answered him in the same way, "So shall it be done for the man who kills him."

28 His eldest brother Eliab heard him talking to the men, and Eliab's anger was kindled against David. He said, "Why have you come down? With whom have you left those few sheep in the wilderness? I know your presumption and the evil of your heart, for you have come down just to see the battle." [29]David said, "What have I done now? It was only a question." [30]He turned away from him toward another and spoke in the same way, and the people answered him again as before.

31 When the words that David spoke were heard, they repeated them before Saul, and he sent for him. [32]David said to Saul, "Let no one's heart fail because of him; your servant will go and fight with this Philistine." [33]Saul said to David, "You are not able to go against this Philistine to fight with him, for you are just a boy, and he has been a warrior from his youth." [34]But David said to Saul, "Your servant used to keep sheep for his father, and whenever a lion or a bear came and took a lamb from the flock, [35]I went after it and struck it down, rescuing the lamb from its mouth, and if it turned against me, I would

y 17.12 Gk Syr: Heb *among men*

---

setting up the contrast between him and David in vv. 38–40. **17:16** *Forty days.* Forty is a frequently used number in the Bible and often signifies a completed cycle of time. **17:17–18** David, like Saul (9:3), is sent on a mission by his father, which will lead toward some fortuitous event. **17:17** *Ephah.* An ancient measure for grain that is equivalent to about 35 liters (8 gallons). **17:20** The journey from Bethlehem to Socoh is about 25 km (15 miles). **17:25** *Give him his daughter.* In the ancient Near East, women were given and received as valuable property, and a king's daughter would normally be given to another king in order to make national alliances. **17:26** *Uncircumcised.* See note on 14:6. **17:28** *Eliab's anger was kindled against David.* Tension among siblings is a biblical theme, and Eliab's anger against his brother recalls the stories of sibling tensions in Genesis, especially between Cain

catch it by the jaw, strike it down, and kill it. [36]Your servant has killed both lions and bears, and this uncircumcised Philistine shall be like one of them, since he has defied the armies of the living God." [37]David said, "The Lord, who saved me from the paw of the lion and from the paw of the bear, will save me from the hand of this Philistine." So Saul said to David, "Go, and may the Lord be with you!"

[38] Saul clothed David with his armor; he put a bronze helmet on his head and clothed him with a coat of mail. [39]David strapped Saul's sword over the armor, and he tried in vain to walk, for he was not used to them. Then David said to Saul, "I cannot walk with these, for I am not used to them." So David removed them. [40]Then he took his staff in his hand and chose five smooth stones from the wadi and put them in his shepherd's bag, in the pouch; his sling was in his hand, and he drew near to the Philistine.

[41] The Philistine came on and drew near to David, with his shield-bearer in front of him. [42]When the Philistine looked and saw David, he disdained him, for he was only a youth, ruddy and handsome in appearance. [43]The Philistine said to David, "Am I a dog, that you come to me with sticks?" And the Philistine cursed David by his gods. [44]The Philistine said to David, "Come to me, and I will give your flesh to the birds of the air and to the wild animals of the field." [45]But David said to the Philistine, "You come to me with sword and spear and javelin, but I come to you in the name of the Lord of hosts, the God of the armies of Israel, whom you have defied. [46]This very day the Lord will deliver you into my hand, and I will strike you down and cut off your head, and I will give the dead bodies of the Philistine army this very day to the birds of the air and to the wild animals of the earth, so that all the earth may know that there is a God in Israel [47]and that all this assembly may know that the Lord does not save by sword and spear, for the battle is the Lord's, and he will give you into our hand."

[48] When the Philistine drew nearer to meet David, David ran quickly toward the battle line to meet the Philistine. [49]David put his hand in his bag, took out a stone, slung it, and struck the Philistine on his forehead; the stone sank into his forehead, and he fell face down on the ground.

[50] So David prevailed over the Philistine with a sling and a stone, striking down the Philistine and killing him; there was no sword in David's hand. [51]Then David ran and stood over the Philistine; he grasped his sword, drew it out of its sheath, and killed him; then he cut off his head with it.

When the Philistines saw that their champion was dead, they fled. [52]The troops of Israel and Judah rose up with a shout and pursued the Philistines as far as Gath[z] and the gates of Ekron, so that the wounded Philistines fell on the way from Shaaraim as far as Gath and Ekron. [53]The Israelites came back from chasing the Philistines, and they plundered their camp. [54]David took the head of the Philistine and brought it to Jerusalem, but he put his armor in his tent.

[55] When Saul saw David go out against the Philistine, he said to Abner, the commander of the army, "Abner, whose son is this young man?" Abner said, "As your soul lives, O king, I do not know." [56]The king said, "Inquire whose son the young man is." [57]On David's return from killing the Philistine, Abner took him and brought him before Saul, with the head of the Philistine in his hand. [58]Saul said to him, "Whose son are you, young man?" And David answered, "I am the son of your servant Jesse the Bethlehemite."

z 17.52 Gk Syr: Heb *a valley*

and Abel (Gen. 4) and Joseph and his brothers (Gen. 37–50). **17:38–40** The description of David removing Saul's armor and choosing to take only the accoutrements of a shepherd onto the battlefield is a direct contrast to Goliath (vv. 4–7), who is a professional warrior, and Saul, a king unwilling to fight for his people. *Sling.* A sling was a legitimate military weapon. **17:43–47** The opponents' insults reveal that this deathmatch is about not only personal bragging rights but also national and religious dominance; it is really a contest of gods, similar to the ones found in Exod. 7–12 and 1 Kgs. 18. **17:50–51** Whether David killed Goliath with his sling or sword has been a long-standing question for interpreters. The fact that David even has a sword, especially in light of vv. 38–40, is surprising. Historical-critical scholars have tried to answer these quandaries by proposing that these verses are an amalgamation of two separate endings to the famous story, which may have been passed down in several different versions itself (see note at the beginning of the chapter).

18

When David[a] had finished speaking to Saul, the soul of Jonathan was bound to the soul of David, and Jonathan loved him as his own soul. ²Saul took him that day and would not let him return to his father's house. ³Then Jonathan made a covenant with David because he loved him as his own soul. ⁴Jonathan stripped himself of the robe that he was wearing and gave it to David and his armor and even his sword and his bow and his belt. ⁵David went out and was successful wherever Saul sent him; as a result, Saul set him over the army. And all the people, even the servants of Saul, approved.

6 As they were coming home, when David returned from killing the Philistine, the women came out of all the towns of Israel, singing and dancing, to meet King Saul, with tambourines, with songs of joy, and with musical instruments.[b] ⁷And the women sang to one another as they made merry,

"Saul has killed his thousands
    and David his ten thousands."

⁸Saul was very angry, for this saying displeased him. He said, "They have ascribed to David ten thousands, and to me they have ascribed thousands; what more can he have but the kingdom?" ⁹So Saul eyed David from that day on.

10 The next day an evil spirit from God rushed upon Saul, and he raved within his house, while David was playing the lyre, as he did day by day. Saul had his spear in his hand, ¹¹and Saul threw the spear, for he thought, "I will pin David to the wall." But David eluded him twice.

12 Saul was afraid of David because the LORD was with him but had departed from Saul. ¹³So Saul removed him from his presence and made him a commander of a thousand, and David marched out and came in, leading the army. ¹⁴David had success in all his undertakings, for the LORD was with him. ¹⁵When Saul saw that he had great success, he stood in awe of him. ¹⁶But all Israel and Judah loved David, for it was he who marched out and came in leading them.

17 Then Saul said to David, "Here is my elder daughter Merab; I will give her to you as a wife; only be valiant for me and fight the LORD's battles." For Saul thought, "I will not raise a hand against him; let the Philistines deal with him." ¹⁸David said to Saul, "Who am I, and who are my kinsfolk, my father's family in Israel, that I should be son-in-law to the king?" ¹⁹But at the time when Saul's daughter Merab should have been given to David, she was given to Adriel the Meholathite as a wife.

20 Now Saul's daughter Michal loved David. Saul was told, and the thing pleased him. ²¹Saul thought, "Let me give her to him that she may be a snare for him and that the hand of the Philistines may be against him." Therefore Saul said to David a second time,[c] "You shall now be my son-in-law." ²²Saul commanded his servants, "Speak to David

a 18.1 Heb *he*   b 18.6 Or *triangles* or *three-stringed instruments*
c 18.21 Heb *by two*

18:1–4 Jonathan's devotion (episode 1). David and Jonathan's intense "soul bond" has been compared to the friendship of Gilgamesh and Enkidu, chronicled in the well-known Mesopotamian Gilgamesh Epic. Both ancient tales have been interpreted through platonic and queer lenses. The entire chronicle of David's supersession of Saul (18:1–19:17) is an exaggerated drama in which David takes Saul's throne by taking his three children. **18:4** Jonathan's transfer of his princely garments and military accouterments to David likely symbolizes his abdication of power to him.

18:5–30 David's success continues, and Saul's anxiety begins. 18:10 *Evil spirit.* See note on 16:14. *He raved* is a biased translation; the word is from the Hebrew verb "nava," to prophesy, and this form indicates that Saul is prophesying reflexively, literally "to himself." Taken more loosely, this may mean that Saul is prophesying internally or is in a kind of ecstatic state (see 19:20–24, where it is translated as "prophetic frenzy"). **18:17** Though a daughter of the king is mentioned as a war prize in 17:25, Merab, Saul's eldest, is not explicitly offered to David until now (vv. 17–19 are not present in the Septuagint). In both stories, she is viewed as property to be traded for military valiance. Saul's attempt to kill David by enemy-combatant proxy foreshadows David's own premeditated murder of Uriah (2 Sam. 11). **18:19** Saul's offer of Merab to David in v. 17 was only a proposal. Nevertheless, giving a betrothed daughter to another man was typically unacceptable and alerts the reader to impending social discord (see also Judg. 15). **18:20–27** The sister-wives motif (i.e., a father giving two daughters to one man) appears several times in the Hebrew Bible (see Gen. 29; Judg. 15) and always leads to family conflict. The motif does not suggest that this was standard practice; on the

in private and say, 'See, the king is delighted with you, and all his servants love you; now then, become the king's son-in-law.' " ²³So Saul's servants reported these words to David in private. And David said, "Does it seem to you a little thing to become the king's son-in-law, seeing that I am a poor man and of no repute?" ²⁴The servants of Saul told him, "This is what David said." ²⁵Then Saul said, "Thus shall you say to David, 'The king desires no marriage present except a hundred foreskins of the Philistines, that he may be avenged on the king's enemies.' " Now Saul planned to make David fall by the hand of the Philistines. ²⁶When his servants told David these words, David was well pleased to be the king's son-in-law. Before the time had expired, ²⁷David rose and went, along with his men, and killed one hundred*d* of the Philistines, and David brought their foreskins, which were given in full number to the king, that he might become the king's son-in-law. Saul gave him his daughter Michal as a wife. ²⁸But when Saul realized that the Lᴏʀᴅ was with David and that Saul's daughter Michal loved him, ²⁹Saul was still more afraid of David. So Saul was David's enemy from that time forward.

30 Then the commanders of the Philistines came out to battle, and as often as they came out, David had more success than all the servants of Saul, so that his fame became very great.

19 Saul spoke with his son Jonathan and with all his servants about killing David. But Saul's son Jonathan took great delight in David. ²Jonathan told David, "My father Saul is trying to kill you; therefore be on guard tomorrow morning; stay in a secret place and hide yourself. ³I will go out and stand beside my father in the field where you are, and I will speak to my father about you; if I learn anything I will tell you." ⁴Jonathan spoke well of David to his father Saul, saying to him, "The king should not sin against his servant David, because he has not sinned against you and because his deeds have been of good service to you, ⁵for he took his life in his hand when he attacked the Philistine, and the Lᴏʀᴅ brought about a great victory for all Israel. You saw it and rejoiced; why then will you sin against an innocent person by killing David without cause?" ⁶Saul heeded the voice of Jonathan; Saul swore, "As the Lᴏʀᴅ lives, he shall not be put to death." ⁷So Jonathan called David and related all these things to him. Jonathan then brought David to Saul, and he was in his presence as before.

8 Again there was war, and David went out to fight the Philistines. He launched a heavy attack on them, so that they fled before him. ⁹Then an evil spirit from the Lᴏʀᴅ came upon Saul as he sat in his house with his spear in his hand, while David was playing music. ¹⁰Saul sought to pin David to the wall with the spear, but he eluded Saul, so that he struck the spear into the wall. David fled and escaped that night.

11 Saul sent messengers to David's house to keep watch over him, planning to kill him in the morning. David's wife Michal told him, "If you do not save your life tonight, tomorrow you will be killed." ¹²So Michal let David down through the window; he fled away and escaped. ¹³Michal took an idol*e* and laid it on the bed; she put a net*f* of goats' hair on its head and covered it with the clothes. ¹⁴When Saul sent messengers to take David, she said, "He is sick." ¹⁵Then Saul sent the messengers to see David for themselves. He said, "Bring him up to me

d 18.27 Gk: Heb *two hundred*   *e* 19.13 Heb *the teraphim*
f 19.13 Meaning of Heb uncertain

contrary, it warns against it. **18:25** *A hundred foreskins of the Philistines.* The Philistines are repeatedly referred to as "uncircumcised" in 1 Samuel (see note on 14:6). Saul presumes David cannot accomplish the outlandish request and will die trying.

19:1–7 Jonathan's devotion (episode 2). Jonathan protects David from his father. Saul acquiesces.

19:8–17 David's success, Saul's assassination attempts, and Michal's intervention. 19:9 *Evil spirit.* See note on 16:14. **19:12** *Let David down through the window.* Reminiscent of the story of Rahab saving the Israelite spies in Jericho (Josh. 2). Like Rahab, Michal also uses deception to save the Israelite protagonist, which is depicted as praiseworthy throughout the Hebrew Bible. **19:13** *Idol.* Ancient Near Eastern peoples worshiped many gods and often made images of them to place in their temples and houses. Both biblical and archaeological evidence confirm that the ancient Israelites worshiped gods other than YHWH, the god of Israel, even though many passages condemn

in the bed, that I may kill him." [16]When the messengers came in, the idol[g] was in the bed, with the covering[h] of goats' hair on its head. [17]Saul said to Michal, "Why have you deceived me like this and let my enemy go, so that he has escaped?" Michal answered Saul, "He said to me, 'Let me go; why should I kill you?'"

18 Now David fled and escaped; he came to Samuel at Ramah and told him all that Saul had done to him. He and Samuel went and settled at Naioth. [19]Saul was told, "David is at Naioth in Ramah." [20]Then Saul sent messengers to take David. When they saw the company of the prophets in a frenzy, with Samuel standing in charge of[i] them, the spirit of God came upon the messengers of Saul, and they also fell into a prophetic frenzy. [21]When Saul was told, he sent other messengers, and they also fell into a frenzy. Saul sent messengers again the third time, and they also fell into a frenzy. [22]Then he himself went to Ramah. He came to the great well that is in Secu; he asked, "Where are Samuel and David?" And someone said, "They are at Naioth in Ramah." [23]He went there, toward Naioth in Ramah, and the spirit of God came upon him. As he was going, he fell into a prophetic frenzy, until he came to Naioth in Ramah. [24]He, too, stripped off his clothes, and he, too, fell into a frenzy before Samuel. He lay naked all that day and all that night. Therefore it is said, "Is Saul also among the prophets?"

20 David fled from Naioth in Ramah. He came before Jonathan and said, "What have I done? What is my guilt? And what is my sin against your father that he is trying to take my life?" [2]He said to him, "Far from it! You shall not die. My father does nothing either great or small without disclosing it to me, and why should my father hide this from me? Never!" [3]But David also swore, "Your father knows well that you like me, and he thinks, 'Do not let Jonathan know this, or he will be grieved.' But truly, as the LORD lives and as you yourself live, there is but a step between me and death." [4]Then Jonathan said to David, "Whatever you say, I will do for you." [5]David said to Jonathan, "Tomorrow is the new moon, and I should not fail to sit with the king at the meal, but let me go, so that I may hide in the field until the third evening. [6]If your father misses me at all, then say, 'David earnestly asked leave of me to run to Bethlehem his city, for there is a yearly sacrifice there for all the family.' [7]If he says, 'Good!' it will be well with your servant, but if he is angry, then know that evil has been determined by him. [8]Therefore deal kindly with your servant, for you have brought your servant into a sacred covenant[j] with you. But if there is guilt in me, kill me yourself; why should you bring me to your father?" [9]Jonathan said, "Far be

g 19.16 Heb *the teraphim*   h 19.16 Meaning of Heb uncertain   i 19.20 Meaning of Heb uncertain   j 20.8 Heb *a covenant of the LORD*

such practices. See **"Apostasy," p. 1238**. **19:17** *Why have you deceived me?* Another woman will ask Saul the same question in 1 Sam. 28:12. The plot of the deceived becoming the deceiver (alongside the sister-wives motif and hiding idols) also appears in the story of Jacob, Laban, Rachel, and Leah (Gen. 29–31; see note on 18:20–27 for sister-wives motif). **19:18** Samuel has been absent from the narrative since he anointed David in chap. 16. The word *Ramah* can mean "high place," but it can also connote "deceit," as it comes from the same root as the word in 19:17 (see note), which has thematic significance. When David gets to Ramah, he tells Samuel *all that Saul had done to him*, which was a large ruse to control or exterminate David. They settle in Naioth, which denotes a place of rest or settling.

19:18–24 David and Saul at Ramah. 19:20–24 *Prophetic frenzy*. The ecstatic state of the group is the same as Saul's in 18:10 (see note on 18:10). This time, when Saul falls into the prophetic state, it is the result of "the spirit of God" rather than an "evil spirit." **19:24** *He, too*. Emphasis is placed on Saul's participation in the prophetic rite; he can still experience the spirit of God and be moved. *Naked*. The connotation of Saul's nakedness is unclear, though context suggests it is not negative—all the prophets stripped off their clothes, and the people conclude Saul is a prophet based on his actions, including this one.

20:1–42 Jonathan's devotion (episode 3). 20:5 *New moon*. The sign of the beginning of a new month; the moon was an important indicator of time in the ancient world, and its rhythms were celebrated (Num. 28:11–15). **20:6** *A yearly sacrifice*. A typical event for a family; one started the book

it from you! If I knew that it was decided by my father that evil should come upon you, would I not tell you?" [10]Then David said to Jonathan, "Who will tell me if your father answers you harshly?" [11]Jonathan replied to David, "Come, let us go out into the field." So they both went out into the field.

12 Jonathan said to David, "By the Lord, the God of Israel! When I have sounded out my father, about this time tomorrow or on the third day, if he is well disposed toward David, shall I not then send and disclose it to you? [13]But if my father intends to do you harm, the Lord do so to Jonathan and more also, if I do not disclose it to you and send you away, so that you may go in safety. May the Lord be with you, as he has been with my father. [14]If I am still alive, show me the faithful love of the Lord, but if I die,[k] [15]never cut off your faithful love from my house, even if the Lord were to cut off every one of the enemies of David from the face of the earth." [16]Thus Jonathan made a covenant with the house of David, saying, "May the Lord seek out the enemies of David." [17]Jonathan made David swear again by his love for him, for he loved him as he loved his own life.

18 Jonathan said to him, "Tomorrow is the new moon; you will be missed because your place will be empty. [19]On the day after tomorrow, you shall go a long way down; go to the place where you hid yourself earlier, and remain beside the stone there.[l] [20]I will shoot three arrows to the side of it, as though I shot at a mark. [21]Then I will send the boy, saying, 'Go, find the arrows.' If I say to the boy, 'Look, the arrows are on this side of you; collect them,' then you are to come, for, as the Lord lives, it is safe for you and there is no danger. [22]But if I say to the young man, 'Look, the arrows are beyond you,' then go, for the Lord has sent you away. [23]As for the matter about which you and I have spoken, the Lord be between you and me forever."

24 So David hid himself in the field. When the new moon came, the king sat at the feast to eat. [25]The king sat upon his seat, as at other times, upon the seat by the wall. Jonathan stood, while Abner sat by Saul's side, but David's place was empty.

26 Saul did not say anything that day, for he thought, "Something has befallen him; he is not clean; surely he is not clean." [27]But on the second day, the day after the new moon, David's place was empty. And Saul said to his son Jonathan, "Why has the son of Jesse not come to the feast, either yesterday or today?" [28]Jonathan answered Saul, "David earnestly asked leave of me to go to Bethlehem; [29]he said, 'Let me go, for our family is holding a sacrifice in the city, and my brother has commanded me to be there. So now, if I have found favor in your sight, let me get away and see my brothers.' For this reason he has not come to the king's table."

30 Then Saul's anger was kindled against Jonathan. He said to him, "You son of a rebellious woman![m] Do I not know that you have chosen the son of Jesse to your own shame and to the shame of your mother's nakedness? [31]For as long as the son of Jesse lives upon the earth, neither you nor your kingdom shall be established. Now send and bring him to me, for he shall surely die." [32]Then Jonathan answered his father Saul, "Why should he be put to death? What has he done?" [33]But Saul threw his spear at him to strike him, so Jonathan knew that it was the decision of his father to put David to death. [34]Jonathan sprang up[n] from the table in fierce anger and ate no food on the second day of the month, for he was grieved for David and because his father had disgraced him.

35 In the morning Jonathan went out into the field to the appointment with David, and with him was a little boy. [36]He said to the boy, "Run and find the arrows that I shoot." As the boy ran, he shot an arrow beyond him. [37]When the boy came to the place where Jonathan's arrow had fallen,

k 20.14 Gk: Meaning of Heb uncertain l 20.19 Meaning of Heb uncertain m 20.30 Cn Compare Q ms Gk: Meaning of MT uncertain n 20.34 Q ms Gk: MT *rose*

of 1 Samuel (1:3). **20:12–17** Jonathan and David swear their love for and commitment to each other once again (see 18:1–5). **20:28–29** Jonathan feeds Saul the lie David concocted in 20:6. Like his sister Michal, Jonathan is willing to deceive his father for David's sake (19:12, 17). **20:30–31** *You son of a rebellious woman . . . the shame of your mother's nakedness.* As the textual footnote indicates, the meaning of the phrase "rebellious woman" (v. 30) is difficult to translate appropriately, but it is most certainly derogatory. Saul is irate and insults his son's mother publicly, a low blow in any culture (see

Jonathan called after the boy and said, "Is the arrow not beyond you?" [38]Jonathan called after the boy, "Hurry, be quick, do not linger." So Jonathan's boy gathered up the arrows and came to his master. [39]But the boy knew nothing; only Jonathan and David knew the arrangement. [40]Jonathan gave his weapons to the boy and said to him, "Go and carry them to the city." [41]As soon as the boy had gone, David rose from beside the stone heap[o] and prostrated himself with his face to the ground. He bowed three times, and they kissed each other and wept with each other; David wept the more.[p] [42]Then Jonathan said to David, "Go in peace, since both of us have sworn in the name of the LORD, saying, 'The LORD shall be between me and you and between my descendants and your descendants forever.'" He got up and left, and Jonathan went into the city.[q]

21 [r]David came to Nob to the priest Ahimelech. Ahimelech came trembling to meet David and said to him, "Why are you alone and no one with you?" [2]David said to the priest Ahimelech, "The king has charged me with a matter and said to me, 'No one must know anything of the matter about which I send you and with which I have charged you.' I have made an appointment[s] with the young men for such and such a place. [3]Now then, what have you at hand? Give me five loaves of bread or whatever is here." [4]The priest answered David, "I have no ordinary bread at hand, only holy bread—provided that the young men have kept themselves from women." [5]David answered the priest, "Indeed, women have been kept from us as always when I go on an expedition; the vessels of the young men are holy even when it is a common journey; how much more today will their vessels be holy?" [6]So the priest gave him the holy bread, for there was no bread there except the bread of the Presence, which is removed from before the LORD, to be replaced by hot bread on the day it is taken away.

7 Now a certain man of the servants of Saul was there that day, detained before the LORD; his name was Doeg the Edomite, the chief of Saul's shepherds.

8 David said to Ahimelech, "Is there no spear or sword here with you? I did not bring my sword or my weapons with me because the king's business required haste." [9]The priest said, "The sword of Goliath the Philistine, whom you killed in the valley of Elah, is here wrapped in a cloth behind the ephod; if you will take that, take it, for there is none here except that one." David said, "There is none like it; give it to me."

o 20.41 Gk: Heb *from beside the south* p 20.41 Vg: Meaning of Heb uncertain q 20.42 This sentence is 21.1 in Heb r 21.1 21.2 in Heb s 21.2 Q ms Vg: Meaning of MT uncertain

Isa. 57:3 for a similar verbal assault). **20:41** *They kissed each other and wept.* Crying and kissing are not gendered behaviors in ancient Israelite culture. It is appropriate for David and Jonathan to express their feelings in this manner.

21:1–9 Ahimelech assists David. David continues to be on the run in 1 Sam. 21, going from place to place to meet other important characters as he did in 19:18 and 20:1. **21:1** *Nob.* David repeats the action of coming to a sacred person in a sacred place (19:18). **21:2** David lies to the priest, which continues the theme of deception. It may be that Ahimelech knows this (or figures it out) and plays along, making him the third person to help David evade Saul via duplicity (Michal and Jonathan do so in chaps. 19–20). **21:4** *Holy bread* is bread that has been sanctified and offered to God (see v. 6). *Young men have kept themselves from women.* A euphemism for refraining from sexual relations. Having sex made someone ritually unprepared to enter a holy place or eat holy food. One needed to be purified, usually by washing oneself, to be ready (Lev. 15, see esp. v. 18). **21:5** David suggests that his men always refrain from sexual relations when they are on a mission. *The vessels.* It is not clear if David is referring to the men and their body parts, their eating utensils, or other items. **21:6** *Bread of the Presence*, literally "bread of the face," is a technical term for the holy bread that is put in the presence (literally "before the face") of God (Lev. 24:6–9). **21:7** A narratorial aside that will become important later in chap. 22, when Doeg will report David's meeting with Ahimelech to King Saul (vv. 9–10). **21:9** The relic-like sword of Goliath now lies in a sacred shrine, wrapped in cloth and curtained by an ephod, a holy garment. Weaponry is highlighted throughout 1 Samuel, but this verse in particular exalts a sword—its famous ownership and exceptional form—a mythic motif in other ancient and medieval literature (e.g., Excalibur, Harpe, Kusanagi-no-Tsurugi, and Zulfiqar).

10 David rose and fled that day from Saul; he went to King Achish of Gath. ¹¹The servants of Achish said to him, "Is this not David the king of the land? Did they not sing to one another of him in dances,

'Saul has killed his thousands
    and David his ten thousands'?"

¹²David took these words to heart and was very much afraid of King Achish of Gath. ¹³So he changed his behavior before them; he pretended to be mad when in their presence.ᵗ He scratched marks on the doors of the gate and let his spittle run down his beard. ¹⁴Achish said to his servants, "Look, you see the man is mad; why then have you brought him to me? ¹⁵Do I lack madmen, that you have brought this fellow to play the madman in my presence? Shall this fellow come into my house?"

22 David left there and escaped to the cave of Adullam; when his brothers and all his father's house heard of it, they went down there to him. ²Everyone who was in distress, and everyone who was in debt, and everyone who was discontented gathered to him, and he became captain over them. Those who were with him numbered about four hundred.

3 David went from there to Mizpeh of Moab. He said to the king of Moab, "Please let my father and mother come to you, until I know what God will do for me." ⁴He left them with the king of Moab, and they stayed with him all the time that David was in the stronghold. ⁵Then the prophet Gad said to David, "Do not remain in the stronghold; leave and go into the land of Judah." So David left and went into the forest of Hereth.

6 Saul heard that David and those who were with him had been located. Saul was sitting at Gibeah, under the tamarisk tree on the height, with his spear in his hand, and all his servants were standing around him. ⁷Saul said to his servants who stood around him, "Hear now, you Benjaminites; will the son of Jesse give every one of you fields and vineyards? Will he make you all commanders of thousands and commanders of hundreds? ⁸Is that why all of you have conspired against me? No one discloses to me when my son makes a league with the son of Jesse; none of you is sorry for me or discloses to me that my son has stirred up my servant against me to lie in wait, as he is doing today." ⁹Doeg the Edomite, who was in charge of Saul's servants, answered, "I saw the son of Jesse coming to Nob, to Ahimelech son of Ahitub; ¹⁰he inquired of the LORD for him, gave him provisions, and gave him the sword of Goliath the Philistine."

11 The king sent for the priest Ahimelech son of Ahitub and for all his father's house, the priests who were at Nob, and all of them came to the king. ¹²Saul said, "Listen now, son of Ahitub." He answered, "Here I am, my lord." ¹³Saul said to him, "Why have you conspired against me, you and the son of

t 21.13 Heb *in their hands*

21:10–15 David seeks refuge with Achish (episode 1). 21:10 Now David has run out of safe persons and places (19:18; 20:1; 21:1). In order to hide from Saul, he attempts to become a refugee in Gath, a city in Philistia. Despite his efforts to appear nonthreatening, he is unwelcome and must leave (22:1). He will later be welcomed (chap. 27).

22:1–2 David gathers supporters. 22:2 Israel is not yet a strong nation-state, and people who are in need turn to charismatic leaders, especially military protectors, for help. The portrayal of David as a captain of the downtrodden reinforces his narrative role as the underdog, who will rise up to save himself and the people.

22:3–5 David's family takes refuge in Moab. 22:3 As in 21:10, David has to seek sanctuary in other countries. Because he is a threat to the king, his family is also at risk. In tribal societies, disputes were not seen as individual affairs but familial. **22:4–5** A *stronghold* was an enclosed and fortified area, designed for protection from external threats. **22:5** The *prophet Gad* first appears here in the Hebrew Bible, and it is unclear whether or not he is an Israelite prophet. Regardless, David trusts the divine messenger and follows his command. See also 2 Sam. 24:11–13, 18.

22:6–23 Saul executes the priests of Nob; Abiathar escapes. 22:6 *Sitting . . . under the tamarisk tree.* Sitting under a tree was common to find respite from the sun, but it may also signal Saul's leadership position (see also 1 Sam. 14:2 and Judg. 4:4–5). **22:9–10** The narratorial aside in 1 Sam. 21:7 now reveals its significance (see note on 21:7) and will lead to the doom of Nob. **22:13** *Why have you conspired against me.* Saul responds to Ahimelech's disloyalty as he did to Michal's (19:17)

Jesse, by giving him bread and a sword and by inquiring of God for him, so that he has risen against me to lie in wait, as he is doing today?"

14 Then Ahimelech answered the king, "Who among all your servants is so faithful as David? He is the king's son-in-law and is quick[u] to do your bidding and is honored in your house. [15]Is today the first time that I have inquired of God for him? By no means! Do not let the king impute anything to his servant or to any member of my father's house, for your servant has known nothing of all this, much or little." [16]The king said, "You shall surely die, Ahimelech, you and all your father's house." [17]The king said to the guard who stood around him, "Turn and kill the priests of the LORD, because their hand also is with David; they knew that he fled and did not disclose it to me." But the servants of the king would not raise a hand to attack the priests of the LORD. [18]Then the king said to Doeg, "You, Doeg, turn and attack the priests." Doeg the Edomite turned and attacked the priests; on that day he killed eighty-five who wore the linen ephod. [19]Nob, the city of the priests, he put to the sword; men and women, children and infants, oxen, donkeys, and sheep, he put to the sword.

20 But one of the sons of Ahimelech son of Ahitub, named Abiathar, escaped and fled after David. [21]Abiathar told David that Saul had killed the priests of the LORD. [22]David said to Abiathar, "I knew on that day, when Doeg the Edomite was there, that he would surely tell Saul. I am responsible[v] for the lives of all your father's house. [23]Stay with me, and do not be afraid, for the one who seeks my life seeks your life; you will be safe with me."

23 Now they told David, "The Philistines are fighting against Keilah and are robbing the threshing floors." [2]David inquired of the LORD, "Shall I go and attack these Philistines?" The LORD said to David, "Go and attack the Philistines and save Keilah." [3]But David's men said to him, "Look, we are afraid here in Judah; how much more then if we go to Keilah against the armies of the Philistines?" [4]Then David inquired of the LORD again. The LORD answered him, "Yes, go down to Keilah, for I will give the Philistines into your hand." [5]So David and his men went to Keilah, fought with the Philistines, brought away their livestock, and dealt them a heavy defeat. Thus David rescued the inhabitants of Keilah.

6 When Abiathar son of Ahimelech fled to David at Keilah, he came down with an ephod in his hand. [7]Now it was told Saul that David had come to Keilah. And Saul said, "God has given[w] him into my hand, for he has shut himself in by entering a town that has gates and bars." [8]Saul summoned all the people to war, to go down to Keilah, to besiege David and his men. [9]When David learned that Saul was plotting evil against

u 22.14 Heb *and turns aside*   v 22.22 Gk Vg: Meaning of Heb uncertain   w 23.7 Gk Tg: Heb *made a stranger of*

and Jonathan's (20:30). All three helped David escape by deceiving the king or his servants (see note on 21:2 for Ahimelech's less obvious trickery). **22:16–19** Saul commits an unconscionable crime by ordering the execution of innocent priests. His servants confirm the heinousness of the act by refusing to do it. Doeg the Edomite is willing, likely because he is not an Israelite. Ironically, even though Doeg is committing a great crime in Israel, he is obeying the command of his master in annihilating a people, which caused Saul to lose his kingship (chap. 15). **22:20** *Abiathar* is the son of Ahimelech who eventually becomes one of David's high priests—a powerful position in the kingdom. *But one . . . escaped*. The escape of one individual from a massacre is a motif in the Hebrew Bible (see, e.g., Judg. 9:5; 2 Kgs. 11:2; Job 1:15–19). In several cases, including this one, the escapee becomes a messenger of the terrible news. **22:22** *I knew on that day*. See notes on 1 Sam. 21:7 and 22:9–10.

23:1–5 David defends Keilah. 23:1 *Keilah* is a Judahite town. *Threshing floors* are areas where gathered grain was processed, separating the grain seeds from the stalks and husks. Robbing a whole town's threshing floors would mean starvation for the community. **23:2** *Inquired of the LORD*. Asking God whether or not one should attack an enemy was common practice in ancient Israel.

23:6–29 Saul pursues David; David escapes. 23:6 *Ephod*. See note on 14:3. **23:7** *For he has shut himself in by entering a town that has gates and bars*. Walled cities were meant to keep enemies out, but they could become traps for those within too. **23:9** *Bring the ephod here*. The ephod

him, he said to the priest Abiathar, "Bring the ephod here." [10]David said, "O LORD, the God of Israel, your servant has heard that Saul seeks to come to Keilah, to destroy the city on my account. [11]And now, will[x] Saul come down as your servant has heard? O LORD, the God of Israel, I beseech you, tell your servant." The LORD said, "He will come down." [12]Then David said, "Will the men of Keilah surrender me and my men into the hand of Saul?" The LORD said, "They will surrender you." [13]Then David and his men, who were about six hundred, set out and left Keilah; they wandered wherever they could go. When Saul was told that David had escaped from Keilah, he gave up the expedition. [14]David remained in the strongholds in the wilderness, in the hill country of the wilderness of Ziph. Saul sought him every day, but the LORD[y] did not give him into his hand.

15 David was in the wilderness of Ziph at Horesh when he learned that[z] Saul had come out to seek his life. [16]Saul's son Jonathan set out and came to David at Horesh; there he strengthened his hand through the LORD.[a] [17]He said to him, "Do not be afraid, for the hand of my father Saul shall not find you; you shall be king over Israel, and I shall be second to you; my father Saul also knows that this is so." [18]Then the two of them made a covenant before the LORD; David remained at Horesh, and Jonathan went home.

19 Then some Ziphites went up to Saul at Gibeah and said, "David is hiding among us in the strongholds of Horesh, on the hill of Hachilah, which is south of Jeshimon. [20]Now, O king, whenever you wish to come down, do so, and our part will be to surrender him into the king's hand." [21]Saul said, "May you be blessed by the LORD for showing me compassion! [22]Go and make sure once more; find out exactly where he is and who has seen him there, for I am told that he is very cunning. [23]Look around and learn all the hiding places where he lurks

and come back to me with sure information. Then I will go with you, and if he is in the land, I will search him out among all the thousands of Judah." [24]So they set out and went to Ziph ahead of Saul.

David and his men were in the wilderness of Maon, in the Arabah to the south of Jeshimon. [25]Saul and his men went to search for him. When David was told, he went down to the rock and stayed in the wilderness of Maon. When Saul heard that, he pursued David into the wilderness of Maon. [26]Saul went on one side of the mountain and David and his men on the other side of the mountain. David was hurrying to get away from Saul, while Saul and his men were closing in on David and his men to capture them. [27]Then a messenger came to Saul, saying, "Hurry and come, for the Philistines have made a raid on the land." [28]So Saul stopped pursuing David and went against the Philistines; therefore that place was called the Rock of Escape.[b] [29c]David then went up from there and lived in the strongholds of En-gedi.

24 When Saul returned from following the Philistines, he was told, "David is in the wilderness of En-gedi." [2]Then Saul took three thousand chosen men out of all Israel and went to look for David and his men in the direction of the Rocks of the Wild Goats. [3]He came to the sheepfolds beside the road, where there was a cave, and Saul went in to relieve himself.[d] Now David and his men were sitting in the innermost parts of the cave. [4]The men of David said to him, "Here is the day of which the LORD said to you, 'I will give your enemy into your hand, and you shall do to him as it seems good to you.'" Then David went and

x 23.11 Q ms Compare Gk: MT *Will the men of Keilah surrender me into his hand? Will* y 23.14 Q ms Gk: MT *God* z 23.15 Or *saw that* a 23.16 Gk Compare Q ms: MT *God* b 23.28 Or *Rock of Division*; meaning of Heb uncertain c 23.29 24.1 in Heb d 24.3 Heb *to cover his feet*

assists David in making contact with the divine and may help protect him. See 14:3, 18–19 and notes. **23:14** *Strongholds.* See note on 22:4–5. *The wilderness of Ziph* is a nearby area in the hill country of Judah. **23:15–18** A short rendezvous between Jonathan and David in which the authors—via the voice of Jonathan—reinforce their perspective: David should be king, not Saul. **23:19–28** Saul continues to pursue David and be thwarted; a doublet of this story (23:19–24:22) appears in chap. 26 (see the introductory note there for details). **23:28** *Therefore that place was called the Rock of Escape.* An etiology (see note on 5:5). **23:29** *Strongholds.* See note on 22:4–5. *En-gedi* is an oasis east of the wildernesses of Ziph and Maon, near the Dead Sea.

24:1–22 David spares and humiliates Saul (episode 1). 24:3 *Sheepfolds* are pens, or gated areas,

stealthily cut off a corner of Saul's cloak. [5]Afterward David was stricken to the heart because he had cut off a corner of Saul's cloak. [6]He said to his men, "The LORD forbid that I should do this thing to my lord, the LORD's anointed, to raise my hand against him, for he is the LORD's anointed." [7]So David rebuked his men severely and did not permit them to attack Saul. Then Saul got up and left the cave and went on his way.

8 Afterward David also rose up and went out of the cave and called after Saul, "My lord the king!" When Saul looked behind him, David bowed with his face to the ground and did obeisance. [9]David said to Saul, "Why do you listen to the words of those who say, 'David seeks to do you harm'? [10]This very day your eyes have seen how the LORD gave you into my hand in the cave, and some urged me to kill you, but I spared[e] you. I said, 'I will not raise my hand against my lord, for he is the LORD's anointed.' [11]See, my father, see the corner of your cloak in my hand, for by the fact that I cut off the corner of your cloak and did not kill you, you may know for certain that there is no wrong or treason in my hands. I have not sinned against you, though you are hunting me to take my life. [12]May the LORD judge between me and you! May the LORD avenge me on you, but my hand shall not be against you. [13]As the ancient proverb says, 'Out of the wicked comes forth wickedness,' but my hand shall not be against you. [14]Against whom has the king of Israel come out? Whom do you pursue? A dead dog? A single flea? [15]May the LORD, therefore, be judge and give sentence between me and you. May he see to it and plead my cause and vindicate me against you."

16 When David had finished speaking these words to Saul, Saul said, "Is this your voice, my son David?" Saul lifted up his voice and wept. [17]He said to David, "You are more righteous than I, for you have repaid me good, whereas I have repaid you evil. [18]Today you have explained how you have dealt well with me, in that you did not kill me when the LORD put me into your hands. [19]For who has ever found an enemy and sent the enemy safely away? So may the LORD reward you with good for what you have done to me this day. [20]Now I know that you shall surely be king and that the kingdom of Israel shall be established in your hand. [21]Swear to me, therefore, by the LORD that you will not cut off my descendants after me and that you will not wipe out my name from my father's house." [22]So David swore this to Saul. Then Saul went home, but David and his men went up to the stronghold.

25 Now Samuel died, and all Israel assembled and mourned for him. They buried him at his home in Ramah.

Then David got up and went down to the wilderness of Paran.

2 There was a man in Maon whose property was in Carmel. The man was very rich; he had three thousand sheep and a

e 24.10 Gk Syr Tg: Heb *it* (my eye) *spared*

for sheep. **24:6** *The LORD's anointed* is a title referring to the king, who is anointed as a symbol of divine appointment. **24:9–15** David chooses to confront Saul publicly, a shrewd political move. In Gen. 38, Tamar similarly uses Judah's personal items to call him out publicly. As a result, both are deemed more righteous by the accused (see v. 17 and Gen. 38:26). **24:12–15** *The LORD judge*. The God of Israel is commonly portrayed as a judge who will listen to arguments and mete out justice, especially to those wrongly accused. Here, David is making his case against Saul for unfairly accusing him of treason and harassment. He calls on the Lord to "avenge" (v. 12) and "vindicate" (v. 15) him from his oppressor. **24:17** *You have repaid me good, whereas I have repaid you evil*. The concept of repaying good and evil will reappear in the next story (25:21, 39), which encourages readers to compare and contrast the characters in each. See also 26:23. **24:21** *Cut off my descendants . . . wipe out my name*. Saul fears that David will massacre everyone in his family, which was not uncommon for kings to do when they took the throne from someone other than their biological father. If the family was eradicated, then a family line (name) would also be lost, which was a tragedy in ancient Israel. **24:22** David swears not to cut off Saul's family completely, but this will not stop him from nearly doing so. In 2 Sam. 21:1–9, he will give seven of Saul's sons to the Gibeonites so they can kill them. *Stronghold*. See note on 22:4–5.
   25:1a Samuel dies. A brief notification of the death of one of the three main characters in 1 Samuel.
   25:1b–42 The parable of Nabal and Abigail. 25:2 *There was a man. . . . The man was very rich*. A typical introduction to a parable or story with a moral (see note on 1:1), many of which feature a rich

thousand goats. He was shearing his sheep in Carmel. [3]Now the name of the man was Nabal, and the name of his wife was Abigail. The woman was clever and beautiful, but the man was surly and mean; he was a Calebite. [4]David heard in the wilderness that Nabal was shearing his sheep. [5]So David sent ten young men, and David said to the young men, "Go up to Carmel, and go to Nabal, and greet him in my name. [6]Thus you shall salute him, 'Peace be to you, and peace be to your house, and peace be to all that you have. [7]I hear that you have shearers; now your shepherds have been with us, and we did them no harm, and they missed nothing all the time they were in Carmel. [8]Ask your young men, and they will tell you. Therefore let my young men find favor in your sight, for we have come on a feast day. Please give whatever you have at hand to your servants and to your son David.'"

9 When David's young men came, they said all this to Nabal in the name of David, and then they waited. [10]But Nabal answered David's servants, "Who is David? Who is the son of Jesse? There are many servants today who are breaking away from their masters. [11]Shall I take my bread and my water and the meat that I have butchered for my shearers and give it to men who come from I do not know where?" [12]So David's young men turned away and came back and told him all this. [13]David said to his men, "Every man strap on his sword!" And every one of them strapped on his sword; David also strapped on his sword, and about four hundred men went up after David, while two hundred remained with the baggage.

14 But one of the young men told Abigail, Nabal's wife, "David sent messengers out of the wilderness to salute our master, and he shouted insults at them. [15]Yet the men were very good to us, and we suffered no harm, and we never missed anything when we were in the fields as long as we were with them; [16]they were a wall to us both by night and by day, all the while we were with them keeping the sheep. [17]Now, therefore, know this and consider what you should do, for evil has been decided against our master and against all his house; he is so ill-natured that no one can speak to him."

18 Then Abigail hurried and took two hundred loaves, two skins of wine, five sheep ready dressed, five measures of parched grain, one hundred clusters of raisins, and two hundred cakes of figs. She loaded them on donkeys [19]and said to her young men, "Go on ahead of me; I am coming after you." But she did not tell her husband Nabal. [20]As she rode on the donkey and came down under cover of the mountain, David and his men came down toward her, and she met them. [21]Now David had said, "Surely it was in vain that I protected all that this fellow has in the wilderness, so that nothing was missed of all that belonged to him, but he has returned me evil for good. [22]God do so to David[f] and more also if by morning I leave so much as one male of all who belong to him."

23 When Abigail saw David, she hurried and dismounted from the donkey and fell before David on her face, bowing to the ground. [24]She fell at his feet and said, "Upon me alone, my lord, be the guilt; please let your servant speak in your ears and hear the words of your servant. [25]My lord, do not take seriously this ill-natured fellow, Nabal, for as his name is, so is he; Nabal[g] is

f 25.22 Gk Compare Syr: Heb *the enemies of David*
g 25.25 That is, *fool*

fool and/or wise hero. Saul's story also begins this way in 9:1, where his father is introduced as a rich man. The reader is implicitly drawn to consider the similarities between the fools, Nabal and Saul, in contrast to the clever schemers, Abigail and David. **25:3** Nabal means "fool" and Abigail means "joy of my father." Their names reinforce the parabolic nature of the story, as do the contrasting descriptions that mirror their names (see previous note). **25:5–8** Requesting hospitality while in someone's territory was common. **25:10–11** Nabal's response is disrespectful by ancient and modern standards. **25:18** Abigail responds with hospitality, though it is arguably a meager meal for six hundred soldiers (see v. 13). That said, she could not have been readily prepared for so many unplanned guests. She may have taken everything she had. *Hurried*. Individuals who "hurry" when showing hospitality are portrayed as virtuous—Abraham and his servant (Gen. 18:6–7), Rebekah (Gen. 24:18, 20, 46), Abigail, and the medium at Endor (1 Sam. 28:24). **25:19** *Did not tell*. See note on 10:16. **25:21** *But he has returned me evil for good*. See note on 24:17. **25:23–31** Abigail, in her great sagacity, shows extreme deference to David and flatters him in order to obtain her desire—the security of her household. **25:25** *Nabal*. See note on

his name, and folly is with him, but I, your servant, did not see the young men of my lord, whom you sent.

26 "Now then, my lord, as the LORD lives and as you yourself live, since the LORD has restrained you from bloodguilt and from taking vengeance with your own hand, now let your enemies and those who seek to do evil to my lord be like Nabal. ²⁷And now let this present that your servant has brought to my lord be given to the young men who follow my lord. ²⁸Please forgive the trespass of your servant, for the LORD will certainly make my lord a sure house, because my lord is fighting the battles of the LORD, and evil shall not be found in you so long as you live. ²⁹If anyone should rise up to pursue you and to seek your life, the life of my lord shall be bound in the bundle of the living under the care of the LORD your God, but the lives of your enemies he shall sling out as from the hollow of a sling. ³⁰When the LORD has done to my lord according to all the good that he has spoken concerning you and has appointed you prince over Israel, ³¹my lord shall have no cause of grief or pangs of conscience for having shed blood without cause or for having saved himself. And when the LORD has dealt well with my lord, then remember your servant."

32 David said to Abigail, "Blessed be the LORD, the God of Israel, who sent you to meet me today! ³³Blessed be your good sense, and blessed be you, who kept me today from bloodguilt and from avenging myself by my own hand! ³⁴For as surely as the LORD the God of Israel lives, who has restrained me from hurting you, unless you had hurried and come to meet me, truly by morning there would not have been left to

Nabal so much as one male." ³⁵Then David received from her hand what she had brought him; he said to her, "Go up to your house in peace; see, I have heeded your voice, and I have granted your petition."

36 Abigail came to Nabal; he was holding a feast in his house like the feast of a king. Nabal's heart was merry within him, for he was very drunk, so she told him nothing at all until the morning light. ³⁷In the morning, when the wine had gone out of Nabal, his wife told him these things, and his heart died within him; he became like a stone. ³⁸About ten days later the LORD struck Nabal, and he died.

39 When David heard that Nabal was dead, he said, "Blessed be the LORD, who has judged the case of Nabal's insult to me and has kept back his servant from evil; the LORD has returned the evildoing of Nabal upon his own head." Then David sent word to Abigail to make her his wife. ⁴⁰When David's servants came to Abigail at Carmel, they said to her, "David has sent us to you to take you to him as his wife." ⁴¹She rose and bowed down, with her face to the ground, and said, "Your servant is a slave to wash the feet of the servants of my lord." ⁴²Abigail got up hurriedly and rode away on a donkey; her five maids attended her. She went after the messengers of David and became his wife.

43 David also married Ahinoam of Jezreel; both of them became his wives. ⁴⁴Saul had given his daughter Michal, David's wife, to Palti son of Laish, who was from Gallim.

26 Then the Ziphites came to Saul at Gibeah, saying, "David is in hiding on the hill of Hachilah, which is opposite

25:3. **25:28** *The LORD will certainly make my lord a sure house* is an implicit nod to David's upcoming kingship. **25:30** *Appointed you prince over Israel* is a more explicit nod to David's supplantation of Saul. **25:32–42** The moralistic tale ends with the wise and foolish persons "getting what they deserve": Abigail, life; and Nabal, death. See note on 24:17. **25:33** *By my own hand.* An ominous detail (see vv. 38–39). **25:39** *To make her his wife.* David is quick to take widows as wives (see 2 Sam. 11:26–27).

25:43–44 David's wives. David strategically marries women from the various lands and tribes. Many ancient leaders did so to secure political alliances. **25:44** *Saul had given his daughter Michal, David's wife.* Earlier (1 Sam. 18:19), Saul had given his elder daughter, Merab, who was promised to David, to Adriel the Meholathite. Here, it says he gives Michal, who is already David's wife, to Palti son of Laish. Later, in 27:3, David takes "his two wives, Ahinoam and Abigail" to Gath (the daughters of Saul are absent from the list of wives). Finally, in 2 Sam. 3:14–16, David takes Michal back from Palti (called Paltiel).

26:1–25 David spares and humiliates Saul (episode 2). A doublet of the episodes in 23:19–24:22. Doublets, two variations of the same story, occur throughout the Hebrew Bible. While some scholars

Jeshimon."[b] [2]So Saul rose and went down to the wilderness of Ziph, with three thousand chosen men of Israel, to seek David in the wilderness of Ziph. [3]Saul encamped on the hill of Hachilah, which is opposite Jeshimon,[i] beside the road. But David remained in the wilderness. When he learned that Saul had come after him into the wilderness, [4]David sent out spies and learned that Saul had indeed arrived. [5]Then David set out and came to the place where Saul had encamped, and David saw the place where Saul lay, with Abner son of Ner, the commander of his army. Saul was lying within the encampment, while the army was encamped around him.

6 Then David said to Ahimelech the Hittite and to Joab's brother Abishai son of Zeruiah, "Who will go down with me into the camp to Saul?" Abishai said, "I will go down with you." [7]So David and Abishai went to the army by night; there Saul lay sleeping within the encampment, with his spear stuck in the ground at his head, and Abner and the army lay around him. [8]Abishai said to David, "God has given your enemy into your hand today; now, therefore, let me pin him to the ground with one stroke of the spear; I will not strike him twice." [9]But David said to Abishai, "Do not destroy him, for who can raise his hand against the LORD's anointed and be guiltless?" [10]David said, "As the LORD lives, the LORD will strike him down, or his day will come to die, or he will go down into battle and perish. [11]The LORD forbid that I should raise my hand against the LORD's anointed, but now take the spear that is at his head and the water jar, and let us go." [12]So David took the spear that was at Saul's head and the water jar, and they went away. No one saw it or knew it, nor did anyone awake, for they were all asleep, because a deep sleep from the LORD had fallen upon them.

13 Then David went over to the other side and stood on top of a hill far away, with a great distance between them. [14]David called to the army and to Abner son of Ner, saying, "Abner! Will you not answer?" Then Abner replied, "Who are you who calls to the king?" [15]David said to Abner, "Are you not a man? Who is like you in Israel? Why then have you not kept watch over your lord the king? For one of the people came in to destroy your lord the king. [16]This thing that you have done is not good. As the LORD lives, you deserve to die because you have not kept watch over your lord, the LORD's anointed. See now, where is the king's spear or the water jar that was at his head?"

17 Saul recognized David's voice and said, "Is this your voice, my son David?" David said, "It is my voice, my lord, O king." [18]And he added, "Why does my lord pursue his servant? For what have I done? What guilt is on my hands? [19]Now, therefore, let my lord the king hear the words of his servant. If it is the LORD who has stirred you up against me, may he accept an offering, but if it is mortals, may they be cursed before the LORD, for they have driven me out today from my share in the heritage of the LORD, saying, 'Go, serve other gods.' [20]Now therefore, do not let my blood fall to the ground away from the presence of the LORD, for the king of Israel has come out to seek a single flea, like one who hunts a partridge in the mountains."

21 Then Saul said, "I have done wrong; come back, my son David, for I will never

b 26.1 Or *opposite the wasteland*   i 26.3 Or *opposite the wasteland*

think this is a literary technique, others believe it is the result of multiple oral (and/or written) variants, derived from one original tradition, being edited together later in time. These two theories need not always be mutually exclusive. **26:6** *Ahimelech the Hittite and to Joab's brother Abishai.* Until now, most of David's men have not been identified. **26:10** *The LORD will strike him down . . . or he will go down into battle and perish.* The first phrase is an allusion to the death of Nabal (who symbolically represents Saul; 1 Sam. 25:38) and the second a foreshadowing of Saul's future (31:4). **26:12** *A deep sleep from the LORD* is a reminder that God is in control of the unfolding events (see also Gen. 2:21; 15:12; Isa. 29:10). **26:13–16** David's public shaming of Abner is an extension of his humiliation of Saul in vv. 18–20; the servant's failure is a reflection on his master, the king. **26:16** *The king's spear or the water jar.* See note on 24:9–15. **26:19** *Driven me out today from my share in the heritage of the LORD, saying, 'Go, serve other gods.'* In the ancient Near East, one worshiped the local gods. Since David is being run out of the land (the heritage), the implication is that he is also being forced to worship the gods of the lands in which he has taken refuge (i.e., not the Lord), neither of which he wants to do.

harm you again, because my life was precious in your sight today; I have been a fool and have made a great mistake." ²²David replied, "Here is the spear, O king! Let one of the young men come over and get it. ²³The LORD rewards everyone for his righteousness and his faithfulness, for the LORD gave you into my hand today, but I would not raise my hand against the LORD's anointed. ²⁴As your life was precious today in my sight, so may my life be precious in the sight of the LORD, and may he rescue me from all tribulation." ²⁵Then Saul said to David, "Blessed be you, my son David! You will do many things and will succeed in them." So David went his way, and Saul returned to his place.

27 David said in his heart, "I shall certainly perish one day by the hand of Saul; there is nothing better for me than to escape to the land of the Philistines; then Saul will despair of seeking me any longer within the borders of Israel, and I shall escape out of his hand." ²So David set out and went over, he and the six hundred men who were with him, to King Achish son of Maoch of Gath. ³David stayed with Achish at Gath, he and his troops, every man with his household, and David with his two wives, Ahinoam of Jezreel and Abigail of Carmel, Nabal's widow. ⁴When Saul was told that David had fled to Gath, he no longer sought for him.

5 Then David said to Achish, "If I have found favor in your sight, let a place be given me in one of the country towns so that I may live there, for why should your servant live in the royal city with you?" ⁶So that day Achish gave him Ziklag; therefore Ziklag has belonged to the kings of Judah to this day. ⁷The length of time that David lived in the country of the Philistines was one year and four months.

8 Now David and his men went up and made raids on the Geshurites, the Girzites, and the Amalekites, for these were the landed settlements from Telam[j] on the way to Shur and on to the land of Egypt. ⁹David struck the land, leaving neither man nor woman alive, but took away the sheep, the oxen, the donkeys, the camels, and the clothing and came back to Achish. ¹⁰When Achish asked, "Against whom[k] have you made a raid today?" David would say, "Against the Negeb of Judah," or "Against the Negeb of the Jerahmeelites," or "Against the Negeb of the Kenites." ¹¹David left neither man nor woman alive to be brought back to Gath, thinking, "They might tell about us and say, 'David has done so and so.'" Such was his practice all the time he lived in the country of the Philistines. ¹²Achish trusted David, thinking, "He has made himself utterly abhorrent to his people Israel; therefore he shall always be my servant."

28 In those days the Philistines gathered their forces for war, to fight against Israel. Achish said to David, "You know, of course, that you and your men are to go out with me in the army." ²David said to Achish, "Very well, then you shall know what your servant can do." Achish said to David, "Very well, I will make you my bodyguard for life."

3 Now Samuel had died, and all Israel had mourned for him and buried him in Ramah,

j 27.8 Compare Gk 15.4: Heb *from of old*   k 27.10 Q ms Gk Vg: MT lacks *whom*

27:1–28:2 David seeks refuge with Achish (episode 2) and acquires Ziklag. 27:2 *King Achish*: David stayed with Achish previously (see 21:10–15). This time, he has a larger retinue and requests land. **27:6** *Therefore Ziklag has belonged to the kings of Judah to this day*. An etiology (see note on 5:5). **27:8** *Amalekites*. Saul supposedly destroyed all the Amalekites (15:8). Such discrepancies are common in the Hebrew Bible, particularly in Joshua–2 Kings. **27:10–12** David tells Achish that he is raiding territories of the Judahites (his own people) and their allies (Jerahmeelites and Kenites) in order to maintain his appearance as a defector, when he is actually raiding enemy territories. In order to keep his secret, he kills everyone who might reveal it. **28:1–2** David has made an alliance with the Philistine king. David verbally affirms his loyalty to Achish by committing to fight against his own people (although see chap. 29).

28:3–25 Saul and the medium at Endor; Samuel prophesies Saul's death. 28:3 *Expelled the mediums and the wizards*. Individuals in the trades of talking to the dead, divining, and giving oracles. These professionals were often otherized in the Hebrew Bible as "religiously foreign" and could be put to death (Lev. 19:31; 20:6, 27; Deut. 18:11). However, as the story suggests, they were living

his own city. Saul had expelled the mediums and the wizards from the land. ⁴The Philistines assembled and came and encamped at Shunem. Saul gathered all Israel, and they encamped at Gilboa. ⁵When Saul saw the army of the Philistines, he was afraid, and his heart trembled greatly. ⁶When Saul inquired of the Lᴏʀᴅ, the Lᴏʀᴅ did not answer him, not by dreams or by Urim or by prophets. ⁷Then Saul said to his servants, "Seek out for me a woman who is a medium, so that I may go to her and inquire of her." His servants said to him, "There is a medium at Endor."

8 So Saul disguised himself and put on other clothes and went there, he and two men with him. They came to the woman by night. And he said, "Consult a spirit for me, and bring up for me the one whom I name to you." ⁹The woman said to him, "Surely you know what Saul has done, how he has cut off the mediums and the wizards from the land. Why then are you laying a snare for my life to bring about my death?" ¹⁰But Saul swore to her by the Lᴏʀᴅ, "As the Lᴏʀᴅ lives, no punishment shall come upon you for this thing." ¹¹Then the woman said, "Whom shall I bring up for you?" He answered, "Bring up Samuel for me." ¹²When the woman saw Samuel, she cried out with a loud voice, and the woman said to Saul, "Why have you deceived me? You are Saul!" ¹³The king said to her, "Have no fear; what do you see?" The woman said to Saul, "I see a divine being*ˡ* coming up out of the ground." ¹⁴He said to her, "What is his appearance?" She said, "An old man is coming up; he is wrapped

in a robe." So Saul knew that it was Samuel, and he bowed with his face to the ground and did obeisance.

15 Then Samuel said to Saul, "Why have you disturbed me by bringing me up?" Saul answered, "I am in great distress, for the Philistines are warring against me, and God has turned away from me and answers me no more, either by prophets or by dreams, so I have summoned you to tell me what I should do." ¹⁶Samuel said, "Why then do you ask me, since the Lᴏʀᴅ has turned from you and become your enemy? ¹⁷The Lᴏʀᴅ has done to you just as he spoke by me, for the Lᴏʀᴅ has torn the kingdom out of your hand and given it to your neighbor, David. ¹⁸Because you did not obey the voice of the Lᴏʀᴅ and did not carry out his fierce wrath against Amalek, therefore the Lᴏʀᴅ has done this thing to you today. ¹⁹Moreover, the Lᴏʀᴅ will give Israel along with you into the hands of the Philistines, and tomorrow you and your sons shall be with me; the Lᴏʀᴅ will also give the army of Israel into the hands of the Philistines."

20 Immediately Saul fell full length on the ground filled with fear because of the words of Samuel, and there was no strength in him, for he had eaten nothing all day and all night. ²¹The woman came to Saul, and when she saw that he was terrified, she said to him, "Your servant has listened to you; I have taken my life in my hand and have listened to what you have said to me. ²²Now, therefore, you also listen to your servant;

ˡ 28.13 Or *a god* or *gods*

within Israel and sought out for their abilities. **28:4** *Shunem* and *Gilboa* are cities in the Jezreel Valley in the north. **28:6** *Not by dreams or by Urim or by prophets.* Saul wants to know what to do, and he is getting desperate. He has tried the standard means of divine inquiry to no avail. *Urim*, often paired with Thummim, is a sacred object used to channel divine messages (see 1 Sam. 14:41–42 and its note). **28:7** *Medium.* The woman at Endor is not just any medium; she is a "baalat ov," literally a "master of spirits" or "lord of ghosts," suggesting she had great powers. *Endor* is a city just north of where the armies are encamped. **28:8** *Saul disguised himself. . . . by night:* Saul does not want to be caught in hypocrisy (v. 3), and he knows he would not be trusted undisguised. **28:12** *Why have you deceived me?* See note on 19:17. **28:13** *Divine being.* Heb. "elohim." See translational note below and note on 4:7–8. This use of "elohim" shows the word's range of meaning. *Coming up out of the ground.* The spirits of the dead—both good and evil—go down into Sheol, which is under the earth. **28:19** *Tomorrow you and your sons shall be with me.* Samuel is foretelling Saul's death and the death of his children. Prophets are well known for bringing devastating news, including death and national defeat, but the fact that Samuel is doing it from the grave is intense. **28:21** *Taken my life in my hand* is an idiomatic expression referring to risking one's life (see also 1 Sam. 19:5). **28:22** The medium exemplifies her kindness and wisdom by offering Saul something to eat and convincing him to take it. Her virtue is accentuated when she prepares the generous meal *quickly* (v. 24) as Abigail did for David (see note on 25:18).

let me set a morsel of bread before you. Eat, that you may have strength when you go on your way." [23]He refused and said, "I will not eat." But his servants, together with the woman, urged him, and he listened to their words. So he got up from the ground and sat on the bed. [24]Now the woman had a fatted calf in the house. She quickly slaughtered it, and she took flour, kneaded it, and baked unleavened cakes. [25]She put them before Saul and his servants, and they ate. Then they rose and went away that night.

29 Now the Philistines gathered all their forces at Aphek, while the Israelites were encamped by the spring that is in Jezreel. [2]As the lords of the Philistines were passing on by hundreds and by thousands and David and his men were passing on in the rear with Achish, [3]the commanders of the Philistines said, "What are these Hebrews doing here?" Achish said to the commanders of the Philistines, "Is this not David, the servant of King Saul of Israel, who has been with me now for days and years? Since he deserted to me I have found no fault in him to this day." [4]But the commanders of the Philistines were angry with him, and the commanders of the Philistines said to him, "Send the man back, so that he may return to the place that you have assigned to him; he shall not go down with us to battle, or else he may become an adversary to us in the battle. For how could this fellow reconcile himself to his lord? Would it not be with the heads of the men here? [5]Is this not David, of whom they sing to one another in dances,

'Saul has killed his thousands
and David his ten thousands'?"

6 Then Achish called David and said to him, "As the LORD lives, you have been honest, and to me it seems right that you should march out and in with me in the campaign, for I have found nothing wrong in you from the day of your coming to me until today. Nevertheless, the lords do not approve of you. [7]So go back now, and go peaceably; do nothing to displease the lords of the Philistines." [8]David said to Achish, "But what have I done? What have you found in your servant from the day I entered your service until now, that I should not go and fight against the enemies of my lord the king?" [9]Achish replied to David, "I know that you are as blameless in my sight as an angel of God; nevertheless, the commanders of the Philistines have said, 'He shall not go up with us to the battle.' [10]Now then, rise early in the morning, you and the servants of your lord who came with you, and go to the place that I appointed for you. As for the evil report, do not take it to heart, for you have done well before me.[m] Start early in the morning, and leave as soon as you have light." [11]So David set out with his men early in the morning, to return to the land of the Philistines. But the Philistines went up to Jezreel.

30 Now when David and his men came to Ziklag on the third day, the Amalekites had made a raid on the Negeb and on Ziklag. They had attacked Ziklag, burned it down, [2]and taken captive the women and all[n] who were in it, both small and great; they killed none of them but carried them off and went their way. [3]When David and his men came to the city, they found it burned down and their wives and sons and daughters taken captive. [4]Then David and the people who were with him raised their voices and wept until they had no more strength to weep. [5]David's two

m 29.10 Gk: Heb lacks *and go to the place . . . done well before me*   n 30.2 Gk: Heb lacks *and all*

29:1–11 Achish relieves David of mercenary duties. 29:3–4 Achish's men have a legitimate concern. David showed disloyalty to Saul by allying with a Philistine, which means he could do so again to Achish. Also, in 14:21, Israelite mercenaries turned on the Philistines during a battle with Saul and joined the ranks of the latter. **29:6** *You have been honest.* Achish has had the wool pulled over his eyes. David is not loyal to Achish or the Philistines. **29:9** *An angel of God.* Heb. "malakh"; "elohim" could also be translated as "messenger of God."

30:1–31 David avenges Ziklag and gathers supporters. 30:2 *Killed none of them.* The conflict between the Israelites and the Amalekites continues (see 15:8–26 and 27:8). In this episode, the Amalekites chose to take persons captive—a current narrative necessity, so that David can heroically save them. In the larger narrative of 1 Samuel, though, it is ironic, since Saul and David were said to have each attacked the Amalekites and left no one alive. **30:5** *David's two wives.*

wives also had been taken captive, Ahinoam of Jezreel and Abigail the widow of Nabal of Carmel. 6David was in great danger, for the people spoke of stoning him because all the people were bitter in spirit for their sons and daughters. But David strengthened himself in the LORD his God.

7 David said to the priest Abiathar son of Ahimelech, "Bring me the ephod." So Abiathar brought the ephod to David. 8David inquired of the LORD, "Shall I pursue this band? Shall I overtake them?" He answered him, "Pursue, for you shall surely overtake and shall surely rescue." 9So David set out, he and the six hundred men who were with him. They came to the Wadi Besor, where those stayed who were left behind. 10But David went on with the pursuit, he and four hundred men; two hundred stayed behind, too exhausted to cross the Wadi Besor.

11 In the open country they found an Egyptian and brought him to David. They gave him bread, and he ate; they gave him water to drink; 12they also gave him a piece of fig cake and two clusters of raisins. When he had eaten, his spirit revived, for he had not eaten bread or drunk water for three days and three nights. 13Then David said to him, "To whom do you belong? Where are you from?" He said, "I am a young man of Egypt, servant to an Amalekite. My master left me behind because I fell sick three days ago. 14We had made a raid on the Negeb of the Cherethites and on that which belongs to Judah and on the Negeb of Caleb, and we burned Ziklag down." 15David said to him, "Will you take me down to this raiding party?" He said, "Swear to me by God that you will not kill me or hand me over to my master, and I will take you down to them."

16 When he had taken him down, they were spread out all over the ground, eating and drinking and dancing, because of the great amount of spoil they had taken from the land of the Philistines and from the land of Judah. 17David attacked them from twilight until the evening of the next day. Not one of them escaped, except four hundred young men, who mounted camels and fled. 18David recovered all that the Amalekites had taken, and David rescued his two wives. 19Nothing was missing, whether small or great, sons or daughters, spoil or anything that had been taken; David brought back everything. 20David also captured all the flocks and herds, which were driven ahead of the other cattle; people said, "This is David's spoil."

21 Then David came to the two hundred men who had been too exhausted to follow David and who had been left at the Wadi Besor. They went out to meet David and to meet the people who were with him. When David drew near to the people, he saluted them. 22Then all the corrupt and worthless fellows among the men who had gone with David said, "Because they did not go with us, we will not give them any of the spoil that we have recovered, except that each man may take his wife and children and leave." 23But David said, "You shall not do so, my brothers, with what the LORD has given us; he has preserved us and handed over to us the raiding party that attacked us. 24Who would listen to you in this matter? For the share of the one who goes down into the battle shall be the same as the share of the one who stays by the baggage; they shall share alike." 25From that day forward he made it a statute and an ordinance for Israel; it continues to the present day.

26 When David came to Ziklag, he sent part of the spoil to his friends, the elders of Judah, saying, "Here is a present for you from the spoil of the enemies of the LORD." 27It was for those in Bethel, in Ramoth of the Negeb, in Jattir, 28in Aroer, in Siphmoth, in Eshtemoa, 29in Racal, in the towns of the Jerahmeelites, in the towns of the Kenites, 30in Hormah, in Bor-ashan, in Athach, 31in Hebron, all the places where David and his men had roamed.

See 25:42–44 and notes. **30:7** *Ephod.* See 23:9 and notes. **30:9–10** Two hundred of David's men stay behind because they are exhausted, likely from the six-day journey to and from Aphek, where they had intended to fight with King Achish. **30:11–15** The literary device of finding an enemy informer is also used in the deuterocanonical/apocryphal book of Judith. See **"Judith as Trickster," p. 1372**. **30:25** An etiology for the equal sharing of the spoil (see note on 5:5). **30:26–31** David is giving diplomatic gifts to appease much-needed allies for his imminent rise to the throne.

31 Now the Philistines fought against Israel, and the men of Israel fled before the Philistines, and many fell[o] on Mount Gilboa. ²The Philistines overtook Saul and his sons, and the Philistines killed Jonathan and Abinadab and Malchishua, the sons of Saul. ³The battle pressed hard on Saul, and the archers found him, and he was badly wounded by them. ⁴Then Saul said to his armor-bearer, "Draw your sword and thrust me through with it, so that these uncircumcised may not come and thrust me through and make sport of me." But his armor-bearer was unwilling, for he was terrified. So Saul took his own sword and fell on it. ⁵When his armor-bearer saw that Saul was dead, he also fell on his sword and died with him. ⁶So Saul and his three sons and his armor-bearer and all his men died together on the same day. ⁷When the men of Israel who were on the other side of the valley and those beyond the Jordan saw that the men of Israel had fled and that Saul and his sons were dead, they forsook their towns and fled, and the Philistines came and occupied them.

8 The next day, when the Philistines came to strip the dead, they found Saul and his three sons fallen on Mount Gilboa. ⁹They cut off his head, stripped off his armor, and sent messengers throughout the land of the Philistines to carry the good news to the houses of their idols and to the people. ¹⁰They put his armor in the temple of Astarte,[p] and they fastened his body to the wall of Beth-shan. ¹¹But when the inhabitants of Jabesh-gilead heard what the Philistines had done to Saul, ¹²all the valiant men set out, traveled all night long, and took the body of Saul and the bodies of his sons from the wall of Beth-shan. They came to Jabesh and burned them there. ¹³Then they took their bones and buried them under the tamarisk tree in Jabesh and fasted seven days.

o 31.1 Heb *and they fell slain*   *p* 31.10 Heb plural

31:1–13 The death and burial of Saul and his sons. **31:2** Samuel's prophecy in 28:19 begins to unfold as Saul's sons die in battle. **31:4** *Draw your sword and thrust me through*. Saul requests to die with dignity rather than be tortured by his enemies. *Uncircumcised*. See note on 14:6. *But his armor-bearer was unwilling*. Like Saul's men who refused to kill the priests at Nob, Saul's armor-bearer is disinclined to kill the king, the LORD's anointed. *So Saul took his own sword and fell on it*. Saul dies by his own hand rather than by the enemy's (cf. 2 Sam. 1:10). The biblical author does not comment on the moral or ethical implications of the act, though interpreters throughout the ages have hotly debated it. The same discussion arises regarding the choice of his armor-bearer (v. 5). **31:8–10** The Philistines desecrate the bodies of the dead and put them on display to intimidate their enemies—a familiar practice among ancient armies. *Astarte* is a local goddess who was associated with war as well as fertility. The Philistines place Saul's armor in her temple as a thanksgiving offering. *Beth-shan* is a nearby city in the Jezreel Valley; it means "house of peace," a tragic irony in this context. **31:11–12** *The valiant men* of Jabesh-Gilead honor the king and the dead. Saul once saved the people of Jabesh-Gilead from the Ammonites (11:1–11). *Burned them there*. The Israelites did not burn their dead; they buried them. It may be that the men wanted to prevent the Philistines from doing further harm. **31:13** *Buried them . . . fasted*. Burying the dead and mourning their loss was the standard custom.

2 SAMUEL

The Goal of 2 Samuel

An important goal of the Former Prophets / Historical Books in general and 2 Samuel in particular is to establish the legitimacy of David's reign and the significance of his dynasty. This last goal looms large in 2 Samuel and is discerned most clearly in 2 Sam. 7: God establishes a covenant with David, promising that a descendant of David will always sit on the throne in Jerusalem. We find explicit and implicit references to this Davidic covenant throughout both the Old and the New Testaments.

Portrayals of David: Different Lenses

The narrative about David extends from 1 Sam. 16 to 1 Kgs. 2, from David's introduction into the court of Saul to his death. The stories about David that we find in 1 Samuel are generally positive, emphasizing David's bravery, his loyalty, his leadership qualities. The portrayal of David that emerges from the stories in 2 Samuel is more complicated. In 2 Samuel, we have stories that depict a heroic David (e.g., 2 Sam. 2:1–7, when David becomes ruler over Judah; or 2 Sam. 12:26–31, when David gains control over the Ammonites) as well as stories that depict David as morally flawed and weak (David sleeping with Bathsheba and David's subsequent murder of Bathsheba's husband, Uriah the Hittite, in 2 Sam. 11; the rape of Tamar and Absalom's revenge in 2 Sam. 13:1–39).

David, on the basis of the stories of 1 Samuel and 2 Samuel, has been praised for his piety and extolled as an ideal king. We see this praise of David elsewhere in the Old Testament; in 1 Chronicles—a much later, postexilic, very positive retelling of the story of David—most of the stories reflecting David's flawed character are left out. Certainly, some of the stories in both 1 and 2 Samuel warrant the assessment of David as a pious, ideal king; the stories provide good reasons that David becomes the gold standard by which other kings are judged. So for example, in 2 Kgs. 22:2, speaking of Josiah, "He did what was right in the sight of the Lord and walked in all the way of his father David; he did not turn aside to the right or to the left." In 2 Sam. 7, the reader learns about God's covenant with David, promising him a descendant on the throne in Jerusalem, and we read of David's pious prayer. One of the more intriguing aspects of the stories in 2 Samuel is this: David is presented as a flawed character, with human faults, although one whom God favors (this is a motif that appears elsewhere in the Bible; for example, Jacob, Abraham's grandson who is not without his flaws, is the inheritor of the covenant made between God and his grandfather).

It is not easy to put David in a particular box on the basis of the 2 Samuel stories. Read with a certain lens, the picture of David in 2 Samuel is a positive one, but we catch glimpses through these twenty-four chapters of implicit (and sometimes explicit) criticisms of the powerful king. One example appears in 2 Sam. 11:1: "In the spring of the year, the time when kings go out to battle, David sent Joab with his officers and all Israel with him; they ravaged the Ammonites and besieged Rabbah. But David remained at Jerusalem." The criticism is clear: David was not doing what kings were supposed to do, and this led to an act of adultery and murder, an act that has consequences for David.

Even the first story of 2 Samuel can be read in different ways. In one reading, David is acting nobly to avenge the death of Saul, "the Lord's anointed" (2 Sam. 1:14), killed by an Amalekite. Read with a different lens (and the gaps in the story allow for this reading), David is working hard to avoid the charge of regicide, of king killing; he works to be seen as someone who honored Saul and respected him, wanting no part in his death. We are not told what David is thinking; we are not told what he considered his motivation; we are told only what he says to his men. From a certain lens, it is obvious that David is making sure—here as well as in the death of Saul's son Ishbaal in 2 Sam. 4—that he appears innocent of the blood of Saul and his son.

In the end, the portrayal of David in 2 Samuel is complex.

Reading Guide

Unlike other sections of the Former Prophets / Historical Books, where the stories often stand alone, the stories of 2 Samuel are a continuous narrative; we need to follow the thread of the stories to make sense of this narrative. David first appears in the middle of 1 Samuel: in the stories in 1 Sam. 16–31, David is introduced into the entourage of Saul; David's power, reputation, and influence grow; and eventually David has a falling out with Saul, but when an opportunity to kill Saul arises, David

does not take advantage of it. In 2 Samuel, the towering figure of David is front and center from the very beginning—stories of his triumphs and troubles are what this book contains. At the beginning of 2 Samuel, Saul has died, and an ambitious David is intent on consolidating his own leadership of the Israelites; this section ends with the capture of Jerusalem in 2 Sam. 5. From this point until the end of 2 Sam. 12, the stories revolve around the centralization of power in Jerusalem. David's trajectory is ever upward, it seems, from the stories in the first part of 2 Samuel. But toward the end of this section focusing on the centralization of power in Jerusalem, we find the story of Bathsheba and Uriah the Hittite, with David sleeping with Bathsheba and then murdering Bathsheba's husband, Uriah. The trials and tribulations that persist for the remainder of David's reign seem to stem from this deeply troubling episode. David repents his actions, prompted to do so by his prophet Nathan, but his adultery with Bathsheba and murder of Uriah stall the ever-upward trajectory of the stories. According to 2 Samuel, the loss of David's kingdom to his son Absalom follows closely upon the story of Bathsheba and Uriah the Hittite. In 2 Samuel, David is presented as a clever politician (2 Sam. 1), as a hero (2 Sam. 5, 6, 8), as an adulterer and a murderer (2 Sam. 11), as a king on the run (2 Sam. 15), as a grieving father (2 Sam. 18–19), and as a victorious warrior (2 Sam. 21). These twenty-four chapters of 2 Samuel contain some of the most dramatic (and disturbing) stories in the entire Hebrew Bible: we find stories of murder, deception, rape, hubris, and warfare, along with the linchpin story of God's covenant with David and his descendants (2 Sam. 7). At the end of 2 Samuel, we are left to wonder: What do we make of David? What do we think about him, as a person? How do these stories depict God?

Deirdre A. Dempsey

1 After the death of Saul, when David had returned from defeating the Amalekites, David remained two days in Ziklag. ²On the third day, a man came from Saul's camp with his clothes torn and dirt on his head. When he came to David, he fell to the ground and did obeisance. ³David said to him, "Where have you come from?" He said to him, "I have escaped from the camp of Israel." ⁴David said to him, "How did things go? Tell me!" He answered, "The army fled from the battle, but also many of the army fell and died, and Saul and his son Jonathan also died." ⁵Then David asked the young man who was reporting to him,

"How do you know that Saul and his son Jonathan died?" ⁶The young man reporting to him said, "I happened to be on Mount Gilboa, and there was Saul leaning on his spear, while the chariots and the horsemen drew close to him. ⁷When he looked behind him, he saw me and called to me. I answered, 'Here, sir.' ⁸And he said to me, 'Who are you?' I answered him, 'I am an Amalekite.' ⁹He said to me, 'Come, stand over me and kill me, for convulsions have seized me, and yet my life still lingers.' ¹⁰So I stood over him and killed him, for I knew that he could not live after he had fallen. I took the crown that was on his head and

1:1 *After the death of Saul, when David had returned from defeating the Amalekites, David remained two days in Ziklag.* According to the Hebrew Bible (HB), the Amalekites, based in the Negev, were longtime enemies of the Israelites (Num. 14:45; 21:3). At the end of 1 Samuel (1 Sam. 30), we read the story of an Amalekite raid on the town of Ziklag and David's subsequent battle against the Amalekites. In the next chapter, 1 Sam. 31, we read the story of the death of Saul at the hands of the Philistines. Second Samuel opens after David has returned to Ziklag after his battle with the Amalekites and after Saul's death at the hands of the Philistines. See **"Saul's Death," p. 424**.

1:2 *On the third day, a man came from Saul's camp.* Later in this chapter (v. 8), this man will identify himself as an Amalekite. Given David's recent battle against the Amalekites (and the fact that the story related by this Amalekite does not match the story of Saul's death related in 1 Sam. 31), we have to ask ourselves: What could this Amalekite have been thinking when he presented himself to David? The narrator leaves this question open, but it seems likely that the Amalekite thought that David might reward him in some way, since according to the Amalekite's story, he was the cause of Saul's death.

1:10 *I took the crown that was on his head and the armlet that was on his arm, and I have brought them here to my lord.* In 1 Sam. 15, Saul is ordered to exterminate all the Amalekites, but he fails to carry out this order; this disobedience results in the loss of his kingdom. Here in 2 Sam. 1, it is an Amalekite who presents the dead king's crown to David.

Going Deeper: Saul's Death (2 Samuel 1)

From the very first chapter, 2 Samuel raises questions that are hard to answer. A reader who comes to 2 Sam. 1 after having read 1 Sam. 31 might be puzzled—in these two chapters, one immediately following the other, the stories told of the death of Saul are different. In 1 Sam. 31:1–5, we find the story of Saul's suicide. Saul asks his armor-bearer to kill him, since he is wounded and does not want to fall into the hands of the Philistines while still alive. His armor-bearer refuses, so Saul then takes his own sword and falls on it. In 2 Sam. 1:9–10, the Amalekite tells David how a mortally wounded Saul asked the Amalekite to kill him, and he did so. There are other differences between the two stories: to name just two, in 1 Sam. 31:2, mention is made of three dead sons of Saul, while only Jonathan's death is mentioned in 2 Sam. 1:4. In 1 Sam. 31:3, Saul is in peril from the archers, while in 2 Sam. 1:6, the danger is from the chariots and the horsemen. Even an inattentive reader would recognize these differences and wonder. Some commentators have suggested that these two stories come from different traditions about the death of Saul—that is, that different stories were told about his death. Certainly, the editor of the narrative about David has combined different traditions elsewhere—for example, we have two stories about David's introduction to Saul's court, 1 Sam. 16 and 1 Sam. 17. Could there be another reason that the editor chose to include a story in 2 Sam. 1 that so obviously conflicts with the story of Saul's death in 1 Sam. 31? Later in 2 Samuel, we will encounter stories about David in which he appears somewhat gullible, not always capable of discerning the truth (2 Sam. 14, for example). Could this first story in 2 Samuel, in which David acts so decisively, be intended to present David on his upward trajectory, before he commits adultery with Bathsheba and murders Uriah the Hittite? Perhaps here, in 2 Sam. 1, the reader is intended to recognize that David immediately knows that he has been lied to, and that the Amalekite has stolen the crown and armlet from the body of Saul, bringing them to David because he assumed he would be rewarded.

Deirdre A. Dempsey

the armlet that was on his arm, and I have brought them here to my lord."

11 Then David took hold of his clothes and tore them, and all the men who were with him did the same. ¹²They mourned and wept and fasted until evening for Saul and for his son Jonathan and for the army of the Lord and for the house of Israel, because they had been struck down*a* by the sword. ¹³David said to the young man who had reported to him, "Where do you come from?" He answered, "I am the son of a resident alien, an Amalekite." ¹⁴David said to him, "Were you not afraid to lift your hand to destroy the Lord's anointed?" ¹⁵Then David called one of the young men and said, "Come here and strike him down." So he struck him down, and he died. ¹⁶David said to him, "Your blood be on your head, for your own mouth has testified against you, saying, 'I have killed the Lord's anointed.'"

a 1.12 Q ms Gk: Heb *had fallen*

1:11 *Then David took hold of his clothes and tore them.* Tearing clothes is a sign of mourning in the Bible (Gen. 37:34; 44:13; 2 Sam. 13:31). Our narrator is developing a theme that will continue in 2 Samuel: David appears loyal to Saul and not implicated in or pleased by Saul's death. And this surface reading might be the most accurate reading. It is also true that, in the course of 2 Samuel, David takes advantage of opportunities to rid himself of Saul's descendants (who would be potential rivals to the throne; 2 Sam. 21).

1:14 *Were you not afraid to lift your hand to destroy the Lord's anointed?* In 1 Sam. 31:4, Saul pleaded with his armor-bearer to kill him; the armor-bearer "was terrified" and refused. Earlier in 1 Samuel, David had used this title ("the Lord's anointed") when he spared Saul's life (1 Sam. 26:9). The reader of 2 Samuel who knows this earlier story in 1 Samuel knows what will happen to the Amalekite in 2 Sam. 1. In the HB, special offices were confirmed by anointing someone's head with oil; to be anointed meant to be designated for a particular task. Prophets were sometimes anointed, and Cyrus, the Persian king who frees the Jews from the Babylonian captivity, was called "anointed" (Isa. 45:1). The title is often used of David and the Davidic kings. "Christ," the title given to Jesus in the NT, comes into English from the Greek word "christos," which means "anointed."

17 David intoned this lamentation over Saul and his son Jonathan. [18](He ordered that The Song of the Bow[b] be taught to the people of Judah; it is written in the Book of Jashar.) He said,

19 "Your glory, O Israel, lies slain upon
    your high places!
  How the mighty have fallen!
20 Tell it not in Gath;
    proclaim it not in the streets of
      Ashkelon,
  or the daughters of the Philistines will
      rejoice;
    the daughters of the uncircumcised
      will exult.

21 You mountains of Gilboa,
    let there be no dew or rain upon you
      nor bounteous fields![c]
  For there the shield of the mighty was
      defiled,
    the shield of Saul, anointed with oil
      no more.

22 From the blood of the slain,
    from the fat of the mighty,
  the bow of Jonathan did not turn back,
    nor the sword of Saul return empty.

23 Saul and Jonathan, beloved and lovely!
    In life and in death they were not
      divided;
  they were swifter than eagles;
    they were stronger than lions.

24 O daughters of Israel, weep over Saul,
    who clothed you with crimson, in
      luxury,
  who put ornaments of gold on your
      apparel.

25 How the mighty have fallen
    in the midst of the battle!

Jonathan lies slain upon your high
    places.
26   I am distressed for you, my brother
      Jonathan;
  greatly beloved were you to me;
    your love to me was wonderful,
      passing the love of women.

27 How the mighty have fallen,
    and the weapons of war perished!"

2 After this David inquired of the LORD, "Shall I go up into any of the cities of Judah?" The LORD said to him, "Go up." David said, "To which shall I go up?" He said, "To Hebron." 2So David went up there, along with his two wives, Ahinoam of Jezreel and Abigail the widow of Nabal of Carmel. 3David brought up the men who were with him, every one with his household, and they settled in the towns of Hebron. 4Then the people of Judah came, and there they anointed David king over the house of Judah.

When they told David, "It was the people of Jabesh-gilead who buried Saul," 5David sent messengers to the people of Jabesh-gilead and said to them, "May you be blessed by the LORD, because you showed this loyalty to Saul your lord and buried him! 6Now may the LORD show steadfast love and faithfulness to you! And I, too, will reward you because you have done this thing. 7Therefore let your hands be strong and be valiant, for Saul your lord is dead, and the house of Judah has anointed me king over them."

b 1.18 Heb *that The Bow*   c 1.21 Meaning of Heb uncertain

1:18 *It is written in the Book of Jashar.* This book, mentioned also in Josh. 10:13, no longer exists. In later biblical books, we find references to other lost royal chronicles (e.g., in 1 Kgs. 14:19, there is mention of "the Book of the Annals of the Kings of Israel").

2:1 *After this David inquired of the LORD.* The first of several occasions in 2 Samuel when David seeks instruction from God. We are not given much detail about how this inquiring of the Lord happened. Perhaps the lots were used (1 Sam. 14:37–42; Jonah 1:7), or the king consulted a seer or a prophet (1 Sam. 28:6; 2 Sam. 7:2–3). There might have been different ways to cast lots—for example, using different marked stones, producing yes or no results.

2:4 *Then the people of Judah came, and there they anointed David king over the house of Judah.* David is anointed king over Judah, not over the territory of all the tribes of Israel. At this point, there are two kings: David and Saul's son, Ishbaal, set on the throne of his father by Abner, Saul's general. *It was the people of Jabesh-gilead who buried Saul.* Perhaps to prove his loyalty to Saul, David reaches out to praise and reward the inhabitants of Jabesh-gilead, who had endangered themselves to provide Saul with an honorable burial (1 Sam. 31:11–13).

8 But Abner son of Ner, commander of Saul's army, had taken Ishbaal[d] son of Saul and brought him over to Mahanaim. [9]He made him king over Gilead, the Ashurites, Jezreel, Ephraim, Benjamin, and all Israel. [10]Ishbaal,[e] Saul's son, was forty years old when he began to reign over Israel, and he reigned two years. But the house of Judah followed David. [11]The time that David was king in Hebron over the house of Judah was seven years and six months.

12 Abner son of Ner and the servants of Ishbaal[f] son of Saul went out from Mahanaim to Gibeon. [13]Joab son of Zeruiah and the servants of David went out and met them at the pool of Gibeon. One group sat on one side of the pool, while the other sat on the other side of the pool. [14]Abner said to Joab, "Let the young men come forward and have a contest before us." Joab said, "Let them come forward." [15]So they came forward and were counted as they passed by, twelve for Benjamin and Ishbaal[g] son of Saul and twelve of the servants of David. [16]Each grasped his opponent by the head and thrust his sword in his opponent's side, so they fell down together. Therefore that place was called Helkath-hazzurim,[h] which is at Gibeon. [17]The battle was very fierce that day, and Abner and the men of Israel were beaten by the servants of David.

18 The three sons of Zeruiah were there, Joab, Abishai, and Asahel. Now Asahel was as swift of foot as a wild gazelle. [19]Asahel pursued Abner, turning neither to the right nor to the left as he followed him. [20]Then Abner looked back and said, "Is it you, Asahel?" He answered, "Yes, it is." [21]Abner said to him, "Turn to your right or to your left, and seize one of the young men, and take his spoil." But Asahel would not turn away from following him. [22]Abner said again to Asahel, "Turn away from following me; why should I strike you to the ground? How then could I show my face to your brother Joab?"

[23]But he refused to turn away. So Abner struck him in the stomach with the butt of his spear, so that the spear came out at his back. He fell there and died where he lay. And all those who came to the place where Asahel had fallen and died stood still.

24 But Joab and Abishai pursued Abner. As the sun was going down they came to the hill of Ammah, which lies before Giah on the way to the wilderness of Gibeon. [25]The Benjaminites rallied around Abner and formed a single band; they took their stand on the top of a hill. [26]Then Abner called to Joab, "Is the sword to keep devouring forever? Do you not know that the end will be bitter? How long will it be before you order your people to turn from the pursuit of their kinsmen?" [27]Joab said, "As God lives, if you had not spoken, the people would have continued to pursue their kinsmen, not stopping until morning." [28]Joab sounded the trumpet, and all the people stopped; they no longer pursued Israel or engaged in battle any further.

29 Abner and his men traveled all that night through the Arabah; they crossed the Jordan, and, marching the whole forenoon,[i] they came to Mahanaim. [30]Joab returned from the pursuit of Abner, and when he had gathered all the people together, there were missing of David's servants nineteen men besides Asahel. [31]But the servants of David had killed of Benjamin three hundred sixty of Abner's men. [32]They took up Asahel and buried him in the tomb of his father, which was at Bethlehem. Joab and his men marched all night, and the day broke upon them at Hebron.

3 There was a long war between the house of Saul and the house of David; David grew stronger and stronger, while

d 2.8 Gk: Heb Ish-bosheth e 2.10 Gk: Heb Ish-bosheth
f 2.12 Gk: Heb Ish-bosheth g 2.15 Gk: Heb Ish-bosheth
h 2.16 That is, field of sword edges i 2.29 Meaning of Heb uncertain

2:8 *But Abner son of Ner, commander of Saul's army, had taken Ishbaal son of Saul and brought him over to Mahanaim.* Ishbaal's name in the Hebrew text is "Ish-bosheth," which means "man of shame." Hebrew scribes, copying down the stories of Saul's son, wanted to avoid the mention of the god Baal that appears in the name Ishbaal. They substituted the Hebrew word meaning "shame," so that instead of "man of Baal," the name reads "man of shame."

2:14 *Let the young men come forward and have a contest before us.* The combat that is described here is puzzling; it seems to be some sort of duel. Because the forces seem equally matched, the ritual ignites a war between David and his supporters on one side and those who still supported Saul's dynasty on the other side.

the house of Saul became weaker and weaker.

2 Sons were born to David at Hebron: his firstborn was Amnon, of Ahinoam of Jezreel; [3]his second was Chileab, of Abigail the widow of Nabal of Carmel; the third was Absalom son of Maacah, daughter of King Talmai of Geshur; [4]the fourth was Adonijah son of Haggith; the fifth was Shephatiah son of Abital; [5]and the sixth was Ithream, of David's wife Eglah. These were born to David in Hebron.

6 While there was war between the house of Saul and the house of David, Abner was making himself strong in the house of Saul. [7]Now Saul had a concubine whose name was Rizpah daughter of Aiah. And Ishbaal[j] said to Abner, "Why have you gone in to my father's concubine?" [8]The words of Ishbaal[k] made Abner very angry; he said, "Am I a dog's head for Judah? Today I keep showing loyalty to the house of your father Saul, to his brothers, and to his friends and have not given you into the hand of David, yet you charge me now with a crime concerning this woman. [9]So may God do to Abner and so may he add to it! For just what the LORD has sworn to David, that will I accomplish for him: [10]to transfer the kingdom from the house of Saul and set up the throne of David over Israel and over Judah, from Dan to Beer-sheba." [11]And Ishbaal[l] could not answer Abner another word because he feared him.

12 Abner sent messengers to David where he was,[m] saying, "To whom does the land belong? Make your covenant with me, and I will give you my support to bring all Israel over to you." [13]He said, "Good; I will make a covenant with you. But one thing I require of you: you shall never appear in my presence unless you bring Saul's daughter Michal when you come to see me." [14]Then David sent messengers to Saul's son Ishbaal,[n] saying, "Give me my wife Michal, to whom I became engaged at the price of one hundred foreskins of the Philistines." [15]Ishbaal[o] sent and took her from her husband Paltiel the son of Laish. [16]But her husband went with her, weeping as he walked behind her all the way to Bahurim. Then Abner said to him, "Go back home!" So he went back.

17 Abner sent word to the elders of Israel, saying, "For some time past you have been seeking David as king over you. [18]Now then bring it about, for the LORD has promised David: Through my servant David I will save my people Israel from the hand of the Philistines and from all their enemies." [19]Abner also spoke directly to the Benjaminites; then Abner went to tell David at Hebron all that Israel and the whole house of Benjamin were ready to do.

20 When Abner came with twenty men to David at Hebron, David made a feast for Abner and the men who were with him. [21]Abner said to David, "Let me go and rally all Israel to my lord the king, in order that they may make a covenant with you and that you may reign over all that your heart desires." So David dismissed Abner, and he went away in peace.

22 Just then the servants of David arrived with Joab from a raid, bringing much spoil with them. But Abner was not with David at Hebron, for David[p] had dismissed him, and he had gone away in peace. [23]When Joab and all the army that was with him came, it

j 3.7 Heb And he   k 3.8 Gk: Heb Ish-bosheth   l 3.11 Heb And he   m 3.12 Meaning of Heb uncertain   n 3.14 Heb Ish-bosheth   o 3.15 Heb Ish-bosheth   p 3.22 Heb he

3:7 *Why have you gone in to my father's concubine?* Ishbaal, growing weaker and weaker politically, is suspicious of Abner's ambitions; he accuses Abner of having sex with one of Saul's concubines (the Hebrew word that is translated as "concubine" is different from the word used for "wife"; a "concubine" did not have the same status in the family as a wife did). Having sex with a concubine of a king would have been a way of claiming political control and would have been an act of treason on Abner's part (2 Sam. 16:21).

3:8 *Am I a dog's head for Judah?* Abner's angry response to Ishbaal's accusation. This term, *dog's head*, occurs only here in the HB. Elsewhere we find "dog" used as a term of self-deprecation (1 Sam. 17:43; 2 Kgs. 8:13). Ishbaal's accusation seems to be the last straw for Abner, who subsequently offers "to bring all Israel" over to David's side (3:12).

3:13 *Saul's daughter Michal.* This request demonstrates David's political abilities. Michal's return (she was taken away from him by Saul in 1 Sam. 25:44) will enable David to rule in her stead and will give him a footing in Saul's dynasty.

was told to Joab, "Abner son of Ner came to the king, and he has dismissed him, and he has gone away in peace." ²⁴Then Joab went to the king and said, "What have you done? Abner came to you; why did you dismiss him, so that he got away? ²⁵You know that Abner son of Ner came to deceive you and to learn your comings and goings and to learn all that you are doing."

26 When Joab came out from David's presence, he sent messengers after Abner, and they brought him back from the cistern of Sirah, but David did not know about it. ²⁷When Abner returned to Hebron, Joab took him aside in the gateway to speak with him privately, and there he stabbed him in the stomach. So he died on account of the blood of Asahel, Joab's*q* brother. ²⁸Afterward, when David heard of it, he said, "I and my kingdom are forever guiltless before the LORD for the blood of Abner son of Ner. ²⁹May the bloodguilt fall on the head of Joab and on all his father's house, and may the house of Joab never be without one who has a discharge, or who has a defiling skin disease, or who holds a spindle, or who falls by the sword, or who lacks food!" ³⁰So Joab and his brother Abishai murdered Abner because he had killed their brother Asahel in the battle at Gibeon.

31 Then David said to Joab and to all the people who were with him, "Tear your clothes, put on sackcloth, and mourn over Abner." And King David followed the bier. ³²They buried Abner at Hebron. The king lifted up his voice and wept at the grave of Abner, and all the people wept. ³³The king lamented for Abner, saying,

"Should Abner die as a fool dies?
³⁴ Your hands were not bound;
    your feet were not fettered;
as one falls before the wicked
    you have fallen."

And all the people wept over him again. ³⁵Then all the people came to persuade David to eat something while it was still day, but David swore, saying, "So may God do to me and more, if I taste bread or anything else before the sun goes down!" ³⁶All the people took notice of it, and it pleased them, just as everything the king did pleased all the people. ³⁷So all the people and all Israel understood that day that the king had no part in the killing of Abner son of Ner. ³⁸And the king said to his servants, "Do you not know that a prince and a great man has fallen this day in Israel? ³⁹Today I am powerless, even though anointed king; these men, the sons of Zeruiah, are too violent for me. The LORD pay back the one who does wickedly in accordance with his wickedness!"

4 When Saul's son Ishbaal*r* heard that Abner had died at Hebron, his courage failed, and all Israel was dismayed. ²Saul's son had two captains of raiding bands; the name of the one was Baanah, and the name of the other was Rechab. They were sons of Rimmon, a Benjaminite from Beeroth, for Beeroth is considered to belong to Benjamin. ³(Now the people of Beeroth had fled to Gittaim and are there as resident aliens to this day.)

4 Saul's son Jonathan had a son who was crippled in his feet. He was five years old

q 3.27 Heb *his*   *r* 4.1 Heb lacks *Ishbaal*

3:27 *And there he stabbed him in the stomach.* Abner had killed Joab's brother Asahel; this is given as the reason Joab killed Abner. The narrator makes a point of emphasizing, in the verses following 3:27, that David knew nothing of Joab's murderous intentions. David curses Joab (3:29) and orders a period of mourning for Abner.

3:29 *Who holds a spindle.* Instead of sword-wielding warriors, Joab's house should have weavers who hold spindles, which are tools for weaving. David is faced with a dilemma when Joab kills Abner. David is eager to make sure that his alliance with Abner will continue, even when the followers of Ishbaal and Abner hear that Abner was killed by Joab, David's general. David declares that he and his kingdom are innocent of Abner's blood; he casts the blame on Joab.

3:33 *The king lamented for Abner, saying, "Should Abner die as a fool dies?"* David maintains, in his lament, that Abner did *not* die as a fool. Abner had returned to Hebron and went with Joab, unforced, into a confined space, circumstances that might suggest that Abner did not pay enough attention to the danger. David emphasizes that Abner died because of the wickedness of Joab. David does convince the people that he is not complicit in the death of Abner (2 Sam. 3:36–37).

4:4 *His name was Mephibosheth.* There are two people in 2 Samuel who have this name. The son of Jonathan is mentioned here and again in 2 Sam. 9:3, 6–7; 16:1–4; 21:7. Another Mephibosheth (the

when the news about Saul and Jonathan came from Jezreel. His nurse picked him up and fled, and in her haste to flee it happened that he fell and became lame. His name was Mephibosheth.

5 Now the sons of Rimmon the Beerothite, Rechab and Baanah, set out, and about the heat of the day they came to the house of Ishbaal[s] while he was taking his noonday rest. [6]They came inside the house as though to take wheat,[t] and they struck him in the stomach; then Rechab and his brother Baanah escaped. [7]Now they had come into the house while he was lying on his couch in his bedchamber; they attacked him, killed him, and beheaded him. Then they took his head and traveled by way of the Arabah all night long. [8]They brought the head of Ishbaal[u] to David at Hebron and said to the king, "Here is the head of Ishbaal[v] son of Saul, your enemy who sought your life; the LORD has avenged my lord the king this day on Saul and on his offspring."

[9] David answered Rechab and his brother Baanah, the sons of Rimmon the Beerothite, "As the LORD lives, who has redeemed my life out of every adversity, [10]when the one who told me, 'See, Saul is dead,' thought he was bringing good news, I seized him and killed him at Ziklag—this was the reward I gave him for his news. [11]How much more, then, when wicked men have killed a righteous man on his bed in his own house! And now shall I not require his blood at your hand and destroy you from the earth?" [12]So David commanded the young men, and they killed them; they cut off their hands and feet and hung their bodies beside the pool at Hebron. But the head of Ishbaal[w] they took and buried in the tomb of Abner at Hebron.

5 Then all the tribes of Israel came to David at Hebron and said, "Look, we are your bone and flesh. [2]For some time, while Saul was king over us, it was you who led out Israel and brought it in. The LORD said to you, 'It is you who shall be shepherd of my people Israel, you who shall be ruler over Israel.' " [3]So all the elders of Israel came to the king at Hebron, and King David made a covenant with them at Hebron before the LORD, and they anointed David king over Israel. [4]David was thirty years old when he began to reign, and he reigned forty years. [5]At Hebron he reigned over Judah seven years and six months, and at Jerusalem he reigned over all Israel and Judah thirty-three years.

6 The king and his men marched to Jerusalem against the Jebusites, the inhabitants of the land, who said to David, "You will not come in here; even the blind and the lame

---

s 4.5 Heb *Ish-bosheth* t 4.6 Meaning of Heb uncertain u 4.8 Heb *Ish-bosheth* v 4.8 Heb *Ish-bosheth* w 4.12 Heb *Ish-bosheth*

---

son of Rizpah, Saul's concubine) is mentioned in 2 Sam. 21:8. Jonathan's son will be found by David, in 2 Sam. 9, and brought to live in Jerusalem.

4:8 *They brought the head of Ishbaal to David at Hebron.* Ishbaal is beheaded by two of his own captains, Baanah and Rechab. The two bring the head to David, clearly expecting David to be pleased with the death of Ishbaal. David reminds the two of what had happened when the Amalekite (2 Sam. 1) had come to David with news of Saul's death. As with that unnamed Amalekite, David orders these two, Baanah and Rechab, to be put to death. The head of Ishbaal is treated with respect.

5:3 *And they anointed David king over Israel.* After a reign of seven years in Hebron, over Judah, David is now anointed king over all Israel. In vv. 1–2, the justification for David's kingship is made explicit: he is an Israelite, and during much of Saul's reign, it was David who led the forces. He will reign another thirty-three years now, over all Israel. According to the narrative, David was thirty years old when he was anointed king of all Israel. This chapter and the next two chapters are arguably the high point of David's kingship. He will move from success to success, until the episode with Bathsheba and Uriah the Hittite in 2 Sam. 11.

5:6 *The king and his men marched to Jerusalem against the Jebusites, the inhabitants of the land.* The choice to conquer Jerusalem and make that city his capital underscores David's political astuteness. Jerusalem, a Canaanite city until David conquers it, did not belong to any of the tribes. No tribe would resent David for taking it as his own capital city, and no tribe would be jealous that David chose the city of another tribe as his capital. *You will not come in here; even the blind and the lame will turn you back.* The Jebusites, non-Israelite inhabitants of Jerusalem, use this phrase to ridicule

will turn you back," thinking, "David cannot come in here." [7]Nevertheless, David took the stronghold of Zion, which is now the city of David. [8]David had said on that day, "Whoever would strike down the Jebusites, let him get up the water shaft to attack the lame and the blind, those whom David hates."[x] Therefore it is said, "The blind and the lame shall not come into the house." [9]David occupied the stronghold and named it the city of David. David built the city all around from the Millo inward. [10]And David became greater and greater, for the LORD of hosts[y] was with him.

11 King Hiram of Tyre sent messengers to David, along with cedar trees and carpenters and masons who built David a house. [12]David then perceived that the LORD had established him king over Israel and that he had exalted his kingdom for the sake of his people Israel.

13 In Jerusalem, after he came from Hebron, David took more concubines and wives, and more sons and daughters were born to David. [14]These are the names of those who were born to him in Jerusalem: Shammua, Shobab, Nathan, Solomon, [15]Ibhar, Elishua, Nepheg, Japhia, [16]Elishama, Eliada, and Eliphelet.

17 When the Philistines heard that David had been anointed king over Israel, all the Philistines went up in search of David, but David heard about it and went down to the stronghold. [18]Now the Philistines had come and spread out in the valley of Rephaim. [19]David inquired of the LORD, "Shall I go up against the Philistines? Will you give them into my hand?" The LORD said to David, "Go up, for I will certainly give the Philistines into your hand." [20]So David came to Baal-perazim, and David defeated them there. He said, "The LORD has burst forth against my enemies before me like a bursting flood." Therefore that place is called Baal-perazim.[z] [21]The Philistines abandoned their idols there, and David and his men carried them away.

22 Once again the Philistines came up and were spread out in the valley of Rephaim. [23]When David inquired of the LORD, he said, "You shall not go up; go around to their rear and come upon them opposite the balsam trees. [24]When you hear the sound of marching in the tops of the balsam trees, then be on the alert, for then the LORD has gone out before you to strike down the army of the Philistines." [25]David did just as the LORD had commanded him, and he struck down the Philistines from Geba all the way to Gezer.

6 David again gathered all the chosen men of Israel, thirty thousand. [2]David and all the people with him set out and went from Baale-judah to bring up from

x 5.8 Q ms Syr Tg: MT *those who hate David*   y 5.10 Q ms Gk: MT *the LORD God of hosts*   z 5.20 That is, *lord of bursting forth*

David. After David's victory, in v. 8, David turns the phrase around and declares that "the blind and the lame shall not come into the house." In Lev. 21:18, the "blind" and the "lame" are named as two groups that are not allowed to participate in religious service at the altar of the temple. Our narrator references a restriction of his own later time to signal the subsequent arrival of the ark in Jerusalem (2 Sam. 6) and the building of the temple (1 Kgs. 5–9; in the HB, the Jerusalem temple is often referred to as "the house").

5:7 *Nevertheless, David took the stronghold of Zion, which is now the city of David.* Jerusalem is often named after its highest point, Mount Zion.

5:17 *When the Philistines heard that David had been anointed king over Israel, all the Philistines went up in search of David.* The first battle in which David participated was against the Philistine champion Goliath (1 Sam. 17). David, just recently established in Jerusalem, now must fight the Philistines again. David had been aligned with Achish, the Philistine ruler of Gath, during the time when David was on the run from Saul. Perhaps the Philistines considered David's kingship as a betrayal of this relationship or as a potential danger to their own territory. The Philistines' aggression is contrasted with Hiram's helpfulness.

5:20 *Therefore that place is called Baal-perazim.* This is a pun in the original Hebrew. "Burst forth" is "paraz" in Hebrew, and "bursting flood" is "perez mayim."

5:24 *When you hear the sound of marching in the tops of the balsam trees.* The signal for David's attack, perhaps the sound of the rustling of the leaves.

6:2 *To bring up from there the ark of God.* David has made Jerusalem his administrative center; he is now going to make Jerusalem an important religious center by bringing the ark, the symbol

there the ark of God, which is called by the name of the Lord of hosts who is enthroned on the cherubim. ³They carried the ark of God on a new cart and brought it out of the house of Abinadab, which was on the hill. Uzzah and Ahio,ᵃ the sons of Abinadab, were driving the new cart ⁴with the ark of God,ᵇ and Ahioᶜ went in front of the ark. ⁵David and all the house of Israel were dancing before the Lord with all their might, with songsᵈ and lyres and harps and tambourines and castanets and cymbals.

6 When they came to the threshing floor of Nacon, Uzzah reached out his hand to the ark of God and took hold of it, for the oxen lurched. ⁷The anger of the Lord was kindled against Uzzah, and God struck him there,ᵉ and he died there beside the ark of God. ⁸David was angry because the Lord had burst forth with an outburst upon Uzzah, so that place is called Perez-uzzahᶠ to this day. ⁹David was afraid of the Lord that day; he said, "How can the ark of the Lord come into my care?" ¹⁰So David was unwilling to take the ark of the Lord into his care in the city of David; instead, David took it to the house of Obed-edom the Gittite. ¹¹The ark of the Lord remained in the house of Obed-edom the Gittite three months, and the Lord blessed Obed-edom and all his household.

12 It was told King David, "The Lord has blessed the household of Obed-edom and all that belongs to him because of the ark of God." So David went and brought up the ark of God from the house of Obed-edom

to the city of David with rejoicing, ¹³and when those who bore the ark of the Lord had gone six paces, he sacrificed an ox and a fatted calf. ¹⁴David danced before the Lord with all his might; David was girded with a linen ephod. ¹⁵So David and all the house of Israel brought up the ark of the Lord with shouting and with the sound of the trumpet.

16 As the ark of the Lord came into the city of David, Michal daughter of Saul looked out of the window and saw King David leaping and dancing before the Lord, and she despised him in her heart.

17 They brought in the ark of the Lord and set it in its place, inside the tent that David had pitched for it, and David offered burnt offerings and offerings of well-being before the Lord. ¹⁸When David had finished offering the burnt offerings and the offerings of well-being, he blessed the people in the name of the Lord of hosts ¹⁹and distributed food among all the people, the whole multitude of Israel, both men and women, to each a cake of bread, a portion of meat,ᵍ and a cake of raisins. Then all the people went back to their homes.

20 David returned to bless his household. But Michal the daughter of Saul came out to meet David and said, "How the king of Israel honored himself today, uncovering himself today before the eyes of his servants' maids,

a 6.3 Or and his brother   b 6.4 Compare Gk: Heb which was on the hill with the ark of God   c 6.4 Or and his brother   d 6.5 Q ms Gk: MT fir trees   e 6.7 Meaning of Heb uncertain   f 6.8 That is, bursting out against Uzzah   g 6.19 Vg: Meaning of Heb uncertain

of God's presence, into the city. According to Exod. 25:10, God ordered the construction of the ark immediately following the ratification of the Mosaic covenant (Exod. 20:22–24:18). Bringing the ark into Jerusalem will enhance David's status with the priesthood and strengthen his control over the tribes. On the ark, see note on 1 Sam. 1:3.

6:7 The anger of the Lord was kindled against Uzzah, and God struck him there, and he died there beside the ark of God. This death causes David to abandon his first attempt to bring the ark into the city. This is a puzzling story; Uzzah seems to be concerned for the safety of the ark and loses his life because of that concern. What is clear from the story is that Uzzah was not supposed to touch the ark, perhaps because it was a symbol of God's holiness. See "Holiness (Exodus)," p. 88.

6:12 So David went and brought up the ark of God. David seems motivated by his desire for the blessings that Obed-edom and his household had received from the ark.

6:14 David was girded with a linen ephod. A priestly garment. On the ephod, see note on 1 Sam. 14:3.

6:16 And she despised him in her heart. Michal, Saul's daughter and David's wife, later confronts David (v. 20), admonishing him for his unkinglike behavior. The chapter ends with the remark that Michal remained childless; in the HB, this is a source of shame (Gen. 30:1–2; 1 Sam. 1:3–11). Some commentators have suggested that David used this opportunity of Michal's disdain to refuse to sleep with her, ensuring that she would not have any child Saul's followers might support, as a direct descendant of Saul.

as any vulgar fellow might shamelessly uncover himself!" [21]David said to Michal, "It was before the Lord, who chose me in place of your father and all his household, to appoint me as prince over Israel, the people of the Lord—I will dance before the Lord. [22]I will make myself yet more contemptible than this, and I will be humbled in my own eyes, but by the maids of whom you have spoken, by them I shall be held in honor." [23]And Michal the daughter of Saul had no child to the day of her death.

7 Now when the king was settled in his house and the Lord had given him rest from all his enemies around him, [2]the king said to the prophet Nathan, "See now, I am living in a house of cedar, but the ark of God stays in a tent." [3]Nathan said to the king, "Go, do all that you have in mind, for the Lord is with you."

[4] But that same night the word of the Lord came to Nathan, [5]"Go and tell my servant David: Thus says the Lord: Are you the one to build me a house to live in? [6]I have not lived in a house since the day I brought up the people of Israel from Egypt to this day, but I have been moving about in a tent and a tabernacle. [7]Wherever I have moved about among all the people of Israel, did I ever speak a word with any of the tribal leaders[b] of Israel, whom I commanded to shepherd my people Israel, saying, 'Why have you not built me a house of cedar?' [8]Now therefore thus you shall say to my servant David: Thus says the Lord of hosts: I took you from the pasture, from following the sheep to be prince over my people Israel, [9]and I have been with you wherever you went and have cut off all your enemies from before you, and I will make for you a great name, like the name of the great ones of the earth. [10]And I will appoint a place for my people Israel and will plant them, so that they may live in their own place and be disturbed no more, and evildoers shall afflict them no more, as formerly, [11]from the time that I appointed judges over my people Israel, and I will give you rest from all your enemies. Moreover, the Lord declares to you that the Lord will make you a house. [12]When your days are fulfilled and you lie down with your ancestors, I will raise up your offspring after you, who shall come forth from your body, and I will establish his kingdom. [13]He shall build a house for my name, and I will

b 7.7 Or *any of the tribes*

7:2 *The king said to the prophet Nathan.* The word we use in English, "prophet," comes from a Greek word meaning "one who speaks for another." In the biblical narratives, the prophet is usually understood as speaking for God. The prophet Nathan appears here in 7:2 for the first time. Nathan, like some other prophets (Elijah and Isaiah), has direct access to the king (cf. 12:1–15). He will appear later when David and Solomon are running the risk of losing the kingdom (1 Kgs. 1). *See now, I am living in a house of cedar, but the ark of God stays in a tent.* King Hiram of Tyre has given David the gift of a cedar house (2 Sam. 5:11). While David is living in comfort in a house, the ark of God is in a tent. Nathan at first confirms David's plan to build a permanent structure (a "house"—that is, the temple) for the ark (the sign of God's presence); the prophet returns the next day to inform David of what he has learned from God about the building of the temple. God will be the initiator of this plan, not David.

7:9 *And I will make for you a great name.* The Hebrew word "shem," translated as "name," can have the meaning of "fame," "reputation," "descendants." In 2 Sam. 8:13, this promise is alluded to again.

7:11 *Moreover, the Lord declares to you that the Lord will make you a house.* This passage is the foundation of the Davidic covenant, important both in Judaism and in Christianity. The Davidic covenant is the divine promise that there will always be a descendant of David on the throne in Jerusalem. The word "house," "bet" in Hebrew, can have a number of meanings: a physical structure—that is, a house—a household, a temple, or a dynasty. God, through Nathan, tells David, "You will not build me a 'house' (a temple); I will build you a 'house' (a dynasty)!" In the New Testament, Jesus is overtly called "son of David" (Matt. 1:1); two of his titles, "Messiah" (from the Hebrew "meshiakh") and "Christ" (from the Greek "christos"), both mean "anointed one," and both are references back to David as the "Lord's anointed." What seems to be an unconditional promise, with no strings attached, in 2 Samuel is made conditional elsewhere in the Hebrew Bible (1 Kgs. 8:25; Ps. 89:38–39). See **"Divine Retribution," p. 339**.

Going Deeper: The Davidic Covenant (2 Samuel 7)

Second Samuel 7 is the high point of the narrative about David. David, sitting in his house (a gift from King Hiram, according to 2 Sam. 5), decides that he should build a "house" (i.e., the temple), to house the ark, the religious relic Moses was commanded to build (Exod. 25:10). This ark (sometimes called "the ark of God," sometimes "the ark of the covenant") accompanied the tribes on their desert wanderings and was a potent symbol of the presence of God with the Israelites; when the Israelites camped during their desert wanderings the ark was placed in a portable structure, a tent with a separate room, the tabernacle (2 Sam. 7:6). David is quickly informed that the building of a house for God is not his decision—God has been content to move about in a tent and a tabernacle that God had dictated be constructed in Exodus. God considers David a bit presumptuous for suggesting that he, David, might build God a house. The expression "thus says the Lord" in v. 8 signals that the prophet Nathan is just the messenger, delivering a message from God. In the phrase in v. 8 translated as "I took you from the pasture," the independent personal pronoun *I* is written out in the Hebrew; this unnecessary use of "I" is a mark of emphasis. God is saying, "*I* did this, David, you did not do it; I am the reason you succeeded." God goes on and promises David that God will build a "house"—that is, a dynasty, for David. And this dynasty, according to v. 16, "shall be made sure before me" and David's throne "shall be established forever." The word "covenant" is not used in 2 Sam. 7, but in 2 Sam. 23:5, in his "last words," David makes a reference to the "everlasting covenant" God has made with him. (See **"Covenant (Genesis)," p. 23**.) Second Samuel 7 is the heart of the Davidic covenant: God promised to keep a descendant of David on the throne in Jerusalem, an eternal, royal line. A reader who knows something about the history of the Davidic dynasty knows that the Babylonian invasion of the sixth century BCE will destroy the Davidic dynasty, leading to the messianic expectation of the Second Temple period (sixth century BCE to 70 CE) that a messiah, an "anointed one" like David, will arise.

Deirdre A. Dempsey

establish the throne of his kingdom forever. [14]I will be a father to him, and he shall be a son to me. When he commits iniquity, I will punish him with a rod such as mortals use, with blows inflicted by human beings. [15]But I will not take[i] my steadfast love from him, as I took it from Saul, whom I put away from before you. [16]Your house and your kingdom shall be made sure forever before me;[j] your throne shall be established forever." [17]In accordance with all these words and with all this vision, Nathan spoke to David.

[18] Then King David went in and sat before the Lord and said, "Who am I, O Lord God, and what is my house, that you have brought me thus far? [19]And yet this was a small thing in your eyes, O Lord God; you have spoken also of your servant's house into the distant future. May this be instruction for the people,[k] O Lord God! [20]And what more can David say to you? For you know your servant, O Lord God! [21]Because of your promise and according to your own heart, you have wrought all this greatness so that your servant may know it. [22]Therefore you are great, O Lord God, for there is no one like you, and there is no God besides you, according to all that we have heard with our ears. [23]Who is like your people, like Israel? Is there another[l] nation on earth whose God went to redeem it as a people and to make a name for himself, doing[m] great and awesome things, driving out[n] nations and their gods before your people, whom you redeemed for yourself from Egypt? [24]And you established your people Israel for yourself to be your people forever, and you, O Lord, became their God. [25]And now, O Lord God, as for the word that you have spoken concerning your servant and concerning his house, confirm it forever; do as you have promised. [26]Thus your name will be magnified forever in the saying, 'The Lord of hosts is God over Israel,' and the house of your servant David will be established before you. [27]For you, O Lord of hosts, the God of Israel, have made this revelation to your servant, saying, 'I will build you a house';

i 7.15 Gk Syr Vg: Heb *shall not depart*   *j* 7.16 Gk Heb mss: MT *before you*   *k* 7.19 Meaning of Heb uncertain   *l* 7.23 Gk: Heb *one*   *m* 7.23 Gk: Heb adds *for you*   *n* 7.23 Gk: Heb *for your land*

7:23 *And to make a name for himself.* The Hebrew word for "name" ("shem"), used in God's speech in 7:13, also occurs several times in David's prayer. Here in David's prayer it has the meaning of "fame," "reputation."

therefore your servant has found courage to pray this prayer to you. [28]And now, O Lord God, you are God, and your words are true, and you have promised this good thing to your servant; [29]now, therefore, may it please you to bless the house of your servant so that it may continue forever before you, for you, O Lord God, have spoken, and with your blessing shall the house of your servant be blessed forever."

8 Some time afterward, David attacked the Philistines and subdued them; David took Metheg-ammah out of the hand of the Philistines.

2 He also defeated the Moabites and, making them lie down on the ground, measured them off with a cord; he measured two lengths of cord for those who were to be put to death and one length[o] for those who were to be spared. And the Moabites became servants to David and brought tribute.

3 David also struck down the king of Zobah, Hadadezer son of Rehob, as he went to restore his monument at the River Euphrates. [4]David took from him one thousand seven hundred horsemen and twenty thousand foot soldiers. David hamstrung all the chariot horses but left enough for a hundred chariots. [5]When the Arameans of Damascus came to help King Hadadezer of Zobah, David killed twenty-two thousand men of the Arameans. [6]Then David put garrisons among the Arameans of Damascus, and the Arameans became servants to David and brought tribute. The Lord gave victory to David wherever he went. [7]David took the gold shields that were carried by the servants of Hadadezer and brought them to Jerusalem. [8]From Betah and from Berothai, towns of Hadadezer, King David took a great amount of bronze.

9 When King Toi of Hamath heard that David had defeated the whole army of Hadadezer, [10]Toi sent his son Joram to King David, to greet him and to congratulate him because he had fought against Hadadezer and defeated him. Now Hadadezer had often been at war with Toi. Joram brought with him articles of silver, gold, and bronze; [11]these also King David dedicated to the Lord, together with the silver and gold that he dedicated from all the nations he subdued, [12]from Edom, Moab, the Ammonites, the Philistines, Amalek, and from the spoil of the king of Zobah, Hadadezer son of Rehob.

13 David won a name for himself. When he returned, he killed eighteen thousand Edomites[p] in the Valley of Salt. [14]He put garrisons in Edom; throughout all Edom he put garrisons, and all the Edomites became David's servants. And the Lord gave victory to David wherever he went.

15 So David reigned over all Israel, and David administered justice and equity to all his people. [16]Joab son of Zeruiah was over the army; Jehoshaphat son of Ahilud was recorder; [17]Zadok son of Ahitub and Ahimelech son of Abiathar were priests; Seraiah was secretary; [18]Benaiah son of Jehoiada was over[q] the Cherethites and the Pelethites; and David's sons were priests.

9 David asked, "Is there still anyone left of the house of Saul to whom I may show kindness for Jonathan's sake?" [2]Now there was a servant of the house of Saul whose name was Ziba, and he was summoned to David. The king said to him, "Are you Ziba?" And he said, "At your service!" [3]The king said, "Is there anyone remaining of the house of Saul to whom I

o 8.2 Heb *one full length*   p 8.13 Gk Syr Heb mss: MT *Arameans*   q 8.18 Syr Tg Vg: Heb lacks *was over*

8:2 *Making them lie down on the ground, measured them off with a cord; he measured two lengths of cord for those who were to be put to death and one length for those who were to be spared.* The meaning of the measuring ceremony in this verse is uncertain; using ropes to determine the fate of prisoners occurs only here in the Bible.

8:11 *These also King David dedicated to the Lord.* David's handling of the spoils of battle is contrasted with Saul; Saul was supposed to dedicate spoils to the Lord but did not, and he consequently lost his throne (1 Sam. 15).

9:1 *David asked, "Is there still anyone left of the house of Saul to whom I may show kindness for Jonathan's sake?"* The story of the bond between David and Jonathan (Saul's son) begins in 1 Sam. 18:1–5. In 1 Sam. 20:42, their covenant is renewed. David is informed in 2 Sam. 9 that Jonathan's son Mephibosheth is still alive. In 2 Sam. 4:4 we learned that Mephibosheth's nurse had escaped with

may show the kindness of God?" Ziba said to the king, "There remains a son of Jonathan; he is crippled in his feet." ⁴The king said to him, "Where is he?" Ziba said to the king, "He is in the house of Machir son of Ammiel, at Lo-debar." ⁵Then King David sent and brought him from the house of Machir son of Ammiel, at Lo-debar. ⁶Mephibosheth son of Jonathan son of Saul came to David and fell on his face and did obeisance. David said, "Mephibosheth!" He answered, "I am your servant." ⁷David said to him, "Do not be afraid, for I will show you kindness for the sake of your father Jonathan; I will restore to you all the land of your grandfather Saul, and you yourself shall eat at my table always." ⁸He did obeisance and said, "What is your servant, that you should look upon a dead dog such as I?"

9 Then the king summoned Saul's servant Ziba and said to him, "All that belonged to Saul and to all his house I have given to your master's grandson. ¹⁰You and your sons and your servants shall till the land for him and shall bring in the produce, so that your master's grandson may have food to eat, but your master's grandson Mephibosheth shall always eat at my table." Now Ziba had fifteen sons and twenty servants. ¹¹Then Ziba said to the king, "According to all that my lord the king commands his servant, so your servant will do." Mephibosheth ate at David's[r] table, like one of the king's sons. ¹²Mephibosheth had a young son whose name was Mica. And all who lived in Ziba's house became Mephibosheth's servants. ¹³Mephibosheth lived in Jerusalem, for he always ate at the king's table. Now he was lame in both his feet.

10 Some time afterward, the king of the Ammonites died, and his son Hanun succeeded him. ²David said, "I will deal loyally with Hanun son of Nahash, just as his father dealt loyally with me." So David sent envoys to console him concerning his father. When David's envoys came into the land of the Ammonites, ³the princes of the Ammonites said to their lord Hanun, "Do you really think that David is honoring your father just because he has sent messengers with condolences to you? Has not David sent his envoys to you to search the city, to spy it out, and to overthrow it?" ⁴So Hanun seized David's envoys, shaved off half the beard of each, cut off their garments in the middle at their waists, and sent them away. ⁵When David was told, he sent to meet them, for the men were greatly ashamed. The king said, "Remain at Jericho until your beards have grown and then return."

6 When the Ammonites saw that they had become odious to David, the Ammonites sent and hired the Arameans of Bethrehob and the Arameans of Zobah, twenty thousand foot soldiers, as well as the king of Maacah, one thousand men, and the men of Tob, twelve thousand men. ⁷When David heard of it, he sent Joab and all the army

r 9.11 Gk: Heb *my*

the then five-year-old Mephibosheth when she heard that Saul and Jonathan had been killed in battle with the Philistines (1 Sam. 31:1–7). During the escape, the boy fell and became crippled. David provides an income for Mephibosheth and brings him to stay at the king's court in Jerusalem. Some commentators have suggested David is ensuring that he can keep a close eye on someone who might, through his kinship with Saul, have a claim to the throne. David's action, on the surface a kind one, places the one remaining male heir of Saul under house arrest. In 2 Sam. 16, it is recorded that Mephibosheth continued to hope that his grandfather's throne might be restored to him (if Ziba's account in 2 Sam. 16:3 can be believed). On Mephibosheth, see note on 4:4.

10:1 *Some time afterward, the king of the Ammonites died, and his son Hanun succeeded him*. Hanun's father, Nahash, had been defeated by Saul. Hanun is an inexperienced king and listens to the bad advice of his advisers (much like Rehoboam in 1 Kgs. 12). There are at least two possible reasons for Hanun's reaction to the envoys: by this time, David's tendency to wage war on his neighbors is probably well known; new kings knew that they were vulnerable to attack as they consolidated power—this vulnerability made them prone to overreaction.

10:4 *So Hanun seized David's envoys, shaved off half the beard of each, cut off their garments in the middle at their waists, and sent them away*. This was a humiliating insult, since beards were marks of masculinity; in addition, the cutting away of the garments probably left the envoys' buttocks exposed.

of the warriors. [8]The Ammonites came out and drew up in battle array at the entrance of the gate, but the Arameans of Zobah and of Rehob and the men of Tob and Maacah were by themselves in the open country.

9 When Joab saw that the battle was set against him both in front and in the rear, he chose some of the picked men of Israel and arrayed them against the Arameans; [10]the rest of the troops he put in the charge of his brother Abishai, and he arrayed them against the Ammonites. [11]He said, "If the Arameans are too strong for me, then you shall help me, but if the Ammonites are too strong for you, then I will come and help you. [12]Be strong, and let us be courageous for the sake of our people and for the cities of our God, and may the Lord do what seems good to him." [13]So Joab and the people who were with him moved forward into battle against the Arameans, and they fled before him. [14]When the Ammonites saw that the Arameans fled, they likewise fled before Abishai and entered the city. Then Joab returned from fighting against the Ammonites and came to Jerusalem.

15 But when the Arameans saw that they had been defeated by Israel, they gathered themselves together. [16]Hadadezer sent and brought out the Arameans who were beyond the River, and they came to Helam, with Shobach the commander of the army of Hadadezer at their head. [17]When it was told David, he gathered all Israel together and crossed the Jordan and came to Helam. The Arameans arrayed themselves against David and fought with him. [18]The Arameans fled before Israel, and David killed of the Arameans seven hundred chariot teams and forty thousand horsemen and wounded Shobach the commander of their army, so that he died there. [19]When all the kings who were servants of Hadadezer saw that they had been defeated by Israel, they made peace with Israel and became subject to them. So the Arameans were afraid to help the Ammonites any more.

11 In the spring of the year, the time when kings go out to battle, David sent Joab with his officers and all Israel with him; they ravaged the Ammonites and besieged Rabbah. But David remained at Jerusalem.

2 It happened, late one afternoon when David rose from his couch and was walking about on the roof of the king's house, that he saw from the roof a woman bathing; the woman was very beautiful. [3]David sent someone to inquire about the woman. It was reported, "This is Bathsheba daughter of Eliam, the wife of Uriah the Hittite." [4]So David sent messengers to get her, and she came to him, and he lay with her. (Now she was purifying herself after her period.) Then she returned to her house. [5]The woman conceived, and she sent and told David, "I am pregnant."

6 So David sent word to Joab, "Send me Uriah the Hittite." And Joab sent Uriah to David. [7]When Uriah came to him, David asked how Joab and the people fared and how the war was going. [8]Then David said to Uriah, "Go down to your house and wash your feet." Uriah went out of the king's house, and there followed him a present

11:1 *In the spring of the year, the time when kings go out to battle.* It was more difficult to fight battles when the ground was wet from the winter rains. This chapter begins with an implicit criticism of David: it is the time for kings to go out to battle, but David has not. He sends his general Joab and his army to fight the Ammonites, but he himself stays in Jerusalem. What follows in chap. 11 is the tragic and troubling story of David's sexual encounter with Bathsheba and his subsequent murder of Uriah the Hittite, one of his officers who was with Joab on campaign. According to Nathan's conversation with David in 2 Sam. 12:1–4, David is completely at fault in the encounter. As the narrative of David's reign has come down to us in 2 Samuel, 2 Sam. 11 marks a turning point: David's steady rise in power and prestige comes to an end.

11:2 *He saw from the roof a woman bathing; the woman was very beautiful.* David is on his roof; no information is given about Bathsheba's location—David might have seen her through a window. In 11:4, we are told that her bath was a postmenstrual ritual purification (Lev. 15:19–24). Given the timing of the sexual encounter, Uriah the Hittite, out on campaign, could not be the father of the child.

11:4 *So David sent messengers to get her, and she came to him, and he lay with her.* The Hebrew here translated as "he lay," "shakav," is used to describe sexual intercourse, without indicating how that intercourse happened. See **"David and Bathsheba," p. 438.**

from the king. [9]But Uriah slept at the entrance of the king's house with all the servants of his lord and did not go down to his house. [10]When they told David, "Uriah did not go down to his house," David said to Uriah, "You have just come from a journey. Why did you not go down to your house?" [11]Uriah said to David, "The ark and Israel and Judah remain in booths,[s] and my lord Joab and the servants of my lord are camping in the open field; shall I then go to my house to eat and to drink and to lie with my wife? As you live and as your soul lives, I will not do such a thing." [12]Then David said to Uriah, "Remain here today also, and tomorrow I will send you back." So Uriah remained in Jerusalem that day. On the next day,[t] [13]David invited him to eat and drink in his presence and made him drunk, and in the evening he went out to lie on his couch with the servants of his lord, but he did not go down to his house.

[14] In the morning David wrote a letter to Joab and sent it by the hand of Uriah. [15]In the letter he wrote, "Set Uriah in the forefront of the hardest fighting, and then draw back from him, so that he may be struck down and die." [16]As Joab kept watch over the city, he assigned Uriah to the place where he knew there were valiant warriors. [17]The men of the city came out and fought with Joab, and some of the servants of David among the people fell. Uriah the Hittite was killed as well. [18]Then Joab sent and told David all the news about the fighting, [19]and he instructed the messenger, "When you

have finished telling the king all the news about the fighting, [20]if the king's anger rises and if he says to you, 'Why did you go so near the city to fight? Did you not know that they would shoot from the wall? [21]Who killed Abimelech son of Jerubbaal?[u] Did not a woman throw an upper millstone on him from the wall, so that he died at Thebez? Why did you go so near the wall?' then you shall say, 'Your servant Uriah the Hittite is dead, too.'"

[22] So the messenger went and came and told David all that Joab had sent him to tell. [23]The messenger said to David, "The men gained an advantage over us and came out against us in the field, but we drove them back to the entrance of the gate. [24]Then the archers shot at your servants from the wall; some of the king's servants are dead, and your servant Uriah the Hittite is dead also." [25]David said to the messenger, "Thus you shall say to Joab, 'Do not let this matter trouble you, for the sword devours now one and now another; press your attack on the city and overthrow it.' And encourage him."

[26] When the wife of Uriah heard that her husband was dead, she made lamentation for him. [27]When the mourning was over, David sent and brought her to his house, and she became his wife and bore him a son. But the thing that David had done displeased the Lord, **12** [1]and the Lord sent Nathan to David. He came to him and said to him, "There were two men in

[s] 11.11 Or *at Succoth* [t] 11.12 Gk ms Syr ms OL ms: Heb *that day and the next* [u] 11.21 Gk Syr: Heb *Jerubbesheth*

11:9 *But Uriah slept at the entrance of the king's house.* David's attempts to cover up the paternity of the child Bathsheba is bearing by allowing Uriah an opportunity to sleep with Bathsheba all fail. Uriah, because of his loyalty to the soldiers he has left behind (see notes on 1 Sam. 21:4–5), does not want to take advantage of the opportunity to have sex with Bathsheba.

11:21 *Your servant Uriah the Hittite is dead, too.* Desperate to hide his crime—adultery was a crime and could threaten not only David's reputation but also his throne—David decides to murder Uriah. Then he can marry Bathsheba, and his crime will go undetected. Joab assumes, in his message back to David, that the king will be more upset by the loss of life (besides the life of Uriah the Hittite) than the king turns out to be. Satisfied that his crime will remain hidden, David brings Bathsheba into his house as a wife.

11:27 *But the thing that David had done displeased the Lord.* This phrase is intended to remind the reader of David's words to Joab in v. 25. A literal translation of the Hebrew there is "Let the thing not be a bad thing in your eyes!" Here in 11:27, we find in the Hebrew, "The thing that David had done was bad in the eyes of the Lord." David might not be upset, but God is, and this will have consequences.

12:1 *And the Lord sent Nathan to David.* We first encountered the prophet Nathan in 2 Sam. 7, when he recounted to David the vision the prophet had received from God. Here in 2 Sam. 12, Nathan begins with a parable about a poor man and a beloved lamb, a lamb like a daughter ("bat" in Hebrew, just like the first part of Bathsheba's name, "bat-shaba").

Going Deeper: David and Bathsheba (2 Samuel 11–12)

For such an important story, David's adultery with Bathsheba is told with very little detail (2 Sam. 11:2–4). The rest of the chapter is devoted to describing in detail David's efforts to cover up the crime, ending with his murder of Bathsheba's husband, Uriah. In 11:1, we read that David has sent his army into the field, but he himself remains in Jerusalem. While he is walking about on the flat roof of his house, he sees from the roof a beautiful woman bathing. He is informed that she is married to one of the officers now off doing battle for David, but he still sends messengers "to get her," and when she comes to David, "he lay with her." The Hebrew word, *shakav*, "he lay," is used to describe sexual intercourse without indicating how that intercourse happened. In other words, there is no indication in this verb that David raped Bathsheba. By contrast, in 13:22, in the story of Amnon's rape of Tamar, the Hebrew word *innah* is used (also in 2 Sam. 13:12, 14, 32), meaning "to force" or "to rape." For centuries, commentators, artists, theologians, and preachers have suggested that Bathsheba was somehow complicit in David's crime, partly due to the use of the word *shakav*. One of the other reasons blame is attributed to Bathsheba is a misreading of the story: it is David who is on the flat roof of his palace; Bathsheba's location is not mentioned. She is not bathing on her roof to seduce David, as is often assumed. She is taking a postmenstrual ritual purification bath (11:4; Lev. 15:19–24); David might have seen her through a window. Leonard Cohen's beautiful song "Hallelujah," in which we hear the line, "You saw her bathing on the roof," is an example of how this misreading persists. David's attempts to get away with his crime seem to have succeeded, but at the very end of 2 Sam. 11 we read, "But the thing that David had done displeased the LORD." In Nathan's speech to David (in which Nathan twice uses the messenger formula, "Thus says the LORD," signaling that God is speaking through the prophet), David alone bears the blame ("You have struck down Uriah the Hittite with the sword and have taken his wife to be your wife," v. 9). In Nathan's parable of the poor man and his ewe lamb, the lamb seems to be Bathsheba. It is David who has exerted his power unjustly, and his crime marks the end of his upward trajectory and ushers in internal strife and conflict for the rest of David's reign.

Deirdre A. Dempsey

a certain city, the one rich and the other poor. ²The rich man had very many flocks and herds, ³but the poor man had nothing but one little ewe lamb that he had bought. He brought it up, and it grew up with him and with his children; it used to eat of his meager fare and drink from his cup and lie in his bosom, and it was like a daughter to him. ⁴Now there came a traveler to the rich man, and he was loath to take one of his own flock or herd to prepare for the wayfarer who had come to him, but he took the poor man's lamb and prepared that for the guest who had come to him." ⁵Then David's anger was greatly kindled against the man. He said to Nathan, "As the LORD lives, the man who has done this deserves to die; ⁶he shall restore the lamb fourfold because he did this thing and because he had no pity."

7 Nathan said to David, "You are the man! Thus says the LORD, the God of Israel: I anointed you king over Israel, and I rescued you from the hand of Saul; ⁸I gave you your master's house and your master's wives into your bosom and gave you the house of Israel and of Judah, and if that had been too little, I would have added as much more. ⁹Why have you despised the word of the LORD, to do what is evil in his sight? You have struck down Uriah the Hittite with the sword and have taken his wife to be your wife and have killed him with the sword of the Ammonites. ¹⁰Now, therefore, the sword

12:6 *He shall restore the lamb fourfold because he did this thing and because he had no pity.* David is furious when he hears the story of the rich man's theft of the poor man's lamb and wants to punish the perpetrator. The mention of "fourfold" anticipates the death of David's four sons during his lifetime: the baby born to David and Bathsheba, Amnon, Absalom, and Adonijah.

12:7 *You are the man!* The rich man had many lambs; David had many wives and concubines but stole the wife of one of his officers.

12:10 *Now, therefore, the sword shall never depart from your house.* The word "sword" is a metaphor for violence. God's promise to David in 2 Sam. 7 is not taken back, but Nathan's words point to long-lasting consequences of David's sin for his descendants.

shall never depart from your house, for you have despised me and have taken the wife of Uriah the Hittite to be your wife. [11]Thus says the LORD: I will raise up trouble against you from within your own house, and I will take your wives before your eyes and give them to your neighbor, and he shall lie with your wives in broad daylight. [12]For you did it secretly, but I will do this thing before all Israel and in broad daylight." [13]David said to Nathan, "I have sinned against the LORD." Nathan said to David, "Now the LORD has put away your sin; you shall not die. [14]Nevertheless, because by this deed you have utterly scorned the LORD,[v] the child born to you shall die." [15]Then Nathan went to his house.

The LORD struck the child whom Uriah's wife bore to David, and it became very ill. [16]David therefore pleaded with God for the child; David fasted and went in and lay all night on the ground. [17]The elders of his house stood beside him urging him to rise from the ground, but he would not, nor did he eat food with them. [18]On the seventh day the child died. And the servants of David were afraid to tell him that the child was dead, for they said, "While the child was still alive, we spoke to him, and he did not listen to us; how then can we tell him the child is dead? He may do himself some harm." [19]But when David saw that his servants were whispering together, he perceived that the child was dead, and David said to his servants, "Is the child dead?" They said, "He is dead."

20 Then David rose from the ground, washed, anointed himself, and changed his clothes. He went into the house of the LORD and worshiped; he then went to his own house, and when he asked, they set food before him, and he ate. [21]Then his servants said to him, "What is this thing that you have done? You fasted and wept for the child while it was alive, but when the child died, you rose and ate food." [22]He said, "While the child was still alive, I fasted and wept, for I said, 'Who knows? The LORD may be gracious to me, and the child may live.' [23]But now he is dead; why should I fast? Can I bring him back again? I shall go to him, but he will not return to me."

24 Then David consoled his wife Bathsheba and went to her and lay with her, and she bore a son, and he named him Solomon. The LORD loved him [25]and sent a message by the prophet Nathan, so he named him Jedidiah[w] because of the LORD.

26 Now Joab fought against Rabbah of the Ammonites and took the royal city. [27]Joab sent messengers to David and said, "I have fought against Rabbah; moreover, I have taken the water city. [28]Now, then, gather the rest of the people together, encamp against the city, and take it, lest I myself take the city and it be called by my name." [29]So David gathered all the people together and went to Rabbah and fought against it and took it. [30]He took the crown of Milcom[x] from his head; the weight of it was a talent of gold, and in it was a precious stone, and it was placed on David's head. He also brought forth the spoil of the city, a very great amount. [31]He brought out the people who were in it and set them to work with saws and iron picks and iron axes or sent them to the brickworks. Thus he did to all the cities of the Ammonites. Then David and all the people returned to Jerusalem.

v 12.14 Cn: Heb *scorned the enemies of the* LORD   w 12.25 That is, *beloved of the* LORD   x 12.30 Gk: Heb *their kings*

12:14 *The child born to you shall die.* David's sin will be transferred to the baby, who will die in David's place (see 12:15–20).

12:20 *Then David rose from the ground, washed, anointed himself, and changed his clothes.* Although David had been warned that the child would die, David lies on the ground, fasts, and weeps. When the child dies, he resumes his normal activities. David might have believed that it was possible that God might allow the child to live. Once the child was dead, David realized and accepted that God had rejected his appeals.

12:28 *Lest I myself take the city and it is called by my name.* David continued to be disengaged from this war with the Ammonites; Joab has to alert him to the fact that the city Rabbah is just about to fall in order to bring David to the battle.

12:30 *Milcom.* Reading with the Greek version of 2 Samuel. The Hebrew reads, "their kings." Milcom is the name or title of the Ammonite god (1 Kgs. 11:33; Jer. 49:1, 3; Zeph. 1:5). The crown might have been on a statue of the god.

13 Some time passed. David's son Absalom had a beautiful sister whose name was Tamar, and David's son Amnon fell in love with her. [2]Amnon was so tormented that he made himself ill because of his sister Tamar, for she was a virgin, and it seemed impossible to Amnon to do anything to her. [3]But Amnon had a friend whose name was Jonadab, the son of David's brother Shimeah, and Jonadab was a very crafty man. [4]He said to him, "O son of the king, why are you so haggard morning after morning? Will you not tell me?" Amnon said to him, "I love Tamar, my brother Absalom's sister." [5]Jonadab said to him, "Lie down on your bed and pretend to be ill, and when your father comes to see you, say to him, 'Let my sister Tamar come and give me something to eat and prepare the food in my sight, so that I may see it and eat it from her hand.'" [6]So Amnon lay down and pretended to be ill, and when the king came to see him, Amnon said to the king, "Please let my sister Tamar come and make a couple of cakes in my sight, so that I may eat from her hand."

7 Then David sent home to Tamar, saying, "Go to your brother Amnon's house and prepare food for him." [8]So Tamar went to her brother Amnon's house, where he was lying down. She took dough, kneaded it, made cakes in his sight, and baked the cakes. [9]Then she took the pan and set them before him, but he refused to eat. Amnon said, "Send out everyone from me." So everyone went out from him. [10]Then Amnon said to Tamar, "Bring the food into the chamber so that I may eat from your hand." So Tamar took the cakes she had made and brought them into the chamber to Amnon her brother. [11]But when she brought them near him to eat, he took hold of her and said to her, "Come, lie with me, my sister." [12]She answered him, "No, my brother, do not force me, for such a thing is not done in Israel; do not do anything so vile! [13]As for me, where could I carry my shame? And as for you, you would be as one of the scoundrels in Israel. Now therefore, I beg you, speak to the king, for he will not withhold me from you." [14]But he would not listen to her, and being stronger than she, he forced her and lay with her.

15 Then Amnon was seized with a very great loathing for her; indeed, his loathing was even greater than the lust he had felt for her. Amnon said to her, "Get out!" [16]But she said to him, "No, my brother,[y] for this wrong in sending me away is greater than the other that you did to me." But he would not

[y] 13.16 Cn Compare Gk Vg: Meaning of Heb uncertain

---

2 Sam. 13 This chapter can be divided into two episodes: the rape of Tamar by her half brother Amnon (vv. 1–22) and Absalom's revenge and flight (vv. 23–39). Amnon's mother was Ahinoam (2 Sam. 3:2); Maacah (2 Sam. 3:3) was the mother of both Tamar and Absalom. Amnon is David's firstborn son, so he would be expected to become king after his father. In the present form of 2 Samuel, this story follows immediately after David's crime and is intended to be seen as evidence of the violence that David's crime brings on his household. The violence begins in 2 Sam. 13 and will continue for much of the remainder of 2 Samuel.

13:1 *David's son Absalom had a beautiful sister whose name was Tamar, and David's son Amnon fell in love with her.* Like Bathsheba (2 Sam. 11:2), Tamar is described as beautiful.

13:3 *And Jonadab was a very crafty man.* Jonadab is Amnon's cousin, a son of David's brother. Jonadab concocts a plan to help Amnon gain access to Tamar. The close relationship (half siblings) of Tamar and Amnon is not explicitly mentioned, although Tamar and Amnon use the words "brother" and "sister" to address each other. In v. 13, in an effort to stop the rape, Tamar suggests that David might allow Amnon to wed her; after the rape, Tamar seems to refer to a law requiring a rapist to marry his victim (cf. Deut. 22:28–29). In the society in which Tamar lived, her rape and loss of virginity resulted in a loss of status.

13:7 *Then David sent home to Tamar, saying, "Go to your brother Amnon's house and prepare food for him."* David is fooled by Amnon into believing that his son is ill, and he unknowingly sends Tamar into the hands of her rapist. After the rape, although David is angry, he makes no effort to punish his firstborn son (2 Sam. 13:21), nor does the story mention any attempt to comfort Tamar or to force Amnon to marry her. Had David acted, he might have avoided the violence and chaos that followed.

13:16 *No, my brother, for this wrong in sending me away is greater than the other that you did to me.* Amnon, after the rape, orders his sister to leave. She stands her ground, insisting that he not do

listen to her. [17]He called the young man who served him and said, "Put this woman out of my presence and bolt the door after her." [18](Now she was wearing an ornamented[z] robe with sleeves, for this is how the virgin daughters of the king were clothed in earlier times.[a]) So his servant put her out and bolted the door after her. [19]But Tamar put ashes on her head and tore the long robe that she was wearing; she put her hand on her head and went away, crying aloud as she went.

20 Her brother Absalom said to her, "Has Amnon your brother been with you? Be quiet for now, my sister; he is your brother; do not take this to heart." So Tamar remained, a desolate woman, in her brother Absalom's house. [21]When King David heard of all these things, he became very angry, but he would not punish his son Amnon because he loved him, for he was his firstborn.[b] [22]But Absalom spoke to Amnon neither good nor bad, for Absalom hated Amnon because he had raped his sister Tamar.

23 After two full years Absalom had sheepshearers at Baal-hazor, which is near Ephraim, and Absalom invited all the king's sons. [24]Absalom came to the king and said, "Your servant has sheepshearers; will the king and his servants please go with your servant?" [25]But the king said to Absalom, "No, my son, let us not all go, or else we will be burdensome to you." He pressed him, but he would not go but gave him his blessing. [26]Then Absalom said, "If not, please let my brother Amnon go with us." The king said to him, "Why should he go with you?" [27]But Absalom pressed him until he let Amnon and all the king's sons go with him.

Absalom made a feast like a king's feast.[c] [28]Then Absalom commanded his servants, "Watch when Amnon's heart is merry with wine, and when I say to you, 'Strike Amnon,' then kill him. Do not be afraid; have I not myself commanded you? Be courageous and valiant." [29]So the servants of Absalom did to Amnon as Absalom had commanded. Then all the king's sons rose, and each mounted his mule and fled.

30 While they were on the way, the report came to David that Absalom had killed all the king's sons, and not one of them was left. [31]The king rose, tore his garments, and lay on the ground, and all his servants who were standing by tore their garments. [32]But Jonadab, the son of David's brother Shimeah, said, "Let not my lord suppose that they have killed all the young men the king's sons; Amnon alone is dead. This has been determined by Absalom from the day Amnon[d] raped his sister Tamar. [33]Now, therefore, do not let my lord the king take it to heart, as if all the king's sons were dead, for Amnon alone is dead."

34 But Absalom fled. When the young man who kept watch looked up, he saw many people coming from the Horonaim road[e] by the side of the mountain. [35]Jonadab said to the king, "See, the king's sons have come; as your servant said, so it has come about." [36]As soon as he had finished speaking, the king's sons arrived and raised their

z 13.18 Meaning of Heb uncertain   a 13.18 Cn: Heb were clothed in robes   b 13.21 Q ms Gk: MT lacks but he would not punish . . . firstborn   c 13.27 Gk Compare Q ms: MT lacks Absalom made a feast like a king's feast   d 13.32 Heb he   e 13.34 Cn Compare Gk: Heb the road behind him

so. According to Deut. 22:28–29, a man who rapes a virgin (and is caught in the act) must pay the woman's father a certain amount of silver and is obligated to marry the woman.

13:22 *For Absalom hated Amnon because he had raped his sister Tamar.* The Hebrew word used is "innah" (also in 2 Sam. 13:12, 14, 32). This word can have a more general sense of "to oppress," "to humiliate," but is used with the meaning of "to rape" here in 2 Sam. 13 and elsewhere (Gen. 34:2; Judg. 19:24; 20:4; Lam. 5:11). Absalom will wait awhile before seeking revenge.

13:27 *But Absalom pressed him until he let Amnon and all the king's sons go with him.* Absalom sets a trap for Amnon as revenge for the trap Amnon set for Tamar. In both cases—Amnon's trap and Absalom's trap—it would have been wise for David to have been more suspicious and cautious. David encourages Tamar to nurse her brother Amnon, and the king allows his firstborn son Amnon to attend the party Absalom throws at the end of the sheep-shearing. Absalom has Amnon murdered during the festivities. It is the "crafty" Jonadab who recognized that Absalom intended revenge on Amnon; David lacked the wisdom to discern this. Absalom initially invited his father, David, to the sheep-shearing celebration (2 Sam. 13:24). This leaves open the question: Was this initial invitation just part of the trap, so that David would relent and send Amnon as his representative, or would Absalom have killed his father if David had said yes to the invitation and attended the party?

Going Deeper: The Rape of Tamar (2 Samuel 13)

The strife foreseen by Nathan in 12:10 is not long in coming. The consequences of Amnon's rape of Tamar almost destroy David's achievements. The story is heartbreaking: Amnon, David's son, "fell in love" with Tamar, his half sister. As an unmarried woman who was a part of the royal household, Tamar would have been closely watched. Amnon had a friend, Jonadab (David's nephew), who is described as "very crafty," and he comes up with a scheme that would give Amnon access to Tamar. In the Hebrew, the word used to describe Jonadab is *khakam*, usually translated as "wise." In English, this descriptive word is always positive, but in the Bible, someone who is *khakam*, "wise," does not always use this wisdom for good. For example, the "wise woman" in 14:2 uses her wisdom to lie to the king, to bring about a reconciliation that will almost destroy David's kingdom. In other words, the word in Hebrew is more morally neutral than "wise" is, in English. In the rest of the stories in 2 Samuel, the question of David's wisdom surfaces. He has shown wisdom earlier, for example, in 2 Sam. 1, but has this wisdom diminished? The king is not wise enough to discern that Tamar is in danger from Amnon, nor does he discern how profoundly affected Absalom, Tamar's brother, is by Tamar's rape. The "wise woman" in chapter 14 calls David "wise" in v. 20, but is he really? It is the "very crafty" Jonadab who, in 13:32–33, recognizes that Absalom has killed Amnon because of Amnon's rape of Tamar; David had not seen this coming.

The Hebrew word *shakav*, "he lay," occurs in this rape story alongside the Hebrew word *innah* in 13:14; otherwise, we find the word *innah* alone (13:12, 22, 32). This word can have a more general sense of "to oppress," "to humiliate," but is used with the meaning of "to rape" here in 2 Sam. 13 and elsewhere (Gen. 34:2; Judg. 19:24; 20:4; Lam. 5:11). David does not move to protect Tamar after Amnon rapes her; she moves into her brother Absalom's house, having lost status because of the rape (2 Sam. 13:16–20). David is angry at Amnon (13:21), but does nothing to either comfort Tamar or punish Amnon. Had the king acted, the tragic events of Absalom's rebellion and eventual death might not have occurred.

Deirdre A. Dempsey

voices and wept, and the king and all his servants also wept very bitterly.

37 But Absalom fled and went to Talmai son of Ammihud, king of Geshur. David mourned for his son day after day. ³⁸Absalom, having fled to Geshur, stayed there three years. ³⁹And the heart of*ᶠ* the king went out, yearning for Absalom, for he was now consoled over the death of Amnon.

14 Now Joab son of Zeruiah perceived that the king's mind was on Absalom. ²Joab sent to Tekoa and brought from there a wise woman. He said to her, "Pretend to be a mourner; put on mourning garments, and do not anoint yourself with oil, but behave like a woman who has been mourning many days for the dead. ³Go to the king and speak to him as follows." And Joab put the words into her mouth.

4 When the woman of Tekoa came*ᵍ* to the king, she fell on her face to the ground and did obeisance and said, "Help, O king!" ⁵The king asked her, "What is your trouble?" She answered, "Alas, I am a widow; my husband is dead. ⁶Your servant had two

sons, and they fought with one another in the field; there was no one to part them, and one struck the other and killed him. ⁷Now the whole family has risen against your servant. They say, 'Give up the man who struck his brother, so that we may kill him for the life of his brother whom he murdered, even if we destroy the heir as well.' Thus they would quench my one remaining ember and leave to my husband neither name nor remnant on the face of the earth."

8 Then the king said to the woman, "Go to your house, and I will give orders concerning you." ⁹The woman of Tekoa said to the king, "On me be the guilt, my lord the king, and on my father's house; let the king and his throne be guiltless." ¹⁰The king said, "If anyone says anything to you, bring him to me, and he shall never touch you again." ¹¹Then she said, "Please, may the king keep the LORD your God in mind, so that the avenger of blood may kill no more and my son not be destroyed." He said, "As the LORD lives, not one hair of your son shall fall to the ground."

ᶠ 13.39 Q ms Gk: MT *And David* *ᵍ* 14.4 Heb mss Gk Syr Vg: MT *said*

13:37 *But Absalom fled and went to Talmai son of Ammihud, king of Geshur.* According to 2 Sam. 3:3, Talmai is Absalom's maternal grandfather. David will show a lack of wisdom when he decides to bring Absalom back from Geshur (chap. 14).

12 Then the woman said, "Please let your servant speak a word to my lord the king." He said, "Speak." [13]The woman said, "Why then have you planned such a thing against the people of God? For in giving this decision the king convicts himself, inasmuch as the king does not bring his banished one home again. [14]We must all die; we are like water spilled on the ground, which cannot be gathered up. But God will not take away a life; he will devise plans so as not to keep an outcast banished forever from his presence.[b] [15]Now I have come to say this to my lord the king because the people have made me afraid; your servant thought, 'I will speak to the king; it may be that the king will perform the request of his servant. [16]For the king will hear and deliver his servant from the hand of the man who would cut both me and my son off from the heritage of God.' [17]Your servant thought, 'The word of my lord the king will set me at rest,' for my lord the king is like the angel of God, discerning good and evil. The LORD your God be with you!"

18 Then the king answered the woman, "Do not withhold from me anything I ask you." The woman said, "Let my lord the king speak." [19]The king said, "Is the hand of Joab with you in all this?" The woman answered and said, "As surely as you live, my lord the king, one cannot turn right or left from anything that my lord the king has said. For it was your servant Joab who commanded me; it was he who put all these words into the mouth of your servant. [20]In order to change the course of affairs your servant Joab did this. But my lord has wisdom like the wisdom of the angel of God to know all things that are on the earth."

21 Then the king said to Joab, "Very well, I grant this; go, bring back the young man Absalom." [22]Joab prostrated himself with his face to the ground and did obeisance and blessed the king, and Joab said, "Today your servant knows that I have found favor in your sight, my lord the king, in that the king has granted the request of his servant." [23]So Joab set off, went to Geshur, and brought Absalom to Jerusalem. [24]The king said, "Let him go to his own house; he is not to come into my presence." So Absalom went to his own house and did not come into the king's presence.

25 Now in all Israel there was no one to be praised so much for his beauty as Absalom; from the sole of his foot to the crown of his head there was no blemish in him. [26]When he cut the hair of his head (for at the end of every year he used to cut it; when it was heavy on him, he cut it), he weighed the hair of his head, two hundred shekels by the king's weight. [27]There were born to Absalom three sons and one daughter whose name was Tamar; she was a beautiful woman.

28 So Absalom lived two full years in Jerusalem without coming into the king's presence. [29]Then Absalom sent for Joab to send him to the king, but Joab would not come to him. He sent a second time, but Joab would not come. [30]Then he said to his servants, "Look, Joab's field is next to mine, and he has barley there; go and set it on fire." So Absalom's servants set the field on fire. [31]Then Joab rose and went to Absalom at his house and said to him, "Why have your servants set my field on fire?" [32]Absalom answered Joab, "Look, I sent word to you. Come here that I may send you to the king with the question, 'Why have I come from Geshur? It would be better for me to be there still.' Now let me go into the king's presence; if there is guilt in me, let him kill

b 14.14 Meaning of Heb uncertain

14:20 *But my lord has wisdom like the wisdom of the angel of God to know all things that are on the earth.* Joab, David's general, deceives David in an attempt to bring about a reconciliation between David and Absalom. He sends a "wise woman" to David with a fake story. The wise woman's fake story is about a legal issue with her sons; she is asking for the king's judgment. Like the story the prophet Nathan told the king in 2 Sam. 12, this woman's story is about David's sons.

14:21 *Bring back the young man Absalom.* David grants the request to bring Absalom back to Jerusalem after three years of exile; Absalom will not be allowed into the king's presence. After two years in Jerusalem, Absalom forces the issue with Joab, who convinces the king to see Absalom. A question that remains in this chapter: Why did Joab want Absalom back? A clue to this might be in v. 7, when the wise woman, using Joab's words, speaks of the destruction of "the heir." Did Joab assume that Absalom would inherit his father's kingdom? Did Joab want to be seen by Absalom as the person upon whom Absalom must depend in order to inherit the kingdom from his father?

me!" [33]Then Joab went to the king and told him, and he summoned Absalom. So he came to the king and prostrated himself with his face to the ground before the king, and the king kissed Absalom.

15 After this Absalom provided for himself a chariot and horses and fifty men to run ahead of him. [2]Absalom used to rise early and stand beside the road into the gate, and when anyone brought a suit before the king for judgment, Absalom would call out and say, "From what city are you?" When the person said, "Your servant is of such and such a tribe in Israel," [3]Absalom would say, "See, your claims are good and right, but there is no one deputed by the king to hear you." [4]Absalom would also say, "If only I were judge in the land! Then all who had a suit or cause might come to me, and I would give them justice." [5]Whenever people came near to do obeisance to him, he would put out his hand and take hold of them and kiss them. [6]Thus Absalom did to every Israelite who came to the king for judgment, so Absalom stole the hearts of the people of Israel.

7 At the end of four[i] years Absalom said to the king, "Please let me go to Hebron and pay the vow that I have made to the LORD. [8]For your servant made a vow while I lived at Geshur in Aram: If the LORD will indeed bring me back to Jerusalem, then I will serve the LORD in Hebron."[j] [9]The king said to him, "Go in peace." So he got up and went to Hebron. [10]But Absalom sent secret messengers throughout all the tribes of Israel, saying, "As soon as you hear the sound of the trumpet, then shout: Absalom has become king at Hebron!" [11]Two hundred men from Jerusalem went with Absalom; they were invited guests, and they went in innocence, knowing nothing of the matter. [12]While Absalom was offering the sacrifices, he sent for[k] Ahithophel the Gilonite, David's counselor, from his city Giloh. The conspiracy grew in strength, and the people with Absalom kept increasing.

13 A messenger came to David, saying, "The hearts of the Israelites have gone after Absalom." [14]Then David said to all his officials who were with him at Jerusalem, "Get up! Let us flee, or there will be no escape for us from Absalom. Hurry, or he will soon overtake us, and bring disaster down upon us, and attack the city with the edge of the sword." [15]The king's officials said to the king, "Your servants are ready to do whatever our lord the king decides." [16]So the king left, followed by all his household, except ten concubines whom he left behind to look after the house. [17]The king left, followed by all the

i 15.7 Gk Syr: Heb *forty*   j 15.8 Gk mss: Heb lacks *in Hebron*
k 15.12 Or *he sent*

15:1 *After this Absalom provided for himself a chariot and horses and fifty men to run ahead of him.* Absalom now sets in motion the first part of his plan to replace his father as king; "himself" in the verse is an indication that this is Absalom's own initiative, taken without the knowledge of his father, David. He has outfitted himself with what a king would have. In 1 Sam. 8, the prophet Samuel warned the people of the dangers of a king; some of the vocabulary of 1 Sam. 8:11 surfaces in 2 Sam. 15:1. In v. 2, Absalom will compare his ability to render wise judgments with the ability of his father (deciding judicial matters was something a king did; see 1 Kgs. 3:16–28).

15:7 *Please let me go to Hebron.* Absalom, as his power grows, keeps his plan for usurping the kingship hidden from his father for four years. Four years seems like a long time to keep a plan like this undercover; perhaps this is also intended to point to David's lack of wisdom? Absalom's plot becomes public when he gathers supporters in Hebron, the city where David first began to rule (2 Sam. 2:4).

15:12 *While Absalom was offering the sacrifices, he sent for Ahithophel the Gilonite, David's counselor.* The offering of sacrifices might have been seen by some of the Israelites as Absalom's fulfillment of his vow (2 Sam. 15:7–8); Absalom, however, intends the offering of sacrifices to be part of his coronation ceremony (in 1 Kgs. 1:9, Adonijah offers sacrifices, proclaiming his intention to become king). See **"Offerings and Sacrifices," p. 146.** *Ahithophel the Gilonite.* The grandfather of Bathsheba (2 Sam. 23:34), who now sides with Absalom.

15:14 *Then David said to all his officials who were with him at Jerusalem.* David makes no attempt to stay and defend himself in Jerusalem; he recognizes that the rebellion is too strong for him to save the city. He abandons Jerusalem in order to prevent its destruction during battle.

15:16 *So the king left, followed by all his household, except ten concubines whom he left behind to look after the house.* These ten concubines (women in David's household who were of a lower status

people, and they stopped at the last house. [18]All his officials passed by him, and all the Cherethites, and all the Pelethites, and all the six hundred Gittites who had followed him from Gath passed on before the king.

19 Then the king said to Ittai the Gittite, "Why are you also coming with us? Go back, and stay with the king, for you are a foreigner and also an exile from your home. [20]You came only yesterday, and shall I today make you wander about with us while I go wherever I can? Go back, and take your kinsfolk with you, and may the LORD show[l] steadfast love and faithfulness to you." [21]But Ittai answered the king, "As the LORD lives and as my lord the king lives, wherever my lord the king may be, whether for death or for life, there also your servant will be." [22]David said to Ittai, "Go then, march on." So Ittai the Gittite marched on, with all his men and all the little ones who were with him. [23]The whole country wept aloud as all the people passed by; the king crossed the Wadi Kidron, and all the people moved on toward the wilderness.

24 Abiathar came up, and Zadok also, with all the Levites, carrying the ark of the covenant of God. They set down the ark of God until the people had all passed out of the city. [25]Then the king said to Zadok, "Carry the ark of God back into the city. If I find favor in the eyes of the LORD, he will bring me back and let me see both it and the place where it stays. [26]But if he says, 'I take no pleasure in you,' here I am, let him do to me what seems good to him." [27]The king also said to the priest Zadok, "Look,[m] go back to the city in peace, you and Abiathar,"[n]

with your two sons, Ahimaaz your son and Jonathan son of Abiathar. [28]See, I will wait at the fords of the wilderness until word comes from you to inform me." [29]So Zadok and Abiathar carried the ark of God back to Jerusalem, and they remained there.

30 But David went up the ascent of the Mount of Olives, weeping as he went, with his head covered and walking barefoot, and all the people who were with him covered their heads and went up, weeping as they went. [31]David was told that Ahithophel was among the conspirators with Absalom. And David said, "O LORD, I pray you, turn the counsel of Ahithophel into foolishness."

32 When David came to the summit, where God was worshiped, Hushai the Archite came to meet him with his coat torn and earth on his head. [33]David said to him, "If you go on with me, you will be a burden to me. [34]But if you return to the city and say to Absalom, 'I will be your servant, O king; as I have been your father's servant in time past, so now I will be your servant,' then you will defeat for me the counsel of Ahithophel. [35]The priests Zadok and Abiathar will be with you there. So whatever you hear from the king's house, tell it to the priests Zadok and Abiathar. [36]Their two sons are with them there, Zadok's son Ahimaaz and Abiathar's son Jonathan, and by them you shall report to me everything you hear." [37]So Hushai, David's friend, came into the city just as Absalom was entering Jerusalem.

---

l 15.20 Cn Compare Gk: Heb lacks *may the LORD show*
m 15.27 Gk: Heb *Are you a seer* or *Do you see?* *n* 15.27 Cn: Heb lacks *and Abiathar*

---

than David's wives) appear again in 2 Sam. 16:21–22, when Absalom has sex with them as a signal of the success of his rebellion. David's abandonment of his concubines recalls Nathan's prediction of David's punishment in 2 Sam. 12:11: "I will take your wives before your eyes and give them to your neighbor, and he shall lie with your wives in broad daylight." In 2 Sam. 20:3, David places these women under house arrest.

15:19 *Then the king said to Ittai the Gittite.* As a non-Israelite, Ittai, who is from the city of Gath, does not need to flee.

15:23 *The whole country wept aloud as all the people passed by.* An indication that David still had a great deal of support.

15:24 *Abiathar came up, and Zadok also, with all the Levites, carrying the ark of the covenant of God.* The king sends the ark back into the city (on *the ark*, see note on 6:2). David phrases his decision as a willingness to accept whatever outcome the Lord wishes. The narrator knows, of course, how the story ends—for this reason, David is referred to as "the king" throughout the story of Absalom's rebellion. Since Absalom is a son of David, the reader who knows the 2 Sam. 7 story of God's promise to David (that his descendants would always rule in Jerusalem) could suppose that it is possible that David will not return to Jerusalem but that the Davidic line will continue to rule. See **"The Davidic Covenant," p. 433**.

16 When David had passed a little beyond the summit, Ziba the servant
of Mephibosheth met him with a couple
of donkeys saddled, carrying two hundred
loaves of bread, one hundred bunches of
raisins, one hundred of summer fruits, and
one skin of wine. [2]The king said to Ziba,
"Why have you brought these?" Ziba answered, "The donkeys are for the king's
household to ride, the bread and summer
fruit are for the young men to eat, and the
wine is for those to drink who faint in the
wilderness." [3]The king said, "And where is
your master's son?" Ziba said to the king,
"He remains in Jerusalem, for he said, 'Today the house of Israel will give me back
my grandfather's kingdom.' " [4]Then the
king said to Ziba, "All that belonged to Mephibosheth is now yours." Ziba said, "I do
obeisance; let me find favor in your sight,
my lord the king."

5 When King David came to Bahurim, a
man of the family of the house of Saul came
out whose name was Shimei son of Gera;
he came out cursing. [6]He threw stones at
David and at all the servants of King David;
now all the people and all the warriors were
on his right and on his left. [7]Shimei shouted while he cursed, "Out! Out! Murderer!
Scoundrel! [8]The LORD has avenged on all of
you the blood of the house of Saul, in whose
place you have reigned, and the LORD has
given the kingdom into the hand of your son
Absalom. See, disaster has overtaken you,
for you are a man of blood."

9 Then Abishai son of Zeruiah said to the
king, "Why should this dead dog curse my
lord the king? Let me go over and take off
his head." [10]But the king said, "What have
I to do with you, you sons of Zeruiah? If
he is cursing because the LORD has said to
him, 'Curse David,' who then shall say, 'Why
have you done so?' " [11]David said to Abishai
and to all his servants, "My own son seeks
my life; how much more now may this Benjaminite! Let him alone, and let him curse,
for the LORD has bidden him. [12]It may be
that the LORD will look on my distress,[o] and
the LORD will repay me with good for this
cursing of me today." [13]So David and his men
went on the road while Shimei went along
on the hillside opposite him and cursed as
he went, throwing stones and flinging dust
at him. [14]The king and all the people who
were with him arrived weary at the Jordan,[p]
and there he refreshed himself.

15 Now Absalom and all the Israelites[q]
came to Jerusalem; Ahithophel was with
him. [16]When Hushai the Archite, David's
friend, came to Absalom, Hushai said to
Absalom, "Long live the king! Long live the
king!" [17]Absalom said to Hushai, "Is this your
loyalty to your friend? Why did you not go
with your friend?" [18]Hushai said to Absalom, "No, but the one whom the LORD and
this people and all the Israelites have chosen, his I will be, and with him I will remain.
[19]Moreover, whom should I serve? Should it
not be his son? Just as I have served your
father, so I will serve you."

20 Then Absalom said to Ahithophel,
"Give us your counsel; what shall we do?"
[21]Ahithophel said to Absalom, "Go in to your
father's concubines, the ones he has left to
look after the house, and all Israel will hear
that you have made yourself odious to your
father, and the hands of all who are with
you will be strengthened." [22]So they pitched
a tent for Absalom upon the roof, and Absalom went in to his father's concubines in
the sight of all Israel. [23]Now in those days
the counsel that Ahithophel gave was as if

o 16.12 Gk Vg: Heb *iniquity* *p* 16.14 Gk ms: Heb lacks *at the Jordan* *q* 16.15 Gk: Heb *all the people, the men of Israel*

16:1 *Ziba the servant of Mephibosheth met him.* Ziba was introduced in 2 Sam. 9; he had been one of Saul's servants. David, in 2 Sam. 9, makes Ziba responsible for the farming that needed to be done on Mephibosheth's land. Here in this chapter, David hears from Ziba that Mephibosheth has betrayed David. The king rewards Ziba for his loyalty, giving him everything that Mephibosheth had owned. On Mephibosheth, see note on 4:4.

16:5 *When King David came to Bahurim, a man of the family of the house of Saul came out whose name was Shimei son of Gera; he came out cursing.* While Ziba shows his support for David, Shimei curses him. Shimei's reaction gives us a window into understanding some of the resentment that had built up toward David, resentment that found an outlet in support of Absalom's rebellion.

16:21 *Go in to your father's concubines.* Having sex with a concubine of a king would have been a way of claiming political control and would have been an act of treason on Absalom's part. In 3:7, Saul's son Ishbaal accuses Abner, his general, of this act of treason.

one consulted the oracle[r] of God, so all the counsel of Ahithophel was esteemed both by David and by Absalom.

17 Moreover Ahithophel said to Absalom, "Let me choose twelve thousand men, and I will set out and pursue David tonight. [2]I will come upon him while he is weary and discouraged and throw him into a panic, and all the people who are with him will flee. I will strike down only the king, [3]and I will bring all the people back to you as a bride comes home to her husband. You seek the life of only one man,[s] and all the people will be at peace." [4]The advice pleased Absalom and all the elders of Israel.

5 Then Absalom said, "Call Hushai the Archite also, and let us hear too what he has to say." [6]When Hushai came to Absalom, Absalom said to him, "This is what Ahithophel has said; shall we do as he advises? If not, you tell us." [7]Then Hushai said to Absalom, "This time the counsel that Ahithophel has given is not good." [8]Hushai continued, "You know that your father and his men are warriors and that they are enraged, like a bear robbed of her cubs in the field. Besides, your father is expert in war; he will not spend the night with the troops. [9]Even now he has hidden himself in one of the pits or in some other place. And when some of our troops[t] fall at the first attack, whoever hears it will say, 'There has been a slaughter among the troops who follow Absalom.' [10]Then even the valiant warrior whose heart is like the heart of a lion will utterly melt with fear, for all Israel knows that your father is a warrior and that those who are with him are valiant warriors. [11]But my counsel is that all Israel be gathered to you, from Dan to Beer-sheba, like the sand by the sea for multitude, and that you go to battle in person. [12]So we shall come upon him in whatever place he may be found, and we shall light on him as the dew falls on the ground, and he will not survive, nor will any of those with him. [13]If he withdraws into a city, then all Israel will bring ropes to that

city, and we shall drag it into the valley until not even a pebble is to be found there." [14]Absalom and all the men of Israel said, "The counsel of Hushai the Archite is better than the counsel of Ahithophel." For the LORD had ordained to defeat the good counsel of Ahithophel, so that the LORD might bring ruin on Absalom.

15 Then Hushai said to the priests Zadok and Abiathar, "Thus and so did Ahithophel counsel Absalom and the elders of Israel, and thus and so I have counseled. [16]Therefore send quickly and tell David, 'Do not lodge tonight at the fords of the wilderness, but by all means cross over, lest the king and all the people who are with him be swallowed up.' " [17]Jonathan and Ahimaaz were waiting at En-rogel; a female slave used to go and tell them, and they would go and tell King David, for they could not risk being seen entering the city. [18]But a young man saw them and told Absalom, so both of them went away quickly and came to the house of a man at Bahurim who had a well in his courtyard, and they went down into it. [19]The man's wife took a covering, stretched it over the well's mouth, and spread out grain on it, and nothing was known of it. [20]When Absalom's servants came to the woman at the house, they said, "Where are Ahimaaz and Jonathan?" The woman said to them, "They have crossed over the brook[u] of water." And when they had searched and could not find them, they returned to Jerusalem.

21 After they had gone, the men came up out of the well and went and told King David. They said to David, "Go and cross the water quickly, for thus and so has Ahithophel counseled against you." [22]So David and all the people who were with him set out and crossed the Jordan; by daybreak not one was left who had not crossed the Jordan.

23 When Ahithophel saw that his counsel was not followed, he saddled his donkey and went off home to his own city. He set his

r 16.23 Heb *word*   s 17.3 Gk: Heb *like the return of the whole (is) the man whom you seek*   t 17.9 Gk mss: Heb *some of them*   u 17.20 Meaning of Heb uncertain

17:1 On *Ahithophel*, see note on 15:12.
17:15 *Then Hushai said to the priests Zadok and Abiathar, "Thus and so did Ahithophel counsel Absalom and the elders of Israel, and thus and so I have counseled."* The narrator is using *thus and so* here to avoid repeating the conversation in the preceding section. This will happen again in 17:21. Hushai is, of course, on David's side, although Absalom does not know that.

house in order and hanged himself; he died and was buried in the tomb of his father.

24 Then David came to Mahanaim, while Absalom crossed the Jordan with all the men of Israel. ²⁵Now Absalom had set Amasa over the army in the place of Joab. Amasa was the son of a man named Ithra the Ishmaelite,ʳ who had married Abigal daughter of Nahash, sister of Zeruiah, Joab's mother. ²⁶The Israelites and Absalom encamped in the land of Gilead.

27 When David came to Mahanaim, Shobi son of Nahash from Rabbah of the Ammonites, and Machir son of Ammiel from Lo-debar, and Barzillai the Gileadite from Rogelim ²⁸brought beds, basins, and earthen vessels, wheat, barley, meal, parched grain, beans and lentils,ʷ ²⁹honey and curds, sheep, and cheese from the herd, for David and the people with him to eat, for they said, "The troops are hungry and weary and thirsty in the wilderness."

18 Then David mustered the men who were with him and set over them commanders of thousands and commanders of hundreds. ²And David sent forth the army: one third under the command of Joab; one third under the command of Abishai son of Zeruiah, Joab's brother; and one third under the command of Ittai the Gittite. The king said to the men, "I myself will also go out with you." ³But the men said, "You shall not go out. For if we flee, they will not care about us. If half of us die, they will not care about us. But you are worth ten thousand of us;ˣ therefore it is better that you send us help from the city."

⁴The king said to them, "Whatever seems best to you I will do." So the king stood at the side of the gate, while all the army marched out by hundreds and by thousands. ⁵The king ordered Joab and Abishai and Ittai, saying, "Deal gently for my sake with the young man Absalom." And all the people heard when the king gave orders to all the commanders concerning Absalom.

6 So the army went out into the field against Israel, and the battle was fought in the forest of Ephraim. ⁷The men of Israel were defeated there by the servants of David, and the slaughter there was great on that day, twenty thousand men. ⁸The battle spread over the face of all the country, and the forest claimed more victims that day than the sword.

9 Absalom happened to meet the servants of David. Absalom was riding on his mule, and the mule went under the thick branches of a great oak. His head caught fast in the oak, and he was left hangingʸ between heaven and earth, while the mule that was under him went on. ¹⁰A man saw it and told Joab, "I saw Absalom hanging in an oak." ¹¹Joab said to the man who told him, "What, you saw him! Why then did you not strike him there to the ground? I would have been glad to give you ten pieces of silver and a belt." ¹²But the man said to Joab, "Even if I felt in my hand the weight of a thousand pieces of silver, I would not raise my hand against the king's son, for in our hearing the king commanded you and Abishai and Ittai,

v 17.25 Gk mss: Heb *Israelite*   w 17.28 Heb *and lentils and parched grain*   x 18.3 Gk Vg Symmachus: Heb *for now there are ten thousand such as we*   y 18.9 Gk Syr Tg: Heb *was put*

18:2 *I myself will also go out with you.* In 2 Sam. 11, David was in Jerusalem while his army was in the field; David's willingness to go out with his army, in this chapter, signals that he is now aware of how precarious his situation is. And is it maybe also a signal that David has changed and grown? His advisers counsel against David's presence on the battlefield because of the danger to him.

18:5 *Deal gently for my sake with the young man Absalom.* Despite Absalom's rebellion, David still loves him. David continues to let his love for his son sway him to make bad (in terms of his kingship) decisions.

18:8 *And the forest claimed more victims that day than the sword.* This puzzling statement probably means that God used the forest to help David's army win. In Isa. 56:9, God summons the wild animals of the forest to "eat" (from the same Hebrew verb translated as *claimed* here) the people; in Josh. 10:11, hailstones sent by God kill the enemy.

18:9 *His head caught fast in the oak, and he was left hanging between heaven and earth.* Absalom's long hair was caught; earlier in 2 Sam. 14:26, mention was made of how much hair Absalom had. In that earlier passage, the narrator might be leading us to think of Samson and his strength-giving hair; this might lead us to think that Absalom will prevail. In 2 Sam. 18, what had been mentioned as something positive earlier becomes the immediate occasion for Absalom's undoing.

saying, 'For my sake protect the young man Absalom!' ¹³On the other hand, if I had dealt treacherously against his life^z (and there is nothing hidden from the king), then you yourself would have stood aloof." ¹⁴Joab said, "I will not waste time like this with you." He took three spears in his hand and thrust them into the heart of Absalom while he was still alive in the oak. ¹⁵And ten young men, Joab's armor-bearers, surrounded Absalom and struck him and killed him.

16 Then Joab sounded the trumpet, and the troops came back from pursuing Israel, for Joab restrained the troops. ¹⁷They took Absalom, threw him into a great pit in the forest, and raised over him a very great heap of stones. Meanwhile all the Israelites fled to their homes. ¹⁸Now Absalom in his lifetime had taken and set up for himself a pillar that is in the King's Valley, for he said, "I have no son to keep my name in remembrance." He called the pillar by his own name; it is called Absalom's Monument to this day.

19 Then Ahimaaz son of Zadok said, "Let me run and carry tidings to the king that the LORD has delivered him from the power of his enemies." ²⁰Joab said to him, "You are not to carry tidings today; you may carry tidings another day, but today you shall not do so because the king's son is dead." ²¹Then Joab said to a Cushite, "Go, tell the king what you have seen." The Cushite bowed before Joab and ran. ²²Then Ahimaaz son of Zadok said again to Joab, "Come what may, let me also run after the Cushite." And Joab said, "Why will you run, my son, seeing that you have no reward^a for the tidings?" ²³"Come what may," he said, "I will run." So he said to him, "Run." Then Ahimaaz ran by the way of the Plain and outran the Cushite.

24 Now David was sitting between the two gates. The sentinel went up to the roof of the gate by the wall, and when he looked up he saw a man running alone. ²⁵The sentinel shouted and told the king. The king said, "If he is alone, there are tidings in his mouth." He kept coming and drew near. ²⁶Then the sentinel saw another man running, and the sentinel called to the gatekeeper and said,

"See, another man running alone!" The king said, "He also is bringing tidings." ²⁷The sentinel said, "I think the first one runs like Ahimaaz son of Zadok." The king said, "He is a good man and comes with good tidings."

28 Then Ahimaaz cried out to the king, "All is well!" He prostrated himself before the king with his face to the ground and said, "Blessed be the LORD your God, who has delivered up the men who raised their hand against my lord the king." ²⁹The king said, "Is it well with the young man Absalom?" Ahimaaz answered, "I saw a great tumult when the king's servant Joab sent your servant, but I do not know what it was." ³⁰The king said, "Turn aside, and stand here." So he turned aside and stood still.

31 Then the Cushite came, and the Cushite said, "Good tidings for my lord the king! For the LORD has vindicated you this day, delivering you from the power of all who rose up against you." ³²The king said to the Cushite, "Is it well with the young man Absalom?" The Cushite answered, "May the enemies of my lord the king and all who rise up to do you harm be like that young man."

33 ^bThe king was deeply moved and went up to the chamber over the gate and wept, and as he went he said, "O my son Absalom, my son, my son Absalom! Would I had died instead of you, O Absalom, my son, my son!"

19 It was told Joab, "The king is weeping and mourning for Absalom." ²So the victory that day was turned into mourning for all the troops, for the troops heard that day, "The king is grieving for his son." ³The troops stole into the city that day as soldiers steal in who are ashamed when they flee in battle. ⁴The king covered his face, and the king cried with a loud voice, "O my son Absalom, O Absalom, my son, my son!" ⁵Then Joab came into the house to the king and said, "Today you have covered with shame the faces of all your officers who have saved your life today, and the lives of your sons and your daughters, and the lives of your wives and your concubines, ⁶for

z 18.13 Another reading is *at the risk of my life*
a 18.22 Meaning of Heb uncertain   b 18.33 19.1 in Heb

18:33 *O my son Absalom, my son, my son Absalom!* David's grief over the death of his son prevents him from rejoicing at his army's hard-fought victory. Joab will reprimand him for this.

19:5–6 *Then Joab came into the house to the king and said, "Today you have covered with shame the faces of all your officers who have saved your life today, and the lives of your sons and your*

love of those who hate you and for hatred of those who love you. You have made it clear today that commanders and officers are nothing to you, for I perceive that, if Absalom were alive and all of us were dead today, then you would be pleased. [7]So go out at once and speak kindly to your servants, for I swear by the Lord, if you do not go, not a man will stay with you this night, and this will be worse for you than any disaster that has come upon you from your youth until now." [8]Then the king got up and took his seat in the gate. The troops were all told, "See, the king is sitting in the gate," and all the troops came before the king.

Meanwhile, all the Israelites had fled to their homes. [9]All the people were disputing throughout all the tribes of Israel, saying, "The king delivered us from the hand of our enemies and saved us from the hand of the Philistines, and now he has fled out of the land because of Absalom. [10]But Absalom, whom we anointed over us, is dead in battle. Now therefore why do you say nothing about bringing the king back?"

[11] King David sent this message to the priests Zadok and Abiathar, "Say to the elders of Judah, 'Why should you be the last to bring the king back to his house? The talk of all Israel has come to the king.[c] [12]You are my kin; you are my bone and my flesh; why then should you be the last to bring back the king?' [13]And say to Amasa, 'Are you not my bone and my flesh? So may God do to me and more, if you are not the commander of my army from now on, in place of Joab.'" [14]Amasa[d] swayed the hearts of all the people of Judah as one, and they sent word to the king, "Return, both you and all your servants." [15]So the king came back to the Jordan, and Judah came to Gilgal to meet the king and to bring him over the Jordan.

[16] Shimei son of Gera, a Benjaminite from Bahurim, hurried to come down with the people of Judah to meet King David; [17]with him were a thousand people from Benjamin. And Ziba, the servant of the house of Saul, with his fifteen sons and his twenty servants, rushed down to the Jordan ahead of the king [18]while the crossing was taking place,[e] to bring over the king's household and to do his pleasure.

Shimei son of Gera fell down before the king as he was about to cross the Jordan [19]and said to the king, "May my lord not hold me guilty or remember how your servant did wrong on the day my lord the king left Jerusalem; may the king not bear it in mind. [20]For your servant knows that I have sinned; therefore, see, I have come this day, the first of all the house of Joseph to come down to meet my lord the king." [21]Abishai son of Zeruiah answered, "Shall not Shimei be put to death for this because he cursed the Lord's anointed?" [22]But David said, "What have I to do with you, you sons of Zeruiah, that you should today become an adversary to me? Shall anyone be put to death in Israel this day? For do I not know that I am this day king over Israel?" [23]The king said to Shimei, "You shall not die." And the king gave him his oath.

[24] Mephibosheth grandson of Saul came down to meet the king; he had not taken care of his feet or trimmed his beard or washed his clothes from the day the king left until the day he came back in safety. [25]When he came from Jerusalem to meet the king, the king said to him, "Why did you not go with me, Mephibosheth?" [26]He answered, "My lord, O king, my servant deceived me, for your servant said to him,

c 19.11 Gk: Heb *to the king, to his house*   d 19.14 Heb *He*
e 19.18 Cn: Heb *the ford crossed*

daughters, and the lives of your wives and your concubines, for love of those who hate you and for hatred of those who love you." Joab reprimands David for allowing his grief at the loss of his son Absalom to be so obvious; Joab argues that David's grief is inappropriate, since his army has endangered their lives to put down Absalom's rebellion. David takes Joab's reprimand to heart and appears before his army. He will, however, later replace Joab as general of his army.

19:13 *So may God do to me and more, if you are not the commander of my army from now on, in place of Joab.* The opening—*So may God do to me and more*—is a common oath formula in the HB. A paraphrase would be "You will most certainly be commander of my army from now on, in place of Joab." Amasa, to whom this is addressed, had been the general over Absalom's army (2 Sam. 17). This replacement is intended as a punishment for Joab, who killed Absalom, but it is also part of David's attempt to smooth out the divisions that had contributed to the near success of Absalom's rebellion.

'Saddle a donkey for me[f] so that I may ride on it and go with the king.' For your servant is lame. ²⁷He has slandered your servant to my lord the king. But my lord the king is like the angel of God; do therefore what seems good to you. ²⁸For all my father's house were doomed to death before my lord the king, but you set your servant among those who eat at your table. What further right have I, then, to appeal to the king?" ²⁹The king said to him, "Why speak any more of your affairs? I have decided: you and Ziba shall divide the land." ³⁰Mephibosheth said to the king, "Let him take it all, since my lord the king has arrived home safely."

31 Now Barzillai the Gileadite had come down from Rogelim; he went on with the king to the Jordan to escort him over the Jordan. ³²Barzillai was a very aged man, eighty years old. He had provided the king with food while he stayed at Mahanaim, for he was a very wealthy man. ³³The king said to Barzillai, "Come over with me, and I will provide for you in Jerusalem at my side." ³⁴But Barzillai said to the king, "How many years have I still to live, that I should go up with the king to Jerusalem? ³⁵Today I am eighty years old; can I discern what is pleasant and what is not? Can your servant taste what he eats or what he drinks? Can I still listen to the voice of singing men and singing women? Why then should your servant be an added burden to my lord the king? ³⁶Your servant will go a little way over the Jordan with the king. Why should the king recompense me with such a reward? ³⁷Please let your servant return, so that I may die in my own town, near the graves of my father and my mother. But here is your servant Chimham; let him go over with my lord the king and do for him whatever seems good to you." ³⁸The king answered, "Chimham shall go over with me, and I will do for him whatever seems good to you, and all that you desire of me I will do for you." ³⁹Then all the people crossed over the Jordan, and the king crossed over; the king kissed Barzillai and blessed him, and he returned to his own home. ⁴⁰The king went on to Gilgal, and Chimham went on with him; all the people of Judah, and also half the people of Israel, brought the king on his way.

41 Then all the people of Israel came to the king and said to him, "Why have our kindred the people of Judah stolen you away and brought the king and his household over the Jordan and all David's men with him?" ⁴²All the people of Judah answered the people of Israel, "Because the king is near of kin to us. Why then are you angry over this matter? Have we eaten at all at the king's expense? Or has he given us any gift?" ⁴³But the people of Israel answered the people of Judah, "We have ten shares in the king, and in David also we have more than you. Why then did you despise us? Were we not the first to speak of bringing back our king?" But the words of the people of Judah were fiercer than the words of the people of Israel.

20 Now a scoundrel named Sheba son of Bichri, a Benjaminite, happened to be there. He sounded the trumpet and cried out,

f 19.26 Gk Syr Vg: Heb *said, 'I will saddle a donkey for myself*

19:30 *Mephibosheth said to the king, "Let him take it all, since my lord the king has arrived home safely."* Mephibosheth, Jonathan's son, had been accused of treason by Ziba, his servant (2 Sam. 16). David had given all that belonged to Mephibosheth to Ziba, who was one of the first to help David when he abandoned Jerusalem. Now David, perhaps to placate supporters of Saul who had joined the rebellion, treats Mephibosheth kindly. Mephibosheth, aware no doubt that it could have gone very badly for him and perhaps aware that Ziba's testimony against him was accurate, decides not to pursue the matter of his property. On Mephibosheth, see note on 4:4.

19:43 *But the people of Israel answered the people of Judah, "We have ten shares in the king, and in David also we have more than you."* This story anticipates the split of the Davidic kingdom detailed in 1 Kgs. 12. In that passage, the northern tribes (Israel) abandon David's grandson Rehoboam, while the southern tribes (Judah and Benjamin) stay with him. This distrust between Israel and Judah, described here in 2 Sam. 19, will explode into a second rebellion in 2 Sam. 20. David has defeated Absalom and his rebellion, but the troubles that began with David's adultery with Bathsheba and with the murder of Uriah continue.

20:1 *We have no portion in David, no share in the son of Jesse! Everyone to your tents, O Israel!* This phrase will be repeated in 1 Kgs. 12:16, when the northern tribes split from the two southern

"We have no portion in David,
no share in the son of Jesse!
Everyone to your tents, O Israel!" ²So all the people of Israel withdrew from David and followed Sheba son of Bichri, but the people of Judah followed their king steadfastly from the Jordan to Jerusalem.

3 David came to his house at Jerusalem, and the king took the ten concubines whom he had left to look after the house and put them in a house under guard and provided for them but did not go in to them. So they were shut up until the day of their death, living as if in widowhood.

4 Then the king said to Amasa, "Call the men of Judah together to me within three days, and be here yourself." ⁵So Amasa went to summon Judah, but he delayed beyond the set time that had been appointed him. ⁶David said to Abishai, "Now Sheba son of Bichri will do us more harm than Absalom; take your lord's servants and pursue him, or he will find fortified cities for himself and escape from us." ⁷Joab's men went out after him, along with the Cherethites, the Pelethites, and all the warriors; they went out from Jerusalem to pursue Sheba son of Bichri. ⁸When they were at the large stone that is in Gibeon, Amasa came to meet them. Now Joab was wearing a soldier's garment, and over it was a belt with a sword in its sheath fastened at his waist; as he went forward, it fell out. ⁹Joab said to Amasa, "Is it well with you, my brother?" And Joab took Amasa by the beard with his right hand to kiss him. ¹⁰But Amasa did not notice the sword in Joab's hand; Joab struck him in the belly so that his entrails poured out on the ground, and he died. He did not strike a second blow.

Then Joab and his brother Abishai pursued Sheba son of Bichri. ¹¹And one of Joab's men took his stand by Amasa and said, "Whoever favors Joab, and whoever is for David, let him follow Joab." ¹²Amasa lay wallowing in his blood on the highway, and the man saw that all the people were stopping. Since he saw that all who came by him were stopping, he carried Amasa from the highway into a field and threw a garment over him. ¹³Once he was removed from the highway, all the people went on after Joab to pursue Sheba son of Bichri.

14 Sheba^g passed through all the tribes of Israel to Abel of Beth-maacah,^b and all the Bichrites^i assembled and followed him inside. ¹⁵Joab's forces^j came and besieged him in Abel of Beth-maacah; they threw up a siege ramp against the city, and it stood against the rampart. Joab's forces were battering the wall to break it down. ¹⁶Then a wise woman called from the city, "Listen! Listen! Tell Joab, 'Come here, I want to speak to you.'" ¹⁷He came near her, and the woman said, "Are you Joab?" He answered, "I am." Then she said to him, "Listen to the words of your servant." He answered, "I am listening." ¹⁸Then she said, "They used to say in the old days, 'Let them inquire at Abel,' and so they would settle a matter. ¹⁹I am one of those who are peaceable and faithful in Israel; you seek to destroy a city that is a mother in Israel; why will you swallow up the heritage of the LORD?" ²⁰Joab answered, "Far be it from me, far be it, that I should swallow up or destroy! ²¹That is not the case!

g 20.14 Heb *He*   h 20.14 Compare 20.15: Heb *and Beth-maacah*   i 20.14 Compare Gk Vg: Heb *Berites*   j 20.15 Heb *They*

tribes and form their own kingdom. It is Sheba, from the tribe of Benjamin, who begins this rebellion, an indication that the small tribe of Benjamin was not fully committed to David. Saul, David's predecessor as the Lord's anointed, had been a member of the tribe of Benjamin.

20:5 *So Amasa went to summon Judah, but he delayed beyond the set time that had been appointed him.* Amasa took more than the three days allotted to him by David. It is not clear that Amasa intends to rebel against David (Amasa does not seem to fear Joab when Joab approaches him in 2 Sam. 20:9), but Joab takes this opportunity to get his revenge on Amasa for taking over the leadership of David's army. In 2 Sam. 20:10, Joab kills Amasa with only one thrust of his sword.

20:18 *Then she said, "They used to say in the old days, 'Let them inquire at Abel.'"* The wise woman is reminding Joab that her city, Abel (Beth-maacah), had been a place where people went to settle disputes because of the wisdom of its people; the inhabitants are not rebels but people with a reputation for common sense.

20:19 *You seek to destroy a city that is a mother in Israel; why will you swallow up the heritage of the LORD?* This term *heritage* occurs frequently in the HB, referring to land given by God to the Israelites (Deut. 4:21; 1 Sam. 10:1).

But a man of the hill country of Ephraim called Sheba son of Bichri has lifted up his hand against King David; give him up alone, and I will withdraw from the city." The woman said to Joab, "His head shall be thrown over the wall to you." ²²Then the woman went to all the people with her wise plan. And they cut off the head of Sheba son of Bichri and threw it out to Joab. So he blew the trumpet, and they dispersed from the city, and all went to their homes, while Joab returned to Jerusalem to the king.

23 Now Joab was in command of all the army of Israel;ᵏ Benaiah son of Jehoiada was in command of the Cherethites and the Pelethites; ²⁴Adoram was in charge of the forced labor; Jehoshaphat son of Ahilud was the recorder; ²⁵Sheva was secretary; Zadok and Abiathar were priests; ²⁶and Ira the Jairite was also David's priest.

21 Now there was a famine in the days of David for three years, year after year, and David inquired of the Lord. The Lord said, "There is bloodguilt on Saul and on his house because he put the Gibeonites to death." ²So the king called the Gibeonites and spoke to them. (Now the Gibeonites were not of the people of Israel but of the remnant of the Amorites; although the people of Israel had sworn to spare them, Saul had tried to wipe them out in his zeal for the people of Israel and Judah.) ³David said to the Gibeonites, "What shall I do for you? How shall I make expiation, that you may bless the heritage of the Lord?" ⁴The Gibeonites said to him, "It is not a matter of silver or gold between us and Saul or his house; neither is it for us to put anyone to death in Israel." He said, "What do you say that I should do for you?" ⁵They said to the king, "The man who consumed us and planned to destroy us so that we should have no place in all the territory of Israel, ⁶let seven of his sons be handed over to us, and we will impale them before the Lord at Gibeon on the mountain of the Lord."ˡ The king said, "I will hand them over."

7 But the king spared Mephibosheth, the son of Saul's son Jonathan, because of the oath of the Lord that was between them, between David and Jonathan son of Saul. ⁸The king took the two sons of Rizpah daughter of Aiah, whom she bore to Saul, Armoni and Mephibosheth; and the five sons of Merabᵐ daughter of Saul, whom she bore to Adriel son of Barzillai the Meholathite; ⁹he gave them into the hands of the Gibeonites, and they impaled them on the mountain before the Lord. The seven of them perished together. They were put to death in the first days of harvest, at the beginning of barley harvest.

10 Then Rizpah the daughter of Aiah took sackcloth and spread it on a rock for

k 20.23 Cn: Heb *Joab to all the army, Israel* l 21.6 Cn Compare: Heb *at Gibeah of Saul, the chosen of the Lord* m 21.8 Heb mss Syr Compare Gk: MT *Michal*

21:1 *And David inquired of the Lord. The Lord said, "There is bloodguilt on Saul and on his house because he put the Gibeonites to death."* The Gibeonites first appear in the HB in Josh. 9–10. The Gibeonites tricked Joshua into thinking that they had journeyed to him from a great distance, so Joshua did not exterminate them as he did other non-Israelite people. Joshua makes a treaty with the Gibeonites, swearing to let them live (Josh. 9:15). Saul's attack on the Gibeonites violated this treaty. *Bloodguilt*. The question of bloodguilt has surfaced before in 2 Samuel. In 2 Sam. 1:16, David declares that he is innocent of the blood of the Amalekite who delivers the news of Saul's death. When Joab murders Abner, David proclaims that he is innocent (2 Sam. 3:28–30). To be guilty of bloodguilt meant that the "avenger of blood" had the right to take the life of the murderer, according to Num. 35:19 and Deut. 19:11–12.

21:7 *But the king spared Mephibosheth, the son of Saul's son Jonathan, because of the oath of the Lord that was between them.* This is a reference to the covenant that Jonathan made with David (1 Sam. 18:3, "Then Jonathan made a covenant with David because he loved him as his own soul"; 1 Sam. 20:42 gives more information on that covenant: "The Lord shall be between me and you and between my descendants and your descendants forever"). There were two descendants of Saul named Mephibosheth; see note on 4:4.

21:9 *The seven of them perished together. They were put to death in the first days of harvest, at the beginning of barley harvest.* The barley harvest would begin in April.

21:10 *Then Rizpah the daughter of Aiah took sackcloth and spread it on a rock for herself, from the beginning of harvest until rain fell on them from the heavens; she did not allow the birds of the air*

herself, from the beginning of harvest until rain fell on them from the heavens; she
did not allow the birds of the air to come
on the bodies[n] by day or the wild animals
by night. [11]When David was told what Rizpah daughter of Aiah, the concubine of
Saul, had done, [12]David went and took the
bones of Saul and the bones of his son Jonathan from the people of Jabesh-gilead, who
had stolen them from the public square of
Beth-shan, where the Philistines had hung
them up, on the day the Philistines killed
Saul on Gilboa. [13]He brought up from there
the bones of Saul and the bones of his son
Jonathan, and they gathered the bones of
those who had been impaled. [14]They buried
the bones of Saul and of his son Jonathan
in the land of Benjamin in Zela, in the tomb
of his father Kish; they did all that the king
commanded. After that, God heeded supplications for the land.

15 The Philistines went to war again with
Israel, and David went down together with
his servants. They fought against the Philistines, and David grew weary. [16]Ishbi-benob,
one of the descendants of the giants, whose
spear weighed three hundred shekels of
bronze and who was fitted out with new
weapons,[o] said he would kill David. [17]But
Abishai son of Zeruiah came to his aid and
attacked the Philistine and killed him. Then
David's men swore to him, "You shall not go
out with us to battle any longer, so that you
do not quench the lamp of Israel."

18 After this a battle took place with the
Philistines at Gob; then Sibbecai the Hushathite killed Saph, who was one of the descendants of the giants. [19]Then there was
another battle with the Philistines at Gob,
and Elhanan son of Jaare-oregim the Bethlehemite killed Goliath the Gittite, the shaft
of whose spear was like a weaver's beam.
[20]There was again war at Gath, where there
was a man of great size who had six fingers
on each hand and six toes on each foot,
twenty-four in number; he, too, was descended from the giants.[p] [21]When he taunted Israel, Jonathan son of David's brother
Shimei killed him. [22]These four were descended from the giants[q] in Gath; they fell
by the hands of David and his servants.

22 David spoke to the LORD the words
of this song on the day when the
LORD delivered him from the hand of all
his enemies and from the hand of Saul. [2]He
said,
　"The LORD is my rock, my fortress, and
　　　my deliverer,
[3]　　my God, my rock in whom I take
　　　refuge,
　my shield and the horn of my salvation,
　　my stronghold and my refuge,
　　my savior; you save me from
　　　violence.
[4] I call upon the LORD, who is worthy to
　　be praised,
　　and I am saved from my enemies.

[5] For the waves of death encompassed
　　me;
　　the torrents of perdition assailed me;
[6] the cords of Sheol entangled me;
　　the snares of death confronted me.

n 21.10 Heb *them*　o 21.16 Heb *was belted anew*　p 21.20 Gk:
Heb *from the Raphah*　q 21.22 Gk: Heb *from the Raphah*

---

to come on the bodies by day or the wild animals by night. Sackcloth is a sign of mourning. Rizpah,
Saul's concubine, is the mother of two of the victims. The desecration of a corpse by a wild animal
was considered the ultimate retribution against an enemy. Goliath threatens David with this (1 Sam.
17:44), and in 2 Kgs. 9:36, this is Jezebel's fate.

　　22:1 *The words of this song.* This entire chapter is a psalm of thanksgiving; it appears also in the
book of Psalms (Ps. 18).

　　22:2 *My rock.* A metaphor used frequently in the HB (2 Sam. 22:3, 47; 23:3).

　　22:3 *The horn of my salvation.* The word "horn" in the HB often appears as a symbol of strength
(1 Kgs. 22:11; Ps. 92:10).

　　22:5 *For the waves of death encompassed me.* Just as in the psalm in Jonah 2, death is equated
with engulfing waters. Given the account of the world's origin that we see in Gen. 1, it seems that
the Israelites (and other ancient Near Eastern people) believed the world to be surrounded, above
and below, by water that was separated by God at the creation. (Gen. 7:11 describes the reversal of
the process of the separation of these original waters.) Consequently, when one was near death and
about to descend to Sheol, the place of the dead, they entered a realm close to the original waters.
See **"Creation," p. 23**.

7 In my distress I called upon the Lord;
    to my God I called.
  From his temple he heard my voice,
    and my cry came to his ears.

8 Then the earth reeled and rocked;
    the foundations of the heavens
      trembled
    and reeled because he was angry.
9 Smoke went up from his nostrils
    and devouring fire from his mouth;
    glowing coals flamed forth from
      him.
10 He bowed the heavens and came down;
    thick darkness was under his feet.
11 He rode on a cherub and flew;
    he was seen upon the wings of the
      wind.
12 He made darkness around him a
      canopy,
    thick clouds, a gathering of water.
13 Out of the brightness before him
    coals of fire flamed forth.
14 The Lord thundered from heaven;
    the Most High uttered his voice.
15 He sent out arrows and scattered them,
    lightning and routed them.
16 Then the channels of the sea were seen;
    the foundations of the world were
      laid bare
  at the rebuke of the Lord,
    at the blast of the breath of his nostrils.

17 He reached from on high; he took me;
    he drew me out of mighty waters.
18 He delivered me from my strong enemy,
    from those who hated me,
    for they were too mighty for me.
19 They came upon me in the day of my
      calamity,
    but the Lord was my stay.
20 He brought me out into a broad place;
    he delivered me because he
      delighted in me.

21 The Lord rewarded me according to my
      righteousness;
    according to the cleanness of my
      hands he recompensed me.

22 For I have kept the ways of the Lord
    and have not wickedly departed
      from my God.
23 For all his ordinances were before me,
    and from his statutes I did not turn
      aside.
24 I was blameless before him,
    and I kept myself from guilt.
25 Therefore the Lord has recompensed
    me according to my
      righteousness,
    according to my cleanness in his
      sight.

26 With the loyal you show yourself loyal;
    with the blameless*r* you show
      yourself blameless;
27 with the pure you show yourself pure,
    and with the crooked you show
      yourself shrewd.
28 You deliver a humble people,
    but your eyes are upon the haughty
      to bring them down.
29 Indeed, you are my lamp, O Lord;
    the Lord lightens my darkness.
30 By you I can outrun a troop,
    and by my God I can leap over a
      wall.
31 This God—his way is perfect;
    the promise of the Lord proves true;
    he is a shield for all who take refuge
      in him.

32 For who is God but the Lord?
    And who is a rock except our God?
33 The God who has girded me with
      strength*s*
    has opened wide my path.*t*
34 He made my feet like the feet of deer
    and set me secure on the heights.
35 He trains my hands for war,
    so that my arms can bend a bow of
      bronze.
36 You have given me the shield of your
      salvation,
    and your help*u* has made me great.

r 22.26 Heb mss Gk: MT *blameless warrior*   s 22.33 Q ms Gk
Syr Vg: MT *God is my strong refuge*   t 22.33 Meaning of Heb
uncertain   u 22.36 Q ms: MT *your answering*

22:9 *Smoke went up from his nostrils and devouring fire from his mouth.* Smoke and fire can accompany the Lord's appearances (Exod. 24:17; Deut. 4:24; Isa. 30:27). Here the Lord is pictured as if he is the fire-breathing Leviathan in Job 41:18–21.

22:11 *He rode on a cherub.* The cherubim (plural of cherub) in the HB are depicted as winged creatures (Exod. 25:20; 1 Kgs. 6:23–24; Ezek. 10:8). See note on 1 Kgs. 6:23.

37 You have made me stride freely,
and my feet do not slip;
38 I pursued my enemies and destroyed them
and did not turn back until they were consumed.
39 I consumed them; I struck them down
so that they did not rise;
they fell under my feet.
40 For you girded me with strength for the battle;
you made my assailants sink under me.
41 You made my enemies turn their backs to me,
those who hated me, and I destroyed them.
42 They looked, but there was no one to save them;
they cried to the LORD, but he did not answer them.
43 I beat them fine like the dust of the earth;
I crushed them and stamped them down like the mire of the streets.

44 You delivered me from strife with the peoples;ᵛ
you kept me as the head of the nations;
people whom I had not known served me.
45 Foreigners came cringing to me;
as soon as they heard of me, they obeyed me.
46 Foreigners lost heart
and came trembling outʷ of their strongholds.

47 The LORD lives! Blessed be my rock,
and exalted be my God, the rock of my salvation,
48 the God who gave me vengeance
and brought down peoples under me,
49 who brought me out from my enemies;
you exalted me above my adversaries;
you delivered me from the violent.

50 For this I will extol you, O LORD, among the nations
and sing praises to your name.
51 He is a tower of salvation for his king
and shows steadfast love to his anointed,
to David and his descendants forever."

23 Now these are the last words of David:
The oracle of David, son of Jesse,
the oracle of the man whom God exalted,ˣ
the anointed of the God of Jacob,
the favorite of the Strong One of Israel:

2 The spirit of the LORD speaks through me;
his word is upon my tongue.
3 The God of Israel has spoken;
the Rock of Israel has said to me:
"One who rules over people justly,
ruling in the fear of God,
4 is like the light of morning,
like the sun rising on a cloudless morning,
gleaming from the rain on the grassy land."

5 Is not my house like this with God?
For he has made with me an everlasting covenant,
ordered in all things and secure.
Will he not cause to prosper
all my help and my desire?

v 22.44 Heb mss Q ms Gk: MT *my people* w 22.46 Meaning of Heb uncertain x 23.1 Q ms: MT *who was raised on high*

23:1 *The anointed of the God of Jacob, the favorite of the Strong One of Israel*. The central metaphor of the poem compares a just ruler to the sun; the effect of a just king's rule is like the beneficial rays of the sun. David has been referred to previously as "the anointed"; this refers back to his anointing as leader by the prophet Samuel (1 Sam. 16:1–13) and his subsequent anointings by the tribes. "Strong One of Israel" with reference to the God of Israel occurs elsewhere in the HB (Isa. 1:24), as does "Strong One of Jacob" (Gen. 49:24; Ps. 132:2, 5; Isa. 49:26; 60:16).

23:3 *The Rock of Israel*. Another metaphor for God, used often of God in the HB (2 Sam. 22:3, 47).

23:5 *For he has made with me an everlasting covenant*. A reference back to God's promise to David in 2 Sam. 7. God has promised to build a dynasty for David, one that would rule forever in Jerusalem (2 Sam. 7:16). The important term *covenant* was not used in 2 Sam. 7 but is used now at the end of the narrative about David. See **"The Davidic Covenant," p. 433.**

6 But the godless[y] are all like thorns that
    are thrown away,
  for they cannot be picked up with
    the hand;
7 to touch them one uses an iron bar
    or the shaft of a spear.
  And they are entirely consumed in
    fire on the spot.[z]

8 These are the names of the warriors whom David had: Josheb-basshebeth a Tahchemonite; he was chief of the Three;[a] he wielded his spear[b] against eight hundred whom he killed at one time.

9 Next to him among the three warriors was Eleazar son of Dodo son of Ahohi. He was with David when they defied the Philistines who were gathered there for battle. The Israelites withdrew, [10]but he stood his ground. He struck down the Philistines until his arm grew weary, though his hand clung to the sword. The LORD brought about a great victory that day. Then the people came back to him—but only to strip the dead.

11 Next to him was Shammah son of Agee the Hararite. The Philistines gathered together at Lehi, where there was a plot of ground full of lentils, and the army fled from the Philistines. [12]But he took his stand in the middle of the plot, defended it, and killed the Philistines, and the LORD brought about a great victory.

13 Toward the beginning of harvest three of the thirty chiefs went down to join David at the cave of Adullam while a band of Philistines was encamped in the valley of Rephaim. [14]David was then in the stronghold, and the garrison of the Philistines was then at Bethlehem. [15]David said longingly, "Oh, that someone would give me water to drink from the well of Bethlehem that is by the gate!" [16]Then the three warriors broke through the camp of the Philistines, drew water from the well of Bethlehem that was by the gate, and brought it to David. But he would not drink of it; he poured it out to the LORD, [17]for he said, "The LORD forbid that I should do this. Can I drink the blood of the men who went at the risk of their lives?" Therefore he would not drink it. The three warriors did these things.

18 Now Abishai son of Zeruiah, the brother of Joab, was chief of the Thirty.[c] With his spear he fought against three hundred men and killed them and won a name beside the Three. [19]He was the most renowned of the Thirty[d] and became their commander, but he did not attain to the Three.

20 Benaiah son of Jehoiada was a valiant warrior[e] from Kabzeel, a doer of great deeds; he struck down two sons of Ariel[f] of Moab. He also went down and killed a lion in a pit on a day when snow had fallen. [21]And he killed an Egyptian, a handsome man. The Egyptian had a spear in his hand, but Benaiah went against him with a staff, snatched the spear out of the Egyptian's hand, and killed him with his own spear. [22]Such were the things Benaiah son of Jehoiada did and won a name beside the three warriors. [23]He was renowned among the Thirty, but he did not attain to the Three. And David put him in charge of his bodyguard.

24 Among the Thirty were Asahel brother of Joab; Elhanan son of Dodo of Bethlehem; [25]Shammah of Harod; Elika of Harod; [26]Helez the Paltite; Ira son of Ikkesh of Tekoa; [27]Abiezer of Anathoth; Mebunnai the Hushathite; [28]Zalmon the Ahohite; Maharai of Netophah; [29]Heleb son of Baanah of Netophah; Ittai son of Ribai of Gibeah of the Benjaminites; [30]Benaiah of Pirathon; Hiddai of the wadis of Gaash; [31]Abi-albon the Arbathite; Azmaveth of Bahurim;[g] [32]Eliahba of Shaalbon; the sons of Jashen: Jonathan [33]son of[h] Shammah the Hararite; Ahiam son of Sharar the Hararite; [34]Eliphelet son of Ahasbai of Maacah; Eliam son of Ahithophel the Gilonite; [35]Hezro[i] of Carmel; Paarai the Arbite; [36]Igal son of Nathan of Zobah; Bani the Gadite; [37]Zelek the Ammonite; Naharai of Beeroth, the armor-bearer of Joab son of Zeruiah; [38]Ira the Ithrite; Gareb the Ithrite; [39]Uriah the Hittite—thirty-seven in all.

24

Again the anger of the LORD was kindled against Israel, and he incited

y 23.6 Heb *worthless*   z 23.7 Heb *in sitting*   a 23.8 Gk Vg: Meaning of Heb uncertain   b 23.8 Meaning of Heb uncertain   c 23.18 Heb mss Syr: MT *Three*   d 23.19 Heb ms Syr: Heb *Was he the most renowned of the Three?*   e 23.20 Another reading is *the son of Ish-hai*   f 23.20 Gk: Heb lacks *sons of*   g 23.31 Cn: Heb *the Barhumite*   h 23.33 Gk: Heb lacks *son of*   i 23.35 Another reading is *Hezrai*

24:1 *Again the anger of the LORD was kindled against Israel, and he incited David against them.* The reason for the "again" is unclear. The reference might be the drought that was brought on by the bloodguilt on Saul's house (2 Sam. 21:1–14). Here in 2 Sam. 24:1 is the only example where God's anger occurs without a specific crime on Israel's part.

David against them, saying, "Go, count the people of Israel and Judah." [2]So the king said to Joab and the commanders of the army[j] who were with him, "Go through all the tribes of Israel, from Dan to Beer-sheba, and take a census of the people, so that I may know how many there are." [3]But Joab said to the king, "May the LORD your God increase the number of the people a hundredfold while the eyes of my lord the king can still see it! But why does my lord the king want to do this?" [4]But the king's word prevailed against Joab and the commanders of the army. So Joab and the commanders of the army went out from the presence of the king to take a census of the people of Israel. [5]They crossed the Jordan and began from[k] Aroer and from the city that is in the middle of the valley, toward Gad and on to Jazer. [6]Then they came to Gilead and to Kadesh in the land of the Hittites,[l] and they came to Dan, and from Dan[m] they went around to Sidon [7]and came to the fortress of Tyre and to all the cities of the Hivites and Canaanites, and they went out to the Negeb of Judah at Beer-sheba. [8]So when they had gone through all the land, they came back to Jerusalem at the end of nine months and twenty days. [9]Joab reported to the king the number of those who had been recorded: in Israel there were eight hundred thousand soldiers able to draw the sword, and those of Judah were five hundred thousand.

[10] But afterward, David was stricken to the heart because he had numbered the people. David said to the LORD, "I have sinned greatly in what I have done. But now, O LORD, I pray you, take away the guilt of your servant, for I have done very foolishly." [11]When David rose in the morning, the word of the LORD came to the prophet Gad, David's seer, saying, [12]"Go and say to David: Thus says the LORD: Three things I offer[n]

you; choose one of them, and I will do it to you." [13]So Gad came to David and told him; he asked him, "Shall seven years of famine come to you on your land? Or will you flee three months before your foes while they pursue you? Or shall there be three days' pestilence in your land? Now consider and decide what answer I shall return to the one who sent me." [14]Then David said to Gad, "I am in great distress; let us fall into the hand of the LORD, for his mercy is great, but let me not fall into human hands."

[15] So the LORD sent a pestilence on Israel from that morning until the appointed time, and seventy thousand of the people died, from Dan to Beer-sheba. [16]But when the angel stretched out his hand toward Jerusalem to destroy it, the LORD relented concerning the evil and said to the angel who was bringing destruction among the people, "It is enough; now stay your hand." The angel of the LORD was standing[o] by the threshing floor of Araunah the Jebusite. David looked up and saw the angel of the LORD standing between earth and heaven and in his hand a drawn sword stretched out over Jerusalem. Then David and the elders, clothed in sackcloth, fell on their faces.[p] [17]When David saw the angel who was destroying the people, he said to the LORD, "I alone have sinned, and I, the shepherd, have done evil,[q] but these sheep, what have they done? Let your hand, I pray, be against me and against my father's house."

[18] That day Gad came to David and said to him, "Go up and erect an altar to the LORD on the threshing floor of Araunah the Jebusite." [19]Following Gad's instructions,

j 24.2 Cn Compare 1 Chr 21.2 Gk: Heb *to Joab the commander of the army* *k* 24.5 Gk mss: Heb *encamped in Aroer south of* *l* 24.6 Gk: Heb *to the land of Tahtim-hodshi* *m* 24.6 Cn Compare Gk: Heb *they came to Dan-jaan and* *n* 24.12 Or *hold over* *o* 24.16 Q ms: MT lacks *standing* *p* 24.16 Q ms Compare 1 Chr 21.16: MT lacks *David looked . . . faces* *q* 24.17 Q ms Gk: MT reads *I alone have done wickedly*

24:2 *And take a census of the people.* Why taking a census should pose a problem is a bit puzzling. A census would be necessary for taxation and military conscription. Some commentators suggest that David seems to be forgoing his usual consultation with God (2 Sam. 2:1) before military endeavors, assuming that with his army he can defeat his enemies without God's intervention.

24:10 *But afterward, David was stricken to the heart.* Perhaps because he had acted without consulting God.

24:11 *The word of the LORD came to the prophet Gad, David's seer.* Unlike in 2 Sam. 12:5–6, in 2 Sam. 24:10, David confesses his sin before "the word of the LORD" comes to his prophet Gad. Perhaps David has changed. This prophet has appeared once before, in 1 Sam. 22:5, when he counseled David to head to Judah.

David went up, as the Lord had command- ed. [20]When Araunah looked down, he saw the king and his servants coming toward him, and Araunah went out and prostrat- ed himself before the king with his face to the ground. [21]Araunah said, "Why has my lord the king come to his servant?" David said, "To buy the threshing floor from you in order to build an altar to the Lord, so that the plague may be averted from the people." [22]Then Araunah said to David, "Let my lord the king take and offer up what seems good to him; here are the oxen for the burnt offer- ing and the threshing sledges and the yokes of the oxen for the wood. [23]All this, O king, Araunah gives to the king." And Araunah said to the king, "May the Lord your God respond favorably to you."

24 But the king said to Araunah, "No, but I will buy them from you for a price; I will not offer burnt offerings to the Lord my God that cost me nothing." So David bought the threshing floor and the oxen for fifty shek- els of silver. [25]David built there an altar to the Lord and offered burnt offerings and of- ferings of well-being. So the Lord answered his supplication for the land, and the plague was averted from Israel.

24:25 *And the plague was averted from Israel.* David follows Gad's order and builds an altar in Jerusalem and offers sacrifices. This altar is the first built in Jerusalem and anticipates the building of the temple by David's son Solomon.

1 KINGS

The Text of 1 Kings

First and 2 Kings constitute one book in the HB (Masoretic Text); the division into two books is a convention of the Septuagint (LXX), the Greek translation of the Hebrew Bible, in which 1–2 Kings is referred to as 3–4 Reigns (with 1–2 Samuel as 1–2 Reigns). There are a few notable differences between the LXX and MT, particularly with respect to order of events; for example, in the LXX, 1 Kgs. 21 comes before 1 Kgs. 20. These differences appear to be largely based on divergent Hebrew manuscripts.

There are at least two major editions of the Deuteronomistic History (DH; see **"The Deuteronomistic History," p. 337**) of which 1 Kings is a part, a preexilic and an exilic version (before and after the fall of Judah to the Babylonians in 587/586 BCE). The preexilic edition of the DH was likely put together during the reign of either Hezekiah or Josiah to promote the centralization and streamlining of YHWH worship to one temple in Jerusalem. With regard to the exilic version of the DH, 2 Kgs. 25:27–30 is a good anchor point for dating when this version was written. Here, the Babylonian king Evil-merodach, or "Evil Marduk" (a corruption of Amel-Marduk, "Marduk's man"), releases the deposed former king, Jehoiachin, from prison. These verses appear to express some hope for an imminent restoration of the Davidic monarchy, suggesting that at least parts of 1–2 Kings were composed at a time when such a restoration was plausible.

Themes in 1 Kings

The book of Kings is less "history," as a modern reader might understand the term, and more what scholarly interpreters would call "historiography." A historiography carefully selects and frames source material—often adding creative and ideological elements—to tell a story with a message. The compilers of 1–2 Kings use source material, which is sometimes named, for example, the Book of the Acts of Solomon (1 Kgs. 11:41), the Book of the Annals of the Kings of Israel (1 Kgs. 14:19), and the Book of the Annals of the Kings of Judah (1 Kgs. 14:29). But Kings appropriates its sources to tell the story of Israel and Judah from a particular theological perspective that speaks to the text's exilic audience. One major agenda of 1–2 Kings is explaining two catastrophes that led to exile: the destruction of the northern kingdom of Israel by the Assyrians (2 Kgs. 17; 722 BCE) and the Babylonian defeat of the southern kingdom of Judah, which included the destruction of Jerusalem and its temple, and the end of the Davidic monarchy (2 Kgs. 24–25; 587/586 BCE).

The book's clear theological viewpoint marks it as part of a larger historiography known as the Deuteronomistic History (see **"The Deuteronomistic History," p. 337**), a literary work that spans from Joshua through 2 Kings. The work as a whole presents Israel's past as a recurring cycle of disobedience to YHWH's commands, especially in matters of worship, and repentance, something certainly reflected in 1 Kings's cyclical framework.

The demise of the northern kingdom and the Babylonian onslaught of Jerusalem were devastating events for the community, as archaeological evidence and other biblical passages can attest (Lam. 1–2). They carried immense theological weight as well. The issues at stake were related to the power of Israel's God. After disaster, should the people continue to trust YHWH (Ps. 137)? Did YHWH fail? Was Marduk, the national god of the Babylonian Empire, more powerful than Israel's God? Did the kingdoms fall because they disobeyed YHWH's covenant? Or did disaster strike because Israel and Judah stopped venerating other gods (Jer. 44:15–19)?

Kings answers these questions decisively. Jeroboam's creation of shrines in the north to rival the YHWH temple in Jerusalem was the main reason for the fall of the northern kingdom of Israel (1 Kgs. 12:26–13:10, 32–34; 14:16; 15:30, 34, etc.), though other religious practices also draw the narrator's ire (1 Kgs. 16:33; 2 Kgs. 13:6; 17:16; 23:15). The kingdom of Judah and David's dynasty fell because of the failure to eliminate religious practices other than the worship of YHWH alone in the Jerusalem temple. With respect to Judah, religious practices the narrator condemns include the following:

- High places, or *bamot*, local cult sites for the worship of either YHWH or other deities (1 Kgs. 3:4; 11:7).
- Baal or "baals," a rival deity of YHWH or perhaps representations of YHWH that too closely resemble the Canaanite storm god, Baal.

- "Sacred poles," or *asherahs*, wooden cult objects that probably represent YHWH's spouse (1 Kgs. 14:15, 23; 15:13; 2 Kgs. 18:4; 21:3; 23:14). The wife of the Canaanite creator god, El, is named Asherah.
- Illicit priests, or *qedeshim*, cult functionaries whose religious practices are unknown (1 Kgs. 14:24; 15:12; 22:46; 2 Kgs. 23:7).
- Child sacrifice (2 Kgs. 16:3; 17:17; 21:6; 23:10).

The narrator gives most monarchs in the book of Kings positive or negative reviews based on the religious practices they allowed, ended, or established. Almost all receive harsh reviews except Judahite kings Asa and Jehoshaphat, despite retaining the high places, and Hezekiah and Josiah, the only kings to institute ideal Deuteronomistic worship in Judah and beyond. Prophetic narratives, such as those featuring Elijah (1 Kgs. 17–19), are also central to articulating the book's theological vision. These earlier narratives (1 Kgs. 17–2 Kgs. 9), possibly composed during the eighth century BCE, were incorporated into the book of Kings perhaps because prophets play an important role in the Deuteronomistic History as transmitters of YHWH's commands (1 Kgs. 19:14; 2 Kgs. 17:13, 23; 21:10). The negative portrayals of northern rulers, especially the Tyrian-influenced Ahab (1 Kgs. 16–19, 21), may have also prompted the inclusion of these prophetic pericopes.

Reading Guide

In the opening chapter of 1 Kings the reader encounters a different King David from the strong, virile, successful king presented in earlier chapters of Samuel. Second Samuel concludes with a desperate ritual by David to end a deadly plague sent by YHWH, sent to punish him for taking a census of the people of Israel and Judah (2 Sam. 24). The plague is last in a series of upheavals during David's tumultuous reign, which begin in 2 Sam. 11 and continue through 2 Sam. 24, including a murderous affair with Bathsheba and the death of the child of that union; a rape and fratricide within his own household; a revolt by his own son, Absalom; and another revolt by Sheba, son of Bichri. As the narrative stands now, the reader is prepared for the first episode of 1 Kings, in which David is extremely weak and seemingly impotent. David has declined from the famed warrior who attracted women (1 Sam. 18; 2 Sam. 6:20–22) to a worn-down man who cannot even get "warm" with the "very beautiful" Abishag (1 Kgs. 1:1–4).

David's decline creates the context for the palace intrigue and violence that would place Solomon, David's son by Bathsheba, on the throne (1 Kgs. 1:4–2:46). From the end of Solomon's problematic reign (1 Kgs. 3–11), the narrative recounts how the kingdoms of Israel and Judah became divided, and highlights certain events in the history of the two kingdoms, until the termination of the Judahite monarchy at the hand of the Babylonian Empire in 2 Kgs. 25. In addition, the book weaves in stories of certain northern prophets to support its overarching narrative.

Brian Rainey

1 King David was old and advanced in years, and although they covered him with clothes, he could not get warm. ²So his servants said to him, "Let a young virgin be sought for my lord the king, and let her wait on the king and be his attendant; let her lie in your bosom, so that my lord the king may be warm." ³So they searched for a beautiful young woman throughout all the territory of Israel and found Abishag the Shunammite and brought her to the king. ⁴The young woman was very

1:1–2:46 Originally, 1 Kgs. 1–2 may have been the conclusion to 2 Sam. 9–20. According to traditional scholarship, these two blocks of text make up the "Succession Narrative" or "Court History," an earlier narrative of David's monarchy used and framed by the Deuteronomistic History (see **"The Deuteronomistic History," p. 337**). Recently, however, scholars have questioned the idea that these texts should be read as a unity with a common theme.

1:1–4 The search for a *young woman* and the intimate physical contact Abishag has with David suggest that virility and impotence are also at issue, not simply physical warmth. The text is sure to remind the reader that there was no intercourse between the two. 1:3 *Abishag the Shunammite.* Probably from Shunem, a town near the Jezreel Valley, in the northern territory of Issachar (Josh. 19:18).

beautiful. She became the king's attendant and served him, but the king did not know her sexually.

5 Now Adonijah son of Haggith exalted himself, saying, "I will be king." He prepared for himself chariots and horsemen, and fifty men to run before him. [6]His father had never at any time reprimanded him by asking, "Why have you done thus and so?" He was also a very handsome man, and he was born next after Absalom. [7]He conferred with Joab son of Zeruiah and with the priest Abiathar, and they supported Adonijah. [8]But the priest Zadok, and Benaiah son of Jehoiada, and the prophet Nathan, and Shammah[a] and his companions,[b] David's own warriors, did not side with Adonijah.

9 Adonijah sacrificed sheep, oxen, and fatted cattle by the stone Zoheleth, which is beside En-rogel, and he invited all his brothers, the king's sons, and all the royal officials of Judah, [10]but he did not invite the prophet Nathan or Benaiah or the warriors or his brother Solomon.

11 Then Nathan said to Bathsheba, Solomon's mother, "Have you not heard that Adonijah son of Haggith has become king and our lord David does not know it? [12]Now therefore come, let me give you advice, so that you may save your own life and the life of your son Solomon. [13]Go in at once to King David and say to him, 'Did you not, my lord the king, swear to your servant, saying, "Your son Solomon shall succeed me as king, and he shall sit on my throne?" Why then is Adonijah king?' [14]Then while you are still there speaking with the king, I will come in after you and confirm your words."

15 So Bathsheba went to the king in his room. The king was very old; Abishag the Shunammite was attending the king. [16]Bathsheba bowed and did obeisance to the king, and the king said, "What do you wish?" [17]She said to him, "My lord, you swore to your servant by the LORD your God, saying, 'Your son Solomon shall succeed me as king, and he shall sit on my throne.' [18]But now suddenly Adonijah has become king, though you, my lord the king, do not know it. [19]He has sacrificed oxen, fatted cattle, and sheep in abundance and has invited all the children of the king, the priest Abiathar, and Joab the commander of the army, but your servant Solomon he has not invited. [20]But you, my lord the king, the eyes of all Israel are on you to tell them who shall sit on the throne of my lord the king after him. [21]Otherwise it will come to pass, when my lord the king sleeps with his ancestors, that my son Solomon and I will be counted offenders."

22 While she was still speaking with the king, the prophet Nathan came in. [23]The king was told, "Here is the prophet Nathan." When he came in before the king, he did obeisance to the king, with his face to the ground. [24]Nathan said, "My lord the king, have you said, 'Adonijah shall succeed me as king, and he shall sit on my throne'? [25]For today he has gone down and has sacrificed

a 1.8 Lucianic: Heb *Shimei*   b 1.8 Lucianic: Heb *Rei*

1:5 According to 2 Sam. 3:1–5, Adonijah precedes Solomon for succession, if going by birth order. Adonijah assembles an entourage to stake his reasonable claim to kingship. Wars for succession by siblings are not uncommon in the wider ancient west Asian and east African world. *Haggith*, one of David's four wives in Hebron (2 Sam. 3:2–5).

1:6 David and Absalom also called *handsome* (2 Sam. 14:25).

1:7–9 The factions in the contest over succession. Many note that the factions divide around who was with David in Hebron and who joined him after he built up Jerusalem as his capital. As with many modern power struggles, securing the support of the military is important. Joab, commander of the army, supports Adonijah, but David's bodyguard and the "warriors" do not. The priesthood is divided as well; of the two priests ministering at the royal shrine in Jerusalem (2 Sam. 15:24–29), Abiathar took Adonijah's side, but Zadok took Solomon's.

Abiathar. Last surviving member of the priestly house of Eli who escaped Saul's massacre of his family and fled to David (1 Sam. 22:7–23). *Benaiah.* Famed warrior, commander of the Cherethites and Pelethites (2 Sam. 8:18; 20:23; 23:20–22; see also note on 1:38).

1:11 *Bathsheba, Solomon's mother.* David acquired Bathsheba by murdering her husband, Uriah the Hittite (2 Sam. 11:2–12:25; see **"David and Bathsheba," p. 438**). Along with the prophet Nathan, she plays a leading role in getting her own son on the throne and also possibly in saving their lives.

oxen, fatted cattle, and sheep in abundance and has invited all the king's children, Joab the commander[c] of the army, and the priest Abiathar, who are now eating and drinking before him, and saying, 'Long live King Adonijah!' [26]But he did not invite me, your servant, and the priest Zadok, and Benaiah son of Jehoiada, and your servant Solomon. [27]Has this thing been brought about by my lord the king and you have not let your servants know who should sit on the throne of my lord the king after him?"

28 King David answered, "Summon Bathsheba to me." So she came into the king's presence and stood before the king. [29]The king swore, saying, "As the LORD lives, who has saved my life from every adversity, [30]as I swore to you by the LORD, the God of Israel, 'Your son Solomon shall succeed me as king, and he shall sit on my throne in my place,' so will I do this day." [31]Then Bathsheba bowed with her face to the ground and did obeisance to the king and said, "May my lord King David live forever!"

32 King David said, "Summon to me the priest Zadok, the prophet Nathan, and Benaiah son of Jehoiada." When they came before the king, [33]the king said to them, "Take with you the servants of your lord and have my son Solomon ride on my own mule and bring him down to Gihon. [34]There let the priest Zadok and the prophet Nathan anoint him king over Israel; then blow the trumpet and say, 'Long live King Solomon!' [35]You shall go up following him. Let him enter and sit on my throne; he shall be king in my place, for I have appointed him to be ruler over Israel and over Judah." [36]Benaiah son of Jehoiada answered the king, "Amen! May the LORD, the God of my lord the king, so ordain. [37]As the LORD has been with my lord the king, so may he be with Solomon and make his throne greater than the throne of my lord King David."

38 So the priest Zadok, the prophet Nathan, Benaiah son of Jehoiada, and the Cherethites and the Pelethites went down and had Solomon ride on King David's mule and led him to Gihon. [39]There the priest Zadok took the horn of oil from the tent and anointed Solomon. Then they blew the trumpet, and all the people said, "Long live King Solomon!" [40]And all the people went up following him, playing on pipes and rejoicing with great joy, so that the earth quaked at their noise.

41 Adonijah and all the guests who were with him heard it as they finished feasting. When Joab heard the sound of the trumpet, he said, "Why is the city in an uproar?" [42]While he was still speaking, Jonathan son of the priest Abiathar arrived. Adonijah said, "Come in, for you are a worthy man and surely you bring good news." [43]Jonathan answered Adonijah, "No, for our lord King David has made Solomon king; [44]the king has sent with him the priest Zadok, the prophet Nathan, Benaiah son of Jehoiada, and the Cherethites and the Pelethites, and they had him ride on the king's mule; [45]the priest Zadok and the prophet Nathan have anointed him king at Gihon, and they have gone up from there rejoicing, so that the city is in an uproar. This is the noise that you heard. [46]Solomon now sits on the royal throne. [47]Moreover, the king's servants came to congratulate our lord King David, saying, 'May God make the name of Solomon more famous than yours and make his throne greater than your throne.' The king bowed in worship on the bed [48]and went on to pray thus, 'Blessed be the LORD, the God of Israel, who today has granted one of my offspring[d] to sit on my throne and permitted me to witness it.'"

49 Then all the guests of Adonijah got up trembling and went their own ways. [50]Adonijah, fearing Solomon, got up and went to grasp the horns of the altar. [51]Solomon was

c 1.25 Gk: Heb *the commanders*   d 1.48 Gk: Heb *one*

1:35 *Ruler.* Hebrew "nagid" is a divinely ordained crown prince. See 1 Sam. 9:16; 10:1; 13:14; 25:30; 2 Sam. 5:2; 6:21; 7:8; 1 Kgs. 14:7; 16:2; 2 Kgs. 20:5. See **"Kingship/Monarchy," p. 390**.

1:38 *Cherethites and the Pelethites.* Philistine mercenaries (1 Sam. 30:14; 2 Sam. 15:18; Ezek. 25:16; Zeph. 2:5). David's personal Philistine military contingent is essential for maintaining his grip on power (2 Sam. 15:17–23; 20:7). *King David's mule.* See Zech. 9:9.

1:41 *Joab.* Commander of the army (2 Sam. 8:16) but also cursed by David for killing Abner, one of Saul's lieutenants (2 Sam. 3:22–30; 1 Kgs. 2:5–6).

1:49–53 *Horns of the altar.* The altar may have functioned like cities of refuge mentioned in Deut. 19:4–7.

informed, "Adonijah is afraid of King Solomon; see, he has laid hold of the horns of the altar, saying, 'Let King Solomon swear to me first that he will not kill his servant with the sword.' " ⁵²So Solomon responded, "If he proves to be a worthy man, not one of his hairs shall fall to the ground, but if wickedness is found in him, he shall die." ⁵³Then King Solomon sent to have him brought down from the altar. He came to do obeisance to King Solomon, and Solomon said to him, "Go home."

2 When David's time to die drew near, he charged his son Solomon, saying: ²"I am about to go the way of all the earth. Be strong, be courageous, ³and keep the charge of the LORD your God, walking in his ways and keeping his statutes, his commandments, his ordinances, and his testimonies, as it is written in the law of Moses, so that you may prosper in all that you do and wherever you turn. ⁴Then the LORD will establish his word that he spoke concerning me: 'If your heirs take heed to their way, to walk before me in faithfulness with all their heart and with all their soul, there shall not fail you a successor on the throne of Israel.'

5 "Moreover, you know also what Joab son of Zeruiah did to me, how he dealt with the two commanders of the armies of Israel, Abner son of Ner and Amasa son of Jether, whom he murdered, retaliating in time of peace for blood that had been shed in war and putting innocent blood*ᵉ* on the belt around my*ᶠ* waist and on the sandals on my*ᵍ* feet. ⁶Act, therefore, according to

your wisdom, but do not let his gray head go down to Sheol in peace. ⁷Deal loyally, however, with the sons of Barzillai the Gileadite, and let them be among those who eat at your table, for with such loyalty they met me when I fled from your brother Absalom. ⁸There is also with you Shimei son of Gera, a Benjaminite from Bahurim, who cursed me with a terrible curse on the day when I went to Mahanaim, but when he came down to meet me at the Jordan, I swore to him by the LORD, 'I will not put you to death with the sword.' ⁹Therefore do not hold him guiltless, for you are a wise man; you will know what you ought to do to him, and you must bring his gray head down with blood to Sheol."

10 Then David slept with his ancestors and was buried in the city of David. ¹¹The time that David reigned over Israel was forty years; he reigned seven years in Hebron and thirty-three years in Jerusalem. ¹²So Solomon sat on the throne of his father David, and his kingdom was firmly established.

13 Then Adonijah son of Haggith came to Bathsheba, Solomon's mother. She asked, "Do you come peaceably?" He said, "Peaceably." ¹⁴Then he said, "May I have a word with you?" She said, "Go on." ¹⁵He said, "You know that the kingdom was mine and that all Israel expected me to reign; however, the kingdom has turned about and become my brother's, for it was his from the LORD. ¹⁶And now I have one request to make of you; do not refuse me." She said to him, "Go on." ¹⁷He said, "Please ask King

e 2.5 Gk: Heb *blood of war*   *f* 2.5 Gk: Heb *his*   *g* 2.5 Gk: Heb *his*

2:1–4 An example of the Deuteronomistic History's theological framework. See **"The Deuteronomistic History," p. 337**. Compare Josh. 1:6–7. The survival of David's dynasty depends on his heirs keeping the commands of YHWH as communicated by Moses.

2:5 *Abner son of Ner.* Stabbed by Joab in the stomach in revenge for his killing of Joab's brother (2 Sam. 3:22–30).

2:7 *Barzillai the Gileadite.* Escorted David, in flight from Saul, over the Jordan River and provided him with food in Mahanaim, a place referenced in the negative comment about Shimei's curse (2 Sam. 19:31–39).

2:8 *Shimei son of Gera.* A relative of Saul who cursed David when he was in flight from Absalom (2 Sam. 16:5–13).

2:13 *Do you come peaceably?* After Adonijah's unsuccessful attempt to take Solomon's throne, Solomon's mother, Bathsheba, who thwarted Adonijah's attempt, asks a reasonable question. She does not know whether Adonijah has come to seek revenge.

2:17 *Give me Abishag the Shunammite.* Access to wives of the king seems to accompany challenges to kingship and is associated with securing the throne (2 Sam. 3:7; 12:8; 16:15–23), which explains how Solomon could interpret Adonijah's request so harshly.

Solomon—he will not refuse you—to give me Abishag the Shunammite as my wife." [18]Bathsheba said, "Very well; I will speak to the king on your behalf."

19 So Bathsheba went to King Solomon, to speak to him on behalf of Adonijah. The king rose to meet her and bowed down to her; then he sat on his throne and had a throne brought for the king's mother, and she sat on his right. [20]Then she said, "I have one small request to make of you; do not refuse me." And the king said to her, "Make your request, my mother, for I will not refuse you." [21]She said, "Let Abishag the Shunammite be given to your brother Adonijah as his wife." [22]King Solomon answered his mother, "And why do you ask Abishag the Shunammite for Adonijah? Ask for him the kingdom as well! For he is my elder brother, and the priest Abiathar and Joab son of Zeruiah are on his side!" [23]Then King Solomon swore by the LORD, "So may God do to me, and more also, for Adonijah has devised this scheme at the risk of his life! [24]Now therefore as the LORD lives, who has established me and placed me on the throne of my father David and who has made me a house as he promised, today Adonijah shall be put to death." [25]So King Solomon sent Benaiah son of Jehoiada; he struck him down, and he died.

26 The king said to the priest Abiathar, "Go to Anathoth, to your estate, for you deserve death. But I will not at this time put you to death because you carried the ark of the Lord GOD before my father David and because you shared in all the hardships my father endured." [27]So Solomon banished Abiathar from being priest to the LORD, thus fulfilling the word of the LORD that he had spoken concerning the house of Eli in Shiloh.

28 When the news came to Joab—for Joab had supported Adonijah though he had not supported Absalom—Joab fled to the tent of the LORD and grasped the horns of the altar. [29]When it was told King Solomon, "Joab has fled to the tent of the LORD and now is beside the altar," Solomon sent Benaiah son of Jehoiada, saying, "Go, strike him down." [30]So Benaiah came to the tent of the LORD and said to him, "The king commands, 'Come out.'" But he said, "No, I will die here." Then Benaiah brought the king word again, saying, "Thus said Joab, and thus he answered me." [31]The king replied to him, "Do as he has said, strike him down and bury him, and thus take away from me and from my father's house the guilt for the blood that Joab shed without cause. [32]The LORD will bring back his bloody deeds on his own head because, without the knowledge of my father David, he attacked and killed with the sword two men more righteous and better than he: Abner son of Ner, commander of the army of Israel, and Amasa son of Jether, commander of the army of Judah. [33]So shall their blood come back on the head of Joab and on the head of his descendants forever, but to David, and to his descendants, and to his house, and to his throne there shall be peace from the LORD forevermore." [34]Then Benaiah son of Jehoiada went up and struck him down and killed him, and he was buried at his own house near the wilderness. [35]The king put Benaiah son of Jehoiada over the army in his place, and the king put the priest Zadok in the place of Abiathar.

36 Then the king sent and summoned Shimei and said to him, "Build yourself a house in Jerusalem and live there, and do

2:20 *Make your request, my mother, for I will not refuse you.* Solomon states that he will grant what Bathsheba asks. This turns out to be false.

2:24 *Today Adonijah shall be put to death.* Solomon concludes that the request for Abishag is a bad-faith request. Solomon stated in 1 Kgs. 1:52 that Adonijah's life depended on his good behavior; because the request is interpreted as an example of "wickedness," Adonijah forfeits his life.

2:26–27 Abiathar the priest loses his position because of his support for Adonijah but keeps his life because of his work as a priest and loyalty to David. **2:27** *The house of Eli in Shiloh.* First Samuel 2:30–36 "foretells" the destruction of the Elides, save one survivor who will then be replaced by a more "faithful priest."

2:31–32 *The blood that Joab shed without cause.* Abner, a relative of Saul, was his army commander (1 Sam. 14:50). After Abner defected to David during the war between the households, Joab killed Abner in revenge for the murder of Joab's brother (2 Sam. 3:26–30). *Amasa.* Absalom's army commander, killed by Joab (2 Sam. 20:4–10).

not go out from there to any place whatever. ³⁷For on the day you go out and cross the Wadi Kidron, know for certain that you shall die; your blood shall be on your own head." ³⁸And Shimei said to the king, "The sentence is fair; as my lord the king has said, so will your servant do." So Shimei lived in Jerusalem many days.

39 But it happened at the end of three years that two of Shimei's slaves ran away to King Achish son of Maacah of Gath. When it was told Shimei, "Your slaves are in Gath," ⁴⁰Shimei arose and saddled a donkey and went to Achish in Gath, to search for his slaves; Shimei went and brought his slaves from Gath. ⁴¹When Solomon was told that Shimei had gone from Jerusalem to Gath and returned, ⁴²the king sent and summoned Shimei and said to him, "Did I not make you swear by the LORD and solemnly adjure you, saying, 'Know for certain that on the day you go out and go to any place whatever, you shall die'? And you said to me, 'The sentence is fair; I accept.' ⁴³Why then have you not kept your oath to the LORD and the commandment with which I charged you?" ⁴⁴The king also said to Shimei, "You know in your own heart all the evil that you did to my father David, so the LORD will bring back your evil on your own head. ⁴⁵But King Solomon shall be blessed, and the throne of David shall be established before the LORD forever." ⁴⁶Then the king commanded Benaiah son of Jehoiada, and he went out and struck him down, and he died.

So the kingdom was established in the hand of Solomon.

3 Solomon made a marriage alliance with Pharaoh king of Egypt; he took Pharaoh's daughter and brought her into the city of David until he had finished building his own house and the house of the LORD and the wall around Jerusalem. ²The people were sacrificing at the high places, however, because no house had yet been built for the name of the LORD.

3 Solomon loved the LORD, walking in the statutes of his father David, except that he sacrificed and offered incense at the high places. ⁴The king went to Gibeon to sacrifice there, for that was the principal high place; Solomon used to offer a thousand burnt offerings on that altar. ⁵At Gibeon the LORD appeared to Solomon in a dream by night, and God said, "Ask what I should give you." ⁶And Solomon said, "You have shown great and steadfast love to your servant my father David because he walked before you in faithfulness, in righteousness, and in uprightness of heart toward you, and you have kept for him this great and steadfast love and have given him a son to sit on his throne today. ⁷And now, O LORD my God, you have made your servant king in place of my father David, although I am only a little child; I do not know how to go out or come in. ⁸And your servant is in the midst of the people whom you have chosen, a great people so numerous they cannot be numbered or counted. ⁹Give your servant, therefore, an understanding mind to govern your people, able to discern between good and evil, for who can govern this great people of yours?"

10 It pleased the Lord that Solomon had asked this. ¹¹God said to him, "Because you have asked this and have not asked for yourself long life or riches or for the life of your enemies but have asked for yourself understanding to discern what is right, ¹²I now do according to your word. Indeed, I give you a wise and discerning mind; no one like you has been before you, and no one like you shall arise after you. ¹³I give you also what you have not asked, both riches and honor all your life; no other king shall

1 Kgs. 3–11 An account of Solomon's reign, which is on the whole positive until 1 Kgs. 11—though some see implicit criticism in the account earlier.

3:1 *Pharaoh king of Egypt*. Solomon's marriage to the daughter of an unnamed pharaoh should be juxtaposed with 1 Kgs. 14:25–28.

3:2–3 *High places*. Hebrew "bamot" are local sites for worship, either for YHWH or for other deities. The Deuteronomistic narrator tolerates pretemple high places but does not approve. High places, as respected cult sites, seem to have intrinsic power; Solomon experiences a theophany at Gibeon, the principal high place.

3:9 *An understanding mind*. Literally "a discerning heart." In the HB, the heart is the seat of not emotion but thought and will.

compare with you. ¹⁴If you will walk in my ways, keeping my statutes and my commandments, as your father David walked, then I will lengthen your life."

15 Then Solomon awoke; it had been a dream. He came to Jerusalem, where he stood before the ark of the covenant of the LORD. He offered up burnt offerings and offerings of well-being and provided a feast for all his servants.

16 Later, two women who were prostitutes came to the king and stood before him. ¹⁷The one woman said, "Please, my lord, this woman and I live in the same house, and I gave birth while she was in the house. ¹⁸Then on the third day after I gave birth, this woman also gave birth. We were together; there was no one else with us in the house; only the two of us were in the house. ¹⁹Then this woman's son died in the night because she lay on him. ²⁰She got up in the middle of the night and took my son from beside me while your servant slept. She laid him at her breast and laid her dead son at my breast. ²¹When I rose in the morning to nurse my son, I saw that he was dead, but when I looked at him closely in the morning, clearly it was not the son I had borne." ²²But the other woman said, "No, the living son is mine, and the dead son is yours." The first said, "No, the dead son is yours, and the living son is mine." So they argued before the king.

23 Then the king said, "The one says, 'This is my son who is alive, and your son is dead,' while the other says, 'Not so! Your son is dead, and my son is the living one.'" ²⁴So the king said, "Bring me a sword," and they brought a sword before the king. ²⁵The king said, "Divide the living boy in two; then give half to the one and half to the other." ²⁶But the woman whose son was alive said to the king, because compassion for her son burned within her, "Please, my lord, give her the living boy; certainly do not kill him!" The other said, "It shall be neither mine nor yours; divide it." ²⁷Then the king responded, "Give her the living boy; do not kill him. She is his mother." ²⁸All Israel heard of the judgment that the king had rendered, and they stood in awe of the king because they perceived that the wisdom of God was in him to execute justice.

4 King Solomon was king over all Israel, ²and these were his high officials: Azariah son of Zadok was the priest; ³Elihoreph and Ahijah sons of Shisha were secretaries; Jehoshaphat son of Ahilud was recorder; ⁴Benaiah son of Jehoiada was in command of the army; Zadok and Abiathar were priests; ⁵Azariah son of Nathan was over the officials; Zabud son of Nathan was priest and king's friend; ⁶Ahishar was in charge of the palace; and Adoniram son of Abda was in charge of the forced labor.

3:14 *If you will walk in my ways.* God reaffirms Deuteronomistic theology here, offering Solomon a long life in exchange for his obedience. See **"Divine Retribution," p. 339**.

3:16–28 Solomon demonstrates his skill in legal matters, an essential element of good kingship and proof that God has answered his prayer for wisdom (2 Sam. 15:1–5). **3:16** *Prostitutes* (Heb. "zonot"). Does not necessarily mean "sex worker" but a generally marginalized social class of women who live and act outside the confines of the patriarchal household. See **"Cult Prostitution," p. 486**. As today, words for "prostitute" may be used of women who act contrary to expected gender roles. For two women to live in a house together would be an uncommon arrangement in ancient Israel. **3:19** The woman speaking assumes that the other woman accidentally smothered her infant son. Since she was asleep at the time, she cannot say how the infant died. **3:24–25** Solomon's proposal acknowledges that in a case of hearsay, he cannot establish parental rights. Therefore, he makes the presumably equitable decision to divide the infant in half, knowing that the infant will not survive the procedure. **3:26** *Because compassion for her son burned within her.* Although the woman wants to parent her child, she would rather relinquish her rights than see him killed. The narrator's addition to the story solves the mystery of who gave birth to the child. **3:27–28** Without knowing the innermost thoughts of the woman, Solomon determines that she is the child's parent. This is proof that *the wisdom of God was in him*.

4:1–19 An account of Solomon's administrative offices. Some argue that Solomon's bureaucracy was influenced by Egyptian practices. Compare 2 Sam. 8:15–18 and 20:23–26. **4:2** *Azariah son of Zadok.* Since Zadok rejected Adonijah's attempt to claim the throne and supported Solomon in 1 Kgs. 1, his son becomes priest alongside his father (v. 4). **4:4** Abiathar is still listed as a priest,

7 Solomon had twelve officials over all Israel who provided food for the king and his household; each one had to make provision for one month in the year. 8These were their names: Ben-hur, in the hill country of Ephraim; 9Ben-deker, in Makaz, Shaalbim, Beth-shemesh, and Elon-beth-hanan; 10Ben-hesed, in Arubboth (to him belonged Socoh and all the land of Hepher); 11Ben-abinadab, in all Naphath-dor (he had Taphath, Solomon's daughter, as his wife); 12Baana son of Ahilud, in Taanach, Megiddo, and all Beth-shean, which is beside Zarethan below Jezreel, and from Beth-shean to Abel-meholah, as far as the other side of Jokmeam; 13Ben-geber, in Ramoth-gilead (he had the villages of Jair son of Manasseh, which are in Gilead, and he had the region of Argob, which is in Bashan, sixty great cities with walls and bronze bars); 14Ahinadab son of Iddo, in Mahanaim; 15Ahimaaz, in Naphtali (he had taken Basemath, Solomon's daughter, as his wife); 16Baana son of Hushai, in Asher and Bealoth; 17Jehoshaphat son of Paruah, in Issachar; 18Shimei son of Ela, in Benjamin; 19Geber son of Uri, in the land of Gilead, the country of King Sihon of the Amorites and of King Og of Bashan. And there was one garrison in the land.

[[20 Judah and Israel were as numerous as the sand by the sea; they ate and drank and were happy. 21bSolomon was sovereign over all the kingdoms from the Euphrates to the land of the Philistines, even to the border of Egypt; they brought tribute and served Solomon all the days of his life.i]]

22 Solomon's provision for one day was thirty cors of choice flour and sixty cors of meal, 23ten fat oxen and twenty pasture-fed cattle, one hundred sheep, besides deer, gazelles, roebucks, and fatted fowl. 24For he had dominion over all the region west of the Euphrates,j and he had peace on all sides. 25During Solomon's lifetime Judah and Israel lived in safety, from Dan even to Beer-sheba, all of them under their vines and fig trees. 26Solomon also had forty thousand stalls of horses for his chariots and twelve thousand horsemen. 27Those officials supplied provisions for King Solomon and for all who came to King Solomon's table, each one in his month; they let nothing be lacking. 28They also brought to the required place barley and straw for the horses and swift steeds, each according to his charge.

29 God gave Solomon very great wisdom, discernment, and breadth of understanding as vast as the sand on the seashore, 30so that Solomon's wisdom surpassed the wisdom of all the people of the East and all the wisdom of Egypt. 31He was wiser than anyone else, wiser than Ethan the Ezrahite and Heman, Calcol, and Darda, children of Mahol; his fame spread throughout all the surrounding nations. 32He composed three thousand proverbs, and his songs numbered a thousand and five. 33He would speak of trees, from the cedar that is in the Lebanon to the hyssop that grows in the wall; he would speak of animals, and birds, and reptiles, and fish. 34People came from all the nations to hear the wisdom of Solomon, from all the kings of the earth who had heard of his wisdom.

b 4.21 5.1 in Heb i 4.20–21 Gk lacks 4.20–21 j 4.24 Gk: Heb adds *from Tiphsah to Gaza, over all the kings west of the Euphrates*

although he lost his position in 1 Kgs. 2. **4:7–19** Solomon divides his kingdom into twelve administrative districts ruled by royally appointed officials ("nitzavim"), overseen by "Azariah son of Nathan" (4:5). This centralization of power is later revealed as a source of resentment (1 Kgs. 12:4–19).

4:20–21 This extremely positive summary of Solomon's reign is absent in the LXX. It suggests Solomon dominated the entire region of Syria-Palestine.

4:20–28 English translation, 4:20–28 = Masoretic Text, 4:20–5:8. **4:22** *Cors* According to Ezek. 45:14, a cor contains ten baths, or approximately fourteen bushels. The daily provision for flour and meal is massive, indicating the size of his court. **4:25** *From Dan even to Beer-sheba* indicates the northern and southern borders of Solomon's kingdom, which encompasses all the land allotted to Israel. *Under their vines and fig trees*, an expression of security and peace (see Mic. 4:4; Zech. 3:10).

4:31 Solomon surpasses all the well-known wise people of his day, though there is no record of these particular wisdom celebrities. Internationally celebrated wise people such as Dan'el/Daniel were common (Ezek. 14:14, 20; 28:3).

4:32 Solomon's skill at composing proverbs may explain why the biblical book of Proverbs was historically attributed to him. See **"Solomon," p. 595.**

5 ᵏNow King Hiram of Tyre sent his servants to Solomon when he heard that they had anointed him king in place of his father, for Hiram had always been a friend to David. ²Solomon sent word to Hiram, saying, ³"You know that my father David could not build a house for the name of the Lord his God because of the warfare with which his enemies surrounded him, until heˡ put them under the soles of his feet.ᵐ ⁴But now the Lord my God has given me rest on every side; there is neither adversary nor misfortune. ⁵So I intend to build a house for the name of the Lord my God, as the Lord said to my father David, 'Your son, whom I will set on your throne in your place, shall build the house for my name.' ⁶Therefore command that cedars from the Lebanon be cut for me. My servants will join your servants, and I will give you whatever wages you set for your servants, for you know that there is no one among us who knows how to cut timber like the Sidonians."

7 When Hiram heard the words of Solomon, he rejoiced greatly and said, "Blessed be the Lord today, who has given to David a wise son to be over this great people." ⁸Hiram sent word to Solomon, "I have heard the message that you have sent to me; I will fulfill all your needs in the matter of cedar and cypress timber. ⁹My servants shall bring it down to the sea from the Lebanon; I will make it into rafts to go by sea to the place you indicate. I will have them broken up there for you to take away. And you shall meet my needs by providing food for my household." ¹⁰So Hiram supplied Solomon's every need for timber of cedar and cypress. ¹¹Solomon, in turn, gave Hiram twenty thousand cors of wheat as food for his household and twenty cors of fine oil. Solomon gave this to Hiram year by year. ¹²So the Lord gave Solomon wisdom, as he had promised him. There was peace between Hiram and Solomon, and the two of them made a treaty.

13 King Solomon conscripted forced labor out of all Israel; the levy numbered thirty thousand men. ¹⁴He sent them to the Lebanon, ten thousand a month in shifts; they would be a month in the Lebanon and two months at home;ⁿ Adoniram was in charge of the forced labor. ¹⁵Solomon also had seventy thousand laborers and eighty thousand stonecutters in the hill country,

k 5.1 5.15 in Heb l 5.3 Gk: Heb the Lord m 5.3 Gk Tg Vg: Heb my feet or his feet n 5.14 Or at his palace

1 Kgs. 5 English translation, 5:1–18 = Masoretic Text, 5:15–32.

1 Kgs. 5–7 These chapters were probably formed from administrative records, particularly building reports, which are common in the official records of ancient west Asia.

5:1 *Friend.* Literally "lover" (Heb. "ohev"). The language of love here is treaty/covenant language; Hiram and David had formed an alliance of equals, not a suzerain-vassal treaty. Treaties are full of familial and emotive language, such as "love" (meaning a positive disposition and actions toward a treaty partner) and "hate" (violating the treaty). Typically, in a suzerain-vassal treaty, the stronger party—the suzerain—will demand complete loyalty and tribute from the vassal state in exchange for "protection." Complete loyalty also means that the vassal will provide military assistance to the suzerain and avoid independent diplomatic relations with other nations, especially rivals. A suzerain-vassal treaty is similar to an organized crime "protection" racket; the vassal pays off the suzerain so that he does not commit acts of violence against the vassal. Treaties, particularly of the Neo-Assyrian type, often contain curses levied against those who violate them. Treaties in ancient west Asia, such as the Aramean Sefire Treaty (mid-eighth century BCE), often hold the parties' descendants responsible for keeping its stipulations. Here, it seems Solomon and Hiram explicitly renew the treaty of equals Hiram and David had (v. 12). See note on 20:32.

5:5 Solomon is ready to fulfill the promise God made to his father, David, in 2 Sam. 7 that David's son would build a house for God. See **"The Davidic Covenant," p. 433**.

5:6 The Lebanon region is well known for its cedars, an important commodity that enriched Phoenician city-states.

5:11 Solomon pays Hiram of Tyre lavishly for the cedar trees needed to build God's house. For *cors*, see note on 4:22.

5:12 Solomon demonstrates wisdom in international affairs.

5:13–18 *Forced labor* (Heb. "mas"). Solomon uses corvée labor from the people of Israel, about which 1 Kings is not consistent (cf. 1 Kgs. 9:20–22). Conscripting "free" royal subjects for building

[16]besides Solomon's three thousand three
hundred supervisors who were over the
work, having charge of the people who did
the work. [17]At the king's command, they
quarried out great, costly stones in order
to lay the foundation of the house with
dressed stones. [18]So Solomon's builders and
Hiram's builders and the Gebalites did the
stonecutting and prepared the timber and
the stone to build the house.

6 In the four hundred eightieth year after the Israelites came out of the land
of Egypt, in the fourth year of Solomon's
reign over Israel, in the month of Ziv, which
is the second month, he began to build the
house of the LORD. [2]The house that King
Solomon built for the LORD was sixty cubits
long, twenty cubits wide, and thirty cubits
high. [3]The vestibule in front of the nave of
the house was twenty cubits wide, across
the width of the house. Its depth was ten
cubits in front of the house. [4]For the house
he made windows with recessed frames.[o]
[5]He also built a structure against the wall
of the house, running around the walls
of the house, both the nave and the inner
sanctuary, and he made side chambers all
around. [6]The lowest story[p] was five cubits
wide, the middle one was six cubits wide,
and the third was seven cubits wide, for
around the outside of the house he made
offsets on the wall in order that the supporting beams should not be inserted into
the walls of the house.
7 The house was built with stone finished
at the quarry so that neither hammer nor ax
nor any tool of iron was heard in the temple
while it was being built.
8 The entrance for the lower[q] story was
on the south side of the house: one went up
by winding stairs to the middle story and
from the middle story to the third. [9]So he
built the house and finished it; he roofed the
house with beams and planks of cedar. [10]He
built the structure against the whole house,
each story[r] five cubits high, and it was
joined to the house with timbers of cedar.
11 Now the word of the LORD came to Solomon, [12]"Concerning this house that you are
building, if you will walk in my statutes, obey
my ordinances, and keep all my commandments by walking in them, then I will establish my promise with you that I made to your
father David. [13]I will dwell among the Israelites and will not forsake my people Israel."
14 So Solomon built the house and finished it. [15]He lined the walls of the house
on the inside with boards of cedar; from
the floor of the house to the rafters of the
ceiling, he covered them on the inside with
wood, and he covered the floor of the house
with boards of cypress. [16]He built twenty
cubits of the rear of the house with boards
of cedar from the floor to the rafters, and
he built this within as an inner sanctuary, as
the most holy place. [17]The house, that is, the
nave in front of the inner sanctuary, was forty cubits long. [18]The cedar within the house
had carvings of gourds and open flowers;
all was cedar; no stone was seen. [19]The inner sanctuary he prepared in the innermost

o 6.4 Gk: Meaning of Heb uncertain *p* 6.6 Gk: Heb *structure* *q* 6.8 Gk Tg: Heb *middle* *r* 6.10 Heb lacks *each story*

projects is fairly common in ancient west Asia, so this would not be out of the ordinary for Solomon's building projects.

6:1–34 Some make a useful distinction between types of work on the temple: Masonry (6:2–14); woodwork (6:15–25), with detailed descriptions of the woodwork of the inner sanctuary (6:16–20), the cherubim (6:23–27), and the doors (6:31–34); and precious metalwork on the wood (6:20, 21, 22, 28, 30, 35). **6:2–3** Measurements show Solomon's temple is a "long-house" sanctuary design: a rectangular structure in which the representation of the god is usually placed at the far end of the temple, away from the entrance, which is located on the narrow side of the building. There have been no temples found in the region that are identical to Solomon's temple, but some are close in design, such as the Late Bronze Age temples found at Hazor and Lachish. Many scholars contend that the eighth-century BCE temple at Tell Tainat (Syria) is the closest to Solomon's temple, though there are still significant differences. **6:7** The stones for the house are prepared *at the quarry*, so that the construction site of the house itself is silent. Cf. Hab. 2:20. A place that will contain God's presence is prepared as reverently and therefore as quietly as possible. **6:11–13** Deuteronomistic foreshadowing that places conditions on the success of the Davidic dynasty and YHWH's continued presence among the people (cf. 2 Sam. 7:14–16). See **"The Deuteronomistic History," p. 337**. **6:19** *The ark of the covenant of the LORD.* The portable house for God that had been in use since its

part of the house, to set there the ark of the covenant of the LORD. ²⁰The interior of the inner sanctuary was twenty cubits long, twenty cubits wide, and twenty cubits high; he overlaid it with pure gold. He also overlaid the altar with cedar.ˢ ²¹Solomon overlaid the inside of the house with pure gold, then he drew chains of gold across, in front of the inner sanctuary, and overlaid it with gold. ²²Next he overlaid the whole house with gold, in order that the whole house might be perfect; even the whole altar that belonged to the inner sanctuary he overlaid with gold.

23 In the inner sanctuary he made two cherubim of olivewood, each ten cubits high. ²⁴Five cubits was the length of one wing of the cherub and five cubits the length of the other wing of the cherub; it was ten cubits from the tip of one wing to the tip of the other. ²⁵The other cherub also measured ten cubits; both cherubim had the same measure and the same form. ²⁶The height of one cherub was ten cubits, and so was that of the other cherub. ²⁷He put the cherubim in the innermost part of the house; the wings of the cherubim were spread out so that a wing of one was touching the one wall and a wing of the other cherub was touching the other wall; their other wings toward the center of the house were touching wing to wing. ²⁸He also overlaid the cherubim with gold.

29 He carved the walls of the house all around about with carved engravings of cherubim, palm trees, and open flowers, in the inner and outer rooms. ³⁰The floor of the house he overlaid with gold, in the inner and outer rooms.

31 For the entrance to the inner sanctuary he made doors of olivewood; the lintel and the doorposts were five-sided.ᵗ ³²He covered the two doors of olivewood with carvings of cherubim, palm trees, and open flowers; he overlaid them with gold and spread gold on the cherubim and on the palm trees.

33 So also he made for the entrance to the nave doorposts of olivewood, four-sided each, ³⁴and two doors of cypress wood; the two leaves of the one door were folding, and the two leaves of the other door were folding. ³⁵He carved cherubim, palm trees, and open flowers, overlaying them with gold evenly applied upon the carved work. ³⁶He built the inner court with three courses of dressed stone to one course of cedar beams.

37 In the fourth year the foundation of the house of the LORD was laid, in the month of Ziv. ³⁸In the eleventh year, in the month of Bul, which is the eighth month, the house was finished in all its parts and according to all its specifications. He was seven years in building it.

7 Solomon was building his own house thirteen years, and he finished his entire house.

2 He built the House of the Forest of the Lebanon one hundred cubits long, fifty cubits wide, and thirty cubits high, built on four rows of cedar pillars, with cedar beams on the pillars. ³It was roofed with cedar on the forty-five rafters, fifteen in each row, which were on the pillars. ⁴There were window frames in the three rows, facing each other in the three rows. ⁵All the doorways and doorposts had four-sided frames, opposite, facing each other in the three rows.

6 He made the Hall of Pillars fifty cubits long and thirty cubits wide. There was a porch in front with pillars and a canopy in front of them.

7 He made the Hall of the Throne where he was to pronounce judgment, the Hall of

ˢ 6.20 Meaning of Heb uncertain   ᵗ 6.31 Meaning of Heb uncertain

construction after the exodus from Egypt. David brought the ark to Jerusalem in 2 Sam. 6. See note on Exod. 25:10–22. **6:20–22** The extensive use of gold indicates the house's significance as God's dwelling place, which must be *perfect*. **6:23** *Cherubim*. Composite beings of animal/human features (Ezek. 1:5–14; 10:12–14, 20–22), not infants with wings. The most common "cherub" found in ancient west Asian iconography is a sphinxlike figure with a human head, lion's body, and eagle's wings. The Renaissance image of the cherub as a winged baby is inspired by Greek and Roman depictions of the god Eros.

7:1 *Thirteen years*. Solomon's palace was finished after the temple, which took seven years.

7:2–6 Neither the House of the Forest of the Lebanon nor the Hall of Pillars has a stated purpose.

7:7 *The Hall of the Throne* appears to be a courthouse, where Solomon can display his famous wisdom (see 1 Kgs. 3).

Justice, covered with cedar from the floor to the rafters.ᵘ

8 His own house where he would reside, in the other court back of the hall, was of the same construction. Solomon also made a house like this hall for Pharaoh's daughter, whom he had taken in marriage.

9 All these were made of costly stones, cut according to measure, sawed with saws, back and front, from the foundation to the coping and from outside to the great court. ¹⁰The foundation was of costly stones, huge stones, stones of eight and ten cubits. ¹¹There were costly stones above, cut to measure, and cedarwood. ¹²The great court had three courses of dressed stone to one layer of cedar beams all around; so had the inner court of the house of the LORD and the vestibule of the house.

13 Now King Solomon invited and received Hiram from Tyre. ¹⁴He was the son of a widow of the tribe of Naphtali, whose father, a man of Tyre, had been an artisan in bronze; he was full of skill, intelligence, and knowledge in working bronze. He came to King Solomon and did all his work.

15 He cast two pillars of bronze. Eighteen cubits was the height of the one, and a cord of twelve cubits would encircle it; the second pillar was the same.ᵛ ¹⁶He also made two capitals of molten bronze to set on the tops of the pillars; the height of the one capital was five cubits, and the height of the other capital was five cubits. ¹⁷There were nets of checker work with wreaths of chain work for the capitals on the tops of the pillars, seven for the one capital and seven for the other capital. ¹⁸He made the columns with two rows around each latticework to cover the capitals that were above the pomegranates; he did the same with the other capital. ¹⁹Now the capitals that were on the tops of the pillars in the vestibule were of lily-work, four cubits high. ²⁰The capitals were on the two pillars and also above the rounded projection that was beside the latticework; there were two hundred pomegranates in rows all around, and so with the other capital. ²¹He set up the pillars at the vestibule of the temple; he set up the pillar on the south and called it Jachin, and he set up the pillar on the north and called it Boaz. ²²On the tops of the pillars was lily-work. Thus the work of the pillars was finished.

23 Then he made the molten sea; it was round, ten cubits from brim to brim, and five cubits high. A line of thirty cubits would encircle it completely. ²⁴Under its brim were gourdsʷ all around it, each of ten cubits, surrounding the sea; there were two rows of gourds,ˣ cast when it was cast. ²⁵It stood on twelve oxen, three facing north, three facing west, three facing south, and three facing east; the sea was set on them. The hindquarters of each were toward the inside. ²⁶Its thickness was a handbreadth; its brim was made like the brim of a cup, like the flower of a lily; it held two thousand baths.ʸ

27 He also made the ten stands of bronze; each stand was four cubits long, four cubits wide, and three cubits high. ²⁸This was the construction of the stands: they had borders; the borders were within the frames; ²⁹on the borders that were set in the frames were lions, oxen, and cherubim. On the frames, both above and below the lions and oxen, there were wreaths of beveled work. ³⁰Each stand had four bronze wheels and axles of bronze; at the four corners were supports for a basin. The supports were cast with wreaths at the side of each. ³¹Its opening was within the crown, whose height was one cubit; its opening was round, as a pedestal is made; it was a cubit and a half wide. At its opening there were carvings; its borders were four-sided, not round. ³²The

u 7.7 Syr Vg: Heb *floor*   v 7.15 Cn: Heb *and a cord of twelve cubits encircled the second pillar*   w 7.24 Meaning of Heb uncertain   x 7.24 Meaning of Heb uncertain   y 7.26 A Heb measure of volume

7:8 Solomon has a palace for himself and a separate one for his wife.

7:9–11 The writer emphasizes the significant cost of the stones used in all Solomon's building projects.

7:13–14 *Hiram from Tyre.* This person may be different from the "King Hiram of Tyre" of 1 Kgs. 5. The narrator notes that Hiram's mother is Israelite, but in a patrilineal descent system, Hiram takes on the Tyrian background of his father.

7:15–45 Hiram personally creates the bronze work for the temple, including its pillars (vv. 15–22), *the molten sea* (a huge pot, vv. 23–26), the bronze stands with supporting wheels (vv. 27–37), ten bronze basins (vv. 38–39), and all other bronze vessels (vv. 40–45).

four wheels were underneath the borders; the axles of the wheels were in the stands; and the height of a wheel was a cubit and a half. [33]The wheels were made like a chariot wheel; their axles, their rims, their spokes, and their hubs were all cast. [34]There were four supports at the four corners of each stand; the supports were of one piece with the stands. [35]On the top of the stand there was a round band half a cubit high; on the top of the stand, its stays and its borders were of one piece with it. [36]On the surfaces of its stays and on its borders he carved cherubim, lions, and palm trees where each had space, with wreaths all around. [37]In this way he made the ten stands; all of them were cast alike, with the same size and the same form.

38 He made ten basins of bronze; each basin held forty baths;[z] each basin measured four cubits; there was a basin for each of the ten stands. [39]He set five of the stands on the south side of the house and five on the north side of the house; he set the sea on the southeast corner of the house.

40 Hiram also made the pots, the shovels, and the basins. So Hiram finished all the work that he did for King Solomon on the house of the LORD: [41]the two pillars, the two bowls of the capitals that were on the tops of the pillars, the two latticeworks to cover the two bowls of the capitals that were on the tops of the pillars; [42]the four hundred pomegranates for the two latticeworks, two rows of pomegranates for each latticework, to cover the two bowls of the capitals that were on the pillars; [43]the ten stands, the ten basins on the stands; [44]the one sea and the twelve oxen underneath the sea.

45 The pots, the shovels, and the basins—all these vessels that Hiram made for King Solomon for the house of the LORD were of burnished bronze. [46]In the plain of the Jordan the king cast them, in the clay ground between Succoth and Zarethan. [47]Solomon left all the vessels unweighed because there were so many of them; the weight of the bronze was not determined.

48 So Solomon made all the vessels that were in the house of the LORD: the golden altar, the golden table for the bread of the Presence, [49]the lampstands of pure gold, five on the south side and five on the north, in front of the inner sanctuary; the flowers, the lamps, and the tongs, of gold; [50]the cups, snuffers, basins, dishes for incense, and firepans, of pure gold; the sockets for the doors of the innermost part of the house, the most holy place, and for the doors of the main hall of the temple, of gold.

51 Thus all the work that King Solomon did on the house of the LORD was finished. Solomon brought in the things that his father David had dedicated, the silver, the gold, and the vessels, and stored them in the treasuries of the house of the LORD.

8 Then Solomon assembled the elders of Israel and all the heads of the tribes, the leaders of the ancestral houses of the Israelites, before King Solomon in Jerusalem, to bring up the ark of the covenant of the LORD out of the city of David, which is Zion. [2]All the people of Israel assembled to King Solomon at the festival in the month Ethanim, which is the seventh month. [3]And all the elders of Israel came, and the priests carried the ark. [4]So they brought up the

z 7.38 A Heb measure of volume

7:47 *The weight of the bronze was not determined* is another sign of the extravagance of the project. No expense was spared.

7:51 In addition to the new objects, Solomon also brought in items *that his father David had dedicated* for the future temple.

8:1–9 *Ark of the covenant of the* LORD. The ark was an important cult object (1 Sam. 4–6), which was transferred to Jerusalem by David (2 Sam. 6). From a Deuteronomistic perspective, this is not just the "ark of the LORD," the "ark of God," or the "ark of the God of Israel" (1 Sam. 5–6) but the "ark of the covenant of the LORD" (Deut. 10:8), making the written covenant the major focus of religious life (Deut. 10:1–5). **8:6** *Underneath the wings of the cherubim.* The ark serves as a footstool or throne for YHWH (Num. 7:89; 1 Sam. 4:4; 2 Sam. 6:2; 2 Kgs. 19:15; Ps. 99:1; Isa. 37:16; Ezek. 9:3), and cherubim serve as a deity's "guardians" (Ezek. 10:18; 41:18). YHWH can also ride a cherub (2 Sam. 22:11; Ps. 18:10); in the iconographies of surrounding cultures, gods often ride or stand on cherubs, lions, or other animals and composite beings. There have been a number of cherubim thrones found in areas in and surrounding ancient Israel, including at Byblos, Hamath, and Megiddo.

ark of the Lord, the tent of meeting, and all the holy vessels that were in the tent; the priests and the Levites brought them up. [5]King Solomon and all the congregation of Israel, who had assembled before him, were with him before the ark, sacrificing so many sheep and oxen that they could not be counted or numbered. [6]Then the priests brought the ark of the covenant of the Lord to its place, in the inner sanctuary of the house, the most holy place, underneath the wings of the cherubim. [7]For the cherubim spread out their wings over the place of the ark, so that the cherubim made a covering above the ark and its poles. [8]The poles were so long that the ends of the poles were seen from the holy place in front of the inner sanctuary, but they could not be seen from outside; they are there to this day. [9]There was nothing in the ark except the two tablets of stone that Moses had placed there at Horeb, where the Lord made a covenant with the Israelites when they came out of the land of Egypt. [10]And when the priests came out of the holy place, a cloud filled the house of the Lord, [11]so that the priests could not stand to minister because of the cloud, for the glory of the Lord filled the house of the Lord.

[12] Then Solomon said,

"The Lord has said that he would dwell
    in thick darkness.
[13] I have built you an exalted house,
    a place for you to dwell forever."

[14] Then the king turned around and blessed all the assembly of Israel, while all the assembly of Israel stood. [15]He said, "Blessed be the Lord, the God of Israel, who with his hand has fulfilled what he promised with his mouth to my father David, saying, [16]'Since the day that I brought my people Israel out of Egypt, I have not chosen a city from any of the tribes of Israel in which to build a house, that my name might be there, nor did I choose anyone to be a ruler over my people Israel. But I have chosen Jerusalem in order that my name may be there,[a] and I have chosen David to be over my people Israel.' [17]My father David had it in mind to build a house for the name of the Lord, the God of Israel. [18]But the Lord said to my father David, 'You did well to consider building a house for my name; [19]nevertheless, you shall not build the house, but your son who shall be born to you shall build the house for my name.' [20]Now the Lord has fulfilled the promise that he made, for I have risen in the place of my father David; I sit on the throne of Israel, as the Lord promised, and have built the house for the name of the Lord, the God of Israel. [21]There I have provided a place for the ark, in which is the covenant of the Lord that he made with our ancestors when he brought them out of the land of Egypt."

[22] Then Solomon stood before the altar of the Lord in the presence of the whole assembly of Israel and spread out his hands to heaven. [23]He said, "O Lord, God of Israel, there is no God like you in heaven above or on earth beneath, keeping covenant and steadfast love with your servants who walk before you with all their heart, [24]the covenant that you kept for your servant my father David as you declared to him; you promised with your mouth and have this day fulfilled with your hand. [25]Therefore, O Lord, God of Israel, keep for your servant my father David that which you promised him, saying, 'There shall never fail you a successor before me to sit on the throne of Israel, if only your children look to their way, to walk before me as you have walked before me.' [26]Therefore, O God of Israel, let your word be confirmed that you promised to your servant my father David.

[27] "But will God indeed dwell on the earth? Even heaven and the highest heaven cannot contain you, much less this house

a 8.16 Cn Compare Q ms and 2 Chr 6.5–6: MT lacks *nor did . . . be there*

8:10–11 Description of YHWH's presence links the Solomonic temple with the tabernacle (Exod. 40:34–35).
8:14–29 Deuteronomistic perspective on the temple, underscoring the proper location of divine worship (8:29), the incomparability of YHWH (Deut. 4:39), the covenant (Deut. 4:5), and the endurance of the Davidic monarchy—with conditions (8:25). See **"The Deuteronomistic History," p. 337**. 8:18–21 Solomon reminds the people that he was chosen to build the temple as a promise God made to David. See 2 Sam. 7:12–13 and **"Covenant (Genesis)," p. 23**. 8:25 Solomon's prayer reaffirms that the success of the monarchy is conditional upon the people's obedience to YHWH.

that I have built! ²⁸Regard your servant's prayer and his plea, O LORD my God, heeding the cry and the prayer that your servant prays to you today, ²⁹that your eyes may be open night and day toward this house, the place of which you said, 'My name shall be there,' that you may heed the prayer that your servant prays toward this place. ³⁰Hear the plea of your servant and of your people Israel when they pray toward this place; O hear in heaven your dwelling place; hear and forgive.

31 "If someone sins against a neighbor and is required to take an oath and comes and swears before your altar in this house, ³²then hear in heaven, and act, and judge your servants, condemning the guilty by bringing their conduct on their own heads and vindicating the righteous by rewarding them according to their righteousness.

33 "When your people Israel, having sinned against you, are defeated before an enemy but turn again to you, confess your name, pray and plead with you in this house, ³⁴then hear in heaven, forgive the sin of your people Israel, and bring them again to the land that you gave to their ancestors.

35 "When heaven is shut up and there is no rain because they have sinned against you and then they pray toward this place, confess your name, and turn from their sin because you punish^b them, ³⁶then hear in heaven and forgive the sin of your servants, your people Israel, when you teach them the good way in which they should walk, and grant rain on your land, which you have given to your people as an inheritance.

37 "If there is famine in the land, if there is plague, blight, mildew, locust, or caterpillar; if their enemy besieges them in any^c of their cities; whatever suffering, whatever sickness there is; ³⁸whatever prayer, whatever plea there is from any individual or from all your people Israel, all knowing the suffering of their own hearts so that they stretch out their hands toward this house; ³⁹then hear in heaven your dwelling place, forgive, act, and render to all whose hearts you know—according to all their ways, for only you know the human heart—⁴⁰so that they may fear you all the days that they live in the land that you gave to our ancestors.

41 "Likewise when foreigners, who are not of your people Israel, come from a distant land because of your name ⁴²—for they shall hear of your great name, your mighty hand, and your outstretched arm—when foreigners come and pray toward this house, ⁴³then hear in heaven your dwelling place and do whatever the foreigners ask of you, so that all the peoples of the earth may know your name and fear you, as do your people Israel, and so they may know that your name has been invoked on this house that I have built.

44 "If your people go out to battle against their enemy, by whatever way you shall send them, and they pray to the LORD toward the city that you have chosen and the house that I have built for your name, ⁴⁵then hear in heaven their prayer and their plea and maintain their cause.

46 "If they sin against you—for there is no one who does not sin—and you are angry with them and give them to an enemy, so that they are carried away captive to the land of the enemy, far off or near, ⁴⁷then if they come to their senses in the land to which they have been taken captive and repent and plead with you in the land of their captors, saying, 'We have sinned and have done wrong; we have acted wickedly,' ⁴⁸if they repent with all their heart and soul in the land of their enemies who took them captive and pray to you toward their land that you gave to their ancestors, the city that you have chosen, and the house that I have built for your name, ⁴⁹then hear in

b 8.35 Or *when you answer*   c 8.37 Gk Syr: Heb *in the land*

8:31 *Required to take an oath.* For example, the scenarios of Exod. 22:7-13.

8:32-40 In a series of possible catastrophes, including defeat in war (vv. 33-34), famine (vv. 35-37), and invasion and illness (v. 37), Solomon prays that if the people repent from the actions that have caused the catastrophes, YHWH will restore them. Cf. Deut. 30:1-10.

8:41-43 The prayer that YHWH will intercede on behalf of *foreigners, who are not of your people Israel*, suggests that the temple will be a place where all can come and pray. Cf. Isa. 56:1-8; Zech. 8:22-23.

8:46-53 The reference to exile is the final possible catastrophe mentioned in the lengthy prayer. See **"Exile (2 Kings)," p. 539**.

heaven your dwelling place their prayer and their plea, maintain their cause, [50]and forgive your people who have sinned against you and all their transgressions that they have committed against you, and grant them compassion in the sight of their captors, so that they may have compassion on them [51](for they are your people and heritage that you brought out of Egypt, from the midst of the iron smelter). [52]Let your eyes be open to the plea of your servant and to the plea of your people Israel, listening to them whenever they call to you. [53]For you have separated them from among all the peoples of the earth to be your heritage, just as you promised through Moses, your servant, when you brought our ancestors out of Egypt, O Lord GOD."

54 Now when Solomon finished offering all this prayer and this plea to the LORD, he arose from facing the altar of the LORD, where he had knelt with hands outstretched toward heaven; [55]he stood and blessed all the assembly of Israel with a loud voice:

56 "Blessed be the LORD, who has given rest to his people Israel according to all that he promised; not one word has failed of all his good promise that he spoke through his servant Moses. [57]The LORD our God be with us, as he was with our ancestors; may he not leave us or abandon us, [58]but incline our hearts to him, to walk in all his ways and to keep his commandments, his statutes, and his ordinances that he commanded our ancestors. [59]Let these words of mine, with which I pleaded before the LORD, be near to the LORD our God day and night, and may he maintain the cause of his servant and the cause of his people Israel, as each day requires, [60]so that all the peoples of the earth may know that the LORD is God; there is no other. [61]Therefore devote yourselves completely to the LORD our God, walking in his statutes and keeping his commandments, as at this day."

62 Then the king and all Israel with him offered sacrifice before the LORD. [63]Solomon offered as sacrifices of well-being to the LORD twenty-two thousand oxen and one hundred twenty thousand sheep. So the king and all the people of Israel dedicated the house of the LORD. [64]The same day the king consecrated the middle of the court that was in front of the house of the LORD, for there he offered the burnt offerings and the grain offerings and the fat pieces of the sacrifices of well-being, because the bronze altar that was before the LORD was too small to receive the burnt offerings and the grain offerings and the fat pieces of the sacrifices of well-being.

65 So Solomon held the festival at that time and all Israel with him—a great assembly, people from Lebo-hamath to the Wadi of Egypt—before the LORD our God, seven days.[d] [66]On the eighth day he sent the people away, and they blessed the king and went to their tents joyful and in good spirits because of all the goodness that the LORD had shown to his servant David and to his people Israel.

9 When Solomon had finished building the house of the LORD and the king's house and all that Solomon desired to build, [2]the LORD appeared to Solomon a second time, as he had appeared to him at Gibeon. [3]The LORD said to him, "I have heard your prayer and your plea that you made before me; I have consecrated this house that you have built and put my name there forever; my eyes and my heart will be there for all time. [4]As for you, if you will walk before me as David your father walked, with integrity of heart and uprightness, doing according to all that I have commanded you and keeping my statutes

d 8.65 Compare Gk: Heb *seven days and seven days, fourteen days*

9:1–9 YHWH's second visitation to Solomon at Gibeon is an obvious Deuteronomistic composition restating that the endurance of David's dynasty, the people's residence on the land, and the temple depend on obedience to YHWH's *statutes* and *ordinances*. See **"The Deuteronomistic History," p. 337**. **9:3** *I have heard your prayer.* YHWH has confirmed not only that the temple is an acceptable home (see 1 Kgs. 8:10–11) but that Solomon's prayer for divine favor for Israel and anyone who comes to the temple has been accepted. **9:4–5** See 1 Kgs. 3:14. **9:6–9** Unlike the earlier positive statement in 1 Kgs. 3, YHWH warns Solomon that disobeying the covenant will lead to negative consequences for all Israel. Even non-Israelites will know that the loss of land and the destruction of the temple will be the direct result of disobedience. The Israelites themselves will become *a proverb and a taunt among all peoples* (cf. Deut. 28:37; Zech. 8:13). See **"Divine Retribution," p. 339**.

and my ordinances, [5]then I will establish your royal throne over Israel forever, as I promised your father David, saying, 'You shall never lack a successor on the throne of Israel.'

6 "If you turn aside from following me, you or your children, and do not keep my commandments and my statutes that I have set before you but go and serve other gods and worship them, [7]then I will cut Israel off from the land that I have given them, and the house that I have consecrated for my name I will cast out of my sight, and Israel will become a proverb and a taunt among all peoples. [8]This house will become a heap of ruins;[e] everyone passing by it will be astonished and will hiss, and they will say, 'Why has the LORD done such a thing to this land and to this house?' [9]Then they will say, 'Because they abandoned the LORD their God, who brought their ancestors out of the land of Egypt, and embraced other gods, worshiping them and serving them; therefore the LORD brought this disaster upon them.'"

10 At the end of twenty years, in which Solomon had built the two houses, the house of the LORD and the king's house, [11]King Hiram of Tyre having supplied Solomon with cedar and cypress timber and gold, as much as he desired, King Solomon gave to Hiram twenty cities in the land of Galilee. [12]But when Hiram came from Tyre to see the cities that Solomon had given him, they did not please him. [13]Therefore he said, "What kind of cities are these that you have given me, my brother?" So they are called the land of Cabul[f] to this day. [14]But Hiram had sent to the king one hundred twenty talents of gold.

15 This is the account of the forced labor that King Solomon conscripted to build the house of the LORD and his own house, the Millo and the wall of Jerusalem, Hazor, Megiddo, Gezer [16](Pharaoh king of Egypt had gone up and captured Gezer and burned it down, had killed the Canaanites who lived in the city, and had given it as dowry to his daughter, Solomon's wife; [17]so Solomon rebuilt Gezer), Lower Beth-horon, [18]Baalath, Tadmor in the wilderness, within the land, [19]as well as all of Solomon's storage cities, the cities for his chariots, the cities for his cavalry, and whatever Solomon desired to build in Jerusalem, in Lebanon, and in all the land of his dominion. [20]All the people who were left of the Amorites, the Hittites, the Perizzites, the Hivites, and the Jebusites, who were not of the people of Israel—[21]their descendants who were still left in the land, whom the Israelites were unable to destroy completely—these Solomon conscripted for slave labor, and so they are to this day. [22]But of the Israelites Solomon made no slaves; they were the soldiers; they were his officials, his commanders, his captains, and the commanders of his chariotry and cavalry.

23 These were the chief officers who were over Solomon's work: five hundred fifty who had charge of the people who carried on the work.

24 But Pharaoh's daughter went up from the city of David to her own house that Solomon had built for her; then he built the Millo.

25 Three times a year Solomon used to offer up burnt offerings and sacrifices of well-being on the altar that he built for the LORD, offering incense[g] before the LORD. So he completed the house.

26 King Solomon built a fleet of ships at Ezion-geber, which is near Eloth on the

e 9.8 Syr OL: Heb *will become high*   f 9.13 Perhaps meaning *as nothing*   g 9.25 Gk: Heb *offering incense with it that was*

9:10–14 This story may downplay the implications of Solomon's transfer of Israelite land to a foreigner. Solomon gave away Israel's land, but it was not that valuable. And he may have even gotten a deal on it (v. 14).

9:13 *Cabul.* Perhaps a play on Hebrew "kebal" ("like nothing").

9:15–22 This passage emphatically asserts that Solomon did not conscript Israelites for forced labor on Solomon's building projects (v. 22), which stands in tension with 5:13–18. This narrator asserts that Solomon drafted only remnants of the Canaanite nations for the corvée (Heb. "mas," forced labor conscripts). According to Lev. 25:44–46, non-Israelites could be enslaved and therefore would be suitable for forced labor. The passage also contradicts Jeroboam's argument for mercy in 1 Kgs. 12:4. On behalf of the northern tribes, he asks Solomon's son Rehoboam, now king, to "lighten the hard service of your father and his heavy yoke that he placed on us."

9:25 Solomon continues to offer proper worship to YHWH at the temple, a sign of obedience.

shore of the Red Sea,[b] in the land of Edom. [27]Hiram sent his servants with the fleet, sailors who were familiar with the sea, together with the servants of Solomon. [28]They went to Ophir and imported from there four hundred twenty talents of gold that they delivered to King Solomon.

10 When the queen of Sheba heard of the fame of Solomon (fame due to[i] the name of the LORD), she came to test him with riddles. [2]She came to Jerusalem with a very great retinue, with camels bearing spices and very much gold and precious stones, and when she came to Solomon, she told him all that was on her mind. [3]Solomon answered all her questions; there was nothing hidden from the king that he could not explain to her. [4]When the queen of Sheba had observed all the wisdom of Solomon, the house that he had built, [5]the food of his table, the seating of his officials, and the attendance of his servants, their clothing, his valets, and his burnt offerings that he offered at the house of the LORD, it took her breath away.

6 So she said to the king, "The report was true that I heard in my own land of your accomplishments and of your wisdom, [7]but I did not believe the reports until I came and my own eyes saw it. Not even half had been told me; your wisdom and prosperity far surpass the report that I had heard. [8]Happy are your wives![j] Happy are these your servants who continually attend you and hear your wisdom! [9]Blessed be the LORD your God, who has delighted in you and set you on the throne of Israel! Because the LORD loved Israel forever, he has made you king to execute justice and righteousness." [10]Then she gave the king one hundred twenty talents of gold, a great quantity of spices, and precious stones; never again did spices come in such quantity as that which the queen of Sheba gave to King Solomon.

11 Moreover, the fleet of Hiram, which carried gold from Ophir, brought from Ophir a great quantity of almug wood and precious stones. [12]From the almug wood the king made supports for the house of the LORD and for the king's house, lyres also and harps for the singers; no such almug wood has come or been seen to this day.

13 Meanwhile, King Solomon gave to the queen of Sheba every desire that she expressed, as well as what he gave her out of Solomon's royal bounty. Then she returned to her own land with her servants.

14 The weight of gold that came to Solomon in one year was six hundred sixty-six talents of gold, [15]besides that which came from the traders and from the business of the merchants and from all the kings of Arabia and the governors of the land. [16]King Solomon made two hundred large shields of beaten gold; six hundred shekels

b 9.26 Or *Sea of Reeds*   i 10.1 Meaning of Heb uncertain   j 10.8 Gk Syr: Heb *men*

9:28 *Ophir*. Unknown location. Some have speculated southern Arabia or east Africa.
10:1–29 These accounts, including the famous narrative about the queen of Sheba (vv. 1–10), boast of Solomon's immense wealth. From a Deuteronomistic standpoint, this is not entirely positive. According to Deut. 17:14–20, the king may not accumulate great wealth or wives. Yet 1 Kgs. 10, a chapter about Solomon's wealth, precedes 1 Kgs. 11, which discusses Solomon's multiple wives (compare Deut. 17:17). **10:1** *The queen of Sheba*. Sheba is usually identified with the kingdom of Saba, which dominated southern Arabia in the tenth century BCE. But many traditions about the queen of Sheba have developed. According to Josephus, the queen of Sheba was Ethiopian, and many have associated her with that area. In the Qur'an (Sura 27:14–44), the queen, named Bilqis, is so impressed with Solomon's opulence that she abandons her own gods to follow Solomon's God. In the *Kebra Negast*, an Ethiopian legend, the queen, named Makeda, converts to Judaism after beholding Solomon's wealth and has a son, Menilek, by him. *She came to test him with riddles*. Cf. 1 Kgs. 4:34, which claims that people everywhere want to hear Solomon's wisdom. **10:6–7** The queen concludes that all she had heard about Solomon is true, because she has seen it for herself. Cf. Job 42:5–6, where Job states that hearing about God is secondary to having seen God for himself. **10:9** *Blessed be the* LORD *your God*. The queen recognizes that Solomon's prosperity is a gift from his God, a common view in the ancient world where each group had its own deity. Cf. 2 Kgs. 18, in which Sennacherib argues that Israel's misfortunes are a result of not following YHWH and that other people's gods have failed to protect them. **10:11–12** *Almug wood*. Mentioned in Ugaritic and Akkadian texts, but species unknown. **10:14–22** An extensive description of Solomon's wealth,

of gold went into each large shield. [17]He made three hundred shields of beaten gold; three minas of gold went into each shield; and the king put them in the House of the Forest of Lebanon. [18]The king also made a great ivory throne and overlaid it with the finest gold. [19]The throne had six steps. The top of the throne was rounded in the back, and on each side of the seat were arm rests and two lions standing beside the arm rests, [20]while twelve lions were standing, one on each end of a step on the six steps. Nothing like it was ever made in any kingdom. [21]All King Solomon's drinking vessels were of gold, and all the vessels of the House of the Forest of Lebanon were of pure gold; none were of silver—it was not considered as anything in the days of Solomon. [22]For the king had a fleet of ships of Tarshish at sea with the fleet of Hiram. Once every three years the fleet of ships of Tarshish used to come bringing gold, silver, ivory, apes, and peacocks.[k]

23 Thus King Solomon excelled all the kings of the earth in riches and in wisdom. [24]The whole earth sought the presence of Solomon to hear his wisdom, which God had put into his mind. [25]Every one of them brought a present, objects of silver and gold, garments, weaponry, spices, horses, and mules, so much year by year.

26 Solomon gathered together chariots and horses; he had fourteen hundred chariots and twelve thousand horses, which he stationed in the chariot cities and with the king in Jerusalem. [27]The king made silver as common in Jerusalem as stone, and he made cedar as plentiful as the sycamores in the Shephelah. [28]Solomon's import of horses was from Egypt and Kue, and the king's traders received them from Kue at a price. [29]A chariot could be imported from Egypt for six hundred shekels of silver and a horse for one hundred fifty, so through the king's traders they were exported to all the kings of the Hittites and the kings of Aram.

11 King Solomon loved many foreign women along with the daughter of Pharaoh: Moabite, Ammonite, Edomite, Sidonian, and Hittite women, [2]from the nations concerning which the Lord had said to the Israelites, "You shall not enter into marriage with them, neither shall they with you, for they will surely incline your heart to follow their gods." Solomon clung to these in love. [3]Among his wives were seven hundred princesses and three hundred concubines, and his wives turned away his heart. [4]For when Solomon was old, his wives turned away his heart after other gods, and his heart was not true to the Lord his God, as was the heart of his father David. [5]For Solomon followed Astarte the goddess of the Sidonians and Milcom the abomination of the Ammonites. [6]So Solomon did what was evil in the sight of the Lord and did not completely follow the Lord, as his father David had done. [7]Then Solomon built a high place for Chemosh the abomination of Moab and for Molech the abomination of the Ammonites on the mountain east of Jerusalem. [8]He did the same for all his foreign wives who offered incense and sacrificed to their gods.

9 Then the Lord was angry with Solomon because his heart had turned away from the Lord, the God of Israel, who had appeared

k 10.22 Or *baboons*

specifically the amount of gold items found in his palaces. **10:26–29** Royal trading in horses is specifically criticized in Deut. 17:16.

11:1–13 Explains the division of the two kingdoms as a result of Solomon's decision to build shrines to the gods of his wives' nations. The shrines set up by Solomon endure to the reign of Josiah (2 Kgs. 23:13). **11:1–2** Deuteronomy 7:1–6 forbids intermarriage with Canaanite nations, but the nations listed in 1 Kgs. 11:1 differ substantially from the list in Deuteronomy. **11:5** *Astarte*. Hebrew "Ashtoret" was a goddess of fertility very popular throughout Syria-Palestine, but here identified as Sidonian. *Milcom*. National god of the Ammonites. *Abomination*. Hebrew "shiqqutz" is the term used of illicit cult objects (Deut. 29:17; Isa. 66:3; Jer. 4:1; 7:30; 13:27; 16:18; 32:34; Ezek. 7:20; 11:18, 21; 20:7, 30; 37:23). **11:7** *Chemosh*. National god of Moab, mentioned in the late-ninth-century BCE Mesha Stele (*Ancient Near Eastern Texts Relating to the Old Testament*, 320). **11:9–10** *The Lord, the God of Israel, who had appeared to him twice and had commanded him concerning this matter*. See 1 Kgs. 3:14 and 9:4–5, in which YHWH links the longevity of the kingdom to Solomon's obedience to the covenant.

to him twice ¹⁰and had commanded him concerning this matter, that he should not follow other gods, but he did not observe what the Lord had commanded. ¹¹Therefore the Lord said to Solomon, "Since this has been your mind and you have not kept my covenant and my statutes that I have commanded you, I will surely tear the kingdom from you and give it to your servant. ¹²Yet for the sake of your father David I will not do it in your lifetime; I will tear it out of the hand of your son. ¹³I will not, however, tear away the entire kingdom; I will give one tribe to your son for the sake of my servant David and for the sake of Jerusalem, which I have chosen."

14 Then the Lord raised up an adversary against Solomon, Hadad the Edomite; he was of the royal house in Edom. ¹⁵For when David was destroying[l] Edom and Joab the commander of the army went up to bury the dead, he killed every male in Edom ¹⁶(for Joab and all Israel remained there six months until he had eliminated every male in Edom), ¹⁷but Hadad fled to Egypt with some Edomites who were servants of his father. He was a young boy at that time. ¹⁸They set out from Midian and came to Paran; they took people with them from Paran and came to Egypt, to Pharaoh king of Egypt, who gave him a house, assigned him an allowance of food, and gave him land. ¹⁹Hadad found great favor in the sight of Pharaoh, so that he gave him his sister-in-law for a wife, the sister of Queen Tahpenes. ²⁰The sister of Tahpenes gave birth by him to his son Genubath, whom Tahpenes weaned in Pharaoh's house; Genubath was in Pharaoh's house among the children of Pharaoh. ²¹When Hadad heard in Egypt that David slept with his ancestors and that Joab the commander of the army was dead, Hadad said to Pharaoh, "Let me depart, that I may go to my own country." ²²But Pharaoh said to him, "What do you lack with me that you now seek to

go to your own country?" And he said, "No, do let me go."

23 God raised up another adversary against Solomon,[m] Rezon son of Eliada, who had fled from his master, King Hadadezer of Zobah. ²⁴He gathered followers around him and became leader of a marauding band, after the killing by David; they went to Damascus, settled there, and made him king in Damascus. ²⁵He was an adversary of Israel all the days of Solomon, making trouble as Hadad did; he despised Israel and reigned over Aram.

26 Jeroboam son of Nebat, an Ephraimite of Zeredah, a servant of Solomon, whose mother's name was Zeruah, a widow, rebelled against the king. ²⁷The following was the reason he rebelled against the king. Solomon built the Millo and closed up the gap in the wall[n] of the city of his father David. ²⁸The man Jeroboam was very able, and when Solomon saw that the young man was industrious, he gave him charge over all the forced labor of the house of Joseph. ²⁹About that time, when Jeroboam was leaving Jerusalem, the prophet Ahijah the Shilonite found him on the road. Ahijah had clothed himself with a new garment. The two of them were alone in the open country ³⁰when Ahijah laid hold of the new garment he was wearing and tore it into twelve pieces. ³¹He then said to Jeroboam, "Take for yourself ten pieces, for thus says the Lord, the God of Israel: See, I am about to tear the kingdom from the hand of Solomon and will give you ten tribes. ³²One tribe will remain his, for the sake of my servant David and for the sake of Jerusalem, the city that I have chosen out of all the tribes of Israel. ³³This is because he has[o] forsaken me, worshiped Astarte the goddess of the Sidonians, Chemosh the god of Moab, and Milcom the god of the Ammonites, and has[p]

l 11.15 Gk Syr: Heb *was in*   m 11.23 Heb *him*   n 11.27 Heb lacks *in the wall*   o 11.33 Gk Syr Vg: Heb *they have*   p 11.33 Gk Syr Vg: Heb *they have*

11:14 *An adversary* (Heb. "satan"). See **"The Satan," p. 687.**
11:15 *Edom.* A small kingdom to the southeast of Judah, subjugated by David (2 Sam. 8:13–14).
11:23 *King Hadadezer of Zobah.* See 2 Sam. 8:3–8.
11:28 *House of Joseph.* Suggests Jeroboam was in charge of forced labor for northern territories.
11:29–39 Ahijah the Shilonite's prophecy seems to fit a pattern in which prophets announce the fall of dynasties and anoint the replacement (1 Sam. 15:24–30; 1 Kgs. 14:7–16; 16:1–7; 19:15–18; 21:17–27). 11:30–31 Similar "tearing" imagery in the prophet Samuel's announcement that Saul's dynasty would end (1 Sam. 15:27–28). 11:32–36 YHWH will give a piece of the kingdom to Solomon's

not walked in my ways, doing what is right in my sight and keeping my statutes and my ordinances, as his father David did. ³⁴Nevertheless, I will not take the whole kingdom away from him but will make him ruler all the days of his life, for the sake of my servant David whom I chose and who did keep my commandments and my statutes, ³⁵but I will take the kingdom away from his son and give it to you—that is, the ten tribes. ³⁶Yet to his son I will give one tribe, so that my servant David may always have a lamp before me in Jerusalem, the city where I have chosen to put my name. ³⁷I will take you, and you shall reign over all that your soul desires; you shall be king over Israel. ³⁸If you will listen to all that I command you, walk in my ways, and do what is right in my sight by keeping my statutes and my commandments, as David my servant did, I will be with you and will build you an enduring house, as I built for David, and I will give Israel to you. ³⁹For this reason I will punish the descendants of David, but not forever." ⁴⁰Solomon sought therefore to kill Jeroboam, but Jeroboam promptly fled to Egypt, to King Shishak of Egypt, and remained in Egypt until the death of Solomon.

41 Now the rest of the acts of Solomon, all that he did as well as his wisdom, are they not written in the Book of the Acts of Solomon? ⁴²The time that Solomon reigned in Jerusalem over all Israel was forty years. ⁴³Solomon slept with his ancestors and was buried in the city of his father David, and his son Rehoboam succeeded him.

12 Rehoboam went to Shechem, for all Israel had come to Shechem to make him king. ²When Jeroboam son of Nebat heard of it (for he was still in Egypt, where he had fled from King Solomon), then Jeroboam remained in Egypt. ³And they sent and called him, and Jeroboam and all the assembly of Israel came and said to Rehoboam, ⁴"Your father made our yoke heavy. Now,

therefore, lighten the hard service of your father and his heavy yoke that he placed on us, and we will serve you." ⁵He said to them, "Go away for three days, then come again to me." So the people went away.

6 Then King Rehoboam took counsel with the older men who had attended his father Solomon while he was still alive, saying, "How do you advise me to answer this people?" ⁷They answered him, "If you will be a servant to this people today and serve them and speak good words to them when you answer them, then they will be your servants forever." ⁸But he disregarded the advice that the older men gave him and consulted with the young men who had grown up with him and now attended him. ⁹He said to them, "What do you advise that we answer this people who have said to me, 'Lighten the yoke that your father put on us'?" ¹⁰The young men who had grown up with him said to him, "Thus you should say to this people who spoke to you, 'Your father made our yoke heavy, but you must lighten it for us'; thus you should say to them, 'My little finger is thicker than my father's loins. ¹¹Now, whereas my father laid on you a heavy yoke, I will add to your yoke. My father disciplined you with whips, but I will discipline you with scorpions.'"

12 So Jeroboam and all the people came to Rehoboam the third day, as the king had said, "Come to me again the third day." ¹³The king answered the people harshly. He disregarded the advice that the older men had given him ¹⁴and spoke to them according to the advice of the young men, "My father made your yoke heavy, but I will add to your yoke; my father disciplined you with whips, but I will discipline you with scorpions." ¹⁵So the king did not listen to the people because it was a turn of affairs brought about by the LORD to fulfill his word that the LORD had spoken by Ahijah the Shilonite to Jeroboam son of Nebat.

16 When all Israel saw that the king

son *for the sake of my servant David.* **11:38** YHWH makes the same offer to Jeroboam that Solomon received—permanent kingship in exchange for obeying the commandments.

12:8 *Young men.* Hebrew "yeladim," "boys," emphasizes the immaturity of Rehoboam and his young advisers.

12:10 *Little finger* (Heb. "qoten"). As in many misogynistic, patriarchal societies, Rehoboam uses phallic language and imagery to assert dominance and control. Other body parts—for example, feet (Ruth 3:7)—can be used as euphemisms for sexual organs.

12:16 Compare the rebel Sheba's similar protest in 2 Sam. 20:1.

would not listen to them, the people answered the king,

> "What share do we have in David?
> We have no inheritance in the son
> of Jesse.
> To your tents, O Israel!
> Look now to your own house,
> O David."

So Israel went away to their tents. [17]But Rehoboam reigned over the Israelites who were living in the towns of Judah. [18]When King Rehoboam sent Adoram, who was taskmaster over the forced labor, all Israel stoned him to death. King Rehoboam then hurriedly mounted his chariot to flee to Jerusalem. [19]So Israel has been in rebellion against the house of David to this day.

20 When all Israel heard that Jeroboam had returned, they sent and called him to the assembly and made him king over all Israel. There was no one who followed the house of David except the tribe of Judah alone.

21 When Rehoboam came to Jerusalem, he assembled all the house of Judah and the tribe of Benjamin, one hundred eighty thousand chosen troops, to fight against the house of Israel, to restore the kingdom to Rehoboam son of Solomon. [22]But the word of God came to Shemaiah the man of God: [23]"Say to King Rehoboam of Judah, son of Solomon, and to all the house of Judah and Benjamin, and to the rest of the people: [24]Thus says the LORD: You shall not go up or fight against your kindred the people of Israel. Let everyone go home, for this thing is from me." So they heeded the word of the LORD and went home again, according to the word of the LORD.

25 Then Jeroboam built Shechem in the hill country of Ephraim and resided there; he went out from there and built Penuel. [26]Then Jeroboam said to himself, "Now the kingdom may well revert to the house of David. [27]If this people continues to go up to offer sacrifices in the house of the LORD at Jerusalem, the heart of this people will turn again to their master, King Rehoboam of Judah; they will kill me and return to King Rehoboam of Judah." [28]So the king took counsel and made two calves of gold. He said to the people,[q] "You have gone up to Jerusalem long enough. Here are your gods, O Israel, who brought you up out of the land of Egypt." [29]He set one in Bethel, and the other he put in Dan. [30]And this thing became a sin, for the people went to worship before the one at Bethel and before the other as far as Dan.[r] [31]He also made houses[s] on high places and appointed priests from among all the people who were not Levites. [32]Jeroboam appointed a festival on the fifteenth day of the eighth month like the festival that was in Judah, and he offered sacrifices on the altar; so he did in Bethel, sacrificing to the calves that he had made. And he placed in Bethel the priests of the high places that he had made. [33]He went up to the altar that he had made in Bethel on the fifteenth day in the eighth month, in the month that he had selected on his own; he appointed a festival for the people of Israel, and he went up to the altar to offer incense.

q 12.28 Gk: Heb *to them*   r 12.30 Compare Gk: Heb *went to the one as far as Dan*   s 12.31 Gk Vg: Heb *a house*

12:19 *To this day* suggests this part of the text was composed before the destruction of the northern kingdom in 722 BCE. See **"Exile (2 Kings)," p. 539**.

12:25–30 Jeroboam builds up shrines at the prestigious cult sites of Shechem (Gen. 32:24–32), Bethel (Gen. 35), and Dan to prevent worshipers from going to the temple in Jerusalem. **12:28** *Two calves of gold.* Most likely represent the presence of YHWH, who is described as a bull (Gen. 49:24; "Mighty One" = Heb. "abbir," "bull," Isa. 1:24; 49:26; 60:16; Ps. 132:2, 5). Like the ark, the calves probably served as a footstool or seat for YHWH (see note on 8:6). *Here are your gods, O Israel.* See Aaron's statement in Exod. 32:4.

12:32–33 The festival Jeroboam desecrates, from a Deuteronomistic viewpoint, is probably Sukkot, or the Festival of Booths, which appears to have developed from a fall harvest festival (Exod. 23:16; Deut. 16:13–15). According to the Holiness Code (Lev. 17–26), the festival should take place on the fifteenth day of the seventh month (Lev. 23:34). Many academic biblical scholars understand the Holiness Code as a separate, exilic or postexilic source with its own Priestly inspired theology expressed in Lev. 17–26—though some notable scholars believe the Holiness Code was written earlier. Because of its possible late date, the Holiness Code may not give an accurate or full picture of how this festival, or something like it, was practiced during Jeroboam's time. Festivals that would define the community—and their appropriate times and practices—were a topic of discussion for

13 A man of God came out of Judah by the word of the LORD to Bethel, while Jeroboam was standing by the altar to offer incense. ²And he cried out against the altar by the word of the LORD and said, "O altar, altar, thus says the LORD: A son shall be born to the house of David, Josiah by name, and he shall sacrifice on you the priests of the high places who offer incense on you, and human bones shall be burned on you." ³He gave a sign the same day, saying, "This is the sign that the LORD has spoken: The altar shall be torn down, and the ashes that are on it shall be poured out." ⁴When the king heard what the man of God cried out against the altar at Bethel, Jeroboam stretched out his hand from the altar, saying, "Seize him!" But the hand that he stretched out against him withered so that he could not draw it back to himself. ⁵The altar also was torn down, and the ashes poured out from the altar, according to the sign that the man of God had given by the word of the LORD. ⁶The king said to the man of God, "Entreat now the favor of the LORD your God, and pray for me, so that my hand may be restored to me." So the man of God entreated the LORD, and the king's hand was restored to him and became as it was before. ⁷Then the king said to the man of God, "Come home with me and dine, and I will give you a gift." ⁸But the man of God said to the king, "If you give me half your kingdom, I will not go in with you, nor will I eat food or drink water in this place. ⁹For thus I was commanded by the word of the LORD: 'You shall not eat food, or drink water, or return by the way that you came.'" ¹⁰So he went another way and did not return by the way that he had come to Bethel.

11 Now there lived an old prophet in Bethel. One of his sons came and told him all that the man of God had done that day in Bethel; the words also that he had spoken to the king, they told to their father. ¹²Their father said to them, "Which way did he go?" And his sons showed him the way that the man of God who came from Judah had gone. ¹³Then he said to his sons, "Saddle a donkey for me." So they saddled a donkey for him, and he mounted it. ¹⁴He went after the man of God and found him sitting under an oak tree. He said to him, "Are you the man of God who came from Judah?" He answered, "I am." ¹⁵Then he said to him, "Come home with me and eat some food." ¹⁶But he said, "I cannot return with you or go in with you, nor will I eat food or drink water with you in this place, ¹⁷for it was said to me by the word of the LORD, 'You shall not eat food or drink water there or return by the way that you came.'" ¹⁸Then the other*ᵗ* said to him, "I also am a prophet as you are, and an angel spoke to me by the word of the LORD, 'Bring him back with you into your house so that he may eat food and drink water.'" But he was deceiving him. ¹⁹Then the man of God*ᵘ* went back with him and ate food and drank water in his house.

20 As they were sitting at the table, the word of the LORD came to the prophet who had brought him back, ²¹and he cried out to the man of God who came from Judah, "Thus says the LORD: Because you have disobeyed the word of the LORD and have not kept the commandment that the LORD your God commanded you ²²but have come back and have eaten food and drunk water in the place of which he said to you, 'Eat no food, and drink no water,' your body shall not come to your ancestral tomb." ²³After the man of God*ᵛ* had eaten food and had drunk, they saddled for him a donkey belonging to the prophet who had brought him back. ²⁴Then as he went away, a lion met him on the road and killed him. His body was thrown in the road, and the donkey stood beside it; the lion also stood beside the body. ²⁵People passed by and saw the body

t 13.18 Heb *he*   *u* 13.19 Heb *he*   *v* 13.23 Heb *he*

exilic and postexilic biblical authors (Lev. 23:1; Zech. 14:16–17; Neh. 8:14–17). According to Neh. 8:17, the Festival of Booths was not celebrated from the time of Joshua until the postexilic period, which conflicts with 1 Kgs. 12:32–33's implication that the festival was celebrated properly in Judah.

13:1–10 An anti-Jeroboam narrative designed to discredit the Bethel shrine. **13:2** *Josiah* will eventually reign over Israel for approximately thirty years. See 2 Kgs. 22–23. **13:4** *Altar at Bethel.* See 12:25–33.

13:11 The unnamed *prophet*—despite his intentions—is also a deceiver (v. 18). See **"Prophecy,"** p. 484.

Focus On: Prophecy (1 Kings 13)

Prophecy constitutes the words in the Hebrew Bible that a man or woman, called a prophet, speaks in God's name. While most prophets are men, Miriam (Exod. 15:20), Deborah (Judg. 4:4), Huldah (2 Kgs. 22:14), and Ezekiel's prophetic enemies in chap. 13 are women. The Prophetic Books (see **"Introduction to the Latter Prophets / Prophetic Books," pp. 9–12**) each begin with an identification of the prophet usually as having received "the word of the Lord"; less commonly, the prophet receives a "vision" (Isa. 1:1; Ezek. 1:1; Obad. 1) or an "oracle" (Nah. 1:1; Hab. 1:1), or in Amos's case, sees words (1:1).

The prophets often encourage the people to make positive changes now to avoid future trouble as a result of current disobedience. The common prophetic argument is that God will reward the righteous and punish the wicked (see **"Divine Retribution," p. 339**). Also, the people must be faithful and worship God alone (see **"Apostasy," p. 1238** and **"Repentance," p. 1245**). Some books describe different political and social problems (for example, foreign alliances in Hosea and economic injustice in Micah), or improper religious practices (delay in rebuilding the temple in Haggai and incorrect sacrifices in Malachi). Nahum and Obadiah are specific prophecies against the non-Israelite areas of Nineveh and Edom, respectively, and Habakkuk is a dialogue between the prophet and God about why the Israelites are suffering. Unlike the other Prophetic Books, which often contain words of warning or comfort preceded by "Thus says the Lord," Jonah is written as a narrative.

Additionally, prophecy is not limited to the books named for particular prophets, and the prophets do not always agree with each other (e.g., Jer. 28). In 1 Kgs. 13, one prophet speaks against an altar at Bethel but is deceived by another prophet and killed as punishment for not obeying God's command to return home immediately. The dead prophet's warning against the altar comes true in 2 Kgs. 23; however, the test of prophecy is not just whether the words spoken actually happen but whether the prophets themselves remain faithful to God. Many prophecies are open-ended with respect to when the events they describe will happen (e.g., Joel 2). Most importantly, the people hearing the prophecies have to decide whether to believe the prophet; in both Jer. 44 and the book of Malachi, the people express skepticism. Contemporary readers also have to decide what the prophecies spoken centuries ago mean today.

Stacy Davis

thrown in the road, with the lion standing by the body. And they came and told it in the town where the old prophet lived.

26 When the prophet who had brought him back from the way heard of it, he said, "It is the man of God who disobeyed the word of the Lord; therefore the Lord has given him to the lion, which has torn him and killed him according to the word that the Lord spoke to him." ²⁷Then he said to his sons, "Saddle a donkey for me." So they saddled one, ²⁸and he went and found the body thrown in the road, with the donkey and the lion standing beside the body. The lion had not eaten the body or attacked the donkey. ²⁹The prophet took up the body of the man of God, laid it on the donkey, and

brought it back to the city*ʷ* to mourn and to bury him. ³⁰He laid the body in his own grave, and they mourned over him, saying, "Alas, my brother!" ³¹After he had buried him, he said to his sons, "When I die, bury me in the grave in which the man of God is buried; lay my bones beside his bones. ³²For the saying that he proclaimed by the word of the Lord against the altar in Bethel and against all the houses of the high places that are in the cities of Samaria shall surely come to pass."

33 Even after this event Jeroboam did not turn from his evil way but made priests for the high places again from among all the people; any who wanted to be priests he

w 13.29 Gk: Heb *he came to the town of the old prophet*

13:22 *Ancestral tomb.* Hebrew "qeber abot," "fathers' tomb." Being buried with ancestors and kinfolk is important (Judg. 8:32; 16:31; 2 Sam. 2:32; 17:23; 21:14; 1 Kgs. 11:43; 2 Kgs. 12:21; 15:7, 22, 38; 22:20), and being denied burial in an ancestral tomb is a harsh punishment (1 Kgs. 14:13; 21:23–24).

13:29–31 The unnamed *man of God* receives a proper burial and is not left out in the open air (cf. 14:11; 21:24).

consecrated for the high places. [34]This matter became sin to the house of Jeroboam, so as to cut it off and to destroy it from the face of the earth.

14 At that time Abijah son of Jeroboam fell sick. [2]Jeroboam said to his wife, "Go, disguise yourself so that it will not be known that you are the wife of Jeroboam, and go to Shiloh, for the prophet Ahijah is there, who said of me that I should be king over this people. [3]Take with you ten loaves, some cakes, and a jar of honey, and go to him; he will tell you what shall happen to the child."

[4] Jeroboam's wife did so; she set out and went to Shiloh and came to the house of Ahijah. Now Ahijah could not see, for his eyes were dim because of his age. [5]But the Lord said to Ahijah, "The wife of Jeroboam is coming to inquire of you concerning her son, for he is sick. Thus and thus you shall say to her when she comes. She will pretend to be another woman."

[6] But when Ahijah heard the sound of her feet as she came in at the door, he said, "Come in, wife of Jeroboam; why do you pretend to be another? For I am charged with heavy tidings for you. [7]Go, tell Jeroboam, 'Thus says the Lord, the God of Israel: Because I exalted you from among the people, made you leader over my people Israel, [8]and tore the kingdom away from the house of David to give it to you, yet you have not been like my servant David, who kept my commandments and followed me with all his heart, doing only that which was right in my sight, [9]but you have done evil above all those who were before you and have gone and made for yourself other gods and cast images, provoking me to anger, and have thrust me behind your back, [10]therefore I will bring evil upon the house of Jeroboam. I will cut off from Jeroboam every male, both bond and free in Israel, and will consume the house of Jeroboam, just as one burns up dung until it is all gone. [11]Anyone belonging to Jeroboam who dies in the city the dogs shall eat, and anyone who dies in the open country the birds of the air shall eat, for the Lord has spoken.' [12]Therefore set out, go to your house. When your feet enter the city, the child shall die. [13]All Israel shall mourn for him and bury him, for he alone of Jeroboam's family shall come to the grave, because in him there is found something pleasing to the Lord, the God of Israel, in the house of Jeroboam. [14]Moreover the Lord will raise up for himself a king over Israel who shall cut off the house of Jeroboam today, even right now![x]

[15] "The Lord will strike Israel as a reed is shaken in the water; he will root up Israel out of this good land that he gave to their ancestors and scatter them beyond the Euphrates, because they have made their sacred poles,[y] provoking the Lord to anger. [16]He will give Israel up because of the sins of Jeroboam, which he sinned and which he caused Israel to commit."

[17] Then Jeroboam's wife got up and went away, and she came to Tirzah. As she came to the threshold of the house, the child died. [18]All Israel buried him and mourned for him, according to the word of the Lord that he spoke by his servant the prophet Ahijah.

[19] Now the rest of the acts of Jeroboam, how he warred and how he reigned, are written in the Book of the Annals of the Kings of Israel. [20]The time that Jeroboam reigned was twenty-two years; then he slept with his ancestors, and his son Nadab succeeded him.

x 14.14 Meaning of Heb uncertain   y 14.15 Or *Asherahs*

14:1 *Abijah.* His illness leads to his eventual death (v. 17).

14:2 *Shiloh* is the central site of Israel's sanctuary (cf. 1 Sam. 1:24; 3:21; 4:3; 1 Kgs. 2:27). For *Ahijah*'s prophecy about Jeroboam's rule, see 11:29–35.

14:7 *Leader.* See note on 1:35.

14:15 *Beyond the Euphrates* is a reference to the destruction of northern kingdom in 722 BCE. The making of the *sacred poles* (Heb. "asherim") is a symbol of Israel's idolatry and provokes YHWH's anger (vv. 15–16). These *poles* are wooden cult objects that may represent YHWH's consort (cf. 1 Kgs. 14:23; 15:13; 2 Kgs. 18:4; 21:3; 23:14).

14:16 The king receives primary blame; he causes the people to sin.

14:19 *The Annals* is one of the sources the author used to construct this account (see **"Introduction to 1 Kings," pp. 460–61**).

Making Connections: Cult Prostitution (1 Kings 14)

In the twentieth century, some scholars thought that the word *qadesh* (translated as "illicit priests," 14:24; 15:12; "serve in an illicit shrine," Deut. 23:17 [Masoretic Text 23:18]), and its feminine counterpart *qedeshah* (translated as "prostitute," Gen. 38:21–22; "serve in an illicit shrine," Deut. 23:17) had something to do with cult prostitution. The translations were based on an assumption that fertility rituals of early ancient west Asian cultures involved "sympathetic magic" in which participants, sometimes imagined to be officiants, sometimes laypeople, participated in sex rituals and orgies to bring about rain and good harvests. Cult prostitution, it was suggested, involved laypeople paying officiants for some kind of sex ritual to bring about positive results. Translations for the masculine *qadesh* of 1 Kings range from "male cult prostitute" to "sodomite." Over time, scholars realized that this picture of ancient religion was built on scant evidence, uncritical readings of Greek and Roman sources like Herodotus and Strabo, and the overactive, Orientalizing imaginations of some biblical scholars.

There is no evidence from ancient west Asia that cult prostitution was practiced, nor are cognate terms such as *qadishtu* (Akkadian) and *qadishu* (Ugaritic) related to cult prostitution or anything sexual. Most often, the female Akkadian *qadishtu* is associated with wet nursing and childbirth, and the function of the Ugaritic male version is unknown. Because of the lack of evidence for "cult prostitution" in the cognate literature, scholars latched onto the biblical association between the words *qedeshah* and *zonah* in Gen. 38:15, 21–22 (and *zonah* does mean sex worker here) to argue that the *qedeshah* had something to do with sex work.

The root *zanah* refers to two very different expressions of women's sexual agency, though they are both related in that they take place outside of the realm of the patriarchal family. Perhaps the *qedeshah* is the same way; it refers to a woman who can act professionally outside of the family structure, but in different ways—by becoming either a cult functionary (Deut. 23:17) or sex worker (Gen. 38:21–22).

Categories in the HB can be blurry, and associations are often made that modern people might not make. Consequently, the most convincing explanation of the totality of the evidence is a social-class-based analysis. In this perspective, the *zonah* and *qedeshah* are closely associated in Gen. 38 not because of "cult prostitution" but because both words refer to types of (somewhat) independent women and their activities. Both *zonah* and *qedeshah* appear together (Hos. 4:14) because they operate outside of the expected norms for wives, mothers, and daughters in ancient west Asia.

Brian Rainey

21 Now Rehoboam son of Solomon reigned in Judah. Rehoboam was forty-one years old when he began to reign, and he reigned seventeen years in Jerusalem, the city that the Lord had chosen out of all the tribes of Israel, to put his name there. His mother's name was Naamah the Ammonite. [22]Judah did what was evil in the sight of the Lord; they provoked him to jealousy with their sins that they committed, more than all that their ancestors had done. [23]For they also built for themselves high places, pillars, and sacred poles[z] on every high hill and under every green tree; [24]there were also illicit priests in the land. They committed all the abominations of the nations that the Lord had driven out before the people of Israel.

25 In the fifth year of King Rehoboam, King Shishak of Egypt came up against Jerusalem; [26]he took away the treasures of the house of the Lord and the treasures of the king's house; he took everything. He also took away all the shields of gold that Solomon had made, [27]so King Rehoboam

z 14.23 Or *Asherahs*

14:21 For the significance of naming the mother, see note at 15:13. Also, her *Ammonite* origin reminds readers of Solomon's interethnic marriages (see 11:1–2).

14:23 On *sacred poles*, see note at 14:15.

14:24 *Illicit priests* (Heb. "qedeshim"). What these particular religious figures did is unknown, but it was probably not related to cult prostitution, as was previously thought. Similar terminology in Mesopotamian sources suggests that a female version of the figure ("qadishtu") may have performed rituals surrounding childbirth. See **"Cult Prostitution," p. 486**.

14:25 *Shishak*. Sheshonq I (945–924 BCE), Libyan founder of the Twenty-Second Dynasty. Sheshonq's relief at Karnak gives an account of his invasion of Israel and Judah.

made shields of bronze instead and committed them to the hands of the officers of the guard who kept the door of the king's house. ²⁸As often as the king went into the house of the LORD, the guard carried them and brought them back to the guardroom.

29 Now the rest of the acts of Rehoboam and all that he did, are they not written in the Book of the Annals of the Kings of Judah? ³⁰There was war between Rehoboam and Jeroboam continually. ³¹Rehoboam slept with his ancestors and was buried with his ancestors in the city of David. His mother's name was Naamah the Ammonite. His son Abijam succeeded him.

15 Now in the eighteenth year of King Jeroboam son of Nebat, Abijam began to reign over Judah. ²He reigned for three years in Jerusalem. His mother's name was Maacah daughter of Abishalom. ³He committed all the sins that his father did before him; his heart was not true to the LORD his God, like the heart of his father David. ⁴Nevertheless, for David's sake the LORD his God gave him a lamp in Jerusalem, setting up his son after him and establishing Jerusalem, ⁵because David did what was right in the sight of the LORD and did not turn aside from anything that he commanded him all the days of his life, except in the matter of Uriah the Hittite. ⁶The war begun between Rehoboam and Jeroboam continued all the days of his life. ⁷The rest of the acts of Abijam and all that he did, are they not written in the Book of the Annals of the Kings of Judah? There was war between Abijam and Jeroboam. ⁸Abijam slept with his ancestors, and they buried him in the city of David. Then his son Asa succeeded him.

9 In the twentieth year of King Jeroboam of Israel, Asa began to reign over Judah; ¹⁰he reigned forty-one years in Jerusalem. His mother's name was Maacah daughter of Abishalom. ¹¹Asa did what was right in the sight of the LORD, as his father David had done. ¹²He put away the illicit priests out of the land and removed all the idols that his ancestors had made. ¹³He also removed his mother Maacah from being queen mother, because she had made an abominable image for Asherah; Asa cut down her image and burned it at the Wadi Kidron. ¹⁴But the high places were not taken away. Nevertheless, the heart of Asa was true to the LORD all his days. ¹⁵He brought into the house of the LORD the votive gifts of his father and his own votive gifts—silver, gold, and utensils.

16 There was war between Asa and King Baasha of Israel all their days. ¹⁷King Baasha of Israel went up against Judah and built Ramah to prevent anyone from going out or coming in to King Asa of Judah. ¹⁸Then Asa took all the silver and the gold that were left in the treasures of the house of the LORD and the treasures of the king's house and gave them into the hands of his servants. King Asa sent them to King Ben-hadad son of Tabrimmon son of Hezion of Aram, who resided in Damascus, saying, ¹⁹"Let there be an alliance between me and

15:4 *A lamp.* Hebrew "nir," can also mean "field" (Prov. 13:23). YHWH promises a small parcel of land—the city of Jerusalem and environs—to David's descendants forever (1 Kgs. 11:36; 15:4; 2 Kgs. 8:19; 2 Chr. 21:7).

15:7 *Book of the Annals of the Kings of Judah.* Perhaps similar format as Mesopotamian royal chronicles. (See **"Introduction to 1 Kings," pp. 460–61**.)

15:12 *Illicit priests.* See note on 1 Kgs. 14:24.

15:13 *Queen mother.* Hebrew "gebirah," "great lady," "mistress." In modern hereditary monarchies, usually a royal title for the widowed mother of the reigning king, but not always. In the ancient Judahite monarchy, the "gebirah" seems to be an official position, since the queen mother can be removed. Some queen mothers—such as Bathsheba, Maacah, and Athaliah—are clearly influential in the royal court. The "gebirah" may have both political and religious functions, as appears to be the case with Maacah. *Asherah.* Here appears to be a direct reference to the goddess Asherah, the spouse of El in Canaanite mythology; but *asherah* can also refer to a wooden cult object that probably represents the goddess. *Wadi Kidron.* A place where Josiah destroys illicit cult objects (2 Kgs. 23:6–12).

15:14 *High places.* See note on 3:2–3.

15:16–22 Asa's alliance with Ben-hadad of Aram creates a problem for Israel on its northeastern flank, forcing Baasha to withdraw from Ramah, a southern Benjaminite city.

you, like that between my father and your father: I am sending you a present of silver and gold; go, break your alliance with King Baasha of Israel, so that he may withdraw from me." ²⁰Ben-hadad listened to King Asa and sent the commanders of his armies against the cities of Israel. He conquered Ijon, Dan, Abel-beth-maacah, and all Chinneroth, with all the land of Naphtali. ²¹When Baasha heard of it, he stopped building Ramah and lived in Tirzah. ²²Then King Asa made a proclamation to all Judah; none was exempt: they carried away the stones of Ramah and its timber with which Baasha had been building; with them King Asa built Geba of Benjamin and Mizpah. ²³Now the rest of all the acts of Asa, all his power, all that he did, and the cities that he built, are they not written in the Book of the Annals of the Kings of Judah? But in his old age he was diseased in his feet. ²⁴Then Asa slept with his ancestors and was buried with his ancestors in the city of his father David; his son Jehoshaphat succeeded him.

25 Nadab son of Jeroboam began to reign over Israel in the second year of King Asa of Judah; he reigned over Israel two years. ²⁶He did what was evil in the sight of the Lord, walking in the way of his ancestor and in the sin that he caused Israel to commit.

27 Baasha son of Ahijah, of the house of Issachar, conspired against him, and Baasha struck him down at Gibbethon, which belonged to the Philistines, for Nadab and all Israel were laying siege to Gibbethon. ²⁸So Baasha killed Nadab*ᵃ* in the third year of King Asa of Judah and succeeded him. ²⁹As soon as he was king, he killed all the house of Jeroboam; he left to the house of Jeroboam not one who breathed, until he had destroyed it, according to the word of the Lord that he spoke by his servant Ahijah

the Shilonite—³⁰because of the sins of Jeroboam that he committed and that he caused Israel to commit and because of the anger to which he provoked the Lord, the God of Israel.

31 Now the rest of the acts of Nadab and all that he did, are they not written in the Book of the Annals of the Kings of Israel? ³²There was war between Asa and King Baasha of Israel all their days.

33 In the third year of King Asa of Judah, Baasha son of Ahijah began to reign over all Israel at Tirzah; he reigned twenty-four years. ³⁴He did what was evil in the sight of the Lord, walking in the way of Jeroboam and in the sin that he caused Israel to commit.

16 The word of the Lord came to Jehu son of Hanani against Baasha, saying, ²"Since I exalted you out of the dust and made you leader over my people Israel, and you have walked in the way of Jeroboam and have caused my people Israel to sin, provoking me to anger with their sins, ³therefore I will consume Baasha and his house, and I will make your house like the house of Jeroboam son of Nebat. ⁴Anyone belonging to Baasha who dies in the city the dogs shall eat, and anyone of his who dies in the field the birds of the air shall eat."

5 Now the rest of the acts of Baasha, what he did, and his power, are they not written in the Book of the Annals of the Kings of Israel? ⁶Baasha slept with his ancestors and was buried at Tirzah, and his son Elah succeeded him. ⁷Moreover, the word of the Lord came by the prophet Jehu son of Hanani against Baasha and his house, both because of all the evil that he did in the sight of the Lord,

a 15.28 Heb *him*

15:23 *Diseased in his feet.* One of three unexplained misfortunes to befall Judahite kings given relatively positive reviews by the Deuteronomistic History (2 Kgs. 15:5; 23:29–30). See **"The Deuteronomistic History," p. 337**. Josiah's death at the hands of Pharaoh Neco II (610–595 BCE) is particularly jarring because he is the ideal Deuteronomistic king. The book of Chronicles, written later during the postexilic period, supplies explanations for these misfortunes (2 Chr. 16:7–12; 26:16–21; 35:21–25).

15:27 *Issachar.* May note a rivalry between the tribes of Issachar and Ephraim, from which Jeroboam and Nadab come.

15:29 See 1 Kgs. 14:10–14.

16:2 *leader.* See note on 1:35.

16:7–19 The instability of monarchy in the north is interpreted theologically. The Omride dynasty emerges victorious from these volatile power struggles (v. 23).

Focus On: Baal (1 Kings 16)

Baal is not a proper name but a generic title that means "lord," which makes identifying the "Baal" condemned by the Deuteronomistic History difficult (Judg. 2:13; 6:25–30; 1 Kgs. 16:31–32; 18; 19:18; 22:53; 2 Kgs. 3:2; 10:18–28; 11:18; 17:16; 21:3–5). In the mythological texts from the ancient city of Ugarit, *Baal* is the most common appellation for the rain, fertility, and storm god, whose proper name is Hadad. The "Baal" of the HB could well be an Israelite version of Hadad, a well-regarded deity in the region. Furthermore, some of the references to "Baal" in the HB make fertility and rain a central topic (1 Kgs. 17–18).

Reading between the lines of the Deuteronomistic History, and looking at archaeological finds from ancient Israel and Judah, it seems the default for Israelite and Judahite religion was "polytheism." Attempts to institute exclusive worship of YHWH, especially concentrated in Jerusalem, were more flashes in the pan than foundational for Israelite religion—at least until the exile. Israelites probably worshiped YHWH as the predominant member of Israel's pantheon along with other deities under YHWH's authority, such as the "host of heaven," which may have included Baal, Asherah, and Astarte. In Ugaritic mythology, Hadad is subordinate to the ultimate king of the pantheon and creator, El, with whom YHWH may have been identified (Gen. 14:22; see **"God's Name," p. 89**).

Some, however, suspect that the "Baal" of the HB might represent a form of YHWH himself, or a popular YHWH cult that Deuteronomists hated. "Baal," or "the Baals" (Judg. 2:11; 3:7; 8:33; 10:6–10; 1 Sam. 7:4; 12:10; 1 Kgs. 18:18), could also possibly refer to YHWH worship centered on local shrines and high places, not the Jerusalem temple. A hypothetical "Baal YHWH" cult might have been targeted because it employed iconography, worship practices, and mythological assumptions Deuteronomists did not like (1 Kgs. 12:28; 18:26–29). Competition could be another reason. Similar to today, religion was not simply a collection of abstract ideas and beliefs; real resources and wealth are deeply involved. Offerings are not just gifts to a deity, but a form of payment to which officiants are entitled. Ancient temples were involved in finance and trade, used and traded in enslaved labor, and served as treasuries. From a practical point of view, centralizing the cult of YHWH in Jerusalem means concentrating and funneling resources and money to one establishment in one locale, something to which officiants and political leaders disadvantaged by this model might object (see note on 12:25–30; **"Cult Centralization," p. 264**).

Whether *Baal* in the HB represents Hadad, YHWH, or either depending on context, it would not be surprising if most Israelites and Judahites had more of a connection with worship traditions surrounding their local shrines than with a royal temple complex in the capital. Monarchs would have a political interest in recognizing this popular cult by building official royal shrines for it (1 Kgs. 16:32; 2 Kgs. 3:2; 11:18; 21:3).

Brian Rainey

provoking him to anger with the work of his hands, in being like the house of Jeroboam, and also because he destroyed it.

8 In the twenty-sixth year of King Asa of Judah, Elah son of Baasha began to reign over Israel in Tirzah; he reigned two years. ⁹But his servant Zimri, commander of half his chariots, conspired against him. When he was at Tirzah drinking himself drunk in the house of Arza, who was in charge of the palace at Tirzah, ¹⁰Zimri came in and struck him down and killed him, in the twenty-seventh year of King Asa of Judah, and succeeded him.

11 When he began to reign, as soon as he had seated himself on his throne, he killed all the house of Baasha; he did not leave him a single male of his kindred or his friends. ¹²Thus Zimri destroyed all the house of Baasha, according to the word of the Lord, which he had spoken against Baasha by the prophet Jehu, ¹³because of all the sins of Baasha and the sins of his son Elah that they committed and that they caused Israel to commit, provoking the Lord God of Israel to anger with their idols. ¹⁴Now the rest of the acts of Elah and all that he did, are they not written in the Book of the Annals of the Kings of Israel?

15 In the twenty-seventh year of King Asa of Judah, Zimri reigned seven days in Tirzah. Now the troops were encamped against Gibbethon, which belonged to the Philistines, ¹⁶and the troops who were encamped heard it said, "Zimri has conspired, and he has killed the king"; therefore all Israel made Omri, the commander of the army, king over Israel that day in the camp. ¹⁷So Omri went up from Gibbethon and all Israel with him, and they besieged Tirzah. ¹⁸When Zimri saw that the city was taken, he went into the citadel of the king's house;

he burned down the king's house over himself with fire and died—[19]because of the sins that he committed, doing evil in the sight of the LORD, walking in the way of Jeroboam, and for the sin that he committed, causing Israel to sin. [20]Now the rest of the acts of Zimri and the conspiracy that he made, are they not written in the Book of the Annals of the Kings of Israel?

21 Then the people of Israel were divided into two parts: half of the people followed Tibni son of Ginath to make him king, and half followed Omri. [22]But the people who followed Omri overcame the people who followed Tibni son of Ginath, so Tibni died, and Omri became king. [23]In the thirty-first year of King Asa of Judah, Omri began to reign over Israel; he reigned for twelve years, six of them in Tirzah.

24 He bought the hill of Samaria from Shemer for two talents of silver; he fortified the hill and called the city that he built Samaria, after the name of Shemer, the owner of the hill.

25 Omri did what was evil in the sight of the LORD; he did more evil than all who were before him. [26]For he walked in all the way of Jeroboam son of Nebat and in the sins that he caused Israel to commit, provoking the LORD, the God of Israel, to anger by their idols. [27]Now the rest of the acts of Omri that he did and the power that he showed, are

they not written in the Book of the Annals of the Kings of Israel? [28]Omri slept with his ancestors and was buried in Samaria; his son Ahab succeeded him.

29 In the thirty-eighth year of King Asa of Judah, Ahab son of Omri began to reign over Israel; Ahab son of Omri reigned over Israel in Samaria twenty-two years. [30]Ahab son of Omri did evil in the sight of the LORD more than all who were before him.

31 And as if it had been a light thing for him to walk in the sins of Jeroboam son of Nebat, he took as his wife Jezebel daughter of King Ethbaal of the Sidonians and went and served Baal and worshiped him. [32]He erected an altar for Baal in the house of Baal that he built in Samaria. [33]Ahab also made a sacred pole.[b] Ahab did more to provoke the anger of the LORD, the God of Israel, than had all the kings of Israel who were before him. [34]In his days Hiel of Bethel built Jericho; he laid its foundation at the cost of Abiram his firstborn and set up its gates at the cost of his youngest son Segub, according to the word of the LORD that he spoke by Joshua son of Nun.

17 Now Elijah the Tishbite, of Tishbe[c] in Gilead, said to Ahab, "As the LORD the God of Israel lives, before whom I stand, there shall be neither dew nor rain these

b 16.33 Or *Asherah*   *c* 17.1 Gk: Heb *of the settlers*

16:23–28 The beginning of the Omride dynasty—which, according to archaeological and extra-biblical textual evidence, presided over a period of great wealth for the north (1 Kgs. 22:39).

16:31 *Jezebel* (Heb. "Izebel"). Proposals for the meaning of the queen's name include a distortion of the Phoenician name "'iy ba'lu" ("where is Baal?") or a form of "'iy zabul(u)" ("where is the exalted one?"). *Baal* and "zabul" are both epithets for the storm god Hadad in Ugaritic mythology. After the death of Hadad in the Baal Cycle, the land dries up and vegetation ceases to grow, prompting the gods to ask, "Where is Mightiest Baal? Where is the Exalted One ['iy zabul(u)], Lord of the Earth?" The mythic themes Jezebel's name references are deeply relevant to the stories in 1 Kgs. 17–19. See **"Baal," p. 489.** *King Ethbaal of the Sidonians.* Perhaps from Phoenician, "'t b'l," "with Baal." Ethbaal (r. 887–855 BCE) probably ruled from Tyre. King Hiram of Tyre refers to his subjects as Sidonian (1 Kgs. 5:6), suggesting that "Sidonian" refers to Phoenician peoples generally (Josh. 13:6) or that Tyre and Sidon were at times interchangeable. This may have been a convention outside of ancient Israel as well. In extrabiblical sources Hiram II (r. 739–730 BCE) is referred to as "Hiram of Tyre" in the annals of Assyrian king Tiglath-pileser III but "king of the Sidonians" in a Cypriot inscription (P. J. Boyles, *BASOR* 365 [2012], 38–39).

16:34 See Josh. 6:26.

17:1 The introduction of Elijah marks the beginning of a series of prophetic stories that will run through 2 Kgs. 9; 1 Kgs. 17–19 focus on Elijah. On Ahab's rise to power, see 16:29–33. Elijah's popularity in Israel's traditions extends beyond the Kings narrative (cf. Mal. 4:5–6; Sir. 48:1–6; Matt. 17:3–4). Contemporary Judaism makes space for the presence of Elijah at the annual Passover Seder.

17:1–7 The story asserts YHWH's power over nature, particularly rain, which is the provenance of the storm god Baal. It prepares readers for the confrontation in 1 Kgs. 18.

years, except by my word." [2]The word of the LORD came to him, saying, [3]"Go from here and turn eastward, and hide yourself by the Wadi Cherith, which is east of the Jordan. [4]You shall drink from the wadi, and I have commanded the ravens to feed you there." [5]So he went and did according to the word of the LORD; he went and lived by the Wadi Cherith, which is east of the Jordan. [6]The ravens brought him bread and meat in the morning and bread and meat in the evening, and he drank from the wadi. [7]But after a while the wadi dried up because there was no rain in the land.

8 Then the word of the LORD came to him, saying, [9]"Go now to Zarephath, which belongs to Sidon, and live there, for I have commanded a widow there to feed you." [10]So he set out and went to Zarephath. When he came to the gate of the town, a widow was there gathering sticks; he called to her and said, "Bring me a little water in a vessel, so that I may drink." [11]As she was going to bring it, he called to her and said, "Bring me a morsel of bread in your hand." [12]But she said, "As the LORD your God lives, I have nothing baked, only a handful of meal in a jar and a little oil in a jug; I am now gathering a couple of sticks so that I may go home and prepare it for myself and my son, that we may eat it and die." [13]Elijah said to her, "Do not be afraid; go and do as you have said, but first make me a little cake of it and bring it to me, and afterward make something for yourself and your son. [14]For thus says the LORD the God of Israel: The jar of meal will not be emptied and the jug of oil will not fail until the day that the LORD sends rain on the earth." [15]She went and did as Elijah said, so that she as well as he and her household ate for many days. [16]The jar of meal was not emptied, neither did the jug of oil fail, according to the word of the LORD that he spoke by Elijah.

17 After this the son of the woman, the mistress of the house, became ill; his illness was so severe that there was no breath left in him. [18]She then said to Elijah, "What have you against me, O man of God? You have come to me to bring my sin to remembrance and to cause the death of my son!" [19]But he said to her, "Give me your son." He took him from her bosom, carried him up into the upper chamber where he was lodging, and laid him on his own bed. [20]He cried out to the LORD, "O LORD my God, have you brought calamity even upon the widow with whom I am staying, by killing her son?" [21]Then he stretched himself upon the child three times and cried out to the LORD, "O LORD my God, let this child's life come into him again." [22]The LORD listened to the voice of Elijah; the life of the child came into him again, and he revived. [23]Elijah took the child, brought him down from the upper chamber into the house, and gave him to his mother; then Elijah said, "See, your son is alive." [24]So the woman said to Elijah, "Now I know that you are a man of God and that the word of the LORD in your mouth is truth."

18 After many days the word of the LORD came to Elijah, in the third year of the drought,[d] saying, "Go, present yourself to Ahab; I will send rain on the earth." [2]So Elijah went to present himself to Ahab. The famine was severe in Samaria. [3]Ahab summoned Obadiah, who was in charge of the palace. (Now Obadiah revered the LORD greatly; [4]when Jezebel was killing off the prophets of the LORD, Obadiah took a hundred prophets, hid them fifty to a cave, and provided them with bread and water.) [5]Then Ahab said to Obadiah, "Go through the land to all the springs of water and to all the wadis; perhaps we may find grass to keep the horses and mules alive and not lose some of the animals." [6]So they divided the land between them to pass through it; Ahab went in one direction by himself, and Obadiah went in another direction by himself.

7 As Obadiah was on the way, Elijah met him; Obadiah recognized him, fell on his face, and said, "Is it you, my lord Elijah?"

---

d 18.1 Heb lacks *of the drought*

17:8–24 In addition to demonstrating YHWH is superior to Baal even in Sidon itself, the stories may also contrast a positive example of a Sidonian woman who recognizes YHWH's power through Elijah, with the Sidonian influence on Ahab. Compare 2 Kgs. 4, a story about Elisha (Elijah's successor) and another widow.

18:1–2 Underscores Baal's failure to provide rain.

18:3 Probably different from the prophet of the book of Obadiah.

⁸He answered him, "It is I. Go, tell your lord that Elijah is here." ⁹And he said, "How have I sinned, that you would hand your servant over to Ahab to kill me? ¹⁰As the LORD your God lives, there is no nation or kingdom to which my lord has not sent to seek you, and when they would say, 'He is not here,' he would require an oath of the kingdom or nation that they had not found you. ¹¹But now you say, 'Go, tell your lord that Elijah is here.' ¹²As soon as I have gone from you, the spirit of the LORD will carry you I know not where; so, when I come and tell Ahab and he cannot find you, he will kill me, although I your servant have revered the LORD from my youth. ¹³Has it not been told my lord what I did when Jezebel killed the prophets of the LORD, how I hid a hundred of the LORD's prophets fifty to a cave and provided them with bread and water? ¹⁴Yet now you say, 'Go, tell your lord that Elijah is here'; he will surely kill me." ¹⁵Elijah said, "As the LORD of hosts lives, before whom I stand, I will surely show myself to him today." ¹⁶So Obadiah went to meet Ahab and told him, and Ahab went to meet Elijah.

17 When Ahab saw Elijah, Ahab said to him, "Is it you, you troubler of Israel?" ¹⁸He answered, "I have not troubled Israel, but you have, and your father's house, because you have forsaken the commandments of the LORD and followed the Baals. ¹⁹Now therefore have all Israel assemble for me at Mount Carmel, with the four hundred fifty prophets of Baal and the four hundred prophets of Asherah who eat at Jezebel's table."

20 So Ahab sent to all the Israelites and assembled the prophets at Mount Carmel. ²¹Elijah then came near to all the people and said, "How long will you go limping with two different opinions? If the LORD is God, follow him, but if Baal, then follow him." The people did not answer him a word. ²²Then Elijah said to the people, "I, even I only, am left a prophet of the LORD, but Baal's prophets number four hundred fifty. ²³Let two bulls be given to us; let them choose one bull for themselves, cut it in pieces, and lay it on the wood but put no fire to it; I will prepare the other bull and lay it on the wood but put no fire to it. ²⁴Then you call on the name of your god, and I will call on the name of the LORD; the god who answers by fire is indeed God." All the people answered, "Well spoken!" ²⁵Then Elijah said to the prophets of Baal, "Choose for yourselves one bull and prepare it first, for you are many; then call on the name of your god, but put no fire to it." ²⁶So they took the bull that was given them, prepared it, and called on the name of Baal from morning until noon, crying, "O Baal, answer us!" But there was no voice and no answer. They limped about the altar that they had made. ²⁷At noon Elijah mocked them, saying, "Cry aloud! Surely he is a god; either he is meditating, or he has wandered away, or he is on a journey, or perhaps he is asleep and must be awakened." ²⁸Then they cried aloud, and, as was their custom, they cut themselves with swords and lances until the blood gushed out over them. ²⁹As midday passed, they raved on until the time of the offering of the oblation, but there was no voice, no answer, and no response.

30 Then Elijah said to all the people, "Come closer to me," and all the people came closer to him. First he repaired the

---

18:8–16 Suggests that Obadiah was expected to apprehend Elijah or act in a way that leads to his capture or death.

18:19 *Mount Carmel.* Hebrew "hakarmel," "the Carmel." A mountain range in northern Israel, where the modern city of Haifa rests. The name *Carmel* ("orchard") probably reflects the greenery that fills the range to this day.

18:27 *A god* (Heb. "Elohim"). Elijah may be poking fun at foreign myths. In the Babylonian myths of Atrahasis and Enuma Elish, gods complain about disrupted sleep. In petitions for deliverance, YHWH himself is sometimes asked to "awake" (Pss. 7:6; 35:23; 59:4–5; Isa. 51:9). In the Marduk Prophecy, the presence of the Babylonian god Marduk leaves his cult statue and goes on a journey. More relevant to 1 Kgs. 18, the Baal Cycle describes Baal going on a journey to different cities.

18:28 Cutting is part of petitionary mourning rituals (Hos. 7:14). The Baal Cycle describes the gods cutting themselves to mourn the dead Baal (see **"Baal," p. 489**). Deut. 14:1 forbids cutting oneself to mourn the dead.

18:29 *Offering of the oblation.* Hebrew "minha" refers to a late afternoon sacrifice used to designate time in some narratives (e.g., 2 Kgs. 3:20; 16:13, 15).

altar of the LORD that had been thrown down; ³¹Elijah took twelve stones, according to the number of the tribes of the sons of Jacob, to whom the word of the LORD came, saying, "Israel shall be your name"; ³²with the stones he built an altar in the name of the LORD. Then he made a trench around the altar, large enough to contain two measures of seed. ³³Next he put the wood in order, cut the bull in pieces, and laid it on the wood. He said, "Fill four jars with water and pour it on the burnt offering and on the wood." ³⁴Then he said, "Do it a second time," and they did it a second time. Again he said, "Do it a third time," and they did it a third time, ³⁵so that the water ran all around the altar and filled the trench also with water.

36 At the time of the offering of the oblation, the prophet Elijah came near and said, "O LORD, God of Abraham, Isaac, and Israel, let it be known this day that you are God in Israel, that I am your servant, and that I have done all these things at your bidding. ³⁷Answer me, O LORD, answer me, so that this people may know that you, O LORD, are God and that you have turned their hearts back." ³⁸Then the fire of the LORD fell and consumed the burnt offering, the wood, the stones, and the dust and even licked up the water that was in the trench. ³⁹When all the people saw it, they fell on their faces and said, "The LORD indeed is God; the LORD indeed is God." ⁴⁰Elijah said to them, "Seize the prophets of Baal; do not let one of them escape." Then they seized them, and Elijah brought them down to the Wadi Kishon and killed them there.

41 Elijah said to Ahab, "Go up, eat and drink, for there is a sound of rushing rain." ⁴²So Ahab went up to eat and to drink. Elijah went up to the top of Carmel; there he bowed himself down upon the earth and put his face between his knees. ⁴³He said to his servant, "Go up now, look toward the sea." He went up and looked and said, "There is nothing." Then he said, "Go again seven times." ⁴⁴At the seventh time he said, "Look, a little cloud no bigger than a person's hand

is rising out of the sea." Then he said, "Go say to Ahab, 'Harness your chariot and go down before the rain stops you.' " ⁴⁵In a little while the heavens grew black with clouds and wind; there was a heavy rain. Ahab rode off and went to Jezreel. ⁴⁶But the hand of the LORD was on Elijah; he girded up his loins and ran in front of Ahab to the entrance of Jezreel.

19 Ahab told Jezebel all that Elijah had done and how he had killed all the prophets with the sword. ²Then Jezebel sent a messenger to Elijah, saying, "So may the gods do to me and more also, if I do not make your life like the life of one of them by this time tomorrow." ³Then he was afraid;^e he got up and fled for his life and came to Beer-sheba, which belongs to Judah; he left his servant there.

4 But he himself went a day's journey into the wilderness and came and sat down under a solitary broom tree. He asked that he might die, "It is enough; now, O LORD, take away my life, for I am no better than my ancestors." ⁵Then he lay down under the broom tree and fell asleep. Suddenly an angel touched him and said to him, "Get up and eat." ⁶He looked, and there at his head was a cake baked on hot stones and a jar of water. He ate and drank and lay down again. ⁷The angel of the LORD came a second time, touched him, and said, "Get up and eat, or the journey will be too much for you." ⁸He got up and ate and drank; then he went in the strength of that food forty days and forty nights to Horeb the mount of God. ⁹At that place he came to a cave and spent the night there.

Then the word of the LORD came to him, saying, "What are you doing here, Elijah?" ¹⁰He answered, "I have been very zealous for the LORD, the God of hosts, for the Israelites have forsaken your covenant, thrown down your altars, and killed your prophets

e 19.3 Gk: Heb *he saw*

19:1 There are *prophets* who work in various quarters (cf. 18:19). These oppose Elijah and function as prophets on behalf of the kingdom. On *Jezebel*, see note at 16:31. See **"Prophecy," p. 484**.

19:3 Elijah is forced to flee far south, to Beer-sheba, which belongs to Judah. The NRSVue follows the Greek text (*he was afraid*) rather than the Hebrew text ("he saw") here.

19:4–10 Similar to Jonah 4:5–10. *Horeb* recalls the place in which YHWH made a covenant with Israel (1 Kgs. 8:9), which leads to Elijah's charge about the covenant (v. 10). The *God of hosts* seems to refer to the deity's militaristic side, as one preparing for battle.

with the sword. I alone am left, and they are seeking my life, to take it away."

11 He said, "Go out and stand on the mountain before the LORD, for the LORD is about to pass by." Now there was a great wind, so strong that it was splitting mountains and breaking rocks in pieces before the LORD, but the LORD was not in the wind, and after the wind an earthquake, but the LORD was not in the earthquake, ¹²and after the earthquake a fire, but the LORD was not in the fire, and after the fire a sound of sheer silence. ¹³When Elijah heard it, he wrapped his face in his mantle and went out and stood at the entrance of the cave. Then there came a voice to him that said, "What are you doing here, Elijah?" ¹⁴He answered, "I have been very zealous for the LORD, the God of hosts, for the Israelites have forsaken your covenant, thrown down your altars, and killed your prophets with the sword. I alone am left, and they are seeking my life, to take it away." ¹⁵Then the LORD said to him, "Go, return on your way to the wilderness of Damascus; when you arrive, you shall anoint Hazael as king over Aram. ¹⁶Also you shall anoint Jehu son of Nimshi as king over Israel, and you shall anoint Elisha son of Shaphat of Abel-meholah as prophet in your place. ¹⁷Whoever escapes from the sword of Hazael, Jehu shall kill, and whoever escapes from the sword of Jehu, Elisha shall kill. ¹⁸Yet I will leave seven thousand in Israel, all the knees that have not bowed to Baal, and every mouth that has not kissed him."

19 So he set out from there and found Elisha son of Shaphat, who was plowing. There were twelve yoke of oxen ahead of him, and he was with the twelfth. Elijah passed by him and threw his mantle over him. ²⁰He left the oxen, ran after Elijah, and said, "Let me kiss my father and my mother, and then I will follow you." Then Elijah*f* said to him, "Go back again, for what have I done to you?" ²¹He returned from following him, took the yoke of oxen, and slaughtered them; using the equipment from the oxen, he boiled their flesh and gave it to the people, and they ate. Then he set out and followed Elijah and became his servant.

20 King Ben-hadad of Aram gathered all his army together; thirty-two kings were with him, along with horses and chariots. He marched against Samaria, laid siege to it, and attacked it. ²Then he sent messengers into the city to King Ahab of Israel and said to him, "Thus says Ben-hadad: ³Your silver and gold are mine; your fairest wives and children also are mine." ⁴The king of Israel answered, "As you say, my lord, O king, I am yours, and all that I have." ⁵The messengers came again and said, "Thus says Ben-hadad: I sent to you, saying, 'Deliver to me your silver and gold, your wives and children'; ⁶now I will send my servants to you tomorrow about this time, and they shall search your house and the houses of your servants and lay hands on whatever pleases them*g* and take it away."

7 Then the king of Israel called all the elders of the land and said, "Look now! See how this man is seeking trouble, for he sent to me for my wives, my children, my silver, and my gold, and I did not refuse him." ⁸Then all the elders and all the people said to him, "Do not listen or consent." ⁹So he said to the messengers of Ben-hadad, "Tell my lord the king: All that you first demanded of your servant I will do, but this thing I cannot do." The messengers left and brought him word again. ¹⁰Ben-hadad sent to him and said, "The gods do so to me and more also, if the dust of Samaria will provide a handful for each of the people who follow me."

f 19.20 Heb *he* *g* 20.6 Gk Syr Vg: Heb *you*

19:11–16 YHWH makes an appearance—*to pass by*—before the prophet, recalling other rare divine manifestations elsewhere (cf. Exod. 3). Following the *sheer silence* (v. 12), YHWH gives Elijah instructions to *anoint* the next round of leadership: kings of the northern and southern kingdoms as well as his successor-prophet. 19:13 Elijah bequeaths this mantle to his successor, Elisha (2 Kgs. 2:8, 13–14).
19:18 *Kissed him* (i.e., Baal) is the only reference to this practice in the book and may be the narrator's rhetorical flourish. The LXX replaces the language of kissing with "worshiping."
20:1 *Ben-hadad* had formed an alliance with King Asa (of Judah) earlier. See 1 Kgs. 15.
20:3 It was common practice to take *wives and children* as war captives, perhaps to use as forced labor (cf. Deut. 20:14).
20:7 For the complicated role the *elders of the land* play as advisers to kings, see 8:1–3; 12:6–8.

[11]The king of Israel answered, "Enough![b] One who puts on armor should not brag like one who takes it off." [12]When Ben-hadad heard this message—now he had been drinking with the kings in the booths—he said to his men, "Take your positions!" And they took their positions against the city.

13 Then a certain prophet came up to King Ahab of Israel and said, "Thus says the LORD: Have you seen all this great multitude? Look, I will give it into your hand today, and you shall know that I am the LORD." [14]Ahab said, "By whom?" He said, "Thus says the LORD: By the young men who serve the district governors." Then he said, "Who shall begin the battle?" He answered, "You." [15]Then he mustered the young men who served the district governors, two hundred thirty-two; after them he mustered all the people of Israel, seven thousand.

16 They went out at noon, while Ben-hadad was drinking himself drunk in the booths, he and the thirty-two kings allied with him. [17]The young men who served the district governors went out first. Ben-hadad had sent out scouts,[i] and they reported to him, "Men have come out from Samaria." [18]He said, "If they have come out for peace, take them alive; if they have come out for war, take them alive."

19 But these had already come out of the city: the young men who served the district governors and the army that followed them. [20]Each killed his man; the Arameans fled, and Israel pursued them, but King Ben-hadad of Aram escaped on a horse with the cavalry. [21]The king of Israel went out, attacked the horses and chariots, and inflicted a massive defeat on the Arameans.

22 Then the prophet approached the king of Israel and said to him, "Come, strengthen yourself, and consider well what you have to do, for in the spring the king of Aram will come up against you."

23 The servants of the king of Aram said to him, "Their gods are gods of the hills, so they were stronger than we, but let us fight against them in the plain, and surely we shall be stronger than they. [24]Also do this: remove the kings, each from his post, and put commanders in place of them; [25]and muster an army like the army that you have lost, horse for horse, and chariot for chariot; then we will fight against them in the plain, and surely we shall be stronger than they." He heeded their voice and did so.

26 In the spring Ben-hadad mustered the Arameans and went up to Aphek to fight against Israel. [27]After the Israelites had been mustered and provisioned, they went out to engage them; the people of Israel encamped opposite them like two little flocks of goats, while the Arameans filled the country. [28]A man of God approached and said to the king of Israel, "Thus says the LORD: Because the Arameans have said, 'The LORD is a god of the hills, but he is not a god of the valleys,' therefore I will give all this great multitude into your hand, and you shall know that I am the LORD." [29]They encamped opposite one another seven days. Then on the seventh day the battle began; the Israelites killed one hundred thousand Aramean foot soldiers in one day. [30]The rest fled into the city of Aphek, and the wall fell on twenty-seven thousand men who were left.

Ben-hadad also fled and entered the city to hide. [31]His servants said to him, "Look, we have heard that the kings of the house of Israel are merciful kings; let us put sackcloth around our waists and ropes on our heads, and go out to the king of Israel; perhaps he will spare your life." [32]So they tied sackcloth around their waists, put ropes on their heads, went to the king of Israel, and said, "Your servant Ben-hadad says, 'Please let me

b 20.11 Gk: Heb *Tell him*   i 20.17 Heb lacks *scouts*

20:11 The NRSVue follows the Greek text (*Enough*) instead of the Hebrew ("Tell him"); scholars debate whether an older Hebrew manuscript lay behind the Greek version of the story.

20:13 The story of another unnamed prophet (cf. 13:11–32) is a narrative device Kings utilizes to move the account forward. It also may indicate a close relationship between prophets and the Deuteronomistic History (see **"Introduction to 1 Kings," pp. 460–61**).

20:21–22 The Kings narrative offers a complicated portrayal of Ahab—one in which the king occasionally obeys YHWH's prophets and receives the deity's support for military victory. But his actions will be called into question again (see vv. 35–43).

20:26 The town of *Aphek* is approximately twenty miles from Samaria.

20:32 *Brother*. By using the treaty language of brotherhood, Ahab signals that he would like to negotiate a pact in which Ben-hadad is an equal, not a vassal. See note at 5:1.

live.'" And he said, "Is he still alive? He is my brother." [33]Now the men were watching for an omen; they quickly took it up from him and said, "Yes, Ben-hadad is your brother." Then he said, "Go and bring him." So Ben-hadad came out to him, and he had him come up into the chariot. [34]Ben-hadad[j] said to him, "I will restore the towns that my father took from your father, and you may establish bazaars for yourself in Damascus, as my father did in Samaria." The king of Israel responded,[k] "I will let you go on those terms." So he made a treaty with him and let him go.

35 At the command of the Lord a certain member of a company of prophets[l] said to another, "Strike me!" But the man refused to strike him. [36]Then he said to him, "Because you have not obeyed the voice of the Lord, as soon as you have left me, a lion will kill you." And when he had left him, a lion met him and killed him. [37]Then he found another man and said, "Strike me!" So the man hit him, striking and wounding him. [38]Then the prophet departed and waited for the king along the road, disguising himself with a bandage over his eyes. [39]As the king passed by, he cried to the king and said, "Your servant went out into the thick of the battle; then a soldier turned and brought a man to me and said, 'Guard this man; if he is missing, your life shall be given for his life, or else you shall pay a talent of silver.' [40]While your servant was busy here and there, he was gone."

The king of Israel said to him, "So shall your judgment be; you yourself have decided it." [41]Then he quickly took the bandage away from his eyes. The king of Israel recognized him as one of the prophets. [42]Then he said to him, "Thus says the Lord: Because you have let the man go whom I had devoted to destruction, therefore your life shall be for his life and your people for his people." [43]The king of Israel set out toward home, resentful and sullen, and came to Samaria.

21 Later the following events took place: Naboth the Jezreelite had a vineyard in Jezreel beside the palace of King Ahab of Samaria. [2]And Ahab said to Naboth, "Give me your vineyard, so that I may have it for a vegetable garden, because it is near my house; I will give you a better vineyard for it, or, if it seems good to you, I will give you its value in money." [3]But Naboth said to Ahab, "The Lord forbid that I should give you my ancestral inheritance." [4]Ahab went home resentful and sullen because of what Naboth the Jezreelite had said to him, for he had said, "I will not give you my ancestral inheritance." He lay down on his bed, turned away his face, and would not eat.

5 His wife Jezebel came to him and said, "Why are you so depressed that you will

j 20.34 Heb *He*   k 20.34 Heb lacks *The king of Israel responded*   l 20.35 Heb *of the sons of the prophets*

20:35 A *company of prophets* attests to the communal nature of this function in ancient Israel (cf. 1 Sam. 10:10; 19:20; 2 Kgs. 2:3; 4:38). See **"Prophecy," p. 484**.

20:42 *Devoted to destruction* (Heb. "herem"). A number of things can be devoted to destruction, such as illegitimate cult objects or people who worship illegitimate deities (Exod. 22:20; Deut. 7:26). In warfare, "herem" is usually a ritualized massacre that involves the destruction of an enemy's entire population (men, women, and children) and animals in a particular territory. The stated purpose for the mass killing and destruction is to dedicate the enemy's plunder to a god (Deut. 2:34; 3:6; 7:2; 13:15–17; Josh. 6–7; 10–11; 1 Sam. 15). There appear to be different kinds of "herem" because in some instances, not all inhabitants of the enemy's territory are killed (Judg. 21:11). Israel was not the only society to promote "herem." In the mid-ninth century, Mesha, king of Moab, bragged about committing "herem" against Israel in his famous stele. Those who do not completely destroy something devoted to destruction face YHWH's punishment (Josh. 7; 1 Sam. 15:25–27). Here, Ben-hadad, an individual, is supposed to be dedicated to destruction, but Ahab allows him to live.

21:3–4 *Ancestral inheritance* (Heb. "nahalat abot"). An Israelite's ancestral estate ("nahalah") is supposed to be kept within tribes (Lev. 25:8–31; Num. 27:1–11; 36:1–12; Deut. 25:5–10; Josh. 17:3–6; Jer. 32:6–12). Ahab's offer, even if generous, demands that Naboth violate a central Israelite principle of land ownership. When the people first demand a king, Samuel warns that royal expropriation of people's land will be an abuse that comes with kingship (1 Sam. 8:14–15). **21:4** *Resentful and sullen* repeats the description of Ahab in 20:43.

21:5 *Jezebel* has been absent from the narrative since 19:2, when she promised to murder Elijah. Elijah, however, has managed to stay alive (see v. 17).

not eat?" ⁶He said to her, "Because I spoke to Naboth the Jezreelite and said to him, 'Give me your vineyard for money, or if you prefer, I will give you another vineyard for it,' but he answered, 'I will not give you my vineyard.' " ⁷His wife Jezebel said to him, "Do you now govern Israel? Get up, eat some food, and be cheerful; I will give you the vineyard of Naboth the Jezreelite."

8 So she wrote letters in Ahab's name and sealed them with his seal; she sent the letters to the elders and the nobles who lived with Naboth in his city. ⁹She wrote in the letters, "Proclaim a fast, and seat Naboth at the head of the assembly; ¹⁰seat two scoundrels opposite him, and have them bring a charge against him, saying, 'You have cursed God and the king.' Then take him out and stone him to death." ¹¹The men of his city, the elders and the nobles who lived in his city, did as Jezebel had sent word to them. Just as it was written in the letters that she had sent to them, ¹²they proclaimed a fast and seated Naboth at the head of the assembly. ¹³The two scoundrels came in and sat opposite him, and the scoundrels brought a charge against Naboth in the presence of the people, saying, "Naboth cursed God and the king." So they took him outside the city and stoned him to death. ¹⁴Then they sent to Jezebel, saying, "Naboth has been stoned; he is dead."

15 As soon as Jezebel heard that Naboth had been stoned and was dead, Jezebel said to Ahab, "Go, take possession of the vineyard of Naboth the Jezreelite, which he refused to give you for money, for Naboth is not alive but dead." ¹⁶As soon as Ahab heard that Naboth was dead, Ahab set out to go down to the vineyard of Naboth the Jezreelite, to take possession of it.

17 Then the word of the LORD came to Elijah the Tishbite, saying, ¹⁸"Go down to meet King Ahab of Israel, who rules*m* in Samaria; he is now in the vineyard of Naboth, where he has gone to take possession. ¹⁹You shall say to him: Thus says the LORD: Have you killed and also taken possession? You shall say to him: Thus says the LORD: In the place where dogs licked up the blood of Naboth, dogs will also lick up your blood."

20 Ahab said to Elijah, "Have you found me, O my enemy?" He answered, "I have found you. Because you have sold yourself to do what is evil in the sight of the LORD, ²¹I will bring disaster on you; I will consume you and will cut off from Ahab every male, bond or free, in Israel, ²²and I will make your house like the house of Jeroboam son of Nebat and like the house of Baasha son of Ahijah, because you have provoked me to anger and have caused Israel to sin. ²³Also concerning Jezebel the LORD said: The dogs shall eat Jezebel within the bounds of Jezreel. ²⁴Anyone belonging to Ahab who dies in the city the dogs shall eat, and anyone of his who dies in the open country the birds of the air shall eat."

25 (Indeed, there was no one like Ahab, who sold himself to do what was evil in the sight of the LORD, urged on by his wife Jezebel. ²⁶He acted most abominably in going after idols, as the Amorites had done, whom the LORD had driven out before the Israelites.)

27 When Ahab heard those words, he tore his clothes and put sackcloth over his bare flesh; he fasted, lay in the sackcloth, and went about dejectedly. ²⁸Then the word of the LORD came to Elijah the Tishbite, ²⁹"Have you seen how Ahab has humbled himself before me? Because he has humbled himself before me, I will not bring the

m 21.18 Heb *who is*

21:8 The *elders* find themselves in another complicated situation (cf. 12:6–8), but here they simply follow the royal command.

21:9 A *fast* indicates a solemn occasion (cf. 21:28; 2 Sam. 12:16).

21:9–12 Jezebel makes sure the accusation can technically stand on legal grounds by having two "witnesses" (Deut. 17:6; 19:15).

21:13 *Cursed God and the king*. See Exod. 22:28.

21:22 On *Jeroboam son of Nebat*, see 11:26–14:20. On *Baasha son of Ahijah*, see 15:27–34.

21:23–24 See note on 13:22.

21:26 *Amorites*. In addition to Canaanite, Amorite is used of the former inhabitants of the land displaced by the Israelites (Gen. 15:16; Josh. 24:15, 18).

21:27 *Sackcloth over his bare flesh* is a sign of Ahab's dejected, mournful, and "humbled" (v. 29) state (cf. 20:31; 2 Kgs. 6:30; 19:1–3). Ahab's humility causes YHWH to revise plans (vv. 28–29).

21:27–29 The Omride dynasty would end during the reign of Ahab's son Jehoram (2 Kgs. 9–10).

disaster in his days, but in his son's days I will bring the disaster on his house."

22 For three years Aram and Israel continued without war. ²But in the third year King Jehoshaphat of Judah came down to the king of Israel. ³The king of Israel said to his servants, "Do you know that Ramoth-gilead belongs to us, yet we are doing nothing to take it out of the hand of the king of Aram?" ⁴He said to Jehoshaphat, "Will you go with me to battle at Ramoth-gilead?" Jehoshaphat replied to the king of Israel, "I am as you are; my people are your people; my horses are your horses."

5 But Jehoshaphat also said to the king of Israel, "Inquire first for the word of the LORD." ⁶Then the king of Israel gathered the prophets together, about four hundred of them, and said to them, "Shall I go to battle against Ramoth-gilead, or shall I refrain?" They said, "Go up, for the LORD will give it into the hand of the king." ⁷But Jehoshaphat said, "Is there no other prophet of the LORD here of whom we may inquire?" ⁸The king of Israel said to Jehoshaphat, "There is still one other by whom we may inquire of the LORD, Micaiah son of Imlah, but I hate him, for he never prophesies anything favorable about me but only disaster." Jehoshaphat said, "Let the king not say such a thing." ⁹Then the king of Israel summoned an officer and said, "Bring quickly Micaiah son of Imlah." ¹⁰Now the king of Israel and King Jehoshaphat of Judah were sitting on their thrones, arrayed in their robes, at the threshing floor at the entrance of the gate of Samaria, and all the prophets were prophesying before them. ¹¹Zedekiah son of

Chenaanah made for himself horns of iron, and he said, "Thus says the LORD: With these you shall gore the Arameans until they are destroyed." ¹²All the prophets were prophesying the same and saying, "Go up to Ramoth-gilead and triumph; the LORD will give it into the hand of the king."

13 The messenger who had gone to summon Micaiah said to him, "Look, the words of the prophets with one accord are favorable to the king; let your word be like the word of one of them, and speak favorably." ¹⁴But Micaiah said, "As the LORD lives, whatever the LORD says to me, that I will speak."

15 When he had come to the king, the king said to him, "Micaiah, shall we go to Ramoth-gilead to battle, or shall we refrain?" He answered him, "Go up and triumph; the LORD will give it into the hand of the king." ¹⁶But the king said to him, "How many times must I make you swear to tell me nothing but the truth in the name of the LORD?" ¹⁷Then Micaiah*ⁿ* said, "I saw all Israel scattered on the mountains like sheep that have no shepherd, and the LORD said, 'These have no master; let each one go home in peace.'" ¹⁸The king of Israel said to Jehoshaphat, "Did I not tell you that he would not prophesy anything favorable about me but only disaster?"

19 Then Micaiah*ᵒ* said, "Therefore hear the word of the LORD: I saw the LORD sitting on his throne, with all the host of heaven standing beside him to the right and to the left of him. ²⁰And the LORD said, 'Who will entice Ahab, so that he may go up and fall at Ramoth-gilead?' Then one said one thing, and another said another, ²¹until a certain spirit came

n 22.17 Heb *he*   *o* 22.19 Heb *he*

22:2 *Jehoshaphat.* See 1 Kgs. 22:41–51; 2 Kgs. 3.

22:3 *Ramoth-gilead.* An important city in the Transjordanian territory of Gad (Deut. 4:43; Josh. 20:8) on the "King's Highway" (Num. 21:22), an important trade route running from Damascus to the Gulf of Aqabah.

22:8 *Micaiah son of Imlah.* Not to be confused with Micah of Moresheth, the prophet for whom the book of Micah is named. According to the superscription of the book of Micah, Micah of Moresheth prophesied at a different time (Mic. 1:1).

22:10 *Threshing floor.* A public site where transactional, cultic, and legal activity takes place (Gen. 50:10–11; Judg. 6:37; 2 Sam. 24; Ruth 3). An outdoor, open space, often at the gate, for separating wheat kernels from stalks.

22:11–12 Performances with props often accompany prophecy (cf. Jer. 28:5–16; Ezek. 4:1–5:4).

22:22 *Entice* (Heb. "patah"). It may have been common for prophets to accuse other prophets of being enticed or deceived by YHWH (Ezek. 14:9). Jeremiah accuses YHWH of "enticing" him (Jer. 20:7).

22:19–23 Representation of the inner workings of YHWH's divine council (Pss. 82:1; 89:6–7; Zech. 3; Job 1–2). It appears as though prophets are thought to appear in YHWH's divine council before pronouncing oracles (Jer. 23:18, 22).

forward and stood before the Lord, saying, 'I will entice him.' ²²'How?' the Lord asked him. He replied, 'I will go out and be a lying spirit in the mouth of all his prophets.' Then the Lord*ᵖ* said, 'You are to entice him, and you shall succeed; go out and do it.' ²³So you see, the Lord has put a lying spirit in the mouth of all these your prophets; the Lord has decreed disaster for you.'

24 Then Zedekiah son of Chenaanah came up to Micaiah, slapped him on the cheek, and said, "Which way did the spirit of the Lord pass from me to speak to you?" ²⁵Micaiah replied, "You will find out on that day when you go in to hide in an inner chamber." ²⁶The king of Israel then ordered, "Take Micaiah, and return him to Amon the governor of the city and to Joash the king's son, ²⁷and say: Thus says the king: Put this fellow in prison, and feed him on reduced rations of bread and water until I come in peace." ²⁸Micaiah said, "If you return in peace, the Lord has not spoken by me." And he said, "Hear, you peoples, all of you!"

29 So the king of Israel and King Jehoshaphat of Judah went up to Ramoth-gilead. ³⁰The king of Israel said to Jehoshaphat, "I will disguise myself and go into battle, but you wear your robes." So the king of Israel disguised himself and went into battle. ³¹Now the king of Aram had commanded the thirty-two captains of his chariots, "Fight with no one small or great but only with the king of Israel." ³²When the captains of the chariots saw Jehoshaphat, they said, "It is surely the king of Israel." So they turned to fight against him, and Jehoshaphat cried out. ³³When the captains of the chariots saw that it was not the king of Israel, they turned back from pursuing him. ³⁴But a certain man drew his bow and unknowingly struck the king of Israel between the scale armor and the breastplate; so he said to the driver of his chariot, "Turn around and carry me out of the battle, for I am wounded." ³⁵The battle grew hot that day, and the king was propped up in his chariot facing the Arameans until at evening he died; the blood from the wound had flowed into the bottom of the chariot. ³⁶Then about sunset a shout went through the army, "Every man to his city, and every man to his country!"

37 So the king died and was brought to Samaria; they buried the king in Samaria. ³⁸They washed the chariot by the pool of Samaria; the dogs licked up his blood, and the prostitutes washed themselves in it,*ᵍ* according to the word of the Lord that he had spoken. ³⁹Now the rest of the acts of Ahab and all that he did and the ivory house that he built and all the cities that he built, are they not written in the Book of the Annals of the Kings of Israel? ⁴⁰So Ahab slept with his ancestors, and his son Ahaziah succeeded him.

41 Jehoshaphat son of Asa began to reign over Judah in the fourth year of King Ahab of Israel. ⁴²Jehoshaphat was thirty-five years old when he began to reign, and he reigned twenty-five years in Jerusalem. His mother's name was Azubah daughter of Shilhi. ⁴³He walked in all the way of his father Asa; he did not turn aside from it, doing what was right in the sight of the Lord, yet the high places were not taken away, and the people still sacrificed and offered incense on the high places. ⁴⁴Jehoshaphat also made peace with the king of Israel.

45 Now the rest of the acts of Jehoshaphat and his power that he showed and how he waged war, are they not written in the Book of the Annals of the Kings of Judah? ⁴⁶The remnant of the illicit priests who remained from the days of his father Asa, he purged from the land.

47 There was no king in Edom; a deputy was king. ⁴⁸Jehoshaphat made ships of the Tarshish type to go to Ophir for gold, but they did not go, for the ships were wrecked at Ezion-geber. ⁴⁹Then Ahaziah son of Ahab said to Jehoshaphat, "Let my servants go with your servants in the ships," but Jehoshaphat was not willing. ⁵⁰Jehoshaphat slept with his ancestors and was buried with his ancestors in the city of his father David; his son Jehoram succeeded him.

51 Ahaziah son of Ahab began to reign over Israel in Samaria in the seventeenth year of King Jehoshaphat of Judah; he reigned two years over Israel. ⁵²He did what was evil in the sight of the Lord and walked in the way of his father and mother and in the way of Jeroboam son of Nebat, who caused Israel to sin. ⁵³He served Baal and worshiped him; he provoked the Lord, the God of Israel, to anger, just as his father had done.

p 22.22 Heb *he*   *q* 22.38 Heb lacks *in it*

2 KINGS

The Traumatic Background of 2 Kings

The book of 2 Kings, the last book of what is known as the Deuteronomistic History (Judges, 1 and 2 Samuel, 1 and 2 Kings; see **"The Deuteronomistic History," p. 337**), concludes the dramatic narrative of the nation of Israel after its settlement in the land of Canaan. This history ends with a disheartening blow as the southern kingdom of Judah is destroyed by the Babylonian Empire, its temple (also called the Temple of Solomon or the First Temple) demolished, and its king and leadership exiled. A cataclysmic event that begins the first exile and diaspora, the destruction of Judah required and led to complex theological explanations as to its meanings and causes—the most prevalent of which was that it was the natural consequence of Israel's continual disregard and contravention of their covenant with YHWH. Despite this explanation, however, a sense of cognitive dissonance and trauma lingers in the text. As suggested by reiterative rumination, the riddle of exile seems to have remained unresolved. Indeed, what can fully and truly explain why YHWH, the God of Israel, allowed the country—the one that God promised to protect and claimed as a special and unique possession—to be destroyed? As such, 2 Kings reflects a complicated and, at times, tortured attempt to explain and understand an ineffable and incomprehensible upheaval.

Structure and Narrative

As in 1 Kings, the chapters of 2 Kings alternate between a description of the situation in the northern kingdom of Israel (also called Samaria or Israel) and that in the southern kingdom of Judah until 2 Kgs. 17:7, which describes the decimation of the north by the Assyrians (722 BCE). Considering that the northern kingdom of Israel is the first to be destroyed, the historical narrative of 2 Kings reflects the bias and proclivities of the writers and editors from Judah, who at some point after the demise of their own country by the Babylonians in 587/586 BCE began to compile, edit, and organize the accounts of these two nations, which were no more. Undoubtedly as a result, the north is usually faulted, and its demise is explained as caused by its heretical, impious tendencies. Hence, the northern kings are nearly universally faulted for their religious misbehavior—namely, their inability to properly and exclusively worship YHWH. A more mixed rating is given to the southern kings. Some kings, such as Hezekiah (2 Kgs. 18–19) and most notably Josiah (2 Kgs. 22–23), are rated positively and even superlatively, while others, such as Manasseh (2 Kgs. 21) and Ahaz (2 Kgs. 16), are paralleled to their northern counterparts and faulted for their lack of faith and piety. At the end, however, despite the reformative actions of periodic pious kings, 2 Kings depicts no one and nothing as able ultimately to halt the end of Judah, which too, like the north, is eventually destroyed by a foreign nation. This disheartening end is hinted at and forewarned by the theological explications, assessments, and foreshadows—likely inserted after the destruction of Judah has occurred—that pockmark the account of 2 Kings.

Reading Guide

Two interrelated questions run throughout 2 Kings, increasing in volume after the demise of the northern kingdom and at the approach of the end of the southern kingdom of Judah: What can the nation do to prevent destruction, and who or what is ultimately responsible for it? At the heart of these questions is the dateless conflict between theology and reality, religion and history. In particular, a specific theological assumption in Judah called Zion theology, which promised God's protection of the Davidic dynasty as well as of Jerusalem (see note for 2 Kgs. 19:34), increasingly came into conflict with historical events. That is, despite the theological assertion that the nations were special—especially to their deity, YHWH—in reality, Israel and Judah, as small ancient Near Eastern states, were mere pawns in a larger power struggle among more powerful empires.

This harsh reality inevitably led to other questions and concerns, which, though addressed more fully in postexilic texts such as Daniel and Esther, nonetheless appear initially in 2 Kings: How do we survive and live in the midst of empire and colonization? The discussions of the cost and gain of anti-imperial coalitions and rebellions (2 Kgs. 16, 18, 24), the attempts to thwart or play one imperial power off another (2 Kgs. 17, 18, 23), the use of tribute as bribery (2 Kgs. 12, 15, 16, 18, 23), and finally, the devastating effects of sieges and attacks, such as famine (2 Kgs. 6, 18, 24, 25)—all manifest the ways in which 2 Kings struggles with this question of empire and survival.

Evident in these struggles, questions, and strategies for survival are the horrendous effects of empire and the colonial enterprise, effects that—then as now—lead to the suffering of so many for the gains of a select few. Indeed, the voices and cries of those suffering, though not loud, are present and detectable. They bubble up or sometimes sigh in the corners of the history recounted in 2 Kings as it describes the hardships and desperation of the powerless and marginalized—the women, children, elderly, and poor who suffer, hunger, are sickened, are enslaved, and are killed in the midst of these needless fights for money, power, and fame. These voices, which sometimes appear only as the "sound of sheer silence" (1 Kgs. 19:12), whisper and nudge us to listen, hear, imagine, lament, and act.

As such, though 2 Kings describes ancient events, this text remains undoubtedly relevant today. We still struggle with how to reconcile the conflict between reality and our core religious assumptions and wishes. We still wonder what to do and how to survive in a difficult world fueled by detrimental and horrific forces of empire, those that thrive on greed, power, trauma, and death. And relatedly, we still wrestle with what to do in the face of so much suffering, especially of the powerless—how to resist, challenge, and act. In so doing, 2 Kings shows us that the questions that we contend with today are not new. They are but echoes of those asked in ancient times. The biblical text not only reflects the deep struggles to understand these perpetual concerns but also offers us an ever-renewable space with which to attempt to address and wrestle with these unanswerable questions anew.

Song-Mi Suzie Park

1 After the death of Ahab, Moab rebelled against Israel.

2 Ahaziah had fallen through the lattice in his upper chamber in Samaria and was injured, so he sent messengers, telling them, "Go, inquire of Baal-zebub, the god of Ekron, whether I shall recover from this injury." 3But the angel of the Lord said to Elijah the Tishbite, "Get up, go to meet the messengers of the king of Samaria and say to them: Is it because there is no God in Israel that you are going to inquire of Baal-zebub, the god of Ekron? 4Now therefore thus says the Lord: You shall not leave the bed to which you have gone, but you shall surely die." So Elijah went.

5 The messengers returned to the king, who said to them, "Why have you returned?" 6They answered him, "There came a man to meet us, who said to us, 'Go back to the king who sent you and say to him: Thus says the Lord: Is it because there is no God in Israel that you are sending to inquire of Baal-zebub, the god of Ekron? Therefore you shall not leave the bed to which you have gone but shall surely die.'" 7He said to them, "What sort of man was he who came to meet you and told you these things?" 8They answered him, "A hairy man with a leather belt around his waist." He said, "It is Elijah the Tishbite."

1:1 Political context. *Moab* is a neighboring country to Israel. Moab's ancestor is said to be the result of an incestuous relationship between Lot, the nephew of Abraham, and Lot's unnamed daughters (Gen. 19:30–38). Moreover, the biblical text portrays Moabite women as a source of sexual temptation and, relatedly, illicit worship (Num. 25:1–2; 1 Kgs. 11:1, 7). However, Moab is said to be a relative of Israel (Gen. 19:37), and the Moabitess Ruth is the ancestor of King David (Ruth 4:17–18). *Rebelled against Israel.* Moab had been subjugated by Israel since the time of David (2 Sam. 8:2). The disparaging stories about Moab likely served to justify Israel's colonization of this country.

1:2–4 Ahaziah's injury and inquiry. 1:2 *Ahaziah*, the son of Ahab and Jezebel, falls *through the lattice*, the roof or part of an upper story balcony, and is injured. His injury, short rule, and heretical behavior after the accident likely defend the embarrassing overthrow of Moab's vassalage. *Baal-zebub, the god of Ekron*—whose name means "lord [*baal*] of flies [*zebub*]," likely a parody of "zebul" (prince)—is the local deity of *Ekron*, one of the five cities of the Philistines (1 Sam. 6:18; 18:30; 29:3, 4, 9), an ancient people of Aegean descent with whom Israel was frequently at war. This deity is referenced in the New Testament (Matt. 10:25; 12:24; Mark 3:22; Luke 11:15–19). **1:3** *Elijah the Tishbite.* A very important prophet whose name means "my God is YHWH" and who becomes the precursor to the messiah in postbiblical traditions.

1:5–8 Elijah's message. 1:8 *Hairy man with a leather belt around his waist.* Elijah is identifiable by his dress and hair, both of which symbolize his outsider status as well as his possible identity as a nazirite (Num. 6:1–21).

9 Then the king sent to him a captain of fifty with his fifty men. He went up to Elijah, who was sitting on the top of a hill, and said to him, "O man of God, the king says: Come down." [10]But Elijah answered the captain of fifty, "If I am a man of God, let fire come down from heaven and consume you and your fifty." Then fire came down from heaven and consumed him and his fifty.

11 Again the king sent to him another captain of fifty with his fifty. He went up[a] and said to him, "O man of God, this is the king's order: Come down quickly!" [12]But Elijah answered him,[b] "If I am a man of God, let fire come down from heaven and consume you and your fifty." Then the fire of God came down from heaven and consumed him and his fifty.

13 Again the king sent the captain of a third fifty with his fifty. So the third captain of fifty went up and came and fell on his knees before Elijah and entreated him, "O man of God, please let my life and the life of these fifty servants of yours be precious in your sight. [14]Look, fire came down from heaven and consumed the two former captains of fifty men with their fifties, but now let my life be precious in your sight." [15]Then the angel of the LORD said to Elijah, "Go down with him; do not be afraid of him." So he set out and went down with him to the king [16]and said to him, "Thus says the LORD: Because you have sent messengers to inquire of Baal-zebub, the god of Ekron—is it because there is no God in Israel to inquire of his word?—therefore you shall not leave the bed to which you have gone, but you shall surely die."

17 So he died according to the word of the LORD that Elijah had spoken. His brother[c] Jehoram succeeded him as king in the second year of King Jehoram son of Jehoshaphat of Judah, because Ahaziah had no son. [18]Now the rest of the acts of Ahaziah that he did, are they not written in the Book of the Annals of the Kings of Israel?

2 Now when the LORD was about to take Elijah up to heaven by a whirlwind, Elijah and Elisha were on their way from Gilgal. [2]Elijah said to Elisha, "Stay here, for the LORD has sent me as far as Bethel." But Elisha said, "As the LORD lives and as you yourself live, I will not leave you." So they went down to Bethel. [3]The company of prophets who were in Bethel came out to Elisha and said to him, "Do you know that today the LORD will take your master away from you?" And he said, "Yes, I know; keep silent."

4 Elijah said to him, "Elisha, stay here, for the LORD has sent me to Jericho." But he said, "As the LORD lives and as you yourself live, I will not leave you." So they came to Jericho. [5]The company of prophets who were at Jericho drew near to Elisha and said to him, "Do you know that today the LORD will take your master away from you?" And he answered, "Yes, I know; keep silent."

6 Then Elijah said to him, "Stay here, for the LORD has sent me to the Jordan." But he said, "As the LORD lives and as you yourself live, I will not leave you." So the two of them went on. [7]Fifty men of the company of prophets also went and stood at some distance from them, as they both were standing by the Jordan. [8]Then Elijah

a 1.11 Gk: Heb *He answered* b 1.12 Gk: Heb *them* c 1.17 Gk Syr: Heb lacks *His brother*

1:9–18 The confirmation of Elijah's message. 1:10, 12, 14 *Fire . . . came down from heaven.* Fire, a feature of a storm deity, signifies God's presence (Exod. 3:2–6; 19:18; 24:17) as well as God's anger (Ps. 89:46; Isa. 66:15; Lam. 2:4; Ezek. 21:31; 22:21) and punishment (Gen. 19:24; Lev. 10:2; Num. 11:1; 16:35; 26:10). **1:17** *So he died according to the word of the* LORD *that Elijah had spoken* confirms the prophetic authority of Elijah.

2:1–8 Elijah's farewell and last miracle. 2:3, 5, 7 *Company of prophets.* A guild or cohort of prophets headed by a leader, such as Elijah. Its members were married (2 Kgs. 4:1), lived in community (2 Kgs. 6), and/or ate together (2 Kgs. 4:38–44). It is unclear whether this guild consisted only of men. **2:8** *Mantle . . . the water was parted.* The mantle, which is thrown on Elisha in 1 Kgs. 19:19 to call him to serve as Elijah's protégé, is used to perform Elijah's final miracle, which mimics Moses's parting of the Reed Sea (Exod. 14) and Joshua's parting of the Jordan (Josh. 3–4).

2:9–12 Elisha's request and Elijah's departure. Elisha witnesses Elijah's departure and inherits Elijah's mantle, the symbol of his authority. **2:9** *Double share of your spirit* references the inheritance meant for the heir (Deut. 21:17) and confirms Elisha as Elijah's successor. It may also refer to Elisha's status as a double of Elijah, as Elisha repeats many of Elijah's miracles (2 Kgs. 4:4–5, 33–35,

took his mantle and rolled it up and struck the water; the water was parted to the one side and to the other, and the two of them crossed on dry ground.

9 When they had crossed, Elijah said to Elisha, "Tell me what I may do for you before I am taken from you." Elisha said, "Please let me inherit a double share of your spirit." ¹⁰He responded, "You have asked a hard thing, yet if you see me as I am being taken from you, it will be granted you; if not, it will not." ¹¹As they continued walking and talking, a chariot of fire and horses of fire separated the two of them, and Elijah ascended in a whirlwind into heaven. ¹²Elisha kept watching and crying out, "Father, father! The chariots of Israel and its horsemen!" But when he could no longer see him, he grasped his own clothes and tore them in two pieces.

13 He picked up the mantle of Elijah that had fallen from him and went back and stood on the bank of the Jordan. ¹⁴He took the mantle of Elijah that had fallen from him and struck the water. He said, "Where is the LORD, the God of Elijah? Where is he?" He struck the water again, and the water was parted to the one side and to the other, and Elisha crossed over.

15 When the company of prophets who were at Jericho saw him at a distance, they declared, "The spirit of Elijah rests on Elisha." They came to meet him and bowed to the ground before him. ¹⁶They said to him, "See now, we have fifty strong men among your servants; please let them go and seek your master; it may be that the spirit of the LORD has caught him up and thrown him down on some mountain or into some valley." He responded, "No, do not send them." ¹⁷But when they urged him to the point of embarrassment, he said, "Send them." So they sent fifty men who searched for three days but did not find him. ¹⁸When they came back to him (he had remained at Jericho), he said to them, "Did I not say to you, 'Do not go'?"

19 Now the people of the city said to Elisha, "The location of this city is good, as my lord sees, but the water is bad, and the land is unfruitful." ²⁰He said, "Bring me a new bowl, and put salt in it." So they brought it to him. ²¹Then he went to the spring of water and threw the salt into it and said, "Thus says the LORD: I have made this water wholesome; from now on neither death nor miscarriage shall come from it." ²²So the water has been wholesome to this day, according to the word that Elisha spoke.

23 He went up from there to Bethel, and while he was going up on the way, some small boys came out of the city and jeered at him, saying, "Go away, baldhead! Go away, baldhead!" ²⁴When he turned around and saw them, he cursed them in the name of the LORD. Then two she-bears came out of the woods and mauled forty-two of the boys. ²⁵From there he went on to Mount Carmel and then returned to Samaria.

3 In the eighteenth year of King Jehoshaphat of Judah, Jehoram son of Ahab became king over Israel in Samaria; he reigned twelve years. ²He did what was

---

43–44; 1 Kgs. 17:14–16, 20–22). **2:11** *A chariot of fire and horses of fire* separate the two prophets. These phrases correlate YHWH's prophets with the heavenly armies, perhaps implying that the prophets and their words are part of Israel's defenses. *Whirlwind.* A manifestation of YHWH as a storm deity (Nah. 1:3; Job 38:1; Ps. 50:3). Because Elijah does not die, he becomes an important figure in Jewish tradition, connected to the advent of the Day of the Lord (Mal. 4:5; see **"The Day of the Lord," p. 1322**) as well as the messianic age (Rev. 11).

2:13–18 Elisha succeeds Elijah. Affirming his position as Elijah's successor, Elisha repeats Elijah's final miracle. His authority, however, is not fully accepted by the other prophets, who question whether Elijah is truly gone.

2:19–22 Elisha's other miracles. Elisha uses a purifying agent, salt, to cleanse the waters. As water symbolizes chaos as well as fertility and life, this miracle affirms Elisha's status as a prophet of the life-giving storm deity YHWH.

2:23–25 Final affirmation. Elisha's status as Elijah's successor is reaffirmed as Elisha sics two she-bears on children who taunt his baldness and command him to "go up" (my translation)—both of which contrast Elisha to his hirsute mentor (1:8), who just ascended (2:1–12).

3:1–3 The reign of Jehoram in Israel. Jehoram's reign over the northern kingdom of Israel is assessed negatively.

evil in the sight of the LORD, though not like his father and mother, for he removed the pillar of Baal that his father had made. ³Nevertheless, he clung to the sin of Jeroboam son of Nebat that he caused Israel to commit; he did not depart from it.

4 Now King Mesha of Moab was a sheep breeder who used to deliver to the king of Israel one hundred thousand lambs and the wool of one hundred thousand rams. ⁵But when Ahab died, the king of Moab rebelled against the king of Israel. ⁶So King Jehoram marched out of Samaria at that time and mustered all Israel. ⁷As he went he sent word to King Jehoshaphat of Judah, "The king of Moab has rebelled against me; will you go with me to battle against Moab?" He answered, "I will; I am as you are; my people are your people; my horses are your horses." ⁸Then he asked, "By which way shall we march?" Jehoram answered, "By the way of the wilderness of Edom."

9 So the king of Israel, the king of Judah, and the king of Edom set out, and when they had made a roundabout march of seven days, there was no water for the army or for the animals that were with them. ¹⁰Then the king of Israel said, "Alas! The LORD has summoned these three kings to hand them over to Moab." ¹¹But Jehoshaphat said, "Is there no prophet of the LORD here through whom we may inquire of the LORD?" Then one of the servants of the king of Israel answered, "Elisha son of Shaphat, who used to pour water on the hands of Elijah, is here." ¹²Jehoshaphat said, "The word of the LORD is with him." So the king of Israel and Jehoshaphat and the king of Edom went down to him.

13 Elisha said to the king of Israel, "What have I to do with you? Go to your father's prophets or to your mother's." But the king of Israel said to him, "No; it is the LORD who has summoned these three kings to hand them over to Moab." ¹⁴Elisha said, "As the LORD of hosts lives, whom I serve, were it not that I have regard for King Jehoshaphat of Judah, I would give you neither a look nor a glance. ¹⁵But get me a musician." And then, while the musician was playing, the hand of the LORD came on him. ¹⁶And he said, "Thus says the LORD: I will make this wadi full of pools. ¹⁷For thus says the LORD: You shall see neither wind nor rain, but the wadi shall be filled with water, so that you shall drink, you, your army,ᵈ and your animals. ¹⁸This is only a trifle in the sight of the LORD, for he will also hand Moab over to you. ¹⁹You shall conquer every fortified city and every choice city; every good tree you shall fell, all springs of water you shall stop up, and every good piece of land you shall ruin with stones." ²⁰The next day, about the time of the morning offering, suddenly water began to flow from the direction of Edom until the country was filled with water.

21 When all the Moabites heard that the kings had come up to fight against them, all who were able to put on armor, from the youngest to the oldest, were called out and were drawn up at the frontier. ²²When they rose early in the morning and the sun shone

d 3.17 Gk: Heb *cattle*

3:4–20 Moab's rebellion. Expanding upon the notice of Moab's rebellion in 2 Kgs. 1, Moab under King *Mesha*—who is also mentioned in the Mesha Stele, or the Moabite Stone (ca. 840 BCE)—rebels against Israelite subjugation. As a result of this rebellion, a joint coalition is formed to recapture and punish Moab.

3:9–12 Elisha consulted. En route, the coalition runs out of water. Jehoshaphat, the king of Judah, suggests that they consult a prophet and is told of the presence of Elisha, *who used to pour water on the hands of Elijah* (v. 11)—a description that affirms Elisha's status as Elijah's successor and a bona fide prophet of YHWH, the storm deity in charge of water. Jehoram, the king of Israel, appears impiously to have failed to consult a deity before going to war (1 Sam. 23:2–4; 2 Sam. 2:1; 5:19; 1 Kgs. 22:5) and is also ignorant of the presence of Elisha. The emphasis on Jehoram's impiety might explain why Elisha's prophecy ultimately fails to come true.

3:13–20 Elisha's prophecy. Using a *musician*, Elisha prophesies that YHWH will provide water and that Moab will be defeated. Music was seen as a conduit to God and therefore as a way to induce prophecy (1 Sam. 10:5; 1 Chr. 25:1).

3:21–27 Warfare and child sacrifice. 3:21–25 The Moabites mistake the pools of water for blood, perhaps as a result of the red-tinted Edomite soil and/or the reflection of the sun. Thinking that the coalition turned against each other, the Moabites rush to loot the camps and are slaughtered by the

upon the water, the Moabites saw the water opposite them as red as blood. ²³They said, "This is blood; the kings must have fought together and killed one another. Now then, Moab, to the spoil!" ²⁴But when they came to the camp of Israel, the Israelites rose up and attacked the Moabites, who fled before them; as they entered Moab, they continued the attack.ᵉ ²⁵The cities they overturned, and on every good piece of land everyone threw a stone until it was covered; every spring of water they stopped up, and every good tree they felled. Only at Kir-hareseth did the stone walls remain until the slingers surrounded and attacked it. ²⁶When the king of Moab saw that the battle was going against him, he took with him seven hundred swordsmen to break through opposite the king of Edom, but they could not. ²⁷Then he took his firstborn son who was to succeed him and offered him as a burnt offering on the wall. And great wrath came upon Israel, so they withdrew from him and returned to their own land.

4 Now the wife of a member of the company of prophets cried to Elisha, "Your servant my husband is dead, and you know that your servant feared the Lord, but a creditor has come to take my two children as slaves." ²Elisha said to her, "What shall I do for you? Tell me, what do you have in the house?" She answered, "Your servant has nothing in the house except a jar of oil." ³He said, "Go outside, borrow vessels from all your neighbors, empty vessels—and not just a few. ⁴Then go in, shut the door behind you and your children, and start pouring into all these vessels; when each is full, set it aside." ⁵So she left him and shut the door behind her and her children; they kept bringing vessels to her, and she kept pouring. ⁶When the vessels were full, she said to her son, "Bring me another vessel." But he said to her, "There are no more." Then the oil stopped flowing. ⁷She came and told the man of God, and he said, "Go sell the oil and pay your debts, and you and your children can live on the rest."

8 One day Elisha was passing through Shunem, where a wealthy woman lived, who urged him to have a meal. So whenever he passed that way, he would stop there for a meal. ⁹She said to her husband, "Look, I am sure that this man who regularly passes our way is a holy man of God. ¹⁰Let us make a small roof chamber with walls and put there for him a bed, a table, a chair, and a lamp, so that he can stay there whenever he comes to us."

11 One day when he came there, he went up to the chamber and lay down there. ¹²He said to his servant Gehazi, "Call the Shunammite woman." When he had called her, she stood before him. ¹³He said to him, "Say to her: Since

e 3.24 Compare Gk Syr: Meaning of Heb uncertain

coalition's soldiers. Water and blood recall childbirth, which is contrasted to the forthcoming death of a child. **3:26–27** The loss of battle imminent, the king of Moab, Mesha, sacrifices his own firstborn son as a *burnt offering*, unleashing a *great wrath*, likely that of Chemosh, the god of the Moabites, which turns the tide of war to Moab's favor, causing the Israelite coalition to retreat. Similar to the story of the sacrifice of Jephthah's daughter (Judg. 11), this story links warfare and child sacrifice, and in so doing, it highlights the unnamed victims of warfare and colonization who are oftentimes the most vulnerable members of society.

4:1–7 Elisha and the poor widow. 4:1–2 Providing a glimpse into the economic difficulties faced by women, especially those married to religious officials, this story centers on an unnamed widow of a *member of the company of prophets* (see note for 2 Kgs. 2:3), who early traditions identify as the wife of Obadiah, a pious servant of Ahab. After her husband's death, she has become so impoverished that creditors are coming to take away her two *children as slaves*, which, though an accepted way to pay off debt in ancient Israel (Exod. 21:7), was, however, condemned by the prophets (Amos 2:6; Mic. 2:9). See **"Human Bondage in Ancient Israel (the Law),"** p. 115. **4:3–7** The life-giving abilities of YHWH are emphasized, as Elisha, the prophet of YHWH, magically regenerates oil for the widow, thereby ensuring that she and her children have sustenance as well as sellable commodities and therefore are safe from enslavement.

4:8–17 Elisha and the great woman of Shunem. 4:8–13 In contrast to the widow, the rich, childless, and married woman of Shunem gifts Elisha meals and housing. Perhaps uncomfortable with this inverted relationship, Elisha asks if anything can be done for her in return. **4:13** *Live among my own people.* She answers that she has no need, as she is well cared for by either her own family

you have taken all this trouble for us, what may be done for you? Would you have a word spoken on your behalf to the king or to the commander of the army?" She answered, "I live among my own people." [14]He said, "What then may be done for her?" Gehazi answered, "Well, she has no son, and her husband is old." [15]He said, "Call her." When he had called her, she stood at the door. [16]He said, "At this season, in due time, you shall embrace a son." She replied, "No, my lord, O man of God; do not deceive your servant."

17 The woman conceived and bore a son at that season, in due time, as Elisha had declared to her.

18 When the child was older, he went out one day to his father among the reapers. [19]He complained to his father, "Oh, my head, my head!" The father said to his servant, "Carry him to his mother." [20]He carried him and brought him to his mother; the child sat on her lap until noon, and he died. [21]She went up and laid him on the bed of the man of God, closed the door on him, and left. [22]Then she called to her husband and said, "Send me one of the servants and one of the donkeys, so that I may quickly go to the man of God and come back again." [23]He said, "Why go to him today? It is neither new moon nor Sabbath." She said, "It will be all right." [24]Then she saddled the donkey and said to her servant, "Urge the animal on; do not hold back for me unless I tell you." [25]So she set out and came to the man of God at Mount Carmel.

When the man of God saw her coming, he said to Gehazi his servant, "Look, there is the Shunammite woman; [26]run at once to meet her and say to her: Are you all right? Is your husband all right? Is the child all right?" She answered, "It is all right." [27]When she came to the man of God at the mountain, she caught hold of his feet. Gehazi approached to push her away, but the man of God said, "Let her alone, for she is in bitter distress; the LORD has hidden it from me and has not told me." [28]Then she said, "Did I ask my lord for a son? Did I not say, 'Do not mislead me?'" [29]He said to Gehazi, "Gird up your loins, and take my staff in your hand, and go. If you meet anyone, give no greeting, and if anyone greets you, do not answer, and lay my staff on the face of the child." [30]Then the mother of the child said, "As the LORD lives and as you yourself live, I will not leave without you." So he rose up and followed her. [31]Gehazi went on ahead and laid the staff on the face of the child, but there was no sound or sign of life. He came back to meet him and told him, "The child has not awakened."

32 When Elisha came into the house, he saw the child lying dead on his bed. [33]So he went in and closed the door on the two of them and prayed to the LORD. [34]Then he got up on the bed[f] and lay upon the child, putting his mouth upon his mouth, his eyes upon his eyes, and his hands upon his hands, and while he lay bent over him, the flesh of the child became warm. [35]He got down, walked once to and fro in the room, then got up again and bent over him; the child sneezed seven times, and the child opened his eyes. [36]Elisha[g] summoned Gehazi and said, "Call the Shunammite woman." So he called her. When she came to him, he said, "Take your son." [37]She came and fell at his feet, bowing to the ground; then she took her son and left.

f 4.34 Heb lacks *on the bed* g 4.36 Heb *He*

or her community. **4:14–17** *She has no son.* Despite the assertions of her self-sufficiency, when the prophet finds out that she is childless, he informs her that she will bear a son. Though this prophecy mimics the promise given to Abraham (Gen. 18:14), the assumption that a woman, no matter her claims, cannot truly be fulfilled without having children, especially a son, can be detected.

4:18–37 The death and resurrection of the woman's son. 4:27 *The LORD has hidden it from me.* When the son dies, the mother obtains help from Elisha, who seems oddly unaware of the death, perhaps setting up for Elisha's first failed attempt at revivification. **4:28** *Did I ask my lord for a son?* The mother's cry emphasizes the burden of Elisha's unrequested gift. **4:29–31** The mother's activity can be juxtaposed with the passivity of Elisha, who initially sends his assistant Gehazi to revive the child on his behalf. **4:32–37** On Elisha's second attempt, he successfully revives the dead child through an act of magical mirroring and touch, by lying on the child, *putting his mouth upon his mouth, his eyes upon his eyes, and his hands upon his hands*, thereby transferring some of the life-giving and duplicating abilities of YHWH embodied by the prophet to the dead child. This causes the child to come back to life and sneeze, perhaps indicating that the soul that has departed has returned to the body.

38 When Elisha returned to Gilgal, there was a famine in the land. As the company of prophets was sitting before him, he said to his servant, "Put the large pot on, and make some stew for the company of prophets." ³⁹One of them went out into the field to gather herbs; he found a wild vine and gathered from it a lapful of wild gourds and came and cut them up into the pot of stew, not knowing what they were. ⁴⁰They served some for the men to eat. But while they were eating the stew, they cried out, "O man of God, there is death in the pot!" They could not eat it. ⁴¹He said, "Then bring some flour." He threw it into the pot and said, "Serve the people and let them eat." And there was nothing harmful in the pot.

42 A man came from Baal-shalishah bringing food from the first fruits to the man of God: twenty loaves of barley and fresh ears of grain in his sack. Elisha said, "Give it to the people and let them eat." ⁴³But his servant said, "How can I set this before a hundred people?" So he repeated, "Give it to the people and let them eat, for thus says the LORD: They shall eat and have some left." ⁴⁴He set it before them; they ate and had some left, according to the word of the LORD.

5 Naaman, commander of the army of the king of Aram, was a great man and in high favor with his master because by him the LORD had given victory to Aram. The man, though a mighty warrior, suffered from a skin disease. ²Now the Arameans on one of their raids had taken a young girl captive from the land of Israel, and she served Naaman's wife. ³She said to her mistress, "If only my lord were with the prophet who is in Samaria! He would cure him of his skin disease." ⁴So Naaman*b* went in and told his lord just what the girl from the land of Israel had said. ⁵And the king of Aram said, "Go, then, and I will send along a letter to the king of Israel."

He went, taking with him ten talents of silver, six thousand shekels of gold, and ten sets of garments. ⁶He brought the letter to the king of Israel, which read, "When this letter reaches you, know that I have sent to you my servant Naaman, that you may cure him of his skin disease." ⁷When the king of Israel read the letter, he tore his clothes and said, "Am I God, to give death or life, that this man sends word to me to cure a man of his skin disease? Just look and see how he is trying to pick a quarrel with me."

8 But when Elisha the man of God heard that the king of Israel had torn his clothes, he sent a message to the king, "Why have you torn your clothes? Let him come to me, that he may learn that there is a prophet in Israel." ⁹So Naaman came with his horses and chariots and halted at the entrance of Elisha's house. ¹⁰Elisha sent a messenger to him, saying, "Go, wash in the Jordan seven times, and your flesh shall be restored, and you shall be clean." ¹¹But Naaman became angry and went away, saying, "I thought that for me he would surely come out and stand and call on the name of the LORD his God and would wave his hand over the spot and cure the skin disease! ¹²Are not Abana*i*

b 5.4 Heb *he*   *i* 5.12 Another reading is *Amana*

4:38–44 Famine and food. Elisha turns a poisonous soup into edible sustenance and magically regenerates food for the hungry, an act mimicked by Jesus (Matt. 14:13–21; 15:32–39; Mark 6:31–44; 8:1–9; Luke 9:12–17).

5:1–7 Naaman and the captive girl. 5:1 *Aram.* A country located north of Israel, with which Israel comes into conflict. Jacob's mother, Rebekah, and his sister-wives, Leah and Rachel, are Aramean, as is his uncle and father-in-law, Laban, with whom he has an ambivalent relationship (Gen. 29–31). *Naaman . . . great man,* whose name means "gracious," is a powerful, foreign general who is contrasted to and saved by a powerless, unnamed Israelite enslaved girl. *Because by him the LORD had given victory.* The only time in the Hebrew text that states that YHWH has given victory to a foreign nation, hinting at YHWH's displeasure with Israel and its leadership. The *skin disease* might be leuke, which causes whitening or discoloration of the skin, instead of Hansen's disease, or leprosy. **5:2** The *young girl captive from the land of Israel* might have been captured during one of Aram's successful campaigns. The seizure of women during war was likely not uncommon (Deut. 20:14; 21:10–14). **5:6–7** When Naaman arrives with a reference letter, the Israelite king, either ignorant of or lacking confidence in Israel's miracle-working prophets, faithlessly declares that this is a trap by the Aramean king.

5:8–19 Naaman is healed. 5:10 *Wash in the Jordan.* Emphasizing his miraculous powers, Elisha tells an incensed Naaman, who expects more fanfare and address, that a simple, repeated bath in

and Pharpar, the rivers of Damascus, better than all the waters of Israel? Could I not wash in them and be clean?" He turned and went away in a rage. [13]But his servants approached and said to him, "Father, if the prophet had commanded you to do something difficult, would you not have done it? How much more, when all he said to you was, 'Wash, and be clean'?" [14]So he went down and immersed himself seven times in the Jordan, according to the word of the man of God; his flesh was restored like the flesh of a young boy, and he was clean.

15 Then he returned to the man of God, he and all his company; he came and stood before him and said, "Now I know that there is no God in all the earth except in Israel; please accept a present from your servant." [16]But he said, "As the LORD lives, whom I serve, I will accept nothing!" He urged him to accept, but he refused. [17]Then Naaman said, "If not, please let two mule loads of earth be given to your servant, for your servant will no longer offer burnt offering or sacrifice to any god except the LORD. [18]But may the LORD pardon your servant on one count: when my master goes into the house of Rimmon to worship there, leaning on my arm, and I bow down in the house of Rimmon, when I do bow down in the house of Rimmon, may the LORD pardon your servant on this one count." [19]He said to him, "Go in peace."

But when Naaman had gone from him a short distance, [20]Gehazi, the servant of Elisha the man of God, thought, "My master has let that Aramean Naaman off too lightly by not accepting from him what he offered. As the LORD lives, I will run after him and get something from him." [21]So Gehazi went after Naaman. When Naaman saw someone running after him, he jumped down from the chariot to meet him and said, "Is

everything all right?" [22]He replied, "Yes, but my master has sent me to say, 'Two members of a company of prophets have just come to me from the hill country of Ephraim; please give them a talent of silver and two changes of clothing.'" [23]Naaman said, "Please accept two talents." He urged him and tied up two talents of silver in two bags, with two changes of clothing, and gave them to two of his servants, who carried them in front of Gehazi.[j] [24]When he came to the citadel, he took the bags[k] from them and stored them inside; he dismissed the men, and they left.

25 He went in and stood before his master, and Elisha said to him, "Where have you been, Gehazi?" He answered, "Your servant has not gone anywhere at all." [26]But he said to him, "Did I not go with you in spirit when someone left his chariot to meet you? Is this a time to accept silver and to accept clothing, olive orchards and vineyards, sheep and oxen, and male and female slaves? [27]Therefore the skin disease of Naaman shall cling to you and to your descendants forever." So he left his presence diseased, as white as snow.

6 Now the company of prophets said to Elisha, "As you see, the place where we live under your charge is too small for us. [2]Let us go to the Jordan, and let us collect logs there, one for each of us, and build a place there for us to live." He answered, "Do so." [3]Then one of them said, "Please come with your servants." And he answered, "I will." [4]So he went with them. When they came to the Jordan, they cut down trees. [5]But as one was felling a log, his ax head fell into the water; he cried out, "Alas, master! It was borrowed." [6]Then the man of God said, "Where did it fall?" When he showed him the place, he cut

j 5.23 Heb *him*   *k* 5.24 Heb lacks *the bags*

---

the Jordan will suffice to heal him of this disease. *Seven times* references the seven sneezes of the Shunammite woman's son who is revived by Elisha (2 Kgs. 4:35). *Seven* is a number of completion (Lev. 14:7, 15–16, 27). **5:14** *Flesh of a young boy* (Heb. "na'ar") alludes to the young captive girl ("na'arah") from Israel who sent Naaman on his journey. **5:15** *Now I know that there is no God in all the earth.* Perhaps this declaration of YHWH's universality signals Naaman's conversion. **5:17** *Two mule loads of earth.* In contrast to his earlier declaration of YHWH's universality, Naaman thinks that YHWH is tied to the land, the soil, of Israel.

5:19–27 Gehazi's greed and comeuppance. In contrast to Naaman's servants, Gehazi, the servant of Elisha, unscrupulously lies to Naaman in order to receive payment that Elisha refuses and inherits Naaman's skin disease as punishment. This negative story does not fit with any other stories about Gehazi and might explain why Gehazi disappears from the narrative and does not succeed Elisha.

6:1–7 The ax miracle. 6:6 *Stick . . . made the iron float.* Elisha again comes to the rescue of the

off a stick and threw it in there and made the iron float. [7]He said, "Pick it up." So he reached out his hand and took it.

8 Once when the king of Aram was at war with Israel, he took counsel with his officers. He said, "At such and such a place shall be my camp." [9]But the man of God sent word to the king of Israel, "Take care not to pass this place, for the Arameans are going down there." [10]The king of Israel sent word to the place of which the man of God spoke. More than once or twice he warned a place[l] so that it was on the alert.

11 The mind of the king of Aram was greatly perturbed because of this; he called his officers and said to them, "Now tell me: Who among us is betraying us to[m] the king of Israel?" [12]Then one of his officers said, "No one, my lord king. It is Elisha, the prophet in Israel, who tells the king of Israel the words that you speak in your bedchamber." [13]He said, "Go and find where he is; I will send and seize him." He was told, "He is in Dothan." [14]So he sent horses and chariots there and a great army; they came by night and surrounded the city.

15 When an attendant of the man of God rose early in the morning and went out, an army with horses and chariots was all around the city. His servant said, "Alas, master! What shall we do?" [16]He replied, "Do not be afraid, for there are more with us than there are with them." [17]Then Elisha prayed, "O Lord, please open his eyes that he may see." So the Lord opened the eyes of the servant, and he saw; the mountain was full of horses and chariots of fire all around Elisha. [18]When the Arameans[n] came down against him, Elisha prayed to the Lord and said, "Strike this people, please, with blindness." So he struck them with blindness as Elisha had asked. [19]Elisha said to them, "This is not the way, and this is not the city; follow me, and I will bring you to the man whom you seek." And he led them to Samaria.

20 As soon as they entered Samaria, Elisha said, "O Lord, open the eyes of these men so that they may see." The Lord opened their eyes, and they saw that they were inside Samaria. [21]When the king of Israel saw them he said to Elisha, "Father, shall I strike them? Shall I strike them?" [22]He answered, "No! Would you strike those whom you have taken captive with your sword and with your bow? Set food and water before them so that they may eat and drink, and let them go to their master." [23]So he prepared for them a great feast; after they ate and drank, he sent them on their way, and they went to their master. And the Arameans no longer came raiding into the land of Israel.

24 Some time later King Ben-hadad of Aram mustered his entire army; he marched against Samaria and laid siege to it. [25]As the siege continued, famine in Samaria became so great that a donkey's head was sold for eighty shekels of silver and one-fourth of

l 6.10 Heb *warned it*   m 6.11 Cn Compare Gk Tg: Heb *among us is with*   n 6.18 Heb *they*

company of prophets (see note on 2 Kgs. 2:3) to retrieve a borrowed ax-head by using the stick to locate it. Iron was expensive and valuable in the ancient world.
6:8–23 The thwarted attack. 6:8–13 Showing how YHWH's prophets better protect the country than human weaponry, Elisha is able to "see" into the military plans of the Arameans and help Israel thwart or avoid their attacks. This infuriates the unnamed *king of Aram*, who thinks it is the work of a spy. When the king is told that the responsible party is the prophet Elisha, who is so magically endowed that he can even hear conversations in the king's *bedchamber*, the king idiotically sends human weapons—*horses and chariots...and a great army*—to kidnap Elisha. **6:16–17** Emphasizing the theme of divine sight and human blindness, Elisha tells his servant, who grows fearful of the approaching Aramean army, to *open his eyes* so that he can see the *horses and chariots of fire*—that is, the much more powerful divine army that surrounds Elisha and that Elisha sees take away Elijah in 2 Kgs. 2. **6:18–19** *Strike...with blindness.* In opposition to opening the eyes of his servant, Elisha now closes the eyes of the Aramean army by striking them with blindness as the angels do to the men of Sodom and Gomorrah (Gen. 19:11). **6:20–22** Instead of the Arameans kidnapping Elisha, he kidnaps them, leading them to Samaria, not to kill them, as the king of Israel desires, but to kill them with kindness, as they are given food and water and then returned, which puts a temporary stop to the raids.
6:24–7:2 The Aramean siege and starving mothers. 6:24 *Ben-hadad...marched against Samaria* describes a second siege of Samaria led by *Ben-hadad of Aram* (1 Kgs. 20:1). **6:25** *Famine...donkey's head...dove's dung.* The siege leads to a severe famine (Deut. 28:56–57; Ezek. 5:10; Lam. 2:20),

a kab of dove's dung for five shekels of silver. ²⁶Now as the king of Israel was walking on the city wall, a woman cried out to him, "Help, my lord king!" ²⁷He said, "If the LORD does not help you, where would my help come from? From the threshing floor or from the winepress?" ²⁸But then the king asked her, "What is your complaint?" She answered, "This woman said to me, 'Give up your son; we will eat him today, and we will eat my son tomorrow.' ²⁹So we cooked my son and ate him. The next day I said to her, 'Give up your son, and we will eat him.' But she has hidden her son." ³⁰When the king heard the words of the woman he tore his clothes—now since he was walking on the city wall, the people could see that he had sackcloth on his body underneath—³¹and he said, "So may God do to me and more, if the head of Elisha son of Shaphat stays on his shoulders today." ³²So he dispatched a man from his presence.

Now Elisha was sitting in his house, and the elders were sitting with him. Before the messenger arrived, Elisha said to the elders, "Are you aware that this murderer has sent someone to take off my head? When the messenger comes, see that you shut the door and hold it closed against him. Is not the sound of his master's feet behind him?" ³³While he was still speaking with them, the king° came down to him and said, "This trouble is from the LORD! Why should I hope

7 in the LORD any longer?" ¹But Elisha said, "Hear the word of the LORD: Thus says the LORD: Tomorrow about this time a measure of choice meal shall be sold for a shekel and two measures of barley for a shekel, at the gate of Samaria." ²Then the captain on whose hand the king leaned said to the man of God, "Even if the LORD were to make windows in the sky, could such a thing happen?" But he said, "You shall see it with your own eyes, but you shall not eat from it."

3 Now there were four men with a defiling skin disease outside the city gate who said to one another, "Why should we sit here until we die? ⁴If we say, 'Let us enter the city,' the famine is in the city, and we shall die there, but if we sit here, we shall also die. Therefore, let us desert to the Aramean camp; if they spare our lives, we shall live, and if they kill us, we shall but die." ⁵So they arose at twilight to go to the Aramean camp, but when they came to the edge of the Aramean camp there was no one there at all. ⁶For the Lord had caused the Aramean army to hear the sound of chariots and of horses, the sound of a great army, so that they said to one another, "The king of Israel has hired the kings of the Hittites and the kings of Egypt to fight against us." ⁷So they fled away in the twilight and abandoned their tents,

o 6.33 Cn: Heb *messenger*

where items that were usually discarded or used by the very poor, such as *dove's dung*—perhaps a husk of a plant or a substance used as salt (*Ant.* 9.62), to plant wheat or corn, or as kindling—are sold for astronomical prices. **6:26–27** The desperate cries of a hungry woman to the Israelite king, perhaps Jehoram, are summarily dismissed by the king, who shirks responsibility. Criticisms of the political system and its leadership, one that ignores or dismisses the cries of the hungry, marginalized, and poor, are undoubtedly present. **6:28–29** Perhaps alluding to the story of Solomon and the prostitutes (1 Kgs. 3:16-28), a woman recounts a harrowing tale whereby she and another woman planned to kill and eat their children. Cannibalism in the midst of war (Deut. 28:53-57; Ezek. 5:10; Lam. 2:20; 4:10) speaks to a society where control, domination, abuse, and leadership deficiencies are widespread. **6:30–32** The Israelite king, who is wearing *sackcloth*, perhaps as a sign of mourning and fasting, blames and threatens to kill Elisha. The voluntary abstinence from food by the powerful, irresponsible king contrasts him with the powerless, desperate starving woman. **6:32–7:2** Elisha, who is sitting with the elders, has foreknowledge that the king, who blames him for the famine, has sent someone to kill him and therefore bars the doors. When the king arrives, he dejectedly replies that he has lost hope, at which point Elisha prophesies that the famine will end tomorrow—a prophecy doubted by the king's captain. Questions are raised as to why Elisha, with his magical powers, failed to do anything to relieve the suffering of the people sooner.

7:3–20 The end of the siege. 7:3–8 As Elisha foretold, the siege comes to an abrupt end as the Lord causes the Aramean army to flee when it hears the sounds of a great approaching army. The first to witness the miraculous desertion of the Arameans and the end of the famine are those on the margins—four men who are impure because of their skin diseases (Lev. 13:46) and therefore

their horses, and their donkeys, leaving the camp just as it was, and fled for their lives. [8]When these diseased men had come to the edge of the camp, they went into a tent, ate and drank, carried off silver, gold, and clothing, and went and hid them. Then they came back, entered another tent, carried off things from it and went and hid them.

9 Then they said to one another, "What we are doing is wrong. This is a day of good news; if we are silent and wait until the morning light, we will be found guilty; therefore let us go and tell the king's household." [10]So they came and called to the gatekeepers of the city and told them, "We went to the Aramean camp, but there was no one to be seen or heard there, nothing but the horses tied, the donkeys tied, and the tents as they were." [11]Then the gatekeepers called out and proclaimed it to the king's household. [12]The king got up in the night and said to his servants, "I will tell you what the Arameans have prepared against us. They know that we are starving, so they left the camp to hide themselves in the open country, thinking, 'When they come out of the city, we shall take them alive and get into the city.'" [13]One of his servants said, "Let some men take five of the remaining horses, since those left here will suffer the fate of the whole multitude of Israel that have perished already;[p] let us send and find out." [14]So they took two mounted men, and the king sent them after the Aramean army, saying, "Go and find out." [15]So they went after them as far as the Jordan; the whole way was littered with garments and equipment that the Arameans had thrown away in their haste. So the messengers returned and told the king.

16 Then the people went out and plundered the camp of the Arameans. So a measure of choice meal was sold for a shekel and two measures of barley for a shekel, according to the word of the LORD. [17]Now the king had appointed the captain on whose hand he leaned to have charge of the gate; the people trampled him to death in the gate, just as the man of God had said when the king came down to him. [18]For when the man of God had said to the king, "Two measures of barley shall be sold for a shekel and a measure of choice meal for a shekel, about this time tomorrow in the gate of Samaria," [19]the captain had answered the man of God, "Even if the LORD were to make windows in the sky, could such a thing happen?" And he had answered, "You shall see it with your own eyes, but you shall not eat from it." [20]It did indeed happen to him; the people trampled him to death in the gate.

8 Now Elisha had said to the woman whose son he had restored to life, "Get up and go with your household and settle wherever you can, for the LORD has called for a famine, and it will come on the land for seven years." [2]So the woman got up and did according to the word of the man of God; she went with her household and settled in the land of the Philistines seven years. [3]At the end of the seven years, when the woman returned from the land of the Philistines, she set out to appeal to the king for her house and her land. [4]Now the king was talking with Gehazi the servant of the man of God, saying, "Tell me all the great things that Elisha has done." [5]While he was

p 7.13 Compare Gk Syr Vg: Meaning of Heb uncertain

have to reside outside of the city. **7:9–15** Finding the Aramean camp deserted, the men start to pillage it until they, perhaps more attuned to the suffering of others as outsiders, realize they need to share the news. Ever faithless, when the king is told of the desertion, he thinks it is a trick by the Arameans despite Elisha's earlier prophecy. **7:16–20** When the hungry and desperate people in the city hear of the departure of the army, they rush to the camps to find food, causing a stampede. The captain who doubted Elisha's message about the famine's end is trampled to death, thereby fulfilling Elisha's prophecy (2 Kgs. 7:2).

8:1–6 The Shunammite woman and the restoration of land. The woman from Shunem, whose son was revived by Elisha, is warned by the prophet to flee the coming famine (see note on 2 Kgs. 4:1–2). When she returns, she goes to the king to appeal to get her house and land back, maybe because it was confiscated by the king, neighbors, or family. When she arrives, Gehazi, Elisha's assistant, is in the midst of telling the king about Elisha's miraculous resurrection of her son, and her land is restored. Her brief story offers an analogy of the loss of property and possession suffered by modern refugees and immigrants.

telling the king how Elisha had restored a dead person to life, the woman whose son he had restored to life appealed to the king for her house and her land. Gehazi said, "My lord king, here is the woman, and here is her son whom Elisha restored to life." [6]When the king questioned the woman, she told him. So the king appointed an official for her, saying, "Restore all that was hers, together with all the revenue of the fields from the day that she left the land until now."

7 Elisha went to Damascus while King Ben-hadad of Aram was ill. When it was told him, "The man of God has come here," [8]the king said to Hazael, "Take a present with you and go to meet the man of God. Inquire of the LORD through him, whether I shall recover from this illness." [9]So Hazael went to meet him, taking a present with him, all kinds of goods of Damascus, forty camel loads. When he entered and stood before him, he said, "Your son King Ben-hadad of Aram has sent me to you, saying, 'Shall I recover from this illness?'" [10]Elisha said to him, "Go, say to him, 'You shall certainly recover,' but the LORD has shown me that he shall certainly die." [11]He fixed his gaze and stared at him to the point of embarrassment. Then the man of God wept. [12]Hazael asked, "Why does my lord weep?" He answered, "Because I know the evil that you will do to the people of Israel; you will set their fortresses on fire; you will kill their young men with the sword, dash in pieces their little ones, and rip up their pregnant women." [13]Hazael said, "What is your servant, who is a mere dog, that he should do this great thing?" Elisha answered, "The LORD has shown me that you are to be king over Aram." [14]Then he left Elisha and went to his master Ben-hadad,[q] who said to him, "What did Elisha say to you?" And he answered, "He told me that you would certainly recover." [15]But the next day he took the bedcover and dipped it in water and spread it over the king's face, until he died. And Hazael succeeded him.

16 In the fifth year of King Joram son of Ahab of Israel,[r] Jehoram son of King Jehoshaphat of Judah began to reign. [17]He was thirty-two years old when he became king, and he reigned eight years in Jerusalem. [18]He walked in the way of the kings of Israel, as the house of Ahab had done, for the daughter of Ahab was his wife. He did what was evil in the sight of the LORD. [19]Yet the LORD would not destroy Judah, for the sake of his servant David, since he had promised to give a lamp to him and to his descendants forever.

20 In his days Edom revolted against the rule of Judah and set up a king of their own. [21]Then Joram crossed over to Zair with all his chariots. He set out by night and attacked the Edomites and their chariot

q 8.14 Heb lacks *Ben-hadad* *r* 8.16 Gk Syr: Heb adds *Jehoshaphat being king of Judah,*

8:7–15 The death of Ben-hadad. 8:7–9 In contrast to the Israelite king, Ahaziah (2 Kgs. 1), the Aramean king, *Ben-hadad,* sends a messenger, *Hazael,* to Elisha to inquire whether he will recover. The sympathetic portrait of *Ben-hadad* contradicts previous descriptions as the king who tried to kidnap Elisha (2 Kgs. 6:8–13) and/or put Samaria under siege (2 Kgs. 6:24). **8:10** *You shall certainly recover . . . he shall certainly die.* Elisha gives a contradictory answer, which suggests that Hazael should lie to Ben-hadad. Later scribes correct Elisha's response as "Go, say, *not* you shall recover." **8:11–13** Elisha, foretelling Hazael's usurpation, states that he will commit vile atrocities as king, elucidating the horrors suffered by the vulnerable during warfare and colonization (cf. Amos 1:13; Hos. 13:16). Though Hazael replies that he is a *mere dog*—that is, a nobody, incapable of *this great thing*—his response shows how anyone, when given a little power, can succumb to using it to inflict great suffering. First Kgs. 19:15–18 has Elijah, not Elisha, appointing Hazael as king. **8:14–15** Elisha's oracle is confirmed as Ben-hadad recovers from the illness, only to die at the hands of Hazael, who either smothers him to death (*Ant.* 9.92) or applies a compress to help him recover. Biblical and ancient Near Eastern sources confirm the usurpation of Hazael, called the "son of nobody" in Assyrian sources, and his expansion of Aram's territories, including the colonization of parts of Israel and Judah (2 Kgs. 10:32–33; 13:3).

8:16–29 The reigns of Jehoram and Ahaziah. The reigns of Jehoram and his successor, Ahaziah, in Judah are described and assessed negatively. The repetition of *Ahab* (2 Kgs. 8:16, 18 [2x], 25, 27 [3x], 28, 29) indicates that these summaries serve as a prelude to 2 Kgs. 9, which describes the fall of the House of Ahab.

commanders who had surrounded him,[s] but his army fled home. [22]So Edom has been in revolt against the rule of Judah to this day. Libnah also revolted at the same time. [23]Now the rest of the acts of Joram and all that he did, are they not written in the Book of the Annals of the Kings of Judah? [24]So Joram slept with his ancestors and was buried with them in the city of David; his son Ahaziah succeeded him.

[25] In the twelfth year of King Joram son of Ahab of Israel, Ahaziah son of King Jehoram of Judah began to reign. [26]Ahaziah was twenty-two years old when he began to reign; he reigned one year in Jerusalem. His mother's name was Athaliah, a granddaughter of King Omri of Israel. [27]He also walked in the way of the house of Ahab, doing what was evil in the sight of the LORD, as the house of Ahab had done, for he was son-in-law to the house of Ahab.

[28] He went with Joram son of Ahab to wage war against King Hazael of Aram at Ramoth-gilead, where the Arameans wounded Joram. [29]King Joram returned to be healed in Jezreel of the wounds that the Arameans had inflicted on him at Ramah, when he fought against King Hazael of Aram. King Ahaziah son of Jehoram of Judah went down to see Joram son of Ahab in Jezreel because he was wounded.

9 Then the prophet Elisha called a member of the company of prophets and said to him, "Gird up your loins; take this flask of oil in your hand, and go to Ramoth-gilead. [2]When you arrive, look there for Jehu son of Jehoshaphat son of Nimshi; go in and get him to leave his companions, and take him into an inner chamber. [3]Then take the flask of oil, pour it on his head, and say, 'Thus says the LORD: I anoint you

king over Israel.' Then open the door and flee; do not linger."

[4] So the young man, the young prophet, went to Ramoth-gilead. [5]He arrived while the commanders of the army were in council, and he announced, "I have a message for you, commander." "For which one of us?" asked Jehu. "For you, commander." [6]So Jehu[t] got up and went inside; the young man poured the oil on his head, saying to him, "Thus says the LORD the God of Israel: I anoint you king over the people of the LORD, over Israel. [7]You shall strike down the house of your master Ahab, so that I may avenge on Jezebel the blood of my servants the prophets and the blood of all the servants of the LORD. [8]For the whole house of Ahab shall perish; I will cut off from Ahab every male, bond or free, in Israel. [9]I will make the house of Ahab like the house of Jeroboam son of Nebat and like the house of Baasha son of Ahijah. [10]The dogs shall eat Jezebel in the territory of Jezreel, and no one shall bury her." Then he opened the door and fled.

[11] When Jehu came back to his master's officers, they said to him, "Is everything all right? Why did that madman come to you?" He answered them, "You know the sort and how they babble." [12]They said, "Liar! Come on, tell us!" So he said, "This is just what he said to me: 'Thus says the LORD, I anoint you king over Israel.'" [13]Then hurriedly they all took their cloaks and spread them for him on the bare[u] steps, and they blew the trumpet and proclaimed, "Jehu is king."

[14] Thus Jehu son of Jehoshaphat son of Nimshi conspired against Joram. Joram with all Israel had been on guard at Ramoth-gilead against King Hazael of Aram, [15]but

s 8.21 Meaning of Heb uncertain   t 9.6 Heb *he*
u 9.13 Meaning of Heb uncertain

9:1–13 The anointing of Jehu. 9:1–7 In fulfillment of the prophecy in 1 Kgs. 19:16, Elisha sends a member of the company of prophets (see note on 2 Kgs. 2:3) to anoint Jehu, Israel's military commander, as the new king over Israel, seemingly encouraging him to launch a coup. **9:7–10** Elisha's proxy parallels the reign of *Ahab* to that of *Jeroboam* and *Baasha*, two kings who displeased YHWH and were removed (1 Kgs. 14:10–11; 16:1–7). Ahab's wife, *Jezebel*, is targeted as Elijah's earlier prophecy about the consumption of her corpse by dogs in Jezreel—the location of the vineyard of Naboth, which Jezebel and Ahab illegally seized (see note on 1 Kgs. 21:3–4)—is repeated. **9:11** *Madman* references the erratic behavior of prophets or their marginal status. It also alludes to Jehu as someone who drives like a *madman* (2 Kgs. 9:20). **9:12–13** Despite calling the prophet a madman, the soldiers instantly accept his word that Jehu is the new king, hinting that the coup was likely planned ahead of time.

9:14–29 The assassination of Joram and Ahaziah. 9:14–16 Jehu launches his coup at a moment

King Joram had returned to be healed in Jezreel of the wounds that the Arameans had inflicted on him when he fought against King Hazael of Aram. So Jehu said, "If this is your wish, then let no one slip out of the city to go and tell the news in Jezreel." [16]Then Jehu mounted his chariot and went to Jezreel, where Joram was lying ill. King Ahaziah of Judah had come down to visit Joram.

17 In Jezreel, the sentinel standing on the tower spied the company of Jehu arriving and said, "I see a company." Joram said, "Take a horseman; send him to meet them, and let him say, 'Is it peace?'" [18]So the horseman went to meet him; he said, "Thus says the king, 'Is it peace?'" Jehu responded, "What have you to do with peace? Fall in behind me." The sentinel reported, saying, "The messenger reached them, but he is not coming back." [19]Then he sent out a second horseman, who came to them and said, "Thus says the king, 'Is it peace?'" Jehu answered, "What have you to do with peace? Fall in behind me." [20]Again the sentinel reported, "He reached them, but he is not coming back. It looks like the driving of Jehu son of Nimshi, for he drives like a maniac."

21 Joram said, "Get ready." And they got his chariot ready. Then King Joram of Israel and King Ahaziah of Judah set out, each in his chariot, and went to meet Jehu; they met him at the property of Naboth the Jezreelite. [22]When Joram saw Jehu, he said, "Is it peace, Jehu?" He answered, "What peace can there be, so long as the many prostitutions[v]

and sorceries of your mother Jezebel continue?" [23]Then Joram reined about and fled, saying to Ahaziah, "Treason, Ahaziah!" [24]Jehu drew his bow with all his strength and shot Joram between the shoulders, so that the arrow pierced his heart, and he sank in his chariot. [25]Jehu said to his aide Bidkar, "Lift him out and throw him on the plot of ground belonging to Naboth the Jezreelite, for remember when you and I rode side by side behind his father Ahab how the LORD uttered this oracle against him: [26]'For the blood of Naboth and for the blood of his children that I saw yesterday, says the LORD, I swear I will repay you on this very plot of ground.' Now, therefore, lift him out and throw him on the plot of ground in accordance with the word of the LORD."

27 When King Ahaziah of Judah saw this, he fled in the direction of Beth-haggan. Jehu pursued him, saying, "Shoot him also!" And they shot him[w] in the chariot at the ascent to Gur, which is by Ibleam. Then he fled to Megiddo and died there. [28]His officers carried him in a chariot to Jerusalem and buried him in his tomb with his ancestors in the city of David.

29 In the eleventh year of Joram son of Ahab, Ahaziah began to reign over Judah.

30 When Jehu came to Jezreel, Jezebel heard of it; she painted her eyes and adorned her head and looked out of the window. [31]As Jehu entered the gate, she said, "Is it peace,

v 9.22 Or *idolatries*   w 9.27 Syr Vg Compare Gk: Heb lacks *and they shot him*

of weakness for the regime as King Joram is recovering from his wounds. **9:17–20** Repeating a three-fold pattern found elsewhere (e.g., 2 Kgs. 1:9, 11, 13; 2:2–3, 4–5, 6), Joram sends three soldiers to ask the charioteer, who is finally identified as Jehu by his maniacal driving as a *madman*, whether everything is shalom (see note on 2 Kgs. 9:22), only to have each soldier join the coup. **9:21** *Naboth the Jezreelite.* See note for 2 Kgs. 9:24–26. **9:22** *Is it peace, Jehu?* Joram, forced to confront Jehu himself, asks him whether it is shalom. Though usually translated as "peace," shalom connotes a state of health, completeness, order, and right relationship with God or between individuals. Different ideas about what constitutes shalom are evident. *Prostitutions and sorceries of . . . Jezebel.* Referring to Jezebel's pious devotion to her god, Baal, which the writers/editors characterize as idolatry and apostasy (see **"Idolatry (Hosea)," p. 2183**; see **"Apostasy," p. 1238**) and which they frequently liken to sexual offenses (Hos. 1–2; Jer. 3; Ezek. 16; 23), Jehu's charge has led to the image of Jezebel as a foreign temptress and a witch (Rev. 2:20–23; 2 Bar. 62:8; b. Sanh. 39B) as well as to the modern misogynistic and racist use of the term "Jezebel" to refer to a sexually promiscuous woman who is usually Black. **9:24–26** Deflecting blame, Jehu turns himself into the restorer of peace who fulfills Elijah's prophecies against Jezebel and Ahab (1 Kgs. 21). **9:27–29** *Ahaziah*, the king of Judah, who was related to and intermarried into Ahab's family, is also assassinated en route to visit his relative. **9:30–37 The death of Jezebel. 9:30** *Painted her eyes . . . adorned her head.* Reflective of the "woman at the window" motif in ancient Near Eastern art, Jezebel's preparations to die with dignity have been misread by interpreters as an attempt to seduce Jehu. **9:31** *Zimri, murderer.* Jezebel

Zimri, murderer of your master?" [32]He looked up to the window and said, "Who is on my side? Who?" Two or three eunuchs looked out at him. [33]He said, "Throw her down." So they threw her down; some of her blood spattered on the wall and on the horses, which trampled on her. [34]Then he went in and ate and drank; he said, "See to that cursed woman and bury her, for she is a king's daughter." [35]But when they went to bury her, they found no more of her than the skull and the feet and the palms of her hands. [36]When they came back and told him, he said, "This is the word of the LORD, which he spoke by his servant Elijah the Tishbite: In the territory of Jezreel the dogs shall eat the flesh of Jezebel; [37]the corpse of Jezebel shall be like dung on the field in the territory of Jezreel, so that no one can say, 'This is Jezebel.'"

10 Now Ahab had seventy sons in Samaria. So Jehu wrote letters and sent them to Samaria, to the rulers of the city,[x] to the elders, and to the guardians of the sons of[y] Ahab, saying, [2]"Since your master's sons are with you and you have at your disposal chariots and horses, a fortified city, and weapons, [3]select the son of your master who is the best qualified, set him on his father's throne, and fight for your master's house." [4]But they were utterly terrified and said, "Look, two kings could not withstand him; how then can we stand?" [5]So the steward of the palace and the governor of the city, along with the elders and the guardians, sent word to Jehu, "We are your servants; we will do anything you say. We will not make anyone king; do whatever you think right." [6]Then he wrote them a

second letter, saying, "If you are on my side and if you are ready to obey me, take the heads of your master's sons and come to me at Jezreel tomorrow at this time." Now the king's sons, seventy persons, were with the leaders of the city, who were charged with their upbringing. [7]When the letter reached them, they took the king's sons and killed them, seventy persons; they put their heads in baskets and sent them to him at Jezreel. [8]When the messenger came and told him, "They have brought the heads of the king's sons," he said, "Lay them in two heaps at the entrance of the gate until the morning." [9]Then in the morning when he went out, he stood and said to all the people, "You are innocent. It was I who conspired against my master and killed him, but who struck down all these? [10]Know, then, that there shall fall to the earth nothing of the word of the LORD that the LORD spoke concerning the house of Ahab, for the LORD has done what he said through his servant Elijah." [11]So Jehu killed all who were left of the house of Ahab in Jezreel, all his leaders, close friends, and priests, until he left him no survivor.

12 Then he set out and went to Samaria. On the way, when he was at Beth-eked of the Shepherds, [13]Jehu met relatives of King Ahaziah of Judah and said, "Who are you?" They answered, "We are kin of Ahaziah; we have come down to visit the royal princes and the sons of the queen mother." [14]He said, "Take them alive." They took them alive and slaughtered them at the pit of Beth-eked, forty-two in all; he spared none of them.

15 When he left there, he met Jehonadab

x 10.1 Lucianic Vg: Heb *of Jezreel*   y 10.1 Gk: Heb lacks *of the sons of*

mockingly insinuates that Jehu will be like Zimri, another usurper who was overthrown seven days later (1 Kgs. 16). **9:32–37** Portrayed as the archenemy and opposite of Elijah, Jezebel—the foreign, female, royal devotee of Baal—is given an opposite conclusion to that of Elijah. While Elijah ascends to heaven (2 Kgs. 2), Jezebel is thrown down, trampled by horses, and eaten by dogs, becoming nothing more than *dung*, with only her *skull*, her *feet*, and the *palms of her hands* remaining to speak of her presence. Her tortured body invites a counter-reading and elucidates the undercurrent of misogyny that runs throughout the biblical text. **10:1–17** The purge of Ahab's descendants and the Baal cult. **10:1** *Seventy* is a symbolic number connoting totality (Judg. 9:5; 12:14). **10:8** *Two heaps at the entrance of the gate.* The severed heads of Ahab's seventy sons are displayed at the gate as a gruesome warning to the royalists. **10:9–10** Jehu declares the people innocent of the coup, hinting that they will not suffer retaliation for their assassinations. Jehu again justifies his coup as the fulfillment of Elijah's prophecy against Ahab and his kin. **10:14** *Forty-two* is a number associated with death. Elisha calls on two she-bears to kill forty-two taunting children (2 Kgs. 2:24), and forty-two judges of the dead are also mentioned in the Egyptian Book of the Dead. **10:15–16** *Jehonadab son of Rechab.* Signifying YHWH's approval

son of Rechab coming to meet him; he greeted him and said to him, "Is your heart as true to mine as mine is to yours?"[z] Jehonadab answered, "It is." Jehu said,[a] "If it is, give me your hand." So he gave him his hand. Jehu took him up with him into the chariot. [16]He said, "Come with me and see my zeal for the Lord." So he[b] had him ride in his chariot. [17]When he came to Samaria, he killed all who were left to Ahab in Samaria, until he had wiped them out according to the word of the Lord that he spoke to Elijah.

18 Then Jehu assembled all the people and said to them, "Ahab offered Baal small service, but Jehu will offer much more. [19]Now therefore summon to me all the prophets of Baal, all his servants, and all his priests; let none be missing, for I have a great sacrifice to offer to Baal; whoever is missing shall not live." But Jehu was acting with cunning in order to destroy the servants of Baal. [20]Jehu decreed, "Sanctify a solemn assembly for Baal." So they proclaimed it. [21]Jehu sent word throughout all Israel; all the servants of Baal came, so that there was no one left who did not come. They entered the temple of Baal until the temple of Baal was filled from wall to wall. [22]He said to the keeper of the wardrobe, "Bring out the vestments for all the servants of Baal." So he brought out the vestments for them. [23]Then Jehu entered the temple of Baal with Jehonadab son of Rechab; he said to the servants of Baal, "Search and see that there is no servant of the Lord here among you but only servants of Baal." [24]Then they proceeded to offer sacrifices and burnt offerings.

Now Jehu had stationed eighty men outside, saying, "Whoever allows any of those to escape whom I deliver into your hands shall forfeit his life." [25]As soon as he had finished presenting the burnt offering, Jehu said to the guards and to the officers, "Come in and kill them; let no one escape." So they put them to the sword. The guards and the officers threw them out and then went into the citadel of the temple of Baal. [26]They brought out the pillar[c] that was in the temple of Baal and burned it. [27]Then they demolished the pillar of Baal and destroyed the temple of Baal and made it a latrine to this day.

28 Thus Jehu wiped out Baal from Israel. [29]But Jehu did not turn aside from the sins of Jeroboam son of Nebat that he caused Israel to commit: the golden calves that were in Bethel and in Dan. [30]The Lord said to Jehu, "Because you have done well in carrying out what I consider right and in accordance with all that was in my heart have dealt with the house of Ahab, your sons of the fourth generation shall sit on the throne of Israel." [31]But Jehu was not careful to follow the law of the Lord the God of Israel with all his heart; he did not turn from the sins of Jeroboam that he caused Israel to commit.

32 In those days the Lord began to trim off parts of Israel. Hazael defeated them throughout the territory of Israel: [33]from the Jordan eastward, all the land of Gilead, the Gadites, the Reubenites, and the Manassites, from Aroer, which is by the Wadi Arnon, that is, Gilead and Bashan. [34]Now the

z 10.15 Gk: Heb *Is it right with your heart, as my heart is with your heart?* a 10.15 Gk: Heb lacks *Jehu said* b 10.16 Gk Syr Tg: Heb *they* c 10.26 Gk Vg Syr Tg: Heb *pillars*

of the coup, Jehonadab meets Jehu en route. The Rechabites ("rechab" means "chariot"), who are described as a nomadic, ascetic group (Jer. 35), might be devotees of YHWH, the "chariot God" (2 Kgs. 2:12; 6:17).

10:18–36 Annihilation of the Baal cult and the assessment of Jehu's reign. 10:13–27 The cult of Baal, an ancient Near Eastern storm god who is worshiped by Jezebel and very similar to and therefore a competitor of YHWH, is destroyed as Jehu gathers the Baal officials on the pretense of celebration and then slaughters them en masse as a kind of human sacrifice to YHWH. See **"Baal," p. 489**. The repetition of *servant(s)* (vv. 19 [2x], 21, 22, 23 [3x]) from "to serve" ("'eved"), which sounds like "to destroy" ("'avad"), hints at Jehu's real intentions. As Jezebel is turned into dung, the temple of her god, Baal, is turned into a *latrine*. Jehu's actions show how religion and religious ideas are used to justify violence. **10:28–36** Despite his zealous actions, Jehu is given an ambivalent assessment. Though his dynasty will continue for four generations, he is said to have been incomplete in his religious fidelity (v. 31), continuing the *sins of Jeroboam* (1 Kgs. 12), and suffers the loss of territories during his reign (v. 32). This aligns historically with the negative economic and political ramifications that followed his coup, as his assassinations severed important political alliances with Judah and Tyre.

rest of the acts of Jehu, all that he did, and all his power, are they not written in the Book of the Annals of the Kings of Israel? ³⁵So Jehu slept with his ancestors, and they buried him in Samaria. His son Jehoahaz succeeded him. ³⁶The time that Jehu reigned over Israel in Samaria was twenty-eight years.

11 Now when Athaliah, Ahaziah's mother, saw that her son was dead, she set about to destroy all the royal family. ²But Jehosheba, King Joram's daughter, Ahaziah's sister, took Joash son of Ahaziah and stole him away from among the king's children who were about to be killed; she put*ᵈ* him and his nurse in a bedroom. Thus she*ᵉ* hid him from Athaliah, so that he was not killed; ³he remained with her six years, hidden in the house of the Lord, while Athaliah reigned over the land.

4 But in the seventh year Jehoiada summoned the captains of the Carites and of the guards and had them come to him in the house of the Lord. He made a covenant with them and put them under oath in the house of the Lord; then he showed them the king's son. ⁵He commanded them, "This is what you are to do: one-third of you, those who go off duty on the Sabbath and guard the king's house ⁶(another third being at the gate Sur and a third at the gate behind the guards), shall guard the palace, ⁷and your two divisions that come on duty in force on the Sabbath and guard the house of the Lord*ᶠ* ⁸shall surround the king, each with weapons in hand, and whoever approaches the ranks is to be killed. Be with the king in his comings and goings."

9 The captains did according to all that the priest Jehoiada commanded; each brought his men who were to go off duty on the Sabbath, with those who were to come on duty on the Sabbath, and came to the priest Jehoiada. ¹⁰The priest delivered to the captains the spears and shields that had been King David's, which were in the house of the Lord; ¹¹the guards stood, every man with his weapons in his hand, from the south side of the house to the north side of the house, around the altar and the house, to guard the king on every side. ¹²Then he brought out the king's son, put the crown on him, and gave him the covenant; they proclaimed him king and anointed him; they clapped their hands and shouted, "Long live the king!"

13 When Athaliah heard the noise of the guard and of the people, she went into the house of the Lord to the people; ¹⁴when she looked, there was the king standing by the pillar, according to custom, with the captains and the trumpeters beside the king, and all the people of the land rejoicing and blowing trumpets. Athaliah tore her clothes and cried, "Treason! Treason!" ¹⁵Then the

d 11.2 Heb lacks *she put*   *e* 11.2 Gk Syr Vg: Heb *they*   *f* 11.7 Heb *the* Lord *to the king*

11:1–3 The reign of Athaliah in Judah. 11:1 The reign of the only queen of Judah—Athaliah, either the daughter (2 Kgs. 8:18) or sister (2 Kgs. 8:26; 2 Chr. 22:2) of Ahab, the hated husband of the even more hated Jezebel, to whom Athaliah is paralleled—begins not with the expected introductory overview but by the shocking statement that she tried *to destroy all the royal family.* This unexplained action, which threatens the promises God made to David (2 Sam. 7), portrays Athaliah as a mad, murdering mother. However, it would have been unlikely for Athaliah, especially as a woman, to obtain the throne without the support of powerful factions. **11:2–3** Befitting the hero myth, a special baby boy, *Joash,* like Moses (Exod. 2), is secreted away and hidden in the temple by *Jehosheba,* the sister of the recently assassinated Ahaziah (2 Kgs. 11:2), the daughter of Jehoram, and likely the daughter of Athaliah.

11:4–21 The coup and end of Athaliah's reign. 11:4–8 When *Joash* is seven years old, *Jehoiada,* the priest who might have been the husband of Jehosheba (2 Chr. 22:11), plans a coup with the help of the guards and the *Carites,* also known as Cherethites (1 Kgs. 1:38), a group of mercenary bodyguards associated with David (1 Sam. 30:14; 2 Sam. 8:18; 15:18; 20:7). **11:9–12** Jehoiada and his allies execute the coup by suddenly crowning Joash when he turns seven. The secrecy of the planning, the mention of mysterious covenants or agreements, the heavy protection surrounding the royal child, and the use of old weaponry, *the spears and shields that had been King David's,* hint at political intrigue and suggest that Athaliah had more support than the text lets on. **11:13–16** Athaliah is caught unawares by the coup and the illegal coronation at the temple, which she rightly deems as *treason.* Before she can say any more or rouse her supporters, she is taken out of the temple and

priest Jehoiada commanded the captains who were set over the army, "Bring her out between the ranks and kill with the sword anyone who follows her." For the priest said, "Let her not be killed in the house of the LORD." [16]So they laid hands on her; she went through the horses' entrance to the king's house, and there she was put to death.

17 Jehoiada made a covenant between the LORD and the king and people, that they should be the LORD's people; also between the king and the people. [18]Then all the people of the land went to the house of Baal and tore it down; his altars and his images they broke in pieces, and they killed Mattan, the priest of Baal, in front of the altars. The priest posted guards over the house of the LORD. [19]He took the captains, the Carites, the guards, and all the people of the land; then they brought the king down from the house of the LORD, marching through the gate of the guards to the king's house. He took his seat on the throne of the kings. [20]So all the people of the land rejoiced, and the city was quiet after Athaliah had been killed with the sword at the king's house.

21 [g]Jehoash was seven years old when he began to reign.

12 In the seventh year of Jehu, Jehoash began to reign; he reigned forty years in Jerusalem. His mother's name was Zibiah of Beer-sheba. [2]Jehoash did what was right in the sight of the LORD all his

days because the priest Jehoiada instructed him. [3]Nevertheless, the high places were not taken away; the people continued to sacrifice and make offerings on the high places.

4 Jehoash said to the priests, "All the silver offered as sacred donations that is brought into the house of the LORD—the census tax, personal redemption payments, and silver from voluntary offerings brought into the house of the LORD—[5]let the priests receive from each of the donors, and let them repair the house wherever any need of repairs is discovered." [6]But by the twenty-third year of King Jehoash the priests had made no repairs on the house. [7]Therefore King Jehoash summoned the priest Jehoiada with the other priests and said to them, "Why are you not repairing the house? Now therefore do not accept any more silver from your donors but hand it over for the repair of the house." [8]So the priests agreed that they would neither accept more silver from the people nor repair the house.

9 Then the priest Jehoiada took a chest, made a hole in its lid, and set it beside the altar on the right side as one entered the house of the LORD; the priests who guarded the threshold put in it all the silver that was brought into the house of the LORD. [10]Whenever they saw that there was a great deal of silver in the chest, the king's secretary and

g 11.21 12.1 in Heb

---

assassinated. **11:17–21** The priest, *Jehoiada*, likely alongside his royal wife, Jehosheba, secures power with the help of the *people of the land*, a group mentioned elsewhere in the Bible (2 Kgs. 21:24; 24:14; 25:12; Jer. 34:18–20; Ezek. 22:29) and whose identity is debated. To secure the new rule and give it a semblance of legitimacy, they make another mysterious *covenant* and tear down the altars to Baal, though there is no mention that Athaliah, whose name contains the theophoric suffix "ya" for YHWH, was a worshiper of Baal. Despite ruling for six years, the absence of a concluding assessment further delegitimizes Athaliah's reign.

12:1–3 The reign of Joash in Judah. 12:1 In contrast to Athaliah, her grandson, Joash, who begins his reign as a child, is given an introductory overview. **12:2** *Because the priest Jehoiada instructed him.* Because the relative pronoun, translated as "because," is ambiguous, it is unclear whether 12:2 means that Joash was well-behaved because of his earlier training by *Jehoiada*, the priest, or whether his good behavior was limited to the time under *Jehoiada*'s supervision. Second Chr. 24:17–22 takes the latter view, stating that after Jehoiada's death, Joash was swayed by impious officials. **12:3** *High places were not taken away.* Local altars that are finally removed by Hezekiah (2 Kgs. 18:4).

12:4–16 Temple renovations. 12:4–8 Joash, who was hidden in the temple, tries to repair it with donations but is thwarted by the priests, who seemingly are keeping the money instead of using it for repairs. The priests likely became accustomed to having the run of the country, as Joash was only seven when he began his rule and therefore likely served as puppet king to Jehoiada. **12:9–16** Because the priests seemingly cannot be trusted with handling the funds for the temple

the high priest went up, cast the silver that was found in the house of the Lord into ingots, and counted it. ¹¹They gave the silver that was weighed out into the hands of the workers who had the oversight of the house of the Lord; then they paid it out to the carpenters and the builders who worked on the house of the Lord, ¹²to the masons and the stonecutters, as well as to buy timber and quarried stone for making repairs on the house of the Lord, as well as for any outlay for repairs of the house. ¹³But for the house of the Lord no basins of silver, snuffers, bowls, trumpets, or any vessels of gold or of silver were made from the silver that was brought into the house of the Lord, ¹⁴for that was given to the workers who were repairing the house of the Lord with it. ¹⁵They did not ask an accounting from those into whose hand they delivered the silver to pay out to the workers, for they dealt honestly. ¹⁶The silver from the guilt offerings and the silver from the sin offerings was not brought into the house of the Lord; it belonged to the priests.

17 At that time King Hazael of Aram went up, fought against Gath, and took it. But when Hazael set his face to go up against Jerusalem, ¹⁸King Jehoash of Judah took all the votive gifts that Jehoshaphat, Jehoram, and Ahaziah, his ancestors, the kings of Judah, had dedicated, as well as his own votive gifts, all the gold that was found in the treasuries of the house of the Lord and of the king's house, and sent these to King Hazael of Aram. Then Hazael withdrew from Jerusalem.

19 Now the rest of the acts of Joash and all that he did, are they not written in the Book of the Annals of the Kings of Judah? ²⁰His servants arose, devised a conspiracy, and killed Joash in the house of Millo, on the way that goes down to Silla. ²¹It was Jozacar son of Shimeath and Jehozabad son of Shomer, his servants, who struck him down, so that he died. He was buried with his ancestors in the city of David; then his son Amaziah succeeded him.

13 In the twenty-third year of King Joash son of Ahaziah of Judah, Jehoahaz son of Jehu began to reign over Israel in Samaria; he reigned seventeen years. ²He did what was evil in the sight of the Lord and followed the sins of Jeroboam son of Nebat that he caused Israel to sin; he did not depart from them. ³The anger of the Lord was kindled against Israel, so he gave them repeatedly into the hand of King Hazael of Aram, then into the hand of Ben-hadad son of Hazael. ⁴But Jehoahaz entreated the Lord, and the Lord heeded him, for he saw the oppression of Israel, how the king of Aram oppressed them. ⁵Therefore the Lord gave Israel a savior, so they escaped from the hand of the Arameans, and the people of Israel lived in their homes as formerly. ⁶Nevertheless, they did not depart from the sins of the house of Jeroboam that he caused Israel to sin but walked*ᵇ* in them; the sacred pole*ⁱ* also remained in Samaria. ⁷So Jehoahaz was left with an army of not more than fifty horsemen, ten chariots,

b 13.6 Gk Syr Tg Vg: Heb *he walked*   *i* 13.6 Or *Asherah*

repairs, the funds are secured in a box and turned over directly to the workers. The repetition of *silver* hints at conflicts between the crown and priests over the money.

12:17–18 The Aramean attack. Criticism of Joash can be detected as Jerusalem is attacked by Hazael of Aram, and Joash is forced to bribe him by raiding the temple he has just refurbished, nullifying the repairs and the major accomplishment of his reign.

12:19–21 The assassination. Hinting at court intrigue, Joash's premature death from an assassination offers an ignoble end to the reign of the special royal child saved from Athaliah's murderous rampage. The naming of the two assassins suggests that they might have been prominent individuals and that Joash's death might have been related to his clash with the priests (cf. 2 Chr. 24:22–25).

13:1–9 The reign of Jehoahaz in Israel. 13:1–2 Jehoahaz of Israel is charged with doing *evil in the sight of the Lord* and committing the *sins of Jeroboam*, the first king of the north (1 Kgs. 12). **13:3** Indicative of divine displeasure, Israel is attacked by Aram. **13:4–5** Likely a later insertion, perhaps referring to the lifting of the Aramean siege in 2 Kgs. 6:24–7:20 or following the cycle of sin-punishment-entreaty-rescue found in Judges. **13:6** A *sacred pole*, or Asherah, was a fertility symbol that resembled either a living tree or the goddess Asherah, who, according to inscriptions from Kuntillet 'Ajrud and Khirbet el-Qom, is said to be a consort of YHWH.

and ten thousand footmen, for the king of Aram had destroyed them and made them like the dust at threshing. ⁸Now the rest of the acts of Jehoahaz and all that he did, including his might, are they not written in the Book of the Annals of the Kings of Israel? ⁹So Jehoahaz slept with his ancestors, and they buried him in Samaria; then his son Joash succeeded him.

10 In the thirty-seventh year of King Joash of Judah, Jehoash son of Jehoahaz began to reign over Israel in Samaria; he reigned sixteen years. ¹¹He also did what was evil in the sight of the LORD; he did not depart from all the sins of Jeroboam son of Nebat that he caused Israel to sin, but he walked in them. ¹²Now the rest of the acts of Joash and all that he did, as well as the might with which he fought against King Amaziah of Judah, are they not written in the Book of the Annals of the Kings of Israel? ¹³So Joash slept with his ancestors, and Jeroboam sat upon his throne; Joash was buried in Samaria with the kings of Israel.

14 Now when Elisha had fallen sick with the illness of which he was to die, King Joash of Israel went down to him and wept before him, crying, "My father, my father! The chariots of Israel and its horsemen!" ¹⁵Elisha said to him, "Take a bow and arrows," so he took a bow and arrows. ¹⁶Then he said to the king of Israel, "Draw the bow," and he drew it. Elisha laid his hands on the king's hands. ¹⁷Then he said, "Open the window eastward," and he opened it. Elisha said, "Shoot," and he shot. Then

he said, "The LORD's arrow of victory, the arrow of victory over Aram! For you shall fight the Arameans in Aphek until you have made an end of them." ¹⁸He continued, "Take the arrows," and he took them. He said to the king of Israel, "Strike the ground with them"; he struck three times and stopped. ¹⁹Then the man of God was angry with him and said, "You should have struck five or six times; then you would have struck down Aram until you had made an end of it, but now you will strike down Aram only three times."

20 So Elisha died, and they buried him. Now bands of Moabites used to invade the land in the spring of the year. ²¹As a man was being buried, a marauding band was seen and the man was thrown into the grave of Elisha; as soon as the man touched the bones of Elisha, he came to life and stood on his feet.

22 Now King Hazael of Aram oppressed Israel all the days of Jehoahaz. ²³But the LORD was gracious to them and had compassion on them; he turned toward them because of his covenant with Abraham, Isaac, and Jacob and would not destroy them, nor has he banished them from his presence until now.

24 When King Hazael of Aram died, his son Ben-hadad succeeded him. ²⁵Then Jehoash son of Jehoahaz took again from Ben-hadad son of Hazael the towns that he had taken from his father Jehoahaz in war. Three times Joash defeated him and recovered the towns of Israel.

13:10–13 The reign of Jehoash in Israel. The reign of Jehoash, or Joash, of Israel is assessed negatively. His conflict with Ahaziah of Judah is likely a later insertion and is repeated verbatim in 2 Kgs. 14:15–16. **13:14–21 The death of Elisha. 13:14** Joash, surprisingly, appears at Elisha's deathbed. He refers to Elisha as *father* and references *the chariots of Israel and its horsemen*, the same phrase uttered by Elisha during Elijah's ascent (2 Kgs. 2:12), which might have been an honorific title likening these prophets to the divine forces protecting Israel (see note on 2 Kgs. 2:11). **13:15–19** Maybe connected to belomancy, or divination by arrows (cf. Ezek. 21:21), Elisha offers a two-part departing gift by ordering Joash to shoot an *arrow of victory* out of the window and then to strike the ground with the arrows. Angered by the weak completion of his command, Elisha declares that Aram will be defeated only three times—the number of times Joash struck the ground. This comports historically, as Aramean hegemony in the Levant waxed and waned in the ninth century with the rise of Assyria. **13:20–21** In contrast to the ascent of his mentor, Elijah, the death and burial of Elisha are anticlimactic. As a result, another miracle is added whereby a corpse thrown into the gravesite of Elisha comes back to life by touching the prophet's bones. **13:22–25 Israel and Aram. 13:23** *Covenant with Abraham, Isaac, and Jacob.* This reference might serve to explain the diminishment of the Aramean threat during the reigns of the impious northern kings Jehoahaz and Joash. **13:25** *Three times.* In fulfillment of Elisha's departing gift to Joash.

14

In the second year of King Joash son of Joahaz of Israel, King Amaziah son of Joash of Judah began to reign. ²He was twenty-five years old when he began to reign, and he reigned twenty-nine years in Jerusalem. His mother's name was Jehoaddin of Jerusalem. ³He did what was right in the sight of the LORD, yet not like his ancestor David; in all things he did as his father Joash had done. ⁴But the high places were not removed; the people still sacrificed and made offerings on the high places. ⁵As soon as the royal power was firmly in his hand, he killed his servants who had murdered his father the king. ⁶But he did not put to death the children of the murderers, according to what is written in the book of the law of Moses, where the LORD commanded, "The parents shall not be put to death for the children or the children be put to death for the parents, but all shall be put to death for their own sins."

7 He killed ten thousand Edomites in the Valley of Salt and took Sela by storm; he called it Jokthe-el, which is its name to this day.

8 Then Amaziah sent messengers to King Jehoash son of Jehoahaz son of Jehu of Israel, saying, "Come, let us look one another in the face." ⁹King Jehoash of Israel sent word to King Amaziah of Judah, "A thornbush on Lebanon sent to a cedar on Lebanon, saying, 'Give your daughter to my son for a wife,' but a wild animal of Lebanon passed by and trampled down the thornbush. ¹⁰You have indeed defeated Edom, and your heart has lifted you up. Be content with your glory and stay at home, for why should you provoke trouble so that you fall, you and Judah with you?"

11 But Amaziah would not listen. So King Jehoash of Israel went up; he and King Amaziah of Judah faced one another in battle at Beth-shemesh, which belongs to Judah. ¹²Judah was defeated by Israel; everyone fled home. ¹³King Jehoash of Israel captured King Amaziah of Judah son of Jehoash son of Ahaziah at Beth-shemesh; he came to Jerusalem and broke down the wall of Jerusalem from the Ephraim Gate to the Corner Gate, a distance of four hundred cubits. ¹⁴He seized all the gold and silver and all the vessels that were found in the house of the LORD and in the treasuries of the king's house, as well as hostages; then he returned to Samaria.

15 Now the rest of the acts that Jehoash did, his might, and how he fought with King Amaziah of Judah, are they not written in the Book of the Annals of the Kings of Israel? ¹⁶Jehoash slept with his ancestors and was buried in Samaria with the kings of Israel; then his son Jeroboam succeeded him.

17 King Amaziah son of Joash of Judah lived fifteen years after the death of King Jehoash son of Jehoahaz of Israel. ¹⁸Now the rest of the deeds of Amaziah, are they not written in the Book of the Annals of the Kings of Judah? ¹⁹They made a conspiracy against him in Jerusalem, and he fled to Lachish. But they sent after him to Lachish and killed him there. ²⁰They brought him on horses; he was buried in Jerusalem with his ancestors in the city of David. ²¹All the people of Judah took Azariah, who was sixteen years old, and made him king to succeed his

---

14:1–22 The reign of Amaziah in Judah. 14:1–4 Amaziah, the son of the assassinated Joash (2 Kgs. 12), ascends the throne and is given a generally positive assessment, though he is faulted for the lack of removal of the high places. **14:5–6** *Book of the law of Moses.* One of Amaziah's first acts is to put to death his father's murderers, though their children are spared, following *the book of the law of Moses.* What this book entails, its relationship to the laws in Deuteronomy, and whether it is a retrojection remain unclear. **14:7** *Killed ten thousand Edomites.* Perhaps an attempt to extend Judah's influence or a setup for Judah's confrontation with Israel. **14:8** *Look one another in the face.* Connoting either a confrontation or an attempt to establish a more equitable relationship, such as an alliance. **14:9–10** Jehoash, the king of Israel, replies to Amaziah's request with an insulting parable that likens Judah to an arrogant thistle, a plant frequently found in Mesopotamian and biblical parables (Judg. 9:14–15), that tries to marry a great cedar (i.e., Israel), only to be trampled by a wild animal. **14:11–14** A battle ensues between the two kingdoms, and the more powerful northern kingdom triumphs as Jehoash takes Amaziah hostage, breaks down a *wall of Jerusalem*, and seizes *all the gold and silver and all the vessels* in the temple and the palace. **14:15–22** Like his father's, Amaziah's reign begins well, only to end disastrously with a military invasion, loss of wealth, and an assassination, perhaps even spearheaded by the same group who murdered his father, Joash (2 Kgs. 12).

father Amaziah. ²²He rebuilt Elath and restored it to Judah, after King Amaziah[j] slept with his ancestors.

23 In the fifteenth year of King Amaziah son of Joash of Judah, King Jeroboam son of Joash of Israel began to reign in Samaria; he reigned forty-one years. ²⁴He did what was evil in the sight of the Lord; he did not depart from all the sins of Jeroboam son of Nebat that he caused Israel to sin. ²⁵He restored the border of Israel from Lebo-hamath as far as the Sea of the Arabah, according to the word of the Lord, the God of Israel, which he spoke by his servant Jonah son of Amittai, the prophet who was from Gath-hepher. ²⁶For the Lord saw that the distress of Israel was very bitter; there was no one left, bond or free, and no one to help Israel. ²⁷But the Lord had not said that he would blot out the name of Israel from under heaven, so he saved them by the hand of Jeroboam son of Joash.

28 Now the rest of the acts of Jeroboam and all that he did, and his might, how he fought, and how he recovered for Israel Damascus and Hamath, which had belonged to Judah, are they not written in the Book of the Annals of the Kings of Israel? ²⁹Jeroboam slept with his ancestors, the kings of Israel; his son Zechariah succeeded him.

15 In the twenty-seventh year of King Jeroboam of Israel, King Azariah son of Amaziah of Judah began to reign. ²He was sixteen years old when he began to reign, and he reigned fifty-two years in Jerusalem. His mother's name was Jecoliah of Jerusalem. ³He did what was right in the sight of the Lord, just as his father Amaziah had done. ⁴Nevertheless, the high places

were not taken away; the people still sacrificed and made offerings on the high places. ⁵The Lord struck the king so that he had a defiling skin disease to the day of his death and lived in a separate house. Jotham the king's son was in charge of the palace, governing the people of the land. ⁶Now the rest of the acts of Azariah and all that he did, are they not written in the Book of the Annals of the Kings of Judah? ⁷Azariah slept with his ancestors; they buried him with his ancestors in the city of David; his son Jotham succeeded him.

8 In the thirty-eighth year of King Azariah of Judah, Zechariah son of Jeroboam reigned over Israel in Samaria six months. ⁹He did what was evil in the sight of the Lord, as his ancestors had done. He did not depart from the sins of Jeroboam son of Nebat that he caused Israel to sin. ¹⁰Shallum son of Jabesh conspired against him and struck him down in Ibleam[k] and killed him and reigned in place of him. ¹¹Now the rest of the deeds of Zechariah are written in the Book of the Annals of the Kings of Israel. ¹²This was the promise of the Lord that he gave to Jehu, "Your sons shall sit on the throne of Israel to the fourth generation." And so it happened.

13 Shallum son of Jabesh began to reign in the thirty-ninth year of King Uzziah of Judah; he reigned one month in Samaria. ¹⁴Then Menahem son of Gadi came up from Tirzah and came to Samaria; he struck down Shallum son of Jabesh in Samaria and killed him; he reigned in place of him. ¹⁵Now the rest of the deeds of Shallum, including the conspiracy that he made, are written in

j 14.22 Heb *the king*   k 15.10 Lucianic: Meaning of Heb uncertain

14:23–29 The reign of Jeroboam II in Israel. 14:23–24 While Amaziah rules in Judah, Jeroboam comes to the throne in Israel and, as expected of northern kings, is assessed negatively. **14:25** *Jonah son of Amittai, the prophet.* The list of Jeroboam's accomplishments undercuts the negative assessment and is said to be the result of the prophet *Jonah*, whose name was likely borrowed for the main character in the book of Jonah.
15:1–7 The reign of Azariah in Judah. Also known as Uzziah (2 Kgs. 15:13, 30, 32, 34; 2 Chr. 26; 27:2; Isa. 1:1; 6:1), Azariah's reign over Judah is assessed positively. Despite his lengthy reign, only his *skin disease* is mentioned. The Chronicler explains his disease as the result of pride (2 Chr. 26:16–20), and postbiblical traditions note that the earthquake mentioned during his reign (Amos 1:1; Zech. 14:5) was caused by YHWH's wrath striking the king (*Ant.* 9.225; cf. Targum to Isa. 28:2).
15:8–31 The reigns of Zechariah, Shallum, Menahem, Pekahiah, and Pekah in Israel. 15:8–12 The northern kingdom of Israel is marked by instability, as Zechariah—who, like all northern kings, is assessed negatively—reigns for only six months before he is assassinated by Shallum in a coup. **15:13–15** Shallum, also assessed negatively, replaces Zechariah on the throne, only to be assassinated

the Book of the Annals of the Kings of Israel. [16]At that time Menahem sacked Tiphsah, all who were in it and its territory from Tirzah on; because they did not open it to him, he sacked it. He ripped open all the pregnant women in it.

17 In the thirty-ninth year of King Azariah of Judah, Menahem son of Gadi began to reign over Israel; he reigned ten years in Samaria. [18]He did what was evil in the sight of the LORD; he did not depart all his days from any of the sins of Jeroboam son of Nebat that he caused Israel to sin. [19]King Pul of Assyria came against the land; Menahem gave Pul a thousand talents of silver, so that he might help him confirm his hold on the royal power. [20]Menahem exacted the silver from Israel, that is, from all the wealthy, fifty shekels of silver from each one, to give to the king of Assyria. So the king of Assyria turned back and did not stay there in the land. [21]Now the rest of the deeds of Menahem and all that he did, are they not written in the Book of the Annals of the Kings of Israel? [22]Menahem slept with his ancestors, and his son Pekahiah succeeded him.

23 In the fiftieth year of King Azariah of Judah, Pekahiah son of Menahem began to reign over Israel in Samaria; he reigned two years. [24]He did what was evil in the sight of the LORD; he did not turn away from the sins of Jeroboam son of Nebat that he caused Israel to sin. [25]Pekah son of Remaliah, his captain, conspired against him with fifty of the Gileadites and attacked him in Samaria, in the citadel of the palace along with Argob and Arieh; he killed him and reigned in place of him. [26]Now the rest of the deeds of Pekahiah and all that he did are written in the Book of the Annals of the Kings of Israel.

27 In the fifty-second year of King Azariah of Judah, Pekah son of Remaliah began to reign over Israel in Samaria; he reigned twenty years. [28]He did what was evil in the sight of the LORD; he did not depart from the sins of Jeroboam son of Nebat that he caused Israel to sin.

29 In the days of King Pekah of Israel, King Tiglath-pileser of Assyria came and captured Ijon, Abel-beth-maacah, Janoah, Kedesh, Hazor, Gilead, and Galilee, all the land of Naphtali, and he carried the people captive to Assyria. [30]Then Hoshea son of Elah made a conspiracy against Pekah son of Remaliah, attacked him, and killed him; he reigned in place of him, in the twentieth year of Jotham son of Uzziah. [31]Now the rest of the acts of Pekah and all that he did are written in the Book of the Annals of the Kings of Israel.

32 In the second year of King Pekah son of Remaliah of Israel, King Jotham son of Uzziah of Judah began to reign. [33]He was twenty-five years old when he began to reign, and he reigned sixteen years in Jerusalem. His mother's name was Jerusha daughter of Zadok. [34]He did what was right in the sight of the LORD, just as his father Uzziah had done. [35]Nevertheless, the high places were not removed; the people still sacrificed and made offerings on the high places. He built the upper gate of the house of the LORD. [36]Now the rest of the acts of Jotham and all that he did, are they not written in the Book of the Annals of the Kings of Judah? [37]In those days the LORD began to send King Rezin of Aram and Pekah son of

and replaced a month later by Menahem. **15:16** Menahem's coup seems to have been extremely violent, as there is mention of Menahem sacking Tiphsah (probably Tappuah) and ripping open *all the pregnant women,* an inhumane act engaged in by foreign enemies (2 Kgs. 8:11–12; Amos 1:13). **15:19–21** *Pul.* Another name for the Assyrian king Tiglath-pileser III (744–727 BCE), whom Menahem bribes to stay on the throne. Under this king, Assyria, a kingdom located in the northern part of Mesopotamia, would greatly expand and colonize much of the Near East in the eighth century BCE. **15:19–22** Menahem's reign, which is assessed negatively, seems to have been somewhat successful, as he is able to pass on the throne to his son, Pekahiah. **15:23–26** Pekahiah, who is assessed negatively, rules for two years before he is assassinated and replaced by Pekah in a coup. **15:27–31** Pekah, who is assessed negatively, rules for twenty years until he is also assassinated and replaced by Hoshea in a coup.

15:32–38 The reign of Jotham in Judah. The reign of Azariah's son, Jotham, in Judah is assessed positively. Though 2 Chr. 27 mentions other construction activities, the specific mention of the renovation of the *upper gate of the house of the LORD* and that his mother was the daughter of the priest Zadok (cf. 1 Kgs. 1:38–39) hints at his affiliation with the priestly class.

Remaliah against Judah. ³⁸Jotham slept with his ancestors and was buried with his ancestors in the city of David, his ancestor; his son Ahaz succeeded him.

16 In the seventeenth year of Pekah son of Remaliah, King Ahaz son of Jotham of Judah began to reign. ²Ahaz was twenty years old when he began to reign; he reigned sixteen years in Jerusalem. He did not do what was right in the sight of the LORD his God, as his ancestor David had done, ³but he walked in the way of the kings of Israel. He even made his son pass through fire, according to the abominable practices of the nations whom the LORD had driven out before the people of Israel. ⁴He sacrificed and made offerings on the high places, on the hills, and under every green tree.

5 Then King Rezin of Aram and King Pekah son of Remaliah of Israel came up to wage war on Jerusalem; they besieged Ahaz but could not conquer him. ⁶At that time King Rezin of Aram recovered Elath for Edom*ˡ* and drove the Judeans from Elath, and the Edomites came to Elath, where they live to this day. ⁷Ahaz sent messengers to King Tiglath-pileser of Assyria, saying, "I am your servant and your son. Come up and rescue me from the hand of the king of Aram and from the hand of the king of Israel, who are attacking me." ⁸Ahaz also

took the silver and gold found in the house of the LORD and in the treasures of the king's house and sent a present to the king of Assyria. ⁹The king of Assyria listened to him; the king of Assyria marched up against Damascus and took it, carrying its people captive to Kir; then he killed Rezin.

10 When King Ahaz went to Damascus to meet King Tiglath-pileser of Assyria, he saw the altar that was at Damascus. King Ahaz sent to the priest Uriah a model of the altar and its pattern exact in all its details. ¹¹The priest Uriah built the altar; in accordance with all that King Ahaz had sent from Damascus, so did the priest Uriah build it, before King Ahaz arrived from Damascus. ¹²When the king came from Damascus, the king viewed the altar. Then the king drew near to the altar, went up on it, ¹³and offered his burnt offering and his grain offering, poured his drink offering, and dashed the blood of his offerings of well-being against the altar. ¹⁴The bronze altar that was before the LORD he removed from the front of the house, from the place between his altar and the house of the LORD, and put it on the north side of his altar. ¹⁵King Ahaz commanded the priest Uriah, saying, "Upon the great altar offer the morning burnt offering and the evening grain offering and the king's burnt offering and his grain offering,

ˡ 16.6 Cn: Heb *Aram*

16:1–20 The reign of Ahaz in Judah. 16:1–3 In stark contrast to the previous four kings of Judah, Ahaz is assessed very negatively, charged with not doing *right in the sight of the LORD*, behaving like the kings of the northern kingdom, and passing his son through the fire—likely a reference to child sacrifice. **16:4** Ahaz is also condemned for the worship of other gods, which is likened to sexual offenses such as adultery in the prophetic texts (Hos. 1–2; Ezek. 23) and which is described as sacrificing and making offerings on the high places, on hills, and under green trees. The expression *under every green tree* (1 Kgs. 14:23; 2 Kgs. 17:10; 2 Chr. 28:4; Isa. 57:5; Jer. 2:20; 3:6; 3:13; 17:2; Ezek. 6:13) might refer to the worship of the goddess Asherah. **16:5–6** The negative appraisal of Ahaz might explain the Syro-Ephraimite War (735–732 BCE), the purpose of which is debated, whereby King Rezin of Damascus (Syria) and King Pekah of Samaria attempted to remove Ahaz and replace him with a puppet king either because he refused to join an anti-Assyrian alliance or because of Judah's territorial expansions. **16:7–8** To remain on the throne, Ahaz calls on Assyria for help by offering a bribe, an act looked down upon in the biblical text (Exod. 23:8; Deut. 16:19; Ps. 15:5; Prov. 17:23; Isa. 5:23; Ezek. 22:12), and by voluntarily submitting to Assyrian rule. **16:9** Assyria, heeding Ahaz's call, destroys and captures Damascus and removes its king. Second Kgs. 17 describes the destruction of Samaria. Historically, an anti-Assyrian coalition that did not include Judah confronted Assyria in a series of military campaigns but ultimately failed to stop its encroachment and colonization. **16:10–20** Ahaz goes to Damascus to meet the Assyrian king, sees an altar there, has a replica of it made, and places it in the temple in Jerusalem. Ahaz also makes other changes to the temple complex supposedly *because of the king of Assyria* (v. 18). The purpose of Ahaz's actions is much debated, as Assyria did not force its vassals to adopt its religion. Also debated is whether these

with the burnt offering of all the people of the land, their grain offering, and their drink offering; then dash against it all the blood of the burnt offering and all the blood of the sacrifice, but the bronze altar shall be for me to inquire by." [16]The priest Uriah did everything that King Ahaz commanded.

17 Then King Ahaz cut off the frames of the stands and removed the laver from them; he removed the sea from the bronze oxen that were under it and put it on a pediment of stone. [18]The covered portal for use on the Sabbath that had been built inside the palace and the outer entrance for the king he removed from[m] the house of the Lord. He did this because of the king of Assyria. [19]Now the rest of the acts of Ahaz that he did, are they not written in the Book of the Annals of the Kings of Judah? [20]Ahaz slept with his ancestors and was buried with his ancestors in the city of David; his son Hezekiah succeeded him.

17 In the twelfth year of King Ahaz of Judah, Hoshea son of Elah began to reign in Samaria over Israel; he reigned nine years. [2]He did what was evil in the sight of the Lord, yet not like the kings of Israel who were before him. [3]King Shalmaneser of Assyria came up against him; Hoshea became his vassal and paid him tribute. [4]But the king of Assyria found treachery in Hoshea, for he had sent messengers to King So of Egypt and offered no tribute to the king of Assyria, as he had done year by year; therefore the king of Assyria confined him and imprisoned him.

[5]Then the king of Assyria invaded all the land and came to Samaria; for three years he besieged it. [6]In the ninth year of Hoshea the king of Assyria captured Samaria; he carried the Israelites away to Assyria. He placed them in Halah, on the Habor, the river of Gozan, and in the cities of the Medes.

[7]This occurred because the people of Israel had sinned against the Lord their God, who had brought them up out of the land of Egypt from under the hand of Pharaoh king of Egypt. They had worshiped other gods [8]and walked in the customs of the nations whom the Lord had driven out before the people of Israel and in the customs that the kings of Israel had introduced.[n] [9]The people of Israel did[o] things that were not right against the Lord their God. They built for themselves high places at all their towns, from watchtower to fortified city; [10]they set up for themselves pillars and sacred poles[p] on every high hill and under every green tree; [11]there they made offerings on all the high places, as the nations did whom the Lord had carried away before them. They did wicked things, provoking the Lord to anger; [12]they served idols, of which the Lord had said to them, "You shall not do this." [13]Yet the Lord warned Israel and

m 16.18 Cn: Heb lacks *from*   n 17.8 Meaning of Heb uncertain   o 17.9 Meaning of Heb uncertain   p 17.10 Or *Asherahs*

changes—which were approved and enacted by Uriah, the priest, who is praised as one of the "faithful witnesses" in Isa. 8:2 KJV—are portrayed as praiseworthy or disgraceful.

17:1–4 The reign of Hoshea in Israel. 17:1–2 Though Hoshea, the last king of Israel, is assessed as better than previous northern kings, Israel is destroyed during his reign. **17:3–4** Initially a loyal vassal, Hoshea tries to obtain Egyptian support from *King So*, possibly a reference to the Egyptian town Sais or a mistake. This leads to his imprisonment and the destruction of the country.

17:5–6 The destruction of the northern kingdom of Israel. The northern kingdom of Israel (Samaria) is destroyed in 722 BCE by Assyria. Conflicting evidence portrays a confusing picture of Samaria's last days, as the inscriptions of the Assyrian king Sargon II boast that he conquered Samaria, while other records, such as the Babylonian Chronicle, state that the conquest occurred during the reign of a different Assyrian king, Shalmaneser V, mentioned in 2 Kgs. 17:3.

17:7–23 The theological justification. The destruction of Israel raised questions about the sovereignty and power of YHWH, the god of Israel, thereby necessitating a lengthy explanation. Under the umbrella charge of worshiping other gods (v. 7), a litany of Israel's sins is presented to justify Israel's destruction as well-deserved. They include building *high places* (i.e., local shrines; v. 9) and making *offerings* on them (v. 11); building *pillars and sacred poles* (i.e., the Asherahs; see note on 2 Kgs. 13:6) *on every hill and under every green tree* (vv. 10, 16; see note on 2 Kgs. 16:4); serving *idols* and other false gods, such as *Baal* and *the host of heaven* (i.e., astral bodies; vv. 12, 15–16); casting images of the *two calves* (v. 16); despising YHWH's *statutes* and *commandments* in violation of their covenant (vv. 15–16); offering child sacrifice (i.e., making *their sons and their daughters pass through fire*; v. 17);

Judah by every prophet and every seer, saying, "Turn from your evil ways and keep my commandments and my statutes, in accordance with all the law that I commanded your ancestors and that I sent to you by my servants the prophets." [14]They would not listen but were stubborn, as their ancestors had been, who did not believe in the LORD their God. [15]They despised his statutes and his covenant that he had made with their ancestors and the warnings that he had given them. They went after false idols and became false; they followed the nations that were around them, concerning whom the LORD had commanded them that they should not do as they did. [16]They rejected all the commandments of the LORD their God and made for themselves cast images of two calves; they made a sacred pole,[q] worshiped all the host of heaven, and served Baal. [17]They made their sons and their daughters pass through fire, used divination and augury, and sold themselves to do evil in the sight of the LORD, provoking him to anger. [18]Therefore the LORD was very angry with Israel and removed them out of his sight; none was left but the tribe of Judah alone.

19 Judah also did not keep the commandments of the LORD their God but walked in the customs that Israel had introduced. [20]The LORD rejected all the descendants of Israel; he punished them and gave them into the hand of plunderers, until he had banished them from his presence.

21 When he had torn Israel from the house of David, they made Jeroboam son of Nebat king. Jeroboam drove Israel from following the LORD and made them commit great sin. [22]The people of Israel continued in all the sins that Jeroboam committed;

they did not depart from them [23]until the LORD removed Israel out of his sight, as he had foretold through all his servants the prophets. So Israel was exiled from their own land to Assyria until this day.

24 The king of Assyria brought people from Babylon, Cuthah, Avva, Hamath, and Sepharvaim and placed them in the cities of Samaria in place of the people of Israel; they took possession of Samaria and settled in its cities. [25]When they first settled there, they did not worship the LORD; therefore the LORD sent lions among them that killed some of them. [26]So the king of Assyria was told, "The nations that you have carried away and placed in the cities of Samaria do not know the law of the god of the land; therefore he has sent lions among them; they are killing them because they do not know the law of the god of the land." [27]Then the king of Assyria commanded, "Send there one of the priests whom you carried away from there; let him[r] go and live there and teach them the law of the god of the land." [28]So one of the priests whom they had carried away from Samaria came and lived in Bethel; he taught them how they should worship the LORD.

29 But every nation still made gods of its own and put them in the shrines of the high places that the people of Samaria had made, every nation in the cities in which they lived; [30]the people of Babylon made Succoth-benoth, the people of Cuth made Nergal, the people of Hamath made Ashima; [31]the Avvites made Nibhaz and Tartak; the Sepharvites burned their children in the fire to Adrammelech and Anammelech, the

q 17.16 Or *Asherah*   r 17.27 Syr Vg: Heb *them*

and using *divination and augury* (v. 17). Considering that YHWH has long warned Israel to turn from their evil ways through the prophets (v. 13), its punishment and destruction is a long time coming. **17:19–20** *Judah also did not keep the commandments of the LORD.* A later insertion explains why Judah was also eventually destroyed. **17:21–23** Israel's apostasy, which caused its destruction, is said to have begun from the moment of its founding by Jeroboam, the first king of the northern kingdom.

17:24–41 Samaria's resettlement and impiety. 17:24 To ensure submission, Assyria deported and resettled some of the conquered population to other places throughout its empire. **17:25–28** These foreigners do not know how to properly worship the god of this land and therefore are attacked by *lions*, following a known narrative motif (1 Kgs. 13:24; 20:36). As a result, an exiled priest from the northern kingdom is sent to teach the resettled population how to properly worship YHWH, a task that ends in failure, as the northerners themselves were exiled because of this inability. **17:29–41** Reflecting anti-Samaritan bias, maybe from growing tensions between Jews and Samaritans in the Persian period, the Samaritans are charged with improper worship of YHWH and behaving like their northern predecessors.

gods of Sepharvaim. ³²They also worshiped the LORD and appointed from among themselves all sorts of people as priests of the high places, who sacrificed for them in the shrines of the high places. ³³So they worshiped the LORD but also served their own gods, after the manner of the nations from among whom they had been carried away. ³⁴To this day they continue to practice their former customs.

They do not worship the LORD, and they do not follow the statutes or the ordinances or the law or the commandment that the LORD commanded the children of Jacob, whom he named Israel. ³⁵The LORD had made a covenant with them and commanded them, "You shall not worship other gods or bow yourselves to them or serve them or sacrifice to them, ³⁶but you shall worship the LORD, who brought you out of the land of Egypt with great power and with an outstretched arm; you shall bow yourselves to him, and to him you shall sacrifice. ³⁷The statutes and the ordinances and the law and the commandment that he wrote for you, you shall always be careful to observe. You shall not worship other gods; ³⁸you shall not forget the covenant that I have made with you. You shall not worship other gods, ³⁹but you shall worship the LORD your God; he will deliver you out of the hand of all your enemies." ⁴⁰They would not listen, however, but continued to practice their former custom.

41 So these nations worshiped the LORD but also served their carved images; to this day their children and their children's children continue to do as their ancestors did.

18 In the third year of King Hoshea son of Elah of Israel, Hezekiah son of King Ahaz of Judah began to reign. ²He was twenty-five years old when he began to reign; he reigned twenty-nine years in Jerusalem. His mother's name was Abi daughter of Zechariah. ³He did what was right in the sight of the LORD, just as his ancestor David had done. ⁴He removed the high places, broke down the pillars, and cut down the sacred pole.ˢ He broke in pieces the bronze serpent that Moses had made, for until those days the people of Israel had made offerings to it; it was called Nehushtan. ⁵He relied on the LORD, the God of Israel, so that there was no one like him among all the kings of Judah after him or among those who were before him. ⁶For he held fast to the LORD; he did not depart from following him but kept the commandments that the LORD had commanded Moses. ⁷The LORD was with him; wherever he went, he prospered. He rebelled against the king of Assyria and would not serve him. ⁸He attacked the Philistines as far as Gaza and its territory, from watchtower to fortified city.

9 In the fourth year of King Hezekiah, which was the seventh year of King Hoshea son of Elah of Israel, King Shalmaneser of Assyria came up against Samaria, besieged it, ¹⁰and at the end of three years took it. In the sixth year of Hezekiah, which was the ninth year of King Hoshea of Israel, Samaria was taken. ¹¹The king of Assyria carried the Israelites away to Assyria and settled them in Halah, on the Habor, the river of Gozan, and in the cities of the Medes, ¹²because they did not obey the voice of the LORD their God but transgressed his

ˢ 18.4 Or *Asherah*

18:1–8 The reign of Hezekiah in Judah. 18:1–2 The negative assessment of King Ahaz (2 Kgs. 16) sets the stage for the reign of his son, Hezekiah, one of the most lauded kings of Judah, who is given a superlative assessment. **18:3** *Just as his ancestor David had done.* Only two kings, Hezekiah and his grandson, Josiah (2 Kgs. 22:2), are compared to David. **18:4** *Removed the high places.* The one thing that all his pious monarchic predecessors failed to do, Hezekiah accomplishes. **18:4–6** *Nehushtan.* Not only is Hezekiah compared to Moses, but he even destroys the bronze serpent, the Nehushtan, made by Moses because people are illegally worshiping it (cf. Num. 21:4–9). **18:5** *There was no one like him.* This superlative assessment will be undermined by other narratives about Hezekiah that follow (2 Kgs. 20). **18:7–8** *Rebelled against the king of Assyria.* Hezekiah's military successes, including his rebellion against Assyria, are the effects of divine favor. However, the account of Sennacherib's invasion that follows undermines this assessment.

18:9–12 The destruction and exile of Israel. The successful reign of the faithful and divinely favored Hezekiah contrasts with the destruction and exile of the impious northern kingdom of Israel for their transgression of the covenant.

Going Deeper: The Survival of Jerusalem (2 Kings 18–19)

In 701 BCE, the mighty Assyrian Empire—having decimated forty-six Judean villages—was poised to destroy Jerusalem. Surprisingly, the army returned home leaving Jerusalem intact, and its survival changed history.

Two decades earlier, the Assyrians had demolished the northern kingdom of Israel so thoroughly that its dispersed and unidentifiable survivors are now regarded as the *lost* tribes of Israel (2 Kgs. 17). Had Jerusalem reached the same fate, its survivors might similarly have dissolved into the world around them, and the Bible, Judaism, Christianity, and Islam might never have existed—at least not in the forms we recognize them. But Jerusalem did survive, and this spurred a zealous faith in YHWH, the God worshiped in the temple in Jerusalem, as uniquely powerful to save. How did they survive?

According to all accounts, the Assyrians attacked Judah because King Hezekiah had rebelled and stopped paying tribute to the empire (18:7). One hypothesis is that Hezekiah, in the wake of disaster, apologized and went back to paying tribute (cf. 18:13–16 and the Annals of Sennacherib, the Assyrian king). One peculiarity of this seemingly prosaic explanation is its uniqueness: Sennacherib allowed no other rebels to apologize and return to paying a tribute.

The Bible also reports that an angel from YHWH killed 185,000 of the Assyrian troops, which caused the survivors to retreat to Assyria (19:35–36). Such a miracle would surely spur great faith in the power of YHWH. In an equally fantastic account, Herodotus says a mischief of mice sabotaged Assyrian weapons. Historians are understandably skeptical of supernatural explanations and conjecture that miraculous accounts mask some natural phenomenon (like an epidemic).

Yet another explanation is that the Cushites who ruled as the twenty-fifth dynasty in Egypt rescued Jerusalem. In order to keep the Assyrian threat from reaching Egyptian soil, it was in their best interest to help rebels in the land of Canaan defeat the Assyrians. Source-critical scholars identify 2 Kgs. 18:17–19:9, 36 as one of three layers that make up this story; when isolated, this account implies that Assyria left Jerusalem in order to fight Tirhakah, king of Cush. If Tirhakah was successful, that would explain why Assyria did not return to the region for decades. Although crediting Africans with Jerusalem's salvation was once popular, the hypothesis nearly disappeared during the height of racist historiography through the nineteenth and twentieth centuries. Only in recent decades has this hypothesis received renewed attention.

Justin Michael Reed

covenant—all that Moses the servant of the Lord had commanded; they neither listened nor obeyed.

13 In the fourteenth year of King Hezekiah, King Sennacherib of Assyria came up against all the fortified cities of Judah and captured them. ¹⁴King Hezekiah of Judah sent to the king of Assyria at Lachish, saying, "I have done wrong; withdraw from me; whatever you impose on me I will bear." The king of Assyria demanded of King Hezekiah of Judah three hundred talents of silver and thirty talents of gold. ¹⁵Hezekiah gave him all the silver that was found in the house of the Lord and in the treasuries of the king's house. ¹⁶At that time Hezekiah stripped the gold from the doors of the temple of the Lord and from the doorposts that King Hezekiah of Judah had overlaid and gave it to the king of Assyria. ¹⁷The king of Assyria sent the Tartan, the Rabsaris, and the Rabshakeh with a great army from Lachish to King Hezekiah at Jerusalem. They went up and came to Jerusalem. When they arrived, they came and stood by the conduit of the upper pool, which is on the highway to the

18:13–19:34 Sennacherib's invasion. The attack by the Assyrian king Sennacherib in 701 BCE—whereby Judah nearly suffered the same fate as its sister-nation, Israel, but for mysterious reasons survived—is a momentous event in Israelite history. Indeed, the conflicting accounts of this attack, variously dated in 2 Kgs. 18:13–19:34, hint at a complex narrative and editorial history of this event.

18:13–16 First account. The first account of the Assyrian attack of Judah in 701, which is viewed as the most historically accurate. Hezekiah, in contrast to his earlier description, immediately relents and pays a bribe to thwart the attack.

18:17–19:9 Second account. Instead of leaving after receiving a bribe, Sennacherib turns to attack the city, which indicates that this is a different account of the 701 attack. **18:17** *The Tartan, the Rabsaris, and the Rabshakeh.* Sennacherib sends three Assyrian emissaries—the chief commander

fuller's field. ¹⁸When they called for the king, there came out to them Eliakim son of Hilkiah, who was in charge of the palace, and Shebnah the secretary, and Joah son of Asaph, the recorder.

19 The Rabshakeh said to them, "Say to Hezekiah: Thus says the great king, the king of Assyria: On what do you base this reliance of yours? ²⁰Do you think that mere words are strategy and power for war? On whom do you now rely, that you have rebelled against me? ²¹See, you are relying now on Egypt, that broken reed of a staff, which will pierce the hand of anyone who leans on it. Such is Pharaoh king of Egypt to all who rely on him. ²²But if you say to me, 'We rely on the LORD our God,' is it not he whose high places and altars Hezekiah has removed, saying to Judah and to Jerusalem, 'You shall worship before this altar in Jerusalem'? ²³Come now, make a wager with my master the king of Assyria: I will give you two thousand horses, if you are able on your part to set riders on them. ²⁴How then can you repulse a single captain among the least of my master's servants when you rely on Egypt for chariots and for horsemen? ²⁵Moreover, is it without the LORD that I have come up against this place to destroy it? The LORD said to me, 'Go up against this land, and destroy it.'"

26 Then Eliakim son of Hilkiah, Shebnah, and Joah said to the Rabshakeh, "Please speak to your servants in the Aramaic language, for we understand it; do not speak to us in the language of Judah within the hearing of the people who are on the wall." ²⁷But the Rabshakeh said to them, "Has my master sent me to speak these words to your master and to you and not to the people sitting on the wall, who are doomed with you to eat their own dung and to drink their own urine?"

28 Then the Rabshakeh stood and called out in a loud voice in the language of Judah, "Hear the word of the great king, the king of Assyria: ²⁹Thus says the king: Do not let Hezekiah deceive you, for he will not be able to deliver you out of my hand. ³⁰Do not let Hezekiah make you rely on the LORD by saying, 'The LORD will surely deliver us, and this city will not be given into the hand of the king of Assyria.' ³¹Do not listen to Hezekiah, for thus says the king of Assyria: Make your peace with me and come out to me; then every one of you will eat from your own vine and your own fig tree and drink water from your own cistern, ³²until I come and take you away to a land like your own land, a land of grain and wine, a land of bread and vineyards, a land of olive oil and honey, that you may live and not die. Do not listen to Hezekiah when he misleads you by saying, 'The LORD will deliver us.' ³³Has any of the gods of the nations ever delivered its land out of the hand of the king of Assyria? ³⁴Where are the gods of Hamath and Arpad? Where are the gods of Sepharvaim, Hena, and Ivvah? Have they delivered Samaria out of my hand? ³⁵Who among all the gods of the countries have delivered their countries out of my hand, that the LORD should deliver Jerusalem out of my hand?"

36 But the people were silent and answered him not a word, for the king's command was, "Do not answer him." ³⁷Then Eliakim son of Hilkiah, who was in charge of the palace, and Shebna the secretary,

(Tartan), the "chief eunuch" (Rabsaris), and the "chief butler" (Rabshakeh). **18:18** The three Assyrian emissaries are met with three Judean officials. **18:19–25** In a devastating diatribe, the Rabshakeh proceeds to name and then eliminate every possible source of rescue for Judah: Judah's ally, Egypt, is an undependable, broken stick that will harm those who lean on it (v. 21); Judah's own military is so weak that it lacks both equipment and cavalry; and finally, Judah's God, YHWH, is so displeased by Hezekiah's reforms of the temple cult (v. 22) that he has even authorized Sennacherib to attack Judah (v. 25). **18:26** *Aramaic language.* The Judean officials pitifully ask that the Rabshakeh speak in Aramaic, the language of diplomacy, instead of the commonly understood Hebrew (*the language of Judah*). Some have wondered whether the Rabshakeh was an Israelite turncoat because of his bilingualism (b. Sanh. 60a). **18:27** *Eat their own dung and . . . drink their own urine.* Rebuffing the request, the Rabshakeh heightens the terror by describing the horrifying effect of a long siege. **18:28–35** The Rabshakeh proceeds to plant doubts about the pious Hezekiah and about YHWH by comparing YHWH to other gods of other cities that have fallen to Assyria. **18:32** *Land of grain and wine . . . bread and vineyards . . . olive oil and honey.* The Rabshakeh's promises parallel language in other parts of the biblical text (Deut. 8:8). **18:36** The people remain silent because they have been

and Joah son of Asaph, the recorder, came to Hezekiah with their clothes torn and told him the words of the Rabshakeh.

19 When King Hezekiah heard it, he tore his clothes, covered himself with sackcloth, and went into the house of the LORD. [2]And he sent Eliakim, who was in charge of the palace, and Shebna the secretary, and the senior priests, covered with sackcloth, to the prophet Isaiah son of Amoz. [3]They said to him, "Thus says Hezekiah: This day is a day of distress, of rebuke, and of disgrace; children have come to the birth, and there is no strength to bring them forth. [4]It may be that the LORD your God heard all the words of the Rabshakeh, whom his master the king of Assyria has sent to mock the living God, and will rebuke the words that the LORD your God has heard; therefore lift up your prayer for the remnant that is left." [5]When the servants of King Hezekiah came to Isaiah, [6]Isaiah said to them, "Say to your master: Thus says the LORD: Do not be afraid because of the words that you have heard, with which the servants of the king of Assyria have reviled me. [7]I myself will put a spirit in him so that he shall hear a rumor and return to his own land; I will cause him to fall by the sword in his own land."

8 The Rabshakeh returned and found the king of Assyria fighting against Libnah, for he had heard that the king had left Lachish. [9]When the king[t] heard concerning King Tirhakah of Cush, "See, he has set out to fight against you," he sent messengers again to Hezekiah, saying, [10]"Thus shall you speak to King Hezekiah of Judah: Do not let your God on whom you rely deceive you by promising that Jerusalem will not be given into the hand of the king of Assyria. [11]See, you have heard what the kings of Assyria have done to all lands, destroying them utterly. Shall you be delivered? [12]Have the gods of the nations delivered them, the nations that my predecessors destroyed: Gozan, Haran, Rezeph, and the people of Eden who were in Telassar? [13]Where is the king of Hamath, the king of Arpad, the king of the city of Sepharvaim, the king of Hena, or the king of Ivvah?"

14 Hezekiah received the letter from the hand of the messengers and read it; then Hezekiah went up to the house of the LORD and spread it before the LORD. [15]And Hezekiah prayed before the LORD and said, "O LORD the God of Israel, who are enthroned above the cherubim, you are God, you alone, of all the kingdoms of the earth; you have made heaven and earth. [16]Incline your ear, O LORD, and hear; open your eyes, O LORD, and see; hear the words of Sennacherib, which he has sent to mock the living God. [17]Truly, O LORD, the kings of Assyria have laid waste the nations and their lands [18]and have hurled their gods into the fire, though they were no gods but the work of human hands—wood and stone—and so they were destroyed. [19]So now, O LORD our God, save us, I pray you, from his hand, so that all the kingdoms of the earth may know that you, O LORD, are God alone."

t 19.9 Heb *he*

---

ordered to do so, which hints at division in the country. **19:1–9** Hezekiah responds by tearing his clothes and putting on sackcloth as a sign of supplication and mourning (Gen. 37:34; 2 Sam. 1:11; Job 1:20), before proceeding to the temple to seek Isaiah, the prophet (vv. 1–2). To Hezekiah's pitiful declaration that perhaps YHWH will be so incensed as to respond (v. 4), Isaiah reassures him that YHWH will cause Sennacherib to hear a rumor and retreat, which immediately happens as Sennacherib, for mysterious reasons, maybe hearing the approach of the Egyptians, suddenly ends the attack (vv. 8–9a). For his incendiary words via the Rabshakeh, Isaiah also promises that Sennacherib will be assassinated when he returns home (v. 7). **19:9** *Tirhakah of Cush.* Likely inaccurate, as he becomes ruler of Egypt, of which Ethiopia was a part, in 689 BCE and is only a child in 701 BCE. See **"The Survival of Jerusalem," p. 528**.

19:9–37 Final source. Instead of retreating, Sennacherib sends another insulting message, indicating that 2 Kgs. 19:9b is the start of another account of the 701 attack. **19:10–13** This time the message is sent via a letter—that is, a scroll—and it focuses on YHWH's ability to save Judah by comparing him to the powerless gods of other conquered nations. **19:14–19** Hezekiah responds more confidently this time. Affirming the monotheistic vision of YHWH as the only God of the earth (v. 15), as opposed to the false, useless idols and gods of other conquered nations (v. 18), Hezekiah implores YHWH to save Judah so that everyone on earth will also understand YHWH's omnipotence (v. 19).

20 Then Isaiah son of Amoz sent to Hezekiah, saying, "Thus says the Lord, the God of Israel: I have heard your prayer to me about King Sennacherib of Assyria. **21**This is the word that the Lord has spoken concerning him:

She despises you; she scorns you—
> virgin daughter Zion;
she tosses her head—behind your back,
> daughter Jerusalem.

22 Whom have you mocked and reviled?
> Against whom have you raised your
> > voice
and haughtily lifted your eyes?
> Against the Holy One of Israel!
23 By your messengers you have mocked
> the Lord,
> and you have said, 'With my many
> > chariots
I have gone up the heights of the
> mountains,
> to the far recesses of Lebanon;
I felled its tallest cedars,
> its choicest cypresses;
I entered its farthest retreat,
> its densest forest.
24 I dug wells
> and drank foreign waters,
I dried up with the sole of my foot
> all the streams of Egypt.'

25 Have you not heard
> that I determined it long ago?
I planned from days of old
> what now I bring to pass,
that you should make fortified cities
> crash into heaps of ruins,
26 while their inhabitants, shorn of
> strength,
> are dismayed and confounded;
they have become like plants of the field
> and like tender grass,

like grass on the housetops
> that is scorched before the east
> > wind."*

27 But I know your sitting
> and your going out and your coming
> > in
> and your raging against me.
28 Because you have raged against me
> and your arrogance has come to my
> > ears,
I will put my hook in your nose
> and my bit in your mouth;
I will turn you back on the way
> by which you came.

29 "And this shall be the sign for you: This year you shall eat what grows of itself and in the second year what springs from that; then in the third year sow, reap, plant vineyards, and eat their fruit. **30**The surviving remnant of the house of Judah shall again take root downward and bear fruit upward, **31**for from Jerusalem a remnant shall go out and from Mount Zion a band of survivors. The zeal of the Lord of hosts will do this.

32 "Therefore thus says the Lord concerning the king of Assyria: He shall not come into this city, shoot an arrow there, come before it with a shield, or cast up a siege ramp against it. **33**By the way that he came, by the same he shall return; he shall not come into this city, says the Lord. **34**For I will defend this city to save it, for my own sake and for the sake of my servant David."

35 That very night the angel of the Lord set out and struck down one hundred eighty-five thousand in the camp of the Assyrians; when morning dawned, they were all dead bodies. **36**Then King Sennacherib of Assyria left, went home, and lived

u 19.26 Cn Compare Isa 37.27 Q ms: Meaning of MT uncertain

19:20–34 YHWH immediately answers Hezekiah's prayer by sending Isaiah with an oracle mocking Assyria's arrogance and promising a humiliating retreat. **19:21** *Virgin daughter Zion* is another name for Jerusalem. Assyria, the unfit suitor, is rejected from his attempt to enter Jerusalem, which, like other cities, is depicted as a female. **19:28** *Put my hook in your nose and my bit in your mouth.* YHWH will treat Assyria like a stubborn, stupid farm animal. **19:29–31** The oracle is confirmed by a sign (Isa. 7:11; 8:1). **19:34** *For the sake of my servant David.* A reference to Zion theology, which entails the divine promises to David concerning his dynasty and YHWH's defense of Jerusalem (2 Sam. 7; Pss. 2; 48; Isa. 33:20–24; 65:17–25). **19:35–37** Isaiah's oracle is immediately fulfilled, as the Assyrian army retreats without taking Jerusalem. Assyrian sources are ambiguous as to what happened at the end of the 701 attack. **19:35–36** As on Passover (Exod. 12), the angel of the Lord decimates the enemy, and Sennacherib, utterly defeated, retreats. The attack becomes remembered

at Nineveh. [37]As he was worshiping in the house of his god Nisroch, his sons Adrammelech and Sharezer killed him with the sword, and they escaped into the land of Ararat. His son Esar-haddon succeeded him.

20

In those days Hezekiah became sick and was at the point of death. The prophet Isaiah son of Amoz came to him and said to him, "Thus says the LORD: Set your house in order, for you shall die; you shall not recover." [2]Then Hezekiah turned his face to the wall and prayed to the LORD, [3]"Remember now, O LORD, I implore you, how I have walked before you in faithfulness with a whole heart and have done what is good in your sight." Hezekiah wept bitterly. [4]Before Isaiah had gone out of the middle court, the word of the LORD came to him, [5]"Turn back and say to Hezekiah prince of my people: Thus says the LORD, the God of your ancestor David: I have heard your prayer, I have seen your tears; indeed, I will heal you; on the third day you shall go up to the house of the LORD. [6]I will add fifteen years to your life. I will deliver you and this city out of the hand of the king of Assyria; I will defend this city for my own sake and for my servant David's sake." [7]Then Isaiah said, "Bring a lump of figs. Let them take it and apply it to the boil, so that he may recover."

8 Hezekiah said to Isaiah, "What shall be the sign that the LORD will heal me and that I shall go up to the house of the LORD on the third day?" [9]Isaiah said, "This is the sign to you from the LORD, that the LORD will do the thing that he has promised: Shall the shadow advance[v] ten intervals, or shall it retreat ten intervals?" [10]Hezekiah answered, "It is normal for the shadow to lengthen ten intervals; rather, let the shadow retreat ten intervals." [11]The prophet Isaiah cried to the LORD, and he brought the shadow back the ten intervals, by which the sun[w] had declined on the dial of Ahaz.

12 At that time King Merodach-baladan son of Baladan of Babylon sent envoys with letters and a present to Hezekiah, for he had heard that Hezekiah had been sick. [13]Hezekiah welcomed them;[x] he showed them all his treasure house, the silver, the gold, the spices, the precious oil, his armory, all that was found in his storehouses; there was nothing in his house or in all his realm that Hezekiah did not show them. [14]Then the prophet Isaiah came to King Hezekiah and said to him, "What did these men say? From where did they come to you?" Hezekiah answered, "They have come from a far country, from Babylon." [15]He said, "What have they seen in your house?" Hezekiah answered, "They have seen all that is in my house; there is nothing in my storehouses that I did not show them."

16 Then Isaiah said to Hezekiah, "Hear the word of the LORD: [17]Days are coming when

v 20.9 Gk Syr Tg: Heb *the shadow has advanced*   w 20.11 Heb *it*   x 20.13 Gk Vg Syr: Heb *When Hezekiah heard about them*

as a miraculous event. **19:37** In fulfillment of Isaiah's oracle, Sennacherib is assassinated at home, an event substantiated by Assyrian sources. See **"The Survival of Jerusalem," p. 528**.

20:1–11 Hezekiah's illness. 20:1–2 Inexplicably, the pious king, Hezekiah, suddenly becomes so sick that Isaiah, the prophet, tells him to prepare for his demise. Considering that sickness is a sign of divine displeasure or punishment (Num. 25:8), some propose an unstated wrongdoing on the part of Hezekiah (*Ag. Ap.* 2.3.22; b. Ber. 10a). **20:3–5** Hezekiah's prayer is enough for YHWH to suddenly reverse course, and Isaiah is sent back, before he has even exited the palace complex, to tell Hezekiah that he will recover. **20:6** *I will deliver you and this city.* This hints that the illness occurred during or before the 701 Assyrian attack, as Hezekiah's body mirrors that of Jerusalem, which is assaulted by the Assyrians. **20:7** A poultice of figs is applied and seems to heal the sick king. **20:8–11** A second account of the illness begins here, as Hezekiah, who should have already been healed, now requests and is given a sign confirming his healing, the reversal of a shadow on the *dial*, or steps, *of Ahaz*, perhaps a sundial.

20:12–19 The visit of the Babylonian envoys. 20:12 Hearing about Hezekiah's illness, King Merodach-baladan of Babylon (721–710 BCE) sends envoys. Some, such as Josephus (*Ant.* 5.30), speculate that the visit was for the purpose of forming a military alliance against Assyria. **20:13** The reason for Hezekiah's display is left unstated, though perhaps it was to prove Judah's military capabilities to a potential ally. **20:14–15** Sexual innuendos about the unveiling of the virgin Zion are present as Isaiah questions Hezekiah about his display of Judah's wealth to the envoys. **20:16–18** Isaiah gives a harsh

all that is in your house and that which your ancestors have stored up until this day shall be carried to Babylon; nothing shall be left, says the LORD. ¹⁸Some of your own sons who are born to you shall be taken away; they shall be eunuchs in the palace of the king of Babylon." ¹⁹Then Hezekiah said to Isaiah, "The word of the LORD that you have spoken is good." For he thought, "Why not, if there will be peace and security in my days?"

20 The rest of the deeds of Hezekiah, all his power, how he made the pool and the conduit and brought water into the city, are they not written in the Book of the Annals of the Kings of Judah? ²¹Hezekiah slept with his ancestors, and his son Manasseh succeeded him.

21 Manasseh was twelve years old when he began to reign; he reigned fifty-five years in Jerusalem. His mother's name was Hephzibah. ²He did what was evil in the sight of the LORD, following the abominable practices of the nations that the LORD drove out before the people of Israel. ³For he rebuilt the high places that his father Hezekiah had destroyed; he erected altars for Baal, made a sacred pole,ʸ as King Ahab of Israel had done, worshiped all the host of heaven and served them. ⁴He built altars in the house of the LORD, of which the LORD had said, "In Jerusalem I will put my name." ⁵He built altars for all the host of heaven in the two courts of the house of the LORD. ⁶He made his son pass through fire; he practiced soothsaying and augury and dealt with mediums and with wizards. He did much evil in the sight of the LORD, provoking him to anger. ⁷The carved image of Asherah that he had made he set in the house of which the LORD said to David and to his son Solomon, "In this house and in Jerusalem, which I have chosen out of all the tribes of Israel, I will put my name forever; ⁸I will not cause the feet of Israel to wander any more out of the land that I gave to their ancestors, if only they will be careful to do according to all that I have commanded them and according to all the law that my servant Moses commanded them." ⁹But they did not listen; Manasseh misled them to do more evil than the nations had done that the LORD destroyed before the people of Israel.

10 The LORD said by his servants the prophets, ¹¹"Because King Manasseh of Judah has committed these abominations, has done things more wicked than all that the Amorites who were before him did, and has caused Judah also to sin with his idols, ¹²therefore thus says the LORD, the God of Israel: I am bringing upon Jerusalem and

y 21.3 Or *Asherah*

prophecy of doom, which foretells the destruction of Judah and the end of the Davidic dynasty. Why the pious Hezekiah is connected to the coming exile and destruction of Judah is unclear. **20:19** Hezekiah gives a mysterious reply to Isaiah's prophecy, which can be read as either selfish indifference to Judah's fate or faithful acceptance of God's plans.

21:1–18 The reign of Manasseh in Judah. In contrast to his father, Hezekiah, Manasseh is touted as the worst king of Judah and blamed for Judah's destruction and exile. Compared to the hated northern king, Ahab, Manasseh contravenes almost all the important laws in Deuteronomy, and the account of his reign consists almost entirely of a list of his wrongdoings. **21:1** *Reigned fifty-five years.* His lengthy reign undermines the negative assessment. **21:3–9** In contrast to his father, Hezekiah, Manasseh rebuilds and reerects the *high places*, *altars for Baal*, and the *sacred poles*, or *Asherahs* (vv. 3, 7; see note on 2 Kgs. 13:6), that his father had demolished (2 Kgs. 18:4). While his father is commended for following the commandments given to Moses (18:6), Manasseh, in contrast, wantonly transgresses these commandments (21:9). Moreover, he also worships the heavenly hosts, the astral bodies, even building altars for them in the midst of the temple (21:3). And like his grandfather, Ahaz, he also passes his son through the fire—that is, practices child sacrifice (2 Kgs. 16:3)—and, going further, practices *soothsaying and augury* in direct violation of Deut. 18:10–11. **21:10–15** This section is likely an insertion after the destruction and exile of Judah in 587/586 BCE blaming Manasseh for the failure of YHWH's promises to David (2 Sam. 7; Ps. 132:11, 13–18; see note on 2 Kgs. 19:34). **21:11** *Amorites* are one of the native people of Canaan whom God disturbingly orders the Israelites to annihilate during their conquest (Exod. 33:2; 34:11; Num. 21; Josh. 2:10) and to whom Manasseh is unfavorably compared. **21:12** *Ears . . . will tingle.* An expression found in other parts of the biblical text to talk about a surprising, sometimes horrifying divine action (1 Sam. 3:11;

Judah such evil that the ears of everyone who hears of it will tingle. ¹³I will stretch over Jerusalem the measuring line for Samaria and the plummet for the house of Ahab; I will wipe Jerusalem as one wipes a dish, wiping it and turning it upside down. ¹⁴I will cast off the remnant of my heritage and give them into the hand of their enemies; they shall become a prey and a spoil to all their enemies ¹⁵because they have done what is evil in my sight and have provoked me to anger, since the day their ancestors came out of Egypt even to this day."

16 Moreover, Manasseh shed very much innocent blood, until he had filled Jerusalem from one end to another, besides the sin that he caused Judah to sin so that they did what was evil in the sight of the Lord.

17 Now the rest of the acts of Manasseh, all that he did and the sin that he committed, are they not written in the Book of the Annals of the Kings of Judah? ¹⁸Manasseh slept with his ancestors and was buried in the garden of his house, in the garden of Uzza. His son Amon succeeded him.

19 Amon was twenty-two years old when he began to reign; he reigned two years in Jerusalem. His mother's name was Meshullemeth daughter of Haruz of Jotbah. ²⁰He did what was evil in the sight of the Lord, as his father Manasseh had done. ²¹He walked in all the way in which his father walked, served the idols that his father served, and worshiped them; ²²he abandoned the Lord, the God of his ancestors, and did not walk in the way of the Lord. ²³The servants of Amon conspired against him and killed the king in his

house. ²⁴But the people of the land killed all those who had conspired against King Amon, and the people of the land made his son Josiah king in place of him. ²⁵Now the rest of the acts of Amon that he did, are they not written in the Book of the Annals of the Kings of Judah? ²⁶He was buried in his tomb in the garden of Uzza; then his son Josiah succeeded him.

22 Josiah was eight years old when he began to reign; he reigned thirty-one years in Jerusalem. His mother's name was Jedidah daughter of Adaiah of Bozkath. ²He did what was right in the sight of the Lord and walked in all the way of his father David; he did not turn aside to the right or to the left.

3 In the eighteenth year of King Josiah, the king sent Shaphan son of Azaliah son of Meshullam, the secretary, to the house of the Lord, saying, ⁴"Go up to the high priest Hilkiah and have him add up the entire sum of the silver that has been brought into the house of the Lord that the keepers of the threshold have collected from the people; ⁵let it be given into the hand of the workers who have the oversight of the house of the Lord; let them give it to the workers who are at the house of the Lord repairing the house, ⁶that is, to the carpenters, to the builders, to the masons; and let them use it to buy timber and quarried stone to repair the house. ⁷But no accounting shall be asked from them for the silver that is delivered into their hand, for they deal honestly."

8 The high priest Hilkiah said to Shaphan the secretary, "I have found the book of the

Jer. 19:3). **21:13–14** *Measuring line . . . plummet.* YHWH, like an urban appraiser or architect (Isa. 34:11; Lam. 2:8; Amos 7:7–9), will construct tools to deconstruct or demolish Judah, wiping it clean like a dish after a meal and even upturning it to make sure nothing remains. **21:16** *Shed . . . innocent blood.* The apex of Manasseh's misdeeds might refer to human sacrifice or the oppression of the poor and marginalized (e.g., Jer. 7:6; 22:3, 17; Ezek. 22:6–7, 12–13, 25–31). In postbiblical traditions, the *innocent blood* includes that of the prophet Isaiah, whom Manasseh murders (b. Sanh. 103b; b. Yebam. 49b; y. Sanh. 10:28c; Tg. Isa. 66:1; Pesiq. Rab. 4:3).

21:19–26 The reign of Amon in Judah. The reign of Manasseh's son, Amon, which is assessed negatively, lasts for only two years before he is assassinated.

22:1–2 The reign of Josiah of Judah. Josiah is depicted as the best king of Judah. However, his early death undermines the positive portrayal of his reign. **22:2** *Did what was right in the sight of the Lord.* A phrase applied only to a few kings (1 Kgs. 15:11; 2 Kgs. 18:3). *Walked in all the way of his father David.* Only Josiah and Hezekiah (2 Kgs. 18:3) are compared to David. *Did not turn aside to the right or to the left*, a phrase used in Deuteronomy (Deut. 2:27; 5:32; 17:20; 28:14) to mark an exceptional and ideal king.

22:3–20 Temple renovation and the discovery of the book. 22:3–7 Recalling Joash's temple renovations (2 Kgs. 12:11–12, 16), Josiah also improves the temple. **22:8** *Book of the law.* Likely some

law in the house of the LORD." When Hilkiah gave the book to Shaphan, he read it. [9]Then Shaphan the secretary came to the king and reported to the king, "Your servants have melted down the silver that was found in the house and have delivered it into the hand of the workers who have oversight of the house of the LORD." [10]Shaphan the secretary informed the king, "The priest Hilkiah has given me a book." Shaphan then read it aloud to the king.

[11] When the king heard the words of the book of the law, he tore his clothes. [12]Then the king commanded the priest Hilkiah, Ahikam son of Shaphan, Achbor son of Micaiah, Shaphan the secretary, and the king's servant Asaiah, saying, [13]"Go, inquire of the LORD for me, for the people, and for all Judah, concerning the words of this book that has been found, for great is the wrath of the LORD that is kindled against us, because our ancestors did not obey the words of this book to do according to all that is written concerning us."

[14] So the priest Hilkiah, Ahikam, Achbor, Shaphan, and Asaiah went to the prophet Huldah the wife of Shallum son of Tikvah son of Harhas, keeper of the wardrobe; she resided in Jerusalem in the Second Quarter, where they consulted her. [15]She declared to them, "Thus says the LORD, the God of Israel: Tell the man who sent you to me: [16]"Thus says the LORD: I will indeed bring disaster on this place and on its inhabitants—all the words of the book that the king of Judah has read. [17]Because they have abandoned me and have made offerings to other gods, so that they have provoked me to anger with all the work of their hands, therefore my wrath will be kindled against this place, and it will not be quenched.' [18]But as to the king of Judah who sent you to inquire of the LORD, thus shall you say to him: 'Thus says the LORD, the God of Israel: Regarding the words that you have heard, [19]because your heart was penitent and you humbled yourself before the LORD, when you heard how I spoke against this place and against its inhabitants, that they should become a desolation and a curse, and because you have torn your clothes and wept before me, I also have heard you, says the LORD. [20]Therefore, I will gather you to your ancestors, and you shall be gathered to your grave in peace; your eyes shall not see all the disaster that I will bring on this place.' " They took the message back to the king.

23 Then the king directed that all the elders of Judah and Jerusalem should be gathered to him. [2]The king went up to the house of the LORD, and with him went all the people of Judah, all the inhabitants of Jerusalem, the priests, the prophets, and all the people, both small and great; he read in their hearing all the words of the book of the covenant that had been found in the house of the LORD. [3]The king stood by the pillar and made a covenant before the LORD, to follow the LORD, keeping his commandments, his decrees, and his statutes, with all his heart and all his soul, to perform the words of this covenant that were written in this book. All the people joined in the covenant.

[4] The king commanded the high priest Hilkiah, the priests of the second order, and the guardians of the threshold to bring out of the temple of the LORD all the vessels made for Baal, for Asherah, and for all the host of heaven; he burned them outside Jerusalem in the fields of the Kidron and

version of the book of Deuteronomy. **22:11–13** Josiah's pious reaction, whereby he tears his clothes in sorrow and mentions God's great wrath against Israel for its long history of disobedience, sets up the success of Josiah's reformations. **22:14–20** God states, however, that the destruction of the country is unstoppable. Because of his piety, Josiah will not see Judah fall and will die in peace—a prophecy that oddly contradicts the description of the king's premature death at 2 Kgs. 23:29. These discrepancies hint that later editors updated Huldah's prophecy. **22:14** *Prophet Huldah* is one of only four named female prophets in the Hebrew Bible and is married to a royal official. The lack of surprise at Huldah's gender might hint that female prophets were not uncommon in ancient Israel.

23:1–27 The reformation of the cult and the celebration of Passover. Despite Huldah's warning about the inevitability of Judah's destruction, Josiah undertakes a complete reformation of the cult. These inconsistencies hint that the text was reworked and edited at a later point. **23:1–3** *All.* The repetition of *all* recalls the language of the original covenant agreement ceremony (Deut. 29:1–27). **23:4–14** Josiah cleans house by removing, destroying, and/or defiling all personnel, items, and altars

carried their ashes to Bethel. [5]He deposed the idolatrous priests whom the kings of Judah had ordained to make offerings in the high places at the cities of Judah and around Jerusalem, those also who made offerings to Baal, to the sun, the moon, the constellations, and all the host of the heavens. [6]He brought out the image of[z] Asherah from the house of the LORD, outside Jerusalem, to the Wadi Kidron, burned it at the Wadi Kidron, beat it to dust, and threw the dust of it upon the graves of the common people. [7]He broke down the houses of the illicit priests who were in the house of the LORD, where the women did weaving for Asherah. [8]He brought all the priests out of the towns of Judah and defiled the high places where the priests had made offerings, from Geba to Beer-sheba; he broke down the high places of the gates that were at the entrance of the gate of Joshua the governor of the city, which were on the left at the gate of the city. [9]The priests of the high places, however, did not come up to the altar of the LORD in Jerusalem but ate unleavened bread among their kindred. [10]He defiled Topheth, which is in the valley of Ben-hinnom, so that no one would make a son or a daughter pass through fire as an offering to Molech. [11]He removed the horses that the kings of Judah had dedicated to the sun at the entrance to the house of the LORD, by the chamber of the eunuch Nathan-melech, which was in the precincts;[a] then he burned the chariots of the sun with fire. [12]The altars on the roof of the upper chamber of Ahaz that the kings of Judah had made and the altars that Manasseh had made in the two courts of the house of the LORD he pulled down from there and broke in pieces and threw the rubble into the Wadi Kidron. [13]The king defiled the high places that were east of Jerusalem, to the south of the Mount of Destruction, which King Solomon of Israel had built for Astarte the abomination of the Sidonians, for Chemosh the abomination of Moab, and for Milcom the abomination of the Ammonites. [14]He broke the pillars in pieces, cut down the sacred poles,[b] and covered the sites with human bones.

15 Moreover, the altar at Bethel, the high place erected by Jeroboam son of Nebat, who caused Israel to sin—he pulled down that altar along with the high place. He burned the high place, crushing it to dust; he also burned the sacred pole.[c] [16]As Josiah turned, he saw the tombs there on the mount, and he sent and took the bones out of the tombs and burned them on the altar and defiled it, according to the word of the LORD that the man of God proclaimed when Jeroboam stood by the altar at the festival; he turned and looked up at the tomb of the man of God who had proclaimed these things.[d] [17]Then he said, "What is that monument that I see?" The people of the city told him, "It is the tomb of the man of God who came from Judah and proclaimed these things that you have done against the altar at Bethel." [18]He said, "Let him rest; let no one move his bones." So they let his bones alone, with the bones of the prophet who came out of Samaria. [19]Moreover, Josiah removed all the shrines of the high places that were in the towns of Samaria that kings of Israel had made, provoking the LORD to anger; he did to them just as he had done at Bethel. [20]He slaughtered on the altars all the priests of the high places who were there and burned human bones on them. Then he returned to Jerusalem.

21 The king commanded all the people, "Keep the Passover to the LORD your God

z 23.6 Heb lacks *image of*   a 23.11 Meaning of Heb uncertain   b 23.14 Or *Asherahs*   c 23.15 Or *Asherah*   d 23.16 Gk: Heb *proclaimed, who had proclaimed these things*

affiliated with other gods or cult sites outside of the temple in Jerusalem. **23:7** *Illicit priests* probably refers to male temple prostitutes (cf. 1 Kgs. 14:24; 15:12; Ezek. 16:16). **23:10** *Topheth* is a place of human and child sacrifice (cf. Jer. 7:31; 19:13), and *Molech* is a god associated with child sacrifice. **23:12** Josiah is the antithesis of and undoes the actions of his predecessors, Ahaz and Manasseh. **23:13** *Astarte*, likely the queen of heaven (cf. Jer. 44), is an important Canaanite goddess associated with sex, fertility, and war. *Chemosh* is the national deity of the Moabites (see notes on 2 Kgs. 3:26–27) and *Milcom*, the Ammonites. **23:14** *Human bones* are used to defile a cult site. **23:15** Josiah undoes the sin of Jeroboam, the founder of the northern kingdom of Israel, who is condemned for erecting a sanctuary at Dan and Bethel (cf. 1 Kgs. 12:29–30). **23:16–18** *Man of God*, who predicted during Jeroboam's reign the future advent of Josiah (1 Kgs. 13:1–3, 30–32). **23:21–23** The cultic reformation is capped off with the celebration of the Passover as directed in Deut. 16:5–6, which has

as prescribed in this book of the covenant." ²²No such Passover had been kept since the days of the judges who judged Israel, even during all the days of the kings of Israel and of the kings of Judah, ²³but in the eighteenth year of King Josiah this Passover was kept to the LORD in Jerusalem.

24 Moreover, Josiah put away the mediums, wizards, teraphim,ᵉ idols, and all the abominations that were seen in the land of Judah and in Jerusalem, so that he established the words of the law that were written in the book that the priest Hilkiah had found in the house of the LORD. ²⁵Before him there was no king like him who turned to the LORD with all his heart, with all his soul, and with all his might, according to all the law of Moses, nor did any like him arise after him.

26 Still the LORD did not turn from the fierceness of his great wrath by which his anger was kindled against Judah because of all the provocations with which Manasseh had provoked him. ²⁷The LORD said, "I will remove Judah also out of my sight, as I have removed Israel, and I will reject this city that I have chosen, Jerusalem, and the house of which I said, 'My name shall be there.'"

28 Now the rest of the acts of Josiah and all that he did, are they not written in the Book of the Annals of the Kings of Judah? ²⁹In his days Pharaoh Neco king of Egypt went up to the king of Assyria to the River Euphrates. King Josiah went to meet him, but when Pharaoh Neco met him at Megiddo, he killed him. ³⁰His servants carried him dead in a chariot from Megiddo, brought

him to Jerusalem, and buried him in his own tomb. The people of the land took Jehoahaz son of Josiah, anointed him, and made him king in place of his father.

31 Jehoahaz was twenty-three years old when he began to reign; he reigned three months in Jerusalem. His mother's name was Hamutal daughter of Jeremiah of Libnah. ³²He did what was evil in the sight of the LORD, just as his ancestors had done. ³³Pharaoh Neco confined him at Riblah in the land of Hamath, so that he might not reign in Jerusalem, and imposed tribute on the land of one hundred talents of silver and a talent of gold. ³⁴Pharaoh Neco made Eliakim son of Josiah king in place of his father Josiah and changed his name to Jehoiakim. But he took Jehoahaz away; he came to Egypt and died there. ³⁵Jehoiakim gave the silver and the gold to Pharaoh, but he taxed the land in order to meet Pharaoh's demand for money. He exacted the silver and the gold from the people of the land, from all according to their assessment, to give it to Pharaoh Neco.

36 Jehoiakim was twenty-five years old when he began to reign; he reigned eleven years in Jerusalem. His mother's name was Zebidah daughter of Pedaiah of Rumah. ³⁷He did what was evil in the sight of the LORD, just as all his ancestors had done.

24 In his days King Nebuchadnezzar of Babylon came up; Jehoiakim became his servant for three years, then

e 23.24 Or household gods

not occurred since Josh. 5:10–11, when the Israelites first entered the land of Canaan. **23:25** Josiah's superlative assessment, which is based on Deut. 6:5, mimics Moses's evaluation in Deut. 34:10 and surpasses that of Hezekiah's (cf. 2 Kgs. 18:5). **23:26–27** Josiah and his reform, however, are said to be insufficient to thwart the destruction of Judah, which is again blamed on Manasseh.

23:28–30 The death of Josiah. In contradiction to Huldah's prophecy, Josiah, for unknown reasons, meets King Neco of Egypt—perhaps to stop him from supporting Assyria, which is in decline—and is killed. The brevity speaks to the horror and the anticlimactic nature of his death.

23:31–24:7 The reigns of Jehoahaz and Jehoiakim of Judah. 23:31–33 Jehoahaz, who is assessed negatively, reigns for three short months before being removed, imprisoned, and replaced by the Egyptian king Neco for unstated reasons. **23:34–24:7** His replacement, Eliakim, who is also assessed negatively and whose name is changed to Jehoiakim by Neco, heavily taxes the country to pay tribute to Egypt until Babylon replaces Egypt as Judah's overlord. Jehoiakim initially submits to the rule of King Nebuchadnezzar of Babylon, only to later rebel. **24:1** *Nebuchadnezzar* II (ruled 605–562 BCE) is the founder of the Neo-Babylonian Empire, of which *Babylon* is the capital city. After Babylon's defeat of Egypt in the battle of Carchemish (605 BCE), it would become the most important imperial power in the ancient Near East in the seventh and sixth centuries BCE.

turned and rebelled against him. [2]He[f] sent against him bands of the Chaldeans, bands of the Arameans, bands of the Moabites, and bands of the Ammonites; he sent them against Judah to destroy it, according to the word of the Lord that he spoke by his servants the prophets. [3]Surely this came upon Judah at the command of the Lord, to remove them out of his sight, for the sins of Manasseh, for all that he had committed, [4]and also for the innocent blood that he had shed, for he filled Jerusalem with innocent blood, and the Lord was not willing to pardon. [5]Now the rest of the deeds of Jehoiakim and all that he did, are they not written in the Book of the Annals of the Kings of Judah? [6]So Jehoiakim slept with his ancestors; then his son Jehoiachin succeeded him. [7]The king of Egypt did not come again out of his land, for the king of Babylon had taken over all that belonged to the king of Egypt from the Wadi of Egypt to the River Euphrates.

8 Jehoiachin was eighteen years old when he began to reign; he reigned three months in Jerusalem. His mother's name was Nehushta daughter of Elnathan of Jerusalem. [9]He did what was evil in the sight of the Lord, just as his father had done.

10 At that time the servants of King Nebuchadnezzar of Babylon came up to Jerusalem, and the city was besieged. [11]King Nebuchadnezzar of Babylon came to the city while his servants were besieging it; [12]King Jehoiachin of Judah gave himself up to the king of Babylon: himself, his mother, his servants, his officers, and his palace officials. The king of Babylon took him prisoner in the eighth year of his reign.

13 He carried off all the treasures of the house of the Lord and the treasures of the king's house; he cut in pieces all the vessels of gold in the temple of the Lord that King Solomon of Israel had made, all this as the Lord had foretold. [14]He carried away all Jerusalem, all the officials, all the warriors, ten thousand captives, all the artisans and the smiths; no one remained except the poorest people of the land. [15]He carried away Jehoiachin to Babylon; the king's mother, the king's wives, his officials, and the elite of the land, he took into captivity from Jerusalem to Babylon. [16]The king of Babylon brought captive to Babylon all the men of valor, seven thousand, the artisans and the smiths, one thousand, all of them strong and fit for war. [17]The king of Babylon made Mattaniah, Jehoiachin's uncle, king in his place and changed his name to Zedekiah.

18 Zedekiah was twenty-one years old when he began to reign; he reigned eleven years in Jerusalem. His mother's name was Hamutal daughter of Jeremiah of Libnah. [19]He did what was evil in the sight of the Lord, just as Jehoiakim had done. [20]Indeed, Jerusalem and Judah so angered the Lord that he expelled them from his presence.

Zedekiah rebelled against the king of
25
Babylon. [1]And in the ninth year of his reign, in the tenth month, on the tenth day of the month, King Nebuchadnezzar of Babylon came with all his army against Jerusalem and laid siege to it; they built siegeworks against it all around. [2]So the city was besieged until the eleventh year of King Zedekiah. [3]On the ninth day of the fourth month, the famine became so severe in the city that there was no food for the people of the land. [4]Then a breach was made in the city wall;[g] the king with all the soldiers fled[h] by night by the way of the gate between the two walls, by the King's

---

f 24.2 Gk: Heb the Lord   g 25.4 Heb lacks wall
h 25.4 Lucianic: Heb lacks the king and fled

24:2 The constant attacks from Judah's neighbors indicate that God has abandoned the country.
24:3 The sins of Manasseh again are used to justify God's abandonment of Judah.
    24:8–17 The reign of Jehoiachin and the capture of Jerusalem. Jehoiachin, who is assessed negatively, ascends the throne only to descend it as his father's rebellion against Babylon leads to a siege in 597 BCE. His capitulation leads to the end of the siege as the temple is stripped of its wealth, and Jehoiachin and his court are exiled (v. 15). Jehoiachin is replaced by his uncle, Mattaniah, whose name is changed to Zedekiah by the king of Babylon.
    24:18–25:21 The reign of Zedekiah and the fall of Judah. 24:18–20 The last king of Judah, Zedekiah, who is assessed negatively, ascends the throne. The account of the fall and destruction of Judah that occurs during his reign is also described in Jer. 52. **24:20** Though the reasons for Zedekiah's rebellion are unstated in the text, turmoil in the Babylonian Empire might have led some states, including Judah, to form a coalition and rebel. **25:1–3** Zedekiah's rebellion leads to another siege,

Going Deeper: Exile (2 Kings 25)

Exile runs like a scarlet thread throughout the Hebrew Bible. Indeed, human society begins with the exile of Adam and Eve (Gen. 3:23-24) and is spread through the forced scattering of the people of Babel (11:8). Later, the ancestors of Israel also experience exile as God calls on Abram (later Abraham) to emigrate from his homeland (12:1-2). This action is repeated by Jacob, who is Abraham's grandson, and Jacob's son Joseph, both of whom are exiled from Canaan (27:41-45; 37:28, 36). Indeed, Joseph persuades his whole family to move to Egypt from Canaan, an exile that lasts several generations until Moses leads the Israelites back toward the promised land in Exodus.

The cycle of exile and return continues even after the Israelites are settled on the land. The northern kingdom of Israel is exiled and destroyed by the Assyrians in 722 BCE. This event leads to the forced migration and resettlement of the northern population to different parts of the Assyrian Empire, resulting in the so-called ten lost tribes of Israel. After the demise of the northern kingdom, the southern kingdom of Judah follows suit at the hands of the Babylonians. Culminating with the destruction of the temple built by Solomon in 586 BCE, portions of Judah's population are exiled in waves of deportations starting in 597 BCE by the Babylonians. Later, the Persian emperor allows a small group of exiled Jews to return to Jerusalem and build the Second Temple in 538 BCE. This structure is eventually destroyed by another imperial power, Rome, in 70 CE, beginning another exile.

Exiles pockmark the history of Israel, and as such, these events left an indelible mark on the imagination and understanding of the writers and editors of the Hebrew Bible. The text reflects their struggles as it debates the possible causes of exile as well as the reforms and requirements needed to bring it to an end (Jer. 24; 31; Ezek. 18; Ps. 137). Indeed, the Hebrew Scriptures—most of which were composed, edited, and collated during the time of exile or shortly thereafter—make up a text of, by, and for exiles. Expressing a gamut of responses about the feelings and struggles of the immigrant experience (cf. Esther, Daniel, and Ezra), the text affirms to those who feel alienated that they too can survive, live, and possibly even thrive in an unknown and challenging context.

Song-Mi Suzie Park

Garden, though the Chaldeans were all around the city. They went in the direction of the Arabah. ⁵But the army of the Chaldeans pursued the king and overtook him in the plains of Jericho; all his army was scattered, deserting him. ⁶Then they captured the king and brought him up to the king of Babylon at Riblah, who passed sentence on him. ⁷They slaughtered the sons of Zedekiah before his eyes, then put out the eyes of Zedekiah; they bound him in fetters and took him to Babylon.

8 In the fifth month, on the seventh day of the month—which was the nineteenth year of King Nebuchadnezzar, king of Babylon—Nebuzaradan, the captain of the bodyguard, a servant of the king of Babylon, came to Jerusalem. ⁹He burned the house of the Lord, the king's house, and all the houses of Jerusalem; every great house he burned down. ¹⁰All the army of the Chaldeans who were with the captain of the guard broke down the walls around Jerusalem. ¹¹Nebuzaradan the captain of the guard carried into exile the rest of the people who were left in the city and the deserters who had defected to the king of Babylon—all the rest of the multitude. ¹²But the captain of the guard left some of the poorest people of the land to be vinedressers and tillers of the soil.

13 The bronze pillars that were in the house of the Lord, as well as the stands and the bronze sea that were in the house of the Lord, the Chaldeans broke in pieces and carried the bronze to Babylon. ¹⁴They took away the pots, the shovels, the snuffers, the dishes for incense, and all the bronze vessels used in the temple service, ¹⁵as well as the firepans and the

which results in a devastating famine (cf. Jer. 37:21). **25:4-6** When the city's wall is breached, Zedekiah attempts to flee, only to be caught, imprisoned, and punished. In an act of total emasculation, Zedekiah's sons, the royal heirs, are killed before him, and Zedekiah is then blinded, a punishment for rebellious slaves. **25:8-12** The temple built by Solomon, called Solomon's temple or the First Temple, is burned, along with the palace and every other large structure; Jerusalem's walls are destroyed; and another group of people is exiled. Scholars debate the size of the deported population, with some arguing that the numbers were minimal. **25:13-17** The artifacts in the temple that

basins. What was made of gold the captain of the guard took away for the gold and what was made of silver for the silver. [16]As for the two pillars, the one sea, and the stands that Solomon had made for the house of the LORD, the bronze of all these vessels was beyond weighing. [17]The height of the one pillar was eighteen cubits, and on it was a bronze capital; the height of the capital was three cubits; latticework and pomegranates, all of bronze, were on the capital all around. The second pillar had the same, with the latticework.

[18] The captain of the guard took the chief priest Seraiah, the second priest Zephaniah, and the three guardians of the threshold; [19]from the city he took an officer who had been in command of the soldiers and five men of the king's council who were found in the city; the secretary who was the commander of the army who mustered the people of the land; and sixty men of the people of the land who were found in the city. [20]Nebuzaradan the captain of the guard took them and brought them to the king of Babylon at Riblah. [21]The king of Babylon struck them down and put them to death at Riblah in the land of Hamath. So Judah went into exile out of its land.

[22] He appointed Gedaliah son of Ahikam son of Shaphan as governor over the people who remained in the land of Judah, whom King Nebuchadnezzar of Babylon had left. [23]Now when all the captains of the forces and their men heard that the king of Babylon had appointed Gedaliah as governor, they came with their men to Gedaliah at Mizpah, namely, Ishmael son of Nethaniah, Johanan son of Kareah, Seraiah son of Tanhumeth the Netophathite, and Jaazaniah son of the Maacathite. [24]Gedaliah swore to them and their men, saying, "Do not be afraid because of the Chaldean officials; live in the land, serve the king of Babylon, and it shall be well with you." [25]But in the seventh month, Ishmael son of Nethaniah son of Elishama, of the royal family, came with ten men; they struck down Gedaliah so that he died, along with the Judeans and Chaldeans who were with him at Mizpah. [26]Then all the people, high and low,[i] and the captains of the forces set out and went to Egypt, for they were afraid of the Chaldeans.

[27] In the thirty-seventh year of the exile of King Jehoiachin of Judah, in the twelfth month, on the twenty-seventh day of the month, King Evil-merodach of Babylon, in the year that he began to reign, released King Jehoiachin of Judah from prison; [28]he spoke kindly to him and gave him a seat above the other seats of the kings who were with him in Babylon. [29]So Jehoiachin put aside his prison clothes. Every day of his life he dined regularly in the king's presence. [30]For his allowance, a regular allowance was given him by the king, a portion every day, as long as he lived.

i 25.26 Or *young and old*

were destroyed or taken (cf. 1 Kgs. 7:15–51) are described in detail. **25:18–21** The religious personnel as well as other community leaders, perhaps members of the anti-Babylonian party, are executed. **25:21** *So Judah went into exile* might be the last line of an earlier version of the book of Kings (see **"Exile (2 Kings)," p. 539**).

25:22–26 Gedaliah and the reverse exodus. 25:22–24 Gedaliah, an important Judean who was the son of the scribe Ahikam (Jer. 40:9), and whose father was a supporter of the prophet Jeremiah (Jer. 26:24), is made governor by the Babylonians. His appointment seems to have been viewed favorably by Jeremiah (Jer. 39:14; 40:1–6) as well as others in the land who hoped it would bring stability. **25:25** Gedaliah, however, is assassinated by a member of the royal family who perhaps hoped to ascend the throne or as a vendetta against a collaborator. His death is mourned by those in exile (Zech. 7:5; 8:19). **25:26** *Went to Egypt.* A nation whose history began with an exodus from Egypt now ends its history with a reverse exodus as people flee and return to Egypt, a consequence warned of in Deut. 17:16 and 28:68.

25:27–30 Jehoiachin released. Scholars debate whether this last description of Jehoiachin's release from prison and his favorable treatment by the new Babylonian king, Evil-merodach or Amel-Marduk, offers hope for the reestablishment of the Davidic dynasty or reflects an updated ideology about how to live and survive in exile.

1 CHRONICLES

Content and Genre

First and Second Chronicles originally constituted a single book that, probably due to its length, was separated into two parts by translators of the Septuagint, the Old Greek translation of the Hebrew text begun in the third century BCE. Splitting the book into two portions eventually became standard practice, but the continuity of the overall narrative remains. Thus, 1 Chronicles is best read in tandem with 2 Chronicles, and these "two books" are often referred to together, singly, as simply Chronicles, with their author conveniently called the Chronicler. To understand Chronicles fully, it is helpful to read it alongside Samuel and Kings, comparing and contrasting it with those other texts.

Chronicles selectively retells key accounts from the monarchic era of ancient Israel's history, reworking and supplementing selections from Genesis, 1–2 Samuel, and 1–2 Kings to present a new narrative with a distinct perspective (see **"Revising/Rewriting the Bible," p. 584**). After nine chapters of genealogies, 1 Chronicles briefly narrates the death of Saul, Israel's first king. The remainder of 1 Chronicles recounts the reign of David, up to and including the accession of his son Solomon to the throne. Chronicles focuses on the public, political history of Israel and Judah's kings while omitting some of the more personal, salacious details found in parallel texts in 1–2 Samuel and 1–2 Kings. For example, in 2 Sam. 11–12, David impregnates Bathsheba and then arranges for her husband, Uriah, to be killed, earning the rebuke of the prophet Nathan. No mention of this incident is included in Chronicles.

First Chronicles places a high premium on the unity of Israel, portraying the twelve tribes as a unified confederation with shared priorities centering on David's kingship. First Chronicles also devotes considerable attention to the organization and functioning of David's military structure and of the temple, including the roles of the Levites as gatekeepers, musicians, and caretakers. Taken together, 1 and 2 Chronicles devote more attention to temple worship than any other theme. The temple is presented in the text as the spiritual and theological center of ancient Israel, something that the Chronicler must have seen as key to Israelite identity in his own day.

In the Old Testament canon, 1 and 2 Chronicles are located between Kings and Ezra-Nehemiah in a partition known as the Historical Books (see **"The Bible as a Collection," pp. 2145–47**). The emphasis on record keeping, administrative practice, and the public actions of the monarchy certainly gives Chronicles a historical flavor. At the same time, Chronicles is no disinterested presentation of the past. Its selective compilation, rearrangement, and supplementation of the monarchic history tell a new story, one that highlights David's successful leadership of Israel as well as his foundational role in organizing the work of the temple, despite the fact that it was constructed after his death.

Dating and Authorship

The precise date of the composition of Chronicles is unknown, but scholars can identify clues to its date in the content of the book itself. For example, 2 Chronicles closes with Cyrus's edict at the end of the Babylonian exile, meaning the text can be from no earlier than 538 BCE. The Chronicler also quotes extensively from several biblical texts in something that seems close to the final forms we have now—including Samuel, Kings, Psalms, and Genesis—which locates Chronicles *after* those books, well into at least the late Persian or early Hellenistic era. Thus, Chronicles was likely written in the late fourth or early third century BCE, although some scholars would push its date even further toward the end of the third century BCE.

Nothing is known about the author of 1 and 2 Chronicles beyond the hints of their interests that can be gleaned from the text itself. The Chronicler is writing extensively about the administration of the first Jerusalem temple at a time long after its destruction, when the Second Temple (finished ca. 515 BCE) is the one presently in use. The Davidic origin of the temple administration that is outlined in 1 Chronicles serves to legitimate (if not also, at times, *de*legitimate or rebuke) aspects of the Second Temple's organization and worship. At the same time, the accomplishments presented in 1 Chronicles reinforce Davidic—and therefore Judean—authority at a time when Judah was ruled by foreign empires. Whether endorsing or critiquing, the Chronicler is interpreting their postexilic present through the lens of a selective, intentionally crafted account of the preexilic past.

Reading Guide

The nine chapters of genealogies opening 1 Chronicles are memorable (if not often enjoyed) for their density, but the narrative portions of 1 Chronicles are also punctuated by other lists of names. The ubiquitous lists may make 1 Chronicles at times feel reminiscent of an attendance roster, but those lists also have significant political undertones. Genealogies can prescribe or authorize social roles, such as those of the priests and Levites (see 9:10–33). Lists of military forces emphasize David's success as commander and the support for him as king (see 12:23–37; 27:1–15), while lists of temple functionaries set in place by David (see 1 Chr. 23–26) showcase his administrative skills and characterize him as a devoted caretaker of Israel's religious life.

Lists can also lend a general air of authority to a text because of their specificity; they give readers the sense that the author is working from "official," fact-based sources. The Chronicler drew from a variety of source documents, including preexisting parts of the Hebrew Bible, to compose the text. The Chronicler also gestures toward other texts, such as the "Annals of King David" (1 Chr. 27:24), "the records of the seer Samuel," "the records of the prophet Nathan," and "the records of the seer Gad" (29:29)—texts whose existence cannot be verified and whose references are particularly plentiful in 2 Chronicles (e.g., 2 Chr. 13:22; 20:34; 24:27). Although the relationship of these resources to the Chronicler's text is unclear, their effect is similar to that of footnotes in a research paper, situating the Chronicler's words as part of a larger, ongoing conversation in the tradition.

Readers will notice that women are largely absent from 1 Chronicles, especially when compared to the many female characters who appear in the Davidic stories in Samuel-Kings. For example, the wives of David who bore him children are listed in 1 Chr. 3:1–9, but the stories about them found in Samuel-Kings do not appear in 1 Chronicles. One of David's wives, Michal, is omitted entirely from the genealogy because she bore David no children, but there is one starkly negative reference to her in 1 Chr. 15:29, where she watches David's dancing with disdain as he returns the ark of the covenant to Jerusalem. The text likely depends on 2 Sam. 6:16, but it is curious that it is included, as Michal is never described in Chronicles as David's wife.

Despite being a densely male-centered text, there are surprising glimmers of female agency and leadership in Chronicles: the mother of Jabez names her son as a reflection of her own experience of pain (1 Chr. 4:9), for example (see **"Prayer of Jabez," p. 548**), and Sheerah, a descendant of Ephraim, is described as a builder of three cities, one of which bears her name (7:24).

Cameron B. R. Howard

1 Adam, Seth, Enosh; ²Kenan, Mahalalel, Jared; ³Enoch, Methuselah, Lamech; ⁴Noah, Shem, Ham, and Japheth.

5 The descendants of Japheth: Gomer, Magog, Madai, Javan, Tubal, Meshech, and Tiras. ⁶The descendants of Gomer: Ashkenaz, Diphath, and Togarmah. ⁷The descendants of Javan: Elishah, Tarshish, Kittim, and Rodanim.

8 The descendants of Ham: Cush and Egypt, Put, and Canaan. ⁹The descendants of Cush: Seba, Havilah, Sabta, Raama, and Sabteca. The descendants of Raama: Sheba and Dedan. ¹⁰Cush became the father of Nimrod; he was the first to be a mighty one on the earth.

11 Egypt became the father of Ludim,

1:1–27 From Adam to Abraham. The book opens with a nine-chapter genealogical prologue. The lists of names in this opening section align closely with genealogies in the Primeval History of the book of Genesis (Gen. 1–11). However, they have been stripped of much of the commentary that accompanies them in Genesis, such as ages or occupations. The abrupt nature of the beginning of 1 Chronicles assumes that its readers are already familiar with those first names and the relationship among them. **1:1–4** This list of descendants is taken from Gen. 5. It is presented linearly, from father to son, beginning with Adam—the first human, according to Gen. 2—through Noah. Cain and Abel, Adam's first two sons, whose stories are told in Gen. 4, are omitted. **1:4** At this point, the genealogy begins to branch, or "segment," following the lineage of one sibling awhile before doubling back to the others. *Shem, Ham, and Japheth* are sons of Noah. **1:5–23** These genealogical lists are derived from Gen. 10, the so-called Table of Nations. The lists associate nations or peoples who occupy particular geographical regions with branches of a lineage that traces back to a single ancestor,

Anamim, Lehabim, Naphtuhim, [12]Pathrusim, Casluhim, and Caphtorim, from whom the Philistines come.*a*

13 Canaan became the father of Sidon his firstborn, and Heth, [14]and the Jebusites, the Amorites, the Girgashites, [15]the Hivites, the Arkites, the Sinites, [16]the Arvadites, the Zemarites, and the Hamathites.

17 The descendants of Shem: Elam, Asshur, Arpachshad, Lud, and Aram. The sons of Aram:*b* Uz, Hul, Gether, and Meshech. [18]Arpachshad became the father of Shelah, and Shelah became the father of Eber. [19]To Eber were born two sons: the name of the one was Peleg (for in his days the earth was divided), and the name of his brother was Joktan. [20]Joktan became the father of Almodad, Sheleph, Hazarmaveth, Jerah, [21]Hadoram, Uzal, Diklah, [22]Ebal, Abimael, Sheba, [23]Ophir, Havilah, and Jobab; all these were the descendants of Joktan.

24 Shem, Arpachshad, Shelah; [25]Eber, Peleg, Reu; [26]Serug, Nahor, Terah; [27]Abram, that is, Abraham.

28 The sons of Abraham: Isaac and Ishmael. [29]These are their genealogies: the firstborn of Ishmael was Nebaioth, then Kedar, Adbeel, Mibsam, [30]Mishma, Dumah, Massa, Hadad, Tema, [31]Jetur, Naphish, and Kedemah. These are the sons of Ishmael. [32]The sons of Keturah, Abraham's concubine: she bore Zimran, Jokshan, Medan, Midian, Ishbak, and Shuah. The sons of Jokshan: Sheba and Dedan. [33]The sons of Midian: Ephah, Epher, Hanoch, Abida, and Eldaah. All these were the descendants of Keturah.

34 Abraham became the father of Isaac. The sons of Isaac: Esau and Israel. [35]The sons of Esau: Eliphaz, Reuel, Jeush, Jalam, and Korah. [36]The sons of Eliphaz: Teman, Omar, Zephi, Gatam, Kenaz, Timna, and Amalek. [37]The sons of Reuel: Nahath, Zerah, Shammah, and Mizzah.

38 The sons of Seir: Lotan, Shobal, Zibeon, Anah, Dishon, Ezer, and Dishan. [39]The sons of Lotan: Hori and Homam; and Lotan's sister was Timna. [40]The sons of Shobal: Alian, Manahath, Ebal, Shephi, and Onam. The sons of Zibeon: Aiah and Anah. [41]The son of Anah: Dishon. The sons of Dishon: Hamran, Eshban, Ithran, and Cheran. [42]The sons of Ezer: Bilhan, Zaavan, and Jaakan.*c* The sons of Dishan:*d* Uz and Aran.

43 These are the kings who reigned in the land of Edom before any king reigned over the Israelites: Bela son of Beor, whose city was called Dinhabah. [44]When Bela died, Jobab son of Zerah of Bozrah succeeded him. [45]When Jobab died, Husham of the land of the Temanites succeeded him. [46]When

a 1.12 Heb *Casluhim, from which the Philistines come, Caphtorim* *b* 1.17 Cn: Heb omits *and Aram. The sons of* *c* 1.42 Or *and Akan* *d* 1.42 Heb *Dishon*

Adam. **1:12** *Caphtorim, from whom the Philistines come.* The Philistines are the featured enemies of Israel in many conflicts depicted in the monarchic histories of the Bible (e.g., 1 Chr. 10). They lived along the Mediterranean Sea on the southwest coast of Palestine, but their association here with Caphtor, modern-day Crete, suggests they migrated across the sea from the Aegean region (see also Amos 9:7). **1:19** *Peleg* means "division" in Hebrew. This quick aside in the genealogy provides a brief etiology, or origin story, for why Peleg was given his name. Such etymological etiologies are particularly common in the book of Genesis, from which this genealogy has been taken. **1:24** The genealogy doubles back to Noah's son Shem again and presents a linear genealogy of fathers and sons from Shem through Arpachshad and down to Abraham, following Gen. 11:10–26. **1:27** *Abram, that is, Abraham.* Abram is renamed Abraham when God makes a covenant with him at Gen. 17:1–8.

1:28–54 From Abraham to Jacob. Having surveyed the primeval origins of civilizations surrounding Israel, the genealogies begin to focus on Israel itself, beginning with the patriarch Abraham. **1:28** *The sons of Abraham: Isaac and Ishmael.* Isaac's mother is Sarah; Ishmael's mother is Hagar. The stories of Abraham's family are found in Gen. 12–25. **1:29–31** Parallel to Gen. 25:13–16a. The Bible associates the twelve tribes of Ishmael with his twelve sons, just as there are twelve tribes of Israel descended from Isaac's son Jacob. Along with the sons of Abraham's second wife, Keturah, the Ishmaelites are presented in the Bible as ancestors of the Arabians. **1:32–33** Parallel to Gen. 25:1–4. **1:34** *The sons of Isaac: Esau and Israel.* Jacob and Esau are Isaac's twin sons by his wife, Rebekah (Gen. 25:19–28). Jacob is renamed *Israel* after wrestling with a mysterious stranger at Peniel (Gen. 32:22–32). **1:35–54** Adapted from Gen. 36:15–43. **1:36** *Timna* is listed as a son of Eliphaz in the Masoretic Text but as a concubine to Eliphaz and the mother of Amalek in the Septuagint and Gen. 36:12. See also 1 Chr. 1:39, where Timna is listed as the sister of Lotan.

Husham died, Hadad son of Bedad, who defeated Midian in the country of Moab, succeeded him, and the name of his city was Avith. ⁴⁷When Hadad died, Samlah of Masrekah succeeded him. ⁴⁸When Samlah died, Shaulᵉ of Rehoboth on the River succeeded him. ⁴⁹When Shaulᶠ died, Baal-hanan son of Achbor succeeded him. ⁵⁰When Baal-hanan died, Hadad succeeded him; the name of his city was Pai, and his wife's name was Mehetabel daughter of Matred daughter of Mezahab. ⁵¹And Hadad died.

The clansᵍ of Edom were: clansʰ Timna, Aliah,ⁱ Jetheth, ⁵²Oholibamah, Elah, Pinon, ⁵³Kenaz, Teman, Mibzar, ⁵⁴Magdiel, and Iram; these are the clansʲ of Edom.

2 These are the sons of Israel: Reuben, Simeon, Levi, Judah, Issachar, Zebulun, ²Dan, Joseph, Benjamin, Naphtali, Gad, and Asher. ³The sons of Judah: Er, Onan, and Shelah; these three the Canaanite woman Bath-shua bore to him. Now Er, Judah's firstborn, was wicked in the sight of the Lord, and he put him to death. ⁴His daughter-in-law Tamar also bore him Perez and Zerah. Judah had five sons in all.

5 The sons of Perez: Hezron and Hamul. ⁶The sons of Zerah: Zimri, Ethan, Heman, Calcol, and Darda,ᵏ five in all. ⁷The son of

Carmi: Achar, the troubler of Israel, who transgressed in the matter of the devoted thing; ⁸and Ethan's son was Azariah.

9 The sons of Hezron who were born to him: Jerahmeel, Ram, and Chelubai.ˡ ¹⁰Ram became the father of Amminadab, and Amminadab became the father of Nahshon, prince of the sons of Judah. ¹¹Nahshon became the father of Salma, Salma of Boaz, ¹²Boaz of Obed, Obed of Jesse. ¹³Jesse became the father of Eliab his firstborn, Abinadab the second, Shimea the third, ¹⁴Nethanel the fourth, Raddai the fifth, ¹⁵Ozem the sixth, David the seventh; ¹⁶and their sisters were Zeruiah and Abigail. The sons of Zeruiah: Abishai, Joab, and Asahel, three. ¹⁷Abigail bore Amasa, and the father of Amasa was Jether the Ishmaelite.

18 Caleb son of Hezron had children by his wife Azubah and by Jerioth;ᵐ these were her sons: Jesher, Shobab, and Ardon. ¹⁹When Azubah died, Caleb married Ephrath, who bore him Hur. ²⁰Hur became the father of Uri, and Uri became the father of Bezalel.

21 Afterward Hezron went in to the daughter of Machir father of Gilead, whom he married when he was sixty years old, and

e 1.48 Or *Saul* f 1.49 Or *Saul* g 1.51 Or *chiefs* h 1.51 Or *chiefs* i 1.51 Or *Alvah* j 1.54 Or *chiefs* k 2.6 Heb mss Gk Vg Syr; MT *Dara* l 2.9 Or *Caleb* m 2.18 Meaning of Heb uncertain

2:1–55 The sons of Israel and the descendants of Judah. 2:1 *Israel*—that is, Jacob. **2:3** Leah is the mother of *Judah* (Gen. 29:31–35), and even though Judah is the fourth of Jacob's twelve sons, the genealogy focuses on him first. This choice is consistent with 1 Chronicles's interest in David, who is a descendant of Judah, as well as in the southern kingdom, where the tribe of Judah had its homeland. In 922 BCE, during the reign of David's grandson Rehoboam, the united kingdom of Israel split into two: the northern kingdom of Israel, with Samaria as its capital, and the southern kingdom of Judah, with its capital at Jerusalem. Chronicles devotes very little attention to the history of the northern kingdom. **2:3–5** *Wicked in the sight of the Lord* (cf. Gen. 38:7) points to the story of Judah and his sons in Gen. 38. After the death of his sons *Er* and *Onan*, Judah refuses to give his youngest son, *Shelah*, to Tamar, who had been married to each man when he died. Thus, Judah shirks the familial duties of levirate marriage, which expected a brother of the deceased to sire children with his widow in order to carry on the name and inheritance of the dead man (cf. Deut. 25:5–10). Tamar then disguises herself as a prostitute in order to have children by Judah, who declares her more righteous than he. The Chronicler's allusion to Gen. 38 without recounting its dramatic details is both an acknowledgment and a citation of that story, not a denial of it. **2:6** *Ethan, Heman, Calcol, and Darda.* Cf. 1 Kgs. 4:31. **2:7** *Achar*—that is, Achan. *Transgressed in the matter of the devoted thing.* See Josh. 7:1–26. Here again Chronicles alludes to a story it assumes its audience knows, giving the original reader a narrative foothold. **2:10** *Nahshon, prince of the sons of Judah.* See Num. 1:7; 2:3; 7:12–17; 10:14. **2:11–12** Cf. Ruth 4:18–21. **2:16** The names of women are relatively rare in the genealogies of 1 Chronicles, but the inclusion of *Zeruiah and Abigail* is particularly striking, since they are presented as the progenitors of their lines. (Similarly, see Keturah in 1 Chr. 1:32–33.) Amasa's father is mentioned only secondarily, and the father of Zeruiah's children is not mentioned at all. **2:21** *Hezron* is the son of Perez from v. 5. Here the genealogy doubles back to

Going Deeper: Women in the Genealogy (1 Chronicles 1–9)

First Chr. 1–9 can be a dull read, and it is tempting to skip these lists and jump to the action beginning in chapter 10. A closer look at these names, though, reveals that they are more than just some dull historical report but reflect a rich and carefully constructed ideology. Genealogies tell stories.

The genealogy in Chronicles begins with Adam and ends with Saul's family. While ostensibly summarizing and repeating prior information from elsewhere in the Bible, Chronicles differs in several ways, demonstrated by a careful reading. First, it contains far more details than other texts. Are these from different sources that are no longer extant? Second, some of the genealogical information differs from what has come before. Are these alternative traditions? Finally, although genealogies usually recount the descent of fathers and sons, the overwhelmingly masculine nature of the records in Chronicles is striking. Many of the passages are just lists of men's names, not interrupted by a word, let alone by a woman. Additionally, the verb that sometimes connects father to son is "to give birth" and not, as it is often elsewhere, "to cause to give birth," which creates the further impression that here men are appropriating women's reproductive power, giving birth to their own sons (see, e.g., 1:10; 1:18). Women are all but erased in Chronicles. This makes the times when women do appear noteworthy, even remarkable.

Keturah, Abraham's second wife, gives birth to a non-Israelite line of sons and is the first woman to appear in 1 Chronicles (1:32; see Gen. 25:1–4). In Esau's line, Timna, sister of Lotan, is noted (1 Chr. 1:39; see Gen. 36:22), which may indicate important traditions about her that have been lost. In one instance, a woman names her son Jabez because she bore him "in pain" (1 Chr. 4:9), thus recentering women's birthing process in the only words spoken by a woman in this passage. There are concentrations of women in David's genealogy (his many wives and Tamar in chap. 3) and in Manasseh's, including the descendants of both his sons and daughters (7:14–19). Sheerah, Ephraim's daughter, is said to build three settlements, a unique statement in the Bible (7:24). Although often not as exciting as other texts, genealogies like those found in Chronicles can provide information about how their writers thought about men and women, families and nations.

Jennifer L. Koosed

she bore him Segub, ²²and Segub became the father of Jair, who had twenty-three towns in the land of Gilead. ²³But Geshur and Aram took from them Havvoth-jair, Kenath and its villages, sixty towns. All these were descendants of Machir, father of Gilead. ²⁴After the death of Hezron in Caleb-ephrathah, Abijah wife of Hezron bore him Ashhur, father of Tekoa.

25 The sons of Jerahmeel, the firstborn of Hezron: Ram his firstborn, Bunah, Oren, Ozem, and Ahijah. ²⁶Jerahmeel also had another wife, whose name was Atarah; she was the mother of Onam. ²⁷The sons of Ram, the firstborn of Jerahmeel: Maaz, Jamin, and Eker. ²⁸The sons of Onam: Shammai and Jada. The sons of Shammai: Nadab and Abishur. ²⁹The name of Abishur's wife was Abihail, and she bore him Ahban and Molid. ³⁰The sons of Nadab: Seled and Appaim; and Seled died childless. ³¹The son of Appaim: Ishi. The son of Ishi: Sheshan. The son of Sheshan: Ahlai. ³²The sons of Jada, Shammai's brother: Jether and Jonathan; and Jether died childless. ³³The sons of Jonathan: Peleth and Zaza. These were the descendants of Jerahmeel. ³⁴Now Sheshan had no sons, only daughters, but Sheshan had an Egyptian slave whose name was Jarha. ³⁵So Sheshan gave his daughter in marriage to his slave Jarha, and she bore him Attai. ³⁶Attai became the father of Nathan, and Nathan of Zabad. ³⁷Zabad became the father of Ephlal, and Ephlal of Obed. ³⁸Obed became the father of Jehu, and Jehu of Azariah. ³⁹Azariah became the father of Helez, and Helez of Eleasah. ⁴⁰Eleasah became the father of Sismai, and Sismai of Shallum. ⁴¹Shallum became the father of Jekamiah, and Jekamiah of Elishama.

42 The sons of Caleb brother of Jerahmeel:

Hezron, listing his children with a second wife. **2:22** *Twenty-three towns in the land of Gilead.* See Num. 32:41; Deut. 3:14. **2:23** *Sixty towns.* See Josh. 13:8–13, 29–31. **2:34** *Sheshan had no sons, only daughters.* This contrasts with v. 31, when Ahlai is named as the son of Sheshan. The discrepancy may be a result either of there being two different persons by the name of Sheshan or of there being two different genealogical traditions about the same Sheshan. **2:35** In a genealogy that is thoroughly patrilineal, it is remarkable to see Sheshan's line perpetuated through his daughter. It may be a reflection of Exod. 21:4, where a wife given to a slave, as well as any children born to them,

Mesha his firstborn, who was father of Ziph. The sons of Mareshah father of Hebron. ⁴³The sons of Hebron: Korah, Tappuah, Rekem, and Shema. ⁴⁴Shema became father of Raham, father of Jorkeam; and Rekem became the father of Shammai. ⁴⁵The son of Shammai: Maon; and Maon was the father of Beth-zur. ⁴⁶Ephah also, Caleb's concubine, bore Haran, Moza, and Gazez; and Haran became the father of Gazez. ⁴⁷The sons of Jahdai: Regem, Jotham, Geshan, Pelet, Ephah, and Shaaph. ⁴⁸Maacah, Caleb's concubine, bore Sheber and Tirhanah. ⁴⁹She also bore Shaaph father of Madmannah, Sheva father of Machbenah and father of Gibea; and the daughter of Caleb was Achsah. ⁵⁰These were the descendants of Caleb.

The sons of Hur the firstborn of Ephrathah: Shobal father of Kiriath-jearim, ⁵¹Salma father of Bethlehem, and Hareph father of Beth-gader. ⁵²Shobal father of Kiriath-jearim had other sons: Haroeh, half of the Menuhoth. ⁵³And the families of Kiriath-jearim: the Ithrites, the Puthites, the Shumathites, and the Mishraites; from these came the Zorathites and the Eshtaolites. ⁵⁴The sons of Salma: Bethlehem, the Netophathites, Atroth-beth-joab, and half of the Manahathites, the Zorites. ⁵⁵The families also of the scribes that lived at Jabez: the Tirathites, the Shimeathites, and the Sucathites. These are the Kenites who came from Hammath, father of the house of Rechab.

3 These are the sons of David who were born to him in Hebron: the firstborn Amnon, by Ahinoam the Jezreelite; the second Daniel, by Abigail the Carmelite; ²the third Absalom, son of Maacah daughter of King Talmai of Geshur; the fourth Adonijah, son of Haggith; ³the fifth Shephatiah, by Abital; the sixth Ithream, by his wife Eglah; ⁴six were born to him in Hebron, where he reigned for seven years and six months. And he reigned thirty-three years in Jerusalem. ⁵These were born to him in Jerusalem: Shimea, Shobab, Nathan, and Solomon, four by Bath-shua daughter of Ammiel; ⁶then Ibhar, Elishama, Eliphelet, ⁷Nogah, Nepheg, Japhia, ⁸Elishama, Eliada, and Eliphelet, nine. ⁹All these were David's sons, besides the sons of the concubines, and Tamar was their sister.

10 The descendants of Solomon: Rehoboam, Abijah his son, Asa his son, Jehoshaphat his son, ¹¹Joram his son, Ahaziah his son, Joash his son, ¹²Amaziah his son, Azariah his son, Jotham his son, ¹³Ahaz his son, Hezekiah his son, Manasseh his son, ¹⁴Amon his son, Josiah his son. ¹⁵The sons of Josiah: Johanan the firstborn, the second Jehoiakim, the third Zedekiah, the fourth Shallum. ¹⁶The descendants of Jehoiakim: Jeconiah his son, Zedekiah his son; ¹⁷and the sons of Jeconiah the captive: Shealtiel his son, ¹⁸Malchiram, Pedaiah, Shenazzar, Jekamiah, Hoshama, and Nedabiah. ¹⁹The sons of Pedaiah: Zerubbabel and Shimei; and the sons of Zerubbabel: Meshullam

remains with the master (see **"Women in the Genealogy," p. 545**). **2:46** The word "pilegesh," translated as *concubine*, refers to a secondary wife.

3:1–24 Descendants of David and Solomon. 3:1–3 Parallel, with variations, to 2 Sam. 3:2–5. **3:5–8** Parallel, with variations, to 2 Sam. 5:14–15. **3:5** *Bath-shua daughter of Ammiel* is Bathsheba daughter of Eliam in 2 Sam. 11 and 1 Kgs. 1–2. The name *Ammiel* is an alternate form of Eliam—a transposition of the first two consonants in the name with the last two. These minor differences suggest the Chronicler may be drawing from a slightly different source tradition than the one behind 2 Samuel. **3:10–14** The genealogy of Solomon becomes starkly linear, one member of each generation, father to son, in what amounts to a dynastic list of the kings of Judah from Rehoboam to Josiah. **3:16** *Jeconiah*—that is, Jehoiachin. The name is Jehoiachin in 2 Kings, Coniah or Jeconiah in Jeremiah, Jeconiah here in 1 Chronicles, and Jehoiachin at 2 Chr. 36:8–9. **3:17** *Jeconiah the captive.* According to 2 Kgs. 24:10–17, Jeconiah/Jehoiachin surrendered to King Nebuchadnezzar during the siege of Jerusalem in 597 BCE and was taken as a captive to Babylon. He was later released from prison (2 Kgs. 25:27–30), which explains how his line—which is also the Davidic dynastic line—could continue into the postexilic period, even when there was no throne for the Davidic descendants to occupy. A cuneiform tablet discovered in Babylon lists rations for Jehoiachin, king of Judah, and his five sons, corroborating his survival and progeny, though Chronicles lists a total of seven sons. **3:19–24** This genealogical information is found only in 1 Chronicles, which continues the Davidic line well into the Persian period, showing its survival into the era of the Chronicler. Although

and Hananiah, and Shelomith was their sister; [20]and Hashubah, Ohel, Berechiah, Hasadiah, and Jushab-hesed, five. [21]The sons of Hananiah: Pelatiah and Jeshaiah, his son Rephaiah, his son Arnan, his son Obadiah, his son Shecaniah. [22]The son of Shecaniah: Shemaiah, and the sons of Shemaiah: Hattush, Igal, Bariah, Neariah, and Shaphat—six. [23]The sons of Neariah: Elioenai, Hizkiah, and Azrikam, three. [24]The sons of Elioenai: Hodaviah, Eliashib, Pelaiah, Akkub, Johanan, Delaiah, and Anani, seven.

4 The sons of Judah: Perez, Hezron, Carmi, Hur, and Shobal. [2]Reaiah son of Shobal became the father of Jahath, and Jahath became the father of Ahumai and Lahad. These were the families of the Zorathites. [3]These were the sons[n] of Etam: Jezreel, Ishma, and Idbash; and the name of their sister was Hazzelelponi, [4]and Penuel was the father of Gedor, and Ezer was the father of Hushah. These were the sons of Hur, the firstborn of Ephrathah, the father of Bethlehem. [5]Ashhur father of Tekoa had two wives, Helah and Naarah; [6]Naarah bore him Ahuzzam, Hepher, Temeni, and Haahashtari.[o] These were the sons of Naarah. [7]The sons of Helah: Zereth, Izhar,[p] and Ethnan. [8]Koz became the father of Anub, Zobebah, and the families of Aharhel son of Harum. [9]Jabez was honored more than his brothers, and his mother named him

Jabez, saying, "Because I bore him in pain." [10]Jabez called on the God of Israel, saying, "Oh, that you would bless me and enlarge my territory and that your hand might be with me and that you would keep me from hurt and harm!" And God granted what he asked. [11]Chelub the brother of Shuhah became the father of Mehir, who was the father of Eshton. [12]Eshton became the father of Beth-rapha, Paseah, and Tehinnah the father of Ir-nahash. These are the men of Recah. [13]The sons of Kenaz: Othniel and Seraiah; and the sons of Othniel: Hathath and Meonothai.[q] [14]Meonothai became the father of Ophrah, and Seraiah became the father of Joab father of Ge-harashim,[r] so-called because they were artisans. [15]The sons of Caleb son of Jephunneh: Iru, Elah, and Naam; and the son of Elah: Kenaz. [16]The sons of Jehallelel: Ziph, Ziphah, Tiria, and Asarel. [17]The sons of Ezrah: Jether, Mered, Epher, and Jalon. These are the sons of Bithiah, daughter of Pharaoh, whom Mered married,[s] and she conceived and bore[t] Miriam, Shammai, and Ishbah father of Eshtemoa. [18]And his Judean wife bore Jered father of Gedor, Heber father of Soco, and Jekuthiel father of Zanoah. [19]The sons of the wife of Hodiah, the sister of

n 4.3 Gk Compare Vg: Heb *the father*   o 4.6 Or *the Ahashtarite*   p 4.7 Or *Zohar*   q 4.13 Gk Vg: Heb lacks *and Meonothai*   r 4.14 That is, *valley of artisans*   s 4.17 The clause: *These are . . . married* is transposed from 4.18   t 4.17 Heb lacks *and bore*

Judah was governed by Persia at the time, illustrating the endurance and legitimacy of the Davidic dynasty—rooted in Adam, the first human, no less (1:1)—showcases the survival of Israelite identity in the face of foreign rule and lays the groundwork for claiming Davidic authorization of postexilic institutions (cf. chaps. 22–28). **3:19** *Zerubbabel* was a governor of Judah in the late sixth to early fifth century who is mentioned many times in Ezra-Nehemiah, Haggai, and Zechariah (e.g., Ezra 5:2; Hag. 1:1; Zech. 4:6). Haggai names him as a son of *Shealtiel*, whereas 1 Chronicles lists him as a son of *Pedaiah*, another of Jeconiah's sons. In either case, Zerubbabel is a descendant of David, which may have given him particular authority in postexilic governance and kept hope alive for reinstating Davidic kingship.

4:1–23 Descendants of Judah. From here through chap. 8, the genealogy will map the descendants of the twelve sons of Jacob, the eponymous ancestors of the twelve tribes of Israel. The genealogy first doubles back to Judah (cf. 2:3) to trace different branches of his lineage. However, this section does not chart easily into a family tree, because it does not always follow linear paths, nor does it even connect each name listed with the greater genealogy of Judah. **4:1** *Sons* is used in the broader sense of "descendants" here, introducing a brief linear genealogy of six generations from Judah to Shobal. **4:9–10** The text does not connect *Jabez* directly to the surrounding genealogical lists. Instead, these two verses read like a colorful side story. The person *Jabez* must have been associated with the tribe of Judah in some way; *Jabez* appears as a Judahite place-name at 2:55. This passage is distinguished from the material surrounding it by its narrative quality, as well as by its theological emphasis; it is the first mention of God in the book of Chronicles. **4:9** *His mother* is the only woman portrayed as speaking in the book of 1 Chronicles. *Pain* in Hebrew ("*ōtseb*") is a

Making Connections: The Prayer of Jabez (1 Chronicles 4:9–10)
In the year 2000, Bruce Wilkinson published a book that launched two verses from 1 Chronicles out of obscurity and into the popular consciousness. *The Prayer of Jabez: Breaking through to the Blessed Life*, based on 1 Chr. 4:9–10, has sold well over ten million copies, nine million of those within the first two years of its publication. It also spawned a wide array of merchandise and spin-off books. Its premise is that praying Jabez's prayer will lead the petitioner to receive blessings from God, particularly financial ones. Critics have decried the book as an example of the "prosperity gospel"—a theological outlook that claims prayer and positivity, if performed correctly, lead to financial prosperity from God—while the book's defenders testify to ways they have seen the prayer work in their lives.

In the context of 1 Chronicles, Jabez's prayer has its own internal logic. The text makes clear that his name (*Ya'bēts*) is meant to be a pun on the Hebrew word *'ōtseb*, which means "pain." In ancient Israel, names were laden with meaning, and a name like "pain" was a harbinger of hardship. Whereas Jabez's mother named him in pain—in Hebrew, "called [*qr'*] his name" (v. 9 KJV)—Jabez "called [*qr'*] on the God of Israel" (v. 10 NRSVue) to counteract the fate his name implied. There is a similar lexical echo at the end of Jabez's prayer, when he prays for God to keep him from "hurt and harm" (v. 10 NRSVue), with the latter word using the same root as "pain" (*'tsb*).

Perhaps especially because of its internal coherence, this brief account of Jabez and his prayer is startling for how it interrupts the terse patterns of the genealogical lists in which it is found. Aside from being the name of a town in 1 Chr. 2:55, the proper noun "Jabez" appears nowhere else in the Bible, and there is no other information about this character. Thus, despite the fame afforded by Wilkinson's book, Jabez and his prayer retain an air of mystery. It is perhaps for this reason that readers, like Wilkinson himself, have returned to this otherwise neglected corner of the Old Testament / Hebrew Bible.

Cameron B. R. Howard

Naham, were the fathers of Keilah the Garmite and Eshtemoa the Maacathite. ²⁰The sons of Shimon: Amnon, Rinnah, Ben-hanan, and Tilon. The sons of Ishi: Zoheth and Ben-zoheth. ²¹The sons of Shelah son of Judah: Er father of Lecah, Laadah father of Mareshah, and the families of the guild of linen workers at Beth-ashbea; ²²and Jokim, and the men of Cozeba, and Joash, and Saraph, who married into Moab but returned to Lehem*ᵘ* (the records*ᵛ* are ancient). ²³These were the potters and inhabitants of Netaim and Gederah; they lived there with the king in his service.

24 The sons of Simeon: Nemuel, Jamin, Jarib, Zerah, Shaul;*ʷ* ²⁵Shallum was his son, Mibsam his son, Mishma his son. ²⁶The sons of Mishma: Hammuel his son, Zaccur his son, Shimei his son. ²⁷Shimei had sixteen sons and six daughters, but his brothers did not have many children, nor did all their family multiply like the Judeans. ²⁸They lived in Beer-sheba, Moladah, Hazar-shual, ²⁹Bilhah, Ezem, Tolad, ³⁰Bethuel, Hormah, Ziklag, ³¹Beth-marcaboth, Hazar-susim, Beth-biri, and Shaaraim. These were their towns until David became king. ³²And their villages were Etam, Ain, Rimmon, Tochen,

u 4.22 Vg Compare Gk: Heb *and Jashubi-lahem*   *v* 4.22 Or *matters*   *w* 4.24 Or *Saul*

slightly forced pun on *Jabez* (Hebrew "*Ya'bēts*"). See **"The Prayer of Jabez," p. 548**. **4:21** *The sons of Shelah son of Judah* doubles back once again to the ancestor *Judah*, son of Jacob (2:3). **4:22** *The records are ancient.* The implications of this note are not clear. It could be an affirmation of those records' authenticity or the opposite: an apology of sorts for their brevity or lack of clarity. The note could have been brought on by the reference to intermarriage with *Moab*, something forbidden in Deuteronomy but portrayed relatively positively in the book of Ruth. This seems less likely, though, since the Chronicler does not demonstrate any particular anxiety about exogamous (outside the clan) marriage in Israel's genealogies (cf. 4:17; 2:3, 34–35; etc.). **4:23** *Potters and inhabitants.* This verse encapsulates two of the explanations genealogies provide: the associations of families with particular social roles and of peoples with certain geographical locations. (So also, similarly, *guild of linen workers* in v. 21.) See **"Women in the Genealogy," p. 545**.
4:24–43 Descendants of Simeon. Having traced many branches of Judah's line, the genealogy returns to the twelve sons of Israel (2:1–2), next with Simeon. Simeon's mother is Leah, and he is the second son of Jacob. **4:27** *Nor did all their family multiply* imparts some editorial judgment by the Chronicler, who elsewhere associates progeny with blessing (e.g., 25:5). **4:28–33** Adapted

and Ashan, five towns, [33]along with all their villages that were around these towns as far as Baal. These were their settlements. And they kept a genealogical record.

34 Meshobab, Jamlech, Joshah son of Amaziah, [35]Joel, Jehu son of Joshibiah son of Seraiah son of Asiel, [36]Elioenai, Jaakobah, Jeshohaiah, Asaiah, Adiel, Jesimiel, Benaiah, [37]Ziza son of Shiphi son of Allon son of Jedaiah son of Shimri son of Shemaiah—[38]these mentioned by name were leaders in their families, and their clans increased greatly. [39]They journeyed to the entrance of Gedor, to the east side of the valley, to seek pasture for their flocks, [40]where they found rich, good pasture, and the land was very broad, quiet, and peaceful, for the former inhabitants there belonged to Ham. [41]These, registered by name, came in the days of King Hezekiah of Judah and attacked their tents and the Meunim who were found there and exterminated them to this day and settled in their place, because there was pasture there for their flocks. [42]And some of them, five hundred men of the Simeonites, went to Mount Seir, having as their leaders Pelatiah, Neariah, Rephaiah, and Uzziel, sons of Ishi; [43]they destroyed the remnant of the Amalekites who had escaped, and they have lived there to this day.

5 The sons of Reuben the firstborn of Israel. (He was the firstborn, but because he defiled his father's bed his birthright was given to the sons of Joseph son of Israel, so that he is not enrolled in the genealogy according to the birthright; [2]though Judah became prominent among his brothers and a ruler came from him, yet the birthright belonged to Joseph.) [3]The sons of Reuben, the firstborn of Israel: Hanoch, Pallu, Hezron, and Carmi. [4]The sons of Joel: Shemaiah his son, Gog his son, Shimei his son, [5]Micah his son, Reaiah his son, Baal his son, [6]Beerah his son, whom King Tiglath-pileser[x] of Assyria carried away into exile; he was a chieftain of the Reubenites. [7]And his kindred by their families, when the genealogy of their generations was reckoned: the chief, Jeiel, and Zechariah, [8]and Bela son of Azaz, son of Shema, son of Joel, who lived in Aroer, as far as Nebo and Baal-meon. [9]He also lived to the east as far as the beginning of the desert this side of the Euphrates, because their cattle had multiplied in the land of Gilead. [10]And in the days of Saul they made war on the Hagrites, who fell by their hand, and they lived in their tents throughout all the region east of Gilead.

11 The sons of Gad lived beside them in the land of Bashan as far as Salecah: [12]Joel

x 5.6 Heb *Tilgath-pilneser*

from Josh. 19:2–8. **4:33** The Hebrew verb translated as *kept a genealogical record* is attested only in the postexilic period and refers specifically to a written ancestry record. **4:38–43** The genealogical format of 1 Chr. 1–9 is interrupted with the longest piece of narrative so far. It explains that the Simeonites were so prolific that they needed more room for their families' flocks, so they overtook the resident settlers at Gedor for the *rich, good pasture.* The narrative stays largely on theme for the genealogies, conveying both a social role (shepherds) and a geographical location (Gedor). **4:41** *These, registered by name*—presumably the Simeonites mentioned in v. 37, though the antecedent is not altogether clear. *Registered* is more woodenly rendered "written." *In the days of King Hezekiah,* who reigned at the end of the eighth and beginning of the seventh centuries BCE. **4:43** *Amalekites* feature in several conflicts with the Israelites throughout biblical history. See especially 1 Sam. 15:1–33 and 1 Sam. 30:1–20.

5:1–10 Descendants of Reuben. 5:1–3 *The sons of Reuben the firstborn of Israel.* These words appear before and after the parenthetical note on Reuben's lost birthright. In the Hebrew text, which contains no such punctuation marks, the repetition itself effectively forms the parentheses around the note, a technique called "resumptive repetition." **5:1** Reuben's mother is Leah, and he is Jacob's *firstborn* son. Traditionally, the firstborn son would receive special status and a double portion of inheritance. *Defiled his father's bed.* See Gen. 35:22; 49:4. **5:3** An identical list is found at Exod. 6:14. **5:6** *Tiglath-pileser* III ruled Assyria from 744 to 727 BCE. His repeated incursions into the northern kingdom of Israel from 734 to 732 inflamed the Syro-Ephraimite War. See 2 Kgs. 15:29–16:20. **5:9** *To the east.* The tribes of Reuben and Gad, as well as half the tribe of Manasseh, settled east of the Jordan River after the conquest of Canaan (Num. 32; Deut. 29:8; Josh. 1:12–16; 13:8–13).

5:11–22 Descendants of Gad. 5:11 Zilpah, Leah's maid, is the mother of *Gad,* and he is Jacob's

the chief, Shapham the second, Janai, and Shaphat in Bashan. [13]And their kindred according to their clans: Michael, Meshullam, Sheba, Jorai, Jacan, Zia, and Eber, seven. [14]These were the sons of Abihail son of Huri, son of Jaroah, son of Gilead, son of Michael, son of Jeshishai, son of Jahdo, son of Buz; [15]Ahi son of Abdiel, son of Guni, was chief in their clan, [16]and they lived in Gilead, in Bashan and in its towns, and in all the pasturelands of Sharon to their limits. [17]All of these were enrolled by genealogies in the days of King Jotham of Judah and in the days of King Jeroboam of Israel.

18 The Reubenites, the Gadites, and the half-tribe of Manasseh had valiant warriors who carried shield and sword and drew the bow, expert in war, forty-four thousand seven hundred sixty, ready for service. [19]They made war on the Hagrites, Jetur, Naphish, and Nodab, [20]and when they received help against them, the Hagrites and all who were with them were given into their hands, for they cried to God in the battle, and he granted their entreaty because they trusted in him. [21]They captured their livestock: fifty thousand of their camels, two hundred fifty thousand sheep, two thousand donkeys, and one hundred thousand captives. [22]Many fell slain because the war was of God. And they lived in their territory until the exile.

23 The members of the half-tribe of Manasseh lived in the land; they were very numerous from Bashan to Baal-hermon, Senir, and Mount Hermon. [24]These were the heads of their clans: Epher,[y] Ishi, Eliel, Azriel, Jeremiah, Hodaviah, and Jahdiel, mighty warriors, famous men, heads of their clans. [25]But they transgressed against the God of their ancestors and prostituted themselves to the gods of the peoples of the land whom God had destroyed before them. [26]So the God of Israel stirred up the spirit of King Pul of Assyria, the spirit of King Tiglath-pileser[z] of Assyria, and he carried them away, namely, the Reubenites, the Gadites, and the half-tribe of Manasseh, and brought them to Halah, Habor, Hara, and the River Gozan, to this day.

6 [a]The sons of Levi: Gershon, Kohath, and Merari. [2]The sons of Kohath: Amram, Izhar, Hebron, and Uzziel. [3]The children of Amram: Aaron, Moses, and Miriam. The sons of Aaron: Nadab, Abihu, Eleazar, and Ithamar. [4]Eleazar became the father of Phinehas, Phinehas of Abishua, [5]Abishua of Bukki, Bukki of Uzzi, [6]Uzzi of Zerahiah, Zerahiah of Meraioth, [7]Meraioth of Amariah, Amariah of Ahitub, [8]Ahitub of Zadok, Zadok of Ahimaaz, [9]Ahimaaz of Azariah, Azariah of Johanan, [10]and Johanan of Azariah (it was he who served as priest in the house that Solomon built in Jerusalem). [11]Azariah became the father of Amariah, Amariah of Ahitub, [12]Ahitub of Zadok, Zadok of Shallum, [13]Shallum of Hilkiah, Hilkiah of Azariah, [14]Azariah of Seraiah, Seraiah of Jehozadak; [15]and Jehozadak went into exile when the LORD sent Judah and Jerusalem into exile by the hand of Nebuchadnezzar.

16 [b]The sons of Levi: Gershom, Kohath, and Merari. [17]These are the names of the sons of Gershom: Libni and Shimei. [18]The sons of Kohath: Amram, Izhar, Hebron, and Uzziel. [19]The sons of Merari: Mahli and

y 5.24 Gk Vg: Heb *and Epher*　z 5.26 Heb *Tilgath-pileser*
a 6.1 5.27 in Heb　b 6.16 6.1 in Heb

seventh son. **5:20** Like Jabez's prayer (4:10), this theological comment within a narrative embedded in the genealogy emphasizes that the petitioner called out or *cried to God* and that God fulfilled the request.

5:23–26 The half tribe of Manasseh. 5:23 *Manasseh* was the firstborn son of Joseph, the youngest of Jacob's children, and his mother was Asenath. In a deathbed blessing, Jacob granted Manasseh and his brother, Ephraim, an inheritance—an allotment of land in Canaan—with the rest of Jacob's sons (Gen. 48:5). **5:25** *Prostituted themselves.* Prostitution is a metaphor for Israel's infidelity to God that is particularly common in the prophetic literature (e.g., Jer. 3:6–8; Hos. 1:2; Ezek. 16). **5:26** *Stirred up the spirit* is a favorite phrase in postexilic texts to describe divine agency working on an individual, including non-Israelite kings like the Assyrian king *Tiglath-pileser* and the Persian king Cyrus (e.g., 2 Chr. 36:22; Ezra 1:1; 1:5; Hag. 1:14; Jer. 51:11). *Pul* is another name for *Tiglath-pileser*; the Chronicler is referring to a single king of Assyria by two different names.

6:1–30 Descendants of Levi. The Hebrew text numbers 6:1–30 as 5:27–6:15. **6:1** *Levi* is the third son of Jacob, and Leah is his mother (Gen. 29:31–35). **6:15** *Jehozadak* is the father of the postexilic high priest Jeshua (see, e.g., Hag. 1:1; Zech. 6:11; Ezra 3:2).

Mushi. These are the clans of the Levites according to their ancestry. ²⁰Of Gershom: Libni his son, Jahath his son, Zimmah his son, ²¹Joah his son, Iddo his son, Zerah his son, Jeatherai his son. ²²The sons of Kohath: Amminadab his son, Korah his son, Assir his son, ²³Elkanah his son, Ebiasaph his son, Assir his son, ²⁴Tahath his son, Uriel his son, Uzziah his son, and Shaul his son. ²⁵The sons of Elkanah: Amasai and Ahimoth, ²⁶Elkanah his son, Zophai his son, Nahath his son, ²⁷Eliab his son, Jeroham his son, Elkanah his son, Samuel his son.^c ²⁸The sons of Samuel: Joel^d his firstborn, the second Abijah.^e ²⁹The sons of Merari: Mahli, Libni his son, Shimei his son, Uzzah his son, ³⁰Shimea his son, Haggiah his son, and Asaiah his son.

31 These are the men whom David put in charge of the service of song in the house of the LORD, after the ark came to rest there. ³²They ministered with song before the tabernacle of the tent of meeting until Solomon had built the house of the LORD in Jerusalem, and they performed their service in due order. ³³These are the men who served, and their sons were: Of the Kohathites: Heman, the singer, son of Joel, son of Samuel, ³⁴son of Elkanah, son of Jeroham, son of Eliel, son of Toah, ³⁵son of Zuph, son of Elkanah, son of Mahath, son of Amasai, ³⁶son of Elkanah, son of Joel, son of Azariah, son of Zephaniah, ³⁷son of Tahath, son of Assir, son of Ebiasaph, son of Korah, ³⁸son of Izhar, son of Kohath, son of Levi, son of Israel; ³⁹and his kinsman Asaph, who stood on his right, namely, Asaph son of Berechiah, son of Shimea, ⁴⁰son of Michael, son of Baaseiah, son of Malchijah, ⁴¹son of Ethni, son of Zerah, son of Adaiah, ⁴²son of Ethan, son of Zimmah, son of Shimei, ⁴³son of Jahath, son of Gershom, son of Levi. ⁴⁴On the left were their kindred the sons of Merari: Ethan son of Kishi, son of Abdi, son of Malluch, ⁴⁵son of Hashabiah, son of Amaziah, son of Hilkiah, ⁴⁶son of Amzi, son of Bani, son of Shemer, ⁴⁷son of Mahli, son of Mushi, son of Merari, son of Levi; ⁴⁸and their kindred the Levites were appointed for all the service of the tabernacle of the house of God.

49 But Aaron and his sons made offerings on the altar of burnt offering and on the altar of incense, doing all the work of the most holy place, to make atonement for Israel, according to all that Moses the servant of God had commanded. ⁵⁰These are the sons of Aaron: Eleazar his son, Phinehas his son, Abishua his son, ⁵¹Bukki his son, Uzzi his son, Zerahiah his son, ⁵²Meraioth his son, Amariah his son, Ahitub his son, ⁵³Zadok his son, Ahimaaz his son.

54 These are their dwelling places according to their settlements within their territories: to the sons of Aaron of the families of Kohathites—for the lot fell to them first—⁵⁵to them they gave Hebron in the land of Judah and its surrounding pasturelands, ⁵⁶but the fields of the city and its villages they gave to Caleb son of Jephunneh. ⁵⁷To the sons of Aaron they gave the cities of refuge: Hebron, Libnah with its pasturelands, Jattir, Eshtemoa with its pasturelands, ⁵⁸Hilen^f with its pasturelands, Debir with its pasturelands, ⁵⁹Ashan with its pasturelands, and Beth-shemesh with its pasturelands. ⁶⁰From the tribe of Benjamin, Geba with its pasturelands, Alemeth with its pasturelands, and Anathoth with its pasturelands. All their towns throughout their families were thirteen.

c 6.27 Gk mss: Heb lacks *Samuel his son*   d 6.28 Gk Syr: Heb lacks *Joel*   e 6.28 Lucianic Syr: Heb *Vashni, and Abijah*   f 6.58 Heb mss: MT *Hilez*

6:31–53 Musicians appointed by David. In the Hebrew text, this is 6:20–38. **6:31** *After the ark came to rest there.* See chap. 15. **6:49** All priests and Levites are descendants of Levi, but only descendants of *Aaron*, great-grandson of Levi (6:1–3), could be priests, who do *all the work of the most holy place*—that is, offering sacrifices. The Levites are elsewhere described as cultic caretakers in perpetual service to the priests (cf. Num. 3:6–9), but in Chronicles, the work of the Levites in the care of the temple and in public liturgical practice receives careful attention and an honored status.

6:54–81 Settlements of the Levites. In Hebrew, this unit is 6:39–66. The Levites were not given allotments of land as an inheritance and were instead to be supported by the tithes of the Israelites (Num. 18:21–24). They did, however, receive particular towns and pasturelands for their settlements, which are enumerated here (cf. Num. 35:1–8; Josh. 21:1–42). **6:54** The distribution of *dwelling places* by *lot* emphasizes the order of distribution was by chance rather than by a hierarchy within the tribe. **6:57** *Cities of refuge* were places where "a slayer who kill[ed] a person without intent" might flee as a "refuge from the avenger . . . until there [was] a trial before the congregation" (Num. 35:11–12).

61 To the rest of the Kohathites were given by lot out of the family of the tribe, out of the half-tribe, the half of Manasseh, ten towns. [62]To the Gershomites according to their families were allotted thirteen towns out of the tribes of Issachar, Asher, Naphtali, and Manasseh in Bashan. [63]To the Merarites according to their families were allotted twelve towns out of the tribes of Reuben, Gad, and Zebulun. [64]So the people of Israel gave the Levites the towns with their pasturelands. [65]They also gave them by lot out of the tribes of Judah, Simeon, and Benjamin these towns that are mentioned by name.

66 And some of the families of the sons of Kohath had towns of their territory out of the tribe of Ephraim. [67]They were given the cities of refuge: Shechem with its pasturelands in the hill country of Ephraim, Gezer with its pasturelands, [68]Jokmeam with its pasturelands, Beth-horon with its pasturelands, [69]Aijalon with its pasturelands, Gath-rimmon with its pasturelands; [70]and out of the half-tribe of Manasseh, Aner with its pasturelands, and Bileam with its pasturelands, for the rest of the families of the Kohathites.

71 To the Gershomites: out of the half-tribe of Manasseh: Golan in Bashan with its pasturelands and Ashtaroth with its pasturelands; [72]and out of the tribe of Issachar: Kedesh with its pasturelands, Daberath[g] with its pasturelands, [73]Ramoth with its pasturelands, and Anem with its pasturelands; [74]out of the tribe of Asher: Mashal with its pasturelands, Abdon with its pasturelands, [75]Hukok with its pasturelands, and Rehob with its pasturelands; [76]and out of the tribe of Naphtali: Kedesh in Galilee with its pasturelands, Hammon with its pasturelands, and Kiriathaim with its pasturelands. [77]To the rest of the Merarites out of the tribe of Zebulun: Rimmono with its pasturelands, Tabor with its pasturelands, [78]and across the Jordan from Jericho, on the east side of the Jordan, out of the tribe of Reuben: Bezer in the steppe with its pasturelands, Jahzah with its pasturelands, [79]Kedemoth with its pasturelands, and Mephaath with its pasturelands; [80]and out of the tribe of Gad: Ramoth in Gilead with its pasturelands, Mahanaim with its pasturelands, [81]Heshbon with its pasturelands, and Jazer with its pasturelands.

7 The sons[b] of Issachar: Tola, Puah, Jashub, and Shimron, four. [2]The sons of Tola: Uzzi, Rephaiah, Jeriel, Jahmai, Ibsam, and Shemuel, heads of their ancestral houses, namely, of Tola, mighty warriors of their generations, their number in the days of David being twenty-two thousand six hundred. [3]The son of Uzzi: Izrahiah. And the sons of Izrahiah: Michael, Obadiah, Joel, and Isshiah, five, all of them chiefs; [4]and along with them, by their generations, according to their ancestral houses, were units of the fighting force, thirty-six thousand, for they had many wives and sons. [5]Their kindred belonging to all the families of Issachar were in all eighty-seven thousand mighty warriors, enrolled by genealogy.

6 The sons of[i] Benjamin: Bela, Becher, and Jediael, three. [7]The sons of Bela: Ezbon, Uzzi, Uzziel, Jerimoth, and Iri, five, heads of ancestral houses, mighty warriors; and their enrollment by genealogies was twenty-two thousand thirty-four. [8]The sons of Becher: Zemirah, Joash, Eliezer, Elioenai, Omri, Jeremoth, Abijah, Anathoth, and Alemeth. All these were the sons of Becher; [9]and their enrollment by genealogies, according to their generations, as heads of their ancestral houses, mighty warriors, was twenty thousand two hundred. [10]The son of Jediael: Bilhan. And the sons of Bilhan: Jeush, Benjamin, Ehud, Chenaanah, Zethan, Tarshish, and Ahishahar. [11]All these were the sons of Jediael according to the heads of their ancestral houses, mighty warriors, seventeen thousand two hundred, ready for service in war. [12]And Shuppim and Huppim were the sons of Ir, Hushim the son of Aher.

g 6.72 Or *Dobrath*   b 7.1 Syr Compare Vg: Heb *And to the sons*   i 7.6 Heb mss Lucianic Vg Tg Syr: MT lacks *sons of*

7:1–5 Descendants of Issachar. 7:1 *Issachar* is the ninth son of Jacob, and his mother is Leah (Gen. 30:14–21). **7:2** *The days of David* were in the early tenth century BCE. This temporal detail, along with the vocabulary of being *enrolled by genealogy* (v. 5), implies these are numbers from David's census (cf. 21:1–17).

7:6–12 Descendants of Benjamin. *Benjamin* is the youngest (twelfth) son of Jacob, and Rachel is his mother. She died giving birth to him (Gen. 35:16–21). **7:12** *Dan*, the fifth son of Jacob and first son of Bilhah, Rachel's maid (Gen. 30:1–8), does not appear in this portion of the genealogy. Some

13 The descendants of Naphtali: Jahziel, Guni, Jezer, and Shallum, the descendants of Bilhah.

14 The sons of Manasseh: Asriel, whom his Aramean concubine bore; she bore Machir the father of Gilead. ¹⁵And Machir took a wife for Huppim and for Shuppim. The name of his sister was Maacah. And the name of the second was Zelophehad; and Zelophehad had daughters. ¹⁶Maacah the wife of Machir bore a son, and she named him Peresh; the name of his brother was Sheresh, and his sons were Ulam and Rekem. ¹⁷The son of Ulam: Bedan. These were the sons of Gilead son of Machir son of Manasseh. ¹⁸And his sister Hammolecheth bore Ishhod, Abiezer, and Mahlah. ¹⁹The sons of Shemida were Ahian, Shechem, Likhi, and Aniam.

20 The sons of Ephraim: Shuthelah, and Bered his son, Tahath his son, Eleadah his son, Tahath his son, ²¹Zabad his son, Shuthelah his son, and Ezer and Elead. Now the people of Gath who were born in the land killed them, because they came down to raid their cattle. ²²And their father Ephraim mourned many days, and his brothers came to comfort him. ²³Ephraimʲ went in to his wife, and she conceived and bore a son, and he named him Beriah,ᵏ because disaster had befallen his house. ²⁴His daughter was Sheerah, who built both Lower and Upper Beth-horon and Uzzen-sheerah. ²⁵Rephah was his son, Resheph his son, Telah his son, Tahan his son, ²⁶Ladan his son, Ammihud his son, Elishama his son, ²⁷Nunˡ his son, Joshua his son. ²⁸Their possessions and settlements were Bethel and its towns, and eastward Naaran, and westward Gezer and its towns, Shechem and its towns, as far as Ayyah and its towns; ²⁹also along the borders of the Manassites, Beth-shean and its towns, Taanach and its towns, Megiddo and its towns, Dor and its towns. In these lived the sons of Joseph son of Israel.

30 The sons of Asher: Imnah, Ishvah, Ishvi, Beriah, and their sister Serah. ³¹The sons of Beriah: Heber and Malchiel, who was the father of Birzaith. ³²Heber became the father of Japhlet, Shomer, Hotham, and their sister Shua. ³³The sons of Japhlet: Pasach, Bimhal, and Ashvath. These are the sons of Japhlet. ³⁴The sons of Shemer: Ahi, Rohgah, Hubbah, and Aram. ³⁵The sons of Helemᵐ his brother: Zophah, Imna, Shelesh, and Amal. ³⁶The sons of Zophah: Suah, Harnepher, Shual, Beri, Imrah, ³⁷Bezer, Hod, Shamma, Shilshah, Ithran, and Beera. ³⁸The sons of Jether: Jephunneh, Pispa, and Ara. ³⁹The sons of Ulla: Arah, Hanniel,

j 7.23 Heb He   k 7.23 In Heb Beriah is related to the word for disaster   l 7.27 Heb Non   m 7.35 Or Hotham

scholars propose that this omission is due to textual corruption and that a brief genealogy for Dan originally appeared here, especially since the Hebrew text names Hushim as the son of Dan at Gen. 46:23. Notably, there is also no genealogy for Zebulun, Leah's sixth and final son and Jacob's tenth.

7:13 Descendants of Naphtali. *Naphtali* is the sixth son of Jacob. He and Dan are the two sons of *Bilhah*, Rachel's maid. This verse is probably dependent on Gen. 46:24, but the inclusion of Naphtali's mother's name is unique among the Chronicler's genealogies of Jacob's sons (see **"Women in the Genealogy," p. 545**).

7:14–19 Descendants of Manasseh. The lineage in this section is particularly difficult to follow due to missing relationships and ambiguous formulations. **7:14** *Manasseh* is the oldest son of Joseph. See the note at 5:23. This portion of Manasseh's genealogy refers to the segment of the tribe that settles west of the Jordan River, whereas the earlier genealogy (5:23–26) refers to the Transjordanian half of the tribe that lives east of the Jordan. Manasseh's *Aramean concubine* is referred to at Gen. 46:20 in the Greek Septuagint but not in the Hebrew text. **7:15** By noting that *Zelophehad had daughters* (cf. Num. 26:33), the text nods to the tradition in which those daughters petitioned Moses for their father's inheritance, since he had no sons. Moses granted their request, under the condition that they marry within their tribe (Num. 27:1–11; 36:1–12; Josh. 17:3–6).

7:20–29 Descendants of Ephraim. 7:20 *Ephraim* is a son of Joseph and his Egyptian wife, Asenath. When Ephraim and Manasseh's grandfather Jacob blesses them (Gen. 48), he crosses his hands so that the younger son, Ephraim, is blessed with Jacob's right hand and receives firstborn status. **7:24** The description of a woman, *Sheerah*, as a builder of cities is remarkable and without parallel in the Hebrew Bible. *Uzzen-sheerah* is named after its builder.

7:30–40 Descendants of Asher. 7:30 *Asher* is the eighth son of Jacob, and his mother is Zilpah, Leah's maid (Gen. 30:9–13).

and Rizia. [40]All of these were men of Asher, heads of ancestral houses, select mighty
warriors, chief of the princes. Their number
enrolled by genealogies, for service in war,
was twenty-six thousand men.

8 Benjamin became the father of Bela his
firstborn, Ashbel the second, Aharah
the third, [2]Nohah the fourth, and Rapha
the fifth. [3]And Bela had sons: Addar, Gera,
Abihud,[n] [4]Abishua, Naaman, Ahoah, [5]Gera,
Shephuphan, and Huram. [6]These are the
sons of Ehud (they were heads of ancestral houses of the inhabitants of Geba,
and they were carried into exile to Manahath): [7]Naaman,[o] Ahijah, and Gera, that is,
Heglam,[p] who became the father of Uzza
and Ahihud. [8]And Shaharaim had sons in
the country of Moab after he had sent away
his wives Hushim and Baara. [9]He had sons
by his wife Hodesh: Jobab, Zibia, Mesha,
Malcam, [10]Jeuz, Sachia, and Mirmah. These
were his sons, heads of ancestral houses.
[11]He also had sons by Hushim: Abitub and
Elpaal. [12]The sons of Elpaal: Eber, Misham,
and Shemed, who built Ono and Lod with
its towns, [13]and Beriah and Shema (they
were heads of ancestral houses of the inhabitants of Aijalon who put to flight the
inhabitants of Gath), [14]and Ahio, Shashak,
and Jeremoth. [15]Zebadiah, Arad, Eder,
[16]Michael, Ishpah, and Joha were the sons
of Beriah. [17]Zebadiah, Meshullam, Hizki,
Heber, [18]Ishmerai, Izliah, and Jobab were
the sons of Elpaal. [19]Jakim, Zichri, Zabdi,
[20]Elienai, Zillethai, Eliel, [21]Adaiah, Beraiah,
and Shimrath were the sons of Shimei.
[22]Ishpan, Eber, Eliel, [23]Abdon, Zichri,
Hanan, [24]Hananiah, Elam, Anthothijah,
[25]Iphdeiah, and Penuel were the sons of
Shashak. [26]Shamsherai, Shehariah, Athaliah, [27]Jaareshiah, Elijah, and Zichri were the
sons of Jeroham. [28]These were the heads of
ancestral houses, according to their generations, chiefs. These lived in Jerusalem.

29 Jeiel[q] the father of Gibeon lived in
Gibeon, and the name of his wife was
Maacah. [30]His firstborn son: Abdon, then
Zur, Kish, Baal, Nadab, [31]Gedor, Ahio, Zech-
er, [32]and Mikloth, who became the father
of Shimeah. Now these also lived opposite
their kindred in Jerusalem, with their kindred. [33]Ner became the father of Kish, Kish
of Saul,[r] Saul[s] of Jonathan, Malchishua,
Abinadab, and Esh-baal; [34]and the son of
Jonathan was Merib-baal; and Merib-baal
became the father of Micah. [35]The sons of
Micah: Pithon, Melech, Tarea, and Ahaz.
[36]Ahaz became the father of Jehoaddah;
and Jehoaddah became the father of Alemeth, Azmaveth, and Zimri; Zimri became
the father of Moza. [37]Moza became the father of Binea; Raphah was his son, Eleasah
his son, Azel his son. [38]Azel had six sons, and
these are their names: Azrikam, Bocheru,[t]
Ishmael, Sheariah, Obadiah, and Hanan; all
these were the sons of Azel. [39]The sons of his
brother Eshek: Ulam his firstborn, Jeush the
second, and Eliphelet the third. [40]The sons
of Ulam were mighty warriors, archers, having many children and grandchildren, one
hundred fifty. All these were Benjaminites.

9 So all Israel was enrolled by genealogies, and these are written in the Book
of the Kings of Israel. And Judah was tak-
en into exile in Babylon because of their

n 8.3 Or *father of Ehud* *o* 8.7 Heb *and Naaman* *p* 8.7 Or *he carried them into exile* *q* 8.29 Heb lacks *Jeiel* *r* 8.33 Or *Shaul* *s* 8.33 Or *Shaul* *t* 8.38 Or *his firstborn*

8:1–40 Descendants of Benjamin. This genealogy of Benjamin differs significantly from the one at 7:6–12, as well as the ones at Gen. 46:21 and Num. 26:38–40, suggesting conflicting traditions as well as change in the tradition(s) over time. **8:8** No reason is given for why Shaharaim *sent away his wives.* **8:28** After the division of the kingdom during the reign of Rehoboam (see the note at 2:3), Benjamin and Judah were the tribes left in the southern kingdom, with *Jerusalem*, part of the tribal land of Benjamin (cf. Josh. 18:28), as its capital.

9:1–2 Although numbered as the beginning of chap. 9, v. 1 provides the conclusion to the genealogical information on the tribes of Israel from chaps. 2–8, while v. 2 pivots forward in time to introduce family lines in the postexilic period (vv. 3–34). **9:1** *All Israel* is a favorite designation of the Chronicler for the unity of the twelve (or rather, thirteen, counting Joseph's two sons in his stead; see note on 5:23) ancestral tribes. *Enrolled by genealogies.* See the note at 4:33. Throughout Chronicles, the text points to other source texts such as *the Book of the Kings of Israel* (cf. 27:24; 29:29–30; 2 Chr. 9:29; 12:15; 13:22; 16:11; 20:34; 24:27; 25:26; 26:22; 27:7; 28:26; 32:32; 33:18; 35:26–27; 36:8). These citations serve several different purposes. First, they may be the names of actual source texts

unfaithfulness. ²Now the first to live again in their possessions in their towns were Israelites, priests, Levites, and temple servants.

3 And some of the people of Judah, Benjamin, Ephraim, and Manasseh lived in Jerusalem: ⁴Uthai son of Ammihud, son of Omri, son of Imri, son of Bani, from the sons of Perez son of Judah. ⁵And of the Shilonites: Asaiah the firstborn and his sons. ⁶Of the sons of Zerah: Jeuel and their kin, six hundred ninety. ⁷Of the Benjaminites: Sallu son of Meshullam, son of Hodaviah, son of Hassenuah, ⁸Ibneiah son of Jeroham, Elah son of Uzzi, son of Michri, and Meshullam son of Shephatiah, son of Reuel, son of Ibnijah; ⁹and their kindred according to their generations, nine hundred fifty-six. All these were heads of families according to their ancestral houses.

10 Of the priests: Jedaiah, Jehoiarib, Jachin, ¹¹and Azariah son of Hilkiah, son of Meshullam, son of Zadok, son of Meraioth, son of Ahitub, the chief officer of the house of God; ¹²and Adaiah son of Jeroham, son of Pashhur, son of Malchijah, and Maasai son of Adiel, son of Jahzerah, son of Meshullam, son of Meshillemith, son of Immer; ¹³besides their kindred, heads of their ancestral houses, one thousand seven hundred sixty, qualified for the work of the service of the house of God.

14 Of the Levites: Shemaiah son of Hasshub, son of Azrikam, son of Hashabiah, of the sons of Merari; ¹⁵and Bakbakkar, Heresh, Galal, and Mattaniah son of Mica, son of Zichri, son of Asaph; ¹⁶and Obadiah son of Shemaiah, son of Galal, son of Jeduthun, and Berechiah son of Asa, son of Elkanah, who lived in the villages of the Netophathites.

17 The gatekeepers were: Shallum, Akkub, Talmon, Ahiman; and their kinsman Shallum was the chief, ¹⁸stationed previously in the king's gate on the east side. These were the gatekeepers of the camp of the Levites. ¹⁹Shallum son of Kore, son of Ebiasaph, son of Korah, and his kindred of his ancestral house, the Korahites, were in charge of the work of the service, guardians of the thresholds of the tent, as their ancestors had been in charge of the camp of the Lord, guardians of the entrance. ²⁰And Phinehas son of Eleazar was chief over them in former times; the Lord was with him. ²¹Zechariah son of Meshelemiah was gatekeeper at the entrance of the tent of meeting. ²²All these who were chosen as gatekeepers at the thresholds were two hundred twelve. They were enrolled by genealogies in their villages. David and the seer Samuel established them in their office of trust. ²³So they and their descendants were in charge of the gates of the house of the Lord, that is, the house of the tent, as guards. ²⁴The gatekeepers were on the four sides: east, west, north, and south; ²⁵and their kindred who were in their villages were obliged to come in every seven days, in turn, to be with them, ²⁶for the four

the Chronicler used, which are no longer extant. Regardless of whether these texts actually existed, they also add an air of authority to the Chronicler's account, especially for the Persian period, an era of emerging bureaucracy when written texts carried particular weight. Finally, the many references to books and annals provide an explanation of sorts for the Chronicler's discriminating presentation of information. The Chronicler makes no secret that what Chronicles presents is a particular, selective account of the history of Israel and Judah; additional sources are the place for interested readers to obtain (presumably) further information.

9:3–9 Inhabitants of Jerusalem after the exile. Having given attention to primeval, ancestral, and Davidic foundations of Israel's leadership, the genealogical prologue of 1 Chr. 1–9 turns next to the postexilic era—the era of the author—to connect the past more explicitly with cultic work in the present (i.e., the Persian period). From chap. 10 onward, the text will continue this work of drawing on the past to authorize the future by turning to the genre of narrative punctuated by lists rather than by genealogical lists punctuated occasionally by narrative, as is the case in chaps. 1–9.

9:10–13 Priestly families. 9:13 *Qualified for the work of the service.* A phrase with military overtones (the Hebrew phrase is "mighty warriors"; see the note at 26:6–8), though it also connotes a more general suitability for service.

9:14–34 Levitical families. 9:22 Again the Chronicler draws on two favorite sources of authorization for postexilic social roles: that these gatekeepers were *enrolled by genealogies* (i.e., by written records) and that *David and the seer Samuel established them*—Samuel being an addition to the more standard appeal to Davidic origins.

chief gatekeepers, who were Levites, were in charge of the chambers and the treasures of the house of God. ²⁷And they would spend the night near the house of God, for on them lay the duty of watching, and they had charge of opening it every morning.

28 Some of them had charge of the utensils of service, for they were required to count them when they were brought in and taken out. ²⁹Others of them were appointed over the furniture and over all the holy utensils, also over the choice flour, the wine, the oil, the incense, and the spices. ³⁰Others of the sons of the priests prepared the mixing of the spices, ³¹and Mattithiah, one of the Levites, the firstborn of Shallum the Korahite, was in charge of making the flat cakes. ³²Also some of their kindred of the Kohathites had charge of the rows of bread, to prepare them for each Sabbath.

33 Now these are the singers, the heads of ancestral houses of the Levites, living in the chambers of the temple free from other service, for they were on duty day and night. ³⁴These were heads of ancestral houses of the Levites, according to their generations; these leaders lived in Jerusalem.

35 In Gibeon lived the father of Gibeon, Jeiel, and the name of his wife was Maacah. ³⁶His firstborn son was Abdon, then Zur, Kish, Baal, Ner, Nadab, ³⁷Gedor, Ahio, Zechariah, and Mikloth; ³⁸and Mikloth became the father of Shimeam; and these also lived opposite their kindred in Jerusalem, with their kindred. ³⁹Ner became the father of Kish, Kish of Saul, Saul of Jonathan, Malchishua, Abinadab, and Esh-baal; ⁴⁰and the son of Jonathan was Merib-baal; and Merib-baal became the father of Micah. ⁴¹The sons of Micah: Pithon, Melech, Tahrea, and Ahaz;ᵘ ⁴²and Ahaz became the father of Jarah, and Jarah of Alemeth, Azmaveth, and Zimri; and Zimri became the father of Moza. ⁴³Moza became the father of Binea; and Rephaiah was his son, Eleasah his son, Azel his son. ⁴⁴Azel had six sons, and these are their names: Azrikam, Bocheru,ᵛ Ishmael, Sheariah, Obadiah, and Hanan; these were the sons of Azel.

10 Now the Philistines fought against Israel, and the men of Israel fled before the Philistines and fell slain on Mount Gilboa. ²The Philistines overtook Saul and his sons, and the Philistines killed Jonathan and Abinadab and Malchishua, the sons of Saul. ³The battle pressed hard on Saul, and the archers found him, and he was wounded by the archers. ⁴Then Saul said to his armor-bearer, "Draw your sword and thrust me through with it, so that these uncircumcised may not come and make sport of me." But his armor-bearer was unwilling, for he was terrified. So Saul took his own sword and fell on it. ⁵When his armor-bearer saw

u 9.41 Heb lacks *and Ahaz* v 9.44 Or *firstborn*

9:35–44 The family of King Saul. This final section of the lengthy genealogies that open Chronicles repeats very closely the lineage of Saul already provided at 8:29–38 and thus functions more as an introduction to 10:1–12 than as a conclusion to the material immediately preceding it.

10:1–12 The death of Saul and his sons. A parallel account of Saul's death is found in 1 Sam. 31:1–13. By choosing to begin the narrative here, without any of the backstory of Saul or the early life of David, the Chronicler achieves several things. First, the undercurrent of skepticism about the monarchy that runs through Samuel-Kings is avoided. That skepticism is established in 1 Sam. 8, where the people ask the prophet Samuel for a king "to govern us, like other nations" (v. 5). God's response through Samuel is that the people will end up regretting their request, since it is a rejection of God as their king, and human kings will take the people's resources. While individual kings are criticized for missteps in Chronicles, it does not present any comparable antimonarchic sentiment. Second, beginning the narrative at Saul's death provides a clean break between Saul and David. The complicated backstory of their relationship—in which David serves Saul, loves Saul's son Jonathan, outshines Saul on the battlefield, is pursued by Saul, and even decides not to kill Saul when he has the opportunity—is not allowed to cloud the stark distinction the Chronicler draws between Saul's defeat and David's leadership. Finally, especially by omitting the tale of David's time among the Philistines as he hid from Saul, the Chronicler sets the tone for the streamlined version of David's story that will be told throughout 1 Chronicles. David's personal biography is not completely suppressed—the Chronicler assumes the ancient audience knows that tradition—but the rhetorical effect of David's pared-down and sanitized story is to emphasize his accomplishments while downplaying any faults or questionable actions. **10:4** A wounded Saul kills himself to avoid being

that Saul was dead, he also fell on his sword and died. ⁶Thus Saul died; he and his three sons and all his house died together. ⁷When all the men of Israel who were in the valley saw that the army*ʷ had fled and that Saul and his sons were dead, they abandoned their towns and fled, and the Philistines came and occupied them.

8 The next day when the Philistines came to strip the dead, they found Saul and his sons fallen on Mount Gilboa. ⁹They stripped him and took his head and his armor and sent messengers throughout the land of the Philistines to carry the good news to their idols and to the people. ¹⁰They put his armor in the temple of their gods and fastened his head in the temple of Dagon. ¹¹But when all Jabesh-gilead heard everything that the Philistines had done to Saul, ¹²all the valiant warriors got up and took away the body of Saul and the bodies of his sons and brought them to Jabesh. Then they buried their bones under the oak in Jabesh and fasted seven days.

13 So Saul died for his unfaithfulness; he was unfaithful to the Lord in that he did not keep the command of the Lord; moreover, he had consulted a medium, seeking guidance, ¹⁴and did not seek guidance from the Lord. Therefore the Lordˣ put him to death and turned the kingdom over to David son of Jesse.

11 Then all Israel gathered together to David at Hebron and said, "Look, we are your bone and flesh. ²For some time now, even while Saul was king, it was you who commanded the army of Israel. The Lord your God said to you, 'It is you who shall be shepherd of my people Israel, you who shall be ruler over my people Israel.' " ³So all the elders of Israel came to the king at Hebron, and David made a covenant with them at Hebron before the Lord. And they anointed David king over Israel, according to the word of the Lord by Samuel.

4 David and all Israel marched to Jerusalem, that is, Jebus, where the Jebusites were, the inhabitants of the land. ⁵The inhabitants of Jebus said to David, "You will not come in here." Nevertheless, David took the stronghold of Zion, now the city of David. ⁶David had said, "Whoever attacks the Jebusites first shall be chief and commander." And Joab son of Zeruiah went up first, so he became chief. ⁷David resided in the stronghold; therefore it was called the city of David. ⁸He built the city all around, from the Millo in complete circuit, and Joab repaired the rest of the city. ⁹And David became greater and greater, for the Lord of hosts was with him.

w 10.7 Heb *they* *x* 10.14 Heb *he*

tortured and killed by the enemy Philistines. **10:9–10** The Philistines' desecration of Saul's body helped give rise to the English term "philistine," a disparaging word meaning a boorish, uncultured person.

10:13–14 So Saul died for his unfaithfulness. The Chronicler adds theological commentary here, pointing very specifically to Saul's consultation of a medium (1 Sam. 28:3–25) as proof of his infidelity to God and God's law. **10:13** *He did not keep the command of the Lord.* Necromancy—consulting with the dead through a medium—is forbidden in Lev. 19:31; 20:6, 27; and Deut. 18:10.

11:1–3 David anointed king. These verses are parallel to 2 Sam. 5:1–3. The Chronicler omits any picture of David as the chieftain of a smaller tribal confederation, such as the fact that David had first ruled over only the house of Judah at Hebron for seven and a half years (2 Sam. 2:11; 5:5). Instead, David's reign begins at the point when "all Israel"—that is, all twelve tribes—submit to his monarchic leadership. Once again, these selective omissions on the part of the Chronicler do not necessarily attempt to erase the past (see, e.g., the nod to David and Saul's conflict at 1 Chr. 12:1) as much as focus on David's greatness and lasting public achievements and so, by extension, serve to endorse the institution of the monarchy itself (see **"David," p. 558**).

11:4–9 Jerusalem captured. Abridged from 2 Sam. 5:6–10. **11:4** *Jebus, where the Jebusites were, the inhabitants of the land.* According to Josh. 15:63 and Judg. 1:21, the Israelites were unable to expel the Jebusites from the land during the conquest of Canaan and thus continued to live among them. **11:5** The *city of David* refers to a subsection of Jerusalem. In the New Testament, Bethlehem is described by the term "city of David" (Luke 2:4), but that referent is not found in the Hebrew Bible. **11:8** *Millo* refers to a structural feature of the city, possibly a terraced support or retaining wall. **11:9** *Lord of hosts*, a title that essentially means "Lord of the heavenly armies," evokes a sense of divine blessing over David's military efforts.

Making Connections: David (1 Chronicles 11)

The stories of David, king of Israel, found in 1 Sam. 16–1 Kgs. 2 have mesmerized and scandalized readers for two millennia. These accounts portray a leader who is at once a zealous warrior, a shrewd politician, a talented musician, a violent womanizer, and a pious devotee of his God. David's character shows the full range of human emotion, from dancing joyfully in front of the ark of the covenant (2 Sam. 6:12–15) to lamenting with overwhelming grief at the death of his son Absalom (2 Sam. 18:33). The result is a deeply complex portrait of David that has inspired diverse—and often very selective—interpretations of his character.

The author of Chronicles is one of David's very first interpreters. This composition downplays many of the more troubling accounts in David's life story, focusing instead on his military successes—though with fewer gory details than Samuel and Kings—and on his administrative accomplishments. As one example of the latter, David's reputation as a musician and composer of psalms finds its way into the Chronicler's account in a bureaucratic mode, as David establishes the rotation for the temple singers.

The New Testament emphasizes Jesus of Nazareth's continuity with the lineage of David, seeing Jesus as a fulfillment of God's promises for a messiah—an anointed liberator-king. Like the Chronicler, the Gospel writers emphasize David's genealogy in order to draw connections from the monarchic era of Israelite history to the writers' own day. The result is a focus more on the office of David than the person of David.

Despite later and apparently flatter representations of Israel's most famous king, David's colorful backstory as found in Samuel and Kings has drawn much attention from interpreters in literature and the arts. These interpretations have often built not only on the biblical story but also on one another (see **"The Bible in Visual Art," pp. 2168–71**). For example, Leonard Cohen's popular song "Hallelujah," which has been covered by a multitude of artists over four decades, invokes David's reputation as a musician. The song also includes a nod to David's relationship with Bathsheba and juxtaposes it with allusions to the story of Delilah in Judg. 16, who bound Samson and cut his hair. Borrowing from Cohen's song, Geraldine Brooks later titled her retelling of the David story *The Secret Chord* (2015).

Cameron B. R. Howard

10 Now these are the chiefs of David's warriors, who gave him strong support in his kingdom, together with all Israel, to make him king, according to the word of the LORD concerning Israel. ¹¹This is an account of David's mighty warriors: Jashobeam, son of Hachmoni,ʸ was chief of the Three;ᶻ he wielded his spear against three hundred whom he killed at one time.

12 And next to him among the three warriors was Eleazar son of Dodo, the Ahohite. ¹³He was with David at Pas-dammim when the Philistines were gathered there for battle. There was a plot of ground full of barley. Now the people had fled from the Philistines, ¹⁴but he and David took their stand in the middle of the plot, defended it, and killed the Philistines, and the LORD saved them by a great victory.

15 Three of the thirty chiefs went down to the rock to David at the cave of Adullam while the army of Philistines was encamped in the valley of Rephaim. ¹⁶David was then in the stronghold, and the garrison of the Philistines was then at Bethlehem. ¹⁷David said longingly, "Oh, that someone would give me water to drink from the well of Bethlehem that is by the gate!" ¹⁸Then the Three broke through the camp of the Philistines and drew water from the well of Bethlehem that was by the gate, and they brought it to David. But David would not drink of it; he poured it out to the LORD

y 11.11 Or *a Hachmonite   z* 11.11 Heb *Thirty*

11:10–47 David's mighty men and their exploits. These verses are largely parallel to 2 Sam. 23:8–39, except 1 Chr. 11:41b–47, which are additions in the Chronicler's account. Whereas 2 Samuel places the warriors' tales after the "last words of David" (23:1) at the end of his life, the Chronicler places them at the beginning of David's kingship, associating them with his accession to the throne. **11:18** *But David would not drink of it.* It may seem insulting to the efforts the warriors made to quench David's thirst for him not to drink the water they brought. But by pouring the water out *to the LORD*, David honors the warriors' risk by devoting the water as a sacrifice to God rather than

[19]and said, "My God forbid that I should do this. Can I drink the blood of these men? For at the risk of their lives they brought it." Therefore he would not drink it. The three warriors did these things.

20 Now Abishai,[a] the brother of Joab, was chief of the Thirty.[b] With his spear he fought against three hundred and killed them and won a name[c] beside the Three. [21]He was the most renowned[d] of the Thirty[e] and became their commander, but he did not attain to the Three.

22 Benaiah son of Jehoiada was a valiant man[f] of Kabzeel, a doer of great deeds; he struck down two sons of[g] Ariel of Moab. He also went down and killed a lion in a pit on a day when snow had fallen. [23]And he killed an Egyptian, a man of great stature, five cubits tall. The Egyptian had in his hand a spear like a weaver's beam, but Benaiah went against him with a staff, snatched the spear out of the Egyptian's hand, and killed him with his own spear. [24]Such were the things Benaiah son of Jehoiada did, and he won a name beside the three warriors. [25]He was renowned among the Thirty, but he did not attain to the Three. And David put him in charge of his bodyguard.

26 The warriors of the armies were Asahel brother of Joab, Elhanan son of Dodo of Bethlehem, [27]Shammoth of Harod,[h] Helez the Pelonite, [28]Ira son of Ikkesh of Tekoa, Abiezer of Anathoth, [29]Sibbecai the Hushathite, Ilai the Ahohite, [30]Maharai of Netophah, Heled son of Baanah of Netophah, [31]Ithai son of Ribai of Gibeah of the Benjaminites, Benaiah of Pirathon, [32]Hurai of the wadis of Gaash, Abiel the Arbathite, [33]Azmaveth of Bahurim, Eliahba of Shaalbon, [34]Hashem[i] the Gizonite, Jonathan son of Shagee the Hararite, [35]Ahiam son of Sachar the Hararite, Eliphal son of Ur, [36]Hepher the Mecherathite, Ahijah the Pelonite, [37]Hezro of Carmel, Naarai son of Ezbai, [38]Joel the brother of Nathan, Mibhar son of Hagri, [39]Zelek the Ammonite, Naharai of Beeroth (the armor-bearer of Joab son of Zeruiah), [40]Ira the Ithrite, Gareb the Ithrite, [41]Uriah the Hittite, Zabad son of Ahlai, [42]Adina son of Shiza the Reubenite, a leader of the Reubenites, and thirty with him, [43]Hanan son of Maacah, and Joshaphat the Mithnite, [44]Uzzia the Ashterathite, Shama and Jeiel sons of Hotham the Aroerite, [45]Jediael son of Shimri and his brother Joha the Tizite, [46]Eliel the Mahavite, and Jeribai and Joshaviah sons of Elnaam, and Ithmah the Moabite, [47]Eliel, and Obed, and Jaasiel the Mezobaite.

12 The following are those who came to David at Ziklag, while he could not move about freely because of Saul son of Kish; they were among the mighty warriors who helped him in war. [2]They were archers and could shoot arrows and sling stones with either the right hand or the left; they were Benjaminites, Saul's kindred. [3]The chief was Ahiezer, then Joash, both sons of Shemaah of Gibeah; also Jeziel and Pelet sons of Azmaveth; Beracah, Jehu of Anathoth, [4]Ishmaiah of Gibeon, a warrior among the Thirty and a leader over the Thirty; Jeremiah,[j] Jahaziel, Johanan, Jozabad of Gederah, [5]Eluzai,[k] Jerimoth, Bealiah, Shemariah, Shephatiah the Haruphite;

a 11.20 Gk Vg Tg: Heb *Abshai*   b 11.20 Syr: Heb *Three*   c 11.20 Gk Vg Tg Syr: Heb *did not attain*   d 11.21 Heb *more renowned among the two*   e 11.21 Syr: Heb *Three*   f 11.22 Syr: Heb *the son of a valiant man*   g 11.22 Lucianic: Heb lacks *sons of*   h 11.27 Heb *the Harorite*   i 11.34 Compare Gk: Heb *the sons of Hashem*   j 12.4 Heb 12.5   k 12.5 Heb 12.6

using it for his own satisfaction. **11:41** *Uriah the Hittite* appears in 2 Sam. 11 as the husband of Bathsheba, whom David impregnates while Uriah is consecrating himself for battle on David's behalf. To cover up his crime, David has Uriah assigned to the front lines of the battlefield, where he dies. This is the only mention of Uriah the Hittite in Chronicles; the larger story, which is deeply unflattering to David and inspires a rebuke of him by the prophet Nathan (2 Sam. 12), is completely omitted. See **"David and Bathsheba," p. 438**.

12:1–22 David's followers in the wilderness. The Chronicler's tendency to double back in the timeline, which was observable in the genealogies of 1 Chr. 1–9, shows up again here. This particular list delineates men loyal to David while Saul was still alive, including people whose tribal loyalties (i.e., *Benjaminites, Saul's kindred*) should have made them supporters of Saul. **12:1** *While he could not move about freely because of Saul son of Kish*—that is, when David took refuge with the Philistines as Saul sought to kill him (1 Sam. 28–30). The Chronicler nods to an episode in David's life that his audience is presumed to know already. **12:2** *With either the right hand or the left.* The ambidexterity of the archers and stone slingers gave them a battlefield advantage, not unlike a

6Elkanah, Isshiah, Azarel, Joezer, and Jashobeam, the Korahites; 7and Joelah and Zebadiah, sons of Jeroham of Gedor.

8 From the Gadites there went over to David at the stronghold in the wilderness mighty and experienced warriors, expert with shield and spear, whose faces were like the faces of lions and who were swift as gazelles on the mountains: 9Ezer the chief, Obadiah second, Eliab third, 10Mishmannah fourth, Jeremiah fifth, 11Attai sixth, Eliel seventh, 12Johanan eighth, Elzabad ninth, 13Jeremiah tenth, Machbannai eleventh. 14These Gadites were officers of the army, the least equal to a hundred and the greatest to a thousand. 15These are the men who crossed the Jordan in the first month, when it was overflowing all its banks, and put to flight all those in the valleys to the east and to the west.

16 Some Benjaminites and Judahites came to the stronghold to David. 17David went out to meet them and said to them, "If you have come to me in friendship, to help me, then my heart will be knit to you, but if you have come to betray me to my adversaries, though my hands have done no wrong, then may the God of our ancestors see and give judgment." 18Then the spirit came upon Amasai, chief of the Thirty, and he said,[l]

"We are yours, O David,
　and with you, O son of Jesse!
Peace, peace to you,
　and peace to the one who helps you!
For your God is the one who helps you."

Then David received them and made them officers of his troops.

19 Some of the Manassites deserted to David when he came with the Philistines for the battle against Saul. (Yet he did not help them, for the rulers of the Philistines took counsel and sent him away, saying, "He will desert to his master Saul at the cost of our heads.") 20As he went to Ziklag these Manassites deserted to him: Adnah, Jozabad, Jediael, Michael, Jozabad, Elihu, and Zillethai, chiefs of the thousands in Manasseh. 21They helped David against the band of raiders,[m] for they were all warriors and commanders in the army. 22Indeed, from day to day people kept coming to David to help him until there was a great army, like an army of God.

23 These are the numbers of the divisions of the armed troops who came to David in Hebron to turn the kingdom of Saul over to him, according to the word of the LORD. 24The people of Judah bearing shield and spear numbered six thousand eight hundred armed troops. 25Of the Simeonites, mighty warriors, seven thousand one hundred. 26Of the Levites four thousand six hundred. 27Jehoiada, leader of the house of[n] Aaron, and with him three thousand seven hundred. 28Zadok, a young warrior, and twenty-two commanders from his own ancestral house. 29Of the Benjaminites, the kindred of Saul, three thousand, of whom the majority had continued to keep their allegiance to the house of Saul. 30Of the Ephraimites, twenty thousand eight hundred, mighty warriors, notables in their ancestral houses. 31Of the half-tribe of Manasseh, eighteen thousand, who were expressly named to come and make David king. 32Of Issachar,

l 12.18 Gk: Heb lacks *and he said*　m 12.21 Or *as officers of his troops*　n 12.27 Vg: Heb lacks *the house of*

baseball player who can hit from either the right or left side of home plate. **12:8** *Like the faces of lions.* In biblical poetry, lions are a recurring symbol of ferocity and stealth (see, e.g., Gen. 49:9; Num. 24:9; Pss. 10:9; 22:13). **12:18** *Then the spirit came upon Amasai.* The visitation by the spirit and the poetic nature of Amasai's utterance imply that he is experiencing a prophetic moment. This is the only place that a reference to God's "spirit" ("ruakh") occurs in 1 Chronicles, although there are several references in 1 and 2 Chronicles related to prophecy. By contrast, both "the spirit of God" and "an evil spirit from the LORD" come and go over Saul multiple times in 1 Samuel's account, sending him alternately into prophetic frenzies and fits of melancholy (e.g., 1 Sam. 10:10; 16:14; 18:10; 19:20). When Samuel anoints David, the spirit of God falls upon David and stays with him (1 Sam. 16:13). In Chronicles, however, Saul's struggles with the spirit are ignored, and David mostly keeps his wits about him, rarely moved to frenzy or to a passion for anything except administering God's kingdom.

12:23–40 David's army at Hebron. A list of warriors spans the entirety of Israel's tribes, underscoring broad-based support for David's kingship across *all Israel.* The Chronicler returns focus to Hebron, forming a kind of envelope structure ("inclusio") with the beginning of chap. 11, thus linking

those who had understanding of the times, to know what Israel ought to do, two hundred chiefs, and all their kindred under their command. ³³Of Zebulun, fifty thousand seasoned troops equipped for battle with all the weapons of war to help David⁰ with singleness of purpose. ³⁴Of Naphtali, a thousand commanders, with whom there were thirty-seven thousand armed with shield and spear. ³⁵Of the Danites, twenty-eight thousand six hundred equipped for battle. ³⁶Of Asher, forty thousand seasoned troops ready for battle. ³⁷Of the Reubenites and Gadites and the half-tribe of Manasseh from beyond the Jordan, one hundred twenty thousand armed with all the weapons of war.

38 All these, warriors arrayed in battle order, came to Hebron with full intent to make David king over all Israel; likewise all the rest of Israel were of a single mind to make David king. ³⁹They were there with David for three days, eating and drinking, for their kindred had provided for them. ⁴⁰And also their neighbors from as far away as Issachar and Zebulun and Naphtali came bringing food on donkeys, camels, mules, and oxen—abundant provisions of meal, cakes of figs, clusters of raisins, wine, oil, oxen, and sheep, for there was joy in Israel.

13 David consulted with the commanders of the thousands and of the hundreds, with every leader. ²David said to the whole assembly of Israel, "If it seems good to you, and if it is the will of the LORD our God, let us send abroad to our kindred who remain in all the land of Israel, including the priests and Levites in the cities that have pasturelands, that they may come together to us. ³Then let us bring again the ark of our God to us, for we did not seek it in the days of Saul." ⁴The whole assembly agreed to do so, for the thing pleased all the people.

5 So David assembled all Israel from the Shihor of Egypt to Lebo-hamath, to bring the ark of God from Kiriath-jearim. ⁶And David and all Israel went up to Baalah, that is, to Kiriath-jearim, which belongs to Judah, to bring up from there the ark of God, the LORD, who is enthroned on the cherubim, which is called by his^p name. ⁷They carried the ark of God on a new cart from the house of Abinadab, and Uzzah and Ahio^q were driving the cart. ⁸David and all Israel were dancing before God with all their might, with songs and lyres and harps and tambourines and cymbals and trumpets.

9 When they came to the threshing floor of Chidon, Uzzah put out his hand to hold the ark, for the oxen lurched. ¹⁰The anger of the LORD was kindled against Uzzah; he struck him down because he put out his hand to the ark, and he died there before God. ¹¹David was angry because the LORD had burst out against Uzzah, so that place is called Perez-uzzah^r to this day. ¹²David

o 12.33 Gk: Heb lacks *David* p 13.6 Heb lacks *his* q 13.7 Or *and his brother* r 13.11 That is, *bursting out against Uzzah*

chaps. 11 and 12 together as a unit. **12:38** *Likewise all the rest of Israel were of a single mind to make David king.* The rhetorical force of vv. 23–40 builds to this moment. Phrases like *to know what Israel ought to do* (v. 32) and *singleness of purpose* (v. 33) accompany the listings of each tribe's warriors, underscoring a nearly unanimous and essentially spontaneous outpouring of support for David's kingship that is not paralleled in 2 Sam. 5.

13:1–14 The ark brought from Kiriath-jearim. 13:1–5 These verses introduce a story culled from 2 Sam. 6:1–11 with a prologue that further underscores the ongoing emphasis on the unity of Israel, culminating in the assertion that the *whole assembly agreed to do so* (i.e., go get the ark), *for the thing pleased all the people.* **13:3** *The ark of our God* is the ark of the covenant, the sacred box on which sits the mercy seat of God and that holds the tablets of the law given to Moses (see Exod. 25:10–21; Deut. 10:1–5). *For we did not seek it in the days of Saul.* The Chronicler takes a passive-aggressive swipe at Saul, implying he did not bother to look for Israel's most sacred cultic object. **13:5** *From the Shihor of Egypt to Lebo-hamath.* This phrase indicates two extreme points on the southwest and northern edges of Israel, used to indicate the totality of the land. The effect would be similar to describing the mainland United States as the land from southern California to Maine. **13:6–14** These verses are parallel to 2 Sam. 6:2–11. **13:10** *Because he put out his hand to the ark.* What might seem like an act of care or devotion is interpreted as disrespect for the ark's holiness and perhaps even a sign of God's discontent with the ark's transfer. **13:11** *Perez-uzzah* means "bursting out against Uzzah" in Hebrew. An etiology for the naming of the city is nestled in a larger story

was afraid of God that day; he said, "How can I bring the ark of God into my care?" [13]So David did not take the ark into his care into the city of David; he took it instead to the house of Obed-edom the Gittite. [14]The ark of God remained with the household of Obed-edom in his house three months, and the LORD blessed the household of Obed-edom and all that he had.

14 King Hiram of Tyre sent messengers to David, along with cedar logs and masons and carpenters to build a house for him. [2]David then perceived that the LORD had established him as king over Israel and that his kingdom was highly exalted for the sake of his people Israel.

3 David took more wives in Jerusalem, and David became the father of more sons and daughters. [4]These are the names of the children whom he had in Jerusalem: Shammua, Shobab, and Nathan; Solomon, [5]Ibhar, Elishua, and Elpelet; [6]Nogah, Nepheg, and Japhia; [7]Elishama, Beeliada, and Eliphelet.

8 When the Philistines heard that David had been anointed king over all Israel, all the Philistines went up in search of David, but David heard about it and went out against them. [9]Now the Philistines had come and made a raid in the valley of Rephaim. [10]David inquired of God, "Shall I go up against the Philistines? Will you give them into my hand?" The LORD said to him, "Go up, and I will give them into your hand." [11]So they went up to Baal-perazim, and David defeated them there. David said, "God has burst forth against my enemies by my hand, like a bursting flood." Therefore that place is called Baal-perazim. [s] [12]They abandoned their gods there, and at David's command they were burned.

13 Once again the Philistines made a raid in the valley. [14]When David again inquired of God, God said to him, "You shall not go up after them; go around and come upon them opposite the balsam trees. [15]When you hear the sound of marching in the tops of the balsam trees, then go out to battle, for God has gone out before you to strike down the army of the Philistines." [16]David did as God had commanded him, and they struck down the Philistine army from Gibeon to Gezer. [17]The fame of David went out into all lands, and the LORD brought the fear of him on all nations.

15 David [t] built houses for himself in the city of David, and he prepared a place for the ark of God and pitched a tent

s 14.11 That is, *lord of bursting forth*   *t* 15.1 Heb *He*

of the ark's journey toward Jerusalem. **13:12** *David was afraid of God that day.* Rattled by the death of Uzzah, David no longer considers it wise to bring the ark into his sector of Jerusalem, so he gives it into the care of *Obed-edom the Gittite* (v. 13). As a Gittite—that is, one from Gath—Obed-edom is presumably a Philistine. However, in subsequent references in 1 Chr. 15, 16, and 26, Obed-edom is named as a Levite (cf. also 2 Chr. 25:24). It is unclear if these are meant to refer to different people or if they are two different traditions about the same person.

14:1–7 David established at Jerusalem. These verses are parallel to 2 Sam. 5:11–16, where they occur earlier in David's story, just after his capture of Jerusalem. If the preceding episode with the ark raised a rare moment of drama and suspicion regarding God's endorsement of David, the ample evidence of blessings in this section, including more children born to David, should put the reader immediately at ease.

14:8–17 Defeat of the Philistines. These verses are parallel to 2 Sam. 5:17–25. The transfer of power from one ruler to the next often creates a prime opportunity for enemy attacks, since the organization of the nation or kingdom is in transition. **14:9** *The valley of Rephaim* is the same place where David's best warriors, the Three, fetched him water from the well of Bethlehem while the Philistines were encamped there (1 Chr. 11:15–19). **14:11** *Baal-perazim* means "lord of bursting forth" in Hebrew. This etiology recalls when God also burst forth against Uzzah (13:11), leading to the place-name *Perez-uzzah*, "bursting out against Uzzah." The same Hebrew verb—"prz," "to burst" or "to breach"—appears in both names. **14:17** Having been affirmed in his leadership by "all Israel" in chaps. 11–13, David's reputation begins to widen: first with King Hiram of Tyre at the beginning of this chapter (v. 1) and now broadening into *all lands* and *all nations*.

15:1–29 The ark brought to Jerusalem. 15:1–24 These verses are the Chronicler's own addition to the ark account, either as a new composition or as an interpolation from an unknown source. After Uzzah's death at the threshing floor of Chidon (13:9–10), David decides to make extensive

for it. [2]Then David commanded that no one but the Levites were to carry the ark of God, for the LORD had chosen them to carry the ark of the LORD and to minister to him forever. [3]David assembled all Israel in Jerusalem to bring up the ark of the LORD to its place, which he had prepared for it. [4]Then David gathered together the descendants of Aaron and the Levites: [5]of the sons of Kohath, Uriel the chief, with one hundred twenty of his kindred; [6]of the sons of Merari, Asaiah the chief, with two hundred twenty of his kindred; [7]of the sons of Gershom, Joel the chief, with one hundred thirty of his kindred; [8]of the sons of Elizaphan, Shemaiah the chief, with two hundred of his kindred; [9]of the sons of Hebron, Eliel the chief, with eighty of his kindred; [10]of the sons of Uzziel, Amminadab the chief, with one hundred twelve of his kindred.

[11] David summoned the priests Zadok and Abiathar and the Levites Uriel, Asaiah, Joel, Shemaiah, Eliel, and Amminadab. [12]He said to them, "You are the heads of families of the Levites; sanctify yourselves, you and your kindred, so that you may bring up the ark of the LORD, the God of Israel, to the place that I have prepared for it. [13]Because you did not carry it[u] the first time,[v] the LORD our God burst out against us because we did not give it proper care." [14]So the priests and the Levites sanctified themselves to bring up the ark of the LORD, the God of Israel. [15]And the Levites carried the ark of God on their shoulders with the poles, as Moses had commanded according to the word of the LORD.

[16] David also commanded the chiefs of the Levites to appoint their kindred as singers to raise loud sounds of joy on musical instruments, on harps and lyres and cymbals. [17]So the Levites appointed Heman son of Joel; and of his kindred Asaph son of Berechiah; and of the sons of Merari, their kindred, Ethan son of Kushaiah; [18]and with them their kindred of the second order, Zechariah, Jaaziel, Shemiramoth, Jehiel, Unni, Eliab, Benaiah, Maaseiah, Mattithiah, Eliphelehu, and Mikneiah, and the gatekeepers Obed-edom and Jeiel. [19]The singers Heman, Asaph, and Ethan were to sound bronze cymbals; [20]Zechariah, Aziel, Shemiramoth, Jehiel, Unni, Eliab, Maaseiah, and Benaiah were to play harps according to Alamoth, [21]but Mattithiah, Eliphelehu, Mikneiah, Obed-edom, Jeiel, and Azaziah were to lead with lyres according to the Sheminith.[w] [22]Chenaniah, leader of the Levites in music, was to direct the music, for he understood it. [23]Berechiah and Elkanah were to be gatekeepers for the ark. [24]Shebaniah, Joshaphat, Nethanel, Amasai, Zechariah, Benaiah, and Eliezer, the priests, were to blow the trumpets before the ark of God. Obed-edom and Jehiah also were to be gatekeepers for the ark.

[25] So David and the elders of Israel and the commanders of the thousands went to bring up the ark of the covenant of the LORD from the house of Obed-edom with rejoicing. [26]And because God helped the Levites who were carrying the ark of the covenant of the LORD, they sacrificed seven bulls and seven rams. [27]David was clothed with a robe of fine linen, as also were all the Levites who

u 15.13 Cn: Heb lacks *carry it*   v 15.13 Meaning of Heb uncertain   w 15.21 Or *set for the eighth* (octave)

preparations to transfer the ark properly. After all, Obed-edom has been blessed after keeping the ark in his house for three months (13:14), so the danger must be not in possessing the ark but rather in how it is handled. **15:2** *No one but the Levites were to carry the ark.* In the wake of Uzzah's death, transporting the ark has become a job for specialists (cf. Num. 7:9). **15:4–10** The Chronicler's love of lists is again on display in these verses: the assembled Levites are numbered and classified according to their lineage. **15:15** The Hebrew word translated as *poles* refers to a yoke that might join together two oxen. This term differs from the one describing the "poles" that were part of the carrying apparatus for the ark (Exod. 25:15)—a curious mismatch of terms for a text trying to demonstrate compliance with Mosaic law. It may be that the shoulder (Num. 7:9), not the poles, is the key issue. **15:20–21** *Alamoth* and *Sheminith* are technical musical terms whose precise meaning is now lost. *Alamoth* (cf. the superscription to Ps. 46) may be related to the Hebrew word for "young woman," indicating a particular tone or style. *Sheminith* (cf. the superscriptions to Pss. 6 and 12) is also the Hebrew word for "eighth," leading scholars to speculate that the term could have some relationship to the octave or perhaps an instrument with eight strings. **15:25–29** These verses are adapted from 2 Sam. 6:12–16. **15:27** In 2 Sam. 6:14, David wears only a linen ephod—that is, a simple loincloth or apron—causing Michal to accost him as one who "might shamelessly uncover himself" (2 Sam. 6:20).

were carrying the ark, and the singers, and Chenaniah the leader of the music of the singers, and David wore a linen ephod. ²⁸So all Israel brought up the ark of the covenant of the LORD with shouting, to the sound of the horn, trumpets, and cymbals, and made loud music on harps and lyres.

29 As the ark of the covenant of the LORD came to the city of David, Michal daughter of Saul looked out of the window and saw King David leaping and dancing, and she despised him in her heart.

16 They brought in the ark of God and set it inside the tent that David had pitched for it, and they offered burnt offerings and offerings of well-being before God. ²When David had finished offering the burnt offerings and the offerings of well-being, he blessed the people in the name of the LORD, ³and he distributed to every person in Israel—man and woman alike—to each a loaf of bread, a portion of meat,ˣ and a cake of raisins.

4 He appointed certain of the Levites as ministers before the ark of the LORD, to invoke, to thank, and to praise the LORD, the God of Israel. ⁵Asaph was the chief, and second to him was Zechariah, Jeiel, Shemiramoth, Jehiel, Mattithiah, Eliab, Benaiah, Obed-edom, and Jeiel, with harps and lyres; Asaph was to sound the cymbals, ⁶and the priests Benaiah and Jahaziel were to blow trumpets regularly before the ark of the covenant of God.

7 Then on that day David first appointed

the singing of praises to the LORD by Asaph and his kindred.

⁸ O give thanks to the LORD, call on his name,
　make known his deeds among the peoples.
⁹ Sing to him, sing praises to him;
　tell of all his wonderful works.
¹⁰ Glory in his holy name;
　let the hearts of those who seek the LORD rejoice.
¹¹ Seek the LORD and his strength;
　seek his presence continually.
¹² Remember the wonderful works he has done,
　his miracles and the judgments he uttered,
¹³ O offspring of his servant Israel,
　children of Jacob, his chosen ones.

¹⁴ He is the LORD our God;
　his judgments are in all the earth.
¹⁵ Remember his covenant forever,
　the word that he commanded for a thousand generations,
¹⁶ the covenant that he made with Abraham,
　his sworn promise to Isaac,
¹⁷ which he confirmed to Jacob as a statute,
　to Israel as an everlasting covenant,
¹⁸ saying, "To you I will give the land of Canaan
　as your portion for an inheritance."

x 16.3 Compare Gk Syr Vg: Meaning of Heb uncertain

The Chronicler adds to David's ensemble a *robe of fine linen* over the linen ephod. **15:29** This lone sentence about David's wife *Michal daughter of Saul* stands out in a book that mentions very few women by name and depicts even fewer as active characters in the narrative (see **"Women in the Genealogy," p. 545**). Given the disappointment in Saul that 1 Chronicles has already displayed (cf. 10:13–14; 13:3), the sentence may be more about Saul than Michal herself: in the face of David's piety, triumph, and joy, Saul's daughter's disdain of David is another subtle reminder of Saul's failures. That Michal is simply a vehicle for the Chronicler's agenda is further supported by the fact that 1 Chronicles does not quote from the longer story at 2 Sam. 6:20–23, in which Michal verbally rebukes David.

　16:1–6 The ark placed in the tent. Verses 1–3 are adapted from 2 Sam. 6:17–19.

　16:7–36 David's psalm of thanksgiving. The long hymn here is actually a mash-up of several psalms attested in the biblical book of Psalms. David is traditionally associated with both the playing of music and the composition of psalms. A young David played his lyre to soothe Saul during the king's bouts of melancholy (1 Sam. 16:23). Dozens of psalms contain the notation "of David"—that is, attributed to, dedicated to, or after the style of David. However, there is nothing in the Chronicler's text to indicate David was involved in the composition or performance of this particular psalm, nor are any of the three psalms incorporated here (Pss. 105, 96, and 106) explicitly associated with either David or Asaph in the Psalter. See **"David," p. 558**. **16:8–22** Parallel to Ps. 105:1–15, a hymn of

19 When they were few in number,
  of little account, and strangers in
    the land,*y*

20 wandering from nation to nation,
  from one kingdom to another
    people,

21 he allowed no one to oppress them;
  he rebuked kings on their account,

22 saying, "Do not touch my anointed ones;
  do my prophets no harm."

23 Sing to the LORD, all the earth.
  Tell of his salvation from day to day.

24 Declare his glory among the nations,
  his marvelous works among all the
    peoples.

25 For great is the LORD and greatly to be
    praised;
  he is to be revered above all gods.

26 For all the gods of the peoples are idols,
  but the LORD made the heavens.

27 Honor and majesty are before him;
  strength and joy are in his place.

28 Ascribe to the LORD, O families of the
    peoples,
  ascribe to the LORD glory and strength.

29 Ascribe to the LORD the glory due his
    name;
  bring an offering and come before
    him.
  Worship the LORD in holy splendor;

30   tremble before him, all the earth.
  The world is firmly established; it
    shall never be moved.

31 Let the heavens be glad, and let the
    earth rejoice,
  and let them say among the nations,
    "The LORD is king!"

32 Let the sea roar and all that fills it;
  let the field exult and everything in it.

33 Then shall the trees of the forest sing
    for joy
  before the LORD, for he comes to
    judge the earth.

34 O give thanks to the LORD, for he is
    good,
  for his steadfast love endures
    forever.

35 Say also,
  "Save us, O God of our salvation,
    and gather and rescue us from
      among the nations,
  that we may give thanks to your holy
    name
  and glory in your praise.

36 Blessed be the LORD, the God of Israel,
  from everlasting to everlasting."

Then all the people said "Amen!" and praised the LORD.

37 David*z* left Asaph and his kinsfolk there before the ark of the covenant of the LORD to minister regularly before the ark as each day required, 38and also Obed-edom and his*a* sixty-eight kinsfolk, while Obed-edom son of Jeduthun and Hosah were to be gatekeepers. 39And he left the priest Zadok and his kindred the priests before the tabernacle of the LORD in the high place that was at Gibeon, 40to offer burnt offerings to the LORD on the altar of burnt offering regularly, morning and evening, according to all that is written in the law of the LORD that he commanded Israel. 41With them were Heman and Jeduthun and the rest of

y 16.19 Heb *in it*   *z* 16.37 Heb *He*   *a* 16.38 Gk Syr Vg: Heb *their*

---

praise that recounts YHWH's past deeds on Israel's behalf. **16:23–33** Parallel to Ps. 96 (with small variations), an enthronement psalm, extolling the praises of YHWH as king. **16:34–36** Parallel to Ps. 106:1, 47–48. The Chronicler does not retain any of the penitential core of the psalm, choosing instead to appropriate the praises at the psalm's beginning and end. **16:36b** This final line is very close to the final line in the Hebrew and Greek versions of Ps. 106, which reads, "And let all the people say, 'Amen.' Praise the LORD!" The Chronicler makes a small adjustment to the line, reworking it as a narrative conclusion to the scene.

16:37–43 Regular worship maintained. This section assumes that there are two cultic sites in operation in Israel: the one in the city of David that David is establishing, focused on the *ark of the covenant* and its tent, and one in *Gibeon*, where *burnt offerings* are being made on a regular schedule. First Chronicles is set before the construction of the Jerusalem temple but is composed during the Second Temple period, which is influenced by Deuteronomy's ideal of centralized worship. The Chronicler seems to hold these two ideas in tension, allowing for a functioning sacrificial site at Gibeon but also taking the return of the ark as a stepping stone toward the construction of the temple in Jerusalem and centralized, exclusive worship there. Notably, David installs musicians

those chosen and expressly named to render thanks to the Lord, for his steadfast love endures forever. [42]Heman and Jeduthun had with them trumpets and cymbals for the music and instruments for sacred song. The sons of Jeduthun were appointed to the gate.

43 Then all the people departed to their homes, and David went home to bless his household.

17 Now when David settled in his house, David said to the prophet Nathan, "I am living in a house of cedar, but the ark of the covenant of the Lord is under a tent." [2]Nathan said to David, "Do all that you have in mind, for God is with you."

3 But that same night the word of God came to Nathan, saying, [4]"Go and tell my servant David: Thus says the Lord: You shall not build me a house to live in. [5]For I have not lived in a house since the day I brought out Israel to this very day, but I have lived in a tent and a tabernacle.[b] [6]Wherever I have moved about among all Israel, did I ever speak a word with any of the judges of Israel, whom I commanded to shepherd my people, saying, 'Why have you not built me a house of cedar?' [7]Now therefore thus you shall say to my servant David: Thus says the Lord of hosts: I took you from the pasture, from following the sheep, to be ruler over my people Israel, [8]and I have been with you wherever you went and have cut off all your enemies before you, and I will make for you a name like the name of the great ones of the earth. [9]I will appoint a place for my people Israel and will plant them, so that they may live in their own place and be disturbed no more, and evildoers shall wear them down no more, as they did formerly, [10]from the time that I appointed judges over my people Israel, and I will subdue all your enemies. Moreover, I declare to you that the Lord will build you a house. [11]When your days are fulfilled to go to be with your ancestors, I will raise up your offspring after you, one of your own sons, and I will establish his kingdom. [12]He shall build a house for me, and I will establish his throne forever. [13]I will be a father to him, and he shall be a son to me. I will not take my steadfast love from him, as I took it from him who was before you, [14]but I will confirm him in my house and in my kingdom forever, and his throne shall be established forever." [15]In accordance with all these words and all this vision, Nathan spoke to David.

16 Then King David went in and sat before the Lord and said, "Who am I, O Lord God, and what is my house, that you have brought me thus far? [17]And even this was a small thing in your sight, O God; you have also spoken of your servant's house into the distant future. You regard me as someone of high rank,[c] O Lord God! [18]And what more can David say to you for honoring your servant? You know your servant. [19]For

---

b 17.5 Gk: Heb *but I have been from tent to tent and from tabernacle*   c 17.17 Meaning of Heb uncertain

---

at both locations, pointing to the importance of instruments and songs in the Chronicler's vision of worship. **16:43** This verse is parallel to 2 Sam. 6:19b–20.

17:1–15 God's covenant with David. Parallel to 2 Sam. 7:1–17. See **"Davidic Covenant," p. 433**. **17:1** *The prophet Nathan.* Thus far prophets have been conspicuously absent from the monarchic story in Chronicles, particularly since in Samuel they push back against both the monarchy (1 Sam. 8) and David's conduct (2 Sam. 12). Although David's desire to build a house for God is denied here, it is presented not as a prophetic rebuke but rather as a promise of continuing greatness for the Davidic family line. **17:10** *The Lord will build you a house.* David already has many physical houses; this *house* will be a dynastic household, generations of rulers descended from David himself. **17:11** *When your days are fulfilled to go to be with your ancestors*—that is, when you die. *One of your own sons*—that is, Solomon. **17:13** *Him who was before you*—that is, Saul. **17:14** *His throne shall be established forever.* The Chronicler affirms this promise, despite the fact that when the Chronicler writes, Judah is ruled by foreign kings, and there is no Davidic monarch on the throne.

17:16–27 David's prayer. Parallel to 2 Sam. 7:18–29. David's prayer responds to the promises of God made through Nathan in the preceding section. It is thick with the same kinds of language in the extended psalm of 1 Chr. 16:7–36: praise of God's greatness, gratitude for God's past works, and extolling the distinctiveness of God's relationship with Israel. David also includes an affirmation of God's promise of a dynastic house for David. In other words, the prayer is a model of the kind of piety that befits a chosen king. **17:16** *Before the Lord*, presumably in front of the ark in its tent.

your servant's sake, O LORD, and according to your own heart, you have done all these great deeds, making known all these great things. ²⁰There is no one like you, O LORD, and there is no God besides you, according to all that we have heard with our ears. ²¹Who is like your people Israel, one nation on the earth whom God went to redeem to be his people, making for yourself a name for great and awesome things, in driving out nations before your people whom you redeemed from Egypt? ²²And you made your people Israel to be your people forever, and you, O LORD, became their God. ²³And now, O LORD, as for the word that you have spoken concerning your servant and concerning his house, let it be established forever, and do as you have promised. ²⁴Thus your name will be established and magnified forever in the saying, 'The LORD of hosts, the God of Israel, is Israel's God,' and the house of your servant David will be established in your presence. ²⁵For you, my God, have revealed to your servant that you will build a house for him; therefore your servant has found it possible to pray before you. ²⁶And now, O LORD, you are God, and you have promised this good thing to your servant; ²⁷therefore may it please you to bless the house of your servant so that it may continue forever before you. For you, O LORD, have blessed and are blessed[d] forever."

18 Some time afterward, David attacked the Philistines and subdued them; he took Gath and its villages from the Philistines.

2 He defeated Moab, and the Moabites became subject to David and brought tribute.

3 David also struck down King Hadadezer of Zobah, toward Hamath,[e] as he went to set up a monument at the River Euphrates. ⁴David took from him one thousand chariots, seven thousand cavalry, and twenty thousand foot soldiers. David hamstrung all the chariot horses but left one hundred of them. ⁵When the Arameans of Damascus came to help King Hadadezer of Zobah, David killed twenty-two thousand Arameans. ⁶Then David put garrisons[f] in Aram of Damascus, and the Arameans became subject to David and brought tribute. The LORD gave victory to David wherever he went. ⁷David took the gold shields that were carried by the servants of Hadadezer and brought them to Jerusalem. ⁸From Tibhath and from Cun, cities of Hadadezer, David took a vast quantity of bronze; with it Solomon made the bronze sea and the pillars and the vessels of bronze.

9 When King Tou of Hamath heard that David had defeated the whole army of King Hadadezer of Zobah, ¹⁰he sent his son Hadoram to King David, to greet him and to congratulate him because he had fought against Hadadezer and defeated him. Now Hadadezer had often been at war with Tou. He sent all sorts of articles of gold, of silver, and of bronze; ¹¹these also King David dedicated to the LORD, together with the silver and gold that he had carried off from all the nations, from Edom, Moab, the Ammonites, the Philistines, and Amalek.

12 Abishai son of Zeruiah killed eighteen thousand Edomites in the Valley of Salt. ¹³He put garrisons in Edom, and all the Edomites became subject to David. And the LORD gave victory to David wherever he went.

14 So David reigned over all Israel, and he administered justice and equity to all his people. ¹⁵Joab son of Zeruiah was over the army; Jehoshaphat son of Ahilud was recorder; ¹⁶Zadok son of Ahitub and Ahimelech son of Abiathar were priests; Shavsha

d 17.27 Or *and it is blessed*   e 18.3 Meaning of Heb uncertain
f 18.6 Gk Vg Compare Syr: Heb lacks *garrisons*

18:1–13 David's kingdom established and extended. Parallel to 2 Sam. 8:1–14. David's victories stretch across an impressive geographical range, underscoring his role as a guardian of Israel's borders and as a caretaker of "all Israel." *Gath* is in the territory of the Philistines southwest of Israel; *Moab* is east of Israel; *Hadadezer of Zobah* and the *Arameans of Damascus* lived north of Israel, in Syria; *Edom* is south of Israel. **18:11** *Dedicated to the LORD*—that is, consecrated for God rather than kept for himself.

18:14–17 David's administration. Parallel to 2 Sam. 8:15–18. **18:14** *All Israel* is a recurring phrase in 1 Chronicles's depiction of David's reign, part of the book's emphasis on the unity of the nation. At the anointing of David at Hebron, *all Israel*—meaning all the tribes—was already gathered to make him king (1 Chr. 11). Now, as David's kingdom continues to grow in strength and in prominence throughout the region, the Chronicler continues to accentuate David's commitment to *all*

was secretary; [17]Benaiah son of Jehoiada was over the Cherethites and the Pelethites; and David's sons were the chief officials in the service of the king.

19

Some time afterward, King Nahash of the Ammonites died, and his son succeeded him. [2]David said, "I will deal loyally with Hanun son of Nahash, for his father dealt loyally with me." So David sent messengers to console him concerning his father. When David's servants came to Hanun in the land of the Ammonites to console him, [3]the officials of the Ammonites said to Hanun, "Do you think, because David has sent consolers to you, that he is honoring your father? Have not his servants come to you to search and to overthrow and to spy out the land?" [4]So Hanun seized David's servants, shaved them, cut off their garments in the middle at their waists, and sent them away, [5]and they departed. When David was told about the men, he sent messengers to them, for they felt greatly humiliated. The king said, "Remain at Jericho until your beards have grown and then return."

[6] When the Ammonites saw that they had made themselves odious to David, Hanun and the Ammonites sent a thousand talents of silver to hire chariots and cavalry from Aram-naharaim, from Aram-maacah, and from Zobah. [7]They hired thirty-two thousand chariots and the king of Maacah with his army, who came and camped before Medeba. And the Ammonites were mustered from their cities and came to battle. [8]When David heard of it, he sent Joab and all the army of the warriors. [9]The Ammonites came out and drew up in battle array at the entrance of the city, and the kings who had come were by themselves in the open country.

[10] When Joab saw that the line of battle was set against him both in front and in the rear, he chose some of the picked men of Israel and arrayed them against the Arameans; [11]the rest of his troops he put in the charge of his brother Abishai, and they were arrayed against the Ammonites. [12]He said, "If the Arameans are too strong for me, then you shall help me, but if the Ammonites are too strong for you, then I will help you. [13]Be strong, and let us be courageous for our people and for the cities of our God, and may the LORD do what seems good to him." [14]So Joab and the troops who were with him advanced toward the Arameans for battle, and they fled before him. [15]When the Ammonites saw that the Arameans fled, they likewise fled before Abishai, Joab's brother, and entered the city. Then Joab came to Jerusalem.

[16] But when the Arameans saw that they had been defeated by Israel, they sent messengers and brought out the Arameans who were beyond the River, with Shophach the commander of the army of Hadadezer at their head. [17]When David was informed, he gathered all Israel together, crossed the

Israel, as well as all Israel's commitment to him. **18:17** 2 Sam. 8:18 specifies that "David's sons were priests." By the time of the Chronicler, priestly duties were undertaken only by members of priestly families—that is, by the descendants of Aaron in the tribe of Levi. David and his sons were from the tribe of Judah. See **"Revising/Rewriting the Bible," p. 584.**

19:1–19 Defeat of the Ammonites and Arameans. Parallel to 2 Sam. 10. **19:1** *Ammonite* territory was east of the river Jordan. **19:2** The language of "loyalty" implies that David and Nahash had been in a treaty relationship and that David wants to continue that relationship with Nahash's son and successor, Hanun—though on what terms the text does not say. **19:3** Especially coming on the heels of David's multidirectional conquests (18:1–13), the Ammonites are skeptical of David's motives. They choose to treat the messengers as enemies rather than diplomats. **19:4–5** Shaving an enemy's beard was an act of violence that brought shame to the man who was *shaved.* Similarly, to *cut off their garments in the middle at their waists* was to leave them exposed and shamed. The statement that *they felt greatly humiliated* confirms the effectiveness of the Ammonites' tactics. **19:6** Realizing they have provoked David's wrath, the Ammonites hire soldiers from allies in Aramean territory north and northeast of Israel. **19:8** The Chronicler has recently noted (18:15) that *Joab* is the head of David's army. In the extended accounts of David's battlefield exploits in 1–2 Samuel, Joab features prominently as a character, whereas in Chronicles, his role, while still vital, is presented more functionally than dramatically. **19:10** *Picked men*—that is, elite soldiers. **19:16** Having faced a loss at the hands of Joab and his brother Abishai, the *Arameans* call in reinforcements from the east.

Jordan, came to them, and drew up his forces against them. When David set the battle in array against the Arameans, they fought with him. [18]The Arameans fled before Israel, and David killed seven thousand Aramean charioteers and forty thousand foot soldiers and also Shophach the commander of their army. [19]When the servants of Hadadezer saw that they had been defeated by Israel, they made peace with David and became subject to him. So the Arameans were not willing to help the Ammonites any more.

20 In the spring of the year, the time when kings go out to battle, Joab led out the army, ravaged the country of the Ammonites, and came and besieged Rabbah. But David remained at Jerusalem. Joab attacked Rabbah and overthrew it. [2]David took the crown of Milcom[g] from his head; he found that it weighed a talent of gold, and in it was a precious stone, and it was placed on David's head. He also brought out the spoil of the city, a very great amount. [3]He brought out the people

who were in it and set them to work[h] with saws and iron picks and axes.[i] Thus David did to all the cities of the Ammonites. Then David and all the people returned to Jerusalem.

[4]After this, war broke out with the Philistines at Gezer; then Sibbecai the Hushathite killed Sippai, who was one of the descendants of the giants, and the Philistines were subdued. [5]Again there was war with the Philistines, and Elhanan son of Jair killed Lahmi the brother of Goliath the Gittite, the shaft of whose spear was like a weaver's beam. [6]Again there was war at Gath, where there was a man of great size who had six fingers on each hand and six toes on each foot, twenty-four in number; he also was descended from the giants.[j] [7]When he taunted Israel, Jonathan son of Shimea, David's brother, killed him. [8]These were descended from the giants[k] in Gath; they fell by the hand of David and his servants.

g 20.2 Gk Vg: Heb *of their king* h 20.3 Heb *and he sawed* i 20.3 Heb *saws* j 20.6 Gk: Heb *from the Raphah* k 20.8 Gk: Heb *from the Raphah*

19:19 David's victory has reaped dividends not only by defeating both the Ammonites and the Arameans but also by breaking up their alliance and forcing the fealty of the Arameans.

20:1–3 Siege and capture of Rabbah. 20:1–2 Verse 1 aligns with 2 Sam. 11:1, while v. 2 is adapted from 2 Sam. 12:26–30. The material excised from 2 Sam. 11:2–12:25 is the story of David's impregnating Bathsheba, his arrangement of her husband Uriah's death on the battlefield, and the prophet Nathan's rebuke of David for his actions. The 2 Samuel story also implicates Joab, who follows David's orders and then uses David's interest in Uriah's death to avoid criticism for a tactical mistake in the siege of Rabbah. These omissions in the narrative are consistent with the sanitized portrait of David offered by 1 Chronicles, which prefers to focus on David's military victories and leadership prowess. See **"David," p. 558. 20:1** *Rabbah* is the city now known as Amman, the capital of Jordan. **20:2** *Milcom* (Heb. "mlkm") is a patron god of the Ammonites (cf. 1 Kgs. 11:5, 33; 2 Kgs. 23:13). However, the same word ("mlkm") could also be read as "their king." *Milcom* is the reading of the Greek Septuagint and the Latin Vulgate; "their king" is the vocalization preserved in the Hebrew text.

20:4–8 Exploits against the Philistines. Adapted from 2 Sam. 21:18–22. In 1 Chronicles, the location of the battle is changed from Gob to Gezer, and the Philistine killed by Elhanan is Goliath's brother Lahmi rather than Goliath himself. The books of Samuel preserve two different traditions about the death of Goliath. In 1 Sam. 17, a young David, too small for a warrior's armor, kills Goliath with a stone and sling. In 2 Sam. 21, "Elhanan son of Jaare-oregim the Bethlehemite" kills Goliath. Both of these accounts from Samuel, like the one in 1 Chronicles, describe Goliath with the phrase "the shaft of whose spear was like a weaver's beam." Despite clearly having access to a version of 1 and 2 Samuel as a source, the Chronicler includes none of the traditions about David's boyhood, such as the Goliath story from 1 Sam. 17. Nevertheless, the adjustments to the Goliath tradition in 1 Chronicles indicate that the Chronicler knew and wanted to preserve the tradition that David killed Goliath. If Elhanan kills Goliath's brother, David's boyhood heroism still stands. **20:4** *Descendants of the giants.* Here and in the parallel Samuel texts, the Hebrew Bible describes the Philistines, or at least a subset of them, as people of extraordinarily large size (see also Deut. 2:20–23; Josh. 11:22; 13:3–4). Scholars have proposed a range of possibilities to explain this literary tradition, from genetic disorders to comparisons with Philistine architectural features, but no physical evidence of the phenomenon has been found; it may be a case, therefore, of hyperbolic rhetoric.

21 Satan stood up against Israel and incited David to count the people of Israel. ²So David said to Joab and the commanders of the army, "Go, number Israel, from Beer-sheba to Dan, and bring me a report, so that I may know their number." ³But Joab said, "May the LORD increase the number of his people a hundredfold! Are they not, my lord the king, all of them my lord's servants? Why then should my lord require this? Why should he bring guilt on Israel?" ⁴But the king's word prevailed against Joab. So Joab departed and went throughout all Israel and came back to Jerusalem. ⁵Joab gave the total count of the people to David. In all Israel there were one million one hundred thousand men who drew the sword, and in Judah four hundred seventy thousand who drew the sword. ⁶But he did not include Levi and Benjamin in the numbering, for the king's command was abhorrent to Joab.

7 But God was displeased with this thing, and he struck Israel. ⁸David said to God, "I have sinned greatly in that I have done this thing. But now, please remove the guilt of your servant, for I have done very foolishly." ⁹The LORD spoke to Gad, David's seer, saying, ¹⁰"Go and say to David: Thus says the LORD: Three things I offer you; choose one of them, so that I may do it to you." ¹¹So Gad came to David and said to him, "Thus says the LORD: Take your choice: ¹²either three years of famine; or three months of devastation by your foes, while the sword of your enemies overtakes you; or three days of the sword of the LORD, pestilence on the land, and the angel of the LORD destroying throughout all the territory of Israel. Now decide what answer I shall return to the one who sent me." ¹³Then David said to Gad, "I am in great distress; let me fall into the hand of the LORD, for his mercy is very great, but let me not fall into human hands."

14 So the LORD sent a pestilence on Israel, and seventy thousand persons fell in Israel. ¹⁵And God sent an angel to Jerusalem to destroy it, but when he was about to destroy it, the LORD took note and relented concerning the calamity; he said to the destroying angel, "Enough! Stay your hand." The angel of the LORD was standing by the threshing floor of Ornan the Jebusite. ¹⁶David looked up and saw the angel of the LORD standing between earth and heaven and in his hand a drawn sword stretched out over Jerusalem. Then David and the elders, clothed in sackcloth, fell on their faces. ¹⁷And David said to God, "Was it not I who gave the command to count the people? It is I who have sinned and done very wickedly. But these sheep, what have they done? Let your hand, I pray, O LORD my God, be against me and against my father's house, but do not let your people be plagued!"

21:1–17 **The census and plague.** Cf. 2 Sam. 24:1–17. 21:1 *Satan* may also be translated as "an adversary." When the Hebrew word "ha-satan" ("the satan" or "the adversary") appears in Zech. 3 and Job 1, it describes a supernatural figure in an antagonistic relationship with YHWH. When the word "satan" ("an adversary") appears without the definite article in military, political, and legal contexts in the Hebrew Bible, such as 1 Sam. 29:4 or 1 Kgs. 11:14, it refers to a human adversary—an enemy or accuser. While "satan" in 1 Chr. 21:1 can be translated as a personal noun referring to a supernatural being, it is equally plausible to understand it as an unidentified human antagonist. Either way, the Chronicler takes the agency for inciting David to conduct the census out of God's hands (see 2 Sam. 24:1) and puts it in the hands of someone else, whether Satan or an unspecified enemy. The reference to God's pre-census anger in 2 Sam. 24:1 is also removed. The effect of the Chronicler's change is to give David unmitigated blame for the census. The Chronicler's motivation for this uncharacteristic aspersion of David is not clear. Perhaps it is to smooth out the theological difficulty of God's acting against David without explicit cause. Or it may be that David's singularly shouldering the blame at the beginning of the story better echoes his request at the end that his people be spared (1 Chr. 21:17), further strengthening the portrayal of his leadership. David's piety is certainly underscored by the story, since he testifies to the mercy of God (21:13). 21:7 1 Chronicles is a book that loves to list and count people, so it is ironic that David's census would anger God. The potential danger of a census is also noted at Exod. 30:12, even as the importance of accounting for taxation and military administration is affirmed there, in Num. 1 and 26, and throughout 1 and 2 Chronicles. See also the note at 1 Chr. 27:23. 21:16 The *angel* with a *drawn sword* recalls the story of Balaam's talking donkey (Num. 22), in which the angel stands in the road as Balaam's adversary (cf. 1 Chr. 21:1). David can see the angel, whereas Balaam could not.

18 Then the angel of the LORD commanded Gad to tell David that he should go up and erect an altar to the LORD on the threshing floor of Ornan the Jebusite. ¹⁹So David went up following Gad's instructions, which he had spoken in the name of the LORD. ²⁰Ornan turned and saw the king,ˡ and while his four sons who were with him hid themselves, Ornan continued to thresh wheat. ²¹As David came to Ornan, Ornan looked and saw David; he went out from the threshing floor and prostrated himself before David with his face to the ground. ²²David said to Ornan, "Give me the site of the threshing floor that I may build on it an altar to the LORD—give it to me at its full price—so that the plague may be averted from the people." ²³Then Ornan said to David, "Take it, and let my lord the king do what seems good to him; see, I present the oxen for burnt offerings and the threshing sledges for the wood and the wheat for a grain offering. I give it all." ²⁴But King David said to Ornan, "No, but I will buy them for the full price. I will not take for the LORD what is yours nor offer burnt offerings that cost me nothing." ²⁵So David paid Ornan six hundred shekels of gold by weight for the site. ²⁶David built there an altar to the LORD and presented burnt offerings and offerings of well-being. He called upon the LORD, and he answered him with fire from heaven on the altar of burnt offering. ²⁷Then the LORD commanded the angel, and he put his sword back into its sheath.

28 At that time, when David saw that the LORD had answered him at the threshing floor of Ornan the Jebusite, he made his sacrifices there. ²⁹For the tabernacle of the LORD that Moses had made in the wilderness and the altar of burnt offering were at that time in the high place at Gibeon, ³⁰but David could not go before it to inquire of God, for he was afraid of the sword of the

22 angel of the LORD. ¹Then David said, "Here shall be the house of the LORD God and here the altar of burnt offering for Israel."

2 David gave orders to gather together the aliens who were residing in the land of Israel, and he set stonecutters to prepare dressed stones for building the house of God. ³David also provided great stores of iron for nails for the doors of the gates and for clamps, as well as bronze in quantities beyond weighing, ⁴and cedar logs without number—for the Sidonians and Tyrians brought great quantities of cedar to David. ⁵For David said, "My son Solomon is young and inexperienced, and the house that is to be built for the LORD must be exceedingly magnificent, famous and glorified throughout all lands; I will therefore make preparation for it." So David provided

ˡ 21.20 Heb ms Gk: MT *angel*

21:18–27 **David's altar and sacrifice.** Cf. 2 Sam. 24:18–25. *Ornan* is called Araunah in 2 Samuel. As a *Jebusite*, Ornan would be associated with the indigenous inhabitants of Jerusalem (see 1 Chr. 11:4). **21:24** As part of shouldering responsibility for God's judgment, David understands that the sacrifices must be entirely his. **21:26** *He answered him with fire from heaven.* The divine response of fire igniting the burnt offerings on the altar echoes Lev. 9:24, Judg. 6:21, and 1 Kgs. 18:36–39 and is a sign of God's affirmation. **21:27** With the verses that follow, this line is an addition in the Chronicler's account.

21:28–22:1 **The place chosen for the temple.** Along with the preceding verse, this section is the Chronicler's addition to the narrative of the census and plague, drawing an etiological line between that story and the establishment of the Jerusalem temple. David sets up an altar and offers his sacrifices *at the threshing floor of Ornan the Jebusite* rather than at Gibeon (cf. 1 Chr. 16:39–40). **22:1** David declares that the altar he has established on the threshing floor will be the site of *the house of the LORD God*—that is, the temple.

22:2–5 **David prepares to build the temple.** Most of the material from this point through the end of 1 Chronicles is without parallel in Samuel-Kings, although it contains ample language borrowed from both Deuteronomic and priestly traditions. The additions, which focus on temple administration, reflect the Chronicler's interest in foregrounding David's multifaceted role in constructing and organizing the Jerusalem temple, despite the fact that the temple will not be built during David's lifetime. **22:5** Here David provides the rationale for his extensive preparations for the temple, even though God has told him he is not to be its builder. His son and successor, Solomon, is *young and inexperienced*, not yet up to the task of building a temple that will be *exceedingly magnificent,*

materials in great quantity before his death.

6 Then he called for his son Solomon and charged him to build a house for the LORD, the God of Israel. ⁷David said to Solomon, "My son, I had planned to build a house to the name of the LORD my God. ⁸But the word of the LORD came to me, saying, 'You have shed much blood and have waged great wars; you shall not build a house to my name because you have shed so much blood in my sight on the earth. ⁹See, a son shall be born to you; he shall be a man of rest. I will give him rest from all his enemies on every side; indeed, his name shall be Solomon, and I will give peace*ᵐ* and quiet to Israel in his days. ¹⁰He shall build a house for my name. He shall be a son to me, and I will be a father to him, and I will establish his royal throne in Israel forever.' ¹¹Now, my son, the LORD be with you, so that you may succeed in building the house of the LORD your God, as he has spoken concerning you. ¹²Only, may the LORD grant you discretion and understanding, so that when he gives you charge over Israel you may keep the law of the LORD your God. ¹³Then you will prosper, if you are careful to observe the statutes and the ordinances that the LORD commanded Moses for Israel. Be strong and of good courage. Do not be afraid or dismayed. ¹⁴With great pains I have provided for the house of the LORD one hundred thousand talents of gold, one million talents of silver, and bronze and iron beyond weighing, for there is so much of it; timber and stone also I have provided. To these you must add more. ¹⁵You have an abundance of workers: stonecutters, masons, carpenters, and all kinds of artisans without number, skilled in working ¹⁶gold, silver, bronze, and iron. Now begin the work, and the LORD be with you."

17 David also commanded all the leaders of Israel to help his son Solomon, saying, ¹⁸"Is not the LORD your God with you? Has he not given you rest on every side? For he has delivered the inhabitants of the land into my hand, and the land is subdued before the LORD and his people. ¹⁹Now set your mind and heart to seek the LORD your God. Go and build the sanctuary of the LORD God so that the ark of the covenant of the LORD and the holy vessels of God may be brought into the house built for the name of the LORD."

23 When David was old and full of days, he made his son Solomon king over Israel.

2 David assembled all the leaders of Israel and the priests and the Levites. ³The Levites, thirty years old and up, were counted, and the total head count of men was thirty-eight thousand. ⁴"Twenty-four thousand of

---

m 22.9 The Heb word for *peace* is related to *Solomon*

---

famous and glorified throughout all lands. This explanation has both political and religious implications in an ancient culture where the two realms were not separate; the fame of the temple would bring recognition both to Israel and to Israel's God.

22:6–19 David's charge to Solomon and the leaders. 22:8 The very type of success that brought David glory—namely, having *waged great wars*—is cited as an impediment to temple building. There is an echo here of 1 Kgs. 5:3–4, but rather than the wars being a drain on David's time and energy, they are recast in terms of David's having *shed much blood*—a question of ethics but one that may also imply ritual uncleanness. Bloodshed is not part of the reasoning relayed to David through Nathan in 1 Chr. 17:3–15. **22:9** In a pun on Solomon's name, God declares that Solomon (Heb. "Shelomoh") will be a man of peace (Heb. "shalom"), in contrast to David's life of war. The contrast drawn between the reigns of David and Solomon—war versus peace—is as much a matter of progress in the stages of kingship as it is a matter of judgment on David: David has made the necessary military conquests to secure the kingdom for his posterity; Solomon will be the king made for peace and prosperity. David has set Solomon up to succeed and continues to do so by initiating the preparations for the temple (see **"Solomon," p. 595**). **22:13** *Be strong and of good courage. Do not be afraid or dismayed.* The Chronicler adopts these phrases from Deuteronomistic literature, where they appear often. See, for example, Deut. 31:6–8 and Josh. 1:6–9. **22:18** *Given you rest* is another favorite Deuteronomistic phrase (e.g., Deut. 12:8–12; Josh. 1:13–15).

23:1–32 Families of the Levites and their functions. 23:1 None of the dramatic conflict surrounding David's old age and the monarchic succession in 1 Kgs. 1–2 is included in 1 Chronicles. **23:2** *Thirty years old and up.* Verses 24 and 27, which reflect back to vv. 2–3 and provide a kind of closing bracket

these," David said, "shall have charge of the work in the house of the Lord, six thousand shall be officers and judges, [5]four thousand gatekeepers, and four thousand shall offer praises to the Lord with the instruments that I have made for praise." [6]And David organized them in divisions corresponding to the sons of Levi: Gershon, Kohath, and Merari.

7 The sons of Gershon[n] were Ladan and Shimei. [8]The sons of Ladan: Jehiel the chief, Zetham, and Joel, three. [9]The sons of Shimei: Shelomoth, Haziel, and Haran, three. These were the heads of families of Ladan. [10]And the sons of Shimei: Jahath, Zina, Jeush, and Beriah. These four were the sons of Shimei. [11]Jahath was the chief and Zizah the second, but Jeush and Beriah did not have many sons, so they were enrolled as a single family.

12 The sons of Kohath: Amram, Izhar, Hebron, and Uzziel, four. [13]The sons of Amram: Aaron and Moses. Aaron was set apart to consecrate the most holy things, so that he and his sons forever should make offerings before the Lord and minister to him and pronounce blessings in his name forever, [14]but as for Moses the man of God, his sons were to be reckoned among the tribe of Levi. [15]The sons of Moses: Gershom and Eliezer. [16]The son of Gershom: Shebuel the chief. [17]The son of Eliezer: Rehabiah the chief; Eliezer had no other sons, but the sons of Rehabiah were very numerous. [18]The son of Izhar: Shelomith the chief. [19]The sons of Hebron: Jeriah the chief, Amariah the second, Jahaziel the third, and Jekameam the fourth. [20]The sons of Uzziel: Micah the chief and Isshiah the second.

21 The sons of Merari: Mahli and Mushi. The sons of Mahli: Eleazar and Kish.

[22]Eleazar died having no sons but only daughters; their kindred, the sons of Kish, married them. [23]The sons of Mushi: Mahli, Eder, and Jeremoth, three.

24 These were the sons of Levi by their ancestral houses, the heads of families as they were enrolled according to the number of the names of the individuals from twenty years old and up who were to do the work for the service of the house of the Lord. [25]For David said, "The Lord, the God of Israel, has given rest to his people, and he resides in Jerusalem forever. [26]And so the Levites no longer need to carry the tabernacle or any of the things for its service"—[27]for according to the last words of David these were the number of the Levites from twenty years old and up—[28]"but their duty shall be to assist the descendants of Aaron for the service of the house of the Lord, having the care of the courts and the chambers, the cleansing of all that is holy, and any work for the service of the house of God; [29]to assist also with the rows of bread, the choice flour for the grain offering, the wafers of unleavened bread, the baked offering, the offering mixed with oil, and all measures of quantity or size. [30]And they shall stand every morning thanking and praising the Lord, and likewise at evening, [31]and whenever burnt offerings are offered to the Lord on Sabbaths, new moons, and appointed festivals, according to the number required of them, regularly before the Lord. [32]Thus they shall keep charge of the tent of meeting and the sanctuary and shall attend the descendants of Aaron, their kindred, for the service of the house of the Lord."

n 23.7 Vg Compare Gk Syr: Heb *to the Gershonite*

for the lists of Levites, say the minimum age for the count was *twenty years.* While the reasons for the discrepancy are not clear, the thirty-year-old minimum seems to be a preexilic precedent (cf. Num. 4:3), while the twenty-year-old minimum aligns better with postexilic expectations (cf. Ezra 3:8; 1 Chr. 27:23). **23:6** David's organization of Levitical duties by family branch calls attention to the fact that genealogies are not simply records of names but also assertions of social roles and dividing lines between insiders and outsiders. See **"Women in the Genealogy," p. 545. 23:13–14** This section of the list points to the key distinction between priests and Levites. Moses and Aaron are both descendants of Levi. However, priests must be descendants of Aaron, whereas Moses's descendants are counted among the rest of the Levites, whose duties span the work of the temple outside of the care of the *most holy things.* **23:22** By marrying as cousins, the *sons of Kish* and the *daughters* of *Eleazar* ensure Eleazar's line continues, since Levitical lineage is traced through the father's family. **23:26** *Carry the tabernacle.* See Num. 1:50. **23:27** The reference to the *last words of David* seems to be a tacit acknowledgment of the discrepancy between twenty years versus thirty years (cf. v. 3) and an endorsement of *twenty years old* as the proper number.

24

The divisions of the descendants of Aaron were these. The sons of Aaron: Nadab, Abihu, Eleazar, and Ithamar. ²But Nadab and Abihu died before their father and had no sons, so Eleazar and Ithamar became the priests. ³Along with Zadok of the sons of Eleazar and Ahimelech of the sons of Ithamar, David organized them according to the appointed duties in their service. ⁴Since more chief men were found among the sons of Eleazar than among the sons of Ithamar, they organized them under sixteen heads of ancestral houses of the sons of Eleazar and eight of the sons of Ithamar. ⁵They organized them by lot, all alike, for there were officers of the sanctuary and officers of God among both the sons of Eleazar and the sons of Ithamar. ⁶The scribe Shemaiah son of Nethanel, a Levite, recorded them in the presence of the king, and the officers, and Zadok the priest, and Ahimelech son of Abiathar, and the heads of ancestral houses of the priests and of the Levites—one ancestral house being chosen for Eleazar and one chosen for Ithamar.

7 The first lot fell to Jehoiarib, the second to Jedaiah, ⁸the third to Harim, the fourth to Seorim, ⁹the fifth to Malchijah, the sixth to Mijamin, ¹⁰the seventh to Hakkoz, the eighth to Abijah, ¹¹the ninth to Jeshua, the tenth to Shecaniah, ¹²the eleventh to Eliashib, the twelfth to Jakim, ¹³the thirteenth to Huppah, the fourteenth to Jeshebeab, ¹⁴the fifteenth to Bilgah, the sixteenth to Immer, ¹⁵the seventeenth to Hezir, the eighteenth to

Happizzez, ¹⁶the nineteenth to Pethahiah, the twentieth to Jehezkel, ¹⁷the twenty-first to Jachin, the twenty-second to Gamul, ¹⁸the twenty-third to Delaiah, the twenty-fourth to Maaziah. ¹⁹These had as their appointed duty in their service to enter the house of the LORD according to the procedure established for them by their ancestor Aaron, as the LORD God of Israel had commanded him.

20 And of the rest of the sons of Levi: of the sons of Amram, Shubael; of the sons of Shubael, Jehdeiah. ²¹Of Rehabiah: of the sons of Rehabiah, Isshiah the chief. ²²Of the Izharites, Shelomoth; of the sons of Shelomoth, Jahath. ²³The sons of Hebron:*ᵒ* Jeriah the chief,*ᵖ* Amariah the second, Jahaziel the third, Jekameam the fourth. ²⁴The sons of Uzziel, Micah; of the sons of Micah, Shamir. ²⁵The brother of Micah, Isshiah; of the sons of Isshiah, Zechariah. ²⁶The sons of Merari: Mahli and Mushi. The sons of Jaaziah: Beno.*ᵍ* ²⁷The sons of Merari: of Jaaziah, Beno,*ʳ* Shoham, Zaccur, and Ibri. ²⁸Of Mahli: Eleazar, who had no sons. ²⁹Of Kish, the sons of Kish: Jerahmeel. ³⁰The sons of Mushi: Mahli, Eder, and Jerimoth. These were the sons of the Levites according to their ancestral houses. ³¹These also cast lots corresponding to their kindred, the descendants of Aaron, in the presence of King David, Zadok, Ahimelech, and the heads of ancestral houses of the priests and of the Levites, the chief as well as the youngest brother.

o 24.23 Heb lacks Hebron   p 24.23 Heb lacks the chief   q 24.26 Or his son: Meaning of Heb uncertain   r 24.27 Or his son: Meaning of Heb uncertain

24:1–19 Divisions of the priests. 24:2 *Nadab and Abihu died.* See Lev. 10:1–3. **24:5** After identifying an organizational scheme of twenty-four families descended from Aaron's sons Eleazar and Ithamar, David, Ahimelech, and Zadok cast lots, letting chance determine the order of the rotation of priests serving in the sanctuary, since the twenty-four divisions were otherwise *all alike.*

24:20–31 Other Levites. Despite being labeled as *the rest of the sons of Levi*, this list duplicates many of the names from 23:7–23 but does not include any descendants of Gershon, only of Kohath and Merari (see 23:6). Since chaps. 24–27 go on to list even more Levites, the idea of this list as *the rest of the sons of Levi* suggests it is a later supplement to vv. 1–19. **24:31** *These also cast lots.* Once again, a method of chance is used to set up a schedule, this time for the Levitical families, emphasizing they are all on equal footing.

25:1–31 The temple musicians. When the ark was returned to Jerusalem, David appointed Levite musicians "to invoke, to thank, and to praise the LORD, the God of Israel" (16:4). Now the musical guilds are appointed to *prophesy with lyres, harps, and cymbals.* The implications of the language of prophecy in this section are not immediately clear; however, it can be helpful to remember that in the ancient Near East, a prophet was understood to be an intermediary between God and humans rather than simply as one who predicts the future. Music and prophecy are closely associated in the Bible, particularly in the early monarchic era, when music was sometimes used to entrance listeners into a prophetic state (1 Sam. 10:5–6; 2 Kgs. 3:15–16). Thus, the temple musicians serve a prophetic role in that their work enables them to communicate with God: they send praise to God but can also

25 David and the officers of the army also set apart for the service the sons of Asaph, and of Heman, and of Jeduthun, who should prophesy with lyres, harps, and cymbals. The list of those who did the work and of their duties was: ²Of the sons of Asaph: Zaccur, Joseph, Nethaniah, and Asarelah, sons of Asaph, under the direction of Asaph, who prophesied under the direction of the king. ³Of Jeduthun, the sons of Jeduthun: Gedaliah, Zeri, Jeshaiah, Shimei,ˢ Hashabiah, and Mattithiah, six, under the direction of their father Jeduthun, who prophesied with the lyre in thanksgiving and praise to the LORD. ⁴Of Heman, the sons of Heman: Bukkiah, Mattaniah, Uzziel, Shebuel, and Jerimoth, Hananiah, Hanani, Eliathah, Giddalti, and Romamti-ezer, Joshbekashah, Mallothi, Hothir, Mahazioth. ⁵All these were the sons of Heman the king's seer, according to the promise of God to exalt him, for God had given Heman fourteen sons and three daughters. ⁶They were all under the direction of their father for the music in the house of the LORD with cymbals, harps, and lyres for the service of the house of God. Asaph, Jeduthun, and Heman were under the order of the king. ⁷They and their kindred, who were trained in singing to the LORD, all of whom were skillful, numbered two hundred eighty-eight. ⁸And they cast lots for their duties, small and great, teacher and pupil alike.

9 The first lot fell for Asaph to Joseph; the second to Gedaliah, to him and his brothers and his sons, twelve; ¹⁰the third to Zaccur, his sons and his brothers, twelve; ¹¹the fourth to Izri, his sons and his brothers, twelve; ¹²the fifth to Nethaniah, his sons and his brothers, twelve; ¹³the sixth to Bukkiah, his sons and his brothers, twelve; ¹⁴the seventh to Jesarelah,ᵗ his sons and his brothers, twelve; ¹⁵the eighth to Jeshaiah, his sons and his brothers, twelve; ¹⁶the ninth to Mattaniah, his sons and his brothers, twelve; ¹⁷the tenth to Shimei, his sons and his brothers, twelve; ¹⁸the eleventh to Azarel, his sons and his brothers, twelve; ¹⁹the twelfth to Hashabiah, his sons and his brothers, twelve; ²⁰to the thirteenth, Shubael, his sons and his brothers, twelve; ²¹to the fourteenth, Mattithiah, his sons and his brothers, twelve; ²²to the fifteenth, to Jeremoth, his sons and his brothers, twelve; ²³to the sixteenth, to Hananiah, his sons and his brothers, twelve; ²⁴to the seventeenth, to Joshbekashah, his sons and his brothers, twelve; ²⁵to the eighteenth, to Hanani, his sons and his brothers, twelve; ²⁶to the nineteenth, to Mallothi, his sons and his brothers, twelve; ²⁷to the twentieth, to Eliathah, his sons and his brothers, twelve; ²⁸to the twenty-first, to Hothir, his sons and his brothers, twelve; ²⁹to the twenty-second, to Giddalti, his sons and his brothers, twelve; ³⁰to the twenty-third, to Mahazioth, his sons and his brothers, twelve; ³¹to the twenty-fourth, to Romamti-ezer, his sons and his brothers, twelve.

ˢ 25.3 Gk ms: MT lacks *Shimei*   ᵗ 25.14 Or *Asarelah*

potentially bring word from God to the people. **25:1** *Asaph* was the chief musician appointed to sound cymbals before the ark of the covenant when it was returned to Jerusalem (15:16–24; 16:4–6). The reputation of *Asaph* as a musician is also attested in the book of Psalms, where a dozen psalms are associated with him (Pss. 50, 73–83). The sons of Asaph also feature in the establishment of Second Temple worship as described in Ezra-Nehemiah (e.g., Ezra 3:10; Neh. 11:22). **25:2** *Under the direction of* is more mechanically rendered "according to the hand of." In the temple's organizational chart, the king supervises *Asaph*, Jeduthun, and Heman, while each of those men supervises his own branch of the family. **25:3** *Jeduthun.* In 1 Chr. 15, the head trio of musicians accompanying the ark includes the name "Ethan" rather than Jeduthun (vv. 17, 19), but the name Jeduthun appears with Heman and Asaph in chap. 16. At 2 Chr. 35:15, Jeduthun, rather than Heman, is called the "king's seer." *Jeduthun* is also mentioned in the superscriptions of three psalms (see Pss. 39, 62, 77). **25:4–6** *Heman* is the grandson of the prophet Samuel, according to 1 Chr. 6:33, further cementing the Chronicler's association of music with prophecy. The mention of Heman's *three daughters* has led some commentators to see them as participants in the musical service at the temple, particularly because the text says *they were all under the direction of their father.* It is more likely, however, that the opening of v. 6 is a case of resumptive repetition—one of the Chronicler's favorite literary techniques (cf. 5:1–3)—picking up from the beginning of v. 5, since both verses begin with the same Hebrew words. Only the sons are named in v. 4. Heman's *fourteen sons and three daughters* are mentioned by quantity as evidence of *the promise of God to exalt him.* Then the text resumes its discussion of the sons' work at the temple: *all these*—that is, the *sons of Heman the king's seer*—were temple musicians.

26

As for the divisions of the gatekeepers: of the Korahites, Meshelemiah son of Kore, of the sons of Asaph. ²Meshelemiah had sons: Zechariah the firstborn, Jediael the second, Zebadiah the third, Jathniel the fourth, ³Elam the fifth, Jehohanan the sixth, Eliehoenai the seventh. ⁴Obed-edom had sons: Shemaiah the firstborn, Jehozabad the second, Joah the third, Sachar the fourth, Nethanel the fifth, ⁵Ammiel the sixth, Issachar the seventh, Peullethai the eighth; for God blessed him. ⁶Also to his son Shemaiah sons were born who exercised authority in their ancestral houses, for they were men of great ability. ⁷The sons of Shemaiah: Othni, Rephael, Obed, and Elzabad, whose brothers were able men, Elihu and Semachiah. ⁸All these, sons of Obed-edom with their sons and brothers, were able men qualified for the service; sixty-two of Obed-edom. ⁹Meshelemiah had sons and brothers, able men, eighteen. ¹⁰Hosah, of the sons of Merari, had sons: Shimri the chief (for though he was not the firstborn, his father made him chief), ¹¹Hilkiah the second, Tebaliah the third, Zechariah the fourth; all the sons and brothers of Hosah totaled thirteen.

12 These divisions of the gatekeepers, corresponding to their leaders, had duties, just as their kindred did, ministering in the house of the LORD, ¹³and they cast lots by ancestral houses, small and great alike, for their gates. ¹⁴The lot for the east fell to Shelemiah. They cast lots also for his son Zechariah, a prudent counselor, and his lot came out for the north. ¹⁵Obed-edom's came out for the south, and to his sons was allotted the storehouse. ¹⁶For Shuppim and Hosah it came out for the west, at the gate of Shallecheth on the ascending road. Guard corresponded to guard. ¹⁷On the east there were six Levites each day,ᵘ on the north four each day, on the south four each day, as well as two and two at the storehouse, ¹⁸and for the colonnadeᵛ on the west there were four at the road and two at the colonnade.ʷ ¹⁹These were the divisions of the gatekeepers among the Korahites and the sons of Merari.

20 And of the Levites, Ahijah had charge of the treasuries of the house of God and the treasuries of the dedicated gifts. ²¹The sons of Ladan, the sons of the Gershonites belonging to Ladan, the heads of families belonging to Ladan the Gershonite: Jehieli.ˣ

22 The sons of Jehieli, Zetham and his brother Joel, were in charge of the treasuries of the house of the LORD. ²³Of the Amramites, the Izharites, the Hebronites, and the Uzzielites: ²⁴Shebuel son of Gershom, son of Moses, was chief officer in charge of the treasuries. ²⁵His brothers: from Eliezer were his son Rehabiah, his son Jeshaiah, his son Joram, his son Zichri, and his son Shelomoth. ²⁶This Shelomoth and his brothers were in charge of all the treasuries of the dedicated gifts that King David, and the heads of families, and the officers of the thousands and the hundreds, and the commanders of the army had dedicated. ²⁷From spoil won in battles they dedicated gifts for the maintenance of the house of the LORD. ²⁸Also all that Samuel the seer, and Saul son of Kish, and Abner son of Ner, and Joab son of Zeruiah had dedicated—all dedicated gifts were in the care of Shelomothʸ and his brothers.

29 Of the Izharites, Chenaniah and his sons were appointed to outside duties for

u 26.17 Gk: Heb lacks *each day*   v 26.18 Meaning of Heb uncertain   w 26.18 Meaning of Heb uncertain   x 26.21 Meaning of Heb uncertain   y 26.28 Gk: Heb *Shelomith*

26:1–19 The gatekeepers. 26:5 *For God blessed him*—that is, Obed-edom's many children are a sign of God's favor, as were Heman's (25:5). Obed-edom's blessing came from keeping the ark of the covenant in his care (13:14). **26:6–8** *Men of great ability* can also be translated as "mighty warriors." Similarly, *able men* can be translated as "strong men," with *able men qualified for the service* as "mighty men with strength for the work." The military language—including the consistent use of the Hebrew word translated as "strength," "valor," or "army"—suggests the gatekeepers served a security function, not just a ceremonial or administrative one. In addition, the clearer language of "guarding" is provided in the descriptions of the gatekeepers at 9:23–27. **26:19** The total number of divisions for the gatekeepers is twenty-four, just as it was for the priests and musicians. The administration of Judah as described in Chronicles is largely organized around multiples of twelve, with twenty-four as the standard number of divisions serving in regular rotations in the temple.

26:20–32 The treasurers, officers, and judges. 26:29 *Outside duties*—that is, some Levites were

Israel, as officers and judges. ³⁰Of the Hebronites, Hashabiah and his brothers, one thousand seven hundred men of ability, had the oversight of Israel west of the Jordan for all the work of the Lord and for the service of the king. ³¹Of the Hebronites, Jerijah was chief of the Hebronites. (In the fortieth year of David's reign search was made of whatever genealogy or family and men of great ability among them were found at Jazer in Gilead.) ³²King David appointed him and his brothers, two thousand seven hundred men of ability, heads of families, to have the oversight of the Reubenites, the Gadites, and the half-tribe of the Manassites for everything pertaining to God and for the affairs of the king.

27 This is the list of the people of Israel, the heads of families, the commanders of the thousands and the hundreds, and their officers who served the king in all matters concerning the divisions that came and went, month after month throughout the year, each division numbering twenty-four thousand:

2 Jashobeam son of Zabdiel was in charge of the first division in the first month; in his division were twenty-four thousand. ³He was a descendant of Perez and was chief of all the commanders of the army for the first month. ⁴Dodai the Ahohite was in charge of the division of the second month; Mikloth was the chief officer of his division. In his division were twenty-four thousand. ⁵The third commander, for the third month, was Benaiah son of the chief priest Jehoiada; in his division were twenty-four thousand. ⁶This is the Benaiah who was a mighty man of the Thirty and in command of the Thirty; his son Ammizabad was in charge of his division.ᶻ ⁷Asahel brother of Joab was fourth, for the fourth month, and his son Zebadiah

after him; in his division were twenty-four thousand. ⁸The fifth commander, for the fifth month, was Shamhuth, the Izrahite; in his division were twenty-four thousand. ⁹Sixth, for the sixth month, was Ira son of Ikkesh the Tekoite; in his division were twenty-four thousand. ¹⁰Seventh, for the seventh month, was Helez the Pelonite, of the Ephraimites; in his division were twenty-four thousand. ¹¹Eighth, for the eighth month, was Sibbecai the Hushathite, of the Zerahites; in his division were twenty-four thousand. ¹²Ninth, for the ninth month, was Abiezer of Anathoth, a Benjaminite; in his division were twenty-four thousand. ¹³Tenth, for the tenth month, was Maharai of Netophah, of the Zerahites; in his division were twenty-four thousand. ¹⁴Eleventh, for the eleventh month, was Benaiah of Pirathon, of the Ephraimites; in his division were twenty-four thousand. ¹⁵Twelfth, for the twelfth month, was Heldai the Netophathite, of Othniel; in his division were twenty-four thousand.

16 Over the tribes of Israel, for the Reubenites, Eliezer son of Zichri was chief officer; for the Simeonites, Shephatiah son of Maacah; ¹⁷for Levi, Hashabiah son of Kemuel; for Aaron, Zadok; ¹⁸for Judah, Elihu, one of David's brothers; for Issachar, Omri son of Michael; ¹⁹for Zebulun, Ishmaiah son of Obadiah; for Naphtali, Jerimoth son of Azriel; ²⁰for the Ephraimites, Hoshea son of Azaziah; for the half-tribe of Manasseh, Joel son of Pedaiah; ²¹for the half-tribe of Manasseh in Gilead, Iddo son of Zechariah; for Benjamin, Jaasiel son of Abner; ²²for Dan, Azarel son of Jeroham. These were the leaders of the tribes of Israel. ²³David did not count those below twenty years of age, for the Lord had promised to make Israel as

z 27.6 Gk Vg: Heb *Ammizabad was his division*

appointed to duties outside of the temple, in greater Israel. **26:31** Despite being set during the reign of David, the idea that one might *search* a *genealogy*—particularly a written record—to identify and authorize social roles is a thoroughly postexilic idea (cf. Ezra 2:62; Neh. 7:64) and underscores the late-Persian-period authorship of 1 Chronicles. **26:32** Cf. the note at 5:9.

27:1–15 The military divisions. 27:1 The organization of the military divisions into twelve echoes the numerical schema of multiples of twelve in the temple. Each division has twenty-four thousand troops and is assigned a month of the year when it *served the king*—that is, provided a fresh stock of troops for any of the king's military needs, particularly in Jerusalem.

27:16–24 Leaders of tribes. 27:23 Here a clearer reason for God's displeasure with census taking is provided (versus 1 Chr. 21:7): to count the exact number of Israelites would be to doubt God's promise to give Abraham so many descendants that they would be impossible to count (Gen. 15:5).

numerous as the stars of heaven. [24]Joab son of Zeruiah began to count them but did not finish, yet wrath came upon Israel for this, and the number was not entered into the account of the Annals of King David.

[25] Over the king's treasuries was Azmaveth son of Adiel. Over the treasuries in the country, in the cities, in the villages and in the towers was Jonathan son of Uzziah. [26]Over those who did the work of the field, tilling the soil, was Ezri son of Chelub. [27]Over the vineyards was Shimei the Ramathite. Over the produce of the vineyards for the wine cellars was Zabdi the Shiphmite. [28]Over the olive and sycamore trees in the Shephelah was Baal-hanan the Gederite. Over the stores of oil was Joash. [29]Over the herds that pastured in Sharon was Shitrai the Sharonite. Over the herds in the valleys was Shaphat son of Adlai. [30]Over the camels was Obil the Ishmaelite. Over the donkeys was Jehdeiah the Meronothite. [31]Over the flocks was Jaziz the Hagrite. All these were stewards of King David's property.

[32] Jonathan, David's uncle, was a counselor, being a man of understanding and a scribe; Jehiel son of Hachmoni attended the king's sons. [33]Ahithophel was the king's counselor, and Hushai the Archite was the king's friend. [34]After Ahithophel came Jehoiada son of Benaiah and Abiathar. Joab was commander of the king's army.

28

David assembled at Jerusalem all the officials of Israel, the officials of the tribes, the officers of the divisions that served the king, the commanders of the thousands, the commanders of the hundreds, the stewards of all the property and cattle of the king, and his sons, together with the palace officials, the mighty warriors, and all the warriors. [2]Then King David rose to his feet and said, "Hear me, my brothers and my people. I had planned to build a house of rest for the ark of the covenant of the LORD, for the footstool of our God, and I made preparations for building. [3]But God said to me, 'You shall not build a house for my name, for you are a warrior and have shed blood.' [4]Yet the LORD God of Israel chose me from all my ancestral house to be king over Israel forever, for he chose Judah as leader, and in the house of Judah my father's house, and among my father's sons

27:24 *Wrath came upon Israel.* This remark refers to the disastrous census attempt recounted in 1 Chr. 21.

27:25-34 **Other civic officials.** 27:32 *Jonathan, David's uncle* may also be translated as "Jonathan, David's beloved." According to Samuel, Saul's son Jonathan loved David as he loved his own soul (1 Sam. 18:1; 20:17), and David describes Jonathan's love as "wonderful, passing the love of women" (2 Sam. 1:26). There is no record of an uncle of David named Jonathan. However, 1 Chr. 10:2 recounts the death of Saul's son Jonathan decades earlier, whereas the setup of the civic administration comes late in David's life. Saul's son Jonathan was a warrior, but this Jonathan is described as *counselor* and *scribe*. David also has a nephew named Jonathan credited with killing a six-fingered, six-toed Philistine giant (1 Chr. 20:7), which suggests that the name was known in the family. The evidence thus leans more toward "uncle" for the translation, but the coincidence of the alternative "beloved" is nonetheless striking. 27:33 The designation of *Hushai the Archite* as the king's *friend* is, unlike most of the surrounding lists, not so much a formal office as an allusion to the tradition of Hushai as a loyal coconspirator of David. Hushai is also described as the king's *friend* at 2 Sam. 15:37 and 16:16. In that story, Hushai shows loyalty to David by feigning loyalty to Absalom and then giving Absalom advice that leads to his defeat (2 Sam. 15:32–18:18). In the same story, *Ahithophel*, David's *counselor*, becomes an ally of Absalom but then hangs himself after Absalom follows Hushai's advice instead (17:23).

28:1-21 **Solomon instructed to build the temple.** David convenes an assembly of Israel's leaders so that he can supervise the transfer of temple and administrative plans to his son and successor, Solomon. Much of what David says to the assembly and to Solomon echoes what he has already said to Solomon in 1 Chr. 22:6–16, followed by the observation "he made his son Solomon king over Israel" (23:1). In this way, the organizational lists of 23:2–27:34 are an interruption to what is essentially the Chronicler's succession narrative, begun at 22:2, which then resumes at 28:1. The Chronicler's succession narrative omits all the intrigue around Adonijah's attempt to take the throne, as told in 1 Kgs. 1–2, and it does not dwell on David's frailty at all (1 Kgs. 1:1–5). Instead, the story forges continuities between David's plans for the temple and Solomon's eventual construction of it, and it depicts a smooth transfer of power from David to Solomon. 28:2 *I had planned.* See 1 Chr. 17:1–15; 22:7.

he took delight in making me king over all Israel. ⁵And of all my sons, for the Lord has given me many, he has chosen my son Solomon to sit upon the throne of the kingdom of the Lord over Israel. ⁶He said to me, 'It is your son Solomon who shall build my house and my courts, for I have chosen him to be a son to me, and I will be a father to him. ⁷I will establish his kingdom forever, if he continues resolute in keeping my commandments and my ordinances, as he is today.' ⁸Now therefore in the sight of all Israel, the assembly of the Lord, and in the hearing of our God, observe and search out all the commandments of the Lord your God, that you may possess this good land and leave it for an inheritance to your children after you forever.

9 "And you, my son Solomon, know the God of your father, and serve him with single mind and willing heart, for the Lord searches every mind and understands every plan and thought. If you seek him, he will be found by you, but if you forsake him, he will abandon you forever. ¹⁰Take heed, now, for the Lord has chosen you to build a house as the sanctuary; be strong, and act."

11 Then David gave his son Solomon the plan of the vestibule and of its houses, its treasuries, its upper rooms, and its inner chambers, and of the room for the cover, ¹²and the plan of all that he had in mind for the courts of the house of the Lord, all the surrounding chambers, the treasuries of the house of God, and the treasuries for dedicated gifts; ¹³for the divisions of the priests and of the Levites, and all the work of the service in the house of the Lord; for all the vessels for the service in the house of the Lord, ¹⁴the weight of gold for all golden vessels for each service, the weight of silver vessels for each service, ¹⁵the weight of the golden lampstands and their lamps, the weight of gold for each lampstand and its lamps, the weight of silver for a lampstand and its lamps, according to the use of each in the service, ¹⁶the weight of gold for each table for the rows of bread, the silver for the silver tables, ¹⁷and pure gold for the forks, the basins, and the cups; for the golden bowls and the weight of each; for the silver bowls and the weight of each; ¹⁸for the altar of incense made of refined gold and its weight; also his plan for the golden chariot of the cherubim that spread their wings and covered the ark of the covenant of the Lord.

19 "All this, in writing at the Lord's direction, he made clear to me—the plan of all the works."

20 David said further to his son Solomon, "Be strong and of good courage, and act. Do not be afraid or dismayed, for the Lord God, my God, is with you. He will not fail you or forsake you, until all the work for the service of the house of the Lord is finished. ²¹Here are the divisions of the priests and the Levites for all the service of the house of God, and with you in all the work will be every volunteer who has skill for any kind of service; also the officers and all the people will be wholly at your command."

29 King David said to the whole assembly, "My son Solomon, whom alone God has chosen, is young and inexperienced, and the work is great, for the temple[a] will not be for mortals but for the Lord God. ²So I have provided for the house of my God, so far as I was able, the gold for the things of gold, the silver for the things of silver, and the bronze for the things of bronze, the iron for the things of iron, and wood for the things of wood, besides great quantities of onyx and stones for setting, antimony, colored stones, all sorts of precious stones, and marble in abundance. ³Moreover, in addition to all that I have provided for the holy house, I have a treasure of my own of gold and silver, and because of my devotion to the house of my God I give it to the house of my God: ⁴three thousand talents of gold, of the gold of Ophir, and seven thousand talents of refined silver, for overlaying the walls of the house, ⁵and for all the work

a 29.1 Heb *fortress*

28:19 *In writing.* The reliance on writing as a tool of both administration and authority is characteristic of Persian-period Israel (cf. the note at 26:31). **28:20–21** Borrowing characteristically Deuteronomic language, David assures Solomon that God will be with him in the construction of the temple (v. 20). David then gestures at the whole bevy of people—organized by David—who will be *at your command.* Thus David reassures Solomon that he has both divine and human support for the task ahead of him.

29:1–9 Offerings for building the temple. 29:5–6 Having listed the materials he has arranged from both the national treasury and his personal wealth for the temple construction, David takes

to be done by artisans, gold for the things of gold and silver for the things of silver. Who then will offer willingly, consecrating themselves today to the LORD?"

6 Then the leaders of ancestral houses made their freewill offerings, as did also the leaders of the tribes of Israel, the commanders of the thousands and of the hundreds, and the officers over the king's work. ⁷They gave for the service of the house of God five thousand talents and ten thousand darics of gold, ten thousand talents of silver, eighteen thousand talents of bronze, and one hundred thousand talents of iron. ⁸Whoever had precious stones gave them to the treasury of the house of the LORD, into the care of Jehiel the Gershonite. ⁹Then the people rejoiced because these had given willingly, for with single mind they had offered freely to the LORD; King David also rejoiced greatly.

10 Then David blessed the LORD in the presence of all the assembly; David said, "Blessed are you, O LORD, the God of our ancestor Israel, forever and ever. ¹¹Yours, O LORD, are the greatness, the power, the glory, the victory, and the majesty, for all that is in the heavens and on the earth is yours; yours is the kingdom, O LORD, and you are exalted as head above all. ¹²Riches and honor come from you, and you rule over all. In your hand are power and might, and it is in your hand to make great and to give strength to all. ¹³And now, our God, we give thanks to you and praise your glorious name.

14 "But who am I, and what is my people, that we should be able to make this freewill offering? For all things come from you, and of your own have we given you. ¹⁵For we are aliens and transients before you, as were all our ancestors; our days on the earth are like a shadow, and there is no hope. ¹⁶O LORD our God, all this abundance that we have provided for building you a house for your holy name comes from your hand and is all your own. ¹⁷I know, my God, that you search the heart and take pleasure in uprightness; in the uprightness of my heart I have freely offered all these things, and now I have seen your people who are present here offering freely and joyously to you. ¹⁸O LORD, the God of Abraham, Isaac, and Israel, our ancestors, keep forever such purposes and thoughts in the hearts of your people, and direct their hearts toward you. ¹⁹Grant to my son Solomon that with single mind he may keep your commandments, your decrees, and your statutes, performing all of them, and that he may build the temple[b] for which I have made provision."

20 Then David said to the whole assembly, "Bless the LORD your God." And all the assembly blessed the LORD, the God of their ancestors, and bowed their heads and prostrated themselves before the LORD and the king. ²¹On the next day they offered sacrifices and burnt offerings to the LORD, a thousand bulls, a thousand rams, and a thousand lambs, with their libations, and sacrifices in abundance for all Israel, ²²and they ate and drank before the LORD on that day with great joy.

They made David's son Solomon king a second time; they anointed him as the LORD's

b 29.19 Heb *fortress*

up a collection for additional funds, asking the gathered leaders for *freewill offerings*—that is, for anything they feel moved to give rather than a designated amount. **29:7** The reference to *darics* is anachronistic; *darics* are Persian coins that were not minted until the end of the sixth century BCE; they take their name from the Persian king Darius. The slip is a further reminder that 1 Chronicles was written well after the events it describes and may be commenting on the state of the Second Temple as much as the first one.

29:10–22a David's praise to God. 29:14 David professes that everything given for the temple already belongs to God, a theological claim found in several places throughout the Hebrew Bible (cf. Lev. 25:23; Deut. 10:14; Ps. 24:1). **29:20** *The LORD, the God of their ancestors.* It can be helpful to remember that everywhere the translation renders LORD in small caps, the underlying Hebrew text has the divine name YHWH. Thus, when the gathered people of Israel bless the LORD here, they make clear that in a world where each city-state or region has its own favorite god(s), they are claiming their own God is the one who was in relationship with their ancestors and the one to whom they continue to give their allegiance. See **"God's Name," p. 89.**

29:22b–25 Solomon anointed king. 29:22 *A second time.* Presumably, the first time was at 23:1, when David makes Solomon king in front of a smaller gathering of the leaders of Israel. Given the

prince and Zadok as priest. [23]Then Solomon sat on the throne of the LORD, succeeding his father David as king; he prospered, and all Israel obeyed him. [24]All the leaders and the mighty warriors and also all the sons of King David pledged their allegiance to King Solomon. [25]The LORD highly exalted Solomon in the sight of all Israel and bestowed upon him such royal majesty as had not been on any king before him in Israel.

26 Thus David son of Jesse reigned over all Israel. [27]The period that he reigned over Israel was forty years; he reigned seven years in Hebron, and thirty-three years in Jerusalem. [28]He died in a good old age, full of days, riches, and honor, and his son Solomon succeeded him. [29]Now the acts of King David, from first to last, are written in the records of the seer Samuel, and in the records of the prophet Nathan, and in the records of the seer Gad, [30]with accounts of all his rule and his might and of the events that befell him and Israel and all the kingdoms of the earth.

more intimate setting of the first coronation, the effect is akin to having a small wedding in the office of the justice of the peace, followed by a large and public party with the community sometime later. The consecration of *Zadok as priest* alongside Solomon as king helps cement the importance of the priestly office for the Second Temple period, a time when priests assumed community leadership roles outside of their temple duties (e.g., Jeshua in Ezra 3–5). **29:24** The idea that *all the sons of King David pledged their allegiance to King Solomon* glosses over the deadly conflict between Solomon and Adonijah, as well as their respective allies, recounted in the succession narrative of 1 Kgs. 1–2. See **"Revising/Rewriting the Bible," p. 584**.

29:26–30 Summary of David's reign. While the closing of 1 Chronicles is in some ways an artificial stopping place, since 1 and 2 Chronicles were originally a single book, the end of David's reign provides a fitting conclusion for this first half of Chronicles. David is the father not only of the line of kings whose accounts are included in 2 Chronicles but also of the temple construction and administration that continue throughout 2 Chronicles and into the Chronicler's own era. A new stage of Israel's life begins at 2 Chronicles, even as David's influence over it never goes away. *Written in the records.* See note on 9:1.

2 CHRONICLES

Content and Purpose

Second Chronicles continues retelling the story of Samuel and Kings from a distinctly postexilic perspective. Like 1 Chronicles, the book draws inspiration from sections of the Pentateuch like Leviticus and Numbers that had little impact on Samuel-Kings. It also punctuates its narrative with prophetic speeches and stories that have no parallel in Samuel-Kings. Finally, like 1 Chronicles, it incorporates portions from Psalms as its worship-filled "soundtrack" for telling the story of God's people. To this extent, 2 Chronicles draws the Law, Prophets, and Writings (the trifold division of Israel's Scriptures) into its liturgical account of the past. After the stories of Solomon (2 Chr. 1–9), the book focuses almost exclusively on Judean kings. Gone are the stories of Elijah and Elisha and the kings of the northern kingdom, not because they were unimportant, but because Chronicles wants to focus on the way that temple worship occupies the center of Israel's life in the past and into the postexilic present. Second Chronicles recounts the rise and fall of God's kingdom mediated through the Davidic monarchy. Solomon sat on the divine throne, according to Chronicles (1 Chr. 28:5; 29:23; 2 Chr. 9:8), as ruler over God's kingdom. While we glimpse the kingdom of God in the days of loyal kings like Hezekiah and Josiah, no future Judean king attains this status. Second Chr. 10–36 tell the story of the kingdom's demise and dissolution but do so in a way that engenders hope and leads to worship of the God who shows covenantal loyalty. To that end, 2 Chronicles also takes us on a journey from the building of the temple and its dedication during Solomon's reign (2 Chr. 2–7) until the edict of Cyrus that the exiles should return and rebuild the temple (36:23).

Reading Guide

The Temple's Grandeur and Divine Presence

The temple towers over the Chronicler's history and plays a significant role as a mediator of divine presence. Uniquely in Chronicles, the sanctuary was made according to a divine "pattern" or "design" (Heb. *tabnit*) that David received from YHWH and gave to Solomon (1 Chr. 28:11, 19). The temple is physically taller in Chronicles than in Kings. Sitting before the ten menorahs are ten tables of shewbread (2 Chr. 4:7–8), instead of the one reported in Kings (1 Kgs. 7:48), representing the people of God basking in God's divine light (represented in the menorah). According to Solomon, the temple's physically grand stature reflected its relationship to YHWH's grandeur. The temple was the site of an angelic appearance to David (1 Chr. 21:16), at which he then offered the first sacrifice on what would become the temple's altar (22:1). It was also built on Mount Moriah, where the angel of YHWH had appeared to Abraham (2 Chr. 3:1; Gen. 22). It was also the site of dramatic appearances of divine glory (2 Chr. 5:11–13; 7:1–6). The temple was *for* God and *about* God (1 Chr. 22:5; 29:1). Solomon expresses the relationship in clear terms: "The house that I am about to build will be great, for our God is greater than other gods" (2 Chr. 2:5). The temple reflected YHWH's own sovereignty over the nations and their gods.

Unity around King and Temple

In addition to expressing YHWH's grandeur, the temple was also a rallying point for YHWH's people. Chronicles regularly highlights the occasions when the temple unified Israel. Moreover, for both 1 and 2 Chronicles, the Judean king was supposed to rally the people to himself *so that* he could direct them toward YHWH. Just as "all Israel" gathered together around David (1 Chr. 11:1, 10; 12:23–38) and joined in the ark's procession to Jerusalem (15:3, 28), so too they all gather with Solomon to worship at the tabernacle (2 Chr. 1:2), dedicate the temple, and declare the steadfast love of YHWH (7:3–8). As 2 Chronicles develops, the phrase "all Israel" usually designates the northern tribes in their rebellion against YHWH (e.g., 10:3, 16; 12:1; 13:4, 15; 18:16). However, kings like Hezekiah (29:24; 30:1–6) and Josiah (35:3) restore unity to God's people through their efforts at reforming the cult and reestablishing YHWH worship at the temple. Even if "all Israel" was no longer an intact reality in the Chronicler's own day, he cast a vision of reforming the people of God in worship around the temple. Thus, "whoever" among "*all* His people" was summoned in the book's final verse to go up to the temple with the knowledge of God's abiding presence (36:23 NASB; italics added).

Prophetic Warnings

Prophets feature prominently in the book. Chronicles introduces several prophetic speeches that are not recorded elsewhere in the Old Testament (1 Chr. 12:18; 2 Chr. 12:5–8; 15:2–7; 16:7–9; 19:2–3; 20:15–17, 37; 21:12–15; 24:20; 25:7–16; 28:9–11; 35:21). Chronicles is especially interested in making sure that readers see history as the fulfillment of the prophetic word.

Prophets also play an important role in interpreting history, warning kings and people, and urging God's people toward covenant fidelity. When Judah faced a threat from an overwhelmingly powerful coalition, King Jehoshaphat urged the people, "Believe in the Lord your God and you will be established; believe his prophets and you will succeed" (2 Chr. 20:20). But the Judean kingdom eventually fell. The people kept "mocking the messengers of God, despising his words, and scoffing at his prophets until the wrath of the Lord against his people became so great that there was no remedy" (36:16). Yet it was through the prophetic words of the pagan ruler Cyrus that the exiles were encouraged to "go up" to Jerusalem and rebuild the temple (36:23).

Exile and Return

Second Chronicles uses a unique pattern of exile and return to tell its history. In this way, the stories of Judah's kings anticipate the Babylonian exile and the summons to return that conclude the book. In some of these "mini exile and return" narratives, the temple plays a central role. When King Jehoram rebelled against YHWH and led Judah astray (2 Chr. 21:11), the Philistines and Arabs came and carried off the king's possessions, "together with his sons and wives" (21:17 NIV). Later, King Amaziah pursued idols (25:14), bringing God's wrath against him (v. 20). Then in battle, King Amaziah was captured, Jerusalem's walls were breached, the temple was pillaged, and captives were taken away (vv. 23–24). King Ahaz worshiped other gods, set up illicit altars, and closed the temple's doors (28:1–4, 22–25). As a result, nearly 120,000 Judeans were killed and many deported (28:5–7). These events anticipate the ultimate exile of Judah's king and the destruction of Jerusalem in 2 Chr. 36. Conversely, Judah's faithful kings instituted "returns from exile" that presage the final return under Cyrus. Hezekiah urged Israelites from the former northern kingdom in this way: "Yield yourselves to the Lord and come to his sanctuary . . . serve the Lord your God." If they did so, their kindred and children would "find compassion with their captors and return to this land" (30:8–9). Though spoken before *the* exile, these words clearly anticipate God's word to the exiles through Cyrus in 2 Chr. 36:23. This exile-and-return pattern reminds us that for Chronicles, worship in God's presence lies at the heart of Israel's future in the land.

Matthew J. Lynch

1 Solomon son of David strengthened himself in his kingdom; the Lord his God was with him and made him exceedingly great.

2 Solomon summoned all Israel, the commanders of the thousands and of the hundreds, the judges, and all the leaders of all Israel, the heads of families. ³Then Solomon

David has now left the stage with the kingdom firmly in Solomon's hand. Second Chronicles 1 foregrounds the beginning of the fulfillment of David's prayer that Solomon would keep torah and build the temple (1 Chr. 29:19). As his first public act as king, Solomon leads all Israel to the tabernacle at Gibeon to seek YHWH. In response to this pursuit and for requesting wisdom, YHWH rewards him with wisdom and wealth, which (in subsequent chapters) he directs toward the establishment of the temple.

1:1 In contrast to Kings, where the transition from David to Solomon was fraught with intrigue and violence (1 Kgs. 1–2), Chronicles highlights the seamless transition of power, where Solomon *strengthened himself* over the kingdom. Verse 1 outlines the chapter's two main themes: God's presence and willingness to make Solomon *great*. Only YHWH can give wealth and thereby make kings "great," as David recognized in the previous chapter (1 Chr. 29:12). Both themes feature heavily in this chapter, raising questions about (a) the ends to which God's presence resides among God's people and (b) the purpose of such greatness (seen through wealth). Chronicles consistently points us toward worship at the Jerusalem temple as the end and purpose of these themes.

1:2–6 Whereas in Kings, Solomon goes alone to the Gibeonite high place, in Chronicles, he leads *all Israel* to worship as his first public act. See **"Revising/Rewriting the Bible," p. 584**. Chronicles

Going Deeper: Revising/Rewriting the Bible (2 Chronicles 1)

The book of Chronicles is the most extensive example of rewriting that we have within the Bible. Chronicles rewrites the story of Samuel-Kings but does so with different emphases and by drawing from a wide range of biblical texts. First, Chronicles incorporates genealogical information from books like Genesis and Numbers and other portions of the Old Testament to connect the people of Israel to their wider human family beginning with Adam (1 Chr. 1) and eventually to Israel's own history (1 Chr. 2–9). Rewriting involves artistry. As the Chronicler revisits genealogical information, he places the tribe of Levi at the structural center of the genealogy (1 Chr. 6) and the tribe of Judah first in the list of tribes (1 Chr. 2). Second, Chronicles weaves priestly law into its narrative. Priestly material from the latter part of Exodus, Leviticus, and portions of Numbers and Ezekiel hardly receives any attention in Samuel-Kings. In Chronicles, we see priestly footprints everywhere (see **"The Bible and Methods," pp. 2148–49**). According to 1 Chr. 15–16 and 23–26, for instance, David arranged the priests and Levites for the Jerusalem temple, allotting them duties as singers and musicians, gatekeepers, maintenance workers, and treasurers. These duties reflect knowledge of priestly literature, especially laws about the roles of Levites (e.g., Num. 3:5–13; 8:5–19). Other features in Chronicles come from priestly texts in the Pentateuch. For instance, we read about the priestly covenant of salt (2 Chr. 13:5; cf. Lev. 2:13; Num. 18:19), the importance of Korah's family (1 Chr. 9; cf. Num. 16; 26), and a concern for purity (2 Chr. 26:16–23; 29; cf. Lev. 8–10; Num. 16). Finally, Chronicles draws extensively from Psalms, Israel's worship and prayer book. First Chr. 16 quotes from sections of Pss. 96, 105, and 106, while 2 Chr. 6:41–42 draws from Ps. 132. Throughout the book, the psalmic "loyalty refrain" ("his love endures forever") appears prominently in various places (2 Chr. 5:13; 7:3, 6; 20:21). David also alludes to Ps. 39:12 in his prayer (1 Chr. 29:15), and his blessing in 1 Chr. 29:10 evokes blessings in Psalms (e.g., 41:13; 72:18; 89:52; 106:48). In addition, when speaking about the temple, Solomon's language in 2 Chr. 2:5 sounds very similar to Ps. 135:5, emphasizing that the temple should be "great," reflecting YHWH's greatness. In sum, Chronicles draws together scriptural threads and, for this reason, offers a fitting conclusion to the Jewish canon (see **"The Bible as a Collection," pp. 2145–47**).

Matthew J. Lynch

and the whole assembly with him went to the high place that was at Gibeon, for God's tent of meeting, which Moses the servant of the Lord had made in the wilderness, was there. ⁴(But David had brought the ark of God up from Kiriath-jearim to the place that David had prepared for it, for he had pitched a tent for it in Jerusalem.) ⁵Moreover, the bronze altar that Bezalel son of Uri son of Hur had made was there in front of the tabernacle of the Lord. And Solomon and the assembly inquired at it. ⁶Solomon went up there to the bronze altar before the Lord, which was at the tent of meeting, and offered a thousand burnt offerings on it.

7 That night God appeared to Solomon and said to him, "Ask what I should give you." ⁸Solomon said to God, "You have shown great and steadfast love to my father David and have made me succeed him as king. ⁹O Lord God, let your promise to my father David now be fulfilled, for you have made me king over a people as numerous as the dust of the earth. ¹⁰Give me now wisdom and knowledge to go out and come in before this people, for who can rule this great people of yours?" ¹¹God answered Solomon, "Because this was in your heart and you have not asked for possessions, wealth, honor, or the life of those

is interested in the unity of God's people around the sanctuary, where the people find their true purpose. Solomon's future success as a leader is signaled here in his desire to *inquire* of the Lord's presence through sacrificial worship. King Saul fell short because of his failure to "seek" the Lord at the ark (1 Chr. 10:14). This scene at Gibeon is transitional. The ark is in Jerusalem, while the tabernacle and altar still reside at Gibeon. Chronicles reminds readers that God is present, since Solomon's sacrifices take place *before the Lord* at the Mosaic bronze altar and tabernacle. These details highlight the continuity between past and present and God's ongoing presence during transitional times. They also create a sense of longing for the unification of worship in Jerusalem.

1:7–13 God's appearance to Solomon (v. 7) is the third reference to divine presence in this chapter (cf. vv. 1, 6), and it anticipates a second divine appearance in 2 Chr. 7:12–22, once the temple is built. To that extent, the divine appearances bookend the accounts of the temporary division of the cult

who hate you and have not even asked for long life but have asked for wisdom and knowledge for yourself that you may rule my people over whom I have made you king, [12]wisdom and knowledge are granted to you. I will also give you riches, possessions, and honor, such as none of the kings had who were before you, and none after you shall have the like." [13]So Solomon came from[a] the high place at Gibeon, from the tent of meeting, to Jerusalem. And he reigned over Israel.

14 Solomon gathered together chariots and horses; he had fourteen hundred chariots and twelve thousand horses, which he stationed in the chariot cities and with the king in Jerusalem. [15]The king made silver and gold as common in Jerusalem as stone, and he made cedar as plentiful as the sycamores of the Shephelah. [16]Solomon's import of horses was from Egypt and Kue; the king's traders received them from Kue at the prevailing price. [17]They imported from Egypt (and then exported) a chariot for six hundred shekels of silver and a horse for one hundred fifty, so through them these were exported to all the kings of the Hittites and the kings of Aram.

2 [b]Solomon decided to build a temple for the name of the LORD and a royal palace for himself. [2c]Solomon conscripted seventy thousand laborers and eighty thousand stonecutters in the hill country, with three thousand six hundred to oversee them.

3 Solomon sent word to King Huram of Tyre, "Once you dealt with my father David and sent him cedar to build himself a house to live in. [4]I am now about to build a house for the name of the LORD my God and dedicate it to him for offering fragrant incense before him, and for the regular offering of the rows of bread, and for burnt offerings morning and evening, on the Sabbaths and the new moons and the appointed festivals of the LORD our God, as ordained forever for Israel. [5]The house that I am about to build will be great, for our God is greater than other gods. [6]But who is able to build him a house, since heaven, even highest heaven, cannot contain him? Who am I to build a house for him except as a place to make offerings before him? [7]So now send me an artisan skilled to work in gold, silver, bronze, and iron and in purple, crimson, and blue fabrics, trained also in engraving, to join the skilled workers who are with me in Judah and Jerusalem, whom my father David provided. [8]Send me also cedar, cypress, and algum timber from Lebanon, for I know that your servants are skilled in cutting Lebanon timber. My servants will work with your servants [9]to prepare timber for me in abundance, for the house I am about to build will be great and wonderful. [10]I will provide for your servants, those who cut the timber, twenty thousand cors of crushed wheat, twenty thousand cors of

a 1.13 Gk Vg: Heb *to*   b 2.1 1.18 in Heb   c 2.2 2.1 in Heb

between Gibeon and Jerusalem and its eventual unification. God's appearance also forms another link with the tabernacle, from which God would appear to Moses and speak to him (Exod. 29:42; 33:9, 11). Solomon prays for wisdom to rule the people, and God grants him wisdom and wealth. In later chapters, we learn that both the wisdom and the wealth given by God find their true purpose in the construction of and worship at the temple.

1:14–17 The final verses of this chapter describe the incredible wealth and power that Solomon accumulated. Notably absent is any reference to his many wives (cf. 1 Kgs. 11:1–3). The reference to Egyptian horses sits uneasily against the backdrop of Deut. 17:16, which explicitly forbids a king from acquiring them.

2:1–2 Solomon gets right to work on the temple, first by conscripting 153,600 temporary residents into labor (cf. vv. 17–18). Like Kings, Chronicles wants to distance Solomon from any hint that he enslaved Israelites (1 Kgs. 9:20–22; 2 Chr. 2:17–18)—in keeping with Israelite law (Lev. 25:39–46)—but the people's subsequent anger at Rehoboam hints that he either enslaved Israelites for building projects (as in 1 Kgs. 5:13–14; cf. 1 Kgs. 12:4; 2 Chr. 10:9) or effectively did so through crushing taxes. Whereas Kings describes the construction of Solomon's palace, Chronicles skips right to the temple.

2:3–10 Solomon requests supplies from the Tyrian king Huram. The region of Tyre was known for its towering cedars. Huram contributed cedars to David's palace earlier (2 Sam. 5:11), and Tyrian cedars later decorated the Second Temple (Ezra 3:7). Solomon's letter to Huram gives an opportunity to emphasize the temple's ritual and theological role. The temple was designed for daily and

barley, twenty thousand baths[d] of wine, and twenty thousand baths[e] of oil."

11 Then King Huram of Tyre answered in a letter that he sent to Solomon, "Because the LORD loves his people, he has made you king over them." [12]Huram also said, "Blessed be the LORD God of Israel, who made heaven and earth, who has given King David a wise son endowed with discretion and understanding who will build a temple for the LORD and a royal palace for himself.

13 "I have dispatched Huram-abi, a skilled artisan endowed with understanding, [14]the son of one of the Danite women, his father a Tyrian. He is trained to work in gold, silver, bronze, iron, stone, and wood and in purple, blue, and crimson fabrics and fine linen and to do all sorts of engraving and execute any design that may be assigned him, with your artisans, the artisans of my lord, your father David. [15]Now, as for the wheat, barley, oil, and wine of which my lord has spoken, let him send them to his servants. [16]We will cut whatever timber you need from Lebanon and bring it to you as rafts by sea to Joppa; you will take it up to Jerusalem."

17 Then Solomon took a census of all the aliens who were residing in the land of Israel, after the census that his father David had taken, and there were found to be one hundred fifty-three thousand six hundred. [18]Seventy thousand of them he assigned as laborers, eighty thousand as stonecutters in the hill country, and three thousand six hundred as overseers to make the people work.

3 Solomon began to build the house of the LORD in Jerusalem on Mount Moriah, where the LORD had appeared to his father David, at the place that David had designated, on the threshing floor of Ornan the Jebusite. [2]He began to build on the second day of the second month of the fourth year of his reign. [3]These are Solomon's measurements[f] for building the house of God: the length, in cubits of the old standard, was sixty cubits and the width twenty cubits. [4]The vestibule in front of the nave of the house was twenty

d 2.10 A Hebrew measure of volume   e 2.10 A Hebrew measure of volume   f 3.3 Syr: Heb *foundations*

seasonal offerings and to establish the supremacy of Israel's God. Through its very construction, the temple was to function like an icon that pointed beyond itself to the supreme God who cannot be contained (vv. 5–6, 9). Solomon also requests a *skilled* (literally "wise") artisan (v. 7), which recalls the inspired artisans Bezalel and Oholiab, who crafted the tabernacle with wisdom (Exod. 31:1–6).

2:11–12 Huram responds favorably to Solomon's request for supplies. Huram also blesses YHWH for his favor toward Solomon. This may reflect (a) the blessing of Melchizedek to God and Abraham (Gen. 14:18–20) and (b) the enactment of hopes that the nations would recognize the blessed state of Israel's king (Ps. 72:17). Huram confirms that Solomon's wisdom, discretion, and understanding were used in the temple's construction (2:12), an idea already foreshadowed in 1:12 (cf. 1 Chr. 22:12). To this extent, the temple and Solomon's wisdom in its construction win international renown.

2:13–16 Huram sends Huram-abi, an artisan of mixed Danite and Tyrian origin. In Kings, the craftsman was of Naphtali descent (1 Kgs. 7:14). Chronicles may be associating Huram-abi more directly with Oholiab, the tabernacle craftsman who was also a Danite (Exod. 31:6; 35:30–36:2). Chronicles wants readers to witness the continuity between the tabernacle and the temple.

2:17–18 Solomon takes a census, which might otherwise evoke memories of David's disastrous census (1 Chr. 21) were it not for the fact that these are temporary foreign workers (*aliens*; cf. 1 Chr. 22:2). The reference to foreigners is curious and not in Chronicles's source texts. Care for the immigrant is central to the Pentateuch's vision of community (Exod. 20:10; 22:21; 23:9; Lev. 25:35; Deut. 10:18–19). Their presence at the temple recalls the conscription of the Gibeonites to serve at the altar (Josh. 9:26–27). Thus, the temple garners the nations' blessings and service, features that appear throughout Israel's prophetic literature (Isa. 49:23; 60:1–16).

3:1–7 Chronicles portrays the sacred geography of the temple's location. Mount Moriah is not mentioned in Kings but is the location of the binding of Isaac in Gen. 22:2, where it is called "the mount of the LORD" (22:14). In both places, an angel of YHWH appeared (Gen. 22:11, 15; 1 Chr. 21:15–18) to prevent disaster and extend mercy. The temple will become associated with appealing to God for those reasons. Moreover, the connection to Moriah reminds us that the temple continues Abrahamic and Davidic traditions (cf. the exodus traditions in 1 Kgs. 6:1). **3:3–5** Chronicles emphasizes the enormous height of the vestibule (120 cubits), giving the temple a grand appearance from

cubits long, across the width of the house,[g] and its height was one hundred twenty cubits. He overlaid it on the inside with pure gold. [5]The great hall he lined with cypress, covered it with fine gold, and made palms and chains on it. [6]He adorned the house with settings of precious stones. The gold was gold from Parvaim. [7]So he lined the house with gold: its beams, its thresholds, its walls, and its doors; and he carved cherubim on the walls.

[8] He made the most holy place; its length, corresponding to the width of the house, was twenty cubits, and its width was twenty cubits; he overlaid it with six hundred talents of fine gold. [9]The weight of the nails was fifty shekels of gold. He overlaid the upper chambers with gold.

[10] In the most holy place he made two carved cherubim and overlaid[h] them with gold. [11]The wings of the cherubim together extended twenty cubits: one wing of the one, five cubits long, touched the wall of the house, and its other wing, five cubits long, touched the wing of the other cherub; [12]and of this cherub, one wing, five cubits long, touched the wall of the house, and the other wing, also five cubits long, was joined to the wing of the first cherub. [13]The wings of these cherubim extended twenty cubits;

the cherubim[i] stood on their feet facing the main hall. [14]And Solomon[j] made the curtain of blue and purple and crimson fabrics and fine linen and worked cherubim into it.

[15] In front of the house he made two pillars thirty-five cubits high, each with a capital of five cubits on its top. [16]He made encircling[k] chains and put them on the tops of the pillars, and he made one hundred pomegranates and put them on the chains. [17]He set up the pillars in front of the temple, one on the right, the other on the left; the one on the right he called Jachin, and the one on the left, Boaz.

4 He made an altar of bronze, twenty cubits long, twenty cubits wide, and ten cubits high. [2]Then he made the molten sea; it was round, ten cubits from rim to rim and five cubits high. A line of thirty cubits would encircle it completely. [3]Under it were figures of bulls all around, each of ten cubits, surrounding the sea; there were two rows of bulls, cast when it was cast. [4]It stood on twelve bulls, three facing north, three facing west, three facing south, and three facing east; the sea was set on them.

g 3.4 Meaning of Heb uncertain   h 3.10 Heb *they overlaid*   i 3.13 Heb *they*   j 3.14 Heb *he*   k 3.16 Cn: Heb *in the inner sanctuary*

the front. In Kings, the vestibule stood a mere thirty cubits, and the rebuilt temple had a sixty-cubit vestibule. This is literally a "great house" (or *great hall*, as translated here). The temple's grandeur receives emphasis throughout chaps. 3–4. It is possible that the Chronicler is using different sources than Kings here, though the result is a more impressive temple. The designs on the inside of the gold-lined hall evoke divine holiness in a forestlike environment. The location of Parvaim is unknown. **3:6** The reference to *precious stones* does not appear in Kings, but in Chronicles, they were plundered (1 Chr. 20:2) and donated by David (1 Chr. 29:2). Aaron's breastplate also holds precious stones (Exod. 28:17; 39:10). **3:7** The gold-lined house would have glowed with the ten seven-branched candelabras (2 Chr. 4:7).

3:8–14 The *most holy place* is a perfect square, viewed from above. Chronicles adds detail about gold nails, perhaps to distinguish them from the iron nails used for the outer gates (1 Chr. 22:3). **3:10–13** The cherubim are hybrid creatures. Their wings spanned the entire twenty-cubit width of the most holy place. Some suggest that these were winged lions, but the emphasis on their widespread wings visually defies ancient iconographic representations of these creatures, and we know from Kings that they were as tall as they were wide (1 Kgs. 6:23–24). They may have been humanlike creatures. **3:14** Cherubim also appear in the temple's blue-purple-crimson curtains, lending them heavenly associations.

3:15–17 Two ornamented freestanding pillars stood at the temple's entrance. *Jachin* and *Boaz* can be translated as "He will establish in strength" and may refer to the temple itself.

4:1–6 This altar replaces Bezalel's bronze altar (1:5) and is enormous (roughly 30′ × 30′ × 15′), a detail Kings omits, making it equal to the most holy place in square footage. **4:2** The *sea* evokes images of a subdued sea over which YHWH is enthroned (Ps. 29:10) and could hold approximately eighteen thousand gallons. With the two pillars (3:15–17), the sea reflects aspects of ancient cosmology (Job 9:6; Ps. 75:3), where deities expressed creational power by calming chaotic waters. **4:4** The twelve *figures of bulls* correspond to the twelve tribes and represent the costliest sacrifices

The hindquarters of each were toward the inside. ⁵Its thickness was a handbreadth; its rim was made like the rim of a cup, like the flower of a lily; it held three thousand baths.ʲ ⁶He also made ten basins in which to wash and set five on the right side and five on the left. In these they were to rinse what was used for the burnt offering. The sea was for the priests to wash in.

7 He made ten golden lampstands as prescribed and set them in the temple, five on the right side and five on the left. ⁸He also made ten tables and placed them in the temple, five on the right side and five on the left. And he made one hundred basins of gold. ⁹He made the court of the priests and the great court and doors for the court; he overlaid their doors with bronze. ¹⁰He set the sea at the southeast corner of the house.

11 And Huram made the pots, the shovels, and the basins. Thus Huram finished the work that he did for King Solomon on the house of God: ¹²the two pillars, the bowls, and the two capitals on the top of the pillars; and the two latticeworks to cover the two bowls of the capitals that were on the top of the pillars; ¹³the four hundred pomegranates for the two latticeworks, two rows of pomegranates for each latticework, to cover the two bowls of the capitals that were on the pillars. ¹⁴He made the stands, the basins on the stands, ¹⁵the one sea, and the twelve bulls underneath it. ¹⁶The pots, the shovels, the forks, and all the equipment for these Huram-abi made of burnished bronze for King Solomon for the house of the Lord. ¹⁷In the plain of the Jordan the king cast them, in the clay ground between Succoth and Zeredah. ¹⁸Solomon made all these things in great quantities, so that the weight of the bronze was not determined.

19 So Solomon made all the things that were in the house of God: the golden altar, the tables for the bread of the Presence, ²⁰the lampstands and their lamps of pure gold to burn before the inner sanctuary, as prescribed; ²¹the flowers, the lamps, and the tongs, of purest gold; ²²the snuffers, basins, ladles, and firepans, of pure gold. As for the entrance to the temple: the inner doors to the most holy place and the doors of the main hall of the temple were of gold.

5 Thus all the work that Solomon did for the house of the Lord was finished. Solomon brought in the things that his father David had dedicated and stored the silver, the gold, and all the vessels in the treasuries of the house of God.

ʲ 4.5 A Hebrew measure of volume

(Lev. 1). **4:6** While the sea provided a place for priests to cleanse themselves ritually, the ten additional basins were for washing items offered as sacrifices.

4:7–10 The Chronicler's temple was well lit, with ten lampstands (five on each side) of gold that illuminated the gold-lined holy place, with its *one hundred basins of gold*, presumably for drink offerings (v. 8; cf. Exod. 27:3). The idea of Israel living in the light of YHWH is a major theme in the Pentateuch (Num. 6:24–26). The temple contains ten tables for the bread of the presence, whereas Kings only reports one (1 Kgs. 7:48). **4:9–10** Less costly metals were used in the priestly court, suggesting that the most valuable items related to the holiness of God's presence and not the priests as such. The location of this court is uncertain but is likely the court where priests carried out their duties.

4:11–18 The account returns to Huram-abi, the craftsman sent by Hiram of Tyre (2:13–14). Huram-abi crafted implements and designs of bronze to be used by the priests and to adorn the temple. He carried out all duties under Solomon's direction (vv. 11, 16, 18) and in such exceeding number that the amount of the bronze could not be weighed (cf. 1 Chr. 22:3, 14). Zeredah is likely a misreading of Zarethan (Josh. 3:16; 1 Kgs. 4:12; 7:46) and may be associated with Tell ed-Dâmiyeh along the clay banks of the Jordan River north of the Dead Sea (near the Jabbok canyon) or Tell Umm Hammad. Archaeologists have found evidence of metal mining in the southern Jordan Valley and copper mining (necessary for bronze) in the eastern Arava desert, at Feinan.

4:19–22 Whereas Huram-abi worked with bronze on items that would lie outside the temple, Solomon constructed items of *gold* for the sanctuary itself. All the items that Solomon made pertained to the golden altar (or altar of incense), tables for the bread of the presence, lampstands (including snuffers), drink offerings (basins), and the entrance itself.

5:1 This verse summarizes the previous section before the narrator transitions to the procession of the temple's most holy item (the ark). Chronicles uses similar summarizing phrases in 1 Chr. 16:2; 2 Chr. 1:1; 2:1; 3:1–2; 4:11; 7:11; 8:1, 16.

2 Then Solomon assembled the elders of Israel and all the heads of the tribes, the leaders of the ancestral houses of the people of Israel, in Jerusalem, to bring up the ark of the covenant of the LORD out of the city of David, which is Zion. ³And all the Israelites assembled before the king at the festival that is in the seventh month. ⁴And all the elders of Israel came, and the Levites carried the ark. ⁵So they brought up the ark, the tent of meeting, and all the holy vessels that were in the tent; the priests and the Levites brought them up. ⁶King Solomon and all the congregation of Israel, who had assembled before him, were before the ark, sacrificing so many sheep and oxen that they could not be numbered or counted. ⁷Then the priests brought the ark of the covenant of the LORD to its place, in the inner sanctuary of the house, in the most holy place, underneath the wings of the cherubim. ⁸For the cherubim spread out their wings over the place of the ark, so that the cherubim made a covering above the ark and its poles. ⁹The poles were so long that the ends of the poles were seen from the holy place*m* in front of the inner sanctuary, but they could not be seen from outside; they are there to this day. ¹⁰There was nothing in the ark except the two tablets that Moses put there at Horeb, where the LORD made a covenant*n* with the people of Israel when they came out of Egypt.

11 Now when the priests came out of the holy place (for all the priests who were present had sanctified themselves, without regard to their divisions), ¹²all the Levitical singers, Asaph, Heman, and Jeduthun, their sons and kindred, arrayed in fine linen, with cymbals, harps, and lyres, stood east of the altar with one hundred twenty priests who were trumpeters. ¹³It was the duty of the trumpeters and singers together to make themselves heard in unison in praise and thanksgiving to the LORD, and when the song was raised, with trumpets and cymbals and other musical instruments, in praise to the LORD,

"For he is good,
   for his steadfast love endures
      forever,"

the house, the house of the LORD, was filled with a cloud, ¹⁴so that the priests could not stand to minister because of the cloud, for the glory of the LORD filled the house of God.

m 5.9 Gk Heb mss: MT *from the ark*   *n* 5.10 Heb lacks *a covenant*

5:2–10. 5:2–3 After *all* (2x) the construction work was completed (v. 1), *all* (3x in vv. 2–4; 9x in chap. 5) the leaders and people of Israel gathered in Zion/Jerusalem to go in procession with the king and the ark, which were meant to be unifying features of Israel's corporate life. This procession occurred during the Succoth Festival, which recalls Israel's and God's wilderness sojourning. Succoth occurs in the seventh month, along with the Feast of Trumpets, or Rosh Hashanah (Lev. 23:24; Num. 29:1), and the Day of Atonement (Lev. 16:29; Num. 29:7). Only Succoth is a multiday festival (2 Chr. 7:8), so that must be in view here. **5:4** Chronicles is careful to note that *the Levites carried the ark*, as required by the law (Num. 4:15; 7:9; Deut. 10:8; cf. 1 Kgs. 8:3). **5:5–6** Alongside the ark and into the temple went the *tent of meeting*, which Chronicles likely associates with the ancient tabernacle. Solomon went before the ark, offering sacrifices like his father, David, did when the ark first went in procession to Jerusalem (1 Chr. 15:25–27). **5:7–10** Here the priests take the ark into the sanctuary. This may imply a different group than the Levites who carried the ark, as only priests entered the sanctuary. However, a resolution is found in Num. 4:15, which stipulates that the only Levites who could carry the ark were the Kohathites. Moreover, only Kohathites could become priests who served in the sanctuary (Num. 4:1–4). So the Levites who carried the ark were likely Kohathites, and thus the priests who brought the ark into the sanctuary were likely the same group. Verse 10 draws attention to the covenant tablets in the ark, providing the theological foundation for Solomon's covenant prayer of dedication in chap. 6.

5:11–14. 5:11 Disregard for divisions is important, for it indicates that *all* priests were present, whether or not they were on duty (cf. 1 Chr. 24). **5:12–13** The music of all singers and musicians accompanied the appearance of YHWH's glory cloud. In Chronicles, music is deeply connected to YHWH's presence, and musical activity forms the logical extension of the Levites' ark-carrying duties (1 Chr. 16:4; 2 Chr. 7:1–6; 20:21–22). As they accompanied God's presence by carrying the ark, so now they accompany God's presence with music. The scene conveys a sense of totality as all praise God *in unison* and recalls the descent of God's presence on the tabernacle when none could

6 Then Solomon said, "The Lord has said that he would reside in thick darkness. ²I have built you an exalted house, a place for you to dwell forever."

3 Then the king turned around and blessed all the assembly of Israel, while all the assembly of Israel stood. ⁴And he said, "Blessed be the Lord, the God of Israel, who with his hand has fulfilled what he promised with his mouth to my father David, saying, ⁵'Since the day that I brought my people out of the land of Egypt, I have not chosen a city from any of the tribes of Israel in which to build a house, so that my name might be there, and I chose no one as ruler over my people Israel, ⁶but I have chosen Jerusalem in order that my name may be there, and I have chosen David to be over my people Israel.' ⁷My father David had it in mind to build a house for the name of the Lord, the God of Israel. ⁸But the Lord said to my father David, 'You did well to consider building a house for my name; ⁹nevertheless, you shall not build the house, but your son who shall be born to you shall build the house for my name.' ¹⁰Now the Lord has fulfilled his promise that he made, for I have succeeded my father David and sit on the throne of Israel, as the Lord promised, and have built the house for the name of the Lord, the God of Israel. ¹¹There I have set the ark, in which is the covenant of the Lord that he made with the people of Israel."

12 Then Solomon⁰ stood before the altar of the Lord in the presence of the whole assembly of Israel and spread out his hands. ¹³Solomon had made a bronze platform five cubits long, five cubits wide, and three cubits high and had set it in the court, and he stood on it. Then he knelt on his knees in the presence of the whole assembly of Israel and spread out his hands toward heaven. ¹⁴He said, "O Lord, God of Israel, there is no God like you in heaven or on earth, keeping covenant and steadfast love with your servants who walk before you with all their heart—¹⁵you who have kept for your servant, my father David, what you promised to him. Indeed, you promised with your mouth and this day have fulfilled with your hand. ¹⁶Therefore, O Lord, God of Israel, keep for your servant my father David that which you promised him, saying, 'There shall never fail you a successor before me to sit on the throne of Israel, if only your children keep to their way, to walk in my law as you have walked before me.' ¹⁷Therefore, O Lord, God of Israel, let your word be confirmed that you promised to your servant David.

18 "But will God indeed dwell with mortals on earth? Even heaven and the highest heaven cannot contain you, much less this house that I have built! ¹⁹Regard your servant's prayer and his plea, O Lord my God, heeding the cry and the prayer that your servant prays to you. ²⁰May your eyes be open day and night toward this house, the place where you promised to set your name,

o 6.12 Heb *he*

enter (Exod. 40:34–35). The refrain *For he is good, for his steadfast love endures forever* occurs elsewhere in Chronicles (1 Chr. 16:34; 2 Chr. 7:3) and throughout Psalms (e.g., 100:5; 136:1).

6:1–11. 6:1–3 Before his prayer of appeal (vv. 12–42), Solomon affirms the importance of God's mysterious presence (*in thick darkness*) and the *exalted* quality of the house. This quality recalls Solomon's words to Huram that the temple would be "great" and reflect YHWH's supremacy over the gods (2 Chr. 2:5). **6:4–11** Solomon's introductory prayer draws an important connection between the temple's construction and God's promises to David through Nathan the prophet. The Davidic covenant (2 Sam. 7) included promises concerning the temple (2 Sam. 7:5–7, 12–13) and, by extension, Jerusalem (1 Kgs. 11:13, 32, 36; 2 Chr. 5:2). See **"Covenant (Genesis)," p. 23**. The emphasis here is on the king's submission to God's presence and a celebration of promises fulfilled.

6:12–17 Solomon's prayer in vv. 12–42 is a prayer of appeal that depends on the promises of God for its justification. So he begins in vv. 14–17 with the Davidic covenant. Standing and then kneeling on a large bronze platform (a detail not mentioned in Kings) before the altar, Solomon utters his prayer. The coordination of prayer and sacrifice is an idea that finds expression in Psalms (e.g., 141:2) and 2 Chronicles (7:1, 12). After thanking God for keeping God's promises, Solomon asks God to continue keeping them. This seeming contradiction gets at the heart of prayer, which often involves asking God to be God, to continue in the steadfast love (v. 14) that defined his actions in the past.

6:18–21 While God is present in the temple, the temple does not constrain God (cf. 2 Chr. 2:6), who also dwells in heaven, from where he hears the prayers of petitioners near and far (vv. 22–42).

and may you heed the prayer that your servant prays toward this place. ²¹And hear the plea of your servant and of your people Israel when they pray toward this place; may you hear from heaven your dwelling place; hear and forgive.

22 "If someone sins against a neighbor and is required to take an oath and comes and swears before your altar in this house, ²³may you hear from heaven, and act, and judge your servants, repaying the guilty by bringing their conduct on their own heads and vindicating the righteous by rewarding them according to their righteousness.

24 "When your people Israel, having sinned against you, are defeated before an enemy but turn again to you, confess your name, pray and plead with you in this house, ²⁵then hear from heaven, forgive the sin of your people Israel, and bring them again to the land that you gave to them and to their ancestors.

26 "When heaven is shut up and there is no rain because they have sinned against you and then they pray toward this place, confess your name, and turn from their sin because you punish them, ²⁷then hear in heaven and forgive the sin of your servants, your people Israel, when you teach them the good way in which they should walk, and grant rain on your land, which you have given to your people as an inheritance.

28 "If there is famine in the land, if there is plague, blight, mildew, locust, or caterpillar; if their enemies besiege them in any of the settlements of the lands; whatever suffering, whatever sickness there is; ²⁹whatever prayer, whatever plea there is from any individual or from all your people Israel, all knowing their own suffering and their own sorrows so that they stretch out their hands toward this house; ³⁰then hear from heaven, your dwelling place, forgive, and render to all whose hearts you know, according to all their ways, for only you know the human heart. ³¹Thus may they fear you and walk in your ways all the days that they live in the land that you gave to our ancestors.

32 "Likewise when foreigners, who are not of your people Israel, come from a distant land because of your great name and your mighty hand and your outstretched arm, when they come and pray toward this house, ³³then hear from heaven your dwelling place and do whatever the foreigners ask of you, so that all the peoples of the earth may know your name and fear you, as do your people Israel, and so they may know that your name has been invoked on this house that I have built.

34 "If your people go out to battle against their enemies, by whatever way you shall send them, and they pray to you toward this city that you have chosen and the house that I have built for your name, ³⁵then hear from heaven their prayer and their plea and maintain their cause.

36 "If they sin against you—for there is no one who does not sin—and you are angry with them and give them to an enemy, so that they are carried away captive to a land far off or near, ³⁷then if they come to their senses in the land to which they have been taken captive and repent and plead with you in the land of their captivity, saying, 'We have sinned and have done wrong; we have acted wickedly,' ³⁸if they repent with all their heart and soul in the land of their captivity, to which they were taken captive, and pray toward their land that you gave

6:22–31 Solomon outlines scenarios, drawn from the Deuteronomic curses (Deut. 28:15–68), in which God's people would face trouble, pray at the temple, and seek God's forgiveness. These include individual *sins against a neighbor* (vv. 22, 29) or corporate sins against God (vv. 24, 26, 29) that bring drought (v. 26), famine (v. 28), plague (v. 28), or distress from enemies (v. 28). Sins against a neighbor (vv. 22–23) necessitate an appeal for forgiveness at the altar, where sacrifices also took place (cf. Exod. 22:7–14; Lev. 6:1–7; Num. 5:11–31). Sins against God necessitate a turn in appeal toward God and a confession of YHWH's name, an expression of allegiance (vv. 24, 26). Solomon also entrusts the people to God's judicial care, asking for just judgments (vv. 23, 30; cf. Deut. 1:17; 10:17; 17:8) such that they will learn God's ways and remain in the land.

6:32–33 The temple is also a "house of prayer for all peoples" (Isa. 56:7), so the foreigner's petition is welcome at the temple.

6:34–39 The last two petitions relate to prayers away from the temple, either when at war (vv. 34–35) or in exile (vv. 36–39). As God's people turn in utter loyalty, they can expect to find God's forgiveness.

to their ancestors, the city that you have chosen, and the house that I have built for your name, [39]then hear from heaven your dwelling place their prayer and their pleas, maintain their cause, and forgive your people who have sinned against you. [40]Now, O my God, let your eyes be open and your ears attentive to prayer from this place.

[41] Now rise up, O LORD God, and go to
your resting place,
you and the ark of your might.
Let your priests, O LORD God, be
clothed with salvation,
and let your faithful rejoice in your
goodness.
[42] O LORD God, do not reject your
anointed one.
Remember your steadfast love for
your servant David."

7 When Solomon had ended his prayer, fire came down from heaven and consumed the burnt offering and the sacrifices, and the glory of the LORD filled the temple. [2]The priests could not enter the house of the LORD because the glory of the LORD filled the LORD's house. [3]When all the people of Israel saw the fire come down and the glory of the LORD on the temple, they bowed down on the pavement with their faces to the ground and worshiped and gave thanks to the LORD, saying,

"For he is good,
for his steadfast love endures
forever."

4 Then the king and all the people offered sacrifice before the LORD. [5]King Solomon offered as a sacrifice twenty-two thousand oxen and one hundred twenty thousand sheep. So the king and all the people dedicated the house of God. [6]The priests stood at their posts, the Levites also, with the instruments for music to the LORD that King David had made for giving thanks to the LORD—for his steadfast love endures forever—whenever David offered praises through their playing. Opposite them the priests sounded trumpets, and all Israel stood.

7 Solomon consecrated the middle of the court that was in front of the house of the LORD, for there he offered the burnt offerings and the fat of the offerings of well-being because the bronze altar Solomon had made could not hold the burnt offering and the grain offering and the fat parts.

8 At that time Solomon held the festival for seven days, and all Israel with him, a very great congregation, from Lebo-hamath to the Wadi of Egypt. [9]On the eighth day they held a solemn assembly, for they had observed the dedication of the altar seven days and the festival seven days. [10]On the twenty-third day of the seventh month he sent the people away to their homes, joyful and in good spirits because of the goodness that the LORD had shown to David and to Solomon and to his people Israel.

11 Thus Solomon finished the house of the LORD and the king's house; all that Solomon had planned to do in the house of the LORD and in his own house he successfully accomplished.

12 Then the LORD appeared to Solomon in the night and said to him, "I have heard

6:40–42 Chronicles evokes Psalms again in reference to the ark's movement (v. 41; cf. 1 Chr. 16:8–36), drawing from Ps. 132:8–10, the only psalm to mention the ark. Solomon prays that God would demonstrate his steadfast love for David by entering—and presumably remaining present in—the temple.

7:1–11 God responds to Solomon's appeals with a dramatic appearance of fire to consume the dedicatory offering and to manifest God's glory in (v. 1) and on (v. 3) the temple. This is the second appearance of God's presence at the temple (5:13–14), and this one also includes a declaration of God's *steadfast love* (v. 3). The emphasis on God's steadfast love (also in v. 6) and presence recalls the scene at Sinai, where God's glory appeared to Moses and God declared God's steadfast love (Exod. 34:6–7). The priests and Levites, with all Israel, gather as Solomon consecrates the court with offerings (v. 7). The gathering includes seven days to dedicate the temple, seven for the Feast of Tabernacles, and a day of *solemn assembly* (v. 9; Lev. 23:23–36; Neh. 8:18).

7:12–22 In the fourth major divine appearance in just four chapters (1:7; 5:13–14; 7:1–2), YHWH brings a word of encouragement and warning for Solomon. As the people humble themselves, seek God, and pray, God will respond and forgive (cf. 6:22–42). Seeking God in petition is a major theme in Chronicles (e.g., 1 Chr. 10:13–14; 16:10–11; 22:19; 2 Chr. 11:16; 15:4; 20:4). It involves petitioning God in times of distress and pursuing God's presence in regular worship. Securing the Davidic promises

your prayer and have chosen this place for myself as a house of sacrifice. ¹³When I shut up the heavens so that there is no rain or command the locust to devour the land or send pestilence among my people, ¹⁴if my people who are called by my name humble themselves, pray, seek my face, and turn from their wicked ways, then I will hear from heaven and will forgive their sin and heal their land. ¹⁵Now my eyes will be open and my ears attentive to the prayer that is made in this place. ¹⁶For now I have chosen and consecrated this house so that my name may be there forever; my eyes and my heart will be there for all time. ¹⁷As for you, if you walk before me as your father David walked, doing according to all that I have commanded you and keeping my statutes and my ordinances, ¹⁸then I will establish your royal throne, as I made a covenant*ᵖ* with your father David saying, 'You shall never lack a successor to rule over Israel.'

19 "But if you*ᵍ* turn aside and forsake my statutes and my commandments that I have set before you and go and serve other gods and worship them, ²⁰then I will pluck you*ʳ* up from the land that I have given you,*ˢ* and this house, which I have consecrated for my name, I will cast out of my sight and will make it a proverb and a byword among all peoples. ²¹And regarding this house, now exalted, everyone passing by will be astonished and say, 'Why has the Lᴏʀᴅ done such a thing to this land and to this house?' ²²Then they will say, 'Because they abandoned the Lᴏʀᴅ the God of their ancestors who brought them out of the land of Egypt,

and they embraced other gods and worshiped them and served them; therefore he has brought all this calamity upon them.'"

8 At the end of twenty years, during which Solomon had built the house of the Lᴏʀᴅ and his own house, ²Solomon rebuilt the cities that Huram had given to him and settled the people of Israel in them.

3 Solomon went to Hamath-zobah and captured it. ⁴He built Tadmor in the wilderness and all the storage towns that he built in Hamath. ⁵He also built Upper Beth-horon and Lower Beth-horon, fortified cities, with walls, gates, and bars, ⁶and Baalath, as well as all Solomon's storage towns, and all the towns for his chariots, the towns for his cavalry, and whatever Solomon desired to build, in Jerusalem, in Lebanon, and in all the land of his dominion. ⁷All the people who were left of the Hittites, the Amorites, the Perizzites, the Hivites, and the Jebusites, who were not of Israel, ⁸from their descendants who were still left in the land, whom the people of Israel had not destroyed—these Solomon conscripted for forced labor, as is still the case today. ⁹But of the people of Israel Solomon made no slaves for his work; they were soldiers and his officers, the commanders of his chariotry and cavalry. ¹⁰These were the chief officers of King Solomon, two hundred fifty of them, who exercised authority over the people.

11 Solomon brought Pharaoh's daughter from the city of David to the house that he

p 7.18 Heb lacks *a covenant*   *q* 7.19 The word *you* in this verse is plural   *r* 7.20 Heb *them*   *s* 7.20 Heb *them*

seems to depend on Solomon's obedience here (vv. 17–18). **7:19–22** Rejecting YHWH by serving idolatry will lead to exile and rejection of the temple. Covenant promises depend on allegiance to YHWH and find expression in temple worship and prayer. See **"Divine Retribution," p. 339.**

8:1–2 Chronicles omits the palace construction account from Kings to keep its focus on the temple (1 Kgs. 7:1–12) and possibly to avoid Kings's implicit critique of Solomon for spending more time on the palace (thirteen years) than the temple (seven years). First Chr. 15:1 refers to David's tents for the ark and himself, which seems to anticipate the temple-palace complex here. In v. 2, Solomon receives cities, which he gave to Huram in Kings (1 Kgs. 9:11–13).

8:3–10 Despite Chronicles's emphasis on Solomon as a man of peace (1 Chr. 22:9), the narrator offers the only biblical account of Solomon's military activities. *Hamath-zobah* (1 Chr. 18:3) may refer to Hamath's envelopment of the old kingdom of Zobah (2 Sam. 8:3, 5). Otherwise, Solomon was a builder who fortified cities to solidify the kingdom, an activity of future kings that Chronicles emphasizes (2 Chr. 11:5–12; 14:6; 17:1–2; 21:3; 26:9). The reference to enslaving the remaining Canaanite peoples (2 Chr. 8:7–8) contrasts with Solomon's refusal to enslave Israelites (v. 9), a point also made in 2 Chr. 2:1–2. See **"Solomon," p. 595.**

8:11 Solomon avoids settling Pharaoh's daughter in sacred space, which may relate to laws regarding uncleanness after sexual relations (Lev. 12, 15) or to her associations with idolatry in Kings

had built for her, for he said, "My wife shall not live in the house of King David of Israel, for the places to which the ark of the Lord has come are holy."

12 Then Solomon offered up burnt offerings to the Lord on the altar of the Lord that he had built in front of the vestibule, ¹³as the duty of each day required, offering according to the commandment of Moses for the Sabbaths, the new moons, and the three annual festivals: the Festival of Unleavened Bread, the Festival of Weeks, and the Festival of Booths. ¹⁴According to the ordinance of his father David, he appointed the divisions of the priests for their service, and the Levites for their offices of praise and ministry alongside the priests as the duty of each day required, and the gatekeepers in their divisions for the several gates, for so David the man of God had commanded. ¹⁵They did not turn away from what the king had commanded the priests and Levites regarding anything at all or regarding the treasuries.

16 Thus all the work of Solomon was accomplished, from' the day the foundation of the house of the Lord was laid until the house of the Lord was finished completely.

17 Then Solomon went to Ezion-geber and Eloth on the shore of the sea, in the land of Edom. ¹⁸Huram sent him, in the care of his servants, ships and servants familiar with the sea. They went to Ophir together with the servants of Solomon and imported from there four hundred fifty talents of gold and brought it to King Solomon.

9 When the queen of Sheba heard of the fame of Solomon, she came to Jerusalem to test him with riddles, having a very great retinue and camels bearing spices and very much gold and precious stones. When she came to Solomon, she discussed with him all that was on her mind. ²Solomon answered all her questions; there was nothing hidden from Solomon that he could not explain to her. ³When the queen of Sheba had observed the wisdom of Solomon, the house that he had built, ⁴the food of his table, the seating of his officials, and the attendance of his servants, and their clothing, his valets, and their clothing, and his burnt offerings" that he offered at the house of the Lord, it took her breath away.

5 So she said to the king, "The report was true that I heard in my own land of your accomplishments and of your wisdom, ⁶but I did not believe the' reports until I came and my own eyes saw it. Not even half of the greatness of your wisdom had been told to me; you far surpass the report that I had heard. ⁷Happy are your people! Happy are these your servants who continually attend you and hear your wisdom! ⁸Blessed be the Lord your God, who has delighted in you and set you on his throne as king for the Lord your God. Because your God loved Israel and would establish them forever, he has made you king over them, that you may execute justice and righteousness." ⁹Then

t 8.16 Gk Syr Vg: Heb to   u 9.4 Gk Syr Vg: Heb ascent   v 9.6 Heb their

(1 Kgs. 11:1–2). In his only brush with foreign women (according to Chronicles), Solomon emerges as a respecter of the temple. See **"Intermarriage," p. 649**.

8:12–15 After the dramatic and unique events of chaps. 6–7, Solomon installs the priestly and Levitical divisions (cf. 2 Chr. 5:11–14; 7:6) and makes provision for the temple's daily and seasonal rhythm of sacrifices, festivals, and music. All was done according to David's instructions (1 Chr. 23–26).

8:17–18 Ezion-geber is likely a fort near Elath (Eloth) and sits at the north end of the Gulf of Aqaba in a region that was frequently contested by Judah and Edom. The location of Ophir is unknown.

9:1–4 This section continues the focus on Solomon's accomplishments and fame begun in 8:16. Sheba is sometimes listed with Raamah of northern Arabia (Gen. 10:7; 1 Chr. 1:9; Ezek. 27:22) and is likely in southern Arabia (modern-day Yemen). The queen of Sheba admires Solomon's wealth but especially his wisdom (also in v. 5) and worship. Her complete admiration is expressed in a list of seven items in vv. 3–4.

9:5–12 The queen of Sheba recognizes Solomon's blessed state and, in one significant change from Kings, observes that Solomon sits on the Lord's throne (v. 8; cf. 1 Kgs. 10:9, which has "throne of Israel"). This accords with David's assessment in 1 Chr. 28:5 and 29:23 and reflects the idea that Solomon's kingdom was an instance of YHWH's kingdom on earth. The lavish gifts from the queen of Sheba are expressed in a series of superlatives in vv. 9–12 (very great quantity, no spices such as those, and never was seen the like of them before). Solomon responds to such gifts with even

Reading through Time: Solomon (2 Chronicles 9)

Like his father, David, the figure of Solomon is remembered differently throughout Israel's biblical traditions, and in early Judaism and Christianity, his memory continues to take shape. Within the Hebrew Bible / Old Testament, Solomon is first presented as a complex character in 1 Kgs. 1–11. He ascends to the throne after a struggle for power with his half brother Adonijah (1 Kgs. 1). Although God grants him great wisdom (1 Kgs. 3), he also violates key aspects of Deuteronomy's royal laws (Deut. 17:14–20). For instance, Israel's kings were not to acquire many wives (17:17), yet Solomon does so (1 Kgs. 11:1). Kings even tells us that although he "loved the LORD" (3:3), he also "loved many foreign women" (11:1) and eventually supported temples to multiple gods. Kings were not to accumulate chariots and horses (Deut. 17:16), yet Solomon does so (1 Kgs. 10:26–28). Finally, although Solomon builds the temple for the Lord, he spends more time building his palace (9:10). It is no wonder that when the queen of Sheba comes to admire his kingdom, she emphasizes how good those in the *palace* have it (10:5, 8) and not how well the *whole people* live. In short, according to Kings, Solomon is a mixed blessing at best, and his reign ends in disaster.

Chronicles offers a very different portrait of Solomon. Gone are references to the violent transfer of power after David. "All Israel" obeyed Solomon, and all its leadership came peacefully under his authority (1 Chr. 29:23). Chronicles never mentions the idolatry that Solomon enables. Chronicles does not whitewash his reign completely (e.g., 2 Chr. 1:16; cf. Deut. 17:16), yet it leaves a rather rosy picture. Solomon even sits on the Lord's own throne (1 Chr. 29:23). It seems that Solomon becomes an *ideal* in Chronicles, even though its readers would also know the *real* Solomon from Kings.

Certain Hebrew Bible books highlight the surpassing wisdom of Solomon. Proverbs solidifies Solomon's link to wisdom and wise sayings (1:1; 10:1). Ecclesiastes hints at a Solomonic connection (1:1), Song of Songs attributes the book to Solomon (1:1), and Pss. 72 and 127 are linked to him. In these varied ways, Solomon becomes the "go-to" wisdom figure in the Old Testament, despite his checkered past.

Matthew J. Lynch

she gave the king one hundred twenty talents of gold, a very great quantity of spices, and precious stones; there were no spices such as those that the queen of Sheba gave to King Solomon.

10 Moreover, the servants of Huram and the servants of Solomon who brought gold from Ophir brought algum wood and precious stones. [11]From the algum wood, the king made steps*w* for the house of the LORD and for the king's house, lyres also and harps for the singers; there never was seen the like of them before in the land of Judah.

12 Meanwhile, King Solomon gave to the queen of Sheba every desire that she expressed, well beyond what she had brought to the king. Then she returned to her own land with her servants.

13 The weight of gold that came to Solomon in one year was six hundred sixty-six talents of gold, [14]besides that which the traders and merchants brought, and all the kings of Arabia and the governors of the land brought gold and silver to Solomon. [15]King Solomon made two hundred large shields of beaten gold; six hundred shekels*x* of beaten gold went into each large shield. [16]He made three hundred shields of beaten

w 9.11 Gk Vg: Meaning of Heb uncertain   *x* 9.15 Heb lacks *shekels*

greater gifts (v. 12). The queen of Sheba's visit captures the imagination of Isaiah in his depiction of the nations streaming to Zion (Isa. 60) and likely influences the portrait of the magi in Matt. 2. See **"Solomon," p. 595**.

9:13–21 The Chronicler draws further attention to the excessive wealth of Solomon's kingdom in these verses, as well as vv. 22 and 27. The numbers are almost certainly hyperbolic, as even silver became worthless. The amount of gold Solomon received in one year would equal the weight of a fire truck or loaded school bus. With this surplus wealth, Solomon decorated his palace, including the armory called the *House of the Forest of Lebanon* (v. 16; cf. Isa. 22:8). The imports from Tarshish (v. 21; in Spain) reflect the astonishing international reach of Solomon's economic ties. The span from Sheba to Tarshish is nearly 3,700 mi. (6,000 km) in a direct line. There is no indication here that such wealth and international influence benefited the people of Israel, a point that emerges clearly in the next chapter. But for this snapshot in time, the wealth reflects what is literally a "golden era" in God's kingdom.

gold; three hundred shekelsʸ of gold went into each shield, and the king put them in the House of the Forest of Lebanon. ¹⁷The king also made a great ivory throne and overlaid it with pure gold. ¹⁸The throne had six steps and a footstool of gold, which were attached to the throne, and on each side of the seat were arm rests and two lions standing beside the arm rests, ¹⁹while twelve lions were standing, one on each end of a step on the six steps. The like of it was never made in any kingdom. ²⁰All King Solomon's drinking vessels were of gold, and all the vessels of the House of the Forest of Lebanon were of pure gold; silver was not considered as anything in the days of Solomon. ²¹For the king's ships went to Tarshish with the servants of Huram; once every three years the ships of Tarshish used to come bringing gold, silver, ivory, apes, and peacocks.ᶻ

22 Thus King Solomon excelled all the kings of the earth in riches and in wisdom. ²³All the kings of the earth sought the presence of Solomon to hear his wisdom, which God had put into his mind. ²⁴Every one of them brought a present, objects of silver and gold, garments, weaponry, spices, horses, and mules, so much year by year. ²⁵Solomon had four thousand stalls for horses and chariots and twelve thousand horses, which he stationed in the chariot cities and with the king in Jerusalem. ²⁶He ruled over all the kings from the Euphrates to the land of the Philistines and to the territory of Egypt.

²⁷The king made silver as common in Jerusalem as stone and cedar as plentiful as the sycamore of the Shephelah. ²⁸Horses were imported for Solomon from Egypt and from all lands.

29 Now the rest of the acts of Solomon, from first to last, are they not written in the history of the prophet Nathan and in the prophecy of Ahijah the Shilonite and in the visions of the seer Iddo concerning Jeroboam son of Nebat? ³⁰Solomon reigned in Jerusalem over all Israel forty years. ³¹Solomon slept with his ancestors and was buried in the city of his father David, and his son Rehoboam succeeded him.

10 Rehoboam went to Shechem, for all Israel had come to Shechem to make him king. ²When Jeroboam son of Nebat heard of it (for he was in Egypt, where he had fled from King Solomon), then Jeroboam returned from Egypt. ³They sent and called him, and Jeroboam and all Israel came and said to Rehoboam, ⁴"Your father made our yoke heavy. Now, therefore, lighten the hard service of your father and his heavy yoke that he placed on us, and we will serve you." ⁵He said to them, "Come to me again in three days." So the people went away.

6 Then King Rehoboam took counsel with the older men who had attended his father Solomon while he was still alive,

ʸ 9.16 Heb lacks *shekels*   ᶻ 9.21 Or *baboons*

9:22–28 These verses display God's faithfulness to God's promises. Solomon's status now exceeds all kings, who process toward Jerusalem to request *the presence* (a phrase otherwise used of God in the Hebrew Bible) of Solomon. Solomon's wealth and wisdom fulfill God's promise of wealth and wisdom in 2 Chr. 1:12 and are yet additional instances of God's loyal love (1 Chr. 16:34, 41; 2 Chr. 5:13; 7:3, 6; 20:21). The extent of Solomon's territory in v. 26 reflects the territory promised to Abraham (Gen. 15:18). The passing reference to horses imported from Egypt is ominous, as Israelite kings were commanded to do no such thing (Deut. 17:16). **9:29–31** Chronicles highlights three otherwise unknown prophetic sources. Nathan's prophetic career overlapped David's and Solomon's. Ahijah's appears next in 2 Chr. 10:15 and refers to a prophecy about Solomon's kingdom only mentioned in Kings (1 Kgs. 11:29–39). Iddo also appears as an author in 2 Chr. 12:15 and 13:22. For Chronicles, prophecy drives history.
2 Chr. 10 begins the second major section of Chronicles, which concludes in chap. 36. Unlike Kings, which recounts the fortunes of Judah and Israel, Chronicles focuses almost exclusively on the Judean kingdom, though it shows interest in the northern population (e.g., 2 Chr. 13).
10:1–5 The coronation of Solomon's son Rehoboam at Shechem was a disaster (cf. 2 Kgs. 12:1–19). Deep in northern Israelite territory, Shechem is the site of Abram's first altar in the land (Gen. 12:6) and Joshua's covenant renewal ceremony (Josh. 24). The Judean Rehoboam likely sought northern support. Jeroboam was formerly in charge of labor in Ephraim and Manasseh, northern tribes (1 Kgs. 11:28), and he fell out with Solomon. Jeroboam here demands relief for laborers.
10:6–11 Rehoboam's failure to listen to the elders shows that he lacks his father's wisdom (cf. Prov. 31:23). Rehoboam not only rejects their advice but follows that of the young men who encourage

saying, "How do you advise me to answer this people?" ⁷They answered him, "If you will be kind to this people and please them and speak good words to them, then they will be your servants forever." ⁸But he rejected the advice that the older men gave him and consulted the young men who had grown up with him and now attended him. ⁹He said to them, "What do you advise that we answer this people who have said to me, 'Lighten the yoke that your father put on us'?" ¹⁰The young men who had grown up with him said to him, "Thus should you speak to the people who said to you, 'Your father made our yoke heavy, but you must lighten it for us'; tell them, 'My little finger is thicker than my father's loins. ¹¹Now, whereas my father laid on you a heavy yoke, I will add to your yoke. My father disciplined you with whips, but I will discipline you with scorpions.'"

12 So Jeroboam and all the people came to Rehoboam the third day, as the king had said, "Come to me again the third day." ¹³The king answered them harshly. King Rehoboam rejected the advice of the older men; ¹⁴he spoke to them in accordance with the advice of the young men, "My father made your yoke heavy, but I will add to it; my father disciplined you with whips, but I will discipline you with scorpions." ¹⁵So the king did not listen to the people because it was a turn of affairs brought about by God so that the LORD might fulfill his word that he had spoken by Ahijah the Shilonite to Jeroboam son of Nebat.

16 When all Israel saw that the king would not listen to them, the people answered the king,

"What share do we have in David?
    We have no inheritance in the son
        of Jesse.
Each of you to your tents, O Israel!
    Look now to your own house,
        O David."

So all Israel departed to their tents. ¹⁷But Rehoboam reigned over the people of Israel who were living in the cities of Judah. ¹⁸When King Rehoboam sent Hadoram, who was taskmaster over the forced labor, the people of Israel stoned him to death. King Rehoboam hurriedly mounted his chariot to flee to Jerusalem. ¹⁹So Israel has been in rebellion against the house of David to this day.

11 When Rehoboam came to Jerusalem, he assembled one hundred eighty thousand chosen troops of the house of Judah and Benjamin to fight against Israel, to restore the kingdom to Rehoboam. ²But the word of the LORD came to Shemaiah the man of God: ³"Say to King Rehoboam of Judah, son of Solomon, and to all Israel in Judah and Benjamin: ⁴Thus says the LORD: You shall not go up or fight against your kindred. Let everyone return home, for this thing is from me." So they heeded the word of the LORD and turned back from the expedition against Jeroboam.

5 Rehoboam resided in Jerusalem, and he built cities for defense in Judah. ⁶He built up

further oppression. The phrase *my little finger* (v. 10), omitted in v. 14, may be a euphemism for Rehoboam's genitals, and *scorpions* may refer to a thorny plant. Rehoboam ends up looking like Pharaoh, who imposed harsher conditions after Moses's request for relief (Exod. 5:6–9).

10:12–15 We hear of God for the first time in the account of Rehoboam's downfall (v. 15). Rehoboam's rejection of the elders' advice fits into a larger pattern of prophetic intervention, fulfillment, and history writing emphasized in Chronicles (e.g., 2 Chr. 9:29; 11:2; 36:22). The Chronicler nowhere else mentions Ahijah's specific prophecy recounted in 1 Kgs. 11.

10:16–19 Rehoboam's hardline policy led to the loss of the northern kingdom of Israel. *The people* of Israel respond in two ways here. They disavow any connection to David, reversing the earlier "bone and flesh" pledge of unity (1 Chr. 11:1; 2 Sam. 5:1). They stone their taskmaster Hadoram (Adoniram in Kings) to death. Verse 19 seems critical of Israel's response, but the context of oppression rationalizes their reaction. The north's *rebellion* contains within it the seeds of hope for reunification.

11:1–4 Rehoboam continues in his obstinance, gathering an unimaginable force to *restore the kingdom* to himself. This event portrays Rehoboam as an attempted unifier, albeit under his own name. While the prophet Shemaiah (mentioned also in 2 Chr. 12:5, 7) forbids military action, he affirms the familial unity between Judah and Israel (*your kindred*).

11:5–12 Chronicles associates building projects with loyal kings (cf. 1 Chr. 11:8–9; 2 Chr. 8:1–6; 14:6; 17:12–13; 26:9–10; 27:4; 32:5), an important feature to highlight in a fragile postexilic context.

Bethlehem, Etam, Tekoa, [7]Beth-zur, Soco, Adullam, [8]Gath, Mareshah, Ziph, [9]Adoraim, Lachish, Azekah, [10]Zorah, Aijalon, and Hebron, fortified cities that are in Judah and in Benjamin. [11]He made the fortresses strong and put commanders in them and stores of food, oil, and wine. [12]He also put large shields and spears in all the cities and made them very strong. So he held Judah and Benjamin.

13 The priests and the Levites who were in all Israel presented themselves to him from all their territories. [14]The Levites had left their pasturelands and possessions and had come to Judah and Jerusalem because Jeroboam and his sons had prevented them from serving as priests of the LORD [15]and had appointed his own priests for the high places and for the goat-demons and for the calves that he had made. [16]Those who had set their hearts to seek the LORD God of Israel came after them from all the tribes of Israel to Jerusalem to sacrifice to the LORD, the God of their ancestors. [17]They strengthened the kingdom of Judah, and for three years they made Rehoboam son of Solomon secure, for they walked for three years in the way of David and Solomon.

18 Rehoboam took as his wife Mahalath daughter of Jerimoth son of David and of Abihail daughter of Eliab son of Jesse. [19]She bore him sons: Jeush, Shemariah, and Zaham. [20]After her he took Maacah daughter of Absalom, who bore him Abijah, Attai, Ziza, and Shelomith. [21]Rehoboam loved Maacah daughter of Absalom more than all his other wives and concubines (he took eighteen wives and sixty concubines and became the father of twenty-eight sons and sixty daughters). [22]Rehoboam appointed Abijah son of Maacah as chief prince among his brothers, for he intended to make him king. [23]He dealt wisely and distributed some of his sons through all the districts of Judah and Benjamin, in all the fortified cities; he gave them abundant provisions and found many wives for them.

12 When the rule of Rehoboam was established and he grew strong, he abandoned the law of the LORD, he and all Israel with him. [2]In the fifth year of King Rehoboam, because they had been unfaithful to the LORD, King Shishak of Egypt came up against Jerusalem [3]with twelve hundred chariots and sixty thousand cavalry. A countless army came with him from Egypt:

Rehoboam's knowledge of the impending attack by Pharaoh Shishak (2 Chr. 12), as well as ongoing concerns about the northern kingdom, may have motivated such activities.
11:13–17 Disaffected priests and Levites migrate south. This scene anticipates 2 Chr. 13, where we learn that because Jeroboam appointed non-Levites as priests and thus rejected YHWH, Judah would defeat them in battle (13:9–12). Levites lived among the tribes except when they served on rotation at the temple (1 Chr. 24–26). Chronicles portrays a mass migration of priests, Levites, and other loyalists toward Jerusalem. This constitutes a mini "return from exile" event that Chronicles sees repeated at various times in Judah's history. *Goat-demons* (v. 15) likely evokes Lev. 17:7, which refers to illicit sacrifices as "sacrifices for goat-demons."
11:18–23 Chronicles seems to associate multiple wives, plentiful children, and wealth with divine favor (cf. 1 Chr. 14:3–7; 2 Chr. 13:21), yet the placement of this detail just before Rehoboam's downfall (chap. 12) raises questions. Rehoboam's love for Maacah above his other wives (v. 21) accounts for his selection of Abijah, her son, as king designate (v. 22). The preferential treatment may allude negatively to Deut. 21:15–17, which prohibits special treatment of the son of a preferred wife over the firstborn, who seems to be Jeush (v. 19).
12:1 Rehoboam's successes were short lived. Chronicles regularly notes the downfall of kings when their power seemed (self-)secure (2 Chr. 26:16; 32:25–26). By forsaking the law, Rehoboam and the people left themselves vulnerable to attack. Religious reform needed to accompany physical fortifications, as demonstrated later by Jehoshaphat (2 Chr. 17:7–9).
12:2–4 Pharaoh Shishak's (who reigned ca. 945–924 BCE) invasion is documented in a Karnak inscription and may be represented pictorially there as well. Shishak's dominance is also evident in a stone pillar found at Megiddo that recognizes Egyptian sovereignty. The Egyptian Third Intermediate period was characterized by less wealth than other eras, so Shishak's ambitions may have been to ravage the temple. Moreover, Shishak held long-term connections with Jeroboam and may have been aiding his ally. Because Shishak came from Libya, the inclusion of *Libyans* and the oft-accompanying *Cushites* (translated elsewhere as "Ethiopians") makes sense.

Libyans, Sukkiim, and Cushites. ⁴He took the fortified cities of Judah and came as far as Jerusalem. ⁵Then the prophet Shemaiah came to Rehoboam and to the officers of Judah who had gathered at Jerusalem because of Shishak and said to them, "Thus says the LORD: You abandoned me, so I have abandoned you to the hand of Shishak." ⁶Then the officers of Israel and the king humbled themselves and said, "The LORD is in the right." ⁷When the LORD saw that they had humbled themselves, the word of the LORD came to Shemaiah, saying, "They have humbled themselves; I will not destroy them, but I will grant them some deliverance, and my wrath shall not be poured out on Jerusalem by the hand of Shishak. ⁸Nevertheless, they shall be his servants, so that they may know the difference between serving me and serving the kingdoms of other lands."

9 So King Shishak of Egypt came up against Jerusalem; he took away the treasures of the house of the LORD and the treasures of the king's house; he took everything. He also took away the shields of gold that Solomon had made, ¹⁰but King Rehoboam made in place of them shields of bronze and committed them to the hands of the officers of the guard who kept the door of the king's house. ¹¹Whenever the king went into the house of the LORD, the guard would come along bearing them and would then bring them back to the guardroom. ¹²Because he humbled himself, the wrath of the LORD turned from him, so as not to destroy them completely; moreover, conditions were good in Judah.

13 So King Rehoboam strengthened himself in Jerusalem and reigned. Rehoboam was forty-one years old when he began to reign; he reigned seventeen years in Jerusalem, the city that the LORD had chosen out of all the tribes of Israel to put his name there. His mother's name was Naamah the Ammonite. ¹⁴He did evil, for he did not set his heart to seek the LORD.

15 Now the acts of Rehoboam, from first to last, are they not written in the records of the prophet Shemaiah and of the seer Iddo, recorded by genealogy? There were continual wars between Rehoboam and Jeroboam. ¹⁶Rehoboam slept with his ancestors and was buried in the city of David, and his son Abijah succeeded him.

13 In the eighteenth year of King Jeroboam, Abijah began to reign over Judah. ²He reigned for three years in Jerusalem. His mother's name was Micaiah daughter of Uriel of Gibeah.

Now there was war between Abijah and Jeroboam. ³Abijah engaged in battle, having

---

12:5–8 The pattern of prophetic judgment, humility, and divine preservation recurs in Chronicles and seems to be exemplary of what the author expects of readers (2 Chr. 7:13–15). To abandon YHWH is to invite ruin. Yet YHWH responds mercifully to those who humble themselves (Ezra 9; Neh. 9; Dan. 9), even though suffering still ensues (2 Chr. 12:9). This passage suggests that while the prophetic word is serious, it is open to revocation in response to those who humble themselves. See **"Divine Retribution," p. 339.**

12:9–12 Sin and judgment in Chronicles frequently impact the temple. The downgraded materials in the king's house (bronze instead of gold) signal Rehoboam's fall from prominence. The king's humility preserved the nation (v. 12). Failure to humble oneself before YHWH results in YHWH humbling the people, usually through other nations (2 Chr. 28:19–20).

12:13–14 In the end, Rehoboam's reign is characterized by the evil he did. Though he *strengthened himself* via fortified cities (11:5–10), he did not *set his heart to seek the LORD*. This latter indictment touches on a key theme in Chronicles that usually relates to reverencing the ark or temple (1 Chr. 13:3; 15:13; 16:11; 2 Chr. 11:16; 19:3).

12:15–16 We learn here that war continued between Rehoboam and Jeroboam, foreshadowing the events of chap. 13. Unlike Kings, Chronicles includes frequent references to its prophetic sources (e.g., 1 Chr. 29:29; 2 Chr. 9:29–31; 13:22; 26:22; 32:32).

13:1–2 Chronicles typically avoids references to contemporary rulers in Israel, as is common in Kings, but here mentions the northern ruler Jeroboam because of the role he plays in the narrative that follows. Abijah commands little attention in Kings (there called Abijam) but becomes the vaunted successor to Solomon in Chronicles because of his devotion to the temple (vv. 10–11). **13:3** The Chronicler uses exaggerated numbers to highlight the insurmountable odds facing God's people and the need for prayer (cf. v. 17; 2 Chr. 14:9).

an army of valiant warriors, four hundred thousand picked men; and Jeroboam drew up his line of battle against him with eight hundred thousand picked mighty warriors. ⁴Then Abijah stood on the slope of Mount Zemaraim that is in the hill country of Ephraim and said, "Listen to me, Jeroboam and all Israel! ⁵Do you not know that the LORD God of Israel gave the kingship over Israel forever to David and his sons by a covenant of salt? ⁶Yet Jeroboam son of Nebat, a servant of Solomon son of David, rose up and rebelled against his lord, ⁷and certain worthless scoundrels gathered around him and defied Rehoboam son of Solomon when Rehoboam was young and irresolute and could not withstand them.

8 "And now you think that you can withstand the kingdom of the LORD in the hand of the sons of David, because you are a great multitude and have with you the golden calves that Jeroboam made as gods for you. ⁹Have you not driven out the priests of the LORD, the descendants of Aaron, and the Levites and made priests for yourselves like the peoples of other lands? Whoever comes to be consecrated with a young bull or seven rams becomes a priest of what are no gods. ¹⁰But as for us, the LORD is our God, and we have not abandoned him. We have priests ministering to the LORD who are descendants

of Aaron and Levites for their service. ¹¹They offer to the LORD every morning and every evening burnt offerings and fragrant incense, set out the rows of bread on the table of pure gold, and care for the golden lampstand so that its lamps may burn every evening, for we keep the charge of the LORD our God, but you have abandoned him. ¹²See, God is with us at our head, and his priests have their battle trumpets to sound the call to battle against you. O Israelites, do not fight against the LORD, the God of your ancestors, for you cannot succeed."

13 Jeroboam had sent an ambush around to come on them from behind; thus his troopsª were in front of Judah, and the ambush was behind them. ¹⁴When Judah turned, the battle was in front of them and behind them. They cried out to the LORD, and the priests blew the trumpets. ¹⁵Then the people of Judah raised the battle shout. And when the people of Judah shouted, God defeated Jeroboam and all Israel before Abijah and Judah. ¹⁶The Israelites fled before Judah, and God gave them into their hands. ¹⁷Abijah and his army defeated them with great slaughter; five hundred thousand picked men of Israel fell slain. ¹⁸Thus the Israelites were subdued at that time,

a 13.13 Heb *they*

13:4 The location of Mount Zemaraim is uncertain, but Josh. 18:21–24 places it in Benjaminite territory, in the vicinity of Abijah's mother's birthplace, Gibeah (v. 2). From here, King Abijah gives a forceful speech.

13:5 The *covenant of salt* likely refers to the enduring (or preserving) qualities of a covenant (cf. Num. 18:19).

13:6–7 Abijah glosses over the oppressive context of Jeroboam's revolt in order to focus on the cultic offenses of the northern kingdom. He also attributes Rehoboam's incompetence to his youthfulness, even though he came to the throne at age forty-one (2 Chr. 12:13).

13:8–12 For Chronicles, YHWH's kingdom is associated with proper worship and the Davidic kingdom and was thus exclusively in Judah (cf. 1 Chr. 17:14; 28:5; 29:23; 2 Chr. 9:8). The conflict that follows is thus a contest of deities and their cultic adherents, akin to Elijah's showdown with the prophets of Baal on Mount Carmel (1 Kgs. 18). Military power meant nothing when cut off from the divine life source. Israel had more troops but had *driven out* the priests and Levites (2 Chr. 13:9), rendering themselves powerless. An illegitimate cult also meant illegitimate gods, even if the northerners purportedly worshiped YHWH by name. Abijah draws a contrast with true YHWH devotion in Judah, demonstrated by the priests' dutiful activities in the temple (vv. 10–12). For the Chronicler's postexilic generation, who lacked a Davidic king, tangible evidence of divine power and faithfulness in the temple was paramount. Nevertheless, the LORD is still *the God of [the Israelites'] ancestors*, suggesting hope that the kingdom might be restored.

13:13–18 Despite Jeroboam's clever military tactics (reminiscent of Joshua's attack on Ai in Josh. 8), Abijah's words hit the mark. A desperate appeal is accompanied by priestly trumpet blasts (vv. 14–15), a scene with parallels in the Jericho attack (Josh. 6), Israel's later encounter with the Transjordanian coalition (2 Chr. 20), and Jesus's conflict with the devil where he insisted on the need to

and the people of Judah prevailed because they relied on the Lord, the God of their ancestors. [19]Abijah pursued Jeroboam and took cities from him: Bethel with its villages and Jeshanah with its villages and Ephron[b] with its villages. [20]Jeroboam did not recover his power in the days of Abijah; the Lord struck him down, and he died. [21]But Abijah strengthened himself. He took fourteen wives and became the father of twenty-two sons and sixteen daughters. [22]The rest of the acts of Abijah, his behavior and his deeds, are written in the story of the prophet Iddo.

14 [a]So Abijah slept with his ancestors, and they buried him in the city of David. His son Asa succeeded him. In his days the land was quiet for ten years. [2][d]Asa did what was good and right in the sight of the Lord his God. [3]He took away the foreign altars and the high places, broke down the pillars, cut down the sacred poles,[e] [4]and commanded Judah to seek the Lord, the God of their ancestors, and to keep the law and the commandment. [5]He also removed from all the cities of Judah the high places and the incense altars. And the kingdom was quiet under him. [6]He built fortified cities in Judah while the land was quiet. He had no war in those years, for the Lord gave him rest. [7]He said to Judah, "Let us build these cities and surround them with walls and towers, gates and bars; the land is still ours because we have sought the Lord our God; we have sought him, and he has given us rest on every side." So they built and prospered. [8]Asa had an army of three hundred thousand from Judah armed with large shields and spears and two hundred eighty thousand troops from Benjamin who carried shields and drew bows; all these were mighty warriors.

9 Zerah the Cushite came out against them with an army of a million men and three hundred chariots and came as far as Mareshah. [10]Asa went out to meet him, and they drew up their lines of battle in the valley of Zephathah at Mareshah. [11]Asa cried to the Lord his God, "O Lord, there is no difference for you between helping the mighty and the weak. Help us, O Lord our God, for we rely on you, and in your name we have come against this multitude. O Lord, you are our God; let no mortal prevail against you." [12]So the Lord defeated the Cushites before Asa and before Judah, and the Cushites fled. [13]Asa and the army with him pursued them as far as Gerar, and the Cushites fell until no one remained alive, for they were broken before the Lord and his army. The people of Judah[f] carried away a great quantity of spoil. [14]They defeated all

b 13.19 Or *Ephrain*   c 14.1 13.23 in Heb   d 14.2 14.1 in Heb
e 14.3 Or *Asherahs*   f 14.13 Heb *They*

"worship the Lord your God, and serve only him" (Luke 4:8; cf. Deut. 6:13). Whereas the north fought against the God of their ancestors (2 Chr. 13:12), Judah relied on the *God of their ancestors* (v. 18).

13:19–22 Recapturing Bethel is cultically significant, since Jeroboam had installed a golden calf there. On wealth and children as signs of divine favor, see comment on 11:18–23.

2 Chr. 14 The Chronicler's account of Asa's reign is far longer than Kings's (2 Chr. 14:1–16:14 compared to 1 Kgs. 15:9–24) and focuses on his cultic activities.

14:1–7 The first ten years of his reign give Asa sufficient peace for him to undertake religious reforms and bulk up his military defenses. The positive evaluation of Asa (v. 2) relates to his removal of illicit *foreign* cultic paraphernalia outside of Jerusalem (v. 5). Presumably, Jerusalem remained cultically orthodox, even during Rehoboam's reign, though the presence of such contraband around Judah is a surprise, given the emphasis on Rehoboam's repentance and Abijah's commendable reign (chap. 13). The emphasis on seeking the Lord (vv. 4, 7) relates to keeping the law (v. 4) and pursuing worship at the temple. The author omits Kings's reference to Asa's ancestors' idols (1 Kgs. 15:12). Asa's large army consists of Judeans and Benjaminites and reflects the incorporation of Benjamin into the territory of Judah (see comment on 13:4).

14:9–15 *Zerah the Cushite* is otherwise unknown in the Old Testament. Biblical "Ethiopia" (Cush in Hebrew) is roughly equivalent to ancient Nubia, or modern Sudan (see 16:8), though it may be associated with Cushan, a region likely in the Sinai Peninsula (cf. Hab. 3:7). Zerah's army is fantastically huge and militarily superior, accentuating the need for another Judean appeal to divine aid (cf. 2 Chr. 13:14). *There is no difference for you* (v. 11) could also be rendered "there is none with you," highlighting YHWH's exclusive power to deliver. Notably, it was not Asa's fortified cities that provided protection but direct divine aid (v. 12). From Mareshah (about twenty-five miles southwest of

the cities around Gerar, for the fear of the LORD was on them. They plundered all the cities, for there was much plunder in them. [15]They also attacked the tents of those who had livestock[g] and carried away sheep and goats in abundance and camels. Then they returned to Jerusalem.

15 The spirit of God came upon Azariah son of Oded. [2]He went out to meet Asa and said to him, "Hear me, Asa, and all Judah and Benjamin: The LORD is with you while you are with him. If you seek him, he will be found by you, but if you abandon him, he will abandon you. [3]For a long time Israel was without the true God and without a teaching priest and without law, [4]but when in their distress they turned to the LORD, the God of Israel, and sought him, he was found by them. [5]In those times it was not safe for anyone to go or come, for great disturbances afflicted all the inhabitants of the lands. [6]They were broken in pieces, nation against nation and city against city, for God troubled them with every sort of distress. [7]But you, take courage! Do not let your hands be weak, for your work shall be rewarded."

8 When Asa heard these words, the prophecy of Azariah son of Oded,[b] he took courage and put away the abominable idols from all the land of Judah and Benjamin and from the towns that he had taken in the hill country of Ephraim. He repaired the altar of the LORD that was in front of the vestibule of the house of the LORD.[i] [9]He gathered all Judah and Benjamin and those from Ephraim, Manasseh, and Simeon who were residing as aliens with them, for great numbers had deserted to him from Israel when they saw that the LORD his God was with him. [10]They were gathered at Jerusalem in the third month of the fifteenth year of the reign of Asa. [11]They sacrificed to the LORD on that day, from the spoil that they had brought, seven hundred oxen and seven thousand sheep. [12]They entered into a covenant to seek the LORD, the God of their ancestors, with all their heart and with all their soul, [13]and whoever would not seek the LORD, the God of Israel, was to be put to death, whether young or old, man or woman. [14]They took an oath to the LORD with a loud voice and with shouting and with trumpets and with horns. [15]All Judah rejoiced over the oath, for they had sworn with all their heart and had sought him with their whole desire, and he was found by them, and the LORD gave them rest all around.

g 14.15 Meaning of Heb uncertain   h 15.8 Compare Syr Vg: Heb *the prophecy, the prophet Oded*   i 15.8 Heb *the vestibule of the LORD*

Jerusalem), Judah drives the Ethiopians back to Gerar (likely near the Egyptian-Philistia border, or about thirty miles southwest of Mareshah). Plundering Gerar (v. 14–15) evokes the story of Abraham gaining great wealth from Abimelech, king of Gerar (Gen. 20:14–16). The wealth gained in this battle is likely the same that is dedicated to the temple (2 Chr. 15:11, 18).

15:1–7 Another previously unknown prophet offers a historical retrospective and warning. The spirit-inspired admonition to *seek* the Lord is central to the Chronicler's view of history (1 Chr. 16:11; 28:9; 2 Chr. 7:14) and frequently relates to temple-focused reform and worship. Other spirit-endowed prophets appear in Chronicles (1 Chr. 12:18; 2 Chr. 20:14; 24:20). The pattern of distress and seeking the Lord draws its primary inspiration from Judges (2:18; 3:9, 15; 4:3; 6:7; 10:10), whose conditions are also outlined in 2 Chr. 15:5–6. Asa's reforms in 14:3–5 focused on Judah (e.g., not including idols), which 15:8–15 may summarize and extend. The exhortation to *take courage* echoes similar encouragement before the Israelite conquest (Josh. 1:7, 9), and the latter half of the verse likely quotes Jer. 31:16, referring to the return from exile. In its postexilic context, the verse offers reward for those who heed Cyrus's later encouragement to participate in the temple's restoration as they return to the land (2 Chr. 36:22–23).

15:8 Asa takes immediate action in removing *abominable idols*, a phrase used to describe the idols removed by Josiah in Kings (2 Kgs. 23:24) and in Ezekiel (11:18–21).

15:9 Asa's altar repairs reflect a pattern in Chronicles that good kings show concern for the temple's upkeep and maintenance. The reform extends into land claimed in the north, beyond the Judean reform outlined in 14:3–5. It anticipates Hezekiah's and Josiah's later reforms (2 Chr. 30:1, 18; 31:1; 34:6, 9) and touches on the theme of "all Israel" that pervades the book.

15:10–15 Gathering in the *third month* may refer to the Festival of Weeks (Pentecost; Exod. 23:16; Lev. 23:15–21; Deut. 16:9–10). This was also the month that Israel arrived at Sinai (Exod. 19:1), rendering this an opportune time to reaffirm covenant commitments by seeking the Lord (2 Chr. 15:12; cf. Deut. 6:5).

16 King Asa even removed his mother Maacah from being queen mother because she had made an abominable image for Asherah. Asa cut down her image, crushed it, and burned it at the Wadi Kidron. [17]But the high places were not taken out of Israel. Nevertheless, the heart of Asa was true all his days. [18]He brought into the house of God the votive gifts of his father and his own votive gifts: silver, gold, and utensils. [19]And there was no more war until the thirty-fifth year of the reign of Asa.

16 In the thirty-sixth year of the reign of Asa, King Baasha of Israel went up against Judah and built Ramah to prevent anyone from going out or coming into the territory of[j] King Asa of Judah. [2]Then Asa took silver and gold from the treasures of the house of the Lord and the king's house and sent them to King Ben-hadad of Aram, who resided in Damascus, saying, [3]"Let there be an alliance between me and you, like that between my father and your father; I am sending to you silver and gold; go, break your alliance with King Baasha of Israel, so that he may withdraw from me." [4]Ben-hadad listened to King Asa and sent the commanders of his armies against the cities of Israel. They conquered Ijon, Dan, Abel-maim, and all the store cities of Naphtali. [5]When Baasha heard of it, he stopped building Ramah and let his work cease. [6]Then King Asa brought all Judah, and they carried away the stones of Ramah and its timber with which Baasha had been building, and with them he built up Geba and Mizpah.

7 At that time the seer Hanani came to King Asa of Judah and said to him, "Because you relied on the king of Aram and did not rely on the Lord your God, the army of the king of Aram has escaped you. [8]Were not the Cushites and the Libyans a huge army with exceedingly many chariots and cavalry? Yet because you relied on the Lord, he gave them into your hand. [9]For the eyes of the Lord range throughout the entire earth to strengthen those whose heart is true to him. You have done foolishly in this, for from now on you will have wars." [10]Then Asa was angry with the seer and put him in the stocks, in prison, for he was in a rage with him because of this. And Asa inflicted cruelties on some of the people at the same time.

11 The acts of Asa, from first to last, are written in the Book of the Kings of Judah

j 16.1 Heb lacks *the territory of*

15:16–19 Asa spared no one in his reforms. He deposed Maacah, the *queen mother* (literally "great lady"), burning her Asherah images as mandated by Deut. 7:25 (cf. 1 Chr. 14:12). King Hezekiah also disposes of illicit cultic items in the Kidron Valley on the eastern side of Jerusalem (2 Chr. 29:16; 30:14). The positive evaluation of Asa, despite his failure to remove high places (yet see 14:3), follows the nuanced interpretation of kings present in the Chronicler's sources. Second Chr. 14:3 reports that Asa had removed high places but only from Judah. Only Hezekiah removes them from all the land. Thus Asa anticipates greater reforms to come.

16:1 Ramah sits between Bethel and Jerusalem in the center of the Benjamin Plateau, and its occupation by Baasha cut off Judah's access to Bethel (as well as the coast and Jordan Valley) from the south and prevented northerners from accessing Jerusalem. Baasha likely sought to reclaim territory annexed by Abijah (13:19) and Asa (15:8).

16:2–3 Instead of seeking the Lord as he did earlier (15:14), Asa strips the temple of its wealth to buy Aramean aid. Chronicles never looks favorably on pillaging the temple for foreign aid, as Rehoboam had done (12:9) and Jehoash (24:23) and Amaziah (25:20–24) would do. Though not explicitly condemned, this event occurs during the negative portion of Asa's reign.

16:4–6 By attacking cities in northern Israel, Ben-hadad relieved pressure on Judah and enabled Asa to fortify the Benjaminite cities of Geba and Mizpah (northeast and northwest of Ramah).

16:7–10 The *seer* (or prophet) Hanani is otherwise unknown, though the "seer" Jehu, son of a man named Hanani, appears in 19:2 and 20:34. Reliance on foreign aid betrays infidelity toward YHWH and the temple (cf. 28:24). Asa failed to learn to trust from the events described in chap. 15, and as a result, Judah would face troubles from Aram as well, as chap. 18 describes. Asa's response mimics the response of the temple chief Pashhur, who put Jeremiah in stocks for his prophecies (Jer. 20:2). Putting false prophets in stocks was a known duty of temple leadership, according to Jer. 29:26.

16:11–14 In the end, the king who sought God when facing an army of over one million soldiers fails to seek God about his own foot disease. Notably, Asa's failure is not in consulting physicians

and Israel. [12]In the thirty-ninth year of his reign Asa was diseased in his feet, and his disease became severe; yet even in his disease he did not seek the LORD but sought help from physicians. [13]Then Asa slept with his ancestors, dying in the forty-first year of his reign. [14]They buried him in the tomb that he had cut out for himself in the city of David. They laid him on a bier that had been filled with various kinds of spices prepared by the perfumer's art, and they made a very great fire in his honor.

17
His son Jehoshaphat succeeded him and strengthened himself against Israel. [2]He placed forces in all the fortified cities of Judah and set garrisons in the land of Judah and in the cities of Ephraim that his father Asa had taken. [3]The LORD was with Jehoshaphat because he walked in the earlier ways of his father;[k] he did not seek the Baals [4]but sought the God of his father and walked in his commandments and not according to the ways of Israel. [5]Therefore the LORD established the kingdom in his hand. All Judah brought tribute to Jehoshaphat, and he had great riches and honor. [6]His heart was courageous

in the ways of the LORD; furthermore, he removed the high places and the sacred poles[l] from Judah.

[7]In the third year of his reign he sent his officials Ben-hail, Obadiah, Zechariah, Nethanel, and Micaiah to teach in the cities of Judah. [8]With them were the Levites Shemaiah, Nethaniah, Zebadiah, Asahel, Shemiramoth, Jehonathan, Adonijah, Tobijah, and Tob-adonijah; and with these Levites the priests Elishama and Jehoram. [9]They taught in Judah, having the book of the law of the LORD with them; they went around through all the cities of Judah and taught among the people.

[10] The fear of the LORD fell on all the kingdoms of the lands around Judah, and they did not make war against Jehoshaphat. [11]Some of the Philistines brought Jehoshaphat presents and silver for tribute, and the Arabs also brought him seven thousand seven hundred rams and seven thousand seven hundred male goats. [12]Jehoshaphat grew steadily greater. He built fortresses and storage cities in Judah. [13]He carried out great works in the cities of

k 17.3 Gk: Heb *his father David*   l 17.6 Or *Asherahs*

but in *only* seeking physicians. Though failing in the end, Asa is nevertheless deemed a good and honorable king. The fire is likely to burn the spices in his honor (cf. Jer. 34:5) and not for cremation.

2 Chr. 17 The Chronicler's account of Jehoshaphat (17:1–21:1a) is far longer than Kings's (1 Kgs. 22:1–36, 40–50; 2 Kgs. 3:4–27) and appears to be styled correspondingly to the account of Asa. See **"Revising/Rewriting the Bible," p. 584**. Like Asa, Jehoshaphat is a reformer who faces major threats from neighboring nations, and his military activities reflect trust as well as mistrust in the Lord.

17:1–2 Jehoshaphat explicitly follows the fortifying policies of his father, Asa (cf. 2 Chr. 14:6–8), as well as Solomon (8:5–6) and Rehoboam (11:5–11) before him. The cities near the border of Benjamin and Ephraim are regularly contested, as seen during the reign of Asa.

17:3–6 Jehoshaphat *sought* YHWH instead of the Baals (also in 19:3 and 20:3). Once again, "seeking" YHWH leads to cultic reforms. His removal of high places and sacred poles might seem unnecessary, given Asa's reforms, though they may have been restored during Asa's final years. On "sacred poles," see note on 1 Kgs. 14:15. Securing the nation militarily is useless without such attention to worship, the true source of Judah's strength.

17:7–9 Jehoshaphat appoints three groups (officials, Levites, and priests) to teach torah throughout Judah, reflecting a postexilic practice known in Ezra 7:25 and Neh. 8:7 and anticipating his later judicial reforms (2 Chr. 19:4–11). Other Hebrew Bible passages associate priests with teaching the law (Lev. 10:11; Deut. 33:10; Hos. 4:6; Mal. 2:7), and Deuteronomy associates law teaching with "Levitical priests" (Deut. 24:8). They bring the *book of the law of the LORD* with them, a phrase also used in 2 Chr. 34:14.

17:10–11 Evidence of the Chronicler's view of power is evident here. Fear of YHWH falls on the surrounding nations after the leaders "fortify" Judah by teaching the law. Tribute comes from the *Philistines* and *Arabs*, the first nations since Solomon to offer it (2 Chr. 9).

17:12–13 Like many other kings in Chronicles, Jehoshaphat was a great builder. *Storage cities* likely refers to cities or forts used to provision troops and sell goods to travelers.

Judah. He had soldiers, mighty warriors, in Jerusalem. ¹⁴This was the muster of them by ancestral houses: Of Judah, the commanders of the thousands: Adnah the commander, with three hundred thousand mighty warriors, ¹⁵and next to him Jehohanan the commander, with two hundred eighty thousand, ¹⁶and next to him Amasiah son of Zichri, a volunteer for the service of the LORD, with two hundred thousand mighty warriors. ¹⁷Of Benjamin: Eliada, a mighty warrior, with two hundred thousand armed with bow and shield, ¹⁸and next to him Jehozabad with one hundred eighty thousand armed for war. ¹⁹These were in the service of the king, besides those whom the king had placed in the fortified cities throughout all Judah.

18 Now Jehoshaphat had great riches and honor, and he made a marriage alliance with Ahab. ²After some years he went down to Ahab in Samaria. Ahab slaughtered an abundance of sheep and oxen for him and for the people who were with him and induced him to go up against Ramoth-gilead. ³King Ahab of Israel said to King Jehoshaphat of Judah, "Will you go with me to Ramoth-gilead?" He answered him, "I am as you are; my people are your people. We will be with you in the war."

4 But Jehoshaphat also said to the king of Israel, "Inquire first for the word of the LORD." ⁵Then the king of Israel gathered the prophets together, four hundred of them, and said to them, "Shall we go to battle against Ramoth-gilead, or shall I refrain?" They said, "Go up, for God will give it into the hand of the king." ⁶But Jehoshaphat said, "Is there no other prophet of the LORD here of whom we may inquire?" ⁷The king of Israel said to Jehoshaphat, "There is still one other by whom we may inquire of the LORD, Micaiah son of Imlah, but I hate him, for he never prophesies anything favorable about me but only disaster." Jehoshaphat said, "Let the king not say such a thing." ⁸Then the king of Israel summoned an officer and said, "Bring quickly Micaiah son of Imlah." ⁹Now the king of Israel and King Jehoshaphat of Judah were sitting on their thrones, arrayed in their robes, and they were sitting at the threshing floor at the entrance of the gate of Samaria, and all the prophets were prophesying before them. ¹⁰Zedekiah son of Chenaanah made for himself horns of iron, and he said, "Thus says the LORD: With these you shall gore the Arameans until they are destroyed." ¹¹All the prophets were prophesying the same and saying, "Go up to Ramoth-gilead and triumph; the LORD will give it into the hand of the king."

12 The messenger who had gone to summon Micaiah said to him, "Look, the words of the prophets with one accord are favorable to the king; let your word be like the word of one of them, and speak favorably." ¹³But Micaiah said, "As the LORD lives, whatever my God says, that I will speak."

14 When he had come to the king, the king said to him, "Micaiah, shall we go to Ramoth-gilead to battle, or shall I refrain?"

17:14–19 Jehoshaphat's troops total 1.16 million soldiers, likely an exaggerated number. Alternatively, the Hebrew word translated as "thousand" may refer to an army unit as small as fourteen or as large as one hundred. The rhetorical point is to emphasize the king's growing stature (v. 12).

18:1–3 Not all records of wealth are positive in Chronicles. Jehoshaphat's alliance by marriage leads to serious troubles, as Ahab draws the Judean king into a conflict with Aram. *Ramoth-gilead* was an important fortress on the route from Damascus south toward Transjordan and was regularly claimed by Aram (yet see 1 Kgs. 4:13).

18:4–7 Jehoshaphat proves spiritually acute, pursuing a policy to *inquire first* (literally "seeking") of YHWH via his prophets. Ahab's four hundred prophets seem like "yes-men" gathered to confirm Ahab's desire for war. Jehoshaphat's question implies that Ahab's prophets were biased, a point confirmed by Ahab himself (vv. 6–7). Once again, Jehoshaphat proves more spiritually attuned (vv. 4, 7), as even antimonarchic prophets could be sent by God.

18:8–9 The Israelite and Judean kings sat enthroned at the threshing floor, seeking prophetic insight. Threshing floors and harvest time are regularly associated with divine presence in the Hebrew Bible (Josh. 3:15; Judg. 6:11–12, 37; 1 Sam. 6:13–15; 2 Sam. 6:6–7, 19; 24:16; 1 Chr. 21:18–27).

18:10–14 Zedekiah's prophetic sign act portrays an ox goring its opponents (cf. Pss. 22:21; 75:10) and commands the support of the other prophets. Micaiah's agreement with these prophets may reflect his skepticism regarding Ahab's truth seeking.

He answered, "Go up and triumph; they will be given into your hand." [15]But the king said to him, "How many times must I make you swear to tell me nothing but the truth in the name of the Lord?" [16]Then Micaiah[m] said, "I saw all Israel scattered on the mountains like sheep without a shepherd, and the Lord said, 'These have no master; let each one go home in peace.'" [17]The king of Israel said to Jehoshaphat, "Did I not tell you that he would not prophesy anything favorable about me but only disaster?"

18 Then Micaiah[n] said, "Therefore hear the word of the Lord: I saw the Lord sitting on his throne, with all the host of heaven standing to the right and to the left of him. [19]And the Lord said, 'Who will entice King Ahab of Israel, so that he may go up and fall at Ramoth-gilead?' Then one said one thing, and another said another, [20]until a certain spirit came forward and stood before the Lord, saying, 'I will entice him.' The Lord asked him, 'How?' [21]He replied, 'I will go out and be a lying spirit in the mouth of all his prophets.' Then the Lord[o] said, 'You are to entice him, and you shall succeed; go out and do it.' [22]So you see, the Lord has put a lying spirit in the mouth of these your prophets; the Lord has decreed disaster for you."

23 Then Zedekiah son of Chenaanah came up to Micaiah, slapped him on the cheek, and said, "Which way did the spirit of the Lord pass from me to speak to you?"

[24]Micaiah replied, "You will find out on that day when you go in to hide in an inner chamber." [25]The king of Israel then ordered, "Take Micaiah, and return him to Amon the governor of the city and to Joash the king's son, [26]and say: Thus says the king: Put this fellow in prison, and feed him on reduced rations of bread and water until I return in peace." [27]Micaiah said, "If you return in peace, the Lord has not spoken by me." And he said, "Hear, you peoples, all of you!"

28 So the king of Israel and King Jehoshaphat of Judah went up to Ramoth-gilead. [29]The king of Israel said to Jehoshaphat, "I will disguise myself and go into battle, but you wear your robes." So the king of Israel disguised himself, and they went into battle. [30]Now the king of Aram had commanded the captains of his chariots, "Fight with no one small or great but only with the king of Israel." [31]When the captains of the chariots saw Jehoshaphat, they said, "It is the king of Israel." So they turned to fight against him, and Jehoshaphat cried out, and the Lord helped him. God drew them away from him, [32]for when the captains of the chariots saw that it was not the king of Israel, they turned back from pursuing him. [33]But a certain man drew his bow and unknowingly struck the king of Israel between the scale armor and the breastplate, so he said to the driver of his chariot, "Turn around, and carry me out of the battle, for

m 18.16 Heb *he*   n 18.18 Heb *he*   o 18.21 Heb *he*

18:15–17 But the truth was not with the majority, and even Ahab suspects so, prompting Micaiah's report of a divine vision. Micaiah's response parallels the words of Israel's prophets (Jer. 10:21; Nah. 3:18) and reflects the ideal of kings as shepherds in the ancient world (Jer. 3:15; 23:1; Ezek. 34). Jesus identifies as a "good shepherd" who gives his life for the sheep (John 10:1–2). Ahab, too, will give his life but not for anyone other than himself.

18:18–22 Micaiah's vision reflects the idea that prophets are privy to the divine council (Isa. 6; Jer. 23:16–22), through whom God enacts God's will. Enticing Ahab through a lying spirit is surprising yet reflects the idea that God uses such spirits to bring judgment and lure powerful kings to their own ruin (cf. 1 Sam. 16:14), as God had done with Pharaoh in Exodus. The passage also reflects the conviction that even non-Yahwistic prophets are within YHWH's sphere of control (cf. Balaam in Num. 22–24).

18:23–24 Zedekiah rightly questions Micaiah. Who is to say that the spirit prompted deceit among the four hundred prophets but truth with Micaiah? The difference, of course, is that only one prophet stood in the divine council. Only future actions would vindicate Micaiah's words (Deut. 18:22).

18:25–27 Like Hanani before him (2 Chr. 16:10), Micaiah's unpopular words lead to his detainment in a scene that anticipates the prophet Zechariah's martyrdom for his prophesying (2 Chr. 24:21). Truthful prophecy often leads to mistreatment (Isa. 53; Jer. 20:2; 38:1–6; Amos 7:12–13; Luke 4:24–30).

18:28–34 Despite the appearance of truth seeking, Ahab thinks he can avoid his fate through disguise. The Arameans mistake Jehoshaphat for *the king of Israel*, a mistitling that proves truer than they know. Jehoshaphat's outcry draws divine aid to his side, a pattern evident throughout

I am wounded." [34]The battle grew hot that day, and the king of Israel propped himself up in his chariot facing the Arameans until evening; then at sunset he died.

19 King Jehoshaphat of Judah returned in peace to his house in Jerusalem. [2]Jehu son of Hanani the seer went out to meet him and said to King Jehoshaphat, "Should you help the wicked and love those who hate the LORD? Because of this, wrath has gone out against you from the LORD. [3]Nevertheless, some good is found in you, for you destroyed the sacred poles[p] out of the land and have set your heart to seek God."

4 Jehoshaphat resided at Jerusalem; then he went out again among the people, from Beer-sheba to the hill country of Ephraim, and brought them back to the LORD, the God of their ancestors. [5]He appointed judges in the land in all the fortified cities of Judah, city by city, [6]and said to the judges, "Consider what you are doing, for you judge not on behalf of humans but on the LORD's behalf; he is with you in giving judgment. [7]Now, let the fear of the LORD be upon you; take care what you do, for there is no perversion of justice with the LORD our God or partiality or taking of bribes."

8 Moreover, in Jerusalem Jehoshaphat appointed certain Levites and priests and heads of families of Israel to give judgment for the LORD and to decide disputed cases. They had their seat at Jerusalem. [9]He charged them, "This is how you shall act: in the fear of the LORD, in faithfulness, and with your whole heart; [10]whenever a case comes to you from your kindred who live in their cities concerning bloodshed, law or commandment, statutes or ordinances, then you shall instruct them, so that they may not incur guilt before the LORD and wrath may not come on you and your kindred. Do so, and you will not incur guilt. [11]See, Amariah the chief priest is over you in all matters of the LORD; and Zebadiah son of Ishmael, the governor of the house of Judah, in all the king's matters; and the Levites will serve you as officers. Deal courageously, and may the LORD be with the good!"

20 After this the Moabites and Ammonites, and with them some of the Meunites,[q] came against Jehoshaphat for battle. [2]Messengers[r] came and told Jehoshaphat, "A great multitude is coming against you from Edom,[s] from beyond the

p 19.3 Or *Asherahs* *q* 20.1 Heb *Ammonites* *r* 20.2 Heb *They* *s* 20.2 Heb ms: MT *Aram*

Chronicles, where prayer is more powerful than weapons of war (1 Chr. 5:20; 2 Chr. 13:14–15; 20:9; 32:20). The seemingly random arrow is divinely directed, proving Micaiah's words and displaying Ahab's folly. Like Saul, Ahab falls in battle from an arrow wound (1 Sam. 31:3; 1 Chr. 10:3).

19:1–3 While not initially condemned, the alliance of chap. 18 appears in a decidedly negative light on the basis of Jehu's prophetic word. As his father, Hanani, opposed Asa for his foreign alliance (16:7–9), so Jehu opposes Jehoshaphat's alliance (19:1–3). Divine *wrath*, which can threaten the community (Num. 1:53; 16:22, 46; 18:5; Deut. 9:7–8, 19, 22), is frequently quelled by prophetic intercession (Exod. 32:11–13, 31–32; Num. 11:2; 12:13; 16:22, 45–47; Ezra 9:6–15)—or in this case, by prior mitigating actions (Asa's dependence on God and Jehoshaphat's reforms).

19:4–7 Jehoshaphat lives up to his name ("YHWH judges") and personally travels the extent of the land, including parts of the northern kingdom (*the hill country of Ephraim*), to enact judicial reforms. These reforms reflect the concerns of Deut. 10:17 (on God as judge) and Deut. 16:18–17:13 (on the need for judges).

19:8–11 A high court in Jerusalem would judge disputed cases (as stipulated in Deut. 17:8–9 and 21:5). The text reflects a distinction among civil cases (2 Chr. 19:10; handled by elders, Levites, and priests), religious matters (v. 11; handled by the chief priest), and royal matters (v. 11; handled by the governor of the king's house). There is no fail-safe judicial system without *fear of the LORD* (vv. 7, 9), recognition of divine *wrath* (v. 10), and courage to pursue justice (v. 11).

2 Chr. 20 This is one of the Chronicler's finest narratives, reflecting the book's concerns for discerning YHWH's power in worship. The story begins with prayer at the temple in Jerusalem (vv. 5–12), advances through prophecy (vv. 13–17), proceeds to its climax in worship (vv. 18–23), and concludes with joyful worship at the temple in Jerusalem (vv. 26–30).

20:1–4 Without any clear provocation, a coalition of three nations (with the third name in dispute; see v. 1 NRSVue note) gathers for war at En-gedi, an abundant spring that feeds into the

sea; already they are at Hazazon-tamar" (that is, En-gedi). ³Jehoshaphat was afraid; he set himself to seek the LORD and proclaimed a fast throughout all Judah. ⁴Judah assembled to seek help from the LORD; from all the towns of Judah they came to seek the LORD.

5 Jehoshaphat stood in the assembly of Judah and Jerusalem, in the house of the LORD, before the new court, ⁶and said, "O LORD, God of our ancestors, are you not God in heaven? Do you not rule over all the kingdoms of the nations? In your hand are power and might, so that no one is able to withstand you. ⁷Did you not, O our God, drive out the inhabitants of this land before your people Israel and give it forever to the descendants of your friend Abraham? ⁸They have lived in it and in it have built you a sanctuary for your name, saying, ⁹"If disaster comes upon us, the sword, judgment,ᶠ or pestilence, or famine, we will stand before this house and before you, for your name is in this house, and cry to you in our distress, and you will hear and save.' ¹⁰See now, the people of Ammon, Moab, and Mount Seir, whom you would not let Israel invade when they came from the land of Egypt and whom they avoided and did not destroy, ¹¹they reward us by coming to drive us out of your possession that you have given us to inherit. ¹²O our God, will you not execute judgment upon them? For we are powerless against this great multitude that is coming against us. We do not know what to do, but our eyes are on you."

13 Meanwhile, all Judah stood before the LORD, with their little ones, their wives, and their children. ¹⁴Then the spirit of the LORD came upon Jahaziel son of Zechariah, son of Benaiah, son of Jeiel, son of Mattaniah, a Levite of the sons of Asaph, in the middle of the assembly. ¹⁵He said, "Listen, all Judah and inhabitants of Jerusalem and King Jehoshaphat: Thus says the LORD to you: Do not fear or be dismayed at this great multitude, for the battle is not yours but God's. ¹⁶Tomorrow go down against them; they will come up by the ascent of Ziz; you will find them at the end of the valley, before the wilderness of Jeruel. ¹⁷This battle is not for you to fight; take your position, stand still, and see the victory of the LORD on your behalf, O Judah and Jerusalem. Do not fear or be dismayed; tomorrow go out against them, and the LORD will be with you."

18 Then Jehoshaphat bowed down with his face to the ground, and all Judah and the inhabitants of Jerusalem fell down before the LORD, worshiping the LORD. ¹⁹And the

f 20.9 Or the sword of judgment

western side of the Dead Sea. One possibility is that the nations gather in response to Asa's alliance with Syria or Judah's alliance with Israel. Jehoshaphat (v. 3) and the community (v. 4) *seek* the Lord, a response to distress that Chronicles is keen to engender (2 Chr. 7:14). Fasts were part of the appeal process throughout the Hebrew Bible (e.g., Joel 2:12–17; Jonah 3:5–8).

20:5–12 Jehoshaphat's prayer at the temple fits the pattern that Solomon envisioned. In times of distress, Israel was to pray at or toward the temple (2 Chr. 6:21, 24–25). God's sovereign power over the nations and God's transcendent uniqueness are common themes in Chronicles (cf. 1 Chr. 16:25; 29:10–12; 2 Chr. 2:5) and form the basis for prayerful appeals. **20:6** Seventeen of the Hebrew Bible's twenty references to *God of our ancestors* occur in Chronicles, highlighting the book's concern to anchor its theology in the oldest of Israel's traditions. **20:10–11** Jehoshaphat's appeal refers back to the inhospitable treatment of Israel when they traveled toward Canaan (cf. Deut. 2). **20:12** The appeal for divine judgment evokes Jehoshaphat's name ("YHWH judges") and the theological conviction that the Lord is involved in judgment.

20:13–17 The line between prophets and priests blurs in Chronicles and the postexilic period more generally. The spirit *came upon* Jahaziel, who descends from the Levitical family of Asaph, known for its musicianship and prophecy (1 Chr. 25:1–2; Pss. 73–83). **20:16** The locations of *Ziz* and *Jeruel* (v. 16) are unknown, but their proximity to Tekoa (v. 20), which sits between Bethlehem and Hebron on the frontier of the wilderness sloping down toward the Dead Sea, suggests approximate locations. **20:17** The admonition to *stand still* and watch the divine victory echoes Israel's stillness as YHWH defeated the Egyptian army (Exod. 14:13–14) and the acknowledgment throughout the Hebrew Bible that YHWH accomplishes victories without the aid of human weapons (Josh. 24:12; 1 Sam. 17:47; Ps. 44:2–3, 6).

20:18–19 Worship and praise constitute Israel's defiant response to the threatening invasion (cf.

Levites of the Kohathites and the Korahites stood up to praise the LORD, the God of Israel, with a very loud voice.

20 They rose early in the morning and went out into the wilderness of Tekoa, and as they went out Jehoshaphat stood and said, "Listen to me, O Judah and inhabitants of Jerusalem! Believe in the LORD your God and you will be established; believe his prophets and you will succeed." ²¹When he had taken counsel with the people, he appointed those who were to sing to the LORD and praise him in holy splendor, as they went before the army, saying,

"Give thanks to the LORD,
    for his steadfast love endures
    forever."

²²As they began to sing and praise, the LORD set an ambush against the Ammonites, Moab, and Mount Seir who had come against Judah, so that they were routed. ²³For the Ammonites and Moab attacked the inhabitants of Mount Seir, destroying them utterly, and when they had made an end of the inhabitants of Seir, they all helped to destroy one another.

24 When Judah came to the watchtower of the wilderness, they looked toward the multitude; they were corpses lying on the ground; no one had escaped. ²⁵When Jehoshaphat and his people came to take the spoil from them, they found livestock^u in great numbers, goods, clothing, and precious things, which they took for themselves until they could carry no more. They spent three days taking the spoil because of its abundance. ²⁶On the fourth day they assembled in the Valley of Beracah, for there they blessed the LORD; therefore that place has been called the Valley of Beracah^v to this day. ²⁷Then all the people of Judah and Jerusalem, with Jehoshaphat at their head, returned to Jerusalem with joy, for the LORD had enabled them to rejoice over their enemies. ²⁸They came to Jerusalem with harps and lyres and trumpets to the house of the LORD. ²⁹The fear of God came on all the kingdoms of the countries when they heard that the LORD had fought against the enemies of Israel. ³⁰And the realm of Jehoshaphat was quiet, for his God gave him rest all around.

31 So Jehoshaphat reigned over Judah. He was thirty-five years old when he began to reign; he reigned twenty-five years in Jerusalem. His mother's name was Azubah daughter of Shilhi. ³²He walked in the way of his father Asa and did not turn aside from it, doing what was right in the sight of the LORD. ³³Yet the high places were not removed; the people had not yet set their hearts upon the God of their ancestors.

34 Now the rest of the acts of Jehoshaphat, from first to last, are written in the Annals of Jehu son of Hanani, which are recorded in the Book of the Kings of Israel.

35 After this King Jehoshaphat of Judah joined with King Ahaziah of Israel, who did wickedly. ³⁶He joined him in building ships to go to Tarshish; they built the ships in Ezion-geber. ³⁷Then Eliezer son of Dodavahu of Mareshah prophesied against Jehoshaphat, saying, "Because you have joined with Ahaziah, the LORD will destroy what you have made." And the ships were wrecked and were not able to go to Tarshish.

u 20.25 Gk: Heb *among them*   v 20.26 That is, *blessing*

Josh. 6). The Kohathites descend from Levi's son Kohath, and the Korahites from Levi's grandson Korah. The Korahites' role as singers appears in several psalms (42–49, 84–85, 87–88).

20:20–21 Jehoshaphat's encouragement to believe in the Lord and the prophets likely refers to YHWH's exclusive action in battle (v. 17). The Levites' *holy splendor* highlights their role in manifesting divine glory. Similar words are attributed to YHWH in Pss. 29:2 and 96:9. The singers' words (2 Chr. 20:21) echo the refrain found in 1 Chr. 16:34, 41; 2 Chr. 5:13; 7:3, 6, and draw their inspiration from Psalms (e.g., Pss. 96; 136).

20:22–23 The Lord unleashes divine power during the people's praise, recalling the descent of the Lord's glory in praise (2 Chr. 5:12–13).

20:24–30 After despoiling the enemy (vv. 24–25), the people gather in the Valley of Beracah (i.e., blessing) to continue in praise and process to Jerusalem.

20:31–37 Though Jehoshaphat failed to remove the high places (v. 33), he receives a positive evaluation from the Chronicler (v. 32). Nevertheless, the concluding assessment (vv. 35–37) casts a shadow over the king. The Chronicler is generally negative about alliances, as expressed through the words of Eliezer, the fourth prophet to appear during Jehoshaphat's reign.

21 Jehoshaphat slept with his ancestors and was buried with his ancestors in the city of David; his son Jehoram succeeded him. ²He had brothers, the sons of Jehoshaphat: Azariah, Jehiel, Zechariah, Azariah, Michael, and Shephatiah; all these were the sons of King Jehoshaphat of Judah.ʷ ³Their father gave them many gifts of silver, gold, and valuable possessions, together with fortified cities in Judah, but he gave the kingdom to Jehoram because he was the firstborn. ⁴Jehoram ascended the throne of his father, and he strengthened himself, and he put all his brothers to the sword, as well as some of the officials of Israel. ⁵Jehoram was thirty-two years old when he began to reign; he reigned eight years in Jerusalem. ⁶He walked in the way of the kings of Israel, as the house of Ahab had done, for the daughter of Ahab was his wife. He did what was evil in the sight of the LORD. ⁷Yet the LORD would not destroy the house of David because of the covenant that he had made with David and since he had promised to give a lamp to him and to his descendants forever.

8 In his days Edom revolted against the rule of Judah and set up a king of their own. ⁹Then Jehoram crossed over with his commanders and all his chariots. He set out by night and attacked the Edomites, who had surrounded him and his chariot commanders. ¹⁰So Edom has been in revolt against the rule of Judah to this day. At that time Libnah also revolted against his rule because he had forsaken the LORD, the God of his ancestors.

11 Moreover he made high places in the hill country of Judah and led the inhabitants of Jerusalem into unfaithfulness and made Judah go astray. ¹²A letter came to him from the prophet Elijah, saying, "Thus says the LORD, the God of your father David: Because you have not walked in the ways of your father Jehoshaphat or in the ways of King Asa of Judah ¹³but have walked in the way of the kings of Israel and have led Judah and the inhabitants of Jerusalem into unfaithfulness, as the house of Ahab led Israel into unfaithfulness, and because you also have killed your brothers, members of your father's house, who were better than you, ¹⁴see, the LORD will bring a great plague on your people, your children, your wives, and all your possessions, ¹⁵and you yourself will have a severe sickness with a disease of your bowels until your bowels come out, day after day, because of the disease."

16 The LORD aroused against Jehoram the anger of the Philistines and of the Arabs who are near the Cushites. ¹⁷They came up against Judah, invaded it, and carried away all the possessions they found that belonged to the king's house, along with his sons and his wives, so that no son was left to him except Jehoahaz, his youngest son.

18 After all this the LORD struck him in his bowels with an incurable disease. ¹⁹In the course of time, at the end of two years, his bowels came out because of the disease, and he died in great agony. His people made no fire in his honor like the fires made for his ancestors. ²⁰He was thirty-two years old when he began to reign; he reigned eight years in Jerusalem. He departed with no one's regret. They buried him in the city of David but not in the tombs of the kings.

w 21.2 Gk Syr: Heb *Israel*

21:1–7 Jehoram slaughters his six brothers, presumably for their wealth or due to political paranoia, a detail not offered in Kings. The narrator associates such evil deeds with his marriage to Ahab's daughter Athaliah (v. 6). This purge will return on Jehoram when Athaliah murders all but one of her grandsons (2 Chr. 22:10).

21:8–10 Troubles beset Jehoram to the east (Edom) and the west (Libnah / Tel Burna).

21:11–15 Jehoram is intent on "leading" Israel into religious infidelity (v. 11). Letter writing becomes especially important in the postexilic era (2 Chr. 36:22; Ezra 1:1; 4; 5; Neh. 2; 6; Esth. 8–9), though not exclusively (1 Kgs. 21:8–14). Elijah, Ahab's longtime nemesis (1 Kgs. 17–19; 2 Kgs. 1–2), appears nowhere else in Chronicles. He pulls no punches and warns him that his murdered brothers were better than him (2 Chr. 21:13). He and the people would suffer a terrible disease (vv. 14–15).

21:16–20 These verses portray the fulfillment of Elijah's words about Jehoram's family and the disease that would ultimately take his life. YHWH's sovereignty over the nations is expressed in the ability (literally) to "stir up"—*The LORD aroused*—the Assyrians (1 Chr. 5:26), Cyrus the Persian (2 Chr. 36:22), and now the Philistines and Arabs. The reference to Jehoahaz prepares us for chap. 22. The absence of a funeral fire (cf. 16:14) distinguishes Jehoram as Judah's most wicked king to date.

22 The inhabitants of Jerusalem made his youngest son Ahaziah king as his successor, for the troops who came with the Arabs to the camp had killed all the older sons. So Ahaziah reigned as king of Judah. ²Ahaziah was forty-two years old when he began to reign; he reigned one year in Jerusalem. His mother's name was Athaliah, a granddaughter of Omri. ³He also walked in the ways of the house of Ahab, for his mother was his counselor in doing wickedly. ⁴He did what was evil in the sight of the LORD like the house of Ahab, for after the death of his father they were his counselors, to his ruin. ⁵He even followed their advice and went with Jehoram son of King Ahab of Israel to make war against King Hazael of Aram at Ramoth-gilead. The Arameans wounded Joram, ⁶and he returned to be healed in Jezreel of the wounds that he had received at Ramah, when he fought King Hazael of Aram. And Ahaziah son of King Jehoram of Judah went down to see Joram son of Ahab in Jezreel because he was sick.

7 But it was ordained by God that the downfall of Ahaziah should come about through his going to visit Joram. For when he came there he went out with Jehoram to meet Jehu son of Nimshi, whom the LORD had anointed to destroy the house of Ahab. ⁸When Jehu was executing judgment on the house of Ahab, he met the officials of Judah and the sons of Ahaziah's brothers, who attended Ahaziah, and he killed them. ⁹He searched for Ahaziah, who was captured while hiding in Samaria and was brought to Jehu and put to death. They buried him, for they said, "He is the grandson of Jehoshaphat, who sought the LORD with all his heart." And the house of Ahaziah had no one able to rule the kingdom.

10 Now when Athaliah, Ahaziah's mother, saw that her son was dead, she set about to destroy all the royal family of the house of Judah. ¹¹But Jehoshabeath, the king's daughter, took Joash son of Ahaziah and stole him away from among the king's children who were about to be killed; she put him and his nurse in a bedroom. Thus Jehoshabeath daughter of King Jehoram and wife of the priest Jehoiada—because she was a sister of Ahaziah—hid him from Athaliah, so that she did not kill him; ¹²he remained with them six years hidden in the house of God, while Athaliah reigned over the land.

23 But in the seventh year Jehoiada strengthened himself and entered into a compact with the commanders of the hundreds, Azariah son of Jeroham, Ishmael son of Jehohanan, Azariah son of Obed, Maaseiah son of Adaiah, and Elishaphat son of Zichri. ²They went around through Judah and gathered the Levites from all the towns of Judah and the heads of families of Israel, and they came to Jerusalem.

22:1–6 *Forty-two.* Greek and Syriac translations read "twenty-two," as also the parallel in Kings (2 Kgs. 8:26). Heeding poor advice lies at the heart of Ahaziah's failure. His mother was his *counselor*, and the house of Ahab was his *counselors*, whose *advice* he heeds. As Jehoshaphat before him (2 Chr. 18), Ahaziah joins the Israelite king in battle, to his own ruin.

22:7–9 *Jehu son of Nimshi* (not the son of Hanani mentioned in 2 Chr. 19:2 and 20:34). Kings gives the full account of his bloody purge (2 Kgs. 9–10), in which he kills King Joram of Israel (also called Jehoram here), Queen Jezebel, Ahaziah of Judah, Baal worshipers, and many others. Hosea is critical of this coup (Hos. 1:4–5). Here Ahaziah is captured in Samaria (v. 9), while Kings reports his fatal wounding and death in Megiddo (2 Kgs. 9:27). Ahaziah's honorable burial is solely on the basis of Jehoshaphat's loyalty (2 Chr. 22:9). Chronicles does not report the location of his burial, though Kings locates it in Jerusalem (2 Kgs. 9:28).

22:10–12 Athaliah's bloody ambition for the throne stands in stark contrast to Jehoshabeath's protective concern for the Davidic heir Joash. Chronicles tells us that Jehoshabeath was the wife of the priest Jehoiada (v. 11), a detail not mentioned in Kings, to explain how Joash found protection in the temple. Her marriage may also reflect the Chronicler's concern for the temple's sanctity (cf. 2 Chr. 8:11). Notably, Chronicles offers no accession formula ("King X was X years old when he became king") for Athaliah, highlighting the illegitimacy of her rule.

23:1–7 The high priest Jehoiada takes the lead in reestablishing the Davidic Joash on the throne. The passage culminates in temple worship and a restored Davidic king (vv. 17–21), two key aspects of the Davidic covenant (1 Chr. 17). **23:1–3** The assembly proclaims Joash as king at the temple, the

³Then the whole assembly made a covenant with the king in the house of God. Jehoiada^x said to them, "Here is the king's son! Let him reign, as the LORD promised concerning the sons of David. ⁴This is what you are to do: one-third of you, priests and Levites, who come on duty on the Sabbath shall be gatekeepers, ⁵one-third shall be at the king's house, and one-third at the Gate of the Foundation, and all the people shall be in the courts of the house of the LORD. ⁶Do not let anyone enter the house of the LORD except the priests and ministering Levites; they may enter, for they are holy, but all the other^y people shall observe the instructions of the LORD. ⁷The Levites shall surround the king, each with his weapons in his hand, and whoever enters the house shall be killed. Stay with the king in his comings and goings."

8 The Levites and all Judah did according to all that the priest Jehoiada commanded; each brought his men who were to come on duty on the Sabbath with those who were to go off duty on the Sabbath, for the priest Jehoiada did not dismiss the divisions. ⁹The priest Jehoiada delivered to the captains the spears and the large and small shields that had been King David's, which were in the house of God, ¹⁰and he set all the people as a guard for the king, everyone with weapon in hand, from the south side of the house to the north side of the house, around the altar and the house. ¹¹Then he brought out the king's son, put the crown on him, and gave him the covenant; they proclaimed him king, and Jehoiada and his sons anointed him, and they shouted, "Long live the king!"

12 When Athaliah heard the noise of the people running and praising the king, she went into the house of the LORD to the people; ¹³when she looked, there was the king standing by his pillar at the entrance, and the captains and the trumpeters beside the king, and all the people of the land rejoicing and blowing trumpets, and the singers with their musical instruments leading in the celebration. Athaliah tore her clothes and cried, "Treason! Treason!" ¹⁴Then the priest Jehoiada brought out the captains who were set over the army, saying to them, "Bring her out between the ranks; anyone who follows her is to be put to the sword." For the priest said, "Do not put her to death in the house of the LORD." ¹⁵So they laid hands on her; she went into the entrance of the Horse Gate of the king's house, and there they put her to death.

16 Jehoiada made a covenant between himself and all the people and the king that they should be the LORD's people. ¹⁷Then all the people went to the house of Baal and tore it down; his altars and his images they broke in pieces, and they killed Mattan, the priest of Baal, in front of the altars. ¹⁸Jehoiada assigned the care of the house of the LORD to the Levitical priests whom David had organized to be in charge of the house of the LORD, to offer burnt offerings to the LORD, as it is written in the law of Moses,

x 23.3 Heb *He*   y 23.6 Heb lacks *other*

customary place for anointing kings (2 Kgs. 11:14). Once again, Chronicles highlights the crucial role of the Levites and community leaders in key events. Here they join the coup in fidelity to the Davidic covenant. **23:4–7** In contrast to Kings, Chronicles highlights the involvement of Levites from all Judah and the priests and Levites' duty to guard the temple (vv. 6–7) against defilement (cf. 2 Kgs. 11:8). They play the role of temple guardians due to their holiness (v. 6), whereas in Kings, the ranks primarily guarded the king and troops. See **"Revising/Rewriting the Bible," p. 584**.

23:8–11 The Levitical temple guards worked on a rotating basis by divisions (1 Chr. 26:1–19), with the guard changes providing an opportunity to gather forces without raising suspicion. The use of David's weapons (to preserve the Davidic dynasty) recalls 1 Chr. 18:7, where David dedicated weapons from his war with Hadadezer of Syria. Jehoiada crowns Joash and gives him *the covenant* (Heb. "testimony"). *The covenant* may refer to the agreement between the king and the people mentioned in v. 1, though using a different word. More often, the term for "testimony" refers to the covenant record placed in the ark (e.g., Exod. 25:16, 21).

23:12–15 Concern for the temple's sanctity continues to Athaliah's bitter end, as she is put to death outside the temple (vv. 14–15). The coronation of Joash takes place with singing and worship (v. 13), a detail not mentioned in Kings.

23:16–21 The high priest proceeds to enact a covenant to *be the LORD's people*, a phrase that evokes the corresponding phrase "I will be [their] God" found several times in the Hebrew Bible

with rejoicing and with singing, according to the order of David. ¹⁹He stationed the gatekeepers at the gates of the house of the LORD so that no one should enter who was in any way unclean. ²⁰And he took the captains, the nobles, the governors of the people, and all the people of the land, and they brought the king down from the house of the LORD, marching through the upper gate to the king's house. They set the king on the royal throne. ²¹So all the people of the land rejoiced, and the city was quiet after Athaliah had been killed with the sword.

24 Joash was seven years old when he began to reign; he reigned forty years in Jerusalem; his mother's name was Zibiah of Beer-sheba. ²Joash did what was right in the sight of the LORD all the days of the priest Jehoiada. ³Jehoiada got two wives for him, and he became the father of sons and daughters.

4 Some time afterward Joash decided to restore the house of the LORD. ⁵He assembled the priests and the Levites and said to them, "Go out to the cities of Judah and gather silver from all Israel to repair the house of your God, year by year, and see that you act quickly." But the Levites did not act quickly. ⁶So the king summoned Jehoiada the chief and said to him, "Why have you not required the Levites to bring in from Judah and Jerusalem the tax levied by Moses, the servant of the LORD, on² the congregation of Israel for the tent of the covenant?" ⁷For the children of Athaliah, that wicked woman, had broken into the house of God

and had even used all the dedicated things of the house of the LORD for the Baals.

8 So the king gave command, and they made a chest and set it outside the gate of the house of the LORD. ⁹A proclamation was made throughout Judah and Jerusalem to bring in for the LORD the tax that Moses the servant of God laid on Israel in the wilderness. ¹⁰All the leaders and all the people rejoiced and brought their tax and dropped it into the chest until it was full. ¹¹Whenever the chest was brought to the king's officers by the Levites, when they saw that there was a large amount of silver in it, the king's secretary and the officer of the chief priest would come and empty the chest and take it and return it to its place. So they did day after day and collected silver in abundance. ¹²The king and Jehoiada gave it to those who had charge of the work of the house of the LORD, and they hired masons and carpenters to restore the house of the LORD and also workers in iron and bronze to repair the house of the LORD. ¹³So those who were engaged in the work labored, and the repairing went forward at their hands, and they restored the house of God to its proper condition and strengthened it. ¹⁴When they had finished, they brought the rest of the silver to the king and Jehoiada, and with it were made utensils for the house of the LORD, utensils for the service and for the burnt offerings, and ladles, and vessels of gold and silver. They offered burnt offerings in the house of the LORD regularly all the days of Jehoiada.

z 24.6 Compare Vg: Heb *and*

(e.g., Exod. 6:7; Lev. 26:12; Jer. 7:23; 30:22). Covenant commitment leads to broad religious reforms (2 Chr. 23:17), the reestablishment of priestly order (vv. 18–19), and the royal house (v. 20).

24:1–3 Joash's obedience lasted only as long as Jehoiada survived (cf. Judg. 2:7), highlighting the important role of the high priest in maintaining loyalty among Davidic kings.

24:4–7 Joash's restoration of the temple follows the removal of idols and illicit altars (23:17) and implies that the temple fell into disrepair when YHWH was not worshiped. The temple's restoration required silver from *all Israel*, recalling the participation of the people in the tabernacle's (Exod. 35:21–29) and the temple's construction (1 Chr. 29:6–9, 17). However, the emphasis on *silver* (also 2 Chr. 24:11) highlights the economic decline of Israel from the days of David and Solomon (cf. 9:13–21). The *tax* refers to the half-shekel tax required for the sanctuary service in Exod. 30:12–16, though that is a onetime tax (not annual; cf. Neh. 10:33).

24:8–10 On the *tax*, see vv. 4–7. The leaders' and people's rejoicing recalls similar rejoicing when gathering material for the temple during David's reign (1 Chr. 29:6–9).

24:11–14 Temple repairs enable the reestablishment of sacrifices on the altar. As was later the case during Joash's reign (v. 18) and Ahaz's reign (28:24), apostasy led to the abandonment of the temple (28:24), while piety involved temple restoration and the return of regular worship (29:3). See **"Apostasy," p. 1238.**

15 But Jehoiada grew old and full of days and died; he was one hundred thirty years old at his death. ¹⁶And they buried him in the city of David among the kings, because he had done good in Israel and for God and his house.

17 Now after the death of Jehoiada the officials of Judah came and did obeisance to the king; then the king listened to them. ¹⁸They abandoned the house of the LORD, the God of their ancestors, and served the sacred poles[a] and the idols. And wrath came upon Judah and Jerusalem for this guilt of theirs. ¹⁹Yet he sent prophets among them to bring them back to the LORD; they testified against them, but they would not listen.

20 Then the spirit of God took possession of[b] Zechariah son of the priest Jehoiada; he stood above the people and said to them, "Thus says God: Why do you transgress the commandments of the LORD, so that you cannot prosper? Because you have forsaken the LORD, he has also forsaken you." ²¹But they conspired against him, and by command of the king they stoned him to death in the court of the house of the LORD. ²²King Joash did not remember the kindness that Jehoiada, Zechariah's father, had shown him but killed his son. As he was dying, he said, "May the LORD see and avenge!"

23 At the end of the year, the army of Aram came up against Joash. They came to Judah and Jerusalem and destroyed all the officials of the people from among them and sent all the spoil they took to the king of Damascus. ²⁴Although the army of Aram had come with few men, the LORD delivered into their hand a very great army because they had abandoned the LORD, the God of their ancestors. Thus they executed judgment on Joash.

25 When they had withdrawn, leaving him severely wounded, his servants conspired against him because of the blood of the son[c] of the priest Jehoiada, and they killed him on his bed. So he died, and they buried him in the city of David, but they did not bury him in the tombs of the kings. ²⁶Those who conspired against him were Zabad son of Shimeath the Ammonite and Jehozabad son of Shimrith the Moabite. ²⁷Accounts of his sons, and of the many oracles against him, and of the rebuilding[d] of the house of God are written in the Commentary on the Book of the Kings. And his son Amaziah succeeded him.

25 Amaziah was twenty-five years old when he began to reign, and he reigned twenty-nine years in Jerusalem. His mother's name was Jehoaddan of Jerusalem. ²He did what was right in the sight of the LORD, yet not with a true heart. ³As soon as the royal power was firmly in his hand, he killed his servants who had murdered his father the king. ⁴But he did not put their children to death, according to what is written in the law, in the book of Moses, where the LORD commanded, "The

a 24.18 Or *Asherahs*   b 24.20 Heb *clothed itself with*
c 24.25 Gk Vg: Heb *sons*   d 24.27 Heb *founding*

24:15–16 Jehoiada's age likely reflects the Chronicler's high estimation of the high priest, not his literal age. He was even buried among kings in Jerusalem.

24:17–19 Embracing idolatry led to the abandonment of the temple. Verses 18–19 summarize a pattern of prophetic intervention and rejection that repeats throughout the monarchy (e.g., 12:5–8; 16:7–10; 36:15–16).

24:20–22 *Took possession* (literally "clothed") recalls the same language as the spirit that "came upon" (i.e., clothed) Amasai in 1 Chr. 12:18. While Zechariah is Jehoiada's son, he may not be a high priest. Here he acts prophetically, issuing a stern rebuke and ultimately an appeal for vengeance (v. 22). The stoning at Joash's behest signals a tragic turn for the one who owed his enthronement to Zechariah's father.

24:23–27 Aram threatened Judah during Asa's reign (2 Chr. 16), was Jehoshaphat's opponent while allied with Ahab (2 Chr. 18), and was Ahaziah's opponent while allied with Jehoram (2 Chr. 22). An Ammonite and a Moabite conspired to avenge Zechariah's death by killing Joash, fulfilling the appeal in v. 22. In contrast to Jehoiada (v. 16), Joash is not buried among Judah's kings.

2 Chr. 25 Like Joash, Amaziah lived faithfully (vv. 5–12) but then fell into apostasy (vv. 13–28). See **"Apostasy," p. 1238**.

25:1–4 Amaziah enacts justice but refuses to extend punishment to the children of guilty parents (Deut. 24:16), a principle of proportionate justice also expressed in Jer. 31:29–30 and Ezek. 18:19–24.

parents shall not be put to death for the children or the children be put to death for the parents, but all shall be put to death for their own sins."

5 Amaziah assembled the people of Judah and set them by ancestral houses under commanders of the thousands and of the hundreds for all Judah and Benjamin. He mustered those twenty years old and up and found that they were three hundred thousand picked troops fit for war, able to handle spear and shield. 6He also hired one hundred thousand mighty warriors from Israel for one hundred talents of silver. 7But a man of God came to him and said, "O king, do not let the army of Israel go with you, for the LORD is not with Israel—all these Ephraimites. 8Rather, go by yourself and act; be strong in battle, or God will fling you down before the enemy, for God has power to help or to overthrow." 9Amaziah said to the man of God, "But what shall we do about the hundred talents that I have given to the army of Israel?" The man of God answered, "The LORD is able to give you much more than this." 10Then Amaziah discharged the army that had come to him from Ephraim, letting them go home again. But they became very angry with Judah and returned home in fierce anger.

11 Amaziah strengthened himself and led out his people; he went to the Valley of Salt and struck down ten thousand men of Seir. 12The people of Judah captured another ten thousand alive, took them to the top of Sela, and threw them down from the top of Sela, so that all of them were dashed to pieces.

13But the men of the army whom Amaziah sent back, not letting them go with him to battle, fell on the cities of Judah from Samaria to Beth-horon; they killed three thousand people in them and took much plunder.

14 Now after Amaziah came from the slaughter of the Edomites, he brought the gods of the people of Seir, set them up as his gods, and worshiped them, making offerings to them. 15The LORD was angry with Amaziah and sent to him a prophet, who said to him, "Why have you resorted to a people's gods who could not deliver their own people from your hand?" 16But as he was speaking, the king*e* said to him, "Have we made you a royal counselor? Stop! Why should you be put to death?" So the prophet stopped but said, "I know that God has determined to destroy you because you have done this and have not listened to my advice."

17 Then King Amaziah of Judah took counsel and sent to King Joash son of Jehoahaz son of Jehu of Israel, saying, "Come, let us look one another in the face." 18King Joash of Israel sent word to King Amaziah of Judah, "A thornbush on Lebanon sent to a cedar on Lebanon, saying, 'Give your daughter to my son for a wife,' but a wild animal of Lebanon passed by and trampled down the thornbush. 19You say, 'See, I*f* have defeated Edom,' and your heart has lifted you up in boastfulness. Now stay at home; why should you provoke trouble so that you fall, you and Judah with you?"

e 25.16 Heb *he*   *f* 25.19 Gk ms OL Tg Vg: Heb *you*

25:5–10 Amaziah musters a Judean and Benjaminite army to confront an enemy, not named until v. 11. The prophetic warning to avoid partnering with Israelite soldiers recalls similar alliances between Judah and Israel (2 Chr. 18; 22). Divine presence is consistently associated with Judah in Chronicles (2 Chr. 13:12; 15:9). Obedience requires a willingness to accept financial losses for the hope of future reward (v. 9).

25:11–13 The brutal assassination of ten thousand Edomites (v. 12) evokes past grievances against Edom in Ps. 137:7, Lam. 4:21, Ezek. 25:12, and Obad. 1:8, 10. Disbanding the northern fighters leads to a slaughter from the northern to southern kingdoms. Though in Judah, Upper and Lower Beth-horon were built by Ephraim's daughter (1 Chr. 7:24; cf. Josh. 16:3, 5).

25:14–16 In a spectacular failure, Amaziah takes and venerates, rather than burns (Deut. 7:25; 1 Chr. 14:12), the gods of Edom. As we often see in Chronicles, the Lord sends a prophet whom the king rejects (see comment on 2 Chr. 24:17–19).

25:17–19 Amaziah stokes war with Israel, presumably in retaliation for the slaughter in v. 13, an act attributed to arrogance (v. 19). The thornbush image occurs in Judg. 9:14 to describe an unqualified "king" whom the people convince to rule and who leads them to their own destruction. Joash of Israel warns Amaziah of a similar fate.

20 But Amaziah would not listen—it was God's doing, in order to hand them over because they had sought the gods of Edom. ²¹So King Joash of Israel went up; he and King Amaziah of Judah faced one another in battle at Beth-shemesh, which belongs to Judah. ²²Judah was defeated by Israel; everyone fled home. ²³King Joash of Israel captured King Amaziah of Judah son of Joash son of Ahaziah at Beth-shemesh; he brought him to Jerusalem and broke down the wall of Jerusalem from the Ephraim Gate to the Corner Gate, a distance of four hundred cubits. ²⁴He seized all the gold and silver, and all the vessels that were found in the house of God, and Obed-edom with them; he seized also the treasuries of the king's house, also hostages; then he returned to Samaria.

25 King Amaziah son of Joash of Judah lived fifteen years after the death of King Joash son of Jehoahaz of Israel. ²⁶Now the rest of the deeds of Amaziah, from first to last, are they not written in the Book of the Kings of Judah and Israel? ²⁷From the time that Amaziah turned away from the LORD, they made a conspiracy against him in Jerusalem, and he fled to Lachish. But they sent after him to Lachish and killed him there. ²⁸They brought him back on horses; he was buried with his ancestors in the city of David.

26 Then all the people of Judah took Uzziah, who was sixteen years old, and made him king to succeed his father Amaziah. ²He rebuilt Eloth and restored it to Judah, after the king slept with his ancestors. ³Uzziah was sixteen years old when he began to reign, and he reigned fifty-two years in Jerusalem. His mother's name was Jecoliah of Jerusalem. ⁴He did what was right in the sight of the LORD, just as his father Amaziah had done. ⁵He set himself to seek God in the days of Zechariah, who instructed him in the fear[g] of God, and as long as he sought the LORD, God made him prosper.

6 He went out and made war against the Philistines and broke down the wall of Gath and the wall of Jabneh and the wall of Ashdod; he built cities in the territory of Ashdod and elsewhere among the Philistines. ⁷God helped him against the Philistines, against the Arabs who lived in Gur-baal, and against the Meunites. ⁸The Ammonites paid tribute to Uzziah, and his fame spread even to the border of Egypt, for he became very strong. ⁹Moreover Uzziah built towers in Jerusalem at the Corner Gate, at the Valley Gate, and at the Angle and fortified them. ¹⁰He built towers in the wilderness and dug out many cisterns, for he had large herds, both in the Shephelah and in the

g 26.5 Gk: Heb *the visions*

25:20–24 The Chronicler attributes Amaziah's refusal to heed the warning to God's judgment for idolatry. He also refused to listen in v. 16, as would Josiah later (35:22). Beth-shemesh (v. 21) is just twenty miles west of Jerusalem. The damage to Jerusalem's walls and the temple plundering presage the city and temple's ultimate destruction (36:19), just as the taking of *hostages* (v. 24) anticipates Judah's ultimate exile. *Obed-edom* was a Levite, according to Chronicles (1 Chr. 15:18), and would have been long dead by this point. The text likely refers to the fact that the vessels were in Obed-edom's care, just as the ark had been in his tent (1 Chr. 13:13). Thus Amaziah, who worshiped the gods of Edom, ended up losing the temple's vessels for which Obed-edom cared.

25:25–28 The Chronicler links the plot to assassinate Amaziah to his apostasy (v. 27). Lachish lies in the Shephelah, the lowlands to the west, about thirty miles from Jerusalem, and was fortified by Rehoboam (11:9).

26:1–5 Uzziah (Azariah in Kings) comes from the Jerusalem side of Amaziah's family, a detail that likely fuels his efforts at fortifying Jerusalem (v. 9) but may also inspire the entitlement he feels toward the temple (vv. 16–21). Eloth (Elath in Kings) sits on the extreme southern end of Judah on the Gulf of Aqaba. Like Joash, Uzziah's pursuit of God and consequent successes are linked to the life of the high priest (v. 5; cf. 24:1–3).

26:6–10 The list of Uzziah's military and infrastructure achievements is impressive and focuses on the expansion toward the south. Chronicles offers little by way of rationale for the war on the Philistines, though control of the Shephelah (the lowlands between Philistia and Judah) for farming purposes (v. 10) was undoubtedly a motive. Whereas Jerusalem was breached during his father's reign (25:23), Uzziah breached the walls of Gath, Jabneh, and Ashdod and repaired Jerusalem. The wilderness towers (v. 10; cf. 1 Chr. 27:25; 2 Chr. 27:4) likely refer to the fortresses that lined the Negev.

plain, and he had farmers and vinedressers in the hills and in the fertile lands, for he loved the soil. ¹¹Moreover, Uzziah had an army of soldiers, fit for war, in divisions according to the numbers in the muster made by the secretary Jeiel and the officer Maaseiah, under the direction of Hananiah, one of the king's commanders. ¹²The whole number of the heads of ancestral houses of mighty warriors was two thousand six hundred. ¹³Under their command was an army of three hundred seven thousand five hundred, who could make war with mighty power to help the king against the enemy. ¹⁴Uzziah provided for all the army the shields, spears, helmets, coats of mail, bows, and stones for slinging. ¹⁵In Jerusalem he set up machines, invented by skilled workers, on the towers and the corners for shooting arrows and large stones. And his fame spread far, for he was marvelously helped until he became strong.

16 But when he had become strong he grew proud, to his destruction. For he acted unfaithfully toward the LORD his God and entered the temple of the LORD to make offering on the altar of incense. ¹⁷But the priest Azariah went in after him, with eighty priests of the LORD who were men of valor; ¹⁸they withstood King Uzziah and said to him, "It is not for you, Uzziah, to make

offering to the LORD, but for the priests the descendants of Aaron, who are consecrated to make offering. Go out of the sanctuary, for you have acted unfaithfully, and it will bring you no honor from the LORD God." ¹⁹Then Uzziah was enraged. Now he had a censer in his hand to make offering, and when he became enraged with the priests a defiling disease broke out on his forehead, in the presence of the priests in the house of the LORD, by the altar of incense. ²⁰When the chief priest Azariah, and all the priests, looked at him, he was diseased on his forehead. They hurried him out, and he himself hurried to get out, because the LORD had struck him. ²¹King Uzziah had a defiling disease to the day of his death, and being diseased lived in a separate house, for he was excluded from the house of the LORD. His son Jotham was in charge of the palace of the king, governing the people of the land.

22 Now the rest of the acts of Uzziah, from first to last, the prophet Isaiah son of Amoz wrote. ²³Uzziah slept with his ancestors; they buried him near his ancestors in the burial field that belonged to the kings, for they said, "He had a defiling disease." His son Jotham succeeded him.

27 Jotham was twenty-five years old when he began to reign; he reigned

In addition to their function as military forts (see vv. 11–15), the towers also provided lookouts for the protection of vineyards, farmlands, and herds (cf. Isa. 5:2). The comment that Uzziah *loved the soil* offers a personal window into his motivations.

26:11–15 With similar detail, the Chronicler outlines Uzziah's military armaments, including the armor and weaponry of individual soldiers (v. 14) and the large machines set up in Jerusalem, which included a catapult (v. 15). With all these achievements, Chronicles is setting us up for his fall (26:16–23).

26:16–20 Chronicles frequently describes the downfall of Judah's kings at the very height of their power: Rehoboam (2 Chr. 12:1–4), Asa (16:9), Jehoshaphat (20:35–36), Hezekiah (32:25), and Josiah (35:21). The story of Uzziah follows this pattern, though it focuses specifically on his cultic infringement. Offering incense on the altar was the exclusive domain of priests, for it resided in the holy place (Exod. 30:7; 40:5; Num. 18:1–7; 2 Chr. 4:19). Accusing Uzziah of acting *unfaithfully* (v. 18) aligns the king with the rebellious northern tribes (1 Chr. 5:25), Saul's rebellion (1 Chr. 10:13), Rehoboam's rebellion (2 Chr. 12:2), Asa's disobedience (2 Chr. 16:12), and even the root cause of Judah's exile (1 Chr. 9:1). Just as Asa suffered a disease for his unfaithfulness (2 Chr. 16:12), so too did Uzziah. His disease instantly put him in a dangerous position (v. 19), for defilement was prohibited in the sanctuary (cf. Lev. 13:46).

26:21–23 Jotham served as a co-regent in Uzziah's final days. Isaiah makes little reference to Uzziah, though his famous temple vision occurs in the "year that King Uzziah died" (Isa. 6:1). Uzziah's burial notice reflects the ambivalence about his character. He is honored among kings but not in their tombs.

27:1–2 The house of Zadok was established as the high priestly family during David's and Solomon's reigns (1 Chr. 29:22; cf. 2 Chr. 31:10), and another priest by that name served in the postexilic

sixteen years in Jerusalem. His mother's name was Jerushah daughter of Zadok. ²He did what was right in the sight of the Lord just as his father Uzziah had done—only he did not enter the temple of the Lord. But the people still followed corrupt practices. ³He built the upper gate of the house of the Lord and did extensive building on the wall of Ophel. ⁴Moreover, he built cities in the hill country of Judah and forts and towers on the wooded hills. ⁵He fought with the king of the Ammonites and prevailed against them. The Ammonites gave him that year one hundred talents of silver, ten thousand cors of wheat, and ten thousand of barley. The Ammonites paid him the same amount in the second and the third years. ⁶So Jotham strengthened himself because he ordered his ways before the Lord his God. ⁷Now the rest of the acts of Jotham and all his wars and his ways are written in the Book of the Kings of Israel and Judah. ⁸He was twenty-five years old when he began to reign; he reigned sixteen years in Jerusalem. ⁹Jotham slept with his ancestors, and they buried him in the city of David, and his son Ahaz succeeded him.

28

Ahaz was twenty years old when he began to reign; he reigned sixteen years in Jerusalem. He did not do what was right in the sight of the Lord, as his ancestor David had done, ²but he walked in the ways of the kings of Israel. He even made cast images for the Baals, ³and he made offerings in the valley of the son of Hinnom and made his sons pass through fire, according to the abominable practices of the nations whom the Lord had driven out before the people of Israel. ⁴He sacrificed and made offerings on the high places, on the hills, and under every green tree.

5 Therefore the Lord his God gave him into the hand of the king of Aram, who defeated him and took captive a great number of his people and brought them to Damascus. He was also given into the hand of the king of Israel, who defeated him with great slaughter. ⁶Pekah son of Remaliah killed one hundred twenty thousand in Judah in one day, all of them valiant warriors, because they had abandoned the Lord, the God of their ancestors. ⁷And Zichri, a mighty warrior of Ephraim, killed the king's son Maaseiah, Azrikam the commander of the palace, and Elkanah the next in authority to the king.

8 The people of Israel took captive two hundred thousand of their kin: women, sons, and daughters; they also took much spoil from them and brought the spoil to Samaria. ⁹But a prophet of the Lord was there whose name was Oded; he went out to meet the army that came to Samaria

---

period (1 Chr. 9:11; Ezra 7:2). It is unclear whether this Zadok (v. 1) is another priest with whom the royal house mixes (cf. 2 Chr. 22:1). As on other occasions, the Chronicler foregrounds the king's relationship to the temple in his evaluative comments. Notably, Chronicles omits the report of Hezekiah entering the temple (2 Kgs. 19:1; 2 Chr. 32:20). The people's persistent sin sets the stage for the corrupt king who follows (2 Chr. 28).

27:3–7 *Ophel* likely refers to the area between the city of David and the Temple Mount, descending south from the east ridge of the Temple Mount. The Ammonites had been subject to Jotham's father, Uzziah (26:8), and apparently rebelled before Jotham resubjugated them. Tribute items reflect the growing potential of Transjordanian Ammon. The reference to tribute in *the second and the third years* (v. 5) could be taken in positive terms (*even* to the third year) or negative terms (for *only* three years).

2 Chr. 28 Chronicles judges Ahaz to be the worst of Judah's kings, most notably for his utter disregard for the temple.

28:1–4 Ahaz's sins follow the ways of Israel's kings (v. 2) and the Canaanite nations (v. 3). The reference to *cast images for the Baals* is not found in the Chronicler's source (2 Kgs. 16:3), but it shows the extent of Ahaz's imitation of Israel (cf. 2 Chr. 13:8–9; 24:17–18).

28:5–7 The joint Aram-Israelite coalition against Israel forms the backdrop to Isa. 7–8, where Ahaz succumbs to the fear of nations rather than the fear of YHWH. The phrase *took captive* (vv. 5, 8, 11, 17) highlights the theme of mini "exiles" that precede Judah's final exile (cf. 2 Chr. 21:17; 30:9). Judah *abandoned the Lord* (v. 6) just as the north had done (2 Chr. 13:11).

28:8–11 The otherwise unknown prophet Oded confronts Israel for their merciless slaughter and enslavement of their Judean *kin* (vv. 8, 10). They exceeded their divine mandate, highlighting the

and said to them, "Because the LORD, the God of your ancestors, was angry with Judah, he gave them into your hand, but you have killed them in a rage that has reached up to heaven. [10]Now you intend to subjugate the people of Judah and Jerusalem, male and female, as your slaves. But what have you except sins against the LORD your God? [11]Now hear me, and send back the captives whom you have taken from your kindred, for the fierce wrath of the LORD is upon you." [12]Moreover, certain chiefs of the Ephraimites, Azariah son of Johanan, Berechiah son of Meshillemoth, Jehizkiah son of Shallum, and Amasa son of Hadlai, stood up against those who were coming from the war [13]and said to them, "You shall not bring the captives in here, for you propose to bring on us guilt against the LORD in addition to our present sins and guilt. For our guilt is already great, and there is fierce wrath against Israel." [14]So the warriors left the captives and the plunder before the officials and all the assembly. [15]Then those who were mentioned by name got up and took the captives, and with the spoil they clothed all who were naked among them; they clothed them, gave them sandals, provided them with food and drink, and anointed them; and carrying all the feeble among them on donkeys, they brought them to their kindred at Jericho, the city of palm trees. Then they returned to Samaria.

16 At that time King Ahaz sent to the king[h] of Assyria for help. [17]For the Edomites had again invaded and defeated Judah and carried away captives. [18]And the Philistines had made raids on the cities in the Shephelah and the Negeb of Judah and had taken Beth-shemesh, Aijalon, Gederoth, Soco with its villages, Timnah with its villages, and Gimzo with its villages, and they settled there. [19]For the LORD brought Judah low because of King Ahaz of Israel, for he had behaved without restraint in Judah and had been faithless to the LORD. [20]So King Tiglath-pileser[i] of Assyria came against him and oppressed him instead of strengthening him. [21]For Ahaz plundered the house of the LORD and the houses of the king and of the officials and gave tribute to the king of Assyria, but it did not help him.

22 In the time of his distress he became yet more faithless to the LORD—this same King Ahaz. [23]For he sacrificed to the gods of Damascus that had defeated him and said, "Because the gods of the kings of Aram helped them, I will sacrifice to them so that they may help me." But they were the ruin of him and of all Israel. [24]Ahaz gathered together the utensils of the house of God and cut in pieces the utensils of the house of God. He shut up the doors of the house of the LORD and made himself altars in every corner of Jerusalem. [25]In every city of Judah he made high places to make offerings to

h 28.16 Gk Syr Vg: Heb *kings*   i 28.20 Heb *Tilgath-pilneser*

point that even agents of divine wrath are held accountable for the extent and nature of their wrath (cf. Isa. 10:6–7). Israel was forbidden from enslaving their "kin" (Lev. 25:39; cf. Neh. 5:5). See **"Human Bondage in Ancient Israel (The Law)," p. 115**.

28:12–15 Remarkably, Chronicles recounts the opposition to this enslavement plan from within Ephraim (i.e., the most prominent northern tribe). Courageous leadership prevents disaster for the north and leads to a humanitarian response (v. 15). The northern admission of guilt and repatriation prepare the way for a unified Israel under Hezekiah. The provision of food, drink, and anointing by those from Samaria, as well as the mention of *Jericho*, suggests this story as a backdrop to the Good Samaritan parable (Luke 10:25–37).

28:16–21 Verse 17 mentions yet another captivity, and Philistine invasions in the Shephelah (see comment on 2 Chr. 25:25–28) prompt an appeal to Assyria. Isaiah considers this appeal contrary to the Lord's purposes (Isa. 8:6–8, 12–15), though in his account, it is the Israelites and Arameans as aggressors. *Tiglath-pileser* (III) ruled Assyria from 744 to 727 BCE and introduced an aggressively expansionistic policy to the Assyrian Empire. Helping Judah with their immediate troubles brought oppression in the form of crushing taxation and tribute. Ahaz's sin is highlighted with the word *faithless* (literally "utterly unfaithful"; v. 19).

28:22–27 *For he sacrificed.* Ahaz's folly finds succinct expression here. Kings details how Ahaz built a Damascene altar in the Jerusalem temple (2 Kgs. 16:10), likely symbolizing his subordination to Assyria. Ahaz's egregious crimes included closing the temple and building idolatrous altars throughout Jerusalem and Judah. Once again, we see that pagan worship led to the cessation of

other gods, provoking to anger the Lord, the God of his ancestors. [26]Now the rest of his acts and all his ways, from first to last, are written in the Book of the Kings of Judah and Israel. [27]Ahaz slept with his ancestors, and they buried him in the city, in Jerusalem, but they did not bring him into the tombs of the kings of Israel. His son Hezekiah succeeded him.

29 Hezekiah began to reign when he was twenty-five years old; he reigned twenty-nine years in Jerusalem. His mother's name was Abijah daughter of Zechariah. [2]He did what was right in the sight of the Lord, just as his ancestor David had done.

3 In the first year of his reign, in the first month, he opened the doors of the house of the Lord and repaired them. [4]He brought in the priests and the Levites and assembled them in the square on the east. [5]He said to them, "Listen to me, Levites! Sanctify yourselves, and sanctify the house of the Lord, the God of your ancestors, and carry out the filth from the holy place. [6]For our ancestors have been unfaithful and have done what was evil in the sight of the Lord our God; they have forsaken him and have turned away their faces from the dwelling of the Lord and turned their backs. [7]They also shut the doors of the vestibule and put out the lamps and have not offered incense or made burnt offerings in the holy place to the God of Israel. [8]Therefore the wrath of the Lord came upon Judah and Jerusalem, and he has made them an object of horror, of astonishment, and of hissing, as you see with your own eyes. [9]Our fathers have fallen by the sword and our sons and our daughters and our wives are in captivity for this. [10]Now it is in my heart to make a covenant with the Lord, the God of Israel, so that his fierce anger may turn away from us. [11]My sons, do not now be negligent, for the Lord has chosen you to stand in his presence to minister to him and to be his ministers and offer incense."

12 Then the Levites arose, Mahath son of Amasai and Joel son of Azariah, of the sons of the Kohathites; and of the sons of Merari, Kish son of Abdi and Azariah son of Jehallel; and of the Gershonites, Joah son of Zimmah and Eden son of Joah; [13]and of the sons of Elizaphan, Shimri and Jeuel; and of the sons of Asaph, Zechariah and Mattaniah; [14]and of the sons of Heman, Jehuel and Shimei; and of the sons of Jeduthun, Shemaiah and Uzziel. [15]They gathered their brothers, sanctified themselves, and went in as the king had commanded, by the words of the Lord, to cleanse the house of the Lord. [16]The priests went into the inner part of the house of the Lord to cleanse it,

worship at the temple (2 Chr. 24:18; 29:3, 6; 33:16). YHWH worship makes a glorious comeback when Hezekiah reopens the temple's doors (29:3).

2 Chr. 29 Whereas the books of Kings and Isaiah focus on the Assyrian threats during Hezekiah's reign, Chronicles focuses on his worship reforms, Passover celebration, and efforts to unify Israel. Hezekiah's reforms occur in three phases and involve the purification of the temple (vv. 12–19), the city (30:14), and the land (31:1), with only the latter mentioned in Kings (2 Kgs. 18:4). See **"Revising/ Rewriting the Bible," p. 584**.

29:1–2 The enthronement notice removes Kings's reference to Hezekiah's idolatrous father, Ahaz (2 Kgs. 18:1), but retains the link to his spiritual and biological ancestor David. Abijah's father (v. 1) may be the same Zechariah mentioned in 2 Chr. 26, the Jerusalem leader mentioned in Isa. 8:1–4, or an otherwise unknown Judahite.

29:3–11 Hezekiah's speech highlights important themes in Chronicles, including the need for Levites and priests to carry out their duties (vv. 5, 11), the acknowledgment of ancestral guilt (v. 6), the link between divine wrath and temple neglect (vv. 6–9), and covenant renewal (v. 10). Each of these themes would have been crucial for the Chronicler's postexilic audience. Reforms begin with the temple on the very first day of Hezekiah's reign, on the first month, and emanate outward. Hezekiah joins ranks with other reformer-kings before him, including Asa (15:9–15), Jehoshaphat (19:8–11), and Joash (24:4–14).

29:12–14 The list includes the major Levitical families (Kohathites, Merarites, and Gershonites) and their musical families of Asaph, Heman, and Jeduthun.

29:15–19 The *Wadi Kidron* (v. 16) is where Asa smashed and burned the Asherah pole remains from Maacah (15:16). Hezekiah also carries forward Asa's removal of high places from Judah (14:3)

and they brought out all the unclean things that they found in the temple of the LORD into the court of the house of the LORD, and the Levites took them and carried them out to the Wadi Kidron. ¹⁷They began to sanctify on the first day of the first month, and on the eighth day of the month they came to the vestibule of the LORD; then for eight days they sanctified the house of the LORD, and on the sixteenth day of the first month they finished. ¹⁸Then they went inside to King Hezekiah and said, "We have cleansed all the house of the LORD, the altar of burnt offering and all its utensils, and the table for the rows of bread and all its utensils. ¹⁹All the utensils that King Ahaz discarded during his reign when he was faithless, we have restored and sanctified; see, they are in front of the altar of the LORD."

20 Then King Hezekiah rose early, assembled the officials of the city, and went up to the house of the LORD. ²¹They brought seven bulls, seven rams, seven lambs, and seven male goats for a sin offering for the kingdom and for the sanctuary and for Judah. He commanded the priests the descendants of Aaron to offer them on the altar of the LORD. ²²So they slaughtered the bulls, and the priests received the blood and dashed it against the altar; they slaughtered the rams, and their blood was dashed against the altar; they also slaughtered the lambs, and their blood was dashed against the altar. ²³Then the male goats for the sin offering were brought to the king and the assembly; they laid their hands on them, ²⁴and the priests slaughtered them and made a sin offering with their blood at the altar, to make atonement for all Israel. For the king commanded that the burnt offering and the sin offering should be made for all Israel.

25 He stationed the Levites in the house of the LORD with cymbals, harps, and lyres, according to the commandment of David and of Gad the king's seer and of the prophet Nathan, for the commandment was from the LORD through his prophets. ²⁶The Levites stood with the instruments of David and the priests with the trumpets. ²⁷Then Hezekiah commanded that the burnt offering be offered on the altar. When the burnt offering began, the song to the LORD began also, and the trumpets, accompanied by the instruments of King David of Israel. ²⁸The whole assembly worshiped, the singers sang, and the trumpeters sounded; all this continued until the burnt offering was finished. ²⁹When the offering was finished, the king and all who were present with him bowed down and worshiped. ³⁰King Hezekiah and the officials commanded the Levites to sing praises to the LORD with the words of David and of the seer Asaph. They sang praises with gladness, and they bowed down and worshiped.

31 Then Hezekiah said, "You have now consecrated yourselves to the LORD; come near and bring sacrifices and thank offerings to the house of the LORD." The assembly brought sacrifices and thank offerings, and all who were of a willing heart brought burnt offerings. ³²The number of the burnt offerings that the assembly brought was seventy bulls, one hundred rams, and two hundred lambs; all these were for a burnt offering to the LORD. ³³The consecrated

by removing them from all the land (31:1). The temple's purification took sixteen days (v. 17), explaining the delay of Passover (30:3), which would have normally taken place on the fourteenth of the first month (Exod. 12:6).

29:20–24 The *sin*, or purification, offering (cf. Lev. 4:4–21) was efficacious for the royal house, the temple, and all people in Judah (v. 21) and Israel (v. 24). Purification was different from moral reckoning in that it focused on enabling the worshiper to enter divine presence or the temple's ability to house divine presence. However, this purification certainly included the removal of contamination from moral sins such as idolatry that hindered such fellowship. See **"Holiness and Purity," p. 158.**

29:25–30 Moses's laws regarding sacrifice (vv. 20–24) parallel David's commands regarding temple worship (vv. 25–30). Chronicles underscores the authority of David's commands by mentioning two prophetic figures, Gad and Nathan (v. 25). Levitical and priestly worship often accompanies the arrival of divine presence in Chronicles (2 Chr. 7:1–6; 20:21–22), which purification would have facilitated (vv. 20–24). The *burnt offering* is frequently associated with praise in the Old Testament.

29:31–36 The people participate with such willingness and joy (cf. 1 Chr. 29:5) that the priests could not keep up (v. 34). Chronicles also signals the need for flexibility in Levitical (i.e., nonpriestly

offerings were six hundred bulls and three thousand sheep. [34]But the priests were too few and could not skin all the burnt offerings, so, until other priests had sanctified themselves, their kindred, the Levites, helped them until the work was finished, for the Levites were more conscientious[j] than the priests in sanctifying themselves. [35]Besides the great number of burnt offerings there was the fat of the offerings of well-being, and there were the drink offerings for the burnt offerings. Thus the service of the house of the LORD was restored. [36]And Hezekiah and all the people rejoiced because of what God had done for the people, for the thing had come about suddenly.

30 Hezekiah sent word to all Israel and Judah and wrote letters also to Ephraim and Manasseh, that they should come to the house of the LORD at Jerusalem, to keep the Passover to the LORD the God of Israel. [2]For the king and his officials and all the assembly in Jerusalem had taken counsel to keep the Passover in the second month [3](for they could not keep it at its proper time because the priests had not sanctified themselves in sufficient number, nor had the people assembled in Jerusalem). [4]The plan seemed right to the king and all the assembly. [5]So they decreed to make a proclamation throughout all Israel, from Beer-sheba to Dan, that the people should come and keep the Passover to the LORD the God of Israel, at Jerusalem, for they had not kept it in great numbers as prescribed. [6]So couriers went throughout all Israel and Judah with letters from the king and his officials, as the king had commanded, saying, "O people of Israel, return to the LORD, the God of Abraham, Isaac, and Israel, so that he may turn again to the remnant of you who have escaped from the hand of the kings of Assyria. [7]Do not be like your ancestors and your kindred, who were faithless to the LORD God of their ancestors, so that he made them a desolation, as you see. [8]Do not now be stiff-necked as your ancestors were, but yield yourselves to the LORD and come to his sanctuary, which he has sanctified forever, and serve the LORD your God, so that his fierce anger may turn away from you. [9]For as you return to the LORD, your kindred and your children will find compassion with their captors and return to this land. For the LORD your God is gracious and merciful and will not turn away his face from you, if you return to him."

10 So the couriers went from city to city through the country of Ephraim and Manasseh, and as far as Zebulun, but they laughed them to scorn and mocked them. [11]Only a few from Asher, Manasseh, and Zebulun humbled themselves and came to Jerusalem. [12]The hand of God was also on Judah to give them one heart to do what the king and the officials commanded by the word of the LORD.

13 Many people came together in Jerusalem to keep the Festival of Unleavened Bread in the second month, a very large assembly. [14]They set to work and removed the

j 29.34 Heb *upright in heart*

Levitical) duties, which here involve the status of the participants in the preparation of the burnt offerings (cf. 2 Chr. 35:11). Leviticus maintains that preparation was the duty of the offerer (Lev. 1:5–6; 3:2). These flexible arrangements anticipate the flexible date of Passover in 2 Chr. 30:1–3 and highlight the tolerance for adaptable worship rituals. *Well-being* and *drink* offerings (v. 35) accompany the burnt and purification offerings already presented. See **"Offerings and Sacrifices," p. 146.**

30:1 Hezekiah sent Passover invitations to all Israel, including northerners who were alienated from Judah after becoming part of the Assyrian Empire (vv. 1–2).

30:2–9 Hezekiah extends an offer to *return to the LORD* (v. 6) and *come to his sanctuary* (v. 8). Just as Joshua celebrated a Passover in the land upon first entry (Josh. 5), so Hezekiah celebrates Passover after the land's purification and the return of many to Judah. The faithlessness of previous generations (v. 7) brought YHWH's *fierce anger* (v. 8). The removal of that wrath depends here on this return to the temple (v. 8). God's *gracious and merciful* character (v. 9) is theologically foundational in the Pentateuch (Exod. 34:6–7) and characteristic of Israel's praise (Pss. 103:8; 111:4; 112:4; 145:8).

30:10–12 The mixed response of the northerners contrasts with Judah's *one heart* response. Earlier, Judah joined with "one heart" to make David king (1 Chr. 12:38) and to build the temple (1 Chr. 29:19).

30:13–14 The *Festival of Unleavened Bread* includes the Passover celebration and the seven-day celebration of unleavened bread (Exod. 12:14–18; Lev. 23:5–6; Num. 28:16–17). Having already

altars that were in Jerusalem, and all the altars for offering incense they took away and threw into the Wadi Kidron. [15]They slaughtered the Passover lamb on the fourteenth day of the second month. The priests and the Levites were ashamed, and they sanctified themselves and brought burnt offerings into the house of the LORD. [16]They took their accustomed posts according to the law of Moses the man of God; the priests dashed the blood that they received[k] from the hands of the Levites. [17]For there were many in the assembly who had not sanctified themselves; therefore the Levites had to slaughter the Passover lamb for everyone who was not clean, to make it holy to the LORD. [18]For a multitude of the people, many of them from Ephraim, Manasseh, Issachar, and Zebulun, had not cleansed themselves, yet they ate the Passover contrary to what was prescribed. But Hezekiah prayed for them, saying, "May the good LORD pardon all [19]who set their hearts to seek God, the LORD the God of their ancestors, even though not in accordance with the sanctuary's rules of cleanness." [20]The LORD heard Hezekiah and healed the people. [21]The people of Israel who were present at Jerusalem kept the Festival of Unleavened Bread seven days with great gladness, and the Levites and the priests praised the LORD day by day, accompanied by loud instruments for the LORD. [22]Hezekiah spoke encouragingly to all the Levites who showed good skill in the service of the LORD. So the people ate the food of the festival for seven days, sacrificing

offerings of well-being and giving thanks to the LORD the God of their ancestors.

23 Then the whole assembly agreed together to keep the festival for another seven days, so they kept it for another seven days with gladness. [24]For King Hezekiah of Judah gave the assembly a thousand bulls and seven thousand sheep for offerings, and the officials gave the assembly a thousand bulls and ten thousand sheep. The priests sanctified themselves in great numbers. [25]The whole assembly of Judah, the priests and the Levites, and the whole assembly that came out of Israel, and the resident aliens who came out of the land of Israel, and the resident aliens who lived in Judah rejoiced. [26]There was great joy in Jerusalem, for since the time of Solomon son of King David of Israel there had been nothing like this in Jerusalem. [27]Then the priests and the Levites stood up and blessed the people, and their voice was heard; their prayer came to his holy dwelling in heaven.

31 Now when all this was finished, all Israel who were present went out to the cities of Judah and broke down the pillars, cut down the sacred poles,[l] and pulled down the high places and the altars throughout all Judah and Benjamin, and in Ephraim and Manasseh, until they had destroyed them all. Then all the people of Israel returned to their cities, all to their individual properties.

k 30.16 Heb lacks *that they received* l 31.1 Or *Asherahs*

purified the temple (2 Chr. 29), the people now remove the altars that Ahaz had installed in Jerusalem (28:24).
    30:15–19 The priests' and Levites' shame may relate to (1) the people's zeal (29:31–36) that they failed to match, (2) the fact that *they* (i.e., the people) slaughtered the sacrifices due to insufficient numbers of priests and Levites, or (3) the uncleanness of the people who should have been sanctified (vv. 17–18). Whatever their shortcomings, Hezekiah's prayer highlights YHWH's mercy and compassion on those who *set their hearts to seek God* (v. 19; cf. v. 9).
    30:20 *Healed* implies that some unknown affliction had beset the people, likely the *fierce anger* (v. 8) or the "wrath" from 29:8.
    30:21–22 Once again, musicians accompany offerings in God's presence (note the reference to God's *face* in v. 9; cf. 7:1–6; 20:21–22; 29:25–30).
    30:23–27 The final flexible arrangement in Hezekiah's celebration reflects an overflow of joy and abundance, which required another seven-day celebration. The unity of Israel takes center stage, as Judeans, Israelites, and foreigners among them (v. 25) celebrate together. This story of unified and inclusive worship at the temple celebrates and reflects God's covenant love and mercy (v. 9; cf. 1 Chr. 16:34; 2 Chr. 5:13).
    31:1 Celebration in Jerusalem leads to popular-led (rather than royal-led) reforms throughout the whole land, including northern tribal regions.

2 Hezekiah appointed the divisions of the priests and of the Levites, division by division, everyone according to his service, the priests and the Levites, for burnt offerings and offerings of well-being, to minister in the gates of the camp of the LORD and to give thanks and praise. ³The contribution of the king from his own possessions was for the burnt offerings: the burnt offerings of morning and evening, and the burnt offerings for the Sabbaths, the new moons, and the appointed festivals, as it is written in the law of the LORD. ⁴He commanded the people who lived in Jerusalem to give the portion due to the priests and the Levites, so that they might devote themselves to the law of the LORD. ⁵As soon as the word spread, the people of Israel gave in abundance the first fruits of grain, wine, oil, honey, and of all the produce of the field, and they brought in abundantly the tithe of everything. ⁶The people of Israel and Judah who lived in the cities of Judah also brought in the tithe of cattle and sheep and the tithe of the dedicated things that had been consecrated to the LORD their God and laid them in heaps. ⁷In the third month they began to pile up the heaps and finished them in the seventh month. ⁸When Hezekiah and the officials came and saw the heaps, they blessed the LORD and his people Israel. ⁹Hezekiah questioned the priests and the Levites about the heaps. ¹⁰The chief priest Azariah, who was of the house of Zadok, answered him, "Since they began to bring the contributions into the house of the LORD, we have had enough to eat and have plenty to spare, for the LORD has blessed his people, so that we have this great supply left over."

11 Then Hezekiah commanded them to prepare store chambers in the house of the LORD, and they prepared them. ¹²Faithfully they brought in the contributions, the tithes, and the dedicated things. The chief officer in charge of them was Conaniah the Levite, with his brother Shimei as second; ¹³while Jehiel, Azaziah, Nahath, Asahel, Jerimoth, Jozabad, Eliel, Ismachiah, Mahath, and Benaiah were overseers assisting Conaniah and his brother Shimei, by the appointment of King Hezekiah and of Azariah the chief officer of the house of God. ¹⁴Kore son of Imnah the Levite, keeper of the east gate, was in charge of the freewill offerings to God, to apportion the contribution reserved for the LORD and the most holy offerings. ¹⁵Eden, Miniamin, Jeshua, Shemaiah, Amariah, and Shecaniah were faithfully assisting him in the cities of the priests, to distribute the portions to their kindred, old and young alike, by divisions, ¹⁶except those enrolled by genealogy, males from three years old and up, all who entered the house of the LORD as the duty of each day required, for their service according to their offices, by their divisions. ¹⁷The enrollment of the priests was according to their ancestral houses; that of the Levites from twenty years old and up was according to their offices, by their divisions. ¹⁸They were enrolled with all their little children, their wives, their sons, and their daughters, the whole multitude, for they were faithful in keeping themselves holy. ¹⁹And for the descendants of Aaron, the priests, who were in the fields of pastureland belonging to their towns, town by town, the people designated by name were to distribute portions to every male among the priests and to everyone among the Levites who was enrolled.

20 Hezekiah did this throughout all Judah; he did what was good and right and faithful

---

31:2–4 Hezekiah is portrayed as a new David/Solomon, appointing priests and Levites (1 Chr. 16:37–40; 23), giving his own resources (1 Chr. 29:1–5), and following the law.

31:5 *The people of Israel gave in abundance.* As with David, popular generosity followed the king's generosity (v. 5; 1 Chr. 29:6–9).

31:6–7 The people bring tithes required in Lev. 27:32–33. The grain harvest ends in the *third* month, and the grape and fruit harvests end in the *seventh* month (cf. Exod. 23:16; 34:22).

31:8–10 Divine generosity exceeds human generosity (cf. Mal. 3:10). Zadok ruled as a high priest alongside David and Solomon. This Azariah appears nowhere else in Chronicles's genealogies.

31:11–19 Contributions to the temple were distributed to the priests and Levites for their personal needs and for offerings to the temple. The list of Levites handling the initial contributions (vv. 12–13) totals twelve. Even contributions given for Levitical benefit were considered sacred and needed to be distributed by those who purified themselves.

31:20–21 The narrator's evaluation is glowing. The highest praise, according to Chronicles, is that

before the LORD his God. ²¹And every work that he undertook in the service of the house of God and in accordance with the law and the commandments, to seek his God, he did with all his heart, and he prospered.

32 After these things and these acts of faithfulness, King Sennacherib of Assyria came and invaded Judah and encamped against the fortified cities, thinking to win them for himself. ²When Hezekiah saw that Sennacherib had come and intended to fight against Jerusalem, ³he planned with his officers and his warriors to stop the flow of the springs that were outside the city, and they helped him. ⁴A great many people were gathered, and they stopped all the springs and the wadi that flowed through the land, saying, "Why should the Assyrian kings come and find water in abundance?" ⁵Hezekiah*ᵐ* strengthened himself and built up the entire wall that was broken down and raised towers on it,*ⁿ* and outside it he built another wall; he also strengthened the Millo in the city of David and made weapons and shields in abundance. ⁶He appointed combat commanders over the people and gathered them together to him in the square at the gate of the city and spoke encouragingly to them, saying, ⁷"Be strong and of good courage. Do not be afraid or dismayed before the king of Assyria and all the horde that is with him, for there is one greater with us than with him. ⁸With him is an arm of flesh, but with us is the LORD our God, to help us and to fight our battles." The people were encouraged by the words of King Hezekiah of Judah.

9 After this, while King Sennacherib of Assyria was at Lachish with all his forces, he sent his servants to Jerusalem to King Hezekiah of Judah and to all the people of Judah who were in Jerusalem, saying, ¹⁰"Thus says King Sennacherib of Assyria: On what are you relying, that you undergo the siege of Jerusalem? ¹¹Is not Hezekiah misleading you, handing you over to die by famine and by thirst, when he tells you, 'The LORD our God will save us from the hand of the king of Assyria'? ¹²Was it not this same Hezekiah who took away his high places and his altars and commanded Judah and Jerusalem, saying, 'Before one altar you shall worship, and upon it you shall make your offerings'? ¹³Do you not know what I and my ancestors have done to all the peoples of other lands? Were the gods of the nations of those lands at all able to save their lands out of my hand? ¹⁴Who among all the gods of those nations that my ancestors utterly destroyed was able to save his people from my hand, that your God should be able to save you from my hand? ¹⁵Now, therefore, do not let Hezekiah deceive you or mislead you in this fashion, and do not believe him, for no god of any nation or kingdom has been able to save his people from my hand or from the hand of my ancestors. How much less will your God save you out of my hand!"

m 32.5 Heb He   n 32.5 Vg: Heb and raised on the towers

---

one "seeks" God. Hezekiah's life manifests such seeking in two crucial ways: (a) faithfulness in temple worship and (b) law keeping that is heartfelt (cf. Deut. 6:5).

32:1 *After . . . these acts of faithfulness.* This first phrase forebodes trouble by suggesting a period *after* faithfulness. The narrator portrays this whole ordeal with Sennacherib as a test of character that he initially passes, only to fall because of his pride (vv. 24–26).

32:2–8 Hezekiah made extensive preparations for the Assyrian siege on Jerusalem. Hezekiah's tunnel brought water from the Gihon Spring into the city via a carved tunnel to the Siloam Pool (vv. 30–31) and is still viewable today. His fortified walls were over twenty feet thick and greatly enlarged the enclosed areas of Jerusalem to protect Judeans and northerners fleeing Assyrian aggression. The *Millo* may refer to the structure that protected the Gihon Spring. Hezekiah's admonition *Be strong* echoes the words of Joshua to the people in Josh. 10:25 (cf. Moses's words in Deut. 31:6 and Jahaziel's words in 2 Chr. 20:15–17) and recognizes YHWH as Israel's source of power (cf. 20:17).

32:9–19 Sennacherib sat at Lachish, having destroyed it (see notes on 25:25–28). The Assyrian king misinterprets the nature of Hezekiah's reforms, which aimed at removing illicit altars (31:1), as a form of weakness. Sennacherib's threats are fundamentally theological. He equates YHWH with the nations' gods. He also wants to set the people against Hezekiah by accusing the king of misleading (vv. 11, 15), weakening YHWH's cultic presence (v. 12), referring to YHWH as *the God of Hezekiah* (v. 17), and speaking in the native Judean tongue (v. 18).

16 His servants said still more against the Lord GOD and against his servant Hezekiah. [17]He also wrote letters to throw contempt on the LORD the God of Israel and to speak against him, saying, "Just as the gods of the nations in other lands did not rescue their people from my hands, so the God of Hezekiah will not rescue his people from my hand." [18]They shouted it with a loud voice in the language of Judah to the people of Jerusalem who were on the wall, to frighten and terrify them, in order that they might take the city. [19]They spoke of the God of Jerusalem as if he were like the gods of the peoples of the earth, which are the work of human hands.

20 Then King Hezekiah and the prophet Isaiah son of Amoz prayed because of this and cried to heaven. [21]And the LORD sent an angel who cut off all the mighty warriors and commanders and officers in the camp of the king of Assyria. So he returned in disgrace to his own land. When he came into the house of his god, some of his own sons struck him down there with the sword. [22]So the LORD saved Hezekiah and the inhabitants of Jerusalem from the hand of King Sennacherib of Assyria and from the hand of all his enemies; he gave them rest[o] on every side. [23]Many brought gifts to the LORD in Jerusalem and precious things to King Hezekiah of Judah, so that he was exalted in the sight of all nations from that time onward.

24 In those days Hezekiah became sick and was at the point of death. He prayed to the LORD, and he answered him and gave him a sign. [25]But Hezekiah did not respond according to the benefit done to him, for his heart was proud. Therefore wrath came upon him and upon Judah and Jerusalem. [26]Then Hezekiah humbled himself for the pride of his heart, both he and the inhabitants of Jerusalem, so that the wrath of the LORD did not come upon them in the days of Hezekiah.

27 Hezekiah had very great riches and honor, and he made for himself treasuries for silver, for gold, for precious stones, for spices, for shields, and for all kinds of costly objects; [28]storehouses also for the yield of grain, wine, and oil; and stalls for all kinds of cattle and sheepfolds.[p] [29]He likewise provided cities for himself and flocks and herds in abundance, for God had given him very great possessions. [30]This same Hezekiah closed the upper outlet of the waters of Gihon and directed them down to the west side of the city of David. Hezekiah prospered in all his works. [31]So also in the matter of the envoys of the officials of Babylon, who had been sent to him to inquire about the sign that had been done in the land, God left him to himself, in order to test him and to know all that was in his heart.

32 Now the rest of the acts of Hezekiah and his good deeds are written in the vision of the prophet Isaiah son of Amoz in the Book of the Kings of Judah and Israel. [33]Hezekiah slept with his ancestors, and they buried him on the ascent to the tombs of the descendants of David, and all Judah and the inhabitants of Jerusalem did him honor at his death. His son Manasseh succeeded him.

o 32.22 Gk Vg: Heb *guided them*   p 32.28 Gk Vg: Heb *flocks for folds*

32:20–23 We see yet another prophetic appearance in Chronicles, this time in joint appeal with the king. Chronicles omits much detail from its sources, though the cultic and political disgrace of Sennacherib being cut down in his own temple is not lost on him. His god Nisroch could not protect him, despite Sennacherib's claims about YHWH's impotence. Chronicles adds a note that nations brought offerings and gifts to YHWH and Hezekiah in response to this spectacular deliverance. The offerings and gifts negate the shameful words against the Lord God and Hezekiah mentioned in v. 16.

32:24–26 This event receives more attention in the Chronicler's sources (2 Kgs. 20:1–11; Isa. 38:1–22). The important detail for Chronicles is the judgment for Hezekiah's pride, which followed this miraculous deliverance (and perhaps the gifts of nations), and the escape from divine wrath because Hezekiah humbled himself. Humbling is a significant theme in Chronicles (2 Chr. 7:14; 12:6–7; 30:11; 33:12, 19, 23; 34:27).

32:27–31 Chronicles returns to the theme of wealth as a sign of divine favor, a theme that links Hezekiah to David, Solomon, and Jehoshaphat before him (cf. 1 Chr. 29:28; 2 Chr. 1:12; 18:1). This great wealth exhibits the principle of humility (v. 26) before honor (vv. 27–29; cf. Prov. 15:33; 18:12). According to Chronicles, the Babylonian envoy came in response to the sign (v. 31) mentioned in v. 24. Foreign alliances were viewed negatively in Chronicles (2 Chr. 18, 19, 22, 24), as elsewhere in the Hebrew Bible.

33 Manasseh was twelve years old when he began to reign; he reigned fifty-five years in Jerusalem. ²He did what was evil in the sight of the Lord, according to the abominable practices of the nations whom the Lord had driven out before the people of Israel. ³For he rebuilt the high places that his father Hezekiah had pulled down and erected altars to the Baals, made sacred poles,*q* worshiped all the host of heaven, and served them. ⁴He built altars in the house of the Lord, of which the Lord had said, "In Jerusalem shall my name be forever." ⁵He built altars for all the host of heaven in the two courts of the house of the Lord. ⁶He made his son pass through fire in the valley of the son of Hinnom, practiced soothsaying and augury and sorcery, and dealt with mediums and with wizards. He did much evil in the sight of the Lord, provoking him to anger. ⁷The carved image of the idol that he had made he set in the house of God, of which God had said to David and to his son Solomon, "In this house, and in Jerusalem, which I have chosen out of all the tribes of Israel, I will put my name forever; ⁸I will never again remove the feet of Israel from the land that I appointed for your ancestors, if only they will be careful to do all that I have commanded them, all the law, the statutes, and the ordinances given through Moses." ⁹Manasseh misled Judah and the inhabitants of Jerusalem, so that they did more evil than the nations whom the Lord had destroyed before the people of Israel.

10 The Lord spoke to Manasseh and to his people, but they gave no heed. ¹¹Therefore the Lord brought against them the commanders of the army of the king of Assyria, who took Manasseh captive in manacles, bound him with fetters, and brought him to Babylon. ¹²While he was in distress, he entreated the favor of the Lord his God and humbled himself greatly before the God of his ancestors. ¹³He prayed to him, and God received his entreaty, heard his plea, and restored him again to Jerusalem and to his kingdom. Then Manasseh knew that the Lord indeed was God.

14 Afterward he built an outer wall for the city of David west of Gihon, in the valley, reaching the entrance at the Fish Gate; he carried it around Ophel and raised it to a very great height. He also put commanders of the army in all the fortified cities in Judah. ¹⁵He took away the foreign gods and the idol from the house of the Lord and all the altars that he had built on the mountain of the house of the Lord and in Jerusalem, and he threw them out of the city. ¹⁶He also restored the altar of the Lord and offered on it sacrifices of well-being and of thanksgiving, and he commanded Judah to serve the Lord the God of Israel. ¹⁷The people, however, still sacrificed at the high places, but only to the Lord their God.

18 Now the rest of the acts of Manasseh, his prayer to his God, and the words of the seers who spoke to him in the name of the

q 33.3 Or *Asherahs*

33:1–9 Despite his lengthy reign, Manasseh failed to maintain covenant fidelity. This offers a counterexample to the idea that Chronicles simplistically equates long life and wealth with divine favor. Like Ahaz (2 Chr. 28:24), Manasseh set up additional (illicit) altars in the temple area (vv. 4–5) and sacrificed his son (v. 6; cf. 28:3). Manasseh's *carved image of the idol* (v. 7) is an image of Asherah, according to 2 Kgs. 21:7 (cf. Ezek. 8:3), and is a direct affront to God's presence via God's *name* in the temple (2 Chr. 6:6).

33:10–13 The story of Manasseh's captivity is unique to Chronicles and reflects the Chronicler's interest in the pattern of mini exiles that foreshadowed the main exile (2 Chr. 11:13–17; 25:20–24; 28:5–7). This specific exile foreshadowed the exile of Judah's king Jehoiakim (36:6–7), a point reinforced by Manasseh's exile to Babylon rather than Nineveh. Manasseh's humility and prayer also offer a pattern for later exilic audiences. The apocryphal Prayer of Manasseh (cf. v. 13) is inspired by this verse and vv. 18–19.

33:14–17 Like the great builder-kings before him, Manasseh restores the city of Jerusalem and reestablishes YHWH's altar. It becomes clear here that his cultic violations (vv. 1–9) included the cessation of worship at YHWH's altar.

33:18–20 Chronicles remembers Manasseh primarily for his prayer and humility, a remarkable reality given his egregious sins (which Chronicles also details). The note about seers in v. 18 informs us that the warnings of v. 10 were prophetic.

LORD God of Israel, these are in the Annals of the Kings of Israel. [19]His prayer, and how God received his entreaty, all his sin and his faithlessness, the sites on which he built high places and set up the sacred poles[r] and the images, before he humbled himself, these are written in the records of the seers.[s] [20]So Manasseh slept with his ancestors, and they buried him in his house. His son Amon succeeded him.

21 Amon was twenty-two years old when he began to reign; he reigned two years in Jerusalem. [22]He did what was evil in the sight of the LORD, as his father Manasseh had done. Amon sacrificed to all the images that his father Manasseh had made and served them. [23]He did not humble himself before the LORD, as his father Manasseh had humbled himself, but this Amon incurred more and more guilt. [24]His servants conspired against him and killed him in his house. [25]But the people of the land killed all those who had conspired against King Amon, and the people of the land made his son Josiah king to succeed him.

34 Josiah was eight years old when he began to reign; he reigned thirty-one years in Jerusalem. [2]He did what was right in the sight of the LORD and walked in the ways of his ancestor David; he did not turn aside to the right or to the left. [3]For in the eighth year of his reign, while he was still a boy, he began to seek the God of his ancestor David, and in the twelfth year he began to cleanse Judah and Jerusalem of the high places, the sacred poles,[t] and the carved and the cast images. [4]In his presence they pulled down the altars of the Baals; he demolished the incense altars that stood above them. He broke down the sacred poles[u] and the carved and the cast images; he made dust of them and scattered it over the graves of those who had sacrificed to them. [5]He also burned the bones of the priests on their altars and cleansed Judah and Jerusalem. [6]In the towns of Manasseh, Ephraim, and Simeon, and as far as Naphtali, in their ruins[v] all around, [7]he broke down the altars, beat the sacred poles[w] and the images into powder, and demolished all the incense altars throughout all the land of Israel. Then he returned to Jerusalem.

8 In the eighteenth year of his reign, when he had cleansed the land and the house, he sent Shaphan son of Azaliah, Maaseiah the governor of the city, and Joah son of Joahaz, the recorder, to repair the house of the LORD his God. [9]They came to the high priest Hilkiah and delivered the silver that had been brought into the house of God, which the Levites, the keepers of the threshold, had collected from Manasseh and Ephraim and from all the remnant of Israel and from all

r 33.19 Or *Asherahs*   s 33.19 Heb ms Gk: MT *of Hozai*
t 34.3 Or *Asherahs*   u 34.4 Or *Asherahs*   v 34.6 Meaning of Heb uncertain   w 34.7 Or *Asherahs*

33:21–25 King Amon reestablishes the images that Manasseh eventually removed and that Josiah will eventually destroy (34:3–7). Unlike Manasseh and Hezekiah, Amon fails to humble himself. The reasons for his assassination are unknown (v. 24), but it gave way to a counterinsurgency and, eventually, the reign of King Josiah (v. 25).

2 Chr. 34 Josiah is the only king besides Hezekiah whom the Chronicler compares positively to David (2 Chr. 29:2; 34:2). Chronicles remembers Josiah as a reformer who, like Hezekiah, initiates a great Passover celebration (chap. 35) but whose life is ultimately cut short, signaling the beginning of the end for Judah.

34:1–7 After Amon's assassination, Josiah was installed as king at a very young age. He underwent some kind of awakening at age sixteen (v. 3) and began reforms at age twenty (v. 3), presumably because that was the age when priests could serve (1 Chr. 23:24; see note on 1 Chr. 23:2). While not a priest himself, it may have been viewed as an appropriate age for cultic reforms. Josiah's reforms, like Hezekiah's before him, included northern regions (v. 6). A comparison with Chronicles's sources reveals an emphasis on Josiah's purification of Jerusalem, Judah, and the whole land before restoring the temple (cf. 2 Kgs. 22–23, where the land's purification occurs after finding the law book).

34:8–13 Chronicles is adamant that the whole people participated in supporting the temple's renewal (v. 9; cf. 2 Kgs. 22:4). Moreover, in contrast to its sources, Chronicles mentions the oversight of Levites in the work (2 Chr. 34:12–13), including the role of musicians in directing physical labor (vv. 12–13). One wonders if they played dance music to motivate workers!

Judah and Benjamin and from the inhabitants of Jerusalem. ¹⁰They delivered it to the workers who had the oversight of the house of the LORD, and the workers who were working in the house of the LORD gave it for repairing and restoring the house. ¹¹They gave it to the carpenters and the builders to buy quarried stone, and timber for binders, and beams for the buildings that the kings of Judah had let go to ruin. ¹²The people did the work faithfully. Over them were appointed the Levites Jahath and Obadiah, of the sons of Merari, along with Zechariah and Meshullam, of the sons of the Kohathites, to have oversight. Other Levites, all skillful with instruments of music, ¹³were over the burden bearers and directed all who did work in every kind of service, and some of the Levites were scribes, and officials, and gatekeepers.

14 While they were bringing out the silver that had been brought into the house of the LORD, the priest Hilkiah found the book of the law of the LORD given through Moses. ¹⁵Hilkiah said to the secretary Shaphan, "I have found the book of the law in the house of the LORD," and Hilkiah gave the book to Shaphan. ¹⁶Shaphan brought the book to the king and further reported to the king, "All that was committed to your servants they are doing. ¹⁷They have emptied out the silver that was found in the house of the LORD and have delivered it into the hand of the overseers and the workers." ¹⁸The secretary Shaphan informed the king, "The priest Hilkiah has given me a book." Shaphan then read it aloud to the king.

19 When the king heard the words of the law, he tore his clothes. ²⁰Then the king commanded Hilkiah, Ahikam son of Shaphan, Abdon son of Micah, the secretary Shaphan, and the king's servant Asaiah, ²¹"Go, inquire of the LORD for me and for those who are left in Israel and in Judah, concerning the words of the book that has been found, for the wrath of the LORD that is poured out on us is great, because our ancestors did not keep the word of the LORD, to act in accordance with all that is written in this book."

22 So Hilkiah and those whom the king had sent went to the prophet Huldah, the wife of Shallum son of Tokhath son of Hasrah, keeper of the wardrobe (who lived in Jerusalem in the Second Quarter) and spoke to her to that effect. ²³She declared to them, "Thus says the LORD, the God of Israel: Tell the man who sent you to me: ²⁴'Thus says the LORD: I will indeed bring disaster upon this place and upon its inhabitants, all the curses that are written in the book that was read before the king of Judah. ²⁵Because they have forsaken me and have made offerings to other gods, so that they have provoked me to anger with all the works of their hands, my wrath will be poured out on this place and will not be quenched.' ²⁶But as to the king of Judah, who sent you to inquire of the LORD, thus shall you say to him: Thus says the LORD, the God of Israel: 'Regarding the words that you have heard, ²⁷because your heart was penitent and you humbled yourself before God when you heard his words against this place and its inhabitants, and you have humbled yourself before me and have torn your clothes and wept before me, I also have heard you, says the LORD. ²⁸I will gather you to your ancestors and you shall be gathered to your grave in peace; your eyes shall not see all the disaster that I will bring on this place and its inhabitants.'" They took the message back to the king.

34:14–21 The *book of the law* may have been some form of Deuteronomy, given the specific reforms that it inspired, which included the centralization of worship (Deut. 12) and the removal of many religious features that Deuteronomy prohibits. The king's response (2 Chr. 34:19) reflects concern over the disasters portended for covenant violations (e.g., Deut. 28). Rather than taking immediate action, Josiah inquires of God through Huldah (2 Chr. 34:22–28).

34:22–28 Huldah is one of the most prominent prophetesses in the Hebrew Bible, alongside notables like Miriam (Exod. 15:20; Num. 12:2), Deborah (Judg. 4:4), Isaiah's wife (Isa. 8:3), and Noadiah (Neh. 6:14). Female prophets also play significant roles in the New Testament and include characters like Anna (Luke 2:36), Mary and other women at Pentecost (Acts 2:17), and Philip's daughters (Acts 21:9). Huldah prophesies the enactment of covenant curses (Deut. 28:15–68) but also their deferral because of Josiah's humble repentance (2 Chr. 34:27). The implication of v. 28 is that judgment will still come unless future generations also turn from their disloyalty.

29 Then the king sent word and gathered together all the elders of Judah and Jerusalem. ³⁰The king went up to the house of the LORD, with all the people of Judah, the inhabitants of Jerusalem, the priests and the Levites, all the people both great and small; he read in their hearing all the words of the book of the covenant that had been found in the house of the LORD. ³¹The king stood in his place and made a covenant before the LORD, to follow the LORD, keeping his commandments, his decrees, and his statutes, with all his heart and all his soul, to perform the words of the covenant that were written in this book. ³²Then he made all who were present in Jerusalem and in Benjamin pledge themselves to it. And the inhabitants of Jerusalem acted according to the covenant of God, the God of their ancestors. ³³Josiah took away all the abominations from all the territory that belonged to the people of Israel and made all who were in Israel serve the LORD their God. All his days they did not turn away from following the LORD the God of their ancestors.

35 Josiah kept a Passover to the LORD in Jerusalem; they slaughtered the Passover lamb on the fourteenth day of the first month. ²He appointed the priests to their offices and encouraged them in the service of the house of the LORD. ³He said to the Levites who taught all Israel and who were holy to the LORD, "Put the holy ark in the house that Solomon son of David, king of Israel, built; you need no longer carry it on your shoulders. Now serve the LORD your God and his people Israel. ⁴Make preparations by your ancestral houses by your divisions, following the written directions of King David of Israel and the written directions of his son Solomon. ⁵Take position in the holy place according to the groupings of the ancestral houses of your kindred the people, and let there be Levites for each division of an ancestral house.ˣ ⁶Slaughter the Passover lamb, sanctify yourselves, and on behalf of your kindred make preparations, acting according to the word of the LORD by Moses."

7 Then Josiah contributed to the people, as Passover offerings for all who were present, lambs and kids from the flock to the number of thirty thousand and three thousand bulls; these were from the king's possessions. ⁸His officials contributed willingly to the people, to the priests, and to the Levites. Hilkiah, Zechariah, and Jehiel, the chief officers of the house of God, gave to the priests for the Passover offerings two thousand six hundred lambs and kids and three hundred bulls. ⁹Conaniah also, and his brothers Shemaiah and Nethanel, and Hashabiah and Jeiel and Jozabad, the chiefs of the Levites, gave to the Levites for the Passover offerings five thousand lambs and kids and five hundred bulls.

10 When the service had been prepared, the priests stood in their place and the Levites in their divisions according to the king's command. ¹¹They slaughtered the Passover lamb, and the priests dashed the blood that

ˣ 35.5 Meaning of Heb uncertain

34:29–33 Josiah follows the Deuteronomic command to read the Torah (Deut. 17:18–20; 31:11–13; cf. Neh. 8:1–8), and in response, he and the people commit themselves *heart and . . . soul* to the covenant (vv. 31–32; cf. Deut. 6:4–5). The inclusion of priests and Levites (v. 30) alongside the whole people highlights the Chronicler's concern to emphasize the nation's unity around the temple and in worship.

35:1–6 Josiah's Passover celebration recalls Hezekiah's great Passover (2 Chr. 30) and accompanies the new start wrought by Josiah's reforms. Josiah and the people follow the Torah's Passover requirements by slaughtering the lamb on the fourteenth of the first month (v. 1; Exod. 12:6) and Davidic and Solomonic commands by gathering in their prescribed groupings (1 Chr. 23–26; 2 Chr. 8). The command to put the ark in the temple (v. 3) suggests that during Manasseh's and Amon's reigns, the ark was also in "exile." Once again, the pattern of exile and return shapes the Chronicler's account of Judah's history, and this verse may voice hope for the ark's eventual return. It is not mentioned again in Chronicles or Ezra-Nehemiah. The Levites play a prominent role by accompanying each family to ensure fidelity to the law (vv. 5–6).

35:7–9 For Chronicles, great wealth should benefit the people in their worship. Josiah, the officials, and Levitical chiefs provide generously for the Passover celebration.

35:10–15 The Chronicler's account builds anticipation. The priests' *place* is the altar, with the Levites on hand until the time comes to slaughter the lamb. Priests handle blood, according to the

they received[y] from them, while the Levites did the skinning. [12]They set aside the burnt offerings so that they might distribute them according to the groupings of the ancestral houses of the people, to offer to the LORD, as it is written in the book of Moses. And they did the same with the bulls. [13]They roasted the Passover lamb with fire according to the ordinance, and they boiled the holy offerings in pots, in caldrons, and in pans and carried them quickly to all the people. [14]Afterward they made preparations for themselves and for the priests, because the priests the descendants of Aaron were occupied in offering the burnt offerings and the fat parts until night, so the Levites made preparations for themselves and for the priests, the descendants of Aaron. [15]The singers, the descendants of Asaph, were in their place according to the command of David, and Asaph, and Heman, and the king's seer Jeduthun. The gatekeepers were at each gate; they did not need to interrupt their service, for their kindred the Levites made preparations for them.

16 So all the service of the LORD was prepared that day, to keep the Passover and to offer burnt offerings on the altar of the LORD, according to the command of King Josiah. [17]The people of Israel who were present kept the Passover at that time and the Festival of Unleavened Bread seven days. [18]No Passover like it had been kept in Israel since the days of the prophet Samuel; none of the kings of Israel had kept such a Passover as was kept by Josiah, by the priests and the Levites, by all Judah and Israel who were present, and by the inhabitants of Jerusalem. [19]In the eighteenth year of the reign of Josiah, this Passover was kept.

20 After all this, when Josiah had set the temple in order, King Neco of Egypt went up to fight at Carchemish on the Euphrates, and Josiah went out against him. [21]But Neco[z] sent envoys to him, saying, "What have I to do with you, king of Judah? I am not coming against you today but against the house with which I am at war, and God has commanded me to hurry. Cease opposing God, who is with me, so that he will not destroy you." [22]But Josiah would not turn away from him but disguised himself in order to fight with him. He did not listen to the words of Neco from the mouth of God but joined battle in the plain of Megiddo. [23]The archers shot King Josiah, and the king said to his servants, "Take me away, for I am badly wounded." [24]So his servants took him out of the chariot and carried him in his second chariot[a] and brought him to Jerusalem. There he died and was buried in the tombs of his ancestors. All Judah and Jerusalem mourned for Josiah. [25]Jeremiah also uttered a lament for Josiah, and all the singing men and singing women have spoken of Josiah in their laments to this day. They made these a custom in Israel; they are recorded in the Laments. [26]Now the rest of the acts of Josiah and his faithful deeds in accordance with what is written in the law of the LORD

y 35.11 Heb lacks *that they received* z 35.21 Heb *he*
a 35.24 Or *the chariot of his deputy*

Torah (e.g., Lev. 1:5, 11). Before the centralization of worship, this entire ceremony would have taken place in homes. The report that the people *roasted the Passover lamb with fire* combines two legal traditions in the Pentateuch, borrowing the "fire" phrase from Exod. 12:8 and the term translated as "roasted" from Deut. 16:7. The sacrificing took place to the tune of Levitical music (cf. 1 Chr. 25:1–6).

35:16–19 Josiah's Passover was unmatched since the days of Samuel (also a Levite). However, Chronicles omits the phrase "kings of Judah" from its source in v. 18 (cf. 2 Kgs. 23:22) in order to maintain the prominence of Hezekiah's great Passover celebration (2 Chr. 30:26). The legacy of this Passover is not only its abundance but also the way it unified the people of Judah and Israel (v. 18).

35:20–27 Once again, pride comes before a fall. Josiah ignored what was apparently a prophetic warning through Pharaoh Neco (v. 21). Like Ahab, he disguised himself to evade his prophesied fate and fell with an archer's shot (cf. 2 Chr. 18:28–34). Pharaoh Neco II was on a campaign to confront an anti-Assyrian coalition. Josiah, like Hezekiah before him, apparently sided with the Babylonians in opposition to the Egyptian-Assyrian alliance. Though he fell ingloriously, he is still remembered as a great king. The lament of Jeremiah (v. 25) receives no mention in Kings, though Jeremiah's words play a significant role in 2 Chr. 36:12, 21–22. Apparently, lamenting Josiah's death became a tradition and may be linked to the downfall of Judah that followed his untimely death. *The Laments* may refer to the book of Lamentations, though Josiah is not mentioned there, and the book deals with Judah's exile and not the late monarchic period.

²⁷and his acts, first and last, are written in the Book of the Kings of Israel and Judah.

36 The people of the land took Jehoahaz son of Josiah and made him king to succeed his father in Jerusalem. ²Jehoahaz was twenty-three years old when he began to reign; he reigned three months in Jerusalem. ³Then the king of Egypt deposed him in Jerusalem and laid on the land a tribute of one hundred talents of silver and one talent of gold. ⁴The king of Egypt made his brother Eliakim king over Judah and Jerusalem and changed his name to Jehoiakim, but Neco took his brother Jehoahaz and carried him to Egypt.

5 Jehoiakim was twenty-five years old when he began to reign; he reigned eleven years in Jerusalem. He did what was evil in the sight of the Lord his God. ⁶Against him King Nebuchadnezzar of Babylon came up and bound him with fetters to take him to Babylon. ⁷Nebuchadnezzar also carried some of the vessels of the house of the Lord to Babylon and put them in his palace in Babylon. ⁸Now the rest of the acts of Jehoiakim and the abominations that he did and what was found against him are written in the Book of the Kings of Israel and Judah, and his son Jehoiachin succeeded him.

9 Jehoiachin was eight years old when he began to reign; he reigned three months and ten days in Jerusalem. He did what was evil in the sight of the Lord. ¹⁰In the spring of the year King Nebuchadnezzar sent and brought him to Babylon, along with the precious vessels of the house of the Lord, and made his brother Zedekiah king over Judah and Jerusalem.

11 Zedekiah was twenty-one years old when he began to reign; he reigned eleven years in Jerusalem. ¹²He did what was evil in the sight of the Lord his God. He did not humble himself before the prophet Jeremiah who spoke from the mouth of the Lord. ¹³He also rebelled against King Nebuchadnezzar, who had made him swear by God; he stiffened his neck and hardened his heart against turning to the Lord, the God of Israel. ¹⁴All the leading priests and the people also were exceedingly unfaithful, following all the abominations of the nations, and they polluted the house of the Lord that he had consecrated in Jerusalem.

15 The Lord, the God of their ancestors, sent persistently to them by his messengers, because he had compassion on his people and on his dwelling place, ¹⁶but they kept mocking the messengers of God, despising his words, and scoffing at his prophets until the wrath of the Lord against his people became so great that there was no remedy.

17 Therefore he brought up against them the king of the Chaldeans, who killed their youths with the sword in the house of their sanctuary and had no compassion on young man or young woman, the aged or the feeble; he gave them all into his hand.

36:1–4 Pharaoh Neco's influence only grew in Judah. Though appointed by the people, Jehoahaz lasted only three months before Pharaoh Neco deposed him and installed his half brother (2 Kgs. 23:36), whom he likely considered more favorable toward an Egyptian-Babylonian coalition. He also gave Eliakim a YHWH-based name, Jehoiakim (literally "YHWH raises up"). See **"God's Name," p. 89**.

36:5–8 Jehoiakim is also exiled, though to Babylon. The temple vessels are of significant interest to the Chronicler (2 Chr. 25:24; 28:24; 36:10, 18) and play an important role in the books of Ezra-Nehemiah and Daniel (e.g., Ezra 1:7–11; Dan. 1:2; 5:2).

36:9–10 The story of Jehoiakim repeats itself with Jehoiachin, who was also exiled to Babylon with temple vessels (this time *precious vessels*). It is hard to imagine the evil accomplished by this eight-year-old in a mere three months. The Greek Septuagint puts his age at eighteen.

36:11–14 Zedekiah provides yet another example of a proud king, yet he fails to humble himself, the prerequisite for deliverance in Chronicles (e.g., 2 Chr. 7:14). His rebellion against Nebuchadnezzar involved appealing to Egypt for protection (Ezek. 17:15). A stiff neck and hard heart are contrary to God's purposes for God's people, who were to remain responsive to God (Deut. 10:16). Chronicles draws special attention to the priests' (and people's) guilt in polluting the temple, rendering it vulnerable to the destruction that follows.

36:15–16 These summary verses draw together the pattern of rejecting prophets, a pattern Jesus also notices in his own ministry (Matt. 5:12; 23:29–38). Jesus also links the persistent rejection of prophetic warnings to the temple's destruction (Matt. 23:38).

36:17–21 God directs the activity of nations in Chronicles (cf. 1 Chr. 5:26; 6:15; 2 Chr. 36:22),

Going Deeper: Historiography (2 Chronicles 36)

Large portions of the Bible concern themselves with stories about the past. The primary narrative that runs from creation (Gen. 1–2) to the exile (2 Kgs. 25) insists that God has been at work in the world throughout history to accomplish God's purposes. Other portions of the Bible like Ezra-Nehemiah and Chronicles supplement that primary historical narrative with additional histories about postexilic life or retell the primary narrative from a distinctly postexilic perspective. However, parsing out how biblical stories *about the past* correspond to reality is sometimes difficult. We rely instead on extrabiblical parallels to determine when a biblical writer might be adapting a known cultural myth (e.g., the creation story or the flood story) and on historical disciplines like archaeology to help determine the degree to which a biblical story might relate to the past. We also depend on genre clues and literary details. For instance, the Gen. 2 creation story hints that it does *not* take place in the known world. The four rivers flowing from Eden go around the eastern portions of Africa and Mesopotamia. No rivers do that. Other stories exhibit some correspondence with the past, even if we cannot pinpoint how closely they do so. For instance, major national events in the books of Samuel and Kings correspond, broadly speaking, to Iron Age II realities in Judah and Israel. Other stories like the exodus from Egypt are hard to prove historically, though aspects of them relate to known enslavement and migration patterns between Egypt and Palestine during the time of Pharaoh Ramesses II. Perhaps it is best to acknowledge that the Hebrew Bible clearly insists that God's intervention in the particulars of history matters a great deal. But the relationship between history and event is akin to the relationship between a work of art and its subject. Some forms of art exhibit a close verisimilitude (e.g., realism), while other art forms still exhibit correspondence but of a different sort (caricature, impressionism). Each art form can convey a truth about God, the world, and humanity, though in different artistic media. In a similar way, biblical history exhibits art forms that range from reworked myths (creation accounts) to realism (portions of Samuel-Kings) to more impressionistic or caricature-like forms of historical art (Chronicles). Unlike modern history writing, ancient history writing exhibited a tolerance for a wide-ranging breadth of artistic historiographic media.

Matthew J. Lynch

[18]All the vessels of the house of God, large and small, and the treasures of the house of the Lord, and the treasures of the king and of his officials, all these he brought to Babylon. [19]They burned the house of God, broke down the wall of Jerusalem, burned all its palaces with fire, and destroyed all its precious vessels. [20]He took into exile in Babylon those who had escaped from the sword, and they became servants to him and to his sons until the establishment of the kingdom of Persia, [21]to fulfill the word of the Lord by the mouth of Jeremiah, until the land had made up for its Sabbaths. All the days that it lay desolate it kept Sabbath, to fulfill seventy years.

[22] In the first year of King Cyrus of Persia, to fulfill the word of the Lord spoken by Jeremiah, the Lord stirred up the spirit of King Cyrus of Persia so that he made a proclamation throughout all his kingdom and also in writing, saying: [23]"Thus says King Cyrus of Persia: The Lord, the God of heaven, has given me all the kingdoms of the earth, and he has charged me to build him a house at Jerusalem, which is in Judah. Let any of those among you who are of his people—may the Lord their God be with them!—go up."

though their violence is not condoned. Once again, the temple vessels receive special attention, as they provide grounds for hope of an eventual return despite the temple's destruction. The people had become *servants* (v. 20)—or perhaps more accurately, "enslaved"—once again. Verse 21 draws together the idea of the land's need for Sabbath rest expressed in the law (cf. Lev. 25:4; 26:34; Deut. 15:1–18; Jer. 25:11) and Jeremiah's prophesied seventy-year exile (Jer. 29:10).

36:22–23 Chronicles ends on a note of prophetic hope, for the Lord had once again stirred the king, this time to initiate the promised return (in 539 BCE). The encouragement that the exiles *go up* (cf. Ezra 1:3) evokes the many psalms of ascent (Pss. 120–134). The famous Cyrus Cylinder reports that the Persian king restored sanctuaries in many regions.

EZRA-NEHEMIAH

The books of Ezra and Nehemiah were originally a single literary work. It may have been written as early as the late Persian period after the reign of Artaxerxes I (465–424 BCE), the emperor who permits Nehemiah to sojourn to Jerusalem, but it is more likely the work was composed in the Hellenistic period, between 332 and 164 BCE when Jerusalem was under Greek rule. Its language, its references to places and peoples not present until the Hellenistic period, and the chronology that places Artaxerxes's rule before Darius (522–486 BCE; Ezra 4) locate it hundreds of years after the events it describes. Both works relate the idealized story of a small Jerusalem temple community's evolution as it formed a unique identity and negotiated the external pressures of imperial repression and the internal politics of religious and political diversity.

Historical Context

After the death of Alexander the Great, his general Ptolemy administered the region of the empire that included Jerusalem. Ptolemy's cosmopolitanism invited many in the Jewish community to wear Greek styles of dress, attend the theater, and participate in the activities of the gymnasium, where, for men, their circumcision was apparent and set them apart. Many elites in Jerusalem readily integrated these Greek cultural markers into their lifestyles. In fact, some began to question whether circumcision was a necessary marker of their identity.

The later Hellenistic period brought the rule of Seleucus, another of Alexander's generals. His successor, Antiochus IV Epiphanes, desecrated the temple by sacrificing swine upon the altar, erecting a statue of Zeus in the most sacred temple quarters, and forcing members of the community into Hellenistic practices that violated their religious and cultural identities. The story of Ezra and Nehemiah spoke its message of unity and resistance with powerful relevance to the community in Jerusalem threatened by Greek rule.

Reading Guide

The similarities between life for the community of Ezra and Nehemiah and life for their descendants who lived during the Hellenistic period are apparent: both communities lived under harsh imperial rule—Persian and Greek. Both communities faced huge challenges as they negotiated pluralism amid the ongoing formation of cultural identity. Nehemiah contended with pro-Persian groups (Sanballat and Tobiah) within the community, while pro- and anti-Greek factions complicated the latter Jerusalem community.

Ezra and Nehemiah both leave centers of the Persian Empire for Jerusalem to organize the community in response to imperial repression. They hail from different locations in society. Ezra is a scribe well-studied in the teachings of Moses. His focus is primarily religious. He works to strengthen the collective's cultural center by organizing the temple, its personnel, and its activities. Nehemiah is an imperial governor. He works toward the same end but brings the authority of the empire.

The story itself, like any history of a people, reflects the complexities and ambiguities of the human condition. The writer begins with a mass return of former captives from Babylon. It is unlikely that many who were taken captive in 597 or 587 survived to return; yet, the writer makes no distinction between the original captives and their descendants, who probably comprise the "returning" group. Using language that simulates an official imperial decree (Ezra 1:2–4), the story attests to Cyrus's policy of populating the far regions of his rapidly expanding empire by sending groups of people "home." By "returning" all formerly captive peoples to their respective homelands, Cyrus engendered, and perhaps coerced, loyalty among local populations. Wherever the groups migrated, they were intended to serve the empire. As Ezra laments, "Here we are, slaves to this day, slaves in the land that you gave to our ancestors to enjoy its fruit and its good gifts" (Neh. 9:36). However, in a powerful demonstration of faith, the writer reframes their oppression and finds God's providence in this political situation. Ezra speaks a word of hope: "Yet our God has not forsaken us in our slavery but has extended to us his steadfast love before the kings of Persia, to give us new life to set up the house of our God, to repair its ruins, and to give us a wall in Judea and Jerusalem" (Ezra 9:9). Reading God's hand in the action of a foreign king meant that YHWH (see **"God's Name," p. 89**) was more than a national deity such as Marduk of Babylon. This was a

bold theological claim for the writer and differed from some preexilic representations of YHWH as only the God of Israel. The writer envisions a universal God whose power, protection, and promise have been present with Israel from captivity to their new life in Jerusalem and who is sovereign even over Babylon and Persia.

While Ezra is intentional about distinguishing himself from imperial authority (Ezra 8:22–23), Nehemiah's authority is primarily imperial. The name "Nehemiah" (literally "YHWH will comfort") reflects the writer's understanding that Nehemiah's activity attends to the suffering and chaos in Jerusalem. Nehemiah's call is fivefold: to reconstruct Jerusalem's walls, end economic exploitation, increase the population, restructure the temple bureaucracy, and expel foreigners. He faces serious resistance from members of the community aligned with rival imperial officials, Tobiah and Sanballat. As Persian officials, Nehemiah, Sanballat, and Tobiah were useful to the empire depending on their ability to maintain order among the populations in the province and to ensure revenue streams continued to flow from the territories to the imperial treasury. Nehemiah's arrival with imperial funding to fortify Jerusalem signaled a shift in imperial support, which threatened the imperial standing of Sanballat and Tobiah. The two joined forces against Nehemiah to protect their own positions. The jurisdictions for the purposes of taxation were often defined by groups rather than territories, since the Persian Empire was loosely organized geographically. Each official could raise funds by coercion or persuasion, but persuasion was far less labor-intensive and more cost-effective. So the competition between the three becomes a contest for influence over the community. Ultimately, Nehemiah prevails, but only temporarily. When Nehemiah returns to the king's court, he finds that Tobiah has gained enough influence to warrant space in the temple, so he returns to Jerusalem to reinforce his earlier work. In the end, Ezra's and Nehemiah's reforms receive no affirmation from the writer. Perhaps this signals the writer's ambivalence to the plurality of cultures in Jerusalem.

Ezra's and Nehemiah's characters resist any easy assessment. Both identify with the Jerusalem collective and its stories, faith, and experience, but they are imperial authorities and loyal to the king of Persia as well. The reforms reflect the same ambiguities. By any assessment, the mass divorces to separate the "holy" community from those who are now deemed "foreign" (Ezra 9:1–4; 10; Neh. 13; see **"Intermarriage," p. 649**) destroyed families and inflicted great violence. Yet Ezra's and Nehemiah's work also created a space of cultural flourishing. Ezra appeals to Moses's historical authority in the community's collective understanding. He fashions Moses's teachings to call the people toward a cultural unity that resists imperial domination. Together, he and Nehemiah call the people to the social organization that gives the province the political stability that the Persian officials desire. By constructing the Second Temple and fortifying the walls of Jerusalem, the community raises its esteem and signals publicly that they are no longer a plundered people. Rebuilding also serves as a sign of a repaired relationship with God. Both are reminders that God's power is greater than the empire's. At a time when Greek forces oppressed the community in Jerusalem, the story of Ezra–Nehemiah offered a testimony of hope; it reminded them that if God rewarded their forebears' faithfulness by sustaining them through Persian repression, then God would not forsake them now.

Herbert Robinson Marbury

1 In the first year of King Cyrus of Persia, to fulfill the word of the LORD from the mouth of Jeremiah, the LORD stirred up the spirit of King Cyrus of Persia so that he made a proclamation throughout all his kingdom and also in writing, saying:

2 "Thus says King Cyrus of Persia: The LORD, the God of heaven, has given me all the kingdoms of the earth, and he has charged me to build him a house at Jerusalem, which is in Judah. ³Let any of those among you who are of his people—may their God be with them!—go up to Jerusalem in Judah and rebuild the house of the LORD, the God of Israel; he is the God who is in Jerusalem. ⁴And let all survivors in whatever place they reside be assisted by the people of their place with silver and gold, with goods, and with livestock, besides freewill offerings for the house of God in Jerusalem."

5 Then the heads of the families of Judah and Benjamin and the priests and the Levites—everyone whose spirit God had stirred—got ready to go up and rebuild the house of the LORD in Jerusalem. ⁶All their neighbors aided them with silver vessels, with gold, with goods, with livestock, and with valuable gifts, besides all that was freely offered. ⁷King Cyrus himself brought out the vessels of the house of the LORD that Nebuchadnezzar had carried away from Jerusalem and placed in the house of his gods. ⁸King Cyrus of Persia had them released into the charge of Mithredath the treasurer, who counted them out to Sheshbazzar the prince of Judah. ⁹And this was the inventory: gold basins, thirty; silver basins, one thousand; knives,ᵃ twenty-nine; ¹⁰gold bowls, thirty; other silver bowls, four hundred ten; other vessels, one thousand; ¹¹the total of the gold and silver vessels was five thousand four hundred. All these Sheshbazzar brought up when the exiles were brought up from Babylonia to Jerusalem.

a 1.9 Vg: Meaning of Heb uncertain

1:1–11 From Babylonian to Persian dominion. The book begins with a grand vision: a return from exile by the survivors of the Babylonian devastation and a promise of rebuilding the temple in Jerusalem. Five motifs show that the writer intends to portray a continuity between those taken captive in Babylon and those journeying to Jerusalem with Ezra. **1:1** First, the writer invokes ancient oral and more contemporaneous literary traditions associated with the prophets and crafts them to give meaning to the context of the Jerusalem community as they interpret God's activity in history. The author alludes to Jeremiah's prophecy of a seventy-year captivity (Jer. 25:11–12) and also a return (Jer. 29:10; 51:1). See for comparison Isa. 45:1 where Cyrus's edict is God's work fulfilling the promise to restore Israel. Second, the writer frames Cyrus's edict as ultimately the work of God; God is the source of this group's redemption from captivity in Babylon. **1:2–4** These verses overlap with and are more extensive than 2 Chr. 36:22–23. **1:4** Third, Cyrus's edict is framed for the audience in Jerusalem using familiar themes from the exodus. The account of the congregation being enriched from the spoils of an evil empire parallels Exod. 12:33–36, where God directs Egyptians to bestow wealth upon the Israelites as they depart. Here, the Israelites benefit from the wealth of the former Babylonian Empire. Both the books of Exodus and Ezra view the respective liberations from captivity, and the wealth that accrued to the Israelites, as the activity of the hand of God (see **"Exile and Restoration Metanarratives," p. 637**). **1:5** Fourth, the writer foregrounds *Judah* and *Benjamin*, the two tribes in the South that were impacted by the Babylonian devastation. Ezra's opening vision promises a new life in Jerusalem for the descendants of those taken captive by Babylon. Cyrus, the king of Persia, has directed all captive peoples to return to their respective "homelands." In other words, this group claims a connection by lineage to those who experienced exile. Such a claim carries weight as this group, among others, contests for land in Jerusalem. Not everyone departed Babylon for Jerusalem; only *everyone whose spirit God had stirred* is redeemed. Those who did not experience an exile but remained in Judah now fall outside of the self-understanding of those returning from exile as "true Israel." **1:7–11** In the fifth motif, those who return travel with the restored temple vessels to Jerusalem. Returning the seized temple vessels legitimates them as "true Israel" by signaling that God has chosen them over other groups—namely, those who did not experience exile—to restore what had been taken from the *house of the LORD*. **1:7–8** *King Cyrus himself brought out the vessels.* Only the Persian Empire could authorize such a transfer of wealth, thus the transfer also vests this group with imperial imprimatur. **1:8** *Sheshbazzar* was appointed governor of Persian Judah by King Cyrus. He was reportedly tasked with leading an early group of people from Babylon to Jerusalem and given gold to fund the work of establishing them as a community loyal to the empire.

Going Deeper: Exile and Restoration Metanarratives (Ezra 1)

Metanarratives are a convenient way to frame complex histories by organizing many disparate narratives into a single overarching story. For example, one metanarrative in the United States understands the country as founded by groups struggling for freedom from the tyranny of European monarchies, becoming God's shining city on a hill, and offering the hope of democracy to the world. In the narrative, the most authentic Americans are those of British ancestry who arrived on the Mayflower at Plymouth Rock. On one hand, the metanarrative does unifying work by inspiring its adherents to a shared identity, shared values, and shared aspirations. On the other hand, the metanarrative does violence by masking or subordinating experiences (races, ethnicities, religious minorities) that are different from those in the overarching story.

Exodus and conquest along with exile and restoration operate as twin metanarratives that shape ancient Israel's identity (see **"The Exodus Event," p. 105**, and **"Conquest," p. 317**). Roughly, the narratives proceed with seven parallel themes:

- All Israel goes into Egypt.
- All Israel goes into Babylon.
- Israel is oppressed 430 years in Egypt.
- Israel is oppressed 48 years in Babylon.
- God sends Moses to defeat Pharaoh.
- God sends Cyrus to defeat the Babylonians.
- Moses leads them out, organizes worship, and gives the Law.
- Ezra leads them out, organizes worship, and gives the Law.
- God appropriates Egyptians' wealth for Israel.
- God appropriates Babylonians' wealth for Israel.
- God purges the faithless in the wilderness.
- God purges the faithless in Babylon.
- God empties the land for the "faithful remnant" who survive the wilderness.
- God empties the land for the "faithful remnant" who survive the exile.

Those experiences that fall outside of this narrative no longer make up the official story. For example, the Babylonians took into captivity about 10 percent or less of the population of Judah. Only those who lived in Jerusalem—who were skilled, wealthy, literate, and loyal to the Davidic king—were a threat to Babylonian rule. These were ones who could foment rebellion. Villages that were miles outside of Jerusalem generally took their identity from their locales rather than some far-off urban center. These people, the 90 percent, mostly lived their lives farming in the same villages where they were born. They were not a threat to the Babylonians. They were left in Judah to work the land for the new Babylonian rulers. Their stories fall outside of exile and restoration, and thus they fall outside of "true Israel." In Ezra–Nehemiah, this group may constitute "the people of the land" or even those deemed "foreign" as the text works to establish the metanarrative.

Herbert Robinson Marbury

2 Now these are the people of the province who came from those captive exiles whom King Nebuchadnezzar of Babylon had carried captive to Babylon; they returned to Jerusalem and Judah, all to their own towns. [2]They came with Zerubbabel, Jeshua, Nehemiah, Seraiah, Reelaiah, Mordecai, Bilshan, Mispar, Bigvai, Rehum, and Baanah.

2:1–35 List of migration to claim legitimation. The list of those making the journey to Jerusalem parallels the list in Neh. 7. The Persians named the *province* Yehud, a part of the large satrapy "Beyond the River" that included Babylonia and Syria-Palestine. Given the vast historical swath that the book covers (539–424 BCE or 398 BCE if Artaxerxes II is the emperor referenced instead of Artaxerxes I) and the huge numbers comprising this inventory of families, this list is likely a composite of several migrations from Babylon to Jerusalem. No stories of any particular group's journey to Jerusalem are recounted. Rather, the lists in Ezra 2 and Neh. 7 are meant to determine who can claim membership in this new community and ultimately tenure to land in Jerusalem and the surrounding areas. In this list, the community may be of mixed ethnicity (see also Exod. 12:38). **2:2** *Bilshan* is a

The number of the Israelite people: [3]the descendants of Parosh, two thousand one hundred seventy-two. [4]Of Shephatiah, three hundred seventy-two. [5]Of Arah, seven hundred seventy-five. [6]Of Pahath-moab, namely, the descendants of Jeshua and Joab, two thousand eight hundred twelve. [7]Of Elam, one thousand two hundred fifty-four. [8]Of Zattu, nine hundred forty-five. [9]Of Zaccai, seven hundred sixty. [10]Of Bani, six hundred forty-two. [11]Of Bebai, six hundred twenty-three. [12]Of Azgad, one thousand two hundred twenty-two. [13]Of Adonikam, six hundred sixty-six. [14]Of Bigvai, two thousand fifty-six. [15]Of Adin, four hundred fifty-four. [16]Of Ater, namely, of Hezekiah, ninety-eight. [17]Of Bezai, three hundred twenty-three. [18]Of Jorah, one hundred twelve. [19]Of Hashum, two hundred twenty-three. [20]Of Gibbar, ninety-five. [21]Of Bethlehem, one hundred twenty-three. [22]The people of Netophah, fifty-six. [23]Of Anathoth, one hundred twenty-eight. [24]The descendants of Azmaveth, forty-two. [25]Of Kiriatharim, Chephirah, and Beeroth, seven hundred forty-three. [26]Of Ramah and Geba, six hundred twenty-one. [27]The people of Michmas, one hundred twenty-two. [28]Of Bethel and Ai, two hundred twenty-three. [29]The descendants of Nebo, fifty-two. [30]Of Magbish, one hundred fifty-six. [31]Of the other Elam, one thousand two hundred fifty-four. [32]Of Harim, three hundred twenty. [33]Of Lod, Hadid, and Ono, seven hundred twenty-five. [34]Of Jericho, three hundred forty-five. [35]Of Senaah, three thousand six hundred thirty.

36 The priests: the descendants of Jedaiah, of the house of Jeshua, nine hundred seventy-three. [37]Of Immer, one thousand fifty-two. [38]Of Pashhur, one thousand two hundred forty-seven. [39]Of Harim, one thousand seventeen.

40 The Levites: the descendants of Jeshua and Kadmiel, of the descendants of Hodaviah, seventy-four. [41]The singers: the descendants of Asaph, one hundred twenty-eight. [42]The descendants of the gatekeepers: of Shallum, of Ater, of Talmon, of Akkub, of Hatita, and of Shobai, in all one hundred thirty-nine.

43 The temple servants: the descendants of Ziha, Hasupha, Tabbaoth, [44]Keros, Siaha, Padon, [45]Lebanah, Hagabah, Akkub, [46]Hagab, Shamlai, Hanan, [47]Giddel, Gahar, Reaiah, [48]Rezin, Nekoda, Gazzam, [49]Uzza, Paseah, Besai, [50]Asnah, Meunim, Nephisim, [51]Bakbuk, Hakupha, Harhur, [52]Bazluth, Mehida, Harsha, [53]Barkos, Sisera, Temah, [54]Neziah, and Hatipha.

55 The descendants of Solomon's servants: Sotai, Hassophereth, Peruda, [56]Jaalah, Darkon, Giddel, [57]Shephatiah, Hattil, Pochereth-hazzebaim, and Ami.

58 All the temple servants and the descendants of Solomon's servants were three hundred ninety-two.

59 The following were those who came up from Tel-melah, Tel-harsha, Cherub, Addan, and Immer, though they could not prove their families or their descent, whether they belonged to Israel: [60]the descendants of Delaiah, Tobiah, and Nekoda, six hundred fifty-two. [61]Also, of the descendants of the priests: the descendants of Habaiah, Hakkoz, and Barzillai (who had married one of the daughters of Barzillai the Gileadite and was called by their name). [62]These looked for their entries in the genealogical records, but they were not found there, so they were excluded from the priesthood as unclean; [63]the governor told them that they were not to partake of the most holy food until there should be a priest to consult Urim and Thummim.

64 The whole assembly together was forty-two thousand three hundred sixty, [65]besides their male and female servants, of whom there were seven thousand three hundred thirty-seven, and they had two hundred male and female singers. [66]They had

---

Babylonian name. *Bigvai* and *Rehum* are Persian names. The listing communicates a vision of broad unity, starting with *Israelite people*, including laypeople (vv. 3–34), various clergy (vv. 36–42), and others who serve in the temple (vv. 43–58). It is a promising vision of inclusion, valuing the work and roles of every member of the community.

2:59–63 *They could not prove their families or their descent.* Some of those returning could not demonstrate their lineage. The priesthood leaves the question open so that if they have erred, they have erred on the side of inclusion. The community did not allow the *genealogical records* to become the final arbiter, which might have excluded these families forever. Rather, a process by which their legitimacy would be ascertained by divination is established. On the *Urim and Thummim*, see note on Exod. 28:30.

seven hundred thirty-six horses, two hundred forty-five mules, ⁶⁷four hundred thirty-five camels, and six thousand seven hundred twenty donkeys.

68 As soon as they came to the house of the LORD in Jerusalem, some of the heads of families made freewill offerings for the house of God, to erect it on its site. ⁶⁹According to their resources they gave to the building fund sixty-one thousand darics of gold, five thousand minas of silver, and one hundred priestly robes.

70 The priests, the Levites, and some of the people, as well as the singers, the gatekeepers, and the temple servants, lived in their towns and all Israel in their towns.

3 When the seventh month came and the Israelites were in their*ᵇ* towns, the people gathered together as one in Jerusalem. ²Then Jeshua son of Jozadak with his fellow priests and Zerubbabel son of Shealtiel with his kin set out to build the altar of the God of Israel, to offer burnt offerings on it, as prescribed in the law of Moses the man of God. ³They set up the altar on its foundation because they were in dread of the people of the lands, and they offered burnt offerings upon it to the LORD, morning and evening. ⁴And they kept the Festival of Booths,*ᶜ* as prescribed, and offered the daily burnt offerings by number according to the ordinance, as required for each day, ⁵and after that the regular burnt offerings, the offerings at the new moon and at all the sacred festivals of the LORD, and the offerings of everyone who made a freewill offering to the LORD. ⁶From the first day of the seventh month they began to offer burnt offerings to the LORD. But the foundation of the temple of the LORD was not yet laid. ⁷So they gave money to the masons and the carpenters, and food, drink, and oil to the Sidonians and the Tyrians to bring cedar trees from Lebanon to the sea, to Joppa, according to the grant that they had from King Cyrus of Persia.

8 In the second year after their arrival at the house of God at Jerusalem, in the second month, Zerubbabel son of Shealtiel and Jeshua son of Jozadak made a beginning, together with the rest of their people, the priests and the Levites and all who had come to Jerusalem from the captivity. They appointed the Levites from twenty years old and up to have the oversight of the work on the house of the LORD. ⁹And Jeshua with his sons and his kin, and Kadmiel and his sons, Binnui and Hodaviah,*ᵈ* along with the sons of Henadad, the Levites, their sons and kin, together took charge of the workers in the house of God.

10 When the builders laid the foundation of the temple of the LORD, the priests in their vestments were stationed to praise the LORD with trumpets, and the Levites, the sons of Asaph, with cymbals, according to the directions of King David of Israel; ¹¹and they sang responsively, praising and giving thanks to the LORD,

"For he is good,
    for his steadfast love endures forever
        toward Israel."

And all the people responded with a great shout when they praised the LORD because the foundation of the house of the LORD had

b 3.1 Heb mss Gk Syr Vg: MT *the*   *c* 3.4 Or *Tabernacles*
d 3.9 Heb *sons of Judah*

2:68 Upon their arrival from Babylon, the heads of the families contribute to the *house of the* LORD (the temple), the central symbol of God's presence and connection with the community. **2:69** The writer lists *darics*, a coin named after a later ruler, Darius the Great (who reigned from 522 to 486 BCE), among the wealth of those who migrated to Jerusalem, which is another clue to the composite nature of the list. **3:1–11 Establishing the work of the temple.** Although more than a year would pass before the temple's construction begins, the community comes together to avail itself of the temple's many purposes, both civil and religious. **3:2** Both the civil (*Zerubbabel*) and the religious (*Jeshua*) leadership join to reestablish the temple's work. **3:8** The new temple's construction begins in earnest with the *priests* and *Levites* leading *all* from *the captivity*. **3:10** Highlighting the ceremonial role of the temple, the people sing *according to the directions of King David*, to whom tradition attributes many of the psalms and who is a lionized figure in ancient Israel's history. Again, the emphasis is on the ways that this new community emulates the community of the First Temple. **3:11** *The foundation of the house of the* LORD is on the same location as the former temple. The foundation for this Second Temple symbolizes the desire for continuity in faith, heritage, and political legitimacy with the First

been laid. ¹²But many of the priests and Levites and heads of families, old people who had seen the first house on its foundations, wept with a loud voice when they saw this house, though many shouted aloud for joy, ¹³so that the people could not distinguish the sound of the joyful shout from the sound of the people's weeping, for the people shouted so loudly that the sound was heard far away.

4 When the adversaries of Judah and Benjamin heard that the returned exiles were building a temple to the Lord, the God of Israel, ²they approached Zerubbabel and the heads of families and said to them, "Let us build with you, for we worship your God as you do, and we have been sacrificing to him ever since the days of King Esar-haddon of Assyria, who brought us here." ³But Zerubbabel, Jeshua, and the rest of the heads of families in Israel said to them, "You shall have no part with us in building a house for our God, but we alone will build for the Lord, the God of Israel, as King Cyrus of Persia has commanded us."

Temple community, even if this community is now a mixed group, most of whom have no memory of the old monarchy. As contemporary religious communities, individuals, families, and congregations evolve, new contexts and new members require new ways of understanding themselves in the present and connecting to their histories. For those who returned from Babylon, this new context in Jerusalem required them to perform the challenging work of finding meaningful ways of integrating the present with the past, of connecting new members with those who have a long record of faithfulness, and of honoring history while embracing change.

3:12 The account of the *old people* weeping carries a poignant double meaning. The elders' disappointment with the new construction is both an unfortunate refusal to embrace the future and a formidable challenge to a new generation that they have much to achieve to rival the community's former glory. Since the elders carry with them the historical memory of the community, they are the only ones who can raise this critique.

3:13 This amalgam of joy and sorrow reflects the multifaceted nature of the community, old and young, Babylonian, Persian, ancient Israelite, lay, and priest accompanied by their differing hopes, fears, and expectations. This group coalesces around its shared interest in establishing itself and creating the stability and security that it lacked in Babylon. They take on a new shared identity as the remnant redeemed, framed by the overarching narrative of exile and return (see **"Exile and Restoration Metanarratives," p. 637**). Such identity formation is analogous to the story of the pilgrims in American history. While most U.S. citizens descend from ancestors who either were indigenous to North America, were kidnaped and brought on slave ships from Africa, emigrated by way of the Pacific Ocean or the Rio Grande, or arrived at Ellis Island, the Plymouth Rock story has served as the primary narrative framing American identity. Similarly, in Jerusalem, out of this group characterized by difference more than similarity, once again, God fashions a new people.

4:1–24 Politics of rebuilding. The chapter presents a repeated cycle of building and cessation in constructing the temple. An attempt to build the temple began with Cyrus the Great (539–530 BCE; see **"Cyrus," p. 991**) and perhaps ceased during the reign of Cambyses (530–522 BCE). Cambyses did not possess the stature of his predecessor, Cyrus, nor of his successor Darius the Great (522–486 BCE). To meet the empire's demand for revenue, Cambyses focused on conquering new territory, particularly Egypt, while Darius focused on financially and administratively organizing the provinces already under imperial control. Constructing temples, such as the one in Jerusalem, which he authorized and completed around 520 BCE, was an important part of Darius's administration. The fortification of the wall of Jerusalem probably began under Xerxes (biblical Ahasuerus, 486–465 BCE) and was completed during Artaxerxes's reign (465–424 BCE) under the governorship of Nehemiah. Temples were important centers for finance and government. A new temple in Jerusalem and a new wall fortifying it meant that the city was gaining stature as an imperial center. **4:1–5** The new community in Jerusalem faced external challenges on two fronts. First, officials of neighboring jurisdictions feared that imperial attention and funding priorities might shift from their jurisdictions to Jerusalem. Second, other groups within the province had reason to resist the temple's construction. The priesthood who occupied the temple would have unmatched access to financial resources and proximity to the imperial officials. Other priesthoods and their communities would be relatively diminished in stature or even deposed. **4:2–4** *Let us build with you* points to other groups, *people of the land* (see **"Exile and Restoration Metanarratives," p. 637**), who first attempted to join the

4 Then the people of the land discouraged the people of Judah and made them afraid to build, [5]and they bribed officials to frustrate their plan throughout the reign of King Cyrus of Persia and until the reign of King Darius of Persia.

6 In the reign of Ahasuerus, in his accession year, they wrote an accusation against the inhabitants of Judah and Jerusalem.

7 And in the days of Artaxerxes, Bishlam and Mithredath and Tabeel and the rest of their associates wrote to King Artaxerxes of Persia; the letter was written in Aramaic and translated.[e] [8]Rehum the royal deputy and Shimshai the scribe wrote a letter against Jerusalem to King Artaxerxes as follows [9](then Rehum the royal deputy, Shimshai the scribe, and the rest of their associates, the judges, the envoys, the officials, the Persians, the people of Erech, the Babylonians, the people of Susa, that is, the Elamites, [10]and the rest of the nations whom the great and noble Osnappar deported and settled in the cities of Samaria and in the rest of the province Beyond the River wrote—and now [11]this is a copy of the letter that they sent):

"To King Artaxerxes: Your servants, the people of the province Beyond the River, send greeting. And now [12]may it be known to the king that the Jews who came up from you to us have gone to Jerusalem. They are rebuilding that rebellious and wicked city; they are finishing the walls and repairing the foundations. [13]Now may it be known to the king that, if this city is rebuilt and the walls finished, they will not pay tribute, custom, or toll, and the royal revenue will be reduced. [14]Now because we share the salt of the palace and it is not fitting for us to witness the king's dishonor, therefore we send and inform the king, [15]so that a search may be made in the

annals of your ancestors. You will discover in the annals that this is a rebellious city, hurtful to kings and provinces, and that sedition was stirred up in it from long ago. On that account this city was laid waste. [16]We make known to the king that, if this city is rebuilt and its walls finished, you will then have no possession in the province Beyond the River."

17 The king sent an answer: "To Rehum the royal deputy and Shimshai the scribe and the rest of their associates who live in Samaria and in the rest of the province Beyond the River, greeting. And now [18]the letter that you sent to us has been read in translation before me. [19]So I made a decree, and someone searched and discovered that this city has risen against kings from long ago and that rebellion and sedition have been made in it. [20]Jerusalem has had mighty kings who ruled over the whole province Beyond the River, to whom tribute, custom, and toll were paid. [21]Therefore issue an order that these people be made to cease and that this city not be rebuilt, until I make a decree. [22]Moreover, take care not to be slack in this matter; why should damage grow to the hurt of the king?"

23 Then when the copy of King Artaxerxes's letter was read before Rehum and the scribe Shimshai and their associates, they hurried to the Jews in Jerusalem and by force and power made them cease. [24]At that time the work on the house of God in Jerusalem stopped and was discontinued until the second year of the reign of King Darius of Persia.

5 Now Haggai the prophet and Zechariah son of Iddo[f] prophesied to the Jews who

e 4.7 Heb adds *in Aramaic*, indicating that 4.8–6.18 is in Aramaic. Another interpretation is *The letter was written in the Aramaic script and set forth in the Aramaic language*
f 5.1 Gk: Aram adds *the prophets*

project in a show of solidarity. When they were rebuffed, they strategized to raise the empire's suspicion about the loyalty of those who had returned from Babylon. **4:6–24** Since the Persian Empire was loosely controlled by the military, fortifying a city with a wall without prior imperial permission would have been considered a treasonous act. Any major construction within the Persian Empire such as a temple or the fortification of a city would need direct imperial consent not to raise great suspicion. These two distinct projects (constructing the temple and rebuilding the wall) with two different timelines are conflated in order to emphasize the magnitude of outside resistance to rebuilding. Despite formidable resistance, the new community was unwavering in its resolve to establish itself and complete the rebuilding. The Jerusalem community's work and faith prevailed. **4:8** As v. 7 indicates, the *letter*—presumably Ezra 4:8–6:18, according to biblical scholarship—is in Aramaic. Ezra 7:12–26 is also composed in Aramaic. Since Aramaic was the lingua franca of the Persian Empire, the Aramaic portions replicate the language and style of official Persian documents. **5:1–17 Another account of rebuilding the temple.** In this account of the temple's reconstruction,

were in Judah and Jerusalem in the name of the God of Israel who was over them. ²Then Zerubbabel son of Shealtiel and Jeshua son of Jozadak set out to rebuild the house of God in Jerusalem, and with them were the prophets of God, helping them.

3 At the same time Tattenai the governor of the province Beyond the River and Shethar-bozenai and their associates came to them and spoke to them thus, "Who gave you a decree to build this house and to finish this structure?" ⁴They⁹ also asked them this, "What are the names of the men who are building this building?" ⁵But the eye of their God was upon the elders of the Jews, and they did not stop them until a report reached Darius and then answer was returned by letter in reply to it.

6 The copy of the letter that Tattenai the governor of the province Beyond the River and Shethar-bozenai and his associates the envoys who were in the province Beyond the River sent to King Darius; ⁷they sent him a report in which was written as follows: "To Darius the king, all peace! ⁸May it be known to the king that we went to the province of Judah, to the house of the great God. It is being built of hewn stone, and timber is laid in the walls; this work is being done diligently and prospers in their hands. ⁹Then we spoke to those elders and asked them, 'Who gave you a decree to build this house and to finish this structure?' ¹⁰We also asked them their names, for your information, so that we might write down the names of the men at their head. ¹¹This was their reply to us: 'We are the servants of the God of heaven and earth, and we are rebuilding the house that was built many years ago, which a great king of Israel built and finished. ¹²But because our ancestors had angered the God of heaven, he gave them into the hand of King Nebuchadnezzar of Babylon, the Chaldean, who destroyed this house and carried away the people to Babylonia. ¹³However, King Cyrus of Babylon, in the first year of his reign, made a decree that this house of God should be rebuilt. ¹⁴Moreover, the gold and silver vessels of the house of God, which Nebuchadnezzar had taken out of the temple in Jerusalem and had brought into the temple of Babylon, these King Cyrus took out of the temple of Babylon, and they were delivered to a man named Sheshbazzar, whom he had made governor. ¹⁵He said to him, "Take these vessels; go and put them in the temple in Jerusalem, and let the house of God be rebuilt on its site." ¹⁶Then this Sheshbazzar came and laid the foundations of the house of God in Jerusalem, and from that time until now it has been under construction, and it is not yet finished.' ¹⁷And now, if it seems good to the king, have a search made in the royal archives there in Babylon, to see whether a decree was issued by King Cyrus for the rebuilding of this house of God in Jerusalem. Let the king send us his pleasure in this matter."

g 5.4 Gk Syr: Aram *We*

the focus is on the leadership of the prophets Haggai and Zechariah (see Hag. 1:1 and Zech. 1:1). **5:5** *Darius* ruled the Persian Empire from 522 to 486 BCE. He increased the revenue of the Persian bureaucracy by organizing and regularizing tax collection. He authorized and funded the construction of temples and other building projects throughout the empire, including the Second Temple in Jerusalem, which served as a central fixture of imperial administration in the province. The temple was simultaneously a bureaucratic center for tax collection for the Persians and a center for religious, cultural, and civic life for the community in Jerusalem. **5:6–17** Local resistance brings political authorities to the building site to challenge the community's authority to build. Through letters, they attempt to verify that the community has imperial permission. **5:11–12** Perhaps relying on stories that they had heard in Babylon of the existence of an earlier temple or based on the older temple's ruins still on the ground, the community reports to the authorities that they are only *rebuilding the house that was built many years ago*. This reference to the First Temple continues the work of legitimizing the new one. More importantly, for the people, the new temple's legitimacy predates Persian sovereignty. By appealing to a time before the Persians, the subtle response makes clear that God's authority overrides any governmental jurisdiction. Their God was even responsible for the temple's earlier destruction; *the God of heaven* was *angered* so they were given *into the hand of King Nebuchadnezzar of Babylon*. **5:17** The letter ends with a request to *search* the *royal archives* for Cyrus's *decree*. The growing power of written language during the Persian period can be seen here (see also Esth. 1:20; 2:23; 3:12–14; 6:1; 8:9–13).

6 Then King Darius made a decree, and they searched the archives where the documents were stored in Babylon. ²But it was in Ecbatana, the capital in the province of Media, that a scroll was found on which this was written: "A record. ³In the first year of his reign, King Cyrus issued a decree: Concerning the house of God at Jerusalem, let the house be rebuilt, the place where sacrifices are offered and burnt offerings are brought;[b] its height shall be sixty cubits and its width sixty cubits, ⁴with three courses of hewn stones and one course of timber; let the cost be paid from the royal treasury. ⁵Moreover, let the gold and silver vessels of the house of God that Nebuchadnezzar took out of the temple in Jerusalem and brought to Babylon be restored and brought back to the temple in Jerusalem, each to its place; you shall put them in the house of God."

6 "Now you, Tattenai, governor of the province Beyond the River, Shethar-bozenai, and you, their associates, the envoys in the province Beyond the River, keep away; ⁷let the work on this house of God alone; let the governor of the Jews and the elders of the Jews rebuild this house of God on its site. ⁸Moreover, I make a decree regarding what you shall do for these elders of the Jews for the rebuilding of this house of God: the cost is to be paid to these people, in full and without delay, from the royal revenue, the tribute of the province Beyond the River. ⁹Whatever is needed—young bulls, rams, or sheep for burnt offerings to the God of heaven, wheat, salt, wine, or oil, as the priests in Jerusalem require—let that be given to them day by day without fail, ¹⁰so that they may offer pleasing sacrifices to the God of heaven and pray for the life of the king and his children.

¹¹Furthermore, I decree that, if anyone alters this edict, a beam shall be pulled out of the house of the perpetrator, who then shall be impaled on it. The house shall be made a dunghill. ¹²May the God who has established his name there overthrow any king or people who shall put forth a hand to alter this or to destroy this house of God in Jerusalem. I, Darius, make a decree; let it be done with all diligence."

13 Then, according to the word sent by King Darius, Tattenai, the governor of the province Beyond the River, Shethar-bozenai, and their associates did with all diligence what King Darius had ordered. ¹⁴So the elders of the Jews built and prospered, through the prophesying of the prophet Haggai and Zechariah son of Iddo. They finished their building by command of the God of Israel and by decree of Cyrus, Darius, and King Artaxerxes of Persia, ¹⁵and this house was finished on the third day of the month of Adar, in the sixth year of the reign of King Darius.

16 The people of Israel, the priests and the Levites, and the rest of the returned exiles celebrated the dedication of this house of God with joy. ¹⁷They offered at the dedication of this house of God one hundred bulls, two hundred rams, four hundred lambs, and as a sin offering for all Israel, twelve male goats, according to the number of the tribes of Israel. ¹⁸Then they set the priests in their divisions and the Levites in their courses for the service of God at Jerusalem, as it is written in the book of Moses.

19 On the fourteenth day of the first month the returned exiles kept the Passover. ²⁰For both the priests and the Levites had purified

b 6.3 Meaning of Aram uncertain

6:1–12 The empire sanctions the temple's construction. When imperial officials find the original decree from Cyrus's reign, Darius reinstates it. **6:3–5** The *decree* of Cyrus is reproduced. It is similar to 1:2–4 but contains additional details concerning the temple's construction and its financing *from the royal treasury*. **6:6–12** Darius ensures that the temple will be rebuilt and that it is well funded, which is evidence of the dual nature of temples in the ancient world. Darius authorizes the construction and provides the resources for a *house of God in Jerusalem* as he did houses of deities in Egypt and Babylon. Since Persian-constructed temples functioned as bureaucratic and financial centers for the province, these temples would have held archives and served as storehouses for taxes. Darius is just as interested in its construction as the people in Jerusalem, which may explain the dire consequences outlined for *anyone* who *alters this edict* (v. 11) or interferes with the completion of the project (v. 12).

6:14–18 While Darius is interested in the temple's civic function in the imperial bureaucracy, the Jerusalem community is eager to reestablish the temple's cultural and religious role. For them, Persian power did not authorize their temple; rather, the temple was completed through *the*

themselves; all of them were clean. So they slaughtered the Passover lamb for all the returned exiles, for their fellow priests, and for themselves. ²¹It was eaten by the people of Israel who had returned from exile and also by all who had joined them and separated themselves from the pollutions of the nations of the land to seek the LORD, the God of Israel. ²²With joy they celebrated the Festival of Unleavened Bread seven days, for the LORD had made them joyful and had turned the heart of the king of Assyria to them, so that he aided them in the work on the house of God, the God of Israel.

7 After this, in the reign of King Artaxerxes of Persia, Ezra son of Seraiah, son of Azariah, son of Hilkiah, ²son of Shallum, son of Zadok, son of Ahitub, ³son of Amariah, son of Azariah, son of Meraioth, ⁴son of Zerahiah, son of Uzzi, son of Bukki, ⁵son of Abishua, son of Phinehas, son of Eleazar, son of the chief priest Aaron—⁶this Ezra went up from Babylonia. He was a scribe skilled in the law of Moses that the LORD the God of Israel had given, and the king granted him all that he asked, for the hand of the LORD his God was upon him.

7 Some of the people of Israel and some of the priests and Levites, the singers and gatekeepers, and the temple servants also went up to Jerusalem in the seventh year of King Artaxerxes. ⁸They came to Jerusalem in the fifth month, which was in the seventh year of the king. ⁹On the first day of the first month the journey up from Babylon was begun, and on the first day of the fifth month he came to Jerusalem, for the gracious hand of his God was upon him. ¹⁰For Ezra had set his heart to study the law of the LORD and to do it and to teach the statutes and ordinances in Israel.

11 This is a copy of the letter that King Artaxerxes gave to Ezra the priest and scribe, a scholar of the words of the commandments of the LORD and his statutes for Israel: ¹²"Artaxerxes, king of kings, to the priest Ezra, the scribe of the law of the God of heaven: Peace.ⁱ And now ¹³I decree that any of the people of Israel or their priests or Levites in my kingdom who freely offers to go to Jerusalem may go with you. ¹⁴For you are sent by the king and his seven counselors to make inquiries about Judah and Jerusalem according to the law of your God, which is in your hand, ¹⁵and also to convey the silver and gold that the king and his counselors have freely offered to the God of Israel,

i 7.12 Syr Vg: Aram *Perfect*

prophesying of the prophet Haggai and Zechariah and according to the *command of the God of Israel*. **6:15–18 Celebrating the temple's completion.** The community finally completes the temple on the third of Adar (February/March) in 516/515 BCE.

6:19–22 With this account of a Passover celebration, the writer again emphasizes the new community's continuity with the former ancient Israel. By the time the book of Ezra–Nehemiah is written, Passover has come to be celebrated on a fixed date and has been consolidated with the Feast of Unleavened Bread. Passover ritualizes the exile-return metanarrative, just as Thanksgiving ritualizes the metanarrative of Plymouth Rock in the United States.

7:1–6 Introducing Ezra. According to his genealogy, Ezra descends from the line of high priests, but Ezra is first described as a *scribe skilled in the law of Moses* (v. 6) rather than a priest. In any ancient agricultural society, only 1–2 percent of the population was literate beyond the proficiency necessary to perform daily tasks, so a scribe was a highly valued position. Because literacy was so scarce and administrative roles were far less specialized than in modern times, Ezra would have performed all the administrative duties that required literacy. Such duties included composing official correspondence, maintaining provincial records and official accounts, and managing inventories. Ezra also will be later called a "priest" (v. 11).

7:10 Ezra's expertise in the Torah of Moses is emphasized as he comes to Jerusalem prepared not only *to study the law* ("torah") *of the LORD* but *to do it* and *to teach* it. Mere knowledge of the sacred teaching was insufficient; Ezra's role called him to interpret the law of Moses for his community, not simply apply it (see Neh. 8:8). The needs of this generation would be vastly different from the needs of those who left Egypt, those who lived under the monarchy, or those who lived in Babylon. Ezra is called to interpret Moses's instructions for this new community, thus establishing the role of the ideal leader in postexilic Judaism.

7:11–26 Imperial support continues. Artaxerxes's Aramaic decree vests Ezra and his work, particularly the construction of the temple, with imperial authority. As an imperial decree, the document's

whose dwelling is in Jerusalem, [16]with all the silver and gold that you shall find in the whole province of Babylonia and with the freewill offerings of the people and the priests, given willingly for the house of their God in Jerusalem. [17]With this money, then, you shall with all diligence buy bulls, rams, and lambs and their grain offerings and their drink offerings, and you shall offer them on the altar of the house of your God in Jerusalem. [18]Whatever seems good to you and your colleagues to do with the rest of the silver and gold, you may do, according to the will of your God. [19]The vessels that have been given you for the service of the house of your God, you shall deliver before the God of Jerusalem. [20]And whatever else is required for the house of your God that you are responsible for providing, you may provide out of the king's treasury.

[21]"I, King Artaxerxes, decree to all the treasurers in the province Beyond the River: Whatever the priest Ezra, the scribe of the law of the God of heaven, requires of you, let it be done with all diligence, [22]up to one hundred talents of silver, one hundred cors of wheat, one hundred baths[j] of wine, one hundred baths[k] of oil, and unlimited salt. [23]Whatever is commanded by the God of heaven, let it be done with zeal for the house of the God of heaven, or wrath will come upon the realm of the king and his heirs. [24]We also notify you that it shall not be lawful to impose tribute, custom, or toll on any of the priests, the Levites, the singers, the doorkeepers, the temple servants, or other servants of this house of God.

[25]"And you, Ezra, according to the God-given wisdom you possess, appoint magistrates and judges who may judge all the people in the province Beyond the River who know the laws of your God, and you shall teach those who do not know them. [26]All who will not obey the law of your God and the law of the king, let judgment be strictly executed on them, whether for death or for banishment or for confiscation of their goods or for imprisonment."

[27]Blessed be the LORD, the God of our ancestors, who put such a thing as this into the heart of the king to glorify the house of the LORD in Jerusalem [28]and who extended to me steadfast love before the king and his counselors and before all the king's mighty officers. I took courage, for the hand of the LORD my God was upon me, and I gathered leaders from Israel to go up with me.

8 These are their family heads, and this is the genealogy of those who went up with me from Babylonia, in the reign of King Artaxerxes: [2]Of the descendants of Phinehas, Gershom. Of Ithamar, Daniel. Of David, Hattush, [3]of the descendants of Shecaniah. Of Parosh, Zechariah, with whom were registered one hundred fifty males. [4]Of the descendants of Pahath-moab, Eliehoenai son of Zerahiah, and with him two hundred males. [5]Of the descendants of Zattu,[l] Shecaniah son of Jahaziel, and with him three hundred males. [6]Of the descendants of Adin, Ebed son of Jonathan, and with him fifty males. [7]Of the descendants of Elam, Jeshaiah son of Athaliah, and with him seventy males. [8]Of the descendants of Shephatiah, Zebadiah son of Michael, and with him eighty males. [9]Of the descendants of Joab, Obadiah son of Jehiel, and with him two hundred eighteen males. [10]Of the descendants of Bani,[m] Shelomith son of Josiphiah, and with him one hundred sixty males. [11]Of the descendants of Bebai, Zechariah son of Bebai, and with him twenty-eight males. [12]Of the descendants of Azgad, Johanan son of Hakkatan, and with him one hundred ten males. [13]Of the descendants of Adonikam,

j 7.22 A Heb measure of volume   *k* 7.22 A Heb measure of volume   *l* 8.5 Gk: Heb lacks *of Zattu*   *m* 8.10 Gk: Heb lacks *Bani*

authority is greater than any resistance to Ezra's work since the entire region was under Persian jurisdiction. For the community, its theological meaning is clear. Although manifestations of Persian imperial power are visible, the power of God is sovereign. In the letter, there is repeated reference to *the law of the God of heaven* (vv. 12, 21) or *the law[s] of your God* (vv. 14, 25, 26), *the God of Israel* (v. 15), and *God in* or *of Jerusalem* (vv. 16, 17, 19). **7:26** *The law of your God* and *the law of the king* are linked, mutually reinforced, and both binding.

8:1–14 List of migration with Ezra to claim legitimation. A list detailing the mass migration from Babylon to Jerusalem with Ezra. The list, based in family *genealogy*, registers those who have access to and can participate in the new community. The twelve lay families and two priestly families, all of whom also had members return earlier according to Ezra 2:3–15, represent the text's vision of what is now "all Israel"—namely, those who left Babylon to emigrate to Jerusalem.

those who came later, their names being Eliphelet, Jeuel, and Shemaiah, and with them sixty males. [14]Of the descendants of Bigvai, Uthai and Zaccur, and with them seventy males.

15 I gathered them by the river that runs to Ahava, and there we camped three days. As I reviewed the people and the priests, I found there none of the descendants of Levi. [16]Then I sent for Eliezer, Ariel, Shemaiah, Elnathan, Jarib, Elnathan, Nathan, Zechariah, and Meshullam, who were leaders, and for Joiarib and Elnathan, who were wise, [17]and sent them to Iddo, the leader at the place called Casiphia, telling them what to say to Iddo and his colleagues the temple servants at Casiphia, namely, to send us ministers for the house of our God. [18]Since the gracious hand of our God was upon us, they brought us a man of discretion, of the descendants of Mahli son of Levi son of Israel, namely, Sherebiah, with his sons and kin, eighteen; [19]also Hashabiah and with him Jeshaiah of the descendants of Merari, with his kin and their sons, twenty; [20]besides two hundred twenty of the temple servants, whom David and his officials had set apart to attend the Levites. These were all mentioned by name.

21 Then I proclaimed a fast there, at the River Ahava, that we might humble ourselves[n] before our God, to seek from him a safe journey for ourselves, our children, and all our possessions. [22]For I was ashamed to ask the king for a band of soldiers and cavalry to protect us against the enemy on our way, since we had told the king that the hand of our God is gracious to all who seek him, but his power and his wrath are against all who forsake him. [23]So we fasted and petitioned our God for this, and he listened to our entreaty.

24 Then I set apart twelve of the leading priests: Sherebiah, Hashabiah, and ten of their kin with them. [25]And I weighed out to them the silver and the gold and the vessels, the offering for the house of our God that the king, his counselors, his lords, and all Israel there present had offered; [26]I weighed out into their hand six hundred fifty talents of silver, and one hundred silver vessels worth . . . talents,[o] and one hundred talents of gold, [27]twenty gold bowls worth a thousand darics, and two vessels of fine polished bronze as precious as gold. [28]And I said to them, "You are holy to the Lord, and the vessels are holy, and the silver and the gold are a freewill offering to the Lord, the God of your ancestors. [29]Guard them and keep them until you weigh them before the chief priests and the Levites and the heads of families in Israel at Jerusalem, within the chambers of the house of the Lord." [30]So the priests and the Levites took over the silver, the gold, and the vessels as they were weighed out, to bring them to Jerusalem, to the house of our God.

31 Then we left the River Ahava on the twelfth day of the first month to go to Jerusalem; the hand of our God was upon us, and he

n 8.21 Or *fast*   o 8.26 The number of talents is lacking

8:15–20 Only from the ranks of those who come from Babylon does Ezra fill all the roles necessary for temple administration. This group is sufficient to do all that God requires in Jerusalem. The Levites are initially absent from Ezra's migration (v. 15), and Ezra must make an extra effort to recruit them. Their apprehension may reflect resistance to the second-class status they would experience in Jerusalem. Throughout the Hebrew Bible, Levites are portrayed as a second-tier clergy to the Zadokites. In this instance, Nehemiah admonishes the priesthood to give the Levites their just portions of land in Neh. 13:5.

8:21–23 Divine instead of imperial protection. With no imperial military, Ezra petitions God for protection. Ezra believes that his mission's legitimacy is based in God's authority rather than imperial power. Reliance upon the imperial military would only appear to weaken his claim of divine authority. His intention is that his journey and his subsequent work should be seen as God's mandate, not an imperial directive. Ezra's leadership testifies to his devout faithfulness; God's power will prove sufficient and a more effective protector than the imperial army.

8:24–30 Nonetheless, Ezra takes seriously the responsibility of guarding the temple vessels. Transporting such wealth from one end of the empire to another was fraught with danger. As a precaution, he distributes the vessels among the priests and expressly charges each with guarding them to ensure their safe delivery to the temple in Jerusalem.

8:31 *The hand of our God was upon us.* Ezra's fast and prayer (as well as his delegation and distribution of the temple vessels) work, and the group arrives in Jerusalem unharmed.

delivered us from the hand of the enemy and from ambushes along the way. ³²We came to Jerusalem and remained there three days. ³³On the fourth day, within the house of our God, the silver, the gold, and the vessels were weighed into the hands of the priest Meremoth son of Uriah, and with him was Eleazar son of Phinehas, and with them were the Levites, Jozabad son of Jeshua and Noadiah son of Binnui. ³⁴The total was counted and weighed, and the weight of everything was recorded.

35 At that time those who had come from captivity, the returned exiles, offered burnt offerings to the God of Israel: twelve bulls for all Israel, ninety-six rams, seventy-seven lambs, and as a sin offering twelve male goats; all this was a burnt offering to the LORD. ³⁶They also delivered the king's commissions to the king's satraps and to the governors of the province Beyond the River, and they supported the people and the house of God.

9 After these things had been done, the officials approached me and said, "The people of Israel, the priests, and the Levites have not separated themselves from the peoples of the lands with their abominations, from the Canaanites, the Hittites, the Perizzites, the Jebusites, the Ammonites, the Moabites, the Egyptians, and the Amorites. ²For they have taken some of their daughters as wives for themselves and for their sons. Thus the holy seed has mixed itself with the peoples of the lands, and in this faithlessness the officials and leaders have led the way." ³When I heard this, I tore my garment and my mantle and pulled hair from my head and beard and sat appalled. ⁴Then all who trembled at the words of the God of Israel because of the faithlessness of the returned exiles gathered around me while I sat appalled until the evening sacrifice.

5 At the evening sacrifice I got up from my fasting, with my garments and my mantle torn, and fell on my knees, spread out my hands to the LORD my God, ⁶and said,

"O my God, I am too ashamed and embarrassed to lift my face to you, my God, for our iniquities have risen higher than our heads, and our guilt has mounted up to the heavens. ⁷From the days of our ancestors to this day we have been deep in guilt, and for our iniquities we, our kings, and our priests have been handed over to the kings of the lands, to the sword, to captivity, to plundering, and to

9–10 Ezra institutes reforms: intermarriage and community survival. See **"Intermarriage,"** p. 649.

9:1 *The peoples of the lands*, people who are not Israelite. The names of Israel's traditional enemies (*the Canaanites, the Hittites, the Perizzites, the Jebusites, the Ammonites, the Moabites, the Egyptians, and the Amorites*) are invoked to characterize the intermarriages even though most of these groups were no longer in the area. The last three names are additions that appear only in this list. The names are a literary allusion to older laws and stories wherein Israel believed these groups threatened its survival (see Deut. 7:1; 23:3–6). To invoke them signals the urgency of the current situation and calls the community to understand themselves as people also facing a threat. To be a people is as much a political designation as it is an inherited one. As Ezra understood it, the community's survival depended on bringing this disparate group together as a people who would see themselves as having a shared history, identity, and aspirations. In fact, it was crucial for Ezra to consolidate this group into a political unity. Otherwise, would they accept his authority, based in Mosaic law? Although they had been devastated by Babylon and were now subjugated by Persia, Ezra refuses to accept their oppression as hopeless.

9:2 *The holy seed* implies that ethnic identity is connected to religious identity. The phrase is found in Isa. 6:13, although compare with Isa. 56:3, 6–7.

9:5–15 Ezra sets a powerful example. He leads the community to accept this new identity, even portions that were obviously painful. By doing so, they claim a communal identity despite disparate backgrounds and stories. **9:6–7** Claiming that the people are *deep in guilt* and *iniquities*, he leads them in a communal confession and lament. *From the days of our ancestors to this day.* Ezra's communal prayer flattens moral standing among the people and unifies the community translocationally (both in Jerusalem and Babylon) and transhistorically. He invites the community to see their part in their own oppression and to take responsibility; they may be oppressed, but they are not helpless. By claiming responsibility, they also claim agency, so responsibility becomes an act

utter shame, as is now the case. [8]But now for a brief moment favor has been shown by the LORD our God, who has left us a remnant and given us a stake in his holy place, in order that he[p] may brighten our eyes and grant us a little sustenance in our slavery. [9]For we are slaves; yet our God has not forsaken us in our slavery but has extended to us his steadfast love before the kings of Persia, to give us new life to set up the house of our God, to repair its ruins, and to give us a wall in Judea and Jerusalem.

[10] "And now, our God, what shall we say after this? For we have forsaken your commandments, [11]which you commanded by your servants the prophets, saying, 'The land that you are entering to possess is a land unclean with the pollutions of the peoples of the lands, with their abominations. They have filled it from end to end with their uncleanness. [12]Therefore, do not give your daughters to their sons, neither take their daughters for your sons, and never seek their peace or prosperity, so that you may be strong and eat the good of the land and leave it for an inheritance to your children forever.' [13]After all that has come upon us for our evil deeds and for our great guilt, seeing that you, our God, have punished us less than our iniquities deserved and have given us such a remnant as this, [14]shall we break your commandments again and intermarry with the peoples who practice these abominations? Would you not be angry with us until you destroy us without remnant or survivor? [15]O LORD, God of Israel, you are just, but we have escaped as a remnant, as is now the case. Here we are before you in our guilt, though no one can face you because of this."

10 While Ezra prayed and made confession, weeping and throwing himself down before the house of God, a very great assembly of men, women, and children gathered to him out of Israel; the people also wept bitterly. [2]Shecaniah son of Jehiel, of the descendants of Elam, addressed Ezra, saying, "We have broken faith with our God and have married foreign women from the peoples of the land, but even now there is hope for Israel in spite of this. [3]So now let us make a covenant with our God to send away all these wives and their children, according to the counsel of my lord and of those who tremble at the commandment of our God, and let it be done according to the law. [4]Take action, for it is your duty, and we are with you; be strong, and do it." [5]Then Ezra stood up and made the leading priests, the Levites, and all Israel swear that they would do as had been said. So they swore.

6 Then Ezra withdrew from before the house of God and went to the chamber of Jehohanan son of Eliashib, where he spent the night.[q] He did not eat bread or drink water, for he was mourning over the faithlessness of the exiles. [7]They made a proclamation throughout Judah and Jerusalem to all the returned exiles that they should assemble at Jerusalem [8]and that, if any did not come within three days, by order of the officials and the elders all their property should be forfeited and they themselves banned from the congregation of the exiles.

9 Then all the people of Judah and Benjamin assembled at Jerusalem within the

p 9.8 Heb *our God*   q 10.6 1 Esdras 9.2: Heb *where he went*

of resistance. **9:8–9** *But now for a brief moment*. After the lament, Ezra reminds the people of God's grace by recasting their servitude as opportunity. Even in the harsh slavery of Persian dominion, Ezra found God working toward liberation. His prayer reframes their enslaved status under the Persians and directs the people to work within the modicum of liberty available. **9:10–11** *For we have forsaken your commandments*. The problem with the intermarriages also seems to be one of improper worship.

10:1–5 After Ezra's lament, the people slowly accept his course of action. *A very great assembly of men, women, and children* also weep. They agree that the exogamous marriages are sinful and enter a public *covenant* to hold one another accountable and *send away all these wives and their children . . . according to the law* (Deut. 24:1–4 allows for divorce). **10:4–5** They agree, and *all Israel swear that they would* divorce. Divorce as a response to exogamous marriage would be unconscionable to most twenty-first-century moral sensibilities (see **"Intermarriage," p. 649**).

10:7–8 Ezra encounters resistance to his reforms and responds with a harsh penalty for noncompliance: property forfeiture and expulsion from the congregation.

10:9–17 The divorce proceedings. There are no easy resolutions. Ezra struggles to navigate his faith and his understanding of the teachings of Moses. However, when he encounters "real-lived"

Going Deeper: Intermarriage (Ezra 9–10)

Two traditions on exogamy, or marriage to foreigners, appear in the Hebrew Bible. One tradition affirms marriage to foreigners. Joseph is married to an Egyptian woman (Gen. 41:45) and their sons Ephraim and Manasseh become the eponymous ancestors of two tribes. In Num. 12, God punishes Miriam and Aaron when they criticize Moses's marriage to an African (Cushite) woman. Ruth, a Moabite, marries Boaz and becomes an ancestor of David and later Jesus. Another more prominent tradition condemns such behavior. In Genesis, Esau's Hittite wives torment Rebekah and Isaac (Gen. 26). Solomon's marriages earn strong critique in 1 Kgs. 11. Ahab's abuses are blamed on his marriage to Jezebel, the daughter of a Sidonian (1 Kgs. 16:31). Proverbs 7 threatens that such marriages result in the demise of Israelite men. Ezra follows this tradition. Exogamy receives passionate condemnation here because of its power to transfer real property. The priesthood relied upon the agricultural produce of the land both for their livelihood and to meet the imperial tax levy. If the tax levy was not met, the empire might have deposed this priesthood and installed another more effective at producing revenue. Each time a member of the community married an outsider, there was the possibility that heirs who inherited the father's property might identify with the culture of the "foreign" parent and transfer their loyalties and financial support from the community in Jerusalem. Economically, the net effect of intermarriage in the Jerusalem aristocracy was to diminish the wealth of those returning from exile. Demographically, these unions diminished the number of adherents to the temple. With each instance of intermarriage, the Second Temple priesthood saw the collective's land base and likewise its own potential revenue and ability to meet the imperial tax levy erode. Each instance of intermarriage potentially threatened both the life of the temple and the community.

Herbert Robinson Marbury

three days; it was the ninth month, on the twentieth day of the month. All the people sat in the open square before the house of God, trembling because of this matter and because of the heavy rain. [10]Then Ezra the priest stood up and said to them, "You have trespassed and married foreign women and so increased the guilt of Israel. [11]Now make confession to the LORD the God of your ancestors and do his will; separate yourselves from the peoples of the land and from the foreign wives." [12]Then all the assembly answered with a loud voice, "It is so; we must do as you have said. [13]But the people are many, and it is a time of heavy rain; we cannot stand in the open. Nor is this a task for one day or for two, for many of us have transgressed in this matter. [14]Let our officials represent the whole assembly, and let all in our towns who have taken foreign wives come at appointed times, and with them the elders and judges of every town, until the fierce wrath of our God on this

account is averted from us." [15]Only Jonathan son of Asahel and Jahzeiah son of Tikvah opposed this, and Meshullam and Shabbethai the Levites supported them.

16 Then the returned exiles did so. Ezra the priest selected men,[r] heads of families, according to their families, each of them designated by name. On the first day of the tenth month they sat down to examine the matter. [17]By the first day of the first month they had come to the end of all the men who had married foreign women.

18 There were found of the descendants of the priests who had married foreign women, of the descendants of Jeshua son of Jozadak and his brothers: Maaseiah, Eliezer, Jarib, and Gedaliah. [19]They pledged themselves to send away their wives, and their guilt offering was a ram of the flock for their guilt. [20]Of the descendants of Immer: Hanani and Zebadiah. [21]Of the descendants of Harim: Maaseiah, Elijah, Shemaiah, Jehiel, and Uzziah. [22]Of the

r 10.16 Syr: Heb *And there were selected Ezra,*

situations of members of the community, what began as a clear directive to instruct this new generation in Torah and to rebuild the temple unravels in the face of marriages and families. If carried out, the reforms would fall with destructive force on real families, particularly women and children, who enjoyed few protections in such a patriarchal society. Even after prayer and fasting for discernment, Ezra offers no better options. He persists in carrying out the reforms as he understands them. The most vulnerable, the women and children who are expelled, have no say in their fate. They also had invested in the life of the Jerusalem community. If Ezra had consulted them, might other options have come to light?

descendants of Pashhur: Elioenai, Maaseiah, Ishmael, Nethanel, Jozabad, and Elasah.

23 Of the Levites: Jozabad, Shimei, Kelaiah (that is, Kelita), Pethahiah, Judah, and Eliezer. [24]Of the singers: Eliashib. Of the gatekeepers: Shallum, Telem, and Uri.

25 And of Israel: of the descendants of Parosh: Ramiah, Izziah, Malchijah, Mijamin, Eleazar, Hashabiah,[s] and Benaiah. [26]Of the descendants of Elam: Mattaniah, Zechariah, Jehiel, Abdi, Jeremoth, and Elijah. [27]Of the descendants of Zattu: Elioenai, Eliashib, Mattaniah, Jeremoth, Zabad, and Aziza. [28]Of the descendants of Bebai: Jehohanan, Hananiah, Zabbai, and Athlai. [29]Of the descendants of Bani: Meshullam, Malluch, Adaiah, Jashub, Sheal, and Jeremoth. [30]Of the descendants of Pahath-moab: Adna, Chelal, Benaiah, Maaseiah, Mattaniah, Bezalel, Binnui, and Manasseh. [31]Of the descendants of Harim: Eliezer, Isshijah, Malchijah, Shemaiah, Shimeon, [32]Benjamin, Malluch, and Shemariah. [33]Of the descendants of Hashum: Mattenai, Mattattah, Zabad, Eliphelet, Jeremai, Manasseh, and Shimei. [34]Of the descendants of Bani: Maadai, Amram, Uel, [35]Benaiah, Bedeiah, Cheluhi, [36]Vaniah, Meremoth, Eliashib, [37]Mattaniah, Mattenai, and Jaasu. [38]Of the descendants of Binnui:[t] Shimei, [39]Shelemiah, Nathan, Adaiah, [40]Machnadebai, Shashai, Sharai, [41]Azarel, Shelemiah, Shemariah, [42]Shallum, Amariah, and Joseph. [43]Of the descendants of Nebo: Jeiel, Mattithiah, Zabad, Zebina, Jaddai, Joel, and Benaiah. [44]All these had married foreign women, and they sent them away with their children.[u]

s 10.25 Gk: Heb *Malchijah*   t 10.38 Gk: Heb *Bani, Binnui*
u 10.44 1 Esdras 9.36; meaning of Heb uncertain

10:44 The book affirms neither the exogamous marriages nor the divorces. The last chapter simply closes with the words *and they sent them away with their children*. It closes as a cautionary tale. It reminds the community of the consequences of policy decisions that occur when the voices that are most marginalized are absent and when one group in a society decides the fate of another.

NEHEMIAH

1 The words of Nehemiah son of Hacaliah. In the month of Chislev, in the twentieth year, while I was in the citadel of Susa, [2]one of my brothers, Hanani, came with certain men from Judah, and I asked them about the Jews who escaped, those who had survived the captivity, and about Jerusalem. [3]They replied, "The remnant there in the province who escaped captivity are in great trouble and shame; the wall of Jerusalem is broken down, and its gates have been destroyed by fire."

4 When I heard these words, I sat down and wept and mourned for days, fasting and praying before the God of heaven. [5]I said, "O Lord God of heaven, the great and awesome God who keeps covenant and steadfast love with those who love him and keep his commandments, [6]let your ear be attentive and your eyes open to hear the prayer of your servant that I now pray before you day and night for your servants, the Israelites, confessing the sins of the Israelites, which we have sinned against you. Both I and my family have sinned. [7]We have offended you deeply, failing to keep the commandments, the statutes, and the ordinances that you commanded Moses your servant. [8]Remember the word that you commanded Moses your servant, 'If you are unfaithful, I will scatter you among the peoples, [9]but if you return to me and keep my commandments and do them, though your outcasts are under the farthest skies, I will gather them from there and bring them to the place where I have chosen to establish my name.' [10]They are your servants and your people whom you redeemed by your great power and your strong hand. [11]O Lord, let your ear be attentive to the prayer of your servant and to the prayer of your servants who delight in revering your name. Give success to your servant today, and grant him mercy in the sight of this man!"

At the time, I was cupbearer to the king.

2 In the month of Nisan, in the twentieth year of King Artaxerxes, when wine was served him, I carried the wine and gave it to the king. Now, I had never been sad in his presence before. [2]So the king said to me, "Why is your face sad, since you are not sick? This can only be sadness of the heart." Then I was very much afraid. [3]I

1:1–3 *The words of Nehemiah* begin in 445 BCE, ninety-four years after Cyrus's edict. The new king is Artaxerxes I (465–424 BCE). Nehemiah, a high-ranking official in the king's court, is attending to official business in the Persian capital of *Susa* when his brother *Hanani* and members of the community in Jerusalem inform him that Jerusalem has been neglected. Persia's ongoing conflict with the Greeks was costly. The needs of cities such as Jerusalem were overlooked as the empire directed most of its resources to support the war effort. Hanani and the others approach Nehemiah because he is a fellow Judean but also a Persian official with access to the king. Nehemiah's first inquiry concerns the well-being of *the Jews who escaped, those who had survived the captivity*. Despite his role as a Persian official, Nehemiah locates his identity and loyalties with the community in Jerusalem.

1:4–11 Nehemiah rejects privilege to serve his people. When he hears of their despicable condition, he fasts and petitions God in a prayer shaped by the stories of his ancestors. He recalls the hopes, expectations, and experiences of his people passed down over generations and expresses them in the prayer as promises to his people. **1:8–9** Alludes to Deut. 30:1–5. **1:11** Nehemiah knows that if his people's circumstance is to be transformed, then he must commit himself to their struggle. See Isaiah's response to God's call (Isa. 6:8). Nehemiah's devotion specifically to Jerusalem also resonates with the psalmist's pledge to not forget Jerusalem in Ps. 137:5–6. As *cupbearer to the king*, Nehemiah lives a comfortable life. Moreover, he resides at the center of imperial power. Generally, the cupbearer is one of the most trusted members of the royal court because he ensures the king's drink is protected from those who would poison him. Nehemiah has no reason to give up a life of affluence, but the luxury of Persia is not worth disobeying God by ignoring the oppression of others.

2:1–5 Nehemiah strategizes in the king's court. The portrait of Nehemiah's loyalty to his

said to the king, "May the king live forever! Why should my face not be sad, when the city, the place of my ancestors' graves, lies waste and its gates have been destroyed by fire?" 4Then the king said to me, "What do you request?" So I prayed to the God of heaven. 5Then I said to the king, "If it pleases the king, and if your servant has found favor with you, I ask that you send me to Judah, to the city of my ancestors' graves, so that I may rebuild it." 6The king said to me (the queen also was sitting beside him), "How long will you be gone, and when will you return?" So it pleased the king to send me, and I set him a date. 7Then I said to the king, "If it pleases the king, let letters be given me to the governors of the province Beyond the River, that they may grant me passage until I arrive in Judah, 8and a letter to Asaph, the keeper of the king's forest, directing him to give me timber to make beams for the gates of the temple fortress and for the wall of the city and for the house that I shall occupy." And the king granted me what I asked, for the gracious hand of my God was upon me.

9 Then I came to the governors of the province Beyond the River and gave them the king's letters. Now the king had sent officers of the army and cavalry with me. 10When Sanballat the Horonite and Tobiah the Ammonite official*a* heard this, it displeased them greatly that someone had come to seek the welfare of the Israelites.

11 So I came to Jerusalem and was there for three days. 12Then I got up during the night, I and a few men with me; I told no one what my God had put into my heart to do for Jerusalem. The only animal I took was the animal I rode. 13I went out by night by the Valley Gate past the Dragon's Spring and to the Dung Gate, and I inspected the walls of Jerusalem that had been broken down and its gates that had been destroyed by fire. 14Then I went on to the Fountain Gate and to the King's Pool, but there was no place for the animal I was riding to continue. 15So I went up by way of the valley by night and inspected the wall. Then I turned back and entered by the Valley Gate and so returned. 16The officials did not know where I had gone or what I was doing; I had not yet told the Jews, the priests, the nobles, the officials, and the rest who were to do the work.

17 Then I said to them, "You see the trouble we are in, how Jerusalem lies in ruins with its gates burned. Come, let us rebuild the wall of Jerusalem, so that we may no longer suffer disgrace." 18I told them that the hand of my God had been gracious upon me and also the words that the king had spoken to me. Then they said, "Let us start building!" So they committed themselves to the common good. 19But when Sanballat the Horonite and Tobiah the Ammonite official*b* and Geshem the Arab heard of it, they mocked and ridiculed us, saying, "What is this that you are doing? Are you rebelling against the king?" 20Then I replied to them, "The God of heaven is the one who will give us success, and we his servants are going to start building, but you have no share or claim or memorial in Jerusalem."

a 2.10 Heb *servant*   *b* 2.19 Heb *servant*

people in Jerusalem is deepened. In fact, he is willing to put himself in danger for the well-being of this community. He had good reason to be fearful. Life at court was always fraught with intrigue and rivalry between officials. One's position was never secure as courtiers plotted against one another for upward mobility. Moreover, given the protracted wars with Greece, any requests to fortify a city on the western frontier of the empire would be met with suspicion and heightened scrutiny. Already Greek coins were in circulation in Yehud, the Persian name for the province of Judah. If the king suspected Nehemiah of conspiring with the Greeks, the consequence might have been death. At the least, the request offered other courtiers an opportunity to exploit any royal suspicion.

2:7–9 Nehemiah is careful to secure documents signed by the king so as to preempt suspicion at every level of the Persian bureaucracy. Persian administration tightly controlled material resources, particularly for building. At each level, Persian administrators were responsible for inventory. The king's query about Nehemiah's return speaks to possible suspicion. A commitment to return to Persia evidences Nehemiah's desire to remain a member of the Persian court. The condition of a city's walls reflected its stature. To see walls in ruins (v. 17) symbolized the condition and the status of its inhabitants.

3 Then the high priest Eliashib set to work with his fellow priests and rebuilt the Sheep Gate. They consecrated it and set up its doors; they consecrated it as far as the Tower of the Hundred and as far as the Tower of Hananel. [2]And the men of Jericho built next to him. And next to them[c] Zaccur son of Imri built.

3 The sons of Hassenaah built the Fish Gate; they laid its beams and set up its doors, its bolts, and its bars. [4]Next to them Meremoth son of Uriah son of Hakkoz made repairs. Next to them Meshullam son of Berechiah son of Meshezabel made repairs. Next to them Zadok son of Baana made repairs. [5]Next to them the Tekoites made repairs, but their nobles would not put their shoulders to the work of their Lord.[d]

6 Joiada son of Paseah and Meshullam son of Besodeiah repaired the Old Gate; they laid its beams and set up its doors, its bolts, and its bars. [7]Next to them repairs were made by Melatiah the Gibeonite and Jadon the Meronothite—the men of Gibeon and of Mizpah—who were under the jurisdiction of[e] the governor of the province Beyond the River. [8]Next to them Uzziel son of Harhaiah, one of the goldsmiths, made repairs. Next to him Hananiah, one of the perfumers, made repairs, and they restored Jerusalem as far as the Broad Wall. [9]Next to them Rephaiah son of Hur, ruler of half the district of[f] Jerusalem, made repairs. [10]Next to them Jedaiah son of Harumaph made repairs opposite his house, and next to him Hattush son of Hashabneiah made repairs. [11]Malchijah son of Harim and Hasshub son of Pahath-moab repaired another section and the Tower of the Ovens. [12]Next to him Shallum son of Hallohesh, ruler of half the district of[g] Jerusalem, made repairs, he and his daughters.

13 Hanun and the inhabitants of Zanoah repaired the Valley Gate; they rebuilt it and set up its doors, its bolts, and its bars and repaired a thousand cubits of the wall, as far as the Dung Gate.

14 Malchijah son of Rechab, ruler of the district of[h] Beth-haccherem, repaired the Dung Gate; he rebuilt it and set up its doors, its bolts, and its bars.

15 And Shallum son of Col-hozeh, ruler of the district of[i] Mizpah, repaired the Fountain Gate; he rebuilt it and covered it and set up its doors, its bolts, and its bars, and he built the wall of the Pool of Shelah of the King's Garden, as far as the stairs that go down from the city of David. [16]After him Nehemiah son of Azbuk, ruler of half the district of[j] Beth-zur, repaired from a point opposite the graves of David, as far as the artificial pool and the House of the Warriors. [17]After him the Levites made repairs: Rehum son of Bani; next to him Hashabiah, ruler of half the district of[k] Keilah, made repairs for his district. [18]After him their kin made repairs: Binnui,[l] son of Henadad, ruler of half the district of[m] Keilah; [19]next to him Ezer son of Jeshua, ruler[n] of Mizpah, repaired another section opposite the ascent to the armory at the Angle. [20]After him Baruch son of Zabbai repaired another section from the Angle to the door of the house of the high priest Eliashib. [21]After him Meremoth son of Uriah son of Hakkoz repaired another section from the door of the house of Eliashib to the end of the house of

c 3.2 Heb him   d 3.5 Or lords   e 3.7 Meaning of Heb uncertain   f 3.9 Or supervisor of half the portion assigned to   g 3.12 Or supervisor of half the portion assigned to   h 3.14 Or supervisor of the portion assigned to   i 3.15 Or supervisor of the portion assigned to   j 3.16 Or supervisor of half the portion assigned to   k 3.17 Or supervisor of half the portion assigned to   l 3.18 Gk Syr: Heb Bavvai   m 3.18 Or supervisor of half the portion assigned to   n 3.19 Or supervisor

3:1–32 Organizing the community and collective work. Those who had returned from Babylon understood themselves as the ones whom God redeemed, while those taken into exile were the generation that had provoked God's wrath. Both Ezra and Nehemiah understood the Babylonian devastation to be the consequence of the rupture of that earlier generation's relationship with God. Rebuilding Jerusalem reflected the people's commitment to rebuilding that relationship. That God would now allow the walls to be reconstructed symbolized their understanding that their penance was complete. At a more practical level, rebuilding the gates of Jerusalem symbolized the city's return to normal functioning. **3:1–2** The *Sheep Gate* was designed for sheepherders to corral their livestock as they brought them into the city. **3:3** The *Fish Gate* was designed for fishmongers to bring their goods for sale. **3:6** The *Old Gate* was located in the northwestern corner of the city's perimeter adjacent to the Fish Gate. **3:13–14** The *Valley Gate* opened to the Valley of Hinnom on the southwestern quadrant. *The Dung Gate* was designed to dispose of the city's waste. **3:15** The *Fountain Gate* gave access to the King's Pool (Upper Pool) and the Pool of Siloam (Lower Pool).

Eliashib. [22]After him the priests, the men of the surrounding area, made repairs. [23]After them Benjamin and Hasshub made repairs opposite their house. After them Azariah son of Maaseiah son of Ananiah made repairs beside his own house. [24]After him Binnui son of Henadad repaired another section, from the house of Azariah to the Angle and to the corner. [25]Palal son of Uzai repaired opposite the Angle and the tower projecting from the upper house of the king at the court of the guard. After him Pedaiah son of Parosh [26]and the temple servants living[o] on Ophel made repairs up to a point opposite the Water Gate on the east and the projecting tower. [27]After him the Tekoites repaired another section opposite the great projecting tower as far as the wall of Ophel.

28 Above the Horse Gate the priests made repairs, each one opposite his own house. [29]After them Zadok son of Immer made repairs opposite his own house. After him Shemaiah son of Shecaniah, the keeper of the East Gate, made repairs. [30]After him Hananiah son of Shelemiah and Hanun sixth son of Zalaph repaired another section. After him Meshullam son of Berechiah made repairs opposite his living quarters. [31]After him Malchijah, one of the goldsmiths, made repairs as far as the house of the temple servants and of the merchants, opposite the Muster Gate,[p] and to the upper room of the corner. [32]And between the upper room of the corner and the Sheep Gate the goldsmiths and the merchants made repairs.

4 [q]Now when Sanballat heard that we were building the wall, he was angry and greatly enraged, and he mocked the Jews. [2]He said in the presence of his associates and of the army of Samaria, "What are these feeble Jews doing? Will they restore it by themselves?[r] Will they offer sacrifice? Will they finish it in a day? Will they revive the stones out of the heaps of rubbish—burned ones at that?" [3]Tobiah the Ammonite was beside him, and he said, "That stone wall they are building—any fox going up on

o 3.26 Cn: Heb *were living* p 3.31 Or *Hammiphkad Gate*
q 4.1 3.33 in Heb r 4.2 Meaning of Heb uncertain

3:26 The *Water Gate* opened to the Gihon Spring on the east side of the city. **3:28–29** The *Horse Gate* and the *East Gate* were both located in the northeastern quadrant of the city. Prior to the fall of the Israelite monarchy, the Horse Gate would have given access to the king's house. Owning a horse in the ancient world was a sign of wealth. Those arriving on horseback would most likely be visitors of the king or the aristocracy. As with other lists of families in Ezra–Nehemiah, the record of names of those participating in the rebuilding of the gates legitimized their standing and stature as families at the time of the book's composition. The story of the fortification of the wall holds powerful symbolic meaning for the hearers in the Hellenistic period. It speaks of a community in solidarity, committed to accomplishing God's plan. The people come together across distinct administrative districts, demonstrating that the connection of their religious heritage could not be impeded by the imperial bureaucracy or by geographic distance.

4:1–3 Intracommunal struggles. The accounts of Sanballat and Tobiah are probably a composite of several conflicts arising from within the community as it learned to both appreciate and reckon with its political diversity. The name *Sanballat* references the Babylonian deity of the moon, the same deity whom Nabonidus, the last king of Babylon, worshiped. Sanballat sees Nehemiah's work as a threat to his stature as an official in the neighboring province of Samaria. Samaria and Jerusalem had a long history of rivalry for the status as capital city of ancient Israel. This conflict may represent an extension of that rivalry. Samaria dominated Jerusalem from the time of Jeroboam until 722 BCE when its destruction left Jerusalem as the major center of YHWH worship in the region. Since the Babylonians destroyed the Jerusalem temple in 586 BCE, Samaria had risen again as the administrative center. In fact, correspondence during the Persian period, written from a Judean community at Elephantine in Egypt to Samaria with questions about celebrating the Passover, may signal that Samaria, more than Jerusalem, functioned as the center for faith and practice. This new investment in Jerusalem threatened Samaria's resurgence. **4:3** *Tobiah*, whose name translates as "YHWH is good," was also an official who opposed rebuilding. His name suggests that he had a cultural and religious connection to the community. His designation as an *Ammonite* suggests the writers attempt to draw distinctions between those who returned from Babylon and others who worshiped YHWH. Tobiah recognizes the power and status that would accrue to Jerusalem and the likely success of Nehemiah's work, since it was authorized by the king.

it would break it down!" ⁴Hear, O our God, for we are despised; turn their taunt back on their own heads, and give them over as plunder in a land of captivity. ⁵Do not cover their guilt, and do not let their sin be blotted out from your sight, for they have raged against the builders.ˢ

6 So we rebuilt the wall, and all the wall was joined together to half its height, for the people had a mind to work.

7 ᵗBut when Sanballat and Tobiah and the Arabs and the Ammonites and the Ashdodites heard that the repairing of the walls of Jerusalem was going forward and the gaps were beginning to be closed, they were very angry ⁸and all plotted together to come and fight against Jerusalem and to cause confusion in it. ⁹So we prayed to our God and set a guard as a protection against them day and night.

10 But Judah said, "The strength of the burden bearers is failing, and there is too much rubbish so that we are unable to work on the wall." ¹¹And our enemies said, "They will not know or see anything before we come upon them and kill them and stop the work." ¹²When the Jews who lived near them came, they said to us ten times, "From all the places where they liveᵘ they will come up against us."ᵛ ¹³So in the lowest parts of the space behind the wall, in open places, I stationed the people according to their families,ʷ with their swords, their spears, and their bows. ¹⁴After I looked these things over, I stood up and said to the nobles and the officials and the rest of the people, "Do not be afraid of them. Remember the LORD, who is great and awesome,

and fight for your kin, your sons, your daughters, your wives, and your households."

15 When our enemies heard that their plot was known to us and that God had frustrated it, we all returned to the wall, each to his work. ¹⁶From that day on, half of my servants worked on construction, and half held the spears, shields, bows, and body-armor, and the leaders posted themselves behind the whole house of Judah ¹⁷who were building the wall. The burden bearers carried their loads in such a way that each labored on the work with one hand and with the other held a weapon. ¹⁸And each of the builders had his sword strapped at his side while he built. The man who sounded the trumpet was beside me. ¹⁹And I said to the nobles, the officials, and the rest of the people, "The work is great and widely spread out, and we are separated far from one another on the wall. ²⁰Rally to us wherever you hear the sound of the trumpet. Our God will fight for us."

21 So we labored at the work, and half of them held the spears from break of dawn until the stars came out. ²²I also said to the people at that time, "Let every man and his servant pass the night inside Jerusalem, so that they may be a guard for us by night and may labor by day." ²³So neither I nor my brothers nor my servants nor the men of the guard who followed me ever took off our clothes; each kept his weapon in his right hand.ˣ

s 4.5 Meaning of Heb uncertain   t 4.7 4.1 in Heb
u 4.12 Cn: Heb *you return*   v 4.12 Compare Gk Syr: Meaning of Heb uncertain   w 4.13 Meaning of Heb uncertain
x 4.23 Cn: Heb *each his weapon the water*

4:4–5 Nehemiah prays about the oppressor. Despite interference from lesser imperial officials, Nehemiah remains resolute about fulfilling his call to repair Jerusalem. Righteous anger and deep frustration give rise to his prayer for God to *give them over as plunder in a land of captivity*. His prayer asks for the privileged to experience what the oppressed endure every day. The image of *captivity* would have been a powerful one for an audience for whom the Babylonian devastation still loomed large. While his prayer may be unsettling for some, it reflects Nehemiah's anguish over Persian repression and his unwavering belief that God had called him to play a key role in restoring Jerusalem. Such a prayer comes from a place that only deep suffering from injustice can shape. See Ps. 137, which begins in anguish in vv. 1–4 but closes with anger in vv. 7–9. Nehemiah felt deeply about the state of his people. As an official in the Persian court, he knew firsthand the harsh nature of imperial administration and thus the repression under which his community suffered. To understand such a prayer that calls God's wrath on one's oppressors, one must understand the pain of oppression.

4:6 Despite the opposition, the people rebuild the wall and prevail.

4:13 Building the wall was a major act of resistance, especially since it now required taking up arms.

4:16–18 The community realizes the forces of repression are always waiting, so they must continue to protect the work with their *spears, shields, bows, and body-armor*. Faithful witness means not only accomplishing gains through progressive resistance but vigilantly safeguarding those hard-won achievements.

5 Now there was a great outcry of the people and of their wives against their Jewish kin. ²For there were those who said, "With our sons and our daughters, we are many; we must get grain, so that we may eat and stay alive." ³There were also those who said, "We are having to pledge our fields, our vineyards, and our houses in order to get grain during the famine." ⁴And there were those who said, "We are having to borrow money on our fields and vineyards to pay the king's tax. ⁵Now our flesh is the same as that of our kindred; our children are the same as their children; and yet we are forcing our sons and daughters to be slaves, and some of our daughters have been ravished; we are powerless, and our fields and vineyards now belong to others."

6 I was very angry when I heard their outcry and these complaints. ⁷After thinking it over, I contended with the nobles and the officials; I said to them, "You are all taking interest from your own people." And I called a great assembly to deal with them ⁸and said to them, "As far as we were able, we have bought back our Jewish kindred who had been sold to other nations, but now you are selling your own kin, who must then be bought back by us!" They were silent and could not find a word to say. ⁹So I said, "The thing that you are doing is not good. Should you not walk in the fear of our God, to prevent the taunts of the nations our enemies? ¹⁰Moreover I and my brothers and my servants are lending them money and grain. Let us stop this taking of interest. ¹¹Restore to them, this very day, their fields, their vineyards, their olive orchards, and their houses, and the interest on money, grain, wine, and oil that you have been exacting from them." ¹²Then they said, "We will restore everything and demand nothing more from them. We will do as you say." And I called the priests and made them take an oath to do as they

5:1–5 The oppressed appeal to Nehemiah. Nehemiah turns to the problem of class conflict within the Jerusalem community. Yehud was a small, poor province. Its population numbered about ten thousand persons. Of that number about 3–5 percent comprised the landholding aristocracy. The remainder of the populace worked the land and were exploited for their labor. The cost of war with the Greeks meant the empire squeezed provinces like Yehud for resources. During Nehemiah's time, tax rates of 30, 40, or even 50 percent were not uncommon. The scarcity of food, Persian economic repression, and the exploitation within Yehud intersected with potentially disastrous consequences for Nehemiah's community. Money was scarce, and most financial transactions, including taxes, were completed in-kind using services or agricultural produce. **5:3** One year's drought threatened *famine* and ruined entire families. **5:4** *We are having to borrow money on our fields and vineyards.* Those whose land was unable to produce enough to meet their tax levy were forced to borrow money from fellow landowners who probably saw their kindred's misfortune as a windfall or an opportunity to shore up their own wealth and protect themselves from the same fate. **5:5** *We are forcing our sons and daughters to be slaves . . . our daughters have been ravished.* Default on a loan entitled the lien holder to demand a son or a daughter's enslavement as payment. While all enslavement is heinous, the enslavement of daughters was particularly distressing because they lost all rights, even over their own bodies, and were subjected to rape.

5:6–13 Nehemiah confronts the upper classes. 5:6 *I was very angry.* An official of the king's court, Nehemiah had not likely experienced the pain of scarcity and could not understand the behavior of his kindred. **5:8** The current economic exploitation is likened to the Babylonian captivity. Living on the edge of survival had forced them to turn on one another in desperation. They had not experienced abundance and could not see beyond self-preservation. **5:10** The community's *taking of interest* should be understood as a natural response to Persian repression. Such behavior was not unique to Jerusalem but replicated throughout the empire as communities were depleted to support the war effort against Greece. **5:11–12** Most people in the ancient world lived with hunger. Women and children were disproportionately represented in this group. Nehemiah addresses the evil of wealth disparity and shows the community that there are resources sufficient for all to have enough. He understood that God has given humanity all it needs to survive and that inequities that create suffering are attributable to human sin. Nehemiah's activity reminds modern faith communities who negotiate global and local economic systems that create suffering of God's call to work toward abundance for all, not merely for a few. In modern political systems that crush the vulnerable, leaving many without health care, education, decent housing, adequate employment,

had promised. ¹³I also shook out the fold of my garment and said, "So may God shake out everyone from house and from property who does not perform this promise. Thus may they be shaken out and emptied." And all the assembly said, "Amen," and praised the LORD. And the people did as they had promised.

14 Moreover, from the time that I was appointed to be their governor in the land of Judah, from the twentieth year to the thirty-second year of King Artaxerxes, twelve years, neither I nor my brothers ate the food allowance of the governor. ¹⁵The former governors who were before me laid heavy burdens on the people and took food and wine from them, besides forty shekels of silver. Even their servants lorded it over the people. But I did not do so because of the fear of God. ¹⁶Indeed, I devoted myself to the work on this wall and acquired no land, and all my servants were gathered there for the work. ¹⁷Moreover, there were at my table one hundred fifty people, Jews and officials, besides those who came to us from the nations around us. ¹⁸Now that which was prepared for one day was one ox and six choice sheep; also fowls were prepared for me, and every ten days skins of

wine in abundance, yet with all this I did not demand the food allowance of the governor, because of the heavy burden of labor on the people. ¹⁹Remember for my good, O my God, all that I have done for this people.

6 Now when it was reported to Sanballat and Tobiah and to Geshem the Arab and to the rest of our enemies that I had built the wall and that there was no gap left in it (though up to that time I had not set up the doors in the gates), ²Sanballat and Geshem sent to me, saying, "Come and let us meet together in one of the villagesʸ in the plain of Ono." But they intended to do me harm. ³So I sent messengers to them, saying, "I am doing a great work, and I cannot come down. Why should the work stop while I leave it to come down to you?" ⁴They sent to me four times in this way, and I answered them in the same manner. ⁵In the same way Sanballat for the fifth time sent his servant to me with an open letter in his hand. ⁶In it was written, "It is reported among the nations—and Geshemᶻ also says it—that you

y 6.2 Or *Chephirim*　z 6.6 Heb *Gashmu*

or nutritious food, Nehemiah's charge is particularly relevant. His radical move to forgive debt is probably most unsettling. Could Western nations forgive the debt of so-called developing countries where much of the indebtedness resulted from colonial practices that enriched the West? Could society provide health care to every person? Or ensure that every child receives nutritious food, decent housing, and education? Nehemiah's response challenges humanity to confront systems that create scarcity and suffering by redistributing the earth's abundance so that what God has given is sufficient for all. **5:13** Nehemiah's statement articulates God's anger toward those who neglect or participate in exploiting the vulnerable. Charity is not Nehemiah's response. Upending systems of exploitation and replacing them with equity is the faithful response.

5:14–19 Nehemiah's work of establishing the reforms within the life of the community is important, but his leadership by example probably made a greater impression on the people. Nehemiah sets an example for community leadership and distinguishes himself from previous governors. Leaving the royal court of Persia for Jerusalem, Nehemiah relinquishes the privileges of his position; he takes neither *food* nor *wine* nor *shekels* from them (v. 15); he *acquired no land* and labored alongside other members of the community (v. 16).

6:1–4 More community opposition. The political intrigue intensifies. Sanballat, Geshem, and Tobiah join forces to impede the rebuilding. Four times they invite Nehemiah to a public confrontation on the plain of Ono. Nehemiah refuses each overture and redoubles his efforts to complete the wall.

6:5 In a fifth letter, Sanballat threatens to report to the king that Nehemiah's activity amounts to treason. If Nehemiah can muster enough support among the community to complete the wall, then he may take from Sanballat's and Tobiah's popularity and their standing within the imperial bureaucracy. The threat recalls the memory of Hezekiah's activity of fortifying the wall in Jerusalem in defiance of Assyria (2 Chr. 32:5). In response to what Assyria saw as treason, Sennacherib humbled Hezekiah by devastating the region.

6:6–14 Nehemiah sees Tobiah and Sanballat as enemies of Judah, but they are officials who also have a strong following among the people. The friction between Nehemiah's group that had come from Babylon and the other YHWH groups supportive of Sanballat and Tobiah was both

and the Jews intend to rebel; that is why you are building the wall; and according to this report you wish to become their king. ⁷You have also set up prophets to proclaim in Jerusalem concerning you, 'There is a king in Judah!' And now it will be reported to the king according to these words. So come, therefore, and let us confer together." ⁸Then I sent to him, saying, "No such things as you say have been done; you are inventing them out of your own mind," ⁹for they all wanted to frighten us, thinking, "Their hands will drop from the work, and it will not be done." But now, strengthen my hands.

10 One day when I went into the house of Shemaiah son of Delaiah son of Mehetabel, who was confined to his house, he said, "Let us meet together in the house of God, within the temple, and let us close the doors of the temple, for they are coming to kill you; indeed, tonight they are coming to kill you." ¹¹But I said, "Should a man like me run away? Would a man like me go into the temple to save his life? I will not go in!" ¹²Then I perceived and saw that God had not sent him at all, but he had pronounced the prophecy against me because Tobiah and Sanballat had hired him. ¹³He was hired for this purpose, to intimidate me and make me sin by acting in this way, and so they could give me a bad name, in order to taunt me. ¹⁴Remember Tobiah and Sanballat, O my God, according to these things that they did, and also Noadiah the prophetess and the rest of the prophets who wanted to make me afraid.

15 So the wall was finished on the twenty-fifth day of the month Elul, in fifty-two days.

¹⁶And when all our enemies heard of it, all the nations around us were afraid[a] and fell greatly in their own esteem, for they perceived that this work had been accomplished with the help of our God. ¹⁷Moreover, in those days the nobles of Judah sent many letters to Tobiah, and Tobiah's letters came to them. ¹⁸For many in Judah were bound by oath to him, because he was the son-in-law of Shecaniah son of Arah, and his son Jehohanan had married the daughter of Meshullam son of Berechiah. ¹⁹Also they spoke of his good deeds in my presence and reported my words to him. And Tobiah sent letters to intimidate me.

7 Now when the wall had been built and I had set up the doors and the gatekeepers, the singers, and the Levites had been appointed, ²I gave my brother Hanani charge over Jerusalem, along with Hananiah the commander of the citadel, for he was a faithful man and feared God more than many. ³And I said to them, "The gates of Jerusalem are not to be opened while the sun is hot; while the gatekeepers[b] are still standing guard, let them shut and bar the doors. Appoint guards from among the inhabitants of Jerusalem, some at their watch posts, and others before their own houses." ⁴The city was wide and large, but the people within it were few, and no houses had been built.

5 Then my God put it into my mind to assemble the nobles and the officials and the people to be enrolled by genealogy. And I

a 6.16 Or saw   b 7.3 Heb while they

religious and political. For Tobiah, Sanballat, and Geshem, rebuilding the wall bolsters Nehemiah's prominence as their rival and may even be an act of treason against Persia. Various groups saw Nehemiah's building project as an attempt to strengthen the Babylonian returnees above their own factions. For Nehemiah and his community, the work both raised Jerusalem's status and was an act of faith, a response to God's call to serve God's people. As with many issues, religious and political motivations overlap, and their complexity is impossible to parse. Contemporary policies to alleviate poverty, instate universal health care, affect climate change, or correct inequities in judicial systems may point to ways politics and religion continue to intersect. 6:7 *You have also set up prophets to proclaim . . . "There is a king in Judah!"* Although meant as a taunt, Sanballat's words articulate the long-held hope of several groups associated with YHWH in Jerusalem to reestablish the autonomy that existed under the monarchy. By the time the book of Nehemiah was completed, the community had achieved such autonomy under the Hasmoneans (ca. 165 BCE). 6:14 *Noadiah* is one of only a few women in the Hebrew Bible called prophetess ("neviah"). The others are the unnamed wife of Isaiah (Isa. 8:3), Huldah (2 Kgs. 22:14; 2 Chr. 34:22), Miriam (Exod. 15:20), and Deborah (Judg. 4:4).

6:15–19 Although Nehemiah completes the wall, many in the community reject him. Many continued to support Tobiah.

7:5 By inviting all the people to participate in the dedication of the newly walled city, Nehemiah instills pride in the community, renews their connection to their faith, and affirms their understanding

found the book of the genealogy of those who were the first to come back, and I found the following written in it:

6 These are the people of the province who came up out of the captivity of those exiles whom King Nebuchadnezzar of Babylon had carried into exile; they returned to Jerusalem and Judah, each to his town. [7]They came with Zerubbabel, Jeshua, Nehemiah, Azariah, Raamiah, Nahamani, Mordecai, Bilshan, Mispereth, Bigvai, Nehum, Baanah.

The number of the Israelite people: [8]the descendants of Parosh, two thousand one hundred seventy-two. [9]Of Shephatiah, three hundred seventy-two. [10]Of Arah, six hundred fifty-two. [11]Of Pahath-moab, namely, the descendants of Jeshua and Joab, two thousand eight hundred eighteen. [12]Of Elam, one thousand two hundred fifty-four. [13]Of Zattu, eight hundred forty-five. [14]Of Zaccai, seven hundred sixty. [15]Of Binnui, six hundred forty-eight. [16]Of Bebai, six hundred twenty-eight. [17]Of Azgad, two thousand three hundred twenty-two. [18]Of Adonikam, six hundred sixty-seven. [19]Of Bigvai, two thousand sixty-seven. [20]Of Adin, six hundred fifty-five. [21]Of Ater, namely, of Hezekiah, ninety-eight. [22]Of Hashum, three hundred twenty-eight. [23]Of Bezai, three hundred twenty-four. [24]Of Hariph, one hundred twelve. [25]Of Gibeon, ninety-five. [26]The people of Bethlehem and Netophah, one hundred eighty-eight. [27]Of Anathoth, one hundred twenty-eight. [28]Of Beth-azmaveth, forty-two. [29]Of Kiriath-jearim, Chephirah, and Beeroth, seven hundred forty-three. [30]Of Ramah and Geba, six hundred twenty-one. [31]Of Michmas, one hundred twenty-two. [32]Of Bethel and Ai, one hundred twenty-three. [33]Of the other Nebo, fifty-two. [34]The descendants of the other Elam, one thousand two hundred fifty-four. [35]Of Harim, three hundred twenty. [36]Of Jericho, three hundred forty-five. [37]Of Lod, Hadid, and Ono, seven hundred twenty-one. [38]Of Senaah, three thousand nine hundred thirty.

39 The priests: the descendants of Jedaiah, namely, the house of Jeshua, nine hundred seventy-three. [40]Of Immer, one thousand fifty-two. [41]Of Pashhur, one thousand two hundred forty-seven. [42]Of Harim, one thousand seventeen.

43 The Levites: the descendants of Jeshua, namely, of Kadmiel of the descendants of Hodevah, seventy-four. [44]The singers: the descendants of Asaph, one hundred forty-eight. [45]The gatekeepers: the descendants of Shallum, of Ater, of Talmon, of Akkub, of Hatita, of Shobai, one hundred thirty-eight.

46 The temple servants: the descendants of Ziha, of Hasupha, of Tabbaoth, [47]of Keros, of Sia, of Padon, [48]of Lebana, of Hagaba, of Shalmai, [49]of Hanan, of Giddel, of Gahar, [50]of Reaiah, of Rezin, of Nekoda, [51]of Gazzam, of Uzza, of Paseah, [52]of Besai, of Meunim, of Nephushesim, [53]of Bakbuk, of Hakupha, of Harhur, [54]of Bazlith, of Mehida, of Harsha, [55]of Barkos, of Sisera, of Temah, [56]of Neziah, of Hatipha.

57 The descendants of Solomon's servants: of Sotai, of Sophereth, of Perida, [58]of Jaala, of Darkon, of Giddel, [59]of Shephatiah, of Hattil, of Pochereth-hazzebaim, of Amon.

60 All the temple servants and the descendants of Solomon's servants were three hundred ninety-two.

61 The following were those who came up from Tel-melah, Tel-harsha, Cherub, Addon, and Immer, but they could not prove their ancestral houses or their descent, whether they belonged to Israel: [62]the descendants of Delaiah, of Tobiah, of Nekoda, six hundred forty-two. [63]Also, of the priests: the descendants of Hobaiah, of Hakkoz, of Barzillai (who had married one of the daughters of Barzillai the Gileadite and was called by their name). [64]These sought their registration among those enrolled in the genealogies, but it was not found there, so they were excluded from the priesthood as unclean; [65]the governor told them that they were not to partake of the most holy

---

that God has remembered and reclaimed them after the Babylonian devastation. It is a religious ceremony that inspires the participants to dedicate themselves to the faith of their ancestors. Much as a celebration of Seven Last Words reminds worshiping communities anew of Christ's passion or a Watch Night service is a reminder of the ancestors' belief in God's faithfulness even during the horrors of slavery, this worship service filled with congregants from Jerusalem and outlying areas connects them to a new history and reminds them of their connection to God.

7:6–73 List of legitimation. Much of Neh. 7:6–73 restates Ezra 2:1–70. The list both constructs and consolidates ethnic identity. See notes on Ezra 2.

food until a priest with Urim and Thummim should come.

66 The whole assembly together was forty-two thousand three hundred sixty, [67]besides their male and female slaves, of whom there were seven thousand three hundred thirty-seven, and they had two hundred forty-five singers, male and female. [68]They had seven hundred thirty-six horses, two hundred forty-five mules,[c] [69][d]four hundred thirty-five camels, and six thousand seven hundred twenty donkeys.

70 Now some of the heads of ancestral houses contributed to the work. The governor gave to the treasury one thousand darics of gold, fifty basins, and five hundred thirty priestly robes. [71]And some of the heads of ancestral houses gave into the building fund twenty thousand darics of gold and two thousand two hundred minas of silver. [72]And what the rest of the people gave was twenty thousand darics of gold, two thousand minas of silver, and sixty-seven priestly robes.

73 So the priests, the Levites, the gatekeepers, the singers, some of the people, the temple servants, and all Israel settled in their towns.

When the seventh month came, the Israelites being settled in their towns, [1]all the people gathered together into the square before the Water Gate. They told Ezra the scribe to bring the book of the law of Moses, which the LORD had given to Israel. [2]Accordingly, Ezra the priest brought the law before the assembly, both men and women and all who could hear with understanding. This was on the first day of the seventh month. [3]He read from it facing the square before the Water Gate from early morning until midday, in the presence of the men and the women and those who could understand, and the ears of all the people were attentive to the book of the law. [4]Ezra the scribe stood on a wooden platform that had been made for the purpose, and beside him stood Mattithiah, Shema, Anaiah, Uriah, Hilkiah, and Maaseiah on his right hand and Pedaiah, Mishael, Malchijah, Hashum, Hash-baddanah, Zechariah, and Meshullam on his left hand. [5]And Ezra opened the book in the sight of all the people, for he was standing above all the people, and when he opened it, all the people stood up. [6]Then Ezra blessed the LORD, the great God, and all the people answered, "Amen, Amen," lifting up their hands. Then they bowed their heads and worshiped the LORD with their faces to the ground. [7]Also the Levites Jeshua, Bani, Sherebiah, Jamin, Akkub, Shabbethai, Hodiah, Maaseiah, Kelita, Azariah, Jozabad, Hanan, Pelaiah helped the people to understand the law, while the people remained in their places. [8]So they read from the book, from the law of God, with interpretation. They gave the sense, so that the people understood the reading.

9 And Nehemiah, who was the governor, and Ezra the priest and scribe, and the Levites who taught the people said to all the people, "This day is holy to the LORD your God; do not mourn or weep." For all the people wept when they heard the words of the law. [10]Then he said to them, "Go your way, eat the fat and drink sweet wine and send portions of them to those for whom nothing is prepared, for this day is holy to our LORD, and do not be grieved, for the joy of the LORD is your strength." [11]So the Levites stilled all the people, saying, "Be quiet, for this day is holy; do not be grieved." [12]And all the people

c 7.68 Gk and margins of some Heb mss: MT lacks *They had…forty-five mules* d 7.69 7.68 in Heb

8:1–8 **Ezra's teaching.** Nehemiah convened *all the people* and *they told Ezra the scribe to bring the book of the law of Moses* (v. 1). The event evokes a strong sense of a spiritual connection with the community's ancestors. Public reading of the law is commanded in Deut. 31:11 and appears in Josh. 8:34–35 and 2 Kgs. 23:1–2 (where Josiah reads the book of the covenant; see also Exod. 24:7). As they gather to hear the reading of the ancient teachings, they are bound to one another, to their ancestors, and to notable times in their history. 8:8 *With interpretation.* Ezra's role as both reader and interpreter is highlighted (see note on Ezra 7:10).

8:9 *For all the people wept.* The ritual evoked such a powerful sense of identity that they began to weep with grief—over the many lost years of exile and dispersion after the Babylonian devastation.

8:10 *The joy of the LORD is your strength.* Grief turns to joy—over the reaffirmation that despite the destruction of Jerusalem and the community's struggles under Babylonian and Persian repression, they were still people of God. The hearing of the law inspired them to know that they are not a conquered people, but rather, they are God's people.

went their way to eat and drink and to send portions and to make great rejoicing, because they had understood the words that were declared to them.

13 On the second day the heads of ancestral houses of all the people, with the priests and the Levites, came together to Ezra the scribe in order to study the words of the law. [14]And they found it written in the law that the LORD had commanded by Moses that the Israelites should live in booths[e] during the festival of the seventh month [15]and that they should publish and proclaim in all their towns and in Jerusalem as follows, "Go out to the hills and bring branches of olive, wild olive, myrtle, palm, and other leafy trees to make booths,[f] as it is written." [16]So the people went out and brought them and made booths[g] for themselves, each on the roofs of their houses, and in their courts and in the courts of the house of God, and in the square at the Water Gate and in the square at the Gate of Ephraim. [17]And all the assembly of those who had returned from the captivity made booths[h] and lived in them, for from the days of Jeshua son of Nun to that day the Israelites had not done so. And there was very great rejoicing. [18]And day by day, from the first day to the last day, Ezra[i] read from the book of the law of God. They kept the festival seven days, and on the eighth day there was a solemn assembly, according to the ordinance.

9 Now on the twenty-fourth day of this month the Israelites were assembled with fasting and in sackcloth and with earth on their heads.[j] [2]Then those of Israelite descent separated themselves from all foreigners and stood and confessed their sins and the iniquities of their ancestors. [3]They stood up in their place and read from the book of the law of the LORD their God for a fourth part of the day, and for another fourth they made confession and worshiped the LORD their God. [4]Then Jeshua, Bani, Kadmiel, Shebaniah, Bunni, Sherebiah, Bani, and Chenani stood on the stairs of the Levites and cried out with a loud voice to the LORD their God. [5]Then the Levites Jeshua, Kadmiel, Bani, Hashabneiah, Sherebiah, Hodiah, Shebaniah, and Pethahiah said, "Stand up and bless the LORD your God from everlasting to everlasting. Blessed be your glorious name, which is exalted above all blessing and praise."

6 And Ezra said,[k] "You are the LORD, you alone; you have made heaven, the heaven of heavens, with all their host, the earth and all that is on it, the seas and all that is in them. To all of them you give life, and the host of heaven worships you. [7]You are the LORD, the God who chose Abram and brought him out of Ur of the Chaldeans and gave him the name Abraham; [8]and you found his heart faithful before you and made with him a covenant to give to his descendants the land of the Canaanite, the Hittite, the Amorite, the Perizzite, the Jebusite, and the Girgashite, and you have fulfilled your promise, for you are righteous.

9 "And you saw the distress of our ancestors in Egypt and heard their cry at the Red Sea.[l] [10]You performed signs and wonders against Pharaoh and all his servants and all the people of his land, for you knew that they acted insolently against our ancestors. You made a name for yourself that remains

e 8.14 Or *tabernacles* f 8.15 Or *tabernacles* g 8.16 Or *tabernacles* h 8.17 Or *tabernacles* i 8.18 Heb *he* j 9.1 Heb *on them* k 9.6 Gk: Heb lacks *And Ezra said* l 9.9 Or *Sea of Reeds*

8:13–18 So moved by the accounts of their ancestors, they felt compelled to celebrate the Feast of Booths (Tabernacles or Sukkot) as Lev. 23:33–43 mandates in the seventh month (Tishrei) as a way of embodying this ancestral connection. The people also celebrate the Feast of Booths when the temple's altar is rebuilt (Ezra 3:4).

Neh. 9 National confession. After the mass assembly and the celebration of the Feast of Booths (Sukkot), Ezra leads the people into a ritual of lament and remembrance.

9:2 *Those of Israelite descent separated themselves from all foreigners.* It is not clear what *Israelite* or *foreigners* might have meant in this circumstance. It is years after the first groups had migrated from Babylon to Jerusalem. Rituals, family lists, and cultural practices have both constructed and reinforced ideas of ethnicity.

9:6–7 Ezra leads the prayer and confession, which begin with an affirmation that YHWH is the creator God, the one who called Abram and *brought him out of Ur of the Chaldeans* (Babylon), mirroring the exile and return of those he addresses (see **"Exile and Restoration Metanarratives," p. 637**).

to this day. [11]And you divided the sea before them, so that they passed through the sea on dry land, but you threw their pursuers into the depths like a stone into mighty waters. [12]Moreover, you led them by day with a pillar of cloud and by night with a pillar of fire, to give them light on the way in which they should go. [13]You came down also upon Mount Sinai and spoke with them from heaven and gave them right ordinances and true laws, good statutes and commandments, [14]and you made known your holy Sabbath to them and gave them commandments and statutes and a law through Moses your servant. [15]For their hunger you gave them bread from heaven, and for their thirst you brought water for them out of the rock, and you told them to go in to possess the land that you swore to give them.

[16] "But they, our ancestors, acted presumptuously and stiffened their necks and did not obey your commandments; [17]they refused to obey and were not mindful of the wonders that you performed among them, but they stiffened their necks and appointed a leader to return to their slavery in Egypt. But you are a God ready to forgive, gracious and merciful, slow to anger and abounding in steadfast love, and you did not forsake them. [18]Even when they had cast an image of a calf for themselves and said, 'This is your God who brought you up out of Egypt,' and had committed great blasphemies, [19]you in your great mercies did not forsake them in the wilderness; the pillar of cloud that led them in the way did not leave them by day nor the pillar of fire by night that gave them light on the way by which they should go. [20]You gave your good spirit to instruct them and did not withhold your manna from their mouths and gave them water for their thirst. [21]Forty years you sustained them in the wilderness so that they lacked nothing; their clothes did not wear out, and their feet did not swell. [22]And you gave them kingdoms and peoples and allotted to them every corner,[m] so they took possession of the land of King Sihon of Heshbon and the land of King Og of Bashan. [23]You multiplied their descendants like the stars of heaven and brought them into the land that you had told their ancestors to enter and possess. [24]So the descendants went in and possessed the land, and you subdued before them the inhabitants of the land, the Canaanites, and gave them into their hands, with their kings and the peoples of the land, to do with them as they pleased. [25]And they captured fortress cities and a rich land and took possession of houses filled with all sorts of goods, hewn cisterns, vineyards, olive orchards, and fruit trees in abundance; so they ate and were filled and became fat and delighted themselves in your great goodness.

[26] "Nevertheless, they were disobedient and rebelled against you and cast your law behind their backs and killed your prophets, who had warned them in order to turn them back to you, and they committed great blasphemies. [27]Therefore you gave them into the hands of their enemies, who made them suffer. Then in the time of their suffering they cried out to you, and you heard them from heaven, and according to your great mercies you gave them saviors who saved them from the hands of their enemies. [28]But after they had rest, they again did evil before you, and you abandoned them to the hands of their enemies, so that they had dominion

m 9.22 Meaning of Heb uncertain

9:16–17 After a review of Israelite salvation history, Ezra turns to confession. The confession of the ancestors' sins along with their own acknowledges the transgenerational effects of corporate sin. Consider, even now, the long-term devastation of the slave trade, the Trail of Tears, Jim Crow, the Holocaust, the internment of Asian Americans in the 1940s, ongoing inequality toward women, and the police brutality toward African Americans and Latinos. Ezra's call to his people is analogous to a national confession followed by acts of repentance. **9:17** *You are a God ready to forgive.* Interwoven with the confession of transgression is Ezra's faith that with repentance comes God's *steadfast love.* Recalling the litany of national sin is not merely a formulaic recitation; rather the very act of recalling this history is painful, eliciting deep emotions ranging from sorrow to anger to pain. Where Nehemiah raised the congregation's sense of cultural esteem by emphasizing their ancestral connection to God, Ezra tempers such national pride by reminding them of their rebellion against God's love. As such, ancient Israel was not unlike the United States or any other nation—unique but flawed and always in need of honest moral self-reflection. In the face of such sin, Ezra reminds the people that despite their actions, God remains faithful.

over them, yet when they turned and cried to you, you heard from heaven, and many times you rescued them according to your mercies. ²⁹And you warned them in order to turn them back to your law, yet they acted presumptuously and did not obey your commandments but sinned against your ordinances, by the observance of which a person shall live. They turned a stubborn shoulder and stiffened their neck and would not obey. ³⁰Many years you were patient with them and warned them by your spirit through your prophets, yet they would not listen. Therefore you handed them over to the peoples of the lands. ³¹Nevertheless, in your great mercies you did not make an end of them or forsake them, for you are a gracious and merciful God.

32 "Now therefore, our God—the great and mighty and awesome God, keeping covenant and steadfast love—do not treat lightly all the hardship that has come upon us, upon our kings, our officials, our priests, our prophets, our ancestors, and all your people, since the time of the kings of Assyria until today. ³³You have been just in all that has come upon us, for you have dealt faithfully and we have acted wickedly; ³⁴our kings, our officials, our priests, and our ancestors have not kept your law or heeded the commandments and the warnings that you gave them. ³⁵Even in their own kingdom, and in the great goodness you bestowed on them, and in the large and rich land that you set before them, they did not serve you and did not turn from their wicked works. ³⁶Here we are, slaves to this day, slaves in the land that you gave to our ancestors to enjoy its fruit and its good gifts. ³⁷Its rich yield goes to the kings whom you have set over us because of our sins; they have power also over our bodies and over our livestock at their pleasure, and we are in great distress."

38 ⁿBecause of all this we make a firm agreement in writing, and on that sealed document are inscribed the names of our officials, our Levites, and our priests.

10 ᵒUpon the sealed document are the names of Nehemiah the governor, son of Hacaliah, and Zedekiah; ²Seraiah, Azariah, Jeremiah, ³Pashhur, Amariah, Malchijah, ⁴Hattush, Shebaniah, Malluch, ⁵Harim, Meremoth, Obadiah, ⁶Daniel, Ginnethon, Baruch, ⁷Meshullam, Abijah, Mijamin, ⁸Maaziah, Bilgai, Shemaiah; these are the priests. ⁹And the Levites: Jeshua son of Azaniah, Binnui of the sons of Henadad, Kadmiel; ¹⁰and their associates Shebaniah, Hodiah, Kelita, Pelaiah, Hanan, ¹¹Mica, Rehob, Hashabiah, ¹²Zaccur, Sherebiah, Shebaniah, ¹³Hodiah, Bani, Beninu. ¹⁴The leaders of the people: Parosh, Pahath-moab, Elam, Zattu, Bani, ¹⁵Bunni, Azgad, Bebai, ¹⁶Adonijah, Bigvai, Adin, ¹⁷Ater, Hezekiah, Azzur, ¹⁸Hodiah, Hashum, Bezai, ¹⁹Hariph, Anathoth, Nebai, ²⁰Magpiash, Meshullam, Hezir, ²¹Meshezabel, Zadok, Jaddua, ²²Pelatiah, Hanan, Anaiah, ²³Hoshea, Hananiah, Hasshub, ²⁴Hallohesh, Pilha, Shobek, ²⁵Rehum, Hashabnah, Maaseiah, ²⁶Ahiah, Hanan, Anan, ²⁷Malluch, Harim, and Baanah.

28 The rest of the people, the priests, the Levites, the gatekeepers, the singers, the temple servants, and all who have separated themselves from the peoples of the lands to adhere to the law of God, their wives, their sons, their daughters, all who have knowledge and understanding, ²⁹join with their kin, their nobles, and enter into a curse and an oath to walk in God's law, which was given by Moses the servant of God, and to observe and do all the commandments of the Lord our Lord and his ordinances and his statutes. ³⁰We will not

ⁿ 9.38 10.1 in Heb   ᵒ 10.1 10.2 in Heb

9:38 After confession, a covenant renewal.

10:1–27 *Upon the sealed document are the names.* Starting with Nehemiah, the names of the signatories to the covenant.

10:28–29 *All who have separated themselves from the peoples of the lands.* See Ezra 6:21; 10:11; Neh. 9:2; 13:3. The requirement to *enter into a curse and an oath* signals the seriousness of the crisis. Usually, oaths with consequences for the entire community are administered only to men. In this instance, *their wives, their sons, their daughters* are also included in responsibility for the crisis.

10:30–39 Connects three motifs: communal survival, intermarriage, and observance of cultural and religious obligations. Each is connected to the community's devotion to *the house of our God* or the temple (v. 32). Devastation by the Babylonians, repression under the Persians, and the challenges presented by negotiating the interests of diverse political groups within the

give our daughters to the peoples of the land or take their daughters for our sons, [31]and if the peoples of the land bring in merchandise or any grain on the Sabbath day to sell, we will not buy it from them on the Sabbath or on a holy day, and we will forego the crops of the seventh year and the exaction of every debt.

32 We also lay on ourselves the obligation to charge ourselves yearly one-third of a shekel for the service of the house of our God: [33]for the rows of bread, the regular grain offering, the regular burnt offering, the Sabbaths, the new moons, the appointed festivals, the sacred donations, and the sin offerings to make atonement for Israel, and for all the work of the house of our God. [34]We have also cast lots among the priests, the Levites, and the people for the wood offering, to bring it into the house of our God, by ancestral houses, at appointed times, year by year, to burn on the altar of the LORD our God, as it is written in the law. [35]We obligate ourselves to bring the first fruits of our soil and the first fruits of all fruit of every tree, year by year, to the house of the LORD; [36]also to bring to the house of our God, to the priests who minister in the house of our God, the firstborn of our sons and of our livestock, as it is written in the law, and the firstlings of our herds and of our flocks;

[37]and to bring the first of our dough, and our contributions, the fruit of every tree, the wine and the oil, to the priests, to the chambers of the house of our God; and to bring to the Levites the tithes from our soil, for it is the Levites who collect the tithes in all our rural towns. [38]And the priest, the descendant of Aaron, shall be with the Levites when the Levites receive the tithes, and the Levites shall bring up a tithe of the tithes to the house of our God, to the chambers of the storehouse. [39]For the Israelites and the sons of Levi shall bring the contribution of grain, wine, and oil to the storerooms where the vessels of the sanctuary are and where the priests who minister and the gatekeepers and the singers are. We will not neglect the house of our God.

11 Now the leaders of the people lived in Jerusalem, and the rest of the people cast lots to bring one out of ten to live in the holy city Jerusalem, while nine-tenths remained in the other towns. [2]And the people blessed all those who willingly offered to live in Jerusalem.

3 These are the leaders of the province who lived in Jerusalem, but in the towns of Judah all lived on their property in their towns: Israel, the priests, the Levites, the temple servants, and the descendants of Solomon's

community most likely precipitated a posture of retrenchment. **10:30** In addition to threatening cultural and religious continuity, intermarriage had the potential of transferring property from one group to another. Intermarriage could also disrupt temple upkeep. A household where a principal member may not have been devoted to the temple could not be counted on to contribute. The priesthood had few means to persuade the non-Israelite landowners to support the temple. These concerns presented existential challenges for the temple community (see v. 32). The oath to exclude foreigners echoes modern immigration "crises." Economic pressures ignite fears of scarcity and often lead the powerful to scapegoat the vulnerable. **10:31** The practice of Sabbath observance strengthened the community's cultural identity and commitment to the survival of the temple. **10:32** The obligation to give one-third of a shekel was a tangible expression of that commitment and ensured that the temple could meet its tax burden. The Jerusalem priesthood occupied a temple whose construction was funded by the Persians. The temple would have been taxed similarly to others throughout the empire. More prominent temples such as the Eanna in Babylon went into debt to pay the Persian tax levy. Such a burden was heavy for the small Jerusalem temple community. The Persian imperial response might have been severe if the community did not meet its obligations. **10:34–39** Provisions are made for the upkeep of the temple and the support of the priesthood. Since the Levites did not own land, their physical needs had to be met by the community.

11:1–2 Populating Jerusalem. Nehemiah 7:4 notes that Jerusalem was sparsely populated; now the people cast lots to move one-tenth of the surrounding populace into the city. Although Samaria was a competing urban center, those who returned from Babylon organized themselves around Jerusalem. Urban centers offer a privileged lifestyle with amenities not available in rural areas. Jerusalem was no different.

servants. [4]And in Jerusalem lived some of the Judahites and the Benjaminites. Of the Judahites: Athaiah son of Uzziah son of Zechariah son of Amariah son of Shephatiah son of Mahalalel, of the descendants of Perez; [5]and Maaseiah son of Baruch son of Col-hozeh son of Hazaiah son of Adaiah son of Joiarib son of Zechariah son of the Shelahnite.[p] [6]All the descendants of Perez who lived in Jerusalem were four hundred sixty-eight valiant warriors.

[7] And these are the Benjaminites: Sallu son of Meshullam son of Joed son of Pedaiah son of Kolaiah son of Maaseiah son of Ithiel son of Jeshaiah. [8]And his brothers[q] Gabbai, Sallai: nine hundred twenty-eight. [9]Joel son of Zichri was their overseer, and Judah son of Hassenuah was second in charge of the city.

[10] Of the priests: Jedaiah son of Joiarib, Jachin, [11]Seraiah son of Hilkiah son of Meshullam son of Zadok son of Meraioth son of Ahitub, officer of the house of God, [12]and their associates who did the work of the house, eight hundred twenty-two; and Adaiah son of Jeroham son of Pelaliah son of Amzi son of Zechariah son of Pashhur son of Malchijah, [13]and his associates, heads of ancestral houses, two hundred forty-two; and Amashsai son of Azarel son of Ahzai son of Meshillemoth son of Immer, [14]and their associates, valiant warriors, one hundred twenty-eight; their overseer was Zabdiel son of Haggedolim.

[15] And of the Levites: Shemaiah son of Hasshub son of Azrikam son of Hashabiah son of Bunni; [16]and Shabbethai and Jozabad, of the leaders of the Levites, who were over the outside work of the house of God; [17]and Mattaniah son of Mica son of Zabdi son of Asaph, who was the leader to begin the thanksgiving in prayer, and Bakbukiah, the second among his associates; and Abda son of Shammua son of Galal son of Jeduthun. [18]All the Levites in the holy city were two hundred eighty-four.

[19] The gatekeepers Akkub, Talmon, and their associates, who kept watch at the gates, were one hundred seventy-two. [20]And the rest of Israel, and of the priests and the Levites, were in all the towns of Judah, all of them in their inheritance. [21]But the temple servants lived on Ophel, and Ziha and Gishpa were over the temple servants.

[22] The overseer of the Levites in Jerusalem was Uzzi son of Bani son of Hashabiah son of Mattaniah son of Mica, of the descendants of Asaph, the singers, in charge of the work of the house of God. [23]For there was a command from the king concerning them and a settled provision for the singers, as was required every day. [24]And Pethahiah son of Meshezabel, of the descendants of Zerah son of Judah, was at the king's hand in all matters concerning the people.

[25] And as for the villages, with their fields, some of the people of Judah lived in Kiriath-arba and its villages, and in Dibon and its villages, and in Jekabzeel and its villages, [26]and in Jeshua and in Moladah and Beth-pelet, [27]in Hazar-shual, in Beer-sheba and its villages, [28]in Ziklag, in Meconah and its villages, [29]in En-rimmon, in Zorah, in Jarmuth, [30]Zanoah, Adullam, and their villages, Lachish and its fields, and Azekah and its villages. So they camped from Beer-sheba to the valley of Hinnom. [31]The people of Benjamin also lived from Geba onward, at Michmash, Aija, Bethel and its villages, [32]Anathoth, Nob, Ananiah, [33]Hazor, Ramah, Gittaim, [34]Hadid, Zeboim, Neballat, [35]Lod, and Ono, the valley of artisans. [36]And certain divisions of the Levites in Judah were joined to Benjamin.

12 These are the priests and the Levites who came up with Zerubbabel son of Shealtiel and Jeshua: Seraiah, Jeremiah, Ezra, [2]Amariah, Malluch, Hattush, [3]Shecaniah, Rehum, Meremoth, [4]Iddo, Ginnethoi,

p 11.5 Cn: Heb *Shilonite*   *q* 11.8 Gk mss: Heb *And after him*

11:4–24 The list outlines who claims residence in Jerusalem. Those who had returned were not the only group claiming Jerusalem, but the stories of the ancestors, Ezra's reading of ancient teachings, and the location of the temple all compelled Nehemiah to claim Jerusalem as the center for this community.

11:25–36 The census continues for the surrounding villages.

12:1–26 List of legitimation: claiming membership in the clergy. The list fills in historical gaps from the first migration under Cyrus to Nehemiah's time. It is primarily concerned with the clergy: *leaders of the priests* (vv. 1–7), *Levites* (vv. 8–11), *priests* (vv. 12–21), and *gatekeepers* (v. 25). The list intends to demonstrate an unbroken line of succession, God's appointment of clergy leadership

Abijah, ⁵Mijamin, Maadiah, Bilgah, ⁶Shemaiah, Joiarib, Jedaiah, ⁷Sallu, Amok, Hilkiah, Jedaiah. These were the leaders of the priests and of their associates in the days of Jeshua.

8 And the Levites: Jeshua, Binnui, Kadmiel, Sherebiah, Judah, and Mattaniah, who with his associates was in charge of the songs of thanksgiving. ⁹And Bakbukiah and Unno their associates stood opposite them in the service. ¹⁰Jeshua was the father of Joiakim, Joiakim the father of Eliashib, Eliashib the father of Joiada, ¹¹Joiada the father of Jonathan, and Jonathan the father of Jaddua.

12 In the days of Joiakim the priests, the heads of the ancestral houses, were: of Seraiah, Meraiah; of Jeremiah, Hananiah; ¹³of Ezra, Meshullam; of Amariah, Jehohanan; ¹⁴of Malluchi, Jonathan; of Shebaniah, Joseph; ¹⁵of Harim, Adna; of Meraioth, Helkai; ¹⁶of Iddo, Zechariah; of Ginnethon, Meshullam; ¹⁷of Abijah, Zichri; of Miniamin, of Moadiah, Piltai; ¹⁸of Bilgah, Shammua; of Shemaiah, Jehonathan; ¹⁹of Joiarib, Mattenai; of Jedaiah, Uzzi; ²⁰of Sallai, Kallai; of Amok, Eber; ²¹of Hilkiah, Hashabiah; of Jedaiah, Nethanel.

22 As for the Levites, in the days of Eliashib, Joiada, Johanan, and Jaddua, there were recorded the heads of ancestral houses, also the priests until the reign of Darius the Persian. ²³The Levites, heads of ancestral houses, were recorded in the Book of the Annals until the days of Johanan son of Eliashib. ²⁴And the leaders of the Levites: Hashabiah, Sherebiah, and Jeshua son of Kadmiel, with their associates over against them, to praise and to give thanks, according to the commandment of David the man of God, section opposite to section. ²⁵Mattaniah, Bakbukiah, Obadiah, Meshullam, Talmon, and Akkub were gatekeepers standing guard at the storehouses of the gates. ²⁶These were in the days of Joiakim son of Jeshua son of Jozadak and in the days of Nehemiah the governor and of Ezra the priest and scribe.

27 Now at the dedication of the wall of Jerusalem they sought out the Levites in all their places, to bring them to Jerusalem to celebrate the dedication with rejoicing, with thanksgivings and with singing, with cymbals, harps, and lyres. ²⁸The companies of the singers gathered together from the circuit around Jerusalem and from the villages of the Netophathites, ²⁹also from Beth-gilgal and from the region of Geba and Azmaveth, for the singers had built for themselves villages around Jerusalem. ³⁰And the priests and the Levites purified themselves, and they purified the people and the gates and the wall.

31 Then I brought the leaders of Judah up onto the wall and appointed two great companies that gave thanks and went in procession. One went to the right on the wall to the Dung Gate, ³²and after them went Hoshaiah and half the officials of Judah, ³³and Azariah, Ezra, Meshullam, ³⁴Judah, Benjamin, Shemaiah, and Jeremiah, ³⁵and some of the young priests with trumpets: Zechariah son of Jonathan son of Shemaiah son of Mattaniah son of Micaiah son of Zaccur son of Asaph, ³⁶and his kindred, Shemaiah, Azarel, Milalai, Gilalai, Maai, Nethanel, Judah, and Hanani, with the musical instruments of David the man of God, and Ezra the scribe went in front of them. ³⁷At the Fountain Gate, in front of them, they went straight up by the stairs of the city of David, at the ascent of the wall, above the house of David, to the Water Gate on the east.

38 The other company of those who gave thanks went to the left,ʳ and I followed them with half of the people on the wall, above the Tower of the Ovens, to the Broad Wall, ³⁹and above the Gate of Ephraim, and by the Old Gate, and by the Fish Gate and the Tower of Hananel and the Tower of the Hundred, to the Sheep Gate, and they came to a halt at the Gate of the Guard. ⁴⁰So both companies of those who gave thanks stood in the house of God, and I and half of the officials with me; ⁴¹and the priests Eliakim, Maaseiah, Miniamin, Micaiah, Elioenai, Zechariah, and Hananiah, with trumpets; ⁴²and Maaseiah, Shemaiah,

r 12.38 Cn: Heb *opposite*

---

from Babylonia to the time of Ezra's and Nehemiah's work. Such a list legitimates the group of clergy functioning at the time of the book's composition in the Hellenistic period. It presents their authority as having extended over centuries. Equally as important, such a claim places on the clergy the awesome responsibility to live up to the mantle that now rests upon their shoulders.

12:27–43 Dedication of the wall with another celebration and ceremony.

Eleazar, Uzzi, Jehohanan, Malchijah, Elam, and Ezer. And the singers sang with Jezrahiah as their leader. ⁴³They offered great sacrifices that day and rejoiced, for God had made them rejoice with great joy; the women and children also rejoiced. The joy of Jerusalem was heard far away.

44 On that day men were appointed over the chambers for the stores, the contributions, the first fruits, and the tithes, to gather into them the portions required by the law for the priests and for the Levites from the fields belonging to the towns, for Judah rejoiced over the priests and the Levites who ministered. ⁴⁵They performed the service of their God and the service of purification, as did the singers and the gatekeepers, according to the command of David and his son Solomon. ⁴⁶For in the days of David and Asaph long ago there was a leader of the singers, and there were songs of praise and thanksgiving to God. ⁴⁷In the days of Zerubbabel and in the days of Nehemiah all Israel gave the daily portions for the singers and the gatekeepers. They set apart that which was for the Levites, and the Levites set apart that which was for the descendants of Aaron.

13 On that day they read from the book of Moses in the hearing of the people, and in it was found written that no Ammonite or Moabite should ever enter the assembly of God, ²because they did not meet the Israelites with bread and water but hired Balaam against them to curse them—yet our God turned the curse into a blessing. ³When

the people heard the law, they separated from Israel all those of foreign descent.

4 Now before this, Eliashib the priest, who was appointed over the chambers of the house of our God and who was related to Tobiah, ⁵prepared for Tobiah a large room where they had previously put the grain offering, the frankincense, the vessels, and the tithes of grain, wine, and oil, which were given by commandment to the Levites, singers, and gatekeepers, and the contributions for the priests. ⁶While this was taking place I was not in Jerusalem, for in the thirty-second year of King Artaxerxes of Babylon I went to the king. After some time I asked leave of the king ⁷and returned to Jerusalem. I then discovered the wrong that Eliashib had done on behalf of Tobiah, preparing a room for him in the courts of the house of God. ⁸And I was very angry, and I threw all the household furniture of Tobiah out of the room. ⁹Then I gave orders, and they cleansed the chambers, and I brought back the vessels of the house of God, with the grain offering and the frankincense.

10 I also found out that the portions of the Levites had not been given to them, so that the Levites and the singers who had conducted the service had gone back to their fields. ¹¹So I contended with the officials and said, "Why is the house of God forsaken?" And I gathered them together and set them in their stations. ¹²Then all Judah brought the tithe of the grain, wine, and oil into the storehouses. ¹³And I appointed as treasurers over the treasuries Shelemiah the priest, Zadok the scribe, and Pedaiah of the Levites, and as

12:45–47 *According to the command of David and his son Solomon.* Connecting this new community with ancient Israel is an important emphasis not just establishing the unbroken line of clergy from the time of the migration from Babylon to Nehemiah's time but also on the *service* the clergy perform (v. 45), the *songs of praise and thanksgiving to God* (v. 46), and stewardship over the resources (v. 47).

13:1–3 *They read from the book of Moses.* Nehemiah oversees several reforms that are linked to ancient practices through Moses's law. The new Jerusalem temple community identifies with those who have returned from Babylon and adopts their customs and religious practices, including the exclusion of those constructed as "foreign." *No Ammonite or Moabite* invokes the traditional enemies of Israel based on Deut. 23:3–5, which references Num. 22–24.

13:4–13 Tobiah, Nehemiah's rival, has been allocated space in the temple. It would not have been unusual for an imperial official to have an "office" or quarters in the temple, since it was a part of the Persian bureaucracy. However, for Nehemiah, Tobiah's presence threatens his vision for the community. Nehemiah probably believed that Tobiah's location there would have given him undue influence over its internal workings. **13:6** Nehemiah has proven his loyalty to Persia and is allowed to return to Jerusalem a second time. Nehemiah's proximity to the king vests him with more authority than Tobiah. **13:8–9** He expels Tobiah. **13:13** Nehemiah installs a bureaucracy more in line with his vision

their assistant Hanan son of Zaccur son of Mattaniah, for they were considered faithful, and their duty was to distribute to their associates. [14]Remember me, O my God, concerning this, and do not wipe out my good deeds that I have done for the house of my God and for his service.

15 In those days I saw in Judah people treading winepresses on the Sabbath and bringing in heaps of grain and loading them on donkeys, and also wine, grapes, figs, and all kinds of burdens that they brought into Jerusalem on the Sabbath day, and I warned them at that time against selling food. [16]Tyrians also, who lived in the city, brought in fish and all kinds of merchandise and sold them on the Sabbath to the people of Judah in Jerusalem. [17]Then I contended with the nobles of Judah and said to them, "What is this evil thing that you are doing, profaning the Sabbath day? [18]Did not your ancestors act in this way, and did not our God bring all this disaster on us and on this city? Yet you bring more wrath on Israel by profaning the Sabbath."

19 When it began to be dark at the gates of Jerusalem before the Sabbath, I commanded that the doors should be shut and gave orders that they should not be opened until after the Sabbath. And I set some of my servants over the gates, to prevent any burden from being brought in on the Sabbath day. [20]Then the merchants and sellers of all kinds of merchandise spent the night outside Jerusalem once or twice. [21]But I warned them and said to them, "Why do you spend the night in front of the wall? If you do so again, I will lay hands on you." From that time on they did not come on the Sabbath. [22]And I commanded the Levites that they should purify themselves and come and guard the gates, to keep the Sabbath day holy. Remember this also in my favor, O my God, and spare me according to the greatness of your steadfast love.

23 In those days also I saw Jews who had married women of Ashdod, Ammon, and Moab, [24]and half of their children spoke the language of Ashdod, and they could not speak the language of Judah but spoke the language of various peoples. [25]And I contended with them and cursed them and beat some of the men and pulled out their hair, and I made them take an oath in the name of God, saying, "You shall not give your daughters to their sons or take their daughters for your sons or for yourselves. [26]Did not King Solomon of Israel sin on account of such women? Among the many nations there was no king like him, and he was beloved by his God, and God made him king over all Israel; nevertheless, foreign women made even him to sin. [27]Shall we then listen to you and do all this great evil and act treacherously against our God by marrying foreign women?"

for the community. He trusts *Shelemiah the priest, Zadok the scribe, and Pedaiah of the Levites,* who are now responsible for carrying out his vision for the temple. The expulsion of Tobiah is a polemic against the Tobiads, one of the priestly families.

13:15–22 Keeping the Sabbath by refraining from work is enjoined in the Ten Commandments (Exod. 20:8–11; Deut. 5:12–15). This practice may have been particularly important to the exiles in Babylon, as it would have marked them as a distinct community and helped them maintain their identity. In ancient communities, commerce was the activity of the wealthy while the poor worked the land. In this case, the wealthy probably believed they were above adhering to Nehemiah's direction (see Neh. 10:31). Nehemiah finds himself required again to enforce the practice of refraining from commerce on the Sabbath.

13:23–29 Similar to Ezra, Nehemiah is determined to carry out this social and political reorganization, which includes an end to intermarriage (see **"Intermarriage," p. 649**). From his vantage, he believes exogamy presents a serious threat to the community's survival. The focus here is language. Children who only knew the language of the "foreign" parent could not participate in the worship or carry out the rituals of the temple. When these children, particularly the oldest son, inherited their father's land, would they identify with the temple community? Would they contribute of its yield to the storehouses that Nehemiah had so meticulously organized? If not, the temple would not meet its tax burden, and the Persians might depose the priesthood and install another one more sympathetic to Persian rule but less loyal to the community. For Nehemiah, the priesthood, and the elites living in Jerusalem, intermarriage in this regard posed the most serious threat to the community's newly formed identity.

28 And one of the sons of Jehoiada, son of the high priest Eliashib, was the son-in-law of Sanballat the Horonite; I chased him away from me. [29]Remember them, O my God, because they have defiled the priesthood, the covenant of the priests and the Levites.

30 Thus I cleansed them from everything foreign, and I established the duties of the priests and Levites, each in his work, [31]and I provided for the wood offering, at appointed times, and for the first fruits. Remember me, O my God, for good.

13:30–31 The mass divorces ripped families apart. Was the institution of the new temple bureaucracy and the establishment of religious regulations worth the cost? Might different decisions have been made? Would it have been so intolerable to preserve these families? In establishing his reforms, Nehemiah makes difficult choices. He believes the sacrifices are for the sake of preserving the community's identity. *Remember me, O my God, for good.* One may not agree with all Nehemiah's decisions, but it is difficult to impugn his motivation. He declares it before God, laying bare his heart. Nehemiah must have understood his own fallibility and the subsequent pain that the people would experience. However, in the end, could anyone do any more than Nehemiah did? He responded to God's call and offered to God to the best of his ability the totality of his labor, commitment, love, service, and sacrifice, praying that in God's grace, God would remember him.

ESTHER

Genre and Historicity

The book of Esther is an artfully crafted narrative that belongs in the genre of Hebrew short story, alongside texts such as Ruth, Jonah, and perhaps the Joseph novella (Gen. 37–50). The structure is highly intentional; the many drinking feasts in the tale create a chiastic framework that leads readers to a central climax in which foreshadowing and dramatic irony produce a "reveal" worthy of contemporary television. Dialogue and description are used to great effect throughout.

These literary features affect the historicity of the text, leading most scholars to conclude that the book is not intended to be read historically. Rather, the book is something of a comedy, satire, or farce, with strong elements of carnivalesque fantasy. It is a book about and for a people living in the Diaspora, under the thumb of political and social powers much stronger than their own. Identity and savvy are more relevant than faith or God, who does not appear in the story.

This anonymous book was likely written between the fifth and second centuries BCE. It references only the exile of Judah, but not their return in 539 BCE, and the characters seem to view their Persian home as permanent. The book of Esther was not found among the manuscripts discovered at the Dead Sea, though the Greek version(s) indicates a complicated history of transmission (see Gk. Esth.).

Characters

Four main characters form the cast of Esther, with help from significant supporting actors. *Esther* is a Jewish orphan first named Hadassah ("myrtle"), who is in Susa under the care of her cousin Mordecai. Esther is not a Hebrew name; it references the Babylonian deity Ishtar (or perhaps the Persian word *stara*, "star"). Other biblical characters bearing non-Hebrew names include Daniel (Belteshazzar), Hananiah (Shadrach), Mishael (Meshach), and Azariah (Abednego; see Dan. 1–6). Esther herself is enigmatic, controlled by the men around her yet displaying wisdom and bravery (not to mention the looks and personality) worthy of a heroine.

Mordecai's name derives from the national god of Babylon, Marduk. We do not know his Hebrew name, though his pedigree is important to the author: Mordecai is a Benjaminite who was exiled with King Jeconiah (Jehoiachin) of Judah (see 2 Kgs. 24:15). This detail would make him well over one hundred years old at the time of Esther, but the book is not concerned with historical accuracy.

King Ahasuerus, traditionally identified as either of the Persian monarchs Xerxes or Artaxerxes, is a relatively flat and indecisive character. He relies extensively on those around him for counsel, and managing the king is something nearly all the other characters do.

Haman is the villain, cast as an evil buffoon who ultimately orchestrates his own downfall. The book describes him as an Agagite, which may (however impossibly) connect him with Israel's enemy from the early days of the Israelite monarchy (see 1 Sam. 15:8).

The eunuchs, whose physical characteristics presumably make them ideal palace servants, play a critical and recurring role in the plot. On several occasions, they convey messages to, offer suggestions to, care for, inform, and even plot to kill other characters.

Reading Guide

Reversal is the dominant theme of the book. The Jewish orphan Esther replaces the noble queen Vashti, the wicked Haman is outdone by Mordecai, and the planned destruction of the Jews is subverted by the Jews' destruction of their enemies. The entire book turns on one sleepless night in which the king is reminded of an obscure event lost in the royal record.

Gender and sexuality are ever-present in the story (see **"The Bible, Gender, and Sexuality," p. 2160–62**). Feminist readers will be heartened by the two queens' fortitude, even while despairing at their treatment and manipulation by the men around them. But Esther games the system in a way that will remind audiences of Ruth and Tamar (Gen. 38). Eunuchs are more significant here than elsewhere in the Bible; their status creates both security for others and opportunity for them. Queer readers have also drawn attention to the presence and significance of eunuchs in the book. The term *eunuchs* likely refers to males castrated prior to puberty but could also include intersex individuals (see **"Eunuchs," p. 672**).

The final reversal in the story is facilitated through an instance of preemptive violence. While this excessive killing is understood by many to be a feature of the carnivalesque nature of the story, the use of violence to combat violence will give many readers pause, as well as an opportunity to consider the role of violence in liberation movements (see **"Violence against the Jews' Enemies," p. 682**).

God is not mentioned in the book, and the setting is wholly secular. Esther fasts and urges others to do the same, but no one so much as prays in the story. Since Esther is successfully hiding her Jewish identity, it is also unlikely that she is keeping kosher or Shabbat. The Hebrew text seems unconcerned with this lack of piety. Later versions sought to rectify this situation, but it is noteworthy that the canonized Hebrew Bible does not contain those later additions. This "god-less" quality, though disconcerting to some, may increase the appeal of Esther to nonbelieving readers.

The book of Esther is read performatively in Jewish communities during the holiday of Purim, celebrated in early spring. The book closes by establishing the holiday and connecting it to the events in the story. This connection is likely not original to the tale; the earliest mention of the holiday refers to "The Day of Mordecai" (2 Macc. 15:36). Because the holiday is postbiblical (and therefore not prescribed in Torah) and mentions neither the Torah nor the temple, the book of Esther was likely critical to the formal, religious acceptance of Purim.

Each of these themes is fitting for a Diaspora text, written and read by those whose identities and customs are out of step with their cultural surroundings. The story of Esther thus communicates across boundaries and cultures, making meaningful points of contact among the disenfranchised and dislocated.

Brian Albert Smith

1 This happened in the days of Ahasuerus, the same Ahasuerus who ruled over one hundred twenty-seven provinces from India to Cush. [2]In those days when King Ahasuerus sat on his royal throne in the citadel of Susa, [3]in the third year of his reign, he gave a banquet for all his officials and ministers. The army of Persia and Media, the nobles, and the governors of the provinces were present, [4]while he displayed the great wealth of his kingdom and the splendor and pomp of his majesty for many days, one hundred eighty days in all.

5 When these days were completed, the king gave for all the people present in the citadel of Susa, both great and small, a banquet lasting for seven days, in the court of the garden of the king's palace. [6]There were white cotton curtains and blue hangings tied with cords of fine linen and purple to silver rings[a] and marble pillars. There were couches of gold and silver on a mosaic pavement of porphyry, marble, mother-of-pearl, and colored stones. [7]Drinks were served in golden goblets, goblets of different kinds, and the royal wine was lavished according to the bounty of the king. [8]Drinking was by ordinance without restraint, for the king had given orders to all the officials of his palace to do as each one desired. [9]Furthermore, Queen Vashti gave a banquet for the women in the palace of King Ahasuerus.

10 On the seventh day, when the king was merry with wine, he commanded Mehuman,

a 1.6 Or *rods*

1:1–12 The first banquet. The opulent banquet that opens the book of Esther introduces the story. Meals will be a recurring motif. Other themes include the king's power and how it is managed and the role of laws and decrees. Eunuchs appear at key moments, anticipated by the list in v. 10. **1:1** *Ahasuerus* has been associated with the historical king Xerxes, who ruled over the Persian Empire in the mid-fifth century BCE. While the description of his empire, *from India to Cush* (perhaps northern Sudan), may correspond to history, little else does. **1:2** *Susa*, in modern-day Iran, was the capital of the Elamite and Persian kingdoms. Exiles from Judea to Babylon may have moved there after the fall of Babylon in 539 BCE (2 Kgs. 25 and 2 Chr. 36:23–24; see also Ezra 4:9; Neh. 1:1; Dan. 8:2). **1:3** *Banquet* comes from the verb meaning "to drink" and hints at the mood of these events. **1:4** *One hundred eighty days in all.* The banquet's excess sets a tone for similar exaggerations throughout the book. **1:5–9** The capital city gets two additional banquets of *seven days* each. At the end, Susa will suffer an additional day of violence (Esth. 9:13). **1:10** *Eunuchs* play an important

Focus On: Eunuchs (Esther 1)

Eunuchs appear in several places throughout the Bible, but nowhere as significantly as in Esther. The term *eunuch* typically refers to a castrated male, but it could also refer to intersex individuals (the Bible does not have terms for intersex persons). Matthew 19:12 identifies three possible ways one might become a eunuch: "nature" (presumably by birth), unwillingly ("by others"), and by choice. All the eunuchs in the book of Esther are serving in the palace, and we do not know how they became eunuchs or whether they are free or enslaved.

Eunuchs are critical to the plot. In chap. 1, seven eunuchs attending King Ahasuerus are commanded to "bring Queen Vashti before the king" (1:10–11). "Hegai the king's eunuch, who had charge of the women" favors the virgin Esther and counsels her on what to "take with her from the harem" when she spends her first night with Ahasuerus (2:13–15). When Mordecai learns of two eunuchs' plot to kill the king, he informs Esther (2:21–22). Mordecai's action eventually leads to one of the story's key plot twists (6:1–3). Esther's own eunuchs inform her of Haman's plot to kill the Jews (4:4–8), and the eunuch Hathach conveys what may be the most famous message of the book: perhaps Esther has become queen "for just such a time as this" (4:14). Eunuchs deliver Haman to Esther's second banquet (6:14). Finally, the eunuch Harbona suggests the mechanism for Haman's execution (7:9).

We should not be surprised that eunuchs play such a key role in Esther. Their presence in sexualized contexts contributes to the book's irony (see 1:10–11 and 2:12–15). The eunuchs' liminal bodily status corresponds to their boundary-crossing: Esther's eunuchs carry her messages beyond the palace walls, and the king's eunuchs travel to fetch Haman (4:4–17 and 6:14). Eunuchs defy categorization and are thus ideal message-bearers, observers, and plot-shapers: on at least two occasions, the eunuchs influence the course of the story (2:21–23 and 7:9–10). The eunuchs' actions also serve to shift power from men to women and from non-Jews to Jews. Their atypical status and function thus invite our attention. Eunuchs will be of particular interest to intersex, queer, and disabled readers. Scholars have noted the consistent presence of eunuchs in a variety of societies. In the book of Esther, these seemingly marginal characters play quite a central role.

Brian Albert Smith

Biztha, Harbona, Bigtha and Abagtha, Zethar and Carkas, the seven eunuchs who attended him, [11]to bring Queen Vashti before the king wearing the royal crown, in order to show the peoples and the officials her beauty, for she was fair to behold. [12]But Queen Vashti refused to come at the king's command conveyed by the eunuchs. At this the king was enraged, and his anger burned within him.

13 Then the king consulted the sages who knew the laws[b] (for this was the king's procedure toward all who were versed in law and custom, [14]and those next to him were Carshena, Shethar, Admatha, Tarshish, Meres, Marsena, and Memucan, the seven officials of Persia and Media who had access to the king and sat first in the kingdom): [15]"According to the law, what is to be done with Queen Vashti because she has not performed the command of King Ahasuerus conveyed by the eunuchs?" [16]Then Memucan said in the presence of the king and the officials, "Queen Vashti has done wrong not only to the king but also to all the officials and all the peoples who are in all the provinces of King Ahasuerus. [17]For this deed of the queen will be

b 1.13 Cn: Heb *times*

role in the story (see **"Eunuchs," p. 672**). **1:11** Many rabbinic interpreters understood the command to *Queen Vashti* to mean that she should appear *wearing* only *the royal crown*. **1:12** Contemporary readers may see agency and virtue in Vashti's refusal. Her actions will find a foil in Esther's unbidden appearance before Ahasuerus later (4:11). The king's *anger* results in the first plot movement. The plot often moves as a direct result of the king's emotions, desire, and power and others' attempts to manage or manipulate him.

1:13–22 Queen Vashti is removed. The king's response is legal. Fearing that a misbehaving queen will lead to misbehaving wives throughout the kingdom, the king's counselors suggest a royal order to ensure Vashti's banishment and women's good behavior. **1:13–15** There are seven trusted *sages* (literally "wise ones"), just as there were seven eunuchs who delivered the order to Vashti. These sit *first in the kingdom*, emphasizing the importance of the *law*, even in domestic affairs. **1:16–20** In Memucan's speech, Vashti is a model for *all women, noble* and common. The royal marriage has

made known to all women, causing them to look with contempt on their husbands, since they will say, 'King Ahasuerus commanded Queen Vashti to be brought before him, and she did not come.' [18]This very day the noble ladies of Persia and Media who have heard of the queen's behavior will rebel against[c] the king's officials, and there will be no end of contempt and wrath! [19]If it pleases the king, let a royal order go out from him, and let it be written among the laws of the Persians and the Medes so that it may not be altered, that Vashti is never again to come before King Ahasuerus, and let the king give her royal position to another who is better than she. [20]So when the decree made by the king is proclaimed throughout all his kingdom, vast as it is, all women will give honor to their husbands, high and low alike."

21 This advice pleased the king and the officials, and the king did as Memucan proposed; [22]he sent letters to all the royal provinces, to every province in its own script and to every people in its own language, declaring that every man should be master in his own house.[d]

2 After these things, when the anger of King Ahasuerus had abated, he remembered Vashti and what she had done and what had been decreed against her. [2]Then the king's servants who attended him said, "Let beautiful young virgins be sought out for the king. [3]And let the king appoint commissioners in all the provinces of his kingdom to gather all the beautiful young virgins to the harem in the citadel of Susa under custody of Hegai, the king's eunuch, who is in charge of the women; let their cosmetic treatments be given them. [4]And let the young woman who pleases the king be queen instead of Vashti." This pleased the king, and he did so.

5 Now there was a Jew in the citadel of Susa whose name was Mordecai son of Jair son of Shimei son of Kish, a Benjaminite, [6]who had been carried away from Jerusalem among the captives carried away with King Jeconiah of Judah, whom King Nebuchadnezzar of Babylon had carried away. [7]He had brought up Hadassah, that is, Esther, his cousin, for she had neither father nor mother; the young woman was fair and beautiful, and when her father and her mother died, Mordecai adopted her as his own daughter. [8]When the king's order and his edict were proclaimed and when many young women were gathered in the citadel of Susa in custody of Hegai, Esther was taken into the king's palace and put in custody of Hegai, who had charge of the women. [9]The young woman pleased him and won his favor, and he quickly provided her with her cosmetic treatments and her portion of food and with seven chosen maids from the king's palace, and he advanced her and her maids to the best place in the harem.

c 1.18 Cn: Heb *will tell*   d 1.22 Compare Gk: Heb adds *and speak according to the language of his people*

become a model for all marriages, *high and low alike.* **1:21–22** The first *letter* goes out *to every province* (see 3:12–15; 8:9–14; 9:20–23). The use of different provincial *scripts* and *languages* indicates the multiethnic nature of the kingdom (see also 3:12 and 8:9). But the patriarchy (royal and common, public and domestic) is established across all the cultures of the empire.

2:1–14 Vashti's replacement. 2:1–2 A change in the king's emotional state leads to the next plot movement, and those around the king offer another suggestion. **2:3** *Hegai,* not mentioned among the eunuchs in 1:10, oversees the king's women before they become part of the royal harem (see 2:14). **2:4** *The young woman who pleases the king. . . . This pleased the king.* As in 1:21, the king's pleasure is achieved, though this time by his "servants," presumably the domestic staff, in contrast to "those next to him" (1:14). Palace intrigue is not limited to those with political or social status; the inversion of power is a recurring theme. **2:5–6** *Mordecai* is a *Jew* with *Benjaminite* heritage. His identity is crucial to the tension in the story; as an exiled Jerusalemite, he has status in the postexilic Jewish community. **2:7** *Hadassah, that is, Esther,* is Mordecai's cousin, though their relationship seems closer to that of niece and uncle or foster father and *daughter.* This has the double effect of establishing both his care for Esther and his power over her, given the national patriarchal hierarchy. Her *fair and beautiful* appearance is a clue that her physical traits will matter later. **2:8** Esther is taken from her adopted home into the *custody* (literally "hand," often a euphemism for power) of Hegai, "who is in charge of the women" (v. 3; literally "keeper" or "watcher"). Both men exercise protection and power over Esther, and contemporary readers may well view this entire episode as human trafficking or slavery. **2:9** Esther *pleased* Hegai, as she will please most everyone. Esther's

¹⁰Esther did not reveal her people or kindred, for Mordecai had charged her not to tell. ¹¹Every day Mordecai would walk back and forth in front of the court of the harem to learn how Esther was and how she fared.

12 The turn came for each young woman to go in to King Ahasuerus, after being twelve months under the regulations for the women, since this was the regular period of their cosmetic treatment: six months with oil of myrrh and six months with perfumes and cosmetics for women. ¹³When the young woman went in to the king, she was given whatever she asked for to take with her from the harem to the king's palace. ¹⁴In the evening she went in; then in the morning she came back to the second harem in custody of Shaashgaz, the king's eunuch who was in charge of the concubines; she did not go in to the king again unless the king delighted in her and she was summoned by name.

15 When the turn came for Esther daughter of Abihail the uncle of Mordecai, who had adopted her as his own daughter, to go in to the king, she asked for nothing except what Hegai the king's eunuch, who had charge of the women, advised. Now Esther was admired by all who saw her. ¹⁶When Esther was taken to King Ahasuerus in his royal palace in the tenth month, which is the month of Tebeth, in the seventh year of his reign, ¹⁷the king loved Esther more than all the other women; of all the virgins she won his favor and devotion, so that he set the royal crown on her head and made her queen instead of Vashti. ¹⁸Then the king gave a great banquet to all his officials and ministers: "Esther's banquet." He also granted a holiday[e] to the provinces and gave gifts with royal liberality.

19 When the virgins were being gathered together,[f] Mordecai was sitting at the king's gate. ²⁰Now Esther had not revealed her kindred or her people, as Mordecai had charged her, for Esther obeyed Mordecai just as when she was brought up by him. ²¹In those days, while Mordecai was sitting at the king's gate, Bigthan and Teresh, two of the king's eunuchs who guarded the threshold, became angry and conspired to kill[g] King Ahasuerus. ²²But the matter came to the knowledge of Mordecai, and he told it to Queen Esther, and Esther told the king in the name of Mordecai. ²³When the affair was investigated and found to be so, both men were hung on the pole. It was recorded in the book of the annals in the presence of the king.

3 After these things King Ahasuerus promoted Haman son of Hammedatha the Agagite and advanced him and set his seat above all the officials who were with him. ²And all the king's servants who were at the king's gate bowed down and did obeisance to Haman, for the king had so commanded concerning him. But Mordecai did not bow down or do obeisance. ³Then the king's

e 2.18 Or *an amnesty* or *a release from taxes*   f 2.19 Heb adds *a second time*   g 2.21 Heb *to lay hands on*

advances in the harem will remind readers of Joseph and Daniel, other attractive captives who rose to prominence (see Gen. 39–41 and Dan. 1–6). **2:10–11** Esther's secret Jewish identity is the plot linchpin; it is also an open secret, given Mordecai's status and daily public displays of concern. **2:12** The twin six-month treatments for women echo the excessive 180-day feast that opened the book. **2:13** *Whatever she asked for.* This cryptic phrase provides the background for Esther's actions in v. 15. **2:14** Once a woman had been with the king, his *delight* alone determined whether she would return, underscoring his control.

2:15–18 Esther becomes queen. 2:15–16 *She asked for nothing except.* Esther's first independent act demonstrates wisdom—she recognizes that Hegai would likely know just how to win the king's affection. **2:17** The king's *love* for Esther seems to be a combination of *favor and devotion*, as well as physical attraction. **2:18** Another *banquet* marks a significant moment, and the *liberality* of the king's *holiday* reminds readers of the lavish feasts in chap. 1.

2:19–23 Mordecai saves the king. This brief scene provides background for events in chap. 6 while foreshadowing identity, loyalty, hanging, and the royal records. **2:19** *At the king's gate* may indicate an official role in court. **2:20** *Esther* continues to be obedient to *Mordecai*. **2:21** Bigthan is "Bigtha" of 1:10. Eunuchs act at another key moment.

3:1–11 Haman's plot. The central conflict is established with the introduction of Haman, an egomaniac whose most dominant characteristic will lead to his mighty downfall. His conflict with Mordecai drives his desire to kill all Jews, just as Vashti's offense led to a decree concerning all women (1:17). **3:1** Haman is an Agagite, perhaps a reference to King Agag, the enemy of Saul in 1 Sam. 15.

servants who were at the king's gate said to Mordecai, "Why do you disobey the king's command?" ⁴When they spoke to him day after day and he would not listen to them, they told Haman, in order to see whether Mordecai's words would stand, for he had told them that he was a Jew. ⁵When Haman saw that Mordecai did not bow down or do obeisance to him, Haman was infuriated. ⁶But he thought it beneath him to kill*ᵇ* only Mordecai. So, having been told who Mordecai's people were, Haman plotted to destroy all the Jews, the people of Mordecai, throughout the whole kingdom of Ahasuerus.

7 In the first month, which is the month of Nisan, in the twelfth year of King Ahasuerus, they cast Pur—which means "the lot"—before Haman for the day and for the month, and the lot fell on the thirteenth day of*ⁱ* the twelfth month, which is the month of Adar. ⁸Then Haman said to King Ahasuerus, "There is a certain people scattered and separated among the peoples in all the provinces of your kingdom; their laws are different from those of every other people, and they do not keep the king's laws, so that it is not appropriate for the king to tolerate them. ⁹If it pleases the king, let a decree be issued for their destruction, and I will pay ten thousand talents of silver into the hands of those who have charge of the king's business, so that they may put it into the king's treasuries." ¹⁰So the king took his signet ring from his hand and gave it to Haman son of Hammedatha the Agagite, the enemy of the Jews. ¹¹The king said to Haman, "The money is given to you,

and the people as well, to do with them as it seems good to you."

12 Then the king's secretaries were summoned on the thirteenth day of the first month, and an edict, according to all that Haman commanded, was written to the king's satraps and to the governors over all the provinces and to the officials of all the peoples, to every province in its own script and every people in its own language; it was written in the name of King Ahasuerus and sealed with the king's ring. ¹³Letters were sent by couriers to all the king's provinces, giving orders to destroy, to kill, and to annihilate all Jews, young and old, children and women, in one day, the thirteenth day of the twelfth month, which is the month of Adar, and to plunder their goods. ¹⁴A copy of the document was to be issued as a decree in every province by proclamation, calling on all the peoples to be ready for that day. ¹⁵The couriers went quickly by order of the king, and the decree was issued in the citadel of Susa. The king and Haman sat down to drink, but the city of Susa was thrown into confusion.

4 When Mordecai learned all that had been done, Mordecai tore his clothes and put on sackcloth and ashes and went through the city, wailing with a loud and bitter cry; ²he went up to the entrance of the king's gate, for no one might enter the king's gate clothed with sackcloth. ³In every province, wherever the king's command and

b 3.6 Heb *lay hands on*   *i* 3.7 Cn Compare Gk and 3.13 below: Heb lacks *the thirteenth day of*

Saul (as well as Mordecai) was a Benjaminite. **3:2–3** Mordecai's refusal to bow recalls Vashti's refusal as well as the Jews' refusal to bow to the statue of Nebuchadnezzar in Dan. 3:12. Mordecai's loyalty, established in Esth. 2:22, is now questioned. **3:4** Mordecai has revealed his identity in contrast to his charge to Esther (2:10, 20). **3:5–6** Haman's fury now drives the plot, and his ego expands his vengeance from one single offending Jew to all. **3:7** The *Pur* was a means of divination; the phrase *"the lot"* indicates that original audiences were unfamiliar with the term. **3:8–9** Haman still needs the king's authority to accomplish his purposes. His accusation is false, but the king accepts it. Haman suggests a decree like the counselors in Esth. 1; he also offers to compensate the treasury. **3:10** The *signet ring* allows Haman to act with the king's authority. *Enemy* occurs five times in this formulation (3:10; 7:6; 8:1; 9:10, 24).

3:12–15 A second decree. 3:12 *Own script . . . own language.* A phrase of inclusivity in 1:22 is now used to announce ethnic cleansing. **3:13** The date is eleven months from the edict's issue. *Plunder* may be a motivation for the killing. **3:15** *Sat down to drink.* Another meal marks another important moment in the story.

4:1–17 Mordecai convinces Esther. While the city reels in confusion, Mordecai sets about convincing Esther that she must help her people. **4:1** Tearing *clothes* and donning *sackcloth* and *ashes* are conventional outward symbols of mourning (see 2 Sam. 13:31; 2 Kgs. 6:30; 19:1; Jonah 3:6–7). **4:3** *Fasting* stands in sharp contrast to the feasts at the beginning of the book and the king's meal

his decree came, there was great mourning among the Jews, with fasting and weeping and lamenting, and most of them lay in sackcloth and ashes.

4 When Esther's maids and her eunuchs came and told her, the queen was deeply distressed; she sent garments to clothe Mordecai, so that he might take off his sackcloth, but he would not accept them. ⁵Then Esther called for Hathach, one of the king's eunuchs who had been appointed to attend her, and ordered him to go to Mordecai to learn what was happening and why. ⁶Hathach went out to Mordecai in the open square of the city in front of the king's gate, ⁷and Mordecai told him all that had happened to him and the exact sum of money that Haman had promised to pay into the king's treasuries for the destruction of the Jews. ⁸Mordecai also gave him a copy of the written decree issued in Susa for their destruction, that he might show it to Esther, explain it to her, and charge her to go to the king to make supplication to him and to entreat him for her people.

9 Hathach went and told Esther what Mordecai had said. ¹⁰Then Esther spoke to Hathach and gave him a message for Mordecai: ¹¹"All the king's servants and the people of the king's provinces know that, if any man or woman goes to the king inside the inner court without being called, there is but one law: to be put to death. Only if the king holds out the golden scepter to someone may that person live. I myself have not been called to come in to the king for thirty days." ¹²When they told Mordecai what Esther had said, ¹³Mordecai told them to reply to Esther, "Do not think that in the king's palace you will escape any more than all the other Jews. ¹⁴For if you keep silent at this time, relief and deliverance will rise for the Jews from another place, but you and your father's family will perish. Who knows? Perhaps you have come to royal dignity for just such a time as this." ¹⁵Then Esther said in reply to Mordecai, ¹⁶"Go, gather all the Jews to be found in Susa, and hold a fast on my behalf, and neither eat nor drink for three days, night or day. I and my maids will also fast as you do. After that I will go to the king, though it is against the law, and if I perish, I perish." ¹⁷Mordecai then went away and did everything as Esther had ordered him.

5 On the third day Esther put on her royal robes and stood in the inner court of the king's palace, opposite the king's hall. The king was sitting on his royal throne inside the palace opposite the entrance to the

with Haman in 3:15. **4:4** Her position in the palace has apparently secluded Esther from the news, but her response is emotional. **4:5–7** *Hathach,* another *eunuch,* will act as a go-between for Esther and Mordecai. It seems that no one in Esther's orbit is aware of the decree. **4:8** To *explain,* literally "to announce." The sense is informing; Esther will have no difficulty understanding. *And charge her.* Mordecai commands Esther (see 2:10, 20). She will obey him again, but not without some convincing. **4:9–10** The repetition heightens the tension and suspense while adding a degree of absurdity. **4:11** When Esther finally speaks, she is direct and decisive (see vv. 16–17). To this point the text has indicated only Esther's indirect speech and what she has *not* said. But her speech will largely direct the action from this point forward. *There is but one law.* While the outside world reels from Haman's edict, Esther's life is dictated by a law within the palace. **4:12–14** *They . . . them.* Presumably, Hathach remains the go-between, but the text moves to a plural form. *Do not think.* Mordecai's language seems initially desperate and harsh. He is asking Esther to act contrary to his previous commands. But his tone shifts, even as he suggests that her silence may be riskier than her speech. *Who knows?* The same question is asked by the prophet Joel (Joel 2:14) and king of Nineveh (Jonah 3:9). *For just such a time as this.* While God is not mentioned in the book, this passage implies belief in a divine ordering of events. We do not know what Esther thought; she has had little choice or agency to this point. Mordecai now encourages her to find a crucial purpose in her life. **4:15–17** Esther's fast brings her behavior into alignment with her kindred's as well as setting the stage for the next act in the plot, in which she will direct the action. *If I perish, I perish.* Esther uses Mordecai's language to demonstrate her resolve. *Ordered.* To this point, Mordecai had commanded Esther. Now he obeys her.

5:1–8 Esther's first feast. Chaps. 5–7 constitute the climax of the story and are structured around two meals hosted by Esther. They do not share the excesses of the opening banquets. Esther's enemy and her cousin move in varied spaces; she must accomplish everything from inside the domestic, if royal, sphere. **5:1** The text paints a picture of someone waiting to be seen without crossing into another's territory. Esther is negotiating a power imbalance by using her position within space. *Put*

palace. ²As soon as the king saw Queen Esther standing in the court, she won his favor, and he held out to her the golden scepter that was in his hand. Then Esther approached and touched the top of the scepter. ³The king said to her, "What is it, Queen Esther? What is your request? Even to half of my kingdom, it shall be given you." ⁴Then Esther said, "If it pleases the king, let the king and Haman come today to a banquet that I have prepared for the king." ⁵Then the king said, "Bring Haman quickly, so that we may do as Esther desires." So the king and Haman came to the banquet that Esther had prepared. ⁶While they were drinking wine, the king said to Esther, "What is your petition? It shall be granted you. And what is your request? Even to half of my kingdom, it shall be fulfilled." ⁷Then Esther answered, "This is my petition and request: ⁸If I have won the king's favor, and if it pleases the king to grant my petition and fulfill my request, let the king and Haman come tomorrow to the banquet that I will prepare for them, and then I will do as the king has said."

9 Haman went out that day happy and in good spirits, but when Haman saw Mordecai in the king's gate and observed that he neither rose nor trembled before him, he was infuriated with Mordecai; ¹⁰nevertheless, Haman restrained himself and went home. Then he sent and called for his friends and his wife Zeresh, ¹¹and Haman recounted to them the splendor of his riches, the number of his sons, all the promotions with which the king had honored him, and how he had advanced him above the officials and the ministers of the king. ¹²Haman added, "Even Queen Esther let no one but myself come with the king to the banquet that she prepared. Tomorrow also I am invited by her, together with the king. ¹³Yet all this does me no good so long as I see Mordecai the Jew sitting at the king's gate." ¹⁴Then his wife Zeresh and all his friends said to him, "Let a pole fifty cubits high be made, and in the morning tell the king to have Mordecai hung on it; then go with the king to the banquet in good spirits." This advice pleased Haman, and he had the pole made.

6 On that night the king could not sleep, and he gave orders to bring the book of records, the annals, and they were read to the king. ²It was found written how Mordecai had told about Bigthana and Teresh, two of the king's eunuchs who guarded the

on her royal robes. Esther dresses intentionally, recalling Tamar's seduction of Judah (Gen. 38:14–15), Ruth's preparation for her visit to Boaz (Ruth 3:3), and Judith's assignation with Holofernes (Jdt. 10:3–4). **5:2** *As soon as the king saw Queen Esther.* Esther continues to please everyone; Haman will be the exception. **5:3** *What is it, Queen Esther?* Her distress may be outwardly visible, or this could be a typical response to someone risking her life by coming to the king without an invitation. *Even to half of my kingdom*, likely a euphemism for a large gift. The king is clearly happy to see Esther. **5:4–5** Esther speaks formally and leverages her request with timeliness (*that I have prepared for the king*). She is as adept as anyone in manipulating the king. **5:6** Repetition heightens the tension. **5:7–8** Esther's own repetition is more complicated. There is no reason she would need a second banquet to achieve her goal, and her hesitation seems risky. But her invitation to a second banquet strokes Haman's ego. The interlude between the meals holds a profound reversal—something neither Esther nor Mordecai could have anticipated, even as it works to their significant advantage.
5:9–14 Haman's subplot. Parallel to the king in Esth. 1, Haman's emotional state is the focus here, as is the counsel he receives. **5:9** Mordecai now does not even stand before Haman. **5:10** *Zeresh.* Women often go unnamed in the Bible, and the inclusion of Zeresh among Haman's counselors may indicate her cooperation in his ambition. **5:11–13** Haman's egomania is on full display; he is also demonstrating characteristics of the braggart soldier. *Mordecai the Jew.* This phrase echoes the description of Haman in 3:10 ("enemy of the Jews") and will recur in the king's speech in the next chapter. **5:14** *Zeresh and all his friends* lead Haman toward his next move as the king's wise counselors directed him in Esth. 1. The height of the pole (some seventy-five feet) is ridiculous. The pole's size may also mock the man who would build such a contraption. But *this advice pleased Haman*, further connecting him to the king (see 1:21 and 2:4).
6:1–14 Reversal of fortunes. 6:1 A seemingly innocuous request for nighttime reading leads to the first of several reversals in the second half of the story. The royal *records* connect 2:19–23 with this passage. This is a second instance in which one might find a divine hand working behind the scenes, though coincidence is clearly the book's preferred modus operandi. **6:2** *The king's eunuchs,*

threshold and who had conspired to kill[j] King Ahasuerus. [3]Then the king said, "What honor or distinction has been bestowed on Mordecai for this?" The king's servants who attended him said, "Nothing has been done for him." [4]The king said, "Who is in the court?" Now Haman had just entered the outer court of the king's palace to speak to the king about having Mordecai hung on the pole that he had prepared for him. [5]So the king's servants told him, "Haman is there, standing in the court." The king said, "Let him come in." [6]So Haman came in, and the king said to him, "What shall be done for the man whom the king wishes to honor?" Haman said to himself, "Whom would the king wish to honor more than me?" [7]So Haman said to the king, "For the man whom the king wishes to honor, [8]let royal robes be brought, which the king has worn, and a horse that the king has ridden, with a royal crown on its head. [9]Let the robes and the horse be handed over to one of the king's most noble officials; let him[k] robe the man whom the king wishes to honor, and let him[l] conduct the man on horseback through the open square of the city, proclaiming before him: 'Thus shall it be done for the man whom the king wishes to honor.' " [10]Then the king said to Haman, "Quickly, take the robes and the horse, as you have said, and do so to Mordecai the Jew who sits at the king's gate. Leave out nothing that you have mentioned." [11]So Haman took the robes and the horse and robed Mordecai and led him riding through the open square of the city, proclaiming, "Thus shall it be done for the man whom the king wishes to honor."

12 Then Mordecai returned to the king's gate, but Haman hurried to his house, mourning and with his head covered. [13]When Haman told his wife Zeresh and all his friends everything that had happened to him, his advisers and his wife Zeresh said to him, "If Mordecai, before whom your downfall has begun, is of the Jewish people, you will not prevail against him but will surely fall before him."

14 While they were still talking with him, the king's eunuchs arrived and hurried Haman off to the banquet that Esther had prepared.

7 [1]So the king and Haman went in to feast with Queen Esther. [2]On the second day, as they were drinking wine, the king again said to Esther, "What is your petition, Queen Esther? It shall be granted you. And what is your request? Even to half of my kingdom, it shall be fulfilled." [3]Then Queen Esther answered, "If I have won your favor, O king, and if it pleases the king, let my life be given me—that is my petition—and the lives of my people—that is my request. [4]For we have been sold, I and my people, to be destroyed, to be killed, and to be annihilated. If we had been sold

j 6.2 Heb *to lay hands on*   k 6.9 Heb *them*   l 6.9 Heb *them*

though not present, are again at work. **6:3** It is difficult to assess the degree to which the king knows *Mordecai*. He seems to be connected to the court (see 2:19), and "Esther told the king in the name of Mordecai" (2:22), but his ethnicity and connection to Esther are still presumably unknown to Ahasuerus. **6:4–5** By ironic coincidence, Haman has *just entered* the court. *The king's servants*, while not explicitly eunuchs, play a similar role. **6:6–9** The king's question gives Haman's ego full rein; Haman's response contains the kind of excessive detail used throughout the story. In a blatant instance of dramatic irony, the reader knows that Haman is describing Mordecai's honoring and not his own. **6:10–11** *Mordecai the Jew*. Ahasuerus uses Haman's own descriptor as if to increase the insult to Haman. Mordecai, having refused Esther's efforts to cover his sackcloth, is now *robed* in royalty. **6:12** In another reversal, Haman is now the one in mourning. **6:13** *Zeresh and all his friends* make explicit to Haman what the reader already hopes Haman knew—that Mordecai was a Jew; the queen's ethnicity is what the reader knows will be Haman's undoing. This is something Haman and his household seem incapable of imagining. **6:14** *While they were still talking*. Nearly identical phrasing is found in Job 1:16–18; it creates hurried pacing. *Eunuchs* again appear at an opportune moment.

7:1–10 Esther's second feast. Esther continues to control the narrative. She leads the king masterfully to the big reveal and gives Haman enough rope to hang himself, both metaphorically and literally. **7:2** *The king again said*. He repeats his offer, nearly verbatim (5:3). **7:3** The queen's opening is poetic, inserting her petition (*my life*) and her request (*my people*) into the king's phrasing. She places herself first (and will again in v. 4) as a way of emphasizing her people's close proximity to the king. **7:4** *Destroyed . . . killed . . . annihilated*. The queen uses the edict's language to announce her peril. *If we had been sold*. Esther raises a less severe hypothetical situation,

merely as slaves, men and women, I would have held my peace, but no enemy can compensate for this damage to the king."[m] [5]Then King Ahasuerus said to Queen Esther, "Who is he, and where is he, who has presumed to do this?" [6]Esther said, "A foe and an enemy, this wicked Haman!" Then Haman was terrified before the king and the queen. [7]The king rose from the feast in wrath and went into the palace garden, but Haman stayed to beg his life from Queen Esther, for he saw that the king had determined to destroy him. [8]When the king returned from the palace garden to the banquet hall, Haman had thrown himself on the couch where Esther was reclining, and the king said, "Will he even violate the queen in my presence, in my own house?" As the words left the mouth of the king, they covered Haman's face. [9]Then Harbona, one of the eunuchs in attendance on the king, said, "Look, the very pole that Haman has prepared for Mordecai, whose word saved the king,[n] stands at Haman's house, fifty cubits high." And the king said, "Hang him on that." [10]So they hung Haman on the pole that he had prepared for Mordecai. Then the anger of the king abated.

8 On that day King Ahasuerus gave to Queen Esther the house of Haman, the enemy of the Jews, and Mordecai came before the king, for Esther had told what he was to her. [2]Then the king took off his signet ring, which he had taken from Haman, and gave it to Mordecai. So Esther set Mordecai over the house of Haman.

3 Then Esther spoke again to the king; she fell at his feet, weeping and pleading with him to avert the evil design of Haman the Agagite and the plot that he had devised against the Jews. [4]The king held out the

m 7.4 Meaning of Heb uncertain   n 7.9 Heb *who spoke well regarding the king*

perhaps as a way of showing that Haman's edict will cost the king an entire people group—which happens to be the queen's own people. Haman is thus a traitor. *As slaves* recalls Israel's history of bondage in Egypt and the tradition that likens exilic captivity to slavery (Isa. 52:1–4; see also Ezra 9:8–9). *No enemy can compensate for this damage to the king.* This phrase is difficult, and as translated here it may mean that Esther is saving the king from financial loss or from the shame of not protecting his own queen. **7:5** *Who is he, and where is he?* The king has not yet connected his queen's announcement to Haman's plot. The close proximity of Haman increases the irony of the king's questions, just as Haman's presence in the court led to the ironic elevation of Mordecai in Esth. 6. **7:6** Haman's identity is announced with *a foe and an enemy*, echoing his earlier moniker, "enemy of the Jews" (3:10). **7:7** The king's anger returns, but rather than seeking counsel as in 1:13–14, he walks away from the scene. This curious move leaves the queen alone with her "foe" and "enemy," but it also allows Haman space to make another mistake. **7:8** How long the king was out of the room is uncertain, but he returns to find that Haman has *thrown himself* (literally "falling") on the queen's couch. Whether Haman's position is one of pleading or seduction, the scene is farcical. The king has no reason to believe that Haman's intentions are sexual, but Haman's blunder gives the king another reason to terminate him. **7:9** *Harbona* the eunuch (see 1:10) observes that Haman's pole (which he *prepared for Mordecai*) was ready and waiting, just as servants announced Haman's presence in the court in 6:4–5. The king again follows the suggestion of another character in the story. **7:10** Killing an enemy with their own weapon is a classic underdog motif (see 1 Sam. 17:51). Haman is hung (or impaled) on a pole he intended for Mordecai, an inverted parallel of Haman bestowing on Mordecai the honor he intended for himself in Esth. 6. *The anger of the king abated*, as it did when Vashti had been banished (2:1). In Esth. 2 Ahasuerus needed a new queen; now he needs a new number two.

8:1–17 Reversals. The reversals in Esther continue with a relatively quick sequence of events that seem to correct the wrongs of the story. The denouement may be characterized as a movement from fear and danger to hope and celebration. **8:1–2** Esther receives the *house of Haman* presumably as compensation, but she immediately gives it to Mordecai, who moves into Haman's position *before the king. Esther had told what he was to her.* If the king had any lingering questions about the queen's identity and relationships, they are answered now. Acquiring the king's *signet ring* completes Mordecai's replacement of Haman. **8:3–14 A third decree.** Haman's edict (3:12–13) cannot be rescinded, though this policy is likely an invention. **8:3–4** Esther returns to the king, presumably risking once again an uninvited audience. She *fell at his feet*, the same verb used to

golden scepter to Esther, and Esther rose and stood before the king. [5]She said, "If it pleases the king, and if I have won his favor, and if the thing seems right before the king, and I have his approval, let an order be written to revoke the letters devised by Haman son of Hammedatha the Agagite, which he wrote giving orders to destroy the Jews who are in all the provinces of the king. [6]For how can I bear to see the calamity that is coming on my people? Or how can I bear to see the destruction of my kindred?" [7]Then King Ahasuerus said to Queen Esther and to Mordecai the Jew, "See, I have given Esther the house of Haman, and they have hung him on the pole because he plotted to kill[o] the Jews. [8]You may write as you please with regard to the Jews, in the name of the king, and seal it with the king's ring, for an edict written in the name of the king and sealed with the king's ring cannot be revoked."

9 The king's secretaries were summoned at that time, in the third month, which is the month of Sivan, on the twenty-third day, and an edict was written, according to all that Mordecai commanded, to the Jews and to the satraps and the governors and the officials of the provinces from India to Cush, one hundred twenty-seven provinces, to every province in its own script and to every people in its own language, and also to the Jews in their script and their language. [10]He wrote letters in the name of King Ahasuerus, sealed them with the king's ring, and sent them by mounted couriers riding on fast steeds bred from the royal herd.[p] [11]By these letters the king allowed the Jews who were in every city to assemble and defend their lives, to destroy, to kill, and to annihilate any armed force of any people or province that might attack them, their children, and their women, and to plunder their goods [12]on a single day throughout all the provinces of King Ahasuerus, on the thirteenth day of the twelfth month, which is the month of Adar. [13]A copy of the writ was to be issued as a decree in every province and published to all peoples, and the Jews were to be ready on that day to take revenge on their enemies. [14]So the couriers, mounted on their royal steeds, hurried out, urged by the king's command. The decree was issued in the citadel of Susa.

15 Then Mordecai went out from the presence of the king, wearing royal robes of blue and white, with a great golden crown and a mantle of fine linen and purple, while the city of Susa shouted and rejoiced. [16]For the Jews there was light and gladness, joy and honor. [17]In every province and in every city, wherever the king's command and his edict came, there was gladness and joy among the Jews, a festival and a holiday. Furthermore, many of the peoples of the country professed to be Jews because the fear of the Jews had fallen upon them.

o 8.7 Heb *to lay hands on* p 8.10 Meaning of Heb uncertain

describe Haman's posture on her couch in 7:8. **8:5–6** While Esther has succeeded in eliminating Haman, his plan to eradicate the Jews remains. This speech is the first time anyone has used *Jew* in the king's presence. His grasp of the situation might still be unclear; Esther must convince him to act. **8:7–8** *See, I have given.* Is the king surprised that more is required beyond eliminating Haman and elevating Mordecai? He acquiesces to Esther's request in a mood similar to that of 3:10–11, when he authorized Haman's decree. The king speaks of *the Jews* but does not refer to them as Esther's "people," language she used in her pleas (7:3–4; 8:6). **8:9–10** This is nearly identical to the language of 3:12–13. *The Jews* are specifically mentioned; one assumes they were part of *every people* in the earlier passage. **8:11–12** The contents of this edict may be as shocking as those of Haman's. This is not a counter-edict so much as a duplication of the first. It raises the question of whether the Jews would have defended themselves were it not for this explicit permission. It also may act as a warning to those who might kill the Jews. **8:13–14** The similarity of the two decrees' language and publication emphasizes the reversal. **8:15** In 3:15 Haman and the king drank as Haman's edict went out, but here Mordecai parades in royal garb. In contrast to the previous confusion of Susa, the city *shouted and rejoiced* at the second edict. **8:17** *Festival.* This is the same word used throughout for banquets and feasts, and it marks another connection between food and drink and the book's structure. *Professed to be Jews.* This is a famous crux; the verb is indeterminate and could also mean "pretended," "identified with," or "made themselves." While conversion is possible, *the fear of the Jews* seems an unlikely motivator. This is another comic reversal.

9 Now in the twelfth month, which is the month of Adar, on the thirteenth day, when the king's command and edict were about to be executed, on the very day when the enemies of the Jews hoped to gain power over them but that had been changed to a day when the Jews would gain power over their foes, ²the Jews gathered in their cities throughout all the provinces of King Ahasuerus to kill*q* those who had sought their ruin, and no one could withstand them, because the fear of them had fallen upon all peoples. ³All the officials of the provinces, the satraps and the governors, and the royal officials were supporting the Jews because the fear of Mordecai had fallen upon them. ⁴For Mordecai was powerful in the king's palace, and his fame spread throughout all the provinces, because the man Mordecai was growing more and more powerful. ⁵So the Jews struck down all their enemies with the sword, slaughtering and destroying them, and did as they pleased to those who hated them. ⁶In the citadel of Susa the Jews killed and destroyed five hundred people. ⁷They killed Parshandatha, Dalphon, Aspatha, ⁸Poratha, Adalia, Aridatha, ⁹Parmashta, Arisai, Aridai, and Vaizatha, ¹⁰the ten sons of Haman son of Hammedatha, the enemy of the Jews, but they did not touch the plunder.

11 That very day the number of those killed in the citadel of Susa was reported to the king. ¹²The king said to Queen Esther, "In the citadel of Susa the Jews have killed and destroyed five hundred people and the ten sons of Haman. What have they done in the rest of the king's provinces? Now what is your petition? It shall be granted you. And what further is your request? It shall be fulfilled." ¹³Esther said, "If it pleases the king, let the Jews who are in Susa be allowed tomorrow also to do according to this day's edict, and let the ten sons of Haman be hung on the pole." ¹⁴So the king commanded this to be done; a decree was issued in Susa, and the ten sons of Haman were hung. ¹⁵The Jews who were in Susa gathered also on the fourteenth day of the month of Adar, and they killed three hundred persons in Susa, but they did not touch the plunder.

16 Now the other Jews who were in the king's provinces also gathered to defend their lives and gained relief from their enemies and killed seventy-five thousand of those who hated them, but they laid no hands on the plunder. ¹⁷This was on the thirteenth day of the month of Adar, and on the fourteenth day they rested and made that a day of feasting and gladness.

18 But the Jews who were in Susa gathered on the thirteenth day and on the fourteenth

q 9.2 Heb *lay hands on*

9:1–17 Jewish victory. Whether or not the second edict was intended as a deterrent, violence breaks out. Mordecai's plan works, and the Jews successfully defend themselves against those who would destroy them. **9:1** *Had been changed.* The text admits to its own theme of reversal. **9:2–3** *The fear* of the Jews, which had led to some professing "to be Jews" in 8:17, now leads to the Jews' military victory. Similarly, *the fear of Mordecai had fallen* on the government. **9:4** While Esther will make two more appearances, Mordecai receives equal attention and seems a more important figure going forward. **9:5** *Slaughtering and destroying.* These two words are from the edict. **9:6** *In the citadel* likely refers to the government; the five hundred killed were probably part of the court. **9:7–10** Haman's children are named and numbered for the first time (see 5:11). The Jews *did not touch the plunder,* though they were permitted to do so (8:11). This may be an indication that the Jews were motivated by self-defense rather than economic gain. The phrase is repeated in vv. 15 and 16. Taking plunder was a common practice in the ancient world, and the spoils of war often included humans (see Num. 14:3, 31; and Judg. 5:30). Perhaps the Jews, being a minority refugee population who have barely escaped extermination, refuse to take possession of other humans, thereby freeing any captives that belong to their enemies. **9:12** *What is your petition?* The king echoes his earlier questions; he does not assume that he has addressed every need. **9:13–14** Esther asks for an additional day of killing in Susa, perhaps in the town itself (not in the citadel, per v. 12). The hanging of Haman's sons is a symbol of disgrace as well as a warning (see 1 Sam. 31:10–12; 2 Sam. 21:5–13). **9:15–17** Over two days in three places, the Jews kill a total of 75,800 people; such a number (like many other numbers in Esther and the Bible) is an exaggeration for effect. The exaggerated number is part of the excesses of the story, a characteristic of carnival literature (see **"Violence against the Jews' Enemies," p. 682**).

9:18–32 A holiday is established. The events of 13–14 Adar are commemorated with more feasting, an empire-wide event (at least for the Jews) that mirrors the feast of Esth. 1. **9:18–19** The

Making Connections: Violence against the Jews' Enemies (Esther 9)

The violence at the end of Esther (9:1–17) is a final reversal in a story of reversals. Mordecai has devised a counterplot to foil Haman's plan: before their enemies can kill them, the Jews have permission to "defend their lives, to destroy, to kill, and to annihilate any armed force of any people or province that might attack" (8:11). The book explicitly connects this saving violence to the Purim festival, during which Jewish communities wear costumes, read Esther in a dramatic fashion, and overindulge as the book's own excesses may warrant. (One famous rabbinic text suggests getting so drunk as to lose the ability to distinguish between "cursed be Haman" and "blessed be Mordecai"!) Such a carnivalesque celebration of the Jews' deliverance may emphasize the farcical nature of the violence. However, even pretend violence is problematic.

Some early rabbis sought to lessen the shock of the bloodshed by emphasizing that it was directed only at those who would oppress the Jews ("any that *might* attack them"), though the number of the slain is hard to soften: 75,000. Readers have also pointed to similarly violent rescues wrought on Israel's behalf: for example, the drowning of the Egyptian army (Exod. 14) or the promise that YHWH will war from "generation to generation" with the Amalekites (Exod. 17:8–16). See **"The Divine Mandate to Exterminate the Canaanites," p. 313.** Early Christian interpreters seem to have largely ignored the violence in Esther, focusing instead on allegorical readings. Some more recent Christian studies emphasize spiritual or moral interpretations, which tend to extol the virtues of Esther (both the character and the book) while overlooking the violence.

The Jewish people have been victims of systematic violence throughout their history, and the violence in Esther should be read in light of that history. Readers should also recall Haman's desire to "destroy, to kill, and to annihilate all Jews, young and old, children and women" (Esth. 3:13) as well as historic and contemporary corollaries to Haman. The book offers an opportunity to reflect on the survival mechanisms that oppressed peoples have at their disposal as well as the sad reality that the oppressed can, in turn, become oppressors. Many contemporary Jews find the violence in Esther deeply problematic, particularly in light of ongoing realities in Israel-Palestine. Careful readings of this story will thoughtfully consider the violence in light of these complicated relationships and realities.

Brian Albert Smith

and rested on the fifteenth day, making that a day of feasting and gladness. [19]Therefore the Jews of the villages, who live in the open towns, hold the fourteenth day of the month of Adar as a day for gladness and feasting, a holiday on which they send gifts of food to one another.

20 Mordecai recorded these things and sent letters to all the Jews who were in all the provinces of King Ahasuerus, both near and far, [21]enjoining them that they should keep the fourteenth day of the month Adar and also the fifteenth day of the same month, year by year, [22]as the days on which the Jews gained relief from their enemies and as the month that had been turned for them from sorrow into gladness and from mourning into a holiday, that they should make them days of feasting and gladness, days for sending gifts of food to one another and presents to the poor. [23]So the Jews adopted as a custom what they had begun to do, as Mordecai had written to them.

24 For Haman son of Hammedatha the Agagite, the enemy of all the Jews, had plotted against the Jews to destroy them and had cast Pur—that is, "the lot"—to crush and to destroy them, [25]but when Esther[r] came before the king, he gave orders in writing that the wicked plot that he had devised against the Jews should come upon his own head and that he and his sons should be hung on the pole. [26]Therefore these days are called Purim, from the word Pur. Thus because of all that was written in this letter and of what they had faced in this matter and of what had happened to them, [27]the Jews established and accepted as a

r 9.25 Heb *she*

holiday was originally celebrated on two different days because of the extended fighting in Susa. **9:20–22** *Letters* are again sent, though these are not official court edicts. Mordecai establishes a religious custom for the Jews, setting the date(s), the purpose behind the party (*sorrow into gladness*), and the festival traditions (*sending gifts of food . . . and presents to the poor*). **9:23** The letters codify what the Jews had already *begun to do*. **9:24–26** This summary of the story provides an explanation of the holiday and its name. **9:27–28** The narrator is clearly invested in establishing the holiday,

custom for themselves and their descendants and all who joined them that without fail they would continue to observe these two days every year, as it was written and at the time appointed. [28]These days should be remembered and kept throughout every generation, in every family, province, and city, and these days of Purim should never fall into disuse among the Jews, nor should the commemoration of these days cease among their descendants.

[29] Queen Esther daughter of Abihail, along with Mordecai the Jew, gave full written authority confirming this second letter about Purim. [30]Letters were sent wishing peace and security to all the Jews, to the one hundred twenty-seven provinces of the kingdom of Ahasuerus, [31]and giving orders that these days of Purim should be observed at their appointed seasons, as Mordecai the

Jew and Queen Esther enjoined on the Jews, just as they had laid down for themselves and for their descendants regulations concerning their fasts and their lamentations. [32]The command of Esther fixed these practices of Purim, and it was recorded in writing.

10 King Ahasuerus laid tribute on the land and on the islands of the sea. [2]All the acts of his power and might, and the full account of the high honor of Mordecai, to which the king advanced him, are they not written in the annals of the kings of Media and Persia? [3]For Mordecai the Jew was next in rank to King Ahasuerus, and he was powerful among the Jews and popular with his many kindred, for he sought the good of his people and interceded for the welfare of all his descendants.

whose focus is on neither Temple nor Torah but on reversal and rescue orchestrated by an unmentioned God. **9:29–32** The queen joins Mordecai in writing a *second letter* to confirm Mordecai's first. This repetition matches other pairs of meals, treatments, and conversations throughout the book.

10:1–3 Coda. Esther is absent in the conclusion about the king and Mordecai. *Are they not written?* While mimicking the books of 1–2 Kings, this rhetorical question is a final reminder to the reader of the role that the *annals of the kings* have played in the story of Esther (see 6:1). *Mordecai the Jew* gets the last mention, a nod to his care for Esther in her childhood, his critical conversation with her in Esth. 4, and his role in establishing Purim.

JOB

The book of Job has been pored over, performed, parodied, and prayed by countless readers whose many points of entry suggest the book is less like a narrative to be interpreted and more like a prism with many surfaces. A book that begins with the council of heaven and an innocent man's loss swells into a lengthy dialogue around God's gamble with Job's life. Ironically, the plot of Job is actually simple in form, but this timeless story seems haunted by its cryptic style and provocative questions.

Wellness, Religion, and Israelite Wisdom

The book begins and ends with a short prose narrative; the central section consists of poetic dialogues, beginning when three sages travel to the side of their suffering friend. They quickly commence a debate about wellness. The friends hold traditional wisdom views that sickness, child-lessness, poverty, a short life, and a shameful death strike those who are wicked and foolish while health, offspring, wealth, long life, and a good death bless those who are righteous and wise (Prov-erbs). Since Job is now childless, homeless, poor, and sick, the friends assume he must be wicked or foolish. But Job takes exception, consistently arguing that his suffering is undeserved. Job is a righteous sufferer according to God (1:8; 2:3; 42:7-8), the narrator (1:1), and Job's own account (6:30; 9:15), and the book's conclusion approves Job's viewpoints at least above the friends' perspectives (42:8). On the one hand, Job is about how human experience ruptures religion. On the other hand, the dialogue form underscores the value of counsel and deliberation (see Prov. 27:17), even as its dialogic challenges are also explored.

Job's Critique of God

Popular imagination sees Job as a model of patience and piety, and he was a christological figure to early Christian writers. But Job is downright acerbic in his prosecution of God, to the point that Judaism's Talmud lists out his blasphemies. God destroyed Job "for no reason" (2:3), and Job seems to discern heaven's hidden cruelty. He accuses God of strong-arm justice (9:3-19), callousness and ridicule of suffering (9:22-24; 16:11), extreme cruelty toward God's creatures (10:3, 8), and direct violence against him, a faithful servant (6:4; 9:17-18; 10:16-17; 16:9-17; 19:6-12). When the Creator finally speaks, God points away from divine assault and toward the fray of nature's fantastic forms. Perhaps shockingly, God twice affirms Job's characterization of God (42:7-8).

Readers seeking a more flattering characterization of God often turn to the divine speeches (chaps. 38-41), assuming these chapters present a high view of God as Creator of the universe. But the divine self-disclosure in the book does not convey as much order, control, intention, and goodness as one might think. As much as God supports the founding of the earth (38:4), the speech points to the natural world's agencies and energies: monstrous bodies (chaps. 40-41), animal scav-engers (39:30), and a laughing warhorse glittering with spears (39:22-23). Meanwhile, the calami-tous east wind is unleashed (38:24), the sons of God shriek with signals of war (38:7), and there is no map to the gates of death (38:17). Rudolf Otto reads Job's God as a *mysterium tremendum*, a holy transcendence that produces both horror and awe.

God does speak directly with Job from a screaming twist in the fabric of the sky. In the end, the dust settles on roughed-up Job who has just listened to visually rich descriptions of earth's diverse material forms. There is little to determine if Job actually submits to God's overpowering violence, if he has bested God by craftily finding an escape from divine affliction, if he found pleasure in the experience of God's whirlwind, or if some other option springs when the reader turns the prism. Job disappears back into his folktale, memorialized as a survivor of a brutal divine hand.

Job in the Modern World

Job has served as an essential touchstone in Western philosophical thought as well as in the liter-ary canon. The irreparable ruin represented in Job has been important to Jewish survivors of the Holocaust. Major themes in post-Holocaust thinking include the senseless cruelty of Job's children's deaths, the question of God's justice, Jewish piety after catastrophe, and the futurity of a survivor's children. Of note are Elie Wiesel's *The Trial of God* and "Job Our Contemporary" and the art of Samuel Bak (see **"The Bible and Visual Art," pp. 2168-71**). Peruvian liberation theologian Gustavo

Gutiérrez also looked to Job. Speaking of the hungry, the poor, and the dead who suffer society's organized, exploitative, and oppressive injustices, Gutiérrez saw growth in Job's character, whose suffering transformed him in prophetic solidarity with others.

Other substantial engagements include Kafka's *The Trial*, Goethe's *Faust*, Melville's *Moby Dick*, Dostoyevsky's "Grand Inquisitor," Pushkin's *The Bronze Horseman*, Beckett's *The Unnamable*, Oosterwijck's *Vanitas Still Life*, Blake's *The Book of Job*, Kant's "On the Failure of All Possible Theodicies," Jung's *Answer to Job*, Morrison's *A Mercy*, Swados's *The Story of Job*, Alvarez's *Afterlife*, Henriques's "Book of Mechtilde," McKibben's *The Comforting Whirlwind*, and the films *The Tree of Life* and *A Serious Man* (see **"The Bible in Literature," pp. 2176–77**, and **"The Bible in Film and Media," pp. 2172–73**).

Reading Guide

The book begins with a narrative tale introducing the main characters and describing Job's catastrophes (chaps. 1–2; see **"The Satan," p. 687**). It then switches to poetry as speeches are exchanged between Job (chaps. 3, 6–7, 9–10, 12–14, 16–17, 19, 21, 23–24, 26–31), Eliphaz (chaps. 4–5, 15, 22), Bildad (chaps. 8, 18, 25), and Zophar (chaps. 11, 20), at which point Job stops talking, and Elihu, a youthful bystander, joins uninvited and receives no response (chaps. 32–37). God's speeches (chaps. 38–41) summon two responses from Job (40:3–5; 42:1–6). Then the book closes in chap. 42 with a return to a narrative tale relaying God's concluding words (vv. 7–8) and Job's return to wealth and fatherhood (vv. 10–16). The poetry of Job is evocative, strange, musical, and surprising. With unique and foreign words, indefinite grammar, and cryptic poetic parallelism, the book is linguistically challenging. Wordplays resist the declarative propositions of philosophy and theology; poetic ambiguity almost ironically accrues (see especially 1:21 and 13:15). Arguably the most consequential poetic ambiguity lies in Job's final response to God (42:6). Does Job repent? Is he fed up? The text says he despises something, but readers have to fill it in . . . himself? God?

Themes in Job's speeches include his call for a trial of God, critiques of traditional wisdom, and experiences of social suffering (mocking, gaslighting, spitting, disgust, blaming). The book presents a phenomenology of Job's illness, and readers could pursue a disability or trauma-informed reading. To evaluate the book's masculine archetype of suffering, one notes especially Job's local honor and wealthy household, shame, and the divine command "Gird up your loins like a man" (38:3; 40:7). An important focus is the abject minor characters, especially the people enslaved in Job's house and maternal bodies. Animals, from maggots to monsters, often figure in the speeches raising themes of death, predation, bodies, and multispecies flourishing. One could extend this topic to representations of the earth's forms and processes, asking contemporary ecological or feminist-materialist questions. It is possible to find comedic layers, while the fantastic, the monstrous, and horror also do a lot of literary work in the book.

Ingrid E. Lilly

1 There was once a man in the land of Uz whose name was Job. That man was blameless and upright, one who feared God and turned away from evil. ²There were born to him seven sons and three daughters. ³He had seven thousand sheep, three thousand camels, five hundred yoke of oxen, five hundred donkeys, and very many servants, so that this man was the greatest of all the people of the East.

1:1–2:13 Prose tale's introduction. A prose tale frames the book of Job with its tightly narrated, plot-driven, candid moral world (chaps. 1–2; 42:7–17). After Job's "once upon a time" introduction (1:1–5), there are two phases of dialogue in heaven (1:6–12; 2:1–6) each resulting in violence on earth, the first attacking Job's family and possessions (1:13–22) and the second attacking Job's body (2:7–13).

1:1 *Uz.* The location is uncertain, but *Job* is non-Israelite. Job's name could be a Hebrew wordplay with "enemy" or "persecuted one," especially if the book is classified as a fable. Symbolic names are pervasive in biblical literature, even ones predictive of catastrophe (e.g., Isa. 8:3). *Blameless* is most often descriptive of bodily perfection in animals "without blemish," applied here to human character. *Blameless . . . upright . . . feared God . . . turned away from evil*, these four traits are unparalleled in the Hebrew Bible and present Job as a moral exemplar for Israelite covenantal religion and wisdom tradition.

1:2–5 Several parallels with 42:11–17. **1:2–3** Elegant multiples of ten (ten children and two times

⁴His sons used to go and hold feasts in one another's houses in turn, and they would send and invite their three sisters to eat and drink with them. ⁵And when the feast days had run their course, Job would send and sanctify them, and he would rise early in the morning and offer burnt offerings according to the number of them all, for Job said, "It may be that my children have sinned and cursed God in their hearts." This is what Job always did.

6 One day the heavenly beings*ᵃ* came to present themselves before the Lᴏʀᴅ, and the accuser*ᵇ* also came among them. ⁷The Lᴏʀᴅ said to the accuser,*ᶜ* "Where have you come from?" The accuser*ᵈ* answered the Lᴏʀᴅ, "From going to and fro on the earth and from walking up and down on it." ⁸The Lᴏʀᴅ said to the accuser,*ᵉ* "Have you considered my servant Job? There is no one like him on the earth, a blameless and upright man who fears God and turns away from evil." ⁹Then the accuser*ᶠ* answered the Lᴏʀᴅ, "Does Job fear God for nothing? ¹⁰Have you not put a fence around him and his house and all that he has, on every side? You have blessed the work of his hands, and his possessions have increased in the land. ¹¹But stretch out your hand now, and touch all that he has, and he will curse you to your face." ¹²The Lᴏʀᴅ said to the accuser,*ᵍ* "Very well, all that he has is in your power; only do not stretch out your

hand against him!" So the accuser*ʰ* went out from the presence of the Lᴏʀᴅ.

13 One day when his sons and daughters were eating and drinking wine in the eldest brother's house, ¹⁴a messenger came to Job and said, "The oxen were plowing and the donkeys were feeding beside them, ¹⁵and the Sabeans fell on them and carried them off and killed the servants with the edge of the sword; I alone have escaped to tell you." ¹⁶While he was still speaking, another came and said, "The fire of God fell from heaven and burned up the sheep and the servants and consumed them; I alone have escaped to tell you." ¹⁷While he was still speaking, another came and said, "The Chaldeans formed three columns, made a raid on the camels and carried them off, and killed the servants with the edge of the sword; I alone have escaped to tell you." ¹⁸While he was still speaking, another came and said, "Your sons and daughters were eating and drinking wine in their eldest brother's house, ¹⁹and suddenly a great wind came across the desert, struck the four corners of the house, and it fell on the young people, and they are dead; I alone have escaped to tell you."

20 Then Job arose, tore his robe, shaved his head, and fell on the ground and worshiped.

a 1.6 Heb *sons of God*   b 1.6 Heb *the satan*   c 1.7 Heb *the satan*
d 1.7 Heb *the satan*   e 1.8 Heb *the satan*   f 1.9 Heb *the satan*
g 1.12 Heb *the satan*   h 1.12 Heb *the satan*

ten thousand animals). The numerals two and four help structure the prose narrative: Job's four virtues conveyed in pairs (1:1), four destructions and four messengers (1:14–19), paired body parts in his affliction (skin for skin, bone and flesh, and foot to crown in 2:4–7), and in the closing tale, his double possessions (42:10, 12), four generations of children, and 140-year life span (42:16). **1:4–5** Job's religious perfection and great wealth are portrayed as a generous but anxious virtue to protect his family from unknown or hidden guilt (see **"Offerings and Sacrifices," p. 146**).

1:6–12 A scene in heaven of the divine council assembling (see 1 Kgs. 22:19–22; Ps. 82:1). *The accuser* serves God by walking throughout the earth, returning to heaven to provide requested reports. He poses a question about righteousness to a fully cooperative God, and Job's plot of suffering begins (see **"The Satan," p. 687**). Everything that takes place in heaven is revealed to the reader but concealed from the human characters in the book. **1:9** *Fear God for nothing?* The accuser implies that Job fears God for a reason, perhaps selfish gain or excessive terror, motivating God's experiment with Job's life to explore the conditions of Job's acts of righteousness. See 2:3. **1:10** Many commentators see an economic theme established here, since the accuser targets Job's possessions. *Put a fence around* is a phrase associated with protection; it is later inverted in Job's description of misery (3:23). **1:11** *Curse* is literally "bless." A common euphemism, both options are in play (see 1 Kgs. 21:13). See also 2:5 and 2:9. **1:12** God accepts the accuser's proposal and verbally invokes the power of God's hand over Job.

1:13–21 Back on earth, four catastrophes ensue from the four cardinal directions: two military invasions (Sabeans and Chaldeans) and two heavenly weather events (fire/lightning and a desert windstorm). The people killed in these catastrophes are Job's children and the people enslaved in Job's house (see **"Human Bondage in Ancient Israel," p. 115**). **1:15** *I alone have escaped to tell*

Focus On: The Satan (Job 1)

The Hebrew Bible never portrays a cosmic being who is totally evil. The Hebrew word *satan* ("accuser") is primarily used for human opponents, anyone from a bully (Ps. 71:13) to a court prosecutor (Ps. 109:6) to an adversary from a partisan faction (1 Sam. 29:4). Thus, the term *satan* rhetorically emerges in literary contexts that depict the social or emotional power of human accusation: intimacy/harm, affiliation/schism, justice/slander, and dominance/insubordination.

Beginning in the sixth century BCE, *satan* is used for a divine member of the heavenly council, but he is a cooperative prosecutor in God's court (Job 1–2; Zech. 3) or an earthly manifestation of God's wrath/will (Num. 22; 1 Chr. 21). Though divine, this is a far cry from Satan as an independent and cosmic author of evil who is at war with God.

Because of internal developments and external influences, by the first century CE, early Jewish literature was rich, diverse, and downright crowded with cosmic villains and evil forces. Healers fought demons, mythic histories of evil were written and rewritten, and factious groups were characterizing their rivals as vicious fiends. Interestingly, the name Satan is rare among this explosion of cosmic evil agents. A rebellious angel named Azazel transgresses heaven to meddle in human affairs in the book of Enoch. A different angel—Belial—is characterized for an entire era as evil in Essene texts among the Dead Sea Scrolls. Calling themselves the "sons of light," these sectarian authors pulled away from wider society to live in community and vilified everyone else as agents of Belial (especially the Pharisees and Sadducees). These strident antagonisms are reflected in the inner-Jewish debates of the Gospel conflict stories where Satan is a full-blown cosmic agent of evil, and the terrible legacy of Christian demonization of Judaism begins (see **"Anti-Judaism," p. 1865**).

Christian religious imaginations conjure the later, more developed character of Satan in readings of the Hebrew Bible. Satan is read into the Genesis snake (Rev. 12:9). Some of history's influential (mis)translations also projected Satan into Scripture: onto Haman (Esth. 7:4) and foreign gods (Ps. 96:5) in the Greek Septuagint or onto a shining star (Isa. 14:12) in the King James Bible. Contemporary scripturalizations of Satan continue to expand his biblical realm to the mental health discourses of the Psalms, texts about female characters or racist geographies, and texts that explore themes of desire, sex, or power.

Ingrid E. Lilly

²¹He said, "Naked I came from my mother's womb, and naked shall I return there; the LORD gave, and the LORD has taken away; blessed be the name of the LORD."

22 In all this Job did not sin or charge God with wrongdoing.

2 One day the heavenly beings*ⁱ* came to present themselves before the LORD, and the accuser*ʲ* also came among them to present himself before the LORD. ²The LORD said to the accuser,*ᵏ* "Where have you come from?" The accuser*ˡ* answered the LORD, "From going to and fro on the earth and from walking up and down on it." ³The LORD said to the accuser,*ᵐ* "Have you considered my servant Job? There is no one like him on the earth, a blameless and upright man who fears God and turns away from evil. He still persists in his integrity, although you incited me against him, to destroy him for no reason." ⁴Then the accuser*ⁿ* answered the LORD, "Skin for skin! All that the man has he will give for his life. ⁵But stretch out your hand now and touch his bone and his flesh, and he will curse you to your face." ⁶The LORD

i 2.1 Heb *sons of God*   *j* 2.1 Heb *the satan*   *k* 2.2 Heb *the satan*
l 2.2 Heb *The satan*   *m* 2.3 Heb *the satan*   *n* 2.4 Heb *the satan*

you. Repeated by messengers in vv. 16, 17, 19. Quoted by Ishmael in the epilogue of Herman Melville's *Moby Dick.* **1:21** Job accepts gains and losses (see **"Poem on the Times," p. 909**), and his response to catastrophe compares with his response to affliction in 2:8–10. *Mother's womb . . . there.* In Hebrew idiom, wombs can be metaphors for a tomb, Sheol, and the earth. Some regional burial practices suggest womb symbolism for death and, in Egyptian culture, even rebirth. A possible wordplay between *there* ("sham") and Sheol (see Eccl. 9:10; see **"Sheol," p. 695**).

2:1–6 The second scene in heaven tightly parallels the first (1:6–12). **2:3** *For no reason* ("for nothing"). The same phrase occurs in 1:9. Either God destroys *for no reason*, or the accuser incites *for no reason.* Word order suggests the former. **2:4–6** *Skin . . . bone . . . flesh . . . life* ("nefesh"). God agrees to another experiment, this time with Job's body. **2:6** YHWH accepts the accuser's proposal and

said to the accuser,ᵒ "Very well, he is in your power; only spare his life."

7 So the accuserᵖ went out from the presence of the LORD and inflicted loathsome sores on Job from the sole of his foot to the crown of his head. ⁸Jobᵍ took a potsherd with which to scrape himself and sat among the ashes.

9 Then his wife said to him, "Do you still persist in your integrity? Curseʳ God and die." ¹⁰But he said to her, "You speak as any foolish woman would speak. Shall we receive good from God and not receive evil?" In all this Job did not sin with his lips.

11 Now when Job's three friends heard of all these troubles that had come upon him, each of them set out from his home— Eliphaz the Temanite, Bildad the Shuhite, and Zophar the Naamathite. They met together to go and console and comfort him. ¹²When they saw him from a distance, they did not recognize him, and they raised their voices and wept aloud; they tore their robes and threw dust in the air upon their heads. ¹³They sat with him on the ground seven days and seven nights, and no one spoke a word to him, for they saw that his suffering was very great.

3 After this Job opened his mouth and cursed the day of his birth. ²Job said:

³ "Let the day perish in which I was born,
  and the night that said,
  'A male is conceived.'
⁴ Let that day be darkness!
  May God above not seek it
  or light shine on it.
⁵ Let gloom and deep darkness claim it.
  Let clouds settle upon it;
  let the blackness of the day terrify it.

o 2.6 Heb *the satan*   p 2.7 Heb *the satan*   q 2.8 Heb *He*
r 2.9 Heb *Bless*

---

verbally puts Job in his hand. *Spare his life* ("guard" or "keep") must be a call for protection through restraint, since what little we know about accusation by humans or angels does not suggest they actively protected people (see **"The Satan," p. 687**, and **"Angels," p. 1346**).

2:7 Unlike the catastrophes in chap. 1, the narrator reports the accuser's agency over Job's initial affliction, a skin disease (see Lev. 13:18–23).

2:8 *Ashes* are associated with practices of lament.

2:9–10 A short dialogue about Job's *integrity* (see also 2:3) invades the prose narrative, foreshadowing the dialogues in chaps. 3–37. *Curse* is literally "bless"; see note on 1:11.

2:11–13 The introduction of Job's three friends who will exchange dialogues with Job in chaps. 3–31 displays both their generosity and their dramatic, visceral reactions to Job's suffering. Their actions resemble Israelite mourning rituals (see Josh. 7:6; Lam. 2:10) and come to be associated with the Jewish practice of sitting shiva for a deceased family member. **2:12** *Dust* is a major theme word, occurring twenty-six times in Job, meaning dry dirt. Dust frequently symbolizes death or despair in Job as the dried form of clay or soil from which humans are made (Gen. 3:19). Dust ("afar") sounds like the "ashes" ("efer") where Job is sitting in v. 8. "Dust and ashes" occur together in 30:19; 42:6; see Gen. 18:27.

3:1–11:20 First cycle of speeches.

3:1–26 Job's first speech. Job's opening speech announces the book's exquisite poetry, which conveys experiences of pain, suffering, and victimization (see **"Hebrew Poetry," p. 741**). Job's first words are a malediction invoked on his birth. With this curse, he expresses a desire for death by threading scenes of burial and childbirth, daylight and nighttime, stillbirth and afterlife. Numerous wordplays crowd this chapter. A cultural irony is present from the start: In Israelite literature, death breaks off the possibility of communication with God, who can hear neither praise nor supplication from beyond the grave (Pss. 6:5; 30:9; 88:5–6). Such a communication breakdown works counter to Job's eventual demand to speak directly to God, which becomes a prominent theme as Job's speeches proceed. **3:1–10** Cursed of its ability to conceive, the night's gloomy, starless cloud mass is called to aggressively overtake the day of Job's birth, erasing his birthday from the calendar. **3:3** See Jer. 20:14–18, where the same curse on the day of the prophet's birth conveys his physical and social suffering. *Male* ("geber") or "valiant man" is a theme word, far more common in Job than any other Hebrew book (see 3:3; 14:14; 36:9; 38:3; 40:7). Associated with the social value of strength from warrior culture, the even stronger term "gibor" only occurs once in Job to describe God as he attacks Job (16:14; see **"The Bible, Gender, and Sexuality," pp. 2160–62**). **3:4** With Job's *day* shrouded in darkness, and demanding that *God . . . not seek it*, he is disappeared into a space of trouble, introducing

⁶ That night—let thick darkness seize it!
    let it not rejoice among the days of the
        year;
    let it not come into the number of the
        months.
⁷ Yes, let that night be barren;
    let no joyful cry be heard^s in it.
⁸ Let those curse it who curse the Sea,^{t}
    those who are skilled to rouse up
        Leviathan.
⁹ Let the stars of its dawn be dark;
    let it hope for light but have
        none;
    may it not see the eyelids of the
        morning—
¹⁰ because it did not shut the doors of my
        mother's womb
    and hide trouble from my eyes.

¹¹ "Why did I not die at birth,
    come forth from the womb and expire?
¹² Why were there knees to receive me
    or breasts for me to suck?
¹³ Now I would be lying down and quiet;
    I would be asleep; then I would be at
        rest
¹⁴ with kings and counselors of the earth
    who rebuild ruins for themselves,
¹⁵ or with princes who have gold,
    who fill their houses with silver.

¹⁶ Or why was I not buried like a stillborn
        child,
    like an infant that never sees the light?
¹⁷ There the wicked cease from troubling,
    and there the weary are at rest.
¹⁸ There the prisoners are at ease together;
    they do not hear the voice of the
        taskmaster.
¹⁹ The small and the great are there,
    and the slaves are free from their
        masters.

²⁰ "Why is light given to one in misery
    and life to the bitter in soul,
²¹ who long for death, but it does not come,
    and dig for it more than for hidden
        treasures;
²² who rejoice exceedingly
    and are glad when they find the grave?
²³ Why is light given to one who cannot see
        the way,
    whom God has fenced in?
²⁴ For my sighing comes like^u my bread,
    and my groanings are poured out like
        water.
²⁵ Truly the thing that I fear comes upon me,
    and what I dread befalls me.
²⁶ I am not at ease, nor am I quiet;
    I have no rest, but trouble comes."

s 3.7 Heb *come*   *t* 3.8 Cn: Heb *day*   *u* 3.24 Heb *before*

how prone he will become to invisible afflictions and mysterious attacks (e.g., 3:25; 6:4). **3:7–10** A different use of night imagery, Job wants to erase himself by withdrawing into an infertile night and returning to the dark womb. **3:8** *Curse the Sea... Leviathan* invokes the mythology of the deified Sea and its primordial monster, which the Canaanite god vanquishes to restore order (see **"Leviathan," p. 735**). *Curse* is a homophone with "light," highlighting the curse that light has become for Job. Light and day are resignified as a mythic adversary. Job's first speech contains several allusions to incantations and spells. **3:10** *Mother's womb* is literally "my womb." The word *mother* is not present in the Hebrew. **3:11–19** Since Job was indeed born, he now wishes for the ease of a quiet, trouble-free afterlife, questioning why he did not die in childbirth. **3:11–12** Job's description of his mother reduces her to body parts: *womb...knees...breasts*. The YHWH speeches in 38:39–39:30 discuss themes of animal birth, nurture, and youth sustenance. **3:18–19** The afterlife depicted here ends the domination of imprisonment and the exploitation of enslavement. It makes rest available to everyone who dies, including the wealthy, weary, and wicked (vv. 14–17). This anticipates a theme in the book: communities in death. See also Eccl. 9:2–3. **3:20–26** Job now voices his misery as a liquid groan longing for death, digging for the grave as *trouble comes*. **3:21** *Treasures* has the same root word as "buried" in v. 16, another example of how Job poetically threads death throughout the speech. **3:24** *Sighing* and *groanings* are trauma-inflected discourse, sounds without language (see 6:4–7; 7:4–5). **3:26** *Not at ease... quiet... rest* contrasts with the theme of death's rest in vv. 17–19. *But trouble* ("rogez") *comes* is an ominous conclusion that poetically resists closure. "Rogez" can mean "wrath" (Hab. 3:2), "thunder" (Job 37:2), "rage" (Job 39:24), or "turmoil" (Isa. 14:3). Such a cluster of meanings demonstrates how unexpected and strange Job's linguistic and cultural world is for modern sensibilities.

3:26–4:1 Several scholars insert 4:12–21 between 3:26 and 4:1 as a transition to Job's eerie visionary experience, an ancient reading already made by Eleazar ben Kalir, a Byzantine Jewish poet, and warranted by internal references (see 33:15 and chaps. 15 and 17).

4 Then Eliphaz the Temanite answered:
² "If one ventures a word with you, will
you be offended?
But who can keep from speaking?
³ See, you have instructed many;
you have strengthened the weak hands.
⁴ Your words have supported those who
were stumbling,
and you have made firm the feeble
knees.
⁵ But now it has come to you, and you are
impatient;
it touches you, and you are dismayed.
⁶ Is not your fear of God your confidence
and the integrity of your ways your
hope?

⁷ "Think now, who that was innocent ever
perished?
Or where were the upright cut off?
⁸ As I have seen, those who plow iniquity
and sow trouble reap the same.
⁹ By the breath of God they perish,
and by the blast of his anger they are
consumed.
¹⁰ The roar of the lion, the voice of the
fierce lion,
and the teeth of the young lions are
broken.
¹¹ The strong lion perishes for lack of
prey,
and the whelps of the lioness are
scattered.

¹² "Now a word came stealing to me;
my ear received the whisper of it.
¹³ Amid thoughts from visions of the night,
when deep sleep falls on mortals,
¹⁴ dread came upon me and trembling,
which made all my bones shake.
¹⁵ A spirit glided past my face;
the hair of my flesh bristled.
¹⁶ It stood still,
but I could not discern its appearance.
A form was before my eyes;
there was silence; then I heard a voice:
¹⁷ 'Can mortals be righteous beforeᵛ God?
Can humans be pure beforeʷ their
Maker?
¹⁸ Even in his servants he puts no trust,
and his angels he charges with error;
¹⁹ how much more those who live in houses
of clay,
whose foundation is in the dust,
who are crushed like a moth.
²⁰ Between morning and evening they are
destroyed;
they perish forever without any
regarding it.
²¹ Their tent cord is plucked up within them,
and they die devoid of wisdom.'

v 4.17 Or more righteous than   w 4.17 Or more pure than

4:1–25:6 Eliphaz, Bildad, and Zophar dialogue with Job. The friends do the work of listening to survivors in their demands for remembering, engagement, attention, and action. Their speeches are the premier example of dialogue in the Bible. Indeed, the Hebrew Bible rarely offers just one perspective on anything. In the first cycle of speeches, the friends offer Job their perspective on hope. In the second cycle, they find him wicked and mostly sling images of devastation at him, hoping to wrest a traditional response from their ill-fated friend. In so doing, they sometimes pitch their rhetoric, overcome with disgust. The dialogues break down in the third cycle. **4:1–5:27 Eliphaz's first speech.** Job's speech in chap. 3 elicits an uninvited response from Eliphaz. Always the first to speak, Eliphaz's speech lays down most of the repertoire taken up in the friends' speeches. Eliphaz, Bildad, and Zophar appeal regularly to aphorisms, traditional maxims, and hymnic fragments, conveying their own authority and reinforcing social tropes that would feel especially true to someone who confirms them with their experiences of well-being. **4:2** After seven days of silence, Eliphaz acknowledges that he was not invited to speak: *if one ventures a word with you, will you be offended?* This dynamic anticipates the dialogic pattern of the friends' advice, unwanted responses to Job's declarations and cries, and begins to signal a failed friendship leading to a collapse of dialogue altogether (31:40–32:1). **4:3–4** Eliphaz refers to Job's previous reputation as a comforter, a theme Job himself will emphasize in his final speech (chap. 29, especially v. 15). **4:5** Eliphaz attempts to shift Job's empathic attention onto the people he helped, inviting him to see himself in their shoes. **4:6–9** Past (vv. 3–4), present (v. 5), and now future, Eliphaz attempts to ground Job's future hope in his own character resources: piety and integrity. If Job uses his integrity and hope, the disaster he suffers could end happily (v. 7). If he does not, the disaster is the end of the story (vv. 8–9). **4:8** Eliphaz uses traditional maxims here and in 5:2, 17. **4:12–20** A common view espoused by the friends, Eliphaz argues that humans are nothing in relation to God. See also

5 "Call now; is there anyone who will
   answer you?
To which of the holy ones will you turn?
² Surely vexation kills the fool,
   and jealousy slays the simple.
³ I have seen fools taking root,
   but suddenly I cursed their dwelling.
⁴ Their children are far from safety,
   they are crushed in the gate,
   and there is no one to deliver them.
⁵ The hungry eat their harvest,
   and they take it even out of the
      thorns,ˣ
   and the thirstyʸ pant after their
      wealth.
⁶ For misery does not come from the earth,
   nor does trouble sprout from the
      ground,
⁷ but humans are born to trouble
   just as sparksᶻ fly upward.

⁸ "As for me, I would seek God,
   and to God I would commit my cause.
⁹ He does great things and unsearchable,
   marvelous things without number.
¹⁰ He gives rain on the earth
   and sends waters on the fields;
¹¹ he sets on high those who are lowly,
   and those who mourn are lifted to
      safety.
¹² He frustrates the devices of the crafty,
   so that their hands achieve no success.
¹³ He takes the wise in their own craftiness,
   and the schemes of the wily are
      brought to a quick end.
¹⁴ They meet with darkness in the daytime
   and grope at noonday as in the night.

¹⁵ But he saves the needy from the sword of
      their mouth,
   from the hand of the mighty.
¹⁶ So the poor have hope,
   and injustice shuts its mouth.

¹⁷ "How happy is the one whom God
      reproves;
   therefore do not despise the discipline
      of the Almighty.ᵃ
¹⁸ For he wounds, but he binds up;
   he strikes, but his hands heal.
¹⁹ He will deliver you from six troubles;
   in seven no harm shall touch you.
²⁰ In famine he will redeem you from death
   and in war from the power of the sword.
²¹ You shall be hidden from the scourge of
      the tongue
   and shall not fear destruction when it
      comes.
²² At destruction and famine you shall laugh
   and shall not fear the wild animals of
      the earth.
²³ For you shall be in league with the stones
      of the field,
   and the wild animals shall be at peace
      with you.
²⁴ You shall know that your tent is safe;
   you shall inspect your fold and miss
      nothing.
²⁵ You shall know that your descendants
      will be many
   and your offspring like the grass of
      the earth.

x 5.5 Meaning of Heb uncertain   y 5.5 Aquila Symmachus Syr Vg: Heb *snare*   z 5.7 Or *birds*; Heb *sons of Resheph*   a 5.17 Traditional rendering of Heb *Shaddai*

15:14–16; 25:4–6. **5:1–27** Eliphaz recommends that Job call on God to protect him from *vexation* (vv. 1–7); *seek God*, otherwise a wise person like Job will get caught in failure (vv. 8–16); find happiness in *discipline* (v. 17); trust that God will *heal* after he *wounds* (v. 18); and live the traditional script of endurance (vv. 19–26) because, by the seventh catastrophe, the long-sufferer can *laugh* (v. 22) and emerge unharmed (v. 19). Generally, Eliphaz advises that divine brutality is purposeful as a tool for developing wisdom, recommending a good attitude during experiences of violence. **5:7** *Born to trouble* could also be read as "beget trouble." The Hebrew "Resheph" may refer to the name of a Canaanite god of pestilence. **5:8** The preposition "el" is used twice, which plays on the word for God (El), reading visually like "I would seek God, God, God, God (Elohim)." **5:9–16** Hymn praising God as the one who *does great things*. **5:17–26** Exemplary suffering culminating in a traditional hymn of praise. The friends offer that practices of piety are therapies for coping with suffering (see chap. 11). **5:17–18** *Discipline* ("musar") was understood to produce wisdom through transformation. The image of God striking wounds indicates Eliphaz's view that being subjected to a wounder/healer can also produce moral education. This is often called "chastisement," but words like thrash, batter, and flog better capture the physical abuse described here. **5:17** On *Almighty*, see note on 6:4. **5:25–26** Eliphaz wades into Job's traumatic loss of his children with fantastic promises for abundant seed using arboreal metaphors for progeny. By this, Job can enter the grave full of vigor (like Moses

²⁶ You shall come to your grave in ripe old
 age,
  as a shock of grain comes up to the
   threshing floor in its season.
²⁷ See, we have searched this out; it is true.
  Hear, and know it for yourself."

6

Then Job answered:
²"O that my vexation were weighed
 and all my calamity laid in the
  balances!
³ For then it would be heavier than the
  sand of the sea;
  therefore my words have been rash.
⁴ For the arrows of the Almighty[b] are in
  me;
  my spirit drinks their poison;
  the terrors of God are arrayed against
   me.
⁵ Does the wild ass bray over its grass
  or the ox low over its fodder?
⁶ Can that which is tasteless be eaten
  without salt,
  or is there any flavor in the juice of
   mallows?[c]
⁷ My appetite refuses to touch them;
  they are like food that is loathsome
   to me.[d]

⁸ "O that I might have my request
  and that God would grant my desire,

⁹ that it would please God to crush me,
  that he would let loose his hand and
   cut me off!
¹⁰ This would be my consolation;
  I would even exult[e] in unrelenting pain,
  for I have not denied the words of the
   Holy One.
¹¹ What is my strength, that I should wait?
  And what is my end, that I should be
   patient?
¹² Is my strength the strength of stones,
  or is my flesh bronze?
¹³ In truth I have no help in me,
  and any resource is driven from me.

¹⁴ "Those who withhold[f] kindness from a
   friend
  forsake the fear of the Almighty.[g]
¹⁵ My companions are treacherous like a
   torrent bed,
  like swollen streams that pass away,
¹⁶ that run dark with ice,
  turbid with melting snow.
¹⁷ In time of heat they disappear;
  when it is hot, they vanish from their
   place.

b 6.4 Traditional rendering of Heb *Shaddai*   c 6.6 Meaning of Heb uncertain   d 6.7 Meaning of Heb uncertain
e 6.10 Meaning of Heb uncertain   f 6.14 Syr Vg Compare
Tg: Meaning of Heb uncertain   g 6.14 Traditional rendering of Heb *Shaddai*

in Deut. 34:7). **5:26** *Grain* can also mean tomb (see 21:32). **5:27** Eliphaz justifies his authority by
describing the "search" he undertook, a theme across the dialogues about the acquisition of wisdom (especially 28:3, 27).

6:1–7:21 Job's second speech.

6:1–13 Job ruminates on his vexation. Announcing his requests and desires, Job ignores Eliphaz
for the moment. **6:2–3** *In the balances* conveys both the theme of justice (fair trade) and Job's
desire for misery to be material and measurable. Perhaps this captures a timeless human experience of invisible pain and hidden illness, considering Job's afflictions will "touch his bone and
his flesh" (2:5). **6:3** *Rash* seems a premature pronouncement for Job to make. The line could also
read, "My words are choked back." **6:4** *Arrows of the Almighty are in me* introduces one of Job's
primary claims, that his symptoms are the result of divine attack (see Deut. 32:23; Lam. 2:4). The
name translated as *Almighty* ("shaddai") is from the root "shadad" meaning "to deal violently" or
"to devastate." Understood here with the word for God in the second half of the verse, we can hear
the common moniker "El Shaddai," which is variously understood as "God of the mountains," "God
of the deities," or even "fertile God" (literally "God with breasts"; see Gen. 49:25). **6:4–7** A concentration of metaphors about drinking and eating, grounding Job's testimony in his embodied experiences (see v. 30). **6:9** Job's desire for death in chap. 3 was imagined as temporal erasure, a return to
the womb, stillbirth, and miserably digging a grave. *Crush me . . . cut me off* now envisions death as
God's attack. See also 9:17–18. **6:10** *Words of the Holy One* lacks a clear referent. **6:11–13** Job audits
his strength to endure and comes up empty, recalling his proposal to weigh his suffering in 6:2–3.

6:14–30 Job shifts attention to his friends. Job's soliloquy contemplates good friendship. He
ultimately scolds his friends for their lack of kindness and courage. Job feels abandoned because
they fear his suffering. **6:15–19** A meditation on betrayal unfolds from sustained attention to a

¹⁸ The caravans turn aside from their
    course;
    they go up into the waste and perish.
¹⁹ The caravans of Tema look;
    the travelers of Sheba hope.
²⁰ They are disappointed because they
    were confident;
    they come there and are confounded.
²¹ Such you have now become to me;*b*
    you see my calamity and are afraid.
²² Have I said, 'Make me a gift'?
    Or, 'From your wealth offer a bribe for
    me'?
²³ Or, 'Save me from an opponent's hand'?
    Or, 'Ransom me from the hand of
    oppressors'?

²⁴ "Teach me, and I will be silent;
    make me understand how I have gone
    wrong.
²⁵ How forceful are honest words!
    But your reproof, what does it reprove?
²⁶ Do you think that you can reprove words,
    as if the speech of the desperate were
    wind?
²⁷ You would even cast lots over the orphan
    and bargain over your friend.

²⁸ "But now, be pleased to look at me,
    for I will not lie to your face.
²⁹ Turn, I pray; let no wrong be done.
    Turn now; my vindication is at stake.
³⁰ Is there any wrong on my tongue?
    Cannot my taste discern calamity?

7 "Do not human beings have a hard
    service on earth,
    and are not their days like the days of
    a laborer?
² Like a slave who longs for the shadow,
    and like laborers who look for their
    wages,
³ so I am allotted months of emptiness,
    and nights of misery are apportioned
    to me.
⁴ When I lie down I say, 'When shall I rise?'
    But the night is long,
    and I am full of tossing until dawn.
⁵ My flesh is clothed with worms and dirt;
    my skin hardens, then breaks out
    again.
⁶ My days are swifter than a weaver's
    shuttle
    and come to their end without hope.*i*

⁷ "Remember that my life is a breath;
    my eye will never again see good.
⁸ The eye that beholds me will see me no
    more;
    while your eyes are upon me, I shall
    be gone.
⁹ As the cloud fades and vanishes,
    so those who go down to Sheol do not
    come up;
¹⁰ they return no more to their houses,
    nor do their places know them any
    more.

b 6.21 Cn Compare Gk Syr: Meaning of Heb uncertain
i 7.6 Or *as the thread runs out*

desert wadi and its seasonal changes. See Jer. 15:18. **6:21** The verbs for seeing and fearing are very similar, a wordplay that here underscores the friends' failure to witness their friend's suffering. **6:22–23** The economic dependency eschewed here is eventually given by supportive friends in 42:11. **6:26** *Reprove words* distills the painful experience of being scolded for one's testimony, which Job claims are "honest words" (v. 25). The friends will repeatedly pathologize Job's trauma and police his speech. **6:28–29** *Be pleased to look at me . . . turn.* Job requests his friends' presence, inviting them to replace their fear with pleasure and twice calling them to *turn*, a term often misread as repentance but that more accurately refers to renewed allegiance and changed behavior.

    7:1–10 Job's illness narrative. Although all Job's speeches use language to navigate misery, here Job begins to narrate his symptoms and feelings of social death. **7:1–3** *Hard service* is a term usually associated with war conscription, but it can also be applied to labor that was forced (known as corvée). *I am allotted months of emptiness* compares Job's experience of time to that produced by degrading forms of labor, including enslaved labor (though Job was a slaveholder; see 1:3 and 31:13). Note all the terms for time in vv. 1–6. **7:4–5** In Job's first description of corporeal symptoms, he complains of difficulty sleeping and describes his skin disease. *Worms and dirt* are both associated with dead flesh. **7:9** *Sheol* is the abode of the dead. Often depicted underground, it can be shadowy, muddy, or watery. *Sheol* can function rhetorically as eviscerating the social privileges of wealth and knowledge (Eccl. 9:10) and can therefore threaten those of status (Isa. 5:14). Job uses *Sheol* here to accept the evanescence of life and to describe his sense of being invisible before his friends' eyes (see **"Sheol," p. 695**).

11 "Therefore I will not restrain my mouth;
   I will speak in the anguish of my
      spirit;
   I will complain in the bitterness of my
      soul.
12 Am I the Sea or the Dragon
   that you set a guard over me?
13 When I say, 'My bed will comfort me,
   my couch will ease my complaint,'
14 then you scare me with dreams
   and terrify me with visions,
15 so that I would choose strangling
   and death rather than this body.
16 I loathe my life; I would not live forever.
   Let me alone, for my days are a breath.
17 What are humans, that you make so
      much of them,
   that you set your mind on them,
18 visit them every morning,
   test them every moment?
19 Will you not look away from me for a
      while,
   let me alone until I swallow my
      spittle?
20 If I sin, what do I do to you, you watcher
   of humanity?

Why have you made me your target?
   Why have I become a burden to you?
21 Why do you not pardon my transgression
   and take away my iniquity?
For now I shall lie in the earth;
   you will seek me, but I shall not be."

8 Then Bildad the Shuhite answered:
2 "How long will you say these things
   and the words of your mouth be a
      great wind?
3 Does God pervert justice?
   Or does the Almighty*j* pervert the
      right?
4 If your children sinned against him,
   he delivered them into the power of
      their transgression.
5 If you will seek God
   and make supplication to the
      Almighty,*k*
6 if you are pure and upright,
   surely then he will rouse himself for
      you
   and restore to you your rightful place.

j 8.3 Traditional rendering of Heb *Shaddai*   *k* 8.5 Traditional rendering of Heb *Shaddai*

7:11–21 Job announces the power of his voice. Job contrasts his visual obscurity with his determination to vocalize. But whether he finds himself in mythic (v. 12) or mundane (v. 13) spaces, Job understands that unrelenting assaults will not end as long as he is a divine *target* (v. 20). **7:12** *The Sea* ("Yam") and *the Dragon* are dealt with by God at creation (see 3:8; 38:8–11; Isa. 51:9–10). The Israelite tradition about Sea as an adversary of God draws on Canaanite mythology about Baal defeating the sea god Yam. The name Yam and several mythic motifs are absorbed by Israel and applied to God in poetic and epic genres. See Exod. 14:21; 15:6–8; Isa. 51:9–15; Jer. 31:35; Pss. 74:13–14; 89:10–14. **7:14** *Dreams . . . visions* recalls 4:12–21. **7:16** *My days are a breath* echoes Ps. 39:5 and uses the less common word for *breath* ("hevel"), which can also mean "fleeting" or "vanity" (see **"All Is Vanity," p. 906**). **7:17–19** An almost certain parody of human preeminence over creation in the hymnic tradition; compare Ps. 8:4–9, in which God pays attention to humans as beings crowned with honor and given dominion over all things. Instead, Job asks why God makes humans great only to test them constantly. *Swallow my spittle* is almost comedic, an utter contrast with Ps. 8's honorifics. **7:20** *Watcher of humanity.* God's searching gaze, called wonderful knowledge in Ps. 139:6, is scrutinized at the end of Job's second speech, anticipating Job's litigation of God in chap. 9. Contrast Ps. 139:1–18. **7:20–21** *If I sin . . . Why do you not pardon?* Job frequently insists on his innocence (6:29–30; 9:17–21; 13:23; 23:4–12). But as here, Job sometimes floats scenarios about hypothetical iniquity (e.g., 13:23–26; 14:16–18).

8:1–22 Bildad's first speech. Bildad opens by affirming the justice of God (v. 3), a very different tack than Eliphaz in chaps. 4–5 who began by affirming Job's personal past, acknowledging his recent experiences of calamity, and lifting up the resources already in his character (4:3–6). But like Eliphaz, Bildad's advice generally recommends traditional scripts that advise someone suffering to transcend their pain. Bildad seems to find Job innocent. **8:3** *Almighty.* See note on 6:4. **8:4** Bildad's first reference to Job's life experience blames Job's deceased children as deserving of their fate, a callousness that grows out of his orientation to divine principles (v. 3). It is possible Bildad meant to be helpful by affirming Job's personal innocence by applying his theology of retributive justice to Job's children. **8:5** The Hebrew looks visually like "If you seek God, God, God, God (Almighty)." See note for 5:8. **8:6** Job was called *upright* by the narrator in 1:1 and by God in 1:8 and 2:3. *Rouse himself*

Focus On: Sheol (Job 7:9)
The idea of an eternal reward in heaven or eternal punishment in hell does not exist in the Hebrew Bible. Instead, the understanding of the afterlife is similar to the Greek concept of Hades as a place where all the dead go regardless of their behavior in this life. In the Hebrew Bible, that place has several names— the Pit, Death, Earth (or the "Underworld"), and Abaddon. But the most prominent of them, occurring sixty-six times, is Sheol (translated "Hades" in the LXX). The word is not attested in any other Semitic language, and its etymology is disputed; it probably comes from the Hebrew verb "to ask," based on "inquiring" of the dead (necromancy), a practice forbidden in Deut. 18:11 (cf. 1 Chr. 10:13).

Absent a detailed description of Sheol, its characterization is based on biblical references to it. Sheol is where all people go upon dying. A gray-headed (= elderly) Jacob anticipates going to Sheol soon and joining his son Benjamin, who he believes preceded him in death (Gen. 37:35; 42:38; 44:29–31). Joab is also old and gray haired, but his journey to Sheol is not "in peace"—that is, from natural causes—but "with blood," by assassination (1 Kgs. 2:6, 9). As in these verses, a person consistently "goes down" to Sheol, indicating that it is located below ground. The rebels in Num. 16 are swallowed alive by the earth (vv. 30, 33). The deceased Samuel is summoned up from the earth (1 Sam. 28:11–14). Sheol is the opposite of heaven and thus the lowest depth in the cosmos (Deut. 32:22; Isa. 7:11; 14:11, 15; Amos 9:2; Job 11:8; Ps. 139:8). Since death is inescapable, Sheol is insatiable (Prov. 27:20; Isa. 5:14; Hab. 2:5). No one comes back up from Sheol (Job 7:9); only God can rescue people from it (1 Sam. 2:6; Job 14:13; 26:6; Prov. 15:11), but these texts use Sheol as a metaphor for catastrophe and do not envision resurrection of the dead. The Hebrew term for Sheol's residents is most often *rephaim*, translated as "shades" (Isa. 14:9; 26:14; Ps. 88:10) and "the dead" (Prov. 9:18). There is some indication that they lack awareness or memory (Ps. 6:5; Eccl. 9:10) and exist (not live) in a mindless state, perhaps something like zombies in modern imagination.

Steven L. McKenzie

7 Though your beginning was small,
    your latter days will be very great.

8 "For inquire now of bygone generations
    and consider what their ancestors
      have found,
9 for we are but of yesterday, and we know
      nothing,
    for our days on earth are but a
      shadow.
10 Will they not teach you and tell you
    and utter words out of their
      understanding?

11 "Can papyrus grow where there is no
      marsh?
    Can reeds flourish where there is no
      water?
12 While yet in flower and not cut down,
    they wither before any other plant.
13 Such are the paths of all who forget God;
    the hope of the godless shall perish.

14 Their confidence is gossamer,
    a spider's house their trust.
15 If one leans against its house, it will not
      stand;
    if one lays hold of it, it will not endure.
16 The wicked thrive[l] before the sun,
    and their shoots spread over the garden.
17 Their roots twine around the stoneheap;
    they live among the rocks.[m]
18 If they are destroyed from their place,
    then it will deny them, saying, 'I have
      never seen you.'
19 See, these are their happy ways,[n]
    and out of the earth still others will
      spring.

20 "See, God will not reject the blameless,
    nor take the hand of evildoers.
21 He will yet fill your mouth with laughter
    and your lips with shouts of joy.

l 8.16 Heb *He thrives*   *m* 8.17 Gk Vg: Meaning of Heb uncertain   *n* 8.19 Meaning of Heb uncertain

is a description of power. **8:7** Bildad's advice is tightly paired: *beginning . . . small / latter days . . . great.* The friends largely describe Job's "healing" in terms of reversing his misfortunes and restoring his place in the social order. **8:8–10** The wisdom of one's ancestors often provides comfort and orientation. **8:11–19** An allegorical narrative, but the Hebrew is riddled so the referent is unstable. The first image warns of the majestic papyrus that can, without water, dry up overnight (vv. 11–15). The second (vv. 16–19) describes persistent garden plants that, though ripped up and disowned by the places they root, can spring up elsewhere (v. 19).

22 Those who hate you will be clothed with
   shame,
      and the tent of the wicked will be no
         more."

9 Then Job answered:
   2 "Indeed, I know that this is so,
      but how can a mortal be just before
         God?
3 If one wished to contend with him,
   one could not answer him once in a
      thousand.
4 He is wise in heart and mighty in
   strength;
      who has resisted him and succeeded?
5 He removes mountains, and they do not
   know it
      when he overturns them in his anger;
6 he shakes the earth out of its place,
   and its pillars tremble;
7 he commands the sun, and it does not
   rise;
      he seals up the stars;
8 he alone stretched out the heavens
   and trampled the waves of the
      Sea;*o*
9 he made the Bear and Orion,
   the Pleiades and the chambers of the
      south;
10 he does great things beyond
   understanding
      and marvelous things without
         number.
11 Look, he passes by me, and I do not see
   him;
      he moves on, but I do not perceive
         him.

12 He snatches away; who can stop
   him?
      Who will say to him, 'What are you
         doing?'
13 "God will not turn back his anger;
   the helpers of Rahab bowed beneath
      him.
14 How then can I answer him,
   choosing my words with him?
15 Though I am innocent, I cannot answer
   him;
      I must appeal to my accuser for my
         right.
16 If I summoned him and he answered me,
   I do not believe that he would listen to
      my voice.
17 For he crushes me with a tempest
   and multiplies my wounds without
      cause;
18 he will not let me get my breath
   but fills me with bitterness.
19 If it is a contest of strength, he is the
   strong one!
      If it is a matter of justice, who can
         summon him?*p*
20 Though I am innocent, my own mouth
   would condemn me;
      though I am blameless, he would
         prove me perverse.
21 I am blameless; I do not know myself;
   I loathe my life.
22 It is all one; therefore I say,
   'He destroys both the blameless and
      the wicked.'

o 9.8 Or *trampled the back of the sea dragon*   *p* 9.19 Compare
Gk: Heb *me*

9:1–10:22 Job's third speech.
   9:1–24 Job contemplates a trial calling God to account. 9:2 *Just*, meaning right or vindicated
in a court of law. **9:3–14 God litigates unfairly.** If brought to court, God would bring unanswerable
charges (v. 3), overpower challengers (v. 4), throw context into chaos (vv. 5–7), confound explanations (v. 10), commit imperceptible acts (vv. 11–12), and intimidate even the strongest adversaries
(v. 13), leading Job to ask *How then can I answer him?* (v. 14). Job will call the trial *a contest of
strength* (v. 19). **9:4** *Succeeded* ("shalam") has a variety of meanings, most of which carry the
sense of wholeness, soundness, welfare, and safety. "Uninjured" is often proposed here. **9:5–10** Job
searches and finds the underside of tradition's pious metaphors of God's power (e.g., Ps. 104).
9:8 On *the Sea*, see note on 7:12. Standing on the back of an enemy signifies triumph (Deut. 33:29).
9:11 Recalls the mysterious theophany in 4:15–21. **9:14–19** Job then personalizes his vision of an
unjust court case, imagining God's unreceptive, then aggressive and violent attack on him in a court
of so-called might makes right (v. 19). **9:17–18** God crushes and repeatedly wounds Job. With this
description of divine attack, Job develops the etiology for his intense symptoms, begun already
in 6:4 and developed further in 10:16–17. **9:20** *My own mouth would condemn me*. Job realizes the
vocal flow from his mouth will betray him, though God himself made Job bitter (v. 18). He makes this
point again in 16:6–8, where Job laments that his pained speech and sick body will testify against

23 When disaster brings sudden death,
  he mocks at the calamity*q* of the
    innocent.
24 The earth is given into the hand of the
    wicked;
  he covers the eyes of its judges—
  if it is not he, who then is it?

25 "My days are swifter than a runner;
  they flee away; they see no good.
26 They go by like skiffs of reed,
  like an eagle swooping on the prey.
27 If I say, 'I will forget my complaint;
  I will put off my sad countenance and
    be of good cheer,'
28 I become afraid of all my suffering,
  for I know you will not hold me
    innocent.
29 I shall be condemned;
  why then do I labor in vain?
30 If I wash myself with soap
  and cleanse my hands with lye,
31 yet you will plunge me into filth,
  and my own clothes will abhor me.
32 For he is not a mortal, as I am, that I
    might answer him,
  that we should come to trial together.
33 There is no mediator*r* between us,
  who might lay his hand on us both.
34 If he would take his rod away from me
  and not let dread of him terrify me,

35 then I would speak without fear of him,
  for I know I am not what I am thought
    to be.*s*

10 "I loathe my life;
  I will give free utterance to my
    complaint;
  I will speak in the bitterness of my soul.
2 I will say to God, 'Do not condemn me;
  let me know why you contend against
    me.
3 Does it seem good to you to oppress,
  to despise the work of your hands
  and favor the schemes of the wicked?
4 Do you have eyes of flesh?
  Do you see as humans see?
5 Are your days like the days of mortals
  or your years like human years,
6 that you seek out my iniquity
  and search for my sin,
7 although you know that I am not guilty,
  and there is no one to deliver out of
    your hand?
8 Your hands fashioned and made me,
  and now you turn and destroy me.*t*
9 Remember that you fashioned me like
    clay,
  and will you turn me to dust again?

*q 9.23 Meaning of Heb uncertain   r 9.33 Another reading
is Would that there were a mediator   s 9.35 Cn: Heb for I am
not so in myself   t 10.8 Cn Compare Gk Syr: Heb made me
together all around, and you destroy me*

him. **9:23** Job accuses God of mocking victims. **9:24** Job accuses God of promoting the hostile actor(s) and impeding human justice (10:3–4).
  9:25–35 Job wishes he had a mediator. 9:26 See Hab. 1:8. Predators are common images in both Job's and God's speeches (especially chaps. 38–39). Job will soon call God "a lion" who hunts him (10:16). **9:27–31** Job considers alternatives to legal complaint, but they lead to fear, condemnation, and malevolent clothing. **9:33** *Mediator.* From a term that could imply several possible legal actions: decide, judge, argue, prove, convict, or reprove. In 16:19, Job will begin to imagine a "witness . . . in heaven," although "witness" and *mediator* are different terms. **9:34** *Rod* is a common metaphor with many possible meanings, probably used here as a symbol of conquest (Num. 24:17; Isa. 10:24), threshing (Isa. 28:27), or chastisement (Lam. 3:1). On divine chastisement, see 5:17–18. **9:35** *Speak without fear.* Job is honest about his experience of fear (3:25) but resists the traditional sense in which his friends recommend "fear of God" (4:6; 15:4; see 1:8–9; 2:3; 28:28).
  10:1–2 Job's bitter voice has pneumatic force. *Give free utterance* implies letting the voice loose or letting its pressure release from his body (see 3:24 and 7:11). **10:2** *Let me know why you contend against me.* Despite having no mediator (9:33) and feeling terrified (9:34), Job continues his legal pursuit.
  10:3 A new prosecution of God: hating what his own hands made. *Oppress* often takes an economic meaning, so perhaps defraud or extort.
  10:7 See 9:33.
  10:9–13 A meditation on how God formed the human, with several unique features (Gen. 2). Goethe's *Faust* parodied the Joban subject with Homunculus, an artificially produced spirit without flesh, a fire in a test tube. Quickly realizing that life requires embodiment, Homunculus sets out to find a body, much like Job's search for a compelling human form. **10:9** Job juxtaposes the *clay* of formation with the *dust* of death (17:16; 20:11; 21:26).

¹⁰ Did you not pour me out like milk
and curdle me like cheese?
¹¹ You clothed me with skin and flesh
and knit me together with bones and
sinews.
¹² You have granted me life and steadfast
love,
and your care has preserved my spirit.
¹³ Yet these things you hid in your heart;
I know that this was your purpose.
¹⁴ If I sin, you watch me
and do not acquit me of my iniquity.
¹⁵ If I am wicked, woe to me!
If I am righteous, I cannot lift up my
head,
for I am filled with disgrace
and look upon my affliction.
¹⁶ Bold as a lion you hunt me;
you repeat your exploits against me.
¹⁷ You renew your witnesses against me
and increase your vexation toward me;
you bring fresh troops against me.ᵘ

¹⁸ " 'Why did you bring me forth from the
womb?
Would that I had died before any eye
had seen me
¹⁹ and were as though I had not been,
carried from the womb to the
grave.
²⁰ Are not the days of my life few?ᵛ
Let me alone, that I may find a little
comfortʷ
²¹ before I go, never to return,
to the land of gloom and deep
darkness,
²² the land of gloomˣ and chaos,
where light is like darkness.' "

11 Then Zophar the Naamathite answered:
²"Should a multitude of words go
unanswered,
and should one full of talk be
vindicated?
³ Should your babble put others to silence,
and when you mock, shall no one
shame you?
⁴ For you say, 'My conductʸ is pure,
and I am clean in God'sᶻ sight.'
⁵ But O that God would speak
and open his lips to you
⁶ and that he would tell you the secrets of
wisdom!
For wisdom is many-sided.ᵃ
Know then that God exacts of you less
than your guilt deserves.

⁷ "Can you find out the deep things of God?
Can you find out the limit of the
Almighty?ᵇ
⁸ It is higher than heavenᶜ—what can you do?
Deeper than Sheol—what can you
know?
⁹ Its measure is longer than the earth
and broader than the sea.
¹⁰ If he passes through and imprisons
and assembles for judgment, who can
hinder him?
¹¹ For he knows those who are worthless;
when he sees iniquity, will he not
consider it?

ᵘ 10.17 Cn Compare Gk: Heb *toward me; changes and a troop are with me*   ᵛ 10.20 Cn Compare Gk Syr: Heb *Are not my days few? Let him cease!*   ʷ 10.20 Heb *that I may brighten up a little*   ˣ 10.22 Heb *gloom as darkness, deep darkness*   ʸ 11.4 Gk: Heb *teaching*   ᶻ 11.4 Heb *your*   ᵃ 11.6 Meaning of Heb uncertain   ᵇ 11.7 Traditional rendering of Heb *Shaddai*   ᶜ 11.8 Heb *The heights of heaven*

10:16–17 In five tight clauses, Job describes God's attack on him, from a *lion . . . hunt* to *fresh troops*. **10:17** *Vexation* as God's punitive rage (Deut. 32:19; 1 Kgs. 15:30; 21:22; 2 Kgs. 23:26; Ps. 85:5), though also Job's suffering (6:2). The last phrase is difficult. *Troops* can mean "hard service" as in 7:1. The term "change" (see textual note) suggests vanishing or vicissitudes. See 14:14, where both terms occur and probably mean "relief from military service." **10:18–19** See chap. 3, especially v. 10. **10:20–22** See 3:7–19 and 7:9. Job's poetics oscillate between his desire for a court appearance and the wish for the comfort of being left alone. Note the recurring narrative of the grave. **11:1–20 Zophar's first speech.** Zophar is the most accusatory so far. He thinks Job is guilty (v. 5) and deserves even more catastrophe than he got (v. 6). In contrast to Eliphaz and Bildad, who both advised Job to "seek God" (5:8; 8:5), Zophar recommends body gestures common in ancient prayer used to direct one's embodied attention to a deity (vv. 13–15). **11:5** *Open his lips* refers to God's mouth in contrast to Job, whom Zophar called "a man of lips" ("full of talk" in v. 2). See YHWH's acceptance of Job's prayer at the end (42:9). **11:6–9** Zophar understands wisdom to be hidden from humans, available only through divine revelation (chap. 28), although the other two friends claim to be the mouthpiece of the true wisdom tradition (5:27). **11:7** On *Almighty*, see note on 6:4. **11:8** On *Sheol*, see

¹² But the stupid will get understanding
  when a wild ass is born human.^d

¹³ "If you direct your heart rightly,
  you will stretch out your hands
    toward him.
¹⁴ If iniquity is in your hand, put it far
    away,
  and do not let wickedness reside in
    your tents.
¹⁵ Surely then you will lift up your face
    without blemish;
  you will be secure and will not fear.
¹⁶ You will forget your misery;
  you will remember it as waters that
    have passed away.
¹⁷ And your life will be brighter than the
    noonday;
  its darkness will be like the
    morning.
¹⁸ And you will have confidence because
    there is hope;
  you will be protected^e and take your
    rest in safety.
¹⁹ You will lie down, and no one will make
    you afraid;
  many will entreat your favor.

²⁰ But the eyes of the wicked will fail;
  all way of escape will be lost to them,
  and their hope is to breathe their last."

12 Then Job answered:
²"No doubt you are the people,
  and wisdom will die with you.
³ But I have understanding as well as you;
  I am not inferior to you.
  Who does not know such things as
    these?
⁴ I am a laughingstock to my friends;
  I, who called upon God and he
    answered me,
  a just and blameless man, I am a
    laughingstock.
⁵ Those at ease have contempt for
    misfortune,^f
  but it is ready for those whose feet are
    unstable.
⁶ The tents of robbers are at peace,
  and those who provoke God are
    secure,
  who bring their god in their hands.^g

d 11.12 Meaning of Heb uncertain *e* 11.18 Or *you will look around* *f* 12.5 Meaning of Heb uncertain *g* 12.6 Or *whom God brought forth by his hand*; meaning of Heb uncertain

note on 7:9. **11:13–15** *Heart . . . hands. . . . face.* These body gestures were common in ancient practices of prayer. **11:13** *Stretch out your hands toward him.* Echoing ancient West Asian prayers (literally "to lift the hand"), lifted hands were depicted in iconography and literary description. Prayer was often associated with a sense of security (vv. 15, 18, 19; see also Pss. 16:8; 23:4, 6; 121). **11:14** *Put it far away* is literally "cause it to be distant" (Isa. 1:15–16; see **"Sin," p. 150**). **11:15** *Blemish* is a term for bodily imperfection, like a spot. See Job's initial skin disease (2:7). Zophar interprets bodily impairment as a moral sign. *Lift up your face.* Compare God's relentless scrutiny, which prevented Job from lifting up his head (10:15b). In the final prose tale, YHWH lifts Job's face (42:9). **11:16–19** Zophar describes psychological relief through religious practices that he believes help process suffering and effect rest, hope, and the softening of night into morning. The cultural ideas in vv. 15–17 speak to the social shame and disempowerment of skin disease. **11:16** *Forget your misery.* Memory plays an important role in the stages of grief and surviving trauma, impacting one's sense of time, orientation, and modes of attention. Expressing a complex idea, Zophar describes how misery is both remembered and forgotten. **11:18–19** Zophar counters Job's language of tossing at night (7:4) and terrifying dreams (7:13–14) with images of secure rest without fear. **11:19b–20** *Many will entreat your favor* is literally "sweeten/seek the favor of your face."
12:1–20:29 Second cycle of speeches.
12:1–14:22 Job's fourth speech. Job has now listened to all three friends advise him to trust God so he can flourish. By now, this is an exhausting rehearsal of traditional wisdom that ignores Job's testimony: God is attacking him for no reason. So Job takes a new tack. He highlights his own knowledge of traditional wisdom by citing and satirizing biblical passages, delivering up mock proverbs, and testing the implications of wisdom's traditional metaphors. **12:2** *Wisdom will die with you.* The friends repeatedly authorize themselves as the mouthpiece of ancestral wisdom, so Job cuts their generational flow in a masterful opening retort. **12:3–4a** Refusing the social death of invisibility he experienced with his friends, Job shows up to address them with new claims: *I have understanding, I am not inferior,* and *I am a laughingstock to my friends.* **12:4b–6** The Hebrew is notoriously difficult, but stylistically, Job begins to speak in proverbs, which are concise and image-rich statements of

7 "But ask the animals, and they will teach
you,
the birds of the air, and they will tell
you;
8 ask the plants of the earth,[b] and they will
teach you,
and the fish of the sea will declare to
you.
9 Who among all these does not know
that the hand of the Lord has done
this?
10 In his hand is the life of every living
thing
and the breath of every human being.
11 Does not the ear test words
as the palate tastes food?
12 Is wisdom with the aged
and understanding in length of days?

13 "With God[i] are wisdom and strength;
he has counsel and understanding.
14 If he tears down, no one can rebuild;
if he shuts someone in, no one can
open up.
15 If he withholds the waters, they dry up;
if he sends them out, they overwhelm
the land.
16 With him are strength and wisdom;
the deceived and the deceiver are his.
17 He leads counselors away stripped
and makes fools of judges.
18 He looses the sash of kings
and binds a waistcloth on their loins.

19 He leads priests away stripped
and overthrows the mighty.
20 He deprives of speech those who are
trusted
and takes away the discernment of the
elders.
21 He pours contempt on princes
and looses the belt of the strong.
22 He uncovers deep things from the
darkness
and brings deep darkness to light.
23 He makes nations great, then destroys
them;
he enlarges nations, then leads them
away.
24 He strips understanding from the
leaders[j] of the earth
and makes them wander in a pathless
waste.
25 They grope in the dark without light;
he makes them stagger like a
drunkard.

13 "Look, my eye has seen all this;
my ear has heard and understood it.
2 What you know, I also know;
I am not inferior to you.
3 But I would speak to the Almighty,[k]
and I desire to argue my case with
God.
4 As for you, you whitewash with lies;
all of you are worthless physicians.

b 12.8 Or *speak to the earth*   i 12.13 Heb *him*   j 12.24 Heb adds
of the people   k 13.3 Traditional rendering of Heb *Shaddai*

commonly held beliefs. Most translators render this passage as a clever critique of the friends. Eliphaz
(5:22) and Bildad (8:21) recommended laughter to Job. **12:7–8** Job appeals to animals and nature,
a traditional source of knowledge in the wisdom tradition. Notice the verbs of pedagogy: *teach, tell,*
and *declare*. Compare with Deut. 32:7, where "your father" and "elders" instruct. **12:7** *Animals*. The
plural for *animals* or "beasts" is the Hebrew word "behemoth," which refers to a land monster in
other biblical texts, including Job 40:15–24. **12:9–25** Job searches traditional aphorisms about God
and sears them with a meditation on God's destructive, abusive, and capricious dealings. Vv. 13–25
parody a hymn of praise with several common and probably even excerpted lines. See Pss. 96–99,
135–36 for examples. **12:12–13** In Israelite culture, wisdom belongs to older males. Eliphaz will agree
in 15:9–10. **12:14** Job juxtaposes the idealization of old age with the fact of irreversible human breakdown. See Eliphaz in 5:18. **12:17–24** God actively subverts the "counsel," "wisdom," "understanding,"
and "strength" of people in positions of authority (v. 13). See Prov. 8:14–16. The list expands from
local roles, probably from Job's lifeworld, to broad categories like nations and leaders of the earth
(vv. 23–25). Ironically, the list of roles does not include the prophet, whose social critiques often
target these same social roles. **13:1–19** Job returns to his legal case against God, announcing his
intentions and demanding his friends' silence so they will stop performing God's judgment. Given the
friends' increasingly vociferous reactions to Job and the fact that twenty-four chapters of dialogue
with them remain, it is safe to say Job's method of solicitation to his friends does not win him their
silence. **13:1–2** Repetition of 12:3, especially *I am not inferior to you*. **13:3** On *Almighty*, see note on
6:4. **13:4** *Whitewash with lies* is the same phrase that describes the defamation of someone who lives
by God's commandments in Ps. 119:69. *Worthless physicians*, Job highlights how sages qua *physicians*

5 If you would only keep silent,
   that would be your wisdom!
6 Hear now my reasoning,
   and listen to the pleadings of my
      lips.
7 Will you speak falsely for God
   and speak deceitfully for him?
8 Will you show partiality toward him;
   will you plead the case for God?
9 Will it be well with you when he
      searches you out?
   Or can you deceive him as one person
      deceives another?
10 He will surely rebuke you
   if in secret you show partiality.
11 Will not his majesty terrify you
   and the dread of him fall upon you?
12 Your maxims are proverbs of ashes;
   your defenses are defenses of clay.

13 "Let me have silence, and I will speak,
   and let come on me what may.
14 I will take my flesh in my teeth
   and put my life in my hand.*l*
15 See, he will kill me; I have no hope;*m*
   but I will defend my ways to his
      face.
16 This will be my salvation,
   that the godless shall not come before
      him.
17 Listen carefully to my words,
   and let my declaration be in your
      ears.

18 I have indeed prepared my case;
   I know that I shall be vindicated.
19 Who is there who will contend with
      me?
   For then I would be silent and die.
20 "Only grant two things to me;
   then I will not hide myself from your
      face:
21 withdraw your hand far from me,
   and do not let dread of you terrify
      me.
22 Then call, and I will answer;
   or let me speak, and you reply to
      me.
23 How many are my iniquities and my sins?
   Make me know my transgression and
      my sin.
24 Why do you hide your face
   and count me as your enemy?
25 Will you frighten a windblown leaf
   and pursue dry chaff?
26 For you write bitter things against me
   and make me reap*n* the iniquities of
      my youth.
27 You put my feet in the stocks
   and watch all my paths;
   you set a bound to the soles of my
      feet.
28 One wastes away like a rotten thing,
   like a garment that is moth-eaten.

l 13.14 Gk: Heb *Why should I take . . . in my hand?*
m 13.15 Or *Though he kill me, yet I will trust in him*
n 13.26 Heb *inherit*

use knowledge as if it were a therapy. But Job points to the fundamental problem with traditional wisdom's *worthless* theory of well-being. Job will aver that silence is also a form of wisdom (vv. 5–6). See Prov. 17:28. **13:6** *Pleadings* in a legal sense, as in dispute, cause, or complaint (Heb. "riv"). **13:9–10** Somewhat anticipates YHWH's address to Eliphaz and the reparative actions the friends must take in 42:7–9. **13:12** Having searched and refuted a host of traditional proverbs and hymns, Job pronounces as dead the aphorisms that the friends used against him. **13:14–15a** What Job wants to do is dangerous and may kill him. **13:15** *I have no hope* can be read as "I hope in him." *No* and "in him" are homophones in Hebrew, which scribes marked as alternative readings (see textual note). The wordplay results in both an affirmation and a denial of Job's trust in God. This famous line has justified numerous theological interpretations of Job's character, but given the parodies in the chapter, the irony of the double entendre seems intentional. **13:16** Blocking false testimony is Job's pragmatic concern. **13:19** The friends will continue to contend with Job, perhaps because he just called them liars, worthless physicians, deceitful litigants, godless, and spokespeople of a dead tradition who are in need of rebuke. **13:20–28** Addressing God directly, Job's mood slides from pragmatically planning for a fair trial (vv. 20–22) to asking God ruminating questions about his misery (vv. 23–25). The etiology at the end develops Job's case that God is the agent of his suffering (vv. 26–28). **13:20–22** Job makes more plans for a fair legal hearing. Having asked his friends to stay silent, he asks God to stop overpowering and intimidating him. **13:21** *Withdraw your hand* refers to God as the cause of affliction. **13:24** *Enemy* ("oyev"), a possible wordplay on Job's name, "iyyov." **13:27** Returning to the theme that God watches people too closely (7:12–21), Job mashes together three phrases about *feet* and walking as symbols of imprisonment and surveillance. **14:1–22** Job just finished calling humans

14 "A mortal, born of woman, few of
days and full of trouble,
² comes up like a flower and withers,
flees like a shadow and does not last.
³ Do you fix your eyes on such a one?
Do you bring me into judgment with
you?
⁴ Who can bring a clean thing out of an
unclean?
No one can.
⁵ Since their days are determined,
and the number of their months is
known to you,
and you have appointed the bounds
that they cannot pass,
⁶ look away from them and desist,ᵒ
that they may enjoy, like laborers,
their days.

⁷ "For there is hope for a tree,
if it is cut down, that it will sprout
again
and that its shoots will not cease.
⁸ Though its root grows old in the earth
and its stump dies in the ground,
⁹ yet at the scent of water it will bud
and put forth branches like a young
plant.
¹⁰ But mortals die and are laid low;
humans expire, and where are they?
¹¹ As waters fail from a lake
and a river wastes away and dries up,
¹² so mortals lie down and do not rise again;
until the heavens are no more, they
will not awake
or be roused out of their sleep.

¹³ O that you would hide me in Sheol,
that you would conceal me until your
wrath is past,
that you would appoint me a set time
and remember me!
¹⁴ If mortals die, will they live again?
All the days of my service I would wait
until my release should come.
¹⁵ You would call, and I would answer you;
you would long for the work of your
hands.
¹⁶ For then you would notᵖ number my steps;
you would not keep watch over my sin;
¹⁷ my transgression would be sealed up in a
bag,
and you would cover over my iniquity.

¹⁸ "But the mountain falls and crumbles
away,
and the rock is removed from its place;
¹⁹ the waters wear away the stones;
the torrents wash away the soil of the
earth;
so you destroy the hope of mortals.
²⁰ You prevail forever against them, and
they pass away;
you change their countenance and
send them away.
²¹ Their children come to honor, and they
do not know it;
they are brought low, and it goes
unnoticed.
²² They feel only the pain of their own
bodies
and mourn only for themselves."

o 14.6 Cn: Heb *that they may desist* p 14.16 Syr: Heb lacks *not*

"dry chaff," "a rotten thing," and "moth-eaten" (13:25–28), a bleak theme that he carries into this chapter's opening statement (vv. 1–2). Job develops his previous argument: despite humans being formed by God (10:9–13; 14:15), God attacks and prevails over them (10:16–17; 14:20). However, Job seems to have subtly shifted his aesthetic values onto an image of the human as an evanescent flower. Thus, in one of Job's more gentle arguments, he asks why God would apply such assiduous scrutiny to this ephemeral creature (vv. 3–6). God's need to prevail against humans begins to look petulant (v. 20). **14:1** *Born of woman.* See chap. 3, especially vv. 11–12. **14:3** *Do you fix your eyes. . . . Do you bring me into judgment?* Rhetorical questions that highlight the absurdity of God's interactions with humans. **14:6** *Laborers* is the term also in v. 14; see also 7:1–2. **14:7–9** Attention to how trees regenerate. **14:8** *In the ground* is literally "dust." The dead tree stump dies in "dust," where it also revives (v. 9); this is also the word translated as "soil" in 14:19. **14:13** Recalls 3:17–19; 7:9; 10:20–22. On *Sheol,* see note on 7:9. **14:14** *Mortals.* See note on 3:3. **14:17** *Cover over* is the same term as "whitewash" from 13:4. **14:18–19** *Mountain, rock, stones,* and *soil,* a sequence that moves from the seemingly majestic and sturdy to the broken-down and carried away. But note that all four are subjected to destructive force (cf. 9:5–6). Ending on *soil* (the term for "dust") compares this material process to human decay (7:5, 21; 10:9; 17:16; see also Gen. 2:7; 3:19). Job's attention to the cycles of nature as a source of knowledge resembles the attention to the cycles of human generations, sun, wind, and water in Eccl. 1. **14:22** The end of Job's fourth speech presents a profound moment of self-awareness

15 Then Eliphaz the Temanite answered:
² "Should the wise answer with windy knowledge
and fill themselves with the east wind?
³ Should they argue in unprofitable talk
or in words that can do no good?
⁴ But you are doing away with the fear of God
and hindering meditation before God.
⁵ For your iniquity teaches your mouth,
and you choose the tongue of the crafty.
⁶ Your own mouth condemns you, not I;
your own lips testify against you.

⁷ "Are you the firstborn of the human race?
Were you brought forth before the hills?
⁸ Have you listened in the council of God?
And do you limit wisdom to yourself?
⁹ What do you know that we do not know?
What do you understand that is not clear to us?
¹⁰ The gray-haired and the aged are on our side,
those older than your father.
¹¹ Are the consolations of God too small for you
or the word that deals gently with you?
¹² Why does your heart carry you away,
and why do your eyes flash,^{q}
¹³ so that you turn your spirit against God,
and let such words go out of your mouth?
¹⁴ What are mortals, that they can be clean?
Or those born of woman, that they can be righteous?

q 15.12 Meaning of Heb uncertain

about a body in pain and mourning, but with a few options for translation, it is difficult to fully grasp what Job realizes. One possibility strikes notes of both continuity and closure: despite the ephemeral body of the human creature (13:25–14:2, 11, 18–19) and the lack of an afterlife (14:5, 12, 14, 20), the embodied human senses and feels it all (14:22).

15:1–21:34 The friends' second speeches (chaps. 15, 18, 20) and Job's eventual response (chap. 21) are focused on the life and fate of the wicked person. The friends' intense images highlight the moment of the person's devastation, generating sequential visual tableaus of terror and dread. Through the assault of these images, they rhetorically convey their tightly focused argument: the wicked person is nothing, has nothing, can do nothing, and eventually but inevitably comes to nothing. They hope Job will change course and receive instruction.

15:1–35 Eliphaz's second speech. Eliphaz changes his mind about Job's innocence (cf. 4:1–5:27), now finding fault in Job's moral arrogance. Responding to Job's dismissive attitude about sages and traditional wisdom (especially 12:2; 13:12), Eliphaz shifts the debate onto traditional wisdom itself, probably upset that Job defies advice and refuses instruction (Prov. 19:20). Dialing up the rhetoric to compel Job's submission, Eliphaz identifies Job's iniquity and describes the fate of the wicked. **15:2–16** Eliphaz disputes Job's claims of wisdom, but comedic irony emerges in light of the prose narrative. **15:4–6** Eliphaz no longer views Job as upright and righteous, assuming iniquity explains Job's offensive complaints. Eliphaz will go even further in his third speech (22:5). **15:4** Eliphaz is worried that Job's complaints are wrecking the religious experience. **15:8–11** Eliphaz presents several concepts related to traditional wisdom: the council of God as a privileged source, the superior pedagogy of age, and the ideal of collective wisdom vs. suspicion of isolated knowledge. He will use the authority of ancestral knowledge to present his views on the fate of the wicked (vv. 17–19). Readers had access to the council of God from the prose narrative (chaps. 1–2), an irony that sharply undercuts Eliphaz's self-perception as an authoritative sage. **15:11** *Consolations of God*. The friends came to Job's side to offer consolation (2:11), and Job is about to dismiss his friends as miserable comforters (16:2) using the same term. Here, Eliphaz claims that the three friends, joined by society's elders, are best fit to offer God's consolation. A wordplay may lead to the questioning of the character of God: the same Hebrew word is translated as *consolations* and "regret"; the phrase "regret of God" occurs roughly forty times in the Hebrew Bible. *Consolations*/regret here invites the question of whether God's regret is too small for the divine affliction he caused in Job's life. Compare the regret of God and the angel of destruction in 1 Chr. 21:15; that narrative draws many comparisons with the prose tale of Job. **15:11–35** Quoted in full by Jamaican artist Anna Ruth Henriques's painting of a tree, her mother's cancer, and the land of Jah's suffering in her series "The Book of Mechtilde." **15:14–16** Eliphaz reiterates his view that humans are nothing in relation to God

¹⁵ God puts no trust even in his holy ones,
  and the heavens are not clean in his
    sight;
¹⁶ how much less one who is abominable
    and corrupt,
  one who drinks iniquity like water!

¹⁷ "I will show you; listen to me—
  what I have seen I will declare—
¹⁸ what sages have told
  and their ancestors have not hidden,
¹⁹ to whom alone the land was given,
  and no stranger passed among them.
²⁰ The wicked writhe in pain all their days,
  through all the years that are laid up
    for the ruthless.
²¹ Terrifying sounds are in their ears;
  in prosperity the destroyer will come
    upon them.
²² They despair of returning from darkness,
  and they are destined for the sword.
²³ They wander abroad for bread, saying,
    'Where is it?'
  They know that a day of darkness is
    ready at hand;
²⁴ distress and anguish terrify them;
  they prevail against them like a king
    prepared for battle.
²⁵ Because they stretched out their hands
    against God
  and bid defiance to the Almighty,ʳ
²⁶ running stubbornly against him
  with a thickly bossed shield;
²⁷ because they have covered their faces
    with their fat
  and gathered fat upon their loins,

²⁸ they will live in desolate cities,
  in houses that no one should inhabit,
  houses destined to become heaps of
    ruins;
²⁹ they will not be rich, and their wealth
    will not endure,
  nor will they strike root in the earth;ˢ
³⁰ they will not escape from darkness;
  the flame will dry up their shoots,
  and their blossomᵗ will be swept away
    by the wind.
³¹ Let them not trust in emptiness,
    deceiving themselves,
  for emptiness will be their
    recompense.
³² It will be paid in full before their time,
  and their branch will not be green.
³³ They will shake off their unripe grape,
    like the vine,
  and cast off their blossoms, like the
    olive tree.
³⁴ For the company of the godless is
    barren,
  and fire consumes the tents of bribery.
³⁵ They conceive mischief and bring forth
    evil,
  and their belly prepares deceit."

16 Then Job answered:
²"I have heard many such things;
  miserable comforters are you all.
³ Have windy words no limit?
  Or what provokes you that you keep
    on talking?

r 15.25 Traditional rendering of Heb *Shaddai*   s 15.29 Vg:
Meaning of Heb uncertain   t 15.30 Gk: Heb *mouth*

(see 4:12–20). **15:17–35** Having just accused Job of iniquity (v. 16), Eliphaz describes the fate of the wicked. **15:20–22** The wicked person is psychically tormented by sounds of impending destruction. **15:23** Vultures eye the wicked person as a potential meal. **15:24–26** The wicked person is attacked by a warrior king, reversing his "playing the hero" against God. **15:25** On *Almighty*, see note on 6:4. **15:27–28** A well-fed hero dwells in a desolate city. **15:29–35** A series of images depicting futility, emptiness, failed fertility, and barrenness.

16:1–17:16 Job's fifth speech. Job conveys more acutely his suffering from social rejection and physical ailments. When he opens his fifth speech directly addressing his friends as *miserable comforters*, Job observes how often people stigmatize and deride victims. Some commenters see Job displaying empathy for his friends; however, his negative portrayal of them intensifies as they cause Job increased misery throughout this speech (16:2, 20; 17:2, 4–5, 8–9). Meanwhile, God's attack and Job's bodily symptoms intensify as well. Job expects that his gaunt body serves as evidence against him. So he announces that his disembodied cry (16:8) offers his best legal chance to succeed in his case before God (16:19–21). Since such a cry is only achieved through death (16:22), chap. 17 sustains another meditation on Job's terminal suffering, although once he mentions *Sheol* and the *Pit* (17:13–14), Job's big plans to decay into a pure scream fade, and his utter hopelessness returns (17:15–16). **16:1–5** After calling them *miserable comforters*, Job turns the tables on the friends, imagining how easily he could make them an object of derision if they were victims of suffering. **16:2** *Miserable comforters.* See "worthless physicians"

⁴ I also could talk as you do,
  if you were in my place;
I could join words together against
    you
  and shake my head at you.
⁵ I could encourage you with my mouth,
  and the solace of my lips would
    assuage your pain.

⁶ "If I speak, my pain is not assuaged,
  and if I refrain, how much of it leaves
    me?
⁷ Surely now God has worn me out;
  he has" made desolate all my
    company.
⁸ And he hasᵛ shriveled me up,
  which is a witness against me;
my leanness has risen up against me,
  and it testifies to my face.
⁹ He has torn me in his wrath and hated
    me;
  he has gnashed his teeth at me;
  my adversary sharpens his eyes
    against me.
¹⁰ They have gaped at me with their
    mouths;
  they have struck me insolently on the
    cheek;
  they mass themselves together against
    me.
¹¹ God gives me up to the evil
  and casts me into the hands of the
    wicked.

¹² I was at ease, and he broke me in two;
  he seized me by the neck and dashed
    me to pieces;
  he set me up as his target;
¹³   his archers surround me.
He slashes open my kidneys and shows
    no mercy;
  he pours out my gall on the ground.
¹⁴ He bursts upon me again and again;
  he rushes at me like a warrior.
¹⁵ I have sewed sackcloth upon my skin
  and have laid my strength in the dust.
¹⁶ My face is red with weeping,
  and deep darkness is on my eyelids,
¹⁷ though there is no violence in my hands,
  and my prayer is pure.

¹⁸ "O earth, do not cover my blood;
  let my outcry find no resting place.
¹⁹ Even now my witness is in heaven,
  and my advocate is on high.
²⁰ My friends scorn me;
  my eye pours out tears to God,
²¹ that he would maintain the right of a
    mortal with God,
  asʷ one does for a neighbor.
²² For when a few years have come,
  I shall go the way from which I shall
    not return.

17 "My spirit is broken; my days are extinct;
  the grave is ready for me.

u 16.7 Heb *you have*   v 16.8 Heb *you have*   w 16.21 Syr Vg
Tg: Heb *and*

in 13:4. **16:4** *Join words together*. Coupled with the image of a shaking head, these utterances seem to invoke a magical practice. **16:5** Job claims he could offer comfort. In the context, this appears to be rhetorical sarcasm (see v. 4b) inviting his friends to experience their own miserable comfort. Later, Job will announce his skill at comforting victims (29:21–25). **16:6** Job describes what it is like to try to put his suffering into words: his pain cannot be relieved; silence does not quell it, yet pain cannot be physically evacuated from the body. **16:7–8** God made Job's body gaunt, which acts as testimony against him (see 9:20). Notice the three words of litigation: *all my company* ("edah"), *witness* ("ed") *against me*, *testifies*. Although *company* is a common term for a general assembly, the pun with *witness* draws it into the drama of litigation (see v. 19). **16:14** *Warrior*, see "male," 3:3. **16:9–17** Job's most visceral description of God's attack so far (see 6:4; 9:17–18; 10:16–17). Using typical language of affliction, Job depicts God's assaults as if they were attacks by various kinds of opponents: a wild animal (vv. 9–10), a traitor (v. 11), and several kinds of direct warrior combatants (vv. 12–14). Compare with Lam. 3:1–20. **16:18** Job wants his cry of distress to outlast him, perhaps similar to Gen. 4:10, where Abel's blood cries out from the ground. See also Ezek. 24:7–8. This verse is inscribed at numerous Holocaust memorials in Poland, Latvia, Germany, and Israel. **16:19** *Advocate* is a term that only occurs here; etymologically it is related to *witness* ("'ed"). Job seems to be saying that his cry (v. 18) is his advocate in heaven. The belief that a cry can reach heaven/God is a Hebrew idiom (e.g., 1 Sam. 7:8–9; Ps. 142:1). Alternatively, it is possible that Job refers to the ancient tradition that heaven and earth, not his cry, will serve as unbiased witnesses (e.g., Deut. 32:1; Isa. 1:2). See also 9:3–13; 13:13–23; 16:18–21; 19:23–27; 23:2–14. **17:1–16** Job's *spirit is broken*. Given the antagonisms of *mockers* (v. 2), *those who denounce friends* (v. 5), the *upright* stirring themselves (v. 8), and

² Surely there are mockers around me,
  and my eye dwells on their
    provocation.

³ "Lay down a pledge for me with yourself;
  who is there who will give surety for
    me?
⁴ Since you have closed their minds to
    understanding,
  therefore you will not let them
    triumph.
⁵ Those who denounce friends for
    reward—
  the eyes of their children will fail.

⁶ "He has made me a byword of the
    peoples,
  and I am one before whom people spit.
⁷ My eye has grown dim from grief,
  and all my members are like a
    shadow.
⁸ The upright are appalled at this,
  and the innocent stir themselves up
    against the godless.
⁹ Yet the righteous hold to their way,
  and they who have clean hands grow
    stronger and stronger.
¹⁰ But you, come back now, all of you,
  and I shall not find a sensible person
    among you.
¹¹ My days are past; my plans are broken
    off,
  the desires of my heart.

¹² They make night into day;
  'The light,' they say, 'is near to the
    darkness.'ˣ
¹³ If I look for Sheol as my house,
  if I spread my couch in darkness,
¹⁴ if I say to the Pit, 'You are my father,'
  and to the worm, 'My mother' or 'My
    sister,'
¹⁵ where then is my hope?
  Who will see my hope?
¹⁶ Will it go down to the bars of Sheol?
  Shall we descend together into the
    dust?"

18 Then Bildad the Shuhite answered:
² "How long will you hunt for
    words?
  Consider, and then we shall speak.
³ Why are we counted as cattle?
  Why are we stupid in your sight?
⁴ You who tear yourself in your anger—
  shall the earth be forsaken because
    of you
  or the rock be removed out of its
    place?

⁵ "Surely the light of the wicked is put out,
  and the flame of their fire does not
    shine.
⁶ The light is dark in their tent,
  and the lamp above them is put out.

x 17.12 Meaning of Heb uncertain

the *righteous* growing stronger (v. 9), as well as the bullying scene described in v. 6, a big theme in this chapter is how acute social suffering can be. **17:8–10** Job is probably parodying the perspective of his friends, who still consider themselves correct about Job and take themselves to be *upright*, *innocent*, and *righteous*. This is a meditation on the injustice of bullying: Self-righteous folk are *appalled* at Job's ghastly body; they *stir themselves* against him and actually *grow stronger* as a result. Job pops that bubble in v. 10, calling them back to themselves with his own derision: there is not a *sensible person among you*. **17:12** Recalls the light/dark, day/night imagery in chap. 3. **17:13–14** *The Pit* is an evocative term used for deceptive or animal traps, often used to describe *Sheol* (see note on 7:9). Having lost his own family, Job imagines death itself in familial terms: *my house, my father, my mother, my sister*. *Worm* signifies death through bodily decomposition, suggesting that the only kinship available to Job is the symbiosis of compost (see "worm" in 7:5; 21:26; 24:20). **17:15–16** Job ends his fifth speech despondently on the *dust* of human dematerialization and wonders if his *hope*, probably his "outcry" (16:18), can be located or seen anywhere after he has decomposed. •

18:1–21 Bildad's second speech. Most of Bildad's speech describes the terrors that await the wicked person (vv. 5–21), a dramatic flip from his first speech (cf. 8:1–22), where he spoke about the possibility of a bright future for Job. The world Bildad constructs suggests he sees Job as a weakly attached person who cannot pitch a tent or secure roots on the earth, and with no one to remember his name (vv. 15–17), he will be forcibly removed: *such are the dwellings of the ungodly* (v. 21). **18:5–6** *Light . . . in their tent.* Often used as a metaphor for Job's body, *tent* is a theme word in Job discussed in seven of the friend speeches. Similarly, *light* is figurative for "vitality" or "life" (see Isa. 10:17; Ps. 4:6; 27:1; 36:9; 56:13; 97:11; Prov. 16:15). See also Bildad's metaphor of "water" in

7 Their strong steps are shortened,
and their own schemes throw them
down.
8 For they are thrust into a net by their
own feet,
and they walk into a pitfall.
9 A trap seizes them by the heel;
a snare lays hold of them.
10 A rope is hid for them in the ground,
a trap for them in the path.
11 Terrors frighten them on every side
and chase them at their heels.
12 Their strength is consumed by hunger,[y]
and calamity is ready for their
stumbling.
13 By disease their skin is consumed;[z]
the firstborn of Death consumes their
limbs.
14 They are torn from the tent in which
they trusted
and are brought to the king of
terrors.
15 In their tents nothing remains;
sulfur is scattered upon their
habitations.
16 Their roots dry up beneath,
and their branches wither above.
17 Their memory perishes from the earth,
and they have no name in the street.
18 They are thrust from light into darkness
and driven out of the world.
19 They have no offspring or descendant
among their people
and no survivor where they used to
live.

20 They of the west are appalled at their
fate,
and horror seizes those of the east.
21 Surely such are the dwellings of the
ungodly;
such is the place of those who do not
know God."

19 Then Job answered:
2 "How long will you torment me
and break me in pieces with words?
3 These ten times you have cast reproach
upon me;
are you not ashamed to wrong me?
4 And even if it is true that I have erred,
my error remains with me.
5 If indeed you magnify yourselves against
me
and make my humiliation an
argument against me,
6 know then that God has put me in the
wrong
and closed his net around me.
7 Even when I cry out, 'Violence!' I am not
answered;
I call aloud, but there is no justice.
8 He has walled up my way so that I
cannot pass,
and he has set darkness upon my
paths.
9 He has stripped my glory from me
and taken the crown from my
head.

y 18.12 Or *Disaster is hungry for them*   z 18.13 Cn: Heb *It
consumes the limbs of his skin*

8:11. **18:7** *Schemes* is a common word in the book of Proverbs where it is positively understood as "advice" (Prov. 8:14; 12:15); instead, in Job, the word is frequently associated with the wicked like here and in the phrase "plans of the wicked" (see 22:18). For Bildad, destruction is not divine punishment; it is self-generated. **18:8–10** The wisdom trope of *feet*, taking steps, and walking the path is applied here to the wicked person whose landscape is riddled with baited traps. **18:11–14** Terror is represented as a ravenous chase on the wicked person's body (*heels, strength, skin, limbs*). With several references to eating, the consumer is consumed. **18:13** *Firstborn of Death* is a plague. **18:15** *Sulfur is scattered.* See Deut. 29:22. **18:17** *No name in the street* is the title of a famous James Baldwin essay. **18:18** *Driven out of the world* indicates that the goal for Bildad has been to purge the livable world of wicked people.

19:1–29 Job's sixth speech. Job's three speeches in this cycle (chaps. 12–19) have focused on his claim that God is the unjust and aggressive agent of his suffering (vv. 6–12). Important themes in Job's perspective were announced in the opening lines of this cycle (12:3–4): "I have understanding," "I am not inferior," and "I am a laughingstock to my friends." Although Bildad just eviscerated Job, suggestively calling him wicked and ungodly in chap. 18, Job stays focused on characterizing his friends as tormentors (19:2), describing the intensity of his social suffering (19:13–22), and defending his understanding of God, making one last appeal for his friends' pity (19:21). Job will not engage traditional teachings about the wicked until chap. 21. **19:1–5** Job's friends *torment* and *break* (v. 2), *cast reproach* and *wrong* (v. 3), and *magnify* themselves against Job (v. 5). **19:6, 8–12** God's attacks

¹⁰ He breaks me down on every side, and I
  am gone;
  he has uprooted my hope like a tree.
¹¹ He has kindled his wrath against me
  and counts me as his adversary.
¹² His troops come on together;
  they have thrown up siegeworks*a*
  against me
  and encamp around my tent.

¹³ "He has put my family far from me,
  and my acquaintances are wholly
  estranged from me.
¹⁴ My relatives and my close friends have
  failed me;
¹⁵   the guests in my house have
  forgotten me;
  my female servants count me as a
  stranger;
  I have become an alien in their eyes.
¹⁶ I call to my servant, but he gives me no
  answer;
  I must myself plead with him.
¹⁷ My breath is repulsive to my wife;
  I am loathsome to my own family.
¹⁸ Even young children despise me;
  when I rise, they talk against me.
¹⁹ All my intimate friends abhor me,
  and those whom I love have turned
  against me.
²⁰ My bones cling to my skin and to my
  flesh,

and I have escaped by the skin of my
  teeth.
²¹ Have pity on me, have pity on me, O you
  my friends,
  for the hand of God has touched me!
²² Why do you, like God, pursue me,
  never satisfied with my flesh?

²³ "O that my words were written down!
  O that they were inscribed in a book!
²⁴ O that with an iron pen and with lead
  they were engraved on a rock
  forever!
²⁵ For I know that my vindicator*b* lives
  and that in the end he will stand upon
  the earth;
²⁶ and after my skin has been destroyed,
  then in my flesh I shall see God,
²⁷ whom I shall see on my side,
  and my eyes shall behold, and not
  another.
  My heart faints within me!
²⁸ If you say, 'How we will persecute him!'
  and, 'The root of the matter is found
  in him,'
²⁹ be afraid of the sword,
  for wrath brings the punishment of
  the sword,
  so that you may know there is a
  judgment."

a 19.12 Cn: Heb *their way*   *b* 19.25 Or *redeemer*

on Job. See also 6:4; 9:17–18; 10:16–17; 16:9–17. **19:13–19** This is Job's most personal and sustained description of social suffering so far, from brothers (v. 13) to loved ones (v. 19). Note that Job makes no distinctions between relationships structured by domination (his enslaved men and women in vv. 15–16) and his other more reciprocal relationships, although power circulates even here (especially through gendered systems of honor in ancient social life). Job is anguished by each of his companions' various acts of forgetting, estrangement, repulsion, and derision. Indeed, the list culminates in an intense description of Job's painful physical symptoms (v. 20). **19:13** *Family* is literally "my brothers." In chap. 1, Job's children and the people enslaved by him die. **19:15b–16** *Female servants* enslaved to Job esteem their former enslaver as a *stranger* and an *alien*. The male enslaved *servant* does not answer Job, even if he begs. **19:17** *My wife*. Job's wife speaks in 2:9 and is referenced again in 31:10. **19:21–22** Remarkably, Job still asks for pity from his friends. **19:23–24** Written words are imagined in a *book* and on a *rock*. **19:24** *Forever* can be read as "for a witness" in Hebrew, in keeping with Job's search for a legal advocate (16:8, 19). **19:25** *Vindicator* is a common word in legal, prophetic, and psalmic literature. Four interpretations for this figure are possible: Job's own inscribed voice (19:23–24; see also 16:18), a living person (Ruth 4:10; Isa. 44:6), a divine being (Job 9:33; 16:19; see also Gen. 48:16), or God (Ps. 69:18; Isa. 50:8). *The earth*, literally "dust," is an important theme word usually associated with death (see note on 2:12). **19:26** *After my skin has been destroyed* is not typical language for death. Given that Job's illness began as a skin disease (2:7), Job's gruesome self-portrait of his eyes in a flayed body is most likely the figurative language of an illness narrative. *Skin . . . flesh*. Job frequently portrays both skin and flesh as clothing (7:5; 10:11; 19:20). **19:29** *Judgment* only translates part of the Hebrew word, and several different readings have been proposed that take the whole word into account, like "overpowering destruction." "Demons" is also possible.

20

Then Zophar the Naamathite answered:

² "Listen! My thoughts urge me to answer
because of the agitation within me.
³ I hear censure that insults me,
and a spirit beyond my understanding
answers me.
⁴ Do you not know this from of old,
ever since mortals were placed on
earth,
⁵ that the exulting of the wicked is short
and the joy of the godless is but for a
moment?
⁶ Even though they mount up high as the
heavens
and their head reaches to the clouds,
⁷ they will perish forever like their own
dung;
those who have seen them will say,
'Where are they?'
⁸ They will fly away like a dream and not
be found;
they will be chased away like a vision
of the night.
⁹ The eye that saw them will see them no
more,
nor will their place behold them any
longer.
¹⁰ Their children will seek the favor of the
poor,
and their hands will give back their
wealth.
¹¹ Their bodies, once full of youth,
will lie down in the dust with them.

¹² "Though wickedness is sweet in their
mouth,
though they hide it under their tongues,
¹³ though they are loath to let it go
and hold it in their mouths,
¹⁴ yet their food is turned in their
stomachs;
it is the venom of asps within them.
¹⁵ They swallow down riches and vomit
them up again;
God casts them out of their bellies.
¹⁶ They will suck the poison of asps;
the tongue of a viper will kill them.
¹⁷ They will not look on the rivers,
the streams flowing with honey and
curds.
¹⁸ They will give back the fruit of their toil
and will not swallow it down;
from the profit of their trading
they will get no enjoyment.
¹⁹ For they have crushed and abandoned
the poor;
they have seized a house that they did
not build.

²⁰ "For they knew no quiet in their
bellies;
in their greed they let nothing escape.
²¹ There was nothing left after they had
eaten;
therefore their prosperity will not
endure.
²² In full sufficiency they will be in distress;
all the force of misery will come upon
them.
²³ To fill their belly to the full,
God^c will send his fierce anger into
them
and rain it upon them as their food.

c 20.23 Heb he

20:1–29 **Zophar's second speech. 20:1–3** Zophar reacts to Job's insulting speech, calling into question, once again, Job's traditional wisdom (v. 4). **20:4–29** Zophar's descriptions of the fate of wicked people especially address Job's examples and the problem of wicked people who are successful and happy. **20:11** The vigorous *bodies* echo themes of fertility, procreation, and offspring, contrasted succinctly here with the *dust* of death and much more vulgar images to come. **20:12–23** Wickedness as a voracious appetite; Zophar makes extensive use of food and belly metaphors. By this point, Zophar combines his economic critique of the success of wicked people with moral disgust at abject bodily images like dung, vomiting, sucking, and euphemisms for semen (see **"Disgust, Defilement, and Impurity," p. 1162**). In a much more staid fashion, Eliphaz described the food of the wicked (15:23) and will accuse Job of denying food and water to people in poverty (22:7). **20:12–16** Various words for venoms represent one of Mesopotamia's oldest "natural" medical discourses. Plenty of nefarious magical agents were associated with venom (e.g., fierce anger in v. 23), but these terms are based loosely on the knowledge that the belly contains gall / bitter juice. **20:19** The friends' speeches do little to explain what actions constitute wickedness, so Zophar's description here is rare. The economic abuse of power crushes and abandons the poor and seizes houses by force; this verse is reflective of Zophar's economic critique.

²⁴ They will flee from an iron weapon;
  a bronze arrow will strike them
    through.
²⁵ It is drawn forth and comes out of their
    body,
  and the glittering point comes out of
    their gall;
  terrors come upon them.
²⁶ Utter darkness is laid up for their
    treasures;
  a fire fanned by no one will devour
    them;
  what is left in their tent will be
    consumed.
²⁷ The heavens will reveal their iniquity,
  and the earth will rise up against
    them.
²⁸ The possessions of their house will be
    carried away,
  dragged off in the day of God's*d* wrath.
²⁹ This is the portion of the wicked from God,
  the heritage decreed for them by God."

21 Then Job answered:
²"Listen carefully to my words,
  and let this be your consolation.
³ Bear with me, and I will speak;
  then after I have spoken, mock on.
⁴ As for me, is my complaint addressed to
    mortals?
  Why should I not be impatient?
⁵ Look at me and be appalled,
  and lay your hand upon your mouth.
⁶ When I think of it I am dismayed,
  and shuddering seizes my flesh.

⁷ Why do the wicked live on,
  reach old age, and grow mighty in
    power?
⁸ Their children are established in their
    presence
  and their offspring before their eyes.
⁹ Their houses are safe from fear,
  and no rod of God is upon them.
¹⁰ Their bull breeds without fail;
  their cow calves and never miscarries.
¹¹ They send out their little ones like a flock,
  and their children dance around.
¹² They sing to the tambourine and the lyre
  and rejoice to the sound of the pipe.
¹³ They spend their days in prosperity,
  and in peace they go down to Sheol.
¹⁴ They say to God, 'Leave us alone!
  We do not desire to know your ways.
¹⁵ What is the Almighty,*e* that we should
    serve him?
  And what profit do we get if we pray
    to him?'
¹⁶ Is not their prosperity indeed their own
    achievement?*f*
  The plans of the wicked are repugnant
    to me.

¹⁷ "How often is the lamp of the wicked
    put out?
  How often does calamity come upon
    them?
  How often does God*g* distribute pains
    in his anger?

---

d 20.28 Heb *his*   *e* 21.15 Traditional rendering of Heb
Shaddai   *f* 21.16 Heb *in their hand*   *g* 21.17 Heb *he*

21:1–27:23 Third cycle of speeches.
21:1–34 Job's seventh speech. Up to this point, Job has defended himself as a righteous sufferer, urging his friends to agree that his illness is caused by senseless divine attack. Job now finally refutes the friends' claims that the wicked cannot prosper and are always met with suffering, especially in responding to Bildad (chap. 18) and Zophar (chap. 20). Instead of misery and hardship, Job argues, the wicked live long, happy, healthy lives (vv. 7–13) and enjoy a good death (vv. 13, 23–24, 32–33). See Jer. 12:1–2. As for his relationship with his friends, Job earlier called them "miserable comforters" (16:2), and he now offers them advice about how they should comfort him (vv. 2, 34). **21:2** Job instructs his friends to console him by listening. *Consolation* is a noun form of the same verb in 2:11; 16:2; and 21:34. **21:3** *Mock on.* Job appears to be resigned to the antagonism of his friends. **21:4** If there was any doubt before, Job explicitly states that he is frustrated to be in dialogue with his friends when he really wants a debate with God. See 13:1–19. **21:7–13** Note the clear theme of well-being through reproduction and offspring (vv. 8, 10, 11). *Houses* (v. 9) can just mean architectural structures, but the emphasis here is on family, household, and probably descendants. *In peace they go down to Sheol* (v. 13) is at least in part enabled by the memorial and veneration practices carried out by the living family (see **"Sheol," p. 695**). **21:7** Job refutes Zophar (20:11). **21:8** Job refutes Bildad (18:19). **21:9** Job refutes Eliphaz (5:24). **21:13** On *Sheol*, see note on 7:9. **21:15** On *Almighty*, see note on 6:4. **21:16–31** Job demands evidence that any traditional aphorisms about the wicked are true. **21:17** Job refutes Bildad (18:5) by naming God's *anger* as the cause of

¹⁸ How often are they like straw before the wind
and like chaff that the storm carries away?
¹⁹ You say, 'God stores up their iniquity for their children.'
Let it be paid back to them, so that they may know it.
²⁰ Let their own eyes see their destruction,
and let them drink of the wrath of the Almighty.^b
²¹ For what do they care for their household after them,
when the number of their months is cut off?
²² Will any teach God knowledge,
seeing that he judges those who are on high?
²³ One dies in full prosperity,
being wholly at ease and secure,
²⁴ his loins full of milk
and the marrow of his bones moist.
²⁵ Another dies in bitterness of soul,
never having tasted of good.
²⁶ They lie down alike in the dust,
and the worms cover them.

²⁷ "Oh, I know your thoughts
and your schemes to wrong me.
²⁸ For you say, 'Where is the house of the prince?
Where is the tent in which the wicked lived?'
²⁹ Have you not asked those who travel the roads,
and do you not accept their testimony,
³⁰ that the wicked are spared in the day of calamity
and are rescued in the day of wrath?
³¹ Who declares their way to their face,
and who repays them for what they have done?
³² When they are carried to the grave,
a watch is kept over their tomb.
³³ The clods of the valley are sweet to them;
everyone will follow after,
and those who went before are innumerable.
³⁴ How then will you comfort me with empty nothings?
There is nothing left of your answers but falsehood."

22 Then Eliphaz the Temanite answered:
² "Can a mortal be of use to God?
Can even the wisest be of service to him?
³ Is it any pleasure to the Almightyⁱ if you are righteous,
or is it gain to him if you make your ways blameless?
⁴ Is it for your piety that he reproves you
and enters into judgment with you?
⁵ Is not your wickedness great?
There is no end to your iniquities.
⁶ For you have exacted pledges from your family for no reason
and stripped the naked of their clothing.

b 21.20 Traditional rendering of Heb *Shaddai*   i 22.3 Traditional rendering of Heb *Shaddai*

the extinguished *lamp*. See Prov. 13:9; 24:20. **21:18** *Straw before the wind*, see Ps. 35:5. *Like chaff that the storm carries away*, see Ps. 1:4. **21:19** *You say* is not in the Hebrew text. It is inserted because Job quotes the views of Bildad in 18:12, 19 and Zophar in 20:20–21. **21:22–26** Since Job's speeches can be read as an illness narrative, this passage stands out as his most straightforward description of healthy bodies and sick bodies. Job attributes no disease agency to morality. Both body images are presented at their moments of death as equally fated to the same processes of decomposition. **21:31** *Who declares . . . ?* Job asks a fresh question. Up to now, Job has asked who would mediate or advocate for the innocent. Now Job asks who confronts the wicked, developing the book's broad theme of unknown or mysterious divine agencies.

22:1–30 Eliphaz's third speech. Eliphaz was initially confident Job was innocent, depicting suffering as an occasion for moral correction (chap. 5). Then Eliphaz found Job's speech offensive, which at least explained the cause of his suffering (chap. 15). Now Eliphaz views Job's suffering as God's judgment on his (alleged) wicked acts. The main topic of recent exchanges has been the fate of the wicked person (Eliphaz in chap. 15, Bildad in chap. 18, Zophar in chap. 20, and Job in chap. 21). **22:2–11** Eliphaz now accuses Job of acts of iniquity, which automatically bring divine judgment. **22:3** On *Almighty*, see note on 6:4. Also vv. 17, 23, 25–26. **22:6–9** The list of accusations echoes Israelite ethical injunctions designed to protect disadvantaged people. **22:6** *For no reason*. God admitted that he destroyed Job "for no

7 You have given no water to the weary to
   drink,
   and you have withheld bread from the
   hungry.
8 The powerful possess the land,
   and the favored live in it.
9 You have sent widows away
   empty-handed,
   and the arms of the orphans you have
   crushed.*j*
10 Therefore snares are around you,
   and sudden terror overwhelms you,
11 or darkness so that you cannot see;
   a flood of water covers you.

12 "Is not God high in the heavens?
   See the highest stars, how lofty they
   are!
13 Therefore you say, 'What does God know?
   Can he judge through the deep
   darkness?
14 Thick clouds enwrap him, so that he
   does not see,
   and he walks on the dome of heaven.'
15 Will you keep to the old way
   that the wicked have trod?
16 They were snatched away before their
   time;
   their foundation was washed away by
   a flood.
17 They said to God, 'Leave us alone,'
   and 'What can the Almighty*k* do to us?'*l*
18 Yet he filled their houses with good
   things—
   but the plans of the wicked are
   repugnant to me.
19 The righteous see it and are glad;
   the innocent laugh them to scorn,
20 saying, 'Surely our adversaries are cut
   off,
   and what they left, the fire has
   consumed.'

21 "Agree with God,*m* and be at peace;
   in this way good will come to you.
22 Receive instruction from his mouth,
   and lay up his words in your heart.
23 If you return to the Almighty,*n* you will
   be restored,
   if you remove unrighteousness from
   your tents,
24 if you treat gold like dust
   and gold of Ophir like the stones of
   the torrent bed,
25 and if the Almighty*o* is your gold
   and your precious silver,
26 then you will delight yourself in the
   Almighty*p*
   and lift up your face to God.
27 You will pray to him, and he will hear
   you,
   and you will pay your vows.
28 You will decide on a matter, and it will
   be established for you,
   and light will shine on your ways.
29 When others are humiliated, you say it is
   pride,
   for he saves the humble.
30 He will deliver even those who are
   guilty;
   they will escape because of the
   cleanness of your hands."*q*

23 Then Job answered:
2 "Today also my complaint is bitter;*r*
   his*s* hand is heavy despite my
   groaning.
3 Oh, that I knew where I might find him,
   that I might come even to his dwelling!

j 22.9 Gk Syr Tg Vg: Heb *were crushed*   *k* 22.17 Traditional rendering of Heb *Shaddai*   *l* 22.17 Gk Syr: Heb
them   *m* 22.21 Heb *him*   *n* 22.23 Traditional rendering
of Heb *Shaddai*   *o* 22.25 Traditional rendering of Heb
Shaddai   *p* 22.26 Traditional rendering of Heb *Shaddai*
q 22.30 Meaning of Heb uncertain   *r* 23.2 Syr Vg Tg: Heb
rebellious   *s* 23.2 Gk Syr: Heb *my*

reason" in 2:3. Israelite laws were strict regarding debts, pledges, and interest, which included clothing, to limit the power of the wealthy over the poor. **22:10–11** The consequences of Job's wickedness,
according to Eliphaz. **22:18** Eliphaz suddenly breaks off, probably because of his repugnance at the
whole topic. The poetic device of aposiopesis foreshadows the breakdown of the dialogues between
Job and his friends (see chap. 25 and 31:40). **22:21** *Agree with God.* The Hebrew term has several
meanings, including "caretake" or "get in harmony" with the disadvantaged. The word *God* is not in the
Hebrew. There is a wordplay between *be at peace* and "pay your vows," advice Eliphaz will give in v. 27.
22:26 *Lift up your face,* see note on 11:15. **22:28–30** Overcoming suffering is imagined as restoration to
a social position of honor and power. See 11:19–20; chap. 29. In this depiction of restored honor, Eliphaz
describes the local "big man," a remarkable role in which Job would function like God.
   23:1–24:25 Job's eighth speech.
   23:3 Job cannot find God's whereabouts. See vv. 8–9.

⁴ I would lay my case before him
and fill my mouth with arguments.
⁵ I would learn what he would answer me
and understand what he would say to
me.
⁶ Would he contend with me in the
greatness of his power?
No, but he would give heed to me.
⁷ There the upright could reason with
him,
and I should be acquitted forever by
my judge.

⁸ "If I go forward, he is not there;
or backward, I cannot perceive him;
⁹ on the left he hides, and I cannot behold
him;
I turn^t to the right, but I cannot see him.
¹⁰ But he knows the way that I take;
when he has tested me, I shall come
out like gold.
¹¹ My foot has held fast to his steps;
I have kept his way and have not
turned aside.
¹² I have not departed from the
commandment of his lips;

I have treasured his words in my
bosom."^u
¹³ But he stands alone, and who can
dissuade him?
What he desires, that he does.
¹⁴ For he will complete what he appoints
for me,
and many such things are in his
mind.
¹⁵ Therefore I am terrified at his presence;
when I consider, I am in dread of
him.
¹⁶ God has made my heart faint;
the Almighty^v has terrified me.
¹⁷ If only I could vanish in darkness,
and thick darkness would cover my
face!^w

24 "Why are times not kept by the
Almighty,^x
and why do those who know him
never see his days?

t 23.9 Syr Vg: Heb *he turns*   *u* 23.12 Gk: Heb *words more than my daily bread*   *v* 23.16 Traditional rendering of Heb *Shaddai*   *w* 23.17 Or *But I am not destroyed by the darkness; he has concealed the thick darkness from me*   *x* 24.1 Traditional rendering of Heb *Shaddai*

23:4–7 Lawsuit against God. In Job's first discussion of a lawsuit against God, he concluded that God litigates unfairly using strong-arm tactics (9:3–19). So Job tries to plan for a fair trial (13:8, 20–22) and considers whether he needs a mediator (9:33), an advocate (16:19), and a vindicator (19:25). Throughout these calls for a trial, Job questions whether his sick voice could adequately testify before God, exploring the perceived capabilities of his options: embodied voice (7:11), disembodied voice (16:8), and written words (19:23–24). Now in 23:4–7, Job seems more confident in his bitter/rebellious complaints (v. 2) and in his mouthful of arguments (v. 4), if only he could find the right place for a trial (v. 7).

23:8–9 Job's description of an imperceptible God in constant watch who hides just outside of view is a great example of the horror themes sometimes found in the book of Job. *Forward . . . backward . . . left . . . right*, these terms can also refer to the cardinal directions: east, west, north, south.

23:8–17 Where can God be found? Terminology and ideas in this passage will be taken up and developed in chap. 28, the poem that asks where the place of understanding is. Chap. 28 culminates in an important concept in later sapiential thought: "fear of God" as the beginning of wisdom (28:28). Here, Job connects understanding and terror of God in v. 15. Other connections: *He is not there . . . he hides* (vv. 8–9; see 28:12, 20, 21, 23); *I cannot perceive* (v. 8; cf. 28:12, 20, 23, 28); *he knows the way* (v. 10; see 28:23); *tested . . . gold* (v. 10; see 28:1–6, 13, 15–19); *from the commandment . . . what he appoints* (vv. 12, 14; see 28:26–27); *I consider* (v. 15; see 28:12, 20, 23, 28); *I am terrified . . . in dread . . . terrified* (vv. 15–16; see 28:28). **23:11–12** Resembles a conventional wisdom psalm (e.g., Ps. 119). **23:13** *But he stands alone* is literally "He is in one." Lacking a verb, several readings are possible: he desires one thing, he chooses one fate, he speaks in one way, he walks one path, and he commits to one action. These options generate a bit of irony in light of the prose tale (chaps. 1–2), where a divine council surrounds God and the accuser sways God's intentions and actions (1:6–12; 2:1–6). **23:15** *At his presence* is literally "from his face." **23:16** On *Almighty*, see note on 6:4. **23:17** There is repeated use of the word *face* in Hebrew: God's face ("presence" in v. 15), the face of darkness (*darkness* in v. 17a), and Job's *face* (v. 17b).

24:1–25 Job describes the violence and embodied experiences of the wicked, especially noting the consequences of their actions on the lives of the innocent poor (especially vv. 3–4, 9, 14, 21; see **"The Bible and Social Justice," pp. 2165–67**). **24:1** *Why are times not kept.* Either "Why have

² The wicked^y remove landmarks;
    they seize flocks and pasture
      them.
³ They drive away the donkey of the
    orphan;
    they take the widow's ox for a pledge.
⁴ They thrust the needy off the road;
    the poor of the earth all hide
      themselves.
⁵ Like wild asses in the desert
    they go out to their toil,
    scavenging in the wasteland
      food for their young.
⁶ They reap in a field not their own,
    and they glean in the vineyard of the
      wicked.
⁷ They lie all night naked, without
    clothing,
    and have no covering in the cold.
⁸ They are wet with the rain of the
    mountains
    and cling to the rock for want of
      shelter.

⁹ "There are those who snatch the orphan
    child from the breast
    and take as a pledge the infant of the
      poor.
¹⁰ They go about naked, without
    clothing;
    though hungry, they carry the sheaves;
¹¹ between their terraces^z they press out
    oil;
    they tread the winepresses but suffer
      thirst.

¹² From the city the dying groan,
    and the throat of the wounded cries
      for help;
    yet God pays no attention to their prayer.

¹³ "There are those who rebel against the
    light,
    who are not acquainted with its ways
    and do not stay in its paths.
¹⁴ The murderer rises at dusk
    to kill the poor and needy
    and in the night is like a thief.
¹⁵ The eye of the adulterer also waits for
    the twilight,
    saying, 'No eye will see me,'
    and he disguises his face.
¹⁶ In the dark they dig through houses;
    by day they shut themselves up;
    they do not know the light.
¹⁷ For deep darkness is morning to all of them;
    for they are friends with the terrors of
      deep darkness.

¹⁸ "Swift are they on the face of the
    waters;
    their portion in the land is cursed;
    no treader turns toward their vineyards.
¹⁹ Drought and heat snatch away the snow
    waters;
    so does Sheol those who have sinned.
²⁰ The womb forgets them;
    the worm finds them sweet;
    they are no longer remembered,
    so wickedness is broken like a tree.

y 24.2 Gk: Heb *they*   *z* 24.11 Meaning of Heb uncertain

the appointed times (for justice) not been kept by the Almighty?" or "Why have the times (of wrath) not been stocked up by the Almighty?" On *Almighty*, see note on 6:4. **24:2–12** Except for v. 12, all the descriptions of the wicked involve agricultural and wilderness settings. **24:2** *Remove landmarks* is literally "boundaries," meaning to seize or exploit other people's land. This act is frequently prohibited in the Hebrew Scriptures (Deut. 19:14; 27:17; Prov. 22:28; 23:10; Hos. 5:10). **24:3** *Orphan . . . widow* are of frequent concern in Torah and prophetic literature (Deut. 24:17–19; Isa. 1:17; Zech. 7:10). *Pledge.* Eliphaz accuses Job of taking pledges from his brothers in a longer set of accusations about Job's wickedness (22:6). **24:4** *The poor of the earth* become destitute (vv. 5–8) because of the exploitive economic practices of the wicked (vv. 2–3). **24:5** *Scavenging . . . for their young.* See 38:39, 41; 39:28, 30. **24:9** *And take as a pledge the infant of the poor.* Children could become enslaved to pay off family debts (2 Kgs. 4:1; Neh. 5:1–5). **24:13** See Job's meditation on day/light in 3:9, 16, 20. **24:16** *They do not know the light.* See 38:15. **24:17** *Deep darkness.* Job's discourse on the wicked led him to the symbols of light, morning, and darkness, the same symbols used when he cursed the day of his birth in chap. 3. **24:18–24** This passage is unusually difficult to translate and seems out of place. Several ideas seem to contradict Job's perspective on the wicked from chap. 21 and instead echo the views of his friends. Some take it as a misplaced response to Job, either adding it to Bildad's truncated speech in chap. 25, placing it after 24:25 as an anonymous response to Job's eighth speech (chaps. 23–24), or taking it as Zophar's missing third speech, which could go somewhere between Bildad and Elihu (chaps. 25–32). **24:19** On *Sheol*, see note on

21 "They harm[a] the childless woman
  and do no good to the widow.
22 Yet God[b] prolongs the life of the mighty
    by his power;
  they rise up when they despair of life.
23 He gives them security, and they are
    supported;
  his eyes are upon their ways.
24 They are exalted a little while and then
    are gone;
  they wither and fade like the mallow;[c]
  they are cut off like the heads of grain.
25 If it is not so, who will prove me a liar
  and show that there is nothing in what
    I say?"

25 Then Bildad the Shuhite answered:
    2 "Dominion and fear are with God;[d]
  he makes peace in his high heaven.
3 Is there any number to his armies?
  Upon whom does his light not arise?
4 How then can a mortal be righteous
    before God?
  How can one born of woman be pure?
5 If even the moon is not bright
  and the stars are not pure in his sight,
6 how much less a mortal, who is a maggot,
  and a human being, who is a worm!"

26 Then Job answered:
    2 "How you have helped one who has
      no power!
  How you have assisted the arm that
    has no strength!
3 How you have counseled one who has no
    wisdom
  and given much good advice!
4 With whose help have you uttered words,
  and whose spirit has come forth from
    you?
5 The shades below tremble,
  the waters and their inhabitants.
6 Sheol is naked before God,
  and Abaddon has no covering.
7 He stretches out Zaphon[e] over the void
  and hangs the earth upon nothing.
8 He binds up the waters in his thick clouds,
  and the cloud is not torn open by them.
9 He covers the face of the full moon
  and spreads over it his cloud.
10 He has described a circle on the face of
    the waters,
  at the boundary between light and
    darkness.

a 24.21 Gk Tg: Heb *feed on* or *associate with*   *b* 24.22 Heb *he*
c 24.24 Gk: Heb *like all others*   *d* 25.2 Heb *him*   *e* 26.7 Or
the North

7:9. **24:25** *In what I say* is literally "my utterance" or "my words." The term is rare outside of Job, but within the book, it occurs thirty-five times. Job critiques his friends for reproving his words (6:26), and their words of torment break him (19:2). Job also wants his words to be heard when he asks for his friends' silence (13:17), seeks the comfort of words being heard (21:2), and wishes that his words could be written down for a permanent testimony (19:23). With similar persistence, Elihu will ask Job to listen to his words in chaps. 32–37 (see 33:1; 34:16; 36:4). **25:1–6 Bildad's third speech.** A truncated speech, lacking an introduction and a conclusion. Zophar will not even speak a third time, making this the final friend speech before Elihu enters in chap. 32. It is very possible that Zophar's and portions of Bildad's speeches were inserted into Job's mouth (especially 24:18–24; 26:5–14; 27:8–23; 28:1–28). Such editorial disruption conveys the breakdown in dialogue, already anticipated in 22:18 and suggested by subtle interventions of the narrator (27:1; 29:1; 31:40). **25:4–6** Like Eliphaz in chaps. 4 and 15, Bildad expresses his view that humans are nothing in relation to God. **25:6** *Maggot.* Job refers to maggots four times, but always relationally, as clothing (7:5), covers (21:26), consumers (24:20), and even family to humans (17:14). **26:1–31:40 Job's ninth and final speech.**
    26:2–4 Job continues to experience his friends' profuse advice as counsel without wisdom (v. 3). **26:4** *Whose spirit has come forth* is a "who" question to identify the speaking subject. This is a typical question posed in cultures of spirit possession.
    26:5–14 These verses are widely viewed as responding to Job and do not represent Job's own words. Most scholars place them in the mouth of Bildad to elongate his speech after he is cut off at 25:6. **26:6** On *Sheol*, see note on 7:9. Job describes *Sheol*, the Israelite underworld and location of all human afterlives, as concealed from God's gaze (e.g., 10:18–22; see also Ps. 139:8, 11; see **"Sheol," p. 695**). *Abaddon* is the realm of oblivion, another name for the realm of the dead (28:22; 31:12). **26:7–14** The Syro-Canaanite myths of Baal, a weather god, complement the weather metaphors (vv. 8–11) and explain the images of mythic combat (vv. 12–13) in these verses. See also 7:12. **26:7** *Zaphon* is the mountain associated with Baal. **26:10** *Described a circle.* From an ancient perspective, the

11 The pillars of heaven tremble
    and are astounded at his rebuke.
12 By his power he stilled the Sea;
    by his understanding he struck down
        Rahab.
13 By his wind the heavens were made fair;
    his hand pierced the fleeing serpent.
14 These are indeed but the outskirts of his
        ways,
    and how small a whisper do we hear
        of him!
    But the thunder of his power who can
        understand?"

27 Job again took up his discourse and
    said:
2 "As God lives, who has taken away my
        right,
    and the Almighty,*f* who has made my
        soul bitter,
3 as long as my breath is in me
    and the spirit of God is in my nostrils,
4 my lips will not speak falsehood,
    and my tongue will not utter deceit.

5 Far be it from me to say that you are
        right;
    until I die I will not put away my
        integrity from me.
6 I hold fast my righteousness and will not
        let it go;
    my heart will not reproach me as long
        as I live.

7 "May my enemy be like the wicked,
    and may my opponent be like the
        unrighteous.
8 For what is the hope of the godless when
        God cuts them off,
    when God takes away their lives?
9 Will God hear their cry
    when trouble comes upon them?
10 Will they take delight in the
        Almighty?*g*
    Will they call upon God at all times?
11 I will teach you concerning the hand of
        God;

f 27.2 Traditional rendering of Heb *Shaddai*   *g* 27.10 Traditional rendering of Heb *Shaddai*

coastal horizon both walls in the ocean to hold its power in place and marks the boundary where light exchanges places with darkness. See 22:14; 38:8–11, 19; Prov. 8:27–29. **26:12** *The Sea . . . Rahab* are names for the sea god who is defeated by Baal, attested in extensive editions of these combat myths. **26:13** *Hand pierced the fleeing serpent*. See 9:8; Isa. 27:1. **26:14** *Small a whisper . . . thunder* is a metaphor for sensory perception about the expanse of the knowable; the human ear would be overwhelmed by God at full volume. See Exod. 20:18–19.

27:1 Each dialogue begins with a short statement that names the speaker. But the longer phrase *again took up his discourse* is a narrator's device, very rare in the poetic dialogues (29:1; 31:40). This is an editorial intervention in a disorganized section of the book and seems to set off Job's last speech, perhaps as a distinct or culminating monologue.

27:2 *As God lives*. Job uses the formal language of an oath, ironically invoking God, whom he wants to prosecute for senselessly attacking him.

27:2, 10, 11, 13 On *Almighty*, see note on 6:4.

27:5–6 In an essay on theodicy (in 1791), Immanuel Kant quotes 27:5–6, writing, "For with this disposition [Job] proved that he did not found his morality on faith, but his faith on morality: in such a case, however weak this faith might be, yet it alone is of a pure and true kind, i.e. the kind of faith that founds not a religion of supplication, but a religion of good life conduct."

27:7 *May my enemy be like the wicked*. Job refuted the traditional sapiential view in chap. 21 that bad things happen to bad people, arguing instead that bad people can enjoy long happy lives. The dialogues about *the wicked* in 24:18–24; 27:8–23 are textually and interpretively confusing. These passages are all usually shifted out of Job's mouth to the speeches of his friends.

27:8–23 An emphatic declaration that the universe reliably punishes the wicked during their lives, these verses strongly contradict Job's point of view (especially in chap. 21). For example, vv. 19–21 claim that when the wicked go to sleep rich, they wake up poor, that they are swept away by floods, whirlwinds, and windstorms as if such natural disasters are morally strategic and targeted. The characterization of Job from all the previous dialogues would argue that a flood is unjust and senseless, sweeping away the righteous and wicked together (see 21:23–26). Since vv. 8–23 more closely echo the views of Job's friends, many assume they are Zophar's missing third speech. See note on 24:18–24. **27:11** *I will teach you*. The claim of access to knowledge about God sounds like the overconfidence of the friends. Job uses the medical idiom *hand of God* to explain and develop

that which is with the Almighty[b] I will
not conceal.
[12] All of you have seen it yourselves;
why then have you become altogether
vain?

[13] "This is the portion of the wicked with
God
and the heritage that oppressors
receive from the Almighty:[i]
[14] If their children are multiplied, it is for
the sword,
and their offspring have not enough
to eat.
[15] Those who survive them the pestilence
buries,
and their widows make no
lamentation.
[16] Though they heap up silver like dust
and pile up clothing like clay,
[17] they may pile it up, but the just will wear
it,
and the innocent will divide the silver.
[18] They build their houses like nests,
like booths made by sentinels of the
vineyard.
[19] They go to bed with wealth but will do
so no more;
they open their eyes, and it is gone.

[20] Terrors overtake them like a flood;
in the night a whirlwind carries them off.
[21] The east wind lifts them up, and they are
gone;
it sweeps them out of their place.
[22] It[j] hurls at them without pity;
they flee from its[k] power in headlong
flight.
[23] It[l] claps its[m] hands at them
and hisses at them from its[n] place.

28

"Surely there is a mine for silver
and a place for gold to be refined.
[2] Iron is taken out of the earth,
and copper is smelted from ore.
[3] Miners put[o] an end to darkness
and search out to the farthest bound
the ore in gloom and deep darkness.
[4] They open shafts in a valley away from
human habitation;
they are forgotten by travelers;
they sway suspended, remote from
people.
[5] As for the earth, out of it comes bread,
but underneath it is turned up as by
fire.

h 27.11 Traditional rendering of Heb *Shaddai* i 27.13 Traditional rendering of Heb *Shaddai* j 27.22 Or *He* (that is, God) k 27.22 Or *his* l 27.23 Or *He* (that is, God) m 27.23 Or *his* n 27.23 Or *his* o 28.3 Heb *He puts*

the divine cause of his illness. See especially 19:21; also 6:9; 12:9; 30:21. **27:14–16** Several images of death are here: *Children . . . offspring* (v. 14) ensure one is sustained in the afterlife by memorializing practices, but the wicked man's children are deceased (vv. 14–15a). *Widows make no lamentation* (v. 15b) indicates another failed memorial practice. *Silver . . . clothing* (v. 16) are described using the materials of bodily decomposition (*dust . . . clay*). **27:17** The just and innocent get the money and clothing from the downfall of the wicked. These verses celebrate just rewards and stand in total contradiction to Job's earlier views that rewards are unfairly distributed and divine attack is random and senseless. **27:23** *Claps its hands . . . hisses at them*, see Lam. 2:15.

28:1–28 A poem celebrating the divine discovery of wisdom, this largely self-contained composition is probably an editorial addition to the book. It was likely added by later sapiential scribes who wanted to repair Job's complete dismantling of traditional wisdom. The chapter resembles later developments in Second Temple wisdom literature, which among other things, viewed wisdom as hidden from humans and only available through heavenly revelation. This is really quite antithetical to the abundantly practical side of the wisdom tradition, where wisdom is available knowledge garnered from observations of natural and social life to help one live a happy, successful life. While the character of Job critiques the moral layers of practical tradition, insisting that a righteous and wise person like himself can absolutely come into a miserable, unsuccessful life, he vociferously defends his ability to apply practical wisdom to his experience of catastrophe: to speak from his body, know his misery, perceive God's hand in suffering, and challenge God's justice. Indeed, Job's critiques of God's senseless attacks and cruel injustice do not exactly anticipate the rapturous celebration of transcendent wisdom found here. See Prov. 8; Sir. 1, 24; Bar. 3:9–4:4 (see **"Wisdom and Creation," p. 1412**). **28:1–6** A substantial poetic meditation on mining, these six verses interweave a rich description of metals, gems, miners, mining technology, and metallurgy with several key words and themes from Job's other speeches: dust, darkness, hidden places, forgotten paths, and the deep darkness under the earth. **28:5** The spatial layers of the ground: soil grows food while the

6 Its stones are the place of sapphires,[p]
and its dust contains gold.
7 "That path no bird of prey knows,
and the falcon's eye has not seen it.
8 The proud wild animals have not
trodden it;
the lion has not passed over it.

9 "They put their hand to the flinty rock
and overturn mountains by the roots.
10 They cut out channels in the rocks,
and their eyes see every precious
thing.
11 The sources of the rivers they probe;[q]
hidden things they bring to light.

12 "But where shall wisdom be found?
And where is the place of
understanding?
13 Mortals do not know the way to it,[r]
and it is not found in the land of the
living.
14 The deep says, 'It is not in me,'
and the sea says, 'It is not with me.'
15 It cannot be gotten for gold,
and silver cannot be weighed out as
its price.
16 It cannot be valued in the gold of Ophir,
in precious onyx or sapphire.[s]
17 Gold and glass cannot equal it,
nor can it be exchanged for jewels of
fine gold.
18 No mention shall be made of coral or of
crystal;
the price of wisdom is above
pearls.
19 The chrysolite of Cush cannot compare
with it,
nor can it be valued in pure gold.

20 "Where then does wisdom come from?
And where is the place of
understanding?
21 It is hidden from the eyes of all living
and concealed from the birds of the
air.
22 Abaddon and Death say,
'We have heard a rumor of it with our
ears.'

23 "God understands the way to it,
and he knows its place.
24 For he looks to the ends of the earth
and sees everything under the
heavens.
25 When he gave to the wind its weight
and apportioned out the waters by
measure,
26 when he made a decree for the rain,
and a way for the thunderbolt,
27 then he saw it and declared it;
he established it and searched it out.
28 And he said to humankind,
'Truly, the fear of the Lord, that is
wisdom;
and to depart from evil is
understanding.'"

p 28.6 Or *lapis lazuli* *q* 28.11 Gk Vg: Heb *bind* *r* 28.13 Gk: Heb *its price* *s* 28.16 Or *lapis lazuli*

layer below is a much more chaotic realm. **28:6** A wordplay between *sapphires* ("sapir") and *dust* ("apar") parallels an earlier wordplay between "dust" and the "gold of Ophir" (22:24). **28:7–8** *Bird of prey . . . falcon . . . wild animals . . . lion* are animals with various predatory skills. See 10:16–17. **28:9–11** Unnamed agents who have extraordinary powers. **28:9–10** *Overturn mountains . . . cut out channels in the rocks* echoes the technologies of miners (v. 4), the force of natural processes (14:18–19), and the destructive powers of God (9:5; 12:13–15). **28:10–11** *Precious thing . . . hidden things* are the gems uncovered by miners, which are visible through cutting a shaft, a method that Job finds dissimilar to the pursuit of wisdom. **28:12** *Wisdom* can be a human capacity (4:21; 12:2, 12; 13:5; 15:8) and transcendent knowledge (11:6; 12:13). *Where shall wisdom be found?* Repeated in v. 20, this speculative wisdom poem scours the expanse but provides no answer, save that God found the way to it (v. 23). See Prov. 8:22–31; 1:28; Bar. 3:31 (see **"Woman Wisdom," p. 872**). **28:15–19** Extensive economic metaphors. **28:22** On *Abaddon*, see note on 26:6. The spaces of death seem to have a better chance of learning wisdom than the land of the living. **28:27** *Saw it and declared it*. God can see wisdom that is hidden from the "eyes of all living" (v. 21). Note that God discovers the presence and behavior of wisdom (compare "God saw" in Gen. 1:4–31). **28:28** *Lord* is used here and in 12:9; it is the personal name for God (YHWH). The dialogues invoke several names for God, and the name YHWH will not occur again until 38:1. See **"God's Name," p. 89**. "Fear of God" as the beginning of wisdom is a major feature of Second Temple wisdom literature, as in Ben Sira, where the phrase occurs over sixty times (e.g., 1:14). See Prov. 9:10; Ps. 111:10.

29

Job again took up his discourse and said:

2 "O that I were as in the months of old,
    as in the days when God watched over
    me,
3 when his lamp shone over my head,
    and by his light I walked through
    darkness,
4 when I was in my prime,
    when the friendship of God was upon
    my tent,
5 when the Almighty[t] was still with me,
    when my children were around me,
6 when my steps were washed with
    milk
    and the rock poured out for me
    streams of oil!
7 When I went out to the gate of the city,
    when I took my seat in the square,
8 the young men saw me and withdrew,
    and the aged rose up and stood;
9 the nobles refrained from talking
    and laid their hands on their mouths;
10 the voices of princes were hushed,
    and their tongues stuck to the roofs of
    their mouths.
11 When the ear heard, it commended me,
    and when the eye saw, it approved,
12 because I delivered the poor who cried
    and the orphan who had no helper.
13 The blessing of the wretched came upon
    me,

and I caused the widow's heart to sing
    for joy.
14 I put on righteousness, and it clothed me;
    my justice was like a robe and a
    turban.
15 I was eyes to the blind
    and feet to the lame.
16 I was a father to the needy,
    and I championed the cause of the
    stranger.
17 I broke the fangs of the unrighteous
    and made them drop their prey from
    their teeth.
18 Then I thought, 'I shall die in my nest,
    and I shall multiply my days like the
    phoenix;[u]
19 my roots spread out to the waters,
    with the dew all night on my
    branches;
20 my glory was fresh with me
    and my bow ever new in my hand.'

21 "They listened to me and waited
    and kept silence for my counsel.
22 After I spoke they did not speak again,
    and my word dropped upon them like
    dew.[v]
23 They waited for me as for the rain;
    they opened their mouths as for the
    spring rain.

---

t 29.5 Traditional rendering of Heb *Shaddai* u 29.18 Or
like sand v 29.22 Heb lacks *like dew*

29:1–25 Job is nostalgic for his old life and relationships. **29:1** *Again took up his discourse.* See note for 27:1. With no address to his friends and no commentary on the effects of their advice, Job appears to deliver a monologue. **29:2** *God watched over me.* Job expresses nostalgia for a time before his misfortunes. Note that after Job's catastrophes, he consistently calls the divine gaze torturous and seeks to escape it. See 7:20; 14:3; 16:9. **29:3** Following on v. 2, the *lamp . . . light* is imagery that became noxious to Job in his suffering (see chap. 3). In this nostalgic chapter, Job praises the light, even comparing his own face to light in v. 24. The couplet of *lamp/light* occurs in 18:6 and 21:17. **29:5** *My children* could refer to Job's deceased sons or function as a paternalistic term for the many people of inferior status Job mentions in vv. 8–25. On *Almighty*, see note on 6:4. **29:7** *Gate of the city . . . seat in the square.* The gate complex served as the city forum and included open spaces for congregating, centering the activity of high-status men who conducted business, took counsel, and settled legal disputes (see Ruth 4:1–12). **29:9** *Nobles.* Even high-status people showed deference to Job. **29:12–17** Job recalls how he protected all those he calls the *prey* of the unrighteous (v. 17): poor people, orphans, those dying, widows, blind people, people with mobility disabilities, and strangers. **29:14** A quick sartorial interruption, Job describes his bodily adornment, perhaps not accidentally right before configuring his abled body as providing repair to others' impairments (v. 15). **29:18–20** Culturally specific language about male strength, honor, and fertility. For example, a taut bow is a royal symbol of defeat while a newly strung bow, as described here, symbolizes a nexus of virility, warrior strength, and health (see **"The Bible, Gender, and Sexuality," pp. 2160–62**). **29:21–23** *My counsel . . . I spoke . . . my word.* In contrast to the silence of even the highest-status people in his lifeworld (vv. 9–10), Job recalls how people, most likely those of vv. 12–17, were fertilized or at least hydrated by his speech.

²⁴ I smiled on them when they had no
confidence,
and the light of my countenance they
did not extinguish."^w
²⁵ I chose what they should do and sat as
chief,
and I lived like a king among his
troops,
like one who comforts mourners.

30 "But now they make sport of me,
those who are younger than I,
whose fathers I would have disdained
to set with the dogs of my flock.
² What could I gain from the strength of
their hands?
All their vigor is gone.
³ Through want and hard hunger
they gnaw the dry and desolate
ground;
⁴ they pick mallow and the leaves of bushes
and to warm themselves the roots of
broom.
⁵ They are driven out from society;
people shout after them as after a
thief.
⁶ In the gullies of wadis they must live,
in holes in the ground and in the
rocks.
⁷ Among the bushes they bray;
under the nettles they huddle
together.
⁸ A senseless, disreputable brood,
they have been whipped out of the
land.
⁹ "And now they mock me in song;
I am a byword to them.

¹⁰ They abhor me; they keep aloof from me;
they do not hesitate to spit at the sight
of me.
¹¹ Because God has loosed my bowstring
and humbled me,
they have cast off restraint in my
presence.
¹² On my right hand the rabble rise up;
they send me sprawling
and build roads for my ruin.
¹³ They break up my path;
they promote my calamity;
no one restrains^x them.
¹⁴ As through a wide breach they come;
amid the crash they roll on.
¹⁵ Terrors are turned upon me;
my honor is pursued as by the wind,
and my prosperity has passed away
like a cloud.

¹⁶ "And now my soul is poured out within
me;
days of affliction have taken hold of me.
¹⁷ The night racks my bones,
and the pain that gnaws me takes no
rest.
¹⁸ With violence he seizes my garment;^y
he grasps me by^z the collar of my tunic.
¹⁹ He has cast me into the mire,
and I have become like dust and ashes.
²⁰ I cry to you, and you do not answer me;
I stand, and you merely look at me.
²¹ You have turned cruel to me;
with the might of your hand you
persecute me.

^w 29.24 Meaning of Heb uncertain   ^x 30.13 Cn: Heb *helps*
^y 30.18 Gk: Heb *my garment is disfigured*   ^z 30.18 Heb *like*

30:1–31 The longest sustained description of social suffering and the pain of affliction with fantastic descriptions of attack on Job's body, which was dissolved by a storm when *evil came* (v. 26). **30:1–10** Job has no kind words for those who *make sport* of him (v. 1), *mock* him (v. 9), and *spit* at him (v. 10), deploying deeply humiliating and obscene images in a revenge fantasy. **30:1** *Dogs* are figurative of rhetorical humiliation. See Ps. 22:16–20; 2 Kgs. 8:13. **30:3–8** Job pictures bullies as miserable outcasts with no means of survival using poetics of wilderness geographies and plant life. See 24:1–12. **30:9–14** Job's bullies assault him in a second fantastic description: Their attacks are verbal (v. 9) and physical (vv. 10–11); they engineer catastrophic ruin (vv. 12–13) like the pernicious outbursts of an assaulting calamity (v. 14). **30:11** *God has loosed*. The written text requires a plural subject, which is consistent with the malicious activity attributed to Job's bullies in the rest of vv. 9–14. God is not invoked or addressed until vv. 19–24. **30:15–18** A chaotic set of assaults. **30:18** *He seizes . . . he grasps* is literally "With great power, my garment is ransacked; similarly the collar of my tunic binds me up." God is not named in this verse, and since the syntax is obscure, no clear agency can be adduced. **30:19–24** Job shifts his description of affliction to God and addresses God with candid and fateful cries. **30:19** *He has cast me*. With a singular subject, this is the beginning of the description and address to God. *Cast* is usually associated with pedagogy, so most often "teach" (see 6:24), which poetically complements the second verb *have become*, related to the word "proverb" (see

²² You lift me up on the wind, you make me
  ride on it,
  and you toss me about in the roar of
  the storm.
²³ I know that you will bring me to death,
  to the house appointed for all living.

²⁴ "Surely one does not turn against the
  needy,ᵃ
  when in disaster they cry for
  help.ᵇ
²⁵ Did I not weep for those whose day was
  hard?
  Was not my soul grieved for the poor?
²⁶ But when I looked for good, evil came,
  and when I waited for light, darkness
  came.
²⁷ My inward parts are in turmoil and are
  never still;
  days of affliction come to meet me.
²⁸ I go about in sunless gloom;
  I stand up in the assembly and cry for
  help.
²⁹ I am a brother of jackals
  and a companion of ostriches.
³⁰ My skin turns black and falls from me,
  and my bones burn with heat.
³¹ My lyre is turned to mourning
  and my pipe to the voice of those who
  weep.

31 "I have made a covenant with my eyes;
  how, then, could I look upon a virgin?
² What would be my portion from God
  above
  and my heritage from the Almightyᶜ
  on high?
³ Does not calamity befall the unrighteous
  and disaster the workers of iniquity?
⁴ Does he not see my ways
  and number all my steps?

⁵ "If I have walked with falsehood,
  and my foot has hurried to deceit—
⁶ let me be weighed in a just balance,
  and let God know my integrity!—
⁷ if my step has turned aside from the way,
  and my heart has followed my eyes,
  and if any spot has clung to my hands,
⁸ then let me sow and another eat,
  and let what grows for me be rooted out.

⁹ "If my heart has been enticed by a woman
  and I have lain in wait at my
  neighbor's door,
¹⁰ then let my wife grind for another,
  and let other men kneel over her.
¹¹ For that would be a heinous crime;
  that would be a criminal offense;

a 30.24 Heb *ruin*   b 30.24 Cn: Meaning of Heb uncertain
c 31.2 Traditional rendering of Heb *Shaddai*

42:5–6). *Dust and ashes.* See 42:6; Gen. 18:27. **30:24–26** Job highlights the emotional sorrow in his response to others' misfortune. V. 24 does double poetic work: it culminates Job's ultimately candid address to God and also snidely chastises God for a callous response to suffering. Compare with Job's magnanimous responses to the suffering of others in 29:12–17. **30:24** *Turn against the needy* can also be translated as "Let loose his power against a heap of ruins." *When in disaster they cry for help* can also be translated as "If it is destroyed therefore it cries out." **30:27–31** A final description of Job's bodily symptoms, this poetic meditation reaches an acute phase of his illness narrative.

31:1–40 Job's final speech of the book ends with a lengthy profession of innocence. Once again, he calls for an audience with God along with written testimony against him (v. 35). Job wants public recognition of his integrity by being weighed on an honest scale (v. 6) while wearing the scroll of (empty) charges against him (v. 36). The court scene also rhetorically frames the main content of Job's final speech in which Job rehearses his own testimony that would socially absolve him, defending himself against several possible charges: looking at a young woman (v. 1); cheating (vv. 5, 7); adultery (v. 9); denying a fair hearing to those enslaved to him (v. 13); depriving the poor, the widow, or the orphan of their needs (vv. 16–23); confidence in wealth (vv. 24–25); adoration of celestial bodies (vv. 26–27); celebrating or causing an enemy's ruin (vv. 29–30); depriving the stranger of food and lodging (vv. 31–32); concealing wrongdoing in fear and withdrawal (vv. 33–34); and violent extortion of the land (vv. 38–39). These pronouncements of innocence are structured by twenty conditional statements often listing consequences if Job is proved false (vv. 7–8, 9–10, 21–22, 28, 38–40). Some clauses lack an apodosis and are posed as rhetorical questions, particularly wrongs against people regarded as inferior (vv. 13, 16, 19). **31:2** On *Almighty*, see note on 6:4. **31:5** The first of twenty conditional statements, which function like oaths. **31:10** *Grind . . . kneel.* Job invokes a punishment that would actually be an assault on his wife, reflecting a paternalistic custom of retaliation against females associated with privileged males. The body posture for grinding flour or coarse

¹² for that would be a fire consuming down
    to Abaddon,
        and it would burn to the root all my
        harvest.

¹³ "If I have rejected the cause of my male
    or female slaves,
        when they brought a complaint
        against me,
¹⁴ what then shall I do when God rises up?
    When he makes inquiry, what shall I
    answer him?
¹⁵ Did not he who made me in the womb
    make them?
        And did not one fashion us in the womb?

¹⁶ "If I have withheld anything that the
    poor desired
        or have caused the eyes of the widow
        to fail
¹⁷ or have eaten my morsel alone
    and the orphan has not eaten from it—
¹⁸ for from my youth I reared the orphanᵈ
    like a father,
        and from my mother's womb I guided
        the widowᵉ—
¹⁹ if I have seen anyone perish for lack of
    clothing
        or a poor person without covering,
²⁰ whose loins have not blessed me,
    and who was not warmed with the
    fleece of my sheep;
²¹ if I have raised my hand against the orphan
    because I saw I had supporters at the
    gate;
²² then let my shoulder blade fall from my
    shoulder,
        and let my arm be broken from its socket.
²³ For I was in terror of calamity from God,
    and I could not have faced his majesty.

²⁴ "If I have made gold my trust
    or called fine gold my confidence,

²⁵ if I have rejoiced because my wealth was
    great
        or because my hand had gotten much,
²⁶ if I have looked at the sunᶠ when it
    shone
        or the moon moving in splendor,
²⁷ and my heart has been secretly enticed,
    and my mouth has kissed my hand,
²⁸ this also would be an iniquity to be
    punished by the judges,
        for I should have been false to God
        above.

²⁹ "If I have rejoiced at the ruin of those
    who hated me
        or exulted when evil overtook them—
³⁰ I have not let my mouth sin
    by asking for their lives with a curse—
³¹ if those of my tent ever said,
    'O that we might be sated with his
    flesh!'ᵍ—
³² the stranger has not lodged in the street;
    I have opened my doors to the
    traveler—
³³ if I have concealed my transgressions as
    others do,ʰ
        by hiding my iniquity in my bosom,
³⁴ because I stood in great fear of the
    multitude,
        and the contempt of families terrified
        me,
        so that I kept silence and did not go
        out of doors—
³⁵ O that I had one to hear me!
    (Here is my signature! Let the
    Almightyⁱ answer me!)
    O that I had the indictment written by
    my adversary!
³⁶ Surely I would carry it on my shoulder;
    I would bind it on me like a crown;

d 31.18 Heb him   e 31.18 Heb her   f 31.26 Heb the light
g 31.31 Meaning of Heb uncertain   h 31.33 Or as Adam did
i 31.35 Traditional rendering of Heb Shaddai

meal is turned into a metaphor for sexual assault. **31:12** On *Abaddon*, see note on 26:6. **31:13–14** Job uses the laws of slavery to suggest he also deserves a fair trial with God. See 7:1–3; 19:15–16. **31:19–20** Job was generous in sharing clothing with those who had none, so much so that covered loins offer a blessing. **31:22** *Let my shoulder blade fall from my shoulder* is another punishment to counterbalance his crime: lifting his hand (v. 21). **31:26** Worship of the sun and moon, symbols of ancient West Asian and North African deities, is prohibited for Israelites. See Deut. 4:19. **31:27** *My mouth has kissed my hand* is a gesture frequently depicted in ancient iconography signifying worship (see **"Worship," p. 761**). **31:28** *To be punished by the judges.* Effectively the exact same phrase occurs in v. 11, where it is translated as "criminal offense." **31:29–30** See imprecatory psalms (e.g., Pss. 69:24; 35:11–26). **31:35** A legal document. On *Almighty*, see note on 6:4. **31:36** *Crown* is well attested in Proverbs, where it is described as the beautiful honorific gift of Wisdom (Prov. 4:9) and is usually

^{37} I would give him an account of all my
  steps;
  like a prince I would approach him.

^{38} "If my land has cried out against me
  and its furrows have wept together,
^{39} if I have eaten its yield without payment
  and caused the death of its owners,
^{40} let thorns grow instead of wheat
  and foul weeds instead of barley."

The words of Job are ended.

32 So these three men ceased to answer Job, because he was righteous in his own eyes. ^{2}Then Elihu son of Barachel the Buzite, of the family of Ram, became angry. He was angry at Job because he justified himself rather than God; ^{3}he was angry also at Job's three friends because they had found no answer, though they had declared Job to be in the wrong.^{j} ^{4}Now Elihu had waited to speak to Job because they were older than he. ^{5}But when Elihu saw that there was no answer in the mouths of these three men, he became angry.

6 Elihu son of Barachel the Buzite answered:

"I am young in years,
  and you are aged;
therefore I was timid and afraid
  to declare my opinion to you.
^{7} I said, 'Let days speak
  and many years teach wisdom.'
^{8} But truly it is the spirit in a mortal,
  the breath of the Almighty^{k} that
  makes for understanding.
^{9} It is not the old^{l} who are wise
  nor the aged who understand what is
  right.
^{10} Therefore I say, 'Listen to me;
  let me also declare my opinion.'

^{11} "See, I waited for your words;
  I listened for your wise sayings
  while you searched out what to say.
^{12} I gave you my attention,
  but there was, in fact, no one who
  confuted Job,
  no one among you who answered his
  words.
^{13} Yet do not say, 'We have found wisdom;
  God may vanquish him, not a human.'

j 32.3 Or *answer, and had put God in the wrong*   *k* 32.8 Traditional rendering of Heb *Shaddai*   *l* 32.9 Gk Syr Vg: Heb *many*

deployed as a symbol for a specific type of honor. See Prov. 12:4; 14:24; 16:31; 17:6. **31:40** *Foul weeds* is a noxious, stinking plant and Job's last word in his speeches in the Hebrew text.

32:1–37:24 Elihu, a new character, delivers the longest speech of the book. Unexpectedly, a new voice inserts itself. The young man Elihu cannot restrain himself from responding to what he has overheard. We immediately learn he is angry at everyone (32:2–5). But Elihu is really optimistic that he can positively impact Job. He presents himself as a mouthpiece for God's voice, but whose humanness will mitigate the divine terror and pressure Job has experienced (33:1–7). He seems to think he presents God's defense given the trial Job wants. Indeed, Elihu finds Job in the wrong (33:12; 34:7–8, 35–37; 35:16), quotes Job directly in order to refute him (33:8–11, 13; 34:5–6; 35:2–3; 36:23), and his speech anticipates the themes, imagery, and even somewhat the style of the YHWH speeches in chaps. 38–41. Elihu is taken by some readers as a mouthpiece of orthodoxy and by others as a demon (including the Testament of Job, which associates him with Satan and casts him into Sheol unpardoned; see **"The Satan," p. 687**). There are several good reasons for viewing Elihu's speeches as later insertions into the book; for example, his name is not listed among the friends at the end (42:9; also 2:11), and his speeches use numerous unique terms.

32:1–6 Prose introduction to Elihu. 32:2 *Elihu* means "he is my God." *Barachel* means "bless God," although see note on 1:21. **32:4** Traditional wisdom is associated with age in 12:12–13; 15:9–10.

32:6–33:33 Elihu's first speech.

32:6 *Timid* can also be translated as "slithered away," which captures this term's association with a snake or worm.

32:7–8 As a youth, with no traditional claims to be the mouth (v. 5) of traditional wisdom, Elihu appeals to a fresh source for sapiential knowledge that Job also seems to affirm: divine *breath* as the *spirit in a mortal* (see also 26:4; 27:3; 33:4; 34:14). Elihu's spirit will struggle in this effort (vv. 18–20). *The breath of the Almighty*, see Gen. 2:7; Isa. 42:5. *Spirit* of understanding, see 34:14; Isa. 11:2; Exod. 31:3; Num. 11:26–30; 27:18.

32:13 *God may vanquish him.* The friends never say this in the speeches of chaps. 4–25, but this statement does somewhat anticipate the YHWH speeches in chaps. 38–41. *God* is literally "El." *Vanquish* is literally "drive away."

¹⁴ He has not directed his words against
me,
and I will not answer him with your
speeches.

¹⁵ "They are dismayed; they answer no
more;
they have not a word to say.
¹⁶ And am I to wait because they do not
speak,
because they stand there and answer
no more?
¹⁷ I also will give my answer;
I also will declare my opinion.
¹⁸ For I am full of words;
the spirit within me constrains me.
¹⁹ My belly is indeed like wine that has no
vent;
like new wineskins, it is ready to burst.
²⁰ I must speak, so that I may find relief;
I must open my lips and answer.
²¹ I will not show partiality to any person
or use flattery toward anyone.
²² For I do not know how to flatter—
or my Maker would soon put an end
to me!

33 "But now, hear my speech, O Job,
and listen to all my words.
² See, I open my mouth;
the tongue in my mouth speaks.
³ My words declare the uprightness of my
heart,
and what my lips know they speak
sincerely.
⁴ The spirit of God has made me,
and the breath of the Almighty*ᵐ* gives
me life.

⁵ Answer me, if you can;
set your words in order before me;
take your stand.
⁶ See, before God I am as you are;
I, too, was formed from a piece of
clay.
⁷ No fear of me need terrify you;
my pressure will not be heavy on you.

⁸ "Surely, you have spoken in my hearing,
and I have heard the sound of your
words.
⁹ You say, 'I am clean, without
transgression;
I am pure, and there is no iniquity in
me.
¹⁰ Look, he finds occasions against me;
he counts me as his enemy;
¹¹ he puts my feet in the stocks
and watches all my paths.'

¹² "But in this you are not right. I will
answer you:
God is greater than any mortal.
¹³ Why do you contend against him,
saying, 'He will answer none of my*ⁿ*
words'?
¹⁴ For God speaks in one way
and in two, though people do not
perceive it.
¹⁵ In a dream, in a vision of the night,
when deep sleep falls on mortals,
while they slumber on their beds,
¹⁶ then he opens their ears
and terrifies them with warnings,

m 33.4 Traditional rendering of Heb *Shaddai*
n 33.13 Compare Gk: Heb *his*

32:15–16 *Have not a word to say* is literally "words have moved past them" and may be a figurative critique of the sayings of sapiential tradition that are no longer applicable, a view similarly
expressed by Job (13:12).
32:18 *Spirit within me* is literally "a wind in my belly." See v. 8.
32:19 Elihu's belly is filled with gaseous, fermenting wine, which raises the question of what is
going to come out of his mouth when he finds "relief" in v. 20.
33:1–33 Elihu describes how to come back from the brink of death by undoing the catalyst of
pride. Most commenters view this speech about redemptive suffering as Elihu's most distinctive
contribution to the dialogue, although the poetry is notably repetitive and lacks style. 33:1–11 Elihu
refers to Job's call for a trial in 13:17–19. 33:4 On *Almighty*, see note on 6:4. *Spirit . . . breath.* See 32:8
and 34:14. 33:6 *I am as you are* is literally "I am like your mouth." Elihu possibly imagines himself
as Job's spokesperson or else as a worthy mouthpiece, like Moses (Exod. 20:19). 33:9–11 Quotes
Job's words, especially from 13:24, 27. 33:13 Refers to Job's first call for a trial in 9:2–4. 33:14 *Do
not perceive it* may be a general statement, introducing the layers of meaning in a nocturnal vision
(vv. 15–18), or referring to two types of divine communication to humans (vv. 15–18, 19–28). 33:15–
18 Elihu asserts that God teaches and warns through dreams. 33:16 *Terrifies* may be a wordplay in
Hebrew with "seals up," perhaps a pun on open/close (see v. 14), or shorthand for a fuller phrase,

¹⁷ that he may turn them aside from their
    deeds
  and keep them from pride,
¹⁸ to spare their souls from the Pit,
  their lives from traversing the River.
¹⁹ They are also chastened with pain upon
    their beds
  and with continual strife in their
    bones,
²⁰ so that their lives loathe bread
  and their appetites dainty food.
²¹ Their flesh is so wasted away that it
    cannot be seen,
  and their bones, once invisible, now
    stick out.
²² Their souls draw near the Pit
  and their lives to those who bring
    death.
²³ Then, if there should be for one of them
    an angel,
  a mediator, one of a thousand,
  one who declares a person upright,
²⁴ and he is gracious to that person and
    says,
  'Deliver him from going down into the
    Pit;
  I have found a ransom;
²⁵ let his flesh become fresh with youth;
  let him return to the days of his
    youthful vigor,'
²⁶ then he prays to God and is accepted by
    him;
  he comes into his presence with joy,
  and God^o repays him for his
    righteousness.

²⁷ That person sings to others and says,
  'I sinned and perverted what was right,
  and it was not paid back to me.
²⁸ He has redeemed my soul from going
    down to the Pit,
  and my life shall see the light.'
²⁹ "God indeed does all these things,
  twice, three times, with mortals,
³⁰ to bring back their souls from the Pit,
  so that they may see the light of life.^p
³¹ Pay heed, Job, listen to me;
  be silent, and I will speak.
³² If you have anything to say, answer me;
  speak, for I desire to justify you.
³³ If not, listen to me;
  be silent, and I will teach you
    wisdom."

34 Then Elihu continued and said:
  ²"Hear my words, you wise men,
  and give ear to me, you who know,
³ for the ear tests words
  as the palate tastes food.
⁴ Let us choose what is right;
  let us determine among ourselves
    what is good.
⁵ For Job has said, 'I am innocent,
  and God has taken away my right;
⁶ in spite of being right I am counted a
    liar;
  my wound is incurable, though I am
    without transgression.'

o 33.26 Heb *he* p 33.30 Syr: Heb *to be lighted with the light of life*

similar to "seal up the torah" (Isa. 8:16) or "seal up the book" (Dan. 12:4). **33:17** A terrifying dream undoes the moral problem of pride (see Dan. 4:3–4, 26–27). **33:19–28** Elihu describes illness and recovery as a body under discipline (v. 19), and with the help of heavenly intervention (vv. 23–25) and prayer (v. 26), the person can experience presence with God (v. 26) and can sing songs of hope (vv. 27–28). **33:18** *River* can mean "weapon" or "stream." For "weapon," see 36:12; Joel 2:8. For "stream," see Ezek. 31:5, 7, 14–15 depicting great waters that feed a river in the underworld. **33:19** On divine chastisement, see note on 5:17–18. *And with continual strife* refers to debate or defense. *Strife* is translated as "contend" in 9:3; 10:2; 13:19; 23:6. The phrase can also read "and the trembling is unrelenting," a pun that plays between Job's physical sickness and his call for a trial. *Bones*, see 2:5. **33:23** *Angel* is literally "messenger" and can be a theophoric heavenly being (Gen. 21:17), a prophet (Mal. 3:1), or a person who delivers a message (Job 1:14). *Mediator*, see Isa. 43:27. Job has repeatedly called for several different kinds of allies (see 9:33; 16:19; 19:25; 21:31). **33:31** See 13:18. **33:31–33** An almost humorous set of flip-flopping commands for Job to both answer and be quiet. Job never acknowledges Elihu but will next respond to YHWH in 40:3–5 (see also 42:1–6).
  34:2–37 Elihu's second speech. Elihu addresses the friends (vv. 2–15), twice appealing to their wisdom (vv. 2, 10). He then addresses Job (vv. 16–37), challenging especially his sarcastic critique of the wisdom tradition from chap. 12, assuming that Job was also mocking God. **34:3** Quotes Job in 12:11. **34:5–6** Elihu supposedly quotes Job, though he seems to mash up several scattered phrases (especially 9:15–20; 27:2). *Wound is incurable* is also "arrow is fatal," see 6:4. See also Jer. 15:18. **34:5** Quotes Job in

7 Who is there like Job,
who drinks up scoffing like water,
8 who goes in company with evildoers
and walks with the wicked?
9 For he has said, 'It profits one nothing
to take delight in God.'

10 "Therefore, hear me, you who have sense;
far be it from God that he should do wickedness
and from the Almighty[q] that he should do wrong.
11 For according to their deeds he will repay them,
and according to their ways he will make it befall them.
12 Of a truth, God will not do wickedly,
and the Almighty[r] will not pervert justice.
13 Who gave him charge over the earth,
and who laid on him[s] the whole world?
14 If he should take back his spirit[t] to himself
and gather to himself his breath,
15 all flesh would perish together,
and all mortals return to dust.

16 "If you have understanding, hear this;
listen to what I say.
17 Shall one who hates justice govern?
Will you condemn one who is righteous and mighty,
18 who says to a king, 'You scoundrel!'
and to princes, 'You wicked men!';
19 who shows no partiality to nobles,
nor regards the rich more than the poor,
for they are all the work of his hands?
20 In a moment they die;
at midnight the people are shaken and pass away,
and the mighty are taken away by no human hand.

21 "For his eyes are upon the ways of mortals,
and he sees all their steps.
22 There is no gloom or deep darkness
where evildoers may hide themselves.
23 For he has not appointed a time[u] for anyone
to go before God in judgment.
24 He shatters the mighty without investigation
and sets others in their place.
25 Thus, knowing their works,
he overturns them in the night, and they are crushed.
26 He strikes them for their wickedness
while others look on,
27 because they turned aside from following him
and had no regard for any of his ways,
28 so that they caused the cry of the poor to come to him,
and he heard the cry of the afflicted—
29 When he is quiet, who can condemn?
When he hides his face, who can behold him?
Whether nation or person, it is the same—
30 so that the godless should not reign
or those who ensnare the people.

31 "For has anyone said to God,
'I have endured punishment; I will not offend any more;
32 teach me what I do not see;
if I have done iniquity, I will do it no more'?
33 Will he then pay back to suit you
because you reject it?
For you must choose and not I;
therefore declare what you know.[v]

q 34.10 Traditional rendering of Heb *Shaddai* *r* 34.12 Traditional rendering of Heb *Shaddai* *s* 34.13 Heb lacks *on him* *t* 34.14 Heb *his heart his spirit* *u* 34.23 Cn: Heb *yet* *v* 34.33 Meaning of Heb of 34.29–33 uncertain

27:2. **34:7** *Scoffing* would be blasphemy against God. A unique term in Job, the book displays an extensive vocabulary for derisive speech. See, for example, Zophar in 11:3. Job feels mocked by his friends (21:3) and accuses God of mocking victims (9:23) but uses several other terms to describe his own speeches, like "complaint" (e.g., 7:13; 23:2), "cry" (e.g., 19:7; 30:28), "grief" (17:7), and "argument" (19:5; 23:4). **34:10–12** Elihu defends divine justice against the suggestion that God is wicked, similar to Bildad's defense in 8:3–4. **34:10** On *Almighty*, see note on 6:4. **34:14** *Spirit* and *breath* form an important word pair for Elihu (see 32:8; 33:4). Job uses the same two terms in 27:3. **34:17–30** Engages Job's argument that God actively subverts the gifts of wisdom exercised by people in various political and social roles (12:17–25). To preserve God's character, Elihu argues that God only ruins rulers who are *scoundrels* and *wicked men* (v. 18). **34:21–22** See Eliphaz in 22:12–14. See Job in note on 29:2.

³⁴ Those who have sense will say to me,
and the wise who hear me will say,
³⁵ 'Job speaks without knowledge;
his words are without insight.'
³⁶ Would that Job were tried to the limit,
because his answers are those of the
wicked.
³⁷ For he adds rebellion to his sin;
he claps his hands among us
and multiplies his words against God."

35

Elihu continued and said:
²"Do you think this to be just?
You say, 'I am in the right before God.'
³ If you ask, 'What advantage have I?
How am I better off than if I had
sinned?'
⁴ I will answer you
and your friends with you.
⁵ Look at the heavens and see;
observe the clouds, which are higher
than you.
⁶ If you have sinned, what do you
accomplish against him?
And if your transgressions are
multiplied, what do you do to him?
⁷ If you are righteous, what do you give to
him,
or what does he receive from your hand?
⁸ Your wickedness affects others like you,
and your righteousness, other human
beings.

⁹ "Because of the multitude of oppressions
people cry out;
they call for help because of the arm
of the mighty.

¹⁰ But no one says, 'Where is God my Maker,
who gives strength in the night,
¹¹ who teaches us more than the animals of
the earth
and makes us wiser than the birds of
the air?'
¹² There they cry out, but he does not
answer,
because of the pride of evildoers.
¹³ Surely God does not hear an empty
cry,
nor does the Almighty*ᵂ* regard it.
¹⁴ How much less when you say that you do
not see him,
that the case is before him and you are
waiting for him!
¹⁵ And now, because his anger does not
punish
and he does not greatly heed
transgression,*ˣ*
¹⁶ Job opens his mouth in empty talk;
he multiplies words without
knowledge."

36

Elihu continued and said:
²"Bear with me a little, and I will
show you,
for I have yet something to say on
God's behalf.
³ I will bring my knowledge from far away
and ascribe righteousness to my
Maker.
⁴ For truly my words are not false;
one who is perfect in knowledge is
with you.

w 35.13 Traditional rendering of Heb *Shaddai*
x 35.15 Meaning of Heb uncertain

35:2–16 Elihu's third speech. 35:2 Elihu echoes Eliphaz (4:17) and Job (9:2). *I am in the right before God* can also read "My righteousness is better than God's righteousness." **35:3–8** Elihu argues that righteousness is not about what it gets Job (v. 3), since it does not affect God one way or the other (vv. 6–7), but righteous and unrighteous actions do have consequences impacting other humans (v. 8). **35:9** *Multitude* ("rov") is a play on words with *mighty* ("rab"), which can also refer to princes or officials (see Jer. 41:1) and echoes 34:17–30, especially v. 28. This verse also echoes Job in 19:7, though with a shift from Job as subject to a plural subject (*they call for help*) and a shift away from God's attack to a more generic agent (*the arm of the mighty*). **35:12–14** *Empty cry* in v. 13 conveys Elihu's sense that he can diagnose the cries of those who suffer or are oppressed based on whether God answers. He assumes that if God does not respond, it is because of *pride* (v. 12), and the sufferer must learn patience (v. 14). **35:13** On *Almighty*, see note on 6:4. **35:14** *Case* refers to Job's call for a trial. See note 23:4–7. **35:16** *Empty talk* ("hebel") is literally "vapor," "breath," or "vanity." The word is quite poetic, suggesting Job's mouth produces feeble breath, picking up on "empty cry" in v. 13. "Hebel" is generally translated as "vanity" and is a theme word in Ecclesiastes (see **"All Is Vanity," p. 906**).

36:1–37:24 Elihu's fourth speech. 36:2–4 Elihu announces the perfection of his knowledge. **36:2** *I have yet something to say on God's behalf* can also be translated as "for God still has more

5 "Surely God is mighty and does not
 despise any;
  he is mighty in strength of understanding.
6 He does not keep the wicked alive
  but gives the afflicted their right.
7 He does not withdraw his eyes from the
 righteous,
  but with kings on the throne
  he sets them forever, and they are
  exalted.
8 And if they are bound in fetters
  and caught in the cords of affliction,
9 then he declares to them their work
  and their transgressions, that they are
  behaving arrogantly.
10 He opens their ears to instruction
  and commands that they return from
  iniquity.
11 If they listen and serve him,
  they complete their days in prosperity
  and their years in pleasantness.
12 But if they do not listen, they shall perish
  by the sword
  and die without knowledge.

13 "The godless in heart cherish anger;
  they do not cry for help when he binds
  them.
14 They die in their youth,
  and their life ends in shame.^{y}
15 He delivers the afflicted by their affliction
  and opens their ear by adversity.
16 He also allured you out of distress
  into a broad place where there was no
  constraint,
  and what was set on your table was
  full of fatness.

17 "But you are obsessed with the case of
 the wicked;
  judgment and justice seize you.

18 Beware that wrath does not entice you
 into scoffing,
  and do not let the greatness of the
  ransom turn you aside.
19 Will your cry avail to keep you from
 distress,
  or will all the force of your strength?
20 Do not long for the night,
  when peoples are cut off in their
  place.
21 Beware! Do not turn to iniquity;
  because of that you have been tried by
  affliction.
22 See, God is exalted in his power;
  who is a teacher like him?
23 Who has prescribed for him his way,
  or who can say, 'You have done
  wrong'?
24 "Remember to extol his work,
  of which mortals have sung.
25 All people have looked on it;
  everyone watches it from far away.
26 Surely God is great, and we do not know
 him;
  the number of his years is
  unsearchable.
27 For he draws up the drops of water;
  he distills^z his mist in rain,
28 which the skies pour down
  and drop upon mortals abundantly.
29 Can anyone understand the spreading of
 the clouds,
  the thunderings of his pavilion?
30 See, he scatters his lightning around him
  and covers the roots of the sea.
31 For by these he governs peoples;
  he gives food in abundance.
32 He covers his hands with the lightning
  and commands it to strike the mark.

y 36.14 Heb *ends among the prostitutes* *z* 36.27 Cn: Heb *they distill*

words." **36:5–6** A thesis for the chapter. **36:7–14** God topples monarchs to teach and discipline them, reminiscent of Eliphaz in 5:17–18. See also 35:9; 34:17–30. **36:9** *Arrogantly* ("gabar") is derived from a common term meaning "strength," "power." See Eliphaz in 15:25. For the closely related term "geber," "valiant man," see note on 3:3. **36:15–16** Elihu describes how God teaches through affliction. On divine chastisement, see note on 5:17–18. **36:15** *Delivers* is literally "pulls out," which could mean "plunders," "equips for battle," "invigorates," or even "makes manful." The more violent meanings echo in the wordplay with *adversity*, which is better translated as "oppression" or "forced pressure." See also "constraint" in v. 16. **36:16–24** Elihu's direct advice to Job: be careful how you respond to adversity; be patient and find God's instruction. **36:22–33** Celebration of God as a storm deity, culminating in the idea that thunder teaches humans, a theme that continues into the metaphor of God's voice in 37:1–5. Compare the human response to the thunderous voice of the ten commandments in Exod. 19:9, 19; 20:1, 18–21. **36:26** *Surely God is great.* A wisdom aphorism. **36:27** *Mist.* The only other place this word occurs is in Gen. 2:6. **36:29** *Pavilion* is God's heavenly dwelling (see

³³ Its crashing^a tells about him;
  he is jealous^b with anger against
    iniquity.

37 "At this also my heart trembles
  and leaps out of its place.
² Listen, listen to the thunder of his
    voice
  and the rumbling that comes from his
    mouth.
³ Under the whole heaven he lets it loose,
  and his lightning to the corners of the
    earth.
⁴ After it his voice roars;
  he thunders with his majestic voice,
  and he does not restrain the
    lightnings^c when his voice is
    heard.
⁵ God thunders wondrously with his
    voice;
  he does great things that we cannot
    comprehend.
⁶ For to the snow he says, 'Fall on the
    earth';
  and the shower of rain, his heavy
    shower of rain,
⁷ serves as a sign on everyone's hand,
  so that all whom he has made may
    know it.^d
⁸ Then the animals go into their lairs
  and remain in their dens.
⁹ From its chamber comes the whirlwind
  and cold from the scattering winds.
¹⁰ By the breath of God ice is given,
  and the broad waters are frozen fast.
¹¹ He loads the thick cloud with
    moisture;
  the clouds scatter his lightning.
¹² They turn round and round by his
    guidance
  to accomplish all that he commands
    them
  on the face of the habitable world.

¹³ Whether for correction or for his land
  or for love, he causes it to happen.

¹⁴ "Hear this, O Job;
  stop and consider the wondrous
    works of God.
¹⁵ Do you know how God lays his command
    upon them
  and causes the lightning of his cloud
    to shine?
¹⁶ Do you know the balancings of the
    clouds,
  the wondrous works of the one whose
    knowledge is perfect,
¹⁷ you whose garments are hot
  when the earth is still because of the
    south wind?
¹⁸ Can you, like him, spread out the
    skies,
  hard as a molten mirror?
¹⁹ Teach us what we shall say to him;
  we cannot draw up our case because
    of darkness.
²⁰ Should he be told that I want to speak?
  Did anyone ever wish to be swallowed
    up?
²¹ Now, no one can look on the light
  when it is bright in the skies,
  when the wind has passed and cleared
    them.
²² Out of the north comes golden splendor;
  around God is awesome majesty.
²³ The Almighty^e—we cannot find him;
  he is great in power and justice,
  and abundant righteousness he will
    not violate.
²⁴ Therefore mortals fear him;
  he does not regard any who are wise
    in their own conceit."

a 36.33 Meaning of Heb uncertain b 36.33 Meaning of Heb uncertain c 37.4 Heb *them* d 37.7 Meaning of Heb of 37.7 uncertain e 37.23 Traditional rendering of Heb *Shaddai*

2 Sam. 22:12). **37:1–24** The conclusion of Elihu's speeches immediately precedes God's speech from a storm wind (chaps. 38–41), anticipating both its nature imagery and its rhetorical questions. **37:1–13** A sapiential nature hymn praising God that began already in 36:24. See chaps. 25–26; and Sir. 42:15–43:33. The meteorological phenomena (*rain* [v. 6], *clouds* [v. 11], *lightning* [v. 3], *thunder* [v. 2], *cold storm winds* [v. 9], *snow* [v. 6], *ice* [v. 10]) are picked up in YHWH's speech (38:22–38). **37:2–5** God's voice is *thunder*. See 36:33. *Rumbling* also means "trouble" (see 3:26). **37:14–20** Rhetorical questions highlighting Job's inability to imitate God or even to know how God works. These questions, as well as the imperative demands to speak, closely imitate the style of YHWH's speech (chaps. 38–41). **37:15–16** See 38:34–35. **37:19** See 38:4. **37:21–24** A concluding comparison of the sun's rays with God's glory. **37:23** On *Almighty*, see note on 6:4. **37:24** *Regard* is literally "see," which invokes the theme of God's gaze, a significant concern of Job in his earliest speeches. See 7:17–19; 10:18–22; 14:16–17. *Wise in their own conceit* is literally "wise of heart."

38

Then the LORD answered Job out of the whirlwind:

² "Who is this that darkens counsel by
    words without knowledge?
³ Gird up your loins like a man;
    I will question you, and you shall
        declare to me.

⁴ "Where were you when I laid the
        foundation of the earth?
    Tell me, if you have understanding.
⁵ Who determined its measurements—
        surely you know!
    Or who stretched the line upon it?
⁶ On what were its bases sunk,
    or who laid its cornerstone

⁷ when the morning stars sang together
    and all the heavenly beings*f* shouted
        for joy?

⁸ "Or who shut in the sea with doors
    when it burst out from the womb,
⁹ when I made the clouds its garment
    and thick darkness its swaddling
        band,
¹⁰ and prescribed bounds for it,
    and set bars and doors,
¹¹ and said, 'Thus far shall you come and no
        farther,
    and here shall your proud waves be
        stopped'?

f 38.7 Heb *sons of God*

38:1–41:34 The Lord's (YHWH's) speeches. Except for a brief interlude (40:1–6), God's voice takes center stage in five topically distinct speeches: 38:4–38 on the cosmic world, 38:39–39:30 on the world of animals, 40:6–14 on God's commands to Job, 40:15–24 on Behemoth, and 41:1–34 on Leviathan. God's speeches are almost entirely visual communications. They present a series of images from the natural and fantastical world with poetic, stylistic, and rhetorical features. One can read these chapters productively on several themes or through various lenses: sapiential meditation on nature; motifs of the divine warrior, masculinity, and male honor; Israelite theophanies; body ideals; disability discourses; illness narratives; ecological visions; fantasy and horror; the sublime; and still more. Notably silent about Job's specific complaints of injustice, God never indicates one way or the other what caused Job's suffering. Indeed, when Job first imagined calling God to trial (chap. 9), his remarks were prescient: "If I summoned him and he answered me, I do not believe that he would listen to my voice" (9:16).

38:1–40:2 The Lord's first speech.

38:1 *The* LORD. Job, his three friends, and Elihu have invoked the divine names "El," "Eloah," "Elohim" (forms of "God"), and "Almighty." *The* LORD (YHWH) occurs in chaps. 1–2 and several times in these final chapters (see **"Emerging Monotheism," p. 1000,** and **"God's Name," p. 89**). *Whirlwind.* Appearing as an ancient storm deity, YHWH's *whirlwind* is typically destructive and terrifying (Jer. 23:19; 30:23; Ezek. 1:4; Amos 1:14). See also Jonah in Jonah 1:4, 12 and Elijah in 2 Kgs. 2:1, 11.

38:2 God's first words ask an existential or potentially even funny question: *Who is this . . . ?* Most read the question rhetorically as a knowing address to Job, the one who speaks *without knowledge* (see also 42:3), or as the divine claim of difference in identity with humans. *Counsel,* meaning "advice" or "deliberation," is often a human activity in wisdom literature (Prov. 15:22; Ps. 1:1). It also describes God (Ps. 119:24; Prov. 8:14; 19:20–21).

38:3 *Gird up your loins like a man.* Jeremiah is the only other character in biblical literature given this divine command (Jer. 1:17; see also Job 40:7). The act of girding loins is typically preparation for combat or lament rituals (girding with sackcloth in Lam. 2:10 and Ezek. 7:18); however, *gird* is especially common in figurative language for acquiring strength (Ps. 18:32). Note the nature imagery in Psalms depicting God girded (Pss. 65:6; 93:1–2). *Man,* see note on 3:3.

38:4–38 On the cosmic world. See **"The Bible, Science, and the Environment," pp. 2180–81. 38:4** If God mounts a defense here, it is not specific to the character of Job. By undermining human understanding, the deity throws out all human testimony and rhetorically excludes any charge of injustice. See 15:7. **38:7** *Shouted for joy* is literally "shout" and most commonly occurs in war contexts to refer to a war cry or victory song (8:21); it is a sudden, pitched outburst, especially as a trumpet. *Joy* is not a word in the Hebrew text but rather one of many possible connotations. **38:8–11** The imagery of the *womb* (v. 8) and making a newborn swaddle (v. 9) depicts God as parenting the *sea* ("yam"), which would supply a surprising backstory for God's combat myth with "Yam" (see note on 7:12). The moral vision is remarkable: God nurtures the antagonistic power of chaos into existence. See 38:39–41; 39:5–8,

¹² "Have you commanded the morning
  since your days began
  and caused the dawn to know its place,
¹³ so that it might take hold of the skirts of
  the earth,
  and the wicked be shaken out of it?
¹⁴ It is changed like clay under the seal,
  and it is dyed^g like a garment.
¹⁵ Light is withheld from the wicked,
  and their uplifted arm is broken.

¹⁶ "Have you entered into the springs of
  the sea
  or walked in the recesses of the deep?
¹⁷ Have the gates of death been revealed to
  you,
  or have you seen the gates of deep
  darkness?
¹⁸ Have you comprehended the expanse of
  the earth?
  Declare, if you know all this.

¹⁹ "Where is the way to the dwelling of light,
  and where is the place of darkness,
²⁰ that you may take it to its territory
  and that you may discern the paths to
  its home?
²¹ Surely you know, for you were born then,
  and the number of your days is great!

²² "Have you entered the storehouses of
  the snow,
  or have you seen the storehouses of
  the hail,
²³ which I have reserved for the time of
  trouble,
  for the day of battle and war?
²⁴ What is the way to the place where the
  light is distributed
  or where the east wind is scattered
  upon the earth?

²⁵ "Who has cut a channel for the torrents
  of rain
  and a way for the thunderbolt,
²⁶ to bring rain on a land where no one lives,
  on the desert, which is empty of
  human life,
²⁷ to satisfy the waste and desolate land,
  and to make the ground put forth grass?

²⁸ "Has the rain a father,
  or who has fathered the drops of dew?
²⁹ From whose womb did the ice come
  forth,
  and who has given birth to the
  hoarfrost of heaven?
³⁰ The waters become hard like stone,
  and the face of the deep is frozen.

³¹ "Can you bind the chains of the
  Pleiades
  or loose the cords of Orion?
³² Can you lead forth the Mazzaroth in
  their season,
  or can you guide the Bear with its
  children?
³³ Do you know the ordinances of the
  heavens?
  Can you establish their rule on the
  earth?

³⁴ "Can you lift up your voice to the
  clouds,
  so that a flood of waters may cover
  you?
³⁵ Can you send forth lightnings, so that
  they may go
  and say to you, 'Here we are'?
³⁶ Who has put wisdom in the inward parts^h
  or given understanding to the mind?ⁱ

g 38.14 Cn: Heb *and they stand forth*   h 38.36 Meaning of
Heb uncertain   i 38.36 Meaning of Heb uncertain

26–30 (see **"Feminine Imagery for God,"** p. 1029). **38:12–15** Wisdom discourse on light. **38:21** *You were born then* is a sarcastic remark. The surrounding imagery echoes chap. 3 where Job cursed the day of his birth: "stars sang" (v. 7; see 3:7), "shut in" (v. 8; see 3:23), "your days began" (v. 12; see 3:1–8), "dawn" (v. 12; see 3:9), "death" (v. 17; see 3:21), "deep darkness" (v. 17; see 3:5), "light" (v. 19; see 3:9), "darkness" (v. 19; see 3:4, 5). **38:22–38** On fantastic and familial snow, hail, winds, rain. **38:23** *For the day of battle and war*. The natural elements are stored up as weapons, descriptions of YHWH as an ancient West Asian combat deity. See v. 33. **38:28–29** The fertility imagery of male reproduction (v. 28) and female reproduction (v. 29) casts God as a fertility god/goddess. While rain is a common ancient West Asian fertility motif (divine semen), ice and frost are not. **38:33** *Heaven* in the Hebrew Bible is not a place for human afterlife but is depicted as a cosmic structure above the dome of the sky where God dwells, and in v. 22, it keeps "storehouses." **38:36** *Inward parts . . . mind.* In this important statement about where wisdom and understanding are found (see 28:12, 20), uncertain Hebrew nouns leave modern interpreters totally guessing, although *inward parts* is possibly a wordplay with the Egyptian god of wisdom, Thoth.

³⁷ Who has the wisdom to number the clouds?
　　Or who can tilt the waterskins of the
　　　heavens
³⁸ when the dust runs into a mass
　　and the clods cling together?

³⁹ "Can you hunt the prey for the lion
　　or satisfy the appetite of the young
　　　lions,
⁴⁰ when they crouch in their dens
　　or lie in wait in their covert?
⁴¹ Who provides for the raven its prey,
　　when its young ones cry to God
　　and wander about for lack of food?

39 "Do you know when the mountain
　　goats give birth?
　　Do you observe the calving of the deer?
² Can you number the months that they
　　fulfill,
　　and do you know the time when they
　　　give birth,
³ when they crouch to give birth to their
　　offspring
　　and are delivered of their young?
⁴ Their young ones become strong; they
　　grow up in the open;
　　they go forth and do not return to them.

⁵ "Who has let the wild ass go free?
　　Who has loosed the bonds of the swift
　　　ass,

⁶ to which I have given the steppe for its
　　home,
　　the salt land for its dwelling place?
⁷ It scorns the tumult of the city;
　　it does not hear the shouts of the
　　　driver.
⁸ It ranges the mountains as its pasture,
　　and it searches after every green
　　　thing.

⁹ "Is the wild ox willing to serve you?
　　Will it spend the night at your crib?
¹⁰ Can you tie it in the furrow with ropes,
　　or will it harrow the valleys after you?
¹¹ Will you depend on it because its
　　strength is great,
　　and will you hand over your labor to
　　　it?
¹² Do you have faith in it that it will return
　　and bring your grain to your threshing
　　　floor?[j]

¹³ "The ostrich's wings flap wildly,
　　though its pinions lack plumage.[k]
¹⁴ For it leaves its eggs to the earth
　　and lets them be warmed on the ground,
¹⁵ forgetting that a foot may crush them
　　and that a wild animal may trample
　　　them.

j 39.12 Heb *your grain and your threshing floor*　k 39.13 Meaning of Heb uncertain

38:39–chap. 39 On the world of animals. All nine animals in this speech are nondomestic, except maybe the horse. The horse is depicted in its role in human affairs but as a warhorse in the wild and chaotic passions of combat. The animals are all found in world regions that were considered hostile to humans—*steppe* and *salt land* (39:6), *mountains* (39:8), and *rock* and *rocky crag* (39:28)—with a culminating landscape that is fitting of a horror movie: *where the slain are, there it is* (39:30). The introduction of the passage is equally terrifying, a stalking lion provisioning its cubs (38:39). Ancient West Asian texts and iconography associate many of these animals with the royal hunt, which was a public display of kingly protection over fantastic and menacing symbols. Yet the speech does not overindulge these cultural fears or claim God's power over them. God explicitly cares for the *raven*, *wild ass*, *hawk*, and *eagle* (38:39–41; 39:5–8, 26–30), which complements the generally celebratory descriptions of animal agencies, especially in experiential spheres like behavior, birth, nurture, and food. The striking image of God nurturing "Yam" in 38:8–11 clearly announces the speech's wider challenge to moral categories of nurture, protection, provision, and predation by decentering human experience and highlighting the fray of creatures, agencies, desires, and ecologies.

38:39–41 *Lion* and *raven*. Introducing the list of animals, a stalking lion is infamously terrifying in Hebrew literature (see Num. 23:24; Ps. 17:12; Isa. 5:29; Nah. 2:12).

39:1–4 *Mountain goats* and *deer*. Descriptions of birth and natal dispersal.

39:5–12 *Wild ass* and *wild ox*. Animals who refuse to serve humans or live in their farms and cities, favoring wild terrains.

39:13–18 With wings that cannot fly, the ostrich is the perfect enemy of the practical wisdom tradition. In modern philosophical terms, the ostrich shows how bodily morphologies, behavioral functions, and social performances are not foundational, nor can they be rationalized or naturalized. Brought to a moral point related to Job, the ostrich lays eggs that die from parental neglect or

¹⁶ It deals cruelly with its young, as if they
were not its own;
though its labor should be in vain, yet
it has no fear;
¹⁷ because God has made it forget wisdom
and given it no share in understanding.
¹⁸ When it spreads its plumes aloft,^{*l*}
it laughs at the horse and its rider.

¹⁹ "Do you give the horse its might?
Do you clothe its neck with mane?
²⁰ Do you make it leap like the locust?
Its majestic snorting is terrible.
²¹ It paws^{*m*} violently, exults mightily;
it goes out to meet the weapons.
²² It laughs at fear and is not dismayed;
it does not turn back from the sword.
²³ Upon it rattle the quiver,
the flashing spear, and the javelin.
²⁴ With fierceness and rage it swallows the
ground;
it cannot stand still at the sound of the
trumpet.
²⁵ When the trumpet sounds, it says 'Aha!'
From a distance it smells the battle,
the thunder of the captains, and the
shouting.

²⁶ "Is it by your wisdom that the hawk soars
and spreads its wings toward the
south?
²⁷ Is it at your command that the eagle
mounts up
and makes its nest on high?
²⁸ It lives on the rock and makes its home
in the fastness of the rocky crag.
²⁹ From there it spies the prey;
its eyes see it from far away.
³⁰ Its young ones suck up blood,
and where the slain are, there it is."

40 And the Lord said to Job:
²"Shall a faultfinder contend with
the Almighty?"^{*n*}
Anyone who argues with God must
respond."

3 Then Job answered the Lord:
⁴ "See, I am of small account; what shall I
answer you?
I lay my hand on my mouth.
⁵ I have spoken once, and I will not answer,
twice but will proceed no further."

6 Then the Lord answered Job out of the
whirlwind:
⁷ "Gird up your loins like a man;
I will question you, and you declare
to me.
⁸ Will you even put me in the wrong?
Will you condemn me that you may be
justified?
⁹ Have you an arm like God,
and can you thunder with a voice like
his?

¹⁰ "Deck yourself with majesty and dignity;
clothe yourself with glory and splendor.
¹¹ Pour out the overflowings of your anger,
and look on all who are proud and
humble them.
¹² Look on all who are proud and bring
them low;
tread down the wicked where they
stand.
¹³ Hide them all in the dust together;
bind their faces in the world below.^{*o*}
¹⁴ Then I will also acknowledge to you
that your own right hand can give you
victory.

l 39.18 Meaning of Heb uncertain   *m* 39.21 Gk Syr Vg:
Heb *they dig*   *n* 40.2 Traditional rendering of Heb *Shaddai*
o 40.13 Heb *the hidden place*

active culling. Both its lack of wisdom and its laughter are celebrated. See 30:29. **39:17** *Wisdom . . .
understanding.* See 23:8–17; 28:1–28; 38:4, 36.

39:19–25 *Horse.* A warhorse's physical and behavioral features.

39:26–30 *Hawk . . . eagle.* Flight and predatory behaviors.

40:2 YHWH addresses Job's call for a trial. See 13:3; 23:4; 31:35; 33:13. On *Almighty*, see note on
6:4.

40:3–5 Job speaks for the first time since 31:40. **40:4** *Lay my hand on my mouth.* See 29:9.
40:5 Job already knew he would not be able to answer, plus he has not learned what caused his
suffering. See 9:3, 15.

40:6–41:34 The Lord's (YHWH's) second speech.

40:6–14 On God's commands to Job. *Whirlwind,* see note on 38:1. **40:7** *Gird up your loins like a
man* is a phrase repeated from 38:3. *Man,* see note on 3:3. **40:9** *Arm . . . voice,* see 37:2–5; see also
Isa. 30:30. **40:11–14** God challenges Job to destroy all who are proud and wicked and deposit them
in the underworld. Rhetorically, God discredits Job for being unable to act on a cosmic stage.

¹⁵ "Look at Behemoth,
which I made just as I made you;
it eats grass like an ox.
¹⁶ Its strength is in its loins
and its power in the muscles of its belly.
¹⁷ It makes its tail stiff like a cedar;
the sinews of its thighs are knit together.
¹⁸ Its bones are tubes of bronze,
its limbs like bars of iron.

¹⁹ "It is the first of the great acts of God;
only its Maker can approach it with
the sword.
²⁰ For the mountains yield food for it
where all the wild animals play.
²¹ Under the lotus plants it lies,
in the covert of the reeds and in the
marsh.
²² The lotus trees cover it for shade;
the willows of the wadi surround it.
²³ Even if the river is turbulent, it is not
frightened;
it is confident though Jordan rushes
against its mouth.
²⁴ Can one take it with hooks^p
or pierce its nose with a snare?

41 ^q"Can you draw out Leviathan with a
fishhook
or press down its tongue with a cord?
² Can you put a rope in its nose
or pierce its jaw with a hook?
³ Will it make many supplications to you?
Will it speak soft words to you?
⁴ Will it make a covenant with you
to be taken as your servant forever?

⁵ Will you play with it as with a bird
or put it on a leash for your young
women?
⁶ Will traders bargain over it?
Will they divide it up among the
merchants?
⁷ Can you fill its skin with harpoons
or its head with fishing spears?
⁸ Lay hands on it;
think of the battle; you will not do it
again!
⁹ ^rAny hope of capturing it^s will be
disappointed;
one is overwhelmed even at the sight
of it.
¹⁰ No one is so fierce as to dare to stir it up.
Who can stand before it?^t
¹¹ Who can confront it^u and be safe?^v
—under the whole heaven, who?^w

¹² "I will not keep silent concerning its limbs
or its mighty strength or its splendid
frame.
¹³ Who can strip off its outer garment?
Who can penetrate its double coat of
mail?^x
¹⁴ Who can open the doors of its face?
There is terror all around its teeth.
¹⁵ Its back^y is made of shields in rows,
shut up closely as with a seal.
¹⁶ One is so near to another
that no air can come between them.

p 40.24 Cn: Heb *in his eyes*   q 41.1 40.25 in Heb   r 41.9 41.1
in Heb   s 41.9 Heb *of it*   t 41.10 Heb *me*   u 41.11 Heb *me*
v 41.11 Gk: Heb *that I shall repay*   w 41.11 Heb *to me*   x 41.13 Gk:
Heb *bridle*   y 41.15 Cn Compare Gk Vg: Heb *pride*

40:15–24 On Behemoth. A fantastic land monster, akin to the hippopotamus, the rhetoric invites Job to compare his strength. **40:15** *Behemoth* is the same word as the plural for "beast," often paired with Leviathan in postbiblical stories and interpretations. **40:15–19** Descriptions emphasizing midbody strength with several euphemisms for genitalia and fertility. There is no known account of Behemoth's creation. **40:20–24** Descriptions of eating, fearlessness, and invulnerability to technologies of human hunting and subjection (see Isa. 37:29).

41:1–34 On Leviathan. The Leviathan is a fantastic sea monster mentioned already in 3:8 and used here to emphasize the theme of terrific, impenetrable aspects of the cosmos that are outside of maybe even God's control. Unlike the rhetorical questions in 40:15–24, which invite Job to compare himself with the Behemoth, these questions initially invite the comparison of Job and God as Leviathan's combatants. Indeed, the sea monster is called *king over all that are proud* (v. 34), reminiscent of God's belittling challenge to Job in 40:11–14 (see **"Leviathan," p. 735**). **41:1–4** A seamless poetic shift to the *Leviathan* using the imagery of hooks and cords (40:24), vv. 1–4 develop the subjugation metaphor (see Neh. 1:5–6) and draw the ludicrous image of Leviathan as religious supplicant (see Pss. 28:6–8; 86:6–8; 130:1–2; 140:6–7). For *covenant* (v. 4), see Gen. 9:15; Exod. 19:5; 2 Kgs. 23:3; Ezek. 34:25. **41:12–25** God describes Leviathan's body, its defenses (vv. 13–17), and its assaults (vv. 18–21). An immovable creature, his dogged acts of terror are almost steadfast. **41:13** The description here justifies proposals that Leviathan can also refer to a crocodile,

Reading through Time: Leviathan (Job 40–41)

Leviathan's fame far exceeds its biblical role. Mentioned by name only six times in the Bible, Leviathan belongs to a class of water monsters (*tannin*) who are divinely created and probe the ocean abyss as their home (Gen. 1:21; Ps. 148:7).

Leviathan is characterized by fascinating contradictions. Praised as a playful creature, Leviathan prompts God to rejoice (Ps. 104:26). Indeed, God's lengthy meditation on Leviathan in Job 41 acclaims him "creature without equal" and reads like an encomium about his physique: eyes that shine like the morning, breath that sparks like fire, and air-tight scales that are "firmly cast." Able to withstand all human attacks, this physiology comes in handy when Leviathan plays the different role of God's combatant (Ps. 74:14; Isa. 27:1).

Jewish tradition characterizes Leviathan as the ultimate sacrificial meat to be slain for the righteous at the end of days. At three hundred miles long, only Jonah has the knowledge to draw him to heaven, where his flesh makes a tremendous heavenly feast and his skin forms a sukkah ("tent"). The Zohar teaches that Leviathan's "tail is placed in its mouth" to suggest a creature without beginning or end, a cryptic secret that will be revealed once the righteous are feasting on his flesh. Although sometimes revered, Christian tradition has largely associated Leviathan with Satan. Pope Gregory describes how each of Leviathan's body parts maps onto the crafts of the antichrist; Christ silences false doctrine by binding the tongue of Leviathan with the cord. In a medieval Christian encyclopedia, the cords become God's fishing rod: the cross is the hook, Christ is the bait, and the string is the line of Jewish kings (see **"Supersessionism," p. 1647**). Leviathan's jaws were frequently portrayed as the gates of hell; Christ conquers the Leviathan, the monstrous Satan, the cosmic enemy of God.

This protean sea monster burst into Western civilization's early writing and visual culture, and it still lurks and surfaces in modern cultural aftershocks. Leviathan crops up in sixteenth-century England as the title of Thomas Hobbes's influential work of political philosophy. The cover references Job 41:33 and portrays a multitude of individual humans who form Leviathan's impenetrable scales. The sovereign is likened, then, to Leviathan, whom Hobbes calls a "mortal god." In the modern world, we can turn to the great whale of *Moby Dick*, who is at once an object of taxonomy and dissection, a butchered commodity of the whaling industry, and a terrifically sublime phantom to those on the Pequod.

Ingrid E. Lilly

¹⁷ They are joined one to another;
  they clasp each other and cannot be
    separated.
¹⁸ Its sneezes flash forth light,
  and its eyes are like the eyelids of the
    dawn.
¹⁹ From its mouth go flaming torches;
  sparks of fire leap out.
²⁰ Out of its nostrils comes smoke,
  as from a boiling pot and burning
    rushes.
²¹ Its breath kindles coals,
  and a flame comes out of its mouth.
²² In its neck abides strength,
  and terror dances before it.
²³ The folds of its flesh cling together;
  it is firmly cast and immovable.
²⁴ Its heart is as hard as stone,
  as hard as the lower millstone.

²⁵ When it raises itself up the gods are
    afraid;
  at the crashing they are beside
    themselves.
²⁶ Though the sword reaches it, it does not
    avail,
  nor does the spear, the dart, or the
    javelin.
²⁷ It counts iron as straw
  and bronze as rotten wood.
²⁸ The arrow cannot make it flee;
  slingstones, for it, are turned to chaff.
²⁹ Clubs are counted as chaff;
  it laughs at the rattle of javelins.
³⁰ Its underparts are like sharp potsherds;
  it spreads itself like a threshing sledge
    on the mire.
³¹ It makes the deep boil like a pot;
  it makes the sea like a pot of ointment.

regionally known from Egypt. **41:18–21** Fantastic descriptions suggesting that Leviathan is akin to a dragon. **41:18** *Eyes are like the eyelids of the dawn.* The same phrase is used to describe the barren night in Job's curse on his birth (3:9). **41:25** *The gods are afraid.* See Exod. 18:11; Ps. 82:1; 96:4. **41:26–29** A long list of weapons that could never vanquish Leviathan. **41:31–32** Three mythological terms symbolizing chaos are invoked: *sea* ("yam"), *deep* ("tehom"), and Leviathan, who is here supreme

³² It leaves a shining wake behind it;
  one would think the deep to be
    white-haired.
³³ On earth it has no equal,
  a creature without fear.
³⁴ It surveys everything that is lofty;
  it is king over all that are proud."

42

Then Job answered the LORD:
²"I know that you can do all things
  and that no purpose of yours can be
    thwarted.
³ 'Who is this that hides counsel without
    knowledge?'
Therefore I have uttered what I did not
    understand,
  things too wonderful for me that I did
    not know.

⁴ 'Hear, and I will speak;
  I will question you, and you declare
    to me.'
⁵ I had heard of you by the hearing of the
    ear,
  but now my eye sees you;
⁶ therefore I despise myself
  and repent in dust and ashes."

7 After the LORD had spoken these words to Job, the LORD said to Eliphaz the Temanite: "My wrath is kindled against you and against your two friends, for you have not spoken of me what is right, as my servant Job has. ⁸Now therefore take seven bulls and seven rams, and go to my servant Job, and offer up for yourselves a burnt offering, and my servant Job shall pray for you, for I will accept his prayer not to deal with you according to your folly, for you have not

among them. Ancient West Asian cultures widely imagined their civilizational origins through divine defeat of agents like these. Battles with the *sea* are found in 7:12; Ps. 74:12–17 (cf. Isa. 51:9–11). The "deep" precedes creation in Gen. 1:2. Leaving them unvanquished and even unchallenged, the poem ends on a destabilizing image of a morally uncertain cosmos as Job watches the stonehearted creature swim through the world, leaving behind a supernally glistening sea. **41:32** *Shining* recalls "eyelids of the dawn" (v. 18). See Num. 6:25; Pss. 18:28; 19:8; 77:18; Eccl. 8:1. **41:33** *On earth it has no equal.* The Latin translation of this phrase is quoted on the frontispiece of Thomas Hobbes's *Leviathan* (see **"Leviathan," p. 735**).

42:1–6 Job's final words could reflect at least four different responses to YHWH: (1) sublime encounter, (2) repentant submission, (3) moody frustration, and (4) critical rejection. **42:2** *Purpose* has a positive sense in Prov. 3:21 (where is it translated as "prudence") but more often has a negative sense, like "scheme" as implied in Pss. 10:4; 139:20; Prov. 24:8. *Thwarted* is literally "restrained" or "withheld." See Gen. 11:6. **42:3** Job repeats God's question in 38:2. *Things too wonderful* is a very common but ambiguous term. It often describes wonderful acts of God (see 1 Chr. 16:9; Ps. 26:7; Isa. 29:14). But it can also refer to afflictions and diseases (Deut. 28:59; Exod. 3:20) or anything incomprehensible (Deut. 30:11; Prov. 30:18; 2 Sam. 1:26). **42:4** Job repeats God's words in 38:3 and 40:7. **42:6** *Despise . . . repent.* The translation reflects the view that Job is apologetic, humbled, and/or acquiescent. However, the Hebrew terms are versatile and may reflect a different response from Job. For example, Job could be expressing general disdain and frustration. The first linguistic challenge is that *despise* or "reject" has no object, so we do not know whom or what Job despises or rejects. The reader must either fill it in, as the printed English above does (*myself*), or render an English verb that does not need an object (i.e., "fed up"); "flow away" is also sometimes proposed. *Repent* is unlikely. A better translation for the Hebrew word is "regret," "feel pity for," or "be consoled by." *Dust and ashes* (see 30:19; Gen. 18:27) could mean "wretched humanity" or "human mortality" or invoke the elements of a lament ritual. With so many options, perhaps this linguistic range is the point.

42:7–17 The prose tale concludes. The prose tale with which the book began (chaps. 1–2) returns. Its simplicity sharply focuses the reader's ethical confrontation with scripts of recovery from catastrophe: ten new children, double possessions, long life, and restorative relationships. The story develops the theme of ethics and life-giving relationships. However, does this ending justify the original bet between God and the accuser? Missing here is any mention of the accuser (1:6, 12; 2:1, 6–7) or how Job was healed of his illness. Also missing are any explicit mentions of Job's wife or whoever birthed Job's ten new children (2:9; 19:17; 31:10) and whether his new, even larger estate still enslaves people (1:3; 7:1–3; 19:13–19). Job's new daughters are included and named in the story (vv. 14–15). **42:7** In a striking return to wrath (cf. chaps. 38–41), God chastises the three friends. Importantly, God takes Job's side and twice criticizes the friends for not speaking what is *right* (also v. 8). *Right* can also mean "sincere," "firm," or "constant." *My servant.* See 1:8; 2:3.

spoken of me what is right, as my servant Job has done." [9]So Eliphaz the Temanite and Bildad the Shuhite and Zophar the Naamathite went and did what the LORD had told them, and the LORD accepted Job's prayer.

10 And the LORD restored the fortunes of Job when he had prayed for his friends, and the LORD gave Job twice as much as he had before. [11]Then there came to him all his brothers and sisters and all who had known him before, and they ate bread with him in his house; they showed him sympathy and comforted him for all the evil that the LORD had brought upon him; and each of them gave him a piece of money[z] and a gold ring. [12]The LORD blessed the latter days of Job more than his beginning, and he had fourteen thousand sheep, six thousand camels, a thousand yoke of oxen, and a thousand donkeys. [13]He also had seven sons and three daughters. [14]He named the first Jemimah, the second Keziah, and the third Keren-happuch. [15]In all the land there were no women so beautiful as Job's daughters, and their father gave them an inheritance along with their brothers. [16]After this Job lived one hundred and forty years and saw his children and his children's children, four generations. [17]And Job died, old and full of days.

z 42.11 Heb *a qesitah*

42:9 *Accepted Job's prayer* is literally "lifted Job." **42:10** Job's restored fortunes (1:1–3) are a double return. If God honored the law of restitution for stolen property (see Exod. 22:3, 6, 8), this would conclude Job's trial of God. **42:11** *Sympathy and comforted* are terms repeated about Eliphaz, Bildad, and Zophar in 2:12 but now fortified by restorative gifts of a meal and financial resources. Compare the American adage after catastrophe, "thoughts and prayers." Themes about being a good ally to those suffering are suggested in Job's speeches about companionship. *The evil that the LORD had brought upon him.* The narrator makes clear what the poetic speech of God largely evaded (chaps. 38–41; cf. 42:7–8; 2:10). **42:15** Job includes his daughters in his *inheritance along with their brothers.* According to custom, daughters did not usually inherit any of the father's estate, though see Num. 27:1–11.

THE PSALMS

The book of Psalms, also called the Psalter, is a collection of smaller poems called psalms. In point of fact, the Psalter is a collection of collections, an anthology of psalms and groups of psalms. At the highest level, it is composed of five "books" (Pss. 1–41, 42–72, 73–89, 90–106, 107–150), each ending with a concluding doxological verse or two or, in the case of Book V and the Psalter as a whole, with an entire psalm (Ps. 150). Smaller subcollections of psalms are also in evidence, however, as, for example, in Pss. 120–134, the Songs of Ascent.

The Psalms, Poetry, and History

The current shape of the Psalter reveals that the book and its constituent parts have a history, only some of which can be reconstructed. A large problem besetting historical certainty is the psalms' poetic nature. The Psalter contains almost no explicit references to key events in Israel's history mentioned in other parts of the Bible or known from the extrabiblical record. The history that lies behind the psalms is thus hard to discern. Said differently, the Psalter is not a history book; indeed, in some ways, the Psalter might be considered nonhistorical or, better, transhistorical. The historical inexactness of these poems is what allows them to transcend specific periods and prove adaptable to readers across time and regions. Even so, the psalms likely fall into three general time frames within Israel's history: premonarchic, monarchic, and exilic/postexilic. It is common to assume that the psalms played important roles in Israelite worship and the temple, but it is also clear that many psalms would have had a place in the context of family and household religion. The common themes of sickness and praise do not require a centralized cult site to be meaningful.

Earlier scholarship often tried to situate the psalms in particular moments of Israel's history. Psalms that mention the king or the city of Zion/Jerusalem likely presuppose the monarchy, for instance. When disaster struck and the city fell to the Babylonians, these psalms were often spiritualized or applied to future realities. Both Pss. 89 and 137 refer to the fall of Jerusalem, for example, and capture some of the trauma associated with that event. One empire was replaced by another, imposing new challenges, and the psalms proved flexible enough to be reapplied to other times and areas. Despite that flexibility, many scholars believe that in its current form, the Psalter has been profoundly shaped by several traumatic episodes—most especially the Babylonian exile in the sixth century BCE. The Babylonian Empire yielded to the Persian Empire, which was followed in turn by the Greek and the Roman Empires. Throughout, the Psalter was an important resource for those who experienced similar or even completely unrelated events.

As a result, interpretation of the psalms must be flexible. Given the problems of history mentioned above, perhaps the best approach to the psalms is a literary one (see below). That said, the poetic nature of the psalms means that much remains elusive historically and literarily. Wise interpreters will refrain from offering blanket judgments about the Psalter. Each psalm demands its own particular attention.

Reading Guide

The 150 psalms in the Psalter come to us in a limited number of literary forms (see **"The Types of the Psalms," p. 742**). These different kinds of psalms afford readers insight into various aspects of ancient Israel, including its theology, religiosity, and even spirituality. Two scholars, Hermann Gunkel and Sigmund Mowinckel, can be credited for shaping modern interpretation of the psalms by combining careful literary analysis of the different psalm types with an understanding of how the psalms functioned in Israel's life and worship. More recent scholarship is less certain than Gunkel and Mowinckel on the life situations that lie behind the psalms as we now have them. Some scholars also question the validity or usefulness of classifying a psalm as this or that type. Even so, the process of classifying the psalms remains a constant in psalm interpretation, as does the ongoing investigation of the place and function of the psalms in ancient Israel. The psalms are best understood as a repository of Israel's religious poetic works that fall into several primary categories.

Hymns of praise express adoration for God and can take various forms. One version celebrates God's good creation (see Pss. 8, 19, 65, 104, 148). Another celebrates God's sovereignty, captured in the idea of divine enthronement (see Pss. 47, 93, 95, 96, 97, 98, 99). The main elements of these

hymns are a call for divine action, a summons to praise, a call to worship, the praise of God, blessings, and the expression of hopes or desires.

Lament psalms are comparable to how W. E. B. Du Bois describes the spirituals as "sorrow songs." This type appears in both individual and communal forms, employing "I" language and "we" language, respectively. The lament type is the most frequently attested in the Psalter, with well over thirty lament psalms appearing therein, the majority of those individual laments. These psalms are sometimes called *complaint psalms* or *prayers for help*. The laments typically include the following elements: invocation, complaint, petition for help, confession of trust, and vow to praise. More recent scholarship has connected the lament psalms to trauma studies.

Thanksgiving songs look back on past trouble that has been resolved in some way. These psalms usually include an invitation to give thanks, followed by the praise of God and acknowledgment of God's salvific work, an offertory formula, and blessings over participation in the ceremony and exhortation. This type of psalm appears in both individual (Pss. 30, 34, 41, 66, 92, 116, 118, 138) and communal (Pss. 67, 75, 107, 124, 129, 136) forms.

Other types of psalms are attested beyond these three major categories, but they are usually identified by content rather than literary form. For example, the *royal psalms* mention the king and afford a glimpse into ancient ideas about the monarch and monarchy. Other psalms reflect processes of pilgrimage to, entrance into, and worship within the temple (see, e.g., Pss. 15, 24, 120–134). *Zion psalms* celebrate the city of Jerusalem as God's holy abode (see Pss. 46, 48, 76, 84, 87, 122, 125, 132). *Torah psalms* highlight the importance and function of the law as crucial for Israel's identity (Pss. 1, 19, 119). *Wisdom psalms* depend on ancient wisdom traditions (see Pss. 32, 37, 49, 73, 78, 112, 127, 128, 133). *Historical psalms* recount Israel's history in poetic form (Pss. 78, 105–106, 135–136).

Psalms that reflect the importance of Zion and the monarchy show that these realities played theological, not just political, roles; at the same time, such psalms show the political ramifications of theological poetry (see Pss. 2, 18, 20, 21, 45, 72, 89, 101, 110, 132). Some of the psalms mentioning the king or Zion may be rightly classified with other types, whether complaint or thanksgiving psalms (e.g., Pss. 89, 144), coronation hymns (Pss. 2, 110), intercessory psalms (Pss. 20, 21), or even a kind of wedding song (Ps. 45). Such "bleed over" shows that the literary genres are somewhat porous and should not be applied too rigidly.

Stephen Breck Reid and W. H. Bellinger, Jr.

BOOK I
(PSALMS 1–41)

PSALM 1

¹ Happy are those
   who do not follow the advice of the wicked
or take the path that sinners tread
   or sit in the seat of scoffers,
² but their delight is in the law of the LORD,
   and on his law they meditate day and night.
³ They are like trees
   planted by streams of water,
which yield their fruit in its season,
   and their leaves do not wither.
In all that they do, they prosper.

Book I: Pss. 1–41 Book I of the Psalter begins with a two-part introduction (Pss. 1–2). The first reference to David in a superscription occurs in what is called the first Davidic Psalter group (Pss. 3–41; cf. also Pss. 51–72 and 138–145). Book I contains several different types of psalms in the following order: laments (Pss. 3–8), an acrostic (Pss. 9–10), more laments (Pss. 11–14), a chiastic subcollection about entrance to the worship site where the various psalms correspond in an envelope-like structure (Pss. 15–24), and more laments (Pss. 25–41).

Ps. 1:1–41 A torah psalm (see also Pss. 19, 119) that draws the reader to the positive function of God's instruction. The Hebrew term "torah" can refer to a specific body of literature or, more generally, to divine teaching. Psalms 1 and 2 function together, with the mentions of *happy* serving as bookends. Psalm 1 focuses on the flourishing life found in God's law and has a four-part structure: a description of the way of the wicked (v. 1), a contrast with a life focused on torah (v. 2), the way of torah (v. 3), and a judgment of the wicked (vv. 4–6). As an introduction to the Psalter and given its understanding of torah, Ps. 1 likely comes from the exilic or postexilic period. **1:1–3** The beatitude *happy* occurs in

⁴ The wicked are not so
　　but are like chaff that the wind drives
　　　away.
⁵ Therefore the wicked will not stand in
　　　the judgment
　　nor sinners in the congregation of the
　　　righteous,
⁶ for the Lord watches over the way of the
　　　righteous,
　　but the way of the wicked will perish.

Psalm 2

¹ Why do the nations conspire
　　and the peoples plot in vain?
² The kings of the earth set themselves,
　　and the rulers take counsel together,
　　against the Lord and his anointed, saying,
³ "Let us burst their bonds apart
　　and cast their cords from us."

⁴ He who sits in the heavens laughs;
　　the Lord has them in derision.
⁵ Then he will speak to them in his wrath
　　and terrify them in his fury, saying,
⁶ "I have set my king on Zion, my holy hill."

⁷ I will tell of the decree of the Lord:
　He said to me, "You are my son;
　　today I have begotten you.

⁸ Ask of me, and I will make the nations
　　your heritage
　and the ends of the earth your
　　possession.
⁹ You shall break them with a rod of iron
　and dash them in pieces like a potter's
　　vessel."

¹⁰ Now therefore, O kings, be wise;
　be warned, O rulers of the earth.
¹¹ Serve the Lord with fear;
　with trembling ¹²kiss his feet,ᵃ
or he will be angry, and you will perish
　in the way,
for his wrath is quickly kindled.

Happy are all who take refuge in him.

Psalm 3

A Psalm of David, when he fled from his son Absalom.
¹ O Lord, how many are my foes!
　Many are rising against me;
² many are saying to me,
　"There is no help for youᵇ in God."
　　　　　　　　　　　　　　　　Selah

³ But you, O Lord, are a shield around me,

ᵃ 2.12 Cn: Meaning of Heb of 2.11b and 12a is uncertain
ᵇ 3.2 Syr: Heb *him*

eighteen psalms. See **"Hebrew Poetry," p. 741**. Vv. 1–3 offer instruction in two ways, that of the righteous and the *wicked*; the latter is a common term for the enemies of God and of the psalmists. The contrast discusses both locations and types of persons. *Trees* function here as an arboreal metaphor for those who are rooted and stable. **1:4–5** The wicked are described with the metaphor of *chaff*, unsubstantial plant refuse. **1:6** There are two ways: one known by God, the other known only by the wicked.

Ps. 2:1–11 The Psalter has several psalms that mention royal figures. Psalm 2 is the first of these royal psalms (see Pss. 18, 20, 21, 45, 72, 89, 101, 110, 132). In these psalms, God is the patron of the king. Psalm 2 has three parts: an initial question (v. 1), a description (vv. 2–9), and imperative commands (vv. 10–12). It is possible that the prominence of the monarch and Zion put the psalm in the tenth century. **2:1–3** Nations aspire to overthrow divine sovereignty. **2:4–9** The king and Zion are dual instruments of God. **2:7** The phrase *You are my son; . . . begotten you* likely expresses the divine adoption of the monarch (cf. 2 Sam. 7:14; Ps. 89:26–27). The New Testament reads this verse christologically (see Mark 1:11; Acts 13:33; Heb. 5:5). **2:10–11** Final admonition and beatitude. Note that *happy* also occurs in Ps. 1:1, binding these two psalms together in an inclusio or envelope structure.

Ps. 3:1–8 Almost half of the psalms in Book I are individual laments. See **"The Types of the Psalms," p. 742**. Psalm 3 has four stanzas: a complaint (vv. 1–2), a confession of trust (vv. 3–4), a second confession of trust (vv. 5–6), and petitions (vv. 7–8). **Superscription.** *A Psalm of David* occurs in multiple superscriptions. Psalm 3's superscription is one of thirteen to mention some aspect of David's life (see also Pss. 7, 18, 34, 51, 52, 54, 56, 57, 59, 60, 63, 142). Other superscriptions say simply "Of David." In this psalm, the story of David and his son Absalom (see 2 Sam. 15–18) reflects a loss of intimacy and the reality of betrayal. **3:1–2** The word *many* occurs three times in the first two verses, and a large crowd is also present in v. 6. The reference to multiple foes is a common element in personal laments. The precise meaning of *Selah* (also vv. 4, 8) is unclear. It may signal some type of musical interlude. **3:3–6** The psalmist offers a first-person expression of trust. **3:3** Laments often address God with the second-person pronoun *you* to underscore the direct relationship. The psalmist refers to divine protection using

Going Deeper: Hebrew Poetry (Psalms 1:1–2 and 24:1)

Hebrew poetry, like other poetries, is an elevated form of speech that is marked by various elements, above all by versification: composition in poetic lines. Poetry also uses language in unusual ways: familiar words might be used unexpectedly, or rare words might be employed. Like most ancient poetry, Hebrew poetry was composed for oral performance and, as a result, often sounds pleasing. Above all, poetry is both spare and dense. Its brevity means it does not and cannot contain all the information incorporated into prose; much is left to the imagination and to interpretation. Precisely because of its economy, poetic language is dense, each word containing within it multiple meanings. While poetry is seldom easy to read or understand, a third or more of the Hebrew Bible is composed in poetic form. This includes not only books like Psalms and Proverbs but also much of the prophetic corpus. The Apocrypha also contains poetic books, some quite lengthy (e.g., Wisdom of Solomon and Sirach). By way of comparison, other than its citations from the Old Testament, the New Testament contains very little poetry. What poetry does appear is embedded within larger prose blocks (e.g., Phil. 2:6–11; Rev. 1:7; 3:7). Poetic inserts are also found in the First Testament (see **"Introduction to the Torah/Pentateuch," pp. 2–4**) and the Apocrypha (e.g., Tob. 3:2–6; Jdt. 16:1–17; 1 Macc. 1:24b–28).

Lacking regular use of meter and rhyme, Hebrew poetry's primary characteristic is *parallelism*, a widespread phenomenon that helps demarcate Hebrew verse. Parallelism refers to the way Hebrew poetry typically situates two lines (or, more rarely, three) into some kind of close relationship. The relationship may be based on content but could also work at grammatical or syntactical levels. Content-based parallelism is often subdivided into affirming (synonymous), oppositional (antithetical), or advancing (synthetic). In the first type, the content of the two (or three) lines is repeated in a similar if not identical fashion (e.g., Ps. 24:1; Jonah 2:2). In the second type, the lines are at odds: the first utters one sentiment, the second something contrary (e.g., Ps. 1:1–2; Prov. 26:4–5). In the third type, the thought of the first line is furthered or developed in what follows (e.g., Ps. 23:4; Lam. 2:6). Parallelism has been found in many of the world's poetries, including English poetry, largely due to the work of the priest-poet Gerard Manley Hopkins (1844–89), who himself was inspired by the biblical poetic style.

Brent A. Strawn

my glory, and the one who lifts up my
head.
⁴ I cry aloud to the Lᴏʀᴅ,
and he answers me from his holy hill.
Selah

⁵ I lie down and sleep;
I wake again, for the Lᴏʀᴅ sustains me.
⁶ I am not afraid of ten thousands of
people
who have set themselves against me
all around.

⁷ Rise up, O Lᴏʀᴅ!
Deliver me, O my God!

For you strike all my enemies on the
cheek;
you break the teeth of the wicked.

⁸ Deliverance belongs to the Lᴏʀᴅ;
may your blessing be on your people!
Selah

Psalm 4

To the leader: with stringed instruments. A Psalm of David.

¹ Answer me when I call, O God of my right!
You gave me room when I was in
distress.
Be gracious to me, and hear my prayer.

the metaphor of a shield. **3:5** Sleep here is an expression of innocence; an absence of fear is another sign of innocence (see Ps. 56:4, 11). **3:7** The divine attack strikes vulnerable body parts: the cheek and teeth (see Ps. 58:6). **3:8** *Selah.* See note on Ps. 3:1–2.

Ps. 4:1–8 A lament regarding personal enemies with a concentric structure opening with a plea for help (v. 1), followed by a complaint about the language of the community (v. 2), words of instruction (vv. 3–5), a second complaint (v. 6), and a concluding confession that parallels the opening plea (vv. 7–8). **Superscription.** *To the leader* occurs in fifty-five superscriptions in the Psalter and probably refers to a musical or liturgical leader. *With stringed instruments.* See Pss. 6, 54, 55, 61, 67, 76. *A Psalm of David.* See note on Ps. 3 superscription. **4:1** *Hear my prayer* is a petition (cf. Pss. 39:12;

Going Deeper: The Types of the Psalms (Psalm 3)

The great German biblical scholar Hermann Gunkel identified five major types of psalms: individual laments, communal laments, hymns of praise, thanksgiving songs, and royal psalms. Two-thirds of the biblical psalms correspond to one of these five major types. Among these five, three—lament, praise, and thanksgiving—are particularly important.

Lament psalms. Individual lament psalms—sometimes called prayers for help—are the most frequently attested type of psalm. The poet uses "I" language, complaining to God and asking for assistance. These psalms typically end up praising God, but two do not (Pss. 39, 88). The problems discussed in these psalms are usually caused by enemies or by God, though in a few cases, the problem is the psalmist's own sin (see Pss. 6, 32, 38, 51, 102, 130, 143; the penitential psalms). Laments also come in communal forms using "we" language (see Pss. 44, 60, 74, 79, 80, 85, 90, 94, 123, 137). Psalms of trust such as Pss. 23, 91, 121, 125, and 131 might be considered with the complaint psalms because they express trust in the midst of trouble.

Praise psalms. This type occurs in four subtypes: general hymns (e.g., Pss. 29, 33), creation psalms (Pss. 8, 19, 65, 104, 148), enthronement psalms celebrating God's reign (Pss. 47, 93, 95, 96, 97, 98, 99), and Zion psalms that memorialize Jerusalem as the abode of God (Pss. 46, 48, 76, 84, 87, 122, 125, 132). Praise psalms laud God for who God is and for what God has done.

Thanksgiving psalms. This type of psalm occurs in individual (see Pss. 30, 34, 41, 66, 92, 116, 118, 138) and communal (see Pss. 67, 75, 107, 124, 129, 136) forms. In these psalms, the poet looks back on past trouble that has been resolved and thanks God for deliverance.

The last third of the psalms belong to other types. Acrostic psalms, for example, are structured by the use of the alphabet (Pss. 25, 34, 37, 111, 112, 119, 145). Entrance liturgies like Pss. 15 and 24 concern the admissibility of worshipers to the temple area. There are psalms with prophetic warnings (Pss. 50, 81, 82) and historical psalms that recount salvation history (Pss. 78, 105, 106). Royal psalms mention the king (Pss. 2, 18, 20, 21, 45, 72, 89, 101, 110, 132, 144), while wisdom psalms reflect wisdom traditions (Pss. 1, 32, 37, 49, 73, 78, 112, 119, 127, 128, 133).

Stephen Breck Reid

²How long, you people, shall my honor
    suffer shame?
  How long will you love vain words and
    seek after lies?   *Selah*
³But know that the LORD has set apart the
    faithful for himself;
  the LORD hears when I call to him.

⁴When you are disturbed,*ᶜ* do not
    sin;
  ponder it on your beds, and be silent.
        Selah
⁵Offer right sacrifices,
  and put your trust in the LORD.

⁶There are many who say, "O that we
    might see some good!

Let the light of your face shine on us,
  O LORD!"
⁷You have put gladness in my heart
  more than when their grain and wine
    abound.

⁸I will both lie down and sleep in
    peace,
  for you alone, O LORD, make me lie
    down in safety.

PSALM 5

To the leader: for the flutes. A Psalm of David.
¹Listen to my words, O LORD;
  attend to my sighing.

c 4.4 Or are angry

54:2; 84:8; 143:1). Tight spaces contrast with the desire to have room (see Pss. 18:19; 31:8); distress is figured as a cramped place. **4:2, 4** *Selah.* See note on Ps. 3:1–2.

Ps. 5:1–12 A lament over personal enemies with three petitions and responses: a petition for divine hearing (vv. 1–3) and a response to the wicked (vv. 4–6), a second petition (vv. 7–8) and a response to the wicked (v. 9), and a third petition (vv. 10–11) with a blessing (v. 12). The reference to God as king may indicate a historical setting during the monarchy. **Superscription.** *For the flutes* is apparently a direction for musical accompaniment. *To the leader* and *A Psalm of David.* See notes on Ps. 3 and 4 superscriptions. **5:1–6** The opening half is a call for divine hearing, including a reference to God as king. The list of vices includes boastful persons and *those who speak lies* and who are *bloodthirsty*

² Listen to the sound of my cry,
  my King and my God,
  for to you I pray.
³ O Lord, in the morning you hear my voice;
  in the morning I plead my case to you
  and watch.

⁴ For you are not a God who delights in
  wickedness;
  evil will not sojourn with you.
⁵ The boastful will not stand before your
  eyes;
  you hate all evildoers.
⁶ You destroy those who speak lies;
  the Lord abhors the bloodthirsty and
  deceitful.

⁷ But I, through the abundance of your
  steadfast love,
  will enter your house;
I will bow down toward your holy
  temple
  in awe of you.
⁸ Lead me, O Lord, in your righteousness
  because of my enemies;
  make your way straight before me.

⁹ For there is no truth in their mouths;
  their hearts are destruction;
their throats are open graves;
  they flatter with their tongues.
¹⁰ Make them bear their guilt, O God;
  let them fall by their own counsels;
because of their many transgressions,
  cast them out,
  for they have rebelled against you.

¹¹ But let all who take refuge in you rejoice;
  let them ever sing for joy.

Spread your protection over them,
  so that those who love your name may
  exult in you.
¹² For you bless the righteous, O Lord;
  you cover them with favor as with a
  shield.

Psalm 6

*To the leader: with stringed instruments; according to
The Sheminith. A Psalm of David.*
¹ O Lord, do not rebuke me in your anger
  or discipline me in your wrath.
² Be gracious to me, O Lord, for I am
  languishing;
  O Lord, heal me, for my bones are
  shaking with terror.
³ My soul also is struck with terror,
  while you, O Lord—how long?

⁴ Turn, O Lord, save my life;
  deliver me for the sake of your
  steadfast love.
⁵ For in death there is no remembrance of
  you;
  in Sheol who can give you praise?

⁶ I am weary with my moaning;
  every night I flood my bed with
  tears;
  I drench my couch with my weeping.
⁷ My eyes waste away because of grief;
  they grow weak because of all my
  foes.

⁸ Depart from me, all you workers of evil,
  for the Lord has heard the sound of
  my weeping.
⁹ The Lord has heard my supplication;
  the Lord accepts my prayer.

and *deceitful.* **5:7–8** The language of entering the house and temple anticipates Pss. 15 and 24. **5:9–12** Metaphors like *throats are open graves* may refer to verbal abuse. **5:11** This verse brings together the idea of taking refuge in God with the worship of song. **5:12** The psalm closes with a final blessing.
Ps. 6:1–10 The first of the seven penitential prayers (see also Pss. 32, 38, 51, 102, 130, 143). Three stanzas cover the following: an initial petition for grace and healing (vv. 1–3), a second petition (vv. 4–7), and an expression of confidence against the psalmist's adversaries (vv. 8–10). **Superscription.** *To the leader* and *with stringed instruments.* See note on Ps. 4 superscription. *Sheminith* is a translit-eration of the Hebrew word; it may mean "according to the eighth," which would likely be a musical reference. *A Psalm of David.* See note on Ps. 3 superscription. **6:1–5** The first half of the psalm is a request for grace and healing. A soul struck by terror requires divine attention; the psalmist begs for God's consideration. The psalmist bargains with God regarding the threat represented by *Sheol* (= the realm of the dead) and by death, which subverts not only life but also the remembrance and praise of God (cf. Pss. 30:9; 88:10–12; Job 10:21–22; Isa. 38:18). **6:6–7** The psalmist provides a self-description of the illness. **6:8–10** The final verses warn the adversaries based on the psalmist's certainty that God has heard the lament.

¹⁰ All my enemies shall be ashamed and
  struck with terror;
    they shall turn back and in a moment
    be put to shame.

PSALM 7

*A Shiggaion of David, which he sang to the LORD
concerning Cush, a Benjaminite.*

¹ O LORD my God, in you I take refuge;
  save me from all my pursuers, and
  deliver me,
² or like a lion they will tear me apart;
  they will drag me away, with no one to
  rescue.

³ O LORD my God, if I have done this,
  if there is wrong in my hands,
⁴ if I have repaid my ally with harm
  or plundered my foe without
  cause,
⁵ then let the enemy pursue and overtake
  me,
  trample my life to the ground,
  and lay my soul in the dust.   *Selah*

⁶ Rise up, O LORD, in your anger;
  lift yourself up against the fury of my
  enemies;
  awake, O my God;*ᵈ* you have
  appointed a judgment.
⁷ Let the assembly of the peoples be
  gathered around you,
  and over it take your seat*ᵉ* on high.
⁸ The LORD judges the peoples;
  judge me, O LORD, according to my
  righteousness
  and according to the integrity that is
  in me.

⁹ O let the evil of the wicked come to an end,
  but establish the righteous,
  you who test the minds and hearts,
  O righteous God.
¹⁰ God is my shield,
  who saves the upright in heart.
¹¹ God is a righteous judge
  and a God who has indignation every
  day.

¹² If one does not repent, God*ᶠ* will whet his
  sword;
  he has bent and strung his bow;
¹³ he has prepared his deadly weapons,
  making his arrows fiery shafts.
¹⁴ See how they conceive evil
  and are pregnant with mischief
  and bring forth lies.
¹⁵ They make a pit, digging it out,
  and fall into the hole that they have
  made.
¹⁶ Their mischief returns upon their own
  heads,
  and on their own heads their violence
  descends.

¹⁷ I will give to the LORD the thanks due to
  his righteousness
  and sing praise to the name of the
  LORD, the Most High.

PSALM 8

*To the leader: according to The Gittith. A Psalm of
David.*

¹ O LORD, our Sovereign,
  how majestic is your name in all the
  earth!

d 7.6 Or *awake for me*   *e* 7.7 Cn: Heb *return*   *f* 7.12 Heb *he*

Ps. 7:1–17 A lament regarding personal enemies arranged in four parts: an appeal for rescue and vow of innocence (vv. 1–5), another appeal for justice and vindication (vv. 6–9), a confession of trust (vv. 10–16), and a closing vow (v. 17). **Superscription.** The details here point to an event not found elsewhere in the Bible. **7:1** The psalmist claims to take refuge in God. **7:2** *Lion.* The psalmists often depict their enemies as predatory animals (cf. Pss. 10:9; 17:12; 22:12–13; 58:3–6). **7:3–5** Arguments for the psalmist's innocence are set off by the word *if.* For *selah,* see note on Ps. 3:1–2. **7:6–8** These verses provide a petition for divine judgment. **7:10–11** God is here figured as a shield (cf. Pss. 18:2; 28:7; 119:114; 144:2) and as a judge (Pss. 50:4, 6; 67:4; 75:2; 82:2, 8; 94:2; 96:10, 13; 98:9; 119:84)—both of which express trust in God. **7:12** God is a shield but also has a sword of vengeance. **7:15–16** The enemies suffer in proportion to their own transgression (see Ps. 141:10; Prov. 26:27; Esth. 6:14–7:10). **7:17** *I will give to the LORD the thanks* is a phrase that expresses a vow (cf. Pss. 9:2; 109:30; 111:1).

Ps. 8:1–9 A hymn of praise (see Pss. 19, 65, 104, 148) laid out in four parts: a statement of praise (v. 1a), a statement of God's glory and the question of human worth (vv. 1b–4), a response to the psalmist's question (vv. 5–8), and a final praise of God (v. 9). **Superscription.** *The Gittith* may be a musical instrument, perhaps from the city of Gath. *To the leader* and *A Psalm of David.* See notes on Pss. 3 and 4 superscriptions. **8:1** The opening statement highlights divine sovereignty.

You have set your glory above the heavens.
²   Out of the mouths of babes and infants
you have founded a bulwark because of
    your foes,
  to silence the enemy and the avenger.

³ When I look at your heavens, the work of
    your fingers,
  the moon and the stars that you have
    established;
⁴ what are humans that you are mindful of
    them,
  mortals*ᵍ* that you care for them?

⁵ Yet you have made them a little lower
    than God*ʰ*
  and crowned them with glory and honor.
⁶ You have given them dominion over the
    works of your hands;
  you have put all things under their feet,
⁷ all sheep and oxen,
  and also the beasts of the field,
⁸ the birds of the air, and the fish of the sea,
  whatever passes along the paths of
    the seas.

⁹ O Lord, our Sovereign,
  how majestic is your name in all the
    earth!

Psalm 9

To the leader: according to Muth-labben. A Psalm of David.
¹ *ⁱ*I will give thanks to the Lord with my
    whole heart;
  I will tell of all your wonderful deeds.

² I will be glad and exult in you;
  I will sing praise to your name, O Most
    High.

³ When my enemies turned back,
  they stumbled and perished before you.
⁴ For you have maintained my just cause;
  you have sat on the throne giving
    righteous judgment.

⁵ You have rebuked the nations; you have
    destroyed the wicked;
  you have blotted out their name
    forever and ever.
⁶ The enemies have vanished in everlasting
    ruins;
  their cities you have rooted out;
  the very memory of them has
    perished.

⁷ But the Lord sits enthroned forever;
  he has established his throne for
    judgment.
⁸ He judges the world with righteousness;
  he judges the peoples with equity.

⁹ The Lord is a stronghold for the oppressed,
  a stronghold in times of trouble.
¹⁰ And those who know your name put
    their trust in you,
  for you, O Lord, have not forsaken
    those who seek you.

g 8.4 Heb *son of man* *h* 8.5 Or *than the divine beings* or *angels* *i* 9.1 Psalms 9–10 were originally one psalm, as in the Greek and Latin traditions. In Hebrew, Psalms 9–10 formed an acrostic.

8:2 *Out of the mouths of babes* has become a colloquial saying in modern parlance. The word *bulwark* translates a Hebrew word that means strength. **8:4** The psalmist raises a question regarding the apparently elevated role of human beings. **8:5** *A little lower than God* renders the Hebrew word "Elohim" as a singular proper noun instead of a generic plural, "gods," which is also possible. **8:6–8** The psalmist acknowledges human dominion over the created realm (see Gen. 1:26–28), though other psalms (e.g., Ps. 104) are far less anthropocentric. The New Testament offers christological readings of this material in 1 Cor. 15:27–28; Heb. 2:6–8. **8:9** The psalm closes with a statement of God's sovereignty that encompasses (v. 1) and thus surpasses all human capacity.

    Pss. 9–10 An acrostic form, where each line begins with a subsequent letter in the Hebrew alphabet, indicates these two psalms are one composition (as they are in the Greek Septuagint). Other acrostic psalms are Pss. 25, 34, 37, 111, 112, 119, and 145. Together, Pss. 9–10 have four large sections: a statement of praise (9:1–12), a petition (9:13–20), a complaint (10:1–11), and a statement of trust (10:12–18). The references to Zion indicate a setting during the monarchy or later. **Superscription.** *Leader.* See note on Ps. 4 superscription. *David.* See note on Ps. 3 superscription. *Muth-labben* is the transliteration of a Hebrew word whose meaning is unclear; it may be a musical reference. The absence of a superscription in Ps. 10, combined with the acrostic form, again suggests that Pss. 9–10 were originally one composition. **9:1–2** *I will give thanks to the Lord* is a phrase that functions as a vow (cf. Pss. 7:17; 109:30; 111:1). **9:3–10** These verses offer an expression of confidence.

¹¹ Sing praises to the L ORD, who dwells in
Zion.
  Declare his deeds among the
    peoples.
¹² For he who avenges blood is mindful of
them;
  he does not forget the cry of the
    afflicted.

¹³ Be gracious to me, O L ORD.
  See what I suffer from those who hate
    me;
  you are the one who lifts me up from
    the gates of death,
¹⁴ so that I may recount all your praises
  and, in the gates of daughter Zion,
    rejoice in your deliverance.

¹⁵ The nations have sunk in the pit that
they made;
  in the net that they hid has their own
    foot been caught.
¹⁶ The L ORD has made himself known; he
has executed judgment;
  the wicked are snared in the work of
    their own hands.   *Higgaion. Selah*

¹⁷ The wicked shall depart to Sheol,
  all the nations that forget God.

¹⁸ For the needy shall not always be
forgotten,
  nor the hope of the poor perish forever.

¹⁹ Rise up, O L ORD! Do not let mortals
prevail;
  let the nations be judged before you.
²⁰ Put them in fear, O L ORD;
  let the nations know that they are only
    human.   *Selah*

P SALM 10

¹ *j* Why, O L ORD, do you stand far off?
  Why do you hide yourself in times of
    trouble?
² In arrogance the wicked persecute the
poor—
  let them be caught in the schemes
    they have devised.

³ For the wicked boast of the desires of
their heart;
  those greedy for gain curse and
    renounce the L ORD.
⁴ In the pride of their countenance the
wicked say, "God will not seek it
out";
  all their thoughts are, "There is no
    God."

⁵ Their ways prosper at all times;
  your judgments are on high, out of
    their sight;
  as for their foes, they scoff at
    them.
⁶ They think in their heart, "We shall not
be moved;
  throughout all generations we shall
    not meet adversity."

⁷ Their mouths are filled with cursing and
deceit and oppression;
  under their tongues are mischief and
    iniquity.
⁸ They sit in ambush in the villages;
  in hiding places they murder the
    innocent.

Their eyes stealthily watch for the
  helpless;
⁹ they lurk in secret like a lion in its
    den;
they lurk that they may seize the
  poor;
  they seize the poor and drag them off
    in their net.

¹⁰ They stoop, they crouch,
  and the helpless fall by their might.
¹¹ They think in their heart, "God has
forgotten;
  he has hidden his face; he will never
    see it."

¹² Rise up, O L ORD; O God, lift up your hand;
  do not forget the oppressed.

j 10.1 Psalms 9–10 were originally one psalm, as in the
Greek and Latin traditions. In Hebrew, Psalms 9–10
formed an acrostic.

9:11 This is a call to praise for Zion's inhabitants. **9:13–14** This is a call for celebration *in the gates
of daughter Zion*, with *daughter Zion* serving as a title for the city. **9:15–18** These verses offer an
expression of confidence. **9:16, 20** *Selah*. See note on Ps. 3:1–2. **9:19–10:15** This section stipulates a prayer that affirms God's concern for the poor and oppressed in the face of the arrogance
of *the wicked* (10:2–4). **10:9** The psalmist utilizes the lion metaphor again (see note on Ps. 7:2).

13 Why do the wicked renounce God
    and say in their hearts, "You will not
        call us to account"?

14 But you do see! Indeed, you note trouble
        and grief,
    that you may take it into your hands;
    the helpless commit themselves to you;
        you have been the helper of the
        orphan.

15 Break the arm of the wicked and
        evildoers;
    seek out their wickedness until you
        find none.
16 The LORD is king forever and ever;
    the nations shall perish from his land.

17 O LORD, you will hear the desire of the
        meek;
    you will strengthen their heart; you
        will incline your ear
18 to do justice for the orphan and the
        oppressed,
    so that those from earth may strike
        terror no more.*k*

PSALM 11

To the leader. Of David.
1 In the LORD I take refuge; how can you
        say to me,
    "Flee like a bird to the mountains,*l*
2 for look, the wicked bend the bow,
    they have fitted their arrow to the
        string,
    to shoot in the dark at the upright in
        heart.

3 If the foundations are destroyed,
    what can the righteous do?"

4 The LORD is in his holy temple;
    the LORD's throne is in heaven.
    His eyes behold; his gaze examines
        humankind.
5 The LORD tests the righteous and the
        wicked,
    and his soul hates the lover of violence.
6 On the wicked he will rain coals of fire
        and sulfur;
    a scorching wind shall be the portion
        of their cup.
7 For the LORD is righteous;
    he loves righteous deeds;
    the upright shall behold his face.

PSALM 12

*To the leader: according to The Sheminith. A Psalm of
David.*
1 Help, O LORD, for there is no longer
        anyone who is godly;
    the faithful have disappeared from
        humankind.
2 They utter lies to each other;
    with flattering lips and a deceitful
        heart they speak.

3 May the LORD cut off all flattering lips,
    the tongue that makes great boasts,
4 those who say, "With our tongues we
        will prevail;
    our lips are our own—who is our
        master?"

k 10.18 Meaning of Heb uncertain   *l* 11.1 Gk Syr Jerome
Tg: Heb *flee to your mountain, O bird*

10:16–18 The (two-chapter) composition ends with a final statement of confidence. The affirmation that *the LORD is king* ensures justice. For this acclamation, see also Pss. 10:16; 93:1; 96:10; 97:1; 99:1.

Ps. 11:1–7 A lament over personal enemies that includes expressions of trust. The psalm has two stanzas, each with two parts: a statement of trust and prediction of the enemies' fate (vv. 1–3) and a second statement of trust followed by divine action against the enemies (vv. 4–7). The mention of the *holy temple* may indicate a setting during the monarchy. **Superscription.** *To the leader.* See note on Ps. 4 superscription. *David.* See note on Ps. 3 superscription. **11:1–3** The metaphor of refuge is a common one (see Pss. 16:1; 18:2; 25:20; 43:2; 71:1; 144:2). The psalmist uses a quotation that evokes the image of a fleeing bird at risk from a hunter (cf. Isa. 16:2; Pss. 102:7; 124:7). The bird's vulnerability leads to a comment on the instability of the foundations (v. 3). **11:4–5** God's location—in both the temple and heaven—acknowledges divine testing of all and includes hatred for those who love violence. **11:6** Fire and sulfur are tools of punishment (cf. Gen. 19:24). The *cup* is a metaphor for judgment (Isa. 51:17; Ps. 23:5b). **11:7** The benefit of righteousness is seeing the face of God.

Ps. 12:1–8 A lament psalm divided into three parts: a plea (vv. 1–4), a divine response (v. 5), and words of assurance, perhaps from a liturgist (vv. 6–8). **Superscription.** *Sheminith.* See note on Ps. 6 superscription. *To the leader* and *A Psalm of David.* See notes on Pss. 3 and 4 superscriptions. **12:2** A *deceitful heart* marks duplicity in speech and action. **12:4** The enemies' question *who is our*

5 "Because the poor are despoiled,
  because the needy groan,
  I will now rise up," says the Lord;
  "I will place them in the safety for
    which they long."
6 The promises of the Lord are promises
    that are pure,
  silver refined in a furnace on the ground,
  purified seven times.

7 You, O Lord, will protect us;
  you will guard us from this generation
    forever.
8 On every side the wicked prowl,
  as vileness is exalted among
    humankind.

Psalm 13

To the leader. A Psalm of David.
1 How long, O Lord? Will you forget me
    forever?
  How long will you hide your face from
    me?
2 How long must I bear pain^m in my soul
  and have sorrow in my heart all day
    long?
  How long shall my enemy be exalted
    over me?

3 Consider and answer me, O Lord my God!
  Give light to my eyes, or I will sleep
    the sleep of death,
4 and my enemy will say, "I have prevailed";
  my foes will rejoice because I am
    shaken.

5 But I trusted in your steadfast love;
  my heart shall rejoice in your salvation.
6 I will sing to the Lord
  because he has dealt bountifully
    with me.

Psalm 14

To the leader. Of David.
1 Fools say in their hearts, "There is no
    God."
  They are corrupt; they do abominable
    deeds;
  there is no one who does good.

2 The Lord looks down from heaven on
    humankind
  to see if there are any who are wise,
  who seek after God.

3 They have all gone astray; they are all
    alike perverse;
  there is no one who does good,
  no, not one.

4 Have they no knowledge, all the
    evildoers
  who eat up my people as they eat
    bread
  and do not call upon the Lord?

5 There they shall be in great terror,
  for God is with the company of the
    righteous.

m 13.2 Syr: Heb *bold counsels*

master? reveals their profound hubris (cf. Pss. 9–10). **12:5** Divine speech answers enemy speech and expresses advocacy for the poor and needy. **12:6–8** These verses contrast the false speech of the powerful and arrogant (vv. 2–4) with the pure and refined promises of God (v. 6). **12:7–8** The psalmist concludes with a statement of assurance.

Ps. 13:1–6 A lament about personal enemies divided into three parts: a complaint (vv. 1–2), a petition (vv. 3–4), and a confession of trust (vv. 5–6). **Superscription.** *To the leader.* See note on Ps. 4 superscription. *A Psalm of David.* See note on Ps. 3 superscription. **13:1–2** The four-time repetition of the question *How long?* captures the distress of the psalmist. **13:3–4** The petition begins with the imperative *consider*; the psalmist demands God's attention. The psalmist worries about death (signaled by means of light and sleep metaphors) and shame (the speech of the enemies). **13:5–6** The psalmist closes with a statement of trust, in strong contrast to the despairing circumstances of the psalmist, along with a promise to sing to God.

Ps. 14:1–7 This psalm is nearly identical to Ps. 53. **Superscription.** *To the leader.* See note on Ps. 4 superscription. *Of David.* See note on Ps. 3 superscription. **14:1–3** The psalmist begins with a quotation from an adversary. *Fools* refers to people with inferior worldviews, not intellectual deficiencies. The heart is the seat of the will as well as affection. The foolish expression *There is no God* is not philosophical atheism but indicative of living a life without attention to God. The statement *there is no one who does good* recurs in v. 3 and frames this unit. **14:4** This question—perhaps from the divine—is about the community of evildoers. **14:5** The psalmist predicts the coming distress for the

⁶ You would confound the plans of the
poor,
but the LORD is their refuge.

⁷ O that deliverance for Israel would come
from Zion!
When the LORD restores the fortunes
of his people,
Jacob will rejoice; Israel will be glad.

PSALM 15

A Psalm of David.

¹ O LORD, who may abide in your tent?
Who may dwell on your holy hill?

² Those who walk blamelessly and do
what is right
and speak the truth from their heart;
³ who do not slander with their tongue
and do no evil to their friends
nor heap shame upon their neighbors;
⁴ in whose eyes the wicked are despised
but who honor those who fear the
LORD;
who stand by their oath even to their
hurt;
⁵ who do not lend money at interest
and do not take a bribe against the
innocent.

Those who do these things shall never be
moved.

PSALM 16

A Miktam of David.

¹ Protect me, O God, for in you I take
refuge.
² I say to the LORD, "You are my Lord;
I have no good apart from you."ⁿ

³ As for the holy ones in the land, they are
the noble ones
in whom is all my delight.

⁴ Those who choose another god multiply
their sorrows;^o
their drink offerings of blood I will
not pour out
or take their names upon my lips.

⁵ The LORD is my chosen portion and my
cup;
you hold my lot.
⁶ The boundary lines have fallen for me in
pleasant places;
I have a goodly heritage.

⁷ I bless the LORD, who gives me counsel;
in the night also my heart instructs
me.
⁸ I keep the LORD always before me;
because he is at my right hand, I shall
not be moved.

n 16.2 Jerome Tg: Meaning of Heb uncertain   *o* 16.4 Cn:
Meaning of Heb uncertain

wicked. **14:6** With the use of a second-person accusation, the psalmist charges the fools on behalf
of the poor. **14:7** The psalm closes with a wish for divine action from Zion that would restore Israel's
fortunes. The mention of *Jacob* and *Israel* evokes God's past actions for the patriarch and his children (see Gen. 32:28).

Pss. 15–24 This subcollection exhibits a chiastic or envelope-like structure: Pss. 15 and 24, both
entrance liturgies, provide the outer structure; Pss. 16 and 23 express trust in God's salvation; Pss. 17
and 22 are pleas for deliverance; Pss. 18 and 20–21 are royal psalms. The centerpiece of this envelope
structure is Ps. 19, a torah psalm. Interpreters can read each of these psalms individually or together
as a collection.

Ps. 15:1–5 An entrance liturgy that has a counterpart in Ps. 24. **Superscription.** *A Psalm of David.*
See note on Ps. 3 superscription. **15:1** The two-part question regarding the tent and the holy hill is
about access to the temple and the divine presence. **15:2–5** The requirements for access include
blamelessness, truth speaking, a disdain for the wicked, and more. **15:5** For the prohibition of interest, see Exod. 22:25; Lev. 25:35–37. The psalm closes with a promise that stability accompanies
righteousness.

Ps. 16:1–11 A song of trust. **Superscription.** The meaning of *Miktam* is uncertain but may refer to
something being inscribed on a stone (cf. Pss. 56, 57, 58, 59, 60). **16:1–2** The psalm opens with a
call for protection and statement of loyalty. **16:3** The psalmist affirms *the holy ones in the land*, presumably the righteous. **16:4** The poet critiques those who *choose another god.* **16:5–6** The psalm
offers a statement of success for those who trust God. *Chosen portion.* See Ps. 73:26; 142:5. The
boundary lines and *goodly heritage* likely refer to the giving of the promised land. **16:7–8** The verbs
bless and *keep* express the psalmist's trust in God. God's closeness is presented as *at my right hand.*

⁹ Therefore my heart is glad, and my soul
  rejoices;
   my body also rests secure.
¹⁰ For you do not give me up to Sheol
    or let your faithful one see the Pit.

¹¹ You show me the path of life.
   In your presence there is fullness of
     joy;
   in your right hand are pleasures
     forevermore.

PSALM 17

A Prayer of David.
¹ Hear a just cause, O Lᴏʀᴅ; attend to my
   cry;
   give ear to my prayer from lips free of
     deceit.
² From you let my vindication come;
   let your eyes see the right.

³ If you try my heart, if you visit me by
   night,
   if you test me, you will find no
     wickedness in me;
   my mouth does not transgress.
⁴ As for what others do, by the word of
   your lips
   I have avoided the ways of the
     violent.
⁵ My steps have held fast to your paths;
   my feet have not slipped.

⁶ I call upon you, for you will answer me,
   O God;
   incline your ear to me; hear my
     words.
⁷ Wondrously show your steadfast love,

O savior of those who seek refuge
   from their adversaries at your right
     hand.

⁸ Guard me as the apple of the eye;
   hide me in the shadow of your wings,
⁹ from the wicked who despoil me,
   my deadly enemies who surround me.
¹⁰ They close their hearts to pity;
    with their mouths they speak
      arrogantly.
¹¹ They flush me out;ᵖ now they surround
    me;
    they set their eyes to cast me to the
      ground.
¹² They are like a lion eager to tear,
    like a young lion lurking in ambush.

¹³ Rise up, O Lᴏʀᴅ, confront them,
    overthrow them!
    By your sword deliver my life from the
      wicked,
¹⁴ from mortals—by your hand, O Lᴏʀᴅ—
    from mortals whose portion in life is
      in this world.
   May their bellies be filled with what you
     have stored up for them;
    may their children have more than
      enough;
    may they leave something over to their
      little ones.

¹⁵ As for me, I shall behold your face in
    righteousness;
    when I awake I shall be satisfied,
      beholding your likeness.

p 17.11 Q ms Gk: MT *Our steps*

16:10 Avoidance of death (*the Pit* is a synonym for *Sheol*; see note on 6:1–5) is an expression of divine protection for which the psalmist is thankful (cf. Pss. 28:1; 30:3, 9; 69:15; 88:4, 6; 103:4; 143:7). **16:11** God's revelation of *the path of life* is the opposite of the path to Sheol (cf. Prov. 15:24).

Ps. 17:1–15 A lament over personal enemies with three interwoven sections of pleas for help (vv. 1–2, 6–9, 13–14) and statements of support (vv. 3–5, 10–12, 15). **Superscription.** *A Prayer of David.* See Ps. 86 superscription. **17:1–5** Like other laments, the psalm begins with a call for God to hear. **17:3–5** These verses request a divine testing, followed by a statement of innocence. **17:6–14** This section calls for a divine hearing. **17:7** *Right hand* refers to the protective power of God (see Ps. 16:8). **17:8** *The apple of the eye* (cf. Deut. 32:10–11) may be the pupil of the eye and likely refers not only to the psalmist but to the people of Israel more broadly. The phrase *shadow of your wings* is an avian metaphor for divine protection (cf. Deut. 32:11); the wings could be God's or the wings of the cherubim in the temple (1 Kgs. 6:27). **17:12** Leonine imagery is often used to describe the predation of the enemy (see Pss. 7:2; 22:13, 21; 91:13). **17:13–15** This section calls for God to confront the enemies. **17:13** The image of the divine sword of retribution also appears in Ps. 7:12. **17:15** The psalmist claims future access to the face and form of God—stunning claims in light of other biblical traditions that suggest beholding God results in death (e.g., Exod. 33:20).

Psalm 18

To the leader. A Psalm of David the servant of the Lord, who addressed the words of this song to the Lord on the day when the Lord delivered him from the hand of all his enemies and from the hand of Saul. He said:

1 I love you, O Lord, my strength.
2 The Lord is my rock, my fortress, and my deliverer,
my God, my rock in whom I take refuge,
my shield, and the horn of my salvation, my stronghold.
3 I call upon the Lord, who is worthy to be praised,
so I shall be saved from my enemies.

4 The cords of death encompassed me;
the torrents of perdition assailed me;
5 the cords of Sheol entangled me;
the snares of death confronted me.

6 In my distress I called upon the Lord;
to my God I cried for help.
From his temple he heard my voice,
and my cry to him reached his ears.

7 Then the earth reeled and rocked;
the foundations also of the mountains trembled
and reeled because he was angry.
8 Smoke went up from his nostrils
and devouring fire from his mouth;
glowing coals flamed forth from him.
9 He bowed the heavens and came down;
thick darkness was under his feet.
10 He rode on a cherub and flew;
he came swiftly upon the wings of the wind.
11 He made darkness his covering around him,
his canopy thick clouds dark with water.
12 Out of the brightness before him
there broke through his clouds
hailstones and coals of fire.
13 The Lord also thundered in the heavens,
and the Most High uttered his voice.[q]
14 And he sent out his arrows and scattered them;
he flashed forth lightnings and routed them.
15 Then the channels of the sea were seen,
and the foundations of the world were laid bare
at your rebuke, O Lord,
at the blast of the breath of your nostrils.

16 He reached down from on high; he took me;
he drew me out of mighty waters.
17 He delivered me from my strong enemy
and from those who hated me,
for they were too mighty for me.
18 They confronted me in the day of my calamity,
but the Lord was my support.
19 He brought me out into a broad place;
he delivered me because he delighted in me.

q 18.13 Gk: Heb adds *hailstones and coals of fire*

Ps. 18:1–50 A royal psalm that is found in almost identical form in 2 Sam. 22. This lengthy poem has an elaborate structure: an opening announcement (vv. 1–3), a description of distress (vv. 4–6), a theophany (vv. 7–15), a statement of rescue (vv. 16–19), a description of the monarch's righteousness (vv. 20–24), a statement of God's faithfulness (vv. 25–30), an offer of praise of God (vv. 31–36), a second statement of rescue (vv. 37–45), and a concluding doxology (vv. 46–50). The psalm likely dates early in the monarchy. **Superscription.** A specific event from the life of David—this time the threat posed by Saul—is mentioned in the superscription (cf. Ps. 3). *To the leader.* See note on Ps. 4 superscription. *A Psalm of David.* See note on Ps. 3 superscription. **18:1–3** The psalm begins with a statement of affection and loyalty. This hymn of praise uses eight divine epithets, most militaristic in nature. The use of first-person speech underscores the psalmist's fidelity to God. The opening phrase ends with a petition to transform the current conflict. **18:4–5** This account of peril is conveyed by the metaphor of the *cords of death* and the *cords of Sheol* (on the latter, see note on 6:1–5). **18:6** The psalmist confesses that redemption comes from God located in the temple. **18:7–15** These verses describe a theophany—appearance of God—as an earthquake and smoke. **18:10** A *cherub* is a composite creature, here associated with the storm cloud (see Ezek. 1:5; Pss. 68:33; 104:3) that serves the deity. **18:16–19** The psalm pivots from a theophany to the redemption of the monarch. The constraining "cords" and "snares" (vv. 4–5) contrast with *a broad place* (v. 19).

20 The LORD rewarded me according to my
    righteousness;
    according to the cleanness of my
      hands he recompensed me.
21 For I have kept the ways of the LORD
    and have not wickedly departed from
      my God.
22 For all his ordinances were before me,
    and his statutes I did not put away
      from me.
23 I was blameless before him,
    and I kept myself from guilt.
24 Therefore the LORD has recompensed me
    according to my righteousness,
    according to the cleanness of my
      hands in his sight.

25 With the loyal you show yourself loyal;
    with the blameless you show yourself
      blameless;
26 with the pure you show yourself pure;
    and with the crooked you show
      yourself shrewd.
27 For you deliver a humble people,
    but the haughty eyes you bring down.
28 It is you who light my lamp;
    the LORD, my God, lights up my
      darkness.
29 By you I can outrun a troop,
    and by my God I can leap over a wall.
30 This God—his way is perfect;
    the promise of the LORD proves true;
    he is a shield for all who take refuge
      in him.

31 For who is God except the LORD?
    And who is a rock besides our God?
32 The God who has girded me with
      strength
    and made my way safe.r
33 He made my feet like the feet of a deer
    and set me secure on the heights.
34 He trains my hands for war,
    so that my arms can bend a bow of
      bronze.
35 You have given me the shield of your
      salvation,
    and your right hand has supported
      me;
    your helps has made me great.

36 You gave me a wide place for my steps
    under me,
    and my feet did not slip.
37 I pursued my enemies and overtook them
    and did not turn back until they were
      consumed.
38 I struck them down so that they were
    unable to rise;
    they fell under my feet.
39 For you girded me with strength for the
      battle;
    you made my assailants sink under me.
40 You made my enemies turn their backs
    to me,
    and those who hated me I destroyed.
41 They cried for help, but there was no one
    to save them;
    they cried to the LORD, but he did not
      answer them.
42 I beat them fine, like dust before the wind;
    I cast them out like the mire of the
      streets.

43 You delivered me from strife with the
    peoples;t
    you made me head of the nations;
    people whom I had not known served
      me.
44 As soon as they heard of me, they obeyed
    me;
    foreigners came cringing to me.
45 Foreigners lost heart
    and came trembling out of their
      strongholds.

46 The LORD lives! Blessed be my rock,
    and exalted be the God of my
      salvation,
47 the God who gave me vengeance
    and subdued peoples under me,
48 who delivered me from my enemies;
    indeed, you exalted me above my
      adversaries;
    you delivered me from the violent.
49 For this I will extol you, O LORD, among
    the nations
    and sing praises to your name.

r 18.32 Meaning of Heb uncertain   s 18.35 Or gentleness
t 18.43 Gk Tg: Heb people

18:20–30 The phrase For I have kept the ways of the LORD justifies God's saving action in light
of the monarch's righteousness. 18:31–50 The psalm closes with a thanksgiving for victory and
concludes with a reference to God's anointed (v. 50; see Ps. 2:2) and David and his descendants
(see 2 Sam. 7).

⁵⁰ Great triumphs he gives to his king
    and shows steadfast love to his
      anointed,
    to David and his descendants forever.

PSALM 19

To the leader. A Psalm of David.

¹ The heavens are telling the glory of
    God,
    and the firmament*ᵘ* proclaims his
      handiwork.
² Day to day pours forth speech,
    and night to night declares
      knowledge.
³ There is no speech, nor are there words;
    their voice is not heard;
⁴ yet their voice*ᵛ* goes out through all the
    earth
    and their words to the end of the
      world.

In the heavens*ʷ* he has set a tent for the
    sun,
⁵ which comes out like a bridegroom from
    his wedding canopy,
    and like a strong man runs its course
      with joy.
⁶ Its rising is from the end of the heavens
    and its circuit to the end of them,
    and nothing is hid from its heat.

⁷ The law of the Lᴏʀᴅ is perfect,
    reviving the soul;
    the decrees of the Lᴏʀᴅ are sure,
      making wise the simple;
⁸ the precepts of the Lᴏʀᴅ are right,
    rejoicing the heart;

the commandment of the Lᴏʀᴅ is clear,
    enlightening the eyes;
⁹ the fear of the Lᴏʀᴅ is pure,
    enduring forever;
    the ordinances of the Lᴏʀᴅ are true
      and righteous altogether.
¹⁰ More to be desired are they than gold,
    even much fine gold;
    sweeter also than honey
      and drippings of the honeycomb.

¹¹ Moreover, by them is your servant
    warned;
    in keeping them there is great
      reward.
¹² But who can detect one's own errors?
    Clear me from hidden faults.
¹³ Keep back your servant also from the
    insolent;*ˣ*
    do not let them have dominion over
      me.
    Then I shall be blameless
    and innocent of great transgression.

¹⁴ Let the words of my mouth and the
    meditation of my heart
    be acceptable to you,
    O Lᴏʀᴅ, my rock and my redeemer.

PSALM 20

To the leader. A Psalm of David.

¹ The Lᴏʀᴅ answer you in the day of
    trouble!
    The name of the God of Jacob protect
      you!

u 19.1 Or *dome*   *v* 19.4 Gk Jerome Compare Syr: Heb *line*
w 19.4 Heb *In them*   *x* 19.13 Or *from proud thoughts*

Ps. 19:1–14 A torah psalm (see Pss. 1, 119) that has three parts: a speech about creation (vv. 1–6), a speech about torah (vv. 7–10), and a statement of loyalty (vv. 11–14). On the superscription, see notes on Pss. 3 and 4 superscriptions. **19:1–6** The psalm opens with the testimony of creation—without having its own organ for speech—to the glory of God (cf. Rom. 10:18). **19:4** The image of *the sun* likely borrows and adapts language venerating the ancient Near Eastern sun god (Shamash) into a testimony for Israel's God. **19:7–10** The middle of the psalm equates the cosmic testimony and the instruction of God. This section contains six synonyms for torah (*law*), each followed by a benefit. **19:9** The *fear of the* Lᴏʀᴅ (cf. Pss. 34:11; 111:10) is a key theme in Wisdom literature (cf. Prov. 1:7; 2:5; 8:13; etc.), which leads some scholars to think that the torah psalms might also (or instead) be considered wisdom psalms. **19:11–13** The function of torah is to address human frailty. Biblical law addresses *errors* and *hidden faults*, which capture sins done and undone, known and unknown (cf. Lev. 4:2; Num. 15:22–26). **19:14** The poet's final wish is for God's acceptance.

Ps. 20:1–9 The first of two consecutive royal psalms. Psalm 20 has four parts: an intercession (vv. 1–4), a cohortative petition (v. 5), an expression of confidence (vv. 6–8), and a closing petition to God as king (v. 9). On the superscription, see notes on Pss. 3 and 4 superscriptions. **20:1–5** The psalm opens with a prayer by the people to *the God of Jacob* (cf. Pss. 46:7, 11; 75:9; 76:6; 81:1, 4; 84:8; 94:7; 114:7; 146:5) to help the king. **20:1** The *name* is a metonym for divine presence (cf. Deut.

2 May he send you help from the
    sanctuary
  and give you support from Zion.
3 May he remember all your offerings
  and regard with favor your burnt
    sacrifices.   *Selah*

4 May he grant you your heart's desire
  and fulfill all your plans.
5 May we shout for joy over your
    victory
  and in the name of our God set up our
    banners.
  May the Lord fulfill all your petitions.

6 Now I know that the Lord will help his
    anointed;
  he will answer him from his holy
    heaven
  with mighty victories by his right
    hand.
7 Some take pride in chariots and some in
    horses,
  but our pride is in the name of the
    Lord our God.
8 They will collapse and fall,
  but we shall rise and stand upright.

9 Give victory to the king, O Lord;
  answer us when we call.[y]

Psalm 21

To the leader. A Psalm of David.
1 In your strength the king rejoices,
    O Lord,
  and in your help how greatly he
    exults!
2 You have given him his heart's desire
  and have not withheld the request of
    his lips.   *Selah*

3 For you meet him with rich blessings;
  you set a crown of fine gold on his
    head.
4 He asked you for life; you gave it to
    him—
  length of days forever and ever.
5 His glory is great through your help;
  splendor and majesty you bestow on
    him.
6 You bestow on him blessings forever;
  you make him glad with the joy of
    your presence.
7 For the king trusts in the Lord,
  and through the steadfast love of the
    Most High he shall not be moved.

8 Your hand will find out all your
    enemies;
  your right hand will find out those
    who hate you.
9 You will make them like a fiery furnace
  when you appear.
  The Lord will swallow them up in his
    wrath,
  and fire will consume them.
10 You will destroy their offspring from the
    earth
  and their children from among
    humankind.
11 If they plan evil against you,
  if they devise mischief, they will not
    succeed.
12 For you will put them to flight;
  you will aim at their faces with your
    bows.

13 Be exalted, O Lord, in your strength!
  We will sing and praise your power.

y 20.9 Gk: Heb *give victory, O Lord; let the King answer us when
we call*

12:5; 1 Kgs. 18:15–30) and thus can refer to the place for sacrifice (v. 3). **20:2** References to the *sanctuary* and to *Zion* assume cult centralization in Jerusalem. **20:3** The memory of God provides a foundation for redemption. *Selah.* See note on Ps. 3:1–2. **20:6–9** The shift to first-person speech may indicate confidence in divine action. **20:7** *In the name of the* Lord will reappear in the Psalter (cf. Pss. 118:10–12; 124:8; 129:8).

Ps. 21:1–13 Another royal psalm that operates in concert with Ps. 20. Chap. 21 has four elements: an address to God on behalf of the king (vv. 1–6), a summary affirmation describing the king's trust (v. 7), an address to the king (vv. 8–12), and a summary of praise (v. 13). On the superscription, see notes on Pss. 3 and 4 superscriptions. **21:1–7** God functions as the patron of the king, who derives strength from God. **21:2** God gives the monarch his *heart's desire* (cf. 1 Kgs. 3:5–9). *Selah.* See note on Ps. 3:1–2. **21:7** Divine patronage requires the monarch to trust God. **21:8–12** Divine speech that may have been uttered by an intermediary (such as a priest) pronounces promises for *you* (the king). **21:11–12** These verses announce the contingency of conflict. **21:13** The final benediction is addressed to God.

PSALM 22

*To the leader: according to The Deer of the Dawn. A
Psalm of David.*

1 My God, my God, why have you forsaken
me?
Why are you so far from helping me,
from the words of my groaning?
2 O my God, I cry by day, but you do not
answer;
and by night but find no rest.

3 Yet you are holy,
enthroned on the praises of Israel.
4 In you our ancestors trusted;
they trusted, and you delivered them.
5 To you they cried and were saved;
in you they trusted and were not put
to shame.

6 But I am a worm and not human,
scorned by others and despised by the
people.
7 All who see me mock me;
they sneer at me; they shake their
heads;
8 "Commit your cause to the LORD; let him
deliver—
let him rescue the one in whom he
delights!"

9 Yet it was you who took me from the
womb;
you kept me safe on my mother's breast.
10 On you I was cast from my birth,
and since my mother bore me you
have been my God.

11 Do not be far from me,
for trouble is near,
and there is no one to help.

12 Many bulls encircle me;
strong bulls of Bashan surround me;
13 they open wide their mouths at me,
like a ravening and roaring lion.

14 I am poured out like water,
and all my bones are out of joint;
my heart is like wax;
it is melted within my breast;
15 my mouth[z] is dried up like a potsherd,
and my tongue sticks to my jaws;
you lay me in the dust of death.

16 For dogs are all around me;
a company of evildoers encircles me;
they bound my hands and feet.[a]
17 I can count all my bones.
They stare and gloat over me;
18 they divide my clothes among
themselves,
and for my clothing they cast lots.

19 But you, O LORD, do not be far away!
O my help, come quickly to my aid!
20 Deliver my soul from the sword,
my life[b] from the power of the dog!
21 Save me from the mouth of the lion!

From the horns of the wild oxen you
have rescued[c] me.

z 22.15 Cn: Heb *strength*   a 22.16 Meaning of Heb uncertain
b 22.20 Heb *my only one*   c 22.21 Heb *answered*

Ps. 22:1–31 A well-known lament psalm attested in the usage of early Christ followers via the Passion Narratives of the New Testament Gospels (cf. Matt. 27:35–44; Mark 15:24–32; Luke 23:34–37; John 19:23–24). The first section begins with a cry for help (vv. 1–2), a declaration of confidence (vv. 3–5), a description of distress (vv. 6–8), and a declaration of confidence (vv. 9–11); the second part of the psalm begins with a description of distress (vv. 12–18), followed by a plea (vv. 19–21a), a declaration of God's intervention (v. 21b), an assurance of hearing (vv. 22–25), and a description of a meal (vv. 26–31). **Superscription.** *The Deer of the Dawn* probably indicates a musical tune to which the psalm was to be sung. See **"Music and the Psalms," p. 764**. *To the leader.* See note on Ps. 4 superscription. *A Psalm of David.* See note on Ps. 3 superscription. **22:1–2** The initial plea describes the absence and distance of God. Jesus quotes the first line of this psalm on the cross (Matt. 27:46; Mark 15:34). **22:3–5** To be *enthroned* connotes divine transcendence as well as loyalty to earlier generations, but the experience of the psalmist is otherwise. **22:6–8** A *worm* contrasts with the height of the enthroned God. **22:9–11** The psalmist proclaims God's beneficial care since birth. **22:12–13** The image of *bulls* is enhanced by the reference to the fertile grazing land of *Bashan*. The verb *surround* is another instance of the constraints the psalmist feels. **22:14–15** These verses describe the harbingers of death. **22:16** The psalmist augments the threat of the bulls (v. 12) with dogs, likely of the scavenger variety. Once again, the psalmist feels dangerously surrounded (vv. 17–18). **22:21–31** The psalmist concludes with a testimony of deliverance.

²² I will tell of your name to my brothers
and sisters;^d
in the midst of the congregation I will
praise you:
²³ You who fear the LORD, praise him!
All you offspring of Jacob, glorify him;
stand in awe of him, all you offspring
of Israel!
²⁴ For he did not despise or abhor
the affliction of the afflicted;
he did not hide his face from me^e
but heard when I^f cried to him.

²⁵ From you comes my praise in the great
congregation;
my vows I will pay before those who
fear him.
²⁶ The poor^g shall eat and be satisfied;
those who seek him shall praise the LORD.
May your hearts live forever!

²⁷ All the ends of the earth shall remember
and turn to the LORD,
and all the families of the nations
shall worship before him.^h
²⁸ For dominion belongs to the LORD,
and he rules over the nations.

²⁹ To him,ⁱ indeed, shall all who sleep in^j
the earth bow down;
before him shall bow all who go down
to the dust,
and I shall live for him.^k
³⁰ Posterity will serve him;
future generations will be told about
the Lord
³¹ and^l proclaim his deliverance to a people
yet unborn,
saying that he has done it.

A Psalm of David.
¹ The LORD is my shepherd; I shall not want.
²   He makes me lie down in green
pastures;
he leads me beside still waters;^m
³   he restores my soul.ⁿ
He leads me in right paths^o
for his name's sake.

⁴ Even though I walk through the darkest
valley,^p
I fear no evil,
for you are with me;
your rod and your staff,
they comfort me.

⁵ You prepare a table before me
in the presence of my enemies;
you anoint my head with oil;
my cup overflows.
⁶ Surely^q goodness and mercy^r shall follow
me
all the days of my life,
and I shall dwell in the house of the LORD
my whole life long.^s

Of David. A Psalm.
¹ The earth is the LORD's and all that is in it,
the world, and those who live in it,

d 22.22 Or *kindred*   *e* 22.24 Heb *him*   *f* 22.24 Heb
he   *g* 22.26 Or *afflicted*   *h* 22.27 Gk Syr Jerome: Heb *you*
i 22.29 Cn: Heb *They have eaten and*   *j* 22.29 Cn: Heb *all the fat
ones*   *k* 22.29 Compare Gk Syr Vg: Heb *and he who cannot keep
himself alive*   *l* 22.31 Compare Gk: Heb *it will be told about the
Lord to the generation,* ³¹*they will come and*   *m* 23.2 Heb *waters of
rest*   *n* 23.3 Or *life*   *o* 23.3 Or *paths of righteousness*   *p* 23.4 Or
the valley of the shadow of death   *q* 23.6 Or *Only*   *r* 23.6 Or
kindness   *s* 23.6 Heb *for length of days*

Ps. 23:1–6 A song of trust (see also Pss. 91, 121, 125, 131) consisting of three speeches: first about the Lord (vv. 1–4b), then to the Lord (vv. 4c–5), and then a concluding address that is again about the Lord (v. 6). **Superscription.** *A Psalm of David.* See note on Ps. 3 superscription. **23:1** The psalm opens with a depiction of God as a good shepherd (cf. Pss. 28:9; 78:71; 80:1) and the psalmist as without any need. **23:2–3** The psalm explains further the role of the shepherd, who provides a bucolic location of still waters and green pastures. **23:4** The psalmist's use of *darkest valley* suggests threat, death, and danger (cf. Job 10:21–22) but does not lead the poet to distrust in God. The term translated as *evil* here may also signify "disaster." **23:5** As host, God sets a table and anoints the visiting guests. **23:6** To *dwell in the house*—an image of a stable location—is matched with temporal stability (*my whole life long*) and proximity to God.

Ps. 24:1–10 An entrance liturgy for the ark of the covenant divided into three sections: a declaration about God as creator (vv. 1–2), a liturgy announcing the entrance of humans into the divine sphere (vv. 3–6), and a liturgy of the entrance of the divine into the human sphere (vv. 7–10). This psalm functions as the closing bookend in the small complex of Pss. 15–24. **Superscription.** *Of David. A Psalm.* See note on Ps. 3 superscription. **24:1–2** The poet recognizes God as the founder of the

² for he has founded it on the seas
  and established it on the rivers.

³ Who shall ascend the hill of the Lord?
  And who shall stand in his holy place?
⁴ Those who have clean hands and pure
    hearts,
  who do not lift up their souls to what
    is false
  and do not swear deceitfully.
⁵ They will receive blessing from the
    Lord
  and vindication from the God of their
    salvation.
⁶ Such is the company of those who seek
    him,
  who seek the face of the God of
    Jacob.^t   Selah

⁷ Lift up your heads, O gates!
  and be lifted up, O ancient doors,
  that the King of glory may come in!
⁸ Who is the King of glory?
  The Lord, strong and mighty,
  the Lord, mighty in battle.
⁹ Lift up your heads, O gates!
  and be lifted up, O ancient doors,
  that the King of glory may come in!
¹⁰ Who is this King of glory?
  The Lord of hosts,
  he is the King of glory.   Selah

Psalm 25

Of David.
¹ To you, O Lord, I lift up my soul.
² O my God, in you I trust;
  do not let me be put to shame;
  do not let my enemies exult over me.

³ Do not let those who wait for you be put
    to shame;
  let them be ashamed who are
    wantonly treacherous.

⁴ Make me to know your ways, O Lord;
  teach me your paths.
⁵ Lead me in your truth and teach me,
  for you are the God of my
    salvation;
  for you I wait all day long.

⁶ Be mindful of your mercy, O Lord, and of
    your steadfast love,
  for they have been from of old.
⁷ Do not remember the sins of my youth or
    my transgressions;
  according to your steadfast love
    remember me,
  for the sake of your goodness, O Lord!

⁸ Good and upright is the Lord;
  therefore he instructs sinners in the
    way.
⁹ He leads the humble in what is right
  and teaches the humble his way.
¹⁰ All the paths of the Lord are steadfast
    love and faithfulness,
  for those who keep his covenant and
    his decrees.

¹¹ For your name's sake, O Lord,
  pardon my guilt, for it is great.
¹² Who are they who fear the Lord?
  He will teach them the way that they
    should choose.

t 24.6 Gk Syr: Heb your face, O Jacob

---

cosmos. See **"Hebrew Poetry," p. 741**. **24:3** The psalmist raises the question about access (cf. Ps. 15:1) to the temple and God. **24:4** The requirements for entry are ethical metaphors: *clean hands* (actions) and *pure hearts* (aspirations). **24:6, 10** *Selah.* See note on Ps. 3:1–2. **24:7–10** The language to *lift up your heads, O gates* (vv. 7, 9) may be a metaphor for lifting the head or an awakening awareness of the believer. Alternatively, the gates are personified and must stretch upward to accommodate the entry of the *King of glory*. This king is *mighty in battle* and none other than *the Lord of hosts. Hosts* here refers to God's (heavenly) armies.

Ps. 25:1–22 A lament over personal enemies in acrostic form (see note on Pss. 9–10) with seven elements: a petition for divine action (vv. 1–3), a request for instruction (vv. 4–7), a description of God as teacher (vv. 8–11), a description of divine action on behalf of the community (vv. 12–14), an appeal for divine salvation and forgiveness (vv. 15–18), and two final petitions for deliverance (vv. 19–21) and redemption (v. 22). **Superscription.** *Of David.* See note on Ps. 3 superscription. **25:1–7** Petitions for divine assistance include hope for deliverance from shame (v. 3) and direction in life (vv. 4–5). **25:6–7** The psalmist prays for divine attentiveness toward mercy and divine forgetfulness toward human transgressions. **25:8–10** The poet describes God as *good and upright* and the *humble* as teachable. **25:11–21** The second half of the chapter lays out a prayer for pardon.

¹³ They will abide in prosperity,
 and their children shall possess the
 land.
¹⁴ The friendship of the Lord is for those
 who fear him,
 and he makes his covenant known to
 them.
¹⁵ My eyes are ever toward the Lord,
 for he will pluck my feet out of the net.

¹⁶ Turn to me and be gracious to me,
 for I am lonely and afflicted.
¹⁷ Relieve the troubles of my heart,
 and bring me^u out of my distress.
¹⁸ Consider my affliction and my trouble,
 and forgive all my sins.

¹⁹ Consider how many are my foes
 and with what violent hatred they
 hate me.
²⁰ O guard my life and deliver me;
 do not let me be put to shame, for I
 take refuge in you.
²¹ May integrity and uprightness preserve
 me,
 for I wait for you.

²² Redeem Israel, O God,
 out of all its troubles.

PSALM 26

Of David.
¹ Vindicate me, O Lord,
 for I have walked in my integrity,
 and I have trusted in the Lord without
 wavering.
² Prove me, O Lord, and try me;
 test my heart and mind.
³ For your steadfast love is before my eyes,
 and I walk in faithfulness to you.^v

⁴ I do not sit with the worthless,
 nor do I consort with hypocrites;
⁵ I hate the company of evildoers
 and will not sit with the wicked.

⁶ I wash my hands in innocence
 and go around your altar, O Lord,
⁷ singing aloud a song of thanksgiving
 and telling all your wondrous
 deeds.

⁸ O Lord, I love the house in which you
 dwell
 and the place where your glory
 abides.
⁹ Do not sweep me away with sinners
 nor my life with the bloodthirsty,
¹⁰ those in whose hands are evil devices
 and whose right hands are full of
 bribes.

¹¹ But as for me, I walk in my integrity;
 redeem me and be gracious to me.
¹² My foot stands on level ground;
 in the great congregation I will bless
 the Lord.

PSALM 27

Of David.
¹ The Lord is my light and my salvation;
 whom shall I fear?
 The Lord is the stronghold^w of my life;
 of whom shall I be afraid?

² When evildoers assail me
 to devour my flesh—
 my adversaries and foes—
 they shall stumble and fall.

u 25.17 Or *The troubles of my heart are enlarged; bring me*
v 26.3 Or *in your faithfulness* *w* 27.1 Or *refuge*

25:14 Friendship with God occurs in parallel with *covenant* and the fear of God. **25:19** The psalmist draws attention to how many adversaries there are. **25:22** The chapter closes with a request that God save (*redeem*) Israel.

 Ps. 26:1–12 A lament over personal enemies with three elements: a plea for divine vindication (vv. 1–3), a statement of the psalmist's innocence (vv. 4–10), and a second statement of innocence parallel to the petition for vindication (vv. 11–12). **Superscription.** *Of David.* See note on Ps. 3 superscription. **26:1–3** In the psalmist's call for God's vindication, it is unclear whose *faithfulness* is at stake (see footnote at 1:3 in the NRSVue). **26:4–7** These verses describe the psalmist's innocence based on his associations (cf. Ps. 1:1). **26:6** *Wash my hands in innocence* (cf. Ps. 73:13) is a metaphor leading to worship, singing, and a recital of God's acts in history. **26:8–10** Unlike *sinners*, the psalmist expresses love for the temple. **26:11–12** The psalm closes with a second and final statement of innocence.

 Ps. 27:1–14 A lament chapter divided into three parts: a statement of trust (vv. 1–6), a plea for deliverance (vv. 7–12), and a concluding expression of trust (vv. 13–14). **Superscription.** *Of David.* See note on Ps. 3 superscription. **27:1–6** The psalmist affirms loyalty to God that rebuts fear (vv.

³ Though an army encamp against me,
my heart shall not fear;
though war rise up against me,
yet I will be confident.

⁴ One thing I asked of the Lord;
this I seek:
to live in the house of the Lord
all the days of my life,
to behold the beauty of the Lord,
and to inquire in his temple.

⁵ For he will hide me in his shelter
in the day of trouble;
he will conceal me under the cover of his
tent;
he will set me high on a rock.

⁶ Now my head is lifted up
above my enemies all around me,
and I will offer in his tent
sacrifices with shouts of joy;
I will sing and make melody to the
Lord.

⁷ Hear, O Lord, when I cry aloud;
be gracious to me and answer me!
⁸ "Come," my heart says, "seek his face!"
Your face, Lord, do I seek.
⁹   Do not hide your face from me.

Do not turn your servant away in
anger,
you who have been my help.
Do not cast me off; do not forsake me,
O God of my salvation!
¹⁰ If my father and mother forsake me,
the Lord will take me up.

¹¹ Teach me your way, O Lord,
and lead me on a level path
because of my enemies.
¹² Do not give me up to the will of my
adversaries,
for false witnesses have risen against me,
and they are breathing out violence.

¹³ I believe that I shall see the goodness of
the Lord
in the land of the living.
¹⁴ Wait for the Lord;
be strong, and let your heart take
courage;
wait for the Lord!

Psalm 28

Of David.
¹ To you, O Lord, I call;
my rock, do not refuse to hear me,
for if you are silent to me,
I shall be like those who go down to
the Pit.
² Hear the voice of my supplication,
as I cry to you for help,
as I lift up my hands
toward your most holy sanctuary.ˣ

³ Do not drag me away with the
wicked,
with those who are workers of
evil,
who speak peace with their neighbors
while mischief is in their hearts.
⁴ Repay them according to their work
and according to the evil of their
deeds;
repay them according to the work of
their hands;
render them their due reward.
⁵ Because they do not regard the works of
the Lord
or the work of his hands,
he will break them down and build them
up no more.

⁶ Blessed be the Lord,
for he has heard the sound of my
pleadings.
⁷ The Lord is my strength and my
shield;
in him my heart trusts;

x 28.2 Heb *your innermost sanctuary*

1, 3). **27:4** This first-person speech functions as a vow. **27:5** The statement of assurance of divine protection uses three metaphors: *shelter, tent*, and *rock*. **27:7–12** These verses provide a second plea. **27:9** The hiding of God's *face* is an image of divine absence (cf. Pss. 69:17; 102:2; 143:7). **27:13–14** The psalmist places hope in the present, *the land of the living* (cf. Pss. 52:5; 116:9).

Ps. 28:1–9 A lament regarding personal enemies that includes two elements: an initial plea (vv. 1–5) and a testimony to a divine hearing (vv. 6–9). **Superscription.** *Of David.* See note on Ps. 3 superscription. **28:1–5** The petition contrasts the rock and *the Pit*, a synonym for Sheol (see note on Ps. 16:10). **28:6–7** For the commonly used phrase *Blessed be the Lord*, see Pss. 31:21; 41:13; 68:19; 72:18;

so I am helped, and my heart exults,
and with my song I give thanks to him.

⁸ The Lord is the strength of his people;
he is the saving refuge of his anointed.
⁹ O save your people and bless your
heritage;
be their shepherd and carry them
forever.

PSALM 29

A Psalm of David.

¹ Ascribe to the Lord, O heavenly beings,ʸ
ascribe to the Lord glory and
strength.
² Ascribe to the Lord the glory of his name;
worship the Lord in holy splendor.

³ The voice of the Lord is over the waters;
the God of glory thunders,
the Lord, over mighty waters.
⁴ The voice of the Lord is powerful;
the voice of the Lord is full of majesty.

⁵ The voice of the Lord breaks the cedars;
the Lord breaks the cedars of
Lebanon.
⁶ He makes Lebanon skip like a calf
and Sirion like a young wild ox.

⁷ The voice of the Lord flashes forth
flames of fire.

⁸ The voice of the Lord shakes the
wilderness;
the Lord shakes the wilderness of
Kadesh.

⁹ The voice of the Lord causes the oaks to
whirlᶻ
and strips the forest bare,
and in his temple all say, "Glory!"

¹⁰ The Lord sits enthroned over the flood;
the Lord sits enthroned as king forever.
¹¹ May the Lord give strength to his people!
May the Lord bless his people with
peace!

PSALM 30

*A Psalm. A Song at the dedication of the temple. Of
David.*

¹ I will extol you, O Lord, for you have
drawn me up
and did not let my foes rejoice over me.
² O Lord my God, I cried to you for help,
and you have healed me.
³ O Lord, you brought up my soul from Sheol,
restored me to life from among those
gone down to the Pit.ᵃ

⁴ Sing praises to the Lord, O you his
faithful ones,
and give thanks to his holy name.

y 29.1 Heb *sons of gods*   *z* 29.9 Or *causes the deer to calve*
a 30.3 Or *that I should not go down to the Pit*

89:52; 106:48; 124:6; 135:21; 144:1. **28:8–9** The final confession describes God as strength, refuge, and shepherd (cf. Ps. 23).

Ps. 29:1–11 A hymn of praise with three elements: a call to praise (vv. 1–2), a description of God's glory in the storm (vv. 3–9), and an announcement of divine reign and promise (vv. 10–11). See **"Worship," p. 761. Superscription.** *A Psalm of David.* See note on Ps. 3 superscription. **29:1–2** The phrase *Ascribe to the Lord* also occurs in Ps. 96:7, 8. The language of *heavenly beings* refers to the members of God's divine council (see Pss. 82:1, 6; 84:7; 86:8; 95:3). **29:3–9** God's *voice* occurs seven times in this section describing elements often associated with the storm god Baal in the ancient Levant. Here the storm god imagery is applied to Israel's God. **29:5** The *cedars of Lebanon* are a well-known lumber resource from a region north of Israel. **29:6** *Sirion* is another name for Mount Hermon. **29:8** *Kadesh* is the name of a city on the Orontes River. **29:10–11** The hymn closes with a description of the Lord *enthroned* as king above the tumult of the storm. On the language of enthronement, see note on 22:3–5.

Ps. 30:1–12 A thanksgiving song divided into five parts: an introductory individual praise (vv. 1–3), a call for communal praise (vv. 4–5), a recollection of crisis (vv. 6–8), a prayer (vv. 9–10), and a concluding individual praise (vv. 11–12). **Superscription.** *A Song at the dedication of the temple* seems out of place with reference to David's life, since he died before the completion of the temple. This psalm has also been attributed to the Festival of Hanukkah and the cleansing of the Second Temple by Judas Maccabeus (164 BCE; 1 Macc. 4:36–58). *A Psalm. . . . Of David.* See note on Ps. 3 superscription. **30:1–3** The psalmist opens with a confession of divine redemption and deliverance from both enemies and death, called both *Sheol* and *the Pit* (see note on 6:1–5). **30:4–5** The hymn shifts to provide

Focus On: Worship (Psalm 29)

Much religion is manifested in worship. In the psalms, God uses worship in the ongoing creation of a people of faith. Worship includes attachment structures uniting God and Israel and the practices that undergird those attachments. Worship in the Psalter occurs in the context of the household, the village, and the tribe, distinct from the congregations more familiar in later Jewish and Christian worship. The ancient Israelite worshiping community included men, women, and children in all major festivals. Despite the emphasis on Zion and Jerusalem, places of worship included regional locations and, later, synagogues and churches.

Worship involves a *recital* of celebrations of God's nature (hymns, Zion songs, royal psalms) that simultaneously provides a *remembrance* that shapes the community. In the psalms, festivals that were once agrarian are transformed into celebrations of salvation history. Three festivals order the liturgical calendar: Passover, the Festival of Weeks (Pentecost), and the Festival of Booths (Sukkoth; see Exod. 23:14-17; 34:18-26a; Lev. 23; Num. 28:16-29; Deut. 16:1-17).

Worship includes rituals and incorporates practices, narratives, and poetry that served as resources for the community during times of joy, such as the exodus, and times of trauma, such as the exile. These rituals included sacrifice and the making of vows. According to Leviticus, there are five primary types of sacrifice: the burnt offering, the grain offering, the peace offering, the sin or purification offering, and the guilt offering (see **"Offerings and Sacrifices," p. 146**). Prayers and vows often contained a proposal to celebrate (see Pss. 40, 50) and were often offered in exchange for divine help.

In its current form, the Psalter is a prayer book with very little commentary indicating its liturgical use, whether back then or now. Interpreters of Psalms must use material from other passages—biblical and extrabiblical—to infer how the various psalms were used. Much remains uncertain, however. So, for example, while there are clear indications that the psalms were often set to music, some of the terms relating to that practice (e.g., *Selah*) remain unclear.

Stephen Breck Reid

---

⁵ For his anger is but for a moment;
    his favor is for a lifetime.
Weeping may linger for the night,
    but joy comes with the morning.

⁶ As for me, I said in my prosperity,
    "I shall never be moved."
⁷ By your favor, O LORD,
    you had established me as a strong
      mountain;
you hid your face;
    I was dismayed.

⁸ To you, O LORD, I cried,
    and to the LORD I made supplication:
⁹ "What profit is there in my death,
    if I go down to the Pit?
Will the dust praise you?
    Will it tell of your faithfulness?

¹⁰ Hear, O LORD, and be gracious to me!
    O LORD, be my helper!"*ᵇ*

¹¹ You have turned my mourning into
      dancing;
you have taken off my sackcloth
    and clothed me with joy,
¹² so that my soul*ᶜ* may praise you and not
    be silent.
O LORD my God, I will give thanks to
    you forever.

PSALM 31

To the leader. A Psalm of David.
¹ In you, O LORD, I seek refuge;
    do not let me ever be put to shame;
    in your righteousness deliver me.

b 30.10 Or *The* LORD *heard and was gracious to me; the* LORD *became my helper* *c* 30.12 Heb *that glory*

---

an imperative and a rationale for praise because of the brevity of divine punishment, expressed as *joy comes with the morning.* **30:6-7** The psalmist recalls a stable position based on divine access and support. **30:8-10** The psalm's petition to God asserts that praise from the living is better than the silence of death. *The Pit* (v. 9). See note on 6:1-5. **30:11-12** The hymn closes with a celebration of divine intervention and human transformation.

     Ps. 31:1-24 A lament composed of two extended prayers: the first prayer (vv. 1-8) has both a plea to God (vv. 1-6) and a statement of trust and thanksgiving (vv. 7-8); the second prayer (vv. 9-24) begins with multiple pleas (vv. 9-13), moves to an expression of trust (vv. 14-18), and concludes with a thanksgiving (vv. 19-24). **Superscription.** *To the leader.* See note on Ps. 4 superscription. *A Psalm*

² Incline your ear to me;
  rescue me speedily.
Be a rock of refuge for me,
  a strong fortress to save me.

³ You are indeed my rock and my fortress;
  for your name's sake lead me and
    guide me;
⁴ take me out of the net that is hidden
    for me,
  for you are my refuge.
⁵ Into your hand I commit my spirit;
  you have redeemed me, O Lord,
    faithful God.

⁶ You hate[d] those who pay regard to
    worthless idols,
  but I trust in the Lord.
⁷ I will exult and rejoice in your steadfast
    love,
  because you have seen my affliction;
  you have taken notice of my
    adversities
⁸ and have not delivered me into the hand
    of the enemy;
  you have set my feet in a broad place.

⁹ Be gracious to me, O Lord, for I am in
    distress;
  my eye wastes away from grief,
  my soul and body also.
¹⁰ For my life is spent with sorrow
  and my years with sighing;
  my strength fails because of my misery,[e]
  and my bones waste away.

¹¹ I am the scorn of all my adversaries,
  a horror[f] to my neighbors,
  an object of dread to my acquaintances;
  those who see me in the street flee
    from me.
¹² I have passed out of mind like one who is
    dead;
  I have become like a broken vessel.
¹³ For I hear the whispering of many—
  terror all around!—

as they scheme together against me,
  as they plot to take my life.

¹⁴ But I trust in you, O Lord;
  I say, "You are my God."
¹⁵ My times are in your hand;
  deliver me from the hand of my
    enemies and persecutors.
¹⁶ Let your face shine upon your
    servant;
  save me in your steadfast love.
¹⁷ Do not let me be put to shame, O Lord,
  for I call on you;
  let the wicked be put to shame;
  let them go dumbfounded to Sheol.
¹⁸ Let the lying lips be stilled
  that speak insolently against the
    righteous
  with pride and contempt.

¹⁹ O how abundant is your goodness
  that you have laid up for those who
    fear you
and accomplished for those who take
    refuge in you,
  in the sight of everyone!
²⁰ In the shelter of your presence you hide
    them
  from human plots;
you hold them safe under your shelter
  from contentious tongues.

²¹ Blessed be the Lord,
  for he has wondrously shown his
    steadfast love to me
  when I was beset as a city under siege.
²² I had said in my alarm,
  "I am driven far[g] from your sight."
But you heard my supplications
  when I cried out to you for help.

²³ Love the Lord, all you his saints.
  The Lord preserves the faithful

d 31.6 Heb ms Gk Syr Jerome: MT *I hate*   e 31.10 Gk Syr:
Heb *my iniquity*   f 31.11 Cn: Heb *exceedingly*   g 31.22 Heb
mss: MT *cut off*

---

of David. See note on Ps. 3 superscription. **31:4** Nets were used for hunting. **31:5** The first line of this verse is uttered by Jesus during his crucifixion (Luke 23:46); Stephen may also allude to it at the time of his own death (Acts 7:59). **31:7–8** The hymn declares the psalmist's trust. **31:8** A *broad place* is an image connoting freedom and space (cf. Pss. 4:1; 18:19). **31:12** *Broken vessel.* See Jer. 22:28; 48:38. **31:13** *Terror all around.* See Jer. 6:25; 20:3, 10; 46:5; 49:29. **31:16** To *let your face shine* is an image signaling God's favor (see Pss. 4:6; 67:1; 80:3, 7, 19; 119:135); it may be an allusion or reference to the priestly blessing of Num. 6:24–26. **31:17** *Sheol.* See note on Ps. 6:1–5. **31:21** *Blessed be the Lord.* See Pss. 28:6; 41:13; 68:19; 72:18; 89:52; 106:48; 124:6; 135:21; 144:1.

but abundantly repays the one who
  acts haughtily.
²⁴ Be strong, and let your heart take
    courage,
  all you who wait for the LORD.

PSALM 32

Of David. A Maskil.
¹ Happy are those whose transgression is
    forgiven,
  whose sin is covered.
² Happy are those to whom the LORD
    imputes no iniquity
  and in whose spirit there is no deceit.

³ While I kept silent, my body wasted
    away
  through my groaning all day long.
⁴ For day and night your hand was heavy
    upon me;
  my strength was dried up*ᵇ* as by the
    heat of summer.   *Selah*

⁵ Then I acknowledged my sin to you,
  and I did not hide my iniquity;
  I said, "I will confess my transgressions
    to the LORD,"
  and you forgave the guilt of my sin.
                                        Selah

⁶ Therefore let all who are faithful
    offer prayer to you;
  at a time of distress,ⁱ the rush of mighty
    waters
  shall not reach them.

⁷ You are a hiding place for me;
  you preserve me from trouble;
  you surround me with glad cries of
    deliverance.   *Selah*

⁸ I will instruct you and teach you the way
    you should go;
  I will counsel you with my eye upon
    you.
⁹ Do not be like a horse or a mule, without
    understanding,
  whose temper must be curbed with bit
    and bridle,
  else it will not stay near you.

¹⁰ Many are the torments of the
    wicked,
  but steadfast love surrounds those
    who trust in the LORD.
¹¹ Be glad in the LORD and rejoice,
    O righteous,
  and shout for joy, all you upright in
    heart.

PSALM 33

¹ Rejoice in the LORD, O you righteous.
  Praise befits the upright.
² Praise the LORD with the lyre;
  make melody to him with the harp of
    ten strings.
³ Sing to him a new song;
  play skillfully on the strings, with loud
    shouts.

b 32.4 Meaning of Heb uncertain   *i* 32.6 Cn: Heb *at a time
of finding only*

Ps. 32:1–11 A song of thanksgiving with five elements: a beatitude of forgiveness (vv. 1–2), a statement of remembrance (vv. 3–5), an invitation to celebrate (vv. 6–7), a confession or vow (vv. 8–9), and a final call to rejoice (vv. 10–11). **Superscription.** *Of David.* See note on Ps. 3 superscription. The meaning of *Maskil* may derive from a word for instruction (cf. 32:8), but the precise meaning is unknown. **32:1–2** *Happy* occurs in didactic exhortations (cf. 1:1; 2:12; 33:12; 34:8). In this verse, happiness comes from an awareness of divine forgiveness. **32:3–5** The hymn offers a testimony about improper silence followed by an appropriate confession of sin. **32:4** The phrase *your hand was heavy upon me* is an image of divine punishment (cf. 1 Sam. 6:5). **32:6–7** A metaphor for chaos, *mighty waters* (Pss. 18:16; 29:3), is juxtaposed to another metaphor—a *hiding place*—which signifies its opposite (Pss. 27:5; 31:20; 61:4; 119:114). *Selah* (vv. 4, 5, 7). See note on Ps. 3:1–2. **32:8–11** The psalmist closes with a commitment to teach, coupled with animal imagery: the *horse* and the *mule* are symbols for the uninformed (cf. Prov. 26:3).

Ps. 33:1–22 An acrostic (see note on Pss. 9–10) hymn of praise. It has four elements: a three-fold call to praise (vv. 1–3), statements on the trustworthiness of God (vv. 4–15), a statement on the untrustworthiness of humans (vv. 16–19), and a conclusion of a renewed prayer of hope (vv. 20–22). Its lack of a superscription is rare in Book I of the Psalter. **33:1–3** The psalmist begins with a call for the righteous to rejoice. **33:2** Two instruments are mentioned: the *lyre*, commonly mentioned elsewhere (Pss. 57:8; 71:22; 81:2), and the *harp of ten strings* (Ps. 144:9). See **"Music and the Psalms," p. 764. 33:3** *Sing . . . a new song.* See Isa. 42:10; Pss. 40:3; 96:1; 98:1; 144:9; 149:1.

Going Deeper: Music and the Psalms (Psalm 33)

Archaeological finds have recovered musical instruments from the ancient Near East. The psalms, too, mention various instruments, suggesting that they were set to and performed with musical accompaniment. Several of the psalmic superscriptions identify the composition as a "song" (see Pss. 48, 83). Several psalms mention "a new song" (see Pss. 33:3; 96:1; 98:1; 144:9; 149:1), and the imperative verb "sing" is also found (see Pss. 33:3; 68:4, 32; 96:1, 2; 105:2; 137:3; 149:1). Music frequently leads to dancing. In the psalms, both women and men dance together as part of celebrations and religious ceremonies. Singers and dancers join in praise of God (see Ps. 87:7).

Dancing is mentioned in context with musical instruments (see Pss. 149:3; 150:4), which are also mentioned in the Psalter. According to various texts, both women and men were trained in music, song, and dance (see Jer. 9:20; 2 Sam. 1:17–27; Ps. 68:25). Various types of musical instruments are known. *Percussion* instruments include cymbals (see Ps. 150:5; cf. 2 Sam. 6:5) and tambourines/timbrels (see Pss. 81:2; 149:3; 150:4). *Stringed* instruments include the harp, lute, and lyre, which were apparently used in two ways: in solo melody and/or as tenor-bass accompaniment. These two were usually performed together (1 Sam. 10:5), creating a balanced proportion of melody and bass instruments in an ensemble. These instruments are also mentioned in the psalms (superscriptions to Pss. 4; 6; 54; 55; 61; 67; 76). The word *shofar* is sometimes translated as "horn" (Ps. 98:6) but other times as "trumpet." Another word for trumpet seems to have specifically been used by priests (1 Chr. 15:24; 16:6). The precise nature of the instrument translated in English as "pipe" is uncertain.

Several of the psalmic superscriptions refer to musical performance (e.g., Pss. 4, 5, 6, 8, 54, 55, 61, 67, 76). This is corroborated in the books of Ezra and 1–2 Chronicles, which mention guild choirs and "the sons of Asaph" and identify Heman and Etan as cymbal players. "According to The Gittith" (Ps. 8:1) might refer to a musical instrument from Gath, but this is unclear. What is certain, regardless, is that the psalms know of, emerge from, and were performed amid song, dance, and musical instrumentation.

Stephen Breck Reid

⁴ For the word of the Lord is upright,
and all his work is done in
faithfulness.
⁵ He loves righteousness and justice;
the earth is full of the steadfast love of
the Lord.

⁶ By the word of the Lord the heavens
were made
and all their host by the breath of his
mouth.
⁷ He gathered the waters of the sea as in a
bottle;
he put the deeps in storehouses.

⁸ Let all the earth fear the Lord;
let all the inhabitants of the world
stand in awe of him,
⁹ for he spoke, and it came to be;
he commanded, and it stood firm.

¹⁰ The Lord brings the counsel of the
nations to nothing;

he frustrates the plans of the
peoples.
¹¹ The counsel of the Lord stands forever,
the thoughts of his heart to all
generations.
¹² Happy is the nation whose God is the
Lord,
the people whom he has chosen as his
heritage.

¹³ The Lord looks down from heaven;
he sees all humankind.
¹⁴ From where he sits enthroned he
watches
all the inhabitants of the earth—
¹⁵ he who fashions the hearts of them
all
and observes all their deeds.
¹⁶ A king is not saved by his great army;
a warrior is not delivered by his great
strength.
¹⁷ The war horse is a vain hope for victory,
and by its great might it cannot save.

33:4–9 The psalm describes the creative power of the divine word. **33:6–7** The hymn points to the divine creation by word (see Gen. 1). **33:10–19** This section acknowledges the power of divine guidance. **33:12** *Happy.* See note on 32:1–2. **33:16–17** The psalmist observes the limits of human

¹⁸ Truly the eye of the Lord is on those who
fear him,
on those who hope in his steadfast
love,
¹⁹ to deliver their soul from death
and to keep them alive in famine.

²⁰ Our soul waits for the Lord;
he is our help and shield.
²¹ Our heart is glad in him
because we trust in his holy name.
²² Let your steadfast love, O Lord, be upon
us,
even as we hope in you.

Psalm 34

*Of David, when he feigned madness before Abimelech, so
that he drove him out, and he went away.*

¹ I will bless the Lord at all times;
his praise shall continually be in my
mouth.
² My soul makes its boast in the Lord;
let the humble hear and be glad.
³ O magnify the Lord with me,
and let us exalt his name together.

⁴ I sought the Lord, and he answered me
and delivered me from all my fears.
⁵ Look to him, and be radiant,
so your*ʲ* faces shall never be ashamed.
⁶ This poor soul cried and was heard by
the Lord
and was saved from every trouble.
⁷ The angel of the Lord encamps
around those who fear him and
delivers them.
⁸ O taste and see that the Lord is good;
happy are those who take refuge in
him.
⁹ O fear the Lord, you his holy ones,
for those who fear him have no
want.

¹⁰ The young lions suffer want and hunger,
but those who seek the Lord lack no
good thing.

¹¹ Come, O children, listen to me;
I will teach you the fear of the Lord.
¹² Which of you desires life
and covets many days to enjoy
good?
¹³ Keep your tongue from evil
and your lips from speaking deceit.
¹⁴ Depart from evil, and do good;
seek peace, and pursue it.

¹⁵ The eyes of the Lord are on the
righteous,
and his ears are open to their cry.
¹⁶ The face of the Lord is against
evildoers,
to cut off the remembrance of them
from the earth.
¹⁷ When the righteous cry for help, the
Lord hears
and rescues them from all their
troubles.
¹⁸ The Lord is near to the brokenhearted
and saves the crushed in spirit.

¹⁹ Many are the afflictions of the righteous,
but the Lord rescues them from them
all.
²⁰ He keeps all their bones;
not one of them will be broken.
²¹ Evil brings death to the wicked,
and those who hate the righteous will
be condemned.
²² The Lord redeems the life of his
servants;
none of those who take refuge in him
will be condemned.

j 34.5 Gk Syr Jerome: Heb *their*

power, both political and militaristic. **33:20–22** The hymn ends with a confession that the power of the community stems from its hope in God.

Ps. 34:1–22 A thanksgiving song in acrostic form (see Pss. 9–10). **Superscription.** An episode from David's biography—*when he feigned madness*—is associated with the psalm (1 Sam. 21:10–15). *Of David.* See note on Ps. 3 superscription. **34:1–3** The psalmist expresses a commitment to praise. **34:4–10** The blessing of v. 1 includes seeking (v. 4). **34:7** *The angel of the Lord* is a manifestation of God's power (cf. Josh. 5:13–15). This figure occurs only here and in Ps. 35:5–6 in the Psalter. **34:8** The psalmist extends double invitations to taste and see the nature of divine goodness accompanied by happiness (see Pss. 1:1; 2:12). **34:11–18** The *fear of the Lord* becomes a kind of curriculum (cf. Pss. 19:9; 111:10). **34:19–22** The hymn closes with a description of the reality of affliction and divine redemption. **34:20** Early Christ followers will recall this verse when reflecting on the death of Jesus (cf. John 19:36).

Psalm 35

Of David.

1 Contend, O Lord, with those who
      contend with me;
   fight against those who fight against
      me!
2 Take hold of shield and buckler,
   and rise up to help me!
3 Draw the spear and javelin
      against my pursuers;
   say to my soul,
      "I am your salvation."

4 Let them be put to shame and dishonor
      who seek after my life.
   Let them be turned back and
      confounded
   who devise evil against me.
5 Let them be like chaff before the
      wind,
   with the angel of the Lord driving
      them on.
6 Let their way be dark and slippery,
   with the angel of the Lord pursuing
      them.

7 For without cause they hid their net[k] for
      me;
   without cause they dug a pit[l] for my
      life.
8 Let ruin come on them unawares,
   and let the net that they hid ensnare
      them;
   let them fall in it—to their ruin.

9 Then my soul shall rejoice in the Lord,
   exulting in his deliverance.
10 All my bones shall say,
      "O Lord, who is like you?
   You deliver the weak
      from those too strong for them,
   the weak and needy from those who
      despoil them."

11 Malicious witnesses rise up;
   they ask me about things I do not
      know.
12 They repay me evil for good;
   my soul is forlorn.
13 But as for me, when they were sick,
   I wore sackcloth;
   I afflicted myself with fasting.
   I prayed with head bowed[m] on my
      bosom,
14   as though I grieved for a friend or a
      brother;
   I went about as one who laments for a
      mother,
   bowed down and in mourning.

15 But at my stumbling they gathered in
      glee;
   they gathered together against me;
   ruffians whom I did not know
      tore at me without ceasing;
16 they impiously mocked more and more,[n]
   gnashing at me with their teeth.

17 How long, O Lord, will you look on?
   Rescue me from their ravages,
      my life from the lions!
18 Then I will thank you in the great
      congregation;
   in the mighty throng I will praise you.

19 Do not let my treacherous enemies
      rejoice over me
   or those who hate me without cause
      wink the eye.
20 For they do not speak peace,
   but they conceive deceitful words
   against those who are quiet in the
      land.

k 35.7 Heb *a pit, their net* l 35.7 The word *pit* is transposed
from the preceding line m 35.13 Or *My prayer turned back*
n 35.16 Cn Compare Gk: Heb *like the profanest of mockers of
a cake*

Ps. 35:1–28 A lament with two long sections. The first part (vv. 1–18) includes petitions to God (vv. 1–3), a petition against enemies (vv. 4–8), an expression of trust (vv. 9–10), a description of the acts of the enemies (vv. 11–16), a plea to God (v. 17), and a promise/vow of thanksgiving (v. 18). The second part begins with general petitions (vv. 19–21), further petitions to God (vv. 22–26), a call to praise (v. 27), and a thanksgiving (v. 28). **Superscription.** *Of David.* See note on Ps. 3 superscription. **35:1–3** The hymn opens with a call to divine action. **35:2–3** The enemies are presented as warriors. **35:4–6** The psalmist wishes for the shame and dishonor of the enemies. **35:5** *Chaff.* See note on 1:4. **35:7–8** The enemies are presented as hunters. *Angel of the Lord.* See note on Ps. 34:7. **35:9–10** The psalmist's *bones* are depicted as speaking. **35:11–18** The hymn continues with a description of the malicious witnesses. **35:17** The lamenting question *How long?* asks for release; the adversaries are presented as *lions. Lions.* See note on Ps. 7:2. **35:19–21** A petition against the enemies who are quoted as saying *"Aha, Aha"* (cf. Pss. 40:15; 70:3).

21 They open wide their mouths against me;
   they say, "Aha, Aha,
   our eyes have seen it."

22 You have seen, O Lord; do not be silent!
   O Lord, do not be far from me!
23 Wake up! Rouse yourself for my defense,
   for my cause, my God and my Lord!
24 Vindicate me, O Lord, my God,
   according to your righteousness,
   and do not let them rejoice over me.
25 Do not let them say to themselves,
   "Aha, we have our heart's desire."
   Do not let them say, "We have swallowed
   you° up."

26 Let all those who rejoice at my calamity
   be put to shame and confusion;
   let those who exalt themselves against
   me
   be clothed with shame and dishonor.

27 Let those who desire my vindication
   shout for joy and be glad
   and say evermore,
   "Great is the Lord,
   who delights in the welfare of his
   servant."
28 Then my tongue shall tell of your
   righteousness
   and of your praise all day long.

Psalm 36

To the leader. Of David, the servant of the Lord.
1 Transgression speaks to the wicked
   deep in their hearts;
   there is no fear of God
   before their eyes.
2 For they flatter themselves in their own
   eyes
   that their iniquity cannot be found out
   and hated.

3 The words of their mouths are mischief
   and deceit;
   they have ceased to act wisely and do
   good.
4 They plot mischief while on their
   beds;
   they are set on a way that is not good;
   they do not reject evil.

5 Your steadfast love, O Lord, extends to
   the heavens,
   your faithfulness to the clouds.
6 Your righteousness is like the mighty
   mountains;
   your judgments are like the great
   deep;
   you save humans and animals alike,
   O Lord.

7 How precious is your steadfast love,
   O God!
   All people may take refuge in the
   shadow of your wings.
8 They feast on the abundance of your
   house,
   and you give them drink from the
   river of your delights.
9 For with you is the fountain of life;
   in your light we see light.

10 O continue your steadfast love to those
   who know you
   and your salvation to the upright of
   heart!
11 Do not let the foot of the arrogant tread
   on me
   or the hand of the wicked drive me
   away.
12 There the evildoers lie prostrate;
   they are thrust down, unable to rise.

o 35.25 Heb *him*

35:22–28 These verses depict a petition to God as judge (cf. Ps. 96) for action coupled with a call to praise and thanksgiving. 35:22 *Do not be silent.* See Ps. 109:1.
   Ps. 36:1–12 While the genre of this psalm is debated, it contains four parts: a description of the wicked (vv. 1–4), a praise of God's character (vv. 5–6), a praise of God's loyalty (vv. 7–9), and a final petition for deliverance from the wicked (vv. 10–12). **Superscription.** *To the leader.* See note on Ps. 4 superscription. *Of David.* See note on Ps. 3 superscription. The addition of *the servant of the Lord* is rare in Book I of the Psalter (see also Ps. 18). 36:1–4 The wicked are those who do not fear God (cf. Ps. 14:1). The *fear of God* (v. 1) occurs only here in Psalms, but it is synonymous with "the fear of the Lord" found elsewhere (cf. Pss. 19:9; 111:10). 36:4 To *plot mischief* while still in bed means the wicked are constantly planning wrongdoing (cf. Mic. 2:1). 36:5–6 The psalmist praises God's character. 36:7–9 The psalmist praises God's faithfulness. 36:8 *Your house* likely refers to the temple. 36:10–12 The hymn closes with a prayer for deliverance.

Psalm 37

Of David.

1 Do not fret because of the wicked;
do not be envious of wrongdoers,
2 for they will soon fade like the grass
and wither like the green herb.

3 Trust in the Lord and do good;
live in the land and enjoy security.
4 Take delight in the Lord,
and he will give you the desires of your heart.

5 Commit your way to the Lord;
trust in him, and he will act.
6 He will make your vindication shine like the light
and the justice of your cause like the noonday.

7 Be still before the Lord, and wait patiently for him;
do not fret over those who prosper in their way,
over those who carry out evil devices.

8 Refrain from anger and forsake wrath.
Do not fret—it leads only to evil.
9 For the wicked shall be cut off,
but those who wait for the Lord shall inherit the land.

10 Yet a little while, and the wicked will be no more;
though you look diligently for their place, they will not be there.
11 But the meek shall inherit the land
and delight themselves in abundant prosperity.

12 The wicked plot against the righteous
and gnash their teeth at them,
13 but the Lord laughs at the wicked,
for he sees that their day is coming.

14 The wicked draw the sword and bend their bows
to bring down the poor and needy,
to kill those who walk uprightly;
15 their sword shall enter their own heart,
and their bows shall be broken.

16 Better is a little that the righteous person has
than the abundance of many wicked.
17 For the arms of the wicked shall be broken,
but the Lord upholds the righteous.

18 The Lord knows the days of the blameless,
and their heritage will abide forever;
19 they are not put to shame in evil times;
in the days of famine they have abundance.

20 But the wicked perish,
and the enemies of the Lord are like the glory of the pastures;
they vanish—like smoke they vanish away.

21 The wicked borrow and do not pay back,
but the righteous are generous and keep giving;
22 surely those blessed by the Lord shall inherit the land,
but those cursed by him shall be cut off.

23 Our steps[p] are made firm by the Lord
when he delights in our[q] way;
24 though we stumble, we[r] shall not fall headlong,
for the Lord holds us[s] by the hand.

25 I have been young and now am old,
yet I have not seen the righteous forsaken
or their children begging bread.

p 37.23 Heb *A man's steps* *q* 37.23 Heb *his* *r* 37.24 Heb *he stumbles, he* *s* 37.24 Heb *him*

Ps. 37:1–40 An acrostic (see note on Pss. 9–10) wisdom psalm that includes five sections: a petition about the response to the wicked (vv. 1–11), a description of the wicked and their fate (vv. 12–15), a wisdom saying on the superiority of the righteous (vv. 16–26), advice to the righteous (vv. 27–33), and a declaration of God's will for the righteous (vv. 34–40). **Superscription.** *Of David.* See note on Ps. 3 superscription. **37:1–11** The hymn opens with an admonition and a promise. **37:2** *Fade like the grass.* Compare vv. 20 and 36; also see Ps. 129:6–7. **37:12–15** The psalmist turns to an imprecation and description of the wicked enemy (vv. 12–13, 14–15, 20). **37:16–26** The psalm provides a lengthy

26 They are ever giving liberally and
  lending,
  and their children become a blessing.

27 Depart from evil, and do good;
  so you shall abide forever.
28 For the LORD loves justice;
  he will not forsake his faithful ones.

The righteous shall be kept safe forever,
  but the children of the wicked shall be
  cut off.
29 The righteous shall inherit the land
  and live in it forever.

30 The mouths of the righteous utter
  wisdom,
  and their tongues speak justice.
31 The law of their God is in their hearts;
  their steps do not slip.

32 The wicked watch for the righteous
  and seek to kill them.
33 The LORD will not abandon them to their
  power
  or let them be condemned when they
  are brought to trial.

34 Wait for the LORD and keep to his way,
  and he will exalt you to inherit the
  land;
  you will look on the destruction of the
  wicked.

35 I have seen the wicked oppressing
  and towering like a cedar of Lebanon.[t]
36 Again I[u] passed by, and they were no
  more;
  though I sought them, they could not
  be found.

37 Mark the blameless and behold the
  upright,
  for there is posterity for the peaceable.
38 But transgressors shall be altogether
  destroyed;

the posterity of the wicked shall be
  cut off.

39 The salvation of the righteous is from the
  LORD;
  he is their refuge in the time of trouble.
40 The LORD helps them and rescues them;
  he rescues them from the wicked and
  saves them
  because they take refuge in him.

PSALM 38

A Psalm of David, for the memorial offering.

1 O LORD, do not rebuke me in your anger
  or discipline me in your wrath.
2 For your arrows have sunk into me,
  and your hand has come down on me.

3 There is no soundness in my flesh
  because of your indignation;
there is no health in my bones
  because of my sin.
4 For my iniquities have gone over my
  head;
  they weigh like a burden too heavy
  for me.

5 My wounds grow foul and fester
  because of my foolishness;
6 I am utterly bowed down and prostrate;
  all day long I go around mourning.
7 For my loins are filled with burning,
  and there is no soundness in my flesh.
8 I am utterly spent and crushed;
  I groan because of the tumult of my
  heart.

9 O Lord, all my longing is known to you;
  my sighing is not hidden from you.
10 My heart throbs; my strength fails me;
  as for the light of my eyes—it also has
  gone from me.
11 My friends and companions stand aloof
  from my affliction,

t 37.35 Gk: Meaning of Heb uncertain   *u* 37.36 Gk Syr
Jerome: Heb *he*

contrast between the righteous and the wicked (cf. Ps. 1). **37:27–40** Similar to the opening, the hymn closes with an admonition and a promise.

Ps. 38:1–22 A prayer for healing—the third of seven penitential psalms (see note on Ps. 6)—with six parts: an appeal for help (vv. 1–2), a description of suffering (vv. 3–8), a wish to God (vv. 9–10), a description of alienation (vv. 11–14), other wishes to God (vv. 15–20), and a final plea for help (vv. 21–22). **Superscription.** *A Psalm of David.* See note on Ps. 3 superscription. The meaning of the addition to the superscription—*for the memorial offering* (see also Ps. 70)—is unclear. **38:1–8** The hymn opens with a plea for help and a description of suffering. **38:9–10** The psalmist's unpronounced

and my neighbors stand far off.

¹² Those who seek my life lay their snares;
   those who seek to hurt me speak of
      ruin
   and meditate on treachery all day long.

¹³ But I am like the deaf; I do not hear;
   like the mute, who cannot speak.
¹⁴ Truly, I am like one who does not hear
   and in whose mouth is no retort.

¹⁵ But it is for you, O LORD, that I wait;
   it is you, O Lord my God, who will
      answer.
¹⁶ For I pray, "Only do not let them rejoice
      over me,
   those who boast against me when my
      foot slips."

¹⁷ For I am ready to fall,
   and my pain is ever with me.
¹⁸ I confess my iniquity;
   I am sorry for my sin.
¹⁹ Those who are my foes without cause*ᵛ*
      are mighty,
   and many are those who hate me
      wrongfully.
²⁰ Those who render me evil for good
   are my adversaries because I follow
      after good.

²¹ Do not forsake me, O LORD;
   O my God, do not be far from me;
²² make haste to help me,
   O Lord, my salvation.

PSALM 39

To the leader: to Jeduthun. A Psalm of David.
¹ I said, "I will guard my ways
   that I may not sin with my tongue;

I will keep a muzzle on my mouth
   as long as the wicked are in my
      presence."
² I was silent and still;
   I held my peace to no avail;
   my distress grew worse;
³   my heart became hot within me.
   While I mused, the fire burned;
   then I spoke with my tongue:

⁴ "LORD, let me know my end
   and what is the measure of my days;
   let me know how fleeting my life is.
⁵ You have made my days a few
      handbreadths,
   and my lifetime is as nothing in your
      sight.
   Surely everyone stands as a mere breath.
                                    Selah
⁶   Surely everyone goes about like a
      shadow.
   Surely for nothing they are in turmoil;
   they heap up and do not know who
      will gather.

⁷ "And now, O Lord, what do I wait for?
   My hope is in you.
⁸ Deliver me from all my transgressions.
   Do not make me the scorn of the fool.
⁹ I am silent; I do not open my mouth,
   for it is you who have done it.
¹⁰ Remove your stroke from me;
   I am worn down by the blows*ʷ* of your
      hand.

¹¹ "You chastise mortals
   in punishment for sin,
   consuming like a moth what is dear to
      them;
   surely everyone is a mere breath.   *Selah*

v 38.19 Q ms: MT *my living foes   w* 39.10 Heb *hostility*

desires are not unknown to God. **38:11–14** The hymn describes longing and alienation. **38:17–22** The psalm closes with a final confession of guilt and plea for help.

Ps. 39:1–13 A prayer for healing with five parts: a description of the psalmist's silence (vv. 1–3b), a description of the psalmist's move to speech (vv. 3c–5), a meditation (vv. 6–8), a renewed speech (vv. 9–11), and a concluding prayer (vv. 12–13). **Superscription.** *To the leader.* See note on Ps. 4 super-scription. *A Psalm of David.* See note on Ps. 3 superscription. *Jeduthun* is likely a temple musician (cf. 1 Chr. 9:16; 16:37–42; Neh. 11:17; superscriptions to Pss. 62; 77). **39:1–3** The hymn begins with a first-person meditation. **39:4–6** The psalmist complains about the brevity of life (cf. Pss. 90, 103). **39:5** The word *handbreadths* occurs only here in parallel with *mere breath* to point to something that is fleeting. *Selah* (vv. 5, 11). See note on Ps. 3:1–2. **39:7–13** The psalmist petitions God for divine attention and mercy. **39:12** *Hear my prayer* is a phrase that marks a petition (cf. Pss. 4:1; 39:12; 54:2; 84:8; 143:1). *Passing guest* and *alien* are terms for temporary residents or immigrants. *My forebears* likely refers to the ancestral traditions recorded in Genesis (Gen. 12–36).

12 "Hear my prayer, O Lord,
 and give ear to my cry;
 do not hold your peace at my tears.
For I am your passing guest,
 an alien, like all my forebears.
13 Turn your gaze away from me, that I may
 smile again,
 before I depart and am no more."

Psalm 40

To the leader. Of David. A Psalm.
1 I waited patiently for the Lord;
 he inclined to me and heard my
 cry.
2 He drew me up from the desolate
 pit,[x]
 out of the miry bog,
and set my feet upon a rock,
 making my steps secure.
3 He put a new song in my mouth,
 a song of praise to our God.
Many will see and fear
 and put their trust in the Lord.

4 Happy are those who make
 the Lord their trust,
who do not turn to the proud,
 to those who go astray after false
 gods.
5 You have multiplied, O Lord my God,
 your wondrous deeds and your
 thoughts toward us;
 none can compare with you.
Were I to proclaim and tell of them,
 they would be more than can be
 counted.

6 Sacrifice and offering you do not
 desire,
 but you have given me an open
 ear.[y]
Burnt offering and sin offering
 you have not required.
7 Then I said, "Here I am;
 in the scroll of the book it is written
 of me.[z]
8 I delight to do your will, O my God;
 your law is within my heart."

9 I have told the glad news of deliverance
 in the great congregation;
see, I have not restrained my lips,
 as you know, O Lord.
10 I have not hidden your saving help
 within my heart;
 I have spoken of your faithfulness and
 your salvation;
 I have not concealed your steadfast love
 and your faithfulness
 from the great congregation.

11 Do not, O Lord, withhold
 your mercy from me;
let your steadfast love and your
 faithfulness
 keep me safe forever.
12 For evils have encompassed me
 without number;
my iniquities have overtaken me
 until I cannot see;
they are more than the hairs of my
 head,
 and my heart fails me.

13 Be pleased, O Lord, to deliver me;
 O Lord, make haste to help me.
14 Let all those be put to shame and
 confusion
 who seek to snatch away my life;
let those be turned back and brought to
 dishonor
 who desire my hurt.
15 Let those be appalled because of their
 shame
 who say to me, "Aha, Aha!"

16 But may all who seek you
 rejoice and be glad in you;
may those who love your salvation
 say continually, "Great is the Lord!"
17 As for me, I am poor and needy,
 but the Lord takes thought for me.
You are my help and my deliverer;
 do not delay, O my God.

x 40.2 Cn: Heb *pit of tumult* y 40.6 Heb *ears you have dug for me* z 40.7 Meaning of Heb uncertain

Ps. 40:1–17 A thanksgiving and prayer for help in three parts: a statement of the psalmist's perseverance (vv. 1–3), a beatitude and song (vv. 4–11), and a renewed prayer (vv. 12–17). **Superscription.** See notes on Pss. 3 and 4 superscriptions. **40:3** *A new song.* See Ps. 33:3. **40:4** *Happy.* See note on 32:1–2. **40:6** According to the psalmist, God prefers obedience over sacrifice. **40:13–17** These verses are nearly identical to Ps. 70. **40:15** *Aha, Aha* is an insulting reproach made by adversaries (cf. Pss. 35:21; 70:3).

PSALM 41

To the leader. A Psalm of David.

¹ Happy are those who consider the poor;*ᵃ*
    the LORD delivers them in the day of
    trouble.
² The LORD protects them and keeps them
    alive;
    they are called happy in the land.
    You do not give them up to the will of
    their enemies.
³ The LORD sustains them on their
    sickbed;
    in their illness you heal all their
    infirmities.*ᵇ*

⁴ As for me, I said, "O LORD, be gracious
    to me;
    heal me, for I have sinned against
    you."
⁵ My enemies wonder in malice
    when I will die and my name
    perish.
⁶ And when they come to see me, they
    utter empty words
    while their hearts gather mischief;
    when they go out, they tell it
    abroad.
⁷ All who hate me whisper together about
    me;
    they imagine the worst for me.

⁸ They think that a deadly thing has
    fastened on me,
    that I will not rise again from where
    I lie.

⁹ Even my close friend in whom I
    trusted,
    who ate of my bread, has lifted the
    heel against me.
¹⁰ But you, O LORD, be gracious to me,
    and raise me up, that I may repay
    them.

¹¹ By this I know that you are pleased with
    me:
    because my enemy has not triumphed
    over me.
¹² But you have upheld me because of my
    integrity
    and set me in your presence forever.

¹³ Blessed be the LORD, the God of Israel,
    from everlasting to everlasting.
        Amen and Amen.

BOOK II
(PSALMS 42–72)

PSALM 42

To the leader. A Maskil of the Korahites.

¹ As a deer longs for flowing streams,
    so my soul longs for you, O God.
² My soul thirsts for God,
    for the living God.
    When shall I come and behold
    the face of God?
³ My tears have been my food
    day and night,

a 41.1 Or *weak*   *b* 41.3 Heb *you change all his bed*

Ps. 41:1–13 A thanksgiving song in three parts: a beatitude (vv. 1–3), a recollection of past prayers for deliverance (vv. 4–10), and a concluding praise (vv. 11–13). **Superscription.** *Leader* and *A Psalm of David.* See notes on Pss. 3 and 4 superscriptions. **41:1–3** A beatitude concerning those who are considerate. **41:1** *Happy.* See 1:1; 2:12; 33:12; 34:8. **41:4–10** A recollection of a past prayer for help. **41:11–12** A concluding petition. **41:13** This verse is the closing doxology for Book I of the Psalter.

Book II: Pss. 42–72 Book II includes the so-called Elohistic Psalter (Pss. 42–83), a group of psalms known for the prominent use of the word "Elohim" (God) rather than "YHWH" (the Lord). Book II also includes a second Davidic collection (Pss. 51–72). Like Book I, Book II is composed mostly of laments.

Pss. 42–43 The lack of a superscription between these psalms, the similarity of the genre (lament), and several repetitions all indicate that Pss. 42 and 43 should be read together as one psalm that begins with words of lament (42:1–4), followed by a refrain (42:5), more lament (42:6–10), another refrain (42:11), more words of lament (43:1–4), and a final refrain (43:5). **Superscription.** *To the leader.* See note on Ps. 4 superscription. *Maskil.* See note on Ps. 32 superscription. Eleven psalms bear superscriptions referring to the *Korahites* (Pss. 42, 44, 45, 46, 47, 48, 49, 84, 85, 87, 88). Korah was a Levite (Num. 16) and a possible patron for temple singers by the same name (2 Chr. 20:19). **42:1–4** The psalm begins with a complaint and description of longing. Deer are an image of natural beauty and vulnerability (cf. Ps. 18:33). **42:2** To *behold the face* may be a technical

while people say to me continually,
  "Where is your God?"

4 These things I remember,
  as I pour out my soul:
how I went with the throng[c]
  and led them in procession to the
    house of God,
with glad shouts and songs of
    thanksgiving,
  a multitude keeping festival.
5 Why are you cast down, O my soul,
  and why are you disquieted within
    me?
Hope in God, for I shall again praise him,
  my help 6and my God.

My soul is cast down within me;
  therefore I remember you
from the land of Jordan and of
    Hermon,
  from Mount Mizar.
7 Deep calls to deep
  at the thunder of your torrents;
all your waves and your billows
  have gone over me.
8 By day the LORD commands his steadfast
    love,
  and at night his song is with me,
  a prayer to the God of my life.

9 I say to God, my rock,
  "Why have you forgotten me?
Why must I walk about mournfully
  because the enemy oppresses me?"
10 As with a deadly wound in my body,
  my adversaries taunt me,
while they say to me continually,
  "Where is your God?"

11 Why are you cast down, O my soul,
  and why are you disquieted within
    me?

Hope in God, for I shall again praise
    him,
  my help and my God.

PSALM 43

1 Vindicate me, O God, and defend my
    cause
  against an ungodly people;
from those who are deceitful and
    unjust,
  deliver me!
2 For you are the God in whom I take
    refuge;
  why have you cast me off?
Why must I walk about mournfully
  because of the oppression of the
    enemy?

3 O send out your light and your truth;
  let them lead me;
let them bring me to your holy hill
  and to your dwelling.
4 Then I will go to the altar of God,
  to God my exceeding joy,
and I will praise you with the harp,
  O God, my God.

5 Why are you cast down, O my soul,
  and why are you disquieted within
    me?
Hope in God, for I shall again praise
    him,
  my help and my God.

PSALM 44

To the leader. Of the Korahites. A Maskil.
1 We have heard with our ears, O God;
  our ancestors have told us
what deeds you performed in their
    days,
  in the days of old:

c 42.4 Meaning of Heb uncertain

term for entering God's sanctuary (cf. Deut. 31:11). **42:4** *Festival* refers to one of Israel's three great pilgrimage festivals (see Deut. 16; Ps. 84:1–2). **42:6** *The land of Jordan and of Hermon* is a reference to the headwaters of the Jordan River. *Mount Mizar* is located in the Anti-Lebanon Mountains. **42:7** *Deep calls to deep* indicates cosmic, chaotic waters of peril. **43:4** The psalmist makes a vow to God. **43:5** The psalmist addresses questions to the self, then issues a call to *hope in God* and an affirmation of God's help.

Ps. 44:1–26 A communal lament (see also Pss. 60, 74, 79, 80, 85, 90, 94, 123, 137) that has three parts: a declaration of praise and rehearsing of God's provision (vv. 1–8), a declaration of innocence and request for divine behavior (vv. 9–22), and a concluding petition (vv. 23–26). **Superscription.** *To the leader.* See note on Ps. 4 superscription. *Korahites.* See note on Pss. 42–43 superscription. *Maskil.* See note on Ps. 32 superscription. **44:1–8** A hymnic remembrance.

² you with your own hand drove out the
   nations,
      but them you planted;
   you afflicted the peoples,
      but them you set free;
³ for not by their own sword did they win
   the land,
      nor did their own arm give them
      victory,
   but your right hand, and your arm,
      and the light of your countenance,
      for you delighted in them.

⁴ You are my King and my God;
   you command*d* victories for
   Jacob.
⁵ Through you we push down our
   foes;
      through your name we tread down
      our assailants.
⁶ For not in my bow do I trust,
      nor can my sword save me.
⁷ But you have saved us from our foes
      and have put to confusion those who
      hate us.
⁸ In God we have boasted continually,
      and we will give thanks to your name
      forever.   *Selah*

⁹ Yet you have rejected us and shamed us
      and have not gone out with our armies.
¹⁰ You made us turn back from the foe,
      and our enemies have gotten spoil.
¹¹ You have made us like sheep for
   slaughter
      and have scattered us among the
      nations.
¹² You have sold your people for a trifle,
      demanding no high price for them.

¹³ You have made us the taunt of our
   neighbors,
      the derision and scorn of those around
      us.
¹⁴ You have made us a byword among the
   nations,
      a laughingstock*e* among the peoples.

¹⁵ All day long my disgrace is before me,
      and shame has covered my face
¹⁶ at the words of the taunters and revilers,
      at the sight of the enemy and the
      avenger.

¹⁷ All this has come upon us,
      yet we have not forgotten you
      or been false to your covenant.
¹⁸ Our heart has not turned back,
      nor have our steps departed from your
      way,
¹⁹ yet you have broken us in the haunt of
   jackals
      and covered us with deep darkness.

²⁰ If we had forgotten the name of our God
      or spread out our hands to a strange
      god,
²¹ would not God discover this?
      For he knows the secrets of the heart.
²² Because of you we are being killed all
   day long
      and accounted as sheep for the
      slaughter.

²³ Rouse yourself! Why do you sleep,
   O Lord?
      Awake, do not cast us off forever!
²⁴ Why do you hide your face?
      Why do you forget our affliction and
      oppression?
²⁵ For we sink down to the dust;
      our bodies cling to the ground.
²⁶ Rise up, come to our help.
      Redeem us for the sake of your
      steadfast love.

PSALM 45

To the leader: according to Lilies. Of the Korahites. A
Maskil. A love song.
¹ My heart overflows with a goodly theme;
      I address my verses to the king;
         my tongue is like the pen of a ready
         scribe.

d 44.4 Gk Syr: Heb *You are my King, O God; command*
e 44.14 Heb *a shaking of the head*

44:8 *Selah.* See note on Ps. 3:1–2. **44:9–16** The middle section of the psalm comprises a complaint. **44:14** Cf. Deut. 28:37.
   Ps. 45:1–17 A royal wedding song that has four parts: a speech of the poet (v. 1), a praise of
the groom (vv. 2–9), a praise of the bride (vv. 10–15), and the concluding words of the poet (v. 17).
Superscription. *To the leader.* See note on Ps. 4 superscription. *According to Lilies* likely refers to a
melody. *Korahites.* See note on Pss. 42–43 superscription. *Maskil.* See note on Ps. 32 superscription.
A love song occurs only here in the Psalter. **45:1** The psalm begins with the self-presentation of the

² You are the most handsome of men;
  grace is poured upon your lips;
  therefore God has blessed you forever.
³ Gird your sword on your thigh, O mighty
    one,
  in your glory and majesty.

⁴ In your majesty ride on victoriously
  for the cause of truth and to defend*
    the right;
  let your right hand teach you dread
    deeds.
⁵ Your arrows are sharp
  in the heart of the king's enemies;
  the peoples fall under you.

⁶ Your throne, O God,* endures forever
    and ever.
  Your royal scepter is a scepter of equity;
⁷ you love righteousness and hate
    wickedness.
  Therefore God, your God, has anointed you
  with the oil of gladness beyond your
    companions;
⁸ your robes are all fragrant with myrrh
  and aloes and cassia.
  From ivory palaces stringed instruments
  make you glad;
⁹ daughters of kings are among your
    ladies of honor;
  at your right hand stands the queen in
    gold of Ophir.

¹⁰ Hear, O daughter, consider and incline
    your ear;
  forget your people and your father's
    house,
¹¹ and the king will desire your beauty.
  Since he is your lord, bow to him;
¹² Daughter Tyre will seek your favor
    with gifts,

the richest of the people ¹³with all
  kinds of wealth.

  The princess is decked in her chamber
    with gold-woven robes;*
¹⁴ in many-colored robes she is led to
    the king;
  behind her the virgins, her
    companions, follow.
¹⁵ With joy and gladness they are led along
  as they enter the palace of the king.

¹⁶ In the place of ancestors you, O king,*
    shall have sons;
  you will make them princes in all the
    earth.
¹⁷ I will cause your name to be celebrated
    in all generations;
  therefore the peoples will praise you
    forever and ever.

PSALM 46

*To the leader. Of the Korahites. According to Alamoth.
A Song.*
¹ God is our refuge and strength,
  a very present* help in trouble.
² Therefore we will not fear, though the
    earth should change,
  though the mountains shake in the
    heart of the sea,
³ though its waters roar and foam,
  though the mountains tremble with its
    tumult.   *Selah*

⁴ There is a river whose streams make glad
    the city of God,
  the holy habitation of the Most High.

---

f 45.4 Cn: Heb *and the meekness of*   *g* 45.6 Or *Your throne is a
throne of God, it*   *h* 45.13 Or *people.* ¹³*All glorious is the princess
within, gold embroidery is her clothing*   *i* 45.16 Heb lacks
O king   *j* 46.1 Or *well proved*

singer. **45:2–9** The psalmist proceeds to praise the king's physical attractiveness, wise speech (v. 2), and military prowess (vv. 3, 4). **45:6** The meaning of this sentence in Hebrew is unclear, but it is quoted in the New Testament (Heb. 1:8). **45:7** *God . . . has anointed* the king (cf. Ps. 2:6–7). **45:10–11** The singer makes an admonition to the bride. **45:12–15** The psalmist goes on to describe the wedding. **45:16–17** The couple is promised progeny.

  Ps. 46:1–11 One of the songs of Zion (Pss. 46, 48, 76, 84, 87, 122) that testify to Zion as the abode of God and the place of Israelite worship. Psalm 46 has three parts: a declaration of God as shelter and refuge (vv. 1–3), a description of the metaphor "city of God" (vv. 4–7), and a prediction (vv. 8–11). **Superscription.** *To the leader.* See note on Ps. 4 superscription. *Korahites.* See note on Pss. 42–43 superscription. *Alamoth* likely refers to the singers or liturgical participants, but it may refer to a musical setting. **46:1–2** The psalm opens with a statement of confidence in God as refuge (cf. Ps. 2:12). **46:3** The psalm gives an account of a chaotic battle. *Selah.* See note on Ps. 3:1–2. **46:4–5** The psalmist makes another statement of confidence. **46:4** *City of God* is a reference to Zion (see also

[5] God is in the midst of the city;[k] it shall
  not be moved;
  God will help it when the morning
  dawns.
[6] The nations are in an uproar; the
  kingdoms totter;
  he utters his voice; the earth melts.
[7] The LORD of hosts is with us;
  the God of Jacob is our refuge.[l]   *Selah*

[8] Come, behold the works of the LORD;
  see what desolations he has brought
  on the earth.
[9] He makes wars cease to the end of the
  earth;
  he breaks the bow and shatters the
  spear;
  he burns the shields with fire.
[10] "Be still, and know that I am God!
  I am exalted among the nations;
  I am exalted in the earth."
[11] The LORD of hosts is with us;
  the God of Jacob is our refuge.[m]
                                  Selah

PSALM 47

To the leader. Of the Korahites. A Psalm.
[1] Clap your hands, all you peoples;
  shout to God with loud songs of
  joy.
[2] For the LORD, the Most High, is
  awesome,
  a great king over all the earth.
[3] He subdued peoples under us
  and nations under our feet.

[4] He chose our heritage for us,
  the pride of Jacob whom he loves.
                                  Selah

[5] God has gone up with a shout,
  the LORD with the sound of a trumpet.
[6] Sing praises to God, sing praises;
  sing praises to our King, sing praises.
[7] For God is the king of all the earth;
  sing praises with a psalm."[n]

[8] God is king over the nations;
  God sits on his holy throne.
[9] The princes of the peoples gather
  as the people of the God of Abraham.
For the shields of the earth belong to
  God;
  he is highly exalted.

PSALM 48

A Song. A Psalm of the Korahites.
[1] Great is the LORD and greatly to be
  praised
  in the city of our God.
His holy mountain, [2]beautiful in elevation,
  is the joy of all the earth,
Mount Zion, in the far north,
  the city of the great King.
[3] Within its citadels God
  has shown himself a sure defense.

[4] Then the kings assembled;
  they came on together.

k 46.5 Heb *of it*   l 46.7 Or *fortress*   m 46.11 Or *fortress*
n 47.7 Heb *Maskil*

Ps. 87:3). **46:6** This verse gives an account of global revolt. **46:7** A refrain recounting God's presence in Zion. *Selah.* See note on Ps. 3:1–2. **46:8–9** A victory hymn. **46:10** The psalmist employs first-person divine speech here (cf. Ps. 37:7). **46:11** Repetition of the refrain recounting divine presence in Zion. *Selah.* See note on Ps. 3:1–2.

Ps. 47:1–9 An enthronement psalm that celebrates God's rule. The hymn has several parts: an imperative with a rationale (vv. 1–5), a second imperative with a rationale (vv. 6–9a), and a concluding ascription to God (v. 9b). **Superscription.** *To the leader.* See note on Ps. 4 superscription. *Korahites.* See note on Pss. 42–43 superscription. **47:1–2** *Clap* and *shout* are imperatives of celebration (cf. Ps. 98:8; Isa. 55:12). **47:3–5** The psalm continues with hymnic assertions about God. **47:4** *Selah.* See note on Ps. 3:1–2. **47:6–8** The psalmist makes a threefold repetition of the affirmation of God as king (vv. 6, 7, 8).

Ps. 48:1–14 A Zion song (see note on Ps. 46) that contains celebrations of the glories of Mount Zion (vv. 1–3) and the invincibility of Zion (vv. 4–8) by the congregation (vv. 9–11) and that ends with an invitation to contemplate Zion and its relationship to God (vv. 12–14). **Superscription.** *Korahites.* See note on Pss. 42–43 superscription. **48:1–3** The psalm opens with a communal praise of the *city of our God* (vv. 1, 8). God's *holy mountain* refers to Zion, the name of the hill on which the temple sits (cf. Ps. 99:9). **48:2** The psalmist uses the phrase *in the far north* to associate Zion with Mount Zaphon, the mountain home of the Canaanite storm god Baal; the mythology of the latter is co-opted and applied to Israel's God alone (cf. Ps. 29). **48:4–7** This section gives an account of battle

5 As soon as they saw it, they were
astounded;
they were in panic; they took to flight;
6 trembling took hold of them there,
pains as of a woman in labor,
7 as when an east wind shatters
the ships of Tarshish.
8 As we have heard, so have we seen
in the city of the LORD of hosts,
in the city of our God,
which God establishes forever. *Selah*

9 We ponder your steadfast love, O God,
in the midst of your temple.
10 Your name, O God, like your praise,
reaches to the ends of the earth.
Your right hand is filled with victory.
11 Let Mount Zion be glad;
let the towns[o] of Judah rejoice
because of your judgments.

12 Walk about Zion; go all around it;
count its towers;
13 consider well its ramparts;
go through its citadels,
that you may tell the next generation
14 that this is God,
our God forever and ever.
He will be our guide forever.

PSALM 49

To the leader. Of the Korahites. A Psalm.

1 Hear this, all you peoples;
give ear, all inhabitants of the world,
2 both low and high,
rich and poor together.
3 My mouth shall speak wisdom;
the meditation of my heart shall be
understanding.
4 I will incline my ear to a proverb;
I will solve my riddle to the music of
the harp.

5 Why should I fear in times of trouble,
when the iniquity of my persecutors
surrounds me,
6 those who trust in their wealth
and boast of the abundance of their
riches?
7 Truly, no ransom avails for one's life;[p]
there is no price one can give to God
for it.
8 For the ransom of life is costly
and can never suffice,
9 that one should live on forever
and never see the Pit.

10 When we look at the wise, they die;
fool and dolt perish together
and leave their wealth to others.
11 Their graves[q] are their homes forever,
their dwelling places to all
generations,
though they named lands their own.
12 Mortals cannot abide in their pomp;
they are like the animals that perish.

13 Such is the fate of the foolhardy,
the end of those[r] who are pleased
with their lot. *Selah*
14 Like sheep they are appointed for Sheol;
Death shall be their shepherd;
straight to the grave they descend,[s]
and their form shall waste away;
Sheol shall be their home.[t]

o 48.11 Heb *daughters* *p* 49.7 Or *no one can ransom a brother* *q* 49.11 Gk Syr Compare Tg: Heb *their inward thought* *r* 49.13 Tg: Heb *after them* *s* 49.14 Cn: Heb *the upright shall have dominion over them in the morning* *t* 49.14 Meaning of Heb uncertain

and victory. Zion instills terror against adversaries. **48:6** The image of *pains as of a woman in labor* suggests the anguish and agony of the political and religious conflict (cf. Exod. 15:14; Jer. 6:24; 22:23; 50:43; Mic. 4:9–10). **48:8** The psalmist offers affirmations of confidence. *Selah.* See note on Ps. 3:1–2. **48:9–11** This psalm continues with communal praise. **48:12–14** A summons to proceed around Zion and consider its architecture leads to a consideration of God.

Ps. 49:1–20 A meditation in three parts that begins with introductory words and a riddle (vv. 1–6), a response to the riddle (vv. 7–12), and a summary (vv. 13–15). **Superscription.** *To the leader.* See note on Ps. 4 superscription. *Korahites.* See note on Pss. 42–43 superscription. **49:1–4** The psalmist begins by presenting the song to *all you peoples*. The references to the *low*, *high*, *rich*, and *poor* indicate a diverse community, all of whom are addressed by the psalm. **49:5–11** This section makes a plaintive meditation on why one might *fear in times of trouble* (v. 5). **49:10** The *wise*, *fool*, and *dolt* alike share a common fate, death. **49:12** This verse is repeated as a refrain in v. 20. Both humans and animals are mortal. **49:13, 15** *Selah.* See note on Ps. 3:1–2. **49:14–15** *Sheol.* See note on Ps. 6:1–5. **49:14** The meaning of this text in Hebrew is very uncertain.

¹⁵ But God will ransom my soul from the
power of Sheol,
for he will receive me.   *Selah*

¹⁶ Do not be afraid when some become
rich,
when the wealth of their houses
increases.
¹⁷ For when they die they will carry
nothing away;
their wealth will not go down after
them.
¹⁸ Though in their lifetime they count
themselves happy
—for you are praised when you do
well for yourself—
¹⁹ they*u* will go to the company of their
ancestors,
who will never again see the light.
²⁰ Mortals cannot abide in their pomp;
they are like the animals that perish.

PSALM 50

A Psalm of Asaph.
¹ The mighty one, God the Lord,
speaks and summons the earth
from the rising of the sun to its
setting.
² Out of Zion, the perfection of beauty,
God shines forth.

³ Our God comes and does not keep silent;
before him is a devouring fire
and a mighty tempest all around him.
⁴ He calls to the heavens above
and to the earth, that he may judge his
people:
⁵ "Gather to me my faithful ones,
who made a covenant with me by
sacrifice!"
⁶ The heavens declare his righteousness,
for God himself is judge.   *Selah*

⁷ "Hear, O my people, and I will speak,
O Israel, I will testify against you.
I am God, your God.
⁸ Not for your sacrifices do I rebuke you;
your burnt offerings are continually
before me.
⁹ I will not accept a bull from your house
or goats from your folds.
¹⁰ For every wild animal of the forest is mine,
the cattle on a thousand hills.
¹¹ I know all the birds of the air,*v*
and all that moves in the field is mine.

¹² "If I were hungry, I would not tell you,
for the world and all that is in it is
mine.
¹³ Do I eat the flesh of bulls
or drink the blood of goats?
¹⁴ Offer to God a sacrifice of
thanksgiving,*w*
and pay your vows to the Most High.
¹⁵ Call on me in the day of trouble;
I will deliver you, and you shall glorify
me."

¹⁶ But to the wicked God says,
"What right have you to recite my
statutes
or take my covenant on your lips?
¹⁷ For you hate discipline,
and you cast my words behind you.
¹⁸ You make friends with a thief when you
see one,
and you keep company with
adulterers.

¹⁹ "You give your mouth free rein for evil,
and your tongue frames deceit.
²⁰ You sit and speak against your kin;
you slander your own mother's child.

u 49.19 Cn: Heb *you*   *v* 50.11 Gk Syr Tg: Heb *mountains*
w 50.14 Or *make thanksgiving your sacrifice to God*

49:15 *Ransom my soul* could refer to life with God beyond the grave (see Gen. 5:24; 2 Kgs. 2:3, 5).
49:20 This verse repeats v. 12 as a refrain that answers the anxiety of the question of v. 5: the times
of trouble will eventually end definitively.

Ps. 50:1–23 A hymn of praise that resembles a covenant lawsuit with prophetic warnings (see
Hos. 4:19; Mic. 6:1–8). It contains four sections: an introduction (vv. 1–6), declarations on proper
sacrifice (vv. 7–15), a declaration of proper life (vv. 16–22), and a conclusion (v. 23). **Superscription.**
Asaph. The name given to a family of musicians commissioned by David (see 1 Chr. 6:39; 15:17;
16:4–6). Additional Psalms of Asaph occur in Pss. 73–83. **50:1–6** *God shines forth* out of Zion as
the perfection of beauty. **50:4** *God calls to the heavens above and to the earth* recalls the role of
these entities in covenant lawsuits where God takes the people to court (see Deut. 31:28; 32:1; Isa.
1:2). **50:6** *Selah.* See note on Ps. 3:1–2. **50:7–15** These verses comprise a divine indictment and
instruction on right sacrifice (cf. Isa. 1:10–17; Amos 5:21–24). **50:16–21** This section includes another

21 These things you have done, and I have
been silent;
you thought that I was one just like
yourself.
But now I rebuke you and lay the charge
before you.

22 "Mark this, then, you who forget God,
or I will tear you apart, and there will
be no one to deliver.
23 Those who bring thanksgiving as their
sacrifice honor me;
to those who go the right way,*
I will show the salvation of God."

PSALM 51

*To the leader. A Psalm of David, when the prophet
Nathan came to him, after he had gone in to Bathsheba.*
1 Have mercy on me, O God,
according to your steadfast love;
according to your abundant mercy,
blot out my transgressions.
2 Wash me thoroughly from my iniquity,
and cleanse me from my sin.

3 For I know my transgressions,
and my sin is ever before me.
4 Against you, you alone, have I sinned
and done what is evil in your sight,
so that you are justified in your sentence
and blameless when you pass
judgment.
5 Indeed, I was born guilty,
a sinner when my mother conceived me.

6 You desire truth in the inward being;*
therefore teach me wisdom in my
secret heart.

7 Purge me with hyssop, and I shall be clean;
wash me, and I shall be whiter than
snow.
8 Let me hear joy and gladness;
let the bones that you have crushed
rejoice.
9 Hide your face from my sins,
and blot out all my iniquities.

10 Create in me a clean heart, O God,
and put a new and right² spirit within me.
11 Do not cast me away from your presence,
and do not take your holy spirit from me.
12 Restore to me the joy of your salvation,
and sustain in me a willing* spirit.

13 Then I will teach transgressors your ways,
and sinners will return to you.
14 Deliver me from bloodshed, O God,
O God of my salvation,
and my tongue will sing aloud of your
deliverance.

15 O Lord, open my lips,
and my mouth will declare your praise.
16 For you have no delight in sacrifice;
if I were to give a burnt offering, you
would not be pleased.
17 The sacrifice acceptable to God* is a
broken spirit;
a broken and contrite heart, O God,
you will not despise.

18 Do good to Zion in your good pleasure;
rebuild the walls of Jerusalem;

x 50.23 Heb *who set a way*   y 51.6 Meaning of Heb uncertain   z 51.10 Or *steadfast*   a 51.12 Or *generous*   b 51.17 Or
My sacrifice, O God,

divine indictment and instruction on right living addressed to the wicked. **50:22–23** The psalmist
ends with a final warning.

   Ps. 51:1–19 This psalm is the most famous of the seven penitential prayers (see also Pss. 6, 32,
38, 102, 130, 143). It contains an introductory plea for mercy (vv. 1–2), words of confession (vv. 3–6),
more petition (vv. 7–12), a vow (vv. 13–15), and a two-part conclusion about the psalmist (vv. 16–
17) and about Zion (vv. 18–19). **Superscription.** *Leader.* See note on Ps. 4 superscription. *A Psalm
of David.* See note on Ps. 3 superscription. The extended biographical detail in this superscription
relates the psalm to David's taking of Bathsheba and Nathan's parable in response (see 2 Sam. 11–
12). **51:1–2** The psalm begins with pleas for mercy. **51:3–5** The psalmist makes a confession of sin.
51:3 The psalmist's sins are recognized as *ever before me.* **51:4** The psalmist recognizes a breach
with God *alone,* with no mention of how transgression might affect other persons involved. **51:5** *Born
guilty* is a powerful image capturing the profundity of the psalmist's sinfulness. **51:6–9** The psalmist
offers a petition for redemption. **51:10–12** Another petition is made. **51:10** God is the only subject
used for the Hebrew verb *create* (see Gen. 1:1). **51:13–17** The psalmist promises to teach *transgressors* and *sinners* about God's *ways.* The only truly acceptable sacrifice is humility and repentance,
described here as *a broken spirit* and *a broken and contrite heart.* **51:18–19** These verses may be

[19] then you will delight in right sacrifices,
  in burnt offerings and whole burnt
    offerings;
  then bulls will be offered on your altar.

PSALM 52

*To the leader. A Maskil of David, when Doeg the Edomite
came to Saul and said to him, "David has come to the
house of Ahimelech."*

[1] Why do you boast, O mighty one,
  of mischief done against the godly?[c]
  All day long [2]you are plotting
    destruction.
  Your tongue is like a sharp razor,
    you worker of treachery.
[3] You love evil more than good
  and lying more than speaking the
    truth.   *Selah*
[4] You love all words that devour,
  O deceitful tongue.

[5] But God will break you down forever;
  he will snatch and tear you from your
    tent;
  he will uproot you from the land of
    the living.   *Selah*
[6] The righteous will see and fear
  and will laugh at the evildoer,[d] saying,
[7] "See the one who would not take
    refuge in God
  but trusted in abundant riches
  and sought refuge in wealth!"[e]

[8] But I am like a green olive tree
  in the house of God.
  I trust in the steadfast love of God
    forever and ever.

[9] I will thank you forever
  because of what you have done.
  In the presence of the faithful
  I will proclaim[f] your name, for it is
    good.

PSALM 53

*To the leader: according to Mahalath.
A Maskil of David.*

[1] Fools say in their hearts, "There is no
    God."
  They are corrupt; they commit
    abominable acts;
  there is no one who does good.

[2] God looks down from heaven on
    humankind
  to see if there are any who are
    wise,
  who seek after God.

[3] They have all fallen away; they are all
    alike perverse;
  there is no one who does good,
  no, not one.

[4] Have they no knowledge, those
    evildoers,
  who eat up my people as they eat
    bread
  and do not call upon God?

[5] There they shall be in great terror,
  in terror such as has not been.

c 52.1 Cn Compare Syr: Heb *the kindness of God*   *d* 52.6 Heb
him   *e* 52.7 Syr Tg: Heb *in his destruction*   *f* 52.9 Cn: Heb
wait for

a later addition that applies the psalm more corporately to Zion and allows for acceptable animal sacrifice after all.

Ps. 52:1–9 A wisdom psalm in three parts: a statement of the opponents of God (vv. 1–4), a pronouncement of God's opinion of the adversaries (v. 5), and a description of the way of the righteous (vv. 6–9). **Superscription.** *To the leader.* See note on Ps. 4 superscription. *Maskil.* See note on Ps. 32 superscription. *Of David.* See note on Ps. 3 superscription. *Doeg the Edomite.* See 1 Sam. 21:1–8; 22:6–19. **52:1–4** The indictment of the enemy includes their boasting and bad speech. *Selah* (vv. 3, 5). See note on Ps. 3:1–2. **52:5–7** The psalmist predicts divine destruction of the wicked. *Land of the living.* See note on Ps. 27:13. **52:8–9** A strong contrast is drawn between the psalmist and the adversaries, not unlike Ps. 1. Indeed, *I am like a green olive tree* recalls the arboreal imagery of Ps. 1:3.

Ps. 53:1–6 A wisdom psalm that is nearly identical to Ps. 14. It is structurally similar to Ps. 52 with three parts: a description of the acts of a fool (vv. 1–4), a divine verdict (v. 5), and a wish for restoration (v. 6). **Superscription.** *Leader.* See note on Ps. 4 superscription. *According to Mahalath* occurs only here and in Ps. 88; it may be a reference to a musical tune or be some sort of liturgical instruction. *Maskil.* See note on Ps. 32 superscription. *Of David.* See note on Ps. 3 superscription. **53:1–4** The accusation *fools say . . . , "There is no God"* is once again not an instance of theoretical atheism but a functional disregard of God (see Ps. 14), which leads to *abominable acts.* **53:2** *God looks down*

For God will scatter the bones of the
ungodly;^g
they will be put to shame,^h for God has
rejected them.

⁶ O that deliverance for Israel would come
from Zion!
When God restores the fortunes of his
people,
Jacob will rejoice; Israel will be glad.

PSALM 54

*To the leader: with stringed instruments. A Maskil of
David, when the Ziphites went and told Saul, "David is in
hiding among us."*
¹ Save me, O God, by your name,
and vindicate me by your might.
² Hear my prayer, O God;
give ear to the words of my mouth.

³ For the insolent have risen against me;
the ruthless seek my life;
they do not set God before them. *Selah*

⁴ But surely, God is my helper;
the Lord is the upholder ofⁱ my life.
⁵ He will repay my enemies for their evil.
In your faithfulness, put an end to
them.

⁶ With a freewill offering I will sacrifice
to you;
I will give thanks to your name,
O LORD, for it is good.

⁷ For he has delivered me from every
trouble,
and my eye has looked in triumph on
my enemies.

PSALM 55

*To the leader: with stringed instruments. A Maskil of
David.*
¹ Give ear to my prayer, O God;
do not hide yourself from my
supplication.
² Attend to me and answer me;
I am troubled in my complaint.
I am distraught ³by the noise of the
enemy,
because of the clamor of the wicked.
For they bring^j trouble upon me,
and in anger they bear a grudge
against me.

⁴ My heart is in anguish within me;
the terrors of death have fallen upon
me.
⁵ Fear and trembling come upon me,
and horror overwhelms me.
⁶ And I say, "O that I had wings like a
dove!
I would fly away and be at rest;
⁷ truly, I would flee far away;
I would lodge in the wilderness; *Selah*

g 53.5 Cn Compare Gk Syr: Heb *him who encamps against you*
h 53.5 Gk: Heb *you have put (them) to shame* *i* 54.4 Gk Syr
Jerome: Heb *is of those who uphold* or *is with those who uphold*
j 55.3 Cn Compare Gk: Heb *they cause to totter*

from heaven. A superior vantage point that demonstrates God's capacity to judge. **53:5–6** God's judgment is enacted in a terrestrial location, Zion. **53:5** *There* likely refers to Zion, mentioned by name in v. 6. **53:6** A hope for deliverance from Zion and God, which will produce joy and gladness.

Ps. 54:1–7 A prayer for deliverance from personal enemies in three parts: a plea (vv. 1–3), an expression of confidence (vv. 4–5), and a thanksgiving and confession (vv. 6–7). **Superscription.** *Leader.* See note on Ps. 4 superscription. *With stringed instruments.* See note on Ps. 4 superscription (also found in Pss. 6, 55, 61, 67, 76 superscriptions). *Maskil.* See note on Ps. 32 superscription. *Of David.* See note on Ps. 3 superscription. The extended superscription relates the psalm to a specific time in David's life (see 1 Sam. 23:15–19). **54:1–3** The psalm opens with a plea for help. *Selah.* See note on Ps. 3:1–2. **54:4–5** The psalmist makes an expression of confidence in God's aid. **54:4** *God is my helper.* See Isa. 41:10, 13. **54:6–7** Freewill offerings are mentioned in Lev. 7:16–17; these verses also include the psalmist's confession of God's good name and saving acts.

Ps. 55:1–23 A lengthy prayer for deliverance from personal enemies that manifests a complex structure: a cry to God (vv. 1–3), a description of divine vengeance on enemies (vv. 4–5), a wish to escape (vv. 6–8), a description of the enemies of the city (vv. 9–11), a description of betrayal (vv. 12–14), a wish against enemies (v. 15), a confession of God's faithfulness (vv. 16–19), another description of betrayal (vv. 20–21), words of encouragement (v. 22), and a confession of belief in God's action (v. 23). **Superscription.** *Leader.* See note on Ps. 4 superscription. *With stringed instruments.* See superscriptions at Pss. 4, 6, 54, 61, 67, 76. *Maskil.* See note on Ps. 32 superscription. *Of David.* See note on Ps. 3 superscription. **55:1–8** The psalmist is overcome with dread. **55:6** *I would fly away.*

8 I would hurry to find a shelter for myself
  from the raging wind and tempest."

9 Confuse, O Lord, confound their speech,
  for I see violence and strife in the city.
10 Day and night they go around it
  on its walls,
and iniquity and trouble are within it;
11   ruin is in its midst;
oppression and fraud
  do not depart from its marketplace.

12 It is not enemies who taunt me—
  I could bear that;
it is not adversaries who deal insolently
  with me—
  I could hide from them.
13 But it is you, my equal,
  my companion, my familiar friend,
14 with whom I kept pleasant company;
  we walked in the house of God with
  the throng.
15 Let death come upon them;
  let them go down alive to Sheol,
  for evil is in their homes and in their
  hearts.

16 But I call upon God,
  and the LORD will save me.
17 Evening and morning and at noon
  I utter my complaint and moan,
  and he will hear my voice.
18 He will redeem me unharmed
  from the battle that I wage,
  for many are arrayed against me.
19 God, who is enthroned from of old,
      Selah

will hear and will humble them,
because they do not change
  and do not fear God.

20 My companion laid hands on a friend
  and violated a covenant with me[k]
21 with speech smoother than butter
  but with a heart set on war,
with words that were softer than oil
  but in fact were drawn swords.

22 Cast your burden[l] on the LORD,
  and he will sustain you;
he will never permit
  the righteous to be moved.

23 But you, O God, will cast them down
  into the lowest pit;
the bloodthirsty and treacherous
  shall not live out half their days.
But I will trust in you.

PSALM 56

To the leader: according to The Dove on Far-off Terebinths. Of David. A Miktam, when the Philistines seized him in Gath.
1 Be gracious to me, O God, for people
  tramble on me;
  all day long foes oppress me;
2 my enemies trample on me all day long,
  for many fight against me.
O Most High, 3when I am afraid,
  I put my trust in you.
4 In God, whose word I praise,
  in God I trust; I am not afraid;

k 55.20 Heb lacks *with me*   *l* 55.22 Or *Cast what he has given you*

The wilderness provides a sense of safety for the psalmist. **55:7** *Selah* (vv. 7, 19). See note on Ps. 3:1–2. **55:9–11** The psalmist names seven personified evils that lurk in the city. **55:12–15** The intimacy of the betrayal confuses and distresses the psalmist. **55:16–19** The psalmist makes a confession of God's faithfulness. *Selah* (vv. 7, 19). See note on Ps. 3:1–2. **55:17** *Evening and morning and at noon* captures all time periods in a kind of comprehensive merism (a way to speak of the whole of something by speaking of two or three of its key parts, especially the beginning and end), but the time periods may also refer to customary times for prayer (Dan. 6:10). **55:20–23** The psalm concludes with a final assurance. The sentiment *cast your burden on the LORD* is mentioned in the New Testament (Matt. 6:25–34; Luke 12:22–31; 1 Pet. 5:7).

Ps. 56:1–13 A prayer for deliverance from personal enemies that, like Ps. 55, has a complex structure that includes a cry for rescue (vv. 1–2), a declaration of trust (vv. 3–4), a description of the crimes of the enemies (vv. 5–9), a second declaration of trust (vv. 10–11), and an offering of thanksgiving for deliverance (vv. 12–13). **Superscription.** *Leader.* See note on Ps. 4 superscription. *The Dove on Far-off Terebinths* likely refers to a musical tune. *Miktam.* See note on Ps. 16 superscription. *Of David.* See note on Ps. 3 superscription. This extended superscription connects the psalm to the time when David was *seized . . . in Gath* (see 1 Sam. 21:10–15). **56:1–2** The psalmist utters a cry to God for rescue. **56:3–4** These verses make a first declaration

what can flesh do to me?

⁵ All day long they seek to injure my cause;
    all their thoughts are against me for
      evil.
⁶ They stir up strife; they lurk;
    they watch my steps,
  as they hoped to take my life.
⁷   Do not deliver them for any reason;ᵐ
    in wrath cast down the peoples, O God!

⁸ You have kept count of my tossings;
    put my tears in your bottle.
    Are they not in your record?
⁹ Then my enemies will retreat
    in the day when I call.
    This I know, thatⁿ God is for me.
¹⁰ In God, whose word I praise,
    in the Lord, whose word I praise,
¹¹ in God I trust; I am not afraid.
    What can a mere mortal do to me?

¹² My vows to you I must perform, O God;
    I will render thank offerings to you.
¹³ For you have delivered my soul from
      death
    and my feet from falling,
  so that I may walk before God
    in the light of life.

PSALM 57

To the leader: Do Not Destroy. Of David. A Miktam,
when he fled from Saul, in the cave.
¹ Be merciful to me, O God; be merciful
    to me,
    for in you my soul takes refuge;

in the shadow of your wings I will take
    refuge,
    until the destroying storms pass by.
² I cry to God Most High,
    to God who fulfills his purpose
      for me.
³ He will send from heaven and save me;
    he will put to shame those who
      trample on me.   *Selah*
God will send forth his steadfast love
    and his faithfulness.

⁴ I lie down among lions
    that greedily devourᵒ human prey;
their teeth are spears and arrows,
    their tongues sharp swords.

⁵ Be exalted, O God, above the
    heavens.
    Let your glory be over all the earth.

⁶ They set a net for my steps;
    my soul was bowed down.
They dug a pit in my path,
    but they have fallen into it themselves.
        Selah
⁷ My heart is steadfast, O God;
    my heart is steadfast.
I will sing and make melody.
⁸   Awake, my soul!
Awake, O harp and lyre!
    I will awake the dawn.

m 56.7 Gk Compare Syr Jerome: Heb *deliver them because*
of their iniquity   n 56.9 Or *because*   o 57.4 Cn: Heb *are*
aflame for

of trust. **56:5–6** The psalmist describes the actions of the enemies. **56:7–9** The psalm shifts to a petition for God to act against the enemies. **56:8** The idea that *my tears* (cf. Pss. 39:12; 42:3) are collected in God's *bottle* and *record* testifies to God's intimate awareness of the psalmist's distress. **56:10–11** The psalmist makes a second declaration of trust. **56:12–13** The psalm closes with a vow of thanksgiving for deliverance.

    Ps. 57:1–11 A prayer for deliverance from personal enemies that includes a cry to God (v. 1), a declaration of trust (vv. 2–3), a description of the atrocities of the enemies (v. 4), a petition to act (v. 5), acts of the enemies (v. 6), another declaration of trust (vv. 7–8), an offering of thanksgiving (vv. 9–10), and a petition for divine action (v. 11). **Superscription.** *Leader.* See note on Ps. 4 superscription. *Do Not Destroy* could be a musical term or some other sort of liturgical notation (cf. Pss. 58–59). *Miktam.* See note on Ps. 16 superscription. *Of David.* See note on Ps. 3 superscription. This psalm is related to the time David *fled from Saul, in the cave* (see 1 Sam. 22–24). **57:1** An initial plea is expressed, similar to Pss. 51 and 56. *In the shadow of your wings* is a metaphor for divine protection (see Pss. 17:8; 36:7; 63:7; cf. Deut. 32:11); the wings could be part of a zoological image of God or a reference to the cherubim in the temple (cf. 1 Kgs. 6:27). **57:2–3** The psalmist issues a petition. *Selah.* See note on Ps. 3:1–2. **57:4** *Lions* are commonly used as images for adversaries (cf. Ps. 7:2). **57:5** The psalmist utters a praise statement that is repeated in v. 11. **57:6** The psalm moves into a complaint using hunting imagery. *Selah.* See note on Ps. 3:1–2. **57:7–8** These verses shift into an

[9] I will give thanks to you, O Lord, among
the peoples;
I will sing praises to you among the
nations.
[10] For your steadfast love is as high as the
heavens;
your faithfulness extends to the
clouds.

[11] Be exalted, O God, above the heavens.
Let your glory be over all the earth.

Psalm 58

To the leader: Do Not Destroy. Of David. A Miktam.

[1] Do you indeed decree what is right, you
gods?
Do you judge people fairly?
[2] No, in your hearts you devise wrongs;
your hands deal out violence on
earth.

[3] The wicked go astray from the womb;
they err from their birth, speaking
lies.
[4] They have venom like the venom of a
serpent,
like the deaf adder that stops its ear,
[5] so that it does not hear the voice of
charmers
or of the cunning enchanter.

[6] O God, break the teeth in their mouths;
tear out the fangs of the young lions,
O Lord!
[7] Let them vanish like water that runs
away;
like grass let them be trodden down[p]
and wither.
[8] Let them be like the snail that dissolves
into slime,
like the untimely birth that never sees
the sun.
[9] Sooner than your pots can feel the heat
of thorns,
whether green or ablaze, may he
sweep them away!

[10] The righteous will rejoice when they see
vengeance done;
they will bathe their feet in the blood
of the wicked.
[11] People will say, "Surely there is a reward
for the righteous;
surely there is a God who judges[q] on
earth."

Psalm 59

To the leader: Do Not Destroy. Of David. A Miktam, when Saul ordered his house to be watched in order to kill him.

[1] Deliver me from my enemies, O my God;
protect me from those who rise up
against me.
[2] Deliver me from those who work evil;
from the bloodthirsty, save me.

[3] Even now they lie in wait for my life;
the mighty stir up strife against me.
For no transgression or sin of mine,
O Lord,

p 58.7 Cn: Meaning of Heb uncertain *q* 58.11 Or *there are gods who judge*

attitude of thanksgiving. **57:9–10** The psalmist makes a vow to thank and praise the Lord. **57:11** The repetition of v. 5 serves as a concluding refrain.

Ps. 58:1–11 An individual lament containing three elements: a description of the enemies (vv. 1–5), a demand for divine action (vv. 6–9), and a statement of rejoicing of the righteous (vv. 10–11). **Superscription.** *Leader.* See note on Ps. 4 superscription. *Do Not Destroy.* See note on Ps. 57 superscription. *Miktam.* See note on Ps. 16 superscription. *Of David.* See note on Ps. 3 superscription. **58:1–5** The psalm begins with an invective against *you gods* (cf. Ps. 82). **58:3** *Astray from the womb* describes the wicked as corrupt from birth (cf. Ps. 51). **58:6–9** The psalmist curses the enemies with seven curses and a variety of metaphors. **58:10–11** *Bathe their feet in the blood of the wicked* is a particularly gruesome military image.

Ps. 59:1–17 A prayer for deliverance from personal enemies that begins with a cry for rescue (vv. 1–5), followed by a metaphorical description of the enemies (vv. 6–7), a statement of trust (vv. 8–10), a wish for the demise of the enemies (vv. 11–13), a second metaphorical description of the enemies (vv. 14–15), and another statement of trust (vv. 16–17). **Superscription.** *Leader.* See note on Ps. 4 superscription. *Do Not Destroy.* See note on Ps. 57 superscription. *Of David.* See note on Ps. 3 superscription. *Miktam.* See note on Ps. 16 superscription. *Saul ordered his house to be watched* relates this psalm to Saul's murderous hunt for David (1 Sam. 19:11–17). **59:1–2** The psalm opens with an initial plea. **59:3–4a** The psalmist makes a complaint along with a declaration of innocence.

4 for no fault of mine, they run and
make ready.

Rouse yourself, come to my help and see!
5 You, LORD God of hosts, are God of
Israel.
Awake to punish all the nations;
spare none of those who
treacherously plot evil.   *Selah*

6 Each evening they come back
howling like dogs
and prowling about the city.
7 There they are, bellowing with their
mouths,
with sharp words[r] on their lips,
for "Who," they think,[s] "will hear us?"

8 But you laugh at them, O LORD;
you hold all the nations in derision.
9 O my strength, I will watch for you,
for you, O God, are my fortress.
10 My God in his steadfast love will meet
me;
my God will let me look in triumph on
my enemies.

11 Do not kill them, or my people may
forget;
make them totter by your power and
bring them down,
O Lord, our shield.
12 For the sin of their mouths, the words of
their lips,
let them be trapped in their pride.
For the cursing and lies that they utter,
13 consume them in wrath;
consume them until they are no
more.

Then it will be known to the ends of the
earth
that God rules over Jacob.   *Selah*

14 Each evening they come back
howling like dogs
and prowling about the city.
15 They roam about for food
and growl if they do not get their fill.

16 But I will sing of your might;
I will sing aloud of your steadfast love
in the morning.
For you have been a fortress for me
and a refuge in the day of my
distress.
17 O my strength, I will sing praises to you,
for you, O God, are my fortress,
the God who shows me steadfast love.

PSALM 60

*To the leader: according to the Lily of the Covenant. A
Miktam of David; for instruction; when he struggled
with Aram-naharaim and with Aram-zobah, and when
Joab on his return killed twelve thousand Edomites in the
Valley of Salt.*

1 O God, you have rejected us, broken our
defenses;
you have been angry; now restore us!
2 You have caused the land to quake; you
have torn it open;
repair the cracks in it, for it is
tottering.
3 You have made your people suffer hard
things;
you have given us wine to drink that
made us reel.

r 59.7 Heb *with swords*   s 59.7 Heb lacks *they think*

59:4b–5 The complaint and declaration are followed by a petition with an invocation (cf. Ps. 44:23; Isa. 51:9). *Selah.* See note on Ps. 3:1–2. **59:6–7** The enemies are depicted as scavenging dogs, an image repeated in vv. 14–15. **59:8–9** The psalmist affirms confidence in God using the metaphor of divine laughter (cf. Ps. 2:4). **59:10–13** The psalmist makes a petition and curses the enemies. *Selah.* See note on Ps. 3:1–2. **59:14–15** Another instance of the enemies portrayed as dogs. **59:16–17** The psalm concludes with a thanksgiving for God's *might*.

Ps. 60:1–12 A communal lament that contains a description of God's rejection (vv. 1–3), a description of God's salvation (vv. 4–5), God's declaration of power (vv. 6–8), a second description of divine rejection (vv. 9–11), and a final cry for deliverance and assurance of trust (v. 12). **Superscription.** *Leader.* See note on Ps. 4 superscription. *According to the Lily of the Covenant* likely refers to a melody. *Miktam.* See note on Ps. 16 superscription. *Of David.* See note on Ps. 3 superscription. The extended superscription includes specific place-names like *Aram-naharaim* and *Aram-zobah* and specific details like *killed twelve thousand Edomites in the Valley of Salt*, which relate the psalm to multiple events in David's life (cf. 2 Sam. 8:3–8; 10:6–18). **60:1–5** The psalmist begins with the accusation that God has rejected Israel (cf. Ps. 43:2; 44:9, 23). **60:3** *Reel* as if drunk on *wine* is a vivid

[4] You have set up a banner for those who
fear you,
to rally to it out of bowshot.[t] *Selah*
[5] Give victory with your right hand and
answer us,[u]
so that those whom you love may be
rescued.

[6] God has promised in his sanctuary,[v]
"With exultation I will divide up
Shechem
and portion out the Vale of Succoth.
[7] Gilead is mine, and Manasseh is mine;
Ephraim is my helmet;
Judah is my scepter.
[8] Moab is my washbasin;
on Edom I hurl my shoe;
over Philistia I shout in triumph."

[9] Who will bring me to the fortified city?
Who will lead me to Edom?
[10] Have you not rejected us, O God?
You do not go out, O God, with our
armies.
[11] O grant us help against the foe,
for human help is worthless.
[12] With God we shall do valiantly;
it is he who will tread down our
foes.

PSALM 61

To the leader: with stringed instruments. Of David.
[1] Hear my cry, O God;
listen to my prayer.

[2] From the end of the earth I call to you,
when my heart is faint.

Lead me to the rock
that is higher than I,
[3] for you are my refuge,
a strong tower against the enemy.

[4] Let me abide in your tent forever,
find refuge under the shelter of your
wings. *Selah*
[5] For you, O God, have heard my vows;
you have given me the heritage of
those who fear your name.

[6] Prolong the life of the king;
may his years endure to all
generations!
[7] May he be enthroned forever before God;
appoint steadfast love and faithfulness
to watch over him!

[8] So I will always sing praises to your
name,
as I pay my vows day after day.

PSALM 62

To the leader: according to Jeduthun. A Psalm of David.
[1] For God alone my soul waits in silence;
from him comes my salvation.
[2] He alone is my rock and my salvation,
my fortress; I shall never be shaken.

t 60.4 Gk Syr Jerome: Heb *because of the truth* *u* 60.5 Or *me*
v 60.6 Or *by his holiness*

image of the stupefying effects of war (cf. Jer. 25:15–16). **60:4** *Set up a banner.* Cf. Jer. 50:2. *Selah.*
See note on Ps. 3:1–2. **60:6–9** A divine oracle from the sanctuary announces victory over *Shechem*
and *the Vale of Succoth.* God claims ownership of Israelite and Transjordanian locations. **60:8** *Hurl
my shoe* is apparently an unclear image of contempt or of victory and control. **60:10–12** The psalmist
complains about divine absence before requesting divine intervention against Israel's adversaries.

Ps. 61:1–8 A prayer for protection containing four elements: a cry for God (vv. 1–2b), a petition
for help (vv. 2c–5), wishes for the king (vv. 6–7), and a final petition (v. 8). **Superscription.** *Leader.*
See note on Ps. 4 superscription. *Stringed instruments.* See note on Ps. 4 superscription. **61:1–3** *Of
David.* See note on Ps. 3 superscription. This call to hear is typical of lament psalms (see Ps. 13).
61:2–3 *From the end of the earth.* See 46:9; Isa. 5:26. God as *rock* and *refuge* connotes divine
power and protection; perhaps they allude in some way also to the temple. **61:4** *Abide* means to
live securely. *Your tent* seems to allude to the temple (see Ps. 27:6). *Selah.* See note on Ps. 3:1–2.
61:5 The psalmist is confident that God has heard. **61:6–7** A prayer is offered for the longevity of
the king (Ps. 72). **61:8** The psalmist promises a response of *praises* and *vows* (see Ps. 116:14, 18).

Ps. 62:1–12 A song of trust with a chiastic or envelope structure (see note on Pss. 15–24): an
affirmation of trust in God (vv. 1–2), a description of the action of the enemies (vv. 3–4), another
statement of trust in God (vv. 5–8), a description of human attributes (vv. 9–10), and a third
reference to trust in God (vv. 11–12). **Superscription.** *Leader.* See note on Ps. 4 superscription. *According to Jeduthun.* See note on Ps. 39 superscription. *A Psalm of David.* See note on Ps. 3 superscription. **62:1–2** This opening affirmation of trust in God will be repeated in vv. 5–6 as a refrain.

³ How long will you assail a person,
  will you batter your victim, all
    of you,
  as you would a leaning wall, a
    tottering fence?
⁴ Their only plan is to bring down a person
    of prominence.
  They take pleasure in falsehood;
they bless with their mouths,
  but inwardly they curse.   *Selah*

⁵ For God alone my soul waits in silence,
  for my hope is from him.
⁶ He alone is my rock and my salvation,
  my fortress; I shall not be shaken.
⁷ On God rests my deliverance and my
    honor;
  my mighty rock, my refuge is in
    God.

⁸ Trust in him at all times, O people;
  pour out your heart before him;
  God is a refuge for us.   *Selah*

⁹ Those of low estate are but a breath;
  those of high estate are a delusion;
in the balances they go up;
  they are together lighter than a
    breath.
¹⁰ Put no confidence in extortion,
  and set no vain hopes on robbery;
  if riches increase, do not set your
    heart on them.

¹¹ Once God has spoken;
  twice have I heard this:
that power belongs to God,
¹²   and steadfast love belongs to you,
    O Lord.
For you repay to all
  according to their work.

PSALM 63

*A Psalm of David, when he was in the Wilderness of
Judah.*

¹ O God, you are my God; I seek you;
  my soul thirsts for you;
my flesh faints for you,
  as in a dry and weary land where
    there is no water.
² So I have looked upon you in the
    sanctuary,
  beholding your power and glory.
³ Because your steadfast love is better
    than life,
  my lips will praise you.
⁴ So I will bless you as long as I live;
  I will lift up my hands and call on your
    name.

⁵ My soul is satisfied as with a rich feast,ʷ
  and my mouth praises you with joyful
    lips
⁶ when I think of you on my bed
  and meditate on you in the watches of
    the night,
⁷ for you have been my help,
  and in the shadow of your wings I sing
    for joy.
⁸ My soul clings to you;
  your right hand upholds me.

⁹ But those who seek to destroy my life
  shall go down into the depths of the
    earth;
¹⁰ they shall be given over to the power of
    the sword;
  they shall be prey for jackals.
¹¹ But the king shall rejoice in God;
  all who swear by him shall exult,
  for the mouths of liars will be stopped.

w 63.5 Heb *with fat and fatness*

62:3–4 The psalmist makes statements of complaint and indictment of the enemies. *Selah.* See note on Ps. 3:1–2. **62:5–6** This refrain repeats the psalmist's trust in God (see vv. 1–2). **62:8** The listeners are called to trust God as refuge. *Selah.* See note on Ps. 3:1–2. **62:9–10** Human beings, regardless of standing (*low estate . . . high estate*), are described as unworthy of trust. **62:11–12** The psalmist ends by affirming that *power belongs to God*, not humans.

  Ps. 63:1–11 A prayer for deliverance from personal enemies with three sections: expressions of trust and longing (vv. 1–4), a description of longevity with God (vv. 5–8), and a description of the end of the enemies (vv. 9–11). **Superscription.** *A Psalm of David.* See note on Ps. 3 superscription. *Wilderness of Judah* puts this psalm in conversation with David's escape from Saul (1 Sam. 23:14–15; 24:1). **63:1–4** The psalmist expresses longing and trust (cf. Ps. 42:1–2). **63:5–8** These verses describe the good life lived with God. **63:9–10** The description of the good life with God is followed by a description of the fate of the enemies. **63:9** *Depths of the earth* probably refers to Sheol, the realm of the dead. **63:11** The psalm concludes with a prayer for the king (cf. Ps. 61:6–8).

PSALM 64

To the leader. A Psalm of David.

[1] Hear my voice, O God, in my
  complaint;
  preserve my life from the dread
  enemy.
[2] Hide me from the secret plots of the
  wicked,
  from the scheming of evildoers,
[3] who whet their tongues like swords,
  who aim bitter words like arrows,
[4] shooting from ambush at the
  blameless;
  they shoot suddenly and without
  fear.
[5] They hold fast to their evil purpose;
  they talk of laying snares secretly,
  thinking, "Who can see us?[x]
[6]   Who can search out our crimes?[y]
  We have thought out a cunningly
  conceived plot."
  For the human heart and mind are
  deep.

[7] But God will shoot his arrow at them;
  they will be wounded suddenly.
[8] Because of their tongue he will bring
  them to ruin;[z]
  all who see them will shake with
  horror.
[9] Then everyone will fear;
  they will tell what God has brought
  about
  and ponder what he has done.

[10] Let the righteous rejoice in the LORD
  and take refuge in him.
  Let all the upright in heart glory.

PSALM 65

To the leader. A Psalm of David. A Song.

[1] Praise is due to you,
  O God, in Zion,
  and to you shall vows be
  performed,
[2]   O you who answer prayer!
  To you all flesh shall come.
[3] When deeds of iniquity overwhelm
  us,
  you forgive our transgressions.
[4] Happy are those whom you choose and
  bring near
  to live in your courts.
  We shall be satisfied with the goodness
  of your house,
  your holy temple.

[5] By awesome deeds you answer us with
  deliverance,
  O God of our salvation;
  you are the hope of all the ends of the
  earth
  and of the farthest seas.
[6] By your[a] strength you established the
  mountains;
  you are girded with might.
[7] You silence the roaring of the seas,
  the roaring of their waves,
  the tumult of the peoples.
[8] Those who live at earth's farthest bounds
  are awed by your signs;
  you make the gateways of the
  morning and the evening shout
  for joy.

x 64.5 Syr Jerome: Heb them   y 64.6 Cn: Heb They search out crimes   z 64.8 Cn: Heb They will bring him to ruin, their tongue being against them   a 65.6 Gk Jerome: Heb his

Ps. 64:1–10 A prayer for deliverance from personal enemies that has four parts: a cry for aid from God (vv. 1–2), a description of the work of the evil ones (vv. 3–6), a description of divine action and human response (vv. 7–9), and a call for righteous praise (v. 10). **Superscription.** *Leader.* See note on Ps. 4 superscription. *A Psalm of David.* See note on Ps. 3 superscription. **64:1–2** A cry to God to *hear*, *preserve*, and *hide*. **64:3–6** The psalmist describes the acts of evildoers, including "the secret plots of the wicked" (v. 2), presented with the aid of militaristic imagery (*swords, arrows, ambush*). Hunting imagery is also used (*laying snares*; cf. Pss. 140:5; 141:9–10). Once again, the wicked think they may act with impunity because no one sees them (cf. Ps. 10:11). **64:7–9** God's response is a militaristic or hunting action (*shoot his arrow*), which leads directly to enemy injury. **64:10** The psalm ends with a call to the righteous to praise God.

Ps. 65:1–13 A thanksgiving for God's presence in Zion due to three acts of forgiveness (vv. 1–4), power (vv. 5–8), and grace (vv. 9–13). **Superscription.** *Leader.* See note on Ps. 4 superscription. *A Psalm of David.* See note on Ps. 3 superscription. **65:1–4** The psalmist describes God's acts of forgiveness in Zion. **65:4** *Happy* occurs elsewhere in the psalms of those who please God or benefit from God's goodness (cf. Pss. 1:1; 2:12; 33:12; 34:8). *Choose* and *bring near* anticipate a good outcome from God. Zion (v. 1) is now spoken of as *house* and *temple*. **65:5–8** The *awesome deeds* of God

⁹ You visit the earth and water it;
    you greatly enrich it;
the river of God is full of water;
    you provide the people with grain,
    for so you have prepared it.
¹⁰ You water its furrows abundantly,
    settling its ridges,
softening it with showers,
    and blessing its growth.
¹¹ You crown the year with your bounty;
    your wagon tracks overflow with
    richness.
¹² The pastures of the wilderness overflow;
    the hills gird themselves with joy;
¹³ the meadows clothe themselves with
    flocks;
    the valleys deck themselves with
    grain;
    they shout and sing together for joy.

PSALM 66

To the leader. A Song. A Psalm.
¹ Make a joyful noise to God, all the earth;
²   sing the glory of his name;
    give to him glorious praise.
³ Say to God, "How awesome are your
    deeds!
    Because of your great power, your
    enemies cringe before you.
⁴ All the earth worships you;
    they sing praises to you,
    sing praises to your name."   *Selah*

⁵ Come and see what God has done:
    he is awesome in his deeds among
    mortals.
⁶ He turned the sea into dry land;
    they passed through the river on
    foot.
There we rejoiced in him,
⁷   who rules by his might forever,
whose eyes keep watch on the nations—

let the rebellious not exalt themselves.
                                        Selah

⁸ Bless our God, O peoples;
    let the sound of his praise be heard,
⁹ who has kept us among the living
    and has not let our feet slip.
¹⁰ For you, O God, have tested us;
    you have tried us as silver is tried.
¹¹ You brought us into the net;
    you laid burdens on our backs;
¹² you let people ride over our heads;
    we went through fire and through
    water;
yet you have brought us out to a spacious
    place.*b*

¹³ I will come into your house with burnt
    offerings;
    I will pay you my vows,
¹⁴ those that my lips uttered
    and my mouth promised when I was
    in trouble.
¹⁵ I will offer to you burnt offerings of
    fatted calves,
    with the smoke of the sacrifice of
    rams;
    I will make an offering of bulls and goats.
                                        Selah

¹⁶ Come and hear, all you who fear God,
    and I will tell what he has done
    for me.
¹⁷ I cried aloud to him,
    and he was extolled with my tongue.
¹⁸ If I had cherished iniquity in my heart,
    the Lord would not have listened.
¹⁹ But truly God has listened;
    he has heard the words of my
    prayer.

b 66.12 Cn Compare Gk Syr Jerome Tg: Heb *to a saturation*

counter the "deeds of iniquity" (v. 3). **65:9–13** The psalm closes with poetic descriptions of God's acts of abundant grace. **65:9** *The river of God* reflects a tradition associating great fertility with Zion (cf. Ps. 46:4; Ezek. 47:1–12). **65:10–13** Creation images are used as a source of praise.

Ps. 66:1–20 A celebration of God's action in history. The first section praises God (vv. 1–12), the second describes sacrifices brought to God (vv. 13–15), and the third tells of God's goodness (vv. 16–20). **Superscription.** *Leader.* See note on Ps. 4 superscription. **66:1–4** The psalmist calls for *all the earth* to *make a joyful noise* (see Pss. 95:1, 2; 98:4, 6; 100:1). **66:4** *Selah.* See note on Ps. 3:1–2. **66:5–7** *Come and see* bids the audience to experience God's goodness directly. *Selah.* See note on Ps. 3:1–2. **66:6** *Turned the sea into dry land* evokes the exodus tradition (Exod. 13–14). **66:8–12** The psalmist offers praise to the God who guides. *Bless our God, O peoples* corresponds to the command that "all the earth" praise God (v. 1). **66:13–15** The psalmist promises to make sacrifices to God. *Burnt offerings* are particularly important (see Lev. 1:3–17; Pss. 50:8; 51:19). *Selah.* See note on Ps. 3:1–2. **66:16–19** *Come and hear*

²⁰ Blessed be God,
  who has not rejected my prayer
  or removed his steadfast love from me.

PSALM 67

*To the leader: with stringed instruments. A Psalm. A
Song.*

¹ May God be gracious to us and bless us
  and make his face to shine upon us,
           Selah
² that your way may be known upon earth,
  your saving power among all nations.
³ Let the peoples praise you, O God;
  let all the peoples praise you.

⁴ Let the nations be glad and sing for joy,
  for you judge the peoples with equity
  and guide the nations upon earth.
          Selah
⁵ Let the peoples praise you, O God;
  let all the peoples praise you.

⁶ The earth has yielded its increase;
  God, our God, has blessed us.
⁷ May God continue to bless us;
  let all the ends of the earth revere him.

PSALM 68

To the leader. Of David. A Psalm. A Song.
¹ Let God rise up; let his enemies be scattered;
  let those who hate him flee before him.

² As smoke is driven away, so drive them
  away;
  as wax melts before the fire,
  let the wicked perish before God.
³ But let the righteous be joyful;
  let them exult before God;
  let them be jubilant with joy.

⁴ Sing to God; sing praises to his name;
  lift up a song to him who rides upon
    the clouds^c—
his name is the LORD—
  be exultant before him.

⁵ Father of orphans and protector of
  widows
  is God in his holy habitation.
⁶ God gives the desolate a home to live in;
  he leads out the prisoners to
    prosperity,
  but the rebellious live in a parched
    land.

⁷ O God, when you went out before your
  people,
  when you marched through the
    wilderness,   *Selah*
⁸ the earth quaked, the heavens poured
  down rain
  at the presence of God, the God of Sinai,

c 68.4 Or *cast up a highway for him who rides through the deserts*

corresponds to the earlier imperatives in v. 5. **66:20** The psalm closes with a final benediction blessing God.

    Ps. 67:1–7 A communal song of thanksgiving with a chiastic or envelope structure (see note on Pss. 15–24): a request for blessing and a result (vv. 1–2), a refrain (v. 3), a confession of God's work for the world (v. 4), a refrain (v. 5), and finally a global result of blessing (vv. 6–7). **Superscription.** *Leader.* See note on Ps. 4 superscription. *With stringed instruments.* See Pss. 4, 6, 54, 55, 61, 76. **67:1–2** The psalm opens with a request for blessing and the beneficent result for *earth* and *all nations.* **67:1** *May God be gracious . . . and bless* is similar to the priestly blessing (cf. Num. 6:24–26; Ps. 31:16). *Selah.* See note on Ps. 3:1–2. **67:3** A liturgical response that is repeated in v. 5 as a refrain. **67:4** The psalmist confesses God's care for and the judgment of the nations of the earth. *Selah.* See note on Ps. 3:1–2. **67:5** A second response repeats v. 3. **67:6–7** The psalmist concludes with a pronouncement of the result of divine blessing with hopes for a continuation of the same.

    Ps. 68:1–35 A communal hymn that is long and complex. A clear structure is difficult to discern. **Superscription.** *Leader.* See note on Ps. 4 superscription. *Of David.* See note on Ps. 3 superscription. **68:1–6** This hymnic introduction resembles Num. 10:35–36. The destruction of the enemies is depicted with similes using *smoke* and *wax.* **68:4** The command to *sing to God* recurs later in the psalm (v. 32). *Who rides upon the clouds* seems to adapt an epithet for the Canaanite storm god (cloud rider) but applies it to Israel's God (cf. Pss. 18:10–13; 104:3); however, the Hebrew text could also be translated as "who rides through the deserts." **68:5** *Father of orphans and protector of widows* affirms God's benevolent and royal care, exercised from *his holy habitation.* **68:7–10** God is described in the wilderness (v. 7), Sinai (v. 8), and the promised land (v. 9). *Selah.* See note on Ps. 3:1–2. **68:8–9** These verses are similar to Judg. 5:4–5.

at the presence of God, the God of
Israel.
⁹ Rain in abundance, O God, you showered
abroad;
you restored your heritage when it
languished;
¹⁰ your flock found a dwelling in it;
in your goodness, O God, you
provided for the needy.

¹¹ The Lord gives the command;
great is the company of those^d who
bore the tidings:
¹² "The kings of the armies, they flee,
they flee!"
The women at home divide the spoil,
¹³ though they stay among the
sheepfolds—
the wings of a dove covered with silver,
its pinions with green gold.
¹⁴ When the Almighty^e scattered kings there,
snow fell on Zalmon.

¹⁵ O mighty mountain, mountain of Bashan;
O many-peaked mountain, mountain
of Bashan!
¹⁶ Why do you look with envy,
O many-peaked mountain,
at the mount that God desired for his
abode,
where the Lord will reside forever?

¹⁷ With mighty chariotry, twice ten
thousand,
thousands upon thousands,
the Lord came from Sinai into the holy
place.^f
¹⁸ You ascended the high mount,
leading captives in your train
and receiving gifts from people,
even from those who rebel against the
Lord God's abiding there.
¹⁹ Blessed be the Lord,
who daily bears us up;
God is our salvation.   Selah
²⁰ Our God is a God of salvation,
and to God, the Lord, belongs escape
from death.

²¹ But God will shatter the heads of his
enemies,
the hairy crown of those who walk in
their guilty ways.
²² The Lord said,
"I will bring them back from Bashan;
I will bring them back from the depths of
the sea,
²³ so that you may bathe^g your feet in blood,
so that the tongues of your dogs may
have their share from the foe."

²⁴ Your solemn processions are seen,^h
O God,
the processions of my God, my King,
into the sanctuary—
²⁵ the singers in front, the musicians last,
between them young women playing
tambourines:
²⁶ "Bless God in the great congregation,
the Lord, O you who are of Israel's
fountain!"
²⁷ There is Benjamin, the least of them, in
the lead,
the princes of Judah in a body,
the princes of Zebulun, the princes of
Naphtali.

²⁸ Summon your might, O God;
show your strength, O God, as you
have done for us before.
²⁹ Because of your temple at Jerusalem,
kings bear gifts to you.
³⁰ Rebuke the wild animals that live among
the reeds,
the herd of bulls with the calves of the
peoples.
Trample^i under foot those who lust after
tribute;
scatter the peoples who delight in war.^j
³¹ Let bronze be brought from Egypt;
let Cush hasten to stretch out its
hands to God.

d 68.11 Or *company of the women*   e 68.14 Traditional
rendering of Heb *Shaddai*   f 68.17 Cn: Heb *The Lord among
them Sinai in the holy* (place)   g 68.23 Gk Syr Tg: Heb *shatter*   h 68.24 Or *have been seen*   i 68.30 Cn: Heb *Trampling*
j 68.30 Meaning of Heb of 68.30 is uncertain

68:17 God's procession *from Sinai into the holy place,* likely the temple. **68:19** *Blessed be the Lord* is the ultimate focus of the psalm's recounting of God's deeds. *Selah.* See note on Ps. 3:1–2. **68:24–27** God is described in a festal procession to Jerusalem. **68:25** The procession has singers in front, musicians in the rear, and girls playing tambourines between the two. **68:26** *Bless God* reprises the confession of v. 19. **68:27** The mentions of Benjamin (see Judg. 5:14–18), Zebulun, Naphtali, and Judah represent a range of tribes. **68:31** The precise meaning

³² Sing to God, O kingdoms of the earth;
  sing praises to the Lord,   *Selah*
³³ O rider in the heavens, the ancient
    heavens;
  listen, he sends out his voice, his
    mighty voice.
³⁴ Ascribe power to God,
  whose majesty is over Israel
  and whose power is in the skies.
³⁵ Awesome is God in his^k sanctuary,
  the God of Israel;
  he gives power and strength to his
    people.

Blessed be God!

PSALM 69

To the leader: according to Lilies. Of David.
¹ Save me, O God,
  for the waters have come up to my
    neck.
² I sink in deep mire,
  where there is no foothold;
  I have come into deep waters,
  and the flood sweeps over me.
³ I am weary with my crying;
  my throat is parched.
  My eyes grow dim
  with waiting for my God.

⁴ More in number than the hairs of my head
  are those who hate me without cause;
  many are those who would destroy me,
  my enemies who accuse me falsely.
  What I did not steal,
  must I now restore?

⁵ O God, you know my folly;
  the wrongs I have done are not hidden
    from you.

⁶ Do not let those who hope in you be put
    to shame because of me,
  O Lord GOD of hosts;
  do not let those who seek you be
    dishonored because of me,
  O God of Israel.
⁷ It is for your sake that I have borne
    reproach,
  that shame has covered my face.
⁸ I have become a stranger to my
    kindred,
  an alien to my mother's children.

⁹ It is zeal for your house that has
    consumed me;
  the insults of those who insult you
    have fallen on me.
¹⁰ When I humbled my soul with
    fasting,^l
  they insulted me for doing so.
¹¹ When I made sackcloth my
    clothing,
  I became a byword to them.
¹² I am the subject of gossip for those who
    sit in the gate,
  and the drunkards make songs
    about me.

¹³ But as for me, my prayer is to you,
  O LORD.

k 68.35 Gk: Heb *from your*   l 69.10 Gk Syr: Heb *I wept, with fasting my soul*, or *I made my soul mourn with fasting*

of the word translated as *bronze* is uncertain; it appears only here. Other translations render it as "ambassadors," "nobles," or even "princes" (cf. KJV). *Let Cush . . . stretch out its hands to God* has been a touch point for African and African American communities who have claimed this passage as prophetic. **68:32** Repetition of the command to *sing to God* (v. 4) is addressed to all *kingdoms of the earth* (cf. Pss. 65–67). *Selah.* See note on Ps. 3:1–2. See **"Music and the Psalms," p. 764.**

Ps. 69:1–36 This is one of the longest individual lament psalms, containing no less than ten stanzas. The structure is complex: a plea (v. 1), a description of distress (vv. 2–4), a personal confession and second plea (vv. 5–6), a second description of distress (vv. 7–12), a third plea (vv. 13–18), a third description of distress (vv. 19–21), a petition for divine retribution against enemies (vv. 22–28), a final petition (v. 29), an individual vow of praise (vv. 30–33), and a final communal vow of praise (vv. 34–36). **Superscription.** *Leader.* See note on Ps. 4 superscription. *According to Lilies.* See note on Ps. 45 superscription. *Of David.* See note on Ps. 3 superscription. **69:1–5** This introductory plea and description of distress is described in terms of the *deep waters* of chaos and death that lead to *crying* (v. 3). **69:3** *My eyes grow dim* refers to the proximity of death. **69:4b–5** The psalmist claims innocence. **69:6–12** This section includes a plea and description of distress that is the direct result of the psalmist's commitment to God (cf. Jer. 20:7–13). **69:9** John 2:17 interprets *zeal for your house* as the reason for Jesus's cleansing of the temple. **69:13–18** Another set of pleas and description

At an acceptable time, O God,
  in the abundance of your steadfast
    love, answer me.
With your faithful help [14]rescue me
  from sinking in the mire;
let me be delivered from my enemies
  and from the deep waters.
[15] Do not let the flood sweep over me
  or the deep swallow me up
  or the Pit close its mouth over me.

[16] Answer me, O Lord, for your steadfast
    love is good;
  according to your abundant mercy,
    turn to me.
[17] Do not hide your face from your
    servant,
  for I am in distress—make haste to
    answer me.
[18] Draw near to me; redeem me;
  set me free because of my
    enemies.

[19] You know the insults I receive
  and my shame and dishonor;
  my foes are all known to you.
[20] Insults have broken my heart,
  so that I am in despair.
I looked for pity, but there was none;
  and for comforters, but I found
    none.
[21] They gave me poison for food,
  and for my thirst they gave me vinegar
    to drink.

[22] Let their table be a trap for them,
  a snare for their allies.
[23] Let their eyes be darkened so that they
    cannot see,
  and make their loins tremble
    continually.
[24] Pour out your indignation upon
    them,
  and let your burning anger overtake
    them.

[25] May their camp be a desolation;
  let no one live in their tents.
[26] For they persecute those whom you have
    struck down,
  and those whom you have wounded
    they attack still more.[m]
[27] Add guilt to their guilt;
  may they have no acquittal from
    you.
[28] Let them be blotted out of the book of
    the living;
  let them not be enrolled among the
    righteous.
[29] But I am lowly and in pain;
  let your salvation, O God, protect
    me.

[30] I will praise the name of God with a
    song;
  I will magnify him with
    thanksgiving.
[31] This will please the Lord more than
    an ox
  or a bull with horns and hoofs.
[32] Let the oppressed see it and be
    glad;
  you who seek God, let your hearts
    revive.
[33] For the Lord hears the needy
  and does not despise his own who are
    in bonds.

[34] Let heaven and earth praise him,
  the seas and everything that moves in
    them.
[35] For God will save Zion
  and rebuild the cities of Judah,
  and his servants shall live[n] there and
    possess it;
[36]   the children of his servants shall
    inherit it,
  and those who love his name shall live
    in it.

m 69.26 Gk Syr: Heb *recount the pain of*   n 69.35 Syr: Heb
and they shall live

of distress. **69:15** *The Pit.* See note on Ps. 16:10. **69:17** *Do not hide your face* is an image describing divine absence (cf. Pss. 27:9; 102:2; 143:7). **69:19–21** The psalmist continues the description of distress. **69:21** *Gave me poison . . . gave me vinegar to drink* is utilized in the passion accounts of the New Testament (see Matt. 27:34, 48; Mark 15:36; Luke 23:36). **69:22–29** The psalmist offers petitions for divine action against the enemies. **69:25** Acts 1:20 quotes this passage. **69:28** The *book of the living* likely refers to a scroll with the names of the righteous (see Isa. 4:3; Dan. 12:1; Mal. 3:16). **69:30–33** These verses make a final plea to God for the relief of the psalmist's distress. **69:34–36** The psalmist expresses the hope that all of creation will praise God because God *will save Zion and rebuild* Judah's cities for habitation and inheritance.

PSALM 70

To the leader. Of David, for the memorial offering.

¹ Be pleased, O God, to deliver me.
　O Lord, make haste to help me!
² Let those be put to shame and confusion
　who seek my life.
　Let those be turned back and brought to
　　dishonor
　who desire to hurt me.
³ Let those who say, "Aha, Aha!"
　turn back because of their shame.

⁴ Let all who seek you
　rejoice and be glad in you.
　Let those who love your salvation
　say evermore, "God is great!"
⁵ But I am poor and needy;
　hasten to me, O God!
　You are my help and my deliverer;
　O Lord, do not delay!

PSALM 71

¹ In you, O Lord, I take refuge;
　let me never be put to shame.
² In your righteousness deliver me and
　　rescue me;
　incline your ear to me and save me.
³ Be to me a rock of refuge,
　a strong fortress*ᵒ* to save me,
　for you are my rock and my fortress.

⁴ Rescue me, O my God, from the hand of
　　the wicked,
　from the grasp of the unjust and
　　cruel.

⁵ For you, O Lord, are my hope,
　my trust, O Lord, from my youth.
⁶ From my birth I have leaned upon you,
　my protector since my mother's
　　womb.*ᵖ*
　My praise is continually of you.

⁷ I have been like a portent to many,
　but you are my strong refuge.
⁸ My mouth is filled with your praise
　and with your glory all day long.
⁹ Do not cast me off in the time of old
　　age;
　do not forsake me when my strength
　　is spent.
¹⁰ For my enemies speak concerning me,
　and those who watch for my life
　　consult together.
¹¹ They say, "Pursue and seize that
　　person
　whom God has forsaken,
　for there is no one to deliver."

¹² O God, do not be far from me;
　O my God, make haste to help me!
¹³ Let my accusers be put to shame and
　　consumed;
　let those who seek to hurt me
　be covered with scorn and disgrace.
¹⁴ But I will hope continually
　and will praise you yet more and
　　more.

o 71.3 Gk: Heb *to come continually you have commanded*
p 71.6 Q ms Gk Jerome: MT *from my mother's womb you took me*

Ps. 70:1–5 A prayer for deliverance from personal enemies with a chiastic structure (see note on Pss. 15–24): a plea for speed (v. 1), a description of the present world (vv. 2–3), a description of the future world (v. 4), another description of the world as it is (v. 5a), and a final plea for hurry (v. 5b). Psalm 70 repeats Ps. 40:13–17. **Superscription.** *Leader.* See note on Ps. 4 superscription. *Of David.* See note on Ps. 3 superscription. *For the memorial offering.* See note on Ps. 38 superscription. **70:1** The psalmist pleads for a speedy deliverance. **70:2–3** These verses describe the psalmist's current life-threatening reality and desire for those *who seek my life* to be thwarted. **70:3** *Aha, Aha* is a cry of derision (see Ps. 35:21; 40:15; Ezek. 25:3; Mark 15:29). **70:4** Reality as the psalmist wishes it would be. **70:5** Because the psalmist is *poor and needy*, the psalmist ends by again requesting that help be quick to come.

Ps. 71:1–24 A prayer for deliverance from personal enemies with a four-part structure: opening petitions to and declarations about God (vv. 1–8), a description of distress (vv. 9–11), a petition and expression of motivation (vv. 12–18), and a final expression of praise and motivation (vv. 19–24). This is one of six psalms in Books I–II that lacks a superscription. **71:1–8** The psalm begins with an opening petition and declaration about God. **71:1** The psalmist makes reference to the psalmist's own potential shame. **71:2, 4** The petition is a request for personal deliverance: *rescue me.* **71:9–11** These verses describe a situation of distress and failing strength. **71:12–18** This section puts forth the psalmist's petition for God to turn back the enemies, along with the motivation to continue to praise God. **71:13** The psalmist makes another reference to shame, this time to that of the accusers.

[15] My mouth will tell of your righteous
acts,
of your deeds of salvation all day long,
though their number is past my
knowledge.
[16] I will come praising the mighty deeds of
the Lord GOD;
I will praise your righteousness, yours
alone.

[17] O God, from my youth you have taught
me,
and I still proclaim your wondrous
deeds.
[18] So even to old age and gray hairs,
O God, do not forsake me,
until I proclaim your might
to all the generations to come.[q]
Your power [19]and your righteousness,
O God,
reach the high heavens.

You who have done great things,
O God, who is like you?
[20] You who have made me see many
troubles and calamities
will revive me again;
from the depths of the earth
you will bring me up again.
[21] You will increase my honor
and comfort me once again.

[22] I will also praise you with the harp
for your faithfulness, O my God;
I will sing praises to you with the
lyre,
O Holy One of Israel.
[23] My lips will shout for joy
when I sing praises to you;
my soul also, which you have rescued.
[24] All day long my tongue will talk of your
righteous help,
for those who tried to do me harm
have been put to shame and disgraced.

PSALM 72

Of Solomon.

[1] Give the king your justice, O God,
and your righteousness to a king's son.
[2] May he judge your people with
righteousness
and your poor with justice.
[3] May the mountains yield prosperity for
the people,
and the hills, in righteousness.
[4] May he defend the cause of the poor of
the people,
give deliverance to the needy,
and crush the oppressor.

[5] May he live[r] while the sun endures
and as long as the moon, throughout
all generations.
[6] May he be like rain that falls on the
mown grass,
like showers that water the earth.
[7] In his days may righteousness flourish
and peace abound, until the moon is
no more.

[8] May he have dominion from sea to sea
and from the River to the ends of the
earth.
[9] May his foes[s] bow down before him,
and his enemies lick the dust.
[10] May the kings of Tarshish and of the isles
render him tribute;

q 71.18 Gk Compare Syr: Heb *to a generation, to all who come*
r 72.5 Gk: Heb *may they fear you* *s* 72.9 Cn: Heb *those who live in the wilderness*

71:19–24 The psalm closes with praise for what God will do for the speaker and motivation to continue to praise God in the future. **71:24** The psalmist makes a third and final reference to shame, that of those who seek to harm the psalmist.

Ps. 72:1–20 A royal psalm (see notes on Ps. 2) containing five stanzas, ending with a doxology: a petition to God on behalf of the king (vv. 1–4), expressions of hopes for the monarch (vv. 5–7), aspirations for international recognition (vv. 8–11), acts of the king (vv. 12–14), additional hopes for the king's reign (vv. 15–17), and a closing doxology for Book II of the Psalter (vv. 18–20). **Superscription.** *Of Solomon.* Psalms 72 and 127 are the only two psalms that mention David's son and successor in the superscription. **72:1–4** The justice of the king derives from the justice of God. Royal care for *the poor* (see also v. 12) and *the needy* (see also vv. 12–13) leads to wishes for prosperity and longevity. **72:5–7** The psalm expresses a wish for the long life of the monarch. **72:8–11** The psalmist also wishes for the king's universal reign, with reference to key points on the compass, including *the River* (Euphrates) and *Tarshish*, a major trading location for Phoenician merchants that represents a distant port (cf. Jonah 1:3). **72:10** *Sheba* (cf. 1 Kgs. 10:1; Isa. 60:6) was apparently located in the

may the kings of Sheba and Seba
      bring gifts.
[11] May all kings fall down before him,
      all nations give him service.

[12] For he delivers the needy when they call,
      the poor and those who have no helper.
[13] He has pity on the weak and the needy
      and saves the lives of the needy.
[14] From oppression and violence he
            redeems their life,
      and precious is their blood in his sight.

[15] Long may he live!
      May gold of Sheba be given to him.
May prayer be made for him continually
      and blessings invoked for him all day
            long.
[16] May there be abundance of grain in the
            land;
      may it wave on the tops of the
            mountains;
      may its fruit be like Lebanon;
and may people blossom in the cities
      like the grass of the field.
[17] May his name endure forever,
      his fame continue as long as the sun.
May all nations be blessed in him;[t]
      may they pronounce him happy.

[18] Blessed be the Lord, the God of Israel,
      who alone does wondrous things.
[19] Blessed be his glorious name forever;
      may his glory fill the whole earth.
            Amen and Amen.

[20] The prayers of David son of Jesse are
            ended.

BOOK III
(PSALMS 73–89)

PSALM 73

A Psalm of Asaph.

[1] Truly God is good to Israel,
      to those who are pure in heart.
[2] But as for me, my feet had almost stumbled;
      my steps had nearly slipped.
[3] For I was envious of the arrogant;
      I saw the prosperity of the wicked.

[4] For they have no pain;
      their bodies are sound and sleek.
[5] They are not in trouble as others are;
      they are not plagued like other people.
[6] Therefore pride is their necklace;
      violence covers them like a garment.
[7] Their eyes swell out with fatness;
      their hearts overflow with follies.
[8] They scoff and speak with malice;
      loftily they threaten oppression.
[9] They set their mouths against heaven,
      and their tongues range over the
            earth.
[10] Therefore the people turn and praise
            them[u]
      and find no fault in them.[v]
[11] And they say, "How can God know?
      Is there knowledge in the Most High?"
[12] Such are the wicked;
      always at ease, they increase in riches.
[13] All in vain I have kept my heart clean
      and washed my hands in innocence.

t 72.17 Or *bless themselves by him*   u 73.10 Cn: Heb *his people
return here*   v 73.10 Cn: Heb *abundant waters are drained by
them*

southwestern parts of Arabia. **72:12–14** These verses repeat the theme of the king's care for the
poor and needy (see vv. 1–4). **72:15–17** This section repeats the speaker's wishes for the monarch's
longevity (vv. 5–7). **72:18–19** This doxology ends Book II of the Psalter (see Pss. 41:13; 89:52; 106:48;
150:1–6). **72:20** A final colophon suggests that this was once the end of a discrete collection. In
point of fact, psalms associated with *David* appear later in the Psalter (next in Ps. 86).

   Book III: Pss. 73–89 Book III marks a shift in the Psalter as a whole. Psalm 73 begins a collection
of the Psalms of Asaph (Pss. 73–83) followed by a collection of Korahite Psalms (Pss. 84–88, but
note that Ps. 86 is Davidic). Psalm 89 concludes the book with a lengthy royal psalm. These subcollections and the themes of the psalms in Book III suggest that the emphasis at this point is shifting
to the impact of defeat and exile on the community.

   Ps. 73:1–28 A Psalm of Asaph, who is listed as a temple musician in 1 Chr. 15:17–19; 16:4–5; and Ezra
3:10. The psalm is an individual reflection on the problem of evil with an emphasis on the prosperity
of the wicked. **73:1–3** The working premise is that God gives prosperity to the righteous (see Ps.
1)—more specifically that God is good to Israel, to those in the covenant community. But the psalmist has come to see the prosperity of the wicked, which causes problems, stumbling, and slipping.
73:4–12 A description of the prosperity of the wicked, who are at ease and popular. **73:13–16** The

¹⁴ For all day long I have been plagued
and am punished every morning.

¹⁵ If I had said, "I will talk on in this way,"
I would have been untrue to the circle
of your children.
¹⁶ But when I thought how to understand
this,
it seemed to me a wearisome task,
¹⁷ until I went into the sanctuary of God;
then I perceived their end.
¹⁸ Truly you set them in slippery places;
you make them fall to ruin.
¹⁹ How they are destroyed in a moment,
swept away utterly by terrors!
²⁰ They are^w like a dream when one
awakes;
on awaking you despise their
phantoms.

²¹ When my soul was embittered,
when I was pricked in heart,
²² I was stupid and ignorant;
I was like a brute beast toward you.
²³ Nevertheless, I am continually with you;
you hold my right hand.
²⁴ You guide me with your counsel,
and afterward you will receive me
with honor.^x
²⁵ Whom have I in heaven but you?
And there is nothing on earth that I
desire other than you.
²⁶ My flesh and my heart may fail,
but God is the strength^y of my heart
and my portion forever.
²⁷ Indeed, those who are far from you will
perish;

you put an end to those who are false
to you.
²⁸ But for me it is good to be near God;
I have made the Lord God my refuge,
to tell of all your works.

PSALM 74

A Maskil of Asaph.
¹ O God, why do you cast us off forever?
Why does your anger smoke against
the sheep of your pasture?
² Remember your congregation, which
you acquired long ago,
which you redeemed to be the tribe of
your heritage.
Remember Mount Zion, where you
came to dwell.
³ Direct your steps to the perpetual ruins;
the enemy has destroyed everything in
the sanctuary.

⁴ Your foes have roared within your holy
place;
they set up their emblems there.
⁵ At the upper entrance they hacked
the wooden trellis with axes.^z
⁶ And then, with hatchets and hammers,
they smashed all its carved work.
⁷ They set your sanctuary on fire;
they desecrated the dwelling place of
your name,
bringing it to the ground.
⁸ They said to themselves, "We will utterly
subdue them";
they burned all the meeting places of
God in the land.

w 73.20 Cn: Heb *Lord*   *x* 73.24 Or *to glory*   *y* 73.26 Heb *rock*
z 74.5 Cn Compare Gk Syr: Meaning of Heb uncertain

psalmist's own experience is contrary to that of the wicked and thus confusing. **73:17** A transformation is experienced, prompted by entrance into the sanctuary of God. **73:18–28** The psalmist now speaks to God. The end result of the wicked is instability (cf. v. 2), but the psalmist is near to God. The movement is thus one from (wicked) prosperity to (righteous) presence. The psalmist had become bitter but is now able to see communion with God as hope for a way forward. The solution to the problem presented in the psalm is nothing less than *it is good to be near God* (v. 28).

Ps. 74:1–23 A communal lament consisting of a petition and complaint with a section of praise included in vv. 12–17. **Superscription.** *Maskil.* See note on Ps. 32 superscription. *Asaph.* See note on Ps. 50 superscription. **74:1–3** The psalm begins with a question that reveals the theme of divine anger and rejection. **74:2** A call for divine remembering among God, the congregation, and *Mount Zion.* Zion was the center of life and of divine presence for ancient Israel. **74:3** The psalmist moves next to recollect the *perpetual ruins* of the sanctuary and to petition God to come and see these ruins that the enemies have destroyed. **74:4–8** These verses describe the devastation of God's sanctuary by those opposed to both God and the psalmist. **74:4** The enemies *set up their emblems*—that is, their banners—as symbols of power in the temple. **74:8** The destruction of the religious center

⁹ We do not see our emblems;
   there is no longer any prophet,
   and there is no one among us who
      knows how long.
¹⁰ How long, O God, is the foe to scoff?
   Is the enemy to revile your name
      forever?
¹¹ Why do you hold back your hand;
   why do you keep your hand in*a* your
      bosom?

¹² Yet God my King is from of old,
   working salvation in the earth.
¹³ You divided the sea by your might;
   you broke the heads of the dragons in
      the waters.
¹⁴ You crushed the heads of Leviathan;
   you gave him as food*b* for the
      creatures of the wilderness.
¹⁵ You cut openings for springs and torrents;
   you dried up ever-flowing streams.
¹⁶ Yours is the day, yours also the night;
   you established the luminaries*c* and
      the sun.
¹⁷ You have fixed all the bounds of the earth;
   you made summer and winter.

¹⁸ Remember this, O Lord, how the enemy
      scoffs,
   and an impious people reviles your
      name.
¹⁹ Do not deliver the soul of your dove to
      the wild animals;
   do not forget the life of your poor
      forever.

²⁰ Have regard for your*d* covenant,
   for the dark places of the land are full
      of the haunts of violence.

²¹ Do not let the downtrodden be put to
      shame;
   let the poor and needy praise your
      name.
²² Rise up, O God, plead your cause;
   remember how the impious scoff at
      you all day long.
²³ Do not forget the clamor of your foes,
   the uproar of your adversaries that
      goes up continually.

Psalm 75

To the leader: Do Not Destroy. A Psalm of Asaph. A Song.
¹ We give thanks to you, O God;
   we give thanks; your name is near.
   People tell of your wondrous deeds.

² At the set time that I appoint,
   I will judge with equity.
³ When the earth totters, with all its
      inhabitants,
   it is I who keep its pillars steady.   *Selah*
⁴ I say to the boastful, "Do not boast,"
   and to the wicked, "Do not lift up your
      horn;
⁵ do not lift up your horn on high
   or speak with insolent neck."

⁶ For not from the east or from the west
   and not from the wilderness comes
      lifting up,
⁷ but it is God who executes judgment,
   putting down one and lifting up
      another.
⁸ For in the hand of the Lord there is a cup
   with foaming wine, well mixed;

a 74.11 Cn: Heb *do you consume your right hand from*
b 74.14 Heb *food for the people*   c 74.16 Or *moon*; Heb *light*
d 74.20 Gk Syr: Heb *the*

achieves the enemies' goal to *utterly subdue* God's people. **74:9–11** A description of the enemies' taunts. The destruction includes the loss of both *emblems* (of God's sanctuary) and prophets. **74:12–17** These verses testify to God's cosmic power. **74:12** *God my King.* See Ps. 68:24. **74:14** *Leviathan* is a primordial monster in Ugaritic literature and is used as an image of chaotic forces (cf. Job 3:8; 41:1; Isa. 27:1). **74:18–19** A call for divine remembrance. **74:19** *Dove* is an image reflecting "the poor and needy" (v. 21), just as *the wild animals* represent the "adversaries" (v. 23). **74:20–23** Covenant making and overturning of the enemies.

Ps. 75:1–10 Communal thanksgiving hymn. The hymn includes prophetic words of judgment, divine speech, thanksgiving, and instruction. **Superscription.** *To the leader.* See note on Ps. 4 superscription. *Asaph.* See note on Ps. 50 superscription. *Do Not Destroy.* See note on Ps. 57 superscription. The language of the psalm connects with Ps. 74; Ps. 75 gives a response to the petitions in the last part of Ps. 74 as it continues in the historical context of the fall of Jerusalem and destruction of the temple in the sixth century BCE. **75:1** Thanksgiving from the congregation (see Ps. 73:28). *Name* indicates divine presence. **75:2–3** A pronouncement of God. **75:3** *Earth totters* is a metaphor for the unsettled foundation (see also Ps. 46:2–3, 6). *Selah.* See note on Ps. 3:1–2. **75:4–9** The psalmist

he will pour a draught from it,
and all the wicked of the earth
shall drain it down to the dregs.
[9] But I will rejoice[e] forever;
I will sing praises to the God of
Jacob.

[10] All the horns of the wicked I will cut off,
but the horns of the righteous shall be
exalted.

PSALM 76

*To the leader: with stringed instruments. A Psalm of
Asaph. A Song.*
[1] In Judah God is known;
his name is great in Israel.
[2] His abode has been established in
Salem,
his dwelling place in Zion.
[3] There he broke the flashing arrows,
the shield, the sword, and the
weapons of war.   *Selah*

[4] Glorious are you, more majestic
than the everlasting mountains.[f]
[5] The courageous were stripped of their
spoil;
they sank into sleep;
none of the troops
was able to lift a hand.
[6] At your rebuke, O God of Jacob,
both rider and horse lay stunned.

[7] But you indeed are awesome!
Who can stand before you
when your anger is roused?
[8] From the heavens you uttered judgment;

the earth feared and was still
[9] when God rose up to establish judgment,
to save all the oppressed of the earth.
Selah

[10] Human wrath serves only to praise you,
when you bind the last bit of your[g]
wrath around you.
[11] Make vows to the LORD your God and
perform them;
let all who are around him bring gifts
to the one who is awesome,
[12] who cuts off the spirit of princes,
who inspires fear in the kings of the
earth.

PSALM 77

To the leader: according to Jeduthun. Of Asaph. A Psalm.
[1] I cry aloud to God,
aloud to God, that he may hear me.
[2] In the day of my trouble I seek the Lord;
in the night my hand is stretched out
without wearying;
my soul refuses to be comforted.
[3] I think of God, and I moan;
I meditate, and my spirit faints.
Selah

[4] You keep my eyelids from closing;
I am so troubled that I cannot speak.
[5] I consider the days of old
and remember the years of long ago.
[6] I commune[b] with my heart in the night;
I meditate and search my spirit:[i]

e 75.9 Gk: Heb *declare* f 76.4 Gk: Heb *the mountains of
prey* g 76.10 Heb lacks *your* h 77.6 Gk Syr: Heb *My music*
i 77.6 Syr Jerome: Heb *my spirit searches*

chides those who *boast*. *Horn* is a symbol of power (Deut. 33:17; 1 Kgs. 22:11; Ps. 89:17). Drinking from the *cup* brings destruction for the wicked (see also Hab. 2:16). **75:10** A final announcement of the stripping of the *wicked* of the symbols of power; the power of the *righteous* will prevail.

Ps. 76:1–12 Song of Zion. See note on Ps. 46. **Superscription.** *To the leader.* See note on Ps. 4 superscription. *With stringed instruments.* See note on Ps. 4 superscription. *Asaph.* See note on Ps. 50 superscription. **76:1–3** The center for divine action. **76:1** *Judah* and *Israel* receive the support of God. **76:2–3** God's home is in *Salem* (an ancient name for Jerusalem) and *Zion* (another name for Jerusalem), from which God breaks the instruments of war. *Selah.* See note on Ps. 3:1–2. **76:4–6** Description of the divine warrior. **76:6** *God of Jacob* (see also Pss. 46:7, 11; 75:9; 76:6; 81:1, 4; 84:8; 94:7; 114:7; 146:5) accents the power of God and the vulnerability of Jacob. **76:7–9** The divine ruler who is known in Israel and at home in Zion rules over all creation and saves *all the oppressed of the earth. Selah.* See note on Ps. 3:1–2. **76:10–12** Recognition of the divine ruler and promises of praise and thanksgiving. God inspires awe and casts down *princes* and *kings* who oppose divine rule.

Ps. 77:1–20 Lament. A complaint that in its second half recounts Israel's salvation history. **Superscription.** *To the leader.* See note on Ps. 4 superscription. *According to Jeduthun.* See note on Ps. 39 superscription. *Asaph.* See note on Ps. 50 superscription. **77:1–3** Cry to God asking for a hearing. The psalmist *refuses to be comforted.* **77:2** *In the day . . . in the night* is a merism connoting

7 "Will the Lord spurn forever
  and never again be favorable?
8 Has his steadfast love ceased forever?
  Are his promises at an end for all
    time?
9 Has God forgotten to be gracious?
  Has he in anger shut up his
    compassion?"   Selah
10 And I say, "It is my grief
  that the right hand of the Most High
    has changed."

11 I will call to mind the deeds of the
    LORD;
  I will remember your wonders
    of old.
12 I will meditate on all your work
  and muse on your mighty deeds.
13 Your way, O God, is holy.
  What god is so great as our God?
14 You are the God who works wonders;
  you have displayed your might among
    the peoples.
15 With your strong arm you redeemed
    your people,
  the descendants of Jacob and Joseph.
                                        Selah

16 When the waters saw you, O God,
  when the waters saw you, they were
    afraid;
  the very deep trembled.

17 The clouds poured out water;
  the skies thundered;
  your arrows flashed on every side.
18 The crash of your thunder was in the
    whirlwind;
  your lightnings lit up the world;
  the earth trembled and shook.
19 Your way was through the sea,
  your path through the mighty waters,
  yet your footprints were unseen.
20 You led your people like a flock
  by the hand of Moses and Aaron.

PSALM 78

A Maskil of Asaph.
1 Give ear, O my people, to my teaching;
  incline your ears to the words of my
    mouth.
2 I will open my mouth in a parable;
  I will utter dark sayings from of old,
3 things that we have heard and known,
  that our ancestors have told us.
4 We will not hide them from their
    children;
  we will tell to the coming
    generation
  the glorious deeds of the LORD and his
    might
  and the wonders that he has done.

5 He established a decree in Jacob
  and appointed a law in Israel,

continual activity. A merism mentions two parts, typically polar opposites that express a totality. **77:3** *Think[ing]* and *meditat[ing]* prompt *moan[ing]* and *faint[ing]*. *Selah*. See note on Ps. 3:1–2. **77:4–6** Description of distress. **77:4** God, who can change things, is addressed as *you*, but the preoccupation continues to be with the troubles of *I*, the speaker. **77:7–9** Questions posed to God about divine redemption. *Selah*. See note on Ps. 3:1–2. **77:8** Has the *steadfast love* of the covenant with God *ceased*? **77:10** The speaker despairs. *Right hand* is a symbol of divine strength. **77:11–12** *Call to mind*, *remember*, and *meditate* point to divine *deeds*, *wonders of old*, *work*, and *mighty deeds*. **77:15** *Descendants of Jacob and Joseph* remind the reader that God delivered those ancient ancestors. *Selah*. See note on Ps. 3:1–2. **77:16–20** Description of God's redemptive acts in history. **77:16** *Waters* allude to primordial chaos before creation and to Israel's crossing of the Sea of Reeds, or Red Sea (Exod. 14). See note at Exod. 13:18. *Deep* refers to creation (see Gen. 1:1). **77:20** *Moses* and *Aaron* function as God's emissaries and shepherds of the people. *Moses* is a symbol of human intercession (see also Pss. 90 superscription; 99:6; 103:7; 105:26; 106:16, 23, 32). The psalm recounts Israel's salvation history in hope of deliverance from the current crisis.

Ps. 78:1–72 Historical psalm. A psalm that teaches lessons from Israel's history and so has connections with wisdom traditions (see also Pss. 105; 106). The three-part introduction (vv. 1–11) leads to two historical remembrances: one on the wilderness tradition (vv. 12–39) and a second on traditions associated with Egypt and Jerusalem (vv. 40–72). Each recital has four movements: divine generosity, human rebellion, divine judgment, and reconciliation of relationship. **Superscription.** *Maskil.* See note on Ps. 32. *Asaph.* See note on Ps. 50 superscription. One theme of the Asaph psalms is memory, a theme continued here from Ps. 77. **78:1–11** Introduction. **78:2** History as *a parable* and *dark sayings*, which are better understood as riddles. **78:4** Generations need to learn the history of *the*

which he commanded our ancestors
    to teach to their children,
6 that the next generation might know
    them,
    the children yet unborn,
  and rise up and tell them to their
    children,
7   so that they should set their hope
    in God,
  and not forget the works of God,
    but keep his commandments;
8 and that they should not be like their
    ancestors,
    a stubborn and rebellious
    generation,
  a generation whose heart was not
    steadfast,
    whose spirit was not faithful to
    God.

9 The Ephraimites, armed with[j] the bow,
    turned back on the day of battle.
10 They did not keep God's covenant
    and refused to walk according to
    his law.
11 They forgot what he had done
    and the miracles that he had shown
    them.
12 In the sight of their ancestors he worked
    marvels
    in the land of Egypt, in the fields of
    Zoan.
13 He divided the sea and let them pass
    through it
    and made the waters stand like a
    heap.
14 In the daytime he led them with a cloud
    and all night long with a fiery light.
15 He split rocks open in the wilderness
    and gave them drink abundantly as
    from the deep.
16 He made streams come out of the rock
    and caused waters to flow down like
    rivers.

17 Yet they sinned still more against him,
    rebelling against the Most High in the
    desert.
18 They tested God in their heart
    by demanding the food they craved.
19 They spoke against God, saying,
    "Can God spread a table in the
    wilderness?
20 Even though he struck the rock so that
    water gushed out
    and torrents overflowed,
  can he also give bread
    or provide meat for his people?"

21 Therefore, when the LORD heard, he was
    full of rage;
    a fire was kindled against Jacob,
    his anger mounted against Israel,
22 because they had no faith in God
    and did not trust his saving power.
23 Yet he commanded the skies above
    and opened the doors of heaven;
24 he rained down on them manna to eat
    and gave them the grain of heaven.
25 Mortals ate of the bread of angels;
    he sent them food in abundance.
26 He caused the east wind to blow in the
    heavens,
    and by his power he led out the south
    wind;
27 he rained flesh upon them like dust,
    winged birds like the sand of the seas;
28 he let them fall within their camp,
    all around their dwellings.
29 And they ate and were well filled,
    for he gave them what they craved.
30 But before they had satisfied their craving,
    while the food was still in their
    mouths,
31 the anger of God rose against them,
    and he killed the strongest of them
    and laid low the flower of Israel.

j 78.9 Heb *armed with shooting*

---

glorious deeds and *the wonders* that God has done. **78:5–8** God's covenant instruction, or "torah," is part of the historical divine salvation history. The call is to keep the covenant instruction, but Israel *was not faithful.* **78:9** *The Ephraimites* refers to the northern kingdom of Israel, but the precise military event is unclear. **78:12–39** First recital, which recounts the wilderness events. **78:12–16** God acts (see Exod. 13:21–22; 17:6). God led them out of oppression, parted the Sea of Reeds, or Red Sea, guided them, and provided water for them. See note at Exod. 13:18. **78:12** *Zoan* is a city in the Nile River delta in Egypt. **78:17–20** Human rebellion (see Exod. 16–17; Num. 20:2–13). These incidents are also recalled in Ps. 106. **78:18** *They tested God* is a metaphor for rebellion. **78:20** The people crave *bread* and *meat* as well as water. **78:21–31** God's response. God *rained down on them manna to eat.* With wind, God brought them winged birds to eat, and they *were well filled.* Still they had to face

³² In spite of all this they still sinned;
 they did not believe in his wonders.
³³ So he made their days vanish like a
 breath
 and their years in terror.
³⁴ When he killed them, they searched for
 him;
 they repented and sought God
 earnestly.
³⁵ They remembered that God was their
 rock,
 the Most High God their redeemer.
³⁶ But they flattered him with their mouths;
 they lied to him with their tongues.
³⁷ Their heart was not steadfast toward
 him;
 they were not true to his covenant.
³⁸ Yet he, being compassionate,
 forgave their iniquity
 and did not destroy them;
 often he restrained his anger
 and did not stir up all his wrath.
³⁹ He remembered that they were but flesh,
 a wind that passes and does not come
 again.
⁴⁰ How often they rebelled against him in
 the wilderness
 and grieved him in the desert!
⁴¹ They tested God again and again
 and provoked the Holy One of
 Israel.
⁴² They did not keep in mind his power
 or the day when he redeemed them
 from the foe,
⁴³ when he displayed his signs in Egypt
 and his miracles in the fields of Zoan.
⁴⁴ He turned their rivers to blood,
 so that they could not drink of their
 streams.
⁴⁵ He sent among them swarms of flies that
 devoured them
 and frogs that destroyed them.
⁴⁶ He gave their crops to the caterpillar
 and the fruit of their labor to the
 locust.

⁴⁷ He destroyed their vines with hail
 and their sycamores with frost.
⁴⁸ He gave over their cattle to the hail
 and their flocks to thunderbolts.
⁴⁹ He let loose on them his fierce anger,
 wrath, indignation, and distress,
 a company of destroying angels.
⁵⁰ He made a path for his anger;
 he did not spare them from death
 but gave their lives over to the plague.
⁵¹ He struck all the firstborn in Egypt,
 the first issue of their strength in the
 tents of Ham.
⁵² Then he led out his people like sheep
 and guided them in the wilderness
 like a flock.
⁵³ He led them in safety so that they were
 not afraid,
 but the sea overwhelmed their
 enemies.
⁵⁴ And he brought them to his holy hill,
 to the mountain that his right hand
 had won.
⁵⁵ He drove out nations before them;
 he apportioned them for a possession
 and settled the tribes of Israel in their
 tents.

⁵⁶ Yet they tested the Most High God
 and rebelled against him.
 They did not observe his decrees
⁵⁷ but turned away and were faithless like
 their ancestors;
 they twisted like a treacherous bow.
⁵⁸ For they provoked him to anger with
 their high places;
 they moved him to jealousy with their
 idols.
⁵⁹ When God heard, he was full of wrath,
 and he utterly rejected Israel.
⁶⁰ He abandoned his dwelling at Shiloh,
 the tent where he dwelt among
 mortals,
⁶¹ and delivered his power to captivity,
 his glory to the hand of the foe.

divine anger because *they had no faith in God*. **78:32–39** Description of God's grace. **78:34** Divine judgment brought repentance. **78:38** God was *compassionate* and forgave their rebellion. Concerns about the people's faithfulness linger. **78:40–72** Second recital, which recounts the plagues in Egypt and the gift of Jerusalem. **78:40–55** Second example of God's acts focusing on the plagues in Egypt (see Exod. 7–12), the exodus from oppression, and the journey through the wilderness. **78:41** Second use of testing as a metaphor for rebellion. **78:54** *Holy hill* often refers to Zion/Jerusalem, but here it likely refers to the entire land of Canaan. **78:56–58** Human rebellion. **78:56** A final occurrence of testing as an expression of rebellion. **78:58** The rebellion involves improper worship and idolatry. **78:59–64** God's response is *wrath*. *Shiloh* was an early sanctuary site for the ark of

⁶² He gave his people to the sword
and vented his wrath on his heritage.
⁶³ Fire devoured their young men,
and their young women had no
marriage song.
⁶⁴ Their priests fell by the sword,
and their widows made no
lamentation.
⁶⁵ Then the Lord awoke as from sleep,
like a warrior shouting because of
wine.
⁶⁶ He put his adversaries to rout;
he put them to everlasting disgrace.

⁶⁷ He rejected the tent of Joseph;
he did not choose the tribe of
Ephraim,
⁶⁸ but he chose the tribe of Judah,
Mount Zion, which he loves.
⁶⁹ He built his sanctuary like the high
heavens,
like the earth, which he has founded
forever.
⁷⁰ He chose his servant David
and took him from the sheepfolds;
⁷¹ from tending the nursing ewes he
brought him
to be the shepherd of his people Jacob,
of Israel, his inheritance.
⁷² With upright heart he tended them
and guided them with skillful hand.

PSALM 79

A Psalm of Asaph.
¹ O God, the nations have come into your
inheritance;

they have defiled your holy temple;
they have laid Jerusalem in ruins.
² They have given the bodies of your
servants
to the birds of the air for food,
the flesh of your faithful to the wild
animals of the earth.
³ They have poured out their blood like
water
all around Jerusalem,
and there was no one to bury them.
⁴ We have become a taunt to our
neighbors,
mocked and derided by those
around us.

⁵ How long, O Lᴏʀᴅ? Will you be angry
forever?
Will your jealous wrath burn like
fire?
⁶ Pour out your anger on the nations
that do not know you
and on the kingdoms
that do not call on your name.
⁷ For they have devoured Jacob
and laid waste his habitation.

⁸ Do not remember against us the
iniquities of our ancestors;
let your compassion come speedily to
meet us,
for we are brought very low.
⁹ Help us, O God of our salvation,
for the glory of your name;
deliver us and forgive our sins,
for your name's sake.

the covenant before David relocated it to Jerusalem (2 Sam. 6). **78:65–72** God's response as *a warrior*. **78:67** Rejection of the northern kingdom of Israel. *Joseph* and *Ephraim* are the names of the primary northern tribes. **78:68–69** The tribe of Judah, the place of Zion/Jerusalem, is chosen by God to be the place of God's dwelling. **78:70–72** David is then selected as God's chosen leader for Judah (2 Sam. 7).

Ps. 79:1–13 Communal lament. A lament of grief and anger at the loss of Jerusalem and the temple in three parts, which is characteristic of the genre: a complaint in vv. 1–5, a petition in vv. 6–12, and a concluding word of hope in the final verse. **Superscription.** *Asaph.* See note on Ps. 50 superscription. **79:1–5** A description of the trauma that was set in motion by the destruction of Jerusalem and the temple by the Babylonians in 587/586 BCE (see also Ps. 74). The Assyrians failed to conquer Judah's capital in an earlier era, but Babylon succeeded. **79:2–3** Description of the annihilation of Jerusalem's leadership (2 Kgs. 25:18–21), which included improper burial as an instrument of shame and national dishonor. **79:5** *How long?* (see also Pss. 13:1; 35:17; 89:46) characterizes the lament tradition. God has apparently failed to keep covenant with Judah, with severe consequences for the community. Zion was the center of the community's world; it did not hold. The lament articulates Judah's raw pain and humiliation. **79:6–12** Urgent pleas that God will bring judgment on *the kingdoms* that have done this destruction. **79:8** Plea for divine remembrance that will bring compassion to Judah and judgment on the nations that have wreaked havoc in the holy city. The verse's last

¹⁰ Why should the nations say,
    "Where is their God?"
Let the avenging of the outpoured blood
    of your servants
    be known among the nations before
    our eyes.

¹¹ Let the groans of the prisoners come
    before you;
    according to your great power,
    preserve those doomed to
    die.
¹² Return sevenfold into the bosom of our
    neighbors
    the taunts with which they taunted
    you, O Lord!
¹³ Then we your people, the flock of your
    pasture,
    will give thanks to you forever;
    from generation to generation we will
    recount your praise.

PSALM 80

To the leader: on Lilies, a Covenant. Of Asaph. A Psalm.
¹ Give ear, O Shepherd of Israel,
    you who lead Joseph like a flock!
You who are enthroned upon the
    cherubim, shine forth
²   before Ephraim and Benjamin and
    Manasseh.
Stir up your might,
    and come to save us!

³ Restore us, O God;
    let your face shine, that we may be
    saved.

⁴ O Lord God of hosts,
    how long will you be angry with your
    people's prayers?
⁵ You have fed them with the bread of
    tears
    and given them tears to drink in full
    measure.
⁶ You make us the scorn*ᵏ* of our neighbors;
    our enemies laugh among themselves.

⁷ Restore us, O God of hosts;
    let your face shine, that we may be
    saved.

⁸ You brought a vine out of Egypt;
    you drove out the nations and planted it.
⁹ You cleared the ground for it;
    it took deep root and filled the land.
¹⁰ The mountains were covered with its
    shade,
    the mighty cedars with its branches;
¹¹ it sent out its branches to the sea
    and its shoots to the River.
¹² Why then have you broken down its walls,
    so that all who pass along the way
    pluck its fruit?

k 80.6 Syr: Heb *strife*

line poignantly characterizes Judah's woe: *for we are brought very low.* **79:10** The enemies use a popular taunt: *Where is their God?* (see also Pss. 42:3, 10; 115:2). **79:12** *Sevenfold* conveys a sense of completeness (see Lev. 26:21, 24, 28). The psalm suggests that the destruction of Jerusalem and the temple tarnishes the divine reputation, and so the plea is for relief for Judah and woe for Babylon and their allies. **79:13** Vow of continued community identity, confidence in God, and praise. The hope is that divine action will bring a resolution of grief and anger to praise and thanksgiving. The shepherd/sheep metaphor occurs in the Asaphite collection (see Pss. 74:1; 77:20; 78:52; 80:1) and other psalms (cf. Pss. 23:1–3; 74:1).

Ps. 80:1–19 Communal lament. The intense language is focused on the relationship with Israel's God. **Superscription.** *To the leader.* See note on Ps. 4 superscription. *Lilies.* See note on Ps. 45 superscription. *Asaph.* See note on Ps. 50 superscription. **80:1–3** Opening petition. **80:1** *Shepherd of Israel* occurs only here, but the shepherd motif occurs elsewhere in the Psalter (see, e.g., Pss. 23:1–3; 74:1; 79:13). *Enthroned upon the cherubim* refers to divine presence above the ark in the temple (see 1 Sam. 4:4). The ark is, then, the footstool of the divine. The plea is for God to hear and deliver the community. **80:3** The first refrain is a plea for restoration, to bring life out of suffering and death. *Face* is the life-giving presence of God; the language is reminiscent of the Aaronic benediction (Num. 6:22–26). **80:4–6** Petition to God with language akin to other pleas in the Psalms of Asaph. God is addressed as Lord *God of hosts* or armies of the heavenly hosts. **80:7** Second refrain: a plea for restoration. *Selah.* See note on Ps. 3:1–2. **80:8–18** Rehearsal of divine participation in the fate of the community. **80:8** *Vine* represents the people. Previous Asaphite psalms have recounted the salvation history of ancient Israel. Here the metaphor of a vine, its growth and spread, is a means to remind the divine of that history of relationship. **80:12–13** *Broken down its walls* suggests the

¹³ The boar from the forest ravages it,
  and all that move in the field feed on it.

¹⁴ Turn again, O God of hosts;
  look down from heaven and see;
have regard for this vine,
¹⁵   the stock that your right hand
    planted.*ˡ*
¹⁶ It has been burned with fire; it has been
    cut down;
  may they perish at the rebuke of your
    countenance.
¹⁷ But let your hand be upon the one at
    your right hand,
  the one whom you made strong for
    yourself.
¹⁸ Then we will never turn back from
    you;
  give us life, and we will call on your
    name.

¹⁹ Restore us, O Lᴏʀᴅ God of hosts;
  let your face shine, that we may be
    saved.

Psalm 81

To the leader: according to The Gittith. Of Asaph.
¹ Sing aloud to God our strength;
  shout for joy to the God of Jacob.
² Raise a song; sound the tambourine,
  the sweet lyre with the harp.
³ Blow the trumpet at the new moon,

at the full moon, on our festal
    day.
⁴ For it is a statute for Israel,
  an ordinance of the God of Jacob.
⁵ He made it a decree in Joseph,
  when he went out over*ᵐ* the land of
    Egypt.

I hear a voice I had not known:
⁶ "I relieved your*ⁿ* shoulder of the burden;
  your*ᵒ* hands were freed from the
    basket.
⁷ In distress you called, and I rescued you;
  I answered you in the secret place of
    thunder;
  I tested you at the waters of Meribah.
              Selah
⁸ Hear, O my people, while I admonish you;
  O Israel, if you would but listen to me!
⁹ There shall be no strange god among you;
  you shall not bow down to a foreign god.
¹⁰ I am the Lᴏʀᴅ your God,
  who brought you up out of the land of
    Egypt.
  Open your mouth wide, and I will
    fill it.

¹¹ "But my people did not listen to my voice;
  Israel would not submit to me.

l 80.15 Heb adds from 80.17 *and upon the one whom you
made strong for yourself* *m* 81.5 Or *against* *n* 81.6 Heb *his*
o 81.6 Heb *his*

destruction of Jerusalem; the community has been savaged by the destruction of the city and the temple. **80:14** The plea is for God to *turn* and *have regard* for the vine, meaning restoration and vindication for Israel. **80:16** The vine has been *cut down*. **80:18** The people vow fidelity to the covenant relationship with God. **80:19** Third and final refrain: a plea for restoration.

  Ps. 81:1–16 Hymn. A call to praise in vv. 1–3 and a reason for praise in vv. 4–5: covenant instruction mandates the praise. Vv. 6–16 A prophetic warning (see also Pss. 50; 95). **Superscription.** *To the leader.* See note on Ps. 4 superscription. *According to The Gittith* possibly refers to a musical instrument or tune. *Asaph.* See note on Ps. 50 superscription. **81:1–5a** Festal announcement and liturgical summons. **81:1–3** The language of the summons is to *shout, sing,* and *raise a song.* The instruments of worship are a *tambourine, lyre, harp,* and *trumpet.* The blowing of the trumpet may refer to the blowing of the shofar at the New Year. *Our festal day* refers to one of the three major observances, possibly the Feast of Tabernacles (see Lev. 23:33–36, 39–43). **81:5b–10** Divine speech or oracle. **81:5b** Prophetic speech introduction. **81:6–10** Recounts Israel's deliverance from Egyptian slavery. **81:6** *Burden* and *basket* point to Israel's slavery while in Egypt. **81:7** Israel cried out to God (Exod. 3:7–9) for deliverance. *Secret place of thunder* refers to the theophany at Mount Sinai (Exod. 19:16–19; 33:17–23). *Waters of Meribah* refer to when the people called out to God for water in the wilderness and God provided (Exod. 17; Num. 20). **81:9–10** The prophetic call is to hearken unto God and remain faithful to the living God revealed to Israel in this historical narrative (Deut. 6:4–6; 30:15–20). The language echoes the prologue to the Ten Commandments (Exod. 20:2–5; Deut. 5:6–9) and calls for the community to worship only the God who delivered them in the exodus. *Open your mouth* could point to food such as God's gift of quail in the wilderness (Num. 11:31–34) or to the praise of God such as this psalm mandates. **81:11–16** The history of Israel with God has been characterized by

¹² So I gave them over to their stubborn
hearts,
to follow their own counsels.
¹³ O that my people would listen to me,
that Israel would walk in my ways!
¹⁴ Then I would quickly subdue their
enemies
and turn my hand against their foes.
¹⁵ Those who hate the LORD would cringe
before him,
and their doom would last forever.
¹⁶ I would feed you*p* with the finest of the
wheat,
and with honey from the rock I would
satisfy you."

PSALM 82

A Psalm of Asaph.

¹ God has taken his place in the divine
council;
in the midst of the gods he holds
judgment:
² "How long will you judge unjustly
and show partiality to the wicked?
Selah
³ Give justice to the weak and the orphan;
maintain the right of the lowly and the
destitute.
⁴ Rescue the weak and the needy;
deliver them from the hand of the
wicked."

⁵ They have neither knowledge nor
understanding;
they walk around in darkness;
all the foundations of the earth are
shaken.

⁶ I say, "You are gods,
children of the Most High, all of you;
⁷ nevertheless, you shall die like mortals
and fall like any prince."*q*

⁸ Rise up, O God, judge the earth,
for all the nations belong to you!

PSALM 83

A Song. A Psalm of Asaph.

¹ O God, do not keep silent;
do not hold your peace or be still,
O God!
² Even now your enemies are in tumult;
those who hate you have raised their
heads.
³ They lay crafty plans against your people;
they consult together against those
you protect.
⁴ They say, "Come, let us wipe them out as
a nation;
let the name of Israel be remembered
no more."

p 81.16 Cn: Heb *he would feed him*   *q* 82.7 Or *fall as one man,
O princes*

unfaithfulness on the people's part. Yet God still calls them *my people.* God had already initiated the covenant relationship with them, and the prophetic oracle in this psalm calls for a renewal of this relationship. *Wheat* and *honey.* See Deut. 32:13–14. The renewed relationship would have powerful consequences for Israel and for Israel's foes.

Ps. 82:1–8 Hymn. Like Ps. 81, this hymn contains prophetic warnings, albeit in a very different form. **Superscription.** *Asaph.* See note on Ps. 50 superscription. **82:1** The scene envisioned is a gathering of the divine council of heavenly beings. In the worldview of ancient Near Eastern cultures, the primary deity was surrounded by a special assembly of other supernatural beings or subordinate gods. Even in Israel's more monotheistic understanding, God has a divine council (cf. Gen. 6:2; Deut. 32:8–9; Job 1:6; Ps. 29). God calls these heavenly beings to accountability in this scene. **82:2–7** Divine judgment of other gods. **82:2** *Selah.* See note on Ps. 3:1–2. **82:3–4** The members of the council are tasked with protecting society's vulnerable populations: the *weak, orphan, lowly, destitute,* and *needy.* **82:5–6** The divine verdict is that these heavenly beings have neither wisdom nor *understanding* but are in the dark. The implication is that they have failed at their task; such injustice threatens *the foundations of the earth. Children of the Most High* refers to members of the divine council; idols who operate in the dark can wreak havoc for the kingdom of heaven. **82:7** Members of the divine council are sentenced to mortality for nonintervention on behalf of those in need. **82:8** God's action on behalf of justice for the oppressed is foundational for life, and the concluding verse calls for God to bring about justice in the whole world.

Ps. 83:1–18 Communal lament. The lament is a national prayer for help. **Superscription.** *Asaph.* See note on Ps. 50 superscription. Divine judgment is a theme of the Asaphite psalms. **83:1–8** The need for divine action. *Selah.* See note on Ps. 3:1–2. **83:1** Opening plea. **83:2–8** The complaint focuses on the *enemies* surrounding Israel; the petitions are for God to defeat the enemies

⁵ They conspire with one accord;
  against you they make a covenant—
⁶ the tents of Edom and the Ishmaelites,
  Moab and the Hagrites,
⁷ Gebal and Ammon and Amalek,
  Philistia with the inhabitants of
    Tyre;
⁸ Assyria also has joined them;
  they are the strong arm of the children
    of Lot. *Selah*

⁹ Do to them as you did to Midian,
  as to Sisera and Jabin at the Wadi
    Kishon,
¹⁰ who were destroyed at En-dor,
  who became dung for the ground.
¹¹ Make their nobles like Oreb and Zeeb,
  all their princes like Zebah and
    Zalmunna,
¹² who said, "Let us take the pastures
  of God
  for our own possession."

¹³ O my God, make them like whirling
    dust,ʳ
  like chaff before the wind.
¹⁴ As fire consumes the forest,
  as the flame sets the mountains
    ablaze,
¹⁵ so pursue them with your tempest
  and terrify them with your hurricane.
¹⁶ Fill their faces with shame,
  so that they may seek your name,
    O LORD.

¹⁷ Let them be put to shame and dismayed
    forever;
  let them perish in disgrace.
¹⁸ Let them know that you alone,
  whose name is the LORD,
  are the Most High over all the earth.

PSALM 84

*To the leader: according to The Gittith. Of the Korahites.
A Psalm.*
¹ How lovely is your dwelling place,
  O LORD of hosts!
² My soul longs, indeed it faints,
  for the courts of the LORD;
  my heart and my flesh sing for joy
    to the living God.

³ Even the sparrow finds a home
  and the swallow a nest for herself,
  where she may lay her young,
  at your altars, O LORD of hosts,
  my King and my God.
⁴ Happy are those who live in your house,
  ever singing your praise. *Selah*

⁵ Happy are those whose strength is in
    you,
  in whose heart are the highways to
    Zion.ˢ
⁶ As they go through the valley of Baca,
  they make it a place of springs;
  the early rain also covers it with pools.

r 83.13 Or *a tumbleweed*   s 84.5 Heb lacks *to Zion*

and deliver Israel. The language is general, so it is difficult to specify a particular historical crisis. **83:6–8** Prophetic oracles castigate ten nations or people groups: *Edom, Ishmaelites, Moab, Hagrites, Gebal, Ammon, Amalek, Philistia, Tyre,* and *Assyria* (for similar oracles, see Isa. 13–23; Jer. 46–51; Ezek. 25–32). *The children of Lot* refers again to the Ammonites and the Moabites. Hagrites (see 1 Chr. 5) and Gebal are rarely named. Suggested locations for the Hagrites include northern Transjordan, and Gebal is placed in Lebanon. The complaint claims that these enemies are covenanting together against Israel (see also Ps. 2). **83:9–18** Rehearsal of the traditions in the book of Judges about the victories by Deborah and Barak over the Canaanites Jabin and Sisera and Gideon over the Midianites (Judg. 4–8). The current enemies seek to destroy Israel and, in turn, their God. **83:13–15** Theophanies of wind and storm now become associated with Israel's God (Job 38; Ps. 29; 68; Hab. 3). **83:16–18** The purpose of coming after Israel's enemies is so they *may seek* God and know that God rules *over all the earth.* **83:17** The plea is for God to destroy Israel's enemies completely.

Ps. 84:1–12 Song of Zion. This psalm reflects a temple pilgrim's perspective (see also Pss. 46, 48, 76, 87, 122). **Superscription.** *To the leader.* See note on Ps. 4 superscription. *According to The Gittith.* See note on Ps. 81 superscription. *Korahites.* See note on Pss. 42–43 superscription. **84:1–4** Praise of divine space: *your dwelling place, courts of the LORD, your altars,* and *your house.* And praise for the worship of the *living God.* **84:3** There is a place in the temple of worship for every living being, from small birds to royalty. *My King and my God* binds divine sovereignty to the place of the temple. **84:4** *Happy* (whole) are those who keep coming to worship in the temple. *Selah.* See note on Ps. 3:1–2. **84:5–7** Whole (*happy*) are those who take the pilgrimage to Zion, as the journey brings

⁷ They go from strength to strength;
  the God of gods will be seen in Zion.

⁸ O Lᴏʀᴅ God of hosts, hear my prayer;
  give ear, O God of Jacob!   *Selah*
⁹ Behold our shield, O God;
  look on the face of your anointed.

¹⁰ For a day in your courts is better
  than a thousand elsewhere.
 I would rather be a doorkeeper in the
    house of my God
  than live in the tents of wickedness.
¹¹ For the Lᴏʀᴅ God is a sun and shield;
  he bestows favor and honor.
 No good thing does the Lᴏʀᴅ withhold
  from those who walk uprightly.
¹² O Lᴏʀᴅ of hosts,
  happy is everyone who trusts in
    you.

Psalm 85

To the leader. Of the Korahites. A Psalm.
¹ Lᴏʀᴅ, you were favorable to your
    land;
  you restored the fortunes of Jacob.
² You forgave the iniquity of your
    people;
  you pardoned all their sin.   *Selah*
³ You withdrew all your wrath;
  you turned from your hot anger.

⁴ Restore us again, O God of our
    salvation,

and put away your indignation
    toward us.
⁵ Will you be angry with us forever?
  Will you prolong your anger to all
    generations?
⁶ Will you not revive us again,
  so that your people may rejoice in
    you?
⁷ Show us your steadfast love, O Lᴏʀᴅ,
  and grant us your salvation.

⁸ Let me hear what God the Lᴏʀᴅ will
    speak,
  for he will speak peace to his people,
  to his faithful, to those who turn to
    him in their hearts.ᵗ
⁹ Surely his salvation is at hand for those
    who fear him,
  that his glory may dwell in our land.

¹⁰ Steadfast love and faithfulness will
    meet;
  righteousness and peace will kiss each
    other.
¹¹ Faithfulness will spring up from the
    ground,
  and righteousness will look down
    from the sky.
¹² The Lᴏʀᴅ will give what is good,
  and our land will yield its increase.
¹³ Righteousness will go before him
  and will make a path for his steps.

t 85.8 Gk: Heb *but let them not turn back to folly*

---

fertility and strength. *Valley of Baca* is unknown. **84:8–9** *Hear my prayer* is a petition for the king, *your anointed* (see also Pss. 4:1; 39:12; 54:2; 143:1). *Selah*. See note on Ps. 3:1–2. **84:10–12** Praise for being in the temple, which is the location of divine presence. Presence there brings joy and hope. Wisdom, justice, and integrity are tied to temple worship.

  Ps. 85:1–13 Communal lament. This lament begins with the historical memory of divine restoration (vv. 1–3), then a petition in vv. 4–7, followed by an expression of faith in the God who hears in vv. 8–13. A petition, spoken in full confidence of faith, predicts peace (v. 8) as much as it asks for it. **Superscription.** *To the leader.* See note on Ps. 4 superscription. *Korahites.* See note on Pss. 42–43 superscription. **85:1–3** Testimony to divine restorative acts, *restored the fortunes* is the general language of deliverance. **85:2** The speaker recounts past acts of divine forgiveness and withdrawal of wrath. The particular event is unspecified, which allows this psalm to be assigned to various occasions. *Selah*. See note on Ps. 3:1–2. **85:4–7** The current plea is based on past divine restoration, and the psalm petitions for deliverance from the current crisis. The verb *restore* (vv. 1, 4, 6) holds the passage together. **85:8–9** *Let me hear* occurs less frequently (Pss. 51:8; 143:8) than the call for God to hear (see, e.g., Ps. 86:1). **85:10–11** Here the synergy of *steadfast love, faithfulness, righteousness,* and *peace* all comes together. The use of the verb *kiss* indicates an intimate relationship between these virtues. *Steadfast love* is love that does not change with external circumstances: that is, it is persistent solidarity (see **"Hesed," p. 375**). *Faithfulness* is trustworthiness, *righteousness* is right relationship, and *peace* is wholeness in life. **85:12–13** The psalm ends with a statement of assurance of and confidence in divine righteousness.

PSALM 86

A Prayer of David.

¹ Incline your ear, O LORD, and answer me,
    for I am poor and needy.
² Preserve my life, for I am devoted to you;
    save your servant who trusts in you.
  You are my God; ³be gracious to me,
    O Lord,
    for to you do I cry all day long.
⁴ Gladden the soul of your servant,
    for to you, O Lord, I lift up my soul.
⁵ For you, O Lord, are good and forgiving,
    abounding in steadfast love to all who
    call on you.
⁶ Give ear, O LORD, to my prayer;
    listen to my cry of supplication.
⁷ In the day of my trouble I call on you,
    for you will answer me.

⁸ There is none like you among the gods,
    O Lord,
    nor are there any works like yours.
⁹ All the nations you have made shall
    come
  and bow down before you, O Lord,
    and shall glorify your name.
¹⁰ For you are great and do wondrous
    things;
    you alone are God.
¹¹ Teach me your way, O LORD,
    that I may walk in your truth;
  give me an undivided heart to revere
    your name.
¹² I give thanks to you, O Lord my God,
    with my whole heart,

and I will glorify your name
    forever.
¹³ For great is your steadfast love
    toward me;
  you have delivered my soul from the
    depths of Sheol.

¹⁴ O God, the insolent rise up against me;
    a band of ruffians seeks my life,
  and they do not set you before
    them.
¹⁵ But you, O Lord, are a God merciful and
    gracious,
  slow to anger and abounding in
    steadfast love and faithfulness.
¹⁶ Turn to me and be gracious to me;
    give your strength to your servant;
    save the child of your maidservant.
¹⁷ Show me a sign of your favor,
    so that those who hate me may see it
    and be put to shame,
  because you, LORD, have helped me
    and comforted me.

PSALM 87

Of the Korahites. A Psalm. A Song.
¹ On the holy mount stands the city he
    founded;
²   the LORD loves the gates of Zion
    more than all the dwellings of Jacob.
³ Glorious things are spoken of you,
    O city of God.   *Selah*

⁴ Among those who know me I mention
    Rahab and Babylon;

Ps. 86:1–17 Lament. This plea is structured in three sections. **Superscription.** *A Prayer of David.* See Ps. 17 superscription. **86:1–7** The opening petition is bracketed with the phrases *incline your ear* (v. 1) and *give ear* (v. 6). The petitions contain persuasive motivational clauses beginning with *for.* **86:1** The psalmist self-defines as *poor and needy.* **86:5** The speaker appeals to God's forgiveness and *steadfast love* (see also v. 13). **86:7** Statement of certainty in God's help. **86:8–13** Incomparability of God (see also Ps. 22:27–28; Isa. 66:18–19; Zech. 14:9). **86:8–11** This section begins with a confession of faith in God as creator and redeemer (vv. 8–10), then continues with petitions for divine instruction, wisdom, and faithfulness (v. 11). **86:13** God has delivered the psalmist from *the depths of Sheol,* meaning here the power of death (see **"Sheol," p. 695**). **86:14–17** More petitions to God. The psalmist's enemies are characterized as *insolent* and *ruffians.* **86:15** There is a possible echo of the "graciousness formula" in Exod. 34:6. The concluding petitions echo the opening section of the psalm.

Ps. 87:1–7 Song of Zion. See note on Ps. 84. This psalm has two parts: vv. 1–3 about the beautiful Zion and vv. 4–7 about the significance of Zion. **Superscription.** *Korahites.* See notes on Pss. 42–43 superscription. **87:1–3** Description of the place of God. **87:1** *Holy mount,* a reference to Zion, is in parallel with *city,* indicating more than the Temple Mount alone but all of Jerusalem. The *city of God* metaphor parallels Ps. 46:4. **87:3** *Selah.* See note on Ps. 3:1-2. **87:4–6** Zion functions as the primordial city from which come all other major cities. The refrain *this one was born there* (vv. 4, 5, 6) indicates their derivative status. The five cities *Rahab* (Egypt), *Babylon, Philistia, Tyre,* and *Cush*

Philistia, too, and Tyre, with Cush—
　"This one was born there," they
　　say.

5 And of Zion it shall be said,
　"This one and that one were born
　　in it,"
　for the Most High himself will
　　establish it.
6 The LORD records, as he registers the
　　peoples,
　"This one was born there."　　*Selah*

7 Singers and dancers alike say,
　"All my springs are in you."

PSALM 88

*A Song. A Psalm of the Korahites. To the leader:
according to Mahalath Leannoth. A Maskil of Heman the
Ezrahite.*

1 O LORD, God of my salvation,
　at night, when I cry out before you,
2 let my prayer come before you;
　incline your ear to my cry.

3 For my soul is full of troubles,
　and my life draws near to Sheol.
4 I am counted among those who go down
　to the Pit;
　I am like those who have no help,
5 like those forsaken among the dead,
　like the slain that lie in the grave,

like those whom you remember no more,
　for they are cut off from your hand.
6 You have put me in the depths of the Pit,
　in the regions dark and deep.
7 Your wrath lies heavy upon me,
　and you overwhelm me with all your
　　waves.　　*Selah*

8 You have caused my companions to
　　shun me;
　you have made me a thing of horror
　　to them.
　I am shut in so that I cannot escape;
9 　my eye grows dim through sorrow.
　Every day I call on you, O LORD;
　I spread out my hands to you.
10 Do you work wonders for the dead?
　Do the shades rise up to praise you?
　　　　　　　　　　　　　　　Selah
11 Is your steadfast love declared in the
　　grave
　or your faithfulness in Abaddon?
12 Are your wonders known in the
　　darkness
　or your saving help in the land of
　　forgetfulness?

13 But I, O LORD, cry out to you;
　in the morning my prayer comes
　　before you.
14 O LORD, why do you cast me off?
　Why do you hide your face from me?

---

point to the great geopolitical powers of the era. Some of these places are enemies of Israel; even these enemies *know* God. **87:6** *This one was born there* repeats the refrain and accents the priority of the persons of Zion. *Selah.* See note on Ps. 3:1–2. **87:7** Musical and liturgical affirmation of the centrality of Zion as the metropolis, including a liturgical procession into the sanctuary. Zion is central to Book III as the special place of divine presence; thus, the destruction of Zion is particularly traumatic. As the site of divine presence and the fount of divine blessings (*springs*), Zion is the center of the universe.

Ps. 88:1–18 Lament. The psalm has three sections: an address and plea in vv. 1–7, the trauma of isolation in vv. 8–12, and a renewed urgent plea in vv. 13–18. **Superscription.** *Korahites.* See notes on Pss. 42–43 superscription. *To the leader.* See note on Ps. 4 superscription. *According to Mahalath Leannoth.* A musical or liturgical term. *Maskil.* See note on Ps. 32 superscription. *Heman the Ezrahite*, like Ethan (Ps. 89 superscription), has a double identity; he is identified as a sage (1 Kgs. 4:31) and a temple musician (1 Chr. 15:17). **88:1–7** Petition and rationale. **88:1** God is addressed as *God of my salvation*. The plea for divine hearing happens *at night*. **88:3–7** An account of a life *full of troubles*. *Sheol.* See note on Ps. 6:1–5 (see **"Sheol," p. 695**). The trouble seems to be that the psalmist is near death, perhaps from an illness or injury. **88:4** *The Pit.* See note on Ps. 16:10. **88:5** The dead are those whom God remembers no more. **88:6** God, not any enemy, is the cause of the psalmist's plight. **88:7** *Waves* is a metaphor for Sheol, sometimes imagined as a watery place (see, e.g., Jonah 2:3; see **"Sheol," p. 695**). The psalmist is devastated, gripped by the power of death. *Selah.* See note on Ps. 3:1–2. **88:8–12** Description of isolation. **88:9** *Eye* is a symbol of the person. *Spread out my hands* is a posture of prayer *every day.* **88:10–12** Assumes negative answers to rhetorical questions. *Selah.* See note on Ps. 3:1–2. **88:13–18** The psalm concludes with a further description of the absence

¹⁵ Wretched and close to death from my
    youth up,
  I suffer your terrors; I am desperate."
¹⁶ Your wrath has swept over me;
  your dread assaults destroy me.
¹⁷ They surround me like a flood all day
    long;
  from all sides they close in on me.
¹⁸ You have caused friend and neighbor to
    shun me;
  my companions are in darkness.

A Maskil of Ethan the Ezrahite.
¹ I will sing of your steadfast love, O Lord,^v
    forever;
  with my mouth I will proclaim your
    faithfulness to all generations.
² I declare that your steadfast love is
    established forever;
  your faithfulness is as firm as the
    heavens.

³ You said, "I have made a covenant with
    my chosen one;
  I have sworn to my servant David:
⁴ 'I will establish your descendants forever
  and build your throne for all
    generations.'"   *Selah*

⁵ Let the heavens praise your wonders,
    O Lord,
  your faithfulness in the assembly of
    the holy ones.
⁶ For who in the skies can be compared to
    the Lord?

Who among the heavenly beings is
    like the Lord,
⁷ a God feared in the council of the holy
    ones,
  great and awesome^w above all who are
    around him?
⁸ O Lord God of hosts,
  who is as mighty as you, O Lord?
  Your faithfulness surrounds you.
⁹ You rule the raging of the sea;
  when its waves rise, you still them.
¹⁰ You crushed Rahab like a carcass;
  you scattered your enemies with your
    mighty arm.
¹¹ The heavens are yours; the earth also is
    yours;
  the world and all that is in it—you
    founded them.
¹² The north and the south^x—you created
    them;
  Tabor and Hermon joyously praise
    your name.
¹³ You have a mighty arm;
  strong is your hand, high your right
    hand.
¹⁴ Righteousness and justice are the
    foundation of your throne;
  steadfast love and faithfulness go
    before you.
¹⁵ Happy are the people who know the
    festal shout,
  who walk, O Lord, in the light of your
    countenance;

u 88.15 Meaning of Heb uncertain v 89.1 Gk: Heb *the steadfast love of the* Lord w 89.7 Gk Syr: Heb *greatly awesome* x 89.12 Or *Zaphon and Yamin*

of God and continued pleas for divine presence and hearing *in the morning.* **88:14** Absence of the face of God. **88:18** The psalmist is isolated not only from God but also from *friend* and *neighbor*. *Darkness* is an unexpected final word. This is the only lament in the book of Psalms with no hopeful conclusion. The psalmist is remarkably candid as the speaker continues to address God with unanswered prayers.

Ps. 89:1–52 Royal psalm of lament. The psalm contains two parts: the divine founding of the Davidic dynasty in vv. 1–37 and a protest against the fall of that kingdom in vv. 38–52. **Superscription.** *Maskil.* See note on Ps. 32. Like Heman (Ps. 88 superscription), *Ethan the Ezrahite* has a double identity as a sage (1 Kgs. 4:31) and a temple musician (1 Chr. 15:17). **89:1–4** Opening description of God's covenant with David (2 Sam. 7:8–16). **89:2** The Davidic covenant is a sign of God's *steadfast love.* **89:3** The Davidic king is understood as God's *chosen one.* **89:4** *Selah.* See note on Ps. 3:1–2. **89:5–12** Hymn of praise. **89:5–7** *Assembly of the holy ones* and *council of the holy ones* refer to the concept of a divine assembly (see note on Ps. 82). **89:8–10** *Hosts,* or armies of heavenly hosts. *Sea* and *Rahab* both represent chaos. Rahab is a chaos monster, sometimes also a name for Egypt (see Ps. 87:4). These verses harken back to other images of chaos tamed by God (see Job 26:12; Ps. 68:22–23; 74:13–14). **89:11–12** Divine worldwide rule. *Tabor* is in lower Galilee, and *Hermon,* the tallest mountain in Israel, is located on Israel's northeast boundary. **89:13–18** Recital of history. **89:15** *Happy* is an element in didactic exhortation (see Pss. 1:1; 2:12;

¹⁶ they exult in your name all day long
    and extol^y your righteousness.
¹⁷ For you are the glory of their strength;
    by your favor our horn is exalted.
¹⁸ For our shield belongs to the Lord,
    our king to the Holy One of Israel.

¹⁹ Then you spoke in a vision to your
    faithful one and said,
    "I have set the crown^z on one who is
    mighty;
    I have exalted one chosen from the
    people.
²⁰ I have found my servant David;
    with my holy oil I have anointed him;
²¹ my hand shall always remain with him;
    my arm also shall strengthen him.
²² The enemy shall not outwit him;
    the wicked shall not humble him.
²³ I will crush his foes before him
    and strike down those who hate
    him.
²⁴ My faithfulness and steadfast love shall
    be with him,
    and in my name his horn shall be
    exalted.
²⁵ I will set his hand on the sea
    and his right hand on the rivers.
²⁶ He shall cry to me, 'You are my Father,
    my God, and the Rock of my
    salvation!'
²⁷ I will make him the firstborn,
    the highest of the kings of the earth.
²⁸ Forever I will keep my steadfast love for
    him,
    and my covenant with him will stand
    firm.
²⁹ I will establish his line forever
    and his throne as long as the heavens
    endure.
³⁰ If his children forsake my law
    and do not walk according to my
    ordinances,
³¹ if they violate my statutes
    and do not keep my commandments,
³² then I will punish their transgression
    with the rod
    and their iniquity with scourges,

³³ but I will not remove from him my
    steadfast love
    or be false to my faithfulness.
³⁴ I will not violate my covenant
    or alter the word that went forth from
    my lips.
³⁵ Once and for all I have sworn by my
    holiness;
    I will not lie to David.
³⁶ His line shall continue forever,
    and his throne endure before me like
    the sun.
³⁷ It shall be established forever like the
    moon,
    an enduring witness in the skies."
                        Selah

³⁸ But now you have spurned and rejected
    him;
    you are full of wrath against your
    anointed.
³⁹ You have renounced the covenant with
    your servant;
    you have defiled his crown in the dust.
⁴⁰ You have broken through all his
    walls;
    you have laid his strongholds in
    ruins.
⁴¹ All who pass by plunder him;
    he has become the scorn of his
    neighbors.
⁴² You have exalted the right hand of his
    foes;
    you have made all his enemies rejoice.
⁴³ Moreover, you have turned back the
    edge of his sword,
    and you have not supported him in
    battle.
⁴⁴ You have removed the scepter from his
    hand^a
    and hurled his throne to the
    ground.
⁴⁵ You have cut short the days of his
    youth;
    you have covered him with shame.
                        Selah

y 89.16 Cn: Heb *are exalted in*   *z* 89.19 Cn: Heb *help*
a 89.44 Cn: Heb *removed his cleanness*

33:12; 34:8). **89:17–18** *Our horn* and *shield* refer to the king. **89:19–37** A divine oracle establishing the house of David. **89:25** The task of subduing chaos falls to God but also God's servant the king. **89:26–27** The king's sonship is signaled by his call to God: *You are my Father* (see 2 Sam. 7:14; Ps. 2:7). **89:28** Davidic kings see the consequences of their unfaithfulness, but the Davidic covenant continues as a sign of God's *steadfast love.* **89:37** *Selah.* See note on Ps. 3:1–2. **89:38–45** The second part of the psalm in which the situation of the Davidic house is reversed. The psalmist protests. **89:45** *Selah.* See

⁴⁶ How long, O Lᴏʀᴅ? Will you hide
    yourself forever?
How long will your wrath burn like
    fire?
⁴⁷ Remember how short my time is—ᵇ
    for what vanity you have created all
    mortals!
⁴⁸ Who can live and never see death?
    Who can escape the power of Sheol?
                                    Selah

⁴⁹ Lord, where is your steadfast love of
    old,
    which by your faithfulness you swore
    to David?
⁵⁰ Remember, O Lord, how your servant is
    taunted,
    how I bear in my bosom the insults of
    the peoples,ᶜ
⁵¹ with which your enemies taunt, O Lᴏʀᴅ,
    with which they taunted the footsteps
    of your anointed.

⁵² Blessed be the Lᴏʀᴅ forever.
    Amen and Amen.

BOOK IV
(PSALMS 90–106)

Pꜱᴀʟᴍ 90

A Prayer of Moses, the man of God.
¹ Lord, you have been our dwelling placeᵈ
    in all generations.

² Before the mountains were brought
    forth
    or ever you had formed the earth and
    the world,
    from everlasting to everlasting you are
    God.

³ You turn usᵉ back to dust
    and say, "Turn back, you mortals."
⁴ For a thousand years in your sight
    are like yesterday when it is past
    or like a watch in the night.

⁵ You sweep them away; they are like a
    dream,
    like grass that is renewed in the
    morning;
⁶ in the morning it flourishes and is
    renewed;
    in the evening it fades and withers.

⁷ For we are consumed by your anger;
    by your wrath we are overwhelmed.
⁸ You have set our iniquities before you,
    our secret sins in the light of your
    countenance.

⁹ For all our days pass away under your
    wrath;
    our years come to an endᶠ like a sigh.

b 89.47 Meaning of Heb uncertain *c* 89.50 Cn: Heb *bosom all of many peoples* *d* 90.1 Or *our refuge* *e* 90.3 Heb *humankind* *f* 90.9 Syr: Heb *we bring our years to an end*

note on Ps. 3:1–2. **89:46–51** Petition in the context of the house of David. *How long?* is the language of lament psalms (see, e.g., Ps. 13). **89:48** *Selah.* See note on Ps. 3:1–2. **89:49–51** Divine *steadfast love* and *faithfulness* have disappeared. The poignant rhetorical question reveals the darkness of the fall of Zion/Jerusalem and the temple and the end of the Davidic kingdom. This expresses a central question for the shape of the Psalter. **89:50–51** Taunting the Davidic ruler is taunting Israel's God. **89:52** A doxology ends Book III (Pss. 73–89), as with the other books (see Pss. 41:13; 72:18–19; 106:48; 150:1–6). This final verse marks the end of Book III and is not necessarily the end of Ps. 89.

Book IV: Pss. 90–106 The destruction of the Davidic kingdom, its central city of Jerusalem, and its temple as a principal place of divine presence hovers darkly over Book III, Pss. 73–89. Psalm 90 begins Book IV with a Prayer of Moses, placing the reader before there was a Davidic reign and perhaps in the wilderness of exile. Psalm 93 quickly introduces a collection (Pss. 93–101) that celebrates the reign of God. Can the community now move into a future on that basis? Psalms 102–106 make clear the reality of exile but do not discount the reign of God.

Ps. 90:1–17 Communal lament. The basis of the lament is the contrast between divine permanence and human frailty (vv. 1–12). The lament ends with a petition (vv. 13–17). **Superscription.** *Prayer of Moses, the man of God* only occurs here. References to Moses occur in Pss. 90–106. *Moses* is a symbol of a human intercessor (see Pss. 77:20; 99:6; 103:7; 105:26; 106:16, 23, 32) and here asks God to turn from wrath as he does in Exod. 32:12. **90:1** God is praised as the *dwelling place.* **90:2** God is preexistent and *everlasting.* **90:3–6** Eternal God and transient human life. **90:3** God *turn[s]* humans *to dust* (see Gen. 3:19). **90:4** There is a contrast between human and divine perceptions of time. **90:5–6** Four similes—*dream, grass, morning,* and *evening*—indicate the transitory nature of life. **90:7–12** God's great

[10] The days of our life are seventy years
    or perhaps eighty, if we are strong;
even then their span[g] is only toil and
        trouble;
    they are soon gone, and we fly away.

[11] Who considers the power of your anger?
    Your wrath is as great as the fear that
        is due you.
[12] So teach us to count our days
    that we may gain a wise heart.

[13] Turn, O Lord! How long?
    Have compassion on your servants!
[14] Satisfy us in the morning with your
        steadfast love,
    so that we may rejoice and be glad all
        our days.
[15] Make us glad as many days as you have
        afflicted us
    and as many years as we have seen evil.
[16] Let your work be manifest to your
        servants
    and your glorious power to their
        children.
[17] Let the favor of the Lord our God be
        upon us
    and prosper for us the work of our
        hands—
    O prosper the work of our hands!

PSALM 91

[1] You who live in the shelter of the Most
        High,
    who abide in the shadow of the
        Almighty,[b]
[2] will say to the Lord, "My refuge and my
        fortress;
    my God, in whom I trust."
[3] For he will deliver you from the snare of
        the hunter
    and from the deadly pestilence;

[4] he will cover you with his pinions,
    and under his wings you will find
        refuge;
    his faithfulness is a shield and
        defense.
[5] You will not fear the terror of the night
    or the arrow that flies by day
[6] or the pestilence that stalks in
        darkness
    or the destruction that wastes at
        noonday.

[7] A thousand may fall at your side,
    ten thousand at your right hand,
    but it will not come near you.
[8] You will only look with your eyes
    and see the punishment of the
        wicked.

[9] Because you have made the Lord your
        refuge,[i]
    the Most High your dwelling place,
[10] no evil shall befall you,
    no scourge come near your tent.

[11] For he will command his angels
        concerning you
    to guard you in all your ways.
[12] On their hands they will bear you up,
    so that you will not dash your foot
        against a stone.
[13] You will tread on the lion and the
        adder;
    the young lion and the serpent you
        will trample under foot.

[14] Those who love me, I will deliver;
    I will protect those who know my
        name.

g 90.10 Cn Compare Gk Syr Jerome Tg: Heb *pride*
h 91.1 Traditional rendering of Heb *Shaddai*   i 91.9 Cn:
Heb *Because you,* Lord, *are my refuge; you have made*

anger with humans. **90:10** The psalmist's assessment of the human life span is *seventy years or perhaps eighty*. **90:12** *Count our days* refers to a strategy to navigate mortality, a wisdom element to the prayer. **90:13–17** Relationship restored. **90:13–14** Request that God *turn* (see v. 3) and bring joy to the community based on divine *steadfast love*.

Ps. 91:1–16 Wisdom psalm. A song to call the community to trust, with poetic images indicating that God is trustworthy. This psalm has no superscription. **91:1–2** *Most High* is the divine name "Elyon" and *Almighty* is "Shaddai" in Hebrew. The psalmist opens with a first-person statement of trust in divine *refuge* and shelter. **91:3–13** The divine action founding the psalmist's trust. **91:3–4** Metaphors like *snare of the hunter* accent wildlife and hunting imagery. *Pinions* is an ornithological metaphor (Deut. 32:11). *Shield* and *defense* point to militaristic metaphors. **91:11** This verse is quoted in the New Testament; see Matt. 4:6; Luke 4:10–11. **91:14–16** God's words of confirmation, with connections to Ps. 90 (see Ps. 90:14, 16).

¹⁵ When they call to me, I will answer them;
  I will be with them in trouble;
  I will rescue them and honor them.
¹⁶ With long life I will satisfy them
  and show them my salvation.

PSALM 92

A Psalm. A Song for the Sabbath Day.
¹ It is good to give thanks to the LORD,
  to sing praises to your name, O Most
  High,
² to declare your steadfast love in the
  morning
  and your faithfulness by night,
³ to the music of the lute and the harp,
  to the melody of the lyre.
⁴ For you, O LORD, have made me glad by
  your work;
  at the works of your hands I sing for
  joy.

⁵ How great are your works, O LORD!
  Your thoughts are very deep!
⁶ The dullard cannot know;
  the stupid cannot understand this:
⁷ though the wicked sprout like grass
  and all evildoers flourish,
  they are doomed to destruction forever,
⁸ but you, O LORD, are on high forever.
⁹ For your enemies, O LORD,
  for your enemies shall perish;
  all evildoers shall be scattered.

¹⁰ But you have exalted my horn like that
  of the wild ox;
  you have anointed me with fresh oil.

¹¹ My eyes have seen the downfall of my
  enemies;
  my ears have heard the doom of my
  evil assailants.

¹² The righteous flourish like the palm tree
  and grow like a cedar in Lebanon.
¹³ They are planted in the house of the LORD;
  they flourish in the courts of our God.
¹⁴ In old age they still produce fruit;
  they are always green and full of sap,
¹⁵ showing that the LORD is upright;
  he is my rock, and there is no
  unrighteousness in him.

PSALM 93

¹ The LORD is king; he is robed in majesty;
  the LORD is robed; he is girded with
  strength.
He has established the world; it shall
  never be moved;
² your throne is established from of old;
  you are from everlasting.

³ The floods have lifted up, O LORD,
  the floods have lifted up their voice;
  the floods lift up their roaring.
⁴ More majestic than the thunders of
  mighty waters,
  more majestic than the waves^j of the sea,
  majestic on high is the LORD!

⁵ Your decrees are very sure;
  holiness befits your house,
  O LORD, forevermore.

j 93.4 Cn: Heb *majestic are the waves*

Ps. 92:1–15 Thanksgiving song. This psalm begins with praise and thanksgiving (vv. 1–6), continues with a description of the *downfall of my enemies* (vv. 7–11), and ends with hope for the righteous community (vv. 12–15). **Superscription.** *A Song for the Sabbath Day* may refer to a psalm set for Sabbath rituals. **92:1–4** Call for thanksgiving to *Most High* (Elyon). **92:3** *Music* of thanksgiving in worship. **92:4** *At the works of your hands* can refer to God's liberative work (Deut. 32:4; Josh. 24:31). It could point to God's act in creation (see Pss. 8:3; 19:1). **92:5–6** Wisdom perspectives in the prayer. **92:6–11** God's victory over the adversaries, described as *dullard, stupid, wicked,* and *evildoers.* **92:10** *Horn* is parallel to *wild ox,* a metaphor for untamed power. The comparable metaphor *fresh oil* points to the anointing (1 Sam. 16). **92:12–15** God's planting of trees is a metaphor for a life well lived in the care of God. **92:12–14** *The righteous* have sustainable stability like a *palm tree* and a *cedar in Lebanon* rooted in the *house of the* LORD. God brings fruit to these trees even *in old age.* **92:15** God as *rock* brings security humans cannot.

Ps. 93:1–5 Enthronement hymn. See note on Ps. 47. **93:1–2** *The* LORD *is king* (see Pss. 10:16; 96:10; 97:1; 99:1) can also be translated as "the Lord rules" or "reigns." God as creator is *everlasting* sovereign over the world. God's robe and *throne* are the trappings of God's kingship. **93:3–4** *The floods* are powerful symbols of chaos, yet God controls these chaotic waters: *floods, mighty waters,* and *the sea.* **93:5** God's reign is stable even in the midst of chaos, perhaps a reference to the experiences of exile.

PSALM 94

¹ O LORD, you God of vengeance,
   you God of vengeance, shine forth!
² Rise up, O judge of the earth;
   give to the proud what they deserve!
³ O LORD, how long shall the wicked,
   how long shall the wicked exult?

⁴ They pour out their arrogant words;
   all the evildoers boast.
⁵ They crush your people, O LORD,
   and afflict your heritage.
⁶ They kill the widow and the stranger;
   they murder the orphan,
⁷ and they say, "The LORD does not see;
   the God of Jacob does not perceive."

⁸ Understand, O dullest of the people;
   fools, when will you be wise?
⁹ He who planted the ear, does he not
   hear?
   He who formed the eye, does he not
   see?
¹⁰ He who disciplines the nations,
   he who teaches knowledge to
   humankind,
   does he not chastise?
¹¹ The LORD knows our thoughts,ᵏ
   that they are but an empty breath.

¹² Happy are those whom you discipline,
   O LORD,
   and whom you teach out of your law,
¹³ giving them respite from days of trouble,
   until a pit is dug for the wicked.
¹⁴ For the LORD will not forsake his people;
   he will not abandon his heritage;

¹⁵ for justice will return to the righteous,
   and all the upright in heart will
   follow it.

¹⁶ Who rises up for me against the wicked?
   Who stands up for me against
   evildoers?
¹⁷ If the LORD had not been my help,
   my soul would soon have lived in the
   land of silence.
¹⁸ When I thought, "My foot is slipping,"
   your steadfast love, O LORD, held me up.
¹⁹ When the cares of my heart are many,
   your consolations cheer my soul.
²⁰ Can wicked rulers be allied with you,
   those who contrive mischief by
   statute?
²¹ They band together against the life of the
   righteous
   and condemn the innocent to death.
²² But the LORD has become my stronghold
   and my God the rock of my refuge.
²³ He will repay them for their iniquity
   and wipe them out for their
   wickedness;
   the LORD our God will wipe them out.

PSALM 95

¹ O come, let us sing to the LORD;
   let us make a joyful noise to the rock
   of our salvation!
² Let us come into his presence with
   thanksgiving;
   let us make a joyful noise to him with
   songs of praise!

ᵏ 94.11 Heb *the thoughts of humankind*

Ps. 94:1–23 Communal lament. This psalm may be positioned before a collection of enthronement hymns (Pss. 95–99) because of its contrast between wicked rulers and God's reign. **94:1–7** Appeal to divine *vengeance* as vindication for God's innocent, suffering people (see also Deut. 32:35; Pss. 18:47; 58:10; 149:7). **94:3** The question *How long?* (see also Pss. 13:1, 2; 35:17; 74:9, 10; 79:5; 80:4; 89:46; 90:13; 119:84) frames the circumstances of the *wicked* (see also Ps. 73:3). **94:4–7** The wicked are those who defy the call to protect the weak: the *widow*, *stranger*, and *orphan*. Even more, the wicked *kill* and *murder* those who should be under special protection (see Exod. 22:21–24). **94:8–15** God's work as teacher empowers the *dullest* and *fools* to be wise. **94:12** *Happy* functions as a moral exhortation. **94:13–14** God is a God of justice, bringing the downfall of *the wicked* and providing refuge for the people, who are God's *heritage*. **94:16–23** God *rises up* and *stands up* to the *wicked* and *evildoers*. God's *steadfast love* brings hope for the upright. God's active work can be trusted even in the face of adversity.

Ps. 95:1–11 Liturgical enthronement hymn. See Pss. 29, 47, 96–99. The hymn contains two calls to worship, one in the courtyard for all creation (vv. 1–5) and another in the sanctuary for the covenant community (vv. 6–7), followed by a prophetic oracle calling for covenant faithfulness (vv. 7–11). **95:1–5** First call to worship. The call is to testify through the verbs *sing* and *make a joyful noise*. **95:2–5** *Joyful noise* is repeated, characterizing the procession into the sanctuary court.

³ For the LORD is a great God
  and a great King above all gods.
⁴ In his hand are the depths of the earth;
  the heights of the mountains are his
    also.
⁵ The sea is his, for he made it,
  and the dry land, which his hands
    have formed.

⁶ O come, let us worship and bow down;
  let us kneel before the LORD, our
    Maker!
⁷ For he is our God,
  and we are the people of his pasture
    and the sheep of his hand.

O that today you would listen to his voice!
⁸   Do not harden your hearts, as at
      Meribah,
  as on the day at Massah in the
    wilderness,
⁹ when your ancestors tested me
  and put me to the proof, though they
    had seen my work.
¹⁰ For forty years I loathed that generation
  and said, "They are a people whose
    hearts go astray,
  and they do not regard my ways."
¹¹ Therefore in my anger I swore,
  "They shall not enter my rest."

PSALM 96

¹ O sing to the LORD a new song;
  sing to the LORD, all the earth.

² Sing to the LORD; bless his name;
  tell of his salvation from day to day.
³ Declare his glory among the nations,
  his marvelous works among all the
    peoples.
⁴ For great is the LORD and greatly to be
    praised;
  he is to be revered above all gods.
⁵ For all the gods of the peoples are
    idols,
  but the LORD made the heavens.
⁶ Honor and majesty are before him;
  strength and beauty are in his
    sanctuary.

⁷ Ascribe to the LORD, O families of the
    peoples,
  ascribe to the LORD glory and strength.
⁸ Ascribe to the LORD the glory due his
    name;
  bring an offering, and come into his
    courts.
⁹ Worship the LORD in holy splendor;
  tremble before him, all the earth.

¹⁰ Say among the nations, "The LORD is
    king!
  The world is firmly established; it
    shall never be moved.
  He will judge the peoples with
    equity."
¹¹ Let the heavens be glad, and let the earth
    rejoice;
  let the sea roar and all that fills it;

95:3–5 The reasons for the praise are marked with *for*: God as *great King above all gods*. God is praised as creator of all. *Depths, heights, sea*, and *dry land* are four points that indicate all of creation. *The sea* stands for chaos over which God is also sovereign. **95:6–7** Second call to *worship* and *bow down* and *kneel*. Bowing and kneeling recognize the sovereignty of the creator. The pastoral imagery indicates the covenant relationship between God and Israel. **95:7–11** Prophetic warning. **95:7** *O that today you would listen to his voice!* opens the warning with a call to hear (see Exod. 19:5; Deut. 6:4). **95:8–9** *Meribah* and *Massah* are places in the wilderness named in Exod. 17:1–7 and Num. 20:1–13. **95:10** *Forty years* in the wilderness was the price for the people's disobedience after the exodus. **95:11** *Rest* refers to the promise of the land. In this psalm, entrance to worship and entrance to the land include both doxological praise and hearing and obeying.

Ps. 96:1–13 Enthronement hymn. See Pss. 29, 47, 95–99. This hymn begins with a summons to praise followed by reasons (vv. 1–6), an intense second call to praise (vv. 7–10), and finally a call to all creation to praise (vv. 11–13). The hymn is likely a postexilic text (see 1 Chr. 16:23–33). **96:1–6** Call to *sing . . . a new song* (see note on Ps. 33:3) and recount the news of God's *salvation*. See **"Music and the Psalms," p. 764**. The audience consists of *all the earth, the nations*, and *all the peoples*. **96:5** Reasons for praise—marked with *for*—include that the gods of other nations are idols. As the one creator, God is the one God. **96:7–10** The imperatives *ascribe* (vv. 7, 8; see also Pss. 29:1, 2; 68:34) and *worship* (v. 9) are addressed to the *families of the peoples*. The commands point to the key testimony: *the LORD is king* (v. 10; see also Pss. 10:16; 93:1; 97:1; 99:1). Israel's God is the creator and therefore also the sovereign and the bringer of justice. **96:11–13** Even the natural world

¹²   let the field exult and everything in it.
    Then shall all the trees of the forest sing
      for joy
¹³   before the LORD, for he is coming,
    for he is coming to judge the earth.
  He will judge the world with
      righteousness
    and the peoples with his truth.

PSALM 97

¹ The LORD is king! Let the earth
    rejoice;
  let the many coastlands be glad!
² Clouds and thick darkness are all
    around him;
  righteousness and justice are the
    foundation of his throne.
³ Fire goes before him
  and consumes his adversaries on
    every side.
⁴ His lightnings light up the world;
  the earth sees and trembles.
⁵ The mountains melt like wax before the
    LORD,
  before the Lord of all the earth.

⁶ The heavens proclaim his righteousness,
  and all the peoples behold his glory.
⁷ All servants of images are put to shame,
  those who make their boast in
    worthless idols;
  all gods bow down before him.
⁸ Zion hears and is glad,
  and the towns*ˡ* of Judah rejoice
  because of your judgments, O God.

⁹ For you, O LORD, are most high over all
    the earth;
  you are exalted far above all gods.

¹⁰ You who love the LORD, hate evil;
    he guards the lives of his faithful;
    he rescues them from the hand of the
      wicked.
¹¹ Light dawns*ᵐ* for the righteous
    and joy for the upright in heart.
¹² Rejoice in the LORD, O you righteous,
    and give thanks to his holy name!

PSALM 98

A Psalm.
¹ O sing to the LORD a new song,
    for he has done marvelous things.
  His right hand and his holy arm
    have gotten him victory.
² The LORD has made known his victory;
    he has revealed his vindication in the
      sight of the nations.
³ He has remembered his steadfast love
    and faithfulness
  to the house of Israel.
  All the ends of the earth have seen
    the victory of our God.

⁴ Make a joyful noise to the LORD, all the earth;
    break forth into joyous song and sing
      praises.
⁵ Sing praises to the LORD with the lyre,
    with the lyre and the sound of melody.

l 97.8 Heb *daughters* *m* 97.11 Gk Syr Jerome: Heb *is sown*

---

recognizes and praises God. The call to the *heavens, earth, sea,* and *field* testifies to the reign of God. **96:12** The trees also sing of the coming judge. **96:13** Anything is possible when God comes to judge *with righteousness.*

Ps. 97:1–12 Enthronement hymn. See Pss. 29, 47, 95–99. This hymn begins with an account of theophany (vv. 1–5), then the response of creation (vv. 6–9), and ends with assurance to the faithful (vv. 10–12). **97:1** *The LORD is king!* (see also Pss. 10:16; 93:1; 96:10; 99:1). The phrase can also be translated as "the Lord reigns." **97:2–5** Theophany, or appearance of the divine king. Biblical writers often use descriptions of clouds, darkness, fire, and lightning related to God's appearances. God appears out of a whirlwind in Job 38. God appears accompanied by clouds, thunder, and lightning at Sinai (see Exod. 19:16–25; Hab. 3:3–12). **97:6–9** Cosmic response. *The heavens proclaim* (see Ps. 19:1–4) the supremacy of God above other deities (see Ps. 115:4–8). **97:8** The cosmic recognition has parallels in the cities of Zion and the towns of Judah. **97:10–12** God's care described as the divine sowing of light for the righteous ones.

Ps. 98:1–9 Enthronement hymn. See Pss. 29, 47, 95–99. **Superscription.** *A Psalm* is a frequent superscription. There is an initial call to praise (vv. 1–3), then a renewed call to praise (vv. 4–6), and a final call of creation to praise the creator (vv. 7–9). **98:1–3** *Sing to the LORD a new song.* See note on Ps. 33:3. *Right hand* brings victory as a witness of divine rule. **98:2–3** *Made known* is God's revelation and parallels God's remembrance of God's *steadfast love and faithfulness.* The message is of the persistent solidarity and trustworthiness of God. **98:4–6** *Make a joyful noise* (see Pss. 66:1; 95:1,

⁶ With trumpets and the sound of the horn
  make a joyful noise before the King,
    the LORD.

⁷ Let the sea roar and all that fills it,
  the world and those who live in it.
⁸ Let the floods clap their hands;
  let the hills sing together for joy
⁹ at the presence of the LORD, for he is
    coming
  to judge the earth.
He will judge the world with
    righteousness
  and the peoples with equity.

PSALM 99

¹ The LORD is king; let the peoples tremble!
  He sits enthroned upon the cherubim;
    let the earth quake!
² The LORD is great in Zion;
  he is exalted over all the peoples.
³ Let them praise your great and awesome
    name.
  Holy is he!
⁴ Mighty King,ⁿ lover of justice,
  you have established equity;
you have executed justice
  and righteousness in Jacob.
⁵ Extol the LORD our God;
  worship at his footstool.
  Holy is he!

⁶ Moses and Aaron were among his priests,
  Samuel also was among those who
    called on his name.
  They cried to the LORD, and he
    answered them.
⁷ He spoke to them in the pillar of cloud;
  they kept his decrees
  and the statutes that he gave them.

⁸ O LORD our God, you answered them;
  you were a forgiving God to them
  but an avenger of their wrongdoings.
⁹ Extol the LORD our God,
  and worship at his holy mountain,
  for the LORD our God is holy.

PSALM 100

A Psalm of thanksgiving.
¹ Make a joyful noise to the LORD, all the earth.
²   Serve the LORD with gladness;
  come into his presence with singing.

³ Know that the LORD is God.
  It is he who made us, and we are his;ᵒ
  we are his people and the sheep of his
    pasture.

⁴ Enter his gates with thanksgiving
  and his courts with praise.

n 99.4 Cn: Heb *And a king's strength*   o 100.3 Or *and not we ourselves*

2; 100:1) extends to the musical instruments *lyre, horn,* and *trumpets.* The music recognizes God as king. **98:7–9** The natural world—*sea, floods,* and *hills*—all testify (see Ps. 19:1–4; 96:11–12) to God as righteous judge of all creation. The righteous one moves to bring all creation into right relationship with the creator and the creation.

Ps. 99:1–9 Enthronement hymn. See Pss. 29, 47, 95–99. Call to praise the divine king (vv. 1–5), followed by memories of faithful figures in Israel's history (vv. 6–9). **99:1–3** *The LORD is king* can also be translated as "God reigns" (see Pss. 10:16; 93:1; 96:10; 97:1). **99:1** *Enthroned upon the cherubim* refers to the divine presence above the ark in the temple (see 1 Sam. 4:4). **99:2** *The LORD is great in Zion* underscores the connection between Jerusalem and God. **99:3** *Holy is he!* Pronouncement of the holiness of God. **99:4–5** The divine king is a *lover of justice.* Sovereignty and justice are linked. **99:5** *Footstool* is either the ark on Mount Zion or Mount Zion itself (1 Chr. 28:2; Ps. 132:7; see also Isa. 66:1). *Holy is he!* Second pronouncement of the holiness of God. **99:6–9** The ancestors of faith—Moses (Exod. 32:11–14; Deut. 9:26–29; see note on Ps. 77:20), Aaron (Num. 6:22–26), and Samuel (1 Sam. 7:9)—represent models of piety and intercession who called on God's name. The attention to history, especially the focus on the wilderness wanderings, may reflect a setting of exile for the writing of the psalm. **99:9** *The LORD our God is holy.* Third pronouncement of the holiness of God.

Ps. 100:1–5 Hymn of praise and thanksgiving. Concluding psalm, ending the section of the enthronement hymns (Pss. 95–99). **Superscription.** *A Psalm of thanksgiving* is distinctive (see v. 4). **100:1–4** Four imperatives—*make a joyful noise, serve, come,* and *know*—introduce the psalm. The setting is a procession to worship. **100:3** *It is he who made us.* God's creation of humanity is the foundation for the relationship between God and the world. *And we are his* may alternatively be read as "and not we ourselves." *Sheep of his pasture.* For the metaphor of God as shepherd and people as sheep, see notes on Pss. 23:1–3; 79:13; 95:6–7. **100:4** Three imperatives—*enter, give thanks,*

Give thanks to him; bless his
name.

⁵ For the Lᴏʀᴅ is good;
his steadfast love endures forever
and his faithfulness to all
generations.

Psalm 101

Of David. A Psalm.

¹ I will sing of loyalty and of justice;
to you, O Lᴏʀᴅ, I will sing.
² I will study the way that is blameless.
When shall I attain it?

I will walk with integrity of heart
within my house;
³ I will not set before my eyes
anything that is base.

I hate the work of those who fall away;
it shall not cling to me.
⁴ Perverseness of heart shall be far from
me;
I will know nothing of evil.

⁵ One who secretly slanders a neighbor
I will destroy.
A haughty look and an arrogant heart
I will not tolerate.

⁶ I will look with favor on the faithful in
the land,
so that they may live with me;
whoever walks in the way that is
blameless
shall minister to me.

⁷ No one who practices deceit
shall remain in my house;
no one who utters lies
shall continue in my presence.

⁸ Morning by morning I will destroy
all the wicked in the land,
cutting off all evildoers
from the city of the Lᴏʀᴅ.

Psalm 102

*A prayer of one afflicted, when faint and pleading before
the* Lᴏʀᴅ.

¹ Hear my prayer, O Lᴏʀᴅ;
let my cry come to you.
² Do not hide your face from me
in the day of my distress.
Incline your ear to me;
answer me speedily in the day when
I call.

³ For my days pass away like smoke,
and my bones burn like a furnace.
⁴ My heart is stricken and withered like
grass;
I am too wasted to eat my bread.
⁵ Because of my loud groaning,
my bones cling to my skin.
⁶ I am like a desert owl*ᵖ* of the wilderness,
like a little owl of the waste places.
⁷ I lie awake;
I am like a lonely bird on the housetop.
⁸ All day long my enemies taunt me;
those who deride me use my name for
a curse.

p 102.6 Meaning of Heb uncertain

and *bless*—conclude the section. **100:5** The nature of God as *good* provides the reason for the praise the imperatives seek. *Steadfast love* and *faithfulness* again characterize the God who reigns.
  Ps. 101:1–8 Royal psalm. This psalm may have functioned as the king's "oath of office." **Superscription.** *Of David.* See note on Ps. 3 superscription. *A Psalm.* See note on Ps. 98 superscription. **101:1** Introduction by the king. The king pledges *loyalty* and *justice* and sings praises to God. **101:2–7** The king vows *integrity*, framed by the metaphor of being in *my house* (vv. 2, 7). **101:3–5** Royal virtue list. See Prov. 6:6–19. **101:8** *Morning by morning* indicates continuous action. The human ruler commits to justice and integrity in the context of relationship with the divine and with other people. Enthronement psalms offer the community hope in the wilderness of exile; likewise, Ps. 101 also offers hope.
  Ps. 102:1–28 Lament. This lament consists of a prayer for help (vv. 1–11), a hymn to God's reign (vv. 12–22), and a conclusion (vv. 23–28). The middle section suggests an exilic setting. **Superscription.** *A prayer of one afflicted* (sick), *when faint* (close to death), and *pleading* (petition). **102:1** *Hear my prayer* is the language of petition (see Pss. 4:1; 39:12; 54:2; 84:8; 143:1). **102:2** *Do not hide your face* is a metaphor for divine absence (see Pss. 13:1; 27:9; 69:17; 143:7). *Incline your ear* is a metaphor for access (see Pss. 31:2; 45:10; 71:2; 86:1; 88:2). **102:3–11** The woeful state of the psalmist shapes the motivation for God to help. The complaint about the illness is physical (vv. 3, 5, 11), emotional (vv.

[9] Indeed, I eat ashes like bread
and mingle tears with my drink,
[10] because of your indignation and anger,
for you have lifted me up and thrown me aside.
[11] My days are like a lengthening shadow;
I wither away like grass.

[12] But you, O LORD, are enthroned forever;
your name endures to all generations.
[13] You will rise up and have compassion on Zion,
for it is time to favor it;
the appointed time has come.
[14] For your servants hold its stones dear
and have pity on its dust.
[15] The nations will fear the name of the LORD
and all the kings of the earth your glory.
[16] For the LORD will build up Zion;
he will appear in his glory.
[17] He will regard the prayer of the destitute
and will not despise their prayer.

[18] Let this be recorded for a generation to come,
so that a people yet unborn may praise the LORD:
[19] that he looked down from his holy height,
from heaven the LORD looked at the earth,
[20] to hear the groans of the prisoners,
to set free those who were doomed to die,
[21] so that the name of the LORD may be declared in Zion
and his praise in Jerusalem,
[22] when peoples gather together,
and kingdoms, to serve the LORD.

[23] He has broken my strength in midcourse;
he has shortened my days.
[24] "O my God," I say, "do not take me away
at the midpoint of my life,
you whose years endure
throughout all generations."

[25] Long ago you laid the foundation of the earth,
and the heavens are the work of your hands.
[26] They will perish, but you endure;
they will all wear out like a garment.
You change them like clothing, and they pass away,
[27] but you are the same, and your years have no end.
[28] The children of your servants shall live secure;
their offspring shall be established in your presence.

PSALM 103

Of David.

[1] Bless the LORD, O my soul,
and all that is within me,
bless his holy name.
[2] Bless the LORD, O my soul,
and do not forget all his benefits—
[3] who forgives all your iniquity,
who heals all your diseases,
[4] who redeems your life from the Pit,
who crowns you with steadfast love and mercy,
[5] who satisfies you with good as long as you live[q]
so that your youth is renewed like the eagle's.

[6] The LORD works vindication
and justice for all who are oppressed.
[7] He made known his ways to Moses,
his acts to the people of Israel.

q 103.5 Meaning of Heb uncertain

4, 9), and social (vv. 6–7). **102:12–22** Prayer for the restoration of Zion as a demonstration of divine rule. **102:25–28** A renewed expression of confidence in God from the creation to the present. The psalm weaves the individual and community together (both suffer and both will be restored) in a kind of model prayer.

Ps. 103:1–22 Song of praise and thanksgiving. This psalm is an extended meditation on Exod. 34:6–7 in continuity with Ps. 102. It begins with a summons to praise and thanksgiving (vv. 1–5), then two characterizations of God (vv. 6–14, 15–18), and ends with a renewed call to praise (vv. 19–22). **Superscription.** *Of David.* See note on Ps. 3 superscription. **103:1–2** *Bless the LORD* is a first-person blessing vow. *Soul* means self. The blessing and praise introduce the psalmist's reflection of the gift of divine presence. **103:3–5** The repetition of the relative particle *who* presents the reasons for praise. God is the founder of forgiveness and healing. **103:4** *The Pit.* See Pss. 16:10; 28:1; 30:9; 69:15; 88:4, 6; 94:13; 143:7. **103:6–14** Description of God. **103:7** *Moses.* See note on Ps. 77:20.

⁸ The LORD is merciful and gracious,
　　slow to anger and abounding in
　　　steadfast love.
⁹ He will not always accuse,
　　nor will he keep his anger forever.
¹⁰ He does not deal with us according to
　　our sins
　　nor repay us according to our
　　　iniquities.
¹¹ For as the heavens are high above the
　　earth,
　　so great is his steadfast love toward
　　　those who fear him;
¹² as far as the east is from the west,
　　so far he removes our transgressions
　　　from us.
¹³ As a father has compassion for his
　　children,
　　so the LORD has compassion for those
　　　who fear him.
¹⁴ For he knows how we were made;
　　he remembers that we are dust.

¹⁵ As for mortals, their days are like grass;
　　they flourish like a flower of the field;
¹⁶ for the wind passes over it, and it is gone,
　　and its place knows it no more.
¹⁷ But the steadfast love of the LORD is from
　　everlasting to everlasting
　　on those who fear him,
　　and his righteousness to children's
　　　children,
¹⁸ to those who keep his covenant
　　and remember to do his
　　　commandments.

¹⁹ The LORD has established his throne in
　　the heavens,
　　and his kingdom rules over all.
²⁰ Bless the LORD, O you his angels,
　　you mighty ones who do his bidding,
　　obedient to his spoken word.

²¹ Bless the LORD, all his hosts,
　　his ministers who do his will.
²² Bless the LORD, all his works,
　　in all places of his dominion.
　　Bless the LORD, O my soul.

PSALM 104

¹ Bless the LORD, O my soul.
　　O LORD my God, you are very great.
　　You are clothed with honor and majesty,
² 　　wrapped in light as with a garment.
　　You stretch out the heavens like a tent;
³ 　　you set the beams of your^r chambers
　　　on the waters;
　　you make the clouds your^s chariot;
　　you ride on the wings of the wind;
⁴ you make the winds your^t messengers,
　　fire and flame your^u ministers.

⁵ You set the earth on its foundations,
　　so that it shall never be shaken.
⁶ You cover it with the deep as with a
　　garment;
　　the waters stood above the mountains.
⁷ At your rebuke they flee;
　　at the sound of your thunder they take
　　　to flight.
⁸ They rose up to the mountains, ran down
　　to the valleys,
　　to the place that you appointed for
　　　them.
⁹ You set a boundary that they may not
　　pass,
　　so that they might not again cover the
　　　earth.

¹⁰ You make springs gush forth in the valleys;
　　they flow between the hills,
¹¹ giving drink to every wild animal;
　　the wild asses quench their thirst.

r 104.3 Heb *his*　s 104.3 Heb *his*　t 104.4 Heb *his*
u 104.4 Heb *his*

103:8 *Steadfast love.* See Exod. 34:6. **103:9–14** Compassion of God for frail humans. **103:11** Second occurrence of God's *steadfast love.* **103:15–18** Second description of God. **103:15–16** Human life is transitory, like "dust" (v. 14) and *grass* (see Ps. 90:5–6; Isa. 40:7-8). **103:17–18** Third occurrence of *steadfast love,* here tied to *his covenant.* **103:19–22** *Bless the LORD* frames the psalm (vv. 1-2, 20-22). Here it is a cosmic blessing vow as the psalmist calls on *angels,* God's *hosts* and *ministers,* and *all his works* to bless God.

　　Ps. 104:1–35 Creation hymn of praise. The psalm has two sections. The first is a celebration of facets of creation (vv. 2–23); the second is the creator's reign (vv. 24–35a). These sections are surrounded by calls to blessing and praise in the first and last lines. The psalm is similar to the Egyptian "Hymn to Aten," the sun god. **104:1** *Bless the LORD.* See note on Ps. 103:1–2. **104:2** Description of God as the creator *wrapped in light. The heavens like a tent* is reminiscent of the tabernacle. **104:5–9** Ancient account of creation. God creates by overcoming the primordial chaos waters (see Pss. 74, 93). **104:10–13** God

¹² By the streams^v the birds of the air have
their habitation;
they sing among the branches.
¹³ From your lofty abode you water the
mountains;
the earth is satisfied with the fruit of
your work.

¹⁴ You cause the grass to grow for the cattle
and plants for people to cultivate,
to bring forth food from the earth
¹⁵ and wine to gladden the human heart,
oil to make the face shine
and bread to strengthen the human
heart.
¹⁶ The trees of the field^w are watered
abundantly,
the cedars of Lebanon that he planted.
¹⁷ In them the birds build their nests;
the stork has its home in the fir trees.
¹⁸ The high mountains are for the wild goats;
the rocks are a refuge for the coneys.
¹⁹ You have made the moon to mark the
seasons;
the sun knows its time for setting.
²⁰ You make darkness, and it is night,
when all the animals of the forest
come creeping out.
²¹ The young lions roar for their prey,
seeking their food from God.
²² When the sun rises, they withdraw
and lie down in their dens.
²³ People go out to their work
and to their labor until the evening.

²⁴ O Lord, how manifold are your works!
In wisdom you have made them all;
the earth is full of your creatures.
²⁵ There is the sea, great and wide;
creeping things innumerable are there,
living things both small and great.

²⁶ There go the ships
and Leviathan that you formed to
sport in it.

²⁷ These all look to you
to give them their food in due season;
²⁸ when you give to them, they gather it up;
when you open your hand, they are
filled with good things.
²⁹ When you hide your face, they are
dismayed;
when you take away their breath,
they die
and return to their dust.
³⁰ When you send forth your spirit,^x they
are created,
and you renew the face of the ground.

³¹ May the glory of the Lord endure
forever;
may the Lord rejoice in his works—
³² who looks on the earth and it trembles,
who touches the mountains and they
smoke.
³³ I will sing to the Lord as long as I live;
I will sing praise to my God while I
have being.
³⁴ May my meditation be pleasing to him,
for I rejoice in the Lord.
³⁵ Let sinners be consumed from the earth,
and let the wicked be no more.
Bless the Lord, O my soul.
Praise the Lord!

Psalm 105

¹ O give thanks to the Lord; call on his
name;
make known his deeds among the
peoples.

v 104.12 Heb *By them* w 104.16 Gk: Heb *trees of the Lord*
x 104.30 Or *your breath*

orders the waters. **104:14–23** God provides water, food, and shelter for all of creation. The order of creation is framed with people at the beginning (v. 14) and end (v. 23). **104:16** *Cedars of Lebanon.* A region north of Israel and west of Syria known for its lumber (see Ps. 29:5). **104:18** *Coneys* are rabbits. **104:24–32** *How manifold are your works* refers to all of God's creation. The focus here is on divine interaction with creation. **104:26** *Leviathan* is the primordial monster of Ugaritic literature, a metaphor for chaotic forces (see Job 3:8; 41:1; Isa. 27:1). Here the image of Leviathan is playful, thus underscoring God's great power (see **"Leviathan," p. 735**). **104:33–35** Announcement of song by the psalmist. **104:35** *Bless the Lord.* The psalm ends similarly to how it begins, with a benediction/blessing of praise.

Ps. 105:1–45 Historical psalm. Psalms 105 and 106 are paired at the end of Book IV. Psalm 105 recounts God's faithfulness to the people of Israel. See also 1 Chr. 16:9, 12, which incorporate these psalms into the Chronicler's work. There is no superscription. The psalm begins with a call to praise (vv. 1–6), followed by a recount of Israel's salvation history (vv. 7–44), and ends with a renewed call to praise (v. 45). **105:1** *O give thanks* is a call to worship (see Pss. 106:1; 107:1; 118:1, 29; 136:1, 2, 3,

2 Sing to him, sing praises to him;
 tell of all his wonderful works.
3 Glory in his holy name;
 let the hearts of those who seek the
 LORD rejoice.
4 Seek the LORD and his strength;
 seek his presence continually.
5 Remember the wonderful works he has
 done,
 his miracles and the judgments he has
 uttered,
6 O offspring of his servant Abraham,[y]
 children of Jacob, his chosen ones.

7 He is the LORD our God;
 his judgments are in all the earth.
8 He is mindful of his covenant forever,
 of the word that he commanded for a
 thousand generations,
9 the covenant that he made with
 Abraham,
 his sworn promise to Isaac,
10 which he confirmed to Jacob as a statute,
 to Israel as an everlasting
 covenant,
11 saying, "To you I will give the land of
 Canaan
 as your portion for an inheritance."

12 When they were few in number,
 of little account and strangers in it,
13 wandering from nation to nation,
 from one kingdom to another people,
14 he allowed no one to oppress them;
 he rebuked kings on their account,
15 saying, "Do not touch my anointed ones;
 do my prophets no harm."

16 When he summoned famine against the
 land
 and cut off every supply of bread,[z]
17 he had sent a man ahead of them,
 Joseph, who had been sold as a slave.

18 His feet were hurt with fetters;
 his neck was put in a collar of
 iron;
19 until what he had said came to pass,
 the word of the LORD kept testing him.
20 The king sent and released him;
 the ruler of the peoples set him free.
21 He made him lord of his house
 and ruler of all his possessions,
22 to instruct[a] his officials at his pleasure
 and to teach his elders wisdom.

23 Then Israel came to Egypt;
 Jacob lived as an alien in the land of
 Ham.
24 And the LORD made his people very fruitful
 and made them stronger than their
 foes,
25 whose hearts he then turned to hate his
 people,
 to deal craftily with his servants.

26 He sent his servant Moses
 and Aaron, whom he had chosen.
27 They performed his signs among them
 and miracles in the land of Ham.
28 He sent darkness and made the land dark;
 they rebelled[b] against his words.
29 He turned their waters into blood
 and caused their fish to die.
30 Their land swarmed with frogs,
 even in the chambers of their kings.
31 He spoke, and there came swarms of flies
 and gnats throughout their country.
32 He gave them hail for rain
 and lightning that flashed through
 their land.
33 He struck their vines and fig trees
 and shattered the trees of their
 country.

y 105.6 Or *Israel*   z 105.16 Heb *staff of bread*   a 105.22 Gk
Syr Jerome: Heb *to bind*   b 105.28 Cn Compare Gk Syr:
Heb *they did not rebel*

26). See **"Worship," p. 761**. **105:5** *Remember the wonderful works* is a reference to what God has done for Israel (see Pss. 105:2; 106:7; 107:8, 15, 21, 31). Remembering includes reenactment in worship. **105:6** *Offspring of his servant Abraham* and *children of Jacob* are designations for the people of Israel. **105:7-15** God's faithfulness. **105:8-10** *Mindful of his covenant* (see Ps. 111:5). God made an ancestral covenant promise of land to Abraham and Sarah, Isaac and Rebecca, Jacob (Israel), Rachel, and Leah. See Gen. 12:1-7; 15:18-21; 26:2-5; 28:13-15. **105:15** The prohibition of attacks on *my anointed ones* and *prophets* indicates that the ancestral figures anticipate religious leaders and maybe messianic figures. **105:16-23** The story of *Joseph* (see Gen. 37, 39-50). **105:23** *Ham* is the son of Noah (Gen. 9:20-26; 10), progenitor of Egypt (Gen. 10:6b; Ps. 78:51). **105:24-36** The story of Hebrew people in Egypt with *Moses and Aaron* with a focus on the plagues, although only eight of the ten plagues (Exod. 7-11) are mentioned. The plagues are also recounted in Ps. 78:44-51 but

³⁴ He spoke, and the locusts came,
  and young locusts without number;
³⁵ they devoured all the vegetation in their
    land
  and ate up the fruit of their ground.
³⁶ He struck down all the firstborn in their
    land,
  the first issue of all their strength.

³⁷ Then he brought Israel^c out with silver
    and gold,
  and there was no one among their
    tribes who stumbled.
³⁸ Egypt was glad when they departed,
  for dread of them had fallen
    upon it.
³⁹ He spread a cloud for a covering
  and fire to give light by night.
⁴⁰ They asked, and he brought quails
  and gave them food from heaven in
    abundance.
⁴¹ He opened the rock, and water gushed
    out;
  it flowed through the desert like a
    river.
⁴² For he remembered his holy promise
  and Abraham, his servant.

⁴³ So he brought his people out with joy,
  his chosen ones with singing.
⁴⁴ He gave them the lands of the nations,
  and they took possession of the
    wealth of the peoples,
⁴⁵ that they might keep his statutes
  and observe his laws.
  Praise the LORD!

PSALM 106

¹ Praise the LORD!
  O give thanks to the LORD, for he is
    good,
  for his steadfast love endures forever.
² Who can utter the mighty doings of the
    LORD
  or declare all his praise?
³ Happy are those who observe justice,
  who do righteousness at all times.

⁴ Remember us,^d O LORD, when you show
    favor to your people;
  help us^e when you deliver them,
⁵ that we may see the prosperity of your
    chosen ones,
  that we may rejoice in the gladness of
    your nation,
  that we may glory in your heritage.

⁶ Both we and our ancestors have sinned;
  we have committed iniquity, have
    done wickedly.
⁷ Our ancestors, when they were in Egypt,
  did not consider your wonderful
    works;
  they did not remember the abundance of
    your steadfast love
  but rebelled against the Most High^f at
    the Red Sea.^g
⁸ Yet he saved them for his name's sake,
  so that he might make known his
    mighty power.

c 105.37 Heb *them*   d 106.4 Heb mss Gk: MT *me*
e 106.4 Heb mss Gk: MT *me*   f 106.7 Cn: Heb *rebelled at the
sea*   g 106.7 Or *Sea of Reeds*

in a different order. **105:37–45** The story of the exodus and the wilderness wanderings, culminating in the giving of the land. There is no negative appraisal of this period, like there is in Ps. 106. God bestowed the gifts of *a cloud, fire, quails* for food, and *water*. **105:37–38** See Exod. 12:35–36. **105:43–44** Abbreviated description of the entry into the land, lacking any of the specific details found in either Joshua or Judges. **105:45** The gift of the land is accompanied by the statutes and laws of God as covenant instruction. Living as a covenant people gives witness to their relationship with the God who provided and was with them throughout this history.

  Ps. 106:1–48 Community lament. This lament recounts the repeated faithlessness of Israel. It is paired with Ps. 105 at the end of Book IV. There is no superscription. It begins with an introduction of praise and thanksgiving (vv. 1–5), followed by a historical recital of the exodus, wilderness wanderings, and entrance into the land (vv. 6–46), concluding with more praise and thanksgiving (vv. 47–48). **106:1** *O give thanks* (see Pss. 105:1; 107:1; 118:1, 29; 136:1, 2, 3, 26) opens the psalm with a call to praise. **106:2** The question of who can recount mighty acts of God's "steadfast love" (v. 1) is answered in the next verse. **106:3** *Happy* is a didactic observation (see Pss. 1:1; 2:12; 33:12; 34:8) and an answer to the previous question: those who live in *justice* and *righteousness*. **106:4** *Remember* is a metaphor for mindfulness and action, either human or divine, that can bring hope for a better future. **106:6** Quick transition to a confession of sin, sins of both the past and present. **106:7–9** Israel's sin and God's faithfulness at the Sea of Reeds, or Red Sea (Exod. 14–15). See note

⁹ He rebuked the Red Sea,ᵇ and it became
    dry;
    he led them through the deep as
        through a desert.
¹⁰ So he saved them from the hand of the foe
    and delivered them from the hand of
        the enemy.
¹¹ The waters covered their adversaries;
    not one of them was left.
¹² Then they believed his words;
    they sang his praise.

¹³ But they soon forgot his works;
    they did not wait for his counsel.
¹⁴ But they had a wanton craving in the
    wilderness
    and put God to the test in the desert;
¹⁵ he gave them what they asked
    but sent a wasting disease among them.

¹⁶ They were jealous of Moses in the camp
    and of Aaron, the holy one of the Lord.
¹⁷ The earth opened and swallowed up
    Dathan
    and covered the faction of Abiram.
¹⁸ Fire also broke out in their company;
    the flame burned up the wicked.

¹⁹ They made a calf at Horeb
    and worshiped a cast image.
²⁰ They exchanged the glory of Godⁱ
    for the image of an ox that eats grass.
²¹ They forgot God, their Savior,
    who had done great things in Egypt,
²² wondrous works in the land of Ham,
    and awesome deeds by the Red Sea.ʲ
²³ Therefore he said he would destroy them—
    had not Moses, his chosen one,
  stood in the breach before him,
    to turn away his wrath from
    destroying them.

²⁴ Then they despised the pleasant land,
    having no faith in his promise.
²⁵ They grumbled in their tents
    and did not obey the voice of the Lord.
²⁶ Therefore he raised his hand and swore
    to them

that he would make them fall in the
    wilderness
²⁷ and would disperseᵏ their descendants
    among the nations,
    scattering them over the lands.

²⁸ Then they attached themselves to the
    Baal of Peor
    and ate sacrifices offered to the dead;
²⁹ they provoked the Lord to anger with
    their deeds,
    and a plague broke out among them.
³⁰ Then Phinehas stood up and interceded,
    and the plague was stopped.
³¹ And that has been reckoned to him as
    righteousness
    from generation to generation forever.

³² They angered the Lordˡ at the waters of
    Meribah,
    and it went ill with Moses on their
    account,
³³ for they made his spirit bitter,
    and he spoke words that were rash.

³⁴ They did not destroy the peoples,
    as the Lord had commanded them,
³⁵ but they mingled with the nations
    and learned to do as they did.
³⁶ They served their idols,
    which became a snare to them.
³⁷ They sacrificed their sons
    and their daughters to the demons;
³⁸ they poured out innocent blood,
    the blood of their sons and daughters,
  whom they sacrificed to the idols of
    Canaan,
    and the land was polluted with blood.
³⁹ Thus they became unclean by their acts
    and prostituted themselves in their
    doings.

⁴⁰ Then the anger of the Lord was kindled
    against his people,
    and he abhorred his heritage;

h 106.9 Or *Sea of Reeds*   *i* 106.20 Compare Gk mss: Heb
exchanged their glory   *j* 106.22 Or *Sea of Reeds*   *k* 106.27 Syr:
Heb *cause to fall*   *l* 106.32 Heb *him*

at Exod. 13:18. **106:13-15** Israel's sin and God's faithfulness during Israel's rebellion in the wilderness (Num. 11). **106:16-18** Rebellion against divine leadership in the wilderness (Num. 16). **106:19-23** Rebellion at Sinai (Exod. 32). **106:24-27** Israel's sin and God's faithfulness in the wilderness (see Num. 14). **106:28-31** The idolatrous transgression at Baal-peor (Num. 25). **106:32-33** Israel's rebellion at Meribah (Num. 20). **106:34-39** Israel's sin and God's faithfulness during the time of the judges. **106:40-46** The faithlessness provokes the exile. The language is also reminiscent of the cycle

⁴¹ he gave them into the hand of the
nations,
so that those who hated them ruled
over them.
⁴² Their enemies oppressed them,
and they were brought into subjection
under their power.
⁴³ Many times he delivered them,
but they were rebellious in their
purposes
and were brought low through their
iniquity.
⁴⁴ Nevertheless, he regarded their distress
when he heard their cry.
⁴⁵ For their sake he remembered his
covenant
and showed compassion according to
the abundance of his steadfast
love.
⁴⁶ He caused them to be pitied
by all who held them captive.

⁴⁷ Save us, O Lord our God,
and gather us from among the
nations,
that we may give thanks to your holy
name
and glory in your praise.

⁴⁸ Blessed be the Lord, the God of Israel,
from everlasting to everlasting.
And let all the people say, "Amen."
Praise the Lord!

BOOK V
(PSALMS 107–150)

Psalm 107

¹ O give thanks to the Lord, for he is good,
for his steadfast love endures forever.
² Let the redeemed of the Lord say so,
those he redeemed from trouble
³ and gathered in from the lands,
from the east and from the west,
from the north and from the south.^m

⁴ Some wandered in desert wastes,
finding no way to an inhabited town;
⁵ hungry and thirsty,
their soul fainted within them.
⁶ Then they cried to the Lord in their
trouble,
and he delivered them from their
distress;
⁷ he led them by a straight way,
until they reached an inhabited town.
⁸ Let them thank the Lord for his steadfast
love,
for his wonderful works to
humankind.
⁹ For he satisfies the thirsty,
and the hungry he fills with good
things.

¹⁰ Some sat in darkness and in gloom,
prisoners in misery and in irons,

m 107.3 Cn: Heb *sea*

in the book of Judges. See Judg. 2:11–16. **106:45** Divine *steadfast love* and *covenant* bring hope for deliverance. **106:47** Petition: *save us* (see Pss. 80:2; 118:25). The current crisis is the Babylonian exile. **106:48** A doxology ends Book IV (Pss. 90–106), as other books (see Pss. 41:13; 72:18–19; 150:1–6).

Book V: Pss. 107–150 Book V contains several collections of psalms, grouped together by genre, content, or association with David. Book V begins with historical songs of thanksgiving (Pss. 107, 108) that are followed by a collection called the Egyptian Hallel (Pss. 113–118), praise psalms associated with the celebration of Passover. In the Jewish tradition, Pss. 113–114 and 115–118 are sung at the Passover Seder (the ritual meal). Framing the Egyptian Hallel, Pss. 111, 112, and 119 share a torah-oriented frame, celebrating divine law. Psalms 120–134 are Songs of Ascent. David does not show up decisively in Books III and IV of the Psalter but appears again in Book V in Pss. 108, 109, and 110 as well as the final Davidic collection, Pss. 138–145. Psalms 146–150 provide the closing doxology, not just for Book V but also for the book of Psalms as a whole.

Ps. 107:1–43 Communal psalm of thanksgiving. The psalm works as a liturgical reflection of divine intervention on behalf of the community of faith. The similarities to passages in the book of Isaiah indicate a likely postexilic date for the psalm, as do the references to gathering in people in v. 3. **107:1** *O give thanks.* See Pss. 105:1; 106:1; 118:1, 29; 136:1, 2, 3, 26. **107:2** *Let the redeemed of the Lord say so* (see Isa. 62:12) refers to those saved by God in the four vignettes that follow the opening call to give thanks. Each vignette includes a description of distress, a prayer to the Lord, details of delivery, and an expression of thanks. **107:4–9** Vignette 1 is a description of the wilderness experience. **107:6** *Then they cried to the Lord* is the first refrain of distress (see vv. 13, 19, 28). **107:8** *Let them thank the Lord* is the first refrain of thanksgiving (see vv. 15, 21, 31). **107:10–16** Vignette 2 concerns prisoners set free and thanks

¹¹ for they had rebelled against the words
  of God
    and spurned the counsel of the Most
    High.
¹² Their hearts were bowed down with
  hard labor;
    they fell down, with no one to help.
¹³ Then they cried to the LORD in their
  trouble,
    and he saved them from their distress;
¹⁴ he brought them out of darkness and
  gloom,
    and broke their bonds apart.
¹⁵ Let them thank the LORD for his steadfast
  love,
    for his wonderful works to
    humankind.
¹⁶ For he shatters the doors of bronze
    and cuts in two the bars of iron.

¹⁷ Some were sick" through their sinful ways
    and because of their iniquities
    endured affliction;
¹⁸ they loathed any kind of food,
    and they drew near to the gates of
    death.
¹⁹ Then they cried to the LORD in their trouble,
    and he saved them from their distress;
²⁰ he sent out his word and healed them
    and delivered them from destruction.
²¹ Let them thank the LORD for his steadfast
  love,
    for his wonderful works to humankind.
²² And let them offer thanksgiving sacrifices
    and tell of his deeds with songs of joy.

²³ Some went down to the sea in ships,
    doing business on the mighty waters;
²⁴ they saw the deeds of the LORD,
    his wondrous works in the deep.
²⁵ For he commanded and raised the
  stormy wind,
    which lifted up the waves of the sea.
²⁶ They mounted up to heaven; they went
  down to the depths;
    their courage melted away in their
    calamity;
²⁷ they reeled and staggered like drunkards
    and were at their wits' end.

²⁸ Then they cried to the LORD in their
  trouble,
    and he brought them out from their
    distress;
²⁹ he made the storm be still,
    and the waves of the sea were hushed.
³⁰ Then they were glad because they had
  quiet,
    and he brought them to their desired
    haven.
³¹ Let them thank the LORD for his steadfast
  love,
    for his wonderful works to humankind.
³² Let them extol him in the congregation
  of the people
    and praise him in the assembly of the
    elders.

³³ He turns rivers into a desert,
    springs of water into thirsty ground,
³⁴ a fruitful land into a salty waste,
    because of the wickedness of its
    inhabitants.
³⁵ He turns a desert into pools of water,
    a parched land into springs of water.
³⁶ And there he lets the hungry live,
    and they establish a town to live in;
³⁷ they sow fields and plant vineyards
    and get a fruitful yield.
³⁸ By his blessing they multiply greatly,
    and he does not let their cattle decrease.

³⁹ When they are diminished and brought
  low
    through oppression, trouble, and
    sorrow,
⁴⁰ he pours contempt on princes
    and makes them wander in trackless
    wastes,
⁴¹ but he raises up the needy out of distress
    and makes their families like flocks.
⁴² The upright see it and are glad,
    and all wickedness stops its mouth.
⁴³ Let those who are wise pay attention to
    these things
    and consider the steadfast love of the
    LORD.

n 107.17 Cn: Heb *fools*

God for God's deliverance. **107:17–22** Vignette 3 is about the sick who are healed by God and give thanks. **107:23–32** Vignette 4 describes a storm at sea and sailors rescued from a shipwreck. **107:30–32** Thanksgiving for those saved from the peril of the sea and a description of the divine power to save the people. **107:33–42** God's saving power is portrayed as divine reversals of fortunes. **107:33** *Rivers into a desert.* See Isa. 35:6b. **107:35** See Isa. 41:17–18. **107:43** Final word of admonition for the *wise*.

PSALM 108

A Song. A Psalm of David.

¹ My heart is steadfast, O God, my heart is
  steadfast;[o]
  I will sing and make melody.
  Awake, my soul![p]
² Awake, O harp and lyre!
  I will awake the dawn.
³ I will give thanks to you, O LORD, among
  the peoples,
  and I will sing praises to you among
  the nations.
⁴ For your steadfast love is higher than the
  heavens,
  and your faithfulness reaches to the
  clouds.

⁵ Be exalted, O God, above the heavens,
  and let your glory be over all the earth.
⁶ Give victory with your right hand, and
  answer me,
  so that those whom you love may be
  rescued.

⁷ God has promised in his sanctuary:[q]
  "With exultation I will divide up
  Shechem
  and portion out the Vale of Succoth.
⁸ Gilead is mine; Manasseh is mine;
  Ephraim is my helmet;
  Judah is my scepter.
⁹ Moab is my washbasin;
  on Edom I hurl my shoe;
  over Philistia I shout in triumph."

¹⁰ Who will bring me to the fortified city?
  Who will lead me to Edom?

¹¹ Have you not rejected us, O God?
  You do not go out, O God, with our
  armies.
¹² O grant us help against the foe,
  for human help is worthless.
¹³ With God we shall do valiantly;
  it is he who will tread down our
  foes.

PSALM 109

To the leader. Of David. A Psalm.

¹ Do not be silent, O God of my praise.
² For wicked and deceitful mouths are
  opened against me,
  speaking against me with lying
  tongues.
³ They surround me with words of hate
  and attack me without cause.
⁴ In return for my love they accuse me,
  even while I make prayer for them.[r]
⁵ So they reward me evil for good
  and hatred for my love.

⁶ They say,[s] "Appoint a wicked man against
  him;
  let an accuser stand on his right.
⁷ When he is tried, let him be found
  guilty;
  let his prayer be counted as sin.
⁸ May his days be few;
  may another seize his position.
⁹ May his children be orphans
  and his wife a widow.

o 108.1 Heb mss Gk Syr: MT lacks *my heart is steadfast*
p 108.1 Cn Compare 57.8: Heb *also my soul*   q 108.7 Or *by
his holiness*   r 109.4 Syr: Heb *I prayer*   s 109.6 Heb lacks
They say

Ps. 108:1–13 Individual thanksgiving psalm and communal lament. Psalm 108 repeats portions of two other psalms: 57:7–11 (an individual psalm of thanksgiving) and 60:5–12 (a communal lament). The intertextuality of Ps. 108 indicates an exilic or postexilic historical context. Psalm 108 also provides a counterpoint to Ps. 107. **Superscription.** *A Song. A Psalm of David.* See note on Ps. 3 superscription. **108:1–5** Parallel to Ps. 57:7–11 is a first-person statement of disposition and singing. **108:6–13** Parallel to Ps. 60:5–12 is a petition to God. The psalmist lists *Shechem, Succoth, Gilead, Manasseh, Ephraim, Judah, Moab, Edom,* and *Philistia* as representations of "the peoples" in v. 3. **108:12** *O grant us help* petitions God as helper, which can have military overtones. Such a plea to God's martial aid would have fit the postexilic period (see also Exod. 18:4; Deut. 33:26; Ps. 33:20). **108:13** A twofold expression of trust. Divine and human alliance will generate strong deeds. The second phrase affirms that God *will tread down our foes.*

Ps. 109:1–31 Lament. This psalm returns to the lament genre with an imprecatory or cursing voice. The combination of lament and cursing fits the historical setting of the return from the Babylonian exile toward the end of the sixth century BCE. **Superscription.** *To the leader. Of David. A Psalm.* See notes on Pss. 3 and 4 superscriptions. **109:1–5** Petition against the adversaries. **109:1** *Do not be silent.* See Pss. 28:1; 35:22; 39:12; 83:1. **109:6–19** Complaint against the psalmist containing a litany of curses, including curses to the children of the psalmist. **109:6–7** The language is of a

¹⁰ May his children wander about and beg;
　　may they be driven out of[t] the ruins
　　　they inhabit.
¹¹ May the creditor seize all that he has;
　　may strangers plunder the fruits of his
　　　toil.
¹² May there be no one to do him a
　　　kindness
　　nor anyone to pity his orphaned
　　　children.
¹³ May his posterity be cut off;
　　may his name be blotted out in the
　　　second generation.
¹⁴ May the iniquity of his father[u] be
　　　remembered before the Lord,
　　and do not let the sin of his mother be
　　　blotted out.
¹⁵ Let them be before the Lord continually,
　　and may his[v] memory be cut off from
　　　the earth.
¹⁶ For he did not remember to show
　　　kindness
　　but pursued the poor and needy
　　and the brokenhearted to their death.
¹⁷ He loved to curse; let curses come on
　　　him.
　　He did not like blessing; may it be far
　　　from him.
¹⁸ He clothed himself with cursing as his
　　　coat;
　　may it soak into his body like water,
　　like oil into his bones.
¹⁹ May it be like a garment that he wraps
　　　around himself,
　　like a belt that he wears every day."

²⁰ May that be the reward of my accusers
　　　from the Lord,
　　of those who speak evil against my
　　　life.
²¹ But you, O Lord my Lord,
　　act on my behalf for your name's
　　　sake;

because your steadfast love is good,
　　deliver me.
²² For I am poor and needy,
　　and my heart is pierced within me.
²³ I am gone like a shadow at evening;
　　I am shaken off like a locust.
²⁴ My knees are weak through fasting;
　　my body has become gaunt.
²⁵ I am an object of scorn to my
　　　accusers;
　　when they see me, they shake their
　　　heads.

²⁶ Help me, O Lord my God!
　　Save me according to your steadfast
　　　love.
²⁷ Let them know that this is your hand;
　　you, O Lord, have done it.
²⁸ Let them curse, but you will bless.
　　Let my assailants be put to shame;[w]
　　may your servant be glad.
²⁹ May my accusers be clothed with
　　　dishonor;
　　may they be wrapped in their own
　　　shame as in a mantle.
³⁰ With my mouth I will give great thanks
　　to the Lord;
　　I will praise him in the midst of the
　　　throng.
³¹ For he stands at the right hand of the
　　　needy,
　　to save them from those who would
　　　condemn them to death.

Psalm 110

Of David. A Psalm.
¹ The Lord says to my lord,
　　"Sit at my right hand
　until I make your enemies your
　　footstool."

t 109.10 Gk: Heb *may they seek*　*u* 109.14 Cn: Heb *fathers*
v 109.15 Gk: Heb *their*　*w* 109.28 Gk: Heb *They have risen up
and have been put to shame*

judicial process where the psalmist is accused and *found guilty.* **109:16** The psalmist is accused of oppressing the poor. **109:17–18** The psalmist is accused of cursing. **109:20–29** The psalmist petitions God for relief. **109:20** The speaker claims that the accusers *speak evil against* him; in other words, they falsely accuse him of wrongdoing. **109:22** *I am poor and needy.* See Pss. 37:14; 40:17; 70:5; 74:21; 86:1. The psalmist uses vulnerability instead of power to convince God of the importance of intervention. **109:30–31** The psalm ends with expressions of trust and praise. **109:30** *I will give great thanks to the Lord* is a typical phrase in the lament genre.

　　Ps. 110:1–7 Royal psalm. See also Pss. 2, 18, 20, 21, 45, 72, 89, 101, 132. Book V of the Psalter is often considered a postexilic collection; however, Ps. 110 probably comes from the monarchy of ancient Israel's history (ca. 900–586 BCE). **Superscription.** *Of David. A Psalm.* See note on Ps. 3 superscription. **110:1–3** A word to the king. **110:1** *The Lord says* is a prophetic formula that often

² The Lord sends out from Zion
    your mighty scepter.
    Rule in the midst of your foes.
³ Your people will offer themselves willingly
    on the day you lead your forces
    on the holy mountains.ˣ
From the womb of the morning,
    like dew, your youthʸ will come to you.
⁴ The Lord has sworn and will not change
    his mind,
    "You are a priest forever according to
        the order of Melchizedek."ᶻ

⁵ The Lord is at your right hand;
    he will shatter kings on the day of his
        wrath.
⁶ He will execute judgment among the
        nations,
    filling them with corpses;
he will shatter heads
    over the wide earth.
⁷ He will drink from the stream by the path;
    therefore he will lift up his head.

Psalm 111

¹ Praise the Lord!
I will give thanks to the Lord with my
        whole heart,
    in the company of the upright, in the
        congregation.
² Great are the works of the Lord,
    studied by all who delight in them.

³ Full of honor and majesty is his work,
    and his righteousness endures forever.
⁴ He has gained renown by his wonderful
        deeds;
    the Lord is gracious and merciful.
⁵ He provides food for those who fear him;
    he is ever mindful of his covenant.
⁶ He has shown his people the power of
        his works,
    in giving them the heritage of the
        nations.
⁷ The works of his hands are faithful and
        just;
    all his precepts are trustworthy.
⁸ They are established forever and ever,
    to be performed with faithfulness and
        uprightness.
⁹ He sent redemption to his people;
    he has commanded his covenant forever.
    Holy and awesome is his name.
¹⁰ The fear of the Lord is the beginning of
        wisdom;
    all those who practice itᵃ have a good
        understanding.
    His praise endures forever.

Psalm 112

¹ Praise the Lord!
    Happy are those who fear the Lord,

*x 110.3 Heb mss Symmachus Jerome: MT in holy splendor
y 110.3 Cn: Heb the dew of your youth   z 110.4 Or forever, a
rightful king by my edict   a 111.10 Gk Syr: Heb them*

introduces an oracle (see, e.g., Amos 1:3). *Right hand* is a place of honor. *Footstool* refers to the practice of victorious kings placing their feet on the backs (or even necks) of captured enemies. The New Testament quotes this verse to refer to the exaltation of Christ; see Acts 2:34; 1 Cor. 15:25; Heb. 1:3, 13. The verse is used by Jesus and his opponents; see Matt. 22:44; Mark 12:36; Luke 20:42. **110:2** *Zion* is the source of divine and royal power. *Scepter* is a metonym for the rule of the monarch. **110:4–7** Declaration of the king's priestly functions and prerogatives (see also 2 Sam. 6:13–14, 18; 8:18; 24:25; 1 Kgs. 3:4; 8:14, 55). **110:4** *Order of Melchizedek.* Melchizedek is a priest-king of Jerusalem (possibly a Jebusite) who encounters Abraham (see Gen. 14:17–20). Jesus is also given a royal and priestly role in Hebrews where this verse is quoted (Heb. 5:6, 10; 6:20–7:10).

Ps. 111:1–10 Hymn of praise and thanksgiving. The psalm is an acrostic with each half line beginning with a letter of the Hebrew alphabet (from "alef" to "tav"; see Pss. 9–10, 25, 34, 37, 112, 145). The acrostic form generally is associated with wisdom traditions because of the likely scribal roots of the genre. Psalms 111, 112, and 119 share an emphasis on reverence for the torah. Psalms 111–118 use the term "hallelujah" (*praise the Lord*) as an introduction or refrain. The use of earlier traditions indicates a psalm shaped in the monarchy or later. **111:1** *Praise the Lord!* This imperative begins or concludes several psalms (e.g., see Pss. 112, 113, 135, 146–150). *I will give thanks to the Lord* is a vow (see note on Ps. 7:17). **111:2–4** Recital of divine deeds praised. **111:4** See Exod. 34:6. **111:5–9** Recital of divine deeds described. **111:10** *The fear of the Lord is the beginning of wisdom* introduces wisdom (see Prov. 9:10; cf. Prov. 1:7; 4:7). *Fear of the Lord.* See note on Ps. 19:9.

Ps. 112:1–10 Wisdom psalm. Like Ps. 111, Ps. 112 is an acrostic (see Pss. 9–10, 25, 34, 37, 145). Wisdom-informed psalms give no data on the historical location. Psalm 112, like Pss. 111–118, uses the term "hallelujah" (*praise the Lord*) as an introduction or refrain. **112:1–4** Description of the upright. **112:1** *Praise the*

who greatly delight in his
commandments.

2 Their descendants will be mighty in the
land;
the generation of the upright will be
blessed.

3 Wealth and riches are in their houses,
and their righteousness endures forever.

4 They rise in the darkness as a light for
the upright;
they are gracious, merciful, and
righteous.

5 It is well with those who deal generously
and lend,
who conduct their affairs with justice.

6 For the righteous will never be moved;
they will be remembered forever.

7 They are not afraid of evil tidings;
their hearts are firm, secure in the Lord.

8 Their hearts are steady; they will not be
afraid;
in the end they will look in triumph on
their foes.

9 They have distributed freely; they have
given to the poor;
their righteousness endures forever;
their horn is exalted in honor.

10 The wicked see it and are angry;
they gnash their teeth and melt away;
the desire of the wicked comes to nothing.

PSALM 113

1 Praise the Lord!
Praise, O servants of the Lord;
praise the name of the Lord.

2 Blessed be the name of the Lord
from this time on and forevermore.

3 From the rising of the sun to its setting,
the name of the Lord is to be
praised.

4 The Lord is high above all nations
and his glory above the heavens.

5 Who is like the Lord our God,
who is seated on high,

6 who looks far down
on the heavens and the earth?

7 He raises the poor from the dust
and lifts the needy from the ash
heap,

8 to make them sit with princes,
with the princes of his people.

9 He gives the barren woman a home,
making her the joyous mother of
children.
Praise the Lord!

PSALM 114

1 ᵇWhen Israel went out from Egypt,
the house of Jacob from a people of
strange language,

2 Judah became God'sᶜ sanctuary,
Israel his dominion.

3 The sea looked and fled;
Jordan turned back.

4 The mountains skipped like rams,
the hills like lambs.

b 114.1 Psalms 114–115 are a single psalm in the earliest
witnesses   c 114.2 Heb *his*

Lord! See note on Ps. 7:17. *Happy*. See note on Ps. 32:1–2. *Fear the Lord* (see note on Ps. 19:9) and *delight* (see Ps. 1) blend together to provide a picture of the righteous. **112:4** The righteous person aspires to reflect the characteristics of God (see Exod. 34:6). **112:5–9** Description of the ones who revere God. Generosity and care for the poor especially mark the righteous person. **112:9** This verse is cited in the New Testament in 2 Cor. 9:9. *Horn*. See Ps. 75:4–5. **112:10** Description of the fate of the *wicked* (see note on Ps. 1:1).

Ps. 113:1–9 Hymn of praise. This psalm, like Pss. 111–118, uses the term "hallelujah" (*praise the Lord*) as an introduction or refrain. Psalms 113–118 are designated as the Egyptian Hallel because the psalms are sung before (Pss. 113–114) and after (Pss. 115–118) the celebration of the Passover meal. The use of the psalms in later Jewish liturgy gives some clue to their function earlier. They likely come from the postexilic context of Passover celebrations. **113:1–4** A meditation on God's name. **113:1** *Praise the Lord!* See note on Ps. 7:17. *Praise the name of the Lord* is repeated in v. 3. **113:2** God's name is also *blessed*. **113:5–6** *Who is like the Lord our God?* is a rhetorical question about the incomparability of God (see Exod. 15:11). God is located *on high*, above *the heavens and the earth*. **113:7–9** Description of God as a champion of justice for *the poor*, *the needy*, and *the barren woman*. The phrase *Praise the Lord!* frames the psalm (see v. 1).

Ps. 114:1–8 Hymn of praise. This psalm celebrates the deliverance from Egypt. Psalm 114 is part of the Egyptian Hallel (see note on Ps. 113:1–9). Like Pss. 111–118, Ps. 114 uses the term "hallelujah" (*praise the Lord*) as an introduction or refrain. The liturgical use of the psalm and the reference to earlier traditions indicate a likely date of the late monarchy or exilic period. **114:1** Recital of the exodus from Egypt. **114:2** See Exod. 19:5–6. **114:3–4** Recital of the crossing of the Sea of Reeds, or Red

⁵ Why is it, O sea, that you flee?
　　O Jordan, that you turn back?
⁶ O mountains, that you skip like rams?
　　O hills, like lambs?

⁷ Tremble, O earth, at the presence of the
　　　Lord,
　　at the presence of the God of Jacob,
⁸ who turns the rock into a pool of water,
　　the flint into a spring of water.

PSALM 115

¹ ^dNot to us, O Lord, not to us, but to your
　　name give glory,
　　for the sake of your steadfast love and
　　your faithfulness.
² Why should the nations say,
　　"Where is their God?"

³ Our God is in the heavens;
　　he does whatever he pleases.
⁴ Their idols are silver and gold,
　　the work of human hands.
⁵ They have mouths, but they do not
　　speak;
　　they have eyes, but they do not see.
⁶ They have ears, but they do not hear;
　　they have noses, but they do not smell.
⁷ They have hands, but they do not feel;
　　they have feet, but they do not walk;
　　they make no sound in their throats.
⁸ Those who make them are like them;
　　so are all who trust in them.

⁹ O Israel, trust in the Lord!
　　He is their help and their shield.
¹⁰ O house of Aaron, trust in the Lord!
　　He is their help and their shield.
¹¹ You who fear the Lord, trust in the Lord!
　　He is their help and their shield.

¹² The Lord has been mindful of us; he will
　　bless us;
　　he will bless the house of Israel;
　　he will bless the house of Aaron;
¹³ he will bless those who fear the Lord,
　　both small and great.

¹⁴ May the Lord give you increase,
　　both you and your children.
¹⁵ May you be blessed by the Lord,
　　who made heaven and earth.

¹⁶ The heavens are the Lord's heavens,
　　but the earth he has given to human
　　beings.
¹⁷ The dead do not praise the Lord,
　　nor do any who go down into silence.
¹⁸ But we will bless the Lord
　　from this time on and forevermore.
Praise the Lord!

PSALM 116

¹ I love the Lord because he has heard
　　my voice and my supplications.

d 115.1 Psalms 114–115 are a single psalm in the earliest
witnesses

Sea (Exod. 14; see note at Exod. 13:18) and the Jordan River (Josh. 3); the mountains and the hills react to divine action (see Ps. 29:6). **114:5** Taunting questions to the waters that receded at God's command. **114:7** Challenge to the natural world. **114:8** Reference to the provision of water in the wilderness. See Num. 20.

Ps. 115:1–18 Liturgical prayer. This psalm, like Pss. 111–118, uses the term "hallelujah" (*praise the Lord*) as an introduction or refrain. The use of multiple alternating voices (antiphonal) indicates that this psalm may be a liturgical piece. It is part of the Egyptian Hallel (see note on Ps. 113). The liturgical use of the psalm and the reference to earlier traditions indicate a likely date of the late monarchy or exilic period. **115:1** Request for God to *give glory* to God's own name. **115:2** *Where is their God?* introduces the next section and may indicate that the people are experiencing distress. See also Pss. 42:3; 79:10; Mic. 7:10. **115:3–8** A confession that contrasts the location of God (heaven) and the futility of idols, which are the products of human hands. **115:9–11** A repeated call for trust *in the Lord* (vv. 9, 10, 11). **115:12–15** A statement of confidence in God's blessing. **115:16–18** Declaration of praise and a description of the three-tiered universe: heaven, earth, and the realm of the dead. **115:18** *Praise the Lord!* concludes the psalm.

Ps. 116:1–19 Thanksgiving psalm. This psalm gives thanks for the healing of an individual. Psalm 116, like Pss. 111–118, uses the term "hallelujah" (*praise the Lord*) as an introduction or refrain. It is part of the Egyptian Hallel (see note on Ps. 113). Like many thanksgiving songs, Ps. 116 contains an introduction (vv. 1–2), a narrative describing the speaker's distress and God's deliverance (vv. 3–11), and a conclusion. The liturgical use of the psalm and the reference to earlier traditions indicate a likely date of the late monarchy or exilic period. **116:1–2** The introduction includes a rationale for thanks:

² Because he inclined his ear to me,
   therefore I will call on him as long as
     I live.
³ The snares of death encompassed me;
   the pangs of Sheol laid hold on me;
   I suffered distress and anguish.
⁴ Then I called on the name of the
   Lord,
   "O Lord, I pray, save my life!"

⁵ Gracious is the Lord and righteous;
   our God is merciful.
⁶ The Lord protects the simple;
   when I was brought low, he saved
     me.
⁷ Return, O my soul, to your rest,
   for the Lord has dealt bountifully
     with you.

⁸ For you have delivered my soul from
   death,
   my eyes from tears,
   my feet from stumbling.
⁹ I walk before the Lord
   in the land of the living.
¹⁰ ᵉI kept my faith, even when I said,
   "I am greatly afflicted";
¹¹ I said in my consternation,
   "Everyone is a liar."

¹² What shall I return to the Lord
   for all his bounty to me?

¹³ I will lift up the cup of salvation
   and call on the name of the Lord;
¹⁴ I will pay my vows to the Lord
   in the presence of all his people.
¹⁵ Precious in the sight of the Lord
   is the death of his faithful ones.
¹⁶ O Lord, I am your servant;
   I am your servant, the child of your
     serving girl.
   You have loosed my bonds.
¹⁷ I will offer to you a thanksgiving sacrifice
   and call on the name of the Lord.
¹⁸ I will pay my vows to the Lord
   in the presence of all his people,
¹⁹ in the courts of the house of the Lord,
   in your midst, O Jerusalem.
   Praise the Lord!

Psalm 117

¹ Praise the Lord, all you nations!
   Extol him, all you peoples!
² For great is his steadfast love toward us,
   and the faithfulness of the Lord
     endures forever.
   Praise the Lord!

Psalm 118

¹ O give thanks to the Lord, for he is
   good;
   his steadfast love endures forever!

e 116.10 Some early witnesses begin a new psalm here

because God *has heard my voice*. **116:3–11** Narrative account of trouble and salvation. **116:3** *Snares of death.* See Ps. 18:4–5. *Sheol.* See note on Ps. 6:1–5; Ps. 18:5; see also **"Sheol," p. 695**. Death is figured as a form of constraint, causing *distress and anguish*. **116:4** *Name of the Lord* is an element of petition (see note on Ps. 113). **116:5–7** Description of God. **116:5** See Exod. 34:6. **116:6** *The simple* is a metaphor for persons without knowledge or understanding (see Pss. 19:7; 119:130). **116:8–11** Account of trouble and salvation. **116:9** *Land of the living* contrasts with "Sheol" (v. 3). See note on Ps. 27:13. **116:11** *Everyone is a liar* likely refers to the distress from slander or false accusation. **116:12–19** Conclusion of vow and fulfillment. **116:16** Account of salvation. **116:17–19** Vow and fulfillment, spoken in front of the congregation, *in the courts of the house of the Lord*.

    Ps. 117:1–2 Communal hymn. This psalm, like Pss. 111–118, uses the term "hallelujah" (*praise the Lord*) as an introduction or refrain. It is the shortest psalm in the collection and part of the Egyptian Hallel (see note on Ps. 113). The liturgical use of the psalm and the reference to earlier traditions indicate a likely date of the late monarchy or exilic period. **117:1** *Praise the Lord.* See note on Ps. 7:17. *All you nations.* See Pss. 9:17; 72:11, 17; 86:9; 113:4; 118:10. In the New Testament, Paul cites Ps. 117:1 in Rom. 15:11. *Extol him* is an imperative that only occurs here in the Psalter. References to *all you nations* and *all you peoples* speak to the exilic challenge to an entire world. **117:2** Description of the character of God focusing on God's *steadfast love* and *faithfulness*. **117:2** *Praise the Lord!* frames the psalm.

    Ps. 118:1–29 Liturgy of thanksgiving. The psalmist thanks God for deliverance from the nations. This psalm, like Pss. 111–118, uses the term "hallelujah" (*praise the Lord*) as an introduction or refrain. It is the last psalm of the Egyptian Hallel (see note on Ps. 113). The liturgical use of the psalm and the reference to earlier traditions indicate a likely date of the late monarchy or exilic period. **118:1–18** Account of distress. **118:1–4** Summons to give thanks and responses. **118:1** *O give thanks.* See

² Let Israel say,
 "His steadfast love endures forever."
³ Let the house of Aaron say,
 "His steadfast love endures forever."
⁴ Let those who fear the LORD say,
 "His steadfast love endures forever."

⁵ Out of my distress I called on the LORD;
 the LORD answered me and set me in a
 broad place.
⁶ With the LORD on my side I do not fear.
 What can mortals do to me?
⁷ The LORD is on my side to help me;
 I shall look in triumph on those who
 hate me.
⁸ It is better to take refuge in the LORD
 than to put confidence in mortals.
⁹ It is better to take refuge in the LORD
 than to put confidence in princes.

¹⁰ All nations surrounded me;
 in the name of the LORD I cut them off!
¹¹ They surrounded me, surrounded me on
 every side;
 in the name of the LORD I cut them off!
¹² They surrounded me like bees;
 they blazed*ᶠ* like a fire of thorns;
 in the name of the LORD I cut them off!
¹³ I was pushed hard,*ᵍ* so that I was falling,
 but the LORD helped me.
¹⁴ The LORD is my strength and my
 might;
 he has become my salvation.

¹⁵ There are glad songs of victory in the
 tents of the righteous:
 "The right hand of the LORD does
 valiantly;
¹⁶ the right hand of the LORD is exalted;
 the right hand of the LORD does
 valiantly."
¹⁷ I shall not die, but I shall live
 and recount the deeds of the LORD.

¹⁸ The LORD has punished me severely,
 but he did not give me over to death.

¹⁹ Open to me the gates of righteousness,
 that I may enter through them
 and give thanks to the LORD.

²⁰ This is the gate of the LORD;
 the righteous shall enter through it.

²¹ I thank you that you have answered me
 and have become my salvation.
²² The stone that the builders rejected
 has become the chief cornerstone.
²³ This is the LORD's doing;
 it is marvelous in our eyes.
²⁴ This is the day that the LORD has
 made;
 let us rejoice and be glad in it.*ʰ*
²⁵ Save us, we beseech you, O LORD!
 O LORD, we beseech you, give us
 success!

²⁶ Blessed is the one who comes in the
 name of the LORD.*ⁱ*
 We bless you from the house of the
 LORD.
²⁷ The LORD is God,
 and he has given us light.
 Bind the festal procession with branches,
 up to the horns of the altar.*ʲ*

²⁸ You are my God, and I will give thanks
 to you;
 you are my God; I will extol you.

²⁹ O give thanks to the LORD, for he is
 good,
 for his steadfast love endures forever.

f 118.12 Gk: Heb *were extinguished* *g* 118.13 Gk Syr
Jerome: Heb *You pushed me hard* *h* 118.24 Or *in him*
i 118.26 Or *Blessed in the name of the LORD is the one who comes*
j 118.27 Meaning of Heb uncertain

Pss. 105:1; 106:1; 107:1; 118:29; 136:1, 2, 3, 26. **118:2–4** See Ps. 115:9–10. **118:5–18** Account of trouble and salvation. **118:8–9** A series of *It is better* proverbs. **118:10–12** *Name of the LORD.* See note on Ps. 20:7. **118:11–12** The metaphor of *surrounded* is a threat parallel to Ps. 22:12, where the threatening animals are bulls. Here the threatening animals are *bees.* **118:15–16** Repetition of the metaphor *the right hand of the LORD* as a symbol of power. **118:19–28** Processional thanksgiving ceremony. **118:19** *Open to me the gates* anticipates "the gate of the LORD" (v. 20), indicating that this section is a processional ceremony. *Give thanks to the LORD.* See vv. 1, 21, 28, 29. **118:22** *The stone that the builders rejected* is quoted in the New Testament to refer to Jesus (Matt. 21:42; Acts 4:11; Eph. 2:20; 1 Pet. 2:7). **118:26–29** The liturgical procession moves to the altar (see Lev. 23:40), and the speaker gives a benediction. **118:26** The New Testament uses this verse in Matt. 21:9; Mark 11:9; and Luke 19:38. **118:28–29** *I will give thanks to you* and *O give thanks to the LORD* echo the beginning of the psalm (v. 1).

PSALM 119

¹ Happy are those whose way is
 blameless,
 who walk in the law of the Lord.
² Happy are those who keep his decrees,
 who seek him with their whole
 heart,
³ who also do no wrong
 but walk in his ways.
⁴ You have commanded your precepts
 to be kept diligently.
⁵ O that my ways may be steadfast
 in keeping your statutes!
⁶ Then I shall not be put to shame,
 having my eyes fixed on all your
 commandments.
⁷ I will praise you with an upright heart,
 when I learn your righteous
 ordinances.
⁸ I will observe your statutes;
 do not utterly forsake me.

⁹ How can young people keep their way
 pure?
 By guarding it according to your
 word.
¹⁰ With my whole heart I seek you;
 do not let me stray from your
 commandments.
¹¹ I treasure your word in my heart,
 so that I may not sin against you.
¹² Blessed are you, O Lord;
 teach me your statutes.
¹³ With my lips I declare
 all the ordinances of your mouth.
¹⁴ I delight in the way of your decrees
 as much as in all riches.
¹⁵ I will meditate on your precepts
 and fix my eyes on your ways.
¹⁶ I will delight in your statutes;
 I will not forget your word.

¹⁷ Deal bountifully with your servant,
 so that I may live and observe your
 word.
¹⁸ Open my eyes, so that I may behold
 wondrous things out of your law.
¹⁹ I live as an alien in the land;
 do not hide your commandments
 from me.
²⁰ My soul is consumed with longing
 for your ordinances at all times.
²¹ You rebuke the insolent, accursed ones,
 who wander from your
 commandments;
²² take away from me their scorn and
 contempt,
 for I have kept your decrees.
²³ Even though princes sit plotting against
 me,
 your servant will meditate on your
 statutes.
²⁴ Your decrees are my delight;
 they are my counselors.

²⁵ My soul clings to the dust;
 revive me according to your word.
²⁶ When I told of my ways, you answered
 me;
 teach me your statutes.
²⁷ Make me understand the way of your
 precepts,
 and I will meditate on your wondrous
 works.
²⁸ My soul melts away for sorrow;
 strengthen me according to your
 word.
²⁹ Put false ways far from me,
 and graciously teach me your law.
³⁰ I have chosen the way of faithfulness;
 I set your ordinances before me.
³¹ I cling to your decrees, O Lord;
 let me not be put to shame.

Ps. 119:1–176 Anthem to the instruction of God. This psalm is the longest canonical psalm, with 176 verses. It is a torah psalm that celebrates God's instruction to the people of faith (Pss. 1, 19). It is also an acrostic (see Pss. 9–10, 25, 34, 37, 111, 112, 145). As an acrostic, the psalm follows an alphabetical pattern. It has twenty-two strophes with eight verses in each strophe for each letter of the Hebrew alphabet. The Hebrew term "torah" (translated as "law" or "instruction") resonates with the many synonyms used in the psalm: *decrees, precepts, statutes, commandments, ordinances, word,* and *promise*. Typical of wisdom psalms, the psalmist sets before the community a binary choice. Failure of obedience means *false ways* (v. 29), *selfish gain* (v. 36), *vanities* (v. 37), *shame* (v. 46), and *double-minded[ness]* (v. 113). Two of the hallmarks of a person who has made the wrong decision are wickedness and arrogance (e.g., see vv. 21, 22–51, 61, 78, 85, 110, 121–122). **119:1–8** The Hebrew letter "alef"; praise for the law and those who keep it. **119:9–16** The Hebrew letter "bet"; petition for help in keeping the law. **119:17–24** The Hebrew letter "gimel"; prayer for help in a foreign land. **119:25–32** The Hebrew letter "dalet"; prayer for revitalization through keeping the law. **119:33–40** The

32 I run the way of your commandments,
    for you enlarge my understanding.

33 Teach me, O LORD, the way of your
    statutes,
    and I will observe it to the end.
34 Give me understanding, that I may keep
    your law
    and observe it with my whole heart.
35 Lead me in the path of your
    commandments,
    for I delight in it.
36 Turn my heart to your decrees
    and not to selfish gain.
37 Turn my eyes from looking at vanities;
    be gracious to me[k] according to your
    word.
38 Confirm to your servant your promise,
    which is for those who fear you.
39 Turn away the disgrace that I dread,
    for your ordinances are good.
40 See, I have longed for your precepts;
    in your righteousness be gracious
    to me.[l]

41 Let your steadfast love come to me,
    O LORD,
    your salvation according to your
    promise.
42 Then I shall have an answer for those
    who taunt me,
    for I trust in your word.
43 Do not take the word of truth utterly out
    of my mouth,
    for my hope is in your ordinances.
44 I will keep your law continually,
    forever and ever.
45 I shall walk at liberty,
    for I have sought your precepts.
46 I will also speak of your decrees before
    kings
    and shall not be put to shame;
47 I find my delight in your
    commandments
    because I love them.
48 I revere your commandments, which I
    love,
    and I will meditate on your statutes.

49 Remember your word to your servant,
    in which you have made me hope.

50 This is my comfort in my distress,
    that your promise gives me life.
51 The arrogant utterly deride me,
    but I do not turn away from your law.
52 When I think of your ordinances from
    of old,
    I take comfort, O LORD.
53 Hot indignation seizes me because of the
    wicked,
    those who forsake your law.
54 Your statutes have been my songs
    wherever I make my home.
55 I remember your name in the night,
    O LORD,
    and keep your law.
56 This blessing has fallen to me,
    for I have kept your precepts.

57 The LORD is my portion;
    I promise to keep your words.
58 I implore your favor with all my heart;
    be gracious to me according to your
    promise.
59 When I think of your ways,
    I turn my feet to your decrees;
60 I hurry and do not delay
    to keep your commandments.
61 Though the cords of the wicked
    ensnare me,
    I do not forget your law.
62 At midnight I rise to praise you,
    because of your righteous ordinances.
63 I am a companion of all who fear you,
    of those who keep your precepts.
64 The earth, O LORD, is full of your
    steadfast love;
    teach me your statutes.

65 You have dealt well with your servant,
    O LORD, according to your word.
66 Teach me good judgment and knowledge,
    for I believe in your commandments.
67 Before I was humbled I went astray,
    but now I keep your word.
68 You are good and do good;
    teach me your statutes.
69 The arrogant smear me with lies,
    but with my whole heart I keep your
    precepts.

k 119.37 Q ms: MT *give me life*   *l* 119.40 Q ms: MT *give me life*

Hebrew letter "he"; appeal for instruction and understanding. **119:41–48** The Hebrew letter "vav";
prayer for God's deliverance. **119:49–56** The Hebrew letter "zayin"; request for God to *remember*.
119:57–64 The Hebrew letter "khet"; promises to keep God's word. **119:65–72** The Hebrew letter

70 Their hearts are thick like fat,[m]
　　but I delight in your law.
71 It is good for me that I was humbled,
　　so that I might learn your statutes.
72 The law of your mouth is better to me
　　than thousands of gold and silver
　　　pieces.

73 Your hands have made and fashioned me;
　　give me understanding that I may
　　　learn your commandments.
74 Those who fear you shall see me and
　　　rejoice,
　　because I have hoped in your word.
75 I know, O LORD, that your judgments are
　　　right
　　and that in faithfulness you have
　　　humbled me.
76 Let your steadfast love become my
　　　comfort
　　according to your promise to your
　　　servant.
77 Let your mercy come to me, that I may
　　　live,
　　for your law is my delight.
78 Let the arrogant be put to shame,
　　for they have subverted me with
　　　guile;
　　as for me, I will meditate on your
　　　precepts.
79 Let those who fear you turn to me,
　　so that they may know your decrees.
80 May my heart be blameless in your
　　　statutes,
　　so that I may not be put to shame.

81 My soul languishes for your salvation;
　　I hope in your word.
82 My eyes fail with watching for your
　　　promise;
　　I ask, "When will you comfort me?"
83 For I have become like a wineskin in the
　　　smoke,
　　yet I have not forgotten your statutes.
84 How long must your servant endure?
　　When will you judge those who
　　　persecute me?
85 The arrogant have dug pitfalls for me;
　　they flout your law.
86 All your commandments are enduring;

I am persecuted without cause; help
　me!
87 They have almost made an end of me on
　　earth,
　　but I have not forsaken your precepts.
88 In your steadfast love spare my life,
　　so that I may keep the decrees of your
　　　mouth.

89 The LORD exists forever;
　　your word is firmly fixed in heaven.
90 Your faithfulness endures to all
　　generations;
　　you have established the earth, and it
　　　stands fast.
91 By your appointment they stand today,
　　for all things are your servants.
92 If your law had not been my delight,
　　I would have perished in my
　　　misery.
93 I will never forget your precepts,
　　for by them you have given me life.
94 I am yours; save me,
　　for I have sought your precepts.
95 The wicked lie in wait to destroy me,
　　but I consider your decrees.
96 I have seen a limit to all perfection,
　　but your commandment is
　　　exceedingly broad.

97 Oh, how I love your law!
　　It is my meditation all day long.
98 Your commandment makes me wiser
　　than my enemies,
　　for it is always with me.
99 I have more understanding than all my
　　teachers,
　　for your decrees are my meditation.
100 I understand more than the aged,
　　for I keep your precepts.
101 I hold back my feet from every evil way,
　　in order to keep your word.
102 I do not turn away from your ordinances,
　　for you have taught me.
103 How sweet are your words to my taste,
　　sweeter than honey to my mouth!
104 Through your precepts I get understanding;
　　therefore I hate every false way.

m 119.70 Meaning of Heb uncertain

"tet"; prayer for instruction from God. **119:73–80** The Hebrew letter "yod"; praise for God's creation and prayer for help understanding God's law. **119:81–88** The Hebrew letter "kaf"; the psalmist describes his distress and the persecution he experiences. **119:89–96** The Hebrew letter "lamed"; praise of God and confidence in God's *faithfulness*. **119:97–104** The Hebrew letter "mem"; praise

105 Your word is a lamp to my feet
    and a light to my path.
106 I have sworn an oath and confirmed it,
    to observe your righteous ordinances.
107 I am severely afflicted;
    give me life, O LORD, according to your
    word.
108 Accept my offerings of praise, O LORD,
    and teach me your ordinances.
109 I hold my life in my hand continually,
    but I do not forget your law.
110 The wicked have laid a snare for me,
    but I do not stray from your precepts.
111 Your decrees are my heritage forever;
    they are the joy of my heart.
112 I incline my heart to perform your
    statutes
    forever, to the end.

113 I hate the double-minded,
    but I love your law.
114 You are my hiding place and my shield;
    I hope in your word.
115 Go away from me, you evildoers,
    that I may keep the commandments of
    my God.
116 Uphold me according to your promise,
    that I may live,
    and let me not be put to shame in my
    hope.
117 Hold me up, that I may be safe
    and have regard for your statutes
    continually.
118 You spurn all who go astray from your
    statutes,
    for their cunning is in vain.
119 All the wicked of the earth I count[n] as
    dross;
    therefore I love your decrees.
120 My flesh trembles for fear of you,
    and I am afraid of your judgments.

121 I have done what is just and right;
    do not leave me to my oppressors.
122 Guarantee your servant's well-being;
    do not let the godless oppress me.
123 My eyes fail from watching for your
    salvation

and for the fulfillment of your
    righteous promise.
124 Deal with your servant according to your
    steadfast love,
    and teach me your statutes.
125 I am your servant; give me
    understanding,
    so that I may know your decrees.
126 It is time for the LORD to act,
    for your law has been broken.
127 Truly I love your commandments
    more than gold, more than fine gold.
128 Truly I direct my steps by all your
    precepts;[o]
    I hate every false way.

129 Your decrees are wonderful;
    therefore my soul keeps them.
130 The unfolding of your words gives light;
    it imparts understanding to the
    simple.
131 With open mouth I pant,
    because I long for your commandments.
132 Turn to me and be gracious to me,
    as is your custom toward those who
    love your name.
133 Keep my steps steady according to your
    promise,
    and never let iniquity have dominion
    over me.
134 Redeem me from human oppression,
    that I may keep your precepts.
135 Make your face shine upon your servant,
    and teach me your statutes.
136 My eyes shed streams of tears
    because your law is not kept.

137 You are righteous, O LORD,
    and your judgments are right.
138 You have appointed your decrees in
    righteousness
    and in all faithfulness.
139 My zeal consumes me
    because my foes forget your words.
140 Your promise is well tried,
    and your servant loves it.

n 119.119 Q ms Gk Vg: MT *you bring to an end*   o 119.128 Gk
Jerome: Meaning of Heb uncertain

for God's law. **119:105–112** The Hebrew letter "nun"; the psalmist pledges to adhere to God's word.
119:105 *Your word is a lamp to my feet and a light to my path* is one of the most recognizable lines of
this psalm, occurring frequently in contemporary Christian contexts. **119:113–120** The Hebrew letter
"samek"; the psalmist contrasts his love for the law with the ways of the wicked. **119:121–128** The Hebrew
letter "ayin"; prayer for help and a lament that begins with a statement of innocence and persecution.
119:129–136 The Hebrew letter "pe"; praise of God's law and plea for help. **119:137–144** The Hebrew

141 I am small and despised,
  yet I do not forget your precepts.
142 Your righteousness is an everlasting
  righteousness,
  and your law is the truth.
143 Trouble and anguish have come upon me,
  but your commandments are my
  delight.
144 Your decrees are righteous forever;
  give me understanding that I may live.

145 With my whole heart I cry; answer me,
  O LORD.
  I will keep your statutes.
146 I cry to you; save me,
  that I may observe your decrees.
147 I rise before dawn and cry for help;
  I put my hope in your words.
148 My eyes are awake before each watch of
  the night,
  that I may meditate on your promise.
149 In your steadfast love hear my voice;
  O LORD, in your justice preserve my
  life.
150 Those who persecute me with evil
  purpose draw near;
  they are far from your law.
151 Yet you are near, O LORD,
  and all your commandments are
  true.
152 Long ago I learned from your decrees
  that you have established them
  forever.

153 Look on my misery and rescue me,
  for I do not forget your law.
154 Plead my cause and redeem me;
  give me life according to your promise.
155 Salvation is far from the wicked,
  for they do not seek your statutes.
156 Great is your mercy, O LORD;
  be gracious to me*p* according to your
  justice.
157 Many are my persecutors and my
  adversaries,
  yet I do not swerve from your decrees.
158 I look at the faithless with disgust
  because they do not keep your
  commands.

159 Consider how I love your precepts;
  be gracious to me*q* according to your
  steadfast love.
160 The sum of your word is truth,
  and every one of your righteous
  ordinances endures forever.

161 Princes persecute me without cause,
  but my heart stands in awe of your
  words.
162 I rejoice at your word
  like one who finds great spoil.
163 I hate and abhor falsehood,
  but I love your law.
164 Seven times a day I praise you
  for your righteous ordinances.
165 Great peace have those who love your
  law;
  nothing can make them stumble.
166 I hope for your salvation, O LORD,
  and I fulfill your commandments.
167 My soul keeps your decrees;
  I love them exceedingly.
168 I keep your precepts and decrees,
  for all my ways are before you.

169 Let my cry come before you, O LORD;
  give me understanding according to
  your word.
170 Let my supplication come before you;
  deliver me according to your
  promise.
171 My lips will pour forth praise,
  because you teach me your statutes.
172 My tongue will sing of your promise,
  for all your commandments are
  right.
173 Let your hand be ready to help me,
  for I have chosen your precepts.
174 I long for your salvation, O LORD,
  and your law is my delight.
175 Let me live that I may praise you,
  and let your ordinances help me.
176 I have gone astray like a lost sheep; seek
  out your servant,
  for I do not forget your
  commandments.

p 119.156 Q ms: MT *give me life*   *q* 119.159 Q ms: MT *give me
life*

letter "tsade"; praise for God's righteousness and justice. **119:145–152** The Hebrew letter "qof";
plea to God for salvation. **119:153–160** The Hebrew letter "resh"; another plea to God for salvation. **119:161–168** The Hebrew letter "sin/shin"; the psalmist is steadfast despite the persecution.
119:169–176 The Hebrew letter "tav"; final petition to God. **119:175–176** The psalm ends with a
petition for life and a confession.

PSALM 120

A Song of Ascents.

¹ In my distress I cry to the LORD,
   that he may answer me:
² "Deliver me, O LORD,
   from lying lips,
   from a deceitful tongue."

³ What shall be given to you?
   And what more shall be done to you,
   you deceitful tongue?
⁴ A warrior's sharp arrows,
   with glowing coals of the broom tree!

⁵ Woe is me, that I am an alien in Meshech,
   that I must live among the tents of
      Kedar.
⁶ Too long have I had my dwelling
   among those who hate peace.
⁷ I am for peace,
   but when I speak,
   they are for war.

PSALM 121

A Song of Ascents.

¹ I lift up my eyes to the hills—
   from where will my help come?
² My help comes from the LORD,
   who made heaven and earth.

³ He will not let your foot be moved;
   he who keeps you will not slumber.
⁴ He who keeps Israel
   will neither slumber nor sleep.

⁵ The LORD is your keeper;
   the LORD is your shade at your right
      hand.
⁶ The sun shall not strike you by day
   nor the moon by night.

⁷ The LORD will keep you from all evil;
   he will keep your life.
⁸ The LORD will keep
   your going out and your coming in
   from this time on and forevermore.

Pss. 120–134 Psalms of Ascent. The fifteen psalms of ascent, united by a common superscription, reflect the poems of pilgrims. The pilgrimage could be actual travel to Jerusalem (Zion) or liturgical and spiritual travel in a symbolic sense. The label "of ascent" may refer to the steplike poetry throughout. Another possibility is that the name comes from pilgrims "going up" to Jerusalem for one of the three pilgrim festivals: Passover / Unleavened Bread, Weeks, and Booths (Exod. 23:17; 34:23; Deut. 16:16). While many of these psalms seem to have the household or family as the central locus, Ps. 132 fuses the house of David and the theme of Zion to reflect the centralizing ethos likely after the rebuilding of Jerusalem and the early postexilic age (see **"Second Temple," p. 1328**).

Ps. 120:1–7 Individual lament. The lament has three parts: an affirmation of trust and petition (vv. 1–2), an expression of vengeance (vv. 3–4), and a proclamation of woe (vv. 5–7). The first psalm of ascent begins in the Diaspora and moves toward Zion and Jerusalem. **Superscription.** *A Song of Ascents.* See note on Pss. 120–134. **120:1–2** Initial petition for divine deliverance. **120:1** *In my distress* connotes constriction. **120:2** *Lying lips* and *deceitful tongue* focus on how the language of the adversaries provokes shame for the psalmist. **120:3–4** Accusation. **120:4** *Sharp arrows* and *coals of the broom tree* were battle implements well attested in textual and iconographic evidence. **120:5** *Meshech* likely refers to an area in the far north (near the Black Sea), and *Kedar* refers to an area in the far south (southern Arabia). Both groups and areas are associated with military might (Isa. 21:16–17; Ezek. 27:13; 32:26; 38:2). The psalmist self-describes as an immigrant in these regions. **120:6–7** Those among whom the psalmist dwells are violent compared to his own aspirations of peace.

Ps. 121:1–8 Psalm of confidence. This psalm has two parts: a confession of trust (vv. 1–2) and a response by the priest or worship officiant (vv. 3–8). The presence of a worship officiant indicates the centralization of worship in the temple in the seventh century BCE or later in the Second Temple period. Psalm 121 functions as a pilgrimage liturgy for postexilic and later worshipers. **Superscription.** *A Song of Ascents.* See note on Pss. 120–134. A common poetic device called "anadiplosis," or stair-step technique, where the vocabulary connects each line as the reader moves through the psalm, is used here. **121:1–2** Affirmation of confidence. **121:1** *I lift up my eyes* implies aspiration and desire. *Hills* likely refers to Zion and nearby hills for the pilgrims. **121:3–8** A cultic official or priest responds with words of assurance. The speech shifts to second-person language (e.g., *your foot, your keeper, your shade*). *Keeps* and *keeper* illustrate anadiplosis, or stair-step technique, connecting vv. 3 and 4 with v. 5. **121:8** *Your going out and your coming* is a merism indicating the continuous protection of God.

PSALM 122

A Song of Ascents. Of David.
¹ I was glad when they said to me,
　"Let us go to the house of the LORD!"
² Our feet are standing
　within your gates, O Jerusalem.

³ Jerusalem—built as a city
　that is bound firmly together.
⁴ To it the tribes go up,
　the tribes of the LORD,
as was decreed for Israel,
　to give thanks to the name of the LORD.
⁵ For there the thrones for judgment were
　set up,
　the thrones of the house of David.

⁶ Pray for the peace of Jerusalem:
　"May they prosper who love you.
⁷ Peace be within your walls
　and security within your towers."
⁸ For the sake of my relatives and friends
　I will say, "Peace be within you."
⁹ For the sake of the house of the LORD our
　God,
　I will seek your good.

PSALM 123

A Song of Ascents.
¹ To you I lift up my eyes,
　O you who are enthroned in the
　　heavens!
² As the eyes of servants
　look to the hand of their master,
as the eyes of a maid
　to the hand of her mistress,
so our eyes look to the LORD our God,
　until he has mercy upon us.

³ Have mercy upon us, O LORD, have mercy
　upon us,
　for we have had more than enough of
　　contempt.
⁴ Our soul has had more than its fill
　of the scorn of those who are at
　　ease,
　of the contempt of the proud.

PSALM 124

A Song of Ascents. Of David.
¹ If it had not been the LORD who was on
　our side
—let Israel now say—

Ps. 122:1–9 Song of Zion. This hymn celebrates Zion as the home of God (see also Pss. 46, 48, 76, 84, 87). The psalm has three sections: an entreaty to go to Jerusalem (vv. 1–2), a description of Jerusalem and the house of David (vv. 3–5), and a prayer for the well-being of Jerusalem (vv. 6–9). The language about Jerusalem indicates the centrality of Jerusalem both during the monarchy and for the exilic communities. Psalm 122 functions as a pilgrimage liturgy for postexilic and later worshipers. **Superscription.** *A Song of Ascents.* See note on Pss. 120–134. *Of David.* See note on Ps. 3 superscription. Three Songs of Ascent have Davidic superscriptions (Pss. 122, 124, 131). **122:1–2** *I was glad* demonstrates that the psalmist orchestrates not just action but also emotions. The goal of pilgrimage is *the house of the* LORD (temple) and *Jerusalem.* **122:3–5** Praise of Jerusalem. **122:5** *Thrones for judgment.* See 1 Kgs. 7:7. **122:6–9** Hymn to Jerusalem. A cultic official invites the people to pray for the prosperity of Jerusalem. **122:9** The repetition of the phrase *house of the* LORD frames the psalm.

Ps. 123:1–4 Communal lament. This short communal lament has two sections: an expression of trust (vv. 1–2) and a petition and complaint (vv. 3–4). There are two communal laments in the Songs of Ascent (Pss. 123, 126). The lack of reference to Jerusalem or Zion could reflect an earlier time period than the other psalms in this collection. **Superscription.** *A Song of Ascents.* See note on Pss. 120–134. **123:1** *I lift up my eyes* implies aspiration and desire. *Enthroned in the heavens* is a reference to God in heaven (Pss. 20:6; 29:10; 113:5–6; see also Ps. 22:3). **123:2** *As the eyes . . . look.* Typical of anadiplosis, or stair-step technique, the "eyes" of v. 1 continue in v. 2. *Servants . . . master.* Pilgrims follow patterns of enslaved persons, who look to their enslavers for clues to acceptable behavior. **123:3–4** Plea for mercy (see also Pss. 51:1; 57:1) followed by a complaint about the ridicule of others, their *contempt* and *scorn.*

Ps. 124:1–8 Communal psalm of thanksgiving. This psalm has three elements: reflections on the remembered past (vv. 1–5), praise for the deliverance of God (vv. 6–7), and a declaration of trust (v. 8). Despite a possible original historical location different from the particular context of pilgrimage, Ps. 124 in its current canonical context functions as a pilgrimage liturgy for postexilic and later worshipers. **Superscription.** *A Song of Ascents.* See note on Pss. 120–134. *Of David.* See note on Ps. 3 superscription. Three Songs of Ascent have Davidic superscriptions (Pss. 122, 124, 131). **124:1–5** A series of conditional statements with responses: *if* (vv. 1, 2) . . . *then* (vv. 3–5). *If it had not*

² if it had not been the Lord who was on
  our side,
  when our enemies attacked us,
³ then they would have swallowed us up
  alive,
  when their anger was kindled against
  us;
⁴ then the flood would have swept us
  away;
  the torrent would have gone
  over us;
⁵ then over us would have gone
  the raging waters.

⁶ Blessed be the Lord,
  who has not given us
  as prey to their teeth.
⁷ We have escaped like a bird
  from the snare of the hunters;
  the snare is broken,
  and we have escaped.

⁸ Our help is in the name of the Lord,
  who made heaven and earth.

Psalm 125

A Song of Ascents.
¹ Those who trust in the Lord are like
  Mount Zion,
  which cannot be moved but abides
  forever.

² As the mountains surround Jerusalem,
  so the Lord surrounds his people
  from this time on and forevermore.
³ For the scepter of wickedness shall not
  rest
  on the land allotted to the righteous,
  so that the righteous might not stretch out
  their hands to do wrong.
⁴ Do good, O Lord, to those who are good
  and to those who are upright in their
  hearts.
⁵ But those who turn aside to their own
  crooked ways,
  the Lord will lead away with evildoers.
  Peace be upon Israel!

Psalm 126

A Song of Ascents.
¹ When the Lord restored the fortunes of
  Zion,ʳ
  we were like those who dream.
² Then our mouth was filled with laughter
  and our tongue with shouts of
  joy;
  then it was said among the nations,
  "The Lord has done great things for
  them."
³ The Lord has done great things for us,
  and we rejoiced.

r 126.1 Or *brought back those who returned to Zion*

been signals divine advocacy of the people, which prompts the liturgical invitation *let Israel now say.* **124:3** *Swallowed us up alive* is a metaphor for Sheol (cf. Isa. 28:15, 18–19; see **"Sheol," p. 695**). **124:6** Statement of benediction for the rescuing God. **124:7** *Like a bird* is a metaphor for the vulnerable community (see Pss. 11:1; 102:7). **124:8** *Name of the Lord.* See note on Ps. 20:7. *Who made heaven and earth* occurs as a title of God in the postexilic period (see Pss. 115:15; 121:2; 146:6).

Ps. 125:1–5 Song of Zion. The expression of trust in this psalm augments the stature of Zion (see note on Ps. 46). The clear reference to Jerusalem reflects the impulse of both the monarchy and those in exile to accentuate Jerusalem as a center of faith and politics. Psalm 125 has a threefold structure: an expression of trust (vv. 1–2), another expression of trust that gestures to petition (v. 3), and a petition moving to a declaration of peace (vv. 4–5). Psalm 125 functions as a pilgrimage liturgy for postexilic and later worshipers. **Superscription.** *A Song of Ascents.* See note on Pss. 120–134. **125:1–2** Zion as a model of stability (see Pss. 46:5; 122:3). **125:3** *Scepter* is a symbol of monarchic rule, usually associated with positive feelings (see Ps. 45:6); however, the *wickedness* indicates that here the symbol points to foreign oppression. **125:4** Petition. **125:5** *Peace be upon Israel!* Concluding prayer (see also Ps. 128:6).

Ps. 126:1–6 Communal lament. This psalm pairs with Ps. 123 as the only other communal lament in the Psalms of Ascent collection. The psalm has a threefold structure: an expression of trust (vv. 1–3), a petition (v. 4), and an expression of praise (vv. 5–6). The reference to Zion indicates an exilic context for the psalm. Psalm 126 functions as a pilgrimage liturgy for postexilic and later worshipers. **Superscription.** *A Song of Ascents.* See note on Pss. 120–134. **126:1–3** Recollection of divine redemption from the Babylonian exile. **126:1** Restore *the fortunes* refers to the end of the exile (see Deut. 30:3; Jer. 32:44; 33:26; Ezek. 16:53). *Dream* could signal that the exile is not yet over (see vv. 4–6) but only a future hope. **126:2** *Shouts of joy* is a liturgical refrain. Part of the joy of return is the witness

⁴ Restore our fortunes, O LORD,
    like the watercourses in the Negeb.
⁵ May those who sow in tears
    reap with shouts of joy.
⁶ Those who go out weeping,
    bearing the seed for sowing,
shall come home with shouts of joy,
    carrying their sheaves.

PSALM 127

A Song of Ascents. Of Solomon.
¹ Unless the LORD builds the house,
    those who build it labor in vain.
Unless the LORD guards the city,
    the guard keeps watch in vain.
² It is in vain that you rise up early
    and go late to rest,
eating the bread of anxious toil,
    for he gives sleep to his beloved.*

³ Sons are indeed a heritage from the
    LORD,
    the fruit of the womb a reward.
⁴ Like arrows in the hand of a warrior
    are the sons of one's youth.
⁵ Happy is the man who has
    his quiver full of them.
He shall not be put to shame

when he speaks with his enemies in
    the gate.

PSALM 128

A Song of Ascents.
¹ Happy is everyone who fears the LORD,
    who walks in his ways.
² You shall eat the fruit of the labor of
    your hands;
you shall be happy, and it shall go well
    with you.

³ Your wife will be like a fruitful vine
    within your house;
your children will be like olive
    shoots
    around your table.
⁴ Thus shall the man be blessed
    who fears the LORD.

⁵ The LORD bless you from Zion.
    May you see the prosperity of
    Jerusalem
    all the days of your life.
⁶ May you see your children's children.
    Peace be upon Israel!

s 127.2 Or *for he provides for his beloved during sleep*

---

it provides to the nations. **126:4–6** Community request. **126:4** The declaration of restoration (v. 1) becomes a petition for restoration. *Watercourses in the Negeb* points to the dry riverbeds that flash flood amid rainstorms. **126:5** *Shouts of joy* is a repetition of the liturgical refrain from v. 2. The reversal of fortunes is here described as *tears* transforming into *joy*. **126:6** A final refrain of *shouts of joy* describes a reversal of fortunes in parallel to v. 5 where *weeping* becomes joy. There is also an agricultural metaphor deployed here of sowing and reaping.

    Ps. 127:1–5 Wisdom psalm. Six psalms in Book V emerge from wisdom traditions (Pss. 112, 119, 127, 128, 133, 145). This psalm reflects on two wisdom metaphors: the house (vv. 1–2) and the children (vv. 3–5). Psalm 127 functions as a pilgrimage liturgy for postexilic and later worshipers. **Superscription.** *A Song of Ascents.* See note on Pss. 120–134. *Of Solomon* is an unusual superscription (see Ps. 72) and may be included here because of Solomon's building of the temple and his association with wisdom (see 1 Kgs. 3:1–15; 6:1–38). **127:1** A proverb. *Unless the LORD* acts in a project—here building a *house* or guarding a *city*—the project fails. **127:2** There is a shift from the urban environment to the farmer's field but with the same premise. *He gives sleep to his beloved* is uncertain in meaning. **127:3–4** Familial metaphor. **127:4** *Like arrows* signals the strength and protection that comes from having children in an agrarian society. **127:5** *Happy.* See note on Ps. 94:12. The metaphor of arrows as children continues as the man has so many of them they fill a *quiver*. Children protect one from shame at the *gate*, a reference to the public forum.

    Ps. 128:1–6 Wisdom psalm. This psalm consists of two parts: a reflection on wisdom (vv. 1–4) and a priestly blessing (vv. 5–6). The explicit reference to *Zion* and *Jerusalem* (v. 5) anchors the psalm in the period of the monarchy or exile. Psalm 128 fits well into the context of a pilgrimage psalm in the postexilic period. **Superscription.** *A Song of Ascents.* See note on Pss. 120–134. **128:1–4** Benefits of wisdom. **128:1** *Happy.* See note on Ps. 94:12. *Fears the LORD* is foundational for one who *walks in [God's] ways* (see also Ps. 111:10); both phrases denote a proper relationship with God. **128:3** *Olive* trees are cultivated from grafting shoots instead of seeds. **128:4** A proverb. **128:5–6** The blessing promised in v. 4 is given. *The prosperity of Jerusalem* is linked to wisdom's blessings of long life and many children.

PSALM 129

A Song of Ascents.

¹ Often have they attacked me from my
youth
—let Israel now say—
² often have they attacked me from my
youth,
yet they have not prevailed against
me.
³ The plowers plowed on my back;
they made their furrows long.
⁴ The LORD is righteous;
he has cut the cords of the wicked.
⁵ May all who hate Zion
be put to shame and turned backward.
⁶ Let them be like the grass on the
housetops
that withers before it grows up,
⁷ with which reapers do not fill their hands
or binders of sheaves their arms,
⁸ while those who pass by do not say,
"The blessing of the LORD be upon you!
We bless you in the name of the LORD!"

PSALM 130

A Song of Ascents.

¹ Out of the depths I cry to you, O LORD.
²   Lord, hear my voice!

Let your ears be attentive
to the voice of my supplications!

³ If you, O LORD, should mark iniquities,
Lord, who could stand?
⁴ But there is forgiveness with you,
so that you may be revered.

⁵ I wait for the LORD; my soul waits,
and in his word I hope;
⁶ my soul waits for the Lord
more than those who watch for the
morning,
more than those who watch for the
morning.

⁷ O Israel, hope in the LORD!
For with the LORD there is steadfast
love,
and with him is great power to
redeem.
⁸ It is he who will redeem Israel
from all its iniquities.

PSALM 131

A Song of Ascents. Of David.

¹ O LORD, my heart is not lifted up;
my eyes are not raised too high;

Ps. 129:1–8 Communal thanksgiving. This psalm has three sections: an account of past suffering (vv. 1–3), an account of divine intervention (v. 4), and imprecatory or cursing words (vv. 5–8). The reference to Zion indicates an exilic setting and fits well with the pilgrimage theme of the collection. **Superscription.** *A Song of Ascents.* See note on Pss. 120–134. **129:1–3** Complaint about the enemies. **129:1** *Let Israel now say* is a liturgical response to the complaint, which is repeated. **129:3** *Plowed on my back* depicts cruelty as perpetrated on enslaved persons. Prophetic oracles use the metaphor of plowing to describe the destruction of Jerusalem (Jer. 26:18; Mic. 3:12). **129:4** God cuts the *cords* that would tether animals or persons to a farmer. **129:5–7** The verbs in vv. 5–6 are in the Hebrew imperfect form, which can indicate incomplete action. Hence, there are several ways these verses can be understood. They may be a wish for the future or a statement about the present. They may have a cursing tone. **129:6** Grass on rooftops lacks the necessary soil to take root. **129:8** *In the name of the LORD.* See note on Ps. 20:7.

Ps. 130:1–8 Penitential prayer. This psalm is the only penitential prayer in the Psalms of Ascent (see Pss. 6, 32, 38, 51, 102, 143). The structure has four two-verse stanzas: a cry for help (vv. 1–2), a statement of trust (vv. 3–4), a statement of hope (vv. 5–6), and an invitation to the community, all Israel (vv. 7–8). No reference to Zion or Jerusalem occurs in this psalm. Nonetheless, like the other psalms of ascent, Ps. 130 reflects the songs of pilgrims to Jerusalem/Zion. **Superscription.** *A Song of Ascents.* See note on Pss. 120–134. **130:1–2** Invocation and initial plea. **130:1** *Depths* is a metaphor that connects to the depths of the seas or of Sheol, which connote death and destruction (see Prov. 9:18; Mic. 7:19). **130:3–4** A second plea confesses human *iniquities* and trust in God's forgiveness (see Exod. 34:6–7). **130:5–6** Personal prayer. The verbs *wait* and *hope* form one act. **130:7–8** The psalmist's hope is now recommended to the entire community of *Israel.* God's redemptive acts will obviate Israel's iniquities.

Ps. 131:1–3 Psalm of trust. This psalm has three parts: a declaration of humility (v. 1), a declaration of trust in God (v. 2), and an exhortation to the community, Israel. The reference to Israel indicates a setting in the period of the monarchy. Nonetheless, like the other psalms of ascent, it could reflect the songs of pilgrims to Jerusalem/Zion. **Superscription.** *A Song of Ascents.* See note on Pss. 120–134. *Of David.* See note on Ps. 3 superscription. **131:1** Three negative statements indicating the

I do not occupy myself with things
  too great and too marvelous for me.
² But I have calmed and quieted my soul,
  like a weaned child with its mother;
  my soul is like the weaned child that is
    with me.ᵗ

³ O Israel, hope in the LORD
  from this time on and forevermore.

PSALM 132

A Song of Ascents.
¹ O LORD, remember in David's favor
  all the hardships he endured;
² how he swore to the LORD
  and vowed to the Mighty One of
    Jacob,
³ "I will not enter my house
  or get into my bed;
⁴ I will not give sleep to my eyes
  or slumber to my eyelids,
⁵ until I find a place for the LORD,
  a dwelling place for the Mighty One
    of Jacob."

⁶ We heard of it in Ephrathah;
  we found it in the fields of Jaar.
⁷ "Let us go to his dwelling place;
  let us worship at his footstool."

⁸ Rise up, O LORD, and go to your resting
    place,
  you and the ark of your might.

⁹ Let your priests be clothed with
    righteousness,
  and let your faithful shout for joy.
¹⁰ For your servant David's sake
  do not turn away the face of your
    anointed one.

¹¹ The LORD swore to David a sure oath
  from which he will not turn back:
  "One of the sons of your body
  I will set on your throne.
¹² If your sons keep my covenant
  and my decrees that I shall teach
    them,
  their sons also, forevermore,
  shall sit on your throne."

¹³ For the LORD has chosen Zion;
  he has desired it for his habitation:
¹⁴ "This is my resting place forever;
  here I will reside, for I have desired it.
¹⁵ I will abundantly bless its provisions;
  I will satisfy its poor with bread.
¹⁶ Its priests I will clothe with salvation,
  and its faithful will shout for joy.
¹⁷ There I will cause a horn to sprout up for
    David;
  I have prepared a lamp for my
    anointed one.
¹⁸ His enemies I will clothe with disgrace,
  but on him, his crown will gleam."

ᵗ 131.2 Or *my soul within me is like a weaned child*

humility of the speaker. **131:2** *Like a weaned child* refers to satisfaction after a feeding. This verse uses maternal metaphors for God. **131:3** Summary advice for Israel: *hope in the LORD.*
  Ps. 132:1–18 Song of Zion and royal psalm. For other songs of Zion, see Pss. 46, 48, 76, 84, 87, 122, 137; for other royal psalms, see Pss. 2, 18, 20, 21, 45, 72, 89, 101, 110. This psalm, the longest in the songs of ascent, presents the rationale for pilgrimage to Zion. It contains a prayer (vv. 1–10) and the response to prayer (vv. 11–18). Psalm 132 reflects the setting of pilgrims coming to Jerusalem/Zion. **Superscription.** *A Song of Ascents.* See note on Pss. 120–134. **132:1–10** A prayer. **132:1–5** Call to God to *remember* David's vow to build the temple (see 2 Sam. 7). **132:2, 5** *Mighty One of Jacob.* See Gen. 49:24; Isa. 1:24; 49:26. **132:6–7** Description of a pilgrimage procession. **132:6** *We found it in the fields of Jaar* is a possible allusion to the recovery of the ark at Kiriath-jearim (1 Sam. 7:1–2). *Ephrathah* is an area inhabited by the Judahite clan by the same name (Gen. 35:16, 19; 48:7), and Kiriath-jearim ("the fields of Jaar") is on the northern border of Judah and the southern border of Benjamin; here the two are joined in poetic parallelism. **132:7** *Footstool.* See note on Ps. 99:5. **132:8–10** Communal prayer. **132:8** *Resting place* possibly refers to Jerusalem, and therefore this verse recounts the movement of the ark from Ephrathah and Kiriath-jearim to Jerusalem. **132:11–18** Response to prayer. **132:11–12** Divine oracle. **132:11** *The LORD swore* refers to the promise to David to establish a Davidic dynasty to rule from Jerusalem forever (2 Sam. 7). **132:12** *If your sons keep my covenant.* Whereas the covenant is eternal in 2 Sam. 7:14–15, here it is conditional. **132:13–18** Divine oracle. **132:13** *For the LORD has chosen Zion* links God's choice of David to God's choice of Jerusalem. **132:17** *I will cause a horn to sprout up* indicates the restoration of strength and royal power. See also Ezek. 29:21. *Lamp.* See 2 Sam. 21:17; 1 Kgs. 11:36.

PSALM 133

A Song of Ascents.

[1] How very good and pleasant it is
    when kindred live together in unity!
[2] It is like the precious oil on the head,
    running down upon the beard,
on the beard of Aaron,
    running down over the collar of his
        robes.
[3] It is like the dew of Hermon,
    which falls on the mountains of Zion.
For there the Lord ordained his
        blessing,
    life forevermore.

PSALM 134

A Song of Ascents.

[1] Come, bless the Lord, all you servants of
        the Lord,
    who stand by night in the house of the
        Lord!
[2] Lift up your hands to the holy place,
    and bless the Lord.

[3] May the Lord, maker of heaven and
        earth,
    bless you from Zion.

PSALM 135

[1] Praise the Lord!
    Praise the name of the Lord;
    give praise, O servants of the Lord,
[2] you who stand in the house of the Lord,
    in the courts of the house of our God.
[3] Praise the Lord, for the Lord is good;
    sing to his name, for he is
        gracious.
[4] For the Lord has chosen Jacob for
        himself,
    Israel as his own possession.

[5] For I know that the Lord is great;
    our Lord is above all gods.
[6] Whatever the Lord pleases he does,
    in heaven and on earth,
    in the seas and all deeps.
[7] He it is who makes the clouds rise at the
        end of the earth;
    he makes lightnings for the rain
    and brings out the wind from his
        storehouses.

[8] He it was who struck down the firstborn
        of Egypt,
    both humans and animals;

Ps. 133:1–3 Wisdom psalm. The short three-verse announcement of blessing begins with an aphorism (v. 1) and two similes, oil (v. 2) and the dew of Hermon (v. 3), and concludes with a promise (v. 3) that parallels the opening statement. The psalm reflects the setting of the songs of pilgrims to Jerusalem/Zion. **Superscription.** *A Song of Ascents.* See note on Pss. 120–134. **133:1** Exclamation. An aphorism or proverb about the goodness of kindred. The Hebrew Bible assumes the custom of family groups settling near one another and accounts for situations when they must separate (see Gen. 13:6 and 36:7 for stories of separation). **133:2** *Precious oil* is used for anointing and medicine; here it is a metaphor for something good. **133:3** *Dew of Hermon.* Mount Hermon is located in the northern region of Israel (northeast of the city of Dan) and is the highest mountain in the region. The moisture, presumably from the snows, provides needed water for agriculture.

Ps. 134:1–3 Song of praise. This psalm marks the end of the songs of ascent with a final blessing. **Superscription.** *A Song of Ascents.* See note on Pss. 120–134. **134:1–2** Call to bless. **134:1** The call is addressed to the *servants of the Lord,* the entire worshiping community. **134:3** Benediction for pilgrims and a closing reference to *Zion.* See Num. 6:24–26.

Ps. 135:1–21 Community hymn of praise. The use of the plague traditions could also classify this as a historical psalm. The phrase *praise the Lord* ("hallelujah") frames the psalm (vv. 1, 21). Following the imperative to praise, the psalmist gives a summons to praise (vv. 1–4). A description of a celebration of God's sovereignty over all other gods (vv. 5–7) introduces a rehearsal of God's interventions on behalf of Israel (vv. 8–14), which is the center of the psalm. The celebration, then, parallels the psalmist's comparison of God and the gods of other nations (vv. 15–18). The summons to praise at the beginning (vv. 1–4) parallels the summons to bless God at the end (vv. 19–21). Psalms 111–118 and 135–136 create an inclusio around the great torah Ps. 119 and the Psalms of Ascent (Pss. 120–134). **135:1–4** Call to praise. **135:1** *Praise the Lord!* Hebrew "hallelujah." See note on Ps. 7:17. *Servants of the Lord.* See note on Ps. 134:1. **135:4** *Jacob* and *Israel* are parallel; Jacob's name is changed to Israel in Gen. 32. Here, the names designate the special possession of the whole people (see also Exod. 19:1–5; Deut. 7:7–8). **135:5** *Above all gods* is a hymnic chant (see Ps. 82:1, 6–7). **135:5–7** God's sovereignty. **135:6** See Ps. 115:3. **135:7** Storm god imagery. **135:8–12** The plagues in Egypt (Exod. 7–12)

⁹ he sent signs and wonders
 into your midst, O Egypt,
 against Pharaoh and all his
 servants.
¹⁰ He struck down many nations
 and killed mighty kings—
¹¹ Sihon, king of the Amorites,
 and Og, king of Bashan,
 and all the kingdoms of Canaan—
¹² and gave their land as a heritage,
 a heritage to his people Israel.

¹³ Your name, O Lᴏʀᴅ, endures forever,
 your renown, O Lᴏʀᴅ, throughout all
 ages.
¹⁴ For the Lᴏʀᴅ will vindicate his people
 and have compassion on his servants.

¹⁵ The idols of the nations are silver and
 gold,
 the work of human hands.
¹⁶ They have mouths, but they do not
 speak;
 they have eyes, but they do not see;
¹⁷ they have ears, but they do not hear,
 a nose, but there is no breath in their
 mouths.
¹⁸ Those who make them
 and all who trust them
 shall become like them.

¹⁹ O house of Israel, bless the Lᴏʀᴅ!
 O house of Aaron, bless the Lᴏʀᴅ!
²⁰ O house of Levi, bless the Lᴏʀᴅ!
 You who fear the Lᴏʀᴅ, bless the
 Lᴏʀᴅ!
²¹ Blessed be the Lᴏʀᴅ from Zion,
 he who resides in Jerusalem.
 Praise the Lᴏʀᴅ!

¹ O give thanks to the Lᴏʀᴅ, for he is good,
 for his steadfast love endures forever.
² O give thanks to the God of gods,
 for his steadfast love endures forever.
³ O give thanks to the Lord of lords,
 for his steadfast love endures forever;

⁴ who alone does great wonders,
 for his steadfast love endures forever;
⁵ who by understanding made the heavens,
 for his steadfast love endures forever;
⁶ who spread out the earth on the waters,
 for his steadfast love endures forever;
⁷ who made the great lights,
 for his steadfast love endures forever;
⁸ the sun to rule over the day,
 for his steadfast love endures forever;
⁹ the moon and stars to rule over the night,
 for his steadfast love endures forever;

¹⁰ who struck Egypt through their firstborn,
 for his steadfast love endures forever;
¹¹ and brought Israel out from among them,
 for his steadfast love endures forever;
¹² with a strong hand and an outstretched
 arm,
 for his steadfast love endures forever;
¹³ who divided the Red Sea*u* in two,
 for his steadfast love endures forever;
¹⁴ and made Israel pass through the midst
 of it,
 for his steadfast love endures forever;
¹⁵ but overthrew Pharaoh and his army in
 the Red Sea,ᵛ
 for his steadfast love endures forever;
¹⁶ who led his people through the wilderness,
 for his steadfast love endures forever;

u 136.13 Or *Sea of Reeds* *v* 136.15 Or *Sea of Reeds*

and victory over the kings east of the Jordan (Num. 21:21–35) are recounted. **135:13** Prayer chant. **135:14** Hymnic chant. See Deut. 32:36. **135:15–18** Polemics against other gods drawing on Ps. 115:4–8. **135:19–21** Summons to praise, adaptation of Ps. 115:9–11. *Praise the Lord!* ("hallelujah") concludes the psalm (see v. 1).

Ps. 136:1–26 Communal thanksgiving. This hymn has a historical component. The psalm begins with the imperative to *give thanks* (vv. 1–3), then is followed by three sections relating why God should be praised: God creates (vv. 4–9), God directs and protects (vv. 10–22), and God provides (vv. 23–25). The psalm ends with a final imperative to *give thanks* to God (v. 26). Throughout, there is an antiphonal call: *for his steadfast love endures forever* (twenty-six times; see **"Hesed,"** p. 375). Other postexilic texts employ this same confession (see 1 Chr. 16:34; 2 Chr. 5:13; Ezra 3:11). **136:1–3** Summons to give thanks. The confession of the supremacy of Israel's God echoes Ps. 135:3–5. **136:1, 2, 3** *O give thanks.* See Pss. 105:1; 106:1; 107:1; 118:1, 29. **136:4–9** Thanks for God's wondrous creation. **136:10–15** Thanks for God's liberation of the Hebrew slaves from Egypt. This historical recital begins with the plague of the firstborn in Egypt (v. 10; see Exod. 12:29–30) and ends with the death of the Egyptian pursuers (v. 15; see Exod. 14:26–30). **136:16–22** Thanks for protection in the wilderness

who made water flow from the rock,
    for his steadfast love endures forever;[w]
[17] who struck down great kings,
    for his steadfast love endures forever;
[18] and killed famous kings,
    for his steadfast love endures forever;
[19] Sihon, king of the Amorites,
    for his steadfast love endures forever;
[20] and Og, king of Bashan,
    for his steadfast love endures forever;
[21] and gave their land as a heritage,
    for his steadfast love endures forever;
[22] a heritage to his servant Israel,
    for his steadfast love endures forever.

[23] It is he who remembered us in our low
    estate,
    for his steadfast love endures forever;
[24] and rescued us from our foes,
    for his steadfast love endures forever;
[25] who gives food to all flesh,
    for his steadfast love endures forever.

[26] O give thanks to the God of heaven,
    for his steadfast love endures forever.

PSALM 137

[1] By the rivers of Babylon—
    there we sat down, and there we
    wept
    when we remembered Zion.

[2] On the willows[x] there
    we hung up our harps.
[3] For there our captors
    asked us for songs,
    and our tormentors asked for mirth,
      saying,
    "Sing us one of the songs of Zion!"

[4] How could we sing the LORD's song
    in a foreign land?
[5] If I forget you, O Jerusalem,
    let my right hand wither!
[6] Let my tongue cling to the roof of my
    mouth,
    if I do not remember you,
    if I do not set Jerusalem
    above my highest joy.

[7] Remember, O LORD, against the
    Edomites
    the day of Jerusalem's fall,
    how they said, "Tear it down! Tear it down!
    Down to its foundations!"
[8] O daughter Babylon, you devastator![y]
    Happy shall they be who pay you back
    what you have done to us!
[9] Happy shall they be who take your little
    ones
    and dash them against the rock!

w 136.16 Gk: Heb lacks *who made water . . . forever*
x 137.2 Or *poplars*   y 137.8 Or *you who are devastated*

136:19–20 See Num. 21:21–35. **136:23–25** Thanks for sustenance. **136:26** A closing imperative of thanksgiving along with the community refrain that God's *steadfast love endures forever* (see also Ps. 150:6).
    Ps. 137:1–9 Communal lament. Note the contrast between the communal thanksgivings of Pss. 135 and 136 and this communal lament. The fourfold structure of the lament is as follows: a description of the setting (vv. 1–3), words of lament (v. 4), an oath (vv. 5–6), and an imprecation (vv. 7–9). The historical setting is the fall of Jerusalem and the forced exile of many Judeans in 586 BCE. This psalm has had a rich interpretive history (see **"Psalm 137 and Music," p. 850**). **137:1–4** Complaint. **137:1** *By the rivers of Babylon* may refer to a system of channels that brought water from the Tigris and Euphrates Rivers to the city of Babylon. **137:3** *Songs of Zion.* See note on Ps. 46. The national songs celebrating Jerusalem have become a cultural artifact. The captors taunt the exiles with the imperative to sing these songs about the now destroyed Jerusalem. See **"Music and the Psalms," p. 764**. **137:5–6** Self-imprecatory vow and two self-imprecations. **137:5** *Right hand* is a metaphor for agency and strength. **137:6** *My tongue* is an expression about communication. The psalmist vows to *remember* Jerusalem lest the ability to move (hand) and speak (tongue) be lost. **137:7–9** Imprecations. **137:7** Command to God to *remember*. *Edomites* are the descendants of Esau, Judah's neighbors to the south. The glee of the Edomites over Jerusalem's destruction is also recounted by the prophet Obadiah (Obad. 1). **137:8–9** *Happy* introduces statements of vengeance. This is the only combination of the statement *happy shall* with an imprecation. Lex talionis (law of retribution) is a legal principle that a criminal should receive punishment appropriate to the action against the victim. Children would have died in the siege of Jerusalem, and the Babylonians would have killed children in the onslaught (see Lam. 2:19–21). Hence the wish to see Babylonian children suffer.

Making Connections: Psalm 137 and Music

One of the most poignant of the psalms is Ps. 137. It expresses the anguish of war refugees: forced into exile, longing for home, fantasizing about revenge. It is one of the only psalms with a clear historical reference. Generally, psalms foreground emotion, giving little if any context; readers can connect with the sentiments expressed no matter their own circumstances. Psalm 137, obviously written in the aftermath of the Babylonian destruction of Jerusalem in 586 BCE, has transcended its original occasion to connect with diverse populations across time and culture.

Psalm 137 has been a favorite in liturgical settings for centuries and has also been a vehicle for political protest. Popular in Renaissance England, it was a rallying cry for both sides during the English Civil War (1642–51 CE), fought in part over religious freedom. Puritans settling in the Americas frequently sang Ps. 137, as it resonated with their experiences as an oppressed minority, exiled from home by an oppressive empire, with Babylon a stand-in for Catholic Rome. Later, William Billings transformed the psalm into a patriotic elegy about the American Revolution ("Lamentation over Boston"; 1778).

For Africans captured and subsequently enslaved in the Americas, Ps. 137 was particularly evocative of their experience, especially being forced to sing for their white captors. Frederick Douglass's powerful sermon "What to the Slave Is the Fourth of July?" (1852) features a long quotation from the psalm. "Lift Every Voice" (James Weldon Johnson; 1900)—sometimes called the Black national anthem—alludes to the psalm in its third verse. More recently, the psalm has had a resurgence in Rastafarian religion and music. The Melodians put the psalm to music in "Rivers of Babylon" (1969), replacing "the Lord's song" with "King Alpha's song"—a reference to the Ethiopian emperor Haile Selassie I, believed to be the Rastafarian messiah. Zion is Africa, specifically Ethiopia. Babylon is everywhere else, especially anywhere where racial injustice and oppression exist. The final verses are also altered—a call to sing songs of freedom instead of dashing babies' heads (the psalm does the same: singing rather than acting)—which is commensurate with the way Rastafarians advance their social justice agenda through spiritual resistance. The song was temporarily banned in Jamaica after its release because of its political implications. Later, a disco version was recorded by Boney M (1978), with the reference to King Alpha removed. The song topped the charts in the United States and in several European countries.

Jennifer L. Koosed

PSALM 138

Of David.

[1] I give you thanks, O LORD,[z] with my
   whole heart;
   before the gods I sing your praise;
[2] I bow down toward your holy temple
   and give thanks to your name for your
   steadfast love and your
   faithfulness,
   for you have exalted your name and
   your word
   above everything.[a]

[3] On the day I called, you answered me;
   you increased my strength of soul.[b]
[4] All the kings of the earth shall praise
   you, O LORD,
   for they have heard the words of your
   mouth.
[5] They shall sing of the ways of the LORD,
   for great is the glory of the LORD.

z 138.1 Q mss Gk. MT lacks *O LORD*   a 138.2 Cn: Heb *you
have exalted your word above all your name*   b 138.3 Syr Compare Gk Tg: Heb *you made me arrogant in my soul with strength*

Pss. 138–145 The Final Book of David. Psalms 138–145 have superscriptions that connect them to David. Psalms 138–143 reflect the individual speaker, Ps. 145 is a wisdom acrostic, and Ps. 144 is the final royal psalm.

Ps. 138:1–8 Individual song of thanksgiving. Psalm 138 is the first psalm of the final Davidic collection of the book of Psalms (Pss. 138–145). This psalm has three parts, typical of an individual hymn of thanksgiving: an introduction that expresses thanks, in this case, in the presence of the gods (vv. 1–3); a call to praise, focused on the kings of the earth (vv. 4–6); and confidence in God in the face of the psalmist's enemies (vv. 7–8). The references to the temple (v. 2) and to kings (v. 4) indicate a monarchy of an exilic or postexilic setting for the psalm. **Superscription.** *Of David.* See note on Ps. 3 superscription. **138:1–3** Expression of thanks. **138:1** *I give you thanks* opens an offertory formula. *Before the gods* refers to the gods of other peoples (see Pss. 115:4–8; 135:15–18). **138:2** *I bow down* begins another offertory formula. **138:3** A general account of salvation. **138:4–5** Summons to praise

⁶ For though the LORD is high, he regards
the lowly,
but the haughty he perceives from far
away.

⁷ Though I walk in the midst of trouble,
you preserve me against the wrath of
my enemies;
you stretch out your hand,
and your right hand delivers me.
⁸ The LORD will fulfill his purpose for
me;
your steadfast love, O LORD, endures
forever.
Do not forsake the work of your
hands.

PSALM 139

To the leader. Of David. A Psalm.
¹ O LORD, you have searched me and
known me.
² You know when I sit down and when I
rise up;
you discern my thoughts from far
away.
³ You search out my path and my lying
down
and are acquainted with all my
ways.
⁴ Even before a word is on my tongue,
O LORD, you know it completely.
⁵ You hem me in, behind and before,
and lay your hand upon me.
⁶ Such knowledge is too wonderful for
me;
it is so high that I cannot attain it.

⁷ Where can I go from your spirit?
Or where can I flee from your
presence?
⁸ If I ascend to heaven, you are there;
if I make my bed in Sheol, you are
there.
⁹ If I take the wings of the morning
and settle at the farthest limits of the
sea,
¹⁰ even there your hand shall lead me,
and your right hand shall hold me fast.
¹¹ If I say, "Surely the darkness shall cover
me,
and night wraps itself around me,"ᶜ
¹² even the darkness is not dark to you;
the night is as bright as the day,
for darkness is as light to you.

¹³ For it was you who formed my inward
parts;
you knit me together in my mother's
womb.
¹⁴ I praise you, for I am fearfully and
wonderfully made.
Wonderful are your works;
that I know very well.
¹⁵ My frame was not hidden from you,
when I was being made in secret,
intricately woven in the depths of the
earth.
¹⁶ Your eyes beheld my unformed substance.
In your book were written
all the days that were formed for me,
when none of them as yet existed.ᵈ

c 139.11 Q ms: MT *and the light around me become night*
d 139.16 Meaning of Heb uncertain

for *all the kings of the earth.* **138:6** Hymnic line describing God as regarding the *lowly* and recognizing the faults of the *haughty*. **138:7–8** Affirmation of confidence in God's saving power. **138:8** *Your steadfast love . . . endures forever.* See Ps. 136. *The work of your hands* refers to the whole community; thus the individual prayer becomes a petition for all.

    Ps. 139:1–24 Meditation. Although this psalm is often labeled a meditation, the form-critical category is difficult to determine. The four stanzas of Ps. 139 describe God's knowledge of the psalmist (vv. 1–6), the psalmist's inability to hide from God (vv. 7–12), a description of God's creation of the psalmist (vv. 13–18), and finally a petition of the psalmist to God (vv. 19–24). The themes of Ps. 139 do not permit a confident dating. **Superscription.** *To the leader. Of David. A Psalm.* See notes on Pss. 3 and 4 superscriptions. **139:1–18** Acknowledgment of divine presence. **139:1–6** Meditative prayer. This prayer contains several examples of merism (see note on Ps. 77:2). Examples include the following: *when I sit down and when I rise up* (v. 2), *my path and my lying down* (v. 3), and *behind and before* (v. 5). The point is that God's knowledge is pervasive. **139:6** *Wonderful* is a rare Hebrew word occurring only here and in Judg. 13:18. A similar word gestures to things too wonderful to understand in Prov. 30:18–19. **139:7–12** Plaintive reflection on God's omnipresence. **139:11–12** *Darkness* can connote chaos and Sheol, but here it simply indicates an absence of light, which is still luminescent to God. **139:13–16** Acknowledgment of God's creation of the human being. **139:16** *Your book* could come from the Mesopotamian notion of tablets or books of fate in which the deities record the preordained

¹⁷ How weighty to me are your thoughts,
O God!
How vast is the sum of them!
¹⁸ I try to count them—they are more than
the sand;
I come to the end^e—I am still with you.

¹⁹ O that you would kill the wicked, O God,
and that the bloodthirsty would
depart from me—
²⁰ those who speak of you maliciously
and lift themselves up against you for
evil!^f
²¹ Do I not hate those who hate you, O Lord?
And do I not loathe those who rise up
against you?
²² I hate them with perfect hatred;
I count them my enemies.
²³ Search me, O God, and know my heart;
test me and know my thoughts.
²⁴ See if there is any wicked^g way in me,
and lead me in the way everlasting.^h

PSALM 140

To the leader. A Psalm of David.
¹ Deliver me, O Lord, from evildoers;
protect me from those who are
violent,
² who plan evil things in their minds
and stir up wars continually.
³ They make their tongue sharp as a snake's,
and under their lips is the venom of
vipers.   *Selah*

⁴ Guard me, O Lord, from the hands of the
wicked;

protect me from the violent
who have planned my downfall.
⁵ The arrogant have hidden a trap for me,
and with cords they have spread a net,ⁱ
along the road they have set snares for
me.   *Selah*

⁶ I say to the Lord, "You are my God;
give ear, O Lord, to the voice of my
supplications."
⁷ O Lord, my Lord, my strong deliverer,
you have covered my head in the day
of battle.
⁸ Do not grant, O Lord, the desires of the
wicked;
do not further their evil plot.^j   *Selah*

⁹ Those who surround me lift up their
heads;^k
let the mischief of their lips
overwhelm them!
¹⁰ Let burning coals fall on them!
Let them be flung into pits, no more
to rise!
¹¹ Do not let the slanderer be established in
the land;
let evil speedily hunt down the violent!

¹² I know that the Lord maintains the cause
of the needy
and executes justice for the poor.

e 139.18 Or *I awake*   f 139.20 Cn: Meaning of Heb uncertain
g 139.24 Heb *hurtful*   h 139.24 Or *the ancient way*   i 140.5 Or
they have spread cords as a net   j 140.8 Heb adds *they are
exalted*   k 140.9 Cn: Heb *those who surround me are uplifted
in head*

lives of people. **139:17–18** Doxological close to the first sixteen verses. **139:19–24** Petition for deliverance. **139:19–20** A wish that God *would kill the wicked*. **139:21–22** A vow that the psalmist is on God's side. *I hate them* (v. 22) refers to the psalmist's attempt to parallel the activities and affections of God (see Deut. 16:21–22). **139:23–24** Petition. **139:23** *Search me* ends the psalm as it began, with a petition for divine scrutiny.

Ps. 140:1–13 Individual lament. Psalms 138 and 139 are individual hymns; Pss. 140–143 also speak with an individual voice but of individual lament. Psalm 140 begins with a complaint and petition (vv. 1–5), followed by an expression of trust (vv. 6–7), another petition (vv. 8–11), and a concluding expression of trust and praise (vv. 12–13). The themes of Ps. 140 do not allow a confident dating of the psalm. **Superscription.** *To the leader. A Psalm of David.* See notes on Pss. 3 and 4 superscriptions. **140:1–5** Invocation and petition. **140:1** *Deliver me* is an imperative. **140:2–3** Complaint against those who *plan evil*. **140:2** *Wars.* See Pss. 56:6; 59:3; 120:7. **140:3** *Tongue* and *lips* indicate the power of speech in a village setting, whether a curse (see Pss. 58, 109) or other malicious speech. *Selah.* See note on Ps. 3:1–2. **140:4** *Guard me* is the second petition imperative. **140:5** Complaint including hunting metaphors (*trap, cords, net, snares*), emphasizing the threat of predatory speech. *Selah.* See note on Ps. 3:1–2. **140:6–7** Invocation and affirmation of confidence. **140:8–11** A petition to God followed by a curse. *Selah.* See note on Ps. 3:1–2. **140:12–13** Affirmation of confidence. **140:12** The psalmist self-describes as *poor* and *needy* (see Pss. 40:17; 86:1).

[13] Surely the righteous shall give thanks to
your name;
the upright shall live in your presence.

PSALM 141

A Psalm of David.

[1] I call upon you, O LORD; come quickly
to me;
give ear to my voice when I call to you.
[2] Let my prayer be counted as incense
before you
and the lifting up of my hands as an
evening sacrifice.

[3] Set a guard over my mouth, O LORD;
keep watch over the door of my lips.
[4] Do not turn my heart to any evil,
to busy myself with wicked deeds
in company with those who work iniquity;
do not let me eat of their delicacies.

[5] Let the righteous strike me;
let the faithful correct me.
Never let the oil of the wicked anoint my
head,[l]
for my prayer is continually[m] against
their wicked deeds.
[6] When they are given over to those who
shall condemn them,
then they shall learn that my words
were pleasant.
[7] Like a rock that one breaks apart and
shatters on the land,
so shall their bones be strewn at the
mouth of Sheol.[n]

[8] But my eyes are turned toward you,
O GOD, my Lord;
in you I seek refuge; do not leave me
defenseless.
[9] Keep me from the trap that they have
laid for me
and from the snares of evildoers.
[10] Let the wicked fall into their own
nets,
while I alone escape.

PSALM 142

A Maskil of David. When he was in the cave. A Prayer.

[1] With my voice I cry to the LORD;
with my voice I make supplication to
the LORD.
[2] I pour out my complaint before him;
I tell my trouble before him.
[3] When my spirit is faint,
you know my way.

In the path where I walk,
they have hidden a trap for me.
[4] Look on my right hand and see:
there is no one who takes notice
of me;
no refuge remains to me;
no one cares for me.

[5] I cry to you, O LORD;
I say, "You are my refuge,
my portion in the land of the living."

l 141.5 Gk: Meaning of Heb uncertain   *m* 141.5 Cn: Heb
for continually and my prayer   *n* 141.7 Meaning of Heb of
141.5–7 is uncertain

Ps. 141:1–10 Individual complaint. This psalm has three sections: a cry for help (vv. 1–2), followed by a petition (vv. 3–7), and finally a plea for preservation (vv. 8–10). The psalm could have been written at an early or late date. **Superscription.** *A Psalm of David.* See note on Ps. 3 superscription. **141:1–2** Invocation and initial plea. **141:1** *I call upon you . . . I call to you* frames the first verse; the phrase typically occurs later in the line (see Pss. 17:6; 31:17; 86:7; 88:9). **141:2** *Incense.* See Exod. 30:8. *Evening sacrifice.* See Exod. 29:38–42. Like smoke rises up, so should the psalmist's prayers. **141:3–4** Petition. **141:4** *Delicacies* refers to the food of the privileged. **141:5–7** Imprecation. The Hebrew text here is difficult to interpret. **141:7** *Sheol.* See note on Ps. 6:1–5. **141:8** Affirmation of confidence. **141:9–10** Complaint including hunting metaphors (*trap, snares, nets*), emphasizing the threat of the predatory behaviors of the enemies (see Ps. 140:5).

Ps. 142:1–7 Individual complaint. See also Pss. 140, 141, and 143. This psalm has three sections, each with an expression of trust: an appeal (vv. 1–3), a complaint (vv. 3–5), and a final petition/ complaint (vv. 6–7). The superscription indicates that the psalm was grafted into its present context, connecting it to David's biography. **Superscription.** *A Maskil of David.* See note on Ps. 32 super-scription. *When he was in the cave. A Prayer.* See note on Ps. 57 superscription. This is one of thir-teen psalms that have specific references to events in the life of David; here, likely a reference to David's flight from Saul. David fled to a cave at En-gedi (1 Sam. 24). **142:1–2** Initial plea. **142:3** *You know my way* is an affirmation of confidence. *Trap.* See Ps. 140:5. **142:3–4** Complaint. **142:4** *Right hand* represents the agency of the psalmist. **142:5** Invocation and affirmation of confidence. *Portion*

⁶ Listen to my cry,
　　for I am brought very low.

Save me from my persecutors,
　　for they are too strong for me.
⁷ Bring me out of prison,
　　so that I may give thanks to your
　　　name.
The righteous will surround me,
　　for you will deal bountifully
　　　with me.

PSALM 143

A Psalm of David.
¹ Hear my prayer, O LORD;
　　give ear to my supplications in your
　　　faithfulness;
　　answer me in your righteousness.
² Do not enter into judgment with your
　　　servant,
　　for no one living is righteous before
　　　you.

³ For the enemy has pursued me,
　　crushing my life to the ground,
　　making me sit in darkness like those
　　　long dead.
⁴ Therefore my spirit faints within me;
　　my heart within me is appalled.

⁵ I remember the days of old;
　　I think about all your deeds;
　　I meditate on the works of your hands.
⁶ I stretch out my hands to you;
　　my soul thirsts for you like a parched
　　　land.　　　　　　　　　　*Selah*

⁷ Answer me quickly, O LORD;
　　my spirit fails.
Do not hide your face from me,
　　or I shall be like those who go down
　　　to the Pit.
⁸ Let me hear of your steadfast love in the
　　　morning,
　　for in you I put my trust.
Teach me the way I should go,
　　for to you I lift up my soul.

⁹ Save me, O LORD, from my enemies;
　　I have fled to you for refuge.^o
¹⁰ Teach me to do your will,
　　for you are my God.
Let your good spirit lead me
　　on a level path.

¹¹ For your name's sake, O LORD, preserve
　　　my life.
In your righteousness bring me out of
　　　trouble.
¹² In your steadfast love cut off my
　　　enemies,
　　and destroy all my adversaries,
　　for I am your servant.

PSALM 144

Of David.
¹ Blessed be the LORD, my rock,
　　who trains my hands for war and my
　　　fingers for battle,
² my rock^p and my fortress,
　　my stronghold and my deliverer,

o 143.9 Heb ms Gk: MT *to you I have hidden*　　*p* 144.2 Cn: Heb *my steadfast love*

---

refers to inheritance (see Pss. 16:5; 17:14; 73:26; 119:57; Lam. 3:24). **142:6–7** Petition and complaint. **142:7** *Prison* is a metaphor for containment (see Isa. 24:22; 42:7) in contrast to the freedom experienced in the "land of the living" (v. 5). *So that I may give thanks to your name* is a vow.

　　Ps. 143:1–12 Individual complaint. This is the last of the penitential psalms (see note on Ps. 6:1–10) with three parts: a description of distress (vv. 1–6) and a petition and expression of trust (vv. 7–12). The psalm could have been written early or late. **Superscription.** *A Psalm of David.* See note on Ps. 3 superscription. **143:1–2** Invocation. **143:2** *Your servant* functions as an inclusion (see v. 12). *No one living is righteous* is a statement of human sinfulness (see also Pss. 50:5; 130:3–4; Rom. 8:20). **143:3–4** Complaint. **143:5–6** Account of praying. **143:5** Imperative verbs of mindfulness: *remember, think, meditate.* **143:6** *My soul thirsts.* See Ps. 42:2. *Selah.* See note on Ps. 3:1–2. **143:7–11** Petition. **143:7** *Answer me* opens a series of imperatives and jussives, each pleading that God intervene (see Pss. 4:1; 39:12; 54:2; 84:8; 143:1). *Do not hide your face* is a metaphor for divine absence (see Pss. 27:9; 69:17). *Pit.* See note on Ps. 16:10. **143:8, 10** *Teach me* is a petition for wisdom. **143:12** *Cut off my enemies* is an imprecation. *Your servant* frames the psalm (see v. 1).

　　Ps. 144:1–15 Hymn of praise. This psalm makes considerable use of other psalms from Book I (especially Pss. 8, 18, 33, 39). The psalm has two sections: a royal complaint (vv. 1–11) and community words of trust (vv. 12–15). The psalm could have been written early or late. **Superscription.** *Of David.* See note on Ps. 3 superscription. **144:1** *Blessed be the LORD* provides a summons to praise (see Pss.

my shield, in whom I take refuge,
who subdues the peoples[q] under me.

[3] O Lord, what are humans that you
regard them,
or mortals that you think of them?
[4] They are like a breath;
their days are like a passing shadow.

[5] Bow your heavens, O Lord, and come
down;
touch the mountains so that they smoke.
[6] Make the lightning flash and scatter
them;
send out your arrows and rout them.
[7] Stretch out your hand from on high;
set me free and rescue me from the
mighty waters,
from the hand of foreigners,
[8] whose mouths speak lies
and whose right hands are false.

[9] I will sing a new song to you, O God;
upon a ten-stringed harp I will play
to you,
[10] the one who gives victory to kings,
who rescues his servant David.
[11] Rescue me from the cruel sword,
and deliver me from the hand of aliens,
whose mouths speak lies,
and whose right hands are false.

[12] May our sons in their youth
be like plants full grown,
our daughters like corner pillars,
cut for the building of a palace.
[13] May our barns be filled
with produce of every kind;
may our sheep increase by thousands,
by tens of thousands in our fields,
[14] and may our cattle be heavy with
young.
May there be no breach in the walls,[r] no
exile,

and no cry of distress in our streets.

[15] Happy are the people to whom such
blessings fall;
happy are the people whose God is
the Lord.

Psalm 145

Praise. Of David.
[1] I will extol you, my God and King,
and bless your name forever and ever.
[2] Every day I will bless you
and praise your name forever and ever.
[3] Great is the Lord and greatly to be praised;
his greatness is unsearchable.

[4] One generation shall extol your works to
another
and shall declare your mighty acts.
[5] They will recount the glorious[s] splendor
of your majesty,
and on your wondrous works I will
meditate.
[6] They will proclaim the might of your
awesome deeds,
and I will declare your greatness.
[7] They shall celebrate the fame of your
abundant goodness
and shall sing aloud of your
righteousness.

[8] The Lord is gracious and merciful,
slow to anger and abounding in
steadfast love.
[9] The Lord is good to all,
and his compassion is over all that he
has made.

[10] All your works shall give thanks to you,
O Lord,
and all your faithful shall bless you.

q 144.2 Q ms Heb mss Syr Aquila Jerome: MT *my people*
r 144.14 Heb lacks *in the walls* s 145.5 Q ms Gk Vg: MT *On the glorious*

28:6; 31:21; 41:13; 89:52; 106:48; 124:6; 135:21). **144:3–4** Declaration that humans are transitory and frail (see Job 7:17–19; Pss. 8:4; 90:5–6). **144:5–8** Petition reworking Ps. 18:7–19; in both psalms, God is a divine warrior fighting to redeem the psalmist. **144:9–11** Vow. **144:9** *I will sing a new song.* See note on Ps. 33:3. **144:12–14** Recital of blessing on the psalmist. The theme of the blessings is human and agricultural fertility. **144:15** *Happy.* See Pss. 1:1; 2:12.
Ps. 145:1–21 Hymn of praise. This psalm is an acrostic (see note on Pss. 9–10). The Hebrew word for "all" occurs seventeen times in the psalm, emphasizing totality. **Superscription.** *Praise. Of David.* See note on Ps. 3 superscription. **145:1** *My God and King.* See Pss. 68:24; 93; 95–99. **145:3** *Great is the Lord* is an affirmation of God's superlative nature (see Ps. 147:5). **145:4–7** God's *works* and *acts* prompt praise. **145:8–9** Affirmations of God. See Exod. 34:6–7. **145:10–13** God is praised because

¹¹ They shall speak of the glory of your
kingdom
and tell of your power,
¹² to make known to all people your^t
mighty deeds
and the glorious splendor of your^u
kingdom.
¹³ Your kingdom is an everlasting kingdom,
and your dominion endures
throughout all generations.

    The LORD is faithful in all his words
and gracious in all his deeds.^v
¹⁴ The LORD upholds all who are falling
and raises up all who are bowed
down.
¹⁵ The eyes of all look to you,
and you give them their food in due
season.
¹⁶ You open your hand,
satisfying the desire of every living
thing.
¹⁷ The LORD is just in all his ways
and kind in all his doings.
¹⁸ The LORD is near to all who call on him,
to all who call on him in truth.
¹⁹ He fulfills the desire of all who fear
him;
he also hears their cry and saves
them.
²⁰ The LORD watches over all who love
him,
but all the wicked he will destroy.

²¹ My mouth will speak the praise of the
LORD,
and all flesh will bless his holy name
forever and ever.

PSALM 146

¹ Praise the LORD!
Praise the LORD, O my soul!
² I will praise the LORD as long as I live;
I will sing praises to my God all my life
long.

³ Do not put your trust in princes,
in mortals, in whom there is no help.
⁴ When their breath departs, they return
to the earth;
on that very day their plans perish.

⁵ Happy are those whose help is the God
of Jacob,
whose hope is in the LORD their God,
⁶ who made heaven and earth,
the sea, and all that is in them;
who keeps faith forever;
⁷   who executes justice for the
oppressed;
who gives food to the hungry.

    The LORD sets the prisoners free;
⁸   the LORD opens the eyes of the blind.
The LORD lifts up those who are bowed
down;
the LORD loves the righteous.
⁹ The LORD watches over the strangers;
he upholds the orphan and the widow,
but the way of the wicked he brings
to ruin.

¹⁰ The LORD will reign forever,
your God, O Zion, for all generations.
Praise the LORD!

t 145.12 Gk Jerome Syr: Heb *his*   *u* 145.12 Heb *his*
v 145.13 Q ms Gk Syr: MT lacks *The* LORD . . . *his deeds*

of God's works in vv. 4–7; here God's *works* offer the praise. **145:13–14** Affirmation of God. **145:15–16** God's providence is figured as God's giving of *food*. **145:17–20** Affirmation of the justice of God. **145:20** The fate of the wicked and the righteous. See Ps. 1:6. **145:21** *My mouth will speak the praise of the* LORD is both a vow and a wish.

    Ps. 146:1–10 Hymn of praise. The last verse of Ps. 145 sums up Ps. 145 and also introduces the message of Ps. 146. The Hebrew term "hallelujah" (translated as *praise the* LORD) is present in all the final praise psalms (Pss. 146–150). Together, they create a doxological conclusion for the entire Psalter. Each psalm includes an opening and closing cheer: *Praise the* LORD! ("hallelujah"). The collection is labeled the Final Hallel. Psalm 146 has a chiastic or envelope structure with five parts: an opening prayer (vv. 1–2), words of wisdom (vv. 3–4), a description of God as creator and redeemer at the center of the psalm (vv. 5–8), followed by a second set of words of wisdom (vv. 8–9), and a closing praise (v. 10). **146:1** *Praise the* LORD! is an opening cheer. **146:2** *I will praise . . . I will sing praises* is a summons to praise. **146:3–4** Admonition to trust God instead of human help. **146:5–9** *Happy* introduces a hymn to the Lord. Nine participial phrases and two additional statements present the character of God. **146:6** *Who made heaven and earth.* See Ps. 124:8. **146:10** *The* LORD *will reign forever* is a concluding statement of God's eternal sovereignty. Closing cheer: *Praise the* LORD!

Psalm 147

¹ Praise the Lord!
How good it is to sing praises to our God,
　　for he is gracious, and a song of praise
　　is fitting.
² The Lord builds up Jerusalem;
　　he gathers the outcasts of Israel.
³ He heals the brokenhearted
　　and binds up their wounds.
⁴ He determines the number of the stars;
　　he gives to all of them their names.
⁵ Great is our Lord and abundant in
　　power;
　　his understanding is beyond
　　measure.
⁶ The Lord lifts up the downtrodden;
　　he casts the wicked to the ground.

⁷ Sing to the Lord with thanksgiving;
　　make melody to our God on the lyre.
⁸ He covers the heavens with clouds,
　　prepares rain for the earth,
　　makes grass grow on the hills.
⁹ He gives to the animals their food
　　and to the young ravens when they
　　cry.
¹⁰ His delight is not in the strength of the
　　horse
　　nor his pleasure in the speed of a
　　runner,ʷ
¹¹ but the Lord takes pleasure in those who
　　fear him,
　　in those who hope in his steadfast
　　love.

¹² Extol the Lord, O Jerusalem!
　　Praise your God, O Zion!

¹³ For he strengthens the bars of your gates;
　　he blesses your children within you.
¹⁴ He grants peaceˣ within your borders;
　　he fills you with the finest of wheat.
¹⁵ He sends out his command to the
　　earth;
　　his word runs swiftly.
¹⁶ He gives snow like wool;
　　he scatters frost like ashes.
¹⁷ He hurls down hail like crumbs—
　　who can stand before his cold?
¹⁸ He sends out his word and melts them;
　　he makes his wind blow, and the
　　waters flow.
¹⁹ He declares his word to Jacob,
　　his statutes and ordinances to Israel.
²⁰ He has not dealt thus with any other
　　nation;
　　they do not know his ordinances.
　　Praise the Lord!

Psalm 148

¹ Praise the Lord!
Praise the Lord from the heavens;
　　praise him in the heights!
² Praise him, all his angels;
　　praise him, all his host!

³ Praise him, sun and moon;
　　praise him, all you shining stars!
⁴ Praise him, you highest heavens
　　and you waters above the heavens!

⁵ Let them praise the name of the
　　Lord,

w 147.10 Heb legs of a person　x 147.14 Or prosperity

Ps. 147:1-20 Hymn of praise. This psalm is the second in the collection of the Final Hallel; see note on Ps. 146. As such, it begins and ends with the imperative *praise the Lord* (Heb. "hallelujah"). The psalm includes three invitations: to sing praises (vv. 1-6), to sing and make music (vv. 7-11), and to give God glory (vv. 12-20). The reference to Jerusalem (vv. 2, 12) indicates a likely postexilic context. **147:1** *Praise the Lord! How good it is to sing praises* opens the introductory hymn. **147:2** God's redemption of the fallen Jerusalem and the gathering of *the outcasts of Israel*, the exiles. **147:5** *Great is our Lord.* See note on Ps. 145:3. **147:7** *Sing to the Lord* begins the second invitation to thanksgiving. **147:11** *Fear him.* See Ps. 34:7 and note on Ps. 111:10. **147:12** The final invitation begins with a call to praise in *Jerusalem* and *Zion*. **147:15-18** Describes the creative power of God's *command* and *word*. See Gen. 1 and Ps. 33:6-9. **147:19-20** See Deut. 4:6-8. Closing cheer: *Praise the Lord!*

Ps. 148:1-14 Hymn of praise. This psalm is the third in the collection of the Final Hallel; see note on Ps. 146. Psalm 148 is a communal hymn that repeats the imperative to praise God twelve times. The structure of the psalm has two elements: praise to God in heaven (vv. 1-6) and praise to God from the earth (vv. 7-14). **148:1-4** Each line begins with a summons to praise (eight times in four verses), building a musical rhythm. **148:1** Opening cheer: *Praise the Lord!* **148:3** The cosmic entities such as *sun, moon,* and *stars,* depicted as deities in other religions, become here an illustration of God's power. **148:4** *Waters above the heavens.* See Gen. 1:6-7. **148:5-6** Hymnic affirmations

for he commanded and they were
    created.
6 He established them forever and
    ever;
    he fixed their bounds, which cannot
    be passed.*y*

7 Praise the LORD from the earth,
    you sea monsters and all deeps,
8 fire and hail, snow and frost,
    stormy wind fulfilling his
    command!

9 Mountains and all hills,
    fruit trees and all cedars!
10 Wild animals and all cattle,
    creeping things and flying birds!

11 Kings of the earth and all peoples,
    princes and all rulers of the
    earth!
12 Young men and women alike,
    old and young together!

13 Let them praise the name of the LORD,
    for his name alone is exalted;
    his glory is above earth and heaven.
14 He has raised up a horn for his
    people,
    praise for all his faithful,
    for the people of Israel who are close
    to him.
Praise the LORD!

PSALM 149

1 Praise the LORD!
    Sing to the LORD a new song,
    his praise in the assembly of the
    faithful.
2 Let Israel be glad in its Maker;
    let the children of Zion rejoice in their
    King.
3 Let them praise his name with
    dancing,
    making melody to him with
    tambourine and lyre.
4 For the LORD takes pleasure in his
    people;
    he adorns the humble with victory.
5 Let the faithful exult in glory;
    let them sing for joy on their
    couches.
6 Let the high praises of God be in their
    throats
    and two-edged swords in their
    hands,
7 to execute vengeance on the nations
    and punishment on the peoples,
8 to bind their kings with fetters
    and their nobles with chains of
    iron,
9 to execute on them the judgment
    decreed.
    This is glory for all his faithful ones.
Praise the LORD!

y 148.6 Or *he set a law that cannot pass away*

describing God's creation of these cosmic entities (see Gen. 1). **148:7–13** Second summons to praise focusing on earthly entities. **148:7** *Sea monsters* are mythic animals, created in Gen. 1:21 (see **"Leviathan," p. 735**). **148:8** *Fire and hail, snow and frost, stormy wind.* All the earth's weather events are called to praise God. **148:9–10** A praise of natural formations and animals. **148:11–12** Powerful people (*kings, princes,* and *rulers*) and regular people (*men and women alike*) praise God. **148:13–14** Hymnic affirmations of God's *glory.* **148:14** *Raised up a horn* indicates strength or protection (see Pss. 75:10; 89:17). Closing cheer: *Praise the LORD!*

Ps. 149:1–9 Hymn of praise. This psalm is the fourth in the collection of the Final Hallel; see note on Ps. 146. This collection contains three community hymns (Pss. 147, 149, 150). The psalm contains two stanzas: praise for the gathering of the faithful community (vv. 1–4) and praise in the context of battle (vv. 5–9). The reference to Zion and the use of the phrase *sing . . . a new song* indicate a postexilic date for the writing of the psalm. **149:1** The opening cheer *Praise the LORD! Sing to the LORD a new song* is a summons to praise and occurs in enthronement psalms (see note on Ps. 33:3; see Pss. 96:1; 98:1). See **"Music and the Psalms," p. 764. 149:2** God is *Maker* and *King;* the people are *glad* and *rejoice. Children of Zion* (see Lam. 4:2) is another name for Israel. **149:4** *Adorns* can also be translated as "crowns" (see Esth. 1:4; Zech. 12:7). *The humble* is a reference to the poor and afflicted. **149:5–9** Prayers for justice. **149:6** Call for the people of God to go into battle with *two-edged swords.* **149:7** *The nations* and *the peoples* will be punished. The image may be of a battle in the end times. **149:8** Constraint (*fetters* and *chains of iron*) on the powerful, the *kings* and *nobles.* Compare the fate of the kings here to the divine justice of Ps. 2. **149:9** Closing cheer: *Praise the LORD!*

Psalm 150

¹ Praise the Lord!
Praise God in his sanctuary;
   praise him in his mighty firmament!ᶻ
² Praise him for his mighty deeds;
   praise him according to his surpassing
      greatness!

³ Praise him with trumpet sound;
   praise him with lute and harp!

⁴ Praise him with tambourine and
      dance;
   praise him with strings and pipe!
⁵ Praise him with clanging cymbals;
   praise him with loud clashing cymbals!
⁶ Let everything that breathes praise the
      Lord!
Praise the Lord!

z 150.1 Or *dome*

Ps. 150:1–6 Hymn of praise. This psalm is the fifth and last in the collection of the Final Hallel; see note on Ps. 146. The editor of the Psalter placed doxologies at the end of each of the books (see Pss. 41:13; 72:18–19; 89:52; 106:48). Psalm 150 provides the ending doxology for both Book V and the entire Psalter. The internal evidence for the date of Ps. 150 is unclear. However, its location in the Final Hallel indicates a late provenance. This psalm has three parts: a praise of the nature of God (vv. 1–2), a praise with musical instruments (vv. 3–5), and a final exhortation to praise (v. 6). The imperative verb *praise* dominates Ps. 150; every half line in the psalm contains the word. **150:1** Opening cheer: *Praise the Lord!* The parallelism of the *sanctuary* and the *firmament*, the heavenly "dome" (Gen. 1:6), gestures to the connection between the heavens and the earth. **150:2** The *mighty deeds* of God and the *greatness* of God are parallel to each other and thus connected. **150:3–5** Instruments of praise, reflecting the range of instruments in an ensemble: *trumpet, lute, harp, tambourine, strings, pipe, cymbals.* **150:6** *Everything that breathes*, all of creation, contributes to the praise. Closing cheer: *Praise the Lord!*

PROVERBS

Sub-Saharan Africa has witnessed significant growth in Christianity. African biblical scholars have revealed apparent points of resemblance between the worldviews of the ancient Israelite people and those of African peoples. However, very few Bible commentaries have been written by scholars of African descent (see **"The Bible in Global Contexts," pp. 2157–59**). My engagement with the material in the book of Proverbs will thus be shaped by my location as an African–South African biblical scholar located on the African continent.

Authorship, Date, and Social Location

My social location will serve, as far as it is possible, as an optic through which I read the book of Proverbs. Proverbs comes from the hands of late exilic and early postexilic editors. Although the exilic period begins in 586 BCE, the collection does contain older material that dates as far back as the preexilic period, perhaps as far back as the tenth century BCE. Unlike the members of the postexilic Judean society—who in the face of the Persians, their colonial masters, were a minority and marginal in many respects—African–South African people are a majority. They are indigenous to the land, which was extorted from their forebears by the colonizers and the architects of the apartheid regime. Although the apartheid regime has ended, its legacies continue to haunt us, and indigenous South Africans are still marginalized in many respects, especially socioeconomically. Consequently, African perspectives continue to have a marginal impact on scholarship, including biblical scholarship whose orientation and perspectives remain basically American- and Eurocentric. Some of the salient features that will, as far as it is possible, shape my reading lens include African folklore (especially proverbs), socioeconomic class, the environment, age, gender (especially masculinities), and the embodiment of wisdom, among others. All these are affected, in one way or another, by colonial histories.

The Purpose of Proverbs

The educational focus of the book of Proverbs is featured right in the opening (purpose) statement (1:2-7) of the book. The words "wisdom" (*hokmah*) and "instruction" (*torah*) form the enclosure of this purpose statement (1:2, 7). In the sage's view, who is depicted as Solomon (1:1), the paragon of Israel's wisdom, the proverbs will enable learning for the simple and the wise, on the nature of wisdom and instruction, while the foolish will "despise wisdom and instruction" (1:7). The instructional setting featured by the editors of Proverbs is reminiscent of the African educational setting in which African folklore (proverbs, riddles, and folktales) was transmitted, particularly to the young, to equip them with the wisdom of African people. The setting could be a family context, an initiation setting, or a royal court, among others. The African proverb *rutang bana ditaola, le se ye natšo badimong* ("teach children divining bones [*ditaola*], and do not take these with, to the ancestors") is on target here. Hence the educational task of transferring wisdom from one generation to the next would be necessitated by the preceding proverb. The tenor underscores the parents' instructional role in their children's lives.

The instructional nature of Proverbs also becomes evident from the book's present structure, beginning with an instruction (Prov. 1-9) and ending with an instruction in Prov. 31:1-9. Whereas the first is framed as "your father's instruction" (1:8), the last comes from the mother of King Lemuel, one different in both gender and ethnicity from the other speakers of the proverbs. The intervening material, Prov. 10:1-30:33—although variegated in form, articulation, and themes—also bears the mark of the wisdom teacher's commitment to communicating the wisdom (*hokmah*) of the Israelite people in its totality.

Genre

As will become clearer in the text of the study notes, the *mashal* in Proverbs—that is, in Hebrew, the short pithy saying—is a genre that resonates with the form of many African proverbs. Indeed, the short pithy saying (captured through the modality of various parallelisms) is the genre that dominates the book. The instructions (Prov. 1-9; 31:1-9) and poems (Prov. 8; 31:10-31) may be compared with some African folktales and African oral poetry. From the latter literary forms as well, the wisdom of African people is embedded.

Reading Guide

A container of several discrete sections, Proverbs is an instructional manual for both the simple and the learned. Proverbs can be divided into the following eight sections:

1. Instructions from a father (or teacher) to a son: Prov. 1–9
2. Proverbs of Solomon: Prov. 10:1–22:16
3. Sayings of the wise: Prov. 22:17–24:22
4. Additional sayings of the wise: Prov. 24:23–34
5. Additional sayings of Solomon, transcribed by Hezekiah's men: Prov. 25–29
6. Words of Agur: Prov. 30
7. Words of Lemuel, teachings of his mother: Prov. 31:1–9
8. Poem of the Woman of Worth / Woman of Valor: Prov. 31:10–31

Running through the book are the following key words that connect the sections and form the vocabulary of those who have embraced wisdom: wisdom, instruction, righteousness, justice, equity, discernment, knowledge, instruction/teaching, fear of the Lord, counsel, reproof/discipline, commandments/words/sayings, precepts, understanding, insight, prudence, intelligence, and discretion. The daily lives of the wise (both young and old) are to manifest these qualities.

The simplistic and optimistic worldview embedded in Proverbs is much like the African worldview(s). In this way, it may be argued that there is a thread that ties the different sayings in Proverbs together with various African contexts. On the one hand, the listeners and/or readers of the Proverbial material are assured of success and prosperity if they adhere to the sayings contained in the book; while on the other hand, those who do not heed the words of the wise (fools), are assured of failure, calamity, and even death. The wise, according to the sage, display the fear of the Lord (see, e.g., Prov. 1:7), a foundational concept. In addition, the male sage counsels the male addressee (the wisdom teacher's student) that the fear of the Lord, rather than beauty, should be sought in a woman especially in chaps. 1–9 but also at the end: "Charm is deceitful and beauty is vain, but a woman who fears the Lord is to be praised" (31:30; see **"Woman of Worth," p. 903**).

In the interest of inclusivity, many modern English translations replace the word "son" (the literal Heb. rendition of the addressee) with "child." However, I prefer to keep to the literal meaning "son" not only to stay faithful to the Hebrew text but also to lay bare the androcentric nature of the text as well as its origins in patriarchal contexts. In the latter contexts, like in traditional African settings, the education of male children was prioritized. My choice of the male term also aligns with my intention to establish the kind of masculinity being formed and nurtured by the sage through his commandments and teaching in Proverbs.

Madipoane Masenya (Ngwan'a Mphahlele)

1

The proverbs of Solomon son of David, king of Israel:

2 For learning about wisdom and instruction,
for understanding words of insight,

3 for gaining instruction in wise dealing,
righteousness, justice, and equity;

4 to teach shrewdness to the simple,
knowledge and prudence to the young—

5 let the wise, too, hear and gain in learning
and the discerning acquire skill,

6 to understand a proverb and a figure,
the words of the wise and their riddles.

7 The fear of the LORD is the beginning of knowledge;
fools despise wisdom and instruction.

8 Hear, my child, your father's instruction,
and do not reject your mother's teaching,

9 for they are a fair garland for your head
and pendants for your neck.

10 My child, if sinners entice you,
do not consent.

11 If they say, "Come with us, let us lie in wait for blood;
let us wantonly ambush the innocent;

12 like Sheol let us swallow them alive
and whole, like those who go down to the Pit.

13 We shall find all kinds of costly things;
we shall fill our houses with spoil.

14 Throw in your lot among us;
we will all have one purse"—

15 my child, do not walk in their way;
keep your foot from their paths,

16 for their feet run to evil,
and they hurry to shed blood.

17 For in vain is the net baited
while the bird is looking on;

18 yet they lie in wait—to kill themselves!
and set an ambush—for their own lives!

19 Such is the end*a* of all who are greedy for gain;
it takes away the life of its possessors.

a 1.19 Gk: Heb are the ways

1:1 Superscription. The proverbs contained in the book of Proverbs are ascribed to the Israelite king Solomon, who has been traditionally linked with wisdom (perhaps because of his preferred choice for wisdom rather than wealth and power when asked by God about his needs at the start of his journey as an Israelite king, 1 Kgs. 3:5, 7–9). From the contents of Proverbs though, it is evident that some of the material originates from later periods in Israelite history; such material could therefore not have come from Solomon's own hand.

1:2–7 Prologue. Introduces the purpose of proverbs. In the instructional setting featured here, *wisdom and instruction* (v. 2) are for *the simple* and *the young* (both male; v. 4); *the wise* and *the discerning* (both male) must also gain wisdom and instruction to be skilled (v. 5). **1:7** *The fear of the LORD is the beginning of knowledge.* Underlying the gaining of wisdom and instruction is the fear of the Lord, acting as a thesis statement for the whole book. Wisdom gained from people's experiences is wrapped with the supernatural. Fools resist wisdom's path.

1:8–19 Warnings against evil companions. The first episode warns the young men against the ways of evildoers. **1:8–9** The purpose statement is immediately followed by the sage's exhortation to the son to heed parental instruction. By first reflecting on the family setting as the basic one in the formation and nurture of the son, the sage foregrounds the importance of the family in the absence of both the court and the temple in postexilic Judean society. The power dynamics regarding age are displayed by the authority of the teacher/parent who gives instructions and imparts wisdom to the young. The embrace of wisdom by the young cannot happen without attentive ears; neither can it be revealed without appropriate behavior. The Northern Sotho expression "o na le tsebe," literally "he or she has an ear," reveals that the specific child not only listens but also acts; the child is obedient. The sage is thus making wise men who display the fear of the Lord by heeding parental authority. Both the *father's instruction* and the *mother's teaching* should adorn his head and neck, thus forming an integral and visible part of his life. **1:10–14** The evil companions against whom the son is warned are intent on shedding the blood of *the innocent* in order to gain possessions. **1:15–16** Contrary to the evil companions' feet, which run to do evil, the son's feet should avoid evil paths. **1:17–19** The underlying simplistic worldview of negative rewards for evildoers and positive rewards for the righteous is already evident here.

²⁰ Wisdom cries out in the street;
  in the squares she raises her voice.
²¹ At the busiest corner she cries out;
  at the entrance of the city gates she speaks:
²² "How long, O simple ones, will you love being simple?
  How long will scoffers delight in their scoffing
  and fools hate knowledge?
²³ Give heed to my reproof;
  I will pour out my thoughts to you;
  I will make my words known to you.
²⁴ Because I have called and you refused,
  have stretched out my hand and no one heeded,
²⁵ and because you have ignored all my counsel
  and would have none of my reproof,
²⁶ I also will laugh at your calamity;
  I will mock when panic strikes you,
²⁷ when panic strikes you like a storm
  and your calamity comes like a whirlwind,
  when distress and anguish come upon you.
²⁸ Then they will call upon me, but I will not answer;
  they will seek me diligently but will not find me.
²⁹ Because they hated knowledge
  and did not choose the fear of the Lord,
³⁰ would have none of my counsel
  and despised all my reproof,
³¹ therefore they shall eat the fruit of their way
  and be sated with their own devices.

³² For waywardness kills the simple,
  and the complacency of fools destroys them;
³³ but those who listen to me will be secure
  and will live at ease without dread of disaster."

2 My child, if you accept my words
  and treasure up my commandments within you,
² making your ear attentive to wisdom
  and inclining your heart to understanding,
³ if you indeed cry out for insight
  and raise your voice for understanding,
⁴ if you seek it like silver
  and search for it as for hidden treasures—
⁵ then you will understand the fear of the Lord
  and find the knowledge of God.
⁶ For the Lord gives wisdom;
  from his mouth come knowledge and understanding;
⁷ he stores up sound wisdom for the upright;
  he is a shield to those who walk blamelessly,
⁸ guarding the paths of justice
  and preserving the way of his faithful ones.
⁹ Then you will understand righteousness and justice
  and equity, every good path,
¹⁰ for wisdom will come into your heart,
  and knowledge will be pleasant to your soul;
¹¹ prudence will watch over you,
  and understanding will guard you.
¹² It will save you from the way of evil,
  from those who speak perversely,

1:20–33 The call of Wisdom. Wisdom is personified as a woman (see **"Woman Wisdom," p. 872**). **1:20–22** As an instructor, she joins hands with the sage and the parents by opening her mouth and inviting the *simple*, the *scoffers*, and the *fools* to embrace her qualities. **1:24–27** Like the sinners who reap accordingly, those who ignore Wisdom's call will necessarily face calamity. **1:29** *They hated knowledge and did not choose the fear of the Lord.* The optimistic and simplistic mentality is repeated (see 1:17–19) here at the beginning of the book: those who embrace Wisdom—that is, those with the fear of the Lord—will of necessity be safe and live, while the wayward and the fools will be killed and destroyed.

2:1–15 The value of wisdom. The son is once more exhorted to embrace wisdom, which is likened to *silver* and *hidden treasures* (v. 4). Wisdom and understanding are gifts from the Lord; note the repetition of *understand* and *understanding* (vv. 2, 3, 5, 6, 9, 11). Wisdom seekers—that is, the just, faithful, upright, and blameless—are positively rewarded with God's protection and preservation. Those who possess knowledge, prudence, understanding, justice, and righteousness will be saved from evil, perverse, crooked, and devious ways. **2:2** The son's *ear* should pay attention to wisdom, while the *heart*, the seat of the volitional and intellectual capacities, should incline to understanding. **2:6** Even the divine *mouth*, not only the human ones, utters knowledge and understanding.

¹³ who forsake the paths of uprightness
    to walk in the ways of darkness,
¹⁴ who rejoice in doing evil
    and delight in the perverseness of evil,
¹⁵ those whose paths are crooked
    and who are devious in their ways.

¹⁶ You will be saved from the loose woman,*b*
    from the adulteress*c* with her smooth
    words,
¹⁷ who forsakes the partner of her youth
    and forgets her sacred covenant,
¹⁸ for her way*d* leads down to death
    and her paths to the shades;
¹⁹ those who go to her never come back,
    nor do they regain the paths of life.

²⁰ Therefore walk in the way of the good,
    and keep to the paths of the just.
²¹ For the upright will abide in the land,
    and the innocent will remain in it,
²² but the wicked will be cut off from the
    earth,
    and the treacherous will be rooted out
    of it.

3 My child, do not forget my teaching,
    but let your heart keep my
    commandments,
² for length of days and years of life
    and abundant welfare they will give you.

³ Do not let loyalty and faithfulness
    forsake you;
    bind them around your neck;
    write them on the tablet of your
    heart.
⁴ Then you will find favor and high regard
    in the sight of God and of people.

⁵ Trust in the LORD with all your heart,
    and do not rely on your own insight.
⁶ In all your ways acknowledge him,
    and he will make straight your paths.
⁷ Do not be wise in your own eyes;
    fear the LORD and turn away from evil.
⁸ It will be a healing for your flesh
    and a refreshment for your body.

⁹ Honor the LORD with your substance
    and with the first fruits of all your
    produce;
¹⁰ then your barns will be filled with
    plenty,
    and your vats will be bursting with
    wine.

¹¹ My child, do not despise the LORD's
    discipline
    or be weary of his reproof,

b 2.16 Heb *strange woman*   *c* 2.16 Heb *alien woman*
d 2.18 Cn: Heb *house*

2:16 The young man who embraces wisdom's ways and walks blamelessly will also be *saved from the loose woman, from the adulteress*.

2:17 Both in the biblical context and in many African patriarchal contexts, extramarital sex was acceptable, as long as the woman involved had no husband. Hence this woman's marital status is defined.

2:18–19 *Her way leads down to death*, like those of the evil male company in chap. 1. The man-in-the-making who is the sage's addressee is thus indirectly encouraged to cling to the wife of his youth as he is directly admonished to defeat the temptation of tampering with another man's wife. The proverb "monna ke thaka, o a naba" is one among several Northern Sotho proverbs that depict the married male's body as a communal space. Such proverbs that link masculinity with virility are antithetical to the kind of masculinity being formed and nurtured here.

2:21–22 The optimistic mentality/worldview of the good life that is rewarded and the negative one that is punished is embedded in the closing verse.

3:1–2 The *length of days* and *abundant welfare* (success) are linked to the son's heeding of the teacher's instruction.

3:3–4 The addressee's *neck* and *heart* are to be the seats of his *loyalty* ("hesed"; see **"Hesed," p. 375**) and *faithfulness*, behaviors that will earn him favor from God and in the community. The African expression "go fa ke go fega" (to give is to invest) suggests that giving to God necessarily leads to more produce (see also 3:9–10). Such a view on life forms the core of the prosperity gospel message from many contemporary African preachers within neo-Pentecostal and charismatic churches.

3:7–8 Wisdom is to be rooted in one's wholehearted trust in God and the *fear of the LORD*. Wisdom is connected to healing and a healthy body. Positive rewards are thus linked to wise living.

3:11 *The LORD's discipline* is an integral part of the sage's instruction. Just as the son heeds his father's teachings, so must he take discipline seriously. Discipline is connected to divine and parental love.

¹² for the LORD reproves the one he loves,
  as a father the son in whom he delights.
¹³ Happy are those who find wisdom
  and those who get understanding,
¹⁴ for her income is better than silver
  and her revenue better than gold.
¹⁵ She is more precious than jewels,
  and nothing you desire can compare
    with her.
¹⁶ Long life is in her right hand;
  in her left hand are riches and honor.
¹⁷ Her ways are ways of pleasantness,
  and all her paths are peace.
¹⁸ She is a tree of life to those who lay hold
    of her;
  those who hold her fast are called
    happy.
¹⁹ The LORD by wisdom founded the earth;
  by understanding he established the
    heavens;
²⁰ by his knowledge the deeps broke open,
  and the clouds drop down the dew.
²¹ My child, do not let these escape from
    your sight:
  keep sound wisdom and prudence,
²² and they will be life for your soul
  and adornment for your neck.
²³ Then you will walk on your way securely,
  and your foot will not stumble.
²⁴ If you sit down,ᵉ you will not be afraid;
  when you lie down, your sleep will be
    sweet.
²⁵ Then you will not be afraid of sudden panic
  or of the storm that strikes the wicked,

²⁶ for the LORD will be your confidence
  and will keep your foot from being
    caught.

²⁷ Do not withhold good from those to
    whom it is due,ᶠ
  when it is in your power to do it.
²⁸ Do not say to your neighbor, "Go and
    come again;
  tomorrow I will give it," when you
    have it with you.
²⁹ Do not plan harm against your neighbor
  who lives trustingly beside you.
³⁰ Do not quarrel with anyone without cause,
  when no harm has been done to you.
³¹ Do not envy the violent,
  and do not choose any of their ways,
³² for the perverse are an abomination to
    the LORD,
  but the upright are in his confidence.
³³ The LORD's curse is on the house of the
    wicked,
  but he blesses the abode of the
    righteous.
³⁴ Toward the scorners he is scornful,
  but to the humble he shows favor.
³⁵ The wise will inherit honor,
  but stubborn fools, disgrace.

4 Listen, children, to a father's
  instruction,
  and be attentive, that you may gainᵍ
    insight,

e 3.24 Gk: Heb *lie down*   *f* 3.27 Heb *from its owners*
g 4.1 Heb *know*

3:13–18 Hymn to Woman Wisdom. Wisdom is once more personified (see **"Woman Wisdom,"
p. 872**). The motif of seeking and finding her is compared with acquiring riches from beneath the
earth (see also 2:4). The latter are found wanting, as Wisdom provides more than material wealth.
Walking in Wisdom's ways enables one to achieve *peace* ("shalom"), which also connotes wholeness. Unlike the primordial couple who was barred from eating from the tree of life (Gen. 3:22–24),
those *who lay hold of* Wisdom obtain the *tree of life*. Wisdom and Torah will be conflated (Sir. 24:23)
in a later passage that also likens Wisdom to a tree (Sir. 24:12–17).
    3:19–20 *Wisdom* and *understanding* are deployed by the Lord in creation. The connection
between wisdom and creation continues especially in 8:20–31. As integral to the created order,
wisdom is accessible to all.
    3:21–22 True security lies in *wisdom* and *prudence*. Inner life (*soul*) is outwardly reflected (*adorn-
ment for your neck*). See also 3:3.
    3:23–26 The body and its deployment reveal and entrench the kind of security offered by wisdom.
    3:27–30 Good neighborliness entails hospitality as well as extending one's hand to the needy.
As in African ethics, the social welfare of disadvantaged community members is not in the hands of
governments but in the hands of good neighbors and family members.
    3:31–35 The chapter ends with blessings for the righteous and curses for the wicked.
    4:1–2 The teacher and the student are male persons. The *instruction* and the *teaching* ("torah")
of the father (cf. 1:8, where the teaching is the mother's) reveal that the kind of masculinity being
nurtured and shaped in this family setting is the work of men.

2 for I give you good precepts:
   do not forsake my teaching.
3 When I was a son with my father,
   tender and my mother's favorite,
4 he taught me and said to me,
   "Let your heart hold fast my words;
   keep my commandments and live.
5 Get wisdom; get insight: do not forget
      nor turn away
   from the words of my mouth.
6 Do not forsake her, and she will keep
      you;
   love her, and she will guard you.
7 The beginning of wisdom is this: get
      wisdom,
   and whatever else you get, get insight.
8 Prize her highly, and she will exalt
      you;
   she will honor you if you embrace her.
9 She will place on your head a fair
      garland;
   she will bestow on you a beautiful
      crown."
10 Hear, my child, and accept my words,
   that the years of your life may be
      many.
11 I have taught you the way of wisdom;
   I have led you in the paths of
      uprightness.
12 When you walk, your step will not be
      hampered,
   and if you run, you will not
      stumble.
13 Keep hold of instruction; do not let go;
   guard her, for she is your life.

14 Do not enter the path of the wicked,
   and do not walk in the way of
      evildoers.
15 Avoid it; do not go on it;
   turn away from it and pass on.
16 For they cannot sleep unless they have
      done wrong;
   they are robbed of sleep unless they
      have made someone stumble.
17 For they eat the bread of wickedness
   and drink the wine of violence.
18 But the path of the righteous is like the
      light of dawn,
   which shines brighter and brighter
      until full day.
19 The way of the wicked is like deep
      darkness;
   they do not know what they stumble
      over.
20 My child, be attentive to my words;
   incline your ear to my sayings.
21 Do not let them escape from your sight;
   keep them within your heart.
22 For they are life to those who find them
   and healing to all their flesh.
23 Keep your heart with all vigilance,
   for from it flow the springs of life.
24 Put away from you crooked speech,
   and put devious talk far from you.
25 Let your eyes look directly forward
   and your gaze be straight before you.
26 Keep straight the path of your feet,
   and all your ways will be sure.
27 Do not swerve to the right or to the left;
   turn your foot away from evil.

4:3 *When I was a son with my father*. The teaching passes through three generations, from grand-father to father to son. This hierarchical setting, just like the African one, reveals age as an important category within the hierarchy. *My mother's favorite*. The sage's relationship with his mother has emotional rather than instructional undertones.

4:6–9 Like the partner of one's youth, wisdom should be loved (v. 6) as well as embraced (v. 8), not forsaken (see 2:17). Like what is usually done by male human beings and the male deity, wisdom keeps and guards those who embrace her. Those who obtain wisdom and insight will be exalted and crowned.

4:10 *Hear* points to an aural instructional setting, one akin to an African one in which the elders transmitted the wisdom traditions of the people. Obedient youth are guaranteed life (see also 4:13).

4:11–12 Wisdom's embrace also enables *uprightness*. The wisdom worldview dictates that there can be no stumbling for the upright.

4:18–19 Choosing righteousness is equated with choosing light; *the way of the wicked* is the way of darkness.

4:20–27 The father challenges his son to use his body accordingly: the ears in being *attentive* (v. 20) and keeping his words (v. 21); the heart in being alert (v. 23); the tongue in avoiding *crooked speech* (v. 24); the eyes in displaying honesty (v. 25); and the feet/foot in walking uprightly (vv. 26–27). Such calculated and responsible use of the body will be rewarded by *life* and *healing to all their flesh* (v. 22).

5

My child, be attentive to my wisdom;
  incline your ear to my understanding,
[2] so that you may hold on to prudence,
  and your lips may guard knowledge.
[3] For the lips of a loose woman[b] drip
  honey,
  and her speech is smoother than oil,
[4] but in the end she is bitter as wormwood,
  sharp as a two-edged sword.
[5] Her feet go down to death;
  her steps follow the path to Sheol.
[6] She does not keep straight to the path of
  life;
  her ways wander, and she does not
  know it.

[7] And now, my child,[i] listen to me,
  and do not depart from the words of
  my mouth.
[8] Keep your way far from her,
  and do not go near the door of her
  house,
[9] lest you give your honor to others
  and your years to the merciless,
[10] and strangers take their fill of your
  wealth,
  and your labors go to the house of an
  alien,
[11] and at the end of your life you groan,
  when your flesh and body are
  consumed,
[12] and you say, "Oh, how I hated discipline,
  and my heart despised reproof!

[13] I did not listen to the voice of my
  teachers
  or incline my ear to my instructors.
[14] Now I am at the point of utter ruin
  in the public assembly."

[15] Drink water from your own cistern,
  flowing water from your own well.
[16] Should your springs be scattered abroad,
  streams of water in the streets?
[17] Let them be for yourself alone
  and not for sharing with strangers.
[18] Let your fountain be blessed,
  and rejoice in the wife of your youth,
[19]   a lovely deer, a graceful doe.
  May her breasts satisfy you at all times;
  may you be intoxicated always by her
  love.
[20] Why should you be intoxicated, my son,
  by another woman
  and embrace the bosom of an
  adulteress?[j]
[21] For human ways are under the eyes of
  the LORD,
  and he examines all their paths.
[22] The iniquities of the wicked ensnare them,
  and they are caught in the coils of
  their sin.
[23] They die for lack of discipline,
  and because of their great folly they
  are lost.

b 5.3 Heb strange woman i 5.7 Gk Vg: Heb children
j 5.20 Heb alien woman

5:1–2 The son is exhorted to embrace *wisdom* and *understanding* with *ear* and *lips*.

5:3 The knowledge-inspired utterances will enable him to resist the luring words of a *loose woman*. The African proverb "se bone thola boreledi, teng ga yona go a baba" (do not be deceived by the looks of a smooth eye-enticing fruit, it is bitter inside) reveals patriarchy's suspicion of the female Other; men are thus warned not to be deceived by beautiful female looks. Here the emphasis is on her deceitful and dangerous words (cf. 31:26).

5:5 The adulteress will lead the young man to death/Sheol (see also 2:16–19), this in contrast to wisdom, which leads to life. See **"Sheol," p. 695**.

5:6 *And she does not know it.* Like the evildoers in 4:19 whose path is darkness and who would thus stumble unknowingly, so for the adulterous woman.

5:7–8 Obeying the instruction of his teachers will keep the son away from the loose woman's house.

5:9–14 Succumbing to the lure of the adulterous woman leads to *utter ruin*: loss of honor (v. 9), wealth (v. 10), health (v. 11), and community standing (v. 14).

5:15 *Drink water from your own cistern*. An ideal man is one whose sexuality is shared only with his wife (v. 18). African proverbs such as "Monna ke thaka, o a naba" (a man is a pumpkin plant, he spreads) and "monna ke tšhwene, o ja ka matsogo a mabedi" (a man is a baboon, he eats with two hands) reveal that manhood should be typified by virility displayed through sex with women other than one's wife.

5:21–23 God sees all *human ways*, including adultery; sin is punished with death. Sexual misconduct becomes a metaphor for folly generally.

6 My child, if you have given your pledge
        to your neighbor,
    if you have bound yourself to another,[k]
2 you are snared by the utterance of your
        lips,[l]
    caught by the words of your mouth.
3 So do this, my child, and save yourself,
        for you have come into your
        neighbor's power:
    go, hurry,[m] and plead with your
        neighbor.
4 Give your eyes no sleep
    and your eyelids no slumber;
5 save yourself like a gazelle from the
        hunter,[n]
    like a bird from the hand of the fowler.

6 Go to the ant, you lazybones;
    consider its ways and be wise.
7 Without having any chief
    or officer or ruler,
8 it prepares its food in summer
    and gathers its sustenance in harvest.
9 How long will you lie there, O lazybones?
    When will you rise from your sleep?
10 A little sleep, a little slumber,
    a little folding of the hands to rest,
11 and poverty will come upon you like a
        robber,
    and want, like an armed warrior.

12 A scoundrel and a villain
    goes around with crooked speech,

13 winking the eyes, shuffling the feet,
        pointing the fingers,
14 with perverted mind devising evil,
        continually sowing discord;
15 on such a one calamity will descend
        suddenly,
    in a moment, damage beyond repair.

16 There are six things that the LORD hates,
        seven that are an abomination to
        him:
17 haughty eyes, a lying tongue,
        and hands that shed innocent blood,
18 a heart that devises wicked plans,
        feet that hurry to run to evil,
19 a lying witness who testifies falsely,
        and one who sows discord in a
        family.

20 My child, keep your father's
        commandment,
    and do not forsake your mother's
        teaching.
21 Bind them upon your heart always;
    tie them around your neck.
22 When you walk, they[o] will lead you;
    when you lie down, they[p] will watch
        over you;
    and when you awake, they[q] will talk
        with you.

k 6.1 Or *a stranger*   l 6.2 Cn Compare Gk Syr: Heb *the words
of your mouth*   m 6.3 Or *humble yourself*   n 6.5 Cn: Heb *from
the hand*   o 6.22 Heb *it*   p 6.22 Heb *it*   q 6.22 Heb *it*

6:1–5 *Given your pledge.* Being a good neighbor entails respecting pledges, which may also include financial entanglements like collateral for a loan. Proverbs's stress on the value of friendship and good neighborliness is resonant with African contexts, as is the tongue's power to enslave its owner, and hence, "molomo o tshela noka e tletše" (a mouth crosses an overflowing river). There is thus a need to take pledges seriously by hastening to reconcile with a wronged neighbor.

6:6–11 Because wisdom is built into the foundations of creation (3:19–20; 8:22–31), proper observation of nature can yield life lessons (see also 30:24–31). 6:6 In warning against laziness, the man-in-the-making must get his cue from the wise ways of the ant ("nemala"), one of the smallest members of the created order. 6:7–8 The ant is portrayed as internally motivated; without any ruler, it is able to ensure sustenance all year. 6:9–11 The son must thus resist laziness and embrace hard work to avoid suffering from poverty. The mentality embedded in the sage's exhortation here overlooks unjust structural systems in which the exploited poor work hard without commensurate rewards. Also overlooked are the many lazy young men who thrive by stealing from others or corrupt rulers in Africa and globally who, though not industrious, are flourishing.

6:12–15 Like the body can be a vehicle for wisdom (3:23–26), the body can be enlisted as an instrument of evil: the mouth (v. 12), *eyes, feet, fingers* (v. 13), and *mind* (v. 14). Such evildoers will not be left unpunished.

6:16–19 A numerical proverb (see also 30:15–31). Again, the focus is on the body being deployed for what *the LORD hates: haughty eyes, a lying tongue,* murderous *hands* (v. 17), a wicked *heart,* and evil-oriented *feet* (v. 18).

6:20 The sage then reverts to parental instruction in the family setting (see also 1:8).

23 For the commandment is a lamp and the
    teaching a light,
  and the reproofs of discipline are the
    way of life,
24 to preserve you from the wife of
    another,ʳ
  from the smooth tongue of the
    adulteress.ˢ
25 Do not desire her beauty in your heart,
  and do not let her capture you with
    her eyelashes,
26 for a prostitute's fee is only a loaf of
    bread,ᵗ
  but the wife of another stalks a man's
    precious life.
27 Can fire be carried in the bosom
  without burning one's clothes?
28 Or can one walk on hot coals
  without scorching the feet?
29 So is he who sleeps with his neighbor's
    wife;
  no one who touches her will go
    unpunished.
30 Thieves are not despised who steal only
  to satisfy their appetite when they are
    hungry.
31 Yet if they are caught, they will pay
    sevenfold;
  they will forfeit all the goods of their
    house.
32 But he who commits adultery has no
    sense;
  he who does it destroys himself.
33 He will get wounds and dishonor,
  and his disgrace will not be wiped
    away.
34 For jealousy arouses a husband's fury,
  and he will show no restraint when he
    takes revenge.

35 He will accept no compensation
  and will refuse a bribe no matter how
    great.

7 My child, keep my words
  and store up my commandments
    with you;
2 keep my commandments and live;
  keep my teachings as the appleᵘ of
    your eye;
3 bind them on your fingers;
  write them on the tablet of your heart.
4 Say to wisdom, "You are my sister,"
  and call insight your intimate friend,
5 that they may keep you from the loose
    woman,ᵛ
  from the adulteressʷ with her smooth
    words.

6 For at the window of my house
  I looked out through my lattice,
7 and I saw among the simple ones,
  I observed among the youths,
  a young man without sense,
8 passing along the street near her corner,
  taking the road to her house
9 in the twilight, in the evening,
  at the time of night and darkness.

10 Then a woman comes toward him
  decked out like a prostitute, with
    hidden intent.
11 She is loud and wayward;
  her feet do not stay at home;
12 now in the street, now in the squares,
  and at every corner she lies in wait.

r 6.24 Gk: MT *the evil woman*   s 6.24 Heb *alien woman*
t 6.26 Cn Compare Gk Syr Vg Tg: Heb *for because of a harlot
to a piece of bread*   u 7.2 Heb *little man*   v 7.5 Heb *strange
woman*   w 7.5 Heb *alien woman*

6:23 If adhered to, such parental instruction will bring positive rewards such as protection; it will also give direction to life.

6:24–35 Once again, a discourse against adultery. The parent's wise words can keep the youth from the attractions of the strange woman. In stressing the jealousy of the adulteress's husband and his refusal to accept any compensation, the sage foregrounds the fact that the sexuality of a married woman is contained and controlled. However, the punishment for adultery in Lev. 20:10 is death for both a man and a woman. This passage suggests that financial restitution was possible.

7:1 The instructional setting returns to a male teacher with male students (see also 7:24, which ends the discourse).

7:4–5 *Sister* indicates a lover, not a sibling (see, e.g., Song 4:9, 10, 12; 5:1); pursue Wisdom intimately instead of the *loose woman . . . the adulteress*. Woman Wisdom is contrasted to the adulteress or foreign woman. In the teacher's efforts to form and nurture an ideal man in a heteropatriarchal context, instruction on how to avoid and resist an adulteress / alien woman is central.

7:10 *A woman comes toward him.* She is a married woman who does not succumb to the patriarchal expectation that her body be controlled by her husband. Her actions problematize the

13 She seizes him and kisses him,
    and with impudent face she says
        to him:
14 "I had to offer sacrifices,
    and today I have paid my vows;
15 so now I have come out to meet you,
    to seek you eagerly, and I have found
        you!
16 I have decked my couch with
        coverings,
    colored spreads of Egyptian linen;
17 I have perfumed my bed with myrrh,
    aloes, and cinnamon.
18 Come, let us take our fill of love until
        morning;
    let us delight ourselves with love.
19 For my husband is not at home;
    he has gone on a long journey.
20 He took a bag of money with him;
    he will not come home until full moon."

21 With much seductive speech she
        persuades him;
    with her smooth talk she compels him.
22 Right away he follows her
    and goes like an ox to the slaughter
    or bounds like a stag toward the trap[r]
23   until an arrow pierces its entrails.
    He is like a bird rushing into a snare,
        not knowing that it will cost him his
        life.

24 And now, my children, listen to me,
    and be attentive to the words of my
        mouth.
25 Do not let your hearts turn aside to her
        ways;
    do not stray into her paths.

26 For many are those she has laid low,
    and numerous are her victims.
27 Her house is the way to Sheol,
    going down to the chambers of
        death.

8 Does not wisdom call
    and understanding raise her voice?
2 On the heights, beside the way,
    at the crossroads she takes her stand;
3 beside the gates in front of the town,
    at the entrance of the portals she cries
        out:
4 "To you, O people, I call,
    and my cry is to all who live.
5 O simple ones, learn prudence;
    acquire intelligence, you who lack it.
6 Hear, for I will speak noble things,
    and from my lips will come what is
        right,
7 for my mouth will utter truth;
    wickedness is an abomination to my
        lips.
8 All the words of my mouth are
        righteous;
    there is nothing twisted or crooked in
        them.
9 They are all straight to one who
        understands
    and right to those who find
        knowledge.
10 Take my instruction instead of silver
    and knowledge rather than choice
        gold,
11 for wisdom is better than jewels,
    and all that you may desire cannot
        compare with her.

x 7.22 Cn Compare Gk: Meaning of Heb uncertain

underlying perception of a heterosexual married man's body as a communal space because it is the woman who leaves her house to make sexual advances.

7:21–22 *She persuades him* and eventually lures him to her marital bed in her house, thus bringing to realization the only Northern Sotho proverb that appears to celebrate female sexual prowess: "monna ke kobo re apolelana" (a man is a blanket that women exchange). The transactional relationship between the young man and the adulteress featured here resonates with the one between the South African female blessers and sugar mammas. These economically independent women hire the services of younger men for companionship and sexual intimacy. In both cases, the woman is the active seeker; the man is portrayed as a helpless victim who has fallen prey to a highly sexualized woman.

7:24–27 The sage admonishes such a foolish, careless young man who refuses to heed his words and commandments. It is always dangerous to be trapped by an adulterous woman; following her can only lead to death.

8:1–36 The speaker shifts from the male sage as an instructor to personified Wisdom / Woman Wisdom (see **"Woman Wisdom," p. 872**). **8:4–5** The call is not made to "my child" but to the *people* and the *simple ones* (see 1:4). **8:6–9** The emphasis on wise and right speech continues through

12 I, wisdom, live with prudence,
  and I attain knowledge and
    discretion.
13 The fear of the LORD is hatred of evil.
  Pride and arrogance and the way of evil
    and perverted speech I hate.
14 I have good advice and sound wisdom;
  I have insight; I have strength.
15 By me kings reign,
  and rulers decree what is just;
16 by me rulers rule,
  and nobles, all who govern rightly.
17 I love those who love me,
  and those who seek me diligently
    find me.
18 Riches and honor are with me,
  enduring wealth and prosperity.
19 My fruit is better than gold, even fine
    gold,
  and my yield than choice silver.
20 I walk in the way of righteousness,
  along the paths of justice,
21 endowing with wealth those who
    love me
  and filling their treasuries.
22 "The LORD created me at the beginning^y
    of his work,^z
  the first of his acts of long ago.

23 Ages ago I was set up,
  at the first, before the beginning of the
    earth.
24 When there were no depths I was
    brought forth,
  when there were no springs
    abounding with water.
25 Before the mountains had been
    shaped,
  before the hills, I was brought
    forth,
26 when he had not yet made earth and
    fields^a
  or the world's first bits of soil.
27 When he established the heavens, I was
    there;
  when he drew a circle on the face of
    the deep,
28 when he made firm the skies above,
  when he established the fountains of
    the deep,
29 when he assigned to the sea its limit,
  so that the waters might not
    transgress his command,
  when he marked out the foundations of
    the earth,

y 8.22 Or *me as the beginning*   z 8.22 Heb *way*   a 8.26 Meaning of Heb uncertain

foregrounding the *lips* and *mouth*. **8:12** Wisdom lives with *prudence*, *knowledge*, and *discretion*. Woman Wisdom can be compared with a contemporary neighborhood counselor, a social worker on a campaign against drug addiction and violence or similar vices that affect present-day communities. **8:14** *I have good advice*. The qualities of Wisdom displayed here accord with those typical of women in the African proverb "monna ke nku, mosadi ke pudi" (a man is a sheep, a woman is a goat). The proverb speaks to a woman's alleged noisy tendencies and incapacity to keep secrets. Like a woman, Wisdom cries out, not out of fear rooted in cowardice but out of her zeal to inform, entice, and assure the simple of how precious she is, more precious than gold (8:18–19). **8:15–16** The mention of *kings*, *rulers*, and *nobles* as Wisdom's beneficiaries points to an elite context. Wisdom literature may have arisen in royal courts (see 1:1; 31:1). **8:19** The value of Wisdom is more than precious minerals. The conjunction of wealth and wisdom underscores elitist class ideologies. The poor, who have been deprived of the proceeds of the minerals from the land of their ancestors by the colonialists and apartheid masters and instead promised futuristic rewards; those who were given the Christian Bible while their land, which was/is rich with minerals, was taken away from them; as well as African men who were exploited through hard labor in the service of their white masters may not be persuaded that the rich minerals of the land are not as important as wisdom. Instead, wisdom's links with concepts such as "righteousness" and "justice" (v. 20) are likely to be embraced by those who were displaced by the returnees from exile—Judahites and South Africans—as well as the Jews who suffered under the Persian colonial masters and the foreign women who suffered under the Ezra–Nehemiah reforms (see **"Intermarriage," p. 649**). **8:22–31 Poem on Wisdom's origins, in creation and relationship with God.** Personified Wisdom is God's first act of creation, and thus she is elevated above other aspects of the created order. She is close to God, albeit not God. Wisdom is God's delight; in turn, she delights in people. The passage could be considered another creation story, connected to yet distinct from Gen. 1, Ps. 8, and Ps. 90. The language about Wisdom here is reminiscent of the language about Logos (Word) in the Gospel of John (see **"Woman Wisdom," p. 872**).

Going Deeper: Woman Wisdom (Proverbs 8–9)

In Prov. 8, a remarkable figure emerges. Wisdom, an aspect frequently found in books like Proverbs, Job, and Ecclesiastes (see **"Introduction to the Writings," pp. 6–9**), is personified. Wisdom, a quality, becomes Wisdom, a woman. In Hebrew, "wisdom" is grammatically feminine. In Proverbs, linguistic potential becomes a full-blown female figure. She stands in various places (8:2–3), calling out to all, urging them to seek her and her instruction. In this way, Wisdom is a public figure who speaks divine truth, like a prophet. She offers prosperity and honor to all who love her (8:18–21). She is contrasted with the loose or "strange" woman of Prov. 7, who also calls to those who pass her by (7:12–20). Those who love her—that is, who commit adultery with her—take the path to death (7:27). To the contrary, those who seek Woman Wisdom find life.

Proverbs 8:22–9:6 is a creation account that features Woman Wisdom (see **"Creation (Genesis)," p. 16**, and **"Wisdom and Creation," p. 1412**). God "creates" or "acquires" Wisdom "at the beginning" (8:22). She is then alongside God in the rest of creation. Wisdom is accessible not through divine revelation but through careful observation of the natural order: wisdom is built into the world because Woman Wisdom helps create the world. Her presentation is comparable to ancient Near Eastern goddesses, especially Egyptian Maat. Maat is the goddess of justice and order, frequently depicted holding an ankh—the Egyptian symbol of life.

In Prov. 9, Woman Wisdom's activities are domestic: building a house, setting a table, and preparing and serving food (9:1–5). This imagery connects with the powerful wife of Prov. 31 (see **"Woman of Worth," p. 903**). Unlike certain modern understandings of a separate and subordinate domestic sphere, women's association with domesticity in ancient Israel aligned them with considerable power and influence. Woman Wisdom inhabits three domains simultaneously—the public, the cosmic, and the domestic—which attests to her ubiquity and authority, second only to God.

The personification of Wisdom continues in the Wisdom of Solomon. Wisdom is equated with Torah in the book of Sirach. In the New Testament, Woman Wisdom appears in Matt. 11:19; Luke 7:35 and 11:49. The creation language of Prov. 8 is ascribed to the Word, identified with Jesus, in John 1. Texts like these from the New Testament show how various understandings of Jesus have been influenced by Woman Wisdom.

Jennifer L. Koosed

30 then I was beside him, like a master
        worker,[b]
    and I was daily his[c] delight,
        playing before him always,
31 playing in his inhabited world
        and delighting in the human race.

32 "And now, my children, listen to me:
        happy are those who keep my ways.
33 Hear instruction and be wise,
        and do not neglect it.
34 Happy is the one who listens to me,
        watching daily at my gates,
        waiting beside my doors.
35 For whoever finds me finds life
        and obtains favor from the LORD,
36 but those who miss me injure themselves;
        all who hate me love death."

9 Wisdom has built her house;
        she has hewn her seven pillars.
2 She has slaughtered her animals; she has
        mixed her wine;
        she has also set her table.
3 She has sent out her female servants; she
        calls
        from the highest places in the town,
4 "You who are simple, turn in here!"
        To those without sense she says,
5 "Come, eat of my bread
        and drink of the wine I have mixed.
6 Lay aside immaturity and live,
        and walk in the way of insight."

b 8.30 Or *little child*   c 8.30 Gk: Heb lacks *his*

9:1–6 Wisdom's feast. A poem featuring Woman Wisdom (see **"Woman Wisdom," p. 872**). Wisdom is depicted as an independent rich woman, probably single. She performs roles usually performed by men: building the house (v. 1) and slaughtering animals for the feast (v. 2). She also performs tasks usually associated with women: preparing wine (vv. 2, 5) and bread (v. 5). At her service are high-quality *female servants* (v. 3). The female performance of traditional male roles problematizes the stereotypes about femininities and masculinities. There are parallels between Woman Wisdom's generosity and hospitality and the ideal wife in Prov. 31.

[7] Whoever corrects a scoffer wins abuse;
   whoever rebukes the wicked gets hurt.
[8] Do not rebuke a scoffer, lest he hate you;
   rebuke the wise, and he will love you.
[9] Give instruction[d] to the wise, and they
      will become wiser still;
   teach the righteous, and they will gain
      in learning.
[10] The fear of the LORD is the beginning of
      wisdom,
   and the knowledge of the Holy One is
      insight.
[11] For by me your days will be multiplied,
   and years will be added to your life.
[12] If you are wise, you are wise for yourself;
   if you scoff, you alone will bear it.
[13] The foolish woman is loud;
   she is ignorant and knows nothing.
[14] She sits at the door of her house,
   on a seat at the high places of the
      town,
[15] calling to those who pass by,
   who are going straight on their way,
[16] "You who are simple, turn in here!"
   And to those without sense she says,
[17] "Stolen water is sweet,

   and bread eaten in secret is pleasant."
[18] But they do not know that the dead[e] are
      there,
   that her guests are in the depths of
      Sheol.

10 The proverbs of Solomon.

   A wise child makes a glad father,
      but a foolish child is a mother's grief.
[2] Treasures gained by wickedness do not
      profit,
   but righteousness delivers from death.
[3] The LORD does not let the righteous go
      hungry,
   but he thwarts the craving of the
      wicked.
[4] A slack hand causes poverty,
   but the hand of the diligent makes
      rich.
[5] A child who gathers in summer is
      prudent,
   but a child who sleeps in harvest
      brings shame.

d 9.9 Heb lacks *instruction*   e 9.18 Heb *shades*

9:7–12 The sage returns to general maxims, warning his listeners to expend their energies not on a *scoffer* or the *wicked* (v. 7) but on the *wise* and *righteous*, as they are teachable (vv. 8–9). The simple, the inexperienced, and the young seem to be teachable (see 1:4 and 8:5); the scoffer and the wicked do not. **9:10** *The fear of the LORD is the beginning of wisdom* is a recurring theme (see 1:7 and 2:5). See note on 1:7.

9:13–18 Folly's invitation. Like the first poem in 9:1–6, this last episode contains an invitation and a promise, but this time by Folly, a female personification. Woman Folly, like Woman Wisdom, is also *loud* but without knowledge, thus opening her mouth in ignorance (v. 13). She also owns a house like Woman Wisdom (v. 14).

9:17 *Stolen water is sweet* is reminiscent of the water that should be drunk only from one's own cistern (5:15). See note on 5:15.

9:18 Woman Folly entices with sweet water and stolen bread, but the end thereof is death.

10:1–22:16 The proverbs of Solomon. The second collection, ascribed to King Solomon (10:1), exhibits a change in form and style from Prov. 1–9, a probable pointer to a change in authorship and date. The addressee is not named. In addition, the content appears timeless and addresses various themes that affect anyone irrespective of gender, age, ethnicity, socioeconomic class, and sexuality. However, with the instructional nature of Proverbs in view, "the son" of the previous collection is the probable recipient of these sayings. The short pithy saying now replaces the instruction and poem genres of Prov. 1–9, similar to the form of many African proverbs: "Ka hlagolela leokana" / "la re go gola la ntlhaba" (I watered and took care of a young thorny plant / when it grew bigger, it pierced me).

10:1–15:33 Many of the sayings in the first part of this second collection use antithetical parallelism, in which one line carries a thought that is contrasted in the next line (see **"Hebrew Poetry," p. 741**). Sometimes, however, the lines do not tally thematically (see, e.g., 10:8).

10:1 The family setting introduces these proverbs. In the worldview of the sage, *a wise child makes a glad father*, while a foolish one causes *a mother's grief* (see also 6:20).

10:3–4 Exemplifies the sage's analysis of class: hunger and poverty are a result of wickedness and laziness. In real life though, such an uncritical and perhaps elitist view on life does not hold

⁶ Blessings are on the head of the
righteous,
but the mouth of the wicked conceals
violence.
⁷ The memory of the righteous is a
blessing,
but the name of the wicked will rot.
⁸ The wise of heart will heed
commandments,
but one with foolish lips will come to
ruin.
⁹ Whoever walks in integrity walks
securely,
but whoever follows perverse ways
will be found out.
¹⁰ Whoever winks the eye causes trouble,
but one who rebukes boldly makes
peace.ᶠ
¹¹ The mouth of the righteous is a fountain
of life,
but the mouth of the wicked conceals
violence.
¹² Hatred stirs up strife,
but love covers all offenses.
¹³ On the lips of one who has
understanding wisdom is found,
but a rod is for the back of one who
lacks sense.
¹⁴ The wise lay up knowledge,
but the mouth of a fool brings ruin
near.
¹⁵ The wealth of the rich is their fortress;
the poverty of the poor is their ruin.
¹⁶ The wage of the righteous leads to
life,
the gain of the wicked to sin.
¹⁷ Whoever heeds instruction is on the path
to life,
but one who rejects a rebuke goes
astray.
¹⁸ Lying lips conceal hatred,
and whoever utters slander is a fool.
¹⁹ When words are many, transgression is
not lacking,
but the prudent are restrained in
speech.

²⁰ The tongue of the righteous is choice
silver;
the mind of the wicked is of little
worth.
²¹ The lips of the righteous feed many,
but fools die for lack of sense.
²² The blessing of the LORD makes rich,
and toil adds nothing to it.
²³ Doing wrong is like sport to a fool,
but wise conduct is pleasure to a
person of understanding.
²⁴ What the wicked dread will come upon
them,
but the desire of the righteous will be
granted.
²⁵ When the tempest passes, the wicked are
no more,
but the righteous are established
forever.
²⁶ Like vinegar to the teeth and smoke to
the eyes,
so are the lazy to their
employers.
²⁷ The fear of the LORD prolongs life,
but the years of the wicked will be
short.
²⁸ The hope of the righteous ends in
gladness,
but the expectation of the wicked
comes to nothing.
²⁹ The way of the LORD is a stronghold for
the upright
but destruction for evildoers.
³⁰ The righteous will never totter,
but the wicked will not remain on the
earth.
³¹ The mouth of the righteous brings forth
wisdom,
but the perverse tongue will be cut
off.
³² The lips of the righteous know what is
acceptable,
but the mouth of the wicked what is
perverse.

ᶠ 10.10 Gk: Heb *but one with foolish lips will come to ruin*

water, especially for those who continue to reap the cruelties of ruthless systems such as colonialism and apartheid, patriarchy, neocapitalism, and corruption from the African rulers who collude with the West. One may work very hard and yet be exploited by unjust employers. One may have the fear of the Lord yet reap the evil repercussions of patriarchy from the male interpreters of sacred texts, including the Hebrew Bible.

10:11 The importance of the mouth/lips as an organ that reveals the inclinations of the heart. See also vv. 13, 18, 19, 20, 21, 31, 32.

10:27 *The fear of the* LORD is a recurring theme. See note on 1:7.

11

A false balance is an abomination to
the Lord,
but an accurate weight is his delight.
² When pride comes, then comes disgrace,
but wisdom is with the humble.
³ The integrity of the upright guides them,
but the crookedness of the
treacherous destroys them.
⁴ Riches do not profit in the day of wrath,
but righteousness delivers from
death.
⁵ The righteousness of the blameless keeps
their ways straight,
but the wicked fall by their own
wickedness.
⁶ The righteousness of the upright saves
them,
but the treacherous are taken captive
by their schemes.
⁷ When the wicked die, hope perishes,
and the expectation of strength comes
to nothing.
⁸ The righteous are delivered from
trouble,
and the wicked come into it instead.
⁹ With their mouths the godless would
destroy their neighbors,
but by knowledge the righteous are
delivered.
¹⁰ When it goes well with the righteous, the
city rejoices,
and when the wicked perish, there is
jubilation.
¹¹ By the blessing of the upright a city is
exalted,
but it is overthrown by the mouth of
the wicked.

¹² Whoever belittles another lacks
sense,
but an intelligent person remains
silent.
¹³ A gossip goes about telling secrets,
but one who is trustworthy in spirit
keeps a confidence.
¹⁴ Where there is no guidance, a nation^g
falls,
but in an abundance of counselors
there is safety.
¹⁵ To guarantee loans for a stranger brings
trouble,
but there is safety in refusing to do so.
¹⁶ A gracious woman gets honor,
but she who hates virtue is covered
with shame.^h
The timid become destitute,^i
but the aggressive gain riches.
¹⁷ Those who are kind reward
themselves,
but the cruel do themselves harm.
¹⁸ The wicked earn no real gain,
but those who sow righteousness get a
true reward.
¹⁹ Whoever is steadfast in righteousness
will live,
but whoever pursues evil will die.
²⁰ Crooked minds are an abomination to
the Lord,
but those of blameless ways are his
delight.
²¹ Be assured, the wicked will not go
unpunished,

g 11.14 Or *an army* h 11.16 Compare Gk Syr: Heb lacks *but
she … shame* i 11.16 Gk: Heb lacks *The timid … destitute*

11:1 *A false balance*. The warning against the use of dishonest scales and weights in business practices corresponds to an African communal value rooted in a theocentric ethic (see also 16:11; 20:23; Job 31:6). *Abomination to the Lord*. Such overt theologically charged language is unusual, although see 11:20.

11:10 It is simplistically assumed that the whole city supports righteous people. Wisdom here is linked to civic order.

11:16 *A gracious woman* who *gets honor* is contrasted with a shameful one who *hates virtue*. One of several proverbs directed to ideal womanhood (see also 11:22).

11:19 Direct connection between righteousness/life and evil/death. No room is given for deviation—for example, the wicked may prosper, while the righteous and the wise may receive unfair treatment and even death. Such a worldview appears to also be communal, for even the city rejoices when the righteous prosper and the wicked perish (see 11:10).

11:21 *Be assured*. The sage seems to acknowledge that these pronouncements do not always accord with reality but here promises that eventually the wicked will be punished. For readers located in unequal global contexts like South Africa, where the rich become richer while the poor become poorer, and for readers who are aware that they are perpetually exploited not only by political leaders but also by religious leaders, these assurances are not heartening.

but those who are righteous will
escape.
22 Like a gold ring in a pig's snout
is a beautiful woman without good
sense.
23 The desire of the righteous ends only in
good,
the expectation of the wicked in wrath.
24 Some give freely yet grow all the richer;
others withhold what is due and only
suffer want.
25 A generous person will be enriched,
and one who gives water will get
water.
26 The people curse those who hold back
grain,
but a blessing is on the head of those
who sell it.
27 Whoever diligently seeks good seeks
favor,
but evil comes to the one who
searches for it.
28 Those who trust in their riches will
wither,*j*
but the righteous will flourish like
green leaves.
29 Those who trouble their households will
inherit wind,
and the fool will be servant to the wise.
30 The fruit of the righteous is a tree of life,
and the wise capture souls.
31 If the righteous are repaid on earth,
how much more the wicked and the
sinner!

12 Whoever loves discipline loves
knowledge,
but those who hate to be rebuked are
stupid.
2 The good obtain favor from the Lord,
but those who devise evil he
condemns.

3 No one finds security by wickedness,
but the root of the righteous will
never be moved.
4 A good wife is the crown of her husband,
but she who brings shame is like
rottenness in his bones.
5 The thoughts of the righteous are just;
the advice of the wicked is
treacherous.
6 The words of the wicked are a deadly
ambush,
but the speech of the upright delivers
them.
7 The wicked are overthrown and are no
more,
but the house of the righteous will
stand.
8 One is commended for good sense,
but a perverse mind is despised.
9 Better to be despised and have produce*k*
than to be self-important and lack
food.
10 The righteous know the needs of their
animals,
but the mercy of the wicked is cruel.
11 Those who till their land will have plenty
of food,
but those who follow worthless
pursuits have no sense.
12 The wicked covet the proceeds of
wickedness,*l*
but the root of the righteous bears
fruit.
13 The evil are ensnared by the
transgression of their lips,
but the righteous escape from trouble.
14 From the fruit of the mouth one is filled
with good things,
and manual labor has its reward.

j 11.28 Cn: Heb *fall*   *k* 12.9 Cn: Heb *servant*   *l* 12.12 Or *covet the catch of the wicked*

11:24–25 Encourages financial generosity. However, being a loyal adherent to the prosperity gospel promulgated by many preachers on the African continent does not necessarily earn the giver great rewards. Likewise, for those who are subjected to exploitative and greedy rulers and employers, hard work is not always commensurate with one's earnings.

11:30 *Tree of life.* See 3:18; 13:12; 15:4.

12:4 Marital relationships are an important theme. The ideal wife enhances her husband's fame while a bad wife destroys him. The theme has a male-oriented slant where the wife's character reflects on her husband but not vice versa.

12:6 Right versus wrong speech is a prevalent theme.

12:13–14 References to the body parts of *mouth, lips* (vv. 13, 19, 22), and "tongue" (vv. 18, 19) express the theme of wise versus wicked speech. The theme connects with agricultural images (*fruit of the mouth*) and, through parallelism, *manual labor*. Both right speech and hard work yield a good harvest. The ecosystem as a whole appears to be aligned with humans in this regard.

[15] Fools think their own way is right,
but the wise listen to advice.
[16] Fools show their anger at once,
but the prudent ignore an insult.
[17] Whoever speaks the truth gives honest evidence,
but a false witness speaks deceitfully.
[18] Rash words are like sword thrusts,
but the tongue of the wise brings healing.
[19] Truthful lips endure forever,
but a lying tongue lasts only a moment.
[20] Deceit is in the mind of those who plan evil,
but those who counsel peace have joy.
[21] No harm happens to the righteous,
but the wicked are filled with trouble.
[22] Lying lips are an abomination to the Lord,
but those who act faithfully are his delight.
[23] One who is clever conceals knowledge,
but the mind of a fool[m] broadcasts folly.
[24] The hand of the diligent will rule,
while the lazy will be put to forced labor.
[25] Anxiety weighs down the human heart,
but a good word cheers it up.
[26] The righteous are released from misfortune,[n]
but the way of the wicked leads them astray.
[27] The lazy do not roast[o] their game,
but the diligent obtain precious wealth.[p]
[28] In the path of righteousness there is life;
in walking its path there is no death.

13 A wise child loves discipline,[q]
but a scoffer does not listen to rebuke.
[2] From the fruit of their words good persons eat good things,
but the desire of the treacherous is for wrongdoing.
[3] Those who guard their mouths preserve their lives;
those who open wide their lips come to ruin.
[4] The appetite of the lazy craves and gets nothing,
while the appetite of the diligent is richly supplied.
[5] The righteous hate falsehood,
but the wicked act shamefully and disgracefully.
[6] Righteousness guards one whose way is upright,
but sin overthrows the wicked.
[7] Some pretend to be rich yet have nothing;
others pretend to be poor yet have great wealth.
[8] Wealth is a ransom for a person's life,
but a poor person pays no attention to a rebuke.
[9] The light of the righteous rejoices,[r]
but the lamp of the wicked goes out.
[10] By insolence the empty-headed person makes strife,
but wisdom is with those who take advice.
[11] Wealth hastily gotten[s] will dwindle,
but those who gather little by little will increase it.
[12] Hope deferred makes the heart sick,
but a desire fulfilled is a tree of life.

m 12.23 Heb *the heart of fools* *n* 12.26 Syr: Meaning of Heb uncertain *o* 12.27 Meaning of Heb uncertain *p* 12.27 Meaning of Heb uncertain *q* 13.1 Cn: Heb *A wise child the discipline of his father* *r* 13.9 Or *shines* *s* 13.11 Gk Vg: Heb *from vanity*

12:17 Truthful speech is opposed to false witness.

12:18 Thoughtless speech is as damaging as a sword; wise words heal.

12:19 *Truthful lips endure forever* may allude to the long life of the righteous and the steadfastness of truth.

12:24 *The lazy will be put to forced labor* implies that lazy people deserve their fate.

12:27 Lazy people will have the privilege to *roast their game*. The translation from the Hebrew is uncertain, and so is its meaning.

13:1–25 The chapter is typified by the same pattern of two-lined sentences either in an antithetical or synthetical style (see **"Hebrew Poetry," p. 741**). On the one hand, the wise are linked with discipline (v. 1), respect for the word/commandment (v. 13), acting intelligently (v. 16), and heeding reproof (v. 18). On the other hand, the wicked, the scoffers, the treacherous, the sinners, and those who despise instruction are rewarded negatively. The worldview is simplistic and optimistic. **13:11** Forbids wealth gotten through dishonest means. **13:12** *Tree of life*. See 3:18; 11:30; 15:4.

¹³ Those who despise a word bring
     destruction on themselves,
   but those who respect a command
     will be rewarded.
¹⁴ The teaching of the wise is a fountain of
     life,
   so that one may avoid the snares of
     death.
¹⁵ Good sense wins favor,
   but the way of the faithless is their
     ruin.ᵗ
¹⁶ The clever do all things intelligently,
   but the fool displays folly.
¹⁷ A bad messenger brings trouble,
   but a faithful envoy, healing.
¹⁸ Poverty and disgrace are for the one who
     ignores instruction,
   but one who heeds reproof is honored.
¹⁹ A desire realized is sweet to the soul,
   but to turn away from evil is an
     abomination to fools.
²⁰ Whoever walks with the wise becomes
     wise,
   but the companion of fools suffers
     harm.
²¹ Misfortune pursues sinners,
   but prosperity rewards the righteous.
²² The good leave an inheritance to their
     children's children,
   but the sinner's wealth is laid up for
     the righteous.
²³ The field of the poor may yield much food,
   but it is swept away through injustice.

²⁴ Those who spare the rod hate their
     children,
   but those who love them are diligent
     to discipline them.
²⁵ The righteous have enough to satisfy
     their appetite,
   but the belly of the wicked is empty.

14 The wise womanᵘ builds her house,
   but the foolish tears it down with her
     own hands.
² Those who walk uprightly fear the Lord,
   but one who is devious in conduct
     despises him.
³ The talk of fools is a rod for their backs,ᵛ
   but the lips of the wise preserve them.
⁴ Where there are no oxen, there is no
     grain;
   abundant crops come by the strength
     of the ox.
⁵ A faithful witness does not lie,
   but a false witness breathes out lies.
⁶ A scoffer seeks wisdom in vain,
   but knowledge is easy for one who
     understands.
⁷ Leave the presence of a fool,
   for there you do not find words of
     knowledge.
⁸ It is the wisdom of the clever to
     understand where they go,
   but the folly of fools misleads.

t 13.15 Cn Compare Gk Syr Vg Tg: Heb *is enduring*
u 14.1 Heb *Wisdom of women*   *v* 14.3 Cn: Heb *a rod of pride*

13:14 An example of synthetic (or formal) parallelism. **13:23** In a rare instance, the sage problematizes the state of the poor. He acknowledges that injustice by the powerful may thwart the hard labors of the poor, thus challenging the simplistic mentality that easily and unproblematically links poverty with laziness (see, e.g., vv. 18 and 25). **13:24** The modern proverb "spare the rod, spoil the child" comes from Samuel Butler's poem "Hudibras" (seventeenth century) and reflects this verse. Whereas violence is condemned in most of Proverbs, family discipline depends on it. See also 23:13 and 29:15. **13:25** The sage can confidently argue that *the righteous have enough to satisfy their appetite*. For the many African Bible readers who are loyal members of the Christian faith and who continue to pledge meager offerings under the pressures of prosperity gospel preachers, the sayings that simplistically link righteousness with wealth, well-being, and success may be disempowering. The Northern Sotho proverb "tšhiwana ye e sa hwego e leta monono" (an orphan who does not die, awaits wealth) also comes to mind here. In real life, an orphan may outlive his or her parents but never get to be wealthy.

14:1 *The wise woman builds her house*. Reminiscent of Woman Wisdom, who builds a house with seven pillars (9:1), she is contrasted with her foolish counterpart who is the house's destroyer. While female voices are hardly heard, the house is linked not to a father but to a mother. *House* can be understood figuratively. The collective wisdom of the foremothers throughout the generations influences the female members of successive generations as they build households, nurture offspring, and pass on their wisdom to their daughters. Implicit in the transmission of wisdom as an aspect of oral pedagogy, which is a combination of tradition and practice, is the fact that even in the patriarchal world, women play a critical role in the formation of men-in-the-making.

9 Fools mock at the guilt offering,[w]
  but the upright enjoy God's favor.
10 The heart knows its own bitterness,
  and no stranger shares its joy.
11 The house of the wicked is destroyed,
  but the tent of the upright flourishes.
12 There is a way that seems right to a
  person,
  but its end is the way to death.[x]
13 Even in laughter the heart is sad,
  and the end of joy is grief.
14 The perverse get what their ways deserve,
  and the good, what their deeds
  deserve.[y]
15 The simple believe everything,
  but the clever consider their steps.
16 The wise are cautious and turn away
  from evil,
  but the fool throws off restraint and is
  careless.
17 One who is quick-tempered acts foolishly,
  and the schemer is hated.
18 The simple are adorned with[z] folly,
  but the clever are crowned with
  knowledge.
19 The evil bow down before the good,
  the wicked at the gates of the righteous.
20 The poor are disliked even by their
  neighbors,
  but the rich have many friends.
21 Those who despise their neighbors are
  sinners,
  but happy are those who are kind to
  the poor.
22 Do not those who plan evil err?
  Those who plan good find loyalty and
  faithfulness.

23 In all toil there is profit,
  but mere talk leads only to poverty.
24 The crown of the wise is their wealth,
  but folly is the garland[a] of fools.
25 A truthful witness saves lives,
  but one who utters lies is a betrayer.
26 In the fear of the LORD one has strong
  confidence,
  and one's children will have a
  refuge.
27 The fear of the LORD is a fountain of life,
  so that one may avoid the snares of
  death.
28 The glory of a king is a multitude of
  people;
  without people a prince is ruined.
29 Whoever is slow to anger has great
  understanding,
  but one who has a hasty temper exalts
  folly.
30 A tranquil mind gives life to the flesh,
  but jealousy makes the bones rot.
31 Those who oppress the poor insult their
  Maker,
  but those who are kind to the needy
  honor him.
32 The wicked are overthrown by their
  evildoing,
  but the righteous find a refuge in their
  integrity.[b]
33 Wisdom is at home in the mind of one
  who has understanding,
  but it is not[c] known in the heart of fools.

w 14.9 Meaning of Heb uncertain x 14.12 Heb *ways of
death* y 14.14 Cn: Heb *from upon him* z 14.18 Or *inherit*
a 14.24 Cn: Heb *is the folly* b 14.32 Gk Syr: Heb *in their death*
c 14.33 Gk Syr: Heb lacks *not*

14:11 The notion of positive and negative rewards is further highlighted, continuing the metaphor of the house.

14:12–13 The problematization of the optimistic wisdom worldview: what may seem right could be wrong; what seems like laughter could be grief. Indeed, "meno a sega ditšhila" (teeth laugh at trash; African proverb).

14:20–21 Other verses that undermine the general wisdom worldview. The poor are disliked (v. 20) presumably because of prejudice, since disliking one's neighbor is a sin and people are thus exhorted to be kind to the poor (v. 21). See also 14:31.

14:23 Even after verses that seem to affirm the poor, poverty is still linked with a lack of industry.

14:26 *The fear of the* LORD is the foundation of the family, one in which children are secured. See note on 1:7.

14:28 The African expression "motho ke motho ka batho" (a human being is one because of others) may be linked with the sage's affirmation that one can only be a king if there are people (subjects), hence "kgoši ke kgoši ka setšhaba" (a traditional leader is one through community; African proverb). See 14:34–35, which commends righteousness and wisdom for such subjects.

14:31 The theme of the poor and poverty is foregrounded here: the oppression of the poor is an insult to *their Maker*.

34 Righteousness exalts a nation,
    but sin is a reproach to any people.
35 A servant who deals wisely has the king's
        favor,
    but his wrath falls on one who acts
        shamefully.

15 A soft answer turns away wrath,
    but a harsh word stirs up anger.
2 The tongue of the wise adorns
        knowledge,
    but the mouths of fools pour out folly.
3 The eyes of the Lord are in every
        place,
    keeping watch on the evil and the
        good.
4 A gentle tongue is a tree of life,
    but perverseness in it breaks the spirit.
5 A fool despises a parent's instruction,
    but the one who heeds admonition is
        prudent.
6 In the house of the righteous there is
        much treasure,
    but trouble befalls the income of the
        wicked.
7 The lips of the wise spread knowledge;
    not so the minds of fools.
8 The sacrifice of the wicked is an
        abomination to the Lord,
    but the prayer of the upright is his
        delight.
9 The way of the wicked is an abomination
        to the Lord,
    but he loves the one who pursues
        righteousness.

10 There is severe discipline for one who
        forsakes the way;
    one who hates a rebuke will die.
11 Sheol and Abaddon lie open before the
        Lord;
    how much more human hearts!
12 Scoffers do not like to be rebuked;
    they will not go to the wise.
13 A glad heart makes a cheerful
        countenance,
    but by sorrow of heart the spirit is
        broken.
14 The mind of one who has understanding
        seeks knowledge,
    but the mouths of fools feed on
        folly.
15 All the days of the poor are hard,
    but a cheerful heart has a continual
        feast.
16 Better is a little with the fear of the
        Lord
    than great treasure and trouble
        with it.
17 Better is a dinner of vegetables where
        love is
    than a fatted ox and hatred with it.
18 Those who are hot-tempered stir up
        strife,
    but those who are slow to anger calm
        contention.
19 The way of the lazy is overgrown with
        thorns,
    but the path of the upright is a level
        highway.

15:1 There is an emphasis on right speech in the opening of this chapter. *Soft answer* indicates a connection between one's ability to control one's emotions and wisdom.

15:2 The body is again foregrounded, especially parts that enable speech, the *tongue* and *mouth*.

15:3 *The eyes of the Lord are in every place*, a theme that points to the sage's conviction that even in the mundane daily activities of humans, God is not detached. God is omnipresent.

15:4 *A gentle tongue is a tree of life*. Right speech is equated with wisdom. See 3:18; 11:30; 13:12. With their perverse tongues, fools break people's spirits. The African expression "molomo o tshela noka e tletše" (a mouth crosses an overflowing river) points to people who cannot discern, nor have the capacity to say the right word at the right time. The wise are thus able to give a fitting answer and cause everyone (except fools) to rejoice.

15:8 Even right ritual will not make up for wickedness. People thus have to walk uprightly to have their sacrifices acceptable to the Lord.

15:11 *Sheol and Abaddon* are both names for the underworld, another way of indicating death (see 27:20). See **"Sheol," p. 695**. Human hearts are known by the Lord.

15:13–15 The state of the *heart* and *mind* (holistic emotional and mental well-being) is part of wisdom.

15:16 *The fear of the Lord*, even when there are no riches, is better than hatred and trouble amid great wealth. See note on 1:7.

15:18 The *hot-tempered* are contrasted with the *slow to anger*. Emotional control is part of wisdom.

20 A wise child makes a glad father,
   but the foolish despise their mothers.
21 Folly is a joy to one who has no sense,
   but a person of understanding walks
      straight ahead.
22 Without counsel, plans go wrong,
   but with many advisers they succeed.
23 To make an apt answer is a joy to anyone,
   and a word in season, how good it is!
24 For the wise the path of life leads
      upward,
   in order to avoid Sheol below.
25 The LORD tears down the house of the
      proud
   but maintains the widow's boundaries.
26 Evil plans are an abomination to the
      LORD,
   but gracious words are pure.
27 Those greedy for unjust gain make
      trouble for their households,
   but those who hate bribes will
      live.
28 The mind of the righteous ponders how
      to answer,
   but the mouth of the wicked pours
      out evil.
29 The LORD is far from the wicked,
   but he hears the prayer of the
      righteous.

30 The light of the eyes rejoices the heart,
   and good news refreshes the body.
31 The ear that heeds wholesome
      admonition
   will lodge among the wise.
32 Those who ignore instruction despise
      themselves,
   but those who heed admonition gain
      understanding.
33 The fear of the LORD is instruction in
      wisdom,
   and humility goes before honor.

16 The plans of the mind belong to
      mortals,
   but the answer of the tongue is from
      the LORD.
2 All one's ways may be pure in one's own
      eyes,
   but the LORD weighs the spirit.
3 Commit your work to the LORD,
   and your plans will be established.
4 The LORD has made everything for its
      purpose,
   even the wicked for the day of trouble.
5 All those who are arrogant are an
      abomination to the LORD;
   be assured, they will not go
      unpunished.

15:20 Parental instruction in a family context, reminiscent of the opening verse of the present collection (10:1).

15:25 God is featured as being on the side of the weak.

15:28 *The righteous* think carefully first before answering. For the wise, the path of life leads upward, while folly will be poured out of the fools' mouths, who on account of their harsh words, will inevitably bring wrath.

15:29 God thus *hears the prayer of the righteous*. The notion of a God who hears prayers may counter the African notion of a faraway God who cannot be approached directly but only through ancestors as mediators, for which subject dares approach the kgoši / traditional leader directly? God is, however, *far from the wicked*.

15:33 Wisdom is again rooted in *the fear of the LORD*. See note on 1:7.

16:1–22:16 In the second part of the second collection, fewer proverbs use antithetical parallelism and more use synthetic parallelism, in which the second line builds on the idea or image of the first (see **"Hebrew Poetry," p. 741**). Like in the collection as a whole, featured are unrelated but powerful sayings that provide the listener/reader with guidance for daily living. There are sayings that reveal the human incapacity to determine his or her fate, thus highlighting the establishment of God's ultimate plans, proverbs that celebrate living in relative scarcity but with peace as opposed to one of plenty amid corrupt and fraudulent ways, as well as advice on the acceptable behavior of royalty. Noting the concentration of sayings concerning kings and their court, sometimes this section is called the Royal Collection.

16:1–4 In the opening verses, the vulnerability and limitedness of humans are compared to the Lord who knows and controls all. God *weighs the spirit* and establishes plans. Everything has a purpose in God's divine scheme. See also 16:9 and 16:11 for similar ideas. The same theme is found in 16:33, thus framing the chapter's contents.

16:5 Arrogance is an *abomination to the Lord*; the arrogant will of necessity be punished.

[6] By loyalty and faithfulness iniquity is
   atoned for,
   and by the fear of the LORD one avoids
   evil.
[7] When the ways of people please the LORD,
   he causes even their enemies to be at
   peace with them.
[8] Better is a little with righteousness
   than large income with injustice.
[9] The human mind plans the way,
   but the LORD directs the steps.
[10] Inspired decisions are on the lips of a
   king;
   his mouth does not sin in judgment.
[11] Honest balances and scales are the
   LORD's;
   all the weights in the bag are his work.
[12] It is an abomination to kings to do evil,
   for the throne is established by
   righteousness.
[13] Righteous lips are the delight of a king,
   and he loves those who speak what is
   right.
[14] A king's wrath is a messenger of death,
   and whoever is wise will appease it.
[15] In the light of a king's face there is life,
   and his favor is like the clouds that
   bring the spring rain.
[16] How much better to get wisdom than
   gold!
   To get understanding is to be chosen
   rather than silver.
[17] The highway of the upright avoids evil;
   those who guard their way preserve
   their lives.
[18] Pride goes before destruction
   and a haughty spirit before a fall.

[19] It is better to be of a lowly spirit among
   the poor
   than to divide the spoil with the proud.
[20] Those who are attentive to a matter will
   prosper,
   and happy are those who trust in the
   LORD.
[21] The wise of heart is called perceptive,
   and pleasant speech increases
   persuasiveness.
[22] Wisdom is a fountain of life to one who
   has it,
   but folly is the punishment of fools.
[23] The mind of the wise makes their speech
   judicious
   and adds persuasiveness to their lips.
[24] Pleasant words are like a honeycomb,
   sweetness to the soul and health to
   the body.
[25] Sometimes there is a way that seems to
   be right,
   but in the end it is the way to death.
[26] The appetite of workers works for them;
   their hunger urges them on.
[27] Scoundrels concoct evil,
   and their speech is like a scorching fire.
[28] A perverse person spreads strife,
   and a whisperer separates close friends.
[29] The violent entice their neighbors
   and lead them in a way that is not
   good.
[30] One who winks the eyes plans[d] perverse
   things;
   one who compresses the lips brings
   evil to pass.

d 16.30 Gk Syr Vg Tg: Heb *to plan*

16:6 *Fear of the* LORD helps one avoid evil. See note on 1:7.

16:8 Like in 15:16, poverty or relative lack is preferred to wealth gained through fraudulent means (see also 16:16 and 16:19). It is thus better for one to have little (material wealth) but be righteous, wise, and have the fear of the Lord.

16:10 The beginning of a collection of proverbs about kings.

16:12–15 The king should rule in righteousness; such will manifest in the utterances from his mouth, which will then encourage his subjects (v. 13). A Sotho proverb says, "lentšu la kgoši le agelwa lešaka" (words from royalty must be respected). A king's attitude can be a matter of life and death; he exudes life amid his subjects, and his favor is to be desired (vv. 14–15).

16:18 The proud and the haughty will be destroyed (see 16:5). This verse is the origin of the saying "Pride goeth before a fall."

16:21–24 A passage that lauds the *pleasant* (vv. 21 and 24) and *judicious* (v. 23) speech of the wise. Such speech will succeed in counseling, which brings healing to the whole body (v. 24). Wisdom is thus celebrated as a *fountain of life* (v. 22). See also 18:4.

16:27–30 Unlike the righteous, whose words have the capacity to bring life, the words of the *perverse* (v. 28) and the *violent* (v. 29) are compared with *scorching fire* (v. 27), spreading strife and destroying close friendships (v. 28); hence, once again, the power of the mouth to build or destroy.

³¹ Gray hair is a crown of glory;
    it is gained in a righteous life.
³² One who is slow to anger is better than
        the mighty,
    and one whose temper is controlled
        than one who captures a city.
³³ The lot is cast into the lap,
    but the decision is the Lord's alone.

17 Better is a dry morsel with quiet
    than a house full of feasting with strife.
² A slave who deals wisely will rule over a
        child who acts shamefully
    and will share the inheritance as one
        of the family.
³ The crucible is for silver and the furnace
        for gold,
    but the Lord tests the heart.
⁴ An evildoer listens to wicked lips,
    and a liar gives heed to a mischievous
        tongue.
⁵ Those who mock the poor insult their
        Maker;
    those who are glad at calamity will
        not go unpunished.
⁶ Grandchildren are the crown of the aged,
    and the glory of children is their
        parents.
⁷ Excess speech is not becoming to a fool;
    still less is false speech to a ruler.^e
⁸ A bribe is like a magic stone in the eyes
        of those who give it;
    wherever they turn they prosper.
⁹ One who forgives an affront fosters
        friendship,
    but one who dwells on disputes will
        alienate a friend.
¹⁰ A rebuke strikes deeper into a discerning
        person
    than a hundred blows into a fool.

¹¹ Evil people seek only rebellion,
    but a cruel messenger will be sent
        against them.
¹² Better to meet a she-bear robbed of its
        cubs
    than to confront a fool immersed in
        folly.
¹³ Evil will not depart from the house
    of one who returns evil for good.
¹⁴ The beginning of strife is like letting out
        water,
    so stop before the quarrel breaks out.
¹⁵ One who justifies the wicked and one
        who condemns the righteous
    are both alike an abomination to the
        Lord.
¹⁶ Why should fools have a price in hand
    to buy wisdom when they have no
        mind to learn?
¹⁷ A friend loves at all times,
    and kinsfolk are born to share
        adversity.
¹⁸ It is senseless to give a pledge,
    to become surety for a neighbor.
¹⁹ One who loves transgression loves strife;
    one who builds a high threshold
        invites broken bones.
²⁰ The crooked of mind do not prosper,
    and the perverse of tongue fall into
        calamity.
²¹ The one who fathers a fool gets trouble;
    the parent of a fool has no joy.
²² A cheerful heart is a good medicine,
    but a downcast spirit dries up the
        bones.
²³ The wicked accept a concealed bribe
    to pervert the ways of justice.

e 17.7 Or *a noble*

16:31 The righteous are also crowned with long life, revealed by *gray hair*.

17:2 Scattered across this chapter are selected proverbs on the family and its significance, including on the theme of parent-child relationships. Badly behaved children are most likely to experience a reversal of fortunes and be ruled by those in the family who are enslaved, who could also share the family's inheritance.

17:4 Another featured theme is wisdom and folly manifested by the utterance of the *lips* and *tongue*. The fool and his actions are foregrounded by the sage as an example not to be emulated but to be shunned. See also 17:5, 7.

17:5 The sage's sense of justice: God is portrayed as being on the side of the poor.

17:6 While grandchildren are the crown of their grandparents, parents are the glory (crown) of the children, hence the interrelationships between people across three generations.

17:16 The fool resists rebuke and discipline (see 12:1); neither is he teachable.

17:18 *Give a pledge . . . become surety* means to guarantee a loan for another, which is considered destructive to social relationships. See 6:1–2; 11:15; 22:26.

17:23 A concern with criminal justice systems. See also 17:26 and 18:5.

24 The discerning person looks to wisdom,
  but the eyes of a fool to the ends of
  the earth.
25 Foolish children are a grief to their
  father
  and bitterness to her who bore them.
26 To impose a fine on the innocent is not
  right
  or to flog the noble for their integrity.
27 One who spares words is knowledgeable;
  one who is cool in spirit has
  understanding.
28 Even fools who keep silent are
  considered wise;
  when they close their lips, they are
  deemed intelligent.

18 The one who lives alone is
  self-indulgent,
  showing contempt for all sound
  judgment.*f*
2 A fool takes no pleasure in
  understanding,
  but only in expressing personal
  opinion.
3 When wickedness comes, contempt
  comes also,
  and with dishonor comes disgrace.
4 The words of the mouth are deep waters;
  the fountain of wisdom is a gushing
  stream.
5 It is not right to be partial to the guilty
  or to subvert the innocent in
  judgment.

6 A fool's lips bring strife,
  and a fool's mouth invites a flogging.
7 The mouths of fools are their ruin,
  and their lips a snare to themselves.
8 The words of a whisperer are like
  delicious morsels;
  they go down into the inner parts of
  the body.
9 One who is slack in work
  is close kin to a vandal.
10 The name of the Lord is a strong tower;
  the righteous run into it and are safe.
11 The wealth of the rich is their strong
  city;
  in their imagination it is like a high
  wall.
12 Before destruction one's heart is
  haughty,
  but humility goes before honor.
13 If one gives answer before hearing,
  it is folly and shame.
14 The human spirit will endure sickness,
  but a broken spirit—who can bear?
15 An intelligent mind acquires knowledge,
  and the ear of the wise seeks
  knowledge.
16 A gift opens doors;
  it gives access to the great.
17 The one who first states a case seems right,
  until the other comes and
  cross-examines.

f 18.1 Meaning of Heb uncertain

17:25 *Foolish children* can only bring grief and bitterness to their parents.

17:26 A concern with criminal justice systems. See also 17:23 and 18:5. Hence a fine cannot be imposed on *the innocent*, nor can one *flog the noble for their integrity*.

17:27 The need to use words economically.

17:28 Even the fool can deploy wisdom if he follows the preceding advice.

18:1–2 The fool's disposition is as a loner; such a person in the solitary space gets self-opinionated and is not guided by understanding and knowledge. Such a person's folly, with no sound understanding, will be revealed by his mouth's utterances. The African proverb "motho ke motho ka batho" (a human being is a human being because of others) speaks to the wisdom of relationships.

18:6–7 Foolish words become a trap for the fools themselves; they also invite both discipline and destruction, because "mokga kgati o a ikgela" (one who prepares a whip [for discipline] does so for himself or herself; African proverb).

18:8 Wise words are whispered; if not blurred by noise and shouts, they have the capacity to filter through to the inner parts of the body in order to bring healing. See 26:22.

18:10 *The name of the Lord is a strong tower.* Those who seek refuge not in material wealth but in God are secure. The celebration of the seeking of refuge in the name of the Lord rather than in material wealth may be viewed by the economically marginal as a pacifying strategy.

18:13 Folly is a rushed answer, one that comes prematurely. Such people jump before the proverbial drum is sounded (African proverb: "ba fofa pele moropa o lla"). The fool's utterances are contrasted with the words of the wise; words inspired by knowledge are as powerful as gushing waters, coming from the heart, which is a fountain of wisdom (18:4).

18 Casting the lot puts an end to disputes
  and decides between powerful
    contenders.
19 An ally offended is stronger than a city;*g*
  such quarreling is like the bars of a
    castle.
20 From the fruit of the mouth one's
    stomach is satisfied;
  the yield of the lips brings satisfaction.
21 Death and life are in the power of the
    tongue,
  and those who love it will eat its fruits.
22 He who finds a wife finds a good thing
  and obtains favor from the Lord.
23 The poor use entreaties,
  but the rich answer roughly.
24 Some*b* friends play at friendship,*i*
  but a true friend sticks closer than
    one's sibling.

19 Better the poor walking in integrity
  than one perverse of speech who is
    a fool.
2 Desire without knowledge is not good,
  and one who moves too hurriedly
    misses the way.
3 One's own folly leads to ruin,
  yet the heart rages against the Lord.
4 Wealth brings many friends,
  but the poor are left friendless.
5 A false witness will not go unpunished,
  and a liar will not escape.
6 Many seek the favor of the generous,
  and everyone is a friend to a giver of
    gifts.

7 If the poor are hated even by their kin,
  how much more are they shunned by
    their friends!
  When they call after them, they are not
    there.*j*
8 To get wisdom is to love oneself;
  to keep understanding is to prosper.
9 A false witness will not go unpunished,
  and the liar will perish.
10 It is not fitting for a fool to live in luxury,
  much less for a slave to rule over princes.
11 Those with good sense are slow to anger,
  and it is their glory to overlook an
    offense.
12 A king's anger is like the growling of a lion,
  but his favor is like dew on the grass.
13 A stupid child is ruin to a father,
  and a wife's quarreling is a continual
    dripping of rain.
14 House and wealth are inherited from
    parents,
  but a prudent wife is from the Lord.
15 Laziness brings on deep sleep;
  an idle person will suffer hunger.
16 Those who keep the commandment will
    live;
  those who are heedless of their ways
    will die.
17 Whoever is kind to the poor lends to the
    Lord
  and will be repaid in full.

g 18.19 Gk Syr Vg Tg: Meaning of Heb uncertain
h 18.24 Syr Tg: Heb *A man of* *i* 18.24 Cn Compare Syr Vg
Tg: Meaning of Heb uncertain *j* 19.7 Meaning of Heb
uncertain

18:20 The power of wise words can be used to satisfy hunger.

18:22 A wife is a *good thing*; compare with 19:13–14 and 31:10.

18:23 The poor (the wise?) are aware of the tongue's power to utter reconciling words, unlike the rich—the economically powerful—who will, to the contrary, use rough words (see also Sir. 13:3). It appears that each person, including the economically marginalized, is left to fend for themselves. Though kindness to inferiors is recommended, even commanded, class distinctions are not only accepted; they are perpetuated. There is no radical change in the situation of the poor. Hence the elitist status quo is embedded in the book of Proverbs.

18:24 The power of the human spirit and true friendship.

19:1–29 Like in the preceding chapters, variegated themes are addressed by the sage, and one finds the same pattern here: the power of the mouth and its ability to display wisdom and foolishness, especially the toxic and destructive nature of what comes from the fool's mouth; the alienation of the poor; and family relations. **19:8** Wisdom is celebrated, as those who have it are lovers of themselves, and those who embrace understanding prosper. **19:11** The wise are *slow to anger*; emotional control is an attribute of wisdom. **19:13–14** *A stupid child is ruin to a father*. Perhaps the concern here is more with the capacity of such a child to end the patriline. In the familial context, it is clear that the adult male (as father and husband) and his concerns are foregrounded. *Quarreling* (v. 13) is a negative quality in a wife, but *a prudent wife is from the* Lord (v. 14). **19:15** Laziness is rebuked. See also 19:24. **19:16** Obedience to the commandments gives life; disobedience leads to death. **19:17** Those who care for the poor do so for the Lord and will thus be rewarded positively.

¹⁸ Discipline your children while there is hope;
  do not set your heart on their destruction.
¹⁹ A violent-tempered person will pay the penalty;
  if you effect a rescue, you will only have to do it again.^k
²⁰ Listen to advice and accept instruction,
  that you may gain wisdom for the future.
²¹ The human mind may devise many plans,
  but it is the purpose of the LORD that will be established.
²² What is desirable in a person is loyalty,
  and it is better to be poor than a liar.
²³ The fear of the LORD is life indeed;
  filled with it one rests secure and suffers no harm.
²⁴ The lazy person buries a hand in the dish
  and will not even bring it back to the mouth.
²⁵ Strike a scoffer, and the simple will learn prudence;
  reprove the intelligent, and they will gain knowledge.
²⁶ Those who do violence to their father
  and chase away their mother
  are children who cause shame and bring reproach.
²⁷ My child, stop ignoring instruction,
  straying^l from words of knowledge.
²⁸ A worthless witness mocks at justice,
  and the mouth of the wicked devours iniquity.
²⁹ Punishments are prepared for scoffers
  and flogging for the backs of fools.

20 Wine is a mocker, strong drink a brawler,
and whoever is led astray by it is not wise.
² The dread anger of a king is like the growling of a lion;
  anyone who provokes him to anger forfeits life itself.
³ It is honorable to refrain from strife,
  but every fool is quick to quarrel.
⁴ The lazy person does not plow in season;
  harvest comes, and there is nothing to be found.
⁵ The purposes in the human mind are like deep water,
  but the intelligent will draw them out.
⁶ Many proclaim themselves loyal,
  but who can find one worthy of trust?
⁷ The righteous walk in integrity—
  happy are the children who follow them!
⁸ A king who sits on the throne of judgment
  winnows all evil with his eyes.
⁹ Who can say, "I have made my heart clean;
  I am pure from my sin"?
¹⁰ Diverse weights and diverse measures
  are both alike an abomination to the LORD.
¹¹ Even children make themselves known by their acts,
  by whether what they do is pure and right.
¹² The hearing ear and the seeing eye—
  the LORD has made them both.
¹³ Do not love sleep, or else you will come to poverty;
  open your eyes, and you will have plenty of bread.

k 19.19 Meaning of Heb uncertain   l 19.27 Cn: Meaning of Heb uncertain

19:18 Children need to be disciplined *while there is hope*, perhaps meaning earlier on in life because "lešepa le kgobja le sa fiša" (make hay while the sun shines; African proverb). **19:27** The concern with children obeying parents continues. The words, commandments, and discipline from the father may not always be fully embraced by the son, hence an exhortation to him to stop ignoring instruction and straying away from the words of knowledge.

20:1 Drunkenness is a sign of folly, and people can be led astray by wine and strong drink. See 23:29–35 and 31:4–7.

20:2 The influence of a king on people's lives is reflected here; see also 19:12 and 20:8.

20:5 While *the purposes in the human mind are like deep water*, the intelligent can discern them.

20:12 Wisdom entails the responsible use of the body: *the hearing ear and the seeing eye*. God creates the body to be used properly.

20:13 *Do not love sleep* means do not be lazy. Those who sleep too much will suffer from poverty, while those who are alert (the industrious) will have plenty of food. However, in real life, the experiences of those who are marginalized on the basis of their race, class, and gender, among other reasons, belie the sage's observations.

¹⁴ "Bad, bad," says the buyer,
    then goes away and boasts.
¹⁵ There is gold and abundance of costly
    stones,
    but the lips informed by knowledge
    are a precious jewel.
¹⁶ Take the garment of one who has given
    surety for a stranger;
    seize the pledge given as surety for
    foreigners.
¹⁷ Bread gained by deceit is sweet,
    but afterward the mouth will be full
    of gravel.
¹⁸ Plans are established by taking advice;
    wage war by following wise guidance.
¹⁹ A gossip reveals secrets;
    therefore do not associate with a
    babbler.
²⁰ If you curse father or mother,
    your lamp will go out in utter
    darkness.
²¹ An estate quickly acquired in the
    beginning
    will not be blessed in the end.
²² Do not say, "I will repay evil";
    wait for the LORD, and he will help
    you.
²³ Differing weights are an abomination to
    the LORD,
    and false scales are not good.
²⁴ All our steps are ordered by the LORD;
    how then can we understand our own
    ways?
²⁵ It is a snare for one to say rashly, "It is
    holy,"

and begin to reflect only after making
    a vow.
²⁶ A wise king winnows the wicked
    and drives the wheel over them.
²⁷ The human spirit is the lamp of the LORD,
    searching every inmost part.
²⁸ Loyalty and faithfulness preserve the
    king,
    and his throne is upheld by
    righteousness.^m
²⁹ The glory of youths is their strength,
    but the beauty of the aged is their
    gray hair.
³⁰ Blows that wound cleanse away evil;
    beatings make clean the innermost
    parts.

21 The king's heart is a stream of water
    in the hand of the LORD;
    he turns it wherever he will.
² All deeds are right in the sight of the doer,
    but the LORD weighs the heart.
³ To do righteousness and justice
    is more acceptable to the LORD than
    sacrifice.
⁴ Haughty eyes and a proud heart—
    the lamp of the wicked—are sin.
⁵ The plans of the diligent lead surely to
    abundance,
    but everyone who is hasty comes only
    to want.
⁶ The getting of treasures by a lying
    tongue
    is a fleeting vapor and a snareⁿ of death.

m 20.28 Gk: Heb *loyalty*   *n* 21.6 Gk: Heb *seekers*

20:16 Warns against guaranteeing a loan for strangers and foreigners. This exhortation is in contrast to the African spirit of hospitality. See also 6:1–5; 17:18; 22:26.

20:17 Wealth through deceit is dangerous.

20:22 Leave revenge to God.

20:23 *Differing weights* and *false scales* are evil. See note on 11:1.

20:26, 28 A king must judge the wicked accordingly. Such a righteous king is preserved.

20:27 *The human spirit* is God's inner illumination. Light is connected to wisdom and knowledge also in 4:18; 6:23; 13:19.

20:29 Age is celebrated across generations: both the glory of young people in their strength as well as the beauty of the aged in their gray hair.

20:30 Physical discipline can have a purging influence.

21:1 The opening saying links the king with God. As in other verses in the Royal Collection, the king should be righteous and must possess a heart that is open to the ways of wisdom, one that is thus aligned with God. See 16:10, 12–15; 20:8, 26, 28. Cf. 8:15–16.

21:2 A human being is insignificant before God. A person's ways are finite, incomplete, and unreliable. Hence people must not be wise in their own eyes. See 16:2 and 24:12 for other images of God using weights to measure human thoughts and actions.

21:4 In their pride, the wicked act contrary to the ways of the wise as they venture to navigate life outside of the Lord.

7 The violence of the wicked will sweep
    them away
because they refuse to do what is
    just.
8 The way of the guilty is crooked,
but the conduct of the pure is right.
9 It is better to live in a corner of the
    housetop
than in a house shared with a
    contentious wife.
10 The souls of the wicked desire evil;
their neighbors find no mercy in their
    eyes.
11 When a scoffer is punished, the simple
    become wiser;
when the wise are instructed, they
    increase in knowledge.
12 The Righteous One observes the house of
    the wicked;
he casts the wicked down to ruin.
13 If you close your ear to the cry of the
    poor,
you will cry out and not be heard.
14 A gift in secret averts anger,
and a concealed bribe, strong wrath.
15 When justice is done, it is a joy to the
    righteous
but dismay to evildoers.
16 Whoever wanders from the way of
    understanding
will rest in the assembly of the dead.
17 Whoever loves pleasure will suffer
    want;
whoever loves wine and oil will not
    be rich.
18 The wicked is a ransom for the
    righteous
and the faithless for the upright.
19 It is better to live in a desert land
than with a contentious and fretful
    wife.

20 Precious treasure remains[o] in the house
    of the wise,
but the fool devours it.
21 Whoever pursues righteousness and
    kindness
will find life[p] and honor.
22 One wise person went up against a city
    of warriors
and brought down the stronghold in
    which they trusted.
23 To watch over mouth and tongue
is to keep out of trouble.
24 The proud, haughty person, named
    Scoffer,
acts with arrogant pride.
25 The craving of the lazy person is
    fatal,
for lazy hands refuse to labor.
26 All day long the wicked covet,[q]
but the righteous give and do not hold
    back.
27 The sacrifice of the wicked is an
    abomination;
how much more when brought with
    evil intent.
28 A false witness will perish,
but a good listener will testify
    successfully.
29 The wicked put on a bold face,
but the upright give thought to[r] their
    ways.
30 No wisdom, no understanding, no
    counsel
can avail against the LORD.
31 The horse is made ready for the day of
    battle,
but the victory belongs to the
    LORD.

o 21.20 Gk: Heb *and oil* p 21.21 Gk: Heb *life and righteousness*
q 21.26 Gk: Heb *all day long one covets covetously* r 21.29 Or
establish

21:7 The wicked *refuse to do what is just.*
21:8 *The pure* pursue justice and righteousness, and their conduct is right.
21:9 This proverb is repeated in 25:24. See also 21:19.
21:10 The wicked do not show mercy to their neighbor.
21:11 When instructed, they increase in knowledge.
21:13–14 In the typical simplistic worldview embedded in Proverbs, people who do not act wisely can expect punishment. The punishment corresponds to the wicked act. See 12:16–17.
21:16–17 Similar to 12:13–14, the punishments fit the crimes.
21:21 *Righteousness and kindness* are rewarded with *life and honor.*
21:22 Even when they are a minority, the wise can win battles.
21:26 The texts dealing with wealth and poverty reveal a concern for justice for the poor while at the same time decrying the oppressive and dishonest means used to acquire wealth.
21:31 *Victory belongs to the* LORD regardless of human efforts.

22

¹ A good name is to be chosen rather
than great riches,
and favor is better than silver or gold.
² The rich and the poor have this in
common:
the Lord is the maker of them all.
³ The clever see danger and hide,
but the simple go on and suffer for it.
⁴ The reward for humility and fear of the
Lord
is riches and honor and life.
⁵ Thorns and snares are in the way of the
perverse;
the cautious will keep far from them.
⁶ Train children in the right way,
and when old, they will not stray.
⁷ The rich rule over the poor,
and the borrower is the slave of the
lender.
⁸ Whoever sows injustice will reap
calamity,
and the rod of anger will fail.
⁹ Those who are generous are blessed,
for they share their bread with the poor.
¹⁰ Drive out a scoffer, and strife goes out;
quarreling and abuse will cease.

¹¹ Those who love a pure heart and are
gracious in speech
will have the king as a friend.
¹² The eyes of the Lord keep watch over
knowledge,
but he overthrows the words of the
faithless.
¹³ The lazy person says, "There is a lion
outside!
I shall be killed in the streets!"
¹⁴ The mouth of a loose womanˢ is a deep pit;
he with whom the Lord is angry falls
into it.
¹⁵ Folly is bound up in the heart of a child,
but the rod of discipline drives it far
away.
¹⁶ Oppressing the poor in order to enrich
oneself,
and giving to the rich, will lead only
to loss.
¹⁷   The words of the wise:

Incline your ear and hear my words*
and apply your mind to my teaching,

s 22.14 Heb *strange woman*   t 22.17 Cn Compare Gk: Heb
Incline your ear, and hear the words of the wise

22:1–16 In this last section of Proverbs's second collection, the sayings are mostly in the style of antithetical parallelism (see **"Hebrew Poetry," p. 741**). In their address of multiple themes, thus entailing multiple lessons for these men-in-the-making, the sayings contained in the collection as a whole are timeless and even universal. The intended audience would have been younger men with the goal of shaping and nurturing ideal masculinities. The content of this collection addresses everyday themes such as family relationships; care for the needy; being a good neighbor; the need for just and righteous governance, especially by royalty; and hard work. Experience as the best teacher has demonstrated that if people adhere to the order set by the Lord (God and the ancestors in the African tradition) and thus follow wisdom's ways, they will be successful. However, deviation from the order established by God that is discernible in societal and natural structures will be punished. This worldview can be challenged by other experiences (especially those of the marginalized) and will be challenged in other biblical books like Ecclesiastes and Job. **22:1** *Good name* means one's reputation. See also Eccl. 7:1. **22:2** The rich are put on equal footing with the poor, as both are created by God (see 29:13). **22:4** *Fear of the Lord* is a recurring theme (see, e.g., 1:7; 10:27; 16:6). See note on 1:7. Riches, honor, and life are rewarded to those who are humble. **22:7** The poor's disadvantaged position vis-à-vis the rich and the lender's vis-à-vis the borrower are highlighted in the context of the embedded power dynamics. **22:9** While wealth is celebrated as the reward for wisdom, the wealthy are called to a responsibility to be generous to the poor. **22:14** *Loose woman* is literally "strange woman" in Hebrew. She is portrayed as an adulteress in 2:16–19. Those not aligned with God get ensnared by her *mouth* (words), which is likened to a *deep pit*, possibly an allusion to the grave and therefore death. Once again, women are portrayed in a negative light, bifurcated between the good wife (see 31:10–31) and the *loose woman*. **22:15** *Folly* in a child can be remedied by the *rod of discipline*, so parents must not shy away from exercising discipline in their efforts to make and shape ideal masculinities in their sons. **22:16** Justice will be served when the poor are not oppressed and the rich are not given more than they already have.

22:17–24:22 Sayings of the wise. Wisdom literature arose in a global context. This third collection in the book of Proverbs appears to be an adaptation of the Egyptian wisdom book, the Instruction of Amenemope, composed sometime between 1300 and 1000 BCE. Even so, it fits with the major themes of Proverbs as a whole. **22:17–21** The opening verses of the third collection return to the style

¹⁸ for it will be pleasant if you keep them
within you,
if all of them are ready on your lips.
¹⁹ So that your trust may be in the LORD,
I have made them known to you today,
yes, to you.
²⁰ Have I not written for you thirty^u sayings
of admonition and knowledge,
²¹ to show you what is right and true,
so that you may give a true answer to
those who sent you?

²² Do not rob the poor because they are poor
or crush the afflicted at the gate,
²³ for the LORD pleads their cause
and despoils of life those who despoil
them.
²⁴ Make no friends with those given to
anger,
and do not associate with hotheads,
²⁵ lest you learn their ways
and entangle yourself in a snare.
²⁶ Do not be one of those who give pledges,
who become surety for debts.
²⁷ If you have nothing with which to pay,
why should your bed be taken from
under you?
²⁸ Do not remove the ancient landmark
that your ancestors set up.
²⁹ Do you see those who are skillful in their
work?
They will serve kings;
they will not serve common people.

23

When you sit down to eat with an
official,
observe carefully what^v is before you,
² and put a knife to your throat
if you have a big appetite.
³ Do not desire an official's^w delicacies,
for they are deceptive food.
⁴ Do not wear yourself out to get rich;
be wise enough to desist.
⁵ When your eyes light upon it, it is gone,
for suddenly it takes wings to itself,
flying like an eagle toward heaven.
⁶ Do not eat the bread of the stingy;
do not desire their delicacies,
⁷ for like a hair in the throat, so are they.^x
"Eat and drink!" they say to you,
but they do not mean it.
⁸ You will vomit up the little you have
eaten,
and you will waste your pleasant
words.
⁹ Do not speak in the hearing of a fool,
who will only despise the wisdom of
your words.
¹⁰ Do not remove an ancient landmark
or encroach on the fields of orphans,
¹¹ for their vindicator^y is strong;
he will plead their cause against you.
¹² Apply your mind to instruction
and your ear to words of knowledge.

u 22.20 Cn: Heb *in the past* or *noble*   v 23.1 Or *who*
w 23.3 Heb *his*   x 23.7 Meaning of Heb uncertain
y 23.11 Or *redeemer*

of the instruction genre of chaps. 1–9. Although the collection is not addressed to the son, as it is presently featured, it may be assumed that the sons remain the addressees. These are exhorted to use the body effectively in their embrace of wisdom and her ways: *ear, mind* (v. 17), and *lips* (v. 18). Cultivating trust in the Lord is the focus, parallel with the fear of the Lord in 1:7. **22:20** *Thirty sayings.* Thirty is the number of chapters in the Egyptian Instruction of Amenemope. See note on 22:17–24:22. **22:22–23** Once more the theme of poverty and concern for the poor is featured, as the Lord takes the side of those who are on the margins of communities. **22:26** Warnings against loans and pledges are common (see 6:1–2; 11:15; 17:18). It is not clear if the exhortations against the giving of pledges and becoming surety for debts are geared at protecting the poor, especially if paired with the next verse (22:27). **22:28** *The ancient landmark* is a boundary marker (see 23:10). The past and those who lived in the past (*your ancestors*) are celebrated, just like in Africa's contexts. In Africa, the ancestors are still viewed as being present in the community. **22:29** Wisdom is evident here in the skills one possesses. Biblical wisdom includes the art of being skillful and successful in one's relationships and responsibilities in life. The distinction between *kings* and *common people* reveals the elitist nature of the content and addressees of the collection. **23:1–3** Whereas references to the lips and mouth are usually about right and wrong speech, here they are a channel through which food is consumed. Proper eating, especially when with someone of a higher rank, is a mark of wisdom. **23:5** Also highlighted are the dangers associated with riches and the delicacies of the rich. **23:6–8** *Do not eat the bread of the stingy.* The attitude of the giver counts as much to the sage as the gift. **23:8** *You will vomit up.* The receiver of a gift given in stinginess may experience the negative impacts of the gift. In the African tradition, such vomiting would not be linked with stinginess; instead, the possibility is

¹³ Do not withhold discipline from your
      children;
   if you beat them with a rod, they will
      not die.
¹⁴ If you beat them with the rod,
   you will save their lives from Sheol.
¹⁵ My child, if your heart is wise,
   my heart also will be glad.
¹⁶ My soul will rejoice
   when your lips speak what is right.
¹⁷ Do not let your heart envy sinners,
   but always continue in the fear of the
      LORD.
¹⁸ Surely there is a future,
   and your hope will not be cut off.

¹⁹ Hear, my child, and be wise,
   and direct your mind in the way.
²⁰ Do not be among winebibbers
   or among gluttonous eaters of meat,
²¹ for the drunkard and the glutton will
      come to poverty,
   and drowsiness will clothe them with
      rags.

²² Listen to your father who begot you,
   and do not despise your mother when
      she is old.
²³ Buy truth, and do not sell it;
   buy wisdom, instruction, and
      understanding.
²⁴ The father of the righteous will greatly
      rejoice;
   he who fathers a wise son will be glad
      in him.
²⁵ Let your father and mother be glad;
   let her who bore you rejoice.

²⁶ My child, give me your heart,
   and let your eyes observe^z my ways.
²⁷ For a prostitute is a deep pit;
   an adulteress^a is a narrow well.
²⁸ She lies in wait like a robber
   and increases the number of the
      faithless.

²⁹ Who has woe? Who has sorrow?
   Who has strife? Who has complaining?
   Who has wounds without cause?
   Who has redness of eyes?
³⁰ Those who linger late over wine,
   those who keep trying mixed wines.
³¹ Do not look at wine when it is red,
   when it sparkles in the cup
   and goes down smoothly.
³² At the last it bites like a serpent
   and stings like an adder.
³³ Your eyes will see strange things,
   and your mind utter perverse things.
³⁴ You will be like one who lies down in the
      midst of the sea,
   like one who lies on the top of a
      mast.^{b}
³⁵ "They struck me," you will say,^{c} "but I
      was not hurt;
   they beat me, but I did not feel it.
   When shall I awake?
   I will seek another drink."

24 Do not envy the wicked,
   nor desire to be with them,
² for their minds devise violence,
   and their lips talk of mischief.

z 23.26 Or *delight in*   a 23.27 Heb *alien woman*
b 23.34 Meaning of Heb uncertain   c 23.35 Gk Syr Vg Tg:
Heb lacks *you will say*

that the giver could be a witch or a wizard. What is aligned between the two worldviews, though, is the causal relationship between the calamity and the attitude of the actor. **23:13-14** As part of parental instruction, the need for disciplining (foolish) children is foregrounded, even to the point of corporal punishment. See 13:24 and 22:15. **23:22-25** The theme of parent-child family relationships is featured here, with the father foregrounded. **23:26-28** *Let your eyes observe my ways*, an exhortation that reveals that through years of experience, the teacher could confidently present himself as a model. The son's eyes are to avoid gazing at the *prostitute* (v. 27)—who is likened to the adulteress (literally "strange woman")—with its consequent dangers. Both lead to death. See 2:16-19; 7:6-27; 22:14. "Moepalebitla o a ikepela" (one who digs a grave is actually digging his own), says an African proverb. **23:29-36** The elaborate exhortations against too much drinking might indicate that drunkenness was a real challenge facing the young male adults in that ancient sociohistorical context. The toxic consequences of those who are controlled by wine are *woe*, *sorrow*, *strife*, *complaining*, *wounds without cause*, and *redness of eyes* (v. 29). The danger of too much wine is compared to a snake (v. 32); waking and immediately seeking another drink sounds like addiction. Ideal manhood is formed by self-control and sobriety. **24:1-2** The opening verse is a prohibition against envying the wicked. Their bodies—*minds* and *lips*—discharge the violence and mischief respectively. The same prohibition *Do not envy the wicked* is repeated toward the end of the collection (24:19-20), thus

³ By wisdom a house is built,
    and by understanding it is established;
⁴ by knowledge the rooms are filled
    with all precious and pleasant riches.
⁵ Wise warriors are mightier than strong
    ones[d]
    and those who have knowledge than
    those who have strength,
⁶ for by wise guidance you can wage your
    war,
    and in abundance of counselors there
    is victory.
⁷ Wisdom is too high for fools;
    in the gate they do not open their
    mouths.

⁸ Whoever plans to do evil
    will be called a mischief-maker.
⁹ The devising of folly is sin,
    and the scoffer is an abomination to all.

¹⁰ If you faint in the day of adversity,
    your strength being small;
¹¹ if you hold back from rescuing those
    taken away to death,
    those who go staggering to the slaughter;
¹² if you say, "Look, we did not know this"—
    does not he who weighs the heart
    perceive it?
    Does not he who keeps watch over your
    soul know it?
    And will he not repay all according to
    their deeds?

¹³ My child, eat honey, for it is good,
    and the drippings of the honeycomb
    are sweet to your taste.

¹⁴ Know that wisdom is such to your
    soul;
    if you find it, you will find a future,
    and your hope will not be cut off.

¹⁵ Do not lie in wait like an outlaw against
    the home of the righteous;
    do no violence to the place where the
    righteous live;
¹⁶ for though they fall seven times, they will
    rise again,
    but the wicked are overthrown by
    calamity.

¹⁷ Do not rejoice when your enemies fall,
    and do not let your heart be glad
    when they stumble,
¹⁸ lest the Lᴏʀᴅ see it and be displeased
    and turn away his anger from them.

¹⁹ Do not fret because of evildoers.
    Do not envy the wicked,
²⁰ for the evil have no future;
    the lamp of the wicked will go out.

²¹ My child, fear the Lᴏʀᴅ and the king,
    and do not disobey either of them,[e]
²² for disaster comes from them suddenly,
    and who knows the ruin that both can
    bring?
²³   These also are sayings of the wise:

    Partiality in judging is not good.
²⁴ Whoever says to the wicked, "You are
    innocent,"

d 24.5 Gk Compare Syr Tg: Heb *A wise man is strength*
e 24.21 Gk: Heb *do not associate with those who change*

forming an inclusio. **24:3–4** The motif of wisdom as a house builder returns (see 9:1–6 and 31:26–27). Wisdom and its twins, knowledge and understanding, are essential to the success of any family. **24:9** For the sage, the *devising of folly* is tantamount to sin. **24:13** The exhortation to *eat honey* is an end not in itself but in the context of its comparison with the value and hope embedded in wisdom. Hence those who find wisdom have a secure future. **24:15–16** Though the righteous may fall multiple times, they will rise. **24:16–17** The prohibition of celebrating the enemy's fall is motivated not by the love of the enemy but by the idea that such celebration may work against the revenge that is supposed to be meted out onto the enemies by the Lord. The lack of celebration is thus meant to ensure that the enemy is eventually punished. **24:19–20** *Do not envy the wicked* mirrors the language in 24:1–2. Unlike those who embrace wisdom, the wicked live without hope, as they *have no future* (v. 20). Wisdom and knowledge will build a family (24:3–4), and thus a future, but evildoers will not. **24:21–22** The motif of God bringing punishment to offenders is repeated in the last two verses of this third collection of Proverbs. A person's relationship with the Lord and the king are parallel, based on fear and obedience lest disaster befalls those who offend both. As for the authority invested in the latter, the Sotho proverb "lentšu la kgoši le agelwa lešaka" (words from royalty must be respected) is resonant.

    24:23–34 Additional sayings of the wise. The opening verse indicates a different collection, the

will be cursed by peoples, abhorred by
nations,
25 but those who rebuke the wicked will
have delight,
and a good blessing will come upon
them.
26 One who gives an honest answer
gives a kiss on the lips.

27 Prepare your work outside;
get everything ready for you in the field;
and after that build your house.

28 Do not be a witness against your
neighbor without cause,
and do not deceive with your lips.
29 Do not say, "I will do to others as they
have done to me;
I will pay them back for what they
have done."

30 I passed by the field of one who was lazy,
by the vineyard of a stupid person,
31 and see, it was all overgrown with thorns;
the ground was covered with nettles,
and its stone wall was broken down.
32 Then I saw and considered it;
I looked and received instruction.

33 A little sleep, a little slumber,
a little folding of the hands to rest,
34 and poverty will come upon you like a
robber,
and want, like an armed warrior.

25 These are other proverbs of Solomon
that the officials of King Hezekiah of
Judah copied.

2 It is the glory of God to conceal things,
but the glory of kings is to search
things out.
3 Like the heavens for height, like the
earth for depth,
so the mind of kings is unsearchable.
4 Take away the dross from the silver,
and the smith has material for a vessel;
5 take away the wicked from the presence
of the king,
and his throne will be established in
righteousness.
6 Do not put yourself forward in the king's
presence
or stand in the place of the great,
7 for it is better to be told, "Come up here,"
than to be put lower in the presence
of a noble.

fourth in the book of Proverbs. A statement of disapproval is used to introduce the collection: *Partiality in judging is not good.* This is then followed by an example in which the wicked are erroneously celebrated as *innocent.* Whoever judges the *wicked* as *innocent* will be *abhorred by nations.* **24:28–29** The *lips* are connected to the condemnation of false witness (v. 28) and the utterance of words of revenge (v. 29). **24:30–32** For the sage, what happens outside is prioritized, as disorder in *the field* or *the vineyard* is an indication of a chaotic state. See also v. 27, where preparing a field precedes the building of a house. Such fields and broken walls are not owned by a wise person; the industrious are able to evade poverty. **24:33–34** A fool who revels in sleep and rest will suffer the severe consequences of laziness—that is, poverty. See note on 20:13 for the connection between sleep and laziness.

25:1–29:27 Additional sayings of Solomon, transcribed by Hezekiah's men. The fifth collection of Proverbs is attributed to Solomon. The first section (chaps. 25–27) is characterized by the frequent use of the word "like" for comparison, which serves as an effective tool to communicate the lessons to young men based on the sage's experiences. In the second section (chaps. 28–29), the sayings are cast mainly in antithetical and synthetic parallelisms (see **"Hebrew Poetry," p. 741**).

25:1 *Solomon.* Like the superscription of the book as a whole, this section also names Solomon as the author; see 1:1. *King Hezekiah of Judah* was king from 715 to 687 BCE; see 2 Kgs. 18:1–20:21. References to the *officials of King Hezekiah,* the purported copiers, indicate to the reader the language of royalty in the opening verses of this collection.

25:2 *The glory of God* and *kings* is compared; God conceals, and the kings *search things out.* *Glory* can also be translated as "honor."

25:5 The king must rule in righteousness and not yield to the wicked's influence.

25:6–7 The reader is informed of the protocol of how one should behave before the king.

25:7–8 Good neighborliness entails settling scores first with a neighbor rather than rushing to the courts. **25:8** The significance of the right speech is foregrounded, especially in the context of dealing with neighbors and in court.

What your eyes have seen
8   do not hastily bring into court,
for[f] what will you do in the end,
        when your neighbor puts you to
        shame?
9 Argue your case with your neighbor
        directly,
    and do not disclose another's secret,
10 or else someone who hears you will
        bring shame upon you,
    and your ill repute will have no end.

11 A word fitly spoken
    is like apples of gold in a setting of
        silver.
12 Like a gold ring or an ornament of gold
    is a wise rebuke to a listening ear.
13 Like the cold of snow in the time of
        harvest
    are faithful messengers to those who
        send them;
    they refresh the spirit of their
        masters.
14 Like clouds and wind without rain
    is one who boasts of a gift never
        given.
15 With patience a ruler may be persuaded,
    and a soft tongue can break bones.
16 If you have found honey, eat only enough
        for you,
    lest, having too much, you vomit it up.
17 Let your foot be seldom in your
        neighbor's house,
    lest the neighbor become weary of
        you and hate you.
18 Like a war club, a sword, or a sharp
        arrow
    is one who bears false witness against
        a neighbor.

19 Like a bad tooth or a lame foot
    is trust in a faithless person in time of
        trouble.
20 Like vinegar on a wound[g]
    is one who sings songs to a heavy
        heart.
Like a moth in clothing or a worm in
        wood,
    sorrow gnaws at the human
        heart.[b]
21 If your enemies are hungry, give them
        bread to eat,
    and if they are thirsty, give them water
        to drink,
22 for you will heap coals of fire on their
        heads,
    and the LORD will reward you.
23 The north wind produces rain,
    and a backbiting tongue, angry looks.
24 It is better to live in a corner of the
        housetop
    than in a house shared with a
        contentious wife.
25 Like cold water to a thirsty soul,
    so is good news from a far country.
26 Like a muddied spring or a polluted
        fountain
    are the righteous who give way before
        the wicked.
27 It is not good to eat much honey
    or to seek honor on top of honor.
28 Like a city breached, without walls,
    is one who lacks self-control.

26 Like snow in summer or rain in
        harvest,
    so honor is not fitting for a fool.

f 25.8 Cn: Heb *or else*   g 25.20 Gk: Heb *Like one who takes off
a garment on a cold day, like vinegar on lye*   h 25.20 Gk Syr Tg:
Heb lacks *Like a moth . . . human heart*

25:11–15 More sayings about right speech, using a variety of metaphors. There is praise for the right word (v. 11) and *wise rebuke* (v. 12). The easy deployment of precious minerals in the comparison may point to the elite context in which the texts were written. In the next couplets, the lessons are communicated in the context of the elements of nature such as *snow* (v. 13) and *clouds and wind without rain* (v. 14). The passage concludes with the power of *a soft tongue*.

25:16 The need for self-restraint in food consumption. See 25:27, where eating too much *honey* is also a metaphor for seeking too much honor.

25:17 Do not be a regular visitor.

25:18 *War club, a sword, or a sharp arrow*. Lying is compared to weapons of war.

25:20 The negative impacts of songs sung from a distressed heart, among others, are also featured.

25:21 Hostility can be countered with acts of kindness like providing food to eat and water to quench an enemy's thirst, which accords with the African spirit of hospitality.

25:26 The righteous should not yield to the wicked.

26:1–28 Continuing the use of comparisons, the sage focuses on the fool, the lazy, and the

² Like a sparrow in its flitting, like a
    swallow in its flying,
        an undeserved curse goes nowhere.
³ A whip for the horse, a bridle for the
    donkey,
        and a rod for the back of fools.
⁴ Do not answer fools according to their
    folly,
        lest you be a fool yourself.
⁵ Answer fools according to their folly,
        lest they be wise in their own eyes.
⁶ It is like cutting off one's foot and
    drinking down violence,
        to send a message by a fool.
⁷ The legs of a lame person hang limp;
        so does a proverb in the mouth of a
        fool.
⁸ It is like binding a stone in a sling
        to give honor to a fool.
⁹ Like a thornbush brandished by the hand
    of a drunkard
        is a proverb in the mouth of a fool.
¹⁰ Like an archer who wounds everybody
        is one who hires a passing fool or
        drunkard.ⁱ
¹¹ Like a dog that returns to its vomit
        is a fool who reverts to his folly.
¹² Do you see people wise in their own
    eyes?
        There is more hope for fools than for
        them.
¹³ The lazy person says, "There is a lion in
    the road!
        There is a lion in the streets!"
¹⁴ As a door turns on its hinges,
        so does a lazy person in bed.

¹⁵ The lazy person buries a hand in the dish
        and is too tired to bring it back to the
        mouth.
¹⁶ The lazy person is wiser in
    self-esteem
        than seven who can answer
        discreetly.
¹⁷ Like someone who takes a passing dog
    by the ears
        is one who meddles in the quarrel of
        another.
¹⁸ Like a maniac who shoots deadly
        firebrands and arrows,
¹⁹ so is one who deceives a neighbor
        and says, "I am only joking!"
²⁰ For lack of wood the fire goes out,
        and where there is no whisperer,
        quarreling ceases.
²¹ As charcoal is to hot embers and wood to
    fire,
        so is a quarrelsome person for
        kindling strife.
²² The words of a whisperer are like
        delicious morsels;
        they go down into the inner parts of
        the body.
²³ Like the glazeʲ covering an earthen vessel
        are smoothᵏ lips with an evil heart.
²⁴ An enemy dissembles in speaking
        while harboring deceit within;
²⁵ when an enemy speaks graciously, do not
    believe it,
        for there are seven abominations
        concealed within;

i 26.10 Meaning of Heb uncertain j 26.23 Cn: Heb *silver of dross* k 26.23 Gk: Heb *burning*

wicked. The lessons on wisdom are thus presented by what one must avoid. **26:4–5** An antithetical presentation of how a fool needs to be answered underscores the important role of the everyday use of speech. The pair of verses is seemingly contradictory. In answering a fool, one must not give an answer; that is, the latter is viewed as also foolish because one might become a fool. Yet fools should be answered lest they become *wise in their own eyes,* in other words, a fool esteems himself (see also 26:9 and 26:12). The African proverb "La hlogo tšhweu le ka rutwa ke la hlogontsho maano" (the gray haired can be taught to devise plans by the dark haired) and its counterpart "la hlogo tšhweu le ruta la hlogontsho maano" (the gray haired teaches the dark haired to devise plans) are resonant, indicating that sometimes the same scenario requires different responses. **26:9** A fool's mouth must not utter proverbs, as such utterances will not benefit the hearers. **26:13–16** Industry is linked with wisdom, while laziness is depicted as folly. Lazy behavior is condemned and mocked. A lazy person can even struggle to get out of bed (v. 14) and struggle to feed himself or herself (v. 15). **26:20–22** Another pair presenting a contradictory message. On the one hand, whispering is featured negatively for causing quarrels (v. 20); on the other hand, *the words of a whisperer are like delicious morsels* (see 18:8). Such an apparent contradiction on how one should answer a fool enables the sage to problematize the simplistic worldview of Proverbs. Alternatively, read in the context of the next verses, *morsels* may appear to be *delicious* but are actually harmful. **26:23–26** Warnings against "judging a book by its cover." **26:24–28** A passage on enemies and deceitful

²⁶ though hatred is covered with guile,
  the enemy's wickedness will be
    exposed in the assembly.
²⁷ Whoever digs a pit will fall into it,
  and a stone will come back on the one
    who starts it rolling.
²⁸ A lying tongue hates its victims,
  and a flattering mouth works ruin.

27 Do not boast about tomorrow,
  for you do not know what a day may
    bring.
² Let another praise you and not your own
    mouth,
  a stranger and not your own lips.
³ A stone is heavy, and sand is weighty,
  but a fool's provocation is heavier
    than both.
⁴ Wrath is cruel, anger is overwhelming,
  but who is able to stand before
    jealousy?
⁵ Better is open rebuke
  than hidden love.
⁶ Well meant are the wounds a friend
    inflicts,
  but profuse are the kisses of an enemy.
⁷ The sated appetite spurns honey,
  but to a ravenous appetite even the
    bitter is sweet.
⁸ Like a bird that strays from its nest
  is one who strays from home.
⁹ Perfume and incense make the heart glad,
  but the soul is torn by trouble.ˡ

¹⁰ Do not forsake your friend or the friend
    of your parent;
  do not go to the house of your kindred
    in the day of your calamity.
  Better is a neighbor who is nearby
    than kindred who are far away.
¹¹ Be wise, my child, and make my heart
    glad,
  so that I may answer whoever
    reproaches me.
¹² The clever see danger and hide,
  but the simple go on and suffer for it.
¹³ Take the garment of one who has given
    surety for a stranger;
  seize the pledge given as surety for
    foreigners.ᵐ
¹⁴ Whoever blesses a neighbor with a loud
    voice,
  rising early in the morning,
    will be counted as cursing.
¹⁵ A continual dripping on a rainy day
  and a contentious wife are alike;
¹⁶ to restrain her is to restrain the wind
  or to grasp oil in the right hand.ⁿ
¹⁷ Iron sharpens iron,
  and one person sharpens the witsᵒ of
    another.
¹⁸ Anyone who tends a fig tree will eat its
    fruit,

l 27.9 Gk: Heb *the sweetness of a friend is better than one's own counsel   m* 27.13 Vg and 20.16: Heb *for a foreign woman   n* 27.16 Meaning of Heb uncertain   *o* 27.17 Heb *face*

speech. The wise discern an evil motive hidden by smooth talk and gracious speech: "le ge o ka e buela leopeng, magokobu a a go bona" (bad things done in secret, will eventually be exposed; African proverb); in other words, secrets cannot be hidden forever. Such will be the case with the enemy who deceives; one can thus never get away with evil (v. 26). The closing verse foregrounds the *tongue* and *mouth* as critical organs (v. 28).

27:1–2 Prohibition against boasting. Like in the preceding chapters, the *mouth* and *lips* are signif-icant for indicating wise speech—in this case, speech that is discreet and cautious. "O se iteleletše phalafala" (one must not sound one's own drum/horn; African proverb).

27:5–6 Prohibition against hypocrisy. The lips that utter an *open rebuke* are celebrated over the silence of one harboring *hidden love*; likewise, *wounds* from a friend are better than *kisses* from an enemy.

27:10 Good friends and good neighbors can be better than family, especially if the latter does not live in close proximity. Forbearance in visiting others is a mark of wisdom; see 25:17.

27:11 A wise son making his father glad is a recurring theme, especially in the second collection (see 10:1). *So that I may answer whoever reproaches me.* The motive behind this exhortation sheds light on the communal nature of the society of the time: "lebadi ge le eya namaneng le a fetiša" (the scar that gets magnified on the calf; African proverb) means that children's traits inherited from their parents tend to be magnified.

27:14 Neighbors have to be treated with caution and respect.

27:15 The wife who is contentious uses her mouth unwisely, a proverbial goat with no capacity to suffer in silence, unlike a proverbial sheep that cries inwardly (African proverb: "monna ke nku, o llela teng").

and anyone who takes care of a
  master will be honored.
¹⁹ Just as water reflects the face,
  so one human heart reflects another.
²⁰ Sheol and Abaddon are never satisfied,
  and human eyes are never satisfied.
²¹ The crucible is for silver, and the furnace
  is for gold,
  so a person is tested[p] by being praised.
²² Crush a fool in a mortar with a pestle
  along with crushed grain,
  but the folly will not be driven out.

²³ Know well the condition of your flocks,
  and give attention to your herds,
²⁴ for riches do not last forever,
  nor a crown for all generations.
²⁵ When the grass is gone, and new growth
  appears,
  and the herbage of the mountains is
  gathered,
²⁶ the lambs will provide your clothing,
  and the goats the price of a field;
²⁷ there will be enough goats' milk for your
  food,
  for the food of your household
  and nourishment for your female
  servants.

28 The wicked flee when no one
  pursues,
  but the righteous are as bold as a lion.
² When a land rebels
  it has many rulers;
  but with an intelligent[q] person, honesty
  endures.

³ A poor person who oppresses the poor
  is a beating rain that leaves no
  food.
⁴ Those who forsake the law praise the
  wicked,
  but those who keep the law struggle
  against them.
⁵ The evil do not understand justice,
  but those who seek the Lord
  understand it completely.
⁶ Better to be poor and walk in
  integrity
  than to be crooked in one's ways even
  though rich.
⁷ Those who keep the law are wise
  children,
  but companions of gluttons shame
  their parents.
⁸ One who augments wealth by exorbitant
  interest
  gathers it for another who is kind to
  the poor.
⁹ When one will not listen to the law,
  even one's prayers are an
  abomination.
¹⁰ Those who mislead the upright into evil
  ways
  will fall into pits of their own making,
  but the blameless will have a goodly
  inheritance.
¹¹ The rich is wise in self-esteem,
  but an intelligent poor person sees
  through the pose.

p 27.21 Heb lacks *is tested*   q 28.2 Heb *intelligent
knowledgeable*

27:20 *Sheol and Abaddon* (meaning death; see 15:11) and *human eyes are never satisfied*. Human nature is insatiable; indeed, "lešaka la pelong ga le tlale" (the kraal of the heart does not get full; African proverb). See **"Sheol," p. 695**.

27:23–27 A poem or story with a lesson featuring the intersection between humanity, ecology, and economics. Being attuned to the seasons and the proper care of one's flock can provide material benefits, despite the temporary nature of riches.

28:1–29:27 The second part of the fifth collection. Variegated themes range from a comparison of the wicked and the righteous, to family relations and parental relationships, justice-seeking rulers, and rewards and punishments.

28:3 The poor should not oppress one another.

28:4 *The law* has to be kept and not forsaken; see 28:7, 9. "Torah" is usually translated as instruction in Proverbs (see, e.g., 1:8), but in this chapter, the word seems to refer to the legal codes that make up the Mosaic covenant.

28:6 Poverty with integrity is preferred to riches acquired through fraudulent means.

28:7 Children are exhorted to keep the law and not *shame their parents* by keeping bad company.

28:8 Interest-taking from the poor is forbidden in Exod. 22:25.

28:11 Another saying praising the poor over the rich. While the rich are *wise in self-esteem* (another way of saying wise in their own eyes; see 26:4–5), *an intelligent poor person* is not fooled by their posturing.

¹² When the righteous rejoice, there is
    great glory,
    but when the wicked prevail, people
        go into hiding.
¹³ No one who conceals transgressions will
        prosper,
    but one who confesses and forsakes
        them will obtain mercy.
¹⁴ Happy is the one who is never without
        fear,
    but one who is hard-hearted will fall
        into calamity.
¹⁵ Like a roaring lion or a charging bear
    is a wicked ruler over a poor
        people.
¹⁶ A ruler who lacks understanding is a
        cruel oppressor,
    but one who hates unjust gain will
        enjoy a long life.
¹⁷ If someone is burdened with the blood of
        another,
    let that killer be a fugitive until death;
    let no one offer assistance.
¹⁸ One who walks in integrity will be safe,
    but whoever follows crooked ways
        will fall into the Pit.ʳ
¹⁹ Anyone who tills the land will have
        plenty of bread,
    but one who follows worthless
        pursuits will have plenty of poverty.
²⁰ The faithful will abound with blessings,
    but one who is in a hurry to be rich
        will not go unpunished.
²¹ To show partiality is not good,
    yet for a piece of bread a person may
        do wrong.
²² The miser is in a hurry to get rich
    and does not know that loss is sure to
        come.

²³ Whoever rebukes a person will
        afterward find more favor
    than one who flatters with the tongue.
²⁴ Anyone who robs father or mother
    and says, "That is no crime,"
    is partner to a thug.
²⁵ The greedy person stirs up strife,
    but whoever trusts in the Lᴏʀᴅ will be
        enriched.
²⁶ Those who trust in their own wits are
        fools,
    but those who walk in wisdom come
        through safely.
²⁷ Whoever gives to the poor will lack
        nothing,
    but one who turns a blind eye will get
        many a curse.
²⁸ When the wicked prevail, people go into
        hiding,
    but when they perish, the righteous
        increase.

29 One who is often reproved, yet
        remains stubborn,
    will suddenly be broken beyond
        healing.
² When the righteous are in authority, the
        people rejoice,
    but when the wicked rule, the people
        groan.
³ A child who loves wisdom makes a
        parent glad,
    but a companion of prostitutes
        destroys wealth.
⁴ By justice a king gives stability to the
        land,
    but one who makes heavy exactions
        ruins it.

r 28.18 Syr: Heb *fall all at once*

28:12 Righteousness is a public good; wickedness produces fear in the community. See 28:28.
28:15–16 Additional sayings about wise rule, especially concerning the poor; see 28:3.
28:17 *Burdened* is literally "oppressed." The punishment for violent crime is death, but it will come of its own accord; see 1:11–12; 1:16–18; 5:22. In the legal materials, cities of refuge are established for people who have killed others unintentionally (Num. 35:6, 11–12; Deut. 4:41–42; 19:2–7).
28:18 The sage is persuaded that *integrity* makes one *safe*, but *whoever follows crooked ways will fall into the Pit*, which indicates death. Such punishment resonates with the African proverb "mokga kgati o a ikgela" (one who gets a stick [with punitive intentions] does so for oneself).
28:19 Hard work will be rewarded by *plenty of bread*, while those following *worthless pursuits* will reap accordingly.
28:24 A son who robs his parents is condemned.
29:1 Those who will not listen to reproof are condemned; the *stubborn* (literally "stiff-necked") are not teachable. See 3:35.
29:2–4 Kings who are *righteous* and seek *justice* not only make the people glad (v. 2) but are assured of stability in the land (v. 4). In v. 4, economic justice is highlighted.

5 Whoever flatters a neighbor
    is spreading a net for the neighbor's
        feet.
6 In the transgression of the evil there is a
        snare,
    but the righteous sing and rejoice.
7 The righteous know the rights of the
        poor;
    the wicked have no such
        understanding.
8 Scoffers set a city aflame,
    but the wise turn away wrath.
9 If the wise go to law with fools,
    there is ranting and ridicule without
        relief.
10 The bloodthirsty hate the blameless,
    and they seek the life of the upright.
11 A fool gives full vent to anger,
    but the wise quietly holds it back.
12 If a ruler listens to falsehood,
    all his officials will be wicked.
13 The poor and the oppressor have this in
        common:
    the LORD gives light to the eyes of both.
14 If a king judges the poor with equity,
    his throne will be established forever.
15 The rod and reproof give wisdom,
    but a mother is disgraced by a
        neglected child.
16 When the wicked are in authority,
    transgression increases,

but the righteous will look upon their
        downfall.
17 Discipline your children, and they will
        give you rest;
    they will give delight to your heart.
18 Where there is no prophecy, the people
        cast off restraint,
    but happy are those who keep the law.
19 By mere words slaves are not disciplined,
    for though they understand, they will
        not give heed.
20 Do you see someone who is hasty in
        speech?
    There is more hope for a fool than for
        anyone like that.
21 A slave pampered from childhood
    will come to a bad end.^{s}
22 One given to anger stirs up strife,
    and the hothead causes much
        transgression.
23 A person's pride will bring humiliation,
    but one who is lowly in spirit will
        obtain honor.
24 To be a partner of a thief is to hate one's
        own life;
    one hears the victim's curse but
        discloses nothing.^{t}
25 The fear of others^u lays a snare,

s 29.21 Vg: Meaning of Heb uncertain   t 29.24 Meaning of
Heb uncertain   u 29.25 Or human fear

29:7 An important component of righteousness is being conscious of *the rights of the poor*.

29:8 *Scoffers*, like the stubborn (29:1), are those who are not teachable; see 15:12. See also Ps. 1:1.

29:13 The poor and (their) oppressors (the rich) are equal, as the elements of nature are gifted to both by God (see 22:2). This may be affirming to the poor in terms of the understanding that before God, his or her human dignity is the same as that of his or her oppressor. One is not sure, though, how comforting such an affirmation may be for the poor who struggle, since the saying does not necessarily change the attitude of the oppressor for the better.

29:14 The king is expected to judge the poor fairly, which would make a material difference in their lives.

29:15 The theme of parent-child relationships especially in the context of discipline returns. The sage foregrounds the benefits that such discipline will proffer to parents: a mother will not be *disgraced*. This is one of the few proverbs in which the mother's role (and not the father's) is solely highlighted.

29:17 Disciplined children will of necessity please their parents' hearts.

29:18 Through parallelism, *prophecy* and *the law* may be equated. The simplistic mentality of positive rewards for good actions is embedded throughout Proverbs.

29:19 Like in 29:15, corporal punishment is the recommended form of discipline, for *slaves* in this case. See also 13:24 and 22:15. The preceding mentality gives room to neither children who may have received discipline but end up in deviant behavior nor wicked parents who may not be excited by disciplined children. The discipline of another category of child, one hardly mentioned in Proverbs, is that of an enslaved child (vv. 19, 21).

29:21 *A slave* who does not receive discipline at an early age will experience a bad end. References to enslaved people and servants (29:19; the Heb. word is the same for both) presuppose an

but one who trusts in the Lord is
secure.
²⁶ Many seek the favor of a ruler,
but it is from the Lord that one gets
justice.
²⁷ The unjust are an abomination to the
righteous,
but the upright are an abomination to
the wicked.

30 The words of Agur son of Jakeh. An
oracle.

Thus says the man: I am weary, O God;
I am weary, O God, and am wasting
away.ᵛ
² Surely I am too stupid to be human;
I do not have human
understanding.
³ I have not learned wisdom,
nor have I knowledge of the holy
ones.ʷ
⁴ Who has ascended to heaven and come
down?
Who has gathered the wind in the
hollow of the hand?
Who has wrapped up the waters in a
garment?
Who has established all the ends of
the earth?
What is the person's name?
And what is the name of the person's
child?
Surely you know!

⁵ Every word of God proves true;
he is a shield to those who take refuge
in him.
⁶ Do not add to his words,
lest he rebuke you, and you be found
a liar.

⁷ Two things I ask of you;
do not deny them to me before I die:
⁸ Remove far from me falsehood and lying;
give me neither poverty nor riches;
feed me with the food that I need,
⁹ lest I be full and deny you
and say, "Who is the Lord?"
or I be poor and steal
and profane the name of my God.

¹⁰ Do not slander a servant to a master,
lest the servant curse you, and you be
held guilty.

¹¹ There are those who curse their fathers
and do not bless their mothers.
¹² There are those who are pure in their
own eyes,
yet are not cleansed of their filthiness.
¹³ There are those—how lofty are their eyes,
how high their eyelids lift!—
¹⁴ there are those whose teeth are swords,
whose teeth are knives
to devour the poor from off the earth,
the needy from among mortals.

v 30.1 Meaning of Heb uncertain   *w* 30.3 Or *Holy One*

elite household/family setting in which the possession of other people by more powerful ones was taken for granted.
30:1–33 Words of Agur. The sixth collection in Proverbs is one of the few that carries the name of a person other than Solomon. **30:1–3** *Agur son of Jakeh.* Nothing is known about this figure. The first three verses may be a window into Agur's identity in the context of wisdom, understanding, and relationship with God. He is open and frank about his limitedness: *I am weary . . . and am wasting away* (v. 1); *I am too stupid* (v. 2); *I have not learned wisdom* (v. 3). Such self-deprecation may be a challenge in a context in which men are not expected to complain, admit failures, or even cry. The African proverb "monna ke nku o llela teng" (a man is a sheep, he cries inwardly), for example, discourages men to admit weakness. It is also not clear how the introductory disclaimer should guide a reader. Are his exhortations reliable? Or is the tone ironic? **30:4** After the disclaimer, the speaker outlines the works of creation by the same God he had claimed he did not know. God asks similar questions to Job in the opening of God's speech from the whirlwind (Job 38:4–11). The answer to these questions here and in Job is no one but God, underscoring the vast gulf between human knowledge and divine power. *Surely you know!* See Job 38:21. **30:7–9** As though in prayer, the speaker requests *two things* from God: to *remove . . . falsehood and lying* from him and to supply provisions of moderate wealth and needed food. In this appeal for moderation, both *poverty* and *riches* lead people astray. **30:10** The speaker foregrounds the power of *a servant.* **30:11–14** A passage that names four kinds of wicked people: those who curse their parents (v. 11), hypocrites (v. 12), arrogant people (v. 13), and those who oppress the poor (v. 14). The body features to communicate

¹⁵ The leech has two daughters;
 "Give, give," they cry.
Three things are never satisfied;
 four never say, "Enough":
¹⁶ Sheol, the barren womb,
 the earth ever-thirsty for water,
 and the fire that never says, "Enough."

¹⁷ The eye that mocks a father
 and scorns to obey a mother
will be pecked out by the ravens of the
 valley
 and eaten by the vultures.

¹⁸ Three things are too wonderful for me;
 four I do not understand:
¹⁹ the way of an eagle in the sky,
 the way of a snake on a rock,
the way of a ship on the high seas,
 and the way of a man with a woman.

²⁰ This is the way of an adulteress:
 she eats and wipes her mouth
 and says, "I have done no wrong."

²¹ Under three things the earth trembles;
 under four it cannot bear up:
²² a slave when he becomes king
 and a fool when glutted with food,
²³ a contemptible woman when she gets a
 husband
 and a maid when she supplants her
 mistress.

²⁴ Four things on earth are small,
 yet they are exceedingly wise:
²⁵ the ants are a people without strength,
 yet they provide their food in the
 summer;
²⁶ the badgers are a people without
 power,
 yet they make their homes in the
 rocks;
²⁷ the locusts have no king,
 yet all of them march in rank;
²⁸ the lizard* can be grasped in the hand,
 yet it is found in kings' palaces.

²⁹ Three things are stately in their stride;
 four are stately in their gait:
³⁰ the lion, which is mightiest among wild
 animals
 and does not turn back before any;
³¹ the strutting rooster,ʸ the he-goat,
 and a king against whom none can
 stand.

³² If you have been foolish, exalting
 yourself,
 or if you have been devising evil,
 put your hand on your mouth.
³³ For as pressing milk produces curds
 and pressing the nose produces
 blood,
 so pressing anger produces strife.

x 30.28 Or *spider*   *y* 30.31 Gk Syr Tg Compare Vg: Meaning
of Heb uncertain

this problematic behavior are especially the *eyes* and the *teeth*. The oppressor's teeth are like *swords* and *knives*, an image that denotes the rapacious consumption of the less privileged. **30:15** The first numerical saying. The creatures of the natural world can provide lessons to the one wise enough to pay them heed (see 6:6–11). **30:18–19** *Three things . . . four.* The first saying uses a three/four formula (see also 30:21–23, 29–31). The four that he does not understand entail movement: *eagle in the sky*, *snake on a rock, ship on the high seas, man with a woman.* Woman ("almah") means a young woman of marriageable age. **30:20** The passage returns to warnings against the adulterous woman. *She eats* is an allusion to sexual congress. See 2:16–19; 5:5–14; 6:24–35; 7:5–27; 22:14; 23:27–28. **30:21–23** The second of the three/four formula sayings. The four items are all in the human domain and address role reversals between an Othered person (*slave, fool, contemptible woman,* and *maid*) and a superior. **30:24–28** Breaking from the three/four formula by just listing four items. As the speaker continues with the marvels of creation and its investment in wisdom, he lists the *small,* yet *exceedingly wise.* This passage exemplifies the idea that, since God created the world, everything in it reflects God in some way (natural theology). In this case, some of the smallest and most humble animals demonstrate proper ways to live, including societal order without hierarchal structures. However, this passage also demonstrates the limits of wisdom's natural theology: while these lessons are purportedly derived from observation of the natural world, they rely more on stereotypes than accurate descriptions of animal behavior. **30:29–31** The third of the three/four formula sayings. Unlike 30:27–28, which seems to advocate for kingless societies, this passage lauds the king.

30:32–33 The collection concludes by condemning the folly of self-exaltation and the uncontrolled anger that gives birth to strife.

31

The words of King Lemuel. An oracle that his mother taught him:

² No, my son! No, son of my womb!
No, son of my vows!
³ Do not give your strength to women,
your ways to those who destroy kings.
⁴ It is not for kings, O Lemuel,
it is not for kings to drink wine
or for rulers to desire² strong drink,
⁵ lest they drink and forget what has been
decreed
and pervert the rights of all the afflicted.
⁶ Give strong drink to one who is perishing
and wine to those in bitter distress;
⁷ let them drink and forget their poverty
and remember their misery no more.
⁸ Speak out for those who cannot speak,
for the rights of all the destitute.ᵃ
⁹ Speak out; judge righteously;
defend the rights of the poor and needy.
¹⁰ A woman of strength who can find?
She is far more precious than jewels.

¹¹ The heart of her husband trusts in her,
and he will have no lack of gain.
¹² She does him good and not harm
all the days of her life.
¹³ She seeks wool and flax
and works with willing hands.
¹⁴ She is like the ships of the merchant;
she brings her food from far away.
¹⁵ She rises while it is still night
and provides food for her household
and tasks for her female servants.
¹⁶ She considers a field and buys it;
with the fruit of her hands she plants
a vineyard.
¹⁷ She girds herself with strength
and makes her arms strong.
¹⁸ She perceives that her merchandise is
profitable.
Her lamp does not go out at night.
¹⁹ She puts her hands to the distaff,
and her hands hold the spindle.

z 31.4 Cn: Heb *where* a 31.8 Heb *all children of passing away*

31:1–9 Words of Lemuel, teachings of his mother. The seventh collection of Proverbs is attributed to a woman, King Lemuel's mother, and addressed to her son. **31:1** *King Lemuel.* Nothing is known about this figure. *An oracle* is usually associated with the prophetic genre but introduces both the sixth (30:1) and seventh collections in Proverbs. *His mother* is otherwise unnamed; although the son is exhorted to listen to the teachings of his mother in 1:8, this is the only passage where a mother's words are recorded. **31:2** The Queen Mother begins with a strong negative, prohibitive statement. **31:3** The mother expresses a negative view of women: women are to be guarded against, as they have the capacity to destroy powerful men. **31:4–5** Strong drink is to be avoided, as it will cause Lemuel to forget about the decrees and *pervert the rights* of *the afflicted* (see 23:29–35). **31:6–7** Rather than challenging structures that perpetuate poverty, the Queen Mother encourages her son to give wine to those who are *perishing* or in intense *distress* so that they can *forget their poverty*. **31:8–9** A king must thus be justice-seeking by judging righteously, defending the rights of the poor and the needy, and speaking for the voiceless.

31:10–31 Poem of the woman of worth. A poem praising the ideal wife ends the book of Proverbs as the eighth collection (see **"Woman of Worth," p. 903**). After the sage's efforts to shape the masculinities of the young men being addressed, with a special focus on the traits of bad women, the sage then concludes the book with a paean in praise of a good woman. This woman of strength parallels the personification of Wisdom as a woman (see **"Woman Wisdom," p. 872**); thus, Proverbs begins and ends with powerful and idealized female figures. **31:10** *A woman of strength.* The Hebrew phrase "eshet hayil" can be translated in various ways; "capable wife," "woman of valor," and "woman of worth" are common renderings. The husband and his words paint the portrait of an ideal heterosexual marriage partner, hence this poem is part of the formation and nurturing of masculinities evident in all the teachings of the sage. **31:11** The husband's *heart*, a critical organ, trusts her. In 28:25 and 29:25, trust in the Lord is commended. **31:13** The wife's *hands* are featured here and in 31:16, 19 (twice), 20 (twice), 31. The word "hand" in Hebrew is often an expression of strength, authority, and power. **31:14–15** One of the ideal wife's important acts is the provision and preparation of food for *her household*. Note that the house is hers and not her husband's, another indication of her centrality. **31:16** *She considers a field and buys it*, indicating that she is involved in the financial management of the household; a family *vineyard* would provide both wine for the household and a product to sell. See also 31:18, 24. **31:17** Like hands, *arms* are also a part of the body associated with power and strength. **31:19** In addition to food, the ideal wife also provides clothing to her family by working the *distaff* and *spindle* well. See also 31:13,

Making Connections: Woman of Worth (Proverbs 31)

Part of the envelope within which the book of Proverbs is enclosed is instructions that contain images of two powerful women: Woman Wisdom (Prov. 1–9) and the Woman of Worth (Prov. 31:10–31), which follows the only instruction by a woman in the whole Hebrew Bible, the teachings of Lemuel's mother (Prov. 31:1–9). Its genre as a poem, and the systematic and coordinated arrangement of each line of the poem, not only speaks volumes to the quality of womanhood (*bosadi* in the African language of Northern Sotho) but also forms a fitting end to this book whose aim is to nurture and form young men.

The portrayal of ideal womanhood in this paean is based on certain expectations about ideal womanhood in the context of its production. Due to the absence of the temple and the court in Judea in the Persian period, the family regained power as the locus of divine authority. Thus, the young male addressees, the would-be husbands, would need instructions concerning the qualities of ideal womanhood. As with any people concerned with issues of identity, which is a preoccupation of those living under colonial rule, the sage's teaching is concerned with proper marriage. Proverbs contains warnings against the lures of strange women (adulterous but also maybe foreign; see **"Intermarriage," p. 649**), comparisons between good and bad wives, and the qualities of an ideal woman, a *mosadi wa bosadi*. The latter would continue the sages' work on the formation and nurture of ideal masculinities that would earn the husband status at the city gates (31:23). These are the questions that I posed to a male audience as a guest speaker in a church setting some years back: Given that men are considered heads of families in this particular ecclesiastical context, and in all patriarchal cultures and religions globally, thus consequently expected to provide for their families' livelihoods (31:13–22, 24, 27), engage in business (31:16), and instill wisdom in children (31:26), what does this favorite text do to their understanding of ideal masculinities? As the Woman of Worth engages in these activities instead of her husband, is there a reversal of gender expectations of some sort here? The Sotho proverbial woman's hands are eaten by hard work (*mosadi ke tšhwene o lewa mabogo*); yet, what kind of masculinities may be nurtured and shaped by a poem that elevates woman as the household manager in a patriarchal context that dictates otherwise?

Madipoane Masenya (Ngwan'a Mphahlele)

20 She opens her hand to the poor
   and reaches out her hands to the needy.
21 She is not afraid for her household when
   it snows,
   for all her household are clothed in
   crimson.
22 She makes herself coverings;
   her clothing is fine linen and purple.
23 Her husband is known in the city gates,
   taking his seat among the elders of the
   land.
24 She makes linen garments and sells them;
   she supplies the merchant with sashes.
25 Strength and dignity are her clothing,
   and she laughs at the time to come.

26 She opens her mouth with wisdom,
   and the teaching of kindness is on her
   tongue.
27 She looks well to the ways of her household
   and does not eat the bread of idleness.
28 Her children rise up and call her happy;
   her husband, too, and he praises her:
29 "Many women have done excellently,
   but you surpass them all."
30 Charm is deceitful and beauty is vain,
   but a woman who fears the LORD is to
   be praised.
31 Give her a share in the fruit of her hands,
   and let her works praise her in the city
   gates.

21, and 24. **31:20** She also takes care of *the poor* and *needy*. Proverbs commends being kind to the poor; see, for example, 14:21, 31; 19:17; 22:9. **31:21** Wise work is aligned with the seasons like the ant in 6:8. **31:22** Only here is the focus of the wife's work on herself and her interests, a rare feature in many patriarchal cultural contexts. **31:26** Not only is she industrious, she is also wise. *Teaching of kindness* translates the Hebrew "torat hesed"; see **"Hesed," p. 375**. **31:28–29** At the end, *her children* and *her husband* use their mouths to celebrate her, thus affirming the truth of the two African proverbs, one on industry and one on deceptive (female) looks. The proverb "mosadi ke tšhwene o lewa mabogo" celebrates the woman who works very hard for the welfare of her whole household and who also satisfies her husband sexually; "se bone thola boreledi, teng ga yona go a baba" means "female looks can be deceptive." **31:30** *Vain* in Hebrew is "hebel"; see **"All Is Vanity," p. 906**. **31:31** In the end, it is indeed fitting that these *hands* she has used successfully for the family's welfare are celebrated by those very close to her, the husband and children, and publicly celebrated *in the city gates*.

ECCLESIASTES

Authorship and Date

Ecclesiastes is a biblical book long associated with King Solomon (tenth century BCE) and has even been attributed to him. The superscription (1:1) and some of the material in the book (especially 1:12 and 2:1–11) hint at such an attribution but never claim it explicitly. Solomon is identified as the writer of Ecclesiastes in the Jewish tradition: For instance Qohelet Rabbah—a collection of rabbinic interpretations of Ecclesiastes—understands Ecclesiastes as the product of an aging Solomon reflecting back on his life. In the Christian tradition, Solomonic authorship was generally, but never universally, accepted. Gregory of Nyssa (fourth century CE) thought someone else wrote the book; Didymus the Blind (fourth century CE) proposed multiple authors. In the book itself, after a few chapters of what is apparently royal pretense, the author drops the Solomonic persona and seems to identify as a teacher instead, albeit one who seems to be associated with the court (see 8:2–3).

Since the nineteenth century, virtually all biblical scholars have rejected Solomonic authorship based on the evidence in the Hebrew text itself. In addition to the fact that the author never quite claims to be Solomon and the royal persona is dropped by the third chapter, there are aspects of the Hebrew language that are simply not compatible with a tenth-century BCE date of composition. Like any other language, Hebrew has changed and developed over time. The Hebrew of Ecclesiastes contains Persian loan words that could have only entered Hebrew after Israel became a part of the Persian Empire in the sixth century BCE. The language of Ecclesiastes also exhibits grammatical constructions that developed long after the tenth century BCE. Because of these linguistic factors, it is clear that Ecclesiastes could not have been written before the sixth century BCE, at least four hundred years after the reign of Solomon. Many scholars have also discerned the influence of Hellenistic philosophy in the book. As a result, some scholars argue for a Persian period date (sixth to fourth century BCE), and others make the case for a Hellenistic period date (fourth to second century BCE).

Though Solomon could not have written the book of Ecclesiastes, its author was nevertheless a highly educated man, a sage and a teacher (12:9), conversant in international literature and maybe even Greek philosophy. Given the complexities of the book's content and its literary form, some scholars discern not a single author but multiple hands at work in the composition of Ecclesiastes—an observation that is as old as Didymus the Blind (see above).

Literary Character

Ecclesiastes defies easy categorization. While it is usually classified among the Wisdom Books (see **"Introduction to the Writings," pp. 6–9**), it contains both traditional wisdom and challenges to traditional understandings of the order of the world. It also does not represent a single genre; rather, it is a mixture of poetry and prose, first-person reflection, third-person commentary, proverbs, and vignettes.

There is also no clear structure to the book. It is neither an ordered presentation of material nor a random assortment of ideas. Rather, certain sections (especially the beginning and the end of the book) seem carefully placed, while others seem haphazard, adhering to no obvious principle (especially the proverbs in chap. 7). Even so, the book displays a certain unity and cohesiveness established through key words and repeated phrases. These include vanity, toil, "under the sun," "chasing after wind," and pleasure/enjoyment.

Whereas complex and contradictory material could easily indicate a composite text that is the product of many hands, the diversity of form and content might also be understood as the product of a single author who is trying to make an important point about the unpredictability and complexity of life.

Reading Guide

How do we live when we know we are going to die? What does justice mean in the face of human suffering and glaring inequalities? We all know good people who have suffered terribly and bad people who live full, rich lives. Nothing is certain, and everything can change in an instant. Where is God in all of this? Perhaps the reason Ecclesiastes resonates so strongly with contemporary readers is that its questions are timeless and its answers multidimensional. Ecclesiastes goes to the heart of our existential questions about the human condition: Why are we here, and what does it matter? Instead of providing simple answers, it draws us into a process of observation and contemplation.

Ecclesiastes is sometimes considered more of a philosophical treatise than a theological discourse, meaning it concerns itself more with humanity than God. Yet while the author does observe life and make recommendations about how to live in this world, there is also theology here as well as ideas about God that do not accord with much of the rest of the Scripture. Language about God in Ecclesiastes is distinct from other biblical books in two important ways. First, the personal name of God is never used. Ecclesiastes is the only biblical book that discusses God yet never uses God's personal name. Second, in almost every mention of God (thirty-two of forty), the word is used with the definite article—"the God" or perhaps "the Deity"—although English translations usually do not render the definite article. This phrasing makes God in Ecclesiastes appear distant and impersonal. There is a sense that God is in control throughout the book, most especially in the epilogue (12:13–14). But in control to what end? There seems to be little comfort in a distant God who controls in ways perceived as capricious at best, sometimes rewarding the wicked (7:15), and ultimately making no distinction between the wise and the foolish (2:15–16). The classical formulation of the question of theodicy (an explanation for evil and suffering in the world) runs as follows: If God is both all-good and all-powerful, why is there evil and suffering in the world? God is either not all-powerful and can do nothing about it, or God is not all-good and does not care. For Ecclesiastes, God's power is clear; it is God's benevolence that is not. In this way, Ecclesiastes probes the limits of traditional theodicy in a manner similar to the book of Job. In Job, however, God is more directly present to the protagonist, appearing to and speaking with Job. The Teacher of Ecclesiastes gets no such audience and does not seem to assume such is even possible.

It would be a mistake, however, to read Ecclesiastes as all doom and gloom. The speaker does recommend ways to live in a world where the only certainty is death. Seven times the speaker recommends eating, drinking, and enjoying one's life; this carpe diem theme weaves a different kind of weft in the warp of the book. There is much in Ecclesiastes that seems to be a counsel of despair; but a closer look reveals how beautiful and joyful the world can be when we embrace uncertainty and relish every fleeting moment, each made more precious because it will soon be all gone.

Jennifer L. Koosed

1 The words of the Teacher, the son of David, king in Jerusalem.
² Vanity of vanities, says the Teacher,
    vanity of vanities! All is vanity.
³ What do people gain from all the toil
    at which they toil under the sun?
⁴ A generation goes, and a generation
        comes,
    but the earth remains forever.

⁵ The sun rises, and the sun goes down
    and hurries to the place where it
        rises.
⁶ The wind blows to the south
    and goes around to the north;
round and round goes the wind,
    and on its circuits the wind returns.
⁷ All streams run to the sea,
    but the sea is not full;

1:1 Superscription. The book is introduced as *the words of the Teacher* (Heb. "Qohelet"). "Qohelet" is possibly a title meaning something like "gatherer" or "assembler." The word is sometimes translated as "Preacher." See Ezra 2:55, 57 and Neh. 7:57, 59 for similar titles in the Persian period, although the NRSVue transliterates the Hebrew words as if they are names: Hassophereth, Pochereth, and Sophereth. Superscriptions are common in other poetic books, including the prophetic material.
1:2–11 Prologue. This poem introduces the major themes of the book, including the futility of human life. In it, human futility is placed within the context of an abiding natural world. In the natural order, time moves in a circular manner: nature is cyclical, and history repeats. **1:2** *Vanity of vanities . . . all is vanity*. The Hebrew word "hevel" is difficult to translate into English (see **"All Is Vanity," p. 906**). The word means "breath" or "wind" and thus indicates something insubstantial. As a proper name, it is "Abel" (Gen. 4). The word is translated differently in different biblical passages and contexts; it is ambiguous. Possible translations include "futile," "absurd," "meaningless," "fleeting," "empty," and "useless." *Vanity* is a traditional English translation originating from the King James Version. **1:3** Another theme of the book is *toil* and whether or not it is valuable; *under the sun* is a reoccurring phrase meaning "everything in this world." **1:4** This verse exemplifies the poem's central message that human life is fleeting, yet the natural world endures. **1:5** Ernest Hemingway's

Going Deeper: All Is Vanity (Ecclesiastes 1:2; 12:8)

What does the Teacher mean when he proclaims that everything is vanity? The Teacher frames his discourse with this arresting phrase; still further, he repeatedly calls different aspects of life, his discoveries, and his observations "vanity" throughout the text. It is the central theme of his thinking, used thirty-nine times in this short book. Not only is "vanity" the most distinctive word in the book of Ecclesiastes; it is also the most vexing. The underlying Hebrew word *hevel* is notoriously difficult to translate. The most common English rendering—"vanity"—does not capture all the different connotations the word has in Hebrew and is also potentially misleading. In contemporary English, "vanity" can be a description of someone who is arrogant or even shallow, especially about their physical appearance. Those are not the connotations of Hebrew *hevel*, however. Woodenly, *hevel* means "wind" or "breathe"; the proper name of Cain's brother, Abel, is a form of this word (see Gen. 4). Ecclesiastes is clearly using the word in a metaphorical or symbolic sense that requires flexibility in understanding if not also translating. Possible renderings include "ephemeral," "fleeting," "absurd," "meaningless," "futile," "incomprehensible," "pointless," "transient," "elusive," and "worthless." The Teacher may also be using *hevel* philosophically, as part of a search for universal meaning and an acknowledgment that such meaning cannot be fully grasped or controlled. At least one scholar has compared *hevel* to the concept of "absurdity" in Albert Camus's existential philosophy—the experience of two equally valid yet contradictory realities. Other scholars hear resonances with Greek Stoicism and Epicureanism. Since no single English word can fully capture the richness of *hevel*, some translate it in different ways in different verses; others choose not to translate it at all and instead retain the Hebrew. Ultimately, the word serves as a summary statement, capturing the Teacher's reflections that good behavior does not always lead to just reward, that God's behavior is inscrutable and even arbitrary, and that human effort ultimately comes to naught. The word *hevel* is as ambiguous and open to different understandings as is life itself. Perhaps this is why the Teacher used it.

Jennifer L. Koosed

to the place where the streams flow,
   there they continue to flow.
[8] All things*a* are wearisome,
   more than one can express;
the eye is not satisfied with seeing
   or the ear filled with hearing.
[9] What has been is what will be,
   and what has been done is what will
      be done;
   there is nothing new under the sun.
[10] Is there a thing of which it is said,
   "See, this is new"?
It has already been
   in the ages before us.
[11] The people of long ago are not
      remembered,
   nor will there be any remembrance

of people yet to come
   by those who come after them.
   12 I, the Teacher, was king over Israel in Jerusalem. [13] I applied my mind to seek and to search out by wisdom all that is done under heaven; it is an unhappy business that God has given to humans to be busy with. [14] I saw all the deeds that are done under the sun, and see, all is vanity and a chasing after wind.
[15] What is crooked cannot be made
      straight,
   and what is lacking cannot be
      counted.
   16 I said to myself, "I have acquired great wisdom, surpassing all who were over

a 1.8 Or *words*

1926 novel *The Sun Also Rises* alludes to this verse. **1:11** The lack of remembrance is a central concern in Ecclesiastes, especially as it is connected to death. Part of the reason human life is vanity (futile) is that no one remembers you after you are gone.

1:12–18 The Teacher introduces himself. **1:12** The only son of David to rule over Israel in Jerusalem was Solomon. Yet the royal persona adopted here will be dropped later in the book, thereby revealing the speaker as a teacher and a sage—perhaps a court functionary—but not a king. **1:13** *I applied my mind* is more woodenly rendered "I gave my heart." In Hebrew, the heart is the seat of cognition. **1:14** Observation and experience are at the core of the Teacher's philosophy. He watches the world and draws his conclusions from those observations. *Chasing after wind* is a repeating phrase, connecting to the imagery of breath or wind implied by *vanity*; the phrase conveys a sense of the futility of all human endeavors. **1:16** *I said to myself* is more woodenly translated as "I said to

Jerusalem before me, and my mind has had great experience of wisdom and knowledge." [17]And I applied my mind to know wisdom and to know madness and folly. I perceived that this also is but a chasing after wind.

[18] For in much wisdom is much vexation,
    and those who increase knowledge
        increase sorrow.

2 I said to myself, "Come now, I will make a test of pleasure; enjoy yourself." But again, this also was vanity. [2]I said of laughter, "It is mad," and of pleasure, "What use is it?" [3]I searched with my mind how to cheer my body with wine—my mind still guiding me with wisdom—and how to lay hold on folly, until I might see what was good for mortals to do under heaven during the few days of their life. [4]I made great works; I built houses and planted vineyards for myself; [5]I made myself gardens and parks and planted in them all kinds of fruit trees. [6]I made myself pools from which to water the forest of growing trees. [7]I bought male and female slaves and had slaves who were born in my house; I also had great possessions of herds and flocks, more than any who had been before me in Jerusalem. [8]I also gathered

for myself silver and gold and the treasure of kings and of the provinces; I got singers, both men and women, and delights of the flesh, many concubines.[b]

9 So I became great and surpassed all who were before me in Jerusalem; also my wisdom remained with me. [10]Whatever my eyes desired I did not keep from them; I kept my heart from no pleasure, for my heart found pleasure from all my toil, and this was my reward from all my toil. [11]Then I considered all that my hands had done and the toil I had spent in doing it, and again, all was vanity and a chasing after wind, and there was nothing to be gained under the sun.

12 So I turned to consider wisdom and madness and folly, for what can the king's successor do? Only what has already been done. [13]Then I saw that wisdom excels folly as light excels darkness.

[14] The wise have eyes in their head,
    but fools walk in darkness.

Yet I perceived that the same fate befalls all of them. [15]Then I said to myself, "What happens to the fool will happen to me also; why then have I been so very wise?" And I said to

b 2.8 Meaning of Heb uncertain

my heart." The heart becomes almost a separate entity as the Teacher converses with it. Note that Solomon is associated with wisdom in 1 Kgs. 3.

2:1–11 Test of pleasure. This passage is an instance of fictional royal autobiography, as it mimics royal testaments from the ancient Near East, which were designed as propaganda to promote a monarch's greatness. Here, the royal testament is undermined, as the outcome of so much power and wealth is vanity. All great works eventually end up as ruin and rubble, including the names of powerful rulers erased by time. **2:1** *I said to myself* in Hebrew is "I, I said to my heart." The repetition of "I" language emphasizes the personal and introspective nature of this section but also the book as a whole. The verse introducing the test already provides the results of the test: it was *vanity*. **2:5** *Parks* is a Persian word, thus indicating that the text was written during or after the Persian period. **2:7** The casual mention of owning other people, men and women who are listed alongside vineyards and herds, remains a moral problem in the midst of sacred scripture (see **"Human Bondage in Ancient Israel," p. 115**). **2:8** *Concubines* is a contested translation, since the meaning of the Hebrew is uncertain. The passage may be talking about women taken as war captives, a form of slavery. Other translations include "coffers," "luxury items," or "public baths." **2:9** Wisdom remains even in this test of pleasure, suggesting that wisdom is not antithetical to decadent wealth, even though it will all be deemed futile in the end. **2:10** The test of pleasure is complete: everything that was desired was pursued and obtained. **2:11** The Teacher brings together three of the book's refrains—*vanity, chasing after wind, nothing to be gained under the sun*—to produce a powerful concluding statement about the futility of hedonism and conspicuous consumption.

2:12–26 Further investigation about the meaning of life. Once the Teacher concludes that wealth and pleasure do not give life meaning, he turns to consider other ways of being in the world, specifically wisdom and work. The outcome of these pursuits is little better than the Teacher's first set of experiments, as these too are declared vanity in the end. **2:13–17** Wisdom is better than folly; at the same time, both the wise person and the fool die. A fundamental characteristic that should distinguish people (wisdom) ultimately does not because all share the same awful fate: death, oblivion in

myself that this also is vanity. [16]For there is no enduring remembrance of the wise or of fools, seeing that in the days to come all will have been long forgotten. How can the wise die just like fools? [17]So I hated life because what is done under the sun was grievous to me, for all is vanity and a chasing after wind.

18 I hated all my toil in which I had toiled under the sun, seeing that I must leave it to my successor, [19]and who knows whether he will be wise or foolish? Yet he will be master of all for which I toiled and used my wisdom under the sun. This also is vanity. [20]So I turned and gave my heart up to despair concerning all the toil of my labors under the sun, [21]because sometimes one who has toiled with wisdom and knowledge and skill must leave all to be enjoyed by another who did not toil for it. This also is vanity and a great evil. [22]What do mortals get from all the toil and strain with which they toil under the sun? [23]For all their days are full of pain, and their work is a vexation; even at night their minds do not rest. This also is vanity.

24 There is nothing better for mortals than to eat and drink and find enjoyment in their toil. This also, I saw, is from the hand of God, [25]for apart from him[c] who can eat or who can have enjoyment? [26]For to the one who pleases him God gives wisdom and knowledge and joy, but to the sinner he gives the work

of gathering and heaping, only to give to one who pleases God. This also is vanity and a chasing after wind.

3 For everything there is a season and a time for every matter under heaven:
[2] a time to be born and a time to die;
a time to plant and a time to pluck up
what is planted;
[3] a time to kill and a time to heal;
a time to break down and a time to build up;
[4] a time to weep and a time to laugh;
a time to mourn and a time to dance;
[5] a time to throw away stones and a time
to gather stones together;
a time to embrace and a time to refrain
from embracing;
[6] a time to seek and a time to lose;
a time to keep and a time to throw away;
[7] a time to tear and a time to sew;
a time to keep silent and a time to speak;
[8] a time to love and a time to hate;
a time for war and a time for peace.

9 What gain have the workers from their toil? [10]I have seen the business that God has given to everyone to be busy with. [11]He has made everything suitable for its time; moreover, he has put a sense of past and future

c 2.25 Gk Syr: Heb *apart from me*

both body and name. **2:16** In other places in the Bible, a good name endures after one's death, but a bad person's name is forgotten (Prov. 10:7); children are a form of immortality because they carry on one's name and memory. The Teacher disputes the contention that good people are remembered, however, by asserting that no one is remembered. After all, how many people remember the names of their great-grandparents, let alone even more distant ancestors? **2:18–23** Is there at least meaningful work? The Teacher's response is negative. Death again disrupts a meaningful life because after death there is no way to control what happens to the fruit of one's labor. **2:23** Work is a hardship even in one's lifetime, and the anxieties of work can lead to insomnia. **2:24–26** Against the backdrop of futility, pain, and death, one can still enjoy life in the simple pleasures of eating, drinking, and enjoying what one does. This is the first instance of the carpe diem theme that runs throughout Ecclesiastes. **2:24** *Mortals* in Hebrew is "ha-adam," which may allude to the first human creature (Adam) formed out of the earth (Heb. "ha-adamah"; see Gen. 2:7). Enjoyment of life is predicated on transience, according to Ecclesiastes.

3:1–8 Poem on the Times. There is an appropriate time for everything. God has determined a natural flow of events, and it is for human beings to discern those times and respond accordingly. There are twenty-eight items/activities grouped in fourteen antithetical pairs. See **"Poem on the Times," p. 909**. **3:2** Birth and death not only mark the beginning and end of a human life but also epitomize that over which people have no control. *A time to die* may indicate that God has fixed the length of every individual's life. *To pluck up* occurs in the context of war in Zeph. 2:4, implying that here it may also be about destruction, not harvesting. **3:5** Some commentators read *stones* as a veiled sexual reference, but this is uncertain.

3:9–15 The Teacher again asks about the benefit of work. This passage has a more positive message about divine order and human endeavor than the previous one in 2:12–26. **3:11** *He has put a*

Reading through Time: Ecclesiastes's Poem on the Times (Ecclesiastes 3:1–8)

The famous poem found in Eccl. 3:1–8 has been understood in many ways: as a counsel of radical acceptance, an assertion that God determines everything, an anthem of human freedom, and advice to always be ready to act at the right moment. Poets have borrowed from the rhythms of Eccl. 3:1–8 in their own meditations about time and human effort. Robert Southwell's (1561–95) poem "Times Go by Turns" draws on the Teacher's reflection on time, including the cyclical changes of the seasons, the role of chance in human life, and the ever-changing fortune of everyone. Southwell's verse is made more poignant by his own life and death, since he was a Catholic priest martyred by the English state. In "The Love Song of J. Alfred Prufrock," T. S. Eliot (1888–1965) employs the refrain "There will be time" ironically; the title character remains mired in indecision, unable to act but only watching as life passes him by. The Israeli poet Yehuda Amichai (1924–2000) challenges the Teacher directly in "A Man in His Life," which denies that there is a time for everything—at least, not until a man dies. Death by suicide dominates Mark Jarman's (1952–) "Questions for Ecclesiastes." In this poem, a preacher is called to a home where a fourteen-year-old girl has just killed herself. Jarman imagines the preacher using the words of Ecclesiastes in an attempt to comfort the parents, thereby underscoring the utter inadequacy of biblical platitudes in the midst of human suffering and God's silence.

In the late 1950s and 1960s, people resonated strongly with this biblical passage, and it frequently found expression in music. Norman Dello Joio wrote "Meditations on Ecclesiastes" for string orchestra, which explores musically each of the experiences the poem catalogs. The piece won the 1957 Pulitzer Prize. Folk musicians turned the poem into the soundtrack of the counterculture. Pete Seeger set Eccl. 3 to music, recording it in 1959 as "Turn, Turn, Turn!" The song lyrics deviate from the biblical poem at the end, where "I swear it's not too late" replaces "a time for war" (v. 9). In this way, the poem was transformed into a hopeful antiwar anthem that captured the zeitgeist of the era. When it was recorded by the Byrds in 1965, it became an international hit, climbing the charts in the United States, Canada, Germany, New Zealand, the Netherlands, and the United Kingdom.

Jennifer L. Koosed

into their minds, yet they cannot find out what God has done from the beginning to the end. [12]I know that there is nothing better for them than to be happy and enjoy themselves as long as they live; [13]moreover, it is God's gift that all should eat and drink and take pleasure in all their toil. [14]I know that whatever God does endures forever; nothing can be added to it nor anything taken from it; God has done this so that all should stand in awe before him. [15]That which is already has been, that which is to be already is, and God seeks out what has gone by.[d]

16 Moreover, I saw under the sun that, in the place of justice, wickedness was there, and in the place of righteousness, wickedness was there as well. [17]I said to myself, "God will judge the righteous and the wicked, for he has appointed a time for every matter and for every work." [18]I said to myself with regard to humans that God is testing[e] them to show that they are but animals. [19]For the fate of humans and the fate of animals is the same; as one dies, so dies the other. They all have the

d 3.15 Heb *what is pursued*   e 3.18 Meaning of Heb uncertain

sense of past and future into their minds is more opaque in Hebrew and might be rendered as "he gives the world [or eternity] into their hearts." The Teacher may be indicating that humanity is caught between finite time and a desire for something that transcends time. **3:12–13** Another affirmation about enjoying life's simple pleasures. **3:15** Human knowledge and wisdom can never fully grasp the ways of God. This verse reinforces the theme that there is a certain determinism in the order of the world, beyond human understanding or control.

3:16 The possible equation between righteousness and reward, wickedness and punishment is challenged by the Teacher's observations.

3:17–18 Other possible explanations to justify injustice.

3:19–21 Again, death is the great leveler. Not only do both the wise and the foolish die (see 2:14–16) but no distinction is made between human and animal. The words *breath* and *spirit* are the same word in Hebrew ("ruach"); *spirit* is not an immortal soul but an animating breath that God gives to all living creatures after the body is formed from the dust (see Gen. 2:7; Ps. 104:29; Job 34:14–15).

same breath, and humans have no advantage over the animals, for all is vanity. [20]All go to one place, all are from the dust, and all turn to dust again. [21]Who knows whether the human spirit goes upward and the spirit of animals goes downward to the earth? [22]So I saw that there is nothing better than that all should enjoy their work, for that is their lot; who can bring them to see what will be after them?

4 Again I saw all the oppressions that are practiced under the sun. Look, the tears of the oppressed—with no one to comfort them! On the side of their oppressors there was power—with no one to comfort them. [2]And I commended the dead, who have already died, more than the living, who are still alive, [3]but better than both is the one who has not yet been and has not seen the evil deeds that are done under the sun.

4 Then I saw that all toil and all skill in work come from one person's envy of another. This also is vanity and a chasing after wind.

[5] Fools fold their hands
    and consume their own flesh.
[6] Better is a handful with quiet
    than two handfuls with toil
    and a chasing after wind.

7 Again, I saw vanity under the sun: [8]the case of solitary individuals, without sons or brothers; yet there is no end to all their toil, and their eyes are never satisfied with riches. "For whom am I toiling," they ask, "and depriving myself of pleasure?" This also is vanity and an unhappy business.

9 Two are better than one because they have a good reward for their toil. [10]For if they fall, one will lift up the other, but woe to one who is alone and falls and does not have another to help. [11]Again, if two lie together, they keep warm, but how can one keep warm alone? [12]And though one might prevail against another, two will withstand one. A threefold cord is not quickly broken.

13 Better is a poor but wise youth than an old but foolish king who will no longer take advice. [14]One can indeed come out of prison to reign, even though born poor in the kingdom. [15]I saw all the living who, moving about under the sun, follow that[f] youth who replaced the king;[g] [16]there was no end to all those people whom he led.[h] Yet those who come later will not rejoice in him. Surely this also is vanity and a chasing after wind.

5 [i]Guard your steps when you go to the house of God; to draw near to listen is better than the sacrifice offered by fools, for they do not know how to keep from doing evil.[j] [2k]Never be rash with your mouth nor

f 4.15 Heb the second   g 4.15 Heb him   h 4.16 Heb who were before them   i 5.1 4.17 in Heb   j 5.1 Cn: Heb they do not know how to do evil   k 5.2 5.1 in Heb

3:22 Death comes for all, so one needs to enjoy life.

4:1 In contrast to the prophets, the Teacher decries the fate of the oppressed but does not call for the end of injustice.

4:2–3 Although many passages commend life even in the face of suffering, injustice, and death, the Teacher seems to contradict those passages here by proclaiming that it is better to be dead, even better never to have been born. The book lacks consistency on this point (and others), perhaps mirroring the inconsistency of life itself. **4:3** *Better than* sayings are common in proverbial wisdom (see 4:6, 13; 7:1–12; Prov. 15:16–17; 16:8; Sir. 29:22).

4:5–6 An arresting image of self-cannibalism along with a metaphor for idleness, self-destruction, and wasted effort.

4:9–12 The value of companionship. The images used here include working together, supporting each other through hardship, sleeping together (which may have sexual connotations), and fighting together. The passage reflects a similar saying in the Epic of Gilgamesh that also lauds companionship. **4:12** *A threefold cord is not quickly broken* seems to be a well-known proverb across the ancient Near East, appearing also in the Gilgamesh epic.

4:13–16 A parable that may reflect a historical situation known to the original audience but lost to readers today. The ideas of radical reversal of fortune and the fleeting and fickle nature of popular support are not bound to any one historical context. Wisdom affords certain advantages, but those advantages are temporary.

5:1–2 The Teacher turns from personal reflection to practical advice, beginning with the best way to approach temple worship: be circumspect, unlike fools. An alternative translation for *they do not know how to keep from doing evil* is that the fool "does not recognize when he does evil."

let your heart be quick to utter a word before God, for God is in heaven and you upon earth; therefore let your words be few.

3 For dreams come with many cares, and a fool's voice with many words.

4 When you make a vow to God, do not delay fulfilling it, for he has no pleasure in fools. Fulfill what you vow. [5]It is better that you should not vow than that you should vow and not fulfill it. [6]Do not let your mouth lead you into sin, and do not say before the messenger that it was a mistake; why should God be angry at your words and destroy the work of your hands?

7 With many dreams come vanities and a multitude of words,[l] but fear God.

8 If you see in a province the oppression of the poor and the violation of justice and right, do not be amazed at the matter, for the high official is watched by a higher, and there are yet higher ones over them. [9]But all things considered, this is an advantage for a land: a king for a plowed field.[m]

10 The lover of money will not be satisfied with money, nor the lover of wealth with gain. This also is vanity.

11 When goods increase, those who eat them increase, and what gain has their owner but to see them with his eyes?

12 Sweet is the sleep of laborers, whether they eat little or much, but the abundance of the rich will not let them sleep.

13 There is a grievous ill that I have seen under the sun: riches were kept by their owners to their hurt, [14]and those riches were lost in a bad venture; though they are parents of children, they have nothing in their hands. [15]As they came from their mother's womb, so they shall go again, naked as they came; they shall take nothing for their toil that they may carry away with their hands. [16]This also is a grievous ill: just as they came, so shall they go, and what gain do they have from toiling for the wind? [17]Besides, all their days they eat in darkness, in much anger and sickness and resentment.

18 This is what I have seen to be good: it is fitting to eat and drink and find enjoyment in all the toil with which one toils under the sun the few days of the life God gives us, for this is our lot. [19]Likewise, all to whom God gives wealth and possessions and whom he enables to enjoy them and to accept their lot and find enjoyment in their toil—this is the gift of God. [20]For they will scarcely brood over the days of

l 5.7 Meaning of Heb uncertain   m 5.9 Meaning of Heb uncertain

The recommendation, in any event, is to approach God quietly and thoughtfully, not with a loud, ostentatious show (see also Matt. 6:7–8).

5:4–5 A general admonition to watch one's mouth in worship contexts focuses in these verses on vows. Using care in vow-making is a common sentiment in proverbial texts (Prov. 20:25; Sir. 18:22–23) and also reflects legal material on vows (Deut. 23:21–23).

5:6 *Messenger* can also be translated as "angel." The sins of the mouth are a particular focus in later Judaism and in Christianity (see Jas. 3:1–12).

5:7 *Fear God* is a theme also in Proverbs, where it is the beginning of wisdom (Prov. 1:7).

5:8 *A province* is an administrative area in an empire. The administrative hierarchy and bureaucracy described here also reflect the governing structures of an empire. Ancient Israel was part of the Persian Empire beginning in the sixth century BCE and then transitioned to Hellenistic rule in the fourth century BCE. The economic inequalities that proliferate when smaller groups are incorporated into larger empires are the focus here.

5:10–17 Counter to the traditional correlation of wisdom with wealth (see, e.g., Prov. 13:21–22), the Teacher focuses on the ways that wealth brings not satisfaction but more worry and anxiety. The rich are not to be envied; workers rest satisfied in the value of a full day's honest labor. The contrast may be between the wealthy and the enslaved. **5:10** See 1 Tim. 6:10, which ascribes all evil to the love of money. **5:13–17** The Teacher describes three scenarios where wealth leads to sorrow: (1) the one who hoards; (2) the one who makes an investment but loses; and (3) death, which comes for all no matter how one has managed one's money. **5:15** See Job 1:21, which also notes that a person is born naked and will die naked. This may have been a common aphorism.

5:18–20 In the midst of sorrow and death, the Teacher recommends finding enjoyment in simple, everyday pleasures and also in work, using the brevity of life and the reality of death to refocus attention on the present moment. There is also a sense here that God has given pleasure and work to distract humanity from the grim reality of death. Other ancient Near Eastern wisdom texts also express this idea.

their lives because God keeps them occupied with the joy of their hearts.

6 There is an evil that I have seen under the sun, and it lies heavy upon humankind: ²those to whom God gives wealth, possessions, and honor, so that they lack nothing of all that they desire, yet God does not enable them to enjoy these things, but a stranger enjoys them. This is vanity; it is a grievous ill. ³A man may father a hundred children and live many years, but however many are the days of his years, if he does not enjoy life's good things or has no burial, I say that a stillborn child is better off than he. ⁴For it comes in vanity and goes in darkness, and in darkness its name is covered; ⁵moreover, it has not seen the sun or known anything, yet it finds rest rather than he. ⁶Even though he should live a thousand years twice over yet enjoy no good—do not all go to one place?

7 All human toil is for the mouth, yet the appetite is not satisfied. ⁸For what advantage have the wise over fools? And what do the poor have who know how to conduct themselves before the living? ⁹Better is the sight of the eyes than the wandering of desire; this also is vanity and a chasing after wind.

10 Whatever has come to be has already been named, and it is known what humans are and that they are not able to dispute with those who are stronger. ¹¹The more words, the more vanity, so how is one the better? ¹²For who knows what is good for mortals while they live the few days of their vain life, which they pass like a shadow? For who can tell them what will be after them under the sun?

7 A good name is better than precious
    ointment,
    and the day of death, than the day of
      birth.
² It is better to go to the house of mourning
    than to go to the house of feasting,
  for this is the end of everyone,
    and the living will lay it to heart.
³ Sorrow is better than laughter,
  for by sadness of countenance the
    heart is made glad.

6:1–2 In these verses, God has given wealth but not the ability to enjoy that wealth. The passage seems to contradict the reflection on wealth and enjoyment that just preceded it. However, 5:18–19 may be regarded as a general rule, with 6:1–2 an exception to that rule. In this way, the Teacher does not allow any general maxim to go unchallenged. Ultimately, life is inexplicable, and one's current good fortune can depart without warning.

6:3–6 An extended metaphor using a stillborn child. Stillbirth is one of life's greatest tragedies, a painful situation for parents where enormous effort comes to naught and where hopeful expectations are dashed. For the child, life is gone before it could even begin. That a stillborn baby could be considered better off than a living person demonstrates the radical nature of the Teacher's thinking. Job's curse of his own birthday, saying it would have been better to have never been conceived, echoes Ecclesiastes (Job 3:1–16). **6:3** In other biblical passages, children are both blessing and reward, a sign of God's favor (Gen. 12; Job 42); a long life is also a reward from God (Job 42). Here, the Teacher severs the connections between many children, a long life, and divine blessing. The Teacher undercuts traditional theodicies that link good behavior with health and material reward.

6:6 Death always comes, and no distinction is made between people in death.

6:7 *Appetite* is a person's "soul" or "self" (Heb. "nefesh"). The image of the insatiable rich is found in other biblical texts (Ps. 73:9) and connects to the insatiable nature of death, consuming all and never satisfied (Hab. 2:5).

6:10 The Teacher returns to the deterministic and cyclical nature of all history. Passive verbal constructions suggest a deity who is distant and unknowable but nevertheless in control.

6:12 Who knows best how to act in the world? The Teacher, despite all the advice that precedes and follows this verse, recognizes the vanity of his own counsel.

7:1–14 Proverbs. A series of wisdom sayings, some of which may be traditional, others of which were likely composed by the author. The word "good" is repeatedly used (often translated *better*), yet most of what the Teacher calls "good" is unexpected. Many of the proverbs draw attention to death, the unrelenting reality of which is a major theme of the book as a whole. **7:1** In the Hebrew text, there is a wordplay between "name" and "ointment" (see Song 1:3 for another association between names and ointments). A good name is a good reputation, and fine oils are a luxury. A good name confers a kind of immortality but is never secure until one dies (see Sir. 11:28). Wealth means nothing after death. **7:2** Recommending the house of mourning may contradict other passages that

4 The heart of the wise is in the house of
mourning,
but the heart of fools is in the house
of mirth.
5 It is better to hear the rebuke of the wise
than to hear the song of fools.
6 For like the crackling of thorns under a
pot,
so is the laughter of fools;
this also is vanity.
7 Surely oppression makes the wise
foolish,
and a bribe corrupts the heart.
8 Better is the end of a thing than its
beginning;
the patient in spirit are better than the
proud in spirit.
9 Do not be quick to anger,
for anger lodges in the bosom of fools.
10 Do not say, "Why were the former days
better than these?"
For it is not from wisdom that you ask
this.
11 Wisdom is as good as an inheritance,
an advantage to those who see the sun.
12 For the protection of wisdom is like the
protection of money,
and the advantage of knowledge is
that wisdom gives life to the one
who possesses it.
13 Consider the work of God;
who can make straight what he has
made crooked?

14 In the day of prosperity, be joyful, and in
the day of adversity, consider: God has made
the one as well as the other, so that mortals
may not find out anything that comes after
them.
15 In my vain life I have seen everything;
there are righteous people who perish in
their righteousness, and there are wicked
people who prolong their life in their evildoing. 16Do not be too righteous, and do not
act too wise; why should you destroy yourself? 17Do not be too wicked, and do not be
a fool; why should you die before your time?
18It is good that you should take hold of the
one without letting go of the other, for the
one who fears God shall succeed with both.
19 Wisdom gives strength to the wise more
than ten rulers who are in a city.
20 Surely there is no one on earth so righteous as to do good without ever sinning.
21 Do not give heed to everything that people say, or you may hear your servant cursing
you; 22your heart knows that many times you
have yourself cursed others.
23 All this I have tested by wisdom; I said,
"I will be wise," but it was far from me. 24That
which is, is far off, and deep, very deep; who
can find it out? 25I turned my mind to know
and to search out and to seek wisdom and the
sum of things and to know that wickedness
is folly and that foolishness is madness. 26I
found more bitter than death the woman who
is a trap, whose heart is nets, whose hands are

advise eating and drinking; however, mourning practices in the ancient world often involved meals.
7:4 Alluding to this verse, Edith Wharton titled her 1905 novel *House of Mirth*. **7:6** The images are
discordant, and in Hebrew, the saying is onomatopoeic. **7:8** This saying mirrors the sense of 7:1 that
there is no security until one has died. **7:13** God is in control even when things seem counter to
human desire. *Crooked* is the same word used in Job 19:6 (see also 8:3; 34:12) where Job complains
about God's making justice "crooked." **7:14** Both good and evil (translated here as *prosperity* and
adversity) come from God; God is thus unpredictable and unknowable. Vv. 13–14 together challenge
the theological presupposition that God is always benevolent.

7:15 The heart of the matter for the Teacher: good people perish, and evil people prosper. Retribution
theology, an idea expressed throughout much of the Bible—that good people are rewarded by God and
bad people punished by God—is directly challenged by the Teacher's own observations and experiences.
Next to the reality of death, the reality of injustice is what results in the conclusion that all is "vanity."

7:16–17 Given life's contradictions and the fact that both the wise and the foolish die, these verses
commend moderation in both righteousness and wickedness. Such a recommendation—*do not be
too wicked*—is startling in philosophical ethics and sacred scripture.

7:18 As the book itself tries to hold contradictions together, here the Teacher recommends his
readers do as well.

7:23–29 Wisdom is ultimately elusive; one can seek it, but it cannot be found. Even the Teacher
fails. The trope of seeking and finding is common in wisdom texts. In Proverbs, wisdom is personified as a woman (see Prov. 8–9), desired and sought by the wise (Prov. 8:35). In Ecclesiastes, wisdom is never personified as a woman. **7:26–28** Vv. 26 and 28 are perhaps the only all-encompassing

fetters; one who pleases God escapes her, but the sinner is taken by her. [27]See, this is what I found, says the Teacher, adding one thing to another to find the sum, [28]which my mind has sought repeatedly, but I have not found. One man among a thousand I found, but a woman among all these I have not found. [29]See, this alone I found, that God made human beings straightforward, but they have devised many schemes.

8

Who is like the wise man?
And who knows the interpretation of
a thing?
Being wise makes one's face shine,
but arrogance changes one's face.

2 Keep[n] the king's command, and because of your sacred oath [3]do not be terrified; go from his presence; do not delay when the matter is unpleasant, for he does whatever he pleases. [4]For the word of the king is powerful, and who can say to him, "What are you doing?" [5]Whoever obeys a command will meet no harm, and the wise mind will know the time and way. [6]For every matter has its time and way, although the troubles of mortals lie heavy upon them. [7]Indeed, they do not know what is to be, for who can tell them how it

will be? [8]No one has power over the wind[o] to restrain the wind[p] or power over the day of death; there is no discharge from the battle, nor does wickedness deliver those who practice it. [9]All this I observed, applying my mind to all that is done under the sun, while one person exercises authority over another to the other's hurt.

10 Then I saw the wicked approaching to sacrifice;[q] they go in and out of the holy place, and they boast[r] in the city that they have done such things. This also is vanity. [11]Because sentence against an evil deed is not executed speedily, the human heart is fully set to do evil. [12]Though sinners do evil a hundred times and prolong their lives, yet I know that it will be well with those who fear God, because they stand in fear before him, [13]but it will not be well with the wicked, neither will they prolong their days like a shadow, because they do not stand in fear before God.

14 There is a vanity that takes place on earth, that there are righteous people who are treated according to the conduct of the wicked and wicked people who are treated

n 8.2 Heb *I keep*   o 8.8 Or *breath*   p 8.8 Or *breath*
q 8.10 Cn: Heb *buried*   r 8.10 Gk: Heb *they were forgotten*

---

misogynistic statements in the Bible, condemning all women, no matter who they are, as worse than death and incapable of wisdom. The language of trapping is reminiscent of the characterization of the adulterous woman in Prov. 7:5–23, and so some commentators have limited the type of women Ecclesiastes is condemning to adulterous women instead of all women. As folly is personified in Proverbs and linked to the adulterous woman, perhaps this woman without wisdom is Folly herself (see Prov. 9:13–18). The more positive statement in Eccl. 9:9 might counter statements denigrating women, but it is possible to have a negative assessment of women while granting exceptions to the rule and loving one's own wife. **7:29** The Teacher concludes with a negative assessment of human character, especially in terms of honesty, transparency, and trustworthiness.

8:1 The first part of the verse implies that the answer to the question is "no one." If read in the context of the following verse, the second half of the verse offers advice for how to appear before a king—always with a happy countenance so as not to provoke the monarch.

8:2–5 The Teacher presents himself as someone who works in the royal court and gives advice about how best to interact with a king, something that other ancient Near Eastern texts also discuss. There may be a parallel to how one should comport oneself before God, as both the monarch and the deity are powerful and unpredictable.

8:6 *For every matter has its time*, see 3:1–8.

8:7 Human knowledge is limited.

8:8 The image of *wind* recalls the theme of "vanity" and the refrain "chasing after wind," both of which indicate human futility. The lack of clear connection between doing good and being rewarded, and doing evil and being punished, is again emphasized.

8:9 A critique of human hierarchy and authority (and perhaps a critique of God).

8:10 The wicked behave with impunity, even appearing to be good.

8:11 Even if there is punishment for sins, since this punishment does not occur in a timely manner, evil endures.

8:12–14 The Teacher's point is that there is something arbitrary about the consequences of good and evil. That does not mean that the wicked are never punished and the good are never rewarded,

according to the conduct of the righteous. I said that this also is vanity. ¹⁵So I commend enjoyment, for there is nothing better for people under the sun than to eat and drink and enjoy themselves, for this will go with them in their toil through the days of life that God gives them under the sun.

16 When I applied my mind to know wisdom and to see the business that is done on earth, how one's eyes see sleep neither day nor night, ¹⁷then I saw all the work of God, that no one can find out what is happening under the sun. However much they may toil in seeking, they will not find it out; even though those who are wise claim to know, they cannot find it out.

9 All this I laid to heart, examining it all, how the righteous and the wise and their deeds are in the hand of God; whether it is love or hate one does not know. Everything that confronts them ²is vanity,ˢ since the same fate comes to all, to the righteous and the wicked, to the good and the evil,ᵗ to the clean and the unclean, to those who sacrifice and those who do not sacrifice. As are the good, so are the sinners; those who

swear are like those who shun an oath. ³This is an evil in all that happens under the sun, that the same fate comes to everyone. Moreover, the hearts of humans are full of evil; madness is in their hearts while they live, and after that they go to the dead. ⁴But whoever is joined with all the living has hope, for a living dog is better than a dead lion. ⁵The living know that they will die, but the dead know nothing; they have no more reward, and even the memory of them is lost. ⁶Their love and their hate and their envy have already perished; never again will they have any share in all that happens under the sun.

7 Go, eat your bread with enjoyment and drink your wine with a merry heart, for God has long ago approved what you do. ⁸Let your garments always be white; do not let oil be lacking on your head. ⁹Enjoy life with the wife whom you love all the days of your vain life that are given you under the sun,ᵘ because that is your portion in life and in your toil at which you toil under the sun. ¹⁰Whatever your hand finds to do, do with

s 9.2 Syr Compare Gk: Heb *Everything that confronts them is everything*   t 9.2 Gk Syr Vg: Heb lacks *and the evil*   u 9.9 Cn: Heb *sun, all the days of your vanity*

however. Sometimes they are, but that further compounds the problem, underscoring the inscrutability of God and the impossibility of controlling life.

8:15 Justice may be unattainable, but the Teacher pivots again to commend enjoyment in the face of futility.

8:16–17 A final statement about the elusiveness of wisdom and the limits of human understanding. Such a situation leads to sleeplessness, another image of anxiety that can torment and lead to insomnia (2:23).

9:1–6 The radical universality of death. **9:1** Human beings cannot know God's work, yet all is in God's hand. This verse links back to the previous verse (8:17) yet also sets up the binary oppositions that will follow, using the antithesis of *love* and *hate*. Love and hate may refer to the attitude of God or human beings. **9:2–3** *The same fate*. No matter how someone lives in the world, they will die. The Teacher does not assume any kind of life after death. As a result, since there is no justice in this world, there is no justice whatsoever. The common fate of all people, in fact, breeds evil because there are no clear negative consequences for wicked acts (see also 8:11). **9:4** *A living dog is better than a dead lion*. Dogs were maligned animals across the ancient world; lions were feared but praised. The animal imagery participates in the binary oppositions set up in this passage. Life and death are not binary oppositions here, as they sometimes are in biblical literature (see Deut. 30:19); rather, life leads to death for everyone. **9:5–6** Life has one distinct advantage over death, and that is the knowledge of death. The dead are just gone and forgotten.

9:7–10 Another advantage that the living have over the dead is the possibility of enjoyment. This leads to the commendation to enjoy life while that is still possible. This passage is another expression of the carpe diem theme, one modeled closely after the Epic of Gilgamesh. There, the tavern keeper Siduri tells Gilgamesh that immortal life is the sole purview of the gods. She recommends that he return to his city, advising him to enjoy life in terms that are almost identical to Eccl. 9. **9:7** The food and drink recommended are specified as *bread* and *wine*. **9:9** *Wife* is the same word used more generically for "woman." **9:10** *Sheol* simply means the grave here, not an underworld where human consciousness and personality persist (see **"Sheol," p. 695**).

your might, for there is no work or thought or knowledge or wisdom in Sheol, to which you are going.

11 Again I saw that under the sun the race is not to the swift, nor the battle to the strong, nor bread to the wise, nor riches to the intelligent, nor favor to the skillful, but time and chance happen to them all. ¹²For no one can anticipate one's time. Like fish taken in a cruel net or like birds caught in a snare, so mortals are snared at a time of calamity, when it suddenly falls upon them.

13 I have also seen this example of wisdom under the sun, and it seemed great to me. ¹⁴There was a little city with few people in it. A great king came against it and besieged it, building great siegeworks against it. ¹⁵Now there was found in it a poor wise man, and he by his wisdom delivered the city. Yet no one remembered that poor man. ¹⁶So I said, "Wisdom is better than might; yet the poor man's wisdom is despised, and his words are not heeded."

¹⁷ The quiet words of the wise are more to
> be heeded
>> than the shouting of a ruler among
>> fools.

¹⁸ Wisdom is better than weapons of war,
> but one bungler destroys much good.

10

Dead flies make the perfumer's
> ointment give off a foul odor;^y
> so a little folly outweighs wisdom and
> honor.

² The heart of the wise inclines to the
> right,
> but the heart of a fool to the left.

³ Even when fools walk on the road, they
> lack sense
> and show to everyone that they are
> fools.

⁴ If the anger of the ruler rises against you,
> do not leave your post,
> for calmness will undo great
> offenses.

5 There is an evil that I have seen under the sun, as great an error as if it proceeded from the ruler: ⁶folly is set in many high places, and the rich sit in a low place. ⁷I have seen slaves on horseback and princes walking on the ground like slaves.

⁸ Whoever digs a pit will fall into it,
> and whoever breaks through a wall
>> will be bitten by a snake.

⁹ Whoever quarries stones will be hurt by
> them,
> and whoever splits logs will be
>> endangered by them.

¹⁰ If the iron is blunt and one does not whet
> the edge,
> then more strength must be
>> exerted,
> but wisdom helps one to succeed.

¹¹ If the snake bites before it is charmed,
> there is no advantage in a charmer.

¹² Words spoken by the wise bring them
> favor,
> but the lips of fools consume them.

¹³ The words of their mouths begin in
> foolishness,

y 10.1 Gk Vg Syr: Meaning of Heb uncertain

9:11–12 No ability or effort can guarantee success. Not only death but also a terrible accident can upend one's life without warning.

9:13–18 This vignette may be a story that was well known to the Teacher's audience, maybe even drawn from a historical event. The story is ambiguous—were the wise man's words heeded or not? The general point remains, regardless: wisdom when heeded has advantages, yet even when wisdom leads to a positive outcome, no one remembers.

10:1 A minor irritant caused by happenstance can ruin a greater effort. This verse is the likely origin of the English idiom "a fly in the ointment."

10:4 The Teacher continues his advice on how to succeed as an official in court. The ruler is perhaps capricious in his emotion but can be met with a calm that defuses the situation (see 5:7–8; 8:2–9; 10:16–20).

10:5–7 These verses assume a certain social order with rulers at the top and slaves at the bottom. It is the inversion of this order that is called *evil*, not the order itself, thus betraying the Teacher's class allegiances. A chaotic social order reflects a breakdown in the cosmic order, and these verses may look ahead to chap. 12.

10:8–10 There is some value in hard work, but it cannot guarantee success. **10:8** Snakes nest in rocks.

10:10–15 There is some advantage in wisdom, but it cannot guarantee success.

and their talk ends in wicked
    madness,
[14] yet fools talk on and on.
    No one knows what is to happen,
    and who can tell anyone what the
        future holds?
[15] The toil of fools wears them out,
    for they do not even know the way to
        town.

[16] Alas for you, O land, when your king is a
        child
    and your princes feast in the morning!
[17] Happy are you, O land, when your king is
        a nobleman,
    and your princes feast at the proper
        time—
    for strength and not for drunkenness!
[18] Through sloth the roof sinks in,
    and through indolence the house
        leaks.
[19] Feasts are made for laughter,
    wine gladdens life,
    and money meets every need.
[20] Do not curse the king, even in your
        thoughts,
    or curse the rich, even in your
        bedroom,
    for a bird of the air may carry your
        voice,

or some winged creature tell the
    matter.

11 Send out your bread upon the waters,
    for after many days you will get it
        back.
[2] Divide your means seven ways, or even
        eight,
    for you do not know what disaster
        may happen on earth.
[3] When clouds are full,
    they empty rain on the earth;
    whether a tree falls to the south or to the
        north,
    in the place where the tree falls, there
        it will lie.
[4] Whoever observes the wind will not sow,
    and whoever regards the clouds will
        not reap.
5 Just as you do not know how the breath
comes to the bones in the mother's womb,
so you do not know the work of God, who
makes everything.
6 In the morning sow your seed, and at
evening do not let your hands be idle, for you
do not know which will prosper, this or that,
or whether both alike will be good.
7 Light is sweet, and it is pleasant for the
eyes to see the sun.
8 Even those who live many years should
rejoice in them all, yet let them remember

10:16–18 Wise and prudent leadership is essential. Eating and drinking are recommended by the Teacher, but the rule is "everything in moderation."

10:20 Prudent speech (and even prudent thought) is important, although this verse seems ironic given the critique of rulers that appears earlier in this chapter (v. 16)—could there be a wry wink at the reader here? The use of spy networks across the empire is attested in the Persian period. *Some winged creature tell the matter* is probably the origin of the English idiom "a little bird told me."

11:1–6 This unit offers practical advice on how to live in the face of uncertainty. **11:1** *Send out your bread* could refer to acts of charity and other good deeds. Good deeds can have a cascading effect, producing benefits in ways not intended or fully understood. Such acts should be done without expectation of reward. The phrase could also refer to financial investments, however. Some read the reference to *the waters* as encouraging international investments in particular. Soaking bread in water is also an ancient beer-brewing technique. **11:2** *Divide your means* may be referring to prudent financial planning, protecting against misfortune by diversification. Another reading is that one must take chances and be ready for whatever opportunities present themselves. **11:3** Natural events are also beyond human control, even human understanding. **11:4** Waiting for perfect conditions often leads to inaction. **11:5** The genesis of life is a mystery. Like natural phenomena ("the wind" in v. 4) and human life (*breath*), so to God. The Teacher emphasizes uncertainty and unknowability and therefore recommends a humble attitude. **11:6** Humility is not the same thing as passivity. One still must work and be ready to act at the right time.

11:7–10 Life should be enjoyed, especially in one's youth. **11:7** Light and sun are pleasant and also metaphors for life (Job 3:16; 33:28, 30; Pss. 36:9; 56:13). Both are also gifts of God (see Gen. 1; Ps. 104). **11:8** *The days of darkness* refers to death. No matter how long one's life is, it is remarkably brief, especially compared to an eternity of death. *Darkness* can also refer to misfortune or old age. Here, as everywhere in Ecclesiastes, *vanity* means something that is brief, ephemeral and that passes

that the days of darkness will be many. All that comes is vanity.

9 Rejoice, young man, while you are young, and let your heart cheer you in the days of your youth. Follow the inclination of your heart and the desire of your eyes, but know that for all these things God will bring you into judgment.

10 Banish anxiety from your mind, and put away pain from your body, for youth and the dawn of life are vanity.

12 Remember your creator in the days of your youth, before the days of trouble come and the years draw near when you will say, "I have no pleasure in them"; ²before the sun and the light and the moon and the stars are darkened and the clouds return with[w] the rain; ³in the day when the guards of the house tremble, and the strong men are bent, and the women who grind cease working because they are few, and those who look through the windows see dimly; ⁴when the doors on the street are shut, and the sound of the grinding is low, and one rises up at the sound of a bird, and all the daughters of song are brought low; ⁵when one is afraid of heights, and terrors are in the road; the almond tree blossoms, the grasshopper drags itself along,[x] and the caper bud falls; because all must go to their eternal home, and the mourners will go about the streets; ⁶before the silver cord is snapped,[y] and the golden bowl is broken, and the pitcher is broken at the fountain, and the wheel broken at the cistern, ⁷and the dust returns to the earth as it was, and the breath[z] returns to God who gave it. ⁸Vanity of vanities, says the Teacher; all is vanity.

w 12.2 Or *after*   x 12.5 Or *is a burden*   y 12.6 Syr Vg Compare Gk: Heb *is removed*   z 12.7 Or *the spirit*

quickly. Youth is fleeting; nothingness follows. **11:9** The Teacher balances hedonism—the pursuit of pleasure—with prudence by recalling the ever-watchful God. The personification of the *heart* connects these verses back to 2:1–3. Another possible reading is that God will judge people who fail to enjoy all that has been arranged for human enjoyment, since life's pleasures are a divine gift.

12:1–8 The Hebrew of these verses is difficult with the images striking and enigmatic. Consequently, there are a number of ways in which this passage has been understood. Some commentators read the images as allegories for the deterioration of the human body as it ages. Others understand it as describing the breakdown of society, the end of human history, or even the end of the cosmos itself. Whether the poem is understood as allegorical or eschatological, it is most certainly about the inevitability of death. Everything—and everyone—comes to an end. **12:1** *Your creator*. Some translators and commentators think the reference to one's creator is not consistent with the Teacher's theology and therefore understand the word to be a reference to health or the grave. **12:2** The darkening of the celestial lights is a common eschatological image (Ezek. 32:7–8; Isa. 13:9–10; Joel 2:10). In allegorical readings of Eccl. 12:1–8, the sun, moon, and stars are parts of the face. The clouds return after the rain, which does not make meteorological sense, but perhaps the chronological reversal is intentional, unsettling the predictability of the natural world (cf. 1:3–11). **12:3** Society breaks down. In eschatological understandings of this passage, fear and terror seize everyone and everyday activities grind to a halt. In allegorical readings, the various figures are thought to be arms, legs, eyes, and teeth. **12:4** The verse is describing depopulated streets with only the sound of the birds. Birdsong can be desolate and eerie and is sometimes associated with end-time scenes (Isa. 13:21; 34:13). Allegorically, these images could refer to the closing of bodily orifices, including all parts of the alimentary canal—mouth, stomach, digestive tract, anus. The voice is also lost as one ages. **12:5** Old people fear going about in the world. Allegorically, the hair turns white, sexual desire wanes, and a man becomes impotent. Eschatologically, even the natural world begins to falter. The imagery contrasts with that found in the opening poem in Eccl. 1, where nature is predictable and enduring. See Amos 5:16 for communal mourning in the end times. **12:6** *Silver cord, golden bowl, pitcher, cistern*, four broken items that symbolize the body's death. *Cistern* is literally "the pit" and may refer to the grave. In the Second Temple period, broken pottery is frequently found in Jewish tombs, which may indicate that the breaking of pots was part of funerary rituals. See also Gen. 2:7 where the man is molded out of earth not unlike how a potter makes a pot. Henry James alludes to this verse in his novel *The Golden Bowl* (1904). **12:7** Allusions to Genesis continue (see Gen. 2:7; 3:19). The *breath* here is not an immortal soul but the animating force bestowed by God. **12:8** As the Teacher began in 1:2, so the Teacher ends, with the very same motto.

9 Besides being wise, the Teacher also taught the people knowledge, weighing and studying and arranging many proverbs. ¹⁰The Teacher sought to find pleasing words, and he wrote words of truth plainly.

11 The sayings of the wise are like goads, and like nails firmly fixed are the collected sayings that are given by one shepherd.ᵃ ¹²Of anything beyond these, my child, beware. Of making many books there is no end, and much study is a weariness of the flesh.

13 The end of the matter; all has been heard. Fear God, and keep his commandments, for that is the whole duty of everyone. ¹⁴For God will bring every deed into judgment, including*ᵇ* every secret thing, whether good or evil.

a 12.11 Meaning of Heb uncertain   b 12.14 Or *into the judgment on*

12:9–14 Epilogue. The epilogue is widely considered to be written by another hand (or possibly two). The superscription in 1:1 and the epilogue frame the body of the book. **12:11** *One shepherd* is unclear. It may refer to God, who is sometimes called a shepherd (Ps. 23:1), or the figure may be the Teacher himself. The reference to a shepherd may conclude the imagery from earlier in this verse where the wise teacher (the shepherd) uses his words (the stick) to drive forward his students (the sheep). **12:12** An ironic note considering the book just made and the study just undertaken. **12:13–14** Even though the Teacher discusses God throughout, sometimes in very traditional terms, summing up the book with such traditional themes has struck many readers as inconsistent with the message of the book as a whole. Like the rest of the epilogue (and the superscription in 1:1), these lines are attributed to someone other than the Teacher, perhaps added as a way of toning down the more radical content of the book or even smoothing its inclusion in the canon.

SONG OF SONGS

Authorship, Date, and Canonicity

The book begins with the words "The Song of Songs, which is Solomon's," and is traditionally held to have been penned by the king, who is associated with many of the book's themes (love, the natural world, literary arts). While some scholars support the attribution—or at least a connection with a Solomonic school—others suggest a later composition date for the book and therefore see Solomon's connection with the text to be pseudepigraphic. The predominant female voice has led a few scholars to propose that a woman authored this text.

It is impossible to date the book reliably. Scholarship of the last century posits either an early date, connecting it with Ugaritic and other ancient Near Eastern (ANE) traditions, or a comparatively late one, noticing how words and features of the Persian and Aramaic languages have been incorporated into the Song's Hebrew. The Song was one of the last books to be included in the canon of the Hebrew Bible, due to its provocative subject matter and its failure to mention God. Its route to canonicity is perhaps captured in the comments of Rabbi Akiva, who declared that the book must not be treated as a secular song to be sung in taverns but who championed it as the "Holy of Holies." The question of canonization appears to have been settled by 160 BCE.

Poetry, Structure, and Textual Features

The Song's superlative poetic nature has been remarked on by many. There is no consensus on how the structure of the book should be understood—specifically, whether it is one poem or a series of interconnected poems. If a series, opinions vary widely on how and on what basis the book should be divided: subject matter, meter, or poetic technique. Readers are perhaps better served by recognizing multiple, sophisticated techniques, which affect the perception of how the Song is structured. More recent commentators have elected to discuss the Song in poetic units that are determined according to the thematic or subject area.

A few important features, however, provide some structure. One is a series of poetic descriptions or *wasfs* (named after the Arabic poetic form) that elaborately describe the body (4:1-6; 5:10-15; 6:4-7; 7:1-10). A second is the presence of extended speeches by both lovers. The third is the presence of two closely related dream sequences (3:1-3 and 5:2-7). Readers might also take note that there is no identifiable plot in the Song (even if the dream sequences suggest some development), though this has not prevented some from trying to impose one to satisfy particular sensibilities (see **"Sex, Desire, and Eroticism," p. 927**).

Song of Songs in Jewish and Christian Traditions

The Song's reception history boasts an enormous variety of interpretive strategies. Discussion must begin with allegorical interpretation, which dominated Jewish and Christian readings until the nineteenth century. The traditions interpreted the book as the story of the relationship between God and the people of Israel (for Jewish interpretations) or God and the church, Mary, or the individual soul (for Christian readings). These exegetical traditions also produced commentary that was sometimes accompanied by cautions directed at uninitiated readers; this suggests that the Song's subject matter was difficult to understand.

In Jewish traditions, allegorical readings tracked the historical events of the story of Israel, making links to significant moments, such as the exodus. As time progressed, readers began to explore the possibility that the individual was reflected in the relationship depicted in the book. Jewish tradition also explored a mystical encounter with God via the Song in the attribution of various emanations or *sephirot* of the divine to specific characters and bodily descriptions in the book. In Jewish mysticism, the Song was also associated with such themes as creation, covenant, and Shabbat. In praxis, the Song (as one of the Megillot; see **"Introduction to the Writings," pp. 6-9**) has had a long-standing role in the observance of Passover.

In Christian allegories, the Song is a wedding story, which tells of the relationship between Christ and the church. Origen (b. ca. 185) influenced generations of thinkers with this framework, along with his demarcation and subsequent restriction of the book as an esoteric text. The book also supported the cult of Mary, especially in the Middle Ages, where it was critical in the development

of Christian mysticism. It is here especially that we hear from women writers, such as Mechthild von Magdeburg, Hildegard of Bingen, and, later in the early modern period, Teresa of Avila. These writers explore an embodied and differently gendered spirituality that would eventually become important for contemporary feminist readings of the Song.

Reading Guide

Readers today should focus on the fact that the Song is love poetry. Its two main characters, a man (Solomon?) and a woman ("the Shulammite" [6:13]?) are deeply immersed in the natural world, and their story is one of longing and of brief or missed encounters. The Song presents some of the societal and environmental challenges that confront the lovers and veils any sexual contact behind spatial and natural metaphors. It presents a stunning array of metaphorical descriptions of the lovers, which may confound contemporary readers as they struggle to determine their significance but also reveal much of the social world behind the book.

These dynamics indicate numerous interpretive possibilities. For example, the metaphorical descriptions make for fruitful intertextual analyses with other ANE poetic traditions. The relational dynamics between the lovers are also fruitful for feminist readings of the Song as they consider the unexpected sexual autonomy of the woman and the predominance of her voice and experience. Finally, queer readers might consider the possibility that the Song's allegorical history is a useful resource for envisioning a queer spirituality.

All this need not mean, however, that it is inadvisable to look for spiritual meaning in the Song's text. Indeed, it is possible to combine contemporary theoretical approaches (such as gender-critical readings) with a deep appreciation for the Song's theological message, which may be taken to explore human love or human and divine relationships such as those of the covenant or church.

Fiona C. Black

1 The Song of Songs, which is Solomon's.
²Let him kiss me with the kisses of his mouth!
For your love is better than wine;
³ your anointing oils are fragrant;
your name is perfume poured out;
therefore the maidens love you.
⁴ Draw me after you; let us make haste.

The king has brought me into his chambers.
We will exult and rejoice in you;
we will extol your love more than wine;
rightly do they love you.

⁵ I am black and beautiful,
O daughters of Jerusalem,

Song 1 The book begins with vibrant, antiphonal exchanges between the lovers. They are deeply immersed in the natural world, moving about in the outdoors, tending flocks and vineyards. But they also connect—at least via metaphor—with the world's riches, as jewels, ornaments, wine, and spices are written on the bodies of the lovers. A nearby group of friends witnesses the lovers' declarations and celebrates their love.

1:1 Superscription. Likely later than the poem itself, this connects the poem with Solomon. While it cannot confirm authorship, Solomon's reputation as a writer of songs (1 Kgs. 4:32) and his many wives and concubines (1 Kgs. 11:3) likely connected the Song with him.

1:2 *Let him kiss me* begins the poem midscene, and its exuberant declaration that the woman desires contact is repetitive, a poetic excess. *Love* is better translated as "embraces" or "caresses." *Better than wine*. In many places, the lovers will compare kisses or lovemaking to wine (4:10; 7:9) or will use it as a celebration in the same (1:4; 8:2).

1:4 *We/you/they.* It is hard to see to whom the pronouns in this verse refer. Probably "we" refers to the lovers, "they" references the maidens in v. 3, and "you" identifies Solomon as the subject of their admiration and love.

1:5 *Black and beautiful*, the woman's first self-description. The conjunction ("waw") connecting the two adjectives means "and" or "but." Traditional readings using "but" have problematically supported racism and colonialism. The text leaves open the question of whether the woman's blackness is a racial designation or an effect of the sun, as per 1:6a.

Reading through Time: Black and Beautiful (Song of Songs 1:5)

"I am black and beautiful" has been used in Jewish and Christian traditions to connect moral and spiritual imperfection with the color black. Imperfection (or sinfulness) was easily transferred onto racialized persons and had particular force throughout Christian colonial undertakings. Song of Songs 1:5a is thus one of a series of scriptural texts that has contributed to the biblical endorsement of the oppression of people of color (see **"The Curse of Canaan," p. 26**, and **"The Bible, Race, and Ethnicity," pp. 2163–64**).

The phrase can be translated in two ways: the conjunction that links the two adjectives means both "and" and "but." Theoretically, the first translation could celebrate blackness, while the second might denigrate it. However, in most allegorical receptions, whether "and" or "but," the notion that blackness was not desirable still obtained. In Jewish interpretation, Song of Songs Rabbah connects the blackness of skin with impurity; the Targum connects physical beauty (and lack thereof) with racial identity. Christian theologians such as Origen and Bernard of Clairvaux envisioned the journey of the soul toward God as one that must contend with sin (here signified by the adjective "black"). Beauty in these translations could therefore be seen as the hope or promise of the soul (a "whitening") that awaited one who overcame sinful failings or imperfections and turned toward God.

The translation of the conjunction as "and" seeks to disassociate the text from this problematic history. Understanding that blackness *and* beauty are connected ideas allows readers to step toward reformulating prior biblical authorization of racial discrimination. Some womanist critics have used this text to reclaim and celebrate Black women's experiences. Other critics have used it to read for African interests in colonial contexts.

All is not entirely settled, however. The woman's subsequent comment in 1:6a ("Do not gaze at me because I am dark, because the sun has gazed on me") complicates this recuperative translation choice. Readers continue to ask whether the woman's blackness in Song 1:5 is actually a racial designation at all or merely an effect of the sun (or whether, as a person of color, her problematic outdoor conduct is further darkening her skin). This verse could be used to destabilize either the problematic "but" of earlier approaches *or* the recuperative "and" of the present. Students of the Song should guard against overly literal readings; at the same time, they must also acknowledge that metaphors continually affect social, cultural, and political practices around race.

Fiona C. Black

like the tents of Kedar,
 like the curtains of Solomon.
⁶ Do not gaze at me because I am dark,
 because the sun has gazed on me.
My mother's sons were angry with me;
 they made me keeper of the vineyards,
 but my own vineyard I have not kept!
⁷ Tell me, you whom my soul loves,
 where you pasture your flock,
 where you make it lie down at noon,
for why should I be like one who is veiled
 beside the flocks of your companions?
⁸ If you do not know,
 O fairest among women,

follow the tracks of the flock
 and pasture your kids
 beside the shepherds' tents.
⁹ I compare you, my love,
 to a mare among Pharaoh's chariots.
¹⁰ Your cheeks are comely with
 ornaments,
 your neck with strings of jewels.
¹¹ We will make you ornaments of gold,
 studded with silver.
¹² While the king was on his couch,
 my nard gave forth its fragrance.
¹³ My beloved is to me a bag of myrrh
 that lies between my breasts.

1:6 *I am dark.* The brothers may be angry because visible signs of outdoor work or freedom of movement might subject her to discrimination (see **"Black and Beautiful," p. 922**). *My mother's sons.* The mention of brothers gestures at the social world of the Song but is also suggestive of the occasional impediments that the couple face. *My own vineyard.* The woman might be speaking of literal work and responsibilities, or "vineyard" might refer to her body, specifically her sexual conduct or virginity.

14 My beloved is to me a cluster of henna
   blossoms
      in the vineyards of En-gedi.

15 Ah, you are beautiful, my love;
      ah, you are beautiful;
      your eyes are doves.
16 Ah, you are beautiful, my beloved,
      truly lovely.
   Our couch is green;
17   the beams of our house are cedar;
      our rafters*a* are pine.

2 I am a rose of Sharon,
   a lily of the valleys.

2 As a lily among brambles,
      so is my love among maidens.

3 As an apple tree among the trees of the
   wood,
      so is my beloved among young men.
   With great delight I sat in his shadow,
      and his fruit was sweet to my taste.
4 He brought me to the banqueting house,
      and his intention toward*b* me was love.
5 Sustain me with raisins,
      refresh me with apples,
      for I am faint with love.
6 O that his left hand were under my head
      and that his right hand embraced me!
7 I charge you, O daughters of Jerusalem,
      by the gazelles or the wild does:
   do not stir up or awaken love
      until it is ready!

8 The voice of my beloved!
      Look, he comes,
   leaping upon the mountains,
      bounding over the hills.
9 My beloved is like a gazelle
      or a young stag.
   Look, there he stands
      behind our wall,
   gazing in at the windows,
      looking through the lattice.
10 My beloved speaks and says to me:
   "Arise, my love, my fair one,
      and come away,
11 for now the winter is past,
      the rain is over and gone.
12 The flowers appear on the earth;
      the time of singing has come,
   and the voice of the turtledove
      is heard in our land.
13 The fig tree puts forth its figs,
      and the vines are in blossom;
      they give forth fragrance.
   Arise, my love, my fair one,
      and come away.
14 O my dove, in the clefts of the rock,
      in the covert of the cliff,
   let me see your face;
      let me hear your voice,
   for your voice is sweet,
      and your face is lovely.
15 Catch us the foxes,
      the little foxes,
   that ruin the vineyards—
      for our vineyards are in blossom."

a 1.17 Meaning of Heb uncertain   *b* 2.4 Heb *banner above*

Song 2 This chapter contains an extended speech of the woman (2:8–3:11) and includes her lover's reported comments. The woman enjoys the presence and attentions of her lover. He calls to her and encourages her to show herself and speak and to come away into the blossoming countryside. The chapter ends with a puzzling episode (2:17), however, which heightens the shifts the lovers experience as they move in and out of each other's company throughout the Song.

2:1 The woman is not understating her beauty as one flower among many but is declaring it to be as spectacular as the exotic flowers she mentions. **2:3–6** This poem is suggestive of a sexual encounter. Physical proximity (v. 3b), fruit and taste (v. 3b), and eating and embrace (vv. 5, 6) gesture toward intimacy but offer only veiled accounts, blurring the lines between events and wishes, images and subjects. **2:4** *Intention* ("banner"). The translation "banner" would continue the idea of the shadow or shelter in which the woman sits (2:3); however, *intention* seems to make better sense of unfolding events. **2:5** The woman is lovesick; though she asks to be sustained with food, the better solution to her affliction is more lovemaking (2:6). **2:7** *Daughters of Jerusalem.* There is no clear identity for these companions, who serve as a chorus. They are also a foil against which the lovers can declare certain precepts, such as the one here: *do no stir up or awaken love . . . !* Repeated in 3:5 (with some variation) and 8:4, this adjuration advises: do not rush love; it will come to you when the time is right. **2:15** *Catch us the foxes.* This odd expression is another instance of potential impediments the lovers face. It may refer to something that troubles the woman's sexual autonomy (cf. her "vineyard"

¹⁶ My beloved is mine, and I am his;
    he pastures his flock among the lilies.
¹⁷ Until the day breathes
    and the shadows flee,
turn, my beloved, be like a gazelle
    or a young stag on the cleft
      mountains.ᶜ

3 Upon my bed at night
    I sought him whom my soul loves;
I sought him but found him not;
    I called him, but he gave no answer.ᵈ
² "I will rise now and go about the city,
    in the streets and in the squares;
I will seek him whom my soul loves."
    I sought him but found him not.
³ The sentinels found me,
    as they went about in the city.
"Have you seen him whom my soul loves?"
⁴ Scarcely had I passed them,
    when I found him whom my soul loves.

I held him and would not let him go
    until I brought him into my mother's
      house
and into the chamber of her that
      conceived me.
⁵ I charge you, O daughters of Jerusalem,
    by the gazelles or the wild does:
do not stir up or awaken love
    until it is ready!
⁶ Who is that coming up from the
      wilderness
    like a column of smoke,
perfumed with myrrh and frankincense,
    with all the fragrant powders of the
      merchant?
⁷ Look, it is the litter of Solomon!
    Around it are sixty mighty men
    of the mighty men of Israel,

c 2.17 Or *on the mountains of Bether*; meaning of Heb uncertain d 3.1 Gk: Heb lacks this line

in 1:6). The verb "catch," though, is noteworthy for its recognition of the woman's ability to manage the factors that threaten her.

2:16 *My beloved is mine, and I am his.* This statement is repeated in 6:3 and, with some modification, in 7:10. It speaks to the exclusive nature of the relationship—at least from the woman's point of view. *He pastures his flock among the lilies.* The phrase is one of many instances of double entendre in the book (see 2:1). The association also prompted some scholars to suggest that the woman's lover was a shepherd, not the king.

2:17 The end of the chapter seems confusing; the woman seems to be either summoning her lover to her or sending him away (*turn, my beloved*). The verse continues the Song's interplay of the themes of seeking, finding, and absence. *Cleft mountains.* The Song makes frequent reference to specific geographical locations, but the meaning of the Hebrew "Mountains of Bether" is uncertain. The mountains could be the woman herself, an attribution suggested later by the man (4:6).

Song 3 The chapter opens with the first of two dream scenes and is followed by a description of the king's approach from the wilderness. The fanciful appearance of the king is a startling contrast with the presentation in Song 2. It should not be taken for granted that a wedding is taking place between the Song's main characters in this chapter. It is more likely that the scene is a fanciful creation by the woman herself. The conflation of coronation, procession, and wedding indicates that the chapter's final scene is recalling a glorious past, not a present event (see **"Sex, Desire, and Eroticism," p. 927**).

3:1–4 The woman, missing her lover, goes out at night to search for him. Unlike the parallel scene in 5:2–7, the scene ends well with the woman taking matters into her own hands and locating her lover. **3:1** *Upon my bed.* The suggestion that the woman is dreaming is not in the text but is a historic assumption that readers have made, perhaps to manage the expectations that young, unmarried women should not go out at night in pursuit of their lovers. Is the woman awake? Thinking of her lover? Is she engaged in self-pleasure? **3:3** *Sentinels.* The watchmen "go around" the city just as the woman goes around it. They do not assist or impede the woman's search (cf. 5:7), and they are unable to answer her question. **3:4** *Mother's house.* The reference to the woman's familial context is important, again assisting with a reconstruction of the social world of the Song. It may be that bringing her lover home allows her to make the relationship public—a factor that is confusingly not possible in 8:2. Readers should not expect a logical plot progression with these two events.

3:7–10 This is a grand and public celebration that takes us momentarily outside of the intimate world of the lovers. It is possible that, instead of imagining the pair in their usual outdoor rendezvous, the woman is depicting the couple in a richly decorated palanquin (vv. 9–10). The descriptions are reminiscent of her envisioning of his body in 5:10–15.

⁸ all equipped with swords
  and expert in war,
each with his sword at his thigh
  because of alarms by night.
⁹ King Solomon made himself a palanquin
  from the wood of Lebanon.
¹⁰ He made its posts of silver,
  its back of gold, its seat of purple;
its interior was inlaid with stone.
  Daughters*ᵉ* of Jerusalem,
¹¹   come out and look*ᶠ*
at King Solomon,
at the crown with which his mother
    crowned him
  on the day of his wedding,
  on the day of the gladness of his heart.

4 How beautiful you are, my love,
  how very beautiful!
Your eyes are doves
  behind your veil.
Your hair is like a flock of goats,
  moving down the slopes of Gilead.
² Your teeth are like a flock of shorn ewes
  that have come up from the washing,
all of which bear twins,
  and not one among them is bereaved.
³ Your lips are like a crimson thread,
  and your mouth is lovely.
Your cheeks are like halves of a
    pomegranate
  behind your veil.

⁴ Your neck is like the tower of David,
  built in courses;
on it hang a thousand bucklers,
  all of them shields of warriors.
⁵ Your two breasts are like two fawns,
  twins of a gazelle,
  that feed among the lilies.
⁶ Until the day breathes
  and the shadows flee,
I will hasten to the mountain of myrrh
  and the hill of frankincense.
⁷ You are altogether beautiful, my love;
  there is no flaw in you.
⁸ Come with me from Lebanon, my bride;
  come with me from Lebanon.
Depart*ᵍ* from the peak of Amana,
  from the peak of Senir and Hermon,
from the dens of lions,
  from the mountains of leopards.

⁹ You have ravished my heart, my sister,
    my bride;
  you have ravished my heart with a
    glance of your eyes,
  with one jewel of your necklace.
¹⁰ How sweet is your love, my sister, my
    bride!
  How much better is your love than
    wine

e 3.10 Cn Compare Gk: Heb *with love from the daughters*
f 3.11 Gk: Heb adds *daughters of Zion* *g* 4.8 Or *Look*

3:10–11 *Daughters of Jerusalem* / "daughters of Zion." The group appears again (see note on 2:7), this time called to witness and celebrate the arrival of Solomon. The latter phrasing is not seen in the Song elsewhere. *Mother.* As with 3:4, one might read a public and familial endorsement of the relationship via the presence of Solomon's mother.

Song 4 The man's lengthy speech is devoted almost entirely to describing and celebrating his beloved. It comprises the first extended description of the woman's body. This type of poem, known as a "wasf," usually describes the beloved's body from head to toe, using elaborate, often challenging images. They are suggestive, locating places on which the senses converge and tracing the social, natural, and political worlds onto the lovers' forms. After the "wasf," the man suggests a much more intimate and sensorial connection than that of 4:1–6. The chapter's final comments seem to indicate an invitation from the woman to her lover for sex (4:16).

4:5 *Breasts.* The images are not consistent or logical: the woman's breasts are compared to fawns feeding among lilies (to which she is often compared), an activity normally attributed to the man (1:7; 2:2, 16; 6:2–3).

4:6 *Mountain.* The man repeats the woman's self-identification in 2:17, this time embellishing it with richly scented spices.

4:8 *Amana, Senir, Hermon.* The poetic reach of the book is broad, encompassing actual geographical places of beauty (to which we need not assume the lovers travel) as well as imaginary ones. *Bride.* The term is not literally meant but perhaps reflects a future wish (see 3:11). It appears also in v. 11 and in combination with "sister" numerous times in this chapter (vv. 9, 10, 12).

4:9 *Ravished,* literally "captured," "stolen," or "wounded." His interaction with her has him overwhelmed. This image suggests that love can have risks; the lions and leopards of v. 8 might also gesture in this direction (cf. 2:15). *Sister, bride.* See also 4:10; 5:1. Lovers refer to each other using

and the fragrance of your oils than
any spice!
[11] Your lips distill nectar, my bride;
honey and milk are under your
tongue;
the scent of your garments is like the
scent of Lebanon.
[12] A garden locked is my sister, my bride,
a garden[b] locked, a fountain sealed.
[13] Your channel[i] is an orchard of
pomegranates
with all choicest fruits,
henna with nard,
[14] nard and saffron, calamus and
cinnamon,
with all trees of frankincense,
myrrh and aloes,
with all chief spices—
[15] a garden fountain, a well of living
water,
and flowing streams from Lebanon.

[16] Awake, O north wind,
and come, O south wind!
Blow upon my garden
that its fragrance may be wafted
abroad.
Let my beloved come to his garden
that he may eat its choicest fruits.

5

[5] I come to my garden, my sister, my bride;
I gather my myrrh with my spice;
I eat my honeycomb with my honey;
I drink my wine with my milk.

Eat, friends, drink,
and be drunk with love.
[2] I was sleeping, but my heart was awake.
The sound of my beloved knocking!
"Open to me, my sister, my love,
my dove, my perfect one,
for my head is wet with dew,
my locks with the drops of the night."
[3] I had put off my garment;
how could I put it on again?
I had bathed my feet;
how could I soil them?
[4] My beloved thrust his hand into the
opening,
and my inmost being yearned for him.
[5] I arose to open to my beloved,
and my hands dripped with myrrh,
my fingers with liquid myrrh,
upon the handles of the bolt.
[6] I opened to my beloved,
but my beloved had turned away and
was gone.

b 4.12 Heb mss Gk Vg Syr: MT *heap of stones*   i 4.13 Meaning of Heb uncertain

---

"brother" or "sister" in Egyptian poetry, so this epithet is not unusual. It does not indicate an actual familial relationship. She does not call him brother, though in 8:1 she wishes he were "like a brother," ostensibly because then she could show him affection in public.

4:12 *Garden locked.* More traditional readings would see this as a statement of the woman's inviolability or virginity. The following descriptions, though, suggest that the man believes that she has made herself exclusively available to him.

4:13 *Channel,* maybe "shoots" or "watercourses." While the meaning of the Hebrew is uncertain, the context suggests that the reference is anatomical, perhaps referring to the woman's vagina.

4:16 *Let my beloved come.* The woman is unequivocal in her positive response to her lover's ruminations about her body and his access.

Song 5 In this chapter, the man responds to the invitation in 4:16, this time knocking at the woman's door but receiving no answer. Erotic imagery is suggestive of sexual contact for some readers and for others the possibility of self-pleasure. A second "dream scene" follows, this time with troubling results. The chapter also contains the only "wasf"-like poem directed at the man, whose body seems to be described using different imagery.

5:2 The connection to dreams and sleep is better articulated here than in 3:1–4, but the scene should not be dismissed as a mere product of the imagination. Typically, the Song denies transparency with poetic excess and ambiguities (*my heart was awake*). It collapses present and future time along with wishes, imagination, and actual events.

5:4–6 *My beloved thrust his hand. . . . I opened to my beloved.* This suggests a physical connection, coital or masturbatory. The *handles, bolt, hands, fingers,* and *myrrh* are double entendre, and therefore it is not advisable to map image to anatomy. What is important is that the scene once again exhibits tensions and interrupted connections between the lovers. The scene complicates the prior events of 4:16–5:1. **5:6** The woman's search for her lover and the patrolling of the sentinels mirror the earlier scene in chap. 3.

Reading through Time: Sex, Desire, and Eroticism (Song of Songs 5)

With the rise of critical biblical scholarship, the Song's sexual and erotic contents came to the fore. Nineteenth-century sensibilities, however, were not quite ready for a sexually autonomous, unmarried woman who voiced and pursued her own desires. Early biblical criticism often made certain narrative impositions, taking advantage of unclear passages. For instance, with the assistance of Song 3:6–11, which contains an invitation to look at Solomon "on the day of his wedding," interpreters reasoned that the marriage of the lovers had taken place, and therefore any sexual contact was appropriate (e.g., the purported marital "consummation" of Song 5:2–6).

The pendulum has hence swung widely, and a range of readings of the Song's sexual subject matter now exist, including feminist and queer perspectives and thematic interrogations that cover a wide range of erotic possibilities. The book has two important features that invite such diversity. The first is that it is mostly first-person discourse, dominated by the woman, who appears to be the primary speaker and agent. Where allegorical readings of the past might have obfuscated her gender identity by seeing her as representative of the more abstract "Israel," "church," or "soul," contemporary readings are interested in her dominant voice and autonomy. Feminist readers have celebrated her as a sexually free and adventurous figure, pondering her agency, sexual proclivities, and ability to consent to a range of sexual experiences. And where it might be hard to imagine how to queer an obviously heterosexual book, this approach has been explored via the Song's interpretive history. Ironically, the allegorical approaches that are now often jettisoned provide rich resources for queer readings since they trouble heteronormative gender patterns.

The second feature that occasions such diversity is the Song's heavily metaphorical nature: sexual activity is rarely explicitly stated. Instead, it is veiled, which leaves much to the imagination and opens up possibilities for readers to pursue any kind of interest, exploit, or desire. It is possible to map the body via the images, seeing it merge erotically with nature, the city, animals, food, and more. These understandings of sex and desire are in contrast to the usual biblical dynamics around human sexuality, which tend to be heteronormative, suppressing the experiences of women and sexual minorities. In this way, the Song is open to exploration and validation of a range of human sexual experiences and erotic encounters.

Fiona C. Black

My soul failed me when he spoke.
I sought him but did not find him;
   I called him, but he gave no answer.
⁷ Making their rounds in the city
   the sentinels found me;
they beat me; they wounded me;
   they took away my mantle,
   those sentinels of the walls.
⁸ I charge you, O daughters of
   Jerusalem,
if you find my beloved,

tell him this:
   I am faint with love.
⁹ What is your beloved more than another
   beloved,
   O fairest among women?
What is your beloved more than another
   beloved,
   that you thus charge us?

¹⁰ My beloved is all radiant and ruddy,
   distinguished among ten thousand.

5:7 Instead of the woman asking the sentinels where her lover is (3:3), here they shockingly treat her with unprovoked violence, beating and wounding her. *My mantle* is possibly a veil or cloak. The nature of the garment is unclear, as is the woman's state of dress (cf. 5:3). It is unlikely that she has been stripped naked, but readers should not miss the violation. Some have proposed that the text relates a risk the woman would be willing to take for love—or an experience that she might even enjoy. In this scene and others, the Song easily allows for a range of sexual interpretations.

5:9 This challenge of the daughters of Jerusalem is the first time the group answers back when addressed (see note on 2:7). It provides a foil for the following extended (and unique) description of the man.

5:10–15 The description suggests different qualities of beauty in the male form. Readers might take an opportunity to note the kinds of referents that are called on (pillars, alabaster, cedars) in addition to more familiar ones (birds, spices, etc.).

¹¹ His head is the finest gold;
   his locks are wavy,
   black as a raven.
¹² His eyes are like doves
   beside springs of water,
bathed in milk,
   fitly set.^j
¹³ His cheeks are like beds of spices,
   yielding fragrance.
His lips are lilies,
   dripping liquid myrrh.
¹⁴ His arms are rounded gold,
   set with jewels.
His body is an ivory panel,^k
   decorated with sapphires.
¹⁵ His legs are alabaster columns,
   set upon bases of gold.
His appearance is like Lebanon,
   choice as the cedars.
¹⁶ His speech is most sweet,
   and he is altogether desirable.
This is my beloved, and this is my friend,
   O daughters of Jerusalem.

6 Where has your beloved gone,
   O fairest among women?
Which way has your beloved turned
   that we may seek him with you?

² My beloved has gone down to his garden,
   to the beds of spices,
to pasture his flock in the gardens
   and to gather lilies.
³ I am my beloved's, and my beloved is mine;
   he pastures his flock among the lilies.
⁴ You are beautiful as Tirzah, my love,
   comely as Jerusalem,

terrible as an army with banners.
⁵ Turn away your eyes from me,
   for they overwhelm me!
Your hair is like a flock of goats,
   moving down the slopes of Gilead.
⁶ Your teeth are like a flock of ewes
   that have come up from the washing;
all of them bear twins,
   and not one among them is bereaved.
⁷ Your cheeks are like halves of a
      pomegranate
   behind your veil.
⁸ There are sixty queens and eighty
      concubines
   and maidens without number.
⁹ My dove, my perfect one, is the only
      one,
   the darling of her mother,
   flawless to her who bore her.
The maidens saw her and called her
      happy;
   the queens and concubines praised
      her.
¹⁰ "Who is this that looks forth like the
      dawn,
   fair as the moon, bright as the sun,
   terrible as an army with banners?"

¹¹ I went down to the nut orchard
   to look at the blossoms of the valley,
to see whether the vines had budded,
   whether the pomegranates were in
      bloom.
¹² Before I was aware, my desire set me
   in a chariot beside my prince.^l

j 5.12 Meaning of Heb uncertain   *k* 5.14 Meaning of Heb
uncertain   *l* 6.12 Cn: Meaning of Heb uncertain

5:16 *Friend.* A unique endearment, part of a collection ("sister," "bride," *beloved*).
   Song 6 The chapter opens (6:2) in what may be the location of the scene in 4:12–16. It contains the second "wasf" (poem) to describe the woman, much of it a quotation of 4:1–5. It ends with an intriguing invitation from the man for the woman to come back from her reverie (6:13) and offer herself to his gaze. The chapter also includes a perplexing title for the woman, *the Shulammite* (v. 13), the only place where she is identified, albeit with little clarity.
   6:4 It is commonplace in both ancient and modern literature for women to be compared to cities; here two royal cities and (former) capitals are named. Jerusalem was especially known for its magnificence (cf. Ps. 48:2). *Terrible as an army with banners.* This odd phrase seems out of context—perhaps the poet imagines the troops mustered in defense of the cities. *Terrible* might make more sense if understood as "awe-inspiring." *Army* is not present in the text, only inferred, leading some to suggest that *banners* might be understood as "splendid things."
   6:5 The man is overcome by his lover's eyes; the experience is (almost) too much for him. Does he want her to look away or to keep his gaze?
   6:12–13 *My desire set me in a chariot.* The Hebrew text is corrupt, and it is hard to make sense of the phrase—or even assign the speaker. If it is the woman speaking (likely; see 6:11 and 7:12), she seems to have been transported elsewhere in her fancy. She is called back in the next verses to her

13 *m*Return, return, O Shulammite!
Return, return, that we may look upon
you.

Why should you look upon the
Shulammite,
as upon a dance before two armies?*n*

7 How graceful are your feet in
sandals,
O queenly maiden!
Your rounded thighs are like jewels,
the work of a master hand.
2 Your navel is a rounded bowl;
may it never lack mixed wine.
Your belly is a heap of wheat,
encircled with lilies.
3 Your two breasts are like two fawns,
twins of a gazelle.
4 Your neck is like an ivory tower.
Your eyes are pools in Heshbon,
by the gate of Bath-rabbim.

Your nose is like a tower of Lebanon,
overlooking Damascus.
5 Your head crowns you like Carmel,
and your flowing locks are like purple;
a king is held captive in the tresses.
6 How fair and pleasant you are,
O loved one, delectable maiden!*o*
7 You are stately*p* as a palm tree,
and your breasts are like its clusters.
8 I said, "I will climb the palm tree
and lay hold of its branches."
O may your breasts be like clusters of the
vine,
and the scent of your breath like apples,
9 and your kisses*q* like the best wine
that goes down*r* smoothly,
gliding over lips and teeth.*s*

m 6.13 7.1 in Heb   *n* 6.13 Or *dance of Mahanaim*   *o* 7.6 Syr:
Heb *in delights*   *p* 7.7 Heb *This your stature is*   *q* 7.9 Heb *palate*
r 7.9 Heb *to my lover*   *s* 7.9 Gk Syr Vg: Heb *lips of sleepers*

lover. *Return, return.* Or "turn, turn!" in keeping with the dance that is described in the later part of the verse. The call to return makes some sense if the woman was absent in the nut garden, even if in a fantasy. *The Shulammite.* The noun has a definite article, so it is not a proper name. Perhaps it is a gentilic appellation (a woman from Shulem/Shunem?) or a nod to Solomon's own name, since both appear to have the same Hebrew root "slm" (cf. the woman's own pun in 8:10). *Dance before two armies?* ("mahanaim"). A military reference (cf. 6:4, 10), it is unclear whether the woman means "Why gaze?"—the looker has no right to look—or whether she asks, "What will you see in the Shulammite?" Vv. 1–7 suggest the latter. It is not clear to what exactly she is comparing herself. Was the "mahanaim" a recognizable dance? Or is she conducting herself (with her company of friends) in such a way as it reminds the poet of two lines of soldiers?

Song 7 The lengthy poem that results from the man's gaze in 6:13 dominates this chapter. Here readers are offered the most extensive description ("wasf") of the woman's body, which builds on some familiar ideas from the earlier iterations in Song 4 and 6 and proceeds in reverse order. The result is a sensate and fulsome tribute, where the man's praise extends into a plan of action. She responds with an offer to accompany him to the fields and vineyards, where she implies that they will move from appreciating nature to appreciating each other. There, she offers that they will make love.

7:2 *Navel.* Many take the navel as a euphemism for the vulva, which makes anatomical sense, given the order of the descriptions so far, its shape, and the fact that it is filled with wine/fluids.

7:4 *Heshbon ... Bath-rabbim ... Damascus ...* "Carmel" (v. 5). A series of geographical locations appears here, even if not always specific. Land signals how frequently the settings of their love—the countryside and its flora and fauna—merge with the lovers themselves. *Bath-rabbim.* The name ("daughter of many") appears to be functioning in the list as a place name, though no specific geographical location is known in the Hebrew Bible. *Nose is like a tower of Lebanon.* This seems a ridiculous image, but as the comparators become less intimate and develop in geographical grandeur, the amusing or even risible understory of the Song's imagery becomes more visible (see also 7:5).

7:5 *Purple.* The richness of the woman's hair is connected to the royal theme (see 3:10), and indeed the king is mentioned immediately after as its captive.

7:6 *Delectable maiden* ("in delights"). The Hebrew is unclear, but even without the emendation, its general sense is clear enough. He delights in her.

7:8–9 The man now turns to exploration. The event (like that in 4:12–5:1) collapses the senses, the body, and the natural world into a heightened erotic moment, which resonates intertextually throughout the book (in this case, it is smell, touch, taste, kisses, wine, grapes, apples; cf. 2:3, 5; 8:5).

7:9 *Lips and teeth.* Hebrew oddly offers "lips of sleepers," which seems antithetical to kissing and

¹⁰ I am my beloved's,
    and his desire is for me.
¹¹ Come, my beloved,
    let us go forth into the fields
    and lodge in the villages;
¹² let us go out early to the vineyards;
    let us see whether the vines have
        budded,
    whether the grape blossoms have
        opened
    and the pomegranates are in bloom.
    There I will give you my love.
¹³ The mandrakes give forth fragrance,
    and over our doors are all choice fruits,
    new as well as old,
    which I have laid up for you, O my
        beloved.

8 O that you were like a brother to me,
    who nursed at my mother's breast!
If I met you outside, I would kiss you,
    and no one would despise me.
² I would lead you and bring you
    into my mother's house
    and into the chamber of the one who
        bore me.^t
I would give you spiced wine to drink,
    from the juice of my pomegranates.
³ O that his left hand were under my head
    and that his right hand embraced me!

⁴ I charge you, O daughters of Jerusalem,
    do not stir up or awaken love
    until it is ready!
⁵ Who is that coming up from the
        wilderness,
    leaning upon her beloved?

Under the apple tree I awakened you.
There your mother was in labor with you;
    there she who bore you was in labor.

⁶ Set me as a seal upon your heart,
    as a seal upon your arm,
for love is strong as death,
    passion fierce as the grave.
Its flashes are flashes of fire,
    a raging flame.
⁷ Many waters cannot quench love,
    neither can floods drown it.
If one offered for love
    all the wealth of one's house,
    it^u would be utterly scorned.

⁸ We have a little sister,
    and she has no breasts.
What shall we do for our sister,
    on the day when she is spoken for?

t 8.2 Gk Syr: Heb *my mother; she* (or *you*) *will teach me*
u 8.7 Or *he*

drinking. Sleeping lips could simply be still lips or something particular to the poetic imagination of which we are unaware.

7:13 *Mandrakes.* Various plants appear in the Song. Some of these were used in the ancient world not only for enjoyment and consumption but as aphrodisiacs (mandrakes) and as contraceptives (cinnamon, pomegranates, spikenard).

Song 8 The closing chapter of the book contains several important features. The well-known tribute to love is here (8:6–7), accompanied by the perplexing term "shalhebetyah" (*a raging flame,* v. 6), which may hint at God's presence. The chapter also contains another self-identifying statement of the woman's; it is bold, assertive, and counters tradition. The chapter ends perplexingly (8:14): is the woman inviting her lover to be with her (cf. 2:17) or to flee? The final note of the book maintains the opacity that has accompanied the couple's relationship all along, keeping their desire alive and the reader's curiosity piqued.

8:1 *Like a brother.* The woman wishes for a different relationship, one that would allow her to display affection in public without any interference or disapproval.

8:2 *Mother's house.* It is unlikely that she would take a lover to her mother's house, but this reference and that in v. 5 relay the importance of family ties and approval of the relationship.

8:5 The same question is asked about Solomon on his approach in 3:6.

8:6 *Set me as a seal.* The woman asks that she be bound to her lover, inscribed on his heart or worn close to it, on his arm; she will be intimately connected to him, an essential part of who he is. *Love is strong as death, passion fierce as the grave.* Seemingly contradictory, the common idea behind these phrases is that both love and death involve the dissolution of the self. *A raging flame.* The ending of this word ("yah") could be a shortened form of the divine name, thus, a "flame of YHWH." Theologically, the appeal of such a translation would be to locate God as the source of love.

8:8–9 The brothers appear again, forming an inclusio with 1:6, reminding us of the limitations that families and patriarchal codes place on the woman.

⁹ If she is a wall,
    we will build upon her a battlement
      of silver,
  but if she is a door,
    we will enclose her with boards of
      cedar.
¹⁰ I was a wall,
    and my breasts were like towers;
  then I was in his eyes
    as one who brings* peace.
¹¹ Solomon had a vineyard at Baal-hamon;
    he entrusted the vineyard to
      keepers;
  each one was to bring for its fruit a
    thousand pieces of silver.
¹² My vineyard, my very own, is for myself;

you, O Solomon, may have the
    thousand
and the keepers of the fruit two
    hundred!

¹³ O you who dwell in the gardens,
    my companions are listening for your
      voice;
  let me hear it.

¹⁴ Make haste, my beloved,
    and be like a gazelle
or a young stag
  upon the mountains of spices!

*v 8.10 Or *finds*

8:10 *I was a wall.* She answers their censure defiantly, though, asserting her own identity and freedom. *Who brings peace.* In the process, she declares via a pun on Solomon's name (root "slm") that she is aligned with him and not her brothers.

ISAIAH

"The wolf shall live with the lamb" (Isa. 11:6). "Every valley shall be lifted up" (40:4). "God will wipe away the tears from all faces" (25:8). Some of the most powerful religious images in Judaism and Christianity come from the book of Isaiah. Named for an eighth-century BCE prophet from Jerusalem, the book's poems and stories were composed, compiled, and edited for at least three to four hundred years. In response to the challenges of those centuries, Isaiah engages and reimagines key ideas from Judah's religious traditions. The result is one of the most distinctive biblical portraits of God, humanity, and the world, which profoundly influenced later Judaism and Christianity.

Structure and Formation

Since the turn of the twentieth century, biblical scholars have identified three major divisions in Isaiah, reflecting different implied settings and audiences. Chaps. 1–39 (sometimes called First Isaiah) contain stories about Isaiah and prophecies attributed to him. Over 150 years later, after the destruction of Jerusalem by the Babylonians, chaps. 40–55 (Second Isaiah) address the city and its deported citizens. Finally, chaps. 56–66 (Third Isaiah) assume the return of some exiles and the resettlement of Jerusalem. Smaller thematic subunits appear within each section, such as the prophecies against foreign nations in chaps. 13–27 or the visions of Jerusalem's future in chaps. 60–62. Scholars used to argue that the book's three parts developed independently. Recent approaches, however, emphasize connections across Isaiah, including a consistent concern for the fate of Jerusalem and the portrayal of YHWH, the God of Israel and Judah, as a worldwide deity.

Historical Context

The earliest dateable event in Isaiah is the death of the Judean king Uzziah (Isa. 6:1), around 740 BCE. Before this time, Israel and Judah had enjoyed a period of prosperity while neighboring kingdoms were relatively weak. During the 730s, however, Assyria (located in modern Iraq) rapidly expanded westward. By 720, it had conquered Israel and resettled much of its population. Judah submitted to Assyrian control until 704, when it allied with Egypt and rebelled. In response, Assyria invaded Judah in 701, squelching the rebellion and bringing Jerusalem to the edge of destruction. As depicted in Isa. 1–39, the prophet Isaiah viewed Assyria as God's instrument for punishing Judah's social and religious failures. He opposed the rebellion but predicted Jerusalem's survival.

A century later, Babylon (also in modern Iraq) had become the dominant power. It invaded Jerusalem in 587 BCE, conquering the city and exiling many of its citizens. The loss of the Davidic monarchy and temple and the seeming failure of divine promises posed a considerable theological challenge to YHWH worshipers. Isaiah 40–55 responds to the doubts of Judean deportees in Babylon after several decades of exile, reassuring them of YHWH's compassion and inviting their trust in the deity.

The exile ended after Persia (located in modern Iran) conquered Babylon in 539 BCE. Over the following decades, Judean deportees returned to Jerusalem and rebuilt the temple. Internal conflicts within this community led to acrimonious divisions, exacerbated by imperial exploitation. Isaiah 56–66 gives voice to Judeans' disappointments and hopes under Persian rule and possibly the beginning of Hellenistic rule, following the conquests of Alexander the Great in 333–330 BCE.

Prophets and Prophetic Books

In contrast to many contemporary Jews or Christians, ancient worshipers did not expect direct communication with their god(s). Instead, divine-human interactions were mediated through religious specialists like prophets, who received messages from a deity and communicated them to human audiences. Prophets were available for professional consultation, and kings sought their advice about divine approval of political and military decisions.

Isaiah prophesied in Jerusalem between 740 and 700 BCE. As portrayed in the book, he was a typical ancient prophet in most ways. He was associated with the Jerusalem temple and advised Judean kings. Although he criticized their policies, he supported the monarchy as an institution. Depending on the situation, his words could be threatening or reassuring. There is no evidence of Isaiah's activity outside the Bible, and scholars debate how much, if anything, we can really know

about him as a historical figure. The book of Isaiah contains echoes of his voice but also moves beyond him.

The earliest version of the book was likely a written collection of Isaiah's prophecies, similar to archival compilations of prophecies from ancient Assyria. Although the prophet may have played some role in their collection, these texts were scribal elaborations of his words rather than direct transcripts. Their rich imagery and open-ended content allowed for reinterpretation in light of later events, especially the Babylonian conquest of Jerusalem. To facilitate this reinterpretation, generations of later scribes edited and expanded older prophecies and appended new ones, until the book reached its present (and complicated!) form.

Such creative reappropriation continued after the book's completion. Just a few centuries later, the Jewish community associated with the Dead Sea Scrolls and the emerging Christian movement both interpreted Isaiah's prophecies as references to their own time. Texts from the book shaped beliefs and liturgical practices in Judaism and Christianity. Isaiah also influenced later art, literature, music, and public discourse, both religious and secular. Its wide influence testifies to the generative potential of classic religious texts across millennia.

Reading Guide

The book of Isaiah is complex ancient literature. Although it contains short narrative interludes in chaps. 6–8, 20, and 36–39, it consists primarily of poetry and largely lacks conventional characters or a linear plot. The tone oscillates between doom and hope, and the imagery engages the readers' senses and emotions as well as intellects. Meaning is not always straightforward; the poems frequently employ ambiguity, sarcasm, and exaggeration. References to specific events or persons assume knowledge of the larger historical context, but the book ultimately constructs its own imaginative literary world. Different voices address the audience—including the prophet, the people, and personified Jerusalem—and the reader should be attentive to changes in speaker. Ultimately, however, the powerful voice of YHWH dominates the book.

Isaiah pairs an exalted view of God with a pessimistic view of humanity. YHWH, the deity of Israel and Judah, occupies a worldwide stage, controlling the actions of empires and governing international events according to an unopposable divine plan. By contrast, humans are mortal, unreliable, and sinful. The book is particularly concerned with social and economic oppression, insincere worship, and idolatry—understood as both the worship of foreign deities and the reliance on humans instead of YHWH. Another important theme is the future of Jerusalem, both as a physical city and as a spiritual community. Its fate is intertwined with the fortunes of the Davidic monarchy, although here the two halves of the book diverge; chaps. 1–39 assign a prominent future role to an ideal king, but hopes for the monarchy are largely absent from chaps. 40–66. Body imagery appears throughout Isaiah. Physical impairment is frequently a symbol for human frailty, while miraculously transformed bodies inhabit the book's imagined future. Even YHWH possesses a body of unimaginable size and power, reinforcing the book's claims of divine sovereignty. Nature imagery also abounds, with frequent portrayals of transformed landscapes and extensive references to animals. Such images demonstrate a concern for the well-being of nonhuman creation, which suffers judgment and experiences restoration along with humans in Isaiah's remarkable vision.

J. Blake Couey

1 The vision of Isaiah son of Amoz, which he saw concerning Judah and Jerusalem in the days of Uzziah, Jotham, Ahaz, and Hezekiah, kings of Judah.

² Hear, O heavens, and listen, O earth,
   for the LORD has spoken:
I reared children and brought
      them up,
   but they have rebelled
      against me.
³ The ox knows its owner
      and the donkey its master's crib,
   but Israel does not know;
      my people do not understand.

⁴ Woe, sinful nation,
      people laden with iniquity,
   offspring who do evil,
      children who act corruptly,
   who have forsaken the LORD,
      who have despised the Holy One of
         Israel,
   [[who are utterly estranged!]]ᵃ

⁵ Why do you seek further beatings?
      Why do you continue to rebel?
   The whole head is injured,
      and the whole heart faint.
⁶ From the sole of the foot to the
      head,
   there is no soundness in it,
      only bruises and sores
   and bleeding wounds;

they have not been drained or
      bound up
   or softened with oil.

⁷ Your country lies desolate;
      your cities are burned with fire;
   in your very presence
      aliens devour your land;
   it is desolate, as overthrown by
      foreigners.
⁸ And daughter Zion is left
      like a booth in a vineyard,
   like a shelter in a cucumber field,
      like a besieged city.
⁹ If the LORD of hosts
      had not left us a few survivors,
   we would have been like Sodom
      and become like Gomorrah.

¹⁰ Hear the word of the LORD,
      you rulers of Sodom!
   Listen to the teaching of our God,
      you people of Gomorrah!
¹¹ What to me is the multitude of your
      sacrifices?
   says the LORD;
   I have had enough of burnt offerings of
      rams
   and the fat of fed beasts;
   I do not delight in the blood of bulls
      or of lambs or of goats.

a 1.4 Gk OL lack: Heb adds *who are utterly estranged*

1:1 This superscription attributes the book's *vision* to *Isaiah son of Amoz* and locates his prophetic activity during the reigns of four eighth-century BCE Judean kings. **1:2–20** Isaiah 1 contains three poems introducing the book's important themes. The first poem describes how Israel and Judah have been punished for offenses against God but have a final opportunity to repent and be restored. **1:2** *Heavens* and *earth* are summoned to witness the rebellion of God's child, Israel. *LORD* (in small capital letters) is the conventional English translation of "YHWH," the name of the God of Israel and Judah. **1:3** *Israel* here refers to God's people as a whole. More often in Isa. 1–39, it designates the northern kingdom of Israel. **1:4** *Holy One of Israel* affirms God's exalted status and close relationship with God's people. It is a favorite divine title in Isaiah, appearing twenty-five times across the book but only six other times in the Hebrew Bible. **1:5–6** Because Israel is metaphorically portrayed as a child, the image of the beaten body has disturbing overtones of child abuse, although the physical punishment of children was acceptable in the ancient world (Prov. 13:24; 23:13). **1:7** The injured body transforms into a ruined landscape after a military invasion. **1:8** *Daughter Zion.* The city of Jerusalem personified as a woman (see **"Daughter Zion," p. 1118**). *Zion* is another name for Jerusalem, often used to emphasize the city's relationship with God. *Booth* and *shelter* were temporary structures for workers. The similes suggest that Jerusalem remains standing but has become isolated and vulnerable, perhaps following the Assyrian invasion of Judah in 701 BCE (see **"Sennacherib's Attack," p. 984**). **1:9** *LORD of hosts* is a common divine title in Isaiah. The *hosts* are stars, imagined as heavenly armies (cf. Judg. 5:20; Joel 2:11). **1:10** By addressing the people and their rulers as *Sodom* and *Gomorrah* (cf. Gen. 18:20; Ezek. 16:49), the poet emphasizes their wickedness and contradicts v. 9. **1:11–15** Similar condemnations

12 When you come to appear before me,[b]
  who asked this from your hand?
  Trample my courts no more!
13 Bringing offerings is futile;
  incense is an abomination to me.
New moon and Sabbath and calling of
    convocation—
  I cannot endure solemn assemblies
    with iniquity.
14 Your new moons and your appointed
    festivals
  my soul hates;
they have become a burden to me;
  I am weary of bearing them.
15 When you stretch out your hands,
  I will hide my eyes from you;
even though you make many prayers,
  I will not listen;
  your hands are full of blood.
16 Wash yourselves; make yourselves clean;
  remove your evil deeds
  from before my eyes;
cease to do evil;
17 learn to do good;
seek justice;
  rescue the oppressed;
defend the orphan;
  plead for the widow.

18 Come now, let us argue it out,
  says the LORD:
If your sins are like scarlet,
  will they become like snow?
If they are red like crimson,
  will they become like wool?
19 If you are willing and obedient,
  you shall eat the good of the land,

20 but if you refuse and rebel,
  you shall be devoured by the sword,
  for the mouth of the LORD has
    spoken.
21 How the faithful city
  has become a prostitute!
  She that was full of justice,
righteousness lodged in her—
  but now murderers!
22 Your silver has become dross;
  your wine is mixed with water.
23 Your princes are rebels
  and companions of thieves.
Everyone loves a bribe
  and runs after gifts.
They do not defend the orphan,
  and the widow's cause does not come
    before them.
24 Therefore says the Sovereign, the LORD of
    hosts, the Mighty One of Israel:
Surely I will pour out my wrath on my
    enemies
  and avenge myself on my foes!
25 I will turn my hand against you;
  I will smelt away your dross as
    with lye
  and remove all your alloy.
26 And I will restore your judges as at the
    first
  and your counselors as at the
    beginning.
Afterward you shall be called the city of
    righteousness,
  the faithful city.

b 1.12 Or *see my face*

of religious rituals appear in Hos. 6:6 and Amos 5:21–24. Although it is possible that these texts completely reject such practices, more likely they are hyperbolic criticisms of the people's focus on ritual to the exclusion of social and economic justice. **1:15** The worshipers' *hands are full of blood* from their sacrifices (v. 11) and their violent crimes. **1:16–17** Moral imperatives clarify what the deity wants instead of, or in addition to, ritual actions. **1:17** *Justice.* See **"Amos and Martin Luther King Jr.," p. 1262.** *Orphan* and *widow* designate vulnerable classes of people whose rights need special protection. **1:20** *For the mouth of the LORD has spoken* (cf. Isa. 40:5; 58:14) echoes "for the LORD has spoken" in v. 2. The repetition at the beginning and end of a poem, known as "inclusio," emphasizes the work's completeness.

1:21–26 The second poem in chap. 1 is framed by the phrase *faithful city* in the first and final verses. It laments Jerusalem's moral degradation but looks forward to the restoration of its faithfulness. **1:21** Laments over destroyed cities sometimes begin with *How* (Jer. 49:25; Lam. 1:1; 2:1). *Prostitute.* Sexual misconduct is a recurring prophetic metaphor for religious or social shortcomings (see **"Slut-Shaming," p. 1148**). **1:22** *Silver* and *wine* are metaphors for Jerusalem's righteousness, which has been compromised by its leaders' corruption. **1:23** *Orphan* and *widow.* See note on 1:17. **1:24** God's *enemies* and *foes* are not foreign rulers, as one might expect, but Jerusalem's corrupt leaders. **1:25** *Smelt* refers to the process of heating silver to remove impurities (*dross, alloy*), reversing v. 22.

²⁷ Zion shall be redeemed by justice,
  and those in her who repent, by
  righteousness.
²⁸ But rebels and sinners shall be destroyed
  together,
  and those who forsake the LORD shall
  be consumed.
²⁹ For you shall be ashamed of the oaks
  in which you delighted,
  and you shall blush for the gardens
  that you have chosen.
³⁰ For you shall be like an oak
  whose leaf withers
  and like a garden without water.
³¹ The strong shall become like tinder
  and their work like a spark;
  they and their work shall burn
  together,
  with no one to quench them.

2 The word that Isaiah son of Amoz saw
concerning Judah and Jerusalem.

² In days to come
  the mountain of the LORD's house
shall be established as the highest of the
  mountains
  and shall be raised above the hills;
all the nations shall stream to it.
³   Many peoples shall come and say,

"Come, let us go up to the mountain of
  the LORD,
  to the house of the God of Jacob,
that he may teach us his ways
  and that we may walk in his paths."
For out of Zion shall go forth instruction
  and the word of the LORD from
  Jerusalem.
⁴ He shall judge between the nations
  and shall arbitrate for many peoples;
they shall beat their swords into
  plowshares
  and their spears into pruning hooks;
nation shall not lift up sword against
  nation;
  neither shall they learn war any more.
⁵ O house of Jacob,
  come, let us walk
in the light of the LORD!
⁶ You have forsaken your people,
  the house of Jacob,
for they are full of diviners^c from the
  East
  and of soothsayers like the
  Philistines,
  and they clasp hands with foreigners.
⁷ Their land is filled with silver and gold,
  and there is no end to their treasures;

c 2.6 Cn: Heb lacks *of diviners*

1:27–31 The third poem of chap. 1 shifts its focus from social injustice to religious offenses. It may have originally promoted the religious reforms of King Hezekiah or Josiah (2 Kgs. 18:3–6; 23:1–24), or it could reflect Second Temple–era cultic conflicts described later in the book (Isa. 57:5; 65:3; 66:17). **1:27–28** Instead of addressing Jerusalem as a unified entity, these verses distinguish between righteous and wicked persons. **1:29** *Oaks* and *gardens* were sites of unsanctioned religious rituals, unlike the acceptable practices criticized in vv. 11–15. **1:30–31** As punishment for worshiping among oaks and in gardens, the worshipers will (metaphorically) become dying *oak[s]* and *garden[s]*. Explicit connections between crime and penalty are common in Isaiah.
2:1 This superscription probably opened an earlier version of the book, before chap. 1 was added to the beginning.
2:2–4 This poem envisions the future submission of nations to YHWH's worldwide rule. It is the first of several passages in Isaiah depicting a pilgrimage of nations to Jerusalem (18:7; 45:14; 60:5–18; 66:23). A nearly identical passage appears in Mic. 4:1–3. See **"Visions of Peace," p. 937**. **2:2** *Mountain of the LORD's house*. The Temple Mount in Jerusalem (elev. 2,430 ft.). Its increased height contrasts with the motif of leveled mountains in Isa. 2:14; 40:4; 45:2. The verb *stream* (Heb. "nahar") could also be translated as "look with joy." Such double meanings occur frequently in Isaiah's poetry. **2:3** *Ways* and *paths* are metaphors for moral conduct. *Word of the LORD*. Prophetic oracles. **2:4** Nations let YHWH *arbitrate* their disputes instead of resorting to violence to solve them. As a result, war becomes less frequent. Joel 3:10 reverses the imagery of this verse.
2:5–22 In contrast to the hopeful future in vv. 1–4, this poem threatens judgment against humans who exalt themselves and rely on false deities. **2:5–6** *House of Jacob* refers to the nation by the name of its ancestor, Jacob. Repeated language from v. 3 (*come, walk, ways*) connects this poem to the preceding one. **2:6–7** In contrast to the peaceful future of v. 4, these verses describe preparations for military action. Such preparations are generally condemned in Isaiah for demonstrating

Reading through Time: Visions of Peace in Isaiah (Isaiah 2)

The early chapters of Isaiah contain two memorable depictions of worldwide peace. In 2:4, nations forswear war by "beat[ing] their swords into plowshares" (cf. Mic. 4:3), while Isa. 11:6–9 envisions a revitalized creation in which former predators and prey coexist harmoniously. These images have become well-recognized symbols of nonviolence.

Both texts have appeared frequently in public discourse since the mid-twentieth century, following the experience of two world wars and a nuclear arms race. U.S. president Dwight Eisenhower alluded to 2:4 in his 1961 speech warning against the "military-industrial complex." Since the early 1980s, an activist group called the Plowshares Movement has performed acts of protest involving the vandalization of nuclear weapons and facilities. An anti-violence organization called RAWtools refashions donated guns into garden tools. Contemporary environmental advocates sometimes appeal to 11:6–9 to advocate for meat-free diets.

Several public artworks are based on the texts. A sculpture titled *Let Us Beat Swords into Plowshares* by Soviet artist Evgeniy Vuchetich was a gift from the Soviet Union to the United Nations in 1959. Isaiah 2:4 is inscribed in Hebrew and Arabic on the Monument of Peace in Jerusalem, erected in 1967. The scene from 11:6–9 appears on the Knesset Menorah by Jewish sculptor Benno Elkan, a gift to Israel from the United Kingdom in 1956. Allusions to the texts appear in popular music, including the African American spiritual "Down by the Riverside"; the traditional Hebrew folk song "Lo Yisa Goy" (Nation shall not lift up); the 1937 song "Peace in the Valley," written by Thomas A. Dorsey for gospel singer Mahalia Jackson and later performed by Elvis Presley; and the 1992 song "Heal the World" by Michael Jackson.

Christians from pacifist denominations have been particularly drawn to the texts. From 1820 to 1850, inspired by Isa. 11, the Quaker artist Edward Hicks created over sixty paintings titled *The Peaceable Kingdom*. Some versions include a bald eagle among the animals, symbolizing the United States; in others, a depiction of the 1682 peace treaty between William Penn and Indigenous Americans appears in the background. U.S. president Richard Nixon, a Quaker, used a family Bible opened to Isa. 2 for his oath of office. Bluffton College, a Mennonite institution in Ohio, hosts the Lion and Lamb Peace Arts Center, and a sculpture titled *Guns into Plowshares* by Esther and Michael Augsburger stands on the campus of Eastern Mennonite University in Virginia.

J. Blake Couey

their land is filled with horses,
    and there is no end to their chariots.
⁸ Their land is filled with idols;
    they bow down to the work of their
        hands,
    to what their own fingers have
        made.
⁹ And so people are humbled,
    and everyone is brought low—
        [[do not forgive them!
¹⁰ Enter into the rock,
    and hide in the dust
from the terror of the Lord
    and from the glory of his majesty.]]*d*

¹¹ The haughty eyes of people shall be
        brought low,

and the pride of everyone shall be
        humbled,
    and the Lord alone will be exalted on
        that day.
¹² For the Lord of hosts has a day
    against all that is proud and lofty,
    against all that is lifted up and high;*e*
¹³ against all the cedars of Lebanon,
    lofty and lifted up;
    and against all the oaks of Bashan;
¹⁴ against all the high mountains
    and against all the lofty hills;
¹⁵ against every high tower
    and against every fortified wall;

d 2.9–10 Q ms lacks *do not forgive . . . majesty*   *e* 2.12 Cn
Compare Gk: Heb *low*

a lack of trust in God (cf. 22:8–11; 30:15–17; 31:1–3). **2:8** *Idols.* See **"Emerging Monotheism," p. 1000.** **2:10** God's *terror* and *majesty* are tangible manifestations of the deity's presence, which humans encounter as dangerous. This verse counters Assyrian imperial propaganda, which claimed that the aura of their deity, Assur, similarly drove enemies away. **2:11–12** YHWH's *day* is a time of future divine destruction (see **"Day of the Lord," p. 1322**). **2:13–16** The objects in this list symbolically threaten YHWH's preeminence by virtue of their height or splendor. **2:13** *Cedars of Lebanon* were renowned for their height and beauty. Both they and *oaks of Bashan* provided prized

16 against all the ships of Tarshish
and against all the highly prized
vessels.
17 The haughtiness of people shall be
humbled,
and the pride of everyone shall be
brought low,
and the LORD alone will be exalted on
that day.
18 The idols shall utterly pass away.
19 Enter the caves of the rocks
and the holes of the ground,
from the terror of the LORD
and from the glory of his majesty,
when he rises to terrify the earth.
20 On that day people will throw away
to the moles and to the bats
their idols of silver and their idols of
gold,
which they made for themselves to
worship,
21 to enter the caverns of the rocks
and the clefts in the crags,
from the terror of the LORD
and from the glory of his majesty,
when he rises to terrify the earth.
22 [[Turn away from mortals,
who have only breath in their nostrils,
for of what account are they?]]*f*

3 For now the Sovereign, the LORD of
hosts,
is taking away from Jerusalem and
from Judah
support and staff—
all support of bread
and all support of water—
2 warrior and soldier,
judge and prophet,
diviner and elder,
3 captain of fifty
and dignitary,
counselor and skillful magician
and expert enchanter.

4 And I will make youths their princes,
and children shall rule over them.
5 The people will be oppressed,
everyone by another
and everyone by a neighbor;
the youth will be insolent to the elder
and the base to the honorable.
6 Someone will seize a relative,
a member of the clan, saying,
"You have a cloak;
you shall be our leader,
and this heap of ruins
shall be under your rule."
7 But the other will cry out on that day,
saying,
"I will not be a healer;
in my house there is neither bread nor
cloak;
you shall not make me
leader of the people."
8 For Jerusalem has stumbled,
and Judah has fallen,
because their speech and their deeds are
against the LORD,
defying his glorious presence.
9 The look on their faces bears witness
against them;
they proclaim their sin like Sodom;
they do not hide it.
Woe to them,
for they have brought evil on
themselves.
10 Tell the innocent how fortunate they are,
for they shall eat the fruit of their
labors.
11 Woe to the guilty! How unfortunate they
are,
for what their hands have done shall
be done to them.

f 2.22 Gk OL lack 2.22

building materials. **2:16** *Ships of Tarshish* were trade vessels that transported expensive, exotic cargo. **2:22** This verse, which emphasizes the unreliability of humanity, bridges chaps. 2–3.

3:1–15 This poem criticizes Jerusalem's oppressive leadership and threatens their removal from power, which will result in social disorder. **3:1** *Support and staff.* The poem depicts Jerusalem and Judah as a lame person and their leaders as a defective crutch. **3:2–3** This list of officials includes several kinds of religious functionaries whose practices were later banned but were apparently acceptable in preexilic Judah (*diviner, magician, enchanter*). **3:4–5** In the hierarchical society of ancient Judah, such social reversals would have been deeply destabilizing. **3:8** With their metaphoric crutch—their leaders—taken away, Jerusalem and Judah have predictably *stumbled* and *fallen*. **3:9** *Sodom.* Cf. Gen. 18:20; Isa. 1:10; Ezek. 16:49. **3:10–11** Unlike the surrounding verses, in which the entire population suffers for the misdeeds of their leaders, these verses emphasize individual

¹² My people—their oppressors extort
them,
and creditors[g] rule over them.
O my people, your leaders mislead you
and confuse the course of your
paths.

¹³ The Lord rises to argue his case;
he stands to judge the peoples.
¹⁴ The Lord enters into judgment
with the elders and princes of his
people:
It is you who have devoured the
vineyard;
the spoil of the poor is in your houses.
¹⁵ What do you mean by crushing my
people,
by grinding the face of the poor? says
the Lord God of hosts.

¹⁶ The Lord said:
Because the daughters of Zion are
haughty
and walk with outstretched necks,
glancing wantonly with their eyes,
mincing along as they go,
tinkling with their feet;
¹⁷ the Lord will afflict with scabs
the heads of the daughters of Zion,
and the Lord will lay bare their scalps
and heads.

18 On that day the Lord will take away the finery of the anklets, the headbands, and the crescents; ¹⁹the pendants, the bracelets, and the scarfs; ²⁰the headdresses, the armlets, the sashes, the perfume boxes, and the amulets; ²¹the signet rings and nose rings; ²²the festal robes, the mantles, the cloaks, and the handbags; ²³the garments of gauze, the linen garments, the turbans, and the veils.
²⁴ Instead of perfume there will be a stench;
and instead of a sash, a rope;
and instead of well-styled hair, baldness;
and instead of a rich robe, a binding
of sackcloth;
instead of beauty, shame.[h]
²⁵ Your men shall fall by the sword
and your warriors in battle.
²⁶ And her gates shall lament and mourn;
desolate, she shall sit upon the ground.

4 Seven women shall take hold of one man on that day, saying,
"We will eat our own bread and wear
our own clothes;
just let us be called by your name;
take away our disgrace."
2 On that day the branch of the Lord shall be beautiful and glorious, and the fruit of the land shall be the pride and glory of the

g 3.12 Gk: Heb *women*   h 3.24 Q ms: MT lacks *shame*

rewards and punishments. **3:12** In Hebrew, the same consonants could spell the word *creditors* ("noshim"), which appears in the Septuagint, or "women" ("nashim"), which appears in Hebrew manuscripts. This is another example of Isaiah's use of wordplay. *Rule* by women would have been viewed quite negatively in a patriarchal society. **3:14** *Vineyard.* A metaphor for the people of Israel and Judah (cf. 5:1–7), who have been *devoured* by the very leaders charged with caring for them.

3:16–4:1 As a counterpart to the preceding critique of male leaders, this poem denounces Jerusalem's elite women. It focuses on economic inequality, but feminist interpreters observe that it fails to acknowledge women's limited agency in a male-dominated society. **3:16** *Daughters of Zion* (plural) are the female citizens of Jerusalem, in contrast to "Daughter Zion" (singular), which designates the personified city itself. The women's actions may have sexual overtones but are more likely displays of ostentatious wealth. **3:17** As punishment, the deity will shave the women's *heads* (cf. v. 24), which was the typical treatment for prisoners of war. Judahite men endure similar humiliation in Isa. 7:20. **3:18–23** Echoing 3:1, God will *take away* the symbols of the women's socioeconomic status. The meaning of many terms in this list of jewelry and clothing is uncertain. Some items may have been associated with illicit religious practices. **3:25** Violence against Jerusalem's women follows the deaths of their male protectors in battle. **3:26** *Her* refers to an unnamed city, perhaps Jerusalem. **4:1** Following Jerusalem's defeat, there are so few male survivors that *seven women* seek to marry *one man* to remove the *disgrace* of their public humiliation and widowhood. This vignette provides a more sympathetic portrayal of vulnerable women in a patriarchal society than the preceding verses.

4:2–6 This prophecy, written in prose, describes the future purification and glorification of Jerusalem. It forms a bookend with Isa. 2:2–4, framing the descriptions of Jerusalem's corruption in 2:5–4:1. **4:2** *On that day.* An undesignated future period, sometimes with implicit eschatological connotations. It often indicates a later composition added to the surrounding material.

survivors of Israel. ³Whoever is left in Zion and remains in Jerusalem will be called holy, everyone who has been recorded for life in Jerusalem, ⁴once the Lord has washed away the filth of the daughters of Zion and cleansed the bloodstains of Jerusalem from its midst by a spirit of judgment and by a spirit of burning. ⁵Then the Lᴏʀᴅ will create over the whole site of Mount Zion and over its places of assembly a cloud by day and smoke and the shining of a flaming fire by night. Indeed, over all the glory there will be a canopy. ⁶It will serve as a pavilion, a shade by day from the heat and a refuge and a shelter from the storm and rain.

5 I will sing for my beloved
    my love song concerning his vineyard:
My beloved had a vineyard
    on a very fertile hill.
² He dug it and cleared it of stones
    and planted it with choice vines;
he built a watchtower in the midst of it
    and hewed out a wine vat in it;
he expected it to yield grapes,
    but it yielded rotten grapes.

³ And now, inhabitants of Jerusalem
    and people of Judah,
judge between me
    and my vineyard.
⁴ What more was there to do for my
        vineyard
    that I have not done in it?

When I expected it to yield grapes,
    why did it yield rotten grapes?

⁵ And now I will tell you
    what I will do to my vineyard.
I will remove its hedge,
    and it shall be devoured;
I will break down its wall,
    and it shall be trampled down.
⁶ I will make it a wasteland;
    it shall not be pruned or hoed,
    and it shall be overgrown with briers
        and thorns;
I will also command the clouds
    that they rain no rain upon it.

⁷ For the vineyard of the Lᴏʀᴅ of hosts
    is the house of Israel,
and the people of Judah
    are his cherished garden;
he expected justice
    but saw bloodshed;
righteousness
    but heard a cry!
⁸ Woe to those who join house to house,
    who add field to field,
until there is room for no one,
    and you are left to live alone
    in the midst of the land!
⁹ The Lᴏʀᴅ of hosts has sworn in my hearing:
Surely many houses shall be desolate,
    large and beautiful houses, without
        inhabitant.

4:3 *Recorded for life* suggests a record of the names of the righteous (cf. Ps. 69:28; Dan. 12:1; Rev. 20:12). **4:4** *Daughters of Zion* were objects of judgment in Isa. 3:16, but here they experience restoration. *Filth* and *bloodstains*. Ritual impurity and moral failures. **4:5** *Site of Mount Zion* and *places of assembly* refer to the temple, now protected by *cloud* and *fire* like the wilderness tabernacle (Exod. 40:38).

5:1–7 This poem cleverly uses the metaphor of God as a winemaker and the people as a vineyard to express divine frustration with the social failures of Israel and Judah. **5:1** The *love song* was a well-known ancient genre. Biblical examples include Ps. 45 and Song of Songs. This verse initially confuses the audience by withholding the identity of the speaker's *beloved*, later revealed to be YHWH. Although a *vineyard* could be an evocative setting for a love song, it is an unusual subject for one. **5:2** The owner cares for the vineyard and prepares for a large harvest but is disappointed. **5:3** The owner makes a legal case against his fruitless vineyard. **5:5–6** Just as v. 2 methodically listed the steps taken to prepare the vineyard, these verses outline the steps taken to destroy it. **5:7** The vineyard is a metaphor for *Israel* and *Judah*, whose unfulfilled harvest is *justice* and *righteousness* (see **"Amos and Martin Luther King Jr.," p. 1262**). The Hebrew words *justice* ("mishpat") and *bloodshed* ("mishpach") look and sound similar, as do *righteousness* ("tsedaqa") and *cry* ("tse'aqa"). Those similarities ironically emphasize the distance between God's expectations and Israel's and Judah's responses.

5:8–30 Six poetic denunciations, introduced by *woe*, illustrate the absence of justice and righteousness in Israel and Judah, as proclaimed in the preceding poem. **5:8** This verse criticizes the large-scale acquisition of property by wealthy landowners, likely through predatory lending or other

[10] For ten acres of vineyard shall yield but
  one bath,
  and a homer of seed shall yield a mere
  ephah.[i]

[11] Woe to those who rise early in the
  morning
  in pursuit of strong drink,
who linger in the evening
  to be inflamed by wine,
[12] whose feasts consist of lyre and harp,
  tambourine and flute and wine,
but who do not regard the deeds of the
  Lord
  or see the work of his hands!
[13] Therefore my people go into exile for
  lack of knowledge;
their nobles are dying of hunger,
  and their multitude is parched with
  thirst.

[14] Therefore Sheol has enlarged its appetite
  and opened its mouth beyond
  measure;
the nobility of Jerusalem[j] and her
  multitude go down,
  her throng and all who exult in her.
[15] People are bowed down, everyone is
  brought low,
  and the eyes of the haughty are
  humbled.
[16] But the Lord of hosts is exalted by
  justice,
  and the Holy God shows himself holy
  by righteousness.
[17] Then the lambs shall graze as in their
  pasture;
  fatted calves and kids[k] shall feed
  among the ruins.

[18] Woe to those who drag iniquity along
  with cords of falsehood,
  who drag sin along as with cart
  ropes,
[19] who say, "Let him make haste;
  let him speed his work
  that we may see it;
let the plan of the Holy One of Israel
  hasten to fulfillment,
  that we may know it!"
[20] Woe to those who call evil good
  and good evil,
who put darkness for light
  and light for darkness,
who put bitter for sweet
  and sweet for bitter!
[21] Woe to those who are wise in their own
  eyes
  and shrewd in their own sight!
[22] Woe to those who are heroes in drinking
  wine
  and valiant at mixing drink,
[23] who acquit the guilty for a bribe
  and deprive the innocent of their
  rights!
[24] Therefore, as the tongue of fire devours
  the stubble
  and as dry grass sinks down in the flame,
so their root will become rotten,
  and their blossom go up like dust,
for they have rejected the instruction of
  the Lord of hosts
  and have despised the word of the
  Holy One of Israel.

[25] Therefore the anger of the Lord was
  kindled against his people,

i 5.10 The Heb *bath*, *homer*, and *ephah* are measures of
quantity   j 5.14 Heb *her nobility*   k 5.17 Gk: Heb *aliens*

oppressive practices. Small-scale landownership within families is the biblical ideal. **5:10** The punishment for the unjust acquisition of land is a decreased agricultural productivity of that land. *One bath.* Approximately twenty-four to thirty-two liters. *Homer.* Approximately one to two hundred liters. *Ephah.* Approximately ten to twenty liters. **5:11** *Inflamed by wine.* Literally "wine inflames them." The drinkers have lost power over their consumption. **5:12** Lavish festivals result from an inequitable distribution of wealth. The charge that the elite do not adequately consider YHWH's prerogatives runs throughout the chapter (vv. 15–16, 19–21, 24). **5:13** Citizens of Israel and Judah were forced into *exile* multiple times by the Assyrians and Babylonians in the eighth through sixth centuries BCE. In another example of poetic justice, *hunger* and *thirst* are punishments for overconsumption. **5:14** *Sheol.* The name of the underworld in the Hebrew Bible. Death was conventionally portrayed as a monster with an insatiable craving in ancient myths. **5:15** Cf. Isa. 2:11, 17. **5:17** *Lambs*, *fatted calves*, and *kids* may be metaphors for the poorer classes of Jerusalem, whose oppression will end after the wealthier classes are exiled. **5:19** God's *plan* is an important theme in Isaiah (14:26; 22:11; 23:9; etc.). **5:22–23** This is a criticism of excessive consumption by the social elite, who benefit from injustice (cf. v. 12). **5:24** Fire is a frequent image of punishment in Isaiah. **5:25** The final two

and he stretched out his hand against
 them and struck them;
the mountains quaked,
and their corpses were like refuse
 in the streets.
For all this his anger has not turned away,
 and his hand is stretched out still.

26 He will raise a signal for a nation far away
 and whistle for a people at the ends of
 the earth.
Here they come, swiftly, speedily!
27 None of them is weary; none stumbles;
 none slumbers or sleeps;
not a loincloth is loose;
 not a sandal strap broken;
28 their arrows are sharp;
 all their bows strung;
their horses' hoofs seem like flint,
 and their wheels like the whirlwind.
29 Their roaring is like a lion;
 like young lions they roar;
they growl and seize their prey;
 they carry it off, and no one can
 rescue.
30 They will roar over it on that day,
 like the roaring of the sea.
And if one look to the land—
 only darkness and distress;
and the light grows dark with its clouds.

6 In the year that King Uzziah died, I
saw the Lord sitting on a throne, high
and lofty, and the hem of his robe filled the

temple. 2Seraphs were in attendance above
him; each had six wings: with two they covered their faces, and with two they covered
their feet, and with two they flew. 3And one
called to another and said,
 "Holy, holy, holy is the LORD of hosts;
 the whole earth is full of his glory."
4The pivots^j on the thresholds shook at the
voices of those who called, and the house
filled with smoke. 5And I said, "Woe is me! I
am lost, for I am a man of unclean lips, and
I live among a people of unclean lips, yet my
eyes have seen the King, the LORD of hosts!"

6 Then one of the seraphs flew to me,
holding a live coal that had been taken from
the altar with a pair of tongs. 7The seraph^m
touched my mouth with it and said, "Now
that this has touched your lips, your guilt has
departed and your sin is blotted out." 8Then
I heard the voice of the Lord saying, "Whom
shall I send, and who will go for us?" And I
said, "Here am I; send me!" 9And he said, "Go
and say to this people:
 'Keep listening, but do not comprehend;
 keep looking, but do not understand.'
10 Make the mind of this people dull,
 and stop their ears,
 and shut their eyes,
so that they may not look with their eyes
 and listen with their ears
and comprehend with their minds
 and turn and be healed."

j 6.4 Meaning of Heb uncertain *m 6.7 Heb He*

lines are a repeated refrain in Isa. 9:8–10:4; this verse may originally have been part of that poem.
5:26 God summons a foreign army to invade Judah as punishment. Originally, the text probably
had Assyria in mind, but its open-endedness allowed for later reinterpretation. **5:27–28** The poem
uses hyperbole to depict the advancing army as unstoppable. **5:29** The Asiatic *lion* is now extinct in
the Middle East, but it was among the most dangerous animals in ancient Israel and Judah. In royal
inscriptions, Assyrian kings compared their prowess to that of lions. **5:30** The lion's *roar* poetically
morphs into the *roaring of the sea*, and the invading army becomes a force of cosmic destruction.
 6:1–13 Isaiah's temple vision. Scholars debate whether this narrative recounts Isaiah's initial call
to become a prophet or a later commission to a new prophetic task. **6:1** *The year that King Uzziah
died.* Ca. 740 BCE. *Throne, high and lofty.* The wings of the cherubim statues in the temple, approximately fifteen feet tall (1 Kgs. 6:23–28), formed the arms of a giant throne on which the deity could
be imagined as sitting. **6:2** *Seraphs.* Literally "fiery serpents." According to 2 Kgs. 18:4, there was
a statue of a snake in the temple at this time, which may have inspired this part of Isaiah's vision.
Winged serpents (cf. Isa. 14:29; 30:6) appear as guardian figures in ancient Egyptian iconography.
Here, by contrast, they *covered their faces* to protect themselves from God's glory. **6:3** This song of
praise has been incorporated into Jewish and Christian liturgy. Early Christian interpreters understood the threefold *holy* as a reference to the Trinity. **6:5** Isaiah fears he will die from seeing God's
glory. For similar objections to God's commission, cf. Exod. 3:11; 4:1; Jer. 1:6. **6:6–7** Isaiah's prophetic
responsibility for proclaiming God's words makes it important that his *mouth* be pure. His fiery purification anticipates the nation's experience in v. 13. **6:9–10** Instead of inspiring repentance, Isaiah's

11 Then I said, "How long, O Lord?" And he
said,
"Until cities lie waste
without inhabitant,
and houses without people,
and the land is utterly desolate;
12 until the LORD sends everyone far away,
and vast is the emptiness in the midst
of the land.
13 Even if a tenth part remain in it,
it will be burned again,
like a terebinth or an oak
whose stump remains standing
when it is felled."[n]
(The holy seed is its stump.)

7 In the days of Ahaz son of Jotham son
of Uzziah, king of Judah, King Rezin
of Aram and King Pekah son of Remaliah
of Israel went up to attack Jerusalem but
could not conquer it. 2 When the house of
David heard that Aram had allied itself with
Ephraim, the heart of Ahaz[o] and the heart
of his people shook as the trees of the forest
shake before the wind.

3 Then the LORD said to Isaiah, "Go out to
meet Ahaz, you and your son Shear-jashub,[p]
at the end of the conduit of the upper pool on
the highway to the fuller's field, 4 and say to
him: Take heed, be quiet, do not fear, and do
not let your heart be faint because of these
two smoldering stumps of firebrands, because of the fierce anger of Rezin and Aram
and the son of Remaliah. 5 Because Aram—
with Ephraim and the son of Remaliah—has
plotted evil against you, saying, 6 'Let us go
up against Judah and terrify it[q] and conquer
it for ourselves and make the son of Tabeel
king in it'; 7 therefore thus says the Lord GOD:
It shall not stand,
and it shall not come to pass.
8 For the head of Aram is Damascus,
and the head of Damascus is Rezin.
(Within sixty-five years Ephraim will be
shattered, no longer a people.)
9 The head of Ephraim is Samaria,
and the head of Samaria is the son of
Remaliah.

n 6.13 Meaning of Heb uncertain *o* 7.2 Heb *his heart* *p* 7.3 That is, *a remnant shall return* *q* 7.6 Or *cut it off*

words will harden the people's hearts so they will not *turn and be healed.* The Septuagint softens this disturbing claim by translating the commands as past-tense verbs, blaming the people for their refusal to listen. The New Testament quotes these verses in association with Jesus's rejection (Matt. 13:14–15; John 12:38–40; Acts 28:25–27). For the implicit blindness and deafness imagery, see **"Isaiah and Disability," p. 974**. **6:11** *How long.* A cry of lament indicating Isaiah's distress at his commission. The people will remain hardened until their cities have been destroyed by military invasion. **6:12** *Far away* and *emptiness* anticipate the exile of Jerusalem's population to Babylon in 587 BCE. **6:13** This verse initially seems to depict total destruction, but the last sentence—which may have been added later—hints at the survival of a righteous remnant from which the nation could be reestablished.

7:1–17 A narrative about Isaiah and King Ahaz. Its third-person narration suggests that it originated separately from the surrounding first-person narratives. Ahaz's negative response to Isaiah's message fulfills 6:9. **7:1** Around 735 BCE, the kings of *Aram* (located in modern Syria) and the northern kingdom of *Israel* joined forces to resist the growing dominance of Assyria. When Ahaz refused to join their alliance, they attempted to invade Jerusalem and depose him. These events, which scholars call the Syro-Ephraimite conflict, are also described in 2 Kgs. 16:5–9. **7:2** Ahaz is referred to by the name of his dynasty, *the house of David*, evoking God's promises to the royal house. *Ephraim.* Another name for the northern kingdom of Israel. **7:3** *Shear-jashub* means "a remnant will return." The names of prophets' children could symbolically reinforce their messages (cf. Hos. 1:4–9). Although the text does not explain the name, it may have referred to the defeat of Israel (cf. Isa. 10:22–23), which should have reassured Ahaz. *Conduit of the upper pool on the highway to the fuller's field.* Ahaz may be inspecting the city's water supply in preparation for being invaded. The only other mention of this location is Isa. 36:2 (= 2 Kgs. 18:17). Hezekiah's faith in that story contrasts with the lack of faith of his father, Ahaz, here. **7:4** *Smoldering stumps of firebrands.* An insignificant and short-lived threat. **7:6** *Son of Tabeel.* The puppet ruler with whom Aram and Israel seek to replace Ahaz. **7:7** *Thus says the Lord.* A formula introducing prophetic speeches as divine messages, modeled after the openings of ancient messages or letters. **7:8** *Damascus.* The capital of Aram. The leaders of Aram and Israel are mere humans, but Ahaz has God on his side. **7:8** *Within sixty-five years.* No known historical event corresponds to this obscure threat. **7:9** Isaiah advises Ahaz to trust

If you do not stand firm in faith,
    you shall not stand at all."

10 Again the LORD spoke to Ahaz, saying,
[11]"Ask a sign of the LORD your God; let it be
deep as Sheol or high as heaven." [12]But Ahaz
said, "I will not ask, and I will not put the
LORD to the test." [13]Then Isaiah[r] said, "Hear
then, O house of David! Is it too little for
you to weary mortals that you weary my
God also? [14]Therefore the Lord himself will
give you a sign. Look, the young woman is
with child and shall bear a son and shall
name him Immanuel.[s] [15]He shall eat curds
and honey by the time he knows how to
refuse the evil and choose the good. [16]For
before the child knows how to refuse the
evil and choose the good, the land before
whose two kings you are in dread will be
deserted. [17]The LORD will bring on you and
on your people and on your ancestral house
such days as have not come since the day
that Ephraim departed from Judah—the
king of Assyria."

18 On that day the LORD will whistle for
the fly that is at the sources of the streams
of Egypt and for the bee that is in the land of
Assyria. [19]And they will all come and settle
in the steep ravines and in the clefts of the
rocks and on all the thornbushes and on all
the watering holes.[t]

20 On that day the Lord will shave with a
razor hired beyond the River—with the king
of Assyria—the head and the hair of the feet,
and it will take off the beard as well.

21 On that day one will keep alive a young
cow and two sheep [22]and will eat curds because of the abundance of milk that they
give, for everyone left in the land shall eat
curds and honey.

23 On that day every place where there used
to be a thousand vines, worth a thousand shekels of silver, will become briers and thorns.
[24]With bow and arrows one will go there, for
all the land will be briers and thorns, [25]and
as for all the hills that used to be hoed with a
hoe, you will not go there for fear of briers and
thorns, but they will become a place where
cattle are let loose and where sheep tread.

8 Then the LORD said to me, "Take a large
    tablet and write on it in common char-
acters, 'Belonging to Maher-shalal-hash-
baz,'[u] [2]and have it attested[v] for me by reliable

r 7.13 Heb he   s 7.14 That is, *God is with us*   t 7.19 Meaning
of Heb uncertain   u 8.1 That is, *the spoil speeds, the prey
hastens*   v 8.2 Q ms Gk Syr: MT *and I caused to be attested*

God rather than military or political plans. *Samaria.* The capital of Israel. **7:12–13** Isaiah interprets
Ahaz's refusal as an act of faithlessness, despite its pious language. **7:14** *Young woman.* Hebrew
"'almah" means a woman of marriageable age, not necessarily a virgin. The Septuagint translates
this word with "parthenos," which can mean "young woman" or "virgin," and Matt. 1:23 quotes this
translation to connect Jesus's virginal conception to this verse. The name *Immanuel* ("God is with
us") reinforces Isaiah's positive message. Some scholars think the promised child is Ahaz's son, possibly Hezekiah. Alternatively, because he has a symbolic name like Shear-jashub, he could be Isaiah's
son. See **"Understanding the Symbolic Emphasis of Children," p. 1229. 7:15–16** *Refuse the evil and
choose the good* could mean the capacity for moral reasoning, but the context suggests it refers to
the ability to distinguish good food from bad. That is, by the time the child can feed himself, Aram
and Israel will have been conquered, so Ahaz has no reason to fear. **7:17** *Ephraim departed from
Judah.* The separation of the kingdoms of Israel and Judah following King Solomon's death (1 Kgs.
12:1–24). This promise could be positive or negative, but *the king of Assyria* clarifies that it is a threat.
According to 2 Kgs. 16:7, Judah became a vassal of Assyria in exchange for defense against Aram
and Israel, which eventually led to Assyria's invasion of Judah in 701 BCE.

7:18–25 Four later prophecies, introduced by "on that day," describe the aftermath of the Assyrian invasion. **7:18–19** At God's command, the Egyptian and Assyrian armies will overwhelm Judah
like swarms of insects. **7:20** Forced shaving was a form of humiliation for military captives. *Razor.*
The king of Assyria is an instrument of YHWH (cf. 10:15). *Hair of the feet.* A euphemism for pubic
hair. **7:21–22** Despite food shortages following the invasion (cf. 1:7), the people will survive on a
limited but miraculously abundant diet. **7:23–25** Land previously used for agriculture will revert to
wilderness.

8:1–4 This narrative recounts the birth of another prophetic child with a symbolic name during
the Syro-Ephraimite conflict. The first-person narration suggests that it comes from a different
source than 7:1–17. **8:1–2** God commands Isaiah to record his future son's name in the presence of
reliable witnesses to provide later verification that the prophecy was not fabricated after the fact.

witnesses, the priest Uriah and Zechariah son of Jeberechiah." ³And I went to the prophetess, and she conceived and bore a son. Then the Lord said to me, "Name him Maher-shalal-hash-baz, ⁴for before the child knows how to call 'My father' or 'My mother,' the wealth of Damascus and the spoil of Samaria will be carried away by the king of Assyria."

5 The Lord spoke to me again: ⁶"Because this people has refused the waters of Shiloah that flow gently and melt in fear before* Rezin and the son of Remaliah, ⁷therefore the Lord is bringing up against it the mighty flood waters of the River, the king of Assyria and all his glory; it will rise above all its channels and overflow all its banks; ⁸it will sweep on into Judah as a flood and, pouring over, will reach up to the neck, and its outspread wings will fill the breadth of your land, O Immanuel.

⁹ Take notice,* you peoples, and be
    dismayed;
  listen, all you far countries;
  gird yourselves and be dismayed!*
¹⁰ Take counsel together, but it shall be
    brought to naught;
  speak a word, but it will not stand,
  for God is with us."

11 The Lord spoke thus to me while his hand was strong upon me and warned me not to walk in the way of this people, saying: ¹²"Do not call conspiracy all that this people calls conspiracy, and do not fear what it fears or be in dread. ¹³But the Lord of hosts, him you shall regard as holy; let him be your fear, and let him be your dread. ¹⁴He will become a sanctuary, a stone one strikes against; for both houses of Israel he will become a rock one stumbles over, a trap and a snare for the inhabitants of Jerusalem. ¹⁵And many among them shall stumble; they shall fall and be broken; they shall be snared and taken."

16 Bind up the testimony; seal the teaching among my disciples. ¹⁷I will wait for the Lord, who is hiding his face from the house of Jacob, and I will hope in him. ¹⁸See, I and the children whom the Lord has given me are signs and portents in Israel from the Lord of hosts, who dwells on Mount Zion. ¹⁹Now if people say to you, "Consult the ghosts and the familiar spirits that chirp and mutter; should not a people consult their gods, the dead on behalf of the living,

w 8.6 Cn: Heb *rejoicing with*   x 8.9 Gk: Heb *Be shattered*
y 8.9 Q mss: MT repeats *gird yourselves and be dismayed!*

8:3 Because the birth has prophetic significance, it is appropriate for the mother to be a *prophetess*. The text gives no indication that she is Isaiah's wife. The child's name, *Maher-shalal-hash-baz*, means "spoil speeds, prey hastens." **8:4** Like Immanuel in Isa. 7:14–16, the child's name and birth promise quick deliverance for Judah.
8:5–10 Following the hopeful message of v. 4, these verses predict an Assyrian invasion of Judah. Like Isa. 7:18–25, they suggest that deliverance from the Syro-Ephraimite threat will only be temporary. **8:6** *Waters of Shiloah* refers to the Gihon Spring outside of Jerusalem, the city's main water source. The waters are a metaphor for God's promised deliverance, which King Ahaz doubted in chap. 7. *Rezin and the son of Remaliah.* The kings of Aram and Israel (cf. 7:1). **8:7** *The River.* The Euphrates, located in Assyria. Because the people did not trust God, they face an even greater danger, *the king of Assyria.* **8:8** Assyrian propaganda depicted its armies as a raging flood. Initially, *fill the breadth of your land* seems to refer to the flood, but *outspread wings* is an image of protection, with God as a mother bird protecting her young (Ruth 2:12; Ps. 36:7; etc.). The hopeful name *Immanuel* further suggests divine deliverance. This line may reflect the survival of Jerusalem after the Assyrian invasion of 701 BCE (see **"Sennacherib's Attack," p. 984**). **8:9–10** A short poem celebrating God's power over the geopolitical realm. *God is with us* are the same Hebrew words that make up the name Immanuel (Isa. 7:14), suggesting that this prophecy may have originally accompanied the child's birth.
8:11–22 These verses continue to criticize the people for rejecting Isaiah's message. **8:12–13** The people may have accused Isaiah of *conspiracy* because he prophesied the nation's downfall. **8:14–15** *Rock one stumbles over* reverses the usual sense of protection behind the divine title *rock* (see note on 26:4). *Both houses of Israel.* The separate kingdoms of Israel and Judah. **8:16** Isaiah should write down and *seal* his *testimony* to confirm its authenticity after his prophecies have come true. Along with 30:8, this text serves as an origin account for the book of Isaiah. Like Elijah and Elisha in 2 Kings, Isaiah apparently had prophetic *disciples*. **8:17** Because his message was rejected, Isaiah will retire from public ministry, just as God *is hiding his face* from the people. **8:18** The names of Isaiah's *children* are reminders of his prophetic message. **8:19–20** Instead of listening to prophets like

[20]for teaching and for instruction?" surely those who speak like this will have no dawn! [21]They will pass through the land,[z] greatly distressed and hungry; when they are hungry, they will be enraged and will curse[a] their king and their gods. They will turn their faces upward, [22]or they will look to the earth, but they will see only distress and darkness, the gloom of anguish, and they will be thrust into thick darkness.[b]

9

[1]But there will be no gloom for those who were in anguish. In the former time he brought into contempt the land of Zebulun and the land of Naphtali, but in the latter time he will make glorious the way of the sea, the land beyond the Jordan, Galilee of the nations.
[2] [d]The people who walked in darkness
  have seen a great light;
 those who lived in a land of deep
   darkness—
  on them light has shined.
[3] You have multiplied exultation;[e]
  you have increased its joy;
 they rejoice before you
  as with joy at the harvest,
  as people exult when dividing
   plunder.
[4] For the yoke of their burden
  and the bar across their shoulders,
  the rod of their oppressor,
  you have broken as on the day of
   Midian.

[5] For all the boots of the tramping
   warriors
  and all the garments rolled in blood
  shall be burned as fuel for the fire.
[6] For a child has been born for us,
  a son given to us;
 authority rests upon his shoulders,
  and he is named
 Wonderful Counselor, Mighty God,
  Everlasting Father, Prince of Peace.
[7] Great will be his authority,[f]
  and there shall be endless peace
 for the throne of David and his kingdom.
  He will establish and uphold it
 with justice and with righteousness
  from this time onward and
   forevermore.
 The zeal of the LORD of hosts will do this.
[8] The Lord sent a word against Jacob,
  and it fell on Israel,
[9] and all the people knew it—
  Ephraim and the inhabitants of
   Samaria—
  but in pride and arrogance of heart
   they said:
[10] "The bricks have fallen,
  but we will build with dressed
   stones;
 the sycamores have been cut down,
  but we will put cedars in their place."

z 8.21 Heb it   a 8.21 Or curse by   b 8.22 Meaning of Heb uncertain   c 9.1 8.23 in Heb   d 9.2 9.1 in Heb   e 9.3 Cn: Heb multiplied the nation not   f 9.7 Gk: Meaning of Heb uncertain

Isaiah, the people turn to necromancy (communication with the dead) to discern God's will. *Ghosts* were believed to *chirp and mutter* (cf. Isa. 29:4). *Gods.* Ghosts could be referred to as "elohim," the usual Hebrew word for god(s); cf. 1 Sam. 28:13. **8:22** Subjection to darkness is a fitting punishment for seeking out dead spirits.

9:1–7 A poem celebrating the reign of a new king, possibly Hezekiah. After the collapse of the monarchy in 587 BCE, the poem would have been interpreted as a prophecy of a future messianic king (see **"Isaiah and Jesus," p. 951**). **9:1** *Gloom* and *anguish* connect this poem to the preceding verses. *Zebulun* and *Naphtali*. Two Israelite tribes, whose land was annexed by Assyria in 732 BCE. **9:3–4** The people *rejoice* after God rescues them from Assyrian oppression, symbolized by instruments used to control domesticated cattle (*yoke, bar, rod*). *Day of Midian.* Gideon's defeat of the Midianites in Judg. 6–7 (cf. Isa. 10:26). **9:5** The poem uses metonymy (*boots, garments*) to describe the defeat of the Assyrians. **9:6** This verse could describe either the birth of a new king or his accession to the throne, at which point he was ritually reborn as God's son (cf. Ps. 2:6–7). The new king receives throne names; it is unclear whether there are four names, as translated here, or only two ("A Wonderful Counselor is the Mighty God" and "An Everlasting Father is the Prince of Peace"). **9:7** Kings were responsible for achieving *justice* and *righteousness* and maintaining *peace* (cf. Ps. 72).

9:8–10:4 A poem depicting past divine judgments against the northern kingdom of Israel. **9:8–9** Israel ignores prophetic warnings, a possible reference to the prophecies of Amos. **9:10** Instead of interpreting disasters as warnings from God, the people vow to rebuild even more affluently.

¹¹ So the Lord raised adversaries[g] against
  them
  and stirred up their enemies,
¹² the Arameans on the east and the
  Philistines on the west,
  and they devoured Israel with open
  mouth.
For all this his anger has not turned
  away;
  his hand is stretched out still.

¹³ The people did not turn to him who
  struck them
  or seek the Lord of hosts.
¹⁴ So the Lord cut off from Israel head and
  tail,
  palm branch and reed in one day—
¹⁵ elders and dignitaries are the head,
  and prophets who teach lies are the
  tail,
¹⁶ for those who led this people led them
  astray,
  and those who were led by them were
  left in confusion.
¹⁷ That is why the Lord did not have pity
  on[h] their young people
  or compassion on their orphans and
  widows,
for everyone was godless and an
  evildoer,
  and every mouth spoke folly.
For all this his anger has not turned
  away;
  his hand is stretched out still.

¹⁸ For wickedness burned like a fire,
  consuming briers and thorns;
  it kindled the thickets of the forest,
  and they swirled upward in a column
  of smoke.

¹⁹ Through the wrath of the Lord of hosts
  the land was burned,
  and the people became like fuel for the
  fire;
  no one spared another.
²⁰ They gorged on the right but still were
  hungry,
  and they devoured on the left but
  were not satisfied;
they devoured the flesh of their own
  kindred;[i]
²¹ Manasseh devoured Ephraim, and
  Ephraim Manasseh,
  and together they were against Judah.
For all this his anger has not turned
  away;
  his hand is stretched out still.

10 Woe to those who make iniquitous
  decrees,
  who write oppressive statutes,
² to turn aside the needy from justice
  and to rob the poor of my people of
  their right,
to make widows their spoil
  and to plunder orphans!
³ What will you do on the day of
  punishment,
  in the calamity that will come from
  far away?
To whom will you flee for help,
  and where will you leave your wealth,
⁴ so as not to crouch among the prisoners
  or fall among the slain?
For all this his anger has not turned away;
  his hand is stretched out still.
⁵ Woe to Assyria, the rod of my anger—
  the club in their hands is my fury!

g 9.11 Cn: Heb *the adversaries of Rezin*   h 9.17 Q ms: MT
rejoice over   i 9.20 Or *arm*

9:12 Despite their alliance with Israel against Assyria, *the Arameans* were traditionally enemies of Israel, like *the Philistines*. The last two lines are a recurring refrain in this poem (cf. Isa. 5:25). They ominously suggest that even worse judgment lies in the future. **9:17** God's shocking disregard for orphans and widows (cf. 1:17, 23; 10:2) illustrates the severity of Israel's sinfulness. **9:18** *Wickedness* becomes its own punishment, symbolized by fire. **9:21** In v. 12, Israel was "devoured" by external enemies, but here its tribes consume one another. *Against Judah.* A likely reference to the Syro-Ephraimite conflict. **10:1** *Iniquitous decrees.* Corrupt leaders turn law into an instrument of injustice. Nineteenth-century North American abolitionists cited this verse to condemn laws demanding the return of enslaved persons. **10:2** *Widows* and *orphans*. See note on 1:17. **10:3–4** A terrifying picture of the future judgment warned against in the refrain.

10:5–19 This poem depicts Assyria as God's instrument for punishing Israel and Judah, before threatening Assyria itself. **10:5** *Woe* connects this poem to the preceding one (cf. v. 1), suggesting that the punishment repeatedly threatened in 9:8–10:4 is the invasion by Assyria. *Rod of my anger.* Assyria is God's instrument. This claim undercuts Assyrian propaganda, in which Assyrian kings

⁶ Against a godless nation I send him,
  and against the people of my wrath I
    command him,
to take spoil and seize plunder,
  and to tread them down like the mire
    of the streets.
⁷ But this is not what he intends,
  nor does he have this in mind,
but it is in his heart to destroy
  and to cut off nations not a few.
⁸ For he says:
"Are not my commanders all kings?
⁹ Is not Calno like Carchemish?
  Is not Hamath like Arpad?
  Is not Samaria like Damascus?
¹⁰ As my hand has reached to the kingdoms
    of the idols
  whose images were greater than those
    of Jerusalem and Samaria,
¹¹ shall I not do to Jerusalem and her idols
  what I have done to Samaria and her
    images?"

12 When the Lord has finished all his work
on Mount Zion and on Jerusalem, he*j* will punish the arrogant boasting of the king of Assyria and his haughty pride. ¹³For he says:
"By the strength of my hand I have done it,
  and by my wisdom, for I have
    understanding;
I have removed the boundaries of peoples
  and have plundered their treasures;
like a bull I have brought down those
  who sat on thrones.
¹⁴ My hand has found, like a nest,
  the wealth of the peoples,
and as one gathers eggs that have been
    forsaken,
  so I have gathered all the earth,

and there was none that moved a
    wing
  or opened its mouth or chirped."

¹⁵ Shall the ax vaunt itself over the one
    who wields it
  or the saw magnify itself against the
    one who handles it?
As if a rod should raise the one who lifts
    it up,
  or as if a staff should lift the one who
    is not wood!
¹⁶ Therefore the Sovereign, the Lord of
    hosts,
  will send wasting sickness among his
    stout warriors,
and under his glory a burning will be
    kindled
  like the burning of fire.
¹⁷ The light of Israel will become a fire
    and his Holy One a flame,
and it will burn and devour
    his thorns and briers in one day.
¹⁸ The glory of his forest and his fruitful
    land
  the Lord will destroy, both soul and
    body,
  and it will be as when an invalid
    wastes away.
¹⁹ The remnant of the trees of his forest
    will be so few
  that a child can write them down.
20 On that day the remnant of Israel and
the survivors of the house of Jacob will no
longer lean on the one who struck them but
will lean on the Lord, the Holy One of Israel,
in truth. ²¹A remnant will return, the remnant

j 10.12 Gk: Heb *I*

wielded the rod of their god, Assur. **10:6** *Spoil . . . plunder.* Cf. 8:1–4. **10:7** Assyria *intends* to conquer *nations not a few*, instead of just the one nation against which God sent them. **10:8** In a bilingual pun, the Hebrew word meaning *commanders* is related to the Assyrian word meaning *kings.*
10:9 This verse lists six cities already conquered by Assyria in the eighth century BCE (cf. 36:19;
37:13), including *Samaria,* the capital of Israel, which fell in 722–720. **10:10–11** The Assyrian king dismisses YHWH as an idol, matching Isaiah's rhetoric for the deities of other nations. **10:13–14** Rather
than acknowledging his subservience to YHWH, the Assyrian king boasts about his own *strength*
and *wisdom,* signaled by the ease with which he conquered *all the earth.* **10:15** The ludicrous image
of an *ax* or *rod* claiming to operate by its own power illustrates the absurdity of Assyria's boasts.
These rhetorical questions rebut those of the Assyrian king in vv. 8–10. **10:16–17** For *fire* as YHWH's
instrument for defeating Assyria, cf. 30:30; 31:9.

10:20–34 Similar to 7:18–25 and 8:5–10, a series of related prophecies have been appended
to the preceding poem. **10:20** The people will no longer rely on their imperial conquerors, *who
struck them,* for support. By contrast, in 9:13, it is God who strikes the people. **10:21** *A remnant will
return.* This verse may originally have been associated with the birth of Shear-jashub (cf. 7:3). *Jacob.*

of Jacob, to the mighty God. [22]For though your people, O Israel, were like the sand of the sea, only a remnant of them will return. Destruction is decreed, an overwhelming verdict. [23]For the Lord GOD of hosts will make a full end, as decreed, in all the earth.[k]

24 Therefore thus says the Lord GOD of hosts: "O my people who live in Zion, do not be afraid of the Assyrians when they beat you with a rod and lift up their staff against you as the Egyptians did. [25]For in a very little while my indignation will come to an end, and my anger will be directed to their destruction." [26]The LORD of hosts will wield a whip against them, as when he struck Midian at the rock of Oreb; his staff will be over the sea, and he will lift it as he did in Egypt. [27]On that day his burden will be removed from your shoulder, and his yoke will be destroyed from your neck.

He has gone up from Samaria;[l]
[28]   he has come to Aiath;
he has passed through Migron;
   at Michmash he stores his baggage;
[29] they have crossed over the pass;
   at Geba they lodge for the night;
Ramah trembles;
   Gibeah of Saul has fled.
[30] Cry aloud, O daughter Gallim!
Listen, O Laishah!
Answer her, O Anathoth!
[31] Madmenah is in flight;
   the inhabitants of Gebim flee for
      safety.
[32] This very day he will halt at Nob;
he will shake his fist
at the mount of daughter Zion,
the hill of Jerusalem.

[33] Look, the Sovereign, the LORD of hosts,
   will lop the boughs with terrifying
      power;
the tallest trees will be cut down,
   and the lofty will be brought low.
[34] He will hack down the thickets of the
      forest with an ax,
   and Lebanon with its majestic trees[m]
      will fall.

11 A shoot shall come out from the stump
      of Jesse,
   and a branch shall grow[n] out of his
      roots.
[2] The spirit of the LORD shall rest on him,
   the spirit of wisdom and
      understanding,
   the spirit of counsel and might,
   the spirit of knowledge and the fear of
      the LORD.
[3] His delight shall be in the fear of the LORD.

He shall not judge by what his eyes see
   or decide by what his ears hear,
[4] but with righteousness he shall judge for
      the poor
   and decide with equity for the
      oppressed of the earth;
he shall strike the earth with the rod of
      his mouth,
   and with the breath of his lips he shall
      kill the wicked.
[5] Righteousness shall be the belt around
      his waist
   and faithfulness the belt around his
      loins.

k 10.23 Or *land*   l 10.27 Cn: Heb *and his yoke from your neck, and a yoke will be destroyed because of fatness*   m 10.34 Cn Compare Gk Vg: Heb *with a majestic one*   n 11.1 Cn Compare Syr: Heb *bear fruit*

The northern kingdom of Israel. **10:22** The *remnant* motif in Isaiah is double-sided, including both future hopes for restoration and present threats of destruction. **10:24** *Rod* and *staff.* Cf. 9:4; 10:5. **10:26** *Rock of Oreb.* The site of Gideon's defeat of *Midian* in Judg. 7 (cf. Isa. 9:4). *Sea . . . Egypt.* God's defeat of Egypt in Exod. 13–14. **10:27** *Burden* and *yoke* are symbols for Assyrian oppression (cf. Isa. 9:4; 14:25). **10:27–32** The itinerary of an unnamed army (cf. Mic. 1:10–15) from *Samaria* to *Jerusalem.* Originally, it may have been associated with the failed invasion by Israel and Aram, but Assyria is the assumed enemy in the present context. **10:32** The enemy will intimidate but not conquer Jerusalem. **10:33–34** Assyrian kings boasted about cutting down cedars of *Lebanon* (cf. Isa. 37:24), but this propaganda is now appropriated for YHWH's defeat of Assyria.

11:1–10 A poem celebrating the reign of a new king. **11:1** Tree imagery connects this poem to the end of the preceding chapter. *Jesse.* The father of King David. The comparison of the Davidic dynasty to a *stump* could suggest a date after 587 BCE, when the monarchy was overthrown, or it could reflect preexilic disillusionment with the Davidic ruler. In Christian interpretation, this verse is associated with the births of the Virgin Mary and Jesus (see **"Isaiah and Jesus," p. 951**). **11:4** For the association between *righteousness* and the Davidic king, cf. Ps. 72:1–2; Isa. 9:7; 32:1. **11:6–8** The

6 The wolf shall live with the lamb;
the leopard shall lie down with the kid;
the calf and the lion will feed[o]
together,
and a little child shall lead them.
7 The cow and the bear shall graze;
their young shall lie down together;
and the lion shall eat straw like the ox.
8 The nursing child shall play over the hole
of the asp,
and the weaned child shall put its
hand on the adder's den.
9 They will not hurt or destroy
on all my holy mountain,
for the earth will be full of the
knowledge of the LORD
as the waters cover the sea.

10 On that day the root of Jesse shall
stand as a signal to the peoples; the nations
shall inquire of him, and his dwelling shall
be glorious.

11 On that day the Lord will again raise[p] his
hand to recover the remnant that is left of his
people, from Assyria, from Egypt, from Pathros, from Cush, from Elam, from Shinar, from
Hamath, and from the coastlands of the sea.

12 He will raise a signal for the nations
and will assemble the outcasts of
Israel
and gather the dispersed of Judah
from the four corners of the earth.
13 The jealousy of Ephraim shall depart;
the hostility of Judah shall be cut off;
Ephraim shall not be jealous of Judah,
and Judah shall not be hostile toward
Ephraim.
14 But they shall swoop down on the backs
of the Philistines in the west;
together they shall plunder the people
of the east.
They shall put forth their hand against
Edom and Moab,
and the Ammonites shall obey them.
15 And the LORD will dry up[q]
the tongue of the sea of Egypt
and will wave his hand over the River
with his scorching wind
and will split it into seven channels
and make a way to cross on foot;
16 so there shall be a highway from Assyria
for the remnant that is left of his
people,
as there was for Israel
when they came up from the land of
Egypt.

12 You will say on that day:
"I will give thanks to you, O LORD,
for though you were angry with me,
your anger turned away,
and you comforted me.

2 Surely God is my salvation;
I will trust and will not be afraid,

o 11.6 Q ms Gk Syr: MT *and the fatted calf* *p* 11.11 Cn Compare Gk: Heb *the Lord will again a second time* *q* 11.15 Gk Syr: Heb *destroy*

king's righteous reign transforms creation. The images of the cohabitation of predators and prey are a metaphor for world peace, possibly reflecting a tradition that all animals were herbivores at the time of creation (Gen. 9:3). These verses reappear in Isa. 65:25. See **"Visions of Peace," p. 937**. **11:9** *My holy mountain.* The Temple Mount in Jerusalem. **11:10** The repetition of *Jesse* frames the poem. *Signal.* Cf. 5:26; 11:12; 49:22. As in Isa. 2:2, nations will process to Jerusalem.

11:11–16 A poem expressing hope for the return of exiled Israelites and Judeans. Its present form likely reflects the sixth-century Babylonian deportations, but an earlier version may have been associated with the eighth-century Assyrian deportations. **11:11** A list of places inhabited by the exiles in North Africa and Mesopotamia. *Coastlands.* A commonly used term in Isa. 40–66. **11:12** *Signal* connects this poem to 11:10. The term sometimes suggests a summons to war (cf. 5:26; 13:2), but here it beckons other nations to release *the outcasts of Israel* and *the dispersed of Judah* (cf. 49:22; 62:10, where it is translated as "ensign"). **11:13** A reversal of the animosity between *Ephraim* (Israel) and *Judah* that characterized the Syro-Ephraimite conflict (cf. 9:21). **11:14** The returned exiles will dominate their former enemies. **11:15–16** Recalling the fabled crossings of the Red Sea and Jordan River (Exod. 14–15; Josh. 1), God will lead the returning exiles across *the sea of Egypt* and Euphrates *River*. The motif of a *highway* for returning exiles appears in other exilic and postexilic texts in Isaiah (35:8; 40:3; 62:10).

12:1–6 The first section of Isaiah (chaps. 1–12) concludes with a song celebrating God's salvation. An individual speaks in vv. 1–2, while vv. 3–6 address a group. (The Heb. verbs are plural.) **12:1** *On that day* connects the hymn to the preceding chapter (11:10, 11). *Your anger turned away* reverses the threats of 5:25; 9:12, 17, 21; 10:4. **12:2** This verse uses the conventional language of praise (cf. Exod.

Making Connections: Isaiah and Jesus (Isaiah 11)

Perhaps no Hebrew Bible text influenced Christian thought more than Isaiah. It is among the biblical books quoted most often in the New Testament, reflecting Christianity's origins among diverse Jewish movements at the turn of the Common Era. By connecting Jesus's birth, life, and death to Isaiah, the first Christians situated their understanding of divine activity within an older religious tradition and thus gained credibility for their fledgling movement.

In Matthew's Gospel alone, explicit quotations from Isaiah appear in the contexts of Jesus's birth (Matt. 1:22–23), ministry by the Sea of Galilee (3:13–14), miracles (8:16–17; 12:15–21), parables (13:13–17), and religious disputes (15:7–9). (Matthew's reliance on Isaiah is commemorated in a thirteenth-century stained glass window in Chartres Cathedral, France, depicting the Gospel writer sitting on the prophet's shoulders.) Isaiah 52:13–53:12 is linked with Jesus's passion in Luke 22:37, Acts 8:32–33, and 1 Pet. 2:21–25 (see **"Servant(s) of YHWH," p. 1011**), which informed later Christian atonement theology. The apocalyptic portrayal of Jesus's second coming in Revelation also draws heavily on Isaiah (e.g., Isa. 11:4 and 63:3 in Rev. 14:19; Isa. 6:3 in Rev. 4:8; Isa. 65:17 in Rev. 21:1).

Encouraged by such connections, early Christian writers found other texts in Isaiah that seemingly foreshadowed Jesus's life. Imagery from Isaiah especially influenced the development of Christmas traditions. Isaiah 1:3, for example, was understood as a prophecy of the ox and donkey at Jesus's manger, while 60:1–6 informed the portrayal of the magi. In Western Christianity, these connections also contributed to the veneration of Mary. Isaiah 7:14 was a proof text for the virgin birth (cf. Matt. 1:22–23), and 11:1 became associated with Mary through a Latin wordplay (*virga*, "branch," and *virgo*, "virgin"). This connection found visual expression in the medieval artistic motif of the Jesse tree. The eighteenth-century oratorio *Messiah* by Handel uses Isaiah extensively, as do many Christmas hymns, and contemporary lectionaries include many readings from Isaiah during Advent. Little wonder that Isaiah has been called Christianity's "fifth gospel"!

The pervasiveness of such interpretations reflects the Hebrew Bible's canonical status in Christianity. At the same time, they have contributed to the sometimes fraught relationship between Christianity and Judaism (see **"Isaiah and Judaism," p. 1014**). For this reason, many Christian interpreters today explicitly highlight the connections between Jesus and Judaism and acknowledge corresponding Jewish understandings of important texts from Isaiah.

J. Blake Couey

for the LORD[r] is my strength and my might;
he has become my salvation."

3 With joy you will draw water from the wells of salvation. ⁴And you will say on that day:
"Give thanks to the LORD;
call on his name;
make known his deeds among the nations;
proclaim that his name is exalted.

⁵ Sing praises to the LORD, for he has done gloriously;
let this be known in all the earth.

⁶ Shout aloud and sing for joy, O royal[s] Zion,
for great in your midst is the Holy One of Israel."

13 The oracle concerning Babylon that Isaiah son of Amoz saw.

² On a bare hill raise a signal;
cry aloud to them;
wave the hand for them to enter the gates of the nobles.

r 12.2 Q ms Heb mss Gk Syr Vg Tg: MT *for Yah,* the LORD
s 12.6 Or *O inhabitant of*

15:2; Ps. 118:14). **12:3** The repetition of *salvation* plays on the name Isaiah, which means "YHWH is salvation." **12:4** Cf. Ps. 105:1; 1 Chr. 16:8. **12:6** The final lines address *Zion*, whose fate is a central concern in Isa. 1–12. *Holy One of Israel.* See note on 1:4.

13:1–22 This poem opens the prophecies about foreign nations in Isa. 13–27 (see **"Oracles against the Nations," p. 1105**). It depicts the *day of the LORD* as a divine war affecting the entire earth (see **"Day of the Lord," p. 1322**), then narrows its focus to Babylon in v. 17. It was likely written late in the exile (587–539 BCE), expressing the deported Judeans' desire for their oppressors' overthrow. **13:1** A superscription introducing Isa. 13:1–14:27; cf. 1:1; 2:1. The title "Oracle concerning X" heads most prophecies in chaps. 13–23. **13:2** *Raise a signal.* A summons to war (cf. 5:26; 18:3).

³ I myself have commanded my
   consecrated ones,
have summoned my warriors, my
   proudly exulting ones,
to execute my anger.ᵗ

⁴ Listen, a tumult on the mountains
   as of a great multitude!
Listen, an uproar of kingdoms,
   of nations gathering together!
The Lᴏʀᴅ of hosts is mustering
   an army for battle.
⁵ They come from a distant land,
   from the end of the heavens,
the Lᴏʀᴅ and the weapons of his
   indignation,
to destroy the whole earth.

⁶ Wail, for the day of the Lᴏʀᴅ is near;
   it will come like destruction from the
   Almighty!ᵘ
⁷ Therefore all hands will be feeble,
   and every human heart will melt,
⁸   and they will be terrified.
Pangs and agony will seize them;
   they will be in anguish like a woman
   in labor.
They will look aghast at one another;
   their faces will be aflame.
⁹ See, the day of the Lᴏʀᴅ is coming,
   cruel, with wrath and fierce anger,
to make the earth a desolation
   and to destroy its sinners from it.
¹⁰ For the stars of the heavens and their
   constellations
   will not give their light;
the sun will be dark at its rising,
   and the moon will not shed its light.

¹¹ I will punish the world for its evil
   and the wicked for their iniquity;
I will put an end to the pride of the
   arrogant
   and lay low the insolence of tyrants.
¹² I will make mortals more rare than fine
   gold
   and humans than the gold of Ophir.
¹³ Therefore I will make the heavens
   tremble,
   and the earth will be shaken out of its
   place
at the wrath of the Lᴏʀᴅ of hosts
   in the day of his fierce anger.
¹⁴ Like a gazelle on the run
   or like sheep with no one to gather them,
all will turn back to their own people,
   and all will flee to their own lands.
¹⁵ Whoever is found will be thrust through,
   and whoever is caught will fall by the
   sword.
¹⁶ Their infants will be dashed to pieces
   before their eyes;
their houses will be plundered
   and their wives raped.
¹⁷ See, I am stirring up the Medes against
   them,
who have no regard for silver
   and do not delight in gold.
¹⁸ Their bows will slaughter the young men;
   they will have no mercy on the fruit of
   the womb;
their eyes will not pity children.
¹⁹ And Babylon, the glory of kingdoms,
   the splendor and pride of the
   Chaldeans,

t 13.3 Gk: Heb *for my anger*   u 13.6 Traditional rendering
of Heb *Shaddai*

13:3 *My consecrated ones.* YHWH's *warriors* are ritually dedicated to battle. 13:4 The title Lᴏʀᴅ *of hosts* (i.e., heavenly armies) is especially appropriate for this poem. 13:5 Earthly conflicts (*a distant land*) mirror heavenly ones (*from the end of the heavens*), a prominent theme in later apocalyptic literature (see **"Apocalypse," p. 1216**). 13:6 *Almighty* is the conventional rendering of the divine name Shaddai (cf. Gen. 17:1; Ruth 1:20–21; Job 23:16), found only here in Isaiah. "Mountain One" or "Destroyer" are also possible translations. "Shaddai" sounds like the Hebrew word for *destruction* ("shod"). 13:7–8 Extreme bodily distress is a typical reaction to bad news in the Bible. 13:10 For the association of the Day of the Lord with darkness, cf. Joel 2:10; Amos 5:18–20; Zeph. 1:15. 13:11 The denunciation of *pride* and arrogance is a common theme in Isaiah (2:12; 16:6; 23:9). 13:12 *Ophir.* An ancient seaport from which gold and other precious objects were imported. Its location remains unknown. 13:13 The cosmic response to God's wrath mirrors that of humans in vv. 7–8. 13:16 Disturbingly, this text implicates God in war crimes, including infanticide and sexual assault. *Infants will be dashed to pieces.* Cf. 2 Kgs. 8:12; Nah. 3:10; Ps. 137:9. *Raped* is the translation of a vulgar Hebrew verb that was replaced with the euphemism "lie with" in later Jewish tradition. 13:17–18 YHWH's divine army morphs into the *Medes*, an ancient kingdom located in modern Iran, who are also associated with the fall of Babylon in Jer. 51:11, 28; Dan. 5:28–31. 13:19 Babylon fell to

will be like Sodom and Gomorrah
  when God overthrew them.
20 It will never be inhabited
  or lived in for all generations;
Arabs will not pitch their tents there;
  shepherds will not make their flocks
  lie down there.
21 But wild animals will lie down there,
  and its houses will be full of howling
  creatures;
there ostriches will live,
  and there goat-demons will dance.
22 Hyenas will cry in its towers
  and jackals in the pleasant palaces;
its time is close at hand;
  and its days will not be prolonged.

14 But the LORD will have compassion on Jacob and will again choose Israel and will settle them in their own land, and aliens will join them and attach themselves to the house of Jacob. 2And the nations will take them and bring them to their place, and the house of Israel will possess the nations[v] as male and female slaves in the LORD's land; they will take captive those who were their captors and rule over those who oppressed them.

3 When the LORD has given you rest from your pain and turmoil and the hard service with which you were made to serve, 4you will take up this taunt against the king of Babylon:

How the oppressor has ceased!
  How his insolence[w] has ceased!
5 The LORD has broken the staff of the
  wicked,
  the scepter of rulers,
6 that struck down the peoples in wrath
  with unceasing blows,
that ruled the nations in anger
  with unrelenting persecution.
7 The whole earth is at rest and quiet;
  they break forth into singing.
8 The cypresses exult over you,
  the cedars of Lebanon, saying,
"Since you were laid low,
  no one comes to cut us down."
9 Sheol beneath is stirred up
  to meet you when you come;
it rouses the shades to greet you,
  all who were leaders of the earth;
it raises from their thrones
  all who were kings of the nations.
10 All of them will speak
  and say to you:
"You, too, have become as weak as we!
  You have become like us!"
11 Your pomp is brought down to Sheol,
  and the sound of your harps;
maggots are the bed beneath you,
  and worms are your covering.

12 How you are fallen from heaven,
  O Morning Star, son of Dawn!
How you are cut down to the ground,
  you who laid the nations low!
13 You said to yourself,
  "I will ascend to heaven;
I will raise my throne
  above the stars of God;
I will sit on the mount of assembly
  on the heights of Zaphon;[x]

v 14.2 Heb *them* w 14.4 Q ms Compare Gk Syr Vg: Meaning of MT uncertain x 14.13 Or *assembly in the far north*

Cyrus of Persia in 539 BCE, not the Medes, and the city was not destroyed. These historical inconsistencies suggest that this poem was written before these events. *Chaldeans.* Inhabitants of ancient Babylonia. **13:20** Babylon's depopulation is permanent; even nomadic tribes like the *Arabs* will not camp in its ruins. **13:21–22** Instead of humans, wild animals inhabit the city (cf. Isa. 14:23; 23:13; 34:11–17; Jer. 50:39; Zeph. 2:14). *Goat-demons.* Cf. Lev. 17:7; 2 Chr. 11:15; Isa. 34:14.

14:1–23 A satirical poetic lament celebrating the downfall of a tyrant (vv. 4b–21). It may have been inspired by the death of the Assyrian king Sargon II in 705 BCE, but its broad language encourages reapplication to other despots. The prose introduction and conclusion (vv. 1–4a, 22–23) associate it with the fall of Babylon, connecting it to chap. 13. **14:1–2** These verses describe the end of exile using language and themes from chaps. 40–66 (cf. 49:13, 22; 54:8; 66:18–20; etc.). **14:4** The exiles gloat over their fallen oppressor, *the king of Babylon. How* is a stereotypical opening for a lament (cf. 1:21). **14:5–6** Assyria is the *staff* and *scepter* that *struck* Judah in 9:4; 10:5, 24. **14:8** Because Assyrian kings boasted about cutting down *cedars of Lebanon* (cf. Isa. 37:24), the trees celebrate the tyrant's death. **14:9** *Sheol.* The realm of the dead, where the tyrant rejoins the kings whom he conquered. *Shades* may allude to ancient myths about divinized rulers in the underworld. **14:12** *Morning Star, son of Dawn.* The planet Venus, as it appears in the early morning sky. **14:13–14** To describe the tyrant's downfall, the poem apparently alludes to a lost ancient myth about a star deity who unsuccessfully

14 I will ascend to the tops of the clouds;
   I will make myself like the Most High."
15 But you are brought down to Sheol,
   to the depths of the Pit.
16 Those who see you will stare at you
   and ponder over you:
"Is this the man who made the earth
      tremble,
   who shook kingdoms,
17 who made the world like a desert
   and overthrew its cities,
   who would not let his prisoners go
      home?"
18 All the kings of the nations lie in glory,
   each in his own tomb,
19 but you are cast out, away from your grave,
   like loathsome carrion,[y]
clothed with the dead, those pierced by
      the sword,
   who go down to the stones of the Pit
   like a corpse trampled underfoot.
20 You will not be joined with them in burial
   because you have destroyed your land;
   you have killed your people.

   May the descendants of evildoers
      nevermore be named!
21 Prepare a place of slaughter for his sons
   because of the guilt of their father.[z]
Let them never rise to possess the earth
   or cover the face of the world with
      cities.

22 I will rise up against them, says the LORD
of hosts, and will cut off from Babylon name
and remnant, offspring and posterity, says
the LORD. 23And I will make it a possession
of the screech owl[a] and pools of water, and I
will sweep it with the broom of destruction,
says the LORD of hosts.
24 The LORD of hosts has sworn:
   As I have designed,
      so shall it be,
   and as I have planned,
      so shall it come to pass:
25 I will break the Assyrian in my land
   and on my mountains trample him
      under foot;
   his yoke shall be removed from them
   and his burden from their
      shoulders.
26 This is the plan that is planned
   concerning the whole earth,
   and this is the hand that is stretched
      out
   over all the nations.
27 For the LORD of hosts has planned,
   and who will annul it?
   His hand is stretched out,
   and who will turn it back?
28 In the year that King Ahaz died this
oracle came:

y 14.19 Cn Compare Gk: Heb *like a loathed branch*
z 14.21 Syr Compare Gk: Heb *fathers*   a 14.23 Meaning of
Heb uncertain

attempted to take over heaven. Later Christian interpreters understood these verses to describe the revolt of the archangel Lucifer (also the Lat. term for Venus), who was cast out of heaven and became Satan, as depicted in John Milton's epic poem *Paradise Lost*. Cf. the similarly mythical portrayal of the king of Tyre in Ezek. 28:1–19. *Zaphon*. Jebel al-'Aqra' in northern Syria, the home of the gods in Canaanite mythology. **14:15** *Pit*. The underworld. **14:17** *Would not let his prisoners go home* refers to the imperial practice of exiling conquered populations. **14:18** The tyrant did not receive a proper burial, possibly reflecting the fact that Sargon II's body was not recovered after his death in battle. **14:20** The tyrant oppressed his own people along with conquered nations. **14:21** A call for the execution of the tyrant's sons, bringing an end to his dynasty. **14:22–23** A prose conclusion threatens Babylon with destruction.

14:24–27 A poem describing God's *plan* to defeat Assyria. The shift from Babylon to Assyria suggests a typological similarity; see **"World Empires," p. 962**. **14:25** The defeat of Assyria happens in Judah (*my land*), perhaps reflecting Jerusalem's survival of the Assyrian invasion of 701 BCE (see **"Sennacherib's Attack," p. 984**). *Yoke . . . burden*. Cf. 9:4; 10:27. **14:26–27** God's plan involves *all the nations*, not just Israel and Judah. *His hand is stretched out*. Cf. 5:25; 9:12, 17, 21; 10:4.

14:28–32 A poem announcing judgment on the Philistines, traditional enemies of Israel and Judah who inhabited the southeastern Mediterranean coast. The historical setting is a revolt against Assyria in 714 BCE by the Philistines, who attempted to persuade Judah to join them (cf. Isa. 20). The poem illustrates the claim in vv. 26–27 that YHWH's plan for the world will not be thwarted. **14:28** *The year that King Ahaz died*. The dates of Ahaz's reign are debated, but he likely died around 715 BCE. This superscription may originally have headed a collection of prophecies from Isaiah's later career; cf. 6:1, which introduces a collection of earlier prophecies from the Syro-Ephraimite

29 Do not rejoice, all you Philistines,
　　that the rod that struck you is broken,
for from the root of the snake will come
　　forth an adder,
　　and its fruit will be a flying fiery
　　　serpent.
30 In my pastures the poor[b] will graze
　　and the needy lie down in safety,
but I will make your root die of famine,
　　and your remnant I[c] will kill.
31 Wail, O gate; cry, O city;
　　melt in fear, O Philistia, all of you!
For smoke comes out of the north,
　　and there is no straggler in its ranks.

32 What will one answer the messengers of
　　the nation?
"The LORD has founded Zion,
　　and the needy among his people
　　will find refuge in her."

15
An oracle concerning Moab.

Because Ar is laid waste in a night,
　　Moab is undone;
because Kir is laid waste in a night,
　　Moab is undone.

2 Daughter Dibon[d] has gone up
　　to the high places to weep;
over Nebo and over Medeba
　　Moab wails.
Every head is shaved;
　　every beard is shorn;
3 in the streets they bind on sackcloth;
　　on the housetops and in the squares
　　everyone wails and melts in tears.
4 Heshbon and Elealeh cry out;
　　their voices are heard as far as Jahaz;
therefore the loins of Moab quiver;[e]
　　his soul trembles.
5 My heart cries out for Moab;
　　his fugitives flee to Zoar,
　　to Eglath-shelishiyah.
For at the ascent of Luhith
　　they go up weeping;
on the road to Horonaim
　　they raise a cry of destruction;
6 the waters of Nimrim
　　are a desolation;
the grass is withered; the new growth fails;
　　vegetation is no more.

b 14.30 Heb mss: MT *the firstborn of the poor*　c 14.30 Q ms
Vg: MT *he*　d 15.2 Cn: Heb *the house and Dibon*　e 15.4 Or *the
armed men of Moab cry aloud*

conflict. **14:29** This verse mixes metaphors of a *rod* and *snake* to depict Judah's hostility toward the Philistines. They should not *rejoice* at Ahaz's death, because his successor (Hezekiah) will treat them more harshly. *Fiery serpent.* The same Hebrew word translated as "seraphs" in 6:2; cf. 30:6. **14:30** The *poor* and *needy* are depicted as domestic livestock, whom the new king will protect, in contrast to his persecution of the Philistines. **14:31** *Smoke comes out of the north.* A metaphor for the Assyrian army, who invaded Philistia in 711 BCE (cf. Isa. 20:1). **14:32** *Messengers of the nation.* Foreign diplomats, likely from Philistia, who sought to persuade Judah to join their rebellion. *The* LORD *has founded Zion.* God will protect God's chosen city from all enemies so that it may remain a *refuge* for the *needy.* For this reason, Judah should not turn to foreign allies.

　　15:1–16:14 A poem depicting God's judgment against *Moab,* a kingdom east of the Dead Sea (modern Jordan) from Israel and Judah. The poem may originally have been intended to dissuade Judah from allying with Moab against Assyria. Frequent references to Moabite cities add geographic specificity to the poem, but the described invasion does not match any known historical events. These chapters reappear in a substantially rewritten form in Jer. 48. **15:1** *Ar* could be a general term for "city" or the name of a specific Moabite city (Num. 21:15, 28; Deut. 2:9, 18). Similarly, *Kir* may be the word for "city wall" or an abbreviated designation for the city of Kir-hareseth/Kir-heres (2 Kgs. 3:25; Isa. 16:7, 11). **15:2** *Daughter Dibon.* A personification of a major Moabite city (cf. "daughter Zion" in Isa. 1:8; 16:1). *High places.* Sites of public worship, typically condemned in the Hebrew Bible. *Nebo* and *Medeba* are Moabite cities. Cutting one's hair and beard is a sign of mourning, along with wearing a "sackcloth" in v. 3. The Hebrew word translated as *head* ("qorchah") sounds similar to Qarchoh, the name of a high place in Dibon mentioned in an ancient Moabite inscription. **15:4** Moab and its cities lament the invasion, from *Heshbon and Elealeh* in the north to *Jahaz* in the east. *Loins* ("chalutsey") sounds similar to "armed men" ("chalatsey") in Hebrew, one of several examples of wordplay in the poem. **15:5** An unidentified speaker—possibly the poet or God—joins the lamentation over Moab's *fugitives,* who have fled to *Zoar* on Moab's southern border. Because Moab was an enemy of Israel and Judah, some interpreters (including Luther and Calvin) think this expression of grief is sarcastic. It is possible, however, to feel genuine sorrow at an enemy's misfortune while also believing it is justified. **15:6** Environmental distress accompanies the

⁷ Therefore the abundance they have
  gained
    and what they have laid up
they carry away
    over the Wadi of the Willows.
⁸ For a cry has gone
    around the land of Moab;
the wailing reaches to Eglaim;
    the wailing reaches to Beer-elim.
⁹ For the waters of Dibon*f* are full of
  blood,
    yet I will bring upon Dibon*g* even
      more—
a lion for those of Moab who escape,
    for the remnant of the land.

16 Send lambs
    to the ruler of the land,
from Sela, by way of the desert,
    to the mount of daughter Zion.
² Like fluttering birds,
    like scattered nestlings,
so are the daughters of Moab
    at the fords of the Arnon.
³ "Give counsel;
    grant justice;
make your shade like night
    at the height of noon;
hide the outcasts;
    do not betray the fugitive;
⁴ let the outcasts of Moab
    settle among you;
be a refuge to them
    from the destroyer."

When the oppressor is no more,
    and destruction has ceased,
and marauders have vanished from the
      land,
⁵ then a throne shall be established in
      steadfast love
    in the tent of David,
    and on it shall sit in faithfulness
a ruler who seeks justice
    and is swift to do what is right.

⁶ We have heard of the pride of Moab
    —how proud he is!—
of his arrogance, his pride, and his
      insolence;
    his boasts are false.
⁷ Therefore let Moab wail;
    let everyone wail for Moab.
Mourn, utterly stricken,
    for the raisin cakes of Kir-hareseth.

⁸ For the fields of Heshbon languish,
    and the vines of Sibmah,
whose clusters once made drunk
    the lords of the nations,
reached to Jazer
    and strayed to the desert;
their shoots once spread abroad
    and crossed over the sea.
⁹ Therefore I weep as Jazer weeps
    for the vines of Sibmah;

f 15.9 Q ms Vg: MT *Dimon*   *g* 15.9 Q ms Vg: MT *Dimon*

military invasion. **15:8** As in v. 4, the lamentation reaches all corners of Moab, from *Eglaim* in the north to *Beer-elim* in the south. **15:9** The fleeing Moabites face additional threats from wild animals. **16:1** *Lambs.* A gift to the Davidic *ruler* in *Zion* to encourage Judah to accept Moabite refugees. *Sela.* A city in Edom, south of Moab and east of Judah, where the refugees have fled. **16:2** The refugees (*daughters of Moab*) are as vulnerable as baby birds that have fallen from a nest. *Arnon.* A river (modern Wadi al-Mujib) that divided northern and southern Moab. **16:3** A plea for asylum for Moabite refugees. Several of the commands are grammatically feminine, suggesting they are addressed to Daughter Zion. *Shade.* A common biblical metaphor for protection, often associated with a mother bird's wings, which resonates with the simile in v. 2. *Hide the outcasts.* Nineteenth-century North American abolitionist writers cited this line as a biblical mandate to provide shelter to persons fleeing enslavement. **16:4–5** The defeat of oppressive world empires will allow the Davidic monarchy to regain prominence. See **"World Empires," p. 962.** For *faithfulness* and *justice* as kingly virtues, cf. Isa. 9:7; 11:3–5; 32:1. **16:6** Despite the compassionate attitude toward Moabite refugees, the poem denigrates Moab as *proud* (cf. 25:11). The denunciation of *pride* and *arrogance* is a common theme in Isaiah (2:12; 13:11; 23:9). **16:7** The poem returns to Moab's calamity, focusing on the destruction of its viticultural industry. **16:8** *Whose clusters once made drunk the lords of the nations.* The Hebrew verb literally means "smash," which could be a euphemism for drunkenness (cf. 28:1), as in contemporary English. Because of the variable word order of Hebrew poetry, this line can also be read as "whose clusters the lords of the nations smashed," a reference to the military destruction of an enemy's agricultural infrastructure. *Strayed* can also mean "staggered" (19:14; 24:20; 28:7), another image of drunkenness. In a hyperbolic description of the spread of Moab's grapevines, *sea*

I drench you with my tears,
O Heshbon and Elealeh,
for the shout over your fruit harvest
and your grain harvest has ceased.
¹⁰ Joy and gladness are taken away
from the fruitful field,
and in the vineyards no exultation is
heard;
no shouts are raised;
no treader treads out wine in the presses;
the vintage shout is hushed.ᵇ
¹¹ Therefore my heart moans like a harp for
Moab
and my very soul for Kir-heres.

12 When Moab presents himself, when he
wearies himself upon the high place, when
he comes to his sanctuary to pray, he will not
prevail.

13 This was the word that the LORD spoke
concerning Moab in the past. ¹⁴But now the
LORD says, "In three years, like the years of
a hired worker, the glory of Moab will be
brought into contempt, in spite of all its
great multitude, and those who survive will
be very few and feeble."

17 An oracle concerning Damascus.

See, Damascus will cease to be a city
and will become a heap of ruins.
² Her towns will be deserted forever;ⁱ
they will be places for flocks,
which will lie down, and no one will
make them afraid.

³ The fortress will disappear from
Ephraim
and the kingdom from Damascus,
and the remnant of Aram will be
like the glory of the people of Israel,
says the LORD of hosts.

⁴ On that day
the glory of Jacob will be brought low,
and the fat of his flesh will grow lean.
⁵ And it shall be as when reapers gather
standing grain
and their arms harvest the ears,
and as when one gleans the ears of grain
in the Valley of Rephaim.
⁶ Gleanings will be left in it,
as when an olive tree is beaten—
two or three berries
in the top of the highest bough,
four or five
on the branches of a fruit tree,
says the LORD God of Israel.

7 On that day people will look to their Maker, with their eyes on the Holy One of Israel;
⁸they will not have regard for the altars, the
work of their hands, and they will not look to
what their own fingers have made, either the
sacred polesʲ or the altars of incense.

9 On that day their fortified cities will be
like the deserted places of the Hivites and

ᵇ 16.10 Cn Compare Gk: Heb *I have hushed* ⁱ 17.2 Cn
Compare Gk: Heb *the cities of Aroer are deserted* ʲ 17.8 Heb
Asherahs

refers to the Dead Sea. **16:10** *Joy and gladness.* The harvest was normally a time of celebration. In a grim pun, the verb translated as *taken away* can also mean "harvest." **16:12** *High place.* See note on 15:2. The ineffectiveness of Moab's prayers reflects the impotence of its gods. **16:13–14** A later update to the prophecy, of uncertain date, acknowledges that Moab has not yet been destroyed but sets a time limit of *three years* for its demise (cf. 21:16–17). *Years of a hired worker.* The meaning of the simile is unclear. Perhaps it suggests years filled with hard labor. **17:1–11** A poetic announcement of the destruction of Damascus and the northern kingdom of Israel, likely during the Syro-Ephraimite conflict, with later additions criticizing the worship of foreign deities. **17:1** *Damascus.* The capital of Aram, Israel's ally during the Syro-Ephraimite con- flict; see note on 7:1. Assyria conquered Damascus in 732 BCE. **17:2** After the death or exile of Damascus's inhabitants, *flocks* of sheep will graze in its ruins (cf. 5:17; 27:10; 32:14). **17:3** *Ephraim.* The northern kingdom of Israel, which was first invaded by Assyria in 732 and then conquered in 722 BCE. **17:4** *Glory* can also be translated as "weight." This verse compares the reduction of Isra- el's population to a sick person's weight loss. *Jacob.* The northern kingdom of Israel. **17:5–6** A new metaphor compares the depopulation of Israel to the harvest of a field or orchard, in which only a little *grain* or a few olives remain. **17:7–8** A prose addition to the poem shifts the focus to illicit worship practices. *Sacred poles* were ritual objects associated with the goddess Asherah. These are forbidden throughout the Hebrew Bible. **17:9** The *Hivites* and *Amorites* were indigenous inhab- itants of the promised land and were driven out by the Israelites, according to Joshua and Judges (see **"Conquest," p. 317**). *Amorites* sounds similar to the word for "highest bough" ("'amir") in v. 6.

the Amorites,[k] which they deserted because of the people of Israel, and there will be desolation.

[10] For you have forgotten God your Savior
  and have not remembered the Rock of
    your refuge;
therefore, though you plant pleasant
    gardens
  and set out branches of a foreign god,
[11] though you make them grow on the day
    that you plant them
  and make them blossom in the
    morning that you sow,
yet the harvest will flee away
  in a day of sickness and incurable pain.

[12] Woe, the thunder of many peoples,
  they thunder like the thundering of
    the sea!
The roar of nations,
  they roar like the roaring of mighty
    waters!
[13] [[When the nations roar like the roaring
    of many waters,]][l]
  he will rebuke them, and they will flee
    far away,
chased like chaff on the mountains
    before the wind
  and like whirling dust before the
    storm.

[14] At evening time, sudden terror!
  Before morning, they are no more.
This is the fate of those who despoil us
  and the lot of those who plunder us.

18 Woe, land of buzzing[m] wings
  beyond the rivers of Cush,
[2] sending ambassadors by the Nile
  in vessels of papyrus on the waters!
Go, you swift messengers,
  to a nation tall and smooth,
to a people feared near and far,
  a nation mighty[n] and conquering,
  whose land the rivers divide.

[3] All you inhabitants of the world,
  you who live on the earth,
when a signal is raised on the mountains,
    look!
  When a trumpet is blown, listen!
[4] For thus the LORD said to me:
"I will quietly look from my dwelling
  like clear heat in sunshine,
  like a cloud of dew in the heat of
    harvest."
[5] For before the harvest, when the blossom
    is over
  and the flower becomes a ripening
    grape,

k 17.9 Cn Compare Gk: Heb *places of the wood and the highest bough* l 17.13 Heb mss Syr lack *When… waters* m 18.1 Meaning of Heb uncertain n 18.2 Meaning of Heb uncertain

17:10 Another denunciation of devotion to *foreign* deities. For *gardens* as sites of forbidden rituals, cf. 1:29–31; 65:3; 66:17.
  17:12–14 A short poem about God's repulsion of an invasion against Jerusalem. The historical situation is uncertain, but it would fit the events of 701 BCE (see **"Sennacherib's Attack," p. 984**). The poem's placement near the center of Isa. 13–23 reinforces the claim of YHWH's sovereignty over all nations. **17:12** A description of an advancing international army. The object of the attack is not specified, but other biblical texts describe a similar gathering of nations against Jerusalem (Ps. 48:4; Zech. 14:2). Elsewhere in the Bible, the *sea* and *mighty waters* symbolize a primordial threat that must be defeated by God (Pss. 89:9; 104:6–7; Hab. 3:8). **17:13** Despite its size, the army retreats at God's mere *rebuke*, proving no more substantial than *chaff* or *whirling dust*. **17:14** The *fate* of the would-be attackers becomes a paradigm for any nation threatening God's people.
  18:1–7 Although this chapter lacks the "oracle against" heading, it contains a separate poem about *Cush*, an ancient African kingdom south of Egypt (modern Sudan) that supported Judah's rebellion against Assyria in 705 BCE. The poem warns that the Cushites are not invincible. **18:1** Cush is depicted as a faraway land filled with noisy insects. The obscure phrase translated as *buzzing wings* could also mean "winged boats," parallel to "vessels of papyrus" in v. 2. **18:2** *Ambassadors* move between Cush and Jerusalem to finalize their political alliance. The description of the Cushites emphasizes their size (*tall*) and beardlessness (*smooth*) but does not mention their complexion (cf. Jer. 13:23). Skin tone was not a central marker of ethnic difference in the ancient Near East. *Mighty.* An obscure Hebrew term ("qaw-qaw") that could also refer to the Cushites' foreign language. *Conquering.* The Cushites conquered and ruled Egypt in the late eighth century BCE. **18:4** God is unmoved by human political machinations. *My dwelling.* Either the temple in Jerusalem or heaven. *Clear heat* and *cloud of dew* are stationary but have powerful environmental effects. **18:5** Despite

he will cut off the shoots with pruning
  hooks,
    and the spreading branches he will
      hew away.
⁶ They shall all be left
    to the birds of prey of the mountains
    and to the animals of the earth.
And the birds of prey will summer on them,
    and all the animals of the earth will
      winter on them.

7 At that time gifts will be brought to the
Lord of hosts from° a people tall and smooth,
from a people feared near and far, a nation
mighty and conquering, whose land the rivers divide, to Mount Zion, the place of the
name of the Lord of hosts.

19 An oracle concerning Egypt.

See, the Lord is riding on a swift cloud
  and comes to Egypt;
the idols of Egypt will tremble at his
    presence,
    and the heart of the Egyptians will
      melt within them.
² I will stir up Egyptians against Egyptians,
    and they will fight, one against the other,
    neighbor against neighbor,
    city against city, kingdom against
      kingdom;
³ the spirit of the Egyptians within them
      will be emptied out,
    and I will confound their plans;
    they will consult the idols and the spirits
      of the dead
    and the ghosts and the familiar spirits;
⁴ I will deliver the Egyptians
    into the hand of a hard master;

a fierce king will rule over them,
    says the Sovereign, the Lord of hosts.

⁵ The waters of the Nile will be dried up,
    and the river will be parched and dry;
⁶ its canals will become foul,
    and the branches of Egypt's Nile will
      diminish and dry up.
Reeds and rushes will rot away,
⁷   the reeds beside the Nile;ᵖ
all that is sown by the Nile will dry up,
    be driven away, and be no more.
⁸ Those who fish will mourn;
    all who cast hooks in the Nile will
      lament,
    and those who spread nets on the
      water will languish.
⁹ The workers in flax will be in despair,
    and the carders and those at the loom
      will grow pale.
¹⁰ Its weavers will be dismayed,
    and all who work for wages will be
      grieved.

¹¹ Clearly the princes of Zoan are foolish;
    the wise counselors of Pharaoh give
      stupid counsel.
How can you say to Pharaoh,
    "I am one of the sages,
    a descendant of ancient kings"?
¹² Where now are your sages?
    Let them tell you and make known
    what the Lord of hosts has planned
      against Egypt.
¹³ The princes of Zoan have become fools,
    and the princes of Memphis are
      deluded;

o 18.7 Q ms Gk Vg: MT *of*   p 19.7 Gk: Heb *beside the Nile,
beside the mouth of the Nile*

their prowess, the Cushites will be defeated as easily as grapevines are pruned. **18:6** The discarded
vines represent dead soldiers *left* on the battlefield to be consumed by scavengers. **18:7** A later
prose addition reworks v. 2 to describe the Cushites' future payment of tribute to Jerusalem, part
of the larger theme of nations submitting to YHWH's sovereignty in Isaiah (2:2–4; 45:14; 60:5–18;
61:5–6). See **"Visions of Peace," p. 937**.
  19:1–15 Under Cushite rule, Egypt supported Judah and its neighbors in their rebellions against
Assyria. This poem seeks to discredit Egypt as an ally to Judah (cf. Isa. 30:1–7; 31:1–3). **19:1** *Riding on a
swift cloud* reflects YHWH's character as a storm god. **19:3** The failure of Egypt's *plans*, in contrast to
God's unstoppable plan for the world, reveals the ineffectiveness of its practices of divination and necromancy (cf. Isa. 8:19–20). **19:4** The word translated as *deliver* could also mean "dam up," anticipating the
drying of the Nile in v. 5. *Hard master.* Likely the king of Assyria. **19:5–7** Egypt's agriculture depended on
the regular flooding of the *Nile* River. For a similar association of military invasion and drought, cf. 15:6.
19:8–10 Industries associated with the Nile become unproductive. **19:11** *Zoan.* Another name for Tanis,
a city near Egypt's border with Judah. Egypt's royal *counselors* were internationally renowned for their
learning, and many ancient works of Wisdom literature were attributed to them. **19:12** The divine plan is

those who are the cornerstones of its
     tribes
  have led Egypt astray.
¹⁴ The Lord has poured into them⁹
     a spirit of confusion;
  and they have made Egypt stagger in all
     its doings
  as a drunkard staggers around in his
     vomit.
¹⁵ Neither head nor tail, palm branch or
     reed,
  will be able to do anything for Egypt.

16 On that day the Egyptians will be like
women and tremble with fear before the hand
that the Lord of hosts raises against them. ¹⁷And
the land of Judah will become a terror' to the
Egyptians; everyone to whom it is mentioned
will fear because of the plan that the Lord of
hosts is planning against them.

18 On that day there will be five cities in
the land of Egypt that speak the language of
Canaan and swear allegiance to the Lord of
hosts. One of these will be called the City of
the Sun.'

19 On that day there will be an altar to the
Lord in the midst of the land of Egypt and
a pillar to the Lord at its border. ²⁰It will be
a sign and a witness to the Lord of hosts in
the land of Egypt; when they cry to the Lord
because of oppressors, he will send them
a savior and will defend and deliver them.
²¹The Lord will make himself known to the

Egyptians, and the Egyptians will know the
Lord on that day and will serve with sacrifice and offerings, and they will make vows to
the Lord and perform them. ²²The Lord will
strike Egypt, striking but healing, so that they
will return to the Lord, and he will listen to
their supplications and heal them.

23 On that day there will be a highway from
Egypt to Assyria, and the Assyrian will come
into Egypt and the Egyptian into Assyria, and
the Egyptians will serve with the Assyrians.

24 On that day Israel will be the third
party with Egypt and Assyria, a blessing in
the midst of the earth, ²⁵whom the Lord of
hosts has blessed, saying, "Blessed be Egypt
my people and Assyria the work of my hands
and Israel my heritage."

20 In the year that the commander-
in-chief, who was sent by King Sargon of Assyria, came to Ashdod and fought
against it and took it—²at that time the Lord
had spoken to Isaiah son of Amoz, saying,
"Go and loose the sackcloth from your loins
and take your sandals off your feet," and he
had done so, walking naked and barefoot.
³Then the Lord said, "Just as my servant
Isaiah has walked naked and barefoot for
three years as a sign and a portent against
Egypt and Cush, ⁴so shall the king of Assyria

q 19.14 Gk Compare Tg: Heb *it*   r 19.17 Gk: Meaning of
Heb uncertain   s 19.18 Q mss Heb mss Tg Vg: MT *city of
destruction*

beyond the grasp of Egypt's famed counselors. **19:14** *As a drunkard staggers.* A frequent image in Isaiah
(24:20; 28:7; 51:17).
     19:16–25 Five prose additions to the prophecy about Egypt, each beginning with *on that day.*
19:16 *Be like women.* This simile, based on the misogynist view that women are inherently weak and
fearful, appears as a curse against enemy troops in ancient Near Eastern treaties. **19:18–19** A likely
reference to Jewish communities in Egypt in the postexilic period. One such community, located at
Elephantine, had its own temple to YHWH. *City of the Sun.* Heliopolis, an ancient religious center in
Egypt. **19:20** Cf. 19:5. **19:23** The *highway* may represent restored trade relations between Assyria
and Egypt, which would benefit Judah. Elsewhere in Isaiah, highway imagery is associated with
the return of exiles (11:16; 35:8; 40:3). **19:24–25** Egypt and Assyria join Israel as God's people. This
remarkably inclusive vision stops short of full religious pluralism by assuming that Egypt and Assyria
worship YHWH instead of their native deities.
     20:1–6 A narrative about Isaiah (cf. Isa. 7–8, 36–39). **20:1** *Commander-in-chief.* An Assyrian
term for a high-ranking military officer. *Sent by King Sargon of Assyria.* This account contradicts
Assyrian sources, which claim that Sargon II led the army himself. *Ashdod.* A major Philistine city.
The Philistines rebelled against Assyria in 714 BCE, with the support of Cushite-controlled Egypt.
Assyria conquered Ashdod in 711 BCE and suppressed the revolt (see notes on 14:31–32). **20:2** The
following verses describe a prophetic symbolic action in which Isaiah visually acts out his prophecy
in a kind of street theater (cf. Jer. 13; 27; Ezek. 3–4). *Sackcloth.* A sign of mourning. **20:3** *Three
years.* Isaiah began performing the symbolic action around the beginning of the Philistine revolt.
See **"Symbolic Actions," p. 1056.** *A sign and a portent.* Cf. Isa. 8:18. **20:4** Isaiah's nudity foreshadows

lead away the Egyptians as captives and the Cushites as exiles, both the young and the old, naked and barefoot, with buttocks uncovered, to the shame of Egypt. ⁵And they shall be dismayed and confounded because of Cush their hope and of Egypt their boast. ⁶On that day the inhabitants of this coastland will say, 'See, this is what has happened to those in whom we hoped and to whom we fled for help and deliverance from the king of Assyria! And we, how shall we escape?'"

21

The oracle concerning the wilderness of the sea.

As whirlwinds in the Negeb sweep on,
  it comes from the desert,
  from a terrible land.
² A stern vision is told to me;
  the betrayer betrays,
  and the destroyer destroys.
Go up, O Elam;
  lay siege, O Media;
all the sighing she has caused
  I bring to an end.
³ Therefore my loins are filled with anguish;
  pangs have seized me
  like the pangs of a woman in labor;

I am bowed down so that I cannot hear;
  I am dismayed so that I cannot see.
⁴ My mind reels; horror has appalled me;
  the twilight I longed for
  has been turned for me into trembling.
⁵ They prepare the table;
  they spread the rugs;
  they eat; they drink.
Rise up, commanders;
  oil the shield!
⁶ For thus the Lord said to me:
"Go, post a lookout;
  let him announce what he sees.
⁷ When he sees riders, horsemen in pairs,
  riders on donkeys, riders on camels,
let him watch closely,
  very closely."
⁸ Then the watcher' called out:
"Upon a watchtower I stand, O Lord,
  continually by day,
and at my post I am stationed
  throughout the night.
⁹ Look, there they come, riders,
  horsemen in pairs!"
Then he responded,
  "Fallen, fallen is Babylon,

t 21.8 Q ms Syr Vg: MT a lion

the Assyrian defeat of Cush and Egypt, after which their captives will be stripped naked and taken into exile. **20:6** *Inhabitants of this coastland* points to the Philistines, whose own defeat will follow that of Cush and Egypt. By visually portraying the failure of the rebellion, this symbolic action warns against joining the Philistines. Judah remained loyal to Assyria in 714 BCE, although it is impossible to know whether Isaiah's actions—if the narrative is historical—affected this outcome. Less than a decade later, Judah did join a revolt against Assyria with the support of Cush/Egypt, with disastrous consequences (see **"Sennacherib's Attack," p. 984**).

21:1–10 This vision of the fall of Babylon is perhaps the most enigmatic poem among the prophecies against foreign nations. It may reflect Assyria's conquest of Babylon in 689 BCE, which meant ongoing Assyrian dominance over Judah, or the Persian conquest of Babylon in 539 BCE, which marked the end of the exile and Babylonian dominance over Judah. The poem's imagery inspired the Bob Dylan song "All Along the Watchtower" (1967). **21:1** *Wilderness of the sea.* The marshy area between the confluence of the Tigris and Euphrates Rivers and the Persian Gulf, known as "Sealand" in Assyrian sources, on the border between Babylon and Elam. *Negeb.* A wilderness region in southwest Judah. The poem creates suspense by delaying the identification of what *comes from the desert* until the next verse. **21:2** The words *betrayer/betrays* ("boged") and *destroyer/destroys* ("shoded") rhyme in Hebrew; cf. 33:1, where *betrayer* is translated as "treacherous one." *Elam* was located in modern Iran, bordering *Media* (see note on 13:17–18). The Elamites and Medes were Babylon's allies against Assyria in 689 BCE but were part of the Persian army that conquered Babylon in 539 BCE. *She* refers to Babylon, but this does not become clear until v. 9. **21:3** This visceral response reflects the conventional reaction to bad news in the Hebrew Bible (cf. 13:7–8). **21:5** The feasters could be the Babylonians, unaware of the impending disaster (cf. Dan. 5), or the invaders, anticipating their victory. **21:6–7** *Lookout* sometimes refers to prophets (Ezek. 3:17; Hos. 9:8; Hab. 2:1). The title of Harper Lee's 2015 novel *Go Set a Watchman* comes from this verse. **21:9** The sentinel sees fugitives from the battle, who convey its outcome (cf. Jer. 48:19; Ezek. 33:21). *Images of her gods.* Sennacherib destroyed Babylon's divine images when he conquered the city in 689 BCE.

Focus On: World Empires in Isaiah (Isaiah 20)

An empire is a geopolitical polity that controls foreign populations through conquest or domination. During the historical periods depicted in Isaiah, Israel and Judah experienced subjugation by the Assyrian (eighth to seventh century BCE), Babylonian (sixth century BCE), and Persian (sixth to fourth century BCE) Empires. Their respective threats correspond roughly to the major divisions of the book (chaps. 1–39, 40–55, and 56–66).

Isaiah poignantly depicts the harshness of life under empires, portraying them as wild animals or monsters (5:29; 27:1; 51:9). Symbols for imperial subjugation include a yoke (9:4; 10:27; 47:6), a flood or storm (8:7–8; 25:4; 28:2), and imprisonment (14:17; 42:7, 22; 49:9). One of Isaiah's central concerns is exile, an imperial strategy to control subjugated populations through forced resettlement, experienced by both Israel and Judah. The book also acknowledges the suffering of other nations under empire (10:13–14; 15:5; 20:6) and gives voice to violent anti-imperial revenge fantasies (13:17–14:23; 30:27–33; 47:1–15).

Isaiah responds to imperial power by emphasizing divine sovereignty. Instead of attributing agency to Assyria, the book credits YHWH with empowering the empire (5:26; 7:17–19; 37:26) and defeating it (10:12; 14:25; 31:8), emphasizing its status as the deity's tool (7:20; 10:5, 15). Assyrian propaganda is appropriated for YHWH (2:10; 10:5, 33–34; 31:9). YHWH also orchestrates Babylon's conquest of Judah (42:24–25; 43:27–28; 47:6), although Babylon is not explicitly depicted as the deity's agent. Surprisingly, Persia is never named in Isaiah, but the text claims that the Persian ruler Cyrus acts at YHWH's behest to defeat Babylon (see **"Cyrus," p. 991**). YHWH's superiority further extends to imperial deities. The book never refers directly to the Assyrian god Assur, refusing to acknowledge his existence as a rival divine power. By contrast, Babylonian deities are named (46:1) but lampooned as powerless (41:23–24; 44:9–20).

Despite the negative portrayal of other empires, Isaiah sometimes endorses Judah's own imperial aspirations. The cessation of war in 2:4 follows other nations' submission to Judahite hegemony. The end of Assyrian oppression is associated with the revitalization of the Davidic monarchy (9:2–7; 16:4–5). Even after the end of the Davidic dynasty, following the Babylonian conquest, the second half of Isaiah fantasizes about foreign nations paying tribute to Jerusalem (49:22–23; 60:3–17; 66:12).

J. Blake Couey

and all the images of her gods
    lie shattered on the ground."
¹⁰ O my threshed and winnowed one,
    what I have heard from the Lord of
        hosts,
    the God of Israel, I announce to
        you.

11 The oracle concerning Dumah.

One is calling to me from Seir,
    "Sentinel, what of the night?
    Sentinel, what of the night?"

¹² The sentinel says:
"Morning comes and also the night.
    If you will inquire, inquire;
    come back again."

13 The oracle concerning the desert plain.

In the scrub of the desert plain you will
    lodge,
    O caravans of Dedanites.
¹⁴ Bring water to the thirsty,
    O inhabitants of the land of Tema;
    meet the fugitive with bread.

More typically, a conquering army would take them as spoil. **21:10** *Threshed and winnowed one.* This address to the prophet's audience, the people of Judah, uses agricultural metaphors to emphasize their ongoing oppression.

21:11–17 A pair of poems set in the Arabian Desert. **21:11** *Dumah.* An oasis in northwest Arabia. In this poem, the name plays on the similar Hebrew word for "silence." Confusingly, the city is not mentioned in the poem itself. In a possible connection to the previous poem, it was invaded by Assyria at the same time as Babylon in 689 BCE. *Seir.* A region in Edom, a kingdom to the southeast of Judah that bordered Arabia. The address to the *sentinel* picks up imagery from the previous poem. The inquiry may concern whether it is safe to travel, or it may be a request for a prophetic message. The inquirer's identity is unclear. **21:12** An evasive and foreboding response. **21:13** *Desert plain.* The Arabian Desert. *Dedanites.* Inhabitants of Dedan, a city on a west-east trade route through Arabia. **21:14** *Tema.* A city on the same trade route as Dedan. As they transport their wares, the Dedanites

¹⁵ For they have fled from the swords,
 from the drawn sword,
from the bent bow,
 and from the stress of battle.

16 For thus the Lord said to me: "Within a year, according to the years of a hired worker, all the glory of Kedar will come to an end, ¹⁷and the remaining bows of Kedar's warriors will be few, for the LORD, the God of Israel, has spoken."

22 The oracle concerning the valley of vision.

What has happened that you have
 gone up,
 all of you, to the housetops,
² city full of shouting,
 tumultuous city, panic-stricken town?
Your slain are not slain by the sword,
 nor are they dead in battle.
³ Your rulers have all fled together;
 they were captured without the use of
 a bow.ᵘ
All of your people who were found were
 captured,
 though they had fled far away.ᵛ
⁴ Therefore I said:
"Look away from me;
 let me weep bitter tears;
do not try to comfort me
 for the destruction of my beloved
 people."

⁵ For the Lord GOD of hosts has a day
 of tumult and trampling and
 confusion
 in the valley of vision,
a battering down of walls
 and a cry for help to the mountains.
⁶ Elam bore the quiver
 with chariots and cavalry,ʷ
 and Kir uncovered the shield.
⁷ Your choicest valleys were full of chariots,
 and the cavalry took their stand at the
 gates.
⁸ He has taken away the covering of Judah.

On that day you looked to the weapons of the House of the Forest, ⁹and you saw that there were many breaches in the city of David, and you collected the waters of the lower pool. ¹⁰You counted the houses of Jerusalem, and you broke down the houses to fortify the wall. ¹¹You made a reservoir between the two walls for the water of the old pool. But you did not look to him who did it or have regard for him who planned it long ago.

¹² On that day the Lord GOD of hosts
 called for weeping and mourning,
 for baldness and putting on sackcloth,
¹³ but instead there was joy and festivity,
 killing oxen and slaughtering sheep,
 eating meat and drinking wine.

u 22.3 Or *without their bows*   v 22.3 Gk Syr Vg: Heb *fled from far away*   w 22.6 Meaning of Heb uncertain

and *inhabitants of the land of Tema* are commanded to offer supplies to *the fugitive* from an unspecified battle (cf. Isa. 16:3–4). **21:16–17** A later prose update to the poem (cf. 16:14). *Kedar.* A powerful northwest Arabian tribe in the first millennium BCE. It is unclear what event this prophecy refers to.
 22:1–14 A poem about Jerusalem's fate during the revolt against Assyria (see **"Sennacherib's Attack," p. 984**). **22:1** Like Isa. 21:1, this title features an evocative geographic reference instead of the name of a city or kingdom. *Valley of vision* is taken from v. 5. **22:2** *Tumultuous city.* Either Jerusalem, following its invasion by Sennacherib in 701 BCE, or more likely Babylon, following its defeat by Sennacherib in 703 BCE. Babylon's defeat had disastrous implications for its ally Judah. **22:4** The prophetic speaker expresses grief over the fate of his *people* (cf. 6:11; 21:3–4). **22:5** *A day.* See **"Day of the Lord," p. 1322**. *Tumult and trampling and confusion.* Hebrew "mehumah umebusah umebukah"; the "m" and "b" sounds evoke the march of an army or the beat of a war drum. *Valley of vision.* The location of the battle, as seen in the speaker's *vision*. **22:6** *Elam.* See note on 21:2. *Kir.* An unknown Mesopotamian location associated with Aram (2 Kgs. 16:9; Amos 1:5; 9:7). Elamites and Arameans fought alongside Babylon against Assyria in 703 BCE. **22:8** *Covering of Judah.* After Babylon's defeat, Judah lost its protection against Assyria. Although the NRSVue formats vv. 8b–11 as prose, the parallelism suggests that these verses are poetry. *On that day.* Following Babylon's defeat, Jerusalem prepares for the inevitable Assyrian attack (cf. 2 Chr. 32:2–5). *House of the Forest.* A royal storeroom. **22:9** *Waters of the lower pool.* The pool of Siloam, connected to the Gihon Spring outside the city by a tunnel constructed during Hezekiah's reign. **22:11** Jerusalem's leaders trust their military preparations rather than God's divine plan (cf. Isa. 22:8–11; 30:15–17; 31:1–3). **22:12–13** Instead of lamenting and repenting, Jerusalem's leaders fatalistically indulge in lavish feasts; cf.

"Let us eat and drink,
 for tomorrow we die."
[14] The LORD of hosts has revealed himself in
     my ears:
"Surely this iniquity will not be forgiven
     you until you die,"
 says the Lord GOD of hosts.

15 Thus says the Lord GOD of hosts: "Go
to the steward Shebna, who is master of
the household, and say to him: [16]What right
do you have here? Who are your relatives
here, that you have cut out a tomb here for
yourself, cutting a tomb[x] on the height and
carving a habitation for yourself[y] in the
rock? [17]The LORD is about to hurl you away
violently, my fellow. He will seize firm hold
on you, [18]whirl you round and round, and
throw you like a ball into a wide land; there
you shall die, and there your splendid chariots shall lie, O you disgrace to your master's
house! [19]I will thrust you from your office,
and you will be pulled down from your post.

20 "On that day I will call my servant
Eliakim son of Hilkiah [21]and will clothe him
with your robe and bind your sash on him. I
will commit your authority to his hand, and
he shall be a father to the inhabitants of Jerusalem and to the house of Judah. [22]I will
place on his shoulder the key of the house of
David; he shall open, and no one shall shut;
he shall shut, and no one shall open. [23]I will
fasten him like a peg in a secure place, and

he will become a throne of honor to his ancestral house. [24]And they will hang on him
the whole weight of his ancestral house, the
offspring and issue, every small vessel, from
the cups to all the flagons. [25]On that day, says
the LORD of hosts, the peg that was fastened
in a secure place will give way; it will be cut
down and fall, and the load that was on it will
perish, for the LORD has spoken."

23 The oracle concerning Tyre.

Wail, O ships of Tarshish,
 for your fortress is destroyed.[z]
When they came in from Cyprus
 they learned of it.
[2] Be still, O inhabitants of the coast,
 O merchants of Sidon;
your messengers crossed over the
 sea[a]
[3]   and were on the mighty waters;
your revenue[b] was the grain of Shihor,
 the harvest of the Nile;
 you were the merchant of the
 nations.
[4] Be ashamed, O Sidon, for the sea has
 spoken,
 the fortress of the sea, saying:

x 22.16 Gk Vg: Heb *his tomb*   y 22.16 Gk Vg: Heb
himself   z 23.1 Cn: Heb *for it is destroyed, without houses*
a 23.2 Q ms: MT *crossing over the sea, they replenished you*
b 23.3 Heb *its*

Isa. 5:11–12. *Let us eat and drink.* Cf. Luke 12:19; 1 Cor. 15:32. **22:14** Although the feasters probably meant "tomorrow we die" ironically, YHWH confirms that they will indeed *die.*

22:15–25 A denunciation of the royal official Shebna. **22:15** Despite the NRSVue's formatting, vv. 15–19 are poetry. *Master of the household.* Literally "over the palace," a high-ranking royal admin- istrative position. **22:16** *Who are your relatives?* Instead of a traditional family tomb, Shebna built an elaborate individual burial chamber like those of Egyptian royalty. A cluster of such tombs from the Iron Age has been excavated at Silwan in Jerusalem, including one with the inscription "master of the household." **22:18** As translated here, Shebna is threatened with exile and death in a foreign land, leaving his tomb empty (cf. Jer. 22:26). Alternatively, *whirl you round* could depict the unwrap- ping of Shebna's burial shroud, suggesting the desecration of his grave. In the world of the poem, either would be an appropriate punishment for his arrogant disregard for burial norms. **22:19** The word *office* could also mean "monument," a pun on Shebna's tomb. **22:20–21** In Isa. 36–37 (= 2 Kgs. 18–19), Eliakim has the title "over the palace" at the time of Sennacherib's invasion, while Shebna is simply called "scribe," indicating the fulfillment of this prediction. **22:22** Jesus alludes to this verse in his promise to Peter in Matt. 16:19. **22:24–25** A later update, cleverly reusing the *peg* metaphor from v. 23, suggesting that Eliakim eventually fell into disgrace through nepotism.

23:1–18 A poem depicting God's judgment against *Tyre,* a Phoenician city-state and seaport. The most likely setting is the widespread rebellion against Assyria in 705 BCE, in which Tyre participated along with Judah (see **"Sennacherib's Attack," p. 984**). **23:1** *Ships of Tarshish.* See note on 2:16. Tyre's destruction will devastate maritime trade. **23:2** *Sidon.* A neighboring Phoenician city-state. **23:3** *Shihor* is an unknown location or waterway in Egypt. As *merchant of the nations,* Tyre and Sidon benefited from trading international goods like Egyptian *grain.* **23:4** *Fortress of the sea.* Tyre,

"I have neither labored nor given birth;
  I have neither reared young men
    nor brought up young women."
5 When the report comes to Egypt,
  they will be in anguish over the report
    about Tyre.
6 Cross over to Tarshish—
  wail, O inhabitants of the coast!
7 Is this your exultant city
  whose origin is from days of old,
    whose feet carried her
      to settle far away?
8 Who has planned this
  against Tyre, the bestower of crowns,
    whose merchants were princes,
      whose traders were the honored of
        the earth?
9 The LORD of hosts has planned it—
  to defile the pride of all glory,
    to shame all the honored of the earth.
10 Cross over to your own land,
  O ships of^c Tarshish;
    this is a harbor^d no more.
11 He has stretched out his hand over the sea;
  he has shaken the kingdoms;
    the LORD has given command concerning
      Canaan,
        to destroy its fortresses.
12 He said:
"You will exult no longer,
  O oppressed virgin daughter Sidon;
    rise, cross over to Cyprus—
      even there you will have no rest."

13 Look at the land of the Chaldeans! This is the people; it was not Assyria. They destined it for wild animals.^{e} They erected their siege towers; they tore down her palaces; they made her a ruin.
14 Wail, O ships of Tarshish,
  for your fortress is destroyed.
15 From that day Tyre will be forgotten for seventy years, the lifetime of one king. At the end of seventy years, it will happen to Tyre as in the song about the prostitute:
16 Take a harp;
  go about the city,
    you forgotten prostitute!
Make sweet melody;
  sing many songs,
    that you may be remembered.
17 At the end of seventy years, the LORD will visit Tyre, and she will return to her trade and will prostitute herself with all the kingdoms of the world on the face of the earth. 18 Her merchandise and her wages will be dedicated to the LORD; her profits^f will not be stored or hoarded, but her merchandise will supply abundant food and fine clothing for those who live in the presence of the LORD.

24 Now the LORD is about to lay waste
  the earth and make it desolate,
    and he will twist its surface and
      scatter its inhabitants.

c 23.10 Cn Compare Gk: Heb *like the Nile, daughter* d 23.10 Cn: Heb *restraint* e 23.13 Or *This is the people that was not. Assyria founded it for its fleet.* f 23.18 Heb *it*

here personified as a childless woman (cf. Isa. 49:21; 54:1). **23:6** *Tarshish.* A distant Mediterranean port with which Tyre traded; its location is unknown. **23:7** *Settle far away* recalls Phoenicia's colonies throughout the Mediterranean. **23:9** Tyre's demise—resulting from its *pride*—is part of YHWH's plan for the earth (cf. 14:26–27). **23:11** *Over the sea.* A possible allusion to the myth of God's conflict with the sea (see note on 17:12). *Canaan* refers here to the region of Phoenicia; the same Hebrew word also means "trader" (cf. v. 8). **23:12** Like other conquered cities, *Sidon* is personified as an *oppressed virgin daughter* (cf. chap. 47). Following the Assyrian invasion of Phoenicia, the leaders of Tyre and Sidon fled to *Cyprus.* **23:13** This obscure verse may refer to Assyria's earlier defeat of Babylon (*land of the Chaldeans*), or it could be a later update reflecting Babylon's sixth-century BCE siege of Tyre. *Wild animals.* Cf. 13:21–22; 14:23; 34:11–15. **23:14** The repetition of the opening lines marks the original end of the poem. **23:15** A later addition predicting Tyre's restoration after *seventy years.* **23:16** An apparent quotation of a popular song of the time. **23:17** Tyre's profitable international trade is compared to prostitution. **23:18** The *profits* of Tyre's trade will support the community of YHWH worshipers in Jerusalem (cf. 18:7; 45:14; 60:5–18; 61:5–6).

24:1–23 Isaiah 24–27 concludes the prophecies against foreign nations. The chapters begin with a description of worldwide judgment, forming a bookend with 13:1–16, then celebrate God's victory over hostile forces and Zion's redemption. They were written after the time of the prophet Isaiah and allude to earlier material in the book, although scholars disagree about their exact date of composition. Some of the poetry may have originally marked the fall of a hostile empire like Assyria or Babylon, but the lack of specific historical references gives the chapters a more universal outlook, which encouraged later readers to interpret them eschatologically. **24:1** *Earth* (or "land") is

² And it shall be, as with the people, so
    with the priest;
as with the male slave, so with his
    master;
as with the female slave, so with her
    mistress;
as with the buyer, so with the seller;
as with the lender, so with the
    borrower;
as with the creditor, so with the debtor.
³ The earth shall be utterly laid waste and
    utterly despoiled,
    for the Lord has spoken this word.

⁴ The earth dries up and withers;
    the world languishes and withers;
    the heavens languish together with
        the earth.
⁵ The earth lies polluted
    under its inhabitants,
    for they have transgressed laws,
    violated the statutes,
    broken the everlasting covenant.
⁶ Therefore a curse devours the earth,
    and its inhabitants suffer for their guilt;
therefore the inhabitants of the earth
    dwindled,
    and few people are left.
⁷ The wine dries up;
    the vine languishes;
    all the merry-hearted sigh.
⁸ The mirth of the timbrels is stilled;
    the noise of the jubilant has ceased;
    the mirth of the lyre is stilled.

⁹ No longer do they drink wine with singing;
    strong drink is bitter to those who
    drink it.
¹⁰ The city of chaos is broken down;
    every house is shut up so that no one
    can enter.
¹¹ There is an outcry in the streets for lack
    of wine;
all joy has reached its eventide;
    the gladness of the earth is banished.
¹² Desolation is left in the city;
    the gates are battered into ruins.
¹³ For thus it shall be on the earth
    and among the nations,
as when an olive tree is beaten,
    as at the gleaning when the grape
    harvest is ended.

¹⁴ They lift up their voices; they sing for joy;
    they shout from the west over the
    majesty of the Lord.
¹⁵ Therefore in the east give glory to the
    Lord;
in the coastlands of the sea glorify the
    name of the Lord, the God of Israel.
¹⁶ From the ends of the earth we hear songs
    of praise,
    of glory to the Righteous One.

But I say, "I pine away;
    I pine away. Woe is me!
For the treacherous deal treacherously;
    the treacherous deal very
    treacherously."

repeated sixteen times in Isa. 24, marking the chapter's main theme. Soundplay is prominent in the poem, such as the similar sounds of *lay waste* ("boqeq") and *make it desolate* ("boleqah"). *Twist its surface* implies an earthquake, one of several forms of environmental destruction depicted in the chapter. **24:2** All socioeconomic classes of people will be affected by the destruction; cf. Hos. 4:9. **24:3** *Utterly laid waste* ("hibboq tibboq") and *utterly despoiled* ("hibboz tibboz") rhyme internally and externally. The spelling of the Hebrew words may have been artificially modified to achieve this effect. **24:4** Earthquake imagery gives way to drought imagery. *Dries up and withers* ("'abelah nabelah") is another example of rhyme, which is typically uncommon in biblical poetry. **24:5** Human wrongdoing is blamed for environmental disaster—a poignant insight in an era of anthropogenic climate change. For the idea that human action can pollute the land, cf. Num. 35:33; Ps. 106:38; Jer. 3:1–2. Given the chapter's universal outlook, *everlasting covenant* likely refers to the covenant "between God and every living creature of all flesh that is on the earth" at the time of Noah (Gen. 9:16). Elsewhere in Isaiah, the phrase refers to the Davidic covenant (55:3) or Abrahamic covenant (61:8). **24:7–9** Cf. Isa. 16:9–10; 32:10–13. **24:10** *City of chaos* is the first of several references in Isa. 24–27 to a destroyed city (25:2; 26:5; 27:10). Originally, it may have referred to Nineveh, Babylon, or perhaps the Assyrian fortress in Judah at Ramat Rahel. The lack of specific details enables it to function as an archetype of a hostile empire in these chapters. *Chaos* ("tohu") refers to primeval disorder prior to creation in Gen. 1:2 (cf. Isa. 45:18). **24:13** Cf. 17:5–6. **24:14–15** The imagery of judgment abruptly gives way to a description of worldwide praise, anticipating God's victory over evil in vv. 21–23. **24:16** By contrast, the prophetic speaker expresses dismay at the ongoing threat of evildoers.

¹⁷ Terror, the pit, and the snare
 are upon you, O inhabitants of the earth!
¹⁸ Whoever flees at the sound of the terror
 shall fall into the pit,
and whoever climbs out of the pit
 shall be caught in the snare.
For the windows of heaven are opened,
 and the foundations of the earth tremble.
¹⁹ The earth is utterly broken;
 the earth is torn apart;
 the earth is violently shaken.
²⁰ The earth staggers like a drunkard;
 it sways like a hut;
its transgression lies heavy upon it,
 and it falls and will not rise again.

²¹ On that day the Lord will punish
 the host of heaven in heaven
 and on earth the kings of the earth.
²² They will be gathered together
 like prisoners in a pit;
they will be shut up in a prison,
 and after many days they will be
 punished.
²³ Then the moon will be abashed
 and the sun ashamed,
for the Lord of hosts will reign
 on Mount Zion and in Jerusalem,
and before his elders he will be glorified.

25 O Lord, you are my God;
 I will exalt you; I will praise your
 name,

for you have done wonderful things,
 plans formed of old, faithful and sure.
² For you have made the city a heap,
 the fortified city a ruin;
the palace of foreigners is a city no
 more;
 it will never be rebuilt.
³ Therefore strong peoples will glorify
 you;
 cities of ruthless nations will fear you.
⁴ For you have been a refuge to the
 poor,
 a refuge to the needy in their distress,
 a shelter from the rainstorm and a
 shade from the heat.
When the blast of the ruthless was like a
 winter rainstorm,
⁵ the noise of foreigners like heat in a
 dry place,
you subdued the heat with the shade of
 clouds;
 the song of the ruthless was stilled.

⁶ On this mountain the Lord of hosts will
 make for all peoples
 a feast of rich food, a feast of
 well-aged wines,
 of rich food filled with marrow, of
 well-aged wines strained clear.
⁷ And he will destroy on this mountain
 the shroud that is cast over all
 peoples,

Woe is me! Cf. 6:5. V. 16b consists of five different forms of the Hebrew root meaning "treachery" ("bagad"); cf. 21:2 (where it is translated as "betrayer"); 33:1. **24:17** *Terror, pit,* and *snare* are an alliterative triad ("pachad," "pachat," "pach"); cf. Jer. 48:43. **24:18** Even if someone eludes one or two threats, they will not escape the third (cf. Amos 5:19). *Windows of heaven are opened* is flood imagery (cf. Gen. 7:11); together with *foundations of the earth tremble*, it suggests the undoing of creation itself. **24:19** *Utterly broken* ("ro'ah hitro'a'ah"), *torn apart* ("por hitporerah"), and *violently shaken* ("mot hitmotetah") rhyme in Hebrew. **24:20** *Staggers like a drunkard.* A frequent image in Isaiah (19:14; 28:7; 51:17). *Falls and will not rise again.* Cf. Amos 5:2. **24:21** *Host of heaven.* Stars and constellations, which were objects of worship by foreign nations. **24:22** This text may have influenced the idea of Satan's thousand-year imprisonment in Rev. 20:1–3. **24:23** The *moon* and *sun* would have been punished with the host of heaven. YHWH's kingship, with *Zion* as the capital, is an important theme in Isaiah (cf. 6:1, 5; 33:22; 41:21; 44:6).
 25:1–10a A poem celebrating God's defeat of evil. **25:1** *Plans formed of old.* Cf. 22:11; 37:26. The pairing of *wonderful things* and *plans* recalls 9:6 and 28:29, where the same word for "plan" is translated, respectively, as "Counselor" and "counsel." **25:2–3** See note on 24:10. The destruction of the *palace of foreigners* leads other *cities of ruthless nations* to acknowledge God's rule. **25:5** The silencing of the *song of the ruthless* contrasts with the songs of God's worshipers in 24:14–15; 26:1. **25:6** The repetition of *all* throughout vv. 6–8 emphasizes the universality of God's actions. *This mountain.* Zion (cf. 24:23). The *feast* for *all peoples* celebrates God's worldwide rule, modeled after a royal victory banquet. This verse inspired the idea of a heavenly banquet at the end of time (Matt. 8:11; Luke 13:29; Rev. 19:9), which in turn influenced Christian eucharistic liturgy. The abundance of *well-aged wines* contrasts with the absence of wine in 24:7–11. **25:7** *Shroud* and *covering* refer to

the covering that is spread over all
nations;
8 he will swallow up death forever.
Then the Lord God will wipe away the
tears from all faces,
and the disgrace of his people he will
take away from all the earth,
for the Lord has spoken.
9 It will be said on that day,
"See, this is our God; we have waited
for him, so that he might save us.
This is the Lord for whom we have
waited;
let us be glad and rejoice in his salvation."
10 For the hand of the Lord will rest on this
mountain.

The Moabites shall be trodden down in
their place
as straw is trodden down in the
manure.
11 Though they spread out their hands in
the midst of it,
as swimmers spread out their hands
to swim,
their pride will be laid low despite the
struggle^g of their hands.
12 The high fortifications of his walls will
be brought down,
laid low, cast to the ground, even to
the dust.

26 On that day this song will be sung in
the land of Judah:
We have a strong city;
he sets up walls and bulwarks as a
safeguard.
2 Open the gates,
so that the righteous nation that
maintains faithfulness
may enter in.
3 Those of steadfast mind you keep in
peace,
in peace because they trust in you.
4 Trust in the Lord forever,
for in the Lord God^h
you have an everlasting rock.
5 For he has brought low
the inhabitants of the height;
the lofty city he lays low.
He lays it low to the ground,
casts it to the dust.
6 The foot tramples it,
the feet of the poor,
the steps of the needy.

7 The way of the righteous is level;
straight is the path of the righteous
that you clear.
8 In the path of your judgments,
O Lord, we have placed hope;

g 25.11 Meaning of Heb uncertain h 26.4 Heb in Yah, the
Lord

burial garments. **25:8** This verse recalls an ancient Ugaritic myth about the conflict between Baal,
the divine king, and the god *death*. The New Testament cites this verse as a prophecy of the resurrection of the dead (1 Cor. 15:54; Rev. 7:17; 21:4). *Swallow.* A reversal of the frequent depiction of
death as the swallower of living things in ancient mythology (cf. Isa. 5:14; Hab. 2:5). *Disgrace of his
people.* Israel and Judah's submission to world empires. **25:9** *Waited.* Cf. Isa. 33:2; 40:31. **25:10a** In
much of Isaiah, the divine *hand* is an image of judgment, but here it symbolizes protection.

25:10b–12 An announcement of judgment against Moab (see note on 15:1–16:14), which may come
from a different prophecy. Although it is unclear why Moab is singled out, these verses add specificity to the otherwise generalized portrayal of enemy nations in Isa. 24–27. The attitude toward Moab
seems much harsher than in chaps. 15–16. **25:10b–11** A revolting image of the Moabites flailing like
swimmers in *manure.* For the association of Moab with *pride*, cf. 16:6. **25:12** Moab's cities will be
destroyed just like the unnamed city in v. 2.

26:1–8 A poem celebrating Jerusalem's restoration. It may have originally followed the depiction
of God's victory feast in the previous chapter, before the insertion of the anti-Moabite prophecy.
26:1 *Strong city.* Jerusalem, whose fate contrasts with that of the enemy city. Despite the triumphal
tone, the need for military fortifications suggests an ongoing threat. **26:2** A call to *open* Jerusalem's
gates for the entrance of God's people (cf. Pss. 24:7–10; 118:19–20). **26:4** *Rock.* A common title for
God in Isaiah (17:10; 30:29; 44:8). **26:5** The destruction of the enemy city (cf. 24:10; 25:2; 27:10). *Low
to the ground* and *dust* anticipate the fate from which Jerusalem is rescued in 29:4–8. **26:6** The city
is destroyed by the *poor* and *needy*, who suffered the most from its oppression. **26:7** A *level* way
and a *straight* path are both metaphors for *righteous* conduct and the reward for such conduct while
also evoking the frequent Isaianic image of a processional highway (35:8; 40:3; 62:10). **26:8** *Placed
hope* is the same verb translated as "waited" in 25:9.

your name and your renown
are the soul's desire.
⁹ My soul yearns for you in the night;
my spirit within me earnestly seeks you.
For when your judgments are in the
earth,
the inhabitants of the world learn
righteousness.
¹⁰ If favor is shown to the wicked,
they do not learn righteousness;
they corrupt what is upright on the earth
and do not see the majesty of the Lord.
¹¹ O Lord, your hand is lifted up,
but they do not see it.
Let them see your zeal for your people
and be ashamed.
Let the fire for your adversaries
consume them.
¹² O Lord, may you ordain peace for us,
for indeed, all that we have done, you
have done for us.
¹³ O Lord our God,
other lords besides you have ruled
over us,
but we acknowledge your name alone.
¹⁴ The dead do not live;
shades do not rise
because you have punished and
destroyed them
and wiped out all memory of them.
¹⁵ But you have increased the nation, O Lord;
you have increased the nation; you are
glorified;
you have enlarged all the borders of
the land.

¹⁶ O Lord, in distress they sought you;
they poured out a prayer*ⁱ*
when your chastening was on
them.
¹⁷ Like a woman with child
about to give birth
writhes and cries out in her pain,
so were we because of you, O Lord;
¹⁸ we were with child; we writhed,
but we gave birth only to wind.
We have won no victories on earth,
and no one is born to inhabit the
world.
¹⁹ Your dead shall live; their corpses*ʲ* shall
rise.
Those who dwell in the dust will
awake and shout for joy!*ᵏ*
For your dew is a radiant dew,
and the earth will give birth to those
long dead.*ˡ*

²⁰ Come, my people, enter your
chambers,
and shut your doors behind you;
hide yourselves for a little while
until the wrath is past.
²¹ For the Lord comes out from his place
to punish the inhabitants of the earth
for their iniquity;
the earth will disclose the blood shed
on it
and will no longer cover its slain.

i 26.16 Meaning of Heb uncertain   *j* 26.19 Cn Compare
Syr Tg: Heb *my corpse*   *k* 26.19 Q ms Compare Gk Syr: MT
dust, awake and shout for joy!   *l* 26.19 Heb *to the shades*

26:9–21 A poetic lament over the ongoing threat of evil, followed by a promise of restoration. It presupposes the defeat of some imperial powers, but the worldwide divine victory of 24:21–23 and 25:6–9 has not yet happened. **26:9** A change in speakers (*we* vs. *I*) marks the beginning of the poem. **26:10–11** Because God's *hand* of judgment is not visible, wickedness persists (cf. 57:11; 64:7). **26:12** In contrast to their prior trust in military strength or idols, the people acknowledge their reliance on God. **26:13** *Other lords.* Imperial oppressors and their deities. **26:14** Denial of an afterlife is common in the Hebrew Bible (Ps. 49:10–11; Job 14:10–12; Isa. 38:18), but this verse specifically refers to defeated oppressors. *Shades.* See note on 14:9. **26:15** *Enlarged all the borders.* The restoration of previously conquered territory. **26:16** The speaker recalls the people's past sufferings, which were punishments from God. **26:18** *Gave birth only to wind.* A powerful metaphor for futility. **26:19** God's response to the prayer for vindication. The resurrection imagery is a metaphor for national restoration (cf. Ezek. 37:11–14), but later interpreters associated it with the eschatological resurrection of individuals (cf. Dan. 12:2). The fate of Judah's dead contrasts with that of its enemies' dead in v. 14. *Give birth to those long dead* reverses the futility metaphor in vv. 17–18. **26:20** God's defeat of evil is imminent (*a little while*), but in the meantime, God's people should *hide* in safety. **26:21** *Disclose the blood shed on it* recalls the image of Abel's blood crying from the ground in Gen. 4:10. *No longer cover its slain.* The bodies of victims of oppression will be uncovered, perhaps in association with the resurrection imagery in v. 19. Discoveries of mass graves can reveal forgotten or suppressed atrocities, such as the abuse of Native American children in boarding schools in the United States and Canada, to name one contemporary example.

27 On that day the LORD with his cruel and great and strong sword will punish Leviathan the fleeing serpent, Leviathan the twisting serpent, and he will kill the dragon that is in the sea.

² On that day:
A pleasant vineyard—sing about it!
³   I, the LORD, am its keeper;
    every moment I water it.
I guard it night and day
    so that no one can harm it;
⁴   I have no wrath.
If it gives me thorns and briers,
    I will march to battle against it.
    I will burn it up.
⁵ Or else let it cling to me for protection;
    let it make peace with me;
    let it make peace with me.

⁶ In days to come*ᵐ* Jacob shall take root;
    Israel shall blossom and put forth
        shoots
    and fill the whole world with fruit.

⁷ Has he struck them down as he struck
        down those who struck them?
    Or have they been killed as their
        killers*ⁿ* were killed?
⁸ By expulsion,*ᵒ* by exile you struggled
        against them;
    with his fierce blast he removed them
        in the day of the east wind.
⁹ Therefore by this the guilt of Jacob will
    be expiated,

and this will be the full fruit of the
    removal of his sin:
when he makes all the stones of the
    altars
    like chalkstones crushed to pieces;
    no sacred poles*ᵖ* or incense altars will
        remain standing.
¹⁰ For the fortified city is solitary,
    a habitation deserted and forsaken,
        like the wilderness;
the calves graze there;
    there they lie down and strip its
        branches.
¹¹ When its boughs are dry, they are
        broken;
    women come and make a fire of
        them.
For this is a people without
        understanding;
    therefore he who made them will not
        have compassion on them;
    he who formed them will show them
        no favor.

12 On that day the LORD will thresh from the channel of the Euphrates to the Wadi of Egypt, and you will be gathered one by one, O people of Israel. ¹³And on that day a great trumpet will be blown, and those who were lost in the land of Assyria and those who were driven out to the land of Egypt will come and worship the LORD on the holy mountain at Jerusalem.

m 27.6 Heb *Those to come*   *n* 27.7 Q ms: MT *his slain ones*
o 27.8 Meaning of Heb uncertain   *p* 27.9 Heb *Asherahs*

27:1–13 A series of prose and poetic appendices to chaps. 24–26, introduced by *on that day*. **27:1** *Leviathan*. A mythical sea monster representing primordial chaos. Although God defeated Leviathan at creation (Ps. 74:14), the ongoing threat of evil means God must defeat it again. *Fleeing serpent, twisting serpent*, and *dragon* are traditional descriptions of Leviathan, attested in prebiblical Ugaritic myths. **27:2–3** A reversal of the song of the vineyard in Isa. 5:1–7. There, God destroyed the vineyard for its failed harvest, a symbol of social injustice in Israel and Judah. Now, God promises to *guard* the vineyard against all threats. **27:4–5** *Thorns and briers.* Cf. 5:6. Although the vineyard may be destroyed again, it has another chance to *make peace* with God. **27:6** A promise of the vineyard's flourishing. It is unclear whether *Jacob/Israel* here refers to the northern kingdom, as in much of chaps. 1–39, or to Judah and its exiles, as in chaps. 40–48. **27:7** A pair of rhetorical questions implying that God's people were not punished as severely as their oppressors. *Struck* refers to Assyrian oppression in 10:20; 14:6. **27:8–9** *Exile* was God's means of removing Jacob's *guilt*, which was incurred through illicit worship practices. **27:10** The depopulated enemy city will revert to a state of nature (cf. 17:2; 13:21–22; 23:13; etc.). **27:11** Although God's disregard for enemy nations seems harsh, withholding *favor* may encourage changed behavior, according to 26:9–10. **27:12** *Thresh* compares God's repatriation of Israelite and Judean exiles from foreign nations to the removal of grain from its husk. *Euphrates . . . Egypt* recalls the extent of the land promised to Abraham (Gen. 15:18) and Solomon's legendary realm (1 Kgs. 4:21). **27:13** Cf. Isa. 11:11–12. God's *holy mountain* is likewise the destination of returning exiles in 66:20.

28

Woe to the proud garland of the
drunkards of Ephraim
and the fading flower of its glorious
beauty,
at the head of the fertile valley,
those overcome with wine!
2 See, the Lord has one who is mighty and
strong,
like a storm of hail, a destroying
tempest,
like a storm of mighty, overflowing waters;
with force he will hurl them down to
the earth.
3 Trampled under foot will be
the proud garland of the drunkards of
Ephraim.
4 And the fading flower of its glorious
beauty,
at the head of the fertile valley,
will be like a first-ripe fig before the
summer;
whoever sees it eats it up
as soon as it comes to hand.

5 On that day the LORD of hosts will be a
garland of glory
and a diadem of beauty to the
remnant of his people
6 and a spirit of justice to the one who sits
in judgment
and strength to those who turn back
the battle at the gate.

7 These also reel with wine
and stagger with strong drink;
the priest and the prophet reel with
strong drink;

they are confused with wine;
they stagger with strong drink;
they err in vision;
they stumble in giving judgment.
8 All tables are covered with filthy
vomit;
no place is clean.

9 "Whom will he teach knowledge,
and to whom will he explain the
message?
Those who are weaned from milk,
those taken from the breast?
10 For it is precept upon precept, precept
upon precept,
line upon line, line upon line,
here a little, there a little."q

11 Truly, with stammering lip
and with another tongue
he will speak to this people,
12 to whom he has said,
"This is rest;
give rest to the weary,
and this is repose,"
yet they would not hear.
13 Therefore the word of the LORD will be to
them,
"Precept upon precept, precept upon
precept,
line upon line, line upon line,
here a little, there a little,"r
in order that they may go and fall
backward
and be broken and snared and taken.

q 28.10 Meaning of Heb of this verse uncertain
r 28.13 Meaning of Heb of this verse uncertain

28:1–6 Isaiah 28 opens a series of chapters beginning with *woe* (28:1; 29:1; 30:1; 31:1; 33:1). The poem in 28:1–6 announces God's judgment against the northern kingdom of Israel, either during the Syro-Ephraimite conflict in 735–732 BCE (see note on 7:1) or during Assyria's conquest of Samaria in 722–720 BCE. **28:1** *Garland* can also be translated as "crown" and likely refers by metonymy to the king of Israel (*Ephraim*). *Fading flower.* An image of transience (cf. 40:8), foreshadowing Israel's demise. **28:2** *One who is mighty.* God's agent for judging Israel, likely Assyria. *Overflowing waters.* Similar language refers to Assyrian invasions in 8:7–8 and 28:17. **28:4** *First-ripe fig.* A metaphor for Israel's judgment, which will be immediate and total. **28:5–6** YHWH is the people's true *glory*, not the king.

28:7–22 A poem announcing God's judgment against Judah during their rebellion against Assyria in 704–701 BCE (see **"Sennacherib's Attack," p. 984**). **28:7** Extending the imagery from vv. 1 and 3, Judah's religious authorities are *also* drunkards. **28:8** The aftermath of a drunken party (cf. 5:11–12). **28:9–10** A putative quotation of Isaiah's opponents, who dismiss his *message*. The Hebrew words translated as *precept upon precept* and *line upon line* are nonsense syllables ("tsaw letsaw," "qaw leqaw"), likely an approximation of baby talk, mocking Isaiah's prophecy. They also sound like the words for "filthy" and "vomit" in v. 8. **28:11–13** YHWH will speak to *this people* with the foreign language (*another tongue*) of their invaders, represented by the same nonsense syllables they used to

¹⁴ Therefore hear the word of the LORD, you
    scoffers
  who rule this people in Jerusalem.
¹⁵ Because you have said, "We have made a
    covenant with death,
  and with Sheol we have an agreement;
when the overwhelming scourge passes
    through
  it will not come to us,
for we have made lies our refuge,
  and in falsehood we have taken shelter";
¹⁶ therefore thus says the Lord GOD,
"See, I am laying* in Zion a foundation
    stone,
  a tested stone,
a precious cornerstone, a sure
    foundation:
  'One who trusts will not panic.'
¹⁷ And I will make justice the line
  and righteousness the plummet;
hail will sweep away the refuge of lies,
  and waters will overwhelm the shelter.
¹⁸ Then your covenant with death will be
    annulled,
  and your agreement with Sheol will
    not stand;
when the overwhelming scourge passes
    through,
  you will be beaten down by it.
¹⁹ As often as it passes through, it will take
    you,
  for morning by morning it will pass
    through,
  by day and by night,
and it will be sheer terror to understand
    the message."
²⁰ For the bed is too short to stretch oneself
    on it,
  and the covering is too narrow to
    wrap oneself in it.

²¹ For the LORD will rise up as on Mount
    Perazim;
  he will rage as in the valley of Gibeon
to do his deed—strange is his deed!—
  and to work his work—alien is his work!
²² Now therefore do not scoff,
  or your bonds will be made stronger,
for I have heard a decree of destruction
  from the Lord GOD of hosts upon the
    whole land.

²³ Listen and hear my voice;
  Pay attention and hear my speech.
²⁴ Do those who plow for sowing plow
    continually?
  Do they continually open and harrow
    their ground?
²⁵ When they have leveled its surface,
  do they not scatter dill, sow cumin,
and plant wheat in rows
  and barley in its proper place*
  and spelt as the border?
²⁶ For they are well instructed;
  their God teaches them.

²⁷ For dill is not threshed with a threshing
    sledge,
  nor is a cart wheel rolled over cumin,
but dill is beaten out with a stick
  and cumin with a rod.
²⁸ Grain is crushed for bread,
  but one does not thresh it forever;
one drives the cart wheel and horses
    over it
  but does not pulverize it.
²⁹ This also comes from the LORD of hosts;
  he is wonderful in counsel
  and excellent in wisdom.

s 28.16 Q mss Compare Syr Tg: MT *he laid* *t* 28.25 Meaning of Heb uncertain

mock Isaiah's speech. **28:14** *Rule* sounds like another verb meaning "make a riddle," reinforcing the charge that Jerusalem's leaders are *scoffers*. **28:15** *Covenant.* Judah's treaty with Egypt, intended to protect them from Assyria (*the overwhelming scourge*) but which Isaiah thinks will lead to their *death.* The Hebrew word *death* sounds like the name of the Egyptian goddess Mut, who may have been invoked in making the treaty. **28:16–17** In contrast to the failed policies of Jerusalem's current leaders, YHWH will establish *a sure foundation* in *Zion* based on *justice* and *righteousness.* **28:17–19** Judah will be devastated by the Assyrian invasion that it sought to forestall. **28:21** *Mount Perazim* and *Gibeon* were sites of victorious battles by King David (2 Sam. 5:20; 1 Chr. 14:11). This time, however, YHWH will *rise up* against his own people, an action that seems *strange* and *alien.*

    28:23–29 A poem describing a farmer's wisdom, which is attributed to divine instruction. **28:24–28** The farmer knows the appropriate methods for planting, harvesting, and processing a variety of crops. Because harvesting is a metaphor for judgment elsewhere in Isaiah, these verses suggest that God's threatened judgment against Judah is likewise measured and just. **28:29** *Wonderful in counsel.* Cf. 9:6. The word translated as *counsel* is the same word used elsewhere for YHWH's "plan."

29

Woe to Ariel, Ariel,
the city where David encamped!
Add year to year;
let the festivals run their round.
2 Yet I will oppress Ariel,
and there shall be moaning and
lamentation,
and you[u] shall be to me like an Ariel.[v]
3 And like David[w] I will encamp against
you;
I will besiege you with towers
and raise siegeworks against you.
4 Then deep from the earth you shall speak;
from low in the dust your words shall
come;
your voice shall come from the ground
like the voice of a ghost,
and your speech shall whisper out of
the dust.

5 But the multitude of your arrogant ones[x]
shall be like fine dust
and the multitude of tyrants like
flying chaff.
And in an instant, suddenly,
6   you will be visited by the LORD of hosts
with thunder and earthquake and great
noise,
with whirlwind and tempest and the
flame of a devouring fire.
7 And the multitude of all the nations that
fight against Ariel,
all that fight against her and her
stronghold and who distress her,
shall be like a dream, a vision of the
night.
8 Just as when a hungry person dreams of
eating
and wakes up still hungry
or a thirsty person dreams of drinking
and wakes up faint, still thirsty,

so shall the multitude of all the nations be
that fight against Mount Zion.

9 Be astounded and stunned;
blind yourselves and be blind!
Be drunk but not from wine;
stagger but not from strong drink!
10 For the LORD has poured out upon you
a spirit of deep sleep;
he has closed your eyes (the prophets)
and covered your heads (the seers).

11 The vision of all this has become for you
like the words of a sealed document. If it is
given to those who can read with the command, "Read this," they say, "We cannot, for
it is sealed." 12And if it is given to those who
cannot read, saying, "Read this," they say,
"We cannot read."

13 The Lord said:
Because these people draw near with
their mouths
and honor me with their lips,
while their hearts are far from me
and their worship of me is a human
commandment learned by rote,
14 so I will again do
amazing things with this people,
shocking and amazing.
The wisdom of their wise shall perish,
and the discernment of the discerning
shall be hidden.

15 Woe to those who hide a plan too deep
for the LORD,
whose deeds are in the dark,
and who say, "Who sees us? Who
knows us?"

u 29.2 Cn Compare Q ms: MT *she*   v 29.2 That is, *altar hearth*   w 29.3 Heb mss Gk: MT *like a circle*   x 29.5 Q ms Compare Gk: MT *strangers*

29:1–8 In this poem, YHWH both initiates and repulses an attack against Jerusalem, likely during the Assyrian invasion in 701 BCE (see **"Sennacherib's Attack," p. 984**). **29:1** *Ariel*. Another name for Jerusalem. It means "lion of God" but sounds similar to "city of God" or "mountain of God." **29:2** *Ariel* also means "altar hearth" (cf. Ezek. 43:15–16), suggesting that Jerusalem will be burned to rubble. **29:3** The poem compares God's attack on Jerusalem to David's capture of the city (2 Sam. 5:6–9). **29:4** Jerusalem is brought to the brink of death. *Voice of a ghost*. Cf. 8:19. **29:5–8** It is ini-tially uncertain whether v. 5 describes Jerusalem or its invaders. By v. 7, however, YHWH has clearly turned against the invaders, whose threat proves as ephemeral as *a dream*.
   29:9–16 A poem threatening the cessation of prophetic visions, possibly to discredit rival proph-ets. **29:10** Instead of sending the divine spirit to inspire prophecy, God sends *a spirit of deep sleep* to prevent prophecy. *Closed your eyes*. See **"Isaiah and Disability," p. 974**. **29:11–12** Two scenarios in which someone cannot read a scroll, illustrating the failure of the prophets. **29:15** *Hide a plan*. Presumably Judah's alliance with Egypt and rebellion against Assyria, which contradict the divine

Making Connections: Isaiah and Disability (Isaiah 29)

References to disability appear throughout Isaiah. They usually function symbolically, without necessarily reflecting the experiences of disabled persons. Throughout chaps. 1–39, a lack of sight and hearing functions as a metaphor for failed divine-human communication (6:9–10; 29:9–10). By contrast, typical sensory perception signals restored divine-human communication in 32:3, likely a direct reversal of 6:9–10. In 29:18, 32:4, and 35:5–6, the removal of disability further symbolizes divine restoration, parallel to the common motif of the fructification of barren landscapes. These texts from Isaiah likely influenced stories of Jesus's healings of disabled persons in the New Testament Gospels. Although other prophetic texts use similar disability imagery, only Isaiah explicitly depicts its healing. This reflects the book's association of return from exile with idealized bodies (cf. 40:31; 65:20; 66:7–8). Thus, in 35:6, lame bodies do not simply enjoy restored mobility; they gain the capacity to "leap like a deer."

Chaps. 40–66 also use disability language. Isaiah 42:7 combines blindness and imprisonment as symbols for exile, and v. 16 associates blindness with the wilderness highway motif (cf. Jer. 31:8–9). Isaiah 42:18 and 43:8 address the audience as "blind" and "deaf" while ironically acknowledging their able-bodiedness. In 42:19–20, YHWH's servant is "blind" and "deaf" (cf. 50:10). The fourth servant song uses language associated with disability elsewhere in the Hebrew Bible (52:14; 53:2–4, 7–9). In 59:10, the people complain that rampant injustice has forced them to "grope like the blind along a wall," emphasizing the effect of sightlessness on mobility (cf. Deut. 28:29; Zeph. 1:17).

Many of these texts reinforce the cultural stigmatization of disability, and depictions of healing imply that disabled persons have no place in a divinely restored world. Other texts, however, imagine disability as a neutral condition requiring accommodations rather than an inherent bodily flaw. Isaiah 3 (vv. 1, 8) portrays the nation of Judah as a lame person, whose faulty metaphorical crutch is its leaders. In 33:23, lame men join other warriors in dividing military plunder. Isaiah 56:4–5 offers a word of comfort to eunuchs, a class of people considered disabled in the ancient world, guaranteeing them access to the temple and compensation for their lack of children. Such portrayals are more consistent with contemporary models of disability that emphasize the interaction between bodies and their environments.

J. Blake Couey

¹⁶ You turn things upside down!
    Shall the potter be regarded as the
        clay?
Shall the thing made say of its maker,
    "He did not make me,"
or the thing formed say of the one who
        formed it,
    "He has no understanding"?
¹⁷ Shall not Lebanon in a very little while
    become a fruitful field
and the fruitful field be regarded as a
        forest?
¹⁸ On that day the deaf shall hear
    the words of a scroll,
and freed from gloom and darkness
    the eyes of the blind shall see.

¹⁹ The meek shall obtain fresh joy in the Lord,
    and the neediest people shall exult in
        the Holy One of Israel.
²⁰ For the tyrant shall be no more,
    and the scoffer shall cease to be;
all those alert to do evil shall be cut
        off—
²¹ those who cause a person to lose a
    lawsuit,
who set a trap for the arbiter in the gate
and undermine justice for the one in
       the right.

22 Therefore thus says the Lord, who redeemed Abraham, concerning the house of Jacob:

plan (cf. 22:11; 30:1). **29:16** *Potter* and *clay* symbolize the divine-human relationship, which Judah's leaders have transgressed (cf. 45:9).

29:17–24 A poem describing a reversal of fortunes for God's people, following the Assyrian and Babylonian invasions. **29:17** *Lebanon.* A region of Phoenicia famous for its cedars (2:13; 10:34; etc.). Its transformed landscape is a metaphor for Israel and Judah's restoration. **29:18** The healing of the *deaf* and *blind* is another image of national renewal; see **"Isaiah and Disability," p. 974**. The phrase *words of a scroll* connects this poem to the preceding one (vv. 11–12). **29:20–21** The city *gate* was a site for settling legal disputes. **29:22** Other allusions to *Abraham* appear in the exilic and postexilic

"No longer shall Jacob be ashamed;
    no longer shall his face grow pale.
²³ For when he sees his children,
    the work of my hands, in his midst,
    they will sanctify my name;
they will sanctify the Holy One of Jacob
    and will stand in awe of the God of
    Israel.
²⁴ And those who err in spirit will come to
    understanding,
    and those who grumble will accept
    instruction."

30 Woe to the rebellious children, says
    the Lord,
who carry out a plan but not mine;
who make an alliance but against my will,
    adding sin to sin;
² who set out to go down to Egypt
    without asking for my counsel,
to take refuge in the protection of
    Pharaoh
and to seek shelter in the shadow of
    Egypt.
³ Therefore the protection of Pharaoh
    shall become your shame,
    and the shelter in the shadow of Egypt
    your humiliation.
⁴ For though his officials are at Zoan
    and his envoys reach Hanes,
⁵ everyone comes to shame
    through a people that cannot profit
    them,
that brings neither help nor profit,
    only shame and disgrace.

6 An oracle concerning the animals of the
Negeb.
Through a land of trouble and distress,
    of lioness and roaring^y lion,
    of viper and flying serpent,
they carry their riches on the backs of
    donkeys
    and their treasures on the humps of
    camels
    to a people that cannot profit them.
⁷ For Egypt's help is worthless and empty;
    therefore I have called her,
    "Rahab who sits still."^z
⁸ Go now, write it before them on a tablet,
    and inscribe it on a scroll,
so that it may be for the time to come
    as a witness forever.
⁹ For they are a rebellious people,
    faithless children,
children who will not hear
    the instruction of the Lord;
¹⁰ who say to the seers, "Do not see,"
    and to the prophets, "Do not prophesy
    to us what is right;
speak to us smooth things;
    prophesy illusions;
¹¹ leave the way; turn aside from the path;
    let us hear no more about the Holy
    One of Israel."
¹² Therefore thus says the Holy One of
    Israel:
Because you reject this word

y 30.6 Cn: Heb *from them* *z* 30.7 Meaning of Heb uncertain

sections of Isaiah (41:8; 51:2; 63:16). *House of Jacob.* See note on 2:5–6. **29:23** *Children* may refer to returning exiles (cf. 49:21–23; 54:1; 60:4). *Holy One of Jacob.* A variant of the more common "Holy One of Israel."

30:1–7 A poem denouncing Judah's alliance with Egypt during its rebellion against Assyria (see **"Sennacherib's Attack," p. 984**). **30:1** Tension between YHWH's *plan* and human plans is a major theme in Isa. 1–39 (cf. 14:26–27; 19:3; 22:11; 29:15). **30:2** The words *protection* (or "refuge"), *shelter*, and *shadow* (or "shade") are elsewhere used of God (cf. 25:4), suggesting that Judah's reliance on *Pharaoh* and *Egypt* is idolatrous. **30:4** *Zoan* and *Hanes* were cities near Egypt's border with Judah, where Egyptian *officials* and *envoys* went to negotiate the alliance. **30:6** *Oracle* also means "burden," anticipating the references to pack animals later in the verse. *Negeb.* The desert between Judah and Egypt (cf. 21:1), through which Judean envoys travel with *treasures* to secure Egypt's military support. *Flying serpent.* Cf. 14:29. **30:7** *Rahab.* A dangerous sea monster (Job 26:12; Ps. 89:10; Isa. 51:9), also associated with Egypt in Ps. 87:4; cf. Ezek. 29:3; 32:2. (It has no connection to the character Rahab in Josh. 2, 6; the two names are spelled differently in Heb.) Despite its fearsome reputation, Egypt will prove *worthless* to Judah as an ally, so the poem sarcastically renames it *Rahab who sits still.*

30:8–17 A poem criticizing the people's rejection of God's word. **30:8** Because Isaiah's contemporaries will not listen, he should *write* down his message for a future generation. Along with 8:16, this text functions as an origin account for the book of Isaiah. **30:10–11** A quotation attributed to the people expressing their disregard for prophecy. **30:12–13** The rejection of God's *word* will prove

and put your trust in oppression and
deceit
and rely on them,
[13] therefore this iniquity shall become for
you
like a break in a high wall, bulging out
and about to collapse,
whose crash comes suddenly, in an
instant;
[14] its breaking is like that of a potter's vessel
that is smashed so ruthlessly
that among its fragments not a sherd is
found
for taking fire from the hearth
or dipping water out of the cistern.

[15] For thus said the Lord God, the Holy One
of Israel:
In returning and rest you shall be saved;
in quietness and in trust shall be your
strength.
But you refused [16]and said,
"No! We will flee upon horses"—
therefore you shall flee!
and, "We will ride upon swift steeds"—
therefore your pursuers shall be swift!
[17] A thousand shall flee at the threat of one;
at the threat of five you shall flee
until you are left
like a flagstaff on the top of a
mountain,
like a signal on a hill.
[18] Therefore the Lord waits to be gracious
to you;
therefore he will rise up to show
mercy to you.
For the Lord is a God of justice;
blessed are all those who wait for him.

[19] O people in Zion, inhabitants of Jerusalem, you shall weep no more. He will surely be gracious to you at the sound of your cry; when he hears it, he will answer you. [20]Though the Lord may give you the bread of adversity and the water of affliction, yet your Teacher will not hide himself any longer, but your eyes shall see your Teacher. [21]And when you turn to the right or when you turn to the left, your ears shall hear a word behind you, saying, "This is the way; walk in it." [22]Then you will defile your silver-covered idols and your gold-plated images. You will scatter them like impure things; you will say to them, "Away with you!"

[23] He will give rain for the seed with which you sow the ground, and grain, the produce of the ground, will be rich and plenteous. On that day your cattle will graze in broad pastures, [24]and the oxen and donkeys that till the ground will eat silage that has been winnowed with shovel and fork. [25]On every lofty mountain and every high hill there will be brooks running with water—on a day of the great slaughter, when the towers fall. [26]Moreover, the light of the moon will be like the light of the sun, and the light of the sun will be sevenfold, like the light of seven days, on the day when the Lord binds up the injuries of his people and heals the wounds inflicted by his blow.
[27] See, the name of the Lord comes from far away,
his anger burning and his burden
heavy;[a]
his lips are full of indignation,
and his tongue is like a devouring fire;

a 30.27 Meaning of Heb uncertain

disastrous, like an untreated crack in a *wall*. **30:14** A different metaphor (a shattered clay pot) expressing the totality of the threatened future disaster. **30:15** Cf. 7:9. **30:16–17** The people rely on military preparedness instead of God (cf. 2:6–8; 22:8–11; 31:3). Military defeat is a fitting punishment for this misplaced trust.

30:18–26 A promise of restoration for the *inhabitants of Jerusalem*, following the end of imperial oppression. **30:18** God *waits to be gracious* until the people *wait for* (or "trust in") God. **30:20** *Bread of adversity* and *water of affliction* recall the meager rations available during a siege. The *Teacher* is likely God, but it could also be the prophet, to whom the people will now listen (cf. vv. 10–11). **30:22** *Idols.* See **"Emerging Monotheism," p. 1000**. *Impure things.* This describes ritual uncleanness resulting from menstruation in Lev. 12:2; 15:33; 20:18. **30:23–24** Future restoration is associated with abundant food (cf. Isa. 1:19; 25:6). **30:25** *Towers* symbolize imperial oppression. **30:26** The promise of healing reverses the imagery of divine injury in 1:5–6; 5:25; 9:13.

30:27–33 A celebration of the fall of Assyria (cf. 10:12; 14:25), reversing imagery used elsewhere for Assyria. The text may reflect hopes for the future from Isaiah's time, or it may have been written a century later when Assyria's downfall was imminent. **30:27** YHWH's personified *name* stands

²⁸ his breath is like an overflowing stream
    that reaches up to the neck—
to sift the nations with the sieve of
    destruction
and to place on the jaws of the peoples
    a bridle that leads them astray.

29 You shall have a song as in the night when a holy festival is kept and gladness of heart, as when one sets out to the sound of the flute to go to the mountain of the LORD, to the Rock of Israel. ³⁰And the LORD will cause his majestic voice to be heard and the descending blow of his arm to be seen, in furious anger and a flame of devouring fire, with a cloudburst and tempest and hailstones. ³¹The Assyrian will be terror-stricken at the voice of the LORD when he strikes with his rod. ³²And every stroke of the staff of punishment*ᵇ* that the LORD lays upon him will be to the sound of timbrels and lyres with dancing;*ᶜ* with brandished arm he will fight with him. ³³For his burning place*ᵈ* has long been prepared, also for the king;*ᵉ* its pyre is made deep and wide, with fire and wood in abundance; the breath of the LORD, like a stream of sulfur, kindles it.

31

Woe to those who go down to Egypt
    for help
and who rely on horses,
who trust in chariots because they are
    many
and in horsemen because they are
    very strong,
but do not look to the Holy One of Israel
    or consult the LORD!

² Yet he is wise and can bring disaster;
    he does not depart from his words
but will rise against the house of the
    evildoers
    and against the helpers of those who
    work iniquity.
³ The Egyptians are human and not
    God;
    their horses are flesh and not spirit.
When the LORD stretches out his hand,
    the helper will stumble, and the one
    helped will fall,
    and they will all perish together.

⁴ For thus the LORD said to me,
"As a lion or a young lion growls over its
    prey
    and, when a band of shepherds is
    called out against it,
is not terrified by their shouting
    or daunted at their noise,
so the LORD of hosts will come down
    to fight upon Mount Zion and upon
    its hill.
⁵ Like birds hovering overhead, so the
    LORD of hosts
    will protect Jerusalem;
he will protect and deliver it;
    he will spare and rescue it."

6 Turn back to him whom you*ᶠ* have deeply betrayed, O people of Israel. ⁷For on that day all of you shall throw away your idols of

b 30.32 Heb mss Syr: MT *foundation*   *c* 30.32 Cn: Heb *and with battles*   *d* 30.33 Or *Topheth*   *e* 30.33 Or *Molech*
f 31.6 Heb *they*

metonymically for the deity. **30:28** Isaiah 8:7–8 compared Assyria to a flood *that reaches up to the neck*. Now YHWH's *breath* is the flood, and Assyria is the victim. **30:29** Judah will celebrate the fall of Assyria as they would a *holy festival. Mountain of the* LORD. Zion, the Temple Mount. *Rock of Israel.* See note on 26:4. **30:31–32** In 10:5, Assyria was YHWH's *rod* and *staff*, but now these weapons are wielded against Assyria. **30:33** *Burning place.* Literally "Topheth," a site outside Jerusalem where children were sacrificed as burnt offerings (cf. 2 Kgs. 23:10; Jer. 7:31–32). *King* may refer to YHWH, who will use the pyre to punish Assyria, or to the Assyrian king, who will be burned upon the pyre. In a pun, the Hebrew word *king* ("melek") sounds like the name of the foreign deity Molech, to whom children were sacrificed at Topheth.

    31:1–9 A poem denouncing Judah's alliance with Egypt, then celebrating YHWH's deliverance of Jerusalem from Assyrian invasion in 701 BCE (see **"Sennacherib's Attack," p. 984**). **31:1** Judah trusts Egyptian military support more than YHWH (cf. 30:15–17). *Consult the* LORD refers to the solicitation of a divine message from a prophet. **31:2** Egypt's celebrated wisdom cannot compare with YHWH's (see note on 19:11). **31:4** YHWH is like a *lion* who will guard *its prey* (Jerusalem) from attempted rescuers. The simile is ambiguous, but it appears to bode ill for Jerusalem. The *shepherds* may represent Egypt, to whom Judah has turned for protection from Assyria. **31:5** A second animal simile compares YHWH to *birds hovering overhead*. The reader might initially think they are birds of prey, but instead, they are mother birds protecting their young (see note on

silver and idols of gold, which your hands
have sinfully made for you.
8 "Then the Assyrian shall fall by a sword
    not of mortals,
  and a sword not of humans shall
    devour him;
  he shall flee from the sword,
    and his young men shall be put to
      forced labor.
9 His rock shall pass away in terror,
    and his officers desert the standard in
      panic,"
  says the LORD, whose fire is in Zion
    and whose furnace is in
      Jerusalem.

32 See, a king will reign in
    righteousness,
  and princes[g] will rule with justice.
2 Each will be like a hiding place from the
    wind,
    a covert from the tempest,
  like streams of water in a dry place,
    like the shade of a great rock in a
      weary land.
3 Then the eyes of those who have sight
    will not be closed,
  and the ears of those who have
    hearing will listen.
4 The minds of the rash will have good
    judgment,
  and the tongues of stammerers will
    speak readily and distinctly.
5 A fool will no longer be called noble
    nor a villain said to be honorable.
6 For fools speak folly,
    and their minds plot iniquity:
  to practice ungodliness,
    to utter error concerning the LORD,

to leave the craving of the hungry
    unsatisfied,
  and to deprive the thirsty of drink.
7 The villainies of villains are evil;
    they devise wicked devices
  to ruin the poor with lying words,
    even when the plea of the needy is
      right.
8 But those who are noble plan noble
    things,
  and by noble things they stand.
9 Rise up, you women who are at ease,
    hear my voice;
  you complacent daughters, listen to
    my speech.
10 In little more than a year
  you will shudder, you complacent
    ones,
  for the vintage will fail;
    the fruit harvest will not come.
11 Tremble, you women who are at ease;
    shudder, you complacent ones;
  strip and make yourselves bare,
    and put sackcloth on your loins.
12 Beat your breasts for the pleasant fields,[b]
    for the fruitful vine,
13 for the soil of my people
    growing up in thorns and briers,
  yes, for all the joyous houses
    in the jubilant city.
14 For the palace will be forsaken,
    the populous city deserted;
  the hill and the watchtower
    will become dens forever,
  the joy of wild asses,
    a pasture for flocks;

g 32.1 Gk: Heb and for princes h 32.12 Gk: Heb on the lamenting breasts

8:8), signaling Jerusalem's deliverance. **31:8** Assyria's defeat will not come through human efforts
like the alliance with Egypt. **31:9** This verse counters Assyria's propagandistic claims that enemy
soldiers fled in terror before their armies. For *fire* as YHWH's instrument for defeating Assyria, cf.
10:16–17; 30:30.

32:1–8 A poem celebrating the future reign of an ideal king (cf. 11:1–10) and his officials, which
implies a critique of current political leadership. **32:1** For *justice* and *righteousness* as kingly virtues,
cf. Isa. 9:7; 11:3–5; 16:5; Ps. 72:1–2. **32:2** These similes, which describe the king and princes' protection of the vulnerable, are often used for divine protection. **32:3** See **"Isaiah and Disability," p. 974**.
32:5 A reversal of 3:5, 12; and 9:16, which depict social and political leadership by unqualified persons. **32:6–8** These contrasting ethical profiles echo themes from Wisdom literature.

32:9–20 A poem calling on women to lament the destruction of agriculture and cities, likely during
Assyria's invasion of Judah in 701 BCE (see **"Sennacherib's Attack," p. 984**). The second half of the
poem promises a peaceful future following the catastrophe. **32:9** Although the *women* and *daughters*
are not directly criticized (cf. Isa. 3:16–24), the descriptors *at ease* and *complacent* may suggest disregard for the suffering of others. **32:10** Cf. 16:9–10; 24:7–9. **32:11** *Sackcloth*. A symbol of mourning.
32:12 In Hebrew, *breasts* ("shadayim") and *fields* ("sedey") sound alike. **32:14** Cf. 17:3; 13:21–22; 23:13;

¹⁵ until a spirit from on high is poured out
on us,
and the wilderness becomes a fruitful
field,
and the fruitful field is deemed a forest.
¹⁶ Then justice will dwell in the wilderness
and righteousness abide in the fruitful
field.
¹⁷ The effect of righteousness will be peace,
and the result of righteousness,
quietness and trust forever.
¹⁸ My people will abide in a peaceful
habitation,
in secure dwellings, and in quiet
resting places.
¹⁹ The forest will disappear completely,ⁱ
and the city will be utterly laid low.
²⁰ Happy will you be who sow beside every
stream,
who let the ox and the donkey range
freely.

33 Woe to the destroyer,
who yourself have not been
destroyed;
you treacherous one,
with whom no one has dealt
treacherously!
When you have ceased to destroy,
you will be destroyed;
and when you have stopped dealing
treacherously,
you will be dealt with treacherously.

² O Lord, be gracious to us; we wait for you.
Be our arm every morning,
our salvation in the time of trouble.

³ At the sound of tumult, peoples fled;
before your majesty, nations scattered.
⁴ Spoil was gathered as the caterpillar gathers;
as locusts leap, they leapedʲ upon it.
⁵ The Lord is exalted; he dwells on high;
he filled Zion with justice and
righteousness;
⁶ he will be the stability of your times,
abundance of salvation, wisdom, and
knowledge;
the fear of the Lord is Zion's treasure.ᵏ

⁷ Listen! The people of Arielˡ cry out in the
streets;
the envoys of peace weep bitterly.
⁸ The highways are deserted;
travelers have quit the road.
The treaty is broken;
its oathsᵐ are despised,
the people are disregarded.
⁹ The land mourns and languishes;
Lebanon is confounded and withers
away;
Sharon is like a desert,
and Bashan and Carmel shake off
their leaves.

¹⁰ "Now I will arise," says the Lord,
"now I will lift myself up;
now I will be exalted.
¹¹ You conceive chaff; you bring forth stubble;
wind like a fireⁿ will consume you.

i 32.19 Meaning of Heb uncertain   *j* 33.4 Meaning of Heb
uncertain   *k* 33.6 Heb *his treasure*   *l* 33.7 Heb mss: Meaning of MT uncertain   *m* 33.8 Q ms: MT *cities*   *n* 33.11 Cn:
Heb *your breath*

34:11–15. **32:15** God's *spirit* brings about a hopeful future, characterized by the transformation of landscapes. **32:16–17** The word pair *justice* and *righteousness* connects this poem to the preceding one
(cf. 32:1). **32:18–20** God's people will dwell in an idyllic rural environment. The lack of cities, with their
defensive fortifications, suggests the absence of enemy threats.
33:1–24 A poem promising deliverance to Jerusalem from its attackers. Most likely, it originally
responded to Sennacherib's invasion in 701 BCE (see **"Sennacherib's Attack," p. 984**), then was
reinterpreted in light of the Babylonian conquest of 587 BCE (see **"Exile (2 Kings)," p. 539**). Some
version of the poem probably concluded a preexilic edition of the book of Isaiah. **33:1** Cf. Isa. 21:2
for the pair *destroyer* and *treacherous one* (or "betrayer"). This enemy figure—either Assyria or
Babylon—will eventually be defeated. **33:2** A prayer for deliverance. **33:3–4** It is unclear whether
these verses recall Jerusalem's past victories (as translated here) or predict its future triumph. In
either case, it contrasts with the city's current state (vv. 7–9). **33:5** Cf. 1:27; 5:16. **33:7** *Ariel.* Another
name for Jerusalem (cf. 29:1). *Envoys of peace.* Attempts to negotiate a peace treaty were unsuccessful. **33:8** *Treaty is broken* may refer to Judah's rebellions against Assyria or Babylon. **33:9** *Lebanon.* See note on 29:17. *Sharon.* A forested region in western Israel, along the Mediterranean coast
south of Mount *Carmel. Bashan.* A region northeast of Israel, across the Jordan Sea. An invading
army would have marched through these regions en route to Jerusalem. **33:10** YHWH promises to
deliver Jerusalem. **33:11–12** A threat against Jerusalem's invaders. *Chaff* ("chashash") and *stubble*

¹² And the peoples will be as if burned to
    lime,
    like thorns cut down that are burned
    in the fire."

¹³ Hear, you who are far away, what I have
    done,
    and you who are near, acknowledge
    my might.
¹⁴ The sinners in Zion are afraid;
    trembling has seized the godless:
  "Who among us can live with the
    devouring fire?
  Who among us can live with
    everlasting flames?"
¹⁵ Those who walk righteously and speak
    uprightly,
    who despise the gain of oppression,
  who wave away a bribe instead of
    accepting it,
    who stop their ears from hearing of
    bloodshed
    and shut their eyes from looking on
    evil,
¹⁶ they will live on the heights;
    their refuge will be the fortresses of
    rocks;
    their food will be supplied, their water
    assured.
¹⁷ Your eyes will see the king in his
    beauty;
    they will behold a land that stretches
    far away.
¹⁸ Your mind will muse on the terror:
  "Where is the one who counted?
  Where is the one who weighed the
    tribute?
  Where is the one who counted the
    towers?"

¹⁹ No longer will you see the insolent
    people,
    the people of an obscure speech that
    you cannot comprehend,
    stammering in a language that you
    cannot understand.
²⁰ Look on Zion, the city of our appointed
    festivals!
  Your eyes will see Jerusalem,
    a quiet habitation, an immovable tent
  whose stakes will never be pulled up
    and none of whose ropes will be
    broken.
²¹ But there the LORD in majesty will be
    for us
    a place of broad rivers and streams
  where no galley with oars can go
    nor stately ship can pass.
²² For the LORD is our judge; the LORD is our
    ruler;
    the LORD is our king; he will save us.

²³ Your rigging hangs loose;
    it cannot hold the mast firm in its
    place
    or keep the sail spread out.

  Then the blind will divide abundant
    spoil,ᵒ
    and the lame will take plunder.
²⁴ And no inhabitant will say, "I am sick";
    the people who live there will be
    forgiven their iniquity.

34 Draw near, O nations, to hear;
    O peoples, give heed!
  Let the earth hear and all that fills it,
    the world and all that comes from it.

o 33.23 Cn: Heb *Then prey and spoil in abundance will be divided*

("qash") rhyme in Hebrew. **33:14** The focus shifts from the fate of Jerusalem as a whole to the fate of *sinners in Zion* (cf. 1:27–28). *Devouring fire* is a metaphor for divine judgment (cf. 29:6; 30:27, 30). **33:15–16** A list of ethical attributes of Jerusalem's ideal future inhabitants (cf. Ps. 15). **33:17** *King* may refer both to the Davidic ruler and to YHWH (cf. Isa. 6:5; 33:22). **33:18–19** The demise of the city's invaders, identified first by their oppressive actions (v. 18) and then by their foreign language (v. 19). **33:20** This verse portrays Jerusalem as invulnerable to future attacks, a belief that emerged following the city's survival in 701 BCE (see **"Sennacherib's Attack," p. 984**). **33:21** Although Jerusalem is not located near a major watercourse, some idealized descriptions of the city include *rivers* (Ps. 46:4; Ezek. 47:1). **33:23** Building on v. 21, the poem imagines a repulsed naval invasion of Jerusalem, which produced *abundant spoil* for the city's inhabitants, including the *lame* (see **"Isaiah and Disability," p. 974**). **33:24** Inhabitants of the idealized Jerusalem will have transformed bodies that do not get *sick* (cf. 65:20). This verse reflects a conventional but problematic theological association between illness and sin.

34:1–17 A poem depicting worldwide divine judgment, with a focus on Edom (cf. Isa. 63:1–6). Chaps. 34–35 were likely composed during the postexilic period to bridge Isa. 1–33 and 40–66.

2 For the LORD is enraged against all the
nations
and furious against all their hordes;
he has doomed them, has given them
over for slaughter.
3 Their slain shall be cast out,
and the stench of their corpses shall rise;
the mountains shall flow with their
blood.
4 All the host of heaven shall rot away,
and the skies roll up like a scroll.
All their host shall wither
like a leaf withering on a vine
or fruit withering on a fig tree.

5 When my sword has drunk its fill in the
heavens,
upon Edom it will fall,
upon the people I have doomed to
judgment.
6 The LORD has a sword; it is sated with
blood;
it is gorged with fat,
with the blood of lambs and goats,
with the fat of the kidneys of rams.
For the LORD has a sacrifice in Bozrah,
a great slaughter in the land of Edom.
7 Wild oxen shall fall with them
and young steers with the mighty bulls.
Their land shall be soaked with blood,
and their soil made rich with fat.

8 For the LORD has a day of vengeance,
a year of vindication for Zion's cause.[p]
9 And the streams of Edom[q] shall be
turned into pitch
and her soil into sulfur;
her land shall become burning pitch.
10 Night and day it shall not be quenched;
its smoke shall go up forever.
From generation to generation it shall lie
waste;
no one shall pass through it forever
and ever.
11 But the desert owl[r] and the screech owl[s]
shall possess it;
the great owl and the raven shall live
in it.
He shall stretch the line of confusion
and the plummet of chaos over it.
12 They shall call its nobles No Kingdom
There,
and all its princes shall be nothing.
13 Thorns shall grow over its strongholds,
nettles and thistles in its fortresses.
It shall be the haunt of jackals,
an abode for ostriches.
14 Wildcats shall meet with hyenas;
goat-demons shall call to each other;
there also Lilith shall repose
and find a place to rest.
15 There shall the owl nest
and lay and hatch and brood in its
shadow;
there also the buzzards shall gather,
each one with its mate.
16 Seek and read from the book of the LORD:
Not one of these shall be missing;
none shall be without its mate.

p 34.8 Or *of recompense by Zion's defender* *q* 34.9 Heb *her streams* *r* 34.11 Meaning of Heb uncertain *s* 34.11 Meaning of Heb uncertain

34:2 *Doomed.* Literally "devoted to total destruction," a practice of killing all living things in a conquered city (cf. Deut. 20:16–17; Josh. 6:21). **34:4** Cosmic devastation parallels earthly destruction. *Host of heaven.* See note on Isa. 24:21. **34:5** YHWH engages in direct combat with a *sword*, which is personified as thirsting for blood. *Edom.* A kingdom south of the Dead Sea, bordering Judah; its people were putatively descended from Jacob's brother Esau. Many postexilic biblical texts display intense animosity toward Edom (e.g., Obad. 1; Ps. 137:7; Mal. 1:2–4). Here, Edom represents all nations opposed to YHWH. **34:6** The poem compares God's *slaughter* ("zebach") of the Edomites to the *sacrifice* ("tebach") of animals, reinforced by the rhyme of the two Hebrew words. *Bozrah.* An important Edomite city. **34:7** *Wild oxen, steers,* and *mighty bulls* extend the metaphor of animal sacrifice from v. 6. They were also conventional metaphors for political and military leaders. **34:8** *Day of vengeance* (cf. 61:2; 63:4) is likely a variation of "the day of the Lord" (see **"Day of the Lord," p. 1322**). **34:9–10** Edom's destruction is like that of Sodom and Gomorrah in Gen. 19:24–28. **34:11** Wild animals inhabit the deserted city of Edom (cf. Isa. 13:22; 14:23; 23:13). *Line* and *plummet* are normally tools for gauging straightness, but here they are ironically associated with *confusion* and *chaos*, words that describe primordial disorder in Gen. 1:2. **34:14** *Goat-demons.* Cf. Lev. 17:7; 2 Chr. 11:15; Isa. 13:21–22. *Lilith.* A demon believed to kill children, known from ancient Mesopotamia and later identified as Adam's first wife in Jewish tradition. **34:16** *Book of the LORD* refers either to some earlier written version of this prophecy or to a record of the names of the righteous (see

For his mouth, it has commanded,
  and his spirit, it has gathered them.
¹⁷ He has cast the lot for them;
  his hand has portioned it out to them
    with the line.
[[They shall possess it;
  from generation to generation they
    shall live in it.

35 The wilderness and the dry land
  shall be glad;
  the desert shall rejoice and blossom;
like the crocus ²it shall blossom
    abundantly
  and rejoice with joy and shouting.
The glory of Lebanon shall be given
    to it,
  the majesty of Carmel and Sharon.
They shall see the glory of the Lᴏʀᴅ,
  the majesty of our God.]]ᵗ

³ Strengthen the weak hands
  and make firm the feeble knees.
⁴ Say to those who are of a fearful
    heart,
  "Be strong, do not fear!
Here is your God.
  He will come with vengeance,
with terrible recompense.
  He will come and save you."

⁵ Then the eyes of the blind shall be
    opened,
  and the ears of the deaf shall be
    opened;
⁶ then the lame shall leap like a deer,
  and the tongue of the speechless sing
    for joy.

For waters shall break forth in the
    wilderness
  and streams in the desert;
⁷ the burning sand shall become a pool
  and the thirsty ground springs of
    water;
the haunt of jackals shall become a
    swamp;ᵘ
  the grass shall become reeds and
    rushes.

⁸ A highway shall be there,ᵛ
  and it shall be called the Holy
    Way;
the unclean shall not travel on it,ʷ
  but it shall be for God's people;ˣ
  no traveler, not even fools, shall go
    astray.
⁹ No lion shall be there,
  nor shall any ravenous beast come up
    on it;
they shall not be found there,
  but the redeemed shall walk there.
¹⁰ And the ransomed of the Lᴏʀᴅ shall
    return
  and come to Zion with singing;
everlasting joy shall be upon their heads;
  they shall obtain joy and gladness,
  and sorrow and sighing shall flee away.

36 In the fourteenth year of King Hezekiah, King Sennacherib of Assyria
came up against all the fortified cities of

ᵗ 34.17–35.2 Q ms lacks 34.17–35.2 Cn: Heb *in the haunt of jackals is her resting place* ᵘ 35.7 Cn: Heb *in the haunt of jackals is her resting place* ᵛ 35.8 Q ms Gk Syr: MT *A highway and a way shall be there* ʷ 35.8 Or *pass it by* ˣ 35.8 Cn: Heb *for them*

note on 4:3), here imagined as including animals. **34:17** *Lot* and *line* were traditional methods of distributing property. **35:1–10** A poem celebrating the restoration of Judah and the return of exiles, with sharply contrasting imagery from the previous poem. It closely resembles Isa. 40, which it may have immediately preceded before chaps. 36–39 were added to the book. **35:1** *Wilderness*, *dry land*, and *desert* are images for Judah's desolation, which will be reversed. **35:2** *Glory of Lebanon.* Cf. Isa. 60:13. For *Lebanon*, see note on 29:17. *Carmel and Sharon.* See note on 33:9. *See the glory of the Lᴏʀᴅ.* Cf. 40:5. **35:4** Cf. 34:8, where divine *vengeance* meant restoration for Zion. **35:5–6** See **"Isaiah and Disability," p. 974**. **35:7** The transformation of barren landscapes is a recurring motif in Isa. 40–55. Contrast this restoration of Judah's land with the degradation of Edom's land in 34:9–10. **35:8** As in 40:3 and 62:10, a *highway* is constructed for the return of God and the *people* to Jerusalem. The designation *Holy* and the absence of the *unclean* (cf. 52:1, 11) suggest that it leads to the temple. **35:9** There will be no threats to the returning exiles, symbolized by *lion* and *ravenous beast*. **35:10** The same lines appear in 51:11. This verse effectively concludes the poem by repeating words from vv. 1–2 (*singing*, *joy*). **36:1–37:38** Isaiah 36–39 contain stories about Isaiah and King Hezekiah that are nearly identical to 2 Kgs. 18:13–20:19. It is unclear whether the Isaiah versions were borrowed from 2 Kings or vice

Judah and captured them. [2]The king of Assyria sent the Rabshakeh with a great army from Lachish to King Hezekiah at Jerusalem. He stood by the conduit of the upper pool on the highway to the fuller's field. [3]And there came out to him Eliakim son of Hilkiah, who was in charge of the palace, and Shebna the secretary, and Joah son of Asaph, the recorder.

4 The Rabshakeh said to them, "Say to Hezekiah: Thus says the great king, the king of Assyria: On what do you base this reliance of yours? [5]Do you think that mere words are strategy and power for war? On whom, then, do you now rely, that you have rebelled against me? [6]See, you are relying on Egypt, that broken reed of a staff, which will pierce the hand of anyone who leans on it. Such is Pharaoh king of Egypt to all who rely on him. [7]But if you say to me, 'We rely on the LORD our God,' [[is it not he whose high places and altars Hezekiah has removed, saying to Judah and to Jerusalem, 'You shall worship before this altar'?]][y] [8]Come now, make a wager with my master the king of Assyria: I will give you two thousand horses, if you are able on your part to set riders on them. [9]How then can you repulse a single captain among the least of my master's servants, when you rely on Egypt for chariots and for horsemen? [10]Moreover, is it without the LORD that I have come up against this land to destroy it? The LORD said to me, Go up against this land, and destroy it."

11 Then Eliakim, Shebna, and Joah said to the Rabshakeh, "Please speak to your servants in Aramaic, for we understand it; do not speak to us in the language of Judah within the hearing of the people who are on the wall." [12]But the Rabshakeh said, "Has my master sent me to speak these words to your master and to you and not to the people sitting on the wall, who are doomed with you to eat their own dung and drink their own urine?"

13 Then the Rabshakeh stood and called out in a loud voice in the language of Judah, "Hear the words of the great king, the king of Assyria! [14]Thus says the king: Do not let Hezekiah deceive you, for he will not be able to deliver you. [15]Do not let Hezekiah make you rely on the LORD by saying, 'The LORD will surely deliver us; this city will not be given into the hand of the king of Assyria.' [16]Do not listen to Hezekiah, for thus says the king of Assyria: Make your peace with me and come out to me; then every one of you will eat from your own vine and your own fig tree and drink water from your own cistern, [17]until I come and take you away to a

_y_ 36.7 Gk lacks: Heb adds _is it not he . . . this altar'?_

versa or whether both sources drew upon a separate collection of stories about Isaiah. In the present form of the book, these chapters bridge Isa. 1–39 and 40–66 by beginning with a depiction of the Assyrian threat and ending with a prediction of the Babylonian threat. Chaps. 36–37 take place during Sennacherib's invasion in 701 BCE (see **"Sennacherib's Attack," p. 984**). These chapters apparently combine two originally independent versions of the story (36:1–37:9a, 37–38 and 37:9b–36), each with its own Assyrian call for surrender, response from Isaiah, and explanation for Assyria's retreat. **36:1** _Fourteenth year of King Hezekiah._ 701 BCE. _Fortified cities._ In his annals, Sennacherib claimed to have conquered forty-six Judean cities. **36:2** Isaiah 36 omits Hezekiah's submission to Sennacherib in 2 Kgs. 18:14–16, presumably to make Hezekiah appear more positive. _Rabshakeh._ A high-ranking Assyrian military official who acts as Sennacherib's representative. _Lachish._ A Judean city conquered by Sennacherib. Monumental portrayals of its conquest adorned the walls of his palace. _Conduit of the upper pool on the highway to the fuller's field._ Cf. Isa. 7:3. The mention of this location connects Isa. 7 and 36–39, encouraging the reader to contrast the responses of Ahaz and Hezekiah to threatened invasions. **36:3** See note on 22:20–21. **36:4** Although addressed to Hezekiah, the message is meant to be overheard by the Jerusalemites and decrease their confidence in their king. **36:6** This negative portrayal of Egypt recalls Isaiah's own critiques in 30:1–5; 31:1–3. **36:7–10** The Rabshakeh claims that Hezekiah's religious reforms (cf. 2 Kgs. 18:3–4) angered YHWH, leading the deity to empower Sennacherib's invasion. **36:11** Recognizing the speech's negative impact on morale, Hezekiah's courtiers ask the Rabshakeh to speak in _Aramaic_, the diplomatic language used by Assyria, so the people would not understand it. **36:12** _Eat their own dung and drink their own urine_ anticipates an extended blockade of Jerusalem, during which food and water supplies would run low. **36:13** Refusing the courtiers' request, the Rabshakeh addresses the people in their own _language_. **36:16–17** In exchange for surrender, the Rabshakeh offers the Jerusalemites

Going Deeper: Sennacherib's Attack on Jerusalem (Isaiah 36)

Widespread revolt followed the unexpected death of Assyria's king Sargon II in 705 BCE. As described in various nonbiblical sources, King Hezekiah of Judah refused to support the Philistines in an earlier rebellion in 714–711 BCE (cf. Isa. 14:28–32; 20:1–6), but he enthusiastically joined this one. He coordinated efforts with King Merodach-baladan of Babylon (cf. Isa. 39) and secured Egyptian support. He even deposed the pro-Assyrian ruler of Ekron, a Philistine city-state, and replaced him with an ally—the same thing that Israel and Assyria had attempted to do to Jerusalem during the Syro-Ephraimite conflict (7:1–6). As depicted in Isa. 28–31, the prophet Isaiah strongly opposed these actions.

Far from proving weak, however, the new Assyrian ruler Sennacherib systematically suppressed the revolt. According to his annals, he reconquered Babylon in 703 BCE (cf. Isa. 22:1–8). In 701 BCE, he subdued the Phoenicians (cf. Isa. 23) and Philistines, restoring the deposed king of Ekron. After repulsing an Egyptian counteroffensive, he conquered forty-seven Judean cities, most notably Lachish, before finally blockading Jerusalem. (Although this action is sometimes referred to as a "siege," there is no evidence of direct offensive action against the city.)

Assyrian and biblical sources offer conflicting accounts of Jerusalem's survival (see **"The Survival of Jerusalem," p. 528**). Sennacherib's annals claim that Hezekiah was trapped "like a bird in a cage," after which he surrendered and paid substantial tribute. Second Kings 18:14–16, which is omitted from the parallel passage in Isa. 36, corroborates this account. From the Assyrian perspective, the campaign was successful because Sennacherib's primary objective was to secure Hezekiah's submission and reduce his power, not to conquer Jerusalem. By contrast, 2 Kgs. 19 / Isa. 37 suggests that Sennacherib intended to destroy Jerusalem but failed. Some historians argue that a second Egyptian counteroffensive—or at least the threat of one (cf. 2 Kgs. 19:9 / Isa. 37:9)—repelled Assyria. Alternatively, the Assyrian army may have been overextended from previous battles or weakened by a pandemic (cf. 2 Kgs. 19:35 / Isa. 37:36). According to the Greek historian Herodotus, the Assyrian encampment was infested with mice on a campaign to Egypt, which may support the latter scenario.

However one reconstructs the historical events, Judah lost significant territory and remained an Assyrian vassal. To Jerusalem's inhabitants, however, the city's survival seemed miraculous, leading to the belief that it could never be conquered. That belief was shattered when Babylon destroyed the city in 587 BCE.

J. Blake Couey

land like your own land, a land of grain and wine, a land of bread and vineyards. ¹⁸Do not let Hezekiah mislead you by saying, 'The Lᴏʀᴅ will deliver us.' Has any of the gods of the nations delivered their land out of the hand of the king of Assyria? ¹⁹Where are the gods of Hamath and Arpad? Where are the gods of Sepharvaim? Have they delivered Samaria out of my hand? ²⁰Who among all the gods of these countries have delivered their countries out of my hand, that the Lᴏʀᴅ should deliver Jerusalem out of my hand?"

21 But they were silent and answered him not a word, for the king's command was, "Do not answer him." ²²Then Eliakim son of Hilkiah, who was in charge of the palace, and Shebna the secretary, and Joah son of Asaph, the recorder, came to Hezekiah with their clothes torn and told him the words of the Rabshakeh.

37 When King Hezekiah heard it, he tore his clothes, covered himself with sackcloth and went into the house of the Lᴏʀᴅ. ²And he sent Eliakim, who was in charge of the palace, and Shebna the secretary, and the senior priests, covered with sackcloth, to the prophet Isaiah son of Amoz. ³They said to him, "Thus says Hezekiah: This day is a day of distress, of rebuke, and of disgrace; children have come to the birth, and there is no strength to bring them forth. ⁴It may be that the Lᴏʀᴅ your God heard the words of the Rabshakeh, whom his master the king of Assyria has sent to mock the living God, and will rebuke the words that the

abundant food and water and portrays exile as desirable. **36:19** Hamath, Arpad, Sepharvaim, and Samaria were cities previously conquered by Assyria (cf. Isa. 10:9–10). YHWH was also worshiped in Samaria, seemingly supporting the Rabshakeh's claim in v. 20 that the deity was incapable of delivering Jerusalem. **37:1** Torn clothes and sackcloth symbolize mourning. **37:3** A childbirth metaphor

LORD your God has heard; therefore lift up your prayer for the remnant that is left."

[[5 When the servants of King Hezekiah came to Isaiah, 6Isaiah said to them, "Say to your master: Thus says the LORD: Do not be afraid because of the words that you have heard, with which the servants of the king of Assyria have reviled me. 7I myself will put a spirit in him, so that he shall hear a rumor and return to his own land; I will cause him to fall by the sword in his own land."]]z

8 The Rabshakeh returned and found the king of Assyria fighting against Libnah, for he had heard that the king had left Lachish. 9Now the kinga heard concerning King Tirhakah of Cush, "He has set out to fight against you." When he heard it, he sent messengers to Hezekiah, saying, 10"Thus shall you speak to King Hezekiah of Judah: Do not let your God on whom you rely deceive you by promising that Jerusalem will not be given into the hand of the king of Assyria. 11See, you have heard what the kings of Assyria have done to all lands, destroying them utterly. Shall you be delivered? 12Have the gods of the nations delivered them, the nations that my predecessors destroyed, Gozan, Haran, Rezeph, and the people of Eden who were in Telassar? 13Where is the king of Hamath, the king of Arpad, the king of Laar, Sepharvaim, Hena, or Ivvah?"

14 Hezekiah received the letter from the hand of the messengers and read it; then Hezekiah went up to the house of the LORD and spread it before the LORD. 15And Hezekiah prayed to the LORD, saying: 16"O LORD of hosts, God of Israel, who are enthroned above the cherubim, you are God, you alone, of all the kingdoms of the earth; you have made heaven and earth. 17Incline your ear,

O LORD, and hear; open your eyes, O LORD, and see; hear all the words of Sennacherib, which he has sent to mock the living God. 18Truly, O LORD, the kings of Assyria have laid waste all the nations and their lands 19and have hurled their gods into the fire, though they were no gods but the work of human hands—wood and stone—and so they were destroyed. 20So now, O LORD our God, save us from his hand, so that all the kingdoms of the earth may know that you alone are the LORD."

21 Then Isaiah son of Amoz sent to Hezekiah, saying: "Thus says the LORD, the God of Israel: Because you have prayed to me concerning King Sennacherib of Assyria, 22this is the word that the LORD has spoken concerning him:

She despises you; she scorns you—
    virgin daughter Zion;
she tosses her head—behind your back,
    daughter Jerusalem.

23 "Whom have you mocked and reviled?
    Against whom have you raised your
    voice
and haughtily lifted your eyes?
    Against the Holy One of Israel!
24 By your servants you have mocked the
    Lord,
    and you have said, 'With my many
    chariots
I have gone up the heights of the
    mountains,
    to the far recesses of Lebanon;
I felled its tallest cedars,
    its choicest cypresses;
I came to its remotest height,

z 37.5–7 Q ms lacks 37.5–7   a 37.9 Heb he

for Jerusalem's inability to repulse the Assyrian attack. **37:6** Cf. 7:4. **37:7** The two parts of Isaiah's prophecy are respectively fulfilled in v. 9 and vv. 37–38. **37:8** *Libnah.* A Judean city between Lachish and Jerusalem. **37:9** This threat is the "rumor" prophesied by Isaiah in v. 7. As depicted here, Egypt's role in Jerusalem's deliverance contradicts the Rabshakeh's claims in 36:6 and, ironically, many of the warnings in Isa. 28–31. *Tirhakah of Cush.* A Cushite prince in Egypt, here anachronistically called *King*, although his reign began in 690 BCE. (Historians conventionally spell his name "Taharqa" or "Taharqo.") **37:10** Sennacherib's message repeats many of the Rabshakeh's claims from 36:4–20. **37:12–13** A list of cities previously conquered by Assyria, similar to 36:19. **37:14** Hezekiah *spread* the letter *before the LORD* so the deity could read it. **37:15** Hezekiah's prayer demonstrates his piety, in contrast to Ahaz's faithlessness in chap. 7. **37:16** *Enthroned above the cherubim.* See note on 6:1. The claim that YHWH *alone . . . made heaven and earth* counters Assyrian claims about the deity's weakness. **37:19** The ineffectiveness of foreign deities demonstrates their lack of reality, not Assyrian power. **37:20** YHWH's own reputation is at stake in Jerusalem's fate. **37:22** *Daughter Zion.* See note on 1:8. **37:23** *Holy One of Israel.* See note on 1:4. **37:24** Assyrian rulers boasted about cutting down

its densest forest.
²⁵ I dug wells
and drank waters;
I dried up with the sole of my foot
all the streams of Egypt.'

²⁶ "Have you not heard
that I determined it long ago?
I planned from days of old
what now I bring to pass,
that you should make fortified cities
crash into heaps of ruins,
²⁷ while their inhabitants, shorn of
strength,
are dismayed and confounded;
they have become like plants of the field
and like tender grass,
like grass on the housetops
that is scorched before the east wind.ᵇ

²⁸ "I know your rising upᶜ and your sitting
down,
your going out and coming in
and your raging against me.
²⁹ Because you have raged against me
and your arrogance has come to my ears,
I will put my hook in your nose
and my bit in your mouth;
I will turn you back on the way
by which you came.

30 "And this shall be the sign for you: This
year eat what grows of itself and in the second year what springs from that; then in the
third year sow, reap, plant vineyards, and eat
their fruit. ³¹The surviving remnant of the
house of Judah shall again take root downward and bear fruit upward, ³²for from Jerusalem a remnant shall go out and from Mount

Zion a band of survivors. The zeal of the Lord
of hosts will do this.

33 "Therefore thus says the Lord concerning the king of Assyria: He shall not come
into this city, shoot an arrow there, come before it with a shield, or cast up a siege ramp
against it. ³⁴By the way that he came, by the
same he shall return; he shall not come into
this city, says the Lord. ³⁵For I will defend this
city to save it, for my own sake and for the
sake of my servant David."

36 Then the angel of the Lord set out
and struck down one hundred eighty-five
thousand in the camp of the Assyrians;
when morning dawned, they were all dead
bodies. ³⁷Then King Sennacherib of Assyria left, went home, and lived at Nineveh.
³⁸As he was worshiping in the house of his
god Nisroch, his sons Adrammelech and
Sharezer killed him with the sword, and
they escaped into the land of Ararat. His
son Esar-haddon succeeded him.

38 In those days Hezekiah became sick
and was at the point of death. The
prophet Isaiah son of Amoz came to him and
said to him, "Thus says the Lord: Set your
house in order, for you shall die; you shall
not recover." ²Then Hezekiah turned his face
to the wall and prayed to the Lord: ³"Remember now, O Lord, I implore you, how I
have walked before you in faithfulness with
a whole heart and have done what is good in
your sight." And Hezekiah wept bitterly.

4 Then the word of the Lord came to Isaiah: ⁵"Go and say to Hezekiah, Thus says the
Lord, the God of your ancestor David: I have

b 37.27 Q ms: MT *and a field before standing grain*   c 37.28 Q
ms Gk: MT lacks *your rising up*

cedars of *Lebanon.* **37:25** Cf. 19:4–6. **37:26** As in chap. 10, Assyria's conquests were foreordained by
YHWH. *Planned from days of old.* Cf. 14:26–27; 22:11; 23:9. **37:29** *Hook in your nose* and *bit in your
mouth* recall Assyria's humiliating treatment of defeated enemies. **37:30** As with Ahaz in 7:14, Isaiah
offers Hezekiah a *sign* with specific time limits. The invasion will prevent agriculture for two years,
but normal activities will resume in year three. **37:32** *Zeal of the Lord of hosts.* Cf. 9:7. **37:35** God's
defense of Jerusalem is motivated by concern for the deity's reputation and earlier promises to
King David (2 Sam. 7:10–16; Ps. 89:19–37). **37:36** This explanation of Assyria's defeat may preserve
the historical memory of a plague that struck the army, although the number of casualties is surely
exaggerated. **37:37** An alternate explanation for Assyria's retreat, fulfilling Isaiah's prophecy in v. 7.
37:38 Sennacherib was in fact assassinated by his sons but not until 681 BCE, two decades after his
invasion of Judah. There is no known Mesopotamian deity called *Nisroch*; the biblical authors may
have intentionally corrupted the name.
38:1–22 A story about Hezekiah's miraculous recovery from illness, contrasting his fate with that
of the Assyrian army and Sennacherib. **38:1** Although not recounted in the story, Hezekiah likely
asked Isaiah about his health. **38:5** God's response is based on Hezekiah's piety and God's promises

heard your prayer; I have seen your tears; I will add fifteen years to your life. 6I will deliver you and this city out of the hand of the king of Assyria and defend this city.

7 "This is the sign to you from the Lord, that the Lord will do this thing that he has promised: 8See, I will make the shadow cast by the declining sun on the dial of Ahaz turn back ten steps." So the sun turned back on the dial the ten steps by which it had declined.*d*

9 A writing of King Hezekiah of Judah, after he had been sick and had recovered from his sickness:
10 I said: In the noontide of my days
      I must depart;
I am consigned to the gates of Sheol
      for the rest of my years.
11 I said, I shall not see the Lord
      in the land of the living;
I shall look upon mortals no more
      among the inhabitants of the world.
12 My dwelling is plucked up and removed
            from me
      like a shepherd's tent;
like a weaver I have rolled up my life;
      he cuts me off from the loom;
from day to night you bring me to an end;
13   I cry for help*e* until morning;
like a lion he breaks all my bones;
      from day to night you bring me to an end.

14 Like a swallow or a crane*f* I clamor;
      I moan like a dove.
My eyes are weary with looking upward.
      O Lord, I am oppressed; be my security!

15 But what can I say? For he has spoken
            to me,
      and he himself has done it.
All my sleep has fled*g*
      because of the bitterness of my soul.

16 O Lord, by these things people live,
      and in all these is the life of my spirit.*b*
Oh, restore me to health and make me
            live!
17 Surely it was for my welfare
      that I had great bitterness,
but you have held back*i* my life
      from the pit of destruction,
for you have cast all my sins
      behind your back.
18 For Sheol cannot thank you;
      death cannot praise you;
those who go down to the Pit cannot hope
      for your faithfulness.
19 The living, the living, they thank you,
      as I do this day;
fathers make known to children
      your faithfulness.

20 The Lord will save me,
      and we will sing to stringed instruments*j*
all the days of our lives,
      at the house of the Lord.

[[21 Now Isaiah had said, "Let them take a lump of figs and apply it to the boil, so that

d 38.8 Meaning of Heb uncertain   *e* 38.13 Cn: Meaning of Heb uncertain   *f* 38.14 Meaning of Heb uncertain   *g* 38.15 Cn Compare Syr: Heb *I will walk slowly all my years*   *h* 38.16 Meaning of Heb uncertain   *i* 38.17 Cn Compare Gk Vg: Heb *loved*   *j* 38.20 Heb *my stringed instruments*

to *David* and his dynasty (cf. Isa. 37:35). **38:6** Hezekiah's recovery parallels Jerusalem's rescue. This reference to the Assyrian threat implies that this story takes place before chaps. 36–37, despite being placed after them. **38:7** In the parallel account in 2 Kgs. 20, Isaiah requests a medicinal poultice, and then Hezekiah asks for a sign. The omission of these details here underscores the miraculousness of the healing and emphasizes Hezekiah's piety. **38:8** As a sign, the evening shadows turn back, ostensibly adding time to the day. The sign parallels the turning back of Hezekiah's death, adding years to his life. **38:9** A psalm of thanksgiving (cf. Pss. 30; 116). Most likely, an originally freestanding prayer was incorporated into the story because of its appropriateness to Hezekiah's situation (cf. Jonah's prayer in Jonah 2:2-9). It is not included in 2 Kgs. 20. **38:10** *Noontide of my days.* Middle age, suggesting that Hezekiah's death would have been premature. *Sheol.* The realm of the dead. **38:12** A series of metaphors for death, comparing life to a fabric or thread (cf. Job 7:6). **38:13** Hezekiah blames YHWH for his illness, comparing the deity to a *lion.* **38:14** *Clamor* (or "chirp") describes the sounds of ghosts in Isa. 8:19 and 29:4, ominously foreshadowing Hezekiah's death. **38:17** For the association of sickness with *sins,* cf. 33:24. **38:18-19** Unlike the dead, Hezekiah can *praise* and *thank* God. By implication, it was in God's interests to heal him (cf. Pss. 6:5; 30:9). **38:21-22** Cf. 2 Kgs. 20:7-10. Although these verses were originally omitted from this version of the story (see note on v. 7), a later scribe must have appended them here.

he may recover." [22]Hezekiah also had said, "What is the sign that I shall go up to the house of the LORD?"]][k]

39 At that time King Merodach-baladan son of Baladan of Babylon sent envoys with letters and a present to Hezekiah, for he heard that he had been sick and had recovered. [2]Hezekiah welcomed them; he showed them his treasure house, the silver, the gold, the spices, the precious oil, his whole armory, all that was found in his storehouses. There was nothing in his house or in all his realm that Hezekiah did not show them. [3]Then the prophet Isaiah came to King Hezekiah and said to him, "What did these men say? From where did they come to you?" Hezekiah answered, "They have come to me from a far country, from Babylon." [4]He said, "What have they seen in your house?" Hezekiah answered, "They have seen all that is in my house; there is nothing in my storehouses that I did not show them."

5 Then Isaiah said to Hezekiah, "Hear the word of the LORD of hosts: [6]Days are coming when all that is in your house and that which your ancestors have stored up until this day shall be carried to Babylon; nothing shall be left, says the LORD. [7]Some of your own sons who are born to you shall be taken away; they shall be eunuchs in the palace of the king of Babylon." [8]Then Hezekiah said to Isaiah, "The word of the LORD that you have spoken is good." For he thought, "There will be peace and security in my days."

40 Comfort, O comfort my people, says your God.
[2] Speak tenderly to Jerusalem,
  and cry to her
that she has served her term,
  that her penalty is paid,
that she has received from the LORD's hand
  double for all her sins.

[3] A voice cries out:
"In the wilderness prepare the way of
  the LORD;
  make straight in the desert a highway
  for our God.
[4] Every valley shall be lifted up,
  and every mountain and hill be made
  low;
the uneven ground shall become level,
  and the rough places a plain.
[5] Then the glory of the LORD shall be
  revealed,
  and all flesh shall see it together,
  for the mouth of the LORD has spoken."

k 38.21–22 Q ms lacks 38.21–22

39:1–8 The final story in the series recounts a visit to Hezekiah by Babylonian emissaries. Like the previous story, it is set before the events in chaps. 36–37. **39:1** *Merodach-baladan* II was the king of Babylon from 722 to 710 BCE, when he was deposed by Sargon II of Assyria. He retook the throne of Babylon in 703 BCE but was quickly defeated by Sennacherib. The stated reason for this visit connects this story to the preceding one. Historically, it likely preserves the memory of the diplomatic exchange between Judah and Babylon at the beginning of the rebellion against Assyria. **39:2** The display of Hezekiah's treasures may be intended to prove he has the resources for a successful rebellion against Assyria. **39:3** Isaiah's ignorance indicates that he was not consulted about the emissaries' visit. **39:5–7** A prophecy about the Babylonian invasion of Jerusalem in 587 BCE and exile. Its placement here in the book of Isaiah anticipates the announcement of the exile's end in the next chapter. Isaiah does not directly blame Hezekiah's actions for the future disaster, but his words may reflect disapproval of the alliance with Babylon. **39:8** Hezekiah's self-focused response to the prophecy is surprising, given his otherwise positive portrayal in these stories.

40:1–31 The opening poem in Isa. 40–55, the exilic portion of the book, introduces major themes from these chapters: the end of exile and a hopeful future for exiled Judeans, the impotence of foreign deities, and the incomparable power of YHWH as the God of all nations. **40:1** God commands an unidentified group (the verbs are plural) to *comfort [his] people*. Contrast the claim in Lam. 1:2, 9, 16–17, 21 that Jerusalem lacked a "comforter" after its destruction by the Babylonians. **40:2** *Term* and *penalty* refer to the exile, which will soon be over. *Double for all her sins* acknowledges that Jerusalem's suffering was deserved but excessive. **40:3** An unidentified voice calls for the construction of a *highway* for God's return to Jerusalem (cf. 35:8; 62:10). In the New Testament, this verse is associated with John the Baptizer (Matt. 3:3; Mark 1:3; Luke 3:4; John 1:23), and the Qumran community cited it as warrant for their retreat to the desert. **40:4** The construction of the highway requires topographical realignment. **40:5** *Glory of the LORD.* YHWH's tangible presence (cf. Isa.

6 A voice says, "Cry out!"
And I said,[l] "What shall I cry?"
All flesh is grass;
their constancy is like the flower of the field.
7 The grass withers; the flower fades,
[[when the breath of the LORD blows upon it;
surely the people are grass.
8 The grass withers; the flower fades,]][m]
but the word of our God will stand forever.
9 Get you up to a high mountain,
O Zion, herald of good news;[n]
lift up your voice with strength,
O Jerusalem, herald of good news;[o]
lift it up, do not fear;
say to the cities of Judah,
"Here is your God!"
10 See, the Lord GOD comes with might,
and his arm rules for him;
his reward is with him
and his recompense before him.
11 He will feed his flock like a shepherd;
he will gather the lambs in his arms
and carry them in his bosom
and gently lead the mother sheep.

12 Who has measured the waters of the sea[p] in the hollow of his hand
and marked off the heavens with a span,
enclosed the dust of the earth in a measure
and weighed the mountains in scales
and the hills in a balance?
13 Who has directed the spirit of the LORD
or as his counselor has instructed him?
14 Whom did he consult for his enlightenment,
and who taught him the path of justice?
[[Who taught him knowledge
and showed him the way of understanding?
15 Even the nations are like a drop from a bucket
and are accounted as dust on the scales;
see, he takes up the isles like fine dust.
16 Lebanon would not provide fuel enough,
nor are its animals enough for a burnt offering.]][q]
17 All the nations are as nothing before him;
they are accounted by him as less than nothing and emptiness.

18 To whom, then, will you liken God,
or what likeness compare with him?
19 An idol? A workman casts it,
and a goldsmith overlays it with gold
and casts for it silver chains.
20 As a gift one chooses mulberry wood[r]
—wood that will not rot—
then seeks out a skilled artisan
to set up an image that will not topple.

21 Have you not known? Have you not heard?
Has it not been told you from the beginning?
Have you not understood from the foundations of the earth?
22 It is he who sits above the circle of the earth,
and its inhabitants are like grasshoppers,
who stretches out the heavens like a curtain
and spreads them like a tent to live in,

l 40.6 Q ms Gk Vg: MT *and he said* *m* 40.7–8 Q ms Gk lack *when the breath . . . flower fades* *n* 40.9 Or *O herald of good news to Zion* *o* 40.9 Or *O herald of good news to Jerusalem* *p* 40.12 Q ms: MT lacks *of the sea* *q* 40.14–16 Q ms lacks *Who taught him . . . burnt offering* *r* 40.20 Meaning of Heb uncertain

2:10; 6:3). Its visibility to *all flesh* (including animals; cf. 43:20) emphasizes the universality of divine action, an important theme in Isa. 40–66. *Mouth of the LORD has spoken.* Cf. 1:20; 58:14. **40:6** *Grass* is a metaphor for human impermanence. **40:7** Cf. Isa. 15:6; 28:1, 4. **40:8** In contrast to mortal humanity, God's *word* is eternal. **40:9** Jerusalem is commissioned to announce God's return to *the cities of Judah*. **40:10–11** Juxtaposed images portray YHWH as both a conquering warrior and a compassionate shepherd. **40:12–14** Rhetorical questions emphasize YHWH's incomparability, appealing to creation as evidence of divine power. **40:16** *Lebanon* was known for its prized forests (cf. 10:34; 14:8; 37:24). **40:17** This message of YHWH's superiority over world *nations* would have resonated powerfully during the exile. *Emptiness.* Hebrew "tohu," which refers to primordial chaos prior to creation in Gen. 1:2 (cf. Isa. 24:10; 45:18). **40:19–20** In contrast to YHWH, an *idol* is constructed by humans, a theme throughout Isaiah (2:8, 20; 31:7; 44:9–17; 45:20; etc.). **40:21** Divine power should be self-evident. **40:22** The words *circle* ("khug") and *grasshoppers* ("khagabim") sound

²³ who brings princes to naught
  and makes the rulers of the earth as
    nothing.

²⁴ Scarcely are they planted, scarcely sown,
  scarcely has their stem taken root in
    the earth,
  when he blows upon them, and they
    wither,
  and the tempest carries them off like
    stubble.

²⁵ To whom, then, will you compare me,
  or who is my equal? says the Holy One.
²⁶ Lift up your eyes on high and see:
  Who created these?
  He who brings out their host and
    numbers them,
  calling them all by name;
  because he is great in strength,
    mighty in power,
  not one is missing.

²⁷ Why do you say, O Jacob,
  and assert, O Israel,
  "My way is hidden from the Lord,
  and my right is disregarded by my
    God"?
²⁸ Have you not known? Have you not
    heard?
  The Lord is the everlasting God,
    the Creator of the ends of the earth.
  He does not faint or grow weary;
    his understanding is unsearchable.
²⁹ He gives power to the faint
  and strengthens the powerless.

³⁰ Even youths will faint and be weary,
  and the young will fall exhausted,
³¹ but those who wait for the Lord shall
    renew their strength;
  they shall mount up with wings like
    eagles;
  they shall run and not be weary;
  they shall walk and not faint.

41 Listen to me in silence, O coastlands;
  let the peoples renew their strength;
  let them approach, then let them speak;
  let us together draw near for
    judgment.

² Who has roused a victor from the east,
  summoned him to his service?
  He delivers up nations to him
  and tramples kings under foot;
  he makes them like dust with his sword,
  like driven stubble with his bow.
³ He pursues them and passes on safely,
  scarcely touching the path with his feet.
⁴ Who has performed and done this,
  calling the generations from the
    beginning?
  I, the Lord, am first
  and will be with the last.
⁵ The coastlands have seen and are afraid;
  the ends of the earth tremble;
  they have drawn near and come.
⁶ Each one helps the other,
  saying to one another, "Take courage!"
⁷ The artisan encourages the goldsmith,
  and the one who smooths with the
    hammer encourages the one who
    strikes the anvil,

alike. **40:23** *Nothing.* Hebrew "tohu"; see note on v. 17. **40:24** As in vv. 6–8, plant imagery illustrates human frailty. **40:26** *Created* is a Hebrew verb ("bara'") that is only used with God as the subject (cf. Gen. 1:1; Isa. 40:28; 41:20; 42:5; etc.). *Host.* Stars and constellations, here portrayed strictly as natural phenomena and not divine armies or potential objects of worship (cf. 24:21). **40:27** The exilic audience is addressed as *Jacob/Israel* throughout chaps. 40–48, reflecting both the change of *Jacob*'s name to *Israel* (Gen. 32:28; 35:10) and *Jacob*'s ancestry of the nation *Israel.* The exiles' complaint of being *disregarded by [their] God* is quoted and rebutted. **40:30** In contrast to God, becoming *faint* or *weary* is part of the human condition. **40:31** Divine assistance enables humans to transcend their inherent frailty. *Wait for the Lord.* Cf. Isa. 25:9; 26:8; 33:2; 49:23.

41:1–7 A poetic dispute between YHWH and the nations over YHWH's omnipotence (cf. 41:21–29; 43:9–13; 44:7–8; 45:20–25). **41:1** *Coastlands* represent the farthest extent of human habitation. They are summoned to witness the *judgment* between God and world nations. **41:2** *Victor from the east.* Cyrus II of Persia. See **"Cyrus," p. 991**. *Makes them like dust.* Cf. 40:15. **41:4** YHWH's ability to summon Cyrus is evidence of divine power. The divine self-identification *I* (am) *the Lord* appears frequently in Isa. 40–48 (42:8; 45:3–8; 48:17; etc.) as a rhetorical strategy for distinguishing YHWH from other so-called deities. The word pair *first . . . last* expresses permanence and uniqueness (cf. 44:6; 48:12). This language is reused in Rev. 1:17; 2:8; 22:13. **41:7** In contrast to YHWH, idols are human fabrications that must be nailed down to keep from falling over.

Reading through Time: Cyrus (Isaiah 41)

Cyrus II (ca. 600–530 BCE) founded the Persian Empire, also known as the Achaemenid Empire. Between 550 and 540 BCE, he gained control of much of modern Iran and Turkey, and in 539 BCE, he took over Babylon. According to Greek sources, he conquered the city in battle. By contrast, the Cyrus Cylinder—a Babylonian text attributed to Cyrus himself—claims that he seized the city peacefully and was welcomed as a liberator. He then repatriated foreign populations conquered by the Babylonians and returned their plundered divine images. Cyrus generally promoted the native religions of the peoples he ruled. As a result, he is sometimes regarded anachronistically as an advocate of religious freedom, but this practice is better understood as a strategy for imperial control.

Cyrus features prominently in Isa. 40–48 as a liberator of the exiles and restorer of Jerusalem (44:28; 45:13). Although no extrabiblical sources mention Cyrus's repatriation of Judeans, it would be consistent with his imperial policies. Both Isa. 40–48 and the roughly contemporary Cyrus Cylinder depict Cyrus's empowerment by foreign deities, respectively YHWH and Marduk, which may reflect pro-Cyrus imperial propaganda. According to Isaiah, YHWH's empowerment of Cyrus's conquest—even though he was not a YHWH worshiper (45:1–5)—demonstrates YHWH's superiority over Babylonian deities (41:2–4, 25–27; 46:8–11). Cyrus is called YHWH's "shepherd" (44:28) and "anointed" (45:1; or "messiah"), suggesting that he has become YHWH's chosen ruler instead of a native Judean king. Despite this positive portrayal, Cyrus is ultimately YHWH's pawn rather than an independent agent in Isaiah (see **"World Empires," p. 962**). The first-century CE Jewish historian Josephus claimed that Cyrus's repatriation of the exiles was motivated by his own reading of prophecies about him in Isaiah.

Similar biblical portrayals of Cyrus in Ezra 1:1–8 and 2 Chr. 36:22–23 emphasize his support for the reconstruction of the Jerusalem temple. Unlike Isaiah, they depict his acknowledgment of YHWH's worldwide rule. Cyrus also appears as a character in Daniel.

Cyrus became a powerful political symbol for subsequent rulers. Alexander the Great paid tribute to him by visiting his tomb in Persia, and Iranian leaders have long claimed him as a forebear. More recently, some U.S. evangelical Christians compared former president Donald Trump to Cyrus, and Israeli prime minister Benjamin Netanyahu endorsed the comparison after Trump moved the American embassy to Jerusalem in 2018.

Henry W. Morisada Rietz

---

saying of the soldering, "It is good,"
  and they fasten it with nails so that it
    cannot be moved.
[8] But you, Israel, my servant,
  Jacob, whom I have chosen,
    the offspring of Abraham, my friend;
[9] you whom I took from the ends of the
    earth
  and called from its farthest corners,
saying to you, "You are my servant;
  I have chosen you and not cast you
    off";
[10] do not fear, for I am with you;
  do not be afraid, for I am your God;
I will strengthen you; I will help you;
  I will uphold you with my victorious
    right hand.

[11] All who are incensed against you
  shall be ashamed and disgraced;
those who strive against you
  shall be as nothing and shall perish.
[12] You shall seek those who contend with
    you,
  but you shall not find them;
those who war against you
  shall be as nothing at all.
[13] For I, the LORD your God,
  hold your right hand;
it is I who say to you, "Do not fear,
  I will help you."

[14] Do not fear, you worm Jacob,
  you maggot[s] Israel!

s 41.14 Cn: Heb *men of*

41:8–20 A poetic exhortation to the exiles. **41:8** *Israel/Jacob.* See note on Isa. 40:27. *My servant.* See **"Servant(s) of YHWH," p. 1011**. The story of *Abraham,* whom God led from Mesopotamia to the promised land, had special resonance for the exiles in Babylon (cf. 29:22; 51:2). *My friend* may refer to either *Israel/Jacob* or *Abraham* (cf. 2 Chr. 20:7). **41:10** *Do not fear* occurs frequently in Isa. 40–66 (41:13–14; 43:1, 5; 44:2, 8; etc.). *I am with you* recalls the symbolic name Immanuel in 7:14; 8:8, 10. **41:11–12** *Be as nothing.* Cf. 40:17, 23. **41:14** *Worm* and *maggot* are symbols of human frailty. *Redeemer* is a metaphor for divine salvation used almost exclusively in Isa. 40–66 (cf. 43:14; 54:5,

I will help you, says the Lord;
  your Redeemer is the Holy One of
  Israel.
[15] I will make of you a threshing sledge,
  sharp, new, and having teeth;
you shall thresh the mountains and
  crush them,
  and you shall make the hills like chaff.
[16] You shall winnow them, and the wind
  shall carry them away,
  and the tempest shall scatter them.
Then you shall rejoice in the Lord;
  in the Holy One of Israel you shall
  glory.
[17] When the poor and needy seek water,
  and there is none,
  and their tongue is parched with
  thirst,
I the Lord will answer them,
  I the God of Israel will not forsake
  them.
[18] I will open rivers on the bare heights
  and fountains in the midst of the
  valleys;
I will make the wilderness a pool of
  water
  and the dry land springs of water.
[19] I will put in the wilderness the cedar,
  the acacia, the myrtle, and the olive;
I will set in the desert the cypress,
  the plane and the pine together,
[20] so that all may see and know,
  all may consider and understand,
that the hand of the Lord has done this,
  the Holy One of Israel has created it.
[21] Set forth your case, says the Lord;
  bring your proofs, says the King of
  Jacob.
[22] Let them bring them and tell us
  what is to happen.
Tell us the former things, what they were,
  so that we may consider them

and that we may know their outcome
  or declare to us the things to come.
[23] Tell us what is to come hereafter,
  that we may know that you are gods;
do good, or do harm,
  that we may be afraid and terrified.
[24] You, indeed, are nothing,
  and your work is nothing at all;
  whoever chooses you is an
  abomination.
[25] I stirred up one from the north, and he
  has come,
  from the rising of the sun he was
  summoned by name.[t]
He shall trample[u] on rulers as on mortar,
  as the potter treads clay.
[26] Who declared it from the beginning, so
  that we might know,
  and beforehand, so that we might say,
  "He is right"?
There was no one who declared it, none
  who proclaimed,
  none who heard your words.
[27] I first have declared it to Zion,[v]
  and I give to Jerusalem a herald of
  good tidings.
[28] But when I look there is no one;
  among these there is no counselor
  who, when I ask, gives an answer.
[29] No, they are all a delusion;
  their works are nothing;
  their images are empty wind.

42 Here is my servant, whom I uphold,
  my chosen, in whom my soul delights;
I have put my spirit upon him;
  he will bring forth justice to the
  nations.
[2] He will not cry out or lift up his voice
  or make it heard in the street;

t 41.25 Compare Q ms Gk: MT *he shall call on my name* u 41.25 Cn: Heb *come* v 41.27 Cn Compare Q ms: Heb *First to Zion—Behold, behold them*

8; 60:16; etc.), often paired with *Holy One of Israel.* The term originally designated a kinsperson responsible for purchasing freedom for enslaved family members. **41:15** *Threshing sledge.* An agricultural implement with *sharp* blades used to separate grain from chaff (cf. 28:27). **41:16** *Holy One of Israel.* See note on 1:4. **41:17–19** The fructification of barren landscapes is a symbol of God's power (cf. 35:7; 43:19–20; 51:3). **41:20** *Created.* See note on 40:26.

41:21–29 A poetic dispute between YHWH and other deities. **41:21–23** YHWH challenges other deities to prove their divinity by predicting the future (*what is to happen*). **41:25** In contrast to the impotent divine rivals, YHWH has *stirred up one from the north* (Cyrus). **41:27** YHWH has *declared* the future to Zion in these very prophecies. *Herald of good tidings.* Cf. 40:9; 52:7.

42:1–12 The first of the four Servant Songs; see **"Servant(s) of YHWH," p. 1011. 42:1** The *servant* is empowered by God's *spirit*, much like the idealized ruler in 11:2. **42:2–4** The servant *faithfully* fulfills

³ a bruised reed he will not break,
and a dimly burning wick he will not
quench;
he will faithfully bring forth justice.
⁴ He will not grow faint or be crushed
until he has established justice in the
earth,
and the coastlands wait for his
teaching.

⁵ Thus says God, the LORD,
who created the heavens and
stretched them out,
who spread out the earth and what
comes from it,
who gives breath to the people upon it
and spirit to those who walk in it:
⁶ I am the LORD; I have called you in
righteousness;
I have taken you by the hand and
kept you;
I have given you as a covenant to the
people,ʷ
a light to the nations,
⁷   to open the eyes that are blind,
to bring out the prisoners from the
dungeon,
from the prison those who sit in
darkness.
⁸ I am the LORD; that is my name;
my glory I give to no other,
nor my praise to idols.
⁹ See, the former things have come to pass,
and new things I now declare;
before they spring forth,
I tell you of them.
¹⁰ Sing to the LORD a new song,
his praise from the end of the earth!
Let the sea roarˣ and all that fills it,

the coastlands and their inhabitants.
¹¹ Let the desert and its towns lift up their
voice,
the villages that Kedar inhabits;
let the inhabitants of Sela shout for joy;
let them shout from the tops of the
mountains.
¹² Let them give glory to the LORD
and declare his praise in the coastlands.
¹³ The LORD goes forth like a soldier;
like a warrior he stirs up his fury;
he cries out; he shouts aloud;
he shows himself mighty against his
foes.

¹⁴ For a long time I have held my peace;
I have kept still and restrained myself;
now I will cry out like a woman in labor;
I will gasp and pant.
¹⁵ I will lay waste mountains and hills
and dry up all their herbage;
I will turn the rivers into islands
and dry up the pools.
¹⁶ I will lead the blind
by a road they do not know;
by paths they have not known
I will guide them.
I will turn the darkness before them into
light,
the rough places into level ground.
These are the things I will do,
and I will not forsake them.
¹⁷ They shall be turned back and utterly
put to shame—
those who trust in carved images,
who say to cast images,
"You are our gods."

w 42.6 Meaning of Heb uncertain   x 42.10 Cn: Heb *Those
who go down to the sea*

his commission to *bring forth justice* by protecting the vulnerable. **42:5** *Created.* See note on 40:26.
The servant's work extends YHWH's creative acts. **42:6** As in v. 4, the servant's mission is international in scope. **42:7** The servant will rescue the exiles, who are depicted as *prisoners* who have
gone *blind* from being confined to *darkness*. See **"Isaiah and Disability," p. 974**. **42:8–9** A reminder
that YHWH, unlike *idols*, can recount the past and predict the future. *Former things* may refer to
the prophecies in Isa. 1–39. **42:10** The poem concludes with a brief hymn to YHWH (cf. 44:23; 45:8;
49:13). *Sing to the* LORD *a new song* (cf. Pss. 33:3; 96:1; 98:1; etc.) reflects the "new things" (v. 9)
that YHWH is doing (Isa. 42:9; 43:19; 48:6). *Coastlands.* See note on 41:1. **42:11** *Kedar* (see note on
21:16–17) and *Sela* (see note on 16:1) are both located in the *desert*. These former objects of YHWH's
judgment now praise the deity.

    42:13–25 A poetic description of YHWH's saving activities. Although it portends the exiles' deliverance, it also depicts their condition as the result of divine punishment. **42:13** YHWH's advance as
a divine *warrior* is a frequent motif in biblical poetry; cf. Judg. 5:4–6; Isa. 30:27–28; Hab. 3:3–6; etc.
42:14 See **"Feminine Imagery for God," p. 1029**. **42:15** In contrast to 41:17–19, YHWH will *dry up*
lush landscapes. **42:16** A combination of images associated with exile: blindness (cf. v. 7) and the

¹⁸ Listen, you who are deaf,
    and you who are blind, look up and
      see!
¹⁹ Who is blind but my servant
    or deaf like my messenger whom I send?
Who is blind like my dedicated one
    or blind like the servant of the LORD?
²⁰ He sees many things, but he does^y not
      observe them;
    his ears are open, but he does not
      hear.
²¹ The LORD was pleased, for the sake of his
      righteousness,
    to magnify his teaching and make it
      glorious.
²² But this is a people robbed and plundered;
    all of them are trapped in holes
    and hidden in prisons;
they have become a prey with no one to
      rescue,
    a spoil with no one to say, "Restore!"
²³ Who among you will give heed to this;
    who will attend and listen for the time
      to come?
²⁴ Who gave up Jacob to the spoiler
    and Israel to the robbers?
Was it not the LORD, against whom they
      sinned,^z
    in whose ways they would not walk,
    and whose law they would not obey?
²⁵ So he poured upon him the heat of his
      anger
    and the fury of war;
it set him on fire all around, but he did
      not understand;
    it burned him, but he did not take it to
      heart.

43 But now thus says the LORD,
    he who created you, O Jacob,
    he who formed you, O Israel:
Do not fear, for I have redeemed you;
    I have called you by name; you are
      mine.
² When you pass through the waters, I will
      be with you,
    and through the rivers, they shall not
      overwhelm you;
when you walk through fire you shall not
      be burned,
    and the flame shall not consume
      you.
³ For I am the LORD your God,
    the Holy One of Israel, your Savior.
I give Egypt as your ransom,
    Cush and Seba in exchange for you.
⁴ Because you are precious in my sight
    and honored and I love you,
I give people in return for you,
    nations in exchange for your life.
⁵ Do not fear, for I am with you;
    I will bring your offspring from the
      east,
    and from the west I will gather you;
⁶ I will say to the north, "Give them up,"
    and to the south, "Do not
      withhold;
bring my sons from far away
    and my daughters from the end of the
      earth—
⁷ everyone who is called by my name,
    whom I created for my glory,
    whom I formed and made."

y 42.20 Heb mss: MT *You see many things but do*   *z* 42.24 Gk
Tg: Heb *we sinned*

wilderness highway (cf. 40:3–5). **42:18** *Blind* and *deaf* recall Isaiah's commission to shut the people's eyes and ears so they would not repent in 6:10, a state that persists in the world of the poem (v. 25). Now the people are called to *look up and see*. See **"Isaiah and Disability," p. 974**. **42:19–20** In contrast to the exiles, YHWH's servant is *blind* and *deaf* in a positive way. The meaning of the image is unclear. It may refer to the servant's exemplary avoidance of idols or his trust in YHWH despite his impaired perception (cf. 50:10). **42:21** YHWH's actions are motivated by the deity's own *righteousness*. **42:22** Metaphors for exile. *Prisons.* Cf. v. 7. **42:24–25** Exile was YHWH's punishment of *Jacob/Israel* for their disobedience (cf. 40:2), but they have not yet realized this (cf. v. 18).

    43:1–6 A poetic promise of deliverance to the exiles. **43:1** *But now* marks a shift from indictment to promise. *Thus says the LORD.* Throughout Isa. 40–55, the prophetic messenger formula (see note on 7:7) is expanded with other divine titles or attributes. *Created.* See note on 40:26. *Jacob/Israel.* See note on 40:27. **43:2** *Waters* and *rivers* symbolize primordial chaos. *Be with you.* See note on 41:10. *Fire* was a recurring metaphor for punishment in Isa. 1–39. **43:3** *Savior* designates a military deliverer. *Cush.* See note on 18:1. *Seba.* An ancient African kingdom associated with wealth in Ps. 72:10. The payment of a *ransom* develops YHWH's claim to have "redeemed" the exiles (Isa. 43:1). **43:5–6** A promise to repatriate the exiles from throughout the earth. **43:7** *Created/formed* echoes v. 1 and thus encloses the poem.

⁸ Bring forth the people who are blind yet
    have eyes,
  who are deaf yet have ears!
⁹ Let all the nations gather together,
    and let the peoples assemble.
  Who among them declared this
    and foretold to us the former things?
  Let them bring their witnesses to justify
    them,
    and let them hear and say, "It is true."
¹⁰ You are my witnesses, says the Lord,
    and my servant whom I have
      chosen,
  so that you may know and believe me
    and understand that I am he.
  Before me no god was formed,
    nor shall there be any after me.
¹¹ I, I am the Lord,
    and besides me there is no savior.
¹² I am the one who declared and saved and
      proclaimed,
    not some strange god among you;
  you are my witnesses, says the Lord,
    and I am God.
¹³ Indeed, since that day I am he;
    there is no one who can deliver from
      my hand;
    I work, and who can hinder it?

¹⁴ Thus says the Lord,
    your Redeemer, the Holy One of
      Israel:
  For your sake I will send to Babylon
    and break down all the bars,
    and the shouting of the Chaldeans
    will be turned to lamentation.ᵃ
¹⁵ I am the Lord, your Holy One,
    the Creator of Israel, your King.

¹⁶ Thus says the Lord,
    who makes a way in the sea,
    a path in the mighty waters,
¹⁷ who brings out chariot and horse,
    army and warrior;
  they lie down; they cannot rise;
    they are extinguished, quenched like
      a wick:
¹⁸ Do not remember the former things
    or consider the things of old.
¹⁹ I am about to do a new thing;
    now it springs forth; do you not
      perceive it?
  I will make a way in the wilderness
    and rivers in the desert.
²⁰ The wild animals will honor me,
    the jackals and the ostriches,
  for I give water in the wilderness,
    rivers in the desert,
  to give drink to my chosen people,
²¹   the people whom I formed for myself
  so that they might declare my praise.

²² Yet you did not call upon me, O Jacob;
    but you have been weary of me,
      O Israel!
²³ You have not brought me your sheep for
      burnt offerings
    or honored me with your sacrifices.
  I have not burdened you with
      offerings
    or wearied you with frankincense.
²⁴ You have not bought me sweet cane with
      money
    or satisfied me with the fat of your
      sacrifices.

ᵃ 43.14 Meaning of Heb uncertain

43:8–13 A poetic dispute between YHWH and the nations. 43:8 The exiles are invited to the legal proceedings. *Blind* and *deaf* are metaphors for spiritual states, not literal references to disability. See **"Isaiah and Disability," p. 974**. 43:9 The *witnesses* for the *nations* are presumably their impotent deities (cf. 41:22–23; 42:9). 43:10a As beneficiaries of divine actions, the audience members are YHWH's *witnesses*. 43:10b–11 The first of several repeated statements of YHWH's sole existence in Isa. 40–48 (see **"Emerging Monotheism," p. 1000**). 43:12–13 Among the world's deities, only YHWH has the power to *deliver*.

43:14–44:5 A poetic promise of deliverance to the exiles, despite their insufficient worship of YHWH. 43:14 The first specific identification of *Babylon* as the exiles' oppressor. *Bars.* The mechanism for locking the city gates to keep out invaders. *Chaldeans.* Inhabitants of Babylonia. 43:16–17 God's defeat of Egypt during the exodus. 43:19 The return from exile will be a *new* and improved exodus. *Way in the wilderness.* Cf. 40:3. 43:20 *Jackals* and *ostriches* are quintessential wilderness animals (cf. 13:21–22; 34:13). *Water in the wilderness* recalls miracles following the exodus (Exod. 17:1–7; Num. 20:1–13). 43:21–22 Despite being *formed* to *declare [the Lord's] praise*, Jacob/Israel has not worshiped YHWH. 43:23–24 In contrast to Isa. 1:11–15, which criticized the people's excessive religiosity, here they have failed to present *sacrifices*, instead offering the deity their *sins* and

Rather, you have burdened me with your
sins;
you have wearied me with your
iniquities.

25 I alone am the one
who blots out your transgressions for
my own sake,
and I will not remember your sins.
26 Accuse me; let us go to trial;
set forth your case, so that you may be
proved right.
27 Your first ancestor sinned,
and your mediators rebelled against
me.
28 Therefore I profaned the princes of the
sanctuary;
I delivered Jacob to utter
destruction
and Israel to reviling.

44 But now hear, O Jacob my servant,
Israel whom I have chosen!
2 Thus says the LORD who made you,
who formed you in the womb and will
help you:
Do not fear, O Jacob my servant,
Jeshurun whom I have chosen.
3 For I will pour water on the thirsty
land
and streams on the dry ground;
I will pour my spirit upon your
descendants
and my blessing on your offspring.
4 They shall spring up like a green
tamarisk,[b]
like willows by flowing streams.

5 This one will say, "I am the LORD's";
another will be called by the name of
Jacob;
yet another will write on the hand, "The
LORD's,"
and adopt the name of Israel.

6 Thus says the LORD, the King of Israel,
and his Redeemer, the LORD of hosts:
I am the first, and I am the last;
besides me there is no god.
7 Who is like me? Let them proclaim it;
let them declare and set it forth before
me.
Who has announced from of old the
things to come?[c]
Let them tell us[d] what is yet to be.
8 Do not fear or be afraid;
have I not told you from of old and
declared it?
You are my witnesses!
Is there any god besides me?
There is no other rock; I know not one.

9 All who make idols are nothing, and the
things they delight in do not profit; their
witnesses neither see nor know, and so they
will be put to shame. 10Who would fashion a
god or cast an image that can do no good?
11All its devotees shall be put to shame; the
artisans, too, are merely human. Let them
all assemble; let them stand up; they shall
be terrified; they shall all be put to shame.

12 The blacksmith works it with a tool
over the coals, shaping it with hammers and

b 44.4 Q ms: MT *in the midst of grass*   c 44.7 Cn: Heb *from my
placing an eternal people and things to come*   d 44.7 Tg: Heb *them*

---

iniquities. *Wearied* is ironically repeated three times across vv. 22–24, each with a different connotation. **43:26** Legal language recalls 41:1–7, 21–29; 43:8–13, but here the disputed question is
YHWH's justification for punishing the exiles. **43:27** *First ancestor* refers to Jacob, although it is
unclear how he *sinned*. The exiles have a long pedigree of rebellion against God; cf. Jer. 31:29–
30 and Ezek. 18:1–22, which blame the exiles' punishment on their own sins, not their ancestors'.
43:28 *Profaned the princes of the sanctuary.* The destruction of the Jerusalem temple by the Babylonians. **44:2** *Jeshurun.* Another name for Jacob that only appears elsewhere in Deut. 32:15; 33:5,
26. **44:3** See note on 41:17–19.

44:6–23 A poetic dispute over YHWH's power. **44:6** *First . . . last.* See note on 41:4. *Besides me
there is no god.* See **"Emerging Monotheism," p. 1000.** **44:7** A challenge to other so-called deities.
Things to come. See note on 41:21–23. **44:8** *You are my witnesses.* See note on 43:10a. *Rock.* See
note on 26:4. **44:9** Some scholars identify vv. 9–20, a diatribe against manufacturers of divine
images, as a later addition to this text, and their presentation as prose in the NRSVue separates
them from their context. It is possible to analyze these verses as poetry, however, and their content
is consistent with other idol polemics in Isa. 40–48. **44:10** A rhetorical question demonstrating the
absurdity of creating a divine image. **44:11** As "witnesses" (vv. 8, 9) for these so-called deities, the
image manufacturers are called to *assemble* for the dispute. **44:12** Vv. 12–17 describe the manufacture of divine images, reflecting some awareness of religious practices in ancient Mesopotamia.

forging it with his strong arm; he becomes hungry, and his strength fails; he drinks no water and is faint. [13]The carpenter stretches a line, marks it out with a stylus, fashions it with planes, and marks it with a compass; he makes it in human form, with human beauty, to be set up in a shrine. [14]He cuts down cedars or chooses a holm tree or an oak and lets it grow strong among the trees of the forest. He plants a cedar and the rain nourishes it. [15]Then it can be used as fuel. Part of it he takes and warms himself; he kindles a fire and bakes bread. Then he makes a god and worships it, makes it a carved image and bows down before it. [16]Half of it he burns in the fire; over this half he roasts meat, eats it,[e] and is satisfied. He also warms himself and says, "Ah, I am warm[f] by the fire!" [17]The rest of it he makes into a god, his idol, bows down to it and worships it; he prays to it and says, "Save me, for you are my god!"

18 They do not know, nor do they comprehend, for their eyes are shut, so that they cannot see, and their minds as well, so that they cannot understand. [19]No one considers, nor is there knowledge or discernment to say, "Half of it I burned in the fire; I also baked bread on its coals; I roasted meat and have eaten. Now shall I make the rest of it an abomination? Shall I fall down before a block of wood?" [20]He feeds on ashes; a deluded mind has led him astray, and he cannot save himself or say, "Is not this thing in my right hand a fraud?"
[21] Remember these things, O Jacob,
    and Israel, for you are my servant;
I formed you, you are my servant;
    O Israel, do not forget me.[g]

[22] I have swept away your transgressions
        like a cloud
    and your sins like mist;
return to me, for I have redeemed you.

[23] Sing, O heavens, for the LORD has done it;
        shout, O depths of the earth;
break forth into singing, O mountains,
        O forest and every tree in it!
For the LORD has redeemed Jacob
        and will be glorified in Israel.

[24] Thus says the LORD, your Redeemer,
        who formed you in the womb:
I am the LORD, who made all things,
        who alone stretched out the heavens,
        who by myself spread out the earth;
[25] who frustrates the omens of soothsayers
        and makes fools of diviners;
who turns back the wise
        and makes their knowledge foolish;
[26] who confirms the word of his servant
        and fulfills the prediction of his
        messengers;
who says of Jerusalem, "It shall be
        inhabited,"
    and of the cities of Judah, "They shall
        be rebuilt,
    and I will raise up their ruins";
[27] who says to the deep, "Be dry—
        I will dry up your rivers";
[28] who says of Cyrus, "He is my shepherd,
        and he shall carry out all my
        purpose";

e 44.16 Cn Compare Gk Syr: Heb *he eats, he roasts a roast*
f 44.16 Q ms: MT *I see*   g 44.21 Q ms Compare Gk Syr Tg:
MT *you will not be forgotten by me*

The human limitations of the *blacksmith* extend to his creation. **44:13** The emphasis on the image's careful construction and its *human form* belies the claim that it is divine (cf. v. 17). **44:14–17** The absurdity of making a "god" from the same wood with which one *roasts meat* and *warms* oneself is obvious (cf. vv. 19–20). The image cannot possibly *save* its maker; YHWH is the only savior (43:11). This polemic does not accurately portray the function of divine images in Mesopotamian religion. Worshipers did not equate the deity with the image; instead, they believed that it focalized divine presence, and special rituals invited the deity to inhabit the image. This poet is not interested in interreligious dialogue, however. The point is to dissuade Judean exiles from imagining that Babylonian gods are superior to YHWH. **44:18** A lack of knowledge or sight is attributed to the idols themselves in other polemics (Pss. 115:4–8; 135:15–18) but here is applied to their manufacturers in language that recalls Isa. 6:9–10. **44:22** Cf. 43:25. *Cloud* and *mist* are symbols of impermanence. **44:23** A hymnic conclusion (cf. 42:10–11; 45:8; 49:13).
44:24–45:8 A poem depicting Cyrus as the exiles' deliverer and declaring YHWH's unsurpassed divinity. **44:24** YHWH's self-identification is followed by fourteen descriptions of divine activity, beginning with creation. **44:25** A polemic against Babylonian omen interpreters (cf. 45:9–13). **44:26–28** God explicitly promises to repopulate *Judah* and rebuild *Jerusalem* and the *temple*. On *Cyrus*, see **"Cyrus," p. 991**. *Shepherd*. An ancient metaphor for kingship (cf. 2 Sam. 7:7; Jer. 23:4).

and who says of Jerusalem, "It shall be
rebuilt,"
and of the temple, "Your foundation
shall be laid."

45 Thus says the LORD to his anointed,
to Cyrus,
whose right hand I have grasped
to subdue nations before him
and to strip kings of their robes,
to open doors before him—
and the gates shall not be closed:
² I will go before you
and level the mountains;*b*
I will break in pieces the doors of
bronze
and cut through the bars of iron;
³ I will give you the treasures of
darkness
and riches hidden in secret places,
so that you may know that it is I, the
LORD,
the God of Israel, who call you by
your name.
⁴ For the sake of my servant Jacob
and Israel my chosen,
I call you by your name;
I give you a title, though you do not
know me.
⁵ I am the LORD, and there is no other;
besides me there is no god.
I arm you, though you do not know
me,
⁶ so that they may know, from the rising of
the sun
and from the west, that there is no one
besides me;
I am the LORD, and there is no other.

⁷ I form light and create darkness,
I make weal and create woe;
I the LORD do all these things.

⁸ Shower, O heavens, from above,
and let the skies rain down
righteousness;
let the earth open, that salvation may
spring up,*i*
and let it cause righteousness to
sprout up also;
I the LORD have created it.

⁹ Woe to those who strive with their
Maker,
earthen vessels with the potter!*j*
Does the clay say to the one who
fashions it, "What are you
making"?
or "Your work has no handles"?
¹⁰ Woe to anyone who says to a father,
"What are you fathering?"
or to a woman, "With what are you in
labor?"
¹¹ Thus says the LORD,
the Holy One of Israel and its
Maker:
Will you question me*k* about my
children
or command me concerning the work
of my hands?
¹² I made the earth
and created humankind upon it;

b 45.2 Q ms Gk: MT *the swellings*   *i* 45.8 Q ms: MT *that
they may bring forth salvation*   *j* 45.9 Cn: Heb *with the
potsherds* or *with the potters*   *k* 45.11 Cn: Heb *Ask me of things
to come*

45:1 *Anointed.* Literally "messiah" (Heb. "meshiakh"), a term used for Davidic monarchs (cf. 2 Sam. 22:51; Ps. 2:2). *Open . . . not be closed.* Cf. Isa. 22:22. **45:2** *Level the mountains.* Cf. 40:4. **45:3** God calls Cyrus *by [his] name*, just like Jacob/Israel in 43:1. **45:4** Events of worldwide significance happen *for the sake of . . . Jacob/Israel.* **45:7** *Create.* See note on 40:26. The claim that God causes evil is theologically disturbing, but it follows logically from the denial of other active powers in the universe. **45:8** A hymnic conclusion (cf. 42:10-11; 44:23; 49:13).

45:9-19 A poetic rebuttal to skepticism about divine actions, anticipating objections to YHWH's choice of Cyrus. **45:9** In contrast to Isa. 1-39, this is one of only two poems in Isa. 40-66 that begin with *woe* (cf. 55:1, where the Heb. word has a neutral sense). For the *potter/clay* metaphor, cf. 29:16; 64:8. **45:10** See **"Feminine Imagery for God," p. 1029.** **45:11-12** Because God *made the earth*, one should no more challenge God's actions in the world than question a potter about their work or a parent about their children. By contrast, other biblical texts like Job affirm humans' right to question divine actions. **45:13** God's actions, including the empowerment of *Cyrus*, are ultimately meant for the exiles' good. **45:14** The motif of Jerusalem receiving foreign wealth appears throughout chaps. 40-66; cf. 18:7, where *Cush* brings tribute. For *Egypt, Cush*, and the *Sabeans*, cf. 43:3. This is the first time in these chapters that any foreign nations recognize YHWH's sole power, after several previous challenges to do so. Egypt similarly recognizes YHWH's supremacy in

it was my hands that stretched out the
heavens,
and I commanded all their host.
13 I have aroused Cyrus[l] in righteousness,
and I will make all his paths straight;
he shall build my city
and set my exiles free,
not for price or reward,
says the LORD of hosts.
14 Thus says the LORD:
The wealth of Egypt and the
merchandise of Cush
and the Sabeans, tall of stature,
shall come over to you and be yours;
they shall follow you;
they shall come over in chains and
bow down to you.
They will make supplication to you, saying,
"God is with you alone, and there is
no other;
there is no god besides him."
15 Truly, you are a God who hides himself,
O God of Israel, the Savior.
16 All of them are put to shame and
confounded;
the makers of idols go in disgrace
together.
17 But Israel is saved by the LORD
with everlasting salvation;
you shall not be put to shame or confounded
ever again.

18 For thus says the LORD,
who created the heavens
(he is God!),
who formed the earth and made it
(he established it;
he did not create it a chaos;
he formed it to be inhabited!):
I am the LORD, and there is no other.
19 I did not speak in secret
in a land of darkness;

I did not say to the offspring of Jacob,
"Seek me in chaos."
I the LORD speak the truth;
I declare what is right.
20 Assemble yourselves and come together;
draw near, you survivors of the
nations!
They have no knowledge—
those who carry about their wooden
idols
and keep on praying to a god
that cannot save.
21 Declare and present your case;
take counsel together![m]
Who told this long ago?
Who declared it of old?
Was it not I, the LORD?
There is no other god besides me,
a righteous God and a Savior;
there is no one besides me.
22 Turn to me and be saved,
all the ends of the earth!
For I am God, and there is no other.
23 By myself I have sworn;
from my mouth has gone forth in
righteousness
a word that shall not return:
"To me every knee shall bow,
every tongue shall swear."

24 Only in the LORD, it shall be said of me,
are righteousness and strength;
all who were incensed against him
shall come to him and be ashamed.
25 In the LORD all the offspring of Israel
shall triumph and glory.

46 Bel bows down; Nebo stoops;
their idols are on beasts and cattle;

l 45.13 Heb *him*   m 45.21 Syr Vg: Heb *let them take counsel*

19.21–25. **45.15** This verse may repeat one of the exiles' complaints about God, as in 40:27. For the motif of divine hiddenness, cf. 8:17; 54:8; 64:5–7. **45:18–19** The orderliness of creation speaks both to YHWH's sole power and to YHWH's beneficence toward *the offspring of Jacob*.

45:20–25 A poetic dispute over YHWH's power (cf. 41:1–7, 21–29; 43:8–13; 44:6–23). **45:20** *Survivors of the nations* may address Judean exiles scattered among the *nations* or the foreign *survivors* of Cyrus's invasions. **45:21** Cf. 41:22–23, 26–27; 44:7–8. **45:22** After repeated calls to acknowledge YHWH's supremacy, the nations are invited to *turn to* YHWH *and be saved*. **45:23** *A word.* Cf. 40:8; 55:10–11. *Every knee shall bow.* Paul quotes this description of universal submission to God in Rom. 14:11; Phil. 2:10–11. **45:24–25** The contrasting fates of *the offspring of Israel* and their enemies.

46:1–13 A poem mocking other deities and comforting the exiles. **46:1–2** *Bel*, the Babylonian word for "lord," is a title for the Babylonian supreme deity Marduk. *Nebo.* Nabu, the Babylonian god of wisdom; the deity's name appears in personal names like "Nebuchadnezzar." Instead of

Going Deeper: Emerging Monotheism (Isaiah 45)

Although the Hebrew Bible insists on the exclusive worship of YHWH, some texts admit that other deities exist (Deut. 32:8–9; Judg. 11:24; Mic. 4:5). Other biblical texts exclude the possibility of other divine powers, including the book of Isaiah. From beginning to end, an exalted view of YHWH characterizes Isaiah. Height imagery depicts the deity's superiority (6:1; 33:5; 57:15). YHWH tolerates no rivals, natural or human (2:11–17; 10:12; 40:23). Powerful nations act only at the deity's bidding (see **"World Empires," p. 962**). This discourse positions YHWH as the single effective power in the universe.

Isaiah denounces the worship of divine images, stressing their materiality. Isaiah 1–39 refers to them as "the work of [human] hands" (2:8; 17:8; 37:19) and emphasizes their construction from precious metals (2:20; 30:22; 31:7). The polemic intensifies in chaps. 40–55. Detailed descriptions of the manufacture of images reflect knowledge of Mesopotamian religious practices (40:19–20; 41:7; 44:12–14). Isaiah 44:15–20 mocks the absurdity of burning half of a log to cook one's dinner while carving the other half into an idol and praying to it. In 46:1–2, the images themselves bow down, as "weary animals" collapse beneath their weight. These chapters highlight the powers demonstrated by YHWH but lacked by idols, such as the ability to create the cosmos (40:25–26; 45:5–8) or announce future events in advance (41:21–29; 48:5). Such texts would have discouraged exiled Judeans from abandoning the worship of YHWH for Babylonian deities. Throughout Isaiah, idols inevitably disappoint the worshipers who depend on them (19:2–3; 45:16; 57:13).

These texts imply that other so-called gods have no real existence outside their humanly constructed images. A repeated Hebrew word for foreign deities in Isa. 1–39 is 'elilim, which sounds like both the generic term for god ('elohim) and an adjective meaning "worthless" ('elil). Clear claims of YHWH's sole existence appear in Isa. 40–55: "Besides me there is no savior [or god]" (43:10–11; 44:6). "Is there any god besides me? There is no other rock; I know not one" (44:8). "Besides me there is no god. . . . There is no one besides me" (45:5–6). "I am the Lord, and there is no other" (45:18). "There is no other god besides me. . . . There is no one besides me" (45:21). "I am God, and there is no other; I am God, and there is no one like me" (46:9). Scholars debate whether such language is primarily heightened rhetoric or reflects an actual belief in the nonexistence of other deities. In either case, the depiction of YHWH's unrivaled supremacy in Isaiah anticipates the characteristic monotheism of the later religions of Judaism, Christianity, and Islam.

J. Blake Couey

these things you carry are loaded
as burdens on weary animals.
² They stoop; they bow down together;
they cannot save the burden
but themselves go into captivity.

³ Listen to me, O house of Jacob,
all the remnant of the house of Israel,
who have been borne by me from your
birth,
carried from the womb;
⁴ even to your old age I am he;
even when you turn gray I will carry you.
I have made, and I will bear;
I will carry and will save.

⁵ To whom will you liken me and make me
equal
and compare me, as though we were
alike?
⁶ Those who lavish gold from the purse
and weigh out silver in the scales—
they hire a goldsmith, who makes it into
a god;
then they fall down and worship!
⁷ They lift it to their shoulders; they carry it;
they set it in its place, and it stands
there;
it cannot move from its place.
If one cries out to it, it does not answer
or save anyone from trouble.

the expected image of worshipers bowing before these deities, *their idols* appear to *bow down* as the *weary animals* carrying them collapse beneath their weight. The poem likely describes the procession of divine images during Babylonian religious festivals, which the exiles may have witnessed. Even as the exiles are delivered, the Babylonian deities *go into captivity*, a reference to Cyrus's anticipated conquest. **46:3–4** YHWH cares for the exiles from *birth* (cf. 44:2, 24) to *old age*; see **"Feminine Imagery for God," p. 1029**. *Carry* is ironically repeated from vv. 1–2. *Turn gray* ("sebah") sounds like the word for "captivity" ("shibyah"), reinforcing God's care for the exiles in their current situation. **46:6** Cf. 40:19; 41:7; 44:12–17. **46:7** Further ironic repetition of *carry* (cf. vv.

⁸ Remember this and consider;ⁿ
   recall it to mind, you transgressors;
⁹   remember the former things of old,
for I am God, and there is no other;
   I am God, and there is no one like me,
¹⁰ declaring the outcome from the
      beginning
   and from ancient times things not yet
      done,
saying, "My purpose shall stand,
   and I will fulfill my intention,"
¹¹ calling a bird of prey from the east,
   the man for my purpose from a far
      country.
I have spoken, and I will bring it to
      pass;
I have planned, and I will do it.

¹² Listen to me, you stubborn of heart,
   you who are far from deliverance:
¹³ I bring near my deliverance; it is not far
      off,
   and my salvation will not tarry;
I will put salvation in Zion,
   for Israel my glory.

47 Come down and sit in the dust,
   virgin daughter Babylon!
Sit on the ground without a throne,
   daughter Chaldea!
For you shall no more be called
   tender and delicate.
² Take the millstones and grind meal;
   remove your veil;
strip off your robe; uncover your legs;
   pass through the rivers.
³ Your nakedness shall be uncovered,
   and your shame shall be seen.

I will take vengeance,
   and I will spare no one.ᵒ
⁴ Our Redeemer—the Lᴏʀᴅ of hosts is his
      name—
   is the Holy One of Israel.

⁵ Sit in silence, and go into darkness,
   daughter Chaldea!
For you shall no more be called
   the mistress of kingdoms.
⁶ I was angry with my people;
   I profaned my heritage;
I gave them into your hand;
   you showed them no mercy;
on the aged you made your yoke
   exceedingly heavy.
⁷ You said, "I shall be mistress forever,"
   so that you did not lay these things to
      heart
   or remember their end.

⁸ Now therefore hear this, you lover of
      pleasures,
   who sit securely,
who say in your heart,
   "I am, and there is no one besides me;
I shall not sit as a widow
   or know the loss of children"—
⁹ both these things shall come upon you
   in a moment, in one day:
the loss of children and widowhood
   shall come upon you in full measure,
in spite of your many sorceries
   and the great power of your
      enchantments.

n 46.8 Meaning of Heb uncertain   *o* 47.3 Meaning of Heb uncertain

1–2). **46:8** *Transgressors* likely refers to the exiles (cf. 43:25; 44:22). **46:10** *Purpose* is the same word used for YHWH's "plan" in chaps. 1–39. **46:11** *Bird of prey* and *man for my purpose* refer to Cyrus. **46:12–13** The exiles' belief that they are *far from deliverance* is mistaken; note the repetition of *far* in vv. 11–13.

    47:1–15 A poetic celebration of the fall of Babylon (cf. Isa. 13–14), personified as a woman. It logically follows the predictions of Cyrus's conquests in chaps. 45–46 and anticipates the vindication of Jerusalem in chaps. 49–55. This text influenced the imagery of the "whore" of Babylon in Rev. 17:1–6. **47:1** *Babylon* is portrayed as a humiliated *virgin daughter* (cf. 23:12). *Chaldea.* Another name for Babylon. Both Babylon and Jerusalem are personified as women in Isa. 40–55 but with opposite fates. Unfortunately, this creates the impression that one woman's liberation requires another woman's oppression. **47:2** Instead of living in luxury, Babylon will perform menial labor (*grind meal*). **47:3** Babylon's conquest is disturbingly compared to sexual violence against women (cf. Nah. 3:4–6). **47:5** Similar language is used for Jerusalem's destruction in Lam. 1:1. **47:6** YHWH allowed Babylon to conquer Jerusalem. The promise to care for the exiles in old age in 46:4 responds to Babylon's persecution of *the aged*. **47:8** *No one besides me* parodies YHWH's claim to sole power in 43:11; 44:6–8; 45:5–6, 21. **47:9** Babylon's *loss of children* and *widowhood* contrast with Jerusalem's restoration of children and remarriage in 49:20–21; 54:1–5. *Sorceries* and *enchantments* refer

¹⁰ You felt secure in your wickedness;
  you said, "No one sees me."
Your wisdom and your knowledge
  led you astray,
and you said in your heart,
  "I am, and there is no one besides me."
¹¹ But evil shall come upon you,
  which you cannot charm away;
disaster shall fall upon you,
  which you will not be able to ward off,
and ruin shall come on you suddenly,
  of which you know nothing.

¹² Stand fast in your enchantments
  and your many sorceries,
  with which you have labored from
    your youth;
perhaps you may be able to succeed;
  perhaps you may inspire terror.
¹³ You are wearied with your many
    consultations;
  let those who study*p* the heavens
stand up and save you,
  those who gaze at the stars
and at each new moon predict
  what*q* shall befall you.

¹⁴ See, they are like stubble;
  the fire consumes them;
they cannot deliver themselves
  from the power of the flame.
No coal for warming oneself is this,
  no fire to sit before!
¹⁵ Such to you are those with whom you
    have labored,
  who have trafficked with you from
    your youth;
they all wander about in their own paths;
  there is no one to save you.

48 Hear this, O house of Jacob,
  who are called by the name of Israel
  and who came forth from the loins*r* of
    Judah,
who swear by the name of the Lord
  and invoke the God of Israel
  but not in truth or right.
² For they call themselves after the holy city
  and lean on the God of Israel;
  the Lord of hosts is his name.

³ The former things I declared long ago;
  they went out from my mouth, and I
    made them known;
  then suddenly I did them, and they
    came to pass.
⁴ Because I know that you are obstinate,
  and your neck is an iron sinew
  and your forehead brass,
⁵ I declared them to you from long ago,
  before they came to pass I announced
    them to you,
so that you would not say, "My idol did
    them;
  my carved image and my cast image
    commanded them."

⁶ You have heard; now see all this;
  and will you not declare it?
From this time forward I tell you new
    things,
  hidden things that you have not known.
⁷ They are created now, not long ago;
  before today you have never heard of
    them,
so that you could not say, "I already
    knew them."

p 47.13 Meaning of Heb uncertain   *q* 47.13 Gk Syr Compare Vg: Heb *from what*   *r* 48.1 Cn: Heb *waters*

disparagingly to Babylonian religious practices. **47:10** Cf. the similar polemic against Egyptian *wisdom* in 19:11–14. **47:13** The polemic against Babylonian divinatory practices, especially the interpretation of astronomical omens, is part of these chapters' discourse about YHWH's sole ability to foretell the future. **47:15** *Those with whom you have labored.* Literally "traders" ("sokharim"), a reference to Babylon's wealth from international commerce (cf. 23:2, 3, 8), which also plays on the similar-sounding word for "charm" ("shakhrah") used in v. 11.

48:1–22 Further poetic argument for YHWH's divine superiority, with an emphasis on the exiles' waywardness. **48:1** Despite using the proper words, the audience's appeals to YHWH are insincere (cf. 29:13). *Loins of Judah* refers to the exiles' descent from Jacob's son, Judah. **48:2** *Holy city.* Jerusalem. **48:3–4** In addition to demonstrating divine superiority (41:21–29; 43:9–13; 46:9–10), YHWH's announcement of future events responds to the exiles' *obstinate* nature. *Iron* and *brass* symbolize stubbornness, and the image of metal body parts recalls the idol polemics (40:19; 41:7; 44:12). *Sinew* alludes to the story of Jacob's change of name to Israel (Gen. 32:32, there translated as "muscle"); cf. "the name of Israel" in v. 1. **48:5** If YHWH's actions had not been announced in advance, the exiles would have attributed them to their *idol*. This verse suggests that Isaiah's idol polemics are meant to dissuade the exiles, not

8 You have never heard; you have never
  known;
  from of old your ear has not been opened.
  For I knew that you would act very
  treacherously
  and that from birth you were called a
  rebel.

9 For my name's sake I defer my anger;
  for the sake of my praise I restrain it
  for you,
  so that I may not cut you off.
10 See, I have refined you but not like[s] silver;
  I have tested you in the furnace of
  adversity.
11 For my own sake, for my own sake, I do it,
  for why should my name[t] be
  profaned?
  My glory I will not give to another.

12 Listen to me, O Jacob,
  and Israel, whom I called:
  I am he; I am the first,
  and I am the last.
13 My hand laid the foundation of the earth,
  and my right hand spread out the
  heavens;
  when I summon them,
  they stand at attention.

14 Assemble, all of you, and hear!
  Who among them has declared these
  things?
  The one the LORD loves shall perform his
  purpose against Babylon,
  and his arm shall be against the
  Chaldeans.
15 I, even I, have spoken and called him;
  I have brought him, and he will
  prosper in his way.

16 Draw near to me; hear this!
  From the beginning I have not spoken
  in secret;
  from the time it came to be I have
  been there.
  And now the Lord GOD has sent me and
  his spirit.

17 Thus says the LORD,
  your Redeemer, the Holy One of Israel:
  I am the LORD your God,
  who teaches you how to succeed,
  who leads you in the way you should go.
18 O that you had paid attention to my
  commandments!
  Then your prosperity would have
  been like a river
  and your success like the waves of the sea;
19 your offspring would have been like the
  sand
  and your descendants like its grains;
  their name would never be cut off
  or destroyed from before me.

20 Go out from Babylon; flee from Chaldea;
  declare this with a shout of joy;
  proclaim it;
  send it forth to the end of the earth;
  say, "The LORD has redeemed his
  servant Jacob!"
21 They did not thirst when he led them
  through the deserts;
  he made water flow for them from the
  rock;
  he split open the rock, and the water
  gushed out.
22 "There is no peace," says the LORD, "for
  the wicked."

s 48.10 Cn: Heb *with*   t 48.11 Gk OL: Heb *for why should it*

necessarily the other nations, from worshiping other deities. **48:8** *Never heard . . . known.* Cf. 40:21, 28.
Ear has not been opened. Cf. 6:9–10. *I knew.* YHWH's foreknowledge extends to the exiles' rebelliousness.
48:9 Out of self-interest, YHWH exercises restraint so as not to destroy the exiles. **48:10** The exile is
compared to smelting ore to extract metal (cf. 1:25; Ezek. 22:17–22), extending the imagery of the exiles'
metal body parts from v. 4. *Not like silver.* Instead of a literal smelter, the exiles were subjected to *the furnace of adversity.* Instead of *tested* ("bakhanti"), many Hebrew manuscripts read "chosen" ("bakharti"),
suggesting a wordplay. **48:12** *First . . . last.* See note on 41:4. **48:14** *One the LORD loves.* Cyrus, whose
rise to power was not predicted by other deities. **48:16** The antecedent of *me* is unclear. It may be the
prophetic speaker or YHWH's servant, or it may be Cyrus accepting his divine call. See **"Cyrus," p. 991.**
48:17 *Redeemer.* See note on 41:14. *Way* recalls the wilderness highway motif in 35:8; 40:3; 43:19; 62:10.
48:18–19 YHWH wishes the exile had not been necessary but insists that Judah's sinfulness demanded
it. **48:20** A command to leave *Babylon/Chaldea* to return to Jerusalem (cf. 52:11). **48:21** Cf. 43:20.
48:22 An ominous ending to the poem, which may have been added later to conclude chaps. 40–48 as
a subunit within Isaiah. An almost identical line serves a similar function in 57:21.

49

Listen to me, O coastlands;
  pay attention, you peoples from far
    away!
The Lord called me before I was born;
  while I was in my mother's womb he
    named me.
[2] He made my mouth like a sharp sword;
  in the shadow of his hand he hid me;
he made me a polished arrow;
  in his quiver he hid me away.
[3] And he said to me, "You are my servant,
  Israel, in whom I will be glorified."
[4] But I said, "I have labored in vain;
  I have spent my strength for nothing
    and vanity;
yet surely my cause is with the Lord
  and my reward with my God."

[5] And now the Lord says,
  who formed me in the womb to be his
    servant,
to bring Jacob back to him,
  and that Israel might be gathered to
    him,
for I am honored in the sight of the Lord,
  and my God has become my strength—
[6] he says,
"It is too light a thing that you should be
    my servant
  to raise up the tribes of Jacob
  and to restore the survivors of Israel;
I will give you as a light to the nations,
  that my salvation may reach to the
    end of the earth."

[7] Thus says the Lord,
  the Redeemer of Israel and his Holy
    One,
to one deeply despised, abhorred by the
    nations,
  the slave of rulers,
"Kings shall see and stand up;
  princes, and they shall prostrate
    themselves,
because of the Lord, who is faithful,
  the Holy One of Israel, who has
    chosen you."
[8] Thus says the Lord:
In a time of favor I have answered you;
  on a day of salvation I have helped you;
I have kept you and given you
  as a covenant to the people,[u]
to establish the land,
  to apportion the desolate heritages,
[9] saying to the prisoners, "Come out,"
  to those who are in darkness, "Show
    yourselves."
They shall feed along the ways;
  on all the bare heights[v] shall be their
    pasture;
[10] they shall not hunger or thirst,
  neither scorching wind nor sun shall
    strike them down,
for he who has pity on them will lead them
  and by springs of water will guide them.
[11] And I will turn all my mountains into a
    road,
  and my highways shall be raised up.
[12] Look, some shall come from far away,
  some from the north and from the west,
  and some from the land of Syene.[w]

[13] Sing for joy, O heavens, and exult, O earth;
  break forth, O mountains, into singing!

u 49.8 Meaning of Heb uncertain   v 49.9 Or the trails
w 49.12 Q ms: MT Sinim

49:1–13 Isaiah 49 begins a new section of Isa. 40–55. Many images and themes continue from Isa. 40–48, but personified Jerusalem replaces Jacob/Israel as the primary addressee of these poems, and there are no more references to Cyrus. Isaiah 49:1–13 is the second servant song; see **"Servant(s) of YHWH," p. 1011. 49:1** The servant speaks in vv. 1–4. *Coastlands.* See note on 41:1. *Called me before I was born* alludes to Jeremiah's call (Jer. 1:5). Cf. 48:8, in which Jacob/Israel "from birth . . . [was] called a rebel." **49:2** As a metaphor for speech, *sword* usually has negative connotations, but here it denotes powerful, effective words (cf. "rod of his mouth," Isa. 11:4). **49:4** Despite self-doubts, the servant trusts God. **49:5–6** Although the servant is identified as "Israel" in v. 3, he is called to restore *the survivors of Israel*—that is, the exiles. His mission also includes making YHWH known to *the nations.* **49:7** Although the servant is *despised . . . by the nations* (cf. 53:3), YHWH's faithfulness to him will impress *kings* and *princes.* **49:8** *Covenant to the people* recalls the servant's international mission. *Desolate heritages.* Family estates abandoned during the exile. **49:9** *Prisoners . . . in darkness.* Cf. 42:7. *Pasture* implies a comparison between the returning exiles and sheep, with YHWH as their shepherd, which continues into v. 10 (cf. Ps. 23:2-3). **49:11** Cf. Isa. 40:3. **49:12** *Syene.* A city in southern Egypt (modern Aswan), likely the southernmost area inhabited by exiles. **49:13** A hymnic conclusion (cf. 42:10-11; 44:23; 45:8).

For the Lord has comforted his people
  and will have compassion on his
    suffering ones.

14 But Zion said, "The Lord has forsaken me;
    my Lord has forgotten me."
15 Can a woman forget her nursing child
    or show no compassion for the child
      of her womb?
  Even these might forget,
    yet I will not forget you.
16 See, I have inscribed you on the palms of
      my hands;
    your walls are continually before me.
17 Your builders outdo your destroyers,ˣ
    and those who laid you waste go away
      from you.
18 Lift up your eyes all around and see;
    they all gather; they come to you.
  As I live, says the Lord,
    you shall put all of them on like an
      ornament,
    and like a bride you shall bind
      them on.

19 For your wastelands, your desolate
      places,
    and your devastated land—
  now you will be too crowded for your
      inhabitants,
    and those who swallowed you up will
      be far away.
20 The children born in the time of your
      bereavement
    will yet say in your hearing:
  "The place is too crowded for me;
    make room for me to settle."
21 Then you will say in your heart,
  "Who has borne me these?

I was bereaved and barren,
    exiled and put away—
  so who has reared these?
I was left all alone—
    where, then, have these come from?"

22 Thus says the Lord God:
I will soon lift up my hand to the nations
    and raise my signal to the
      peoples,
  and they shall bring your sons in their
      bosom,
    and your daughters shall be carried on
      their shoulders.
23 Kings shall be your foster fathers
    and their queens your nursing
      mothers.
  With their faces to the ground they shall
      bow down to you
    and lick the dust of your feet.
  Then you will know that I am the Lord;
    those who wait for me shall not be put
      to shame.

24 Can the prey be taken from the mighty
    or the captives of a tyrantʸ be
      rescued?
25 But thus says the Lord:
Even the captives of the mighty will be
      taken,
    and the prey of the tyrant will be
      rescued,
  for I will contend with those who
      contend with you,
    and I will save your children.
26 I will make your oppressors eat their
      own flesh,

x 49.17 Or *Your children come swiftly; your destroyers*
y 49.24 Q ms Syr Vg: MT *of a righteous person*

49:14–50:3 A poetic promise of restoration for Zion. **49:14** Like Jacob/Israel in 40:27, personified *Zion* complains of being *forgotten* by God. **49:15** Divine compassion is even greater than that of a mother (see **"Feminine Imagery for God," p. 1029**). Note the threefold repetition of *forget* in response to Zion's complaint. **49:16** Jerusalem's *walls are . . . before [the Lord]* even though they remained destroyed (cf. 52:9; 60:10). **49:17** As indicated by the alternate translation (see NRSVue footnote), this verse plays on the similar sounds of *builders* ("bonayik") and *children* ("benayik"), a metaphor for Jerusalem's exiles. **49:18** *Bride* anticipates Zion's remarriage to YHWH in 54:4–8; 62:4–5. **49:19** *Far away.* Jerusalem's exiles (cf. v. 12) switch places with her enemies. **49:20–21** Having given up hope for her exiled *children*, Jerusalem is surprised by their return in such numbers. **49:22** See note on 11:12. **49:23** Instead of oppressing the exiles, foreign rulers will be their *foster* parents (cf. 60:16). They will *bow down* to Jerusalem, not vice versa. *Wait.* Cf. 25:9; 26:8; 33:2; 40:31. **49:24–25** As in v. 15, YHWH's actions are not limited by human norms. **49:26** *Your oppressors eat their own flesh.* YHWH fittingly punishes Jerusalem's conquerors for forcing its citizens to resort to cannibalism during the siege in 587 BCE (cf. Lam. 2:20; 4:10). *I am the Lord.* See note on 41:4. *Savior.* A military deliverer. *Redeemer.* See note on 41:14. *Mighty One of Jacob.* A divine title attested in Gen. 49:24; Ps. 132:2, 5; Isa. 60:16;

and they shall be drunk with their
 own blood as with wine.
Then all flesh shall know
 that I am the LORD your Savior
 and your Redeemer, the Mighty One
 of Jacob.

50 Thus says the LORD:
 Where is your mother's bill of
 divorce
 with which I dismissed her?
Or which of my creditors is it
 to whom I have sold you?
No, because of your sins you were sold,
 and for your transgressions your
 mother was dismissed.
2 Why was no one there when I came?
 Why did no one answer when I called?
Is my arm powerless to redeem?
 Or have I no strength to deliver?
By my rebuke I dry up the sea;
 I make the rivers a desert,
so that their fish stink for lack of water
 and die of thirst.*z*
3 I clothe the heavens with blackness
 and make sackcloth their covering.
4 The Lord GOD has given me
 a trained tongue,*a*
that I may know how to sustain
 the weary with a word.
Morning by morning he wakens,
 wakens my ear
to listen as those who are taught.
5 The Lord GOD has opened my ear,
 and I was not rebellious;
 I did not turn backward.

6 I gave my back to those who struck me
 and my cheeks to those who pulled
 out the beard;
I did not hide my face
 from insult and spitting.
7 The Lord GOD helps me;
 therefore I have not been disgraced;
therefore I have set my face like flint,
 and I know that I shall not be put to
 shame;
8 he who vindicates me is near.
Who will contend with me?
 Let us stand in court together.
Who are my adversaries?
 Let them confront me.
9 It is the Lord GOD who helps me;
 who will declare me guilty?
All of them will wear out like a garment;
 the moth will eat them up.

10 Who among you fears the LORD
 and obeys the voice of his servant,
who walks in darkness
 and has no light,
yet trusts in the name of the LORD
 and relies upon his God?
11 But all of you are kindlers of fire,
 lighters of firebrands.*b*
Walk in the flame of your fire
 and among the brands that you have
 kindled!
This is what you shall have from my hand:
 you shall lie down in torment.

*z 50.2 Or die on the thirsty ground   a 50.4 Cn: Heb of those who
are taught   b 50.11 Syr: Heb you gird yourselves with firebrands*

cf. "Mighty One of Israel" in 1:24. **50:1** *Divorce* and *sold* to *creditors* (cf. 2 Kgs. 4:1) are metaphors for YHWH's abandonment of Jerusalem and the exiles. Those actions were not initiated by the deity; they responded to the people's *sins*. **50:2–3** YHWH's capacity to *dry up* bodies of water (cf. Isa. 19:5–7; 42:15) and darken *the heavens* (cf. 13:10; 24:23) proves that the exile did not result from divine powerlessness. The attitude of victim blaming in these verses is deeply problematic, but the poet is attempting to restore the audience's confidence in YHWH's power so they can hope for a better future. **50:4–11** The third servant song models the appropriate response to exile, from which the audience should learn; see **"Servant(s) of YHWH," p. 1011. 50:4** Although the speaker in vv. 4–9 is not identified, v. 10 suggests that it is the servant. The effectiveness of the servant's speech (*trained tongue*) echoes 49:2. *Weary* likely refers to the exiles (cf. 40:28–31). **50:5** The servant's *opened . . . ear* sets him apart from the recalcitrant exiles; cf. 6:9–10; 48:8. **50:6** The servant willingly submits to acts of abuse, which symbolize the degradations of exile. **50:7** *Face like flint* expresses the servant's unwavering faith, in contrast to 48:4, where the exiles' iron neck and brass forehead express their obstinance. **50:8** Like YHWH in 41:1–7, 21–29; 43:9–13; 45:20–25, the servant challenges his *adversaries* to a legal dispute. **50:9** Cf. 51:6, 8. **50:10** The servant trusts God even when the outcome is uncertain (cf. 49:4). *Walks in darkness.* Cf. 9:2. **50:11** *Firebrands* symbolize evildoers' attacks against the righteous (cf. Prov. 26:18). In contrast to the servant, who "walks in darkness" but receives vindication, evildoers seem to *walk* in light but ultimately receive *torment*.

51

Listen to me, you who pursue
    righteousness,
  you who seek the Lord.
Look to the rock from which you were
    hewn
  and to the quarry from which you
    were dug.
2 Look to Abraham your father
  and to Sarah, who bore you,
for he was but one when I called him,
  but I blessed him and made him many.
3 For the Lord will comfort Zion;
  he will comfort all her waste places
and will make her wilderness like Eden,
  her desert like the garden of the Lord;
joy and gladness will be found in her,
  thanksgiving and the voice of song.

4 Listen to me, my people,
  and give heed to me, my nation,
for a teaching will go out from me
  and my justice for a light to the
    peoples.
5 I will bring near my deliverance swiftly;
  my salvation has gone out,
  and my arms will rule the peoples;
the coastlands wait for me,
  and for my arm they hope.
6 Lift up your eyes to the heavens
  and look at the earth beneath,
for the heavens will vanish like smoke,
  the earth will wear out like a garment,

and those who live on it will die like
    gnats,c
but my salvation will be forever,
  and my deliverance will never be
    ended.

7 Listen to me, you who know
    righteousness,
  you people who have my teaching in
    your hearts;
do not fear the reproach of others,
  and do not be dismayed when they
    revile you.
8 For the moth will eat them up like a
    garment,
  and the worm will eat them like wool,
but my deliverance will be forever
  and my salvation to all generations.

9 Awake, awake, put on strength,
  O arm of the Lord!
Awake, as in days of old,
  the generations of long ago!
Was it not you who cut Rahab in
    pieces,
  who pierced the dragon?
10 Was it not you who dried up the sea,
  the waters of the great deep;
who made the depths of the sea a way
  for the redeemed to cross over?

c 51.6 Or *in like manner*

51:1–8 A poem announcing salvation for Jerusalem and the world. 51:1 *Righteousness* is one of several repeated terms in this poem, along with "deliverance," "salvation," and "teaching." Unlike Isa. 48:1, this poem assumes that the audience members sincerely *seek the Lord. Rock* and *quarry* are metaphors for ancestry, as becomes clear in the next verse. 51:2 *Abraham.* See note on 41:8. The naming of *Sarah* as an ancestor alongside her husband continues the emphasis on women in Isa. 40–55. 51:3 *Comfort.* Cf. 40:1. *Her wilderness like Eden.* See note on 41:17–19. 51:4 Jerusalem's vindication foreshadows worldwide divine rule. *Teaching will go out.* Cf. 2:3. *Light to the peoples.* Cf. 49:6. Allusions to the Servant Songs in vv. 4–6 connect this poem to the fulfillment of the servant's mission (see **"Servant(s) of YHWH," p. 1011**). 51:5 *Salvation* denotes military deliverance rather than strictly spiritual liberation. YHWH's *arms* are a metonymy for divine power (cf. 40:10). *Coastlands wait.* Cf. 42:4. 51:6 Like the divine word in 40:8, the permanence of God's *salvation/deliverance* contrasts with the impermanence of creation. 51:8 The audience need not fear their detractors, who are mere mortals. Cf. 50:8.

51:9–52:12 A long poem announcing the defeat of Jerusalem's enemies and the end of the exile. It is held together by references to the divine "arm" near the beginning and end (51:9; 52:10) and repeated imperatives in 51:9, 17; 52:1, 11 (cf. "I, I" in 51:12). The double commands recall the repeated "comfort, O comfort" in Isa. 40:1. 51:9 A prayer for deliverance by the exiles. *Arm.* See note on 51:5. *Awake, as in days of old* implies that the deity is currently inactive. *Rahab* and the *dragon* were primordial monsters whom God defeated at creation; the text implicitly connects them with Babylon's oppressive power (cf. 30:7, where *Rahab* symbolizes Egypt). 51:10 *Sea* and *great deep* further allude to creation (cf. Gen. 1:2), while the second half of the verse refers to God's defeat of Egypt at the Red Sea. As in Isa. 43:16–19, the exiles fail to recognize that God is already doing something greater.

¹¹ So the ransomed of the LORD shall return
and come to Zion with rejoicing;
everlasting joy shall be upon their heads;
they shall obtain joy and gladness,
and sorrow and sighing shall flee
away.

¹² I, I am he who comforts you;
why then are you afraid of a mere
mortal who must die,
a human being who fades like grass?
¹³ You have forgotten the LORD, your Maker,
who stretched out the heavens
and laid the foundations of the earth.
You fear continually all day long
because of the fury of the
oppressor,
who is bent on destruction.
But where is the fury of the
oppressor?
¹⁴ The oppressed shall speedily be released;
they shall not die and go down to the
Pit,
nor shall they lack bread.
¹⁵ For I am the LORD your God,
who stirs up the sea so that its waves
roar—
the LORD of hosts is his name.
¹⁶ I have put my words in your mouth
and hidden you in the shadow of my
hand,
stretching out^d the heavens
and laying the foundations of the
earth
and saying to Zion, "You are my
people."

¹⁷ Rouse yourself, rouse yourself!
Stand up, O Jerusalem,
you who have drunk at the hand of the
LORD
the cup of his wrath,

who have drunk to the dregs
the cup of staggering.
¹⁸ There is no one to guide her
among all the children she has borne;
there is no one to take her by the hand
among all the children she has
brought up.
¹⁹ These two things have befallen you
—who will grieve with you?—
devastation and destruction, famine and
sword.
Who will comfort you?^e
²⁰ Your children have fainted;
they lie at the head of every street
like an antelope in a net;
they are full of the wrath of the LORD,
the rebuke of your God.

²¹ Therefore hear this, you who are
wounded,^f
who are drunk but not with wine:
²² Thus says your Sovereign, the LORD,
your God who pleads the cause of his
people:
See, I have taken from your hand the cup
of staggering;
you shall drink no more
from the cup of my wrath.
²³ And I will put it into the hand of your
tormentors,
who have said to you,
"Bow down, that we may walk on
you,"
and you have made your back like the
ground
and like the street for them to walk on.

52 Awake; awake;
put on your strength, O Zion!
Put on your beautiful garments,
O Jerusalem, the holy city,

d 51.16 Syr: Heb *planting*   *e* 51.19 Q ms Gk Syr Vg: MT *how
may I comfort you?*   *f* 51.21 Or *humbled*

51:11 The crossing of the Red Sea prefigures the exiles' *return . . . to Zion.* **51:12** *Fades like grass.* Cf.
40:6–8. **51:13–14** YHWH's power as creator—to which the exiles appealed in vv. 9–10—guarantees
the defeat of the *oppressor* and liberation of the *oppressed. Pit* refers to the underworld (cf. 14:15).
51:15 An affirmation of divine power over the sea/chaos. **51:16** *Put my words in your mouth* assigns a
prophetic function to the liberated exiles (cf. Deut. 18:18; Jer. 1:9). God's choice of *Zion* as his *people*
parallels God's acts of creation. **51:17** The destruction of personified *Jerusalem* is compared to the
forced consumption of an alcoholic beverage (cf. Jer. 25:15). **51:18** Vv. 18–20 describe Jerusalem's
current depopulation, depicted as the loss of *children.* **51:19** The poem has already answered the
question *Who will comfort you?* in v. 12 (cf. 49:13; 51:3). **51:20** *Fainted . . . at the head of every street.*
Cf. Lam. 2:19. **51:21–23** Using the *cup* metaphor from v. 17, the poem describes how Jerusalem's enemies will suffer the same fate they inflicted upon the city. **52:1** The imperatives addressed to YHWH
by the exiles in Isa. 51:9 are now addressed to *Zion. Beautiful garments* contrast with mourning

for the uncircumcised and the unclean
    shall enter you no more.
[2] Shake yourself from the dust; rise up,
    O captive[g] Jerusalem;
loose the bonds from your neck,
    O captive daughter Zion!

3 For thus says the LORD: You were sold for nothing, and you shall be redeemed without money. [4]For thus says the Lord GOD: Long ago, my people went down into Egypt to reside there as aliens; the Assyrian, too, has oppressed them without cause. [5]Now therefore what am I doing here, says the LORD, seeing that my people are taken away without cause? Their rulers howl, says the LORD, and continually, all day long, my name is despised. [6]Therefore my people shall know my name; on[b] that day they shall know that it is I who speak—it is I!

[7] How beautiful upon the mountains
    are the feet of the messenger who
      announces peace,
who brings good news,
    who announces salvation,
    who says to Zion, "Your God reigns."
[8] Listen! Your sentinels lift up their
    voices;
together they shout for joy,
for in plain sight they see
    the return of the LORD to Zion.

[9] Break forth; shout together for joy,
    you ruins of Jerusalem,
for the LORD has comforted his
      people;
    he has redeemed Jerusalem.
[10] The LORD has bared his holy arm
    before the eyes of all the nations,
and all the ends of the earth shall see
    the salvation of our God.

[11] Depart, depart, go out from there!
    Touch no unclean thing;
go out from the midst of it; purify
      yourselves,
    you who carry the vessels of the
      LORD.
[12] For you shall not go out in haste,
    and you shall not go in flight,
for the LORD will go before you,
    and the God of Israel will be your rear
      guard.
[13] See, my servant shall prosper;
    he shall be exalted and lifted up
    and shall be very high.
[14] Just as there were many who were
      astonished at him[i]
    —so marred was his appearance,
      beyond human semblance,
and his form beyond that of
      mortals—

g 52.2 Cn: Heb *rise up, sit*   h 52.6 Q ms Syr Vg Tg: MT *therefore on*   i 52.14 Syr Tg: Heb *you*

clothes. *Uncircumcised* and *unclean* refer to Jerusalem's invaders. **52:2** Contrast the fate of personified Babylon in 47:1. **52:3** *Sold for nothing* suggests that Jerusalem's destruction was gratuitous but also that God did not benefit from it. **52:4** The exile is the climax of a long history of oppression of God's people. **52:5** The deity acknowledges the people's confusion about divine intentions. **52:6** By restoring Jerusalem, YHWH will rehabilitate the divine *name* or reputation. **52:7** Cf. 40:9. **52:8** This depiction of Jerusalem's *sentinels* is imaginative, since its walls have been destroyed. For other imagery of *sentinels*, cf. 21:6–9, 11–12. **52:9** The poet acknowledges the reality of the *ruins of Jerusalem*. Similar calls to praise were addressed to nature in 42:10; 44:23; 45:8; 49:13. *Comforted* and *redeemed* are major themes in Isa. 40–55. **52:10** *Arm.* Cf. 40:10; 51:9, 11. Universal recognition of YHWH's power is another important theme in these chapters (40:5; 41:5; 45:22). **52:11** As in 48:20, the exiles are urgently commanded to leave Babylon. The temple *vessels* had been taken as spoil by the Babylonians (2 Kgs. 25:14–16). Ezra 1:7–10, 5:14–15, and 6:5 report their repatriation by Cyrus. **52:12** *Not go out in haste* further distinguishes the return from exile from the exodus.

    52:13–53:12 The fourth servant song (see **"Servant(s) of YHWH," p. 1011**) emphasizes the servant's suffering and attributes redemptive effects to it. This poem has been the basis for many proposals identifying the servant with a specific figure outside the text, but it remains more helpful to understand the figure as a poetic personification through whom the exiles may gain a new perspective on their own suffering. This poem is connected to Jesus's death in the Christian tradition (see **"Isaiah and Jesus," p. 951**). **52:13** *My* marks vv. 13–15 as divine speech. *Exalted, lifted up,* and *high* are typically characteristics of God in Isaiah (cf. 2:11; 6:1; 33:5) but here attributed to the servant. **52:14** *Marred.* The poem repeatedly describes the servant's mutilated appearance using terms associated with disability (cf. 53:2–3; see **"Isaiah and Disability," p. 974**). This disfigurement results from

[15] so he shall startle[j] many nations;
kings shall shut their mouths because
of him,
for that which had not been told them
they shall see,
and that which they had not heard
they shall contemplate.

53
Who has believed what we have
heard?
And to whom has the arm of the Lord
been revealed?
[2] For he grew up before him like a young
plant
and like a root out of dry ground;
he had no form or majesty that we
should look at him,
nothing in his appearance that we
should desire him.
[3] He was despised and rejected by others;
a man of suffering[k] and acquainted
with infirmity,
and as one from whom others hide their
faces[l]
he was despised, and we held him of
no account.

[4] Surely he has borne our infirmities
and carried our diseases,
yet we accounted him stricken,
struck down by God, and afflicted.
[5] But he was wounded for our
transgressions,
crushed for our iniquities;
upon him was the punishment that made
us whole,
and by his bruises we are healed.
[6] All we like sheep have gone astray;

we have all turned to our own way,
and the Lord has laid on him
the iniquity of us all.

[7] He was oppressed, and he was afflicted,
yet he did not open his mouth;
like a lamb that is led to the slaughter
and like a sheep that before its
shearers is silent,
so he did not open his mouth.
[8] By a perversion of justice he was taken
away.
Who could have imagined his future?
For he was cut off from the land of the
living,
stricken for the transgression of my
people.
[9] They made his grave with the wicked
and his tomb[m] with the rich,[n]
although he had done no violence,
and there was no deceit in his mouth.

[10] Yet it was the will of the Lord to crush
him with affliction.
When you make his life an offering for
sin,[o]
he shall see his offspring and shall
prolong his days;
through him the will of the Lord shall
prosper.
[11] Out of his anguish he shall see;
he shall find satisfaction through his
knowledge.

j 52.15 Meaning of Heb uncertain   k 53.3 Or a man of
sorrows   l 53.3 Or as one who hides his face from us   m 53.9 Q
ms: MT and in his death   n 53.9 Cn: Heb with a rich person
o 53.10 Meaning of Heb uncertain

his submission to violence. **52:15** The servant's suffering brings *nations* to new awareness, fulfilling his mission to be a "light to the nations" (42:6; 49:6). Their shocked silence anticipates the servant's own silence in 53:7. **53:1** An unidentified *we* voice speaks in vv. 1–6, likely either the nations or the exiles. *Arm of the Lord* connects this poem with the preceding one (51:9; 52:10). **53:2** Plant imagery depicts the servant as fragile. **53:4–5** Graphic language expresses the brutality of the servant's suffering. Although the speakers initially attribute his victimization to divine judgment, they realize he suffers the consequences of their own *transgressions* in an expression of solidarity. **53:6–7** *Sheep* imagery characterizes both the speakers' rebellion against God and the servant's silence in the face of suffering. Despite the comparison to a *lamb*, the poem does not use explicit sacrificial language for the servant (except possibly v. 10). On the contrary, it portrays the servant's disfigurement with terms that elsewhere describe animals unfit for sacrifice (Exod. 12:5; Lev. 22:18–25). **53:8–9** These verses may suggest that the servant dies from his injuries, but more likely, they hyperbolically depict the extent of his suffering. **53:10** Vv. 10–12 describe the servant's vindication. The attribution of suffering to YHWH's *will* could problematically imply that victims of violence should not seek relief from it. At the same time, the poem may have therapeutic value by insisting that undeserved suffering need not be meaningless. **53:11** *My* marks the poem's final verses as divine speech, just like its opening verses. In Isa. 52:14, "many . . . were astonished" by the servant; now, *many* are made

Going Deeper: The Servant(s) of YHWH (Isaiah 53)

An enigmatic figure called YHWH's "servant" appears throughout Isa. 40–55. Repeatedly, the deity addresses Jacob/Israel as "my servant" (41:8–9; 44:1–2, 21; 45:4; etc.), often paired with the word "chosen." Four texts, which scholars call the Servant Songs, depict the servant in greater detail (42:1–7; 49:1–7; 50:4–10; 52:13–53:12). YHWH sets him apart before birth (49:1) and charges him to "bring forth justice to the nations" (42:1). Paradoxically, he is both identified as Israel (49:3) and given responsibility for "gather[ing]" Israel (49:5). The servant voluntarily submits to violent persecution (50:6; 53:3–5), by which others are made righteous (53:4–6, 11). God ultimately rewards and vindicates him (53:12).

The servant's identity has been a scholarly preoccupation, with dozens of proposed identifications, but he need not be associated with an individual outside the text. Rather, he is a poetic construct, as becomes clear from the juxtaposition of speeches by the servant and personified Zion in Isa. 49. He symbolizes God's activity in the world, which the text invites the audience to participate in and bear witness to (43:10). The figure of the servant recontextualizes the exiles' suffering in a larger frame of worldwide redemption. In this way, the servant informs the New Testament's portrayal of Jesus's miracles (Matt. 8:16–17; 12:15–21) and death (Acts 8:32–33; 1 Pet. 2:21–25), as well as Paul's mission to the Gentiles (Rom. 15:20–21; Gal. 1:15–16).

Isaiah 61:1–3 is sometimes associated with the Servant Songs, but otherwise, the servant disappears after chap. 53. Instead, the text begins referring to YHWH's "servants," suggesting that the audience has claimed this identity for themselves. These servants may be the "offspring" of the servant mentioned in 53:10. Isaiah 56:6 defines the category inclusively, inviting foreigners "who keep the Sabbath . . . and hold fast [the Lord's] covenant" to become YHWH's servants. By contrast, in the book's final chapters, the servants are a distinct group within the postexilic Jewish community, perhaps reflecting conflicts over control of the newly rebuilt temple. Isaiah 65:13–15 and 66:14 threaten the servants' opponents with suffering but promise rewards for them. Despite these exclusivist overtones, 65:8 declares that the entire community will be saved "for my servants' sake," calling them a "blessing" within it. In this way, the mission of both the servant and the servants ultimately benefits others in Isaiah.

J. Blake Couey

The righteous one,[p] my servant, shall make many righteous,
and he shall bear their iniquities.
[12] Therefore I will allot him a portion with the great,
and he shall divide the spoil with the strong,
because he poured out himself to death and was numbered with the transgressors,
yet he bore the sin of many and made intercession for the transgressors.

54 Shout for joy, O barren one who has borne no children;
burst into song and shout, you who have not been in labor!
For the children of the desolate woman will be more
than the children of the one who is married, says the Lord.
[2] Enlarge the site of your tent, and let the curtains of your habitations be stretched out;
do not hold back; lengthen your cords and strengthen your stakes.
[3] For you will spread out to the right and to the left,
and your descendants will possess nations and will settle desolate towns.

p 53.11 Or *and he shall find satisfaction. Through his knowledge, the righteous one*

righteous by his suffering. The poem never explains how this will happen. Rather than providing a precise theology of atonement, it encourages the exiles to find meaning in their own suffering by situating it within God's larger work. **53:12** *Divide the spoil* associates the servant's vindication with military victory.

54:1–17 A poem promising a reversal of fortunes for personified Zion, using parenthood and marriage metaphors. **54:1** Childlessness is a recurring metaphor for Jerusalem's depopulation in Isa. 40–66, but in 49:20–21, the city's children have been killed. Here, by contrast, the city is depicted as *barren*, recalling the ancestral figure Sarah (cf. 51:2). **54:2–3** Jerusalem will require expansion to

⁴ Do not fear, for you will not be ashamed;
    do not be discouraged, for you will
        not suffer disgrace,
  for you will forget the shame of your
      youth,
  and the disgrace of your widowhood
      you will remember no more.
⁵ For your Maker is your husband;
    the Lord of hosts is his name;
  the Holy One of Israel is your Redeemer;
    the God of the whole earth he is called.
⁶ For the Lord has called you
    like a wife forsaken and grieved in
      spirit,
  like the wife of a man's youth when she
      is cast off,
    says your God.
⁷ For a brief moment I abandoned you,
    but with great compassion I will
      gather you.
⁸ In overflowing wrath for a moment
    I hid my face from you,
  but with everlasting love I will have
      compassion on you,
    says the Lord, your Redeemer.

⁹ This is like the days of Noah to me:
    Just as I swore that the waters of Noah
    would never again go over the earth,
  so I have sworn that I will not be angry
      with you
    and will not rebuke you.
¹⁰ For the mountains may depart
    and the hills be removed,
  but my steadfast love shall not depart
      from you,
  and my covenant of peace shall not be
      removed,

says the Lord, who has compassion
    on you.

¹¹ O afflicted one, storm-tossed and not
    comforted,
  I am about to set your stones in
      antimony
  and lay your foundations with
      sapphires.^q
¹² I will make your pinnacles of rubies,
    your gates of jewels,
  and all your wall of precious stones.
¹³ All your children shall be taught by the
    Lord,
  and great shall be the prosperity of
      your children.
¹⁴ In righteousness you shall be
    established;
  you shall be far from oppression;
    indeed, you shall not fear;
  and from terror; indeed, it shall not
    come near you.
¹⁵ If anyone stirs up strife,
    it is not from me;
  whoever stirs up strife with you
    shall fall because of you.
¹⁶ See, it is I who have created the smith
    who blows the fire of coals
  and produces a weapon fit for its
    purpose;
  I have also created the ravager to
    destroy.
¹⁷ No weapon that is fashioned against
    you shall prosper,
  and you shall confute every tongue
    that rises against you in judgment.

q 54.11 Or *lapis lazuli*

accommodate its restored inhabitants. **54:4–6** Mixing metaphors, the poem depicts Jerusalem as a widowed/divorced woman whom YHWH will marry. Prophetic literature frequently depicts Israel or Jerusalem as YHWH's wife, often with overtones of spousal abuse (e.g., Hos. 2; Ezek. 16; 23). **54:8** *Overflowing wrath* rhymes in Hebrew ("shetsep qetsep"). The poem acknowledges divine anger against Jerusalem, which resulted in the city's destruction and its inhabitants' exile, but contrasts the brevity of divine anger with the permanence of divine favor. *Compassion* and *love* are emphatically repeated in vv. 7–8, 10. Although it is a reassuring message within the world of the poem, it disturbingly echoes many abusers' failed promises to have changed. **54:9** To support YHWH's promise not to destroy Jerusalem again, the poem appeals to the similar promise following Noah's flood (Gen. 8:21–22; 9:11–16). **54:10** God's promise is more permanent than *mountains* and *hills*—which, ironically, are *removed* elsewhere in Isaiah (2:14; 40:4). **54:11** *Not comforted*. Cf. 40:1; 49:13; 51:3; etc. **54:12** The promise to rebuild Jerusalem's walls with fine gemstones suggests the future will be even better than the past. This verse influenced the depiction of the new Jerusalem in Rev. 21:18–21. **54:13** Like YHWH's servant (50:4), the returning exiles (i.e., *your children*) will *be taught by the* Lord. **54:16** As the one who created the *smith*, God is greater than any weapon manufactured by humans. **54:17** *Servants of the* Lord. This verse marks the transition from YHWH's

This is the heritage of the servants of the
  Lord
and their vindication from me, says
  the Lord.

55 Hear, everyone who thirsts;
    come to the waters;
and you who have no money,
  come, buy and eat!
Come, buy wine and milk
  without money and without price.
2 Why do you spend your money for that
    which is not bread
  and your earnings for that which does
    not satisfy?
Listen carefully to me, and eat what is good,
  and delight yourselves in rich food.
3 Incline your ear, and come to me;
  listen, so that you may live.
I will make with you an everlasting
    covenant,
  my steadfast, sure love for David.
4 See, I made him a witness to the peoples,
  a leader and commander for the peoples.
5 Now you shall call nations that you do
    not know,
  and nations that do not know you
    shall run to you,
because of the Lord your God, the Holy
    One of Israel,
  for he has glorified you.

6 Seek the Lord while he may be found;
  call upon him while he is near;
7 let the wicked forsake their way
  and the unrighteous their thoughts;

let them return to the Lord, that he may
    have mercy on them,
  and to our God, for he will abundantly
    pardon.
8 For my thoughts are not your thoughts,
  nor are your ways my ways, says the
    Lord.
9 For as the heavens are higher than the
    earth,
  so are my ways higher than your ways
  and my thoughts than your thoughts.

10 For as the rain and the snow come down
    from heaven
  and do not return there until they
    have watered the earth,
making it bring forth and sprout,
  giving seed to the sower and bread to
    the eater,
11 so shall my word be that goes out from
    my mouth;
  it shall not return to me empty,
but it shall accomplish that which I
    purpose
  and succeed in the thing for which I
    sent it.

12 For you shall go out in joy
  and be led back in peace;
the mountains and the hills before you
    shall burst into song,
  and all the trees of the field shall clap
    their hands.
13 Instead of the thorn shall come up the
    cypress;

servant as a singular idealized figure to a plural identity claimed by the audience (see **"Servant(s) of YHWH," p. 1011**).

55:1–13 The final poem of the exilic section of Isaiah reprises many themes from Isa. 40–54. Frequent imperatives create a sense of urgency, calling on the exiles to embrace their restoration. **55:1** A universal invitation to a free banquet; cf. 25:6. The availability of food contrasts with food shortages experienced during the Babylonian invasion of Jerusalem. *No money.* Cf. 52:3. **55:2** *Eat what is good* recalls 1:19. *Rich food.* Literally "fatness," suggesting meat, which was reserved for special occasions in antiquity. **55:3** God's *covenant* with David is called *everlasting* in 2 Sam. 23:5. This allusion emphasizes God's faithfulness to the exiles; cf. Isa. 61:8. Elsewhere in Isaiah, *everlasting covenant* refers to divine laws broken by the inhabitants of earth, leading to worldwide judgment (24:5). **55:4–5** As God's covenant partner, the exiles bear *witness* to the *nations* concerning God's power (cf. 43:10, 12; 44:8), just as David had done (cf. 11:10). Although the text does not explicitly depict the replacement of the old Davidic covenant, hopes for the restoration of the monarchy are strikingly absent from Isa. 40–66, in contrast to chaps. 1–39. **55:6–7** A call to repentance, contrasting a sense of urgency with a promise of lavish forgiveness. **55:8–9** Height imagery frequently connotes God's superiority over humans in Isaiah. **55:9–11** Nature imagery provides an analogy to the effectiveness of God's *word* (cf. 40:8). *Bread* recalls the promise of abundant food in v. 1. **55:12** The exiles' ecstatic, safe return to Jerusalem evokes the praise of nature (cf. 43:20; 44:23). **55:13** For reforestation as an image of renewal, cf. 41:19; 44:4. *Memorial, everlasting,* and *not be cut off* anticipate the next poem (cf. 56:5).

Reading through Time: Isaiah and Judaism (Isaiah 56)

Isaiah has long been influential within Judaism. The Dead Sea Scrolls—the library of a pre-Christian, Jewish sectarian community—include over twenty copies of Isaiah, more than any book besides Psalms or Deuteronomy. Jewish legends recount how the prophet was sawed in half inside a hollow log by King Manasseh, which the Talmud interprets as punishment for his disparaging of Israel in Isa. 6:5. This ambivalence about Isaiah may reflect discomfort with the book's influence on Christian anti-Judaism. The New Testament used 6:9–10 to explain the Jewish rejection of Christianity (John 12:39–40; Acts 28:25–28). Prophetic critiques such as Isa. 1:3, 29:13, and 65:1 contributed to the stereotype of the perpetual Jewish rebellion against God. Christological interpretations of Isaiah (see **"Isaiah and Jesus," p. 951**) led to claims that Jews ignored their scriptures and rejected their own messiah. The prophet even appeared as a character in medieval plays castigating Jews for not believing his words.

Despite this weaponization of the book, Judaism did not cede Isaiah to Christianity. Interpreters defended alternative readings of texts favored by Christians, identifying Immanuel in 7:14 with Hezekiah and the suffering servant in 52:13–53:12 with Israel rather than Jesus. Such conclusions anticipated later historical-critical biblical scholarship. The twelfth-century Jewish commentator Abraham Ibn Ezra even argued for an exilic setting for chaps. 40–66, over five hundred years before Christian scholars made similar proposals.

Language from Isaiah abounds in Jewish liturgy. More haftarot—assigned synagogue readings from prophetic books—come from Isaiah than any other text, including readings from chaps. 40–66 on seven consecutive Sabbaths (the Sabbaths of consolation; cf. 40:1) following the commemoration of the destructions of the temples on Tisha B'Av. Isaiah 6:3 appears in a prominent Jewish prayer called the Kedushah ("holiness"), a version of which is included in the daily prayer known as the Amidah, along with other references from the book.

Isaiah is also prominent in the modern nation of Israel. Depictions of the return to Jerusalem from Isa. 40–66 significantly informed modern Zionism, and many Israeli place-names come from the book. An entire wing of Israel's national museum, the Shrine of the Book, hosts the Great Isaiah Scroll from the Dead Sea Scrolls. In Jerusalem, scenes from Isaiah adorn public art (see **"Visions of Peace," p. 937**), and the name of the Holocaust memorial, Yad Vashem, comes from 56:5 ("a monument and a name").

J. Blake Couey

---

instead of the brier shall come up the
    myrtle,
and it shall be to the LORD for a memorial,
    for an everlasting sign that shall not
    be cut off.

56 Thus says the LORD:
    Maintain justice, and do what is
    right,
for soon my salvation will come
    and my deliverance be revealed.

[2] Happy is the mortal who does this,
    the one who holds it fast,

who keeps the Sabbath, not profaning it,
    and refrains from doing any evil.

[3] Do not let the foreigner joined to the
    LORD say,
"The LORD will surely separate me
    from his people,"
and do not let the eunuch say,
    "I am just a dry tree."
[4] For thus says the LORD:
To the eunuchs who keep my Sabbaths,
    who choose the things that please me
    and hold fast my covenant,

56:1–8 This poem opens the postexilic section of Isaiah in chaps. 56–66. It assumes the temple has been rebuilt, suggesting a date after 515 BCE, but its inclusion of "foreigners" contrasts with other postexilic texts like Ezra 9 and Neh. 13. **56:1** This verse integrates Isa. 1–39 and 40–55 by playing on multiple meanings of the repeated Hebrew word "tsedaqah" ("righteousness"). *Right*, paired with *justice*, echoes the use of the term in chaps. 1–39 (1:26; 9:7; etc.), while *deliverance*, paired with *salvation*, matches its usual meaning in chaps. 40–55 (46:13; 51:5–6; etc.). **56:2** *Sabbath* observance was an important marker of Jewish identity in the postexilic period, but this verse offers blessings to any *mortal* who *keeps* it (cf. vv. 4, 6). See **"Isaiah and Judaism," p. 1014. 56:3** *Foreigner[s]* and *eunuch[s]* were both banned from the temple in Deut. 23:1–3, which this text may directly subvert. *Dry tree*, a metaphor for the eunuch's lack of reproductive potency, recalls the recurring negative

⁵ I will give, in my house and within my walls,
  a monument and a name
  better than sons and daughters;
I will give them an everlasting name
  that shall not be cut off.

⁶ And the foreigners who join themselves
    to the LORD,
  to minister to him, to love the name of
    the LORD,
  and to be his servants,
all who keep the Sabbath and do not
    profane it
  and hold fast my covenant—
⁷ these I will bring to my holy mountain
  and make them joyful in my house of
    prayer;
their burnt offerings and their sacrifices
  will be accepted on my altar,
for my house shall be called a house of
    prayer
  for all peoples.
⁸ Thus says the Lord GOD,
  who gathers the outcasts of Israel:
I will gather others to them
  besides those already gathered.ʳ
⁹ All you wild animals,
  all you wild animals in the forest,
  come to devour!
¹⁰ Israel'sˢ sentinels are blind;
  they are all without knowledge;

they are all silent dogs
  that cannot bark,
dreaming, lying down,
  loving to slumber.
¹¹ The dogs have a mighty appetite;
  they never have enough.
The shepherds also have no
    understanding;
  they have all turned to their own
    way,
  to their own gain, one and all.
¹² "Come," they say, "let usᵗ get wine;
  let us fill ourselves with strong drink.
And tomorrow will be like today,
  great beyond measure."

57 The righteous perish,
  and no one considers why;
the devout are taken away,
  while no one understands
  that it is due to evil that the righteous
    are taken away.
² Those who walk uprightly enter into
    peace
  and rest on their couches.
³ But as for you, come here,
  you children of a sorceress,
  you offspring of an adulterer and a
    prostitute.ᵘ

r 56.8 Heb *besides his gathered ones*   s 56.10 Heb *His*
t 56.12 Q ms Syr Vg Tg: MT *me*   u 57.3 Heb *an adulterer and*
she prostitutes herself

image of barren landscapes in Isaiah. **56:5** Although eunuchs could achieve social prominence in the ancient world, their inability to reproduce denied them the functional afterlife of having descendants to remember their *name*. To compensate, God will memorialize their names in the temple. Despite the poem's positive portrayal of eunuchs, it cannot resist puns on their lack of genitals. The word translated as *monument* ("yad"; literally "hand") is also a euphemism for "penis," and *cut off* refers to castration in Deut. 23:1. **56:7** *My holy mountain.* The Temple Mount in Jerusalem. Jesus quotes the last line of this verse, along with Jer. 7:11, after removing the money changers from the temple in Matt. 21:13; Mark 11:17; Luke 19:46. **56:8** The inclusion of foreigners and eunuchs in the worshiping community extends God's *gather[ing]* of exiles.

56:9–57:2 A poetic critique of failed community leadership. **56:9** *Wild animals* symbolize external threats to the postexilic Judean community. They can *devour* it because of the failures of its leaders. **56:10** *Sentinels* refers to prophets (cf. 21:6, 11), who are called *blind* because they no longer receive accurate visions (cf. 29:10). Although *dogs* elsewhere denote threat (e.g., 1 Kgs. 14:11; Ps. 22:16), these failed prophets are compared to harmless animals. **56:11** *Mighty appetite* implies the practice of extortion. The community's political leaders are symbolized as ineffective *shepherds* (cf. Ezek. 34:1–16). **56:12** Cf. 5:11, 22–23. **57:1** The failure of community leadership allows *evil* to thrive, to the detriment of *the righteous*. **57:2** This promise appears to contradict the preceding verse. It may refer to the *peace* achieved by the persecuted righteous after their deaths (cf. Gen. 15:15; 2 Kgs. 22:20). *Couches* can refer to funeral "biers" (2 Chr. 16:14) or graves (Ezek. 32:25, where it is translated as "bed").

57:3–21 A poem denouncing forbidden rituals (cf. 65:2–7; 66:17) and contrasting the fates of the righteous and wicked, with YHWH as the speaker. It is unclear whether the poem reflects actual practices or uses exaggerated language to criticize a rival religious group. Although addressed to the rivals, it functions as encouragement to the in-group. **57:3** For the combined charges of sorcery

⁴ Whom are you mocking?
  Against whom do you open your
    mouth wide
  and stick out your tongue?
Are you not children of transgression,
  the offspring of deceit—
⁵ you who burn with lust among the oaks,
    under every green tree;
you who slaughter your children in the
    valleys,
  under the clefts of the rocks?
⁶ Among the smooth stones of the valley is
    your portion;
  it is they who are your lot;
to them you have poured out a drink
    offering;
  you have brought a grain offering.
  Should these acts cause me to relent?
⁷ Upon a high and lofty mountain
  you have set your bed,
  and there you went up to offer sacrifice.
⁸ Behind the door and the doorpost
  you have set up your symbol,
for in deserting me^v you have uncovered
    your bed;
  you have gone up to it;
  you have made it wide;
and you have made a bargain for
    yourself with them;
  you have loved their bed;
  you have gazed on their nakedness.^w
⁹ You journeyed to Molech^x with oil
  and multiplied your perfumes;
you sent your envoys far away
  and sent them down to Sheol.

¹⁰ You grew weary from your many
    wanderings,
  but you did not say, "It is no use!"
You found your desire rekindled,
  and so you did not weaken.

¹¹ Whom did you dread and fear
  so that you lied
and did not remember me
  or give me a thought?
Have I not kept silent and closed my eyes,^y
  and so you do not fear me?
¹² I will announce your verdict,
  and the objects you made will not help
    you.
¹³ When you cry out, let your collection of
    idols deliver you!
  The wind will carry them off;
  a breath will take them away.
But whoever takes refuge in me shall
    possess the land
  and inherit my holy mountain.
¹⁴ It shall be said,
"Build up, build up, prepare the way;
  remove every obstruction from my
    people's way."
¹⁵ For thus says the high and lofty one
  who inhabits eternity, whose name is
    Holy:
I dwell in the high and holy place
  and also with those who are contrite
    and humble in spirit,

v 57.8 Meaning of Heb uncertain   *w* 57.8 Or *phallus*; Heb *hand*   *x* 57.9 Or *the king*   *y* 57.11 Gk Vg: Heb *silent even for a long time*

and promiscuity, cf. 2 Kgs. 9:22; Nah. 3:4. *Adulterer* and *prostitute* are frequent prophetic metaphors for religious apostasy. **57:5** For *oaks* as sites of illicit religious practices, cf. Isa. 1:29–30; Hos. 4:13. The word for *oaks* ("elim") sounds identical to a word for "gods" or "dead spirits," recalling the critique of necromancy in Isa. 8:19–22. *Every green tree.* Cf. 1 Kgs. 14:23; Ezek. 6:13; etc. Metaphorical promiscuity is also associated with child sacrifice in Ezek. 16:20–21; 23:39. **57:6** Although unmarked in English translation, the pronouns shift from masculine plural to feminine singular, suggesting that the poem now addresses the "sorceress/adulteress" herself. This feminine poetic figure—likely the personification of the denounced religious sect—recalls personified Babylon in Isa. 47, who is also accused of practicing magic. **57:7** *Bed* (literally "couch") has overtones of both sexual promiscuity, as developed in the next verse, and death (see note on 57:2). **57:8** *Symbol.* An image for a foreign deity. *Deserting me* (i.e., YHWH) makes clear that sexual infidelity symbolizes religious apostasy. *Nakedness.* Literally "hand," a euphemism for penis (see note on 56:5). **57:9** *Molech.* A deity to whom children were sacrificed. The dispatch of *envoys* to *Sheol* refers to necromancy while also recalling the "agreement with Sheol" in Isa. 28:18 (see also 28:15). **57:10** The apostates' attraction to false deities is insatiable, like nymphomania (cf. Ezek. 16:28–29; see **"Slut-Shaming," p. 1148**). **57:11** For divine hiddenness as a cause of sin, cf. Isa. 64:7. **57:13** Unlike *idols*, YHWH alone provides true *refuge. My holy mountain.* The Temple Mount in Jerusalem. **57:14** Repeated imperatives echo 40:1; 51:9, 17; 52:1, 11; 62:10. *Way* refers to the highway for returning exiles (cf. 35:8; 40:3; 62:10) and to ethical conduct (cf. v. 18). **57:15** The depiction of YHWH as *high* and *holy* is characteristic of Isaiah,

to revive the spirit of the humble
and to revive the heart of the contrite.
¹⁶ For I will not continually accuse,
nor will I always be angry,
for then the spirits would grow faint
before me,
even the souls that I have made.
¹⁷ Because of their wicked covetousness I
was angry;
I struck them; I hid and was angry,
but they kept turning back to their
own ways.
¹⁸ I have seen their ways, but I will heal
them;
I will lead them and repay them with
comfort,
¹⁹ creating for their mourners the fruit of
the lips.ᶻ
Peace, peace, to the far and the near,
says the Lord,
and I will heal them.
²⁰ But the wicked are like the tossing sea
that cannot keep still;
its waters toss up mire and mud.
²¹ There is no peace, says my God, for the
wicked.

58 Shout out; do not hold back!
Lift up your voice like a trumpet!
Announce to my people their rebellion,
to the house of Jacob their sins.
² Yet day after day they seek me
and delight to know my ways,

as if they were a nation that practiced
righteousness
and did not forsake the ordinance of
their God;
they ask of me righteous judgments;
they want God on their side.ᵃ
³ "Why do we fast, but you do not see?
Why humble ourselves, but you do not
notice?"
Look, you serve your own interest on
your fast day
and oppress all your workers.
⁴ You fast only to quarrel and to fight
and to strike with a wicked fist.
Such fasting as you do today
will not make your voice heard on
high.
⁵ Is such the fast that I choose,
a day to humble oneself?
Is it to bow down the head like a
bulrush
and to lie in sackcloth and ashes?
Will you call this a fast,
a day acceptable to the Lord?

⁶ Is not this the fast that I choose:
to loose the bonds of injustice,
to undo the straps of the yoke,
to let the oppressed go free,
and to break every yoke?

z 57.19 Meaning of Heb uncertain a 58.2 Or *they delight to draw near to God*

but divine supremacy does not preclude sympathy for the *humble/contrite.* **57:16** *Not continually accuse.* Cf. Ps. 103:9. YHWH must restrain divine anger because frail created beings cannot long tolerate it. **57:17–18** Cf. Isa. 54:6–7. *Struck them.* Cf. 1:5; 5:25; 9:13; etc. YHWH forgives humans despite their failure to repent. **57:19** *Fruit of the lips* may refer to hymns of praise. **57:20** By their very nature, the *wicked* cannot find peace or security. **57:21** An almost identical line appears in 48:22, marking chaps. 49–57 as a unit.

58:1–14 A poem denouncing religious fasts that are not accompanied by just actions. Although Isaiah frequently condemns forbidden religious rituals, as in the preceding chapter, acceptable rituals do not necessarily guarantee divine favor (cf. 1:11–17). Similar critiques of fasting appear in Zech. 7:1–14 and Matt. 6:16–18. **58:1** *Shout out.* The Hebrew verb "qara ʾ," also translated as "call," appears throughout the poem (vv. 1, 5, 9, 12–13). **58:2** Acknowledgment of the people's piety is ironically framed by denunciations of their sinfulness. **58:3** *Fast.* Self-denial of food as a gesture of devotion or repentance. In the postexilic period, annual days of fasting commemorated the destruction of Jerusalem (cf. Zech. 7). Many Jews, Christians, and Muslims practice fasting today during religious holidays, frequently accompanied by acts of charity. In this verse, the people accuse God of ignoring their fasting, perhaps reflecting the ongoing difficulties of life in postexilic Jerusalem. The deity responds that their rituals are self-serving and do not benefit others. In a wordplay, the words *fast* ("tsom") and *serve* ("timtse'u") sound similar. **58:4** Ironically, *fight* ("matsa") also sounds like *fast* ("tsom") in Hebrew. **58:5** A series of rhetorical questions. *Bow down the head* and *lie in sackcloth and ashes* are gestures of mourning that accompanied fasting. *Bulrush.* A marshy reed that is easily blown over in the wind. **58:6** Further rhetorical questions clarify the divine expectation that fasting be accompanied by just actions. *Bonds of injustice* and *straps of the yoke* metonymically suggest

7 Is it not to share your bread with the
    hungry
  and bring the homeless poor into your
    house;
  when you see the naked, to cover them
    and not to hide yourself from your
    own kin?
8 Then your light shall break forth like the
    dawn,
  and your healing shall spring up
    quickly;
  your vindicator[b] shall go before you;
    the glory of the LORD shall be your
    rear guard.
9 Then you shall call, and the LORD will
    answer;
  you shall cry for help, and he will say,
    "Here I am."

  If you remove the yoke from among you,
    the pointing of the finger, the
    speaking of evil,
10 if you offer your food to the hungry
    and satisfy the needs of the afflicted,
  then your light shall rise in the darkness
    and your gloom be like the noonday.
11 The LORD will guide you continually
    and satisfy your needs in parched places
    and make your bones strong,
  and you shall be like a watered garden,
    like a spring of water
    whose waters never fail.
12 Your ancient ruins shall be rebuilt;
    you shall raise up the foundations of
    many generations;
  you shall be called the repairer of the
    breach,
    the restorer of streets to live in.

13 If you refrain from trampling the
    Sabbath,
  from pursuing your own interests on
    my holy day;
  if you call the Sabbath a delight
    and the holy day of the LORD
    honorable;
  if you honor it, not going your own ways,
    serving your own interests or pursuing
    your own affairs;
14 then you shall take delight in the LORD,
    and I will make you ride upon the
    heights of the earth;
  I will feed you with the heritage of your
    ancestor Jacob,
    for the mouth of the LORD has spoken.

59 See, the LORD's arm is not too short
    to save,
    nor his ear too dull to hear.
2 Rather, your iniquities have been
    barriers
    between you and your God,
  and your sins have hidden his face from
    you
    so that he does not hear.
3 For your hands are defiled with blood
    and your fingers with iniquity;
  your lips have spoken lies;
    your tongue mutters wickedness.
4 No one brings suit justly;
    no one goes to law honestly;
  they rely on empty pleas; they speak lies,
    conceiving mischief and bearing
    iniquity.
5 They hatch adders' eggs
    and weave the spider's web;

b 58.8 Or *vindication*

unjust imprisonment or servitude, perhaps due to oppressive debt (cf. Neh. 5:2–5). **58:7** *Bread avoided during a fast should be share[d] . . . with the hungry.* The word *poor* ("'aniyim") is related to "humble" ("'inninu") in Isa. 58:3. **58:8** *Light.* Cf. 9:2; 42:16; 60:1. *Rear guard.* Cf. 52:12. **58:11** *Water* imagery recalls the motif of revitalized desertscapes in Isa. 40–55. **58:12** *Ruins* and *breach* allude to the incomplete reconstruction of Jerusalem in the early postexilic period. **58:13** *Sabbath* observance (see note on 56:2) should be accompanied by concern for others, as made clear in the Sabbath commandments in Exod. 20:10; Deut. 5:14–15. **58:14** The reference to *Jacob* echoes the beginning of the poem. *Mouth of the* LORD *has spoken.* Cf. Isa. 1:20; 40:5.
    59:1–21 A three-part poem addressing the difficulties of postexilic life. In vv. 1–8, the prophet blames those difficulties on the people's sins. The people confess their sins in vv. 9–15a, and the prophet responds with a promise of divine vindication in vv. 15b–21. **59:1** Cf. 50:2. The prophet denies that the audience's suffering results from divine weakness. **59:2** Human sinfulness prevents God from answering prayers. Cf. 64:7, where the *hidden* divine *face* is the cause of sin. **59:3** Here and in vv. 6–7, specific human body parts are associated with ethical misdeeds (cf. Prov. 6:16–18). *Defiled with blood.* Cf. Isa. 1:15. **59:4** The people metaphorically give birth to sinfulness. **59:5–6** Building on v. 4's birth imagery, ethical misdeeds are compared to *adders' eggs*, which bring death, and a

whoever eats their eggs dies,
and the crushed egg hatches out a
viper.
⁶ Their webs cannot serve as clothing;
they cannot cover themselves with
what they make.
Their works are works of iniquity,
and deeds of violence are in their
hands.
⁷ Their feet run to evil,
and they rush to shed innocent blood;
their thoughts are thoughts of iniquity;
desolation and destruction are in their
highways.
⁸ The way of peace they do not know,
and there is no justice in their ways.
Their roads they have made crooked;
no one who walks in them knows
peace.

⁹ Therefore justice is far from us,
and deliverance does not reach us;
we wait for light, but there is only
darkness;
and for brightness, but we walk in
gloom.
¹⁰ We grope like the blind along a wall,
groping like those who have no eyes;
we stumble at noon as in the twilight,
among the vigorous*c* as though we
were dead.
¹¹ We all growl like bears;
like doves we moan mournfully.
We wait for justice, but there is none;
for salvation, but it is far from us.
¹² For our transgressions before you are
many,
and our sins testify against us.
Our transgressions indeed are with us,
and we know our iniquities:
¹³ transgressing and denying the LORD
and turning away from following our
God,

talking oppression and revolt,
conceiving lying words and uttering
them from the heart.
¹⁴ Justice is turned back,
and deliverance stands at a distance,
for truth stumbles in the public
square,
and uprightness cannot enter.
¹⁵ Truth is lacking,
and whoever turns from evil is
despoiled.

The LORD saw it, and it displeased him
that there was no justice.
¹⁶ He saw that there was no one
and was appalled that there was no
one to intervene,
so his own arm brought him victory,
and his righteousness upheld him.
¹⁷ He put on righteousness like a
breastplate
and a helmet of salvation on his head;
he put on garments of vengeance for
clothing
and wrapped himself in fury as in a
mantle.
¹⁸ According to their deeds, so will he
repay
wrath to his adversaries, requital to
his enemies;
to the coastlands he will render
requital.
¹⁹ So those in the west shall fear the name
of the LORD,
and those in the east, his glory,
for he will come like a pent-up stream
that the wind of the LORD drives on.

²⁰ And he will come to Zion as Redeemer,
to those in Jacob who turn from
transgression, says the LORD.

c 59.10 Meaning of Heb uncertain

---

spider's web, which cannot provide protection. **59:7–8** Drawing on the metaphor of *way* as moral conduct, these verses use four different terms for roadways. **59:9** The people compare their disillusionment to *darkness.* In the preceding verses, *justice* referred to legal equity; here, it denotes divine *deliverance.* **59:10** *Like the blind.* See **"Isaiah and Disability," p. 974.** **59:11** *Like doves.* Cf. 38:14. *Far from us.* Cf. 46:13. **59:12–13** Agreeing with vv. 1–8, the people acknowledge their sinfulness. **59:14** *Justice, deliverance,* and *truth* are personified. **59:15** The prophet resumes speaking in v. 15b. **59:16** In the absence of human action, God acts to bring *victory.* **59:17** As the divine warrior, God wears armor, with each piece associated with a divine attribute. **59:18** *Coastlands.* See note on 41:1. **59:19** Cf. 24:14–15. In 8:7, the advancing Assyrian army was compared to a flood; here the metaphor is applied to YHWH's appearance. **59:20** *Redeemer.* See note on 41:14. Unlike Isa. 40–55, where divine redemption was universal, here it is limited to *those . . . who turn from transgression* (cf. 1:27).

[21]And as for me, this is my covenant with them, says the Lord: my spirit that is upon you and my words that I have put in your mouth shall not depart out of your mouth or out of the mouths of your children or out of the mouths of your children's children, says the Lord, from now on and forever.

60

Arise, shine, for your light has come, and the glory of the Lord has risen upon you.

[2] For darkness shall cover the earth
  and thick darkness the peoples,
but the Lord will arise upon you,
  and his glory will appear over you.
[3] Nations shall come to your light
  and kings to the brightness of your
    dawn.

[4] Lift up your eyes and look around;
  they all gather together; they come
    to you;
your sons shall come from far away,
  and your daughters shall be carried in
    their nurses' arms.
[5] Then you shall see and be radiant;
  your heart shall thrill and rejoice,[d]
because the abundance of the sea shall
    be brought to you;
  the wealth of the nations shall come
    to you.
[6] A multitude of camels shall cover you,
  the young camels of Midian and
    Ephah;

all those from Sheba shall come.
  They shall bring gold and frankincense
    and shall proclaim the praise of the
      Lord.
[7] All the flocks of Kedar shall be gathered
    to you;
  the rams of Nebaioth shall minister to
    you;
they shall be acceptable on my altar,[e]
  and I will glorify my glorious
    house.

[8] Who are these that fly like a cloud
  and like doves to their windows?
[9] For the coastlands shall wait for me,
  the ships of Tarshish first,
to bring your children from far away,
  their silver and gold with them,
for the name of the Lord your God
  and for the Holy One of Israel,
  because he has glorified you.
[10] Foreigners shall build up your walls,
  and their kings shall minister to you,
for in my wrath I struck you down,
  but in my favor I have had mercy
    on you.
[11] Your gates shall always be open;
  day and night they shall not be shut,
so that nations shall bring you their
    wealth,
  with their kings led in procession.

d 60.5 Heb *be enlarged*   *e* 60.7 Q ms Heb mss Gk Syr Tg: MT *will ascend on the favor of my altar*

This narrower perspective will return in 65–66. **59:21** YHWH reaffirms the *covenant* with the people (cf. 55:3–4; 61:8) and the permanence of the divine *word* (cf. 40:8).

60:1–22 The poems in Isa. 60–62 closely resemble chaps. 40–55. Their extravagant rhetoric counters the audience's disillusionment that prior prophetic promises have not been fulfilled. Many scholars view these chapters as the earliest texts within chaps. 56–66. Their positive view of the future contrasts with the surrounding chapters. **60:1** A pair of imperatives addressed to personified Zion (cf. 51:17; 52:1; 54:1). **60:2** The contrast between "light" (v. 1) and *darkness* connects this poem to the preceding one (cf. 59:9). **60:4** As in 49:20–22 and 54:1, returning exiles are depicted as Zion's children. *Nurses' arms.* Cf. 49:23. **60:5** Along with the repatriated exiles, Jerusalem will receive economic support from foreign nations (cf. 18:7; 45:14). This verse supplied the title of Adam Smith's treatise on capitalism, *The Wealth of Nations* (cf. 61:6; 66:12). **60:6** *Midian* and *Sheba* were Arabian tribes that traded widely with neighboring kingdoms; the location of *Ephah* is uncertain. *Gold and frankincense.* This verse influenced the tradition of the magi's gifts for the infant Jesus in Matt. 2:11. **60:7** *Kedar.* See note on Isa. 21:16–17. *Rams* is a metaphor for political or military leaders (see note on 34:7). *Nebaioth.* A place of uncertain location, possibly in Edom. *Acceptable on my altar.* Cf. 56:7. Despite their foreign origins, these animals are suitable for sacrifice in YHWH's *glorious house.* It is unclear whether this verse presupposes or anticipates the rebuilding of the temple, which was completed circa 515 BCE (cf. v. 14). **60:9** *Coastlands shall wait.* Cf. 42:4; 51:5. *Ships of Tarshish.* See note on 2:16. *The Lord your God . . . has glorified you.* Cf. 55:5. **60:10** Just as foreigners destroyed Jerusalem's *walls,* now they will *build* them. For the contrast between YHWH's *wrath* and *mercy,* cf. 54:8. **60:11** Jerusalem's *gates* can remain *open* because there are no longer military threats.

¹² For the nation and kingdom
that will not serve you shall perish;
those nations shall be utterly laid waste.
¹³ The glory of Lebanon shall come to you,
the cypress, the plane, and the pine,
to beautify the place of my sanctuary,
and I will glorify where my feet rest.
¹⁴ The descendants of those who oppressed
you
shall come bending low to you,
and all who despised you
shall bow down at your feet;
they shall call you the City of the LORD,
the Zion of the Holy One of Israel.
¹⁵ Whereas you have been forsaken and
hated,
with no one passing through,
I will make you majestic forever,
a joy from age to age.
¹⁶ You shall suck the milk of nations;
you shall suck the breasts of kings,
and you shall know that I, the LORD, am
your Savior
and your Redeemer, the Mighty One
of Jacob.

¹⁷ Instead of bronze I will bring gold;
instead of iron I will bring silver;
instead of wood, bronze;
instead of stones, iron.
I will appoint Peace as your overseer
and Righteousness as your taskmaster.
¹⁸ Violence shall no more be heard in your
land,
devastation or destruction within your
borders;

you shall call your walls Salvation
and your gates Praise.
¹⁹ The sun shall no longer be
your light by day,
nor for brightness shall the moon
give light to you by night,ᶠ
but the LORD will be your everlasting
light,
and your God will be your glory.
²⁰ Your sun shall no more go down
or your moon withdraw itself,
for the LORD will be your everlasting
light,
and your days of mourning shall be
ended.
²¹ Your people shall all be righteous;
they shall possess the land forever.
They are the shoot that I planted, the
work of my hands,
so that I might be glorified.
²² The least of them shall become a clan
and the smallest one a mighty nation;
I am the LORD;
in its time I will accomplish it quickly.

61 The spirit of the Lord GOD is upon me
because the LORD has anointed me;
he has sent me to bring good news to the
oppressed,
to bind up the brokenhearted,
to proclaim liberty to the captives
and release to the prisoners,
² to proclaim the year of the LORD's favor
and the day of vengeance of our God,
to comfort all who mourn,

ᶠ 60.19 Q ms Gk OL Tg: MT lacks *by night*

60:12 Although this verse's xenophobia is troubling, it responds to centuries of domination of Jerusalem by other nations. **60:13** *Glory of Lebanon* (cf. 35:2) recalls the use of imported cedars in the construction of the First Temple (1 Kgs. 5:8–10). *Cypress . . . plane . . . pine.* Cf. 41:19. For the temple as YHWH's footstool, cf. Pss. 99:5; 132:7; cf. Isa. 66:1. **60:14** Cf. 49:23. **60:15** *Forsaken.* Cf. 49:14; 54:6; 62:4. **60:16** The nations' tribute is compared to a mother's *milk*, which Jerusalem will *suck*; cf. 49:23. *Mighty One of Jacob.* See note on 49:26. **60:17** Instead of foreign rulers, personified *Peace* and *Righteousness* will govern Jerusalem. **60:18** In other biblical texts, Jerusalem's *walls* and *gates* have more pedestrian names (cf. Neh. 12:38–39; Ezek. 48:30–35). **60:19–20** This verse influenced the depiction of the new Jerusalem in Rev. 21:23; 22:5. **60:21** *Your people shall all be righteous* contrasts with the distinction between the righteous and wicked elsewhere in Isa. 56–66. **60:22** Jerusalem's glorious restoration will happen *quickly* but only *in its time*—an unspecified point in the future. See **"Visions of Peace," p. 937**.

61:1–11 Extending the promises of Isa. 60, this poem alternates between the voices of a poetic figure (vv. 1–4, 10–11), whose words echo the servant's speeches from chaps. 40–55, and YHWH (vv. 8–9). It is unclear who speaks in vv. 5–7. **61:1** Jesus quotes vv. 1–2 in his first public speech in Luke 4:16–21 (see **"Isaiah and Jesus," p. 951**). *Spirit . . . upon me.* Cf. 42:1. *Anointed* recalls Cyrus's mission in 45:1. See **"Cyrus," p. 991**. *Release to the prisoners.* Cf. 42:7; 49:9. *Captives* and *prisoners* were likely victims of debt enslavement (cf. Neh. 5:2–5). **61:2** *Year of the LORD's favor* refers to

3 to provide for those who mourn in
Zion—
to give them a garland instead of
ashes,
the oil of gladness instead of mourning,
the mantle of praise instead of a faint
spirit.
They will be called oaks of
righteousness,
the planting of the LORD, to display his
glory.
4 They shall build up the ancient ruins;
they shall raise up the former
devastations;
they shall repair the ruined cities,
the devastations of many generations.

5 Strangers shall stand and feed your
flocks;
foreigners shall till your land and
dress your vines,
6 but you shall be called priests of the
LORD;
you shall be named ministers of our
God;
you shall enjoy the wealth of the nations,
and in their riches you shall glory.
7 Because their[g] shame was double
and dishonor was proclaimed as
their lot,
therefore in their land they shall possess
a double portion;
everlasting joy shall be theirs.

8 For I, the LORD, love justice,
I hate robbery and wrongdoing;[h]
I will faithfully give them their
recompense,
and I will make an everlasting
covenant with them.
9 Their descendants shall be known
among the nations
and their offspring among the peoples;
all who see them shall acknowledge
that they are a people whom the LORD
has blessed.
10 I will greatly rejoice in the LORD;
my whole being shall exult in my God,
for he has clothed me with the garments
of salvation;
he has covered me with the robe of
righteousness,
as a bridegroom decks himself with a
garland
and as a bride adorns herself with her
jewels.
11 For as the earth brings forth its shoots
and as a garden causes what is sown
in it to spring up,
so the Lord GOD will cause righteousness
and praise
to spring up before all the nations.

62 For Zion's sake I will not keep silent,
and for Jerusalem's sake I will not
rest,
until her vindication shines out like the
dawn
and her salvation like a burning torch.
2 The nations shall see your vindication
and all the kings your glory,

g 61.7 Heb *your* *h* 61.8 Or *robbery with a burnt offering*

designated times for debt forgiveness and manumission of enslaved persons (Lev. 25:10–55; Deut. 15:1–18). *Day of vengeance.* See note on Isa. 34:8. Although *vengeance* may seem out of place here, these verses insist that social justice and retributive justice belong together; that is, the liberation of the "oppressed" (v. 1) requires the disempowerment of the oppressors. This connection is reinforced by the similar sounds of *vengeance* ("naqam") and *comfort* ("nakham"). **61:3** Mourning rites give way to expressions of joy. The similar sounds of *garland* ("pe'er") and *ashes* ("'eper") ironically reinforce the contrast between them. *Planting of the LORD* connects this poem with the preceding one (60:21; cf. 5:7). **61:4** Cf. 58:12. **61:5** In addition to rebuilding Jerusalem's walls (60:10), *foreigners* will perform agricultural labor for the postexilic community. **61:6** The postexilic community will act as *priests* toward other nations (cf. Exod. 19:5–6). *Wealth of the nations.* See note on Isa. 60:5. **61:7** *Shame was double.* Cf. 40:2. *Everlasting joy.* Cf. 35:10; 51:11. **61:8** YHWH affirms the divine commitment to *justice*. Given the promise of land in v. 7, *everlasting covenant* (cf. 24:5; 55:3) probably recalls God's promises to Abraham (Gen. 17:7). **61:9** Zion's restoration leads to worldwide recognition of YHWH's power (cf. Isa. 55:5). **61:10** The voice from vv. 1–4 returns with a hymn of thanksgiving. *Garland* echoes v. 3. **61:11** Plant imagery serves as a metaphor for worldwide praise of YHWH.

62:1–12 A poem about Jerusalem's future restoration. **62:1** Although the speaker is not explicitly identified, it is presumably the same voice from Isa. 61. The pledge to intercede tirelessly for *Zion* suggests a prophetic role. **62:2** In the ancient world, a person's *name* was tied to their reputation

and you shall be called by a new name
    that the mouth of the Lord will give.
³ You shall be a beautiful crown in the
    hand of the Lord
  and a royal diadem in the hand of
    your God.
⁴ You shall no more be termed Forsaken,
  and your land shall no more be termed
    Desolate,
  but you shall be called My Delight Is in
    Her
  and your land Married,
  for the Lord delights in you,
    and your land shall be married.
⁵ For as a young man marries a young
    woman,
  so shall your builder*i* marry you,
  and as the bridegroom rejoices over the
    bride,
  so shall your God rejoice over you.
⁶ Upon your walls, O Jerusalem,
    I have posted sentinels;
  all day and all night
    they shall never be silent.
  You who remind the Lord,
    take no rest,
⁷ and give him no rest
    until he establishes Jerusalem
  and makes it renowned throughout
    the earth.

⁸ The Lord has sworn by his right hand
    and by his mighty arm:
I will not again give your grain
    to be food for your enemies,
and foreigners shall not drink the
    wine
  for which you have labored,
⁹ but those who harvest it shall eat it
    and praise the Lord,
and those who gather it shall drink it
    in my holy courts.

¹⁰ Go through, go through the gates;
    prepare the way for the people;
build up, build up the highway;
    clear it of stones;
  lift up an ensign over the peoples.
¹¹ The Lord has proclaimed
    to the end of the earth:
Say to daughter Zion,
    "Look, your savior comes;
his reward is with him
    and his recompense before him."
¹² They shall be called, "The Holy
    People,
  The Redeemed of the Lord,"
and you shall be called, "Sought Out,
  A City Not Forsaken."

i 62.5 Cn: Heb *your sons*

and identity. A change of fortunes might be marked by receiving a *new name* (e.g., Abram/Abraham and Sarai/Sarah in Gen. 17:5, 15; Jacob/Israel in Gen. 32:28; 35:10). **62:3** The restored Jerusalem will be a sign of YHWH's divine kingship. A *crown* could also be associated with a royal wedding (Song 3:11), anticipating the marital imagery of the next verses. **62:4** The change in names promised in v. 2. *Forsaken* (Heb. "Azubah") was the name of two women in the Bible, one of whom was King Jehoshaphat's mother (1 Kgs. 22:42; 1 Chr. 2:18–19). The term is associated with Jerusalem in Isa. 49:14; 54:6; 60:15. *Desolate.* Cf. 1:7; 6:11; 54:1, 3. *My Delight Is in Her* (Heb. "Hephzibah") was the name of King Manasseh's mother (2 Kgs. 21:1). A character named Hephzibah appears in George Eliot's 1861 novel *Silas Marner*, and it was a popular name for churches in the nineteenth century, especially in the southern United States. This verse picks up the marital metaphor in chap. 54, although here not only the city but also its *land shall be married.* **62:5** The Hebrew text reads "your sons" ("banayik") will *marry you*, but the original reading was possibly *your builder* ("bonek"), as NRSVue translates. There may be a wordplay combining the motifs of the returning exiles as Jerusalem's children and the deity as Jerusalem's husband (cf. 49:18). In Hebrew, the "b" sound appears in every word of v. 5a. **62:6** It is unclear whether this verse assumes that Jerusalem's walls have been rebuilt or imagines a counterfactual situation. *Sentinels.* Cf. 52:8. Elsewhere in Isaiah, "sentinel" or "watcher" is a metaphor for a prophet (21:6–8, 11; 56:10). Although this verse uses a different Hebrew word, it seems to refer to a prophet who will intercede on Jerusalem's behalf (cf. v. 1). **62:7** This verse implies that YHWH has been slow to fulfill the promises of restoration for Jerusalem, but the deity can be pressured by human action. **62:8** A divine oath demonstrates the seriousness of this promise. Vv. 8–9 overturn a curse found in Deut. 28:30, 33. **62:10** Repeated imperatives connect this text to 40:1; 52:11; 57:14 (cf. 48:20). *Prepare the way.* Cf. 40:3. The images of *highway* and *ensign* (or "signal") are associated with the return from exile in chaps. 1–55. **62:11** Cf. 40:10. **62:12** Additional new names for Zion and its inhabitants (cf. vv. 2, 4).

63

"Who is this coming from Edom,
from Bozrah in garments stained
crimson?
Who is this so splendidly robed,
marching in his great might?"

"It is I, announcing vindication,
mighty to save."

2 "Why are your robes red
and your garments like theirs who
tread the winepress?"

3 "I have trodden the winepress alone,
and from the peoples no one was
with me;
I trod them in my anger
and trampled them in my wrath;
their juice spattered on my garments,
and I stained all my robes.
4 For the day of vengeance was in my
mind,
and the year for my redeeming work
had come.
5 I looked, but there was no helper;
I was abandoned, and there was no
one to sustain me,
so my own arm brought me victory,
and my wrath sustained me.
6 I trampled down peoples in my anger;
I crushed them[j] in my wrath,

and I poured out their lifeblood on the
earth."
7 I will recount the gracious deeds of the
LORD,
the praiseworthy acts of the LORD,
because of all that the LORD has done for us
and the great favor to the house of
Israel
that he has shown them according to his
mercy,
according to the abundance of his
steadfast love.
8 For he said, "Surely they are my people,
children who will not act deceitfully,"
and he became their savior
9 in all their distress.
It was no messenger or angel
but his presence that saved them;
in his love and pity it was he who
redeemed them;
he lifted them up and carried them all
the days of old.

10 But they rebelled
and grieved his holy spirit;
therefore he became their enemy;
he himself fought against them.
11 Then they[k] remembered the days of old,
of Moses his servant.[l]

j 63.6 Heb mss: MT *I made them drunk*   k 63.11 Heb *he*
l 63.11 Cn: Heb *his people*

63:1–6 A short poem depicting divine judgment against Edom (cf. 34:1–17). Its distinctive question-and-answer style may have been influenced by 21:11–12. The depiction of YHWH as a divine warrior forms a bookend with 59:15b–21, framing the promises of Jerusalem's restoration in chaps. 60–62. **63:1** The questioner's identity is unclear. For *Edom* and *Bozrah*, see notes on 34:5–6. *Edom* is the location from which YHWH marches as a divine warrior in Judg. 5:4. *Garments stained crimson* recalls "garments of vengeance" in 59:17. **63:2** A play on the similar sounds of Hebrew "'adom" (*red*) and "Edom" (cf. Gen. 25:30). **63:3** In a gruesome metaphor, YHWH's garments have been stained red with the blood of the deity's enemies, just like a laborer's garments are stained by stomping grapes in a *winepress* to extract their *juice*. (For blood as a metaphor for grape juice, cf. Gen. 49:11; Sir. 50:15.) This verse inspired the imagery of Rev. 14:18–20, to which the phrase "grapes of wrath" alludes in Julia Ward Howe's "Battle Hymn of the Republic" (1861); that allusion in turn supplied the title of John Steinbeck's 1939 novel *The Grapes of Wrath*. **63:4** *Day of vengeance.* Cf. Isa. 34:8; 61:2. *Year for my redeeming work* recalls "year of the LORD's favor" in 61:2, reinforcing the connection between retributive justice and social justice assumed in these chapters. **63:5** Cf. 59:15–16. **63:6** The reference to *peoples* makes clear that divine wrath is directed against not solely Edom but all nations that have oppressed God's people.

63:7–64:12 A communal prayer of confession and lament (cf. Pss. 60; 79–80; etc.), echoing Isa. 59:9–15a. **63:7** The poem begins by recounting the past relationship between YHWH and the people. In Hebrew, the first and last word of the verse is "hesed" ("gracious deeds, steadfast love"). The individual speaking voice represents the entire community. **63:8** *Savior* designates a military deliverer. **63:9** In the past, YHWH acted directly to redeem the people. **63:10** Vv. 10–11 contain two of the only three references to the *holy spirit* in the Hebrew Bible (cf. Ps. 51:11). *He himself fought against them.* The counterpart to YHWH's direct intervention for the people's good in v. 9. **63:11–14** A series of questions recalling

Where is the one who brought them up
       out of the sea
   with the shepherds of his flock?
Where is the one who put within them
       his holy spirit,
¹² who caused his glorious arm
       to march at the right hand of Moses,
   who divided the waters before them
       to make for himself an everlasting
           name,
¹³   who led them through the depths?
   Like a horse in the desert,
       they did not stumble.
¹⁴ Like cattle that go down into the valley,
       the spirit of the LORD gave them rest.
   Thus you led your people,
       to make for yourself a glorious name.
¹⁵ Look down from heaven and see,
       from your holy and glorious
           habitation.
   Where are your zeal and your might?
       Your great pity and your compassion
       are withheld from me.
¹⁶ For you are our father,
       though Abraham does not know us
   and Israel does not acknowledge us;
   you, O LORD, are our father;
       our Redeemer from of old is your
           name.
¹⁷ Why, O LORD, do you let us stray from
           your ways
   and let our heart harden, so that we
       do not fear you?
   Turn back for the sake of your
       servants,
       the tribes that are your heritage.
¹⁸ Your holy people took possession for a
       little while,
   but now our adversaries have
       trampled down your sanctuary.

¹⁹ We have long been like those whom you
       do not rule,
   like those not called by your name.

64

O that you would tear open the
heavens and come down,
   so that the mountains would quake at
       your presence—
² ᵐas when fire kindles brushwood
       and the fire causes water to boil—
   to make your name known to your
       adversaries,
   so that the nations might tremble at
       your presence!
³ When you did awesome deeds that we
       did not expect,
   you came down; the mountains
       quaked at your presence.
⁴ From ages past no one has heard,
       no ear has perceived,
   no eye has seen any God besides you,
       who works for those who wait for
           him.
⁵ You meet those who gladly do right,
       those who remember you in your
           ways.
   But you were angry, and we sinned;
       because you hid yourself we
           transgressed.ⁿ
⁶ We have all become like one who is
       unclean,
   and all our righteous deeds are like a
       filthy cloth.
   We all fade like a leaf,
       and our iniquities, like the wind, take
           us away.
⁷ There is no one who calls on your name
       or attempts to take hold of you,

m 64.2 64.1 in Heb   n 64.5 Meaning of Heb uncertain

---

the exodus and asking why YHWH does not act similarly in the present. Vv. 11–12 are the only references to *Moses* in Isaiah. **63:15** The poem turns to directly addressing the deity. *Look down from heaven.* Cf. Ps. 80:14. The destruction of the temple (Isa. 63:18; 64:11) led to an increased emphasis on *heaven* as YHWH's *habitation* (cf. 57:15; 66:1), which reinforces the sense of distance between YHWH and the people in this poem. **63:16** As the people's *father*, YHWH's faithfulness exceeds that of their ancestors *Abraham* and *Israel* (Jacob); cf. 49:15. *Redeemer.* See note on 41:14. **63:17** YHWH is blamed for the people's sins (cf. 64:5, 7). *Servants* includes all the people, as opposed to chaps. 65–66, where it designates a righteous subset of the people. **63:18** In contrast with the present exile, the six hundred years of *possession* of the promised land seems like only *a little while. Trampled down your sanctuary.* The destruction of the temple by the Babylonians. **64:1–3** Past manifestations of divine presence included storms, earthquakes, and fire, which caused other *nations* to *tremble* (cf. Exod. 15:14–15; Hab. 3:6–7). **64:4** Paul quotes this verse in 1 Cor. 2:9. *Wait.* Cf. Isa. 8:17; 26:8; 33:2; 40:31; etc. **64:5** Here and in v. 7, YHWH is blamed for human sinfulness (cf. 63:17). *Hid yourself.* Cf. 8:17; 45:15; 54:8; 57:17. **64:6** *Filthy cloth.* Literally a menstrual rag, a symbol of ritual impurity. *Fade*

for you have hidden your face from us
    and have delivered[o] us into the hand
        of our iniquity.
⁸ Yet, O LORD, you are our Father;
    we are the clay, and you are our
        potter;
    we are all the work of your hand.
⁹ Do not be exceedingly angry, O LORD,
    and do not remember iniquity forever.
    Now consider, we are all your people.
¹⁰ Your holy cities have become a
        wilderness;
    Zion has become a wilderness,
    Jerusalem a desolation.
¹¹ Our holy and beautiful house,
    where our ancestors praised you,
has been burned by fire,
    and all our pleasant places have
        become ruins.
¹² After all this, will you restrain yourself,
        O LORD?
    Will you keep silent and punish us so
        severely?

65 I was ready to be sought out by
        those who did not ask,
    to be found by those who did not seek
        me.
    I said, "Here I am, here I am,"
        to a nation that did not call on my name.
² I held out my hands all day long
        to a rebellious people,
    who walk in a way that is not good,
        following their own devices;
³ a people who provoke me
        to my face continually,

sacrificing in gardens
    and offering incense on bricks;
⁴ who sit inside tombs
    and spend the night in secret places;
who eat the flesh of pigs,
    with broth of abominable things in
        their vessels;
⁵ who say, "Keep to yourself;
    do not come near me, for I am too holy
        for you."
These are a smoke in my nostrils,
    a fire that burns all day long.
⁶ See, it is written before me:
    I will not keep silent, but I will repay;
I will indeed repay into their laps
⁷   their[p] iniquities and their[q] ancestors'
        iniquities together,
                                    says the LORD;
because they offered incense on the
        mountains
    and reviled me on the hills,
I will measure into their laps
    full payment for their actions.
⁸ Thus says the LORD:
As the wine is found in the cluster,
    and they say, "Do not destroy it,
        for there is a blessing in it,"
so I will do for my servants' sake
    and not destroy them all.
⁹ I will bring forth descendants from
        Jacob
    and from Judah inheritors of my
        mountains;

o 64.7 Gk Syr OL Tg: Heb *melted*   p 65.7 Gk Syr: Heb *your*
q 65.7 Gk Syr: Heb *your*

---

like a leaf. Cf. 40:8. **64:8** *Our Father.* Cf. 63:16. *Clay . . . potter.* A reversal of 29:16; 45:9. **64:9** *We are all your people* recalls the covenant formula in which YHWH is Israel's god and Israel is YHWH's people (Exod. 6:7; Lev. 26:12; etc.). **64:10–11** Jerusalem and the temple remain in *ruins*, suggesting that this poem dates to the exilic period, which would make it earlier than the rest of chaps. 56–66. **64:12** Although some communal laments end with statements of hope (cf. Pss. 60:12; 79:13), this one ends with uncertainty (cf. Lam. 5:22).

65:1–25 This poem contains alternating statements of condemnation and blessing for rival religious communities, culminating in a description of the eschatological restoration of Jerusalem. **65:1** Responding to the previous poem, YHWH claims to have been *ready* to answer the people's prayers. **65:2** This verse uses the common metaphor of behavior as a path (*way*). **65:3** Vv. 3–4 accuse a rival religious group of performing forbidden rituals (cf. 57:3–13; 66:3, 17). *Gardens.* Cf. 1:29; 17:10; 66:17. It is unclear why the speaker disapproves of *offering incense on bricks*. **65:4** *Tombs* were sites of necromantic practices (cf. 8:19–22; 57:6, 9) and sources of ritual uncleanness, along with *the flesh of pigs* (cf. Lev. 11:7) and *broth of abominable things*. **65:5** As translated here, the rival group considers themselves *too holy* for the speaker's group and avoids them. Alternatively, *keep to yourself* could be addressed to YHWH because the apostates are dedicated (*holy*) to different deities. **65:6** *Into their laps.* An idiom meaning "in full measure." **65:7** *Mountains . . . hills.* Cf. Deut. 12:2; Ezek. 6:13; etc. **65:8** The postexilic community is like a grape *cluster* with both good and bad fruit. YHWH resolves not to *destroy* the entire community and to preserve his *servants*, the righteous

my chosen shall inherit it,
and my servants shall settle there.
[10] Sharon shall become a pasture for flocks
and the Valley of Achor a place for
herds to lie down,
for my people who have sought me.
[11] But you who forsake the LORD,
who forget my holy mountain,
who set a table for Fortune
and fill cups of mixed wine for Destiny,
[12] I will destine you to the sword,
and all of you shall bow down to the
slaughter;
because, when I called, you did not
answer,
when I spoke, you did not listen,
but you did what was evil in my sight
and chose what I did not delight in.
[13] Therefore thus says the Lord GOD:
My servants shall eat,
but you shall be hungry;
my servants shall drink,
but you shall be thirsty;
my servants shall rejoice,
but you shall be put to shame;
[14] my servants shall sing with gladness of
heart,
but you shall cry out in pain of heart
and shall wail in anguish of spirit.
[15] You shall leave your name to my chosen
to use as a curse,
and the Lord GOD will put you to death,
but to his servants he will give a
different name.
[16] Then whoever invokes a blessing in the
land
shall bless by the God of faithfulness,
and whoever takes an oath in the land
shall swear by the God of faithfulness,
because the former troubles are forgotten
and are hidden from my sight.
[17] For I am about to create new heavens
and a new earth;

the former things shall not be
remembered
or come to mind.
[18] But be glad and rejoice forever
in what I am creating,
for I am about to create Jerusalem as a joy
and its people as a delight.
[19] I will rejoice in Jerusalem
and delight in my people;
no more shall the sound of weeping be
heard in it
or the cry of distress.
[20] No more shall there be in it
an infant who lives but a few days
or an old person who does not live out
a lifetime,
for one who dies at a hundred years will
be considered a youth,
and one who falls short of a hundred
will be considered accursed.
[21] They shall build houses and inhabit
them;
they shall plant vineyards and eat
their fruit.
[22] They shall not build and another inhabit;
they shall not plant and another eat,
for like the days of a tree shall the days
of my people be,
and my chosen shall long enjoy the
work of their hands.
[23] They shall not labor in vain
or bear children for calamity,[r]
for they shall be offspring blessed by the
LORD—
and their descendants as well.
[24] Before they call I will answer,
while they are yet speaking I will hear.
[25] The wolf and the lamb shall feed
together;
the lion shall eat straw like the ox,
but the serpent—its food shall be dust!

r 65.23 Or *sudden terror*

subset among the people. **65:10** *Sharon* (see note on Isa. 33:9) and *Valley of Achor* are the western and eastern ends of the promised land. **65:11** The text addresses the religious apostates of vv. 3–7. *My holy mountain.* The Temple Mount in Jerusalem. *Fortune* and *Destiny* were rival deities to YHWH. **65:12** *When I called.* Cf. v. 1. **65:13** The fates of the apostates and servants are contrasted in vv. 13–15, reflecting schisms among the postexilic religious community in Jerusalem. Similar but even more pronounced in-group/out-group distinctions appear in later apocalyptic texts like Daniel and Revelation. **65:15** *Different name.* See note on 62:2. **65:17** *Create.* See note on 40:26. *Former things.* Cf. 43:18. **65:19** Cf. 25:8. **65:20** *Infant* mortality was extremely high in the ancient world. Radically extended life-spans (cf. Gen. 6:3; Ps. 90:10) are another example of Isaiah's association between superhuman bodies and the restored Jerusalem (see **"Isaiah and Disability," p. 974**). **65:21–22** Contrast the curses in Deut. 28:30; Amos 5:11; Zeph. 1:13. **65:25** An adapted quotation of Isa. 11:6–9. The

They shall not hurt or destroy
　　on all my holy mountain,
　　　　　　　　says the LORD.

66 Thus says the LORD:
　　Heaven is my throne,
　and the earth is my footstool;
　so what kind of house could you build
　　　for me,
　what sort of place for me to rest?
[2] All these things my hand has made,
　　so all these things are mine,[s]
　　　　　　　　says the LORD.
But this is the one to whom I will look,
　to the humble and contrite in spirit
　who trembles at my word.

[3] Whoever slaughters an ox is like one
　　who kills a human,
　whoever sacrifices a lamb like one
　　who breaks a dog's neck,
　whoever presents a grain offering like
　　one who offers pig's blood,
　whoever makes a memorial offering of
　　frankincense like one who blesses
　　an idol.
Just as these have chosen their own ways
　and in their abominations they take
　delight,
[4] so I will choose their punishments
　and bring upon them what they fear,
because, when I called, no one
　answered,
　when I spoke, they did not listen,
but they did what was evil in my sight
　and chose what did not please me.
[5] Hear the word of the LORD,
　you who tremble at his word:

Your own people who hate you
　and reject you for my name's sake
have said, "Let the LORD be glorified,
　so that we may see your joy,"
　but it is they who shall be put to
　shame.

[6] Listen, a roar from the city!
　A voice from the temple!
The voice of the LORD,
　dealing retribution to his enemies!

[7] Before she was in labor
　she gave birth;
before her pain came upon her
　she delivered a son.
[8] Who has heard of such a thing?
　Who has seen such things?
Shall a land be born in one day?
　Shall a nation be delivered in one
　moment?
Yet as soon as Zion was in labor
　she delivered her children.
[9] Shall I open the womb and not
　deliver?
　says the LORD;
shall I, the one who delivers, shut the
　womb?
　says your God.

[10] Rejoice with Jerusalem, and be glad for
　her,
　all you who love her;
rejoice with her in joy,
　all you who mourn over her—

s 66.2 Gk Syr: Heb *these things came to be*

---

exclusion of the serpent from the peaceable kingdom is influenced by Gen. 3:14; it also reflects the dualism between the servants and apostates in this chapter.

66:1–16 A poem promising vindication for YHWH's servants and the restoration of Jerusalem. **66:1** *Heaven is my throne.* See note on 63:15. The ark of the covenant, which was likely lost when the First Temple was destroyed, was previously considered YHWH's *footstool* (1 Chr. 28:2). *What kind of house?* This rhetorical question counters overly literal claims about the Second Temple as YHWH's home (cf. 1 Kgs. 8:27). **66:2** *Humble and contrite.* Cf. Isa. 57:15. *Trembles at my word.* Another designation for YHWH's "servants." **66:3** The first half of v. 3 juxtaposes four acceptable worship practices with four violent actions or illicit rituals. NRSVue adds *is like* in its translation, suggesting criticism of the sacrificial system itself. More likely, the juxtaposition criticizes the perceived hypocrisy of the temple's leadership. *Their own ways.* Cf. 65:2. **66:4** *Called . . . answered.* Cf. 65:1. **66:5** An address to YHWH's servants, acknowledging their ostracization by their opponents. **66:6** Appropriately, the *temple* is the source of punishment for those who have corrupted it. **66:7–8** For motherhood and childbirth as metaphors for Jerusalem's restoration, cf. 49:20–23; 54:1–3; 60:4. These verses attribute superhuman capacities to personified Jerusalem's female body (see **"Isaiah and Disability," p. 974**). **66:9** YHWH is depicted as a midwife (cf. Pss. 22:9; 71:6; see **"Feminine Imagery for God," p. 1029**). **66:10** Vv. 10–14 address YHWH's servants, who are identified as

Going Deeper: Feminine Imagery for God (Isaiah 66)

The predominance of masculine images for God in the Hebrew Bible (king, warrior, father, etc.) reflects the biblical writers' cultural norms. Gods and goddesses were gendered in the polytheistic world of the ancient Near East, and YHWH was regarded as male. Men held most positions of authority in ancient Israel and Judah, so masculine imagery seemed appropriate for depicting YHWH as a powerful deity. Despite these tendencies, a few feminine images for YHWH are attested in the Bible, and more of them occur in Isa. 40–66 than anywhere else.

Not surprisingly for a predominantly patriarchal society, Isaiah's feminine divine images are associated with childbirth. Isaiah 46:3, 49:15, and 66:13 compare YHWH's compassion and nurturance to that of a mother. A parental analogy for the deity's treatment of the exiles in 45:10–11 specifically names both father and mother. Isaiah 66:9 imagines YHWH as a midwife, which was a woman's occupation in the ancient world. A less conventional feminine image for the deity appears in 42:13–14. V. 13 compares divine power to that of a "soldier" and "warrior." The metaphor shifts in v. 14, in which YHWH speaks directly: "Now I will cry out like a woman in labor; I will gasp and pant." Both images focus on sound, respectively depicting a warrior's battle cry and a birthing woman's yells. This similarity makes clear that the image of a woman in labor connotes power, acknowledging the bodily strength required to give birth. This positive depiction of birthing women stands out in Isaiah; childbirth is an image of weakness and instability in 13:8 and 21:3.

The relative frequency of feminine divine imagery is consistent with these chapters' interest in women and women's experiences, such as the repeated personification of Jerusalem as a wife and mother (54:1; 62:4–5; 66:11; etc.) or the naming of Sarah alongside Abraham (51:2). It may also reflect Isaiah's developing rhetoric of YHWH's supremacy (see **"Emerging Monotheism," p. 1000**). It is likely no coincidence that these texts come from a period when goddess worship was becoming increasingly unacceptable for ancient Judeans, in contrast to the preexilic period (cf. Jer. 44:15–19). As the sole divine power in the universe, YHWH assumes the characteristics of other gods and goddesses.

J. Blake Couey

---

11 that you may nurse and be satisfied
   from her consoling breast,
that you may drink deeply with delight
   from her glorious bosom.

12 For thus says the LORD:
I will extend prosperity to her like a river
   and the wealth of the nations like an
      overflowing stream,
and you shall nurse and be carried on
      her arm
   and bounced on her knees.
13 As a mother comforts her child,
   so I will comfort you;
   you shall be comforted in Jerusalem.
14 You shall see, and your heart shall
      rejoice;

your bodies*t* shall flourish like the
      grass,
and it shall be known that the power of
   the LORD is with his servants,
   and his indignation is against his
      enemies.
15 For the LORD will come in fire
   and his chariots in a whirlwind,*u*
to vent his anger in fury
   and his rebuke in flames of fire.
16 For by fire will the LORD execute
      judgment,
   and by his sword on all flesh;
   and those slain by the LORD shall be
      many.

t 66.14 Heb *bones*   *u* 66.15 Q ms: MT *like a whirlwind*

Jerusalem's children. 66:11 In 49:23 and 60:16, Jerusalem's inhabitants metaphorically *nurse* at the breasts of the nations. Here, Jerusalem herself provides maternal nourishment. **66:12** *Wealth of the nations.* See note on 60:5. Elsewhere in Isaiah, *overflowing stream* has threatening connotations (8:7–8; 30:28). **66:13** The image of Jerusalem as mother shifts to YHWH as mother (see **"Feminine Imagery for God," p. 1029**). *Comfort* has been an important theme in chaps. 40–66. **66:14** An ironic fulfillment of the enemies' sarcastic prayer in v. 5. *Flourish like the grass.* Cf. 40:6–8. **66:15** *Fire* is a frequent image of divine judgment in Isaiah. **66:16** *Sword.* Cf. 34:5–6.

17 Those who sanctify and purify themselves to go into the gardens, following the one in the center, eating the flesh of pigs, vermin, and rodents, shall come to an end together, says the Lord, [18] for I know[v] their works and their thoughts.

I am[w] coming to gather all nations and tongues, and they shall come and shall see my glory, [19] and I will set a sign among them. From them I will send survivors to the nations, to Tarshish, Put,[x] and Lud, to Meshech,[y] Tubal, and Javan, to the coastlands far away that have not heard of my fame or seen my glory, and they shall declare my glory among the nations. [20] They shall bring all your kindred from all the nations as an offering to the Lord, on horses, and in chariots, and in litters, and on mules, and on dromedaries, to my holy mountain Jerusalem, says the Lord, just as the Israelites bring a grain offering in a clean vessel to the house of the Lord. [21] And I will also take some of them as priests and as Levites, says the Lord.

22 For as the new heavens and the new
    earth,
    which I will make,
shall remain before me, says the Lord,
    so shall your descendants and your
    name remain.
23 From new moon to new moon
    and from Sabbath to Sabbath,
all flesh shall come to worship before me,
    says the Lord.

24 And they shall go out and look at the dead bodies of the people who have rebelled against me, for their worm shall not die, their fire shall not be quenched, and they shall be an abhorrence to all flesh.

v 66.18 Gk Syr: Heb lacks *know*   w 66.18 Gk Syr Vg Tg: Heb *it is*   x 66.19 Gk: Heb *Pul*   y 66.19 Gk: Heb *those drawing the bow*

66:17–24 A series of prose prophecies that oscillate between visions of worldwide judgment and salvation, suggesting that they were added over time as contrasting endings to Isaiah. Vv. 23–24 establish a sense of closure for the book by echoing language from chap. 1 (e.g., "new moon," "Sabbath," "rebelled," "fire," "quenched"). **66:17** A threat of judgment against religious apostates (cf. 57:3–13; 65:2–7, 11; 66:3). *One in the center.* An elliptical reference to the foreign deity worshiped by the apostates. **66:18** *See my glory.* Cf. 40:5. **66:19** Recalling the commission of YHWH's servant (42:6; 49:6), this verse depicts a global mission to proselytize distant nations. *Tarshish.* See note on 23:6. *Put.* A location in Africa, possibly modern Somalia. *Lud.* Either a location in Africa (possibly modern Libya) or ancient Lydia in west Asia Minor (modern Turkey). *Meshech, Tubal.* Locations in Asia Minor. *Javan.* Ancient Greece. *Coastlands.* See note on 41:1. **66:20** Foreign proselytes will repatriate the remaining Judean exiles as a ritual *offering to the Lord.* **66:21** *Them* may refer either to the repatriated exiles or to the foreign proselytes, which would extend the radically inclusive perspective of 56:3–7. **66:22** *New heavens . . . new earth.* Cf. 65:17. **66:23** A vision of universal worship in the Jerusalem temple. *All flesh.* Cf. 40:5. See **"Visions of Peace," p. 937. 66:24** The book of Isaiah ends on a gruesome note, as worshipers view the corpses of YHWH's defeated enemies (cf. v. 16). Mark 9:48 alludes to this verse in a description of hell. In Jewish Bibles, v. 23 is typically reprinted a second time after v. 24 to create a more hopeful conclusion.

JEREMIAH

Historical Backdrop

The superscription of the book of Jeremiah says that Jeremiah's prophetic career spans forty years (627–587 BCE), coinciding with the reigns of Kings Josiah, Jehoiakim, and Zedekiah of Judah (cf. Jer. 1:1–3). This was a chaotic and tumultuous time of war in the ancient Near East. The decline of the Assyrian Empire and the geopolitical volleying of Babylonian and Egyptian leaders made this an unstable time to live in Judah, which was geographically caught between these superpowers. Judeans contended with political, social, ecological, economic, and theological instability, and these realities are reflected in the book of Jeremiah. The book includes descriptive images of a land under siege and in ruins during multiple invasions, and it offers a window into the psychological turmoil that befell the people of Judah and the prophet himself. The volatility of the land and the tragedy of a fallen religious center and kingdom influenced the content of the book.

Literary and Compositional Features

Jeremiah includes several types of literature, such as poetic oracles, sermons, prayers, and prose narratives. At times, these literary styles are woven together, sometimes with short prose texts embedded within poetic passages. Some texts may have circulated independently, such as Jeremiah's laments (scattered throughout Jer. 11–20), the Book of Consolation (Jer. 30–31), and the oracles against the nations (Jer. 46–51). The book contains multiple layers of tradition that do not often fit neatly or chronologically in order. The style of the first twenty-five chapters is largely poetic oracles of judgment. The latter half of the book is predominantly prose narrative and focuses on Jeremiah's life; his relationship with his scribe, Baruch; and Jeremiah's encounters with political and religious officials who were often hostile toward him.

The book has literary echoes from other traditions in the Hebrew Bible, especially the Deuteronomistic History (see **"Deuteronomistic History," p. 337**) and the prophetic books of Hosea and Ezekiel. The imagery, especially in the poetic oracles, is vivid and sometimes troubling. Motifs using ecological images and women or feminine literary characters are pervasive in the book, sometimes with graphic content to convey the horror of destruction.

Another notable literary feature is the image of Jeremiah as the weeping prophet, which is an image that has been influential in religious depictions of Jeremiah throughout the ages. The book is filled with tears and mourning, and the prophet is sometimes described as weeping and reacting emotionally to his circumstance. At times, Jeremiah's prophetic tears seem to represent and depict divine mourning and sadness over the state of affairs. Unlike most other prophetic books of the Hebrew Bible, Jeremiah offers many personal reflections from the prophet's perspective. His anger at YHWH is present, as well as his anger at his community. Moreover, Jeremiah frequently laments even being called upon as a prophet.

Like most books in the Hebrew Bible, Jeremiah was originally written in Hebrew (the Masoretic Text, or MT) and then translated into Greek (the Septuagint, or LXX). For most books in the Hebrew Bible, the Hebrew and Greek manuscripts are similar in content and organization, but this is not the case with Jeremiah. The Greek text is about one-eighth shorter than the Hebrew, and the order of content is notably different. The oracles against the nations are at the end of the Hebrew manuscript, but they follow Jer. 25 in the Greek, suggesting the texts may have been a literary unit of their own before their incorporation in the Jeremiah manuscript tradition. The Greek tradition has several parallels with the Hebrew manuscripts of Jeremiah found at Qumran (the Dead Sea Scrolls, or DSS). The Hebrew of the DSS and the Greek of the LXX have many commonalities in order and length, which suggests that the original edition of Jeremiah may have been shorter and then was expanded into what is preserved in the Hebrew Bible today. The book itself references different scrolls of Jeremiah, which offers clues about the development of the book.

Theological Features

Much of Jeremiah reflects a prophet and a community of scribes who try to comprehend the realities of war and a shifting relationship with God that requires a new theology and a new understanding of what it means to be in a covenantal relationship. The instability of the kingdom is viewed as a

divine reaction to people's failures to keep their covenantal obligations, such as worshiping YHWH alone, promoting justice, and caring for vulnerable groups like widows and orphans. Judeans have failed in all of these regards, and the book of Jeremiah uses those failures to explain the fall of the kingdom as a divine reaction that humans brought on themselves. The language of provoking YHWH to anger is prevalent in the book and is used to offer a theological explanation for the fall of Jerusalem and Judah.

While much of the book is focused on calamity, there are glimmers of hope. The book is about suffering but also survival during periods of trauma. There are images of hope, restoration, and renewal after suffering. The most sustained discussion of restoration comes in the Book of Consolation and its surrounding texts, Jer. 30–33. In this central section, the language of a new covenant is promoted to reimagine and strengthen the human-divine relationship. The covenants of old had been repeatedly broken, so Jeremiah offers a new, more personal view of covenantal theology.

Reading Guide

Jeremiah is the longest book of the Bible, with fifty-two chapters and over 1,300 verses. The content is robust and at times unwieldy. The book opens with the prophet's call from within his mother's womb, followed by his commissioning to prophesy to nations and kingdoms (Jer. 1:1–19). The chapters that follow include dynamic oracles of judgment that explain the disconnect between YHWH and the people of Israel and Judah, using the metaphor of marriage and related language of infidelity to frame the downfall of this relationship and family (2:1–3:24). The metaphor sets the stage for the judgment oracles that follow (4:1–6:30), along with Jeremiah's temple sermon (7:1–34), in which the prophet calls out the shortcomings of the people and proclaims their impending doom.

Oracles of judgment continue with multiple references to mourning over the destruction and preparing for exile. There are also prophetic sermons and symbolic actions that express doom (8:1–19:15). Jeremiah uses his words and actions as prophetic tools of communication, so he sometimes performs acts to prophesy judgment and punishment to the people.

Jeremiah is also imprisoned during his ministry and contends with false prophets who are hostile toward him. Jeremiah's career puts him in precarious situations, and he frequently curses his prophetic calling (20:1–29:32).

There is a brief respite of sustained, hopeful discussion of a postexilic period of restoration in which the exiles are invited to return to Israel and Judah, though this is framed as Jeremiah's dream (30:1–33:26). As the book continues, there are several longer prose narratives that describe the dangers of the prophetic life and Jeremiah's confrontations with religious and political leaders, imprisonment, abduction / forced exile, and ongoing isolation from leaders who do not want to hear or heed his words (34:1–44:30). At the end of the book, there are several oracles of judgment against the nations, including Judah's most immediate neighbors and an extended oracle against the Babylonians, who facilitate the devastation until their eventual decline under Persian expansion and rule (46:1–51:64). The book ends with a review and retelling of the destruction of Jerusalem (52:1–34). A study of Jeremiah reveals a complex, repetitive, thought-provoking, and chilling text. Its disarray, mixing of ideas and metaphors, and contradictory ideas are a beautiful reflection of the chaotic circumstances under which these texts were written.

Jaime L. Waters

1 The words of Jeremiah son of Hilkiah, of the priests who were in Anathoth in the land of Benjamin, ²to whom the word of the LORD came in the days of King Josiah son of Amon of Judah, in the thirteenth year of his reign. ³It came also in the days of King Jehoiakim son of Josiah of Judah until the end of the eleventh year of King Zedekiah son of Josiah of Judah, until the captivity of Jerusalem in the fifth month.

4 Now the word of the LORD came to me saying,

⁵ "Before I formed you in the womb I knew you,
and before you were born I consecrated you;
I appointed you a prophet to the nations."

⁶Then I said, "Ah, Lord GOD! Truly I do not know how to speak, for I am only a boy." ⁷But the LORD said to me,

"Do not say, 'I am only a boy,'
for you shall go to all to whom I send you,
and you shall speak whatever I command you.

⁸ Do not be afraid of them,
for I am with you to deliver you,
says the LORD."

⁹Then the LORD put out his hand and touched my mouth, and the LORD said to me,

"Now I have put my words in your mouth.

¹⁰ See, today I appoint you over nations and over kingdoms,
to pluck up and to pull down,
to destroy and to overthrow,
to build and to plant."

11 The word of the LORD came to me, saying, "Jeremiah, what do you see?" And I said, "I see a branch of an almond tree." ¹²Then the LORD said to me, "You have seen well, for I am watching*a* over my word to perform it." ¹³The word of the LORD came to me a second time, saying, "What do you see?" And I said, "I see a boiling pot, tilted away from the north."

14 Then the LORD said to me: "Out of the north disaster shall break out on all the inhabitants of the land. ¹⁵For now I am calling all the tribes of the kingdoms of the north, says the LORD, and they shall come, and all of them shall set their thrones at the entrance of the gates of Jerusalem, against all its surrounding walls and against all the cities

a 1.12 In Heb the word for *almond* resembles the word for *watching*

1:1–3 The book of Jeremiah begins with a superscription containing introductory material about the prophet's lineage and historical context. These verses locate Jeremiah's prophetic career during the reigns of Kings Josiah, Jehoiakim, and Zedekiah of Judah. Biographical information about Jeremiah's priestly lineage and hometown of Anathoth, a village outside of Jerusalem, gives insights into Jeremiah's perspective and social location (see **"Priests (Leviticus 21)," p. 176**). Jeremiah is from outside the central place of power and cult, and his prophetic messages will be particularly critical of the political and religious leaders in Jerusalem.

1:4–5 Jeremiah is called to be a prophet from within his mother's womb. Jeremiah's mother and her central role in his prophetic career is a recurring motif in the book (15:10; 20:14), as Jeremiah at times despises his calling, his parents, and his birth, often bemoaning how he was treated by his community, who rejected him and his prophecies.

1:6–8 Jeremiah objects to his calling, noting that he is only a boy, although his precise age is not specified. The divine response to Jeremiah's hesitancy is to give Jeremiah assurance that he should not fear his call; rather, he should speak what God has commanded.

1:9 The intimate connection between God and Jeremiah is highlighted again. Beyond the calling from the womb, God touches Jeremiah's mouth, which is his primary prophetic instrument, symbolically putting divine words on his lips.

1:10 Jeremiah is appointed *to pluck up and to pull down, to destroy and to overthrow, to build and to plant*. These verbs represent dimensions of what it means for Jeremiah to be a prophet. Most of his oracles, sermons, and symbolic acts critique and condemn the actions of Israel, Judah, and surrounding nations. Prophecies in Jer. 30–31 focus on rebuilding and planting after destruction.

1:11–19 Following his commissioning, Jeremiah receives symbolic visions and additional details about the forthcoming destruction from the north, an image that recurs in Jer. 4–10 to represent the Babylonian invasion, conquest, and exile. Jeremiah is warned that the forthcoming time will be arduous, and he should be prepared. Despite opposition from community members, royal officials, and religious leaders, Jeremiah will endure the difficulties with divine support. The ominous ending of Jeremiah's call and commission sets the tone for conflicts that emerge in the book.

of Judah. [16]And I will utter my judgments against them for all their wickedness in forsaking me; they have made offerings to other gods and worshiped the works of their own hands. [17]But you, gird up your loins; stand up and tell them everything that I command you. Do not break down before them, or I will break you before them. [18]And I for my part have made you today a fortified city, an iron pillar, and a bronze wall against the whole land, against the kings of Judah, its officials, its priests, and the people of the land. [19]They will fight against you, but they shall not prevail against you, for I am with you, says the LORD, to deliver you."

2 The word of the LORD came to me, saying: [2]Go and proclaim in the hearing of Jerusalem, Thus says the LORD:
I remember the devotion of your youth,
    your love as a bride,
how you followed me in the wilderness,
    in a land not sown.
[3] Israel was holy to the LORD,
    the first fruits of his harvest.
All who ate of it were held guilty;
    disaster came upon them,
               says the LORD.

4 Hear the word of the LORD, O house of Jacob, and all the families of the house of Israel. [5]Thus says the LORD:
What wrong did your ancestors find in
    me
    that they went far from me
and went after worthless things and
    became worthless themselves?

[6] They did not say, "Where is the LORD,
    who brought us up from the land of
      Egypt,
who led us in the wilderness,
    in a land of deserts and pits,
in a land of drought and deep darkness,
    in a land that no one passes through,
    where no one lives?"
[7] I brought you into a plentiful land
    to eat its fruits and its good things.
But when you entered you defiled my
    land
    and made my heritage an abomination.
[8] The priests did not say, "Where is the
    LORD?"
Those who handle the law did not
    know me;
the rulers[b] transgressed against me;
    the prophets prophesied by Baal
and went after things that do not
    profit.

[9] Therefore once more I accuse you,
               says the LORD,
    and I accuse your children's children.
[10] Cross to the coasts of Cyprus and look;
    send to Kedar and examine with care;
    see if there has ever been such a thing.
[11] Has a nation changed its gods,
    even though they are no gods?
But my people have changed their glory
    for something that does not profit.
[12] Be appalled, O heavens, at this;
    be shocked; be utterly desolate,
               says the LORD,

b 2.8 Heb *shepherds*

2:1–8 These verses introduce the language of marriage to characterize the human-divine relationship. The marriage metaphor depicts Israel and Judah as a wife/bride and God as the husband/groom. This metaphor occurs in multiple prophetic books (cf. Hos. 1–3; Ezek. 16). It reflects the close intimacy that is envisioned between the people of Israel and Judah and God. However, the metaphor itself can be problematic, as the wife is blamed and shamed for infidelity, berated, and even metaphorically abused by her husband, God. The imagery that unfolds in the book may be jarring for modern audiences, as it likely was in antiquity. **2:2–7** The wilderness period refers to the time when the Israelites were led out of slavery in Egypt. The wilderness represents a time of challenge and growth when the people received laws that would unite them around the worship of one God. The period is remembered as a time of drought, and the land that they are promised and led to is one overflowing with water. **2:8** The Israelites are going to be accused of unfaithfulness by worshiping other gods, such as Baal. Priests, rulers, and prophets in the community are blamed for misleading the people; see **"Apostasy," p. 1238.**

    2:9–13 Since the relationship is framed as a legal marriage, the accusation of infidelity is characterized as a legal indictment. Using rhetorical questions, God asks how the people could worship other gods. YHWH is called *the fountain of living water*, reiterating the importance of YHWH in sustaining the life of the people. The climate in ancient Israel and Judah was arid, so water was an

Focus On: Sexually Abusive Language in the Prophets (Jeremiah 2–3)

Sexually abusive language is found in multiple places in the prophetic books, including Isa. 3:17–26 and 23:15–17, Jer. 2–3 and 13, Ezek. 16 and 23, Hos. 1–3, and Nah. 3:1–7; similar imagery occurs in Lam. 1 and 2 (a book traditionally associated with Jeremiah). The most extreme examples occur in Ezekiel (see **"Slut-Shaming," p. 1148**). Typically, sexually abusive language comes from God and is directed, via a prophet, at a female target—usually a metaphorical entity such as a nation or city but sometimes a real woman or women.

Sexually abusive language takes multiple forms. Often, the shaming begins with the female body, which is described as unclean and violated (Lam. 1:9–10). Stripping and exposing the female genitals is another common type of sexual humiliation: in Isa. 3, for example, God threatens to afflict haughty women "with scabs" and "lay bare their scalps and heads" (see also Hos. 2, Nah. 3, and Ezek. 16). In other texts, rape is presented as a punishment for sexual impropriety or promiscuity: a woman who "prostitute[s] herself" (e.g., Hos. 2:5) will be punished with sexual humiliation and rape, often by God (who is represented as male).

The scenes of sexual punishment in prophetic literature are part of what is known as the "marriage metaphor." As the name suggests, the marriage metaphor describes Israel and Judah's relationship with God as a marriage, in which God plays the role of the husband, Israel/Judah/Jerusalem is his wife, and the other gods whom Israel worships are illicit lovers. The worship of other gods becomes equated with adultery and is punished with sexual abuse and humiliation (even though these are not the punishments prescribed in biblical laws concerning adultery).

It is not only Israel or the Israelites who are subjected to sexual abuse. Foreign cities and nations are also represented as female and threatened with sexual punishments, including rape. The siege of a city is also described as a rape and often associated with sexual humiliation and shame. Babylon is subjected to especially extreme violence.

While some interpreters seek to dismiss or downplay the sexually abusive language as "merely metaphor," feminist interpreters have argued that we must reckon with the texts and their legacy of justifying abuse. With their undeniable misogyny and violence, these passages are truly "texts of terror," a phrase used to refer to especially violent and misogynistic texts. The challenge is to find ways to read them that take seriously their violence.

Rhiannon Graybill

13 for my people have committed two evils:
　　they have forsaken me,
　the fountain of living water,
　　and dug out cisterns for themselves,
　cracked cisterns
　　that can hold no water.

14 Is Israel a slave? Is he a homeborn
　　servant?
　Why then has he become plunder?
15 The lions have roared against him;
　　they have roared loudly.
　They have made his land a waste;
　　his cities are in ruins, without inhabitant.

16 Moreover, the people of Memphis and
　　Tahpanhes
　have broken the crown of your head.
17 Have you not brought this upon yourself
　　by forsaking the Lord your God,
　　while he led you in the way?
18 What then do you gain by going to
　　Egypt,
　　to drink the waters of the Nile?
　Or what do you gain by going to Assyria,
　　to drink the waters of the Euphrates?
19 Your wickedness will punish you,
　　and your faithlessness will convict
　　you.

especially prized resource. When they lack water, this is interpreted as a sign that they have been unfaithful to God, who provides water.

2:14–29 These verses include mixed metaphors that critique the behaviors of the people of Judah and figuratively describe some of their hardships. References to slavery in vv. 14 and 20 express the constraints and domination that Judah faces while living during a period of unrest due to Babylonian expansion. Rhetorical questions are used as a way to challenge Judah's associations with foreign powers, especially Egypt and Assyria. These relationships are highlighted as introducing the worship of other gods—that is, lusting for / loving strangers—which brings condemnation and suffering in the land. Ecological imagery is also used to symbolize human behaviors.

Know and see that it is evil and bitter
    for you to forsake the Lᴏʀᴅ your God;
the fear of me is not in you,
        says the Lord Gᴏᴅ of hosts.

20 For long ago you broke your yoke
    and burst your bonds,
    and you said, "I will not serve!"
On every high hill
    and under every green tree
    you sprawled and prostituted yourself.
21 Yet I planted you as a choice vine
    from the purest stock.
How then did you turn degenerate
    and become a wild vine?
22 Though you wash yourself with lye
    and use much soap,
    the stain of your guilt is still before me,
        says the Lord Gᴏᴅ.
23 How can you say, "I am not defiled;
    I have not gone after the Baals"?
Look at your way in the valley;
    know what you have done:
a restive young camel interlacing her
    tracks,
24   a wild ass at home in the
      wilderness
in her heat sniffing the wind!
    Who can restrain her lust?
None who seek her need weary
    themselves;
    in her month they will find her.
25 Keep your feet from going bare
    and your throat from thirst.
But you said, "It is no use,
    for I have loved strangers,
    and after them I will go."

26 As a thief is shamed when caught,
    so the house of Israel shall be shamed:
they, their kings, their officials,
    their priests, and their prophets,
27 who say to a tree, "You are my father,"
    and to a stone, "You gave me birth."
For they have turned their backs to me
    and not their faces.
But in the time of their trouble they say,
    "Come and save us!"

28 But where are your gods
    that you made for yourself?
Let them come, if they can save you,
    in your time of trouble,
for you have as many gods
    as you have towns, O Judah.

29 Why do you complain against me?
    You have all rebelled against me,
        says the Lᴏʀᴅ.
30 In vain I have struck down your children;
    they accepted no correction.
Your own sword devoured your prophets
    like a ravening lion.
31 And you, O generation, behold the word
    of the Lᴏʀᴅ![c]
Have I been a wilderness to Israel
    or a land of thick darkness?
Why then do my people say, "We are
    free;
    we will come to you no more"?
32 Can a young woman forget her
    ornaments
    or a bride her attire?
Yet my people have forgotten me,
    days without number.

33 How well you direct your course
    to seek lovers!
So that even to wicked women
    you have taught your ways.
34 Also on your skirts is found
    the lifeblood of the innocent poor,
    though you did not catch them breaking
      in.
    Yet in spite of all these things[d]
35 you say, "I am innocent;
    surely his anger has turned from me."
Now I am bringing you to judgment
    for saying, "I have not sinned."
36 Why do you go about so much
    to change your way?
You shall be put to shame by Egypt
    as you were put to shame by Assyria.
37 From there also you will come away
    with your hands on your head,

c 2.31 Meaning of Heb uncertain   d 2.34 Meaning of Heb uncertain

2:30–34 Jeremiah 2 begins and ends with clear marriage and wilderness language. The depiction of Judah as a bride preparing for marriage is juxtaposed to the fallout and failures of a marriage gone awry. The blood of the poor people in the community is on the bride's skirt, suggesting that social injustice and war have impacted the poor and vulnerable populations in the land. There are also continued critiques against Judah's behavior, which is considered shameful for worshiping other gods, and this action leads to their rejection by YHWH.

for the LORD has rejected those in whom
  you trust,
  and you will not prosper through
  them.

3 If[e] a man divorces his wife
  and she goes from him
and becomes another man's wife,
  will he return to her?
Would not such a land be greatly
  polluted?
You have prostituted yourself with many
  lovers,
  and would you return to me?

says the LORD.

[2] Look up to the bare heights[f] and see!
  Where have you not been lain
    with?
By the waysides you sat waiting for
    lovers,
  like a nomad in the wilderness.
You have polluted the land
  with your prostitutions and
    wickedness.
[3] Therefore the showers have been
    withheld,
  and the spring rain has not come,
yet you have the forehead of a prostitute;
  you refuse to be ashamed.
[4] Have you not just now called to me,
  "My Father, you are the friend of my
    youth—
[5] will he be angry forever,
  will he be indignant to the end?"

This is how you have spoken,
  but you have done all the evil that you
    could.

6 The LORD said to me in the days of King
Josiah: Have you seen what she did, that
faithless one, Israel, how she went up on every high hill and under every green tree and
prostituted herself there? [7]And I thought,
"After she has done all this she will return
to me," but she did not return, and her false
sister Judah saw it. [8]She[g] saw that for all the
adulteries of that faithless one, Israel, I had
sent her away with a decree of divorce, yet
her false sister Judah did not fear, but she
also went and prostituted herself. [9]Because
she took her prostitution so lightly, she polluted the land, committing adultery with
stone and tree. [10]Yet for all this her false
sister Judah did not return to me with her
whole heart but only in pretense, says the
LORD.

11 Then the LORD said to me: Faithless Israel has shown herself less guilty than false
Judah. [12]Go and proclaim these words toward
the north, and say:
  Return, faithless Israel,

says the LORD.

  I will not look on you in anger,
    for I am merciful,

says the LORD;

  I will not be angry forever.

e 3.1 Gk Syr: Heb *Saying, If* f 3.2 Or *the trails* g 3.8 Gk mss
Syr: Heb *I*

3:1–5 These verses build on the marriage metaphor introduced in the previous chapter. The language is graphic, comparing the people of Israel (the wife) to an adulterous woman with many lovers. Multiple times her actions are compared to a prostitute, which is a metaphor for disloyalty to YHWH (cf. Hos. 1–3). There are continued allusions to the wilderness period following the exodus. In addition to the husband/wife metaphor, the image of God as father and the people of Israel as his children is also used to characterize the relationship. **3:1** *If a man divorces his wife.* This stipulation about divorce may have Deut. 24:4 as its source. *Polluted* refers to ritual impurity. Its association with divorce occurs only here.

3:6–10 The theme of returning to God and repentance is prominent in this chapter. The language of returning, Hebrew "shub," signifies an interest in turning away from sinful behavior and turning back toward the relationship with YHWH; see **"Repentance," p. 1245**. The relationship between Judah and Israel is also characterized as a familial one, as Israel and Judah are sisters. These verses allude to the fall of Israel in 722 BCE, which is framed as a divorce, as Israel is seen as abandoning YHWH for the worship of other gods. The reference to Israel's fate is meant to compel Judah to return and repent so that it does not suffer a similar fate. **3:7** *False sister.* Ezek. 23 also uses the imagery of Israel and Judah as sisters.

3:11–25 Details about repentance are found in these verses. The people must acknowledge their guilt, declaring that they did not obey or listen to the divine voice, a recurring theme in the book. The metaphors of parent-child and husband-wife are used to show the intimate relationship and also the pain in its breakdown. **3:11** *Toward the north.* Jeremiah consistently speaks of exile as proceeding toward the north, though Assyria and Babylon lay to the east, because this was the

¹³ Only acknowledge your guilt,
  that you have rebelled against the
    LORD your God
and scattered your favors among
    strangers under every green tree
and have not obeyed my voice,
                says the LORD.
¹⁴ Return, O faithless children,
                says the LORD,
  for I am your husband;
I will take you, one from a city and two
    from a family,
  and I will bring you to Zion.

15 I will give you shepherds after my own
heart who will feed you with knowledge and
understanding. ¹⁶And when you have multiplied
and increased in the land, in those days, says the
LORD, they shall no longer say, "The ark of the
covenant of the LORD." It shall not come to mind
or be remembered or missed, nor shall another
one be made. ¹⁷At that time Jerusalem shall be
called the throne of the LORD, and all nations
shall gather to it, to the presence of the LORD in
Jerusalem, and they shall no longer stubborn-
ly follow their own evil will. ¹⁸In those days the
house of Judah shall join the house of Israel, and
together they shall come from the land of the
north to the land that I gave your ancestors for
a heritage.

¹⁹ I thought
    how I would set you among my
      children
  and give you a pleasant land,
    the most beautiful heritage of all the
      nations.
And I thought you would call to me, "My
    Father,"
  and would not turn from following me.
²⁰ Instead, as a faithless wife leaves her
      husband,
  so you have been faithless to me,
    O house of Israel,
                says the LORD.

²¹ A voice on the bare heights^h is heard,
    the plaintive weeping of Israel's
      children,
because they have perverted their way;
    they have forgotten the LORD their God:
²² Return, O faithless children,
    I will heal your faithlessness.

"Here we come to you,
    for you are the LORD our God.
²³ Truly the hills areⁱ a delusion,
    a tumult on the mountains.
Truly in the LORD our God
    is the salvation of Israel.

24 "But from our youth the shameful thing
has devoured all for which our ancestors had
labored, their flocks and their herds, their
sons and their daughters. ²⁵Let us lie down
in our shame, and let our dishonor cover us,
for we have sinned against the LORD our God,
we and our ancestors, from our youth even to
this day, and we have not obeyed the voice of
the LORD our God."

4 If you return, O Israel,
                says the LORD,
  if you return to me,
if you remove your abominations from
    my presence
    and do not waver,
² and if you swear, "As the LORD lives!"
    in truth, in justice, and in uprightness,
  then nations shall be blessed^j by you,^k
    and by you^l they shall boast.
3 For thus says the LORD to the people of
Judah and to the inhabitants of Jerusalem:
  Break up your fallow ground,
    and do not sow among thorns.
⁴ Circumcise yourselves to the LORD;
    remove the foreskin of your hearts,
  O people of Judah and inhabitants of
      Jerusalem,

h 3.21 Or *the trails*   i 3.23 Gk Syr Vg: Heb *Truly from the
bills is*   j 4.2 Or *shall bless themselves*   k 4.2 Cn: Heb *him*
l 4.2 Cn: Heb *him*

direction from which invading armies arrived. **3:13** *Strangers under every green tree* refers to acts of
worship in open-air shrines to deities other than YHWH. **3:16** *The ark of the covenant* was a wooden
box overlaid with gold housed in the innermost part of the Jerusalem temple. YHWH's invisible
presence was thought to sit enthroned atop it.
    4:1–4 The theme of repentance is prominent in this poem. The themes of justice and upright-
ness are crucial, showing the multiple dimensions of societal and religious issues in Judah. One of
the primary critiques in the judgment of the people concerns their worship of other gods. These
verses also highlight societal failings related to truth, justice, and uprightness. **4:4** The language
of circumcision is an allusion to the Abrahamic covenant, in which the foreskin was removed from

or else my wrath will go forth like fire
    and burn with no one to quench it,
    because of the evil of your doings.
5 Declare in Judah, and proclaim in Jerusalem, and say:
    Blow the trumpet through the land;
        shout aloud[m] and say,
    "Gather together, and let us go
        into the fortified cities!"
[6] Raise a standard toward Zion;
        flee for safety; do not delay,
    for I am bringing evil from the north
        and a great destruction.
[7] A lion has gone up from its thicket;
        a destroyer of nations has set out;
        he has gone out from his place
    to make your land a waste;
        your cities will be ruins
        without inhabitant.
[8] Because of this put on sackcloth,
        lament and wail:
    "The fierce anger of the Lord
        has not turned away from us."

[9]On that day, says the Lord, courage shall fail the king and the officials; the priests shall be appalled and the prophets astounded. [10]Then I said, "Ah, Lord God, how utterly you have deceived this people and Jerusalem, saying, 'It shall be well with you,' even while the sword is at the throat!"

11 At that time it will be said to this people and to Jerusalem: A hot wind comes from me out of the bare heights[n] in the desert toward the daughter of my people, not to winnow or cleanse, [12]a wind too strong for that. Now it is I who speak in judgment against them.
[13] Look! He comes up like clouds,
        his chariots like the whirlwind;
    his horses are swifter than eagles—
        woe to us, for we are ruined!
[14] O Jerusalem, wash your heart clean of
        wickedness
    so that you may be saved.
How long shall your evil schemes
        lodge within you?
[15] For a voice declares from Dan
        and proclaims disaster from Mount
        Ephraim.
[16] Tell the nations, "Here they are!"
        Proclaim against Jerusalem,
    "Besiegers come from a distant land;
        they shout against the cities of Judah.
[17] They have closed in around her like
        watchers of a field
    because she has rebelled against me,
                says the Lord.
[18] Your ways and your doings
        have brought this upon you.
This is your doom; how bitter it is!
        It has reached your very heart."
[19] My anguish, my anguish! I writhe in pain!
        Oh, the walls of my heart!
My heart is beating wildly;
        I cannot keep silent,
for I[o] hear the sound of the trumpet,
        the alarm of war.
[20] Disaster overtakes disaster;
        the whole land is laid waste.

m 4.5 Or *shout, take your weapons*: Heb *shout, fill* (your hand)
n 4.11 Or *the trails*   o 4.19 Or *for you, O my soul,*

the penis to ritually shed blood to enter the covenantal community (cf. Gen. 17:9–27). Jeremiah references circumcision as a metaphorical rather than literal practice and shifts attention to the heart (Heb. "leb," which was thought to be the center for thinking; i.e., the mind) rather than the male organ. Elsewhere, Jeremiah will revisit the metaphor (9:25–26). The mention of the circumcision of the heart could metaphorically allow women members of the community to be more directly connected. In the New Testament, this imagery is reused by Paul in his interpretation of circumcision (cf. Rom. 2:25–29).

4:5–10 The image of the enemy from the north recurs again, which was mentioned at the beginning of the book. This is an allusion to the Neo-Babylonian Empire and its expansion in the Near East. Because of the invasion and destruction, the people are told to put on sackcloth to mourn. The prophet's perspective is included, as he questions divine deception in the midst of destruction. The kings, officials, priests, and prophets are astounded by the realities.

4:11–18 The invasion is described using evocative, ecological images. The repentance language uses the cleaning of the heart to describe how the people of Jerusalem should amend their ways to be saved from destruction. Yet even though these verses suggest that repentance is possible, the following verses emphasize the inevitability of disaster.

4:19–31 Anguish over the circumstances is palpable with a mix of divine and prophetic pain. The heavens and the earth are impacted by the conditions, and the birds respond to the situation by

Suddenly my tents are destroyed,
my curtains in a moment.
²¹ How long must I see the standard
and hear the sound of the trumpet?
²² "For my people are foolish;
they do not know me;
they are stupid children;
they have no understanding.
They are skilled in doing evil
but do not know how to do good."

²³ I looked on the earth, and it was
complete chaos,
and to the heavens, and they had no
light.
²⁴ I looked on the mountains, and they
were quaking,
and all the hills moved to and fro.
²⁵ I looked, and there was no one at all,
and all the birds of the air had fled.
²⁶ I looked, and the fruitful land was a
desert,
and all its cities were laid in ruins
before the Lord, before his fierce
anger.
27 For thus says the Lord: The whole land
shall be a desolation, yet I will not make a
full end.
²⁸ Because of this the earth shall
mourn
and the heavens above grow black,
for I have spoken; I have purposed;
I have not relented, nor will I turn
back.

²⁹ At the noise of horseman and archer
every town takes to flight;
they enter thickets; they climb among
rocks;
all the towns are forsaken,
and no one lives in them.

³⁰ And you, O desolate one,
what do you mean that you dress in
crimson,
that you deck yourself with
ornaments of gold,
that you enlarge your eyes with paint?
In vain you beautify yourself.
Your lovers despise you;
they seek your life.
³¹ For I heard a cry as of a woman in labor,
anguish as of one bringing forth her
first child,
the cry of daughter Zion gasping for
breath,
stretching out her hands,
"Woe is me! I am fainting before killers!"

5 Run to and fro through the streets of
Jerusalem,
look around and take note!
Search its squares and see
if you can find one person
who acts justly
and seeks truth—
so that I may pardon Jerusalem.ᵖ
² Although they say, "As the Lord lives,"
yet they swear falsely.
³ O Lord, do your eyes not look for truth?
You have struck them,
but they felt no anguish;
you have consumed them,
but they refused to take correction.
They have made their faces harder than
rock;
they have refused to turn back.

⁴ Then I said, "These are only the poor;
they have no sense,
for they do not know the way of the Lord,
the law of their God.

ᵖ 5.1 Heb *it*

---

fleeing the land laid waste. **4:30–31** The feminine imagery related to apostasy and suffering is used again, as the people of Judah are likened to a woman finely and beautifully dressed as she prepares to metaphorically commit adultery—that is, worship other gods. Another feminine image is invoked to describe her suffering and anguish as a woman in labor. Jeremiah routinely uses women and images of women's bodies to vividly express contempt, and modern readers encounter and must address the unfortunate risks that come from the repeated associations of women and negative actions. See **"Sexually Abusive Language in the Prophets," p. 1035.**

5:1–17 YHWH instructs Jeremiah to run through the streets looking for anyone who behaves justly and has repented from sinful behavior. This attempt at finding at least one righteous person echoes the story of Sodom and Gomorrah, in which Abraham asks YHWH not to destroy the cities if there is a righteous person present (Gen. 18:22–33). The imagery in much of this oracle again includes language of infidelity, with multiple ecological images. **5:2** *As the Lord lives* was an oath formula, something like the modern English "I swear." **5:4** *These are only the poor.* Jeremiah seems to imply

⁵ Let me go to the rich^q
and speak to them;
surely they know the way of the Lord,
the law of their God."
But they all alike had broken the yoke;
they had burst the bonds.

⁶ Therefore a lion from the forest shall kill
them;
a wolf from the desert shall destroy
them.
A leopard is watching against their
cities;
everyone who goes out of them shall
be torn in pieces,
because their transgressions are many;
their faithlessness is great.

⁷ How can I pardon you?
Your children have forsaken me
and have sworn by those who are no
gods.
When I fed them to the full,
they committed adultery
and trooped to the houses of
prostitutes.
⁸ They were well-fed lusty stallions,
each neighing for his neighbor's wife.
⁹ Shall I not punish them for these things?
says the Lord,
and shall I not bring retribution
on a nation such as this?

¹⁰ Go up through her vine rows and
destroy,
but do not make a full end;
strip away her branches,
for they are not the Lord's.
¹¹ For the house of Israel and the house of
Judah
have been utterly faithless to me,
says the Lord.
¹² They have spoken falsely of the Lord
and have said, "He will do nothing.
No evil will come upon us,
and we shall not see sword or famine."

¹³ The prophets are nothing but wind,
for the word is not in them.
Thus shall it be done to them!

¹⁴ Therefore thus says the Lord, the God of
hosts:
Because you have spoken this word,
I am now making my words in your
mouth a fire
and this people wood, and the fire
shall devour them.
¹⁵ I am going to bring upon you
a nation from far away, O house of
Israel,
says the Lord.
It is an enduring nation;
it is an ancient nation,
a nation whose language you do not
know,
nor can you understand what they say.
¹⁶ Their quiver is like an open tomb;
all of them are mighty warriors.
¹⁷ They shall eat up your harvest and your
food;
they shall eat up your sons and your
daughters;
they shall eat up your flocks and your herds;
they shall eat up your vines and your
fig trees;
they shall destroy with the sword
your fortified cities in which you trust.

18 But even in those days, says the Lord, I
will not make a full end of you. ¹⁹And when
your people say, "Why has the Lord our God
done all these things to us?" you shall say to
them, "As you have forsaken me and served
foreign gods in your land, so you shall serve
strangers in a land that is not yours."

²⁰ Declare this in the house of Jacob;
proclaim it in Judah:
²¹ Hear this, O foolish and senseless people,
who have eyes but do not see,
who have ears but do not hear.

q 5.5 Or *the great*

that the poor might lack moral knowledge enjoyed by the wealthy (literally the "great"). **5:12** *He will do nothing.* According to Jeremiah, many, including prophets, anticipated no response from YHWH to their actions. **5:15–17** The image of invasion and its effects is clear, as the foreign nation *whose language [the people] do not know* will attack and consume food, flocks, vines, and sons and daughters, describing the multiple levels of destruction.

5:18–31 The inability of the people to fully comprehend what they have done wrong and what they experienced through invasion and destruction is highlighted. **5:18** *I will not make a full end of you*—that is, the destruction and exile will not be the end of Judah's story. **5:21** *Eyes but do not*

22 Do you not fear me? says the Lord;
 Do you not tremble before me?
I placed the sand as a boundary for the
  sea,
 a perpetual barrier that it cannot pass;
though the waves toss, they cannot
  prevail;
 though they roar, they cannot pass
  over it.
23 But this people has a stubborn and
  rebellious heart;
 they have turned aside and gone
  away.
24 They do not say in their hearts,
 "Let us fear the Lord our God,
who gives the rain in its season,
 the autumn rain and the spring rain,
and keeps for us
 the weeks appointed for the harvest."
25 Your iniquities have turned these away,
 and your sins have deprived you of
  good.
26 For the wicked are found among my
  people.
 They lie in wait like hunters;
destroyers,ʳ they catch humans.
27 Like a cage full of birds,
 their houses are full of treachery;
therefore they have become great and
  rich;
28 they have grown fat and sleek.
 They know no limits in deeds of
  wickedness;
 they do not judge with justice
the cause of the orphan, to make it
  prosper,
 and they do not defend the rights of
  the needy.
29 Shall I not punish them for these things?
          says the Lord,
 and shall I not bring retribution
on a nation such as this?

30 An appalling and horrible thing
 has happened in the land:
31 the prophets prophesy falsely,
 and the priests rule as the prophets
  direct;ˢ
my people love to have it so,
 but what will you do when the end
  comes?

6 Flee for safety, O children of Benjamin,
 from the midst of Jerusalem!
Blow the trumpet in Tekoa,
 and raise a signal on Beth-haccherem,
for evil looms out of the north
 and great destruction.
2 I have likened daughter Zion
 to the loveliest pasture.ᵗ
3 Shepherds with their flocks shall come
  against her.
 They shall pitch their tents around her;
 they shall pasture, all in their places.
4 "Prepare war against her;
 up, and let us attack at noon!"
"Woe to us, for the day declines;
 the shadows of evening lengthen!"
5 "Up, and let us attack by night,
 and destroy her palaces!"
6 For thus says the Lord of hosts:
Cut down her trees;
 cast up a siege ramp against
  Jerusalem.
This is the city that must be punished;ᵘ
 there is nothing but oppression within
  her.
7 As a well keeps its water fresh,
 so she keeps fresh her wickedness;
violence and destruction are heard
  within her;
 sickness and wounds are ever before
  me.

r 5.26 Meaning of Heb uncertain   s 5.31 Or rule by their
own authority   t 6.2 Or I will destroy daughter Zion, the loveliest
pasture   u 6.6 Or the city of license

see . . . ears but do not hear. Cf. Isa. 6:9–10. 5:22 Images of YHWH as the creator are often invoked by biblical writers to assert divine power. 5:27–29 A society with moral failures is described, as injustice is widespread. The basic requirements of a just society—meeting the needs of those on the economic and social margins (e.g., orphans)—are not being met. 5:31 Failed leadership is another major cause of the problems, as prophets and priests are condemned for their bad actions. Prophetic conflict is a major element in Jeremiah (see **"Prophetic Conflict," p. 1079**).

6:1–8 The image of invasion is intense in these verses, and the impact on the people and the land is notable. Violence and sickness plague the cities, and people are advised to flee from Jerusalem, as the city is under siege. 6:1 *Benjamin.* A territory just to the north of Jerusalem. After Jerusalem's destruction, the Babylonians governed the region from there. 6:3 *Shepherds with their flocks*—that is, foreign kings and their armies. 6:6 *Siege ramp.* Used often in ancient warfare because many cities, like Jerusalem, were built atop hills, making them difficult to attack.

8 Take warning, O Jerusalem,
  or I shall turn from you in disgust
and make you a desolation,
  an uninhabited land.

9 Thus says the LORD of hosts:
Glean[v] thoroughly as a vine
  the remnant of Israel;
like a grape gatherer, pass your hand
  again
  over its branches.

10 To whom shall I speak and give warning,
  that they may hear?
See, their ears are closed;[w]
  they cannot listen.
The word of the LORD is to them an object
  of scorn;
  they take no pleasure in it.
11 But I am full of the wrath of the LORD;
  I am weary of holding it in.

Pour it out on the children in the
  street
  and on the gatherings of young men
  as well;
both husband and wife shall be taken,
  the elderly and those full of days.
12 Their houses shall be turned over to
  others,
  their fields and wives together;
for I will stretch out my hand
  against the inhabitants of the land,
            says the LORD.

13 For from the least to the greatest of
  them,
  everyone is greedy for unjust gain;
and from prophet to priest,
  everyone deals falsely.
14 They have treated the wound of my
  people carelessly,
  saying, "Peace, peace,"

when there is no peace.
15 They acted shamefully; they committed
  abomination,
  yet they were not ashamed;
  they did not know how to blush.
Therefore they shall fall among those
  who fall;
  at the time that I punish them, they
  shall be overthrown,
            says the LORD.
16 Thus says the LORD:
Stand at the crossroads and look,
  and ask for the ancient paths,
where the good way lies; and walk in it,
  and find rest for your souls.
But they said, "We will not walk in it."
17 Also I raised up sentinels for you:
  "Give heed to the sound of the
  trumpet!"
But they said, "We will not give heed."
18 Therefore hear, O nations,
  and know, O congregation, what will
  happen to them.
19 Hear, O earth; I am going to bring
  disaster on this people,
  the fruit of their schemes,
because they have not given heed to my
  words,
  and as for my teaching, they have
  rejected it.
20 Of what use to me is frankincense that
  comes from Sheba
  or sweet cane from a distant land?
Your burnt offerings are not acceptable,
  nor are your sacrifices pleasing to me.
21 Therefore thus says the LORD:
See, I am laying before this people
  stumbling blocks against which they
  shall stumble;
parents and children together,
  neighbor and friend shall perish.

v 6.9 Cn Compare Gk: Heb *They shall glean*   w 6.10 Heb *are uncircumcised*

6:9–21 The fallout of war is described, as inhabitants are on the receiving end of divine wrath for their ongoing failure to listen to divine teachings and follow covenantal obligations. **6:10–11a** Something like a prophetic aside interrupting the prophetic oracle. **6:11, 21** Families and people at all different stages of life are impacted: husbands and wives, young and elderly, parents and children, neighbors and friends all feel the effects of war. **6:12** *Stretch out my hand.* An image personifying divine power. **6:13** *Greedy for unjust gain* points to economic injustice as one aspect of Jeremiah's indictment of his contemporaries. **6:14** *Peace, peace.* Jeremiah charges community leaders with offering a false sense of peace and safety in a moment of political upheaval. **6:17** *Sentinels* were military personnel, but the term was sometimes used to refer to prophets (cf. Isa. 52:8; 56:10; Ezek. 3:17; 33:6, 7; Hos. 9:8). **6:20** *Frankincense that comes from Sheba* apparently refers to the practice of importing some raw material used in the temple worship rituals.

[22] Thus says the LORD:

See, a people is coming from the land of
the north;
a great nation is stirring from the
farthest parts of the earth.
[23] They grasp the bow and the javelin;
they are cruel and have no mercy;
their sound is like the roaring sea;
they ride on horses,
equipped like a warrior for battle,
against you, O daughter Zion!

[24] "We have heard news of them;
our hands fall helpless;
anguish has taken hold of us,
pain as of a woman in labor.
[25] Do not go out into the field
or walk on the road,
for the enemy has a sword;
terror is on every side."

[26] O daughter of my people, put on sackcloth
and roll in ashes;
make mourning as for an only child,
most bitter lamentation,
for suddenly the destroyer
will come upon us.

[27] I have made you a tester and a refiner[x]
among my people
so that you may know and test their ways.
[28] They are all stubbornly rebellious,
going about with slanders;
they are bronze and iron;
all of them act corruptly.
[29] The bellows blow fiercely;
the lead is consumed by the fire;[y]

in vain the refining goes on,
for the wicked are not removed.
[30] They are called "rejected silver,"
for the LORD has rejected them.

7 The word that came to Jeremiah from the LORD: [2]Stand in the gate of the LORD's house, and proclaim there this word, and say, Hear the word of the LORD, all you people of Judah, you who enter these gates to worship the LORD. [3]Thus says the LORD of hosts, the God of Israel: Amend your ways and your doings, and let me dwell with you[z] in this place. [4]Do not trust in these deceptive words: "This is[a] the temple of the LORD, the temple of the LORD, the temple of the LORD."

5 For if you truly amend your ways and your doings, if you truly act justly one with another, [6]if you do not oppress the alien, the orphan, and the widow or shed innocent blood in this place, and if you do not go after other gods to your own hurt, [7]then I will dwell with you[b] in this place, in the land that I gave to your ancestors forever and ever.

8 Here you are, trusting in deceptive words to no avail. [9]Will you steal, murder, commit adultery, swear falsely, make offerings to Baal, and go after other gods that you have not known [10]and then come and stand before me in this house, which is called by my name, and say, "We are safe!"—only to go on doing all these abominations? [11]Has this house, which is called by my name, become a den of robbers in your sight? I, too, am watching,

x 6.27 Or *a fortress*   y 6.29 Cn: Heb *lead from their fire*
z 7.3 Or *and I will let you dwell*   a 7.4 Heb *They are*   b 7.7 Or
and I will let you dwell

6:22–26 The experience and conditions of war are vivid, as the sounds of advancing armies are like the roaring sea. The battle imagery conveys the horror of war, and the anguish of the conditions is again likened to a woman in labor. **6:22** *Land of the north*—that is, Babylon. **6:25** An ominous command not to enter the field or road because of the enemy and the sword. The field and road show the expansiveness of the war, as both city and countryside or urban and rural spaces are unsafe. **6:26** *Put on sackcloth and roll in ashes.* Actions of lament and mourning, here because of the imminent destruction.

6:27–30 The imagery of metallurgy is used, as Jeremiah is instructed to test the value and authenticity of the people, and they are unfortunately inauthentic, rejected silver.

7:1–4 Jeremiah delivers a sermon at the temple in judgment of the people of Judah and their actions. The sermon critiques religious and social practices and reminds the people to not be too comfortable in feeling protected by YHWH. An abbreviated version of the sermon is found in Jer. 26.

7:5–7 Recurring calls for justice are proclaimed. The people of Judah should not oppress those who are most vulnerable in society: aliens, orphans, and widows. These groups were protected categories in biblical law (cf. Deut. 10:18–19; 24:17–22; 27:19).

7:8–15 Several of the Ten Commandments (see **"Law/Decalogue," p. 112**) are mentioned in this sermon. Jeremiah admonishes the people for their theft, murder, adultery, false testimony, and

says the LORD. [12]Go now to my place that was in Shiloh, where I made my name dwell at first, and see what I did to it for the wickedness of my people Israel. [13]And now, because you have done all these things, says the LORD, and when I spoke to you persistently, you did not listen, and when I called you, you did not answer, [14]therefore I will do to the house that is called by my name, in which you trust, and to the place that I gave to you and to your ancestors just what I did to Shiloh. [15]And I will cast you out of my sight, just as I cast out all your kinsfolk, all the offspring of Ephraim.

16 As for you, do not pray for this people, do not raise a cry or prayer on their behalf, and do not intercede with me, for I will not hear you. [17]Do you not see what they are doing in the towns of Judah and in the streets of Jerusalem? [18]The children gather wood, the fathers kindle fire, and the women knead dough, to make cakes for the queen of heaven, and they pour out drink offerings to other gods, to provoke me to anger. [19]Is it I whom they provoke? says the LORD. Is it not themselves, to their own hurt? [20]Therefore thus says the Lord GOD: My anger and my wrath shall be poured out on this place, on humans and animals, on the trees of the field and the fruit of the ground; it will burn and not be quenched.

21 Thus says the LORD of hosts, the God of Israel: Add your burnt offerings to your sacrifices, and eat the flesh. [22]For in the day that I brought your ancestors out of the land of Egypt, I did not speak to them or command

them concerning burnt offerings and sacrifices. [23]But this command I gave them, "Obey my voice, and I will be your God, and you shall be my people; walk only in the way that I command you, so that it may be well with you." [24]Yet they did not obey or incline their ear, but, in the stubbornness of their evil will, they walked in their own counsels and looked backward rather than forward. [25]From the day that your ancestors came out of the land of Egypt until this day, I have persistently sent all my servants the prophets to them, day after day, [26]yet they did not listen to me or pay attention, but they stiffened their necks. They did worse than their ancestors did.

27 So you shall speak all these words to them, but they will not listen to you. You shall call to them, but they will not answer you. [28]You shall say to them: This is the nation that did not obey the voice of the LORD their God and did not accept discipline; truth has perished; it is cut off from their lips.

[29] Cut off your hair and throw it away;
   raise a lamentation on the bare
     heights,[c]
for the LORD has rejected and forsaken
   the generation that provoked his wrath.

30 For the people of Judah have done evil in my sight, says the LORD; they have set their abominations in the house that is called by my name, defiling it. [31]And they go on building the high place[d] of Topheth, which is in

c 7.29 Or *the trails*   d 7.31 Gk Tg Vg: Heb *high places*

worship of Baal and other gods (see **"Baal," p. 489**). These violations and additional wickedness are framed as the cause of the civil and political instability. **7:14** Shiloh was a religious center north of Jerusalem that was destroyed centuries earlier. It is mentioned as an ominous reminder of divine judgment at cultic sites. The setting for Jeremiah's temple sermon is the temple in Jerusalem, and the Shiloh reference would likely invoke fear of temple destruction.

7:16-20 Jeremiah is told not to intercede on behalf of the people, which is one of the primary roles connected to being a prophet. The call not to pray shows how angry and dismissive YHWH is toward the people, as even a divinely appointed intermediary cannot dissuade YHWH from judgment. This theme of not praying will occur again in Jeremiah (cf. Jer. 14:11–12). Forbidden religious practices, such as offering food and drink to the queen of heaven, are blamed for causing the judgment. **7:18** *Queen of heaven* is a title used for an ancient Near Eastern goddess. The reference could be to goddesses such as Anat, Ishtar, Astarte, or Asherah (cf. Jer. 44:15–30).

7:21-34 The people's tendency not to listen is highlighted. Even as Jeremiah is to deliver this sermon at the temple, YHWH tells him that they still will not listen. The failure to listen again is explicitly linked with the current circumstances. Images of child sacrifice are mentioned to show the level of corruption in the land. The punishments for these actions are that the people will be food for the animals and the sounds of marriage will no longer be in the streets. This is a powerful and ironic curse. The human-divine relationship is framed as a marriage, and as a result of Judah's infidelity, there will not be human marriages and their related gladness and joy in the land (cf. Jer. 25:10).

the valley of the son of Hinnom, to burn their sons and their daughters in the fire—which I did not command, nor did it come into my mind. [32]Therefore the days are surely coming, says the LORD, when it will no more be called Topheth or the valley of the son of Hinnom but the valley of Slaughter, for they will bury in Topheth until there is no more room. [33]The corpses of this people will be food for the birds of the air and for the animals of the earth, and no one will frighten them away. [34]And I will bring to an end the sound of mirth and gladness, the voice of the bride and bridegroom in the cities of Judah and in the streets of Jerusalem, for the land shall become a waste.

8 At that time, says the LORD, the bones of the kings of Judah, the bones of its officials, the bones of the priests, the bones of the prophets, and the bones of the inhabitants of Jerusalem shall be brought out of their tombs, [2]and they shall be spread before the sun and the moon and all the host of heaven, which they have loved and served, which they have followed, and which they have inquired of and worshiped, and they shall not be gathered or buried; they shall be like dung on the surface of the ground. [3]Death shall be preferred to life by all the remnant that remains of this evil family in all the places where I have driven them, says the LORD of hosts.

[4] You shall say to them, Thus says the
LORD:
When people fall, do they not get up
    again?
If they go astray, do they not turn
    back?
[5] Why then has this people[e] turned away
    in perpetual faithlessness?
They have held fast to deceit;
    they have refused to return.
[6] I have given heed and listened,
    but they do not speak honestly;

no one repents of wickedness,
    saying, "What have I done!"
All of them turn to their own course
    like a horse plunging headlong into
    battle.
[7] Even the stork in the heavens
    knows its times,
and the turtledove, swallow, and crane[f]
    observe the time of their coming,
but my people do not know
    the ordinance of the LORD.

[8] How can you say, "We are wise,
    and the law of the LORD is with us,"
when, in fact, the false pen of the scribes
    has made it into a lie?
[9] The wise shall be put to shame;
    they shall be dismayed and taken;
since they have rejected the word of the
    LORD,
    what wisdom is in them?
[10] Therefore I will give their wives to others
    and their fields to conquerors,
because from the least to the greatest
    everyone is greedy for unjust gain;
from prophet to priest,
    everyone deals falsely.
[11] They have treated the wound of the
    daughter of my people carelessly,
    saying, "Peace, peace,"
    when there is no peace.
[12] They acted shamefully; they committed
    abomination,
    yet they were not at all ashamed;
    they did not know how to blush.
Therefore they shall fall among those
    who fall;
at the time when I punish them, they
    shall be overthrown,
                    says the LORD.
[13] I will surely gather them,[g] says the LORD;
    there are no grapes on the vine
    nor figs on the fig tree;

e 8.5 Heb ms Gk: MT *this people, Jerusalem*, *f* 8.7 Meaning of Heb uncertain *g* 8.13 Or *make an end to them*

8:1–3 The image of the bones of leaders being disinterred might refer to a practice that shames leaders when treaty obligations were violated (cf. 2 Kgs. 23:16, in which Josiah desecrates kings' tombs at Bethel). Although the people are told to lament for their actions, they will not be mourned, and their leaders' bodies are even desecrated. **8:4–17** The animals in the land speak and understand what is happening in the context of the destruction. While the people do not fully comprehend the destruction, the birds know what is happening. Likewise, the sounds of horses serve as another notice of the arrival of invading troops, who are compared to snakes. **8:8** *False pen of the scribes.* Jeremiah accuses scribes of altering YHWH's teaching, though how is unclear. **8:10–12** *From the least to the greatest . . . they shall be overthrown*

even the leaves are withered,
and what I gave them has passed away
from them.[b]

[14] Why do we sit still?
Gather together; let us go into the
fortified cities
and perish there,
for the Lord our God has doomed us to
perish
and has given us poisoned water to drink
because we have sinned against the
Lord.
[15] We look for peace but find no good,
for a time of healing, but there is
terror instead.

[16] The snorting of their horses is heard
from Dan;
at the sound of the neighing of their
stallions
the whole land quakes.
They come and devour the land and all
that fills it,
the city and those who live in it.
[17] See, I am letting snakes loose among you,
adders that cannot be charmed,
and they shall bite you,
says the Lord.
[18] My joy is gone; grief is upon me;
my heart is sick.
[19] Listen! The cry of the daughter of my
people
from far and wide in the land:

"Is the Lord not in Zion?
Is her King not in her?"
("Why have they provoked me to anger
with their images,
with their foreign idols?")
[20] "The harvest is past, the summer is
ended,
and we are not saved."
[21] For the brokenness of the daughter of my
people I am broken,
I mourn, and horror has seized me.

[22] Is there no balm in Gilead?
Is there no physician there?
Why then has the health of the daughter
of my people
not been restored?

9 [i]O that my head were a spring of
water
and my eyes a fountain of tears,
so that I might weep day and night
for the slain of the daughter of my
people!
[2] [j]O that I had in the desert
a traveler's lodging place,
that I might leave my people
and go away from them!
For they are all adulterers,
a band of traitors.
[3] They bend their tongues like bows;
they have grown strong in the land for
falsehood and not for truth,

b 8.13 Meaning of Heb uncertain   i 9.1 8.23 in Heb
j 9.2 9.1 in Heb

repeats 6:13–15. **8:14–15** *Why do we sit still?* These verses portray the community (*we*) as responding to Jeremiah's words of judgment not in repentance but in resignation. **8:14** The people are said to be given poisoned water, noting the ecological impacts of invasion. This is also another water reference that is a reminder that the people did not pursue the fountain of living water of YHWH (cf. Jer. 2:13), so they now experience poisoned water.

8:18–22 The mourning in these verses is overwhelming, and at times, it is difficult to determine whether this is divine or prophetic mourning for the people and the land. **8:20** *The summer is ended, and we are not saved* suggests the people expected their dire condition to be remedied quickly. **8:22** *Balm in Gilead* refers to a resin or gum from a plant or tree associated with Gilead, a region in Transjordan. The evocative, rhetorical question has become a powerful biblical image used to represent divine healing throughout history. The question posed influenced the Negro spiritual "Balm in Gilead," although the question is rephrased as a declaration: there is a balm in Gilead. Spirituals were songs by enslaved African people, many of whom adopted Christianity and reframed biblical traditions to express faith in healing and hope, and the balm of Gilead is a biblical image invoked to represent divine healing.

9:1–11 These verses build on the images of destruction and judgment described in the previous chapter. The poetry is an exchange between God and Jeremiah where the two voices are intermixed. At times, it is difficult to detect who is speaking. **9:1–2** On multiple occasions, there is mourning and grief over the suffering of the people of Judah. Daughter language is used in v. 1 and later in v. 7. Using familial, feminine imagery was a common ancient practice when referring to cities. **9:3–6** One of the recurring problems during Jeremiah's time is lying. Some people speak falsely about what is happening

for they proceed from evil to evil,
and they do not know me, says the
LORD.

4 Beware of your neighbors,
and put no trust in any of your
kin,
for all your kin are supplanters,
and every neighbor goes around like a
slanderer.
5 They all deceive their neighbors,
and no one speaks the truth;
they have taught their tongues to speak
lies;
they commit iniquity and are too
weary to repent.[k]
6 Oppression upon oppression, deceit[l]
upon deceit!
They refuse to know me, says the
LORD.

7 Therefore thus says the LORD of hosts:
I will now refine and test them,
for what else can I do with the
daughter of my people?
8 Their tongue is a deadly arrow;
it speaks deceit through the
mouth.
They all speak friendly words to their
neighbors
but inwardly are planning to lay an
ambush.
9 Shall I not punish them for these things?
says the LORD,
and shall I not bring retribution
on a nation such as this?

10 Take up[m] weeping and wailing for the
mountains
and a lamentation for the pastures of
the wilderness,
because they are laid waste so that no
one passes through,
and the lowing of cattle is not heard;
both the birds of the air and the
animals
have fled and are gone.
11 I will make Jerusalem a heap of ruins,
a lair of jackals,
and I will make the towns of Judah a
desolation,
without inhabitant.

12 Who is wise enough to understand this? To whom has the mouth of the LORD spoken, so that they may declare it? Why is the land ruined and laid waste like a wilderness, so that no one passes through? 13And the LORD says: Because they have forsaken my law that I set before them and have not obeyed my voice or walked in accordance with it 14but have stubbornly followed their own hearts and have gone after the Baals, as their ancestors taught them. 15Therefore thus says the LORD of hosts, the God of Israel: I am feeding this people with wormwood and giving them poisonous water to drink. 16I will scatter them among nations that neither they nor their ancestors have known, and I will send the sword after them until I have consumed them.

k 9.5 Cn Compare Gk: Heb *they weary themselves with iniquity.*
[l] *Your dwelling* l 9.6 Cn Compare Gk: Heb *Your dwelling in the midst of deceit* m 9.10 Gk Syr: Heb *I will take up*

in the land. Some slander their neighbors, speaking false statements against people in the community. The language of oppression could suggest financial and social misuse and abuse of power. Jeremiah's community is in disarray, with much corruption and discord in the land. Modern readers might unfortunately find some parallels to their own experiences, especially on the societal damage of false statements, deception, and oppression. **9:7–9** These verses depict God speaking in rhetorical questions, pondering how to address, correct, or punish the people for their corruption. **9:10–11** The physical destruction caused by war and the sociological destruction caused by the breakdown of the community have impacts on the people, land, and animals. These verses highlight the reactions of the earth and animal life. Mourning and grief are connected to the suffering in the land, and ecological features respond to the corruption and destruction in the land. Animals also respond to the land's destruction. The land's silence signals that animals have died, fled, or been taken captive as booty during war. Jackals (wild dogs) benefit from these circumstances and are often referenced in biblical texts as a sign of destruction.

9:12–16 The prophet shows the difficulty he has in processing the destruction in the land. God declares that the people's actions in disobeying the law have caused the devastation, offering a theological explanation for the historical and social realities. The worship of Baal is explicitly linked with the situation of the day, which builds on the ongoing claims of apostasy in the land (cf. Jer. 7:8).

[17] Thus says the Lord of hosts:
Consider and call for the mourning
women to come;
send for the skilled women to come;
[18] let them quickly raise a dirge over us,
so that our eyes may run down with tears
and our eyelids flow with water.
[19] For a sound of wailing is heard from Zion:
"How we are ruined!
We are utterly shamed
because we have left the land,
because they have cast down our
dwellings."

[20] Hear, O women, the word of the Lord,
and let your ears receive the word of
his mouth;
teach to your daughters a dirge
and each to her neighbor a lament.
[21] "Death has come up into our windows;
it has entered our palaces
to cut off the children from the streets
and the young men from the squares."
[22] Speak! Thus says the Lord:
"Human corpses shall fall
like dung upon the open field,
like sheaves behind the reaper,
and no one shall gather them."

[23] Thus says the Lord: Do not let the
wise boast in their wisdom; do not let the
mighty boast in their might; do not let
the wealthy boast in their wealth; [24]but let
those who boast boast in this, that they understand and know me, that I am the Lord;
I act with steadfast love, justice, and righteousness in the earth, for in these things I
delight, says the Lord.

[25] The days are surely coming, says the
Lord, when I will attend to all those who are
circumcised only in the foreskin: [26]Egypt,
Judah, Edom, the Ammonites, Moab, and all
those with shaved temples who live in the
desert. For all these nations are uncircumcised, and all the house of Israel is uncircumcised in heart.

10 Hear the word that the Lord speaks to
you, O house of Israel. [2]Thus says the
Lord:
Do not learn the way of the nations
or be dismayed at the signs of the
heavens,
for the nations are dismayed at them.
[3] For the customs of the peoples are
false:
a tree from the forest is cut down
and worked with an ax by the hands
of an artisan;
[4] they deck it with silver and gold;
they fasten it with hammers and nails
so that it cannot move.
[5] Their idols[n] are like scarecrows in a
cucumber field,
and they cannot speak;
they have to be carried,
for they cannot walk.
Do not be afraid of them,
for they cannot do evil,
nor is it in them to do good.

[6] There is none like you, O Lord;
you are great, and your name is great
in might.

n 10.5 Heb They

9:17–22 Mourning women and skilled (Heb. "hokmah," or "wise") women are called to lead
the community in mourning for the loss of life and destruction in the land. Professional mourners
expressed the pain and heartache that many in the community struggled to process. The wise
women understand, lament, and teach others to respond, whereas Jeremiah (in v. 12) and the community (in vv. 23–24) do not fully comprehend the events.
9:23–26 Additional destruction is promised to Judah's neighbors. *Those who are circumcised
only in the foreskin* likely refers to people in the regions listed in v. 26. *Uncircumcised in heart* likely
means that despite the ritual action, the people of Israel (and Judah) are not living out the other
covenantal requirements. Despite being circumcised, their disobedience and disregard for the law
(see vv. 13–14) have led to their judgment and destruction.
10:1–5 The problems of idolatry are highlighted. YHWH mocks idols and those who create them,
noting they decorate elements that cover a hollow interior. Jeremiah and other prophets associate
their use with the religious practices of other nations. YHWH affirms that idols are worthless, so they
cannot be good or evil because they are nothing. **10:3–4** A partial description of how images and
cult statues—that is, idols—were constructed (cf. v. 9; Isa. 44:12–17).
10:6–8 These verses constitute a fragment of a hymn to YHWH. They are found in the Masoretic

7 Who would not fear you, O King of the
    nations?
  For that is your due;
among all the wise ones of the nations
  and in all their kingdoms
  there is no one like you.
8 They are both stupid and foolish;
  the instruction given by idols
  is no better than wood!*o*
9 Beaten silver is brought from Tarshish
  and gold from Uphaz.
They are the work of the artisan and of
    the hands of the goldsmith;
  their clothing is blue and purple;
  they are all the product of skilled
    workers.
10 But the Lord is the true God;
  he is the living God and the
    everlasting King.
At his wrath the earth quakes,
  and the nations cannot endure his
    indignation.*p*

11 Thus shall you say to them: The gods
who did not make the heavens and the earth
shall perish from the earth and from under
the heavens.*q*

12 It is he who made the earth by his power,
  who established the world by his
    wisdom
  and by his understanding stretched
    out the heavens.
13 When he utters his voice, there is a
    tumult of waters in the heavens,
  and he makes the mist rise from the
    ends of the earth.
He makes lightning for the rain

and brings out the wind from his
    storehouses.
14 Everyone is stupid and without
    knowledge;
  goldsmiths are all put to shame by
    their idols,
  for their images are false,
  and there is no breath in them.
15 They are worthless, a work of delusion;
  at the time of their punishment they
    shall perish.
16 The portion of Jacob is not like these,
  for he is the one who formed all
    things,
  and Israel is the tribe of his inheritance;
  the Lord of hosts is his name.
17 Gather up your bundle from the
    ground,
  O you who live under siege!
18 For thus says the Lord:
I am going to sling out the inhabitants of
    the land
  at this time,
and I will bring distress on them,
  so that they shall feel it.

19 Woe is me because of my hurt!
  My wound is severe.
But I said, "Truly this is my punishment,
  and I must bear it."
20 My tent is destroyed,
  and all my cords are broken;
my children have gone from me,
  and they are no more;
there is no one to spread my tent again
  and to set up my curtains.

o 10.8 Q ms Gk lack 10.6–8   p 10.10 Q ms Gk lack 10.10
q 10.11 This verse is in Aramaic

Hebrew canon but not in the Greek manuscript of Jeremiah or in the Hebrew manuscripts of Jeremiah found in the Dead Sea Scrolls. They were likely a late addition to the book.

10:10 The false power of idols is contrasted with the true, real power of YHWH.

10:11 This verse is written in Aramaic rather than Hebrew, which could suggest it is an addition to the text. Its placement near another section that is not found in the Greek text or the Hebrew manuscripts among the Dead Sea Scrolls suggests that this chapter may have originally been shorter. Although the language is different, the sentiment fits the context, affirming that false gods/idols are powerless.

10:12–16 The prophet extols YHWH and highlights the stupidity of the people for creating and worshiping idols. These verses are repeated verbatim in 51:15–19. **10:12–13** YHWH's ability to create the cosmos contrasts with the powerless images of other deities.

10:17–25 The threat and promise of exile are reiterated, and the image of siege is evident. The failure to know and listen is present as another explanation for why destruction and exile are punishments leveled at this people. See **"Exile (2 Kings)," p. 539. 10:18** *I am going to sling out the inhabitants of the land.* A violent image portraying YHWH as the cause of the people's forced exile. **10:19–21** Personified Zion laments her destruction and the exile of her inhabitants.

21 For the shepherds are stupid
  and do not inquire of the Lord;
therefore they have not prospered,
  and all their flock is scattered.

22 Hear, a noise! Listen, it is coming—
  a great commotion from the land of
    the north
to make the cities of Judah a desolation,
  a lair of jackals.

23 I know, O Lord, that the way of humans
    is not in their control,
  that mortals as they walk cannot
    direct their steps.
24 Correct me, O Lord, but in just measure;
    not in your anger, or you will bring me
    to nothing.

25 Pour out your wrath on the nations that
    do not know you
  and on the peoples that do not call on
    your name,
for they have devoured Jacob;
  they have devoured him and
    consumed him
  and have laid waste his habitation.

11 The word that came to Jeremiah from the Lord: 2"Hear the words of this covenant, and speak to the people of Judah and the inhabitants of Jerusalem. 3You shall say to them, Thus says the Lord, the God of Israel: Cursed be anyone who does not heed the words of this covenant, 4which I commanded your ancestors when I brought them out of the land of Egypt, from the iron smelter, saying, 'Listen to my voice, and do all that I command you. So shall you be my people, and I will be your God, 5that I may perform the oath that I swore to your ancestors, to give them a land flowing with milk and honey, as at this day.'" Then I answered, "So be it, Lord."

6 And the Lord said to me: Proclaim all these words in the cities of Judah and in the streets of Jerusalem: Hear the words of this covenant and do them. 7For I solemnly warned your ancestors when I brought them up out of the land of Egypt, warning them persistently, even to this day, saying, "Obey my voice." 8Yet they did not obey or incline their ear, but everyone walked in the stubbornness of an evil will. So I brought upon them all the words of this covenant, which I commanded them to do, but they did not.

9 And the Lord said to me: Conspiracy exists among the people of Judah and the inhabitants of Jerusalem. 10They have turned back to the iniquities of their ancestors of old, who refused to heed my words; they have gone after other gods to serve them; the house of Israel and the house of Judah have broken the covenant that I made with their ancestors. 11Therefore, thus says the Lord, assuredly I am going to bring disaster upon them that they cannot escape; though they cry out to me, I will not listen to them. 12Then the cities of Judah and the inhabitants of Jerusalem will go and cry out to the gods to whom they make offerings, but they will never save them in the time of their trouble. 13For your gods have become as many as your towns, O Judah, and as

---

10:22 *Hear, a noise*—that is, the approaching Babylonian army. 10:23–24 A prayer for YHWH's gracious correction. 10:25 The prophet pleads with YHWH to punish the nations that have destroyed Judah.

11:1–5 The style of this chapter shifts to a prose sermon that explains the exile using language similar to both the poetic oracles of the previous chapters and the book of Deuteronomy. 11:2 *Words of this covenant.* Cf. Deut. 29:9; 2 Kgs. 23:3. 11:3 *Cursed.* A malediction on those who fail to heed the covenant; cf. Deut. 28:20–46. 11:5 *A land flowing with milk and honey* is a reminder of the covenantal promises associated with Abraham and Moses (cf. Gen. 12:1, 7; 15:18–21; Exod. 3:7–8; 13:5; 33:3; Deut. 6:3; 11:9; 26:9, 15; 27:3; 31:20).

11:6–13 The covenantal language continues to be prominent, as the stipulations of the covenant are mentioned. The statement about Egypt is another clear reminder of the salvation that came through the exodus. The prevalence of multiple gods being worshiped is highlighted. The text helps create a picture of a community who is actively worshiping other gods, building altars to them and making sacrificial offerings. 11:9 *Conspiracy.* To this point, the chapter has focused on the people's disobedience to the covenant. Here, disobedience in the form of venerating other deities is likened to political treason. 11:11 *I will not listen to them.* The people's unwillingness to "listen to" YHWH's covenant results in YHWH's refusal to listen to them when they fall into distress. 11:13 *Baal.* While the text speaks of the worship of several deities, only Baal is mentioned by name. See **"Baal," p. 489.**

many as the streets of Jerusalem are the altars to shame you have set up, altars to make offerings to Baal.

14 As for you, do not pray for this people or lift up a cry or prayer on their behalf, for I will not listen when they call to me in the time of their trouble. [15]What right has my beloved in my house, when she has done vile deeds? Can vows[r] and sacrificial flesh avert your doom? Can you then exult? [16]The LORD once called you, "A green olive tree, fair with goodly fruit," but with the roar of a great tempest he will set fire to it, and its branches will be consumed. [17]The LORD of hosts, who planted you, has pronounced evil against you because of the evil that the house of Israel and the house of Judah have done, provoking me to anger by making offerings to Baal.

[18] It was the LORD who made it known to
  me, and I knew;
  then you showed me their deeds.
[19] But I was like a gentle lamb
  led to the slaughter.
And I did not know it was against me
  that they devised schemes, saying,
"Let us destroy the tree with its fruit;
  let us cut him off from the land of the
    living,
  so that his name will no longer be
    remembered!"
[20] But you, O LORD of hosts, who judge
  righteously,
  who try the heart and the mind,
let me see your retribution upon them,
  for to you I have committed my cause.

21 Therefore thus says the LORD concerning the people of Anathoth who seek your life and say, "You shall not prophesy in the name of the LORD, or you will die by our hand"— [22]therefore thus says the LORD of hosts: I am going to punish them; the young men shall die by the sword; their sons and their daughters shall die by famine, [23]and not even a remnant shall be left of them. For I will bring disaster upon the people of Anathoth, the year of their punishment.

12

You will be in the right, O LORD,
  when I lay charges against you,
  but let me put my case to you.
Why does the way of the guilty prosper?
  Why do all who are treacherous
    thrive?
[2] You plant them, and they take root;
  they grow and bring forth fruit;
you are near in their mouths
  yet far from their hearts.
[3] But you, O LORD, know me;
  you see me and test me; my heart is
    with you.
Pull them out like sheep for the slaughter,
  and set them apart for the day of
    slaughter.
[4] How long will the land mourn
  and the grass of every field wither?
For the wickedness of those who live in it,
  the animals and the birds are swept
    away,
  and because people said, "He is blind
    to our ways."[s]

r 11.15 Gk: Heb *Can many*   s 12.4 Gk: Heb *to our future*

11:14–17 As with the temple sermon in Jer. 7, the prophet is once again told not to intercede on behalf of this people (cf. Jer. 7:16; 14:11). 11:17 The language of planting is another use of ecological imagery. Here it is to suggest that YHWH originally planted this community and nurtured its growth. Now, however, because of their apostasy, evil has fallen upon the land.

11:18–23 Jeremiah is often associated with mourning, weeping, and lamenting, and these verses are the first of seven so-called laments in the book (11:18–23; 12:1–6; 15:10–21; 17:14–18; 18:18–23; 20:7–12; 20:14–18). The laments—or more generally, prayers—depict Jeremiah's precarious circumstances as a prophet and his request for divine retribution. Each usually includes a divine response. See **"Prayer and Prophetic Intercession," p. 1053**. 11:21–23 The divine response is to condemn the people of Anathoth, people in Jeremiah's hometown who are attacking him. YHWH insists that they will die by famine, which is described in Jer. 14.

12:1–4 The second of Jeremiah's personal prayers, or laments, continues with the prophet questioning YHWH's actions. Jeremiah accuses YHWH of being unjust, since he sees the land suffering along with the people. 12:1 *When I lay charges against you.* Jeremiah's complaint about YHWH's failure to ensure justice uses language associated with legal proceedings. *Why does the way of the guilty prosper?* A scenario implying that YHWH is negligent in his moral oversight of the community. The nineteenth-century priest and poet Gerard Manley Hopkins opened his "Sonnet 74" with these words. 12:3 *Like sheep for the slaughter.* An image Jeremiah used of himself in the previous chapter.

Going Deeper: Prayer and Prophetic Intercession (Jeremiah 11:18–23)

Unlike most other prophetic books in the Hebrew Bible, Jeremiah offers a detailed and robust presentation of the prophet's life, including his external and internal conflicts. Jeremiah's prayers, which are sometimes called his Laments or Confessions, show the prophet's reactions to his circumstances and his requests for divine help, relief, and vengeance. In addition, Jeremiah's prayers reflect his anger toward God, as the prophet sometimes feels abandoned, tricked, and violated during his moments of struggle.

Jeremiah's prayers are found in 11:18–23, 12:1–6, 15:10–21, 17:14–18, 18:18–23, and 20:7–18. They reveal that he was mocked and threatened by opponents who disagreed with his prophecies. He prays and reflects on his disdain for his prophetic calling and his life: "Why did I come forth from the womb to see toil and sorrow and spend my days in shame?" (20:18). His prayers reference his mother and her womb, language that recalls his prophetic calling *in utero* (1:5). In addition, his prayers are sometimes imprecatory, meaning that they ask God to punish and curse his enemies and their families because of how they treat him: "Give their children over to famine; hurl them out to the power of the sword" (18:21a).

Jeremiah's emotional and psychological state is also evident, and he bluntly calls out YHWH when he feels vulnerable and under attack. He calls YHWH a "deceitful brook" who has not been honest or effective in protecting him (15:18). He even uses language associated with rape, as he says he feels enticed and overpowered by YHWH (20:7).

In addition to his personal prayers, Jeremiah should be praying for his community, as being a mediator and intercessory is a principal aspect of being a prophet. However, YHWH tells Jeremiah not to pray: "As for you [Jeremiah], do not pray for this people, do not raise a cry or prayer on their behalf, and do not intercede with me, for I will not hear you" (7:16; cf. 11:14; 14:11). The Judean community is accused of repeatedly violating their covenantal obligations, and for this reason, prophetic intercession is rejected. Once the Babylonian exile happens, Jeremiah writes to a community in exile and tells them to pray. After they endure exile, they are encouraged to call on YHWH, who will then hear their prayers (29:7, 12).

Jaime L. Waters

⁵ If you have raced with runners and they
　　have wearied you,
　　how will you compete with horses?
And if you trust in a safe land,
　　how will you fare in the thickets of the
　　　Jordan?
⁶ For even your kinsfolk and your own
　　family,
　　even they have dealt treacherously
　　　with you;
　　they are in full cry after you;
do not believe them,
　　though they speak friendly words to
　　you.

⁷ I have forsaken my house;
　　I have abandoned my heritage;
I have given the beloved of my heart
　　into the hands of her enemies.
⁸ My heritage has become to me
　　like a lion in the forest;

she has lifted up her voice against
　　me—
　　therefore I hate her.
⁹ Is the hawk hungry for my heritage?
　　Are the vultures all around her?
Go, assemble all the wild animals;
　　bring them to devour her.
¹⁰ Many shepherds have destroyed my
　　vineyard;
　　they have trampled down my
　　portion;
they have made my pleasant portion
　　a desolate wilderness.
¹¹ They have made it a desolation;
　　desolate, it mourns to me.
The whole land is made desolate,
　　but no one lays it to heart.
¹² Upon all the bare heights' in the desert,
　　spoilers have come,

t 12.12 Or the trails

12:5–13 YHWH's initial response in v. 5 to Jeremiah's complaint in the previous verses does not directly address the issue he raises. Instead, God warns Jeremiah that the persecution that he experiences will persist. **12:7** *I have forsaken my house* assumes YHWH's divine presence no longer dwells in the Jerusalem temple. *I have given.* Babylon's capture of Jerusalem and Judah is understood as YHWH's doing. Divine punishment is also coupled with divine weeping and regret over the circumstances. Again animals are invoked as metaphorical and perhaps literal enemies who attack and devour the land.

for the sword of the LORD devours
   from one end of the land to the other;
   no one shall be safe.
[13] They have sown wheat and have reaped
   thorns;
   they have tired themselves out but
   profit nothing.
They shall be ashamed of their^u harvests
   because of the fierce anger of the
   LORD.

14 Thus says the LORD concerning all my evil neighbors who touch the heritage that I have given my people Israel to inherit: I am about to pluck them up from their land, and I will pluck up the house of Judah from among them. [15] And after I have plucked them up, I will again have compassion on them, and I will bring them again to their heritage and to their land, every one of them. [16] And then, if they will diligently learn the ways of my people, to swear by my name, "As the LORD lives," as they taught my people to swear by Baal, then they shall be built up in the midst of my people. [17] But if any nation will not listen, then I will completely uproot it and destroy it, says the LORD.

13 Thus said the LORD to me, "Go and buy yourself a linen loincloth and put it on your loins, but do not dip it in water." [2] So I bought a loincloth according to the word of the LORD and put it on my loins. [3] And the word of the LORD came to me a second time, saying, [4] "Take the loincloth that you bought and are wearing, and go now to the Euphrates,^v and hide it there in a cleft of the rock." [5] So I went and hid it by the Euphrates,^w as the LORD commanded me. [6] And after many days the LORD said to me, "Go now to the Euphrates,^x and take from there the loincloth that I commanded you to hide there." [7] Then I went to the Euphrates^y and dug, and I took the loincloth from the place where I had hidden it. But now the loincloth was ruined; it was good for nothing.

8 Then the word of the LORD came to me: [9] Thus says the LORD: Just so I will ruin the pride of Judah and the great pride of Jerusalem. [10] This evil people, who refuse to hear my words, who stubbornly follow their own will and have gone after other gods to serve them and worship them, shall be like this loincloth, which is good for nothing. [11] For as the loincloth clings to one's loins, so I made the whole house of Israel and the whole house of Judah cling to me, says the LORD, in order that they might be for me a people, a name, a praise, and a glory. But they would not listen.

12 You shall speak to them this word: Thus says the LORD, the God of Israel: Every wine jar should be filled with wine. And they will say to you, "Do you think we do not know that every wine jar should be filled with wine?" [13] Then you shall say to them: Thus says the LORD: I am about to fill all the inhabitants of this land—the kings who sit on David's throne, the priests, the prophets, and all the

u 12.13 Heb *your*   v 13.4 Or *to Parah*   w 13.5 Or *by Parah*
x 13.6 Or *to Parah*   y 13.7 Or *to Parah*

12:14–17 Enemies of Judah are targets of this section, which shares some similarities with the oracles against the nations at the end of the book (chaps. 46–51). See **"The Oracles against the Nations," p. 1105**. This short oracle depicts YHWH in relation to Judah's neighbors. As in the case of Judah, exile is threatened, followed by gracious restoration. The surrounding peoples will be shown compassion if they worship the God of Israel and Judah. The oracle, however, notes that these neighbors will suffer and be uprooted and destroyed if they do not listen to YHWH. **12:14** *I am about to pluck them up from their land* draws on language from Jeremiah's commissioning (1:10). **12:15** *I will bring them.* YHWH promises to restore Judah's enemies to their own lands.

13:1–11 Jeremiah is instructed to perform a symbolic act involving a linen loincloth. The final condition of the cloth is comparable to what will happen after the destruction of the kingdom and the exile. See **"Symbolic Actions," p. 1056**. **13:4** Jeremiah is depicted going to the Euphrates River, which is one of the two major rivers in Babylonia. This might suggest that this text stems from the exilic period, when people of Judah were living in Babylonia along the Euphrates. **13:9** The ruined loincloth is comparable to the people's ruined pride, which might refer to Judah's faulty understanding of its own invincibility.

13:12–14 Jeremiah delivers a speech that includes a symbolic act involving wine jars. The drunkenness that comes from wine consumption is used as a metaphor for impending destruction. This symbolic image is echoed in Jer. 25, in which punishment is compared to a poisoned wine that is forced upon inhabitants of the land.

inhabitants of Jerusalem—with drunkenness. [14] And I will dash them one against another, parents and children together, says the Lord. I will not pity or spare or have compassion when I destroy them.

[15] Hear and give ear; do not be haughty,
   for the Lord has spoken.
[16] Give glory to the Lord your God
      before he brings darkness
   and before your feet stumble
      on the mountains at twilight;
   while you look for light,
      he turns it into gloom
   and makes it deep darkness.
[17] But if you will not listen,
      my soul will weep in secret for your
         pride;
   my eyes will weep bitterly and run down
      with tears
   because the Lord's flock has been
      taken captive.

[18] Say to the king and the queen mother:
   "Take a lowly seat,
   for your beautiful crown
      has come down from your head."[z]
[19] The towns of the Negeb are shut up,
      with no one to open them;
   all Judah is taken into exile,
      wholly taken into exile.

[20] Lift up your eyes and see
      those who come from the north.
   Where is the flock that was given you,
      your beautiful flock?
[21] What will you say when they set as head
         over you
      those whom you have trained
   to be your allies?

Will not pangs seize you
   like those of a woman in labor?
[22] And if you say in your heart,
   "Why have these things come upon
      me?"
it is for the greatness of your iniquity
   that your skirts are lifted up
   and you are violated.
[23] Can Cushites change their skin
   or leopards their spots?
Then also you can do good,
   who are accustomed to do evil.
[24] I will scatter you[a] like chaff
   driven by the wind from the
      desert.
[25] This is your lot,
   the portion I have measured out to
      you, says the Lord,
because you have forgotten me
   and trusted in lies.
[26] I myself will lift up your skirts over your
      face,
   and your shame will be seen.
[27] I have seen your abominations,
   your adulteries and neighings, your
      shameless prostitutions
   on the hills of the countryside.
Woe to you, O Jerusalem!
   How long will it be
   before you are made clean?

14 The word of the Lord that came to Jeremiah concerning the drought:
[2] Judah mourns,
   and her gates languish;
they lie in gloom on the ground,
   and the cry of Jerusalem goes up.

z 13.18 Gk Syr Vg: Meaning of Heb uncertain   a 13.24 Gk mss: Heb *them*

13:15–27 Exile is envisioned again. **13:18** The king and queen mother (likely King Jehoiachin and his mother, Nehushta, who went into exile in 597) are told to prepare to lose their political power. **13:19** *The towns of the Negeb*. The wilderness area to the south of Jerusalem. **13:21** Suffering is again described using rhetorical questions and the imagery of a woman suffering. **13:22, 26** This literary woman is sexually violated with her skirt lifted up. Publicly lifting the woman's skirt shows the goal of intense shame and humiliation, making the woman an embarrassment and a mockery. The image builds on the recurring tendency to use and misuse women's bodies as a feature of Jeremiah's book. YHWH even declares, *I myself will lift up your skirts over your face, and your shame will be seen.* This graphic imagery fits the husband-wife metaphor, as the failed marriage is now coupled with physical and sexual abuse. Modern readers must grapple with this damaging imagery. See **"Sexually Abusive Language in the Prophets," p. 1035**. **13:23** *Cushites* are from near modern Ethiopia.

14:1–6 These verses offer a window into ancient ecological instability that resembles some of the challenges of today. Judah experiences a drought, and it triggers physical and psychological reactions from the land, people, and animals. The text shows the interconnections among the earth, humans, and animal life and the negative effects that humans can have on the larger earth

Focus On: Symbolic Actions (Jeremiah 13)

Prophets in the Hebrew Bible were men and women who communicated messages from God to various human audiences. Normally, prophecy was an oral phenomenon in which prophets spoke on behalf of YHWH. This is implied in the dozens of instances in which prophetic oracles include the phrase "thus says the LORD." But prophets communicated messages in other ways as well. Occasionally, prophets "performed" their message through symbolic actions that dramatized the divine message.

The prophetic books contain numerous literarily stylized accounts of symbolic actions. Hosea 1–3 includes a report in which the prophet's marriage and the naming of his three children dramatize the fractious relationship between YHWH and Israel. Isaiah 7–8 also contains three accounts in which three children's names symbolize YHWH's intentions. In Isa. 20, the prophet goes about naked and barefoot for three years as a sign of impending Assyrian exile. Ezekiel undertakes symbolic actions as well, including several that depict Babylon's siege and destruction of Jerusalem in the early sixth century BCE (Ezek. 4:1–5:17) and the ensuing exile (12:1–20). Symbolic acts can be used to convey messages of both critique and hope, as several passages in Isaiah, Jeremiah, and Ezekiel demonstrate.

Jeremiah includes reports of the prophet's symbolic actions as well. In 16:1–13, the prophet is instructed not to marry or have children, not to mourn the dead, and not to enter the "house of feasting." Each of these disrupts an aspect of normal life and symbolizes how the looming Babylonian destruction promises to wreak havoc. In 13:1–11, YHWH commands the prophet to hide an undergarment near the Euphrates River (in Babylon). After some time, Jeremiah is told to retrieve the item, only to discover it is now ruined. This symbolizes how Babylon will ruin the "pride of Judah and the great pride of Jerusalem." In 51:59–64, the prophet instructs Seraiah to read a prophetic scroll and then toss it in the Euphrates River, symbolizing the role these words have in "sinking" Babylon. Jeremiah buys a family field in chap. 32, an act symbolizing future hope after the Babylonian destruction and exile. Actions undertaken by others could have symbolic meanings ascribed to them as well. In 18:1–11, Jeremiah observes the work of a potter working at his wheel. His ability to create and re-create symbolizes YHWH's ability to fashion either positive or negative futures for Judah.

Sometimes "actions speak louder than words." In the case of the prophets, the two work in tandem.

J. Todd Hibbard

---

³ Her[b] nobles send their servants for water;
　they come to the cisterns;
they find no water;
　they return with their vessels empty.
They are ashamed and dismayed
　and cover their heads,
⁴ because the ground is cracked.
　Because there has been no rain on the land,
the farmers are dismayed;
　they cover their heads.
⁵ Even the doe in the field forsakes her newborn fawn
　because there is no grass.
⁶ The wild asses stand on the bare heights;[c]
　they pant for air like jackals;
their eyes fail
　because there is no herbage.

⁷ Although our iniquities testify against us,
　act, O LORD, for your name's sake;
our rebellions indeed are many,
　and we have sinned against you.
⁸ O hope of Israel,
　its savior in time of trouble,
why should you be like a stranger in the land,
　like a traveler turning aside for the night?
⁹ Why should you be like someone confused,
　like a mighty warrior who cannot give help?
Yet you, O LORD, are in the midst of us,
　and we are called by your name;
　do not forsake us!

b 14.3 Gk: Heb *their*　c 14.6 Or *the trails*

community. **14:3–4** The people are ashamed and upset by the condition of the earth. Farmers cover their heads as a sign of mourning. The land reveals the damage from the lack of water, as it is dried and cracked. **14:5–6** Animals react and adapt to the lack of water and, by extension, the lack of food. Mother deer abandon their offspring; donkeys pant and die without sustenance.

　14:7–9 The people of Judah recognize their failings. The shame of vv. 3–4 propels them to acknowledge that they have rebelled against God, and they request help and relief. Despite the damage done to the earth and animals, the people pray only for themselves.

¹⁰ Thus says the LORD concerning this
people:
Truly they have loved to wander;
they have not restrained their feet;
therefore the LORD does not accept
them;
now he will remember their iniquity
and punish their sins.

11 The LORD said to me: Do not pray for the
welfare of this people. ¹²Although they fast, I
do not hear their cry, and although they offer
burnt offering and grain offering, I do not accept them, but by the sword, by famine, and
by pestilence I consume them.
13 Then I said: "Ah, Lord GOD! Here are
the prophets saying to them, 'You shall
not see the sword, nor shall you have famine, but I will give you true peace in this
place.' " ¹⁴And the LORD said to me: "The
prophets are prophesying lies in my name;
I did not send them, nor did I command
them or speak to them. They are prophesying to you a lying vision, worthless divination, and the deceit of their own minds.
¹⁵Therefore thus says the LORD concerning
the prophets who prophesy in my name
though I did not send them and who say,
'Sword and famine shall not come on this
land': By sword and famine those prophets shall be consumed. ¹⁶And the people to
whom they prophesy shall be thrown out
into the streets of Jerusalem, victims of
famine and sword. There shall be no one to
bury them—themselves, their wives, their
sons, and their daughters—for I will pour
out their wickedness upon them."

¹⁷ You shall say to them this word:
Let my eyes run down with tears night
and day,
and let them not cease,
for the virgin daughter of my people is
struck down with a crushing blow,
with a very grievous wound.
¹⁸ If I go out into the field,
look—those killed by the sword!
And if I enter the city,
look—those sick with^d famine!
For both prophet and priest ply their
trade throughout the land
and have no knowledge.
¹⁹ Have you completely rejected Judah?
Does your heart loathe Zion?
Why have you struck us down
so that there is no healing for us?
We look for peace but find no good,
for a time of healing, but there is
terror instead.
²⁰ We acknowledge our wickedness,
O LORD,
the iniquity of our ancestors,
for we have sinned against you.
²¹ Do not spurn us, for your name's sake;
do not dishonor your glorious
throne;
remember and do not break your
covenant with us.
²² Can any idols of the nations bring rain,
or can the heavens give showers?
Is it not you, O LORD our God?
We set our hope on you,
for it is you who do all this.

d 14.18 Heb *look—the sicknesses of*

14:10–12 God is not interested in the people's acknowledgment and rejects them. God also instructs Jeremiah not to pray for the people, threatening more suffering instead. In addition to drought, God threatens to inflict sword (war), famine (lack of food), and pestilence (disease). Punishment by sword, famine, and pestilence is a common triad in Jeremiah (cf. 21:9; 24:10; 27:8, 13; 29:17, 18; 32:24, 36; 38:2; 42:17, 22; 44:13).

14:13–18 Jeremiah and God denounce the false prophets of the day. These verses reveal Jeremiah's context and the conflicting messages that people were proclaiming. Jeremiah lives during a period of historical, political, theological, and ecological instability. Yet people in the community (called false or lying prophets) insisted that things were just fine, and there was no cause for concern. **14:17** *Virgin daughter of my people.* God refers to the people of Judah using sexually charged, familial language.

14:19–22 These verses focus on mercy and remorse. The people plead for healing and peace, imploring God to remember their covenant relationship. The people's religious failures are interpreted as causing God to punish them with drought, sword, famine, and pestilence. The depiction of a God who is punitive may be troubling, but it reflects an attempt at rationalizing the catastrophic devastation in Judah. Modern readers, like ancient communities, must contend with the images of a vengeful God.

15

Then the LORD said to me: Though Moses and Samuel stood before me, yet my heart would not turn toward this people. Send them out of my sight, and let them go! ²And when they say to you, "Where shall we go?" you shall say to them: Thus says the LORD:

Those destined for pestilence, to
    pestilence,
and those destined for the sword, to
    the sword;
those destined for famine, to famine,
and those destined for captivity, to
    captivity.

³And I will appoint over them four kinds of destroyers, says the LORD: the sword to kill, the dogs to drag away, and the birds of the air and the wild animals of the earth to devour and destroy. ⁴I will make them a horror to all the kingdoms of the earth because of what King Manasseh son of Hezekiah of Judah did in Jerusalem.

⁵ Who will have pity on you, O Jerusalem,
    or who will bemoan you?
Who will turn aside
    to ask about your welfare?
⁶ You have rejected me, says the LORD;
    you are going backward,
so I have stretched out my hand against
    you and destroyed you—
    I am weary of relenting.
⁷ I have winnowed them with a
    winnowing fork
    in the gates of the land;

I have bereaved them; I have destroyed
    my people;
    they did not turn from their ways.
⁸ Their widows became more numerous
    than the sand of the seas;
I have brought against the mothers of
    youths
    a destroyer at noonday;
I have made anguish and terror
    fall upon her suddenly.
⁹ She who bore seven has languished;
    she has swooned away;
her sun went down while it was yet day;
    she has been shamed and disgraced.
And the rest of them I will give to the
    sword
    before their enemies,
                        says the LORD.

10 Woe is me, my mother, that you ever bore me, a man of strife and contention to the whole land! I have not lent, nor have I borrowed, yet all of them curse me. ¹¹The LORD said: Surely I have intervened in your life*e* for good; surely I have brought enemies upon you*f* in a time of trouble and in a time of distress. ¹²Can one break iron, iron from the north, and bronze?

13 Your wealth and your treasures I will give as plunder, without price, for all your sins, throughout all your territory. ¹⁴I will make you serve your enemies in a land that you do not know, for in my anger a fire is kindled that shall burn against you.

e 15.11 Meaning of Heb uncertain   *f* 15.11 Meaning of Heb uncertain

15:1–4 These verses vividly depict what divine punishment and judgment look like on the ground. Pestilence, sword, and famine are highlighted again. These verses also reference two significant prophets from Israel's history, Moses and Samuel. Moses is often highlighted as a prophet par excellence. The passage assumes they are interceding for Israel, but as with Jeremiah in chap. 11, they are rejected. **15:3** Animals are depicted as participants in punishing the people of Judah. **15:4** *Because of what King Manasseh . . . did.* Though the passage does not identify what Manasseh, who reigned decades beforehand, did, here he is blamed for the destruction befalling Jerusalem and Judah (see also 2 Kgs. 21:1–16; 24:3–4).

15:5–9 Another graphic image of war is described here. YHWH's full disdain for the people is evident, as they are not pitied because of their rejection. The destruction of war is visible through the lives that are negatively impacted and ruined. In particular, women, again, are the window into suffering, as the number of widows increases during this period. **15:5** *Who will have pity on you, O Jerusalem?* This and the next two questions are rhetorical. No one will console Jerusalem. **15:8** *Widows became more numerous than the sand of the seas* because their husbands have fled, died, or been captured and taken into exile. The widows also suffer and languish at the loss of multiple children.

15:10–21 This is the third of Jeremiah's laments. Jeremiah emotionally complains about his prophetic calling, first by lamenting his mother for giving birth to him. His *woe is me* attitude can seem off-putting, especially as the previous verse highlights how many mothers have lost their sons due to war. Jeremiah's complaint is a connection back to his prophetic calling from within his mother's

¹⁵ O Lord, you know;
  remember me and visit me,
  and bring down retribution for me on
    my persecutors.
In your forbearance do not take me away;
  know that on your account I suffer
    insult.
¹⁶ Your words were found, and I ate them,
  and your words became to me a joy
  and the delight of my heart,
for I am called by your name,
  O Lord, God of hosts.
¹⁷ I did not sit in the company of
    merrymakers,
  nor did I rejoice;
under the weight of your hand I sat
    alone,
  for you had filled me with indignation.
¹⁸ Why is my pain unceasing,
  my wound incurable,
  refusing to be healed?
Truly, you are to me like a deceitful brook,
  like waters that fail.

¹⁹ Therefore thus says the Lord:
If you turn back, I will take you back,
  and you shall stand before me.
If you utter what is precious and not
    what is worthless,
  you shall serve as my mouth.
It is they who will turn to you,
  not you who will turn to them.
²⁰ And I will make you to this people
  a fortified wall of bronze;
they will fight against you,
  but they shall not prevail over you,

for I am with you
  to save you and deliver you,
            says the Lord.
²¹ I will deliver you out of the hand of the
    wicked
  and redeem you from the grasp of the
    ruthless.

16 The word of the Lord came to me: ²You shall not take a wife, nor shall you have sons or daughters in this place. ³For thus says the Lord concerning the sons and daughters who are born in this place and concerning the mothers who bear them and the fathers who father them in this land: ⁴They shall die of deadly diseases. They shall not be lamented, nor shall they be buried; they shall become like dung on the surface of the ground. They shall perish by the sword and by famine, and their dead bodies shall become food for the birds of the air and for the wild animals of the earth.

5 For thus says the Lord: Do not enter the house of mourning or go to lament or bemoan them, for I have taken away my peace from this people, says the Lord, my steadfast love and mercy. ⁶Both great and small shall die in this land; they shall not be buried, and no one shall lament for them; there shall be no gashing, no shaving of the head for them. ⁷No one shall break bread*g* for the mourner, to offer comfort for the dead, nor shall anyone give them the cup of consolation to drink for their fathers or their mothers. ⁸You shall not go into the house of feasting to sit with them,

g 16.7 Gk: Heb *break for them*

womb in Jer. 1. His prophetic career forces him to contend with enemies, and he questions God's actions and failure to heal his pain. **15:16** *Your words . . . I ate them.* A metaphor for God placing the prophetic word in the prophet's mouth (cf. Ezek. 2:8–3:3). **15:18** *Deceitful brook.* Perhaps a dry creek bed or wadi. Jeremiah's complaint ends with a serious charge. **15:19** YHWH is not depicted as sympathetic. Rather, YHWH encourages Jeremiah to stop saying things that are *worthless*. Moreover, the divine response is reassurance that God is with Jeremiah, protecting him from enemies and providing messages to declare within the chaos.

16:1–13 Jeremiah receives three prohibitions in these verses. Each outlines a symbolic action followed by a divine oracle of explanation. See **"Symbolic Actions," p. 1056.** First, he is to neither marry nor have a family. The act speaks to the impending doom in the land, which will make the area unviable and dangerous for a family. **16:4** *They shall not be lamented, nor shall they be buried.* The deceased will be denied the customary rites associated with death. To deny someone burial was to disturb their transition to the afterlife. **16:5** The second prohibition Jeremiah receives is not to enter the *house of mourning*, or the "house of the mourning feast" ("marzeah"). This rare term might point to the existence of some type of group who regularly gathered to feast and mourn the dead (cf. Amos 6:7). In Jer. 14, the prophet is restricted from praying for the people, and here Jeremiah is restricted from lamenting for multidimensional suffering and destruction. **16:8** Finally, Jeremiah is prohibited from going to the *house of feasting*, a sign that community celebration will

to eat and drink. ⁹For thus says the Lord of hosts, the God of Israel: I am going to banish from this place, in your days and before your eyes, the voice of mirth and the voice of gladness, the voice of the bridegroom and the voice of the bride.

10 And when you tell this people all these words, and they say to you, "Why has the Lord pronounced all this great evil against us? What is our iniquity? What is the sin that we have committed against the Lord our God?" ¹¹then you shall say to them: It is because your ancestors have forsaken me, says the Lord, and have gone after other gods and have served and worshiped them and have forsaken me and have not kept my law, ¹²and because you have behaved worse than your ancestors, for here you are, every one of you, following your stubborn evil will, refusing to listen to me. ¹³Therefore I will hurl you out of this land into a land that neither you nor your ancestors have known, and there you shall serve other gods day and night, for I will show you no favor.

14 Therefore, the days are surely coming, says the Lord, when it shall no longer be said, "As the Lord lives who brought the people of Israel up out of the land of Egypt," ¹⁵but "As the Lord lives who brought the people of Israel up out of the land of the north and out of all the lands where he had driven them." For I will bring them back to their own land that I gave to their ancestors.

16 I am now sending for many fishermen, says the Lord, and they shall catch them, and afterward I will send for many hunters, and they shall hunt them from every mountain and every hill and out of the clefts of the rocks. ¹⁷For my eyes are on all their ways; they are not hidden from my presence, nor is their iniquity concealed from my sight. ¹⁸And*ᵇ* I will doubly repay their iniquity and their sin because they have polluted my land with the carcasses of their detestable idols and have filled my inheritance with their abominations.

¹⁹ O Lord, my strength and my stronghold,
    my refuge in the day of trouble,
to you shall the nations come
    from the ends of the earth and say:
"Our ancestors have inherited nothing
        but lies,
    worthless things in which there is no
        profit.
²⁰ Can mortals make for themselves gods?
    Such are no gods!"

21 "Therefore I am surely going to teach them, this time I am going to teach them my power and my might, and they shall know that my name is the Lord."

17 The sin of Judah is written with an iron pen; with a diamond point it is engraved on the tablet of their hearts and on the horns of their altars, ²while their children remember their altars and their sacred poles*ⁱ*

b 16.18 Gk: Heb *And first*   *i* 17.2 Or *Asherahs*

cease. **16:9** Jeremiah's prohibition is connected to the earlier statement that there will not be the joy of hearing married couples in the land, which is also included in this sermon. **16:10** The people will inevitably wonder why YHWH is so negatively predisposed to them. **16:13** *I will hurl you.* Like a ball tossed across a field, YHWH will throw the people out of the land, another image of impending exile.

16:14–15 The return from exile is envisioned as a second exodus (cf. Isa. 40). This oracle is repeated with slight variations in 23:7–8.

16:16 The imagery of fishers and hunters expresses the invasion in the land.

16:18 YHWH agrees to *doubly repay their iniquity and their sin*, affirming that the destruction should feel heavy-handed (cf. Isa. 40:1–2).

16:19–20 A fragment of a hymn that recognizes divine strength, critiques the veneration of other gods, and asserts that the people will be taught about YHWH's power through these events. **16:20** *No gods.* See 2:11; 5:7. **16:21** YHWH answers the hymn of vv. 19–20.

17:1–4 The sinful actions of Judah are *written with an iron pen*, a stylus used for engraving stone and metal, and *engraved on the tablet of their hearts* (cf. Prov. 3:3; 7:3), imagery that will occur again in the new covenant (cf. Jer. 31:31). *Horns of their altars* refers to four raised corners on the tops of the altars. The ways that Judah has been violating the covenant are explicated as constructing open-air altars and sacred poles (Heb. "asherim") and worshiping under trees, on hills, and on mountains. These are all violations because they are associated with the veneration of other deities, but Judah should be worshiping YHWH alone and only in the temple.

beside every green tree and on the high hills, ³on the mountains in the open country. Your wealth and all your treasures I will give for spoil as the price of your sin^j throughout all your territory. ⁴By your own act you shall lose the heritage that I gave you, and I will make you serve your enemies in a land that you do not know, for in my anger a fire is kindled that shall burn forever.

⁵ Thus says the LORD:
Cursed are those who trust in mere
 mortals
 and make mere flesh their strength,
 whose hearts turn away from the
 LORD.
⁶ They shall be like a shrub in the desert
 and shall not see when relief comes.
They shall live in the parched places of
 the wilderness,
 in an uninhabited salt land.

⁷ Blessed are those who trust in the
 LORD,
 whose trust is the LORD.
⁸ They shall be like a tree planted by
 water,
 sending out its roots by the stream.
It shall not fear when heat comes,
 and its leaves shall stay green;
in the year of drought it is not anxious,
 and it does not cease to bear fruit.

⁹ The heart is devious above all else;
 it is perverse—
 who can understand it?
¹⁰ I the LORD test the mind
 and search the heart,
to give to all according to their ways,
 according to the fruit of their doings.

¹¹ Like the partridge hatching what it did
 not lay,
 so are all who amass wealth unjustly;
in midlife it will leave them,
 and at their end they will prove to be
 fools.

¹² O glorious throne, exalted from the
 beginning,
 shrine of our sanctuary!
¹³ O hope of Israel! O LORD!
 All who forsake you shall be put to
 shame;
those who turn away from you^k shall be
 recorded in the underworld,^{l}
 for they have forsaken the fountain of
 living water, the LORD.
¹⁴ Heal me, O LORD, and I shall be healed;
 save me, and I shall be saved,
 for you are my praise.
¹⁵ See how they say to me,
 "Where is the word of the LORD?
 Let it come!"
¹⁶ But I have not run away from being a
 shepherd^m in your service,
 nor have I desired the fatal day.
You know what came from my lips;
 it was before your face.
¹⁷ Do not become a terror to me;
 you are my refuge in the day of
 disaster;
¹⁸ Let my persecutors be shamed,
 but do not let me be shamed;
let them be dismayed,
 but do not let me be dismayed;
bring on them the day of disaster;
 destroy them with double
 destruction!

j 17.3 Cn: Heb *spoil, your high places for sin* k 17.13 Heb *me*
l 17.13 Or *in the earth* m 17.16 Meaning of Heb uncertain

17:5–8 This psalm expresses blessings on the one who trusts in YHWH and curses on the one who trusts in human beings. The imagery of water scarcity and cursing and water abundance and blessing is another connection to the assertion of YHWH as the fountain of living water (Jer. 2:13). The imagery of the *tree planted by water*, firm and fruitful, recalls Ps. 1 and portions of the Egyptian composition *Amen-em-opet* (chap. iv).

17:9–10 This short poetic fragment links with the previous psalm through its focus on the human *heart*, which YHWH knows.

17:11 A short proverb meant to illustrate deviousness. *Partridge hatching what it did not lay*. The imagery suggests those enriching themselves by taking what is not theirs.

17:12 *O glorious throne.* YHWH's throne in the temple.

17:13 *Underworld.* Literally "the earth."

17:14–18 Another of Jeremiah's laments. The trials and tribulations of the prophetic calling are also revisited in another prayerful lament by the prophet. See **"Prayer and Prophetic Intercession," p. 1053. 17:14** Jeremiah requests healing within the context of persecution.

19 Thus said the Lord to me: Go and stand in the People's Gate, by which the kings of Judah enter and by which they go out, and in all the gates of Jerusalem, ²⁰and say to them: Hear the word of the Lord, you kings of Judah, and all Judah, and all the inhabitants of Jerusalem who enter by these gates. ²¹Thus says the Lord: For the sake of your lives, take care that you do not bear a burden on the Sabbath day or bring it in by the gates of Jerusalem. ²²And do not carry a burden out of your houses on the Sabbath or do any work, but keep the Sabbath day holy, as I commanded your ancestors. ²³Yet they did not listen or incline their ear; they stiffened their necks and would not hear or receive instruction.

24 But if you listen to me, says the Lord, and bring in no burden by the gates of this city on the Sabbath day but keep the Sabbath day holy and do no work on it, ²⁵then there shall enter by the gates of this city kings*ⁿ* who sit on the throne of David, riding in chariots and on horses, they and their officials, the people of Judah and the inhabitants of Jerusalem, and this city shall be inhabited forever. ²⁶And people shall come from the towns of Judah and the places around Jerusalem, from the land of Benjamin, from the Shephelah, from the hill country, and from the Negeb, bringing burnt offerings and sacrifices, grain offerings and frankincense, and bringing thank offerings to the house of the Lord. ²⁷But if you do not listen to me, to keep the Sabbath day holy and to carry in no burden through the gates of Jerusalem on the Sabbath day,

then I will kindle a fire in its gates; it shall devour the palaces of Jerusalem and shall not be quenched.

18 The word that came to Jeremiah from the Lord: ²"Come, go down to the potter's house, and there I will let you hear my words." ³So I went down to the potter's house, and there he was working at his wheel. ⁴The vessel he was making of clay was spoiled in the potter's hand, and he reworked it into another vessel, as seemed good to him.

5 Then the word of the Lord came to me: ⁶Can I not do with you, O house of Israel, just as this potter has done? says the Lord. Just like the clay in the potter's hand, so are you in my hand, O house of Israel. ⁷At one moment I may declare concerning a nation or a kingdom that I will pluck up and break down and destroy it, ⁸but if that nation, concerning which I have spoken, turns from its evil, I will change my mind about the disaster that I intended to bring on it. ⁹And at another moment I may declare concerning a nation or a kingdom that I will build and plant it, ¹⁰but if it does evil in my sight, not listening to my voice, then I will change my mind about the good that I had intended to do to it. ¹¹Now, therefore, say to the people of Judah and the inhabitants of Jerusalem: Thus says the Lord: Look, I am a potter shaping evil against you and devising a plan against you. Turn now, all of you, from your evil way, and amend your ways and your doings.

n 17.25 Cn: Heb *kings and officials*

17:19–27 Jeremiah is instructed to give another sermon at the *People's Gate*, which is likely a gate of the temple. The Sabbath sermon offers the possibility of restoring the kingdom if people observe the Sabbath. The Sabbath command is integral to the Mosaic covenant (see Exod. 16:23; 20:8–11; Deut. 5:12–15). By highlighting the Sabbath, the sermon gives another cultic practice that can help restore the damaged relationship between YHWH and the people of Judah. Failure to keep the Sabbath is also linked with further destruction in Jerusalem.

18:1–11 Jeremiah performs another symbolic act by visiting a potter who is creating a vessel out of clay. See **"Symbolic Actions," p. 1056.** YHWH will outline two possible futures for Judah and Jerusalem. **18:7** Although the surrounding oracles have focused on *pluck[ing] up and break[ing] down*, the image here is of "build[ing] and plant[ing]" (v. 9), all verbs from Jeremiah's call and commissioning (Jer. 1). YHWH is compared to a potter. **18:8** *I will change my mind.* Literally "I will repent." The language here and in v. 10 suggests YHWH's intentions could be altered based on human actions. The verse is reminiscent of Nineveh (Assyria) in the book of Jonah (Jonah 3:6–10). **18:11** The Hebrew root for "potter" and "to fashion" (Heb. "ytsr") means to form. It has echoes of YHWH forming ("ytsr") the first human in the garden of Eden (cf. Gen. 2:7) and Jeremiah being formed ("ytsr") in the womb for his calling (cf. Jer. 1:5). Here, however, YHWH as a potter is forming an evil plan against the people unless they repent and amend their actions.

12 But they say, "It is no use! We will follow our own plans, and each of us will act according to the stubbornness of our evil will."

13 Therefore thus says the LORD:
   Ask among the nations:
      Who has heard the like of this?
   The virgin Israel has done
      a most horrible thing.
14 Does the snow of Lebanon leave
      the crags of Sirion?[o]
   Do the mountain[p] waters run dry,[q]
      the cold flowing streams?
15 But my people have forgotten me;
      they burn offerings to a delusion;
   they have stumbled[r] in their ways,
      in the ancient roads,
   and have gone into bypaths,
      not the highway,
16 making their land a horror,
      a thing to be hissed at forever.
   All who pass by it are horrified
      and shake their heads.
17 Like the wind from the east,
      I will scatter them before the
         enemy.
   I will show them my back, not my face,
      in the day of their calamity.

18 Then they said, "Come, let us make plots against Jeremiah, for instruction shall not perish from the priest, nor counsel from the wise, nor the word from the prophet. Come, let us bring charges against him,[s] and let us not heed any of his words."

19 Give heed to me, O LORD,
      and listen to what my adversaries say!
20 Is evil a recompense for good?
      Yet they have dug a pit for my life.

Remember how I stood before you
   to speak good for them,
   to turn away your wrath from them.
21 Therefore give their children over to
      famine;
   hurl them out to the power of the
      sword;
let their wives become childless and
      widowed.
   May their men meet death by
      pestilence,
   their youths be slain by the sword in
      battle.
22 May a cry be heard from their
      houses
   when you bring the marauder
      suddenly upon them!
For they have dug a pit to catch me
      and laid snares for my feet.
23 Yet you, O LORD, know
      all their plotting to kill me.
Do not forgive their iniquity;
      do not blot out their sin from your
         sight.
Let them be tripped up before you;
      deal with them while you are
         angry.

19 Thus said the LORD: Go and buy a potter's earthenware jug. Take with you[t] some of the elders of the people and some of the senior priests, 2and go out to the valley of the son of Hinnom at the entry of the Potsherd Gate, and proclaim there the words that I tell you. 3You shall say: Hear the word of the LORD, O kings of Judah and inhabitants

o 18.14 Cn: Heb *of the field*   p 18.14 Cn: Heb *foreign*
q 18.14 Cn: Heb *Are . . . plucked up?*   r 18.15 Gk Syr Vg: Heb
they made them stumble   s 18.18 Heb *strike him with the tongue*
t 19.1 Syr Tg Compare Gk: Heb lacks *take with you*

18:12–17 The stubbornness of the people, their foolish abandoning of YHWH, and their idolatry are highlighted again. Their punishment will be their scattering, a reference to exile. **18:14** Two rhetorical questions about certainties in the natural world, here meant to demonstrate the absurdity of Judah's actions. **18:17** *I will show them my back, not my face.* YHWH turns his back on the people, withholding divine help.

18:18–23 Jeremiah details the risks involved with being a prophet, as he is targeted by adversaries. Jeremiah makes prayers for vengeance, called imprecatory prayers, which wish harm on enemies. Jeremiah prays that those who attack him will feel the divine wrath in a similar way to the people of Judah. Jeremiah prays that they experience famine, widowhood, pestilence, and robbery because they are actively plotting to kill him. **18:18** There is no clear antecedent for *they*, though Jeremiah has no shortage of opponents in the book. *Instruction . . . prophet.* The phrase references three categories of learned teachers (*the priest, the wise, the prophet*) and the types of teaching with each (*instruction, counsel, the word*).

19:1–15 The pottery image is reused in this prose text with another symbolic act. Jeremiah

of Jerusalem. Thus says the Lord of hosts, the God of Israel: I am going to bring such disaster upon this place that the ears of everyone who hears of it will tingle. ⁴Because the people have forsaken me and have profaned this place by making offerings in it to other gods whom neither they nor their ancestors nor the kings of Judah have known, and because they have filled this place with the blood of the innocent ⁵and gone on building the high places of Baal to burn their children in the fire as burnt offerings to Baal, which I did not command or decree, nor did it enter my mind, ⁶therefore the days are surely coming, says the Lord, when this place shall no more be called Topheth or the valley of the son of Hinnom but the valley of Slaughter. ⁷And in this place I will make void the plans of Judah and Jerusalem and will make them fall by the sword before their enemies and by the hand of those who seek their life. I will give their dead bodies for food to the birds of the air and to the wild animals of the earth. ⁸And I will make this city a horror, a thing to be hissed at; everyone who passes by it will be horrified and will hiss because of all its disasters. ⁹And I will make them eat the flesh of their sons and the flesh of their daughters, and all shall eat the flesh of their neighbors in the siege and in the distress with which their enemies and those who seek their life afflict them.

10 Then you shall break the jug in the sight of those who go with you ¹¹and shall say to them: Thus says the Lord of hosts: So will I break this people and this city as one breaks a potter's vessel, so that it can never be mended. In Topheth they shall bury until there is no more room to bury. ¹²Thus will I do to this place, says the Lord, and to its inhabitants, making this city like Topheth. ¹³And the houses of Jerusalem and the houses of the kings of Judah shall be defiled like the place of Topheth—all the houses upon whose roofs offerings have been made to the whole host of heaven and libations have been poured out to other gods.

14 When Jeremiah came from Topheth, where the Lord had sent him to prophesy, he stood in the court of the Lord's house and said to all the people: ¹⁵Thus says the Lord of hosts, the God of Israel: I am now bringing upon this city and upon all its towns all the disaster that I have pronounced against it, because they have stiffened their necks, refusing to hear my words.

20 Now the priest Pashhur son of Immer, who was chief officer in the house of the Lord, heard Jeremiah prophesying these things. ²Then Pashhur struck the prophet Jeremiah and put him in the stocks that were in the upper Benjamin Gate of the house of the Lord. ³The next morning when Pashhur released Jeremiah from the stocks, Jeremiah said to him, "The Lord has named you not Pashhur but 'Terror-all-around.' ⁴For thus says the Lord: I am making you

purchases a potter's earthenware jug and then breaks it in the sight of the people to symbolize their destruction. **19:2** *Valley of the son of Hinnom.* A valley running on the western and southern edges of Jerusalem (see also 7:31). *Potsherd Gate.* Located in the southernmost portion of the city of David. It might have been where broken pottery was dumped, making it an appropriate location for Jeremiah's symbolic act. See **"Symbolic Actions," p. 1056. 19:3–9** Images of illicit cultic practices are highlighted, especially child sacrifice, which was also highlighted in the temple sermon (Jer. 7:30–34). **19:6** Topheth is the location associated with this practice, and it will be renamed the valley of Slaughter because of these actions (cf. 7:31; 2 Kgs. 23:10). **19:9** Horrific imagery of cannibalism, standard curse language in ancient Near Eastern treaties (cf. also Deut. 28:53–57; Lev. 26:29). *Siege.* The Babylonians laid siege to Jerusalem as part of their final assault on the city; cf. Jer. 52:5; 2 Kgs. 24:10; 25:2. **19:10** *Break the jug* symbolizes YHWH's destruction of the people and the city by means of the Babylonians. **19:13** *Defiled.* Because Topheth is turned into a graveyard, it is rendered ritually impure—that is, defiled. *Upon whose roofs offerings have been made.* House rooftops were occasionally used as places for worship; cf. 32:29; 2 Kgs. 23:12; Zeph. 1:5. **19:14** *Court of the Lord's house.* Cf. 26:2.

20:1–6 The risks of prophecy are highlighted with a narrative from the life of Jeremiah in which he is persecuted publicly by the priest Pashhur. **20:2** Jeremiah is beaten and imprisoned in the stockade, which gives an insight into the public aspect of punishment and shaming. Jeremiah's treatment, especially by a priest, shows how hostile his community is toward his messages, which repeatedly condemn their actions and prophesy destruction. **20:3** *Not Pashhur but "Terror-all-around."*

a terror to yourself and to all your friends, and they shall fall by the sword of their enemies while you look on. And I will give all Judah into the hand of the king of Babylon; he shall carry them captive to Babylon and shall kill them with the sword. ⁵I will give all the wealth of this city, all its gains, all its prized belongings, and all the treasures of the kings of Judah into the hand of their enemies, who shall plunder them and seize them and carry them to Babylon. ⁶And you, Pashhur, and all who live in your house, shall go into captivity, and to Babylon you shall go; there you shall die, and there you shall be buried, you and all your friends, to whom you have prophesied falsely."

⁷ O Lᴏʀᴅ, you have enticed me,
    and I was enticed;
you have overpowered me,
    and you have prevailed.
I have become a laughingstock all day
    long;
    everyone mocks me.
⁸ For whenever I speak, I must cry out;
    I must shout, "Violence and
        destruction!"
For the word of the Lᴏʀᴅ has become for
    me
    a reproach and derision all day long.
⁹ If I say, "I will not mention him
    or speak any more in his name,"
then within me there is something like a
    burning fire
    shut up in my bones;
I am weary with holding it in,
    and I cannot.

¹⁰ For I hear many whispering:
    "Terror is all around!
Denounce him! Let us denounce him!"
    All my close friends
    are watching for me to stumble.
"Perhaps he can be enticed,
    and we can prevail against him
    and take our revenge on him."
¹¹ But the Lᴏʀᴅ is with me like a terrifying
    warrior;
    therefore my persecutors will stumble,
    and they will not prevail.
They will be greatly shamed,
    for they will not succeed.
Their eternal dishonor
    will never be forgotten.
¹² O Lᴏʀᴅ of hosts, you test the
    righteous;
    you see the heart and the mind;
let me see your retribution upon them,
    for to you I have committed my cause.

¹³ Sing to the Lᴏʀᴅ;
    praise the Lᴏʀᴅ!
For he has delivered the life of the needy
    from the hands of evildoers.

¹⁴ Cursed be the day
    on which I was born!
The day when my mother bore me,
    let it not be blessed!
¹⁵ Cursed be the man
    who brought the news to my father,
        saying,
    "A child is born to you, a son,"
        making him very glad.

Symbolic names appear elsewhere in the prophetic literature (cf. Isa. 7–8; Hos. 1, 3). Here, the Hebrew word for terror rhymes with Pashhur, creating a wordplay of sorts. "Terror is all around" appears as an exclamation in Jer. 20:10; 46:5; 49:29 (see also 6:25; Ps. 31:13). **20:4** *Babylon* is named for the first time in the book as Judah's foe and place of exile. **20:6** Jeremiah predicts that Pashhur and all his family will go into exile, where Pashhur will die.

20:7–18 The last two of Jeremiah's personal laments in Jer. 11–20. Jeremiah again laments his life as a prophet, detailing the embarrassment and mockery he encounters. **20:7** The language has echoes of rape, with YHWH *entic[ing]*, *overpower[ing]*, and *prevail[ing]* over Jeremiah, and the prophet responds to the rape by crying out against the violence. **20:8** *Reproach and derision.* The prophetic message makes Jeremiah an object of ridicule. **20:11** Despite Jeremiah's experience of violation, he affirms that he is confident that his persecutors will not succeed. Having experienced the negative aspects of divine power, Jeremiah realizes that it will protect his life from those who wish him harm. **20:13** *Sing.* A hymnic fragment rounds out Jeremiah's lament. **20:14–18** Jeremiah returns to lamenting and bemoans his prophetic calling. **20:14** *Cursed be the day on which I was born!* Like Job, Jeremiah wishes he had never been born (Job 3:1–3). *My mother.* He brings up his mother again, as her womb was the place of his calling. See note on 1:4–5. **20:15–17** He curses the person who announced to his father that he was born. He also curses whoever did not kill him in the womb, wishing his mother's pregnancy had been terminated so he would not have been born

¹⁶ Let that man be like the cities
    that the Lord overthrew without pity;
  let him hear a cry in the morning
    and an alarm at noon,
¹⁷ because he did not kill me in the
    womb;
  so my mother would have been my
    grave
  and her womb forever pregnant.
¹⁸ Why did I come forth from the womb
    to see toil and sorrow
  and spend my days in shame?

21 This is the word that came to Jeremiah from the Lord, when King Zedekiah sent to him Pashhur son of Malchiah and the priest Zephaniah son of Maaseiah, saying, ²"Please inquire of the Lord on our behalf, for King Nebuchadrezzar of Babylon is making war against us; perhaps the Lord will perform a wonderful deed for us, as he has often done, and Nebuchadrezzar[u] will withdraw."

3 Then Jeremiah said to them: ⁴Thus you shall say to Zedekiah: Thus says the Lord, the God of Israel: I am going to turn back the weapons of war that are in your hands and with which you are fighting against the king of Babylon and against the Chaldeans who are besieging you outside the walls, and I will bring them together into the center of this city. ⁵I myself will fight against you with outstretched hand and mighty arm, in anger, in fury, and in great wrath. ⁶And I will strike

down the inhabitants of this city, both humans and animals; they shall die of a great pestilence. ⁷Afterward, says the Lord, I will give King Zedekiah of Judah and his servants and the people in this city—those who survive the pestilence, sword, and famine—into the hands of King Nebuchadrezzar of Babylon, into the hands of their enemies, into the hands of those who seek their lives. He shall strike them down with the edge of the sword; he shall not pity them or spare them or have compassion.

8 And to this people you shall say: Thus says the Lord: See, I am setting before you the way of life and the way of death. ⁹Those who stay in this city shall die by the sword, by famine, and by pestilence, but those who go out and surrender to the Chaldeans who are besieging you shall live and shall have their lives as a prize of war. ¹⁰For I have set my face against this city for evil and not for good, says the Lord; it shall be given into the hands of the king of Babylon, and he shall burn it with fire.

11 To the house of the king of Judah say: Hear the word of the Lord, ¹²O house of David! Thus says the Lord:

Execute justice in the morning,
  and deliver from the hand of the
    oppressor
  anyone who has been robbed,
or else my wrath will go forth like fire
  and burn, with no one to quench it,
  because of their evil doings.

u 21.2 Heb *he*

into this prophetic lifestyle. Such a painfully tragic attitude speaks to the misery that Jeremiah feels during his persecution.

21:1–10 This narrative is set during the reign of King Zedekiah (ca. 597–587 BCE), a time of Babylonian expansion led by King Nebuchadrezzar of Babylon. Nebuchadrezzar installed Zedekiah as king after his nephew Jehoiachin was deposed and imprisoned in exile. During the siege, Zedekiah sends two officials to *inquire of the Lord*, which means he consults a prophet to determine what to do and what will happen. The outcome is not favorable. Not only does YHWH refuse to protect Jerusalem from Babylonian aggression; he pledges to *fight against* them. This inverts the idea of YHWH as a divine warrior who fights on behalf of his people. **21:1** *Pashhur son of Malchiah.* A different person named Pashhur from the priest of the same name in Jer. 20 (cf. 38:1–6). **21:2** *Nebuchadrezzar* is an alternate spelling of Nebuchadnezzar (cf. Jer. 27–29). *Wonderful deed.* Reminiscent of the exodus (e.g., Exod. 3:20; 34:10; Pss. 78:11; 106:22). **21:4** *Chaldeans.* Used synonymously with "Babylonians" in Jeremiah. Chaldea was a region in southern Mesopotamia comprising part of the Neo-Babylonian state. **21:6–7** They will experience the triad of curses: sword, famine, and pestilence. **21:9** The people who surrender to the Chaldeans (Babylonians) will live, so this is an instruction to acquiesce to the Babylonians, who are delivering the divine judgment against the land. **21:10** *I have set my face.* An expression of determination.

21:11–14 The *house of David* is addressed, which gives this oracle a precise target: the monarchy in Jerusalem, understood to be descended from David; see **"Davidic Covenant," p. 433**. **21:11** *Execute justice.* The basic requirement of the king. *Deliver from the hand of the oppressor.* "Executing justice"

[13] See, I am against you, O inhabitant of the valley,
O rock of the plain,
          says the LORD;
you who say, "Who can come down against us,
or who can enter our places of refuge?"
[14] I will punish you according to the fruit of your doings,
          says the LORD;
I will kindle a fire in its forest,
and it shall devour all that is around it.

22 Thus says the LORD: Go down to the house of the king of Judah, and speak there this word, [2]and say: Hear the word of the LORD, O king of Judah sitting on the throne of David—you, and your servants, and your people who enter these gates. [3]Thus says the LORD: Act with justice and righteousness and deliver from the hand of the oppressor anyone who has been robbed. And do no wrong or violence to the alien, the orphan, and the widow, or shed innocent blood in this place. [4]For if you will indeed obey this word, then through the gates of this house shall enter kings who sit on the throne of David, riding in chariots and on horses—they, their servants, and their people. [5]But if you will not heed these words, I swear by myself, says the LORD, that this house shall become a desolation. [6]For thus says the LORD concerning the house of the king of Judah:

You are like Gilead to me,
like the summit of Lebanon,

but I swear that I will make you a desert, uninhabited cities.
[7] I will prepare destroyers against you,
all with their weapons;
they shall cut down your choicest cedars and cast them into the fire.

[8] And many nations will pass by this city, and all of them will say one to another, "Why has the LORD dealt in this way with that great city?" [9]And they will answer, "Because they abandoned the covenant of the LORD their God and worshiped other gods and served them."

[10] Do not weep for him who is dead,
nor bemoan him;
weep rather for him who goes away,
for he shall return no more
to see his native land.

[11] For thus says the LORD concerning Shallum son of King Josiah of Judah, who succeeded his father Josiah and who went away from this place: He shall return here no more, [12]but in the place where they have carried him captive he shall die, and he shall never see this land again.

[13] Woe to him who builds his house by unrighteousness
and his upper rooms by injustice,
who makes his neighbors work for nothing
and does not give them their wages,
[14] who says, "I will build myself a spacious house
with large upper rooms,"

requires delivering the oppressed, an act of kindness and grace. Failure to deliver the vulnerable endangers the existence of the Davidic kingship, now under siege centuries after David's reign.

22:1–10 Jeremiah is instructed to tell the king to act with justice and righteousness, encouraging care and protection for aliens, orphans, widows, and innocent people. Images of destruction envision the desolation of the land. **22:10** A poetic statement against weeping for the person who has died is included, which could have a specific person in mind, such as King Shallum (Jehoahaz), the king who reigned for only three months before being deposed and imprisoned in Egypt. Shallum is mentioned in the verses that follow, which could support this interpretation. The references and order of events are not chronological, as Jer. 21 is set during Zedekiah's reign, which is over ten years after the reign of Shallum. It is also possible that the instruction not to weep could be generic to refer to all who will die in the siege. There is an instruction to weep for those who go away in exile, which could refer to King Jehoiachin, who is deposed and exiled for thirty-seven years in Babylon.

22:11–23 King Shallum (Jehoahaz) is found in other texts (see Ezek. 19:2–4—the reference to "one of her cubs" in 19:3 is usually interpreted as Shallum; 2 Kgs. 23:34). He was deposed by the Egyptian king Neco II and died in Egyptian exile. After his reign, Eliakim (Jehoiakim) was established as king, although he switched allegiance between the Egyptians and the Babylonians, trying to strategically side with whoever was strongest at a given time. This disloyalty led to him being killed during the

and who cuts out windows[v] for it,
  paneling it with cedar
  and painting it with vermilion.
[15] Are you a king
  because you compete in cedar?
Did not your father eat and drink
  and do justice and righteousness?
  Then it was well with him.
[16] He judged the cause of the poor and
  needy;
  then it was well.
Is not this to know me?
says the LORD.
[17] But your eyes and heart
  are only on your dishonest gain,
for shedding innocent blood,
  and for practicing oppression and
  violence.
[18] Therefore thus says the LORD concerning
King Jehoiakim son of Josiah of Judah:
They shall not lament for him, saying,
  "Alas, my brother!" or "Alas, sister!"
They shall not lament for him, saying,
  "Alas, lord!" or "Alas, his majesty!"
[19] With the burial of a donkey he shall be
  buried:
  dragged off and thrown out beyond
  the gates of Jerusalem.

[20] Go up to Lebanon and cry out,
  and lift up your voice in Bashan;
cry out from Abarim,
  for all your lovers are crushed.
[21] I spoke to you in your prosperity,
  but you said, "I will not listen."
This has been your way from your
  youth,
  for you have not obeyed my voice.
[22] The wind shall shepherd all your
  shepherds,
  and your lovers shall go into captivity;

then you will be ashamed and dismayed
  because of all your wickedness.
[23] O inhabitant of Lebanon,
  nested among the cedars,
how you will groan[w] when pangs come
  upon you,
  pain as of a woman in labor!
24 As I live, says the LORD, even if King
Coniah son of Jehoiakim of Judah were the
signet ring on my right hand, even from
there I would tear you off [25]and give you
into the hands of those who seek your life,
into the hands of those whom you fear, even
into the hands of King Nebuchadrezzar of
Babylon and into the hands of the Chaldeans. [26]I will hurl you and the mother who
bore you into another country, where you
were not born, and there you shall die. [27]But
they shall not return to the land to which
they long to return.
[28] Is this man Coniah a despised broken
  pot,
  a vessel no one wants?
Why are he and his offspring hurled out
  and cast away in a land that they do
  not know?
[29] O land, land, land,
  hear the word of the LORD!
[30] Thus says the LORD:
Record this man as childless,
  a man who shall not succeed in his
  days,
for none of his offspring shall succeed
  in sitting on the throne of David
  and ruling again in Judah.

23 Woe to the shepherds who destroy
and scatter the sheep of my pasture!
says the LORD. [2]Therefore thus says the LORD,

v 22.14 Gk Vg Syr Tg: MT *my windows* w 22.23 Gk Vg Syr:
Heb *will be pitied*

Babylonian siege. Unlike his father—the reforming king Josiah, known for his justice and execution of the law—Jehoiakim is condemned and not lamented.
  22:24–30 Coniah (Jehoiachin) is also judged and given into Babylonian hands. **22:26** The lan-guage echoes Jeremiah's call, as YHWH says that Jehoiachin and *the mother who bore [him]* will be taken to another country to die. This signals that the king and queen mother were exiled into Babylon, losing political authority, as his signet ring is torn off. This attitude is contrary to Jer. 28:4, which is much more favorable toward Jehoiachin, seeing him as the legitimate king, even while exiled for thirty-seven years. **22:28** Jehoiachin is also compared to the broken vessel used in one of Jeremiah's symbolic acts (cf. Jer. 19).
  23:1–8 A vision of restoration follows the depiction of leaders in exile. Faithful shepherds (lead-ers) who execute justice will be raised up after the exile. **23:1** *Shepherds . . . sheep.* Standard imag-ery for political leaders and the people they lead. **23:2** *You who have scattered my flock.* Jeremiah alternates between blaming political elites for "scattering" the people (i.e., the exile) and claiming

the God of Israel, concerning the shepherds who shepherd my people: It is you who have scattered my flock and have driven them away, and you have not attended to them. So I will attend to you for your evil doings, says the LORD. ³Then I myself will gather the remnant of my flock out of all the lands where I have driven them, and I will bring them back to their fold, and they shall be fruitful and multiply. ⁴I will raise up shepherds over them who will shepherd them, and they shall no longer fear or be dismayed, nor shall any be missing, says the LORD.

5 The days are surely coming, says the LORD, when I will raise up for David a righteous Branch, and he shall reign as king and deal wisely and shall execute justice and righteousness in the land. ⁶In his days Judah will be saved, and Israel will live in safety. And this is the name by which he will be called: "The LORD is our righteousness."

7 Therefore the days are surely coming, says the LORD, when it shall no longer be said, "As the LORD lives who brought the people of Israel up out of the land of Egypt," ⁸but "As the LORD lives who brought out and led the offspring of the house of Israel out of the land of the north and out of all the lands where he* had driven them." Then they shall live in their own land.

9 Concerning the prophets:
My heart is crushed within me;
    all my bones shake;
I have become like a drunkard,
    like one overcome by wine,
because of the LORD
    and because of his holy words.
¹⁰ For the land is full of adulterers;
    because of the curse the land mourns,
    and the pastures of the wilderness are
        dried up.

Their course has been evil,
    and their might is not right.
¹¹ Both prophet and priest are ungodly;
    even in my house I have found their
        wickedness,
                                says the LORD.
¹² Therefore their way shall be to them
    like slippery paths in the darkness,
    into which they shall be driven and
        fall,
for I will bring disaster upon them
    in the year of their punishment,
                                says the LORD.
¹³ In the prophets of Samaria
    I saw a disgusting thing:
they prophesied by Baal
    and led my people Israel astray.
¹⁴ But in the prophets of Jerusalem
    I have seen a more shocking thing:
they commit adultery and walk in lies;
    they strengthen the hands of
        evildoers,
    so that no one turns from wickedness;
all of them have become like Sodom
    to me
    and its inhabitants like Gomorrah.
¹⁵ Therefore thus says the LORD of hosts
    concerning the prophets:
I am going to make them eat wormwood
    and give them poisoned water to
        drink,
for from the prophets of Jerusalem
    ungodliness has spread throughout
        the land.

16 Thus says the LORD of hosts: Do not listen to the words of the prophets who prophesy to you; they are deluding you. They speak visions of their own minds, not from the mouth of the LORD. ¹⁷They keep saying to those who

x 23.8 Gk: Heb *I*

that YHWH has scattered the people (Jer. 9:16; 30:11; cf. 23:3). *Righteous Branch.* Cf. Zech. 3:8; 6:12; Isa. 11:1–9. **23:5** *I will raise up for David.* The promise of a new king implies the current king has failed. **23:6** *The LORD is our righteousness.* This is perhaps a play on the name Zedekiah, Judah's last king, whose name means "Yah (YHWH) is my righteousness." **23:7–8** The restoration and return from exile will supplant the exodus as the seminal event in Israel's religious mythos.

23:9–40 An extended denunciation of prophets with whom Jeremiah disagrees. These figures prophesy hope when destruction fills the land. See **"Prophetic Conflict," p. 1079**. **23:9** *I have become like a drunkard* seems to reflect the overpowering experience of receiving the prophetic message for Jeremiah. **23:11** *Both prophet and priest are ungodly.* In other words, the entire religious establishment is defiled, a reference to their ritual impurity. **23:13** *Samaria.* The capital of the northern kingdom of Israel, destroyed in the late 720s BCE. **23:14** *But in the prophets of Jerusalem.* In other words, the prophets of Jerusalem are worse than the Baal-prophesying prophets of Samaria in Jeremiah's eyes. *Sodom . . . Gomorrah.* See Gen. 18–19. **23:15** *Ungodliness.* The Hebrew term

despise the word of the Lord,[y] "It shall be well with you," and to all who stubbornly follow their own stubborn hearts, they say, "No calamity shall come upon you."

18 For who has stood in the council of the
        Lord
    so as to see and to hear his word?
    Who has given heed to his word so as
        to proclaim it?
19 Look, the storm of the Lord!
    Wrath has gone forth,
  a whirling tempest;
    it will burst upon the head of the
        wicked.
20 The anger of the Lord will not turn back
    until he has executed and
        accomplished
    the intents of his mind.
  In the latter days you will understand it
        clearly.

21 I did not send the prophets,
    yet they ran;
  I did not speak to them,
    yet they prophesied.
22 But if they had stood in my council,
    then they would have proclaimed my
        words to my people,
  and they would have turned them from
        their evil way
  and from the evil of their doings.

23 Am I a God near by, says the Lord, and not a God far off? 24Who can hide in secret places so that I cannot see them? says the Lord. Do I not fill heaven and earth? says the Lord. 25I have heard what the prophets have said who prophesy lies in my name, saying, "I have dreamed! I have dreamed!" 26How long? Will the hearts of the prophets ever turn back—those who prophesy lies and who prophesy the deceit of their own heart? 27They plan to make my people forget my name by their dreams that they tell

one another, just as their ancestors forgot my name for Baal. 28Let the prophet who has a dream tell the dream, but let the one who has my word speak my word faithfully. What has straw in common with wheat? says the Lord. 29Is not my word like fire, says the Lord, and like a hammer that breaks a rock in pieces? 30See, therefore, I am against the prophets, says the Lord, who steal my words from one another. 31See, I am against the prophets, says the Lord, who use their own tongues and say, "Says the Lord." 32See, I am against those who prophesy lying dreams, says the Lord, and who tell them and who lead my people astray by their lies and their recklessness, when I did not send them or command them, so they do not profit this people at all, says the Lord.

33 When this people or a prophet or a priest asks you, "What is the burden of the Lord?" you shall say to them, "You are the burden.[z] I will cast you off, says the Lord." 34And as for the prophet, priest, or the people who say, "The burden of the Lord," I will punish them and their households. 35Thus shall you say to one another, among yourselves, "What has the Lord answered?" or "What has the Lord spoken?" 36But "the burden of the Lord" you shall mention no more, for the burden is everyone's own word, and so you pervert the words of the living God, the Lord of hosts, our God. 37Thus you shall ask the prophet, "What has the Lord answered you?" or "What has the Lord spoken?" 38But if you say, "the burden of the Lord," thus says the Lord: Because you have said these words, "the burden of the Lord," when I sent to you, saying, "You shall not say, 'the burden of the Lord,'" 39therefore, I will surely lift you up[a] and cast you away from my presence, you and the city that I gave to you and your ancestors. 40And I will bring upon you everlasting disgrace and perpetual shame that shall not be forgotten.

y 23.17 Gk Syr: Heb *despise me, the* Lord *has spoken*
z 23.33 Heb ms Gk Syr: MT *What burden?*   a 23.39 Heb mss Gk Vg: MT *forget you*

occurs only here in the Hebrew Bible. **23:18** *Council of the* Lord—that is, the heavenly divine council where the prophetic word originates (cf. 1 Kgs. 22:19–23; Isa. 6:1–8). **23:21** YHWH is explicit in saying that these false prophets were not authorized to speak on behalf of YHWH. The imagery suggests that of the royal messenger speaking on behalf of a king. **23:25** *Dreamed.* Dreams are considered a common form of divine communication. In these verses, however, the dreams are nonrevelatory. **23:33** *Burden of the* Lord seems to connote an oracle of doom. **23:39–40** As a result of listening to these deceptive voices, the people and the land are not only destroyed but an *everlasting disgrace and perpetual shame*, noting the long-term damage that is done and the public humiliation associated with defeat.

24

The LORD showed me two baskets of figs placed before the temple of the LORD. This was after King Nebuchadrezzar of Babylon had taken into exile from Jerusalem King Jeconiah son of Jehoiakim of Judah, together with the officials of Judah, the artisans, and the smiths, and had brought them to Babylon. ²One basket had very good figs, like first-ripe figs, but the other basket had very bad figs, so bad that they could not be eaten. ³And the LORD said to me, "What do you see, Jeremiah?" I said, "Figs—the good figs very good and the bad figs very bad, so bad that they cannot be eaten."

4 Then the word of the LORD came to me: ⁵Thus says the LORD, the God of Israel: Like these good figs, so I will regard as good the exiles from Judah whom I have sent away from this place to the land of the Chaldeans. ⁶I will set my eyes upon them for good, and I will bring them back to this land. I will build them up and not tear them down; I will plant them and not pluck them up. ⁷I will give them a heart to know that I am the LORD, and they will be my people, and I will be their God, for they will return to me with their whole heart.

8 But thus says the LORD: Like the bad figs that are so bad they cannot be eaten, so will I treat King Zedekiah of Judah, his officials, the remnant of Jerusalem who remain in this land, and those who live in the land of Egypt. ⁹I will make them a horror, an evil thing, to all the kingdoms of the earth—a disgrace, a byword, a taunt, and a curse in all the places where I shall drive them. ¹⁰And I will send sword, famine, and pestilence upon them until they are utterly destroyed from the land that I gave to them and their ancestors.

25

The word that came to Jeremiah concerning all the people of Judah, in the fourth year of King Jehoiakim son of Josiah of Judah (that was the first year of King Nebuchadrezzar of Babylon), ²which the prophet Jeremiah spoke to all the people of Judah and all the inhabitants of Jerusalem: ³For twenty-three years, from the thirteenth year of King Josiah son of Amon of Judah to this day, the word of the LORD has come to me, and I have spoken persistently to you, but you have not listened. ⁴And though the LORD persistently sent you all his servants the prophets, you have neither listened nor inclined your ears to hear ⁵when they said, "Turn now, every one of you, from your evil way and wicked doings, and you will remain

24:1-4 This vision uses baskets of figs as symbolic representations of groups of people. YHWH shows Jeremiah the vision and then explains its significance for helping him reflect on people who are exiled in Babylonia and those who do not go into exile. See **"Symbolic Actions," p. 1056**. 24:1 Jeconiah is an alternate spelling for Jehoiachin.

24:5-6 The good figs symbolize people who are sent away from Judah into Babylonia. Their exile will be temporary, and they are promised to return to the land.

24:7 *I will give them a heart to know* and *they will be my people, and I will be their God* are statements using covenantal language. This language confirms the special, legally binding relationship between YHWH and the people of Israel and Judah. The *heart* (Heb. "leb") was considered the center of thinking in ancient Israel (rather than the center of feeling, as it is often used today). These formulaic statements and images are reused throughout Jeremiah and are central to the prophet's theology and understanding of the events before, during, and after exile (cf. Jer. 7:23; 11:4; 30:22; 31:1, 33-34; 32:38-39).

24:8 The bad figs symbolize people who remain in Judah or travel to Egypt during the exile, and King Zedekiah and his officials are highlighted in this category, showing the disdain for them held by many Judeans.

24:9-10 The recurring curses appear here reiterating that failed leadership is one of the contributing factors causing the exile. The destruction of the kingdom brings chaos into the land, which has physical and psychological impacts, as the people are considered a disgrace. The triad of curses—sword, famine, and pestilence—shows the multidimensional aspects of destruction.

25:1-7 Like many chapters, Jer. 25 has a mix of prose narratives that help situate the historical context and poetic prophetic oracles that reflect on the realities of the time. The opening verses situate Jeremiah's prophecies in this chapter to the fourth year of the reign of King Jehoiakim (ca. 609-598 BCE) of Judah and the first year of the reign of King Nebuchadrezzar of Babylon. The Babylonian exile is explained as a punishment orchestrated by YHWH because the Judeans have repeatedly failed to listen to and follow divine teachings and laws.

on the land that the LORD has given to you and your ancestors from of old and forever; [6]do not go after other gods to serve and worship them, and do not provoke me to anger with the work of your hands. Then I will do you no harm." [7]Yet you did not listen to me, says the LORD, and so you have provoked me to anger with the work of your hands to your own harm.

8 Therefore thus says the LORD of hosts: Because you have not obeyed my words, [9]I am going to send for all the tribes of the north, says the LORD, even for King Nebuchadrezzar of Babylon, my servant, and I will bring them against this land and its inhabitants and against all these nations around; I will utterly destroy them and make them an object of horror and of hissing and an everlasting disgrace.[b] [10]And I will banish from them the sound of mirth and the sound of gladness, the voice of the bridegroom and the voice of the bride, the sound of the millstones and the light of the lamp. [11]This whole land shall become a ruin and a waste, and these nations shall serve the king of Babylon seventy years. [12]Then after seventy years are completed, I will punish the king of Babylon and that nation, the land of the Chaldeans, for their iniquity, says the LORD, making the land an everlasting waste. [13]I will bring upon that land all the words that I have uttered against it, everything written in this book that Jeremiah prophesied against all the nations. [14]For many nations and great kings shall make slaves of them also, and I will repay them according to their deeds and the work of their hands.

15 For thus the LORD, the God of Israel, said to me: Take from my hand this cup of the wine of wrath, and make all the nations to whom I send you drink it. [16]They shall drink and stagger and go out of their minds because of the sword that I am sending among them.

17 So I took the cup from the LORD's hand and made all the nations to whom the LORD sent me drink it: [18]Jerusalem and the towns of Judah, its kings and officials, to make them a desolation and a waste, an object of hissing and of cursing, as they are today; [19]Pharaoh king of Egypt, his servants, his officials, and all his people; [20]all the mixed people;[c] all the kings of the land of Uz; all the kings of the land of the Philistines—Ashkelon, Gaza, Ekron, and the remnant of Ashdod; [21]Edom, Moab, and the Ammonites; [22]all the kings of Tyre, all the kings of Sidon, and the kings of the coastland across the sea; [23]Dedan, Tema, Buz, and all who have shaved temples; [24]all the kings of Arabia and all the kings of the mixed peoples[d] that live in the desert; [25]all the kings of Zimri, all the kings of Elam, and all the kings of Media; [26]all the kings of the north, far and near, one after another, and all the kingdoms of the world that are on the

b 25.9 Gk Compare Syr: Heb *and everlasting desolations*
c 25.20 Meaning of Heb uncertain   d 25.24 Meaning of Heb uncertain

25:8–14 The fall of the Judean kingdom, the destruction of the temple, and the Babylonian exile were devastating events. The book of Jeremiah tries to rationalize such catastrophes, offering theological explanations for historical realities. These verses frame destructions as embarrassing divine punishments brought on by human misdeeds. **25:9** The Babylonian king Nebuchadrezzar (also spelled Nebuchadnezzar) is called YHWH's servant, indicating that he is an instrument for divine retribution. This is similar to Isa. 45:1–7, in which the Persian king Cyrus is called YHWH's "anointed," as the end of the Babylonian exile occurs under his reign. **25:11** The length of the exile is said to be seventy years (see also Jer. 29:10), which is not likely the exact time spent in exile. The time under Babylonian siege and exile might have been sixty-six years (605–539 BCE), so the seventy years might be rounding up. The length of seventy years could also be symbolic of a full lifetime or generation that endured exile. Expressing a precise end time could be interpreted as offering hope that the period of domination was fixed and limited.

25:15–29 God's out-of-control anger is highlighted in these verses, as punishment is imagined as a metaphorical poisonous cup of wine that causes intoxication. The book of Ezekiel uses similar imagery to describe punishment. The graphic text depicts people being forced to consume the laced beverage, which is symbolic of devastation and destruction that is hard to swallow. The surrounding peoples are also targeted along with Judah. **25:20, 23–24** Several groups are noted for their physical and ethnic differences, such as the ones with shaved temples and mixed peoples. Mixed peoples are likely groups of diverse cultural and ethnic backgrounds living in Egypt and Arabia. **25:26** *Sheshach.* A cryptogram for Babylon using a technique known as athbash, in which letters are used in reverse alphabetic order (i.e., a = z, b = y, etc.).

face of the earth. And after them the king of Sheshach[e] shall drink.

27 Then you shall say to them, Thus says the Lord of hosts, the God of Israel: Drink; get drunk and vomit; fall and rise no more because of the sword that I am sending among you.

28 And if they refuse to accept the cup from your hand to drink, then you shall say to them: Thus says the Lord of hosts: You must drink! 29See, I am beginning to bring disaster on the city that is called by my name, and how can you possibly avoid punishment? You shall not go unpunished, for I am summoning a sword against all the inhabitants of the earth, says the Lord of hosts.

30 You, therefore, shall prophesy to them all these words and say to them:

The Lord will roar from on high
    and from his holy habitation utter his
      voice;
he will roar mightily against his fold
    and shout like those who tread grapes
    against all the inhabitants of the
      earth.
31 The clamor will resound to the ends of
      the earth,
    for the Lord has an indictment against
      the nations;
he is entering into judgment with all flesh,
    and the guilty he will put to the
      sword,

                  says the Lord.

32 Thus says the Lord of hosts:
See, disaster is spreading
    from nation to nation,
and a great tempest is stirring
    from the farthest parts of the earth!

33 Those slain by the Lord on that day shall extend from one end of the earth to the other. They shall not be lamented or gathered or buried; they shall become dung on the surface of the ground.

34 Wail, you shepherds, and cry out;
    roll in ashes, you lords of the flock,
for the days of your slaughter have
      come—and your dispersions,[f]
and you shall fall like a choice vessel.
35 Flight shall fail the shepherds,
    and there shall be no escape for the
      lords of the flock.
36 Listen! The cry of the shepherds
    and the wail of the lords of the flock!
For the Lord is despoiling their pasture,
37   and the peaceful folds are devastated
    because of the fierce anger of the
      Lord.
38 Like a lion he has left his den,
    for their land has become a waste
because of the cruel anger
    and because of his fierce anger.

26 At the beginning of the reign of King Jehoiakim son of Josiah of Judah, this word came from the Lord: 2Thus says the Lord: Stand in the court of the Lord's house and speak to all the cities of Judah that come to worship in the house of the Lord; speak to them all the words that I command you; do not hold back a word. 3It may be that they will listen and will turn from their evil way, that I may change my mind about the disaster that I intend to bring on them because of their evil doings. 4You shall say to them: Thus says the Lord: If you will not listen to me, to walk in my law that I have set before you 5and to heed the words of my servants the prophets whom I send to you urgently—though you have not heeded—6then I will make this house like Shiloh, and I will make this city a curse for all the nations of the earth.

7 The priests and the prophets and all the people heard Jeremiah speaking these words in the house of the Lord. 8And when Jeremiah had finished speaking all that the Lord had

e 25.26 That is, Babylon   f 25.34 Meaning of Heb uncertain

25:30–38 Divine destruction is compared to a lion roaring, imagery that heightens the intensity of YHWH's anger and the fear the people should feel over their destruction. **25:33** The recurring curse that the people will not be lamented, gathered, or buried occurs here (cf. Jer. 8:1–2; 9:22; 16:4). **26:1–24** Much of this chapter mirrors the temple sermon of Jer. 7, especially the location at the temple and the call for repentance. The sequence of events is out of order with the previous chapters, as this is located during the reign of Jehoiakim. **26:2–8** Jeremiah prophesies against the temple and the city of Jerusalem, saying that they will be destroyed. **26:3** *I may change my mind* suggests YHWH might call off the national disaster; cf. Jer. 18:8. **26:6** *Shiloh.* Cf. Jer. 7:12, 14. **26:8** *You shall die!* In response to Jeremiah's prophecy, priests and prophets insist that he should be sentenced to death. This might be because they seek to impose the penalty for presumptuous prophecy in Deut. 18:20 or

commanded him to speak to all the people, then the priests and the prophets and all the people laid hold of him, saying, "You shall die! [9]Why have you prophesied in the name of the LORD, saying, 'This house shall be like Shiloh, and this city shall be desolate, without inhabitant'?" And all the people gathered around Jeremiah in the house of the LORD.

10 When the officials of Judah heard these things, they came up from the king's house to the house of the LORD and took their seat in the entry of the New Gate of the LORD. [11]Then the priests and the prophets said to the officials and to all the people, "This man deserves the sentence of death because he has prophesied against this city, as you have heard with your own ears."

12 Then Jeremiah spoke to all the officials and all the people, saying, "It is the LORD who sent me to prophesy against this house and this city all the words you have heard. [13]Now therefore amend your ways and your doings, and obey the voice of the LORD your God, and the LORD will change his mind about the disaster that he has pronounced against you. [14]But as for me, here I am in your hands. Do with me as seems good and right to you. [15]Only know for certain that if you put me to death, you will be bringing innocent blood upon yourselves and upon this city and its inhabitants, for in truth the LORD sent me to you to speak all these words in your ears."

16 Then the officials and all the people said to the priests and the prophets, "This man does not deserve the sentence of death, for he has spoken to us in the name of the LORD our God." [17]And some of the elders of the land arose and said to all the assembled people, [18]"Micah of Moresheth, who prophesied during the days of King Hezekiah of Judah, said to all the people of Judah: 'Thus says the LORD of hosts,

Zion shall be plowed as a field;
    Jerusalem shall become a heap of ruins
        and the mountain of the house a
            wooded height.'

[19]"Did King Hezekiah of Judah and all Judah actually put him to death? Did he not fear the LORD and entreat the favor of the LORD, and did not the LORD change his mind about the disaster that he had pronounced against them? But we are about to bring great disaster on ourselves!"

20 There was another man prophesying in the name of the LORD, Uriah son of Shemaiah from Kiriath-jearim. He prophesied against this city and against this land in words exactly like those of Jeremiah. [21]And when King Jehoiakim, with all his warriors and all the officials, heard his words, the king sought to put him to death, but when Uriah heard of it, he was afraid and fled and escaped to Egypt. [22]Then King Jehoiakim sent[g] Elnathan son of Achbor and men with him to Egypt, [23]and they took Uriah from Egypt and brought him to King Jehoiakim, who struck him down with the sword and threw his dead body into the burial place of the common people.

24 But the hand of Ahikam son of Shaphan was with Jeremiah so that he was not given over into the hands of the people to be put to death.

27 In the beginning of the reign of King Zedekiah[b] son of Josiah of Judah, this word came to Jeremiah from the LORD. [2]Thus

g 26.22 Heb adds *men to Egypt*   b 27.1 Heb mss Syr: MT *Jehoiakim*

because they think he is guilty of treason (or both). **26:10** This appears to be a trial scene in which officials are seated in the *New Gate*. Gates are commonly depicted as locations for judicial proceedings in the biblical literature (cf. Isa. 29:21; Amos 5:12, 15; Zech. 8:16). **26:15** Jeremiah insists on his innocence and affirms the divine origins of his prophecies. **26:18–23** Two prophets are highlighted who delivered prophecies of judgment, Micah of Moresheth and Uriah of Kiriath-jearim. Micah prophesied before Jeremiah during the reign of Hezekiah. His prophecies (found within the book of Micah) did not result in his death. He is used here as a precedent not to kill a prophet because of his prophecies. Yet Uriah the prophet was put to death during the reign of Jehoiakim. The story of Uriah, who would be a contemporary of Jeremiah, shows the risks associated with prophesying at this time. **26:18** *Zion shall be plowed as a field.* The quotation is from Mic. 3:12. This is the only case in the Hebrew Bible of one prophetic book quoting from another by name. **26:21** *Escaped to Egypt.* Jeremiah himself will be forcibly taken to Egypt later (cf. Jer. 43:6–7). **26:24** *Ahikam*, a royal official, intercedes on behalf of Jeremiah and ensures his safety during this precarious situation. The Shaphan family from which Ahikam came was a powerful, elite family in the latter years of Judah's existence (cf. 2 Kgs. 22). **27:1–22** This chapter is set during the reign of Zedekiah, and it includes another sign act.

the Lord said to me: Make for yourself yoke straps and bars and put them on your neck. ³Send them to the king of Edom, the king of Moab, the king of the Ammonites, the king of Tyre, and the king of Sidon by the hand of the envoys who have come to Jerusalem to King Zedekiah of Judah. ⁴Give them this charge for their masters: Thus says the Lord of hosts, the God of Israel: This is what you shall say to your masters: ⁵It is I who by my great power and my outstretched arm have made the earth, with the people and animals that are on the earth, and I give it to whomever I please. ⁶Now I have given all these lands into the hand of King Nebuchadnezzar of Babylon, my servant, and I have given him even the wild animals of the field to serve him. ⁷All the nations shall serve him and his son and his grandson, until the time of his own land comes; then many nations and great kings shall make him their slave.

8 But if any nation or kingdom will not serve this king, Nebuchadnezzar of Babylon, and put its neck under the yoke of the king of Babylon, then I will punish that nation with the sword, with famine, and with pestilence, says the Lord, until I have completed its destruction by his hand. ⁹You, therefore, must not listen to your prophets, your diviners, your dreamers,ⁱ your soothsayers, or your sorcerers, who are saying to you, "You shall not serve the king of Babylon." ¹⁰For they are prophesying a lie to you, with the result that you will be removed far from your land; I will drive you out, and you will perish. ¹¹But any

nation that will bring its neck under the yoke of the king of Babylon and serve him, I will leave on its own land, says the Lord, to till it and to live there.

12 I spoke to King Zedekiah of Judah in the same way: Bring your necks under the yoke of the king of Babylon, and serve him and his people, and live. ¹³Why should you and your people die by the sword, by famine, and by pestilence, as the Lord has spoken concerning any nation that will not serve the king of Babylon? ¹⁴Do not listen to the words of the prophets who are saying to you, "You shall not serve the king of Babylon," for they are prophesying a lie to you. ¹⁵I have not sent them, says the Lord, but they are prophesying falsely in my name, with the result that I will drive you out, and you will perish, you and the prophets who are prophesying to you.

16 Then I spoke to the priests and to all this people, saying, Thus says the Lord: Do not listen to the words of your prophets who are prophesying to you, saying, "The vessels of the Lord's house will soon be brought back from Babylon," for they are prophesying a lie to you. ¹⁷Do not listen to them; serve the king of Babylon and live. Why should this city become a desolation? ¹⁸If indeed they are prophets and the word of the Lord is with them, then let them intercede with the Lord of hosts, that the vessels left in the house of the Lord, in the house of the king of Judah, and in Jerusalem may not go to Babylon. ¹⁹For thus says the Lord of hosts concerning

i 27.9 Gk Syr Tg: Heb *dreams*

Jeremiah is instructed to put a yoke of straps and bars on his neck to encourage the king to prepare to be yoked under Babylonian authority. See **"Symbolic Actions," p. 1056**. Yokes were commonly used to bind and control animals, especially in agricultural contexts, as well as prisoners. **27:3** Jeremiah's yoke sends a message to the political leaders of the surrounding kingdoms. **27:5** YHWH asserts authority over all the kingdoms of the earth, not just Judah. **27:6** Nebuchadnezzar is again called YHWH's servant (see Jer. 25:9). This depiction of the Babylonian king suggests that the successful expansion of the Neo-Babylonian Empire was divinely ordained retribution against Judah. **27:9** Other kingdoms had their own intermediaries who counseled their kings. **27:11** *I will leave on its own land*—that is, they will not suffer exile. **27:12–15** Jeremiah turns his attention to Judah and Jerusalem, encouraging King Zedekiah not to listen to prophets who speak favorably about the outcome. Again, Jeremiah insists that Zedekiah's only path to survival is to surrender to the Babylonians. **27:14** *They are prophesying a lie to you* is a common refrain in Jeremiah; see Jer. 5:31; 14:14; 20:6; 23:14, 25; etc. **27:15** *I have not sent them*—unlike Jeremiah (26:12). **27:16–22** Jeremiah turns his attention to *the priests and to all this people*, delivering the same message that his prophetic opponents are wrong. **27:18** *Let them intercede.* Jeremiah points to another important role the prophetic intermediary should play: intercessor. YHWH earlier told him not to intercede on behalf of the people (Jer. 7:16). **27:19–22** The kingdom will fall, and the sacred items of the temple will be looted, shattered, and taken to Babylon. Capturing sacred items used in temples was common in ancient warfare. **27:19** *Pillars, the sea, the stands, and the rest of the vessels.* Sacred items associated with

the pillars, the sea, the stands, and the rest of the vessels that are left in this city, ²⁰which King Nebuchadnezzar of Babylon did not take away when he took into exile from Jerusalem to Babylon King Jeconiah son of Jehoiakim of Judah and all the nobles of Judah and Jerusalem—²¹thus says the LORD of hosts, the God of Israel, concerning the vessels left in the house of the LORD, in the house of the king of Judah, and in Jerusalem: ²²They shall be carried to Babylon, and there they shall stay, until the day when I give attention to them, says the LORD. Then I will bring them up and restore them to this place.

28 In that same year, at the beginning of the reign of King Zedekiah of Judah, in the fifth month of the fourth year, the prophet Hananiah son of Azzur, from Gibeon, spoke to me in the house of the LORD, in the presence of the priests and all the people, saying, ²"Thus says the LORD of hosts, the God of Israel: I have broken the yoke of the king of Babylon. ³Within two years I will bring back to this place all the vessels of the LORD's house, which King Nebuchadnezzar of Babylon took away from this place and carried to Babylon. ⁴I will also bring back to this place King Jeconiah son of Jehoiakim of Judah and all the exiles from Judah who went to Babylon, says the LORD, for I will break the yoke of the king of Babylon."

5 Then the prophet Jeremiah spoke to the prophet Hananiah in the presence of the priests and all the people who were standing in the house of the LORD, ⁶and the prophet Jeremiah said, "Amen! May the LORD do so; may the LORD fulfill the words that you have prophesied and bring back to this place from Babylon the vessels of the house of the LORD and all the exiles. ⁷But listen now to this word that I speak in your hearing and in the hearing of all the people. ⁸The prophets who preceded you and me from ancient times prophesied war, famine, and pestilence against many countries and great kingdoms. ⁹As for the prophet who prophesies peace, when the word of that prophet comes true, then it will be known that the LORD has truly sent the prophet."

10 Then the prophet Hananiah took the yoke from the neck of the prophet Jeremiah and broke it. ¹¹And Hananiah spoke in the presence of all the people, saying, "Thus says the LORD: This is how I will break the yoke of King Nebuchadnezzar of Babylon from the neck of all the nations within two years." At this, the prophet Jeremiah went his way.

12 Sometime after the prophet Hananiah had broken the yoke from the neck of the prophet Jeremiah, the word of the LORD came to Jeremiah: ¹³Go, tell Hananiah, Thus says the LORD: You have broken wooden bars only to forge iron bars in place of them! ¹⁴For thus says the LORD of hosts, the God of Israel:

the temple. See 1 Kgs. 7:15–37. **27:20** *When he took into exile* refers to the earlier assault on Jerusalem by Nebuchadnezzar in 597 BCE. *King Jeconiah*—that is, Jehoiachin. He was still in Babylon under house arrest several decades later (cf. 2 Kgs. 25:27–30).

28:1–17 Jeremiah faces opposition from the prophet Hananiah about the meaning of the yoke sign act from the previous chapter. The interaction between Jeremiah and Hananiah shows the prophetic conflict that recurs in the book. Such conflict is unsurprising, as Jeremiah prophesies destruction, while Hananiah and other prophets in and around Jerusalem deliver more favorable prophecies. See **"Prophetic Conflict," p. 1079.** **28:1** The Hebrew text appears to be corrupted here, since it leads to a contradictory chronology. The Septuagint does not include *at the beginning of the reign of King Zedekiah* but contains only a reference to the *fourth year*—that is, 594/593 BCE. *Gibeon* is modern el-Jib, about five and a half miles northwest of Jerusalem. *The priests and all the people.* See 27:16–22. **28:2–4** Hananiah, whose name means "YHWH is gracious," prophesies that the yoke of Babylon has been broken and the temple vessels and the exiled king Jehoiachin will be returned from Babylon *within two years*, a very specific and short time frame. **28:6** *Amen! May the LORD do so.* Jeremiah's response might express his real hopes, or more likely, he might be mocking Hananiah. **28:7** *Listen now to this word that I speak.* What follows is not a prophetic oracle but an instruction on how to evaluate prophets and prophecy. **28:8–9** Jeremiah suggests that the prophetic statements of old were primarily condemnations and punishments, while statements of peace, such as those of Hananiah, are only true if they come to pass. Deuteronomy 18:20–22 likely influences these statements, as it gives guidance on assessing the validity of a prophet. **28:10** Hananiah breaks the yoke on Jeremiah's neck. **28:14** Jeremiah delivers a message that, despite Hananiah's breaking

I have put an iron yoke on the neck of all these nations so that they may serve King Nebuchadnezzar of Babylon, and they shall indeed serve him; I have even given him the wild animals. ¹⁵And the prophet Jeremiah said to the prophet Hananiah, "Listen, Hananiah, the LORD has not sent you, and you made this people trust in a lie. ¹⁶Therefore thus says the LORD: I am going to send you off the face of the earth. Within this year you will be dead, for you have spoken rebellion against the LORD."

17 In that same year, in the seventh month, the prophet Hananiah died.

29 These are the words of the letter that the prophet Jeremiah sent from Jerusalem to the remaining elders among the exiles and to the priests, the prophets, and all the people whom Nebuchadnezzar had taken into exile from Jerusalem to Babylon. ²This was after King Jeconiah and the queen mother, the court officials, the leaders of Judah and Jerusalem, the artisans, and the smiths had departed from Jerusalem. ³The letter was sent by the hand of Elasah son of Shaphan and Gemariah son of Hilkiah, whom King Zedekiah of Judah sent to Babylon to King Nebuchadnezzar of Babylon. It said: ⁴Thus says the LORD of hosts, the God of Israel, to all the exiles whom I have sent into exile from Jerusalem to Babylon: ⁵Build houses and live in them; plant gardens and eat what they produce. ⁶Take wives and have sons and daughters; take wives for your sons, and give your daughters in marriage, that they may bear sons and daughters; multiply there, and do not decrease. ⁷But seek the welfare of the city where I have sent you into exile, and pray to the LORD on its behalf, for in its welfare you will find your welfare. ⁸For thus says the LORD of hosts, the God of Israel: Do not let the prophets and the diviners who are among you deceive you, and do not listen to your dreams that you dream, ⁹for it is a lie that they are prophesying to you in my name; I did not send them, says the LORD.

10 For thus says the LORD: Only when Babylon's seventy years are completed will I visit you, and I will fulfill to you my promise and bring you back to this place. ¹¹For surely I know the plans I have for you, says the LORD, plans for your welfare and not for harm, to give you a future with hope. ¹²Then when you call upon me and come and pray to me, I will hear you. ¹³When you search for me, you will find me; if you seek me with all your heart, ¹⁴I will let you find me, says the LORD, and I will restore your fortunes and gather you from all the nations and all the places where I have driven you, says the LORD, and I will bring you back to the place from which I sent you into exile.

15 Because you have said, "The LORD has raised up prophets for us in Babylon," ¹⁶thus says the LORD concerning the king who sits on the throne of David and concerning all the

of the yoke, the yoke of Babylon will remain strong and mighty on the people of Judah. Jeremiah's wooden yoke is "replaced" with an unbreakable iron yoke. **28:16** *Within this year you will be dead.* The death sentence certain leaders sought against Jeremiah in chap. 26 is announced for Hananiah. **28:17** *In the seventh month, the prophet Hananiah died*—that is, two months later. The text implies that YHWH killed him.

29:1–23 Jeremiah addresses a letter to people in exile instructing them to be realistic and recognize that the exile will not end soon. He calls out some of the false prophets by name, asserting that their messages will not match reality. Communication between those in exile and those who remained in Jerusalem and Judah was likely common. The letter was delivered by members of two powerful families: one of Shaphan's sons and one of the high priest Hilkiah's sons. This implies that Jeremiah was supported by important elites. The placement of this chapter after chap. 28 is meant to demonstrate how wrong the prophet Hananiah had been. **29:5–6** Jeremiah urges the exiles to make lives for themselves there because they will not be returning anytime soon. **29:7** *Seek the welfare of the city.* The exiles' success hinges on Babylon's success. **29:8–9** *The prophets and the diviners who are among you* makes clear that the exilic community included intermediaries, some of whom disagreed with Jeremiah. The prophet Ezekiel, Jeremiah's younger contemporary, was taken to Babylon. **29:9** *I did not send them.* Cf. Jer. 23:21, 32; 27:15; 28:15, 16. **29:10** *Babylon's seventy years.* See the note on 25:11. *Bring you back to this place*—that is, the return from exile will occur but not for a long time. **29:11** *Plans for your welfare and not for harm.* YHWH intends for the exiles to prosper while in exile—that is, it will not be a place of desolation. **29:16–20** These verses are not

people who live in this city, your kinsfolk who did not go out with you into exile: [17]Thus says the LORD of hosts: I am going to let loose on them sword, famine, and pestilence, and I will make them like rotten figs that are so bad they cannot be eaten. [18]I will pursue them with the sword, with famine, and with pestilence and will make them a horror to all the kingdoms of the earth, to be an object of cursing and horror and hissing and a derision among all the nations where I have driven them, [19]because they did not heed my words, says the LORD, when I persistently sent to them my servants the prophets, but you would not listen, says the LORD. [20]But now, all you exiles whom I sent away from Jerusalem to Babylon, hear the word of the LORD: [21]Thus says the LORD of hosts, the God of Israel, concerning Ahab son of Kolaiah and Zedekiah son of Maaseiah, who are prophesying a lie to you in my name: I am going to deliver them into the hand of King Nebuchadrezzar of Babylon, and he shall kill them before your eyes. [22]And on account of them this curse shall be used by all the exiles from Judah in Babylon: "The LORD make you like Zedekiah and Ahab, whom the king of Babylon roasted in the fire," [23]because they have perpetrated outrage in Israel and have committed adultery with their neighbors' wives and have spoken in my name lying words that I did not command them; I am the one who knows and bears witness, says the LORD.

[24]To Shemaiah of Nehelam you shall say: [25]Thus says the LORD of hosts, the God of Israel: In your own name you sent letters to all the people who are in Jerusalem and to the priest Zephaniah son of Maaseiah and to all the priests, saying, [26]The LORD himself has made you priest instead of the priest Jehoiada, so that there may be officers in the house of the LORD to control any madman who plays the prophet, to put him in the stocks and the collar. [27]So now why have you not rebuked Jeremiah of Anathoth, who plays the prophet for you? [28]For he has actually sent to us in Babylon, saying, "It will be a long time; build houses and live in them, and plant gardens and eat what they produce."

29 The priest Zephaniah read this letter in the hearing of the prophet Jeremiah. [30]Then the word of the LORD came to Jeremiah: [31]Send to all the exiles, saying, Thus says the LORD concerning Shemaiah of Nehelam: Because Shemaiah has prophesied to you, though I did not send him, and has led you to trust in a lie, [32]therefore thus says the LORD: I am going to punish Shemaiah of Nehelam and his descendants; he shall not have anyone living among this people to see[j] the good that I am going to do to my people, says the LORD, for he has spoken rebellion against the LORD.

30

The word that came to Jeremiah from the LORD: [2]Thus says the LORD, the God of Israel: Write in a book all the words that I have spoken to you. [3]For the days are surely coming, says the LORD, when I will restore the fortunes of my people, Israel and Judah, says the LORD, and I will bring them back to the land that I gave to their ancestors, and they shall take possession of it.

4 These are the words that the LORD spoke concerning Israel and Judah:

[5] Thus says the LORD:
We have heard a cry of panic,
   of terror, and no peace.
[6] Ask now and see:
   Can a man bear a child?
Why then do I see every man
   with his hands on his loins like a
      woman in labor?
Why has every face turned pale?

j 29.32 Gk: Heb *and he shall not see*

in the Septuagint. The text seems to read more smoothly without them. **29:17** *Rotten figs.* Cf. Jer. 24:8–10. **29:21** *Ahab* and *Zedekiah* are two prophets among the exiles in Babylon. Nothing more is known about them.

29:24–32 In a second letter, another prophet in Babylon, Shemaiah, is condemned for countering Jeremiah's message to the exiles. He had sent letters to the community in Jerusalem designed to silence Jeremiah. See **"Prophetic Conflict," p. 1079**. **29:25** *Zephaniah.* Cf. Jer. 21:1. **29:26** *Madman.* An unflattering term used for other prophets (2 Kgs. 9:11; Hos. 9:7). **29:31** *Shemaiah* is condemned for his actions, as YHWH declares he did not send him. He and his descendants would feel divine wrath for his deception.

30:1–31:40 The texts of Jer. 30–31 (sometimes Jer. 30–33) are often read as a collection of prose and poetic texts about hope and salvation after the exile. These texts are sometimes called the Book of Consolation, Comfort, or Restoration. **30:1–9** *Book,* better "scroll" (cf. Jer. 25:13; 36:2), for

Making Connections: Prophetic Conflict (Jeremiah 29)

Prophecy in ancient Israel was inherently contentious. Prophets claimed to receive messages from deities, but no visible or audible evidence existed to justify their claims. When a prophet exclaimed "thus says the LORD," the audience could either trust or distrust, but immediate proof that the prophet had, in fact, received a message from their god could not be marshaled. Because prophetic messages often involved some element of prediction—even if only about what was to happen in the near term—audiences sought confirmation, but none was usually forthcoming. Consequently, prophets spoke conflicting messages. While it was not surprising that prophets speaking in the name of different deities (e.g., YHWH and Baal) differed, in the Hebrew Bible, prophets who exclaimed messages from YHWH did not always agree.

Conflict among prophets who announced contradictory messages from YHWH was common. The Hebrew Bible usually only preserves one side of these scenarios. For example, prophetic "winners" are those for whom books are named, persons like Jeremiah or Ezekiel. The prophecies announced by their opponents are only known to the extent that they have been preserved in these books. Unsurprisingly, the rhetoric about prophetic opposition is not neutral or disinterested. On the contrary, it is polemical and designed to delegitimize prophets whose prophecies differed from their own. They prophesy lies (Jer. 5:31; 14:14; 20:6; 23:25, 26, 32; 27:10, 14, 16; 29:9, 21, 31) and are not sent from the Lord (e.g., 14:14). Furthermore, they are charged with prophesying only for personal financial gain and tailoring messages to their audience's wishes (Mic. 3:5). Such language suggests these prophets were actively deceptive and immoral, but the reality was more complex.

The book of Jeremiah includes several passages outlining his conflict with other prophets of YHWH. For example, in 29:24–32, Jeremiah denounces Shemaiah (whose name means "the Lord has heard"), a prophet among the exiles in Babylon. Jeremiah had sent a letter to the Judean exiles in Babylon advising them to settle down and make a life for themselves there; they should not expect to return to Judah soon (29:1–23). In response, Shemaiah sent a letter to the Jerusalem priests objecting to Jeremiah's message and asking why they had not silenced him. When Jeremiah learned of this, he proclaimed a prophetic oracle denouncing Shemaiah as an illegitimate prophet. Both were prophets of YHWH, but they had decidedly different prophetic understandings of the duration of the exile. This undoubtedly created problems for the community as they tried to discern YHWH's will. Unfortunately, prophetic agreement proved illusory.

J. Todd Hibbard

---

⁷ Alas! that day is so great
 there is none like it;
it is a time of distress for Jacob,
 yet he shall be rescued from it.

8 On that day, says the LORD of hosts, I will break his yoke from off your neck, and I will burst your bonds, and strangers shall no more make a servant of him. ⁹But they shall serve the LORD their God and David their king, whom I will raise up for them.

¹⁰ But as for you, have no fear, my servant
 Jacob, says the LORD,
 and do not be dismayed, O Israel,
for I am going to save you from far
 away

and your offspring from the land of
 their captivity.
Jacob shall return and have quiet and ease,
 and no one shall make him afraid.
¹¹ For I am with you, says the LORD, to save
 you;
I will make an end of all the nations
 among which I scattered you,
 but of you I will not make an end.
I will chastise you in just measure,
 and I will by no means leave you
 unpunished.

¹² For thus says the LORD:
Your hurt is incurable;
 your wound is grievous.

---

future consultation. **30:8** *I will break his yoke.* The divine judgment and exile will come to an end. **30:9** *David their king* envisions a restoration of the Davidic dynasty (cf. 23:5–6; 33:15–22). **30:10–24** The end of the exile is described, as the people who were scattered will return. **30:10** *Have no fear* is a phrase used numerous times by the anonymous exilic prophet whose words are preserved in Isa. 40–55. *My servant Jacob.* A phrase used only by exilic-period prophets. **30:11** *In just measure*

¹³ There is no one to uphold your cause,
   no medicine for your wound,
   no healing for you.
¹⁴ All your lovers have forgotten you;
   they care nothing for you,
for I have dealt you the blow of an
      enemy,
   the punishment of a merciless foe,
because your guilt is great,
   because your sins are so
      numerous.
¹⁵ Why do you cry out over your hurt?
   Your pain is incurable.
Because your guilt is great,
   because your sins are so numerous,
   I have done these things to you.
¹⁶ Therefore all who devour you shall be
      devoured,
   and all your foes, every one of them,
      shall go into captivity;
those who plunder you shall be
      plundered,
   and all who prey on you I will make a
      prey.
¹⁷ For I will restore health to you,
   and your wounds I will heal,
                        says the LORD,
because they have called you an outcast:
   "It is Zion; no one cares for her!"

¹⁸ Thus says the LORD:
I am going to restore the fortunes of the
      tents of Jacob
   and have compassion on his dwellings;
the city shall be rebuilt upon its
      mound
   and the citadel set on its rightful site.
¹⁹ Out of them shall come thanksgiving
   and the sound of merrymakers.
I will make them many, and they shall
      not be few;
   I will make them honored, and they
      shall not be disdained.

²⁰ Their children shall be as of old;
   their congregation shall be established
      before me,
   and I will punish all who oppress
      them.
²¹ Their prince shall be one of their own;
   their ruler shall come from their
      midst;
I will bring him near, and he shall
      approach me,
   for who would otherwise dare to
      approach me?
                        says the LORD.
²² And you shall be my people,
   and I will be your God.

²³ Look, the storm of the LORD!
   Wrath has gone forth,
   a whirling^k tempest;
   it will burst upon the head of the
      wicked.
²⁴ The fierce anger of the LORD will not turn
      back
   until he has executed and
      accomplished
   the intents of his mind.
In the latter days you will understand
      this.

31 At that time, says the LORD, I will be
   the God of all the families of Israel,
and they shall be my people.
² Thus says the LORD:
The people who survived the sword
   found grace in the wilderness;
when Israel sought for rest,
³   the LORD appeared to him^l from far
      away.^{m}
I have loved you with an everlasting love;
   therefore I have continued my
      faithfulness to you.

k 30.23 Meaning of Heb uncertain   l 31.3 Gk: Heb *me*
m 31.3 Or *to him long ago*

implies that divine judgment has limits and is not just punitive in Jeremiah's view. **30:14** The metaphorical language associated with marriage and infidelity is reversed in the oracle of restoration
as *all your lovers have forgotten you.* This is a reminder that the veneration of other deities in the
past has not served the people well. **30:16** *All who devour you shall be devoured.* A reminder that
the punishers will themselves be punished. Texts like this emphasized that though Babylon had
prevailed over Jerusalem, its victory was temporary. **30:18** Jerusalem will be rebuilt. **30:19** Despite
the looting and plunder that has occurred in Judah, YHWH commits to restoring their fortunes and
sound of joy. The somber and sad atmosphere will be restored to a place of merriment. **30:23–
24** Cf. 23:19–20. The anger of YHWH will not return, as the people are able to return home. *In
the latter days you will understand this.* A recognition that the text is puzzling and enigmatic to
its immediate audience. **31:1–14** The image of restoration is lively, filled with music, dancing, and

⁴ Again I will build you, and you shall be
  built,
    O virgin Israel!
Again you shall adorn yourself with your
  tambourines
and go forth in the dance of the
  merrymakers.
⁵ Again you shall plant vineyards
  on the mountains of Samaria;
the planters shall plant
and shall enjoy the fruit.
⁶ For there shall be a day when sentinels
  will call
  in the hill country of Ephraim:
"Come, let us go up to Zion,
  to the LORD our God."

⁷ For thus says the LORD:
Sing aloud with gladness for Jacob,
  and raise shouts for the chief of the
  nations;
proclaim, give praise, and say,
  "Save, O LORD, your people,
  the remnant of Israel."
⁸ See, I am going to bring them from the
  land of the north
  and gather them from the farthest
  parts of the earth,
among them the blind and the lame,
  those with child and those in labor
  together;
a great company, they shall return here.
⁹ With weeping they shall come,
  and with consolations" I will lead
  them back;
I will let them walk by brooks of water,
  in a straight path where they shall not
  stumble,
for I have become a father to Israel,
  and Ephraim is my firstborn.

¹⁰ Hear the word of the LORD, O nations,
  and declare it in the coastlands far away;

say, "He who scattered Israel will gather
  him
  and will keep him as a shepherd does
  a flock."
¹¹ For the LORD has ransomed Jacob
  and has redeemed him from hands too
  strong for him.
¹² They shall come and sing aloud on the
  height of Zion,
  and they shall be radiant over the
  goodness of the LORD,
over the grain, the wine, and the oil,
  and over the young of the flock and
  the herd;
their life shall become like a watered
  garden,
  and they shall never languish again.
¹³ Then shall the young women rejoice in
  the dance,
  and the young men and the old shall
  be merry.ᵒ
I will turn their mourning into joy;
  I will comfort them and give them
  gladness for sorrow.
¹⁴ I will give the priests their fill of fatness,
  and my people shall be satisfied with
  my bounty,
                            says the LORD.

¹⁵ Thus says the LORD:
A voice is heard in Ramah,
  lamentation and bitter weeping.
Rachel is weeping for her children;
  she refuses to be comforted for her
  children,
  because they are no more.
¹⁶ Thus says the LORD:
Keep your voice from weeping
  and your eyes from tears,
for there is a reward for your work,
                            says the LORD:

n 31.9 Gk: Heb *supplications*   o 31.13 Cn: Heb *old together*

merrymaking as the exiles are depicted returning home. **31:8** When describing who is at this festive community party, a few groups are highlighted—people who have difficulty seeing and walking and women who are pregnant and in labor. The assumption might be that these groups could have difficulty traveling home from exile, so their inclusion highlights God's special care for people in need of assistance. In addition, these groups are sometimes overlooked and excluded from certain actions, so this is a positive step to envision a full community returning home. **31:9–12** Fittingly, the image of restoration uses water imagery, as the people now will enjoy the land that is compared to a watered garden. They are now back in relationship with YHWH, who is living water, so their return gives them water access again. **31:15–26** In the midst of restoration, there are images of sadness, especially with Rachel weeping for her children. Rachel, one of the matriarchs and the mother of Jacob's sons Joseph and Benjamin (see Gen. 30:22–24; 35:16–20), weeps bitterly for her children. The image is

they shall come back from the land of
the enemy;
[17] there is hope for your future,
says the LORD:
your children shall come back to their
own country.

[18] Indeed, I heard Ephraim pleading:
"You disciplined me, and I took the
discipline;
I was like an untrained calf.
Bring me back; let me come back,
for you are the LORD my God.
[19] For after I had turned away I repented,
and after I was discovered, I struck my
thigh;
I was ashamed, and I was dismayed
because I bore the disgrace of my youth."
[20] Is Ephraim my dear son?
Is he the child in whom I delight?
As often as I speak against him,
I still remember him.
Therefore I am deeply moved for him;
I will surely have mercy on him,
says the LORD.

[21] Set up road markers for yourself;
make yourself signposts;
consider well the highway,
the road by which you went.
Return, O virgin Israel,
return to these your cities.
[22] How long will you waver,
O faithless daughter?
For the LORD has created a new thing on
the earth:
a woman encompasses[p] a man.

23 Thus says the LORD of hosts, the God of
Israel: Once more they shall use these words

in the land of Judah and in its towns when I
restore their fortunes:
"The LORD bless you, O abode of
righteousness,
O holy hill!"
[24]And Judah and all its towns shall live there
together, and the farmers and those who
wander with their flocks.
[25] I will satisfy the weary,
and all who are faint I will replenish.
26 Thereupon I awoke and looked, and my
sleep was pleasant to me.
27 The days are surely coming, says the
LORD, when I will sow the house of Israel and
the house of Judah with the seed of humans
and the seed of animals. [28]And just as I have
watched over them to pluck up and break
down, to overthrow, destroy, and bring evil,
so I will watch over them to build and to
plant, says the LORD. [29]In those days they shall
no longer say:
"The parents have eaten sour grapes,
and the children's teeth are set on
edge."
[30]But all shall die for their own sins; the
teeth of the one who eats sour grapes shall
be set on edge.
31 The days are surely coming, says the
LORD, when I will make a new covenant with
the house of Israel and the house of Judah. [32]It
will not be like the covenant that I made with
their ancestors when I took them by the hand
to bring them out of the land of Egypt—a
covenant that they broke, though I was their
husband, says the LORD. [33]But this is the covenant that I will make with the house of Israel
after those days, says the LORD: I will put my
law within them, and I will write it on their

p 31.22 Meaning of Heb uncertain

a reminder that even though restoration is happening, lives have been lost. **31:21–22** The meaning
of *a woman encompasses a man* is difficult and unclear. It might have in mind a woman taking on
authority that would typically belong to a man. It could also mean that the adulterous woman who
abandoned YHWH is replaced with virgin Israel who is devoted to YHWH. **31:26** The vision of restoration is described as a dream, likely to keep the date of the text during Jeremiah's lifetime. It might
be a postexilic text that is already aware of the end of exile and return to Judah. **31:27–40** Echoes
of Jeremiah's call are found, but now the focus shifts to individual action. Restoration also includes
a vision of a rebuilt and expanded Jerusalem. **31:31** Jeremiah's new covenant builds on covenantal
theology in new ways in which there is no longer a central covenantal figure, such as Abraham or
Moses, but rather each individual makes a covenant. This envisions a personal transformation of the
heart (mind), when the covenant is engraved on the heart, an image used earlier in the book. It also
suggests a critique of those charged with teaching the content of the covenant—that is, priests and
prophets. The New Testament includes several references and expansions of this vision of a new
covenant (e.g., Heb. 8:1–13; see **"New Covenant," p. 1083**).

Focus On: New Covenant (Jeremiah 31)

The theme of covenant permeates much of the Hebrew Bible, as the connection between YHWH and the people of Israel and Judah is framed as a sacred, legally binding relationship. In Jeremiah, many oracles of judgment highlight how the people of Judah have broken the covenant because they failed to keep their obligations. In particular, they worshiped other gods and committed social evils against one another.

For centuries, people were selected to facilitate and mediate the covenant on behalf of the community. Noah, Abraham, and Moses are three important covenantal partners. Jeremiah 31 presents a new idea of the covenant that is more personal than the previous covenants: "I will put my law within them, and I will write it on their hearts, and I will be their God, and they shall be my people" (31:33b). This new covenant highlights each individual's ability to understand and follow the law because it is metaphorically inscribed within the heart, which was considered the center of reason and understanding.

In the New Testament, Jeremiah's language of a new covenant is reinterpreted and reframed in light of Jesus. For instance, in Luke's account of the Last Supper, when Jesus takes wine, he says that the cup is the "new covenant in [his] blood" (Luke 22:20; cf. 1 Cor. 11:25). The sermon to the Hebrews, similarly, interprets Jesus as the mediator of a new covenant, quoting Jer. 31:31–34 and encouraging listeners to connect Jeremiah's six-hundred-year-old prophecy with Jesus. Hebrews states that the new covenant makes the old covenant obsolete in order to affirm the significance of Jesus and his ministry (Heb. 8:6–7, 13). It is important to recognize that the language of a new covenant does not mean that the old covenant is superseded. The long-standing covenantal relationship with the ancestors and people of Israel and Judah is not eliminated. Instead, Jeremiah offers, for Jewish and Christian communities, more intimate language and imagery for reflecting on the nature of the human-divine relationship.

Jaime L. Waters

hearts, and I will be their God, and they shall be my people. ³⁴No longer shall they teach one another or say to each other, "Know the LORD," for they shall all know me, from the least of them to the greatest, says the LORD, for I will forgive their iniquity and remember their sin no more.

³⁵ Thus says the LORD,
who gives the sun for light by day
and the fixed order of the moon and
the stars for light by night,
who stirs up the sea so that its waves roar—
the LORD of hosts is his name:
³⁶ If this fixed order were ever to cease
from my presence, says the LORD,
then also the offspring of Israel would
cease
to be a nation before me forever.

³⁷ Thus says the LORD:
If the heavens above can be measured
and the foundations of the earth
below can be explored,

then I will reject all the offspring of Israel
because of all they have done,
says the LORD.

38 The days are surely coming, says the LORD, when the city shall be rebuilt for the LORD from the tower of Hananel to the Corner Gate. ³⁹And the measuring line shall go out farther, straight to the hill Gareb, and shall then turn to Goah. ⁴⁰The whole valley of the dead bodies and the ashes and all the fields as far as the Wadi Kidron, to the corner of the Horse Gate toward the east, shall be sacred to the LORD. It shall never again be uprooted or overthrown.

32 The word that came to Jeremiah from the LORD in the tenth year of King Zedekiah of Judah, which was the eighteenth year of Nebuchadrezzar. ²At that time the army of the king of Babylon was besieging Jerusalem, and the prophet Jeremiah was confined in the court of the guard that was in the palace of the king of Judah, ³where King Zedekiah of Judah had

32:1–44 The chapter narrates another symbolic act. While in custody, Jeremiah is visited and offered the right to redeem his family field, showing that the land is under threat during the siege on Jerusalem. 32:1 The narrative is set in 588/587 BCE, when the Babylonian siege of Jerusalem had already begun. 32:2 *Court of the guard.* A location in the palace complex where prisoners were held. All references but one to this location occur in Jeremiah (cf. 32:8, 12; 33:1; 37:21; 38:6, 13, 28; 39:14–15; Neh. 3:25). 32:3 *Why do you prophesy?* Zedekiah wants to know why Jeremiah predicts the

confined him. Zedekiah had said, "Why do you prophesy and say: Thus says the Lord: I am going to give this city into the hand of the king of Babylon, and he shall take it; ⁴King Zedekiah of Judah shall not escape out of the hands of the Chaldeans but shall surely be given into the hands of the king of Babylon and shall speak with him face to face and see him eye to eye, ⁵and he shall take Zedekiah to Babylon, and there he shall remain until I attend to him, says the Lord; though you fight against the Chaldeans, you shall not succeed?"

6 Jeremiah said, "The word of the Lord came to me: ⁷Hanamel son of your uncle Shallum is going to come to you and say, 'Buy my field that is at Anathoth, for the right of redemption by purchase is yours.'" ⁸Then my cousin Hanamel came to me in the court of the guard, in accordance with the word of the Lord, and said to me, "Buy my field that is at Anathoth in the land of Benjamin, for the right of possession and redemption is yours; buy it for yourself." Then I knew that this was the word of the Lord.

9 And I bought the field at Anathoth from my cousin Hanamel and weighed out the silver to him, seventeen shekels of silver. ¹⁰I signed the deed, sealed it, got witnesses, and weighed the silver on scales. ¹¹Then I took the sealed deed of purchase containing the terms and conditions and the open copy, ¹²and I gave the deed of purchase to Baruch son of Neriah son of Mahseiah, in the presence of my cousin𝑞 Hanamel, in the presence of the witnesses who signed the deed of purchase, and in the presence of all the Judeans who were sitting in the court of the guard. ¹³In their presence I charged Baruch, saying, ¹⁴"Thus says the Lord of hosts, the God of Israel: Take these deeds, both this sealed deed of purchase and this open deed, and put them in an earthenware jar, in order that they

may last for a long time. ¹⁵For thus says the Lord of hosts, the God of Israel: Houses and fields and vineyards shall again be bought in this land."

16 After I had given the deed of purchase to Baruch son of Neriah, I prayed to the Lord, saying: ¹⁷"Ah Lord God! It is you who made the heavens and the earth by your great power and by your outstretched arm! Nothing is too hard for you. ¹⁸You show steadfast love to the thousandth generation𝑟 but repay the guilt of parents into the laps of their children after them, O great and mighty God whose name is the Lord of hosts, ¹⁹great in counsel and mighty in deed, whose eyes are open to all the ways of mortals, rewarding all according to their ways and according to the fruit of their doings. ²⁰You showed signs and wonders in the land of Egypt and to this day in Israel and among all humankind and have made yourself a name that continues to this very day. ²¹You brought your people Israel out of the land of Egypt with signs and wonders, with a strong hand and outstretched arm, and with great terror, ²²and you gave them this land, which you swore to their ancestors to give them, a land flowing with milk and honey, ²³and they entered and took possession of it. But they did not obey your voice or follow your laws; of all you commanded them to do, they did nothing. Therefore you have made all these disasters come upon them. ²⁴See, the siege ramps have been cast up against the city to take it, and the city, faced with sword, famine, and pestilence, has been given into the hands of the Chaldeans who are fighting against it. What you spoke has happened, as you yourself can see. ²⁵Yet you, O Lord God, have said to me, 'Buy the field for silver and get witnesses,' though the city has been given into the hands of the Chaldeans."

𝑞 32.12 Gk Syr Vg: Heb *my uncle* 𝑟 32.18 Or *to thousands*

city's demise and the king's capture. **32:7** *Anathoth* is Jeremiah's hometown and a source of fierce opposition to him (cf. Jer. 1:1; 11:21, 23). *Right of redemption* was a means to save a family property that could be lost (cf. Lev. 25:25–28). **32:9** *Seventeen shekels* refers to weight, not coins (which were not used until the Persian era). **32:12** Baruch, Jeremiah's scribe, is present to help facilitate and witness the purchase. **32:14** *Sealed deed . . . and this open deed.* Two deeds were prepared. One deed was filed away, and the other was "open" so it could be referenced. **32:15, 44** Purchasing the land serves to save the property. It is also a symbolic act that reveals that the land will still remain after the siege, and it signals that land will be purchased again after the siege. It also proves Jeremiah's ownership should landownership become contested in the aftermath of the Babylonian invasion. **32:16–25** After making the purchase, Jeremiah seeks clarity and understanding. His prayer also revisits past instances of divine salvation and the promise of a land flowing with milk and honey; cf. Neh. 9:6–38. **32:18** Cf. Exod. 34:7.

26 The word of the Lord came to Jeremiah: 27See, I am the Lord, the God of all flesh; is anything too hard for me? 28Therefore, thus says the Lord: I am going to give this city into the hands of the Chaldeans and into the hand of King Nebuchadrezzar of Babylon, and he shall take it. 29The Chaldeans who are fighting against this city shall come, set this city on fire, and burn it, with the houses on whose roofs offerings have been made to Baal and libations have been poured out to other gods, to provoke me to anger. 30For the people of Israel and the people of Judah have done nothing but evil in my sight from their youth; the people of Israel have done nothing but provoke me to anger by the work of their hands, says the Lord. 31This city has aroused my anger and wrath, from the day it was built until this day, so that I will remove it from my sight 32because of all the evil of the people of Israel and the people of Judah that they did to provoke me to anger—they, their kings and their officials, their priests and their prophets, the people of Judah and the inhabitants of Jerusalem. 33They have turned their backs to me, not their faces; though I have taught them persistently, they would not listen and accept correction. 34They set up their abominations in the house that bears my name and defiled it. 35They built the high places of Baal in the valley of the son of Hinnom, to offer up their sons and daughters to Molech, though I did not command them, nor did it enter my mind that they should do this abomination, causing Judah to sin.

36 Now therefore thus says the Lord, the God of Israel, concerning this city of which you say, "It is being given into the hand of the king of Babylon by the sword, by famine, and by pestilence": 37See, I am going to gather them from all the lands to which I drove them in my anger and my wrath and in great indignation; I will bring them back to this place, and I will settle them in safety. 38They shall be my people, and I will be their God. 39I will give them one heart and one way, that they may fear me for all time, for their own good and the good of their children after them. 40I will make an everlasting covenant with them, never to draw back from doing good to them, and I will put the fear of me in their hearts, so that they may not turn from me. 41I will rejoice in doing good to them, and I will plant them in this land in faithfulness, with all my heart and all my soul.

42 For thus says the Lord: Just as I have brought all this great disaster upon this people, so I will bring upon them all the good fortune that I now promise them. 43Fields shall be bought in this land of which you are saying, "It is a desolation, without humans or animals; it has been given into the hands of the Chaldeans." 44Fields shall be bought for silver, and deeds shall be signed and sealed and witnessed in the land of Benjamin, in the places around Jerusalem, and in the cities of Judah, of the hill country, of the Shephelah, and of the Negeb, for I will restore their fortunes, says the Lord.

33

The word of the Lord came to Jeremiah a second time while he was still confined in the court of the guard: 2Thus says the Lord who makes it, the Lord who forms it to establish it—the Lord is his name: 3Call to me, and I will answer you and will tell you great and hidden things that you have not known. 4For thus says the Lord, the God of Israel, concerning the houses of this city and the houses of the kings of Judah that were torn down to make a defense against the siege ramps and before the sword: *s* 5They are coming to fight the Chaldeans and to fill them with the dead bodies of those whom I shall strike down in my anger and my wrath, for I have hidden my face from this city because of all their

s 33.4 Meaning of Heb uncertain

32:34 *Abominations* refers to images and cultic objects associated with other deities. 32:36–44 The message of doom and destruction turns to one of hope and restoration. 32:39–40 Similar to Jer. 31:31, the people are promised restoration and a new covenant, here called an *everlasting covenant* (Heb. "berit olam"). 32:44 The sign act of buying the field is made clear.

33:1–26 This oracle builds on the ideas of hope and healing. Although destruction is depicted in detail, restoration, songs of thanks, and joy and merriment will eventually come. This chapter is significantly shorter in the Septuagint, which could suggest this vision of restoration is a later expansion in the text. 33:2 *It.* Perhaps the earth is intended. 33:4 The stones used for houses in Jerusalem were repurposed to make defensive structures. 33:5 *Fight the Chaldeans . . . I shall strike down.* No distinction

wickedness. [6]I am going to bring it recovery and healing; I will heal them and reveal to them abundance[t] of prosperity and security. [7]I will restore the fortunes of Judah and the fortunes of Israel and rebuild them as they were at first. [8]I will cleanse them from all the guilt of their sin against me, and I will forgive all the guilt of their sin and rebellion against me. [9]And this city[u] shall be to me a name of joy, a praise, and a glory before all the nations of the earth who shall hear of all the good that I do for them; they shall fear and tremble because of all the good and all the prosperity I provide for it.

[10] Thus says the LORD: In this place of which you say, "It is a waste without humans or animals," in the towns of Judah and the streets of Jerusalem that are desolate, without inhabitants, human or animal, there shall once more be heard [11]the voice of mirth and the voice of gladness, the voice of the bridegroom and the voice of the bride, the voices of those who sing as they bring thank offerings to the house of the LORD:

"Give thanks to the LORD of hosts,
    for the LORD is good,
    for his steadfast love endures forever!"
For I will restore the fortunes of the land as at first, says the LORD.

[12] Thus says the LORD of hosts: In this place that is waste, without humans or animals, and in all its towns there shall again be pasture for shepherds resting their flocks. [13]In the towns of the hill country, of the Shephelah, and of the Negeb, in the land of Benjamin, the places around Jerusalem, and in the towns of Judah, flocks shall again pass under the hands of the one who counts them, says the LORD.

[14] The days are surely coming, says the LORD, when I will fulfill the promise I made to the house of Israel and the house of Judah. [15]In those days and at that time I will cause a righteous Branch to spring up for David, and he shall execute justice and righteousness in the land. [16]In those days Judah will be saved, and Jerusalem will live in safety. And this is the name by which it will be called: "The LORD is our righteousness."

[17] For thus says the LORD: David shall never lack a man to sit on the throne of the house of Israel, [18]and the Levitical priests shall never lack a man in my presence to offer burnt offerings, to make grain offerings, and to make sacrifices for all time.

[19] The word of the LORD came to Jeremiah: [20]Thus says the LORD: If any of you could break my covenant with the day and my covenant with the night, so that day and night would not come at their appointed time, [21]only then could my covenant with my servant David be broken, so that he would not have a son to reign on his throne, and my covenant with my ministers the Levites. [22]Just as the host of heaven cannot be numbered and the sands of the sea cannot be measured, so I will increase the offspring of my servant David and the Levites who minister to me.

[23] The word of the LORD came to Jeremiah: [24]Have you not observed how these people say, "The two families that the LORD chose have been rejected by him," and how they hold my people in such contempt that they no longer regard them as a nation? [25]Thus says the LORD: Only if I had not established my covenant with day and night and the ordinances of heaven and earth [26]would I reject the offspring of Jacob and of my servant David and not choose any of his descendants as rulers over the offspring of Abraham, Isaac, and Jacob. For I will restore their fortunes and will have mercy upon them.

34

The word that came to Jeremiah from the LORD, when King Nebuchadrezzar of Babylon and all his army and

---

t 33.6 Meaning of Heb uncertain   *u* 33.9 Heb *And it*

---

is made between the efforts of the Babylonians and YHWH. **33:10–13** The complete destruction of the city and the surrounding land is presumed. **33:14–26** An oracle of salvation, an expansion of Jer. 23:5–6, is given to offer further details about the promised restoration. The covenantal language used in Jeremiah is referenced here in connection to the Davidic covenant, which persists, even without a king in the line of David on the throne. Abraham, Isaac, and Jacob are also invoked, again linking the period of restoration with the covenants of old. **33:17** The hopes for a restoration of the Davidic monarchy continued into the restoration era; cf. Zech. 12:7, 8, 10, 12; 13:1. **33:18** *Levitical priests.* A reference to priests in their association with the Israelite ancestor, Levi; cf. Deut. 18:1–8; 33:8–11. **33:22** A reuse of language from the promise to Abraham in Gen. 22:17–18.

34:1–7 Judgment against Zedekiah. The oracle predicts that Zedekiah will be captured during

all the kingdoms of the earth and all the peoples under his dominion were fighting against Jerusalem and all its cities: ²Thus says the Lord, the God of Israel: Go and speak to King Zedekiah of Judah and say to him: Thus says the Lord: I am going to give this city into the hand of the king of Babylon, and he shall burn it with fire. ³And you yourself shall not escape from his hand but shall surely be captured and handed over to him; you shall see the king of Babylon eye to eye and speak with him face to face, and you shall go to Babylon. ⁴Yet hear the word of the Lord, O King Zedekiah of Judah! Thus says the Lord concerning you: You shall not die by the sword; ⁵you shall die in peace. And as spices were burnedᵛ for your ancestors, the earlier kings who preceded you, so they shall burn spicesʷ for you and lament for you, saying, "Alas, lord!" For I have spoken the word, says the Lord.

6 Then the prophet Jeremiah spoke all these words to Zedekiah king of Judah, in Jerusalem, ⁷when the army of the king of Babylon was fighting against Jerusalem and against all the cities of Judah that were left, Lachish and Azekah, for these were the only fortified cities of Judah that remained.

8 The word that came to Jeremiah from the Lord, after King Zedekiah had made a covenant with all the people in Jerusalem to make a proclamation of liberty to them, ⁹that all should set free their Hebrew slaves, male and female, so that no one should hold another Judean in slavery. ¹⁰And they obeyed, all the officials and all the people who had

entered into the covenant that all would set free their slaves, male or female, so that they would not be enslaved again; they obeyed and set them free. ¹¹But afterward they turned around and took back the male and female slaves they had set free and brought them again into subjection as slaves. ¹²The word of the Lord came to Jeremiah from the Lord: ¹³Thus says the Lord, the God of Israel: I myself made a covenant with your ancestors when I brought them out of the land of Egypt, out of the house of slavery, saying, ¹⁴"Every seventh year each of you must set free any Hebrews who have been sold to you and have served you six years; you must set them free from your service." But your ancestors did not listen to me or incline their ears to me. ¹⁵You yourselves recently repented and did what was right in my sight by proclaiming liberty to one another, and you made a covenant before me in the house that is called by my name, ¹⁶but then you turned around and profaned my name when each of you took back your male and female slaves, whom you had set free according to their desire, and you brought them again into subjection to be your slaves. ¹⁷Therefore, thus says the Lord: You have not obeyed me by granting a release to your neighbors and friends; I am going to grant a release to you, says the Lord—a release to the sword, to pestilence, and to famine. I will make you a horror to all the kingdoms of the earth. ¹⁸And those who transgressed my covenant and did not keep the terms of the covenant that they made

v 34.5 Heb as there was burning   w 34.5 Heb shall burn

the siege on Jerusalem, which is described in Jer. 39:7. Despite his capture, suffering, and exile, he will be mourned with honorary funeral practices. According to Jer. 52:11, Zedekiah was captured, blinded, and taken to Babylon, where he remained imprisoned until his death. **34:7** *Lachish and Azekah* are two towns within eye contact in the Shephelah, southwest of Jerusalem. Both are mentioned in a letter found in Lachish dating to the period of the Babylonian destruction.

34:8–22 The context is still the siege on Jerusalem, and Zedekiah had entered a covenant to free enslaved people in an attempt to gain divine favor and help against the Babylonians. The shift to the practice of slavery, even temporary, offers insight into the cultural context of the passage. The legal corpus has extensive laws regulating slavery and requiring the release from enslavement at appointed times (cf. Exod. 21:2; Deut. 15:1, 12). The act seems to offer temporary help because once the Babylonians lifted the siege, the people re-enslave those who were freed, which is interpreted as a negative and deceptive act. See **"Human Bondage in Ancient Israel," p. 115. 34:8** *To make a proclamation of liberty.* Literally "to proclaim liberty." Cf. Lev. 25:10; Isa. 61:1. **34:14** *Every seventh year.* Cf. Deut. 15:1, 12. **34:15** *You yourselves recently repented* suggests that the covenantal requirement of release from slavery was not being observed. **34:16** Exactly how they *took back* those they had formerly enslaved is not made clear. **34:17** The prophetic message plays on the idea of *release*, in one case to freedom. **34:18–19** In response to their reneging, they are threatened with passing

before me, I will make like[x] the calf when they cut it in two and passed between its parts: [19]the officials of Judah, the officials of Jerusalem, the eunuchs, the priests, and all the people of the land who passed between the parts of the calf [20]shall be handed over to their enemies and to those who seek their lives. Their corpses shall become food for the birds of the air and the wild animals of the earth. [21]And as for King Zedekiah of Judah and his officials, I will hand them over to their enemies and to those who seek their lives, to the army of the king of Babylon, which has withdrawn from you. [22]I am going to command, says the LORD, and will bring them back to this city, and they will fight against it and take it and burn it with fire. The towns of Judah I will make a desolation without inhabitant.

35 The word that came to Jeremiah from the LORD in the days of King Jehoiakim son of Josiah of Judah: [2]Go to the house of the Rechabites, and speak with them, and bring them to the house of the LORD, into one of the chambers; then offer them wine to drink. [3]So I took Jaazaniah son of Jeremiah son of Habazziniah and his brothers and all his sons and the whole house of the Rechabites. [4]I brought them to the house of the LORD into the chamber of the sons of Hanan son of Igdaliah, the man of God, which was near the chamber of the officials, above the chamber of Maaseiah son of Shallum, keeper of the threshold. [5]Then I set before the Rechabites pitchers full of wine and cups, and I said to them, "Have some wine." [6]But they answered, "We will drink no wine, for our ancestor

Jonadab son of Rechab commanded us, 'You shall never drink wine, neither you nor your children, [7]nor shall you ever build a house or sow seed, nor shall you plant a vineyard or even own one, but you shall live in tents all your days, that you may live many days in the land where you reside.' [8]We have obeyed the charge of our ancestor Jonadab son of Rechab in all that he commanded us, to drink no wine all our days, ourselves, our wives, our sons, or our daughters, [9]and not to build houses to live in. We have no vineyard or field or seed, [10]but we have lived in tents and have obeyed and done all that our ancestor Jonadab commanded us. [11]But when King Nebuchadrezzar of Babylon came up against the land, we said, 'Come, and let us go to Jerusalem for fear of the army of the Chaldeans and the army of the Arameans.' That is why we are living in Jerusalem."

12 Then the word of the LORD came to Jeremiah: [13]Thus says the LORD of hosts, the God of Israel: Go and say to the people of Judah and the inhabitants of Jerusalem, Can you not learn a lesson and obey my words? says the LORD. [14]The command has been carried out that Jonadab son of Rechab gave to his descendants to drink no wine, and they drink none to this day, for they have obeyed their ancestor's command. But I myself have spoken to you persistently, and you have not obeyed me. [15]I have sent to you all my servants the prophets, sending them persistently, saying, "Turn now every one of you from your evil way, and amend your doings, and do not go after other gods to serve them, and then

x 34.18 Cn: Heb lacks *like*

between the parts of the calf, which is an allusion to the covenantal ritual of cutting an animal in half and passing through it as a curse if the covenant is broken. The practice occurs in the covenant made between YHWH and Abraham (cf. Gen. 15:7–21). **34:22** *Bring them back* indicates that this took place during a time when the Babylonian army had retreated from Jerusalem, possibly because the Egyptian army had advanced toward the city to provide aid.

35:1–19 This chapter is earlier than the siege described in the previous chapter, as this is set during the reign of Jehoiakim (609–598). The covenantal loyalty of the Rechabites—a nonpriestly religious group who abstained from certain practices, such as drinking alcohol and farming—is invoked. The Rechabites are named after their eponymous founder Rechab, a Kenite whose son Jehonadab was a supporter of Jehu (2 Kgs. 10:15–31). The Rechabites are highlighted here to show how loyalty is rewarded, whereas the disingenuous action of Zedekiah in the previous chapter contributes to the siege. **35:11** As tent-dwelling nomads, their presence in Jerusalem requires an explanation. **35:15** Cf. Jer. 7:3, 5; 18:11; 26:13. **35:17–19** The people once again are reminded that they did not listen, but the Rechabites, on the other hand, obeyed earlier commands and are promised an everlasting place in service of YHWH.

you shall live in the land that I gave to you and your ancestors." But you did not incline your ear or obey me. [16]The descendants of Jonadab son of Rechab have carried out the command that their ancestor gave them, but this people has not obeyed me. [17]Therefore, thus says the LORD, the God of hosts, the God of Israel: I am going to bring on Judah and on all the inhabitants of Jerusalem every disaster that I have pronounced against them, because I have spoken to them and they have not listened, I have called to them and they have not answered.

18 But to the house of the Rechabites Jeremiah said: Thus says the LORD of hosts, the God of Israel: Because you have obeyed the command of your ancestor Jonadab and kept all his precepts and done all that he commanded you, [19]therefore thus says the LORD of hosts, the God of Israel: Jonadab son of Rechab shall not lack a descendant to stand before me for all time.

36 In the fourth year of King Jehoiakim son of Josiah of Judah, this word came to Jeremiah from the LORD: [2]Take a scroll and write on it all the words that I have spoken to you against Israel and Judah and all the nations, from the day I spoke to you, from the days of Josiah until today. [3]It may be that, when the house of Judah hears of all the disasters that I intend to do to them, all of them may turn from their evil ways, so that I may forgive their iniquity and their sin.

4 Then Jeremiah called Baruch son of Neriah, and Baruch wrote on a scroll at Jeremiah's dictation all the words that the LORD had spoken to him. [5]And Jeremiah ordered Baruch, saying, "I am prevented from entering the house of the LORD, [6]so you go, and on a fast day in the hearing of the people in the LORD's house you shall read the words of the LORD from the scroll that you have written at my dictation. You shall read them also in the hearing of all the people of Judah who come up from their towns. [7]It may be that their plea will come before the LORD and that all of them will turn from their evil ways, for great is the anger and wrath that the LORD has pronounced against this people." [8]And Baruch son of Neriah did all that the prophet Jeremiah ordered him about reading from the scroll the words of the LORD in the LORD's house.

9 In the fifth year of King Jehoiakim son of Josiah of Judah, in the ninth month, all the people in Jerusalem and all the people who came from the towns of Judah to Jerusalem proclaimed a fast before the LORD. [10]Then, in the hearing of all the people, Baruch read the words of Jeremiah from the scroll, in the house of the LORD, in the chamber of Gemariah son of Shaphan the secretary, which was in the upper court, at the entry of the New Gate of the LORD's house.

11 When Micaiah son of Gemariah son of Shaphan heard all the words of the LORD from the scroll, [12]he went down to the king's house, into the secretary's chamber, and all the officials were sitting there: Elishama the secretary, Delaiah son of Shemaiah, Elnathan son of Achbor, Gemariah son of Shaphan, Zedekiah son of Hananiah, and all the officials.

36:1–32 The chapter offers insights into how the book of Jeremiah may have been composed and arranged, assuming there might be some historicity embedded within this chapter (see **"Written Prophecy and Scrolls," p. 1090**). The two scrolls of Baruch might speak to at least two versions or editions of Jeremiah. There are similar allusions to multiple scrolls in Jer. 25:1-14. **36:1** *Fourth year of King Jehoiakim*—605 BCE, an important year in the book of Jeremiah (cf. Jer. 25:1; 45:1; 46:2). This was also the year of the battle of Carchemish, when the Babylonian domination of West Asia began. **36:2** *Days of Josiah*, who died in 609 BCE. The first scroll has the words that are spoken to Israel, Judah, and the nations, the oracles of judgment that dominate the beginning and very end of the book. **36:4** *Baruch*. Jeremiah's scribe. A seal impression bearing his name was recovered in a royal archive, suggesting he was a royal scribe. The seal reads, "to/from Baruch son of Neriah, the scribe." **36:5** Jeremiah instructs Baruch to go to the temple to deliver his prophetic words because the prophet is forbidden entry. **36:6** *On a fast day.* Days of public fasts were held in times of national distress. This would have increased the number of people in attendance. **36:9** The people declare a public fast during the disaster in order to repent from their actions and hope for divine favor. *Fifth year of King Jehoiakim*—604 BCE, which is also when Nebuchadrezzar advanced against the Philistine town of Ashkelon. **36:11–19** When the officials hear the ominous prophecies of Jeremiah via Baruch, they question whether they should inform the king, and they instruct Baruch and Jeremiah

Going Deeper: Written Prophecy and Scrolls (Jeremiah 36)

Prophecy in the ancient world was normally an oral phenomenon. Prophets generally spoke their prophecies verbally to their audiences—customarily the king, priests, social elites, or the people in the community. However, the Hebrew Bible has preserved prophetic *books*. How did an originally oral phenomenon ultimately yield a literary result?

Despite the abundance of prophetic material in the Hebrew Bible, little evidence exists for how this material was composed. Isaiah 8 and 30 both speak about preserving prophecies by writing them on a scroll or a tablet. Isaiah 8:16 also preserves a command to "bind up the testimony; seal the teaching among [Isaiah's] disciples." This might indicate that prophecies were preserved by prophetic followers so that they could be consulted later.

Jeremiah 36 might provide another angle from which to think about this. According to the book bearing his name, Jeremiah was like most prophets—he delivered his prophetic messages orally to various audiences. In this chapter, YHWH gives him a divine directive to commit to writing all the prophetic warnings conveyed to him over a period of several years (ca. 627–605 BCE). He calls on the scribe Baruch to write on a scroll everything he dictates. Upon the scroll's completion, he instructs Baruch to take it to the temple courts in Jerusalem and read the prophecies to the people there in hopes that they will respond appropriately to his warnings. The chapter does not specify exactly what is on the scroll, but many scholars think it contained an early version of what became the book of Jeremiah.

Members of the royal court hear what Baruch reads in the temple courts and decide to report its contents to King Jehoiakim. The process by which Jeremiah's prophecies were ultimately made known to the king is similar to how the words of Neo-Assyrian prophets were reported to their kings nearly a century earlier. Scribes committed their oral proclamations to writing, after which they were sent to the palace. In Jer. 36, the king's reaction to the scroll is preserved: King Jehoiakim responds forcefully by burning the scroll column by column as it is read to him. Undeterred, Jeremiah dictates another with additional material, presumably aimed at Jehoiakim. While this chapter is a theologized account meant to demonstrate the king's foolish rejection of Jeremiah's prophecies, the narrative's report of how the prophecies were textualized and made available to the king seems historically likely.

J. Todd Hibbard

---

¹³And Micaiah told them all the words that he had heard when Baruch read the scroll in the hearing of the people. ¹⁴Then all the officials sent Jehudi son of Nethaniah son of Shelemiah son of Cushi to say to Baruch, "Bring the scroll that you read in the hearing of the people, and come." So Baruch son of Neriah took the scroll in his hand and came to them. ¹⁵And they said to him, "Sit down and read it to us." So Baruch read it to them. ¹⁶When they heard all the words, they turned to one another in alarm and said to Baruch, "We certainly must report all these words to the king." ¹⁷Then they questioned Baruch, "Tell us now, how did you write all these words? Was it at his dictation?" ¹⁸Baruch answered them, "He dictated all these words to me, and I wrote them with ink on the scroll." ¹⁹Then the officials said to Baruch, "Go and hide, you and Jeremiah, and let no one know where you are."

20 Leaving the scroll in the chamber of Elishama the secretary, they went to the court of the king, and they reported all the words in the hearing of the king. ²¹Then the king sent Jehudi to get the scroll, and he took it from the chamber of Elishama the secretary, and Jehudi read it in the hearing of the king and all the officials who stood beside the king. ²²Now the king was sitting in his winter apartment (it was the ninth month), and there was a fire burning in the brazier before him. ²³As Jehudi read three or four columns, he would cut them off with a penknife and throw them into the fire in the brazier, until the entire scroll was consumed in the fire that was in the brazier. ²⁴Yet neither the king nor any of his servants who heard all these words was alarmed, nor did they tear their garments. ²⁵Even when Elnathan and Delaiah and Gemariah urged the king not to burn the scroll, he would not listen to them. ²⁶And the king commanded Jerahmeel the king's son and Seraiah son of Azriel and Shelemiah son of Abdeel to arrest the

---

to hide. **36:17** *At his dictation.* Literally "from his mouth." **36:20–26** Jehudi, a royal official, reads the scroll aloud to the king, and he destroys it by cutting it and then throwing it in a fire. **36:24** Neither the king nor his servants respond to the scroll as its words suggest they should. **36:26** The king

secretary Baruch and the prophet Jeremiah. But the Lord hid them.

27 Now after the king had burned the scroll with the words that Baruch wrote at Jeremiah's dictation, the word of the Lord came to Jeremiah: ²⁸Take another scroll and write on it all the former words that were in the first scroll, which King Jehoiakim of Judah has burned. ²⁹And concerning King Jehoiakim of Judah you shall say: Thus says the Lord, You have burned this scroll, saying, "Why have you written in it that the king of Babylon will certainly come and destroy this land and will cut off from it human beings and animals?" ³⁰Therefore thus says the Lord concerning King Jehoiakim of Judah: He shall have no one to sit upon the throne of David, and his dead body shall be cast out to the heat by day and the frost by night. ³¹And I will punish him and his offspring and his servants for their iniquity; I will bring on them and on the inhabitants of Jerusalem and on the people of Judah all the disasters with which I have threatened them, but they would not listen.

32 Then Jeremiah took another scroll and gave it to the secretary Baruch son of Neriah, who wrote on it at Jeremiah's dictation all the words of the scroll that King Jehoiakim of Judah had burned in the fire, and many similar words were added to them.

37 Zedekiah son of Josiah, whom King Nebuchadrezzar of Babylon made king in the land of Judah, succeeded Coniah son of Jehoiakim. ²But neither he nor his servants nor the people of the land listened to the words of the Lord that he spoke through the prophet Jeremiah.

3 King Zedekiah sent Jehucal son of Shelemiah and the priest Zephaniah son of Maaseiah to the prophet Jeremiah, saying, "Please pray for us to the Lord our God." ⁴Now Jeremiah was still going in and out among the people, for he had not yet been put in prison. ⁵Meanwhile, the army of Pharaoh had come out of Egypt, and when the Chaldeans who were besieging Jerusalem heard news of them, they withdrew from Jerusalem.

6 Then the word of the Lord came to the prophet Jeremiah: ⁷Thus says the Lord, God of Israel: This is what you shall say to the king of Judah, who sent you to me to inquire of me: Pharaoh's army, which set out to help you, is going to return to its own land, to Egypt. ⁸And the Chaldeans shall return and fight against this city; they shall take it and burn it with fire. ⁹Thus says the Lord: Do not deceive yourselves, saying, "The Chaldeans will surely go away from us," for they will not go away. ¹⁰Even if you defeated the whole army of Chaldeans who are fighting against you and there remained of them only wounded men in their tents, they would rise up and burn this city with fire.

11 Now when the Chaldean army had withdrawn from Jerusalem at the approach of Pharaoh's army, ¹²Jeremiah set out from Jerusalem to go to the land of Benjamin to receive his share of property^y among the people there. ¹³When he reached the Benjamin Gate, a sentinel there named Irijah son of Shelemiah son of Hananiah arrested the prophet Jeremiah saying, "You are deserting to the Chaldeans." ¹⁴And Jeremiah said, "That is a lie; I am not deserting to the

y 37.12 Or *to slip away*

calls for Baruch and Jeremiah to be arrested, but YHWH hides them. **36:27–32** Jeremiah dictates another scroll, and *many similar words were added to them*, which speaks to the way the content may have evolved over time. **36:30** *He shall have no one to sit upon the throne of David.* Jehoiakim's son Jehoiachin succeeded him but reigned for only three months before being taken to Babylon. Jehoiakim's ultimate fate is unclear (cf. 2 Kgs. 24:6; 2 Chr. 36:6).

37:1–10 The Egyptian advance and the Babylonian threats are highlighted, and King Zedekiah asks for prophetic intercession. YHWH delivers a word declaring that Egypt will retreat and Babylon will lay siege to Jerusalem. **37:5** *Army of Pharaoh.* Pharaoh Hophra began to reign in 589 BCE, though exactly when his army offered a show of might that prompted Babylonian withdrawal from Jerusalem in order to confront the Egyptians is unclear. **37:8–10** The strength of the Babylonian army is emphasized, as is the inevitability of Jerusalem's destruction.

37:11–21 The leaders question Jeremiah's loyalty based on his words and actions, so he is imprisoned in the cistern house, ironically, since the people earlier are accused of making faulty cisterns (2:13). **37:12** *To receive his share of property.* Likely not connected with his land purchase in chap. 32. **37:13** *You are deserting to the Chaldeans.* A justifiable conclusion given Jeremiah's pro-Babylonian

Chaldeans." But Irijah would not listen to him and arrested Jeremiah and brought him to the officials. [15]The officials were enraged at Jeremiah, and they beat him and imprisoned him in the house of the secretary Jonathan, for it had been made a prison. [16]Thus Jeremiah was put in the cistern house, in the cells, and remained there many days.

17 Then King Zedekiah sent for him and received him. The king questioned him secretly in his house and said, "Is there any word from the LORD?" Jeremiah said, "There is!" Then he said, "You shall be handed over to the king of Babylon." [18]Jeremiah also said to King Zedekiah, "What wrong have I done to you or your servants or this people, that you have put me in prison? [19]Where are your prophets who prophesied to you, saying, 'The king of Babylon will not come against you and against this land'? [20]Now please hear me, my lord king: be good enough to listen to my plea, and do not send me back to the house of the secretary Jonathan to die there." [21]So King Zedekiah gave orders, and they committed Jeremiah to the court of the guard, and a loaf of bread was given him daily from the bakers' street, until all the bread of the city was gone. So Jeremiah remained in the court of the guard.

38 Now Shephatiah son of Mattan, Gedaliah son of Pashhur, Jucal son of Shelemiah, and Pashhur son of Malchiah heard the words that Jeremiah was saying to all the people: [2]"Thus says the LORD: Those who stay in this city shall die by the sword, by famine, and by pestilence, but those who go out to the Chaldeans shall live; they shall have their lives as a prize of war and live. [3]Thus says the LORD: This city shall surely

be handed over to the army of the king of Babylon, and he will take it." [4]Then the officials said to the king, "This man ought to be put to death because he is discouraging the soldiers who are left in this city and all the people by speaking such words to them. For this man is not seeking the welfare of this people, but their harm." [5]King Zedekiah said, "Here he is; he is in your hands, for the king is powerless against you." [6]So they took Jeremiah and threw him into the cistern of Malchiah, the king's son, which was in the court of the guard, letting Jeremiah down by ropes. Now there was no water in the cistern but only mud, and Jeremiah sank in the mud.

7 Ebed-melech the Cushite, a eunuch in the king's house, heard that they had put Jeremiah into the cistern. The king happened to be sitting at the Benjamin Gate, [8]So Ebed-melech left the king's house and spoke to the king, [9]"My lord king, these men have acted wickedly in all they did to the prophet Jeremiah by throwing him into the cistern to die there of hunger, for there is no bread left in the city." [10]Then the king commanded Ebed-melech the Cushite, "Take three[z] men with you from here, and pull the prophet Jeremiah up from the cistern before he dies." [11]So Ebed-melech took the men with him and went to the house of the king, to a wardrobe of[a] the storehouse, and took from there old rags and worn-out clothes, which he let down to Jeremiah in the cistern by ropes. [12]Then Ebed-melech the Cushite said to Jeremiah, "Just put the rags and clothes between your armpits and the ropes." Jeremiah did so. [13]Then they

z 38.10 Cn: Heb *thirty* a 38.11 Cn: Heb *to under*

position. **37:17–21** Though Jeremiah is in prison ostensibly for desertion, Zedekiah still values his advice. His request for a prophetic word is likely in the hope that it will be positive. Instead, Jeremiah predicts that Zedekiah will be handed over to the Babylonians. **37:19** *Where are your prophets?* Those who prophesied peace and safety in the face of Babylonian aggression. **37:20–21** Jeremiah pleads with Zedekiah to release him from prison. He is transferred to the *court of the guard* and receives daily bread as long as it lasts.

　　38:1–13 A group of pro-Egyptian officials demands Jeremiah's execution because his message of doom about Jerusalem's fate disheartens Judah's military (cf. Jer. 26). Zedekiah, in a weakened position, relents, and Jeremiah is arrested and thrown into a cistern full of mud. **38:7** Ebed-melech, whose ethnicity is either Ethiopian or Nubian (Heb. "Cushite"), hears of Jeremiah's circumstances and implores the king to save him. Ebed-melech is apparently not from the land of Judah, although he lives and works there and is familiar with Jeremiah. He knows they plan to let Jeremiah starve. **38:10** The king gives instructions to take three men to go rescue Jeremiah. **38:11** The men tie clothes from the royal wardrobe and drop them into the cistern to pull him out. **38:13** *Remained in the court of the guard.* Jeremiah is rescued from the cistern, but he remains under arrest apparently.

drew Jeremiah up by the ropes and pulled him out of the cistern. And Jeremiah remained in the court of the guard.

14 King Zedekiah sent for the prophet Jeremiah and received him at the third entrance of the temple of the LORD. The king said to Jeremiah, "I have something to ask you; do not hide anything from me." [15]Jeremiah said to Zedekiah, "If I tell you, you will put me to death, will you not? And if I give you advice, you will not listen to me." [16]So King Zedekiah swore an oath in secret to Jeremiah, "As the LORD lives, who gave us our lives, I will not put you to death or hand you over to these men who seek your life."

17 Then Jeremiah said to Zedekiah, "Thus says the LORD, the God of hosts, the God of Israel: If you will only surrender to the officials of the king of Babylon, then your life shall be spared, and this city shall not be burned with fire, and you and your house shall live. [18]But if you do not surrender to the officials of the king of Babylon, then this city shall be handed over to the Chaldeans, and they shall burn it with fire, and you yourself shall not escape from their hand." [19]King Zedekiah said to Jeremiah, "I am afraid of the Judeans who have deserted to the Chaldeans, for I might be handed over to them, and they would abuse me." [20]Jeremiah said, "That will not happen. Just obey the voice of the LORD in what I say to you, and it shall go well with you, and your life shall be spared. [21]But if you are determined not to surrender, this is what the LORD has shown me: [22]a vision of all the women remaining in the house of the king of Judah being led out to the officials of the king of Babylon and saying,

'Your trusted friends have seduced you
   and have overcome you.
Now that your feet are stuck in the mud,
   they desert you.'

[23]"All your wives and your children shall be led out to the Chaldeans, and you yourself shall not escape from their hand but shall be seized by the king of Babylon, and this city shall be burned with fire."

24 Then Zedekiah said to Jeremiah, "Do not let anyone else know of this conversation, or you will die. [25]If the officials should hear that I have spoken with you and come and say to you, 'Just tell us what you said to the king; do not conceal it from us, or we will put you to death. What did the king say to you?' [26]then you shall say to them, 'I was presenting my plea to the king not to send me back to the house of Jonathan to die there.'" [27]All the officials did come to Jeremiah and questioned him, and he answered them in the very words the king had commanded. So they stopped questioning him, for the conversation had not been overheard. [28]And Jeremiah remained in the court of the guard until the day that Jerusalem was taken.

39 This is how Jerusalem was captured:[b] in the ninth year of King Zedekiah of Judah, in the tenth month, King Nebuchadrezzar of Babylon and all his army came against Jerusalem and besieged it; [2]in the eleventh year of Zedekiah, in the fourth month, on the ninth day of the month, a breach was made in the city. [3]Then all the officials of the king of Babylon came and sat in the middle gate: Nergal-sharezer, Samgarnebo, Sarsechim the Rabsaris, Nergal-sharezer the Rabmag, with all the rest of the officials of the king of Babylon. [4]When King Zedekiah of Judah and all the soldiers saw them, they fled, going out of the city at night by way of the King's Garden through the gate between the two walls, and they went

b 39.1 In Heb, this clause appears at the end of 38.28

38:14–28 This is the final private interaction between Jeremiah and Zedekiah. 38:15–16 Jeremiah remains unconvinced that Zedekiah will not execute him. Zedekiah promises not to do so, but his promise is made *in secret*, revealing that he is concerned about his own safety (v. 19). 38:17–18 The only way to avoid destruction and death is to surrender. 38:21–23 Jeremiah says that the city will fall to the Babylonians, and he instructs the king to surrender, despite the hostility that will come from pro-Egyptian officials.

39:1–10 The report of Jerusalem's fall. Some of the content is repeated at the end of the book and also in the summary of the siege in 2 Kings (cf. Jer. 52:4–16; 2 Kgs. 25:1–12; see **"Exile (2 Kings)," p. 539**). Unfortunately, the Babylonian text, which might have included an account of Nebuchadrezzar's capture of Jerusalem, is broken and does not contain the relevant portion. 39:2 This day is commemorated in the fast of Tisha B'Av in modern Judaism, a day on which the destruction of both the first and second Jerusalem temples is remembered (among other historical losses). 39:4 *Arabah*. The wilderness to the

toward the Arabah. [5]But the army of the Chaldeans pursued them and overtook Zedekiah in the plains of Jericho, and when they had taken him, they brought him up to King Nebuchadrezzar of Babylon, at Riblah, in the land of Hamath, and he passed sentence on him. [6]The king of Babylon slaughtered the sons of Zedekiah at Riblah before his eyes; also the king of Babylon slaughtered all the nobles of Judah. [7]He put out the eyes of Zedekiah and bound him in fetters to take him to Babylon. [8]The Chaldeans burned with fire the king's house and the houses of the people and broke down the walls of Jerusalem. [9]Then Nebuzaradan the captain of the guard exiled to Babylon the rest of the people who were left in the city, those who had deserted to him, and the rest of the people who remained. [10]Nebuzaradan the captain of the guard left in the land of Judah some of the poor people who owned nothing and gave them vineyards and fields at the same time.

11 King Nebuchadrezzar of Babylon gave command concerning Jeremiah through Nebuzaradan, the captain of the guard, saying, [12]"Take him, look after him well, and do him no harm, but deal with him as he may ask you." [13]So Nebuzaradan the captain of the guard, Nebushazban the Rabsaris, Nergal-sharezer the Rabmag, and all the chief officers of the king of Babylon sent [14]and took Jeremiah from the court of the guard. They entrusted him to Gedaliah son of Ahikam son of Shaphan to be brought home. So he stayed with his own people.

15 The word of the Lord came to Jeremiah while he was confined in the court of the guard: [16]Go and say to Ebed-melech the Cushite: Thus says the Lord of hosts, the God of Israel: I am going to fulfill my words against

this city for evil and not for good, and they shall be accomplished in your presence on that day. [17]But I will save you on that day, says the Lord, and you shall not be handed over to those whom you dread. [18]For I will surely save you, and you shall not fall by the sword, but you shall have your life as a prize of war, because you have trusted in me, says the Lord.

40 The word that came to Jeremiah from the Lord after Nebuzaradan the captain of the guard had let him go from Ramah, when he took him bound in fetters along with all the captives of Jerusalem and Judah who were being exiled to Babylon. [2]The captain of the guard took Jeremiah and said to him, "The Lord your God threatened this place with this disaster, [3]and now the Lord has brought it about and has done as he said, because all of you sinned against the Lord and did not obey his voice. Therefore this thing has come upon you. [4]Now look, I have just released you today from the fetters on your hands. If you wish to come with me to Babylon, come, and I will take good care of you, but if you do not wish to come with me to Babylon, you need not come. See, the whole land is before you; go wherever you think it good and right to go. [5]If you remain,[c] then return to Gedaliah son of Ahikam son of Shaphan, whom the king of Babylon appointed governor of the towns of Judah, and stay with him among the people, or go wherever you think it right to go." So the captain of the guard gave him an allowance of food and a present and let him go. [6]Then Jeremiah went to Gedaliah son

c 40.5 Syr: Meaning of Heb uncertain

south and east of Jerusalem. **39:5** *Riblah.* A city on the east bank of the Orontes River in the Beqaa Valley. It was on a major highway that ran from Egypt to Mesopotamia. **39:6–8** Zedekiah's sons are slaughtered, and the king is blinded and taken into exile. The palace is burned, along with many other houses and the walls of Jerusalem.

39:11–18 Jeremiah is freed from confinement in the royal court, and he remembers Ebed-melech, who had saved him when he was thrown in the cistern. He promises that Ebed-melech will not fall by the sword, but his life will be a *prize of war*, noting that he will survive the siege. Once again, Jeremiah's connection with the powerful Shaphan family appears when he is entrusted to Shaphan's grandson, Gedaliah.

40:1–6 An alternative account to Jer. 39:11–14 of Jeremiah's release from prison. **40:2–3** The text has the Babylonian official Nebuzaradan express a theological interpretation of Jerusalem's destruction that matches Jeremiah's. **40:4–5** *If you wish to come with me to Babylon.* Jeremiah is given the choice of joining the exile in Babylon or remaining in Judah. **40:6** He chooses to remain, which, in light of the good fig / bad fig message of Jer. 24, might be considered unexpected.

of Ahikam at Mizpah and stayed with him among the people who were left in the land.

7 When all the leaders of the forces in the open country and their troops heard that the king of Babylon had appointed Gedaliah son of Ahikam governor in the land and had committed to him men, women, and children, those of the poorest of the land who had not been taken into exile to Babylon, [8]they went to Gedaliah at Mizpah—Ishmael son of Nethaniah, Johanan[d] son of Kareah, Seraiah son of Tanhumeth, the sons of Ophai the Netophathite, Jezaniah son of the Maacathite, they and their troops. [9]Gedaliah son of Ahikam son of Shaphan swore to them and their troops, saying, "Do not be afraid to serve the Chaldeans. Stay in the land and serve the king of Babylon, and it shall go well with you. [10]As for me, I am staying at Mizpah to represent you before the Chaldeans who come to us, but as for you, gather wine and summer fruits and oil, and store them in your vessels, and live in the towns that you have taken over." [11]Likewise, when all the Judeans who were in Moab and among the Ammonites and in Edom and in other lands heard that the king of Babylon had left a remnant in Judah and had appointed Gedaliah son of Ahikam son of Shaphan as governor over them, [12]then all the Judeans returned from all the places to which they had been scattered and came to the land of Judah, to Gedaliah at Mizpah, and they gathered wine and summer fruits in great abundance.

13 Now Johanan son of Kareah and all the leaders of the forces in the open country came to Gedaliah at Mizpah [14]and said to him, "Are you at all aware that Baalis king of the Ammonites has sent Ishmael son of Nethaniah to take your life?" But Gedaliah son of Ahikam would not believe them. [15]Then Johanan son of Kareah spoke secretly to Gedaliah at Mizpah, "Please let me go and kill Ishmael son of Nethaniah, and no one else will know. Why should he take your life, so that all the Judeans who are gathered around you would be scattered and the remnant of Judah would perish?" [16]But Gedaliah son of Ahikam said to Johanan son of Kareah, "Do not do such a thing, for you are telling a lie about Ishmael."

41 In the seventh month, Ishmael son of Nethaniah son of Elishama, of the royal family, one of the chief officers of the king, came with ten men to Gedaliah son of Ahikam, at Mizpah. As they ate bread together there at Mizpah, [2]Ishmael son of Nethaniah and the ten men with him got up and struck down Gedaliah son of Ahikam son of Shaphan with the sword and killed him, whom the king of Babylon had appointed governor in the land. [3]Ishmael also killed all the Judeans who were with Gedaliah at Mizpah and the Chaldean soldiers who happened to be there.

4 On the day after the murder of Gedaliah, before anyone knew of it, [5]eighty men arrived from Shechem and Shiloh and Samaria with their beards shaved and their clothes torn and their bodies gashed, bringing grain offerings and incense to present at the temple of the LORD. [6]And Ishmael son of Nethaniah came out from Mizpah to meet them, weeping as he came. As he met them, he said to

d 40.8 Gk: Heb *Johanan, Jonathan*

40:7–18 Gedaliah is appointed by the Babylonians as the governor of Judah after the siege on Jerusalem. Judah becomes a part of the Neo-Babylonian Empire. **40:8** *Mizpah.* Perhaps modern Tell en-Nasbeh, about eight miles north of Jerusalem. **40:9** Gedaliah tries to convince the people to serve the Babylonians, who are now in power. **40:10** *Live in the towns that you have taken over.* Those who remained, identified as the "poorest of the land" (v. 7), found themselves in possession of towns and lands previously belonging to others. **40:12** *All the Judeans returned.* Those who had fled to neighboring lands during the Babylonian assault now return. **40:14–16** Gedaliah hears that some of Judah's neighbors, such as Moab, Ammon, and Edom, are not simply accepting Babylonian rule. When he is informed about a potential insurrectionist, Ishmael, Gedaliah does not believe the information.

41:1–3 Ishmael, a member of the Judean royal family and allied with the Ammonite royal family, leads an insurrection, killing Gedaliah and all in his entourage, including Judeans and Chaldean soldiers.

41:4–10 Pilgrims from the former northern kingdom of Israel preparing to perform cultic rituals of lamentation on the site of the destroyed temple were also killed. The corpses were thrown in a cistern, showing the disregard for the people. He also took some of the leaders as captives.

them, "Come to Gedaliah son of Ahikam." [7]When they reached the middle of the city, Ishmael son of Nethaniah and the men with him slaughtered them and threw them[e] into a cistern. [8]But there were ten men among them who said to Ishmael, "Do not kill us, for we have stores of wheat, barley, oil, and honey hidden in the fields." So he refrained and did not kill them along with their companions.

9 Now the cistern into which Ishmael had thrown all the bodies of the men whom he had struck down alongside Gedaliah was the one that King Asa had made for defense against King Baasha of Israel; Ishmael son of Nethaniah filled that cistern with those whom he had killed. [10]Then Ishmael took captive all the rest of the people who were in Mizpah, the king's daughters and all the people who were left at Mizpah, whom Nebuzaradan, the captain of the guard, had committed to Gedaliah son of Ahikam. Ishmael son of Nethaniah took them captive and set out to cross over to the Ammonites.

11 But when Johanan son of Kareah and all the leaders of the forces with him heard of all the crimes that Ishmael son of Nethaniah had done, [12]they took all their men and went to fight against Ishmael son of Nethaniah. They came upon him at the great pool that is in Gibeon. [13]And when all the people who were with Ishmael saw Johanan son of Kareah and all the leaders of the forces with him, they were glad. [14]So all the people whom Ishmael had carried away captive from Mizpah turned around and came back and went to Johanan son of Kareah. [15]But Ishmael son of Nethaniah escaped from Johanan with eight men and went to the Ammonites. [16]Then Johanan son of Kareah and all the leaders of the forces with him took all the rest of the people whom he had recovered from Ishmael son of Nethaniah from Mizpah after he had slain Gedaliah son of Ahikam—soldiers,

women, children, and eunuchs, whom Johanan[f] brought back from Gibeon.[g] [17]And they set out and stopped at Geruth Chimham near Bethlehem, intending to go to Egypt [18]because of the Chaldeans, for they were afraid of them, because Ishmael son of Nethaniah had killed Gedaliah son of Ahikam, whom the king of Babylon had made governor over the land.

42 Then all the commanders of the forces, and Johanan son of Kareah and Jezaniah son of Hoshaiah, and all the people from the least to the greatest approached [2]the prophet Jeremiah and said, "Be good enough to listen to our plea, and pray to the LORD your God for us—for all this remnant. For there are only a few of us left out of many, as your eyes can see. [3]Let the LORD your God show us where we should go and what we should do." [4]The prophet Jeremiah said to them, "Very well: I am going to pray to the LORD your God as you request, and whatever the LORD answers you I will tell you; I will keep nothing back from you." [5]They in their turn said to Jeremiah, "May the LORD be a true and faithful witness against us if we do not act according to everything that the LORD your God sends us through you. [6]Whether it is good or bad, we will obey the voice of the LORD our God to whom we are sending you, in order that it may go well with us when we obey the voice of the LORD our God."

7 At the end of ten days the word of the LORD came to Jeremiah. [8]Then he summoned Johanan son of Kareah and all the commanders of the forces who were with him and all the people from the least to the greatest [9]and said to them, "Thus says the LORD, the God of Israel, to whom you sent me to present your

e 41.7 Syr: Heb lacks *and threw them* f 41.16 Heb *he*
g 41.16 Meaning of Heb uncertain

41:9 *King Asa* and *King Baasha.* A Judean king and an Israelite king, both of whom ruled centuries before the current period. **41:11–18** Ishmael is intercepted by Johanan, who frees those Ishmael had kidnaped. However, Ishmael escapes to the Ammonites. Johanan and those he rescues intend *to go to Egypt* because Ishmael's actions will undoubtedly provoke a Babylonian response. Consequently, the insurrection after the siege only adds to the trauma and instability that plague the region. **41:17** *Bethlehem.* About four miles south of Jerusalem. **42:1–22** The commanders and officials reach out to Jeremiah to discern what they should do in the context of more instability, war, and insurrection. **42:4** Prophetic intercession for the people takes the form of prophetic inquiry. **42:7–22** Jeremiah advises the people to remain in the land and try to rebuild, but the community thinks this is bad advice and instead wants to flee to

plea before him: ¹⁰If you will only remain in this land, then I will build you up and not pull you down; I will plant you and not pluck you up, for I am sorry for the disaster that I have brought upon you. ¹¹Do not be afraid of the king of Babylon, as you have been; do not be afraid of him, says the Lord, for I am with you, to save you and to rescue you from his hand. ¹²I will grant you mercy, and he will have mercy on you and restore you to your native soil. ¹³But if you continue to say, 'We will not stay in this land,' thus disobeying the voice of the Lord your God ¹⁴and saying, 'No, we will go to the land of Egypt, where we shall not see war or hear the sound of the trumpet or be hungry for bread, and there we will stay,' ¹⁵then hear the word of the Lord, O remnant of Judah. Thus says the Lord of hosts, the God of Israel: If you are determined to enter Egypt and go to settle there, ¹⁶then the sword that you fear shall overtake you there, in the land of Egypt, and the famine that you dread shall follow close after you into Egypt, and there you shall die. ¹⁷All the people who have determined to go to Egypt to settle there shall die by the sword, by famine, and by pestilence; they shall have no remnant or survivor from the disaster that I am bringing upon them.

18 "For thus says the Lord of hosts, the God of Israel: Just as my anger and my wrath were poured out on the inhabitants of Jerusalem, so my wrath will be poured out on you when you go to Egypt. You shall become an object of execration and horror, of cursing and ridicule. You shall see this place no more. ¹⁹The Lord has said to you, 'O remnant of Judah, Do not go to Egypt.' Be well aware that I have warned you today ²⁰that you have made a fatal mistake. For you yourselves sent me to the Lord your God, saying, 'Pray for us to the Lord our God, and whatever the Lord our God says, tell us, and we will do it.' ²¹So I have told you today, but you have not obeyed the voice of the Lord your God in anything that he sent me to tell you. ²²Be well aware, then, that you shall die by the sword, by famine, and by pestilence in the place where you desire to go and settle."

43 When Jeremiah finished speaking to all the people all the words of the Lord their God, with which the Lord their God had sent him to them, all these words, ²Azariah son of Hoshaiah and Johanan son of Kareah and all the other insolent men said to Jeremiah, "You are telling a lie. The Lord our God did not send you to say, 'Do not go to Egypt to settle there,' ³but Baruch son of Neriah is inciting you against us, to hand us over to the Chaldeans, in order that they may kill us or take us into exile in Babylon." ⁴So Johanan son of Kareah and all the commanders of the forces and all the people did not obey the voice of the Lord to stay in the land of Judah. ⁵But Johanan son of Kareah and all the commanders of the forces took all the remnant of Judah who had returned to settle in the land of Judah from all the nations to which they had been driven—⁶the men, the women, the children, the princesses, and everyone whom Nebuzaradan the captain of the guard had left with Gedaliah son of Ahikam son of Shaphan, also the prophet Jeremiah and Baruch son of Neriah. ⁷And they came into the land of Egypt, for they did not obey the voice of the Lord. And they arrived at Tahpanhes.

8 Then the word of the Lord came to Jeremiah in Tahpanhes: ⁹Take some large stones

Egypt. Jeremiah informs them that fleeing to Egypt will bring about divine anger, and the people will continue to be cursed with sword, famine, and pestilence in Egypt. The critique against fleeing to Egypt might reflect geopolitical realities, as Egypt did not assist Judah against Babylonian invasions. **42:10** *I will build you up.* Language from Jeremiah's commission; cf. 1:10. *I am sorry.* The Hebrew text recalls the scenario envisioned in the potter's house lesson where YHWH expresses the possibility of changing his mind; cf. 18:8.

43:1–7 Jeremiah is accused of being a false prophet by *telling a lie* and not being sent by YHWH. These are the charges Jeremiah leveled against his prophetic opponents earlier in the book (e.g., Jer. 14:14). See **"Prophetic Conflict," p. 1079. 43:3** *Baruch . . . is inciting you against us.* Why the people think this is a possibility is unclear. **43:5–7** Despite the divine command not to go to Egypt, people fled to Egypt. Jeremiah and Baruch are taken against their will to Egypt with the refugees fleeing Judah. **43:7** *Tahpanhes.* Modern Tell Defenneh in the northeastern Delta region of Egypt; cf. 2:16.

43:8–13 Jeremiah performs another symbolic act, burying large stones as a statement that the Babylonians will indeed conquer Egypt. See **"Symbolic Actions," p. 1056.** Nebuchadrezzar's

in your hands, and bury them in the clay pavement[b] that is at the entrance to Pharaoh's palace in Tahpanhes. Let the Judeans see you do it, [10]and say to them, "Thus says the LORD of hosts, the God of Israel: I am going to send and take my servant King Nebuchadrezzar of Babylon, and I will set his throne above these stones that I have buried, and he will spread his royal canopy over them. [11]He shall come and ravage the land of Egypt, giving

those who are destined for pestilence, to
pestilence,
and those who are destined for
captivity, to captivity,
and those who are destined for the
sword, to the sword.

[12]"I shall kindle a fire in the temples of the gods of Egypt, and he shall burn them and carry them away captive, and he shall pick clean the land of Egypt as a shepherd picks his cloak clean of vermin, and he shall depart from there safely. [13]He shall break the obelisks of Heliopolis, which is in the land of Egypt, and the temples of the gods of Egypt he shall burn with fire."

44 The word that came to Jeremiah for all the Judeans living in the land of Egypt, at Migdol, at Tahpanhes, at Memphis, and in the land of Pathros: [2]Thus says the LORD of hosts, the God of Israel: You yourselves have seen all the disaster that I have brought on Jerusalem and on all the towns of Judah. Look at them; today they are a desolation, without an inhabitant in them, [3]because of the wickedness that they committed, provoking me to anger, in that they went to make offerings to and serve other gods that they had not known, neither they, nor you, nor your ancestors. [4]Yet I persistently sent to you all my servants the prophets, saying, "I beg you not to do this abominable thing that I hate!" [5]But they did not listen or incline their ear, to turn from their wickedness and make no offerings to other gods. [6]So my wrath and my anger were poured out and kindled in the towns of Judah and in the streets of Jerusalem, and they became a waste and a desolation, as they still are today. [7]And now thus says the LORD God of hosts, the God of Israel: Why are you doing such great harm to yourselves, to cut off man and woman, child and infant, from the midst of Judah, leaving yourselves without a remnant? [8]Why do you provoke me to anger with the works of your hands, making offerings to other gods in the land of Egypt, where you have come to settle? Will you be cut off and become an object of cursing and ridicule among all the nations of the earth? [9]Have you forgotten the crimes of your ancestors, of the kings of Judah, of their[i] wives, your own crimes and those of your wives, which they committed in the land of Judah and in the streets of Jerusalem? [10]They have shown no contrition or fear to this day, nor have they walked in my law and my statutes that I set before you and before your ancestors.

11 Therefore thus says the LORD of hosts, the God of Israel: I am determined to bring disaster on you, to bring all Judah to an end. [12]I will take the remnant of Judah who are determined to come to the land of Egypt to settle, and they shall perish, everyone; in the land of Egypt they shall fall; by the sword and by famine they shall perish; from the least to the greatest, they shall die by the sword and by famine; and they shall become an object of execration and horror, of cursing and ridicule. [13]I will punish those who live in the land of Egypt as I have punished Jerusalem, with the sword, with famine, and with pestilence, [14]so that none of the remnant of Judah who have come to settle in the land of Egypt shall escape or survive or return to the land of Judah. Although they long to go back to live there, they shall not go back, except some fugitives.

b 43.9 Meaning of Heb uncertain   *i* 44.9 Heb *his*

expansion will bring the destruction of Egyptian people, land, and architecture, making this area no safer than Judah. Nebuchadrezzar invaded Egypt in 568/567 BCE and engaged Pharaoh Amasis in battle, but the outcome is unknown. **43:13** *Heliopolis*, also known as On, is modern Tell Hisn and Matariyeh, a few miles north of downtown Cairo.

44:1–14 Jeremiah delivers a sermon against the Judean refugees who have left their homeland. He argues (again) that the Babylonian destruction was the result of the Judeans' insistence on worshiping other deities, even though the prophets had warned them against this. In light of this, Jeremiah wonders why these same practices persist in Egypt. It will only provoke threats of further destruction. **44:14** Any desire to return from "exile" to Egypt will be futile, unlike the eventual restoration from Babylon.

15 Then all the men who were aware that their wives had been making offerings to other gods and all the women who stood by, a great assembly, all the people who lived in Pathros in the land of Egypt, answered Jeremiah: 16"As for the word that you have spoken to us in the name of the LORD, we are not going to listen to you. 17Instead, we will do everything that we have vowed, make offerings to the queen of heaven and pour out libations to her, just as we and our ancestors, our kings and our officials, used to do in the towns of Judah and in the streets of Jerusalem. We used to have plenty of food and prospered and saw no misfortune. 18But from the time we stopped making offerings to the queen of heaven and pouring out libations to her, we have lacked everything and have perished by the sword and by famine." 19And the women said,ʲ "Indeed we will go on making offerings to the queen of heaven and pouring out libations to her; do you think that we made cakes for her, marked with her image, and poured out libations to her without our husbands' being involved?"

20 Then Jeremiah said to all the people, men and women, all the people who were giving him this answer: 21"As for the offerings that you made in the towns of Judah and in the streets of Jerusalem, you and your ancestors, your kings and your officials, and the people of the land, did not the LORD remember them? Did it not come into his mind? 22The LORD could no longer bear the sight of your evil doings, the abominations that you committed; therefore your land became a desolation and a waste and a curse, without inhabitant, as it is to this day. 23It is because you burned offerings and because you sinned against the LORD and did not obey the voice of the LORD or walk in his law and in his statutes and in his decrees that this disaster has befallen you, as is still evident today."

24 Jeremiah said to all the people and all the women, "Hear the word of the LORD, all you Judeans who are in the land of Egypt, 25Thus says the LORD of hosts, the God of Israel: You and your wives have accomplished in deeds what you declared in words, saying, 'We are determined to perform the vows that we have made, to make offerings to the queen of heaven and to pour out libations to her.' By all means, keep your vows and make your libations! 26Therefore hear the word of the LORD, all you Judeans who live in the land of Egypt: I swear by my great name, says the LORD, that my name shall no longer be pronounced on the lips of any of the people of Judah in all the land of Egypt, saying, 'As the Lord GOD lives.' 27I am going to watch over them for harm and not for good; all the people of Judah who are in the land of Egypt shall perish by the sword and by famine until not one is left. 28And those who escape the sword shall return from the land of Egypt to the land of Judah, few in number, and all the remnant of Judah who have come to the land of Egypt to settle shall know whose words will stand, mine or theirs! 29This shall be the sign to you, says the LORD, that I am going to punish you in this place, in order that you may know that my words of disaster against you will surely be carried out: 30Thus says the LORD, I am going to give Pharaoh Hophra, king of Egypt, into the hands of his enemies, those who seek his life, just as I gave King Zedekiah of Judah into the hand of King Nebuchadrezzar of Babylon, his enemy who sought his life."

ʲ 44.19 Gk: Heb lacks *And the women said*

44:15–20 The people respond to Jeremiah's explanation of the cause of the exile with one of their own. When they ceased making offerings to the *queen of heaven*, who was also mentioned in the temple sermon earlier in the book (cf. Jer. 7:18), all their troubles began. Consequently, the Judeans in Egypt will resume food and libation offerings to her in the hopes that their circumstances will change for the better. This alternative explanation for the Babylonian conquest inverts the usual understanding expressed by the prophets of YHWH. To the degree that this episode is historical, it demonstrates that the theological interpretation of the Babylonian destruction and exile was a contested issue. **44:19** *Without our husbands' being involved* is meant to refute the idea that only women were venerating this goddess.

44:20–30 Predictably, Jeremiah rejects their argument and condemns the people, especially the women who are very vocal about their devotion to the queen of heaven. **44:26** YHWH declares that the divine name will not be pronounced by those in exile in Egypt. **44:27** *I am going to watch over them for harm and not for good*, unlike the exiles; cf. Jer. 1:12; 31:28. **44:28** A few people will survive and flee to Judah, but most will die in Egypt when Nebuchadrezzar assaults the land.

45

The word that the prophet Jeremiah spoke to Baruch son of Neriah, when he wrote these words in a scroll at the dictation of Jeremiah, in the fourth year of King Jehoiakim son of Josiah of Judah: [2]Thus says the Lord, the God of Israel, to you, O Baruch: [3]You said, "Woe is me! The Lord has added sorrow to my pain; I am weary with my groaning, and I find no rest." [4]Thus you shall say to him, "Thus says the Lord: I am going to break down what I have built and pluck up what I have planted—that is, the whole land. [5]And you, do you seek great things for yourself? Do not seek them, for I am going to bring disaster upon all flesh, says the Lord, but I will give you your life as a prize of war in every place to which you may go."

46

The word of the Lord that came to the prophet Jeremiah concerning the nations.

2 Concerning Egypt, about the army of Pharaoh Neco, king of Egypt, which was by the River Euphrates at Carchemish and which King Nebuchadrezzar of Babylon defeated in the fourth year of King Jehoiakim son of Josiah of Judah:

[3] Prepare buckler and shield,
    and advance for battle!
[4] Harness the horses;
    mount the steeds!
Take your stations with helmets on,
    whet the lances,
    put on coats of mail!
[5] Why do I see them terrified?
    They have fallen back;
their warriors are beaten down
    and have fled in haste.
They do not look back—
    terror is all around!
                    says the Lord.
[6] The swift cannot flee away,
    nor can the warrior escape;
in the north by the River Euphrates
    they have stumbled and fallen.

[7] Who is this, rising like the Nile,
    like rivers whose waters surge?
[8] Egypt rises like the Nile,
    like rivers whose waters surge.
It said, "Let me rise; let me cover the earth;
    let me destroy cities and their
        inhabitants."
[9] Advance, O horses,
    and dash madly, O chariots!
Let the warriors go forth:
    Cush and Put, who carry the
        shield,
    the Ludim, who draw[k] the bow.
[10] That day is the day of the Lord God of
        hosts,
    a day of retribution,
    to gain vindication from his foes.
The sword shall devour and be sated
    and drink its fill of their blood.
For the Lord God of hosts holds a
        sacrifice
    in the land of the north by the River
        Euphrates.
[11] Go up to Gilead, and take balm,
    O virgin daughter Egypt!
In vain you have used many medicines;
    there is no healing for you.
[12] The nations have heard of your shame,
    and the earth is full of your cry,
for warrior has stumbled against warrior;
    both have fallen together.

13 The word that the Lord spoke to the prophet Jeremiah about the coming of King Nebuchadrezzar of Babylon to attack the land of Egypt:

[14] Declare in Egypt and proclaim in Migdol;
    proclaim in Memphis and Tahpanhes;
Say, "Take your stations and be ready,
    for the sword shall devour those
        around you."
[15] Why has Apis[l] fled?
    Why did your bull not stand?
Because the Lord thrust him down.

k 46.9 Cn: Heb *who grasp, who draw*   l 46.15 Gk: Heb *mighty ones*

45:1–5 Jeremiah speaks to Baruch, his companion and scribe, during a period of intense invasion. A version of Jeremiah's prophetic commission to break down, build up, pluck, and plant (see Jer. 1:10) is referenced. Despite the difficult circumstances, Jeremiah says that YHWH will give his life as a *prize of war*, suggesting he will survive the invasions.

46:1–28 Judgment against Egypt. The oracle against Egypt names the Egyptian king Neco II and the Babylonian king Nebuchadrezzar. **46:2–12** The focus is on Egypt's defeat by Babylon at the battle of Carchemish. **46:9** *Cush* (Ethiopia), *Put* (Libya), and *Ludim* (people from North Africa) all fought with Egypt. **46:11** *Go up to Gilead, and take balm.* See the note on 8:22. **46:13–26** Anticipates or celebrates Nebuchadrezzar successfully invading Egypt. **46:15** *Apis.* The sacred bull god

¹⁶ Your multitude stumbled^m and fell,
  and one said to another,
"Come, let us go back to our own people
  and to the land of our birth,
  because of the destroying sword."
¹⁷ Give Pharaoh, king of Egypt, the
    name
  "Braggart who missed his chance."

¹⁸ As I live, says the King,
  whose name is the LORD of hosts,
one is coming
  like Tabor among the mountains
  and like Carmel by the sea.
¹⁹ Pack your bags for exile,
  sheltered daughter Egypt!
For Memphis shall become a waste,
  a ruin, without inhabitant.

²⁰ A beautiful heifer is Egypt—
  a gadfly from the north lights upon
    her.
²¹ Even her mercenaries in her midst
  are like fatted calves;
they, too, have turned and fled together;
  they did not stand,
for the day of their calamity has come
    upon them,
  the time of their punishment.

²² She makes a sound like a snake gliding
    away,
  for her enemies march in force
and come against her with axes,
  like those who fell trees.
²³ They shall cut down her forest,
            says the LORD,
  though it is impenetrable,
because they are more numerous
  than locusts;
  they are without number.
²⁴ Daughter Egypt shall be put to shame;
  she shall be handed over to a people
    from the north.

25 The LORD of hosts, the God of Israel,
said: See, I am bringing punishment upon
Amon of Thebes and Pharaoh and Egypt and
her gods and her kings, upon Pharaoh and
those who trust in him. ²⁶I will hand them
over to those who seek their life, to King Nebuchadrezzar of Babylon and his servants.
Afterward Egypt shall be inhabited as in the
days of old, says the LORD.
²⁷ But as for you, have no fear, my servant
    Jacob,
  and do not be dismayed, O Israel,
for I am going to save you from far away
  and your offspring from the land of
    their captivity.
Jacob shall return and have quiet and
    ease,
  and no one shall make him afraid.
²⁸ As for you, have no fear, my servant
    Jacob,
              says the LORD,
  for I am with you.
I will make an end of all the nations
  among which I have banished you,
  but I will not make an end of you!
I will chastise you in just measure,
  and I will by no means leave you
    unpunished.

47 The word of the LORD that came to
the prophet Jeremiah concerning the
Philistines, before Pharaoh attacked Gaza:
² Thus says the LORD:
See, waters are rising out of the north
  and shall become an overflowing
    torrent;
they shall overflow the land and all that
    fills it,
  the city and those who live in it.
People shall cry out,
  and all the inhabitants of the land
    shall wail.

m 46.16 Gk: Heb *the stumblers multiplied*

of Egypt associated with fertility. **46:17** Prophets often assign people symbolic names; cf. Isa. 7:1–8:4; Hos. 1–3. **46:19** Like Judah, exile awaits Egypt. **46:24** Similar to Daughter Zion, Egypt is called *Daughter Egypt*, which shows the convention of using feminine markers for geographic locations. **46:25** *Amon.* An Egyptian sun god associated with a temple at Karnak in *Thebes*. **46:27–28** This oracle of salvation for Israel mirrors Jer. 30:10–11. Its placement after the curse of Egypt helps frame the historical realities as divine acts on behalf of Israel. See **"The Oracles against the Nations,"** p. 1105.

47:1–7 Judgment against the Philistines. The prose narrative implies an imminent attack on Gaza by an unnamed Pharaoh, perhaps by Neco II in 609 BCE (reported by Herodotus). However, *waters are rising out of the north* suggests Babylon is the attacker. If so, the oracle might reflect

³ At the noise of the stamping of the hoofs
　　of his stallions,
　at the clatter of his chariots, at the
　　rumbling of their wheels,
　parents do not turn back for children,
　　so feeble are their hands,
⁴ because of the day that is coming
　　to destroy all the Philistines,
　to cut off from Tyre and Sidon
　　every helper that remains.
　For the Lord is destroying the
　　Philistines,
　the remnant of the coastland of
　　Caphtor.
⁵ Baldness has come upon Gaza;
　Ashkelon is silenced.
　O remnant of Anakim!ⁿ
　How long will you gash yourselves?
⁶ Ah, sword of the Lord!
　How long until you are quiet?
　Put yourself into your scabbard;
　rest and be still!
⁷ How can itᵒ be quiet,
　when the Lord has given it an order?
　Against Ashkelon and against the
　　seashore—
　there he has appointed it.

48 Concerning Moab.

Thus says the Lord of hosts, the God of
Israel:
　Alas for Nebo, it is laid waste!
　　Kiriathaim is put to shame; it is
　　　taken;
　the fortress is put to shame and broken
　　down;
²　the renown of Moab is no more.
　In Heshbon they planned evil against her:
　　"Come, let us cut her off from being a
　　　nation!"
　You also, O Madmen, shall be brought to
　　silence;ᵖ
　the sword shall pursue you.

³ Listen! A cry goes up from Horonaim:
　　"Desolation and great destruction!"
⁴ "Moab is destroyed!"
　her little ones cry out.
⁵ For at the ascent of Luhith
　they goᵍ up weeping bitterly;
　for at the descent of Horonaim
　　they have heard the distressing cry of
　　　anguish.
⁶ Flee! Save yourselves!
　Be like a wild assʳ in the desert!

⁷ Surely, because you trusted in your
　　strongholdsˢ and your treasures,
　you also shall be taken;
　Chemosh shall go out into exile,
　　with his priests and his attendants.
⁸ The destroyer shall come upon every
　　town,
　and no town shall escape;
　the valley shall perish,
　and the plain shall be destroyed,
　　as the Lord has spoken.

⁹ Set aside salt for Moab,
　for she will surely fall;
　her towns shall become a desolation,
　　with no inhabitant in them.

10 Accursed is the one who is slack in doing
the work of the Lord, and accursed is the one
who keeps back the sword from bloodshed.

¹¹ Moab has been at ease from his youth,
　　settled like wineᵗ on its dregs;
　he has not been emptied from vessel to
　　vessel,
　nor has he gone into exile;
　therefore his flavor has remained,
　　and his aroma is unspoiled.

n 47.5 Gk: Heb *their valley*　o 47.7 Gk Vg: Heb *you*
p 48.2 The place name *Madmen* sounds like the Hebrew
verb *to be silent*　q 48.5 Syr Tg: Heb *he goes*　r 48.6 Gk: Heb
like Aroer　s 48.7 Gk: Heb *works*　t 48.11 Heb lacks *like wine*

Nebuchadrezzar's invasion of Philistia in 604 BCE. The imagery includes similar signs of invasion
noted in the book, such as the sounds of animals and the disarray in families. **47:6** *Sword of the
Lord.* This is ultimately YHWH's doing.
　48:1–47 Judgment against Moab. The oracle describes the imminent threat of the destruction of
Moab by the Babylonians and features several cases of borrowing from other oracles about Moab
(e.g., Isa. 15–16). Moab lies to the east of Judah in the Transjordan. Ancestral narratives associate it
with Abraham's nephew Lot (Gen. 19:30–38), but it was historically an enemy of Israel and Judah.
The oracle mentions several towns in Moab, not all of which can be located. **48:1** *Nebo.* Here the
town, not the mountain. It is probably modern Khirbet Mekhayyet. **48:2** *Heshbon.* Modern Tell
Hesban. *Madmen.* Here a city, though the text is problematic. **48:7** *Chemosh.* The national Moabite

12 Therefore, the time is surely coming, says the LORD, when I shall send to him decanters to decant him and empty his vessels and break his jars in pieces. [13]Then Moab shall be ashamed of Chemosh, as the house of Israel was ashamed of Bethel, their confidence.

[14] How can you say, "We are heroes
and mighty warriors"?
[15] Moab is destroyed, and his towns have
gone up,
and the choicest of his young men
have gone down to slaughter,
says the King, whose name is the LORD
of hosts.
[16] The calamity of Moab is near at hand,
and his doom approaches swiftly.
[17] Mourn over him, all you his neighbors,
and all who know his name;
say, "How the mighty scepter is broken,
the glorious staff!"

[18] Come down from glory
and sit on the parched ground,
enthroned daughter Dibon!
For the destroyer of Moab has come up
against you;
he has destroyed your strongholds.
[19] Stand by the road and watch,
you inhabitant of Aroer!
Ask the man fleeing and the woman
escaping;
say, "What has happened?"
[20] Moab is put to shame, for it is broken
down;
wail and cry!
Tell it by the Arnon
that Moab is laid waste.

21 Judgment has come upon the tableland, upon Holon, and Jahzah, and Mephaath, [22]and Dibon, and Nebo, and Beth-diblathaim, [23]and Kiriathaim, and Beth-gamul, and Beth-meon, [24]and Kerioth, and Bozrah, and all the towns of the land of Moab, far and near. [25]The horn of Moab is cut off, and his arm is broken, says the LORD.

26 Make him drunk because he magnified himself against the LORD; let Moab wallow in his vomit; he, too, shall become a laughingstock. [27]Israel was a laughingstock for you, though he was not caught among thieves, but whenever you spoke of him you shook your head!

[28] Leave the towns, and live on the rock,
O inhabitants of Moab!
Be like the dove that nests
on the sides of the mouth of a gorge.
[29] We have heard of the pride of Moab—
he is very proud—
of his loftiness, his pride, and his
arrogance,
and the haughtiness of his heart.
[30] I myself know his insolence, says the LORD;
his boasts are false;
his deeds are false.
[31] Therefore I wail for Moab;
I cry out for all Moab;
for the people of Kir-heres I mourn.
[32] More than for Jazer I weep for you,
O vine of Sibmah!
Your branches crossed over the sea,
reached as far as Jazer;[u]
upon your summer fruits and your
vintage
the destroyer has fallen.
[33] Gladness and joy have been taken away
from the fruitful land of Moab;
I have stopped the wine from the
winepresses;
no one treads them with shouts of joy;
the shouting is not the shout of joy.

34 From the cry of Heshbon to Elealeh as far as Jahaz they utter their voice, from Zoar to Horonaim and Eglath-shelishiyah. For even the waters of Nimrim have become desolate. [35]And I will bring to an end in Moab, says the LORD, those who offer sacrifice at a high place and make offerings to their gods. [36]Therefore my heart moans for Moab like a flute, and my heart moans like a flute for the people of Kir-heres, for the riches they gained have perished.

37 For every head is shaved and every beard cut off; on all the hands there are

u 48.32 Heb mss: MT *the sea of Jazer*

deity. **48:13** *Bethel* refers to the Israelite sanctuary in this town; cf. 1 Kgs. 12:25–33; Amos 7:10–17. **48:18** Daughter language again is used to refer this time to the city of Dibon, modern Dhiban. **48:19** *Aroer.* Modern Khirbet Ara'ir on the Arnon River. **48:20** Shame is also put upon the Moabites, who face destruction. **48:29–45** Lament over the destruction is prominent. **48:31** *Kir-heres.* A

gashes and on the loins sackcloth. [38]On all the housetops of Moab and in the squares there is nothing but lamentation, for I have broken Moab like a vessel that no one wants, says the LORD. [39]How it is broken! How they wail! How Moab has turned his back in shame! So Moab has become a derision and a horror to all his neighbors.

[40] For thus says the LORD:
Look, he shall swoop down like an eagle
    and spread his wings against Moab;
[41] the towns[v] shall be taken
    and the strongholds seized.
The hearts of the warriors of Moab, on
        that day,
    shall be like the heart of a woman in
        labor.
[42] Moab shall be destroyed as a people,
    because he magnified himself against
        the LORD.
[43] Terror, pit, and trap
    are before you, O inhabitants of Moab!
                        says the LORD.
[44] Everyone who flees from the terror
    shall fall into the pit,
and everyone who climbs out of the pit
    shall be caught in the trap.
For I will bring these things[w] upon Moab
    in the year of their punishment,
                        says the LORD.

[45] In the shadow of Heshbon
    fugitives stop exhausted,
for a fire has gone out from Heshbon,
    a flame from the house of Sihon;
it has destroyed the forehead[x] of Moab,
    the scalp of the people of tumult.[y]
[46] Woe to you, O Moab!
    The people of Chemosh have perished,
for your sons have been taken captive
    and your daughters into captivity.
[47] Yet I will restore the fortunes of Moab
    in the latter days, says the LORD.
Thus far is the judgment on Moab.

49 Concerning the Ammonites.

Thus says the LORD:
    Has Israel no sons?
        Has he no heir?
    Why then has Milcom[z] dispossessed Gad
        and his people settled in its towns?
[2] Therefore, the time is surely coming,
        says the LORD,
    when I will sound the battle alarm
        against Rabbah of the Ammonites;
    it shall become a desolate mound,
        and its villages shall be burned with fire;
    then Israel shall dispossess those who
            dispossessed him,
        says the LORD.

[3] Wail, O Heshbon, for Ai is laid waste!
        Cry out, O daughters[a] of Rabbah!
    Put on sackcloth,
        lament, and slash yourselves with whips![b]
    For Milcom[c] shall go into exile,
        with his priests and his attendants.
[4] Why do you boast in your strength?
        Your strength is ebbing,
    O faithless daughter.
        Who trusted in her treasures, saying,[d]
        "Who will attack me?"
[5] I am going to bring terror upon you,
        says the Lord GOD of hosts,
        from all your neighbors,
    and you will be scattered, each headlong,
        with no one to gather the fugitives.

6 But afterward I will restore the fortunes of the Ammonites, says the LORD.

7 Concerning Edom.

Thus says the LORD of hosts:
    Is there no longer wisdom in Teman?
        Has counsel perished from the prudent?

v 48.41 Or *Kerioth*   w 48.44 Gk Syr: Heb *bring upon it*
x 48.45 Or *borderland*   y 48.45 Or *of Shaon*   z 49.1 Gk Vg
Syr: Heb *their king*   a 49.3 Or *villages*   b 49.3 Cn: Meaning
of Heb uncertain   c 49.3 Gk Vg Syr: Heb *their king*
d 49.4 Gk: Heb lacks *saying*

capital city of Moab; modern el-Kerak. **48:45–47** After the lament for the destruction, the oracle ends with a promise that Moab will be destroyed. These verses are not found in the Septuagint, which suggests that they are a later addition. **48:47** *Thus far is the judgment on Moab.* A conclusion that anticipates updates.

49:1–6 Judgment against the Ammonites. Similar to the oracle against the Philistines, this oracle is against an ethnic group rather than a geographic region, such as Edom and Damascus later in the chapter. The Ammonites are targets of the Babylonians, especially since they supported the Judean efforts that were opposed to Babylonia (cf. Jer. 27:3). Terror, lament, and mourning come upon the Ammonites. **49:6** This verse, as at the end of the oracle against Moab, is not in the Septuagint.

49:7–22 Judgment against Edom. Echoes of this oracle are found in the book of Obadiah (cf.

Going Deeper: The Oracles against the Nations (Jeremiah 46–51)

The oracles against the nations are a style of writings found within multiple prophetic books. As the name suggests, these oracles depict YHWH judging, condemning, and punishing the neighbors of Israel and Judah. In Jeremiah, chaps. 46–51 contain oracles of judgment targeting multiple cities, nations, and people groups, with the longest and most detailed judgment made against Babylon, whose leaders and armies were responsible for the fall of Judah and the exile. The placement of these texts at the end of the Hebrew manuscript of Jeremiah differs from the Greek manuscript tradition, where they appear in the middle of the book. This suggests that the oracles against the nations may have developed as their own literary unit originally separate from the larger book.

Other prophetic books in the Hebrew Bible contain collections of oracles against the nations: Isaiah, Ezekiel, Amos, Obadiah, Nahum, Zephaniah, and Zechariah. Like Jeremiah, the others usually cluster the oracles together as a unit. The abundance of these oracles in prophetic literature suggests that this genre was important within prophetic traditions. Their purpose, in addition to judging the enemies of Israel and Judah, was to show YHWH's power and control over all the world.

Like judgment oracles against Israel and Judah, the oracles against the nations frequently use graphic language, vivid metaphorical imagery, poetic devices, and prose statements to communicate bold judgments. Statements that affirm the suffering of the nations are sometimes juxtaposed to the restoration and salvation of YHWH's people. Historical figures, ethnic groups, and regional names are often used to add specificity to who is being targeted. Contemporary as well as past enemies of Israel and Judah are often targets of divine wrath, showing YHWH's strength and judgment over all the world for all time. The violent imagery in the oracles against the nations can make reading them difficult. Nonetheless, as a literary device, the oracles against the nations served the prophetic agenda and interest in affirming divine control over everyone and everything.

Jaime L. Waters

Has their wisdom vanished?
⁸ Flee; turn back; get down low,
   inhabitants of Dedan!
For I will bring the calamity of Esau
   upon him,
   the time when I punish him.
⁹ If grape gatherers came to you,
   would they not leave gleanings?
If thieves came by night,
   even they would pillage only what
     they wanted.
¹⁰ But as for me, I have stripped Esau bare;
   I have uncovered his hiding places,
   and he is not able to conceal himself.
His offspring are destroyed, his kinsfolk
   and his neighbors, and he is no more.
¹¹ Leave your orphans; I will keep them
   alive,
   and let your widows trust in me.

12 For thus says the LORD: If those who do not deserve to drink the cup still have to drink it, shall you be the one to go unpunished? You shall not go unpunished; you must drink it. ¹³For by myself I have sworn, says the LORD, that Bozrah shall become an object of horror and ridicule, a waste, and an

object of cursing, and all her towns shall be perpetual wastes.
¹⁴ I have heard tidings from the LORD,
   and a messenger has been sent among
     the nations:
"Gather yourselves together and come
     against her,
   and rise up for battle!"
¹⁵ For I will make you least among the
     nations,
   despised by humankind.
¹⁶ The terror you inspire
   and the pride of your heart have
     deceived you,
you who live in the clefts of the rock,^e
   who hold the height of the hill.
Although you make your nest as high as
     the eagle's,
   from there I will bring you down,
            says the LORD.

17 Edom shall become an object of horror; everyone who passes by it will be horrified and will hiss because of all its disasters. ¹⁸As when Sodom and Gomorrah and their

e 49.16 Or *of Sela*

Obad. 1–6). **49:18** The destruction of Sodom and Gomorrah is invoked to explain the horror that will befall Edom, and the image of animals and a woman in labor is also used to visualize the destruction.

neighbors were overthrown, says the Lord, no one shall live there, nor shall anyone settle in it. [19]Like a lion coming up from the thickets of the Jordan to a perennial pasture, I will suddenly chase Edom[f] away from it, and I will appoint over it whomever I choose.[g] For who is like me? Who can summon me? Who is the shepherd who can stand before me? [20]Therefore hear the plan that the Lord has made against Edom and the purposes that he has formed against the inhabitants of Teman: Surely the little ones of the flock shall be dragged away; surely their fold shall be appalled at their fate. [21]At the sound of their fall the earth shall tremble; the sound of their cry shall be heard at the Red Sea.[h] [22]Look, he shall mount up and swoop down like an eagle and spread his wings against Bozrah, and the heart of the warriors of Edom on that day shall be like the heart of a woman in labor.

23 Concerning Damascus.

Hamath and Arpad are confounded,
    for they have heard bad news;
they melt in fear; they are troubled like
        the sea[i]
    that cannot be quiet.
[24] Damascus has become feeble; she turned
        to flee,
    and panic seized her;
anguish and pangs seize her,
    as of a woman in labor.
[25] How is the famous city not forsaken,[j]
    the town of my joy?[k]
[26] Therefore her young men shall fall in her
        squares,
    and all her soldiers shall be destroyed
        on that day,
                says the Lord of hosts.
[27] And I will kindle a fire at the wall of
        Damascus,
    and it shall devour the strongholds of
        Ben-hadad.

28 Concerning Kedar and the kingdoms of Hazor that King Nebuchadrezzar of Babylon defeated.

Thus says the Lord:
Rise up; advance against Kedar!
    Destroy the people of the east!
[29] They take their tents and their flocks,
    their curtains and all their goods;
they carry off their camels for themselves,
    and a cry shall go up: "Terror is all
        around!"
[30] Flee; wander far away; hide in deep
        places,
    O inhabitants of Hazor!
                says the Lord.
For King Nebuchadrezzar of Babylon
    has made a plan against you
    and formed a purpose against you.

[31] Rise up; advance against a nation at ease,
    that lives secure,
                says the Lord,
that has no gates or bars,
    that lives alone.
[32] Their camels shall become plunder;
    their herds of cattle a spoil.
I will scatter to every wind
    those who have shaved temples,
and I will bring calamity
    against them from every side,
                says the Lord.
[33] Hazor shall become a lair of jackals,
    an everlasting waste;
no one shall live there,
    nor shall anyone settle in it.

34 The word of the Lord that came to the prophet Jeremiah concerning Elam, at the beginning of the reign of King Zedekiah of Judah.

35 Thus says the Lord of hosts: I am going to break the bow of Elam, the mainstay of their might, [36]and I will bring upon Elam the four winds from the four quarters of heaven, and I will scatter them to all these winds, and there shall be no nation to which

f 49.19 Heb him g 49.19 Meaning of Heb uncertain h 49.21 Or Sea of Reeds i 49.23 Cn: Heb there is trouble in the sea j 49.25 Vg: Heb is not forsaken k 49.25 Syr Vg Tg: Heb the town of my joy

49:23–27 Judgment against Damascus. The horror in the Syrian city is also vividly described as a city in panic, displaying anguish again like a woman in labor. Armies are destroyed, and fire devours the land.

49:28–33 Judgment against Kedar and Hazor. These Arabian desert cities are also conquered by Nebuchadrezzar, showing the range and scope of the Neo-Babylonian Empire. No one is spared, large nations and small cities alike.

49:34–39 Judgment against Elam. The style of this oracle is prose rather than poetry, but the images and outcomes are the same. The imagery is different, focused on the scattering and exile

the exiles from Elam shall not come. [37]I will terrify Elam before their enemies and before those who seek their life; I will bring disaster upon them, my fierce anger, says the LORD. I will send the sword after them until I have consumed them, [38]and I will set my throne in Elam and destroy their king and officials, says the LORD.

39 But in the latter days I will restore the fortunes of Elam, says the LORD.

50

The word that the LORD spoke concerning Babylon, concerning the land of the Chaldeans, by the prophet Jeremiah:

[2] Declare among the nations and proclaim;
set up a banner and proclaim;
do not conceal it, say:
"Babylon is taken;
Bel is put to shame;
Merodach is dismayed.
Her images are put to shame;
her idols are dismayed."

3 For out of the north a nation has come up against her; it shall make her land a desolation, and no one shall live in it; both humans and animals shall flee away.

4 In those days and in that time, says the LORD, the people of Israel shall come, they and the people of Judah together; they shall come weeping as they seek the LORD their God. [5]They shall ask the way to Zion, with faces turned toward it, and they shall come and join themselves to the LORD by an everlasting covenant that will never be forgotten.

6 My people have been lost sheep; their shepherds have led them astray, turning them away on the mountains; from mountain to hill they have gone, they have forgotten their fold. [7]All who found them have devoured them, and their enemies have said,

"We are not guilty, because they have sinned against the LORD, the true pasture, the LORD, the hope of their ancestors."

8 Flee from Babylon, and go out of the land of the Chaldeans, and be like male goats leading the flock. [9]For I am going to stir up and bring against Babylon a company of great nations from the land of the north, and they shall array themselves against her; from there she shall be taken. Their arrows are like the arrows of a skilled warrior who does not return empty-handed. [10]Chaldea shall be plundered; all who plunder her shall be sated, says the LORD.

[11] Though you rejoice, though you exult,
O plunderers of my heritage,
though you frisk about like a heifer on
the grass
and neigh like stallions,
[12] your mother shall be utterly shamed,
and she who bore you shall be
disgraced.
She shall be the last of the nations,
a wilderness, dry land, and a desert.
[13] Because of the wrath of the LORD, she
shall not be inhabited
but shall be an utter desolation;
everyone who passes by Babylon shall be
appalled
and hiss because of all her wounds.
[14] Take up your positions around Babylon,
all you who bend the bow;
shoot at her; spare no arrows,
for she has sinned against the LORD.
[15] Raise a shout against her from all sides,
"She has surrendered;
her bulwarks have fallen;
her walls are thrown down."
For this is the vengeance of the LORD:
take vengeance on her;
do to her as she has done.

of Elamites. **49:37** The judgment of Elam and all these places and peoples is framed as a divine demonstration of wrath.

50:1–46 Judgment against Babylon. After an extensive depiction of the destruction caused by Babylon, Jer. 50–51 offers a detailed depiction of how Babylon will itself fall. While its king was previously depicted as YHWH's servant (cf. Jer. 25:9; 27:6), the time has come for Babylon to be judged. **50:2** *Bel.* One of the names for Marduk, the chief Babylonian deity. *Merodach.* The biblical spelling of Marduk. **50:3, 9** The language of a nation (or nations) coming from the north harkens back to the foe of the north (cf. Jer. 1:13–15; 4:6; 6:1, 22; 10:22). Here it may anticipate Babylon's foes, the Medes and Persians. Graphic depictions of suffering and oppression by the Babylonians are described, with people finally recognizing the divine vengeance. **50:4–5** An expectation of future restoration for Zion. **50:11–16** The desolate image of Jerusalem is applied to Babylon.

¹⁶ Cut off from Babylon the sower
  and the wielder of the sickle in time of
    harvest;
because of the destroying sword,
  all of them shall return to their own
    people,
  and all of them shall flee to their own
    land.

17 Israel is a hunted sheep driven away by lions. First the king of Assyria devoured it, and now at the end King Nebuchadrezzar of Babylon has gnawed its bones. ¹⁸Therefore, thus says the LORD of hosts, the God of Israel: I am going to punish the king of Babylon and his land as I punished the king of Assyria. ¹⁹I will restore Israel to its pasture, and it shall feed on Carmel and in Bashan, and on the hills of Ephraim and in Gilead its hunger shall be satisfied. ²⁰In those days and at that time, says the LORD, the iniquity of Israel shall be sought, and there shall be none, and the sins of Judah, and none shall be found, for I will pardon the remnant that I have spared.

²¹ Go up to the land of Merathaim;ˡ
  go up against her,
and attack the inhabitants of Pekodᵐ
  and utterly destroy the last of
    them,ⁿ
                              says the LORD;
  do all that I have commanded you.
²² The noise of battle is in the land
  and great destruction!
²³ How the hammer of the whole earth
  is cut down and broken!
How Babylon has become
  a horror among the nations!
²⁴ I set a snare for you, and you were
    caught, O Babylon,
  but you did not know it;
you were discovered and seized
  because you challenged the LORD.
²⁵ The LORD has opened his armory
  and brought out the weapons of his
    wrath,
for the Lord GOD of hosts has a task
  in the land of the Chaldeans.
²⁶ Come against her from every quarter;
  open her granaries;

pile her up like heaps of grain, and
    destroy her utterly;
  let nothing be left of her.
²⁷ Kill all her bulls;
  let them go down to the slaughter.
Alas for them, their day has come,
  the time of their punishment!

28 Listen! Fugitives and refugees from the land of Babylon are coming to declare in Zion the vengeance of the LORD our God, vengeance for his temple.

29 Summon archers against Babylon, all who bend the bow. Encamp all around her; let no one escape. Repay her according to her deeds; just as she has done, do to her—for she has arrogantly defied the LORD, the Holy One of Israel. ³⁰Therefore her young men shall fall in her squares, and all her soldiers shall be destroyed on that day, says the LORD.

³¹ I am against you, O arrogant one,
  says the Lord GOD of hosts,
for your day has come,
  the time when I will punish you.
³² The arrogant one shall stumble and fall,
  with no one to raise him up,
and I will kindle a fire in his cities,
  and it will devour everything around him.

33 Thus says the LORD of hosts: The people of Israel are oppressed, and so also are the people of Judah; all their captors have held them fast and refuse to let them go. ³⁴Their Redeemer is strong; the LORD of hosts is his name. He will surely plead their cause, that he may give rest to the earth but unrest to the inhabitants of Babylon.

³⁵ A sword against the Chaldeans, says the
    LORD,
  and against the inhabitants of Babylon
  and against her officials and her
    sages!
³⁶ A sword against the diviners,
  so that they may become fools!
A sword against her warriors,
  so that they may be dismayed!

l 50.21 Or *of Double Rebellion*   *m* 50.21 Or *of Punishment*
n 50.21 Tg: Heb *destroy after them*

50:17–18 *King of Assyria* likely refers to Sennacherib; cf. Isa. 36:1–37:35. **50:21** The two names are wordplays. **50:26–27** An expectation that Babylon's food supply will be decimated. **50:35–37** The repeated imagery of the *sword* paints a picture of complete destruction.

[37] A sword against her[o] horses and against
    her[p] chariots
    and against all the foreign troops in
        her midst,
    so that they may become women!
A sword against her treasures,
    that they may be plundered!
[38] A drought against her waters,
    that they may be dried up!
For it is a land of images,
    and they go mad over idols.

39 Therefore wild animals shall live with
hyenas in Babylon,[q] and ostriches shall inhabit her; she shall never again be peopled or
inhabited for all generations. [40]As when God
overthrew Sodom and Gomorrah and their
neighbors, says the LORD, so no one shall live
there, nor shall anyone settle in her.

[41] Look, a people is coming from the
    north;
    a mighty nation and many kings
    are stirring from the farthest parts of
        the earth.
[42] They wield bow and spear;
    they are cruel and have no mercy.
The sound of them is like the roaring sea;
    they ride upon horses,
set in array as a warrior for battle,
    against you, O daughter Babylon!

[43] The king of Babylon heard news of them,
    and his hands fell helpless;
anguish seized him,
    pain like that of a woman in labor.

44 Like a lion coming up from the thickets
of the Jordan to a perennial pasture, I will
suddenly chase them away from her, and I
will appoint over her whomever I choose.[r]
For who is like me? Who can summon me?
Who is the shepherd who can stand before
me? [45]Therefore hear the plan that the LORD
has made against Babylon and the purposes
that he has formed against the land of the
Chaldeans: Surely the little ones of the flock
shall be dragged away; surely the fold shall
be appalled at their fate. [46]At the sound of the

capture of Babylon the earth shall tremble,
and a cry shall be heard among the nations.

51 Thus says the LORD:
    I am going to stir up a destructive wind[s]
    against Babylon
    and against the inhabitants of
        Leb-qamai,[t]
[2] and I will send winnowers to Babylon,
    and they shall winnow her.
They shall empty her land
    when they come against her from
        every side
    on the day of trouble.
[3] Let not the archer bend his bow,
    and let him not array himself in his
        coat of mail.
Do not spare her young men;
    utterly destroy her entire army.
[4] They shall fall down slain in the land of
        the Chaldeans
    and wounded in her streets.
[5] Indeed, Israel and Judah have not been
        forsaken
    by their God, the LORD of hosts,
though their land is full of guilt
    before the Holy One of Israel.

[6] Flee from the midst of Babylon;
    save your lives, each of you!
Do not perish because of her guilt,
    for this is the time of the LORD's
        vengeance;
    he is repaying her what is due.
[7] Babylon was a golden cup in the LORD's
        hand,
    making all the earth drunken;
the nations drank of her wine,
    and so the nations went mad.
[8] Suddenly Babylon has fallen and is
        shattered;
    wail for her!
Bring balm for her wound;
    perhaps she may be healed.
[9] We tried to heal Babylon,
    but she could not be healed.

o 50.37 Syr: Heb *his*   p 50.37 Syr: Heb *his*   q 50.39 Heb
lacks *in Babylon*   r 50.44 Meaning of Heb uncertain
s 51.1 Or *stir up the spirit of a destroyer*   t 51.1 That is, Chaldea

---

51:1–64 Judgment against Babylon continued. Judgment against Babylon continues. **51:1** *Leb-
qamai,* "heart of those who rise against me," is another example of an athbash cryptogram; see note
on 25:26. **51:7** The cup of wine is an allusion to YHWH forcing Judah and neighboring peoples to
drink a cup of poisoned wine as a signal of divine wrath. **51:8–9** The language of Babylon's healing
seems sarcastic within the context of destruction. **51:9–10** *We, our, us.* The exilic community's voice.

Forsake her, and let each of us go
　to our own country,
for her judgment has reached up to
　heaven
　and has been lifted up even to the
　　skies.
[10] The LORD has brought forth our
　vindication;
　come, let us declare in Zion
　the work of the LORD our God.

[11] Sharpen the arrows!
　Fill the quivers!

The LORD has stirred up the spirit of the
kings of the Medes because his purpose
concerning Babylon is to destroy it, for that
is the vengeance of the LORD, vengeance for
his temple.
[12] Raise a standard against the walls of
　Babylon;
　make the watch strong;
　post sentinels;
　prepare the ambushes;
for the LORD has both planned and done
　what he spoke concerning the
　　inhabitants of Babylon.
[13] You who live by mighty waters,
　rich in treasures,
your end has come;
　the thread of your life is cut.
[14] The LORD of hosts has sworn by himself:
Surely I will fill you with troops like a
　swarm of locusts,
　and they shall raise a shout of victory
　　over you.

[15] It is he who made the earth by his
　power,
　who established the world by his
　　wisdom
and by his understanding stretched out
　the heavens.
[16] When he utters his voice there is a
　tumult of waters in the heavens,
　and he makes the mist rise from the
　　ends of the earth.
He makes lightnings for the rain,
　and he brings out the wind from his
　　storehouses.

[17] Everyone is stupid and without
　knowledge;
　goldsmiths are all put to shame by
　　their idols,
for their images are false,
　and there is no breath in them.
[18] They are worthless, a work of delusion;
　at the time of their punishment they
　　shall perish.
[19] Not like these is the portion of Jacob,
　for he is the one who formed all
　　things,
and Israel is the tribe of his
　inheritance;
　the LORD of hosts is his name.
[20] You are my war club, my weapon of
　battle:
with you I smash nations;
　with you I destroy kingdoms;
[21] with you I smash the horse and its rider;
　with you I smash the chariot and the
　　charioteer;
[22] with you I smash man and woman;
　with you I smash the old man and the
　　boy;
with you I smash the young man and the
　girl;
[23] 　with you I smash shepherds and their
　　flocks;
with you I smash farmers and their
　teams;
　with you I smash governors and
　　deputies.

24 I will repay Babylon and all the inhabitants of Chaldea before your very eyes for all
the wrong that they have done in Zion, says
the LORD.

[25] I am against you, O destroying mountain,
　　　　　　　　　　　　　says the LORD,
　that destroys the whole earth;
I will stretch out my hand against you
　and roll you down from the crags
　and make you a burned-out mountain.
[26] No stone shall be taken from you for a
　corner
　and no stone for a foundation,
but you shall be a perpetual waste,
　says the LORD.

51:11 *Medes.* A people located in northwest Iran. They allied with Babylon to defeat Assyria in the late seventh century but by the sixth century had become Babylon's enemy. The Persians turned Media into a province, and they contributed to the overthrow of Babylon. **51:15–19** Cf. 10:12–16. **51:20–23** Now Israel, not Babylon, is the divine instrument who destroys kingdoms, reversing the

27 Raise a standard in the land;
    blow the trumpet among the nations;
prepare the nations for war against her;
    summon against her the kingdoms,
    Ararat, Minni, and Ashkenaz;
appoint a marshal against her;
    bring up horses like bristling locusts.
28 Prepare the nations for war against her,
    the kings of the Medes, with their
        governors and deputies,
    and every land under their dominion.
29 The land trembles and writhes,
    for the Lord's purposes against
        Babylon stand,
to make the land of Babylon a desolation,
    without inhabitant.
30 The warriors of Babylon have given up
        fighting;
    they remain in their strongholds;
their strength has failed;
    they have become women;
her buildings are set on fire;
    her bars are broken.
31 One runner runs to meet another,
    and one messenger to meet another,
to tell the king of Babylon
    that his city is taken from end to end:
32 the fords have been seized,
    the marshes have been burned with
        fire,
    and the soldiers are in panic.
33 For thus says the Lord of hosts, the God
        of Israel:
Daughter Babylon is like a threshing floor
    at the time when it is trodden;
yet a little while
    and the time of her harvest will come.

34 "King Nebuchadrezzar of Babylon has
        devoured me;
    he has crushed me;
he has made me an empty vessel;
    he has swallowed me like a monster;
he has filled his belly with my delicacies;
    he has spewed me out.
35 May my torn flesh be avenged on
        Babylon,"
    the inhabitants of Zion shall say.

"May my blood be avenged on the
        inhabitants of Chaldea,"
    Jerusalem shall say.
36 Therefore thus says the Lord:
I am going to defend your cause
    and take vengeance for you.
I will dry up her sea
    and make her fountain dry,
37 and Babylon shall become a heap of
        ruins,
    a den of jackals,
an object of horror and of hissing,
    without inhabitant.

38 Like lions they shall roar together;
    they shall growl like lions' whelps.
39 When they are inflamed, I will set out
        their drink
    and make them drunk, until they
        become merry
and then sleep a perpetual sleep
    and never wake, says the Lord.
40 I will bring them down like lambs to the
        slaughter,
    like rams and goats.

41 How Sheshach*u* is taken;
    the pride of the whole earth seized!
How Babylon has become
    an object of horror among the nations!
42 The sea has risen over Babylon;
    she has been covered by its
        tumultuous waves.
43 Her cities have become an object of
        horror,
    a land of drought and a desert,
a land in which no one lives
    and through which no mortal passes.
44 I will punish Bel in Babylon
    and make him disgorge what he has
        swallowed.
The nations shall no longer stream to him;
    the wall of Babylon has fallen.

45 Come out of her, my people!
    Save your lives, each of you,

u 51.41 That is, Babylon

---

image of Nebuchadrezzar as a divine instrument. **51:27** *Ararat.* Urartu, a people who lived in a region in eastern Turkey near Lake Van. *Minni.* A group who lived near Lake Urmia in modern Iraq. *Ashkenaz.* Probably the Scythians who lived in present-day Armenia. **51:29** The disaster that fills the land causes it to writhe and tremble. **51:30** Warriors are called women whose strength has failed, another unfortunate depiction of women, this time to emasculate Babylonian soldiers. **51:41** *Sheshach*—that is, Babylon; see note on 25:26. **51:42** *The sea has risen over Babylon.* The city was not near an

from the fierce anger of the Lord!
⁴⁶ Do not be fainthearted or fearful
　　at the rumors heard in the land—
one year one rumor comes,
　　the next year another,
rumors of violence in the land
　　and of ruler against ruler.

⁴⁷ Assuredly, the days are coming
　　when I will punish the images of
　　　　Babylon;
her whole land shall be put to shame,
　　and all her slain shall fall in her midst.
⁴⁸ Then the heavens and the earth
　　and all that is in them
shall shout for joy over Babylon,
　　for the destroyers shall come against
　　　　her out of the north,
　　　　　　　　　says the Lord.
⁴⁹ Babylon must fall for the slain of Israel,
　　as the slain of all the earth have fallen
　　　　because of Babylon.

⁵⁰ You survivors of the sword,
　　go; do not linger!
Remember the Lord in a distant land,
　　and let Jerusalem come into your
　　　　mind:
⁵¹ We are put to shame, for we have heard
　　insults;
　　dishonor has covered our faces,
for aliens have come
　　into the holy places of the Lord's
　　　　house.

⁵² Therefore the time is surely coming, says
　　the Lord,
　　when I will punish her idols,
and through all her land
　　the wounded shall groan.
⁵³ Though Babylon should mount up to
　　heaven,
　　and though she should fortify her
　　　　strong height,
from me destroyers would come upon
　　her,
says the Lord.

⁵⁴ Listen!—a cry from Babylon!
　　A great crashing from the land of the
　　　　Chaldeans!
⁵⁵ For the Lord is laying Babylon waste
　　and stilling her loud clamor.
Their waves roar like mighty waters;
　　the sound of their clamor
　　　　resounds,
⁵⁶ for a destroyer has come against her,
　　against Babylon;
her warriors are taken;
　　their bows are broken,
for the Lord is a God of recompense;
　　he will repay in full.
⁵⁷ I will make her officials and her sages
　　drunk,
　　also her governors, her deputies, and
　　　　her warriors;
they shall sleep a perpetual sleep and
　　never wake,
　　says the King, whose name is the Lord
　　　　of hosts.

⁵⁸ Thus says the Lord of hosts:
The broad wall of Babylon
　　shall be leveled to the ground,
and her high gates
　　shall be burned with fire.
The peoples exhaust themselves for
　　nothing,
　　the nations only for fire,
　　and they have become weary.

59 The word that the prophet Jeremiah commanded Seraiah son of Neriah son of Mahseiah, when he went with King Zedekiah of Judah to Babylon, in the fourth year of his reign. Seraiah was the quartermaster. ⁶⁰Jeremiah wrote in aᵛ scroll all the disasters that would come on Babylon, all these words that are written concerning Babylon. ⁶¹And Jeremiah said to Seraiah: "When you come to Babylon, see that you read all these words, ⁶²and say, 'O Lord, you yourself threatened to destroy this place so that neither humans nor animals shall live in it, and

v 51.60 Or *one*

actual sea. The reference is to the sea as a mythic symbol of chaos. **51:59–64** *In the fourth year of his reign*—that is, 593 BCE. Jeremiah commands Seraiah, Baruch's brother, to deliver the oracle of judgment in Babylon, reading it aloud and then symbolically throwing it into the Euphrates River. As the written oracle sinks, so Babylon will sink. The attitude against Babylon is notably different from Jeremiah's statements to not fight Babylon. The historical circumstances could be the cause of the shift, or this text may be an anti-Babylonian text added to the book. See **"The Oracles against the Nations," p. 1105.**

it shall be desolate forever.' ⁶³When you finish reading this scroll, tie a stone to it, and throw it into the middle of the Euphrates, ⁶⁴and say, 'Thus shall Babylon sink, to rise no more, because of the disasters that I am bringing on her.' "^w

Thus far are the words of Jeremiah.

52

Zedekiah was twenty-one years old when he began to reign; he reigned eleven years in Jerusalem. His mother's name was Hamutal daughter of Jeremiah of Libnah. ²He did what was evil in the sight of the LORD, just as Jehoiakim had done. ³Indeed, Jerusalem and Judah so angered the LORD that he expelled them from his presence.

Zedekiah rebelled against the king of Babylon. ⁴And in the ninth year of his reign, in the tenth month, on the tenth day of the month, King Nebuchadrezzar of Babylon came with all his army against Jerusalem, and they laid siege to it; they built siegeworks against it all around. ⁵So the city was besieged until the eleventh year of King Zedekiah. ⁶On the ninth day of the fourth month the famine became so severe in the city that there was no food for the people of the land. ⁷Then a breach was made in the city wall,^x and all the soldiers fled and went out from the city by night by the way of the gate between the two walls, by the King's Garden, though the Chaldeans were all around the city. They went in the direction of the Arabah. ⁸But the army of the Chaldeans pursued the king and overtook Zedekiah in the plains of Jericho, and all his army was scattered, deserting him. ⁹Then they captured the king and brought him up to the king of Babylon at Riblah in the land of Hamath, and he passed sentence on him. ¹⁰The king of Babylon killed the sons of Zedekiah before his eyes and also killed all the officers of Judah at Riblah. ¹¹He put out the eyes of Zedekiah and bound him in fetters, and the king of Babylon took him to Babylon and put him in prison until the day of his death.

¹²In the fifth month, on the tenth day of the month—which was the nineteenth year of King Nebuchadrezzar, king of Babylon— Nebuzaradan, the captain of the bodyguard who served the king of Babylon, entered Jerusalem. ¹³He burned the house of the LORD, the king's house, and all the houses of Jerusalem; every great house he burned down. ¹⁴All the army of the Chaldeans who were with the captain of the guard broke down all the walls around Jerusalem. ¹⁵Nebuzaradan the captain of the guard carried into exile some of the poorest of the people and the rest of the people who were left in the city and the deserters who had defected to the king of Babylon, together with the rest of the artisans. ¹⁶But Nebuzaradan the captain of the guard left some of the poorest people of the land to be vinedressers and tillers of the soil.

¹⁷The pillars of bronze that were in the house of the LORD, and the stands and the bronze sea that were in the house of the LORD, the Chaldeans broke in pieces and carried all the bronze to Babylon. ¹⁸They took away the pots, the shovels, the snuffers, the basins, the ladles, and all the vessels of bronze used in the temple service. ¹⁹The captain of the guard took away the small bowls also, the firepans, the basins, the pots, the lampstands, the ladles, and the bowls for libation, both those of gold and those of silver. ²⁰As for the two pillars, the one sea, the twelve bronze bulls that were under the stands, which King Solomon had made for the house of the LORD, the bronze of all these vessels was beyond weighing. ²¹As for the pillars, the height of the one pillar was eighteen cubits; its circumference was twelve cubits; it was hollow, and its thickness was four fingers. ²²Upon it was a capital of bronze; the height of the capital was five cubits; latticework and pomegranates, all of bronze, encircled the top of the capital. And the second pillar had the same, with pomegranates. ²³There were ninety-six pomegranates on the sides; all the pomegranates encircling the latticework numbered one hundred.

²⁴The captain of the guard took the chief priest Seraiah, the second priest Zephaniah,

w 51.64 Gk: Heb *on her. And they shall weary themselves*
x 52.7 Heb lacks *wall*

52:1–34 A historical appendix. Much of this chapter comes from 2 Kgs. 24:18–25:30 and includes details surrounding Zedekiah's reign and demise, the siege and fall of Jerusalem, and the exile. There are slight differences in the dates of the exile and significant differences in the numbers of Judeans exiled. Jeremiah states a total of 4,600 people were exiled, while 2 Kgs. 24 says 18,000 people. The differences could reflect varying traditions or ways of counting (perhaps excluding or including women and children). The differences could also reflect an interest in downplaying or

and the three guardians of the threshold. [25]From the city he took an officer who had been in command of the soldiers, seven men of the king's council who were found in the city; the secretary of the commander of the army who mustered the people of the land; and sixty men of the people of the land who were found inside the city. [26]Then Nebuzaradan the captain of the guard took them and brought them to the king of Babylon at Riblah. [27]And the king of Babylon struck them down and put them to death at Riblah in the land of Hamath. So Judah went into exile out of its land.

[28] This is the number of the people whom Nebuchadrezzar took into exile: in the seventh year, three thousand twenty-three Judeans; [29]in the eighteenth year of Nebuchadrezzar he took into exile from Jerusalem eight hundred thirty-two persons; [30]in the twenty-third year of Nebuchadrezzar, Nebuzaradan the captain of the guard took into exile of the Judeans seven hundred forty-five persons; all the persons were four thousand six hundred.

[31] In the thirty-seventh year of the exile of King Jehoiachin of Judah, in the twelfth month, on the twenty-fifth day of the month, King Evil-merodach of Babylon, in the year he began to reign, showed favor to King Jehoiachin of Judah and brought him out of prison; [32]he spoke kindly to him and gave him a seat above the seats of the other kings who were with him in Babylon. [33]So Jehoiachin put aside his prison clothes, and every day of his life he dined regularly at the king's table. [34]For his allowance, a regular daily allowance was given him by the king of Babylon, as long as he lived, up to the day of his death.

amplifying the impact of exile on the Judean community. **52:28–30** The description of waves of deportations dates to 597, 587, and 582 BCE. **52:31–34** King Jehoiachin, who lived in exile for thirty-seven years, is released from prison at the end of the book.

LAMENTATIONS

Date and Authorship

Lamentations is a book about war. It is a poetic response to the catastrophic events in Judah at the beginning of the sixth century BCE. Between 597 and 587 BCE, the Babylonians invaded and conquered Judah. As part of the conquest, the Babylonians deposed the Judean king, laid siege to Jerusalem, and ultimately destroyed the city and its temple as well as other cities in Judah. During this period, many Judeans died from military violence and famine and sickness related to siege warfare. While some scholars think Lamentations was written shortly after the catastrophe by Judean exiles in Babylonia (see **"Exile (2 Kings)," p. 539**), others date its composition to Judah decades later.

Literary Character and Context

Biblical poetry seems designed to speak to our emotions. Much like contemporary music, it uses all the tools of its genre—including imagery, wordplay, and metaphors—to encourage the audience to empathize with the speaker and to share their experience (see **"Hebrew Poetry," p. 741**).

Each chapter of Lamentations is a complete poem expressing a particular perspective on the war and its aftermath. The speakers take us on a heartbreaking tour of the destroyed city and make us witnesses to the suffering of those who died and those who survived. Chaps. 1 and 2 express the perspective of Daughter Zion (see **"Daughter Zion," p. 1118**) and of an unnamed witness to Zion's experience. Chap. 3 is spoken by "the man"—an individual who expresses suffering and tentative faith and hope in God. Chap. 4 returns mainly to the perspective of a third-person witness. Chap. 5 speaks as "we"—expressing the experience of the community.

While the chapters share some literary and thematic features, they probably originated as separate poems that were edited into the current collection. This collection invites readers both to read the chapters as individual poems and to reflect on the additional meanings that arise when read in their canonical order. Key features of the poems include the multiplicity of voices, the personification of Jerusalem, and the acrostic structure (in chaps. 1–4, each line or stanza begins with one of the twenty-two successive letters of the Hebrew alphabet; chap. 5 also has twenty-two verses). Together, the poems function as a portrait gallery, sharing different responses to catastrophe and different understandings of the role of God in individual and national suffering.

Lamentations also shares features with common genres in the Bible and beyond, especially dirges and laments. The similarity to dirges—poems or songs of mourning for individuals—would have encouraged ancient audiences to transfer the experiences of personal grief to their experience of the national loss of Jerusalem. The resemblance to poems and songs of lament, which usually begin with expressions of pain and suffering and transition to expressions of hope and faith, would have highlighted the ways in which Lamentations diverges from this pattern by returning time and again to expressions of suffering, pain, and isolation from God.

Lamentations in Jewish and Christian Contexts

In Judaism and Christianity, worshiping communities have been invited to share in this cry of pain. Traditionally, Jews recite Lamentations on Tisha B'Av, the solemn holiday that commemorates the destructions of the first and second temples as well as other tragedies in Jewish history (as one of the Megillot; see **"Introduction to the Writings," pp. 6–9**). Also in Judaism, the collection of interpretations called Lamentations Rabbah uses Lamentations as an occasion not only to reiterate and amplify the pain and suffering expressed in Lamentations but also to imagine God's emotional experience during and after the war, destruction, and exile. In some Roman Catholic communities, Lamentations is recited during Holy Week, inviting worshipers to reexperience the tragic death of Jesus before celebrating the resurrection.

Reading Guide

The events of 597–586 challenged core Judean theological beliefs. Before the conquest, many people thought that Jerusalem was invincible because it housed God's temple. The destruction of Jerusalem raised devastating theological questions: Did it mean that God was less powerful than the Babylonians? Did the tragic suffering of the people mean that God had abandoned them? These

questions hover in the background of much of the Hebrew Bible. One response, which probably had roots in preexilic Judah and was prominent in the postexilic period, argues that God and Israel are in a covenantal relationship that determines Israel's (Judah's) fate. If the people obey the covenant, God will protect them and grant them blessings. If they disobey, they will suffer environmental and political catastrophe. According to this perspective, the destruction and exile are not signs of God's powerlessness but rather signs that the covenant is operating as designed. National catastrophe means that Israel sinned and is being punished. If Israel returns to obedience, God will return its fortunes. This perspective appears in the third chapter of Lamentations and occasionally in the other chapters. However, the rest of Lamentations challenges it. Rather than offering Israel's guilt as the full explanation for the tragedies, Lamentations testifies to the vast suffering of the people and demands that God witness and respond to the suffering. God is not presented as an impartial judge meting out consequences. Rather, God is portrayed as a raging and violent enemy. While covenantal theology always holds out the possibility of restoration, the end of Lamentations is deeply uncertain about this possibility, asking whether God will return.

In recent decades, Lamentations has emerged as a valuable resource for dealing with catastrophe and trauma. The voice of Daughter Zion can serve as a model for survivorship—her refusal to accept abuse and violence as legitimate punishment and her consistent demand that the source of power and authority (God) hear her voice and bear witness to her suffering have emerged as a biblical model for cathartic lament and protest. At the same time, the absence of a divine response and the lack of closure in the book can validate the experience of many survivors of trauma for whom conventional explanations of causality are insufficient and for whom the feelings of isolation, anger, despair, and defiance expressed in the book are very real.

Elsie R. Stern

1 How lonely sits the city
    that once was full of people!
How like a widow she has become,
    she that was great among the nations!
She that was a princess among the
      provinces
    has become subject to forced labor.

2 She weeps bitterly in the night,
    with tears on her cheeks;
among all her lovers,
    she has no one to comfort her;
all her friends have dealt treacherously
      with her;
    they have become her enemies.

3 Judah has gone into exile with suffering
    and hard servitude;
she lives now among the nations;
    she finds no resting place;
her pursuers have all overtaken her
    in the midst of her distress.

4 The roads to Zion mourn,
    for no one comes to the festivals;
all her gates are desolate;
    her priests groan;
her young girls grieve,[a]
    and her lot is bitter.

a 1.4 Meaning of Heb uncertain

Lam. 1 is structured as a dialogue. In vv. 1–11 and 17, an observer describes the city's devastation and the suffering of its residents. In vv. 12–16 and 18–22, the city, personified as a woman, describes her suffering and pleads for comfort and vengeance. The repeated contrasts between Zion's former glory and present suffering add to the pathos. The poem is an acrostic. The verses begin with the letters of the Hebrew alphabet in order. While this may have been a memory aid, it also suggests the all-encompassing (A to Z) nature of Zion's suffering.

1:1 *How* ("ekah") communicates despair, horror, and bewilderment: "How can this be?" *Like a widow.* Zion is personified as a woman (see **"Daughter Zion," p. 1118**; see also Isa. 1:8; Zeph. 3:14). In ancient Israel, widows not only experienced grief; they were also vulnerable socially and economically.

1:4 The gates of the city were a gathering place and site for commerce, legal, and other proceedings. Their desolation underscores the end of all normal urban activity.

⁵ Her foes have become the masters;
   her enemies prosper
because the Lord has made her suffer
   for the multitude of her transgressions;
her children have gone away,
   captives before the foe.

⁶ From daughter Zion has departed
   all her majesty.
Her princes have become like stags
   that find no pasture;
they fled without strength
   before the pursuer.

⁷ Jerusalem remembers[b] all the precious
      things
   that were hers in days of old.
When her people fell into the hand of
      the enemy
   and there was no one to help her,
the enemy looked on;
   they mocked over her downfall.

⁸ Jerusalem sinned grievously,
   so she has become a filthy thing;
all who honored her despise her,
   for they have seen her nakedness;
she herself groans
   and turns her face away.

⁹ Her uncleanness was in her skirts;
   she took no thought of her future;
her downfall was appalling,
   with none to comfort her.
Look, O Lord, at my affliction,
   for the enemy has triumphed!

¹⁰ Enemies have stretched out their hands
   over all her precious things;
she has even seen the nations
   invade her sanctuary,
those whom you forbade
   to enter your congregation.

¹¹ All her people groan
   as they search for bread;
they trade their treasures for food
   to revive their lives.
Look, O Lord, and see
   how worthless I have become.

¹² Is it nothing to you,[c] all you who pass by?
   Look and see
if there is any sorrow like my sorrow,
   which was brought upon me,
which the Lord inflicted
   on the day of his fierce anger.

¹³ From on high he sent fire;
   it went deep into my bones;
he spread a net for my feet;
   he turned me back;
he has left me stunned,
   faint all day long.

¹⁴ My transgressions were bound[d] into a
      yoke;
   by his hand they were fastened together;
they weigh on my neck,
   sapping my strength;

b 1.7 Q ms: MT adds *in the days of her affliction and wandering*
c 1.12 Meaning of Heb uncertain   d 1.14 Meaning of Heb
uncertain

1:5 The speaker identifies Zion's suffering as punishment for multiple unnamed transgressions. This explanation for national catastrophe, which is prominent in Deuteronomy and many prophetic books, is challenged by Zion in 1:12–15.

1:8–10 Zion's sins lead to her shame. V. 10 uses the language of rape and sexual violence to describe the invasion of Jerusalem and the temple. This encourages the audience to transfer the feelings of horror, shame, and pain associated with sexual violence to their understanding of the impact of the destruction of the temple. At the same time, it taps into the troubling use of metaphors of adultery and domestic violence to describe the relationship between God and Israel in the prophetic literature (see Jer. 2:20–25; Hos. 2).

1:11b–16 *Look, O Lord.* Zion interrupts the speaker and gives a counterperspective to his account of her suffering. While acknowledging wrongdoing, Zion describes God as acting out of fierce anger, not judicious punishment. She repeatedly beseeches humans and God to serve as witnesses to her suffering and to comfort her. These desires mirror therapeutic and pastoral approaches to trauma that center on bearing witness to the survivor's suffering and accompanying them through the emotional journey of survival. **1:13–14** God is portrayed as a military enemy, using the tactics of siege, exile, and enslavement against Zion. The mention of young men and women, priests, and elders emphasizes that no segment of the population escapes the suffering. After decrying the mocks and taunts of the enemies, Zion challenges God to punish them for their wrongdoing just as God has punished Zion.

Going Deeper: Daughter Zion (Lamentations 1)

The figure of Daughter Zion appears in chaps. 1, 2, and 4 of Lamentations. The figure is a personification of Jerusalem who represents the experience of the city's residents and, more abstractly, of the city itself. Her voice encompasses the city's community and collective identity—including its buildings, its history, and its social fabric. Some scholars have posited a connection between Daughter Zion in Lamentations and city goddesses who mourn the destruction of their cities in Mesopotamian city laments. Daughter Zion also resonates with a long tradition of urban and national personification. Statements like "the city celebrated the Super Bowl victory" or "the nation mourned the death of its leader" are part of this rhetorical tradition.

Lamentations takes personification further by creating a character who represents the city. This strategy encourages the audience to empathize with the city as if it were an individual. Furthermore, the gender of Zion engages three different aspects of the social reality of women in the ancient Near East. First, the poet uses the social, military, and economic vulnerability of women as well as the intense feelings of attachment and protection associated with motherhood to enhance the pathos of the city. The audience is likely to sympathize with the city as a grieving widow and mother as she laments her isolation, her suffering, and the suffering of her children. Second, the poet deploys common ideas about women's sexuality. The use of images of sexual violence to describe the destruction of Jerusalem likely encouraged a potent mixture of shame and horror in ancient audiences, and these feelings are then transferred to the experience of the city. At the same time, the few references to Zion's "promiscuity" likely encouraged feelings of blame and shame, reinforcing the covenantal paradigm in which Zion's suffering was punishment for unspecified sins (see **"Sexually Abusive Language in the Prophets," p. 1035**). Third, the poet incorporates women's role as ritual mourners and lamenters. In the ancient Near East, lamenting the dead was a ritualized part of death and mourning rituals, and women were often the designated mourners. In this role, women could give voice both to the community's grief over the loss and to feelings of anger and despair that are often catalyzed by death. By assigning women to be the designated mourners, women become the mouthpieces for communally held expressions of defiance and anger against God—a role that is at once necessary, powerful, and potentially dangerous.

Elsie R. Stern

the Lord handed me over
to those whom I cannot withstand.

¹⁵ The Lord has rejected
all my warriors in the midst of me;
he proclaimed a time against me
to crush my young men;
the Lord has trodden as in a winepress
the virgin daughter Judah.

¹⁶ For these things I weep;
my eyes^e flow with tears;
for a comforter is far from me,
one to revive my courage;
my children are desolate,
for the enemy has prevailed.

¹⁷ Zion stretches out her hands,
but there is no one to comfort her;
the Lord has commanded against Jacob
that his neighbors should become his foes;
Jerusalem has become
a filthy thing among them.

¹⁸ The Lord is in the right,
for I have rebelled against his word;
but hear, all you peoples,
and behold my suffering;
my young women and young men
have gone into captivity.

¹⁹ I called to my lovers,
but they deceived me;
my priests and elders
perished in the city
while seeking food
to revive their lives.

²⁰ Look, O Lord, at how distressed I am;
my stomach churns;
my heart is wrung within me
because I have been very rebellious.
In the street the sword bereaves;
in the house it is like death.

²¹ They heard how I was groaning,
with no one to comfort me.

e 1.16 Heb *my eye, my eye*

All my enemies heard of my trouble;
　　they are glad that you have done it.
Bring on the day that you have announced,
　　and let them be as I am.

²² Let all their evildoing come before you,
　　and deal with them
as you have dealt with me
　　because of all my transgressions;
for my groans are many,
　　and my heart is faint.

2 How the Lord in his anger
　　has humiliated*f* daughter Zion!
He has thrown down from heaven to earth
　　the splendor of Israel;
he has not remembered his footstool
　　in the day of his anger.

² The Lord has destroyed without mercy
　　all the dwellings of Jacob;
in his wrath he has broken down
　　the strongholds of daughter Judah;
he has brought down to the ground in
　　dishonor
　　the kingdom and its rulers.

³ He has cut down in fierce anger
　　all the might of Israel;
he has withdrawn his right hand from them
　　in the face of the enemy;
he has burned like a flaming fire in Jacob,
　　consuming all around.

⁴ He has bent his bow like an enemy,
　　with his right hand set like a foe;
he has killed all those
　　in whom we took pride
in the tent of daughter Zion;
　　he has poured out his fury like fire.

⁵ The Lord has become like an enemy;
　　he has destroyed Israel.
He has destroyed all its palaces,
　　laid in ruins its strongholds,
and multiplied in daughter Judah
　　mourning and lamentation.

⁶ He has broken down his booth like a
　　garden;
　　he has destroyed his tabernacle;
the Lord has abolished in Zion
　　festival and Sabbath
and in his fierce indignation has spurned
　　king and priest.

⁷ The Lord has scorned his altar,
　　disowned his sanctuary;
he has delivered into the hand of the
　　enemy
　　the walls of her palaces;
a clamor was raised in the house of the
　　Lord
　　as on a day of festival.

⁸ The Lord determined to lay in ruins
　　the wall of daughter Zion;
he stretched the line;
　　he did not withhold his hand from
　　destroying;
he caused rampart and wall to lament;
　　they languish together.

⁹ Her gates have sunk into the ground;
　　he has ruined and broken her bars;
her king and princes are among the nations;
　　guidance is no more,
and her prophets obtain
　　no vision from the Lord.

f 2.1 Meaning of Heb uncertain

Lam. 2 The poem has three parts. In vv. 1–17, an observer describes the brutal destruction of Jerusalem and casts God as the destroying enemy. In vv. 18–19, this speaker exhorts Zion to cry out to God. In vv. 20–22, Zion implores God to witness and respond to the suffering of her people. The verses begin with the letters of the Hebrew alphabet in order.
2:1–8 These verses focus on God's merciless destruction of the temple and Jerusalem. Repeated references to anger, wrath, and violent destruction encourage the audience to experience the devastation of the physical city and to imagine God as a vehemently destructive force. **2:1** The terms *splendor of Israel* and *his footstool* are references to the temple. **2:3** *He has withdrawn his right hand.* The destruction of Jerusalem raised doubts about the power of YHWH. In the ancient Near East, the destruction of a temple and its city often signaled the weakness of the patron god and its inability to protect its earthly dwelling. Lamentations circumvents this challenge by stating that YHWH withdrew protection from the city voluntarily, allowing it to be destroyed. This assertion is sandwiched between descriptions of God as the destroyer—another attempt to preserve God's power despite the destruction of God's temple, city, and people. **2:6–7** YHWH was expected to have a special relationship with the kings and priests; the spurning of *king and priest* is a particularly strong reversal.

¹⁰ The elders of daughter Zion
    sit on the ground in silence;
they have thrown dust on their heads;
    they put on sackcloth;
the young women of Jerusalem
    have bowed their heads to the ground.

¹¹ My eyes are spent with weeping;
    my stomach churns;
my bile is poured out on the ground
    because of the destruction of my
      people,*
because infants and babes faint
    in the streets of the city.

¹² They cry to their mothers,
    "Where is bread and wine?"
as they faint like the wounded
    in the streets of the city,
as their life is poured out
    on their mothers' bosoms.

¹³ What can I say for you, to what compare
    you,
    O daughter Jerusalem?
To what can I liken you, that I may
    comfort you,
    O virgin daughter Zion?
For vast as the sea is your ruin;
    who can heal you?

¹⁴ Your prophets have seen for you
    false and deceptive visions;
they have not exposed your iniquity
    to restore your fortunes
but have seen oracles for you
    that are false and misleading.

¹⁵ All who pass along the way
    clap their hands at you;
they hiss and wag their heads
    at daughter Jerusalem:

"Is this the city that was called
    the perfection of beauty,
    the joy of all the earth?"

¹⁶ All your enemies
    open their mouths against you;
they hiss, they gnash their teeth,
    they cry: "We have devoured her!
Ah, this is the day we longed for;
    at last we have seen it!"

¹⁷ The LORD has done what he purposed;
    he has carried out his threat;
as he ordained long ago,
    he has demolished without pity;
he has made the enemy rejoice over you
    and exalted the might of your foes.

¹⁸ Cry aloud* to the Lord!
    O wall of daughter Zion!
Let tears stream down like a torrent
    day and night!
Give yourself no rest,
    your eyes no respite!

¹⁹ Arise, cry out in the night,
    at the beginning of the watches!
Pour out your heart like water
    before the presence of the Lord!
Lift your hands to him
    for the lives of your children,
who faint for hunger
    at the head of every street.

²⁰ Look, O LORD, and consider!
    To whom have you done this?
Should women eat their offspring,
    the children they have borne?
Should priest and prophet be killed
    in the sanctuary of the Lord?

g 2.11 Heb *the daughter of my people*　h 2.18 Cn: Heb *Their heart cried*

2:11–12 Lamentations repeatedly describes the starvation and death of babies and children. This reflects the reality of siege and war and also underscores the suffering of innocents, challenging the interpretation of the destruction as deserved punishment.

2:15–16 Shame is a recurring theme in Lamentations.

2:18–19 The speaker exhorts Zion to cry out her grief and suffering to God. This advice assumes that God shares the human emotions of pity and empathy and will be moved by those feelings to act on behalf of Zion and her people.

2:20–22 Zion heeds the speaker's advice and cries out to God. Unlike the speaker, who laments the destruction of the physical city and its political and religious structures, Zion laments the suffering and death of her people. **2:20** The image of women eating their children is common in ancient literature about siege and warfare. Regardless of the historicity, these verses express the utter devastation and extreme suffering of the Judean population.

²¹ The young and the old are lying
  on the ground in the streets;
my young women and my young men
  have fallen by the sword;
in the day of your anger you have killed
    them,
  slaughtering without mercy.

²² You invited my enemies from all around
  as if for a day of festival;
and on the day of the anger of the Lord,
  no one escaped or survived;
those whom I bore and reared,
  my enemy has destroyed.

3 I am one who has seen affliction
  under the rod of God's[i] wrath;
² he has driven and brought me
  into darkness without any light;
³ against me alone he turns his hand,
  again and again, all day long.

⁴ He has made my flesh and my skin waste
    away;
  he has broken my bones;
⁵ he has besieged and enveloped me
  with bitterness and tribulation;
⁶ he has made me sit in darkness
  like the dead of long ago.

⁷ He has walled me about so that I cannot
    escape;
  he has put heavy chains on me;
⁸ though I call and cry for help,
  he shuts out my prayer;
⁹ he has blocked my ways with hewn stones;
  he has made my paths crooked.

¹⁰ He is a bear lying in wait for me,
  a lion in hiding;
¹¹ he led me off my way and tore me to pieces;
  he has made me desolate;

¹² he bent his bow and set me
  as a mark for his arrow.
¹³ He shot into my vitals
  the arrows of his quiver;
¹⁴ I have become the laughingstock of all
    my people,
  the object of their taunt songs all day long.
¹⁵ He has filled me with bitterness;
  he has sated me with wormwood.

¹⁶ He has made my teeth grind on gravel;
  he has made me cower in ashes;
¹⁷ my soul is bereft of peace;
  I have forgotten what happiness is;
¹⁸ so I say, "Gone is my glory
  and all that I had hoped for from the
  Lord."

¹⁹ The thought of my affliction and my
    homelessness
  is wormwood and gall!
²⁰ My soul continually thinks of it
  and is bowed down within me.
²¹ But this I call to mind,
  and therefore I have hope:

²² The steadfast love of the Lord never ceases,[j]
  his mercies never come to an end;
²³ they are new every morning;
  great is your faithfulness.
²⁴ "The Lord is my portion," says my soul,
  "therefore I will hope in him."

²⁵ The Lord is good to those who wait for him,
  to the soul that seeks him.
²⁶ It is good that one should wait quietly
  for the salvation of the Lord.
²⁷ It is good for one to bear
  the yoke in youth,

i 3.1 Heb *his* *j* 3.22 Syr Tg: Heb Lord, *we are not cut off*

Lam. 3 does not refer explicitly to the events of 597–587. Instead, it deploys the conventional language of suffering. It is also the only chapter that engages the possibility of hope and faith in God. The acrostic structure continues, but here each Hebrew letter begins three successive verses.
3:2–20 The male speaker deploys metaphors of danger and assault common to psalms of lament—including darkness, entrapment, attack by wild animals, military attack, and the taunting of enemies—to express his suffering. Many of these images resonate with other descriptions of deportation and exile and are also reversals of common images of God's redemptive and protective acts. **3:2** *He has driven . . . me.* The Hebrew is usually translated as "led." The language of leadership (shepherding) is usually employed in reference to God's protection, but this verse describes God leading the speaker into darkness and suffering. **3:18** *From the Lord.* The Hebrew can also mean "because of the Lord." This verse offers two possibilities simultaneously—because of his suffering, the speaker has lost hope or because of God, the speaker has lost hope.
3:21–40 In the midst of his lament, the speaker recites core elements of Israel's theology.

²⁸ to sit alone in silence
  when the Lord*ᵏ* has imposed it,
²⁹ to put one's mouth to the dust
  (there may yet be hope),
³⁰ to give one's cheek to the smiter
  and be filled with insults.

³¹ For the Lord will not
  reject forever.
³² Although he causes grief, he will have
    compassion
  according to the abundance of his
    steadfast love;
³³ for he does not willingly afflict
  or grieve anyone.

³⁴ When all the prisoners of the land
  are crushed under foot,
³⁵ when justice is perverted
  in the presence of the Most High,
³⁶ when one's case is subverted—
  does the Lord not see it?

³⁷ Who can command and have it done,
  if the Lord has not ordained it?
³⁸ Is it not from the mouth of the Most High
  that evil and good come?
³⁹ Why should any who draw breath
    complain
  about the punishment of their sins?

⁴⁰ Let us test and examine our ways
  and return to the Lord.
⁴¹ Let us lift up our hearts as well as our
    hands
  to God in heaven.
⁴² We have transgressed and rebelled,
  and you have not forgiven.

⁴³ You have wrapped yourself with anger
    and pursued us,
  killing without pity;
⁴⁴ you have wrapped yourself with a cloud
  so that no prayer can pass through.
⁴⁵ You have made us filth and rubbish
  among the peoples.

⁴⁶ All our enemies
  have opened their mouths against us;
⁴⁷ panic and pitfall have come upon us,
  devastation and destruction.
⁴⁸ My eyes flow with rivers of tears
  because of the destruction of my people.*ˡ*

⁴⁹ My eyes will flow without ceasing,
  without respite,
⁵⁰ until the Lord from heaven
  looks down and sees.
⁵¹ My eyes cause me grief
  at the fate of all the young women in
    my city.

⁵² Those who were my enemies without cause
  have hunted me like a bird;
⁵³ they flung me alive into a pit
  and hurled stones on me;
⁵⁴ water closed over my head;
  I said, "I am lost."

⁵⁵ I called on your name, O Lord,
  from the depths of the pit;
⁵⁶ you heard my plea, "Do not close your ear
  to my cry for help, but give me relief!"
⁵⁷ You came near when I called on you;
  you said, "Do not fear!"

k 3.28 Heb *he* *l* 3.48 Heb *the daughter of my people*

3:32 *Steadfast love.* The Hebrew term "hesed" denotes positive actions that arise out of obligation (see **"Hesed," p. 375**). God's commitment to the covenant with the house of David and the people of Israel means that God's anger cannot last forever. Commitment to the covenant necessitates a return to compassion. **3:34–36** These verses draw on a belief in divine justice. **3:37–39** *Who can command?* These verses insist that God controls the forces of history.

3:40–41 The speaker exhorts and enacts repentance, inviting his community to pray to God and confess their sins.

3:42 The Hebrew can be translated as "and" or "but." In one of the most shocking moments of the poem, the speaker confesses on behalf of his community, but God still does not forgive. This refusal counters the widespread theology, articulated repeatedly in the prophetic books, that if the people repent, God will forgive.

3:43–54 In similar psalms of lament, the speaker's statement of faith and prayer for help concludes with a praise of God. Here, the poet breaks with that convention and returns to the description of suffering. However, the poem does shift to "we" language, describing collective rather than individual suffering.

3:55–61 The divine actions are translated in the past tense here, suggesting that God's prior actions of protection and salvation are grounds for hope. However, several interpreters have

58 You have taken up my cause, O Lord;
   you have redeemed my life.
59 You have seen the wrong done to me,
      O Lord;
   judge my cause.
60 You have seen all their malice,
   all their plots against me.

61 You have heard their taunts, O Lord,
   all their plots against me.
62 The whispers and murmurs of my assailants
   are against me all day long.
63 Whether they sit or rise—see,
   I am the object of their taunt songs.

64 Pay them back for their deeds, O Lord,
   according to the work of their hands!
65 Give them anguish of heart;
   your curse be on them!
66 Pursue them in anger and destroy them
   from under the Lord's heavens.

4 How the gold has grown dim;
   how the pure gold is changed!
The sacred stones lie scattered
   at the head of every street.

2 The precious children of Zion,
   worth their weight in fine gold—
how they are reckoned as earthen pots,
   the work of a potter's hands!

3 Even the jackals offer the breast
   and nurse their young,
but my people has become cruel,
   like the ostriches in the wilderness.

4 The tongue of the infant sticks
   to the roof of its mouth for thirst;
the children beg for food,
   but there is nothing for them.

5 Those who feasted on delicacies
   perish in the streets;
those who were brought up in purple
   cling to ash heaps.

6 For the chastisement of my people has
      been greater
   than the punishment of Sodom,
which was overthrown in a moment,
   though no hand was laid on it.ᵐ

7 Her princes were purer than snow,
   whiter than milk;
their bodies were more ruddy than coral,
   their form cut like sapphire.ⁿ

8 Now their visage is blacker than soot;
   they are not recognized in the streets.
Their skin has shriveled on their bones;
   it has become as dry as wood.

9 Happier were those pierced by the sword
   than those pierced by hunger,
whose life drains away, deprived
   of the produce of the field.

10 The hands of compassionate women
   have boiled their own children;
they became their food
   in the destruction of my people.

11 The Lord gave full vent to his wrath;
   he poured out his hot anger
and kindled a fire in Zion
   that consumed its foundations.

12 The kings of the earth did not believe,
   nor did any of the inhabitants of the
      world,

m 4.6 Meaning of Heb uncertain   n 4.7 Or lapis lazuli

suggested that the verbs should be translated as "supplications," beseeching God to attend to Israel's suffering and vindicate its case (vv. 58–60).

Lam. 4 contains the most graphic descriptions of the people's suffering during the siege and military conquest, emphasizing the contrast between Jerusalem's glorious past and abject present (vv. 1, 2, 5, 7–8). The verses begin with the letters of the Hebrew alphabet in order.

4:3 *Even the jackals.* Jackals and ostriches were known as scavengers associated with desolate places (Isa. 34:13; Mic. 1:8). Ostriches were thought to callously abandon their eggs (Job 39:13–17).

4:6 Elsewhere, the destruction of Sodom is the epitome of destruction (Deut. 29:22–23). Here, Sodom is luckier than Jerusalem because its destruction occurs without prolonged suffering.

4:8 *Now their visage.* This blackness refers to the darkening of the skin from dirt, scabs, and illness, not to melanin.

4:9–10 As is the case today, wars often caused famine in the ancient world. Death by starvation was drawn out and brutal and affected all segments of the population. Cannibalism is a stock image in texts prophesying or describing sieges and famines. However, it is unknown how commonly it

that foe or enemy could enter
    the gates of Jerusalem.

¹³ It was for the sins of her prophets
    and the iniquities of her priests,
who shed the blood of the righteous
    in her midst.

¹⁴ Blindly they wandered through the
    streets,
    so defiled with blood
that no one was able
    to touch their garments.

¹⁵ "Away! Unclean!" people shouted at
    them;
    "Away! Away! Do not touch!"
So they became fugitives and wanderers;
    it was said among the nations,
    "They shall stay here no longer."

¹⁶ The Lord himself has scattered them;
    he will regard them no more;
no honor was shown to the priests,
    no favor to the elders.

¹⁷ Our eyes failed, ever watching
    vainly for help;
we were watching eagerly
    for a nation that could not save.

¹⁸ They dogged our steps
    so that we could not walk in our streets;
our end drew near; our days were
    numbered,
    for our end had come.

¹⁹ Our pursuers were swifter
    than the eagles in the heavens;
they chased us on the mountains;
    they lay in wait for us in the wilderness.

²⁰ The Lord's anointed, the breath of our life,
    was taken in their pits—
the one of whom we said, "Under his shadow
    we shall live among the nations."

²¹ Rejoice and be glad, O daughter Edom,
    you that live in the land of Uz;
but to you also the cup shall pass;
    you shall become drunk and strip
    yourself bare.

²² The punishment of your iniquity,
    O daughter Zion, is accomplished;
    he will keep you in exile no longer;
but your iniquity, O daughter Edom, he
    will punish;
    he will uncover your sins.

5 Remember, O Lord, what has befallen us;
    look, and see our disgrace!

occurred. The image of mothers consuming their own children is probably a hyperbolic image designed to arouse horror (cf. 2:20).

4:14 It is unclear whether this verse refers to the prophets and priests, the righteous, or the people in general.

4:15 *Away!* This verse alludes to Lev. 13:45, in which the leper is instructed to cry out "Unclean, unclean" to warn others about his state. The language of purity and impurity is multilayered in the Hebrew Bible. In Leviticus, there are clear distinctions between ritual impurity, which is morally neutral, and ethical impurity (see **"Holiness and Purity," p. 158**). In other contexts, the morally neutral category of ritual impurity becomes a negative category. Here it serves as a metaphor for extreme suffering and social isolation. This resonates with contemporary culture, where morally neutral categories of disability, such as blindness or deafness, become negatively charged when used metaphorically.

4:17 *Our eyes failed.* The speaking voice switches to the first-person plural, joining the experience of the besieged and conquered community.

4:20 *The Lord's anointed* probably refers to King Zedekiah, the last king of Judah, who attempted to resist the Babylonians and was blinded and taken captive into Babylonia (2 Kgs. 24:20; 25:6–7).

4:22 *The punishment of your iniquity.* The words translated here as past tense can also be understood as supplications, which better fits the context of ongoing suffering (see note on 3:55–61).

Lam. 5 is not an acrostic, unlike the other chapters, and has a more regular meter and more balanced symmetry. It also conforms more closely to a conventional pattern of communal laments that begin with a cry to God, continue with descriptions of current suffering, and end with a praise of God and appeal for help. Most strikingly, this poem speaks explicitly in the voice of the community, adding a communal voice to Lamentations's tapestry of perspectives on the war, conquest, and exile.

5:1 In Hebrew, words referring to "we/us" end in the same sound: "anu." That sound occurs thirty-four times in this poem, emphasizing the communal nature of this closing voice.

² Our inheritance has been turned over to
  strangers,
    our homes to aliens.
³ We have become orphans, fatherless;
    our mothers are like widows.
⁴ We must pay for the water we drink;
    the wood we get must be bought.
⁵ With a yoke*ᵒ* on our necks we are hard
  driven;
    we are weary; we are given no rest.
⁶ We have made a pact with*ᵖ* Egypt and
  Assyria
    to get enough bread.
⁷ Our ancestors sinned; they are no more,
    and we bear their iniquities.
⁸ Slaves rule over us;
    there is no one to deliver us from their
  hand.
⁹ We get our bread at the peril of our lives,
    because of the sword in the
  wilderness.
¹⁰ Our skin is black as an oven
    from the scorching heat of famine.
¹¹ Women are raped in Zion,
    young women in the towns of Judah.
¹² Princes are hung up by their hands;
    no respect is shown to the elders.
¹³ Young men are compelled to grind,
    and boys stagger under loads of wood.

¹⁴ The old men have left the city gate,
    the young men their music.
¹⁵ The joy of our hearts has ceased;
    our dancing has been turned to
  mourning.
¹⁶ The crown has fallen from our head;
    woe to us, for we have sinned!
¹⁷ Because of this our hearts are sick;
    because of these things our eyes have
  grown dim:
¹⁸ because of Mount Zion, which lies
  desolate;
    jackals prowl over it.

¹⁹ But you, O LORD, reign forever;
    your throne endures to all
  generations.
²⁰ Why have you forgotten us completely?
    Why have you forsaken us these many
  days?
²¹ Restore us to yourself, O LORD, that we
    may be restored;
    renew our days as of old—
²² unless you have utterly rejected us
    and are angry with us beyond
  measure.

o 5.5 Symmachus: Heb lacks *With a yoke*   *p* 5.6 Heb *have
given the hand to*

5:2–3 These verses describe the breakdown of family and inheritance structures that were the backbone of Judean society.

5:4–6 The economy has been destroyed, and the most available commodities now bear a cost.

5:11–14 Every segment of society suffers, and all conventional norms of status and role are overturned.

5:15–16 These verses refer not only to personal emotional experiences but also to the loss of the temple and monarchy. The destruction of the temple ended the dancing and joy associated with the sacrificial rituals.

5:19 This is a statement of the widespread belief in the stability and eternity of God's reign, which are usually invoked to offer comfort and hope.

5:22 *Unless.* The verse can also be translated as "but rather, you have utterly rejected us." These two translations underscore the dynamics of hope and despair throughout the book. Do the speakers feel that God's enmity is permanent and there is no hope of repair, or does their current suffering allow them to hope for repair even as they fear it may not be possible? Both possibilities resonate with human experience, and Lamentations bears witness to this reality even as the despair and hopelessness challenge fundamental convictions that run throughout the Hebrew Bible. Isaiah 40–55 is the Bible's most direct response to the despair expressed in Lamentations. Those chapters address directly the feelings of anger and abandonment, attempting to reassure the exiled Judeans that divine reconciliation is not only possible but imminent.

EZEKIEL

Overview

The book of Ezekiel relates the prophetic experiences and activities of an elite priest who had been exiled to Babylon ten years prior to the fall of Jerusalem to the Babylonians. These specific elements shape the theology of the book. The fate of the temple takes center stage, while sin is described with the cultic language of purity and abomination. The book captures the experience of the city's fall for elite males.

Literary Structure

Three visions that take place in YHWH's temple provide the backbone of this prophetic collection (chaps. 1, 8–11, and 40–48). In each of the visions, a divine power transports Ezekiel into the temple, where he sees YHWH sitting on a movable throne, surrounded by a retinue of divine beings. These visions capture the ancient Near Eastern view that temples housed an aspect of the god worshiped there, as seen, for example, also in the vision of God in Isa. 6. In the first vision, Ezekiel sees God in the temple of Jerusalem. In 8–11, he witnesses God abandoning that temple because of the defilement of that sacred space by the sins of Judeans. The book ends with a nine-chapter description of a perfect temple and the return of YHWH to the literal center of all Israel.

Many of the prophetic texts in the book are dated (e.g., 8:1), which provides structure to the book as a whole. Most of these indicate that the book is generally preserved in chronological order. In general, chaps. 2–7 pertain to Jerusalem when there was still hope for repentance and salvation, while chaps. 12–24 describe the hopelessness of the city once God left the temple. With the announcement of the destruction of Jerusalem in 24:19–27 and 33:21–22, which bookend a section of oracles condemning Judah's neighbors (chaps. 25–32), in chaps. 33–39, the texts become increasingly optimistic about a restored future for Judah's former elites, culminating in an Edenic vision of a perfect temple and perfect state.

Date and Authorship

Most scholars date much of the book to the late exilic period (ca. 550–500; see **"Exile (2 Kings),"** **p. 539**). The book's dated oracles include a later revision of an earlier oracle that incorrectly predicted that Babylon would conquer Egypt (26:19–21 and 29:17–20), yet this revision still does not accord with the fate of Egypt vis-à-vis the Babylonians, as it was neither conquered nor plundered. In addition, the description of the perfect temple in chaps. 40–48 not only does not align with the Second Temple, built after the exile, but also shows no evidence of the tensions involved in its rebuilding. For many of these scholars, Ezekiel contains material stemming from a historical person living in the exile and able to produce this highly literary text.

Other scholars, noting the intricate literary character of the book, assert that it could not have been produced by an exiled figure, with few material resources or communal support. For these scholars, the character of Ezekiel reflects the author's retrospective on the impact of the city's fall on subsequent generations. While the material may be associated with a historical person, the final form of the book shows evidence of a later narrative frame, most evident in the references to dates in the book's introduction and the date citations inserted throughout the texts.

Whether the book was written during the late exilic or early Persian period, it was certainly preserved by Judeans in the Persian period. This indicates that it spoke to later generations as a book that captured their own intergenerational experience of a collective trauma that threatened the preservation of a unique Israelite cultural and religious identity. Later scribes who produced the final form of the book would have adapted their received text to make the connections to their present audience clearer.

Reading Guide

The book of Ezekiel is about God. Every element in the book, including the portrayal of Ezekiel, functions to keep the focus on YHWH's divine prerogative to act as God wills. The result is a rather uncomfortable view of God's character. Not once in the book does God act out of love; the closest the book comes is in 39:25, where God feels compassion or mercy. God is the agent of destruction;

the Babylonian army is a mere pawn in the divine plan. That destruction has as its main goal the shaming of Jerusalem's former elite, depicted through images of degradation and disgust, often portrayed in gendered ways: the elite are depicted as active agents of willful desecration both through visions of idolatry in the temple (chap. 8) and through metaphors likening them to a sexually depraved woman (chaps. 16 and 23).

Ezekiel's defeated elites have no hope of repentance and play no role in their restoration. They are like dead bones strewn across a desolate field or sheep wandering around without sense. In the texts of restoration, YHWH is the sole actor, purifying them from their former sins. The promised restoration has nothing to do with some kind of inner conversion of the people; it is solely an act of divine prerogative. God chooses this people *because* they do not deserve it (36:16–36).

Why such a stark theology whose main purpose is to shame God's people? To modern ears, such a theology may make little sense. Within the exilic and Persian periods, however, such a theology addressed Judea's central concern. The fall of Jerusalem and the subsequent failure of the Second Temple, built during the Persian period, to restore a divinely sanctioned monarchy suggested that Israel's God was either weak or capricious—either way, unworthy of worship and certainly not a foundation for collective identity. The author(s) of the book of Ezekiel addresses this problem head-on. The book utilizes Israel's religious traditions but transforms them into a divine manifesto. For example, chap. 20 recounts God's delivery of the Jews from slavery in Egypt as purely an act of divine choosing. In fact, the whole point of choosing this people is that they were so debased, their establishment as God's nation would prove to the world YHWH's power. Exodus, then, can function no longer as evidence of Israel's righteousness but only as proof of God's authority in world events.

Shame, then, connotes the basic recognition that humans are not God. Within ancient society, which was arranged hierarchically, "shame" denoted that someone recognized their place with respect to someone they should serve or acquiesce to. Wives had "shame" with respect to the male head of household, for example. We might use the word *deference*, but the book of Ezekiel uses the word *shame* for its visceral quality. The book is looking not for intellectual assent but for an utterly interior change that requires the subject to see the world and their place in it in a whole new light.

Exile did that. The fall of Jerusalem caused the former elite to viscerally view their world and their place in it in a whole new way, a way that revealed their own contributions to the fate they now suffered. Shame captures the collective experience of the loss of identity through this ethnic-based trauma. The collective trauma was passed down through the generations for both those living in exile and those "restored" to a nation under the control of foreign overlords. Shame was not an optional state of being; it captured their own experience. The book of Ezekiel gives this shame theological meaning and purpose.

Corrine L. Carvalho

1 In the thirtieth year, in the fourth month, on the fifth day of the month, as I was among the exiles by the River Chebar, the heavens were opened, and I saw visions of God. ²On the fifth day of the month (it was the fifth year of the exile of King Jehoiachin), ³the word of the LORD came to the priest Ezekiel son of Buzi in the land of the Chaldeans by the River Chebar, and the hand of the LORD was on him there.

1:1–3 The book of Ezekiel uses the convention of locating the authorizing prophet chronologically and physically, with a few subtle but important deviations. **1:1** *In the thirtieth year.* While the other dates in the book are figured from the exile of King Jehoiachin, this one has no point of reference. It may refer to the prophet's age. *I was among the exiles.* This brief first-person statement by Ezekiel marks him as one of the former elites of Jerusalem who now lives in exile in a foreign land. **1:2** *On the fifth day.* The first of thirteen dates in the book, here June/July 593 BCE. **1:3** *The priest Ezekiel* indicates that the book will reflect on the fall of Jerusalem from a religious perspective. *The River Chebar* was a canal that branched off the Euphrates River near Nippur. Archaeological remains in this area attest to the presence of a Jewish community during this time period; see **"Diaspora," p. 1338**. *Chaldeans* is a designation for the Babylonians.

4 As I looked, a stormy wind came out of the north: a great cloud with brightness around it and fire flashing forth continually and in the middle of the fire something like gleaming amber. [5]In the middle of it was something like four living creatures. This was their appearance: they were of human form. [6]Each had four faces, and each of them had four wings. [7]Their legs were straight, and the soles of their feet were like the sole of a calf's foot, and they sparkled like burnished bronze. [8]Under their wings on their four sides they had human hands. And the four had their faces and their wings thus: [9]their wings touched one another; each of them moved straight ahead, without turning as they moved. [10]As for the appearance of their faces: the four had the face of a human being, the face of a lion on the right side, the face of an ox on the left side, and the face of an eagle; [11]such were their faces. Their wings were spread out above; each creature had two wings, each of which touched the wing of another, while two covered their bodies. [12]Each moved straight ahead; wherever the spirit would go, they went, without turning as they went. [13]In the middle of[a] the living creatures there was something that looked like burning coals of fire, like torches moving to and fro among the living creatures; the fire was bright, and lightning issued from the fire. [14]The living creatures darted to and fro, like a flash of lightning.

15 As I looked at the living creatures, I saw a wheel on the earth beside the living creatures, one for each of the four of them.[b] [16]As for the appearance of the wheels and their construction: their appearance was like the gleaming of beryl, and the four had the same form, their construction being something like a wheel within a wheel. [17]When they moved, they moved in any of the four directions without veering as they moved. [18]Their rims were tall and awesome, for the rims of all four were full of eyes all around. [19]When the living creatures moved, the wheels moved beside them, and when the living creatures rose from the earth, the wheels rose. [20]Wherever the spirit would go, they went, and the wheels rose along with them, for a living spirit was in the wheels. [21]When they moved, the others moved; when they stopped, the others stopped; and when they rose from the earth, the wheels rose along with them, for a living spirit was in the wheels.

22 Over the heads of the living creatures there was something like a dome, shining like crystal,[c] spread out above their heads. [23]Under the dome their wings were stretched out straight, one toward another, and each of the creatures had two wings covering its body. [24]When they moved, I heard the sound of their wings like the sound of mighty waters, like the thunder of the Almighty,[d] a sound of tumult like the sound of an army; when they stopped, they let down their wings. [25]And there came a voice from above the dome over their heads; when they stopped, they let down their wings.

26 And above the dome over their heads there was something like a throne, in

a 1.13 Gk OL: Heb *And the appearance of*   b 1.15 Heb *of their faces*   c 1.22 Gk: Heb *like the awesome crystal*   d 1.24 Traditional rendering of Heb *Shaddai*

1:4–28 Returning to first-person speech, these verses attempt to describe a complex vision of God's presence, which will be reprised in chaps. 8–11 and 40–48. The description includes fantastical elements, which signal their visionary character, combining images derived from storms, heavenly beings, precious gems, and imperial power. They parallel the vision of God described in Isa. 6:1–7, with significant expansions. 1:4 *Something like.* This phrase occurs throughout the vision's description to signal that the account combines extraordinary detail with indescribable phenomena. 1:10 *The appearance of their faces.* The first creatures that the vision describes—whom the reader later learns bear the throne upon which God sits and are identified as "cherubim" in Ezek. 10:1—resemble similar divine attendants in Mesopotamian art. They are "mixed" creatures, whose body parts resemble various animals. Ezekiel's version of the animals has four faces on a single head, representing their ability to move in any direction. 1:15–21 A *wheel* accompanies each creature, signifying the portability of the deity that they carry. The use of *eyes* set into the rims of the wheels symbolizes their ability to move effortlessly in any direction. The imagery indicates a type of heavenly chariot attended to and moved by heavenly beings. 1:24–25 The vision is not just visual; it is also auditory. The sound of a storm brackets the vision of the moving chariot. 1:26–28 The vision now moves above the creatures to a throne mounted above the wheels with a humanlike being seated upon the throne. Before the prophet can look above this being's belt, he is overcome with awe. *Bow* may be either a rainbow or a weapon. *Glory* indicates the awesomeness of God's presence.

appearance like sapphire,[e] and seated above the likeness of the throne was something that seemed like a human form. [27]Upward from what appeared like the loins I saw something like gleaming amber, something that looked like fire enclosed all around, and downward from what looked like the loins I saw something that looked like fire, and there was a splendor all around. [28]Like the bow in a cloud on a rainy day, such was the appearance of the splendor all around. This was the appearance of the likeness of the glory of the LORD.

When I saw it, I fell on my face, and I heard the voice of someone speaking.

2 He said to me: "O mortal,[f] stand up on your feet, and I will speak with you." [2]And when he spoke to me, a spirit entered into me and set me on my feet, and I heard him speaking to me. [3]He said to me, "Mortal, I am sending you to the people of Israel, to a nation[g] of rebels who have rebelled against me; they and their ancestors have transgressed against me to this very day. [4]The descendants are impudent and stubborn. I am sending you to them, and you shall say to them, 'Thus says the Lord GOD.' [5]Whether they hear or refuse to hear (for they are a rebellious house), they shall know that there has been a prophet among them. [6]And you, O mortal, do not be afraid of them, and do not be afraid of their words, though briers and thorns surround you and you live among scorpions; do not be afraid of their words, and do not be dismayed at their looks, for they are a rebellious house. [7]You shall speak my words to them, whether they hear or refuse to hear, for they are a rebellious house.

[8] "But you, mortal, hear what I say to you; do not be rebellious like that rebellious house; open your mouth and eat what I give you." [9]I looked, and a hand was stretched out to me, and a written scroll was in it. [10]He spread it before me; it had writing on the front and on the back, and written on it were words of lamentation and mourning and woe.

3 He said to me, "O mortal, eat what is offered to you; eat this scroll, and go, speak to the house of Israel." [2]So I opened my mouth, and he gave me the scroll to eat. [3]He said to me, "Mortal, eat this scroll that I give you and fill your stomach with it." Then I ate it, and in my mouth it was as sweet as honey.

4 He said to me, "Mortal, go to the house of Israel and speak my very words to them. [5]For you are not sent to a people of obscure speech and difficult language but to the house of Israel, [6]not to many peoples of obscure speech and difficult language whose words you cannot understand. Surely, if I sent you to them, they would listen to you. [7]But the house of Israel will not be willing to listen to you, for they are not willing to listen to me, because all the house of Israel have a hard forehead and a stubborn heart. [8]See, I have made your face hard against their faces and your forehead hard against their foreheads. [9]Like the hardest stone, harder than flint, I have made your forehead; do not fear them or be dismayed at their looks, for they are a rebellious house." [10]He said to me, "Mortal, all my words that I shall speak to you receive in your heart and hear with your ears; [11]then go to the exiles, to your people, and speak to

e 1.26 Or *lapis lazuli*   f 2.1 Heb *son of man* (and so throughout the book when Ezekiel is addressed)   g 2.3 Syr: Heb *to nations*

2:1–3:11 Ezekiel hears God speaking from the midst of the throne. The speech contains the description of the Israelites as *rebellious* and God's command to the prophet to eat a scroll containing the divine message Ezekiel must relay. See **"Ezekiel, the Hybrid Exile," p. 1130. 2:1** *Mortal*. While the literal translation of the Hebrew is "son of man," here it is not an honorific but connotes the wide gap between God and the prophet. This phrase serves as Ezekiel's epithet. **2:2** *Spirit*, introduced in 1:12, functions as God's agent. For spirits and prophecy, see, for example, 1 Kgs. 22:22–23 and Joel 2:28–29. **2:3** *Rebels* echoes the characterization of the Israelites during the wilderness period in Exodus, Numbers, and Deuteronomy. **2:4** *Lord GOD* is the divine epithet used throughout the book. The first word translates the Hebrew word for "master." The second word is the divine name (the consonants YHWH), which in other books in this translation is rendered "LORD." **2:6** *Briers, thorns,* and *scorpions* are metaphors for prophesying, suggesting that the experience was not only painful but also life-threatening. **2:9** *Written scroll* emphasizes the written character of Ezekiel's prophetic activity as opposed to the public pronouncement of a figure like Amos (7:12–13). **2:10** *Words of lamentation and mourning and woe.* Ezekiel's charge resembles Isaiah's in Isa. 6:11–13—that is, the announcement of total disaster. **3:11** *Whether they*

Focus On: Ezekiel, the Hybrid Exile (Ezekiel 2)

On a surface reading of the book of Ezekiel, the characterization of the main protagonist seems rather straightforward. He speaks very little, has a clear prophetic function, and attempts to conserve Judah's traditions. The odd things that he does here and there are unavoidable, commanded by God. It does not take much digging, though, to see the complexities behind his characterization, actions, and words.

The book starts by introducing him as a priest, a status he reinforces with his focus on the temple and its laws. His actions, however, are strictly those of a prophet: he sees visions, hears voices, acts out divine pronouncements, relays divine speech, and so on. The elders even consult him, as they would a prophet. He never performs a priestly ritual, even those allowed outside the temple, such as intoning a psalm, providing a blessing, or performing circumcision. These two major elements of his characterization (a prophet who uses priestly theology) make him a hybrid of the two roles.

His actions also exhibit hybridity. God renders him speechless, but the book is filled with his songs and speeches. His body is bound yet travels impossible lengths in his visions. Sometimes he claims that God will not punish the innocent, but in other places, the innocent suffer because of the sins of the leaders.

The words that come from Ezekiel's open and shut mouth exhibit a deep cultural hybridity as well. On the one hand, the language and imagery throughout the book demonstrate expert knowledge of Israelite intellectual traditions. His speeches utilize motifs found in the Pentateuch or in other prophets, but they do not simply reuse them; they push the concepts into new territory. On the other hand, the images also resonate with motifs found in foreign cultures. The oracles against Tyre, for example, play with Tyre's own mythic tropes. The most prominent elements of extra-Israelite motifs are those coming from Babylon, including the descriptions of the cherubim, the glory emanating from God, and the concept of a world tree.

This cultural hybridity should be expected. Postcolonial studies have shown that people who experience forced migration and/or colonization develop a hybrid culture: one that merges images from the dominant culture with the subject's indigenous culture. This often helps colonized peoples undermine the hegemonic use of colonizing images. The hybridity of the book of Ezekiel, then, reflects the colonized setting of the book by making Ezekiel the prophet a thoroughly hybrid figure.

Corrine L. Carvalho

them. Say to them, 'Thus says the Lord God,' whether they hear or refuse to hear."

12 Then the spirit lifted me up, and as the glory of the Lord rose[h] from its place, I heard behind me the sound of loud rumbling; [13]it was the sound of the wings of the living creatures brushing against one another and the sound of the wheels beside them that sounded like a loud rumbling. [14]The spirit lifted me up and bore me away; I went in bitterness in the heat of my spirit, the hand of the Lord being strong upon me. [15]I came to the exiles at Tel-abib, who lived by the River Chebar.[i] And I sat there among them, stunned, for seven days.

16 At the end of seven days, the word of the Lord came to me: [17]Mortal, I have made you a sentinel for the house of Israel; whenever you hear a word from my mouth, you shall give them warning from me. [18]When I say to the wicked, "You shall surely die," and you give them no warning and do not speak to warn the wicked from their wicked way in order to save their lives, those wicked persons shall die for their iniquity, but their blood I will require at your hand. [19]But if you warn the wicked and they do not turn from their wickedness or from their wicked way,

h 3.12 Cn: Heb *and blessed be the glory of the Lord*   i 3.15 Heb mss Syr: MT *Chebar, and to where they lived*

hear or refuse to hear. The prophet is only responsible for delivering God's message, not for the reaction of its audience.

3:12–21 The account of Ezekiel's first vision ends with his return to the physical reality of life in exile. **3:12–13** *Rumbling*, or earthquake. **3:17** *Sentinel.* The prophetic office is likened to a guard on the city walls who has the responsibility of sounding a warning about an approaching enemy. The concept is repeated and expanded in chap. 33. **3:18, 21** *You shall surely die* and *They shall surely live* are formal, binding oaths.

they shall die for their iniquity, but you will have saved your life. ²⁰Again, if the righteous turn from their righteousness and commit iniquity and I lay a stumbling block before them, they shall die; because you have not warned them, they shall die for their sin, and their righteous deeds that they have done shall not be remembered, but their blood I will require at your hand. ²¹If, however, you warn the righteous not to sin and they do not sin, they shall surely live because they took warning, and you will have saved your life.

22 Then the hand of the Lᴏʀᴅ was upon me there, and he said to me, "Rise up, go out into the valley, and there I will speak with you." ²³So I rose up and went out into the valley, and the glory of the Lᴏʀᴅ stood there, like the glory that I had seen by the River Chebar, and I fell on my face. ²⁴The spirit entered into me and set me on my feet, and he spoke with me and said to me: "Go, shut yourself inside your house. ²⁵As for you, mortal, cords shall be placed on you, and you shall be bound with them so that you cannot go out among the people, ²⁶and I will make your tongue cling to the roof of your mouth so that you shall be speechless and unable to reprove them, for they are a rebellious house. ²⁷But when I speak with you, I will open your mouth, and you shall say to them, 'Thus says the Lord Gᴏᴅ'; let those who will hear, hear, and let those who refuse to hear, refuse, for they are a rebellious house.

4 "And you, O mortal, take a brick and set it before you. On it portray a city,

Jerusalem, ²and put siegeworks against it, and build a siege wall against it, and cast up a ramp against it; set camps also against it, and plant battering rams against it all around. ³Then take an iron plate and place it as an iron wall between you and the city; set your face toward it, and let it be in a state of siege, and press the siege against it. This is a sign for the house of Israel.

4 "Then lie on your left side and place the guilt of the house of Israel upon it; you shall bear their guilt for the number of the days that you lie there. ⁵For I assign to you a number of days, three hundred ninety days, equal to the number of the years of their guilt, and so you shall bear the guilt of the house of Israel. ⁶When you have completed these, you shall lie down a second time, but on your right side, and bear the guilt of the house of Judah; forty days I assign you, one day for each year. ⁷You shall set your face toward the siege of Jerusalem, and with your arm bared you shall prophesy against it. ⁸See, I am putting cords on you so that you cannot turn from one side to the other until you have completed the days of your siege.

9 "And you, take wheat and barley, beans and lentils, millet and spelt; put them into one vessel and make bread for yourself. During the number of days that you lie on your side, three hundred ninety days, you shall eat it. ¹⁰The food that you eat shall be twenty shekels a day by weight; at fixed times you shall eat it. ¹¹And you shall drink water by measure, one-sixth of a hin; at fixed times you shall drink. ¹²You shall eat it as a barley cake,

3:22–4:16 Ezekiel's first messages are relayed in silence, as he performs the fate that awaits the city: siege and starvation (see **"Symbolic Actions," p. 1056**). **3:22** *Valley*, or plain—that is, outside the inhabited settlement. **3:23** *Fell on my face.* This act of deep reverence occurs four times in Ezekiel (1:28; 3:23; 9:8; 11:13). **3:25** *Cords*, or ropes, indicate he is bound up and unable to move. **3:26** *You shall be speechless.* An odd move considering God has commanded Ezekiel to speak. **3:27** *I will open your mouth* addresses the oddity: the prophet can only speak messages from God. From this point until chap. 24, everything that Ezekiel speaks is divine speech. **4:1** *Brick.* The common building material used in Babylonia. This brick represents the Israelite cities besieged by the Assyrians and Babylonians. **4:3** *Set your face* occurs eleven times in the book. It both captures the physical orientation of the prophet and focuses on the target of the pronouncement. **4:4** *House of Israel.* Although in Ezekiel "Israel" usually designates all twelve tribes, here it refers to the northern kingdom that was besieged and destroyed by the Assyrians in 722 BCE. **4:5** *Three hundred ninety days* denotes a much longer time for Israel's exile than for Judah's, indicating that their sins had been graver. **4:6** *House of Judah; forty days.* Judah, the southern kingdom that survived the Assyrian siege, fell to the Babylonians in 587 BCE. *Forty* days/years is probably symbolic, meaning either "a long time" or the length of two generations. **4:10** *Twenty shekels.* About five pounds. **4:11** *One-sixth of a hin.* About 1.29 pints. In other words, Ezekiel lives on meager rations, just as the people will during the siege. **4:12** *Human dung.* While animal feces was commonly used to make fires,

baking it in their sight on human dung." [13]The LORD said, "Thus shall the people of Israel eat their bread, unclean, among the nations to which I will drive them." [14]Then I said, "Ah Lord GOD! I have never defiled myself; from my youth up until now I have never eaten what died of itself or was torn by animals, nor has carrion flesh come into my mouth." [15]Then he said to me, "See, I will let you have cow's dung instead of human dung, on which you may prepare your bread."

16 Then he said to me, "Mortal, I am going to cut off the supply of bread[j] in Jerusalem; they shall eat bread by weight and with fearfulness, and they shall drink water by measure and in dismay. [17]Lacking bread and water, they will look at one another in dismay and waste away under their punishment.

5 "And you, O mortal, take a sharp sword; use it as a barber's razor and run it over your head and your beard; then take balances for weighing, and divide the hair. [2]One third of the hair you shall burn in the fire inside the city when the days of the siege are completed; one third you shall take and strike with the sword all around the city;[k] and one third you shall scatter to the wind, and I will unsheathe the sword after them. [3]Then you shall take from these a small number and bind them in the hem of your robe. [4]From these, again, you shall take some, throw them into the fire and burn them up; from there a fire will come out against all the house of Israel.

5 "Thus says the Lord GOD: This is Jerusalem; I have set her in the center of the nations, with countries all around her. [6]But she has rebelled against my ordinances and my statutes, becoming more wicked than the nations and the countries all around her, rejecting my ordinances and not following my statutes. [7]Therefore thus says the Lord GOD: Because you are more turbulent than the nations that are all around you and have not followed my statutes or kept my ordinances and have not even acted according to the ordinances of the nations that are all around you, [8]therefore thus says the Lord GOD: I, I myself, am coming against you; I will execute judgments among you in the sight of the nations. [9]And because of all your abominations, I will do to you what I have never yet done and the like of which I will never do again. [10]Surely, parents shall eat their children in your midst, and children shall eat their parents; I will execute judgments on you, and any of you who survive I will scatter to every wind. [11]Therefore, as I live, says the Lord GOD, surely, because you have defiled my sanctuary with all your detestable things and with all your abominations, therefore I will withdraw; my eye will not spare, and I will have no pity. [12]One third of you shall die of pestilence or be consumed by famine among you; one third shall fall by the sword around you; and one third I will scatter to every wind and will unsheathe the sword after them.

j 4.16 Heb *staff of bread*   k 5.2 Heb *it*

especially in places with few trees, such as Mesopotamia, human dung was avoided if possible. This was especially true for priests, who had to maintain elevated levels of ritual purity. **4:14** *I have never eaten* emphasizes Ezekiel's priestly status. See **"Ezekiel, the Hybrid Exile," p. 1130. 4:15** *Cow's dung.* God allows for the more common source of fuel.

5:1–4 God tells Ezekiel to perform another oracle. This time, both the act of shaving and the treatment of the shaved hair symbolize the fate of the besieged inhabitants of Jerusalem. See **"Textual, Performative, and Visual Art," p. 1134. 5:1** *Head . . . beard.* Israelite males were usually bearded with longer hair. Shaving could indicate a state of mourning. Priests also shaved (Ezek. 44:20). **5:2** *In the fire inside the city.* When an army breached the city walls, they would burn down the city. *Strike with the sword.* This incongruous image highlights the symbolic function of the shaven hair; just like the hair, people will die from fire and military attack, while the survivors will flee their homeland. **5:3–4** *A small number.* Only a few will survive, but even they will undergo repeated catastrophes.

5:5–17 God claims agency for Jerusalem's siege and fall. **5:5** *Her*—that is, the city, following the gender of the Hebrew noun "city." **5:9** *Abominations.* This is the first use of the word *abominations*, which appears a total of thirty-four times in the book. It refers to something that is ritually defiling or impure. **5:10** *Parents shall eat their children.* A common threat in siege warfare, representing the horror of starvation. **5:11** *Detestable things.* Objects or actions that impart serious defilement, such as corpse contamination or worshiping idols. See **"Disgust, Defilement, and Impurity," p. 1162.** *My*

13 "My anger shall spend itself, and I will vent my fury on them and satisfy myself, and they shall know that I, the LORD, have spoken in my jealousy when I spend my fury on them. [14]Moreover, I will make you a desolation and an object of mocking among the nations around you, in the sight of all who pass by. [15]You shall be[l] a mockery and a taunt, a warning and a horror, to the nations around you when I execute judgments on you in anger and fury and with furious punishments—I, the LORD, have spoken—[16]when I loose against you[m] my deadly arrows of famine, arrows for destruction, which I will let loose to destroy you, and when I bring more and more famine upon you and cut off your supply of bread.[n] [17]I will send famine and wild animals against you, and they will rob you of your children; pestilence and bloodshed shall pass through you, and I will bring the sword upon you. I, the LORD, have spoken."

6 The word of the LORD came to me: [2]O mortal, set your face toward the mountains of Israel and prophesy against them [3]and say: You mountains of Israel, hear the word of the Lord GOD! Thus says the Lord GOD to the mountains and the hills, to the ravines and the valleys: I, I myself, will bring a sword upon you, and I will destroy your high places. [4]Your altars shall become desolate, and your incense stands shall be broken, and I will throw down your slain in front of your idols. [5]I will lay the corpses of the people of Israel in front of their idols, and I will scatter your bones around your altars. [6]Wherever you live, your towns shall be waste and your high places ruined, so that your altars will be waste and ruined,[o] your idols broken and destroyed, your incense stands cut down, and your works wiped out. [7]The slain shall fall in your midst; then you shall know that I am the LORD.

8 But I will spare some. Some of you shall escape the sword among the nations and be scattered through the countries. [9]Your survivors shall remember me among the nations where they are carried captive, how I was crushed by their wanton heart that turned away from me and their wanton eyes that turned after their idols. Then they will be loathsome in their own sight for the evils that they have committed, for all their abominations. [10]And they shall know that I am the LORD; I did not threaten in vain to bring this disaster upon them.

11 Thus says the Lord GOD: Strike your hands together and stamp your foot and say Alas! for all the vile abominations of the house of Israel. For they shall fall by the sword, by famine, and by pestilence. [12]Those far off shall die of pestilence, those nearby shall fall by the sword, and any who are left and are spared shall die of famine. Thus I will spend my fury upon them. [13]And you shall know that I am the LORD when their slain lie among their idols around their altars, on every high hill, on all the mountaintops, under every green tree, and under every leafy oak, wherever they offered pleasing odor to all their idols. [14]I will stretch out my hand against them and make the land

l 5.15 Q ms Gk Syr Vg Tg: MT *It shall be*   m 5.16 Heb *them* n 5.16 Heb *staff of bread*   o 6.6 Syr Vg Tg: Heb *and will bear their punishment*

eye will not spare. A stock phrase meaning God will take notice. **5:13** The Hebrew word for *jealousy* is difficult to translate into English. It can mean the anger when one partner betrays another but also the anger arising from personal insult. **5:15** *A mockery and a taunt, a warning and a horror.* Jerusalem's destruction shall be so public and shocking that it will become iconic even for other nations.

6:1–14 Although this section begins with an address to the mountains, the chapter explicitly designates sites outside of Jerusalem as additional targets for God's wrath. **6:2** *Mountains of Israel* has multiple meanings. The use of the designation "Israel" in this book means the totality of those who would trace their lineage back to Jacob. The "mountains" can mean physical mountains, like the central highlands, but it can also designate a sacred site. **6:3** *Hills*, *ravines*, and *valleys* match the inclusiveness of the term "Israel." This speech is directed to the whole nation. *High places*, which echoes the "mountains" of v. 2, is a common term for temples and shrines outside of Jerusalem. **6:4** *Idols.* The book of Ezekiel uses a relatively uncommon word to refer to the images of other gods. While scholars debate its precise meaning, it has a deliberately polemical undertone. **6:5** *Corpses . . . bones.* Dead bodies defiled sacred space; cf. 2 Kgs. 23:16. **6:9** *Wanton.* The word's root meaning includes adultery and prostitution. **6:10** *I did not threaten in vain* anticipates 12:21–28, where the people assume God has made empty threats. **6:14** *Riblah*, or Diblah.

Focus On: Textual, Performative, and Visual Art (Ezekiel 6)

The book of Ezekiel functions as a multimedia art installation. While this may not be the traditional way of reading a biblical book, this approach better fits the ancient context for prophetic literature, before "books" were invented and when most people had only a functional level of literacy.

Specially trained scribes would have been the primary "readers" of prophetic scrolls, given the complexity of the material. The people at large had access to a book like Ezekiel through its public performance. We do not know what this might have looked like, whether it involved someone acting as Ezekiel, or whether it entailed a rote proclamation of parts of the scroll. Features within Ezekiel suggest that its performance allowed the performer some leeway to adapt, update, and change emphasis. One modern parallel might be slam poetry, where poets spontaneously change material as they perform it.

Given that much of the poetic material in the Prophets would have been sung, however, remixing and sampling might be a better parallel. The one performing as "Ezekiel" sampled bits of other prophets, like Isaiah's vision in the temple, improvising, riffing, and expanding it, mixing in other traditions as the performance proceeded. The number of references to singing in the book of Ezekiel makes this second model a viable fit.

Ezekiel's own pantomimes that act out divine pronouncements also point to the expectation of a performance. The preserved words assume accompanying actions—some ritual but others provocative, like performance art found today in museums of modern art. Given Ezekiel's roles as priest and prophet, the original performance would have been viewed as a divinatory ritual that brought into reality the pronouncement being performed.

The book of Ezekiel has many visual elements as well. His visions, which are elaborately described, for example, structure the book, as do the allegories of trees, vines, and lions, to name a few. Although the performance probably did not include creating these visual elements, they do stimulate the visual imagination. For a nonliterate audience, some of the images served to remind them of a text they heard performed but could not read.

The book of Ezekiel, then, like many other prophetic collections, combines various artistic media for an audience with various levels and methods of engagement. Approaching it as art fits its author's (or authors') aims.

Corrine L. Carvalho

desolate and waste, throughout all their settlements, from the wilderness to Riblah.*p* Then they shall know that I am the LORD.

7 The word of the LORD came to me: [2]You, O mortal, thus says the Lord GOD to the land of Israel:

An end! The end has come
    upon the four corners of the land.
[3] Now the end is upon you;
    I will let loose my anger upon you;
    I will judge you according to your ways;
    I will punish you for all your
        abominations.
[4] My eye will not spare you; I will have no
        pity.
    I will punish you for your ways

while your abominations are among
        you.
Then you shall know that I am the LORD.
    5 Thus says the Lord GOD:
Disaster after disaster! See, it comes.
[6]   An end has come; the end has come.
    It has awakened against you; see, it
        comes!
[7] Your doom*q* has come to you,
        O inhabitant of the land.
    The time has come; the day is near—
        of tumult, not of reveling on the
        mountains.
[8] Soon now I will pour out my wrath upon
        you;
    I will spend my anger against you.

p 6.14 Cn: Heb *Diblah*   *q* 7.7 Meaning of Heb uncertain

7:1–27 Several short prophetic speeches compose this chapter. The clipped speech creates the breathlessness of panic, denoting that the time for judgment is upon them. **7:2** *Four corners* indicates total destruction. **7:5** *Disaster.* This poem echoes the "end" of vv. 2–4. **7:7** *Doom.* This is the first of several places in the chapter where the Hebrew is unclear, as the notes indicate. It could be that the author has used rare words in these poems or that the nonsensical wording replicates inexpressible horror. **7:8** *Soon now* emphasizes again that the end is near.

I will judge you according to your ways
  and punish you for all your
    abominations.
⁹ My eye will not spare; I will have no pity.
  I will punish you according to your
    ways
  while your abominations are among
    you.
Then you shall know that it is I the LORD who
strike.
¹⁰ See, the day! See, it comes!
  Your doom' has gone out.
  The rod has blossomed; pride has
    budded.
¹¹   Violence has grown into a rod of
    wickedness.
  None of them shall remain,
    not their abundance, not their wealth;
    no preeminence among them.'
¹² The time has come; the day draws near;
    let not the buyer rejoice nor the seller
      mourn,
    for wrath is upon all their multitude.
¹³For the sellers shall not return to what has
been sold as long as they remain alive. For
the vision concerns all their multitude; it
shall not be revoked. Because of their iniquity, they cannot maintain their lives.'
¹⁴ They have blown the horn and made
    everything ready,
    but no one goes to battle,
    for my wrath is upon all their
      multitude.
¹⁵ The sword is outside; pestilence and
    famine are inside;
    those in the field die by the sword;
    those in the city—famine and
      pestilence devour them.
¹⁶ If any survivors escape,
    they shall be found on the mountains
    like doves of the valleys,
    all of them moaning over their iniquity.
¹⁷ All hands shall grow feeble,
    all knees turn to water.

¹⁸ They shall put on sackcloth;
    horror shall cover them.
  Shame shall be on all faces,
    baldness on all their heads.
¹⁹ They shall fling their silver into the
    streets;
    their gold shall be treated as
      unclean.
Their silver and gold cannot save them on
the day of the wrath of the LORD. They shall
not satisfy their hunger or fill their stomachs with it. For it was the stumbling block
of their iniquity. ²⁰From their" beautiful
ornament, in which they took pride, they
made their abominable images, their detestable things; therefore I will make of it an unclean thing to them.
²¹ I will hand it over to strangers as
    plunder,
    to the wicked of the earth as spoil;
    they shall profane it.
²² I will avert my face from them
    so that they may profane my
      treasured' place;
  the violent shall enter it;
    they shall profane it.
²³ Make a chain!"
  For the land is full of bloody crimes;
    the city is full of violence.
²⁴ I will bring the worst of the nations
    to take possession of their houses.
  I will put an end to the arrogance of the
    strong,
    and their holy places shall be
      profaned.
²⁵ When anguish comes, they will seek
    peace,
    but there shall be none.
²⁶ Disaster comes upon disaster;
    rumor follows rumor;

r 7.10 Meaning of Heb uncertain   s 7.11 Meaning of
Heb uncertain   t 7.13 Gk: Meaning of Heb uncertain   u 7.20 Syr Symmachus: Heb *its*   v 7.22 Or *secret*
w 7.23 Meaning of Heb uncertain

7:10 *The day* might be an oblique reference to "the day of the LORD" seen in other prophetic texts (cf. Amos 5:18). What follows through v. 13 remains unclear. **7:14** *Blown the horn*, which was used to warn of an advancing enemy and to signal the start of a battle. **7:17** *Hands* usually symbolized power. The image is ironic, accompanied by *knees* turning to *water*. **7:18** *Sackcloth* and *baldness* indicate mourning for the dead. **7:20** *Ornament.* A metaphor for the temple in Jerusalem, although not specifically named in these verses. The poet contrasts the true value of the temple with the vain attempts to find safety through worshiping other gods. **7:22** *Treasured* or "secret" place refers to the innermost part of the temple. **7:26** *Rumor follows rumor.* The news of Jerusalem's destruction will become a media sensation. *Vision*, *instruction*, and *counsel* signal the failure of every source of security for the city. Nobody will be able to stop God's judgment.

they shall keep seeking a vision from the
prophet;
instruction shall perish from the priest
and counsel from the elders.
²⁷ The king shall mourn,
the prince shall be wrapped in
despair,
and the hands of the people of the
land shall tremble.
According to their way I will deal with
them;
according to their own judgments I
will judge them.
And they shall know that I am the LORD.

8 In the sixth year, in the sixth month, on
the fifth day of the month, as I sat in my
house with the elders of Judah sitting before
me, the hand of the Lord GOD fell upon me
there. ²I looked, and there was a figure that
looked like a man;ˣ below what appeared to
be its loins the figure was fire, and above the
loins it was like the appearance of brightness, like gleaming amber. ³It stretched out
the form of a hand and took me by a lock of
my head, and the spirit lifted me up between
earth and heaven and brought me in visions
of God to Jerusalem, to the entrance of the
gateway of the inner court that faces north,
to the seat of the image of jealousy that provokes to jealousy. ⁴And the glory of the God
of Israel was there, like the vision that I had
seen in the valley.

5 Then Godʸ said to me, "O mortal, lift up
your eyes now in the direction of the north."
So I lifted up my eyes toward the north, and
there, north of the altar gate, in the entrance,
was this image of jealousy. ⁶He said to me,
"Mortal, do you see what they are doing, the
great abominations that the house of Israel
are committing here, to drive me far from
my sanctuary? Yet you will see still greater
abominations."

7 And he brought me to the entrance of the
court; I looked, and there was a hole in the
wall. ⁸Then he said to me, "Mortal, dig through
the wall," and when I dug through the wall,
there was an entrance. ⁹He said to me, "Go in
and see the vile abominations that they are
committing here." ¹⁰So I went in and looked;
there, portrayed on the wall all around, were
all kinds of creeping things and loathsome animals and all the idols of the house of Israel.
¹¹Before them stood seventy of the elders of the
house of Israel, with Jaazaniah son of Shaphan
standing among them. Each had his censer in
his hand, and the fragrant cloud of incense
was ascending. ¹²Then he said to me, "Mortal,
have you seen what the elders of the house of
Israel are doing in the dark, each in his room of
images? For they say, 'The LORD does not see us;
the LORD has forsaken the land.'" ¹³He said also
to me, "You will see still greater abominations
that they are committing."

x 8.2 Gk: Heb *like fire*   y 8.5 Heb *he*

8:1–11:25 The next section of the text returns to Ezekiel's vision in chap. 1. The throne bearing
God's glory ascends out of the temple and makes its way step by step out of the city. This slow
movement gives the people in the city the final hours to repent before the city becomes defenseless
to the military attack.

8:1–18 This chapter opens with exiled male leaders (*elders*) seeking a prophetic message from
Ezekiel. He experiences a second prophetic vision of Jerusalem leading to God's abandonment
of the city. **8:1** *In the sixth year . . . month.* August or September 592 BCE, four years before the
city's fall. *The hand of the Lord,* or the power of God, overcame the prophet. **8:3** *A lock of my
head.* A detail not contained in chap. 1. *The spirit.* Hebrew has simply "a spirit." Prophecy was often
attributed to the influence of spirits (cf. 1 Sam. 10:6; 1 Kgs. 22:21). *Entrance of the gateway.* Ezekiel's
travels take him to various parts of the temple structure, growing ever closer to the sanctuary building, which housed God's presence. *The image of jealousy.* A phrase found only in Ezekiel designating
an idol whose worship makes God jealous (cf. Ps. 78:58). **8:4** *The glory of the God of Israel.* God's
radiant presence. **8:6** *To drive me far from my sanctuary* posits God's forced abandonment of the
temple and its city. **8:7** *A hole in the wall.* It is unclear why Ezekiel must dig through a hole again
rather than coming through the gate. Perhaps it indicates his clandestine witness. **8:10** *All kinds of
creeping things and loathsome animals* probably recalls the religious art of both Babylon and Egypt.
The wording of this text stresses that they provoke disgust, not glory. **8:11** *Seventy of the elders . . .
with Jaazaniah.* Although the exact identities of these participants are not clear, they represent elite
males who controlled the city. *Censer . . . incense.* See, for example, Isa. 17:8; 27:9; Hos. 2:13; 11:2.
8:12 *In the dark.* Although sanctuaries had lamps, generally they were unlit, symbolizing the deity

14 Then he brought me to the entrance of the north gate of the house of the LORD; women were sitting there weeping for Tammuz. [15]Then he said to me, "Have you seen this, O mortal? You will see still greater abominations than these."

16 And he brought me into the inner court of the house of the LORD; there, at the entrance of the temple of the LORD, between the porch and the altar, were about twenty-five men with their backs to the temple of the LORD and their faces toward the east, prostrating themselves to the sun toward the east. [17]Then he said to me, "Have you seen this, O mortal? Is it not bad enough that the house of Judah commits the abominations done here? Must they fill the land with violence and provoke my anger still further? See, they are putting the branch to their nose! [18]Therefore I will act in wrath; my eye will not spare, nor will I have pity, and though they cry in my hearing with a loud voice, I will not listen to them."

9 Then he cried in my hearing with a loud voice, saying, "Draw near, you executioners of the city, each with his destroying weapon in his hand." [2]And six men came from the direction of the upper gate, which faces north, each with his weapon for slaughter in his hand; among them was a man clothed in linen with a writing case at his side. They went in and stood beside the bronze altar.

3 Now the glory of the God of Israel had gone up from the cherub on which it rested to the entryway of the temple. The LORD[z] called to the man clothed in linen who had the writing case at his side [4]and said to him, "Go through the city, through Jerusalem, and put a mark on the foreheads of those who sigh and groan over all the abominations that are committed in it." [5]To the others he said in my hearing, "Pass through the city after him and kill; your eye shall not spare, and you shall show no pity. [6]Cut down old men, young men and young women, little children and women, but touch no one who has the mark. And begin at my sanctuary." So they began with the elders who were in front of the house. [7]Then he said to them, "Defile the house and fill the courts with the slain. Go!" So they went out and killed in the city.

z 9.3 Heb *he*

at rest. This text's use of "darkness" adds a tone of secrecy and foreboding. **8:14** *Weeping for Tammuz.* Tammuz was a Babylonian mythological figure connected with the goddess Ishtar. The myths about his dying and rising represent the changing of the seasons. **8:16** *Between the porch and the altar.* Just outside the sanctuary building with the Holy of Holies. *Their backs to the temple.* These worshipers are inside the large temple complex but in a place reserved only for priests. Their stance (turning their backs on God) depicts their desecration as socially abhorrent. *Prostrating themselves to the sun.* Babylonians and Egyptians both participated in sun worship. The vision has gone from the human-made idols of v. 10 to the worship of the sun as the source of brilliance rather than God's own glory. **8:17** *Violence* includes total social collapse. *Putting the branch to their nose.* Egyptian wall paintings depict worshipers smelling lotus blossoms. **8:18** *Nor will I have pity.* God sums up the ritual abominations with a final judgment of unstoppable divine wrath.

9:1–11 This chapter registers the prophet's horror as the divinely sanctioned execution begins. **9:1–2** *Destroying weapon* and *weapon for slaughter* are two different terms that both indicate fatal bloodshed. **9:1** *Executioners* are called to carry out the death penalty pronounced by God even before the Lord entirely abandons the city. This vision replaces the Babylonian army as the weapon of mass destruction with God's heavenly executioners. **9:2** *A man clothed in linen.* This man and the six executioners are part of God's heavenly bureaucracy. The creature dressed in linen with a writing case determines who is condemned under God's sentence. Linen clothing often signified a priest (e.g., Lev. 16:4; Ezek. 44:17–18) who would determine who was guilty of violating divine law. **9:3** *The glory of the God of Israel . . . cherub.* God's movement away from the temple commences. In this first step, God leaves the Holy of Holies and comes to the exterior door of the sanctuary building. **9:4** *Put a mark* refers in Hebrew to the letter "tau," which was shaped like an "x." This detail shows that God's execution was not an unbridled killing spree but a deliberate sentence on the guilty. *Sigh and groan* describes the sounds of the rituals for which they are judged. **9:5** *You shall show no pity.* God's lack of mercy is transferred onto the executioners. **9:6** *Old men . . . women* signals the totality of the judgment. *The elders who were in front of the house*—that is, those worshiping the sun. **9:7** *Defile the house.* The whole temple complex was made ritually defiled by the presence

⁸While they were killing and I was left alone, I fell prostrate on my face and cried out, "Ah Lord God! Will you destroy all who remain of Israel as you pour out your wrath upon Jerusalem?" ⁹He said to me, "The guilt of the house of Israel and Judah is exceedingly great; the land is full of bloodshed and the city full of perversity, for they say, 'The Lord has forsaken the land, and the Lord does not see.' ¹⁰As for me, my eye will not spare, nor will I have pity, but I will bring down their deeds upon their heads."

11 Then the man clothed in linen with the writing case at his side brought back word, saying, "I have done as you commanded me."

10 Then I looked, and above the dome that was over the heads of the cherubim there appeared above them something like a sapphire,ᵃ in form resembling a throne. ²He said to the man clothed in linen, "Go within the wheelwork underneath the cherubim; fill your hands with burning coals from among the cherubim, and scatter them over the city." He went in as I looked on. ³Now the cherubim were standing on the south side of the house when the man went in, and a cloud filled the inner court. ⁴Then the glory of the Lord rose up from the cherub to the entryway of the temple; the house was filled with the cloud, and the court was full of the brightness of the glory of the Lord. ⁵The sound of the wings of the cherubim was heard as far as the outer court, like the voice of God Almightyᵇ when he speaks.

6 When he commanded the man clothed in linen, "Take fire from within the wheelwork, from among the cherubim," he went in and stood beside a wheel. ⁷And a cherub stretched out his hand from among the cherubim to the fire that was among the cherubim, took some of it, and put it into the hands of the man clothed in linen, who took it and went out. ⁸The cherubim appeared to have the form of a human hand under their wings.

9 I looked, and there were four wheels beside the cherubim, one beside each cherub, and the appearance of the wheels was like gleaming beryl. ¹⁰And as for their appearance, the four looked alike, something like a wheel within a wheel. ¹¹When they moved, they moved in any of the four directions without veering as they moved, but in whatever direction the front wheel faced, the others followed without veering as they moved. ¹²Their entire bodies—backs, hands, and wings—were covered with eyes all around, as were the wheels of the four of them. ¹³As for the wheels, they were called in my hearing "the wheelwork." ¹⁴Each one had four faces: the first face was that of the cherub, the second

a 10.1 Or *lapis lazuli*   b 10.5 Traditional rendering of Heb *El Shaddai*

of corpses. Cf. 2 Kgs. 23:16. **9:8** *I was left alone* could be translated "As they performed their executions, I was the only one left." Otherwise, nowhere in the chapter does it say whether anyone earned a sparing mark on their forehead. *I fell prostrate . . . and cried out*, thus doing what those in Jerusalem had not done. The figure of Ezekiel gives full voice to those who could not stop the disaster. **9:9** *The Lord has forsaken the land.* Ironically, the people justify their worship of other gods by asserting that God had already abandoned them, not seeing that God had been there all along.

10:1–22 The narrative of the chapter describes God's first attack: fiery coals scattered over the city by the linen-clad divine figure simultaneously with God's movements toward the outer court of the temple complex. The chapter also includes more details about the creatures that support God's throne, here explicitly named as cherubim (plural of cherub). **10:1–2** *Dome.* See Ezek. 1:22. It recalls the dome God creates in Gen. 1:14. *Cherubim.* Although 9:3 contains a brief mention of a cherub below God, this chapter provides more detail about these figures. Cherubim, common in Near Eastern iconography, were mixed creatures who guarded the main deity. They were often carved into doorways and thrones. Compared to chap. 1, these creatures have additional details of hands under the wings and burning coal among the wheels, bringing them closer to the vision of seraphim with fiery coals in Isa. 6:1–7. Here the coals purge the city of defilement by setting it aflame. **10:4** *Entryway* picks up the narrative thread from 9:3, where God has just moved to the door of the sanctuary building. *The house was filled with . . . glory.* Ezekiel associates God's presence with both obscurity (a cloud) and brightness (glory), reflecting the connection between fire and smoke; see, for example, Num. 9:15–22. **10:5** *Like the voice of God Almighty.* This phrase echoes Ezek. 1:24, which likens the sound of the wings to roaring water, thunder, and an army. The divine title "Almighty" is used in Ezekiel only here and in 1:24. **10:12** *Covered with eyes all around.* In Ezek. 1:18, the eyes are only on the wheels, while here they cover the cherubim as well.

face was that of a human, the third that of a lion, and the fourth that of an eagle.

15 The cherubim rose up. These were the living creatures that I saw by the River Chebar. ¹⁶When the cherubim moved, the wheels moved beside them, and when the cherubim lifted up their wings to rise up from the earth, the wheels at their side did not veer. ¹⁷When they stopped, the others stopped, and when they rose up, the others rose up with them, for a living spirit was in them.

18 Then the glory of the LORD went out from the entryway of the temple and stopped above the cherubim. ¹⁹The cherubim lifted up their wings and rose up from the earth in my sight as they went out with the wheels beside them. They stopped at the entrance of the east gate of the house of the LORD, and the glory of the God of Israel was above them.

20 These were the living creatures that I saw underneath the God of Israel by the River Chebar, and I knew that they were cherubim. ²¹Each had four faces, each four wings, and underneath their wings something like human hands. ²²As for what their faces were like, they were the same faces whose appearance I had seen by the River Chebar. Each one moved straight ahead.

11 The spirit lifted me up and brought me to the east gate of the house of the LORD, which faces east. There, at the entrance of the gateway, were twenty-five men; among them I saw Jaazaniah son of Azzur and Pelatiah son of Benaiah, officials of the people. ²He said to me, "Mortal, these are the men who devise iniquity and who give wicked counsel in this city; ³they say, 'The time is not near to build houses; this city is the pot, and we are the meat.' ⁴Therefore prophesy against them; prophesy, O mortal."

5 Then the spirit of the LORD fell upon me, and he said to me, "Say, Thus says the LORD: This is what you think, O house of Israel; I know the things that come into your mind. ⁶You have killed many in this city and have filled its streets with the slain. ⁷Therefore thus says the Lord GOD: The slain whom you have placed within it are the meat, and this city is the pot, but you shall be taken out of it. ⁸You have feared the sword, and I will bring the sword upon you, says the Lord GOD. ⁹I will take you out of it and give you over to the hands of foreigners and execute judgments upon you. ¹⁰You shall fall by the sword; I will judge you at the border of Israel. And you shall know that I am the LORD. ¹¹This city shall not be your pot, and you shall not be the meat inside it; I will judge you at the border of Israel. ¹²Then you shall know that I am the LORD, whose statutes you have not followed and whose ordinances you have not kept, but you have acted according to the ordinances of the nations that are around you."

13 Now, while I was prophesying, Pelatiah

10:14 *Four faces.* See note at 1:10. **10:17** *A living spirit* continues the use of the word *spirit* to indicate God as the source of an activity or phenomenon. **10:21** *Each had . . . hands* summarizes the description of the cherubim.

11:1–25 This chapter narrates the end of Ezekiel's second vision. God characterizes those left in the city as unfaithful and arrogant. Once again, Ezekiel's brief lament and sudden return to his reality in Babylon remind the audience of the visionary nature of the preceding chapters and the horror at the heart of that vision. Even the famous promise of a new heart and new spirit insinuates the inherent wretchedness of the people of Jerusalem. **11:1** *The spirit lifted me up* resumes the narrative of Ezekiel's vision by repeating part of Ezek. 8:3. *Jaazaniah son of Azzur and Pelatiah son of Benaiah* are not clearly identified. Hananiah son of Azzur dies in Jer. 28:17, while Jaazaniah son of Shaphan is mentioned in Ezek. 8:11. **11:3** *The time is not near.* The speech attributed to the residents of Jerusalem is enigmatic. Earlier in the book, the people seemed unfazed by the threat of a siege, but here it appears they are preparing for a long siege, presumably one they feel they can survive. *This city is the pot.* Later in the book (Ezek. 24:6–8), the bloody pot is a symbol of the destruction of the city, but here it represents safety for the *meat* or people inside of it, expressing their belief that they will survive the siege. **11:6** *You have killed many in this city* refers to the officials' decisions that led to the deaths of many in the city. **11:7** *Meat . . . pot . . . taken out.* The metaphor of the city as a cooking vessel returns, transforming the metaphor from a symbol of safety in v. 3 to that of destruction here: those killed off by the officials are now the meat. The officials are "taken out" of that city, not as an act of salvation but as the first steps in forced exile. **11:9** *To the hands of foreigners* indicates exile to a foreign land. **11:10** *At the border of Israel.* The sentence of exile begins when those captured pass outside their ancestral land. **11:13** *Pelatiah.* See note on 11:1. *I fell down on my face, cried. . . . You*

son of Benaiah died. Then I fell down on my face, cried with a loud voice, and said, "Ah Lord God! You are finishing off the remnant of Israel!"

14 Then the word of the Lord came to me: [15]Mortal, your kinsfolk, your own kin, your fellow exiles,[c] the whole house of Israel, all of them, are those of whom the inhabitants of Jerusalem have said, "Stay far from the Lord; to us this land is given for a possession." [16]Therefore say: Thus says the Lord God: Though I removed them far away among the nations and though I scattered them among the countries, yet I have been a sanctuary to them for a little while[d] in the countries where they have gone. [17]Therefore say: Thus says the Lord God: I will gather you from the peoples and assemble you out of the countries where you have been scattered, and I will give you the land of Israel. [18]When they come there, they will remove from it all its detestable things and all its abominations. [19]I will give them one heart and put a new spirit within them;[e] I will remove the heart of stone from their flesh and give them a heart of flesh, [20]so that they may follow my statutes and keep my ordinances and obey them. Then they shall be my people, and I will be their God. [21]But as for those whose heart goes after their detestable things and their abominations,[f] I will bring their deeds upon their own heads, says the Lord God.

22 Then the cherubim lifted up their wings, with the wheels beside them, and the glory of the God of Israel was above them. [23]And the glory of the Lord ascended from the middle of the city and stopped on the mountain east of the city. [24]The spirit lifted me up and brought me in a vision by the spirit of God into Chaldea, to the exiles. Then the vision that I had seen left me. [25]And I told the exiles all the things that the Lord had shown me.

12

The word of the Lord came to me: [2]Mortal, you are living in the midst of a rebellious house who have eyes to see but do not see, who have ears to hear but do not hear, [3]for they are a rebellious house. Therefore, mortal, prepare for yourself an exile's baggage, and go into exile by day in their sight; you shall go like an exile from your place to another place in their sight. Perhaps they will understand, though they are a rebellious house. [4]You shall bring out your baggage by day in their sight, as baggage for exile, and you shall go out yourself at evening in their sight, as those do who go into exile. [5]Dig through the wall in their sight, and carry the baggage through it. [6]In their sight you shall lift the baggage on your shoulder and carry it out in the dark; you shall cover your face, so that you may not see the land, for I have made you a sign for the house of Israel.

c 11.15 Gk Syr: Heb *people of your kindred* d 11.16 Or *a little sanctuary* e 11.19 Heb mss Gk Syr Vg: MT *you* f 11.21 Cn: Heb *And to the heart of their detestable things and their abominations their heart goes*

are finishing off the remnant of Israel. Ezekiel's brief moment of independent speech captures the emotions that the visionary report intends to evoke. **11:15–16** *To us this land is given for a possession.* God responds to Ezekiel's fear by reassuring him that the first group of exiles will return from exile, perhaps with all those *scattered* in the various exiles of Israel's history. **11:16** *I have been a sanctuary.* Although this phrase can be translated in a variety of ways, it depicts God as not completely abandoning the exiles. **11:17** *I will gather you* depicts God actively reassembling the exiles from the various places of the Diaspora. **11:19** *One heart . . . a new spirit.* This phrase indicates an internal conversion that God orchestrates. The new spirit connotes a divine power that animates all the people. The "one" heart suggests a collective ethos that will characterize this reconstituted Israel. The contrast of the heart of stone versus one of flesh uses images of death and life to symbolize this restoration. **11:23** *The mountain east of the city.* God finally departs from the city of Jerusalem, moving onto the Mount of Olives.

12:1–16 Chap. 12 has two distinct parts: a symbolic act and a refutation of popular thought. In the first part, Ezekiel acts out fleeing a besieged city before it falls. He leaves at night after digging a hole in the city wall to avoid notice from the enemy. The description contains elements found in the account of Zedekiah's attempted escape in 2 Kgs. 25:4–7. **12:2** *Rebellious* is the same word used to describe the people of Judah in chaps. 2–3. *Eyes to see . . . not hear.* Isaiah 6:10 also depicts the Israelites as metaphorically visually and hearing impaired. **12:5** *Dig through the wall.* Similar to Ezek. 8:8. The word "wall" appears forty-three times in the book; walls, which should have provided safety, here impede escape and later hem in a captive populace. **12:6** *Sign.* A sign was usually a

7 I did just as I was commanded. I brought out my baggage by day, as baggage for exile, and in the evening I dug through the wall with my own hands; I brought it out in the dark, carrying it on my shoulder in their sight.

8 In the morning the word of the Lord came to me: [9]Mortal, has not the house of Israel, the rebellious house, said to you, "What are you doing?" [10]Say to them, "Thus says the Lord God: This oracle concerns the prince in Jerusalem[g] and all the house of Israel in it."[b] [11]Say, "I am a sign for you: as I have done, so shall it be done to them; they shall go into exile, into captivity." [12]And the prince who is among them shall lift his baggage on his shoulder in the dark and shall go out; he[i] shall dig through the wall and carry it through; he shall cover his face so that he may not see the land with his eyes. [13]I will spread my net over him, and he shall be caught in my snare, and I will bring him to Babylon, the land of the Chaldeans, yet he shall not see it, and he shall die there. [14]I will scatter to every wind all who are around him, his helpers and all his troops, and I will unsheathe the sword behind them. [15]And they shall know that I am the Lord when I disperse them among the nations and scatter them through the countries. [16]But I will let a few of them escape from the sword, from famine and pestilence, so that they may tell of all their abominations among the nations where they go; then they shall know that I am the Lord.

17 The word of the Lord came to me: [18]Mortal, eat your bread with quaking and drink your water with trembling and with fearfulness; [19]and say to the people of the land: "Thus says the Lord God concerning the inhabitants of Jerusalem in the land of Israel: They shall eat their bread with fearfulness and drink their water in dismay, because their land shall be stripped of all it contains, on account of the violence of all those who live in it. [20]The inhabited cities shall be laid waste, and the land shall become a desolation, and you shall know that I am the Lord."

21 The word of the Lord came to me: [22]Mortal, what is this proverb of yours about the land of Israel that says, "The days are prolonged, and every vision comes to nothing"? [23]Tell them therefore, "Thus says the Lord God: I will put an end to this proverb, and they shall use it no more as a proverb in Israel." But say to them: "The days are near, and the fulfillment of every vision. [24]For there shall no longer be any false vision or flattering divination within the house of Israel. [25]But I the Lord will speak the word that I speak, and it will be fulfilled. It will no longer be delayed, but in your days, O rebellious house, I will speak the word and fulfill it, says the Lord God."

26 The word of the Lord came to me: [27]Mortal, the house of Israel is saying, "The vision that he sees is for many years ahead;

g 12.10 Tg: Meaning of Heb uncertain   h 12.10 Heb in them   i 12.12 Gk Syr: Heb they

visible event that authenticated a prophecy. It could be a prophet acting out an oracle (Isa. 20:3) or the presence of a particular person or group (Isa. 8:18). Ezekiel also has both meanings of the word; here the enactment of the oracle is a sign, while in 24:24, the prophet himself is the sign. **12:10** *Prince.* The book of Ezekiel consistently uses this title for Zedekiah, since the exiled Jehoiakim was the legitimate king. **12:13** *He shall not see it.* This may reflect the blinding of Zedekiah when he was captured (2 Kgs. 25:7). **12:14–15** *Scatter to every wind.* These verses use agricultural images to describe the exile. **12:16** *Among the nations.* The Judeans exiled to Babylonia lived among other exiled groups. Thus the plight of Judah would have been witnessed by both the Babylonians and other exiled groups.

12:17–28 The second half of the chapter depicts those left in Jerusalem citing traditional sayings to bolster their belief that there was no imminent danger. There are two versions of this story. Vv. 17–25 contain an improperly applied proverb, and vv. 26–28 summarize what the people believed. In both cases, God insists that the destruction is closing in on them. **12:19** *Inhabitants of Jerusalem in the land of Israel* indicates a specific target of the oracle. These are Jerusalemites not already in exile. **12:22** *Proverb* can also be translated as "allegory," "saying," "metaphor," or "riddle." The word is used eight times in the book of Ezekiel, sometimes as a description of his own words but other times as an occasion to refute the proverb. **12:24** *False vision or flattering divination.* Here false prophets are those who have lying visions (see 1 Kgs. 22:19–23) or who are sought by elites to tell them what they want to hear. Cf. Ezek. 13. **12:27** *The vision . . . for distant times.* While the use of the

he prophesies for distant times." ²⁸Therefore say to them, "Thus says the Lord GOD: None of my words will be delayed any longer, but the word that I speak will be fulfilled, says the Lord GOD."

13 The word of the LORD came to me: ²Mortal, prophesy against the prophets of Israel who are prophesying; say to those who prophesy out of their own imaginations: "Hear the word of the LORD!" ³Thus says the Lord GOD: Alas for the senseless prophets who follow their own spirit and have seen nothing! ⁴Your prophets have been like jackals among ruins, O Israel. ⁵You have not gone up into the breaches or repaired a wall for the house of Israel, so that it might stand in battle on the day of the LORD. ⁶They have envisioned falsehood and lying divination; they say, "Says the LORD," when the LORD has not sent them, and yet they wait for the fulfillment of their word! ⁷Have you not seen a false vision or uttered a lying divination when you have said, "Says the LORD," even though I did not speak?

8 Therefore thus says the Lord GOD: Because you have uttered falsehood and envisioned lies, I am against you, says the Lord GOD. ⁹My hand will be against the prophets who see false visions and utter lying divinations; they shall not be in the council of my people nor be enrolled in the register of the house of Israel, nor shall they enter the land of Israel, and you shall know that I am the Lord GOD. ¹⁰Because, in truth, because they have misled my people, saying, "Peace," when there is no peace, and because, when the people build a flimsy wall, these prophets^j smear whitewash on it. ¹¹Say to those who smear whitewash on it that it shall fall. There will be a deluge of rain,^k great hailstones will fall, and a stormy wind will break out. ¹²When the wall falls, will it not be said to you, "Where is the whitewash you smeared on it?" ¹³Therefore thus says the Lord GOD: In my wrath I will make a stormy wind break out, and in my anger there shall be a deluge of rain and hailstones in wrath to destroy it. ¹⁴I will break down the wall that you have smeared with whitewash and bring it to the ground, so that its foundation will be laid bare; when the city falls, you shall perish within it, and you shall know that I am the LORD. ¹⁵Thus I will spend my wrath upon the wall and upon those who have smeared it with whitewash, and I will say to you, "The wall is no more, nor those who smeared it—¹⁶the prophets of Israel who prophesied concerning Jerusalem and saw visions of peace for it when there was no peace, says the Lord GOD."

17 As for you, mortal, set your face against the daughters of your people who prophesy out of their own imaginations; prophesy against them ¹⁸and say: Thus says the Lord GOD: Woe to the women who sew bands on all wrists and make veils for the heads of

j 13.10 Heb *they*   *k* 13.11 Heb *rain and you*

proverb in v. 22 accuses Ezekiel of being a false prophet, here the people assert that he is describing a far-off doomsday.

13:1–23 YHWH condemns prophets who have assured those in Jerusalem that the city would remain safe. **13:2** *Imaginations*, or in Hebrew, "heart." The idea is that the messages that the false prophets deliver come from their own internal thoughts, not from an external divine communication. **13:3** *Senseless*, or "foolish." *Spirit.* True prophecy was often attributed to a divine spirit that possessed the human messenger; here the passage accuses the false prophets of having only their own internal spirit. **13:5** *Wall.* The metaphor of a whitewashed or plaster wall symbolizes the emptiness of the false prophets' predictions. Whitewash can cover fatal defects, and a wall made of plaster cannot withstand a siege. The metaphor means that while the messages of these prophets look good, they cover up the impending disaster of the breach of the city walls. **13:6** *Envisioned . . . divination.* The two means of revelation mentioned here are visions and divination (usually reading omens), but the phrase is meant to include all forms of prophecy. **13:9** *Council of my people . . . enrolled in the register.* They will lose their social status as elites and membership as part of Israel. **13:10** *Because . . . because.* The repetition is in the Hebrew, stressing the reason for the divine wrath. *Peace.* The false prophets deny an impending military defeat. **13:11** *Hailstones . . . stormy wind* adds to the metaphor of the flimsy wall. Here the attack on the city by the Babylonians, which is attributed to God's fury, is represented by tornado-like storms that tear down structures and wreak havoc. **13:14** *Foundation* of the city's walls—that is, total destruction. **13:17** *Imaginations* echoes v. 2; female false prophets receive the same condemnation as their male counterparts. **13:18** *Sew bands . . . make veils.* Vv. 18–20

persons of every height, in the hunt for lives! Will you hunt down lives among my people and maintain your own lives? ¹⁹You have profaned me among my people for handfuls of barley and for pieces of bread, putting to death those who should not die and keeping alive those who should not live, by your lies to my people, who listen to lies.

20 Therefore thus says the Lord God: I am against your bands with which you hunt lives;ⁱ I will tear them from your arms and let the lives go free, the lives that you hunt down like birds. ²¹I will tear off your veils and save my people from your hands; they shall no longer be prey in your hands, and you shall know that I am the Lord. ²²Because you have disheartened the righteous falsely, although I have not disheartened them, and you have encouraged the wicked not to turn from their wicked way and save their lives, ²³therefore you shall no longer see false visions or practice divination; I will save my people from your hand. Then you will know that I am the Lord.

14 Certain elders of Israel came to me and sat down before me. ²And the word of the Lord came to me: ³Mortal, these men have taken their idols into their hearts and placed their iniquity as a stumbling block before them; shall I let myself be consulted by them? ⁴Therefore speak to them, and say to them: Thus says the Lord God: Any

of those of the house of Israel who take their idols into their hearts and place their iniquity as a stumbling block before them and yet come to the prophet, I the Lord will answer those who come with the multitude of their idols, ⁵in order that I may take hold of the hearts of the house of Israel, all of whom are estranged from me through their idols.

6 Therefore say to the house of Israel: Thus says the Lord God: Repent and turn away from your idols, and turn away your faces from all your abominations. ⁷For any of those of the house of Israel or of the aliens who reside in Israel who separate themselves from me, taking their idols into their hearts and placing their iniquity as a stumbling block before them and yet come to a prophet to inquire of me by him, I the Lord will answer them myself. ⁸I will set my face against them; I will make them a sign and a byword and cut them off from the midst of my people, and you shall know that I am the Lord.

9 If a prophet is deceived and speaks a word, I, the Lord, have deceived that prophet, and I will stretch out my hand against him and will destroy him from the midst of my people Israel. ¹⁰And they shall bear their punishment—the punishment of the inquirer and the punishment of the prophet shall be the same—¹¹so that the house of Israel may no longer go astray from me nor defile

l 13.20 Gk Syr: Heb *lives for birds*

refer to prophetic rituals otherwise unknown. These actions might be related to prophetic cursing. It is not clear whether this type of cursing was limited to female prophets or just another example of false prophecy. **13:19** *Handfuls of barley*—that is, motivated by personal gain. Note, however, that the payment in food would have been particularly precious during the famine of the siege. **13:20** *Like birds* occurs twice in this verse. The Hebrew text has "for the birds"; a common trope in postbattle scenes depicts carrion birds feasting on the slain.

14:1–11 These verses also address the role of a prophet when asked to serve as an intermediary with God by sinful people. The narrative focuses on God's anger at this hypocritical request. The final three verses return to the question of a false prophet addressed in chap. 13. **14:1** *Elders* were originally male landowners and, therefore, heads of households. They apparently retained some of their former status among the Judeans in exile. **14:3** *Their idols . . . stumbling block* is repeated three times in this short passage (vv. 3, 4, 7). Taking the idols *into their hearts* connotes a deep interior devotion to that deity. The elders are ironically creating their own *stumbling block*, which keeps them from thriving. **14:4** *Prophet.* Although this word appears seventeen times in the book of Ezekiel, only four times is it used to designate Ezekiel (2:5; 14:4, 7; 33:33), who is normally titled "Mortal." **14:7** *I . . . will answer them myself* through the disaster that is their punishment. **14:8** *A sign and a byword.* Their fate will become legendary. **14:9** *I . . . have deceived that prophet . . . and will destroy him.* God is both the agent of their deception and the punisher for that deception. While the concept may be illogical, it artistically represents divine right over anything resembling human agency, capturing the feeling of being trapped in an inescapable problem. **14:11** *They shall be my people, and I will be their God.* A statement that is found four times in Ezekiel (11:20; 14:11; 37:23, 27)

themselves any more with all their transgressions. Then they shall be my people, and I will be their God, says the Lord God.

12 The word of the Lord came to me: [13]Mortal, when a land sins against me by acting faithlessly and I stretch out my hand against it and cut off its supply of bread[m] and send famine upon it and cut off from it humans and animals, [14]even if Noah, Daniel,[n] and Job, these three, were in it, they would save only their own lives by their righteousness, says the Lord God. [15]If I send wild animals through the land to ravage it so that it is made desolate and no one may pass through because of the animals, [16]even if these three men were in it, as I live, says the Lord God, they would save neither sons nor daughters; they alone would be saved, but the land would be desolate. [17]Or if I bring a sword upon that land and say, "Let a sword pass through the land," and I cut off humans and animals from it, [18]though these three men were in it, as I live, says the Lord God, they would save neither sons nor daughters, but they alone would be saved. [19]Or if I send a pestilence into that land and pour out my wrath upon it with blood, to cut off humans and animals from it, [20]even if Noah, Daniel,[o] and Job were in it, as I live, says the Lord God, they would save neither son nor daughter; they would save only their own lives by their righteousness.

21 Therefore thus says the Lord God: How much more when I send upon Jerusalem my four deadly acts of judgment, sword, famine, wild animals, and pestilence, to cut off humans and animals from it! [22]Yet survivors shall be left in it, sons and daughters who will be brought out; they will come out to you. When you see their ways and their deeds, you will be consoled for the evil that I have brought upon Jerusalem, for all that I have brought upon it. [23]They shall console you when you see their ways and their deeds, and you shall know that it was not without cause that I did all that I have done in it, says the Lord God.

15 The word of the Lord came to me: [2]O mortal, how does the wood of
the vine surpass all other wood,
the vine branch that is among the
trees of the forest?
[3]Is wood taken from it to make anything?
Does one take a peg from it on which
to hang any object?
[4]It is put in the fire for fuel;
when the fire has consumed both ends
of it
and the middle of it is charred,
is it useful for anything?
[5]When it was whole it was used for
nothing;
how much less—when the fire has
consumed it,
and it is charred—
can it ever be used for anything!

m 14.13 Heb *staff of bread* n 14.14 Or *Danel* o 14.20 Or *Danel*

and is found only in other postmonarchic prophets (Jer. 31:33; 32:38; Zech. 8:8). The closest parallel in the Pentateuch is Exod. 29:45.

14:12–23 These verses pose a hypothetical situation: Would God spare the city of Jerusalem for the sake of the righteous people who dwell there? The hypothetical picks three paragons of righteousness: Noah, who was saved from the devastation of the global flood; Job, who did not curse God even though he suffered unjustly; and a "Daniel" or "Dan-el," who was a righteous ancient king known from myths found outside of Israel. The repetitiveness of the hypothetical situation stresses the fact that no one's righteousness will save anyone else, let alone the city as a whole (cf. Gen. 18:16–32). **14:13** *Famine* is the first of four disasters with which God punishes the community for sins. The others are "wild animals" (v. 15), military attack ("sword" in v. 17), and disease ("pestilence" in v. 19). **14:14** *Save only their own lives* indicates that God would not punish the innocent, a statement that implies that no one was innocent when Jerusalem fell. **14:22** *Survivors shall be left.* While some people did survive the fall of Jerusalem, it was not because they were more righteous. They survived merely to serve another divine purpose. *Come out to you.* The pronoun *you* here is plural, meaning that they will join the exiles in Babylon. *Consoled.* The current exiles will take comfort from the survival of even a few of the Judahites.

15:1–8 This short chapter takes a well-known metaphor for the nation of Judah as a vine (e.g., Isa. 5:1–2; 27:1–3; Jer. 2:21; Hos. 10:1) and turns it on its head by comparing it to another metaphor: the nation as a large tree. In passages where the vine is a symbol of election, the grapes take center stage. Here, the poem focuses on the wood of the vine, which is worthless compared to the wood

6 Therefore thus says the Lord G<small>OD</small>: Like the wood of the vine among the trees of the forest, which I have given to the fire for fuel, so I will give up the inhabitants of Jerusalem. ⁷I will set my face against them; although they escape from the fire, the fire shall still consume them, and you shall know that I am the L<small>ORD</small> when I set my face against them. ⁸And I will make the land desolate because they have acted faithlessly, says the Lord G<small>OD</small>.

16 The word of the L<small>ORD</small> came to me: ²Mortal, make known to Jerusalem her abominations ³and say: Thus says the Lord G<small>OD</small> to Jerusalem: Your origin and your birth were in the land of the Canaanites; your father was an Amorite and your mother a Hittite. ⁴As for your birth, on the day you were born your navel cord was not cut, nor were you washed with water to cleanse you, nor rubbed with salt, nor wrapped in cloths. ⁵No eye pitied you to do any of these things for you out of compassion for you, but you were thrown out in the open field, for you were abhorred on the day you were born.

6 I passed by you and saw you flailing about in your blood. As you lay in your blood, I said to you, "Live!*^p*and grow up*^p* like a plant of the field." You grew up and became tall and arrived at full womanhood;*^q* your breasts were formed, and your hair had grown, yet you were naked and bare.

8 I passed by you again and looked on you; you were at the age for love. I spread the edge of my cloak over you and covered your nakedness: I pledged myself to you and entered into a covenant with you, says the Lord G<small>OD</small>, and you became mine. ⁹Then I bathed you with water and washed off the blood from you and anointed you with oil. ¹⁰I clothed you with embroidered cloth and with sandals of fine leather; I bound you in fine linen and covered you with rich fabric.*^r* ¹¹I adorned you with ornaments: I put bracelets on your arms, a chain on your neck, ¹²a ring on your nose, earrings in your ears, and a beautiful crown upon your head. ¹³You were adorned with gold and silver, while your clothing was of fine linen, rich fabric,*^s* and embroidered cloth. You had choice flour and honey and oil for food. You grew exceedingly beautiful, fit to be a queen. ¹⁴Your fame spread among the nations on account of your beauty, for it was perfect because of my splendor that I had bestowed on you, says the Lord G<small>OD</small>.

15 But you trusted in your beauty and prostituted yourself because of your fame and lavished your prostitutions on any passerby.*^t* ¹⁶You took some of your garments and made for yourself colorful high places and

p 16.7 Gk Syr: Heb *Live! I made you a myriad*   *q* 16.7 Cn: Heb *ornament of ornaments*   *r* 16.10 Meaning of Heb uncertain   *s* 16.13 Meaning of Heb uncertain   *t* 16.15 Heb adds *Let it be his*

from stately trees. The contrast of the vine and the tree then stems from these two plant symbols, deliberately pulling the rug out from under Judah's confidence in its election by the very symbol used to represent it.

16:1–58 While the book of Ezekiel contains many metaphors, the ones in this chapter (and chap. 23), which compare the nation to an adulterous woman, are the longest in the book. Like the image of the vine in chap. 15, this metaphor has two sources. First, it builds on the common designation of Jerusalem as "Daughter Zion," a title often used to personify the city as empathetic and that its covenant with God was like a marriage. Earlier prophets, however, had used this same image to represent the sinfulness of the city (e.g., Jer. 2:20; Hos. 4:10). The only difference between Ezekiel and other prophetic books is the expansion of this metaphor into an angry tirade by a deity depicted as a raging husband. **16:1–43a** This is the first of two oracles describing Jerusalem as an adulterous wife. **16:3** *Canaanites, Amorite,* and *Hittite* all indicate the diverse origins of the people who eventually made up the nation of Israel. Here *Hittite* refers not to the ancient nation located in modern-day Turkey but rather to one of the small city-states in the Levant. **16:4** *Navel cord . . . wrapped in cloths* summarizes the rituals performed on a newborn baby. **16:5** *Thrown out in the open field* indicates that the Israelites were rejected by the groups they came from. **16:6** *Flailing about in your blood.* The placental blood that would have normally been washed off the infant. **16:8–14** *I spread the edge of my cloak over you* introduces a number of actions through which God claims the infant both as a daughter and as a wife. This odd combination of rituals reminds the reader that this chapter is an extended metaphor and not a description of regular human relationships. **16:8** *Covenant* can also include a marital vow. **16:15** *Prostituted* in Hebrew covers any variety of illicit sexual interactions, including premarital sex and adultery. **16:16–22** These verses combine ritual metaphors with those of adultery, again signaling that these are metaphors and not actual rituals. **16:16** *High places*

on them prostituted yourself; nothing like this has ever been or ever shall be."[17]You also took your beautiful jewels of my gold and my silver that I had given you and made for yourself male images and with them prostituted yourself, [18]and you took your embroidered garments to cover them and set my oil and my incense before them. [19]Also my bread that I gave you—I fed you with choice flour and oil and honey—you set it before them as a pleasing odor, and so it was, says the Lord God. [20]You took your sons and your daughters, whom you had borne to me, and these you sacrificed to them to be devoured. As if your prostitutions were not enough! [21]You slaughtered my children and delivered them up as an offering to them. [22]And in all your abominations and your prostitutions you did not remember the days of your youth, when you were naked and bare, flailing about in your blood.

23 After all your wickedness (woe, woe to you! says the Lord God), [24]you built yourself a platform and made yourself a lofty place in every square; [25]at the head of every street you built your lofty place and prostituted your beauty, offering yourself[v] to every passer-by and multiplying your prostitution. [26]You prostituted yourself with the Egyptians, your lustful neighbors,[w] multiplying your prostitution, to provoke me to anger. [27]Therefore I stretched out my hand against you, reduced your rations, and gave you up to the will of your enemies, the daughters of the Philistines, who were ashamed of your lewd behavior. [28]You prostituted yourself with the Assyrians because you were insatiable; you prostituted yourself with them, and still you were not satisfied. [29]You multiplied your prostitution with Chaldea, the land of merchants, and even with this you were not satisfied.

30 How sick is your heart,[x] says the Lord God, that you did all these things, the deeds of a brazen prostitute, [31]building your platform at the head of every street and making your lofty place in every square! Yet you were not like a prostitute because you scorned payment. [32]Adulterous wife who receives strangers instead of her husband! [33]Gifts are given to all prostitutes, but you gave your gifts to all your lovers, bribing them to come to you from all around for your prostitutions. [34]So you were different from other women in your prostitutions: no one solicited you to prostitute yourself, and you gave payment, while no payment was given to you; you were different.

35 Therefore, O prostitute, hear the word of the Lord: [36]Thus says the Lord God: Because your lust was poured out and your nakedness uncovered in your prostitution with your lovers, and because of all your abominable idols, and because of the blood of your children that you gave to them, [37]therefore, I will gather all your lovers with whom you took pleasure, all those you loved and all those you hated; I will gather them against you from all around and will uncover your nakedness to them so that they may see all your nakedness. [38]I will judge you as women who commit adultery and shed blood are judged and bring blood upon you in wrath and jealousy. [39]I will deliver you into their hands, and they shall throw down your platform and break down your lofty places; they shall strip you of your clothes and take your beautiful objects and leave you naked and bare. [40]They shall bring up a mob against you, and they shall stone you and cut you to pieces with their swords. [41]They shall burn your houses and execute judgments on you in the sight of many women; I will stop you from prostituting yourself, and you shall also make no more payments. [42]So I will satisfy my fury on you, and my jealousy shall turn away from you; I will be calm and will be angry no longer. [43]Because you have not remembered the days of your youth but have enraged me

u 16.16 Meaning of Heb uncertain   v 16.25 Heb *spreading your legs*   w 16.26 Heb *large-membered neighbors*   x 16.30 Or *How furious I am with you*

usually refer to open-air sanctuaries, not brothels. **16:17** *Male images*, or phallic symbols. **16:19–22** *A pleasing odor* begins a series of ritual images, such as offerings of food, incense, and precious items, culminating with child sacrifice. **16:24** *Platform.* Again, not associated with a brothel but indicating the public aspect of Jerusalem's rejection of YHWH. **16:26–29** *Egyptians*, *Assyrians*, and *Chaldea* all vied for control of monarchic Judah. The passage depicts Judah's attempts to make alliances with these nations as infidelity to God, thus adultery. **16:31** *Not like a prostitute* because these attempted alliances were initiated by Judah, who had to pay tribute to the overlords. **16:38–43a** These verses liken the fate of Jerusalem to the punishment for adultery and murder. While each of those was a

with all these things, therefore I have returned your deeds upon your head, says the Lord God.

Have you not committed lewdness beyond all your abominations? [44]See, everyone who uses proverbs will use this proverb about you, "Like mother, like daughter." [45]You are the daughter of your mother, who loathed her husband and her children, and you are the sister of your sisters, who loathed their husbands and their children. Your mother was a Hittite and your father an Amorite. [46]Your big sister is Samaria, who lived with her daughters to the north of you; your little sister, who lived to the south of you, is Sodom with her daughters. [47]You not only followed their ways and acted according to their abominations; within a very little time you were more corrupt than they in all your ways. [48]As I live, says the Lord God, your sister Sodom and her daughters have not done as you and your daughters have done. [49]This was the guilt of your sister Sodom: she and her daughters had pride, excess of food, and prosperous ease but did not aid the poor and needy. [50]They were haughty and did abominable things before me; therefore I removed them when I saw it. [51]Samaria has not committed half your sins; you have committed more abominations than they and have made your sisters appear righteous by all the abominations that you have committed. [52]Bear your disgrace, you also, for you have brought about for your sisters a more favorable judgment; because of your sins in which you acted more abominably than they, they are more in the right

than you. So be ashamed, you also, and bear your disgrace, for you have made your sisters appear righteous.

53 I will restore their fortunes, the fortunes of Sodom and her daughters and the fortunes of Samaria and her daughters, and I will restore your own fortunes along with theirs, [54]in order that you may bear your disgrace and be ashamed of all that you have done, becoming a consolation to them. [55]As for your sisters, Sodom and her daughters shall return to their former state; Samaria and her daughters shall return to their former state, and you and your daughters shall return to your former state. [56]Was not your sister Sodom a byword in your mouth in the day of your pride, [57]before your wickedness was uncovered? Now you are a mockery to the daughters of Edom[y] and all her neighbors and to the daughters of the Philistines, those all around who despise you. [58]You must bear the penalty of your lewdness and your abominations, says the Lord.

59 Yes, thus says the Lord God: I will deal with you as you have done, you who have despised the oath, breaking the covenant, [60]yet I will remember my covenant with you in the days of your youth, and I will establish with you an everlasting covenant. [61]Then you will remember your ways and be ashamed when you receive your older and younger sisters and I give them to you as daughters, but not on account of my[z] covenant with you. [62]I will establish my covenant with you,

y 16.57 Heb mss Syr: MT *Aram*   z 16.61 Heb lacks *my*

capital offense in ancient Israel, the means of execution differed. **16:43b–52** These verses probably stemmed from an originally separate oracle that uses the imagery of sisters to compare Judah to other noted sinners in Israel's history. **16:44** *Proverb.* The passage expands on another common saying to serve a rhetorical function. **16:46** *Samaria* was the capital of the kingdom of Israel, destroyed in 722 BCE. *Sodom* was on the coast of the Dead Sea, within the kingdom of Judah. It was legendarily destroyed by a natural disaster in prehistoric times. **16:49** *Did not aid the poor and needy.* In the book of Genesis, the sin of Sodom was represented by the attempted gang rape of male outsiders seeking shelter, with no mention of economic injustice. Sodom came to symbolize wickedness, but Jerusalem's sins were far greater, a point made in v. 51's depiction of Samaria's sins as "half" of Jerusalem's. **16:52** *You have made your sisters appear righteous* in comparison to the sinfulness of Jerusalem. *Be ashamed*, repeated in v. 54, would signal Judah's acceptance of its guilt. **16:53–57** *Consolation, byword*, and *mockery* indicate the very public nature of Judah's fate, not as an example of tragedy, but as a symbol of justified divine punishment. Like Sodom, Jerusalem will be remembered for how much it deserved its fall. **16:53** *I will restore their fortunes.* The sister cities will be pardoned to make room for a better example of wickedness: Jerusalem.

16:59–63 The chapter abruptly shifts to God's promise of an eternal covenant with Judah. The language in these verses explicitly connects to the previous material through its insistence on perpetual shame as the desired outcome. **16:60** *I will remember* refers to the covenant God had initiated

Going Deeper: Slut-Shaming as Prophetic Discourse (Ezekiel 16)

The f-bomb is quite ubiquitous in American colloquial conversation. While its origin denotes illicit or unsavory sexual acts, its use as a swear word functions beyond its narrow semantics. Something that is "f——ed" is awry, messed up, unjust, or unbelievable in its egregiousness, to name just a few of its nuances.

The Hebrew word often translated into English as "adulterous woman" (*zonah*) has a similar breadth of meaning. At its root, it refers to female sexual acts outside the norm of socially acceptable behavior, at least for women attached to an elite male. It can mean adultery in our sense of the term, but our concept of a prostitute is not an exact match. Prostitutes were acceptable in ancient Israel, although they came from lower classes. Translations of the word as "whore" get closer to one of its connotations as designating female promiscuity.

This Hebrew word might better parallel the colloquialism *slut* today, a term bent on shaming its female designee not just for multiple sexual acts but also through body-shaming via references to clothing and by censoring her exercise of agency represented by socially unacceptable behaviors such as excessive flirting or the initiation of intimacy. While within a heterosexual context, this behavior represents a male's view of female behavior (or a female's assessment of rival female behavior), slut-shaming can occur in any gendered context. At its base, however, the criticized behavior is depicted within the confines of intimate relationships.

The use of this Hebrew term for adultery, whoring, or prostitution in the Prophets can best be approached through the lens of contemporary slut-shaming. The authors do not always have a specific sexual act in mind. They use sexualized language to represent repulsive and socially unacceptable behavior. In Ezek. 16 and 23, the male leaders of Judah are slut-shamed for seeking economic and political relationships with foreign nations, thus violating their expected sole intimate relationship with YHWH.

Corrine L. Carvalho

---

and you shall know that I am the Lord, ⁶³in order that you may remember and be confounded and never open your mouth again because of your shame, when I forgive you all that you have done, says the Lord God.

17 The word of the Lord came to me: ²O mortal, propound a riddle and speak an allegory to the house of Israel. ³Say: Thus says the Lord God:

A great eagle with great wings and long pinions,
      rich in plumage of many colors,
      came to the Lebanon.

He took the top of the cedar,
⁴   broke off its topmost shoot;
he carried it to a land of trade,
      set it in a city of merchants.
⁵ Then he took a seedling from the land,
      placed it in fertile soil;
a plant*ᵃ* by abundant waters,
      he set it like a willow twig.
⁶ It sprouted and became a vine
      spreading out but low;
its branches turned toward him;
      its roots remained where it stood.

a 17.5 Meaning of Heb uncertain

---

with this nation. *An everlasting covenant* occurs in the book only here and in 37:26. **16:63** *In order that you may remember . . . your shame* indicates two things. First, the eternal covenant will still not be a reward for righteous behavior. Second, it is granted simply to make the recipients realize how unworthy they are and how dependent they remain on God.

17:1–24 This chapter contains another extended metaphor of a vine and a tree (see Ezek. 15). Here, while the vine represents something more "lowly," it is not described as worthless. The metaphor embeds a lengthy explanation of its symbolism in vv. 11–21, tying the metaphoric narrative to Judah's history. **17:2** *Riddle* and *allegory* are two terms indicating the symbolic nature of the material that follows. **17:3** *Eagle*. The first eagle represents Babylon (v. 12), which besieged Jerusalem twice and exiled many of the elites. *Cedar*, which was a valued tree, represents King Jehoiachin, who was exiled by the Babylonians in 597 BCE. **17:6** *It sprouted and became a vine* combines tree and vine imagery. The vine comes from the tree and is lower than it, symbolizing Jehoiachin's exiled status. Even so, this sprig/king flourishes by accepting its/his fate (see 2 Kgs. 25:27–30).

So it became a vine;
    it brought forth branches,
    put forth foliage.

[7] There was another great eagle
    with great wings and much plumage.
And see! This vine stretched out
    its roots toward him;
it shot out its branches toward him
    from the bed where it was planted
    so that he might water it.
[8] It had been transplanted
    to good soil by abundant waters,
so that it might produce branches
    and bear fruit
    and become a noble vine.
[9] Say: Thus says the Lord God:
    Will it prosper?
Will he not pull up its roots,
    cause its fruit to rot[b] and wither,
    its fresh sprouting leaves to fade?
No strong arm or mighty army will be
    needed
    to pull it from its roots.
[10] Look, it has been transplanted. Will it
    thrive?
When the east wind strikes it,
    will it not utterly wither,
    wither on the bed where it grew?

[11] Then the word of the Lord came to me:
[12] Say now to the rebellious house: Do you not
know what these things mean? Tell them:
The king of Babylon came to Jerusalem, took
its king and its officials, and brought them
back with him to Babylon. [13] He took one of
the royal offspring and made a covenant
with him, putting him under oath (he had
taken away the chief men of the land), [14] so
that the kingdom might be humble and not
lift itself up and that by keeping his covenant

it might stand. [15] But he rebelled against him
by sending ambassadors to Egypt, that they
might give him horses and a large army. Will
he succeed? Can one escape who does such
things? Can he break the covenant and yet
escape? [16] As I live, says the Lord God, surely
in the place where the king resides who made
him king, whose oath he despised and whose
covenant with him he broke—in Babylon he
shall die. [17] Pharaoh with his mighty army
and great company will not help him in war,
when ramps are cast up and siege walls built
to cut off many lives. [18] Because he despised
the oath and broke the covenant, because
he gave his hand and yet did all these things,
he shall not escape. [19] Therefore thus says the
Lord God: As I live, I will surely return upon
his head my oath that he despised and my
covenant that he broke. [20] I will spread my net
over him, and he shall be caught in my snare;
I will bring him to Babylon and enter into
judgment with him there for the treason he
has committed against me. [21] All the pick[c] of
his troops shall fall by the sword, and the survivors shall be scattered to every wind, and
you shall know that I, the Lord, have spoken.

22 Thus says the Lord God:
    I myself will take a sprig
        from the lofty top of the cedar;
    I will set it out.
    I will break off a tender shoot
        from the topmost of its young twigs;
    I myself will transplant it
        on a high and lofty mountain.
[23] On the mountain height of Israel
    I will transplant it,
    and it will produce boughs and bear fruit
        and become a noble cedar.

b 17.9 Gk: Meaning of Heb uncertain   c 17.21 Or *fugitives*

Him—that is, the king of Babylon, Nebuchadnezzar. **17:7** *Another great eagle.* The king of Egypt, Psammetichus II, who supported Judah's rebellion against the Babylonians. **17:9** *Will he not pull up its roots?* The alliance with Egypt that Zedekiah pursued led to the second siege of Jerusalem and its ultimate destruction. **17:10** *Will it thrive?* The poet plays with the vulnerability of transplantation. **17:12** *What [do] these things mean?* Further identifies this poem as a riddle. *Its king.* Nebuchad- nezzar. **17:13** *One of the royal offspring.* Zedekiah, who was an uncle of the legitimate king, Jehoia- chin. **17:15** *He rebelled* by seeking an alliance with Egypt. **17:16** *In the place where the king resides* contrasts the legitimate king, Jehoiachin, with the "royal offspring" (v. 13), Zedekiah. Jehoiachin is said to flourish in Babylon, while Zedekiah dies there. **17:19** *Return upon his head my oath.* When oaths were sworn, they usually laid out the consequences of betrayal. **17:20** *Net[s]* were used to catch dangerous animals. **17:22** *I myself will take a sprig.* God transforms the metaphor from one of ambiguity to a symbol of security. The new sprig may refer to one of Jehoiachin's descendants. **17:23** *Become a noble cedar*, thus regaining the exiled monarchy's status. *Every kind of bird.* Smaller kingdoms dependent on this vine-turned-cedar.

Under it every kind of bird will live;
in the shade of its branches will nest
winged creatures of every kind.
24 All the trees of the field shall know
that I am the LORD.
I bring low the high tree;
I make high the low tree;
I dry up the green tree
and make the dry tree flourish.
I the LORD have spoken;
I will accomplish it.

18 The word of the LORD came to me: 2What do you mean by repeating this proverb concerning the land of Israel, "The parents have eaten sour grapes, and the children's teeth are set on edge"? 3As I live, says the Lord GOD, this proverb shall no more be used by you in Israel. 4Know that all lives are mine; the life of the parent as well as the life of the child is mine: it is only the person who sins who shall die.

5 If a man is righteous and does what is lawful and right—6if he does not eat upon the mountains or lift up his eyes to the idols of the house of Israel, does not defile his neighbor's wife or approach a woman during her menstrual period, 7does not oppress anyone but restores to the debtor his pledge, commits no robbery, gives his bread to the hungry and covers the naked with a garment, 8does not take advance or accrued interest, withholds his hand from iniquity, executes true justice between contending parties, 9follows my statutes, and is careful to observe my ordinances, acting faithfully—such a one is righteous; he shall surely live, says the Lord GOD.

10 If he has a son who is violent, a shedder of blood, 11who does any of these things (though his father*d* does none of them), who

eats upon the mountains, defiles his neighbor's wife, 12oppresses the poor and needy, commits robbery, does not restore the pledge, lifts up his eyes to the idols, commits abomination, 13takes advance or accrued interest, shall he then live? He shall not. He has done all these abominable things; he shall surely be put to death; his blood shall be upon himself.

14 But if this son has a son who sees all the sins that his father has done, considers, and does not do likewise, 15who does not eat upon the mountains or lift up his eyes to the idols of the house of Israel, does not defile his neighbor's wife, 16does not wrong anyone, exacts no pledge, commits no robbery but gives his bread to the hungry and covers the naked with a garment, 17withholds his hand from iniquity,*e* takes no advance or accrued interest, observes my ordinances, and follows my statutes, he shall not die for his father's iniquity; he shall surely live. 18As for his father, because he practiced extortion, robbed his brother, and did what is not good among his people, he died for his iniquity.

19 Yet you say, "Why should not the son suffer for the iniquity of the father?" When the son has done what is lawful and right and has been careful to observe all my statutes, he shall surely live. 20The person who sins shall die. A child shall not suffer for the iniquity of a parent nor a parent suffer for the iniquity of a child; the righteousness of the righteous shall be their own, and the wickedness of the wicked shall be their own.

21 But if the wicked turn away from all their sins that they have committed and keep all my statutes and do what is lawful and right, they shall surely live; they shall not die.

d 18.11 Heb *he*   *e* 18.17 Gk: Heb *the poor*

18:1–32 This chapter explicitly addresses the central question of the book: Does God punish the innocent? This is a question not of individual innocence, however, but of intergenerational guilt. Although some biblical texts allow for intergenerational punishment for grave sins, Ezekiel is among many postexilic texts, such as Jeremiah and Chronicles, that reject this explanation. The book of Ezekiel holds those living in Jerusalem at the time of its fall responsible for the disaster. **18:2** *Proverb.* God again addresses a common saying within Judean culture (see 12:22 and 16:44). The skill of a speaker of proverbs depends on using the correct proverb for the situation. In these cases, God denies the legitimacy of the use of these traditional sayings. *The parents have eaten sour grapes* represents the intergenerational effect of family trauma and dysfunction. This proverb is also refuted in Jer. 31:29–30. **18:6** *If he does not.* The actions that are listed are examples. **18:9** *Statutes . . . ordinances* indicates that the previous list was not exhaustive. **18:10** *Son.* In the theoretical discussion that follows, "son" represents anyone in a later generation, while "father" refers to the previous generation. **18:19** *Why should not the son suffer for the iniquity of the father?* The notion of intergenerational punishment was deeply rooted in that culture, and it allowed those

²²None of the transgressions that they have committed shall be remembered against them, for the righteousness that they have done they shall live. ²³Have I any pleasure in the death of the wicked, says the Lord God, and not rather that they should turn from their ways and live? ²⁴But when the righteous turn away from their righteousness and commit iniquity and do the same abominable things that the wicked do, shall they live? None of the righteous deeds that they have done shall be remembered, for the treachery of which they are guilty and the sin they have committed, they shall die.

25 Yet you say, "The way of the Lord is unfair." Hear now, O house of Israel: Is my way unfair? Is it not your ways that are unfair? ²⁶When the righteous turn away from their righteousness and commit iniquity, they shall die for it; for the iniquity that they have committed, they shall die. ²⁷Again, when the wicked turn away from the wickedness they have committed and do what is lawful and right, they shall save their life. ²⁸Because they considered and turned away from all the transgressions that they had committed, they shall surely live; they shall not die. ²⁹Yet the house of Israel says, "The way of the Lord is unfair." O house of Israel, are my ways unfair? Is it not your ways that are unfair?

30 Therefore I will judge you, O house of Israel, all of you according to your ways, says the Lord God. Repent and turn from all your transgressions; otherwise iniquity will be your ruin.ᶠ ³¹Cast away from you all the transgressions that you have committed against me, and get yourselves a new heart and a new spirit! Why will you die, O house of Israel? ³²For I have no pleasure in the death of anyone, says the Lord God. Turn, then, and live.

19

As for you, raise up a lamentation for the princes of Israel, ²and say:
What a lioness was your mother
    among lions!
She lay down among young lions,
    rearing her cubs.
³ She raised up one of her cubs;
    he became a young lion,
and he learned to catch prey;
    he devoured humans.
⁴ The nations heard about him;
    he was caught in their pit,
and they brought him with hooks
    to the land of Egypt.
⁵ When she saw that she was thwarted,
    that her hope was lost,
she took another of her cubs
    and made him a young lion.
⁶ He prowled among the lions;
    he became a young lion,
and he learned to catch prey;
    he devoured people.

ƒ 18.30 Or *so that they shall not be a stumbling block of iniquity to you*

living in Jerusalem when the city fell to claim that they were innocent sufferers. **18:23** *Have I any pleasure in the death of the wicked?* This statement counters the notion that the book presents a bloodthirsty God. **18:25** *The way of the Lord is unfair* accurately captures the reconfiguring of ethical norms that followed the fall of the city. **18:30** *Therefore . . . according to your ways.* Although God does not delight in the fall of the city, criminals and sinners must be held accountable. *House of Israel.* It is unclear whether this would include those already living in exile or if it only addresses those living in Israel at the time of the siege. **18:31** *A new heart and a new spirit.* In Ezek. 11:19, God gives the people "one heart" and a "new spirit." In 36:26, God gives them "a new heart . . . and a new spirit." Here the people are told to get themselves a *new heart and a new spirit.* All three refer to an inner transformation of the ethical and emotional character necessary for restoration.

19:1–14 This chapter consists of a funeral song, utilizing a standard structure with short parallel lines. These dirges were used to commemorate national disasters; Lamentations contains five dirges for Jerusalem. The irony in this chapter is that the person being eulogized is still alive. **19:1** *Princes* were those in the succession line of the royal family. **19:2** *Lioness . . . lions.* Symbols of the royal family—found, for example, on Judean coins. The extended metaphor outlines the succession of kings following the death of Josiah. **19:3** *One of her cubs.* Jehoahaz, who was the son of Josiah and Hamutal. **19:4** *Brought him . . . to the land of Egypt.* He was removed by the Egyptians after only three months on the throne (2 Kgs. 23:31–34). **19:5** *Another of her cubs.* This section of the song combines the fates of two kings. The first is Eliakim, whose name is changed to Jehoiachim, also a son of Josiah, but his mother's name was Zebidah (2 Kgs. 34–37). The second was Jehoiachim's son, Jehoiachin, whose mother was Nehushta (2 Kgs. 24:8). These royal genealogies suggest that

7 And he ravaged their strongholds[g]
   and laid waste their towns;
the land was appalled, and all in it,
   at the sound of his roaring.
8 The nations set upon him
   from the provinces all around;
they spread their net over him;
   he was caught in their pit.
9 With hooks they put him in a neck collar
   and brought him to the king of
     Babylon;
   they brought him into custody,
so that his voice should be heard no
     more
   on the mountains of Israel.
10 Your mother was like a vine in a
     vineyard[b]
   transplanted by the water,
fruitful and full of branches
   from abundant water.
11 Its strongest stem became
   a ruler's scepter;[i]
it towered aloft
   among the clouds;
it stood out in its height
   with its mass of branches.
12 But it was plucked up in fury,
   cast down to the ground;
the east wind dried it up;
   its fruit was stripped off;
its strong stem was withered;
   the fire consumed it.
13 Now it is transplanted into the
     wilderness,
   into a dry and thirsty land.
14 And fire has gone out from its stem,
   has consumed its branches and fruit,

so that there remains in it no strong stem,
   no scepter for ruling.

This is a lamentation, and it is used as a lamentation.

20 In the seventh year, in the fifth month, on the tenth day of the month, certain elders of Israel came to consult the LORD and sat down before me. 2And the word of the LORD came to me: 3Mortal, speak to the elders of Israel, and say to them: Thus says the Lord GOD: Why are you coming? To consult me? As I live, says the Lord GOD, I will not be consulted by you. 4Will you judge them, mortal; will you judge them? Then let them know the abominations of their ancestors 5and say to them: Thus says the Lord GOD: On the day when I chose Israel, I swore to the offspring of the house of Jacob—making myself known to them in the land of Egypt—I swore to them, saying, "I am the LORD your God." 6On that day I swore to them that I would bring them out of the land of Egypt into a land that I had searched out for them, a land flowing with milk and honey, the most glorious of all lands. 7And I said to them, "Cast away the detestable things on which your eyes feast, every one of you, and do not defile yourselves with the idols of Egypt; I am the LORD your God." 8But they rebelled against me and would not listen to me; not one of them cast away the detestable things on which their eyes feasted, nor did they forsake the idols of Egypt.

g 19.7 Tg: Heb *his widows*   h 19.10 Cn: Heb *in your blood*
i 19.11 Heb *Its strongest stems became rulers' scepters*

the "lioness" represents the feminized city rather than the queen mother. **19:9** *Brought him to the king of Babylon* during the first siege of Jerusalem in 597. While the Babylonians did install on the throne Jehoiachin's uncle, Zedekiah, who actually was a son of Hamutal (2 Kgs. 24:18), the book of Ezekiel does not recognize him as a legitimate king. **19:10** *Like a vine.* The metaphor shifts to a vine, symbolizing the feminized subject of the poem (probably the city). **19:14** *No scepter for ruling.* The destruction of the royal line, even though the poem was pronounced when Zedekiah was still on the throne and Jehoiachin was still alive.

20:1–32 Chap. 20 contains three distinct sections: Israel's history of sin (vv. 1–32), the nation's restoration (vv. 33–44), and a condemnation of the area south of Jerusalem called the *Negeb* (vv. 45–49). **20:1** *In the seventh year.* July/August 591. *Came to consult.* See Ezek. 14:1–3. **20:4** *Abominations.* Violations of the law that also cause defilement. See **"Disgust, Defilement, and Impurity,"** **p. 1162**. **20:5** *On the day . . . in the land of Egypt.* Although the patriarch Jacob is mentioned in this chapter, it dates the commencement of the covenant between God and Israel to the exodus from Egypt. **20:6** *Milk and honey* represents a land that is bountiful. **20:7** *The idols of Egypt.* This is the only place in the Hebrew Bible that accuses the future Israelites of worshiping Egyptian deities (contra Exod. 3–4). **20:8** *Rebelled.* See the note at Ezek. 2:3. This begins a repetitive section that traces Israel's history as a series of disobedience to divinely revealed law.

Then I thought I would pour out my wrath upon them and spend my anger against them in the midst of the land of Egypt. ⁹But I acted for the sake of my name, that it should not be profaned in the sight of the nations among whom they lived, in whose sight I made myself known to them in bringing them out of the land of Egypt. ¹⁰So I led them out of the land of Egypt and brought them into the wilderness. ¹¹I gave them my statutes and showed them my ordinances, by whose observance everyone shall live. ¹²Moreover, I gave them my Sabbaths, as a sign between me and them, so that they might know that I the Lord sanctify them. ¹³But the house of Israel rebelled against me in the wilderness; they did not observe my statutes but rejected my ordinances, by whose observance everyone shall live, and my Sabbaths they greatly profaned.

Then I thought I would pour out my wrath upon them in the wilderness, to make an end of them. ¹⁴But I acted for the sake of my name, so that it should not be profaned in the sight of the nations, in whose sight I had brought them out. ¹⁵Moreover, I swore to them in the wilderness that I would not bring them into the land that I had given them, a land flowing with milk and honey, the most glorious of all lands, ¹⁶because they rejected my ordinances and did not observe my statutes and profaned my Sabbaths, for their heart went after their idols. ¹⁷Nevertheless, my eye spared them, and I did not destroy them or make an end of them in the wilderness.

18 I said to their children in the wilderness, "Do not follow the statutes of your parents, nor observe their ordinances, nor defile yourselves with their idols. ¹⁹I the Lord am your God; follow my statutes, be careful to observe my ordinances, ²⁰and hallow my Sabbaths that they may be a sign between me and you, so that you may know that I the Lord am your God." ²¹But the children rebelled against me; they did not follow my statutes and were not careful to observe my ordinances, by whose observance everyone shall live; they profaned my Sabbaths.

Then I thought I would pour out my wrath upon them and spend my anger against them in the wilderness. ²²But I withheld my hand and acted for the sake of my name, so that it should not be profaned in the sight of the nations, in whose sight I had brought them out. ²³Moreover, I swore to them in the wilderness that I would scatter them among the nations and disperse them through the countries, ²⁴because they had not executed my ordinances but had rejected my statutes and profaned my Sabbaths, and their eyes were set on their ancestors' idols. ²⁵Moreover, I gave them statutes that were not good and ordinances by which they could not live. ²⁶I defiled them through their very gifts, in their offering up all their firstborn, in order that I might horrify them, so that they might know that I am the Lord.

27 Therefore, mortal, speak to the house of Israel and say to them: Thus says the Lord God: In this again your ancestors blasphemed me by dealing treacherously with me. ²⁸For when I had brought them into the land that I swore to give them, then wherever they saw

---

20:9 *For the sake of my name.* God acts because the divine reputation is being damaged. **20:11** *Statutes . . . ordinances.* Divinely revealed law. The Pentateuch depicts the Hebrews led through "the wilderness" (v. 10), where the revelation of divine laws occurs at three points (before they commit idolatry with the golden calf, after the destruction of the golden calf, and right before they enter the land God gives them). Ezekiel 20's repetition makes the point that the people were given plenty of opportunity to avoid national catastrophe. **20:12** *Sabbaths* serve as the paradigmatic law in this chapter. The Sabbath provided formerly enslaved persons with legislated days off from hard labor. To ignore their observance made no rational sense, since it was a benefit to them. **20:17** *My eye spared them* undercuts what might appear to be a bloodthirsty God. The emphasis here is on God's intergenerational patience throughout Israel's history. **20:18** *Children,* like chap. 18, depicts rebellion as an intergenerational phenomenon that warranted repeated judgment. **20:25** *Statutes that were not good.* Since giving the people laws that would benefit them was not effective, God gives them laws that would harm them. Ironically, the Israelites do follow these laws, thus incurring more guilt. **20:26** *Offering up all their firstborn.* Child sacrifice was performed by nations surrounding Israel, including Phoenicia and Moab (e.g., 2 Kgs. 3:26–27). Other biblical texts assert that sometimes Israelites practiced this ritual as well (see, e.g., 1 Kgs. 11:7). Most of these texts describe it as idolatry, meaning the children were offered to a god other than YHWH. This passage suggests that at one time, Israelite laws allowed the sacrifice of children to YHWH (e.g., Exod. 13:2). **20:28** *High hill . . . leafy*

any high hill or any leafy tree, there they offered their sacrifices and presented the provocation of their offering; there they sent up their pleasing odors, and there they poured out their drink offerings. ²⁹(I said to them, "What is the high place to which you go? So it is called Bamah^j to this day.") ³⁰Therefore say to the house of Israel: Thus says the Lord GOD: Will you defile yourselves after the manner of your ancestors and go astray after their detestable things? ³¹When you offer your gifts and make your children pass through the fire, you defile yourselves with all your idols to this day. And shall I be consulted by you, O house of Israel? As I live, says the Lord GOD, I will not be consulted by you.

32 What is in your mind shall never happen—the thought, "Let us be like the nations, like the tribes of the countries, and worship wood and stone."

33 As I live, says the Lord GOD, surely with a mighty hand and an outstretched arm and with wrath poured out, I will be king over you. ³⁴I will bring you out from the peoples and gather you out of the countries where you are scattered, with a mighty hand and an outstretched arm and with wrath poured out, ³⁵and I will bring you into the wilderness of the peoples, and there I will enter into judgment with you face to face. ³⁶As I entered into judgment with your ancestors in the wilderness of the land of Egypt, so I will enter into judgment with you, says the Lord GOD. ³⁷I will make you pass under the staff and will bring you within the bond of the covenant. ³⁸I will purge out the rebels among you and those who transgress

against me; I will bring them out of the land where they reside as aliens, but they shall not enter the land of Israel. Then you shall know that I am the LORD.

39 As for you, O house of Israel, thus says the Lord GOD: Go serve your idols, every one of you now and hereafter, if you will not listen to me, but my holy name you shall no more profane with your gifts and your idols.

40 For on my holy mountain, the mountain height of Israel, says the Lord GOD, there all the house of Israel, all of them, shall serve me in the land; there I will accept them, and there I will require your contributions and the choicest of your gifts, with all your sacred things. ⁴¹As a pleasing odor I will accept you, when I bring you out from the peoples and gather you out of the countries where you have been scattered, and I will manifest my holiness among you in the sight of the nations. ⁴²You shall know that I am the LORD when I bring you into the land of Israel, the country that I swore to give to your ancestors. ⁴³There you shall remember your ways and all the deeds by which you have polluted yourselves, and you shall loathe yourselves for all the evils that you have committed. ⁴⁴And you shall know that I am the LORD when I deal with you for my name's sake, not according to your evil ways or corrupt deeds, O house of Israel, says the Lord GOD.

45 ^kThe word of the LORD came to me: ⁴⁶Mortal, set your face toward the south, preach against the south, and prophesy against the forest land in the Negeb; ⁴⁷say to the forest of the Negeb: Hear the word of the LORD: Thus says the Lord GOD: I will

j 20.29 That is, *high place* *k* 20.45 21.1 in Heb

---

tree. These outdoor spaces were associated with the worship of other deities. The *high hill* echoes the shrines called "high places," where stone stelae were often used to represent the gods worshiped there, while the *leafy tree* may connect to the worship of a nature deity, usually gendered as female. **20:31** *I will not be consulted by you.* Wording similar to Ezek. 14:3. **20:32** *Worship wood and stone* echoes the rituals of high places and forests in v. 28.

20:33–44 In this second section, God swears an oath, introduced by *As I live*, to restore Israel. This section also contains echoes of their earlier exodus from slavery in Egypt. **20:33** *With a mighty hand and an outstretched arm* is a phrase found five times in the book of Deuteronomy (4:34; 5:15; 7:19; 11:2; 26:8; with one variant in 9:29) in reference to the exodus, casting the return from exile as a new exodus. **20:35** *Into the wilderness.* Another echo of the exodus narrative. **20:37** *Pass under the staff* probably references a ritual in which a lesser king swears loyalty and subservience to a more powerful king. **20:38** *Aliens* are those who are not full citizens of the place where they live. Exiled Judeans would be classified as "aliens" in Babylon.

20:45–49 The short oracle in vv. 45–48 seems to predict punishment for the area south of Jerusalem. In the Hebrew text, the oracle comes in the following chapter. It is not clear why it is placed here. The chapter ends with one of the few times in the book that Ezekiel initiates dialogue. **20:46** *Negeb* is the biblical name for the arid land south of Jerusalem. **20:47** *The forest of the*

kindle a fire in you, and it shall devour every green tree in you and every dry tree; the blazing flame shall not be quenched, and all faces from south to north shall be scorched by it. ⁴⁸All flesh shall see that I the LORD have kindled it; it shall not be quenched. ⁴⁹Then I said, "Ah Lord GOD! They are saying of me, 'Is he not a maker of allegories?'"

21 ¹ᵗThe word of the LORD came to me: ²Mortal, set your face toward Jerusalem and preach against the sanctuaries; prophesy against the land of Israel ³and say to the land of Israel: Thus says the LORD: I am coming against you and will draw my sword out of its sheath and will cut off from you both righteous and wicked. ⁴Because I will cut off from you both righteous and wicked, therefore my sword shall go out of its sheath against all flesh from south to north, ⁵and all flesh shall know that I the LORD have drawn my sword out of its sheath; it shall not be sheathed again. ⁶Moan, therefore, mortal; moan with body collapsed and bitter grief before their eyes. ⁷And when they say to you, "Why do you moan?" you shall say, "Because of the news that has come. Every heart will melt, and all hands will be feeble, every spirit will be faint, and all knees will turn to water. See, it comes and it will be fulfilled," says the Lord GOD.

8 And the word of the LORD came to me: ⁹Mortal, prophesy and say: Thus says the Lord; say:

A sword, a sword is sharpened;
    it is also polished;
¹⁰ it is sharpened for slaughter,
    honed to flash like lightning!

How can we make merry?
    You have despised the rod
    and all discipline."ᵐ
¹¹ The swordⁿ is given to be polished
    to be grasped in the hand;
    it is sharpened; the sword is polished
    to be placed in the slayer's hand.
¹² Cry and wail, O mortal,
    for it is against my people;
    it is against all Israel's princes;
    they are thrown to the sword,
    together with my people.
    Ah! Strike the thigh!
¹³For consider: What! If you despise the rod, will it not happen?ᵒ says the Lord GOD.
¹⁴ And you, mortal, prophesy;
    strike hand to hand.
Let the sword fall twice, thrice;
    it is a sword for killing.
A sword for great slaughter—
    it surrounds them;
¹⁵ therefore hearts melt,
    and many stumble.
At all their gates I have set
    the pointᵖ of the sword.
Ah! It is made for flashing;
    it is drawn for slaughter.
¹⁶ Attack to the right!
    Engage to the left!
    —wherever your edge is directed.
¹⁷ I, too, will strike hand to hand;
    I will satisfy my fury;
    I the LORD have spoken.
18 The word of the LORD came to me: ¹⁹Mortal, mark out two roads for the sword of the

---

l 21.1 21.6 in Heb   *m* 21.10 Meaning of Heb uncertain
n 21.11 Heb *It*   *o* 21.13 Meaning of Heb uncertain
p 21.15 Meaning of Heb uncertain

Negeb. While the Negeb contains plant life, trees other than palm trees are currently rare. In ancient times, however, some of these areas did have trees. *I will kindle a fire in you.* The tense of the Hebrew in this verse is ambiguous, although probably connoting an imminent future event. *20:49 Is he not a maker of allegories?* A question that fits the prominence of figurative speech throughout the book so far. This is one of two places in the book where Ezekiel's profession is called into question (cf. Ezek. 33:32).

21:1–32 Although this chapter combines separate oracles, God's sword connects them all. In the ancient world, divine warriors, male or female, accompanied armies into battle. The *sword* in these verses symbolizes YHWH's warrior aspect. **21:1–17** This section praises YHWH's swordsmanship, but here the warrior turns against the group that expects protection. *Sanctuaries* could be places where other gods were worshiped or smaller shrines for YHWH. **21:3** *Both righteous and wicked.* In contrast to chap. 18, God's wrath will be directed against the whole community. While this does not make logical sense, it accurately reflects the horrors of war. **21:6** *Moan.* A reaction of deep grief. **21:10** *Rod.* An instrument of discipline, so their despisal of it signaled their disobedience. **21:12** *Strike the thigh* appears only here and in Jer. 31:19. **21:18–27** The second section focuses on the Babylonian conqueror of Zedekiah. **21:19** *The sword of the king of Babylon.* The transition

king of Babylon to come; both of them shall issue from the same land. And make a signpost; make it for a fork in the road leading to a city; ²⁰mark out the road for the sword to come to Rabbah of the Ammonites or to Judah and to*ᵍ* Jerusalem the fortified. ²¹For the king of Babylon stands at the parting of the way, at the fork in the two roads, to use divination; he shakes the arrows; he consults the teraphim;*ʳ* he inspects the liver. ²²Into his right hand comes the lot for Jerusalem, to set battering rams, to call out for slaughter, for raising the battle cry, to set battering rams against the gates, to cast up ramps, to build siege towers. ²³But to them it will seem like a false divination; they have sworn solemn oaths, but he brings their guilt to remembrance, bringing about their capture.

24 Therefore thus says the Lord God: Because you have brought your guilt to remembrance, in that your transgressions are uncovered, so that in all your deeds your sins appear—because you have come to remembrance, you shall be taken in hand.*ˢ*

²⁵ As for you, vile, wicked prince of Israel,
　　you whose day has come,
　　the time of final punishment,
²⁶ thus says the Lord God:
　Remove the turban, take off the crown;
　　things shall not remain as they are.
　Exalt that which is low;
　　humble that which is high.
²⁷ A ruin, a ruin, a ruin—
　　I will make it!
　　(Such has never occurred.)
　Until he comes whose right it is;
　　to him I will give it.

28 As for you, mortal, prophesy, and say: Thus says the Lord God concerning the Ammonites and concerning their reproach; say:
　A sword, a sword! Drawn for slaughter,
　　polished to consume,*ᵗ* to flash like
　　lightning.
²⁹ Offering false visions for you,
　　divining lies for you,
　they place you over the necks
　　of the vile, wicked ones—
　those whose day has come,
　　the time of final punishment.
³⁰ Return it to its sheath!
　In the place where you were created,
　　in the land of your origin,
　　I will judge you.
³¹ I will pour out my indignation upon you;
　　with the fire of my wrath
　　I will blow upon you.
　I will deliver you into brutish hands,
　　those skillful to destroy.
³² You shall be fuel for the fire,
　　your blood shall enter the earth;
　you shall be remembered no more,
　　for I the Lord have spoken.

22 The word of the Lord came to me: ²You, mortal, will you judge, will you judge the bloody city? Then declare to it all its abominable deeds. ³You shall say: Thus says the Lord God: A city! Shedding blood within itself; its time has come; making its idols, defiling itself. ⁴You have become guilty by the blood that you have shed and defiled by the idols that you have made; you have

q 21.20 Gk Syr: Heb *Judah in*　*r* 21.21 Or *the household gods*
s 21.24 Or *be taken captive*　*t* 21.28 Cn: Heb *to contain*

from YHWH's sword to the enemy's implies that the Babylonian army enacted the divinely decreed slaughter of the city. 21:20 *Mark out the road.* The armies had two choices: attack Rabbah, east of the Jordan River, or Jerusalem. 21:21 *Divination,* such as using portable idols and inspecting the livers of sacrificed sheep, was a ritual to discern the divine will. 21:22 *Lot.* A token used in divination (see, e.g., 1 Sam. 10:20–21; Neh. 11:1). 21:23 *Them.* The people of Jerusalem. 21:24 *To remembrance,* or simply "Because you have remembered your guilt." 21:25 *Vile, wicked prince of Israel.* Zedekiah. 21:27 *Until he comes whose right it is.* Either Jehoiachin or one of his descendants. 21:28–32 This oracle against Ammon, a nation east of the Jordan River, would fit better in chaps. 25–32, oracles against foreign nations, which begin with another oracle against Ammon. See **"Oracles against the Nations," p. 1105**. 21:29 *False visions . . . divining lies* attests to the ubiquity of prophecy, especially in times of crisis.

22:1–16 Chap. 22 has three sections, the first one echoed by chap. 24. The Israelites viewed blood as a powerful element, and in ritual texts, it had the power to both purify and defile. "Blood" was also a synonym for violent crimes. 22:2 *The bloody city* can mean a city full of victims of violence, but this passage makes the city the agent of the bloodshed. 22:3 *Shedding blood.* Since the Hebrew word for "city" is grammatically feminine, the pronouns throughout this passage are she/her/hers. For females, defiling blood referred to menstruation, thus the author plays with a third connotation

brought your days near; the appointed time of your years has come. Therefore I have made you a disgrace before the nations and a mockery to all the countries. ⁵Those who are near and those who are far from you will mock you, you infamous one, full of tumult.

6 The princes of Israel in you, everyone according to his power, have been bent on shedding blood. ⁷Father and mother are treated with contempt in you; the alien residing within you suffers extortion; the orphan and the widow are wronged in you. ⁸You have despised my holy things and profaned my Sabbaths. ⁹In you are those who slander to shed blood, those in you who eat upon the mountains, who commit lewdness in your midst. ¹⁰In you they uncover their fathers' nakedness; in you they violate women during their menstrual periods. ¹¹One commits abomination with his neighbor's wife; another lewdly defiles his daughter-in-law; another in you defiles his sister, his father's daughter. ¹²In you, they take bribes to shed blood; you take both advance interest and accrued interest and make gain of your neighbors by extortion, and you have forgotten me, says the Lord God.

13 See, I strike my hands together at the dishonest gain you have made and at the blood that has been shed within you. ¹⁴Can your courage endure, or can your hands remain strong in the days when I shall deal with you? I the Lord have spoken, and I will do it. ¹⁵I will scatter you among the nations and disperse you through the countries, and I will purge your filthiness out of you. ¹⁶And you shall be profaned within yourself in the sight of the nations, and you shall know that I am the Lord.

17 The word of the Lord came to me: ¹⁸Mortal, the house of Israel has become dross to me; all of them, silver,ᵘ bronze, tin, iron, and lead. In the smelter they have become dross. ¹⁹Therefore thus says the Lord God: Because you have all become dross, I will gather you into the midst of Jerusalem. ²⁰As one gathers silver, bronze, iron, lead, and tin into a smelter, to blow the fire upon them in order to melt them, so I will gather you in my anger and in my wrath, and I will put you in and melt you. ²¹I will gather you and blow upon you with the fire of my wrath, and you shall be melted within it. ²²As silver is melted in a smelter, so you shall be melted in it, and you shall know that I the Lord have poured out my wrath upon you.

23 The word of the Lord came to me: ²⁴Mortal, say to it: You are a land that is not cleansed, not rained upon in the day of indignation. ²⁵Its princesᵛ within it are like a roaring lion tearing the prey; they have devoured human lives; they have taken treasure and precious things; they have made many widows within it. ²⁶Its priests have done violence to my teaching and have profaned my holy things; they have made no distinction between the holy and the common, neither have they taught the difference between the unclean and the clean, and they have disregarded my Sabbaths, so that I am profaned among them. ²⁷Its officials within it are like wolves tearing the prey, shedding blood,

u 22.18 Transposed from the end of the verse   v 22.25 Gk: Heb A conspiracy of its prophets

of the phrase. **22:6–12** These verses have a list of sins similar to Ezek. 18:5, including economic, ritual, and sexual violations. **22:7** *The orphan and the widow.* There is no single word in English for either of these terms. In general, the words are used for people who do not belong to a male-led household. **22:8** *Sabbaths.* See note at Ezek. 20:12. **22:9** *Slander* includes both lies and solicited information. *Eat upon the mountains.* Probably a reference to worship at high places. **22:10** *Uncover their fathers' nakedness* includes sexual acts with someone within the household who is the exclusive wife/partner of the head of the household. **22:12** *Interest* was forbidden between Israelite males. **22:16** *Within yourself.* The addressee is the city, whose fate was the result of their own doing.

22:17–22 The next verses use metalworking to represent the coming disaster, since successful sieges ended with burning the city. A *smelter* was a vat for melting raw ore to separate the precious metal from the *dross*, or impurities in which it is embedded. In this metaphor, the burning of the city results only in the worthless dross.

22:23–31 The final section has echoes of other texts from previous material in Ezekiel. The divine speech condemns every elite male position within Judean society for failing in their responsibilities. **22:25** *Princes* refers primarily to the royal family, who have become the enemy of the very people they should protect. **22:26** *Priests* protected the city from ritual defilement by teaching people how to avoid defilement and encouraging participation in proper rituals. **22:27** *Officials*, or the elite class,

destroying lives to get dishonest gain. [28]Its prophets have smeared whitewash on their behalf, seeing false visions and divining lies for them, saying, "Thus says the Lord GOD," when the LORD has not spoken. [29]The people of the land have practiced extortion and committed robbery; they have oppressed the poor and needy and have extorted from the alien without justice. [30]And I sought for anyone among them who would repair the wall and stand in the breach before me on behalf of the land, so that I would not destroy it, but I found no one. [31]Therefore I have poured out my indignation upon them; I have consumed them with the fire of my wrath; I have returned their conduct upon their heads, says the Lord GOD.

23 The word of the LORD came to me: [2]Mortal, there were two women, the daughters of one mother; [3]they prostituted themselves in Egypt; they prostituted themselves in their youth; their breasts were caressed there, and their virgin bosoms were fondled. [4]Oholah was the name of the older and Oholibah the name of her sister. They became mine, and they bore sons and daughters. As for their names, Oholah is Samaria, and Oholibah is Jerusalem.

[5] Oholah prostituted herself while she was mine; she lusted after her lovers the Assyrians, warriors[w] [6]clothed in blue, governors and commanders, all of them handsome young men, mounted horsemen. [7]She bestowed her sexual favors upon them, the choicest men of Assyria all of them, and she defiled herself with all the idols of everyone for whom she lusted. [8]She did not give up her prostitutions that she had practiced since Egypt, for in her youth men had lain with her and fondled her virgin bosom and poured out their lust upon her. [9]Therefore I delivered her into the hands of her lovers, into the hands of the Assyrians, for whom she lusted. [10]These uncovered her nakedness; they seized her sons and her daughters, and they killed her with the sword. Judgment was executed upon her, and she became a byword among women.

[11] Her sister Oholibah saw this, yet she was more corrupt than she in her lusting and in her prostitutions, which were worse than those of her sister. [12]She lusted after the Assyrians, governors and commanders, warriors[x] clothed in full armor, mounted horsemen, all of them handsome young men. [13]And I saw that she was defiled; they both took the same way. [14]But she carried her prostitutions further; she saw male figures carved on the wall, images of the Chaldeans

w 23.5 Meaning of Heb uncertain   x 23.12 Meaning of Heb uncertain

such as landowners and respected elders. They are accused of using their prestige for their own self-interest. **22:28** *Prophets* are accused of false visions and divination, similar to chap. 13. **22:30** *Repair the wall and stand in the breach.* Since siege warfare resulted in breaking through vulnerable parts of the city walls, vulnerable spots had to be guarded. In this metaphor, the one who repairs the wall would be someone who could stem the sins of the inhabitants.

23:1–49 This chapter returns to the same metaphoric language of chap. 16: depicting a city as a sexually promiscuous female (see **"Slut-Shaming," p. 1148; "Sexually Abusive Language in the Prophets," p. 1035**). There are two significant differences between the two chapters. First, this chapter discusses the capitals of both the northern kingdom of Israel, Samaria, and the southern kingdom of Judah, Jerusalem. Both cities were destroyed by armies from Mesopotamia (the Assyrians and the Babylonians). Second, the subject of this chapter focuses on the alliances both kingdoms pursued in vain. For the book of Ezekiel, this was blasphemy, exhibiting a lack of faith in the warrior YHWH and swearing oaths to gods of other countries. **23:2** *Two women, the daughters of one mother* uses gendered figurative language to retell the history of Israel. **23:3** *Prostituted themselves in Egypt.* Although idolatry is mentioned, the focus is on the Israelites ingratiating themselves to greater powers. **23:4** *Oholah* can be translated as "her/its tent," the pronoun referring to the city. *Oholibah* is "her/its tent is in her/it." The tent refers to the central temples located in the capitals of Samaria and Jerusalem. **23:5** *Assyrians* in their quest for empire besieged both Samaria and Jerusalem as they advanced toward Egypt. Samaria's attempts to save itself were unsuccessful, and the city fell in 722 BCE. **23:10** *Uncovered her nakedness . . . became a byword.* The fall of Samaria symbolized the futility of resisting such a powerful enemy. **23:12** *Lusted after the Assyrians.* The king in Jerusalem paid tribute to end the siege of the city. The book of Ezekiel, however, portrays this appeasement as a betrayal of YHWH. **23:14** *Male figures carved on the wall.* Both the Assyrians

portrayed in vermilion, [15]with belts around their waists, with flowing turbans on their heads, all of them looking like officers—a picture of Babylonians whose native land was Chaldea. [16]When she saw them she lusted after them and sent messengers to them in Chaldea. [17]And the Babylonians came to her into the bed of love, and they defiled her with their lust, and after she defiled herself with them, she turned from them in disgust. [18]When she carried on her prostitutions so openly and flaunted her nakedness, I turned in disgust from her, as I had turned from her sister. [19]Yet she increased her prostitutions, remembering the days of her youth, when she prostituted herself in the land of Egypt [20]and lusted after her paramours there, whose members were like those of donkeys and whose emission was like that of stallions. [21]Thus you longed for the lewdness of your youth, when the Egyptians[y] fondled your bosom and caressed[z] your young breasts.

22 Therefore, O Oholibah, thus says the Lord God: I will rouse against you your lovers from whom you turned in disgust, and I will bring them against you from every side: [23]the Babylonians and all the Chaldeans, Pekod and Shoa and Koa, and all the Assyrians with them, handsome young men, governors and commanders all of them, officers and select leaders, all of them riding on horses. [24]They shall come against you from the north[a] with chariots and wagons and a host of peoples; they shall set themselves against you on every side with buckler, shield, and helmet, and I will commit the judgment to them, and they shall judge you according to their ordinances. [25]I will direct my indignation against you, in order that they may deal with you in fury. They shall cut off your nose

and your ears, and your survivors shall fall by the sword. They shall seize your sons and your daughters, and your survivors shall be devoured by fire. [26]They shall also strip you of your clothes and take away your fine jewels. [27]So I will put an end to your lewdness and your prostitution brought from the land of Egypt; you shall not long for them or remember Egypt any more. [28]For thus says the Lord God: I will deliver you into the hands of those whom you hate, into the hands of those from whom you turned in disgust, [29]and they shall deal with you in hatred and take away all the fruit of your labor and leave you naked and bare, and the nakedness of your prostitutions shall be exposed. Your lewdness and your prostitutions [30]have brought this upon you, because you prostituted yourself with the nations and polluted yourself with their idols. [31]You have gone the way of your sister; therefore I will give her cup into your hand. [32]Thus says the Lord God:

You shall drink your sister's cup,
    deep and wide;
it will bring scorn and derision;
    it holds so much.
[33] You shall be filled with drunkenness and
    sorrow.
A cup of horror and desolation
    is the cup of your sister Samaria;
[34] you shall drink it and drain it out
    and gnaw its sherds
    and tear out your breasts,

for I have spoken, says the Lord God. [35]Therefore thus says the Lord God: Because you have forgotten me and cast me behind your back, therefore bear the consequences of your lewdness and prostitutions.

y 23.21 Heb mss: MT *from Egypt* *z* 23.21 Cn: Heb *for the sake of* *a* 23.24 Gk: Meaning of Heb uncertain

and the Babylonians utilized wall art to glorify their warrior kings and gods. The *Chaldeans* are the Babylonians. **23:17** *She turned from them in disgust.* After the Babylonians had exiled the elites in 597, they installed Zedekiah as king, who had probably sworn allegiance to them. That is the period of Jerusalem's prostitution to the Chaldeans. Zedekiah eventually broke that oath and made an alliance with Egypt, represented here. **23:20** *Lusted after her paramours there* means the Egyptian military force, represented by their phallic *members*. **23:23** *Pekod and Shoa and Koa* were smaller tribes in Mesopotamia. **23:24** *From the north.* The route used by Mesopotamian armies had them entering the Levant from the north. *I will commit the judgment to them*—that is, they will be God's instrument to punish Jerusalem for its disobedience. **23:25** *Cut off your nose* begins a brief description of what happened to victims of siege. Conquerors used body mutilation to mark someone as a permanently enslaved person, obtained as plunder. Children (*sons* and *daughters*) were targeted, since they would have a longer length of servitude. Stripping of clothes and jewelry also indicated enslaved status. **23:32** *Cup* is a metaphor for fate. This poem depicts Jerusalem's fate as the same

36 The Lord said to me: Mortal, will you judge Oholah and Oholibah? Then declare to them their abominable deeds. [37]For they have committed adultery, and blood is on their hands; with their idols they have committed adultery, and they have even offered up to them for food the children whom they had borne to me. [38]Moreover, this they have done to me: they have defiled my sanctuary on the same day and profaned my Sabbaths. [39]For when they had slaughtered their children for their idols, on the same day they came into my sanctuary to profane it. This is what they did in my house.

40 They even sent for men to come from far away, to whom a messenger was sent, and they came. For them you bathed yourself, painted your eyes, and decked yourself with ornaments; [41]you sat on a stately couch, with a table spread before it on which you had placed my incense and my oil. [42]The sound of a raucous multitude was around her, with many of the rabble brought in drunken from the wilderness, and they put bracelets on the arms of the women and beautiful crowns upon their heads.

43 Then I said, "Ah, she is worn out with adulteries, but they carry on their sexual acts with her." [44]They have[b] gone in to her as one goes in to a prostitute. Thus they went in to Oholah and to Oholibah, wanton women. [45]But righteous judges shall declare them guilty of adultery and of bloodshed, because they are adulteresses, and blood is on their hands.

46 For thus says the Lord God: Bring up an assembly against them, and make them an object of terror and of plunder. [47]The assembly shall stone them, and with their swords they shall cut them down; they shall kill their sons and their daughters and burn up their houses. [48]Thus will I put an end to lewdness in the land, so that all women may take warning and not commit lewdness as you have done. [49]They shall repay you for your lewdness, and you shall bear the penalty for your sinful idolatry, and you shall know that I am the Lord God.

24 In the ninth year, in the tenth month, on the tenth day of the month, the word of the Lord came to me: [2]Mortal, write down the name of this day, this very day. The king of Babylon has laid siege to Jerusalem this very day. [3]And utter an allegory to the rebellious house and say to them: Thus says the Lord God:

Set on the pot; set it on;
  pour in water also;
[4] put in it the pieces,
  all the good pieces, the thigh and the
    shoulder;
  fill it with choice cuts.
[5] Take the choicest one of the flock;
  pile the logs[c] under it;
  boil its pieces;[d]
  seethe[e] also its bones in it.

6 Therefore thus says the Lord God:
Woe to the bloody city,
  the pot whose crud is in it,
  whose crud has not gone out of it!
Empty it piece by piece,
  making no choice at all.[f]

b 23.44 Q ms: MT *he has* c 24.5 Heb *the bones* d 24.5 Heb mss: MT *its boilings* e 24.5 Cn: Heb *its bones seethe* f 24.6 Heb *piece, no lot has fallen on it*

as Samaria's. **23:37** *Offered up . . . the children.* A reference to child sacrifice, which might be literal or figurative. **23:38** *Defiled my sanctuary . . . profaned my Sabbaths.* The book of Ezekiel maintains its focus on the theological implications of political decisions by casting them in ritual terms. These decisions are not just unwise; they insult God. **23:40** *Sent for men* means they actively sought these alliances. **23:41** *My incense and my oil.* Often, heavy tribute was paid in large part with the treasures of the national temple, such as the gold plating of temple walls, precious votive items, and money garnered through temple taxes. **23:48** *All women may take warning.* While this may indicate that the author views Israelite women as particularly lusty, in keeping with the metaphor that dominates the whole chapter, the *women* here are more probably metaphors for Judean elite males.

24:1–14 This oracle utilizes another allegory to describe the siege of the city. The walled city is likened to a large cooking pot used for certain types of animal sacrifices. **24:1** *Ninth year.* January 588. **24:3** *Allegory*, or metaphor. *Pot* large enough to hold a whole butchered sheep. **24:4** *Pieces* represent various elite groups in the city. **24:5** *Choicest one of the flock.* Probably Zedekiah. **24:6** *The bloody city* echoes the imagery in chap. 22, where the blood referred to violent crimes. Here, it merges violence with the blood of a sacrifice. *Crud.* Any contamination of the pot that requires purification. *Empty it piece by piece* connotes the randomness of the disaster that Jerusalem now faces.

⁷ For the blood she shed is inside it;
   she placed it on a bare rock;
she did not pour it out on the ground,
   to cover it with earth.
⁸ To rouse my wrath, to take
      vengeance,
   I have placed the blood she shed
   on a bare rock,
   so that it may not be covered.
⁹Therefore thus says the Lord God:
   Woe to the bloody city!
   I will even make the pile great.
¹⁰ Heap up the logs; kindle the fire;
   boil the meat well; boil down the
      broth;ᵍ
   let the bones be burned.
¹¹ Stand it empty upon the coals,
   so that it may become hot, its copper
      glow,
   its filth melt in it, its crud be
      consumed.
¹² In vain I have wearied myself;ʰ
   its thick crud does not depart.
   To the fire with its crud!
¹³ Yet when I cleansed you in your filthy
      lewdness,
   you did not become clean from your
      filth;
   you shall not again be cleansed
   until I have satisfied my fury upon
      you.
¹⁴I the Lord have spoken; the time is coming;
I will act. I will not refrain; I will not spare; I
will not relent. According to your ways and
your doings I will judge you, says the Lord
God.
   15 The word of the Lord came to me:
¹⁶Mortal, with one blow I am about to take

away from you the delight of your eyes, yet
you shall not mourn or weep, nor shall your
tears run down. ¹⁷Groan quietly; make no
mourning for the dead. Bind on your turban, and put your sandals on your feet; do
not cover your upper lip or eat the bread
of mourners.ⁱ ¹⁸So I spoke to the people in
the morning, and at evening my wife died.
And on the next morning I did as I was
commanded.

19 Then the people said to me, "Will you
not tell us what these things mean for us,
that you are acting this way?" ²⁰Then I said
to them, "The word of the Lord came to me:
²¹Say to the house of Israel: Thus says the
Lord God: I will profane my sanctuary, the
pride of your power, the delight of your eyes,
and your heart's desire, and your sons and
your daughters whom you left behind shall
fall by the sword. ²²And you shall do as I have
done; you shall not cover your upper lip or
eat the bread of mourners.ʲ ²³Your turbans
shall be on your heads and your sandals on
your feet; you shall not mourn or weep, but
you shall pine away in your iniquities and
groan to one another. ²⁴Thus Ezekiel shall be
a sign to you; you shall do just as he has done.
When this comes, then you shall know that I
am the Lord God."

25 And you, mortal, on the day when I
take from them their stronghold, their joy
and glory, the delight of their eyes and their
heart's affection, and alsoᵏ their sons and
their daughters, ²⁶on that day, one who has
escaped will come to you to report to you

g 24.10 Gk: Heb *mix in the spices* h 24.12 Cn: Meaning of
Heb uncertain i 24.17 Vg Tg: Heb *of men* j 24.22 Vg Tg:
Heb *of men* k 24.25 Heb lacks *and also*

24:7 *Placed it on a bare rock.* There were protocols for disposing ritual items. Liquids should be poured out onto dirt to seep in rather than displayed publicly. **24:11** *Its filth melt in it.* The sacrificial pot would be ritually cleansed in fire. This marks the turning point in the allegory where the city as a pot full of body pieces becomes the defiled city in need of purging. In this allegory, the burning of the city at the end of the siege becomes an agent for the ritual purification of Jerusalem. See **"Disgust, Defilement, and Impurity," p. 1162**.
   24:15–27 This passage refers to the fall of the city after an eighteen-month siege, which it paral-lels with the death of a spouse. Ezekiel's bereavement personifies the emotional devastation of the fall of the city. **24:16** *The delight of your eyes.* The marital metaphor here compares the fall of the temple to the death of an adored wife. *You shall not mourn.* A lack of mourning would be shockingly abnormal, compounding the tragedy. **24:21** *I will profane my sanctuary.* Just as Ezekiel cherished his wife, so too the Judeans cherished their temple. Witnessing its destruction was tantamount to watching your spouse die. **24:22** *Do as I have done*—that is, not mourn for this horrendous loss. **24:24** *Ezekiel shall be a sign to you* again reinforces that Ezekiel's experience reveals the emotional impact of the fall of the temple. **24:26** *One who has escaped.* News of the city's fall would take time to arrive to the exiles. This eyewitness's testimony would convey the emotional impact of the

Making Connections: Disgust, Defilement, and Impurity (Ezekiel 24)
The book of Ezekiel is filled with disgusting images as well as the vocabulary of defilement. This intentional rhetorical move serves the book's attempt to elicit a visceral reaction that creates empathy with the divine agent of Jerusalem's fall. When contemporary audiences reject the portrayal of God in the book, they exhibit the same resistance to the book's theology that probably many in the original audience felt as well.

The most prominent feature of the book's terminology is its use of ritual categories of purity/defilement and holy/profane (see **"Holiness and Purity," p. 158**). Both the narrative and the divine speeches do not just charge people with impurity; they illustrate them with cases that also evoke disgust. One of these comes early in the book when the priest Ezekiel is commanded to cook his food over human feces (4:12), a horror symbolizing the disgusting ways people are driven to eat during famine, siege, warfare, and enslavement. Blood also becomes a metaphor for the inescapable ways both internal social injustice and external war mark everyone, across all social structures and throughout multiple generations. The city as a bloody pot in chap. 24 captures the emotional view of the besieged city as a disgusting pile of meat contained within its own filth. The use of menstrual blood in 36:17 as a metaphor for the Israelites' defiling behavior makes the disgust evoked by their punishment less than the disgust at their own behavior. God's repeated call for shame as a pious response flows directly from representing sin with disgusting images.

Defilement is described using the word "abomination," which appears thirty-four times in the book. It suggests an action that elicits revulsion. This characterizes Judean behavior not just as "rebellious" but as so inherently bad that even they should be repulsed by it. In this way, the book utilizes strategies similar to political cartoons, such as Adam Zyglis's "A Brief History of the Black Man's Neck" (*Buffalo News*, 2020).

The specific Hebrew word used most often for idols in the book of Ezekiel (*gillul*) also contains a note of disgust. It is not the common word for idol, but Ezekiel uses it three times more than the rest of the Hebrew Bible (thirty-six times in Ezekiel; twelve times outside of Ezekiel). It also connotes disgust because it rhymes with a word meaning something detestable (*shiqquts*). Some scholars connect it to a ball of dung.

Corrine L. Carvalho

the news. ²⁷On that day your mouth shall be opened to the one who has escaped, and you shall speak and no longer be silent. So you shall be a sign to them, and they shall know that I am the Lord.

25 The word of the Lord came to me: ²Mortal, set your face toward the Ammonites and prophesy against them. ³Say to the Ammonites: Hear the word of the Lord God: Thus says the Lord God: Because you said, "Aha!" over my sanctuary when it was profaned and over the land of Israel when it was made desolate and over the house of Judah when it went into exile, ⁴therefore I am handing you over to the people of the

devastation. **24:27** *Your mouth shall be opened.* God had "closed" Ezekiel's mouth in 3:26–27 so that he could only communicate God's messages. Here he is released from that restriction, signifying a major narrative shift from oracles of future devastation to materials read in light of the city's fall. *You shall be a sign . . . they shall know.* From the perspective of the exiles, Ezekiel's miraculous cure from his bodily restrictions proves that the city's fall was not caused by divine weakness.

Ezek. 25–32 The next nine chapters focus on pronouncements or oracles condemning nations other than Judah and Israel. Oracles against foreign nations can be found in several prophetic collections, including Amos 1–2; Isa. 13–23; 34; and Jer. 46–51. See **"Oracles against the Nations," p. 1105**. While in the narrative the prophet addresses those nations, the real audience was the Judeans, whose history had been and would continue to be tied up in theirs. The images used in these poems have both motifs from the targeted nations and ones resonating with Israelite traditions. Seven nations are condemned, and the final section addressed to Egypt has seven oracles. Most of the pronouncements are dated within two years of Jerusalem's fall.

25:1–17 The first chapter contains diatribes against four groups whose territories bordered that of Israel: Ammon, Moab, and Edom to the east and the Philistines to the west. **25:1–7** Ammon, across the Jordan River from Israel, was condemned for celebrating when Jerusalem fell. **25:4** *The people of*

East for a possession. They shall set their encampments among you and pitch their tents in your midst; they shall eat your fruit, and they shall drink your milk. [5]I will make Rabbah a pasture for camels and Ammon a fold for flocks. Then you shall know that I am the LORD. [6]For thus says the Lord GOD: Because you have clapped your hands and stamped your feet and rejoiced with all the malice within you against the land of Israel, [7]therefore I have stretched out my hand against you and will hand you over as plunder to the nations. I will cut you off from the peoples and will make you perish out of the countries; I will destroy you. Then you shall know that I am the LORD.

[8]Thus says the Lord GOD: Because Moab[l] said, "The house of Judah is like all the other nations," [9]therefore I will lay open the flank of Moab from the towns[m] on its frontier, the glory of the country, Beth-jeshimoth, Baal-meon, and Kiriathaim. [10]I will give it along with Ammon to the people of the East as a possession. Thus Ammon shall be remembered no more among the nations, [11]and I will execute judgments upon Moab. Then they shall know that I am the LORD.

[12]Thus says the Lord GOD: Because Edom acted revengefully against the house of Judah and has grievously offended in taking vengeance upon them, [13]therefore thus says the Lord GOD: I will stretch out my hand against Edom and cut off from it humans and animals, and I will make it desolate; from Teman even to Dedan they shall fall by the sword. [14]I will lay my vengeance upon Edom by the hand of my people Israel, and they shall act in Edom according to my anger and according to my wrath, and they shall know my vengeance, says the Lord GOD.

[15]Thus says the Lord GOD: Because with unending hostilities the Philistines acted in vengeance and with malice of heart took revenge in destruction, [16]therefore thus says the Lord GOD: I will stretch out my hand against the Philistines, cut off the Cherethites, and destroy the rest of the seacoast. [17]I will execute great vengeance on them with wrathful punishments. Then they shall know that I am the LORD, when I lay my vengeance on them.

26 In the twelfth year,[n] in the eleventh[o] month, on the first day of the month, the word of the LORD came to me: [2]Mortal, because Tyre said concerning Jerusalem,

"Aha, broken is the gateway of the
  peoples;
  it has swung open to me;
I shall be replenished,
  now that it is wasted,"

l 25.8 Gk OL: Heb Moab and Seir   m 25.9 Heb towns from its towns   n 26.1 Gk ms: Heb eleventh year   o 26.1 Cn: Heb lacks eleventh

the East. The Babylonians. **25:5** Rabbah. One of the main cities of Ammon. **25:7** You shall know. Each of the pronouncements judging the foreign nations ends with their "knowledge" of YHWH, indicating that the issue addressed in these oracles is the apparent weakness of YHWH. **25:8–11** Moab, south of Ammon, across the Dead Sea from Judah, is unmoved by Jerusalem's fall. **25:9** Beth-jeshimoth, Baal-meon, and Kiriathaim were prominent Moabite cities. **25:12–14** Edom, southwest of Moab and south of Judah, participated in the destruction of Judah, a betrayal that also informs the second oracle against Edom in Ezek. 35. **25:12** Revengefully implies the Edomites took advantage of Judah's fall. **25:14** By the hand of my people Israel. In Isa. 34 and 63, God exacts punishment on Edom, while here that privilege is reserved for the restored Israelites. **25:15–17** These verses contain a proclamation against the Philistines, who held territory on the southern Mediterranean coast, west of Judah. **25:15** Unending hostilities. In the historical narratives of the premonarchic period (Judges, 1 and 2 Samuel), the Philistines became the quintessential enemy of nascent Israel. Although there are fewer accounts of hostility during the period of the monarchy, the reference here shows continued Judean hostility toward them. **25:16** Cherethites. Perhaps people from Crete.

26:1–28:24 These chapters contain pronouncements against Israel's northern neighbors. Most of this material addresses the seacoast city of Tyre, which had prospered economically during the Assyrian period. The end of the section briefly addresses Sidon, further inland. See **"Oracles against the Nations," p. 1105**.

26:1–21 The proclamations against Tyre begin with three distinct sections connected by phraseology. This chapter has the most generic pronouncements of the ones devoted to Tyre, paralleling the material in chap. 25. **26:1** In the twelfth year. January/February 586. **26:2** I shall be replenished. A personification of the city suggesting that Tyre economically benefited from Jerusalem's fall.

3 therefore, thus says the Lord God:
See, I am against you, O Tyre!
I will hurl many nations against you,
as the sea hurls its waves.
4 They shall destroy the walls of Tyre
and break down its towers.
I will scrape its soil from it
and make it a bare rock.
5 It shall become, in the midst of the sea,
a place for spreading nets.
I have spoken, says the Lord God.
It shall become plunder for the
nations,
6 and its daughter towns inland
shall be killed by the sword.
Then they shall know that I am the Lord.

7 For thus says the Lord God: I will bring against Tyre from the north King Nebuchadrezzar of Babylon, king of kings, together with horses, chariots, cavalry, and a great and powerful army.

8 Your daughter towns inland
he shall put to the sword.
He shall set up a siege wall against you,
cast up a ramp against you,
and raise a roof of shields against you.
9 He shall direct the shock of his battering
rams against your walls
and break down your towers with his
axes.
10 His horses shall be so many
that their dust shall cover you.
At the noise of cavalry, wheels, and
chariots
your very walls shall shake
when he enters your gates
like those entering a breached city.
11 With the hoofs of his horses
he shall trample all your streets.
He shall put your people to the sword,
and your strong pillars shall fall to the
ground.
12 They will take your riches
and plunder your merchandise;
they shall break down your walls
and destroy your fine houses.
Your stones and timber and soil
they shall cast into the water.
13 I will silence the music of your songs;
the sound of your lyres shall be heard
no more.
14 I will make you a bare rock;
you shall be a place for spreading
nets.
You shall never again be rebuilt,
for I the Lord have spoken,
says the Lord God.

15 Thus says the Lord God to Tyre: Shall
not the coastlands shake at the sound of your
fall, when the wounded groan, when slaughter goes on within you?
16 Then all the princes
of the sea shall step down from their thrones;
they shall remove their robes and strip off
their embroidered garments. They shall
clothe themselves with trembling and shall sit
on the ground; they shall tremble every moment and be appalled at you.
17 And they shall
raise a lamentation over you and say to you:

"How you have vanished[p] from the seas,
O city renowned,
once mighty on the sea,
you and your inhabitants,[q]

p 26.17 Gk OL Aquila: Heb *have vanished, O inhabited one,*
q 26.17 Heb *it and its inhabitants*

26:3 *As the sea hurls its waves.* Tyre was built on a small island connected to the mainland only during low tide. The ground was rocky, and the city was surrounded by the sea. **26:5** *A place for spreading nets.* Fishing, an important industry for the city, utilized nets that had to be dried in the sun. **26:6** *Its daughter towns* were smaller communities, probably unwalled, that provided food to the city. People in these communities would have taken refuge in the "mother" city when an invading army approached. **26:7–14** The chapter turns to Babylon's long unsuccessful siege of Tyre, which lasted more than a decade. **26:7** *From the north.* See the note at 23:24. *Nebuchadrezzar,* or Nebuchadnezzar. *King of kings.* An emperor who had subject kings governing their own areas. **26:8–13** *Set up a siege wall.* This poem reflects many of the elements of siege warfare, including the *roof of shields* that would have protected those attacking the city from things hurled from the city walls, such as slingshots, torches, and rocks. **26:14** *A bare rock . . . nets* echoes the image earlier in the chapter (vv. 4–5). This proclamation did not come true, as Ezek. 29:18 attests. **26:15–21** The final part of the chapter anticipates how the fall of Tyre would create panic in the surrounding area. **26:15** *Coastlands* would include the "daughter towns" of v. 6 but also other self-standing walled cities, such as the harbors belonging to the Philistines farther south. **26:16** *They shall remove their robes* describes the official mourning that Tyre's allies would perform at its demise. **26:17** *Raise a lamentation,* or a funeral dirge. Laments for fallen cities were common throughout ancient West

who imposed your[r] terror
    on all the mainland![s]
[18] Now the coastlands tremble
    on the day of your fall;
the coastlands by the sea
    are dismayed at your passing."

19 For thus says the Lord GOD: When I make you a city laid waste, like cities that are not inhabited, when I bring up the deep over you and the great waters cover you, [20]then I will thrust you down with those who descend into the Pit, to the people of long ago, and I will make you live in the world below, among primeval ruins, with those who go down to the Pit, so that you will not be inhabited or have a place[t] in the land of the living. [21]I will bring you to a dreadful end, and you shall be no more; though sought for, you will never be found again, says the Lord GOD.

27

The word of the LORD came to me: [2]Now you, mortal, raise a lamentation over Tyre, [3]and say to Tyre, which sits at the entrance to the sea, merchant of the peoples on many coastlands: Thus says the Lord GOD:

O Tyre, you have said,
    "I am perfect in beauty."
[4] Your borders are in the heart of the seas;
    your builders made perfect your
        beauty.
[5] They made all your planks
    of fir trees from Senir;
they took a cedar from Lebanon
    to make a mast for you.
[6] From oaks of Bashan
    they made your oars;

they made your deck of pines[u]
    from the coasts of Cyprus,
    inlaid with ivory.
[7] Of fine embroidered linen from Egypt
    was your sail,
    serving as your ensign;
blue and purple from the coasts of
    Elishah
    was your awning.
[8] The inhabitants of Sidon and Arvad
    were your rowers;
skilled men of Zemer[v] were within you;
    they were your pilots.
[9] The elders of Gebal and its artisans were
    within you,
    caulking your seams;
all the ships of the sea with their sailors
    were within you,
    to barter for your wares.
[10] Paras[w] and Lud and Put
    were in your army,
    your mighty warriors;
they hung shield and helmet in you;
    they gave you splendor.
[11] Men of Arvad and Helech[x]
    were on your walls all around;
    men of Gamad were at your towers.
They hung their quivers all around your
    walls;
    they made perfect your beauty.

12 Tarshish did business with you out of the abundance of your great wealth; silver, iron, tin, and lead they exchanged for your wares. [13]Javan, Tubal, and Meshech traded

r 26.17 Heb *their* s 26.17 Cn: Heb *its inhabitants* t 26.20 Gk: Heb *I will give beauty* u 27.6 Or *boxwood* v 27.8 Cn: Heb *your skilled men, O Tyre* w 27.10 Or *Persia* x 27.11 Or *and your army*

Asia. **26:19** *The deep* are the primordial waters out of which God created the world. **26:20** *The Pit* occurs ten times in the proclamations against Tyre and Egypt. It designates the place of the dead. *Primeval ruins*—that is, failures that go back to the beginning of time.

27:1–36 In this piece, Tyre is compared to a large merchant ship, whose maritime economy flourished prior to the Babylonian ascendancy. This poem combines the geographical location of Tyre (an island in the Mediterranean) with the symbol of its economic status (a well-appointed merchant ship). As a lament, the poem begins by eulogizing or praising the dead whom the poem honors (vv. 3–25) before lamenting its death (vv. 26–36). **27:3** *At the entrance to the sea* references Tyre's safe port for large ships. *Merchant* governs the use of trade images throughout the chapter. *I am perfect in beauty* is repeated in vv. 4 and 11. This poem does not refute this claim; in fact, it illustrates it. **27:5** *Planks* begins the metaphor of the ship by listing a ship's many features. *Senir.* The detailed list of ship features is outdone by the list of foreign countries that traded with Tyre found in the rest of the chapter. While some locations are known, others are not. What is clear is that the poem refers to trade throughout the Mediterranean rim, the ancient Near East, West Africa, and the Arabian Peninsula. **27:7** *Ensign*, or insignia on a ship's sails. *Purple.* Tyre was also famous for the dyes, some of which could only be manufactured in this region. **27:9** *All the ships of the sea* is a metaphor for other nations. **27:11** *Quivers.* Sailors shot arrows at enemy

with you; they exchanged human beings and vessels of bronze for your merchandise. [14]Beth-togarmah exchanged for your wares horses, war horses, and mules. [15]The Rhodians[y] traded with you; many coastlands were your own special markets; they brought you in payment ivory tusks and ebony. [16]Edom[z] did business with you because of your abundant goods; they exchanged for your wares turquoise, purple, embroidered work, fine linen, coral, and rubies. [17]Judah and the land of Israel traded with you; they exchanged for your merchandise wheat from Minnith, millet,[a] honey, oil, and balm. [18]Damascus traded with you for your abundant goods—because of your great wealth of every kind—wine of Helbon and wool of Zahar. [19]Vedan and Javan from Uzal[b] entered into trade for your wares; wrought iron, cassia, and sweet cane were bartered for your merchandise. [20]Dedan traded with you in saddlecloths for riding. [21]Arabia and all the princes of Kedar were your favored dealers in lambs, rams, and goats; in these they did business with you. [22]The merchants of Sheba and Raamah traded with you; they exchanged for your wares the best of all kinds of spices and all precious stones and gold. [23]Haran, Canneh, Eden, the merchants of Sheba, Asshur, and Chilmad traded with you. [24]These traded with you in choice garments, in clothes of blue and embroidered work, and in carpets of colored material, bound with cords and made secure; in these they traded with you.[c] [25]The ships of Tarshish traveled for you in your trade.

So you were filled and heavily laden
  in the heart of the seas.
[26] Your rowers have brought you
    into the high seas.
The east wind has wrecked you
    in the heart of the seas.
[27] Your riches, your wares, your
      merchandise,
    your sailors and your pilots,
  your caulkers, your dealers in
      merchandise,

and all your warriors within you,
  with all the company
    that is with you,
  sink into the heart of the seas
    on the day of your ruin.
[28] At the sound of the cry of your pilots
    the pasturelands shake,
[29] and down from their ships
    come all who handle the oar.
The sailors and all the pilots of the sea
    stand on the shore
[30] and wail aloud over you
    and cry bitterly.
They throw dust on their heads
    and wallow in ashes;
[31] they make themselves bald for you
    and put on sackcloth,
and they weep over you in bitterness of
      soul,
    with bitter mourning.
[32] In their wailing they raise a lamentation
      for you
    and lament over you:
"Who was ever destroyed[d] like Tyre
    in the midst of the sea?
[33] When your wares came from the seas,
    you satisfied many peoples;
with your abundant wealth and
      merchandise
    you enriched the kings of the earth.
[34] Now you are wrecked by the seas,
    in the depths of the waters;
your merchandise and all your crew
    have sunk with you.
[35] All the inhabitants of the coastlands
    are appalled at you,
and their kings are horribly afraid;
    their faces are convulsed.
[36] The merchants among the peoples hiss at
      you;
    you have come to a dreadful end
    and shall be no more forever."

y 27.15 Gk: Heb *The Dedanites* z 27.16 Heb mss Syr Aquila: MT *Aram* a 27.17 Meaning of Heb uncertain b 27.19 Meaning of Heb uncertain c 27.24 Cn: Heb *in your market* d 27.32 Tg Vg: Heb *silenced*

ships. **27:17** *Judah* is listed as just one of many nations trading with Tyre. **27:19** *Cassia* is a spice similar to cinnamon. **27:25** *You were filled.* Both the metaphorical ship and the actual city represented by that ship. The city of Tyre prospered in this era. **27:26** *The east wind has wrecked you.* An apt metaphor for the anticipated fall of the city. No matter how much treasure a ship/city has accumulated, both are vulnerable to natural disasters. **27:30–32** *Throw dust on their heads* refers to rituals performed when someone died or a community suffered disasters. See **"Textual, Performative, and Visual Art,"** p. 1134. **27:35** *Convulsed*, or distorted in their terror. **27:36** *Hiss at you.* Similar to booing today.

28

The word of the LORD came to me: [2]Mortal, say to the prince of Tyre: Thus says the Lord GOD:

Because your heart is proud
  and you have said, "I am a god;
I sit in the seat of the gods,
  in the heart of the seas,"
yet you are but a mortal and no god,
  though you compare your mind
  with the mind of a god.
[3] You are indeed wiser than Daniel;[e]
  no secret is hidden from you;
[4] by your wisdom and your understanding
  you have amassed wealth for yourself
and have gathered gold and silver
  into your treasuries.
[5] By your great wisdom in trade
  you have increased your wealth,
  and your heart has become proud in
  your wealth.
[6] Therefore thus says the Lord GOD:
Because you compare your mind
  with the mind of a god,
[7] therefore, I will bring strangers against
  you,
  the most terrible of the nations;
they shall draw their swords against the
  beauty of your wisdom
  and defile your splendor.
[8] They shall thrust you down to the Pit,
  and you shall die a violent death
  in the heart of the seas.
[9] Will you still say, "I am a god,"
  in the presence of those who kill you,
though you are but a mortal and no god,
  in the hands of those who pierce
  you?
[10] You shall die the death of the
  uncircumcised
  by the hand of foreigners,
  for I have spoken, says the Lord GOD.

[11] Moreover the word of the LORD came to me: [12]Mortal, raise a lamentation over the king of Tyre, and say to him: Thus says the Lord GOD:

You were the signet of perfection,[f]
  full of wisdom and perfect in beauty.
[13] You were in Eden, the garden of God;
  every precious stone was your
  covering,
carnelian, chrysolite, and moonstone,
  beryl, onyx, and jasper,
sapphire,[g] turquoise, and emerald;
  and worked in gold were your
  settings
  and your engravings.[h]
On the day that you were created
  they were prepared.
[14] You were a cherub;[i]
  I placed you on the holy mountain of
  God;
  you walked among the stones of fire.
[15] You were blameless in your ways
  from the day that you were created,
  until iniquity was found in you.

e 28.3 Or *Danel*   f 28.12 Meaning of Heb uncertain
g 28.13 Or *lapis lazuli*   h 28.13 Meaning of Heb uncertain
i 28.14 Gk: Heb adds *anointed guardian*

28:1–19 The tirade now focuses on Tyre's royal leader, who represents the elite of the city. Like the previous chapter, the poetry acknowledges Tyre's financial success, which is attributed to the skill of its leaders. The admiration parallels the good relationship between Tyre and Israel throughout much of their history. This poem focuses instead on Tyre's confidence, depicted as hubris. **28:1–10** The first part of the chapter describes the reasons God will punish the king of Tyre. **28:2** *Proud.* The first verse of the poem introduces this theme of pride. *I am a god.* There is no direct evidence that Tyre's kings claimed divine status, like the Egyptian pharaohs, so this claim may be more metaphoric than historical. **28:3** *Wiser than Daniel*, or Dan-el, a wise king featured in the myths of those living in or near Tyre. See comment on 14:12–23. **28:5** *And* could be translated as "but," which would fit the context better. **28:10** *Uncircumcised.* A derogatory term Israelites sometimes used to refer to foreigners. It will be used repeatedly in chap. 32. **28:11–19** The second poem in this chapter, a lamentation, uses other mythic motifs to describe the rise and fall of Tyre's fortunes. While much of this imagery seems to echo the creation of Adam in Gen. 2–3, it is more probable that both this chapter and Genesis engage similar mythic tropes in distinct ways independently of each other. **28:12** A *signet* was a special seal that verified the authenticity of a communication or contract, often found as part of a ring or necklace. *Perfect in beauty* is repeated throughout this section. **28:13** *Eden, the garden of God.* This parallels Gen. 2:8, 15; Eden was the place not where Adam was created but where God located him after his creation. *Every precious stone was your covering.* The description of Aaron's breastplate or ephod utilized similar imagery (Exod. 28:6–14). **28:14** *You were a cherub.* See note at 1:10. *On the holy mountain of God* depicts Eden as part of God's mountainous

¹⁶ In the abundance of your trade
    you were filled with violence, and you
      sinned,
so I cast you as a profane thing from the
    mountain of God,
    and I drove you out, O guardian
      cherub,
    from among the stones of fire.
¹⁷ Your heart was proud because of your
      beauty;
    you corrupted your wisdom for the
      sake of your splendor.
I cast you to the ground;
    I exposed you before kings,
    to feast their eyes on you.
¹⁸ By the multitude of your iniquities,
    in the unrighteousness of your
      trade,
    you profaned your sanctuaries.
So I brought out fire from within you;
    it consumed you,
and I turned you to ashes on the earth
    in the sight of all who saw you.
¹⁹ All who know you among the
      peoples
    are appalled at you;
you have come to a dreadful end
    and shall be no more forever.
20 The word of the LORD came to me:
²¹Mortal, set your face toward Sidon, and
prophesy against it, ²²and say: Thus says the
Lord GOD:
I am against you, O Sidon,
    and I will gain glory in your midst.
They shall know that I am the LORD
    when I execute judgments in it
    and manifest my holiness in it;
²³ for I will send pestilence into it,
    and bloodshed into its streets;
and the dead shall fall in its midst,
    by the sword that is against it on every
      side.
And they shall know that I am the LORD.
24 The house of Israel shall no longer find a pricking brier or a piercing thorn among all their neighbors who have treated them with contempt. And they shall know that I am the Lord GOD.

25 Thus says the Lord GOD: When I gather the house of Israel from the peoples among whom they are scattered and manifest my holiness in them in the sight of the nations, then they shall settle on their own soil that I gave to my servant Jacob. ²⁶They shall live in safety in it and shall build houses and plant vineyards. They shall live in safety when I execute judgments upon all their neighbors who have treated them with contempt. And they shall know that I am the LORD their God.

---

domain. **28:15** *You were blameless . . . until iniquity was found in you.* Similar to the narrative arc of Adam's rise and fall. **28:16** *Abundance . . . violence.* Although most of the chapter focuses on the king's pride, here the poem depicts trade as tantamount to violence, suggesting Tyre exploited the people with whom they traded. *I drove you out, O guardian cherub.* In Gen. 3:23–24, God exiles Adam and Eve from the garden for their iniquities and places a cherub at the garden's gate so they cannot return. The material here conflates the human figure with that of the divine cherub. *From among the stones of fire.* The king is also relieved of his gemmed breastplate. **28:17** *I cast you to the ground* makes the king subservient to YHWH. **28:18** *Unrighteousness of your trade*, thus its comparison to "violence" in v. 16. *Fire from within you* suggests that the anticipated fall of Tyre would include internal revolt. **28:19** *All . . . are appalled at you* indicates a global public reaction to the exposure of the beloved city's faults.

28:20–24 This text contains a brief oracle against Sidon, another prominent city north of Israel. During the Assyrian period, Tyre was the wealthier of the two cities; the length of the proclamation against Sidon suggests its importance on the world stage was similar to that of Ammon, Moab, Edom, and Philistia. This oracle does not outline its iniquities and uses stock tropes of divine punishment. **28:24** *Pricking brier or a piercing thorn* depicts the opposition to Judah by smaller nations as more annoyances than fatal threats.

28:25–26 This passage creates a brief pause in the condemnation of foreign nations before the final four chapters devoted to Egypt. These two verses point forward to images of restoration in the last part of the book; see **"Holiness and Purity," p. 158**. **28:25** *From the peoples* includes the restoration of those exiled by the Assyrians as well as those who fled to Egypt and other areas in the wake of the fall of Jerusalem. *Jacob* connotes the restoration of all twelve tribes of Israel, not just Judah. **28:26** *When I execute judgments upon all their neighbors* ties the proclamations against foreign nations directly to the restoration of Israel.

29 In the tenth year, in the tenth month, on the twelfth day of the month, the word of the LORD came to me: [2]Mortal, set your face against Pharaoh king of Egypt, and prophesy against him and against all Egypt; [3]speak and say: Thus says the Lord GOD:

I am against you,
    Pharaoh king of Egypt,
the great dragon sprawling
    in the midst of its channels,
saying, "My Nile is my own;
    I made it for myself."
[4] I will put hooks in your jaws
    and make the fish of your channels
      stick to your scales.
I will draw you up from your channels,
    with all the fish of your channels
      sticking to your scales.
[5] I will fling you into the wilderness,
    you and all the fish of your channels;
you shall fall in the open field
    and not be gathered or picked up.
To the animals of the earth and to the
      birds of the air
    I have given you as food.
[6] Then all the inhabitants of Egypt shall know
    that I am the LORD,
because you[j] were a staff of reed
    to the house of Israel;
[7] when they grasped you with the hand,
    you broke
    and tore all their shoulders,
and when they leaned on you, you broke
    and made all their legs give way.[k]

[8] Therefore, thus says the Lord GOD: I will bring a sword upon you and will cut off from you human and animal, [9]and the land of Egypt shall be a desolation and a waste. Then they shall know that I am the LORD.

Because you[l] said, "The Nile is mine, and I made it," [10]therefore, I am against you and against your channels, and I will make the land of Egypt an utter waste and desolation, from Migdol to Syene, as far as the border of Cush. [11]No human foot shall pass through it, and no animal foot shall pass through it; it shall be uninhabited forty years. [12]I will make the land of Egypt a desolation among desolated countries, and her cities shall be a desolation forty years among cities that are laid waste. I will scatter the Egyptians among the nations and disperse them among the countries.

13 Further, thus says the Lord GOD: At the end of forty years I will gather the Egyptians from the peoples among whom they were scattered, [14]and I will restore the fortunes of Egypt and bring them back to the land of Pathros, the land of their origin, and there they shall be a lowly kingdom. [15]It shall be the most lowly of the kingdoms and never again exalt itself above the nations, and I will make them so small that they will never again rule over the nations. [16]The Egyptians[m] shall never again be the reliance of the house of Israel; they will recall their iniquity when they turned to them for aid. Then they shall know that I am the Lord GOD.

17 In the twenty-seventh year, in the first month, on the first day of the month, the word of the LORD came to me: [18]Mortal, King Nebuchadrezzar of Babylon made his army

j 29.6 Gk Syr Vg: Heb they   k 29.7 Syr: Heb stand   l 29.9 Gk Syr Vg: Heb he   m 29.16 Heb It

29:1–16 The oracles against foreign nations end with a four-chapter section addressed to Egypt because Judah had turned to Egypt for support to withstand the Babylonian siege, the ultimate rebellion against God. See **"Oracles against the Nations," p. 1105.** The material in this section reverses Egypt's own symbols of their strength. **29:1–7** The first section of the chapter consists of a poem focused on Pharaoh. **29:1** *Tenth year.* January 587. **29:3** *Dragon.* The Hebrew here can also mean "serpent," or a reptilian monster, including a crocodile or the uraeus serpents that adorned pharaohs' crowns. *Channels,* or rivers. The northern part of the Nile branches out into a wide delta. **29:6** *Staff of reed.* A pun on the "staff of bread" or food supply chain that made a nation economically secure. Here a staff made of reeds cannot be leaned on, thus dooming those who rely on it. **29:8–12** The poem is followed by a prose pronouncement against Pharaoh's pride, which outstrips the hubris of the king of Tyre. **29:9** *I made it.* Egyptian pharaohs claimed to be demigods. **29:10** *Migdol to Syene* represented two ends of the Nile. *Cush,* or Ethiopia. **29:11** *Forty years,* or "a long time." **29:13–16** The third section of the chapter promises restoration for Egypt. **29:14** *Pathros.* A region of Egypt south of Memphis.

29:17–21 The last section in this chapter is set off by a date formula, the most recent date in the whole book. Two of its features suggest it was a late addition to the book. First, it contradicts the predictions that Babylon was going to sack Tyre. Second, the date of the oracle is out of sequence (see note at 26:7–14). **29:17** *In the twenty-seventh year.* March/April 571, the latest date in the book chronologically. **29:18** *Nebuchadrezzar.* See note at 26:7. *Every head was made bald* from the long

labor hard against Tyre; every head was made bald and every shoulder was rubbed bare, yet neither he nor his army got anything from Tyre to pay for the labor that he had expended against it. [19]Therefore thus says the Lord God: I will give the land of Egypt to King Nebuchadrezzar of Babylon, and he shall carry off its wealth and despoil it and plunder it, and it shall be the wages for his army. [20]I have given him the land of Egypt as his payment for which he labored, because they worked for me, says the Lord God.

21 On that day I will cause a horn to sprout up for the house of Israel, and I will open your lips among them. Then they shall know that I am the Lord.

30

The word of the Lord came to me: [2]Mortal, prophesy, and say: Thus says the Lord God:

Wail, "Alas for the day!"
[3]   For a day is near,
    the day of the Lord is near;
it will be a day of clouds,
    a time of doom[n] for the nations.
[4] A sword shall come upon Egypt,
    and anguish shall be in Cush,
when the slain fall in Egypt,
    and its wealth is carried away,
    and its foundations are torn down.
[5]Cush and Put and Lud and all the mixed populations and Libya[o] and the people of the allied land[p] shall fall with them by the sword.

[6] Thus says the Lord:
Those who support Egypt shall fall,
    and its proud might shall come down;
from Migdol to Syene
    they shall fall within it by the sword,

says the Lord God.
[7] They shall be desolated among other
        desolated countries,
    and their cities shall lie among cities
        laid waste.
[8] Then they shall know that I am the Lord,
    when I have set fire to Egypt,
    and all who help it are broken.
9 On that day, messengers shall go out from me in ships to terrify the secure Cushites, and anguish shall come upon them on the day of Egypt's doom,[q] for it is coming!

10 Thus says the Lord God:
I will put an end to the hordes of Egypt,
    by the hand of King Nebuchadrezzar
        of Babylon.
[11] He and his people with him, the most
        terrible of the nations,
    shall be brought in to destroy the
        land,
    and they shall draw their swords against
        Egypt
    and fill the land with the slain.
[12] I will dry up the channels of the Nile
    and will sell the land into the hand of
        evildoers;
    I will bring desolation upon the land and
        everything in it
    by the hand of foreigners;
    I the Lord have spoken.

13 Thus says the Lord God:
I will destroy the idols
    and put an end to the images in
        Memphis;

n 30.3 Heb lacks *of doom*   o 30.5 Compare Gk Syr Vg: Heb *Cub*   p 30.5 Meaning of Heb uncertain   q 30.9 Heb *the day of Egypt*

effort. *To pay for the labor.* These verses are concerned that the soldiers get paid. Although military personnel were fed and housed, extra pay came solely from the plunder they collected when a city was conquered. Many soldiers (as opposed to officers) would have come from poorer economic backgrounds, including refugees, militiamen, and former prisoners of war. Archaeological evidence from Egypt confirms that Judeans served as militiamen in foreign armies. **29:19** *The wages for his army* reinforces the focus on the soldiers. **29:21** *A horn to sprout up.* An image indicating a new king. *I will open your lips* is also foreshadowed in 24:27.

30:1–4 The pronouncements against Egypt continue with a lamentation over its predicted fall. There is no new date formula until v. 20, which suggests that this material belongs to the late addition. **30:3** *The day of the Lord* is a phrase found throughout the prophetic literature generally referring to God's appearance among the people, either to reward or to punish. Here it spells disaster for the Egyptians.

30:5–19 The material after the lament describes the destruction of Egypt city by city and its effects on neighboring lands. **30:5** *Cush, Put, Lud,* and *Libya* are nations neighboring Egypt. **30:6** *Migdol to Syene.* See note at 29:10. **30:13–18** These verses contain a list of pronouncements against important Egyptian locations, although in no particular order.

there shall no longer be a prince in the
  land of Egypt,
    so I will put fear in the land of Egypt.
[14] I will make Pathros a desolation
    and will set fire to Zoan
    and will execute acts of judgment on
      Thebes.
[15] I will pour my wrath upon Pelusium,
    the stronghold of Egypt,
    and will cut off the hordes of Thebes.
[16] I will set fire to Egypt;
    Pelusium shall be in great agony;
  Thebes shall be breached
    and Memphis face adversaries by day.
[17] The young men of On and of Pi-beseth
    shall fall by the sword,
    and the cities themselves[r] shall go into
      captivity.
[18] At Tehaphnehes the day shall be dark,
    when I break there the dominion of
      Egypt,
  and its proud might shall come to an
    end;
    the city[s] shall be covered by a cloud,
    and its daughter towns shall go into
      captivity.
[19] Thus I will execute acts of judgment on
    Egypt.
    Then they shall know that I am the
      LORD.

20 In the eleventh year, in the first month,
on the seventh day of the month, the word
of the LORD came to me: [21]Mortal, I have broken the arm of Pharaoh king of Egypt; it has
not been bound up for healing or wrapped
with a bandage, so that it may become
strong to wield the sword. [22]Therefore thus
says the Lord GOD: I am against Pharaoh
king of Egypt and will break his arms, both
the strong arm and the one that was broken, and I will make the sword fall from his
hand. [23]I will scatter the Egyptians among
the nations and disperse them throughout the lands. [24]I will strengthen the arms
of the king of Babylon and put my sword
in his hand, but I will break the arms of

Pharaoh, and he will groan before him with
the groans of one mortally wounded. [25]I will
strengthen the arms of the king of Babylon,
but the arms of Pharaoh shall fall. And
they shall know that I am the LORD when I
put my sword into the hand of the king of
Babylon. He shall stretch it out against the
land of Egypt, [26]and I will scatter the Egyptians among the nations and disperse them
throughout the countries. Then they shall
know that I am the LORD.

31 In the eleventh year, in the third
month, on the first day of the month,
the word of the LORD came to me: [2]Mortal,
say to Pharaoh king of Egypt and to his
hordes:
  Whom are you like in your greatness?
[3]   Consider Assyria, a cedar of Lebanon,
  with fair branches and forest shade,
    and of great height,
    its top among the clouds.
[4] The waters nourished it;
    the deep made it grow tall,
  flowing with its rivers
    around the place it was planted,
  sending forth its streams
    to all the trees of the field.
[5] So it towered high
    above all the trees of the field;
  its boughs grew large
    and its branches long,
    from abundant water in its shoots.
[6] All the birds of the air
    made their nests in its boughs;
  under its branches all the animals of the
    field
    gave birth to their young,
  and in its shade
    all great nations lived.
[7] It was beautiful in its greatness,
    in the length of its branches,
  for its roots went down
    to abundant water.

r 30.17 Heb *and they*   s 30.18 Heb *she*

30:20–26 These verses focus on one of the symbols used by Egyptian pharaohs to represent
military strength: a flexed arm. These verses subvert the image by breaking the arm of Pharaoh and
strengthening that of the Babylonian leader. **30:20** *In the eleventh year.* March/April 587.
  31:1–18 Egypt is compared to Assyria via the metaphor of an immense cedar. Trees were used as
symbols of abundance, and gardens were a luxury item, especially in arid areas. The cedar forests
that once covered Lebanon provided the most coveted building material in the ancient Near East.
Within the metaphor, the height of the tree indicates the status of the nation that it represents.
31:1 *In the eleventh year.* May/June 587. **31:3** *Assyria, a cedar of Lebanon.* Assyria was not located in

⁸ The cedars in the garden of God could
   not rival it
   nor the fir trees equal its boughs;
the plane trees were as nothing
   compared with its branches;
no tree in the garden of God
   was like it in beauty.
⁹ I made it beautiful
   with its mass of branches,
   the envy of all the trees of Eden
      that were in the garden of God.

10 Therefore thus says the Lord GOD: Because it* towered high and set its top among the clouds and its heart was proud of its height, ¹¹I gave it into the hand of the prince of the nations; he has dealt with it as its wickedness deserves. I have cast it out. ¹²Foreigners from the most terrible of the nations have cut it down and left it. On the mountains and in all the valleys its branches have fallen, and its boughs lie broken in all the watercourses of the land, and all the peoples of the earth went away from its shade and left it.

¹³ On its fallen trunk settle
   all the birds of the air,
   and among its boughs lodge
      all the wild animals.

¹⁴All this is in order that no trees by the waters may grow to lofty height or set their tops among the clouds and that no trees that drink water may reach up to them in height.

For all of them are handed over to death,
   to the world below;
along with mortals,
   with those who go down to the Pit.

15 Thus says the Lord GOD: On the day it went down to Sheol I closed the deep over it and covered it; I restrained its rivers, and its mighty waters were checked. I clothed Lebanon in gloom for it, and all the trees of the field fainted because of it. ¹⁶I made the nations quake at the sound of its fall, when I cast it down to Sheol with those who go down to the Pit, and all the trees of Eden, the choice and best of Lebanon, all that were well watered, were consoled in the world below. ¹⁷They also went down to Sheol with it, to those killed by the sword, along with its allies,* those who lived in its shade among the nations.

18 Which among the trees of Eden was like you in glory and in greatness? Now you shall be brought down with the trees of Eden to the world below; you shall lie among the uncircumcised, with those who are killed by the sword. This is Pharaoh and all his horde, says the Lord GOD.

32 In the twelfth year, in the twelfth month, on the first day of the month, the word of the LORD came to me: ²Mortal, raise a lamentation over Pharaoh king of Egypt and say to him:

You consider yourself a lion among the
   nations,
   but you are like a dragon in the seas;
you thrash about in your streams,
   trouble the water with your feet,
      and foul your* streams.

t 31.10 Syr Vg: Heb *you*   *u* 31.17 Heb *its arms*   *v* 32.2 Heb *their*

Lebanon but did control the area during their advance on the Levant. **31:8** *The cedars in the garden of God could not rival it.* God's garden is Eden, and the trees there would be those chosen by God, such as Judah, a relatively small nation or tree. Assyria grew outside the garden and therefore did not have a covenant with God. But it was still the largest tree / most powerful nation. **31:9** *I made it beautiful.* Even though Assyria was not part of God's inner circle, it still owed its abundance to God. **31:10** *Its heart was proud* because it did not recognize that YHWH had blessed it with riches. **31:12** *Cut it down.* Assyria fell to the Babylonians circa 612 BCE. **31:14** *No trees . . . may grow to lofty height,* not even Egypt. *The Pit,* or the land of the dead. **31:15** *Sheol.* Another name for the place of the dead. *The deep* refers to the primordial waters that the Israelites believed surrounded the world. **31:17** *They also went down to Sheol.* The antecedent of *they* in v. 16 is the trees of Eden, meaning nations like Judah. **31:18** *Now you shall be brought down* speaks directly to Egypt. *The uncircumcised.* Egyptians did practice circumcision, so this statement could indicate they were among those whom the Egyptians also viewed as unclean.

32:1–16 The proclamations against Egypt return to the metaphor that they began with: Egypt as an animal hunted down and slaughtered by God. **32:1** *In the twelfth year.* February/March 585. **32:2** *Lamentation.* This poem and the next are laments for Egypt's downfall. *A lion . . . a dragon in the seas.* Both the lion and the serpentine dragon symbolized royalty. *In the seas.* In Ezek. 29, the dragon was in the midst of the Nile River. Here the symbol of Egypt starts in the center of the seas,

³ Thus says the Lord GOD:
   In an assembly of many peoples
   I will throw my net over you,
   and I[w] will haul you up in my dragnet.
⁴ I will throw you on the ground;
   on the open field I will fling you
and will cause all the birds of the air to
      settle on you,
   and I will let the wild animals of the
      whole earth gorge themselves on
      you.
⁵ I will strew your flesh on the mountains
   and fill the valleys with your carcass.[x]
⁶ I will drench the land with your flowing
      blood
   up to the mountains,
   and the watercourses will be filled
      with you.
⁷ When I blot you out, I will cover the
      heavens
   and make their stars dark;
I will cover the sun with a cloud,
   and the moon shall not give its light.
⁸ All the shining lights of the heavens
   I will darken above you
   and put darkness on your land,
                     says the Lord GOD.
⁹ I will trouble the hearts of many peoples
   as I carry you captive[y] among the
      nations,
   into countries you have not known.
¹⁰ I will make many peoples appalled at you;
   their kings shall shudder because of you.
When I brandish my sword before them,
   they shall tremble every moment
for their lives, each one of them,
   on the day of your downfall.
¹¹ For thus says the Lord GOD:
The sword of the king of Babylon shall
   come against you.

¹² I will cause your hordes to fall
   by the swords of mighty ones,
   all of them most terrible among the
      nations.
They shall bring to ruin the pride of
      Egypt,
   and all its hordes shall perish.
¹³ I will destroy all its livestock
   from beside abundant waters,
and no human foot shall trouble them
      any more,
   nor shall the hoofs of cattle trouble
      them.
¹⁴ Then I will make their waters clear
   and cause their streams to run like oil,
      says the Lord GOD.
¹⁵ When I make the land of Egypt desolate
   and when the land is stripped of all
      that fills it,
   when I strike down all who live in it,
   then they shall know that I am the
      LORD.
¹⁶ This is a lamentation; it shall be chanted.
   The women of the nations shall
      chant it.
Over Egypt and all its hordes they shall
      chant it,
   says the Lord GOD.

17 In the twelfth year, in the first month,[z] on the fifteenth day of the month, the word of the LORD came to me: ¹⁸ Mortal, wail over the hordes of Egypt
   and send them down,
with Egypt[a] and the daughters of
      majestic nations,
   to the world below,
   with those who go down to the Pit.

w 32.3 Gk Vg: Heb *they*   x 32.5 Symmachus Syr Vg:
Heb *your height*   y 32.9 Gk: Heb *bring your destruction*
z 32.17 Gk: Heb lacks *in the first month*   a 32.18 Heb *it*

stressing its international and cosmic significance. *Thrash about* symbolizes Egypt's attempts to thwart Babylon's advance. **32:3** *I will throw my net over you.* Nets were used to subdue wild animals, such as a lion. The verses that follow describe such a hunt. **32:7–9** *Cover the heavens.* The whole cosmos reacts to the tragedy of Egypt's demise. **32:10** *Many peoples [will be] appalled at you.* The defeat of Egypt would shock the world. **32:11** *The sword of the king of Babylon* indicates that God uses Babylon to bring down Egypt. **32:16** *This is a lamentation . . . the nations shall chant it.* The repetition in this verse stresses the mournful effect of Egypt's fall.

32:17–32 The pronouncements against foreign nations end with Ezekiel sounding a lament that creates a tableau of Egypt surrounded by the political powers of the ancient Near East in the land of the dead (*the Pit* and *Sheol*). See **"Oracles against the Nations," p. 1105.** This macabre portrait captures the futility of worldwide war. The language is repetitive; the repetition of *sword* indicates death in battle, as do the charges that these nations *spread terror*. The overall picture connotes not just the death of Egypt but also its shame in sharing the same fate as these other peoples. **32:17** *In the twelfth year.* February/March 585.

¹⁹ "Whom do you surpass in beauty?
Go down! Be laid to rest with the
uncircumcised!"

²⁰They shall fall among those who are killed by the sword. Egypt[b] has been handed over to the sword; both it and its hordes will be carried away.[c] ²¹The mighty chiefs shall speak of them, with their helpers, out of the midst of Sheol: "They have come down; they lie still, the uncircumcised, killed by the sword."

22 Assyria is there and all its company, their graves all around it, all of them killed, fallen by the sword. ²³Their graves are set in the uttermost parts of the Pit. Its company is all around its grave, all of them killed, fallen by the sword, who spread terror in the land of the living.

24 Elam is there and all its hordes around its grave, all of them killed, fallen by the sword, who went down uncircumcised into the world below, who spread terror in the land of the living. They bear their shame with those who go down to the Pit. ²⁵They have made Elam[d] a bed among the slain with all its hordes, their graves all around it, all of them uncircumcised, killed by the sword, for terror of them was spread in the land of the living, and they bear their shame with those who go down to the Pit; they are placed among the slain.

26 Meshech and Tubal are there, and all their multitude, their graves all around them, all of them uncircumcised, pierced by the sword, for they spread terror in the land of the living. ²⁷And they do not lie with the fallen warriors of long ago[e] who went down to Sheol with their weapons of war, whose swords were laid under their heads and whose shields[f] are upon their bones; for the terror of the warriors was in the land of the living. ²⁸So you shall be broken and lie among the uncircumcised, with those who are killed by the sword.

29 Edom is there, its kings and all its princes, who for all their might are laid with those who are killed by the sword; they lie with the uncircumcised, with those who go down to the Pit.

30 The princes of the north are there, all of them, and all the Sidonians, who have gone down in shame with the slain, for all the terror that they caused by their might; they lie uncircumcised with those who are killed by the sword and bear their shame with those who go down to the Pit.

31 When Pharaoh sees them, he will be consoled for all his hordes—Pharaoh and all his army, killed by the sword, says the Lord God. ³²For he[g] spread terror in the land of the living; therefore he shall be laid to rest among the uncircumcised, with those who are slain by the sword—Pharaoh and all his multitude, says the Lord God.

33

The word of the Lord came to me: ²O mortal, speak to your people and say to them: If I bring the sword upon a land and the people of the land take one of their number as their sentinel, ³and if the sentinel sees the sword coming upon the land and blows the trumpet and warns the people, ⁴then if any who hear the sound of the trumpet do not take warning and the sword comes and takes them away, their blood shall be upon their own heads. ⁵They heard the sound of the trumpet and did not take warning; their blood shall be upon themselves. But if they had taken warning, they would have saved their lives. ⁶But if the sentinel sees the sword coming and does not blow the trumpet so that the people are not warned, and the sword comes and takes any of them, they are taken away in their iniquity, but their blood I will require at the sentinel's hand.

7 So you, mortal, I have made a sentinel for the house of Israel; whenever you hear a word from my mouth, you shall give them warning from me. ⁸If I say to the wicked, "O wicked ones, you shall surely die," and

b 32.20 Heb *It*   c 32.20 Cn: Heb *carry away both it and its hordes*   d 32.25 Heb *it*   e 32.27 Gk OL: Heb *of the uncircumcised*   f 32.27 Cn: Heb *iniquities*   g 32.32 Cn: Heb *I*

33:1–20 Ezekiel 33 bridges between the material set in the period preceding the fall of Jerusalem and the material set after that disaster. At this pivotal moment, the book zeros in on the central question: Did Jerusalem fall because God is cruel and unethical? This question is answered in two parts. **33:1–9** The first answer comes in a repetition of the metaphor that the prophet is like a sentinel, giving a fair warning of danger approaching (see Ezek. 3:16–21) in almost identical language, so that Ezekiel's role as unheeded savior frames the material leading up to the city's eventual collapse. **33:8** *Warn the wicked to turn from their ways* sums up a prophet's purpose. They warned

you do not speak to warn the wicked to turn from their ways, the wicked shall die in their iniquity, but their blood I will require at your hand. ⁹But if you warn the wicked to turn from their ways and they do not turn from their ways, the wicked shall die in their iniquity, but you will have saved your life.

10 Now you, mortal, say to the house of Israel: Thus you have said: "Our transgressions and our sins weigh upon us, and we waste away because of them; how then can we live?" ¹¹Say to them: As I live, says the Lord GOD, I have no pleasure in the death of the wicked but that the wicked turn from their ways and live; turn back, turn back from your evil ways, for why will you die, O house of Israel? ¹²And you, mortal, say to your people: The righteousness of the righteous shall not save them when they transgress, and as for the wickedness of the wicked, it shall not make them stumble when they turn from their wickedness, and the righteous shall not be able to live by their righteousness*ᵇ* when they sin. ¹³Though I say to the righteous that they shall surely live, yet if they trust in their righteousness and commit iniquity, none of their righteous deeds shall be remembered, but in the iniquity that they have committed they shall die. ¹⁴Again, though I say to the wicked, "You shall surely die," yet if they turn from their sin and do what is lawful and right—¹⁵if the wicked restore the pledge,

give back what they have taken by robbery, and walk in the statutes of life, committing no iniquity—they shall surely live; they shall not die. ¹⁶None of the sins that they have committed shall be remembered against them; they have done what is lawful and right; they shall surely live.

17 Yet your people say, "The way of the Lord is not just," when it is their own way that is not just. ¹⁸When the righteous turn from their righteousness and commit iniquity, they shall die for it.*ⁱ* ¹⁹And when the wicked turn from their wickedness and do what is lawful and right, they shall live by it.*ʲ* ²⁰Yet you say, "The way of the Lord is not just." O house of Israel, I will judge all of you according to your ways!

21 In the twelfth year of our exile, in the tenth month, on the fifth day of the month, someone who had escaped from Jerusalem came to me and said, "The city has fallen." ²²Now the hand of the LORD had been upon me the evening before the fugitive came, and he opened my mouth when the fugitive came in the morning, so my mouth was opened, and I was no longer unable to speak.

23 The word of the LORD came to me: ²⁴Mortal, the inhabitants of these waste places in the land of Israel keep saying, "Abraham was only one man, yet he got

b 33.12 Heb *by it*   *i* 33.18 Heb *them*   *j* 33.19 Heb *them*

communities of the consequences of various decisions. Since Ezekiel has performed his duty, the metaphor reiterates that the people had ample time to avoid disaster, placing the blame squarely on their shoulders. **33:10–20** The second section addresses God's ethical character. The theoretical discussion mirrors the rhetorical style of Ezek. 18, which queried whether God held people accountable for the sins of earlier generations. Here the ethical question is whether a person's past deeds determine their fate, for good or for ill. The answer is no; past behavior does not negate present responsibility. Such an answer can be hopeful for those who despair but serves as a warning for those who think they are above the law. **33:11** *I have no pleasure in the death of the wicked.* The wording insinuates that people viewed God as gleefully vengeful. **33:15** *Restore the pledge* refers to collateral for either a loan or part of a sworn oath. *Statutes of life.* Laws that, when obeyed, guarantee protection and bounty from the lawgiver—in this case, God. **33:17** *The way of the Lord is not just* summarizes the accusation against God: innocent people suffered and died when the city fell.

33:21–33 This section picks up the narrative arc from Ezek. 24:25–27, where Ezekiel's wife has just died, which God compares to the fall of Jerusalem and tells the prophet that a messenger will come to report the news. That messenger arrives in this chapter, followed quickly by the reactions of both those still alive amid the rubble and Ezekiel's exiled comrades. **33:21** *In the twelfth year.* January 585. **33:22** *Before the fugitive came* can also be translated as "in the presence of the entering fugitive." *My mouth was opened.* See the comment at Ezek. 3:26 and 24:27. **33:24** *These waste places* can refer to the dry wilderness but also to depopulated areas, such as the ruins in and around Jerusalem. The image is that of a postapocalyptic wasteland with survivors inhabiting barren urban and rural areas. *Abraham was only one man.* These "new" inhabitants, who lay claim to the land legally belonging to those who traced their land ownership over generations, take their

possession of the land, but we are many; the land is surely given us to possess." [25]Therefore say to them: Thus says the Lord GOD: You eat flesh with the blood and lift up your eyes to your idols and shed blood; shall you then possess the land? [26]You depend on your swords, you commit abominations, and each of you defiles his neighbor's wife; shall you then possess the land? [27]Say this to them: Thus says the Lord GOD: As I live, surely those who are in the waste places shall fall by the sword, and those who are in the open field I will give to the wild animals to be devoured, and those who are in strongholds and in caves shall die by pestilence. [28]I will make the land a desolation and a waste, and its proud might shall come to an end, and the mountains of Israel shall be so desolate that no one will pass through. [29]Then they shall know that I am the LORD, when I have made the land a desolation and a waste because of all their abominations that they have committed.

30 As for you, mortal, your people who talk together about you by the walls and at the doors of the houses say to one another, each to a neighbor, "Come and hear what the word is that comes from the LORD." [31]They come to you as people come, and they sit before you as my people, and they hear your words, but they will not obey them. For flattery is on their lips, but their heart is set on their gain.[k] [32]To them you are like a singer of love songs,[l] one who has a beautiful voice and plays well on an instrument; they hear what you say, but they will not do it. [33]When this comes—and come it will!—then they shall know that a prophet has been among them.

34

The word of the LORD came to me: [2]Mortal, prophesy against the shepherds of Israel; prophesy and say to them: To the shepherds—thus says the Lord GOD: Woe, you shepherds of Israel who have been feeding yourselves! Should not shepherds feed the sheep? [3]You eat the fat; you clothe yourselves with the wool; you slaughter the fatted calves, but you do not feed the sheep. [4]You have not strengthened the weak; you have not healed the sick; you have not bound up the injured; you have not brought back the strays; you have not sought the lost, but with force and harshness you have ruled them. [5]So they were scattered because there was no shepherd, and scattered they became food for all the wild animals. [6]My sheep were scattered; they wandered over all the mountains and on every high hill; my sheep were scattered over all the face of the earth, with no one to search or seek for them.

7 Therefore, you shepherds, hear the word of the LORD: [8]As I live, says the Lord GOD, because my sheep have become a prey and my sheep have become food for all the wild animals, since there was no shepherd, and

k 33.31 Meaning of Heb uncertain   l 33.32 Cn: Heb *like a love song*

own survival as evidence that the covenant now falls to them. **33:25** *Eat flesh with the blood.* According to Israelite dietary laws, meat needed to be drained of all blood before eating. Following this is a series of accusations that depict these squatters as ineligible for the covenant. **33:27** *Sword . . . wild animals . . . pestilence.* The squatters will be subject to the same punishments as those living in Jerusalem before its fall. **33:28** *The mountains of Israel.* See the comment at 6:2. **33:30–32** The chapter ends with a glimpse of how the exiles react to Ezekiel's pronouncements: they are merely entertained. **33:30** *Talk together about you.* Ezekiel has become a topic of discussion rather than a voice to be obeyed. **33:32** *To them you are like a singer of love songs.* The word translated here as *love* is not the emotion. It means erotic songs, not surprising given the lurid imagery in chaps. 16 and 23. **33:33** *Then they shall know that a prophet has been among them.* The wording equates the recognition of the true prophet with the recognition of the truth about God.

34:1–31 This chapter utilizes the trope that a king's rule over the people should be like that of a shepherd tending his flock. Here the leaders of Judah are described as bad shepherds because they did not protect the Judeans from war, famine, or exile. Unlike other passages in Ezekiel, this chapter depicts the people as innocent; the blame for Jerusalem's disasters falls to the leaders. **34:1–10** This section describes the selfish behavior of Judah's leaders, including that of Zedekiah, who failed to protect the city. **34:2** *Shepherds* is used as a metaphor for kings in, for example, 2 Sam. 7:7; 24:17; and 1 Kgs. 22:17. *Feeding yourselves* as opposed to *feed[ing] the sheep*—both metaphorically by putting the people in the city on the walls and other vulnerable locations, while the elites had more safety in the interior of the city, and literally by controlling the food stores during the siege. **34:5** *Scattered*

because my shepherds have not searched for my sheep, but the shepherds have fed themselves and have not fed my sheep, [9]therefore, you shepherds, hear the word of the LORD: [10]Thus says the Lord GOD: I am against the shepherds, and I will hold them accountable for my sheep and put a stop to their feeding the sheep; no longer shall the shepherds feed themselves. I will rescue my sheep from their mouths, so that they may not be food for them.

[11] For thus says the Lord GOD: I myself will search for my sheep and will sort them out. [12]As shepherds sort out their flocks when they are among scattered sheep,[m] so I will sort out my sheep. I will rescue them from all the places to which they have been scattered on a day of clouds and thick darkness. [13]I will bring them out from the peoples and gather them from the countries and bring them into their own land, and I will feed them on the mountains of Israel, by the watercourses, and in all the inhabited parts of the land. [14]I will feed them with good pasture, and the mountain heights of Israel shall be their pasture; there they shall lie down in good grazing land, and they shall feed on rich pasture on the mountains of Israel. [15]I myself will be the shepherd of my sheep, and I will make them lie down, says the Lord GOD. [16]I will seek the lost, and I will bring back the strays, and I will bind up the injured, and I will strengthen the weak, but the fat and the strong I will destroy. I will feed them with justice.

[17] As for you, my flock, thus says the Lord GOD: I shall judge between sheep and sheep, between rams and goats: [18]Is it not enough for you to feed on the good pasture, but you must tread down with your feet the rest of your pasture? When you drink of clear water, must you foul the rest with your feet? [19]And must my sheep eat what you have trodden with your feet and drink what you have fouled with your feet?

[20] Therefore, thus says the Lord GOD to them: I myself will judge between the fat sheep and the lean sheep. [21]Because you pushed with flank and shoulder and butted at all the weak animals with your horns until you scattered them far and wide, [22]I will save my flock, and they shall no longer be ravaged, and I will judge between sheep and sheep.

[23] I will set up over them one shepherd, my servant David, and he shall feed them; he shall feed them and be their shepherd. [24]And I the LORD will be their God, and my servant David shall be prince among them; I the LORD have spoken.

[25] I will make with them a covenant of peace and banish wild animals from the land, so that they may live in the wild and sleep in the woods securely. [26]I will make them and the region around my hill a blessing, and I will send down the showers in their season; they shall be showers of blessing. [27]The trees of the field shall yield their fruit, and the

m 34.12 Cn: Heb *their scattered sheep*

sheep refers to those exiled as the result of the siege. *Food for all the wild animals*, or victims of attacks by a series of invaders. **34:11–16** Just as God was the true king, with the human king functioning as God's representative, so too God is the true shepherd who takes over for the failing shepherds. **34:11** *I myself will search for my sheep*. A message of hope for the restoration of the nation after exile. **34:13** *Peoples... countries* indicates that God will bring all Israelites back to the land. This would include those exiled by the Assyrians during the time of Hezekiah, as well as those who became refugees in places like Egypt. *Mountains of Israel*, not literal mountains, but a reference to Israel as God's dwelling place and therefore sacred land (cf. note on 6:2). **34:17–22** These verses return to God's judgment of the wicked shepherds or leaders. See **"Shepherds, Bones, and Monsters," p. 1178**. The repetitions in these verses (*sheep and sheep, rams and goats, the fat sheep and the lean sheep*) keep the focus on clashes within Judean society. The moral narrative focuses on wicked leaders and innocent sheep. **34:23–31** The chapter ends with an idyllic pastoral scene that is a metaphor for a righteous government. First, God puts a good ruler on the throne, and with that reign, all nature responds in harmonious abundance. **34:23** *One shepherd, my servant David*. In this vision of Israel's future, the text depicts a single kingdom (not the dual kingdoms of Israel and Judah) governed by a Davidic king—that is, someone who is a legitimate heir in the lineage of David. **34:24** *Prince*. The most common term used in the book for Judah's ruler. The reticence to use "king" indicates to the audience that God will remain the true king in the future utopia. **34:25** *Covenant of peace* or well-being. The passage goes on to describe what that might look like. No *wild* animals—that is, foreign invaders—will harm them, and they can return to their homes outside the city's walls. **34:27** *Break the bars of their yoke* refers to their exile and servitude

Reading through Time: Shepherds, Bones, and Monsters (Ezekiel 34)
The book of Ezekiel has had less impact in the history of interpretation than, say, Isaiah or the Psalms. It is cited less often by New Testament authors, except in the book of Revelation, for example, and had fewer commentaries written on it during the patristic and medieval periods of Christianity and in postbiblical Judaism. There are, however, three images from Ezekiel that do reappear in art, music, and liturgy: the story of the good shepherd in chap. 34, the revivification of the dry bones in chap. 37, and the image of the enthroned God that structures the book. Each of these has two trajectories within Judaism and Christianity.

The good shepherd was a symbol of the idealized restored Davidic king, as the text explicitly states. The king as a shepherd was not Ezekiel's invention, but the book uses it to demonstrate both the good and the bad sides of the monarchy. In the end, God promises the return of an ideal king who will gather and heal the sheep. When the Davidic monarchy was not restored after the exile (see **"Exile (2 Kings),"** **p. 539**), some Jewish groups continued to hope for a righteous messiah (or anointed king) who would restore them. Christians, on the other hand, eventually transferred that language onto Jesus, whom they titled the Messiah (or "Christ" in Gk.). In both cases, the good shepherd became a utopian figure.

Ezekiel's prophetic revival of the valley of dry bones served as a potent image not just for the book's original audience, for whom it represented restoration after the exile, but for continued audiences. It fed into the concept of a bodily resurrection after death, especially because of the reference to the opening of graves in v. 12. For Christian readers, this paralleled the narrative of Jesus's empty tomb, which signaled his bodily resurrection, but this interpretation was already part of the pre-Christian Jewish engagement with the book. Oppressed peoples also found hope in this metaphor for communal restoration. For example, the spiritual "Dem Bones," written by J. W. Johnson and J. R. Johnson in the early twentieth century, resonated with the African American community supposedly released from slavery but still legally subordinate through racism and Jim Crow laws. Much of the visual art based on Ezekiel, such as *The Vision of Ezekiel* by Fontana (1579), includes skeletons rising from their graves.

The descriptions of the God enthroned above the cherubim inform a long tradition within Judaism called *merkabah* mysticism. Within this tradition, the vision's details represent various aspects of the divine being. Some of this influenced Christian mysticism as well, but the most prominent Christian interpretation is the association of the four writers of the Gospels with each of the cherubim's faces, which is found throughout Christian art and architecture.

Corrine L. Carvalho

earth shall yield its increase. They shall be secure on their soil, and they shall know that I am the LORD when I break the bars of their yoke and save them from the hands of those who enslaved them. [28]They shall no more be plunder for the nations, nor shall the animals of the land devour them; they shall live in safety, and no one shall make them afraid. [29]I will provide for them a splendid vegetation so that they shall no more be consumed with hunger in the land and no longer suffer the insults of the nations. [30]They shall know that I, the LORD their God, am with them and that they, the house of Israel, are my people, says the Lord GOD. [31]You are my sheep, the sheep of my pasture,[n] and I am your God, says the Lord GOD.

35 The word of the LORD came to me: [2]Mortal, set your face against Mount Seir and prophesy against it, [3]and say to it: Thus says the Lord GOD:

I am against you, Mount Seir;
    I stretch out my hand against you
    to make you a desolation and a waste.
[4] I lay your towns in ruins;
    you shall become a desolation,
    and you shall know that I am the LORD.

n 34.31 Gk OL: Heb pasture, you are people

under the Babylonians. **34:28–29** These verses describe the common elements of siege warfare, such as *plunder* and famine that led to citizens *consumed with hunger*.

35:1–15 This chapter seems oddly placed. It contains a pronouncement against Edom, which would seem to fit better with the oracle in 25:12–14. This one has more details that make it closer to charges against Edom in Isa. 34:5–15, Ps. 137:7, and the book of Obadiah. These passages depict this neighbor of Judah as aiding the Babylonians and taking advantage of Judah's fall. **35:2** *Mount Seir.*

5Because you cherished an ancient enmity and gave over the people of Israel to the power of the sword at the time of their calamity, at the time of their final punishment, 6therefore, as I live, says the Lord God, I will make you bloody, and blood shall pursue you; since you did not hate bloodshed, bloodshed will pursue you. 7I will make Mount Seir a waste and a desolation, and I will cut off from it all who come and go. 8I will fill its mountains with the slain; on your hills and in your valleys and in all your watercourses those killed with the sword shall fall. 9I will make you a perpetual desolation, and your cities shall never be inhabited. Then you shall know that I am the Lord.

10 Because you said, "These two nations and these two countries shall be mine, and we will take possession of them"—although the Lord was there—11therefore, as I live, says the Lord God, I will deal with you according to the anger and envy that you showed because of your hatred against them, and I will make myself known among you*o* when I judge you. 12You shall know that I, the Lord, have heard all the abusive speech that you uttered against the mountains of Israel, saying, "They are laid desolate; they are given us to devour." 13And you magnified yourselves against me with your mouth and multiplied your words against me; I heard it. 14Thus says the Lord God: As the whole earth rejoices, I will make you desolate. 15As you rejoiced over the inheritance of the house of Israel because it was desolate, so I will deal with you; you

shall be desolate, Mount Seir and all Edom, all of it. Then they shall know that I am the Lord.

36 And you, mortal, prophesy to the mountains of Israel and say: O mountains of Israel, hear the word of the Lord. 2Thus says the Lord God: Because the enemy said of you, "Aha!" and, "The ancient heights have become our possession," 3therefore prophesy and say: Thus says the Lord God: Because they made you desolate indeed and crushed you from all sides, so that you became the possession of the rest of the nations and an object of gossip and slander among the people, 4therefore, O mountains of Israel, hear the word of the Lord God: Thus says the Lord God to the mountains and the hills, the watercourses and the valleys, the desolate wastes and the deserted towns, which have become a source of plunder and an object of derision to the rest of the nations all around; 5therefore thus says the Lord God: I am speaking in my hot jealousy against the rest of the nations and against all Edom, who, with wholehearted joy and utter contempt, took my land as their possession, because of its pasture, to plunder it. 6Therefore prophesy concerning the land of Israel and say to the mountains and hills, to the watercourses and valleys: Thus says the Lord God: I am speaking in my jealous wrath because you have suffered the insults of the nations; 7therefore thus says the Lord God:

o 35.11 Gk: Heb *them*

A mountainous area south of the Dead Sea that comprised a prominent geological feature of Edom. **35:5** *Because.* This verse outlines Edom's crime of siding with the Babylonians to save their own country. **35:9** *Perpetual desolation.* The predicted punishment would have been more powerful in ancient times, when there was more rainfall in the area than there is now. **35:10** *These two nations—* that is, the northern kingdom of Israel and the southern kingdom of Judah. *Although the Lord was there.* This statement depicts God still residing in the land even after Jerusalem fell, a concept that seems to contradict the visions of God leaving and returning to the city. **35:12** *The mountains of Israel.* See the comment at 6:2. **35:14** *As the whole earth rejoices, I will make you desolate.* This phrase may tie back to the image of God's covenant of peace in 34:24–29, which here contrasts with Edom's uninhabitable fate. **35:15** *The inheritance of the house of Israel* refers to God's permanent gift of the land to the various tribes and families of Israel. Even if the elites have been exiled, they had legal rights to their ancestral land.

36:1–15 The next divine speech centers on the restoration of Israel characterized as the renewal of its land from the ravages of war. The verses contain further indictments of Edom along with recompense for the Babylonian army's destruction. **36:1** *Mountains of Israel.* See 6:2. **36:2** *Enemy.* Babylon, here unnamed. **36:3** *From all sides.* Babylon from the north and Edom from the south. *Possession of the rest of the nations* who occupied and settled in the depopulated areas. **36:4** *Mountains . . . towns* expands the victimhood of the land from the national center to the whole land. **36:5** *Edom.*

I swear that the nations that are all around you shall themselves suffer insults.

8 But you, O mountains of Israel, shall shoot out your branches and yield your fruit to my people Israel, for they shall soon come home. [9]See now, I am for you; I will turn to you, and you shall be tilled and sown, [10]and I will multiply your population, the whole house of Israel, all of it; the towns shall be inhabited and the waste places rebuilt, [11]and I will multiply humans and animals upon you. They shall increase and be fruitful, and I will cause you to be inhabited as in your former times and will do more good to you than ever before. Then you shall know that I am the LORD. [12]I will lead people upon you—my people Israel—and they shall possess you, and you shall be their inheritance. No longer shall you bereave them of children.

13 Thus says the Lord GOD: Because they say to you, "You devour people, and you bereave your nation of children," [14]therefore you shall no longer devour people and no longer bereave your nation of children, says the Lord GOD, [15]and no longer will I let you hear the insults of the nations; no longer shall you bear the disgrace of the peoples, and no longer shall you cause your nation to stumble, says the Lord GOD.

16 The word of the LORD came to me: [17]Mortal, when the house of Israel lived on their own soil, they defiled it with their ways and their deeds; their conduct in my sight was like the uncleanness of a menstrual period. [18]So I poured out my wrath upon them for the blood that they had shed upon the land and for the idols with which they had defiled it. [19]I scattered them among the nations, and they were dispersed through the countries; in accordance with their conduct and their deeds I judged them. [20]But when they came to the nations, wherever they came, they profaned my holy name, in that it was said of them, "These are the people of the LORD, yet they had to go out of his land." [21]But I had concern for my holy name, which the house of Israel had profaned among the nations to which they came.

22 Therefore say to the house of Israel: Thus says the Lord GOD: It is not for your sake, O house of Israel, that I am about to act but for the sake of my holy name, which you have profaned among the nations to which you came. [23]I will sanctify my great name, which has been profaned among the nations and which you have profaned among them, and the nations shall know that I am the LORD, says the Lord GOD, when through you I display my holiness before their eyes. [24]I will take you from the nations and gather you from all the countries and bring you into your own land. [25]I will sprinkle clean water upon you, and you shall be clean from all your uncleannesses, and from all your idols I will cleanse you. [26]A new heart I will give you, and a new spirit I will put within you, and I will remove from your body the heart of stone and give you a heart of flesh. [27]I will

---

The only named enemy in this passage. **36:8** *They shall soon come home*, returning from exile. **36:9** *I am for you*, or "I am on your side." **36:12–15** *You*. It is not clear who is addressed here: while the reader might expect it to be Judah's enemies, the addressee devours its own children, like the Judean bad shepherds in 34:2.

36:16–38 The chapter turns again to a depiction of the restoration of Israel using images found in other parts of the book, including defilement and purification, the transplant of a new heart, and the restoration of God's flock. The one thing that unifies all these verses is that in every case, God is the agent of the action, and Israel is merely acted upon. In this way, even restoration is fully under the control and command of God. **36:17** *Uncleanness of a menstrual period.* While contact with blood could cause ritual contamination, the gendered quality of this blood recalls the metaphors of the city as a defiling wife in chaps. 16 and 23. See **"Slut-Shaming," p. 1148. 36:20** *Profaned my holy name.* To profane something is to remove its sacred character from it. Here the exile of Judah led other nations to conclude that their God was weak, was incompetent, or simply did not exist, making YHWH seem less holy. **36:21** *Concern for my holy name.* God now must rehabilitate this divine reputation. **36:22** *I am about to act.* This time not through more violent punishment but through a completely unwarranted restoration of the exiles to their homeland. **36:23** *I display my holiness.* This divine beneficence will demonstrate the power and nature of Israel's God. **36:25** *I will sprinkle clean water upon you.* The exiles are inherently defiled (see, e.g., 16:4–6), not made more defiled by living in a foreign land. Their continued state of uncleanness is represented by the worship of idols. **36:26** *A new heart . . . a new spirit* indicates a complete change of the human person. **36:27** *I will . . . make you follow my statutes* indicates that with this change

put my spirit within you and make you follow my statutes and be careful to observe my ordinances. ²⁸Then you shall live in the land that I gave to your ancestors, and you shall be my people, and I will be your God. ²⁹I will save you from all your uncleannesses, and I will summon the grain and make it abundant and lay no famine upon you. ³⁰I will make the fruit of the tree and the produce of the field abundant, so that you may never again suffer the disgrace of famine among the nations. ³¹Then you shall remember your evil ways and your dealings that were not good, and you shall loathe yourselves for your iniquities and your abominable deeds. ³²It is not for your sake that I will act, says the Lord GOD; let that be known to you. Be ashamed and dismayed for your ways, O house of Israel.

33 Thus says the Lord GOD: On the day that I cleanse you from all your iniquities, I will cause the towns to be inhabited, and the waste places shall be rebuilt. ³⁴The land that was desolate shall be tilled, instead of being the desolation that it was in the sight of all who passed by. ³⁵And they will say, "This land that was desolate has become like the garden of Eden, and the waste and desolate and ruined towns are now inhabited and fortified." ³⁶Then the nations that are left all around you shall know that I, the LORD, have rebuilt the ruined places and replanted that which was desolate; I, the LORD, have spoken, and I will do it.

37 Thus says the Lord GOD: I will also let the house of Israel ask me to do this for them: to multiply their people like sheep. ³⁸Like a consecrated flock, like the flock at Jerusalem during her appointed festivals, so shall the ruined towns be filled with flocks of people. Then they shall know that I am the LORD.

37 The hand of the LORD came upon me, and he brought me out by the spirit of the LORD and set me down in the middle of a valley; it was full of bones. ²He led me all around them; there were very many lying in the valley, and they were very dry. ³He said to me, "Mortal, can these bones live?" I answered, "O Lord GOD, you know." ⁴Then he said to me, "Prophesy to these bones and say to them: O dry bones, hear the word of the LORD. ⁵Thus says the Lord GOD to these bones: I will cause breath^p to enter you, and you shall live. ⁶I will lay sinews on you and will cause flesh to come upon you and cover you with skin and put breath^q in you, and you shall live, and you shall know that I am the LORD."

7 So I prophesied as I had been commanded, and as I prophesied, suddenly there was a noise, a rattling, and the bones came together, bone to its bone. ⁸I looked, and there were sinews on them, and flesh had come upon them, and skin had covered them, but there was no breath in them. ⁹Then he said to me, "Prophesy to the breath, prophesy, mortal, and say to the breath:^r Thus says the Lord GOD: Come from the four winds, O breath,^s and breathe upon these slain, that

p 37.5 Or wind or spirit   q 37.6 Or wind or spirit   r 37.9 Or wind or spirit   s 37.9 Or wind or spirit

in anthropology, humans will lose their free will, Israel's last hope for not rebelling against divine decrees. **36:31** *You shall loathe yourselves.* The heart transplant will be a welcome change because the people will no longer desire to return to their old ways. They will inherently know that God's decrees bring the future that they hope for. **36:37** *Multiply their people like sheep* brings in the imagery of the divine good shepherd and the covenant of peace of chap. 34.

37:1–28 This chapter contains three more pronouncements of Israel's restoration: one using the metaphor of revivified corpses (vv. 1–14), the next a metaphor of a reunited broken twig (15–23), and the final speech the promise of a restored Davidic king and rebuilt temple (24–28). Their depictions of a bright and blessed future contrast with the darkness of divine punishment that has characterized much of the book up to this point. **37:1–14** Ezekiel's vision of a valley full of dry bones has had a rich history of influence in Christian and Jewish interpretations, some related to the concept of a bodily resurrection (see **"Shepherds, Bones, and Monsters," p. 1178**). The image here, though, is not about the postmortem state but a metaphor for the hopeless condition of the exiles. **37:1** *Hand of the LORD came upon me.* Ezekiel again has a vision of being transported to another place, here an unspecified *valley . . . full of bones.* The image suggests a battlefield where unburied corpses have been picked clean by scavenger animals and the sun has desiccated them. **37:3** *You know.* An enigmatic statement that may be a sign of courtesy toward someone with much higher status and power. **37:5** *Breath.* These verses play with the various connotations of a single word in Hebrew, which can be translated as "wind," "spirit," or "breath." **37:9** *Four winds, O breath*—or "four winds,

they may live." [10]I prophesied as he commanded me, and the breath came into them, and they lived and stood on their feet, a vast multitude.

11 Then he said to me, "Mortal, these bones are the whole house of Israel. They say, 'Our bones are dried up, and our hope is lost; we are cut off completely.' [12]Therefore prophesy and say to them: Thus says the Lord GOD: I am going to open your graves and bring you up from your graves, O my people, and I will bring you back to the land of Israel. [13]And you shall know that I am the LORD when I open your graves and bring you up from your graves, O my people. [14]I will put my spirit within you, and you shall live, and I will place you on your own soil; then you shall know that I, the LORD, have spoken and will act, says the LORD."

15 The word of the LORD came to me: [16]Mortal, take a stick and write on it, "For Judah and the Israelites associated with it"; then take another stick and write on it, "For Joseph (the stick of Ephraim) and all the house of Israel associated with it"; [17]and join them together into one stick, so that they may become one in your hand. [18]And when your people say to you, "Will you not show us what you mean by these?" [19]say to them, "Thus says the Lord GOD: I am about to take the stick of Joseph (which is in the hand of Ephraim) and the tribes of Israel associated with it, and I will put the stick of Judah upon it[t] and make them one stick, in order that they may be one in my hand." [20]When the sticks on which you write are in your hand before their eyes, [21]then say to them, "Thus says the Lord GOD: I will take the people of Israel from the nations among which they have gone and will gather them from every quarter and bring them to their own land. [22]I will make them one nation in the land, on the mountains of Israel, and one king shall be king over them all. Never again shall they be two nations, and never again shall they be divided into two kingdoms. [23]They shall never again defile themselves with their idols and their detestable things or with any of their transgressions. I will save them from all the apostasies into which they have fallen[u] and will cleanse them. Then they shall be my people, and I will be their God.

24 "My servant David shall be king over them, and they shall all have one shepherd. They shall follow my ordinances and be careful to observe my statutes. [25]They shall live in the land that I gave to my servant Jacob, in which your ancestors lived; they and their children and their children's children shall live there forever, and my servant David shall be their prince forever. [26]I will make a covenant of peace with them; it shall be an everlasting covenant with them, and I will

t 37.19 Heb *I will put them upon it* *u* 37.23 Cn: MT *from all the settlements in which they have sinned*

O wind," capturing the wordplay in the original text. **37:10** *A vast multitude.* The word here can be translated as "army," "large group," or "host." **37:11** *The whole house of Israel* is emphasized in vv. 15–23. *Our hope is lost* indicates that the bones are a metaphor for the hopelessness the exiles have experienced. **37:12** *Open your graves* continues the metaphor, the *graves* symbolizing living in exile. **37:14** *Put my spirit within you* resonates with the restoration of a new spirit in 36:27. **37:15–23** Here the prophet acts out God's message by symbolically grafting two sticks into a single branch. This material stresses that the restoration will return Israel to its composition under David: twelve tribes governed by a single divinely appointed king. Such a restoration would have been quite improbable given the fact that the populations from the northern kingdom had been exiled about two centuries prior and had not retained a distinct identity in their Diaspora. **37:16** *A stick . . . another stick,* one for the southern kingdom of Judah and the other for the northern kingdom of Israel. *Joseph, Ephraim,* and *Israel* are all names for that northern kingdom based on the genealogies of some of the more prominent tribes that composed that kingdom. **37:21** *From every quarter* indicates the widespread displacement of the northern populations. **37:22** *One king.* A reunification of the twelve tribes into a single political entity. *Never again* indicates that this will be their perpetual configuration. **37:24–28** These verses tie this restoration to the renewal of a Davidic leader and a rebuilt temple. **37:24** *One shepherd* replicates the Davidic shepherd of 34:23. **37:25** *My servant Jacob.* In Genesis, he was the father of the twelve men who founded the twelve tribes of Israel. **37:26** *A covenant of peace* echoes the covenant described in 34:25–29. **37:26–28** *Forevermore* appears twice in these verses, applied to the restoration of the people and the rebuilt temple or *sanctuary,* which would be God's permanent *dwelling place.*

bless[v] them and multiply them and will set my sanctuary among them forevermore. [27]My dwelling place shall be over them, and I will be their God, and they shall be my people. [28]Then the nations shall know that I the Lord sanctify Israel, when my sanctuary is among them forevermore."

38 The word of the Lord came to me: [2]Mortal, set your face toward Gog, of the land of Magog, the chief prince of Meshech and Tubal. Prophesy against him [3]and say: Thus says the Lord God: I am against you, O Gog, chief prince of Meshech and Tubal; [4]I will turn you around and put hooks into your jaws, and I will lead you out with all your army, horses and horsemen, all of them clothed in full armor, a great company, all of them with shield and buckler, wielding swords. [5]Paras, Cush, and Put are with them, all of them with buckler and helmet; [6]Gomer and all its troops; Beth-togarmah from the remotest parts of the north with all its troops—many peoples are with you.

7 Be ready and keep ready, you and all the companies that are assembled around you, and take command of them.[w] [8]After many days you shall be mustered; in the latter years you shall go against a land restored from war, a land where people were gathered from many nations on the mountains of Israel, which had long lain waste; its people were brought out from the nations and now are living in safety, all of them.

[9]You shall advance, coming on like a storm; you shall be like a cloud covering the land, you and all your troops and many peoples with you.

10 Thus says the Lord God: On that day thoughts will come into your mind, and you will devise an evil scheme. [11]You will say, "I will go up against the land of unwalled villages; I will fall upon the quiet people who live in safety, all of them living without walls and having no bars or gates, [12]to seize spoil and carry off plunder, to assail the waste places that are now inhabited and the people who were gathered from the nations, who are acquiring cattle and goods, who live at the center[x] of the earth." [13]Sheba and Dedan and the merchants of Tarshish and all its young warriors[y] will say to you, "Have you come to seize spoil? Have you assembled your horde to carry off plunder, to carry away silver and gold, to take away cattle and goods, to seize a great amount of spoil?"

14 Therefore, mortal, prophesy and say to Gog: Thus says the Lord God: On that day when my people Israel are living securely, you will rouse yourself[z] [15]and come from your place out of the remotest parts of the north, you and many peoples with you, all of them riding on horses, a great horde, a mighty army; [16]you will come up against my people Israel like a cloud covering the earth.

v 37.26 Tg: Heb *give*   w 38.7 Cn: Heb *hold yourselves in reserve for them*   x 38.12 Heb *navel*   y 38.13 Heb *young lions*   z 38.14 Gk: Heb *will you not know?*

38:1–39:29 These two chapters contain a series of vignettes of a restored Israel attacked by a large army composed of warriors across the known world. This battle is a hypothetical case and therefore contains hyperbole to contrast the evil and might of the enemy with the defenselessness and devotion of restored Israel. The point of God's rescue of Israel in this case is to demonstrate that God can save anyone, no matter the strength of the enemy. Therefore, the destruction of Judah by the Babylonians was warranted; God chose not to rescue them. **38:2–16** The first scene depicts God's mustering of a great enemy to attack a peaceful, restored Israel. **38:2** *Gog, of the land of Magog* is a hypothetical future enemy. *Meshech and Tubal* were in Asia Minor. **38:4** *I will turn you* means that the whole scenario is purposefully scripted by God. **38:5–6** *Paras . . . Beth-togarmah* represent countries far removed from Israel in various directions. **38:6** *Many peoples are with you.* Gog's army contains mercenaries from all parts of the world. **38:8** *In the latter years*—that is, in some unspecified future. *A land restored from war*—that is, Israel. **38:11** *The land of unwalled villages* is an important detail. This restored land is so safe and secure that they need no defenses against foreign enemies. In addition, the fact that Gog brings such a large army against a weaponless people adds to his characterization as evil. **38:12** *Center of the earth*, or more literally its navel, represents this spot as the location for creation. **38:16** *So that the nations may know me.* Israel's safety connotes that restored Israel "knows" YHWH and therefore has divine protection. The purpose of this narrative is to prove to the rest of the world that Israel's God is a mighty God.

In the latter days I will bring you against my land, so that the nations may know me, when through you, O Gog, I display my holiness before their eyes.

17 Thus says the Lord GOD: Are you he of whom I spoke in former days by my servants the prophets of Israel, who in those days prophesied for years that I would bring you against them? 18On that day, when Gog comes against the land of Israel, says the Lord GOD, my wrath shall be aroused. 19For in my jealousy and in my blazing wrath I declare: On that day there shall be a great shaking in the land of Israel; 20the fish of the sea and the birds of the air and the animals of the field and all creeping things that creep on the ground and all humans who are on the face of the earth shall quake at my presence, and the mountains shall be thrown down, and the cliffs shall fall, and every wall shall tumble to the ground. 21I will summon the sword against Gog[a] in[b] all my mountains, says the Lord GOD; the swords of all will be against their comrades. 22With pestilence and bloodshed I will enter into judgment with him, and I will pour down torrential rains and hailstones, fire and sulfur upon him and his troops and the many peoples who are with him. 23So I will display my greatness and my holiness and make myself known in the eyes of many nations. Then they shall know that I am the LORD.

39 And you, mortal, prophesy against Gog and say: Thus says the Lord GOD: I am against you, O Gog, chief prince of Meshech and Tubal! 2I will turn you around and drive you forward and bring you up from the remotest parts of the north and lead you against the mountains of Israel. 3I will strike your bow from your left hand and will make your arrows drop out of your right hand. 4You shall fall on the mountains of Israel, you and all your troops and the peoples who are with you; I will give you to birds of prey of every kind and to the wild animals to be devoured. 5You shall fall in the open field, for I have spoken, says the Lord GOD. 6I will send fire on Magog and on those who live securely in the coastlands, and they shall know that I am the LORD.

7 My holy name I will make known among my people Israel, and I will not let my holy name be profaned any more, and the nations shall know that I am the LORD, the Holy One in Israel. 8It has come! It has happened, says the Lord GOD. This is the day of which I have spoken.

9 Then those who live in the towns of Israel will go out and make fires of the weapons and burn them—bucklers and shields, bows and arrows, clubs and spears—and they will make fires of them for seven years. 10They will not need to take wood out of the field or cut down any trees in the forests, for they will make their fires of the weapons; they will despoil those who despoiled them and plunder those who plundered them, says the Lord GOD.

11 On that day I will give to Gog a place for burial in Israel, the Valley of the Travelers[c] east of the sea; it shall block the path of the travelers, for there Gog and all his

a 38.21 Heb *him*   b 38.21 Heb *to* or *for*   c 39.11 Or *of the Abarim*

38:17–23 Although the battle between God and Gog is not spelled out, these verses describe that clash in epic terms: the earth and all that is in it shakes with fear as the battle ensues. **38:17** *Are you he of whom I spoke* probably refers to other prophetic pronouncements of an enemy horde coming from the north, such as Jer. 1:14–15. Originally, these references applied to either Assyria or Babylon, but they became the paradigmatic origin of epic enemies. **38:21** *I will summon the sword against Gog* is the closest the passage comes to describing the battle. **38:23** *The eyes of many nations* reinforces the purpose of this future display of divine power: to convince the world of God's power. **39:1–20** The next vignette contains a series of postbattle panels: the ravishing of the corpses by carrion birds and wild animals, the despoliation of the defeated through the stripping and burning of their weapons, the mass burial, and finally a glimpse of the divine warrior in this postbattle scene. **39:4–5** *I will give you. . . . You shall fall in the open field* resonates with the depiction of a valley filled with bleached bones in 37:1. **39:9** *Make fires . . . for seven years* provides another detail demonstrating the gigantic size of Israel's enemy. **39:10** *Plunder those who plundered them* represents the irony of the situation. **39:11** *Block the path.* There are so many dead enemies that their corpses block public

horde will be buried; it shall be called the Valley of Hamon-gog.*d* ¹²Seven months the house of Israel shall spend burying them, in order to cleanse the land. ¹³All the people of the land shall bury them, and it will bring them honor on the day that I show my glory, says the Lord God. ¹⁴They will set apart men to pass through the land regularly and bury any invaders*ᵉ* who remain on the face of the land, so as to cleanse it; for seven months they shall make their search. ¹⁵As the searchers*ᶠ* pass through the land, anyone who sees a human bone shall set up a sign by it until the buriers have buried it in the Valley of Hamon-gog.*ᵍ* ¹⁶(A city Hamonah*ʰ* is there also.) Thus they shall cleanse the land.

17 As for you, mortal, thus says the Lord God: Speak to the birds of every kind and to all the wild animals: Assemble and come, gather from all around to the sacrificial feast that I am preparing for you, a great sacrificial feast on the mountains of Israel, and you shall eat flesh and drink blood. ¹⁸You shall eat the flesh of the mighty and drink the blood of the princes of the earth—of rams, of lambs, and of goats, of bulls, all of them fatted calves of Bashan. ¹⁹You shall eat fat until you are filled and drink blood until you are drunk, at the sacrificial feast that I am preparing for you. ²⁰And you shall be filled at my table with horses and chariots, with warriors and all kinds of soldiers, says the Lord God.

21 I will display my glory among the nations, and all the nations shall see my judgment that I have executed and my hand that I have laid on them. ²²The house of Israel shall know that I am the Lord their God from that day forward. ²³And the nations shall know that the house of Israel went into captivity for their iniquity, because they dealt treacherously with me. So I hid my face from them and gave them into the hand of their adversaries, and they all fell by the sword. ²⁴I dealt with them according to their uncleanness and their transgressions and hid my face from them.

25 Therefore thus says the Lord God: Now I will restore the fortunes of Jacob and have mercy on the whole house of Israel, and I will be jealous for my holy name. ²⁶They shall bear their shame, and all the treachery they have practiced against me, when they live securely in their land with no one to make them afraid, ²⁷when I have brought them back from the peoples and gathered them from their enemies' lands and through them have displayed my holiness in the sight of many nations. ²⁸Then they shall know that I am the Lord their God because I sent them into exile among the nations and then gathered them into their own land. I will leave none of them behind, ²⁹and I will never again hide my face from them, when I pour out my spirit upon the house of Israel, says the Lord God.

d 39.11 That is, *the horde of Gog*   *e* 39.14 Heb *travelers*
f 39.15 Heb *travelers*   *g* 39.15 That is, *the horde of Gog*
h 39.16 That is, *the horde*

throughways. **39:12** *Seven months* will be the length of time to bury all the corpses, a process necessary to avoid ritual contamination from the dead bodies. Again, this detail contributes further to the characterization of this mythic enemy as epic. **39:15** *Anyone who sees a human bone* depicts the entire population involved in this purification in one way or another. The details of despoliation and burial characterize restored Israel as wholly obedient to God's statutes and ordinances. **39:17–20** The next scene depicts God setting up a sacrificial feast for the unclean animals who were not allowed to be sacrificed in the temple. This inversion of sacrificial order and object provides another ironic twist to the battle motif. Rather than depicting the victorious human warriors performing thanksgiving sacrifices to the warrior deity, here that deity prepares a sacrifice for the lowliest of animals as an act of purification. **39:23** *The house of Israel went into captivity for their iniquity* serves as the punchline for this two-chapter metaphor. The point of this chain of events is not to save an innocent people per se but to show that God can save anyone, no matter the relative imbalance of power. So if God did not save Judah from destruction by the Babylonians, it must have been because they deserved it as punishment for sins against God. **39:26** *They shall bear their shame . . . when they live securely in their land.* In addition, restored Israel will also experience a renewal of their own shame as they too realize how evil they must have become.

40 In the twenty-fifth year of our exile, at the beginning of the year, on the tenth day of the month, in the fourteenth year after the city was struck down, on that very day, the hand of the LORD was upon me, and he brought me there. [2]He brought me, in visions of God, to the land of Israel and set me down upon a very high mountain on which was a structure like a city to the south. [3]When he brought me there, a man was there whose appearance shone like bronze, with a linen cord and a measuring reed in his hand, and he was standing in the gateway. [4]The man said to me, "Mortal, look closely and listen attentively, and set your mind on all that I shall show you, for you were brought here in order that I might show it to you; declare all that you see to the house of Israel."

5 Now there was a wall all around the outside of the temple area. The length of the measuring reed in the man's hand was six long cubits, each being a cubit and a handbreadth in length, so he measured the thickness of the wall, one reed, and the height, one reed. [6]Then he went into the gateway facing east, going up its steps, and measured the threshold of the gate, one reed deep.[i] There were [7]recesses, and each recess was one reed wide and one reed deep, and the space between the recesses, five cubits, and the threshold of the gate by the vestibule of

i 40.6 Heb *deep, and one threshold, one reed deep*

40–48 The book of Ezekiel ends with a long description of Ezekiel's final visionary journey. Once again, he is transported from Babylon to the main temple of Israel, but here it is contrary to fact; the building and its surroundings have no reflex in Israelite history. Ezekiel, along with the reader, is led through this space by a heavenly architect and tour guide, and Ezekiel is commanded to report what he sees to the whole of Israel. This suggests one of two possibilities that probably coexist in this narrative. First, the temple description comprises the ideal layout for the rebuilding of the sanctuary once Israel is restored (43:11). Similarly, the prophet may be touring the heavenly temple, of which the earthly temple is merely a shadow. Some of the elements in the vision resonate with other Israelite temple descriptions, including the general layout of areas of the sanctuary complex. Others are not only different from other descriptions but also unachievable, such as the fructifying river in chap. 47. See **"Minecraft, the Temple, and Spatial Icons," p. 1197**.

40:1–42:20 The vision commences with a tour of the visionary temple. Major temples, like this one, were walled complexes with many buildings, such as treasury rooms, storage areas, places to prepare the sacrifices, and wardrobe rooms for the priestly vestments. The main building was a sanctuary that was described as the deity's abode. This divine home had an entry porch, an interior audience hall, and an inner room where the divine presence dwelled, thus replicating the three main parts of a king's residence. This sanctuary was surrounded by courtyards where servants/priests prepared the meals/sacrifices and people could approach the king/god with requests and/or gifts. **40:1** *Twenty-fifth year of our exile.* March/April 573. *The hand of the LORD . . . brought me there* connects this vision with those in chaps. 1 and 8–11. **40:2** *To the land of Israel* distinct from "Jerusalem" in 8:3. Jerusalem is never mentioned in this vision. *A very high mountain* as opposed to the phrase "the mountains of Israel" used to designate the nation in other parts of the book. This mountain is the "highest," signifying it as holier than all other parts of the nation. *A structure like a city* with a series of defensible walls, large buildings, and an active support staff. **40:3** *A man . . . whose appearance shone like bronze* indicates that this being had a humanlike form but was made of precious metal. The use of bronze indicates his celestial origin but does not put him among the most elite heavenly figures, which would have had the appearance of silver and gold. *A linen cord.* Cords or belts were often symbols of rank, as was linen, which was the fabric required for priests. *A measuring reed* would have had a similar function as a tape measure today. **40:4** *Declare all that you see to the house of Israel.* This command will be repeated by God in 43:10. **40:5** *Temple.* This is the first time in this vision that the complex is explicitly identified as a temple. Sometimes "temple" refers to the whole temple complex, and other times it designates only the sanctuary building where God's presence resides. *Six long cubits.* There were two standard lengths of cubit. One was the length of just the forearm, about twelve inches. The author makes clear that the temple envisioned here assumes the length of the longer cubit, which included the hand, or about an additional six inches. The measuring reed that the man carried was the length of this longer cubit. **40:6** *Steps.* The temple tour not only moves from outside to inside, but each area was higher than the previous,

the gate at the inner end was one reed deep. [8]Then he measured the inner vestibule of the gateway, one reed. [9]Then he measured the vestibule of the gateway, eight cubits, and its posts, two cubits, and the vestibule of the gate was at the inner end. [10]There were three recesses on either side of the east gate; the three were of the same size, and the posts on either side were of the same size. [11]Then he measured the width of the opening of the gateway, ten cubits, and the width of the gateway, thirteen cubits. [12]There was a barrier before the recesses, one cubit on either side, and each recess was six cubits square. [13]Then he measured the gate from the back[j] of the one recess to the back[k] of the other, a width of twenty-five cubits from wall to wall.[l] [14]He measured[m] the vestibule (sixty cubits) and the gate next to the post on every side of the court.[n] [15]From the front of the gate at the entrance to the end of the inner vestibule of the gate was fifty cubits. [16]The recesses and their posts had windows, with shutters[o] on the inside of the gateway all around, and the vestibules also had windows on the inside all around, and on the posts were palm trees.

17 Then he brought me into the outer court; there were chambers there and a pavement all around the court; thirty chambers fronted on the pavement. [18]The pavement ran along the side of the gates, corresponding to the length of the gates; this was the lower pavement. [19]Then he measured the distance from the inner front of[p] the lower gate to the outer front of the inner court, one hundred cubits.[q]

20 Then he measured the gate of the outer court that faced north—its depth and width. [21]Its recesses, three on either side, and its posts and its vestibule were of the same size as those of the first gate; its depth was fifty cubits and its width twenty-five cubits. [22]Its windows, its vestibule, and its palm trees were of the same size as those of the gate that faced toward the east. Seven steps led up to it, and its vestibule was on the inside.[r] [23]Opposite the gate on the north, as on the east, was a gate to the inner court; he measured from gate to gate, one hundred cubits.

24 Then he led me toward the south, and there was a gate on the south, and he measured its posts and its vestibule; they had the same dimensions as the others. [25]There were windows all around in it and in its vestibule, like the windows of the others; its depth was fifty cubits and its width twenty-five cubits. [26]There were seven steps leading up to it; its vestibule was on the inside.[s] It had palm trees on its posts, one on either side. [27]There was a gate on the south of the inner court, and he measured from gate to gate toward the south, one hundred cubits.

28 Then he brought me to the inner court by the south gate, and he measured the south gate; it was of the same dimensions as the others. [29]Its recesses, its posts, and its vestibule were of the same size as the others, and there were windows all around in it and in its vestibule; its depth was fifty cubits and its width twenty-five cubits. [30]There were vestibules all around the inner court,[t] twenty-five cubits deep and five cubits wide. [31]Its vestibule faced the outer court, and palm trees were on its posts, and its stairway had eight steps.

32 Then he brought me to the inner court on the east side, and he measured the gate; it was of the same size as the others. [33]Its recesses, its posts, and its vestibule were of the same dimensions as the others, and there were windows all around in it and in its vestibule; its depth was fifty cubits and its width twenty-five cubits. [34]Its vestibule faced the outer court, and it had palm trees on its posts, on either side, and its stairway had eight steps.

35 Then he brought me to the north gate, and he measured it; it had the same dimensions as the others. [36]Its recesses, its posts, and its vestibule were of the same size as the others,[u] and it had windows all around. Its depth was fifty cubits and its width twenty-five cubits. [37]Its vestibule[v] faced the outer court, and it had palm trees on its posts, on either side, and its stairway had eight steps.

j 40.13 Gk: Heb *roof*   *k* 40.13 Gk: Heb *roof*   *l* 40.13 Heb *opening facing opening*   *m* 40.14 Heb *made*   *n* 40.14 Meaning of Heb uncertain   *o* 40.16 Meaning of Heb uncertain   *p* 40.19 Compare Gk: Heb *from before*   *q* 40.19 Heb adds *the east and the north*   *r* 40.22 Gk: Heb *before them*   *s* 40.26 Gk: Heb *before them*   *t* 40.30 Meaning of Heb uncertain   *u* 40.36 Heb ms: MT lacks *were of the same size as the others*   *v* 40.37 Gk Vg: Heb *posts*

creating an architectural mount. **40:16** *Palm trees*, probably date palms, were an important source of sugar. **40:38** *The burnt offering* consisted in burning up an entire animal corpse as a gift that goes up to God in the form of smoke. The sacrificial priests slit these animals' throats and drained as much blood as possible from them before butchering and performing the sacrificial rituals.

38 There was a chamber with its door in the vestibule of the gate[w] where the burnt offering was to be washed. [39]And in the vestibule of the gate were two tables on either side on which the burnt offering and the purification offering and the guilt offering were to be slaughtered. [40]On the outside of the vestibule, where one goes up to the entrance of the north gate, were two tables, and on the other side of the vestibule of the gate were two tables. [41]Four tables were on one side and four tables on the other side of the gate, eight tables, on which the sacrifices were to be slaughtered. [42]There were also four tables of hewn stone for the burnt offering, a cubit and a half long, and one cubit and a half wide, and one cubit high, on which the instruments were to be laid with which the burnt offerings and the sacrifices were slaughtered. [43]There were pegs one handbreadth long fastened all around the inside. And on the tables the flesh of the offering was to be laid.

44 On the outside of the inner gateway there were two chambers[x] in the inner court, one[y] at the side of the north gate facing south, the other at the side of the south[z] gate facing north. [45]He said to me, "This chamber that faces south is for the priests who have charge of the temple, [46]and the chamber that faces north is for the priests who have charge of the altar; these are the descendants of Zadok, who alone among the descendants of Levi may come near to the Lord to minister to him." [47]He measured the court, one hundred cubits deep and one hundred cubits wide, a square, and the altar was in front of the temple.

48 Then he brought me to the vestibule of the temple and measured the posts of the vestibule, five cubits deep on either side, and the width of the gate between the posts[a] was fourteen cubits, and the shoulders of the gate were three cubits wide on either side.[b] [49]The width of the vestibule was twenty cubits and the depth twelve[c] cubits; ten steps led up[d] to it, and there were pillars beside the posts on either side.

41 Then he brought me to the nave and measured the posts; on each side six cubits was the depth of the posts.[e] [2]The width of the entrance was ten cubits, and the sidewalls of the entrance were five cubits on either side. He measured the length of the nave, forty cubits, and its width, twenty cubits. [3]Then he went into the inner room and measured the posts of the entrance, two cubits, and the width of the entrance, six cubits, and the sidewalls[f] of the entrance, seven cubits. [4]He measured the depth of the room, twenty cubits, and its width, twenty cubits, beyond the nave. And he said to me, "This is the most holy place."

5 Then he measured the wall of the temple, six cubits thick, and the width of the side chambers, four cubits, all around the temple. [6]The side chambers were in three stories, one over another, thirty in each story. There were offsets[g] all around the wall of the temple to serve as supports for the side chambers so that they should not be supported by the wall of the temple. [7]The passageway[h] of the side chambers widened from story to story, for the structure was supplied with a stairway all around the temple. For this reason the

w 40.38 Cn: Heb *at the posts of the gates*   x 40.44 Gk: Heb *chambers for the singers*   y 40.44 Heb lacks *one*   z 40.44 Gk: Heb *east*   a 40.48 Gk: Heb lacks *between the posts*   b 40.48 Gk: Heb *and the width of the gate was three cubits*   c 40.49 Gk: Heb *eleven*   d 40.49 Gk: Heb *and by steps that went up*   e 41.1 Compare Gk: Heb *tent*   f 41.3 Gk: Heb *width*   g 41.6 Gk: Heb *they entered*   h 41.7 Cn: Heb *it was surrounded*

40:39 *Purification offering and the guilt offering* were partially consumed by the priests (42:13; 44:29). **40:43** *Pegs* are not given a function here, but they may have been where carcasses were hung to allow for the blood to drain out. **40:46** *The descendants of Zadok . . . among the descendants of Levi.* According to the Pentateuch, while the whole tribe of Levi had priestly status, serving at temples and shrines, not all clans within that tribe were allowed to perform sacrifices. While the Pentateuch reserves that right to the descendants of Aaron, the book of Ezekiel puts the clan of Zadok in that role. **41:1** *The nave* was the long interior hall of the sanctuary building. In a king's palace, this would have functioned as an audience hall where elite outsiders would present gifts to the king. In a temple, these gifts take the form of offerings, like produce, breads and cakes, oil, wine, incense, or votive items such as gold bowls and cups. **41:4** *The room . . . beyond the nave . . . is the most holy place.* Sometimes translated as "Holy of Holies." In the palace, the king would have private rooms that only his family and close servants could enter. This private, interior space for God is a perfect cube, devoid of windows to symbolize it as a place of rest and privacy.

structure became wider from story to story. One ascended from the bottom story to the uppermost story by way of the middle one. [8]I saw also that the temple was on a raised platform all around; the foundations of the side chambers measured a full reed of six long cubits high. [9]The thickness of the outer wall of the side chambers was five cubits, and the free space between the side chambers of the temple [10]and the chambers of the court was a width of twenty cubits all around the temple on every side. [11]The side chambers opened onto the area left free, one door toward the north and another door toward the south, and the width of the part that was left free was five cubits all around.

12 The building that was facing the temple yard on the west side was seventy cubits deep, and the wall of the building was five cubits thick all around and its width ninety cubits.

13 Then he measured the temple, one hundred cubits deep, and the yard and the building with its walls, one hundred cubits deep, [14]also the width of the east front of the temple and the yard, one hundred cubits.

15 Then he measured the width of the building facing the yard at the west, together with its galleries[i] on either side, one hundred cubits.

The nave of the temple's interior and the outer[j] vestibule [16]were paneled,[k] and all around all three had windows with recessed[l] frames. Facing the threshold, the temple was paneled with wood all around, from the floor up to the windows (now the windows were covered). [17]On the space above the door, even to the inner room, and on the outside and on all the walls all around in the inner room and the nave there was a pattern.[m] [18]It was formed of cherubim and palm trees, a palm tree between cherub and cherub. Each cherub had two faces: [19]a human face turned toward the palm tree on the one side, and the face of a young lion turned toward the palm tree on the other side. They were carved on the whole temple all around; [20]from the floor to the area above the door, cherubim and palm trees were carved on the wall.[n]

21 The doorposts of the nave were square. In front of the holy place was something resembling [22]an altar of wood, three cubits high, two cubits long, and two cubits wide;[o] its corners, its base,[p] and its walls were of wood. He said to me, "This is the table that stands before the LORD." [23]The nave and the holy place had each a double door. [24]The doors had two leaves apiece, two swinging leaves for each door. [25]On the doors of the nave were carved cherubim and palm trees, such as were carved on the walls, and there was a canopy of wood in front of the vestibule outside. [26]And there were recessed windows and palm trees on either side, on the sidewalls of the vestibule.[q]

42 Then he led me out into the outer court toward the north, and he brought me to the chambers that were opposite the temple yard and opposite the building on the north. [2]The length of the building that was on the north side[r] was[s] one hundred cubits and the width fifty cubits. [3]Facing the twenty cubits that belonged to the inner court and facing the pavement that belonged to the outer court, the chambers rose[t] gallery[u] by gallery[v] in three

i 41.15 Cn: Meaning of Heb uncertain   j 41.15 Gk: Heb of the court   k 41.16 Gk: Heb the thresholds   l 41.16 Cn Compare Gk: Meaning of Heb uncertain   m 41.17 Heb measures   n 41.20 Cn: Heb and the wall   o 41.22 Gk: Heb lacks two cubits wide   p 41.22 Gk: Heb length   q 41.26 Cn: Heb vestibule. And the side chambers of the temple and the canopies   r 42.2 Gk: Heb door   s 42.2 Gk: Heb before the length   t 42.3 Heb lacks the chambers rose   u 42.3 Meaning of Heb uncertain   v 42.3 Meaning of Heb uncertain

41:8 *The temple was on a raised platform*, which ensured that it was symbolically the highest point in the city. **41:12** *The building* behind the temple is given no function in this narrative and does not correspond to any element in other Israelite temple descriptions. **41:13** *One hundred cubits.* Much of the larger spaces in this vision come in multiples of fifty and one hundred. **41:16** *Paneled.* The First Temple was paneled with fragrant cedar wood. **41:18** *A palm tree between cherub and cherub.* Here the symbol of fertility, the palm tree, alternates with representations of the divine bodyguards, the cherubim. *Each cherub had two faces.* While the cherubim that Ezekiel saw in his second vision had four faces, probably the two-dimensional surface of the wall elicits the use of two faces to symbolize their ability to see danger from any direction. **41:22** *An altar of wood*, so not suitable for burnt animal sacrifices. Other offerings would have been placed on these tables. **42:1–12** This section describes the outer court, creating three distinct spaces within the temple complex: an outer court that Israelites could enter, an inner court that was only accessible to priests, and then the sanctuary

stories. ⁴Amid the chambers was an interior passage, ten cubits wide and one hundred cubits deep,ʷ and itsˣ entrances were on the north. ⁵Now the upper chambers were narrower, for the galleriesʸ took more away from them than from the lower and middle chambers in the building. ⁶For they were in three stories, and they had no pillars like the pillars of the outerᶻ court; for this reason the upper chambers were set back from the ground more than the lower and the middle ones. ⁷There was a wall outside parallel to the chambers, toward the outer court, opposite the chambers, fifty cubits long. ⁸For the chambers on the outer court were fifty cubits long, while those opposite the temple were one hundred cubits long. ⁹At the foot of these chambers ran a passage that one entered from the east in order to enter them from the terrace space outside. ¹⁰The entrance was aligned with the start of the wallᵃ toward the court.

On the southᵇ also, opposite the vacant area and opposite the building, there were chambers ¹¹with a passage in front of them; they were similar to the chambers on the north, of the same length and width, with the same exitsᶜ and arrangements and doors. ¹²So the entrances of the chambers to the south were entered through the entrance at the head of the corresponding passage, from the east, along the matching wall.ᵈ

13 Then he said to me, "The north chambers and the south chambers opposite the vacant area are the holy chambers where the priests who approach the LORD shall eat the most holy offerings; there they shall deposit the most holy offerings—the grain offering, the purification offering, and the guilt offering—for the place is holy. ¹⁴When the priests enter

the holy place, they shall not go out of it into the outer court without laying there the vestments in which they minister, for these are holy; they shall put on other garments before they go near to the area open to the people."

15 When he had finished measuring the interior of the temple area, he led me out by the gate that faces east and measured the temple area all around. ¹⁶He measured the east side with the measuring reed, five hundred cubits by the measuring reed. ¹⁷Then he turned and measuredᵉ the north side, five hundred cubits by the measuring reed. ¹⁸Then he turned and measuredᶠ the south side, five hundred cubits by the measuring reed. ¹⁹Then he turned to the west side and measured, five hundred cubits by the measuring reed. ²⁰He measured it on the four sides. It had a wall around it, five hundred cubits long and five hundred cubits wide, to make a separation between the holy and the common.

43

Then he brought me to the gate, the gate facing east. ²And there the glory of the God of Israel was coming from the east; the sound was like the sound of mighty waters, and the earth shone with his glory. ³Theᵍ vision I saw was like the vision that I had seen when he came to destroy the city andᵇ like the vision that I had seen by the River Chebar, and I fell upon my face. ⁴As the glory of the LORD entered the temple by the gate facing east, ⁵the spirit lifted me up

w 42.4 Gk Syr: Heb *a way of one cubit*   x 42.4 Heb *their*   y 42.5 Meaning of Heb uncertain   z 42.6 Gk: Heb lacks *outer*   a 42.10 Compare Gk: Heb *in the thickness of the wall*   b 42.10 Gk: Heb *east*   c 42.11 Heb *and all their exits*   d 42.12 Meaning of Heb uncertain   e 42.17 Gk: Heb *measuring reed all around. He measured*   f 42.18 Gk: Heb *measuring reed all around. He measured*   g 43.3 Gk: Heb *Like the vision*   h 43.3 Syr: Heb *and the visions*

building with a porch, a nave, and the holiest place. In Ezekiel's plan, no human enters that inner building once God's throne is installed and the deity takes up residence. **42:13** *Priests . . . shall eat the most holy offerings.* While a whole burnt offering was completely consumed by fire, priests and sometimes laity ate portions of other offerings (cf. 1 Sam. 1:3). **42:14** *The vestments*, which the priests wore when making offerings in the inner court, could not be worn outside that holy area, so they had changing rooms before going out to the less holy outer court. **42:20** *Five hundred cubits long and five hundred cubits wide* is larger than could be accommodated on the site of the First Temple.

43:1–12 These verses describe God taking up residence in this temple. In the narratives describing the founding of the First Temple by King Solomon, the glory of God appears after the ark of the covenant is placed beneath the cherubim wings (1 Kgs. 8:11; 2 Chr. 5:14). The book of Ezekiel contains no mention of the ark, but the return of the chariot throne has the same function. **43:2** *The glory of the God of Israel* replicates the light that surrounded the great gods in the ancient Near East. *From the east*, where God had traveled to in Ezek. 11:23. **43:3** *Like the vision[s]* described in chaps. 1 and 8–11, including the same sounds and divine spirit. **43:5** *The spirit . . . brought me into the inner court.*

and brought me into the inner court, and the glory of the LORD filled the temple.

6 While the man was standing beside me, I heard someone speaking to me out of the temple. ⁷He said to me: "Mortal, this is the place of my throne and the place for the soles of my feet, where I will reside among the people of Israel forever. The house of Israel shall no more defile my holy name, neither they nor their kings, by their prostitution and by sacrificing to their kings*ⁱ* at their death.*ʲ* ⁸When they placed their threshold by my threshold and their doorposts beside my doorposts, with only a wall between me and them, they were defiling my holy name by their abominations that they committed; therefore I have consumed them in my anger. ⁹Now let them put away their idolatry and sacrifices to their kings*ᵏ* far from me, and I will reside among them forever.

10 "As for you, mortal, describe the temple to the house of Israel, and let them measure the pattern, and let them be ashamed of their iniquities. ¹¹When they are ashamed of all that they have done, make known to them the plan of the temple, its arrangement, its exits and its entrances, and its whole form— all its ordinances and its entire plan and all its laws; and write it down in their sight so that they may observe and follow the entire plan and all its ordinances. ¹²This is the law of the temple: the whole territory on the top of the mountain all around shall be most holy. This is the law of the temple.

13 "These are the dimensions of the altar by long cubits in which each is a cubit and a handbreadth: its base shall be one cubit high*ˡ* and one cubit wide, with a rim of one span around its edge. This shall be the height of the altar: ¹⁴from the base on the ground to the lower ledge, two cubits, with a width of one cubit, and from the lower ledge to the upper ledge, four cubits, with a width of one cubit, ¹⁵and the altar hearth, four cubits, and from the altar hearth projecting upward, four horns. ¹⁶The altar hearth shall be square, twelve cubits long by twelve wide. ¹⁷The ledge also shall be square, fourteen cubits long by fourteen wide, with a rim around it half a cubit high, and its surrounding base, one cubit. Its steps shall face east."

18 Then he said to me: "Mortal, thus says the Lord GOD: These are the ordinances for the altar: On the day when it is erected for offering burnt offerings upon it and for dashing

i 43.7 Or *the corpses of their kings* *j* 43.7 Or *on their high places* *k* 43.9 Or *the corpses of their kings* *l* 43.13 Gk: Heb lacks *high*

Not so far of a journey as in previous transportation scenes. The agency of the spirit counteracts Ezekiel's own stance of obeisance. **43:6** *Out of the temple* or sanctuary building where priests could not enter. **43:7** *This is the place . . . where I will reside . . . forever.* God makes a permanent covenant with all Israel. They, in turn, *shall no more defile [his] holy name*, either because God will have removed their free will (36:27) or because they will be struck with such great awe, like Ezekiel, that they will be a changed people. **43:8** *Their threshold by my threshold.* In the ancient Near East, many kings showed their piety by locating the temple and the palace adjacent to each other. In this vision, not only is the temple moved away from the royal residence, but it is also located outside of the city itself. **43:10** *Describe the temple to the house of Israel* repeats the command to communicate this plan to the people at the start of the vision (40:4). *Be ashamed of their iniquities.* A common refrain in the book, but here it includes dissatisfaction with the First Temple. **43:11** *All its ordinances and its entire plan and all its laws.* The tabernacle plan described in Exod. 25–31 contains laws after the description of the space. This pattern of first describing the indwelling of the deity followed by laws related to the maintenance of that space also appears here; Ezek. 43:13–48:35 contain various statutes and land divisions. The command to *write it down* marks this material as an official decree. **43:12** *The whole . . . top of the mountain . . . shall be most holy.* While this may contradict the gradations of holiness in the plan's description, these chapters consistently portray the area in and immediately surrounding the temple as a holy space and therefore governed by strict laws of access.
43:13–27 This passage describes the construction of the large altar that stood in the inner court in front of the sanctuary building on which animal sacrifices were performed—first designating the size of this altar, followed by the rituals that changed it from a profane edifice to a holy altar. **43:13** *Rim[s]* probably carried away any juices produced by the burning of a sacrifice. **43:15** *Hearth*, or the place for the fire. *Four horns* or protrusions from the altar base, one on each corner. **43:17** *Its steps shall face east* so that as the priests went up to place the animal on the fire, their backs would not be turned to God, like the sinners in Ezek. 8:16. **43:18–21** *Ordinances for the altar* consist of the

blood against it, [19]you shall give to the Levitical priests of the family of Zadok, who draw near to me to minister to me, says the Lord God, a bull of the herd for a purification offering. [20]And you shall take some of its blood and put it on the four horns of the altar and on the four corners of the ledge and upon the rim all around; thus you shall purify it and make atonement for it. [21]You shall also take the bull of the purification offering, and it shall be burnt in the appointed place belonging to the temple, outside the sacred area.

[22] "On the second day you shall offer a male goat without blemish for a purification offering, and the altar shall be purified, as it was purified with the bull. [23]When you have finished purifying it, you shall offer a bull of the herd without blemish and a ram from the flock without blemish. [24]You shall present them before the Lord, and the priests shall throw salt on them and offer them up as a burnt offering to the Lord. [25]For seven days you shall provide daily a goat for a purification offering; also a bull of the herd and a ram from the flock, without blemish, shall be provided. [26]Seven days shall they make atonement for the altar and cleanse it and so consecrate it. [27]When these days are over, then from the eighth day onward the priests shall offer upon the altar your burnt offerings and your offerings of well-being, and I will accept you, says the Lord God."

44

Then he brought me back to the outer gate of the sanctuary that faces east, and it was shut. [2]The Lord said to me: "This gate shall remain shut; it shall not be opened, and no one shall enter by it, for the Lord, the God of Israel, has entered by it; therefore it shall remain shut. [3]Only the prince, because he is a prince, may sit in it to eat food before the Lord; he shall enter by way of the vestibule of the gate and shall go out by the same way."

[4] Then he brought me by way of the north gate to the front of the temple, and I looked, and the glory of the Lord filled the temple of the Lord, and I fell upon my face. [5]The Lord said to me: "Mortal, mark well, look closely, and listen attentively to all that I shall tell you concerning all the ordinances of the temple of the Lord and all its laws, and mark well the entrances[m] to the temple and all the exits of the sanctuary. [6]Say to the rebellious house,[n] to the house of Israel: Thus says the Lord God: O house of Israel, let there be an end to all your abominations [7]in admitting foreigners, uncircumcised in heart and flesh, to be in my sanctuary, profaning my temple when you offer to me my food, the fat and the blood. You[o] have broken my covenant with all your abominations. [8]And you have not kept charge of my sacred offerings,

m 44.5 Syr Tg Vg: Heb *entrance*   n 44.6 Gk: Heb lacks *house*
o 44.7 Gk Syr Vg: Heb *They*

weeklong purification rituals required to make it an acceptable place for sacrifice. *Dashing blood against it*. See, for example, Lev. 1:5. The description of the rituals for the first day, which are more detailed, focuses on the use of the bull's blood as a purifying agent. There are no goat or ram offerings on the first day. **43:22–26** The rituals on days two through seven: offerings of a ram and a bull, along with salt. These whole burnt offerings were also purification offerings, thus removing anything profane or ritually unclean from the altar before a regular schedule of offerings could be instituted. **43:27** *When these days are over*, then the regular temple rituals could commence, including the daily, Sabbath, and new moon offerings.

44:1–31 This chapter resumes the narrative of God's settlement within the temple, followed immediately by the distribution of duties to the Levites and the Zadokites. **44:1** *The outer gate . . . that faces east . . . was shut* resumes the storyline of 43:5. Ezekiel is moved first to the east gate of the inner court through which God had entered the temple. That gate is now closed. **44:2** *This gate shall remain shut*, ensuring both that no danger to God's presence can enter the inner court and that God will never leave the sanctuary again. **44:3** *Only the prince* or royal leader can enter the gateway of the east gate, but he cannot go all the way through it. He must turn around and exit back into the outer court. He still gets the best "seat" in the temple of all laypersons but is not allowed into the inner court of the temple. **44:4** *He brought me by way of the north gate*. Ezekiel is in the inner court, but to leave that area, now that the east gate is closed, he must go to the north gate and circle back to the east entrances at the *front of the temple*. From that vantage point, he witnesses God's glory filling the sanctuary. **44:7** *Admitting foreigners*. The passage alludes to the sins committed in the previous temple. While idolatry is still among these violations, this chapter adds the utilization of nonqualified people to serve as priests. The *foreigners* here may be non-Israelites, or they could also

but you have appointed foreigners[p] to act for you in keeping my charge in my sanctuary.

9 "Thus says the Lord GOD: No foreigner, uncircumcised in heart and flesh, of all the foreigners who are among the people of Israel, shall enter my sanctuary. [10]But the Levites who went far from me, going astray from me after their idols when Israel went astray, shall bear their punishment. [11]They shall be ministers in my sanctuary, having oversight at the gates of the temple and serving in the temple; they shall slaughter the burnt offering and the sacrifice for the people, and they shall attend on them and serve them. [12]Because they ministered to them before their idols and made the house of Israel stumble into iniquity, therefore I have sworn concerning them, says the Lord GOD, that they shall bear their punishment. [13]They shall not come near to me, to serve me as priest, nor come near any of my sacred offerings, the things that are most sacred, but they shall bear their shame and the consequences of the abominations that they have committed. [14]Yet I will appoint them to keep charge of the temple, to do all its chores, all that is to be done in it.

15 "But the Levitical priests, the descendants of Zadok, who kept the charge of my sanctuary when the people of Israel went astray from me, shall come near to me to minister to me, and they shall attend me to offer me the fat and the blood, says the Lord GOD. [16]It is they who shall enter my sanctuary; it is they who shall approach my table to minister to me, and they shall keep my charge. [17]When they enter the gates of the inner court, they shall wear linen vestments; they shall have nothing of wool on them while they minister at the gates of the inner court and within the temple. [18]They shall have linen turbans on their heads and linen undergarments on their loins; they shall not bind themselves with anything that causes sweat. [19]When they go out into the outer court to the people, they shall remove the vestments in which they have been ministering and lay them in the holy chambers, and they shall put on other garments, so that they may not communicate holiness to the people with their vestments. [20]They shall not shave their heads or let their locks grow long; they shall only trim the hair of their heads. [21]No priest shall drink wine when he enters the inner court. [22]They shall not marry a widow or a divorced woman but only a virgin of the stock of the house of Israel or a widow who is the widow of a priest. [23]They shall teach my people the difference between the holy and the common and show them how to distinguish between the unclean and the clean. [24]In a dispute they shall act as judges, and they shall decide it according to my judgments. They shall keep my laws and my statutes regarding all my appointed festivals, and they shall keep my Sabbaths holy. [25]They shall not defile themselves by going near a dead person; for father or mother, however, and for son or daughter and for brother or unmarried sister they may defile themselves. [26]After he has become clean, they shall count seven days for him. [27]On the day that he goes into the holy place, into the inner court, to minister in the holy place, he shall offer his purification offering, says the Lord GOD.

28 "This shall be their inheritance: I am their inheritance, and you shall give them no holding in Israel; I am their holding. [29]They shall eat the grain offering, the purification

be Israelites outside the tribe of Levi. See v. 9 as well. *The fat and the blood.* These two items were always reserved for God. **44:9–14** Outlines the duties of the Levitical priests. Since these duties precluded them from entering the inner court, they had a lower status than the Zadokites. **44:10** *The Levites* begins a long section that distinguishes between Levitical and Zadokite priests. In ancient Israel, priesthood was hereditary. According to 1 Kgs. 1:34–35, David commissions Zadok to serve as a priest in anointing Solomon, a tradition that associates the Zadokite priests with the Davidic dynasty. That tradition also informs the hierarchy of priesthood here. **44:15–27** Lists the duties of the Zadokite priests who performed the rituals in the inner court. Because of that closeness to the sanctuary building, there are further restrictions on their clothing (linen to absorb sweat, vv. 17–19), hairstyle (20), alcohol consumption (21), spouse (22), and mourning rituals (25–27). In addition to burning the animal sacrifices, they also provide ritual instruction to the people at large, adjudicate some judgments, and maintain the ritual calendar, which was based in part on the movements of the moon (23–24). **44:28** *I am their inheritance.* These high-ranking priests lived with their families on temple-owned land. **44:29** *They shall eat* any sacrificial food that was not consumed by fire.

offering, and the guilt offering, and every devoted thing in Israel shall be theirs. ³⁰The first of all the first fruits of all kinds and every offering of all kinds from all your offerings shall belong to the priests; you shall also give to the priests the first of your dough, in order that a blessing may rest on your house. ³¹The priests shall not eat of anything, whether bird or animal, that died of itself or was torn by animals.

45 "When you allot the land as an inheritance, you shall set aside for the Lord a portion of the land as a holy district, twenty-five thousand cubits long and twenty*q* thousand cubits wide; it shall be holy throughout its entire extent. ²Of this, a square plot of five hundred by five hundred cubits shall be for the sanctuary, with fifty cubits for an open space around it. ³In the holy district you shall measure off a section twenty-five thousand cubits long and ten thousand wide, in which shall be the sanctuary, the most holy place. ⁴It shall be a holy portion of the land; it shall be for the priests who minister in the sanctuary and approach the Lord to minister to him, and it shall be both a place for their houses and a holy place for the sanctuary. ⁵Another section, twenty-five thousand cubits long and ten thousand cubits wide, shall be for the Levites who minister at the temple, as their holding for cities to live in.*r*

6 "Alongside the portion set apart as the holy district you shall assign as a holding for the city an area five thousand cubits wide and twenty-five thousand cubits long; it shall belong to the whole house of Israel.

7 "And to the prince shall belong the land on both sides of the holy district and the holding of the city, alongside the holy district and the holding of the city, on the west and on the east, corresponding in length to one of the tribal portions and extending from the western to the eastern boundary ⁸of the land. It is to be his property in Israel. And my princes shall no longer oppress my people, but they shall let the house of Israel have the land according to their tribes.

9 "Thus says the Lord God: Enough, O princes of Israel! Put away violence and oppression, and do what is just and right. Cease your evictions of my people, says the Lord God.

10 "You shall have honest balances, an honest ephah, and an honest bath.*s* ¹¹The ephah and the bath shall be of the same measure, the bath containing one-tenth of a homer and the ephah one-tenth of a homer; the homer shall be the standard measure. ¹²The shekel shall be twenty gerahs. Twenty shekels, twenty-five shekels, and fifteen shekels shall make a mina for you.

13 "This is the offering that you shall make: one-sixth of an ephah from each homer of wheat, and one-sixth of an ephah from each homer of barley, ¹⁴and as the fixed portion of oil*t* one-tenth of a bath*u* from each cor (the cor,*v* like the homer, contains ten baths), ¹⁵and one sheep from every flock of two hundred from the pastures of

q 45.1 Gk: Heb *ten*   *r* 45.5 Gk: Heb *as their holding, twenty chambers*   *s* 45.10 A Heb measure of volume   *t* 45.14 Cn: Heb *oil, the bath the oil*   *u* 45.14 A Heb measure of volume   *v* 45.14 Vg: Heb *homer*

44:30 *First fruits.* They also benefited from other offerings, such as thank offerings for harvests, and other votive gifts to the temple. **44:31** *Anything . . . that died of itself* seems out of place here. It is another prohibition for these priests.

45:1–46:25 A collection of ritual laws that cover a variety of topics. These start with the location of this visionary temple but move into an abbreviated ritual calendar, the responsibilities of nonpriestly persons for the sacrificial system, and a few remaining items pertaining to the layout of the temple complex. Some of these may have been expansions by later scribes as the sacrificial service was reinstated during the Persian period. **45:1–9** Bridges the description of the temple complex and the division of the nation in 47–48. These verses envision a temple separate from both the royal holdings and the city. The priestly families inhabit a buffer zone between holy and profane areas. **45:2** *For the sanctuary.* Actually, the whole temple complex, given the measurements in this verse. **45:6** *The city . . . shall belong to the whole house of Israel* as opposed to Jerusalem, which belonged to the tribe of Judah. This notice, along with the final verse of the book, clearly distinguishes between the old city of Jerusalem and this newly envisioned capital of the reunified tribes. **45:7** *To the prince shall belong the land on both sides* of the holy area. This proximity to the temple marks his elite status among the laity, but it also precludes a king's desire to acquire better landholdings. **45:10–12** Set up a nationwide standard for weight, volume, and monetary value. **45:13–18** Outline who provides for which offerings across the ritual calendar.

Israel. This is the offering for grain offerings, burnt offerings, and offerings of well-being, to make atonement for them, says the Lord God. ¹⁶All the people of the land shall join in making this offering in Israel through the prince. ¹⁷This shall be the obligation of the prince regarding the burnt offerings, grain offerings, and drink offerings, at the festivals, the new moons, and the Sabbaths, all the appointed festivals of the house of Israel: he shall provide the purification offerings, the grain offerings, the burnt offerings, and the offerings of well-being, to make atonement for the house of Israel.

18 "Thus says the Lord God: In the first month, on the first day of the month, you shall take a bull of the herd without blemish and purify the sanctuary. ¹⁹The priest shall take some of the blood of the purification offering and put it on the doorposts of the temple, the four corners of the ledge of the altar, and the posts of the gate of the inner court. ²⁰You shall do the same on the seventh day of the month for anyone who has sinned through error or ignorance; so you shall make atonement for the temple.

21 "In the first month, on the fourteenth day of the month, you shall celebrate the Festival of the Passover, and for seven days unleavened bread shall be eaten. ²²On that day the prince shall provide for himself and all the people of the land a bull for a purification offering. ²³And during the seven days of the festival he shall provide as a burnt offering to the Lord seven bulls and seven rams without blemish, on each of the seven days, and a male goat daily for a purification offering. ²⁴He shall provide as a grain offering an ephah for each bull, an ephah for each ram, and a hin of oil to each ephah. ²⁵In the seventh month, on the fifteenth day of the month and for the seven days of the festival, he shall make the same provision for purification offerings, burnt offerings, and grain offerings and for the oil.

46 "Thus says the Lord God: The gate of the inner court that faces east shall remain closed on the six working days, but on the Sabbath day it shall be opened, and on the day of the new moon it shall be opened. ²The prince shall enter by the vestibule of the gate from outside and shall take his stand by the post of the gate. The priests shall offer his burnt offering and his offerings of well-being, and he shall bow down at the entryway of the gate. Then he shall go out, but the gate shall not be closed until evening. ³The people of the land shall bow down at the entrance of that gate before the Lord on the Sabbaths and on the new moons. ⁴The burnt offering that the prince offers to the Lord on the Sabbath day shall be six lambs without blemish and a ram without blemish, ⁵and the grain offering with the ram shall be an ephah, and the grain offering with the lambs shall be as much as he wishes to give, together with a hin of oil to each ephah. ⁶On the day of the new moon he shall offer a bull of the herd without blemish and six lambs and a ram, which shall be without blemish; ⁷as a grain offering he shall provide an ephah with the bull and an ephah with the ram and with the lambs as much as he wishes, together with a hin of oil to each ephah. ⁸When the prince enters, he shall come in by the vestibule of the gate, and he shall go out by the same way.

9 "When the people of the land come before the Lord at the appointed festivals, whoever enters by the north gate to worship shall go out by the south gate, and whoever enters by the south gate shall go out by the north gate: they shall not return by way of the gate by which they entered but shall go out straight ahead. ¹⁰When they come in, the prince shall come in with them, and when they go out, he shall go out.

11 "At the festivals and the appointed seasons the grain offering with a bull shall be an ephah and with a ram an ephah and with the lambs as much as one wishes to give, together with a hin of oil to an ephah. ¹²When the prince provides a freewill offering, either a burnt offering or offerings of well-being as a freewill offering to the Lord, the gate facing

45:18–25 Describe the observance of only two of Israel's major holy days: New Year's and Passover. It is not clear if the text promotes the observance of only these two feast days or if the list is incomplete. The rituals for both feasts focus on purification rites. 46:1–8 Pays greater attention to the observation of the Sabbath, a weekly holy day. In 46:1–15, the laws describe what the laity must do on each occasion. 46:9–10 Describe how the laity should move through the outer court. 46:11–15 Gives a brief overview of which elements of a sacrifice were the responsibility of the prince and which of the

east shall be opened for him, and he shall offer his burnt offering or his offerings of well-being as he does on the Sabbath day. Then he shall go out, and after he has gone out the gate shall be closed.

13 "You shall provide a lamb, a yearling, without blemish, for a burnt offering to the LORD daily; morning by morning you shall provide it. [14]And you shall provide a grain offering with it morning by morning regularly, one-sixth of an ephah and one-third of a hin of oil to moisten the choice flour, as a grain offering to the LORD; this is the ordinance for all time. [15]Thus the lamb and the grain offering and the oil shall be provided, morning by morning, as a regular burnt offering.

16 "Thus says the Lord GOD: If the prince makes a gift to any of his sons out of his inheritance,[w] it shall belong to his sons; it is their holding by inheritance. [17]But if he makes a gift out of his inheritance to one of his servants, it shall be his to the year of liberty; then it shall revert to the prince; only his sons may keep a gift from his inheritance. [18]The prince shall not take any of the inheritance of the people, thrusting them out of their holding; he shall give his sons their inheritance out of his own holding, so that none of my people shall be dispossessed of their holding."

19 Then he brought me through the entrance, which was at the side of the gate, to the north row of the holy chambers for the priests, and there I saw a place at the extreme western end of them. [20]He said to me, "This is the place where the priests shall boil the guilt offering and the purification offering and where they shall bake the grain offering, in order not to bring them out into the outer court and so communicate holiness to the people."

21 Then he brought me out to the outer court and led me past the four corners of the court, and in each corner of the court there was a court: [22]in the four corners of the court were small[x] courts, forty cubits long and thirty wide; the four were of the same size. [23]On the inside, around each of the four courts,[y] was a row of masonry, with hearths made at the bottom of the rows all around. [24]Then he said to me, "These are the kitchens where those who serve at the temple shall boil the sacrifices of the people."

47 Then he brought me back to the entrance of the temple; there water was flowing from below the entryway of the temple toward the east (for the temple faced east), and the water was flowing down from below the south side of the temple, south of the altar. [2]Then he brought me out by way of the north gate and led me around on the outside to the outer gate that faces toward the east,[z] and the water was trickling out on the south side.

3 Going on eastward with a cord in his hand, the man measured one thousand cubits and then led me through the water, and it was ankle-deep. [4]Again he measured one thousand and led me through the water, and it was knee-deep. Again he measured one thousand and led me through the water, and it was up to the waist. [5]Again he measured one thousand, and it was a river that I could not cross, for the water had risen; it was deep enough to swim in, a river that could not be crossed. [6]He said to me, "Mortal, have you seen this?"

Then he led me back along the bank of the river. [7]As I came back, I saw on the bank of the river a great many trees on the one side and

w 46.16 Gk: Heb *it is his inheritance*   x 46.22 Gk Syr Vg: Meaning of Heb uncertain   y 46.23 Heb *the four of them*   z 47.2 Meaning of Heb uncertain

people. **46:16–18** Attempt to preserve the property belonging to the royal family. The *prince* cannot gift inheritable items to nonfamily members. Similarly, the prince cannot take ancestral property from any other Israelite family. **46:19–24** Ends this section of the laws by returning to the temple complex, describing the locations of ovens and hearths for the preparation of other offerings.

47:1–12 In Ezekiel's final scene, he goes on another tour with his heavenly guide, this time outside of the temple complex into the bountiful land. Ezekiel is led through the waters of a miraculous river that makes the lands south of the temple into a type of new Eden. **47:1** *The entrance of the temple.* Probably the sanctuary building, since Ezekiel proceeds from here to the outer court and then outside the temple complex. *Flowing . . . south.* Although the river leaves through the east gate, it flows south from there. **47:3** *Cord* or measuring stick to measure the buildings. This records the increasing depth of the river. **47:5** *A river that could not be crossed.* Until this point, Ezekiel has been walking through the river. **47:6** *Have you seen this?* can also be translated as "Do you see?" *He led me . . . along the bank* now that the water was too deep for Ezekiel to walk through. **47:7** *A great many trees*

Going Deeper: Minecraft, the Temple, and Spatial Icons (Ezekiel 40–48)

Readers of the book of Ezekiel have long struggled to agree on the purpose of the temple tour in chaps. 40–48. Is it a blueprint for a rebuilt temple? The command for the prophet to write it down seems to suggest so, but the details become uncreatable. Is it a vision of Ezekiel having been transported into a heavenly edifice? That would make sense of the perfections and miraculous elements but does not accord with the command to hold the people responsible for following what Ezekiel writes.

When we look for contemporary parallels to Ezekiel's architectural utopia, a new way to appreciate this material arises. One of the most popular franchises in video games has been *Minecraft*, a virtual version of Legos giving the builder's avatar the ability to walk through the created spaces. A visit to Legoland or a browse through *Minecraft* sites reveals the overwhelming effort put into these miniaturized virtual spaces.

Ezekiel 40–48 is a virtual version of the temple. Like a *Minecraft* re-creation of a physical space—for instance, the Eiffel Tower—the re-creation attempts enough resonance with the original to be recognizable. But the artist also tries to evoke the emotion(s) tied to that space: perhaps awe in this version. Rituals often create virtual spaces that vary depending on the goal of the ritual. During Holy Week in a Catholic church, for example, the interior of the church transforms from the streets of Jerusalem on Palm Sunday to the upper room on Holy Thursday, the site of the cross on Good Friday, and the joy of the empty tomb on Easter Sunday. In a more general context, the virtual space of a wedding differs from that of a funeral even if it occurs in the same physical location.

Ezekiel 40–48 requires the reader to enter the tour of the temple alongside Ezekiel with the appropriate suspension of disbelief. Smell the meat roasting on the sacrificial fire, feel your leg muscles as you mount the final stairs into the inner court, and feel the coolness of the water as you walk in the non-Dead Sea. What the text tells the audience, then, is that the virtual *is* the reality.

Corrine L. Carvalho

on the other. [8]He said to me, "This water flows toward the eastern region and goes down into the Arabah, and when it enters the sea, the sea of stagnant waters, the water will become fresh. [9]Wherever the river goes,[a] every living creature that swarms will live, and there will be very many fish once these waters reach there. It will become fresh, and everything will live where the river goes. [10]People will stand fishing beside the sea[b] from En-gedi to En-eglaim; it will be a place for the spreading of nets; its fish will be of a great many kinds, like the fish of the Great Sea. [11]But its swamps and marshes will not become fresh; they are to be left for salt. [12]On the banks, on both sides of the river, there will grow all kinds of trees for food. Their leaves will not wither nor their fruit fail, but they will bear fresh fruit every month, because the water for them flows from the sanctuary. Their fruit will be for food and their leaves for healing."

13 Thus says the Lord God: These are the boundaries by which you shall divide the land for inheritance among the twelve tribes of Israel. Joseph shall have two portions. [14]You shall divide it equally; I swore to give it to your ancestors, and this land shall fall to you as your inheritance.

15 This shall be the boundary of the land: On the north side, from the Great Sea by way of Hethlon to Lebo-hamath and on to Zedad,[c] [16]Berothah, Sibraim (which lies between the border of Damascus and the border of Hamath), as far as Hazer-hatticon, which is on the border of Hauran. [17]So the boundary shall run from the sea to Hazar-enon, which

a 47.9 Gk Syr Vg Tg: Heb *the two rivers go*   b 47.10 Heb *it*
c 47.15 Gk: Heb *Lebo-zedad,* [16]*Hamath*

represent the magical properties of the temple-based water. The image of lushness in this part of the vision continues through v. 12. **47:8** *Arabah*, or the dry land south of Jerusalem. *The sea of stagnant waters*, or the Dead Sea, the lowest point on earth and the saltiest body of water. **47:9** *Wherever the river goes.* Its waters and its banks teem with life and abundance. **47:10** *The Great Sea*, or the Mediterranean. **47:11** *Its swamps and marshes . . . are to be left for salt*, which was required as part of the sacrifices (43:24). **47:12** *Fresh fruit every month* symbolizes the utopian element of this vision. *Leaves for healing.* Every part of these trees is life-giving. Ezekiel's tour ends here; what follows is divine speech outlining the boundaries of the country and each tribe.

47:13–23 The chapter moves to the outer boundaries of the nation of Israel as a whole. The most notable element in this plan is that none of the land east of the Jordan River is included in Israel's

is north of the border of Damascus, with the border of Hamath to the north.[d] This shall be the north side.

18 On the east side, between Hauran and Damascus; along the Jordan between Gilead and the land of Israel; to the eastern sea and as far as Tamar.[e] This shall be the east side.

19 On the south side, it shall run from Tamar as far as the waters of Meribath-kadesh, from there along the Wadi of Egypt[f] to the Great Sea. This shall be the south side.

20 On the west side, the Great Sea shall be the boundary to a point opposite Lebo-hamath. This shall be the west side.

21 So you shall divide this land among you according to the tribes of Israel. [22]You shall allot it as an inheritance for yourselves and for the aliens who reside among you and have fathered children among you. They shall be to you as native-born of Israel; with you they shall be allotted an inheritance among the tribes of Israel. [23]In whatever tribe aliens reside, there you shall assign them their inheritance, says the Lord GOD.

48

These are the names of the tribes: Beginning at the northern border, on the Hethlon road,[g] to Lebo-hamath, as far as Hazar-enon (which is on the border of Damascus, with Hamath to the north), and[h] extending from the east side to the west,[i] Dan, one portion. [2]Adjoining the territory of Dan, from the east side to the west, Asher, one portion. [3]Adjoining the territory of Asher, from the east side to the west, Naphtali, one portion. [4]Adjoining the territory of Naphtali, from the east side to the west, Manasseh, one portion. [5]Adjoining the territory of Manasseh, from the east side to the west, Ephraim, one portion. [6]Adjoining the territory of Ephraim, from the east side to the west, Reuben, one portion. [7]Adjoining the territory of Reuben, from the east side to the west, Judah, one portion.

8 Adjoining the territory of Judah, from the east side to the west, shall be the portion that you shall set apart, twenty-five thousand cubits in width, and in length equal to one of the tribal portions, from the east side to the west, with the sanctuary in the middle of it. [9]The portion that you shall set apart for the LORD shall be twenty-five thousand cubits in length and twenty[j] thousand in width. [10]These shall be the allotments of the holy portion: the priests shall have an allotment measuring twenty-five thousand cubits on the northern side, ten thousand cubits in width on the western side, ten thousand in width on the eastern side, and twenty-five thousand in length on the southern side, with the sanctuary of the LORD in the middle of it. [11]As for the consecrated priests, the descendants[k] of Zadok who kept my charge, who did not go astray when the people of Israel went astray, as the Levites did, [12]they shall have a special portion from the holy portion of the land, a most holy place, adjoining the territory of the Levites. [13]Alongside the territory of the priests, the Levites shall have an allotment twenty-five thousand cubits in length and ten thousand in width. The whole length shall be twenty-five thousand cubits and the width twenty[l] thousand. [14]They shall not sell or exchange any of it; they shall not transfer this choice portion of the land, for it is holy to the LORD.

15 The remainder, five thousand cubits in width and twenty-five thousand in length, shall be for ordinary use for the city, for dwellings and for pasturelands. In the middle

d 47.17 Meaning of Heb uncertain   e 47.18 Compare Syr: Heb *you shall measure*   f 47.19 Heb lacks *of Egypt* g 48.1 Cn: Heb *by the side of the way*   h 48.1 Cn: Heb *and they shall be his*   i 48.1 Gk: Heb *the east side the west*   j 48.9 Cn: Heb *ten*   k 48.11 Heb ms Gk: MT *of the descendants* l 48.13 Gk: Heb *ten*

territory. **47:22** *The aliens who reside among you . . . shall be to you as native-born of Israel. Aliens* refers to the class of people who lived within the boundaries of Israel but were not among the landowners (those whose genealogies could be traced back to one of the founding members of the tribe). This statement that they shall inherit land continues the vision's utopian nature.

48:1–35 Describe the landholdings of each individual tribe, except for Levi, whose land was included in the description of the temple lands. Here the surprising element is that each tribe is accorded an equal rectangle of land, with six tribes to the north of the city and five to the south. On contemporary maps, such divisions may not look equal, since the width of the land would differ for each group, but this utopian vision may be assuming equal borders on the east and west as well. **48:1–7** Allocates land to Dan, Asher, Naphtali, Manasseh, Ephraim, Reuben, and Judah. **48:8–22** Recapitulates the landholdings of the capital city, the temple complex, and the priestly and

of it shall be the city, [16]and these shall be its dimensions: the north side four thousand five hundred cubits, the south side four thousand five hundred, the east side four thousand five hundred, and the west side four thousand five hundred. [17]The city shall have pasturelands: on the north two hundred fifty cubits, on the south two hundred fifty, on the east two hundred fifty, on the west two hundred fifty. [18]The remainder of the length alongside the holy portion shall be ten thousand cubits to the east and ten thousand to the west, and it shall be alongside the holy portion. Its produce shall be food for the workers of the city. [19]The workers of the city, from all the tribes of Israel, shall cultivate it. [20]The whole portion that you shall set apart shall be twenty-five thousand cubits square, that is, the holy portion together with the property of the city.

[21] What remains on both sides of the holy portion and of the property of the city shall belong to the prince. Extending from the twenty-five thousand cubits of the holy portion to the east border and westward from the twenty-five thousand cubits to the west border, parallel to the tribal portions, it shall belong to the prince. The holy portion with the sanctuary of the temple in the middle of it, [22]and the property of the Levites and of the city, shall be in the middle of that which belongs to the prince. The portion of the prince shall lie between the territory of Judah and the territory of Benjamin.

[23] As for the rest of the tribes: from the east side to the west, Benjamin, one portion. [24]Adjoining the territory of Benjamin, from the east side to the west, Simeon, one portion. [25]Adjoining the territory of Simeon, from the east side to the west, Issachar, one portion. [26]Adjoining the territory of Issachar, from the east side to the west, Zebulun, one portion. [27]Adjoining the territory of Zebulun, from the east side to the west, Gad, one portion. [28]And adjoining the territory of Gad to the south, the boundary shall run from Tamar to the waters of Meribath-kadesh, from there along the Wadi of Egypt[m] to the Great Sea. [29]This is the land that you shall allot as an inheritance among the tribes of Israel, and these are their portions, says the Lord God.

[30] These shall be the exits of the city: On the north side, which is to be four thousand five hundred cubits by measure, [31]three gates: the gate of Reuben, the gate of Judah, and the gate of Levi, the gates of the city being named after the tribes of Israel. [32]On the east side, which is to be four thousand five hundred cubits, three gates: the gate of Joseph, the gate of Benjamin, and the gate of Dan. [33]On the south side, which is to be four thousand five hundred cubits by measure, three gates: the gate of Simeon, the gate of Issachar, and the gate of Zebulun. [34]On the west side, which is to be four thousand five hundred cubits, three gates:[n] the gate of Gad, the gate of Asher, and the gate of Naphtali. [35]The circumference of the city shall be eighteen thousand cubits. And the name of the city from that time on shall be, The Lord Is There.

m 48.28 Heb lacks *of Egypt*   n 48.34 Heb ms Gk Syr: MT *their gates three*

princely lands. Cf. 45:1–9. **48:23–28** Lists the holdings of Benjamin, Simeon, Issachar, Zebulun, and Gad. **48:30–35** Returns to the description of the city (as opposed to the temple complex). Each of the gates on the four sides of the city is named for Israelite tribes. **48:35** *The circumference* suggests a round city, as opposed to the perfectly square temple complex. *The name of the city . . . shall be, The Lord Is There*, pronounced "YHWH-shamah." In this vision, then, the city of Jerusalem is not restored. It is replaced with a city in proper alignment with the temple. See **"Minecraft, the Temple, and Spatial Icons," p. 1197.**

DANIEL

Historical Background

In 587 BCE, King Nebuchadnezzar destroyed Jerusalem and exiled many residents of Judah to Babylon. Some Judahites fled elsewhere in the Mediterranean region, starting a widespread network of Jewish communities. Despite pressures to assimilate, Jewish identity survived. This persistence of minoritized ethnic identity across a geographic expanse is called a "diaspora" (see **"Diaspora,"** **p. 1338**). When the Persian Empire later conquered the ancient Near East (see **"Cyrus," p. 991**), communities of Diaspora Jews were flourishing as mercenaries, traders, farmers, and bureaucrats.

Diasporic Jewish scribes wrote and collected stories of virtuous Jews surviving in the dominant culture while retaining their distinct cultural and religious identities, despite threats to their existence. These stories, called "court tales," include Dan. 1–6, Esther, Joseph (Gen. 37–50), and Nehemiah. They depict the particular struggles of displaced peoples by following the tumultuous careers of Jews in the courts of foreign kings. In them, Jewish exemplars demonstrate successful strategies for negotiating their identities with integrity and loyalty.

In the wake of Alexander the Great's conquest and sudden death in 323 BCE, his generals divided his territory. The ensuing century was tumultuous: wars raged throughout Palestine between the Seleucid Empire, which ruled Alexander's former territories stretching from present-day Afghanistan to Syria and Turkey, and the Ptolemaic Empire, which controlled Egypt. Jerusalem was often involved in severe fighting. Around 300 BCE, Mesopotamian Jews edited Daniel in an attempt to offer a new theological perspective on the rapidly changing situation. They predicted God's direct intervention in the chaos that followed Alexander's death and asserted YHWH's authority over foreign empires (see **"Four Kingdoms," p. 1205**).

Around 200 BCE, the Seleucid Empire conquered Palestine and was welcomed by the inhabitants of Jerusalem as liberators. But in 175 BCE, a series of disputes arose concerning the appointment of the high priest and the establishment of Greek cultural and political institutions in Jerusalem (see **"The Bible in Its Ancient Contexts," pp. 2150–52**). Near 167 BCE, the Seleucid king, Antiochus IV, misinterpreted a violent conflict in Jerusalem between supporters of two rival claimants to the high priesthood as a rebellion against the Seleucid Empire. According to Jewish sources, Antiochus IV attacked Jerusalem, converted the city into a Greek-style *polis* (city), and settled a colony of foreign soldiers, giving them access to the temple to worship their gods. Antiochus IV then forced the residents of Judah to abandon their traditions (including circumcision, the worship of YHWH, and the reading of the Torah) and participate in Greek rituals and customs (1 Macc. 1:29–64). A popular revolt led by the Jewish Hasmonean family—Judah (nicknamed Maccabee, meaning "the Hammer"; see **"Judas Maccabeus," p. 1541**), Jonathan, and Simon—eventually succeeded in reconquering Jerusalem and rededicating the temple to YHWH in 164 BCE (see **"Hanukkah," p. 1544**). They established the Hasmonean dynasty, which ruled Israel until 63 BCE.

During the tumultuous years of 167–164 BCE, Jewish scribes living in Jerusalem updated Dan. 7 to reflect the new conflict and provide encouragement and support to the afflicted. They composed and edited three apocalyptic visions (see **"Apocalypse," p. 1216**), found in chaps. 8, 9, and 10–12. These visions were described as divine revelations to Daniel during the time of the exile, and they encouraged Jews suffering from oppression to remain steadfast in loyalty to God. Other Jews in Jerusalem supported open rebellion, but the authors of Dan. 7–12 believed that God would act decisively to end the conflict without human help (8:25). Chaps. 1 and 8–12 of Daniel are written in Hebrew, suggesting that near 167 BCE, Jewish scribes were relearning Hebrew as a way of reclaiming their ethnic and religious identity in response to Seleucid oppression.

Reading Guide

The book of Daniel is written in two different genres (court stories in chaps. 1–6 and apocalyptic visions in chaps. 7–12) and in two different languages (Ar. in 2:4–7:28 and Heb. in 1:1–2:4 and 8:1–12:13). The book also reflects two very different geographical locations and time periods (in Diaspora, 500–300 BCE; in Jerusalem, 167–164 BCE). Despite these differences, the book responds to

one question: How can a Jew survive as a conquered subject and yet retain identity, integrity, and faith in YHWH?

According to Dan. 1–6, God allowed Jerusalem and the Jewish people to be conquered by Babylon (1:2), and so God remains sovereign over the world even when the Jewish people do not have political sovereignty. These court tales encourage diasporic Jews to worship only the Jewish deity (3:18), to maintain distinctive practices of Jewish prayer (6:10), and to refuse to participate in anything that they perceive to be morally or religiously defiling (1:8). Jews may help the empire function (6:1–5), but they also have the opportunity to educate the empire about YHWH, which has potential impacts not only for Jews but for the world (4:35–37; 6:25–27). The foreign kings and their various responses to the Jewish faith are a primary focus of Dan. 1–6. Chaps. 1–4 in particular trace King Nebuchadnezzar's gradual recognition of the Jewish deity's power, while chap. 5 depicts King Belshazzar's contrasting failure. Taken together, chaps. 1–6 suggest that faithful Jews have the ability to affect the empire in positive ways, at times through example and at times through resistance. Through these stories, diasporic Jews were encouraged to protect themselves with shrewd political maneuvering (1:11–16) and to seek wisdom from YHWH, who grants special knowledge (2:17–19) and delivers the faithful from danger (6:20–23).

Chaps. 7–12 also focus on the nature of God's sovereignty over a world dominated by a foreign power, but the acute crisis of Antiochus IV's persecution of Jews in 167–164 BCE makes survival within the empire and its administrative system untenable. Hence, the apocalyptic visions tear it all down. While the authors of Dan. 7–12 rejected Seleucid rule over Jerusalem, they did not advocate for armed rebellion. Rather, they advocated a faithful posture of expectation, trusting that God would soon intervene decisively in world history, destroying Antiochus IV and the power of world empires before founding a new sovereign Jewish community (7:14, 26–27). Daniel 7–12 is the only apocalyptic text in the Hebrew Bible and is unique for its depiction of named angels (Gabriel in 8:16; 9:21; Michael in 10:13, 21; 12:1) and the resurrection of the righteous and the wicked (12:2–3; see **"Resurrection (Daniel)," p. 1224**).

Some ancient versions of the book of Daniel contained the stories of Susanna and Bel and the Dragon, as well as the additional poems of the Prayer of Azariah and the Song of the Three Jews (both in chap. 3, after v. 23), and strikingly different versions of the stories in chaps. 4–6. Today, Roman Catholic and Orthodox Christian communities include these stories and poems, whereas Jewish and Protestant Christian communities do not (see **"The Bible as a Collection," pp. 2145–47**, and **"Canon (2 Esdras)," p. 1677**). Among the Dead Sea Scrolls are additional materials telling stories related to Daniel, demonstrating ancient forms of scriptural composition and interpretation. Many early Jews and Christians understood Daniel to be a prophet; in the Christian canon, Daniel is the last of the major prophetic books. In the Jewish canon, Daniel is found in the Writings, among other stories of Diaspora.

Brennan Breed

1 In the third year of the reign of King Jehoiakim of Judah, King Nebuchadnezzar of Babylon came to Jerusalem and besieged it. ²The Lord gave King Jehoiakim of Judah into his power, as well as some of the vessels of the house of God. These he brought to the land of Shinar,ᵃ and he placed the vessels in the treasury of his gods.

3 Then the king commanded his palace master Ashpenaz to bring some of the Israelites of the royal family and of the nobility: ⁴young men without physical defect and handsome, versed in every branch of wisdom, endowed with knowledge and insight, and competent to serve in the king's palace; they were to be taught the literature and language of the Chaldeans. ⁵The king assigned them a daily portion of the royal rations of food and wine. They were to be educated for three years, so that at the end of that time they could be stationed in the king's court. ⁶Among them were Daniel, Hananiah, Mishael, and Azariah, from the tribe of Judah. ⁷The palace master gave them other names: Daniel he called Belteshazzar, Hananiah he called Shadrach, Mishael he called Meshach, and Azariah he called Abednego.

8 But Daniel resolved that he would not defile himself with the royal rations of food and wine, so he asked the palace master to allow him not to defile himself. ⁹Now God granted Daniel favor and compassion from the palace master. ¹⁰The palace master said to Daniel, "I am afraid of my lord the king; he has appointed your food and your drink. If he should see you in poorer condition than the other young men of your age, you would endanger my head with the king." ¹¹Then Daniel asked the guard whom the palace master had appointed over Daniel, Hananiah, Mishael, and Azariah: ¹²"Please test your servants for ten days. Let us be given vegetables to eat and water to drink. ¹³You can then compare our appearance with the appearance of the young men who eat the royal rations and deal with your

a 1.2 Gk: Heb adds *to the house of his own gods*

1:1–21 Introduction. Daniel and his three companions are deportees working in the court of King Nebuchadnezzar of Babylon after the destruction of Jerusalem. The exile challenged much of ancient Israelite religious thought and practice, and Dan. 1–6 offers a theological, ritual, and ethical response focusing on the sovereignty, wisdom, and faithfulness of the Jewish God. **1:1** *Third year of . . . King Jehoiakim.* The year 606 BCE, but Nebuchadnezzar was not king until 605 and only captured Jerusalem in 597. This verse attempts to reconcile older sources with different dates (2 Chr. 36:5–7; 2 Kgs. 24). **1:2** *The Lord gave.* God decided to place Jerusalem under Nebuchadnezzar's power and so remains sovereign. Sin is not here named as a cause of the exile (see 2 Kgs. 24:1–4). *Vessels.* Precious items used in temple worship, representing the presence of the deity. Seizing them symbolized God's submission to the victorious gods of Babylon. *Shinar.* Babylon. **1:3** *Palace master* designates a high-ranking official, sometimes a eunuch, working in the court of a king (Esth. 1:10; see **"Eunuchs," p. 672**). Daniel and his companions are from the *royal family* or the *nobility* (see Isa. 39:7). **1:4** *Without physical defect.* Required of both priests and sacrificial animals, symbolizing purity (Lev. 21:17–23; 22:19–21); also reflects the seeming perfection of the royal court. *Chaldeans* often refers to Babylonians in general, but here, specialized omen interpreters and diviners. **1:5** *Portion.* A Persian term for distributing prized *royal rations* to ensure loyalty. **1:6–7** The youth have both Hebrew and foreign names, like Hadassah is Esther (Esth. 2:7) and Joseph is Zaphenath-paneah (Gen. 41:45). The new names mark their high status and their need to conform to dominant cultural expectations. The Jewish youth negotiate the tensions of living double identities within a system of foreign power. **1:8** The youth accept Babylonian education, language, names, and positions in the royal court (see Jer. 29:1–14), but Daniel rejects royal food. *Resolved* is the same Hebrew word as "gave" in v. 7; Ashpenaz "sets" new names on them, but Daniel "sets" his intention not to *defile* himself. *Defile* refers to ritual impurity, not cleanliness or moral concerns. Certain animals may not be eaten, according to Lev. 11, dietary regulations that form the basis of later kosher rules. Postexilic Jews had a wide array of opinions about eating Gentile food (see Esth. 5:4–8; Tob. 1:10–11). **1:10** The *palace master* Ashpenaz does not outright grant Daniel's request; Ashpenaz subtly hints that he will not get involved if Daniel remains healthy. **1:11** Daniel asks the low-level *guard*, not Ashpenaz, to withhold the food. **1:12** *Vegetables* (literally "seeds") and *water*. A diet presumed to lead to languishing compared to meat and wine. Daniel's thriving is attributed to divine intervention.

servants according to what you observe." ¹⁴So he agreed to this proposal and tested them for ten days. ¹⁵At the end of ten days it was observed that they appeared better and fatter than all the young men who had been eating the royal rations. ¹⁶So the guard continued to withdraw their royal rations and the wine they were to drink and gave them vegetables. ¹⁷To these four young men God gave knowledge and skill in every aspect of literature and wisdom; Daniel also had insight into all visions and dreams.

18 At the end of the time that the king had set for them to be brought in, the palace master brought them into the presence of Nebuchadnezzar, ¹⁹and the king spoke with them. Among them all, no one was found to compare with Daniel, Hananiah, Mishael, and Azariah; therefore they were stationed in the king's court. ²⁰In every matter of wisdom and understanding concerning which the king inquired of them, he found them ten times better than all the magicians and enchanters in his whole kingdom. ²¹And Daniel continued there until the first year of King Cyrus.

2 In the second year of Nebuchadnezzar's reign, Nebuchadnezzar dreamed such dreams that his spirit was troubled and his sleep left him. ²So the king commanded that the magicians, the enchanters, the sorcerers, and the Chaldeans be summoned to tell the king his dreams. When they came in and stood before the king, ³he said to them, "I have had such a dream that my spirit is troubled by the desire to understand it." ⁴The Chaldeans said to the king (in Aramaic),ᵇ "O king, live forever! Tell your servants the dream, and we will reveal the interpretation." ⁵The king answered the Chaldeans, "This is a public decree: if you do not tell me both the dream and its interpretation, you shall be torn limb from limb, and your houses shall be laid in ruins. ⁶But if you do tell me the dream and its interpretation, you shall receive from me gifts and rewards and great honor. Therefore tell me the dream and its interpretation." ⁷They answered a second time, "Let the king first tell his servants the dream, then we can give its interpretation." ⁸The king answered, "I know with certainty that you are trying to gain time because you see the decree from me is firm: ⁹if you do not tell me the dream, there is but one verdict for you. You have agreed to speak lying and misleading words to me until things take a turn. Therefore, tell me the dream, and I shall know that you can give me its interpretation." ¹⁰The Chaldeans answered the king, "There is no one on earth who can reveal what the king demands! In fact, no king, however great and powerful, has ever asked such a thing of any magician or enchanter or Chaldean. ¹¹The thing that the king is asking is too difficult, and no one can reveal it to the king except the gods, whose dwelling is not with mortals."

b 2.4 The text from this point through 7.28 is in Aramaic

1:14–15 Perhaps the earliest known use of comparing a control group with an experimental group. 1:16 The *guard* keeps the valuable *royal rations* in exchange for his cooperation. 1:20 *Magicians.* Skilled dream interpreters (2:2; Gen. 41:8) and miracle workers (Exod. 8:18–19). *Enchanters.* Exorcists who healed the sick through incantations.

2:1 *Second year of Nebuchadnezzar's reign.* The year 604 BCE, which conflicts with the three-year period mentioned in 1:5. The scribes responsible for compiling Dan. 1–6 did not synthesize the various timelines.

2:2 *Magicians . . . enchanters.* See note on 1:20. *Chaldeans.* See note on 1:4. *To tell the king his dreams.* Certain ancient experts in omen reading were trained in dream interpretation, but there are no examples of ancient scholars guessing the content of dreams.

2:4 *Aramaic.* A scribal note indicating that the text shifts to Aramaic from Hebrew; it will remain in Aramaic until 8:1. Aramaic was the administrative language of the Persian Empire, in which these stories were composed.

2:5–7 The Chaldeans misunderstood the king's request, but Nebuchadnezzar devises a deadly contest to make sure the Chaldeans are not tricking him (literally "You will be made into pieces and your houses into public latrines").

2:8 *Gain time.* Not "stall" but rather "gain the upper hand."

2:10–11 The nervous Chaldeans ironically reveal that power and knowledge belong only to the divine.

12 Because of this the king flew into a violent rage and commanded that all the wise men of Babylon be destroyed. [13]The decree was issued, and the wise men were about to be executed, and they looked for Daniel and his companions, to execute them. [14]Then Daniel responded with prudence and discretion to Arioch, the king's chief executioner, who had gone out to execute the wise men of Babylon; [15]he asked Arioch, the royal official, "Why is the decree of the king so urgent?" Arioch then explained the matter to Daniel. [16]So Daniel went in and requested that the king give him time and he would tell the king the interpretation.

17 Then Daniel went to his home and informed his companions, Hananiah, Mishael, and Azariah, of the matter [18]and told them to seek mercy from the God of heaven concerning this mystery, so that Daniel and his companions might not perish with the rest of the wise men of Babylon. [19]Then the mystery was revealed to Daniel in a vision of the night, and Daniel blessed the God of heaven.

[20] Daniel said:

"Blessed be the name of God from age
   to age,
   for wisdom and power are his.
[21] He changes times and seasons,
   deposes kings and sets up kings;
he gives wisdom to the wise
   and knowledge to those who have
      understanding.
[22] He reveals deep and hidden things;
   he knows what is in the darkness,
   and light dwells with him.
[23] To you, O God of my ancestors,
   I give thanks and praise,
for you have given me wisdom and
   power

and have now revealed to me what
   we asked of you,
for you have revealed to us what the
   king ordered."

24 Therefore Daniel went to Arioch, whom the king had appointed to destroy the wise men of Babylon, and said to him, "Do not destroy the wise men of Babylon; bring me in before the king, and I will give the king the interpretation."

25 Then Arioch quickly brought Daniel before the king and said to him: "I have found among the exiles from Judah a man who can tell the king the interpretation." [26]The king said to Daniel, whose name was Belteshazzar, "Are you able to tell me the dream that I have seen and its interpretation?" [27]Daniel answered the king, "No wise men, enchanters, magicians, or diviners can show to the king the mystery that the king is asking, [28]but there is a God in heaven who reveals mysteries, and he has disclosed to King Nebuchadnezzar what will happen at the end of days. Your dream and the visions of your head as you lay in bed were these: [29]To you, O king, as you lay in bed, came thoughts of what would be hereafter, and the revealer of mysteries disclosed to you what is to be. [30]But as for me, this mystery has not been revealed to me because of any wisdom that I have more than any other living being, but in order that the interpretation may be known to the king and that you may understand the thoughts of your mind.

31 "You were looking, O king, and there appeared a great statue. That statue was huge, its brilliance extraordinary; it was standing before you, and its appearance was frightening. [32]The head of that statue was of fine gold, its chest and arms of

---

2:13–23 Discrepancies among vv. 1–12, 13–23, and 24–30 suggest that 13–23 are an addition; Daniel seems unknown to the king in v. 25. **2:14** *Prudence and discretion.* Daniel wisely interrupts the slaughter with his open-ended question in v. 15. **2:18** *God of heaven.* A Persian term that can refer equally to Israel's God and the Persian high god Ahuramazda (see Ezra 1:2; 5:12; Neh. 1:4; Jdt. 5:8). *Mystery.* A Persian term referring to cosmic secrets accessible only through divine revelation. **2:19** *Vision of the night.* A dream (see Gen. 46:2); Daniel redreams Nebuchadnezzar's dream. **2:20–23** This poetic prayer's themes are *wisdom* and *power*, which belong to and are dispensed by God alone.

2:24–25 See note on 2:13–23.

2:28 *End of days* initially meant "the future," but Hellenistic scribes later understood it to mean "the end of history," which led to an updating of Dan. 2 and the subsequent production of apocalyptic literature in Dan. 7.

2:31–33 This idol-like *statue* represents human kingdoms that are surprisingly weak, made of four metals of diminishing value, ending in *iron* mixed with baked *clay*.

Focus On: Four Kingdoms (Daniel 2 and 7)

People look for patterns in history to give meaning and order to the otherwise chaotic events of life. The authors of the book of Daniel sought to comprehend the dual crises of the exile (587 BCE) and the persecution of Antiochus IV (167 BCE) by generating new historical patterns, giving readers hope that God is sovereign despite the dominance of foreign empires.

In Dan. 2 and 7, Jewish scribes fashioned one of the most powerful, influential, and long-lasting historical patterns. They repurposed older Persian imperial propaganda that claimed to describe the history of the world as a sequence of three major empires, positioning the Persians as inevitable conquerors: first Assyria, then Media, then Persia. The propaganda effort was incredibly effective. Several Greek historians borrowed the schema to help structure their own histories, and it appears in Tob. 14:4. Roman historians borrowed this pattern, adding Alexander's Greek kingdom as a fourth power following Persia. The Romans interpreted their own rise as a continuation of Alexander's fourth kingdom. Daniel 2 and 7, however, adapted the four kingdoms pattern but changed the ending: divine judgment falls on the empires and God saves the oppressed.

After Constantine (ca. 330 CE), the Roman Empire understood itself as Daniel's fourth kingdom. When Rome fell in 476 CE, the Eastern Roman Empire declared itself the continuation of the fourth kingdom. Various western European kings starting with Charlemagne (ca. 800) argued that the fourth kingdom status had migrated to their local region, which explains why the "Holy Roman Empire" was a wholly German kingdom. France, England, Spain, and Portugal also claimed standing as the fourth kingdom, officially inheriting Rome's status as world ruler; rhetoric from Dan. 2 and 7 suffused the era of colonial exploration. When Constantinople fell to the Turkish army in 1453, the Russian kingdom claimed the title of the fourth kingdom. Even in the twenty-first century, the rhetoric of Dan. 2 and 7 pervades the propaganda and foreign policy of Vladimir Putin.

Persecuted peoples find a source of hope in Dan. 2 and 7. Jews like the eighth-century poet Pinhas the Priest, Monophysite Christians under Byzantine rule, the Black liberation activist Anna Julia Cooper, and the liberation theologian Pablo Richard all have interpreted Dan. 2 and 7 as an affirmation that divine power will one day overthrow the forces of imperialism and establish a new world of peace and equity.

Brennan Breed

silver, its midsection and thighs of bronze, [33]its legs of iron, its feet partly of iron and partly of clay. [34]As you looked on, a stone was cut out, not by human hands, and it struck the statue on its feet of iron and clay and broke them in pieces. [35]Then the iron, the clay, the bronze, the silver, and the gold were all broken in pieces and became like the chaff of the summer threshing floors, and the wind carried them away, so that not a trace of them could be found. But the stone that struck the statue became a great mountain and filled the whole earth.

[36] "That was the dream; now we will tell the king its interpretation. [37]You, O king, the king of kings—to whom the God of heaven has given the kingdom, the power, the might, and the glory, [38]into whose hand he has given human beings wherever they live, the wild animals of the field, and the birds of the air and whom he has established as ruler over them all—you are the head of gold. [39]After you shall arise another kingdom inferior to yours and yet a third kingdom of bronze, which shall rule over the whole earth. [40]And there shall be a fourth kingdom, strong as iron; just as iron crushes and smashes everything,[c] it shall crush and shatter all these. [41]As you saw the feet and toes partly of potter's clay and

c 2.40 Gk Theodotion Syr Vg: Aram adds *and like iron that crushes*

2:34 The *stone* was not crafted by *human hands*, suggesting divine involvement (Ps. 118:22).

2:35 *Chaff.* The inedible by-product of wheat cultivation (Isa. 41:15). *Great mountain.* Symbolic of God's sovereign power and presence (Deut. 32:4), as on Mount Zion (Isa. 2:2).

2:36–43 *Head of gold* represents Nebuchadnezzar's Neo-Babylonian Empire, succeeded by the *inferior* silver Median kingdom, then the *bronze* Persian Empire. The fourth *iron* empire represents the kingdom of Alexander the Great, which fractured after Alexander's death, represented by baked clay.

partly of iron, it shall be a divided kingdom, but some of the strength of iron shall be in it, as you saw the iron mixed with the clay. [42]As the toes of the feet were part iron and part clay, so the kingdom shall be partly strong and partly brittle. [43]As you saw the iron mixed with clay, so will they mix with one another in marriage,[d] but they will not hold together, just as iron does not mix with clay. [44]And in the days of those kings the God of heaven will set up a kingdom that shall never be destroyed, nor shall this kingdom be left to another people. It shall crush all these kingdoms and bring them to an end, and it shall stand forever, [45]just as you saw that a stone was cut from the mountain not by hands and that it crushed the iron, the bronze, the clay, the silver, and the gold. The great God has informed the king what shall be hereafter. The dream is certain and its interpretation trustworthy."

46 Then King Nebuchadnezzar fell on his face, worshiped Daniel, and commanded that a grain offering and incense be offered to him. [47]The king said to Daniel, "Truly, your God is God of gods and Lord of kings and a revealer of mysteries, for you have been able to reveal this mystery!" [48]Then the king promoted Daniel, gave him many great gifts, and made him ruler over the whole province of Babylon and chief prefect over all the wise men of Babylon. [49]Daniel made a request of the king, and he appointed Shadrach, Meshach, and Abednego over the affairs of the province of Babylon. But Daniel remained at the king's court.

3 King Nebuchadnezzar made a golden statue whose height was sixty cubits and whose width was six cubits; he set it up on the plain of Dura in the province of Babylon. [2]Then King Nebuchadnezzar sent for the satraps, the prefects, and the governors, the counselors, the treasurers, the justices, the magistrates, and all the officials of the provinces to assemble and come to the dedication of the statue that King Nebuchadnezzar had set up. [3]So the satraps, the prefects, and the governors, the counselors, the treasurers, the justices, the magistrates, and all the officials of the provinces assembled for the dedication of the statue that King Nebuchadnezzar had set up. When they were standing before the statue that Nebuchadnezzar had set up, [4]the herald proclaimed aloud, "You are commanded, O peoples, nations, and languages, [5]that when you hear the sound of the horn, pipe, lyre, trigon, harp, drum, and entire musical ensemble, you are to fall down and worship the golden statue that King Nebuchadnezzar has set up. [6]Whoever does not fall down and worship shall immediately be thrown into a furnace of blazing fire." [7]Therefore, as soon as all the peoples heard the sound of the horn, pipe, lyre, trigon, harp, drum,[e] and entire musical ensemble, all the peoples, nations, and languages fell down and worshiped the golden statue that King Nebuchadnezzar had set up.

8 Accordingly, at this time certain Chaldeans came forward and denounced the

d 2.43 Aram *by human seed*   e 3.7 Aram mss Gk Vg: MT lacks *drum*

2:44 *Kingdom* refers to either the Jewish God ruling the earth or a newly established Jewish kingdom (see 7:27).

2:47 *Your God* shows that Nebuchadnezzar does not identify with but respects Daniel's God. *Lord of kings* is a Persian title for universal sovereignty, and *revealer of mysteries* shows that Nebuchadnezzar recognizes the Jewish God's control of knowledge.

2:48–49 Daniel's rise to power is similar to Joseph's (Gen. 41:37–45).

3:1 The *golden statue* depicts either the king or a god; Jews considered bowing to either idolatrous. *Dura.* A generic place-name for any fortified enclosure, similar to "fort" in English.

3:2–5 Various lists appear in vv. 2–3, 4–5, 7, 10, 15, 21, which symbolize the completeness and universal control desired by Nebuchadnezzar but frustrated by God. **3:2** *Satraps.* Powerful regional governors in the Persian Empire. **3:4** *Peoples, nations, and languages.* The various ethnicities of Persian subjects demonstrate the empire's universal rule. **3:5** Some of the exotic instruments' names are taken from Greek (*lyre, harp,* and *drum*). *Fall down and worship.* Repeated in vv. 6, 11, 15. Diasporic Jews often accommodated themselves to dominant religious practices, but see Deut. 5:6–10.

3:6 Execution by burning and punishment for refusal to worship are exceedingly rare in the ancient world but heighten the drama and highlight the themes.

3:8 *Chaldeans.* See note on 1:4. *Denounced.* Literally "They ate the pieces," an attempt to destroy rivals.

Jews. ⁹They said to King Nebuchadnezzar, "O king, live forever! ¹⁰You, O king, have made a decree, that everyone who hears the sound of the horn, pipe, lyre, trigon, harp, drum, and entire musical ensemble, shall fall down and worship the golden statue, ¹¹and whoever does not fall down and worship shall be thrown into a furnace of blazing fire. ¹²There are certain Jews whom you have appointed over the affairs of the province of Babylon: Shadrach, Meshach, and Abednego. These men pay no heed to you, O king. They do not serve your gods, and they do not worship the golden statue that you have set up."

13 Then Nebuchadnezzar in furious rage commanded that Shadrach, Meshach, and Abednego be brought in, so they brought those men before the king. ¹⁴Nebuchadnezzar said to them, "Is it true, O Shadrach, Meshach, and Abednego, that you do not serve my gods and you do not worship the golden statue that I have set up? ¹⁵Now if you are ready, when you hear the sound of the horn, pipe, lyre, trigon, harp, drum, and entire musical ensemble, you should fall down and worship the statue that I have made. But if you do not worship, you shall immediately be thrown into a furnace of blazing fire, and who is the god who will deliver you out of my hands?"

16 Shadrach, Meshach, and Abednego answered the king, "O Nebuchadnezzar, we have no need to present a defense to you in this matter. ¹⁷If our God whom we serve is able to deliver us from the furnace of blazing fire and out of your hand, O king, let him deliver us.ᶠ ¹⁸But if not, be it known to you, O king, that we will not serve your gods

and we will not worship the golden statue that you have set up."

19 Then Nebuchadnezzar was so filled with rage against Shadrach, Meshach, and Abednego that his face was distorted. He ordered the furnace heated up seven times more than was customary ²⁰and ordered some of the strongest guards in his army to bind Shadrach, Meshach, and Abednego and to throw them into the furnace of blazing fire. ²¹So the men were bound, still wearing their tunics,ᵍ their trousers,ᵇ their hats, and their other garments, and they were thrown into the furnace of blazing fire. ²²Because the king's command was urgent and the furnace was so overheated, the raging flames killed the men who lifted Shadrach, Meshach, and Abednego. ²³But the three men, Shadrach, Meshach, and Abednego, fell down, bound, into the furnace of blazing fire.

24 Then King Nebuchadnezzar was astonished and rose up quickly. He said to his counselors, "Was it not three men that we threw bound into the fire?" They answered the king, "True, O king." ²⁵He replied, "But I see four men unbound, walking in the middle of the fire, and they are not hurt, and the fourth has the appearance of a god."ⁱ ²⁶Nebuchadnezzar then approached the door of the furnace of blazing fire and said, "Shadrach, Meshach, and Abednego, servants of the Most High God, come out! Come here!" So Shadrach, Meshach, and Abednego came out from the fire. ²⁷And the satraps, the prefects, the governors, and the king's counselors gathered together

ƒ 3.17 Or *If our God whom we serve is able to deliver us, he will deliver us from the furnace of blazing fire and out of your hand, O king.* g 3.21 Meaning of Aram uncertain h 3.21 Meaning of Aram uncertain i 3.25 Aram *a son of the gods*

3:12 *They do not serve.* A reference to the Jewish worship of one deity.

3:15 *Who . . . hands?* See 2 Kgs. 18:19–35, in which the Assyrian king asks the same ironically hubristic question and fails to conquer Jerusalem, and Deut. 32:39.

3:16–18 The three friends refuse to answer Nebuchadnezzar's question, and neither do they declare that their God will surely save them. Instead, their faith consists in respecting the sovereign power of God to choose to save them—or allow them to perish. Though Nebuchadnezzar reckons himself the universal sovereign, he is unable to make the friends *serve* his gods or *worship* the statue.

3:25 *A god.* Literally "like a son of the gods," or a lesser divine being that serves YHWH, known as "messengers" in Hebrew, later translated with the Greek word "angel." This figure approximates the "angel [or messenger] of the LORD" in Exod. 3:1–3 (see Gen. 16:7).

3:26 *Most High God.* A generic name for the most powerful deity, which could refer to the Jewish God (see Gen. 14:19–20).

and saw that the fire had not had any power over the bodies of those men; the hair of their heads was not singed, their tunics[j] were not scorched, and not even the smell of fire came from them. [28]Nebuchadnezzar said, "Blessed be the God of Shadrach, Meshach, and Abednego, who has sent his angel and delivered his servants who trusted in him. They disobeyed the king's command and yielded up their bodies rather than serve and worship any god except their own God. [29]Therefore I make a decree: Any people, nation, or language that utters blasphemy against the God of Shadrach, Meshach, and Abednego shall be torn limb from limb and their houses laid in ruins, for there is no other god who is able to deliver in this way." [30]Then the king promoted Shadrach, Meshach, and Abednego in the province of Babylon.

4 [k]King Nebuchadnezzar to all peoples, nations, and languages that live throughout the earth: May you have abundant prosperity! [2]The signs and wonders that the Most High God has worked for me I am pleased to recount.

[3] How great are his signs,
   how mighty his wonders!
His kingdom is an everlasting
      kingdom,
   and his sovereignty is from
      generation to generation.

4 [l]I, Nebuchadnezzar, was living at ease in my home and prospering in my palace. [5]I saw a dream that frightened me; my fantasies in bed and the visions of my head terrified me. [6]So I made a decree that all the wise men of Babylon should be brought before me, in order that they might tell me the interpretation of the dream. [7]Then the magicians, the enchanters, the Chaldeans, and the diviners came in, and I told them the dream, but they could not tell me its interpretation. [8]At last Daniel came in before me—he who was named Belteshazzar after the name of my god and who is endowed with a spirit of the holy gods[m]—and I told him the dream: [9]"O Belteshazzar, chief of the magicians, I know that you are endowed with a spirit of the holy gods[n] and that no mystery is too difficult for you. Hear[o] the dream that I saw, and tell me its interpretation.

[10] [p]Upon my bed this is what I saw:
   there was a tree at the center of the
      earth,
   and its height was great.
[11] The tree grew great and strong,
   its top reached to heaven,
   and it was visible to the ends of the
      whole earth.
[12] Its foliage was beautiful,
   its fruit abundant,
   and it provided food for all.
The animals of the field found shade
      under it,
   the birds of the air nested in its
      branches,
   and from it all living beings were
      fed.

j 3.27 Meaning of Aram uncertain   *k* 4.1 3.31 in Aram   *l* 4.4 4.1 in Aram   *m* 4.8 Or *a holy, divine spirit*   *n* 4.9 Or *a holy, divine spirit*   *o* 4.9 Theodotion: Aram *The visions of*   *p* 4.10 Theodotion Syr Compare Gk: Aram adds *The visions of my head*

3:29 Nebuchadnezzar threatens to kill anyone who blasphemes God—something the friends refused to do in v. 16, suggesting Nebuchadnezzar has more to learn.

4:1 A first-person proclamation from King Nebuchadnezzar (4:1–3) addressed to *all peoples, nations, and languages* (see note on 3:4) that seemingly confesses the sovereignty of the Jewish God (see note on 3:26).

4:2 *Signs and wonders* evokes the exodus tradition (see Exod. 7:3; Deut. 6:22).

4:4 The first-person dream report begins here. Nebuchadnezzar's *palace*; see v. 29.

4:7 *Magicians . . . enchanters . . . diviners.* See note on 1:20. *Chaldeans.* See note on 1:4.

4:8 *Belteshazzar.* See 1:7. *Spirit* here and in v. 9 describes Daniel's skill in dream interpretation, given by God; see v. 18.

4:9 *Mystery.* See note on 2:18.

4:10 The *tree at the center of the earth* refers to the ancient image of the cosmic tree, symbolizing the stability and flourishing of the world. The king was tasked with nourishing it, which meant ruling the kingdom wisely (see Ezek. 31; Isa. 10:33–11:5).

4:11 The tree symbolizes the strength but also the hubris of the king who claims to rule *the whole earth* (see Isa. 14:13–14; Ezek. 31:3; Gen. 11:4).

13 "I continued looking, in the visions of my head as I lay in bed, and there was a holy watcher coming down from heaven. [14]He cried aloud and said:

'Cut down the tree and chop off its
    branches;
    strip off its foliage and scatter its
    fruit.
Let the animals flee from beneath it
    and the birds from its branches.
[15] But leave its stump and roots in the
    ground,
    with a band of iron and bronze,
    in the tender grass of the field.
Let him be bathed with the dew of
    heaven,
    and let his lot be with the animals
    in the grass of the earth.
[16] Let his mind be changed from that of a
    human,
    and let the mind of an animal be
    given to him.
And let seven times pass over him.
[17] The sentence is rendered by decree of
    the watchers,
    the decision is given by order of the
    holy ones,
in order that all who live may know
    that the Most High is sovereign over
    the kingdom of mortals;
he gives it to whom he will
    and sets over it the lowliest of human
    beings.'

18 "This is the dream that I, King Nebuchadnezzar, saw. Now you, Belteshazzar, declare the interpretation, since all the wise men of my kingdom are unable to tell me the interpretation. You are able, however, for you are endowed with a spirit of the holy gods."[q]

19 Then Daniel, whose name was Belteshazzar, was severely distressed for a while. His thoughts terrified him. The king said, "Belteshazzar, do not let the dream or the interpretation terrify you." Belteshazzar answered, "My lord, may the dream be for those who hate you and its interpretation for your enemies! [20]The tree that you saw, which grew great and strong so that its top reached to heaven and was visible to the whole earth, [21]whose foliage was beautiful and its fruit abundant, and which provided food for all, under which animals of the field lived and in whose branches the birds of the air had nests—[22]it is you, O king! You have grown great and strong. Your greatness has increased and reaches to heaven, and your sovereignty to the ends of the earth. [23]And whereas the king saw a holy watcher coming down from heaven and saying, 'Cut down the tree and destroy it, but leave its stump and roots in the ground, with a band of iron and bronze, in the grass of the field, and let him be bathed with the dew of heaven, and let his lot be with the animals of the field, until seven times pass over him'—[24]this is the interpretation, O king, and it is a decree of the Most High that has come upon my lord the king: [25]You shall be driven away from human society, and your dwelling shall be with the wild animals. You shall be made to eat grass like oxen, you shall be bathed with the dew of heaven, and seven times shall pass over you, until you have learned that the Most High has sovereignty over the kingdom of mortals and gives it to whom he will. [26]As it was commanded to leave the stump and roots of the tree, your kingdom shall be reestablished for you from the time that you learn that Heaven is sovereign. [27]Therefore, O king, may my counsel be acceptable to you: atone for[r] your sins with righteousness and your iniquities with mercy to the oppressed, so that your prosperity may be prolonged."

q 4.18 Or a holy, divine spirit   r 4.27 Aram break off

4:13 Holy watcher. A divine servant of God (see note on 3:25; 8:13).

4:15 Stump and roots. Nebuchadnezzar will be left with some hope of renewal (see Isa. 11:1). Iron and bronze. Shackled Nebuchadnezzar will live outdoors, acting like the animals.

4:16 Nebuchadnezzar loses the power of human cognition and thinks with the mind of an animal for seven times, or seven years.

4:17 This verse summarizes the central claim of the book of Daniel (see Jer. 27:5–6).

4:26 Heaven here, and nowhere else in the Hebrew Bible, means "God" (see note on 4:37).

4:27 Righteousness typically means "behaving rightly" in the Hebrew Bible, but here it signifies almsgiving, as in mercy to the oppressed (see Tob. 4:5–10; Sir. 3:30). Here, atone is more literally translated as "break off," as in "chip away at some of your sins," to delay judgment.

28 All this came upon King Nebuchadnezzar. ²⁹At the end of twelve months he was walking on the roof of the royal palace of Babylon, ³⁰and the king said, "Is this not magnificent Babylon, which I have built as a royal capital by my mighty power and for my glorious majesty?" ³¹While the words were still in the king's mouth, a voice came down from heaven: "O King Nebuchadnezzar, to you it is declared: The kingdom is taken from you! ³²You shall be driven away from human society, and your dwelling shall be with the animals of the field. You shall be made to eat grass like oxen, and seven times shall pass over you, until you have learned that the Most High has sovereignty over the kingdom of mortals and gives it to whom he will." ³³Immediately the sentence was fulfilled against Nebuchadnezzar. He was driven away from human society, he ate grass like oxen, and his body was bathed with the dew of heaven, until his hair grew as long as eagles' feathers and his nails became like birds' claws.

34 When that period was over, I, Nebuchadnezzar, lifted my eyes to heaven, and my reason returned to me.

I blessed the Most High
and praised and honored the one
who lives forever.
For his sovereignty is an everlasting
sovereignty,
and his kingdom endures from
generation to generation.
³⁵ All the inhabitants of the earth are
accounted as nothing,

and he does what he wills with the
host of heaven
and the inhabitants of the earth.
There is no one who can stay his hand
or say to him, "What have you done?"
³⁶At that time my reason returned to me, and my majesty and splendor were restored to me for the glory of my kingdom. My counselors and my lords sought me out, I was reestablished over my kingdom, and still more greatness was added to me. ³⁷Now I, Nebuchadnezzar, praise and extol and honor the King of heaven,

for all his works are truth,
and his ways are justice;
he is able to bring low
those who walk in pride.

5 King Belshazzar made a great feast for a thousand of his lords, and he was drinking wine in the presence of the thousand.

2 Under the influence of the wine, Belshazzar commanded that they bring in the vessels of gold and silver that his father Nebuchadnezzar had taken out of the temple in Jerusalem, so that the king and his lords, his wives, and his concubines might drink from them. ³So they brought in the vessels of gold that had been taken out of the temple, the house of God in Jerusalem, and the king and his lords, his wives, and his concubines drank from them. ⁴They drank the wine and praised the gods of gold and silver, bronze, iron, wood, and stone.

4:29 *Twelve months.* Nebuchadnezzar delayed his judgment with almsgiving.

4:30 Nebuchadnezzar's pride in his architecture echoes ancient royal propaganda; he claims all *power* and *majesty* for himself, which triggers divine judgment.

4:33 *Hair* like *eagles' feathers* and *nails* like *birds' claws* signify both animal existence and ancient imagery of the dead in the underworld.

4:34 When the seven years are complete, Nebuchadnezzar looks upward to show his newfound knowledge of God's universal sovereignty. Then his human capacity for thought returns, and he praises God's *everlasting* reign (see vv. 1–3).

4:37 The only occurrence of the phrase *King of heaven* in the Hebrew Bible (see note on 4:26), but see related terms in the New Testament: "kingdom of heaven" (Matt. 3:2) and "kingdom of God" (Mark 1:15).

5:1 *Belshazzar* only temporarily ruled Babylon while his father, King Nabonidus, sojourned in the desert oasis of Tema from 553 to 543 BCE. It is unclear why Dan. 1–6 does not mention Nabonidus, who was Babylon's last king (see v. 31). *Thousand . . . lords* conveys the feast's immense size (see Esth. 1:1–8).

5:2 *Under the influence.* Belshazzar is intoxicated. *Vessels . . . temple.* See note on 1:2. Belshazzar disrespects the vessels by using them for banqueting. *Wives, and . . . concubines.* Women of different statuses living in the palace are present. Compare to Esth. 1:9.

5:4 *The gods of gold and silver . . . , and stone.* Condemning idol worship (see Deut. 4:28; Isa. 44:9–20; Jer. 10:3–5).

5 Immediately the fingers of a human hand appeared and began writing on the plaster of the wall of the royal palace, next to the lampstand. The king was watching the hand as it wrote. ⁶Then the king's face turned pale, and his thoughts terrified him. His limbs gave way, and his knees knocked together. ⁷The king cried aloud to bring in the enchanters, the Chaldeans, and the diviners, and the king said to the wise men of Babylon, "Whoever can read this writing and tell me its interpretation shall be clothed in purple, have a chain of gold around his neck, and rank third in the kingdom." ⁸Then all the king's wise men came in, but they could not read the writing or tell the king the interpretation. ⁹Then King Belshazzar became greatly terrified, and his face turned pale, and his lords were perplexed.

10 The queen, when she heard the discussion of the king and his lords, came into the banquet hall. The queen said, "O king, live forever! Do not let your thoughts terrify you or your face grow pale. ¹¹There is a man in your kingdom who is endowed with a spirit of the holy gods.ˢ In the days of your father he was found to have enlightenment, understanding, and wisdom like the wisdom of the gods. Your father, King Nebuchadnezzar, made him chief of the magicians, enchanters, Chaldeans, and diviners,ᵗ ¹²because an excellent spirit, knowledge, and understanding to interpret dreams, explain riddles, and solve problems were found in this Daniel, whom the king named Belteshazzar. Now let Daniel be called, and he will reveal the interpretation."

13 Then Daniel was brought in before the king. The king said to Daniel, "So you are Daniel, one of the exiles of Judah, whom my father the king brought from Judah? ¹⁴I have heard of you that a spirit of the godsᵘ is in you and that enlightenment, understanding, and excellent wisdom are found in you. ¹⁵Now the wise men, the enchanters, have been brought in before me to read this writing and tell me its interpretation, but they were not able to reveal the interpretation of the matter. ¹⁶But I have heard that you can give interpretations and solve problems. Now if you are able to read the writing and tell me its interpretation, you shall be clothed in purple, have a chain of gold around your neck, and rank third in the kingdom."

17 Then Daniel answered in the presence of the king, "Let your gifts be for yourself, or give your rewards to someone else! Nevertheless I will read the writing to the king and let him know the interpretation. ¹⁸As for you, O king, the Most High God gave your father Nebuchadnezzar kingship, greatness, glory, and majesty. ¹⁹And because of the greatness that he gave him, all peoples, nations, and languages trembled and feared before him. He killed those he wanted to kill, kept alive those he wanted to keep alive, honored those he wanted to honor, and degraded those he wanted to degrade. ²⁰But when his heart was lifted up and his spirit was hardened so that he acted proudly, he was deposed from his kingly throne, and his glory was stripped from him. ²¹He was driven from human society, and his mind was made like that of an animal. His dwelling was with the wild asses, he was fed grass like oxen, and his body was bathed with the dew of heaven, until he learned that the Most High God has sovereignty over the kingdom of mortals and

s 5.11 Or *a holy, divine spirit*   t 5.11 Aram adds *the king your father*   u 5.14 Or *a divine spirit*

5:5 A disembodied *hand* writes a message on the *plaster* wall. *Writing* was imbued with mysterious power in the ancient world; written curses and condemnations were feared.

5:6 *Limbs gave way.* Literally "The knots of his groin untied," either legs collapsing or uncontrolled excretion. "Untie knots" also means "solve riddles" and describes Daniel in v. 12.

5:7 Belshazzar thinks the writing is a cryptic divine message. *Enchanters . . . diviners.* See note on 1:20. *Chaldeans.* See note on 1:4. *Purple.* Reserved for elites. *Chain.* A sign of status; see Gen. 41:42.

5:9 Failure to understand an omen threatened the king's death or the destruction of the kingdom.

5:10 *Queen.* Possibly Belshazzar's wise mother or grandmother. She remembers court history, wields influence, and was absent from the festival, which was attended by Belshazzar's wives (see 5:2).

5:11 *Spirit.* See note on 4:8.

5:12 *Solve problems.* Literally "untie knots"; see note on 5:6.

5:17–21 See 4:22–33.

sets over it whomever he will. ²²And you, Belshazzar his son, have not humbled your heart, even though you knew all this! ²³You have exalted yourself against the Lord of heaven! The vessels of his temple have been brought in before you, and you and your lords, your wives, and your concubines have been drinking wine from them. You have praised the gods of silver and gold, of bronze, iron, wood, and stone, which do not see or hear or know, but the God in whose power is your very breath and to whom belong all your ways, you have not honored.

24 "So from his presence the hand was sent and this writing was inscribed. ²⁵And this is the writing that was inscribed: MENE,ᵛ TEKEL, and PARSIN. ²⁶This is the interpretation of the matter: MENE: God has numbered the days ofʷ your kingdom and brought it to an end; ²⁷TEKEL: you have been weighed on the scales and found wanting; ²⁸PERES:ˣ your kingdom is divided and given to the Medes and Persians."

29 Then Belshazzar gave the command, and Daniel was clothed in purple, a chain of gold was put around his neck, and a proclamation was made concerning him that he should rank third in the kingdom.

30 That very night Belshazzar, the Chaldean king, was killed. ³¹ʸAnd Darius the Mede received the kingdom, being about sixty-two years old.

6 ²It pleased Darius to set over the kingdom one hundred twenty satraps, stationed throughout the whole kingdom, ²and over them three administrators, one of whom was Daniel; to these the satraps gave account, so that the king might suffer no loss. ³Soon Daniel distinguished himself above the other administrators and satraps because an excellent spirit was in him, and the king planned to appoint him over the whole kingdom. ⁴So the administrators and the satraps tried to find grounds for complaint against Daniel in connection with the kingdom. But they could find no grounds for complaint or any corruption, because he was faithful, and no negligence or corruption could be found in him. ⁵The men said, "We shall not find any ground for complaint against this Daniel unless we find it in connection with the law of his God."

6 So the administrators and satraps conspired and came to the king and said to him, "O King Darius, live forever! ⁷All the administrators of the kingdom, the prefects and the satraps, the counselors and

v 5.25 Gk Vg: Aram reads MENE, MENE,   w 5.26 Aram lacks *the days of*   x 5.28 The singular of *Parsin*   y 5.31 6.1 in Aram   z 6.1 6.2 in Aram

5:25 Each word could be understood as either a weight or an action. MENE means "a mina" (500 g) and "to count." TEKEL means "a shekel" (8 g) and "to weigh." PARSIN means "half-minas" (250 g) and "to divide" but also sounds like "Persian."

5:26 *Numbered* in the sense of "set an endpoint" (see Ps. 90:12).

5:27 TEKEL also sounds like the Hebrew and Aramaic word "qelal," meaning "to be light," which Daniel adds to the interpretation.

5:28 Daniel uses both the verb "divide" and "Persia" to interpret PERES.

5:31 *Darius the Mede* is a fictional character. Cyrus the Persian ruled Media when he conquered Babylon in 539 BCE, and three Persian kings named Darius ruled after the time of Cyrus. The Medians were ruled by the Persians since 550 BCE.

6:1 *Darius.* See note on 5:31. *Satraps.* First established by Darius I; see note on 3:2. The number 120 is hyperbolic (see Esth. 1:1); Persians administered between twenty and thirty satrapies.

6:2 *Three administrators*, including Daniel (see 5:29), audit the satraps to limit mismanagement.

6:3 *Daniel distinguished himself* by identifying corruption and thus made many enemies who feared the king's plan to *appoint him over the whole kingdom. Spirit.* See note on 4:8.

6:4 A conspiracy of administrators digs for political dirt on Daniel but finds none.

6:5 The conspiracy believes that Daniel's vulnerability is his extreme faithfulness to the *law of his God*, which here means his religious commitments and practices rather than the written Torah. Like 3:8–12, minoritized religious fidelity that contrasts with the majority population seems like a weakness but is found, after testing, to be a core strength.

6:7 The courtiers propose an outlandish *ordinance*, or law, that contrasts with the "law" of Daniel's God (v. 5), creating a conflict of sovereignty. Throwing people into a *den of lions* is unprecedented as an ancient punishment; often, lions represent royal power.

the governors are agreed that the king should establish an ordinance and enforce an interdict, that whoever prays to any god or human, for thirty days, except to you, O king, shall be thrown into the den of lions. [8]Now, O king, establish the interdict and sign the document, so that it cannot be changed, according to the law of the Medes and the Persians, which cannot be revoked." [9]Therefore King Darius signed the document and interdict.

10 Although Daniel knew that the document had been signed, he continued to go to his house, which had windows in its upper room open toward Jerusalem, and to get down on his knees three times a day to pray to his God and praise him, just as he had done previously. [11]Then those men watched[a] and found Daniel praying and seeking mercy before his God. [12]Then they approached the king and said concerning the interdict, "O king! Did you not sign an interdict, that anyone who prays to any god or human, within thirty days, except to you, O king, shall be thrown into the den of lions?" The king answered, "The thing stands fast, according to the law of the Medes and Persians, which cannot be revoked." [13]Then they responded to the king, "Daniel, one of the exiles from Judah, pays no attention to you, O king, or to the interdict you have signed, but he is saying his prayers three times a day."

14 When the king heard the charge, he was very much distressed. He was determined to save Daniel, and until the sun went down he made every effort to rescue him. [15]Then the conspirators came to the king and said to him, "Know, O king, that it is a law of the Medes and Persians that no interdict or ordinance that the king establishes can be changed."

16 Then the king gave the command, and Daniel was brought and thrown into the den of lions. The king said to Daniel, "May your God, whom you faithfully serve, deliver you!" [17]A stone was brought and laid on the mouth of the den, and the king sealed it with his own signet ring and with the signet ring of his lords, so that nothing might be changed concerning Daniel. [18]Then the king went to his palace and spent the night fasting; no entertainment was brought to him, and sleep fled from him.

19 Then at dawn, the king got up and at first light hurried to the den of lions. [20]When he came near the den where Daniel was, he cried out anxiously to Daniel, "O Daniel, servant of the living God, has your God whom you faithfully serve been able to deliver you from the lions?" [21]Daniel then said to the king, "O king, live forever! [22]My God sent his angel and shut the lions' mouths so that they would not hurt me, because I was found blameless before him; also before you, O king, I have done no wrong." [23]Then the king was exceedingly glad and commanded that Daniel be taken up out of the den. So Daniel was taken up out of the den, and no kind of harm was found on him because he had trusted in his God. [24]The king gave a command, and those who had maliciously accused Daniel were brought and thrown into the den of lions—they, their children, and their wives. Before they reached the bottom of the den, the lions overpowered them and broke all their bones in pieces.

a 6.11 Gk Theodotion Syr: Aram *rushed in*

6:8 Persian kings did not issue laws *which cannot be revoked*, though the motif occurs in other stories to emphasize the power of written language and the inescapable limits on royal power (see Esth. 1:19; 3:8–10; 8:8–10).

6:10 Praying *toward Jerusalem* and, when in private, on one's *knees* became important after the exile (1 Kgs. 8:35–44, 54). Praying *three times a day* developed in the Second Temple period (Jdt. 9:1; Acts 3:1; m. Ber. 4:5).

6:18 *Fasting.* Religious abstention from food and pleasure to gain sympathy from a god; see also 9:3.

6:20 *Living God* contrasts with lifeless idols (see Josh. 3:10; Jer. 10:10). *Been able to deliver.* See 3:16–18.

6:22 *Angel.* See note on 3:25. Daniel insists on his *blameless* behavior with God and that he avoided *wrong* to the king, even if he did break the royal law.

6:24 The conspirators receive precisely what they devised for Daniel. Biblical texts are divided on the vicarious punishment of family members like *children* and *wives* (see Num. 16:27–33; Josh. 7:10–26; but Deut. 24:16; 2 Kgs. 14:6).

25 Then King Darius wrote to all peoples and nations of every language throughout the whole world: "May you have abundant prosperity! 26I make a decree, that in all my royal dominion people shall tremble and fear before the God of Daniel:

For he is the living God,
  enduring forever.
His kingdom shall never be destroyed,
  and his dominion has no end.
27 He delivers and rescues;
  he works signs and wonders in
    heaven and on earth;
  he has saved Daniel
    from the power of the lions."

28So this Daniel prospered during the reign of Darius and the reign of Cyrus the Persian.

7 In the first year of King Belshazzar of Babylon, Daniel had a dream and visions of his head as he lay in bed. Then he wrote down the dream:*b* 2I,*c* Daniel, saw in my vision by night the four winds of heaven stirring up the great sea, 3and four great beasts came up out of the sea, different from one another. 4The first was like a lion and had eagles' wings. Then, as I watched, its wings were plucked off, and it was lifted up from the ground and made to stand on two feet like a human being, and a human mind was given to it. 5Another beast appeared, a second one, that looked like a bear. It was raised up on one side, had three tusks*d* in its mouth among its teeth, and was told, "Arise, devour many bodies!" 6After this, as I watched, another appeared, like a leopard. The beast had four wings of a bird on its back and four heads, and dominion was given to it. 7After this I saw in the visions by night a fourth beast, terrifying and dreadful and exceedingly strong. It had great iron teeth and was devouring, breaking in pieces, and stamping what was left with its feet. It was different from all the beasts that preceded it, and it had ten horns. 8I was considering the horns when another horn appeared, a little one that came up among them. Three of the original horns were plucked up from before it. There were eyes like human eyes in this horn and a mouth speaking arrogantly.

9 As I watched,
  thrones were set in place,
    and an Ancient One*e* took his throne;

b 7.1 Q ms Theodotion: MT adds *the beginning of the words; he said*   *c 7.2* Theodotion: Aram *Daniel answered and said, I*   *d 7.5* Or *ribs*   *e 7.9* Aram *an Ancient of Days*

6:25–27 Darius praises the Jewish God as a universally sovereign God who *delivers* through *wonders* (see note on 4:2).

6:28 This verse concluded an early version of the book. Apocalyptic visions in Dan. 7–12 were added later. *Cyrus* conquered Babylon in 539 BCE and allowed Jewish exiles to return to Jerusalem (see Isa. 45:1).

7:1–12:13 Apocalyptic visions. Written mostly between the years of 167 and 164 BCE, during the persecutions of Antiochus IV in Jerusalem (see **"Apocalypse," p. 1216**).

7:1 Though 6:28 ends with King Cyrus of Persia sometime after 539 BCE, chap. 7 moves back to the *first year of King Belshazzar of Babylon* (see note on 5:1). Daniel *wrote down* the content as a first-person narration; writing and scribal identity are central themes in Dan. 7–12.

7:2 The *four winds of heaven* symbolize the cosmic totality of divine forces at work in creation (Gen. 1:2). The *great sea* often appears in ancient Near Eastern creation stories wherein a divine warrior destroys chaos monsters (see Job 26:12–13; Ps. 74:13–17; Isa. 27:1).

7:3 *Four great beasts.* Each beast represents a world empire (see Dan. 2 and **"Four Kingdoms," p. 1205**).

7:4 *First* is the Neo-Babylonian Empire (2:37–38). Mythological composite creatures such as a *lion* with *eagles' wings* were associated with divine power and presence. The humanization of the first beast refers to Nebuchadnezzar (see Dan. 4).

7:5 The *bear*like second beast refers to Media, a regional power absorbed into the Persian Empire in 550 BCE. *Raised up.* Poised to pounce. *Tusks.* Literally "ribs," the bones of its prey.

7:6 *Leopard.* Persia. *Four wings* and *four heads* represent the speed, vast expanse, and seemingly universal scope of Persia's rise to power. *Dominion* is the theme of the chapter: YHWH has allowed foreign powers to rule the world for a limited time.

7:7 The *fourth beast* is Alexander the Great's empire. *Ten horns* represent the rulers of the Seleucid Empire, the Greek state that ruled Judea after 200 BCE.

his clothing was white as snow
and the hair of his head like pure
wool;
his throne was fiery flames,
and its wheels were burning fire.
¹⁰ A stream of fire issued
and flowed out from his presence.
A thousand thousands served him,
and ten thousand times ten thousand
stood attending him.
The court sat in judgment,
and the books were opened.
¹¹I watched then because of the noise of the arrogant words that the horn was speaking. And as I watched, the beast was put to death and its body destroyed and given over to be burned with fire. ¹²As for the rest of the beasts, their dominion was taken away, but their lives were prolonged for a season and a time. ¹³As I watched in the night visions,

I saw one like a human being*ᶠ*
coming with the clouds of heaven.
And he came to the Ancient One*ᵍ*
and was presented before him.
¹⁴ To him was given dominion
and glory and kingship,
that all peoples, nations, and languages
should serve him.
His dominion is an everlasting
dominion
that shall not pass away,

and his kingship is one
that shall never be destroyed.

15 As for me, Daniel, my spirit was troubled within me,*ʰ* and the visions of my head terrified me. ¹⁶I approached one of the attendants to ask him the truth concerning all this. So he said that he would disclose to me the interpretation of the matter: ¹⁷"As for these four great beasts, four kings shall arise out of the earth. ¹⁸But the holy ones of the Most High shall receive the kingdom and possess the kingdom forever—forever and ever."

19 Then I desired to know the truth concerning the fourth beast, which was different from all the rest, exceedingly terrifying, with its teeth of iron and claws of bronze, and which devoured and broke in pieces and stamped what was left with its feet; ²⁰and concerning the ten horns that were on its head, and concerning the other horn that came up and before which three others had fallen—the horn that had eyes and a mouth that spoke arrogantly and that seemed greater than the others. ²¹As I looked, that horn made war with the holy ones and was prevailing over them, ²²until the Ancient One*ⁱ* came; then judgment was given for the

f 7.13 Aram *one like a son of man*   g 7.13 Aram *the Ancient of Days*   h 7.15 Aram *troubled in its sheath*   i 7.22 Aram *the Ancient of Days*

7:8 The *little* horn with *human eyes* and a *mouth speaking arrogantly* represents King Antiochus IV (175–164 BCE), who usurped the throne (*plucked up*) and was reviled in Judea and Syria for sacking temples.

7:9–14 A judgment scene involving the divine court. **7:9** *Thrones.* Suggesting that God will reclaim rule over the earth. *Ancient One.* Literally "ancient of days," emphasizing the everlasting nature of God; see Isa. 40:28. *White as snow . . . like pure wool.* Bright light emanates from divine beings (Num. 6:25). *Throne.* See Ezek. 1:13–21. **7:10** *Fire* is associated with divinity (see Exod. 3:2; Deut. 4:15–19). *Thousand thousands.* The angelic host (Ps. 68:17). *Books.* Divine records consulted for judgment (see Exod. 32:32–33; Mal. 3:16). **7:11–12** Because of the *horn* (Antiochus IV), the fourth *beast* is completely *destroyed*, unlike the other kingdoms, which continue for an unspecified amount of *time*. **7:13** *One like a human being.* Traditionally translated as "like a son of man," the phrase highlights the humanity of the being descending *with the clouds of heaven*, contrasting with the four beasts. It is not a gender-specific reference; see Ezek. 3:1–10, where "son of man" is better translated as "mortal." This figure has been understood as the archangel Michael (10:13, 21; 12:1) and a renewed kingdom of Israel (vv. 18, 27). Christians later associate the term with Jesus (Mark 13:26; 14:62; see **"Son of God vs. Son of Man," p. 1774**). **7:14** The humanlike figure is given eternal *dominion* and so parallels the fifth kingdom in Dan. 2. *Serve.* See Isa. 2:2–5; 49:22–23.

7:16 Daniel needs the help of angelic *interpretation* in the apocalyptic visions.

7:18 *Holy ones.* Angels (see 8:10–13; Job 15:15; see **"Angels," p. 1346**).

7:21 *War with the holy ones.* The assault of Antiochus IV on the Jerusalem temple and Jewish faith.

7:22 The vision predicts divine judgment on Antiochus IV and political liberation for Jerusalem.

Focus On: Apocalypse (Daniel 7)

The term *apocalypse* comes from the ancient Greek word *apokalypsis*, meaning "unveiling"; the term begins the New Testament book of Revelation (Rev. 1:1). Scholars use *apocalypse* to describe the genre of ancient Jewish literature exemplified by Revelation and Dan. 7–12, as well as 1 Enoch, 4 Ezra, and 2 Baruch. An apocalypse describes a revelation of divine mysteries about the truth of history, including the end of historical time, and the truth about the world, including the disclosure of supernatural places such as heaven.

Some apocalypses focus more on history, such as Revelation and Dan. 7–12, while others, such as the Astronomical Book found in 1 En. 72–82, focus more on cosmology. Historical apocalypses such as Dan. 7–12 and Revelation explain the meaning and ultimate purpose of catastrophes such as the persecution of Antiochus IV (167–164 BCE) and the Roman destruction of Jerusalem (70 CE) by reinterpreting the past and pointing to an alternative future. Apocalypses are typically written in the names of extraordinary figures, like Enoch (Gen. 5:21–24) and Daniel (Dan. 7:1), who were ancient even at the time of the composition of the apocalypse. These historical summaries reveal a deep plan behind history's seeming chaos: evil is seemingly victorious, but God will soon directly intervene in world affairs, defeat the forces of evil, and bring an end to history and the world as we know it.

Apocalyptic literature imagines the entire cosmos as a battleground between the forces of good and evil. At history's climax, God will bring judgment, punish evildoers, re-create the world, and form a new people and kingdom constituted by the righteous. These teachings are presented as mysteries that can be interpreted only with the help of divine guidance, which reveals the secret meanings behind the striking imagery and numerological puzzles that are common in apocalypses. Apocalypses draw on ancient Near Eastern creation mythologies, so the end of history mirrors its beginning, including echoes of mythological battles between creator gods and chaos monsters.

Apocalyptic thinking is rare in the Hebrew Bible, but the New Testament is suffused with an apocalyptic worldview. In addition to the apocalypse Revelation, Jesus is depicted as an apocalyptic preacher (Matt. 10:26; 11:25; 13:10–37; 24:1–25; Mark 13:1–37) and Paul interprets the world in apocalyptic ways (2 Cor. 12:2–4) and expects the imminent return of Christ (1 Cor. 7:29–31).

Brennan Breed

holy ones of the Most High, and the time arrived when the holy ones gained possession of the kingdom.

23 This is what he said: "As for the fourth beast,
   there shall be a fourth kingdom on earth
      that shall be different from all the other kingdoms;
   it shall devour the whole earth
      and trample it down and break it to pieces.
24 As for the ten horns,
   out of this kingdom ten kings shall arise,
      and another shall arise after them.
This one shall be different from the former ones
      and shall put down three kings.
25 He shall speak words against the Most High,

shall wear out the holy ones of the Most High,
   and shall attempt to change the ritual calendar and the law,
and they shall be given into his power
      for a time, two times,*j* and half a time.
26 Then the court shall sit in judgment,
      and his dominion shall be taken away,
   to be consumed and totally destroyed.
27 The kingship and dominion
      and the greatness of the kingdoms under the whole heaven
   shall be given to the people of the holy ones of the Most High;
      their kingdom shall be an everlasting kingdom,
   and all dominions shall serve and obey them."

j 7.25 Aram a time, times

7:25 *Change the ritual calendar and the law.* Antiochus's attempt to ban Sabbath and feasts (1 Macc. 1:1–53). *Time . . . half a time.* Each "time" consisted of a year, so three and a half years, roughly the time of Antiochus's persecution until the rededication of the temple.

7:27 *People of the holy ones.* The Jewish people.

28 Here the account ends. As for me, Daniel, my thoughts greatly terrified me, and my face turned pale, but I kept the matter in my mind.

8 In the third year of the reign of King Belshazzar a vision appeared to me, Daniel, after the one that had appeared to me at first. [2]In the vision[k] I saw myself in Susa the capital, in the province of Elam,[l] and I was by the Ulai Gate.[m] [3]I looked up and saw a ram standing beside the gate.[n] It had two horns. Both horns were long, but one was longer than the other, and the longer one came up second. [4]I saw the ram charging westward and northward and southward. All beasts were powerless to withstand it, and no one could rescue from its power; it did as it pleased and became strong.

5 As I was watching, a male goat appeared from the west, coming across the face of the whole earth without touching the ground. The goat had a horn[o] between its eyes. [6]It came toward the ram with the two horns that I had seen standing beside the gate,[p] and it ran at it with savage force. [7]I saw it approaching the ram. It was enraged against it and struck the ram, breaking its two horns. The ram did not have power to withstand it; it threw the ram down to the ground and trampled upon it, and there was no one who could rescue the ram from its power. [8]Then the male goat grew exceedingly great, but at the height of its power the great horn was broken, and in its place there came up four prominent horns toward the four winds of heaven.

9 Out of one of them came another[q] horn, a little one, which grew exceedingly great toward the south, toward the east, and toward the beautiful land. [10]It grew as high as the host of heaven. It threw down to earth some of the host and some of the stars and trampled on them. [11]Even against the prince of the host it acted arrogantly; it took the regular burnt offering away from him and overthrew the place of his sanctuary. [12]Because of wickedness, the host was given over to it together with the regular burnt offering;[r] it cast truth to the ground and kept prospering in what it did. [13]Then I heard a holy one speaking, and another holy one said to the one who spoke, "For how long is this vision concerning the regular burnt offering, the transgression that makes desolate, and the giving over of the sanctuary and host to be trampled?"[s] [14]And he answered him,[t] "For two thousand three hundred evenings and mornings; then the sanctuary shall be restored to its rightful state."

k 8.2 Syr Vg: Heb *vision I was looking and*   l 8.2 Gk Theodotion: Heb repeats *in the vision I was looking*   m 8.2 Gk Syr Vg: Heb *River Ulai*   n 8.3 Or *river*   o 8.5 Theodotion: Heb *a horn of vision*   p 8.6 Or *river*   q 8.9 Cn: Heb *one*   r 8.12 Meaning of Heb uncertain   s 8.13 Meaning of Heb uncertain   t 8.14 Gk Theodotion Syr Vg: Heb *me*

8:1–12:13 The remainder of the book is written in somewhat clumsy Hebrew instead of the imperial language of Aramaic, apparently an act of resistance.

8:1 *Third year.* Two years after 7:1.

8:2 *Susa.* A Persian capital located in *Elam* (Esth. 1:2). *Ulai gate.* Likely the Ulai canal, outside of Susa, like the location of Ezekiel's vision in Ezek. 1:1.

8:3 *Ram . . . two horns.* Media and Persia (v. 20). *Longer one.* Persia absorbed the Median Empire in 550 BCE.

8:5 *Goat.* The Macedonian army. *Horn.* Alexander the Great (v. 21).

8:7 *Struck the ram.* Between 332 and 330 BCE, Alexander soundly defeated the Persian Empire.

8:8 *Height of its power.* Alexander died suddenly in 323 BCE. *Four prominent horns.* The successor states of Alexander's empire.

8:9 *A little one.* Antiochus IV; see notes on 7:8, 21. *South.* Egypt. *East.* Parthia. *Beautiful land.* Judea (11:41, 45).

8:10 Antiochus IV's persecution of Judaism is depicted as a war against heaven. *Host.* The divine army.

8:11 *Prince of the host.* Michael. *Regular burnt offering . . . sanctuary.* Antiochus suspended sacrifices to YHWH; see 1 Macc. 1:41–59.

8:12 *Truth.* Right worship of YHWH.

8:13 *Transgression that makes desolate.* The foreign altar erected in the temple (1 Macc. 1:54–60) and a pun on the names of deities worshiped by the Seleucid army in the temple.

8:14 *Two thousand three hundred evenings and mornings.* Or 1,150 days, about three and a half years (see 7:25; 12:7), roughly the length of the persecution.

15 When I, Daniel, had seen the vision, I tried to understand it. Then someone appeared standing before me, having the appearance of a man, [16]and I heard a human voice by the Ulai, calling, "Gabriel, help this man understand the vision." [17]So he came near where I stood, and when he came, I became frightened and fell prostrate. But he said to me, "Understand, O mortal,[u] that the vision is for the time of the end."

18 As he was speaking to me, I fell into a trance, face to the ground; then he touched me and set me on my feet. [19]He said, "Listen, and I will tell you what will take place later in the period of wrath, for it refers to the appointed time of the end. [20]As for the ram that you saw with the two horns, these are the kings of Media and Persia. [21]The male goat[v] is the king of Greece, and the great horn between its eyes is the first king. [22]As for the horn that was broken, in place of which four others arose, four kingdoms shall arise from his[w] nation but not with his power.

[23] At the end of their rule,
> when the transgressions have
> > reached their full measure,
> a king of bold countenance shall arise,
> > skilled in intrigue.

[24] He shall grow strong in power,[x]
> shall cause fearful destruction,
> and shall succeed in what he does.
He shall destroy the powerful
> and the people of the holy ones.

[25] By his cunning
> he shall make deceit prosper under
> > his hand,
> and in his own mind he shall be great.
Without warning he shall destroy many
> and shall even rise up against the
> > Prince of princes.
But he shall be broken, and not by
> human hands.

[26]"The vision of the evenings and the mornings that has been told is true. As for you, seal up the vision, for it refers to many days from now."

27 So I, Daniel, was overcome and lay sick for some days; then I arose and went about the king's business. But I was dismayed by the vision and did not understand it.

9 In the first year of Darius son of Ahasuerus, by birth a Mede, who became king over the realm of the Chaldeans, [2]I,[y] Daniel, perceived in the books the number of years that, according to the word of the LORD to the prophet Jeremiah, must be fulfilled for the devastation of Jerusalem, namely, seventy years.

3 Then I turned to the Lord God to seek an answer by prayer and supplication with fasting and sackcloth and ashes. [4]I prayed to the LORD my God and made confession, saying,

"Ah, Lord, great and awesome God, keeping covenant and steadfast love with those who love you[z] and keep your[a] commandments, [5]we have sinned and done wrong, acted wickedly and rebelled, turning aside from your commandments and ordinances. [6]We have not listened to your servants the prophets, who spoke in your name to our kings, our princes, and our ancestors, and to all the people of the land.

7 "Righteousness is on your side, O Lord, but open shame, as at this day, falls on us, the people of Judah, the inhabitants of Jerusalem, and all Israel, those who are near and those who are far away, in all the lands to which you have driven them because of

---

u 8.17 Heb *son of man*   v 8.21 Or *shaggy male goat*   w 8.22 Gk Theodotion Vg: Heb *the*   x 8.24 Gk Theodotion: Heb *power, but not with his power*   y 9.2 Theodotion: Heb *in the first year of his reign, I*   z 9.4 Heb *him*   a 9.4 Heb *his*

8:16 *Gabriel.* The first named angel in the Hebrew Bible (Luke 1:19); see note on 3:25.

8:17 *Mortal.* Traditionally translated as "son of man," here emphasizing Daniel's mortality; see note on 7:13; Ezek. 3:1. *Time of the end.* The end of the persecution; this vision does not describe an eternal kingdom.

8:19 *Period of wrath.* Antiochus's persecution.

8:25 *Prince of princes.* God. *Not by human hands.* God will defeat Antiochus without human armies (2:45).

9:1 *Darius.* See note on 5:31.

9:2 *Seventy years.* Jeremiah's predicted duration of the Babylonian exile (Jer. 25:11–12; 29:10). Daniel reapplies this prediction to the events of 167 BCE.

9:4–19 After reading Jer. 29:10–14, Daniel *prayed* a communal *confession* of sin, likely borrowed from an earlier source heavily influenced by Deuteronomy, similar to 1 Kgs. 8:23–53; Ezra 9:6–15;

the treachery that they have committed against you. ⁸Open shame, O Lᴏʀᴅ, falls on us, our kings, our princes, and our ancestors because we have sinned against you. ⁹To the Lord our God belong mercy and forgiveness, but we have rebelled against him ¹⁰and have not obeyed the voice of the Lᴏʀᴅ our God by following his laws, which he set before us by his servants the prophets.

11 "All Israel has transgressed your law and turned aside, refusing to obey your voice. So the curse and the oath written in the law of Moses, the servant of God, have been poured out upon us because we have sinned against you. ¹²He has confirmed his words that he spoke against us and against our rulers by bringing upon us a calamity so great that what has been done against Jerusalem has never before been done under the whole heaven. ¹³Just as it is written in the law of Moses, all this calamity has come upon us. We did not entreat the favor of the Lᴏʀᴅ our God, turning from our iniquities and reflecting on his*b* fidelity. ¹⁴So the Lᴏʀᴅ kept watch over this calamity until he brought it upon us. Indeed, the Lᴏʀᴅ our God is right in all that he has done, for we have disobeyed his voice.

15 "And now, O Lord our God, who brought your people out of the land of Egypt with a mighty hand and made your name renowned even to this day—we have sinned, we have done wickedly. ¹⁶O Lord, in view of all your righteous acts, let your anger and wrath, we pray, turn away from your city Jerusalem, your holy mountain; because of our sins and the iniquities of our ancestors, Jerusalem and your people have become a disgrace among all our neighbors. ¹⁷Now therefore, O our God, listen to the prayer of your servant and to his supplication, and for your own sake, Lord,*c* let your face shine upon your desolated sanctuary. ¹⁸Incline your ear, O my God, and hear. Open your eyes and look at our desolation and the city that bears your name. We do not present our supplication before you on the ground of our righteousness but on the ground of your great mercies. ¹⁹O Lord, hear; O Lord, forgive; O Lord, listen and act and do not delay! For your own sake, O my God, because your city and your people bear your name!"

20 While I was speaking and was praying and confessing my sin and the sin of my people Israel and presenting my supplication before the Lᴏʀᴅ my God on behalf of the holy mountain of my God, ²¹while I was speaking in prayer, the man Gabriel, whom I had seen before in a vision, came to me in swift flight at the time of the evening sacrifice. ²²He came*d* and said to me, "Daniel, I have now come out to give you wisdom and understanding. ²³At the beginning of your supplications a word went out, and I have come to declare it, for you are greatly beloved. So consider the word and understand the vision:

24 "Seventy weeks are decreed for your people and your holy city: to finish the transgression, to put an end to sin, and to atone for iniquity, to bring in everlasting righteousness, to seal both vision and prophet, and to anoint a most holy place.*e* ²⁵Know therefore and understand: from the time that the word went out to restore and rebuild Jerusalem until the time of an

b 9.13 Heb *your*   c 9.17 Theodotion Vg Compare Syr: Heb *for the Lord's sake*   d 9.22 Gk Syr: Heb *He made to understand*   e 9.24 Or *thing* or *one*

and Neh. 9:6–37. Confession is not found elsewhere in Daniel (see note on 1:2). **9:11** *Law of Moses.* The covenant is a contract with consequences, stipulated in Deut. 28:15–68 and Lev. 26:27–45. **9:12** *Calamity.* The exile and destruction of Jerusalem (587 BCE) but also the persecution of Antiochus IV (167 BCE). **9:15** *Now.* Daniel shifts from confession to supplication. *Land of Egypt.* Reference to God's saving power in Exod. 1–15. **9:17** *Face shine.* See Num. 6:24–26. **9:18** *City.* Jerusalem.

9:21 *Gabriel.* See note on 8:16. *Evening sacrifice.* See Exod. 29:38–42.

9:23 *Word went out.* See Isa. 55:11.

9:24 *Seventy weeks are decreed.* Jeremiah's seventy years are interpreted as seventy groups of seven-year cycles (see Lev. 25:8), totaling 490 years in all. The revelation divides the seventy weeks into three unequal parts.

9:25 *Seven weeks.* Or forty-nine years, roughly the amount of time between the destruction of Jerusalem (587 BCE), when God began the plan to *restore and rebuild Jerusalem*, and the time of the *anointed prince*, or the ordination of the new high priest Joshua in the newly rebuilt Jerusalem, in 539 BCE (Ezra 3:2). *Troubled time.* The chaotic early Hellenistic period.

anointed prince, there shall be seven weeks, and for sixty-two weeks it shall be built again with streets and moat, but in a troubled time. ²⁶After the sixty-two weeks, an anointed one shall be cut off and shall have nothing, and the troops of the prince who is to come shall destroy the city and the sanctuary. Its*f* end shall come with a flood, and to the end there shall be war. Desolations are decreed. ²⁷He shall make a strong covenant with many for one week, and for half of the week he shall make sacrifice and offering cease, and in their place*g* shall be a desolating sacrilege until the decreed end is poured out upon the desolator."

10 In the third year of King Cyrus of Persia a word was revealed to Daniel, who was named Belteshazzar. The word was true, and it concerned a great conflict. He understood the word, having received understanding in the vision.

2 At that time I, Daniel, had been mourning for three weeks. ³I had eaten no rich food, no meat or wine had entered my mouth, and I had not anointed myself at all, for the full three weeks. ⁴On the twenty-fourth day of the first month, as I was standing on the bank of the great river (that is, the Tigris), ⁵I looked up and saw a man clothed in linen, with a belt of gold from Uphaz around his waist. ⁶His body was like

beryl, his face like lightning, his eyes like flaming torches, his arms and legs like the gleam of burnished bronze, and the sound of his words like the roar of a multitude. ⁷I, Daniel, alone saw the vision; the people who were with me did not see the vision, though a great trembling fell upon them, and they fled and hid themselves. ⁸So I was left alone to see this great vision. My strength left me, and my complexion grew deathly pale, and I retained no strength. ⁹When*b* I heard the sound of his words, I fell into a trance, face to the ground.

10 But then a hand touched me and roused me to my hands and knees. ¹¹He said to me, "Daniel, greatly beloved, pay attention to the words that I am going to speak to you. Stand on your feet, for I have now been sent to you." So while he was speaking this word to me, I stood up trembling. ¹²He said to me, "Do not fear, Daniel, for from the first day that you set your mind to gain understanding and to humble yourself before your God, your words have been heard, and I have come because of your words. ¹³But the prince of the kingdom of Persia opposed me twenty-one days. So Michael, one of the chief princes, came to help me, and I left him there with the prince of the

f 9.26 Or *His* g 9.27 Cn: Meaning of Heb uncertain
b 10.9 Gk Syr: Heb *Then I heard the sound of his words, and when*

9:26 *Sixty-two weeks.* Roughly 539–172 BCE, the time between the end of exile (forty-nine years, or seven "weeks") and the seven years (one "week") of turmoil under Antiochus IV. The math is imprecise, perhaps intentionally so. *Anointed one shall be cut off.* The high priest Onias III was deposed in 175 and then murdered in 172 BCE. *Destroy the city.* Antiochus IV, the *prince*, attacked Jerusalem and gave the temple to Syrian soldiers for their worship of Baal Shamem in 167 BCE.

9:27 *A strong covenant.* Antiochus made an alliance with Judean supporters of the usurper high priests, Jason and then Menelaus. *Half of the week.* Three and a half years; see note on 7:25. *Desolating sacrilege.* See note on 8:13. *Decreed end.* God will put an end to the persecution, but what comes next is unclear.

10:1–12:13 The final three chapters form one extended vision.

10:1 *Third year.* The year 536 BCE, seventy years after 1:1.

10:2–3 *No rich food.* See note on 6:18. Fasting could prepare one for revelation.

10:4 The date of Passover. *River.* See note on 8:2; Ezek. 1:1.

10:5 The description draws from Ezek. 1; 9–11. *Linen.* Priestly and angelic garb. *Uphaz.* Likely a scribal error for Ophir (Job 28:16).

10:6 *Beryl.* See Ezek. 1:16. *Lightning . . . torches.* Divine beings emanate light; see Ezek. 1:13. *Bronze.* See Ezek. 1:7; Rev. 1:15. *Roar.* See Ezek. 1:24.

10:12 *Do not fear.* Often introduces oracles of salvation (Isa. 7:4; 41:10, 13; 43:5; Jer. 30:10; 46:27–28).

10:13 *Prince of . . . Persia.* The divine being responsible for Persia (Deut. 32:8–9). *Opposed me.* Divine conflicts reflect human ones (see Isa. 36:18–20). *Michael.* Israel's divine guardian (10:21; 12:1) and one of the *chief princes*, four archangels, including Gabriel (1 En. 9).

kingdom of Persia[i] [14]and have come to help you understand what is to happen to your people at the end of days. For there is a further vision for those days."

15 While he was speaking these words to me, I turned my face toward the ground and was speechless. [16]Then one in human form touched my lips, and I opened my mouth to speak and said to the one who stood before me, "My lord, because of the vision such pains have come upon me that I retain no strength. [17]How can my lord's servant talk with my lord? For I am exhausted;[j] no strength remains in me, and no breath is left in me."

18 Again one in human form touched me and strengthened me. [19]He said, "Do not fear, greatly beloved; you are safe. Be strong and courageous!" When he spoke to me, I was strengthened and said, "Let my lord speak, for you have strengthened me." [20]Then he said, "Do you know why I have come to you? Now I must return to fight against the prince of Persia, and when I am through with him, the prince of Greece will come. [21]But I am to tell you what is inscribed in the book of truth. There is no one with me who contends against these princes except

11 Michael, your prince. [1]As for me, in the first year of Darius the Mede, I stood up to support and strengthen him.

2 "Now I will announce the truth to you. Three more kings shall arise in Persia. The fourth shall be far richer than all of them, and when he has become strong through his riches, he shall stir up all against the kingdom of Greece. [3]Then a warrior king shall arise who shall rule with great dominion and take action as he pleases. [4]And while still rising in power, his kingdom shall be broken and divided toward the four winds of heaven but not to his posterity nor according to the dominion with which he ruled, for his kingdom shall be uprooted and go to others besides these.

5 "Then the king of the south shall grow strong, but one of his officers shall grow stronger than he and shall rule a realm greater than his own realm. [6]After some years they shall make an alliance, and the daughter of the king of the south shall come to the king of the north to ratify the agreement. But she shall not retain her power, and his offspring shall not endure. She shall be given up, she and her attendants and her child and the one who supported her.

"In those times [7]a branch from her roots shall rise up in his place. He shall come against the army and enter the fortress of the king of the north, and he shall take action against them and prevail. [8]Even their gods, with their idols and with their precious vessels of silver and gold, he shall carry off to Egypt as spoils of war. For some

i 10.13 Gk Theodotion: Heb *I was left there with the kings of Persia* *j* 10.17 Gk: Heb *from now*

10:14 *End of days.* The vision in Dan. 10–12 describes the end of history, going *further* than Dan. 8 and 9.

10:16 *Touched my lips.* See Isa. 6:7; Jer. 1:9.

10:20 *Prince of Greece.* Michael and Gabriel will soon struggle against the angelic guardian of Alexander the Great.

10:21 *Book of truth.* A divine foretelling of history.

11:1 *First year of Darius.* See note on 5:31.

11:2–12:4 A detailed historical summary of the events of 332–164 BCE, focusing on the Seleucids and Ptolemies, two kingdoms at war during the years 300–200 BCE. These intricate political details mattered deeply to Jerusalem because the wars ravaged the city numerous times. The *king of the north* represents the Seleucid dynasty in Syria, which includes Antiochus IV, and the *king of the south* represents the Ptolemaic dynasty in Egypt.

11:2 Prior to Alexander, Persia ruled the ancient Near East and warred with the Greek city-states.

11:3 *Warrior king.* Alexander the Great.

11:4 *Broken and divided.* The sudden death of Alexander and the fracturing of his empire in 323 BCE.

11:5 *King of the south.* Ptolemy I of Egypt, whose officer was Seleucus I, founder of the Seleucid kingdom in Syria.

11:6 *They.* Seleucids and Ptolemies. *Alliance.* A marriage alliance that failed when Queen Berenice was murdered in 246 BCE.

11:7 *Branch.* Ptolemy III, brother of Berenice, attacked the Seleucid Empire in response.

years he shall refrain from attacking the king of the north; [9]then the latter shall invade the realm of the king of the south but will return to his own land.

10 "His sons shall wage war and assemble a multitude of great forces that shall advance like a flood and pass through and again shall carry the war as far as his fortress. [11]Moved with rage, the king of the south shall go out and do battle against the king of the north, who shall muster a great multitude, but the multitude shall be given over to his hand. [12]When the multitude has been carried off, his heart shall be exalted, and he shall overthrow tens of thousands, but he shall not prevail. [13]For the king of the north shall again raise a multitude larger than the former, and after some years[k] he shall advance with a great army and abundant supplies.

14 "In those times many shall rise against the king of the south. The lawless among your own people shall lift themselves up in order to fulfill the vision, but they shall fail. [15]Then the king of the north shall come and throw up siegeworks and take a well-fortified city. And the forces of the south shall not stand, not even his picked troops, for there shall be no strength to resist. [16]But he who comes against him shall take the actions he pleases, and no one shall withstand him. He shall take a position in the beautiful land, and all of it shall be in his power. [17]He shall set his face to come with the strength of his whole kingdom. He shall

make peace with him and shall give him a woman in marriage, in order to destroy the kingdom,[l] but it shall not succeed or be to his advantage. [18]Afterward he shall turn to the coastlands and shall capture many, but a commander shall put an end to his insolence; indeed,[m] he shall turn his insolence back upon him. [19]Then he shall turn back toward the fortresses of his own land, but he shall stumble and fall and shall not be found.

20 "Then shall arise in his place one who shall send an official for the glory of the kingdom, but within a few days he shall be broken, though not in anger or in battle.[n] [21]In his place shall arise a contemptible person on whom royal majesty had not been conferred; he shall come in suddenly and seize the kingdom through intrigue. [22]Armies shall be utterly swept away and broken before him, and the prince of the covenant as well. [23]And after an alliance is made with him, he shall act deceitfully and become strong with a small party. [24]Suddenly he shall come into the richest parts[o] of the province and do what none of his predecessors had ever done, lavishing plunder, spoil, and wealth on them. He shall devise plans against strongholds but only for a time. [25]He shall stir up his power and determination against the king of the south with a great army, and the king of the south shall

k 11.13 Heb *and at the end of the times years* l 11.17 Heb *it* m 11.18 Meaning of Heb uncertain n 11.20 Meaning of Heb uncertain o 11.24 Or *among the richest men*

11:9 Seleucus II fails in a retaliatory attack on Egypt.

11:11–12 Ptolemy IV defeats the Seleucids at Raphia in 217 BCE, but the Ptolemies lose Palestine within two decades.

11:14 *Many shall rise.* Rebellions in both kingdoms. *Lawless among your own people.* Jewish supporters of the Seleucid king Antiochus III.

11:15–16 Antiochus III captures Palestine, including Jerusalem, the *beautiful land*, at Panion in 200 BCE and takes Sidon, the *well-fortified city* of Phoenicia.

11:17 Another misguided marriage alliance between Ptolemies and Seleucids.

11:18 *A commander.* Roman general Scipio defeated Antiochus III at Magnesia, putting financial pressure on the Seleucids that leads to the plundering of temples.

11:19 *Fall.* Antiochus III dies in 187 after robbing a temple.

11:20 *One who shall send an official.* Seleucus IV sends Heliodorus to raid the temple treasury in Jerusalem (2 Macc. 3).

11:21 *Contemptible person.* Antiochus IV, a usurper.

11:22 *The prince of the covenant.* High Priest Onias III; see note on 9:26.

11:24 See 1 Macc. 3:30, which describes this practice of Antiochus IV.

11:25–28 Antiochus IV initiated a successful, but costly, campaign against Egypt. *Set against the holy covenant.* Antiochus plots against Jerusalem and Judaism.

11:29 Antiochus's disastrous final campaign against Egypt begins.

wage war with a much greater and stronger army. But he shall not succeed, for plots shall be devised against him. 26Those who eat of the royal rations shall break him, his army shall be swept away, and many shall fall slain. 27The two kings, their minds bent on evil, shall sit at one table and exchange lies. But it shall not succeed, for there remains an end at the time appointed. 28He shall return to his land with great wealth, but his heart shall be set against the holy covenant. He shall work his will and return to his own land.

29 "At the time appointed he shall return and come into the south, but this time it shall not be as it was before. 30For ships of Kittim shall come against him, and he shall lose heart and withdraw. He shall be enraged and take action against the holy covenant. He shall turn back and come to an understanding with those who forsake the holy covenant. 31Forces sent by him shall occupy and profane the temple and fortress. They shall abolish the regular burnt offering and set up the desolating sacrilege. 32He will flatter with smooth words those who violate the covenant, but the people who are loyal to their God shall stand firm and take action. 33The wise among the people shall give understanding to many; for some days, however, they shall fall by sword and flame and suffer captivity and plunder. 34When they fall, they shall receive a little help, and many shall join them insincerely. 35Some of the wise shall fall, so that they may be refined, purified, and cleansed,ᵖ until the time of the end, for there is still an interval until the time appointed.

36 "The king shall act as he pleases. He shall exalt himself and consider himself greater than any god and shall speak horrendous things against the God of gods. He shall prosper until the period of wrath is completed, for what is determined shall be done. 37He shall pay no respect to the gods of his ancestors or to the one beloved by women; he shall pay no respect to any other god, for he shall consider himself greater than all. 38He shall honor the god of fortresses instead of these; a god whom his ancestors did not know he shall honor with gold and silver, with precious stones and costly gifts. 39He shall deal with the strongest fortresses with the help of a foreign god. Those who acknowledge him he shall make more wealthy and shall appoint them as rulers over many and shall distribute the land for a price.

40 "At the time of the end the king of the south shall attack him. But the king of the north shall rush upon him like a whirlwind, with chariots and horsemen and with many ships. He shall advance against countries and pass through like a flood. 41He shall come into the beautiful land, and tens of thousands shall fall victim, but Edom and Moab and the main part of the Ammonites shall escape from his power. 42He shall stretch out his hand against the countries, and the land of Egypt shall not escape. 43He shall gain control of the treasures of gold and of silver and all the riches of Egypt, and the Libyans and the Cushites shall follow in his train. 44But reports from the east and the north shall alarm him, and he shall go out with great fury to bring ruin and complete destruction to many. 45He shall pitch his palatial tents between the sea and the beautiful holy mountain. Yet he shall come to his end, with no one to help him.

p 11.35 Heb *made them white*

11:30 *Kittim.* The Roman army, intervening in 168 BCE. *Against the holy covenant.* Antiochus invades Jerusalem in 167 BCE (1 Macc. 1:29–32). *Forsake.* See 2 Macc. 4.

11:31 See note on 8:13; 1 Macc. 1:41–64.

11:33 *Wise.* The group responsible for Dan. 7–12.

11:35 *Refined.* See note on 12:4.

11:36–39 Antiochus's activities in Jerusalem.

11:40 Prediction of a massive battle between the Seleucids and Ptolemies culminating in a brief victory for Antiochus, which did not occur.

11:41 *Beautiful land.* Jerusalem.

11:45 *Between the sea and . . . mountain.* A prediction that Antiochus will die between Mount Zion and the Mediterranean; though he died in Persia, the date of his death (164) roughly corresponds to the predictions found in Dan. 7–12.

Focus On: Resurrection (Daniel 12)

While the Hebrew Bible contains several stories of miraculous resuscitation (1 Kgs. 17:17–24; 2 Kgs. 4:8–37; 13:21), it offers no clear reference to everlasting life after death outside of Dan. 12:2–3. Ancient Israelites, like other peoples of the ancient Near East, generally thought of death as a subterranean realm with minimal activity. In Israel, this place was sometimes called Sheol. Depending on the circumstances of death, one could go "down to Sheol" in sorrow (Gen. 37:35; Ezek. 31:15) or in peace (1 Kgs. 2:6; Job 21:13). In all cases, those in Sheol had a shadowy existence, or perhaps no existence at all (Eccl. 9:5, 10). See **"Sheol," p. 695.**

Several prophetic texts envisioned the restoration of the conquered nations of Israel and Judah as a metaphorical revivification and re-enfleshment of dead bodies (Hos. 6:1–3; Ezek. 37:1–14; Isa. 26:19), and others described the punishments meted out on the bodies of those who died in their rebellion against God (Isa. 66:24). Later apocalyptic rereadings of these texts understood these prophecies as literal descriptions of the resurrection of the righteous and the wicked in the end times. Other texts from the third and second centuries BCE, such as Dan. 12, described a bodily resurrection of the righteous, especially those who suffered and died for their faith (see 2 Macc. 7:9–14, 23), and of unpunished sinners. Jubilees 23:11–31, however, describes the immortality of souls but not a bodily resurrection (also see Wis. 1–6). Other voices argue against any life after death (Eccl. 3:16–22; Sir. 41:4), revealing a lively intra-Jewish debate that continued throughout the Roman period (Mark 12:18–23).

By the beginning of the Common Era, some Jewish apocalyptic groups were expecting an imminent end to history followed by the general resurrection of humanity. The New Testament assumes these apocalyptic Jewish beliefs but understands them in light of the individual resurrection of Jesus (see **"Resurrection in the Gospels," p. 1767**).

Paul proclaimed the resurrection of the crucified Jesus (1 Cor. 15:3–8) and interpreted the event as a vindication and exaltation of Jesus (Rom. 1:3–4), an initiation of the end of time (1 Cor. 15:22–24), a preview of the general resurrection to come (1 Cor. 15:12–22), and an act of salvation for the entire cosmos (Rom. 8:17–23). Rabbinic Judaism later developed extensive reflections on resurrection and the "world to come."

Brennan Breed

12 "At that time Michael, the great prince, the protector of your people, shall arise. There shall be a time of anguish such as has never occurred since nations first came into existence. But at that time your people shall be delivered, everyone who is found written in the book. ²Many of those who sleep in the dust of the earth*q* shall awake, some to everlasting life and some to shame and everlasting contempt. ³Those who are wise shall shine like the brightness of the sky,*r* and those who lead the many to righteousness, like the stars forever and ever. ⁴But you, Daniel, keep the words secret and the book sealed until the time of the end. Many shall be running back and forth,*s* and evil*t* shall increase."

5 Then I, Daniel, looked, and two others appeared, one standing on this bank of the stream and one on the other. ⁶One of them said to the man clothed in linen, who was upstream, "How long shall it be until the end of these wonders?" ⁷The man clothed in linen, who was upstream, raised his

q 12.2 Or *the land of dust*   r 12.3 Or *dome*   s 12.4 Meaning of Heb uncertain   t 12.4 Gk: Heb *knowledge*

12:1 *At that time.* After Antiochus's death and the end of history. *Michael.* See note on 10:13. *The book.* The Book of Life (Ps. 69:28).

12:2 *Many.* Not all the dead who *sleep in the . . . earth* will *awake* in resurrection: only those who receive *everlasting life* and those who will receive *everlasting contempt.* See **"Resurrection (Daniel)," p. 1224.**

12:3 The *wise* (see note on 11:33) who taught *righteousness* will *shine* like angels; see note on 10:6.

12:4 A command to keep the teaching secret between the time of Daniel (536 BCE; see 10:1) and the persecution of Antiochus IV in 167.

12:5 *Two others.* Angels.

12:6 *How long.* From the time of the persecution until the end of time.

12:7 *A time . . . time.* See note on 7:25.

right hand and his left hand toward heaven. And I heard him swear by the one who lives forever that it would be for a time, two times, and half a time*u* and that when the shattering of the power of the holy people comes to an end all these things would be accomplished. [8]I heard but could not understand, so I said, "My lord, what shall be the outcome of these things?" [9]He said, "Go your way, Daniel, for the words are to remain secret and sealed until the time of the end. [10]Many shall be purified, cleansed, and refined, but the wicked shall continue to act wickedly. None of the wicked shall understand, but those who are wise shall understand. [11]From the time that the regular burnt offering is taken away and the desolating sacrilege is set up, there shall be one thousand two hundred ninety days. [12]Happy are those who persevere and attain the thousand three hundred thirty-five days. [13]But you, go your way,*v* and rest; you shall rise for your reward at the end of the days."

u 12.7 Heb *a time, times, and a half*   *v* 12.13 Gk Theodotion: Heb adds *to the end*

12:11 A more concrete prediction of 1,290 days; see 8:14 for a slightly shorter prediction.

12:12 An upwardly revised prediction of 1,335 days, suggesting another emendation to account for an unsatisfactory prediction.

12:13 *Rest.* Daniel will die but *rise* in resurrection for a *reward* at the *end of the days.*

HOSEA

Introduction

One of the twelve "minor prophets," designated as such due to their shorter lengths, Hosea can be separated into two main sections: chaps. 1–3 and 4–14. The former emphasizes sexual and marital metaphors to describe the relationship between YHWH and Israel. The latter varies its metaphors with a primary focus on judgment. While its principal focus is Israel, it also addresses Judah (cf. 4:15; 5:5, 12–14; 6:4; 11:12).

Dating

Hosea's superscription (see also note on 1:1) dates the work to around the eighth century BCE, around the time of the Assyrian Empire's defeat of Israel, the northern kingdom (722 BCE). According to its description, the prophet was active during the reigns of Uzziah, Jotham, Ahaz, and Hezekiah, all of whom were kings in the southern kingdom of Judah. However, it refers to only one king of Israel, Jeroboam II. Tentatively, this would date his activity between 781 and 687 BCE. If we consider Uzziah's (Azariah; possibly mentioned in the inscriptions of Tiglath-pileser III) reign lasted approximately 781–740 BCE, it overlapped that of Jeroboam II, circa 783–743 BCE. If we include Jotham, Ahaz, and Hezekiah, who reigned after Uzziah, we can be fairly confident that Hosea's activity included the last days of Jeroboam's and Uzziah's reigns. What is interesting is that there were more Israelite kings after Jeroboam, but they are unmentioned in the superscript. It is not clear if that shows that Hosea's text originally only referred to Jeroboam and possibly Uzziah, with the other three southern kings added by a later southern editor, or if its author was from the southern kingdom of Judah. If the latter, then perhaps the author halted the northern chronology of kings at Jeroboam II to portray the northern kingdom coming full circle, from Jeroboam to Jeroboam. That would make sense, since Jeroboam I was a despised figure among Judean literati (cf. 1 Kgs. 11:26–12:20).

Given what appears to be a reliance upon southern kings for its dating schema, some scholars see the work as intended for a southern audience. That would make sense if the speeches were written after Israel's defeat in 722 BCE. Perhaps, then, references to Israel were "proof" the message was authentic (cf. Deut. 18:21–22), with Israel's defeat providing evidence. If that was the case, a final redaction may be dated to the sixth century BCE with the backdrop of imperial defeat, first by Assyria (Israel; 722 BCE), then by Babylonia (Judah; 597 and 586 BCE). That would make the text part of the tradition in which Judean scribes preserved cultural memories in texts that would become the backbone of the Bible. This push by the intelligentsia correlated with the rise of early synagogues, which included ritualized engagements with the written word, reinforcing memory and identity. Within that context, Hosea's emphasis on punishment followed by restored relationship would find a place in the collective hope for a restored kingdom.

Metaphors

Hosea's metaphors usually target the ruling aristocracy, criticizing its conduct in the affairs of the kingdom. The work conveys attempted alliances with foreign powers, referred to as *ba'alim* ("Baals"), in terms of infidelity and with sexual idioms reminiscent of a fertility cult. Like a jealous husband, or provider, YHWH will punish Israel. For example, "I will uncover her shame in the sight of her lovers" (2:10; see **"Sexually Abusive Language in the Prophets," p. 1035**). This is not a condemnation of literal lovers. Rather, it condemns the kingdom's pursuit of other economic and political powers. Israel's rulers had depended upon them in a time of regional uncertainty, but that was not enough to prevent its defeat.

Hosea 1 introduces Gomer, a figure who might have been Hosea's wife. Some scholars speculate that she was a priestess or temple prostitute. It is an intriguing idea that draws a direct reference to fertility cults, but it lacks firm evidence beyond the modern tendency to see the prophets as focused primarily on monotheistic fidelity rather than being social and political critics. But the idea of monotheism that modern readers are familiar with was not one the biblical authors understood. Though it has been traditional to assume that Hosea and Gomer were married, matching metaphorical descriptions of YHWH and Israel as being married, it is not clear they were (see also notes for 1:2, 3).

While Gomer symbolizes the political and cultural philandering of the political leaders, her children symbolize judgment and a future political life (cf. 2:22–23). Once doomed, Lo-ammi ("not my people") will become Ammi ("my people"). Lo-ruhamah ("no compassion") will become Ruhamah ("compassion"). Jezreel—a fertile valley region that linked trade routes between Asia Minor, the Mediterranean coast, and Mesopotamia—will become a central hub of administration and governance, similar to its previous status as an economic and military center for the northern kingdom (see also note on 1:4–9). In its past, Jezreel was also the center of a bloody coup (cf. 2 Kgs. 9–10).

Literary Traditions

Hosea weaves several literary traditions into its message. It frequently refers to the northern kingdom and its rulers as "Ephraim" (cf. 4:17; 5:3, 11–14; 6:4; though also sometimes alongside Israel; cf. 5:5). This metonym may correlate to a version of the story about Ephraim as Joseph's son. Jacob (Israel) claimed Ephraim and Manasseh (Joseph's sons born in Egypt) as his own (designating them as tribes of Israel). Instead of Manasseh, who was older, Jacob blessed Ephraim (see Gen. 48:15–20). His explanation loosely parallels the Abrahamic covenant (cf. Gen. 12:1–3). The descendants of Ephraim, he promises, will be many. Just as Jacob, the younger brother of Esau, received Isaac's blessing (Gen. 27:27–34), Ephraim receives Jacob's. This theme of the younger overcoming the older, or the lesser overcoming the greater (as a vassal king might overcome its imperial overlord, perhaps), is prominent in books such as Genesis, Exodus, Judges, and the Prophets.

Reading Guide

Whoever is wise will discern meaning, and whoever discerns meaning will understand (14:9). Hosea's focus is not on foretelling the future but on demanding change in the author's present circumstances. It challenges the status quo of Israel's and Judah's leaders, using a combination of religious, sexual, economic, and political critiques (see **"Idolatry in Social-Political Terms," p. 1234**). But it also reimagines a restored society in which the sources of social and political problems are removed. In that, perhaps it is not unlike some forms of protest in the modern world.

Jeremiah W. Cataldo

1 The word of the LORD that came to Hosea son of Beeri, in the days of Kings Uzziah, Jotham, Ahaz, and Hezekiah of Judah and in the days of King Jeroboam son of Joash of Israel.

2 When the LORD first spoke through Hosea, the LORD said to Hosea, "Go, take for yourself a wife of prostitution and have children of prostitution, for the land commits great prostitution by forsaking the LORD." ³So he went and took Gomer daughter of Diblaim, and she conceived and bore him a son.

1:1 Superscription. "In the days of [king's name]" was a common dating schema (cf. Isa. 1:1). Uzziah r. 781–740 BCE, Jotham r. 740–736 BCE, Ahaz r. 736–716 BCE, Hezekiah r. 716–687 BCE, and Jeroboam (II) r. 783–743 BCE. Identification of Jeroboam only, and no Israelite kings after him, was likely a political statement by the author linking Jeroboam II with his namesake, Jeroboam I (ca. 930–910 BCE), the first king of Israel after Solomon's reign over confederated Israelite and Judean kingdoms (see also **"Introduction to Hosea," pp. 1226–27**).
1:2–9 Sexual infidelity and relationship. Scholars debate whether Gomer was a promiscuous woman, a prostitute, or prone to adultery. Sexual and gendered imagery conveys Hosea's assessment of Israel's political and economic defeat. Misdirected sexuality conveys a pursuit of other masculine political authorities and a disregard for fertility that belonged to a single masculine authority. Rather than preserve the economic well-being of the kingdom, Israel's political authorities relied upon foreign providers. Often in the Prophets, the relational aspect of sex symbolizes hierarchies of authority, while references to fertility symbolize economic issues. **1:2** *Wife [or woman] of prostitution.* The Hebrew term "ishah" can mean either "wife" or "woman." Hosea condemns not prostitution but the woman, or kingdom, seeking relationships with other providers through political alliances. **1:3** The Hebrew term "laqah" (to take) can refer to buying or taking a wife (cf. Deut. 20:7). Since Hosea uses marriage as a metaphor for politics, "wife" (but see v. 2 and the **"Introduction to**

4 And the LORD said to him, "Name him Jezreel,[a] for in a little while I will punish the house of Jehu for the blood of Jezreel, and I will put an end to the kingdom of the house of Israel. [5]On that day I will break the bow of Israel in the Valley of Jezreel."

6 She conceived again and bore a daughter. Then the LORD said to him, "Name her Lo-ruhamah,[b] for I will no longer have pity on the house of Israel or forgive them. [7]But I will have pity on the house of Judah, and I will save them by the LORD their God; I will not save them by bow or by sword or by war or by horses or by horsemen."

8 When she had weaned Lo-ruhamah, she conceived and bore a son. [9]Then the LORD said, "Name him Lo-ammi,[c] for you are not my people, and I am not your God."[d]

10 [e]Yet the number of the people of Israel shall be like the sand of the sea, which can be neither measured nor numbered, and in the place where it was said to them, "You are not my people," it shall be said to them,

"Children of the living God." [11]The people of Judah and the people of Israel shall be gathered together, and they shall appoint for themselves one head, and they shall rise up from the land, for great shall be the day of Jezreel.

2

[f]Say to your brothers, "Ammi,"[g] and to your sisters, "Ruhamah."[b]

[2] Plead with your mother, plead—
for she is not my wife,
and I am not her husband—
that she put away her prostitution from her face
and her adultery from between her breasts,
[3] or I will strip her naked
and expose her as in the day she was born

a 1.4 That is, *God sows*   b 1.6 That is, *not pitied*   c 1.9 That is, *not my people*   d 1.9 Heb *I am not yours*   e 1.10 2.1 in Heb   f 2.1 2.3 in Heb   g 2.1 That is, *my people*   h 2.1 That is, *pitied*

Hosea," pp. 1226–27) fits the context. **1:4–9** *Jezreel* ("God sows") was an important Israelite economic and political center and the site of Jehu's coup (2 Kgs. 9–10). *Lo-ruhamah* (v. 6) means "no pity." YHWH will have no pity for the nation overwhelmed by foreign empires. *Lo-ammi* ("not my people") implies that YHWH has disowned the people. The children symbolize the consequences of ill-advised political and economic decisions. But note two important elements: they (1) have names and (2) are living (cf. the fate of the nameless child in 2 Sam. 12:15–23). Both elements imply a future, which is a theme Hosea will revisit at multiple points (cf. 2:14–23).

1:10–11 Restoration. 1:10 *Sand of the sea.* The imagery invokes the Abrahamic covenant (cf. Gen. 22:17; also Gen. 32:12 and 1 Kgs. 3:8). **1:11** Judah and Israel will inhabit the land as a unified kingdom and reverse the breaking of Jezreel (cf. v. 4). The children renamed symbolize a renewed relationship between God and people.

2:1–13 Sexual infidelity. The metaphor criticizes Israel and Judah for economic and political relationships with foreign kingdoms (see **"Idolatry in Social-Political Terms," p. 1234**). The "woman" (symbolizing leaders of Israel and Judah) pursues other lovers (Heb. "ba'alim," a play on Baal), or economic and political "providers." In v. 8, the people are accused of giving silver and gold to Baal, prioritizing him as the national deity and provider rather than YHWH. YHWH's response to the woman is portrayed in terms that can be described as misogynist and abusive (cf. 2:3, 6, 10; see **"Sexually Abusive Language," p. 1035**). This makes the symbolism of a marital relationship, in which the woman cannot escape what could appear as an abusive relationship, difficult for readers. **2:1** When gathered together, the people (cf. 1:11) will be renamed from Lo-ammi ("not my people") to Ammi ("my people") for the men of the society and from Lo-ruhamah ("no compassion") to Ruhamah ("compassion") for the women of the society. Making "Ammi" refer to "brothers" refers to a renewal of patriarchal lineages, whereas "Ruhamah" describes the people's subordinate relationship to YHWH. Both changes result from the victory in Jezreel (1:11). **2:2** The command *plead with your mother* metaphorically separates the audience from the promiscuous woman, but only temporarily so (cf. v. 16). *Not my wife . . . not her husband* suggests a broken contract or covenant. *Prostitution from her face* can refer to seduction, such as with the eyes, or a commitment to something (cf. Ezek. 7:22, in which YHWH turns his face *from* the people, leading to its defeat). *Between her breasts.* A sexual parallel between the kingdom's actions and those of prostitutes (contrast sexual imagery in Song 8:10). **2:3** *I will strip her naked.* What YHWH provided will be taken away: land, economic prosperity, and political independence (cf. Ezek. 16:7, 22, 39; Isa. 32:13–14). A parched

Going Deeper: Understanding the Symbolic Emphasis of Children (Hosea 1 and 2)

In Hos. 1:2, YHWH commands the prophet to take a "wife of prostitution" (the meaning of the phrase is ambiguous) and have "children of prostitution." The text uses the same verbal root, *laqah* (to take), in both vv. 2 and 3. While the act of taking on the part of the patriarchal male could precede a marriage, that was not always the case. Consequently, it is not clear that Gomer and Hosea ever married or whether he simply took her as a sexual object. Also uncertain is how the language of sexual infidelity identifies her: Was she a prostitute or sex worker? A promiscuous woman? An adulterous woman *after* marriage, if one took place? None of that is entirely clear (but see also **"Slut-Shaming as Prophetic Discourse," p. 1148**; 1:2–9; note on 4:14), and that uncertainty influences how to interpret the children. Who, for instance, is their father? Hosea? Other lovers?

Despite the uncertainty of their paternal lineage, the children are given symbolic names. Their names carry negative connotations at first (such as "*not* my people"); however, they are subsequently changed to symbolize hope (cf. Hos. 2:23). The prophet Isaiah also had symbolically named children, including his son Shear-jashub ("a remnant will return"; Isa. 7:3). He had a second child named Maher-shalal-hash-baz, whose name signified the quick demise of Judah's political enemies and the possibility of restoration (Isa. 8:3; cf. 8:17–18; 9:6–7).

In Hosea and Isaiah, the children reflect the political situations of their audiences while symbolizing the future of the kingdom. That future was put at risk when its leaders sought economic and political alliances with other kingdoms, behaving like a promiscuous woman seeking provisions from other providers (cf. Hos. 2:5; Isa. 8:3). The initial benefit and satisfaction of these alliances turned into despair when those kingdoms changed the nature of the relationship. We are left to ask, Is defeat and despair the fate of the nation? Or, as Jacob was renamed Israel (cf. Gen. 32:28), which emphasized a future through his children (the twelve tribes of Israel), Is the future found in children's names? After all, Hosea's are renamed, and Isaiah's named, to encourage hope beyond the despair of each prophet's audience (cf. Hos. 1:11; Isa. 8:18). The prophets, it would seem, imagined a newly formed Israel in the symbolism of children.

Jeremiah W. Cataldo

and make her like a wilderness
and turn her into a parched land
and kill her with thirst.
[4] Upon her children also I will have no
pity,
because they are children of
prostitution.
[5] For their mother has prostituted
herself;
she who conceived them has acted
shamefully.

For she said, "I will go after my lovers;
they give me my bread and my
water,
my wool and my flax, my oil and my
drink."
[6] Therefore I will hedge up her[i] way with
thorns,
and I will build a wall against her
so that she cannot find her paths.

i 2.6 Gk Syr: Heb *your*

land invokes a lifeless and chaotic context, or the wilderness. But the wilderness is also a place of renewal (cf. vv. 14–15), like nation narratives such as Exod. 14:11–13; Num. 1:1–19; and Lev. 7:37–38, including its emphasis upon rituals as social frameworks. Even if posed as metaphors, the actions directed at the woman in this verse, stripping her and killing her with thirst, are violent and abusive. **2:4–5** *No pity.* A play on Lo-ruhamah. But also a threat, as 2:1 already stated that Lo-ruhamah will become Ruhamah ("pity"). This fits the typical prophetic pattern of alternating between absolute condemnation and possible redemption. The children (the future of the people) are called to argue with, even accuse, their mother, the latter of whom symbolizes the ruling authorities. *My lovers.* The leaders pursued other providers for economic stability rather than YHWH. Provision in those areas is symbolized by "clothing," the prosperity of the kingdom, which hides one's nakedness or shame, but which will be stripped off (cf. vv. 9–10). **2:6–7** *Build a wall.* Walls can be symbols of divine protection (cf. Mic. 7:11; Zech. 2:5; Ps. 91:4; Ezra 9:9), but here they ensnare. *Pursue . . . but not overtake.* Alliances will be broken (see also note on 2:13). *My first husband.* The people will return to YHWH, who represents the foundation of national identity, when other nations have abandoned (or conquered)

⁷ She shall pursue her lovers
  but not overtake them,
and she shall seek them
  but shall not find them.
Then she shall say, "I will go
  and return to my first husband,
  for it was better with me then than
    now."
⁸ She did not know
  that it was I who gave her
  the grain, the wine, and the oil
and who lavished upon her silver
  and gold that they used for Baal.
⁹ Therefore I will take back
  my grain in its time
  and my wine in its season,
and I will take away my wool and my flax,
  which were to cover her nakedness.
¹⁰ Now I will uncover her shame
  in the sight of her lovers,
  and no one shall rescue her out of my
    hand.
¹¹ I will put an end to all her mirth,
  her festivals, her new moons, her
    Sabbaths,
  and all her appointed festivals.
¹² I will lay waste her vines and her fig trees,
  of which she said,
"These are my pay,
  which my lovers have given me."
I will make them a forest,

and the wild animals shall devour
  them.
¹³ I will punish her for the festival days of
  the Baals,
to whom she offered incense
  and decked herself with her rings and
    jewelry
and went after her lovers
  and forgot me, says the LORD.

¹⁴ Therefore, I will now allure her
  and bring her into the wilderness
  and speak tenderly to her.
¹⁵ From there I will give her her vineyards
  and make the Valley of Achor a door
    of hope.
There she shall respond as in the days
  of her youth,
  as at the time when she came out of
    the land of Egypt.
¹⁶On that day, says the LORD, you will call
me "my husband," and no longer will you
call me "my Baal."ʲ ¹⁷For I will remove the
names of the Baals from her mouth, and
they shall be mentioned by name no more.
¹⁸I will make for youᵏ a covenant on that day
with the wild animals, the birds of the air,
and the creeping things of the ground, and
I will abolishˡ the bow, the sword, and war

j 2.16 That is, *"my master"* ǀ k 2.18 Heb *them* ǀ l 2.18 Heb *break*

them. **2:8** *She did not know.* Frequently, "to know" ("yada") refers to an intimate knowledge and can refer to sexual relations (cf. Gen. 4:1). Here, it is a play on both ideas: the woman (Israel's leaders) did not know her husband (YHWH) was providing for her. **2:9–10** *Take back.* The people will have nothing to support their cohesion as a people. *Nakedness.* The Hebrew term is more graphic, meaning "pudenda." The imagery invokes the idea of Israel's leaders giving themselves and the kingdom over to foreign authorities. **2:11** The festivals marking agricultural seasons will be stopped, as also agricultural production (contrast Deut. 11:13–17). In the wilderness, uncertainty, chaos, and lack (see also note on 2:9–10) will characterize the woman's reality. The lack of Sabbaths suggests no rest from that (cf. Lev. 16:31; Deut. 5:14). **2:13** A play on "ba'alim" as "owners, husbands, lords," who are a family's providers, and Baals as foreign deities, which also symbolize foreign powers. Cf. 2:16–17, in which YHWH will be called no longer "my master" ("ba'al") but "my husband" ("ish"), which is meant to invoke a more intimate relationship. The names of other masters ("ba'alim") with whom the woman engaged in sexual activity will be forgotten, which is necessary for the renewal in vv. 14–23.

2:14–23 Renewal in the wilderness. The place of judgment will become one of renewal. **2:14** *Speak tenderly* suggests renewal (see also Isa. 40:3; 41:19; 43:19–20; Ezek. 20:33–38), symbolized as a courtship. **2:15** Overgrown vineyards (cf. v. 12) will be returned, invoking a bridal gift (based on v. 14). *Valley of Achor.* Joshua 7:21–26 explains Joshua's defeat by the inhabitants of Canaan. The youthful woman symbolizes a maturing people ready for marriage (cf. Ezek. 16:8), or political and economic independence, a parallel to the Hebrews departing Egypt (cf. Exod. 13:17–22). **2:16–17** The title change shows a renewed relationship. YHWH will not be like the foreign masters ("ba'alim") the woman pursued (see note on 2:13); he will be her husband (see note on 2:1). But perhaps one who ensures loyalty through threats (cf. 2:3, 6, 10). **2:18** *Covenant* invokes the imagery of a marriage covenant (cf. Job 5:23; Isa. 11:6–9; also Gen. 1:30). YHWH will reverse the defeat in 1:5.

from the land, and I will make you[m] lie down in safety. [19]And I will take you for my wife forever; I will take you for my wife in righteousness and in justice, in steadfast love and in mercy. [20]I will take you for my wife in faithfulness, and you shall know the LORD.

[21] On that day I will answer, says the LORD,
    I will answer the heavens,
    and they shall answer the earth,
[22] and the earth shall answer the grain,
        the wine, and the oil,
    and they shall answer Jezreel,[n]
[23]   and I will sow him[o] for myself in the land.
    And I will have pity on Lo-ruhamah,[p]
    and I will say to Lo-ammi,[q] "You are my people,"
    and he shall say, "You are my God."

3 The LORD said to me again, "Go, love a woman who has a lover and is an adulteress, just as the LORD loves the people of Israel, though they turn to other gods and love raisin cakes." [2]So I bought her for fifteen shekels of silver and a homer of barley and a measure of wine.[r] [3]And I said to her, "You must remain as mine for many days; you shall not prostitute yourself; you shall not have intercourse with a man, nor I with you." [4]For the Israelites shall remain many days without king or prince, without sacrifice or pillar, without ephod or teraphim. [5]Afterward the Israelites shall return and seek the LORD their God and David their king; they shall come in awe to the LORD and to his goodness in the latter days.

4 Hear the word of the LORD, O people of Israel,
    for the LORD has an indictment
        against the inhabitants of the land.
There is no faithfulness or loyalty
    and no knowledge of God in the land.
[2] Swearing, lying, and murder,
    and stealing and adultery break out;
    bloodshed follows bloodshed.
[3] Therefore the land mourns,
    and all who live in it languish;
together with the wild animals
    and the birds of the air,
    even the fish of the sea are perishing.

[4] Yet let no one contend,
    and let none accuse,
    for with you is my contention, O priest.[s]

m 2.18 Heb *them*   n 2.22 That is, *God sows*   o 2.23 Cn: Heb *her*   p 2.23 That is, *not pitied*   q 2.23 That is, *not my people*   r 3.2 Gk: Heb *a homer of barley and a lethek of barley*   s 4.4 Cn: Meaning of Heb uncertain

2:19–20 *I will take you . . . and you shall know the LORD.* Cf. Isa. 62:4, which also describes a change in status from abandoned to a community and its land in which YHWH again resides. **2:21–23** The land will again provide with the certainty of seasons. *Jezreel.* The nuance "God sows" is clear. YHWH will "sow" the renewed kingdom in the land, and the land will produce, providing economic and political independence (cf. Jer. 31:32–33; Zech. 13:7–9).

3:1–5 This section either repeats 1:2 or describes additional infidelity, as it does not mention Gomer specifically. If Hosea is commanded to love another woman, then his actions mimic those of the woman. The command is *not* explicitly "Go, love *your* wife." It is simply *Go, love a woman [or wife]*, without specificity. **3:1** *Raisin cakes* refers to either sacrificial offerings or fine foods (cf. Song 2:5; 2 Sam. 6:19; 1 Chr. 16:3; Isa. 16:7). The Hebrew is not entirely clear whether it is the gods or the people who love raisin cakes. **3:2** Hosea exchanged *fifteen shekels of silver, a homer of barley,* and *a measure of wine* for the woman. A homer is equivalent to six bushels, or approximately 230 liters. Based on v. 3, the trade seems to be for a limited time, which led some scholars to suggest that Hosea redeems his woman, or wife, from slavery, based on the price. But that is not clear from the text. **3:3** The woman shall not have sex with other men or with Hosea. This parallels the wilderness experience of 2:3–5. **3:4** The wilderness experience of the people refers to a period without a king or the national cult. The *pillar* ("matsebah") may refer to a monument (cf. 2 Sam. 18:18) or a sacred pillar (cf. 1 Kgs. 14:23; 2 Kgs. 10:26–27). **3:5** After not having intercourse (v. 3), symbolizing the lack of a monarchy and national cult (v. 4), the people will return to YHWH and the Davidic monarchy (cf. 1 Kgs. 2:45; 9:5).

4:1–10 Yahweh accuses Israel. The indictment against Israel builds on the covenantal theme that permeates Hosea. **4:1** The Hebrew term for *indictment* ("rib"; v. 1) refers to a dispute, frequently public (cf. Deut. 17:8; 2 Sam. 22:44; Gen. 13:7; Jer. 15:10). **4:2** This list of activities emphasizes chaos. In contrast, a stable society relies on direct speech, truth, the preservation of life, and respect for (private) property. **4:3** Israel exists as a kingdom while its people are in the land. That *the land*

5 You shall stumble by day;
   the prophet also shall stumble with
     you by night,
   and I will destroy your mother.
6 My people are destroyed for lack of
     knowledge!
   Because you have rejected knowledge,
   I reject you from being a priest to me;
and since you have forgotten the law of
     your God,
   I also will forget your children.

7 The more they increased,
   the more they sinned against me;
   they changed*f* their glory into
     shame.
8 They feed on the sin of my people;
   they are greedy for their iniquity.
9 And it shall be like people, like priest;
   I will punish them for their ways
   and repay them for their deeds.
10 They shall eat but not be satisfied;
   they shall prostitute themselves but
     not multiply,
because they have forsaken the LORD
   to devote themselves to 11prostitution.

Wine and new wine
   take away the understanding.
12 My people consult a piece of wood,
   and their divining rod gives them
     oracles.
For a spirit of prostitution has led them
     astray,
   and they have prostituted
     themselves, forsaking their
     God.
13 They sacrifice on the tops of the
     mountains
   and make offerings upon the hills,
under oak, poplar, and terebinth
   because their shade is good.

Therefore your daughters prostitute
     themselves,
   and your daughters-in-law commit
     adultery.
14 I will not punish your daughters when
     they prostitute themselves
   nor your daughters-in-law when
     they commit adultery,

f 4.7 Tg Syr: MT *I will change*

mourns symbolizes the defeat of its monarchy and the displacement of its people. *All . . . languish* in a reversal of creation (cf. Gen. 1:20–25) because the kingdom's leaders pursue self-gain rather than the kingdom's stability (cf. Jer. 4:27–28; Zeph. 1:2–5). **4:5** *Destroy your mother.* A likely reference to the kingdom and its leaders, including the Yahwistic cult. But "mother" should be read with the children in mind (cf. Hos. 1–2). The kingdom will be defeated, but as the children will be renamed, there is hope (cf. 1:11; 2:22–23). **4:6** The relationship with the provider and protector will be lost, jeopardizing economic and political stability (cf. Jer. 6:2). The metaphor of the people as a wife dependent upon her husband for her well-being should be read here. Because the priests did not advise by the *law,* the future of the kingdom is in jeopardy (cf. 2 Kgs. 22:8–11; Mal. 2:7–8). **4:7** *Glory into shame.* Parallels the contrast between a woman adorned and provided for (cf. 2:8–9) and one whose nudity is shamefully exposed (cf. 2:3, 10). **4:8** Yahwistic priests were fed in part by sacrifices offered at the national temple (cf. Lev. 6:24–30). The prophet accuses the priests of encouraging sacrifices but failing to offer proper guidance. **4:9–10** That the priests are also guilty implies that all governing institutions have been corrupted. The wilderness experience of the people (2:3), which parallels that of the exodus tradition (cf. Exod. 14:10–13), will be one devoid of institutional structure and authority, which are necessary for any nation. *Prostitute . . . but not multiply.* The leaders cannot ensure the future of the kingdom because its economic and political well-being is under the control of foreign powers.

4:11–19 Wine and sexual infidelity. The accusation against the people focuses specifically on drunkenness, sexual activity, and divination. These symbolize the political inadequacies that led to the kingdom's defeat. **4:11** A condemnation not of drinking wine but of wine making people more malleable to priestly suggestion without proper discernment. **4:12** The reference here may be to the pillars of 10:1–2. *A piece of wood.* The Hebrew reads "in his wood." In parallel with *rod* ("maqqel"), "'ets" (*wood*) may refer to a staff. As sexual metaphors, they may also refer to male and female deities, with Asherah portrayed as a sacred pillar (cf. 2 Kgs. 10:26–27; 17:10; 18:4) and with a phallus, or "rod," representing YHWH or another male deity (cf. Hab. 2:11, 19, in which "'ets" and "'eben" ["stone"] may refer to idols). **4:13** The reference is to high places (cf. Num. 33:52; Deut. 12:2) and sacred orchards (cf. Isa. 1:29). **4:14** Some scholars have translated the Hebrew

for the men themselves go aside with
    prostitutes
  and sacrifice with female attendants;
thus a people without understanding
    comes to ruin.

¹⁵ Though you prostitute yourself,
    O Israel,
  do not let Judah become guilty.
Do not enter into Gilgal
    or go up to Beth-aven,
  and do not swear, "As the LORD lives."
¹⁶ Like a stubborn heifer,
    Israel is stubborn;
  can the LORD now feed them
    like a lamb in a broad pasture?

¹⁷ Ephraim is joined to idols—
    let him alone.
¹⁸ When their drinking is ended, they
    indulge in sexual orgies;
  they love lewdness more than their
    glory.^u
¹⁹ A wind has wrapped them^v in its
    wings,
  and they shall be ashamed because
    of their altars.^w

5 Hear this, O priests!
  Give heed, O house of Israel!

Listen, O house of the king!
  For the judgment pertains to you,
for you have been a snare at Mizpah
  and a net spread upon Tabor
² and a pit dug deep in Shittim,^x
  but I will punish all of them.

³ I know Ephraim,
  and Israel is not hidden from me,
for now, O Ephraim, you have
    prostituted yourself;
  Israel is defiled.
⁴ Their deeds do not permit them
  to return to their God.
For the spirit of prostitution is within
    them,
  and they do not know the LORD.

⁵ Israel's pride testifies against him;
  Ephraim^y stumbles in his guilt;
  Judah also stumbles with them.
⁶ With their flocks and herds they shall go
  to seek the LORD,
but they will not find him;
  he has withdrawn from them.
⁷ They have dealt faithlessly with the
    LORD,

u 4.18 Cn Compare Gk: Meaning of Heb uncertain
v 4.19 Heb *her*   w 4.19 Gk Syr: Heb *sacrifices*   x 5.2 Cn:
Meaning of Heb uncertain   y 5.5 Heb *Israel and Ephraim*

"qadesh" (*female attendants*) as "temple prostitute," but there is no evidence temple prostitution was practiced during this time. **4:15** *Gilgal* may refer to a location near the border between Benjamin and Judah (cf. Josh. 15:7), which had a shrine and altar (cf. 1 Sam. 10:8; Judg. 3:19). The word is also a play on "roll away" ("galal"), like the disgrace of Egypt being removed from the Hebrews (Josh. 5:9). *Beth-aven.* "House of wickedness." Likely a surrogate for Bethel. **4:16** Heifer ("parah"), or cow, can highlight the cow as a well-fed or fertile mother (cf. Gen. 41:2, 3, 26; Job 21:10; 1 Sam. 6:10). The term occurs in Amos 4:1 as a symbolic reference to economic status and neglect of responsibilities. In the situation described in Hos. 4:16, Israel has attributed its economic well-being to providers other than YHWH. **4:17** *Ephraim.* A reference to the northern kingdom of Israel. **4:18** See also v. 14. The reference here is not to sexual orgies but, based on previous uses of sexual metaphors, to the economic and political prostitution of the kingdom and its land by the people's rulers. **4:19** Cf. the "east wind" that refers to the foreign powers from Mesopotamia (Assyria and Babylonia; 12:1). Foreign power has bound the people up *in its wings* (cf. the correlation of wings and power in Exod. 19:4).

5:1–2 *Hear, give heed,* and *listen* represent part of a prophetic formula invoking obligation (cf. Isa. 66:5; Jer. 2:4; Ezek. 34:7, 9), whether of obedience (cf. Deut. 6:4), the acceptance of one's fate (cf. Ps. 92:12), or favorable action as a response (cf. 1 Sam. 15:22). *Priests, Israel,* and *king* identify those held responsible for Israel. *Mizpah* refers to either a location in Gilead (cf. 2 Kgs. 10:33) or a "watchtower," possibly on Mount Tabor. *Shittim* may refer to "revolters" or, with modification, a location (cf. Num. 25:1; Mic. 6:5 describes a journey from Shittim to Gilgal).

5:3–4 To *know* also describes sexual encounters (cf. Gen. 4:1; see also the note on 2:8), which fits the sexual metaphors of Hos. 1–4, and Israel's spirit of sexual infidelity (v. 4).

5:5–7 Sacrifices will not be accepted, and Judah too will stumble. *Illegitimate children* can be translated as "foreign children" and is not an obvious reference to Jezreel, Lo-ammi, and Lo-ruhamah.

Focus On: Idolatry in Social-Political Terms (Hosea 5)

In the ancient world, gods and cults reflected the political identities of their kingdoms. Their cultures did not separate religion from politics, and both reinforced national identity. That explains in part why biblical authors decried intermixing with foreigners (cf. Deut. 23:3; Neh. 13:1). It also provides a better context for Hosea's declaration that Israel would live without a king, a prince, a pillar, and idols (see notes on Hos. 3:4; 4:12). Of that list, "pillar" was likely a reference to a sacred pillar, many times associated with the goddess Asherah (cf. Deut. 12:3; 1 Kgs. 14:23; 2 Kgs. 17:10; 18:4; 23:14). The symbolism was not strictly religious but rather reflected political aspects of an ideal national identity.

In Hosea, the kingdom's pursuit of other "providers" (political authorities) should be read alongside Hosea's comments about idols and pillars. Accusations of idolatry were critiques of political and economic decisions and actions that diminished the uniqueness of Israelite identity by building dependencies upon foreign authorities, which were symbolized by their own deities. Recall the condemnation of the woman's pursuit of other *ba'alim* ("Baals"; cf. 2:17). The term may refer to a plurality of Baal figures, or it can refer to husbands, providers, or rulers. While the former sense loosely fits the religious context of Hosea, the latter reinforces Hosea's political concerns, which he expresses through sexual, possibly marital, metaphors (cf. Hos. 1–4; see **"Symbolic Emphasis of Children," p. 1229**). Perhaps the ambiguity was intentional: the fluidity of the term illustrates the ease with which one could combine religious, social, economic, and political critiques.

Promiscuity and idolatry are parallel metaphors in Hosea, as in other prophetic works, that converge on Israel's political defeat (cf. 5:2–5). Israel's leaders sought political alliances that not only subordinated the kingdom to foreign authorities but led to its downfall. In addition, accusations of idolatry put into tension the strife and struggle between two social, economic, and political institutions of authority: the monarchy and the cult. A kingdom's defeat was also its god's, and it explains the tension in Hosea, among other biblical books: with the fall of Israel, YHWH either had been defeated or was controlling foreign empires to exercise national judgment (cf. Hos. 5:14–15; see Jer. 23:1–4). Hosea hoped that if the latter, that same power would rebuild the defeated kingdom, one whose national identity was firmly rooted in the symbol of its own national deity.

Jeremiah W. Cataldo

for they have borne illegitimate
children.
Now the new moon shall devour
them along with their fields.

[8] Blow the horn in Gibeah,
the trumpet in Ramah.
Sound the alarm at Beth-aven;
look behind you, Benjamin!
[9] Ephraim shall become a desolation
in the day of punishment;
among the tribes of Israel
I declare what is sure.
[10] The princes of Judah have become
like those who remove the landmark;

on them I will pour out
my wrath like water.
[11] Ephraim is oppressed, crushed in
judgment,
because he was determined to go
after vanity.[z]
[12] Therefore I am like maggots to Ephraim
and like rottenness to the house of
Judah.
[13] When Ephraim saw his sickness
and Judah his wound,
then Ephraim went to Assyria
and sent to the great king.[a]

z 5.11 Gk: Meaning of Heb uncertain   *a* 5.13 Cn: Heb *to a king who will contend*

5:8 *Beth-aven* ("house of wickedness") may be a pejorative reference to Bethel (see 4:15). If Beth-aven (cf. 4:15; 5:8; 10:5) differed from Bethel, it may have been a place between Bethel and Ai (cf. Josh. 7:2). Even if they were two different locations, their proximity and their wordplay ("house of God" and "house of wickedness") suggest why Hosea conflates them.

5:9 Cf. 1 Chr. 12:30; Ps. 60:7; see also Hos. 9:16.

5:10 *Those who remove the landmark* do not respect private property. The princes of Judah are guilty of ceding YHWH's property to foreign powers. See also Deut. 19:14; 27:17; Job 24:2; Prov. 22:28; 23:10.

5:12 Inverting the role of a provider, YHWH becomes the rottenness that destroys provisions.

5:13 *Went to Assyria* should be read with the metaphor of sexual infidelity. Ephraim sought another "provider," but Assyria cannot cure the rottenness of YHWH (v. 12).

But he is not able to cure you
    or heal your wound.
[14] For I will be like a lion to Ephraim
    and like a young lion to the house of
        Judah.
    I myself will tear and go away;
        I will carry off, and no one shall
            rescue.
[15] I will return again to my place
    until they acknowledge their guilt
        and seek my face.
    In their distress they will beg my
        favor:

6 "Come, let us return to the Lord,
    for it is he who has torn, and he will
        heal us;
    he has struck down, and he will bind
        us up.
[2] After two days he will revive us;
    on the third day he will raise us up,
        that we may live before him.
[3] Let us know, let us press on to know the
        Lord;
    his appearing is as sure as the dawn;
    he will come to us like the showers,
        like the spring rains that water the
            earth."

[4] What shall I do with you, O Ephraim?
    What shall I do with you, O Judah?

Your love is like a morning cloud,
    like the dew that goes away early.
[5] Therefore I have hewn them by the
        prophets;
    I have killed them by the words of
        my mouth,
    and my[b] judgment goes forth as the
        light.
[6] For I desire steadfast love and not
        sacrifice,
    the knowledge of God rather than
        burnt offerings.

[7] But at[c] Adam they transgressed the
        covenant;
    there they dealt faithlessly with me.
[8] Gilead is a city of evildoers,
    tracked with blood.
[9] As robbers lie in wait[d] for someone,
    so the priests are banded together;[e]
    they murder on the road to Shechem;
    they commit a monstrous crime.
[10] In the house of Israel I have seen a
        horrible thing;
    Ephraim's prostitution is there; Israel
        is defiled.

[11] For you also, O Judah, a harvest is
        appointed.

b 6.5 Gk Syr: Heb *your*   c 6.7 Cn: Heb *like*   d 6.9 Cn:
Meaning of Heb uncertain   e 6.9 Syr: Heb *are a company*

5:14–15 *Like a lion* symbolizes overwhelming might and destruction (cf. Isa. 5:29; Jer. 2:15; Mic. 5:8; Ps. 35:17), which can be avoided if the people return to YHWH (see also Zech. 10:9–12).

6:1 The community responds to being *torn* by YHWH (see 5:14) by announcing their intention to *return to the Lord*.

6:2 Important occurrences on the *third day* fit a literary pattern of emphasis: this, this, and then this (cf. Gen. 22:4; Exod. 19:11; 1 Kgs. 12:12; Amos 4:4; see also Matt. 17:23).

6:3 In context (cf. Hos. 1–3), *know[ing]* entails a dependent relationship with mutual benefit: the people are provided for, and in turn, their future generations commit to YHWH to ensure their well-being (cf. Isa. 37:20; Ezek. 29:21; 35:15; 36:11–12; Zech. 6:15). YHWH's *appearing* brings fertility (cf. Song 2:11–13), which facilitates economic and political stability (cf. Ps. 71:5–8). *Spring rains* matured crops, occurring approximately March–April.

6:4 As a contrast to Judah, *Ephraim* refers to Israel. This series of questions highlights not only frustration but also the obligation of relationship (cf. 11:8). *Your love is like.* As the morning cloud dissipates and the dew evaporates early, so does the people's commitment (v. 5; 13:3).

6:5 The prophets declare judgment against the monarchy and temple (cf. 4:4–9). *Light* exposes what is hidden, making it known (cf. Job 12:22; Matt. 4:16). Judgment is linked to the appearance of YHWH (v. 3; contrast Amos 5:20).

6:6 Relationship along with ritual (see also Ezek. 16:8; Mic. 6:6–8).

6:7–11 *Adam* was a city in the Jordan River Valley (cf. Josh. 3:16). *Gilead* is sometimes an attributive, identifying different cities as part of a district, such as in Ramoth-gilead (cf. 1 Kgs. 22:29) or Jabesh-gilead (cf. Judg. 21:12). *Shechem* was a major town in Ephraim (cf. Josh. 20:7; 1 Kgs. 12:25). The covenant between YHWH and the Israelite tribes was declared there under Joshua (Josh. 24:25). It is also where Joseph's bones were said to have been buried (Josh. 24:32). **6:10** Sexually illicit behavior

When I would restore the fortunes of
my people,

7 ¹when I would heal Israel,
the corruption of Ephraim is revealed,
and the wicked deeds of Samaria,
for they deal falsely;
the thief breaks in,
and the bandits raid outside.
² But they do not consider
that I remember all their
wickedness.
Now their deeds surround them;
they are before my face.
³ By their wickedness they make the king
glad,
and the officials by their treachery.
⁴ They are all adulterers;
they are like a heated oven
whose baker does not need to stir the fire
from the kneading of the dough until
it is leavened.
⁵ On the day of our king the officials
became sick with the heat of wine;
he stretched out his hand with
mockers.
⁶ For they are kindled*f* like an oven; their
heart burns within them;
all night their anger smolders;

in the morning it blazes like a
flaming fire.
⁷ All of them are hot as an oven,
and they devour their rulers.
All their kings have fallen;
none of them calls upon me.

⁸ Ephraim mixes himself with the
peoples;
Ephraim is a cake not turned.
⁹ Foreigners devour his strength,
but he does not know it;
gray hairs are sprinkled upon him,
but he does not know it.
¹⁰ Israel's pride testifies against*g* him;
yet they do not return to the LORD
their God
or seek him, for all this.

¹¹ Ephraim has become like a dove,
silly and without sense;
they call upon Egypt, they go to
Assyria.
¹² As they go, I will cast my net over them;
I will bring them down like birds of
the air;

f 7.6 Gk Syr: Heb *brought near*   *g* 7.10 Or *humbles*

is set up as the contrast to covenant fidelity (v. 7), symbolized in the prophetic metaphor of marriage (cf. Ezek. 16:8; but see also Prov. 2:17).

7:2 *I remember* can mean the remembering of a jealous husband or an accounting in crimes for a court case over a broken covenant.

7:3 *Make the king glad* refers to actions that benefited the king, and his officials, rather than the nation.

7:4–5 *Adulterers* should be read in light of the previous accusation (v. 3). Reliance upon foreign political authorities was likened to adultery against YHWH. *Stir the fire* plays on the intensity of the sexual drive. Baking leavened bread requires constant high heat. On *heat of wine*, see also Isa. 28:1.

7:6 *Kindled like an oven* continues vv. 4–5. The officials are duplicitous. They seduce the king into trusting them, but the fire that burns within is really their own aspirations (cf. v. 4 with v. 6). With the dawn (the sun exposes), their fire will consume like anger (contrast 6:3 and notes on the verse).

7:7 *Devour their rulers.* Literally "judges." Those who could judge the officials' actions are removed (see also 5:1–5). Consequently, officials can move against their kings, who do not call upon YHWH (cf. 1 Kgs. 15:8–12).

7:8–10 While treating foreigners fairly is encouraged (cf. Deut. 10:17–19), mixing bloodlines is condemned (cf. Ezra 10:10; Deut. 7:1–6). *Pride.* See also 5:5.

7:11 Israel sought Egypt and Assyria as political and economic benefactors (cf. 2 Kgs. 15:19–20; 17:3–6). But doing so is deemed *silly*, reflecting the low intellect of a *dove* (cf. Ps. 55:5–7; Nah. 2:7; Ezek. 7:16), which is also a sacrificial animal. Israel/Ephraim sacrifices itself through poor political and economic decisions resulting in dependency upon foreign kingdoms (cf. Gen. 15:9–10).

7:12 *Cast my net.* The people will be gathered together and held for judgment, perhaps in contrast to YHWH's actions in Exod. 19:4. Regarding *assembly* and its context, the Hebrew is unclear. It reads, "as a report to their assembly/congregation." The references to the report and assembly/congregation lack specificity. They may refer to the "devoured" judges (v. 7), who fatefully gave their report.

I will discipline them according to
the report made to their assembly.[b]
[13] Woe to them, for they have strayed
from me!
Destruction to them, for they have
rebelled against me!
I would redeem them,
but they speak lies against me.

[14] They do not cry to me from the heart,
but they wail upon their beds;
they gash themselves for grain and
wine;
they rebel against me.
[15] It was I who trained and strengthened
their arms,
yet they plot evil against me.
[16] They turn to that which does not profit;[i]
they have become like a defective
bow;
their officials shall fall by the sword
because of the rage of their tongue.
So much for their babbling in the land
of Egypt.

8 Set the trumpet to your lips!
One like a vulture[j] is over the house
of the LORD,
because they have broken my covenant
and transgressed my law.
[2] They cry to me,
"My God, we know you!"[k]

[3] Israel has spurned the good;
the enemy shall pursue him.
[4] They made kings but not through me;
they set up princes but without my
knowledge.
With their silver and gold they made idols
for their own destruction.
[5] Your calf is rejected, O Samaria.
My anger burns against them.
How long will they be incapable of
innocence?
[6] For it is from Israel,
an artisan made it;
it is not God.
The calf of Samaria
shall be broken to pieces.

[7] For they sow the wind,
and they shall reap the whirlwind.
The standing grain has no heads;
it shall yield no meal;
if it were to yield,
foreigners would devour it.
[8] Israel is swallowed up;
now they are among the nations
as a useless vessel.
[9] For they have gone up to Assyria,
a wild ass wandering alone;

b 7.12 Meaning of Heb uncertain   i 7.16 Cn: Meaning of
Heb uncertain   j 8.1 Meaning of Heb uncertain   k 8.2 Gk
Syr: Heb adds *Israel*

7:13 Cf. Isa. 45:19; Jer. 5:1.

7:14–16 *Upon their beds* may be a reference to sexual infidelity (and its consequences; v. 4). *Grain and wine*, which the people will no longer be provided, were important economic products in Israel and Judah. *Babbling in . . . Egypt.* The Hebrew for *babbling* ("la'ag") can also be read as "mocking" or "stammering" (see also Ps. 123:4; Isa. 28:11). This may refer to the actions of King Hoshea (2 Kgs. 17:4), whose pursuit of Egyptian support led to his arrest and Assyria's siege of Samaria for three years (2 Kgs. 17:5).

8:1 The *trumpet* (Heb. "shofar") was used in battle (cf. Judg. 7:8; Isa. 58:1). Its use, though infrequent, as a sacred instrument developed later. *Vulture* is possibly a griffon vulture or eagle. The reference is to a bird with a large wingspan, which, as a metaphor, denotes power (cf. Jer. 4:13; Lam. 4:19; Deut. 28:49; also YHWH's actions, Exod. 19:4).

8:2 *Know* may be a double entendre (see also note for 6:3; Gen. 4:1; 1 Sam. 1:19; Judg. 19:25; 1 Kgs. 1:4). The Hebrew adds "Israel" after *My God, we know you,* but its grammatical purpose is not clear.

8:4 In the ancient Near East, a high priest of the national cult or a prophet of the national deity often coronated a king.

8:5–6 *Calf* is a likely reference to the temples in Bethel and Dan that Jeroboam set up when Israel abandoned its confederacy with Judah (1 Kgs. 12:26–30). Hosea's focus on Bethel/Beth-aven is likely still at work here (4:15; 5:8; 10:5, 15; 12:4).

8:7–10 *Whirlwind* is a symbol of power and destruction (cf. Job 21:18; Ps. 11:6; Jer. 4:13; Nah. 1:3). To *reap the whirlwind* implies futile actions resulting in destruction. The Assyrian Empire defeated Israel circa 722 BCE (cf. v. 8). *Wild ass.* See also Jer. 2:24. The Hebrew for *bargain with the nations* literally reads "hire themselves out," as though a prostitute (cf. 2:2–5).

Focus On: Apostasy (Hosea 8)

Apostasy refers to the rejection of one's religion. In the Hebrew Bible, apostasy is closely linked to idolatry. The first and second commandments (Exod. 20:2–6 // Deut. 5:6–10) state that the Israelites must not have any gods before God and must not create any image or idol for worship.

For a number of prophets, apostasy is the primary reason for God's anger, and the prophets warn that unless the people return to God, disaster will result. Hosea argues that the northern kingdom will fall because of idolatry (3:1; 4:12; 8:1–14) and improper worship of God through the creation of golden calves (chaps. 10 and 13). Jeremiah 7 concludes that God will punish with exile those in Judah who make offerings to other gods yet also claim to worship God. Some texts talk about apostasy in terms of marriage, where God is the husband and Israel is God's unfaithful wife, including Hos. 2, Jer. 2–3, and Ezek. 16 and 23. This metaphor describes Israel's punishment in terms of domestic violence and sexual assault (see **"Sexually Abusive Language," p. 1035**).

Even after the Babylonian exile, which the earlier prophets blamed on apostasy and idolatry, prophets continued to warn about both. In Jer. 44, the exiles in Egypt resist Jeremiah's argument that the worship of the Queen of Heaven will lead to the people's demise. Third Isaiah insists that the denial of God for other gods will lead to the idols' destruction, along with their worshipers' (chaps. 57, 65–66). The book of Malachi argues that improper sacrifices will bring punishment to the priests unless they change their ways.

The Shema (Deut. 6:4), one of the most important prayers in Judaism, asserts that God is *ehad*. *Ehad* may be translated as the number "one" or the word "alone." In both senses, the Israelites assert that God is their God and the only one they will worship. The idea of combining the worship of God with the worship of other deities or religious practices (syncretism) was not considered an acceptable idea by the biblical writers. While syncretism is more common today, debates about such practices still occur. For example, some Christians question if they can practice yoga or Buddhist meditation. The state of Alabama did not lift its ban on teaching yoga in public schools until 2021, although Sanskrit words such as *om* and *namaste* remain prohibited in these classes.

Stacy Davis

Ephraim has bargained for lovers.
¹⁰ Though they bargain with the nations,
    I will now gather them up.
They shall soon writhe
    under the burden of kings and
      princes.

¹¹ When Ephraim multiplied altars to
    expiate sin,
    they became to him altars for
      sinning.
¹² Though I write for him the multitude of
    my instructions,
    they are regarded as a strange thing.
¹³ Though they offer choice sacrifices,^{*l*}
    though they eat flesh,
    the LORD does not accept them.

Now he will remember their iniquity
    and punish their sins;
    they shall return to Egypt.
¹⁴ Israel has forgotten his Maker
    and built palaces,
and Judah has multiplied fortified cities,
    but I will send a fire upon his cities,
    and it shall devour his strongholds.

9 Do not rejoice, O Israel!
    Do not exult^{*m*} as other nations do,
for you have prostituted yourself,
    departing from your God.
You have loved a prostitute's pay
    on all threshing floors.

l 8.13 Cn: Meaning of Heb uncertain   *m* 9.1 Gk: Heb *To exultation*

8:12 Those who regard YHWH's instructions as strange are the rulers and officials (see also the subject of v. 9). Like women (continuing v. 9), they will be subordinated to the authority of other kings and princes (v. 10).

8:13 *Return to Egypt*—that is, from one foreign power to another (cf. 2 Kgs. 17:4; cf. Hos. 7:11; 11:11; Lam. 5:6; Deut. 17:16; but cf. Isa. 19:22–25).

8:14 This verse does not fit cleanly with the previous material. The coda on Judah may, however, be a call to a southern audience to learn from Israel's fate.

9:1 *As other nations do* highlights Israel's lack of national identity and loyalty to YHWH. Israel is YHWH's; other nations have their own deities. *Prostitute's pay.* Cf. Deut. 23:18; Isa. 23:18; Mic. 1:7.

² Threshing floor and wine vat shall not
   feed them,
  and the new wine shall fail them.
³ They shall not remain in the land of the
   Lord,
  but Ephraim shall return to Egypt,
  and in Assyria they shall eat unclean
   food.

⁴ They shall not pour drink offerings of
   wine to the Lord,
  and their sacrifices shall not please
   him.
Such sacrifices shall be like mourners'
   bread;
  all who eat of it shall be defiled,
for their bread shall be for their hunger
   only;
  it shall not come to the house of the
   Lord.

⁵ What will you do on the day of
   appointed festival
  and on the day of the festival of the
   Lord?
⁶ For even if they escape destruction,
  Egypt shall gather them;
  Memphis shall bury them.
Nettles shall possess their precious
   things of silver;ⁿ
  thorns shall be in their tents.

⁷ The days of punishment have come;
  the days of recompense have
   come.
  Israel will cry out,ᵒ

"The prophet is a fool;
  the man of the spirit is mad!"
Because of your great iniquity,
  your hostility is great.
⁸ The prophet is a sentinel for my God
   over Ephraim,
yet a hunter's snare is on all his ways
  and hostility in the house of his God.
⁹ They have deeply corrupted themselves
  as in the days of Gibeah;
he will remember their iniquity;
  he will punish their sins.

¹⁰ Like grapes in the wilderness,
  I found Israel.
Like the first fruit on the fig tree,
  in its first season,
  I saw your ancestors.
But they came to Baal-peor
  and consecrated themselves to a
   thing of shame
  and became detestable like the thing
   they loved.
¹¹ Ephraim's glory shall fly away like a bird—
  no birth, no pregnancy, no
   conception!
¹² Even if they bring up children,
  I will bereave them until no one is left.
Woe to them indeed
  when I depart from them!
¹³ Once I saw Ephraim as a young palm
  planted in a lovely meadow,ᵖ
  but now Ephraim must lead out his
   children for slaughter.

n 9.6 Meaning of Heb uncertain   o 9.7 Or *will know*
p 9.13 Meaning of Heb uncertain

9:2–3 Israel's fate includes a loss of economic stability. The *land* of Israel was metaphorically the home of YHWH. But like an offended husband, YHWH will drive the "prostituting" people from his "house." While important for their economic function, threshing floors were also locations where prostitutes would sometimes provide their services. *Unclean food.* Cf. Ezek. 4:12–13.

9:4 *Pour drink offerings of wine* is literally "pour out wine" (see also Exod. 30:9). The same action casts graven images (cf. Isa. 40:19; 44:10). The Hebrew phrase "bread of wickedness" ("lehem onim" [from "aven"]) plays on Beth-aven ("house of wickedness"; see also notes to 4:15; 5:8).

9:5–6 Memphis was the capital city of Lower Egypt. *Thorns.* What was once a place of habitation will be no longer (see also v. 3). Their tents (cities), once places of "sexual infidelity," will be overgrown (see 2:3).

9:7–9 *Israel will cry out.* The Hebrew has "will know" (cf. 6:3). With punishment, the people will know that the prophet with only positive messages was foolish. *Sentinel.* While a (true) prophet speaks judgment, like a "shofar" (8:1), he also sounds the alarm before the nation's enemies (cf. 5:8; 8:1).

9:10 *Baal-peor* was the place where, according to Num. 25:1–9, Hebrew men had sex with Moabite women, leading to their participation in Moabite cultic practices. They were executed (see also Deut. 4:3).

9:11–12 *No birth.* A possible play on Hosea's children as symbolic of the people's fate (Hos. 1–2). Children make the people's future possible, which YHWH promises to prevent.

¹⁴ Give them, O Lord—
  what will you give?
Give them a miscarrying womb
  and dry breasts.

¹⁵ Every evil of theirs began at Gilgal;
  there I came to hate them.
Because of the wickedness of their deeds
  I will drive them out of my house.
I will love them no more;
  all their officials are rebels.

¹⁶ Ephraim is stricken,
  their root is dried up,
  they shall bear no fruit.
Even though they give birth,
  I will kill the cherished offspring of
    their womb.
¹⁷ Because they have not listened to him,
  my God will reject them;
  they shall become wanderers among
    the nations.

10 Israel is a luxuriant vine
  that yields its fruit.
The more his fruit increased,
  the more altars he built;
as his country improved,
  he improved his pillars.
² Their heart is false;
  now they must bear their guilt.
The Lord^q will break down their altars
  and destroy their pillars.

³ For now they will say:
  "We have no king,
for we do not fear the Lord,
  and a king—what could he do for us?"
⁴ They utter mere words;
  with empty oaths they make covenants;
so litigation springs up like poisonous
    weeds
  in the furrows of the field.
⁵ The inhabitants of Samaria tremble
  for the calf^r of Beth-aven.
Its people shall mourn for it,
  and its idolatrous priests shall wail^s
    over it,
  over its glory that has departed
    from it.
⁶ The thing itself shall be carried to
    Assyria
  as tribute to the great king.^t
Ephraim shall be put to shame,
  and Israel shall be ashamed of his
    idol.^u

⁷ Samaria's king shall perish
  like a chip on the face of the waters.
⁸ The high places of Aven, the sin of
    Israel,
  shall be destroyed.
Thorn and thistle shall grow up
  on their altars.

q 10.2 Heb *he*   r 10.5 Gk Syr: Heb *calves*   s 10.5 Cn: Heb
exult   t 10.6 Cn: Heb *to a king who will contend*   u 10.6 Cn:
Heb *plan*

9:14 Cf. Ezek. 23:34. The breasts Ephraim offered its lovers will be dried and its womb a place of death. This metaphor emphasizes both a lack of fertility and a lack of appeal to foreign powers. Ephraim's economic and political stability will be undercut through its rejection by its previous lovers, or foreign providers.

9:15 *My house* likely refers to the land (see also v. 3). *Gilgal* is where the Israelite monarchy was established (in 1 Sam. 11:14). See also 1 Sam. 13:15; 2 Kgs. 2:1; note on 4:15.

9:16 See also v. 14. Killing children jeopardizes Ephraim's future.

10:1–2 Israel's prosperity gave it a false sense of security. *Pillars*, or sacred pillars (cf. Exod. 24:4; Hos. 3:4; Isa. 19:19), may be dedicated to YHWH or another deity. *Heart is false.* The Hebrew emphasizes "smooth," possibly as the type of speech meant to seduce (cf. Prov. 7:21).

10:3–6 *No king* represents a conceivable reference to the Assyrian conquest of Israel, but it may also imply a rejection of appointed kings (see also note on 8:4). *Empty oaths* signal a lack of covenantal commitment, which was earlier symbolized as sexual infidelity (cf. Hos. 1–2). Like a wife, Israel should be faithful to the ideal YHWH represents (see also 9:15 note). *Beth-aven.* Likely Bethel, where Jeroboam set up a calf in the temple, presumably as the deity's pedestal (1 Kgs. 12:31–33). Since Israel also worshiped YHWH, this may have functioned like the ark in Judah (cf. Exod. 25:22). *Glory that has departed.* Because of the actions of Israel's rulers, YHWH has departed, signaling defeat (cf. 1 Sam. 4:22; Ezek. 10:18). *Carried to Assyria.* It was common to carry off or destroy gods of defeated peoples as a political statement (see **"Idolatry in Social-Political Terms," p. 1234**).

10:7–8 *Samaria's king.* Cf. v. 3. *Chip.* A "splinter" separated from a main trunk, symbolizing a politically helpless king (cf. v. 1) who will perish in the turbulent political waters.

They shall say to the mountains, "Cover
us,"
and to the hills, "Fall on us."

9 Since the days of Gibeah you have
sinned, O Israel;
there they have continued.
Shall not war overtake them in
Gibeah?
10 I will come[v] against the wayward
people to punish them,
and nations shall be gathered against
them
when they are punished[w] for their
double iniquity.

11 Ephraim was a trained heifer
that loved to thresh,
and I spared her fair neck,
but I will make Ephraim break the
ground;
Judah must plow;
Jacob must harrow for himself.
12 Sow for yourselves righteousness;
reap steadfast love;
break up your fallow ground,
for it is time to seek the LORD,
that he may come and rain
righteousness upon you.

13 You have plowed wickedness;
you have reaped injustice;
you have eaten the fruit of lies.
Because you have trusted in your
chariots,[x]
in the multitude of your warriors,

14 therefore the tumult of war shall rise
against your people,
and all your fortresses shall be
destroyed,
as Shalman destroyed Beth-arbel on
the day of battle,
when mothers were dashed in pieces
with their children.
15 Thus it shall be done to you,
O Bethel,
because of your great wickedness.
At dawn the king of Israel
shall be utterly cut off.

11 When Israel was a child, I loved him,
and out of Egypt I called my son.
2 The more I[y] called them,
the more they went from me;[z]
they kept sacrificing to the Baals
and offering incense to idols.

3 Yet it was I who taught Ephraim to
walk;
I took them up in my[a] arms,
but they did not know that I healed
them.
4 I led them with cords of human
kindness,
with bands of love.
I was to them like those
who lift infants to their cheeks.[b]
I bent down to them and fed them.

v 10.10 Cn Compare Gk: Heb *In my desire* w 10.10 Gk:
Heb *bound* x 10.13 Gk: Heb *your way* y 11.2 Gk: Heb *they*
z 11.2 Gk: Heb *them* a 11.3 Gk Syr Vg: Heb *his* b 11.4 Or
who ease the yoke on their jaws

10:9–10 *Gibeah* (cf. Judg. 19–21), where the Israelites defeated the Benjaminites.

10:11–12 *Trained heifer.* One of the inconsistent metaphors in chap. 10; others include a fertile vine and a depiction of a masculine Israel as a contrast to a feminine one. The context suggests the heifer rejects its training, acting belligerently. *Spared her fair neck*, the meaning of which is unclear. The suggestion seems to be that the heifer was special to YHWH but rebelled (see also 4:16).

10:13–15 *Shalman destroyed Beth-arbel* is possibly a reference to Shalmaneser III's campaign, who fought Ahab in 853 BCE.

11:1 *Son* conveys not only lineage but also a loyal political relationship (cf. Exod. 4:22), symbolizing a future hope. *Out of Egypt.* A reference to the exodus tradition (cf. Exod. 12:29–42).

11:2 *Sacrificing to the Baals* is possibly a reference to sacrifices offered to Baal idols, here in parallel with incense or smoke offerings. The Hebrew term "ba'alim" can also be a plural form of "lords," "owners," or "husbands" (cf. Deut. 24:4; Exod. 21:29; Isa. 1:3). It may associate the pursuit of other gods with that of other "lords," or political and economic providers (see also 2:13 note).

11:3–4 That "ba'alim" (see v. 2) might be read as "owner" or "lord" may find support in this description of YHWH's actions: teaching, comforting, healing, demonstrating kindness, and feeding. These are actions of a provider, husband, and father. They also support justice and welfare, attributes often claimed by rulers (cf. Code of Hammurabi; see also Exod. 6:6; Isa. 51:5). This would be consistent with the reference to "son" in v. 1.

⁵ They shall return to the land of Egypt,
  and Assyria shall be their king,
  because they have refused to return
    to me.
⁶ The sword rages in their cities;
  it consumes their oracle priests
  and devours because of their
    schemes.
⁷ My people are bent on turning away
    from me.
  To the Most High they call,
  but he does not raise them up at all.ᶜ

⁸ How can I give you up, Ephraim?
  How can I hand you over, O Israel?
  How can I make you like Admah?
  How can I treat you like Zeboiim?
My heart recoils within me;
  my compassion grows warm and
    tender.
⁹ I will not execute my fierce anger;
  I will not again destroy Ephraim,
for I am God and no mortal,
  the Holy One in your midst,
  and I will not come in wrath.ᵈ

¹⁰ They shall go after the Lord,
  who roars like a lion;

when he roars,
  his children shall come trembling
    from the west.
¹¹ They shall come trembling like birds
    from Egypt
  and like doves from the land of
    Assyria,
  and I will return them to their homes,
    says the Lord.

¹² ᵉEphraim has surrounded me with
    lies
  and the house of Israel with deceit,
but Judah still walksᶠ with God
  and is faithful to the Holy One.

12 Ephraim herds the wind
  and pursues the east wind all day
    long;
  they multiply falsehood and violence;
  they make a treaty with Assyria,
  and oil is carried to Egypt.

² The Lord has an indictment against
    Judah
  and will punish Jacob according to
    his ways

c 11.7 Meaning of Heb uncertain   d 11.9 Meaning of Heb
uncertain   e 11.12 12.1 in Heb   f 11.12 Heb *roams* or *rules*

11:5–7 Hosea mentions Egypt and Assyria as contrasting imagery to YHWH and an independent Israel, who should not be dependent upon either of the former. But Israel's leaders do depend on them (in contrast to vv. 3–4), which undermines the status of YHWH among the nations. See also 8:13; 9:3; 10:6.

11:8–9 *Admah . . . Zeboiim.* These cities, allied with Sodom and Gomorrah, were defeated by a coalition including Amraphel, king of Shinar, or northern and southern Babylonia (cf. Gen. 14:1–2). According to Deut. 29:23, they were destroyed with Sodom and Gomorrah. *I will not* signals that YHWH will not destroy Ephraim like Admah and Zeboiim. This presumes the response in v. 10.

11:10–12 While the lion's roar is terrifying (cf. Isa. 5:29; Amos 3:8; Ps. 22:13), here it summons YHWH's *children* (cf. Joel 3:16). *Children* may be a link to Hosea's renamed children (1:11–2:1) or to the son of v. 1. *From the west.* Probably Egypt. Assyria and Babylonia were east. *But Judah.* A contrast that would have been apparent after Israel's defeat by the Assyrian Empire (ca. 722 BCE). Judah existed as a kingdom until 586 BCE. It is possible that this message, or a portion of it, was directed to Judah's rulers.

12:1. *Herds the wind.* An expression of futility (cf. note on 8:7–10). *East wind.* A reference to the Assyrian Empire, with whom they made treaties. *Oil is carried to Egypt.* One type of economic exchange and partnership.

12:2–6 *Indictment.* A legal charge for a broken agreement (see also note on 4:1), including political and economic alliances, such as between a suzerain and a vassal (see also Hos. 4:1; Mic. 6:2; Deut. 17:8). *Jacob.* The patriarch whose sons became the tribes of Israel and Judah (cf. Gen. 46:1–34; see also Exod. 1:5; 3:15–16; Sir. 36:13). *Womb . . . supplant.* Jacob clutched Esau's heel at birth (Gen. 25:24–26), later stealing his birthright and blessing (Gen. 27:30–36). Jacob *strove with God* at Penuel, where Jacob was renamed Israel (Gen. 32:24–30). *Bethel.* After fleeing Esau, Jacob dreamed of a ladder or stairway to the heavens at Bethel (Gen. 28:10–22), in which the Abrahamic covenant (cf. Gen. 12:1–8) was restated. He later built an altar at Bethel, confirming it as a sacred space (Gen. 35:1). See also note on 5:8.

and repay him according to his
    deeds.
[3] In the womb he tried to supplant his
    brother,
    and in his manhood he strove with
      God.
[4] He strove with the angel and prevailed;
    he wept and sought his favor;
  he met him at Bethel,
    and there he spoke with him.[g]
[5] The LORD the God of hosts,
    the LORD is his name!
[6] But as for you, return to your God;
    hold fast to love and justice,
    and wait continually for your God.

[7] A trader in whose hands are false
    balances,
    he loves to oppress.
[8] Ephraim has said, "Ah, I am rich;
    I have gained wealth for myself;
  in all of my gain
    no offense has been found in me
    that would be sin."[h]
[9] I am the LORD your God
    from the land of Egypt;
  I will make you live in tents again,
    as in the days of the appointed festival.

[10] I spoke to the prophets;
    it was I who multiplied visions,
    and through the prophets I will bring
      destruction.
[11] In[i] Gilead there is iniquity;
    they shall surely come to nothing.
  In Gilgal they sacrifice bulls,
    so their altars shall be like stone heaps

    on the furrows of the field.
[12] Jacob fled to the land of Aram;
    there Israel served for a wife,
    and for a wife he guarded sheep.[j]
[13] By a prophet the LORD brought Israel up
    from Egypt,
    and by a prophet he was guarded.
[14] Ephraim has given bitter offense,
    so his Lord will bring his crimes
      down on him
    and pay him back for his insults.

13 When Ephraim spoke, there was
    trembling;
  he was exalted in Israel,
    but he incurred guilt through Baal
    and died.
[2] And now they keep on sinning
    and make a cast image for
      themselves,
  idols of silver made according to their
    understanding,
    all of them the work of artisans.
  "Sacrifice to these," they say.[k]
    People are kissing calves!
[3] Therefore they shall be like the
    morning mist
    or like the dew that goes away early,
  like chaff that swirls from the threshing
    floor
    or like smoke from a window.

[4] Yet I have been the LORD your God
    ever since the land of Egypt;

g 12.4 Gk Syr: Heb *us* h 12.8 Meaning of Heb uncertain
i 12.11 Syr: Heb *If* j 12.12 Heb lacks *sheep* k 13.2 Cn Compare Gk: Heb *To these they say sacrifices of people*

12:7–9 Ephraim's self-confidence (cf. v. 8), or that of its leaders, has changed it. *Tents* invokes the tradition of the exodus (cf. Lev. 23:42–43; Neh. 8:17).

12:10–14 *Spoke to the prophets*, which ones are not specified, nor whether they listened (cf. Jer. 23:9; Hos. 4:5; Ezek. 22:28; see also 9:7–9 note). *Gilead . . . Gilgal.* The reason Gilead is listed is not clear. It could be its association with Jacob, where he camped after Rachel stole her father's household idols (Gen. 31:19; see also 31:21–25). Joshua set up memorials of the escape from Egypt in Gilgal (Josh. 4:20; 5:9), which was also his base of operations for some time (cf. Josh. 10:7, 15, 43; 14:6; see also note on Hos. 4:15). *By a prophet*—that is, Moses (Deut. 34:10).

13:1–3 Israel controlled the intersection of trade routes in the Jezreel Valley (see the **"Introduction to Hosea," pp. 1226–27**; note on 1:4–9). *Guilt through Baal.* Here "ba'al" is singular, prefixed with a preposition and a definite article. The preceding verb, "'asham" (be guilty), does not expect a preposition. Rather, the preposition attached to "ba'al" seems to mark a location, with "ba'al" being a shortened form of Baal-peor (cf. Hos. 9:10; Num. 25:3, 5; Deut. 4:3). *Kissing calves* refers to the calves Jeroboam commissioned (see note for 10:3–6; also 1 Kgs. 12:28–29). Kissing invokes Hosea's prostitution metaphors.

13:4–8 Jeroboam's calves (in Bethel and Dan) were associated with a deity who liberated the people from *Egypt* (again, 1 Kgs. 12:28–29). YHWH was worshiped in the northern kingdom, so the calves

you know no God but me,
and besides me there is no savior.
[5] It was I who fed[l] you in the
wilderness,
in the land of drought.
[6] When I fed[m] them, they were satisfied;
they were satisfied, and their heart
was proud;
therefore they forgot me.
[7] So I will become like a lion to them;
like a leopard I will lurk beside the
way.
[8] I will fall upon them like a bear robbed
of her cubs
and will tear open the covering of
their heart;
there I will devour them like a lion,
as a wild animal would mangle them.

[9] I will destroy you, O Israel;
who can help you?[n]
[10] Where now is[o] your king, that he may
save you?
Where in all your cities are your
rulers,
of whom you said,
"Give me a king and rulers"?
[11] I gave you a king in my anger,
and I took him away in my wrath.

[12] Ephraim's iniquity is bound up;
his sin is kept in store.
[13] The pangs of childbirth come for him,
but he is an unwise son,
for at the proper time he does not
present himself

at the mouth of the womb.

[14] Shall I ransom them from the power of
Sheol?
Shall I redeem them from Death?
O Death, where are[p] your plagues?
O Sheol, where is[q] your destruction?
Compassion is hidden from my eyes.

[15] Although he may flourish among
rushes,[r]
the east wind shall come, a blast
from the LORD,
rising from the wilderness,
and his fountain shall dry up;
his spring shall be parched.
It shall strip his treasury
of every precious thing.
[16] [s]Samaria shall bear her guilt
because she has rebelled against her
God;
they shall fall by the sword;
their little ones shall be dashed in
pieces,
and their pregnant women ripped
open.

14 Return, O Israel, to the LORD your
God,
for you have stumbled because of
your iniquity.

l 13.5 Gk Syr: Heb *knew* *m* 13.6 Cn: Heb *according to
their pasture* *n* 13.9 Gk Syr: Heb *for in me is your help*
o 13.10 Gk Syr Vg: Heb *I will be* *p* 13.14 Gk Syr: Heb *I will
be* *q* 13.14 Gk Syr: Heb *I will be* *r* 13.15 Or *among brothers*
s 13.16 14.1 in Heb

may have been associated with him (see also notes for 10:3–6; 13:1–3). *Savior*, or "liberator," one who
ensures victory (cf. Deut. 20:4; Judg. 3:9; 2 Kgs. 19:34). *Fed you.* See also Exod. 16:8–35. *Lion, leopard,*
and *bear* are predatory animals, here used as metaphors of judgment (see also Hos. 5:14).

13:9–13 Poor political and economic decisions undermined Israel's royal institution. *Mouth of the
womb.* A reminder that birthing complications posed a high risk for both mother and child (see also
"Symbolic Emphasis of Children," p. 1229). Contrast Jer. 30:6.

13:14–16 *Sheol.* Cf. Pss. 6:5; 9:17; 30:3; Isa. 28:15; 28:18. *O Death, where are your plagues?* Possibly a
reference to a rival god, Mot (Death), associated with the underworld, infertility, and drought, which
were consequences of his plagues (cf. Exod. 9:15). Mot is powerless before YHWH, who devours the
people (v. 8). *East wind.* A reference to the empires from Mesopotamia. YHWH is credited with controlling the actions of the empires (see 12:1). YHWH will exercise judgment *from the wilderness* and
rekindle a relationship with the people (2:14). A kingdom's *treasury* or wealth was controlled by its
rulers. Conquering armies would often destroy its next generation, here signified by *little ones* and
pregnant women (cf. 2 Kgs. 8:12; Nah. 3:10; Isa. 13:8), jeopardizing the kingdom's future (cf. notes on
1:4–9; 9:11–12, 14, 16; see **"Symbolic Emphasis of Children," p. 1229**).

14:1–3 Israel's former "lovers" cannot save it. *Take words* is an awkward phrase that seems associated with *the fruit of our lips. Words* may also refer to a covenant with YHWH (cf. Exod. 24:3).
Orphan finds mercy. Perhaps a play on the metaphor of Hosea's relationship with Gomer (cf. Hos.

Focus On: Repentance (Hosea 14)

Repentance, or expressing remorse to God through word and action for bad behavior, is the primary solution for any problem in prophetic books. According to Deut. 28–30, God rewards obedience and punishes disobedience; however, even during punishment, if the people "return to the Lord [their] God," then punishment will end (Deut. 30:2). The word translated as "repent" or "repentance" in the Hebrew Bible comes from the word *shuv*, meaning "to return" or "to turn back." Repentance in theory means turning away from what is wrong and turning toward what is right.

What repentance looks like in practice depends on the prophetic book and its context. In Hosea, the people are called to abandon idolatry and an alliance with Assyria (14:1–3). Jeremiah argues that if the people repent and leave their idols behind, then they will avoid God's wrath (4:1–4). While this does not happen in time to avoid exile, the prophet notes that the people's repentance after exile will lead to its eventual end (Jer. 31:19–26). Ezekiel 13 states that those prophets who do not encourage people to repent when it is necessary will be punished themselves. In Malachi, the speaker calls for the people to return to God by obeying, among other things, the laws for proper sacrifice and giving offerings (Mal. 1:6–14; 3:8–12).

Perhaps most importantly, prophets call for repentance because they believe in God's love and mercy. Joel asks the people to fast and pray that God will remove the locust plague from the land. The locust plague does not appear to be a punishment for wrongdoing, but the prophet concludes that it cannot hurt to repent anyway: "Return to the Lord your God, for he is gracious and merciful, slow to anger, abounding in steadfast love, and relenting from punishment" (2:13). Jonah quotes the same passage when the prophet complains about God sparing the Ninevites when they engage in an all-out fast in the hopes that God will pardon them (3:7–9; 4:2). And it is this hope of God's kindness that motivates calls to repent, such as the one in Isaiah: "Seek the Lord while he may be found; call upon him while he is near; let the wicked forsake their way and the unrighteous their thoughts; let them return to the Lord, that he may have mercy on them, and to our God, for he will abundantly pardon" (55:6–7).

Stacy Davis

---

² Take words with you
　and return to the Lord;
say to him,
　"Take away all guilt;
accept that which is good,
　and we will offer
　the fruit*ᵗ* of our lips.
³ Assyria shall not save us;
　we will not ride upon horses;
we will say no more, 'Our God,'
　to the work of our hands.
In you the orphan finds mercy."

⁴ I will heal their disloyalty;
　I will love them freely,
　for my anger has turned from them.

⁵ I will be like the dew to Israel;
　he shall blossom like the lily;
　he shall strike root like the forests of
　　Lebanon.*ᵘ*
⁶ His shoots shall spread out;
　his beauty shall be like the olive tree
　and his fragrance like that of
　　Lebanon.
⁷ They shall again live beneath my*ᵛ*
　　shadow;
　they shall flourish as a garden;*ʷ*
they shall blossom like the vine;
　their fragrance shall be like the wine
　　of Lebanon.

t 14.2 Gk Syr: Heb *bulls*　*u* 14.5 Cn: Heb *like Lebanon*
v 14.7 Heb *his*　*w* 14.7 Cn: Heb *they shall grow grain*

1–2). It implies the loss of the interest and provision of the foreign power, also of the "mother," Israel's ruling authorities. The term for mercy comes from the same Hebrew root as the term for one of Hosea's children (Lo-)Ruhamah. The orphaned child symbolizes hope, which would suggest that the child also symbolizes the remnant of the nation.

14:4–7 *Blossom* and *strike root*. After the wilderness period (cf. 2:3), the people will be cultivated into a kingdom. *Fragrance like that of Lebanon*. Perhaps the scent of the forests, which included olive and cedar trees (see also Song 4:11). The reference may also include the crocus plant, from which saffron, with its powerful aroma, is produced. *Beneath my shadow* refers to protection, like the shadows of a city wall (cf. Jer. 48:45; Ps. 91:1; but see also the shadow under wings, Pss. 17:8;

⁸ O Ephraim, what have Iˣ to do with
    idols?
  It is I who answer and look after you.ʸ
  I am like an evergreen cypress;
    your fruit comes from me.
⁹ Those who are wise understand these
    things;

those who are discerning know
    them.
For the ways of the Lord are right,
  and the upright walk in them,
  but transgressors stumble in them.

x 14.8 Or *What more has Ephraim* *y* 14.8 Heb *him*

36:7; 57:1; 63:7; see also note on Hos. 4:19). *Live, flourish, blossom.* A reversal of the people's promised destruction (cf. 4:6; 13:4–8). *Fragrance . . . like the wine of Lebanon.* Good wine that has not spoiled has a powerful aroma.

14:8 *It is I.* YHWH reminds the people that he, not any foreign power, was Israel's provider. *Evergreen cypress,* or "luxuriant cypress." The appeal of Lebanon's forests, and the economic promise they offer, is claimed by YHWH, who makes things grow in the wilderness (cf. Isa. 41:19; 55:13).

14:9 A call for wisdom and understanding to discern what has been written (cf. Ps. 107:43). This may refer to the sentiment expressed in Deut. 1:13 that wise men with understanding should be leaders. That would be consistent with the view that Hosea's primary audience is the ruling aristocracy. Consequently, new leaders should learn from the mistakes of those past.

JOEL

Authorship, Date, and Literary History

Joel's author is unknown, as "Joel son of Pethuel" (1:1) may not refer to an actual person. While the precise date is also unclear, the context suggests a date in the postexilic period (539–333 BCE), when Israel was under the control of the Persian Empire. Because the temple, or "the house of the LORD your God" (1:14; cf. 1:16; 2:17), exists, the earliest date would be after the completed reconstruction of the Second Temple in 515 BCE. The reference to Israelites being sold to the Greeks suggests a later postexilic date in the fifth or fourth century. The book describes a locust plague using apocalyptic and eschatological (end of the world) language, which also suggests a later date (see **"Apocalypse," p. 1216**).

Intertextuality in Joel

The book includes a description of mourning rituals (fasting and wearing of sackcloth) that appears in other biblical books such as Isa. 58 and Jonah 3. The "day of the LORD" (Joel 1:15), an eschatological reference, also appears in the books of Zephaniah, Zechariah, and Malachi, with varying emphases on divine judgment on the wicked, followed by divine rewarding of the righteous (see **"The Day of the Lord," p. 1322**).

Joel in Jewish Tradition

Joel 2:15–27, an ultimately successful call for fasting in the hope that God will show mercy in the face of the locust plague, is read on Shabbat Shuvah, the Sabbath service between Rosh Hashanah (the Jewish New Year) and Yom Kippur (the Day of Atonement). These days are known as the Days of Awe, a time in which Jews reflect on the previous year and make whatever amends are necessary for mistakes against others and God. *Shuvah* in Hebrew means to return or to repent, so it is a time for turning from one's mistakes and turning toward better conduct. Theologically, the word refers to conversion, a change in one's religious life, ideally for the better.

Reading Guide

The primary issue in the book of Joel is how to get rid of a massively destructive locust plague. While such plagues are common in the Middle East and Africa, from the author's perspective, this one is so severe that it is almost apocalyptic, with God apparently leading the locust army (2:11). Such an infestation can only signal the end of the world, since the army is literally causing earthquakes and blocking every source of natural light (2:2, 10). Therefore, everyone in the community must pray for relief—farmers, priests, the old, the young, the newlyweds. The author describes the loss of crops and the risk to humans and animals, making prayer and fasting even more urgent activities.

The community comes together "with fasting, with weeping, and with mourning" (2:12). The people trust in the goodness of God, described as "gracious and merciful, slow to anger, abounding in steadfast love, and relenting from punishment" (2:13). While the prophet never says what the people have done to be punished with locusts, the solution is to ask God for help as the end of time approaches.

Once God answers the people's prayer and destroys the locusts, however, the text turns to the final judgment, which will be a violent and catastrophic one. Darkness will fall again, and God will employ strict retribution against all Israel's enemies, even becoming a trader of enslaved people (3:8). Israel will win the final battle and live in safety because God "will avenge their blood, and [God] will not clear the guilty" (3:21).

The theme of apocalyptic eschatology, while a part of the Hebrew Bible (see Zechariah for one example), has a particular view of the world that may be disturbing to contemporary readers. Specifically, the idea that God will destroy the lands and lives of those who act against God's chosen people is a reminder that in many biblical texts, God is not the God of everyone. The gracious God of Joel 2 is gracious to God's people and absolutely ruthless toward those who are not God's

people. The view of divine retribution, where God rewards the righteous and punishes the wicked, while common in the Hebrew Bible, is not a part of contemporary Jewish theology today. Apocalyptic eschatology can best be described as a cry of the oppressed (for one such cry, see Ps. 137). Those who have been crushed in life long to have their fortunes restored in a later and better world, where "the mountains shall drip sweet wine, the hills shall flow with milk, and all the streambeds of Judah shall flow with water" (Joel 3:18). While such a desire may be natural, the idea that God favors some above others has had devastating historical consequences, from justifying Christian anti-Judaism for centuries to declaring Native Americans and Africans as not fully human in early modern American theology. When reading Joel, one should be aware of the longing for freedom that those under the rule of the Persian Empire may have experienced while recognizing that such longing can be expressed in violent ways. The reader has to decide what type of eschatology they would like, if any.

Stacy Davis

1 The word of the Lord that came to Joel son of Pethuel:

² Hear this, O elders;
give ear, all inhabitants of the land!
Has such a thing happened in your days
or in the days of your ancestors?
³ Tell your children of it,
and let your children tell their children,
and their children another generation.

⁴ What the cutting locust left,
the swarming locust has eaten;
what the swarming locust left,
the hopping locust has eaten;
and what the hopping locust left,
the destroying locust has eaten.

⁵ Wake up, you drunkards, and weep,
and wail, all you wine drinkers,
over the sweet wine,
for it is cut off from your mouth.
⁶ For a nation has invaded my land,
powerful and innumerable;
its teeth are lions' teeth,
and it has the fangs of a lioness.
⁷ It has laid waste my vines
and splintered my fig trees;
it has stripped off their bark and thrown it down;
their branches have turned white.

⁸ Lament like a virgin dressed in sackcloth
for the husband of her youth.
⁹ The grain offering and the drink offering are cut off
from the house of the Lord.
The priests mourn,
the ministers of the Lord.
¹⁰ The fields are devastated,
the ground mourns,
for the grain is destroyed,
the wine dries up,
the oil fails.

1:1 The prophetic call. Joel receives *the word of the Lord*, which designates him as a prophet.
1:2–12 Problem. Many prophetic books address a particular ethical or social dilemma. In Joel's context, the problem is a natural disaster, specifically a plague of locusts. **1:4** *Cutting locust . . . swarming locust . . . hopping locust . . . destroying locust.* There are four Hebrew words for locusts, "gazam," "arbeh," "yelek," and "hasil"; while they are translated as "cutting," "swarming," "hopping," and "destroying," those translations are based on the destructive nature of any locust infestation. Using all of the Hebrew words suggests the severity of the problem and the large number of locusts plaguing the land. **1:5–12** The locust attack has caused an agricultural catastrophe, destroying vines and fruit trees, grain and barley. As a result, everyone suffers, from those who enjoy a good drink on occasion to priests, who can no longer receive the sacrifices they need to survive because the people have nothing to give (see Lev. 21–22). The prophet calls for people to *wail* in vv. 5 and 11 (Heb. "yalal," or "howl") for their losses, the way a woman would cry if her fiancé died before their wedding. **1:10** *The fields are devastated, the ground mourns.* Even the earth cries out because of the locusts' destruction (cf. Hos. 4:3).

¹¹ Be dismayed, you farmers;
    wail, you vinedressers,
over the wheat and the barley,
    for the crops of the field are ruined.
¹² The vine withers;
    the fig tree droops.
Pomegranate, palm, and apple—
    all the trees of the field are
        dried up;
surely, joy withers away
    among the people.

¹³ Put on sackcloth and lament, you
        priests;
    wail, you ministers of the altar.
Come, pass the night in sackcloth,
    you ministers of my God!
Grain offering and drink offering
    are withheld from the house of
        your God.

¹⁴ Consecrate a fast;
    call a solemn assembly.
Gather the elders
    and all the inhabitants of the land
to the house of the Lord your God,
    and cry out to the Lord.

¹⁵ Alas for the day!
For the day of the Lord is near,
    and as destruction from the
        Almighty*a* it comes.
¹⁶ Is not the food cut off
    before our eyes,
joy and gladness
    from the house of our God?

¹⁷ The seed shrivels under the clods;*b*
    the storehouses are desolate;

the granaries are ruined
    because the grain has withered.
¹⁸ How the animals groan!
    The herds of cattle wander about
because there is no pasture for
        them;
    even the flocks of sheep are
        perishing.

¹⁹ To you, O Lord, I cry,
    for fire has devoured
        the pastures of the wilderness,
and flames have burned
    all the trees of the field.
²⁰ Even the wild animals cry to you
    because the watercourses are
        dried up,
and fire has devoured
    the pastures of the wilderness.

2 Blow the trumpet in Zion;
    sound the alarm on my holy
        mountain!
Let all the inhabitants of the land
        tremble,
    for the day of the Lord is coming, it
        is near—
² a day of darkness and gloom,
    a day of clouds and thick
        darkness!
Like blackness spread upon the
        mountains,
    a great and powerful army comes;
their like has never been from of old,
    nor will be again after them
    in ages to come.

a 1.15 Traditional rendering of Heb *Shaddai* *b* 1.17 Meaning of Heb uncertain

1:13–20 Possible solution. Under these circumstances, the prophet calls for rituals of mourning in hopes of gaining God's attention because the situation is so dire. Even the animals are crying out in distress because they do not have sufficient food and water (vv. 18 and 20). **1:13** *Put on sackcloth and lament, you priests; wail, you ministers of the altar.* Sackcloth is an itchy material worn as a sign of repentance. **1:14** *Consecrate a fast; call a solemn assembly.* Similarly, fasting, the intentional abstaining from food, is also a sign of repentance. Note, however, that the prophet does not indicate that the people have committed any sin that would have brought the locusts upon them and therefore would require repentance. **1:15** *The day of the Lord.* The phrase usually has an eschatological (end of the world) meaning (see **"The Day of the Lord," p. 1322**). In this case, the locusts are so numerous that the prophet thinks they must be a sign that the world is about to end. The phrase reappears in chaps. 2 and 3.

2:1–11 The locust invasion. The text describes the locusts as an unprecedented attacking army, destroying every natural resource, that signals the end of time. The locusts are called *war horses*, a *powerful army, warriors,* and *soldiers* (vv. 4, 5, and 7). They move in formation and systematically destroy everything in sight. **2:2** *For the day of the Lord is coming, it is near—a day of darkness and*

³ Fire devours in front of them,
    and behind them a flame burns.
Before them the land is like the garden
    of Eden,
    but after them a desolate wilderness,
    and nothing escapes them.

⁴ They have the appearance of horses,
    and like war horses they charge.
⁵ As with the rumbling of chariots,
    they leap on the tops of the mountains,
like the crackling of a flame of fire
    devouring the stubble,
like a powerful army
    drawn up for battle.

⁶ Before them peoples are in anguish;
    all faces grow pale.^c
⁷ Like warriors they charge;
    like soldiers they scale the wall.
Each keeps to its own course;
    they do not swerve from their paths.
⁸ They do not jostle one another;
    each keeps to its own track;
they burst through the weapons
    and are not halted.
⁹ They leap upon the city;
    they run upon the walls;
they climb up into the houses;
    they enter through the windows like
    a thief.

¹⁰ The earth quakes before them;
    the heavens tremble.

The sun and the moon are darkened,
    and the stars withdraw their shining.
¹¹ The LORD utters his voice
    at the head of his army;
how vast is his host!
    Numberless are those who obey his
    command.
Truly the day of the LORD is great,
    terrible indeed—who can endure it?

¹² Yet even now, says the LORD,
    return to me with all your heart,
with fasting, with weeping, and with
    mourning;
¹³   rend your hearts and not your
    clothing.
Return to the LORD your God,
    for he is gracious and merciful,
slow to anger, abounding in steadfast
    love,
    and relenting from punishment.
¹⁴ Who knows whether he will not turn
    and relent
    and leave a blessing behind him,
a grain offering and a drink offering
    for the LORD your God?

¹⁵ Blow the trumpet in Zion;
    consecrate a fast;
call a solemn assembly;
¹⁶   gather the people.
Consecrate the congregation;
    assemble the aged;

c 2.6 Meaning of Heb uncertain

gloom, a day of clouds and thick darkness! Like blackness spread upon the mountains, a great and powerful army comes; their like has never been from of old, nor will be again after them in ages to come. The number of locusts is so great that they literally appear to block out natural light. **2:10** *The earth quakes before them; the heavens tremble. The sun and the moon are darkened, and the stars withdraw their shining.* The disasters are another eschatological sign, specifically an apocalyptic one, in which the upcoming end of the world brings an upheaval of the natural order (see **"Apocalypse," p. 1216**). **2:11** *The LORD utters his voice at the head of his army; how vast is his host! . . . Truly the day of the LORD is great, terrible indeed—who can endure it?* The acknowledgment that God is responsible for the locust plague explains the call to prayer and mourning in chap. 1 and the repeated call in the next set of verses. Because the Hebrew Bible does not have a concept of a devil or evil spirits that cause disaster (see **"The Satan," p. 687**), such troubles either come directly from God (as in this case) or happen with God's full knowledge (see Job 1–2).

2:12–17 Call to prayer. The prophet, speaking in God's name, tells the people to repent completely and wholeheartedly, with a community-wide fast, in the hopes that God will remove the locusts not only for the people's sake but for the sake of God's own reputation. **2:13** *Return to the LORD your God, for he is gracious and merciful, slow to anger, abounding in steadfast love, and relenting from punishment.* This divine description, seen in Exod. 34:6 and Jonah 4:2, gives the people hope that God will spare them. **2:16** *Assemble the aged; gather the children, even infants at the breast. Let the bridegroom leave his room and the bride her canopy.* Groups that are typically excluded from fasting must now participate, another example of the seriousness of the locust infestation.

gather the children,
even infants at the breast.
Let the bridegroom leave his room
and the bride her canopy.

[17] Between the vestibule and the altar,
let the priests, the ministers of the
LORD, weep.
Let them say, "Spare your people,
O LORD,
and do not make your heritage a
mockery,
a byword among the nations.
Why should it be said among the
peoples,
'Where is their God?'"

[18] Then the LORD became jealous for his
land
and had pity on his people.
[19] In response to his people the LORD said:
"I am sending you
grain, wine, and oil,
and you will be satisfied;
and I will no more make you
a mockery among the nations.

[20] I will remove the northern army far
from you
and drive it into a parched and
desolate land,
its front into the eastern sea
and its rear into the western sea;
its stench and foul smell will rise up."
Surely he has done great things!

[21] Do not fear, O soil;
be glad and rejoice,
for the LORD has done great things!
[22] Do not fear, you animals of the field,
for the pastures of the wilderness are
green;
the tree bears its fruit;
the fig tree and vine give their full
yield.

[23] O children of Zion, be glad,
and rejoice in the LORD your God,

for he has given the early rain[d] for your
vindication;
he has poured down for you
abundant rain,
the early and the later rain, as before.
[24] The threshing floors shall be full of
grain;
the vats shall overflow with wine and
oil.

[25] I will repay you for the years
that the swarming locust has eaten,
the hopper, the destroyer, and the
cutter,
my great army that I sent against you.

[26] You shall eat in plenty and be satisfied
and praise the name of the LORD your
God,
who has dealt wondrously with you.
And my people shall never again be put
to shame.
[27] You shall know that I am in the midst of
Israel
and that I, the LORD, am your God
and there is no other.
And my people shall never again be put
to shame.

[28] [e]Then afterward
I will pour out my spirit on all flesh;
your sons and your daughters shall
prophesy,
your old men shall dream dreams,
and your young men shall see visions.
[29] Even on the male and female slaves,
in those days I will pour out my spirit.

30 I will show portents in the heavens
and on the earth, blood and fire and columns of smoke. [31]The sun shall be turned to
darkness and the moon to blood, before the
great and terrible day of the LORD comes.
[32]Then everyone who calls on the name of
the LORD shall be saved, for in Mount Zion
and in Jerusalem there shall be those who

d 2.23 Meaning of Heb uncertain   e 2.28 3.1 in Heb

2:18–27 Prayer answered. God decides to restore the people's land, removing the locusts and giving the animals back their food and water. The drought will end, and the people will praise God for their restored crops.

2:28–32 The apocalypse begins. Once the land is restored, the end of the present world order can begin. The signs will include universal prophecy (vv. 28–29; see Acts 2) and worldwide darkness. At that point, *everyone who calls on the name of the LORD shall be saved* (v. 32).

escape, as the LORD has said, and among the survivors shall be those whom the LORD calls.

3 [f]For then, in those days and at that time, when I restore the fortunes of Judah and Jerusalem, [2]I will gather all the nations and bring them down to the valley of Jehoshaphat, and I will enter into judgment with them there, on account of my people and my heritage Israel, because they have scattered them among the nations. They have divided my land [3]and cast lots for my people and traded boys for prostitutes and sold girls for wine and drunk it down.

4 What are you to me, O Tyre and Sidon, and all the regions of Philistia? Are you paying me back for something? If you are paying me back, I will turn your deeds back upon your own heads swiftly and speedily. [5]For you have taken my silver and my gold and have carried my rich treasures into your temples.[g] [6]You have sold the people of Judah and Jerusalem to the Greeks, removing them far from their own border. [7]But now I will rouse them to leave the places to which you have sold them, and I will turn your deeds back upon your own heads. [8]I will sell your sons and your daughters into the hand of the people of Judah, and they will sell them to the Sabeans, to a nation far away, for the LORD has spoken.

[9] Proclaim this among the nations:
Consecrate yourselves for war;
   stir up the warriors.
Let all the soldiers draw near;
   let them come up.
[10] Beat your plowshares into swords
   and your pruning hooks into spears;
   let the weakling say, "I am a
     warrior."

[11] Come quickly,[b]
   all you nations all around;
   gather yourselves there.
Bring down your warriors, O LORD.
[12] Let the nations rouse themselves
   and come up to the valley of
     Jehoshaphat,
for there I will sit to judge
   all the neighboring nations.

[13] Put in the sickle,
   for the harvest is ripe.
Go in, tread,
   for the winepress is full.
The vats overflow,
   for their wickedness is great.

[14] Multitudes, multitudes,
   in the valley of decision!
For the day of the LORD is near
   in the valley of decision.
[15] The sun and the moon are darkened,
   and the stars withdraw their
     shining.

[16] The LORD roars from Zion
   and utters his voice from
     Jerusalem,
and the heavens and the earth
     shake.
But the LORD is a refuge for his people,
   a stronghold for the people of Israel.

[17] So you shall know that I, the LORD your
     God,
   dwell in Zion, my holy mountain.
And Jerusalem shall be holy,
   and strangers shall never again pass
     through it.

f 3.1 4.1 in Heb   g 3.5 Or *palaces*   h 3.11 Meaning of Heb uncertain

3:1–8 Divine justice for God's people. According to the prophet, the apocalypse will bring a reversal of fortune for Israel. All the nations that have sold their children into slavery and plundered their goods will in turn have their children enslaved. This retribution is God's doing, according to the prophet.

3:9–16 The final battle. Israel must now prepare to fight the nations. Just as God led the locusts, however, God will now lead God's people. **3:10** *Beat your plowshares into swords and your pruning hooks into spears.* Farmers must now turn their tools into weapons, the opposite of the peaceful eschatological future described in Isa. 2:4 and Mic. 4:3. **3:15** *The sun and the moon are darkened, and the stars withdraw their shining.* Again, one of the main signs of the apocalypse is terrifying darkness. **3:16** *The LORD roars from Zion and utters his voice from Jerusalem, and the heavens and the earth shake.* Just as God led the locusts in chap. 2 with a shout, God will give another battle shout in this decisive battle.

3:17–21 Israel's perfect postapocalyptic future. After the battle, Jerusalem will be free from outside invaders, and the people's enemies will be destroyed. **3:18** *In that day the mountains shall*

[18] In that day
the mountains shall drip sweet wine,
the hills shall flow with milk,
and all the streambeds of Judah
shall flow with water;
a fountain shall come forth from the
house of the LORD
and water the Wadi Shittim.

[19] Egypt shall become a desolation
and Edom a desolate wilderness,

because of the violence done to the
people of Judah,
in whose land they have shed
innocent blood.
[20] But Judah shall be inhabited forever
and Jerusalem to all generations.
[21] I will avenge their blood, and I will not
clear the guilty,[i]
for the LORD dwells in Zion.

i 3.21 Gk Syr: Heb *I will hold innocent their blood that I have not held innocent*

drip sweet wine, the hills shall flow with milk, and all the streambeds of Judah shall flow with water; a fountain shall come forth from the house of the LORD and water the Wadi Shittim. The land that had previously struggled with locusts and drought will now spontaneously produce not only water but milk and wine without the people's labor.

AMOS

Authorship, Dates, and Literary History

According to its superscription (1:1), the book of Amos originated with an eponymous shepherd from the Judean town of Tekoa and contains words that he saw concerning the northern kingdom of Israel during the reigns of two eighth-century BCE kings. Much, but not all, of the book's contents are consistent with this historical and geographical context. The forty-year reign of the northern king Jeroboam II (787–748 BCE) was a time of economic prosperity and political stability for Israel. With the Assyrian Empire focused on Damascus, Israel was able to recover territory it had lost to its regional rival and grow its economy without direct imperial pressure. Leaving his home in the southern kingdom of Judah, Amos traveled to Israel to expose the unequal distribution of this economic prosperity, to condemn the hollowness of Israel's worship in the face of such disparity, and to tell them that Assyria's imperial gaze would soon turn to them and threaten Israel's destruction.

The oracles of Amos were preserved by his followers and even later communities because his words continued to resonate in contexts beyond their initial setting. Part of this preservation involved organizing his oracles into groups and minicollections. The structure and order of the book of Amos as we know it reflect the work of these later scribes rather than the prophet himself. These scribes also supplemented Amos's words. The third-person references to Amos (1:1; 7:10–17) were written by someone other than the prophet and at some point added to the emerging collection of his oracles. Later scribes also updated the prophetic collection with oracles that brought Amos's vision to bear on their Judean context and Babylon's coming conquest of the southern kingdom (2:4–5; 6:1). The last verses of the book (9:11–15) date to the exilic (586–539 BCE) or postexilic period following Babylon's conquest and are among its latest additions. Thus, the book of Amos began with the eighth-century BCE prophet but did not end with him. That his words spoke to subsequent communities who were inspired to expand his vision to their own contexts is a testament to the enduring power of his prophetic witness.

Reading Guide

The book of Amos breaks neatly into four sections, each distinguished by patterned language within the section. The first consists of oracles against the nations (chaps. 1–2), which all open with the same punishment formula. The second section (3:1–5:17) is three collections of oracles that begin with the summons to "hear this word" of the Lord (3:1; 4:1; 5:1). The third section (5:18–6:14) is punctuated by cries of "woe" at various groups (5:18; 6:1, 4). The last section (chaps. 7–9) contains five visions, the first four of which begin the same way (7:1, 4, 7; 8:1). The prose narrative about Amos (7:10–17) was inserted into this final section, and the postexilic vision of restoration (9:11–15) was attached to the book's ending.

The primary themes of the book are divine outrage at the social injustice (2:6–7; 3:15; 4:1; 5:7, 10–15, 24; 6:1–7; 8:4–6), the shortcomings of Israel's worship (2:8; 4:4–5; 5:4–5, 21–23; 8:14), and the ambivalent meaning of the exodus tradition (2:10; 3:2; 4:10; 5:25; 9:7). What are largely missing from the book are calls for repentance. Three calls to "seek" the Lord (5:4, 6, 14) notwithstanding, Amos is a wrecking ball who condemns the injustice and corruption taking place in Israel and announces the dreadful consequences of this intolerable and unsustainable iniquity.

The most prominent feature of Amos's prophetic style is the way he twists familiar genres and concepts for rhetorical effect. Examples of such reversal include the oracles against foreign nations redirected at Judah and Israel (2:4–16), a parody of a call to worship (4:4–5), a mock lamentation (5:1–2), doxologies that highlight YHWH's destructive power (5:8–9; 9:5–6), the "day of the Lord" as a day of darkness instead of vindication (5:18–20; see **"The Day of the Lord," p. 1322**), a satirical vignette of carefree excess (6:1–7), a plumb line used for destruction rather than building (7:7–9), joyful songs replaced by lamentation (8:3, 10), oaths sarcastically sworn by divinized pride instead of a deity (8:7), and feasts that turn into mourning (8:10). This distinctive prophetic style parallels the social and religious problems diagnosed in the book. Amos's creative reversals mirror the distortions of justice and righteousness he has seen throughout the land (5:7; 6:12).

Andrew R. Davis

1 The words of Amos, who was among the shepherds of Tekoa, which he saw concerning Israel in the days of King Uzziah of Judah and in the days of King Jeroboam son of Joash of Israel, two years[a] before the earthquake.

2 And he said:

The LORD roars from Zion
    and utters his voice from Jerusalem;
the pastures of the shepherds wither,
    and the top of Carmel dries up.

3 Thus says the LORD:
For three transgressions of Damascus,
    and for four, I will not revoke the
        punishment,[b]
because they have threshed Gilead
    with threshing sledges of iron.
4 So I will send a fire on the house of
        Hazael,
    and it shall devour the strongholds of
        Ben-hadad.
5 I will break the gate bars of Damascus
    and cut off the inhabitants from the
        Valley of Aven
and the one who holds the scepter from
        Beth-eden,
    and the people of Aram shall go into
        exile to Kir,
                    says the LORD.

6 Thus says the LORD:
For three transgressions of Gaza,
    and for four, I will not revoke the
        punishment,[c]
because they carried into exile entire
        communities,
    to hand them over to Edom.
7 So I will send a fire on the wall of Gaza,
    and it shall devour its strongholds.
8 I will cut off the inhabitants from
        Ashdod
    and the one who holds the scepter
        from Ashkelon;
I will turn my hand against Ekron,
    and the remnant of the Philistines
        shall perish,
                    says the Lord GOD.

9 Thus says the LORD:
For three transgressions of Tyre,
    and for four, I will not revoke the
        punishment,[d]
because they delivered entire
        communities over to Edom
    and did not remember the covenant
        of kinship.
10 So I will send a fire on the wall of Tyre,
    and it shall devour its strongholds.

a 1.1 Or *during two years*   b 1.3 Heb *cause it to return*
c 1.6 Heb *cause it to return*   d 1.9 Heb *cause it to return*

1:1 Superscription. A heading by a later editor attributes the following words to Amos, whose name means "the one who is supported (by YHWH)." It establishes his occupation (shepherd; cf. 7:14; 2 Kgs. 3:4), home (Tekoa in Judah), target (Israel), and time frame according to kings' reigns (786–742 BCE). Archaeological evidence of an *earthquake* circa 760 BCE corresponds to this dating. In style and content, the superscription matches those of Hosea, Amos, and Zephaniah and suggests the same editorial hand.

1:2 YHWH, like Amos, is based in the south and has a withering message for the north. *Roars.* See also 3:4, 8.

1:3–2:16 Oracles against the nations. Oracles announcing YHWH's punishment of Israel's foreign enemies are a standard feature of prophetic books (Isa. 13–23; Jer. 46–51; Ezek. 25–32; Zeph. 2). The first five oracles in Amos 1–2 concern foreign nations, but the series culminates with oracles against Judah and Israel. The foreign nations are condemned for their violation of international order, but Israel and Judah are indicted for domestic transgressions. *For three . . . and for four* are not exact counts but poetic parallelisms indicating "several" (Prov. 6:16; Job 33:14).

1:3–5 *Damascus* was the capital of Aram and an occasional threat on Israel's northern border (1 Kgs. 22). *Hazael* and *Ben-hadad* were Aramean kings who seized Israelite territory in the early eighth century BCE (2 Kgs. 13:3–5). *Strongholds* is a recurrent word in Amos (1:4, 7, 10, 12, 14; 2:2, 5; 3:9, 11; 6:8). *Exile to Kir.* Cf. 9:7; 2 Kgs. 16:9.

1:6–8 Four cities of the Philistine pentapolis—*Gaza, Ashdod, Ashkelon,* and *Ekron*—are condemned for slave trading with Edom, a kingdom in southern Transjordan. Ashdod was the largest among them in the eighth century (3:9). It is unclear if Edom was the recipient of the slaves, perhaps used to work in its copper mines, or a broker of them.

1:9–12 The oracles against *Tyre* and *Edom* are likely later additions. Like the oracle against Judah, they end without "says the Lord," and Tyre's oracle repeats much of Gaza's. Tyre was a seaport and

¹¹ Thus says the LORD:
  For three transgressions of Edom,
    and for four, I will not revoke the
      punishment,*
  because he pursued his brother with
      the sword
    and cast off all pity;
  he maintained his anger perpetually*
    and kept his wrath* forever.
¹² So I will send a fire on Teman,
    and it shall devour the strongholds of
      Bozrah.

¹³ Thus says the LORD:
  For three transgressions of the
      Ammonites,
    and for four, I will not revoke the
      punishment,*
  because they have ripped open
      pregnant women in Gilead
    in order to enlarge their territory.
¹⁴ So I will kindle a fire against the wall of
      Rabbah,
    and it shall devour its strongholds,
  with shouting on the day of battle,
    with a storm on the day of the
      whirlwind;
¹⁵ then their king shall go into exile,
    he and his officials together,
                              says the LORD.

2 Thus says the LORD:
  For three transgressions of Moab,
    and for four, I will not revoke the
      punishment,*
  because he burned to lime

the bones of the king of Edom.
² So I will send a fire on Moab,
    and it shall devour the strongholds of
      Kerioth,
  and Moab shall die amid uproar,
    amid shouting and the sound of the
      trumpet;
³ I will cut off the ruler from its midst
    and will kill all its officials with him,
                              says the LORD.

⁴ Thus says the LORD:
  For three transgressions of Judah,
    and for four, I will not revoke the
      punishment,*
  because they have rejected the
      instruction of the LORD
    and have not kept his statutes,
  but they have been led astray by the
      same lies
    after which their ancestors walked.
⁵ So I will send a fire on Judah,
    and it shall devour the strongholds of
      Jerusalem.

⁶ Thus says the LORD:
  For three transgressions of Israel,
    and for four, I will not revoke the
      punishment,*
  because they sell the righteous for
      silver
    and the needy for a pair of sandals—

e 1.11 Heb *cause it to return* f 1.11 Syr Vg: Heb *and his
anger tore perpetually* g 1.11 Gk Syr Vg: Heb *and his wrath
kept* h 1.13 Heb *cause it to return* i 2.1 Heb *cause it to return*
j 2.4 Heb *cause it to return* k 2.6 Heb *cause it to return*

commercial center (Isa. 23; Ezek. 26–28). *Covenant of kinship* (literally "of brothers") refers to treaty partners. Edom was a kingdom in southern Transjordan, which did not develop established cities until the seventh century BCE. *Brother* again denotes a treaty partner.

1:13–15 The *Ammonites'* transgression is against Israel, their northern neighbor. Their horrific treatment of pregnant women is sadly not unique (2 Kgs. 8:12; 15:16).

2:1–3 *Moab's* transgression involves disinterring an Edomite king and desecrating his bones (2 Kgs. 23:16). *Lime* is the chalky residue left when bones are burned.

2:4–5 Divine punishment turns to *Judah.* Insofar as their transgressions have made them an enemy of YHWH, they will be punished like foreign enemies. This oracle is probably a later addition by an editor who updated the collection for a Judean audience by inserting Judah before the original climactic oracle against Israel. The reference to *rejected . . . instruction* (Heb. "torah") and *not kept . . . statutes* may reflect Deuteronomistic influence (cf. 2 Kgs. 17:15).

2:6–16 Israel's injustice and sacrilege have made it no less an enemy of YHWH than the foreign nations, and their transgressions will likewise be punished. Unlike the oracles against the nations, which focus on transgressions between kingdoms, this oracle highlights domestic problems. What all the oracles share is divine outrage at the way economic interests and exploitation violate human dignity. **2:6** *They sell . . . the needy for a pair of sandals.* Later the needy are bought for the same (8:6). This trafficking of the poor into debt slavery is a chilling echo of the slave trade mentioned

[7] they who trample the head of the poor
　　into the dust of the earth
　　and push the afflicted out of the way;
father and son go in to the same young
　　woman,
　　so that my holy name is profaned;
[8] they lay themselves down beside every
　　altar
　　on garments taken in pledge;
and in the house of their God they
　　drink
　　wine bought with fines they imposed.

[9] Yet I destroyed the Amorite before
　　them,
　　whose height was like the height of
　　　cedars
　　and who was as strong as oaks;
I destroyed his fruit above
　　and his roots beneath.
[10] Also I brought you up out of the land of
　　Egypt
　　and led you forty years in the
　　　wilderness,
　　to possess the land of the Amorite.
[11] And I raised up some of your children
　　to be prophets
　　and some of your youths to be
　　　nazirites.
　　Is it not indeed so, O people of Israel?
　　　　　　　　　says the Lord.

[12] But you made the nazirites drink wine
　　and commanded the prophets,
　　saying, "You shall not prophesy."

[13] So, I will press you down in your place,
　　just as a cart presses down
　　when it is full of sheaves.[l]
[14] Flight shall perish from the swift,
　　and the strong shall not retain their
　　　strength,

nor shall the mighty save their lives;
[15] those who handle the bow shall not
　　stand,
　　and those who are swift of foot shall
　　not save themselves,
　　nor shall those who ride horses save
　　their lives;
[16] and those who are stout of heart among
　　the mighty
　　shall flee away naked on that day,
　　　　　　　　　says the Lord.

3 Hear this word that the Lord has spoken against you, O people of Israel, against the whole family that I brought up out of the land of Egypt:
[2] You only have I known
　　of all the families of the earth;
therefore I will punish you
　　for all your iniquities.

[3] Do two walk together
　　unless they have made an
　　　appointment?
[4] Does a lion roar in the forest
　　when it has no prey?
Does a young lion cry out from its den
　　if it has caught nothing?
[5] Does a bird fall into a snare on the
　　earth
　　when there is no trap for it?
Does a snare spring up from the ground
　　when it has taken nothing?
[6] Is a trumpet blown in a city,
　　and the people are not afraid?
Does disaster befall a city
　　unless the Lord has done it?
[7] Surely the Lord God does nothing
　　without revealing his secret
　　to his servants the prophets.

l 2.13 Meaning of Heb uncertain

in 1:6, 9. **2:7** The *young woman* is not a prostitute. Heb. "na'arah" may imply her status as a servant within the household whose males are exploiting her. **2:8** *Garments taken in pledge* is a violation of the covenant (Exod. 22:25; Deut. 24:17). **2:10** Amos engages the exodus tradition also in 3:2 and 9:7. **2:11–12** Nazirites were forbidden to drink (Num. 6:2–3; Judg. 13:5), and prophets were expected to prophesy. YHWH's plans for Israel have been turned upside down (cf. Mic. 2:6; Isa. 30:10; Jer. 5:31).
　3:1–5:17 Three summons. This section consists of various oracles organized into three collections, each beginning with the command "Hear this word" (3:1; 4:1; 5:1).
　3:1–2 The first command to *hear* is addressed to all the people of Israel, who have covenanted with YHWH. The exodus tradition alludes to this covenant (2:10; 9:7), as does the verb "to know," which implies not just cognitive knowledge but relational knowledge (Gen. 18:19; Exod. 6:7; 10:2).
　3:7–8 After a series of rhetorical questions whose implied answer is no, Amos asks who can resist a prophetic word from YHWH. Implied answer: no one (7:15). This irresistibility stands in tension with

⁸ The lion has roared;
    who will not fear?
The Lord GOD has spoken;
    who can but prophesy?

⁹ Proclaim to the strongholds in
        Ashdod
    and to the strongholds in the land of
        Egypt,
    and say, "Assemble yourselves on
        Mount^m Samaria,
    and see what great tumults are
        within it
    and what oppressions are in its
        midst."
¹⁰ They do not know how to do right, says
        the LORD,
    those who store up violence and
        robbery in their strongholds.
¹¹ Therefore thus says the Lord GOD:
    An adversary shall surround the land
        and strip you of your defense,
    and your strongholds shall be
        plundered.

12 Thus says the LORD: As the shepherd
rescues from the mouth of the lion two legs
or a piece of an ear, so shall the people of
Israel who live in Samaria be rescued, with
the corner of a couch and part^n of a bed.

¹³ Hear and testify against the house of
        Jacob,
    says the Lord GOD, the God of hosts:

¹⁴ On the day I punish Israel for its
        transgressions,
    I will punish the altars of Bethel,
    and the horns of the altar shall be cut
        off
    and fall to the ground.
¹⁵ I will tear down the winter house as
        well as the summer house,
    and the houses of ivory shall perish,
    and the great houses^o shall come to an
        end,
                            says the LORD.

4 Hear this word, you cows of Bashan
    who are on Mount Samaria,
who oppress the poor, who crush the
        needy,
    who say to their husbands, "Bring
        something to drink!"
² The Lord GOD has sworn by his
        holiness:
    The time is surely coming upon you
    when they shall take you away with
        hooks,
    even the last of you with fishhooks.
³ Through breaches in the wall you shall
        leave,
    each one straight ahead,
    and you shall be flung out into
        Harmon,^p
                            says the LORD.

m 3.9 Gk Syr: Heb *the mountains of*   n 3.12 Meaning of Heb
uncertain   o 3.15 Or *many houses*   p 4.3 Meaning of Heb
uncertain

the people's desire to silence prophets (2:12) and Amos's eschewal of the designation "prophet" (7:14). *His servants the prophets* has a Deuteronomistic ring (2 Kgs. 21:10) and may be a later addition. *The lion has roared.* See 1:2.

3:9–11 The multiple addressees in this passage make it hard to understand its audiences. *Strongholds* is a favorite word of Amos, occurring twelve times in the book. *Ashdod.* See 1:8.

3:12 This prose line provides a link between the three-verse poems before and after it. The reference to Samaria looks back to vv. 9–11, and the furniture anticipates the luxurious houses in v. 15. The pastoral imagery recalls Amos's occupation (1:1; 7:14).

3:14 Although *Bethel* is remembered positively in Genesis (28:10–17; 35:1–15), in 1 Kgs. 12:28–13:10 and 2 Kgs. 23:15–20, the sanctuary exemplifies illicit worship. Located just eleven miles north of Jerusalem, Bethel was the capital's closest and most formidable rival. The *horns of the altar*, one at each of its four corners, are mentioned in 1 Kgs. 2:28–34 and attested in altars found through archaeological excavation.

3:15 On the multiple *houses* of kings in ancient Israel, including Ahab's ivory house, see 1 Kgs. 21:1; 22:39; Jer. 36:22.

4:1–3 The second summons to *hear* goes to wealthy women of Samaria, who are compared to cows in Bashan, a fertile region in northern Transjordan (Ps. 22:12). The comparison identifies them as a part of a well-fed class used to enjoying fine and abundant food. The meaning of *hooks . . . fishhooks* is debated, but along with *breaches in the wall*, they depict the population of a besieged city sent into exile.

⁴ Come to Bethel—and transgress;
  to Gilgal—and multiply
    transgression;
bring your sacrifices every morning,
  your tithes every three days;
⁵ bring a thank offering of leavened
    bread
  and proclaim freewill offerings,
    publish them;
  for so you love to do, O people of
    Israel!
                    says the Lord GOD.

⁶ I gave you cleanness of teeth in all your
    cities
  and lack of bread in all your places;
yet you did not return to me,
                    says the LORD.

⁷ And I also withheld the rain from you
  when there were still three months
    to the harvest;
I would send rain on one city
  and send no rain on another city;
one field would be rained upon,
  and the field on which it did not rain
    withered;
⁸ so two or three towns wandered to one
    town
  to drink water and were not
    satisfied;
yet you did not return to me,
                    says the LORD.

⁹ I struck you with blight and mildew;
  I laid waste*q* your gardens and your
    vineyards;

the locust devoured your fig trees
  and your olive trees;
yet you did not return to me,
                    says the LORD.

¹⁰ I sent among you a pestilence after the
    manner of Egypt;
  I killed your young men with the
    sword;
I carried away your horses;*r*
  and I made the stench of your camp
    go up into your nostrils;
yet you did not return to me,
                    says the LORD.

¹¹ I overthrew some of you
  as when God overthrew Sodom and
    Gomorrah,
  and you were like a brand snatched
    from the fire;
yet you did not return to me,
                    says the LORD.

¹² Therefore thus I will do to you, O Israel;
  because I will do this to you,
    prepare to meet your God, O Israel!

¹³ For the one who forms the mountains,
    creates the wind,
  reveals his thoughts to mortals,
makes the morning darkness,
  and treads on the heights of the
    earth—
  the LORD, the God of hosts, is his
    name!

q 4.9 Cn: Heb *the multitude of*   r 4.10 Heb *with the captivity of your horses*

4:4–5 In this parody, Amos adopts the voice of a priest calling pilgrims to worship (cf. Hos. 4:15), but instead of bringing them close to YHWH, their offerings compound their *transgression*. As with the oracles against foreign nations in chaps. 1–2, Amos has taken a familiar genre and turned it into a prophetic condemnation. Like *Bethel* (see 3:14), *Gilgal* is remembered positively in some biblical texts (Josh. 4:20; 5:9; 1 Sam. 7:16) and negatively in others (Amos 5:5; Hos. 9:15; 12:11).

4:6–12 Each oracle in this collection ends with a statement of not returning to YHWH and the oracular formula *says the LORD*. The oracles describe divine reprimand in the form of plagues, and the litany of nonrepentance culminates in a declaration of punishment (v. 12; cf. Isa. 9:8–21). The plagues resemble treaty curses that would take effect if the treaty were breached (cf. Lev. 26:14–39; Deut. 28:15–68; 1 Kgs. 8:35–40). **4:7–8** YHWH also *withheld the rain* in 1 Kgs. 17–18. **4:10** The *pestilence after the manner of Egypt* recalls Exod. 9:3–6. **4:11** *Overthrew* (Heb. "hpk") is the same verb used to describe YHWH's destruction of *Sodom and Gomorrah* and the cities of the plain in Gen. 19:25, 29. See also Isa. 1:9–10.

4:13 The first of three doxologies (5:8–9; 9:5–6). These hymns of praise to YHWH are identifiable by their use of participles, which give the poetry a lively tempo. This doxology offers the expected praise of YHWH's creative power, but in the other two, Amos transforms the genre into a "praise" of YHWH's destructive power (cf. Job 5:9–16; 9:5–12).

5 Hear this word that I take up over you
in lamentation, O house of Israel:
² Fallen, no more to rise,
is maiden Israel;
forsaken on her land,
with no one to raise her up.

³ For thus says the Lord GOD:
The city that marched out a thousand
shall have a hundred left,
and that which marched out a hundred
shall have ten left.*

⁴ For thus says the LORD to the house of
Israel:
Seek me and live,
⁵ but do not seek Bethel,
and do not enter into Gilgal
or cross over to Beer-sheba,
for Gilgal shall surely go into exile,
and Bethel shall come to nothing.

⁶ Seek the LORD and live,
or he will break out against the
house of Joseph like fire,
and it will devour Bethel, with no
one to quench it.
⁷ Ah, you who turn justice to wormwood
and bring righteousness to the ground!

⁸ The one who made the Pleiades and
Orion
and turns deep darkness into the
morning
and darkens the day into night,
who calls for the water of the sea
and pours it out on the surface of the
earth,
the LORD is his name,

⁹ who makes destruction flash out
against the strong,
so that destruction comes upon the
fortress.

¹⁰ They hate the one who reproves in the
gate,
and they abhor the one who speaks
the truth.
¹¹ Therefore because you trample on the
poor
and take from them levies of grain,
you have built houses of hewn stone,
but you shall not live in them;
you have planted pleasant vineyards,
but you shall not drink their wine.
¹² For I know how many are your
transgressions
and how great are your sins—
you who afflict the righteous, who take
a bribe
and push aside the needy in the gate.
¹³ Therefore the prudent will keep silent
in such a time,
for it is an evil time.

¹⁴ Seek good and not evil,
that you may live,
and so the LORD, the God of hosts, will
be with you,
just as you have said.
¹⁵ Hate evil and love good,
and establish justice in the gate;
it may be that the LORD, the God of
hosts,
will be gracious to the remnant of
Joseph.

s 5.3 Heb adds *to the house of Israel*

5:1–17 This section's position at the center of the book of Amos is underscored by its chiastic structure: (A) lament (vv. 1–3); (B) exhortation to *seek* (vv. 4–6); (C) injustice condemned (v. 7); (D) doxology (vv. 8–9); (C') injustice condemned (vv. 10–12); (B') exhortation to *seek* (vv. 14–15); (A') lamentation (vv. 16–17). At the center of this centerpiece is the power of YHWH, which expands into outrage at injustice, the need for repentance, and lamentation over present and future suffering. **5:1–3** The third summons (see 3:1; 4:1) is for the house of Israel, who are told to hear a song of *lamentation*, which turns out to be a dirge for Israel itself. Typically, a dirge was sung for someone who had died (2 Sam. 1:17–27; 3:33–34). Amos's use of the genre here implies that the people of Israel are "dead men walking." **5:4–7** A rare call for repentance in the book (also 5:14–15). The preceding lamentation implies that Israel's fate is sealed, but this passage leaves open the possibility of continued life with YHWH. For *justice/righteousness*, see 5:24. **5:8–9** The second of three doxologies (see 4:13). *Pleiades* and *Orion* are mentioned together in Job 9:9 and 38:31 as symbols of divine creative power. **5:10–13** The city *gate* served as the court of law (Ruth 4) and a marketplace (2 Kgs. 7:1, 18), but Amos sees it as a place of suppressed justice (5:15) and unfair taxation (8:5). The *vineyards* and *wine* lost by the wealthy are given to the people of Israel in the book's concluding

¹⁶ Therefore thus says the Lord, the God
of hosts, the Lord:
In all the squares there shall be wailing,
and in all the streets they shall say,
"Alas! Alas!"
They shall call the farmers to
mourning
and those skilled in lamentation to
wailing;
¹⁷ in all the vineyards there shall be
wailing,
for I will pass through the midst of
you,
says the Lord.

¹⁸ Woe to you who desire the day of the
Lord!
Why do you want the day of the
Lord?
It is darkness, not light,
¹⁹   as if someone fled from a lion
and was met by a bear
or went into the house and rested a
hand against the wall
and was bitten by a snake.
²⁰ Is not the day of the Lord darkness, not
light,
and gloom with no brightness in it?

²¹ I hate, I despise your festivals,
and I take no delight in your solemn
assemblies.
²² Even though you offer me your
burnt offerings and grain
offerings,
I will not accept them,
and the offerings of well-being of your
fatted animals
I will not look upon.
²³ Take away from me the noise of your
songs;
I will not listen to the melody of your
harps.
²⁴ But let justice roll down like water
and righteousness like an
ever-flowing stream.

25 Did you bring to me sacrifices and
offerings the forty years in the wilderness, O house of Israel? ²⁶You shall take
up Sakkuth your king and Kaiwan your
star god, your images,^t which you made
for yourselves; ²⁷therefore I will take you
into exile beyond Damascus, says the Lord,
whose name is the God of hosts.

t 5.26 Heb *your images, your star god*

vision of restoration (9:14). **5:16–17** *Squares* (Heb. "hutsot") denoting a marketplace (1 Kgs. 20:34) and *vineyards* reprise locales from preceding verses. Here they have become places of lamentation.

5:18–6:14 Woe oracles. This section is punctuated by declarations of "woe" (Heb. "hoy") against various groups (5:18; 6:1, 4). "Hoy" is a cry of mourning (e.g., 1 Kgs. 13:30; Jer. 22:18), which is used in the prophetic literature of the Hebrew Bible to announce judgment.

5:18–20 The first woe is a reversal of the *day of the Lord*. This day was thought to be the time when YHWH would vindicate Israel against its enemies, but as in chaps. 1–2, Amos insists that because Israel has made itself an enemy of YHWH, it will be a day of punishment instead (cf. Zeph. 1:14–18; Joel 1:15). See **"The Day of the Lord," p. 1322**.

5:21–24 YHWH rejects any worship that is divorced from *justice* and *righteousness* (Mic. 6:6–8; Isa. 1:10–17). **5:21** *Festivals* (Heb. "haggim") involved a pilgrimage to a major sanctuary, such as the temple in Jerusalem (Deut. 16:16), but they also took place in other cities (Judg. 21:19; 1 Kgs. 12:32–33). **5:22** *Burnt offerings*, *grain offerings*, and *offerings of well-being* were standard sacrifices within Israelite worship (cf. Lev. 1, 6–7). **5:24** *Justice/righteousness* is a common hendiadys in the prophetic books (Hos. 2:19; Mic. 7:9; Isa. 1:21, 27; 5:7; et al.). Justice (Heb. "mishpat") is from the verb "to judge" and refers to the power to adjudicate, and righteousness (Heb. "tsedaqah") refers to right relationship. Combined in hendiadys, the terms call for Israelites to use whatever "mishpat" they have to bring about "tsedaqah" among themselves and between themselves and YHWH. As the God of Israel, YHWH exemplifies this justice-for-righteousness (cf. Isa. 5:16), and the king has more power than most to imitate this divine power (cf. Isa. 9:7), but everyone has power in some sphere and should use that power for right relationship. An *ever-flowing stream* is one fed by steady springs (like the Jordan River) rather than a wadi that only runs during the rainy season.

5:25 The *wilderness* journey after the exodus is idealized, as in Hos. 2:15; Jer. 2:2–3; but contrast Pss. 78:40–42; 106:25–33.

5:26 *Sakkuth* and *Kaiwan* do not refer to celestial bodies, as previously thought. Their meaning is unknown, but their association with *images* suggests cultic paraphernalia.

Making Connections: Amos and Martin Luther King Jr. (Amos 5)

The prophet Amos was a strong voice in eighth-century Israel for the powerless against the powerful. He denounced the Israelite king and other social elites who exploited the powerless through land expropriation and the perversion of the judicial process. In his view, divine retribution awaited those who did not protect the most economically vulnerable in society. While he supported YHWH religion centered on the Jerusalem temple, Amos felt that attention to justice was as important as religious ritual. Nowhere is this clearer than in Amos 5:21–24, which declares that YHWH despises the practice of religion—festivals, sacrificial offerings, and music—absent justice. The passage concludes with a well-known refrain that has been cited often: "But let justice roll down like water and righteousness like an ever-flowing stream" (v. 24). The water imagery associated with justice and righteousness in this verse describes them as powerful and unending forces in society. As water flows unstoppably and works its way into every place it can, the text hopes for a society overrun by justice.

The words of this verse were especially important to Dr. Martin Luther King Jr. In notes he wrote on the passage as a doctoral student, he called Amos 5:21–24 the key passage in the book, noting that these verses depict God as interested above all else in justice and righteousness. He saw the demand for justice as one of what he called the divine foundations of society. As such, it provided an important theological grounding for his civil rights work throughout the South. In 1963, he penned his famous "Letter from Birmingham Jail," and Amos appears again. King cites Amos 5:24 as evidence that Amos was an "extremist" like Jesus, Paul, and himself, and in the prophet's case, an extremist for justice. He also used Amos's language for rhetorical effect. In his well-known 1963 "I Have a Dream" speech delivered in Washington, D.C., he again quotes the prophet: "We will not be satisfied until 'justice rolls down like waters, and righteousness like a mighty stream.'" Here the prophet's words express the goal to which the civil rights movement aspired.

Amos was not working to overcome injustice known principally through racism. Nevertheless, as King knew well, injustice takes many forms. Were Amos alive today, one could easily imagine him still calling for a wave of justice to wipe out social ills.

J. Todd Hibbard

6 Woe to those who are at ease in Zion
 and for those who feel secure on
  Mount Samaria,
 the notables of the first of the nations,
  to whom the house of Israel resorts!
² Cross over to Calneh and see;
  from there go to Hamath the great;
  then go down to Gath of the
   Philistines.
 Are you better*ᵘ* than these kingdoms?
  Or is your*ᵛ* territory greater than
   their*ʷ* territory,
³ you who put far away the evil day
  and bring near a reign of violence?

⁴ Woe to those who lie on beds of ivory
  and lounge on their couches
and eat lambs from the flock
  and calves from the stall,
⁵ who sing idle songs to the sound of the
  harp
 and like David improvise on
  instruments of music,
⁶ who drink wine from bowls
  and anoint themselves with the finest
   oils
 but are not grieved over the ruin of
  Joseph!
⁷ Therefore they shall now be the first to
  go into exile,
 and the revelry of the loungers shall
  pass away.

u 6.2 Or Are they better   v 6.2 Heb their   w 6.2 Heb your

6:1–7 *Woe* (see 5:18–6:14) is twice announced for elites of *Zion* and *Samaria* who enjoy carefree luxury and ignore the ruin outside their insular lifestyle. *First* (v. 1), *finest* (v. 6), and *first* (v. 7) are the same word in the Hebrew; this leading class will lead the way into exile. **6:2** *Gath* was destroyed at the end of the ninth century BCE and serves as an example of a once great city that suffered a precipitous fall. **6:4–6** This scene of excess engages all the reader's senses, evoking the sensual pleasures of the revelry itself: the sight of the ivory beds, the taste of the lamb and wine, the sound of the harp, the smell and feel of the oil. **6:7** *Revelry* stands for Heb. "mirzah," which was an upper-class religious gathering with lots of alcohol. It may have been part of funerary practices (Jer. 16:5).

⁸ The Lord God has sworn by himself
  (says the Lord, the God of hosts):
I abhor the pride of Jacob
  and hate his strongholds,
  and I will deliver up the city and all
    that is in it.

9 If ten people remain in one house, they shall die. ¹⁰And if a relative, one who burns it,ˣ takes up the body to bring it out of the house and says to someone in the innermost parts of the house, "Is anyone else with you?" the answer will come, "No." Then the relativeʸ shall say, "Hush! We must not mention the name of the Lord."

¹¹ For the Lord commands,
  and he will shatter the great house
    to bits
  and the little house to pieces.
¹² Do horses run on rocky crags?
  Does one plow the sea with oxen?ᶻ
But you have turned justice into
    poison
  and the fruit of righteousness into
    wormwood,
¹³ you who rejoice in Lo-debar,ᵃ
  who say, "Have we not by our own
    strength
  taken Karnaimᵇ for ourselves?"
¹⁴ Indeed, I am raising up against you a
    nation,

O house of Israel, says the Lord, the
    God of hosts,
and they shall oppress you from
    Lebo-hamath
  to the Wadi Arabah.

7 This is what the Lord God showed me: he was forming locusts at the time the latter growth began to sprout (it was the latter growth after the king's mowings). ²When they had finished eating the grass of the land, I said,
  "O Lord God, forgive, I beg you!
  How can Jacob stand?
  He is so small!"
³ The Lord relented concerning this;
  "It shall not be," said the Lord.

4 This is what the Lord God showed me: the Lord God was calling for judgment by fire, and it devoured the great deep and was eating up the land. ⁵Then I said,
  "O Lord God, cease, I beg you!
  How can Jacob stand?
  He is so small!"
⁶ The Lord relented concerning this;
  "This also shall not be," said the Lord
    God.

x 6.10 Meaning of Heb uncertain   y 6.10 Heb *he*   z 6.12 Or *Does one plow them with oxen*   a 6.13 Or *in a thing of nothingness*   b 6.13 Or *horns*

6:8–14 This section is framed by the oracular formula *says the Lord, the God of hosts* in vv. 8 and 14. Within that frame is a loose collection of oracles that cohere around the theme of divine destruction. **6:8** Oaths were sworn by a deity who guaranteed the oath. When YHWH swears an oath, he can only do so *by himself* (Isa. 45:23; Jer. 51:14). Cf. 8:7. **6:9–10** In the aftermath of destruction, family members dispose of corpses and search for survivors. The fate of *ten people* recalls the escalating decimation in 5:3. **6:11–14** This oracle is framed by ruined houses—literal *house[s]* in v. 11 and the *house of Israel* in v. 14. In between are rhetorical questions that expose the absurdity of Israel's corruption and quotations that exemplify Israel's oblivious arrogance. **6:12** For *justice/righteousness* and *wormwood*, see 5:7. **6:14** The oppressing *nation* against Israel is the Assyrian Empire, which conquered Israel in 722 BCE. *Lebo-hamath* and *Wadi Arabah* represent the expansion of Israel under Jeroboam II (2 Kgs. 14:25). Those gains will soon be lost to the Assyrians.

7:1–9:6 Vision reports. Amos sees five visions of destruction, and for the first two, he intercedes on behalf of Israel (cf. Exod. 32:7–14). For the last three, however, there is no intercession, and destruction proceeds.

7:1–3 Amos intercedes and gets YHWH to stop the destructive locusts (Isa. 33:4; Nah. 3:17; Joel 1:4). Cf. Exod. 10:12–19, where Moses's intercession brings an end to the plague of locusts. *Latter growth* is the late crop that begins to sprout in late winter / early spring. *The Lord relented*—that is, changed his mind (Exod. 32:12–14; 34:14).

7:4–6 Amos intercedes again but this time only asks YHWH to *cease*, not to "forgive," as in v. 2. The *fire* is so great, it consumes the primordial waters of creation (Heb. "tehom"; Gen. 1:2; 7:11; Prov. 8:24, 27–28; Job 38:16). YHWH changes his mind again because of Amos's intercession.

Focus On: Speaking Truth to Power (Amos 7)

Confronting powerful people can be risky, something prophets in ancient Israel and Judah knew well. In their role as divine messengers, prophets often found themselves addressing social, religious, and political elites who were displeased by the prophetic proclamations. For example, the eighth-century prophet Amos, who hailed from the kingdom of Judah, spent much time denouncing elites—including the king—in the kingdom of Israel. In Amos 7:10–17, he entered the state temple at Bethel and announced the impending death of King Jeroboam and the exile of the populace by the Assyrians. The priest in charge of the temple, Amaziah, kicked Amos out and debarred him from ever returning. Amos's message had amounted to sedition against the kingdom. Undeterred, Amos reiterated his message of Israel's demise.

The prophets frequently challenged elites for abusing their positions of power, exacerbating inequalities in a society that was already deeply unequal. Economic practices like land expropriation (Isa. 5:8), charging exorbitant interest rates (Ezek. 18:8) and fines (Amos 2:8), and using rigged scales to weigh out silver and gold for payment (Mic. 6:11) drew prophetic ire. Priestly teaching that tilted the balance of power toward the temple by placing an excessive economic burden on worshipers prompted prophetic censure (Hos. 5:1). Failure to ensure fair judicial proceedings prompted prophetic rebukes of those in power (Amos 5:12, 15). Royal policies that compelled subjects to do work on behalf of the king elicited harsh prophetic reprimand (Jer. 22:13). In these and numerous other instances, prophets defended the powerless, marginalized, and vulnerable against the whims and wishes of kings, royal officials, priests, and the wealthy.

Criticizing the powerful could come with serious consequences for prophets. Several prophets were imprisoned for speaking out against royal policies. For example, Jeremiah was arrested and thrown in prison because, contrary to most of the royal establishment, he advised surrender to the Babylonians to avoid destruction (Jer. 37:11–16; 38:1–6). The prophet Micaiah was imprisoned for prophesying the death of the Israelite king, Ahab (1 Kgs. 22:27). King Asa put the prophet Hanani in stocks in prison for criticizing him over a political alliance with the king of Aram (2 Chr. 16:10). To avoid imprisonment (or execution), the otherwise powerful prophet Elijah fled on foot from Queen Jezebel after having prophets allied with her killed (1 Kgs. 19:1–3). Nevertheless, the biblical prophets remained steadfast in their commitment to challenging economic, political, and social power even when doing so proved dangerous.

J. Todd Hibbard

7 This is what he showed me: the Lord was standing beside a wall built with a plumb line, with a plumb line in his hand. [8]And the Lord said to me, "Amos, what do you see?" And I said, "A plumb line." Then the Lord said,

"See, I am setting a plumb line
  in the midst of my people Israel;
  I will spare them no longer;
[9] the high places of Isaac shall be made
    desolate,

and the sanctuaries of Israel shall be
    laid waste,
and I will rise against the house of
  Jeroboam with the sword."

10 Then Amaziah, the priest of Bethel, sent to King Jeroboam of Israel, saying, "Amos has conspired against you in the very center of the house of Israel; the land is not able to bear all his words. [11]For thus Amos has said,

7:7–8 This vision follows the pattern of introduction but lacks the prophetic intercession and divine repentance. A new element is YHWH's question to Amos (see 8:2; Jer. 1:11–14). *Plumb line* is a translation based on context; they are standing by a wall, and YHWH is holding a metal (cf. LXX) implement, which he will set against the people in judgment. This reading presumes a lead implement, but the best cognate for Heb. "'anak" is Akk. "annaku," meaning "tin."

7:9 This verse previews language in 7:10–17 (*Isaac, sanctuaries, Jeroboam, sword*) and was probably added by an editor to connect the prose narrative to the preceding vision.

7:10–17 An interruption in the series of visions, this narrative shifts the text from poetry to prose and from the first-person voice of the prophet to a third-person story about the prophet. The scene

'Jeroboam shall die by the sword,
and Israel must go into exile
away from his land.'"

¹²And Amaziah said to Amos, "O seer, go, flee away to the land of Judah, earn your bread there, and prophesy there, ¹³but never again prophesy at Bethel, for it is the king's sanctuary, and it is a temple of the kingdom."

14 Then Amos answered Amaziah, "I am*c* no prophet nor a prophet's son, but I am*d* a herdsman and a dresser of sycamore trees, ¹⁵and the LORD took me from following the flock, and the LORD said to me, 'Go, prophesy to my people Israel.'

¹⁶ "Now therefore hear the word of the
LORD.
You say, 'Do not prophesy against Israel,
and do not preach against the house
of Isaac.'

¹⁷ Therefore thus says the LORD:
Your wife shall become a prostitute in
the city,
and your sons and your daughters
shall fall by the sword,
and your land shall be parceled out
by line;
you yourself shall die in an unclean
land,
and Israel shall surely go into exile
away from its land."

8 This is what the Lord GOD showed me: a basket of summer fruit. ²He said, "Amos,

what do you see?" And I said, "A basket of summer fruit." Then the LORD said to me,
"The end*e* has come upon my people
Israel;
I will spare them no longer.
³ The songs of the temple*f* shall become
wailings on that day,"
says the Lord GOD;
"the dead bodies shall be many,
cast out in every place. Be silent!"

⁴ Hear this, you who trample on the needy,
and bring to ruin the poor of the
land,
⁵ saying, "When will the new moon be
over
so that we may sell grain,
and the Sabbath,
so that we may offer wheat for sale?
We will make the ephah smaller and
the shekel heavier
and practice deceit with false balances,
⁶ buying the poor for silver
and the needy for a pair of sandals
and selling the sweepings of the
wheat."

⁷ The LORD has sworn by the pride of
Jacob:
Surely I will never forget any of their
deeds.

c 7.14 Or *was*   d 7.14 Or *was*   e 8.2 In Heb the word for *end* is related to the word for *summer fruit*   f 8.3 Or *palace*

takes place at *Bethel* (see 3:14; 4:4; 5:5), which was established as a *king's sanctuary* and a *temple of the kingdom* by the founder of the northern kingdom of Israel (and *Jeroboam* II's namesake) Jeroboam I (1 Kgs. 12:28–33). The narrative has numerous parallels with 1 Kgs. 13. **7:12** *Seer* (Heb. "hozeh") may have institutional connotations (cf. 2 Sam. 24:11), which would explain Amos's reply denying any professional status as a prophet. **7:14** *I am no prophet nor a prophet's son* (cf. Zech. 13:5) means that Amos is not part of a professional guild of prophets (1 Sam. 10:5; 1 Kgs. 22:6; cf. Mic. 3:5–8, 11). For *prophet's son*, see 2 Kgs. 2:3, 5, 15; 4:1; 6:1. For *herdsman*, cf. 1:1. A *dresser of sycamore trees* was one who incised the tree's fruit to hasten its ripening. **7:15** The phrase *took me from following the flock* is said of David in 2 Sam. 7:8. **7:17** This curse recycles language from 7:11, turning that oracle against king and nation into a personal one against Amaziah.

8:1–3 After the interruption of 7:10–17, the visions resume. Like the third vision (7:7–8), this fourth one includes YHWH's question to Amos and lacks his intercession. *Summer fruit* (Heb. "qayits") is a pun on *end* (Heb. "qets"). These fruits were the second crop of figs during the year; an earlier crop occurred in winter (Hos. 9:10).

8:4–6 A scene of economic exploitation in the marketplace (see 5:11). For the *new moon*, see Num. 28:11–15. An *ephah* is a dry goods measure between ten and twenty liters. To make it *smaller* and the *shekel heavier* is to charge more for less. Other fraudulent practices involve *false balances* and the substitution of *sweepings* (chaff) for wheat. *Buying the poor* refers again to debt slavery (cf. 2:6).

8:7–8 In a sarcastic oath, YHWH swears *by the pride of Jacob*, which in 6:8 was an object of divine hatred. The object of *by* should be the deity who guarantees the oath. The substitution of Jacob's arrogance implies that it has grown to cosmic proportions. The *Nile* flooded and subsided annually,

8 Shall not the land tremble on this
        account,
    and everyone mourn who lives in it,
and all of it rise like the Nile,
        and be tossed about and sink again,
        like the Nile of Egypt?

9 On that day, says the Lord GOD,
    I will make the sun go down at noon
    and darken the earth in broad daylight.
10 I will turn your feasts into mourning
    and all your songs into lamentation;
I will bring sackcloth on all loins
    and baldness on every head;
I will make it like the mourning for an
        only son
    and the end of it like a bitter day.

11 The time is surely coming, says the Lord
        GOD,
    when I will send a famine on the land,
not a famine of bread or a thirst for water,
    but of hearing the words of the LORD.
12 They shall wander from sea to sea
    and from north to east;
they shall run to and fro, seeking the
        word of the LORD,
    but they shall not find it.

13 On that day the beautiful young women
        and the young men
    shall faint for thirst.
14 Those who swear by Ashimah of Samaria
    and say, "As your god lives, O Dan,"

and, "As the way of Beer-sheba lives"—
    they shall fall and never rise again.

9 I saw the LORD standing beside[g] the al-
    tar, and he said:
Strike the capitals until the thresholds
        shake
    and shatter them on the heads of all
        the people,[b]
and those who are left I will kill with
        the sword;
    not one of them shall flee away,
    not one of them shall escape.

2 Though they dig into Sheol,
    from there shall my hand take them;
though they climb up to heaven,
    from there I will bring them down.
3 Though they hide themselves on the top
        of Carmel,
    from there I will search out and take
        them;
and though they hide from my sight at
        the bottom of the sea,
    there I will command the serpent,
        and it shall bite them.
4 And though they go into captivity in
        front of their enemies,
    there I will command the sword, and
        it shall kill them;
and I will fix my eyes on them
    for harm and not for good.

g 9.1 Or on   b 9.1 Heb all of them

providing water for irrigation (9:5; Jer. 46:7–8). Amos uses the comparison to envision a destructive flood (cf. Isa. 8:7–8). **8:9–10** A solar eclipse was a sign of looming disaster (Isa. 13:10; Ezek. 32:7; Joel 2:10, 31; 3:15; cf. Amos 5:18–20). It also demonstrates YHWH's power over celestial bodies (5:8). As in 8:3, joyful *songs* will turn into *lamentation* (also 5:16–17). *Sackcloth* and *baldness* were signs of mourning (Isa. 22:12). **8:11–12** Unlike the literal hunger and thirst mentioned in 4:6–8, this *famine* is metaphorical and refers to the lack of YHWH's *word* in the land. **8:14** *Ashimah* (with a different spelling) is mentioned in 2 Kgs. 17:30 as a Syrian deity, but the name also sounds like the Hebrew word for "guilt" ("'asham"). Like the "pride of Jacob" in 8:7, the name seems to be used sarcastically, here serving as the divine guarantor of the oath. This role implies the apotheosis of Israel's pride. It is unclear why *Dan* (a tribe and city in Israel) and *way* (a common noun) are invoked in mock oaths. *Dan* and *Beer-sheba* occur together as a merism indicating the full extent of Israel (Judg. 20:1; 1 Sam. 3:20; 2 Sam. 17:11). **9:1–4** The last vision breaks the patterned introduction of the first four but shares with them the verb "ra'ah," "to see" (to show = to cause to see). The vision of YHWH in a temple making the *thresholds shake* recalls Isa. 6:4. The imagery may be related to the earthquake mentioned in the superscription (1:1). **9:2–4** Scenes of flight from the earthquake alternate between low places (*Sheol, the bottom of the sea*) and high places (*heaven, the top of Carmel*). Neither extreme escapes the divine gaze. *Sheol* was a place of death where one was separated from family and God (Ps. 6:5; Ezek. 32:17–32). *The serpent . . . shall bite.* Cf. 5:19.

5 The Lord, GOD of hosts,
  he who touches the earth and it melts,
    and all who live in it mourn,
  and all of it rises like the Nile
    and sinks again, like the Nile of Egypt,
6 who builds his upper chambers in the
    heavens
  and founds his vault upon the earth,
  who calls for the waters of the sea
    and pours them out upon the surface
      of the earth—
  the LORD is his name.

7 Are you not like the Cushites to me,
  O people of Israel? says the LORD.
  Did I not bring Israel up from the land
    of Egypt
  and the Philistines from Caphtor and
    the Arameans from Kir?
8 The eyes of the Lord GOD are upon the
    sinful kingdom,
  and I will destroy it from the face of
    the earth
  —except that I will not utterly
    destroy the house of Jacob,
                    says the LORD.

9 For I will command
  and shake the house of Israel among
    all the nations,
  as one shakes with a sieve
  but no pebble shall fall to the ground.
10 All the sinners of my people shall die by
    the sword,
  who say, "Evil shall not overtake or
    meet us."

11 On that day I will raise up
  the booth of David that is fallen
  and repair its[i] breaches
  and raise up its[j] ruins
  and rebuild it as in the days of old,
12 in order that they may possess the
    remnant of Edom
  and all the nations who are called by
    my name,
  says the LORD who does this.

13 The time is surely coming, says the
    LORD,
  when the one who plows shall catch
    up with the one who reaps
  and the treader of grapes with the
    one who sows the seed;
  the mountains shall drip sweet
    wine,
  and all the hills shall flow with it.
14 I will restore the fortunes of my people
    Israel,
  and they shall rebuild the ruined
    cities and inhabit them;
  they shall plant vineyards and drink
    their wine,
  and they shall make gardens and eat
    their fruit.
15 I will plant them upon their land,
  and they shall never again be
    plucked up
  out of the land that I have given
    them,
              says the LORD your God.

i 9.11 Gk: Heb *their*   j 9.11 Gk: Heb *his*

9:5–6 The last of three doxologies (also 4:13; 5:8–9) is framed by the divine name and highlights YHWH's power of creation. *Like the Nile.* Cf. 8:8. *Upper chambers* (cf. Ps. 104:3, 13) is the result of deleting the first letter of a word that would otherwise denote "stairs." *Vault* translates a Hebrew word that describes something held tightly together. Here it refers to the band that separates the earth from the cosmic waters above (cf. Gen. 1:6–8; Prov. 8:27).

9:7–8 In a startling twist on the exodus tradition already cited in the book (3:2), Israel's claim to a special relationship with YHWH is rejected. *Caphtor* refers to Crete (cf. Jer. 47:4). For *Kir*, see 1:5. The *sinful kingdom* in v. 8 is unspecified and could refer to any of these nations mentioned in v. 7 (or chaps. 1–2). Only *the house of Jacob* will be spared total destruction.

9:11–15 Addendum of restoration. This concluding vision is a late addition to the book, whose hopeful outlook contrasts with the earlier material. **9:11–12** The rebuilding of the *booth of David*, its *breaches*, and its *ruins* presumes the fall of Jerusalem and the Davidic monarchy and is evidence of a date after 586 BCE. Further evidence is *Edom*, which was despised for looting Judah after its fall (Obad. 1–15; Ps. 137:7). **9:13–15** In this vision of restoration, the crops will be so abundant that the *one who reaps* will still be gathering fruit when it becomes time again to plow and sow seed (cf. Lev. 26:5). Normally, the two activities would be at least a month apart. For *mountains shall drip sweet wine*, see Joel 3:18. *Plant vineyards and drink their wine* reverses the judgment in 5:11.

OBADIAH

Authorship, Dates, and Literary History

Just a single chapter nestled between the books of Amos and Jonah, the book of Obadiah is the shortest in the Hebrew Bible. With only the name Obadiah in the superscription (1) and no clues about his identity in the book itself, we know nothing about Obadiah. We are not even sure if "Obadiah," which means "servant of YHWH," is a proper name; like Malachi ("my messenger"), it could be a designation.

We are on firmer ground when it comes to dating. The condemnation of Edom for looting Jerusalem after its fall (11–14; cf. Ps. 137:7; Lam. 4:21; Ezek. 35:5–6) situates the book in the aftermath of the city's destruction by Babylon in 586 BCE.

The most striking aspect of the book's composition is its parallels with other prophetic books: vv. 1b–4 // Jer. 49:14–16; v. 5 // Jer. 49:9; v. 6 // Jer. 49:10a; v. 8 // Jer. 49:7; v. 17a // Joel 2:32. These sometimes verbatim parallels show considerable use of existing prophetic traditions and compound the challenge of identifying a distinct perspective that can be attributed to Obadiah.

Reading Guide

The book's brevity affords little opportunity to discern an overall design, but there is a clear movement from divine judgment on Edom (1–4), the depiction of its punishment (5–9), the listing of its crimes (10–14), the "day of the LORD" against all nations (15–16; see **"The Day of the Lord," p. 1322**), and the vindication of Zion (17–21). The book of Obadiah is best understood in the tradition of the "oracles against the nations" found in many prophetic books (e.g., Amos 1–2; Isa. 13–23; Jer. 46–51; Ezek. 25–32; Zeph. 2); see **"The Oracles against the Nations," p. 1105**. Within this corpus, Edom is a regular target (Amos 1:11–12; Isa. 21:11–12; Jer. 49:7–22; Ezek. 35; see also Isa. 34; Joel 3:19; Mal. 1:2–5).

Andrew R. Davis

1 The vision of Obadiah.

Thus says the Lord GOD concerning Edom:
We have heard a report from the LORD,
  and a messenger has been sent
    among the nations:
"Rise up! Let us rise against it for battle!"
² I will surely make you least among the
  nations;
  you shall be utterly despised.
³ Your proud heart has deceived you,
  you who live in the clefts of the rock,[a]
  whose dwelling is in the heights.

You say in your heart,
  "Who will bring me down to the
    ground?"
⁴ Though you soar aloft like the eagle,
  though your nest is set among the
    stars,
  from there I will bring you down,
        says the LORD.
⁵ If thieves came to you,
  if plunderers by night
  —how you have been destroyed!—

a 3 Or clefts of Sela

1a Superscription. This editorial addition identifies the work as Obadiah's *vision* (see Isa. 1:1; Nah. 1:1). Like the book it introduces, this superscription is the shortest of the prophetic books. It contains no information about the date or background of *Obadiah*, whose name means "servant of YHWH." Like Malachi ("my messenger"), Obadiah could be a designation rather than a proper name.

1b–14 Doom for Edom. Like other prophetic books, Obadiah declares an oracle against the nation of Edom (cf. Amos 1:11–12; Isa. 21:11–12; 34; Jer. 49:7–22; Ezek. 35; Joel 3:19; Mal. 1:2–5). **1b–4** Framed by a messenger formula (*Thus says the Lord GOD*) and an oracular formula (*says the LORD*), this section declares divine judgment on Edom. The parallels with Jer. 49:14–16 are almost verbatim. The minor differences between the two texts suggest not dependency between them but independent use of the same preexisting oracle. Two unique features in Obadiah are the end of v. 3 (*You say in your heart*) and *set among the stars* in v. 4 (cf. Isa. 14:13). These added details underscore Edom's *proud heart.* **5–9** Edom's punishment involves being *pillaged*, *deceived* by its allies (literally "men of

would they not steal only what they
   wanted?
If grape gatherers came to you,
   would they not leave gleanings?
⁶ How Esau has been pillaged,
   his treasures searched out!
⁷ All your allies have deceived you;
   they have driven you to the
      border;
your confederates have prevailed
   against you;
those who ate your food have set a
   trap for you—
there is no understanding.
⁸ On that day, says the Lord,
   I will destroy the wise out of Edom
   and understanding out of Mount
      Esau.
⁹ Your warriors shall be shattered,
   O Teman,
so that everyone from Mount Esau
   will be cut off.

¹⁰ For the slaughter and violence done to
   your brother Jacob,
shame shall cover you,
   and you shall be cut off forever.
¹¹ On the day that you stood aside,
   on the day that strangers carried off
      his wealth
and foreigners entered his gates
   and cast lots for Jerusalem,
   you, too, were one of them.
¹² But you should not have gloated over*ᵇ
   your brother
   on the day of his misfortune;
you should not have rejoiced over the
   people of Judah
   on the day of their ruin;
you should not have boasted
   on the day of distress.

¹³ You should not have entered the gate of
   my people
   on the day of their calamity;
you should not have joined in the
   gloating over Judah'sᶜ disaster
   on the day of his calamity;
you should not have stolen his goods
   on the day of his calamity.
¹⁴ You should not have stood at the
   crossings
   to cut off his fugitives;
you should not have handed over his
   survivors
   on the day of distress.

¹⁵ For the day of the Lord is near against
   all the nations.
As you have done, it shall be done to
   you;
   your deeds shall return on your own
      head.
¹⁶ For as you have drunk on my holy
   mountain,
   all the nations shall drink
      continually;
they shall drink and gulp downᵈ
   and shall be as though they had
      never been.

¹⁷ But on Mount Zion there shall be those
   who escape,
   and it shall be holy,
and the house of Jacob shall take
   possession of those who
      dispossessed them.
¹⁸ The house of Jacob shall be a fire,
   the house of Joseph a flame,
   and the house of Esau stubble;

b 12 Heb *on the day of*   *c* 13 Heb *his*   *d* 16 Meaning of Heb
uncertain

your covenant"; cf. Amos 1:11), and *shattered*. For v. 5, cf. Jer. 49:9. *Esau* was the eponymous ancestor of the Edomites (Gen. 25:30; 36:1). For *the wise out of Edom*, cf. Jer. 49:7. *Teman* refers to the northernmost part of Edom (see Amos 1:12; Ezek. 25:13). **10–14** Having envisioned the doom to come for Edom, Obadiah names the crimes that have occasioned its ruin. The prophet accuses Edom of joining forces with Babylon and looting Jerusalem after its fall (Ps. 137:7; Lam. 4:22; Ezek. 35:5–6).
   15–21 The Day of YHWH. The scope expands from Edom to *all the nations*. The *day of the Lord* was thought to be the time when YHWH would vindicate Israel and punish its enemies (cf. Amos 5:18–20; Zeph. 1:14–18; Joel 1:15). See **"The Day of the Lord," p. 1322. 15–16** Although the Day of YHWH is directed at *all the nations*, the *you* is still singular and suggests a continued focus on Edom. For *drink[ing]* as a prophetic metaphor of punishment, see Isa. 51:17; Jer. 25:15; 49:12; Ezek. 23:31–34. **17–21** The focus returns to *Jacob* (Israel/Judah) and *Esau* (Edom), with special attention to *those . . . saved* on *Mount Zion*, an image that frames the section (see Joel 2:32). *Take possession* (Heb. "yarash") occurs four times in these verses, as Israel reclaims lost territory and more.

they shall burn them and consume
them,
and there shall be no survivor of the
house of Esau,
for the LORD has spoken.
¹⁹ Those of the Negeb shall possess Mount
Esau,
and those of the Shephelah the land
of the Philistines;
they shall possess the land of
Ephraim and the land of
Samaria,
and Benjamin shall possess Gilead.

²⁰ The exiles of the Israelites who are in
Halah*e*
shall possess*f* Phoenicia as far as
Zarephath,
and the exiles of Jerusalem who are in
Sepharad
shall possess the towns of the Negeb.
²¹ Those who have been saved*g* shall go up
to Mount Zion
to rule Mount Esau,
and the kingdom shall be the LORD's.

e 20 Cn: Heb *in this army*   *f* 20 Cn: Meaning of Heb uncertain   *g* 21 Gk Syr: Heb *Saviors*

JONAH

Introduction

The book of Jonah is unique in the Hebrew Bible. It is located among other prophetic books. In fact, it is part of a collection known as the Book of the Twelve (Prophets) or the Minor Prophets. But while other prophetic books consist mainly of prophetic oracles in poetic form, Jonah is a short story in narrative prose. It contains a single oracle of only five words in Hebrew (3:4). The character of Jonah is also unique as a prophet. He is the only prophet in the Hebrew Bible who directly disobeys God and tries to run away from his commission. Yet Jonah is uniquely successful in his mission, and the entire city of Nineveh repents after his prophecy. While such success would be the envy of other prophets, Jonah is uniquely angry about Nineveh's response and pardon, complaining that it was what motivated him to flee in the first place (4:2). Even Jonah's ending is almost unique; only the book of Nahum (also about Nineveh) ends with a question the way Jonah does.

Jonah as a Prophet

The book of Jonah never actually calls Jonah a prophet. The facts that the word of the Lord comes to him (1:1; 3:1) and that he prophesies (3:4) show that he was a prophet. There is also a Jonah who is mentioned as a prophet in 2 Kgs. 14:25, and since both of them are called the son of Amittai, it seems clear that they are intended to be the same person. The story in 2 Kgs. 14:25 takes place during the reign of Jeroboam II, king of Israel, in the first half of the eighth century BCE (ca. 790–750), and this is when the story in the book of Jonah is set. However, the book of Jonah was probably written considerably later. While the matter is debated among scholars, the book is commonly dated to the time of the Persian Empire (ca. 539–333 BCE). Reasons for this dating include the book's language, information that does not fit what we know of the Near East in the eighth century, and citations and allusions to other biblical texts that postdate the eighth century.

The Composition of Jonah

Another topic that has engendered much debate among scholars is the composition of Jonah. The psalm that serves as Jonah's prayer in chap. 2 is commonly, though not universally, considered distinct in origin from the prose narrative, whether it was incorporated by the author of that narrative or added to it later. While the prose story is often treated as a unit, there are tensions within it that might indicate reworking (see especially 4:5).

Literary Features

Among the literary features of Jonah that stand out are its use of hyperbole or exaggeration and its out-of-the-ordinary characterizations. Hyperbole is most apparent in the repeated use of the word "great" or "large," which occurs fourteen times in Jonah's four chapters, far more than in any other text of comparable size in the Hebrew Bible. The city of Nineveh is consistently called the "great city," and the "great wind," "great storm," and "great fish" play important roles. The two main characters are Jonah and God. As hinted above, Jonah is a kind of anti-hero or anti-prophet. He is by turns disobedient, sullen and morose, and angry and argumentative. God is YHWH, the God of Israel, the Lord of land and sea and all creation, but in Jonah, God is a micromanager who personally engages Jonah, hurls the wind on the sea, and appoints the fish, the plant, and the worm. Other characters include the sailors and the Ninevites, non-Israelite adherents of other gods, who nonetheless contrast with Jonah in the speed and ease with which they comply with what they perceive to be God's will. Strikingly, animals are characters in Jonah. The fish and the worm serve as instruments to accomplish God's purposes, just as Jonah does. The animals in Nineveh repent, as do its human inhabitants, and are instrumental in motivating God's pardon for the city. Finally, the narrator is an important character in Jonah, apparent in the framing of the story, what information is divulged and when, the creation of the dialogue between characters, and leaving the entire book unresolved by concluding it with an unanswered question.

HEBREW BIBLE | 1271

Reading Guide

The book of Jonah consists of just four chapters. In chap. 1, Jonah is called as a prophet and attempts to flee from God. He is then swallowed by a large fish. Chap. 2 consists of Jonah's prayer psalm from the belly of the fish, followed by the fish vomiting him out. Chap. 3 describes Jonah's mission to Nineveh and his successful prophesying there, as the people repent and God spares the city. Chap. 4 chronicles Jonah's anger at the pardon of Nineveh and God's response to Jonah. The greatest challenge of the book of Jonah is probably the question of how to understand its nature or genre and why it was written. The book is widely considered satire or parody based on its transparent ridicule of Jonah. Christian interpreters often see Jonah as a type of Christ (Matt. 12:39–41) and the story about him as a critique of bigotry and an endorsement of God's universal concern for all people regardless of ethnicity or nationality. Jews, however, focus on Jonah's role as a prophet and highlight the tension in the book between justice and mercy. Particularly in a post-Holocaust world, the book raises the question whether forgiveness is always possible or even appropriate. In both cases, this seemingly simple story touches on weighty theological issues.

Rhiannon Graybill, John Kaltner, and Steven L. McKenzie

1 Now the word of the Lord came to Jonah son of Amittai, saying, ²"Go at once to Nineveh, that great city, and cry out against it, for their wickedness has come up before me." ³But Jonah set out to flee to Tarshish from the presence of the Lord. He went down to Joppa and found a ship going to Tarshish; so he paid his fare and went on board, to go with them to Tarshish, away from the presence of the Lord.

4 But the Lord hurled a great wind upon the sea, and such a mighty storm came upon the sea that the ship threatened to break up. ⁵Then the sailors were afraid, and each cried to his god. They threw the cargo that was in the ship into the sea, to lighten it for them. Jonah, meanwhile, had gone down into the hold of the ship and had lain down and was fast asleep. ⁶The captain came and said to him, "What are you doing sound asleep? Get up; call on your god!

Perhaps the god will spare us a thought so that we do not perish."

7 The sailors[a] said to one another, "Come, let us cast lots, so that we may know on whose account this calamity has come upon us." So they cast lots, and the lot fell on Jonah. ⁸Then they said to him, "Tell us why this calamity has come upon us. What is your occupation? Where do you come from? What is your country? And of what people are you?" ⁹"I am a Hebrew," he replied. "I worship the Lord, the God of heaven, who made the sea and the dry land." ¹⁰Then the men were even more afraid and said to him, "What is this that you have done!" For the men knew that he was fleeing from the presence of the Lord, because he had told them so.

11 Then they said to him, "What shall we do to you, that the sea may quiet down for us?" For the sea was growing more and

a 1.7 Heb *They*

1 **Jonah's call and attempted flight. 1:1** *Jonah son of Amittai* is mentioned in 2 Kgs. 14:25, where he is identified as a prophet from Gath-hepher. *Jonah* means "dove." **1:2** *Nineveh* was the capital of the Assyrian Empire until its destruction in 612 BCE. This is the first of fourteen appearances of the adjective *great* in the book and the first of ten occurrences of the Hebrew root that the word translated as *wickedness* comes from. **1:3** *Tarshish* is likely Tartessos in southern Spain, the opposite direction from Nineveh. **1:4** *Threatened.* Literally "thought about" or "considered." **1:5** *His god* might also be translated as "his gods." The mention of Jonah's descent *into the hold of the ship* uses the same Hebrew verb that describes his actions in v. 3 as he "went down to Joppa" and "went on board" the ship. **1:6** This is the only reference to *the captain* in the chapter. *Your god* might also be translated as "your gods." **1:7** The casting of *lots* is mentioned elsewhere in the Bible, but the precise nature of the objects and how they were used remain unknown (1 Sam. 10:20–21; 14:36–46; Acts 1:21–26). **1:10** This is the second of three references to the sailors' fear in the chapter (vv. 5, 16), and Jonah uses the same Hebrew verb in the previous verse to describe his "worship" of YHWH. **1:11** The final part of the verse might be translated as "for the sea is growing more and more tempestuous"

Reading through Time: Jonah's Fish (Jonah 1)

Jonah's fish is one of the most famous animals in the entire Bible. The Hebrew word that describes it (*dag*) refers simply to a fish or a fishlike aquatic creature without specifying its type. Its traditional identification as a whale is understandable considering its size. The Greek translation of the word in the Septuagint as "whale" (*kētos*) undoubtedly played an important role in this (mis)identification. However, *kētos* can also mean "sea monster," and the designation "fish" downplays its probable mythological background, in which the creature may have been a monster symbolizing the Northwest Semitic sea god Yamm. The motif of a person trapped inside an aquatic monster is found in ancient literature and folklore, as seen in the example of the Greek myth about Herakles's rescue of Hesione. Jonah's three-day imprisonment in the sea creature also finds similarities in the journeys to the underworld undertaken by other literary figures like Inanna/Ishtar, Enkidu, Dumuzi, Persephone, Demeter, Odysseus, and Orpheus. Indeed, the psalm in Jonah 2 identifies its author's location as Sheol, the underworld in the Hebrew Bible. The text tells us very little about the fish, aside from the mention of its great size. The Hebrew adjective "great" (*gadol*) is used elsewhere in the story to describe the evil of the city of Nineveh (1:2), the storm (1:4, 12), the sailors' fear (1:10, 16), the dimensions of Nineveh (3:2–3), and Jonah's anger (4:1).

An unusual aspect of the fish is that it changes grammatical gender in Hebrew, as it is twice described as male (*dag*; 2:1, 11 [Eng. 1:17; 2:10]) and once as female (*daga*; 2:2 [Eng. 2:1]). Various explanations for this oddity have been proposed, including editorial error, grammatical necessity, evidence of multiple literary sources, and the presence of two fish in the story, but the reason for the gender shift remains a mystery. YHWH's appointing of the fish anticipates a set of similar divine actions that take place in the book's fourth chapter, as the same Hebrew verb is used to describe how the deity appoints the plant (4:6), the worm (4:7), and the wind (4:8). In this way, the fish and these other nonhuman actors are the instruments and means by which YHWH interacts with the natural world and the divine will is realized. Their compliance thus contrasts sharply with Jonah's disobedience.

Rhiannon Graybill

more tempestuous. ¹²He said to them, "Pick me up and throw me into the sea; then the sea will quiet down for you, for I know it is because of me that this great storm has come upon you." ¹³Nevertheless, the men rowed hard to bring the ship[b] back to land, but they could not, for the sea grew more and more stormy against them. ¹⁴Then they cried out to the Lord, "Please, O Lord, we pray, do not let us perish on account of this man's life. Do not make us guilty of innocent blood, for you, O Lord, have done as it pleased you." ¹⁵So they picked Jonah up and threw him into the sea, and the sea ceased from its raging. ¹⁶Then the men feared the Lord even more, and they offered a sacrifice to the Lord and made vows.

17 [c]But the Lord provided a large fish to swallow up Jonah, and Jonah was in the belly of the fish three days and three nights.

2 Then Jonah prayed to the Lord his God from the belly of the fish, ²saying,

b 1.13 Heb lacks *the ship*   c 1.17 2.1 in Heb

and therefore continue the sailors' speech, but it is more likely a narratorial comment. **1:12** Jonah's request that they *throw* him into the water uses the same Hebrew verb that describes YHWH hurling the wind on the sea (v. 4) and the sailors tossing their cargo overboard (v. 5). **1:14** This is the first time that the men utter the name of Jonah's God (YHWH), and their supplication adopts the standard three-part structure of ancient Near Eastern prayers: (1) address, (2) petition(s), and (3) motivation. The phrase *innocent blood* indicates that they should not be considered guilty for what they are about to do to Jonah, and it makes no claim that he is innocent. **1:16** The sequence of three verbs in quick succession continues the sense of swiftness and urgency that began in the previous verse. The description of the men's fear is identical to what is found in v. 10, but this time its object is specified as YHWH. **1:17** The Hebrew text begins chap. 2 at 1:17 and is one verse ahead of the English throughout the chapter. *Three days and three nights* designates a relatively long time under unpleasant conditions. See **"Jonah's Fish," p. 1273.**

2 Jonah's prayer psalm from the belly of the fish. **2:1** *From the belly of the fish.* The Hebrew uses a feminine form here as opposed to the masculine in the previous verse. There is no clear explanation for the change in gender. Because the fish is feminine, *belly* might be rendered as "womb" in addition to "bowels" or "entrails." **2:2** The psalm in this chapter was probably added later. It is a psalm of

"I called to the Lord out of my distress,
    and he answered me;
out of the belly of Sheol I cried,
    and you heard my voice.
³ You cast me into the deep,
    into the heart of the seas,
    and the flood surrounded me;
all your waves and your billows
    passed over me.
⁴ Then I said, 'I am driven away
    from your sight;
how^d shall I look again
    upon your holy temple?'
⁵ The waters closed in over me;
    the deep surrounded me;
weeds were wrapped around my
    head
⁶   at the roots of the mountains.
I went down to the land
    whose bars closed upon me forever;
yet you brought up my life from the Pit,
    O Lord my God.
⁷ As my life was ebbing away,
    I remembered the Lord,

and my prayer came to you,
    into your holy temple.
⁸ Those who worship vain idols
    forsake their true loyalty.
⁹ But I with the voice of thanksgiving
    will sacrifice to you;
what I have vowed I will pay.
    Deliverance belongs to the Lord!"
¹⁰Then the Lord spoke to the fish, and it
vomited Jonah out onto the dry land.

3 The word of the Lord came to Jonah
a second time, saying, ²"Get up, go to
Nineveh, that great city, and proclaim to it
the message that I tell you." ³So Jonah set out
and went to Nineveh, according to the word
of the Lord. Now Nineveh was an exceedingly large city, a three days' walk across.
⁴Jonah began to go into the city, going a
day's walk. And he cried out, "Forty days
more, and Nineveh shall be overthrown!"
⁵And the people of Nineveh believed God;

d 2.4 Theodotion: Heb *surely*

thanksgiving for rescue from a crisis situation that is described using metaphors of death and drown-ing. It is used to depict Jonah's experience in the sea, although its expression of thanks is not entirely appropriate for Jonah, who does not know if he will survive the fish. The Hebrew for *belly* here is dif-ferent from the word translated as "belly" in 1:17 and 2:1. *Sheol.* The underworld, the place of the dead. The psalm begins by depicting the psalmist's *distress* in terms of dying. **2:3** The psalm transitions from the metaphor of death to that of drowning in the sea. YHWH, named in 2:2, is addressed in the second person as the one who *cast* the psalmist into the sea, while the sailors threw Jonah overboard in 1:15. **2:4** This verse reflects a different setting from the Jonah story, since Jonah was not *driven away* from God but ran away. Also, the *temple* was in Jerusalem, the capital of Judah, rather than Israel, where Jonah was from (2 Kgs. 14:25). The psalm here seems to presuppose exile. **2:5** *Weeds* or "reeds" might mean "end" or "extinction" here. **2:6** *Land* or "earth" and *Pit* are other names for the underworld, which is here envisioned as a city entered at the foot of mountains that is locked from the outside to keep its residents in. *You brought up my life from the Pit* praises YHWH for rescue from crisis and may mark an older ending of the psalm. **2:7** As in 2:4, the *temple* here does not fit with the Jonah story. **2:8** This harsh condemnation of idol worshipers contrasts with the positive portrayal of the sailors. *Their true loyalty* may allude to God. **2:9** *Deliverance belongs to the Lord.* A concluding benediction (Ps. 3:8). **2:10** The *fish* is grammatically masculine again. *Vomited* suggests distastefulness.

3 Jonah's mission to Nineveh. 3:1 *A second time.* See 1:1. **3:2** *Message that I tell you.* It is not clear whether God supplies the exact words or the gist; the nature of the oracle in 3:4 suggests the latter. **3:3** *Exceedingly.* Literally "to God"—interpreted as a superlative, similar to the way English can use "divine." *Three days' walk across.* About fifty miles, a hyperbole. The excavated city walls of ancient Nineveh are about seven and a half miles in circumference. **3:4** *Began to go.* The phrase suggests that in a version of the story before the addition of the hyperbole about its size, Jonah barely set foot inside the city gate when he delivered his oracle. *Forty days.* A round number for a significant period of testing or decision (Exod. 16:35; 24:18; Num. 32:13; 1 Kgs. 19:8; etc.). *Over-thrown* is reminiscent of what is said of Sodom and Gomorrah (Jer. 49:18; Gen. 19), but the verb might mean "overturned," suggesting repentance. It is not clear how Jonah communicated with the people of Nineveh, who did not speak Hebrew. **3:5** *Sackcloth.* Literally "sacks" for transporting grain (Gen. 42:35); presumably made of cheap, rough cloth and therefore appropriate as clothing for demonstrating penitence. *Everyone, great and small.* A reference to social status or wealth.

they proclaimed a fast, and everyone, great and small, put on sackcloth.

6 When the news reached the king of Nineveh, he rose from his throne, removed his robe, covered himself with sackcloth, and sat in ashes. [7]Then he had a proclamation made in Nineveh: "By the decree of the king and his nobles: No human or animal, no herd or flock, shall taste anything. They shall not feed, nor shall they drink water. [8]Humans and animals shall be covered with sackcloth, and they shall cry mightily to God. All shall turn from their evil ways and from the violence that is in their hands. [9]Who knows? God may relent and change his mind; he may turn from his fierce anger, so that we do not perish."

10 When God saw what they did, how they turned from their evil ways, God changed his mind about the calamity that he had said he would bring upon them, and he did not do it.

4 But this was very displeasing to Jonah, and he became angry. [2]He prayed to the LORD and said, "O LORD! Is not this what I said while I was still in my own country? That is why I fled to Tarshish at the beginning, for I knew that you are a gracious and merciful God, slow to anger, abounding in steadfast love, and relenting from punishment. [3]And now, O LORD, please take my life from me, for it is better for me to die than to live." [4]And the LORD said, "Is it right for you to be angry?" [5]Then Jonah went out of the city and sat down east of the city and made a booth for himself there. He sat under it in the shade, waiting to see what would become of the city.

6 The LORD God appointed a bush and made it come up over Jonah, to give shade over his head, to save him from his discomfort, so Jonah was very happy about the bush. [7]But when dawn came up the next day, God appointed a worm that attacked the bush, so that it withered. [8]When the sun rose, God prepared a sultry east wind, and the sun beat down on the head of Jonah so that he was faint and asked that he might die. He said, "It is better for me to die than to live."

9 But God said to Jonah, "Is it right for you to be angry about the bush?" And he said, "Yes, angry enough to die." [10]Then the LORD said, "You are concerned about the bush, for which you did not labor

However, as the story stands, the king is not included yet (3:6). **3:6** *Sat in ashes.* Another sign of repentance, along with fasting and wearing sacks. **3:7** *Decree.* Literally "taste," a pun on the occurrence of the same word later in the verse. *Nor shall they drink water* indicates that the fast lasted much less than forty days before God responded. **3:8** In the LXX, this verse seems to continue the report of the people's activities in v. 5 rather than the king's decree in v. 7. *Violence.* The only concrete indication of the nature of Nineveh's evil. **3:9** *Who knows? God may relent and change his mind.* Identical to Joel 2:14. Cf. 2 Sam. 12:22; Esth. 4:14. The question expresses hope that God will respond in forgiveness to their acts of repentance and will not destroy the city. **3:10** *Calamity.* The same word translated as *evil* earlier in the verse. Together they form a wordplay. Because the Ninevites turn from their evil ways, God turns from enacting the evil (disaster) intended for the city as punishment.

4 Jonah's anger at the pardon of Nineveh and God's response to Jonah. 4:1 *This was very displeasing to Jonah.* Jonah is angry that the city has not been destroyed. *He became angry.* Jonah's anger at God recalls other biblical characters who display raw emotions, including Moses (Exod. 32:19), Elijah (1 Kgs. 19:10), and Job (Job 3). *He prayed to the LORD and said.* This is Jonah's second prayer, following the psalm in the fish. While Jonah was relatively taciturn in Nineveh (chap. 3), he now speaks freely. **4:2** *A gracious and merciful God, slow to anger.* Cf. Exod. 34:6–7a. **4:5** *East of the city.* Having traveled east to Nineveh, Jonah now travels farther east. *A booth.* A temporary structure. This verse may be a later addition: it is not clear why Jonah needs the shade of the bush (4:6) if he already has built a booth (4:5). **4:6** *The LORD God appointed.* This is the first of three consecutive acts of appointing: the bush (4:6), the worm (4:7), and the wind (4:8). In addition, a different variation of God's name is given in each. *A bush.* Heb. "qiqayon." The species of plant is unknown; interpreters have suggested a castor bean plant (*Ricinus communis*) or a gourd vine (reflecting the Gk. translation). **4:7** *A worm.* Like the plant, the species is unknown. **4:8** *A sultry east wind.* There are several famous winds in the Middle East, including the sirocco and the khamsin. It is not clear,

Going Deeper: The Genre of Jonah (Jonah 4)

What sort of story is the book of Jonah? Is it a prophetic tale? A moral lesson? A parable? Satire? Does it resemble other texts in the Hebrew Bible, or is it something unique? All these are questions about genre, a topic that has generated much lively discussion among biblical scholars but has yet to produce a definitive consensus.

The most common perspective on Jonah's genre is that it represents an anti-prophetic satire. Perhaps prophecy was satirized because during the Persian period when the book was likely written (ca. 539–333 BCE), the role of the prophet in society had begun to change and was being called into question. In many ways, Jonah is a terrible prophet: he flees from God, is swallowed by the fish, and only reluctantly prophesies at all; when his halfhearted prophecy succeeds, his response is not gratitude but extreme anger. In his success, Jonah inverts the typical biblical prophetic pattern—the failure of the prophet is a common biblical motif—and the result is a satirical account. Related to the satire argument, some readers describe the book of Jonah as a parody (a deliberate exaggeration of the typical prophetic story for comedic effect).

Not all scholars agree that the book of Jonah is satirical. Some classify the text as a "prophetic tale," pointing to similar examples in other biblical texts, such as the stories of Elijah and Elisha in the book of Kings. There is a brief mention of "Jonah ben Amittai" in 2 Kgs. 14 that might support this position, and Islamic tradition has a collection of "Stories of the Prophets" that includes Jonah (Yunus). However, this view does not account for the obvious hyperbole in Jonah (the word "great" is used fourteen times) or other elements that are humorous or unrealistic, such as the animals in Nineveh repenting. Also, while the events of Jonah 1 have parallels in Hellenistic seafaring tales that might be seen to resemble prophetic tales, these tales are patently mythological, and they date from considerably later than the early eighth-century setting of 2 Kgs. 14.

Still another possibility is to treat Jonah as didactic literature. Scholars have proposed that the text is a parable (Heb. *mashal*) or moral lesson. Interpreters who take this route generally focus on Jonah 4 and the book's challenging ending, treating God's final unanswered question to Jonah as an invitation to reflect on the issues the book raises. A final suggestion is that the book of Jonah does not represent an existing genre of literature at all and is, instead, a unique work.

Rhiannon Graybill

and which you did not grow; it came into being in a night and perished in a night. ¹¹And should I not be concerned about Nineveh, that great city, in which there are more than a hundred and twenty thousand persons who do not know their right hand from their left and also many animals?"

however, if the author intends an actual weather formation. **4:11** *And should I not be concerned?* God's question seems to be intended to instruct Jonah, but the precise meaning intended is not clear. *More than a hundred and twenty thousand persons.* The number 120,000 is not an exact figure but rather a symbolically large number. *Who do not know their right hand from their left.* An expression meaning that they are foolish. *And also many animals?* The animals refer back to Jonah 3:7–8. See **"The Genre of Jonah," p. 1276.**

MICAH

Authorship, Date, and Major Events

Micah was a contemporary of Isaiah of Jerusalem. He was active from approximately 760 to 700 BCE, during the reigns of the Judean kings Jotham, Ahaz, and Hezekiah. He reflects on two major events in Israelite and Judean history: the fall of the capital of Israel, Samaria, to the Assyrians (722 BCE) and the siege of Jerusalem, the capital of Judah, by the Assyrian king Sennacherib (701 BCE). These events are recounted in 2 Kgs. 17–19.

In other biblical books, the fall of Samaria in contrast with Jerusalem's survival of the Assyrian siege are interpreted together to affirm Zion theology, which is the idea that Jerusalem is inviolable due to God's presence there (Ps. 46:5). Micah's message is striking in that he denies this sense of security. Later, the prophet Jeremiah presents a position similar to Micah's. The story of Jeremiah even features elders quoting from a prophet named Micah (literally "Micaiah") from Moresheth to support their position: "Micah of Moresheth, who prophesied during the days of King Hezekiah of Judah, said to all the people of Judah: 'Thus says the LORD of hosts, Zion shall be plowed as a field; Jerusalem shall become a heap of ruins and the mountain of the house a wooded height.' . . . Did [King Hezekiah] not fear the LORD and entreat the favor of the LORD, and did not the LORD change his mind about the disaster that he had pronounced against them?" (Jer. 26:18–19). The account in Jeremiah suggests the possibility that Hezekiah considered Micah's message and, rather than rejecting it, listened to him and made a seemingly successful supplication to God to save the people.

Micah as a Prophet

The book of Micah is among the Book of the Twelve. As far as literary genre, Micah is certainly in line with other examples of biblical prophets. See **"The Bible as a Collection," pp. 2145–47.** At the same time, themes such as social justice, covenant, divine favor, and good leadership span throughout the biblical anthology.

Several details in the book raise the question of how Micah might have understood his role relative to other prophets. The book does not feature a call narrative for Micah, and he does not use the formula "thus says YHWH." This is reminiscent of Amos stating that he is not a prophet (Amos 7:14). As an individual, Micah contrasts himself with prophets, seers, and diviners (3:5–8). He criticizes them, saying that God will not answer them, whereas Micah successfully receives God's messages. He says that the prophets lead the people astray (3:5), take money in exchange for divine messages (3:11), and alter their messages to be positive or negative depending on how they benefit (3:5). He says that God will neither communicate with them nor respond to them due to unjust behaviors (3:6–7). Micah recalls the foundational prophets Moses, Aaron, and Miriam by name along with Balaam, whose prophetic messages honored YHWH (Num. 22–24; Mic. 6:4–5). Drawing positively on this prophetic tradition sharpens Micah's critique of corrupt prophets. His critiques of prophets and powerful elites might indicate that he presents himself not as a prophet per se but perhaps simply as a representative of his rural contingency.

Reading Guide

Micah, the Covenant, and Leadership

Micah utilizes a framework for his message that is based on the covenant lawsuit (6:1–2). The covenant is an agreement between the people and God (see **"Covenant (Genesis)," p. 23**). The prophets blame misfortune on the people, saying that while God upholds God's covenant, the people have not upheld their part of the deal, specifically due to what they deem as corrupt behaviors. God's suit or contention (*rib*) is that the people have not upheld standards of fairness. Within this metaphorical lawsuit framework, because of the people's corruption, God does not want their offerings (6:6–8). Moreover, God will punish them. This theological explanation is unflattering for the people, but it serves rhetorically to protect God's reputation. That is, misfortune is not explained as God's weakness or inability to protect God's people. In fact, Micah characterizes God as having such expansive authority that God can utilize the Assyrians to punish Israel and Judah. Micah's immediate audience seems to be the rulers and elites of Samaria and Jerusalem. Like the books of Amos and Hosea as well as portions of Isaiah, the book of Micah speaks to Judeans by utilizing the Assyrian destruction

of Samaria as a lesson for the people of Jerusalem and Judah, prior to the Babylonians destroying Jerusalem in 586 BCE.

Micah and Social Justice

Micah raises issues in critique of elites, leaders, and prophets, holding that justice is required for God to communicate with God's people, such that the people cannot rely solely on offering sacrifices to God to ensure favor and protection (6:6-8). This is comparable to the sentiment in Amos 5:21-24, from which Martin Luther King Jr. quoted in support of the modern civil rights movement in the United States. See **"Bible and Social Justice," pp. 2165-67, and "Amos and Martin Luther King Jr.," p. 1262**. He shows particular concern for injustices against rural inhabitants and farmers, which would be in line with his town of origin. He criticizes the elites of Samaria and Jerusalem in a manner similar to Amos (Amos 4-5). Micah accuses creditors and oppressors of seizing fields, foreclosing on farms, taking rural properties, using false weights and measures, and corrupting the justice system. Despite direct challenges to leaders, priests, and prophets, it is interesting to notice that Micah does not critique the Judean monarchy itself. Rather, he foretells a ruler from Bethlehem (5:2). Compared to the prophet Isaiah, who interacts extensively with the Judean kings Ahaz and Hezekiah, the book of Micah does not feature interaction with specific kings.

The book of Micah is organized with an introductory superscription (1:1), followed by a series of oracles that alternate between messages of judgment and restoration, and finally a concluding lament and liturgical prayer. There are indications that the book of Micah was edited after the destruction of Jerusalem in 586 BCE, with possible references to exile (4:10) as well as the later rebuilding of Jerusalem's walls at the time of Nehemiah (7:11; Neh. 2:17). Editorial activity is further indicated by the shared text exhibited in Mic. 4:1-4 and Isa. 2:2-4. Editors possibly used material from other sources to supplement a series of original oracles attributed to Micah.

Debra Scoggins Ballentine

1 The word of the Lord that came to Micah of Moresheth in the days of Kings Jotham, Ahaz, and Hezekiah of Judah, which he saw concerning Samaria and Jerusalem.

² Hear, you peoples, all of you;
  listen, O earth, and all that is in it,
and let the Lord God be a witness
  against you,
  the Lord from his holy temple.

³ For the Lord is coming out of his place
  and will come down and tread upon
    the high places of the earth.
⁴ Then the mountains will melt under him,
  and the valleys will burst open
like wax near the fire,
  like waters poured down a slope.
⁵ All this is for the transgression of Jacob
  and for the sins of the house of Israel.
  What is the transgression of Jacob?
  Is it not Samaria?

1:1 Superscription. The introductory superscription locates Micah's career during the reigns of the Judean kings Jotham, Ahaz, and Hezekiah, which date to the second half of the eighth century BCE. The superscription identifies Micah as being from a town called Moresheth, so Micah appears to be from Judah, about twenty-five miles southwest of Jerusalem. While Micah is from a more rural setting, his audience appears to be urban populations, as the superscription indicates that the messages YHWH provides to Micah concern the cities of Samaria, the capital of Israel, and Jerusalem, the capital of Judah. Micah's hometown is also referenced in 1:14 as Moresheth-gath among locations that have suffered misfortunes. **1:2-2:11 Oracle of judgment.** The book of Micah presents oracles that alternate between the themes of judgment and restoration. **1:2** Micah uses the phrase *Hear, you peoples, all of you*. Micaiah son of Imlah also uses this exact phrase (1 Kgs. 22:28), suggesting they might be the same individual. Micah is a shortened form of the name Micaiah, meaning "Who is like YHWH?" The rhetorical question "Who is a God like you?" (7:18) similarly communicates the theological claim that no other divine beings are adequately comparable to YHWH. **1:3-4 Theophany.** YHWH appears, emerging from his temple to witness against the people. The impact of YHWH appearing is described as physically destructive in melting mountains and cleaving valleys. **1:5** YHWH as "witness" (1:2) blames

And what is the high place[a] of Judah?
Is it not Jerusalem?
6 Therefore I will make Samaria a heap in
the open country,
a place for planting vineyards.
I will pour down her stones into the valley
and uncover her foundations.
7 All her images shall be beaten to
pieces,
all her wages shall be burned with
fire,
and all her idols I will lay waste;
for as the wages of a prostitute she
gathered them,
and as the wages of a prostitute they
shall again be used.

8 For this I will lament and wail;
I will go barefoot and naked;
I will make lamentation like the jackals
and mourning like the ostriches.
9 For her wound[b] is incurable.
It has come to Judah;
it has reached to the gate of my people,
to Jerusalem.

10 Tell it not in Gath;
weep not at all;
in Beth-leaphrah
roll yourselves in the dust.
11 Pass on your way,
inhabitants of Shaphir,
in nakedness and shame;
the inhabitants of Zaanan
do not come forth;
Beth-ezel is wailing
and shall remove its support from you.
12 For the inhabitants of Maroth
wait anxiously for good,

yet disaster has come down from the
Lord
to the gate of Jerusalem.
13 Harness the steeds to the chariots,
inhabitants of Lachish;
it was the beginning of sin
to daughter Zion,
for in you were found
the transgressions of Israel.
14 Therefore you shall give parting gifts
to Moresheth-gath;
the houses of Achzib shall be a deception
to the kings of Israel.
15 I will again bring a conqueror upon you,
inhabitants of Mareshah;
the glory of Israel
shall come to Adullam.
16 Make yourselves bald and cut off your
hair
for your pampered children;
make yourselves as bald as the eagle,
for they have gone from you into exile.

2 Woe to those who devise wickedness
and evil deeds[c] on their beds!
When the morning dawns, they
perform it,
because it is in their power.
2 They covet fields and seize them,
houses and take them away;
they oppress householder and house,
people and their inheritance.
3 Therefore thus says the Lord:
Now, I am devising against this family
an evil
from which you cannot remove your
necks,

a 1.5 Heb *what are the high places*   b 1.9 Gk Syr Vg: Heb
wounds   c 2.1 Cn: Heb *work evil*

the capital city Samaria for Israel's wrongs, and the oracle draws a parallel between Samaria and Jerusalem. Both Samaria and Jerusalem will be punished, as in 2:3. **1:6** The destruction of Samaria occurred in 722 BCE. **1:7** *Images* and *idols* refer to icons that the author regards as illegitimate. The translation as *idols* echoes the biblical polemic. **1:8–9** YHWH mourns for Samaria and regards her demise as final and unpreventable. YHWH anticipates the arrival of her incurable wound to God's people in Jerusalem. **1:8** The prophet Isaiah performs a sign act of walking through Jerusalem naked (Isa. 20:1–6). **1:10–16** This list of towns, including Micah's hometown in v. 14, names locations that have already suffered destruction and captivity. They exhibit many gestures of mourning as they *weep, wail, roll . . . in the dust*, experience *nakedness* and *shame*, and *cut off [their] hair*. **1:12–13** YHWH is credited with the suffering of these towns and blames Israel for the wrongdoings. While the exact locations of some of these towns are unknown, it seems they are in the area through which the Assyrian king Sennacherib campaigned in 701 BCE (2 Kgs. 18–19; Isa. 36–37). **2:1–2** The narrator cites complaints of oppressive and corrupt behaviors by those in power who seize people's properties. **2:3** *This family*, later referenced as "house of Jacob" and "Jacob" (2:7, 12), indicates Israel. YHWH will punish them for the wrongdoings YHWH accuses them of having done, as foreshadowed

and you shall not walk arrogantly,
  for it will be an evil time.
⁴ On that day they shall take up a taunt
    song against you
  and wail with bitter lamentation
and say, "We are utterly ruined;
    the Lord*d* alters the inheritance of my
    people;
  how he removes it from me!
    Among our captors*e* he parcels out
    our fields."
⁵ Therefore you will have no one in the
    Lord's assembly
  to allot you a piece of land.

⁶ "Do not preach"—thus they preach—
  "one should not preach of such things;
  disgrace will not overtake us."
⁷ Should this be said, O house of Jacob?
  Is the Lord's patience exhausted?
  Are these his doings?
Do not my words do good
  to one who walks uprightly?
⁸ But you rise up against my people*f* as
    an enemy;
  you strip the robe from the peaceful,*g*
from those who pass by trustingly
  with no thought of war.
⁹ The women of my people you drive out
    from their pleasant houses;
from their young children you take away
  my glory forever.
¹⁰ Arise and go,
    for this is no place to rest,
because of uncleanness that destroys
  with a violent destruction.
¹¹ If someone were to go about uttering
    empty falsehoods,
  saying, "I will preach to you of wine
    and strong drink,"
such a one would be the preacher for
    this people!

¹² I will surely gather all of you, O Jacob;
  I will gather the survivors of Israel;
I will set them together
  like sheep in a fold,
like a flock in its pasture;
  it will resound with people.
¹³ The one who breaks out will go up
    before them;
  they will break through and pass the
    gate,
  going out by it.
Their king will pass on before them,
  the Lord at their head.

3 And I said:
  Listen, you heads of Jacob
    and rulers of the house of Israel!
  Should you not know justice?—
²   you who hate the good and love the
      evil,
  who tear the skin off my people*b*
    and the flesh off their bones,
³ who eat the flesh of my people,
    flay their skin off them,
  break their bones in pieces,
    and chop them up like meat*i* in a
      kettle,
    like flesh in a caldron.

⁴ Then they will cry to the Lord,
    but he will not answer them;
  he will hide his face from them at that
    time
    because they have acted wickedly.

⁵ Thus says the Lord concerning the
    prophets
  who lead my people astray,
  who cry "Peace"

d 2.4 Heb *he*   *e* 2.4 Cn: Heb *the rebellious*   *f* 2.8 Cn: Heb *But
yesterday my people rose*   *g* 2.8 Cn: Heb *from before a garment*
b 3.2 Heb *from them*   *i* 3.3 Gk: Heb *as*

in 1:2–4. **2:4** The fate of the people is made more explicit, as deserving of taunting, wailing, and
lamenting. YHWH will divide their fields among their captors. **2:5** They will have no representation
and no access to YHWH's assembly. **2:6–11** Those who *preach* are identified as the enemy of God's
people for advising them wrongly by reassuring them. Micah suggests that his message would not
bother upright people, as opposed to the corrupt people who do not like his criticisms.

2:12–13 Oracle of restoration. God will gather surviving Israelites and lead them as their shepherd
and king.

3:1–12 Oracle of judgment. 3:1–4 The critique of leaders is communicated by featuring the deity
directly blaming them for harming God's people. Micah states that God will not answer their invocations. This contrasts with biblical scenes in which YHWH does respond to cries for help (Exod.
2:23; 3:7–9; Judg. 3:9). **3:5–8** Micah contrasts himself with prophets, seers, and diviners. He criticizes
them, saying that whereas God will not answer them, Micah receives messages from God. **3:5** Micah

when they have something to eat
but declare war against those
who put nothing into their mouths.
[6] Therefore it shall be night to you,
without vision,
and darkness to you, without
revelation.
The sun shall go down upon the prophets,
and the day shall be black over them;
[7] the seers shall be disgraced
and the diviners put to shame;
they shall all cover their lips,
for there is no answer from God.
[8] But as for me, I am filled with power,
with the spirit of the LORD,
and with justice and might,
to declare to Jacob his transgression
and to Israel his sin.

[9] Hear this, you rulers of the house of
Jacob
and chiefs of the house of Israel,
who abhor justice
and pervert all equity,
[10] who build Zion with blood
and Jerusalem with wrong!
[11] Its rulers give judgment for a bribe;
its priests teach for a price;
its prophets give oracles for money;
yet they lean upon the LORD and say,
"Surely the LORD is with us!
No harm shall come upon us."
[12] Therefore because of you
Zion shall be plowed as a field;
Jerusalem shall become a heap of ruins,
and the mountain of the temple a
wooded height.

4

In days to come
the mountain of the LORD's temple
shall be established as the highest of
the mountains
and shall be raised up above the
hills.
Peoples shall stream to it,
[2]   and many nations shall come and
say:
"Come, let us go up to the mountain of
the LORD,
to the house of the God of Jacob,
that he may teach us his ways
and that we may walk in his paths."
For out of Zion shall go forth
instruction,
and the word of the LORD from
Jerusalem.
[3] He shall judge between many
peoples
and shall arbitrate between strong
nations far away;
they shall beat their swords into
plowshares
and their spears into pruning
hooks;
nation shall not lift up sword against
nation;
neither shall they learn war any
more;
[4] but they shall all sit under their own
vines and under their own fig
trees,
and no one shall make them afraid,
for the mouth of the LORD of hosts
has spoken.

[5] For all the peoples walk,
each in the name of its god,
but we will walk in the name of the
LORD our God
forever and ever.

says that the prophets lead the people astray by altering their messages to be positive or negative depending on how they benefit. **3:6–7** Micah says that God will neither communicate with them nor respond to them due to unjust behaviors. **3:10** *Zion* is a poetic name for Jerusalem. **3:9–12** The fall of Jerusalem is attributed to the leadership being corrupt. Micah denies Zion theology (Ps. 46:5). **3:11** He accuses priests of corruptly taking money in exchange for teaching and likewise accuses prophets of taking money in exchange for delivering messages as if they are from God.

4:1–5:15 Oracle of restoration. The community and temple will be restored in the future. **4:1–5** This is an idealized view of YHWH's mountain as the highest among all mountains. **4:1–3** This passage is parallel with Isa. 2:2–4 regarding the end of warcraft among nations as a result of torah, as the word of YHWH, dispersing from Jerusalem. **4:2** *Instruction.* Heb. "torah." **4:4** The image of sitting under one's own fig tree depicts an ideal of farmers being able to sit peacefully with their crops and enjoy them. George Washington cited this image, and many have echoed Washington's use in critique of the impacts of war and imperial oppression. **4:5** This reflects the common ancient Near Eastern theological idea that each group of people has its own patron god. Among the various gods

⁶ On that day, says the LORD,
    I will assemble the lame
and gather those who have been driven
    away
    and those whom I have afflicted.
⁷ The lame I will make the remnant,
    and those who were cast off, a strong
    nation,
and the LORD will reign over them in
    Mount Zion
    now and forevermore.

⁸ And you, O tower of the flock,
    hill of daughter Zion,
to you it shall come,
    the former dominion shall come,
    the sovereignty of daughter
    Jerusalem.

⁹ Now why do you cry aloud?
    Is there no king in you?
Has your counselor perished,
    that pangs have seized you like a
    woman in labor?
¹⁰ Writhe and groan,ʲ O daughter Zion,
    like a woman in labor,
for now you shall go forth from the city
    and camp in the open country;
    you shall go to Babylon.
There you shall be rescued;
    there the LORD will redeem you
    from the hands of your enemies.

¹¹ Now many nations
    are assembled against you,
saying, "Let her be profaned,
    and let our eyes gaze upon Zion."
¹² But they do not know
    the thoughts of the LORD;
they do not understand his plan,
    that he has gathered them as sheaves
    to the threshing floor.
¹³ Arise and thresh,
    O daughter Zion,
for I will make your horn iron
    and your hoofs bronze;
you shall beat in pieces many peoples
    and shallᵏ devote their gain to the
    LORD,
    their wealth to the Lord of the whole
    earth.

5 ˡNow you are walled around with a
    wall;ᵐ
siege is laid against us;
with a rod they strike the ruler of Israel
    upon the cheek.

² ⁿBut you, O Bethlehem of Ephrathah,
    who are one of the little clans of
    Judah,
from you shall come forth for me
    one who is to rule in Israel,
whose origin is from of old,
    from ancient days.
³ Therefore he shall give them up until
    the time

j 4.10 Meaning of Heb uncertain *k* 4.13 Gk Syr Tg: Heb *and I will* *l* 5.1 4.14 in Heb *m* 5.1 Cn Compare Gk: Meaning of Heb uncertain *n* 5.2 5.1 in Heb

and peoples, YHWH is the patron God of Israel and Judah (Deut. 32:8–9). **4:6–8** *On that day* suggests a utopian or idealized future accomplished by YHWH gathering and then preserving and strengthening the *lame*, the *cast off*, and those God has afflicted, ultimately to reign over them. Both YHWH and Jerusalem will have dominion and sovereignty. **4:9–10** In contrast with the idealized view, the current extent of suffering is depicted with imagery of a woman in the pangs of labor. She has no king and her *counselor* has perished, but she is to go to Babylon, where YHWH will redeem her. The reference to Babylon suggests an awareness of the later Judean exile to Babylon in 586 BCE. **4:11–13** These verses suggest that God has subjected the people's enemies to a trap. While the nations are assembled against Zion, predicting her defilement, God plans to enable God's people to defeat the nations and bring them as conquered spoils to God. All the nations are to be beaten into pieces. This anticipated killing and subjugation to God is presented as a means to achieve an idealized social and political status quo in favor of the position of God. **5:1** Some power has laid siege, presumably Assyria, as mentioned in 5:5. Assyrian kings laid siege to Samaria before Israel's fall in 722 BCE. The Assyrian king Sennacherib laid siege to Jerusalem in 701 BCE. In addition to the accounts in 2 Kings, Assyrian inscriptions describe siege activities with graphic detail. **5:2** Micah states that a ruler will come from Bethlehem, as had David (1 Sam. 17:12). In the Christian New Testament, Matt. 2:5–6 references this statement from Micah as a proof text to bolster claims about Jesus, and John 7:42 describes people being familiar with the statement. **5:3** The people will be subject to the siege until the woman who is currently in labor gives birth to the child. It is unclear what the time schema is meant to be, and

when she who is in labor has brought
forth;
then the rest of his kindred shall return
to the people of Israel.
[4] And he shall stand and feed his flock in
the strength of the LORD,
in the majesty of the name of the
LORD his God.
And they shall live secure, for now he
shall be great
to the ends of the earth,
[5] and he shall be the one of peace.

If the Assyrians come into our land
and tread upon our soil,[o]
we will raise against them seven
shepherds
and eight rulers.
[6] They shall rule the land of Assyria with
the sword
and the land of Nimrod with the
drawn sword;[p]
they[q] shall rescue us from the Assyrians
if they come into our land
or tread within our border.

[7] Then the remnant of Jacob,
surrounded by many peoples,
shall be like dew from the LORD,
like showers on the grass,
which do not depend upon people
or wait for any mortal.
[8] And among the nations the remnant of
Jacob,
surrounded by many peoples,
shall be like a lion among the animals
of the forest,

like a young lion among the flocks of
sheep,
which, when it goes through, treads
down
and tears in pieces, with no one to
deliver.
[9] Your hand shall be lifted up over your
adversaries,
and all your enemies shall be cut off.

[10] On that day, says the LORD,
I will cut off your horses from among
you
and will destroy your chariots;
[11] and I will cut off the cities of your land
and destroy all your strongholds;
[12] and I will cut off sorceries from your
hand,
and you shall have no more
soothsayers;
[13] and I will cut off your images
and your pillars from among you,
and you shall bow down no more
to the work of your hands;
[14] and I will uproot your sacred poles[r]
from among you
and destroy your towns.
[15] And in anger and wrath I will execute
vengeance
on the nations that did not obey.

6 Hear what the LORD says:
Rise, plead your case before the
mountains,
and let the hills hear your voice.

o 5.5 Gk: Heb *in our palaces*   p 5.6 Cn: Heb *in its entrances*
q 5.6 Heb *he*   r 5.14 Or *Asherahs*

this notion is similar to what is seen in Isa. 7:14 regarding the pregnancy of the Judean queen and her baby Hezekiah, the next Judean king. A remnant of people will return to the Israelites. **5:4** The new ruler will have worldwide renown. **5:5–6** Assyrian oppression and presence in the land will be overturned, the Assyrians will be defeated, and the people will be delivered by a collection of new rulers. The poetic number pairing of *seven shepherds* with *eight rulers* communicates that there will be a sufficiently abundant number of leaders. Historically, Babylonian forces overtook Assyria in 612 BCE. *Nimrod* is featured in the biblical foundational story of the origins of all the nations and neighbors of Israel and Judah. *Nimrod* is a mighty hunter before YHWH, and he founds major cities in Assyria and rules there (Gen. 10:8–12). **5:7–9** The *remnant of Jacob* will be among the peoples and nations and wield victorious power over them that is characterized quite violently. This raises questions regarding who benefits from the reversal of fortunes and at what cost—that is, who suffers in this reversal of fortunes? The idealized future is not beneficial for everyone. **5:10–15** *On that day* before restoration, YHWH will destroy the people's chariotry and fortifications, along with the cultic objects that have angered YHWH. The people will be forced to comply with cultic practices that YHWH purportedly prefers. These standards align with Deuteronomy's depiction of proper worship and honoring of YHWH (Deut. 18:9–14), which King Hezekiah followed (2 Kgs. 18:4).
6:1–16 Oracle of judgment. 6:1–2 Mountains, hills, and earthly foundations are summoned to

² Hear, you mountains, the case of the
      LORD,
   and you enduring foundations of the
      earth,
   for the LORD has a case against his
      people,
   and he will contend with Israel.

³ "O my people, what have I done to you?
   In what have I wearied you? Answer
      me!
⁴ For I brought you up from the land of
      Egypt
   and redeemed you from the house of
      slavery,
   and I sent before you Moses,
      Aaron, and Miriam.
⁵ O my people, remember now what King
      Balak of Moab devised,
   what Balaam son of Beor answered
      him,
   and what happened from Shittim to
      Gilgal,
   that you may know the saving acts of
      the LORD."

⁶ "With what shall I come before the LORD
   and bow myself before God on high?
   Shall I come before him with burnt
      offerings,
   with calves a year old?
⁷ Will the LORD be pleased with
      thousands of rams,
   with ten thousands of rivers of oil?

Shall I give my firstborn for my
      transgression,
   the fruit of my body for the sin of my
      soul?"
⁸ He has told you, O mortal, what is good,
   and what does the LORD require of
      you
   but to do justice and to love kindness
   and to walk humbly with your God?

⁹ The voice of the LORD cries to the city
   (and he shall save those who fear his
      nameˢ):
   Hear, O tribe and assembly of the city!ᵗ
¹⁰   Can I forgetᵘ the treasures of
         wickedness in the house of the
         wicked
   and the despicable false measure?
¹¹ Can I tolerate wicked scales
   and a bag of dishonest weights?
¹² Yourᵛ wealthy are full of violence;
   yourʷ inhabitants speak lies
   with tongues of deceit in their mouths.
¹³ Therefore I have begunˣ to strike you
      down,
   making you desolate because of your
      sins.
¹⁴ You shall eat but not be satisfied,
   and there shall be a gnawing hunger
      within you;

ˢ 6.9 Gk: Meaning of Heb uncertain   ᵗ 6.9 Cn Compare
Gk: Heb *tribe, and who has appointed it yet?*   ᵘ 6.10 Cn:
Meaning of Heb uncertain   ᵛ 6.12 Heb *Whose*   ʷ 6.12 Heb
whose   ˣ 6.13 Gk Syr Vg: Heb *have made sick*

hear YHWH's case against Israel. **6:3–4** YHWH claims innocence relative to the covenant relationship. As evidence for YHWH's innocence, the oracle cites saving the people from Egypt as well as sending Moses, Aaron, and Miriam. This draws on the story of Exodus as a paradigmatic example of YHWH responding to the people's suffering in order to rescue them. The inclusion of Miriam along with her brothers is noteworthy, since most biblical recollections of the Exodus story fail to include her. This is the only reference to her in the prophetic books of the Hebrew Bible. **6:5** *Balaam* is a figure known from Num. 22–24 as well as from an eighth-century BCE inscription discovered at Tell Deir 'Allā in modern Jordan. Even when hired to curse Israel, YHWH has Balaam bless Israel instead. This story is cited here to provide more evidence in favor of YHWH's case against the people. **6:6–8** *Kindness.* Heb. "khesed," "covenant loyalty." Social justice is a requisite for God to be willing to communicate with the people. This message is similar to Amos 5:21–24, which Dr. Martin Luther King Jr. quoted often. This is not a wholesale critique of the sacrificial system but rather a statement about the reciprocal relationship between the people and God, and it builds on and reinforces the logic undergirding the sacrificial system. The example of offering the *firstborn* is included in a list of grand and costly offerings. The rhetorical point is that such extreme offerings are not required, but rather God requires justice, covenant loyalty, and humility. This passage is useful for studying ancient Near Eastern human ritual killing, along with legislation about the firstborn belonging to YHWH (e.g., Exod. 13:1–2; 22:29–30) and the stories in Gen. 22 and 2 Kgs. 3:27. **6:9–16** YHWH speaks directly to the city about its corrupt, wicked, wealthy inhabitants. YHWH accuses the people of injustices and sentences them to destruction, desolation, starvation, violence, lack of goods, and

you shall put away but not save,
and what you save, I will hand over
to the sword.
15 You shall sow but not reap;
you shall tread olives but not anoint
yourselves with oil;
you shall tread grapes but not drink
wine.
16 For you have kept the statutes of Omri[y]
and all the works of the house of
Ahab,
and you have followed their counsels.
Therefore I will make you a desolation
and your[z] inhabitants an object of
hissing,
so you shall bear the scorn of my
people.

7 Woe is me! For I have become like one
who,
after the summer fruit has been
gathered,
after the vintage has been gleaned,
finds no cluster to eat;
there is no first-ripe fig for which I
hunger.
2 The faithful have disappeared from the
land,
and there is no one left who is upright;
they all lie in wait for blood,
and they hunt each other with nets.
3 Their hands are skilled to do evil;
the official and the judge ask for a
bribe,
and the powerful dictate what they
desire;
thus they pervert justice.[a]
4 The best of them is like a brier,
the most upright of them a thorn
hedge.
The day of their[b] sentinels, of their[c]
punishment, has come;
now their confusion is at hand.

5 Put no trust in a friend;
have no confidence in a loved one;
guard the doors of your mouth
from her who lies in your embrace,
6 for the son treats the father with
contempt,
the daughter rises up against her
mother,
the daughter-in-law against her
mother-in-law;
your enemies are members of your
own household.
7 But as for me, I will look to the LORD;
I will wait for the God of my
salvation;
my God will hear me.

8 Do not rejoice over me, my enemies;[d]
when I fall, I shall rise;
when I sit in darkness,
the LORD will be a light to me.
9 I must bear the indignation of the LORD
because I have sinned against him,
until he takes my side
and executes judgment for me.
He will bring me out to the light;
I shall see his vindication.
10 Then my enemies[e] will see,
and shame will cover those[f] who said
to me,
"Where is the LORD your God?"
My eyes will see their[g] downfall;[h]
now they[i] will be trodden down
like the mire of the streets.

11 A day for the building of your walls!
On that day the boundary shall be far
extended.

y 6.16 Gk Syr Vg Tg: Heb *the statutes of Omri are kept*
z 6.16 Heb *its*   a 7.3 Cn: Heb *they weave it*   b 7.4 Heb
your   c 7.4 Heb *your*   d 7.8 Heb *enemy*   e 7.10 Heb *enemy*
f 7.10 Heb *she*   g 7.10 Heb *her*   h 7.10 Heb lacks *downfall*
i 7.10 Heb *she*

scorn. 6:16 *Omri* and *Ahab* were kings of Israel (1 Kgs. 16:21–34). In the account in Kings, the fall of Israel is partially blamed on all of Israel's kings leading the people to displease God.

7:1–7 Lament. *Woe is me.* Micah responds to social disintegration by proposing trust in YHWH for *salvation.* The extent of social disintegration is exhibited with images of a scarcity of food, the disappearance of good people, and an abundance of dishonest people. Micah suggests not trusting even one's closest friends and family.

7:8–20 Concluding liturgy. 7:8–10 This is a first-person lament for the destruction of Jerusalem, which occurred in 586 BCE. Whether the first-person perspective represents the city or the people, the subject admits guilt and willingness to bear punishment while awaiting YHWH to execute judgment and be vindicated. The idea of enemies taunting by asking *"Where is the* LORD *your God?"* is reminiscent of Ps. 115:2. 7:11–13 Restoration. The walls of Jerusalem were rebuilt under

¹² On that day they will come to you
   from Assyria to[j] Egypt
and from Egypt to the River,
   from sea to sea and from mountain
      to mountain.
¹³ But the earth will be desolate
   because of its inhabitants,
      for the fruit of their doings.

¹⁴ Shepherd your people with your staff,
   the flock that belongs to you,
which lives alone in a forest
   in the midst of a garden land;
let them feed in Bashan and Gilead
   as in the days of old.
¹⁵ As in the days when you came out of
      the land of Egypt,
   show us[k] marvelous things.
¹⁶ The nations shall see and be ashamed
   of all their might;
they shall lay their hands on their
      mouths;
   their ears shall be deaf;
¹⁷ they shall lick dust like a snake,
   like the crawling things of the earth;

they shall come trembling out of their
   fortresses;
they shall turn in dread to the LORD
   our God,
and they shall stand in fear of you.

¹⁸ Who is a God like you, pardoning
      iniquity
   and passing over the transgression
      of the remnant of his possession?
He does not retain his anger forever
   because he delights in showing
      steadfast love.
¹⁹ He will again have compassion
      upon us;
   he will tread our iniquities under
      foot.
You will cast all our[l] sins
   into the depths of the sea.
²⁰ You will show faithfulness to Jacob
   and steadfast love to Abraham,
as you have sworn to our ancestors
   from the days of old.

j 7.12 Heb ms: MT *Assyria and cities of* k 7.15 Cn: Heb *I will show him* l 7.19 Gk Syr Vg Tg: Heb *their*

the leadership of Nehemiah (Neh. 2:17–20). *From Assyria to Egypt, sea to sea, mountain to mountain.* These phrases indicate the extent of the full Fertile Crescent, encompassing Israel and Judah's primary geopolitical context. **7:14–20** The liturgical prayer is hopeful, affirming the covenant and YHWH's leadership and care for the people. **7:14** Bashan and Gilead were fertile areas in the Transjordan. **7:19** *Cast all our sins into the depths of the sea* possibly reflects a ritual disposal of *iniquities* and *sins*. **7:20** *Abraham* and *Jacob*. The book ends by citing the covenants God made with Abraham and Jacob. The future tense is hopeful and communicates that God will abide by former promises to these foundational figures (Gen. 12:1–3; 17:6–8; 28:13–15). These covenants are cited when YHWH protects Israel from destruction (2 Kgs. 13:23).

NAHUM

Author, Dates, Context, Unique Features, and Genres

Nahum—identified as an Elkoshite, meaning from an unidentifiable place named Elkosh—is unknown apart from the work that bears this name. Nothing else is known of this person. As is common among prophetic texts, the title is imposed by a secondary narrating hand. The name likely stems from the verbal root that means to "comfort" or "regret," "compassion" or "revenge."

The work can be reasonably dated between 663 BCE, when Assyria conquered and occupied the Egyptian city of Thebes referenced in 3:8, and the eventual destruction of the Assyrian Empire in 612 BCE. The text can be read as a prophetic prediction of the inevitable fall of Nineveh, the capital of the Assyrian Empire, receiving final form after Nineveh's fall, likely accounting for some of the detail about the fall.

The sociopolitical context of the book is the aftermath of the Assyrian decimation of the northern Israelite monarchy in 723/722 BCE, with the southern kingdom Judah mentioned once, in 1:15. Jerusalem is not named. Assyrian occupation was brutal, violent, and costly; Judah and its monarchs were regularly humiliated and required to pay such heavy tribute that they ransacked their own temple in order to comply (2 Kgs. 18:15–16). The Assyrians documented their legendary brutality in images that survive to the present: depictions of them peeling the skin off their prisoners and cutting them open down to the bone and placing them on sharp sticks to fall to their penetrating deaths. (The latter tactic would be adopted by the notorious Vlad the Impaler.)

Nahum is unique among the prophetic books in being presented as a literary work (1:1). The collection is also distinguished by addressing an audience, Nineveh and its inhabitants, with no indication that the contents would be communicated to them.

The book is composed of poetic verse with the exception of the narrating introduction, likely by a second hand. There is a partial acrostic in the first eight verses that may have its origins in the earliest layer of the work. Chap. 1:2–11 may be read discretely as an independent psalm and may have functioned in a liturgy marking the downfall of Nineveh. The book is characterized by repeated shifts between topics and subjects of address that are difficult to identify and follow when reading in English but are more clearly indicated by the use of gendered language in Hebrew. The book may be organized according to the themes of its units, or it may be subdivided into individual oracles facilitated by internal markers in the Hebrew text that identify each oracle.

In addition to being part of the prophetic genre, the book could be considered an epistle to Nineveh; it could also be understood as the script for a public performance with the intended audience the surviving remnant of Israel and Judah and not the Ninevites. Other genres include lament and taunting.

Theological Issues

Nahum is a challenging book for its depiction of an angry, vengeful, wrathful God; the sexually violent language attributed to God and God's prophet; and the ethical issues arising from the book—namely, the condemnation of Nineveh for turning away from the God of Israel, with whom they historically had no prior relationship. Unsurprisingly, the text is not represented among any of the major Christian lectionaries or in the prophetic readings that accompany the Torah in Jewish contexts.

Reading Guide

While contemporary readers may struggle with the language of Nahum, the rage to which it gives voice is more familiar, the rage of a people long oppressed and subject to unimaginable brutality. Nahum's verbal violence may be read in conversation with the Watts riots of 1965, the 1968 riots in the District of Columbia after the assassination of Rev. Dr. Martin Luther King Jr., the 1992 riots in Los Angeles after the arrest of Rodney King, and the many riots stemming from and occurring alongside Black Lives Matter movement protests between 2014 and 2020 in particular, each giving voice to incandescent rage. The images of unburied bodies in the streets have an even more recent parallel in the photos of the war dead in the wake of the Russian invasion of Ukraine in the early spring of 2022. However, no amount of rage, however righteous, justifies the violent sexual language or the acts it evokes.

The contemporary reader will have to contend with the portrait of Nahum's God. Even with an understanding of the social, cultural, political, and emotional forces and the catastrophic violence that combine to shape the production of these verses, many readers may well find this deity difficult to engage.

Wil Gafney

1 An oracle concerning Nineveh. The book of the vision of Nahum of Elkosh.

² A jealous and avenging God is the LORD;
   the LORD is avenging and wrathful;
the LORD takes vengeance on his
      adversaries
   and prolongs it against his enemies.
³ The LORD is slow to anger but great in
      power,
   and the LORD will by no means clear
      the guilty.

His way is in whirlwind and storm,
   and the clouds are the dust of his feet.
⁴ He rebukes the sea and makes it dry,
   and he dries up all the rivers;
Bashan and Carmel wither,
   and the bloom of Lebanon fades.
⁵ The mountains quake before him,
   and the hills melt;
the earth heaves before him,
   the world and all who live in it.

⁶ Who can stand before his indignation?
   Who can endure the heat of his
      anger?

His wrath is poured out like fire,
   and by him the rocks are broken in
      pieces.
⁷ The LORD is good,
   a stronghold in a day of trouble;
he protects those who take refuge in him,
⁸   even in a rushing flood.
He will make a full end of his adversaries[a]
   and will pursue his enemies into
      darkness.
⁹ Why do you plot against the LORD?
   He will make an end;
   no adversary will rise up twice.
¹⁰ Like thorns they are entangled;
   like drunkards they are drunk;
   they are consumed like dry straw.
¹¹ From you one has gone out
   who plots evil against the LORD,
   one who counsels wickedness.

¹² Thus says the LORD:
Though they are at full strength and
      many,[b]
   they will be cut off and pass away.
Though I have afflicted you,
   I will afflict you no more.

a 1.8 Gk: Heb *of her place*   b 1.12 Meaning of Heb uncertain

1:1 More important than the prophet is the target of the coming diatribe, Nineveh, whose name is given before his. Nineveh will also be named in each of the next two chapters as well, in 2:8 and 3:7.

1:2–3 God is *jealous*, vengeful, wrathful, and unforgiving. In the Torah, God's jealousy is tied to the worship of other gods (Exod. 20:5; 34:14; Num. 5:30; Deut. 4:24; 5:9; 6:15; 32:19). The distinct spelling of the word for *jealous* is shared with Josh. 24:19, where God will not forgive transgressions or sins. God's relationship with Israel is regularly articulated within a marriage metaphor characterized by jealousy. The divine wrath in v. 2 has a corollary in Ezek. 25:17. Here, God is styled as the "lord" or "master" of wrath, invoking and usurping the title of Baal (lord/master). Combined with the use of El in v. 1, Nahum's rhetoric subordinates the gods of Canaan to the God of Israel, indicating the fate of Nineveh and its gods. V. 3 cites Num. 14:18, which has been edited to remove the language about God being loving and forgiving. **1:3b** This portrait of God contains some of the classical storm elements of a theophany, the technical term for an appearance of God associated with the Canaanite deity Baal.

1:4–5 Bashan and Carmel represent food production; threatening them means threatening hunger.

1:7–11 The use of gendered language marks shifts in Nahum's address that are not easy to follow in translation. God's goodness *in a day of trouble* in v. 7 can also be understood as God's goodness in the day "of an adversary." The word recurs in v. 9, where it is indeed translated as *adversary*. The feminine gender of the word suggests it is in reference to Nineveh given ancient cities were presented as female, or it could be a veiled reference to Ishtar, the primary goddess of Nineveh.

1:12–13 These two verses are arguably an independent unit of prophecy addressing a completely different audience, Jerusalem in particular or Judah as a whole.

¹³ And now I will break off his yoke from
    you
  and snap the bonds that bind you.

¹⁴ The LORD has commanded concerning you:
  Your name shall be perpetuated no
    longer;
  from the house of your gods I will cut off
    the carved image and the cast image.
  I will prepare your grave, for you are
    worthless.

¹⁵ ᶜLook! On the mountains the feet of one
  who brings good tidings,
  who proclaims peace!
  Celebrate your festivals, O Judah;
    fulfill your vows,
  for never again shall the wicked invade
    you;
  they are utterly cut off.

2 A scatterer has come up against you.
  Guard the ramparts;
  watch the road;
gird your loins;
  collect all your strength.

² (For the LORD is restoring the majesty of
  Jacob,
  as well as the majesty of Israel,

  though ravagers have ravaged them
  and ruined their branches.)

³ The shields of his warriors are red;
  his soldiers are clothed in crimson.
  The metal on the chariots flashes
  on the day when he musters them;
  the chargersᵈ prance.
⁴ The chariots race madly through the
    streets;
  they rush to and fro through the
    squares;
  their appearance is like torches;
  they dart like lightning.
⁵ He calls his officers;
  they stumble as they come forward;
  they hasten to the wall,
  and the screenᵉ is set up.
⁶ The river gates are opened;
  the palace trembles.
⁷ It is decreedᶠ that the cityᵍ be exiled,
  its slave women led away,
  moaning like doves
  and beating their breasts.
⁸ Nineveh is like a pool
  whose watersʰ run away.

c 1.15 2.1 in Heb   d 2.3 Cn Compare Gk Syr: Heb *cypresses*
e 2.5 Meaning of Heb uncertain   f 2.7 Meaning of Heb
uncertain   g 2.7 Heb *it*   h 2.8 Cn Compare Gk: Heb *a pool,
from the days that she has become, and they*

1:14 The dramatic shift in v. 14 back to Nineveh likely addresses its monarch, given the masculine language. The eradication of his name is the ancient way of wiping him off the face of the earth in every way. The language is agricultural and reproductive; his name will no longer be "sown" or "implanted," marking the end of his dynasty and family line. Rather, he will be planted in the ground, in his grave. **1:15** Nahum 1:15 in Christian Bibles is 2:1 in Hebrew and in Jewish Bibles in English and other languages. This verse marks the first place Nahum addresses Judah by name. Freedom from Assyrian oppression means that the Judeans can return to their religious festivals without the shadow of war or conquest constraining their joy. The promise that never again would the *wicked* or worthless invade Judah and, by inference, Jerusalem and its temple will be short-lived. **2:1** The proclamation moves quickly and repeatedly between Judah and Nineveh. "You" in the previous verse referred to Judah and Jerusalem. In this verse, it refers to Nineveh, which will need all its strength for what God has planned next. **2:2** Almost as an aside, a rationale is provided for what God intends to do. It is to restore *the majesty of Jacob* representing Israel constituted by whoever survived the earlier Assyrian decimation and the Judeans. **2:3–13** This unit is composed of a graphic and dramatic telling of the bloody fate of Nineveh and its people at the hand of the God of Israel, seemingly for a public performance. These verses will be expanded upon in the following and final chapter of the book. **2:3–4** The scene opens with the impressive array of the dashing Assyrian army in their *crimson* uniforms, with their shining *chariots* and their prancing horses. **2:5** *He* is either the commander of this unit or all the nation's forces or the unspecified monarch. Something has gone wrong for the sumptuously arrayed army. Their officers stumble about at their defenses. **2:6** The *river gates* refer to all the water control measures on and around the Tigris. The flood language may be intended to invoke God's mighty power over water referenced at the beginning of the book, Nah. 1:4–5. **2:7** The warriors of vv. 3–5 are now joined by enslaved women

"Halt! Halt!"—
  but no one turns back.
⁹ "Plunder the silver;
  plunder the gold!
There is no end of treasure!
  An abundance of every precious thing!"

¹⁰ Devastation, desolation, and destruction!
  Hearts faint and knees tremble;
all loins quake;
  all faces grow pale!
¹¹ What became of the lions' den,
  the cave of the young lions,
where the lion goes,
  and the lion's cubs, with no one to
  disturb them?
¹² The lion has torn enough for his whelps
  and strangled prey for his lionesses;
he has filled his caves with prey
  and his dens with torn flesh.

13 See, I am against you, says the LORD of hosts, and I will burn your[i] chariots in smoke, and the sword shall devour your young lions; I will cut off your prey from the earth, and the voice of your messengers shall be heard no more.

3 Woe, city of bloodshed,
  utterly deceitful, full of plunder—
  no end to the prey!
² The crack of whip and rumble of wheel,
  galloping horse and bounding
  chariot!
³ Horsemen charging,
  flashing sword and glittering spear,
piles of dead,
  heaps of corpses,
dead bodies without end—
  they stumble over the bodies!
⁴ Because of the countless debaucheries
    of the prostitute,
  gracefully alluring, mistress of sorcery,
who enslaves[j] nations through her
  debaucheries
  and peoples through her sorcery,
⁵ I am against you,
  says the LORD of hosts,
  and will lift up your skirts over your
  face,
and I will let nations look on your
  nakedness
  and kingdoms on your shame.

i 2.13 Heb *her*   *j* 3.4 Heb *sells*

in v. 7 who should be read as all the women of the city and not just those previously enslaved. There is in v. 7 a series of actions performed on Nineveh or, in some readings, her queen. There is also a double entendre in that to be *exiled* is also to be "uncovered"—that is, stripped naked, evoking the sexual violence that accompanies war and the only explicit mention of *women* in the book. **2:9** In v. 9, the Babylonian army is given permission to loot Nineveh and her precious treasures, which would have included physical and sexual violence against women and men, indiscriminate slaughter, enslavement, and for women encumbered with young children, infanticide. **2:10** This single verse provides a lament for the fallen city. **2:11–12** This section forms a distinct subunit within vv. 3–13 mocking the unnamed Assyrian monarch and his family stylized as a pride of *lions*. The *cubs* no longer have a place to play. The taunt builds in v. 12 mentioning his *lionesses*, queens, and *caves* in which they could shelter and hide, but alas, there is no hiding place. **2:13** In the final verse of the chapter, God pronounces judgment against the city and her royals, specifically targeting the next generation. First came the flood; now comes the fire. The formulaic language of this pronouncement will recur in 3:5.

3:1 The final chapter, a single oracular unit, presents the devastation of the fallen city of Nineveh as the physical and sexual violence that occurs to women in captured and conquered cities.

3:3 The slaughter is epic. The *bodies* pile up in the street, unburied.

3:4 In v. 4, God through Nahum speaks to the city as a woman using sexualized language to blame her for the violence that did and will happen to her. She is charged with "whoredom," a slur, rather than for selling sex, as misconstrued by the translation *prostitute*. This is the rhetoric of slut-shaming (see **"Slut-Shaming as Prophetic Discourse," p. 1148**). Similarly, calling her a witch is not a charge of engaging in arcane practices. Nineveh's military and economic might is constructed as the fruit of her whoredom, translated here as *debaucheries*. The language begs the question of what relationship is imagined between God and Nineveh to account for this retaliation. The rhetoric is bombastic and theologically impoverished, conjuring a God who could be bested by foreign sorcery. The combination of the two charges, selling sex and sorcery, invokes Jezebel in 2 Kgs. 9:22.

3:5–6 Having named her a whore, God now treats her like one. In an act of divine savagery, it is God in the first person who physically assaults the city-as-woman by stripping her in public, exposing

⁶ I will throw filth at you
  and treat you with contempt
  and make you a spectacle.
⁷ Then all who see you will shrink from
    you and say,
  "Nineveh is devastated; who will
    bemoan her?"
  Where shall I seek comforters for you?

⁸ Are you better than Thebes[k]
  that sat by the Nile,
with water around her,
  her rampart a sea,
  water her wall?
⁹ Cush was her strength,
  Egypt, too, and that without limit;
  Put and the Libyans were her[l] helpers.

¹⁰ Yet she became an exile;
  she went into captivity;
even her infants were dashed in pieces
  at the head of every street;
lots were cast for her nobles;
  all her dignitaries were bound in fetters.
¹¹ You also will be drunken;
  you will go into hiding;[m]
you will seek
  a refuge from the enemy.
¹² All your fortresses are like fig trees
  with first-ripe figs—
if shaken they fall
  into the mouth of the eater.
¹³ Look at your troops:
  they are women in your midst.
The gates of your land
  are wide open to your foes;
  fire has devoured the bars of your gates.

¹⁴ Draw water for the siege;
  strengthen your forts;
trample the clay;
  tread the mortar;
  take hold of the brick mold!
¹⁵ There the fire will devour you;
  the sword will cut you off.
  It will devour you like the locust.

Multiply yourselves like the locust;
  multiply like the grasshopper!
¹⁶ You increased your merchants
  more than the stars of the heavens.
  The locust sheds its skin and flies
    away.
¹⁷ Your guards are like grasshoppers,
  your scribes like swarms[n] of locusts
settling on the fences
  on a cold day—
when the sun rises, they fly away;
  no one knows where they have gone.
¹⁸ Your shepherds are asleep,
  O king of Assyria;
  your nobles slumber.
Your people are scattered on the
    mountains
  with no one to gather them.
¹⁹ There is no assuaging your hurt;
  your wound is mortal.
All who hear the news about you
  clap their hands over you.
For who has ever escaped
  your endless cruelty?

k 3.8 Or *No-amon*   *l* 3.9 Gk Syr: Heb *your*   *m* 3.11 Meaning of Heb uncertain   *n* 3.17 Meaning of Heb uncertain

her vulva. The assault would have been understood as a sexual one by Nahum's hearers and readers. This grotesque sexualized violence is not an isolated episode in the Scriptures. See **"Sexually Abusive Language in the Prophets," p. 1035**. In v. 6, the word for *filth* refers to religious artifacts prohibited for Israelite use; she is stoned with her own sacred objects, indicating the looting of her temples.

3:7 V. 7 makes it clear that Nineveh's treatment at God's hand is a successful object lesson and no other nation will offer her aid or comfort.

3:8–10 In a series of taunts whose introduction may best be heard as "Who do you think you are?" God and Nahum compare Assyria to *Thebes*, the capital of Egypt. Even with the help of the Nubians from the south and the *Libyans* to the west, Egypt and her capital were no match for the Assyrians. V. 10 details the fate of the people of Thebes at its conquest, suggestive of the fate of the Ninevites.

3:11–19 In the final verses, God speaks to the city directly in a merciless taunt song. There is no compassion for the women, children, or men of the city who are not responsible for its political policies or military maneuvers. **3:13** God and the prophet return to sexualized language, emasculating Nineveh's warriors by comparing them to *women*, and then paint a portrait of the city gates *wide open*, evoking the legs of a woman. **3:18–19** His *shepherds* in v. 18 likely refer to the monarch's officers or officials. All levels of his society are devastated, the people, the *nobles*, the royals. There was no one left to shepherd or *gather* them.

HABAKKUK

Author, Dates, and Context

The name Habakkuk lacks any identifying information, and as is common, "prophet" is supplied by the narrator's hand in secondary editorial inscriptions in 1:1 and 3:1. The name itself has too many letters to fit neatly in the Semitic triliteral root system, leading some to surmise an Akkadian root. The liturgical instructions for the psalm in the third chapter have led some to conclude that the author was connected to the Jerusalem temple.

Habakkuk is among a very small number of literate prophets. Like Isaiah (8:1), he is told to write in 2:2 (cf. Jeremiah, who needs Baruch to read and write for him in Jer. 36:4–10). Clearly identifiable dating information is lacking from the volume. The only contextual information is the mention of the Chaldeans (Babylonians) in 1:6. They do not yet appear to be the dominant force they will become, so the work can be placed before the rise of the Babylonian Empire in the seventh century BCE, arguably before or just after their defeat of the Egyptians in 605 BCE. Unnamed, the Assyrians appear to be the villains in the text, as the ascendant empire of this time period. Curiously, neither "Israel" nor "Judah" are mentioned; however, it would appear that the temple is still standing given the liturgical instructions of 3:1, placing this work before the temple's fall to the Babylonians in 586 BCE. In spite of or because of this lack of specificity, Habakkuk enjoys a literary life beyond the book. He appears in Bel and the Dragon, one of the Greek sections of Daniel without a corresponding Hebrew text, now included in the deuterocanonical books. He also appears in the Pseudepigrapha, noncanonical religious works written between 300 BCE and 300 CE. The volume of Habakkuk is also represented among the Qumran community (a Jewish sect from the second century BCE–first century CE), where it became the subject of a specialized commentary called a pesher.

Genres and Distinguishing Features

The book consists of two broad divisions, chaps. 1–2 and chap. 3. The first section (chaps. 1–2) is dialogical, consisting of a conversation between Habakkuk and God, and a second section blends the dialogue with a collection of oracles. These sections do not exactly correlate with the division between the first two chapters. A psalm comprises chap. 3. The first two chapters wrestle with theodicy (here, violence in the world), calling upon God for an explanation and action and sharing parallels with Job. Habakkuk joins a long list of characters who have their say with God: Abraham (Gen. 18:22–33), Rebekah (Gen. 25:22), Moses (Num. 11:10–15), and Job (e.g., 7:17–21). Additionally, Habakkuk's prophetic discourse can be understood as a prayer for understanding and intervention. His two discourses may be read as the biblical exemplar of speaking truth to the ultimate power.

Habakkuk distinguishes itself and its prophet by starting with not a message from God to or through the prophet but rather a message from the prophet to God, thus demonstrating the breadth of prophetic discourse. Unlike Job, God is readily engaged by Habakkuk and does not intimidate the prophet with a theophanic display. *Theophany* is the technical term for an appearance of God, usually with storm elements such as clouds and lightning and thunder.

Reading Guide

Habakkuk may be experienced as a balm for the souls of folk who have been told "You can't pray that way!" or "You can't question God!" Indeed, his question "O LORD, how long?" (1:2) is a staple of Psalms. The opening verses held and continue to hold significance for many in the Black Lives Matter movement for articulating a moral struggle against corrupt legal practices.

Habakkuk's language is insistent, urgent, devoid of flowery praise. He needs, if not answers, then a response, a change in his people's circumstances. He is a "people's prophet." The text is an invitation for people to bring their concerns to God and a model of prayer that is conversational, suggesting a devotional practice of sitting and listening after having one's say. It is also a surprisingly confrontational model of prayer. And God accepts it without rebuke. The concluding psalm is an "I will praise God anyhow" psalm. Habakkuk is not bargaining with God, using the praises of God as currency; rather, he is faithfully giving thanks in spite of all that is not well in his world.

Wil Gafney

1
The oracle that the prophet Habakkuk saw.

2 O Lord, how long shall I cry for help,
   and you will not listen?
Or cry to you "Violence!"
   and you will not save?
3 Why do you make me see wrongdoing
   and look at trouble?
Destruction and violence are before me;
   strife and contention arise.
4 So the law becomes slack,
   and justice never prevails.
The wicked surround the righteous;
   therefore judgment comes forth
      perverted.

5 Look at the nations and see!
   Be astonished! Be astounded!
For a work is being done in your days
   that you would not believe if you
      were told.
6 For I am rousing the Chaldeans,
   that fierce and impetuous nation,
who march through the breadth of the
      earth
   to seize dwellings not their own.
7 Dread and fearsome are they;
   their justice and dignity proceed
      from themselves.
8 Their horses are swifter than leopards,
   more menacing than wolves at dusk;
   their horses charge.
Their horsemen come from far away;
   they fly like an eagle swift to devour.
9 They all come for violence,
   with faces pressing[a] forward;
   they gather captives like sand.
10 At kings they scoff,
   and of rulers they make sport.
They laugh at every fortress
   and heap up earth to take it.
11 Then they sweep by like the wind;
   they transgress and become guilty;
   their own might is their god!

12 Are you not from of old,
   O Lord my God, my Holy One?
You[b] shall not die.
O Lord, you have marked them for
      judgment,
   and you, O Rock, have established
      them for punishment.
13 Your eyes are too pure to behold evil,
   and you cannot look on wrongdoing;
why do you look on the treacherous
   and are silent when the wicked
      swallow
   those more righteous than they?
14 You have made people like the fish of
      the sea,
   like crawling things that have no
      ruler.

a 1.9 Meaning of Heb uncertain   b 1.12 Or We

1:1 Habakkuk's prophetic methodology is oracular speech, one of the dominant forms of prophecy and described as having been "envisioned," distinct from seeing with the human eye.

1:2–2:6 There is scholarly disagreement over how much of chap. 2 to group with chap. 1. Some extend the unit to 2:8. The dialogical nature of the opening unit makes it especially suitable for public performance, with the narrator setting the stage with the superscription. Habakkuk's first speech is in 1:2–4.

1:2 Habakkuk has questions for God about the violent state of the world that lay responsibility for its violent state at God's feet, where God's failure to *save* is both a statement and an accusation.

1:3 Habakkuk's language becomes stronger. God forces him to look at the *violence*, *trouble*, and *wrongdoing* that God does not prevent and from which God does not deliver.

1:4 In a charge that otherwise might be addressed to the people or their leaders, Habakkuk proclaims that the *law*, the torah as religious teaching and civil law, has become ineffectual, leading to a perversion of *justice*—without quite blaming God.

1:5–11 God responds to Habakkuk in 1:5–11. The divine response is perplexing. God is going to add the *Chaldeans*, the Babylonians, to the situation. They are terrifying, *dread and fearsome*. One of Habakkuk's complaints was about *violence*, and now the Babylonians, who do not even acknowledge God but rather worship *their own might*, will bring more of it.

1:12–2:1 Habakkuk's response in 1:12–2:1 understandably indicates his dissatisfaction.

1:12 While the Hebrew text says "We *shall not die*," most understand the primary reference to be God, meaning that whatever happens, God's life is not at stake like Habakkuk's and his people.

1:13 Habakkuk tells God that God is not behaving according to Habakkuk's theological understanding of God, *too pure to behold evil* yet *silent* in the face of *wrongdoing* by the *wicked*.

¹⁵ He brings all of them up with a hook;
  he drags them out with his net;
he gathers them in his seine,
  so he rejoices and exults.
¹⁶ Therefore he sacrifices to his net
  and makes offerings to his seine,
for by them his portion is lavish,
  and his food is rich.
¹⁷ Is he then to keep on emptying his net
  and destroying nations without mercy?

2 I will stand at my watchpost
  and station myself on the rampart;
I will keep watch to see what he will
    say to me
and what heᶜ will answer concerning
    my complaint.
² Then the Lord answered me and said:
  Write the vision;
    make it plain on tablets,
    so that a runner may read it.
³ For there is still a vision for the
    appointed time;
    it speaks of the end and does not lie.
If it seems to tarry, wait for it;
    it will surely come; it will not delay.
⁴ Look at the proud!
  Their spirit is not right in them,
  but the righteous live by their
    faithfulness.

⁵ Moreover, wealthᵈ is treacherous;
  the arrogant do not endure.
They open their throats wide as Sheol;
  like Death they never have enough.
They gather all nations for themselves
  and collect all peoples as their own.
6 Shall not everyone taunt such people and, with mocking riddles, say about
them,
  "Alas for you who heap up what is not
    your own!"
How long will you load yourselves
    with goods taken in pledge?
⁷ Will not your own creditors suddenly
    rise
  and those who make you tremble
    wake up?
Then you will be plunder for them.
⁸ Because you have plundered many
    nations,
  all who survive of the peoples shall
    plunder you—
because of human bloodshed and
    violence to the earth,
  to cities and all who live in them.

⁹ "Alas for you who get evil gain for your
    house,

c 2.1 Syr: Heb *I*   d 2.5 Q mss: MT *wine*

1:15–17 After describing the Babylonians as scooping up nations and people like fish in a *seine* or net, Habakkuk asks if God will continue to permit them to destroy *nations without mercy*.

2:1–5 The numbering of chapters and verses can be arbitrary. At a minimum, the first five verses of chap. 2 are a literary continuation of chap. 1. **2:1** Having made his case, Habakkuk takes a "wait-and-see" approach. *Complaint* is a technical term for an argument, more in the sense of a debate than a legal proceeding. As translated, Habakkuk is waiting *to see* God's response to his argument, but in the text, he is waiting to form his own response. **2:2** God's response opens a second round of dialogue showing that God is in conversation with Habakkuk, seeking to be understood rather than simply making pronouncements. God's less-than-direct response is directed to Habakkuk personally, to *me*. God tells Habakkuk to *write the vision*, placing him in the company of Isaiah (8:1) and Nahum (1:1) as the rare examples of literate prophets; see also Moses (Exod. 17:14; 34:1, 27; Num. 17:2) and Ezekiel (Ezek. 24:2; 37:16, 20; 43:11). **2:4–5** An important correction to the traditional translation of v. 4, *the righteous live by their faithfulness* removes the anachronistic Christian concept of "faith," restoring the Hebrew biblical concept of *faithfulness* as something one does, not what one believes. See Rom. 1:17 and **"Faith of Jesus Christ," p. 1938**. The *righteous* are distinguished from the *proud* and *arrogant*, who by v. 5 are apparently the Babylonians, where gathering *nations* and collecting *peoples* echo 1:15. However, the critique against them is a common one against economic injustice within Israel and Judah; the ambiguity may be intentional.

2:6–20 Vv. 6 through 20 are a clearly distinguishable unit consisting of oracles that begin with the word "woe" or *alas* after a brief introduction. **2:6** The economic critique suggests an occupation phase rather than active war or conquest. Again, the behaviors have often been critiqued in Israel and Judah by their own prophets: abusing the poor by holding on to the collateral *pledge* of an indebted person. **2:7–8** These verses pronounce an eye for an eye, judgment in which they— the ambiguity between Israel and Babylon is maintained—will be at the mercy of their merciless

setting your nest on high
to be safe from the reach of harm!"
¹⁰ You have devised shame for your house
by cutting off many peoples;
you have forfeited your life.
¹¹ The very stones will cry out from the
wall,
and the rafter will respond from the
woodwork.

¹² "Alas for you who build a town by
bloodshed
and found a city on iniquity!"
¹³ Is it not from the LORD of hosts
that peoples labor only to feed the
flames
and nations weary themselves for
nothing?
¹⁴ But the earth will be filled
with the knowledge of the glory of
the LORD,
as the waters cover the sea.

¹⁵ "Alas for you who make your neighbors
drink,
pouring out your wrath until they are
drunk,
in order to gaze on their nakedness!"
¹⁶ You will be sated with contempt
instead of glory.
Drink, you yourself, and stagger!ᵉ
The cup in the LORD's right hand
will come around to you,

and shame will come upon your
glory!
¹⁷ For the violence done to Lebanon will
overwhelm you;
the destruction of the animals will
terrify you—ᶠ
because of human bloodshed and
violence to the earth,
to cities and all who live in them.

¹⁸ What use is an idol
once its maker has shaped it—
a cast image, a teacher of lies?
For its maker trusts in what has been
made,
though the product is only an idol
that cannot speak!
¹⁹ Alas for you who say to the wood,
"Wake up!"
to silent stone, "Rouse yourself!"
Can it teach?
See, it is gold and silver plated,
and there is no breath in it at all.

²⁰ But the LORD is in his holy temple;
let all the earth keep silence before
him!

3 A prayer of the prophet Habakkuk according to Shigionoth.

ᵉ 2.16 Q ms Gk: MT *be uncircumcised*   ᶠ 2.17 Gk Syr: Heb *terrify them*

creditors, and those who *plunder* will in turn be plundered. **2:12** This verse applies to a colonizing empire like Babylon more than to Israel or Judah in their state at the presumptive time of the compilation of the text. **2:14** This verse is a near duplicate of the latter half of Isa. 11:9. The bloody efforts of the colonizing empire in 2:12 will be for naught; their empire will not cover the face of the earth, but rather *the knowledge of the glory of the* LORD will. That *knowledge* suggests intimacy; the *glory* could be perceived by those at a distance. God's glory is an extension of God's self that is visible to select people granted intimate access. *Knowledge* speaks of relationship and access. Covering the *earth* includes all nations and all peoples. **2:17** The sudden appearance of *Lebanon* is not explained. One possibility is that the *violence* refers to the near extinction of the famed cedars of Lebanon cut down in a construction project for Nebuchadnezzar. Deforestation would lead to the *destruction* of *animals.* **2:18–19** Vv. 18 and 19 mock idols and their worship, focusing on their construction from dead materials such as *wood* and *stone* and *gold* and *silver.* **2:20** V. 20 calls for silence in the presence of God, leading some to speculate about the role of silence in the worship occurring in the Jerusalem temple.

3:1–19 The psalm in chap. 3 has its own superscription, or introduction (separate from Hab. 1:1), allowing it to have circulated independently; its opening and concluding verses frame it in the liturgical and musical traditions of Psalms. While not directly linked to the preceding chapters, it may nonetheless be read as a response to them. Though the composition bears the name of Habakkuk, there is some scholarship indicating it is older than the rest of the work and possibly the composition of a woman, indicated by feminine language describing the psalmist/composer. **3:1** *Prayer* as a literary genre, descriptor, and title characterizes Pss. 72, 102, and 142; *Shigionoth* (left untranslated)

² O Lᴏʀᴅ, I have heard of your renown,
and I stand in awe, O Lᴏʀᴅ, of your
work.
In our own time revive it;
in our own time make it known;
in wrath may you remember mercy.
³ God came from Teman,
the Holy One from Mount Paran.
                                                    Selah

His glory covered the heavens,
and the earth was full of his praise.
⁴ The brightness was like the sun;
rays came forth from his hand,
where his power lay hidden.
⁵ Before him went pestilence,
and plague followed close behind.
⁶ He stopped and shook the earth;
he looked and made the nations
tremble.
The eternal mountains were shattered;
along his ancient pathways
the everlasting hills sank low.
⁷ I saw the tents of Cushan under affliction;
the tent curtains of the land of
Midian trembled.
⁸ Was your wrath against the rivers,ᵍ
O Lᴏʀᴅ,
or your anger against the riversʰ
or your rage against the sea,ⁱ
when you drove your horses,
your chariots to victory?
⁹ You brandished your naked bow;
satedʲ were the arrows at your
command.ᵏ   Selah
You split the earth with rivers.
¹⁰ The mountains saw you and writhed;
a torrent of water swept by;
the deep gave forth its voice.
The sun raised high its hands;
¹¹ the moon stood still in its exalted place,
at the light of your arrows speeding by,
at the gleam of your flashing spear.
¹² In fury you marched on the earth;
in anger you trampled nations.
¹³ You came forth to save your people,
to save your anointed.
You crushed the head of the wicked
house,
laying it bare from foundation to
roof.ˡ   Selah
¹⁴ You pierced with theirᵐ own arrows the
head of his warriors,ⁿ
who came like a whirlwind to scatter
us,ᵒ

g 3.8 Or *against River*   h 3.8 Or *against River*   i 3.8 Or *against Sea*   j 3.9 Heb mss: MT *oaths*   k 3.9 Meaning of Heb uncertain   l 3.13 Heb *neck*   m 3.14 Heb *his*   n 3.14 Gk Vg Syr: Meaning of Heb uncertain   o 3.14 Heb *me*

also occurs in Ps. 7 in the singular form. While various definitions have been proposed, it can only be said with certainty the terms represent a musical subgenre. **3:2** The language of *awe* in v. 2 connects the psalm to the end of chap. 2. Similarly, the prayer that God *revive* the divine *work* can be understood as a response to the dialogue of Hab. 1–2 and the prophet's preferred response to his opening petition. *In our own time* provides the desired framework now. **3:3–15** The majority of this psalm is in praise and awe of God configured as the Divine Warrior, an ancient theological genre preceding the Israelites, found across the ancient Afro-Asiatic world. Much of this language existed earlier in the hymnic traditions of Baal. **3:3** The interjection *Selah* occurs in vv. 3, 9, and 13 (and in Pss. 3–4, 7, 9, 20–21, 24, 32, 39, 44, 46–50, 52, 54–55, 57, 59–62, 66–68, 75–77, 81–85, 87–89, 140, and 143). In each place in Habakkuk, it marks a dramatic act of God, suggesting it was a musical sound, perhaps some form of percussion (in other places, it may have been a moment of silence). Here it is a divine procession resulting in God's *glory* being displayed across the *heavens*. The geographical references, *Teman* and *Mount Paran*, present God as coming up from the south, likely to the unnamed Judah and Jerusalem. **3:4–6** *Brightness . . . like the sun* and *plague* and *pestilence* signify the danger of God's holiness; as with radiation, one cannot stand in its immediate presence without risking extraordinary harm. Geological upheavals are a traditional response to a theophany, an appearance of God. **3:7** *Midian* and Kush (Nubia), represented here by *the tents of Cushan*, are in the south in keeping with previous geographical references in v. 3. **3:8–15** In these anthropomorphic verses, God performs the physical actions of an ancient monarch leading his people to war from the front: riding on *chariots* pulled by *horses* (v. 8); loosing *arrows* from a *bow* (v. 9); crushing the *head* (skull) of the enemy (v. 13), usually with a war club or by stomping (see v. 10); and executing the enemy *head* or commander (v. 14). **3:8** In Canaanite and later Israelite epic poetry, *rivers*, floods, waters, and *the sea* are elements of chaos subdued by the gods demonstrating mastery. Echoes of this can be seen in the first Genesis creation narrative (Gen. 1:2–10) and in the flood stories of the Hebrew Bible (Gen. 6–8) and the Gilgamesh Epic. **3:11** The moon—or in many manuscripts, the sun and moon—stands

gloating as if ready to devour the
poor who were in hiding.
[15] You trampled the sea with your horses,
churning the mighty waters.

[16] I hear, and I tremble within;
my lips quiver at the sound.
Rottenness enters into my bones,
and my steps tremble[p] beneath me.
I wait quietly for the day of calamity
to come upon the people who attack us.

[17] Though the fig tree does not blossom
and no fruit is on the vines;
though the produce of the olive fails
and the fields yield no food;

though the flock is cut off from the
fold
and there is no herd in the stalls,
[18] yet I will rejoice in the LORD;
I will exult in the God of my
salvation.
[19] GOD, the Lord, is my strength;
he makes my feet like the feet of a
deer
and makes me tread upon the
heights.[q]

To the leader: with stringed[r]
instruments.

p 3.16 Cn Compare Gk: Meaning of Heb uncertain
q 3.19 Heb *my heights* *r* 3.19 Heb *my stringed*

still, evoking the divine warrior poem in Josh. 10:12–13. **3:16** The prophet's response to this awesome display is tremulous, evoking Job after the whirlwind speech; see Job 40:4. **3:17–18** These verses of praise may be read in conversation with Hab. 1–2 so that Habakkuk's praise is not dependent on God responding to his petition. Here the difficulty is an ecological and agricultural catastrophe with no reason given. It may be the result of war, but that is not specified. **3:19** The final verse is a confession of trust in God. In it, the author uses the image of a female *deer*, a doe, to represent themselves, suggesting to some an original author. The concluding liturgical instruction to the *leader* specifies *stringed instruments*, and based on the Hebrew reading, the instruments belong to the author.

ZEPHANIAH

Introduction

"A text without a context is a pretext." This contemporary proverb is a useful reminder when reading a prophetic collection like Zephaniah, generated in response to specific events in a specific place. Even when reading this work long after those circumstances have been resolved one way or another, that historical and cultural framework is important for making sense of the volume. Zephaniah begins with "the day of the LORD" (1:7). That is an apocalyptic day, meaning one on which all things will be revealed. It is usually a day of judgment and, often, destruction. Sometimes the day concludes with restoration and re-creation. It is a day with no expected date and is a regular feature of Israelite prophetic poetry (see Isa. 13:6, 9; 58:13; Jer. 46:10; Ezek. 13:5; 30:3; Joel 1:15; 2:1, 11, 31; 3:14; Amos 5:18, 20; Obad. 15; Mal. 4:5) that continues into the New Testament (1 Cor. 5:5; 2 Cor. 1:14; 1 Thess. 5:2; 2 Thess. 2:2; 2 Pet. 3:10). The timing of the day varies among the books of Scripture; in Zephaniah, it is at hand and coming soon. The Day of the Lord is also characterized by the survival of a faithful remnant in Zephaniah and elsewhere. See **"The Day of the Lord," p. 1322**.

Author, Dates, Context, and Genre

Zephaniah has the longest genealogy of any prophetic figure in all the prophetic books. He is identified with specificity back to the great king Hezekiah and as the son of someone with an African Nubian name: Cushi—all that in just the first verse. (See **"Ethnicity," p. 1300**.) The context of the writing is provided both geographically, with reference to the southern monarchy of Judah and Jerusalem (1:4), and temporally, during the reign of Josiah of Judah (1:1). In spite of the opening reference to King Josiah, there is no evidence Zephaniah ever spoke to the king, whose prophet of record was the prophetess Huldah; see 2 Kgs. 22:14 and 2 Chr. 34:22. The oracles in Zephaniah also address a wide array of international audiences: the four major Philistine cities, Gaza, Ashkelon, Ashdod, and Ekron (2:4); the Cherethites (or Cretans) and Canaan (2:5); Moab and Ammon (2:8–9); Nubia (Cush; 2:12); and Nineveh and Assyria (2:13).

The late-seventh-century setting places it in conversation with Nahum and Jeremiah; Zephaniah grapples with political and social upheaval as the Assyrian Empire declined and the Babylonian Empire gathered power. Owing to the "Day of the Lord" material, the primary content genre of the book is apocalyptic; the primarily literary genre consists of oracles. (See **"The Day of the Lord," p. 1322**.) Within the poetic verses, there are a significant number of literary techniques employed: alliteration, assonance, double entendres, puns, and other wordplay. As is the case with Habakkuk, there are specialized commentaries called pesharim on Zephaniah from the Jewish community at Qumran (second century BCE–first century CE), in addition to at least one pseudepigraphic (noncanonical) version of the volume, written in the first century CE.

Reading Guide

Jewish and Christian readers come to the book of Zephaniah with multiple perspectives on whether they are expecting a transformational messianic age or a final judgment; those perspectives shape how the book is read, especially interpretations of how and why divine judgment is to take place.

It is dangerous to use the sort of rhetoric that appears in Zephaniah as a rationale for modern politics or international borders. There are those who claim that the Palestinians broadly and Gazans in particular should be "pushed into the Sea" in order that the borders of Israel conform with "biblical prophecy," citing verses like Zeph. 2:4–7 where the rhetoric calls for the divine destruction of the Palestinian territory of Gaza and a significant portion of the kingdom of Jordan in 2:5–11, in addition to parts of Ethiopia and Sudan (2:12) and Iraq (2:13–15).

Understanding the literary and rhetorical genres of the book and their originating context helps the contemporary reader make sense of this volume and avoid misapplying the texts. It is apocalyptic, anticipating a cataclysm yet to come. It stands in the company of other biblical books with similar and contrasting visions of the day God takes the world in hand. These apocalyptic prophecies find their origin after the fall of Samaria, the capital of the northern Israelite monarchy, to the Assyrians in 722 BCE. Its destruction and the dispersal of its people resulted in the loss of ten of the tribes of Israel and their greatest geographical footprint. It was a devastating loss. These verses, and to

some degree the entirety of the Hebrew Bible, are trauma literature responding to that loss and the arguably even more devastating loss of the southern monarchy of Judah, Jerusalem, the temple, and the ability to be self-governing, due to the Babylonian conquest in 587/586 BCE. These two events frame the collection of the individual books that would become the Hebrew Bible. It is also useful to remember that literalism—taking statements as factually true and unfolding in a historical time and place—is a postbiblical reading strategy and not the framework of the ancient people who spoke, wrote, and preserved these texts. Besides this, the future that the prophet describes is not one that will be brought about by human intervention.

Wil Gafney

1 The word of the Lord that came to Zephaniah son of Cushi son of Gedaliah son of Amariah son of Hezekiah, in the days of King Josiah son of Amon of Judah.

2 I will utterly sweep away everything
    from the face of the earth, says the Lord.
3 I will sweep away humans and animals;
    I will sweep away the birds of the air
    and the fish of the sea.
    I will make the wicked stumble.[a]
    I will cut off humanity
    from the face of the earth, says the Lord.
4 I will stretch out my hand against Judah
    and against all the inhabitants of
        Jerusalem,
and I will cut off from this place every
        remnant of Baal
    and the name of the idolatrous
        priests,[b]
5 those who bow down on the roofs
    to the host of the heavens,

those who bow down and swear to the
        Lord
    but also swear by Milcom,[c]
6 those who have turned back from
        following the Lord,
    who have not sought the Lord or
        inquired of him.

7 Be silent before the Lord God,
    for the day of the Lord is at hand!
The Lord has prepared a sacrifice;
    he has consecrated his guests.
8 And on the day of the Lord's sacrifice
    I will punish the officials and the king's
        sons
    and all who dress themselves in
        foreign attire.
9 On that day I will punish
    all who leap over the threshold,

a 1.3 Cn: Heb *and those who cause the wicked to stumble*
b 1.4 Compare Gk: Heb *the idolatrous priests with the priests*
c 1.5 Gk mss Syr Vg: Heb *their king*

1:1 Zephaniah's genealogy spans five generations. His father's African name occurs as a personal name and an indicator of ancestry; see Isa. 18:1, 7; Jer. 36:14; and the superscription to Ps. 7. Cush overlaps Ethiopia and Sudan. Israelite identity is determined by the father, meaning when Israelites had non-Israelite mothers, their children would be counted as Israelites. Amariah, Hezekiah's son, and Gedaliah, Hezekiah's grandson, are otherwise unknown. As with the majority of prophets, the title is imposed by the narrator's pen.
1:2–9 This first unit consists of two parts: God speaks in the first person and the prophet responds. **1:2** This opening verse is a succinct prophecy that may have circulated independently; it calls for the extinction of all life on *the face of the earth*. **1:3–6** These verses expand upon 1:2, progressing in greater detail. Humankind and animal-kind will be destroyed, including those not on the face of the earth, *the birds of the air and the fish of the sea*. The targets for extermination move from larger to smaller: from *Judah* to *Jerusalem* to idolaters. *Baal* is the major Canaanite deity whose worship persisted and whose title was also used for the Israelite God (Hos. 2:16; see **"Baal," p. 489**). *Milcom* is the chief God of the Ammonites on Israel's eastern border; however, the Hebrew text more properly says, "their king." **1:6** To fail to inquire of God is to fail to seek God through a prophet. That specific verb is professional terminology, just as "to diagnose" means to have gotten a medical opinion. **1:7** The demand for silence may anticipate public outcry at a performance. It is in the third person, suggesting Zephaniah responding to God. The cry is urgent, *for the day of the Lord is at hand*. **1:8–9** The speaking voice returns to the first person, signifying God. The *king's sons* here is an inclusive plural; only sexism and poor translation erase the possibility of the king's daughters being included. **1:9** This obscure expression may refer to entering idolatrous temples.

Reading through Time: Ethnicity (Zephaniah 1)

The book of Zephaniah begins as follows: "The word of the LORD that came to Zephaniah son of Cushi" (1:1). In Hebrew, *Cushi* comes from the word *Cush*, which refers to the land south of Egypt (Isa. 11:11; 18:1; 20:3, 5; 43:3; 45:14; Ezek. 29:10; 30:4, 5; Nah. 3:9; Zeph. 3:10), inhabited by Africans, a term usually translated as "Cushites" (Isa. 20:4; Jer. 13:23; Ezek. 30:9; Amos 9:7; Zeph. 2:12) but in the (older) NRSV translated as "Ethiopians." In almost all these examples, Cushi has a negative connotation; the land or its people will be punished or even traded in exchange for the chosen Israelites. The Hebrew Bible consistently characterizes non-Israelites negatively. The incestuous conception of the Ammonites and Moabites in Gen. 19 and the portrayal of the Edomites as a consistent enemy of Israel in Ps. 137 and Mal. 1 provide two examples. Complicating the situation, however, is that all three groups are related to the Israelites; the Ammonites and Moabites are descended from Abraham's nephew Lot, and the Edomites come from Esau, Jacob's twin brother. Ethnic hierarchy is linked to family disputes. In the case of Cush, however, the ethnic diversity has significant historical consequences. According to Gen. 10, Cush is one of the sons of Ham. While Ham's son Canaan receives a curse in Gen. 9:25 because Ham looked at his naked father, Noah, early modern and modern biblical interpreters collapsed both chapters into a justification for African slavery. The biblical emphasis on ethnicity became a modern one about race.

That modern emphasis shapes how the prophet Zephaniah, the son of Cushi, is described. While Ebed-Melech, who rescues Jeremiah (Jer. 38), is described as *ha-Cushi* (translated as "the Cushite"), Zephaniah typically is not. Just like "Jehudi son of Nethaniah son of Shelemiah son of Cushi" (Jer. 36:14), Zephaniah son of Cushi is not linked to Ethiopia or Ethiopians in most scholarly discourse or biblical translations. Some Hebrew Bible dictionaries suggest that *Cushi* could mean *Cushite* in these cases, like it does everywhere else. The scholarly insistence that it is a proper name, however, masks the fact that the name has clear ethnic connotations. Zephaniah might have had Cushite ancestry, and simply acknowledging this possibility can shape how non-Israelite groups are interpreted. If the word of the Lord can come to someone with a Cushite ancestor, then the Israelites by definition are more ethnically diverse than they may appear.

Stacy Davis

who fill their master's house
with violence and fraud.

10 On that day, says the LORD,
a cry will be heard from the Fish
Gate,
a wail from the Second Quarter,
a loud crash from the hills.
11 The inhabitants of the Mortar wail,
for all the traders have perished;
all who weigh out silver are cut off.
12 At that time I will search Jerusalem
with lamps,
and I will punish the people
who settle like dregs in wine,
those who say in their hearts,
"The LORD will not do good,
nor will he do harm."

13 Their wealth shall be plundered
and their houses laid waste.
Though they build houses,
they shall not inhabit them;
though they plant vineyards,
they shall not drink wine from
them.

14 The great day of the LORD is near,
near and hastening fast;
the sound of the day of the LORD is
bitter;
the warrior cries aloud there.
15 That day will be a day of wrath,
a day of distress and anguish,
a day of ruin and devastation,
a day of darkness and gloom,
a day of clouds and thick darkness,

1:10–13 The unit begun in 1:10 continues through 1:18. Vv. 10 through 13 address Jerusalem with great specificity, naming wealthy neighborhoods and locations: *the Fish Gate, Second Quarter,* and *the Mortar.* The prophet Huldah lives in the *Second Quarter* at this time; see 2 Kgs. 22:14; 2 Chr. 34:22.

1:14–16 *The great day of the LORD* has moved from "at hand" in 1:7 to *near and hastening fast.* It is so terrible it will reduce warriors to tears, best characterized by chaos and terror. These lines form the basis of the hymn *Dies Irae,* "Day of Wrath." The language *day of clouds* is shared with Ezek. 30:3; 34:12; and Joel 2:2.

16   a day of trumpet blast and battle cry
        against the fortified cities
        and against the lofty battlements.

17 I will bring such distress upon people
        that they shall walk like the blind;
        because they have sinned against the
          Lord,
      their blood shall be poured out like dust
      and their flesh like dung.
18 Neither their silver nor their gold
        will be able to save them
        on the day of the Lord's wrath;
      in the fire of his passion
        the whole earth shall be consumed,
      for a full, a terrible end
        he will make of all the inhabitants of
         the earth.

2 Gather together, gather,
     O shameless nation,
2 before you are driven away[d]
        like the drifting chaff,[e]
    before there comes upon you
        the fierce anger of the Lord,
    before there comes upon you
        the day of the Lord's wrath.
3 Seek the Lord, all you humble of the land
        who do his commands;

      seek righteousness, seek humility;
        perhaps you may be hidden
        on the day of the Lord's wrath.
4 For Gaza shall be deserted,
        and Ashkelon shall become a
         desolation;
    Ashdod's people shall be driven out at
         noon,
        and Ekron shall be uprooted.
5 Woe, inhabitants of the seacoast,
        you nation of the Cherethites!
    The word of the Lord is against you,
        O Canaan, land of the Philistines,
        and I will destroy you until no
         inhabitant is left.
6 And you, O seacoast, shall be pastures,
        meadows for shepherds,
        and folds for flocks.
7 The seacoast shall become the possession
        of the remnant of the house of Judah,
      on which they shall pasture,
    and in the houses of Ashkelon
        they shall lie down at evening.
    For the Lord their God will be mindful
        of them
        and restore their fortunes.

d 2.2 Cn: Heb *before a decree is born*   *e* 2.2 Cn: Heb *like chaff a day has passed away*

1:17 The speech returns to the first person briefly, and a rationale is given for the devastation. The people have *sinned*; no details are provided.

1:18 The chapter ends where it began; *the whole earth shall be consumed.* The first half of the verse is duplicated in Ezek. 7:19.

2:1–3 This brief oracle warns an unnamed nation to change its ways before *the day of the Lord's wrath*, which is a slight modification of "the day of the Lord." The word *nation* is generally used for non-Israelite peoples, but in 2:1 and 2:9, it clearly refers to Judah. The *humble of the land* (or humble-poor) refers to the poor of Israel, particularly those left behind during the deportations and exile to Babylon. **2:3** The *humble of the land* combined with those who observe and fulfill God's *commands* indicates the nation is indeed Judah. In spite of the fact that everyone and everything is under the threat of destruction in 1:2 and 1:18, there is a possibility of survival for those who seek *righteousness* and *humility.*

2:4–15 The rest of the chapter declares God's sovereignty over all peoples of the earth, citing nations and far-flung empires, including some of Israel's historic enemies in its Afro-Asiatic geographical context. (Israel forms the land bridge between Africa and Asia, with the bulk of the nation, ancient and modern, on the African continental plate.) **2:4** Scholars debate whether to include v. 4 with 2:1–3. The opening conjunction, *for,* suggests reading v. 4 as a warning of the consequences for failing to seek "righteousness" and "humility" in 2:3. **2:4–7** Gaza, Ashkelon, Ashdod, and Ekron are the four major cities of Philistia, located on Israel's left flank, offering direct access to a significant stretch of the Mediterranean coastline. Not even during its greatest periods of stability, during the reigns of David and Solomon, was Israel ever able to capture this most valuable territory. The *Cherethites* are understood to be the Cretans by the translators of the Septuagint (the Gk. version of the Hebrew Bible) and by subsequent contemporary interpreters. The Aegean island of Crete was believed to have been the ancestral home of the Philistines (see Gen. 10:14; Deut. 2:23; Jer. 47:4; Amos 9:7; and 1 Chr. 1:12). One way of reading v. 7 is that it would take an act of God—that is, the

⁸ I have heard the taunts of Moab
    and the revilings of the Ammonites,
how they have taunted my people
    and made boasts against their
        territory.
⁹ Therefore, as I live, says the LORD of
        hosts,
    the God of Israel,
Moab shall become like Sodom
    and the Ammonites like Gomorrah,
a land possessed by nettles and salt pits
    and a waste forever.
The remnant of my people shall
        plunder them,
    and the survivors of my nation shall
        possess them.
¹⁰ This shall be their lot in return for their
        pride,
    because they scoffed and boasted
against the people of the LORD of
        hosts.
¹¹ The LORD will be terrible against them;
    he will shrivel all the gods of the
        earth,
and to him shall bow down
        each in its place,
    all the coasts and islands of the nations.

¹² You also, O Cushites,
    shall be killed by my sword.

¹³ And he will stretch out his hand against
        the north
    and destroy Assyria,

and he will make Nineveh a desolation,
    a dry waste like the desert.
¹⁴ Herds shall lie down in it,
    every wild animal of the earth;ᶠ
the desert owlᵍ and the screech owlʰ
    shall lodge on its capitals;
the owlⁱ shall hoot at the window,
    the ravenʲ croak on the threshold,
    for its cedar work will be laid bare.
¹⁵ Is this the exultant city
    that lived secure,
that said to itself,
    "I am, and there is no one else"?
What a desolation it has become,
    a lair for wild animals!
Everyone who passes by it
    hisses and shakes the fist.

3 Woe, soiled, defiled,
    oppressing city!
² It has listened to no voice;
    it has accepted no correction.
It has not trusted in the LORD;
    it has not drawn near to its God.

³ The officials within it
    are roaring lions;
its judges are evening wolves
    that leave nothing until the morning.
⁴ Its prophets are reckless,
    faithless persons;

f 2.14 Gk: Heb *nation*   g 2.14 Meaning of Heb uncertain
h 2.14 Meaning of Heb uncertain   i 2.14 Cn: Heb *a voice*
j 2.14 Gk Vg: Heb *desolation*

wrath of God—to pry the coastline away from the Philistines. **2:8-11** The subject of the prophetic address moves to Israel's eastern border: *Moab* and *the Ammonites*. They are charged with making *boasts* against Israelite *territory*. That territory was a matter of some dispute. Israel regularly pushed into Ammon, Edom, and Moab, and they regularly pushed back, which Israel referred to as "rebellion." *As I live* is a regularly occurring oath formula that God uses to guarantee whatever is being promised. The oath is as sure as God is eternal. This certainty is the destruction of these nations in the same way as *Sodom* and *Gomorrah*, leaving them uninhabited and available for Israelite migration and occupation. **2:12** Moving to the west again, the prophecy speaks to the African nation of Cush, Nubia (called Ethiopia in the original NRSV translation). The nation has already fallen; the Hebrew text uses an adjective, not a future-oriented verb. Given that Cush fell to Egypt and Egypt is not condemned by Zephaniah, Egypt is God's *sword* here. **2:13-15** The final verses deal with *Assyria* and its capital city, *Nineveh*. It will be depopulated, a refuge for domesticated and *wild animals*, particularly nonkosher animals that are not suitable for sacrifice upon the altars of God. In contemporary terms, the city will become a laughingstock, a punch line.

3:1-13 The third chapter of Zephaniah consists of two portions. The first is a "woe" oracle to an unnamed city. In its anonymity, the city could be Nineveh, continuing the theme of the previous units condemning Israel's enemies, or it could be Jerusalem, using the anonymity to demonstrate how much like other cities it is. **3:3-4** The presence of *judges* and *prophets* characterizes Israel and Judah as well as their neighbors in the wider Afro-Asiatic world. Zephaniah uses an explicitly masculine expression to describe the prophets as *faithless persons*, excluding women who were

its priests have profaned what is sacred;
  they have done violence to the law.
[5] The LORD within it is righteous;
  he does no wrong.
Every morning he renders his judgment,
  each dawn without fail,
  but the unjust knows no shame.

[6] I have cut off nations;
  their battlements are in ruins;
I have laid waste their streets
  so that no one walks in them;
their cities have been made desolate,
  without people, without inhabitants.
[7] I said, "Surely the city[k] will fear me;
  it will accept correction;
it will not lose sight[l]
  of all that I have brought upon it."
But they were the more eager
  to make all their deeds corrupt.

[8] Therefore wait for me, says the LORD,
  for the day when I arise as a witness.
For my decision is to gather nations,
  to assemble kingdoms,
to pour out upon them my indignation,
  all the heat of my anger,
for in the fire of my passion
  all the earth shall be consumed.

[9] At that time I will change the speech of
    the peoples
  to a pure speech,

that all of them may call on the name of
    the LORD
  and serve him with one accord.
[10] From beyond the rivers of Cush
  my suppliants, my scattered ones,
  shall bring my offering.

[11] On that day you shall not be put to
    shame
  because of all the deeds by which
    you have rebelled against me;
for then I will remove from your midst
  your proudly exultant ones,
and you shall no longer be haughty
  in my holy mountain.
[12] For I will leave in the midst of you
  a people humble and lowly.
They shall seek refuge in the name of
    the LORD—
[13]   the remnant of Israel;
they shall do no wrong
  and utter no lies,
nor shall a deceitful tongue
  be found in their mouths.
Then they will pasture and lie down,
  and no one shall make them afraid.

[14] Sing aloud, O daughter Zion;
  shout, O Israel!
Rejoice and exult with all your heart,
  O daughter Jerusalem!

k 3.7 Heb *it* l 3.7 Gk Syr: Heb *its dwelling will not be cut off*

prophets at the time whom he would likely have heard of, such as King Josiah's prophet, Huldah (2 Kgs. 22:14; 2 Chr. 34:22), and the woman with whom Isaiah had at least one child (Isa. 8:3; see Isa. 7:3 for Isaiah's other child). However, *law*, torah, is unique to Israel, though other nations have laws. These charges occur nearly exactly in Ezek. 22:23–28. **3:5** By v. 5, it is clear that Jerusalem is the referent even if Nineveh was intended in 3:1 because the God of Israel dwells *within* Jerusalem, within its temple. **3:6–13** God speaks in the first person as the destroyer of *nations* and the one who depopulates their cities. The *city* in 3:7 is anonymous; the following verses should be read with regard to both Jerusalem and its enemies. Sometimes one will be more clearly indicated than another. **3:8–10** God demonstrates sovereignty over all *nations* and *kingdoms*, and the oracle returns to the previous apocalyptic language in which the *earth* will be *consumed*. Also echoing the previous chapter (2:7), some remnant will remain. God will transform the language of this remnant *to a pure speech*, meaning "plain" speech to facilitate multinational, multiethnic worship. That would mean that God's *suppliants* and *scattered ones* include people from foreign nations, particularly Egypt and Cush (or Ethiopia) given the reference to the two major sections of the Nile, and from Israel and Judah. **3:11–13** Speaking directly to Jerusalem, indicated by the use of the second-person feminine (the nation is addressed with masculine language), God promises not to *shame* her for her past *deeds* and to remove the troublemakers from her *midst*. The *holy mountain* in v. 11 is Zion, the hill on which Jerusalem sits. In 3:13, the remnant is finally explicitly identified as *the remnant of Israel* who will be tended like sheep by God.

3:14–20 The conclusion of the third chapter is a poem to *daughter Zion* and *daughter Jerusalem*, pet names for Jerusalem (the same expression can also mean a woman from Zion/Jerusalem). There

15 The LORD has taken away the judgments
        against you;
    he has turned away your enemies.
    The king of Israel, the LORD, is in your
        midst;
    you shall fear disaster no more.
16 On that day it shall be said to Jerusalem:
    "Do not fear, O Zion;
        do not let your hands grow weak.
17 The LORD, your God, is in your midst,
        a warrior who gives victory;
    he will rejoice over you with gladness;
        he will renew you*m* in his love;
    he will exult over you with loud singing
18   as on a day of festival."*n*
    I will remove disaster from you,*o*
        so that you will not bear reproach
            for it.

19 I will deal with all your oppressors
        at that time.
    And I will save the lame
        and gather the outcast,
    and I will change their shame into
        praise
        and renown in all the earth.
20 At that time I will bring you home,
        at the time when I gather you;
    for I will make you renowned and
        praised
        among all the peoples of the
            earth,
    when I restore your fortunes
        before your eyes, says the LORD.

m 3.17 Gk Syr: Heb *he will be silent*   *n* 3.18 Gk Syr: Meaning
of Heb uncertain   *o* 3.18 Cn: Heb *I will remove from you;*
they were

is no language of destruction in these verses; indeed, Zion/Jerusalem need not *fear disaster* any longer (3:15, 18). The day of wrath is passed. Thus Zion is called to *sing, rejoice,* and *exult* (celebrate; 3:14). In a rare move, God will also *sing, rejoice,* and *exult* over Jerusalem in 3:17–18. God's presence in the *midst* of the city in v. 17 should be regarded not as physical but as the presence of God's name, which represents God's self as in 3:12. The poem ends repeating some of its opening themes, an end to *shame* and *disaster* (3:18–19). The concluding image is of a God who *gather[s]* those who have been scattered by disaster, such as the Assyrian conquest and deportations and the Babylonian conquest and exile. On the other side of the Day of the Lord, Israel, Judah, and, to some degree, the rest of the world will experience a reversal of fortune.

HAGGAI

Authorship, Date, and Literary History

Haggai is a little-known prophet who lived in the small province of Yehud, formerly Judah and which would later become Judea, during the early years of the Persian Empire's rule in the ancient Near East. The dating of the oracles, in the second year of the reign of Darius I (520 BCE), indicates that Haggai prophesied nearly twenty years after the original return of Jews from the Babylonian exile. The book of Haggai records four sermons addressed to key leaders of Yehud—Zerubbabel the governor and Joshua the high priest—and the people of the land across about a five-month period. As the book portrays it, the main focus of Haggai's preaching is on rebuilding the temple that had been destroyed in 587 BCE. The focus on the temple coincides with the only other references to Haggai in the Old Testament. In the book of Ezra, Haggai appears alongside Zechariah as the two of them exhort the people to finish rebuilding the temple. Interestingly, the book of Haggai does not mention Zechariah, nor does the book of Zechariah mention Haggai.

Reading Guide

The book of Haggai does not end with a celebration of the people having finished rebuilding the temple. All that the book reports is that the people finished laying the temple's foundation (2:18). Therefore, it seems likely that this collection of prophecies originally aimed to motivate the people of Jerusalem and Yehud to finish what they started.

The structure of the book of Haggai revolves around four sermons. Part one (1:1–15) tells the story of Haggai's first sermon and the people's response. Haggai accuses the people of claiming that the time has not yet come to rebuild the temple, even though the date of this sermon indicates that eighteen years have elapsed since the original return of the exiles who, according to the book of Ezra, came with the intention of rebuilding the temple (see Ezra 1). Haggai follows up this accusation with a declaration that the sufferings that the people have endured represent God's judgment against their poor logic, as God withheld the rains necessary to sustain their agricultural economy. In a rare moment within all of the prophetic literature, Zerubbabel, Joshua, and the people actually obey the command of God and start to rebuild the temple. The first section ends with a final exhortation to sustain the people in their work, assuring them that God is with them.

Part two records a second sermon delivered just a little over a month after the first (2:1–9). The prophet responds to the fact that people in the older generation that returned from the exile remember the glorious First Temple built by Solomon and look at the freshly built temple foundation with sorrow rather than joy. The goal of Haggai's sermon is to motivate the people to keep working, despite initial feelings of disappointment, exhorting them to "take courage" (literally "be strong") and giving them a vision of a (near) future when the wealth of the nations will come and contribute to an even more splendid Second Temple.

According to the book of Haggai, the last two sermons occur on the same day. In part three, the prophet offers a second sermon encouraging the people to complete their work of rebuilding the temple (2:10–19). Haggai draws out two analogies based on texts in the Law of the Old Testament declaring that the people's offerings at the temple were unacceptable, just as they would be if the people brought sacrifices to God in a state of uncleanness. However, now that they have finished laying the temple's foundation, they and their land will garner God's blessing if they continue to rebuild.

Part four ends the book with a sermon directed at a key individual: Zerubbabel the governor of Yehud (2:20–23). Nevertheless, the prophet still seeks to encourage the people to finish the work, this time by promising that God will overthrow Yehud's overlords and that Zerubbabel, as God's "chosen one," will mediate the relationship between God and the people.

Many readers in the West, especially those with Protestant roots, may have difficulty appreciating a whole book of the Bible focused on the temple. But one major way people honored God in the ancient world was through the sacrificial rituals (the other was through obeying the commandments that regulate society). Moreover, according to the Hebrew Bible, God selected Jerusalem as the special place in which to build the house of God, the temple (2 Sam. 7). To understand the importance of Jerusalem and the temple for Jewish identity, we may draw an analogy with the Great Mosque

that surrounds the Kaaba in Mecca in relation to Muslim identity. Not only do Muslims in Mecca come to offer prayers to Allah as a community, but millions of Muslims from around the world come for the great pilgrimage, the Hajj, once a year to perform rituals reenacting moments in their sacred history tied to Adam, Abraham, Hagar, Ishmael, and Muhammad. If anything were to happen to the Great Mosque and the Kaaba, Muslims worldwide would feel devastated. And we can easily imagine that Muslims worldwide would do everything they could to rebuild the Great Mosque and Kaaba. The prophecies of the book of Haggai indicate that the prophet felt that the returning exiles did not act as quickly as one would expect given the centrality of the temple for the identity of the residents of Jerusalem and Yehud (formerly Judah) for nearly four hundred years before it was destroyed.

Robert L. Foster

1 In the second year of King Darius, in the sixth month, on the first day of the month, the word of the LORD came by the prophet Haggai to Zerubbabel son of Shealtiel, governor of Judah, and to Joshua son of Jehozadak, the high priest: ²"Thus says the LORD of hosts: These people say the time has not yet come to rebuild the LORD's house." ³Then the word of the LORD came by the prophet Haggai, saying: ⁴"Is it a time for you yourselves to live in your paneled houses, while this house lies in ruins? ⁵Now therefore thus says the LORD of hosts: Consider how you have fared. ⁶You have sown much and harvested little; you eat, but you never have enough; you drink, but you never have your fill; you clothe yourselves, but no one is warm; and you that earn wages earn wages to put them into a bag with holes.

7 "Thus says the LORD of hosts: Consider how you have fared. ⁸Go up to the hills and bring wood and build the house, so that I may take pleasure in it and be honored, says the LORD. ⁹You have looked for much, but it came to little, and when you brought it home, I blew it away. Why? says the LORD of hosts. Because my house lies in ruins, while all of you hurry off to your own houses. ¹⁰Therefore the heavens above you have withheld the dew, and the earth has withheld its produce. ¹¹And I have called for a drought*ᵃ* on the land and the hills, on the grain, the new wine, the oil, on what the soil produces, on humans and animals, and on all their labors."

12 Then Zerubbabel son of Shealtiel and Joshua son of Jehozadak, the high priest, with all the remnant of the people, obeyed the voice of the LORD their God and the words of the prophet Haggai, as the LORD

a 1.11 Or *ruin*

1:1 *In the second year of King Darius* marks the time of Haggai's prophecy by the regnal year of the king of Persia, the empire ruling the land of Yehud (formerly Judah) at this time. Invoking Darius I's reign in each section also foreshadows the later prophecy promising God will overthrow the "throne of kingdoms"—that is, Darius's throne (2:21–22).

1:2 *The LORD of hosts* invokes the description of God in the book of Exodus, who led out the "hosts" of Israel from Egypt (e.g., Exod. 12:37–42). The population of the tiny province of Yehud is hardly a large "host." But using *the LORD of hosts* assures the audience that the God addressing them is the same one who delivered the Israelites from Egypt.

1:4 *Is it a time for you yourselves to live in your paneled houses?* The word *paneled* is used in describing the building of the First Temple, Solomon's temple, particularly the temple roof (1 Kgs. 7:3, 7). The contrast points out the irony that people have finished building their homes—they have roofs—but have not even begun rebuilding God's house, the temple. See **"Second Temple," p. 1328**.

1:8 *That I may ... be honored* invokes a common conception of temples in the ancient world: people build magnificent structures for their gods in order to evoke the awe and reverence their gods deserve. The Exodus story claims that after the people finished building the original house of God, the tabernacle, God ensured its glory by filling the house with God's own glory (Exod. 40:34–38).

1:12 *All the remnant of the people, obeyed,* first of all, recognizes that the prophet's audience in Yehud is small, just a remnant of the preexile population. This verse also notes the people's obedience, a rarity in the prophetic books of the Old Testament. The other three sermons in the book of Haggai assume that this first positive step has occurred.

their God had sent him, and the people feared the Lord. [13]Then Haggai, the messenger of the Lord, spoke to the people with the Lord's message, saying, "I am with you, says the Lord." [14]And the Lord stirred up the spirit of Zerubbabel son of Shealtiel, governor of Judah, and the spirit of Joshua son of Jehozadak, the high priest, and the spirit of all the remnant of the people, and they came and worked on the house of the Lord of hosts, their God, [15]on the twenty-fourth day of the month, in the sixth month.

2 In the second year of King Darius, [1]in the seventh month, on the twenty-first day of the month, the word of the Lord came by the prophet Haggai, saying: [2]"Speak now to Zerubbabel son of Shealtiel, governor of Judah, and to Joshua son of Jehozadak, the high priest, and to the remnant of the people, and say: [3]Who is left among you who saw this house in its former glory? How does it look to you now? Is it not in your sight as nothing? [4]Yet now take courage, O Zerubbabel, says the Lord; take courage, O Joshua, son of Jehozadak, the high priest; take courage, all you people of the land, says the Lord; work, for I am with you, says the Lord of hosts, [5]according to the promise that I made you when you came out of Egypt. My spirit abides among you; do not fear. [6]For thus says the Lord of hosts: Once again, in a little while, I will shake the heavens and the earth and the sea and the dry land, [7]and I will shake all the nations, so that the treasure of all nations will come, and I will fill this house with splendor, says the Lord of hosts. [8]The silver is mine, and the gold is mine, says the Lord of hosts. [9]The latter splendor of this house shall be greater than the former, says the Lord of hosts, and in this place I will give prosperity, says the Lord of hosts."

10 On the twenty-fourth day of the ninth month, in the second year of Darius, the word of the Lord came to the prophet Haggai, saying: [11]"Thus says the Lord of hosts: Ask the priests for a ruling: [12]If one carries consecrated meat in the fold of one's garment and with the fold touches bread, or stew, or wine, or oil, or any kind of food, does it become holy?" The priests answered, "No." [13]Then Haggai said, "If one who is unclean by contact with a dead body touches any of these, does it become unclean?" The priests answered, "Yes, it becomes unclean." [14]Haggai then said, "So is it with this people and with this nation before me, says the Lord, and so with every work of their hands; what they offer there is unclean. [15]But now, consider what will come to pass from this day on. Before a stone was placed upon a stone in the Lord's temple, [16]how did you fare?[b] When one came to a heap of twenty measures, there were but ten; when one came to the wine vat to draw fifty measures, there were but twenty. [17]I struck you and every work of your hands with blight and mildew and hail, yet you did not return

b 2.16 Gk: Heb *since they were*

1:14 *And the Lord stirred up the spirit of Zerubbabel . . . the spirit of Joshua . . . and the spirit of all the remnant* echoes language in the book of Exodus when everyone with a willing "spirit" donated personal riches toward building the tabernacle (Exod. 35:20–29).

2:3 *Is it not in your sight as nothing?* By this time, the temple consists of only its foundation (Hag. 2:18). The book of Ezra records that the people who remembered the glory of Solomon's temple wept when they saw the foundation of the Second Temple (Ezra 3:12). Here it seems the prophet simply acknowledges their sorrow.

2:4–5 *I am with you . . . according to the promise that I made you when you came out of Egypt.* This explicit reference to the exodus invokes God's promise to the hosts of Israel to bring them out of Egypt, keeping the promise made to Abraham, Isaac, and Jacob to give their descendants the land of Canaan (Exod. 6:2–8).

2:7 *I will shake all the nations, so that the treasure of all nations will come* presents God as a king conquering nations and plundering their goods. Once again, the book echoes the Exodus story where Israel "plundered" the Egyptians as they exited Egypt (Exod. 11:1–3; 12:33–36).

2:14 *What they offer there is unclean* indicates that for eighteen years, the people offered sacrifices on the temple site, looking for God's benefactions, without honoring God by rebuilding the temple.

2:17 *I struck you and every work of your hands* highlights that just because the temple had not been rebuilt did not mean God was not present—and responding—to the people's inaction. Instead

to me, says the LORD. [18]Consider from this day on, from the twenty-fourth day of the ninth month. Since the day that the foundation of the LORD's temple was laid, consider: [19]Is there any seed left in the barn? Do the vine, the fig tree, the pomegranate, and the olive tree still yield nothing? From this day on I will bless you."

20 The word of the LORD came a second time to Haggai on the twenty-fourth day of the month: [21]"Speak to Zerubbabel, governor of Judah, saying: I am about to shake the heavens and the earth [22]and to overthrow the throne of kingdoms; I am about to destroy the strength of the kingdoms of the nations and overthrow the chariots and their riders, and the horses and their riders shall fall, every one by the sword of a comrade. [23]On that day, says the LORD of hosts, I will take you, O Zerubbabel my servant, son of Shealtiel, says the LORD, and make you like a signet ring; for I have chosen you, says the LORD of hosts."

of giving benefactions, God disciplined the people because they had not honored God by rebuilding the temple.

2:19 *From this day on I will bless you.* The temple rebuilding now begun elicits God's promise to give the people the benefactions that they looked for in their sacrifices.

2:21–22 *I am about . . . to overthrow the throne of kingdoms* uses the singular "throne," implying the throne of Darius, who sits on the throne ruling the kingdoms subject to the Persian Empire. **2:22** *Overthrow the chariots and their riders, and the horses and their riders shall fall* invokes Exodus imagery, when the Egyptian armies and their chariots pursued the fleeing Israelites but were overthrown in the Sea of Reeds (Exod. 15:1, 21).

2:23 *I will take you, O Zerubbabel . . . and make you like a signet ring.* The signet ring metaphor suggests that Zerubbabel will authenticate God's will in the world, much like a signet ring impressed into a seal confirms that a document comes from the king and contains the king's directives. On the other hand, the word for *signet ring*, more generically, refers to an "inscription." It seems likely that this final verse offers one last reference to the book of Exodus, particularly to the diadem the high priest wore with its seal, "Holy to the LORD." In this case, Zerubbabel, like the high priest, takes on the guilt of the people so that God will accept their sacrifices (Exod. 28:36–38).

ZECHARIAH

Literary History

Zechariah is the eleventh member of the Book of the Twelve (Hosea–Malachi). The book of Zechariah connects to its predecessor Haggai not only by the relationship of their supposed authors (Ezra 5:1; 6:14) but also by the careful chronological association of their contents. The beginning oracle of Zechariah is set in October–November 520 BCE, fitting it between the oracles in Hag. 1:1–2:9 and those in 2:10–23. Zechariah's visions occur on February 15, 519 BCE (1:7), about two months after the final oracles in Haggai. In short, it appears that either the author or an editor wished these texts to be read together.

Zechariah also demonstrates connections to the book that follows it, Malachi. Zechariah 9, Zech. 12, and Malachi begin with the word "oracle" (*massaʾ*). This suggests these blocks of material— Zech. 9–11, Zech. 12–14, and Malachi—are to be read as related to one another and not to Zech. 1–8. In addition, Zech. 1–8 contrasts strongly in style and structure with Zech. 9–14. While Zech. 1–8 follows a clear sequence of visions, Zech. 9–14 has little coherent structure. Almost all scholars thus see Zech. 1–8 and Zech. 9–14 as separate entities, originating in different contexts. Some designate Zech. 9–14 as Deutero-Zechariah (meaning second). Others divide chaps. 9–14 into Deutero-Zechariah (chaps. 9–11) and Trito-Zechariah (chaps. 12–14), respectively. In this introduction, I will treat Zech. 1–8 and 9–14 separately.

Authorship and Date

Zechariah 1–8. Most of Zech. 1–8 probably originated with Zechariah the prophet. Ezra notes that Zechariah, whose name means "YHWH has remembered," supported the rebuilding of the temple of YHWH in Jerusalem (5:1; 6:14). But while the book of Haggai shows a clear emphasis on rebuilding, Zechariah focuses on the preparations for the new temple and what it would mean for Jerusalem and Judah. Nehemiah 12:16 mentions a Zechariah as the head of the priestly house of Iddo. If this Zechariah is the author, then he was a priest returning from exile. According to the dates provided in the book (1:1, 7; 7:1), Zechariah was active at least from late 520 BCE to late 518 BCE. The great majority of his surviving work is a series of visions (1:7–6:8) that took place on February 15, 519 BCE.

Zechariah 9–14. Given the diversity of material and perspective found in Zech. 9–14, it is difficult to assert a single author. Rather, there were likely multiple authors and editors who produced the various pieces and gathered them together. There is little scholarly consensus on when these chapters were written and edited, with suggestions ranging from the time of Josiah to the Hellenistic and Maccabean periods (fourth to first century BCE). The chapters may allude to historical events, but these allusions are usually so vague that precise identifications are questionable. Given the association of Zech. 9–11 and 12–14 with Malachi, a text that is more confidently dated to the early to mid-Persian period (sixth to fifth century BCE), it is probably best to posit that Zech. 9–14 emerged and was edited in that same period.

Reading Guide

Zechariah 1–8. A series of eight symbolic visions (1:7–6:8) dominate this section. Such visions appear in other, earlier prophetic literature (Amos 7:7–9; 8:1–3; Jer. 1:11–19; Ezek. 1:1; 8:2). In these visions, objects become symbols. A woman in a basket represents the wickedness of the people (Zech. 5:5–11). Joshua's filthy clothes represent his inability to preside at the temple (3:1–5).

Zechariah introduces a new and more complicated use of visions. The visions feature interrelated subjects and language, inviting the reader to find as many points of contact as possible. Zechariah is also innovative in the use of angels, who function as mediators and explicators, drawing the prophet's attention to certain objects and then explaining their symbolic import. While these visions may strike the modern reader as odd, it is important to note that in Zech. 1–8, they include both mundane items (the prophet himself, horses, baskets, scrolls, and clothing) and otherworldly settings (the mysterious glen in 1:8–11, a meeting of the Divine Council in 3:1–5, and the heavens in 1:18, 5:1, and 5:5). Later apocalyptic visions will focus more on the otherworldly (cf. Dan. 7), though continuity between Zechariah and apocalyptic thought cannot be denied (see **"Apocalypse," p. 1216**).

Zechariah 1–8 also includes oracles, statements supposed to be directly from the deity and often couched in poetry. Several oracles expand on the visions. For example, Zech. 2:6–13 calls the exiles

to return after a vision described the rebuilding of a safe and secure Jerusalem (also see 3:6–10; 4:6–10a). Chaps. 7–8 feature a collection of oracles, structured by a question about fasting (7:2–3) and its answer (8:18–19). YHWH rehearses the disobedience of the ancestors (7:8–14) but then closes the section with a series of oracles affirming the future of Jerusalem (8:1–23).

The visions construct a new relationship and a new reality. Jerusalem will be restored and secure (2:1–5). The temple, priesthood, and Jerusalem will be renewed by the removal of ritual uncleanness (3:1–10) and human wickedness (5:1–11). A Davidic governor and a proper high priest will lead (4:1–14; 6:9–14). YHWH is moving forward (1:7–17; 6:1–8). The concluding oracles (7:1–8:23) build the case that the past will resolve into a prosperous future for Jerusalem.

Zechariah 9–14. These chapters appear to be a hodgepodge of various prophetic forms of literature. They resist simple classifications. Some scholars read Zech. 9–14 as an anthology, a loosely connected collection of varied prophetic literature with little sense of coherence. Others claim that there is a discernible cohesion provided by linkages between and among these chapters. For example, the metaphor of the people as sheep links chaps. 9, 10, and 13, while horses appear in 10, 12, and 14.

Another feature that suggests some coherence in this collection is their almost complete absence of questions. The only question is indirect (13:6). Haggai, Malachi, and Zech. 1–8 make frequent use of questions (forty-eight), so the lack of questions sets these chapters apart from other literature while presenting an assertive, direct style.

Zechariah 9–14 is also noted for its frequent references to other biblical literature, especially to the book of Jeremiah. While other works of the Persian period also exemplify the use of other texts, these chapters feature much more frequent allusions. Some of these are mentioned in the study notes. These allusions mean that Zech. 9–14 should be seen not as derivative but as a creative reframing of older texts.

Donald C. Polaski

1 In the eighth month, in the second year of Darius, the word of the LORD came to the prophet Zechariah son of Berechiah son of Iddo, saying: [2]"The LORD was very angry with your ancestors. [3]Therefore say to them: Thus says the LORD of hosts: Return to me, says the LORD of hosts, and I will return to you, says the LORD of hosts. [4]Do not be like your ancestors, to whom the former prophets proclaimed, 'Thus says the LORD of hosts: Return from your evil ways and from your evil deeds.' But they did not hear or heed me, says the LORD. [5]Your ancestors, where are they? And the prophets, do they live forever? [6]But my words and my statutes, which I commanded my servants the prophets, did they not overtake your ancestors? So they repented and said, 'The LORD of hosts has dealt with us according to our ways and deeds, just as he planned to do.'"

7 On the twenty-fourth day of the eleventh month, the month of Shebat, in the second year of Darius, the word of the LORD came to the prophet Zechariah son of Berechiah son of Iddo: [8]In the night I saw a man mounted on a red horse! He was standing among the myrtle trees in the shadows,[a] and behind him were red, sorrel, and white horses. [9]Then I said, "What are these, my lord?" The angel who spoke with me said

a 1.8 Gk Syr: Meaning of Heb uncertain

1:1–6 Introduction to the prophet Zechariah. For Zechariah, the return to YHWH is essential to the restoration of the temple. **1:1** October–November 520 BCE. Nehemiah 12:16 mentions a Zechariah as the head of the priestly house of Iddo. If he is the author, he was a priest returning from exile. **1:3–4** *Return* translates the Hebrew "shub," which often implies repentance. **1:6** The people who repent ("shub") here are probably Zechariah's audience—the "you" of *your ancestors*.

1:7–17 The first vision. Zechariah sees a man on horseback, part of YHWH's force providing information on the state of the world. The lack of activity ("peace") is not good, as it indicates YHWH has not yet taken action to support his people. YHWH vows to take action through the building of the temple. **1:7** January–February 519 BCE. The repetition of a date and the prophetic genealogy set the visions off from the introduction. **1:8–11** The colors of the horses are probably not symbolic but represent typical colors for horses. The presence of myrtles with their bright green leaves indicates

to me, "I will show you what they are." [10]So the man who was standing among the myrtle trees answered, "They are those whom the LORD has sent to patrol the earth." [11]Then they spoke to the angel of the LORD who was standing among the myrtle trees, "We have patrolled the earth, and the whole earth remains at peace." [12]Then the angel of the LORD said, "O LORD of hosts, how long will you withhold mercy from Jerusalem and the cities of Judah, with which you have been angry these seventy years?" [13]Then the LORD replied with gracious and comforting words to the angel who spoke with me. [14]So the angel who spoke with me said to me, "Proclaim this message: Thus says the LORD of hosts: I am very zealous for Jerusalem and for Zion, [15]and I am extremely angry with the nations that are at ease, for while I was only a little angry, they made the disaster worse. [16]Therefore, thus says the LORD: I have returned to Jerusalem with compassion; my house shall be built in it, says the LORD of hosts, and a measuring line shall be stretched out over Jerusalem. [17]Proclaim further: Thus says the LORD of hosts: My cities shall again overflow with prosperity; the LORD will again comfort Zion and again choose Jerusalem."

[18] [b]And I looked up and saw four horns. [19]I asked the angel who spoke with me, "What are those?" And he answered me, "Those are the horns that have scattered Judah, Israel, and Jerusalem." [20]Then the LORD showed me four blacksmiths. [21]And I asked, "What are they coming to do?" He answered, "Those are the horns that scattered Judah, so that no head could be raised, but these have come to terrify them, to strike down the horns of the nations that lifted up their horns against the land of Judah to scatter its people."[c]

2 [d]I looked up and saw a man with a measuring line in his hand. [2]Then I asked, "Where are you going?" He answered me, "To measure Jerusalem, to see how wide and how long it is." [3]Then the angel who spoke with me came forward, and another angel came forward to meet him [4]and said to him, "Run, say to that young man: Jerusalem shall be inhabited like unwalled villages because of the multitude of people and animals in it. [5]For I will be a wall of fire all around it, says the LORD, and I will be the glory within it."

b 1.18 2.1 in Heb   *c* 1.21 Heb *it*   *d* 2.1 2.5 in Heb

---

a pleasant area (cf. Isa. 41:19; 55:13). The Persian Empire was famous for the speed and efficiency of its communication by horsemen. **1:12** The *seventy years* are the period when Judahites lacked a temple, 586–520 BCE. **1:13** As claimed in 1:3, YHWH now expresses mercy, perhaps due to the people's turning toward YHWH in 1:6. The conversation among YHWH, angels, and a prophet indicates a meeting of the Divine Council (1 Kgs. 22:19–23; Isa. 6:1–8). **1:14** *Zealous* ("qone"), often rendered as "jealous," denotes YHWH's emotional relationship to the people. *Zealous* better communicates that YHWH intends to act decisively, involving disturbing the peace. **1:16** The *measuring line* indicates the temple project, the renewal of Jerusalem, is beginning (see 2:1 and contrast with Jer. 31:38–39; Ezek. 47:3).

1:18–21 The second vision. Zechariah sees horns and asks what they are. The angel claims they represent the nations who have punished Israel and Judah and who now will themselves be punished by YHWH. **1:18** What Zechariah sees is not immediately clear. They could be a pair of horned animals, horns on war helmets, or the four horns on the altar in Jerusalem. *Four* probably represents totality. **1:19** The angel links the horns to the destruction of Israel, Judah, and Jerusalem. Horns represent power elsewhere (Deut. 33:17; Ps. 132:17; Jer. 48:25; Ezek. 29:21; Dan. 7:7–8; 8:1–14). **1:20–21** The *blacksmiths*, perhaps better understood as generic artisans, possess the metaphorical ability to destroy the horns, though how that process works is not at all clear.

2:1–5 The third vision. Rejecting a typical reconstruction, YHWH insists the new Jerusalem will lack walls and be able to welcome masses of people. **2:1–2** The *measuring line* establishes boundaries and assists in parceling land out. **2:4** Other prophets claimed that the restored land would feature a large population (Isa. 49:19; 54:3) of people and animals (Jer. 31:27; Ezek. 36:11), but Zechariah focuses only on Jerusalem, not the whole land. **2:5** The Persian capital city Pasargadae, lacking walls and surrounded by fire altars, was an apt model for Zechariah's restored Jerusalem. Unlike other prophets, Zechariah claims YHWH's *glory* will dwell in Jerusalem as a whole, not only within the temple (Ezek. 43:1–9).

6 Up, up! Flee from the land of the north, says the LORD, for I have spread you abroad like the four winds of heaven, says the LORD. ⁷Up! Escape to Zion, you who live with daughter Babylon. ⁸For thus said the LORD of hosts after his glory sent me to the nations who plundered you: Truly, one who touches you touches the apple of my eye.ᵉ ⁹For I am going to raiseᶠ my hand against them, and they shall become plunder for their own slaves. Then you will know that the LORD of hosts has sent me. ¹⁰Sing and rejoice, O daughter Zion! For I will come and dwell in your midst, says the LORD. ¹¹Many nations shall join themselves to the LORD on that day and shall be my people, and I will dwell in your midst. And you shall know that the LORD of hosts has sent me to you. ¹²The LORD will inherit Judah as his portion in the holy land and will again choose Jerusalem.

13 Be silent, all flesh, before the LORD, for he has roused himself from his holy dwelling.

3 Then he showed me the high priest Joshua standing before the angel of the LORD and the accuserᵍ standing at his right hand to accuse him. ²And the LORD said to the accuser,ʰ "The LORD rebuke you,

O accuser!ⁱ The LORD who has chosen Jerusalem rebuke you! Is not this man a brand plucked from the fire?" ³Now Joshua was wearing filthy clothes as he stood before the angel. ⁴The angelʲ said to those who were standing before him, "Take off his filthy clothes." And to him he said, "See, I have taken your guilt away from you, and I will clothe you with festal apparel." ⁵And he said,ᵏ "Let them put a clean turban on his head." So they put a clean turban on his head and clothed him with apparel, and the angel of the LORD was standing by.

6 Then the angel of the LORD warned Joshua, saying ⁷"Thus says the LORD of hosts: If you will walk in my ways and keep my requirements, then you shall rule my house and have charge of my courts, and I will give you the right of access among those who are standing here. ⁸Now listen, Joshua, high priest, you and your colleagues who sit before you! For they are an omen of things to come: I am going to bring my servant the Branch. ⁹For on the stone that I have set before Joshua, on a single stone with seven facets, I will engrave its inscription, says the

e 2.8 Heb *his eye* f 2.9 Or *wave* g 3.1 Heb *the satan*
h 3.2 Heb *the satan* i 3.2 Heb *the satan* j 3.4 Heb *He*
k 3.5 Syr Vg Tg: MT *I said*

2:6–13 **Oracles on the repopulation of Jerusalem. 2:6–7** While the scattering of the people was YHWH's doing and was universal, involving *the four winds*, he now urges that they escape to Jerusalem, especially those exiled to Babylon. **2:9** The punishment of the plunderers will be soon, as it will certify Zechariah's status as a prophet. **2:10** *Daughter Zion* describes Jerusalem in the Hebrew Bible (see especially Lam.). Here she contrasts with "daughter Babylon," the doomed oppressor (v. 7). See **"Daughter Zion," p. 1118. 2:11** See Isa. 60:8–16 (the nations will come to Jerusalem, give over their wealth, and serve Israel) and Isa. 56:1–8 (foreigners can "join themselves" to YHWH). Zechariah moves beyond Isa. 56 by suggesting the other nations will be one people with Israel. **2:12** *Holy land* appears only here in the Hebrew Bible. Zechariah here claims *the holy land*, especially Judah, is set apart, fit for divine use and ownership. **2:13** This call is both universal (*all flesh*) and particular (*his holy dwelling*); cf. Hab. 2:20. This dwelling may be in Jerusalem or in the heavens (Ps. 11:4). Isaiah 26:21 and Mic. 1:2–4 note that YHWH, as Divine Warrior, will leave his abode to do battle for his people.

3:1–5 The fourth vision. YHWH asserts that Joshua the high priest is ritually fit to serve. **3:1** *The accuser* translates the Hebrew "hassatan," often rendered as "the Satan" or "Satan." He functions as YHWH's prosecutor, accusing people of wrongdoing (see Job 1–2 and **"The Satan," p. 687**). Joshua is the high priest who returned from exile with Zerubbabel (Hag. 1:1; Ezra 3:2; 5:2; Sir. 49:12). **3:2–4** *Brand plucked from the fire* symbolizes Joshua's life in exile. His *filthy clothes* represent his lacking the ritual purity needed to preside at the temple. This defective ritual state, not moral failure, is Joshua's *guilt*. See **"Holiness and Purity," p. 158. 3:5** Joshua's new apparel represents the establishment of his ritual purity, necessary for the renewed temple to function.

3:6–10 Four responses to the renewal of Joshua. 3:6–7 Joshua's role will include having *access among those who are standing here*, the Divine Council. **3:8** *Branch* ("tsemakh") denotes a coming Davidic ruler (Jer. 23:5–6; 33:14–16; cf. Isa. 11:1; Ps. 132:17). Zechariah associates the image with Zerubbabel. **3:9–10** The engraved stone is probably the golden rosette worn by the high priest. It symbolizes the high priest's power to remove the people's ritual and moral faults (Exod. 28:36–38).

LORD of hosts, and I will remove the guilt of this land in a single day. [10]On that day, says the LORD of hosts, you shall invite each other to come under your vine and fig tree."

4 The angel who spoke with me came again and wakened me, as one is wakened from sleep. [2]He said to me, "What do you see?" And I said, "I see a lampstand all of gold, with a bowl on the top of it; there are seven lamps on it, with seven lips on each of the lamps that are on the top of it. [3]And by it there are two olive trees, one on the right of the bowl and the other on its left." [4]I said to the angel who spoke with me, "What are these, my lord?" [5]Then the angel who spoke with me answered me, "Do you not know what these are?" I said, "No, my lord." [6]He said to me, "This is the word of the LORD to Zerubbabel: Not by might, nor by power, but by my spirit, says the LORD of hosts. [7]What are you, O great mountain? Before Zerubbabel you shall become a plain, and he shall bring out the top stone amid shouts of 'Grace, grace to it!'"

8 Moreover, the word of the LORD came to me, saying, [9]"The hands of Zerubbabel have laid the foundation of this house; his hands shall also complete it. Then you will know that the LORD of hosts has sent me to you. [10]For whoever has despised the day of small things shall rejoice and shall see the plummet in the hand of Zerubbabel.

"These seven are the eyes of the LORD that range through the whole earth." [11]Then I said to him, "What are these two olive trees on the right and the left of the lampstand?" [12]And a second time I said to him, "What are these two branches of the olive trees that pour out the oil[/] through the two golden pipes?" [13]He said to me, "Do you not know what these are?" I said, "No, my lord." [14]Then he said, "These are the two anointed ones who stand by the Lord of the whole earth."

5 Again I looked up and saw a flying scroll. [2]And he said to me, "What do you see?" I answered, "I see a flying scroll; its length is twenty cubits and its width ten cubits." [3]Then he said to me, "This is the curse that goes out over the face of the whole land, for everyone who has stolen, as is forbidden on one side, has gone unpunished, and everyone who has sworn falsely,[m] as is forbidden on the other side,

[/] 4.12 Cn: Heb gold   [m] 5.3 The word *falsely* added from verse 4

Renewing the high priesthood will provide a paradisial life *under your vine and fig tree*, commonly associated with the rule of YHWH and/or the monarch (1 Kgs. 4:25; Mic. 4:4; 1 Macc. 14:12). **4:1–14 The fifth vision.** A lampstand and two olive trees indicate that Zerubbabel and Joshua would share power. **4:1–5** The vision describes a golden lampstand (menorah) flanked by two olive trees. The lampstand does not resemble the familiar seven-branched menorah of later Jewish tradition. This stand has no branches but features a bowl with seven indentations for wicks. The bowl would have been filled with olive oil as fuel, explaining the presence of the olive trees. **4:6–10a** Rather than explain the items seen, the angel focuses on Zerubbabel. Zerubbabel will build the new temple, relying on YHWH's spirit in the face of the might and power of opponents (v. 6; cf. Ezra 4:1–5, 11–16). While a *great mountain* may oppose him, Zerubbabel will bring forth *the top stone* (v. 7), signaling his responsibility for the temple project (vv. 8–9) and causing those disappointed in the project, the despisers of *the day of small things* (Ezra 3:11; Hag. 2:3), to rejoice. **4:10b** The explanation of the vision begins. YHWH's eyes symbolize YHWH's control over the earth, reflecting the use of the term "eyes" to refer to participants in imperial domestic intelligence (cf. 2 Chr. 16:9; Ezra 5:5). **4:11–14** The olive trees are the *two anointed ones* ("sons of oil" in Heb.): Zerubbabel and Joshua. Kings as well as priests were anointed in ancient Israel. The proper operation of the restored Jerusalem requires a Davidic governor and a Zadokite high priest working as corulers. While this never becomes a political reality (see below, chap. 6), it does inform "dual messianism," the notion that the end of the age would involve two messiahs, seen especially in the Dead Sea Scrolls (1QS 9:11; 1QSa 2:11–21; CD 12:23–13:1). **5:1–4 The sixth vision.** A flying scroll indicates wrongdoing in the community. **5:1–2** A flying scroll is decidedly odd. The scroll, apparently unrolled, also has a strange shape: 30′ × 15′, a 2 × 1 rectangle. Actual scrolls could be quite long but were much narrower. **5:3** The angel claims the scroll is a curse intended for *the whole land* ("kol ha'arets"), implying it involves only the area around Jerusalem. Elsewhere in Zechariah, however, the phrase is rendered as "the whole earth," suggesting a

has gone unpunished. 4 I have sent it out,
says the LORD of hosts, and it shall enter the
house of the thief and the house of anyone who swears falsely by my name, and it
shall abide in that house and consume it,
both timber and stones."

5 Then the angel who spoke with me
came forward and said to me, "Look up
and see what this is that is coming out."
6 I said, "What is it?" He said, "This is a
basket[n] coming out." And he said, "This is
their iniquity[o] in the whole land." 7 Then
a leaden cover was lifted, and there was
a woman sitting in the basket![p] 8 And he
said, "This is Wickedness." So he thrust
her back into the basket[q] and pressed the
leaden weight down on its mouth. 9 Then
I looked up and saw two women coming
forward. The wind was in their wings;
they had wings like the wings of a stork,
and they lifted up the basket[r] between
earth and sky. 10 Then I said to the angel
who spoke with me, "Where are they
taking the basket?"[s] 11 He said to me, "To
the land of Shinar, to build a house for it,
and when this is prepared, they will set it
down there on its base."

6 And again I looked up and saw four
chariots coming out from between
two mountains—mountains of bronze.
2 The first chariot had red horses, the second chariot black horses, 3 the third chariot white horses, and the fourth chariot
dappled gray[t] horses. 4 Then I said to the
angel who spoke with me, "What are
these, my lord?" 5 The angel answered
me, "These are the four winds[u] of heav-
en going out, after presenting themselves
before the Lord of the whole earth. 6 The
chariot with the black horses goes toward
the north country, the white ones go toward the west country,[v] and the dappled
ones go toward the south country." 7 When
the steeds came out, they were impatient
to get off and patrol the earth. And he
said, "Go, patrol the earth." So they patrolled the earth. 8 Then he cried out to
me, "See, those who go toward the north
country have set my spirit at rest in the
north country."

n 5.6 Heb *ephah* *o* 5.6 Gk Compare Syr: Heb *their eye* *p* 5.7 Heb *ephah* *q* 5.8 Heb *ephah* *r* 5.9 Heb *ephah* *s* 5.10 Heb *ephah* *t* 6.3 Meaning of Heb uncertain *u* 6.5 Or *spirits* *v* 6.6 Cn: Heb *go after them*

universal role (1:11; 4:10b; 6:5). The curse addresses theft and false testimony, violations drawn from covenantal traditions (Exod. 20:15–16). The curse will apply to all Jews, in the land and in the Diaspora, who have evaded punishment. **5:4** YHWH's curse will punish even those who commit secret violations, an ideal form of law enforcement.

5:5–11 The seventh vision. A woman in a basket signifies wickedness and its fate. **5:5–6** This *basket* ("'efah") holds about two-thirds of a bushel. Its lead lid indicates something more substantial than a basket. **5:6** The *basket* represents the *iniquity* ("'avon") of the people of *the whole land* ("kol ha'arets"), paralleling the "'avon" ("guilt") of Joshua in 3:4. The people suffer from a lack of ritual purity, symbolized as the *basket*. **5:7–8** No woman could fit in a *basket* this size, adding to the oddness of the vision. She symbolizes the moral faults of the people. Perhaps a woman is chosen to represent wickedness because men viewed women as tempting them to adultery and apostasy (Prov. 2:16; 5:3, 20; 7:5; Exod. 34:11–16; Deut. 7:3–4; 17:17; Judg. 3:6; 1 Kgs. 11:1–8; Ezra 9:1–4). See **"Apostasy," p. 1238**. **5:9** The women with wings like storks add one more odd element. Why these creatures were chosen for this duty is unclear, but their purpose is certain: the *basket* and its contents are a danger to the community as it begins a renewed life. The *basket*, with its passenger, must be removed. **5:10–11** They take this dangerous object to *Shinar*, a term for Babylon that conjures up the story of Babel (Gen. 11:1–9). While the land around Jerusalem and its new temple would be holy (2:12), Babylon would own only ritual and moral fault, demonstrated by the *basket*'s placement in a new shrine there.

6:1–8 The eighth vision. The visions conclude with the dawn of a new age. **6:1–6** The two bronze mountains may allude to the going forth of the Mesopotamian sun god Shumash, casting this final night vision of Zechariah at dawn. The four colors, chariots, and horses here represent *the four winds of heaven*. These represent universal extent (2:6; Dan. 8:8) as well as YHWH's power (Jer. 49:36; Ezek. 37:9; Dan. 7:2). **6:7** The horses *patrol* the earth, as in 1:10–11. The threefold use of the verb "halakh" (to walk about) adds emphasis, while the translation of the verb as *patrol* adds a military dimension to gathering information. **6:8** In the first vision, the patrol informed YHWH that the world was "at peace," indicating his people needed relief (1:11–12). Now YHWH's *spirit* (or wind) has *rest in*

9 The word of the LORD came to me: ¹⁰"Collect silver and gold" from the exiles— from Heldai, Tobijah, and Jedaiah—who have arrived from Babylon, and go the same day to the house of Josiah son of Zephaniah. ¹¹Take the silver and gold and make a crown* and set it on the head of the high priest Joshua son of Jehozadak; ¹²say to him: Thus says the LORD of hosts: Here is a man whose name is Branch, for he shall branch out in his place, and he shall build the temple of the LORD. ¹³It is he who shall build the temple of the LORD; he shall bear royal honor and shall sit upon his throne and rule. There shall be a priest by his throne, with peaceful understanding between the two of them. ¹⁴And the crown* shall be in the care of Heldai,* Tobijah, Jedaiah, and Josiah* son of Zephaniah, as a memorial in the temple of the LORD.

15 "Those who are far off shall come and help to build the temple of the LORD, and you shall know that the LORD of hosts has sent me to you. This will happen if you diligently obey the voice of the LORD your God."

7 In the fourth year of King Darius, the word of the LORD came to Zechariah on the fourth day of the ninth month, which is Chislev. ²Now the people of Bethel had sent Sharezer and Regem-melech and their men to entreat the favor of the LORD ³and to ask the priests of the house of the LORD of hosts and the prophets, "Should I mourn and practice abstinence in the fifth month, as I have done for so many years?" ⁴Then the word of the LORD of hosts came to me: ⁵"Say to all the people of the land and the priests: When you fasted and lamented in the fifth month and in the seventh for these seventy years, was it for me that you fasted? ⁶And when you eat and when you drink, do you not eat and drink only for yourselves? ⁷Were not these the words that the LORD proclaimed by the former prophets, when Jerusalem was inhabited and in prosperity, along with the towns around it, and when the Negeb and the Shephelah were inhabited?"

w 6.10 Heb lacks silver and gold   x 6.11 Gk mss Syr Tg: Heb crowns   y 6.14 Gk Syr: Heb crowns   z 6.14 Syr: Heb Helem   a 6.14 Syr: Heb Hen

the north country (Babylon), showing that the calm enforced by Babylon is now over. The world is now ordered in a way that will benefit YHWH's people.

6:9–15 An oracle elaborating proper rule in Jerusalem. This oracle appears to have been adjusted by a later editor to reflect a change in government. **6:9–10** Zechariah receives a direct divine command, not a vision. *Heldai, Tobijah, Jedaiah,* and *Josiah son of Zephaniah* are otherwise unknown. The *same day* indicates the urgency of this project. **6:11** The Hebrew indicates "crowns" ("'atarot") are to be made, suggesting that the author initially thought of two rulers, but only one ruler (the high priest Joshua) came to power. The plural "crowns" also appears in v. 14. **6:12– 15** YHWH speaks of Joshua in ways used previously for Zerubbabel: the title *Branch* (3:8) and the sole responsibility for building the temple (4:6–10). Acquiring royal glory and ruling from a throne would characterize a king, not a priest. The text notes that a priest would stand beside this throne, not sit on it. It is best to surmise an early version of this oracle understood "crowns" would be made for Joshua and Zerubbabel and they would rule together, as in 4:11–14. But Zerubbabel disappeared, leading to his erasure from the oracle and Joshua's assumption of his description. Perhaps royal hopes attached to Zerubbabel (Hag. 2:20–23) upset the Persian authorities, who then removed Zerubbabel.

7:1–7 Introduction to a series of oracles addressing the effects of the restoration of the temple (7:1–8:23). 7:1 December 7, 518 BCE, about two years after Zechariah had his visions, a clear beginning to this section. **7:2–3** *Bethel* was a major shrine to YHWH in the northern kingdom. Worship of YHWH apparently continued there during the exile, including mourning and fasting to mark the destruction of the temple. The delegation wonders whether to continue this, given the restoration of the temple. To *entreat the favor of the LORD* often marks requests of particular gravity and urgency (Deut. 3:23; 1 Kgs. 13:6; 2 Chr. 33:12–13; Ezra 8:23; Jer. 26:19). **7:4–6** Zechariah claims that their fasting has not moved YHWH (cf. Isa. 58:1–9a), perhaps because they were fasting out of the same self-interest seen in feasting. The fast in the seventh month probably mourned the assassination of Gedaliah (Jer. 41:1–3). **7:7** Zechariah claims he is simply repeating the warnings of the former prophets. *The Negeb and the Shephelah* were south and southwest of Jerusalem. Their inhabitation signifies prosperity, prosperity lost when the former prophets were ignored (see 1:4–6).

8 The word of the LORD came to Zechariah, saying: ⁹"Thus says the LORD of hosts: Render true judgments, show kindness and mercy to one another; ¹⁰do not oppress the widow, the orphan, the alien, or the poor; and do not devise evil in your hearts against one another. ¹¹But they refused to listen and turned a stubborn shoulder and stopped their ears in order not to hear. ¹²They made their hearts adamant in order not to hear the law and the words that the LORD of hosts had sent by his spirit through the former prophets. Therefore great wrath came from the LORD of hosts. ¹³Just as, when Iᵇ called, they would not hear, so, when they called, I would not hear, says the LORD of hosts, ¹⁴and I scattered them with a whirlwind among all the nations that they had not known. Thus the land they left was desolate, so that no one went to and fro, and a pleasant land was made desolate."

8 The word of the LORD of hosts came to me, saying: ²"Thus says the LORD of hosts: I am zealous for Zion with great zeal, and I am zealous for her with great wrath. ³Thus says the LORD: I will return to Zion and will dwell in the midst of Jerusalem; Jerusalem shall be called the faithful city, and the mountain of the LORD of hosts shall be called the holy mountain. ⁴Thus says the LORD of hosts: Old men and old women shall again sit in the streets of Jerusalem, each with staff in hand because of their great age. ⁵And the streets of the city shall be full of boys and girls playing in its streets. ⁶Thus says the LORD of hosts: Even though it seems impossible to the remnant of this people in these days, should it also seem impossible to me, says the LORD of hosts? ⁷Thus says the LORD of hosts: I will save my people from the east country and from the west country, ⁸and I will bring them to live in Jerusalem. They shall be my people and I will be their God, in faithfulness and in righteousness."

9 "Thus says the LORD of hosts: Let your hands be strong—you who have recently been hearing these words from the mouths of the prophets who were present when the foundation was laid for the rebuilding of the temple, the house of the LORD of hosts. ¹⁰For before those days there were no wages for people or for animals, nor was there any safety from the foe for those who went out or came in, and I set them all against one another. ¹¹But now I will not deal with the remnant of this people as in the former

b 7.13 Heb *he*

7:8–14 An oracle explaining YHWH's displeasure. The previous oracle hinted at self-interest as a problem in the relationship with YHWH. Here Zechariah expands on this reason in terms reminiscent of the former prophets. **7:8–10** Instructions common in the Torah and the Prophets. For *do not oppress the widow, the orphan, the alien, or the poor*, see Deut. 24:17–22; Isa. 1:17–23; Jer. 7:1–11; Ezek. 22:7; and Mal. 3:5. **7:11–14** As in 1:1–6, the ancestors provide a negative example. YHWH will treat the people as they have treated YHWH. The picture of an utterly uninhabitable land is hyperbolic. The land was indeed inhabited between the destruction of the temple and its rebuilding.

8:1–8 Five brief oracles addressing life in the restored Jerusalem. 8:1–2 YHWH is again *zealous* for his people and wrathful (1:14–15). It is best to assume Israel's oppressors are in view here as in the first vision. See Ezek. 36:5–6 and Nah. 1:2. **8:3** As in 1:16, YHWH promises to dwell in Jerusalem. The holiness of *the mountain of the LORD* is an especially frequent topic in Isaiah (11:9; 27:13; 56:7; 57:13; 65:11, 25; 66:20). **8:3–6** The streets of Jerusalem will again be filled with both the aged and children, an indication of inclusive well-being, extending to young, old, male, and female. YHWH affirms this *impossible* future, despite possible doubts from *the remnant*. Calling them a remnant emphasizes their smallness and lack of power (Isa. 10:21–22) but also frames their very survival and restoration as a gift from YHWH (Isa. 11:10–11). **8:7–8** Having dealt with the north (6:8), YHWH now rescues Jews east and west (cf. Isa. 43:5). *They shall be my people and I will be their God* is a common summary of YHWH's covenant with the people in Jeremiah and Ezekiel (Jer. 24:7; 31:1, 33; 32:38; Ezek. 11:20; 14:11; 37:23, 27). Formulated there as the future, here it is seen as a more immediate reality.

8:9–13 An oracle calling the people to work, featuring a reversal of fortune. 8:9–10 The oracle emphasizes work on restoration, beginning and ending with a call to *let your hands be strong*. The audience, those who have been listening to Haggai and Zechariah (*the prophets*), is reminded of the economic distress (Hag. 1:5–11) caused by YHWH's creation of social conflict. **8:11–13** YHWH will deal with the people who remain (8:6) differently, with special reference to agriculture (even *peace*

days, says the LORD of hosts. ¹²For there shall be a sowing of peace; the vine shall yield its fruit, the ground shall give its produce, and the skies shall give their dew, and I will cause the remnant of this people to possess all these things. ¹³Just as you have been a cursing among the nations, O house of Judah and house of Israel, so I will save you, and you shall be a blessing. Do not be afraid, but let your hands be strong."

14 "For thus says the LORD of hosts: Just as I purposed to bring disaster upon you when your ancestors provoked me to wrath, and I did not relent, says the LORD of hosts, ¹⁵so again I have purposed in these days to do good to Jerusalem and to the house of Judah; do not be afraid. ¹⁶These are the things that you shall do: speak the truth to one another, render in your gates judgments that are true and make for peace, ¹⁷do not devise evil in your hearts against one another, and love no false oath, for all these are things that I hate, says the LORD."

18 The word of the LORD of hosts came to me, saying: ¹⁹"Thus says the LORD of hosts: The fast of the fourth month, and the fast of the fifth, and the fast of the seventh, and the fast of the tenth shall be seasons of joy and gladness and cheerful festivals for the house of Judah; therefore love truth and peace."

20 "Thus says the LORD of hosts: Peoples shall yet come, the inhabitants of many cities; ²¹the inhabitants of one city shall go to another, saying, 'Come, let us go to entreat the favor of the LORD and to seek the LORD of hosts; I myself am going.' ²²Many peoples and strong nations shall come to seek the LORD of hosts in Jerusalem and to entreat the favor of the LORD. ²³Thus says the LORD of hosts: In those days ten men from nations of every language shall take hold of a Jew, grasping his garment and saying, 'Let us go with you, for we have heard that God is with you.'"

9 An Oracle.

The word of the LORD is against the land of Hadrach
    and will rest upon Damascus.
For to the LORD belongs the capital[c] of Aram,[d]
    as do all the tribes of Israel;

c 9.1 Heb *eye*   d 9.1 Cn: Heb *of Adam* (or *of humankind*)

is sown), neatly reversing the distress mentioned by Haggai (Hag. 1:5–11). YHWH also will reverse the way Israel and Judah are perceived: they have been seen by the nations as cursed but will be seen as blessed. **8:13** *Do not be afraid* often begins oracles of salvation, implying that salvation is at hand (see Isa. 41:10, 13, 14; 43:1, 5; 44:2, 8; 54:4).

8:14–17 Another oracle featuring a reversal of fortune. 8:14–15 YHWH relentlessly punished the ancestors (1:2–6) and will now be just as relentless in offering blessing. YHWH says, *Do not be afraid*, so salvation is once more at hand. **8:16–17** Judah and Jerusalem must maintain ethical standards mandated before: truth telling (5:3–4), fair judgments (7:9), and refusing to do evil against a neighbor (7:10).

8:18–19 A final oracle. Fasting reappears from the first unit (7:1–7) of this series, setting off 7:1–8:19 as a distinct section. **8:19** The author adds more fasts, producing a narrative of Jerusalem's destruction: the tenth month (the siege begins), the fourth month (the first attack on the city), the fifth month (the destruction of the temple and fall of the city), and the seventh month (the assassination of Gedaliah). Another reversal: fasts will now become times of good cheer. The three nouns that replace the four fasts—*joy* ("sason"), *gladness* ("simkhah"), and *festivals* ("mo'edim")—are elsewhere associated with feasting (e.g., Exod. 23:15; Lev. 23:4; Num. 9:2–3; Esth. 8:16–17; 9:16–22; Jer. 33:11).

8:20–23 Oracles summarizing restoration. 8:20–22 People from Bethel came to *entreat the favor* of YHWH (7:2). Now that vision expands to include many more peoples. **8:23** This final oracle is even more universal in scope, speaking of *nations of every language*. This phrase describes the supposed universal extent of an empire (Dan. 3:7; 4:1; 5:19; 6:25; 7:14). The ten men grasping a Jew's clothes demonstrate a kind of desperation among non-Jews to be in God's presence (see Isa. 4:1).

9:1–8 YHWH will soon establish authority over other nations in the region. 9:1 *Oracle* ("massa'") serves here and in 12:1 to mark chaps. 9–11 as a distinct block of material, often called Deutero-Zechariah. YHWH begins with *Damascus*, northeast of Israel, the capital of modern Syria. *Hadrach* is otherwise unknown. The Hebrew here may be read as "YHWH has an eye on humanity and on all

2 Hamath also, which borders on it,
  Tyre and Sidon, though they are very
  wise.
3 Tyre has built itself a rampart
  and heaped up silver like dust
  and gold like the dirt of the streets.
4 But now, the Lord will strip it of its
  possessions
  and hurl its wealth into the sea,
  and it shall be devoured by fire.

5 Ashkelon shall see it and be afraid;
  Gaza, too, and shall writhe in
  anguish;
  Ekron also, because its hopes are
  withered.
  The king shall perish from Gaza;
  Ashkelon shall be uninhabited;
6 a mongrel people shall settle in Ashdod,
  and I will make an end of the pride of
  Philistia.
7 I will take away its blood from its
  mouth
  and its abominations from between
  its teeth;
  it, too, shall be a remnant for our God;
  it shall be like a clan in Judah,
  and Ekron shall be like the Jebusites.
8 Then I will encamp at my house as a
  guard,
  so that no one shall march to and fro;
  no oppressor shall again overrun them,
  for now I have seen with my own
  eyes.

9 Rejoice greatly, O daughter Zion!
  Shout aloud, O daughter Jerusalem!
  See, your king comes to you;
  triumphant and victorious is he,
  humble and riding on a donkey,
  on a colt, the foal of a donkey.
10 He*e* will cut off the chariot from
  Ephraim
  and the war horse from Jerusalem;
  and the battle bow shall be cut off,
  and he shall command peace to the
  nations;
  his dominion shall be from sea to sea
  and from the River to the ends of the
  earth.

11 As for you also, because of the blood of
  my covenant with you,
  I will set your prisoners free from the
  waterless pit.
12 Return to your stronghold, O prisoners
  of hope;
  today I declare that I will restore to
  you double.
13 For I have bent Judah as my bow;
  I have made Ephraim its arrow.*f*
  I will arouse your sons, O Zion,
  against your sons, O Greece,
  and wield you like a warrior's sword.

14 Then the Lord will appear over them,
  and his arrow go forth like lightning;

e 9.10 Gk: Heb *I*   *f* 9.13 Meaning of Heb uncertain

the tribes of Israel" (see notes c and d), a fit introduction to chaps. 9–11. **9:2–4** YHWH will proceed from *Hamath* (near Damascus) to the coast of Phoenicia (modern Lebanon). Tyre's destruction may allude to Alexander's siege of 332 BCE, but it probably reflects earlier prophecies (see especially Ezek. 26–28). **9:5–7** YHWH will move south along the coast to Philistine cities. After punishing them, YHWH will remove unclean food (*blood* and *abominations*) from their mouth, implying that they are now clean (cf. 3:4) and will be part of YHWH's rule. The *Jebusites*, earlier Canaanite inhabitants of Jerusalem, had already been incorporated into Israel (Josh. 15:63; Judg. 1:21). **9:8** YHWH *will encamp* (a military image) at the temple, promising vigilant protection (cf. 2:10). On YHWH's *eyes*, see 9:1.

9:9–17 A king will enter Jerusalem and restore the people. 9:9 For *daughter Zion*, see above at 2:10. "Tsaddiq" (*triumphant*) and "nosa'" (*victorious*) may also be rendered as "righteous" and "saved," a better fit with humility. For connections between royal authority and riding a donkey or a mule, see 2 Sam. 13:29; 18:9; 19:26; 1 Kgs. 1:33–44. This text was used later in Matt. 21:5–6 as the basis for the odd image of Jesus entering Jerusalem astride two animals. **9:10** The bounds of the kingdom could include the whole world. Capitalizing *River* suggests a particular river (the Euphrates) is in view, limiting the scope. See Ps. 72:8. **9:11–12** *You* is feminine, thus Zion/Jerusalem. The *blood of my covenant* probably refers to the covenant ceremony in Exod. 24:3–8. The *prisoners* here are exiles who, once freed from the pit, will return to their *stronghold* and will then be *prisoners* in their hoped-for home, Zion. On *double*, see Isa. 61:7. **9:13–16** Judah and Ephraim will serve as YHWH's war implements. Greeks rarely appear in the Hebrew Bible, so the reason for this hostility is uncertain.

the Lord God will sound the trumpet
  and march forth in the whirlwinds of
    the south.
¹⁵ The Lord of hosts will protect them,
  and they shall consume and conquer
    the slingers;ᵍ
they shall drink their bloodʰ like wine
  and be full like a bowl,
  drenched like the corners of the
    altar.

¹⁶ On that day the Lord their God will
    save them,
  for they are the flock of his people,
for like the jewels of a crown
  they shall shine on his land.
¹⁷ For what goodness and beauty are his!
  Grain shall make the young men
    flourish,
  and new wine the young women.

10 Ask rain from the Lord
  in the season of the spring rain,
from the Lord who makes the storm
    clouds,
  who gives showers of rain to you,ⁱ
  the vegetation in the field to
    everyone.
² For the teraphimʲ utter nonsense,
  and the diviners see lies;
the dreamers tell false dreams
  and give empty consolation.
Therefore the peopleᵏ wander like sheep;
  they suffer for lack of a shepherd.

³ My anger is hot against the shepherds,
  and I will punish the leaders,ˡ

for the Lord of hosts cares for his flock,
    the house of Judah,
  and will make them like his proud
    war horse.
⁴ Out of them shall come the
    cornerstone,
  out of them the tent peg,
  out of them the battle bow,
  out of them every commander.
⁵ Together they shall be like warriors in
    battle,
  trampling the foe in the mud of the
    streets;
they shall fight, for the Lord is with them,
  and they shall put to shame the
    riders on horses.

⁶ I will strengthen the house of Judah,
  and I will save the house of Joseph.
I will bring them back because I have
    compassion on them,
  and they shall be as though I had not
    rejected them,
for I am the Lord their God, and I will
    answer them.
⁷ Then the people of Ephraim shall
    become like warriors,
  and their hearts shall be glad as with
    wine.
Their children shall see it and rejoice;
  their hearts shall exult in the Lord.

⁸ I will signal for them and gather them in,
  for I have redeemed them,

g 9.15 Cn: Heb *the slingstones*   h 9.15 Gk: Heb *they roared*
i 10.1 Heb *them*   j 10.2 Or *household gods*   k 10.2 Heb *they*
l 10.3 Or *male goats*

The imagery draws on Divine Warrior traditions (Ps. 18:6–15; Deut. 33:2; Judg. 5:4–5; Hab. 3:3–6). The *trumpet* (shofar) can both announce YHWH's presence (Exod. 19:13–19) and presage military action (Josh. 6:4–20; Judg. 3:27). *Them* in vv. 14–15 refers to the sons of Zion. They are YHWH's sword (v. 13) that will *drink* the *blood* of the enemies and be *drenched* in it (Isa. 34:5–6; Jer. 46:10). **10:1–12 YHWH empowers the people, both Judah and Ephraim (Israel). 10:1–2** Rain at the proper time was essential to agriculture, especially at the rainy season's end (spring) and beginning (autumn, often marked by thunderstorms). *Teraphim* could be used in divination (Judg. 18). *Diviners* are regarded negatively in the Hebrew Bible (1 Sam. 15:23; 2 Kgs. 23:24; but note Hos. 3:4). Dreaming was an approved way of divine communication (Gen. 41:25; Dan. 1:17), but here the results are false (Deut. 13:1–5; Jer. 23:32). The people, like a wandering flock, have lacked proper leadership. **10:3–5** The scene shifts, with YHWH attacking *shepherds* and *leaders* (literally "he-goats"; see Isa. 14:9; Jer. 50:8; Ezek. 34:17), likely a reference to poor local leadership. YHWH's service as Judah's shepherd implies that the wandering sheep represent the northern tribes, Israel. *Cares for* ("paqad") could be rendered as "muster": YHWH of Hosts calls forth Judah as an army. In any case, Judah will be marked by strong leadership, described metaphorically. **10:6–7** Strengthening Judah saves Israel. Unlike in the past when Israel did not seek YHWH correctly (10:2), YHWH will now answer them. Like Judah, they will become warriors. **10:8** The signal, either whistling or hissing, continues

and they shall be as numerous as
   they were before.
⁹ Though I scattered them among the
   nations,
   yet in far countries they shall
      remember me,
   and they shall rear their children and
      return.
¹⁰ I will bring them home from the land of
      Egypt
   and gather them from Assyria;
I will bring them to the land of Gilead
      and to Lebanon,
   until there is no room for them.
¹¹ They*m* shall pass through the sea of
      distress,
   and the waves of the sea shall be
      struck down,
   and all the depths of the Nile dried up.
The pride of Assyria shall be laid low,
   and the scepter of Egypt shall depart.
¹² I will make them strong in the LORD,
   and they shall walk in his name,
                              says the LORD.

11

Open your doors, O Lebanon,
   so that fire may devour your cedars!
² Wail, O cypress, for the cedar has fallen,
   for the glorious trees are ruined!

Wail, oaks of Bashan,
   for the thick forest has been felled!
³ Listen, the wail of the shepherds,
   for their glory is despoiled!
Listen, the roar of the lions,
   for the thickets of the Jordan are
      destroyed!

4 "Thus says the LORD my God: Be a
shepherd of the flock doomed to slaughter. ⁵Those who buy them kill them and go
unpunished, and those who sell them say,
'Blessed be the LORD, for I have become
rich,' and their own shepherds have no pity
on them. ⁶For I will no longer have pity on
the inhabitants of the earth, says the LORD. I
will cause them, every one, to fall each into
the hand of a neighbor and each into the
hand of the king, and they shall devastate
the earth, and I will deliver no one from
their hand."

7 So on behalf of the sheep merchants,*n* I
became the shepherd of the flock doomed
to slaughter. I took two staffs; one I named
Favor, the other I named Unity, and I tended
the sheep. ⁸In one month I disposed of the
three shepherds, for I had become impatient with them, and they also detested me.

m 10.11 Gk: Heb *He*   *n* 11.7 Gk: Meaning of Heb uncertain

the flock imagery (Judg. 5:16). **10:9–10** The Assyrians had relocated the northern tribes among various ethnic groups throughout the empire. That area is extended to include even the *far countries*.
Judeans were treated differently by the Babylonians, who settled them in distinct communities.
Israelites lived in Egypt as emigrants, not exiles (e.g., the Jewish colony at Elephantine). The author
imagines a universal return of all Israel, from Egypt to the south and west and Assyria to the north
and east. Their large numbers will necessitate their living beyond the typical bounds of the land,
completely filling *Lebanon* (the interior of present-day Lebanon) and *Gilead* (a part of present-day
Jordan). **10:11–12** Seas and rivers being subjugated indicates the return of the northern tribes would
be like the exodus from Egypt (Exod. 14:21–29), the entry into the land (Josh. 4:19–24), and, perhaps,
a new creation (Gen. 1:1–10; Ps. 74:12–17).

   11:1–3 A change in tone. This unit shifts away from the hopeful tone of the previous two chapters:
the trees themselves wail a lament. *Bashan* was northwest of the Sea of Galilee, while the *thickets of
the Jordan* refer to the junglelike area along the Jordan River. This oracle suggests massive changes
coming with the end of the age, especially to nature, but offers no clear evaluation of them.

   11:4–17 The story of the shepherd. This unit, in prose, ends the poetry that began with chap. 9.
Its interpretation is notoriously uncertain. **11:4–5** YHWH assigns the prophet a hopeless task (cf.
prophetic futility in Isa. 6:9–13). The three groups involved may represent the powerful in Judean
society who fail to use their power for the flock. **11:6** YHWH, like the unconcerned shepherds, will
have no pity for the flock. *The inhabitants of the earth* implies a universal judgment. Left to their own
devices, they will oppress one another, destroying the earth. **11:7** The *sheep merchants* are the pro-
spective buyers and sellers of the doomed flock. The prophet will shepherd the flock with two symbolically named staffs, beginning a symbolic prophetic action (cf. Ezek. 37:15–23). *Favor* ("no'am")
could refer to a pleasant state of being (note the connection with the name Naomi ["no'omi"] in
Ruth 1:20). *Unity* ("hobelim"), actually the Hebrew word for "bonds," describes a state of being
bound together. **11:8** A baffling account. The conflict may reflect actual events, though identifying

9 So I said, "I will not be your shepherd. What
is to die, let it die; what is to be destroyed,
let it be destroyed; and let those that are left
devour the flesh of one another!" 10 I took
my staff Favor and broke it, annulling the
covenant that I had made with all the peoples. 11 So it was annulled on that day, and
the sheep merchants[o] who were watching
me knew that it was the word of the LORD.
12 I then said to them, "If it seems right to you,
give me my wages, but if not, keep them." So
they weighed out as my wages thirty shekels
of silver. 13 Then the LORD said to me, "Throw
it into the treasury"[p]—this lordly price at
which I was valued by them. So I took the
thirty shekels of silver and threw them into
the treasury[q] in the house of the LORD. 14 Then
I broke my second staff Unity, annulling the
family ties between Judah and Israel.

15 Then the LORD said to me: "Take once
more the implements of a worthless shepherd. 16 For I am now raising up in the land
a shepherd who does not care for the perishing, or seek the wandering,[r] or heal the
maimed, or nourish the healthy,[s] but devours the flesh of the fat ones, tearing off
even their hoofs.

17 Oh, my worthless shepherd,
    who deserts the flock!
May the sword strike his arm
    and his right eye!
Let his arm be completely withered,
    his right eye utterly blinded!"

12 An Oracle.
The word of the LORD concerning Israel:
Thus says the LORD, who stretched out the
heavens and founded the earth and formed
the human spirit within: 2 See, I am about
to make Jerusalem a cup of reeling for all
the surrounding peoples; it will be against
Judah also in the siege against Jerusalem.
3 On that day I will make Jerusalem a heavy
stone for all the peoples; all who lift it shall
grievously hurt themselves. And all the
nations of the earth shall come together
against it. 4 On that day, says the LORD, I will
strike every horse with panic and its rider
with madness. But on the house of Judah I

o 11.11 Gk: Meaning of Heb uncertain *p* 11.13 Syr: Heb *it to the potter* *q* 11.13 Syr: Heb *it to the potter* *r* 11.16 Syr Compare Gk Vg: Heb *the youth* *s* 11.16 Meaning of Heb uncertain

the players is mere guesswork. Reading it symbolically hardly clarifies matters. **11:9** The prophet resigns his symbolic commission. Like YHWH in v. 6, he abandons the flock to its fate, though the mention of cannibalism makes the scene more graphic (cf. Mic. 3:1–3). **11:10** The breaking of *Favor* symbolizes YHWH's annulment of the covenant. The *covenant that I had made with all the peoples* probably refers to the Noahic covenant (Gen. 9:8–17). YHWH had promised never to destroy people again, but now he will allow humans to destroy themselves. **11:11–13** It is not clear whether *thirty shekels of silver* are a fair wage or a calculated insult. If the latter, then the mention of a *lordly price* would be sarcastic. This passage informs accounts of Judas in the Gospels (see especially Matt. 27:3–10, where it is ascribed incorrectly to Jeremiah). **11:14** The prophet symbolically breaks *the family ties between Judah and Israel*. The sense here is still covenantal. The ties between Judah and Israel are both ethnic (the covenant with Abraham; Gen. 15:18–21; 17:19–21) and political (the covenant with David as ruler of both kingdoms; Ps. 89:3–4). **11:15–16** A new prophetic action. The precise *implements* are not stated, but they are part of the prophet's impersonation of a *worthless* or "foolish" ("'evili") shepherd. As a fool, the shepherd would reject wisdom (Prov. 1:7) and lack morals (Ps. 107:17). The prophet's performance indicates the advent of an incompetent, neglectful leader. He will greedily devour (raw?) animals down to the hooves, an alarming image of abusive power (cf. Ezek. 34:1–10). **11:17** The word translated as *oh* ("hoi") often means "woe," suggesting this verse is a woe oracle that concludes the impersonation of the worthless ("'elil") shepherd. It includes a curse that mandates a violent end to abusive leadership.

12:1–13:1 Seven oracles. They promise victory for Judah and Jerusalem *on that day*, the Day of YHWH. See **"The Day of the Lord," p. 1322**. **12:1** As in 9:1, *oracle* ("massa'") begins a distinct section, chaps. 12–14, often called Trito-Zechariah. The prophet poetically notes YHWH's power as creator (cf. Gen. 2:7). **12:2** YHWH announces war between Judah/Jerusalem and the other nations. The *cup of reeling* makes the nations drunk (Isa. 51:17, 22; Jer. 25:15–29; Obad. 16; Hab. 2:16). It is unclear whether Judah will be with or against Jerusalem. **12:3 Oracle 1.** The nations will not injure themselves because of the stone's weight but will cut themselves on it. **12:4–5 Oracle 2.** YHWH fights for the people by disrupting their enemies. The *clans of Judah* ("'allupe," perhaps leaders)

Focus On: The Day of the Lord (Zechariah 12:1–13:1)

In Israel's prophetic tradition, the Day of YHWH was a coming day of YHWH's decisive intervention in the life of Israel. This intervention could favor Israel or harm Israel. It could be described in limited, more realistic terms (a military invasion) or in more expansive terms (a cosmic catastrophe). This tradition develops imagery that will inform apocalyptic thought, which features an imminent end of the present age (see **"Apocalypse," p. 1216**).

The Day of YHWH tradition probably began in oracles against other nations. In these oracles, prophets proclaimed disaster for nations such as Egypt (Isa. 19:16), Moab (Jer. 48:22), and Babylon (Jer. 50:27–31). YHWH would come forth as a warrior to defeat the enemy and vindicate the people. Eventually, prophets applied this imagery to all nations, as in Zeph. 1:2: "I will utterly sweep away everything from the face of the earth, says the Lord." Prophets also turned the Day of YHWH against Israel and Judah, reading YHWH's day of intervention as bringing woe, not delight, as in Amos's famous reversal: "Woe to you who desire the day of the Lord! Why do you want the day of the Lord? . . . Is not the day of the Lord darkness, not light, and gloom with no brightness in it?" (Amos 5:18, 20).

This use of the Day of YHWH is common in prophetic literature, and as in the "day of deliverance" model above, it develops into a time of cosmic judgment against the people. Thus Joel's picture of a punishing locust plague develops from a description of a plague (Joel 1:4–7) into YHWH leading a massive locust army on the Day of YHWH: "The Lord utters his voice at the head of his army; how vast is his host! Numberless are those who obey his command. Truly the day of the Lord is great, terrible indeed—who can endure it?" (Joel 2:11).

Elements of this tradition appear in Zechariah. For example, Zech. 12:1–9 deploys the language in Judah's favor, with YHWH throwing all enemies into a panic. But in chap. 14, we find a searing image of cosmic defeat for Jerusalem (14:1–2) followed by YHWH fighting for Jerusalem, enacting cosmic revenge against all other nations (14:3, 12–15). This leads to the nations participating in the Feast of Booths (14:16–19). So here the author presents a variety of possible meanings of the Day of YHWH.

Donald C. Polaski

will keep a watchful eye, when I strike every horse of the peoples with blindness. ⁵Then the clans of Judah shall say to themselves, "The inhabitants of Jerusalem have strength through the Lord of hosts, their God."

6 On that day I will make the clans of Judah like a blazing pot on a pile of wood, like a flaming torch among sheaves, and they shall devour to the right and to the left all the surrounding peoples, while Jerusalem shall again be inhabited in its place, in Jerusalem.

7 And the Lord will save the tents of Judah first, that the glory of the house of David and the glory of the inhabitants of Jerusalem may not be exalted over that of Judah. ⁸On that day the Lord will shield the inhabitants of Jerusalem so that the feeblest among them on that day shall be like David, and the house of David shall be like God, like the angel of the Lord, at their head. ⁹And on that day I will seek to destroy all the nations that come against Jerusalem.

10 And I will pour out a spirit of compassion and supplication on the house of David and the inhabitants of Jerusalem so that, when they look on the one^t whom they

t 12.10 Heb on me

recognize YHWH's empowerment of Jerusalem. **12:6–7 Oracle 3.** Not a pot on a fire, but more likely a pot of hot coals in a thicket of trees, having the same effect as a torch among sheaves (cf. Judg. 15:4–5). Judah's leaders will be a flaming, destructive force. The author's concern for equality of glory appears to be rooted in the sociopolitical realities of his time, but little can be said beyond that. **12:8 Oracle 4.** On the day of battle, even the weakest warrior will be a David, while the house of David itself will be in some sense divine. The second claim is not new (Pss. 2:6–8; 110:1–3). The first suggests that all Jerusalemites (even the weakest) will relate to YHWH as the house of David has done in the past, redistributing the Davidic covenant (see Isa. 55:3). **12:9–10 Oracle 5.** YHWH will *seek to destroy* all the enemies of Jerusalem, reiterating the preceding verses. The rest is obscure. It may refer to an unknown historical conflict resulting in the stabbing of a leader. The Hebrew briefly shifts to the first person, reading "on me whom they have pierced" (see note t), suggesting that YHWH is the one stabbed, an unclear metaphor. Whatever the precise sense, YHWH

have pierced, they shall mourn for him as one mourns for an only child and weep bitterly over him as one weeps over a firstborn. [11]On that day the mourning in Jerusalem will be as great as the mourning for Hadad-rimmon in the plain of Megiddo. [12]The land shall mourn, each family by itself; the family of the house of David by itself and their wives by themselves; the family of the house of Nathan by itself and their wives by themselves; [13]the family of the house of Levi by itself and their wives by themselves; the family of the Shimeites by itself and their wives by themselves; [14]and all the families that are left, each by itself and their wives by themselves.

13

On that day a fountain shall be opened for the house of David and the inhabitants of Jerusalem, to cleanse them from sin and impurity.

2 On that day, says the LORD of hosts, I will cut off the names of the idols from the land, so that they shall be remembered no more, and also I will remove from the land the prophets and the unclean spirit. [3]And if any prophets appear again, their fathers and mothers who bore them will say to them, "You shall not live, for you speak lies in the name of the LORD," and their fathers and their mothers who bore them shall pierce them through when they prophesy. [4]On that day the prophets will be ashamed, every one, of their visions when they prophesy; they will not put on a hairy mantle in order to deceive, [5]but each of them will say, "I am no prophet; I am a tiller of the soil, for the land has been my possession[u] since my youth." [6]And if anyone asks them, "What are these wounds on your chest?"[v] the answer will be "The wounds I received in the house of my friends."

[7] "Awake, O sword, against my shepherd,
    against the man who is my
        associate,"
                    says the LORD of hosts.
 "Strike the shepherd, that the sheep
        may be scattered;
  I will turn my hand against the little
        ones.
[8] In the whole land, says the LORD,
        two-thirds shall be cut off and perish,
        and one-third shall be left alive.
[9] And I will put this third into the fire,
        refine them as one refines silver,
        and test them as gold is tested.

u 13.5 Cn: Heb *for humankind has caused me to possess*
v 13.6 Heb *wounds between your hands*

will give the leaders of Jerusalem the ability to have compassion on someone they have wounded (killed?), mourning him in the most extreme terms. Deaths of firstborn or only children were especially grievous (e.g., Exod. 12:29–32; Judg. 11:34–40). The text does not suggest the one pierced is a martyr or messianic figure, but later readers make that connection (John 19:37; b. Sukkah 52a). **12:11–14 Oracle 6.** *Hadad-rimmon* is perhaps a Semitic dying-and-rising deity, suggesting annual mourning rituals, while *the plain of Megiddo* may allude to such rituals for Josiah (2 Chr. 35:20–25). Women held special roles in mourning (2 Chr. 35:25; Jer. 9:17–26; Ezek. 32:16). *Nathan* could refer to David's prophet (2 Sam. 7:2–3) or David's son (2 Sam. 5:14), *Levi* to the ancestor of cultic functionaries (Exod. 32:26–28), and Shimei to an ancestor of a priestly clan (Num. 3:14–22). **13:1 Oracle 7.** The *fountain* refers to water at the temple that cleanses moral and ritual fault (Lev. 15; Num. 8:5–7; 19:10b–13) and the cosmic waters of life present in Jerusalem (Ezek. 47:1–12; Joel 3:18; Zech. 14:8).

13:2–6 A prose oracle against religious practices in Judah. 13:2 *Names of the idols* are gods worshiped via idolatry. The *prophets* could be associated with other gods, but the author appears to attack prophetic practice in general as false (cf. 1 Kgs. 22:21–23). **13:3** The parents, not YHWH, will exterminate falsehood. Compare the child who suggests worshiping other gods (Deut. 13:6–11) or who is rebellious (Deut. 21:18–21). *Pierce them through* suggests a connection of the conflict in 12:6 with prophecy. **13:4–6** *On that day* prophets will vanish due to social stigmatization (shame). Visions deceive, in contrast to chaps. 1–8. The *mantle* alludes to Elijah and Elisha (1 Kgs. 19:13, 19; 2 Kgs. 2:8–15), while *I am no prophet* quotes Amos (Amos 7:14). The prophet has wounds, perhaps the result of self-flagellation (1 Kgs. 18:28), but would rather people think he was beaten by his friends or lovers.

13:7–9 A poetic oracle announcing judgment. The *shepherd*, a leader, is on intimate terms with YHWH but fails. The people are *scattered*, a familiar theme (Deut. 4:27; 28:64; Jer. 9:16; 13:24; Ezek. 11:16–17; Neh. 1:8). For YHWH's testing as metallurgical, see Jer. 6:29 and Isa. 1:25. Psalm 66:10–11, Isa. 48:10, and Job 23:10 associate fire with suffering. The purified will have a covenant with YHWH (Exod. 6:7; Hos. 2:23; and note Zech. 10:6).

Going Deeper: The End of Prophecy (Zechariah 13:4–6)

The book of Zechariah presents contradictory evaluations of prophecy. It extols the "former prophets" as exemplars ignored by the people at their peril (1:4–6; 7:7, 12). It assigns Zechariah the role of prophet (1:4; 8:9), a role that appears honorable. But in 13:1–5, we learn that YHWH will remove prophets from the land, the parents of prophets will be glad to kill them, and the prophets will be ashamed of their role. Basically, the prophets are a bunch of liars.

Why the change? What we can see here is the erosion of prophecy as a social phenomenon. Prophecy can only exist where people believe it to be valid. We can already see in Zech. 1–8 that the author is working on the issue of authority. Zechariah emphasizes YHWH's spirit as the driving force in human affairs: "This is the word of the LORD to Zerubbabel: Not by might, nor by power, but by my spirit, says the LORD of hosts" (4:6).

This same spirit inspired the former prophets as well as Zechariah (7:12). The mention of the "former prophets," unique to Zechariah, is also a claim of authority. Zechariah claims continuity with them, demanding his audience attend to his message, lest they suffer the same fate as previous generations: "Thus says the LORD of hosts: Return to me, says the LORD of hosts, and I will return to you, says the LORD of hosts. Do not be like your ancestors, to whom the former prophets proclaimed, 'Thus says the LORD of hosts: Return from your evil ways and from your evil deeds.' But they did not hear or heed me, says the LORD" (Zech. 1:3–4). Zechariah also claims continuity with the prophetic tradition of visions and dreams, seen, for example, in Isa. 6 and Ezek. 1. Amos provides a parallel: his visions are interpreted by YHWH (Amos 7:1–9; 8:1–3). Zechariah apparently needed to buttress his authority in the face of skepticism.

That skepticism appears to have grown much stronger by the time Zech. 13 was written. Granted, the author of this passage could also claim authority. Jeremiah was famous for accusing prophets of lacking authority, lying, and not following God's spirit (23:16–17, 21–32). For whatever reasons, prophecy was losing the social prerequisites it needed to survive. The book of Zechariah may be the final text written in a continuous tradition of Israelite prophecy.

Donald C. Polaski

They will call on my name,
    and I will answer them.
I will say, 'They are my people,'
    and they will say, 'The LORD is our
      God.'"

14 See, a day is coming for the LORD, when the plunder taken from you will be divided in your midst. ²For I will gather all the nations against Jerusalem to battle, and the city shall be taken and the houses plundered and the women raped; half the city shall go into exile, but the rest of the people shall not be cut off from the city. ³Then the LORD will go forth and fight against those nations as when he fights on a day of battle. ⁴On that day his feet shall stand on the Mount of Olives, which lies before Jerusalem on the east, and the Mount of Olives shall be split in two from east to west by a very wide valley, so that one half of the mount shall withdraw northward and the other half southward. ⁵And you shall flee by the valley of the LORD's mountain,ʷ for the valley between the mountains shall reach to Azal,ˣ and you shall flee as you fled from the earthquake in the days of King Uzziah of Judah. Then the LORD my God will come and all the holy ones with him.

6 On that day there shall not beʸ either cold or frost.ᶻ ⁷And there shall be continuous

w 14.5 Heb *my mountains*   x 14.5 Meaning of Heb uncertain
y 14.6 Cn: Heb *there shall not be light*   z 14.6 Compare Gk
Syr Vg Tg: Meaning of Heb uncertain

14:1–21 The Day of YHWH in Jerusalem. This section often evades understanding. **14:1–3** *A day is coming* implies it is coming very soon (Joel 1:15), heightening the sense of urgency. YHWH *will gather all the nations*, a Day of YHWH motif (Joel 3:2; Zeph. 3:8; Matt. 25:32), but here resulting not in their judgment but in Jerusalem's fall and the exile of half its population. **14:4–5** *The Mount of Olives*, east of Jerusalem, runs north to south and was divided from the temple by a deep valley (see map: *Jerusalem from the Time of David to the Maccabees*). YHWH will create an escape route by splitting the mountain in two. *Azal's* location is unknown. The *holy ones* are the Divine Council (Deut. 33:2–3; Ps. 89:5–7). **14:6–9** YHWH will eliminate severe cold and the possibility of drought, removing the risks of agriculture and suggesting paradise (Gen. 2:10–14; Ezek. 47:1–12; Joel 3:18). Constant light on the Day of YHWH reverses claims that the day would bring darkness (Joel 2:1–2;

day (it is known to the LORD), not day and not night, for at evening time there shall be light.

8 On that day living water shall flow out from Jerusalem, half of it to the eastern sea and half of it to the western sea; it shall continue in summer as in winter.

9 And the LORD will become king over all the earth; on that day the LORD will be one and his name one.

10 The whole land shall be turned into a plain from Geba to Rimmon south of Jerusalem. But Jerusalem*a* shall remain aloft on its site from the Gate of Benjamin to the place of the former gate, to the Corner Gate, and from the Tower of Hananel to the king's winepresses. [11]And it shall be inhabited, for never again shall it be doomed to destruction; Jerusalem shall abide in security.

12 This shall be the plague with which the LORD will strike all the peoples who wage war against Jerusalem: their flesh shall rot while they are still on their feet, their eyes shall rot in their sockets, and their tongues shall rot in their mouths. [13]On that day a great panic from the LORD shall fall on them, so that each will seize the hand of a neighbor, and the hand of the one will be raised against the hand of the other; [14]even Judah will fight at Jerusalem. And the wealth of all the surrounding nations shall be collected: gold, silver, and garments in great abundance. [15]And a plague like this plague shall fall on the horses, the mules, the camels, the donkeys, and whatever animals may be in those camps.

16 Then all who survive of the nations that have come against Jerusalem shall go up year after year to worship the King, the LORD of hosts, and to keep the Festival of Booths.*b* [17]If any of the families of the earth do not go up to Jerusalem to worship the King, the LORD of hosts, there will be no rain upon them. [18]And if the family of Egypt do not go up and present themselves, there will be no rain for them; there will be the plague that the LORD inflicts on the nations that do not go up to keep the Festival of Booths.*c* [19]Such shall be the punishment of Egypt and the punishment of all the nations that do not go up to keep the Festival of Booths.*d*

20 On that day there shall be inscribed on the bells of the horses, "Holy to the LORD." And the cooking pots in the house of the LORD shall be as holy as*e* the bowls in front of the altar, [21]and every cooking pot in Jerusalem and Judah shall be holy to the LORD of hosts, so that all who sacrifice may come and use them to boil the flesh of the sacrifice. And there shall no longer be traders*f* in the house of the LORD of hosts on that day.

a 14.10 Heb *it*   *b* 14.16 Or *Tabernacles*   *c* 14.18 Or *Tabernacles*   *d* 14.19 Or *Tabernacles*   *e* 14.20 Heb *shall be like*   *f* 14.21 Or *Canaanites*

Zeph. 1:14–18; Amos 5:18), while YHWH's claim to rule redirects hopes for Davidic rule expressed earlier (3:8; 4:8–10; 9:9–10). **14:10–11** *Geba* and *Rimmon* are probably villages located respectively north and south of Jerusalem. Identification of the various towers and gates of Jerusalem remains speculative. See map: *Jerusalem from the Time of David to the Maccabees.* The area around Jerusalem will sink down and become a plain, while the city itself will be elevated (Ps. 48:2; Isa. 2:2; Mic. 4:1). The city's security and inhabitation are now certain, reversing 14:1–2. **14:12–15** YHWH conquers not in battle but through *plague* (Exod. 7–11; 2 Kgs. 19:35–36) and *panic* (Exod. 14:24; Josh. 10:10; Judg. 4:15). Earlier imagery (11:6; 12:4) used against the people now applies to enemies. For acquiring the wealth of other nations, see Isa. 60:5–16; 61:6; 66:12. **14:16–19** The remnant of the nations will come to Jerusalem for pilgrimage, not battle, reversing the concern with the remnant of Israel (8:6, 11–12; 13:8; 14:2). The *Festival of Booths* (Sukkot) began as a fall harvest festival, later becoming associated with Israel's wilderness wanderings. The feast was also linked to the dedication of the temple (1 Kgs. 8:2) and public reading of the Torah (Neh. 7:73b–8:1). Its connection to YHWH's rule as king, a major emphasis here, remains unclear. The threat of drought is the enforcement mechanism (Deut. 28:22; Amos 4:7; Hag. 1:9–11). Egypt is an exemplary transgressor, perhaps because of the traditions of the plagues and the hardening of Pharaoh's heart. **14:20–21** The temple's holiness will expand. Horse gear will be inscribed like the turban of the high priest (Exod. 28:36). The pots used in the temple precincts will have their holiness made equal to that of the basins used at the altar itself, while household pots will also be holy to YHWH. The holiness of the temple forecloses economic activity. *Traders* ("kena'ani") suggests the ethnic term "Canaanites."

MALACHI

Authorship, Date, and Literary History

The book of Malachi is the last of the twelve minor prophets (or, in Jewish tradition, the Book of the Twelve) and thus serves also as the final book of the Old Testament for Christians. The word *mal'akhi* means "my messenger" in Hebrew, and this fact, combined with the general use of the term "messenger" (Heb. *mal'akh*) elsewhere in the book (2:7; 3:1), as well as the lack of information regarding a personage named Malachi from the relevant time period, has led to speculation that it is a pseudonym. Indeed, this may have been the interpretation of the ancient Greek translators of the Septuagint (an early translation of the Hebrew Bible), who rendered the word *mal'akhi* in 1:1 as "*his* messenger" (Gk. *angelou autou*). Another tradition of Jewish Aramaic translation identifies the figure as Ezra the scribe. But it is just as plausible that Malachi was, in fact, the name of the prophet (perhaps representing a slightly shortened form of a longer name Mal'akhyahu—i.e., "messenger of YHWH").

While there are no explicit indications of a date in the book, the references to a functioning sacrificial cult suggest a time after 515 BCE, the date given to the completion of the Second Temple based on Ezra 6:15. Given that much of Malachi's critique of the temple cult seems to presuppose an overall attitude of complacency, scholars have tended to favor a date for the book closer to 450 BCE—that is, at some remove from the initial rebuilding and restoration of temple practices. But plausible arguments can be offered for a date of composition at any time in the fifth century BCE. The use of the term "governor" (Heb. *pekhah*) in 1:8, being a foreign loanword from Akkadian, is further evidence of the book's origins in the Persian period.

Interpreters have noted a close connection between Malachi and the preceding books of Haggai and Zechariah on both historical and thematic grounds. Since Malachi evinces a fairly consistent style throughout, scholars have tended not to posit overly complex accounts of composition for the book, though there is general agreement that one or more passages in the conclusion (4:4–6; perhaps also 4:1–3) represent later insertions by a different author or authors. In fact, Mal. 4:4–6 offers a rather fitting conclusion not only to Malachi but to the entire Book of the Twelve.

Reading Guide

The book of Malachi is often understood as consisting of six major speeches (1:2–5; 1:6–2:9; 2:10–16; 2:17–3:5; 3:6–12; 3:13–4:3) plus a conclusion (4:4–6) that mentions both Moses and Elijah and has an eschatological orientation. A regular pattern in the speeches is that of an initial statement (e.g., "'I have loved you,' says the LORD" [1:2]), followed by a question (e.g., "But you say, 'How have you loved us?'" [1:2]), then a prophetic response (e.g., "'Is not Esau Jacob's brother?' says the LORD. 'Yet I have loved Jacob, but I have hated Esau'" [1:2–3]). However, there are slight variations of this pattern throughout the book. This overall structure contributes to the book's distinctive dialogical character. Scholars who emphasize the content of the prophetic responses would describe the book as "hortatory"—that is, having the nature of an exhortation or encouragement. Others would describe the book as disputational in order to highlight the framing of the content as a debate between the prophet and the people: the questions of the interlocutors, in particular, are presented in an implicit tone of disagreement or protest, lending urgency to the prophet's responses.

In terms of the message, the book confronts the faithlessness and corruption of the people of the time, with a special emphasis on matters relating to the institution of the temple, from improper sacrifices to the giving of tithes. This would be especially pertinent if Mal. 2:10–16 (the third speech of the book) is taken to be an extended metaphor for the practice of idolatry, though it is also possible that the language is literal and is in fact speaking against foreign intermarriage (see **"Intermarriage," p. 649**). Throughout the book, the prophet observes that the people's behavior arises out of a failure to recognize the true character of the Lord as deserving of respect (1:6), a great King (1:14), the father and creator of all (2:10), unchanging (3:6), and capable of granting abundant blessing (3:10). Moreover, the prophetic voice of the book consciously situates itself in a certain time period in the history of the nation, frequently appealing to events and promises of the past (e.g., 1:2–3; 2:4, 10; 3:6–7) while also evincing a concern with future judgment (3:1–5; 3:16–4:6).

Joseph Lam

1 An oracle. The word of the Lord to Israel by Malachi.[a]

2 "I have loved you," says the Lord. But you say, "How have you loved us?" "Is not Esau Jacob's brother?" says the Lord. "Yet I have loved Jacob, [3]but I have hated Esau; I have made his hill country a desolation and his heritage a desert for jackals. [4]If Edom says, 'We are shattered but we will rebuild the ruins,' the Lord of hosts says: They may build, but I will tear down, until they are called the wicked country, the people with whom the Lord is angry forever. [5]Your own eyes shall see this, and you shall say, 'Great is the Lord beyond the borders of Israel!'"

6 A son honors his father and a servant his master. If then I am a father, where is the honor due me? And if I am a master, where is the respect due me? says the Lord of hosts to you, O priests, who despise my name. You say, "How have we despised your name?" [7]By offering polluted food on my altar. And you say, "How have we polluted it?"[b] By thinking that the Lord's table may be despised. [8]When you offer blind animals in sacrifice, is that not wrong? And when you offer those that are lame or sick, is that not wrong? Try presenting that to your governor; will he be pleased with you or show you favor? says the Lord of hosts. [9]And now implore the favor of God, that he may be gracious to us. The fault is yours. Will he show favor to any of you? says the Lord of hosts. [10]Oh, that someone among you would shut the temple[c] doors, so that you would not kindle fire on my altar in vain! I have no pleasure in you, says the Lord of hosts, and I will not accept an offering from your hands. [11]For from the rising of the sun to its setting my name is great among the nations, and in every place incense is offered to my name and a pure offering, for my name is great among the nations, says the Lord of hosts. [12]But you profane it when you say that the Lord's table is polluted and its food[d] may be despised. [13]"What a weariness this is," you say, and you sniff at it,[e] says the Lord of hosts. You bring what has been taken by violence or is lame or sick, and this you bring as your offering! Shall I accept that from your hand? says the Lord. [14]Cursed be the cheat who has a male in the flock and vows to give it and yet sacrifices to

a 1.1 Or *by my messenger*   *b* 1.7 Gk: Heb *you*   *c* 1.10 Heb lacks *temple*   *d* 1.12 Cn: Heb *its fruit, its food*   *e* 1.13 Or *at me*

1:1 *An oracle.* The Hebrew word "massa'" is sometimes translated as "burden" and is a relatively common designation for a prophetic pronouncement. The particular combination of titles here (*An oracle. The word of the Lord*), however, appears elsewhere only in Zech. 9:1 and 12:1.

1:2–5 Speech 1: The Lord's covenantal love for Israel. The terms "love" and "hate" should be understood as covenantal language, with "love" denoting the favor displayed by a suzerain king toward a vassal. In the ancient Near East, kings of individual cities (i.e., vassals) would regularly enter into political arrangements with a more powerful king (the suzerain) who would provide protection for the vassal in exchange for the vassal's loyalty and regular gifts (tribute). In light of this concept, the message here is that though both Israel and Edom have experienced destruction, it is the Lord's exclusive covenant with Jacob/Israel that provides the basis for a hope of restoration. See **"Covenant (Genesis)," p. 23**. **1:3** The mention of the desolation of Edom, personified as Esau (Gen. 36:1), probably alludes to the takeover of Edomite territory by the Nabateans following the Babylonian exile of Judah (see Obad. 1–21).

1:6–2:9 Speech 2: The failure of the priests. 1:6 The proper attitude of a son toward a father and a servant toward a master provides comprehensible analogies for the respect that one should give to the Lord. **1:8** *When you offer blind animals in sacrifice.* In Leviticus, it is explicitly stated that any animal offered for sacrifice is to be without blemish (Lev. 22:17–25), based on the principle that it is, at some level, understood to be a food-gift to the Lord (e.g., Lev. 3:11; see also 1:12 below). Thus, to offer animals that are blind, lame, or sick goes against both the letter and the spirit of the sacrificial laws. Note that while it is strictly speaking the task of the offerer and not the priest to perform the slaughter of the animal (e.g., Lev. 1:3–5), the extent of the corruption here described could not have taken place without the priests allowing it. See **"Offerings and Sacrifices," p. 146**. **1:12–13** While one might want to read *the Lord's table* and *its food* as referring to the table containing the bread of the presence (Exod. 25:23–30), the exclusive focus on animal offerings in the present context suggests instead that it is the priests' share in the temple sacrifices that are in view (e.g., Lev. 6:14–18; 7:29–36) and that the altar is being likened to a table for divine food. Not only do the priests permit defective sacrifices, but they disdain the portions that they receive from them. **1:14** The withholding of a *male in the flock* (that is presumably unblemished) while offering *what is blemished* reveals the hypocritical and self-interested attitude of the people

Focus On: Second Temple (Malachi 1)

The term "Second Temple" refers to the temple that was rebuilt in Jerusalem following the return of Jews from exile in the sixth century BCE. According to the biblical description (1 Kgs. 6:1; 2 Chr. 3:1–2), Solomon built the First Temple, which stood until its destruction by the Babylonians in 586 BCE (2 Kgs. 25:8–16; 2 Chr. 36:17–19). Some decades later, Cyrus, the Persian king who overthrew the Babylonians, issued a decree allowing the return of exiles to Jerusalem for the purposes of rebuilding a temple to YHWH (2 Chr. 36:22–23; Ezra 1:1–4), the process of which is narrated in Ezra 1–6. The date of completion of the Second Temple is recorded as "the third day of the month of Adar, in the sixth year of the reign of King Darius" (Ezra 6:15), which corresponds to 515 BCE. Scholars generally understand this first iteration of the rebuilt temple to have been relatively modest in size and appearance (Hag. 2:2–3).

Although the sacrificial laws in Leviticus are, strictly speaking, a description of what took place in the wilderness tabernacle, they are often understood as reflecting the rites of either the First or the Second Temple (or both). The other literary sources we possess from the period of the Second Temple confirm its role as the location of the sacrificial cult, a destination for pilgrimage festivals, and an institution that was central to Jewish life and identity. The deuterocanonical book of 1 Maccabees narrates how the Seleucid king Antiochus IV Epiphanes profaned the temple by "erect[ing] a desolating sacrilege on the altar of burnt offering" (1 Macc. 1:54), prompting the Maccabean Revolt of 167–164 BCE. The temple was completely transformed under Herod the Great in the second half of the first century BCE through an expansion of its platform area and a rebuilding of the sanctuary itself, making it one of the most impressive religious complexes in the Roman world—it was this temple that stood in the time of Jesus. Work on the temple complex continued until not long before its final destruction by the Romans in 70 CE during the Great Jewish Revolt.

Joseph Lam

the Lord what is blemished, for I am a great King, says the Lord of hosts, and my name is reverenced among the nations.

2 And now, O priests, this command is for you. [2]If you will not listen, if you will not lay it to heart to give glory to my name, says the Lord of hosts, then I will send the curse on you, and I will curse your blessings; indeed, I have already cursed them[f] because you do not lay it to heart. [3]I will rebuke your offspring and spread dung on your faces, the dung of your offerings, and I will put you out of my presence.[g]

4 Know, then, that I have sent this command to you, that my covenant with Levi may hold, says the Lord of hosts. [5]My covenant with him was a covenant of life and well-being, which I gave him; this called for reverence, and he revered me and stood in awe of my name. [6]True instruction was in his mouth, and no wrong was found on his lips. He walked with me in integrity and uprightness, and he turned many from iniquity. [7]For the lips of a priest should guard knowledge, and people should seek instruction from his mouth, for he is the messenger of the Lord of hosts. [8]But you have turned aside from the way; you have caused many to stumble by your instruction; you have corrupted the covenant of Levi, says the Lord of hosts, [9]so I make you despised and humbled before all the people, inasmuch as you have not kept my ways but have shown partiality in your instruction.

f 2.2 Heb *it*   *g* 2.3 Cn Compare Gk Syr: Heb *and he shall bear you to it*

toward sacrifice. **2:3** According to Leviticus, the dung of an animal sacrifice was to be burned in an ash heap outside the camp (Lev. 4:11–12). **2:6–7** *True instruction was in his mouth . . . and people should seek instruction from his mouth.* These phrases have a proverbial character in that they adhere to the patterns of poetic parallelism (i.e., the regular correspondence in Hebrew poetry of two or more successive line segments in terms of grammar, word order, meaning, or other linguistic features; see **"Hebrew Poetry," p. 741**) and articulate a principle that is applicable widely. Note that the book of Proverbs is also characterized by poetic parallelism as well as by a general orientation in its content. In light of the proverbial nature of 2:6–7, it is possible that these verses represent a previously known saying that was incorporated into the present context. The addition of *for he is the messenger of the Lord of hosts*, with its use of the term "mal'akh" ("messenger"), harks back to the name of the book. **2:9** *Shown partiality*, literally "lifted up [the] face," is the same idiom as that which is translated as "show you favor" in 1:8 and simply denotes the expression of pleasure toward another person. The negative connotation in the present context arises from the unfairness by which the Levite priests presumably exercised their favor.

10 Have we not all one father? Has not one God created us? Why then are we faithless to one another, profaning the covenant of our ancestors? ¹¹Judah has been faithless, and abomination has been committed in Israel and in Jerusalem, for Judah has profaned the sanctuary of the LORD, which he loves, and has married the daughter of a foreign god. ¹²For the one who does this, may the LORD cut off any witness[b] or advocate from the tents of Jacob or anyone who could bring an offering to the LORD of hosts.

13 And this you do as well: You cover the LORD's altar with tears, with weeping and groaning because he no longer regards the offering or accepts it with favor at your hand. ¹⁴You ask, "Why does he not?" Because the LORD was a witness between you and the wife of your youth, to whom you have been faithless, though she is your companion and your wife by covenant. ¹⁵Did God[i] not make them one, flesh with spirit in it? And what does the one desire? Godly offspring. So look to yourselves, and do not let anyone be faithless to the wife of his youth.[j] ¹⁶For I hate[k] divorce, says the LORD, the God of Israel, and covering one's garment with violence, says the LORD of hosts. So take heed to yourselves and do not be faithless.

17 You have wearied the LORD with your words. Yet you say, "How have we wearied him?" By saying, "All who do evil are good in the sight of the LORD, and he delights in them." Or by asking, "Where is the God of justice?"

3 See, I am sending my messenger to prepare the way before me, and the Lord whom you seek will suddenly come to his temple. The messenger of the covenant in whom you delight—indeed, he is coming, says the LORD of hosts. ²But who can endure the day of his coming, and who can stand when he appears?

For he is like a refiner's fire and like washers' soap; ³he will sit as a refiner and purifier of silver, and he will purify the descendants of Levi and refine them like gold and silver, until they present offerings to the LORD in righteousness.[l] ⁴Then the offering of Judah and Jerusalem will be pleasing to the LORD, as in the days of old and as in former years.

5 Then I will draw near to you for judgment; I will be swift to bear witness against the sorcerers, against the adulterers, against those who swear falsely, against those who oppress the hired workers in their wages, the widow, and the orphan, against those who thrust aside the alien and do not fear me, says the LORD of hosts.

b 2.12 Q ms Compare Gk: MT *arouse*   *i* 2.15 Heb *he*
j 2.15 Meaning of Heb uncertain   *k* 2.16 Cn: Heb *he hates*
l 3.3 Or *right offerings to the* LORD

2:10–16 Speech 3: The faithlessness of Judah. 2:10 The references to God as father and creator are reminiscent of Deut. 32:6 and Isa. 64:8. **2:11** *Has married the daughter of a foreign god.* Two interpretations of this phrase are possible: (1) it could be a metaphorical way of describing acts of idolatry in the temple; or (2) it could refer to literal intermarriage between the men of Judah and women of other nations. Option 1 would entail taking the subsequent mentions of the wife of one's youth and of divorce (2:14–16) as part of the same extended metaphor, while option 2 would lead to a literal interpretation of 2:14–16, envisioning a situation in which men of Judah were divorcing their wives in order to marry foreign women (see **"Intermarriage," p. 649**). In the present verse, option 1 seems preferable because it is *Judah* collectively who is said to have entered into the illicit marriage (and not "the men of Judah"). (But see note on 2:15.) **2:15** *Did God not make them one, flesh with spirit in it?* This is certainly reminiscent of Gen. 2:24 but falls short of an exact quotation (especially since the word for "flesh" here is different from the one in Gen. 2:24). *So look to yourselves.* Notwithstanding the note on 2:11 regarding the plausibility of taking marriage to a foreign daughter as a metaphor, here the use of the second-person plural *yourselves*, plus the injunction for individuals not to be *faithless to the wife of [one's] youth*, work in favor of a literal interpretation of foreign marriage.

2:17–3:5 Speech 4: The judgment of the Lord. 2:17 Despite the chapter division falling immediately after this verse, preserving the book's overall statement-question-response pattern requires connecting 2:17 with what follows. **3:1** *See, I am sending my messenger* is similar in wording to Exod. 23:20. The word "mal'akhi" ("my messenger") indicates a play on the same word in 1:1 (regardless of whether it is taken as a pseudonym or not). *Prepare the way.* The same phrasing is found in Isa. 40:3; 57:14; and 62:10. **3:2–3** The dual metaphors of smelting and of cleansing cloth are employed here to describe the corrective transformation of the Levites that is necessary.

6 For I the Lord do not change; therefore you, O children of Jacob, have not perished. [7]Ever since the days of your ancestors you have turned aside from my statutes and have not kept them. Return to me, and I will return to you, says the Lord of hosts. But you say, "How shall we return?"

8 Will anyone rob God? Yet you are robbing me! But you say, "How are we robbing you?" In your tithes and offerings! [9]You are cursed with a curse, for you are robbing me—the whole nation of you! [10]Bring the full tithe into the storehouse, so that there may be food in my house, and thus put me to the test, says the Lord of hosts; see if I will not open the windows of heaven for you and pour down for you an overflowing blessing. [11]I will rebuke the locust[m] for you, so that it will not destroy the produce of your soil, and your vine in the field shall not be barren, says the Lord of hosts. [12]Then all nations will count you happy, for you will be a land of delight, says the Lord of hosts.

13 You have spoken harsh words against me, says the Lord. Yet you say, "How have we spoken against you?" [14]You have said, "It is vain to serve God. What do we profit by keeping his command or by going about as mourners before the Lord of hosts? [15]Now we count the arrogant happy; evildoers not only prosper, but when they put God to the test they escape."

16 Then those who revered the Lord spoke with one another. The Lord took note and listened, and a book of remembrance was written before him of those who revered the Lord and thought on his name. [17]They shall be mine, says the Lord of hosts, my special possession on the day when I act, and I will spare them as parents spare their children who serve them. [18]Then once more you shall see the difference between the righteous and the wicked, between one who serves God and one who does not serve him.

4 "See, the day is coming, burning like an oven, when all the arrogant and all evildoers will be stubble; the day that comes shall burn them up, says the Lord of hosts, so that it will leave them neither root nor branch. [2]But for you who revere my name the sun of righteousness shall rise, with healing in its wings. You shall go out leaping like calves from the stall. [3]And you shall tread down the wicked, for they will be ashes under the soles of your feet, on the day when I act, says the Lord of hosts.

4 Remember the teaching of my servant Moses, the statutes and ordinances that I commanded him at Horeb for all Israel.

5 See, I will send you the prophet Elijah before the great and terrible day of the Lord comes. [6]He will turn the hearts of parents to their children and the hearts of children to their parents, so that I will not come and strike the land with a curse.[o]

m 3.11 Heb *devourer*   n 4.1 3.19 in Heb   o 4.6 Or *a ban of utter destruction*

3:6–12 Speech 5: Proper tithes and offerings. 3:7 *Return to me, and I will return to you.* See also Zech. 1:3. **3:8** The Israelite tithe as described in Lev. 27:30–32 is presented as an obligatory payment extracted from both the fruit of the land and the livestock. Thus, to withhold the payment is akin to robbing God. **3:10–11** These verses set forth the positive motivation for paying the full tithe—the Lord challenges the people to test to see if they would indeed receive material blessings to compensate for their perceived loss.

3:13–4:3 Speech 6: The fate of the righteous and the wicked. 3:14 In Hebrew, the word *serve* is also used to describe the act of worship. **3:15** While in 3:10 the Lord calls the people to test the limits of divine blessing regarding the tithe, here we see *evildoers . . . put[ting] God to the test* in disobedience while ostensibly getting away with it. **3:16** The Hebrew phrase for *book of remembrance* is unique to this passage, but other similar phrases relate to practices of recordkeeping and evince a strong emphasis on the importance of memory (e.g., Exod. 17:14; 32:32–33; Isa. 30:8; Ps. 69:28). **3:17** On the term *special possession*, see also Exod. 19:5; Deut. 7:6; 14:2; 26:18; Ps. 135:4. **4:2** For the phrase *the sun of righteousness*, compare Isa. 60:19–20. *Leaping like calves from the stall.* A calf that is confined for fattening leaps with vigor when released.

4:4–6 Conclusion. 4:4 *Teaching* is the Hebrew term "torah." The phrase "law ['torah'] of Moses" is also found in Josh. 8:31–32; 23:6; 2 Kgs. 14:6; 23:25; and Neh. 8:1. **4:5–6** If Moses represents the "torah," then Elijah represents the ideal prophet, here representing the sign of the coming of the *day of the Lord* that is mentioned in other prophetic contexts (e.g., Isa. 13:6, 9; Amos 5:18, 20; Joel 1:15; 2:1, 11; 3:14; Obad. 15; Zeph. 1:7, 14). See **"The Day of the Lord," p. 1322.**

The Deuterocanonical/Apocryphal Books Variously Included in Roman Catholic, Greek, and Slavonic Bibles

New Revised Standard Version Updated Edition

Introduction to the Deuterocanonical/Apocryphal Books

Collections of Books

There is a wide range of books collected under the category of deuterocanonical/apocryphal books. The books gathered here are those that are not in the version of the Hebrew Bible we use today but in the Greek translation (known as the Septuagint) of older versions of the Jewish Scriptures, or in the Old Latin and Vulgate translations, or both. They were composed by Jews (with the exception of 2 Esd. 1–2, 15–16), but they are not authoritative in the Jewish tradition or in most Protestant Christian traditions. Most, but not all, are authoritative in Roman Catholic and Orthodox Christian churches and are interspersed within their Old Testaments (see **Canonical Orders of the Books of the Bible, p. xxi–xxv**; **"The Bible as a Collection," pp. 2145–47**, and **"Canon," p. 1677**). This edition of the Bible follows the Protestant Christian practice of grouping the deuterocanonical/apocryphal books separately from the Hebrew Bible (if they are included in Protestant Bibles at all).

The word *apocryphal* comes from a Greek term that means "hidden things." Although these books were not "hidden" or "secret," Protestant Christians use the term *apocryphal* to refer to the compositions they may deem to be valuable but not authoritative or canonical. The term *deuterocanonical* is used in the Roman Catholic Church to refer to those books affirmed as canonical at the Council of Trent in 1546 (Tobit; Judith; 1–2 Maccabees; Wisdom of Solomon; Sirach; Baruch, including Letter of Jeremiah; and Additions to Esther and Daniel). In the Roman Catholic tradition, the deuterocanonical books are no less authoritative than the protocanonical books (i.e., the books in the Hebrew Bible also recognized by Jews and Protestants); the term simply indicates that their authority was settled later. In this study bible, the terms *deuterocanonical* and *apocryphal books* are used as convenient ways of referring to this collection of documents but are not intended to convey a judgment on whether they are or should be considered religiously authoritative.

Most of these documents were composed during the Second Temple period after the Babylonian exile, whether in Israel-Palestine or in the diaspora of Jewish people following the exile, with the earliest composition possibly dating to the fourth or third century BCE (Letter of Jeremiah) and the latest after the first century CE (2 Esdras, including the Christian additions). Some were composed in Hebrew or Aramaic and then translated into Greek, while others were original Greek compositions. There are scholarly debates about what the original language was for many of the compositions. (For discussions of the dates, original languages, and places of composition, see the introductions to each book.)

Many of the documents were popular during the Second Temple period, which lasted until 70 CE, when the temple in Jerusalem was destroyed. Manuscript copies of several of these compositions have been found among the Dead Sea Scrolls in the caves used by the Jewish community at Qumran between the second century BCE and the first century CE (including Sirach, Tobit, Letter of Jeremiah, Psalm 151) and in the possession of the Jews who fled to Masada at the time of the first Jewish revolt against Rome sometime between 66 and 74 CE (Sirach). The Jewish historian Josephus (first century CE) used the Septuagintal traditions, including the Additions to Esther as well as 1 Esdras and 1 Maccabees, as sources.

After the destruction of the Second Temple in 70 CE, Jews collected the various sayings, interpretations, and traditions of their teachers, the rabbis. They were eventually codified in the Mishnah (ca. 200 CE) and the Talmud (ca. 500 CE). These rabbinic sources show familiarity with several of the deuterocanonical/apocryphal books or their traditions. The festival celebrating the "dedication"—in Hebrew, *Hanukkah*—of the Jerusalem temple is discussed in the Mishnah (m. Bik. 1:16; m. Roš Haš. 1:3; m. Ta'an. 2:10; m. Meg. 3:4, 6; m. Mo'ed Qaṭ. 3:9; m. B. Qam. 6:6). The story behind Hanukkah itself is recounted in 1–2 Maccabees but not in the Mishnah, perhaps indicating how well known it was. Passages from Sirach appear in the Talmud, although the rabbis eventually would not deem it as authoritative, along with other books (b. Sanh. 100b; t. Yad. 2:13). Several copies of Sirach in its original Hebrew were also found in a storehouse (*genizah*) of a synagogue in Cairo (the Cairo Genizah). Although Judith is not mentioned in the rabbinic sources, references to her appear in later commentaries on the Talmud.

Scholars have noticed echoes of Sirach, Tobit, and Wisdom of Solomon in some of the early sayings of Jesus, the Gospels, the writings of Paul, and the book of James. Many early Christian writers such as Clement of Rome and the author of the *Didache* quote and allude to passages in the deuterocanonical/apocryphal books. As the Greek translations of the Hebrew Bible (Septuagint) were used by Greek-speaking Christians, the Greek versions of books like Esther and Daniel as well as most of the deuterocanonical/apocryphal books, which were circulating in Greek, became authoritative to Christians. As the Christian Old Testament was translated into other languages such as Latin, Slavonic, and Syriac—often dependent on Greek translations—these books were often included in those Bibles and became authoritative in those churches as well (see **"The Bible as a Collection," pp. 2145–47**, and **"Canon," p. 1677**).

The compositions in the deuterocanonical/apocryphal books provide insights into the lives, thoughts, hopes, and struggles of the Jews during the Second Temple period, out of which both Rabbinic Judaism and early Christianity emerged.

Reading Guide

The diversity of these books as well as the canons that include them makes it difficult to generalize about the overall view of God or religious practices within the deuterocanonical/apocryphal books. Instead, within Christian churches for which these books are canonical, they may be read within the context of the sections of the canon in which they are placed. More often, however, in those churches, these texts will be heard as they are read in religious services as part of the set readings (called a lectionary) from the Bible for that day (see **"The Bible in Religious Interpretation and Practice," pp. 2155–56**).

As with other documents in the Bible, an important way of reading these books is to understand them as individual compositions. Here one seeks to discern the particular historical and cultural situations that each book addresses and the various themes and ideas that it contains. Many of the books tell stories (e.g., Tobit, Judith, Additions to Esther, Additions to Daniel, Baruch, 1 Maccabees, 2 Maccabees, 1 Esdras, 3 Maccabees), so one can analyze the structure of the narrative, plot development, and characters.

The documents collected in the deuterocanonical/apocryphal books were composed over a span of more than four to five hundred years, some in Israel/Palestine and others in the Jewish diaspora. Thus, these books may be read alongside other documents considering similar historical situations and contexts to see how different authors understood and responded to those conditions. Many of the narrative books reflect on and interpret the events of the Maccabean Revolt of 167–164 BCE for their current context (e.g., Judith, Baruch, Additions to Daniel, 1 Maccabees, 2 Maccabees). Other books reflect the concerns of Jews in the diaspora and strategies of how to live as a minoritized people (e.g., Additions to Daniel, Additions to Esther, Wisdom of Solomon, 4 Maccabees; cf. Daniel, Esther). Although it is important to recognize the diversity of experiences in the diaspora over many centuries (see **"The Bible in Its Ancient Contexts," pp. 2150–52**; **"Diaspora," p. 1338**; these books give us insights into different aspects of people's lives (see **"Jewish Women in the Diaspora," p. 1525**; **"Masculinity," p. 1701**.

Many of these documents are read in relationship to their literary genres or forms. There are historical narratives (e.g., 1 Maccabees, 2 Maccabees, 1 Esdras; see **"Introduction to the Former Prophets / Historical Books," pp. 4–6**) and folktales (Tobit, Judith, Additions to Esther, Additions to Daniel), although the lines between these categories are not sharp (see **"Court Tales," p. 1608**). Some of the documents are expansions of earlier versions of the books. Thus, it is interesting to compare and contrast the Hebrew and Greek versions of Esther as well as the book of Daniel with and without the Additions to Daniel (Prayer of Azariah, Song of the Three Young Men, Susanna, Bel and the Dragon). (The Hebrew/Aramaic versions appear in the Hebrew Bible, while the Greek versions appear in the deuterocanonical/apocryphal books.) Since 1 Esdras draws heavily from 2 Chronicles and Ezra–Nehemiah, one might compare how its author used those sources to reinterpret those stories and create new meanings (see **"Rewriting the Bible," p. 584**).

The book of 2 Esdras contains three different compositions that have been added together. Since these writings were originally separate, scholars also refer to them by different titles: 4 Ezra, 5 Ezra, and 6 Ezra. The earliest composition is 2 Esd. 3–14, which is also known as 4 Ezra. This Jewish apocalypse was written after the destruction of Jerusalem in 70 CE (for other apocalypses, see

Daniel and Revelation; see also **"Apocalypse," p. 1216**). Christian writers added two other sections to this book over the next few hundred years. Second Esdras 1–2 is one composition, which scholars also call 5 Ezra, and 2 Esd. 15–16 is another one, also known as 6 Ezra.

Many of the documents in the deuterocanonical/apocryphal books are poetic in form. Some of these are or contain songs or liturgical texts (Psalm 151, Prayer of Manasseh, Prayer of Azariah, Song of the Three Young Men, Baruch). These compositions may be profitably compared and contrasted with other songs and prayers in both the Hebrew Bible (e.g., the Psalms) and the Christian Scriptures as well as other early Jewish sources such as those found among the Dead Sea Scrolls (see **"Worship," p. 761**; **"Types of Psalms," p. 742**; **"Hebrew Poetry," p. 741**). Other poetic books, such as Sirach and Wisdom of Solomon, contain collections of sayings and admonitions (see the discussion of Proverbs in **"Introduction to the Writings," pp. 6–9**). These compositions often include images, themes, and ideas that developed over time (e.g., see **"Wisdom and Creation," p. 1412**).

In addition, one might read these books in light of later artistic representations to consider how artists have interpreted them. Characters and scenes from the deuterocanonical/apocryphal books appear in paintings, engravings, and other visual arts. Some of the more popular subjects include Susanna, Tobit with the angel Raphael, and Judith (see **"Judith in Art," p. 1376**). The deutero-canonical/apocryphal books are also represented in other media—for example, the lyrics to George Frideric Handel's 1746 oratorio *Judas Maccabaeus* written by Thomas Morell, which are based on 1 Maccabees.

The reader is invited into these different reading strategies and contexts in order to continue to make the literature in the deuterocanonical/apocryphal books meaningful. We might ask ourselves, How do the ways that the authors drew upon their traditions, expanding and rewriting their sources, suggest ways that we might deal with our own traditions or even invent new narratives? How might the poetry, prayers, and songs of these books inspire new compositions? In all, these books welcome readers to ask broader humanistic questions that have long been posed to these ancient texts: What is wisdom, love, and devotion? How do we make sense of war, destruction, and atrocities? How should we resist structures and cultures that minoritize and oppress people? How do we live good and virtuous lives?

Henry W. Morisada Rietz

TOBIT

Authorship, Date of Composition, and Language

The book of Tobit is named after the narrator, Tobit (from Heb. *tobith*, "goodness"), or its protagonist, Tobias (Heb. *tob-yah*, "the Lord is good"). The document was originally written in a Semitic language, either Hebrew or Aramaic. Although the story is set after the Assyrian conquest of the northern kingdom of Israel in 722 BCE, the book was composed by an anonymous author in the second or third century BCE during the Hellenistic period.

The purpose of the book is to exhort Jews living in the Diaspora to adhere to their Jewish identity as the people of God through strict observance of the Torah. The author provides models of behavior for the Diaspora community that include prayer, fear of God, almsgiving, family life, avoiding mixed marriages, care for the deceased, suffering, gender inequality, and banquets. Fragments of Tobit in Aramaic and Hebrew were found among the Dead Sea Scrolls. The story is preserved in three Greek recensions (G^I, G^{II}, and G^{III}). The Greek text was included in the Septuagint, an early translation of the Hebrew Bible by the Greek-speaking Jews of the Diaspora. Tobit is one of the seven deuterocanonical/apocryphal books recognized as inspired by the Roman Catholic and Greek Orthodox Churches. Protestant churches do not accept it as canonical but hold the text to have value to the reader.

The author appears to have been familiar with the book of Ahiqar ("Ahikar" in Tobit). This classic work is a folktale of Babylonian or Persian origin about a wise and moral man who served as chief counselor of Sennacherib, king of Assyria (704–681 BCE). The author of Tobit presents Ahikar as a pious Jew who is the nephew of Tobit and whose life imitates the vicissitudes of Tobit (1:21–22; 14:10).

Literary Characteristics

The placement of Tobit among the historical books in Roman Catholic and Greek Orthodox canons suggests that it is a historical text. However, many scholars today classify it as a novella or folktale about the past incorporating different literary genres and traditions from the Hebrew Bible (see **"Court Tales," p. 1608**; **"Historical Fiction," p. 1635**). Several features in the narrative betray the patriarchal orientation of the book of Genesis. Tobias's trip, the search for a wife, the marriage of Tobias and Sarah, and the reencounter of Tobit with Tobias parallel the stories of the marriages of Isaac and Rebekah and Jacob and Rachel (Gen. 24, 29). Tobit 1 recalls the fall of Israel to the Assyrians and the people being exiled to Assyria (2 Kgs. 17). From the prophets, the author cites Amos (Tob. 2:6) and Nahum's prophecy about the fate of Nineveh (Tob. 14:4), and alludes to the hymns of Jerusalem's restoration in Isa. 60–62 (Tob. 13:11, 14; 14:6–7). Elements of Wisdom literature are found in Tobit's fidelity and patience in his suffering (cf. Job 1–2) and in his counsel to Tobias (Tob. 4:3–19; 14:8–11).

Reading Guide

The book narrates the family drama of Tobit, his son Tobias, and their relative Sarah along with the demon Asmodeus and the angel Raphael. Tobit is a pious and just Jew living in Nineveh, the capital of Assyria, who sends his son Tobias to Media to reclaim money he left there. Along the way, Tobias meets Sarah, who is badgered by the demon Asmodeus. The plot of Tobit may be divided into three parts: (1) chaps. 1–4, (2) chaps. 5–10, and (3) chaps. 11–14. The first section (chaps. 1–4) introduces the characters and their situations. Ironically, Tobit's blindness and poverty are caused by his pious care for the dead. Since corpses were considered unclean, he sleeps outside his home to preserve its ritual purity (see Num. 19:14–16). When he loses his sight after bird droppings fall on his eyes and is unable to work, his wife, Anna, takes on the role of provider, diligently working to support her family. Poor, blind, and unable to fulfill his duty as provider for his family, Tobit prays for death. The narrative then introduces the situation of Sarah, a young virgin living in Ecbatana. She is afflicted by the demon Asmodeus (the name is either from a Hebrew word meaning "destroyer" or from Aeshma Daeva, the Persian demon of lust), who has killed seven of her husbands on their wedding night. Dispirited, she,

like Tobit, prays for death. The two parallel stories of affliction culminate in God hearing their pleas and sending the angel Raphael (meaning "God has healed") "to heal both of them" (3:17).

In the second part (chaps. 5-10), Tobit wants to send Tobias to Rages in Media to collect the money he left with Gabael, his cousin. Tobias, however, needs a guide for the journey and meets the angel Raphael, who identifies himself as Azariah. On their way to Media, Tobias and Raphael (called Azariah) camp along the Tigris River, where a fish leaps out of the waters to devour Tobias. Raphael orders Tobias to gut it and preserve its heart, liver, and gall for their healing powers (6:1-9). As they enter Media, Raphael tells Tobias that they need to visit their relative Raguel and that Tobias is to take Raguel's daughter Sarah as his wife and fulfill his legal duties of the nearest kinsman-redeemer. Tobias is reluctant, having heard that her previous husbands "died in the bridal chamber" (6:14). Tobias worries about how his aged parents will fare if he suffers the same fate as Sarah's previous husbands. Raphael tells him that by burning the fish's liver and heart in the bridal chamber and praying to God, the demon Asmodeus will not harm him. Arriving in Ecbatana, Tobias and Raphael find hospitality in the home of Raguel and Edna, Sarah's parents, and Tobias asks for Sarah's hand in marriage. Raguel agrees and writes a marriage contract according to the law of Moses. As Edna prepares Sarah in the bridal chamber, both weep. When Tobias enters the bridal chamber with his bride, he burns the fish's liver and heart, and the demon Asmodeus is immediately driven away by the odor to a remote part of Egypt. There Raphael binds him, "hand and foot" (8:3). The couple pray to God and ask for a union based on love and not on lust. The next morning, Raguel prepares a lavish wedding banquet for the couple and promises that after fourteen days of celebration, they can return to Nineveh with half his property (8:19-21). Meanwhile, Tobias commissions Raphael to collect the money from Gabael's house (9:1-6). Back in Nineveh, Tobit and Anna become increasingly worried about Tobias's delay (10:1-7). Every morning, Anna gazes down the road hoping for his arrival but thinking Tobias is dead.

The third part of the story (chaps. 11-14) narrates Tobias's return to Nineveh with his wife, Sarah, and Tobias's healing of his father's blindness with the gall of the fish. In response to being healed, Tobit erupts in a hymn of praise to God. When Tobias seeks to pay Azariah for all he has done, Azariah reveals his real identity as the angel Raphael and then disappears. After Tobit and Anna die, Tobias and Sarah move to Media based on Nahum's prophecies of the destruction of Nineveh.

J. L. Manzo

1 The book of the words of Tobit son of Tobiel son of Hananiel son of Aduel son of Gabael son of Raphael son of Raguel of the descendants[a] of Asiel, of the tribe of Naphtali, ²who in the days of King Shalmaneser[b] of the Assyrians was taken into captivity from Thisbe, which is to the south of Kedesh Naphtali in Upper Galilee, above Asher toward the west, and north of Phogor.

3 I, Tobit, walked in the ways of truth and righteousness all the days of my life. I performed many acts of charity for my kindred and my nation who had gone with me in exile to Nineveh in the land of the Assyrians. ⁴When I was in my own country, in the land of Israel, while I was still a young man, the whole tribe of my ancestor Naphtali deserted the house of David and Jerusalem. This city had been chosen from among all the tribes of Israel, where all the tribes of Israel should offer sacrifice and where the temple, the dwelling of God, had been consecrated and established for all generations forever.

5 All my kindred and my ancestral house of

a 1.1 Other ancient authorities lack *of Raphael son of Raguel of the descendants*   b 1.2 OL: Gk *Enemessaros*

1:1-2 Prologue. The *book of the words* (Gk. "biblos logōn") tells the story of Tobit, a Jew. *The tribe of Naphtali* was part of the northern kingdom of Israel, which was conquered by Assyria in 722 BCE. Tobit's family was captured in his hometown of Thisbe in upper Galilee and exiled to Nineveh, the capital of the Assyrian Empire.

1:3-9 Tobit's way of life in Israel. 1:3 *Walked in the ways of truth and righteousness* means he is observing God's commandments in the Torah. **1:4-5** The ancestral tribe of *Naphtali deserted the house of David and Jerusalem* refers to the division of the country into two kingdoms in 922 BCE: the kingdom of Israel in the north and the kingdom of Judah in the south. Jeroboam I, king of Israel,

Going Deeper: Diaspora (Tobit 1)

Diaspora is the Greek word for "dispersion," referring to Jewish communities outside the land of Israel. The Hebrew words *galut* and *golah*, or "exile," carry a negative charge. For much of history, including the Roman period, more Jews lived outside the land of Israel than in it. They were spread throughout the Mediterranean because of expulsions, military service, colonization, economic opportunity, seafaring, and international trade. Two traumas forced some Jews from their land—the deportation of Judahites to Babylon around the destruction of the First Jerusalem Temple in 587/586 BCE and the taking of captive Jews to Rome after the destruction of the Second Temple in 70 CE. Jews were expelled from Jerusalem after the Bar Kokhba revolt (132–135/136 CE) and suffered intermittent expulsions from Rome and other places.

Despite the implication of early Jewish sources that diaspora/*galut* was a calamity, Jews flourished in other places. Papyri, epigraphy, and literary works show Jews as a part of military and civic affairs and intellectual life, from a military settlement in Egypt in the fifth century BCE to the philosopher Philo in first-century Alexandria, Egypt, who claims a million Jews resided there (*Flacc.* 43). A temple for Jewish worship and sacrifice operated at Leontopolis in the Nile Delta. In Rome they suffered temporary expulsions but were also given privileges by Julius Caesar, including exemption from sacrifice to the Roman gods. Jewish catacombs in Rome are extant today, and in Asia Minor remains of synagogues are visible at Sardis (Turkey). There are several sites in present-day Tunisia (Hammam-Lif, Kelibia) and Dura-Europos (Syria). Inscriptions at Aprodisias (Turkey) appear to include non-Jewish donors to the synagogue. Acts attests to Paul visiting several diaspora synagogues. Farther east, some Jewish exiles remained in Babylonia, forming the core of a community where rabbinic activity flourished, ultimately producing the Babylonian Talmud. Jews seemed to retain dual loyalties, both to the land and God of Israel and to their lands of birth and residence. Acts 2:5–11 refers to "Jews from every people under heaven," while Philo cites Jews as having mother cities and fatherlands (*Flacc.* 46).

In New Testament texts "diaspora" is often symbolic. In John 7:35 it functions as a metaphor for the non-Jewish world, a place to encounter gentiles. In other instances, diaspora is social and theological, suggesting believers are in the world but are not at home there (Jas. 1:1; 1 Pet. 1:1) versus their "citizenship" in heaven (Phil. 3:20).

Claudia Setzer

Naphtali sacrificed upon all the mountains of Galilee to the calf that King Jeroboam of Israel had erected in Dan and on all the mountains of Galilee. ⁶But I alone went often to Jerusalem for the festivals, as it is prescribed for all Israel by an everlasting decree. I would hurry off to Jerusalem with the first fruits of the crops and the firstlings of the flock, the tithes of the cattle, and the first shearings of the sheep. ⁷I would give these to the priests, the sons of Aaron, at the altar, likewise the tenth of the grain, wine, olive oil, pomegranates, figs, and the rest of the fruits to the sons of Levi who ministered at Jerusalem. Also every six years I would save up a second tenth in money and go and distribute it each year in Jerusalem, ⁸giving it to the orphans and widows and to the converts who had attached themselves to the Israelites. In the third year I would bring it and give it to them, and we would eat it according to the ordinance decreed concerning it in the law of Moses and according to the instructions of Deborah, the mother of my father Tobiel,ᶜ for my father had died and left me an orphan. ⁹When I became a man I married a woman,ᵈ a member of our own family, and by her I became the father of a son whom I named Tobias.

10 After I was carried away captive to Assyria and came as a captive to Nineveh,

c 1.8 OL: Gk *Hananiel* d 1.9 Other ancient authorities add *Anna*

made Dan a center of worship (cf. 1 Kgs. 12:25–33). **1:6–8** *To Jerusalem for the festivals* refers to the three pilgrimage festivals: Passover, the Festival of Weeks, and the Festival of Booths (Exod. 23:14–17; Deut. 14:22–27; 16:16), which every male was expected to observe in Jerusalem (Deut. 12:10–11). **1:8** *Converts.* See **"Gentile Conversion," p. 1530**. **1:9** *I married a woman, a member of our own family.* Endogamy was encouraged in the Diaspora to preserve cultural, religious, and economic autonomy.
 1:10–15 Tobit's way of life in Nineveh. **1:10–11** Tobit observes the dietary laws by refusing to eat

everyone of my kindred and my people ate the food of the nations, [11]but I kept myself from eating the food of the nations. [12]Because I was mindful of God with all my heart, [13]the Most High gave me favor and good standing with Shalmaneser,[e] and I used to buy everything he needed. [14]Until his death I used to go into Media to buy for him there, and I left in trust bags holding ten talents of silver with Gabael, the brother of Gabri, in the country of Media. [15]But when Shalmaneser[f] died and his son Sennacherib reigned in his place, Median roads became lawless, and I could no longer travel to Media.

16 In the days of Shalmaneser[g] I performed many acts of charity to my kindred, those of my people. [17]I would give my food to the hungry and my clothing to the naked, and if I saw the dead body of any of my nation thrown out behind the wall of Nineveh, I would bury it. [18]I also buried any whom King Sennacherib put to death when he came fleeing from Judea in those days of judgment that the King of heaven executed upon him because of his blasphemies. For in his anger he put to death many Israelites, but I would secretly remove the bodies and bury them. So when Sennacherib looked for them he could not find them. [19]Then one of the Ninevites went and informed the king about me, that I was burying them, so I hid myself. But when I realized that the king knew about me and that I was being searched for to be put to

death, I was afraid and ran away. [20]Then all my property was confiscated; nothing was left to me that was not taken into the royal treasury except my wife Anna and my son Tobias.

21 But not forty days passed before two of Sennacherib's[h] sons killed him, and when they fled to the mountains of Ararat, his son Esar-haddon[i] reigned after him. He appointed Ahikar, the son of my brother Hanael,[j] over all the accounts of his kingdom, and he had authority over the entire administration. [22]Ahikar interceded for me, and I returned to Nineveh. Now Ahikar was chief cupbearer, keeper of the signet, and in charge of administration and accounts under King Sennacherib of Assyria, so Esar-haddon[k] appointed him as second-in-command. He was my nephew[l] and so a close relative.

2 In the days of[m] Esar-haddon[n] I returned home, and my wife Anna and my son Tobias were restored to me. At our Festival of Pentecost, which is the sacred Festival of Weeks, a good dinner was prepared for me, and I reclined to eat. [2]When the table had been set for me and an abundance of food placed before me, I said to my son Tobias, "Go, my son, and bring whatever poor person you may find of our kindred among the

e 1.13 OL: Gk *Enemessaros* f 1.15 OL: Gk *Enemessaros* g 1.16 OL: Gk *Enemessaros* h 1.21 Gk *his* i 1.21 Gk *Sacherdonos* j 1.21 Other authorities read *Hananael* k 1.22 Gk *Sacherdonos* l 1.22 Q ms adds *a member of my father's household* m 2.1 Q ms: S *Then under* n 2.1 Gk *Sacherdonos*

unclean food (cf. Lev. 11:1–47; Deut. 14:1–29). **1:12–13** God blesses Tobit by raising him to the position of buyer of provisions in Shalmaneser's government. **1:14** As Shalmaneser's agent, Tobit travels to Media—a site of Assyrian Israelite settlement—to supply the king's needs. The deposit with Gabael of *ten talents of silver* weighed about 750 pounds. This vast amount of money indicates God's blessings. **1:15** The identification of *Sennacherib* as Shalmaneser's son and successor is historically inaccurate. Shalmaneser V was succeeded by his brother Sargon II (722–705 BCE). Sennacherib was Sargon II's son and successor.

1:16–22 Tobit's charity. 1:16–17 Tobit continues feeding the hungry, clothing the naked, and burying the dead (cf. Deut. 14:28–29; 21:23). Many Jews faced extreme poverty in the exile, prompting affluent Jews to help the poor and afflicted. **1:18–20** Tobit buries those killed by the king and whose bodies were left exposed as signs of contempt. When a Ninevite reports his actions, Tobit's property is confiscated. **1:21–22** After the death of Sennacherib, Tobit obtains a pardon with the help of *Ahikar*, here portrayed as Tobit's nephew. Ahikar was a powerful official under both Shalmaneser and Sennacherib and is a protagonist in the Assyrian wisdom folktale the book of Ahiqar.

2:1–10 The *Festival of Weeks*, known in Greek as *Pentecost* because it is observed fifty days after the Passover (Deut. 16:9–12; Lev. 23:16), was a pilgrimage festival to be celebrated in Jerusalem to commemorate the wheat harvest. After the destruction of the Jerusalem temple in 587 BCE, it was celebrated with a special meal. **2:2** Tobit fulfills the principal requirement of the Festival of Weeks—solidarity with the alien, the orphan, and the widow—by inviting them to sit at his table (see Deut.

exiles in Nineveh who is wholeheartedly mindful of God,[o] and he shall eat together with me. I will wait for you, my son, until you come back." [3]So Tobias went to look for some poor person of our kindred. When he had returned he said, "Father!" And I replied, "Here I am, my son." Then he went on to say, "Look, father, one of our own nation has been killed and thrown into the marketplace, and now he lies there strangled." [4]Then I sprang up, left the dinner before even tasting it, and removed him from the square and laid him in one of the outbuildings at my home until sunset, when I might bury him. [5]When I returned, I washed myself and ate my food in sorrow. [6]Then I remembered the prophecy of Amos, how he said against Bethel,

> "Your festivals shall be turned into
>   mourning
> and all your songs[p] into
>   lamentation."

And I wept.

[7] When the sun had set, I went and dug a grave and buried him. [8]And my neighbors laughed and said, "Is he still not afraid? He has already been hunted down to be put to death for doing this, and he ran away, yet here he is again burying the dead!" [9]That same night I washed myself and went into my courtyard and lay down by the wall of the courtyard; my face was uncovered because of the heat. [10]I did not know that there were sparrows on the wall; their fresh droppings fell into my eyes and produced white films. I went to physicians to be healed, but the more they treated me with ointments, the more my vision was obscured by the white films, until I became completely blind. For four years I remained unable to see. All my kindred were sorry for me, and Ahikar took care of me for two years before he went to Elymais.

[11] At that time my wife Anna earned money at women's work. [12]She used to send what she made to the owners, and they would pay wages to her. One day, the seventh of Dystrus, when she cut off a piece she had woven and sent it to the owners, they paid her full wages and also gave her a young goat for a meal. [13]When it came toward me, the goat began to bleat, so I called her and said, "Where did you get this goat? It is surely not stolen, is it? Return it to the owners, for we have no right to eat anything stolen." [14]But she said to me, "It was given to me as a gift in addition to my wages." But I did not believe her and told her to return it to the owners. I became flushed with anger against her over this. Then she replied to me, "Where are your acts of charity? Where are your righteous deeds? These things are known about you!"[q]

o 2.2 OL: S lacks *of God*   p 2.6 OL mss: S reads *ways*
q 2.14 Or *to you*; Gk *with you*

16:14). **2:3** News that *one of our own nation has been killed . . . and now he lies* at the marketplace *strangled* prompts Tobit to rise quickly from the meal table, retrieve the body, and hide it until it could be buried at sunset, most likely to prevent retaliation from the authorities (Deut. 21:22–23). **2:5** *I washed myself.* Touching a dead body was a source of ritual defilement (Num. 19:14–16). **2:6** The interruption of the meal prompts Tobit to recall Amos's dire words: *Your festivals shall be turned into mourning . . . your songs into lamentation*, an oracle originally referring to the inhabitants of Bethel who would be punished for exploiting the poor (Amos 8:10; cf. 8:4–6). **2:9** Because of his ritual impurity, Tobit sleeps in the courtyard with his face uncovered—that is, without covering his body—because it is warm. **2:10** Sparrows' droppings fall into his eyes, causing him to become blind. Tobit's reward for observing the Torah is suffering, a contradiction to the principle that God blesses those who keep God's commandments (Deut. 28). Ahikar looks after him before traveling to Elymais, a Persian region known as Elam.

2:11–14 Anna earns a living. 2:12 *Dystrus* is a month in the Macedonian calendar corresponding to late February or early March. Anna is paid for weaving clothing and given a *goat for a meal*. Women contributed to the economy of the household by manufacturing textiles, pottery, baskets, and other goods. **2:13–14** Tobit accuses Anna of theft (*we have no right to eat anything stolen*) and of lying (*I did not believe her*). Tobit's anger may arise from knowing the goat was given so that she could feed him. In a patriarchal system, "There is wrath and impudence and great disgrace when a wife supports her husband" (Sir. 25:22). Anna responds by asking, *Where are your acts of charity? Where are your righteous deeds?* Tobit has shown great concern for the needs of others but expresses no gratitude for his wife's good deeds.

3 Then with much grief and anguish of heart I wept, and with groaning I began to pray:

² "You are righteous, O Lord,
and all your deeds are just;
all your ways are mercy and truth;
you judge the world.ʳ

³ And now, O Lord, may you be mindful of me
and look favorably upon me.
Do not punish me for my sins
or for my unwitting offenses
or for those of my ancestors.
They sinned against you

⁴ and disobeyed your commandments.
So you gave us over to plunder, exile, and death,
to become the talk, the byword, and an object of reproach
among all the nations among whom you have dispersed us.

⁵ And now your many judgments are true
in dealing with me according to my sins.
For we have not kept your commandments
and have not walked in accordance with truth before you.

⁶ So now deal with me as you will;
command my spirit to be taken from me,
so that I may be released from the face of the earth and become dust.
For it is better for me to die than to live,
because I have had to listen to undeserved insults,
and great is the sorrow that attends me.
Command, O Lord, that I be released from this distress;
release me to go to the place of eternity,
and do not, O Lord, turn your face away from me.
For it is better for me to die
than to see so much distress in my life
and better not to listen to insults."

7 On the same day, at Ecbatana in Media, it also happened that Sarah, the daughter of Raguel, was reproached by one of her father's female slaves. ⁸For she had been married to seven husbands, and the wicked demon Asmodeus had killed each of them before they had been with her as is customary for wives. So the female slave said to her, "You are the one who killsˢ your husbands! See, you have already been married to seven husbands and have not borne the nameᵗ a single one of them. ⁹Why do you beat us? Because your husbands are dead? Go with them! May we never see a son or daughter of yours!"

10 Overcome with emotion at that time, she wept and went up to her father's upper room, intending to hang herself. But she thought it over and said, "Let no one ever reproach my father, saying to him, 'You had only one beloved daughter, and she hanged herself out of distress!'ᵘ I would bring my father in his old age down in sorrow to Hades. It is better for me not to hang myself but to beg the Lord that I may die, so that I will not have to listen to these reproaches for the rest of my life." ¹¹At that same time, with hands outstretched toward the window, she prayed and said,

r 3.2 Other ancient authorities read *you render true and righteous judgment forever* s 3.8 Other ancient authorities read *strangles* t 3.8 Other ancient authorities read *have had no benefit from* u 3.10 Other ancient authorities lack *out of distress*

3:1–6 Tobit's suffering and prayer. Tobit prays for death. **3:2** The doxology addresses God as a righteous, just, merciful, and true judge. **3:3–4** Liability for the sins of the ancestors is tied to the idea that the exile is punishment for disobeying God's commandments (Exod. 20:5–6). **3:6** The repeated requests for death (*command my spirit to be taken from me, so that I may be released from the face of the earth and become dust . . . release me to go to the place of eternity*—that is, the grave, or Hades) capture the bitter despair of a person who sees death as preferable to living in suffering.

3:7–15 Sarah's suffering and prayer. 3:7 The author introduces Sarah, the daughter of Raguel, a close relative of Tobit. **3:8** Sarah is oppressed by the demon Asmodeus (the name is either from Heb. "destroyer" or a form of "Aeshma Daeva," the Persian demon of lust), who has killed her seven husbands on their wedding nights. *Have not borne the name.* She has been unable to fulfill her social role as a wife and mother. **3:9** *Why do you beat us?* indicates how Sarah takes out her frustration on her "female slaves" (v. 7). They retaliate by unjustly accusing her of murdering her husbands and wishing her dead. **3:10** She contemplates hanging herself, but knowing that suicide would grieve her father, she prays for death instead. By petitioning God for death, Sarah acknowledges God as

"Blessed are you, merciful God!
    Blessed is your name[v] forever;
    let all your works bless you forever.
[12] And now,[w] my face is toward you,
    and I have raised my eyes.
[13] Command that I be released from the
    earth
    and not listen to such reproaches any
      more.
[14] You know, O Master, that I am
    innocent[x]
    of any defilement with a man
[15] and that I have not disgraced my name
    or the name of my father in the land of
      my exile.
I am my father's only child;
    he has no other child to be his heir,
and he has no close relative or other
    kindred
    for whom I should keep myself as
      wife.
Already seven husbands of mine have
    died.
    Why should I still live?
But if it is not pleasing to you, O Lord, to
    take my life,
    hear me in my disgrace."

16 At that very moment, the prayers of both of them were heard in the glorious presence of God. [17]So Raphael was sent to heal both of them: Tobit by removing the white films from his eyes, so that he might see God's light with his eyes,[y] and Sarah, daughter of Raguel, by giving her in marriage to Tobias son of Tobit, and by setting her free from the wicked demon Asmodeus. For Tobias was entitled to have her before all others who had desired to marry her. At the same time that Tobit returned from the courtyard into his house, Sarah daughter of Raguel came down from her upper room.

4 That same day Tobit remembered the money that he had left in trust with Gabael at Rages in Media, [2]and he said to himself, "Now that I have asked for death, why do I not call my son Tobias and explain to him about this money before I die?" [3]Then he called his son Tobias, and when he came to him he said, "Give[z] me a proper burial. Honor your mother and do not abandon her all the days of her life. Do whatever pleases her, and do nothing that makes her unhappy. [4]Remember her, my son, because she faced many dangers for you[a] while you were in her womb. And when she dies, bury her beside me in the same grave.

5 "Be mindful of the Lord all your days, my son, and refuse to sin or to transgress his commandments. Do what is right all the days of your life, and do not walk in the ways of wrongdoing, [6]for those who act honestly will prosper in all their activities. To all those who practice righteousness,[b] [7]give alms according to your circumstances, my son, and do not turn your face away from anyone who is poor. Then the face of God will not be turned away from you. [8]Act according to what you have, my son. If you have much, give alms from it; if you have little, give alms in accordance with what you have. Do not be afraid,

v 3.11 Other ancient authorities add *holy and honorable*
w 3.12 Other ancient authorities add *Lord* x 3.14 Q ms adds *in my bones* y 3.17 Other ancient authorities lack *with his eyes* z 4.3 Other ancient authorities read *My son, when I die, give* a 4.4 Q ms adds *and carried you* b 4.6 S lacks 4.6–19, reading *To those who practice righteousness* [19]*the Lord will give good counsel*; 4.7–18 supplied here from another Gk ms

the one who gives life and who takes it away (cf. Job 1:21). **3:13** She, like Tobit, asks for death to end being reproached. **3:14** *I am innocent of any defilement with a man* indicates that her marriages were not consummated. **3:15** *I am my father's only child; he has no other child to be his heir.* She grieves being unable to bear offspring and provide her father with progeny. In a patriarchal society, this was seen as disgraceful.

3:16–17 God hears their prayers and sends Raphael (Heb., meaning "God heals") *to heal* them of their afflictions.

4:1–19 The way of wisdom. Tobit remembers the money he deposited with Gabael. Before sending Tobias to collect it, Tobit delivers a farewell discourse that serves as a sapiential exhortation on how Tobias is to conduct his affairs. **4:2–4** Tobit, who buried the dead, asks Tobias for a *proper burial* and care for his wife: *honor your mother* (cf. Exod. 20:12). Taking care of a widow was a filial duty. **4:5–6** Tobias is urged to *do what is right . . . not walk in the ways of wrongdoing* in order to *prosper* in life. Tobit's words reflect the idea that good conduct is rewarded (cf. Deut. 27–28). **4:7–8** *Give alms according to your circumstances* establishes the principle that even small contributions are significant. *Do not turn your face away . . . then the face of God will not be turned away from*

my son, to give alms. [9]You will be laying up a good treasure for yourself against a day of need. [10]For almsgiving delivers from death and keeps you from going into the darkness. [11]Indeed, almsgiving, for all who practice it, is an excellent offering in the presence of the Most High.

[12] "Beware, my son, of every kind of sexual immorality. First of all, marry a woman from among the descendants of your ancestors; do not marry a foreign woman, who is not of your father's tribe, for we are the descendants of prophets and true-born sons of prophets. The first prophet was[c] Abraham, then Isaac and Jacob, our ancestors of old. Remember, my son, that these all took wives from among their kindred. They were blessed in their children, and their posterity will inherit the land. [13]So now, my son, love your kindred, and in your heart do not be so arrogant against the daughters of the members of your people as to refuse to take one of them as a wife. For in arrogance there is ruin and great confusion, and in idleness there is loss and dire poverty, because idleness is the mother of famine.

[14] "Do not keep over until the next day the wages of those who work for you, but pay them their wages the same day, and let not the pay of those among you be delayed overnight. Your pay will not be kept over if you serve God faithfully. Watch yourself, my son, in everything you do, and discipline yourself in all your conduct. [15]And what you hate, do not do to anyone. May[d] no evil go with you on any of your way. [16]Give some of your food to the hungry and some of your clothing to the naked. Give all your surplus as alms, my son, and do not let your eye begrudge your giving of alms. [17]Pour out your food and your wine on the grave of the righteous, but do not give it to sinners. [18]Seek advice from every wise person, and do not be disdainful, since any counsel is useful. [19]At all times bless God and ask him that your ways may be made straight and that all your paths and plans may prosper. For no nation has good counsel, but the Lord himself gives it. Whom he wants to, he exalts, and whom he wants to, he casts down to Hades below. So now, my son, remember these commandments of mine, and do not let them be erased from your heart.

[20] "And now, my son, let me explain to you that I left ten talents of silver in trust with Gabael son of Gabrias, at Rages in Media. [21]Do not be afraid, my son, because we have become poor. You have great wealth if you fear God and flee from every sin and do what is good in the sight of the Lord your God."

5 Then Tobias answered his father Tobit, "I will do everything that you have commanded me, father, [2]but how can I obtain the money[e] from him, since he does not know me and I do not know him? What evidence[f] am I to give him so that he will recognize and trust me and give me the money? Also, I do not know the roads to Media or how to get there." [3]Then Tobit answered his son Tobias, "He gave me his bond, and I gave

c 4.12 Other ancient authorities add *Noah, then* d 4.15 Other ancient authorities read *Do not drink wine to excess, and may* e 5.2 Gk *it* f 5.2 Gk *sign*

you emphasizes again that good deeds are rewarded. **4:9–10** *Almsgiving delivers from death*—that is, from premature death. **4:11** *Almsgiving . . . is an excellent offering*, taking the place of expiatory sacrifices in the temple for Israelites living in the Diaspora. **4:12–13** *Beware . . . of sexual immorality* (Gk. "porneias"—that is, all sexual activity outside of marriage) is followed by the call to practice endogamy to preserve their identity. **4:14** To delay paying a laborer is an act of injustice. **4:15** Tobias is urged to adhere to what is later called the Golden Rule: *what you hate, do not do to anyone* (cf. Matt. 7:12; Luke 6:31). **4:16** *Do not let your eye begrudge your giving of alms* shows that charity should be offered with a sincere heart. **4:17** *Pour out your food and your wine on the grave of the righteous* refers to giving alms to the family of the deceased who were righteous. **4:18–19** Tobias is to seek good counsel and worship God as the basis for his upright life. *For no nation has good counsel* may be an assertion that only Israel has received God's wisdom in the Torah. Tobit then stresses God's sovereignty and control over human life.

4:20–21 Final instructions. 4:20 *Ten talents of silver*, see note on 1:14. **4:21** True *wealth*, however, consists in avoiding *sin* and doing *good in the sight of the Lord*.

5:1–3 Tobias worries about the trip. 5:2 The series of doubts—*how can I obtain the money . . . ? What evidence am I to give him . . . ? I do not know the roads*—shows his concerns about the journey to see Gabael. **5:3** Tobias's claim over the money will be verified by presenting half of the bond. A

him my bond. I[g] divided his in two; we each took one part, and I put one with the money. And now twenty years have passed since I left this money in trust. So now, my son, find yourself a trustworthy man to go with you, and we will pay him wages until you return. But get back the money from Gabael."[b]

4 So Tobias went out to look for a man to go with him to Media, someone who was acquainted with the way. He went out and found the angel Raphael standing in front of him, but he did not perceive that he was an angel of God. [5]Tobias[i] said to him, "Where do you come from, young man?" "From the Israelites, your kindred," he replied, "and I have come here to work." Then Tobias[j] said to him, "Do you know the way to go to Media?" [6]"Yes," he replied, "I have been there many times; I am acquainted with it and know all the roads. I have often traveled to Media and would stay with our kinsman Gabael who lives in Rages of Media. It is a journey of two days from Ecbatana to Rages, for it lies in a mountainous area, while Ecbatana is in the middle of the plain." [7]Then Tobias said to him, "Wait for me, young man, until I go in and tell my father, for I do need you to travel with me, and I will pay you your wages." [8]He replied, "All right, I will wait, but do not take too long."

9 So Tobias went in to tell his father Tobit and said to him, "I have just found a man who is one of our own Israelite kindred!" He replied, "Call the man in so that I may learn about his people and to what tribe he belongs and whether he is trustworthy enough to go with you, my son."

10 Then Tobias went out and called him and said, "Young man, my father is calling for you." So he went in to him, and Tobit greeted him first. He replied, "Many greetings to you!" But Tobit retorted, "What is left for me to greet any more? I am a man without eyesight; I cannot see the light of heaven, but I lie in darkness like the dead who no longer see the light. Although still alive, I am among the dead. I hear people's voices, but I cannot see them." But the young man[k] said, "Take courage; the time is near for God to heal you; take courage." Then Tobit said to him, "My son Tobias wishes to go to Media. Can you accompany him and guide him? I will pay your wages, brother." He answered, "I can go with him, and I know all the roads. I have often gone to Media, have crossed all its plains, and am familiar with its mountains and all of its roads."

11 Then Tobit[l] said to him, "Brother, of what family are you and from what tribe? Tell me, brother." [12]He replied, "Why do you need to know my tribe and lineage? Are you seeking an employee or a tribe and lineage?"[m] But Tobit[n] said, "I want to be sure, brother, whose son you are and what your name is." [13]He replied, "I am Azariah, the son of the elder Hananiah, one of your relatives." [14]Then Tobit[o] said to him, "You are very welcome, brother. Do not feel bitter toward me, brother, because I wanted to be sure about your family. It turns out that you are a kinsman and of good and noble lineage. For I knew Hananiah and Nathan, the two sons of the elder Shemeliah,[p] and they used to go with me to Jerusalem and worship with me there; they were not led astray. Your kindred are good people; you are of good stock. Welcome!"

15 Then he added, "I will pay you a drachma a day as wages, as well as expenses for

g 5.3 Other authorities read He   h 5.3 Gk from him
i 5.5 Gk He   j 5.5 Gk he   k 5.10 Gk he   l 5.11 Gk he
m 5.12 OL: S lacks and lineage? Are you seeking an employee or a tribe and lineage?   n 5.12 Gk he   o 5.14 Gk he   p 5.14 Other ancient authorities read Shemaiah

bond was a legal document written twice and signed by both parties, here cut into two pieces that can be matched. Tobit's suggestion, *find . . . a trustworthy man*, anticipates Raphael's appearance.

5:4–8 Tobias finds Raphael. 5:4–5 The *young man*—the angel Raphael in disguise—identifies himself as an Israelite, from Tobias's kindred. **5:6–8** Raphael claims extensive knowledge about the way to Media, and he says that he would even *stay with our kinsman Gabael*.

5:9–17 The angel meets Tobit. 5:10 The upbeat greeting of the *young man*—*Many greetings to you!*—is initially rejected by Tobit because of his blindness, but it is in fact foreshadowing the blessings that are to come, for *the time is near for God to heal you*. **5:11–12** After the initial greeting, Tobit ensures that the young man is not only a suitable guide to lead Tobias to Media but also a Jew. **5:13** The young man claims to be *Azariah* (Heb., meaning "the LORD has helped") *son of the elder Hananiah* (Heb., meaning "the LORD is merciful"). Tobit understands the names as proof of family ancestry, but the reader may also see them as signs of God's providence. **5:15–16** The "young man" is then offered *a drachma a day*, roughly the equivalent of a skilled worker's daily pay, to accompany

yourself and my son. So go with my son, [16]and I will add something to your wages." Raphael[q] answered, "I will go with him, so do not fear. We shall leave in good health and return to you in good health because the way is safe." [17]So Tobit[r] said to him, "Blessings be upon you, brother."

Then he called his son and said to him, "Make preparations for the journey, my son, and set out with your brother. May God in heaven bring you safely there and return you in good health to me, and may his angel, my son, accompany you both for your safety."

Before he[s] went out to start his journey, he kissed his father and mother. Tobit then said to him, "Have a safe journey."

18 But his mother began to weep and said to Tobit, "Why is it that you have sent my son away? Is he not the staff of our hand as he goes in and out before us? [19]Do not heap money upon money, but let it be a ransom for our son. [20]The life that is given to us by the Lord is enough for us." [21]Tobit[t] said to her, "Do not worry; our son will leave in good health and return to us in good health. Your eyes will see him on the day when he returns to you in good health. Say no more! Do not fear for them, my sister, [22]for a good angel will accompany him; his journey will be successful, and he will come back in good health." [1]So she stopped weeping.

6 The young man went out, and the angel went with him, [2]and the dog came out with him and went along with them. So they both journeyed along, and when the first night overtook them they camped by the Tigris River. [3]Then the young man went down to wash his feet in the Tigris River, and a large fish leaped up from the water and tried to swallow the young man's foot, and he cried out. [4]But the angel said to the young man, "Catch hold of the fish and hang on to it!" So the young man grasped the fish and drew it up on the land. [5]Then the angel said to him, "Cut open the fish and take out its gall, heart, and liver. Keep them with you, but throw away the intestines. For its gall, heart, and liver are useful as medicine." [6]So after cutting open the fish the young man gathered together the gall, heart, and liver; then he roasted and ate some of the fish and kept some to be salted for the journey.[u]

The two continued on their way together until they were near Media. [7]Then the young man questioned the angel and said to him, "Azariah, my brother, what medicinal value is there in the fish's heart and liver and in the gall?" [8]He replied, "As for the fish's heart and liver, you must burn them to make a smoke in the presence of a man or woman afflicted by a demon or evil spirit, and every affliction will flee away and never remain with that person any longer. [9]And as for the gall, anoint a person's eyes where white films have appeared on them; blow upon them, upon the white films, and the eyes[v] will be healed."

10 When they entered Media and were already approaching Ecbatana, [11]Raphael said to the young man, "Tobias, my brother." "Here I am," he answered. Then Raphael[w] said to him, "We must stay this night in the home of Raguel. That man is your relative, and he has a daughter named Sarah. [12]He has

q 5.16 Gk *He* r 5.17 Gk *he* s 5.17 Other ancient authorities read *So he made preparations for the journey and* t 5.21 Gk *He* u 6.6 Q ms: S lacks *for the journey* v 6.9 Gk *they* w 6.11 Gk *he*

Tobias to Media. 5:17 There is irony in Tobit's blessing upon the young man and Tobias in his petition that God's *angel . . . accompany you both* on the way, since God has sent the "young man," God's angel Raphael, in disguise.

5:18–6:1a Anna weeps. 5:18–19 *Why is it that you have sent my son away?* expresses Anna's love, concern, and disapproval of Tobit sending her only child to a distant land on a task that may not be successful. **5:20–22** Tobit ironically assures her of God's care: *a good angel will accompany him.*

6:1b–9 Journey to Rages. 6:1b–2 Tobias *and the angel* are accompanied by a *dog* (cf. 11:4) and spend the first night by the Tigris River. **6:3** *A large fish leaped up . . . and tried to swallow the young man's foot.* Feet are a euphemism for the genitals in the Bible. If the fish tried to swallow Tobias's genitals, the incident foreshadows Asmodeus's attempt to kill him to prevent the consummation of the marriage with Sarah. **6:7–8** The foul-smelling smoke will be used to release Sarah from Asmodeus in 6:17–18 (cf. 2 Kgs. 20:7). **6:9** *Gall,* a digestive liquid produced in the liver and stored in the gallbladder, was used to treat blindness in the ancient Near East (see Pliny, *Nat. Hist.* 33.24).

6:10–13 Raphael encourages Tobias to marry Sarah. 6:12 Raguel *has no male heir . . . and you, as next of kin to her, have . . . a hereditary claim on her.* According to the law of levirate marriage

Reading through Time: Angels (Tobit 6)

Angels appear throughout the Bible. They are called sons of God, heavenly host, cherubim, and seraphim. Four angels are named in the Hebrew Bible, deuterocanonical/apocryphal books, or Christian Scriptures: Gabriel, Michael, Raphael, and Uriel. The endings of their names, el (Heb., meaning "God"), indicate their closeness to the deity. Angels are spirit beings that can assume a temporary physical appearance to carry out God's mission.

Raphael (Heb., meaning "God heals") exemplifies his ministry in healing, protecting, and guiding in the book of Tobit (cf. 1 En.). Raphael's healing work includes curing Tobit from blindness (6:9; 11:7) and releasing Sarah from the power of the demon Asmodeus (6:8; 12:14). Raphael makes Tobit's and Sarah's prayers known to God (12:12). Raphael appears to the other characters in Tobit as a "young man" who identifies himself as Azariah (Heb., meaning "YHWH's help"), a kinsman to Tobit, and offers to guide and protect Tobias on his journey to Ecbatana. Raphael's presence indicates that God accompanies God's people in times of suffering, persecution, illness, and fear. The idea that angels protect people is also attested in the New Testament. Jesus's words—"in heaven their [children's] angels continually see the face of my Father in heaven" (Matt. 18:10)—give rise to the Christian idea of "guardian angels."

Michael (Heb., meaning "who is like God") is "one of the chief princes" of a battalion of angels (Dan. 10:13). The book of Daniel mentions him frequently as the angel that will have a significant role in the end-time events (Dan. 12:1). In Revelation, Michael leads a host of angels in a victorious war over Satan and his demons (Rev. 12). The angel Gabriel (Heb., meaning "strength of God") announces the impending births of John and Jesus in Luke's Gospel (Luke 1:8-20, 26-38). Uriel (Heb., meaning "fire of God") instructs Ezra in 2 Esdras (4:1-4; 10:29-59) and is portrayed elsewhere as the angel of repentance and of the damned (Apoc. Pet. 4, 6).

Some traditions mention seven angels (Tob. 12:15; Rev. 8:2). First Enoch lists the four biblical angels along with three others: Reuel/Raguel, Sariel/Sarakiel, and Remiel (1 En. 20:1-8). These and other angels are developed in later Jewish and Christian traditions.

J. L. Manzo

---

no male heir and no daughter except Sarah only, and you, as next of kin to her, have before all other men a hereditary claim on her. Also, it is right for you to inherit her father's possessions. Moreover, the young woman is intelligent, brave, and very beautiful, and her father is a good man." [13]He continued, "You have every right to take her in marriage. So listen to me, brother; tonight I will speak to her father about the young woman, so that we may take her to be your bride. When we return from Rages[x] we will celebrate her marriage. For I know that Raguel can by no means keep her from you or promise her to another man without incurring the penalty of death according to the decree of the book of Moses. Indeed, he knows that you, rather than any other man, are entitled to marry his daughter. So now listen to me, brother, and tonight we shall speak concerning the young woman and arrange her engagement

to you. And when we return from Rages, we will take her and bring her back with us to your house."

[14] Then Tobias said in answer to Raphael, "Azariah, my brother, I have heard that she already has been married to seven husbands and that they died in the bridal chamber. On the night when they went in to her, they would die. And I have heard some say that a demon kills them.[y] [15]It does not harm her, but it kills anyone who desires to approach her. So now, since I am the only son my father has, I am afraid that I may die and bring my father's and mother's lives down to their graves, grieving for me—and they have no other son to bury them."

[16] But Raphael[z] said to him, "Do you not remember your father's orders when he commanded you to take a wife from your father's

x 6.13 OL: S reads *Raguel*   y 6.14 Other ancient authorities lack *And I... kills them*   z 6.16 Gk *he*

(Deut. 25:5-10), if a man dies childless, his next of kin marries his widow, and they bear children to perpetuate the name of the deceased and protect inheritance rights.

6:14-19 Tobias's hesitation. 6:14-15 Tobias, an *only son*, is fearful of leaving his parents destitute in their old age if he dies. **6:16** *Do you not remember your father's orders . . . to take a wife from*

house? Now listen to me, brother, and say no more about this demon. Take her. I know that this very night she will be given to you in marriage. [17]When you enter the bridal chamber, take some of the fish's liver and heart and put them on the embers of the incense. An odor will be given off; [18]the demon will smell it and flee and will never be seen near her any more. Now when you are about to go to bed with her, both of you must first stand up and pray, imploring the Lord of heaven that mercy and safety may be granted to you. Do not be afraid, for she has always been set apart for you. You will save her, and she will go with you. I know that you will have children by her, and they will be as brothers and sisters to you. Now say no more!" When Tobias heard the words of Raphael and learned that she was his sister, related through his father's lineage, he loved her very much, and his heart was drawn to her.

7 Now when they[a] entered Ecbatana, Tobias[b] said to him, "Azariah, my brother, take me straight to our brother Raguel." So he took him to Raguel's house, where they found him sitting beside the courtyard door. They greeted him first, and he replied, "Many greetings, my brothers; welcome and good health!" Then he brought them into his house. [2]He said to his wife Edna, "How much this young man resembles my kinsman Tobit!" [3]Then Edna questioned them, saying, "Where are you from, my brothers?" They answered her, "We belong to the descendants of Naphtali who are exiles in

Nineveh." [4]She said to them, "Do you know our kinsman Tobit?" And they replied, "Yes, we know him." Then she asked them, "Is he in good health?" [5]They replied, "He is alive and in good health." And Tobias added, "He is my father!" [6]At that Raguel jumped up and kissed him and wept. [7]He also spoke to him as follows, "Blessings on you, my son, offspring of a good and noble father! O most miserable of calamities that such an upright and beneficent man has become blind!" He then embraced his kinsman Tobias and wept. [8]His wife Edna also wept for him, and their daughter Sarah likewise wept. [9]Then Raguel[c] slaughtered a ram from the flock and received them very warmly.

When they had bathed and washed themselves and had reclined to dine, Tobias said to Raphael, "Azariah, my brother, ask Raguel to give me my sister Sarah." [10]But Raguel overheard it and said to the young man, "Eat and drink, and be merry tonight. For no one except you, brother, has the right to marry my daughter Sarah. Likewise I am not at liberty to give her to any other man than you because you are my nearest relative. But let me explain to you the true situation more fully, my son. [11]I have given her to seven men of our kinsmen, and all died on the night when they went in to her. But now, my son, eat and drink, and the Lord will act on behalf of you both." But Tobias said, "I will neither eat nor drink anything until you settle the

a 7.1 Q ms OL: S *he*   *b* 7.1 Gk *he*   *c* 7.9 Gk *he*

your father's house recalls Tobit's earlier instruction (4:12). **6:17–18a** Raphael provides instructions on how to dispel the demon. **6:18b** Raphael's command to accompany the ritual with prayer attributes the healing properties of the fish organs to God. That *she has always been set apart for you* expresses the unique idea in the Bible that God has predestined their union.

7:1–9a At Ecbatana. 7:1 Ecbatana is the capital of Media. Tobias addresses Raphael as *Azariah*, the name Raphael used to identify himself to Tobit (5:13). Raguel's salutation, *many greetings*, echoes the angel's earlier greeting to Tobit (5:10). **7:2** Raguel notices Tobias's uncanny resemblance to his kinsman Tobit. **7:3** The name Edna comes from a Hebrew word meaning "pleasure" or "delight." *Descendants of Naphtali*, one of the twelve tribes of Israel, captured by the Assyrians in 722 BCE. *Nineveh* was located on the Tigris River and was the capital of the Assyrian Empire. **7:5** Raguel and Edna learn that Tobias is the son of Tobit, Raguel's kinsman. **7:7–9a** *That such an upright and beneficent man has become blind* goes against the concept of retributive justice (cf. Deut. 27:11–28:68). Their tears express joy in meeting Tobias and Azariah (that is, Raphael), who are readily welcomed with a sumptuous meal.

7:9b–14 The marriage arrangement. 7:10–11a *Eat and drink, and be merry tonight* may express Raguel's benign way of saying "eat, drink, and be merry, for tomorrow you will die" (cf. Isa. 22:13) or perhaps an attempt to calm Tobias's eagerness, as he refuses to eat or drink until the marriage arrangements are settled. **7:11b** *She is given to you in accordance with the decree in the book of*

things that pertain to me." So Raguel said, "I will do so. She is given to you in accordance with the decree in the book of Moses, and it has been decreed from heaven that she be given to you. Take your sister; from now on you are her brother, and she is your sister. She is given to you from today and forever. May the Lord of heaven, my son, guide and prosper you both this night and grant you mercy and peace." [12]Then Raguel summoned his daughter Sarah. When she came to him, he took her by the hand and gave her to Tobias,[d] saying, "Take her to be your wife in accordance with the law and decree written in the book of Moses. Take her and bring her safely to your father. And may the God of heaven let your journey go smoothly and in his peace." [13]Then he called her mother and told her to bring writing material, and he wrote out a copy of a marriage contract, to the effect that he gave her to him as wife according to the decree of the law of Moses.[e] [14]Then they began to eat and drink.

[15] Raguel called his wife Edna and said to her, "Sister, get the other room ready, and take her there." [16]So she went and made the bed in the room as he had told her and brought Sarah[f] there. She wept for her daughter.[g] Then, wiping away the tears, she said to her, "Take courage, my daughter; the Lord of heaven grant you joy in place of your sorrow. Take courage, my daughter." Then she went out.

8 When they had finished eating and drinking, they wanted to retire, so they took the young man and brought him into the bedroom. [2]Then Tobias remembered the words of Raphael, and he took the fish's liver and heart out of the bag where he had them and put them on the embers of the incense. [3]The odor of the fish so repelled the demon that he fled to the remotest parts[h] of Egypt. But Raphael followed him and at once bound him there hand and foot.

4 When the parents[i] had gone out and shut the door of the room, Tobias got out of bed and said to Sarah,[j] "Sister, get up, and let us pray and implore our Lord that he grant us mercy and safety." [5]So she got up, and they began to pray and implore that they might be kept safe. Tobias[k] began by saying,

"Blessed are you, O God of our
    ancestors,
    and blessed is your name in all
    generations forever.
Let the heavens and the whole creation
    bless you forever.
[6] You made Adam, and for him you made
    his wife Eve
    as a helper and support.
    From the two of them the human race
    has sprung.

d 7.12 Gk *him*   e 7.13 Other ancient authorities add *and put his seal to it*   f 7.16 Gk *her*   g 7.16 Gk *her*   h 8.3 Gk *fled through the air to the parts*   i 8.4 Gk *they*   j 8.4 Gk *her*   k 8.5 Gk *He*

Moses is likely a reference to the law of levirate marriage (Deut. 25:5–10). See note on 6:12. **7:12** *He took her by the hand and gave her to Tobias* is a legal gesture denoting the transfer of the woman from the father's authority to that of the husband (Exod. 21:7; 22:16). **7:13** The *marriage contract* probably expressed Raguel's consent to give Sarah in marriage to Tobias.

7:15–16 The wedding preparation. 7:15 Raguel asks Edna to prepare a special room for the wedding night. **7:16** Edna weeps in anticipation for what she believes will be another night of mourning. Edna's wish that *the Lord of heaven grant you joy in place of your sorrow* expresses her hope that this night will be different from Sarah's previous wedding nights.

8:1–9a The wedding night. 8:2 Following Raphael's earlier instructions (6:17–18a), Tobias *took the fish's liver and heart . . . and put them on the embers of the incense.* **8:3** In the ancient Near East, the burning of the fish's organs was thought to have an apotropaic function of warding off evil or a means to enhance sexual potency. Here, the foul smell produced by the burned organs *so repelled the demon that he fled to the remotest parts of Egypt.* That Raphael *at once bound him . . . hand and foot* may rely on Jewish traditions that attribute to angels the subjugation of the leader of demons (1 En. 10:4). **8:4–5** As previously directed by Raphael (6:18), the couple prays for God's protection. **8:6–7** *You made Adam, and for him you made his wife Eve as a helper and support.* Tobias's prayer recalls the creation account in Gen. 2. *It is not good that the man should be alone; let us make a helper for him like himself* is a variation of Gen. 2:18: "It is not good that the man should be alone; I will make him a helper as his partner." Tobias emphasizes that he is marrying Sarah *not for sexual gratification, but with sincerity.*

You said, 'It is not good that the man
should be alone;
let us make a helper for him like
himself.'
⁷ I now am taking this sister of mine,
not for sexual gratification,
but with sincerity.
Grant that she and I may find mercy
and that we may grow old
together."
⁸And they both together said, "Amen, Amen."
⁹Then they went to sleep for the night.

But Raguel arose and called his servants
to him, and they went and dug a grave, ¹⁰for
he said, "It is possible that he will die, and
we will become an object of ridicule and
derision." ¹¹When they had finished digging
the grave, Raguel went into his house and
called his wife, ¹²saying, "Send one of the female slaves and have her go in to see if he is
alive. But if he is dead, let us bury him without anyone knowing it." ¹³So they sent the female slave, lit a lamp, and opened the door;
and she went in and found them lying in bed
asleep together. ¹⁴Then the female slave came
out and informed them that he was alive and
that nothing was wrong. ¹⁵So they blessed the
God of heaven, and Raguel⁽ˡ⁾ said,

"Blessed are you, O God, with every pure
blessing;
let all your chosen ones bless you.⁽ᵐ⁾
Let them bless you forever.
¹⁶ Blessed are you because you have made
me glad.
It has not turned out as I expected,
but you have dealt with us according
to your great mercy.
¹⁷ Blessed are you because you had
compassion
on two only children.
Be merciful to them, O Master, and keep
them safe;
bring their lives to fulfillment
in happiness and mercy."
¹⁸Then he ordered his servants to fill in the
grave before daybreak.

19 After this he asked his wife to bake
many loaves of bread, and he went out to
the herd and brought two steers and four
rams and ordered them to be slaughtered.
So they began to make preparations. ²⁰Then
he called for Tobias and⁽ⁿ⁾ said to him: "You
shall not leave here for fourteen days but
shall stay here eating and drinking with me,
and you shall cheer up my daughter, who
has been depressed. ²¹Take at once half of
what I own and return in safety to your father; the other half will be yours when my
wife and I die. Take courage, my son. I am
your father, and Edna is your mother, and
we belong to you as well as to your sister
now and forever. Take courage, my son."

9 Then Tobias called Raphael and said
to him, ²"Azariah, my brother, take
four servants and two camels with you and
travel to Rages. Go to the home of Gabael,
give him the bond, get the money, and then

l 8.15 Gk *they* *m* 8.15 Other ancient authorities lack this
line *n* 8.20 OL reads *swore on oath, saying*

8:9b–18 Tobias survives. 8:9b–10 Tobias's trust in God is contrasted with Raguel's instruction to his servants to dig a grave for Tobias in the middle of the night. **8:12** *See if he is alive* captures Raguel's hope that Tobias is alive while anticipating his death. **8:14–17** Upon hearing *that he was alive*, Raguel praises God. Raguel emphasizes that both Tobias and Sarah are *only children*. **8:18** The filling of the *grave before daybreak* covers up Raguel's earlier doubts that Tobias would live.
8:19–21 The wedding celebration. 8:19 The wedding celebration is an elaborate banquet of many loaves of bread and many slaughtered animals. **8:20** For *fourteen days*, twice the time of a usual wedding celebration, Raguel invites Tobias to eat and drink and to *cheer up* Sarah. Raguel wants to see Sarah happy before she departs from them. **8:21** Take . . . *half of what I own* is Sarah's dowry, given to Tobias as Sarah's husband. Since Sarah was an only child, she would inherit the rest of her parents' fortune upon their death. *I am your father, and Edna is your mother* expresses Raguel's familial affection for Tobias.
9:1–6 Raphael collects the money. 9:1–2 *Then Tobias called Raphael* during the celebration to carry out the original purpose of their trip, the collection of the ten talents of silver (4:20). Tobias tells Raphael, whom he calls Azariah, to travel to Rages with *four servants and two camels*. Rages is about two hundred miles northeast of Ecbatana; therefore, the camels were needed to carry the ten talents of silver and other provisions needed for the trip. Tobias further instructs Raphael to present the *bond* to Gabael. The *bond*—a legal document written twice with matching signatures, or a document written twice and then cut into two matching pieces, with each party keeping a

bring him with you to the wedding celebration. [4]For you know that my father must be counting the days, and if I delay even one day I will upset him very much. [3]You are witness to the oath Raguel has sworn, and I cannot violate his oath."[o] [5]So Raphael with the four servants and two camels went to Rages in Media and stayed with Gabael. Raphael[p] gave him the bond and informed him that Tobit's son Tobias had married and was inviting him to the wedding celebration. So Gabael[q] got up and counted out to him the money bags, with their seals intact, and they put them together. [6]In the morning they both got up early and went to the wedding celebration. When they came into Raguel's house, they found Tobias reclining at table. He sprang up and greeted Gabael,[r] who wept and blessed him with the words, "Good and noble son of a father good and noble, upright and generous! May the Lord grant the blessing of heaven to you and your wife and to your father and to the mother of your wife. Blessed be God, for I see in Tobias the very image of my cousin Tobit."

10 Now day by day Tobit kept counting how many days Tobias[s] would need

for going and for returning. And when the days had passed and his son did not appear, [2]he said, "Is it possible that he has been detained? Or that Gabael has died, and there is no one to give him the money?" [3]And he began to worry. [4]His wife Anna said, "My son has perished and is no longer among the living." And she began to weep and mourn for her son, saying, [5]"Woe to me, my child, the light of my eyes, that I let you make the journey." [6]But Tobit kept saying to her, "Be quiet and stop worrying, my sister; he is all right. Something must have happened to delay them. The man who went with him is trustworthy and is one of our own kin. Do not grieve for him, my sister; he will be here soon." [7]She answered him, "Be quiet yourself! Stop trying to deceive me! My son has perished." She would rush out every day and watch the road her son had taken and would heed no one.[t] When the sun had set she would go in and mourn and weep all night long, getting no sleep.

Now when the fourteen days of the wedding celebration had ended that Raguel had

---

o 9.3 In other ancient authorities 9.3 precedes 9.4
p 9.5 Gk *He*   q 9.5 Gk *he*   r 9.6 Gk *him*   s 10.1 Gk *he*
t 10.7 Other ancient authorities read *would eat nothing*

---

copy—authenticates the right of claim over the money. **9:3–4** Tobias expresses his eagerness to return to his parents, who must be worried about his whereabouts; at the same time, he wishes to remain in Ecbatana for the fourteen days of the marriage celebration as Raguel promised (8:20). **9:5** Raphael presents Gabael with the *bond*, and immediately he turns over the bags with their original seal. Thus, Gabael is portrayed as a person of utmost integrity. **9:6** *In the morning they both got up early and went to the wedding celebration* envisions a one-day trip back to Ecbatana. The trip, however, would have taken at least twelve days. When they enter Raguel's house, they find Tobias *reclining at table*. In the ancient Near East, people typically ate reclining on the left side on cushions with the right hand free to dip from a common dish. Gabael weeps because he is overjoyed to see Tobias. Gabael characterizes Tobit as being a person of integrity and Tobias as mirroring his father in character and appearance.

   10:1–7a Tobias's parents worry. 10:1 *Tobit kept counting how many days Tobias would need for going and for returning.* This juxtaposes Tobit's unease with the joyful mood of the wedding celebration in the previous scene. **10:2** Tobit's questions—*Is it possible that he has been detained? Or that Gabael has died, and there is no one to give him the money?*—depict his anxiety over the success of Tobias's journey, but he does not question whether his son has died. **10:4–5** Anna presents a more pessimist outlook. *My son has perished . . . the light of my eyes* captures her motherly concern over her only child, whom she believes to be dead. She even blames herself, saying, *woe to me . . . that I let you make the journey* (contrast 5:18, where Tobit sends the son). **10:6** Tobit's words, *be quiet and stop worrying*, echo his argument with Anna about sending Tobias on the journey in the first place (5:21–22). His attempt to console Anna—*something must have happened to delay them*—is an ironic reminder that something unexpected has already happened: God, who sent Raphael to protect Tobias's life on the journey and success in the task, has also given him a virtuous, beautiful wife. **10:7a** Anna rejects Tobit's words of consolation because she believes Tobias is already dead. Nevertheless, every day she would *watch the road* Tobias had taken hoping for his safe return.

   10:7b–10 Tobias remembers his parents. Tobias seeks to return to Nineveh after *the fourteen days*

sworn to observe for his daughter, Tobias came to him and said, "Send me back, for I know that my father and mother do not believe that they will see me again. So I beg of you, father, to let me go so that I may return to my own father. I have already explained to you how I left him." [8]But Raguel said to Tobias, "Stay, my son, stay with me; I will send messengers to your father Tobit, and they will inform him about you." [9]But he said to him, "No! I beg you to send me back to my father." [10]So Raguel stood and gave Tobias his wife Sarah, as well as half of all his property: male and female slaves, oxen and sheep, donkeys and camels, clothing, money, and household goods. [11]Then he saw them safely off; he embraced Tobias[u] and said to him, "Farewell, my son; have a safe journey. The Lord of heaven prosper you and your wife Sarah, and may I see children of yours before I die." [12]Then he said to his daughter Sarah, "My daughter, go to your father-in-law and your mother-in-law,[v] since from now on they are as much your parents as those who gave you birth. Go in peace, daughter, and may I hear a good report about you as long as I live." Then he bade them farewell and let them go. Then Edna said to Tobias, "My child and dear brother, the Lord of heaven bring you back safely, and may I live long enough to see children from you and of my daughter Sarah before I die. In the sight of the Lord I entrust my daughter to you; do nothing to make her unhappy all the days of your life. Go in peace, my son. From now on I am your mother, and Sarah is your sister. May we all prosper together all the days of our lives." Then she kissed them both and saw them safely off. [13]Tobias parted from Raguel with happiness and joy, praising the Lord of heaven and earth, King over all, because he had made his journey a success, and he blessed Raguel and his wife Edna and said,[w] "May it come to pass that I honor[x] them all the days of their lives."[y]

11 When they came near to Kaserin, which is opposite Nineveh, Raphael said, [2]"You are aware of how we left your father. [3]Let us run ahead of your wife and prepare the house while they are still on the way." [4]As they went on together, Raphael[z] said to him, "Have the gall ready in your hand." And the dog[a] went along behind them.

5 Meanwhile Anna sat looking intently down the road by which her son would come. [6]When she caught sight of him coming, she said to his father, "Look, your son is coming, and the man who went with him!"

7 Raphael said to Tobias before he had approached his father, "I know that his eyes will be opened. [8]Smear the gall of the fish on his eyes; the medicine will make the white films shrink and peel off from his eyes, and your father will regain his sight and see the light."

u 10.11 Gk *him*   v 10.12 Other ancient authorities lack parts of *Then . . . mother-in-law*   w 10.13 OL: S *And he said to him*   x 10.13 Cn: S *May it go well for you to honor*   y 10.13 OL: Meaning of Gk uncertain   z 11.4 Gk *he*   a 11.4 OL: S reads *And the Lord*

of the wedding celebration had ended, despite Raguel's insistence to delay the trip. **10:10** *Raguel . . . gave Tobias his wife Sarah . . . half of all his property: male and female slaves, oxen and sheep, donkeys and camels, clothing, money, and household goods.* The dowry (Heb. "mohar") described here is the property the bride brings to her husband's home for the economic stability of the marriage and to solidify family ties. For commandments regarding enslaved people, see Exod. 21:2–11, 20–21; Lev. 25:47–55; Deut. 15:12–18. See **"Human Bondage in Ancient Israel (The Law)," p. 115.**

10:11–13 Farewells. 10:12 *My daughter, go to your father-in-law and your mother-in-law.* Sarah is now a member of Tobias's family and must honor her in-laws as her own parents. Edna addresses Tobias as *my child and dear brother*, or kinsman, to express their familial relationship. After petitioning the *Lord of heaven* to grant her the joy of seeing her future grandchildren, she invokes the Lord as witness of having placed Sarah under Tobias's care.

11:1–6 Tobias's return. 11:1–3 *When they came near to Kaserin . . . opposite Nineveh,* Raphael suggests traveling ahead of the caravan to prepare the house for Sarah's arrival. **11:4** *Have the gall ready* anticipates Raphael's intention to complete his second assigned task, healing Tobit (3:17; 6:9). While dogs are often portrayed negatively in the Bible, here *the dog* that *went along* is a symbol of faithful companionship (cf. 6:2). **11:5** Despite believing that Tobias has perished (10:4, 7), *Anna sat looking intently down the road*, desperately hoping for his return.

11:7–14a Tobit's healing. 11:7–8 Before Tobias sees his father, Raphael reassures him that Tobit's *eyes will be opened*. The passive voice implies that God is the one who will restore Tobit's sight.

9 Then Anna ran up to her son and threw her arms around her son, saying, "Now that I have seen you, my son, I am ready to die." And she wept. [10]Then Tobit got up and came stumbling out through the courtyard door. Tobias went up to him, [11]with the gall of the fish in his hand, and blew it into his eyes, then took hold of him, saying, "Take courage, father." With this he applied the medicine on his eyes, [12]and it stung.[b] [13]Next, with both his hands he peeled off the white films from the corners of his eyes. Then Tobit[c] threw his arms around him, [14]and he wept and said to him, "I see you, my son, the light of my eyes!" Then he said,

"Blessed be God.
   May his great name be upon us,
   and blessed be all the angels[d]
   throughout all the ages.
[15] Though he afflicted me,[e]
   now I see my son Tobias!"

So Tobit went in rejoicing and praising God at the top of his voice. Tobias reported to his father that his journey had been successful, that he had brought the money, that he had married Raguel's daughter Sarah, and that she was, indeed, on her way there, very near to the gate of Nineveh.

16 Then Tobit,[f] rejoicing and praising God, went out to meet his daughter-in-law at the gate of Nineveh. When the people of Nineveh saw him coming, walking along in full vigor and with no one leading him, they were amazed. [17]Before them all, Tobit acknowledged that God had been merciful to him and had restored his sight. When Tobit met Sarah the wife of his son Tobias, he blessed her, saying, "Come in, my daughter, and be welcome. Blessed be your God who has brought you to us, my daughter. Blessed be your father and your mother, blessed be my son Tobias, and blessed be you, my daughter. Come in now to your home, and be welcome, with blessing and joy. Come in, my daughter." So on that day there was rejoicing among all the Jews who were in Nineveh. [18]Ahikar and his nephew Nadab were also present to share Tobit's joy.[g]

12 When the wedding celebration was ended, Tobit called his son Tobias and said to him, "My son, see to paying the wages of the man who went with you, and give him a bonus as well." [2]He replied, "Father, how much shall I pay him? It would do me no harm to give him half of the possessions brought back with me. [3]For he has led me back safely, cured my wife, brought the money back with me, and healed you. How much extra shall I give him as a bonus?" [4]Tobit replied, "He deserves, my son, to receive

b 11.12 Cn: S *and applied*   c 11.13 Gk *he*   d 11.14 Other ancient authorities lack *May his great . . . angels*   e 11.15 OL adds *he has had mercy upon me*   f 11.16 Gk *he*   g 11.18 Other ancient authorities add *With merriment they celebrated Tobias's wedding feast for seven days, and many gifts were given to him*

Tobias follows Raphael's instruction to smear the fish's gall on his father's eyes. **11:9** Tobit's healing is momentarily interrupted by Anna's emotional reunion with Tobias. **11:10–12** Tobias approaches his father and applies the gall by blowing it into his father's eyes. **11:13–14a** Removing the *white films* from his eyes, Tobit exclaims, *I see you, my son, the light of my eyes*. He has gone from being in a state of blindness and anger to one of sight and joy.

11:14b–15 The doxology. Tobit praises God for regaining his sight and the safe return of his son. *Angels* are appropriately blessed because of Raphael's intervention. *Though he afflicted me, now I see my son Tobias* is Tobit's recognition of God's sovereignty over life.

11:16–18 Tobit meets Sarah. 11:16 Tobit meets Sarah to the amazement of the people who see him walking unassisted. **11:17** *Before them all*, Tobit announces that God has healed him (cf. 12:6). Tobit also blesses Sarah and welcomes her into the family. *Among all the Jews* is an anachronistic reference that reflects the period in which the book of Tobit was composed (second or third century BCE) rather than the narrative setting after the fall of the northern kingdom of Israel in 722 BCE. Joining the celebration are Tobit's nephew Ahikar and Nadab, Ahikar's nephew (see 14:10). According to the book of Ahiqar, Nadab betrays his uncle Ahikar.

12:1–5 Raphael's wages paid. 12:1 *When the wedding celebration was ended*, Tobit instructs Tobias to pay Azariah's *wages* and to include *a bonus*. Earlier Tobit had agreed to pay Azariah a drachma a day, the standard wage for a skilled laborer's day's work, and promised, "I will add something to your wages" (5:15–16). **12:2–3** *How much shall I pay him?* Azariah has done much more than just guide Tobias on the journey; he brought Tobias back safely with the money, and he healed Tobit and Sarah. Tobias suggests *to give him half of the possessions brought back with me*. **12:4–5** Tobit agrees, indicating their generosity and righteousness.

half of all that he brought back." [5]So Tobias[b] called him and said, "Take for your wages half of all that you brought back, and farewell."

6 Then Raphael[i] called the two of them privately and said to them, "Bless God and acknowledge him in the presence of all the living for the good things he has done for you. Bless and sing praise to his name. With fitting honor declare to all people the deeds[j] of God. Do not be slow to acknowledge him. [7]It is good to conceal the secret of a king and to acknowledge and reveal the works of God with proper honor. Do good, and evil will not overtake you. [8]Prayer with fidelity is good, and almsgiving with righteousness is better than wealth with injustice. It is better to give alms than to lay up gold, [9]for almsgiving saves from death and purges away every sin. Those who give alms will enjoy a full life, [10]but those who commit sin and do wrong are their own enemies.

11 "I will now declare the whole truth to you and will conceal nothing from you. Already I have declared it to you when I said, 'It is good to conceal the secret of a king but to reveal with due honor the works of God.' [12]So now when you and Sarah prayed, it was I who brought the record of your prayers before the glory of the Lord, and likewise whenever you would bury the dead. [13]And that time when you did not hesitate to get up and leave your dinner to go and lay out that corpse, [14]I was sent to you to test you. And at the same time God sent me to heal you and Sarah your daughter-in-law. [15]I am Raphael, one of the seven angels who stand ready and enter before the glory of the Lord."

16 The two of them were shaken and threw themselves face down, for they were afraid. [17]But he said to them, "Do not be afraid; peace be with you. Bless God forevermore. [18]As for me, when I was with you, I was not acting on my own will but by the will of God. Bless him each and every day; sing his praises. [19]When you were watching me, I was not really eating[k] anything, but what you saw was a vision. [20]So now bless the Lord on the earth[l] and acknowledge God. See, I am ascending to him who sent me. Write down all these things that have happened to you." And he ascended. [21]Then they stood up and could see him no more. [22]They kept blessing God and singing his praises, and they acknowledged God for these marvelous deeds of his, that an angel of God had appeared to them.

b 12.5 Gk *he*   i 12.6 Gk *he*   j 12.6 Gk *words*; other ancient authorities read *words of the deeds*   k 12.19 Other ancient authorities add *and drinking*   l 12.20 Other ancient authorities read *get up from the ground*

12:6–10 Raphael's instructions. 12:6 Raphael summons Tobit and Tobias privately and instructs them to praise and honor God *in the presence of all the living.* **12:7** *It is good to conceal the secret of a king* (cf. Sir. 27:16) but appropriate *to acknowledge and reveal the works of God.* **12:8** *Prayer with fidelity is good, and almsgiving with righteousness is better than wealth with injustice* are pillars of Jewish practice. In the Diaspora, private and public fasting became more prominent (1 Macc. 3:44–48; Esth. 4:1–3, 15–17). **12:9** That *almsgiving saves from death* is a reference not to eternal life but rather to protection from premature death (see also 4:10). **12:10** Raphael's closing words remind sinners that they condemn themselves by their actions.

12:11–15 Raphael's identity is revealed. 12:11 Raphael is about to reveal *the whole truth* about his identity. The repetition of v. 7 (slightly altered wording) suggests that he has faithfully hidden the secrets of the heavenly king. **12:12** *It was I who brought the record of your prayers* shows Raphael's intermediary role in securing divine help for Tobit and Sarah. *Likewise whenever you would bury the dead* recalls the accounts of Tobit burying the destitute (1:16–20). **12:13** *And that time* refers to the story in 2:1–6. **12:14** *I was sent . . . to test you* reflects the idea that God tests the fidelity of the faithful in times of trials (Job 1:9–12). **12:15** *I am Raphael, one of the seven angels.* Azariah's real identity as the angel Raphael is finally revealed to Tobit and Tobias. Seven angels are also mentioned in Rev. 8:2 (see **"Angels,"** p. 1346).

12:16–22 Raphael's departure. 12:16 Being shaken, throwing oneself face down, and being afraid are typical reactions to a theophany in the biblical narratives (e.g., Exod. 3:6). **12:17–18** The angel's words, *do not be afraid; peace be with you,* seek to ease their fears. Raphael credits God for his actions: *I was not acting on my own will but by the will of God.* **12:19** *I was not really eating anything* affirms Raphael's heavenly nature (cf. Luke 24:36–41). **12:20–21** *I am ascending to him who sent me.* The Gospel of John has Jesus use similar words in John 16:5. **12:22** Tobit and Tobias respond by *blessing God and singing his praises* for all that God has done, including sending them an angel.

13

Then Tobit[m] said:
"Blessed be God who lives forever,
and blessed be his kingdom.

² For he afflicts, and he shows mercy;
he leads down to Hades in the lowest
regions of the earth,
and he brings up from the great abyss,
and there is nothing that can escape
his hand.

³ Acknowledge him before the nations,
O children of Israel,
for he has scattered you among them.

⁴ He has shown you his greatness even
there.
Exalt him in the presence of every living
being,
because he is our[n] Lord, and he is our
God;
he is our Father, and he is God forever.

⁵ He will afflict[o] you for your iniquities,
but he will again show mercy on all
of you.
He will gather you from all the nations
among whom you have been scattered.

⁶ If you turn to him with all your heart and
with all your soul,
to do what is true before him,
then he will turn to you
and will no longer hide his face from
you.
So now see what he has done for you;
acknowledge him at the top of your
voice.

Bless the Lord of righteousness,
and exalt the King of the ages.[p]
In the land of my exile I acknowledge him
and show his power and majesty to a
nation of sinners:
'Turn back, you sinners, and do what is
right before him;
perhaps he may look with favor upon
you and show you mercy.'

⁷ As for me, I exalt my God,
and my soul rejoices in the King of
heaven.

⁸ Let all people speak of his majesty
and acknowledge him in Jerusalem.

⁹ O Jerusalem, the holy city,
he afflicted[q] you for the deeds of your
hands[r]
but will again have mercy on the
children of the righteous.

¹⁰ Acknowledge the Lord worthily,
and bless the King of the ages,
so that your tent[s] may be rebuilt for
you[t] with joy.
May he cheer all those within you who
are captives
and love all those within you who are
distressed,
to all generations forever.

m 13.1 Gk *he*   n 13.4 Q mss read *your*   o 13.5 Other ancient
authorities read *He afflicted*   p 13.6 S lacks 13.6b–10a and
is filled in from other ancient authorities   q 13.9 Other
ancient authorities read *will afflict*   r 13.9 Other ancient
authorities read *your children*   s 13.10 Or *tabernacle*
t 13.10 Q ms: Gk reads *in you*

13:1–18 Tobit thanks God and hopes for Jerusalem's restoration. 13:1 *Blessed be God who lives
forever* fulfills Raphael's exhortation to "bless God" (12:6). **13:2–3** *For he afflicts . . . leads down to
Hades . . . he has scattered* indicates how God's sovereignty allots different trials to humans but also
shows mercy . . . brings up from the great abyss. **13:4** *Exalt him in the presence of every living being*
echoes Raphael's instructions to him (12:6) to "bless God and acknowledge him in the presence of
all the living." **13:5** *He will gather you from all the nations* reflects the hopes of both the exiles after
722 BCE and Jews in the Diaspora in the third and second centuries BCE that God will return them
to the promised land. **13:6–7** Restoration requires that Israel *turn to him with all your heart and with
all your soul* (cf. Deut. 30:1–2). The focus on sin, punishment, repentance, and salvation presupposes
the idea of blessings and curses (see Deut. 27–28). The diasporic community would have seen the
exile as punishment for their disobedience to God's word but also God's mercy if they turn to God.
13:9 *O Jerusalem, the holy city, he afflicted you for the deeds of your hands.* In the Zion theology of
the southern kingdom of Judah, Jerusalem is the holy city chosen by God for the temple (see 1 Kgs.
8). Note that the character of Tobit is from the northern tribe of Naphtali in the years soon after the
fall of the northern kingdom in 722 BCE. The anachronistic reference to Jerusalem *afflicted* refers
to the destruction of Jerusalem centuries later by the Babylonians (587 BCE). Similar to some other
exilic and postexilic writings, the destruction of Jerusalem is seen as punishment for Judah's *deeds*
and "iniquities" (e.g., 1 Kgs. 8:46; Lam. 1:18). **13:10–11** *Acknowledge the Lord . . . so that your tent may
be rebuilt for you with joy.* The tent or tabernacle, God's portable habitation in the wilderness, is conflated with the rebuilding of the temple. Tobit envisions an eschatological future in which the rebuilt
temple will be a sight of joy for the exiles and the place God will be worshiped by all the *inhabitants*

[11] A bright light will shine to all the
remotest parts of the earth;
many nations will come to you from
far away,
the inhabitants of the ends of the earth
to your holy name,
bearing gifts in their hands for the
King of heaven.
Generation after generation will give
joyful praise in you;
the name of the chosen city will
endure forever.
[12] Cursed are all who reject you
and all who blaspheme you;
cursed are all who hate you[u]
and all who speak a harsh word
against you;
cursed are all who conquer you
and pull down your walls,
all who overthrow your towers
and set your homes on fire.
But blessed forever will be all who
build you up.[v]
[13] Rejoice,[w] then, and exult over the
children of the righteous,
for they will all be gathered together
and will bless the Lord of the ages.
[14] Happy will be those who love you,
and happy are those who will rejoice
in your peace.
Happy also all people who grieve with you
because of your afflictions,
for they will rejoice with you
and witness all your joy forever.
[15] My soul blesses[x] the Lord, the great King,
[16] for Jerusalem will be rebuilt as his
house for all ages.
How happy I will be if a remnant of my
descendants should survive
to see your glory and acknowledge the
King of heaven.

The gates of Jerusalem will be built with
sapphire and emerald
and all your walls with precious
stones.
The towers of Jerusalem will be built
with gold
and their battlements with pure gold.
[17] The streets of Jerusalem will be paved
with ruby and with stones of Ophir.
[18] The gates of Jerusalem will sing hymns
of joy,
and all her houses will cry, 'Hallelujah!
Blessed be the God of Israel!'—
and the blessed will bless the holy
name forever and ever."

14 So ended Tobit's words of praise. 2 He died in peace when he was one hundred twelve years old and was buried with great honor in Nineveh. He was fifty-eight[y] years old when he lost his eyesight, and after regaining it he lived in prosperity, giving alms. He continued to bless God and to acknowledge God's greatness.

3 When he was about to die, he called his son Tobias and his seven children[z] and gave this command: "My son, take your children 4and escape off to Media, for I believe the word of God that Nahum spoke about Nineveh, that all these things will occur and will happen to Assyria and Nineveh. Indeed, everything that was spoken by the prophets of Israel whom God sent will occur. None of all their words will fail, but all will come true at their appointed times. So it will be safer in Media than among the Assyrians or in Babylon. For I know and believe that whatever

u 13.12 Q ms: S lacks *reject . . . hate you* v 13.12 OL: S *who fear you* w 13.13 Q mss: S *Go* x 13.15 OL reads *O my soul, bless* y 14.2 Q mss OL: S *sixty-two* z 14.3 OL: S lacks *and his seven children*

of the ends of the earth forever. See **"Gentile Conversion," p. 1530. 13:12–14** *Cursed are all* who seek the destruction of Jerusalem, but *blessed* and *happy* are they who *love* Jerusalem, *grieve* for its demise, and *rejoice* over its restoration (cf. Isa. 66:10). See the curses and blessings in Deut. 27–28. **13:15–17** Tobit *blesses the Lord* because *Jerusalem will be rebuilt as his house for all ages.* Jerusalem will be rebuilt with gates made of *sapphire and emerald*, towers of *gold*, and streets paved *with ruby and with stones of Ophir.* The metals represent beauty, permanence, and durability. **13:18** *The gates of Jerusalem will sing hymns of joy*, and *houses* will praise God with a *Hallelujah.*

14:1–11a Tobit's farewell discourse. **14:2** Tobit dies *in peace* at the age of *one hundred twelve years old*, a long life that is a sign of God's blessings for his fidelity and charity. **14:3** *When he was about to die*, Tobit summons his son Tobias and his seven grandsons to deliver a farewell discourse to instruct them about their future conduct and prophesy about the future. Deathbed speeches, or testaments, were a common literary form in the ancient Near East (e.g., Gen. 48–49). **14:4** *I believe the word of God that Nahum spoke about Nineveh.* Tobit cites Nahum's prophecy regarding

God has said will be fulfilled and will occur; not a single word of the prophecies will fail. All of our kindred, inhabitants of the land of Israel, will be counted and taken as captives from the good land, and the whole land of Israel will be desolate; even Samaria and Jerusalem will be desolate. And the temple of God in it will be burned to the ground and will be desolate for a while.[a]

5 "But God will again have mercy on them, and God will bring them back into the land of Israel, and they will rebuild the temple but not like the first one until the appointed time is completed. After this they all will return from their exile and will rebuild Jerusalem in splendor, and in it the temple of God will be rebuilt, just as the prophets of Israel have said concerning it. [6]Then all the nations in the whole world will all be converted and will truly fear God. They will all abandon all their idols who deceitfully have led them into their error, [7]and in righteousness they will praise the eternal God. All the Israelites who are saved in those days and are truly mindful of God will be gathered together; they will go to Jerusalem and live in safety forever in the land of Abraham, and it will be given over to them. Those who sincerely love God will rejoice, but those who commit sin and injustice will vanish from all the earth.

9 "So now, my children, I command you, serve God faithfully and do what is pleasing in his sight. Your children are also to be commanded to do what is right and to give alms and to be mindful of God and to bless his name at all times with sincerity and with all their strength. [8]So now, my son, leave Nineveh; do not remain here.[b] [10]On whatever day you bury your mother beside me, do not stay overnight within the confines of the city, for I see that there is much injustice within it and that much deceit is practiced within it, while the people are without shame. See, my son, what Nadab did to Ahikar, who had reared him. Was he not, while still alive, brought down into the earth? For God repaid him to his face for this shameful treatment. Ahikar came out into the light, but Nadab went into the eternal darkness because he tried to kill Ahikar. Because he gave alms, he escaped the fatal trap that Nadab had set for him, but Nadab fell into it himself and was destroyed. [11]So now, my children, see what almsgiving accomplishes and what injustice does—it brings death! But now my breath fails me."

Then they laid him on his bed, and he died, and he received an honorable funeral. [12]When Tobias's mother died, he buried her beside his father. Then he and his wife[c] returned to Media and settled in Ecbatana with Raguel his father-in-law. [13]He looked after his parents-in-law[d] with great respect in their old age and buried them in Ecbatana of Media. He inherited both the property of Raguel and that of his father

a 14.4 OL: Other ancient authorities read *of God will be in distress and will be burned for a while* b 14.8 In other ancient authorities 14.8 precedes 14.9 c 14.12 Other ancient authorities add *and children* d 14.13 Gk *them*

Nineveh's destruction, which was sacked in 612 BCE by a coalition of armies under the leadership of Babylon. *All of our kindred . . . will be . . . taken as captives . . . Samaria and Jerusalem will be desolate* reflects the destruction of Israel by the Assyrians in 722 BCE and of Judah by the Babylonians in 587 BCE. While the narrative is set before these events, the book of Tobit was composed much later in the second or third century BCE. **14:5** *But God will again have mercy . . . and God will bring them back* is Tobit's confidence in the return of the exiles and the restoration of Israel. Israel will gather in Jerusalem to rebuild its temple. **14:6–7** *The nations . . . will all be converted* from idolatry to praise the God of Israel *in righteousness*. Israelites *mindful of God* will return to Jerusalem and *live in safety forever in the land of Abraham*. Tobit's words echo God's promise of safety and rest in Deut. 12:10–12 for the first Israelites whom Joshua led into the promised land. **14:8–9** Reflecting the narrative setting after 722 BCE, Tobias and his children are instructed to *do what is right and . . . give alms* and *leave Nineveh*. **14:10** That *there is much injustice* in Nineveh contrasts the righteous conduct Tobit is commanding. Tobit illustrates his instructions with the story of the righteous Ahikar, who was saved from Nadab's plot to kill him *because he gave alms*.
    14:11b–15 Death of Tobit and Anna. 14:11b *Honorable funeral.* The book, which began by describing Tobit's courage and generosity in burying others, now ends with the burial of Tobit. The passage also recalls 4:3, when Tobit first asked Tobias, "Give me a proper burial." **14:12–13** *When Tobias's mother died, he buried her* next to Tobit as instructed in 14:10. Tobias and Sarah then travel to Media to live in Ecbatana with Sarah's parents, whom he *looked after*. The passage also recalls 4:3,

Tobit. [14]He died highly respected at the age of one hundred seventeen years. [15]Before he died he saw and heard[e] of the destruction of Nineveh, and he saw its prisoners being led into Media, those whom King Cyaxares[f] of Media had taken captive. Tobias[g] blessed God for all he had done to the people of Nineveh and Assyria; before he died he rejoiced over Nineveh, and he blessed the Lord God forever and ever. Amen.

e 14.15 Other ancient authorities lack *saw and*   f 14.15 Cn: S *Ahikar*   g 14.15 Gk *He*

where Tobit instructs Tobias to take care of Anna after his death. When Raguel dies, Tobias inherits Raguel's estate. **14:14** *He died highly respected at the age of one hundred seventeen years*, surpassing his father. **14:15** *Before he died*, he learned of the destruction of Nineveh and Assyria and praised God for its destruction.

JUDITH

Judith is one of the rare books from Israelite and Jewish antiquity in which the protagonist is a woman, moreover one whose actions confound conventional gender expectations of the time (see **"Jewish Women in the Diaspora," p. 1525; "Masculinity," p. 1701**). The action-packed narrative is driven by the ambitious quest of King Nebuchadnezzar and his Assyrian army to conquer all the peoples of the Tigris-Euphrates region and the seacoast of Syria-Palestine. The Israelite heroine Judith invents a plan to foil the invading army by seducing and beheading its Assyrian general, Holofernes. This straightforward plot is made engaging by virtue of its vivid characters and the suspenseful unfolding of its carefully crafted narrative.

Genre, Original Language, and Date
Along with other works written during the Hellenistic period—such as Tobit and the different versions of Daniel and Esther, 3 Maccabees, and Joseph and Aseneth—the genre of Judith can be considered a fictive novella. While it appears to be a historical account, there are obvious historical errors like portraying Babylonian Nebuchadnezzar as the king over the Assyrians in Nineveh (see **"Historical Fiction," p. 1635**). The story is set immediately after the end of the exile (538 BCE), though the Persian king Cyrus defeated Nebuchadnezzar in 539 BCE. The towns mentioned are often geographically misplaced or otherwise unknown.

The original language of Judith has been debated. Unlike the book of Tobit, no Hebrew or Aramaic fragments of Judith have been found at Qumran among the Dead Sea Scrolls or elsewhere. It thus may have originally been written in Greek, containing Hebraisms. The composition of Judith is dated to the late second century or early first century BCE. The foreign threat to the people and especially the central concern for maintaining the sanctity of the temple as a sacrificial worship site would link it to the desecration of the temple by the Seleucid king Antiochus Epiphanes IV in 164 BCE. Judith is often thought to have been written during the time of the Hasmoneans after Jews had regained their independence from Greek hegemony. There are signs of anti-Samaritan polemic, and the fictive town of Bethulia is set near Shechem in Samaritan country, so that may suggest a date prior to John Hyrcanus's destruction of the Samaritan temple at Mount Gerizim in 112/111 BCE.

Literary Character and Themes
The Jewish literature of the Hellenistic period shows a marked tendency to allude to or otherwise engage earlier scriptural motifs and characters. Judith may be the most "intertextual" of all the books in the deuterocanonical/apocryphal books with many biblical echoes. The figure of Judith and her actions in slaying Holofernes resemble the story of Deborah, Jael, and Sisera in Judges. Her seductive wiles are like the femme fatale Delilah or the Strange Woman of Proverbs. She employs trickery like her ancestor Jacob but plays the role of savior of her people like Moses (see **"Judith as Trickster," p. 1372**). Judith is rich in prayers and clearly draws on biblical models. The composition of her prayer in chap. 9 is scripturalized, drawing on interpretive traditions related to Gen. 34, Isa. 36–39, and the Song of Moses in Exod. 15. More broadly, the story can be read allegorically as a David-and-Goliath tale of the victory of the oppressed righteous over the powerful wicked. Literary motifs, such as "the hand of Judith" or true and false speech, recur in the narrative, while the theological perspectives appear most clearly in the speeches and prayers. The issue of right worship is central to the book. Who deserves worshipful fear/awe: Nebuchadnezzar or Israel's God? Fear can also be understood as a wisdom motif from the frequent proverb anchoring the biblical wisdom tradition: the fear of the Lord is the beginning of wisdom. Like most of the Wisdom literature, God does not speak directly as in the prophets or appear as a deus ex machina. Alongside the many echoes of the Hebrew Bible in Judith are Greek thematic influences as found in the classic Greek writers Herodotus, Ctesias, and Xenophon. Judith is similar to several warrior queens who rule and make important political decisions such as Herodotus's Tomyris or Artemisia.

Afterlife in Judaism and Christianity
In Christianity, engagement with Judith has been continuous. She is frequently mentioned in the writings of the early church, where she is lauded for her virtues of modesty, chastity, and justice,

perhaps because the abbreviated Latin version irons out some of the story's more morally ambiguous elements. The story and figure of Judith became particularly popular in European art of the Renaissance and Byzantine eras (see **"Judith in Art," p. 1376**). Whereas in early Christianity she was a type of the church, in Renaissance Europe she came to be seen as embodying civic virtues. While Judith was not included in the Hebrew Bible (Tanakh), the story was known in the Jewish tradition, as medieval works attest. There are multiple Judith midrashim (Ma'aseh Yehudit) and liturgical poems (*piyyutim*) that engage the legend. Jewish tradition associates Judith with the Maccabees and the festival of Hanukkah (see **"Hanukkah," p. 1544**).

Reading Guide

Judith is structured in two parts. Each half of the book contains its own threefold chiastic structure. The first chapters (1:1–7:32) detail the "Assyro-Babylonian" campaign against all the western nations. The hubristic King Nebuchadnezzar launches a military campaign by ordering his general Holofernes to lead the armies against the nations. Holofernes delivers the ultimatum that all must worship Nebuchadnezzar as god or else they will scorch and burn their territories. The massive array of troops terrorizes all in their path until all the nations capitulate and only Israel is left refusing to worship Nebuchadnezzar. Holofernes learns about the Israelites from his ally Achior the Ammonite. Achior relates the history of Israel from their origins in Ur of the Chaldees up until the present day and their ongoing relationship to their God. He tells them that the Israelites can be defeated only if they sin against their God; otherwise, they are invincible. The second half of the book (8:1–16:25) introduces Judith, who plays the commanding lead in the rest of the story. The leaders of Judith's hometown of Bethulia are ready to submit to the Assyrians, but Judith chastises them for their lack of faith in God. She devises a secret plan to deliver them. The prayer she offers (Jdt. 9:2–14) before leaving on her mission stands at the very center of the book and contains central affirmations of divine omniscience and omnipotence. In the unfolding drama, Judith transforms herself from a drably clothed widow into a perfumed, bright, and bejeweled temptress dressed to kill. Leaving Bethulia with her maid, she gives herself over to the Assyrian forces and claims to be a traitor. Struck by her beauty and wise speech, they take her to Holofernes, in whose camp she remains, all the while observing the Jewish dietary commandments (i.e., keeping kosher) and praying and bathing nightly. Invited to a private drinking party by the lustful Holofernes, Judith finally seizes the moment to kill the drunken general by hewing off his head. The tale continues with a complete routing of the Assyrians and a celebratory march to Jerusalem, where they offer a song of praise. Then Judith returns to her life of quiet domesticity and lives a long life.

Judith H. Newman

1 It was the twelfth year of the reign of Nebuchadnezzar, who ruled over the Assyrians in the great city of Nineveh. In those days Arphaxad ruled over the Medes in Ecbatana. ²He built walls around Ecbatana with hewn stones three cubits thick and six cubits long; he made the walls seventy cubits high and fifty cubits wide. ³At its gates he raised towers one hundred cubits high and sixty cubits wide at the foundations. ⁴He made its gates seventy cubits high and forty cubits wide to allow his armies to march out in force and his infantry to form their ranks. ⁵Then King Nebuchadnezzar made

1:1–7:32 "Assyro-Babylonian" Empire threatens Israel and the region.

1:1–6 Arphaxad fortifies his capital. 1:1 *Nebuchadnezzar* is introduced as the ruler of the Assyrians in their capital Nineveh. This is a historical error equivalent to calling Napoleon the king of the British in London. Nebuchadnezzar was the king of Babylon (605–562 BCE) whose army destroyed Jerusalem, the capital city of Judah, in 586 BCE. Nineveh was defeated in 612 BCE by the Babylonians and Medes. Such a mix-up of the most well-known enemies of Israel would have been recognized by contemporary Jewish readers as a sign that the tale was fictional (see **"Historical Fiction," p. 1635**). *Arphaxad*, identified as the ruler of the Medes, is otherwise unknown. **1:2** *Ecbatana* lay east of the Zagros mountains in what is now modern Iran. Like much else in this chapter, the fortifications described are exaggerated. A cubit is the length of a forearm, about eighteen inches, so the wall would be thirty-five yards high and twenty-five yards thick. **1:3** The *towers* would be fifty yards high and thirty yards wide. **1:5** *Ragau*, referred to as Rages in Tobit (cf. 4:1), is 185 miles

war against King Arphaxad in the great plain that is on the borders of Ragau. ⁶There rallied to him all the people of the hill country and all those who lived along the Euphrates, the Tigris, and the Hydaspes, and, on the plain, Arioch, king of the Elymeans. Thus many nations joined the forces of the Cheleoudites.ᵃ

7 Then Nebuchadnezzar, king of the Assyrians, sent messengers to all who lived in Persia and to all who lived in the west, those who lived in Cilicia and Damascus, Lebanon and Antilebanon, and all who lived along the seacoast, ⁸and those among the nations of Carmel and Gilead, and Upper Galilee and the great plain of Esdraelon, ⁹and all who were in Samaria and its towns, and beyond the Jordan as far as Jerusalem and Bethany and Chelous and Kadesh and the river of Egypt, and Tahpanhes and Raamses and the whole land of Goshen, ¹⁰even beyond Tanis and Memphis, and all who lived in Egypt as far as the borders of Ethiopia. ¹¹But all who lived in the whole region showed contempt for the summons of Nebuchadnezzar, king of the Assyrians, and refused to join him in the war, for they were not afraid of him but regarded him as only one man.ᵇ So they sent back his messengers empty-handed and in disgrace.

12 Then Nebuchadnezzar became very angry with this whole region and swore by his throne and kingdom that he would take revenge on the whole territory of Cilicia and Damascus and Syria, that he would kill with his sword also all the inhabitants of the land of Moab, and the people of Ammon, and all Judea, and every one in Egypt, as far as the coasts of the two seas.

13 In the seventeenth year he led his forces against King Arphaxad and defeated him in battle, overthrowing the whole army of Arphaxad and all his cavalry and all his chariots. ¹⁴Thus he took possession of his towns and came to Ecbatana, captured its towers, plundered its markets, and turned its glory into disgrace. ¹⁵He captured Arphaxad in the mountains of Ragau and struck him down with his spears, thus destroying him once and for all. ¹⁶Then he returned to Nineveh, he and all his combined forces, a vast body of troops, and there he and his forces rested and feasted for one hundred twenty days.

2 In the eighteenth year, on the twenty-second day of the first month, there was talk in the palace of Nebuchadnezzar, king of the Assyrians, about carrying out his revenge on the whole region, just as he had said. ²He summoned all his attendants and all his nobles and set before them his secret plan and recounted fully, with his own lips, all the wickedness of the region.ᶜ ³They decided that all who had not obeyed his command should be destroyed.

a 1.6 Syr: Gk *Chaldeans*   b 1.11 Or *a man*   c 2.2 Meaning of Gk uncertain

---

northeast of Ecbatana, near modern Teheran. It is the place where Arphaxad is killed (1:15). **1:6** For *Cheleoudites*, the Greek reads "Chaldeans" who would be the neo-Babylonians. This alliance of peoples from a broad geographic range reaching India is exaggerated for effect.

1:7–11 Other nations spurn Nebuchadnezzar's calls for help. Nebuchadnezzar sends messengers to the west and to the south through Syria, Lebanon, Palestine, Egypt, and Ethiopia. **1:8** *Esdraelon*, formerly called Jezreel (Judg. 6:33), is the broad plain in northern Israel just north of Mount Carmel. **1:9** *The river of Egypt* is not the Nile but the Wadi el-Arish, which separates Egypt and Palestine. **1:10** *Tanis* (Zoan) was a city in Lower Egypt on the east Delta. **1:11** *For they were not afraid of him* introduces the theme of fear, which laces throughout the book. Fear paralyzes many nations and individuals. The only one who is not afraid but acts on the courage of her convictions is Judith.

1:12–16 Nebuchadnezzar vows revenge. 1:12 *Nebuchadnezzar became very angry*. The topos of the excessive anger of a hubristic eastern king is found elsewhere: Ahasuerus (Esth. 1:12) and a different "Nebuchadnezzar" in Daniel (Dan. 2:12; 3:13, 19). Narcissistic leaders, then and now, pose threats if their power is unchecked. **1:16** *Feasted for one hundred twenty days*. This celebration at the end of Nebuchadnezzar's victory occurs exactly one year before the celebration of Judith and her people in 16:20.

2:1–20 The "Assyro-Babylonians" prepare for war. 2:1 The date, the twenty-second day of Nisan, is the day after Passover, the same date when Pharaoh and the Egyptians were drowned at the Red Sea. This is the first of a number of connections to Exodus in the book of Judith. **2:2** *With his own lips*, literally "from his mouth," is repeated in the Greek of 2:3 and 2:6 (although not translated) to emphasize his own command has not been heeded. **2:3** *All who had not obeyed.* The Greek phrase

4 When he had completed his plan, Nebuchadnezzar, king of the Assyrians, called Holofernes, the chief general of his army, second only to himself, and said to him, 5"Thus says the Great King, the lord of the whole earth: Leave my presence and take with you men confident in their strength, one hundred twenty thousand foot soldiers and twelve thousand cavalry. 6March out against all the land to the west, because they disobeyed my orders. 7Tell them to prepare earth and water, for I am coming against them in my anger and will cover the whole face of the earth with the feet of my troops, to whom I will hand them over to be plundered. 8Their wounded shall fill their ravines and gullies, and the swelling river shall be filled with their dead. 9I will lead them away captive to the ends of the whole earth. 10You shall go and seize all their territory for me in advance. They must yield themselves to you, and you shall hold them for me until the day of their punishment. 11But to those who resist, show no mercy but hand them over to slaughter and plunder throughout your whole region. 12For as I live and by the power of my kingdom, what I have spoken I will accomplish by my own hand. 13And you—take care not to transgress any of your lord's commands, but carry them out exactly as I have ordered you; do it without delay."

14 So Holofernes left the presence of his lord and summoned all the commanders, generals, and officers of the Assyrian army. 15He mustered the picked troops by divisions as his lord had ordered him to do, one hundred twenty thousand of them, together with twelve thousand archers on horseback, 16and he organized them as a great army is marshaled for a campaign. 17He took along a vast number of camels and donkeys and mules for transport and innumerable sheep and oxen and goats for food, 18also ample rations for everyone and a huge amount of gold and silver from the royal palace.

19 Then he set out with his whole army to go ahead of King Nebuchadnezzar and to cover the whole face of the earth to the west with their chariots and cavalry and picked foot soldiers. 20Along with them went a mixed crowd like a swarm of locusts, like the dustd of the earth, a multitude that could not be counted.

21 They marched for three days from Nineveh to the plain of Bectileth and camped opposite Bectileth near the mountain that is to the north of Upper Cilicia. 22From there Holofernese took his whole army, the infantry, cavalry, and chariots, and went up into the hill country. 23He ravaged Put and Lud and plundered all the Rassisites and the Ishmaelites on the border of the desert, south of the country of the Chelleans. 24Then he followedf the Euphrates and passed through Mesopotamia and destroyed all the fortified towns along the Wadi Abron, as far as the sea. 25He also seized the territory of Cilicia

d 2.20 Gk sand   e 2.22 Gk he   f 2.24 Or crossed

translated as all is literally "all flesh," perhaps an echo of Gen. 6:12 or Isa. 40:5, in order to compare Nebuchadnezzar to God, who governs and reveals glory to "all flesh." 2:5 The lord of the whole earth. In the only time he speaks, Nebuchadnezzar uses self-aggrandizing terms typical of ancient kings. The phrase recurs (6:4; cf. 11:1, 7) and contrasts with the "real" Lord of the whole earth, Israel's God. A similar contrast occurs between Pharaoh and YHWH in the exodus story. One hundred twenty thousand foot soldiers and twelve thousand cavalry. The size of the army approximates that of Antiochus IV in 1 Macc. 15:13. 2:7 Prepare earth and water. This phrase, which was a sign of surrender, is known only from the Greek historian Herodotus. The author of Judith must have been familiar with his work. 2:12 By my own hand. Nebuchadnezzar's claim that he will inflict vengeance by his own hand is an arrogant boast. He soon disappears from the narrative. Judith, by contrast, will save her people by her own "hand" (8:33; 9:9–10). 2:17 The massive amount of provisions contrasts with Judith's preparation for her own mission (10:4–5). She takes only a small supply of food and her expectation that God is with her.

2:21–28 The conquests of Holofernes. 2:21 They marched for three days is an exaggerated pace. The distance from Nineveh to upper Cilicia could not be covered in that time. 2:23–24 The Rassisites, Chelleans, and the Wadi Abron are otherwise unknown. 2:24 He followed or crossed the Euphrates is the third time he would have crossed the river. The progression of the army is circuitous and backtracking. This pseudogeography, like the pseudohistory, was probably written to give the impression of a devastating and brutal campaign. Royal inscriptions, like Sennacherib's First Campaign, often

and killed everyone who resisted him. Then he came to the southern borders of Japheth, facing Arabia. 26He surrounded all the Midianites and burned their tents and plundered their sheepfolds. 27Then he went down into the plain of Damascus during the wheat harvest and burned all their fields and destroyed their flocks and herds and sacked their towns and ravaged their lands and put all their young men to the sword.

28 So fear and dread of him fell upon all the people who lived along the seacoast, at Sidon and Tyre, and those who lived in Sur and Ocina and all who lived in Jamnia. Those who lived in Azotus and Ascalon feared him greatly.

3 They therefore sent messengers to him to sue for peace in these words: 2"We, the servants of Nebuchadnezzar, the Great King, lie prostrate before you. Do with us whatever you will. 3See, our buildings and all our land and all our wheat fields and our flocks and herds and all our encampmentsᵍ lie before you; do with them as you please. 4Our towns and their inhabitants are also your slaves; come and deal with them as you see fit."

5 The men came to Holofernes and told him all this. 6Then he went down to the seacoast with his army and stationed garrisons

in the fortified towns and took picked men from them as auxiliaries. 7These people and all in the countryside welcomed him with garlands and dances and tambourines. 8Yet he demolished all their shrinesᵇ and cut down their sacred groves, for he had been commissioned to destroy all the gods of the land, so that all nations should worship Nebuchadnezzar alone and that all their dialects and tribes should call upon him as a god.

9 Then he came toward Esdraelon, near Dothan, facing the great ridge of Judea; 10he camped between Geba and Scythopolis and remained for a whole month in order to collect all the supplies for his army.

4 When the Israelites living in Judea heard of everything that Holofernes, the general of Nebuchadnezzar, the king of the Assyrians, had done to the nations and how he had plundered and destroyed all their temples, 2they were therefore greatly terrified at his approach; they were alarmed both for Jerusalem and for the temple of the Lord their God. 3For they had only recently returned from exile, and all the people of Judea had just now gathered together, and the sacred vessels and the altar and the temple had been consecrated after their

g 3.3 Gk *all the sheepfolds of our tents*   h 3.8 Syr: Gk *borders*

included exaggerated accounts of vicious actions of war to make a fearful impression. **2:28** *So fear and dread.* The rampages of his warriors have their desired terrorizing effect.

3:1–10 The peoples along the seacoast plead for peace. 3:2–4 Some cities in antiquity greeted victors with welcome. The abject language of the coastal cities—which would include Tyre, Sidon, Jamnia, and Ascalon—and the prostration of their inhabitants emphasize servility. *Servants* or *slaves* is repeated at the beginning and end of their speech to emphasize submission. **3:7** Victorious armies were often greeted with such celebration (cf. 2 Sam. 6:14–16; 2 Chr. 20:21–22, 28). The mention of dancing and music here is nonetheless surprising, but the festivities will be reversed when Judith is greeted as a victor (Jdt. 15:12). **3:8** While most conquering armies would burn civic buildings and dwellings, Holofernes only destroys places concerned with worship. Holofernes's focus on places of worship anticipates the focus on the Jerusalem temple and the competition throughout the book over who should be worshiped as god: Nebuchadnezzar or Israel's God. The expectation that all should worship Nebuchadnezzar is reminiscent of Dan. 3. **3:9** While many of the locations in the first part of the book are invented or not portrayed accurately, the sites in Judah are more accurate. The plain of *Esdraelon*, first mentioned in 1:8, lies between the highlands of Galilee and Samaria and Judea. **3:10** *Scythopolis.* This city identified by its Greek name is also known in Hebrew as Beth Shean. The campsite is strategically located in northern Israel between the Jezreel and Jordan Valleys. A *whole month* allows the great army to regroup and for word of the army's fierce destruction to spread.

4:1–7 The Israelites prepare for war. 4:1–2 Having heard of Holofernes's scorched earth campaign targeting worship sites, the Israelites living in Judea are terrified. Their concern for the preservation of their temple in Jerusalem is paramount. **4:3** *Only recently returned from exile.* The Babylonian exile ended in 538 BCE when the Persian king Cyrus II permitted Jews to return to their homeland.

profanation. ⁴So they sent word to every district of Samaria, and to Kona, Beth-horon, Belmain, and Jericho, and to Choba and Aesora, and the valley of Salem. ⁵They immediately seized all the high hilltops and fortified the villages on them and stored up food in preparation for war, since their fields had recently been harvested.

6 The high priest Joakim, who was in Jerusalem at the time, wrote to the people of Bethulia and Betomesthaim, which faces Esdraelon opposite the plain near Dothan, ⁷ordering them to seize the mountain passes, since by them Judea could be invaded, and it would be easy to stop any who tried to enter, for the approach was narrow, wide enough for only two at a time to pass.

8 So the Israelites did as they had been ordered by the high priest Joakim and the council of the whole people of Israel, in session at Jerusalem. ⁹And every man of Israel cried out to God with great fervor, and they humbled themselves with much fasting. ¹⁰They and their wives and their children and their cattle and every resident alien and hired laborer and purchased slave—they all put sackcloth around their waists. ¹¹And all the Israelite men, women, and children

living at Jerusalem prostrated themselves before the temple and put ashes on their heads and spread out their sackcloth before the Lord. ¹²They even draped the altar with sackcloth and cried out in unison, praying fervently to the God of Israel not to allow their infants to be carried off and their wives to be taken as plunder, and the towns they had inherited to be destroyed, and the sanctuary to be profaned and desecrated to the malicious joy of the nations.

13 The Lord heard their prayers and had regard for their distress, for the people fasted many days throughout Judea and in Jerusalem before the sanctuary of the Lord Almighty. ¹⁴The high priest Joakim and all the priests who stood before the Lord and ministered to the Lord, with sackcloth around their loins, offered the daily burnt offerings, the votive offerings, and freewill offerings of the people. ¹⁵With ashes on their turbans, they cried out to the Lord with all their might to look with favor on the whole house of Israel.

5 It was reported to Holofernes, the general of the Assyrian army, that the people of Israel had prepared for war and had

---

This anachronistic reference to their return is another sign that the book is a fictional novella (see **"Historical Fiction," 1635**). **4:4** *Samaria* was the name of both a city and a region in antiquity. The city of Shechem was in this region, and the story of Dinah's rape by Shechem (Gen. 34) is interpreted in Judith's prayer (Jdt. 9). During the time when Judith was written, the Samaritans who had their own temple in Gerizim near Shechem would have been rivals to Judeans. The Hasmonean high priest and ruler John Hyrcanus defeated Samaria in 107 BCE and destroyed its temple. **4:6** *The high priest Joakim* is otherwise unknown. There is a high priest Joiakim mentioned in Neh. 12:26, but he did not have military authority. There is no mention in Judith of a king nor hope for the future restoration of the Davidic monarchy.

4:8–15 The Israelites offer prayers and penance to their god. 4:8 The political leadership of the *council* (Gk. "gerousia"), which met in Jerusalem (mentioned also in 11:14; 15:8), may offer another clue to the dating of the book. "Gerousia" was the usual term in Hellenistic cities for the governing body. John Hyrcanus II instituted the Sanhedrin (Gk. "synedrion") in 67 BCE. **4:9–11** This fervent public performance of prayer and fasting was a ritualized way of externalizing a response to the terror they were experiencing. The entire population—including women and children, landless residents, enslaved persons, and even cattle—joins in the activity by putting ashes on their heads and wearing sackcloth. Cattle also wear sackcloth in Jonah 3:7–8, and there ultimately the entire city of Nineveh—with its cattle—is spared. **4:12** The population prays with passion knowing what is at stake is not only the destruction of their ancestral land but also the abduction and worse of women and infants and the desecration of their temple. **4:13** Although the Lord is said to have heard their prayers, the narrative never includes a direct divine response or speech. **4:14** *The daily burnt offerings, the votive offerings, and freewill offerings.* The priestly offerings in the temple are specified (cf. Exod. 29:38–42; Lev. 7:11–17; Deut. 27:7) and indicate the importance of the continuity of the sacrificial system as a regular divine tribute that must not be interrupted. **4:15** *Turbans.* The Persian word used is "kidaris," which would be the linen headcloth of the priests (Ezek. 44:18).

5:1–4 Holofernes gathers information about the Israelites. The general Holofernes now acts as

closed the mountain passes and fortified all the high hilltops and set up barricades in the plains. ²In great anger he called together all the princes of Moab and the commanders of Ammon and all the governors of the coastland ³and said to them, "Tell me, you Canaanites, what people is this that lives in the hill country? What towns do they inhabit? How large is their army, and in what does their power and strength consist? Who rules over them as king and leads their army? ⁴And why have they alone, of all who live in the west, refused to come out and meet me?"

5 Then Achior, the leader of all the Ammonites, said to him, "May my lord please listen to a report from the mouth of your servant, and I will tell you the truth about this people that lives in the mountain district near you. No falsehood shall come from your servant's mouth. ⁶These people are descended from the Chaldeans. ⁷At one time they lived in Mesopotamia because they did not wish to follow the gods of their ancestors who were in Chaldea. ⁸Since they had abandoned the ways of their ancestors and worshiped the God of heaven, the God they had come to know, their ancestors^i drove them out from the presence of their gods. So they fled to Mesopotamia and lived there for a long time. ⁹Then their God commanded them to leave the place where they were

living and go to the land of Canaan. There they settled and grew very prosperous in gold and silver and very much livestock. ¹⁰When a famine spread over the land of Canaan they went down to Egypt and lived there as long as they had food. There they became so great a multitude that their number could not be counted. ¹¹So the king of Egypt became hostile to them; he exploited them and forced them to make bricks, reducing them to slaves. ¹²They cried out to their God, and he afflicted the whole land of Egypt with incurable plagues. So the Egyptians drove them out of their sight. ¹³Then God dried up the Red Sea before them, ¹⁴and he led them by the way of Sinai and Kadesh-barnea. They drove out all the people of the desert ¹⁵and took up residence in the land of the Amorites and by their might destroyed all the inhabitants of Heshbon, and crossing over the Jordan they took possession of all the hill country. ¹⁶They drove out before them the Canaanites, the Perizzites, the Jebusites, the Shechemites, and all the Gergesites and lived there a long time.

17 "As long as they did not sin against their God they prospered, for the God who hates iniquity is with them. ¹⁸But when they departed from the way he had prescribed for

i 5.8 Gk *they*

an enraged tyrant. **5:2** *Moab.* The region immediately to the east of the Dead Sea. **5:3** *Ammon,* north of Moab. *Canaanites* is another anachronism. *Canaanites* is a term for the preexilic peoples of the land. Holofernes asks strategic questions about the people he wants to defeat. He is puzzled that the people of Israel are the only holdouts who will not welcome him and submit to his army.

5:5–23 Achior recounts the history of the Israelites. Other such historical surveys appear in Josh. 24:1–15; Neh. 9:6–37; cf. Deut. 26:6–9; 1 Sam. 12:6–17; 2 Kgs. 17:7–23; Pss. 78; 105; 106. **5:5** *Tell you the truth.* The contrast between true and false speech is a theme played out in the book. Judith will deceive Holofernes with speech she declares as true but that readers know is false. Even though Achior declares himself to be a servant of Holofernes, his speech reflects the Israelite view of God, history, and Deuteronomic theology. **5:7** *The gods of their ancestors* is an allusion to the origins of Abraham in Ur of the Chaldeans (Gen. 11:27–31). The tradition about Abraham as the first monotheist not wishing to follow alien gods in favor of the "God of heaven" is a theme developed in contemporaneous literature (Jub. 11–12; LAB 23:5; Josephus, *Ant.* 1.154–157). **5:10** *Their number could not be counted* is a reference to part of God's blessing to the ancestors, first pronounced to Abram in Gen. 12:1–3. Joseph went down into Egypt and his descendants became numerous (Exod. 1:7), thus realizing part of the divine promise but at the same time proving a threat to Pharaoh (Exod. 1:9). **5:12** *They cried out to their God.* Just like the Israelites in their current crisis, the Israelites in Egypt clamored to God about their suffering (Exod. 3:7–9), so God sent plagues against the Egyptians to liberate them. **5:16** The list of peoples driven out by the Israelites differs from the preexilic lists, which usually include six or seven nations (Exod. 3:8; Josh. 9:1; Judg. 3:5; Deut. 7:1-2; Josh. 3:10) ending with the Jebusites, the inhabitants of Jerusalem before King David conquered it. The list here includes the *Shechemites*—that is, the Samaritans. Their mention anticipates Judith's focus on Shechem in her prayer (chap. 9). **5:18–19** Achior includes a description of the exile as punishment

them, they were utterly defeated in many battles and were led away captive to a foreign land. The temple of their God was razed to the ground, and their towns were occupied by their enemies. [19]But now they have returned to their God and have come back from the places where they were scattered and have occupied Jerusalem, where their sanctuary is, and have settled in the hill country, because it was uninhabited.

20 "So now, my master and lord, if there is any oversight in this people and they sin against their God and we find out their offense, then we can go up and defeat them. [21]But if they are not a guilty nation, then let my lord pass them by, for their Lord and God will defend them, and we shall become the laughingstock of the whole world."

22 When Achior had finished saying these things, all the people standing around the tent began to complain; Holofernes's officers and all the inhabitants of the seacoast and Moab insisted that he should be cut to pieces. [23]They said, "We are not afraid of the Israelites; they are a people with no strength or power for making war. [24]Therefore let us go ahead, Lord Holofernes, and your vast army will swallow them up."

6 When the disturbance made by the people outside the council had died down, Holofernes, the commander of the Assyrian army, said to Achior[j] in the presence of all the foreign contingents:

2 "Who are you, Achior and you mercenaries of Ephraim, to prophesy among us as you have done today and tell us not to make war against the people of Israel because their God will defend them? What god is there except Nebuchadnezzar? He will send his forces and destroy them from the face of the earth. Their God will not save them; [3]we the king's[k] servants will destroy them as one person. They cannot resist the might of our cavalry. [4]We will overwhelm them;[l] their mountains will be drunk with their blood, and their fields will be full of their dead. Not even their footprints will survive our attack; they will utterly perish. So says King Nebuchadnezzar, lord of the whole earth. For he has spoken; none of his words shall be in vain.

5 "As for you, Achior, you Ammonite mercenary, you have said these words in a moment of perversity; you shall not see my face again from this day until I take revenge on this people that came out of Egypt. [6]Then at my return the sword of my army and the spear[m] of my servants shall pierce your sides, and you shall fall among their wounded. [7]Now my slaves are going to take you back into the hill country and put you in one of the towns beside the passes. [8]You will not die until you perish along with them. [9]If you really hope in your heart that they will not be taken, then do not look downcast! I have spoken, and none of my words shall fail to come true."

10 Then Holofernes ordered his slaves who waited on him in his tent to seize Achior and

j 6.1 Other ancient authorities add and to all the Moabites k 6.3 Gk his l 6.4 Other ancient authorities add with it m 6.6 OL Syr: Gk people

for sin and the postexilic return. **5:23** Continuing the theme of fear vs. courage, Holofernes's entourage claims not to fear even after hearing Achior's truthful account of the power of Israel's God.

6:1–13 The Assyrians turn Achior over to the Israelites. 6:2–4 This scene is reminiscent of the address of the Rabshakeh, the envoy of the Assyrian king Sennacherib before the siege of Jerusalem (Isa. 36:1–20 // 2 Kgs. 18:17–35). It may also reflect a comparison between Nebuchadnezzar and the Seleucid king Antiochus IV and his claim to be divine. Holofernes reaffirms his belief in Nebuchadnezzar as a divine sovereign whose armies can conquer anything. Although Achior did not claim to be a prophet, Holofernes elevates his speech to that level and contrasts it with the words of Nebuchadnezzar, an echo of 2:5. **6:4** *They will utterly perish.* The language of total destruction is harsh. Wiping from the face of the earth can only be accomplished by God elsewhere in the Bible (Gen. 6:7; 7:4; 1 Kgs. 9:7; Amos 9:8; etc.). **6:5–9 Holofernes threatens Achior. 6:5** *Mercenary.* Achior had joined the army simply for pay. *Shall not see my face again.* In fact, Achior will see Holofernes's face again once the tables have turned (14:6). **6:10–13 Achior is delivered to the Israelites. 6:10** *Slaves* (Gk. "douloi") are likely enslaved attendants. They would hold a lower status than servants (Gk. "paides"; cf. 3:2), who would be officials on the king's payroll. The NRSVue is not consistent in translating these Greek words as distinct from each other in the book of Judith. The city *Bethulia* is otherwise unknown but is here situated by a strategic pass on the way to Jerusalem. The name is likely a play on the Hebrew "betulah," meaning "young woman."

take him away to Bethulia and hand him over to the Israelites. [11]So the slaves took him and led him out of the camp into the plain, and from the plain they went up into the hill country and came to the springs below Bethulia. [12]When the men of the town saw them," they seized their weapons and ran out of the town to the top of the hill, and all the slingers kept them from coming up by throwing stones at them. [13]So having taken shelter below the hill, they bound Achior and left him lying at the foot of the hill and returned to their master.

14 Then the Israelites came down from their town and found him; they untied him and brought him into Bethulia and placed him before the magistrates of their town, [15]who in those days were Uzziah son of Micah, of the tribe of Simeon, and Chabris son of Gothoniel, and Charmis son of Melchiel. [16]They called together all the elders of the town, and all their young men and women ran to the assembly. They set Achior in the midst of all their people, and Uzziah questioned him about what had happened. [17]He answered and told them what had taken place at the council of Holofernes, and all that he had said in the presence of the Assyrian leaders, and all that Holofernes had boasted he would do against the house of Israel. [18]Then the people fell down and worshiped God and cried out:

19 "O Lord God of heaven, see their arrogance, and have pity on our people in their humiliation, and look kindly today on the faces of those who are consecrated to you."

20 Then they reassured Achior and praised him highly. [21]Uzziah took him from the assembly to his own house and gave a banquet for the elders, and all that night they called on the God of Israel for help.

7 The next day Holofernes ordered his whole army and all the allies who had joined him to break camp and move against Bethulia and seize the passes up into the hill country and make war on the Israelites. [2]So all their warriors marched off that day; their fighting forces numbered one hundred seventy thousand infantry and twelve thousand cavalry, not counting the baggage and the foot soldiers handling it, a very great multitude. [3]They encamped in the valley near Bethulia, beside the spring, and they spread out in breadth over Dothan as far as Balbaim and in length from Bethulia to Cyamon, which faces Esdraelon.

4 When the Israelites saw their vast numbers, they were greatly terrified and said to one another, "They will now strip clean the whole land; neither the high mountains nor the valleys nor the hills will bear their weight." [5]Yet they all seized their weapons, and when they had kindled fires on their towers, they remained on guard all that night.

6 On the second day Holofernes led out all his cavalry in full view of the Israelites in Bethulia. [7]He reconnoitered the approaches to their town and visited the springs that supplied their water; he seized them and set guards of soldiers over them and then returned to his army.

n 6.12 Other ancient authorities add *on the top of the hill*

6:14–21 The scene shifts to the Israelites of Bethulia. 6:15 Among the magistrates is Uzziah *of the tribe of Simeon*, Judith's lineage, which she will mention in her prayer (chap. 9). The leadership and the townspeople of Bethulia debrief Achior about the plans of Holofernes. **6:18–19** The Bethulians again display their piety by prostrating themselves and petitioning for mercy to their god, addressed as the "God of heaven," an address not found in the Hebrew Bible. The gesture of lowering oneself to the ground suggests submission to a higher power, whether divine, as in this case, or human. **6:20–21** After the elders praise Achior and Uzziah hosts a *banquet* (Gk. "poton"; literally "drinking party") for him, they resume their prayers to God for help.

7:1–7 The Assyrians prepare for war. 7:1–3 The plan of attack is toward the south from the Esdraelon plain (cf. note on 1:8). **7:2** The numbers of the army are quite specific: 170,000 infantry and 12,000 cavalry. When Holofernes left Nineveh, he commanded 120,000 troops, which suggests that they added 50,000 allies. This massed army preparing to attack is intended to be both terrifying and demoralizing to vulnerable Bethulia. **7:3** *Near Bethulia, beside the spring.* Springs would have provided the water source for the townspeople. **7:6–7** Holofernes acts like the leader of an army by going before his troops, commandeering the town's water supply, and appointing guards. This is the last time he appears as a military man. Later, he appears lounging in his tent, eating and drinking and hoping for pleasure with Judith (10:20–22).

8 Then all the chieftains of the Edomites and all the leaders of the Moabites and the commanders of the coastland came to him and said, 9"Listen to what we have to say, my lord, and your army will suffer no losses. 10This people, the Israelites, do not rely on their spears but on the height of the mountains where they live, for it is not easy to reach the tops of their mountains. 11Therefore, my lord, do not fight against them in regular formation, and not a man of your army will fall. 12Remain in your camp, and keep all the men in your forces with you; let your servants take possession of the spring of water that flows from the foot of the mountain, 13for this is where all the people of Bethulia get their water. So thirst will destroy them, and they will surrender their town. Meanwhile, we and our people will go up to the tops of the nearby mountains and camp there to keep watch to see that no one gets out of the town. 14They and their wives and children will waste away with famine, and before the sword reaches them they will be strewn about in the streets where they live. 15Thus you will pay them back with evil because they rebelled and did not receive you peaceably."

16 These words pleased Holofernes and all his attendants, and he gave orders to do as they had said. 17So the army of the Ammonites moved forward, together with five thousand Assyrians, and they encamped in the valley and seized the water supply and the springs of the Israelites. 18And the Edomites and Ammonites went up and encamped in the hill country opposite Dothan, and they sent some of their men toward the south and the east, toward Egrebeh, which is near Chusi beside the Wadi Mochmur. The rest of the Assyrian army encamped in the plain and covered the whole face of the land. Their tents and supply trains spread out in great number, and they formed a vast multitude.

19 The Israelites then cried out to the Lord their God, for their courage failed, because all their enemies had surrounded them, and there was no way of escape from them. 20The whole Assyrian army, their infantry, chariots, and cavalry, surrounded them for thirty-four days, until all the water containers of every inhabitant of Bethulia were empty; 21their cisterns were going dry, and on no day did they have enough water to drink, for their drinking water was rationed. 22Their children were listless, and the women and young men fainted from thirst and were collapsing in the streets of the town and in the gateways; they no longer had any strength.

23 Then all the people, the young men, the women, and the children, gathered around Uzziah and the rulers of the town and cried out with a loud voice and said before all the elders, 24"Let God judge between you and us! You have done us a great injury in not making peace with the Assyrians. 25For now we have no one to help us; God has sold us into their hands to be strewn before them in thirst and exhaustion. 26Now summon them and surrender the whole town as plunder to the army of Holofernes and to all his forces. 27For it would be better for us to be captured by them.° We shall indeed become slaves, but our lives will be spared, and we shall not witness our little ones dying before our eyes and our wives and children drawing their last breath. 28We call to witness against you heaven and earth and our God, the Lord of our ancestors, who punishes us for our sins and the sins of our ancestors; do today the things that we have described!"

29 Then great and general lamentation arose throughout the assembly, and they cried out to the Lord God with a loud voice.

o 7.27 Other ancient authorities add *than to die of thirst*

7:8–18 Neighbors provide strategy to Holofernes. 7:8–14 Moabites have already been mentioned (1:12; 5:22; 6:1; 7:8), as have the coastland peoples (2:28). Edomites are here mentioned for the first time. All are traditional neighbors and enemies of Israel. They know the lay of the land and are eager to provide strategic advice to Holofernes. **7:16–18** Following their advice and with their assistance, Holofernes seizes the water supply with the Ammonite army and just five thousand of his Assyrian troops. **7:18** Egrebeh, Chusi, and the Valley of Mochmur are not mentioned in the Bible, though they may be southeast of Shechem.

7:19–32 Israelites experience famine and great distress. 7:20–22 By the time the siege of Bethulia had lasted thirty-four days, all their cisterns containing water had dried up resulting in widespread weakness. **7:23–27** The residents urge the leaders of Bethulia to surrender. **7:28** *Punishes us for our sins and the sins of our ancestors* reflects a Deuteronomistic perspective; that is, they believe

³⁰But Uzziah said to them, "Courage, my brothers and sisters! Let us hold out for five days more; by that time the Lord our God will turn his mercy to us again, for he will not forsake us utterly. ³¹But if these days pass by and no help comes for us, I will do as you say."

32 Then he dismissed the people to their various posts, and they went up on the walls and towers of their town. The women and children he sent home. In the town they were in great misery.

8 Now in those days Judith heard about these things: she was the daughter of Merari son of Ox son of Joseph son of Oziel son of Elkiah son of Ananias son of Gideon son of Raphain son of Ahitub son of Elijah son of Hilkiah son of Eliab son of Nathanael son of Salamiel son of Sarasadai son of Israel. ²Her husband Manasseh, who belonged to her tribe and family, had died during the barley harvest. ³For as he stood overseeing those who were binding sheaves in the field, he was overcome by the burning heat and took to his bed and died in his town Bethulia. So they buried him with his ancestors in the field between Dothan and Balamon.

⁴Judith remained as a widow for three years and four months ⁵at home, where she set up a tent for herself on the roof of her house. She put sackcloth around her waist and dressed in widow's clothing. ⁶She fasted all the days of her widowhood except the day before the Sabbath and the Sabbath itself, the day before the new moon and the day of the new moon, and the festivals and days of rejoicing of the house of Israel. ⁷She was beautiful in appearance and was very lovely to behold. Her husband Manasseh had left her gold and silver, male and female slaves, livestock, and fields, and she maintained this estate. ⁸No one spoke ill of her, for she feared God with great devotion.

9 When Judith heard the harsh words spoken by the people against the ruler because they were faint for lack of water, and when she heard all that Uzziah said to them and how he promised them under oath to surrender the town to the Assyrians after five days, ¹⁰she sent her maid in charge of all she possessed to summon Uzziah and* Chabris and Charmis, the elders of her

p 8.10 Other ancient authorities lack *Uzziah and*

they are now suffering because of their ancestors' sins and their own. **7:30** *Courage, my brothers and sisters!* While Uzziah's exhortation sounds at first like Moses or Joshua, his leadership is not strong. He is urging them to wait only five more days and test God to deliver them.

8:1–16:25 Judith saves her people.

8:1–3 Judith finally enters the scene. 8:1 This is the first mention of Judith, who will dominate the action from this point on. Her name is the grammatically feminine form of "Jew" or "Judean," thus representing the people as a whole. The list of her ancestors is much longer than any woman in the Bible. Even male figures are usually introduced with at most four or five generations. These family connections traced all the way to Israel/Jacob indicate Judith's importance, honoring the heroine of the story. **8:2** Judith's *husband Manasseh*, of the same Simeonite tribe as Judith, is introduced to situate her as a widow. He died of sunstroke during the barley harvest, perhaps to suggest a weak disposition. The barley harvest is however the temporal setting for two other stories of powerful, bereaved women (2 Sam. 21:9; Ruth 1:22), and this brief description contains echoes of both the stories of Rizpah and Ruth. Widow is one of the three categories of most vulnerable people in ancient Israel along with the orphan and the resident alien.

8:4–8 Judith lives as a secluded widow. 8:4 *Three years and four months* equals forty months, a significant number. The Israelites spent forty years in the wilderness (Num. 32:13); Jonah gives Nineveh forty days to repent (Jonah 3:4); the city of Bethulia was under siege for forty days. Judith is ascetic in her dress and her dietary practices and pious in her behavior. In contrast to the Israelites who fast and don sackcloth in the face of an emergency (Jdt. 9; 4:9–13), Judith fasts regularly as a sign of mourning except on Sabbaths and festival days when fasting was prohibited. **8:8** *No one spoke ill of her.* Judith's reputation was safeguarded by her devotion to God. Her "fear" in the sense of awe and worship is directed toward the right object.

8:9–27 Judith reproaches the leaders of Bethulia. 8:10 *Maid.* The Greek term here ("abra") is relatively rare. The common terms for enslaved females are "paidiskē" and "doulē." "Abra" seems to be used for a favorite female domestic servant owned by a woman. Although she goes unnamed and never speaks, she plays an important role in overseeing Judith's estate and accompanying her

town. [11]They came to her, and she said to them,

"Listen to me, rulers of the people of Bethulia! What you have said to the people today is not right; you have even sworn and pronounced this oath between God and you, promising to surrender the town to our enemies unless the Lord turns and helps us within so many days. [12]Who are you to put God to the test today and to set yourselves up in the place of[q] God in human affairs? [13]You are putting the Lord Almighty to the test, but you will never learn anything! [14]You cannot plumb the depths of the human heart or understand the workings of the human mind; how do you expect to search out God, who made all these things, and find out his mind or comprehend his thought? No, my brothers, do not anger the Lord our God. [15]For if he does not choose to help us within these five days, he has power to protect us within any time he pleases or even to destroy us in the presence of our enemies. [16]Do not try to bind the purposes of the Lord our God, for God is not like a human being, to be threatened, or like a mere mortal, to be won over by pleading. [17]Therefore, while we wait for his deliverance, let us call upon him to help us, and he will hear our voice, if it pleases him.

[18] "For never in our generation nor in these present days has there been any tribe or family or people or town of ours that worships gods made with hands, as was done in days gone by. [19]That was why our ancestors were handed over to the sword and to pillage, and so they suffered a great catastrophe before our enemies. [20]But we know no other god but him, and so we hope that he will not disdain us or any of our people. [21]For if we are captured, all Judea will fall, and our sanctuary will be plundered, and he will make us pay for its desecration with our blood. [22]The slaughter of our kindred and the captivity of the land and the desolation of our inheritance—all this he will bring on our heads among the nations, wherever we serve as slaves, and we shall be an offense and a disgrace in the eyes of those who acquire us. [23]For our slavery will not bring us into favor, but the Lord our God will turn it to dishonor.

[24] "Therefore, my brothers, let us set an example for our kindred, for their lives depend upon us, and the sanctuary—both the temple and the altar—rests upon us. [25]In spite of everything, let us give thanks to the Lord our God, who is putting us to the test as he did our ancestors. [26]Remember what he did with Abraham and how he tested Isaac and what happened to Jacob in Syrian Mesopotamia, while he was tending the sheep of Laban, his mother's brother. [27]For he has not tried us with fire, as he did them, to search their hearts, nor has he taken vengeance on us, but the Lord scourges those who are close to him in order to admonish them."

[28] Then Uzziah said to her, "All that you have said was spoken out of a true heart, and there is no one who can deny your words. [29]Today is not the first time your wisdom has been shown, but from the beginning of your life all the people have recognized your understanding, for your heart's disposition is right. [30]But the people were so thirsty that they compelled us to do for them what we have promised and made us take an oath that we cannot break. [31]Now since you are a God-fearing woman, pray for us, so that the Lord may send us rain to fill our cisterns. Then we will no longer feel faint from thirst."

[32] Then Judith said to them, "Listen to me. I am about to do something that will go down through all generations of our people. [33]Stand at the town gate tonight so that I may go out with my maid, and within the days

q 8.12 Or *above*

on her mission. Her role is similar to Bagoas, Holofernes's servant. **8:11b–27** Judith's speech accuses the leaders of putting God *to the test* (cf. Moses in Exod. 17:2–7; Deut. 6:16; see also Ps. 95:8–9). God who created all cannot be known fully by mortals. She warns them of the consequences of idolatry and reminds them that if they endure their "testing," God will be faithful to them. **8:26** *Abraham.* See Gen. 22. This passage likely refers to the tradition that *Isaac* was the one tested, not Abraham (4 Macc. 13:12; LAB 32:2–3). *Jacob* and *Laban.* See Gen. 29:9–30.
8:28–35 Uzziah and Judith converse. 8:29 Uzziah recognizes Judith's wise words. Her *wisdom* is like the earlier Israelite wisdom tradition in that God does not make an overt appearance but works in the background as a providential Creator. Wisdom is also shown through fearing God and prayer. **8:32–35** Judith promises divine deliverance through her secret plan that will go down in history. She and her maid depart with the blessing of Uzziah and the elders.

after which you have promised to surrender the town to our enemies, the Lord will deliver Israel by my hand. [34]Only, do not try to find out what I am doing, for I will not tell you until I have finished what I am about to do."

35 Uzziah and the rulers said to her, "Go in peace, and may the Lord God go before you, to take vengeance on our enemies." [36]So they returned from the tent and went to their posts.

9 Then Judith prostrated herself, put ashes on her head, and uncovered the sackcloth she was wearing. At the very time when the evening incense was being offered in the house of God in Jerusalem, Judith cried out to the Lord with a loud voice and said,

2 "O Lord God of my ancestor Simeon, to whom you gave a sword to take revenge on those strangers who had torn off a virgin's clothing[r] to defile her and exposed her thighs to put her to shame and profaned her womb to disgrace her, for you said, 'It shall not be done'—yet they did it, [3]so you gave up their rulers to be killed, and their bed, which was ashamed of the deceit they had practiced, was stained with blood, and you struck down slaves along with princes and princes on their thrones. [4]You gave up their wives for plunder and their daughters to captivity and all their spoils to be divided among your beloved children who burned with zeal for you and abhorred the pollution of their blood and called on you for help. O God, my God, hear me also, a widow.

5 "For you have done these things and those that went before and those that followed. You have designed the things that are now and those that are to come. What you had in mind has happened; [6]the things you decided on presented themselves and said, 'Here we are!' For all your ways are prepared in advance, and your judgment is with foreknowledge.

7 "Here now are the Assyrians, a greatly increased force, priding themselves in their horses and riders, boasting in the strength of their foot soldiers, and trusting in shield and spear, in bow and sling. They do not know that you are the Lord who crushes wars; the Lord is your name. [8]Break their strength by your might, and bring down their power in your anger, for they intend to profane your sanctuary and to pollute the tabernacle where your glorious name resides and to break off the horns[s] of your altar with the sword. [9]Look at their pride, and send your wrath upon their heads. Give to me, a widow, the strong hand to do what I plan. [10]By the deceit of my lips strike down the slave with the prince and the prince with his attendant; crush their arrogance by the hand of a woman.

---

r 9.2 Cn: Gk *loosed her womb*   s 9.8 Syr: Gk *horn*

9:1–14 Judith prays to God. 9:1 *Uncovered the sackcloth.* Judith's preparations for prayer are similar to 4:11. She must have worn sackcloth underneath her widow's garments. *Time when the evening incense was being offered.* For prayer coinciding with the timing of temple sacrifice, see also Ezra 9:5; Dan. 9:20–21; 1 Kgs. 18:36; Luke 1:10; Rev. 8:3. **9:2** *God of my ancestor Simeon.* Prayers typically address the "God of our ancestors" or "God of Abraham, Isaac, and Jacob." Her unique address highlights not only her affiliation with the tribe of Simeon but his actions taken on behalf of Dinah (Gen. 34). **9:2–3** In an honor-shame culture, *shame* has a strong negative connotation. **9:4** *Who burned with zeal.* This is an interpretive recasting of the rape of Dinah story. Neither Dinah nor Shechem is named but both Simeon and Levi are blamed for their violence by their father, Jacob (Gen. 34:30; 49:5–6; see also Jub. 30; T. Levi). The language of pollution and defilement is here applied to both Dinah's womb and the potential violation of the temple's inner sanctuary. Other sources legitimating violent acts also refer to Phinehas, who was rewarded for his zeal in preventing idolatry by killing an Israelite man having exogamous intercourse with a Moabite (Num. 25; 1 Macc. 2). **9:5–6** As in her speech to the Bethulians (8:11–27), Judith displays her theological knowledge, affirming God's providence and omniscience. **9:7–10** Judith describes the Assyrian threat drawing on language from the Song of the Sea (Exod. 15). Hekeziah's prayer when facing Sennacherib's siege of Jerusalem also serves as a model (2 Kgs. 19:15–19 // Isa. 37:16–20). **9:7** *Horses and riders.* Exodus 15:1, 21. *The Lord who crushes wars.* This is the same language as the Greek Septuagint (Exod. 15:3). **9:8** Judith has already made clear to the Bethulians what was at stake if the Assyrians conquered them (8:24). **9:10** *Deceit of my lips.* She will lie in order to beguile her enemy (see **"Judith as Trickster," p. 1372**). *By the hand of a woman.* Being killed by a woman was considered a disgrace

11 "For your strength does not depend on numbers nor your might on the powerful. But you are the God of the lowly, helper of the oppressed, upholder of the weak, protector of the forsaken, savior of those without hope. [12]Please, please, God of my father, God of the heritage of Israel, Lord of heaven and earth, Creator of the waters, King of all your creation, hear my prayer! [13]Make my deceitful words bring wound and bruise on those who have planned cruel things against your covenant and against your sacred house and against Mount Zion and against the house your children possess. [14]Let your whole nation and every tribe know and understand that you are God, the God of all power and might, and that there is no other who protects the people of Israel but you alone!"

10 When Judith[t] had stopped crying out to the God of Israel and had ended all these words, [2]she rose from where she lay prostrate. She called her maid and went down into the house where she lived on Sabbaths and on her festal days. [3]She removed the sackcloth she had been wearing, took off her widow's garments, bathed her body with water, and anointed herself with precious ointment. She combed her hair, put on a tiara, and dressed herself in the festive attire that she used to wear while her husband Manasseh was living. [4]She put sandals on her feet and put on her anklets, bracelets, rings, earrings, and all her other jewelry. Thus she made herself very beautiful, to entice the eyes of all the men who might see her. [5]She gave her maid a skin of wine and a flask of oil and filled a bag with roasted grain, dried fig cakes, and fine bread;[u] then she wrapped up all her dishes and gave them to her to carry.

6 Then they went out to the town gate of Bethulia and found Uzziah standing there with the elders of the town, Chabris and Charmis. [7]When they saw her transformed in appearance and dressed differently, they were very greatly astounded at her beauty and said to her, [8]"May the God of our ancestors grant you favor and fulfill your plans, so that the people of Israel may glory and Jerusalem may be exalted." She bowed down to God.

9 Then she said to them, "Order the gate of the town to be opened for me so that I may go out and accomplish the things you have just said to me." So they ordered the young men to open the gate for her, as she requested. [10]When they had done this, Judith went out, accompanied by her maid. The men of the town watched her until she had gone down the mountain and passed through the valley, where they lost sight of her.

11 As the women[v] were going straight on through the valley, an Assyrian patrol met her [12]and took her into custody. They asked her, "To what people do you belong, and where are you coming from, and where are you going?" She replied, "I am a daughter

t 10.1 Gk *she* u 10.5 Other ancient authorities add *and cheese* v 10.11 Gk *they*

(Judg. 9:53–54). Here she links herself to her murderous ancestor Simeon, who wielded a sword. **9:11–12** Long lists of divine epithets are frequent in Jewish prayers from the Greco-Roman era (cf. 2 Macc. 1:24–25; 3 Macc. 2:2–3; 6:2). Judith trusts that God will side with the oppressed against the aggressor. The widow's strength comes from this prayerful conviction.

10:1–5 Judith prepares for her mission. 10:3–4 Similar to Esther, Judith gets ready by bathing, primping herself, and donning festive clothes and jewelry in order to transform her appearance. Tamar (Gen. 38:14, 19) and Ruth (Ruth 3:3) also prepare to entice heterosexual men. Judith's actions are also like those of Hera as she gets ready to seduce Zeus (Homer, *Il.* 14.166–86). **10:5** In addition to her external appearance, she prepares her own sustenance with special foods. *Fine bread*, literally "pure bread"—that is, kosher food. She observes the Jewish dietary laws.

10:6–10 The elders give their blessing. 10:6–7 The *town gate* is the site of public activity dominated by men. Dressed to kill, Judith is entering their arena. From now on, her efforts to transform herself prove successful, and there are frequent references to her beautiful appearance. **10:8** The elders offer their blessing. Even though they do not know the details, they trust that it is for the glory of Israel and Jerusalem. Judith's response is to acknowledge God rather than the men's reaction. **10:10** Leaving the town gate, they are entering a vulnerability zone.

10:11–19 The Assyrians capture Judith. A patrol encounters Judith and peppers her with questions. **10:12a** *Where are you coming from, and where are you going?* These are the same questions the angel poses to the enslaved Egyptian Hagar, who is in a similarly vulnerable position (Gen. 16:8). **10:12b–13** This

Focus On: Judith as Trickster (Judith 10:6–12:20)

In the middle of her long prayer to gain strength for her mission, Judith petitions God: "By the deceit of my lips strike down the slave with the prince and the prince with his attendant; crush their arrogance by the hand of a woman" (Jdt. 9:10). Modern readers might recoil that Judith prays to be a successful liar in order to save her people, but if we think of Judith as a trickster figure, her actions make more sense within her culture. The figure of the trickster was first conceived in the study of folklore and anthropology. The trickster is found in many cultures, like the Coyote figure in native cultures of North America, the Tar Baby found in the Brer Rabbit tales of enslaved African Americans, or early stories of Robin Hood in England. In antiquity, Prometheus, Hermes, and Hera of Greek mythology have also been understood as tricksters.

The chief characteristic of the trickster is to be one who deceives, who crafts a ruse or "trick" that plays a central role in the unfolding action among characters. Trickster stories are meant to amuse their audience and are laced with humor as the antics and actions unfold. A number of trickster stories are contained in the book of Genesis. Jacob plays the trickster in his deceitful behavior of tricking his father, Isaac, out of his older brother's, Esau's, birthright and blessing as the firstborn. Rachel plays the trickster in her escape from Laban. Tamar, too, plays the trickster as a prostitute in exposing the hypocrisies of her father-in-law, Judah. The tricksters in Genesis also exemplify the national character. In that regard, Judith not only plays a central role in the narrative, but her name (Heb. *Yehudit*) suggests she serves as an ideal embodiment of the nation.

Judith's ruse is her mission to slay Holofernes, during which she deceives her Assyrian interlocutors (Jdt. 10:12–13; 11:5–19). She also speaks with a "forked tongue" by which her words have two meanings. She tells Holofernes shortly before decapitating him, "I will gladly drink, my lord, because today is the greatest day in my whole life" (Jdt. 12:18). We as readers know that "lord" does not mean Holofernes but Israel's Lord God.

But tricksters are also truth-tellers, at least through the results of their actions. They can reveal the problems at work in the larger social or political order. This small but courageous nation, epitomized by Judith, could seem an underdog among its alpha-dog neighbors, but it still could achieve victory through fidelity to YHWH.

Judith H. Newman

of the Hebrews, but I am fleeing from them, for they are about to be handed over to you to be devoured. [13]I am on my way to see Holofernes the commander of your army, to give him a true report; I will show him a way by which he can go and capture all the hill country without losing one of his men, captured or slain."

14 When the men heard her words and observed her face—she was in their eyes marvelously beautiful—they said to her, [15]"You have saved your life by hurrying down to see our lord. Go at once to his tent; some of us will escort you and hand you over to him. [16]When you stand before him, have no fear in your heart, but tell him what you have just said, and he will treat you well."

17 They chose from their number a hundred men to accompany her and her maid, and they brought them to the tent of Holofernes. [18]There was great excitement in the whole camp, for her arrival was reported from tent to tent. They came and gathered around her as she stood outside the tent of Holofernes, waiting until they told him about her. [19]They marveled at her beauty and admired the Israelites, judging them by her. They said to one another, "Who can despise these people, who have women like this among them? It is not wise to leave one of their men alive, for if we let them go they will be able to beguile the whole world!"

20 Then the guards of Holofernes and all his attendants came out and led her into the tent. [21]Holofernes was resting on his bed under a canopy that was woven with purple, gold, emeralds, and other precious stones. [22]When they told him of her, he came to the

is the first of Judith's deceptions. **10:14** Just like the Israelite elders, the Assyrian soldiers cannot take their eyes off Judith. **10:17** The large escort of *a hundred men* was unnecessary and suggests the effect that Judith's appearance has had on them.

10:20–23 Judith appears before Holofernes. 10:21 When Judith first meets Holofernes, he is reclining on his bed, the place where he will meet his fateful end. Holofernes's tent and its canopy

front of the tent, with silver lamps carried before him. [23]When Judith came into the presence of Holofernes[w] and his attendants, they all marveled at the beauty of her face. She prostrated herself and did obeisance to him, but his slaves raised her up.

11 Then Holofernes said to her, "Take courage, woman, and do not be afraid in your heart, for I have never hurt anyone who chose to serve Nebuchadnezzar, king of all the earth. [2]Even now, if your people who live in the hill country had not slighted me, I would never have lifted my spear against them. They have brought this on themselves. [3]But now tell me why you have fled from them and have come over to us. In any event, you have come to safety. Take courage! You will live tonight and ever after. [4]No one will hurt you. Rather, all will treat you well, as they do the servants of my lord King Nebuchadnezzar."

[5]Judith answered him, "Accept the words of your slave, and let your servant speak in your presence. I will say nothing false to my lord this night. [6]If you follow the words of your servant, God will accomplish something through you, and my lord will not fail to achieve his purposes. [7]By the life of Nebuchadnezzar, king of the whole earth, and by the power of him who has sent you to direct every living being! Not only do humans serve him because of you, but also the animals of the field and the cattle and the birds of the air will live because of your power, under Nebuchadnezzar and all his house. [8]For we have heard of your wisdom and skill, and it is

reported throughout the whole world that you alone are the best in the whole kingdom, the most informed and the most astounding in military strategy.

[9]"Now as for Achior's speech in your council, we have heard his words, for the people of Bethulia spared him and he told them all he had said to you. [10]Therefore, lord and master, do not disregard what he said, but keep it in your mind, for it is true. Indeed, our people cannot be punished nor can the sword prevail against them unless they sin against their God.

[11]"But now, in order that my lord may not be defeated and his purpose frustrated, death will fall upon them, for a sin has overtaken them by which they are about to provoke their God to anger when they do what is wrong. [12]Since their food supply is exhausted and their water has almost given out, they have planned to kill their livestock and have determined to use all that God by his laws has forbidden them to eat. [13]They have decided to consume the first fruits of the grain and the tithes of the wine and oil, which they had consecrated and set aside for the priests who minister in the presence of our God in Jerusalem—things it is not lawful for any of the people even to touch with their hands. [14]Since even the people in Jerusalem have been doing this, they have sent messengers there in order to bring back permission from the council of the elders. [15]When the response reaches them and they act upon it, on that very day they will be handed over to you to be destroyed.

w 10.23 Gk *him*

are very opulent. Ahasuerus's palace is also described as luxurious (Esth. 1:6–7). The audience knows Judith's true feelings about the Assyrians and their leaders, so they can recognize her ironic and two-faced gesture of prostration.

11:1–4 Holofernes reassures Judith. 11:1 *Do not be afraid.* Like the soldiers in his patrol (10:15–16), Holofernes underestimates Judith and her fearlessness. His claim that he has never hurt anyone contradicts his destruction of the submissive coastal peoples (3:1–8). *Nebuchadnezzar, king of all the earth.* Compare 2:5; 6:4; and 11:7. Readers know that Judith views God as king of all creation (9:12).

11:5–19 Judith responds to Holofernes. Her speech is full of deception and double entendres. **11:5** *Nothing false* echoes Achior's statement (5:5). *My lord.* Does Judith mean her God or Nebuchadnezzar? **11:7–8** Judith's flattery of Holofernes as the best military strategist is contradicted by his lax attitude toward military discipline. Similar situational irony is depicted in 2 Sam. 11:1, where it was the time of the year when kings go out to battle, but King David stayed home and launched an affair and raped Bathsheba. **11:11–15** *Sin has overtaken them.* Judith's false account of the Bethulians' sin is meant to jibe with Achior's account. *First fruits of the grain and the tithes of the wine and oil.* Deuteronomy 18:4; Neh. 10:39; Num. 18:21–24. Holofernes would not have known the details of Israelite sacrificial practices, but she intends to convince him they are bound for destruction because of

16 "So when I, your slave, learned all this, I fled from them. God has sent me to accomplish with you things that will astonish the whole world wherever people shall hear about them. ¹⁷Your servant is indeed God-fearing and serves the God of heaven night and day. So, my lord, I will remain with you, but every night your servant will go out into the valley and pray to God. He will tell me when they have committed their sins. ¹⁸Then I will come and tell you, so that you may go out with your whole army, and not one of them will be able to withstand you. ¹⁹Then I will lead you through Judea until you come to Jerusalem; there I will set your throne.ˣ You will drive them like sheep that have no shepherd, and no dog will so much as growl at you. For this was told me to give me fore-knowledge; it was announced to me, and I was sent to tell you."

20 Her words pleased Holofernes and all his attendants. They marveled at her wisdom and said, ²¹"No other woman from one end of the earth to the other looks so beautiful or speaks so wisely!" ²²Then Holofernes said to her, "God has done well to send you ahead of the people, to strengthen our hands and bring destruction on those who have despised my lord. ²³You are not only beautiful in appearance but wise in speech. If you do as you have said, your God shall be my God, and you shall live in the palace of King Nebuchadnezzar and be renowned throughout the whole world."

12 Then he commanded them to bring her in where his silver dinnerware was kept and ordered them to set a table for her with some of his own delicacies and with some of his own wine to drink. ²But Judith said, "I cannot partake of them, or it will be an offense, but I will have enough with the things I brought with me." ³Holofernes said to her, "If your supply runs out, where can we get you more of the same? For none of your people are here with us." ⁴Judith replied, "As surely as you live, my lord, your servant will not use up the supplies I have with me before the Lord carries out by my hand what he has determined."

5 Then the attendants of Holofernes brought her into the tent, and she slept until midnight. Toward the morning watch she got up ⁶and sent this message to Holofernes: "Let my lord now give orders to allow your servant to go out and pray." ⁷So Holofernes commanded his guards not to hinder her. She remained in the camp three days. She went out each night to the valley of Bethulia and bathed at the spring in the camp.ʸ ⁸After bathing, she prayed the Lord God of Israel to direct her way for the triumph of hisᶻ people.

x 11.19 Or *chariot*   y 12.7 Other ancient authorities lack *in the camp*   z 12.8 Other ancient authorities read *her*

their lawlessness; compare 5:17–18. **11:16** *Things that will astonish the whole world.* More irony erupts. Judith has something very different in mind from what Holofernes might imagine. Here she presents herself as a prophet with foreknowledge of divine plans. While she does not receive revelatory oracles, in other ways she resembles women prophets like Miriam (Exod. 15:20) and Deborah (Judg. 4:4). The prophet Anna is modeled in certain ways after Judith (Luke 2:36). **11:17–19** Judith plans to leave the camp every night to purify herself by bathing, eat her kosher food, and pray.

11:20–23 Holofernes's reaction. Like Achior, Holofernes and his servants recognize Judith's wisdom. Through her speech and actions, she embodies an amalgam of two female figures encountered in Wisdom literature. She is the virtuous Woman Wisdom of Prov. 9 but also the Strange Woman who seduces men through her sexuality and smooth words (Prov. 7:5, 21–22; cf. Sir. 24 and Wis. 7:7–9:18). **11:23** *Your God shall be my God.* Shifting homelands meant shifting allegiance to gods. The same words are spoken by Ruth the Moabite to her Israelite mother-in-law, Naomi (Ruth 1:16).

12:1–4 Judith dines with Holofernes. 12:2 *An offense* (Gk. "skandalon"). Just as Daniel and his friends restrict their diet to vegetables and water according to their ancestral laws (Dan. 1:5–16), Judith refuses the food offered to her by Holofernes. For other cases of avoiding gentile food, see Tobit (Tob. 1:10–11) and Greek Esther (Gk. Esth. 14:17). Refusing to eat pork resulted in the deaths of the martyrs Eleazar and the mother and her seven sons (2 Macc. 6:18–31; 7:1–42; 4 Macc. 5:1–6:30). **12:4** *Carries out by my hand* echoes 9:10 and anticipates Holofernes's death.

12:5–9 Judith stays in the camp for three days abiding by her own rules. 12:5 *Morning watch.* There are three watches in the night: the first (Lam. 2:19) from sunset to ten o'clock, the middle watch (Judg. 7:19) from ten until two o'clock, and the morning watch (Exod. 14:24; 1 Sam. 11:11) from two o'clock to sunrise. **12:8** *After bathing.* This purification rite was widespread in the Hellenistic-Roman

⁹Then she returned purified and stayed in the tent until she ate her food toward evening.

10 On the fourth day Holofernes held a banquet for his slaves only and did not invite any of his officers. ¹¹He said to Bagoas, the eunuch who had charge of his personal affairs, "Go and persuade the Hebrew woman who is in your care to join us and to eat and drink with us. ¹²For it would be a disgrace if we let such a woman go without being intimate with her. If we do not seduce her, she will laugh at us."

13 So Bagoas left the presence of Holofernes and approached her and said, "Let this pretty servant not hesitate to come to my lord to be honored in his presence and to enjoy drinking wine with us and to become today like one of the Assyrian women who serve in the palace of Nebuchadnezzar." ¹⁴Judith replied, "Who am I to refuse my lord? Whatever pleases him I will do at once, and it will be a joy to me until the day of my death." ¹⁵So she proceeded to dress herself in all her woman's finery. Her maid went ahead and spread for her on the ground before Holofernes the lambskins she had received from Bagoas for her daily use in reclining.

16 Then Judith came in and lay down. Holofernes's heart was ravished with her and his passion was aroused, for he had been waiting for an opportunity to be with her from the day he first saw her. ¹⁷So Holofernes said to her, "Have a drink and be merry with us!" ¹⁸Judith said, "I will gladly drink, my lord, because today is the greatest day in my whole life." ¹⁹Then she took what her maid had prepared and ate and drank before him. ²⁰Holofernes was greatly pleased with her and drank a great quantity of wine, much more than he had ever drunk in any one day since he was born.

13 When evening came, his slaves quickly withdrew. Bagoas closed the tent from outside and shut out the attendants from his master's presence. They went to bed, for they all were weary because the banquet had lasted so long. ²But Judith was left alone in the tent, with Holofernes stretched out on his bed, for he was dead drunk.

3 Now Judith had told her maid to stand outside the bedchamber and to wait for her to come out, as she did on the other days, for she said she would be going out for her prayers. She had said the same thing to Bagoas. ⁴So everyone went out, and no one, either small

era as part of household Judaism. Many "miqva'ot" (ritual baths) have been uncovered at archaeological sites in Syria-Palestine, including plastered stepped pools at Qumran, Magdala, and Sepphoris. Judith seems to have bathed in a freshwater spring rather than a "miqveh."

12:10–12 Holofernes holds a private banquet. **12:10** *Banquet*, literally a "drinking party" (Gk. "poton"; cf. 6:21). His officers are excluded, perhaps because they might be rivals for Judith's attention. **12:11** *Bagoas* is a Persian name and one that is particularly associated with eunuchs. Eunuchs often supervised harems. The book of Esther includes three named eunuchs who attended to the harem: Hegai, Shaashgaz, and Hathach. For other eunuchs named Bagoas, see Ovid, *Am.* 2.2.1; Lucian, *Eunuch* 47.4; Heliodorus, *Aeth.* 8.2.3. Like Judith's maid, Bagoas plays a domestic role in charge of household affairs. Bagoas, however, is involved in the dialogue, unlike Judith's silent maid. **12:12** Holofernes crudely contemplates the sexual assault of a captive woman, reflecting the tragic pattern of abuse and rape that has occurred to subjugated women during war throughout the ages.

12:13–15 Bagoas speaks to Judith privately and more politely to procure her for Holofernes's sexual pleasure. **12:13** *Like . . . the Assyrian women.* These women would constitute the palace harem. **12:14** *To refuse my lord.* Judith responds with another double entendre. She would never refuse her God's requests, but she will spurn Holofernes.

12:16–20 The seduction scene offers a strong contrast between Holofernes and Judith. He is an undisciplined military man with unbridled lust who drinks himself into a stupor. She remains in full possession of all her senses, steeling herself for the right moment to kill him. **12:18** *The greatest day in my whole life.* Judith speaks with a forked tongue. The drunken Holofernes may not have registered the words, but here she gives her consent—not to the limp lord but to her God. It will be the greatest day if she can defeat the general and the army that wished to ravish her body, her temple, and her people.

13:1–10 Judith seizes the initiative to slay Holofernes. **13:3** She tells both domestic servants the same thing so that she can accomplish the feat unimpeded. The interaction of a man and a woman in a private and secluded place was a liminal space of potential grave consequence. **13:4** *Said in*

Reading through Time: Judith in Art (Judith 13)

The book of Judith has an engaging plot with enough action and intrigue to fill many seasons of an internet miniseries, with military battles, sex, and violence along with a cast of lively and morally ambiguous characters. It is thus not surprising that Judith has had a rich reception history in the arts in literary, visual, and musical forms. While literary dramatizations or musical renditions of Judith could include the entire story, visual depictions of Judith have to be more selective, typically singling out one view. Although Judith's long prayer lies at the center of the book, visual artists have overwhelmingly ignored that tame scene and chosen to depict instead the erotic and violent decapitation of the Assyrian general Holofernes. There was an especially explosive interest in Judith in the art of the European Renaissance and Baroque periods. Two examples from Roman Catholic Italy demonstrate how the signification of Judith's triumphant decapitation could change given different political and cultural circumstances. The Renaissance artist Donatello brought Judith to life in Florence as a bronze sculpture in which she holds a sword high in one hand and, with the other, grasps the hair of Holofernes, ready to sever his head from his limp, drunken body. Judith does not represent the defense of Jerusalem so much as civic virtue and liberation from the tyranny of the Medici dynasty as the Florentines established their republic. The significance of the decapitation scene would shift again a century later in the work of Artemisia Gentileschi, a Baroque artist following the style of Caravaggio. Gentileschi survived a rape by the friend of her father and the subsequent trial after which she, the rape victim, was tortured. Her personal trauma thus underlies the three vivid and violent paintings she made of a vehement Judith, accompanied by her faithful maid, and the decapitated Holofernes gruesomely displayed. Gentileschi's story itself has been interpreted in several films, providing yet more lenses on Judith as the interpretive process of Scripture continues on in many forms through the ages.

Judith H. Newman

or great, was left in the bedchamber. Then Judith, standing beside his bed, said in her heart, "O Lord God of all might, look in this hour on the work of my hands for the exaltation of Jerusalem. ⁵Now indeed is the time to help your heritage and to carry out my design to destroy the enemies who have risen up against us."

6 She went up to the bedpost near Holofernes's head and took down his sword that hung there. ⁷She came close to his bed, took hold of the hair of his head, and said, "Give me strength today, O Lord God of Israel!" ⁸Then she struck his neck twice with all her might and cut off his head. ⁹Next she rolled his body off the bed and pulled down the canopy from the posts. Soon afterward she went out and gave Holofernes's head to her maid, ¹⁰who placed it in her food bag.

Then the two of them went out together, as they were accustomed to do for prayer.

They passed through the camp, circled around the valley, went up the mountain to Bethulia, and came to its gates. ¹¹From a distance Judith called out to the sentries at the gates, "Open, open the gate! God, our God, is with us, still showing his power in Israel and his strength against our enemies, as he has done today!"

12 When the people of her town heard her voice, they hurried down to the town gate and summoned the elders of the town. ¹³They all ran together, both small and great, for it seemed unbelievable that she had returned. They opened the gate and welcomed them. Then they lit a fire to give light and gathered around them. ¹⁴Then she said to them with a loud voice, "Praise God, O praise him! Praise God, who has not withdrawn his mercy from the house of Israel but has destroyed our enemies by my hand this very night!"

her heart. Prayers were generally said aloud. One of the exceptions is the barren Hannah, who prays for a son (1 Sam. 1) and who is then accused of being drunk by the priest Eli. Judith prays not for herself but for Jerusalem and for her people to destroy the aggressor who threatens their existence. **13:5** *To carry out my design.* Judith takes credit for the plan. **13:7** Her final prayer begins not with an invocation of God but with an urgent petition. **13:10** *Placed it in her food bag* is a bit of dry humor. Surely Holofernes's head would not be considered part of a kosher diet.

13:11–16 Judith and her maid return to Bethulia. 13:13 *Small and great,* literally "from small to big," is a Hebrew expression translated into Greek. **13:14** Judith credits God with the victory in her

15 Then she pulled the head out of the bag and showed it to them and said, "See here, the head of Holofernes, the commander of the Assyrian army, and here is the canopy beneath which he lay in his drunken stupor. The Lord has struck him down by the hand of a woman. ¹⁶As the Lord lives, who has protected me in the way I went, I swear that it was my face that seduced him to his destruction and that he committed no sin with me, to defile and shame me."

17 All the people were greatly astonished. They bowed down and worshiped God and said with one accord, "Blessed are you, our God, who have this day humiliated the enemies of your people."

18 Then Uzziah said to her, "O daughter, you are blessed by the Most High God above all other women on earth, and blessed be the Lord God, who created the heavens and the earth, who has guided you to cut off the head of the leader of our enemies. ¹⁹Your hope*a* will never depart from the hearts of those who remember the power of God. ²⁰May God grant this to be a perpetual honor to you, and may he reward you with blessings because you risked your own life when our people was brought low, and you averted our ruin, walking in the straight path before our God." And all the people said, "Amen. Amen."

14 Then Judith said to them, "Listen to me, my friends. Take this head and hang it upon the parapet of your wall. ²As soon as day breaks and the sun rises on the earth, each of you take up your weapons, and let every able-bodied man go out of the town; set a captain over them, as if you were going down to the plain against the Assyrian outpost; only do not go down. ³Then they will seize their arms and go into the camp and rouse the officers of the Assyrian army. They will rush into the tent of Holofernes and will not find him. Then panic will come over them, and they will flee before you. ⁴Then you and all who live within the borders of Israel will pursue them and cut them down in their tracks. ⁵But before you do all this, bring Achior the Ammonite to me so that he may see and recognize the man who despised the house of Israel and sent him to us as if to his death."

6 So they summoned Achior from the house of Uzziah. When he came and saw the head of Holofernes in the hand of one of the men in the assembly of the people, he fell down on his face in a faint. ⁷When they raised him up he threw himself at Judith's feet and did obeisance to her and said, "Blessed are you in every tent of Judah! In every nation those who hear your name will be alarmed. ⁸Now tell me what you have done during these days."

So Judith told him in the presence of the people all that she had done from the day she left until the moment she began speaking to them. ⁹When she had finished, the people raised a great shout and made a joyful noise in their town. ¹⁰When Achior saw all that the God of Israel had done, he believed firmly in

a 13.19 Other ancient authorities read *praise*

jubilant exhortation to praise. Such repeated calls to praise are also found in Psalms (e.g., Pss. 148:1–3; 150:1–6). **13:15** *By the hand of a woman.* The decapitation of an enemy was a symbolic castration. For a woman to do this would be especially humiliating (see **"Masculinity," p. 1701**). **13:16** *Defile and shame me.* Judith makes clear she has not been shamed, continuing the theme of honor vs. shame, purity vs. defilement. Her *face* seduced Holofernes; her body remained undefiled.

13:17–20 The people respond with blessings. Nebuchadnezzar had expected his military power could force people to worship him. Instead, the Israelites orient their blessings toward their own God. **13:17** *Blessed are you, our God.* While we might expect a blessing over Judith, she credits God working through her for the victory. Tobit 8:5; 11:14 contains the same form of blessing. **13:18** Uzziah takes the opportunity to bless Judith herself. Here is another echo of the story of Jael's killing of Sisera. Jael is blessed by Deborah for killing the Canaanite general (Judg. 5:24).

14:1–5 Judith directs the military strategy. Adopting the role of military leader, Judith directs the Israelites to rout the Assyrians. First, she summons Achior.

14:6–10 Achior joins the house of Israel. Achior's eyes and ears lead him to acknowledge the God of Israel. **14:10** *Believed firmly in God.* Although he at first prostrated himself before Judith, he now orients himself toward the God of Israel. This entails circumcision, a necessary condition for joining the covenant people (Gen. 17), although Deut. 23:3 prohibits Ammonites from joining. For other gentiles becoming circumcised and adopting Jewish practices, see Josephus, *Ant.* 20.139, *Vita.* 113.

God. So he was circumcised and joined the house of Israel, remaining so to this day.

11 As soon as it was dawn, they hung the head of Holofernes on the wall. Then they all took their weapons and went out in companies to the mountain passes. [12]When the Assyrians saw them, they sent word to their commanders, who then went to the generals and the captains and to all their other officers. [13]They came to Holofernes's tent and said to the steward in charge of all his personal affairs, "Wake up our lord, for the slaves have been so bold as to come down against us to give battle, to their utter destruction."

14 So Bagoas went in and knocked at the entry of the tent, for he supposed that he was sleeping with Judith. [15]But when no one answered, he opened it and went into the bedchamber and found him dead, sprawled over the footstool, with his head missing. [16]He cried out with a loud voice and wept and groaned and shouted and tore his clothes. [17]Then he went to the tent where Judith had stayed, and when he did not find her, he rushed out to the people and shouted, [18]"The slaves have foiled us! One Hebrew woman has brought disgrace on the house of King Nebuchadnezzar. Look, Holofernes is lying on the ground, and his head is missing!"

19 When the leaders of the Assyrian army heard this, they tore their tunics and were greatly dismayed, and their loud cries and shouts rose up throughout the camp.

15 When the men in the tents heard it, they were amazed at what had happened. [2]Overcome with fear and trembling, they did not wait for one another, but with one impulse all rushed out and fled by every path across the plain and through the hill country. [3]Those who had camped in the hills around Bethulia also took to flight. Then the Israelites, everyone who was a soldier, rushed out upon them. [4]Uzziah sent men to Betomasthaim[b] and Choba and Kola and to all the frontiers of Israel to tell what had taken place and to urge all to rush out upon the enemy to destroy them. [5]When the Israelites heard it, with one accord they fell upon the enemy[c] and cut them down as far as Choba. Those in Jerusalem and all the hill country also came, for they were told what had happened in the camp of the enemy. The men in Gilead and in Galilee outflanked them with great slaughter, even beyond Damascus and its borders. [6]The rest of the people

b 15.4 Other ancient authorities add *and Bebai*   c 15.5 Gk *them*

The author of Jubilees holds a different view and only accepted descendants of Abraham who were circumcised on the eighth day (Jub. 15:25–34).

14:11–13 The head of Holofernes is displayed. This gruesome ritual of war was common in antiquity. For the exhibition of other decapitated heads or bodies, see Goliath (1 Sam. 17:57), Saul (1 Sam. 31:9–10), and Ahab's family (2 Kgs. 10:7–8). Contemporaneous to Judith is the display of Nicanor's head (1 Macc. 7:47; 2 Macc. 15:35). The head of John the Baptist meets a somewhat different fate (Matt. 14:8).

14:14–19 Bagoas and the Assyrian army react to Holofernes's murder. 14:16 Crying out in distress is a recurrent theme, but elsewhere, it is Israelites who cry out to God (see 4:9, 12, 15; 5:12; 6:18; 7:19, 23, 29; 9:1). Here Bagoas cries out and laments because his "lord" has been killed. **14:18** The use of *slaves* and a *Hebrew woman* evokes the status of Israel as Hebrew slaves in Egypt. The typological pattern is reinscribed in the narrative: Israel's God cares about the oppressed and will save them. *Brought disgrace.* Judith escaped disgrace, inflicting shame instead on the house of Nebuchadnezzar.

15:1–7 The Assyrians flee in terror. 15:2 *With fear and trembling.* This is a reversal of 2:28. Judith prophetically predicted that the Assyrians would be fearful once they learned of Holofernes's death (14:3). The people are depicted as each going their own way in a panicked dispersion. **15:4** Uzziah reenters the story by ordering vengeful attacks. **15:5** While the exact locations of some cities are unknown (Betomasthaim, Choba, Kola), the mentions of Gilead and Galilee suggest the military excursions of the Maccabees (1 Macc. 5:9–64), which align with the borders at the time of King David. Just as they have worshiped *with one accord* (13:17; 15:9), so too did the Israelites demonstrate a unified purpose in relation to their enemies. Having faced a vicious invader, they are united in their vicious reprisal. The Israelites seem to follow the rules of "herem," holy war, described in two kinds in Deut. 20:10–18. **15:6–7** The plundering of the Assyrians may evoke the plundering of the Egyptians during the exodus (Exod. 12:35–36). In contrast to the modern era in which international law might require war reparations, in antiquity, plunder and looting were common practices that could restore lost property as recompense.

of Bethulia fell upon the Assyrian camp and plundered it, acquiring great riches. ⁷And the Israelites, when they returned from the slaughter, took possession of what remained. Even the villages and towns in the hill country and in the plain got a great amount of plunder, since there was a vast quantity of it.

8 Then the high priest Joakim and the council of the Israelites who lived in Jerusalem came to witness the good things that the Lord had done for Israel and to see Judith and to wish her well. ⁹When they met her, they all blessed her with one accord and said to her, "You are the glory of Jerusalem, you are the great boast of Israel, you are the great pride of our people! ¹⁰You have done all this with your own hand; you have done great good to Israel, and God is well pleased with it. May the Almighty Lord bless you forever!" And all the people said, "Amen."

11 All the people plundered the camp for thirty days. They gave Judith the tent of Holofernes and all his silver dinnerware, his beds, his bowls, and all his furniture. She took them and loaded her mules and hitched up her carts and piled the things on them.

12 All the women of Israel gathered to see her and blessed her, and some of them performed a dance in her honor. She took ivy-wreathed wands in her hands and distributed them to the women who were with her, ¹³and she and those who were with her crowned themselves with olive wreaths. She went before all the people in the dance,

leading all the women, while all the men of Israel followed, bearing their arms and wearing garlands and singing hymns.

14 Judith began this thanksgiving before all Israel, and all the people loudly sang this song of praise. ¹And Judith said,

16

"Begin a song to my God with
  tambourines;
  sing to my Lord with cymbals.
Raise to him a new psalm;ᵈ
  exalt him and call upon his name.
² For the Lord is a God who crushes wars;
  he sets up his camp among his people;
  he delivered me from the hands of my
    pursuers.
³ The Assyrian came down from the
    mountains of the north;
  he came with myriads of his warriors;
  their numbers blocked up the wadis,
  and their cavalry covered the hills.
⁴ He boasted that he would burn up my
    territory
  and kill my young men with the
    sword
and dash my infants to the ground
  and seize my children as plunder
  and take my virgins as spoil.

⁵ "But the Lord Almighty has foiled them
  by the hand of a woman.ᵉ
⁶ For their mighty one did not fall by the
    hands of the young men,

---

d 16.1 Other ancient authorities read *a psalm and praise*
e 16.5 Other ancient authorities add *he has confounded them*

15:8–13 Judith is honored on returning to Jerusalem. 15:8 *The high priest Joakim.* Abraham is likewise met by a priest after returning from his military victory (Gen. 14:17–18). **15:12** Like the victory celebration after the crossing of the Red Sea, women *performed a dance.* **15:13** *Olive wreaths.* This was a Greek practice after military victory; see also 2 Macc. 10:7; 3 Macc. 7:16; Wis. 2:8.

15:14 Judith leads the thanksgiving. Like the prophetess Miriam after God's victory over the Egyptians (Exod. 15:21), Judith begins a song of praise and thanksgiving. See too Judg. 11:34; 1 Sam. 18:6–7. Reworked Pentateuchᶜ (4Q365) preserves a longer song of Miriam.

16:1–17 Judith's new song of deliverance. The victory hymn is patterned after the Song of Moses (Exod. 15) with resonances with the Song of Deborah (Judg. 5). See also the Song of Simon (1 Macc. 14:4–15) and **"Hebrew Poetry," p. 741. 16:1** Like Miriam and her band of women (Exod. 15:21), they use *tambourines.* Singing in unison further enhances community cohesion. **16:2** *The Lord is a God who crushes wars.* This phrase from the Song of Moses also appears in Judith's earlier prayer (9:7–8). **16:4** *My young men . . . my infants . . . my children . . . my virgins.* The stakes of losing to the invading Assyrians are made clear through the use of the first person pronominal adjectives. **16:5** *By the hand of a woman.* This is the tenth mention of Judith's hand in the book. Her hand that decapitated the threat to Israel's well-being is a recurrent motif (2:12; 8:33; 9:9, 10; 12:4; 13:14, 15; 15:10). Compare Judg. 4:9 and the retelling of the Judges story in LAB 31:1, 7, which emphasizes the disparity of strength. The weak can conquer the powerful when empowered by divine help. **16:6** *Sons of the Titans.* These Greek mythic deities are mentioned also in the Septuagint in 2 Sam. 5:18, 22. *Tall giants* is likely a reference to the Nephilim known from Gen. 6:4. Compare 3 Macc. 2:4; Bar. 3:26–28.

nor did the sons of the Titans strike
  him down,
nor did tall giants set upon him,
but Judith daughter of Merari
  with the beauty of her countenance
  undid him.

[7] "For she put away her widow's clothing
  to exalt the oppressed in Israel.
She anointed her face with perfume;
[8]   she fastened her hair with a tiara
  and put on a linen gown to beguile
  him.
[9] Her sandal ravished his eyes,
  her beauty captivated his mind,
  and the sword severed his neck!
[10] The Persians trembled at her boldness;
  the Medes were daunted at her daring.

[11] "Then my oppressed people shouted;
  my weak people cried out,[f] and the
  enemy[g] trembled;
  they lifted up their voices, and the
  enemy[h] were turned back.
[12] Sons of female slaves pierced them
  through
  and wounded them like the children
  of fugitives;
  they perished before the army of my
  Lord.

[13] "I will sing to my God a new song:
O Lord, you are great and glorious,
  wonderful in strength, invincible.
[14] Let all your creatures serve you,
  for you spoke, and they were made.
You sent forth your spirit,[i] and it formed
  them;[j]
  there is none that can resist your
  voice.
[15] For the mountains shall be shaken to
  their foundations with the waters;
before your glance the rocks shall
  melt like wax.

But to those who fear you
  you show mercy.
[16] For every sacrifice as a fragrant offering
  is a small thing,
  and the fat of all whole burnt offerings
  to you is a very little thing,
but whoever fears the Lord is great
  forever.

[17] "Woe to the nations that rise up against
  my people!
The Lord Almighty will take vengeance
  on them in the day of judgment;
he will send fire and worms into their
  flesh;
  they shall weep in pain forever."

[18] When they arrived at Jerusalem, they worshiped God. As soon as the people were purified, they offered their burnt offerings, their freewill offerings, and their gifts. [19]Judith also dedicated to God all the possessions of Holofernes that the people had given her, and the canopy that she had taken for herself from his bedchamber she gave as a votive offering. [20]For three months the people continued feasting in Jerusalem before the sanctuary, and Judith remained with them.

[21] After this they all returned home to their own inheritances. Judith went to Bethulia and remained on her estate. For the rest of her life she was honored throughout the whole country. [22]Many desired to marry her, but she gave herself to no man all the days of her life after her husband Manasseh died and was gathered to his people. [23]She became more and more famous and grew old in her husband's house, reaching the age of one hundred five. She set her maid free. She died in Bethulia, and they buried her in the cave of her husband Manasseh,

f 16.11 Other ancient authorities read *feared* g 16.11 Gk
they h 16.11 Gk *they* i 16.14 Or *breath* j 16.14 Other
ancient authorities read *they were created*

16:10 *Persians . . . Medes.* As in the Song of Moses (Exod. 15:14–15), foreign nations are understood to have witnessed the saving event. **16:13** *A new song.* See Pss. 33:3; 144:9; 149:1; Isa. 42:10. This may indicate the hymn is composite. **16:14** *For you spoke.* The reference to God whose speech brought creation into being evokes Gen. 1 as well as Judith's emphasis on the divine creator (8:14; 9:5–6, 12; 13:18).

16:18–25 The people return to their customary life. 16:18 *Worshiped God.* In this book in which rightly directed worship is emphasized, their activities at the Jerusalem temple are highly significant. *Burnt offerings . . . freewill offerings, and . . . gifts* are the same offerings made by the high priest Joakim in 4:14. **16:19** *Judith . . . dedicated* to the temple her share of all the plunder taken from Holofernes, including the bejeweled canopy of his bed. **16:21–22** Judith returns to a life of celibacy and asceticism. **16:23** *Set her*

24and the house of Israel mourned her for seven days. Before she died she distributed her property to all those who were next of kin to her husband Manasseh and to her own nearest kindred. 25No one ever again spread terror among the Israelites during the lifetime of Judith or for a long time after her death.

maid free. This unnamed woman is manumitted. **16:24** *Seven days* is the customary period of mourning (Gen. 50:10; 1 Sam. 31:13; Sir. 22:12). To have all Israel mourn for a woman is unprecedented. Although she dies childless, the heroine has been memorialized in this tale, so her memory endures in those who read it.

ESTHER

(The Greek Version Containing

the Additional Chapters)

God is never explicitly mentioned in the older, Hebrew version of Esther that became the canonical form of the book in Jewish and Protestant circles. One senses the hand of providence behind the action, but the author is unusually reticent to speak of God directly. Moreover, the Jewish protagonists, Esther and Mordecai, do not exhibit any particularly Jewish forms of piety. By the time Esther was translated into Greek—the form in which it circulated among Jews in the Mediterranean Diaspora (see **"Diaspora," p. 1338**) and became known in the early church—its character had been radically changed. Esther had become an explicitly religious tale in which God plays a prominent role, and the leading Judean characters seek God's help and show themselves explicitly to maintain their commitment to the law of Moses.

Significance

Greek Esther is an important companion to the older version of Esther in a number of respects. First, it bears witness to the values that were of such importance in some Jewish circles that their absence in the older Hebrew version of Esther could not be allowed to stand. The latter version, of course, continued to be embraced without alterations in other Jewish circles and eventually "triumphed" as *the* canonical form of the book. Nevertheless, Esther is one of the few books of the Hebrew Bible whose canonicity was explicitly questioned in rabbinic circles (along with Ecclesiastes and Sirach). It was perhaps this marginal status that both led to its expansion in more explicitly religious directions and allowed for such free reimagining of the text. The Greek version displays what some Jews considered to be indispensable elements in a contender for the status of canonical Scripture. Second, it bears explicit witness to the tensions that existed between Jews and non-Jews in the Hellenistic period and to the spectrum of situations that Jews might face as a result—from being lauded as benefactors and pillars of government to being hunted as suspected subversives (see **"Court Tales," p. 1608**). Third, it was the form in which the book of Esther was overwhelmingly read and engaged in the early church at least until the time of Jerome's careful work consulting Hebrew versions of Old Testament texts and making distinctions between Hebrew and Greek text traditions.

Origins

Greek Esther concludes with a note (colophon) documenting its pedigree. According to this note, a Greek-speaking Jew named Lysimachus translated the work in Jerusalem, and another Jew named Dositheus, a priest accompanied by his son Ptolemy, brought the translated work to Egypt, presumably to the authorities within the large Jewish community in Alexandria. This took place "in the fourth year of the reign of Ptolemy and Cleopatra" (11:1). While every Macedonian king of Egypt took the name Ptolemy, only three of them had wives named Cleopatra *and* reigned for four years or more. The translation's arrival in Egypt can therefore be dated to 114 BCE, 78 BCE, or 48 BCE. Scholars tend to favor one of the first two of these dates. The two additions containing the reconstructed edicts, however, may well have been freshly composed and added any time after the original translation but before 90 CE or so, when Josephus used the final form of Greek Esther as a source for his *Antiquities*.

The chapter numbers in the text that follows are the result of Jerome's editorial work in the preparation of his Latin translation, the Vulgate, at the turn of the fifth century CE. Jerome observed that the Greek version contained substantial material absent from the Hebrew. Because he privileged the Hebrew text, he removed the "additions" from the running text and grouped them all together at the end. When chapter numbers were eventually added, the additions were numbered as chaps. 10–16. They are restored here to their proper place in the flow of Greek Esther.

Reading Guide

The transformation of Esther into a book that more explicitly reflects Jewish convictions and practices was brought about first by the addition of four large blocks of new material. Addition A (11:2–12:6) and Addition F (10:4–11:1) frame the original work between an episode in which Mordecai has a mysterious dream prior to any of the story's action and an episode in which Mordecai recalls this dream and interprets it in light of the events that have transpired. Another addition (Addition C [13:8–14:19]) provides both Mordecai and Esther with lengthy prayers calling upon God to intervene to save God's people. A fourth addition (Addition D [15:1–16]) expands the episode of Esther's uninvited appearance before the king, augmenting the drama and narrating God's intervention to change the king's heart. There are also multiple small alterations and brief additions to Hebrew Esther, interjecting acknowledgments of God and of pious Jewish practice throughout the narrative.

These four major additions might have already existed in the Hebrew version of Esther that Lysimachus translated into Greek. Two further additions purport to provide the decree to exterminate the Jewish population (Addition B [13:1–7]) and the decree allowing the Jews to defend themselves and urging those loyal to the king to protect their Jewish neighbors (Addition E [16:1–24]). These two give every indication of having been composed originally in Greek. Although the editors and/or translator responsible for the Greek version had also sought to condense the Hebrew narrative, Greek Esther is 70 percent longer than Hebrew Esther.

The reader's experience is dramatically altered. Mordecai's dream (Addition A) and his interpretation (Addition F) provide a framing narrative that emphasizes God's providential oversight from the outset. The reader is left in no doubt: the remainder of the book will reveal "what God had determined to do" (11:12). Additions C and D shift the center of the story's gravity from Esther's dinner with Haman and the king to Mordecai's and Esther's prayers to God and Esther's courageous entrance before the king. Additions B and E, introducing the edicts, intensify first the complication and then the resolution that drive the story while also heightening the impression that the work is a piece of historiography rather than legend (see **"Historical Fiction," p. 1635**).

David A. deSilva

Note: The deuterocanonical portions of the book of Esther are several additional passages found in the Greek translation of the Hebrew book of Esther, a translation that differs also in other respects from the Hebrew text (the latter is translated in the NRSVue Old Testament). The disordered chapter numbers come from the displacement of the additions to the end of the canonical book of Esther by Jerome in his Latin translation and from the subsequent division of the Bible into chapters by Stephen Langton, who numbered the additions consecutively as though they formed a direct continuation of the Hebrew text. So that the additions may be read in their proper context, the whole of the Greek version is here translated, though certain familiar names are given according to their Hebrew rather than their Greek form, for example, Mordecai and Vashti instead of Mardocheus and Astin. The order followed is that of the Greek text, but the chapter and verse numbers conform to those of the King James, or Authorized, Version. The additions, conveniently indicated by the letters A–F, are located as follows: A before 1.1; B after 3.13; C and D after 4.17; E after 8.12; F after 10.3.

ADDITION A

11 ^{2a}In the second year of the reign of Artaxerxes the Great, on the first day of Nisan, Mordecai son of Jair son of Shimei son of Kish, of the tribe of

a 11.2 11.2–12.6 corresponds to A 1–17 in some translations.

11:2–12:6 (Addition A) Mordecai's dream and discovery of a treasonous plot.
11:2–12 Mordecai's dream. The opening dream report announces the plot of the book as demonstrating God's control of events (cf. 11:12). Mordecai will offer an interpretation of the dream in 10:4–13. Together with Addition F, this framing narrative recalls Joseph's dreams at the outset of his story that are fulfilled by the end of the saga (Gen. 37:6–10; 42:9), portraying the working out of God's providential design. **11:2** *In the second year* of Artaxerxes's (Xerxes I's) reign places the episode in 485 BCE. *Nisan* corresponds to the second half of March and the first half of April. Mordecai's

Benjamin, had a dream. ³He was a Jew living in the city of Susa, a great man serving in the court of the king. ⁴He was one of the captives whom King Nebuchadnezzar of Babylon had taken captive from Jerusalem with King Jeconiah of Judea. And this was his dream: ⁵Noises[b] and confusion, thunder and earthquake, tumult on the earth! ⁶Then two great dragons came forward, both ready to fight, and they roared terribly. ⁷At their roaring every nation prepared for war, to fight against a nation of righteous people. ⁸It was a day of darkness and gloom, of tribulation and distress, affliction and great tumult on the earth! ⁹And the whole righteous nation was troubled; they feared the evils that threatened them[c] and were ready to perish. ¹⁰Then they cried out to God, and at their outcry, as though from a tiny spring, there came a great river with abundant water; ¹¹light came, and the sun rose, and the lowly were exalted and devoured those held in honor.

12 Mordecai saw in this dream what God had determined to do, and after he awoke he had it on his mind, seeking all day to understand it in every detail.

12 Now Mordecai took his rest in the courtyard with Gabatha and Tharra, the two eunuchs of the king who kept watch in the courtyard. ²He overheard their conversation and inquired into their purposes and learned that they were preparing to lay hands on King Artaxerxes, and he informed the king concerning them. ³Then the king examined the two eunuchs, and after they had confessed it, they were led away. ⁴The king wrote these things down as a commemoration, and Mordecai wrote an account of them. ⁵And the king ordered Mordecai to serve in the court and rewarded him for these things. ⁶But Haman son of Hammedatha, a Bougean, who was in great honor with the king, determined to injure Mordecai and his people because of the two eunuchs of the king.

END OF ADDITION A

---

b 11.5 Or *Voices*   c 11.9 Gk *their own evils*

---

dream thus falls on the Persian New Year's Day. *Mordecai* is not a typical Judean name, being built upon the name of the Babylonian god Marduk. It may have been an adopted name, even as Esther (cf. the goddess Ishtar) also bore the Hebrew name Hadassah (Heb. Esth. 2:7). **11:3** *Jew* indicates here a member of the ethnic group hailing from Judea ("Yehud" in the Persian period). *Susa* was the westernmost of several capital cities in the Persian Empire. **11:4** *Nebuchadnezzar* deported Judeans to Babylon in 597 and 586 BCE (see **"Exile (2 Kings)," p. 539**). The Greek does not here specifically say that Mordecai was *one of the captives*, but that he was "of the captivity" or "captive population." When Mordecai is (re)introduced in 2:5–6, however, he is explicitly said to have been brought to Babylon by Nebuchadnezzar, an anachronism if he is still alive in 485 BCE. **11:6** As *dragons* are generally negative figures in prophetic and apocalyptic texts (see Isa. 27:1; Ezek. 29:3; 32:2; Rev. 12:3), this detail seems not to fit the story of Mordecai and Haman, suggesting that the vision might have been composed independently. The dream might have originally suggested the warring of the Ptolemaic and Seleucid monarchs over Judea and the deliverance brought by the growing Maccabean Revolt (see 1 Macc., 2 Macc.). **11:8** The language is typical for prophetic visions of forthcoming calamity (cf. Isa. 13:4; 22:5; Ezek. 7:7; Amos 5:20; Joel 2:2; Zeph. 1:15). **11:10** Calling upon God for help is a prominent feature of Greek Esther (especially Addition C). **11:11** The theme of reversal occurs frequently in Scripture (cf. 1 Sam. 2:7–8; Prov. 3:34; Luke 1:52; 1 Pet. 5:5–6), but the explicit, violent participation of the *lowly* in devouring their enemies is unusual (see **"Reversal," p. 1642**). The reappearance of *light* or morning after darkness is a common image for divine deliverance (cf. Pss. 97:11; 118:25–27; Isa. 9:2; 58:8–10; 60:1–3; 62:1). **11:12** The dream vision at the opening of Greek Esther establishes a God-centered frame for the forthcoming story. The Providence at work in the shadows of Hebrew Esther emerges center stage from the outset in the Greek version.

12:1–6 Mordecai foils a plot against the king. The invention of an earlier plot against the king (cf. 2:21–23) allows for the introduction of Mordecai and Haman prior to any other action in the story. **12:1** *Eunuchs*, men deprived of their testicles and thus reproductive capabilities, were entrusted with a variety of sensitive functions in Babylonian and Persian courts. Their incapacity to bear children was thought to render them less ambitious and more devoted to the regent and his or her line. See **"Eunuchs," p. 672**. **12:6** Greek Esther introduces *Haman* earlier in the story and supplies an

1 It was after this that the following things happened in the days of Artaxerxes, the same Artaxerxes who ruled over one hundred twenty-seven provinces from India to Ethiopia.[d] ²In those days, when King Artaxerxes was enthroned in the city of Susa, ³in the third year of his reign, he gave a banquet for his Friends and other persons of various nations, the Persians and Median nobles, and the governors of the satrapies. ⁴After this, when he had displayed to them the riches of his kingdom and the splendor of his bountiful celebration during the course of one hundred eighty days, ⁵at the end of the wedding feast the king gave a drinking party for the people of various nations who lived in the city. This was held for six days in the courtyard of the royal palace, ⁶which was adorned with curtains of fine linen and cotton, held by cords of linen and purple fabric attached to gold and silver blocks on pillars of marble and other stones. Gold and silver couches were placed on a mosaic floor of emerald, mother-of-pearl, and marble. There were coverings of gauze, embroidered in various colors, with roses scattered around them. ⁷The cups were of gold and silver, and a miniature cup was displayed, made of ruby, worth thirty thousand talents. There was abundant sweet wine, such as the king himself drank. ⁸This drinking party was not in accordance with established custom, but the king wished to have it so, and he commanded his stewards to comply with his pleasure and with that of the guests.

9 Meanwhile, Queen Vashti gave a drinking party for the women in the palace where King Artaxerxes was.

10 On the seventh day, when the king was in good humor, he told Haman, Bazan, Tharra, Boraze, Zatholtha, Abataza, and Tharaba, the seven eunuchs who served King Artaxerxes, ¹¹to escort the queen to him in order to proclaim her as queen and to place the diadem on her head and to have her display her beauty to all the governors and the people of various nations, for she was indeed a beautiful woman. ¹²But Queen Vashti refused to obey him and would not come with the eunuchs. This offended the king, and he became furious. ¹³He said to his Friends, "This is how Vashti has answered me.[e] Give, therefore, your ruling and judgment on this matter." ¹⁴Arkesaeus, Sarsathaeus, and Malesear, the governors of the Persians and Medes who were closest to the king, who sat beside him in the chief seats, came to him ¹⁵and told him what, according to the law, was to be done to Queen Vashti for not obeying the order that the king had sent her by the eunuchs. ¹⁶Then Muchaeus said to the king and the governors, "Queen Vashti has wronged not only the king but also all the king's governors and officials"

d 1.1 Other ancient authorities lack to Ethiopia e 1.13 Gk has said thus and so

additional motive for his hostility toward Mordecai and the Jewish people, hinting that Haman was behind the eunuch's conspiracy (see also 16:10, 14). The meaning of the term *Bougean* is unclear, though it is a term of reproach (essentially a "blowhard") in Homer, *Od.* 18.79.

1:1–22 Artaxerxes's banquet and the dismissal of Vashti. 1:1 In the Persian period, *Ethiopia* also encompassed what is now Sudan. **1:3** The *third year* would begin in 484 BCE. The king's *Friends* were privileged vassals and clients. *Satrapies* is here a synonym for "provinces" in 1:1. **1:4–7** The king's display of wealth is complemented by expenditure on his vassals, a performance of both power and beneficence that served to bind them to their patron. **1:7** The *cup . . . made of ruby* is absent from the Hebrew. **1:8** *Established custom* would have all the guests drink only when—and as often as—the king drank (Herodotus, *Hist.* 1.33). Artaxerxes relaxes this rule so that his guests may enjoy as much or as little as they desire. **1:9** Before the Roman period, it was customary for wives not to accompany their husbands at banquets, for whom other female companionship was often provided (with whom husbands would also not wish their own wives to be confused by other guests). **1:10** *Haman* is surprisingly presented as one of the eunuchs in the Greek (as opposed to the Hebrew), despite having sired ten sons (9:13–14, 25). *Tharra* had already been executed in Addition A (12:1–3). **1:11** Greek Esther adds an honorable motive behind the summoning of Vashti, namely, *to proclaim her as queen.* This might suggest on the editor's part a growing sensitivity to, and embarrassment over, the king's objectification of Vashti in the Hebrew version. **1:12** Vashti is caught between conflicting values. While submissiveness and obedience toward their husbands were valued in wives, so was modesty. **1:14–16** Apparently *Muchaeus* offers a suggestion that goes beyond

[17](for he had reported to them what the queen had said and how she had defied the king). "And just as she defied King Artaxerxes, [18]so now the other noble wives of the Persian and Median governors, on hearing what she has said to the king, will likewise dare to dishonor their husbands. [19]If, therefore, it pleases the king, let him issue a royal decree, inscribed in accordance with the laws of the Medes and Persians so that it may not be altered, that the queen may no longer come into his presence, and let the king give her royal rank to a woman better than she. [20]Let whatever law the king enacts be proclaimed in his kingdom, and thus all women will give honor to their husbands, rich and poor alike." [21]This speech pleased the king and the governors, and the king did as Muchaeus had recommended. [22]The king sent the decree[f] into all his kingdom, to every province in its own language, so that men would be feared in their households.

2 After these things, the king's anger abated, and he no longer remembered Vashti or remembered what he[g] had said and how he had condemned her. [2]Then the king's servants said, "Let beautiful and virtuous young women be sought out for the king. [3]The king shall appoint officers in all the provinces of his kingdom, and they shall select beautiful young virgins to be brought to the harem in the city of Susa. Let them be entrusted to the king's eunuch who is in charge of the women, and let ointments and whatever else they need be given them. [4]And the woman who pleases the king shall be queen instead of Vashti." This pleased the king, and he did so.

5 Now there was a Jew in the city of Susa whose name was Mordecai son of Jair son of Shimei son of Kish, of the tribe of Benjamin; [6]he had been taken captive from Jerusalem among those whom King Nebuchadnezzar of Babylon had captured. [7]And he had a foster child, the daughter of his father's brother, Aminadab, and her name was Esther. When her parents died, he brought her up as a wife for himself. The young woman was beautiful in appearance. [8]So when the decree of the king was proclaimed and many young women were gathered in the city of Susa in custody of Gai, Esther also was brought to Gai, who had custody of the women. [9]The young woman pleased him and won his favor, and he quickly provided her with ointments and her portion of food,[b] as well as seven young women chosen from the palace; he treated her and her maids with special favor in the harem. [10]Now Esther had not disclosed her people or country, for Mordecai had commanded her not to make it known. [11]And every day Mordecai walked in the courtyard of the harem, to see what would happen to Esther.

12 Now the period after which a young woman was to go to the king was twelve

f 1.22 Gk lacks *the decree* g 2.1 Or *she* h 2.9 Gk lacks *of food*

---

what *was to be done to Queen Vashti* in strict legal terms. **1:18–20** Vashti's dismissal is to serve as a warning to all wives concerning submission to their husbands' commands. The authority of the male head of the household over the wife, children, and enslaved persons was the cornerstone of domestic order in Persian, Greek, Roman, and Jewish cultures. **1:19** The unalterable nature of the *laws of the Medes and Persians* emerges also in Dan. 6:8, 15. It may receive confirmation from a report by Diodorus Siculus (*Bib. Hist.* 17.30) concerning Darius III's alleged inability to commute a sentence passed upon a man who was later proven innocent, though Herodotus reports that the Persian king was free to do as he pleased (*Bib. Hist.* 3.31).

2:1–18 Esther becomes queen. 2:1 The search for a new queen is motivated by the king's inability to forget Vashti in the Hebrew version. **2:3** Entrusting the harem to a *eunuch* avoided awkward complications in the royal house (see **"Eunuchs," p. 672**). **2:5–6** See note on 11:4. The introduction of Mordecai is redundant in light of Addition A, showing the secondary character of that Addition. **2:7** The Hebrew text notes that Esther also had a Hebrew name, Hadassah. In the Hebrew, Mordecai had only intended to raise Esther as his own daughter and not, as in the Greek, to make her his *wife.* **2:9** While the main text retains the detail from the Hebrew that Esther received *her portion of food* from the eunuch in charge of the harem, which was presumably not kosher, Addition C will stress her commitment to observing the dietary laws of the Torah to the extent possible (14:17; see **"Diet," p. 268**). **2:10** Esther's silence about her ethnicity is essential to the plot. **2:12** While candidates for the positions of concubine and queen spent a year in a day spa, one should observe that the isolation from former social networks and resocialization into the court ensured the allegiances of these

months. During this time the days of cosmetic treatment are completed: six months while they are anointing themselves with oil of myrrh and six months with spices and ointments for women. [13]Then she goes in to the king; she is handed to the person appointed and goes with him from the harem to the king's palace.[i] [14]In the evening she enters, and in the morning she departs to the second harem, where Gai the king's eunuch is in charge of the women, and she does not go in to the king again unless she is summoned by name.

15 When the time was fulfilled for Esther daughter of Aminadab, the brother of Mordecai's father, to go in to the king, she neglected none of the things that the eunuch in charge of the women had commanded. For Esther found favor in the eyes of all who saw her. [16]So Esther went in to King Artaxerxes in the twelfth month, which is Adar, in the seventh year of his reign. [17]And the king loved Esther passionately, and she found favor beyond all the other virgins, and he put on her the queen's diadem. [18]Then the king gave a drinking party lasting seven days for all his Friends and the officers to celebrate his marriage to Esther, and he granted a remission of taxes to those who were under his rule.

19 Meanwhile Mordecai was serving in the court. [20]Esther had not disclosed her country, for thus Mordecai had instructed her to fear God and keep his laws, just as she had done when she was with him. So Esther did not change her way of life.

21 Now two of the king's eunuchs, who were chief bodyguards, were upset because of Mordecai's advancement, and they plotted to kill King Artaxerxes. [22]The matter became known to Mordecai, and he warned Esther, who in turn revealed the plot to the king. [23]He investigated the two eunuchs and hanged them. Then the king ordered that a record commemorating Mordecai's goodwill be deposited in the royal archive.

3 After these events King Artaxerxes honored Haman son of Hammedatha, a Bougean, and exalted him, and would seat him first among all the king's[j] Friends. [2]So all who were at court used to do obeisance to Haman,[k] for so the king had commanded to be done. Mordecai, however, did not do obeisance. [3]Then the king's courtiers said to Mordecai, "Mordecai, why do you disobey the king's command?" [4]Day after day they spoke to him, but he would not listen to them. Then they informed Haman that Mordecai was resisting the king's command. Mordecai had told them that he was a Jew. [5]So when Haman learned that Mordecai was not doing obeisance to him, he became furiously angry [6]and resolved to destroy all the Jews under Artaxerxes's rule.

7 In the twelfth year of the reign of Artaxerxes, Haman[l] came to a decision and cast lots, taking the days and the months one by one, to fix on one day to destroy the whole people of Mordecai. The lot fell on the fourteenth[m] day of the month of Adar.

---

i 2.13 Meaning of Gk uncertain   j 3.1 Gk all his   k 3.2 Gk him   l 3.7 Gk he   m 3.7 Other ancient witnesses read thirteenth

---

women who would have intimate access to the king. **2:14** A foreshadowing of the danger Esther believes herself to face in 15:1–7 (Addition D). **2:16** *Adar* is the last month in the Persian calendar. The action is set here in mid-479 BCE. **2:18** This *drinking party* recalls the earlier one that resulted in the dismissal of Vashti (1:5, 10).

2:19–23 Mordecai saves Artaxerxes from a second plot. **2:20** The Greek version emphasizes that Esther, like Daniel (cf. Dan. 1:8), did not compromise her obedience to the Torah after her introduction to the court. **2:21** In the Hebrew version, the cause of the eunuchs' anger is unspecified. **2:23** *Investigated*, more probably "examined" under torture. When used to indicate a mode of execution, the verb rendered *hanged* refers not to strangling but rather impaling or crucifixion.

3:1–13 Mordecai snubs Haman, who plans his revenge. **3:1** The relative honor in which people were held was often exhibited in seating arrangements throughout the Mediterranean and Levant. People were competitive when it came to claiming precedence over one another (cf. Ps. 110:1; Mark 10:37; Luke 14:8–11). **3:2** *Obeisance* refers to the low bow that might even place one prostrate before a superior. Greeks frowned upon it as undignified, but it was typical in the Levant. **3:4** Mordecai might have revealed *that he was a Jew* by way of explanation for his refusal to do obeisance to Haman. Addition C (13:12–14) makes his rationale explicit. **3:5–6** Haman's plan to gain satisfaction for the slight is out of proportion to Mordecai's challenge. **3:7** The *twelfth year* places these events in 475–474 BCE. The *fourteenth* rather than the thirteenth of Adar is highlighted in the Hebrew of

8 Then Haman[n] said to King Artaxerxes, "There is a certain nation scattered among the other nations in all your kingdom; their laws are different from those of every other nation, and they do not keep the laws of the king. It is not expedient for the king to tolerate them. ⁹If it pleases the king, let him decree that they are to be destroyed, and I will pay ten thousand talents of silver into the king's treasury." ¹⁰So the king took off his signet ring and gave it to Haman to seal the decree[o] that was to be written against the Jews. ¹¹The king told Haman, "Keep the money, and do whatever you want with that nation."

12 So on the thirteenth day of the first month the king's secretaries were summoned, and in accordance with Haman's instructions they wrote in the name of King Artaxerxes to the magistrates and the governors in every province from India to Ethiopia, one hundred twenty-seven provinces in all, and to the governors of the nations, each in his own language. ¹³Instructions were sent by couriers throughout all the empire of Artaxerxes to destroy the Jewish people in a single day of the twelfth month, which is Adar, and to plunder their goods.

Addition B

13 [p]This is a copy of the letter: "The Great King, Artaxerxes, writes the following to the governors of the hundred twenty-seven provinces from India to Ethiopia and to the officials under them:

2 "Having become ruler of many nations and master of the whole world (not elated with presumption of authority but always acting reasonably and with kindness), I have determined to settle the lives of my subjects in lasting tranquility and, in order to make my kingdom peaceable and open to travel throughout all its extent, to restore the peace desired by all people.

3 "When I asked my counselors how this might be accomplished, Haman—who excels among us in sound judgment and is distinguished for his unchanging goodwill and steadfast fidelity and has attained the second place of honor in the kingdom—⁴pointed out to us that among all the nations in the world there is scattered a certain hostile people who have laws contrary to those of every nation and continually disregard the ordinances of kings, so that the unifying of the kingdom that we honorably intend cannot be brought about. ⁵We understand that this people, and it alone, stands constantly in opposition to all humanity, perversely following a strange manner of life and laws, and is ill-disposed to our interests, doing all the

n 3.8 Gk *he o* 3.10 Gk lacks *the decree p* 13.1 13.1–7 corresponds to B 1–7 in some translations.

---

this verse (as in both Heb. and Gk. Esth. 8:12). **3:9** A *talent* was a measure of weight equivalent to twenty-six kilograms in the Persian period. Extravagant "gifts" often accompanied requests for royal concessions (cf. 2 Macc. 4:7–9, 23–25). This does not alter its character as essentially a massive bribe. The king's refusal (v. 11) shows his high-mindedness in one respect, at least. **3:10** A *signet ring* bore a stone with a distinctive carving. When this stone was pressed into clay or soft wax, it left an impression identifying the person and authority behind a document. **3:13** The Jews are to be treated as enemies about to be conquered rather than as citizens or tolerated residents with civic rights.

13:1–7 (Addition B) The text of the king's edict. This addition shows parallels with the edict issued by a gentile king in 3 Macc. 3:12–29. Whether or not this indicates a literary relationship, it reflects the broader experience and fears of the Jewish minority culture. Both charge Jewish subjects with antisocial behavior (13:4–5; cf. 3 Macc. 3:19–24), issue an extermination order (13:6; cf. 3 Macc. 3:25), and propose that greater peace and stability will result (13:7; cf. 3 Macc. 3:26). The rhetoric of scapegoating is evident in both texts. **13:1** Inscriptions witness that Xerxes was known as *the Great King* as well as the "king of kings." **13:2** Note the contrast between the praise of the king and the actual character of his actions. Dismissing Vashti and giving Haman carte blanche can hardly be considered to show reasonableness and concern for one's subjects. That the ruler of the Persian Empire is called *master of the whole world* exemplifies the tendency of ancient empires to exaggerate their dominion. **13:3** Contrast the presentation of Haman in the decree with his covert disloyalty elsewhere (12:6; 16:10–14). Within the narrative world, the verbiage of the edict is Haman's own, since the king had simply given Haman his signet ring and, with it, his authority to issue the edict (see, explicitly, 8:5). Thus, Haman lavishes (unmerited) praise upon himself. **13:4–5** The Jewish people's commitment to following the Torah made them stand out and apart from their non-Jewish neighbors. The Letter of Aristeas ascribes a social engineering intent to the Torah: it established social boundaries between

harm they can so that our kingdom may not
attain stability.
6 "Therefore we have decreed that those
indicated to you in the letters written by
Haman, who is in charge of affairs and is
our second father, shall all—wives and children included—be utterly destroyed by the
swords of their enemies, without pity or restraint, on the fourteenth day of the twelfth
month, Adar, of this present year, [7]so that
those who have long been hostile and remain
so may in a single day go down in violence
to Hades and leave our interests secure and
untroubled hereafter."

END OF ADDITION B

---

3 [14]Copies of the letter were posted in every province, and all the nations were
ordered to be prepared for that day. [15]The
matter was expedited also in Susa. And
while the king and Haman caroused together, the city was thrown into confusion.

4 When Mordecai learned of all that had
been done, he tore his clothes, put on
sackcloth, and sprinkled himself with ashes; then he rushed through the street of the
city, shouting loudly: "An innocent nation is
being destroyed!" [2]He got as far as the king's
gate, and there he stopped, because no one
was allowed to enter the courtyard clothed
in sackcloth and ashes. [3]And in every province where the letter had been posted there
was crying, lamentation, and great mourning among the Jews, and they put on sackcloth and ashes. [4]When the queen's[q] maids
and eunuchs came and told her, she was
deeply troubled by what she heard had
happened and sent instructions to clothe
Mordecai and to remove his sackcloth, but
he would not consent. [5]Then Esther summoned Hachratheus, the eunuch who attended her, and dispatched him to get accurate information for her from Mordecai.[r]
7 So Mordecai told him what had happened and about the promise that Haman
had promised the king: ten thousand talents
for the royal treasury to bring about the destruction of the Jews. [8]He also gave him a
copy of what had been posted in Susa for
their destruction, to show to Esther, and he
told him to charge her to go in to the king
and plead for his favor in behalf of the people. "Remember," he said, "the days when
you were an ordinary person, being brought
up under my care, for Haman, who is second
to the king, has spoken against us and demands our death. Call upon the Lord; then
speak to the king in our behalf and save us
from death."
9 Hachratheus went in and told her all
these things. [10]And Esther said to him, "Go to
Mordecai and say: [11]All nations of the realm
know that if any man or woman goes to the
king inside the inner court without being
called, there is no escape for that person.
Only the one to whom the king stretches out
the golden scepter is safe—and it is now thirty days since I myself was called to go to the
king."
12 So Hachratheus delivered Esther's entire message to Mordecai, [13]and then Mordecai said to Hachratheus, "Go and say
to her: Esther, do not say to yourself that

q 4.4 Gk *When her* *r* 4.5 Other ancient witnesses add [6]*So Hachratheus went out to Mordecai in the street of the city opposite the city gate.*

Jews and their neighbors, protecting Jews from gentiles' erroneous views (139–42). As a result, Jews were frequently accused of not showing solidarity with their gentile neighbors and even of harboring hostility against them. Jewish communities living in predominantly gentile cities experienced sporadic pogroms during the Hellenistic and Roman periods. Diversity is often viewed as a threat to social cohesiveness and solidarity. **13:7** *Hades* is the Greek term for the underworld. It reflects a three-tiered cosmology of heaven (or sky), earth, and underworld.

3:14–4:4 Word of the extermination order spreads. 4:1 Tearing one's garments, wearing rough sackcloth, and applying ash and other signs of self-abasement reflect widespread ancient practice (see Gen. 37:34; 1 Kgs. 21:27; 2 Kgs. 19:1; Dan. 9:3; Jonah 3:5–8; Jdt. 4:10–14; 10:3; 1 Macc. 2:14; 3:47; Matt. 11:21). The content of Mordecai's outcry is absent in the Hebrew. **4:4** The reason for this is unclear. Esther may wish to see Mordecai personally, which would be impossible for him while thus clad (see v. 2), or she may wish for Mordecai to hide the fact that the decree affects him as a Jew.

4:5–17 Mordecai charges Esther to deliver their people. 4:8 Mordecai's speech is only reported in the Hebrew, not quoted. The instruction to *call upon the Lord* sets the stage for Addition C. **4:13–14** Mordecai suggests that Esther bears a responsibility to use her privileged position to help her

you alone among all the Jews in the realm will escape alive. [14]For if you take no heed at such a time as this, help and protection will come to the Jews from another quarter, but you and your father's family will perish. And who knows whether it was not for such a time as this that you were made queen?" [15]Then Esther gave the messenger this answer to take back to Mordecai: [16]"Go and gather the Jews who are in Susa and fast on my behalf; for three days and nights do not eat or drink, and my maids and I will also go without food. After that I will go to the king, contrary to the law, even if I must die." [17]So Mordecai went away and did what Esther had told him to do.

ADDITION C

13 [8s]Then Mordecai[t] prayed to the Lord, calling to remembrance all the works of the Lord.

9 He said, "O Lord, Lord, King of all powers, for the universe is in your power and there is no one who can oppose you when it is your will to save Israel, [10]for you have made heaven and earth and every wonderful thing under heaven. [11]You are Lord of all, and there is no one who can resist you, the Lord. [12]You know all things; you know, O Lord, that it was not in insolence or pride or for any love of glory that I did this and refused to bow down to this proud Haman, [13]for I would have been willing to kiss the soles of his feet to save Israel! [14]But I did this so that I might not set human glory above the glory of God, and I will not bow down to anyone but you, who are my Lord, and I will not do these things in pride. [15]And now, O Lord God and King, God of Abraham, spare your people, for the eyes of our foes are upon us[u] to annihilate us, and they desire to destroy the inheritance that has been yours from the beginning. [16]Do not neglect your portion, which you redeemed for yourself out of the land of Egypt. [17]Hear my prayer and have mercy upon your inheritance; turn our mourning into feasting that we may live and sing praise to your name, O Lord; do not destroy the lips[v] of those who praise you."

18 And all Israel cried out with all their might, for their death was before their eyes.

s 13.8 13.8–15.16 corresponds to C 1–30 and D 1–16 in some translations.   t 13.8 Gk *he*   u 13.15 Gk *for they are eying us*   v 13.17 Gk *mouth*

people rather than insulate herself from danger. **4:14** The closest that the Hebrew version comes to speaking about God is this claim that the Jews will receive help *from another quarter*. Just as Joseph's vicissitudes positioned him to deliver Egypt and his own family from a seven-year famine (cf. Gen. 50:20), Mordecai suggests Esther's life had taken the course it did to position her similarly. **4:16** Esther involves the people in fasting and, presumably, prayer as a means of securing God's help for the dangerous course she has chosen. On fasting, see also Judg. 20:26–28; 2 Sam. 12:16, 21–22; Ezra 8:21–23; Dan. 9:3; Jonah 3:5–8; Jdt. 4:9–13.

13:8–14:19 (Addition C) Mordecai's and Esther's prayers. While these prayers are well integrated into, and clearly composed for, Esther's story, they also bear parallels to other prayers from the Second Temple period (cf. Neh. 9; Dan. 9:4–19; Jdt. 9:7–14).

13:8–18 Mordecai's prayer. 13:9–11 The prayer supplies the explicit profession of God, perceived to be lacking in the Hebrew. **13:10** The God of Israel is frequently distinguished from the gods of nations as the true creator of *heaven and earth.* See Jer. 10:1–10. **13:12–14** The addition allows Mordecai to reject pride and personal rivalry, which the Hebrew text could lead readers to suspect was indeed Mordecai's motive, as the cause of his people's danger. His affront to Haman was the consequence of his commitment to distinguish between the honors due to God and the honors due to humans. This was a lively concern in Greek and Roman environments, where a ruler cult was the norm. However, the patriarchs and other Jews appear to have had no issues with bowing in reverence before a human authority (cf. Gen. 23:7; 33:1–3; 43:26, 28; 1 Sam. 24:8; 25:23; 28:14; 2 Sam. 1:2; 9:6; 14:1–4; 1 Kgs. 1:16, etc.). **13:15–17** Mordecai emphasizes God's selection of Israel as God's *inheritance* and *portion* among all the nations of the earth and thus God's particular relationship with this one nation (cf. Deut. 7:6–8; 1 Kgs. 3:8; Pss. 105:6, 43; 106:4–5; Isa. 42:1; 43:20). **13:16** Redemption from slavery in *Egypt* is foundational to Israel's identity (see Exod. 1–15). **13:17** Turning *mourning into feasting* is a common motif of Jewish liturgical and prophetic texts (see Ps. 30:11; Isa. 61:3; Jer. 31:13). God was frequently urged to intervene by the consideration that God's honor was promoted by *the lips* of Israelites (see Pss. 6:5; 115:17; Sir. 17:28). **13:18** Not only the protagonists but all the people of Israel pray to God to intervene. "Crying out" is a common expression for calling for divine help (see Exod. 2:23; 1 Sam. 7:8; Pss. 17:6; 18:6; 22:2; 27:7; 28:1, etc.).

14 Then Queen Esther, seized with mortal anguish, fled to the Lord. ²She took off the garments of her honor and put on the garments of distress and mourning, and instead of costly perfumes she covered her head with ashes and dung, and she utterly humbled her body; every part that she loved to adorn she covered with her tangled hair. ³She prayed to the Lord God of Israel and said: "O my Lord, you alone are our king; help me, who am alone and have no helper but you, ⁴for my danger is in my hand. ⁵Ever since I was born I have heard in the tribe of my family that you, O Lord, took Israel out of all the nations and our ancestors from among all their forebears for an everlasting inheritance and that you did for them all that you said. ⁶And now we have sinned before you, and you have delivered us into the hands of our enemies ⁷because we glorified their gods. You are righteous, O Lord! ⁸And now they are not satisfied that we are in bitter slavery, but they have set their hands on the hands of their idols ⁹to abolish what your mouth has ordained and to destroy your inheritance, to stop the mouths of those who praise you and to quench your altar and the glory of your house, ¹⁰to open the mouths of the nations for the praise of vain idols and to magnify forever a mortal king.

¹¹ "O Lord, do not surrender your scepter to what has no being, and do not let them laugh at our downfall, but turn their plan against them and make an example of him who began this against us. ¹²Remember, O Lord; make yourself known in this time of our affliction and give me courage, O King of the gods and Master of all dominion! ¹³Put eloquent speech in my mouth before the lion and turn his heart to hate the man who is fighting against us, so that there may be an end of him and those who agree with him. ¹⁴But save us by your hand and help me, who am alone and have no helper but you, O Lord. You have knowledge of all things, ¹⁵and you know that I hate the splendor of the lawless and abhor the bed of the uncircumcised and of any alien. ¹⁶You know my necessity, that I abhor the sign of my proud position that is upon my head on days when I appear in public. I abhor it like a menstrual cloth, and I do not wear it on the days when I am at rest. ¹⁷And your servant has not eaten at Haman's table, and I have not honored the king's feast or drunk the wine of libations. ¹⁸Your servant has had no joy since the day that I was brought here until now, except in you, O Lord God of Abraham. ¹⁹O God, whose might is over all, hear the voice of the despairing and

14:1–19 Esther's prayer. This addition made a strong impact on the early church, which remembered Esther as a model of prayer and trust in God (1 Clem. 55.6; Clement of Alexandria, *Strom.* 4.19). **14:1–2** See note on 4:1. **14:3** The conviction that Israel has no king but God would fuel revolutionary movements throughout the Roman period. It suggests that Jewish monolatry is not without political ramifications. **14:5** On God's choice of Israel, see Lev. 20:22–26; Deut. 4:20, 34; 32:7–12; Josh. 24:2–3. **14:6–7** Esther nods to Deuteronomy's theology of history by citing Israel's idolatry, and thus its disloyalty to the covenant, as the cause of their exile (cf. Deut. 28:47–68; Jer. 25:1–14). In this she agrees with contemporary prayers that also own Israel's responsibility for its plight (cf. Dan. 9:3–19; Bar. 1:15–3:8; Pr. Azar. 3–22). **14:8** *Slavery* is here figurative, referring to gentile domination in the exilic period and beyond. **14:9–12** God should suspend God's just judgment and intervene to help Israel, since Israel alone witnesses to the honor of the one, true God. The extermination of the Jewish people would lead the nations to conclude that their false gods were stronger than Israel's God (cf. Ps. 79:9–11). **14:9** God's *altar* and *house*—that is, the temple in Jerusalem—were destroyed already in 587 BCE by Nebuchadnezzar. **14:12** Esther's prayer for *courage* (cf. vv. 4, 19) heightens the dramatic significance of the action to follow in 15:1–7. Psalm 95:3 also celebrates God as "a great King above all gods" (see also Deut. 10:17; Ps. 136:2–3). **14:13** *Lion* as a metaphor for Artaxerxes may evoke a parallel between Esther's uninvited audience with the king and Daniel's courage in the lions' den (Dan. 6:10–13). **14:15** Intermarriage between Jews and gentiles was discouraged in many Jewish circles (cf. Deut. 7:3–4; Ezra 9:1–4; 10:1–5; Tob. 4:12–13; see **"Intermarriage," p. 649**). Esther's harsh language may suggest her lack of consent to becoming queen. It certainly reflects the author's sentiments toward gentiles and mixed unions. **14:16** *Menstrual* blood was ritually defiling (cf. Lev. 15:19–24). To speak of her royal turban as a *menstrual cloth* expresses Esther's disgust at her place in the royal court. **14:17** The readers are again assured that Esther has kept kosher and avoided idolatry (cf. Jdt. 12:1–2), topics conspicuously absent from the Hebrew version of Esther. *Libations* involve the pouring out of a small amount of wine in honor of one or more gods.

save us from the hands of evildoers. And save me from my fear!"

15 On the third day, when she ended her prayer, she took off the garments in which she had worshiped and arrayed herself in the garments of her honor. ²Then, majestically adorned, after invoking the aid of the all-seeing God and Savior, she took two maids with her; ³on one she leaned gently for support, ⁴while the other followed, carrying her train. ⁵She was radiant with perfect beauty, and she looked happy, as if beloved, but her heart was frozen with fear. ⁶When she had gone through all the doors, she stood before the king. He was seated on his royal throne, clothed in the full array of his majesty, all covered with gold and precious stones. He was most terrifying.

7 Lifting his face, ablaze with glory, he looked at her in fierce anger. The queen faltered, turned pale and faint, and collapsed on the head of the maid who went in front of her. ⁸Then God changed the spirit of the king to gentleness, and in alarm he sprang from his throne and took her in his arms until she came to herself. He comforted her with soothing words and said to her, ⁹"What is it, Esther? I am your kin."ʷ Take courage. ¹⁰You shall not die, for our law applies only to our subjects.ˣ Come near."

11 Then he raised the golden scepter and touched her neck with it; ¹²he embraced her and said, "Speak to me." ¹³She said to him, "I saw you, my lord, like an angel of God, and my heart was shaken with fear at your glory. ¹⁴For you are wonderful, my lord, and your countenance is full of grace." ¹⁵And while she was speaking, she fainted and fell. ¹⁶Then the king was agitated, and all his attendants tried to comfort her.

5 ³ʸThe king said to her, "What do you wish, Esther? What is your request? It shall be yours, even to half of my kingdom." ⁴And Esther said, "Today is a special day for me. If it pleases the king, let him and Haman come to the banquet that I shall prepare today." ⁵Then the king said, "Bring Haman quickly, so that we may do as Esther desires." So they both came to the banquet that Esther had spoken about. ⁶While they were drinking wine, the king said to Esther, "What is it, Queen Esther? It shall be granted you." ⁷She said, "My petition and request is: ⁸if I have found favor in the sight of the king, let the king and Haman come again tomorrow to the banquet that I shall prepare them, and tomorrow I will do the same."

9 So Haman went out from the king joyful and glad of heart. But when he saw Mordecai the Jew in the courtyard, he was filled with anger. ¹⁰Nevertheless, he went home and summoned his friends and his wife Zosara. ¹¹And he told them about his riches and the honor that the king had bestowed on him and how he had advanced him to be the first in the kingdom. ¹²And Haman said, "The queen did not invite anyone to the banquet with the king except me, and I am invited again tomorrow. ¹³But these things give me no pleasure as long as I see

---

w 15.9 Gk *brother*   x 15.10 Meaning of Gk uncertain
y 5.3 In Greek, Addition D replaces 5.1–2 in Hebrew.

15:1–16 (Addition D) Esther's unscheduled audience with the king. Addition D serves as an extended replacement for the scene in Heb. Esth. 5:1–2. There is more drama in the Greek surrounding Esther's entrance before the king, his reaction, and her potential fate, making this episode the turning point here. **15:2** The *two maids* appear never to have been given a choice in regard to facing the danger of entering uninvited. **15:8** In Greek Esther, God acts directly upon the king to transform his angry annoyance into solicitous concern. **15:9** In the Greek, the king calls himself Esther's "brother" rather than the generic *kin*. Spouses referring to one another as brother or sister reflect ancient terms of endearment (cf. Song 4:10; 5:2) as well as the fact that the sibling relationship was generally held to be the most reliable among ancient cultures. **15:13** King David is also compared to *an angel of God* (1 Sam. 29:9; 2 Sam. 14:17, 20; 19:27).

5:3–8 Esther invites Haman and the king to a banquet. After the drama of Addition D, Esther's request is anticlimactic. Deferring her real request, however, makes room in the narrative for Haman to become self-assured through this double invitation to dine privately with the king and queen (see 5:12), setting him up for his downfall.

5:9–14 Haman's anger at Mordecai is renewed. 5:9 The honors Haman thinks he will enjoy make

Mordecai the Jew in the courtyard." ¹⁴His wife Zosara and his friends said to him, "Let a pole be cut, fifty cubits high, and in the morning tell the king and have Mordecai hung on it. Then, go with the king to the banquet and enjoy yourself." This advice pleased Haman, so the pole was prepared.

6 That night the Lord took sleep from the king, so he told his teacher to bring the book of daily records and to read to him. ²He found the words written about Mordecai, how he had told the king about the two royal eunuchs who were on guard and sought to lay hands on Artaxerxes. ³The king said, "What honor or favor did we bestow on Mordecai?" The king's servants said, "You have not done anything for him." ⁴While the king was inquiring about the goodwill shown by Mordecai—Look! Haman was in the courtyard. The king asked, "Who is in the courtyard?" Now Haman had come to speak to the king about hanging Mordecai on the pole that he had prepared. ⁵The servants of the king said, "Look! Haman is standing in the courtyard." And the king said, "Summon him." ⁶Then the king said to Haman, "What shall I do for the person whom I wish to honor?" And Haman said to himself, "Whom would the king wish to honor more than me?" ⁷So he said to the king, "For a person whom the king wishes to honor, ⁸let the king's servants bring out the fine linen robe that the king wears and the horse on which the king rides, ⁹and let them be given to one of the king's honored Friends,

and let him robe the person whom the king loves and mount him on the horse, and let him proclaim through the open square of the city, saying, 'Thus shall it be done to everyone whom the king honors.' " ¹⁰Then the king said to Haman, "You have spoken well! Do just as you have said for Mordecai the Jew who serves at court. And let not a word of what you have said be omitted." ¹¹So Haman got the robe and the horse; he put the robe on Mordecai, mounted him on the horse, and went through the open square of the city, proclaiming, "Thus shall it be done to everyone whom the king wishes to honor." ¹²Then Mordecai returned to the courtyard, but Haman returned home, mourning and with his head covered. ¹³Haman told his wife Zosara and his friends what had befallen him. His friends and his wife said to him, "If Mordecai is of the Jewish people and you have begun to be humiliated before him, you will surely fall. You will not be able to defend yourself, because a living god is with him."

14 While they were still talking, the eunuchs arrived and hurriedly brought Haman to the drinking party that Esther had **7** prepared. ¹So the king and Haman went in to drink with the queen. ²And the second day, as they were drinking wine, the king said, "What is it, Queen Esther? What is your petition, and what is your request? It shall be granted to you, even to half of my kingdom." ³She answered and said, "If I have found favor with the king, let my life be granted me at my petition and my people at my request. ⁴For we have been sold, I and

him sensitive to recollections of Mordecai's denying Haman that honor. **5:14** The height of the *pole* (over twenty meters) will allow those who have witnessed Mordecai's elevation at court to witness his degradation. The anticipated method of execution involves impalement in some fashion. Ironically, Haman is preparing his own instrument of execution.
6:1–13 Artaxerxes orders Haman to honor Mordecai. 6:1 The Greek version attributes the king's inability to sleep to God's intervention, leading to Mordecai being awarded new honors. Herodotus refers to Persian kings keeping records of their subordinates' service (see *Hist.* 7.100; 8.85, 90). **6:3** Reciprocity was a core social value in the Persian, Greek, Roman, and Judean cultures. The king is, of course, a general benefactor of all his subjects, but significant services such as Mordecai performed require some *honor or favor* in return. **6:6** Haman emerges as a case study in the perils of prideful presumption. **6:8** The highest honors are represented by close association with the king, even being invested with the king's wardrobe and riding upon the king's horse. **6:12** To be forced to act as the agent of a hated rival's exaltation—all the more when this rival had shown one significant disrespect (3:1–6)—would have been mortifying in the honor-sensitive culture of Persia (and subsequent empires). For covering one's head as a sign of mourning, see 2 Sam. 15:30. **6:13** Even Haman's wife makes a confession of faith (absent from the Hebrew).
6:14–7:10 Esther confronts Haman before the king. 7:4 *Sold* is metaphorical (though see 3:9 and note). *Our adversary brings shame on*, or more transparently, "the slanderer is not worthy of," the

my people, to be destroyed, plundered, and made slaves—we and our children—male and female slaves. I took no heed, but now our adversary brings shame on[z] the king's court." ⁵Then the king said, "Who is the person who would dare to do this thing?" ⁶Esther said, "Our enemy is this evil man Haman!" At this, Haman was terrified in the presence of the king and queen.

7 The king rose from the banquet and went into the garden, and Haman began to beg for his life from the queen, for he saw that he was in serious trouble. ⁸When the king returned from the garden, Haman had thrown himself on the couch, pleading with the queen. The king said, "Will you dare even assault my wife in my own house?" Haman, when he heard, turned away his face. ⁹Then Bugathan, one of the eunuchs, said to the king, "Look, Haman has even prepared a pole for Mordecai, who gave information of concern to the king; it is standing at Haman's house, a pole fifty cubits high." So the king said, "Let Haman be executed on that." ¹⁰So Haman was hung on the pole that had been prepared for Mordecai. With that the anger of the king abated.

8 On that very day King Artaxerxes granted to Esther all the property of the adversary Haman. Mordecai was summoned by the king, for Esther had told the king[a] that he was related to her. ²The king took his ring, which he had taken back from Haman, and gave it to Mordecai, and Esther set Mordecai over everything that had been Haman's.

3 Then she spoke once again to the king, and, falling at his feet, she asked him to avert all the evil that Haman had planned against the Jews. ⁴The king extended his golden scepter to Esther, and she rose and stood before the king. ⁵Esther said, "If it pleases you, and if I have found favor, let an order be sent rescinding the letters that Haman wrote and sent to destroy the Jews in your kingdom. ⁶How can I look on the ruin of my people? How can I be safe if my ancestral nation[b] is destroyed?" ⁷The king said to Esther, "Now that I[c] have granted all of Haman's property to you and have hung him on a pole because he laid hands on the Jews, what else do you request? ⁸Write in my name what you think best and seal it with my ring, for whatever is written at the king's command and sealed with my ring cannot be contravened."

9 The secretaries were summoned on the twenty-third day of the first month, that is, Nisan, in the same year, and all that she commanded with respect to the Jews was given in writing to the administrators and governors of the satrapies from India to Ethiopia, one hundred twenty-seven satrapies, to each province in its own language. ¹⁰The edict was written[d] with the king's authority and sealed with his ring, and they sent out the letters by couriers. ¹¹He ordered the Jews[e] in every city

z 7.4 Gk *is not worthy of*   a 8.1 Gk *him*   b 8.6 Gk *country*   c 8.7 Gk *If I*   d 8.10 Gk *It was written*   e 8.11 Gk *them*

king's court. Misrepresentation and failure to seek justice demean the king's government. **7:8** For Haman to assault the queen would have been a grievous injury to the king's honor, hence the king's summary decision about Haman's fate. The Greek translator missed an opportunity here when rendering the Hebrew "they covered Haman's face" as *Haman . . . turned away his face*. The Hebrew version recalls Haman's mourning "with his head covered" after Mordecai had begun to be honored above him (6:12), which Haman's wife interpreted as foreshadowing his downfall. **7:9–10** *Let . . . be executed* reflects the standard Greek verb for impalement or crucifixion. Thus *hung* should be heard more as "suspended" than strangled.

8:1–12 The king rescinds the former edict. 8:1 The Greek word rendered *adversary* connotes slanderer or accuser in a court of law, an appropriate summary of Haman's activity toward the Jewish people. Haman's fate is poetically just, as he suffered what he had planned for the target of his accusations, namely, Mordecai. **8:2** Mordecai is elevated to the position of vizier vacated by Haman ("second" in authority only to the king according to 13:3; cf. 16:11). **8:8** Authority to issue decrees with the king's authority passes to Esther and Mordecai (in the Gk., it is clear that the king addresses a plural "you"). **8:9** In the Greek, only ten days have passed since Haman's composition of his edict in the king's name (see 3:12) and the rescinding of that edict. The date for the execution of Haman's original decree and the Jews' newly authorized resistance against anyone who would act upon that decree remains almost a year off (v. 12). **8:11** The Greek adds the stipulation that the Jews should *observe their laws*. Jewish authors throughout the Greek and Roman periods were interested in documenting their gentile overlords' permission to live in line with the Torah.

to observe their laws, to defend themselves, and to act as they wished against their opponents and enemies [12]on a single day, the thirteenth of the twelfth month, which is Adar, throughout all the kingdom of Artaxerxes.

ADDITION E

16 [f]The following is a copy of this letter: "The Great King, Artaxerxes, to the governors of the provinces from India to Ethiopia, one hundred twenty-seven provinces, and to those who are loyal to our government, greetings.

2 "Many people, the more they are honored with the most generous kindness of their benefactors, the more proud do they become, [3]and not only seek to injure our subjects, but in their inability to stand prosperity, they even undertake to scheme against their own benefactors. [4]They not only take away thankfulness from others, but, carried away by the boasts of those who know nothing of goodness, they even assume that they will escape the evil-hating justice of God, who always sees everything. [5]And often many of those who are set in places of authority have been made in part responsible for the shedding of innocent blood and have been involved in irremediable calamities, by the persuasion of friends who have been entrusted with the administration of public affairs, [6]when these persons by the false trickery of their evil natures beguile the sincere goodwill of their sovereigns.

7 "What has been wickedly accomplished through the pestilent behavior of those who exercise authority unworthily can be seen not so much from the more ancient records that we hand on as from investigation of matters close at hand.[g] [8]In the future we will take care to render our kingdom quiet and peaceable for all, [9]by changing our methods and always judging what comes before our eyes with more equitable consideration. [10]For Haman son of Hammedatha, a Macedonian (really an alien to the Persian blood and quite devoid of our kindliness), having become our guest, [11]enjoyed so fully the goodwill that we have for every nation that he was called our father and was continually bowed down to by all as the person second to the royal throne. [12]But, unable to restrain his arrogance, he undertook to deprive us of our kingdom and our life[h] [13]and with intricate craft and deceit asked for the destruction of Mordecai, our savior and perpetual benefactor, and of Esther, the blameless partner of our kingdom, together with their whole nation. [14]He thought that by these methods he would catch us undefended and would transfer the kingdom of the Persians to the Macedonians.

15 "But we find that the Jews, who were consigned to annihilation by this thrice-accursed man, are not evildoers but are governed by most righteous laws [16]and are children of the living God, most high, most mighty,[i] who has directed the kingdom both for us and for our ancestors in the most excellent order.

17 "You will therefore do well not to put in execution the letters sent by Haman son

f 16.1 16.1–24 corresponds to E 1–24 in some translations. *g* 16.7 Gk *matters beside* (your) *feet*   *h* 16.12 Gk *our spirit*   *i* 16.16 Gk *greatest*

16:1–24 (Addition E) The edict rescinding the extermination order. In the narrative world, it is Esther and Mordecai who are responsible for the wording of the new edict (8:8), even as Haman had been responsible for the verbiage of the extermination order (3:10–12). The professions of God's intervention in and providence over Persian rule might be more properly attributed to them rather than to the king's own (alleged) religious enlightenment. **16:2–4** Benefactors were held to merit loyalty, gratitude, and service. To return treachery for a benefactor's favor would rate among the grossest violations of the virtue of *justice*. **16:9** This amounts to an implicit admission that the king had not exercised due diligence before giving Haman carte blanche in regard to his Jewish subjects. **16:10–14** *Haman* has become a *Macedonian* in Greek Esther (see also 9:24). The Macedonians will conquer Persia under the leadership of Alexander the Great between the years 334–331 BCE. Greek Esther makes Mordecai and Esther heroes who preserve Persia from Macedonian machinations for another century and a half. This suggests that a ruler's Jewish subjects, far from being hostile to his or her rule, may prove essential to preserving it. **16:13** *Savior* is not an uncommon honorific title for rulers and benefactors. **16:15** The story becomes a vindication of the particularities of the Jewish way of life. The distinctive practices of the Jewish people, and any restrictions on interethnic social interaction, are not to be interpreted as posing any danger to the well-being of the state. **16:16** Compare Matt. 5:44–45, where people become *children* of God by imitating God's character and not by virtue of belonging to

of Hammedatha, [18]since he, the one who did these things, has been executed at the gates of Susa with all his household—for God, who rules over all things, has speedily inflicted on him the punishment that he deserved.

19 "Therefore post a copy of this letter publicly in every place and permit the Jews to live according to their own customs. [20]And lend them support, so that on the thirteenth day of the twelfth month, Adar, on that very day, they may defend themselves against those who attack them at the time of affliction. [21]For God, who rules over all things, has made this day to be a joy for his chosen people instead of a day of destruction for them.

22 "Therefore you shall observe this with all good cheer as a notable day among your commemorative festivals, [23]so that both now and hereafter it may represent deliverance for us and for those loyal to the Persians but a reminder of destruction for those who plot against us.

24 "Every city and country, without exception, that does not act accordingly shall be destroyed in wrath with spear and fire. It shall be made not only impassable for humans but also most hateful to wild animals and birds for all time.

END OF ADDITION E

8 [13]"Let copies of the decree be posted conspicuously in all the kingdom, and let all the Jews be ready on that day to fight against their enemies."

14 So the messengers on horseback set out with all speed to perform what the king had commanded, and the decree was posted also in Susa. [15]Mordecai went out dressed in the royal robe and wearing a gold crown and a turban of purple linen. The people in Susa rejoiced on seeing him. [16]And the Jews had light and gladness [17]in every city and province wherever the decree was published; wherever the proclamation was made, the Jews had joy and gladness, a banquet and a holiday. And many of the nations were circumcised and became Jews out of fear of the Jews.

9 Now on the thirteenth day of the twelfth month, which is Adar, the letter written by the king arrived. [2]On that same day the enemies of the Jews perished; no one resisted, because they feared them. [3]The governors of the satrapies, the princes, and the royal secretaries were paying honor to the Jews, because fear of Mordecai weighed upon them. [4]The king's decree required that Mordecai's name be held in honor throughout the kingdom.[j] [6]Now in the city of Susa the Jews killed five hundred men, [7]including Pharsannestain, Delphon, Phasga, [8]Pharadatha, Barea, Sarbacha, [9]Marmasima, Aruphaeus, Arsaeus, Zabutheus, [10]the ten sons of Haman son of Hammedatha, the Bougean, the enemy of the Jews—and they indulged themselves in plunder.

11 That same day, the number of those killed in Susa was reported to the king. [12]The king said to Esther, "In the city of Susa, the Jews have destroyed five hundred people. What do you suppose they have done in the surrounding countryside? Whatever more you ask will be done for you." [13]And Esther said to the king, "Let the Jews be allowed to

j 9.4 Meaning of Gk uncertain. Some ancient authorities add 9.5, So the Jews struck down all their enemies with the sword, killing and destroying them, and they did as they pleased to those who hated them.

a particular ethnic group. See also Hos. 1:10; 2:1. On God's providence over international affairs, see also Dan. 4:34–37. **16:18** The notice that Haman's household had been executed contradicts the slaughter of Haman's ten sons ten months later in 9:6–10, 13–14. **16:19** The author voices the hope shared by diasporic Jews in the Hellenistic and Roman periods that they would be permitted to practice the Torah without slander, suspicion, or worse. **16:21** See note on 13:15–17. **16:23** The well-being of the Jews and their Persian neighbors are closely linked. Showing support for their Jewish neighbors when attacked by their enemies within the empire is also promoted as the course of action that *loyal . . . Persians* will pursue (cf. v. 20). Such sentiments reflect the hopes of diasporic Jews throughout the Greco-Roman world, who faced too frequent pogroms at the hands of sectors of the gentile population.

8:13–17 The new edict is disseminated. 8:13 Edicts were "published" in the form of inscriptions in public spaces. **8:17** The detail concerning the gentiles' circumcision is absent from the Hebrew. Here many of their neighbors become full converts to Judaism (contrast Heb. Esth. 8:17).

9:1–19 The Jews destroy their enemies. 9:2 While Addition E (see also Heb. Esth. 8:11–12) appears to have authorized self-defense, it is difficult to avoid the impression that the Jews of Susa and its provinces took preemptive action against known enemies (9:2, 5–6, 15–16). See **"Violence against the Jews' Enemies," p. 682. 9:13** The display of corpses was an act of degradation meant either to

do the same tomorrow. Also, hang up the bodies of Haman's ten sons." [14]So he permitted this to be done and handed over to the Jews of the city the bodies of Haman's sons to hang up. [15]The Jews who were in Susa gathered on the fourteenth and killed three hundred men but took no plunder.

16 Now the other Jews in the kingdom gathered to defend themselves and got relief from their enemies. They destroyed fifteen thousand of them on the thirteenth of Adar but did not engage in plunder. [17]On the fourteenth day of the same month they rested and kept it as a day of rest with joy and gladness. [18]The Jews who were in the city of Susa came together also on the fourteenth but did not rest. They celebrated the fifteenth with joy and gladness. [19]On this account, then, the Jews who are scattered around the countryside keep the fourteenth of Adar as a joyful holiday and send presents of food to one another, while those who live in the large cities keep the fifteenth day of Adar as their joyful holiday, also sending presents to one another.

20 Mordecai recorded these things in a book and sent it to the Jews in the kingdom of Artaxerxes both near and far, [21]to institute these days as holidays and to keep the fourteenth and fifteenth days of Adar, [22]for on these days the Jews got relief from their enemies. The whole month (namely, Adar) in which their condition had been changed from sorrow into gladness and from a time of distress to a holiday was to be celebrated as a time for feasting[k] and gladness and for sending presents of food to their friends and to the poor.

23 So the Jews accepted what Mordecai had written to them: [24]how Haman son of Hammedatha, the Macedonian, fought against them, how he made a decree and cast lots[l] to destroy them, [25]and how he went in to the king, telling him to hang Mordecai, but the wicked plot he had devised against the Jews came back upon himself, and he and his sons were hanged. [26]Therefore these days were called "Purim," because of the lots (for in their language this is the word that means "lots"). And so, because of what was written in this letter and because of what they had experienced in this affair and what had befallen them, Mordecai established this festival,[m] [27]and the Jews took upon themselves, upon their descendants, and upon all who would join them to observe it without fail.[n] These days of Purim should be a memorial and kept from generation to generation, in every city, family, and country. [28]These days of Purim shall be observed for all time, and the commemoration of them shall never cease among their descendants.

29 Then Queen Esther daughter of Aminadab along with Mordecai the Jew wrote down what they had done and gave full authority to the letter about Purim.[o] [31]And Mordecai and Queen Esther established this decision on their own responsibility, pledging their own well-being to the plan.[p] [32]Esther established it by a decree forever, and it was written for a memorial.

k 9.22 Gk *of weddings*   l 9.24 Gk *a lot*   m 9.26 Gk *he established* (it)   n 9.27 Meaning of Gk uncertain   o 9.29 9.30 in Heb is lacking in Gk: *Letters were sent to all the Jews, to the one hundred twenty-seven provinces of the kingdom of Ahasuerus, in words of peace and truth.*   p 9.31 Meaning of Gk uncertain

repair the honor of those harmed by those executed or to deter viewers from following the example of those thus displayed (or both). There were limitations on how long corpses could be displayed in ancient Israel (see Deut. 21:22–23), but not in most cultures. **9:16** The Greek lowers the number of gentile casualties from the seventy-five thousand in the Hebrew.

9:20–32 The Festival of Purim is established. 9:20 The *book* indicates the text of Esther, the festal scroll read at (and authorizing) the Feast of Purim (see 9:26, 29; 11:1; see **"Bible in Religious Interpretation," pp. 2155–56**). **9:21** The two-day slaughter in Susa and the second-day slaughter throughout the empire account for the fact that the Festival of Purim extends over two days rather than falling on one or the other. The fourteenth of Adar is referred to as "Mordecai's day" in 2 Macc. 15:36. **9:22** Sending food to the poor is in keeping with almsgiving in Jewish piety (see Sir. 3:30; 7:10; 12:1–7; 29:7–13; Tob. 4:6b–11, 16–17; 12:8–9; 14:2, 9–11). **9:25** Esther is strangely absent from the summary here (contrast Heb. Esth. 9:25), with Mordecai foregrounded instead. This may reflect the influence of the framing vision (Addition A) and its interpretation (Addition F), which foreground the conflict between Haman and Mordecai. Wicked plots returning to plague the inventor is a motif in the Jewish Scriptures (cf. Ps. 7:16; 1 Sam. 25:39; 1 Kgs. 2:32–33). **9:26** The Hebrew word for "lot" here is "pur" (plural, "purim"), a loan word from Babylonian. But see 10:10–13 for a later, more nationalistic explanation of the *lots* behind the Festival of Purim.

10

The king levied a tax upon his kingdom both by land and sea. ²And as for his power and bravery and the wealth and glory of his kingdom, they were recorded in the annals of the kings of the Persians and the Medes. ³Mordecai succeeded King Artaxerxes and was great in the kingdom, as well as honored by the Jews. His way of life was such as to make him beloved to his whole nation.

ADDITION F

4 ᵠAnd Mordecai said, "These things have come from God, ⁵for I remember the dream that I had concerning these matters, and none of them has failed to be fulfilled. ⁶There was the little spring that became a river, and there was light and sun and abundant water. The river is Esther, whom the king married and made queen. ⁷The two dragons are Haman and myself. ⁸The nations are those that gathered to destroy the name of the Jews. ⁹And my nation, this is Israel, who cried out to God and was saved. The Lord has saved his people; the Lord has rescued us from all these evils; God has done great signs and wonders, wonders that have never happened among the nations. ¹⁰For this purpose he made two lots, one for the people of God and one for all the nations, ¹¹and these two lots came to the hour and moment and to the day of judgment before God and among all the nations. ¹²And God remembered his people and vindicated his inheritance. ¹³So they will observe these days in the month of Adar, on the fourteenth and fifteenthʳ of that month, with an assembly and joy and gladness before God, from generation to generation forever among his people Israel."

11

¹In the fourth year of the reign of Ptolemy and Cleopatra, Dositheus, who said that he was a priest and a Levite,ˢ and his son Ptolemy brought to Egyptᵗ the preceding letter about Purim, which they said was authentic and had been translated by Lysimachus son of Ptolemy, one of the residents of Jerusalem.

END OF ADDITION F

---

q 10.4 10.4–13 and 11.1 correspond to F 1–11 in some translations.   r 10.13 Other ancient authorities lack *and fifteenth*   s 11.1 Or *priest, and Levitas*   t 11.1 Cn: Gk *brought in*

10:1–3 Epilogue. 10:2 A reference to additional deeds in *the annals* is a stereotypical way to close the account of a reign (see 1 Kgs. 14:19, 29; 15:7, 23, 31, etc.). **10:3** *Succeeded.* Hebrew Esther left Mordecai merely "next in rank" to Artaxerxes (Heb. Esth. 10:3).

10:4–11:1 (Addition F) Mordecai interprets his dream. This addition underscores the antagonism between non-Jewish nations and the Jewish people in a tale that formerly highlighted the antagonism of two individuals, Haman and Mordecai. **10:5** It has been ten years since Mordecai had this *dream* (11:1; 3:7). Compare Gen. 42:9. **10:7** See note on 11:6. **10:8** The image of the destruction of the *name of the Jews* suggests that Haman's plan had been to so thoroughly extinguish the Jewish people that their very memory would be obliterated (see Ps. 83:4). **10:9** *Signs and wonders* recall God's deliverance of Israel from Egypt (Exod. 7:3–4; Deut. 4:34; 6:22; 7:19, etc.). **10:10–12** The *lots* that gave Purim its name are reimagined not merely as the lots Haman cast to determine the date on which to execute the extermination order but as the two destinies that God has set for the Jewish nation versus all the non-Jewish nations lumped together. "Lot" is also used metaphorically for destiny in Jer. 13:25 and frequently in the Dead Sea Scrolls. The precision of God's predetermination shown by the setting of *the hour and moment and . . . day* for intervention is an apocalyptic motif appropriate to the dream vision and its interpretation (see Rev. 9:15). **11:1 Colophon.** A colophon is a short note at the end of a document giving information about its source, production, and transmission. The colophon suggests that Esther had been translated into Greek in Jerusalem and then brought to the diasporic community in Egypt. To the extent that the colophon is reliable, it provides some support for the theory that Additions A, C, D, and F had already been added to one version of Esther in Hebrew. The colophon provides evidence for the presence of scribes well-trained in Greek in the capital of Judea. *Ptolemy and Cleopatra.* See introduction. Other Jews were known to bear the name *Dositheus* (see 2 Macc. 12:19, 24, 35; 3 Macc. 1:3). The name means "gift of God" and may represent a translation of an original Hebrew name like Jehonathan ("God gave"). Both languages favored names related in some way to a deity. The phrase *which they said was authentic* leads some scholars to think that the writer of the colophon distances himself from the claims made by Dositheus and Ptolemy concerning the document. It could also be read simply as neutral reporting.

WISDOM OF SOLOMON

Authorship, Date, and Setting

The Wisdom of Solomon (Wisdom) opens a window into the world of those who devoted their lives to a deeper understanding of life's mysteries in ancient Israel and the larger Jewish Diaspora. It is a miscellany of guidance to those seeking to live faithfully and safely while mitigating the social, political, and religious disruptions accompanying life in an at times perplexing and hostile Mediterranean world. It is an anonymous work, though one in which the author seeks subtle authority for its message by hinting at authorship by Solomon, son of David, legendary king of Jerusalem. The material in 6:21–9:18, which focuses specifically on protocols for wise governance, and the extensive prayer that closes this section (9:1–18), with its reference to the construction of a temple (9:7–8), are reminiscent of Solomon's dream at Gibeon (1 Kgs. 3:5–15), where he requests "an understanding mind" (3:9) from YHWH, as well as the prayer credited to him at the dedication of the Jerusalem temple (1 Kgs. 8:22–53). These internal references were likely included to bolster claims to Solomonic authorship and to enhance Wisdom's overall message. However, many of the book's distinguishing themes suggest that the actual author was a member of the Jewish diasporic community living, perhaps, in Alexandria, Egypt. The book is difficult to date, though a time of composition between the third and first centuries BCE seems plausible.

Timeless Guidelines for Godly Living

Wisdom foregrounds the quest for knowledge, righteousness, and kindness and centers them as the most crucial elements in the known world. It shows that they are so integrally related as to be almost mirror images of one another. To seek one is, in some sense, to embody them all. They are aligned with the transcendent Sophia (Gk. word for "wisdom"), which is the force that sets in order and sustains everything. Its collection of advice and lore reflects an array of influences: Greek, Egyptian, Hebrew, Canaanite, and Mesopotamian.

The book also juxtaposes those who pursue these virtues as godly and those who reject them as ungodly. The gulf separating their respective worlds is vast. God's power and majesty envelop the former. Theirs are the gifts of life and flourishing. The ungodly have a contract with death. They are fated for suffering and trouble. The faithful, especially those in positions of power, are admonished to take heed. While the courting of wisdom and righteousness as well as the pragmatic and cosmic dimensions thereof are the primary foci of the book, it utilizes stories from Israel's past—especially the exodus from Egypt and wilderness sojourn—as illustrative of how God protects and provides for the righteous. In this way, Wisdom offers a theological reinterpretation of these venerable traditions as a way of demonstrating God's supremacy over adversaries, the forces of nature, and Egyptian hegemony.

The author takes on the roles of king, prophet, elder, philosopher, and sage in reflecting on the realities of life in an unstable world in which one is deemed an "outsider" and "at a distance from" one's homeland—whether that homeland is actual, imagined, or teleological. Wisdom aims to be an authoritative guide to a multigenerational, heterogeneous, and widely dispersed Jewish community embedded within a largely Hellenized culture. The author reflects on Israel's past with an eye toward the present and the eschatological fulfillment of God's plan. At the same time, Wisdom discloses—to an intended audience of (no doubt) elite males navigating the challenges of life in Diaspora—those hidden and straightforward competencies that the righteous, those in positions of power, and those seeking friendship with God must possess.

Searching for Wisdom in a Time of Disruption

It is interesting to think about the Wisdom of Solomon within the larger literary sphere of so-called success literature. Twenty-first-century experts offering advice on how to achieve fame and fortune in, or navigate the at times intractable difficulties of, life abound. All seem to promise answers to perennial questions and pathways to lives filled with wealth, meaning, safety, and prominence. Modern sages continue to proliferate, particularly in a global context where information of all kinds is commoditized and access to it is deemed essential for survival. This is particularly true in the United States, where there is an extensive corpus of literature touting the benefits of hard work,

positive thinking, and prayer on material wealth and social advancement. Many of these works draw on themes found in sapiential biblical and deuterocanonical/apocryphal books like the Wisdom of Solomon.

Three of the book's facets can be commended to modern readers. The first is its emphasis on discerning and acting in accord with the highest and most noble of human aspirations. Among those elevated by Wisdom is kindness (12:19), a divine attribute to which humanity should aspire. The second is awareness of how the refashioning of old stories can create opportunities for individuals and social groups experiencing trauma to foster safety and wholeness while mitigating harm. We see this in the author's recapitulation of high points of Israel's history in chaps. 10–12. Finally is the book's profile of skills possessed by the sage (7:17–21), a collection of competencies including both the mundane and the mysterious. They encourage one to consider the aptitudes promoted by today's purveyors of success and to ponder those capacities required for meaningful living and where they can be found.

Reading Guide

There is no scholarly consensus about Wisdom's structure. It is most useful to describe its themes sequentially. It opens with an appeal to righteousness, wisdom, and kindness (1:1–11); reflections on the power of God and righteousness as a divine creation (1:12–15); and an account of the ungodly and their covenant with death (1:16–2:24). The next several chapters focus on the righteous and the benefits they enjoy (3:1–9), the troubles experienced by the ungodly (3:10–12), the blessings bestowed on childless women and eunuchs (3:13–14), the rewards linked to good work and understanding (3:15), children of adulterers (3:16–18), the fate of an unrighteous generation (3:19–4:6), and the destiny of the righteous in life and death (4:7–14a). The author then addresses the mystery of how the righteous flourish (4:14b–5:16) and God's protection against the unrighteous (5:17–23). Chaps. 6–8 deal with the responsibilities of kings (6:1–11), the beauty and source of wisdom (6:12–25), the life of the sage (7:1–22a), wisdom's traits (7:22b–8:1), and the rewards of attending the quest for wisdom (8:2–21). Chap. 9 offers an illustrative paradigm for prayer, a sage's most important endeavor. This is followed by a section detailing the role of wisdom in Israel's history (10:1–12:27) and the plight of the ignorant (13:1–9). The remainder of chap. 13 and chaps. 14–16 contain admonitions against the worship and manufacture of idols (13:10–14:31); reminders of God's kindness, sustenance, and healing power (15:1–3; 16:13–29); and cautions against idol worship (15:4–16:12). The final section contains musings on God's judgments, protection of the faithful, superiority over Egyptian power, and deliverance of the faithful in Egypt (17:1–19:21). It concludes with a doxology (19:22). Wisdom begins with counsel and concludes with praise.

Hugh R. Page, Jr.

1 Love righteousness, you rulers of the
earth;
think of the Lord in goodness
and seek him with sincerity of heart,
2 because he is found by those who do not
put him to the test
and manifests himself to those who do
not distrust him.
3 For perverse thoughts separate people
from God,
and when his power is tested, it exposes
the foolish,
4 because wisdom will not enter a
deceitful soul
or dwell in a body enslaved to sin.
5 For a holy and disciplined spirit will flee
from deceit
and will leave foolish thoughts
behind
and will be ashamed at the approach of
unrighteousness.

6 For wisdom is a kindly spirit,
but it will not free blasphemers from the
guilt of their words,
because God is witness of their inmost
feelings
and a true observer of their hearts and a
hearer of their tongues.
7 Because the spirit of the Lord has filled
the world

and that which holds all things together
knows what is said,
8 therefore those who utter
unrighteous things will not
escape notice,
and justice, when it punishes, will not
pass them by.
9 For inquiry will be made into the
counsels of the ungodly,
and a report of their words will come to
the Lord,
to convict them of their lawless
deeds,
10 because a jealous ear hears all things,
and the sound of grumbling does not go
unheard.
11 Beware, then, of useless grumbling,
and keep your tongue from slander,
because no secret word is without
result,[a]
and a lying mouth destroys the soul.

12 Do not court death by the error of your
life
or bring on destruction by the works of
your hands,
13 because God did not make death,
and he does not delight in the
destruction of the living.

a 1.11 Or *will go unpunished*

1:1–11 Appeal to righteousness, wisdom, and kindness. 1:1–5 While the target audience of the book appears to be those with political authority, its maxims and moral guidance also have value for all who trust the Lord. The idea of testing connotes challenging authority, a trope that would make sense to those in positions of power. In this instance, it also raises a question as to the role this anthology is intended to play in the intellectual and moral formation of ancient and modern audiences. Should reading lead to reflection and thoughtful querying or elicit immediate obedience? The book's content and tone do not appear to signal a desire for facile reception. Rather, they encourage deep and sustained engagement in orienting one's heart toward *righteousness* and the quest for *wisdom* as well as in avoiding ways of thinking and acting that would be deemed—considering the author's understanding—*perverse* and show one to be *foolish*. The key is to situate oneself appropriately on an ethical continuum where wisdom and folly represent polar extremes, while at the same time eschewing *sin* and cultivating a *disciplined spirit.* **1:6** *A kindly spirit.* This sentence calls attention to wisdom's generosity and discerning nature. **1:7** *That which holds all things together* is perhaps another description of wisdom that emphasizes its all-encompassing and omnipresent essence. **1:8** Wisdom is aware of all utterances and ensures just recompense for all thoughts and actions. **1:9–11** Given their mundane and spiritual power, words issued in public or harbored in secret do not escape divine scrutiny. A record is kept of all things said. **1:11** *Secret word* stands in parallel with earlier mentions of *grumbling* and *slander*. All three are types of speech with the power to cause harm and are to be avoided by the righteous.
   1:12–15 God as creative force and righteousness as divine creation. There is a single cosmos. The human and divine realms intersect in that cosmos, and the forces of life and death coexist, albeit in separate, permeable realms. **1:12** *Error* in this instance stands for everything opposed to righteous living. It is the pathway to death. **1:13** God is not responsible for creating death and does not delight

14 For he created all things so that they
     might exist;
the generative forces[b] of the world are
     wholesome,
and there is no destructive poison in
     them,
and the dominion[c] of Hades is not on
     earth.
15 For righteousness is immortal.[d]
16 But the ungodly by their words and
     deeds summoned death;[e]
considering him a friend, they pined away
and made a covenant with him,
because they are fit to belong to his
     company.

2 For they reasoned unsoundly, saying to
     themselves,
"Short and sorrowful is our life,
and there is no remedy when a life comes
     to its end,
and no one has been known to return
     from Hades.
2 For we were born by mere chance,
and hereafter we shall be as though we
     had never been,
for the breath in our nostrils is smoke,
and reason is a spark kindled by the
     beating of our hearts;
3 when it is extinguished, the body will
     turn to ashes,
and the spirit will dissolve like empty air.
4 Our name will be forgotten in time,
and no one will remember our works;

our life will pass away like the traces of
     a cloud
and be scattered like mist
that is chased by the rays of the sun
and overcome by its heat.
5 For our allotted time is the passing of a
     shadow,
and there is no return from our death,
because it is sealed up and no one turns
     back.

6 "Come, therefore, let us enjoy the good
     things that exist
and make use of the creation to the full
     as in youth.
7 Let us take our fill of costly wine and
     perfumes,
and let no flower of spring pass us by.
8 Let us crown ourselves with rosebuds
     before they wither.
9 Let no meadow be free from our revelry;
everywhere let us leave signs of
     enjoyment,
because this is our portion, and this our
     lot.
10 Let us oppress the righteous poor man;
let us not spare the widow
or regard the gray hairs of the aged.
11 But let our might be our law of right,
for what is weak proves itself to be
     useless.

b 1.14 Or *the creatures*   c 1.14 Or *palace*   d 1.15 OL adds *but
unrighteousness is the acquisition of death*   e 1.16 Gk *him*

in its ravages. **1:14–15** By contrast, God has created all *wholesome* things including *righteousness*, which is, like God and wisdom itself, eternal. Here and elsewhere, views of death—that is, as a physical entity, a physical state of being, and a philosophy—converge. The same is true of righteousness, the pursuit of which yields concrete outcomes in the day-to-day lives of people and the larger life that extends beyond physical mortality. Thus, one's embrace or rejection of righteousness in the here and now determines whether one enjoys the immediate and continuing benefits of either immortality or death.

1:16–2:24 The ungodly and their covenant with death. The ungodly are chastised for courting a relationship and making a *covenant* with death through their actions. **2:1–5** The ungodly have a fatalistic vision of human life. They believe it is subject to chance, is devoid of purpose, ends at the grave, and holds no promise of longevity even through the memories of others. **2:6–9** Given the fleeting and vapid nature of daily existence, the ungodly focus on pure physical enjoyment. Their way of life is reminiscent of that advocated by the Greek philosopher Epicurus (ca. fourth to third centuries BCE). They become consumers of the finest things available: for example, *costly wine*, *perfumes*, and *rosebuds*. *This is our portion, and this our lot* indicates that the ungodly feel a sense of entitlement to these precious goods. Rather than appreciating them as gifts to be cherished, they treat them as commodities for personal use. **2:10** The ungodly treat in a comparable way *the righteous poor man*, *the widow*, and *the aged*, all of whom are without a proper social safety net and are vulnerable to attack from or neglect by those enjoying social and other forms of privilege. A complete absence of respect for life is indicative of their alignment and friendship with death. **2:11** *What is weak proves itself to be useless* suggests that righteousness is no match for physical

¹² "Let us lie in wait for the righteous man,
  because he is inconvenient to us and
    opposes our actions;
  he reproaches us for sins against the law
  and accuses us of sins against our
    training.
¹³ He professes to have knowledge of God
  and calls himself a child of the Lord.
¹⁴ He became to us a reproof of our
    thoughts;
  the very sight of him is a burden to us,
¹⁵ because his manner of life is unlike that
    of others,
  and his ways are strange.
¹⁶ We are considered by him as something
    base,
  and he avoids our ways as unclean;
  he calls the last end of the righteous
    happy
  and boasts that God is his father.
¹⁷ Let us see if his words are true,
  and let us test what will happen at the
    end of his life,
¹⁸ for if the righteous man is God's child, he
    will help him
  and will deliver him from the hand of his
    adversaries.
¹⁹ Let us test him with insult and torture,
  so that we may find out how reasonable
    he is
  and make trial of his forbearance.

²⁰ Let us condemn him to a shameful
    death,
  for, according to what he says, he will be
    protected."
²¹ Thus they reasoned, but they were led
    astray,
  for their wickedness blinded them,
²² and they did not know the secret
    purposes of God,
  nor hoped for the wages of holiness,
  nor discerned the prize for blameless
    souls,
²³ for God created us for incorruption
  and made us in the image of his own
    eternity,ᶠ
²⁴ but through an adversary'sᵍ envy death
    entered the world,
  and those who belong to his company
    experience it.

3 But the souls of the righteous are in the
    hand of God,
  and no torment will ever touch them.
² In the eyes of the foolish they seemed to
    have died,
  and their departure was thought to be a
    disaster
³ and their going from us to be their
    destruction,
  but they are at peace.

f 2.23 Other ancient authorities read nature   *g 2.24 Or a*
devil's

strength, which is the *law* by which the unrighteous live. It is interesting to compare this with the Pauline notion that power is perfected in weakness (1 Cor. 1:25; 2 Cor. 12:9). **2:12** *He reproaches us.* The righteous are targeted for punishment because they shame the unrighteous. **2:15** *His ways are strange* is perhaps equivalent to modern colloquial expressions indicative of outsider status—for example, "they are weird" or "they are not like us." In a social world where group belonging ensured safety and protection, and where various social groups were in competition for adherents, insults of this kind would have been common. **2:16** *Boasts that God is his father.* A claim of divine protection and patronage would lend credence and moral authority to the truth claims of the righteous. **2:17** *Let us test what will happen at the end of his life.* Testing, trying, or proving the legitimacy of claims made by the righteous is a means of justifying harsh treatment by the unrighteous. One sees this theme of testing the righteous in the story of Jesus's crucifixion in the Synoptic Gospels (see Matt. 27:49; Mark 15:36). **2:22** *The secret purposes of God . . . the wages of holiness . . . the prize for blameless souls.* These allude to the hidden dimensions of God's plans for the righteous. The unrighteous have no knowledge of what God intends for the righteous, even during times of persecution. **2:23–24** The timeless mystery empowering the righteous is that God created humanity for immortality and that death finds its way into the human realm through the envy of *an adversary.* This is the esoteric truth that enables them to thrive in a world subject to the torment of the unrighteous and escape the power of death, cast here as a divine opponent.

3:1–9 Blessings of the righteous. The righteous have no reason to fear. They are and will remain in God's care. **3:1** *The souls of the righteous* refers to that part of the human person representing their essence and character. **3:2** The foolish are misled because their view of human life is narrow. It fails to take into consideration that life has meaningful dimensions on both sides of the grave. **3:3** *They are at peace* refers to the present and the future dispositions of the

⁴ For though in the sight of others they
    were punished,
  their hope is full of immortality.
⁵ Having been disciplined a little, they will
    receive great good,
  because God tested them and found
    them worthy of himself;
⁶ like gold in the furnace he tried them,
  and like a sacrificial burnt offering he
    accepted them.
⁷ In the time of their visitation they will
    shine forth
  and will run like sparks through the
    stubble.
⁸ They will govern nations and rule over
    peoples,
  and the Lord will reign over them forever.
⁹ Those who trust in him will understand
    truth,
  and the faithful will abide with him in love,
  because grace and mercy are upon his
    holy ones,
  and he watches over his elect.^b
¹⁰ But the ungodly will be punished as their
    reasoning deserves,
  those who disregarded the righteousⁱ
  and rebelled against the Lord,
¹¹ for those who despise wisdom and
    instruction are miserable.
  Their hope is vain, their labors are
    unprofitable,
  and their works are useless.

¹² Their wives are foolish and their
    children evil;
  their offspring are accursed.
¹³ For blessed is the barren woman who is
    undefiled,
  who has not entered into a sinful union;
  she will have fruit when God examines
    souls.
¹⁴ Blessed also is the eunuch whose hands
    have done no lawless deed
  and who has not devised wicked things
    against the Lord,
  for special favor will be shown him for
    his faithfulness
  and a place of great delight in the temple
    of the Lord.
¹⁵ For the fruit of good labors is renowned,
  and the root of understanding does not
    fail.
¹⁶ But children of adulterers will not come
    to maturity,
  and the offspring of an unlawful union
    will perish.
¹⁷ Even if they live long they will be held of
    no account,
  and finally their old age will be without
    honor.
¹⁸ If they die young, they will have no hope
  and no consolation on the day of
    judgment.

b 3.9 Text of this line uncertain; omitted by some ancient
authorities   i 3.10 Or what is right

righteous. **3:4** *Their hope is full of immortality.* Even during periods of distress in their current life, the righteous possess a more expansive sense of their destiny, which has an eternal scope. **3:5–7** The author draws on images from the worlds of metallurgy and worship, where fire is used respectively to refine ore and to make burnt offerings. The lives of the righteous, however troubled, are akin to one of the ancient world's most precious metals and flash like sparks from the burned tinder of an altar fire. They are an offering acceptable and pleasing to God. **3:8–9** The righteous ultimately enjoy a reversal of fortune, though it is unclear what the time horizon will be. Ultimately, they will be in positions of authority within a divinely constituted hierarchy, with God at the pinnacle. Trust and faith in God will yield true knowledge and an abiding relationship with the divine.

3:10–12 The troubles of the ungodly. The lives of the ungodly are fraught. Just as material rewards accompany the quest for righteousness, misery is associated with poor reasoning, the rejection of wisdom, and rebellion against what is right and just.

3:13–15 Blessings on childless women and eunuchs. There is good news for those considered devoid of divine favor (barren widows) or who do not conform to priestly purity codes because they are eunuchs. Both are accorded favor for aligning themselves with the moral touchstones articulated by the author. Appropriate behavior and avoidance of wickedness ensure blessings. **3:15** *The root of understanding does not fail* suggests that the source of peace and prosperity for everyone is proper knowledge and the actions that emerge from such knowledge.

3:16–18 Children of adulterers. This concern with the offspring of those deemed unrighteous may reflect tensions within the author's community concerning the maintenance of cultural boundaries or practices related to separation from those considered ritually impure.

¹⁹ For the end of an unrighteous generation
is grievous.

4 Better than this is childlessness with
virtue,
for in the memory of virtue*j* is
immortality,
because it is known both by God and by
mortals.
² When it is present, people imitate*k* it,
and they long for it when it has gone;
throughout all time it marches, crowned
in triumph,
victor in the contest for prizes that are
undefiled.
³ But the prolific brood of the ungodly
will be of no use,
and none of their illegitimate seedlings
will strike a deep root
or take a firm hold.
⁴ For even if they put forth boughs for a
while,
standing insecurely they will be shaken
by the wind,
and by the violence of the winds they
will be uprooted.
⁵ The branches will be broken off before
they come to maturity,
and their fruit will be useless,
not ripe enough to eat and good for
nothing.
⁶ For children born of unlawful unions
are witnesses of evil against their
parents when God examines them.*l*
⁷ But the righteous, even if they die early,
will be at rest.
⁸ For old age is not honored for length of
time
or measured by number of years,
⁹ but understanding is gray hair for anyone,
and a blameless life is ripe old age.
¹⁰ There was one who pleased God and was
loved by him
and while living among sinners was
taken up.
¹¹ He was caught up so that evil might not
change his understanding
or guile deceive his soul.
¹² For the fascination of wickedness
obscures what is good,
and roving desire perverts the innocent
mind.
¹³ Being perfected in a short time, he
fulfilled long years,
¹⁴ for his soul was pleasing to the Lord;
therefore he hastened him from the
midst of wickedness.
Yet the peoples saw and did not
understand
or take such a thing to heart,
¹⁵ that God's grace and mercy are with his
elect
and that he watches over his holy ones.
¹⁶ The righteous who have died will
condemn the ungodly who are
living,
and youth that is quickly perfected*m* will
condemn the prolonged old age of
the unrighteous.
¹⁷ For they will see the end of the wise
and will not understand what the Lord
purposed for them
and for what he kept them safe.

j 4.1 Gk *it*   *k* 4.2 Other ancient authorities read *honor*
l 4.6 Gk *at their examination*   *m* 4.16 Or *ended*

3:19–4:6 The fate of an unrighteous generation. The unrighteous, however fruitful they might be in terms of offspring, are anything but blessed. They may have many descendants to remember their deeds but have little merit when compared to what the righteous leave as a legacy, which endures into eternity. Thus, it is better to have no children than to have those lacking virtue. **4:1** *In the memory of virtue is immortality.* Virtuous actions endure not just in the sight of the public but in the presence of God. **4:3–6** The children of the unrighteous are like plants that are neither firmly rooted nor fruitful. They witness to the corruption of their parents.

4:7–14a The fate of the righteous in life and death. The righteous are an enigma. Their lives cannot be judged using ordinary criteria. They can only be understood by God's own standards. Length of life is not an accurate measure because virtuous living can result in early death if it is part of God's plan. **4:10** *While living among sinners was taken up* may be a reference to the enigmatic story of Enoch (Gen. 5:18–24).

4:14b–5:16 The mystery of righteous flourishing. How is it that the righteous thrive in the face of difficulty? How is it that even when they appear not to have enjoyed the benefit of long years or renown among peers, they can be said to enjoy God's favor and protection? The sage reflects on such apparent oddities. **4:15** *God's grace and mercy are with his elect*, ensuring that despite

18 The unrighteous[n] will see and will have
   contempt for them,
but the Lord will laugh them to scorn.
19 After this they will become dishonored
   corpses
and an outrage among the dead forever,
because he will dash them speechless to
   the ground
and shake them from the foundations;
they will be left utterly dry and barren,
and they will suffer anguish,
and the memory of them will perish.
20 They will come with dread when their
   sins are reckoned up,
and their lawless deeds will convict them
   to their face.

5 Then the righteous will stand with great
   confidence
in the presence of those who have
   oppressed them
and those who make light of their
   labors.
2 When the unrighteous[o] see them, they
   will be shaken with dreadful fear,
and they will be amazed at the
   unexpected salvation of the
   righteous.
3 They will speak to one another in
   repentance,
and in anguish of spirit they will groan,
4 "These are persons whom we once held
   in derision
and made a byword of reproach—fools
   that we were!
We thought that their lives were
   madness
and that their end was without honor.
5 Why have they been numbered among
   the children of God?
And why is their lot among the holy ones?
6 So it was we who strayed from the way
   of truth,
and the light of righteousness did not
   shine on us,
and the sun did not rise upon us.
7 We took our fill of the paths of
   lawlessness and destruction,

and we journeyed through trackless
   deserts,
but the way of the Lord we have not
   known.
8 What has our arrogance profited us?
And what good has our boasted wealth
   brought us?

9 "All those things have vanished like a
   shadow
and like a rumor that passes by;
10 like a ship that sails through the billowy
   water,
and when it has passed no trace can be
   found,
no track of its keel in the waves;
11 or as, when a bird flies through the air,
no evidence of its passage is found;
the light air, lashed by the beat of its
   pinions
and pierced by the force of its rushing
   flight,
is traversed by the movement of its wings,
and afterward no sign of its coming is
   found there;
12 or as, when an arrow is shot at a target,
the air, thus divided, comes together at
   once,
so that no one knows its pathway.
13 So we also, as soon as we were born,
   ceased to be,
and we had no sign of virtue to show
but were consumed in our wickedness."
14 Because the hope of the ungodly is like
   thistledown[p] carried by the wind
and like a light frost[q] driven away by a
   storm;
it is dispersed like smoke before the
   wind,
and it passes like the remembrance of a
   guest who stays but a day.
15 But the righteous live forever,
and their reward is with the Lord;
the Most High takes care of them.

n 4.18 Gk *They*   o 5.2 Gk *they*   p 5.14 Other ancient
authorities read *dust*   q 5.14 Other ancient authorities
read *spider's web*

circumstances or appearances to the contrary, God favors the righteous. **4:18–19** *The Lord will laugh them to scorn. . . . he will dash them speechless to the ground.* The language here is reminiscent of Ps. 2:4, 9. **5:2** *They will be amazed at the unexpected salvation of the righteous.* This amazement is due to the inability of the unrighteous to grasp the scope of God's plan, which extends beyond the grave. **5:14** *The hope of the ungodly is like thistledown carried by the wind.* Such hopes are insubstantial and fleeting—easily carried away. **5:15–16** *The righteous live forever, and their reward is with the Lord.* It is interesting to think of this blessed state as beginning during the mortal existence of

¹⁶ Therefore they will receive a glorious
        crown
    and a beautiful diadem from the hand of
        the Lord,
    because with his right hand he will cover
        them,
    and with his arm he will shield them.
¹⁷ The Lord^r will take his zeal as his whole
        armor
    and will arm all creation to repel^s his
        enemies;
¹⁸ he will put on righteousness as a
        breastplate
    and wear impartial justice as a helmet;
¹⁹ he will take holiness as an invincible
        shield
²⁰ and sharpen stern wrath for a sword,
    and the world will join him to fight
        against the senseless.
²¹ Shafts of lightning will fly with true aim
    and will leap from the clouds to the
        target, as from a well-drawn bow,
²² and hailstones full of wrath will be
        hurled as from a catapult;
    the water of the sea will rage against them,
    and rivers will relentlessly overwhelm
        them;
²³ a mighty wind will rise against them,
    and like a tempest it will winnow them
        away.
    Lawlessness will lay waste the whole
        earth,
    and evildoing will overturn the thrones
        of rulers.

6 Listen therefore, O kings, and understand;
    learn, O judges of the ends of the earth.

² Give ear, you who rule over multitudes
    and boast of many nations.
³ For your dominion was given you from
        the Lord
    and your sovereignty from the Most High;
    he will search out your works and
        inquire into your plans.
⁴ Because as servants of his kingdom you
        did not rule rightly
    or keep the law
    or walk according to the purpose of God,
⁵ he will come upon you terribly and
        swiftly,
    because severe judgment falls on those in
        high places.
⁶ For the lowliest may be pardoned in
        mercy,
    but the mighty will be mightily tested.
⁷ For the Lord of all will not stand in awe
        of anyone
    or show deference to greatness,
    because he himself made both small and
        great,
    and he takes thought for all alike.
⁸ But a strict inquiry is in store for the
        mighty.
⁹ To you then, O monarchs, my words are
        directed,
    so that you may learn wisdom and not
        transgress.
¹⁰ For they will be made holy who observe
        holy things in holiness,
    and those who have been taught them
        will find a defense.

r 5.17 Gk He   s 5.17 Or punish

those living righteously and continuing after their earthly sojourn concludes. Eternal life begins in the here and now and continues as one transitions after death and obtains *a glorious crown and a beautiful diadem from the hand of the Lord.*

5:17–23 God's power and protection against the unrighteous. The language here has apocalyptic overtones similar to those found in some biblical texts describing the Lord as a divine warrior marching out in defense of Israel (see, for example, Hab. 3:3–15). It is included here, perhaps, to highlight the cosmic scope of the battle against the unrighteous and God's ultimate victory over them.

6:1–11 An admonition to monarchs. The author offers specific advice to kings relating to expectations for the exercise of their authority. It applies, by extension, to all in positions of power, within communities of the dispersed faithful and beyond. The admonitions face both inwardly and externally. **6:2** *You who rule over multitudes and boast of many nations.* The focus is on all with responsibility. One can imagine those under the author's tutelage would have seen themselves destined for such roles. **6:3** *He will search out your works and inquire into your plans.* Everything one does is within God's purview. Therefore, those in authority need to know that their actions will be under divine scrutiny. **6:8** *A strict inquiry is in store for the mighty.* The powerful are held to a higher standard than others in evaluating the quality of their governance. **6:10** *They will be made holy who observe holy things in holiness.* Association with holiness begets holiness. This is critical for those in power to comprehend, given that they are in fact being judged by one whose holiness is without

¹¹ Therefore set your desire on my words;
   long for them, and you will be instructed.
¹² Wisdom is radiant and unfading,
   and she is easily discerned by those who
      love her
   and is found by those who seek her.
¹³ She hastens to make herself known to
      those who desire her.
¹⁴ One who rises early to seek her will have
      no difficulty,
   for she will be found sitting at the gate.
¹⁵ To fix one's thought on her is perfect
      understanding,
   and one who is vigilant on her account
      will soon be free from care,
¹⁶ because she goes about seeking those
      worthy of her,
   and she graciously appears to them in
      their paths
   and meets them in every thought.

¹⁷ The beginning of wisdom^t is the most
      sincere desire for instruction,
¹⁸ and concern for instruction is love of her,
   and love of her is the keeping of her
      laws,
   and giving heed to her laws is assurance
      of immortality,
¹⁹ and immortality brings one near to God,
²⁰ so the desire for wisdom leads to a
      kingdom.

²¹ Therefore if you delight in thrones and
      scepters, O monarchs over the
      peoples,
   honor wisdom, so that you may reign
      forever.
²² I will tell you what wisdom is and how
      she came to be,
   and I will hide no secrets from you,
   but I will trace her course from the
      beginning of creation
   and make knowledge of her clear,
   and I will not pass by the truth,
²³ nor will I travel in the company of sickly
      envy,
   for envy^u does not associate with
      wisdom.
²⁴ The multitude of the wise is the salvation
      of the world,
   and a sensible king is the stability of any
      people.
²⁵ Therefore be instructed by my words,
      and you will profit.

7 I also am mortal like everyone else,
   a descendant of the first-formed child
      of earth,
   and in the womb of a mother I was
      molded into flesh,
² within the period of ten months,
      compacted with blood,

---

t 6.17 Gk *Her beginning* u 6.23 Gk *this*

---

parallel. **6:11** *Set your desire on my words.* The ultimate curriculum for effective rule consists of God's instruction, no doubt read and understood according to the interpretive guidelines set out by this book's author.

6:12–25 The beauty, awe, allure, and source of Wisdom. Wisdom here is personified as a woman. These reflections on the salutary traits of Wisdom are meant to inspire and encourage those seeking to find and embrace her. She meets those who are sincere in their pursuit of her and does not disappoint when they encounter her. **6:13** *She hastens to make herself known to those who desire her.* Wisdom is responsive to those seeking connection to and relationship with her. **6:17** *The beginning of wisdom is the most sincere desire for instruction.* A recurring theme elsewhere in biblical and deuterocanonical/apocryphal books dealing with wisdom has to do with whence the quest to obtain it begins. Positions proposed include "fear of the Lᴏʀᴅ" (Ps. 111:10; Prov. 1:7; 9:10), "to fear the Lord" (Sir. 1:14), and to "get wisdom" (Prov. 4:7). **6:18** *Love of her is the keeping of her laws, and giving heed to her laws is assurance of immortality.* Understanding Wisdom's precepts, perhaps as the author has articulated them in this book, leads to eternal life. **6:22** *I will tell you what wisdom is and how she came to be, and I will hide no secrets from you.* Perhaps the most profound of mysteries has to do with Wisdom's cosmic point of origin, which the author promises to reveal clearly. **6:24** *The multitude of the wise is the salvation of the world.* The suggestion here is, perhaps, of a complementary relationship between monarchs and sages in maintaining social stability. **6:25** *Be instructed by my words, and you will profit.* The implication here is that advice offered in this anthology of wise counsel is superior to that of others.

7:1–22a The birth and life of the sage. The author offers personal biographical reflections and, perhaps, a general overview of how those seeking to be sages should view themselves and approach their pilgrimage toward knowledge. **7:1** *I also am mortal like everyone else.* The sage is

from the seed of a man and the pleasure
of marriage.
³ And when I was born, I began to breathe
the common air
and fell upon the kindred earth;
my first sound was a cry, as is true of all.
⁴ I was nursed with care in swaddling
cloths.
⁵ For no king has had a different beginning
of existence;
⁶ there is for all one entrance into life and
one way out.
⁷ Therefore I prayed, and understanding
was given me;
I called on God, and the spirit of wisdom
came to me.
⁸ I preferred her to scepters and thrones,
and I accounted wealth as nothing in
comparison with her.
⁹ Neither did I liken to her any priceless gem,
because all gold is but a little sand in her
sight,
and silver will be accounted as clay
before her.
¹⁰ I loved her more than health and beauty,
and I chose to have her rather than light
because her radiance never ceases.
¹¹ All good things came to me along with her,
and in her hands uncounted wealth.
¹² I rejoiced in them all because wisdom
leads them,
but I did not know that she was their
mother.
¹³ I learned without guile, and I impart
without grudging;
I do not hide her wealth,

¹⁴ for it is an unfailing treasure for
mortals;
those who get it obtain friendship with
God,
commended for the gifts that come from
instruction.
¹⁵ May God grant me to speak with
judgment
and to have thoughts worthy of what I
have received,
for he is the guide even of wisdom
and the corrector of the wise.
¹⁶ For both we and our words are in his
hand,
as are all understanding and skill in
crafts.
¹⁷ For it is he who gave me unerring
knowledge of what exists,
to know the structure of the world and
the activity of the elements,
¹⁸ the beginning and end and middle of
times,
the alternations of the solstices and the
changes of the seasons,
¹⁹ the cycles of the year and the
constellations of the stars,
²⁰ the natures of animals and the tempers
of wild animals,
the powers of spirits' and the thoughts of
human beings,
the varieties of plants and the virtues of
roots;
²¹ I learned both what is secret and what is
manifest,

v 7.20 Or *winds*

not superhuman but a normal human being like those to whom counsel is given. **7:6** *There is for all one entrance into life* emphasizes that all, even the wise, come into the world in the same way. **7:7** *I prayed, and understanding was given me; I called on God, and the spirit of wisdom came to me.* Here one learns the secret of the sage's skill. Prayer opens the portal for the relationship with wisdom to begin. **7:13** *I learned without guile, and I impart without grudging; I do not hide her wealth.* This sage is not a teacher of mysteries creating conundrums to be pondered. Instead, this possessor of wisdom's spirit reveals willingly and in a straightforward manner its treasures. **7:14** *Friendship with God* suggests that it is not simply the possession of a body of knowledge that makes one wise but the realization that there is a relational dimension that one is to seek with God. **7:15** *He is the guide even of wisdom and the corrector of the wise*: an affirmation that God is superior to—indeed, the steward of—wisdom as well as the one responsible for the sage. **7:16** *All understanding and skill in crafts* refers to the totality of applied and practical proficiencies. **7:17–20** This is a self-disclosure of the sage's portfolio of essential skills. It is inclusive of matters structural, elemental, celestial, terrestrial (including flora and fauna), meteorological, spiritual, and intellectual. For aspiring sages, this is part of the curriculum by which they are formed and about which only hints are written in the book itself. **7:21** *What is secret and what is manifest.* In other words, the sage has been taught what might be called esoteric (*secret*) and exoteric (*what is manifest*) things. Such comprehensive knowledge, as is noted in the next verse, is bestowed by "wisdom, the fashioner of all things" (v. 22a).

²² for wisdom, the fashioner of all things,
  taught me.
  There is in her a spirit that is intelligent,
    holy,
  unique, manifold, subtle,
  agile, clear, unpolluted,
  distinct, invulnerable, loving the good,
    keen,
²³ irresistible, beneficent, humane,
  steadfast, sure, free from anxiety,
  all-powerful, overseeing all,
  and penetrating through all spirits
  that are intelligent, pure, and altogether
    subtle.
²⁴ For wisdom is more mobile than any
    motion;
  because of her pureness she pervades
    and penetrates all things.
²⁵ For she is a breath of the power of God
  and a pure emanation of the glory of the
    Almighty;
  therefore nothing defiled gains entrance
    into her.
²⁶ For she is a reflection of eternal light,
  a spotless mirror of the working of God,
  and an image of his goodness.
²⁷ Although she is but one, she can do all
    things,
  and while remaining in herself, she
    renews all things;
  in every generation she passes into holy
    souls
  and makes them friends of God and
    prophets,
²⁸ for God loves nothing so much as the
    person who lives with wisdom.
²⁹ She is more beautiful than the sun
  and excels every constellation of the
    stars.
  Compared with the light she is found to
    be more radiant,

³⁰ for it is succeeded by the night,
  but against wisdom evil does not prevail.
8 She reaches mightily from one end of
    the earth to the other,
  and she orders all things well.
² I loved her and sought her from my
    youth;
  I desired to take her for my bride
  and became enamored of her beauty.
³ She glorifies her noble birth by living
    with God,
  and the Lord of all loves her.
⁴ For she is an initiate in the knowledge of
    God
  and an associate in his works.
⁵ If riches are a desirable possession in life,
  what is richer than wisdom, the active
    cause of all things?
⁶ And if understanding is effective,
  who more than she is fashioner of what
    exists?
⁷ And if anyone loves righteousness,
  her labors are virtues,
  for she teaches self-control and
    prudence,
  justice and courage;
  nothing in life is more profitable for
    mortals than these.
⁸ And if anyone longs for wide experience,
  she knows the things of old and infers
    the things to come;
  she understands turns of speech and the
    solutions of riddles;
  she has foreknowledge of signs and
    wonders
  and of the outcome of seasons and times.
⁹ Therefore I determined to take her to live
    with me,
  knowing that she would give me good
    counsel
  and encouragement in cares and grief.

7:22b–8:1 The essential traits of Wisdom. True to his earlier promise, the author presents tantalizing insights on the nature of wisdom, though they invite readers to ponder a reality that is ultimately unfathomable. **7:25** *She is a breath of the power of God and a pure emanation of the glory of the Almighty.* Wisdom is not identical to but issues from God. **7:27** *In every generation she passes into holy souls and makes them friends of God and prophets* asserts that Wisdom inhabits those who are holy, thereby fostering close relationship with the divine and empowering them to be inspired spokespersons. Wisdom is, therefore, the source of prophecy. **8:1** *She orders all things well.* Wisdom is the entity through which all facets of the created world are set in place.

8:2–21 The quest for wisdom and its rewards. The pilgrimage in search of wisdom has its immediate and longer-term benefits, some of the more important of which are enumerated here. **8:4** *She is an initiate in the knowledge of God and an associate in his works.* Like a devotee in a Greek mystery school, Wisdom herself has been initiated into the realm of God's own knowledge. **8:8** *She knows the things of old and infers the things to come.* The scope of Wisdom's knowledge encompasses the

¹⁰ Because of her I shall have glory among
    the multitudes
  and honor in the presence of the elders,
    though I am young.
¹¹ I shall be found keen in judgment,
  and in the sight of rulers I shall be
    admired.
¹² When I am silent they will wait for me,
  and when I speak they will give heed;
  if I speak at greater length,
  they will put their hands on their
    mouths.
¹³ Because of her I shall have immortality
  and leave an everlasting remembrance to
    those who come after me.
¹⁴ I shall govern peoples,
  and nations will be subject to me;
¹⁵ dread monarchs will be afraid of me
    when they hear of me;
  among the people I shall show myself
    capable and courageous in war.
¹⁶ When I enter my house, I shall find rest
    with her,
  for companionship with her has no
    bitterness,
  and life with her has no pain but
    gladness and joy.
¹⁷ When I considered these things inwardly
  and pondered in my heart
  that in kinship with wisdom there is
    immortality,
¹⁸ and in friendship with her, pure delight,
  and in the labors of her hands, unfailing
    wealth,
  and in the experience of her company,
    understanding,
  and renown in sharing her words,

I went about seeking how to get her for
    myself.
¹⁹ As a child I was naturally gifted,
  and a good soul fell to my lot,
²⁰ or rather, being good, I entered an
    undefiled body.
²¹ But I perceived that I would not possess
    wisdom unless God gave her to me—
  and it was a mark of insight to know
    whose gift she was—
  so I appealed to the Lord and implored
    him,
  and with my whole heart I said,

9 "O God of my ancestors and Lord of
    mercy,
  who have made all things by your word
² and by your wisdom have formed
    humankind
  to have dominion over the creatures you
    have made
³ and rule the world in holiness and
    righteousness
  and pronounce judgment in uprightness
    of soul,
⁴ give me the wisdom that sits by your
    throne,
  and do not reject me from among your
    children.
⁵ For I am your servant, the son of your
    female servant,
  a man who is weak and short-lived,
  with little understanding of judgment
    and laws,
⁶ for even one who is perfect among
    humans
  will be regarded as nothing without the
    wisdom that comes from you.

temporal sweep of all that has been or will be. **8:13** *Because of her I shall have immortality.* Perhaps the most important reward is that of eternal life that comes from being in Wisdom's presence. **8:16** *Companionship with her has no bitterness, and life with her has no pain.* The sense here is that one receives those elements associated with a good life, one free of discomfort. **8:20** *Being good, I entered an undefiled body* alludes to the idea of a soul's preexistence and the impact of its character on the nature of its incarnation at birth. We can see here the confluence of ideas from the Jewish and larger Mediterranean religious realms in shaping this author's ideas. **8:21** *I perceived that I would not possess wisdom unless God gave her to me.* The sage realized, early on, that wisdom was a gift that must be solicited from God and, as a result, turns to the only means through which it could be petitioned.

9:1–18 A prayer for wisdom. Among those spiritual matters with which sages must be familiar is that of the architecture and content of prayer, which are here modeled for all to see. **9:1** *God of my ancestors and Lord of mercy.* Acknowledgment of the historical scope of the sage's community with God, and its essential attributes, is critical. **9:2** *By your wisdom have formed humankind.* The sage once again acknowledges the role wisdom plays in the created order. **9:3** *Rule the world in holiness and righteousness.* The relationship between wisdom—as eternal truth—and both holiness and righteousness as instruments of governance is articulated. **9:4** *Give me the wisdom that sits by*

Focus On: Wisdom and Creation (Wisdom of Solomon 9)

Stories about creation, or "cosmogonies," are a well-known category of folklore from around the world. They help explain astronomical, meteorological, and geographical features. They account for flora, fauna, and other natural phenomena. They offer rationales for political structures and social mores. They may also be related to or complement narratives about the birth of deities, sometimes referred to as "theogonies." Most creation accounts are concerned with identifying the forces responsible for making or setting in order those things that exist, both tangible and unseen; detailing the essential features of the cosmos; and identifying those principles governing human interactions. Whether ancient or modern, mythological or scientific, they employ language that is highly evocative, imaginative, and at points speculative.

In the ancient Near Eastern and Greco-Roman worlds, intelligence and sound judgment were attributes ascribed to many deities, among which were Athena (Greece), Thoth (Egypt), Enki (Sumer), El (Ugarit), and Ea (Mesopotamia). Wisdom was also an attribute of YHWH, God of Israel. In the wisdom traditions of the Second Temple and Hellenistic periods, wisdom (Heb. *hokma*; Gk. *sophia*) was the first of God's creations (Sir. 1:4). Wisdom is present with God at the creation of the world (Wis. 9:9) and, in some instances, seen as a companion or "initiate" of God (Wis. 8:3–4). In some texts, wisdom is a veritable hypostasis—or alter ego—of God (Prov. 9:1; Wis. 7:25–27; 10:1–19; see **"Woman Wisdom," p. 872**). Wisdom is the power through which all things are made, set in place (Wis. 9:18), and sustained (Prov. 3:19; Wis. 7:22; 8:1).

Wisdom was, for many Jewish sages, the cosmic mystery whose secrets the righteous sought to discern. In many respects, their goal was to make sense of the innumerable conundrums that they encountered each day. In the modern scientific field of cosmology, the "Big Bang," radioactive residue, black holes, event horizons, and exoplanets are part of the vocabulary deployed in engaging some of these same oddities and new riddles that perplex us. Twenty-first-century scholars and sages, like their ancient counterparts, focus their energies on understanding how the universe came into existence. All recognize that the stories we tell about our origins are efforts to grapple with realities that are ultimately beyond our full comprehension in ways that enable us to live meaningfully and with hope for the future.

Hugh R. Page, Jr.

⁷ You have chosen me to be king of your
    people
and to be judge over your sons and
    daughters.
⁸ You have given command to build a
    temple on your holy mountain
and an altar in the city of your
    habitation,
a copy of the holy tent that you prepared
    from the beginning.
⁹ With you is wisdom, she who knows
    your works
and was present when you made the
    world;
she understands what is pleasing in your
    sight

and what is right according to your
    commandments.
¹⁰ Send her forth from the holy heavens,
and from the throne of your glory send
    her,
that she may labor at my side
and that I may learn what is pleasing to
    you.
¹¹ For she knows and understands all things,
and she will guide me wisely in my actions
and guard me with her glory.
¹² Then my works will be acceptable,
and I shall judge your people justly
and shall be worthy of the throne^w of my
    father.

w 9.12 Gk *thrones*

your throne. Here, elsewhere in this prayer, and throughout the book, mythological, philosophical, and ethical language coalesce in describing wisdom. Wisdom is at once a cosmic entity, a knowledge system, and a way of life with an ethic based on right relationship with the one true God. **9:7–8** These verses reference traditions about King Solomon and give the impression that he is the author of the book (cf. 2 Sam. 7:12–17). **9:9** *With you is wisdom, she who knows your works and was present when you made the world.* Cosmic and instrumental language referring to Wisdom's role in

¹³ For who can learn the counsel of God?
  Or who can discern what the Lord wills?
¹⁴ For the reasoning of mortals is worthless,
  and our designs are likely to fail,
¹⁵ for a perishable body weighs down the
    soul,
  and this earthy tent burdens the
    thoughtful* mind.
¹⁶ We can hardly guess at what is on earth,
  and what is at hand we find with labor,
  but who has traced out what is in the
    heavens?
¹⁷ Who has learned your counsel
  unless you have given wisdom
  and sent your holy spirit from on high?
¹⁸ And thus the paths of those on earth
    were set right,
  and people were taught what pleases you
  and were saved by wisdom."

10 Wisdom*ʸ* protected the first-formed
    father of the world,
  when he alone had been created;
  she delivered him from his transgression
² and gave him strength to rule all things.
³ But when an unrighteous man departed
    from her in his anger,
  he perished because in rage he killed his
    brother.

⁴ When the earth was flooded because of
    him, wisdom again saved it,
  steering the righteous man by a paltry
    piece of wood.

⁵ Wisdom*ᶻ* also, when the nations in
    wicked agreement had been put to
    confusion,
  recognized the righteous man and
    preserved him blameless before God
  and kept him strong in the face of his
    compassion for his child.

⁶ Wisdom*ᵃ* rescued a righteous man when
    the ungodly were perishing;
  he escaped the fire that descended on
    the Five Cities.*ᵇ*
⁷ Evidence of their wickedness still
    remains:
  a continually smoking wasteland,
  plants bearing fruit that does not ripen,
  and a pillar of salt standing as a
    monument to an unbelieving soul.
⁸ For because they passed wisdom by,
  they not only were hindered from
    recognizing the good

x 9.15 Or *anxious* y 10.1 Gk *She* z 10.5 Gk *She* a 10.6 Gk
She b 10.6 Or *on Pentapolis*

---

creation are combined. **9:15** *A perishable body weighs down the soul, and this earthy tent burdens the thoughtful mind.* One sees here the idea that the human body is an impediment to the soul's intellectual and spiritual activities. **9:18** *People were taught what pleases you and were saved by wisdom.* Wisdom has soteriological dimensions; through it, salvation is secured.

  10:1–12:27 Wisdom's role in Israel's history. Living at a distance from home—whether that home is an actual, imagined, or hoped-for place of residence—is disorienting. It can generate feelings of rootlessness, disconnection from familiar persons and places, the fragmenting of community, and the shattering of personal identity. Survival and thriving in such an environment can be aided by the gathering and curation of artifacts, among which are stories of the past. This process of remembering—of reassembling broken, lost, or forgotten things—is a way of mitigating the disruptive impact of the Diaspora, situating oneself safely in the present moment, embracing and reframing stories of the past, and envisioning a hopeful future. Here, the author begins a selective retelling of Israel's history, recounting important episodes in it that extend from the travails of primordial humanity to the entry of God's people, newly liberated from Egypt, into the "holy land" (12:3). The narrative pays particular attention to the role that Wisdom has played in that saga. The moral tone of this philosophical midrash calls attention to the "backstory" of Israel's history, those devotees of wisdom that are its leading lights, and the antiheroes whose errors should be avoided. It subtly urges those reading or hearing this history to be vigilant in their pursuit of righteousness and avoidance of "detestable practices" (12:4) in their day. **10:1** *The first-formed father of the world* is a reference to the story of Adam (Gen. 2:5–3:24). **10:3** *An unrighteous man*: a reference to Cain and the murder of his brother, Abel (Gen. 4:1–16). **10:4** *A paltry piece of wood* refers to the ark constructed by Noah and the story of the great flood (Gen. 6:5–9:17). **10:5** *The nations . . . had been put to confusion* refers to the story of the confusion of languages at Babel (Gen. 11:1–9). *Kept him strong in the face of his compassion for his child* appears to be a reference to the story of Abraham and God's directive to sacrifice Isaac (Gen. 22). **10:6–8** The destruction of Sodom and Gomorrah, the rescue of Lot and the monument testifying to his wife's disobedience, and the perpetual ruin of "the land of the

but also left for humankind a reminder
of their folly,
so that their failures could never go
unnoticed.

9 Wisdom rescued from troubles those
who served her.
10 When a righteous man fled from his
brother's wrath,
she guided him on straight paths;
she showed him the kingdom of God
and gave him knowledge of holy things;
she prospered him in his labors
and increased the fruit of his toil.
11 When his oppressors were covetous,
she stood by him and made him rich.
12 She protected him from his enemies
and kept him safe from those who lay in
wait for him;
in his arduous contest she declared him
victorious,
so that he might learn that godliness is
more powerful than anything else.

13 When a righteous man was sold,
wisdom[c] did not desert him
but delivered him from sin.
14 She descended with him into the
dungeon,
and when he was in prison she did not
leave him,
until she brought him the scepter of a
kingdom
and authority over his masters.
Those who accused him she showed to
be false,
and she gave him everlasting honor.
15 Holy people and blameless offspring
wisdom[d] delivered from a nation of
oppressors.
16 She entered the soul of a servant of the
Lord

and withstood dread kings with wonders
and signs.
17 She gave to holy people the reward of
their labors;
she guided them along a marvelous way
and became a shelter to them by day
and a starry flame through the night.
18 She brought them over the Red Sea
and led them through deep waters,
19 but she drowned their enemies
and cast them up from the depth of the
sea.
20 Therefore the righteous plundered the
ungodly;
they sang hymns, O Lord, to your holy
name
and praised with one accord your
defending hand,
21 for wisdom opened the mouths of those
who were mute
and made the tongues of infants speak
clearly.

11 Wisdom[e] prospered their works by the
hand of a holy prophet.
2 They journeyed through an uninhabited
wilderness
and pitched their tents in untrodden
places.
3 They withstood their enemies and fought
off their foes.
4 When they were thirsty, they called upon
you,
and water was given them out of flinty
rock
and from hard stone a remedy for their
thirst.
5 For through the very things by which
their enemies were punished,
they themselves received benefit in their
need.

c 10.13 Gk she   d 10.15 Gk she   e 11.1 Gk She

plain" (Gen. 19:1–29) are the focus here. **10:10–12** The story of Wisdom's guidance of Jacob during
his difficulties with Esau, his brother (Gen. 27:41), is recounted. *Kingdom of God* and *holy things*, no
doubt, refer to the matters disclosed to Jacob in his vision at Bethel (Gen. 28). **10:13–14** These lines
revisit the story of Joseph (Gen. 37–50). **10:15–19** Wisdom's role in the exodus from Egypt and the
miraculous encounter at the *Red Sea* (or Sea of Reeds) receives comment (Exod. 1–14). **10:20** *They
sang hymns, O Lord, to your holy name and praised with one accord your defending hand* may be a
reference to the so-called Song of the Sea (Exod. 15:1–18, 21) led by Moses and Miriam. The author
attributes inspiration for what some consider one of the earliest biblical poems to Wisdom herself.
11:1 *The hand of a holy prophet* calls attention to Moses and his leadership of the liberated community through their wilderness sojourn. **11:4** *Water was given them out of flinty rock* references
Wisdom's role behind the scenes at Massah and Meribah (Exod. 17:1–7). **11:5–14** A retrospective is
offered on the slaughter of Israelite male children as a means of political subjugation and population

⁶ Instead of the fountain of an ever-
    flowing river,
  stirred up and defiled with blood
⁷ in rebuke for the decree to kill the infants,
  you gave them abundant water
    unexpectedly,
⁸ showing by their thirst at that time
  how you punished their enemies.
⁹ For when they were tried, though they
    were being disciplined in mercy,
  they learned how the ungodly were
    tormented when judged in wrath.
¹⁰ For you tested them as a parent[f] does in
    warning,
  but you examined the ungodly[g] as a stern
    king does in condemnation.
¹¹ Whether absent or present, they were
    equally distressed,
¹² for a twofold grief possessed them
  and a groaning at the memory of what
    had occurred.
¹³ For when they heard that through their
    own punishments
  the righteous[h] had received benefit, they
    perceived it was the Lord's doing.
¹⁴ For though they had mockingly rejected
    him who long before had been cast
    out and exposed,
  at the end of the events they marveled
    at him,
  when they felt thirst in a different way
    from the righteous.
¹⁵ In return for their foolish and wicked
    thoughts,
  which led them astray to worship
    irrational serpents and worthless
    animals,
  you sent upon them a multitude of
    irrational creatures to punish them,

¹⁶ so that they might learn that one is
    punished by the very things by
    which one sins.
¹⁷ For your all-powerful hand,
  which created the world out of formless
    matter,
  did not lack the means to send upon
    them a multitude of bears or bold
    lions
¹⁸ or newly created unknown beasts full of
    rage
  or such as breathe out fiery breath
  or belch forth a thick pall of smoke
  or flash terrible sparks from their eyes;
¹⁹ not only could the harm they did destroy
    people,[i]
  but the mere sight of them could kill by
    fright.
²⁰ Even apart from these, people[j] could fall
    at a single breath
  when pursued by justice
  and scattered by the breath of your
    power.
  But you have arranged all things by
    measure and number and weight.
²¹ For it is always in your power to show
    great strength,
  and who can withstand the might of
    your arm?
²² Because the whole world before you is
    like a speck that tips the scales
  and like a drop of morning dew that falls
    on the ground.
²³ But you are merciful to all, for you can
    do all things,
  and you overlook people's sins, so that
    they may repent.

f 11.10 Gk *a father*   g 11.10 Gk *those*   h 11.13 Gk *they*
i 11.19 Gk *them*   j 11.20 Gk *they*

control (Exod. 1:8–22). This was one of many acts of state-sponsored terror countered by divinely ordered plagues, the first of which was the despoliation of Egypt's source of water and commerce, the Nile (Exod. 7:14–25). The author juxtaposes this tragic punishment with the miraculous quenching of the community's thirst with water from a legendary rock in "the wilderness of Sin" (Exod. 17:1). The testing of the righteous and the ungodly—identified in this instance with the larger Egyptian populace—are juxtaposed. The former is like parental instruction, the latter akin to firm monarchic rule (v. 10). In the end, Moses, the once-rejected Egyptian insider, is recognized by those who cast him out as they come to terms with their own misery and thirst. Recompense, satiation, and the hidden dimensions of divine chastisement, through the agency of oppressors, are part of wisdom's strange logic. **11:15–12:2** The breadth and scope of divine compassion, forbearance, and love—even toward the unrighteous—are engaged. A message of this kind may be intended to encourage those living in the Diaspora to think of God's care in more inclusive terms: to consider righteousness as a growth process rather than a fixed state of being and to imagine theirs as a blended community—a "mixed crowd" (Exod. 12:38)—planted permanently in a new adopted homeland. In such light, even the religious traditions of the Egyptians and other peoples can be seen as the result of

²⁴ For you love all things that exist
and detest none of the things that you
have made,
for you would not have formed anything
if you had hated it.
²⁵ How would anything have endured if
you had not willed it?
Or how would anything not called forth
by you have been preserved?
²⁶ You spare all things, for they are yours,
O Lord, you who love the living.

12 For your immortal spirit is in all
things.
² Therefore you correct little by little
those who trespass,
and you remind and warn them of the
things through which they sin,
so that they may be freed from
wickedness and put their trust in
you, O Lord.
³ Those who lived long ago in your holy land
⁴ you hated for their detestable practices,
their works of sorcery and unholy rites,
⁵ their merciless slaughter*ᵏ* of children,
and their sacrificial feasting on human
flesh and blood.
These initiates from the midst of a
bloody revelry,*ˡ*
⁶ these parents who murder helpless lives,
you willed to destroy by the hands of our
ancestors,
⁷ so that the land most precious of all to you
might receive a worthy colony of the
children of God.
⁸ But even these you spared, since they
were but mortals,
and sent wasps*ᵐ* as forerunners of your
army
to destroy them little by little,

⁹ though you were not unable to give
the ungodly into the hands of the
righteous in battle
or to destroy them at one blow by dread
wild animals or your stern word.
¹⁰ But judging them little by little you gave
them an opportunity to repent,
though you were not unaware that their
origin*ⁿ* was evil
and their wickedness inborn
and that their way of thinking would
never change.
¹¹ For their offspring were accursed from
the beginning,
and it was not through fear of anyone
that you left them unpunished for
their sins.
¹² For who will say, "What have you done?"
or will resist your judgment?
Who will accuse you for the destruction
of nations that you made?
Or who will come before you to plead as
an advocate for the unrighteous?
¹³ For neither is there any god besides you
whose care is for all people,*ᵒ*
to whom you should prove that you have
not judged unjustly,
¹⁴ nor can any king or monarch confront
you about those whom you have
punished.
¹⁵ You are righteous, and you rule all things
righteously,
deeming it alien to your power
to condemn anyone who does not
deserve to be punished.
¹⁶ For your strength is the source of
righteousness,

k 12.5 Gk slaughterers   l 12.5 Meaning of Gk uncertain
m 12.8 Or hornets   n 12.10 Or nature   o 12.13 Or all things

erroneous thinking and subject to change. **11:26** *You spare all things, for they are yours, O Lord, you who love the living* is the incontrovertible truth, the driving force for God's compassionate care of everyone. One wonders, then, about the mission of wisdom's adherents. Is it to be actively involved in modeling lives dedicated to righteousness and understanding? Should it entail ongoing encounters with those who reject such values? Should it consist of establishing a life separate from Greek culture? These are questions that the author seems subtly to weave into the fabric of this chapter and elsewhere in the book. **12:1** *Your immortal spirit is in all things* is another of the author's essential takeaways for those seeking to understand God's relationship to the world and its inhabitants. Everything has an eternal spiritual core that gives it inestimable value and worth. **12:2** *You correct little by little those who trespass* and *that they may be freed from wickedness* set out the strategy and basic objective of God's behavioral interventions. Ultimately, the goal is liberation—not from an oppressive political regime but from *wickedness*. **12:3–27** The historical midrash continues with the Israelites' journey to Canaan and encounter with the land's inhabitants. The author understands this to be a legitimate colonization, justified by the unseemly religious practices found there. The narrative reflects knowledge of traditions found in Deuteronomy, Joshua, and Judges. It also incorporates

and your sovereignty over all causes you
to spare all.
17 For you show your strength when people
doubt the completeness of your
power,
and you rebuke any insolence among
those who know it.[p]
18 Although you are sovereign in strength,
you judge fairly,
and with great forbearance you govern
us,
for you have power to act whenever you
choose.
19 Through such works you have taught
your people
that the righteous must be kind,
and you have filled your children with
good hope,
because you give repentance for sins.
20 For if you punished with such great care
and indulgence[q]
the enemies of your children and those
deserving of death,
granting them time and opportunity to
give up their wickedness,
21 with what strictness you have judged
your children,[r]
to whose ancestors you gave oaths and
covenants full of good promises!
22 So while chastening us you scourge
our enemies ten thousand times
more,
so that when we judge we may meditate
upon your goodness,
and when we are judged we may expect
mercy.
23 Therefore those who lived unrighteously,
in a life of folly,
you tormented through their own
abominations.
24 For they went far astray on the paths of
error,
accepting as gods those animals that
even their enemies[s] despised;
they were deceived like foolish infants.
25 Therefore, as though to children who
cannot reason,
you sent your judgment to mock them.
26 But those who have not heeded the
warning of mild rebukes
will experience the deserved judgment
of God.
27 For when in their suffering they became
incensed
at those creatures that they had thought
to be gods, being punished by
means of them,
they saw and recognized as the true
God the one whom they had before
refused to know.
Therefore the utmost condemnation
came upon them.

13 For all people who were ignorant of
God were foolish by nature,
and they were unable from the good
things that are seen to know the
one who exists,
nor did they recognize the artisan while
paying heed to his works;

p 12.17 Meaning of Gk uncertain *q* 12.20 Other ancient authorities lack *and indulgence*; others read *and entreaty* *r* 12.21 Gk *sons* *s* 12.24 Gk *they*

hyperbolic language that portrays those practices in a completely negative manner. It attributes the incompleteness of the occupation to God's desire for repentance of the land's inhabitants, who are deemed *evil* (v. 10) and *accursed* (v. 11). Though the theological rationale given for the dispossession of Indigenous populations here differs slightly in emphasis from that found elsewhere (Deut. 9:4–5; Josh. 1:3–9; 24:1–28; and Judg. 2), accounts like these cannot help but be jarring to modern sensibilities. Awareness of the atrocities accompanying European colonization of Africa and elsewhere; the seizing of lands, abrogation of rights, and genocide of Indigenous peoples in the United States; and the Russian Republic's military incursion into Ukraine during 2022 should caution against facile reading and encourage careful assessment of why narratives like these are produced and how they can be critically engaged at a time when serious efforts are being made to alleviate the corrosive effects of colonialism, xenophobia, and religious persecution globally. It is crucial to keep in mind that the conceptions of the divine, wisdom, righteousness, evil, holiness, and so on are the product of a specific author (or authors) living in a specific place and time and dealing with a vexing set of existential crises. Such context-specific knowledge requires culturally competent and disciplined engagement to fully understand and frame it for modern consumption.

13:1–9 The plight of the ignorant. This extended reflection focuses on those whose limited vision prevents them from appreciating the hand of God at work in the world. **13:1** *The one who exists* and *the artisan* are evocative divine epithets that center God's presence and creative capacities.

² but they supposed that either fire or
   wind or swift air
or the circle of the stars or turbulent
   water
or the luminaries of heaven were the
   gods that rule the world.
³ If through delight in the beauty of these
   things people assumed them to be
   gods,
let them know how much better than
   these is their Lord,
for the author of beauty created them.
⁴ And if people[t] were amazed at their
   power and working,
let them perceive from them
how much more powerful is the one who
   formed them.
⁵ For from the greatness and beauty of
   created things
comes a corresponding perception of
   their Creator.
⁶ Yet these people are little to be blamed,
for perhaps they go astray
while seeking God and desiring to find
   him.
⁷ For while they live among his works,
   they keep searching
and trust in what they see because
   the things that are seen are
   beautiful.
⁸ Yet again, not even they are to be
   excused,
⁹ for if they had the power to know so
   much
that they could investigate the world,
how did they not more quickly find the
   Lord of these things?
¹⁰ But miserable, with their hopes set on
   dead things, are those

who give the name "gods" to the works
   of human hands,
gold and silver fashioned with skill
and likenesses of animals
or a useless stone, the work of an ancient
   hand.
¹¹ A skilled woodcutter may saw down a
   tree easy to handle
and skillfully strip off all its bark
and then with pleasing workmanship
make a useful vessel that serves life's
   needs
¹² and burn the cast-off pieces of his work
to prepare his food and eat his fill.
¹³ But a cast-off piece from among them,
   useful for nothing,
a stick crooked and full of knots,
he takes and carves with care in his
   leisure
and shapes it with skill gained in
   idleness;[u]
he forms it in the likeness of a human
   being
¹⁴ or makes it like some worthless animal,
giving it a coat of red paint and coloring
   its surface red
and covering every blemish in it with
   paint;
¹⁵ then he makes a suitable niche for it
and sets it in the wall and fastens it there
   with iron.
¹⁶ He takes thought for it so that it may not
   fall,
because he knows that it cannot help
   itself,
for it is only an image and has need of
   help.

t 13.4 Gk *they*   *u* 13.13 Other ancient authorities read *with
intelligent skill*

13:4 *If people were amazed at their power and working, let them perceive from them how much
more powerful is the one who formed them.* The polemic against worshiping celestial and natural
phenomena, instead of their creator, is pointed. However, it is interesting to note that the author
does not deny that these forces have power, a belief that was common in the ancient Mediterranean
world. **13:7** *Trust in what they see because the things that are seen are beautiful.* The implication is
that appearances can be deceptive and that the sense of awe elicited by any aspect of nature should
not mislead someone to see it as divine. **13:9** *How did they not more quickly find the Lord of these
things?* This is an incisive critique of those who fail to grasp that planets, stars, and other elements
of nature are subject to God's dominion.

   13:10–14:31 The folly of idol worship. Especially biting is this polemic against the worship of idols,
which is reminiscent of equally stinging remarks found in prophetic books such as Isaiah (40:18–20;
44:9–20), Jeremiah (10:2–5), and Habakkuk (2:18). The degree of vitriol is much stronger than that
expressed for those that acknowledge the power of natural forces, perhaps because idols are *the
works of human hands*. **13:10–19** The author goes to great lengths to illustrate the uselessness of
idols in obtaining personal assistance such as support of family or life's necessities, health or safe

¹⁷ When he prays about possessions and his
marriage and children,
he is not ashamed to address a lifeless
thing.
For health he appeals to a thing that is
weak;
¹⁸ for life he prays to a thing that is dead;
for aid he entreats a thing that is utterly
inexperienced;
for a prosperous journey, a thing that
cannot take a step;
¹⁹ for money-making and work and success
with his hands,
he asks strength of a thing whose hands
have no strength.

14 Again, one preparing to sail and
about to voyage over raging
waves
calls upon a piece of wood more fragile
than the ship that carries him.
² For it was desire for gain that planned
that vessel,
and wisdom was the artisan who
built it,
³ but it is your providence, O Father, that
steers its course,
because you have given it a path in the
sea
and a safe way through the waves,
⁴ showing that you can save from every
danger,
so that even a person who lacks skill may
put to sea.
⁵ It is your will that works of your wisdom
should not be without effect;
therefore people trust their lives even to
the smallest piece of wood,

and passing through the billows on a raft
they come safely to land.
⁶ For even in the beginning, when arrogant
giants were perishing,
the hope of the world took refuge on a
raft
and guided by your hand left to the
world the seed of a new generation.
⁷ For blessed is the wood by which
righteousness comes.
⁸ But the idol made with hands is
accursed, and so is the one who
made it—
he for having made it, and the perishable
thing because it was named a god.
⁹ For equally hateful to God are the
ungodly and their ungodliness,
¹⁰ for what was done will be punished
together with the one who did it.
¹¹ Therefore there will be a visitation also
upon the idols of the nations,
because, though part of what God
created, they became an
abomination,
stumbling blocks for human souls
and a trap for the feet of the foolish.
¹² For the idea of making idols was the
beginning of sexual immorality,
and the invention of them was the
corruption of life,
¹³ for they did not exist from the beginning,
nor will they last forever.
¹⁴ For through human vanity they entered
the world,
and therefore their speedy end has been
planned.

travels, or material prosperity. **14:6** *In the beginning, when arrogant giants were perishing, the hope of the world took refuge on a raft* concludes an impassioned plea about the ineffectiveness of idols in protecting those on perilous sea voyages. It makes reference to the story of the "sons of God," "daughters of humans," and their offspring—"the heroes that were of old"—and the "wickedness of humans" (Gen. 6:4–5) that resulted in the great flood. The ark that carried Noah is juxtaposed with the wood used in the fashioning of an idol. It is through the former that hope for the future was secured. **14:7** *Blessed is the wood by which righteousness comes.* The author shows great devotion to Noah and the ark he builds at God's command (Gen. 6:14–16) as a sacred artifact and vehicle through which God's righteousness is made known. **14:8** The condemnation of idols and those making them is particularly strong, perhaps because of how they came to be part of the religious landscape, which is explained later. **14:11** *Though part of what God created, they became an abomination, stumbling blocks for human souls and a trap for the feet of the foolish* responds to possible questions about why idols, if they are made from materials created by God, should be condemned. **14:12** *The idea of making idols was the beginning of sexual immorality, and the invention of them was the corruption of life* advances the idea that idols are deceptive and lead one away from an accurate understanding of God's activity in the world and toward an inauthentic existence. **14:14** *Through human vanity they entered the world.* As human fabrications, idols are not deserving of the reverence due

¹⁵ For a father, consumed with grief at an
    untimely bereavement,
made an image of his child, who had
    been suddenly taken from him;
he now honored as a god what was once
    a dead human being
and handed on to his dependents secret
    rites and initiations.
¹⁶ Then the ungodly custom, grown strong
    with time, was kept as a law,
and at the command of monarchs carved
    images were worshiped.
¹⁷ When people could not honor monarchs^v
    in their presence, since they lived at
    a distance,
they imagined their appearance far away
and made a visible image of the king
    whom they honored,
so that by their zeal they might flatter
    the absent one as though present.

¹⁸ Then the ambition of the artisan impelled
even those who did not know the king^w
    to intensify their worship.
¹⁹ For he, perhaps wishing to please his
    ruler,
skillfully forced the likeness to take
    more beautiful form,
²⁰ and the multitude, attracted by the
    charm of his work,
now regarded as an object of worship the
    one whom shortly before they had
    honored as a human.

²¹ And this became a hidden trap for
    humankind,
because people, in bondage to
    misfortune or to royal authority,
bestowed on objects of stone or wood the
    name that ought not to be shared.

²² Then it was not enough for them to err
    about the knowledge of God,
but though living in great strife due to
    ignorance,
they call such great evils peace.
²³ For whether they kill children in their
    initiations or celebrate secret
    mysteries
or hold frenzied revels with strange
    customs,
²⁴ they no longer keep either their lives or
    their marriages pure,
but they either treacherously kill one
    another or grieve one another by
    adultery,
²⁵ and all is a raging riot of blood
    and murder, theft and deceit,
    corruption, faithlessness, tumult,
    perjury,
²⁶ confusion over what is good,
    forgetfulness of favors,
defiling of souls, sexual perversion,
    disorder in marriages, adultery, and
    debauchery.

v 14.17 Gk *them*   *w* 14.18 Gk lacks *the king*

to God. **14:15–20** Responsibility is traced to four sources for the establishment and promulgation of idol worship: a grieving *father*, unscrupulous *monarchs*, zealous citizens, and enterprising artisans. The source of these stories is not known. They may be part of a body of lore curated by the author and redeployed in this book. They may also have been the result of the author's own creative imagination. **14:21** *People, in bondage to misfortune or to royal authority, bestowed on objects of stone or wood the name that ought not to be shared.* The political sentiments expressed here are surprisingly antimonarchic and sensitive to the realities people dealing with difficult circumstances face. Such would include persons all along the social spectrum. **14:22** *Though living in great strife due to ignorance, they call such great evils peace.* This is another strong indictment of the deceptive nature of devotion to idols, this time linked to enduring—but not appropriately naming or calling out—difficult realities. The author does not want readers to be misled by erroneous claims about foreign gods and the images representing them nor by false notions that they can be safe and whole entrusting their lives to them. **14:23** *Initiations*, *secret mysteries*, and *frenzied revels with strange customs.* The specific rituals and practices to which reference is made are not known. **14:24–29** The worship of idols leads to complete social collapse, as evidenced by violence, impiety, and a host of moral failures. **14:30** *Because they thought wrongly about God in devoting themselves to idols and because in deceit they swore unrighteously through contempt for holiness.* As one would expect, given what the author has said throughout the book about the alignment of wisdom and righteousness, incorrect thinking and impiety are the two things that prove most harmful for idol worshipers. A possible message here is that swearing an oath by an idol is harmful because it is an unwise act that is an affront to wisdom and a sin against a righteous God.

27 For the worship of idols not to be named
   is the beginning and cause and end of
      every evil.
28 For their worshipers[x] either rave in
      exultation
   or prophesy lies or live unrighteously or
      readily commit perjury,
29 for because they trust in lifeless idols
   they swear wicked oaths and expect to
      suffer no harm.
30 But just penalties will overtake them on
      two counts:
   because they thought wrongly about
         God in devoting themselves to idols
   and because in deceit they swore
      unrighteously through contempt
      for holiness.
31 For it is not the power of the things by
      which people swear[y]
   but the just penalty for those who sin
   that always pursues the transgression of
      the unrighteous.

15 But you, our God, are kind and true,
   patient, and ruling all things[z] in
      mercy.
2 For even if we sin we are yours, knowing
      your power;
   but we will not sin because we know that
      you acknowledge us as yours.
3 For to know you is complete
      righteousness,
   and to know your power is the root of
      immortality.
4 For neither has the evil intent of human
      art misled us,

nor the fruitless toil of painters,
   a figure stained with varied colors,
5 whose appearance arouses yearning in
      fools,
   so that they desire[a] the lifeless form of a
      dead image.
6 Lovers of evil things and fit for such
      objects of hope[b]
   are those who either make or desire or
      worship them.
7 A potter kneads the soft earth
   and laboriously molds each vessel for
      our service,
   fashioning out of the same clay
   both the vessels that serve clean uses
   and those for contrary uses, making all
      alike,
   but which shall be the use of each of them
   the worker in clay decides.
8 With misspent toil, these workers form a
      futile god from the same clay—
   these mortals who were made of earth a
      short time before
   and after a little while go to the earth
      from which all mortals are taken,
   when the time comes to return the souls
      that were borrowed.
9 But the workers are not concerned that
      mortals are destined to die
   or that their life is brief,
   but they compete with workers in gold
      and silver

x 14.28 Gk *they*   y 14.31 Or *of the oaths people swear*   z 15.1 Or
ruling the universe   a 15.5 Gk *and he desires*   b 15.6 Gk *such
hopes*

15:1–3 God's kindness and power. The polemic against idol worship continues but makes a slight turn toward recognition of God's benevolence and genuineness: two characteristics that inanimate representations of deities are incapable of displaying. **15:3** *To know you is complete righteousness, and to know your power is the root of immortality.* This is a confident affirmation that a relationship with God and a deep appreciation of the essence, potential, and tangible manifestations of divine power—all of which the Greek term "kratos," translated as "power," connotes—are the sources of eternal life.

15:4–19 Admonitions against the manufacture and worship of idols. Idol manufacture and commerce are the focus here. **15:5** The foolish are susceptible to manipulation by the palpable beauty of *the lifeless form of a dead image.* It is this kind of deception that the author finds so troubling. **15:6** The author calls readers to reject the production, longing for, and veneration of idols, which are judged to be *evil things.* **15:7** The artists involved in the making of objects designate them for *clean* or unclean uses, distinguished by whether they are to be dedicated for service to God. **15:8** *Misspent toil.* The labor of potters that make idols is without reward or benefit because it is invested in the creation of an object devoid of power. They fail to recognize that they are manufacturing objects of the same substance from which they themselves have been made—a real irony. The image of humans being formed from the ground to which they will return when they die is from Gen. 2–3 (see 2:7; 3:19; cf. Eccl. 3:20; 12:7). **15:9** *But the workers are not concerned that mortals are destined to die or that their life is brief.* The author presumes callousness on the part of idol makers and a concern

and imitate workers in copper,
and they count it a glorious thing to
mold counterfeit gods.

[10] Their heart is ashes, their hope is
cheaper than dirt,
and their lives are of less worth than
clay,

[11] because they failed to know the one who
formed them
and inspired them with active souls
and breathed a living spirit into them.

[12] But they considered our existence an
idle game
and life a festival held for profit,
for they say one must get money
however one can, even by base
means.

[13] For these persons, more than all others,
know that they sin
when they make from earthy matter
fragile vessels and carved images.

[14] But most foolish and more miserable
than an infant
are all the enemies who oppressed your
people.

[15] For they thought that all the idols of the
nations were gods,
though these have neither the use of
their eyes to see with,
nor nostrils with which to draw breath,
nor ears with which to hear,
nor fingers to feel with,
and their feet are of no use for walking.

[16] For a human made them,
and one whose spirit is borrowed formed
them,
for none can form gods that are like
themselves.

[17] People are mortal, and what they make
with lawless hands is dead,
for they are better than the objects they
worship,
since[c] they have life, but the idols[d] never
had.

[18] Moreover, they worship even the most
hateful animals,
which are worse than all others when
judged by their lack of intelligence,

[19] and even as animals they are not so
beautiful in appearance that one
would desire them,
but they have escaped both the praise of
God and his blessing.

16 Therefore those people[e] were
deservedly punished through such
creatures
and were tormented by a multitude of
animals.

[2] Instead of this punishment you showed
kindness to your people,
and you prepared quails to eat,
a delicacy to satisfy the desire of
appetite,

[3] in order that those people, when they
desired food,

c 15.17 Other ancient authorities read *of which*   d 15.17 Gk
but they   e 16.1 Gk *they*

with their own economic welfare given competition in the market for sacred objects. **15:11** *They failed to know the one who formed them and inspired them with active souls.* The criticism here is striking because the author seems to speak not simply as a sage but as an artist—one with a deep appreciation for the eternal source that fires imagination and creativity. **15:12** *They considered our existence an idle game and life a festival held for profit.* To make light of the serious matter that is life, in the interest of material gain, is abhorrent for this author. There is an underlying ethic that informs the work of the artisan. The same is true of the sage. Both must be dedicated to truth and the cultivation of life rather than to profit. **15:13** *For these persons, more than all others, know that they sin.* "Making," whether with clay and pigment or with words and sound guidance, requires a commitment to honesty and human thriving. To profit from the vision, insight, and inspiration that fuel creativity in service to wisdom and righteousness is an affront to God. **15:14–19** While the preceding anti-idol commentary appears to be directed largely toward those inside the author's immediate community, this denunciation is targeted toward those producing and worshiping images of foreign gods. They use idols to justify their ill-treatment of God's people. **15:16** *None can form gods that are like themselves.* This is the essential problem for all who make or venerate images of deities. Mortals are incapable of creating things that are immortal. **15:18** *They worship even the most hateful animals.* Earlier, the author acknowledges the deceptive beauty of idols (e.g., 14:20). In this instance, those who make images of animals considered unattractive or loathsome by God are scorned.

16:1–12 Punishment of idol worshipers and salvation of the righteous in the wilderness. The point of reference shifts once again to the story of the exodus from Egypt and the sojourn in the

might lose the least remnant of appetite[f]
because of the odious creatures sent to
    them,
while your people,[g] after suffering want
    a short time,
might partake of delicacies.
⁴ For it was necessary that upon those
    oppressors inescapable want should
    come,
while to these others it was merely
    shown how their enemies were
    being tormented.

⁵ For when the terrible rage of wild
    animals came upon your people[b]
and they were being destroyed by the
    bites of writhing serpents,
your wrath did not continue to the end;
⁶ they were troubled for a little while as a
    warning
and received a symbol of deliverance
    to remind them of your law's
    command.

⁷ For the one who turned toward it was
    saved not by the thing that was
    beheld
but by you, the Savior of all.
⁸ And by this also you convinced our
    enemies
that it is you who deliver from every
    evil.
⁹ For they were killed by the bites of
    locusts and flies,
and no healing was found for them
because they deserved to be punished by
    such things.
¹⁰ But your children were not conquered
    even by the fangs of venomous
    serpents,
for your mercy came to their help and
    healed them.
¹¹ To remind them of your oracles they
    were bitten
and then were quickly delivered,

so that they would not fall into deep
    forgetfulness
and become unresponsive[i] to your
    kindness.
¹² For neither herb nor poultice cured
    them,
but it was your word, O Lord, that heals
    all people.
¹³ For you have power over life and death;
you lead mortals down to the gates of
    Hades and back again.
¹⁴ A person in wickedness kills another
but cannot bring back the departed spirit
or set free the imprisoned soul.
¹⁵ To escape from your hand is impossible,
¹⁶ for the ungodly, refusing to know you,
were flogged by the strength of your
    arm,
pursued by unusual rains and hail and
    relentless storms
and utterly consumed by fire.
¹⁷ For—most incredible of all—in water,
    which quenches all things,
the fire had still greater effect,
for the universe defends the righteous.
¹⁸ At one time the flame was restrained,
so that it might not consume the
    creatures sent against the ungodly,
but that seeing this they might know
that they were being pursued by the
    judgment of God,
¹⁹ and at another time even in the midst of
    water it burned more intensely than
    fire,
to destroy the crops of the unrighteous
    land.
²⁰ Instead of these things you gave your
    people food of angels,
and without their toil you supplied them
    from heaven with bread ready to
    eat,
providing every pleasure and suited to
    every taste.

*f 16.3 Gk loathed the necessary appetite   g 16.3 Gk they
h 16.5 Gk them   i 16.11 Meaning of Gk uncertain*

wilderness. **16:5–12** A reference, perhaps, to the encounter with serpents in the wilderness (Num. 21:6–9).

16:13–29 God's capacity to heal and sustain the faithful. The evidence of history confirms the idea that God's power supports the faithful and never fails. **16:13** *You have power over life and death; you lead mortals down to the gates of Hades and back again.* God has power that extends from the land of the living to the place of the dead. This statement is reminiscent of that made in Deut. 30:15–20, where life and blessing from keeping the covenant are juxtaposed with death and accursedness. **16:20** *You gave your people food of angels* is a reference to the feeding of Israel in the wilderness with manna (see Exod. 16:31; Num. 11:7; Deut. 8:3). The phrasing here is similar to that found in Ps.

21 For your sustenance manifested your
   sweetness toward your children,
and the bread, ministering[j] to the desire
   of the one who took it,
was changed to suit everyone's liking.
22 Snow and ice withstood fire without
   melting,
so that they might know that the crops
   of their enemies
were being destroyed by the fire that
   blazed in the hail
and flashed in the showers of rain;
23 whereas the fire,[k] in order that the
   righteous might be fed,
even forgot its native power.

24 For creation, serving you who made it,
exerts itself to punish the unrighteous
and in kindness relaxes on behalf of
   those who trust in you.
25 Therefore at that time also, changed into
   all forms,
it served your all-nourishing bounty,
according to the desire of those who had
   need,[l]
26 so that your children, whom you loved,
   O Lord, might learn
that it is not the production of crops that
   feeds humankind
but that your word sustains those who
   trust in you.
27 For what was not destroyed by fire
was melted when simply warmed by a
   fleeting ray of the sun,
28 to make it known that one must rise
   before the sun to give you
   thanks
and must pray to you at the dawning of
   the light,
29 for the hope of an ungrateful person will
   melt like wintry frost
and flow away like wastewater.

17 Great are your judgments and hard to
   describe;

therefore uninstructed souls have gone
   astray.
2 For when lawless people supposed that
   they held the holy nation in their
   power,
they themselves lay as captives of
   darkness and prisoners of long
   night,
shut in under their roofs, exiles from
   eternal providence.
3 For thinking that in their secret sins they
   were unobserved
behind a dark curtain of forgetfulness,
they were scattered, terribly[m] alarmed
and appalled by specters.
4 For not even the inner chamber that held
   them protected them from fear,
but terrifying sounds rang out around
   them,
and dismal phantoms with gloomy faces
   appeared.
5 And no power of fire was able to give
   light,
nor did the brilliant flames of the stars
   avail to illumine that hateful night.
6 Nothing was shining through to them
except a dreadful, self-kindled fire,
and in terror they deemed the things that
   they saw
to be worse than that unseen
   appearance.
7 The delusions of their magic art lay
   humbled,
and their boasted wisdom was scornfully
   rebuked.
8 For those who promised to drive off the
   fears and disorders of a sick soul
were sick themselves with ridiculous fear.
9 For even if nothing disturbing frightened
   them,

j 16.21 Gk *and it, ministering*   k 16.23 Gk *this*   l 16.25 Or
who made supplication   m 17.3 Other ancient authorities
read *unobserved, they were darkened behind a dark curtain of
forgetfulness, terribly*

78:25; 2 Esd. 1:19; and John 6:31. **16:24** *For creation, serving you who made it, exerts itself to punish the unrighteous.* The sage understands that those things made by divine command also have the ability to administer divine justice. **16:26** *Your word sustains those who trust in you.* Ultimately, this is the key lesson to be derived from the preceding narrative. Here, it is the word of God, the recounting of the sacred narrative, and the sage's commentary on both that constitute the nurturing utterances.

17:1–21 The magnitude and mystery of God's judgments and their superiority over Egypt's powers. The superiority of God's power and wisdom is made known in the liberation of Israel from Egyptian subjugation. **17:1** *Great are your judgments and hard to describe.* This is the reason one requires the presence of those devoted to the search for wisdom and the teaching of its precepts. **17:7** *The delusions of their magic art lay humbled.* In the contest between Israel's God and Egypt's

yet, scared by the passing of wild
      animals and the hissing of snakes
[10] they perished in trembling fear,
      refusing to look even at the air, though it
      nowhere could be avoided.
[11] For wickedness is a cowardly thing,
      condemned by its own testimony;[n]
      distressed by conscience, it has always
      exaggerated[o] the difficulties.
[12] For fear is nothing but a giving up of the
      helps that come from reason,
[13] and hope, being weaker, prefers ignorance
      of what causes the torment.
[14] But throughout the night, which was
      really powerless
      and which came upon them from the
      recesses of powerless Hades,
      they all slept the same sleep
[15] and now were driven by monstrous
      specters
      and now were paralyzed by their souls'
      surrender,
      for sudden and unexpected fear
      overwhelmed them.
[16] And whoever was there fell down
      and thus was kept shut up in a prison not
      made of iron;
[17] for whether they were farmers or
      shepherds
      or workers who toiled in the wilderness,
      they were seized and endured the
      inescapable fate,
      for with one chain of darkness they all
      were bound.
[18] Whether there came a whistling wind,
      or a melodious sound of birds in wide-
      spreading branches,
      or the rhythm of violently rushing water,
[19] or the harsh crash of rocks hurled down,
      or the unseen running of leaping animals,

or the sound of the most savage roaring
      beasts,
      or an echo thrown back from a hollow of
      the mountains,
      it paralyzed them with terror.
[20] For the whole world was illumined with
      brilliant light
      and went about its work unhindered,
[21] while over those people alone heavy
      night was spread,
      an image of the darkness that was
      destined to receive them,
      but still heavier than darkness were they
      to themselves.

18 But for your holy ones there was very
      great light.
      Their enemies[p] heard their voices but did
      not see their forms
      and counted them happy for not having
      suffered
[2] and were thankful that your holy ones,[q]
      though previously wronged, were
      doing them no injury,
      and they begged their pardon for having
      been at variance with them.[r]
[3] Therefore you provided a flaming pillar
      of fire
      as a guide for your people's[s] unknown
      journey
      and a harmless sun for their glorious
      wandering.
[4] For their enemies[t] deserved to be
      deprived of light and imprisoned in
      darkness,
      those who had kept your children
      imprisoned,

n 17.11 Meaning of Gk uncertain   *o* 17.11 Other ancient
authorities read *anticipated*   *p* 18.1 Gk *They*   *q* 18.2 Meaning of Gk uncertain   *r* 18.2 Meaning of Gk uncertain
s 18.3 Gk *their*   *t* 18.4 Gk *those persons*

deities, the Egyptian wise ones' mystical capacities are shown to be without true power. **17:12** *Fear is nothing but a giving up of the helps that come from reason.* Thus reason is, presumably, the outgrowth of both righteous living and the quest for wisdom. **17:21** *Over those people alone heavy night was spread.* Only those Egyptians aligned against Israel and its God were without literal and intellectual illumination.

18:1–25 God's protection of the faithful in Egypt. While those responsible for the victimization of God's faithful in Egypt suffered greatly, those within the soon-to-be-freed community benefited from the Lord's care. The recounting of God's actions in the past may provide hope for the readers in the author's immediate audience—living perhaps in diasporic communities within a city like Alexandria. **18:1** *For your holy ones there was very great light.* There is illumination—actual and metaphorical, past and present—for the Lord's faithful. **18:3** *A flaming pillar of fire as a guide for your people's unknown journey* is a reference to the account in Exod. 13:21–22. **18:4** *The imperishable light of the law was to be given to the world.* The illuminating wisdom of the Torah was given at Sinai. The commandments (Exod. 20:1–17) contain, for many, its basic precepts. Here, the author is likely referring

through whom the imperishable light
of the law was to be given to the
world.
⁵ When they had resolved to kill the
infants of your holy ones,
and one child had been abandoned and
rescued,
you in punishment took away a
multitude of their children,
and you destroyed them all together by a
mighty flood.
⁶ That night was made known beforehand
to our ancestors
so that they might rejoice in sure
knowledge of the oaths in which
they trusted.
⁷ The deliverance of the righteous and the
destruction of their enemies
were expected by your people.
⁸ For by the same means by which you
punished our enemies
you called us to yourself and glorified us.
⁹ For in secret the holy children of good
people offered sacrifices
and with one accord agreed to the divine
law,
so that the holy ones would share alike
the same things,
both blessings and dangers,
and already they were singing the praises
of the ancestors."
¹⁰ But the discordant cry of their enemies
echoed back,
and their piteous lament for their
children was spread abroad.
¹¹ The slave was punished with the same
penalty as the master,
and the commoner suffered the same
loss as the king,
¹² and they all together by the one formʸ of
death
had corpses too many to count.
For the living were not sufficient even to
bury them,
since in one instant their most valued
children had been destroyed.

¹³ For though they had disbelieved
everything because of their magic
arts,
yet when their firstborn were destroyed
they acknowledged your people to
be God's child.
¹⁴ For while gentle silence enveloped all
things
and night in its swift course was now
half-gone,
¹⁵ your all-powerful word leaped from
heaven, from the royal throne,
into the midst of the land that was
doomed,
a stern warrior
¹⁶ carrying the sharp sword of your
authentic command,
and stood and filled all things with
death
and touched heaven while standing on
the earth.
¹⁷ Then at once apparitions in dreadful
dreams greatly troubled them,
and unexpected fears assailed them,
¹⁸ and one here and another there, hurled
down half-dead,
made known why they were dying,
¹⁹ for the dreams that disturbed them
forewarned them of this,
so that they might not perish without
knowing why they suffered.
²⁰ The experience of death touched also
the righteous,
and a plague came upon the multitude in
the desert,
but the wrath did not long continue.
²¹ For a blameless man was quick to act as
their champion;
he brought forward the shield of his
ministry,
prayer and propitiation by incense;
he withstood the anger and put an end to
the disaster,
showing that he was your servant.

u 18.9 Other ancient authorities read *dangers, the ancestors
already leading the songs of praise*   y 18.12 Gk *name*

to the entirety of the scriptural and interpretive traditions considered authoritative by the author.
18:5 *One child had been abandoned and rescued* is a reference to the rescue of the baby Moses
(Exod. 2:1–6). **18:15** *Your all-powerful word leaped from heaven . . . a stern warrior.* God's word, issued
from God's throne, is the source of divine punishment. **18:20** *Experience of death touched also the
righteous, and a plague came upon the multitude in the desert.* It is difficult to identify with certainty
the story being referred to here, though it appears to be linked to the sojourn in the wilderness (e.g.,
Num. 16:41–50). **18:21** *A blameless man was quick to act* is a possible reference to Aaron, brother of
Moses, and his interventions (cf. Num. 16:47–50).

22 He conquered the wrath[w] not by strength
of body,
not by force of arms,
but by his word he subdued the avenger,
appealing to the oaths and covenants
given to our ancestors.
23 For when the dead had already fallen on
one another in heaps,
he intervened and held back the assault
and cut off its way to the living.
24 For on his long robe the whole world was
depicted,
and the glories of the ancestors were
engraved on the four rows of stones,
and your majesty was on the diadem
upon his head.
25 To these the destroyer yielded, these he[x]
feared,
for merely to test the wrath was enough.

19 But the ungodly were assailed to the
end by pitiless anger,
for God[y] knew in advance even their
future actions:
2 how, though they themselves had
permitted[z] your people to depart
and hastily sent them out,
they would change their minds and
pursue them.
3 For while they were still engaged in
mourning
and were lamenting at the graves of their
dead,
they reached another foolish decision
and pursued as fugitives those whom
they had begged and compelled to
leave.
4 For the fate they deserved drew them on
to this end
and made them forget what had happened,
in order that they might fill up the
punishment that their torments still
lacked
5 and that your people might experience[a]
an incredible journey,
but they themselves might meet a
strange death.
6 For the whole creation in its nature was
fashioned anew,
complying with your commands,
so that your children might be kept
unharmed.

7 The cloud was seen overshadowing the
camp
and dry land emerging where water had
stood before,
an unhindered way out of the Red Sea
and a grassy plain out of the raging
waves,
8 where those protected by your hand
passed through as one nation,
after gazing on marvelous wonders.
9 For they ranged like horses
and leaped like lambs,
praising you, O Lord, who delivered them.
10 For they still recalled the events of their
sojourn,
how instead of producing animals the
earth brought forth gnats,
and instead of fish the river spewed out
vast numbers of frogs.
11 Afterward they saw also a new kind of
bird,
when desire led them to ask for
luxurious food,
12 for, to give them relief, quails came up
from the sea.
13 The punishments did not come upon the
sinners
without prior signs in the violence of
thunder,
for they justly suffered because of their
wicked acts,
for they practiced a more bitter hatred of
strangers.
14 Others had refused to receive strangers
when they came to them,
but these made slaves of guests who
were their benefactors.
15 And not only so, but while punishment
of some sort will come upon the
former
for having received strangers with
hostility,
16 the latter, having first received them
with festal celebrations,
afterward afflicted with terrible sufferings
those who had already shared the same
rights.

w 18.22 Cn: Gk *multitude*   x 18.25 Other ancient authorities
read *they*   y 19.1 Gk *he*   z 19.2 Other ancient authorities
read *had changed their minds to permit*   a 19.5 Other ancient
authorities read *accomplish*

19:1–21 Escape from Egypt, deliverance at the Red Sea, and the wilderness sojourn. The remarkable journey from Egypt is creatively retold, with emphasis placed on the divine favor enjoyed by
the faithful. **19:5** The author acknowledges that this is *an incredible journey*—one resulting in life

17 They were stricken also with loss of
    sight—
just as were those at the door of the
    righteous man—
when, surrounded by yawning darkness,
all of them tried to find the way through
    their own doors.
18 For the elements changed[b] places with
    one another,
as on a harp the notes vary the nature of
    the rhythm,
while each note remains the same.[c]
This may be clearly inferred from the
    sight of what took place.
19 For land animals were transformed into
    water creatures,
and creatures that swim moved over to
    the land.

20 Fire even in water retained its normal
    power,
and water forgot its fire-quenching
    nature.
21 Flames, on the contrary, failed to
    consume
the flesh of perishable creatures that
    walked among them,
nor did they melt[d] the crystalline,
    quick-melting kind of heavenly
    food.
22 For in everything, O Lord, you have
    exalted and glorified your people,
and you have not neglected to help
    them at all times and in all places.

b 19.18 Gk *changing*   c 19.18 Meaning of Gk uncertain
d 19.21 Cn: Gk *nor could be melted*

for themselves and death for their tormentors. **19:17** *They were stricken also with loss of sight—just as were those at the door of the righteous man.* The episode at Sodom (Gen. 19:11) in which angels blinded those seeking to assail Lot's guests is used here as a reference to the blindness visited upon those in Egypt who oppressed the faithful during their sojourn there.

19:22 Concluding doxology. The author concludes with a hopeful message for those living in Diaspora then and now: the Lord remembers and supports the faithful. In this context, words like *exalted* and *glorified* denote material support required to endure challenging circumstances. The reference made to God's support *at all times and in all places* would have had particular poignance for those experiencing the social and psychological disorientation that typifies life as an outsider. This final word rings true for those absent places to call home, ostracized, or on the move across time and space.

ECCLESIASTICUS, OR THE WISDOM OF JESUS SON OF SIRACH

Author and Date

Originally written in Hebrew, the book called Ecclesiasticus in Christian Bibles is an ancient Jewish compilation of teachings and prayers compiled in the name of a scribe who lived and taught in the land of Israel in the second century BCE, commonly called Ben Sira (i.e., the Heb. equivalent of the Gk. "son of Sirach"). At the end of the book, which is also called "Sirach," the author identifies himself by name, and he describes his aim as providing "instruction in understanding and knowledge" that leads to wisdom, "fear of the Lord," and prosperity (50:27–51:29). He reveals himself to be a head of a "house of instruction" in Jerusalem (51:23). References within the book point to its initial composition after the death of the high priest Simon II (219–196 BCE) but before the Maccabean Revolt (167–164 BCE). Scholars typically date it to 180 BCE.

Historical Context

Ben Sira presents himself as a traditionalist, but his work is highly innovative. Like other Hellenistic-era Jewish sources, the work repackages Israel's ancestral traditions for an era marked by the growing prominence of Greek *paideia* (i.e., elite literate education) among even non-Greek elites in Ptolemaic, Seleucid, and other empires. See **"The Bible in Its Ancient Contexts," pp. 2150–52** for more on Hellenism. To the totalizing claims made for Greek knowledge in Hellenistic empires, Ben Sira offers a Jewish *paideia* that answers the same questions but claims a unique connection to God as the creator. Similar concerns are expressed in Jewish apocalypses of the third and second centuries BCE, such as Daniel, the Book of the Watchers (1 En. 1–36), and the Epistle of Enoch (1 En. 91–107). Ben Sira shares their celebration of professional scribes as custodians of Israel's ancestral wisdom, experts in cosmology, and recipients of divine knowledge. Yet he expresses caution about dream visions and hidden knowledge. Only passing allusion is made to angels and the end times. His work is not just for other scribes but also for others who need their counsel.

Audience and Aims

Sirach is aimed toward a narrow audience: Jewish men of moderate means, neither poor nor powerful. It is to this audience that Ben Sira offers practical advice on topics like wealth, health, gift-giving, loans, and banquets. Caution and moderation are counseled throughout. Many of his teachings presume an orderly arithmetic of reciprocity both among people and with God. Unlike Ecclesiastes, Ben Sira does not present the prosperity of the wicked as beyond human understanding. Unlike Daniel, he does not forestall the vindication of the righteous to the end times. Like the Greek *paideia* of the time, his instruction is for men and excludes women. He outlines an ideal of Jewish masculinity characterized by sense-based discernment, an ethics of caution, and the regulation of emotions. One discerns the character of others through one's eyes and ears. One must be cautious with one's tongue and mouth. Proper speech is a special concern throughout Sirach.

Literary Structure and Textual Witnesses

Like much Hellenistic literature, Sirach circulates under the name of an author. It may be the oldest known Hebrew text to do so. In form, however, it is a compilation of sayings, poems, and prayers loosely structured around themes. Partly as a result, materials continued to be added and shifted during its transmission, both in Hebrew and in Greek. The main form in which we know the text is the Greek translation, which the Prologue dates to 132 BCE and which came to be transmitted primarily by Christians. Parts of the Hebrew are preserved in ancient manuscripts from the Dead Sea Scrolls and Masada as well as in medieval Jewish manuscripts from Cairo Genizahs. Like the Greek manuscript tradition, Hebrew witnesses exhibit significant variance.

Significance and Reception

In scholarship on ancient Judaism, Sirach is most famous for its references to the law, command-ments, and Israel's ancestors. These references are often read as evidence for an early stage in the development of what came to be the Tanakh / Old Testament. Some concern with Scripture is evident in the translator's Prologue. Ben Sira's work, however, exhibits surprisingly little concern for scripturality. If anything, it is a window onto a precanonical vision of Jewish learning. Even despite the elevation of the scribe, and the likelihood that the author himself was a scribe, his focus falls on oral teaching and proper behavior. Learning is not framed in terms of scriptural interpretation but rather in terms of listening to experts, observing the cosmos, practicing commandments, praying to God, and culling Israel's past for great men to emulate. In Greek versions transmitted by Chris-tians, the Prologue reframes Ben Sira's concerns with a focus on books and reading. Its Jewish transmission in Hebrew, however, was marked by its atomization into sayings and its mining for liturgical materials. Not only are Hebrew manuscripts preserved in Cairo Genizahs, but Sirach is the only work in the deuterocanonical/apocryphal books quoted in the Babylonian Talmud and other rabbinic literature. The book opens a window into everyday life in Jerusalem in the second century BCE while also pointing to those elements of Second Temple Judaism that continued to resonate in both Judaism and Christianity.

Reading Guide

Most of Sirach is taken up with practical advice about social and economic interactions, focusing on everyday situations and experiences. Topics range from proper comportment when walking, to caution when taking out a loan, to the etiquette of attending a banquet. Sirach extends the Isra-elite Wisdom traditions best known from Proverbs, Job, and Ecclesiastes. It also bears the marks of the Hellenistic period. During the author's lifetime, the land of Israel passed from the control of the Ptolemies to the Seleucids (ca. 200–198 BCE). If there is a response to Hellenism, however, it is subtle rather than combative. The Hellenistic period saw the intensification of local claims among Greeks and non-Greeks alike. Ben Sira offers a poignant Jerusalemite example. He celebrates the cosmic power of Israel's God and wisdom. Yet he insists on their special connection to the people of Israel and the city of Jerusalem. He lavishes attention on the Jerusalem temple and the high priest. Even as he lauds God's wisdom as accessible through observed cycles of creation, he argues for its localization in the temple, law, commandments, and ancestors of Israel.

Liane M. Feldman and Annette Yoshiko Reed

THE PROLOGUE

1 Many great teachings have been given to us through the Law and the Prophets [2]and the others[a] that followed them, [3]and for these we should praise Israel for instruction and wisdom. [4]Now those who read them must not only themselves understand them [5]but must also as lovers of learning be able through [6]both speaking and writing to help

a P.2 Or *other books*

P:1–36 Prologue. The Prologue is not by the author of the rest of Sirach (i.e., Ben Sira). Rather, it was written by the translator of the text from Hebrew into Greek. He does not give his name, but he refers to Ben Sira as his "grandfather" (v. 7). Likely written in Alexandria around 132 BCE, the Pro-logue speaks to the early reception of Ben Sira's instruction outside of the land of Israel. Almost fifty years later, the translator has a different notion of what "instruction and wisdom" entail. Whereas Ben Sira celebrates wisdom's localization in Jerusalem and the land of Israel, his grandson focuses on Israel's literary heritage. There are more references to "books" in the Prologue than in the rest of the work combined. But there is not a single reference to "fear of the Lord," a major theme in the rest of the book (see 50:29 and notes on 1:11–20; 21:11–22:2; 23:27). Different cultural contexts may help account for this difference: Ben Sira lived in Jerusalem, while the translator wrote in Egypt, far from Jerusalem and within a Ptolemaic intellectual culture marked by an especially sharp concern for textuality. **P:1–3** *The Law and the Prophets and the others that followed them.* This list telegraphs the totality of Israel's literary heritage. The first two elements find some parallel in the Dead Sea Scrolls and New Testament (Matt. 5:17; Luke 24:44). The third element, *the others*, is open-ended (cf. vv. 8–10, 24–25). The threefold structure presages the much later anthologizing of Jewish Scriptures

the outsiders. [7]So my grandfather Jesus, who had devoted himself especially [8]to the reading of the Law [9]and the Prophets [10]and the other books of our ancestors [11]and had acquired considerable proficiency in them, [12]was himself also led to write something pertaining to instruction and wisdom, [13]so that by becoming familiar also with his book[b] those who love learning [14]might make even greater progress in living according to the law.

15 You are invited, therefore, [17]to read it [16]with goodwill and attention [18]and to be indulgent [19]in cases where we may seem [20]to have rendered some phrases imperfectly, despite our diligent labor in translating. [21-22]For what was originally expressed in Hebrew does not have exactly the same effect when translated into another language. [23]Not only this book, [24]but even the Law itself, the Prophets,[c] [25]and the rest of the books [26]differ not a little when read in the original.

27 In the thirty-eighth year of the reign of Euergetes, [28]when I came to Egypt and stayed for some time, [29]I found a copy affording[d] no little instruction. [30]It seemed highly necessary that I should myself devote some diligence and labor to the translation of this book. [31-32]During that time I have applied my skill day and night [33]to complete and publish the book [34]for those living abroad who wish to gain learning and are [35]preparing [36]to live according to the law.

1

All wisdom is from the Lord,
  and with him it remains forever.
[2] The sand of the sea, the drops of rain,
  and the days of eternity—who can
    count them?
[3] The height of heaven, the breadth of the
    earth,
  the abyss, and wisdom[e]—who can
    search them out?
[4] Wisdom was created before all things
  and prudent understanding from
    eternity.[f]
[6] The root of wisdom—to whom has it
    been revealed?
  Her subtleties—who knows them?[g]

b P.13 Gk *with these things* c P.24 Gk *prophecies*
d P.29 Other ancient authorities read *found opportunity for* e 1.3 Other ancient authorities read *the depth of the abyss* f 1.4 Other ancient authorities add as 1.5: *The source of wisdom is God's word in the highest heaven, and her ways are the eternal commandments.* g 1.6 Other ancient authorities add as 1.7: *The knowledge of wisdom—to whom was it manifested? And her abundant experience—who has understood it?*

into a tripartite compilation (i.e., Tanakh = Torah, Nevi'im, Ketuvim; cf. b. Baba Batra 16a). It stands in contrast, however, to the much broader description of the scope of Jewish scribal knowledge in the rest of the book (see especially chaps. 39 and 51). **P:7-10** *Reading . . . books of our ancestors.* The translator depicts Ben Sira's wisdom as rooted in *reading* and *books,* in contrast to Ben Sira's own emphasis on what one sees, hears, learns, and speaks, together with the power of prayer (another topic wholly unmentioned in the Prologue). Contrast Ben Sira's view of "law," which is not yet bookish. **P:12-14** The translator frames Ben Sira's writing as a response to his reading. Contrast Ben Sira's autobiographical comments in chap. 51. **P:21-22** This passage speaks poignantly to the challenges of translation. The translator knows of the translation of other Jewish Scriptures into Greek, a process attested for the Torah/Pentateuch in the Letter of Aristeas. **P:27** *Thirty-eighth year of the reign of Euergetes.* The translator does not hesitate to use a non-Jewish imperial system of dating. This reference to a known Ptolemaic king points to his Egyptian setting and allows us to date the Prologue and translation with unusual precision (ca. 132 BCE). **P:34** *Living abroad.* In contrast to the Hebrew, the Greek translation is meant for Jews living outside the land of Israel (see **"Diaspora," p. 1338**). **P:35-36** *Live according to the law.* To a much greater degree than Ben Sira's own book, the translator's Prologue identifies wisdom with *law.* For Ben Sira, by contrast, "law" is only one element in his localization of wisdom as an inheritance of Israel; he also, for instance, identifies wisdom with the Jerusalem temple (e.g., 14:24-27; 24:10; 51:14).

1:1-10 Wisdom. Ben Sira's own work begins with the first of a series of poems on seeking and finding wisdom (see 14:20-15:10; 24; 38:24-39:11; cf. Prov. 8; Bar. 3:9-4:4). Wisdom is introduced as the totality of knowledge. Its fullness is beyond human understanding, but it is nevertheless described in numerical terms, as measured by God. Numerical language—"count," "height," "breadth," "measure"— suggests the positive valuation of mathematical reasoning in the construction of knowledge, reminiscent of Greek "paideia." **1:3** Human beings are here invited to seek out wisdom alongside and within the physical world. **1:4** The association of wisdom and cosmology is developed in 16:24-18:14 and 42:15-43:33 (see **"Wisdom and Creation," p. 1412**). **1:6** Behind the Greek term *subtleties* is likely

⁸ There is but one who is wise, greatly to
   be feared,
   seated upon his throne: the Lord.
⁹ It is he who created her;
   he saw her and took her measure;
   he poured her out upon all his works,
¹⁰ upon all the living according to his gift;
   he lavished her upon those who love
   him.ᵇ
¹¹ The fear of the Lord is glory and exultation
   and gladness and a crown of rejoicing.
¹² The fear of the Lord delights the heart
   and gives gladness and joy and long
   life.ⁱ
¹³ Those who fear the Lord will have a
   happy end;
   on the day of their death they will be
   blessed.

¹⁴ To fear the Lord is the beginning of
   wisdom;
   she is created with the faithful in the
   womb.
¹⁵ She madeʲ among humans an eternal
   foundation,
   and among their descendants she will
   abide faithfully.
¹⁶ To fear the Lord is fullness of wisdom;
   she inebriates mortals with her fruits;
¹⁷ she fills theirᵏ whole house with
   desirable goods
   and theirˡ storehouses with her produce.
¹⁸ The fear of the Lord is the crown of wisdom,
   making peace and perfect health to
   flourish.ᵐ

¹⁹ She rained down knowledge and
   discerning comprehension,
   and she heightened the glory of those
   who held her fast.
²⁰ To fear the Lord is the root of wisdom,
   and her branches are long life.ⁿ

²² Unjust anger cannot be justified,
   for anger tips the scale to one's ruin.
²³ Those who are patient stay calm until the
   right moment,
   and then cheerfulness comes back to
   them.
²⁴ They hold back their words until the
   right moment,
   and then the lips of many tell of their
   good sense.

²⁵ In the treasuries of wisdom is insightful
   analogy,
   but godliness is an abomination to a
   sinner.
²⁶ If you desire wisdom, keep the
   commandments,
   and the Lord will lavish her upon
   you.

b 1.10 Other ancient authorities add *Love of the Lord is glorious wisdom; to those to whom he appears he apportions her, that they may see him.*   *i* 1.12 Other ancient authorities add *The fear of the Lord is a gift from the Lord; also for love he makes firm paths.*   *j* 1.15 Gk *made as a nest*   *k* 1.17 Other ancient authorities read *her*   *l* 1.17 Other ancient authorities read *her*   *m* 1.18 Other ancient authorities add *Both are gifts of God for peace; exultation opens out for those who love him. He saw her and took her measure.*   *n* 1.20 Other ancient authorities add as 1.21: *The fear of the Lord drives away sins, and where it abides, it will turn away all anger.*

the Hebrew term "moftim," "great deeds." **1:9–10** The language of pouring out combined with *gift* evokes sacrificial offerings. Interestingly, the dynamics are inverted here: God makes the offering to *those who love him*. The use of *love* is likely here covenantal language. On wisdom as God's creation, compare Prov. 8:22–31 and Wis. 9:9.

1:11–20 Fear of the Lord. As in Prov. 1:7, wisdom is equated with *fear of the Lord* (also 19:20; 21:11; cf. 25:10–11). The question of what this entails is a recurrent concern (e.g., 1:27–30; 2:7–10, 15–18; 9:16; 10:22, 24; 15:1; 16:2; 19:20; 21:11; 23:27; 25:6, 10–11; 27:3; 33:1; 40:26–27; 50:29). Here, it is explored through imagery associating wisdom with kingship and nature, both of which are characterized with fullness and excess. **1:11** The imagery of *glory and exultation* echoes the description of high-priestly garments in Exod. 28. *Crown of rejoicing* is royal imagery (also v. 18). **1:16** *Inebriates.* Wisdom is likened to a mind-altering substance, again with language of excess. **1:17** Wisdom is likened to agricultural crops necessary for physical survival. **1:18** Along with guaranteeing health, *making peace* is a hallmark of the ideal king. **1:20** Wisdom and long life are here the visible elements of the metaphor of a tree; fear of the Lord is what sustains both below the surface.

1:22–27 Reciprocity. Advice about social reciprocity is paired with advice about divine reciprocity. **1:22–24** Patience is necessary in choosing one's moment and not reacting impulsively. **1:22** The imagery of *the scale* evokes the public square and economic transactions as well as interpersonal relationships. **1:25** Further economic imagery is used in relation to wisdom. **1:26** A reciprocal covenantal payoff: if one keeps the commandments, God will reward that person with an

27 For the fear of the Lord is wisdom and
   discipline;
   fidelity and humility are his delight.

28 Do not disobey the fear of the Lord;
   do not approach him with a divided
   mind.
29 Do not be a hypocrite before others,
   and keep watch over your lips.
30 Do not exalt yourself, or you may fall
   and bring dishonor upon yourself.
   The Lord will reveal your secrets
   and overthrow you before the whole
   congregation,
   because you did not come in the fear of
   the Lord,
   and your heart was full of deceit.

2 My child, when you come to serve the
   Lord,
   prepare yourself for testing.*o*
2 Set your heart right and be steadfast,
   and do not be impetuous in time of
   calamity.
3 Cling to him and do not depart,
   so that your last days may be prosperous.
4 Accept whatever befalls you,
   and in times of humiliation be patient.
5 For gold is tested in the fire,
   and those found acceptable, in the
   furnace of humiliation.*p*

6 Trust in him, and he will help you;
   make your ways straight and hope in
   him.

7 You who fear the Lord, wait for his mercy;
   do not stray, or else you may fall.
8 You who fear the Lord, trust in him,
   and your reward will not be lost.
9 You who fear the Lord, hope for good
   things,
   for lasting joy and mercy.*q*
10 Consider the generations of old and see:
   Has anyone trusted in the Lord and
   been disappointed?
   Or has anyone persevered in the fear of
   the Lord*r* and been forsaken?
   Or has anyone called upon him and
   been neglected?
11 For the Lord is compassionate and
   merciful;
   he forgives sins and saves in time of
   distress.

12 Woe to timid hearts and to slack hands
   and to the sinner who walks a double
   path!

o 2.1 Or *trials*   *p* 2.5 Other ancient authorities add *in
sickness and poverty put your trust in him*   *q* 2.9 Other ancient
authorities add *for his reward is an everlasting gift with joy*
r 2.10 Gk *of him*

excess of wisdom. **1:27** The Greek word translated here and elsewhere as *discipline* or "education"
is "paideia"—the technical term for those forms of Greek literate education that were central to
shaping elite manhood under the Hellenistic empires of Ben Sira's time (and later under the Roman
Empire as well). The Hebrew equivalent, attested for 21:19, is "musar."

1:28–30 Admonishments against disobedience. 1:30 *Reveal your secrets.* Compare 1:6, where
wisdom is characterized in terms of being revealed. Here the motif is reversed: if one disobeys, the
threat is that God will reveal something that one may want to keep hidden, resulting in public shame
and communal dishonor.

2:1–6 Restraint. This section is marked by the theme of God testing people, not only for their
loyalty or faithfulness, but also for their ability to behave rightly and with self-restraint. **2:1** *My child.*
Israelite and other instruction literature often uses the framing device of a father speaking to his
sons (e.g., Prov. 1:8, 10, 15; 4:10). Ben Sira similarly addresses the reader as "my child" in 3:12; 3:17;
4:1; 6:18; 6:32; 10:28; 11:10; 14:11; 18:15; 21:1; 31:22; 37:27; 38:9; 38:16; 40:28. **2:2** *Do not be impetuous.*
Thoughtful and restrained action is advocated even in the face of disaster. **2:4** *Be patient.* Even the
possibility of public shame is no reason for impulsive behavior. **2:5** This image of passing through
fire and being *found acceptable* has resonances of sacrificial offerings, which were burned to be
accepted by God. The Israelites' time in Egypt is likened to a *furnace* that they passed through in
order to become God's people (Deut. 4:20; cf. Wis. 3:6). **2:6** *Make your ways straight and hope in
him.* Other manuscripts read "hope in him and he will make your ways straight," implying causality
between hoping and receiving assistance from God.

2:10 *Consider the generations of old.* This verse introduces the past as a source of didactic examples, a theme most fully realized in chaps. 44–49.

2:12–14 Woes. With the common prophetic formula, *woe to . . . ,* Ben Sira adopts the voice of a
prophet as well as a teacher (cf. 24:33). **2:12** *A double path.* The problem is not halfheartedness but

¹³ Woe to the fainthearted who have no
trust!
  Therefore they will have no shelter.
¹⁴ Woe to you who have lost patience!
  What will you do when the Lord's
    reckoning comes?

¹⁵ Those who fear the Lord will not disobey
    his words,
  and those who love him will keep his
    ways.
¹⁶ Those who fear the Lord will seek his
    favor,
  and those who love him will be filled
    with his law.
¹⁷ Those who fear the Lord will prepare
    their hearts
  and will humble themselves before
    him.
¹⁸ Let us fall into the hands of the Lord
  but not into the hands of mortals,
  for equal to his majesty is his mercy.ˢ

3 Listen to me your father, O children;
  act accordingly, that you may be safe.
² For the Lord honors a father above his
    children,
  and he confirms a mother's judgment
    over her sons.

³ Those who honor their father atone for
    sins,
⁴   and those who respect their mother
    are like those who lay up treasure.
⁵ Those who honor their father will have
    joy in their children,
  and when they pray they will be
    heard.
⁶ Those who respect their father will have
    long life,
  and those who honorᵗ their mother
    obey the Lord;ᵘ
⁷   they will serve their parents as their
    masters.ᵛ
⁸ Honor your father by word and deed,
  that his blessing may come upon you.
⁹ For a father's blessing strengthens the
    houses of the children,
  but a mother's curse uproots their
    foundations.
¹⁰ Do not glorify yourself by your father's
    dishonor,
  for your father's dishonor is no glory
    to you.

s 2.18 Syr adds *and equal to his name are his works* *t* 3.6 Heb:
Other ancient authorities read *comfort* *u* 3.6 Heb: Gk
and those who obey the Lord honor their mother *v* 3.7 In other
ancient authorities this line is preceded by *Those who fear
the Lord honor their father,*

rather trying to go in two directions at once; later, Ben Sira similarly critiques those who are "double-tongued" (e.g., 5:14; 6:1).

2:15–18 Fear of the Lord. As a point of contrast with the preceding "woes," this section returns to the pattern of repetition in 1:11–20, expounding wisdom by describing *those who fear the Lord*. On this major theme, see also notes on 21:11–22:2; 23:27. **2:16** *Filled with his law;* that is, filled to overflowing. This verse is the first mention of *law* in the book itself (i.e., in contrast to the Prologue). Whereas the Prologue describes *law* as written and read, it is here a broader category, not centered on books—in this case, it is what is given as a reward for loyalty. See notes on 15:1; 21:11; 24:23; 32:14–33:15. **2:17–18** *Humble themselves . . . fall into the hands.* This is a variation of the common biblical formula of humbling oneself and falling on one's face in worship (1 Chr. 21:13; cf. 1 En. 14). Anthropomorphizing language is used for God.

3:1–16 Parents. Unlike the Pentateuchal commandment to honor one's father and mother (Exod. 20:12; Deut. 5:16), this poem prioritizes honoring the father. This is consistent with Ben Sira's treatment of women as inferior to men. **3:1** *Listen to me your father.* As in 2:1, Ben Sira casts himself in the role of a father, passing on wisdom to his progeny (cf. 3:1; 6:23; 16:24; 23:7). It is a common sapiential trope to address the reader like a father. In the Second Temple period, in particular, this trope may have taken on further significance due to the proliferation of testamentary texts and traditions that claim to record the deathbed teachings that figures from Israel's past passed along to their children (e.g., Enoch to Methuselah in 1 En.; Amram to Moses and Aaron in Visions of Amram, etc.). In this poem, it is especially fitting since the topic is proper behavior toward one's parents. **3:2** Honoring and respecting one's parents is an act of "imitatio Dei," imitating God. **3:3–4** Here, Ben Sira begins to construct a credit theology, wherein people incur debts through their sins but can also store up credits for the future. *Atone for sins.* Honoring one's father is a necessary act in order to maintain a relationship with God. *Lay up treasure.* Respecting one's mother is not essential but adds to one's heavenly "credit." **3:8–11** Ben Sira consistently presents honoring the father as generating "joy," *blessing,* and prosperity, while framing references to the mother in terms of what happens if she

[11] The honor of one's father is one's own
glory,
and a mother dishonored is a disgrace
to her children.

[12] My child, help your father in his old age,
and do not grieve him as long as he
lives;

[13] even if his mind fails, be patient with him;
do not despise him because you have
all your faculties.

[14] For kindness to a father will not be
forgotten
and will be credited to you against
your sins;

[15] in the day of your distress it will be
remembered in your favor;
like frost in fair weather, your sins will
melt away.

[16] Whoever forsakes a father is like a
blasphemer,
and whoever angers a mother is
cursed by the Lord.

[17] My child, perform your tasks with
humility;
then you will be loved more than a
giver of gifts.[w]

[18] The greater you are, the more you must
humble yourself;
so you will find favor in the sight of
the Lord.[x]

[20] For great is the might of the Lord,
but by the humble he is glorified.

[21] Neither seek what is too difficult for you
nor investigate what is beyond your
power.

[22] Reflect upon what you have been
commanded,
for what is hidden is not your concern.

[23] In matters greater than your own affairs,
do not meddle,
for things beyond human
understanding have been shown
you.

[24] For their conceit has led many astray,
and wrong opinion has impaired their
judgment.

[25] Without eyes there is no light;
without knowledge there is no
wisdom.[y]

[26] A stubborn mind will fare badly at the end,
and whoever loves danger will perish
in it.

[27] A stubborn mind will be burdened by
troubles,
and the sinner adds sin to sins.

[28] When calamity befalls the proud, there
is no healing,
for an evil plant has taken root in him.

[29] The mind of the intelligent appreciates
proverbs,

w 3.17 Heb Syr: Gk *more than an acceptable person*
x 3.18 Other ancient authorities add as 3.19, *Many are
lofty and renowned, but to the humble he reveals his secrets.*
y 3.25 Heb: Other ancient authorities lack 3.25

is disrespected—namely, cursing and disgrace. **3:12–13** The instruction to honor one's father is not predicated on his continued wisdom. **3:14** *Be forgotten.* Some manuscripts have the imagery of "blotting out," evoking the physical act of removing ink from parchment. *Credited to you.* Here we find an explicit expression of Ben Sira's credit theology: he positions God as keeping a divine ledger for each individual.

3:17–29 Humility. This poem explores *humility* with a focus on knowledge. **3:21** For *what is beyond your power*, some manuscripts read "what is concealed from you," suggesting that not all knowledge is available or accessible to everyone. In most of the book, the rhetoric of hiddenness pertains to human secrets kept—or not kept—among friends (e.g., 8:17–19; 13:12; 19:4–17; 22:22; 27:16–21); here, this rhetoric is used in relation to divine secrets. Jewish apocalypses of the time claim to reveal divine or heavenly secrets about the cosmos and the end of time; Ben Sira may answer and attenuate such claims. In stark contrast to the Book of the Watchers (1 En. 1–36) and other early material in 1 Enoch, for instance, Ben Sira expresses a concern for human overreaching more akin to Job 28. **3:22** The verb in the phrase *what you have been commanded* can also be translated as "permitted." These verses reflect on the different forms of knowledge and the proper limitations to knowledge-seeking. This and the preceding verse are quoted to make a similar point in the Talmud and other rabbinic sources (y. Hagigah 2:1/77c; b. Hagigah 13a; Genesis Rabbah 8:2). **3:25** *Without eyes.* The metaphor is a reminder that the acquisition of knowledge is an embodied practice reliant on multiple senses. **3:26–27** For *stubborn mind*, some manuscripts read "hardened heart," evoking Pharaoh in the story of the exodus (Exod. 7:14; 8:32). Contrast "mind of the intelligent" in v. 29. **3:29** *Attentive ear.* Bodily language underscores the connection between listening and wisdom.

and an attentive ear is the desire of
the wise.
30 As water extinguishes a blazing fire,
so almsgiving atones for sin.
31 Those who repay favors give thought to
the future;
when they fall they will find support.

4 My child, do not cheat the poor of their
living,
and do not keep needy eyes waiting.
2 Do not grieve the hungry
or anger one in need.
3 Do not add to the troubles of the angry
or delay giving to the needy.
4 Do not reject a suppliant in distress
or turn your face away from the poor.
5 Do not avert your eye from the needy,
and give no one reason to curse
you,
6 for if in bitterness of soul some should
curse you,
their Creator will hear their prayer.

7 Endear yourself to the congregation;
bow your head low to the great.
8 Give a hearing to the poor,
and return their greeting kindly.
9 Rescue the oppressed from the
oppressor,
and do not be hesitant in giving a
verdict.

10 Be a father to orphans,
and be like a husband to their mother;
you will then be like a son of the Most
High,
and he will love you more than does
your mother.
11 Wisdom teaches[z] her children
and takes hold of those who seek her.
12 Whoever loves her loves life,
and those who seek her from early
morning will be filled with joy.
13 Whoever holds her fast inherits glory,
and the Lord blesses the place she[a]
enters.
14 Those who serve her minister to the Holy
One;
the Lord loves those who love her.
15 Whoever obeys her will judge the nations,
and whoever listens to her will live
securely.
16 If they remain faithful, they will inherit
her;
their descendants will also obtain her.
17 For at first she will walk with them in
disguise;
she will bring fear and dread upon
them
and will torment them by her discipline
until she trusts them,[b]

z 4.11 Heb Syr: Gk *exalts*   a 4.13 Or *he*   b 4.17 Or *until they remain faithful in their heart*

3:30–4:10 The poor. This poem focuses on one's duties toward the poor. Cf. Tob. 4:7–11; Epistle of Enoch (1 En. 91–107). **3:30** The Hebrew for *almsgiving* is "tzedakah," which can connote right behavior as well as almsgiving. Note the sacrificial language *atones for sin*, here used apart from the offering of sacrifices. *Almsgiving*, like honoring one's father, can atone for sin. **4:1–10** The oppressed are sorted into four categories: widows, orphans, foreigners, and the poor. Cf. 35:16–19; Exod. 22:21–22; Deut. 14:29; 24:17–22; Jer. 7:6; 22:3; Ezek. 22:7; Ps. 146:9; Tob. 1:3, 8. **4:1** *Needy eyes.* Although eyes can be likened to knowledge, they also express physical needs. **4:2–4** The language used in this section evokes a credit/debt model. In this case, the tally concerns the troubles of the oppressed and the duty to lessen that number. The language *turn your face away* is often used to describe God's display of displeasure or disfavor to the people. Some Hebrew manuscripts read "do not despise the requests of the poor." **4:5** *Avert your eye.* Seeing is knowing. The injunction is not to ignore what becomes known to you. **4:8** *Give a hearing.* Hearing, like seeing, is again presented as behavior that leads to right action. **4:10** *Be a father . . . more than does your mother.* This verse evokes the poem in 3:1–10 about honoring one's parents, again with different approaches to fathers and mothers.

4:11–19 Wisdom. Wisdom is personified as a female teacher (cf. chap. 24), with a focus on love of her and obedience to her (see **"Woman Wisdom," p. 872**). **4:11** For *takes hold of those who seek her*, some Hebrew manuscripts read "understand her." A reciprocal model requires an investment in order to receive help. **4:14** The verb translated as *minister* is typically used in ritual and temple contexts. **4:15** For *live securely*, some Hebrew manuscripts read "will settle in the chambers of the temple," suggesting physical proximity to God; cf. her "house" in Prov. 9:1. **4:17–18** The acquisition of Wisdom is presented as a difficult path. Compare the metaphor of paths and the persistent testing required to walk alongside Wisdom in Wis. 6:15–16. Here too, seekers of Wisdom must prove themselves worthy.

and she will test them with her
ordinances.
¹⁸ Then she will come straight back to them
again and gladden them
and will reveal her secrets to them.
¹⁹ If they go astray, she will forsake them
and hand them over to their ruin.

²⁰ Watch for the opportune time, and
beware of evil,
and do not be ashamed to be yourself.
²¹ For there is a shame that leads to sin,
and there is a shame that is glory and
favor.
²² Do not show partiality to your own harm
or deference to your downfall.
²³ Do not refrain from speaking at the
proper moment,ᶜ
and do not hide your wisdom.ᵈ
²⁴ For wisdom becomes known through
speech
and education through the words of
the tongue.
²⁵ Never speak against the truth,
but be ashamed of your ignorance.
²⁶ Do not be ashamed to confess your
sins,
and do not try to stop the current of
a river.
²⁷ Do not subject yourself to a fool
or show partiality to a ruler.
²⁸ Fight to the death for truth,
and the Lord God will fight for you.

²⁹ Do not be reckless in your speech
or sluggish and remiss in your deeds.
³⁰ Do not be like a lion in your home
or suspicious of your slaves.

³¹ Do not let your hand be stretched out to
receive
and closed when it is time to give back.
5 Do not rely on your wealth
or say, "I have enough."
² Do not follow your inclination and
strength
in pursuing the desires of your heart.
³ Do not say, "Who can have power over
me?"
for the Lord will surely punish you.

⁴ Do not say, "I sinned, yet what has
happened to me?"
for the Lord is slow to anger.
⁵ Do not be so confident of forgivenessᵉ
that you add sin to sins.
⁶ Do not say, "His mercy is great;
he will forgiveᶠ the multitude of my
sins,"
for both mercy and wrath are with him,
and his anger will rest on sinners.
⁷ Do not delay to turn back to the Lord,
and do not postpone it from day to day,
for suddenly the wrath of the Lord will
come forth,
and at the time of punishment you
will perish.
⁸ Do not rely on dishonest wealth,
for it will not benefit you on the day of
calamity.

⁹ Do not winnow in every wind
or follow every path.ᵍ

c 4.23 Heb: Gk *at a time of salvation*   d 4.23 Other ancient
authorities lack *and do not hide your wisdom*   e 5.5 Heb: Gk
atonement   f 5.6 Heb: Gk *he* (or *it*) *will atone for*   g 5.9 Gk
adds *so it is with the double-tongued sinner*

4:20–31 Proper behavior. This poem focuses on behavior, specifically with respect to speech. This is yet another case in which Ben Sira addresses concerns that are common within Greek "paideia" as well. **4:24** This verse presumes an oral context for the acquisition of knowledge; contrast the focus on reading in the translator's Prologue. **4:27–30** These verses emphasize restraint, both from speaking rashly or in anger and from procrastinating action.

5:1–9 Sin and punishment. This poem emphasizes the punishment of sins, especially in the case of arrogance that leads to sin. Each verse is a negative command (*Do not . . .*). **5:1** The presumption is that Ben Sira's audience has some measure of *wealth* that distinguishes them from "the poor" (cf. 4:1–10). **5:2** For *your inclination and strength*, some Hebrew manuscripts have "your heart and your eyes," again invoking the embodiment of knowledge. **5:3** Wealth does not grant unchecked *power*; God can and will *punish* the rich who sin. **5:4** Ben Sira here addresses the phenomena of sinners who are nonetheless prosperous, assuring the reader of the inevitability of punishment. Contrast Ecclesiastes, which laments how the wicked continue to prosper (Eccl. 7:15; 8:14). **5:5** *Forgiveness* of sins is not a given. While there is a divine ledger, God can choose not to follow it strictly. **5:7** *Do not delay.* Avoid procrastination when acting rightly (cf. 4:23). **5:9** *Winnow in every wind.* Not all paths are meant for Ben Sira's audience to follow in the pursuit of wisdom (cf. 3:23–24).

¹⁰ Stand firm in what you know,
  and let your speech be consistent.
¹¹ Be quick to hear,
  and utter a reply patiently.
¹² If you understand, answer your neighbor,
  but if not, put your hand over your
    mouth.

¹³ Honor and dishonor come from
    speaking,
  and the tongue of mortals may be
    their downfall.
¹⁴ Do not be called double-tongued[b]
  and do not lay traps with your tongue,
  for shame comes to the thief
  and severe condemnation to the
    double-tongued.
¹⁵ In great and small matters cause no
    harm,[i]

6 ¹and do not become an enemy instead
    of a friend,
  for a bad name incurs shame and
    reproach;
  so it is with the double-tongued
    sinner.

² Do not fall into the grip of passion,[j]
  or you may be torn apart as by a
    bull.[k]
³ Your leaves will be devoured and your
    fruit destroyed,
  and you will be left like a withered
    tree.
⁴ Strong passion[l] destroys those who
    have it
  and makes them the laughingstock of
    their enemies.

⁵ Pleasant speech multiplies friends,
  and a gracious tongue multiplies
    courtesies.
⁶ Let those who are at peace with you be
    many,
  but let your advisers be one in a
    thousand.
⁷ When you gain friends, gain them
    through testing,
  and do not trust them hastily.
⁸ For there are friends who are such when
    it suits them,
  but they will not stand by you in time
    of trouble.
⁹ And there are friends who turn to enmity
  and tell of the quarrel to your disgrace.
¹⁰ And there are friends who are
    companions at the table,
  but they will not stand by you in time
    of trouble.
¹¹ When you are prosperous, they become
    your second self
  and boldly command your slaves,
¹² but if you are brought low, they turn
    against you
  and hide themselves from you.
¹³ Keep away from your enemies,
  and be on guard with your friends.

¹⁴ Faithful friends are a sturdy shelter;
  whoever finds one has found a
    treasure.
¹⁵ Faithful friends are beyond price;
  no amount can balance their worth.

b 5.14 Heb: Gk *a slanderer* *i* 5.15 Heb Syr: Gk *be ignorant*
j 6.2 Heb: Meaning of Gk uncertain *k* 6.2 Meaning of Gk
uncertain *l* 6.4 Heb: Gk *An evil soul*

5:10–6:4 Speech. The poem shifts here to positive instructions, again with a focus on the power of speech. **5:14** *Double-tongued*—that is, slanderous and deceitful speech. This language picks up on the double path imagery in 2:12; just as the audience must choose one path and not follow them all, so they should be consistent (cf. 5:10) in their speech as well. **5:15–6:1** *A bad name.* A man's reputation is dependent on how one speaks of him. The concern here is for damaging one's reputation through deceitful speech (cf. 20:24). One's social status is tied to one's reputation. On one's reputation as what survives after death, see also 11:33. **6:2** *Torn apart as by a bull* is a vivid illustration of what kind of damage can happen in the absence of restraint.

6:5–17 Friendship. This poem warns about the dangers of false friends and highlights some of the risks of deceitful representations of people, tying it to the previous poem in 5:10–6:4. The themes of false friends and the difficulty in finding trustworthy friends are also found throughout Hellenistic literature. It is a recurrent concern in Sirach (9:10; 11:29–14:2; 22:19–26; 37:1–6). **6:6** A pleasant demeanor and speech should yield one many acquaintances, but the warning here is that most of those acquaintances will not be true friends. **6:7** *Through testing.* There is a parallel in Ben Sira's thought between the acquisition of wisdom and the acquisition of *friends*: both are to be gained slowly and are to be tested in the process (cf. 4:17–18). **6:10–12** This cluster of instructions ends with warnings against people who would befriend you only for what you can give them.

¹⁶ Faithful friends are life-saving medicine,
and those who fear the Lord will find
them.
¹⁷ Those who fear the Lord direct their
friendship aright,
for as they are, so are their neighbors
also.
¹⁸ My child, from your youth choose
discipline,
and when you have gray hair you will
find wisdom.
¹⁹ Come to her like one who plows and
sows,
and wait for her good harvest.
For when you cultivate her you will toil
but little,
and soon you will eat of her produce.
²⁰ She seems very harsh to the
undisciplined;
fools will not remain with her.
²¹ She will be like a heavy stone to test
them,
and they will not delay in casting her
aside.
²² For wisdom is like her name;
she is not readily perceived by many.

²³ Listen, my child, and accept my
judgment;
do not reject my counsel.
²⁴ Put your feet into her fetters
and your neck into her collar.
²⁵ Bend your shoulder and carry her,
and do not become angry with her
bonds.
²⁶ Come to her with all your soul,
and keep her ways with all your might.
²⁷ Search out and seek, and she will
become known to you,

and when you get hold of her, do not
let her go.
²⁸ For at last you will find her rest,
and she will be changed into joy for
you.
²⁹ Then her fetters will become for you a
strong defense,
and her collar a glorious robe.
³⁰ Her yoke*^m* is a golden ornament
and her bonds a purple cord.
³¹ You will wear her like a glorious robe
and put her on like a splendid crown.*ⁿ*

³² If you are willing, my child, you can be
disciplined,
and if you apply yourself you will
become clever.
³³ If you love to listen you will accept
discipline,
and if you pay attention you will
become wise.
³⁴ Stand in the company of the elders.
Who is wise? Attach yourself to such
a one.
³⁵ Be ready to listen to every godly
discourse,
and let no wise proverbs escape you.
³⁶ If you see an intelligent person, rise early
to visit him;
let your foot wear out his doorstep.
³⁷ Reflect on the statutes of the Lord,
and meditate at all times on his
commandments.
It is he who will give insight to*^o* your
mind,
and your desire for wisdom will be
granted.

*m 6.30 Heb: Gk Upon her   n 6.31 Heb: Gk crown of gladness
o 6.37 Heb: Gk will confirm*

6:18–37 Wisdom. Returning to the theme of wisdom, this poem reiterates the labor and discipline required to attain it. It uses agricultural imagery of sowing, toiling, and cultivating—metaphors commonly used in Greek literature to refer to education. **6:18–19** Patience and time are essential components of acquiring wisdom. **6:23–31** Two different social stations are contrasted in these two stanzas. In the first, the process of acquiring wisdom is likened to that of an enslaved person in *fetters*, a *collar*, and *bonds* (vv. 23–27). In the second, the acquisition of wisdom is likened to the garments of the high priest, one of the most powerful positions in society at this time (vv. 28–31; see **"Priests and Temple," p. 1479**). **6:30–31** *Glorious robe . . . splendid crown.* See 50:11 for these described as the garments of the high priest Simon II; also 45:7-12 for the description of Aaron's garments. **6:32–37** This stanza emphasizes the value and necessity of listening and paying attention in order to gain wisdom. It imagines a student in the context of many elders and teachers. **6:35** One should not pursue every path (cf. 2:12; 5:9) but rather *every godly* path. **6:37** *Meditate at all times on his commandments.* The acquisition of wisdom is a continual process that requires constant attention; for similar language, see Ps. 1:2. Ultimately it is God, not human teachers, who grants wisdom to an individual who seeks it.

7 Do no evil, and evil will never overtake
you.
[2] Stay away from wrong, and it will turn
away from you.
[3] Do[p] not sow in the furrows of injustice,
and you will not reap a sevenfold crop.

[4] Do not seek from the Lord high office
or the seat of honor from the king.
[5] Do not assert your righteousness before
the Lord
or display your wisdom before the king.
[6] Do not seek to become a judge,
or you may be unable to root out
injustice;
perhaps you will fear the powerful
and so mar your integrity.
[7] Commit no offense against the public,
and do not disgrace yourself among
the people.

[8] Do not commit a sin twice;
even for one you will not go
unpunished.
[9] Do not say, "He will consider the great
number of my gifts,
and when I make an offering to the
Most High God, he will accept it."
[10] Do not grow weary when you pray;
do not neglect to give alms.

[11] Do not ridicule a person who is
embittered in spirit,
for there is one who humbles and exalts.
[12] Do not devise[q] a lie against your brother
or do the same to a friend.
[13] Refuse to utter any lie,
for it is a habit that results in no good.
[14] Do not babble in the company of the
elders,
and do not repeat yourself when you
pray.
[15] Do not hate hard labor
or farm work, which was created by
the Most High.
[16] Do not enroll in the ranks of sinners;
remember that retribution will not
delay.
[17] Humble yourself to the utmost,
for the punishment of the ungodly is
fire and worms.[r]
[18] Do not exchange a friend for money
or a real brother for the gold of Ophir.
[19] Do not dismiss[s] a wise and good wife,
for her charm is worth more than gold.
[20] Do not abuse slaves who work faithfully
or hired laborers who give of themselves.

*p 7.3 Gk My child, do   q 7.12 Heb: Gk plow   r 7.17 Heb for
the expectation of mortals is worms   s 7.19 Heb: Gk deprive
yourself of*

7:1–9:12 Negative commands. What follows is a long series of negative commands, most of
which begin with the injunction *do not*. They do not follow a thematic or other structure but function to introduce key topics later explored in more detail. In addition, several themes emerge: the
need to avoid political offices of any kind (7:4–7), the need to avoid arrogance and laziness (7:5–17),
the importance of proper treatment of people of all social classes (7:18–8:19), and the challenge of
dealing with women (9:1–9). **7:3** *Do not sow.* Ben Sira returns to agricultural imagery, now applied
to interpersonal relationships rather than to the acquisition of wisdom. **7:4–5** These verses warn
against obtaining *high office* or seeking to impress a *king* with one's wisdom. Contrast the Letter of
Aristeas, also written in the second century BCE, wherein the translators spend days impressing the
Ptolemaic king with their wisdom. **7:6** *Or you may be unable to root out injustice.* There is a recognition that obtaining an official office may impede someone from acting justly because the powerful
are able to reward a judgment in their favor. **7:9** *He will consider the great number of my gifts.* The
text stresses again that wealth cannot buy favor with God, even as it can with earthly judges (cf. 5:1,
3). **7:10** *Do not grow weary.* The Hebrew verb here can also mean "do not shorten"—that is, warning
against laziness in prayer. **7:12–14** These verses pick up the theme of deceitful speech from 5:10–6:4,
adding the idea of babbling and repetitive speech to the list of unacceptable speech behaviors.
7:16 The assertion *retribution will not delay* seems to go against the idea in 5:4 that sometimes
punishment for sin is not immediate. **7:17** *Humble yourself . . . fire and worms.* This same aphorism is
attributed to R. Levitas of Yavneh in m. Avot 4:4. That version has *worms* but not *fire*. The surviving
Hebrew for this verse is the same. Whereas the Greek version seems to allude to an afterlife judgment, the Hebrew versions evoke death as decay. Compare also Jdt. 16:17, which has both fire and
worms on the day of judgment, possibly influenced by Hellenistic eschatologies.

7:18–8:19 Relations with others. The focus of these two stanzas is on the proper treatment of members
of one's immediate household, both human and animal. **7:20–21** *Do not abuse slaves.* The assumption

21 Let your soul love intelligent slaves;[t]
    do not withhold from them their
      freedom.

22 Do you have cattle? Look after them;
    if they are profitable to you, keep
      them.
23 Do you have children? Discipline them,
    and make them obedient[u] from their
      youth.
24 Do you have daughters? Be concerned
    for their chastity,[v]
  and do not show yourself too
    indulgent with them.[w]
25 Give a daughter in marriage, and you
    complete a great task,
  but give her to a sensible man.
26 Do you have a wife who pleases you?[x] Do
    not divorce her,
  but do not trust yourself to one whom
    you detest.

27 With all your heart honor your father,
    and do not forget the birth pangs of
      your mother.
28 Remember that it was of your parents[y]
    you were born;
  how will you repay what they have
    given to you?

29 With all your soul fear the Lord
    and revere his priests.
30 With all your might love your Maker,
    and do not neglect his ministers.
31 Fear the Lord and honor the priest,
    and give him his portion, as you have
      been commanded:
  the first fruits, the purification offering,
    the gift of the shoulders,
  the sacrifice of sanctification, and the
    first fruits of the holy things.

32 Stretch out your hand to the poor,
    so that your blessing may be complete.
33 Give graciously to all the living;
    do not withhold kindness even from
      the dead.
34 Do not lag behind those who weep,
    but mourn with those who mourn.
35 Do not hesitate to visit the sick,
    because for such deeds you will be
      loved.
36 In all you do, remember the end of your
    life,
  and then you will never sin.

8 Do not contend with the powerful,
    or you may fall into their hands.
2 Do not quarrel with the rich,
    in case their resources outweigh
      yours,
  for gold has ruined many
    and has perverted the minds of kings.
3 Do not argue with the loud of mouth,
    and do not heap wood on their fire.

4 Do not make fun of one who is
    uneducated,
  or your ancestors may be insulted.
5 Do not reproach one who is turning away
    from sin;
  remember that we all deserve
    punishment.
6 Do not disdain one who is old,
    for some of us are also growing old.
7 Do not rejoice over anyone's death;
    remember that we must all die.

8 Do not slight the discourse of the sages,
    but turn to their maxims,

t 7.21 Heb *Love a wise slave as yourself* u 7.23 Gk *bend their necks* v 7.24 Gk *body* w 7.24 Gk *do not brighten your face toward them* x 7.26 Heb Syr lack *who pleases you* y 7.28 Gk *them*

here is that Ben Sira's audience is from a social class that could purchase enslaved people and hired laborers. See further 33:25–33. **7:22** *Do you have cattle?* The fact that this is phrased as a question suggests that some but not all of the intended audience would have owned livestock. **7:23–26** The question format continues with respect to children, daughters, and a pleasing wife. Not all of these were a given; if one had them, they were to be valued. **7:29–31** Moving outside the home, the focus shifts to God, priests, and the proper offering of sacrifices to show them honor. **7:31** This list of sacrifices is eclectic and does not correspond to any known schema of sacrificial offerings. **8:1–19** The text turns to potentially harmful relationships with people in both higher and lower social classes. **8:1–2** The potential for great wealth or power to lead to corruption or downfall is a concern present here and elsewhere in literature of this period (e.g., Eccl. 5:11–13). **8:3** *Loud of mouth* in Hebrew is literally "a man of tongue"—referring to someone who is likely to spread gossip or speak deceitfully. The Greek verb here also has a connotation of slanderous speech. **8:4** *Ancestors* is in Hebrew "nobles." **8:5–7** There is a focus in these verses on what all people share despite differences in social class: sin, growing old, and death. **8:8–9** *Discourse of the*

because from them you will learn
discipline
and how to serve the great.
⁹ Do not ignore the discourse of the aged,
for they themselves learned from their
parents;ᶻ
from them you learn how to understand
and to give an answer when the need
arises.

¹⁰ Do not kindle the coals of sinners,
or you may be burnedᵃ in their flaming
fire.
¹¹ Do not let the insolent bring you to your
feet,
or they may lie in ambush against your
words.
¹² Do not lend to one who is stronger than
you,
but if you do lend anything, count it
as a loss.
¹³ Do not give surety beyond your means,
but if you give surety be prepared to
pay.

¹⁴ Do not go to law against a judge,
for the decision will favor him because
of his standing.
¹⁵ Do not travel on the road with the reckless,
or your troubles may become
burdensome,
for they will act as they please,
and through their folly you will perish
with them.

¹⁶ Do not pick a fight with the
quick-tempered,
and do not journey with them through
a deserted region,
because bloodshed means nothing to
them,
and where no help is at hand they will
strike you down.
¹⁷ Do not consult with fools,
for they cannot keep a secret.
¹⁸ In the presence of strangers do nothing
that is to be kept secret,
for you do not know what they will
divulge.ᵇ
¹⁹ Do not reveal your thoughts to anyone,
or you may drive away your
happiness.ᶜ

9 Do not be jealous of the wife whom you
embrace,
or you will teach her an evil lesson to
your own hurt.
² Do not give yourself to a woman
and let her trample down your
strength.
³ Do not go near a loose woman,ᵈ
or you may fall into her snares.
⁴ Do not dally with a female singer,
or you may be caught in her activities.
⁵ Do not look intently at a virgin,
or you may stumble and incur
penalties for her.

z 8.9 Or *ancestors*   a 8.10 Heb: Gk *do not get burned*
b 8.18 Or *it will bring forth*   c 8.19 Heb: Gk *and let him not
return a favor to you*   d 9.3 Heb *strange woman*

sages . . . discourse of the aged. In both cases, the focus is on the intergenerational transmission of knowledge (cf. Deut. 6:4–7; Prov. 4:1–4). **8:10** *Do not kindle.* There is here a reminder to exercise restraint in
speech lest one incite someone to further sin and become entangled in it oneself. **8:11** *Bring you to your
feet.* Bodily restraint is paired with the restraint of speech. **8:12–13** *Do not give surety.* Power dynamics
are here explored with respect to loans. Those with more power can refuse to pay back loans taken from
those beneath them in a social hierarchy, but one in a subservient position cannot refuse to pay back
loans taken from someone above them. See also 29:14–20. **8:17–19** These verses focus on the ability to
keep a secret or control speech; one should assume that everything said or done will be made public. On
secrets, see 13:12; 19:4–17; 22:22; 27:16–21. **8:19** *Drive away your happiness.* Being happy is closely tied to
maintaining one's privacy.

9:1–9 Women. Nearing the end of this long section of negative commands (*Do not . . .*), the focus
turns to women. Up to this point, Ben Sira has expressed some passing reservations about women.
This is his first extended discussion of women, and it is clear that he views them as dangerous. His
disdain for women goes beyond the caution expressed in Ecclesiastes, Proverbs, or the Wisdom of
Solomon; compare, however, 4Q184. **9:1** *Do not be jealous.* A man's jealousy of his wife can lead to
his own downfall. Contrast Num. 5:5–31, where the repercussions fall only on the wife. **9:2** *Do not
give yourself to a woman.* This verse serves as an introduction and summary of the prohibitions in
vv. 3–9. **9:3–9** Two different behaviors are prohibited in these verses: giving oneself to a woman
and looking at a woman. **9:3** *A loose woman* is in Hebrew "an unknown woman." **9:5** *Do not look.*
Looking leads to action. This is another instance of Ben Sira linking sight with the acquisition of

⁶ Do not give yourself to prostitutes,
  or you may lose your inheritance.
⁷ Do not look around in the streets of a
    city
  or wander about in its deserted
    sections.
⁸ Turn away your eyes from a shapely
    woman,
  and do not gaze at beauty belonging
    to another;
many have been seduced by a woman's
    beauty,
  and by it passion is kindled like a
    fire.
⁹ Never dine^e with another man's wife
  or revel with her at wine,
or your heart may turn aside to her,
  and in blood^f you may plunge into
    destruction.
¹⁰ Do not abandon old friends,
  for new ones cannot equal them.
A new friend is like new wine;
  when it has aged, you will drink it
    with pleasure.

¹¹ Do not envy the notoriety of
    sinners,
  for you do not know what their end
    will be like.
¹² Do not delight in what pleases the
    ungodly;^g
  remember that they will not be held
    guiltless until Hades.

¹³ Keep far from those who have power to
    kill,
  and you will not be haunted by the
    fear of death.
But if you approach them, make no
    misstep,
  or they may rob you of your life.
Know that you are stepping among
    snares
  and that you are walking on the city
    battlements.

¹⁴ As much as you can, aim to know your
    neighbors,
  and consult with the wise.
¹⁵ Let your conversation be with intelligent
    people,
  and let all your discussion be about
    the law of the Most High.
¹⁶ Let the righteous be your dinner
    companions,
  and let your boast be in the fear of the
    Lord.
¹⁷ A work is praised for the skill of the
    artisan,
  so a people's leader is proved wise by
    his words.
¹⁸ The loud of mouth are feared in their
    city,
  and the one who is reckless in speech
    is hated.

e 9.9 Heb: Gk *sit down*   f 9.9 Heb: Gk *by your spirit*
g 9.12 Gk: Heb *the success of the arrogant*

knowledge (in this case, illicit knowledge). **9:6** *Lose your inheritance.* One of the greatest threats of women, according to Ben Sira, is their capacity to lead men to financial ruin. Cf. Prov. 29:3. **9:8** Prolonged looking can lead a man to unrestrained action. *Kindled like a fire.* Ben Sira often uses fire metaphors when discussing sinful behavior (e.g., 8:3, 10). **9:9** The phrase *in blood* is only in the Hebrew and possibly refers to the death penalty for adultery (cf. Lev. 20:10; Deut. 22:22). The Greek has "by your spirit" here.

9:10–16 Friends. The focus shifts to which types of people one should associate with and how. The final set of negative commands (*Do not . . .*) in the extended section that began with 7:1 concerns friendship. **9:10** *When it has aged.* The text continues with the theme of patience and the need to wait for something to come to maturity before enjoying it (cf. 2:1–6; 4:17–18; 6:7, 18–19). **9:12** The Hebrew lacks *Hades* here, instead reading only "remember that at the time of death they will not be unpunished." For other references to Hades in the Greek, see note on 14:12. Compare 7:17 for another instance of divergent views of the afterlife in the Hebrew and Greek versions. **9:15** *Let all your discussion.* The text here returns to the theme of proper discourse (cf. 6:35).

9:17–10:5 Rulers. This section focuses on a description of the ideal ruler (cf. Deut. 17:14–20; Prov. 25:4–5; 28:3). Compare the seven symposia in the Letter of Aristeas devoted to kingship (§§187–292). The land of Israel was not ruled by a native king at the time Ben Sira was writing; in fact, the region had been under foreign imperial rule for over three centuries (i.e., under Achaemenid Persian, Ptolemaic, then Seleucid rule). The high priest was the primary political leader (see **"Priests and Temple," p. 1479**). Although elsewhere lauded (e.g., 45:25), high priests are not mentioned in this section. **9:18** *Loud of mouth* is in Hebrew "man of tongue" (cf. 8:3).

10

A wise magistrate educates his people,
and the rule of an intelligent person is well ordered.

² As the people's judge is, so are his officials;
as the ruler of the city is, so are all its inhabitants.

³ An undisciplined king ruins his people,
but a city becomes fit to live in through the understanding of its rulers.

⁴ The government of the earth is in the hand of the Lord,
and over it he will raise up the right leader for the time.

⁵ Human success is in the hand of the Lord,
and it is he who confers honor upon the lawgiver.ᵇ

⁶ Do not get angry with your neighbor for every injury,
and do not resort to acts of insolence.

⁷ Arrogance is hateful to the Lord and to mortals,
and injustice is outrageous to both.

⁸ Sovereignty passes from nation to nation
on account of injustice and insolence and wealth.ⁱ

⁹ How can dust and ashes be proud?
Even in life the human body is infested with worms.ʲ

¹⁰ A long illness mocks the physician;
the king of today will die tomorrow.

¹¹ For when humans die
they inherit maggots and verminᵏ and worms.

¹² The beginning of human pride is to forsake the Lord;
the heart has withdrawn from its Maker.

¹³ For the beginning of pride is sin,
and the one who clings to it pours out abominations.
Therefore the Lord brought upon them unheard-of calamities
and destroyed them completely.ˡ

¹⁴ The Lord overthrew the thrones of rulers
and enthroned the lowly in their place.

¹⁵ The Lord plucked up the roots of the nationsᵐ
and planted the humble in their place.

¹⁶ The Lord laid waste the lands of the nations
and destroyed them to the foundations of the earth.

¹⁷ He removed some of them and destroyed them
and erased the memory of them from the earth.

¹⁸ Pride was not created for human beings
or violent anger for those born of women.

¹⁹ Whose offspring are worthy of honor?
Human offspring.
Whose offspring are worthy of honor?
Those who fear the Lord.
Whose offspring are unworthy of honor?
Human offspring.
Whose offspring are unworthy of honor?
Those who break the commandments.

²⁰ Among family members their leader is worthy of honor,

b 10.5 Heb: Gk *scribe* *i* 10.8 Other ancient authorities add here or after 10.9a: *Nothing is more wicked than one who loves money, for such a person puts his own soul up for sale.* *j* 10.9 Heb: Meaning of Gk uncertain *k* 10.11 Heb: Gk *wild animals* *l* 10.13 Gk: Heb *brings upon them . . . destroys them* *m* 10.15 Other ancient authorities read *proud nations*

10:6–18 Pride. The focus shifts to the threat of pride and arrogance, picking up on and expanding warnings from 5:1–9 and 7:5–17. **10:8** Some versions include an additional verse after this discussing the power of wealth to corrupt one's integrity (cf. 8:1–2). **10:9–11** Death is certain for all humankind, including the most educated (e.g., the physician) and the most powerful (e.g., the king); cf. 8:5–7; 41:1–13. This may be partly a response to Ptolemaic and Seleucid kings claiming divine status and establishing ruler cults. Compare Wis. 7:5–6 on the inevitability of Solomon's death and the death of all rulers. **10:14** *Overthrew the thrones of the rulers.* Pride leads to sin in all humans, but it has especially dire consequences for kings. *Enthroned the lowly in their place.* This can lead to a complete overturning of the social order. **10:15** *Plucked* and *planted* return to the agricultural imagery (cf. 1:17; 6:18–37; 7:3).

10:19–25 Honor. The first of a two-part discourse on honor and humility focuses on honor, specifically honoring *those who fear the Lord*. **10:19** *Whose offspring are worthy of honor?* This question is repeated as a refrain four times, twice with *worthy* and twice with *unworthy*. Here, *human offspring*

but those who fear the Lord are
worthy of honor in his eyes."
22 The guest and the stranger° and the poor—
their boast is the fear of the Lord.
23 It is not right to despise one who is
intelligent but poor,
and it is not proper to honor one who
is sinful.
24 The prince and the judge and the ruler
are honored,
but none of them is greater than the
one who fears the Lord.
25 Free people will serve a wise slave,
and an intelligent person will not
complain.
26 Do not make a display of your wisdom
when you do your work,
and do not extol yourself when you
are in difficulty.
27 Better those who work and have plenty
than those who boast and lack bread.

28 My child, honor yourself with humility,
and give yourself the esteem you deserve.
29 Who will acquit those who condemn^p
themselves,
and who will honor those who
dishonor themselves?^q
30 The poor are honored for their knowledge,
while the rich are honored for their
wealth.
31 One who is honored in poverty, how
much more in wealth!
And one dishonored in wealth, how
much more in poverty!

11 The wisdom of the humble lifts their
heads high

and seats them among the great.
2 Do not praise individuals for their good
looks
or loathe anyone because of
appearance alone.
3 The bee is small among flying creatures,
but what it produces is the origin of
sweet things.
4 Do not mock those wearing only a
loincloth
or make fun of those whose day is
bitter,^r
for the works of the Lord are
wonderful
and his works are concealed from
humans.
5 Many oppressed have sat upon a throne,^s
and one whom no one expected has
worn a crown.
6 Many rulers have been utterly disgraced,
and the honored have been handed
over to others.
7 Do not find fault before you investigate;
examine first and then criticize.
8 Do not answer before you listen,
and do not interrupt when another is
speaking.
9 Do not argue about a matter that does
not concern you,
and do not sit with sinners when they
judge a case.

n 10.20 Other ancient authorities add as 10.21: *The fear of
the Lord is the beginning of acceptance; obduracy and pride are the
beginning of rejection.*   o 10.22 Heb: Gk *The rich and the eminent*   p 10.29 Heb: Gk *sin against*   q 10.29 Heb Lat: Gk *their
own life*   r 11.4 Heb: Gk *Do not boast about wearing fine clothes,
and do not exalt yourself when you are honored*   s 11.5 Heb: Gk
Many sovereigns have sat on the ground

are deemed *worthy* or *unworthy* depending on how they choose to act. **10:22** The Hebrew rendered
the guest and the stranger and the poor is in Greek "the rich and the eminent and the poor." The
Hebrew has a focus on lower social classes (cf. 4:1–10), while the Greek includes all social classes.
10:24 *None of them is greater.* Apart from the social hierarchy at this time, Ben Sira argues that the
highest honor belongs to *one who fears the Lord.*

10:26–11:6 Humility. The second part of the two-part discourse on honor and humility focuses on
the need for humility and its relationship to honor. **10:26–27** *Do not make a display . . . do not extol
yourself.* Humility involves self-restraint in one's behavior (cf. 2:1–6; 4:27–30; 8:10–11). **10:30** *The rich
are honored for their wealth* cautions that wealth can generate false honor, just as it can generate
false friends (cf. 6:10–12). **11:1–6** Just as speech can be deceitful and create false impressions of people (cf. 6:5–17), so too with appearances. This short poem warns not to rely solely on how someone
appears when judging them. **11:1** This verse is quoted in rabbinic literature as "written in the book of
ben Sira" (y. Berakhot 7:2/11b; y. Nazir 5:3/54b; cf. b. Berakhot 48a; Genesis Rabbah 91:4). **11:3** The
metaphor of *the bee* finds parallel in Egyptian wisdom traditions (Papyrus Insinger 25.2).

11:7–28 Patience. Four stanzas develop a theme of patience and the need to examine, test, and
cultivate things over time. **11:7** The text advises restraint until a matter has been analyzed fully.
11:8 *Do not answer . . . do not interrupt* is a further reminder of the importance of listening before

¹⁰ My child, do not busy yourself with
  many matters;
  if you multiply activities, you will not
  be held blameless.
If you pursue, you will not overtake,
  and by fleeing you will not escape.
¹¹ There are those who work and struggle
  and hurry
  but are so much the more in want.
¹² There are others who are slow and need
  help,
  who lack strength and abound in
  poverty,
but the eyes of the Lord look kindly
  upon them;
  he lifts them out of their lowly condition
¹³ and raises up their heads
  to the amazement of the many.

¹⁴ Good things and bad, life and death,
  poverty and wealth, come from the
  Lord.ᵗ
¹⁷ The Lord's gift remains with the devout,
  and his favor brings lasting success.
¹⁸ A person becomes rich through diligence
  and self-denial,
  and the reward allotted to him is this:
¹⁹ when he says, "I have found rest,
  and now I shall feast on my goods!"
he does not realize how time passes by;
  he will leave them to others and will die.

²⁰ Stand by your agreement and attend to it,
  and grow old in your work.
²¹ Do not wonder at the works of a sinner,
  but trust in the Lord and keep at your
  job,

for it is easy in the sight of the Lord
  to make the poor person suddenly
  rich, in an instant.
²² The blessing of the Lord isᵘ the reward of
  the pious,
  and quickly his blessing flourishes.
²³ Do not say, "What do I need,
  and what further benefit can be
  mine?"
²⁴ Do not say, "I have enough,
  and what harm can come to me
  now?"
²⁵ In the day of prosperity, adversity is
  forgotten,
  and in the day of adversity, prosperity
  is not remembered.
²⁶ For it is easy for the Lord on the day of
  death
  to reward individuals according to
  their conduct.
²⁷ An hour's misery makes one forget
  delights,
  and at the close of one's life one's
  deeds are revealed.
²⁸ Call no one happy before his death;
  by how he ends, a person becomes
  known.ᵛ
²⁹ Do not invite everyone into your home,
  for many are the tricks of the crafty.
³⁰ Like a decoy partridge in a cage, so is the
  mind of the proud,

---

t 11.14 Other ancient authorities add as 11.15–16: ¹⁵Wisdom, understanding, and knowledge of the law come from the Lord; affection and the ways of good works come from him. ¹⁶Error and darkness were created with sinners; evil grows old with those who take pride in malice. u 11.22 Heb: Gk is in v 11.28 Heb: Gk and through his children a person becomes known

---

speaking (cf. 3:29; 6:32–37). **11:10** *Do not busy yourself with many matters.* Ben Sira again prefers his students to have a single focus rather than attempting to pursue many paths (5:9). **11:14** Cf. Isa. 45:7. All things in life are imagined to come from the divine—both good and bad. This reinforces Ben Sira's discussion of punishment for sin in 5:1–9. Some manuscripts have additional verses that qualify the idea that evil and bad things come from God, attributing them instead to sinners. **11:19** One should not rest from right behavior and enjoy their accumulated wealth. That wealth may be passed to others to enjoy when one dies. On wealth passing on to others, see Eccl. 2:18–23; the author of Ecclesiastes encourages his audience to enjoy what they have while they live. Compare 14:11 and 30:18–25. **11:20** *Grow old in your work.* Retirement from one's labor is not a possibility for Ben Sira; one must work into old age to attain wisdom and maintain the fear of the Lord (cf. 6:18–19; 25:3–6). **11:27** *One's deeds are revealed* may be a reference to the idea of a divine ledger where one's good and bad deeds in life are given a final tally (cf. 3:3–4); it is not clear whether the idea of an afterlife is here presumed. Generally, Ben Sira tends to focus on the continuance of one's reputation and progeny on earth (e.g., 11:33; 30:6; 37:25–26) rather than postmortem afterlife or end-time judgment (cf. chap. 28; 36:1–22).

11:29–12:18 Friends. A concern with friendship marks the book throughout, and it is among the themes that Ben Sira shares with Egyptian wisdom traditions (e.g., Papyrus Insinger 11.22–12.25). Here, he offers further advice on choosing one's friends and navigating relationships. **11:30** *Like spies.*

and like spies they observe your
weakness,^{w}

^{31} for they lie in wait, turning good into
evil,

and to worthy actions they attach
blame.

^{32} From a spark many coals are kindled,
and a sinner lies in wait to shed blood.

^{33} Beware of scoundrels, for they devise
evil,

and they may ruin your reputation
forever.

^{34} Receive strangers into your home, and
they will stir up trouble for you

and will make you a stranger to your
own family.

12

If you do good, know to whom you
do it,

and you will be thanked for your good
deeds.

^{2} Do good to the devout, and you will be
repaid—

if not by them, certainly by the Most
High.

^{3} No good comes to one who persists in
evil

or to one who does not give alms.

^{4} Give to the devout, but do not help the
sinner.

^{5} Do good to the humble, but do not
give to the ungodly;

hold back their bread, and do not give it
to them,

for by means of it they might subdue
you;

then you will receive twice as much evil
for all the good you have done to them.

^{6} For the Most High also hates sinners
and will inflict punishment on the
ungodly.^{x}

^{7} Give to the one who is good, but do not
help the sinner.

^{8} A friend is not known^y in prosperity,
nor is an enemy hidden in adversity.

^{9} One's enemies are friendly^z when one
prospers,

but in adversity even one's friend
disappears.

^{10} Never trust your enemy,
for like corrosion in copper, so is his
wickedness.

^{11} Even if he humbles himself and walks
bowed down,

take care to be on your guard against
him.

Be to him like one who polishes a mirror,
to be sure it does not become
completely tarnished.

^{12} Do not put him next to you,
or he may overthrow you and take
your place.

Do not let him sit at your right hand,
or else he may try to take your own
seat,

and at last you will acknowledge my words
and be stung by what I have said.

^{13} Who pities a snake charmer when he is
bitten

or all those who go near wild animals?

^{14} So no one pities people who associate
with sinners

and become involved in their sins.

^{15} They stand by you for a while,
but if you falter, they will not be there.

^{16} Enemies speak sweetly with their lips,
but in their hearts they plan to throw
you into a pit;

enemies may have tears in their eyes,
but if they find an opportunity they
will never have enough of your
blood.

^{17} If evil comes upon you, you will find
them there ahead of you;

pretending to help, they will trip you up.

w 11.30 Heb: Gk *downfall*   *x* 12.6 Other ancient authorities add *and he is keeping them for the day of their punishment*
y 12.8 Other ancient authorities read *punished*   *z* 12.9 Heb:
Gk *grieved*

One should always expect that strangers or false friends will reveal that which you do not want to
be revealed (cf. 8:17–19). **11:32** *From a spark many coals are kindled.* Fire metaphors are again tied
to sinful behavior (cf. 8:3, 10; 9:8). **11:33** *Ruin your reputation forever.* What one keeps after death is
one's reputation. **12:1–5** In a brief reflection on where one should focus their efforts to do good, Ben
Sira argues that one should do good only for those who fear the Lord and act rightly, echoing his
earlier discussion of who deserves honor (10:19). **12:5** *Hold back their bread.* Helping or associating
with a sinner may lead one to sin—a concept repeated several times already in this text (7:16; 8:10;
11:9). **12:10–12** An enemy should not be kept close because that gives them an opportunity to *overthrow you* (cf. 6:13).

¹⁸ Then they will shake their heads and
   clap their hands
   and whisper much and show their
   true faces.

13 Whoever touches pitch gets dirty,
   and whoever associates with the
   proud will become like them.
² Do not lift a weight too heavy for
   you
   or associate with one mightier and
   richer than you.
   How can the clay pot associate with the
   iron kettle?
   The pot will strike against it and be
   smashed.
³ A rich person does wrong and even adds
   insults;
   a poor person suffers wrong and must
   add apologies.
⁴ Rich people*ᵃ* will exploit you*ᵇ* if you can
   be of use to them,
   but if you are in need they will
   abandon you.
⁵ If you own something, they will live with
   you;
   they will drain your resources without
   a qualm.
⁶ When they need you, they will deceive
   you
   and will smile at you and encourage
   you;
   they will speak to you kindly and say,
   "What do you need?"
⁷ They will embarrass you with their
   delicacies,
   until they have drained you two or
   three times,
   and finally they will laugh at you.

Should they see you afterwards, they will
   pass you by
   and shake their heads at you.

⁸ Take care not to be led astray
   and humiliated when you are enjoying
   yourself.*ᶜ*
⁹ When the influential invite you, be
   reserved,
   and they will invite you more insistently.
¹⁰ Do not be forward, or you may be
   rebuffed;
   do not stand aloof, or you will be
   forgotten.
¹¹ Do not try to treat them as equals
   or trust their lengthy conversations,
   for they will test you by prolonged talk,
   and while they smile they will be
   examining you.
¹² Cruel are those who do not keep your
   secrets;
   they will not spare you harm or
   imprisonment.
¹³ Be on your guard and very careful,
   for you are walking about with your
   own downfall.*ᵈ*

¹⁵ Every creature loves its like
   and every person a neighbor.
¹⁶ All living beings associate with their
   own kind,
   and people stick close to those like
   themselves.

a 13.4 Gk *He*   *b* 13.4 Heb: Gk *work with you*   *c* 13.8 Other ancient authorities read *in your folly*   *d* 13.13 Other ancient authorities add as 13.14: *When you hear these things in your sleep, wake up! During all your life love the Lord, and call on him for your salvation.*

13:1–24 Caution. Ben Sira's characteristic ethics of caution is here extended to social relationships. There are indications in the poem's framing that Ben Sira is here speaking of a well-off scribe's relationships with his far richer patrons (cf. vv. 1, 26; see **"Scribes and Scribalism," p. 1486**). The contrast between the experiences of the poor and the experiences of the rich is here used to develop the recurrent themes of humility and behavioral restraint. **13:1** *Pitch* was a viscous black material that was a by-product of the production of ink. Scribes would have dealt it with frequently. This proverb is later picked up and used by Shakespeare in *Much Ado about Nothing* and *Henry IV, Part I.* **13:4** The behavior of the rich is likened to that of a false friend (cf. 6:10). **13:8–10** These three verses emphasize behavioral restraint; the first and third warn against impulsive or proactive behavior around the rich, while the second counsels a posture of reticence toward their invitations. **13:10** *Do not stand aloof.* One cannot completely avoid the rich and must be noticed by them. **13:11** *Do not try to treat them as equals.* This phrase begins a section where Ben Sira reminds his students not to forget their place in the social hierarchy. **13:15** For *every person a neighbor*, the Hebrew reads "every person someone who is like himself"; the concern is not with those who live near one another but with those of the same social status. **13:16** *People stick close to those like themselves.* The rich will not associate with those of other social classes, even as they may make use of them for

17 What does a wolf have in common with
     a lamb?
   No more has a sinner with the devout.
18 What peace is there between a hyena
     and a dog,
   and what peace between the rich and
     the poor?
19 Wild asses in the wilderness are the prey
     of lions;
   likewise the poor are feeding grounds
     for the rich.
20 Humility is an abomination to the proud;
   likewise the poor are an abomination
     to the rich.

21 When the rich person totters, he is
     supported by friends,
   but when the humble[e] falls, he is
     pushed away by friends.
22 If the rich person slips, many come to the
     rescue;
   he speaks unseemly words, but they
     justify him.
   If the humble person slips, they even
     criticize him;
   he talks sense but is not given a
     hearing.
23 The rich person speaks, and all are
     silent;
   they extol to the clouds what he says.
   The poor person speaks, and they say,
     "Who is this fellow?"
   And should he stumble, they push him
     down.
24 Riches are good if they are free from sin;
   poverty is evil only in the opinion of
     the ungodly.

25 The heart changes the countenance
     either for good or for evil.[f]

26 The sign of a happy heart is a cheerful
     face,
   but to devise proverbs requires
     strenuous thinking.

14 Happy are those who do not blunder
     with their lips
   and are not stricken with grief for sin.
2 Happy are those whose hearts do not
     condemn them
   and who have not given up their hope.
3 Riches are inappropriate for the
     small-minded,
   and of what use is wealth to misers?
4 What they deny themselves they collect
     for others,
   and others will live in luxury on their
     goods.
5 If they are mean to themselves, to whom
     will they be generous?
   They will not enjoy their own riches.
6 No one is worse than those who are
     grudging to themselves;
   this is the repayment for their meanness.
7 If ever they do good, it is by mistake,[g]
   and in the end they reveal their
     meanness.
8 Misers are evil people;
   they turn away and disregard people.
9 The eyes of the greedy are not satisfied
     with their share;
   greedy injustice withers the soul.
10 Misers begrudge bread,
   and it is lacking at their tables.

11 My child, treat yourself well, according
     to your means,
   and present worthy offerings to the Lord.

e 13.21 Other ancient authorities read *poor*   f 13.25 Other
ancient authorities add *and a glad heart makes a cheerful
countenance*   g 14.7 Syr: Gk *through forgetfulness*

their own gain or entertainment (cf. vv. 4–7, 19). **13:17** For the *wolf* and *lamb* as opposites, see Isa.
11:6. **13:20** *Humility is an abomination to the proud.* The parallelistic structure of this verse equates
humility with the poor and pride with the rich. **13:21–23** The complaint in these verses is that the
behaviors of the rich are justified, no matter how unseemly, while even the sensible speech of the
humble is ignored (v. 22) or rejected (v. 23). **13:24** *Riches are good.* Wealth is not a problem in itself.
The problem is wealth gained through, or used to justify, sinful behavior. On wealth, see 14:3–19 and
31:5–11.
   13:25–14:2 Happiness. This short poem reflects on happiness, a theme that will be discussed in
relation to wisdom in 14:20–27. **13:26** *A cheerful face . . . strenuous thinking.* Some of the work of a
scribe is to *devise proverbs*, which might suggest a scribe cannot always have a happy heart.
   14:3–19 Wealth. Picking up from 13:24, this poem elaborates on the proper use of wealth as well
as death and the transmission of wealth. **14:8** *Misers are evil people.* One who has wealth should use
it for himself and for the benefit of others, rather than simply hoarding it. **14:11** Enjoying one's wealth
is not evil, as long as such enjoyment is within one's means (cf. Eccl. 2:24). *Present worthy offerings.*

¹² Remember that death does not tarry,
 and the decree[b] of Hades has not been
  shown to you.
¹³ Do good to friends before you die,
 and reach out and give to them as
  much as you can.
¹⁴ Do not deprive yourself of a day's
  enjoyment;
 do not let your share of desired good
  pass by you.
¹⁵ Will you not leave the fruit of your
  labors to another,
 and what you acquired by toil to be
  divided by lot?
¹⁶ Give and take and indulge yourself,
 because in Hades one cannot look for
  luxury.
¹⁷ All living beings become old like a
  garment,
 for the decree[i] from of old is, "You
  must die!"
¹⁸ Like abundant leaves on a spreading tree
  that sheds some and puts forth others,
 so are the generations of flesh and
  blood:
 one dies, and another is born.
¹⁹ Every work decays and ceases to exist,
 and the one who made it will pass
  away with it.

²⁰ Happy are those who meditate on[j]
  wisdom
 and who reason intelligently,
²¹ who reflect in their hearts on her ways
 and ponder her secrets,
²² pursuing her like a hunter
 and lying in wait on her paths;
²³ who peer through her windows
 and listen at her doors;
²⁴ who camp near her house
 and fasten their tent pegs to her walls;
²⁵ who pitch their tents near her
 and so occupy an excellent lodging
  place;
²⁶ who place their children under her
  shelter
 and lodge under her boughs;
²⁷ who are sheltered by her from the heat
 and dwell in the midst of her glory.

15 Whoever fears the Lord will do this,
 and whoever holds to the law will
  obtain wisdom.[k]
² She will come to meet him like a
  mother,
 and like a young bride she will
  welcome him.

b 14.12 Heb Syr: Gk *covenant*   *i* 14.17 Heb: Gk *covenant*
j 14.20 Other ancient authorities read *die in*   *k* 15.1 Gk *her*

Those with wealth must also share it with the Lord by making offerings. Compare 31:5–11. **14:12** For *Hades*, the Hebrew here reads "Sheol," which is often imagined as a deep pit in the ground people are said to go to after they die (cf. Gen. 37:35; Num. 16:30, 33; 2 Sam. 22:6; Isa. 5:14; Ezek. 31:15–16). **14:15** *Divided by lot* was one way of apportioning inheritances among ancient Jews. **14:16–17** One Hebrew manuscript contains an additional verse between v. 16 and v. 17, qualifying that indulging oneself is good, so long as what is done is "beautiful before God," thus calling back to the idea that one's pursuits must always be godly (cf. 6:35; 9:15).

14:20–15:10 Wisdom. Returning to the theme of happiness in 13:25–14:2, the focus turns again to Wisdom, here personified as a woman (cf. chap. 24; see **"Woman Wisdom," p. 872**). **14:22** *Pursuing her like a hunter.* The image of the man who pursues Wisdom in these verses is aggressive and perhaps even abusive—a stark contrast from the imagery of sowing and cultivating used earlier. **14:23** *Who peer through her windows.* Ben Sira tends to objectify women (cf. 9:1–9), and his treatment of Wisdom is no exception. **14:24–27** The imagery shifts in these verses to liken the pursuit of Wisdom to a pilgrimage to a temple. **14:24** *Camp near her house.* Several ancient sources depict pilgrims camping near the sanctuary for the duration of some festivals (e.g., Lev. 23:42–43; Deut. 16:13–15; Zech. 14:16; Ezra 3:1–6). **14:26** *Under her boughs.* Wisdom is depicted as a tree, as in 1:20 and 24:13–17. **14:27** *And dwell in the midst of her glory.* The Hebrew does not have "glory" here, instead saying only "and dwell in her dwelling place." The phrase *in the midst of her glory* evokes a temple context, since God's glory is often imagined as residing at a temple (cf. 36:19). **15:1–10** There is a shift in perspective in this poem from the one seeking Wisdom (14:20–27) to her response. There is a special concern for what she will give to those who seek her. **15:1** *The law* in Hebrew is "torah" (literally "teaching"). This term eventually comes to denote the five books of what we now know as the Torah/Pentateuch (i.e., Genesis, Exodus, Leviticus, Numbers, Deuteronomy). Here and elsewhere in the body of Ben Sira's book, *law* bears a broader sense, typically focused on oral teachings and proper behavior marked by discipline and restraint. See notes on 21:11; 24:23; 32:14–33:15. Contrast the Prologue. **15:2** Cf. Wis. 7:12; 8:2.

³ She will feed him with the bread of
understanding
and give him the water of wisdom to
drink.
⁴ He will lean on her and not fall,
and he will rely on her and not be put
to shame.
⁵ She will exalt him above his neighbors
and will open his mouth in the midst
of the assembly.
⁶ Gladness[l] and a crown of rejoicing
and an everlasting name he will
inherit.
⁷ The foolish will not obtain her,
and sinners will not see her.
⁸ She is far from arrogance,
and liars will never think of her.
⁹ Praise is unseemly on the lips of a sinner,
for it has not been sent from the Lord.
¹⁰ For in wisdom must praise be uttered,
and the Lord will make it prosper.
¹¹ Do not say, "It was the Lord's doing that I
fell away,"
for he does not do[m] what he hates.
¹² Do not say, "It was he who led me
astray,"
for he has no need of the sinful.
¹³ The Lord hates all abominations;
such things are not loved by those
who fear him.
¹⁴ It was he who created humans in the
beginning,
and he left them in the power of their
own inclinations.[n]

¹⁵ If you choose, you can keep the
commandments,
and to act faithfully is a matter of
your choice.
¹⁶ He has placed before you fire and water;
stretch out your hand for whichever
you choose.
¹⁷ Before each person are life and death,
and whichever one chooses will be
given.
¹⁸ For great is the wisdom of the Lord;
he is mighty in power and sees
everything;
¹⁹ his eyes are on those who fear him,
and he knows every human action.
²⁰ He has not commanded anyone to be
ungodly,
and he has not given anyone
permission to sin.

16 Do not desire a multitude of
worthless[o] children,
and do not rejoice in ungodly offspring.
² If they multiply, do not rejoice in them,
unless the fear of the Lord is in them.
³ Do not trust in their survival
or rely on their numbers,[p]
for one can be better than a thousand,
and to die childless is better than to
have ungodly children.

l 15.6 Other ancient authorities read *He will find gladness*
m 15.11 Heb: Gk *you ought not to do* n 15.14 Heb: Gk *deliberation* o 16.1 Heb: Gk *unprofitable* p 16.3 Other ancient
authorities add *for you will groan in untimely mourning, and
will know of their sudden end*

15:3 *Bread of understanding . . . water of wisdom.* Metaphors of physical sustenance are again used to allude to the embodiment of knowledge (cf. 1:3, 17; 4:1; 5:2). **15:5** *Open his mouth in the midst of the assembly.* One of wisdom's rewards is public recognition—something that in 13:21–23 is said to elude the humble. So too Wis. 8:10–12. **15:7** Wisdom can only be attained by those who fear God (10:19–25).

15:11–20 *Sin.* This section turns to the issue of the origins of sin: is it from God or is it because of the free will of human beings? Ben Sira argues that sin originates in the choices made by people (cf. 11:14; cf. **"Sin," p. 150**). He does not explain, however, why God gave people free choice. There are some parallels to the speeches by Job's friends found in Job 4–31. Contrast the depiction of a super-natural cause of human sin in 1 En. 6–16. **15:14** *In the beginning.* One of the Hebrew manuscripts seems to evoke Gen. 1:1 in its phrasing here. But other Hebrew manuscripts read "he first created humankind." **15:16** Cf. 8:3, 10; 9:8; 11:32. **15:18** In order for Ben Sira's credit theology (cf. 3:3–4, 14) to function properly, God must be able to see and therefore know everything that transpires among human beings. Divine omniscience is a recurrent theme (e.g., 16:17–23; 17:15; 23:19; 39:19; 42:18). **15:20** *He has not commanded.* God does not desire human beings to sin, but there are those who choose wrongly.

16:1–23 *Punishment.* Human beings are free to choose sin, but this poem makes clear that such choices will be punished by God. It makes three main arguments. First, the proliferation of sinners does not ensure their survival (16:1–4). Second, past exempla demonstrate the certainty of punish-ment (16:5–14). Third, one cannot hide from God's sight (16:17–23). **16:3** *To die childless is better.*

⁴ For through one intelligent person a city
  can be filled with people,
  but through a clan of outlaws it
    becomes desolate.

⁵ Many such things my eye has seen,
  and my ear has heard things more
    striking than these.
⁶ In an assembly of sinners a fire is
    kindled,
  and in a disobedient nation wrath has
    blazed up.
⁷ He did not forgive the ancient giants*q*
  who revolted in their might.
⁸ He did not spare the neighbors of Lot,
  whom he loathed on account of their
    arrogance.
⁹ He showed no pity on the doomed
    nation,
  on those dispossessed because of their
    sins,*r*
¹⁰ or on the six hundred thousand foot
    soldiers
  who assembled in their stubbornness.*s*
¹¹ Even if there were only one stiff-necked
    person,
  it would be a wonder if he remained
    unpunished.
  For mercy and wrath are with the Lord;*t*
  he acquits and forgives,*u* but he also
    pours out wrath.
¹² Great as is his mercy, so also is his
    chastisement;
  he judges people according to their
    deeds.
¹³ The sinner will not escape with plunder,
  and the patience of the godly will not
    be frustrated.

¹⁴ He makes room for every act of
    almsgiving;
  everyone receives in accordance with
    his or her deeds.*v*

¹⁷ Do not say, "I am hidden from the Lord,
  and who from on high has me in
    mind?
  Among so many people I am unknown,
  for what am I in a boundless creation?
¹⁸ Look, heaven and the highest heaven,
  the abyss and the earth tremble at his
    visitation!*w*
¹⁹ Together the mountains and the
    foundations of the earth
  shake and tremble when he looks
    upon them.
²⁰ But no human mind can grasp this,
  and who can comprehend his ways?
²¹ Like a tempest that no one can see,
  so most of his works are concealed.*x*
²² Who is to announce his acts of justice?
  Or who can await them? For his
    decree*y* is far off."*z*
²³ Such are the thoughts of one devoid of
    understanding;

q 16.7 Gk: Heb *princes*   *r* 16.9 Other ancient authorities
add *all these things he did to the hard-hearted nations, and by the
multitude of his holy ones he was not appeased*   *s* 16.10 Other
ancient authorities add *chastising, showing mercy, striking,
healing, the Lord persisted in mercy and discipline*   *t* 16.11 Gk
him   *u* 16.11 Heb: Gk *a master of propitiations*   *v* 16.14 Other
ancient authorities add 16.15–16: *¹⁵The Lord hardened
Pharaoh so that he did not recognize him, in order that his works
might be known under heaven. ¹⁶His mercy is manifest to the whole
of creation, and he apportioned his light and darkness to Adam.*
w 16.18 Other ancient authorities add *The whole world past
and present is in his will.*   *x* 16.21 Meaning of Gk uncertain:
Heb Syr *If I sin, no eye can see me, and if I am disloyal all in secret,
who is to know?*   *y* 16.22 Heb: Gk *the covenant*   *z* 16.22 Other
ancient authorities add *and a scrutiny for all comes at the end*

Dying childless was a serious concern in the ancient world, where one's name was carried on by one's sons. Ben Sira's claim here is radical: no children to carry on your name is better than children who will ruin it by being ungodly; compare 30:1–13 on the challenges of a wicked son. A similar but more negative view can be found in Wis. 4:1–6. **16:5** Knowledge is linked again to sight and hearing (cf. 3:29; 4:8; 5:11). **16:7** *The ancient giants.* Cf. 1 En. 6–16; Qumran Book of the Giants; also Gen. 6:1–4. **16:8** *Neighbors of Lot.* Cf. Gen. 18:16–19:29; also Ezek. 16:49–50. Lot's neighbors are here condemned for the sin of arrogance (cf. 5:1–9; 7:4–7). The didactic use of these figures as negative exempla in summaries of Israel's past is also attested in Wis. 10:7. **16:10** *Six hundred thousand.* This number refers to the Israelites in the wilderness, numbered as six hundred thousand in Exod. 12:37. **16:11** *Even if there were only one.* God's punishment is presented as a certainty, down to the level of each individual person. **16:14** The godly are rewarded and the ungodly punished based on their *deeds* (cf. 11:26–28). **16:17** *In a boundless creation.* Beginning in this section, there is a shift to cosmological imagery to express the totality of God's sight and knowledge (cf. 42:15–43:33). Nothing and no one can go unseen. See also 23:19. **16:19** Even the cosmos fears God's gaze. **16:22** Some manuscripts add "and a scrutiny for all comes at the end" after this verse, echoing some Hebrew versions of 9:12 and 11:26–28.

a senseless and misguided person
        thinks foolishly.
²⁴ Listen to me, my child, and acquire
        knowledge,
    and pay close attention to my words.
²⁵ I will impart discipline precisely*ᵃ*
    and declare knowledge accurately.

²⁶ When the Lord created*ᵇ* his works from
        the beginning
    and, in making them, determined their
        boundaries,
²⁷ he arranged their works in an eternal
        order
    and their dominion*ᶜ* for all
        generations.
    They neither hunger nor grow weary,
    and they do not abandon their tasks.
²⁸ They do not crowd one another,
    and they never disobey his word.
²⁹ Then the Lord looked upon the earth
    and filled it with his good things.
³⁰ With all kinds of living beings he
        covered its surface,
    and into it they must return.

17 The Lord created humans out of
        earth
    and makes them return to it again.
² He gave them a fixed number of days
    but granted them authority over
        everything on the earth.*ᵈ*
³ He endowed them with strength like his
        own*ᵉ*
    and made them in his own image.

⁴ He put the fear of them*ᶠ* in all living
        beings
    and gave them dominion over beasts
        and birds.*ᵍ*
⁶ Discretion and tongue and eyes,
    ears and a mind for thinking he gave
        them.
⁷ He filled them with knowledge and
        understanding
    and showed them good and evil.
⁸ He put the fear of him into*ʰ* their hearts
    to show them the majesty of his
        works.*ⁱ*
¹⁰ And they will praise his holy name,
⁹   to proclaim the grandeur of his works.
¹¹ He bestowed knowledge upon them
    and allotted to them the law of life.*ʲ*
¹² He established with them an eternal
        covenant
    and revealed to them his decrees.
¹³ Their eyes saw his glorious majesty,
    and their ears heard the glory of his
        voice.
¹⁴ He said to them, "Beware of all
        iniquity."
    And he gave commandment to each of
        them concerning the neighbor.

a 16.25 Gk *by weight*   *b* 16.26 Heb: Gk *judged*   *c* 16.27 Or
elements   *d* 17.2 Lat: Gk *it*   *e* 17.3 Lat: Gk *proper to them*
f 17.4 Syr: Gk *him*   *g* 17.4 Other ancient authorities add
as 17.5: *They obtained the use of the five faculties of the Lord;
as sixth he distributed to them the gift of mind, and as seventh,
reason, the interpreter of one's faculties.*   *h* 17.8 Other ancient
authorities read *He set his eye upon*   *i* 17.8 Other ancient
authorities add *and he gave them to boast of his marvels forever*
j 17.11 Other ancient authorities add *so that they may know
that they who are alive now are mortal*

16:24–18:14 Creation. Wisdom is not just associated with law; it is also communicated through the cosmos. Compare 1 En. 2–5. **16:24** Knowledge is acquired through careful attention and listening. **16:25** Precision and accuracy in the transmission of knowledge mirror the precision and accuracy of God's creation of the cosmos. **16:26–27** *Determined their boundaries.* An essential element of creation was God's separation and ordering of different elements (cf. Gen. 1:1–2:4). **17:1–24** The discussion of God's orderly cosmos continues with the creation of human beings, delving into their nature and their relationship to good and evil. This account seems to draw on some (but not all) of the traditions found also in Gen. 1–3, seemingly favoring the priestly ideas therein. **17:1** *Out of earth . . . makes them return to it.* By this account, human beings were always meant to be mortal (cf. Gen. 2:7; 3:19); a limited life-span is not the result of sin. **17:3** *Strength like his own.* The Greek has "proper to them," suggesting discomfort with equating human and divine strength. *In his own image.* Cf. Gen. 1:26–27. **17:6** *Discretion and tongue and eyes, ears and a mind.* This list may reflect one understanding of a human's five senses, which were not identical to the five senses as we now conceive of them. An additional verse (17:5) appears in some Greek manuscripts prior to this one, claiming a gift of five faculties plus a sixth "gift of mind" and a seventh of "reason" and/or "speech." **17:7** In Ben Sira's account of the creation of humankind, God gave human beings knowledge of *good and evil* from the start. This fits with his earlier claim that sin exists because of free will (15:11–20). **17:11–14** The *law of life*, along with the eternal covenant, and God's decrees are given to human beings at the time of their creation; a similar concept is expressed in Jubilees, another Hebrew text

15 Their ways are always before him;
    they will not be hidden from his eyes.^{k}
17 He appointed a ruler for every nation,
    but Israel is the Lord's own portion.^{l}
19 All their works are as the sun before him,
    and his eyes are ever upon their ways.
20 Their iniquities are not hidden from him,
    and all their sins are before the Lord.^{m}
22 One's almsgiving is like a signet ring with
    the Lord,^{n}
    and he will keep a person's kindness
    like the apple of his eye.^{o}
23 Afterward he will rise up and repay them,
    and he will bring their recompense on
    their heads.
24 Yet to those who repent he grants a
    return,
    and he encourages those who are
    losing hope.
25 Turn back to the Lord and forsake your
    sins;
    pray in his presence and lessen your
    offense.
26 Return to the Most High and turn away
    from iniquity^p
    and hate intensely what is abhorrent.
27 Who will sing praises to the Most High in
    Hades
    in place of the living who give thanks?
28 From the dead, as from one who does
    not exist, thanksgiving has ceased;
    those who are alive and well sing the
    Lord's praises.
29 How great is the mercy of the Lord
    and his forgiveness for those who
    return to him!
30 For not everything is within human
    capability,
    since human beings are not immortal.

31 What is brighter than the sun? Yet it can
    be eclipsed.
    So flesh and blood devise evil.
32 He marshals the host of the height of
    heaven,
    but all humans are dust and ashes.

18 He who lives forever created the
    whole universe;
2   the Lord alone will be justified.^{q}
4 To none has he given power to proclaim
    his works,
    and who can search out his mighty
    deeds?
5 Who can measure his majestic power,
    and who can fully recount his mercies?
6 It is not possible to diminish or increase
    them,
    nor is it possible to fathom the
    wonders of the Lord.
7 When humans have finished, they are
    just beginning,
    and when they stop, they are still
    perplexed.
8 What are humans, and of what use are
    they?
    What is good in them, and what is evil?

k 17.15 Other ancient authorities add *^{16}Their ways from youth tend toward evil, and they are unable to make for themselves hearts of flesh in place of their stony hearts. ^{17}For in the division of the nations of the whole earth,* l 17.17 Other ancient authorities add as 17.18: *whom, being his firstborn, he brings up with discipline, and allotting to him the light of his love, he does not neglect him.* m 17.20 Other ancient authorities add as 17.21: *But the Lord, who is gracious and knows how they are formed, has neither left them nor abandoned them but has spared them.* n 17.22 Gk *him* o 17.22 Other ancient authorities add *apportioning repentance to his sons and daughters* p 17.26 Other ancient authorities add *for he will lead you out of darkness to the light of health.* q 18.2 Other ancient authorities add *and there is no other beside him; ^{3}he steers the world with the span of his hand, and all things obey his will, for he is king of all things by his power, separating among them the holy things from the profane.*

from the second century BCE. **17:17** *A ruler for every nation*—that is, except Israel. When Ben Sira was writing, the land of Israel was not under native rule but rather part of a Hellenistic empire (i.e., Seleucids). *Israel is the Lord's own portion.* Cf. Deut. 32:8–9. This idea is explored in a number of writings from the second century BCE, including the "Animal Apocalypse" (1 En. 89:59–70) and Jub. 15:31–32—albeit there with a sense of the rulers of each non-Israelite nation as angels or demons. **17:19–20** Picking up on the theme of v. 15, this verse returns to God's ability to see everything done by human beings. Compare Jub. 5:13, where divine omniscience is used to stress that "there is no injustice." **17:24–32 Repentance.** Ben Sira here introduces the possibility of repentance for sin (cf. 21:1). **17:25** *Lessen your offense.* Repentance may not entirely erase your sin, but it can mitigate at least part of it. **17:30** *Not everything is within human capability.* Because of their mortality, human beings are not able to acquire knowledge or skill in everything. Such a process takes much time, and their time is limited. See 6:18–19; 11:20 for growing old in the pursuit of knowledge. See 2:12; 5:9; 6:35; 11:10 for the necessity of choosing only one path to pursue. **18:1–14 Divine majesty.** The theme of creation continues with a poem contrasting the vastness and immeasurability of God with the fragility and weakness of human beings. **18:2** *The Lord alone will be justified.* Cf. 7:6; 8:14; 10:2;

⁹ The number of days in their life is great
     if they reach one hundred years.ʳ
¹⁰ Like a drop of water from the sea and a
     grain of sand,
     so are a few years among the days of
         eternity.
¹¹ That is why the Lord is patient with them
     and pours out his mercy upon them.
¹² He sees and recognizes that their end is
     miserable;
     therefore he grants his forgiveness all
         the more.
¹³ The compassion of humans is for their
     neighbors,
     but the compassion of the Lord is for
         every living thing.
   He rebukes and trains and teaches them
     and turns them back, as a shepherd
         his flock.
¹⁴ He has compassion on those who accept
     his discipline
   and who are eager for his decrees.
¹⁵ My child, do not mix reproach with your
     good deeds
     or harsh words with any gift.
¹⁶ Does not the dew give relief from the
     scorching heat?
     So a word is better than a gift.
¹⁷ Indeed, does not a word surpass a good
     gift?
     Both are to be found in a gracious
         person.
¹⁸ A fool will rebuke ungraciously,
     and the gift of a grudging giver makes
         the eyes weary.
¹⁹ Before you speak, learn,
     and before you fall ill, take care of
         yourself.
²⁰ Before judgment comes, examine yourself,
     and at the time of scrutiny you will
         find forgiveness.

²¹ Before falling ill, humble yourself,
     and when you have sinned, repent.
²² Let nothing hinder you from paying a
     vow promptly,
     and do not wait until death to be
         released from it.
²³ Before making a vow, prepare yourself;
     do not be like one who puts the Lord
         to the test.
²⁴ Think of his wrath on the day of death
     and of the moment of vengeance
         when he turns away his face.
²⁵ In the time of plenty think of the time of
     hunger;
     in days of wealth think of poverty and
         need.
²⁶ From morning to evening conditions
     change;
     all things move swiftly before the Lord.

²⁷ One who is wise is cautious in
     everything;
     when sin is all around, one guards
         against wrongdoing.
²⁸ Every intelligent person knows wisdom
     and praises the one who finds her.
²⁹ Those who are skilled in words become
     wise themselves
     and pour forth apt proverbs.ˢ

SELF-CONTROLᵗ
³⁰ Do not follow your base desires
     but restrain your appetites.
³¹ If you allow your soul to take pleasure in
     base desire,
     it will make you the laughingstock of
         your enemies.

r 18.9 Other ancient authorities add *but the death of each one
is beyond the calculation of all*   s 18.29 Other ancient authorities add *Better is confidence in a single master than clinging with
a dead heart to a dead one.*   t 18.30 This heading is included
in the Gk text.

11:9. **18:12** *Their end is miserable.* When human beings come to the end of their lives, we remain
perplexed (v. 7). We never achieve genuine happiness or understanding; our mortality limits our
knowledge, in turn generating God's pity and mercy. **18:13** *For their neighbors.* People only care
about those who are like them; see 13:15–20 and notes there.

18:15–18 Giving. These verses begin a series of poems on the relationship between speech and
behavior—here with respect to gift-giving. **18:18** *Makes the eyes weary.* This is a euphemism for
blindness, suggesting that grudgingly giving a gift can impede the pursuit of knowledge and wisdom. Earlier, knowledge is linked in part to the ability to see and observe (cf. 4:5; 11:1–6).

18:19–19:3 Self-control. A need for self-reflection and self-awareness is highlighted in these
verses. **18:22–23** In some traditions, a *vow* was considered to be a binding act and a delay or
failure to fulfill it was a serious sin (cf. Lev. 27; Num. 30; Deut. 23:21). **18:30** Self-control is a common theme in Hellenistic literature. Compare also Wis. 8:7; 4 Macc. 1:18. In what follows, Ben Sira
stresses the need for self-control both with respect to desires (18:30–19:3) and with respect to

³² Do not revel in great luxury,
  or you may become impoverished by
    contact with it.
³³ Do not become a beggar by feasting with
    borrowed money,
  when you have nothing in your purse.ᵘ

19 The one who does thisᵛ will not
    become rich;
  one who despises small things will fail
    little by little.
² Wine and women lead intelligent men
    astray,
  and the man who consorts with
    prostitutes is reckless.
³ Decay and worms will take possession of
    him,
  and the reckless person will be
    snatched away.
⁴ One who trusts quickly has a shallow mind,
  and one who sins does wrong to
    himself.
⁵ One who rejoices in wickednessʷ will be
    condemned,ˣ
⁶   but one who hates discussion lacks
    understanding.
⁷ Never repeat a conversation,
  and you will lose nothing at all.
⁸ With friend or foe do not report it,
  and unless it would be a sin for you do
    not reveal it,
⁹ for someone may have heard you and
    watched you
  and in time will hate you.
¹⁰ Have you heard something? Let it die
    with you.
  Be brave; it will not make you burst!

¹¹ Having heard something, the fool suffers
    birth pangs
  like a woman in labor with a child.
¹² Like an arrow stuck in a person's thigh,
  so is gossip in the belly of a fool.
¹³ Question a friend; perhaps he did not do it;
  or if he did, so that he may not do it
    again.
¹⁴ Question a neighbor; perhaps he did not
    say it;
  or if he said it, so that he may not
    repeat it.
¹⁵ Question a friend, for often it is slander;
  so do not believe every word.
¹⁶ A person may make a slip without
    intending it.
  Who has not sinned with his tongue?
¹⁷ Question your neighbor before you
    threaten him,
  and make room for the law of the
    Most High.ʸ
²⁰ The whole of wisdom is fear of the Lord,
  and in all wisdom there is the
    fulfillment of the law.ᶻ

u 18.33 Other ancient authorities add *for you will be
plotting against your own life*   *v* 19.1 Heb: Gk *A worker who
is a drunkard*   *w* 19.5 Other ancient authorities read
heart*   *x* 19.5 Other ancient authorities add *but one who
withstands pleasures crowns his life.* *⁶One who controls the tongue
will live without strife,*   *y* 19.17 Other ancient authorities
add *and do not be angry.* *¹⁸The fear of the Lord is the beginning
of acceptance, and wisdom obtains his love.* *¹⁹The knowledge of the
Lord's commandments is life-giving discipline, and those who do
what is pleasing to him enjoy the fruit of the tree of immortality.*
z 19.20 Other ancient authorities add *and the knowledge of his
omnipotence.* *²¹When a slave says to his master, "I will not act as you
wish," even if later he does it, he angers the one who supports him.*

speech (19:4–17; also Wis. 8:7–8). **18:32** *Do not revel in great luxury.* The caution is against indulging
in excess. Ben Sira is not promoting asceticism or suggesting that people must restrain themselves
from all pleasure. A measured level of indulgence is acceptable (cf. 14:3–19). On moderation, see
chap. 31. **19:2** Both *wine and women* challenge a man's ability to exercise restraint. On women, see
also 9:1–9; on wine, see 31:25–31.

  19:4–17 Speech. Up to this point, Ben Sira's concern has been to warn his students not to trust that
others will keep their secrets and that false friends would gossip and spread lies about them (cf. 5:10–
6:4; 7:12–14; 8:3). Here, his concern shifts to his students' ability to keep secrets. **19:7** *Never repeat a
conversation.* Spreading gossip can harm the gossiper, as one can never know who overhears a conversation and could hold a grudge (v. 9). **19:11** *The fool suffers birth pangs.* The fool is naturally unable
to keep a secret, whereas one with wisdom and right behavior will not act on their natural instincts.
19:13–17 Ben Sira's advice is to *question* everything that one hears. Listening is essential, but analyzing, testing, and verifying are even more important (cf. 11:7–28). One should go directly to one's friend
or neighbor and ask about what has been heard, both to test the claim and to offer them a chance to
improve their behavior if the report is true; for a similar idea, see Lev. 19:17–18; also 1QS col. 6.

  19:20–30 Wisdom. This poem aims to make a distinction between true wisdom and mere cleverness. One who is truly wise is one who fears the Lord and does not transgress his law. **19:20** *The
whole of wisdom is fear of the Lord.* So too 1:14–16; 21:11; Prov. 1:7. But contrast the suggestion in

²² The knowledge of wickedness is not
    wisdom,
    nor is there prudence in the counsel of
    sinners.
²³ There is a cleverness that is detestable,
    and there is a fool who merely lacks
    wisdom.
²⁴ Better are the God-fearing who lack
    understanding
    than the highly intelligent who
    transgress the law.
²⁵ There is a cleverness that is exact but unjust,
    and there are people who abuse favors
    to gain a verdict.ᵃ
²⁶ There are villains bowed down in
    mourning,
    but inwardly they are full of deceit.
²⁷ They hide their faces and pretend not to
    hear,
    but when no one notices, they will
    take advantage of you.
²⁸ Even if lack of strength keeps them from
    sinning,
    they will nevertheless do evil when
    they find the opportunity.
²⁹ People will be known by their appearances,
    and sensible people will be known
    when first met face to face.
³⁰ People's attire and hearty laughter
    and the way they walk proclaim
    things about them.

20 There is a rebuke that is untimely,
    and there is the person who is wise
    enough to keep silent.
² How much better it is to rebuke than to
    fume!
³ And the one who admits his fault will be
    kept from ridicule.
⁴ Like a eunuch lusting to violate a young
    woman

is the person who makes decisions
    under compulsion.
⁵ Some people keep silent and are foundᵇ
    to be wise,
    while others are detested for being
    talkative.
⁶ Some people keep silent because they
    have nothing to say,
    while others keep silent because they
    know when to speak.
⁷ The wise remain silent until the right
    moment,
    but the arrogant and the fool miss the
    right moment.
⁸ Whoever talks too much is detested,
    and whoever pretends to authority is
    hated.ᶜ
⁹ There may be good fortune for a person
    in adversity,
    and a windfall may result in a loss.
¹⁰ There is the gift that profits you nothing
    and the gift to be paid back double.
¹¹ There are losses for the sake of glory,
    and there are some who have
    raised their heads from humble
    circumstances.
¹² Some buy much for little
    but pay for it seven times over.
¹³ The wise make themselves beloved by
    only few words,ᵈ
    but the courtesies of fools are wasted.
¹⁴ A fool's gift will profit you nothing,ᵉ
    for he looks for recompense
    sevenfold.ᶠ

a 19.25 Other ancient authorities add *and the one who
justifies is wise in judgment.*   b 20.5 Gk: Heb *thought*
c 20.8 Other ancient authorities add *How good it is to show
repentance when you are reproved, for so you will escape deliberate
sin!*   d 20.13 Heb: Gk *by words*   e 20.14 Other ancient
authorities add *so it is with the envious who give under compulsion*   f 20.14 Syr: Gk *he has many eyes instead of one*

25:10–11 that fearing the Lord surpasses wisdom. **19:24** Intelligence is not identical to wisdom, since one can still behave wrongly by transgressing the law. **19:26** This verse warns again of trusting appearances (cf. 11:1–6)—in this case, the appearance of piety. Simply because someone performs piety does not mean they are pious. **19:29–30** Despite prior warnings against judging someone on the basis of their appearance, Ben Sira here claims that a person can be known by how they look, what they wear, how they walk, and how they laugh. Physiognomy was among the technical arts commonly valued in Hellenistic culture, and its adaptation by Jews is attested in the Dead Sea Scrolls (4Q186, 4Q561). Learning proper comportment, including walking, formed part of elite masculinity in Greek "paideia."

    20:1–31 Speech. Proper speech is a recurrent concern in the book (cf. 5:10–6:4). **20:1** *Rebuke* can be necessary (cf. 19:13–17), but it must be delivered at the proper time. **20:3** Accountability and self-awareness are valuable in an individual (cf. 18:19–21). **20:5–8** It is not always possible to infer whether a person is wise from their silence; the key is the appropriate timing of one's speech. **20:9–17** Here Ben Sira makes use of the themes of wealth and gift-giving to explore the

¹⁵ He gives little and insults much;
    he opens his mouth like a town crier.
Today he lends, and tomorrow he asks it
    back;
    such a one is hateful.^g
¹⁶ The fool says, "I have no friends,
    and I get no thanks for my good
    deeds."
    Those who eat his bread are
    evil-tongued.
¹⁷ How many will ridicule him, and how
    often!^b
¹⁸ A slip on the pavement is better than a
    slip of the tongue;
    the downfall of the wicked will occur
    just as speedily.
¹⁹ A coarse person is like an inappropriate
    story,
    continually on the lips of the ignorant.
²⁰ A proverb from a fool's lips will be
    rejected,
    for he does not tell it at the proper
    time.

²¹ One may be prevented from sinning by
    poverty,
    so when he rests he feels no remorse.
²² One may lose his life through shame
    or lose it because of a foolish person.ⁱ
²³ One may make promises to a friend out
    of shame
    and so make an enemy for nothing.
²⁴ A lie is an ugly blot on a person;
    it is continually on the lips of the
    ignorant.
²⁵ A thief is preferable to a habitual liar,
    but both will inherit ruin.
²⁶ The character of liars leads to disgrace,
    and their shame is ever with them.

PROVERBIAL SAYINGS^j
²⁷ Wise persons advance themselves by
    their words,

and those who are sensible please the
    great.
²⁸ Those who cultivate the soil heap up
    their harvest,
    and those who please the great atone
    for injustice.
²⁹ Favors and gifts blind the eyes of the
    wise;
    like a muzzle on the mouth they stop
    reproofs.
³⁰ Hidden wisdom and unseen treasure—
    of what value is either?
³¹ Better are those who hide their folly
    than those who hide their wisdom.^k

21 Have you sinned, my child? Do so no
    more,
    but ask forgiveness for your past sins.
² Flee from sin as from a snake,
    for if you approach sin it will bite you.
Its teeth are lion's teeth
    and can destroy human lives.
³ All lawlessness is like a two-edged
    sword;
    there is no healing for the wound it
    inflicts.

⁴ Panic and insolence will waste away
    riches;
    thus the house of the proud will be
    uprooted.^l
⁵ The prayer of the poor goes from their
    lips to the ears of God,^m
    and his judgment comes speedily.
⁶ Those who hate reproof walk in the
    sinner's steps,

---

g 20.15 Other ancient authorities add *to God and humans*
h 20.17 Other ancient authorities add *for he has not honestly
received what he has, and what he does not have is unimportant
to him*   i 20.22 Other ancient authorities read *human
respect*   j 20.27 This heading is included in the Gk text.
k 20.31 Other ancient authorities add 20.32: *Unwearied
endurance in seeking the Lord is better than a masterless charioteer
of one's own life.*   l 21.4 Other ancient authorities read *laid
waste*   m 21.5 Gk *his ears*

---

distinction between a wise person and a fool. For more on gift-giving, see 18:15–18. **20:18** *A slip on the pavement.* Physical injury is better than inappropriate speech. **20:24** *Continually on the lips.* Like improper action (cf. 20:19), deceitful speech is more likely to be repeated and passed around among the fools who do not know how to hold their tongues (cf. 19:4–17). **20:25** *A thief is preferable.* As in v. 18, Ben Sira suggests that physical harm—in this case: loss of property—is preferable to the damage to one's reputation that can be caused by deceitful speech.

21:1–20 Sins. 21:1 *Ask forgiveness.* A second reminder in this text that repentance is possible (cf. 17:24). **21:5** Here, it seems as though *the poor* are being preferred by God, but this is not quite what Ben Sira suggests elsewhere. Throughout this book, he argues that wealth corrupts and leads to sin. God's preference for the poor is not because of their poverty per se; it is because they have fewer opportunities to sin. For wealth as a cause of sin, see 8:1–2; 13:24. For righteousness among the

but those who fear the Lord repent in
their heart.
7 The mighty in speech are widely known;
when they slip, the sensible person
knows it.

8 Those who build their houses with other
people's money
are like those who gather stones for
their own burial mounds.
9 An assembly of the lawless is like a
bundle of tinder,
and their end is a blazing fire.
10 The way of sinners is paved with smooth
stones,
but at its end is the pit of Hades.
11 Those who keep the law control their
thoughts,
and the fulfillment of the fear of the
Lord is wisdom.
12 Those who are not clever cannot be
taught,
but there is a cleverness that increases
bitterness.
13 The knowledge of the wise will increase
like a flood
and their counsel like a life-giving
spring.
14 The mind[n] of a fool is like a broken jar;
it can hold no knowledge.

15 When intelligent people hear a wise
saying,
they praise it and add to it;
when fools[o] hear it, they laugh at[p] it
and throw it behind their backs.

16 The chatter[q] of fools is like a burden on a
journey,
but delight is found in the speech of
the intelligent.
17 The utterance of sensible people is
sought in the assembly,
and they ponder their words in their
minds.

18 Like a house in ruins is wisdom to a fool,
and the knowledge of the ignorant is
meaningless talk.
19 To the senseless, education is fetters on
their feet
and like manacles on their right
hands.
20 Fools raise their voices when they laugh,
but the wise[r] smile quietly.
21 To the sensible, education is like a
golden ornament
and like a bracelet on the right arm.

22 The foot of a fool rushes into a house,
but an experienced person waits
respectfully outside.
23 A boor peers into the house from the
door,
but a cultivated person remains
outside.
24 It is ill-mannered for a person to listen at
a door;
the discreet would be grieved by the
disgrace.

n 21.14 Syr Lat: Gk *entrails* o 21.15 Syr: Gk *revelers*
p 21.15 Syr: Gk *dislike* q 21.16 Syr: Gk *explanation*
r 21.20 Syr Lat: Gk *clever*

wealthy as especially laudable as a result, see 31:9–11. **21:8** *With other people's money.* Once again, Ben Sira cautions against borrowing money and living beyond one's means (cf. 8:12–13; 29:1–28). He returns to the topic of loans in 29:1–28.

21:11–22:2 Wisdom and folly. 21:11 Here the *fear of the Lord* is expressed by actions, specifically the keeping of God's *law* (cf. 15:1; 23:27). There is no indication, however, that this *law* is equated with the written Torah/Pentateuch. Here as elsewhere in the body of the book, the term *law* refers to a broader set of precepts including cautious social behavior, proper comportment, and the regulation of one's thoughts and emotions—that is, what one might call Ben Sira's Jewish "paideia." See notes on 15:1; 24:23; 32:14–33:15 on *law.* See notes on 1:11–20 and 23:27 on *fear of the Lord.* **21:12** *A cleverness that increases bitterness.* Cf. Eccl. 1:18. **21:15** *Throw it behind their backs.* Literally, the fool puts the wise saying in a place where he cannot "see" it. As throughout the book, vision is a key manner of expressing the acquisition of knowledge. **21:19** *Education.* In the Greek, "paideia" (which is also translated as "discipline"; e.g., 1:27); in the Hebrew, "musar." The two words have slightly different nuances. Both, however, convey learning and self-discipline. See 6:23–31 for a description of the process of acquiring wisdom as akin to being in *fetters.* **21:22** *The foot of a fool rushes into a house.* Compare 6:36 where the one seeking wisdom should wear out the wise person's doorstep. Ben Sira again advocates for discretion and restraint. **21:23** *A boor peers into the house from the door.* Compare 14:23 where Ben Sira likens the pursuit of wisdom to peering into the windows of a house.

²⁵ The lips of babblers speak of what is not
    their concern,^s
  but the words of the prudent are
    weighed in the balance.
²⁶ The mind of fools is in their mouth,
  but the mouth of the wise is in^t their
    mind.
²⁷ When ungodly people curse an
    adversary,
  they curse themselves.
²⁸ Whisperers degrade themselves
  and are hated in their
    neighborhoods.

22 The idler is like a filthy stone,
    and every one hisses at his disgrace.
² The idler is like a lump of dung;
  anyone who picks it up will shake it
    off his hand.
³ It is a disgrace to be the father of an
    undisciplined son,
  and the birth of a daughter is a loss.
⁴ A sensible daughter obtains a husband of
    her own,
  but one who acts shamefully is a grief
    to her father.
⁵ An impudent daughter disgraces father
    and husband
  and is despised by both.
⁶ Like music in time of mourning is
    ill-timed conversation,
  but a thrashing and discipline are at
    all times wisdom.^u
⁹ Whoever teaches a fool is like one who
    glues potsherds together
  or who rouses a sleeper from deep
    slumber.
¹⁰ Whoever tells a story to a fool tells it to a
    drowsy man,
  and at the end he will say, "What is
    it?"
¹¹ Weep for the dead, for they have left the
    light behind,

and weep for the fool, for they have
    left intelligence behind.
Weep less bitterly for the dead, for they
    are at rest,
  but the life of the fool is worse than
    death.
¹² Mourning for the dead lasts seven days,
  but for the foolish or the ungodly it
    lasts all the days of their lives.

¹³ Do not talk much with senseless people
    or visit unintelligent people.^v
Stay clear of them, or you may have
    trouble
  and be spattered when they shake
    themselves off.
Avoid them and you will find rest,
  and you will never be wearied by their
    lack of sense.
¹⁴ What is heavier than lead?
  And what is its name except "Fool"?
¹⁵ Sand, salt, and a piece of iron
  are easier to bear than a stupid person.

¹⁶ A wooden beam firmly bonded into a
    building
  is not loosened by an earthquake;
so the mind firmly resolved after due
    reflection
  will not be afraid in a crisis.
¹⁷ A mind settled on an intelligent thought
  is like plaster decoration that makes a
    wall smooth.
¹⁸ Fences^w set on a high place
  will not stand firm against the wind;

s 21.25 Other ancient authorities read *The lips of strangers
speak of these things*   *t* 21.26 Other ancient authorities omit
in   *u* 22.6 Other ancient authorities add 22.7–8: ⁷*Children
who are brought up in a good life conceal the lowly birth of their
parents.* ⁸*Children who glory in contempt and ignorance stain the
nobility of their kindred.*   *v* 22.13 Other ancient authorities
add *For being without sense he will despise everything about you*
w 22.18 Other ancient authorities read *Pebbles*

22:1–2 In Ben Sira's view, one must work continually for the acquisition of wisdom; there should be
no opportunity to cease from it.
  22:3–6 Children. Another passage, like 16:3, that laments children who behave in unrestrained
ways (cf. 7:24–25; 30:1–13; 42:9–14). Just as Ben Sira treats fathers as superior to mothers, so he here
focuses less on wayward sons (cf. 30:1–13) and more on the shame brought upon men by daughters
(cf. 26:10–12; 42:9–14). **22:6** *Thrashing.* Cf. 30:1, 12; Prov. 13:24.
  22:9–18 Wisdom and folly. 22:9 *Glues potsherds together.* This would result in a pot unable
to hold water effectively; cf. 21:14. **22:12** A *mourning* period of *seven days* is also reflected in Gen.
50:10 and Jdt. 16:24. A seven-day purification period after coming into contact with a dead body
can be found in Num. 19. Later, Ben Sira suggests taking only a day or two (38:17). **22:16–18** These
verses praise the stability of a wise person's thoughts, almost certainly because they have been
constructed slowly and correctly and tested over time (cf. 4:17–18; 6:7).

so a timid mind with a fool's resolve
    will not stand firm against any fear.
¹⁹ One who pricks the eye brings tears,
    and one who pricks the heart makes
        clear its feelings.
²⁰ One who throws a stone at birds scares
        them away,
    and one who reviles a friend destroys
        a friendship.
²¹ Even if you draw your sword against a
        friend,
    do not despair, for there is a way back.
²² If you open your mouth against your
        friend,
    do not worry, for reconciliation is
        possible.
But as for reviling, arrogance,
    disclosure of secrets, or a
        treacherous blow—
in these cases any friend will take to
    flight.

²³ Gain the trust of your neighbor in his
        poverty,
    so that you may rejoice[x] with him in
        his prosperity.
Stand by him in time of distress,
    so that you may share with him in his
        inheritance.[y]
²⁴ The vapor and smoke of the furnace
        precede the fire;
    so insults precede bloodshed.
²⁵ I am not ashamed to shelter a friend,
    and I will not hide from him,
²⁶ but if harm should come to me because
        of him,
    whoever hears of it will beware of
        him.
²⁷ Who will set a guard over my mouth
    and an effective seal upon my lips,
so that I may not fall because of them
    and my tongue may not destroy me?

23 O Lord, Father and Master of my life,
    do not abandon me to their designs,
    and do not let me fall among them!
² Who will set whips over my thoughts
    and the discipline of wisdom over my
        mind,
so as not to spare me in my errors
    and not overlook my[z] sins?
³ Otherwise my mistakes may be
        multiplied,
    and my sins may abound,
and I may fall before my adversaries,
    and my enemy may rejoice over me.[a]
⁴ O Lord, Father and God of my life,
    do not give me haughty eyes,
⁵   and remove desire from me.
⁶ Let neither gluttony nor lust overcome me,
    and do not give me over to shameless
        passion.

DISCIPLINE OF THE TONGUE[b]
⁷ Listen, my children, to instruction
        concerning the mouth;
    the one who observes it will never be
        caught.
⁸ Sinners are overtaken through their lips;
    by them the reviler and the arrogant
        are tripped up.
⁹ Do not accustom your mouth to oaths
    nor habitually utter the name of the
        Holy One,
¹⁰ for as a slave who is constantly under
        scrutiny
    will not lack bruises,
so also the person who always swears
        and utters the Name
    will never be cleansed[c] from sin.

x 22.23 Other ancient authorities read *you also may be filled*
y 22.23 Other ancient authorities add *For one should not always despise restricted circumstances or admire a rich person who has no resolve.* z 23.2 Gk *their* a 23.3 Other ancient authorities add *From them the hope of your mercy is remote* b 23.7 This heading is included in the Gk text. c 23.10 Syr *be free*

22:19–26 Friendship. Another discussion on friendship (cf. 6:5–17; 11:28–12:18). Here, the focus falls on the possibility of reconciliation if a friend acts wrongly.

22:27–23:6 Prayer for self-control. Sirach is best known for its instructions, but it also includes prayers and hymns. This brief prayer beseeches God for aid in self-control over the impulses. The opening plea for control of speech echoes Ps. 141:3 (cf. Prov. 21:23). As in Hellenistic education, the ideal of discipline spans mouth, mind, and body, and bodily control pertains to food, sex, and emotion. On control of the thoughts, see also 21:11.

23:7–15 Discipline of the tongue. The heading used for this cluster of instructions in Greek manuscripts aptly describes its theme. Proper speech is a recurring theme throughout the book. Extending the themes of the preceding prayer, this cluster of instructions focuses first on oaths, warning against their habitual overuse (vv. 7–11) due to the danger of dishonoring the divine name (cf. Exod. 20:7; Deut. 5:11). Then it turns to curses (vv. 12–15), invoking the danger of dishonoring one's parents

11 The one who swears many oaths is full of
iniquity,
and the scourge will not leave his
house.
If he swears in error, his sin remains on
him,
and if he disregards it, he sins doubly;
if he swears a false oath, he will not be
justified,
for his house will be filled with
calamities.
12 There is a manner of speaking
comparable to death;[d]
may it never be found in the
inheritance of Jacob!
Such conduct will be far from the godly,
and they will not wallow in sins.
13 Do not accustom your mouth to lewd
ignorance,
for it involves sinful speech.
14 Remember your father and mother
when you sit among the great,
or you may forget yourself in their
presence,
and behave like a fool through habit;
then you will wish that you had never
been born,
and you will curse the day of your
birth.
15 Those who are accustomed to using
abusive language
will never become disciplined as long
as they live.
16 Two kinds of individuals multiply sins,
and a third incurs wrath.
Hot passion that blazes like a fire
will not be quenched until it burns
itself out;
those who commit incest with their near
of kin
will never cease until the fire burns
them up.

17 To the sexually immoral all bread is
sweet;
he will never weary until he dies.
18 The one who sins against his marriage
bed
says to himself, "Who can see me?
Darkness surrounds me, the walls hide
me,
and no one sees me. Why should I
worry?
The Most High will not remember my
sins."
19 His fear is confined to human eyes,
and he does not realize that the eyes
of the Lord
are ten thousand times brighter than
the sun;
they look upon every aspect of human
behavior
and see into hidden corners.
20 Before the universe was created, it was
known to him,
and so it is since its completion.
21 This man will be punished in the streets
of the city,
and where he least suspects it he will
be seized.

22 So it is with a woman who leaves her
husband
and presents him with an heir by
another man.
23 For, first of all, she has disobeyed the law
of the Most High;
second, she has committed an offense
against her husband;
and third, through sexual immorality she
has committed adultery
and brought forth children by another
man.

d 23.12 Other ancient authorities read *clothed about with
death*

(cf. 3:1–10; 4:10). **23:12** *Inheritance of Jacob.* This is the first mention of Jacob in the text (cf. Gen. 25–
32). The second half of the book increasingly depicts wisdom as an *inheritance* unique to the people
Israel, and Jacob's name occurs frequently (24:8, 23; 36:13; 44:23; 45:5, 17; 46:14; 47:22; 48:10; 49:10).
23:16–27 Lust. Returning to the theme of bodily self-control in vv. 4–6, this cluster of instructions
warns about lust. **23:16** *Two kinds.* These are incest and a man's act of adultery (cf. Lev. 18), as discussed in vv. 17–21. *A third.* This is a woman's act of adultery, as discussed in vv. 22–27. Women are
condemned to a greater degree than men, even for the same acts. **23:19** Human sight is contrasted
with divine sight, and the latter is depicted as total (cf. 39:19–20). God is described as omniscient
and concerned with individual acts (cf. 16:17–23; see note on 15:18). **23:20** As in many Jewish writings from the Hellenistic period (e.g., 1 En. 1–36), creation is evoked as exemplary of divine knowledge, particularly to warn against the human temptation to sin (e.g., 1 En. 2–5). **23:23** *The law of
the Most High.* This verse presumes a precept such as is found in Exod. 20:14 and Deut. 5:18. The

24 She herself will be brought before the
assembly,
and her punishment will extend to her
children.
25 Her children will not take root,
and her branches will not bear fruit.
26 She will leave behind an accursed
memory,
and her disgrace will never be blotted
out.
27 Those who survive her will recognize
that nothing is better than the fear of
the Lord
and nothing sweeter than to heed the
commandments of the Lord.*e*

THE PRAISE OF WISDOM*f*

24 Wisdom praises herself
and tells of her glory in the midst of
her people.
2 In the assembly of the Most High she
opens her mouth,
and in the presence of his hosts she
tells of her glory:
3 "I came forth from the mouth of the
Most High
and covered the earth like a mist.
4 I encamped in the heights,
and my throne was in a pillar of cloud.
5 Alone I compassed the vault of heaven
and traversed the depths of the abyss.
6 Over waves of the sea, over all the earth,
and over every people and nation I
have held sway.*g*

7 Among all these I sought a resting place;
in whose inheritance should I abide?

8 "Then the Creator of all things gave me a
command,
and my Creator pitched my tent.
He said, 'Encamp in Jacob,
and in Israel receive your inheritance.'
9 Before the ages, in the beginning, he
created me,
and for all the ages I shall not cease
to be.
10 In the holy tent I ministered before him,
and so I was established in Zion.
11 Thus in the beloved city he gave me a
resting place,
and in Jerusalem was my domain.
12 I took root in an honored people;
in the portion of the Lord is my
inheritance.

13 "I grew tall like a cedar in Lebanon
and like a cypress on the heights of
Hermon.
14 I grew tall like a palm tree in En-gedi*h*
and like rosebushes in Jericho;
like a fair olive tree in the field
and like a plane tree beside water*i* I
grew tall.

e 23.27 Other ancient authorities add as 23.28: *It is a
great honor to follow God, and to be received by him is long
life.   f* 24.1 This heading is included in the Gk text.
g 24.6 Other ancient authorities read *I have acquired a
possession   h* 24.14 Other ancient authorities read *on the
beaches   i* 24.14 Other ancient authorities omit *beside water*

transgression of divine law, however, is only one of three arguments against a woman bearing a child
with a man other than her spouse. Consistent with the book's concern for social relationships, her
sin is also described in terms of the effects on her husband and her children. **23:27** *Fear of the Lord*
is explored throughout the book, mostly with variations on its traditional association with wisdom
(especially 1:11–20, 27–30; 19:20; 25:11; 40:26–27; cf. Prov. 1:7). This verse is the first to parallel *fear
of the Lord* with *commandments of the Lord* (cf. 21:11). Elsewhere it is associated with a variety of
virtues, including self-control (21:11) and experience (25:6).

    24:1–22 Praise of Wisdom. This is one of the most celebrated sections of the book. Wisdom is
here personified (cf. 14:23), and she speaks in the first person praising herself, in a speech recalling
Prov. 8–9 in particular (cf. Job 28; Wis. 7–8; Bar. 3:9–4:4; see **"Woman Wisdom," p. 872**). Compared
to Proverbs, however, the focus falls less on Wisdom's accessibility to all and more on articulating
her special relationship with Israel. The location of her speech is *in the midst of her people* and *in
the assembly of the Most High* (v. 1) rather than along crossroads and at the gates of the city as in
Prov. 8:2–3. **24:3–17** Wisdom's speech begins with her association with creation (vv. 3–5; cf. Gen. 1:2;
Prov. 8:22–31; see **"Wisdom and Creation," p. 1412**). Yet her sway *over every people and nation* (v. 6)
is here invoked to emphasize God's selection of Israel as her dwelling (v. 8) and Jerusalem as her
resting place and *domain* (v. 11; cf. 1 En. 42:8–12). Wisdom pertains to all people and places. Yet she
is an *inheritance* unique to the people Israel and coterminous with chosenness (v. 8; see **"Election,"
p. 31**). The specific geography and vegetation of the land of Israel are cited to describe Wisdom's
localized flourishing (vv. 13–17).

¹⁵ Like cassia and camel's thorn I gave forth
    perfume,
  and like choice myrrh I spread my
    fragrance,
  like galbanum, onycha, and stacte,
    and like the odor of incense in the tent.
¹⁶ Like a terebinth I spread out my branches,
    and my branches are glorious and
    graceful.
¹⁷ Like the vine I bud forth delights,
    and my blossoms become glorious and
    abundant fruit.ʲ

¹⁹ "Come to me, you who desire me,
    and eat your fill of my fruits.
²⁰ For the memory of me is sweeter than
    honey
  and the possession of me sweeter than
    the honeycomb.
²¹ Those who eat of me will hunger for more,
    and those who drink of me will thirst
    for more.
²² Whoever obeys me will not be put to shame,
    and those who work with me will not
    sin."
²³ All this is the book of the covenant of the
    Most High God,
  the law that Moses commanded us

as an inheritance for the
    congregations of Jacob.ᵏ
²⁵ It becomes full, like the Pishon, with
    wisdom
  and like the Tigris at the time of the
    spring harvest.
²⁶ It fills up, like the Euphrates, with
    understanding,
  and like the Jordan at harvest time.
²⁷ It pours forth instruction like the Nile,ˡ
    like the Gihon at the time of vintage.
²⁸ The first man did not know wisdomᵐ
    fully,
  nor will the last one fathom her.
²⁹ For her thoughts are more abundant
    than the sea
  and her counsel deeper than the great
    abyss.

³⁰ I came forth like a canal from a river,
    like a water channel into a garden.

j 24.17 Other ancient authorities add as 24.18: *I am the
mother of beautiful love, of fear, of knowledge, and of holy hope;
I give to all my children; these things are eternal for those who are
named by him.* k 24.23 Other ancient authorities add as
24.24: *Do not cease to be strong in the Lord, cling to him so that he
may strengthen you; the Lord Almighty alone is God, and besides
him there is no savior.* l 24.27 Syr: Gk *It makes instruction shine
forth like light* m 24.28 Gk *her*

24:23–34 Wisdom and law. 24:23 Cf. Exod. 24:7. Whereas the translator's Prologue describes
Israel's ancestral tradition in terms of books and describes learning in terms of reading, the body
of the work includes only two references to books—the other of which is Ben Sira's own (50:27).
The reference here to *the book of the covenant of the Most High God* recalls the ratification of the
Sinaitic covenant through Moses's acts of writing and reading in Exod. 24. In addition, the *book of the
covenant* is here paralleled with *the law that Moses commanded us* and *an inheritance for the congregations of Jacob*, recalling the words of Moses's deathbed blessing of the Israelites in Deut. 33:4. The
emphasis is similarly on God's chosenness of Israel—a theme here expressed through the claim that
Wisdom uniquely dwells among this people, consistent with the repeated concern throughout the
work to depict the Jewish observance of commandments as an important component of proper ethical action (e.g., 1:26; 6:37; 7:31; 10:19; 15:15; 17:14; 23:27). There is thus an association of Wisdom with
Moses's "torah" in the sense of "teaching" (i.e., the literal meaning of the Heb. term translated by Gk.
"nomos" and Eng. "law") but not yet any explicit reference to Torah/Pentateuch as a set of written
Scriptures. See notes on 15:1; 21:11; 32:14–33:15. **24:25–27** Six rivers are mentioned here by name, four
of which are also named in Gen. 2:10–14 in relation to Eden. To the famed Mesopotamian rivers of the
Tigris and *Euphrates* are here added the Levantine *Jordan* and the Egyptian *Nile*—both prominent in
the geography of Jewish life in the Hellenistic period. **24:28–31** Whereas the covenantal associations
of v. 23 convey Wisdom's special relationship to Israel, the shift to water imagery in the rest of the
chapter (vv. 25–34) turns to emphasize its much broader impact. Divine wisdom may be centered
in one earthly place and housed among one people, but it surpasses all human understanding and
extends even beyond human history. **24:30–34** Just as Wisdom's first-person speech combines an
emphasis on her cosmic relevance with her local and historical association with Israel, the chapter
ends with first-person comments from Ben Sira that make a similar point. He likens his own relationship to wisdom to a *canal* (v. 30) that channels a broader flow of water, not just to his own *garden*
(v. 31) and for his own benefit (v. 34), but also out to the *sea* and with an impact even *far away* (v. 32),
for all who seek wisdom (v. 34). He likens the enduring value of wisdom to *prophecy* (v. 33).

31 I said, "I will water my garden
  and drench my flower beds."
And look, my canal became a river
  and my river a sea.
32 I will again make instruction shine forth
  like the dawn,
  and I will make it clear from far away.
33 I will again pour out teaching like prophecy
  and leave it to all future generations.
34 Observe that I have not labored for
  myself alone
  but for all who seek wisdom."

25 I take pleasure in three things,
  and they are beautiful in the sight of
  God and of mortals:[o]
agreement among brothers and sisters,
  friendship among neighbors,
  and a wife and a husband who live in
  harmony.
2 I hate three kinds of people,
  and I loathe their manner of life:
a pauper who boasts, a rich person who
  lies,
  and an old adulterer who lacks sense.

3 If you gathered nothing in your youth,
  how can you find anything in your old
  age?
4 How attractive is sound judgment in
  gray-haired women
  and for aged men to possess good
  counsel!
5 How attractive is wisdom in the aged
  and understanding and counsel in the
  venerable!

6 Rich experience is the crown of the aged,
  and their boast is the fear of the Lord.

7 I can think of nine whom I would call
  happy,
  and a tenth my tongue proclaims:
a man who can rejoice in his children,
  who lives to see the downfall of his
  foes.
8 Happy the man who lives with a sensible
  wife
  and who does not plow with ox and
  ass together,[p]
who does not slip with the tongue
  and who has not become enslaved to
  an inferior.
9 Happy is the one who finds good sense
  and the one who speaks to attentive
  listeners.
10 How great is the one who finds
  wisdom!
  But none is superior to the one who
  fears the Lord.
11 Fear of the Lord surpasses everything;
  to whom can we compare the one
  who has it?[q]
13 Any wound, but not a wound of the
  heart!
  Any wickedness, but not the
  wickedness of a woman!

n 24.34 Gk her o 25.1 Syr Lat: Gk *In three things I was
beautiful, and I stood in beauty before the Lord and mortals*
p 25.8 Heb Syr: Gk lacks *and the one who does not plow with
ox and ass together* q 25.11 Other ancient authorities add
as 25.12: *The fear of the Lord is the beginning of love for him, and
faith is the beginning of clinging to him.*

25:1–2 Relations with others. After the focused reflection on wisdom in chap. 24, Ben Sira returns
to the practical wisdom about social relationships that forms the focus of the majority of the book.
His depiction of his own role as akin to a "canal" channeling wisdom in 24:30–34, however, is echoed
in his passing reference to the shared assessment of beauty by divine and human eyes. When read
in the context of the preceding chapter, the effect is to associate his own assessments with wisdom.
Even as Ben Sira describes his judgments in terms of his visceral emotional reactions (e.g., *pleasure*,
hate) to various people, they take on the authority of divinely sanctioned instruction. His reactions
are conveyed in two numbered lists that telegraph the importance of harmony between people
(siblings, friends, spouses) while condemning causes of disharmony (boasting, lying, adultery).

25:3–6 Experience. The value of old age is lauded over youth. The experience that comes with age
is elevated through its association with *the fear of the Lord* (v. 6)—a phrase used throughout the book
to celebrate what is most exemplary of wisdom (e.g., 1:11–20, 27–30; 19:20; 23:27; 25:11; 40:26–27).

25:7–11 Beatitude. The didactic form of the numbered list is here paired with the liturgical structure of a beatitude ("Happy/blessed are . . ."; cf. 14:20–27). The beatitude structure has precedents
in Psalms (e.g., Pss. 1:1; 2:12; 32:1; 112:1; cf. Isa. 56:2). It is also found in other Second Temple Jewish
literature (e.g., 4Q525, 2 En. 42:6), although now most famous from the Sermon on the Mount (Matt.
5:3–12; cf. Luke 6:20–23) as well as the Jewish "Ashrei" prayer.

25:13–26:27 Women. 25:13–26 Ben Sira's infamous hostility toward women is here on display
in his vivid condemnation of female wickedness, which includes the blaming of womankind for the

14 Any suffering, but not suffering from
those who hate!
And any vengeance, but not the
vengeance of enemies!
15 There is no venom[r] worse than a snake's
venom,[s]
and no anger worse than a woman's[t]
wrath.
16 I would rather live with a lion and a
dragon
than live with an evil woman.
17 A woman's wickedness changes her
appearance
and darkens her face like that of a
bear.
18 Her husband sits[u] among the neighbors,
and he cannot help sighing[v] bitterly.
19 Any iniquity is small compared to a
woman's iniquity;
may a sinner's lot befall her!
20 A sandy ascent for the feet of the aged—
such is a garrulous wife to a quiet
husband.
21 Do not be ensnared by a woman's beauty,
and do not desire a woman for her
possessions.[w]
22 There is wrath and impudence and great
disgrace
when a wife supports her husband.
23 Dejected mind, gloomy face,
and wounded heart come from an evil
wife.
Drooping hands and weak knees
come from the wife who does not
make her husband happy.
24 From a woman sin had its beginning,
and because of her we all die.
25 Allow no outlet to water
and no boldness of speech to an evil
wife.
26 If she does not go as you direct,
separate her from yourself.

26 Happy is the husband of a good
wife;
the number of his days will be
doubled.
2 A courageous wife brings joy to her
husband,
and he will complete his years in
peace.
3 A good wife is a good portion;
she will be granted as a portion to the
man who fears the Lord.
4 Whether rich or poor, his heart is
content,
and at all times his face is cheerful.
5 Of three things my heart is frightened,
and of a fourth I am in great fear:[x]
slander in the city, the gathering of a mob,
and false accusation—all these are
worse than death.
6 But it is heartache and sorrow when a
wife has a rival,
and a tongue-lashing makes it known
to all.
7 A bad wife is a chafing yoke;
taking hold of her is like grasping a
scorpion.
8 A drunken wife arouses great anger;
she cannot hide her shame.
9 The haughty stare betrays a sexually
immoral wife;
her eyelids give her away.
10 Keep strict watch over a headstrong
daughter,
or else, when she finds liberty, she will
make use of it.
11 Be on guard against her impudent eye,
and do not be surprised if she sins
against you.
12 As a thirsty traveler opens his mouth
and drinks from any water near him,

r 25.15 Syr: Gk *head*   s 25.15 Syr: Gk *head*   t 25.15 Other
ancient authorities read *an enemy's*   u 25.18 Heb Syr: Gk
loses heart   v 25.18 Other ancient authorities read *and lis-*
tening he sighs   w 25.21 Heb Syr: Gk lacks *for her possessions*
x 26.5 Syr: Meaning of Gk uncertain

origins of both sin and death (v. 24)—a trope that recalls Jewish and Christian traditions about Eve
(2 Cor. 11:3; 1 Tim. 2:14; cf. Gen. 3:6) but also Greek traditions about Pandora. **26:1–27** Ben Sira's
diatribe against wicked women is interlaced with verses noting the qualities of a good wife as loyal,
modest, beautiful, and silent. Far more detail is lavished, however, on her wicked counterparts—
including wives who are bad, drunken, haughty, and unchaste (vv. 7-9) and daughters who are
headstrong, impudent, and sinful (vv. 10-12); cf. 4Q184. **26:5** *Of three things . . . and of a fourth.* Many
of Ben Sira's instructions are structured as numbered lists, geared toward ease of memorization and
suggesting an oral setting and didactic use. This chapter includes examples of the more specific
structure "Of X things . . . of X + 1 . . ." (i.e., vv. 5 and 28); cf. 50:25–26; Amos 1:3, 6, 11, 13; 2:1, 4, 6;
Prov. 30:18–19, 21–23. This form is found in later rabbinic literature as well. It is here used to depict a

so she will sit in front of every tent peg
and open her quiver to the arrow.

13 A wife's charm delights her husband,
and her skill puts flesh on his bones.

14 A silent wife is a gift from the Lord,
and nothing is so precious as her
self-discipline.

15 A modest wife adds charm to charm,
and no scales can weigh the value of
her self-control.

16 Like the sun rising in the heights of the
Lord,
so is the beauty of a good wife in her
well-ordered home.

17 Like the shining lamp on the holy
lampstand,
so is a beautiful face on a stately
figure.

18 Like golden pillars on silver bases,
so are shapely legs upon steadfast
feet.

———————

Other ancient authorities add verses 19–27:

19 *My child, keep sound the bloom of your youth,*
and do not give your strength to strangers.

20 *Seek a fertile field within the whole plain,*
and sow it with your own seed, trusting in
your fine stock.

21 *So your offspring will prosper,*
and, having confidence in their good descent,
will grow great.

22 *A prostitute is regarded as spittle*
and a married woman as a tower of death to
her lovers.

23 *A godless wife is given as a portion to a lawless*
man,
but a pious wife is given to the man who
fears the Lord.

24 *A shameless woman constantly acts*
disgracefully,

but a modest daughter will even be
embarrassed before her husband.

25 *A headstrong wife is regarded as a dog,*
but one who has a sense of shame will fear
the Lord.

26 *A wife honoring her husband will seem wise to*
all,
but if she dishonors him in her pride she will
be known to all as ungodly.
Happy is the husband of a good wife,
for the number of his years will be
doubled.

27 *A loud-voiced and garrulous wife is like a*
trumpet sounding the charge,
and every person like this lives in the anarchy
of war.

———————

28 At two things my heart is grieved,
and because of a third anger comes
over me:
a warrior in want through poverty,
intelligent men who are treated
contemptuously,
and a man who turns back from
righteousness to sin—
the Lord will prepare him for the
sword!

29 A merchant can hardly keep from
wrongdoing,
nor is a tradesman innocent of sin.

27 Many have committed sin for
gain,[y]
and those who seek to get rich will
avert their eyes.

2 As a stake is driven firmly into a fissure
between stones,
so sin is wedged in between selling
and buying.

y 27.1 Other ancient authorities read *a trifle*

jealous woman as worse than slander, mobs, and false accusations. **26:19–27** The anthological form of this book, as more compilation than treatise, seems to have made it especially permeable to additions and omissions during the course of its transmission. This unit is found in some Greek and Syriac manuscripts but missing from the Hebrew and other Greek manuscripts. Scholars debate whether this variance is the result of addition or omission. It shares with vv. 1–18 the sorting of women into the binary of bad and good, with godless, loud, and headstrong wives and shameless women thus contrasted with pious and honorable wives and modest daughters. **26:26** *Happy is the husband of a good wife.* This refrain repeats v. 1.

26:28 *At two things . . . because of a third.* A form parallel to v. 5 is here used to add a point unrelated to women. Two examples of men who act well but suffer are contrasted with the case of men who act well and then fall into error.

26:29–27:3 Commerce. **26:29** *A merchant.* This verse begins a new cluster of instructions, dedicated to the theme of commerce. **27:1–3** Commerce inevitably brings the danger of *sin.* But *fear of the Lord* has a protective effect (cf. 1:18; 33:1).

³ If a person is not steadfast in the fear of
    the Lord,
    his house will be quickly overthrown.
⁴ When a sieve is shaken, the refuse appears;
    so does a person's waste when he speaks.
⁵ The kiln tests the potter's vessels,
    and the test of a person is in his
    conversation.
⁶ Its fruit discloses the cultivation of a tree;
    so does speech[z] the thoughts of the
    human mind.
⁷ Do not praise anyone before he speaks,
    for this is the way people are tested.
⁸ If you pursue justice, you will attain it
    and wear it like a glorious robe.
⁹ Birds roost with their own kind,
    so honesty comes home to those who
    practice it.
¹⁰ A lion lies in wait for prey;
    so does sin for evildoers.
¹¹ The conversation of the godly is always
    wise,
    but the fool changes like the moon.
¹² Among stupid people limit your time,
    but among thoughtful people linger on.
¹³ The talk of fools is offensive,
    and their laughter is wantonly sinful.
¹⁴ Their cursing and swearing make one's
    hair stand on end,
    and their quarrels make others stop
    their ears.

¹⁵ The strife of the proud leads to bloodshed,
    and their abuse is grievous to hear.
¹⁶ Whoever betrays secrets destroys
    confidence
    and will never find a congenial friend.
¹⁷ Love your friends and keep faith with
    them,
    but if you betray their secrets, do not
    follow after them.
¹⁸ For as a person destroys an enemy,[a]
    so you have destroyed the friendship
    of your neighbor.
¹⁹ And as you allow a bird to escape from
    your hand,
    so you have let your neighbor go and
    will not catch him again.
²⁰ Do not go after him, for he is too far off
    and has escaped like a gazelle from a
    snare.
²¹ For a wound may be bandaged,
    and there is reconciliation after abuse,
    but whoever has betrayed secrets is
    without hope.
²² Whoever winks the eye plots harm,
    and those who know such a one will
    keep their distance.
²³ In your presence their mouths are all
    sweetness,
    and they admire your words,

z 27.6 Other ancient authorities read *reasoning*
a 27.18 Other ancient authorities read *corpse*

27:4–7 Speech. The book returns to the theme of speech (e.g., 5:10–6:4; 20:1–31). In this case, the speech in question is not oaths or curses (cf. 23:7–15) but everyday conversation. The focus falls not on the one who speaks but on the one who listens. The observation of everyday phenomena like sieves, kilns, and fruit trees offers metaphors to connect speech to a person's mind and character. The implication is that wisdom extends to the discernment of clues to character even in ordinary interactions. Just as one's vision should become attuned to the physical comportment of other people (19:29–30), so one's ears should become honed as well. Through one's senses, one tests others. Part of wisdom is choosing apt associates (so too, e.g., Letter of Aristeas 130; see also 3 Macc. 6:22–24 on the dangers of choosing false friends who give bad advice).

27:8–10 Reciprocity. Three short aphorisms express how those who seek out a virtue or vice will find it.

27:11–15 Speech. The concern with the power of speech is further explored with a focus on what is at stake in learning to discern character from conversation. Association with pious people means hearing wise words. The dangers of hearing the words, laughter, and cursing of stupid people range from wasting one's time to risking bloodshed.

27:16–21 Secrets. The power of speech—and the importance of control over one's speech—is exemplified by the broken secret. The danger of associating with those who cannot keep secrets had been stressed in 8:17; 13:12; and 22:22 (cf. Prov. 20:19). Here the focus is on keeping the secrets of one's friends, lest one lose those friendships forever.

27:22–29 Hypocrisy. The concern for proper speech continues with a turn toward hypocrisy, or twisted speech—which is here condemned with a special hate. Ben Sira's emotional reaction of hate is here underlined by the claim of a divine counterpart: *even the Lord hates* those who *twist their speech* (vv. 23–24).

but later they will twist their speech
and with your own words they will
cause a scandal.

²⁴ I have hated many things but them above
all;
even the Lord hates them.

²⁵ Those who throw a stone straight up
throw it on their own heads,
and a treacherous blow opens up
many wounds.

²⁶ Whoever digs a pit will fall into it,
and whoever sets a snare will be
caught in it.

²⁷ If people do evil, it will roll back upon
them,
and they will not know where it came
from.

²⁸ Mockery and abuse issue from the proud,
but vengeance lies in wait for them
like a lion.

²⁹ Those who rejoice in the fall of the godly
will be caught in a snare,
and pain will consume them before
their death.

³⁰ Anger and wrath, these also are
abominations,
yet a sinner holds on to them.

28 The vengeful will face the Lord's
vengeance,
for he keeps a strict account of[b] their
sins.

² Forgive your neighbor the wrong he has
done,
and then your sins will be pardoned
when you pray.

³ Does anyone harbor anger against
another
and expect healing from the Lord?

⁴ If people have no mercy toward those
like themselves,
can they then seek pardon for their
own sins?

⁵ If mere mortals harbor wrath,
who will make an atoning sacrifice for
their sins?

⁶ Remember the end of your life and set
enmity aside;
remember corruption and death and
be true to the commandments.

⁷ Remember the commandments and
do not be angry with your
neighbor;
remember the covenant of the Most
High and overlook faults.

⁸ Refrain from strife, and your sins will be
fewer,
for the hot-tempered kindle strife

⁹ and the sinner disrupts friendships
and sows discord among those who
are at peace.

¹⁰ In proportion to the fuel, so will the fire
burn,
and in proportion to the obstinacy, so
will strife increase;[c]
in proportion to people's strength will be
their anger,
and in proportion to their wealth they
will increase their wrath.

¹¹ A hasty quarrel kindles a fire,
and a hasty dispute sheds blood.

¹² If you blow on a spark, it will glow;
if you spit on it, it will be put out,
yet both come out of your mouth.

b 28.1 Other ancient authorities read *for he firmly establishes*
c 28.10 Other ancient authorities read *burn*

27:30–28:11 Emotions. To the potentially positive value of the emotions of the wise, which issue forth from their skills of discerning character, Ben Sira shifts to the danger of unregulated emotions. Hate might be warranted at times, but *anger* brings multiple sorts of danger. The text moves through these dangers from the divine to the social. Human vengeance risks sparking divine vengeance and a dearth of divine mercy (vv. 1–3), for instance, but it also risks an escalation of social conflicts that might lead to discord and bloodshed (vv. 8–11). **28:2** *When you pray.* Consistent with the text's emphasis on the efficacy of prayer (cf. 21:5; 34:29; 35:16–21; 37:15; 38:9; 51:11), it is here associated with the pardoning of sins. **28:6–7** *Remember.* Four exhortations to remember here introduce arguments specific to Israel into the discussion of the dangers of anger. The first two pertain to recollecting one's mortality, first in relation to one's postmortem fate (cf. vv. 21–22) and then in relation to the *commandments.* The second two are reminders of the *commandments* and *the covenant,* here associated with refraining from anger and overlooking faults (cf. Lev. 19:18).

28:12–26 Speech. 28:12 The metaphor of the *mouth* is used to convey the doubled power of speech: one can *blow on a spark* to stoke it or use *spit* to put it out, just as one's choice of words can either escalate or cease strife. This saying is quoted in Leviticus Rabbah 33.1, attributed to "bar

13 Curse the gossips and the
  double-tongued,
    for they destroy the peace of many.
14 Slander[d] has shaken many
  and scattered them from nation to
    nation;
  it has destroyed strong cities
  and overturned the houses of the
    great.
15 Slander[e] has driven courageous women
  from their homes
  and deprived them of the fruit of their
    toil.
16 Those who pay heed to slander[f] will not
  find rest,
  nor will they settle down in peace.
17 The blow of a whip raises a welt,
  but a blow of the tongue crushes the
    bones.
18 Many have fallen by the edge of the
  sword,
  but not as many as have fallen because
    of the tongue.
19 Happy is the one who is protected
  from it,
  who has not been exposed to its
    anger,
  who has not borne its yoke,
  and who has not been bound with its
    fetters.
20 For its yoke is a yoke of iron,
  and its fetters are fetters of bronze;
21 its death is an evil death,
  and Hades is preferable to it.
22 It has no power over the godly;
  they will not be burned in its flame.

23 Those who forsake the Lord will fall into
  its power;
  it will burn among them and will not
    be put out.
  It will be sent out against them like a lion;
  like a leopard it will mangle them.
24a Look! Fence in your property with
  thorns,
25b   and make a door and a bolt for your
    mouth.
24b Lock up your silver and gold,
25a   and make balances and scales for your
    words.
26 Take care not to err with your tongue[g]
  and fall victim to one lying in wait.

29 The merciful lend to their neighbors;
  by holding out a helping hand they
    keep the commandments.
2 Lend to your neighbor in his time of need;
  repay your neighbor when a loan falls
    due.
3 Keep your word and be honest with him,
  and on every occasion you will find
    what you need.
4 Many regard a loan as a windfall
  and cause trouble to those who help
    them.
5 One kisses another's hands until he gets
  a loan
  and is deferential in speaking of his
    neighbor's money,
  but at the time for repayment he delays
  and pays back with empty promises
  and finds fault with the time.

d 28.14 Gk *A third tongue*   *e* 28.15 Gk *A third tongue*
f 28.16 Gk *it*   *g* 28.26 Gk *with it*

Sira" in the context of a discussion of Lev. 25:1–14. **28:13** *Curse the gossips.* What is negative in most cases has its place when done by the wise and in the correct context. Hypocrisy, earlier deemed to rightly inspire hate (27:24), also warrants cursing, which is otherwise discouraged (23:12–15). **28:14–15** *Slander* is literally a third tongue—even worse than the doubled tongue of hypocrisy in v. 13. The power of speech, in this case, extends to unwarranted dispersion, destruction of the mighty, and shaming of pious women. **28:21–22** *An evil death.* The text here appears to presume some sort of belief in afterlife judgment—a concept not explicitly attested in earlier biblical literature but increasingly discussed in the Second Temple period. It is unclear whether the judgment by fire, to which the Greek seems to allude, occurs directly postmortem or awaits end-time resurrection. On the use of "Hades" in the Greek in relation to the likely Hebrew "Sheol," see 9:12; 14:12; see also note on 7:17. **28:24–26** Control of speech is likened to fencing in one's property and locking up one's riches.

29:1–28 **Loans.** This chapter is a focused discussion of practicalities with respect to loans. The advice is detailed and presumes a lived situation in which loans, surety, and debt were commonplace. Whereas much of the book focuses on friendship, the focus here is primarily on neighbors (see note on 13:15). **29:1–7** Exhortations to be generous to one's neighbors are here associated with *the commandments* (v. 1; cf. Deut. 15:7–11). The main focus of this section, however, is arguing for generosity in relation to the social value of reciprocity among equals. The assumed situation is one in which people lend one another funds in their times of need, such that honesty, gratitude,

⁶ If he can pay, his creditor[b] will hardly get
    back half
    and will regard that as a windfall.
If he cannot pay, the borrower[i] has
    robbed the other of his money,
    and he has needlessly made him an
    enemy;
he will repay him with curses and
    reproaches
    and instead of glory will repay him
    with dishonor.
⁷ Many refuse to lend, not because of
    meanness,
    but from fear[j] of being defrauded
    needlessly.

⁸ Nevertheless, be patient with someone in
    humble circumstances,
    and do not keep him waiting for your
    alms.
⁹ Help the poor for the commandment's sake,
    and in their need do not send them
    away empty-handed.
¹⁰ Lose your silver for the sake of a brother
    or a friend,
    and do not let it rust under a stone and
    be lost.
¹¹ Lay up your treasure according to the
    commandments of the Most High,
    and it will profit you more than gold.
¹² Store up almsgiving in your treasury,
    and it will rescue you from every
    disaster;
¹³ better than a stout shield and a sturdy
    spear,
    it will fight for you against the enemy.
¹⁴ A good person will be surety for his
    neighbor,
    but the one who has lost all sense of
    shame will fail him.

¹⁵ Do not forget the kindness of your
    guarantor,
    for he has given his life for you.
¹⁶ A sinner wastes the property of his
    guarantor,
¹⁷   and the ungrateful person abandons
    his rescuer.
¹⁸ Being surety has ruined many who were
    prosperous
    and has tossed them about like waves
    of the sea;
it has driven the influential into exile,
    and they have wandered among
    foreign nations.
¹⁹ The sinner comes to grief through
    surety;
    his pursuit of gain involves him in
    lawsuits.
²⁰ Assist your neighbor to the best of your
    ability,
    but be careful not to fall yourself.
²¹ The necessities of life are water, bread,
    and clothing,
    and also a house to assure
    privacy.
²² Better is the life of the poor under their
    own crude roof
    than sumptuous food in the house of
    strangers.
²³ Be content with little or much,
    and you will hear no reproach for
    being a guest.[k]
²⁴ It is a miserable life to go from house to
    house;
    as a guest you should not open your
    mouth;

b 29.6 Gk *he*   *i* 29.6 Gk *he*   *j* 29.7 Other ancient authorities read *many refuse to lend, therefore, because of such meanness; they are afraid*   *k* 29.23 Lat: Gk *reproach from your family*; other ancient authorities lack this line

care in spending a loan, and quick repayment are all pressing. One is exhorted to be generous as a creditor, but one is also warned to act properly as a lender with the understanding that creditors are sometimes warranted in refusing to lend (v. 7). **29:8–13** The text turns from a situation of reciprocal lending among neighbors to a situation of charitable giving to the poor. *The commandments* are invoked as rationale (vv. 9, 11), in part through another level of reciprocity; charitable actions will be rewarded with protection against disaster, such that alms can be likened to weapons (vv. 12–13; cf. 3:30–31). This advice extends the earlier discussion of proper action toward the poor (see 3:30–4:10 and note on 21:5). **29:14–20** Returning to neighbors and social reciprocity, Ben Sira discusses the practicalities of serving as a *guarantor* and being grateful to those who do the same for you; contrast Prov. 6:1–5. Ben Sira tempers the call for generosity with an acknowledgment of the dangers of lending and putting up surety; special care must be given because of the risk of ruin, lawsuits, and even exile. **29:21–28** From the dangers of lending money and putting up surety for others, the text turns to emphasize the importance of ensuring one is able to have one's own house—however modest—rather than be forced to stay with others.

25 you will play the host and provide drink without being thanked,
and besides this you will hear rude words like these:
26 "Come here, stranger, prepare the table;
let me eat what you have there."
27 "Be off, stranger, for an honored guest is here;
my brother has come for a visit, and I need the house."
28 It is hard for a sensible person to bear scolding about lodging[l] and the insults of the moneylender.

CONCERNING CHILDREN[m]

30 He who loves his son will whip him often,
so that he may rejoice at the way he turns out.
2 He who disciplines his son will profit by him
and will boast of him among acquaintances.
3 He who teaches his son will make his enemies envious
and will glory in him among his friends.
4 When the father dies, he will not seem to be dead,
for he has left behind him one like himself,
5 whom in his life he looked upon with joy
and at death, without grief.
6 He has left behind him an avenger against his enemies
and one to repay the kindness of his friends.

7 Whoever cherishes his son will bind up his wounds,
and at every cry his heart will be troubled.

8 An unbroken horse turns out stubborn,
and an unchecked son turns out headstrong.
9 Pamper a child, and he will terrorize you;
play with him, and he will grieve you.
10 Do not laugh with him, or you will have sorrow with him,
and in the end you will gnash your teeth.
11 Give him no freedom in his youth;[n]
12 beat his sides while he is young,
or else he will become stubborn and disobey you.[o]
13 Discipline your son and make his yoke heavy,[p]
so that you may not be offended by his shamelessness.

14 Better off poor, healthy, and fit than rich and afflicted in body.
15 Health and fitness are better than any gold
and a robust body[q] than countless riches.
16 There is no wealth better than health of body
and no gladness above joy of heart.
17 Death is better than a life of misery
and eternal sleep[r] than chronic sickness.

CONCERNING FOODS[s]

18 Good things poured out upon a mouth that is closed

l 29.28 Or *scolding from the household*   *m* 30.1 This heading is included in the Gk text.   *n* 30.11 Other ancient authorities add *and do not ignore his errors. Bow down his neck in his youth,*   *o* 30.12 Other ancient authorities add *and you will have sorrow of soul from him*   *p* 30.13 Heb: Gk *take pains with him*   *q* 30.15 Gk: Syr Heb read *spirit*   *r* 30.17 Other ancient authorities lack *eternal sleep*   *s* 30.18 This heading is included in the Gk text; other ancient authorities place the heading before 30.16

30:1–13 Sons. Paralleling the use of binary contrasts to discuss women in chap. 26, this cluster of instructions juxtaposes its ideal of a disciplined son (vv. 1–6) with cautions about a spoiled son (vv. 9–13; cf. Prov. 29:15). Fatherhood is here associated with violence (vv. 1, 12; cf. 22:6; Prov. 13:24; 23:13–24). The aim is less to raise a pious or wise child than to enable boasting to the father's friends and inspire envy among his enemies (vv. 2–3), while also continuing relationships of friendship and enmity even after one's own death (v. 6). The ideal son is one who exactly replicates the father (v. 4). Compare the instructions for a son's behavior toward his father in 3:1–16.

30:14–17 Wealth and health. This cluster of teachings cautions against valuing wealth over health. It escalates into an assertion that living with chronic illness is worse than death. On illness in relation to his advice to make sure to heed the expertise of physicians and pharmacists, see 38:1–15.

30:18–25 Enjoyment. 30:18–20 After the denigration of a life of chronic illness in v. 17, it is stressed that a good life should not go unappreciated. Ben Sira makes this point with three metaphors: food offerings to the dead, sacrifice to an idol, and the embrace of a woman to a eunuch.

are like offerings of food placed upon
a grave.
[19] Of what use to an idol is a sacrifice?
For it can neither eat nor smell.
So is the one punished by the Lord;
[20] he sees with his eyes and groans
as a eunuch groans when embracing a
young woman.[t]

[21] Do not give yourself over to sorrow,
and do not distress yourself
deliberately.
[22] A joyful heart is life itself,
and rejoicing lengthens one's life span.
[23] Indulge yourself[u] and take comfort,
and remove sorrow far from you,
for sorrow has destroyed many,
and no advantage ever comes from it.
[24] Jealousy and anger shorten life,
and anxiety brings on premature old
age.
[25] Those who are cheerful and merry at table
will benefit from their food.

31 Wakefulness over wealth wastes away
one's flesh,
and anxiety about it drives away sleep.
[2] Wakeful anxiety prevents slumber,
and a severe illness carries off sleep.[v]
[3] Rich people toil to amass possessions,
and when they rest, they fill
themselves with their delicacies.
[4] Poor people toil to make a meager living,
and if ever they rest, they become
needy.

[5] Those who love gold will not be
justified;
those who pursue money will be led
astray[w] by it.
[6] Many have come to ruin because of
gold,
and their destruction has met them
face to face.
[7] It is a stumbling block to those who are
avid for it,
and every fool will be taken captive
by it.
[8] Blessed are the rich who are found
blameless
and who do not go after gold.
[9] Who are they, that we may call them
happy?
For they have done wonders among
their people.
[10] Who has been tested by it and been
found perfect?
Let it be for them a ground for
boasting.
Who has had the power to transgress
and did not transgress
and to do evil and did not do it?
[11] Their prosperity will be established,[x]
and the assembly will proclaim their
acts of charity.

t 30.20 Other ancient authorities add *So is the person who does right under compulsion* *u* 30.23 Other ancient authorities read *Beguile yourself* *v* 31.2 Other ancient authorities read *sleep carries off a severe illness* *w* 31.5 Heb Syr: Gk *pursues destruction will be filled* *x* 31.11 Other ancient authorities add *because of this*

The first two invoke values lauded within earlier biblical literature but not necessarily shared by the broader Hellenistic culture of Ben Sira's time. **30:21–25** Despite Ben Sira's emphasis on various other sorts of bodily self-control, he here calls for savoring food (cf. Eccl. 9:7) and enjoying life (cf. Eccl. 11:9–10). Significantly, however, the focus again falls on the regulation of emotions. As in chap. 28, there is a caution against uncontrolled *anger*; here, the same is said for *jealousy* and *anxiety* (v. 24). In addition, the reader is warned against wallowing in *sorrow* or deliberately distressing oneself (v. 21) in light of the destructive effects of such sadness in itself (v. 23). Conversely, *rejoicing* is said to lengthen *one's life span* (v. 22).

31:1–2 Anxiety. The concern for regulating one's anxiety in 30:24 is here extended with a pair of verses that associate anxiety over money, in particular, with sleeplessness and illness. Anxiety is similarly a concern in Egyptian wisdom texts (e.g., Papyrus Insinger 19.7–8).

31:3–4 Work. The toil of the rich is contrasted with the toil of the poor; both work (cf. 40:1), but only the former can rest.

31:5–11 Wealth. That the implied audience of the book includes well-off Jews is suggested by the treatment of wealth in this cluster of instructions. It begins with truisms about the dangers of greed (vv. 5–7). Far from critiquing the rich, it continues with a sketch of the ideal rich man, who uses his stature to benefit his people (v. 9), who is all the more celebrated for resisting the temptations to evil that come with wealth (v. 10), and who takes his own prosperity to give to his community (v. 11; cf. 29:8–13). Wealth poses a danger to ethics, but this danger can be defused by communal engagement and generosity. Compare the approach to rich and poor in the Epistle of Enoch (1 En. 91–107).

¹² ʸAre you seated at the table of the great?ᶻ
  Do not be greedy at it,
  and do not say, "How much food there
    is here!"
¹³ Remember that a greedy eye is a bad
    thing.
  What has been created more greedy
    than the eye?
  Therefore it covers the face with tears.
¹⁴ Do not reach out your hand for
    everything you see,
  and do not crowd your neighborᵃ at
    the dish.
¹⁵ Judge your neighbor's feelings by your
    own,
  and in every matter be thoughtful.
¹⁶ Eat what is set before you like a well
    brought-up person,ᵇ
  and do not chew greedily, or you will
    be despised.
¹⁷ Be the first to stop, as befits good manners,
  and do not be insatiable, or you will
    give offense.
¹⁸ If you are seated among many persons,
  do not help yourselfᶜ before they do.
¹⁹ How ample a little is for the
    well-disciplined!
  They do not breathe heavily when in
    bed.
²⁰ Healthy sleep depends on moderate
    eating;
  they rise early and feel fit.

The distress of sleeplessness and of
    nausea
  and colic are with the glutton.
²¹ If you are overstuffed with food,
  get up to vomit, and you will have
    relief.
²² Listen to me, my child, and do not
    disregard me,
  and in the end you will appreciate my
    words.
  In everything you do be moderate,ᵈ
  and no sickness will overtake you.
²³ People bless those who are liberal with
    food,
  and the testimony to their generosity
    is trustworthy.
²⁴ The city complains of those who are
    stingy with food,
  and the testimony to their stinginess is
    accurate.
²⁵ Do not try to prove your strength by
    wine-drinking,
  for wine has destroyed many.
²⁶ As the furnace tests the work of the smith,ᵉ
  so wine tests hearts when the insolent
    quarrel.
²⁷ Wine is very life to humans
  if taken in moderation.

y 31.12 Some ancient authorities add the title *Concerning Food* z 31.12 Heb Syr: Gk *at a great table* a 31.14 Gk *him* b 31.16 Heb: Gk *like a human being* c 31.18 Gk *reach out your hand* d 31.22 Heb Syr: Gk *industrious* e 31.26 Heb: Gk *tests the hardening of steel by dipping*

31:12–18 Table etiquette. The implied audience of the book is not the elite per se but rather men with some degree of wealth who thus need advice about how best to navigate encounters with those who have power over them. This encompasses matters of etiquette when dining with the powerful—a common topic in sapiential literature (cf. Prov. 23:1–3). The implication is that the reader's everyday manners might not suffice when *seated at the table of the great.* Most of the advice pertains to restraint. One should not take too much food or crowd the others at the table. One should *be the first to stop* but not the first to start. Caution in such settings encompasses attention to how one chews.

31:19–24 Eating. The recurrent theme of self-control continues with a cluster of instructions about moderation in eating. As in vv. 1–2, sleeplessness is a special concern (vv. 19–21). Overeating is deemed bad for one's health (vv. 20–22), while *stinginess* with food is deemed bad for one's reputation (vv. 23–24). **31:22** *Listen to me, my child.* See notes on 2:1 and 3:1.

31:25–31 Drinking. The concern with the regulation of eating in chaps. 30–31 is here extended to drinking wine. Here too, the emphasis falls on *moderation* (v. 27). Too much *wine-drinking* can be destructive, leading to *bitterness, anger,* and strife (vv. 25–26, 29–30; cf. Prov. 20:1). The danger lies in uncontrolled emotions and the social tensions that can result. But wine can also foster the positive emotions that Ben Sira encourages in 30:21–25. In the Hellenistic period, questions about propriety around wine-drinking may have become more prominent due to the popularity of the symposium, a period of drinking after a banquet. Compare also the narratives about excessive wine-drinking leading to political foul play and assassinations in 1 Macc. 16:15–17 (for Simon, son of Mattathias) and Jdt. 13:1–8 (for Holofernes).

What is life to one who is without wine?
  It has been created to make people
    happy.
[28] Wine drunk at the proper time and in
    moderation
  is rejoicing of heart and gladness of
    soul.
[29] Wine drunk to excess leads to bitterness
    of spirit,
  to quarrels and stumbling.
[30] Drunkenness increases the anger of fools
    to their own hurt,
  reducing their strength and adding
    wounds.
[31] Do not reprove your neighbors at a
    banquet of wine,
  and do not despise them in their
    merrymaking;
speak no word of reproach to them,
  and do not distress them by making
    demands of them.

32 If they make you master of the feast,
    do not exalt yourself;
  be among them as one of their
    number.
Take care of them first and then sit
    down;
[2]   when you have fulfilled all your
    duties, take your place,
so that you may be merry along with
    them
  and receive a wreath for your
    excellent leadership.

[3] Speak, you who are older, for it is your
    right,
  but with accurate knowledge, and do
    not interrupt the music.

[4] Where there is entertainment, do not
    pour out talk;
  do not display your cleverness at the
    wrong time.
[5] A ruby seal in a setting of gold
  is a concert of music at a banquet of
    wine.
[6] A seal of emerald in a rich setting of gold
  is the melody of music with good
    wine.

[7] Speak, you who are young, if you are
    obliged to,
  but no more than twice and only if
    asked.
[8] Be brief; say much in few words;
  be as one who knows and can still
    hold his tongue.
[9] Among the great do not act as their equal;
  and when another is speaking, do not
    babble.
[10] Lightning travels ahead of the thunder,
  and approval goes before one who is
    modest.
[11] Leave in good time and do not be the last;
  go home quickly and do not linger.
[12] Amuse yourself there to your heart's
    content,
  but do not sin through proud speech.
[13] But above all bless your Maker,
  who intoxicates you with his good gifts.
[14] The one who seeks God[f] will accept his
    discipline,
  and those who rise early to seek him[g]
    will find favor.

f 32.14 Heb: Gk *who fears the Lord*   g 32.14 Other ancient
authorities lack *to seek him*

32:1–13 Table etiquette. Advice for attending a banquet continues, picking up the theme raised in 31:12. **32:1–2** *Master of the feast.* Cf. John 2:9–10. Although advice about dining with the powerful is among the traditional topics of sapiential literature in Israel and the Near East, the reference to this position suggests that Ben Sira's focus on this issue also reflects his Hellenistic context. **32:3–9** Etiquette is here distinguished by age, along a binary contrast of young and old. Whereas Ben Sira had advised care in speech for all in 20:5–7, he here specifies that older men should speak to display their knowledge at banquets, as long as they do not interrupt the music or entertainment. By contrast, younger men should keep their speech to a minimum and make sure not to talk over others. **32:10–13** Just as etiquette includes when to start and stop eating (31:17–18), so it also includes when to leave. Such opportunities are tricky to navigate but should be enjoyed with gratitude to the divine.

32:14–33:19 Seeking the divine. So far, in the chapters following the discussion of Wisdom in chap. 24, only passing reference has been made to God, the law, and the commandments. In this passage, the focus shifts somewhat abruptly from eating and drinking to questions about the divine. Seeking God is directly paralleled with seeking *the law*. Here too, what is meant is not "law" (Heb. "torah," Gk. "nomos") in the sense of those Scriptures that we now call the Torah/Pentateuch but

15 The one who seeks the law will be filled
   with it,
   but the hypocrite will stumble at it.
16 Those who fear the Lord will form true
   judgments,
   and they will kindle righteous deeds
   like a light.
17 Sinners will shun reproof
   and will find a decision according to
   their liking.

18 A sensible person will not overlook a
   thoughtful suggestion;
   an insolent[b] and proud person will not
   be deterred by fear.[i]
19 Do nothing without deliberation,
   but when you have acted do not
   regret it.
20 Do not go on a path full of hazards,
   and do not stumble at an obstacle
   twice.[j]
21 Do not be overconfident on a smooth[k]
   road,
22   and give good heed to your paths.[l]
23 Guard[m] yourself in every act,
   for this is the keeping of the
   commandments.

24 The one who keeps the law preserves
   himself,[n]
   and the one who trusts the Lord will
   not suffer loss.

33 No evil will befall the one who fears
   the Lord,
   but in trials such a one will be rescued
   again and again.
2 The wise will not hate the law,
   but the one who is hypocritical about
   it is like a boat in a storm.
3 The sensible person will trust in the law,[o]
   for such a one the law is as
   dependable as a divine oracle.

4 Prepare what to say, and then you will be
   listened to;
   draw upon your training and give your
   answer.

5 The heart of a fool is like a cart wheel
   and his thoughts like a turning axle.
6 A mocking friend is like a stallion
   that neighs no matter who the rider is.
7 Why is one day more important than
   another,
   when all the daylight in the year is
   from the sun?
8 By the Lord's wisdom they were
   distinguished,
   and he appointed the different
   seasons and festivals.
9 Some days he exalted and hallowed,
   and some he made ordinary days.
10 All humans come from the ground,
   and humankind[p] was created out of
   the dust.
11 In the fullness of his knowledge the Lord
   distinguished them
   and appointed their different ways.
12 Some he blessed and exalted,
   and some he made holy and brought
   near to himself,
   but some he cursed and brought low
   and turned them out of their place.
13 Like clay in the hand of the potter,
   to be molded as he pleases,
   so are humans in the hand of their Maker,
   to be given whatever he decides.

14 Good is the opposite of evil
   and life the opposite of death;
   so the sinner is the opposite of the
   godly.
15 Look at all the works of the Most High;
   they come in pairs, one the opposite of
   the other.

16 Now I was the last to keep vigil;
   I was like a gleaner following the
   grape-pickers;

b 32.18 Heb: Gk *alien*   i 32.18 Or *cower in fear*; other ancient
authorities add *and after acting, with him, without delibera-*
tion   j 32.20 Heb: Gk *stumble on stony ground*   k 32.21 Or
an unexplored   l 32.22 Heb Syr: Gk *and beware of your*
children   m 32.23 Heb Syr: Gk *Trust*   n 32.24 Heb: Gk *who*
believes the law heeds the commandments   o 33.3 Heb *a word*
p 33.10 Heb: Gk *Adam*

rather the broader set of precepts for action described throughout the book, which include discernment (32:16–18) and self-control (v. 23); see notes on 15:1; 21:11; 24:23. Everyday advice—such as to
wake up early (32:14) and listen to others' suggestions (v. 18)—is here interwoven with calls to seek
God and *the law* (vv. 14–15). The recurrent theme of self-control is here linked to *the commandments*
(v. 23). **32:24–33:1** An apotropaic rationale is here given for following the law (i.e., to ward off evil):
it protects one from *loss* and *trials*. **33:2–3** The *law* is likened to a *divine oracle* in terms of its trustworthiness. **33:16–19** As in 24:30–34 Ben Sira speaks in the first person to explain his relationship to

¹⁷ by the blessing of the Lord I arrived first,
and like a grape-picker I filled my
winepress.
¹⁸ Consider that I have not labored for
myself alone
but for all who seek instruction.
¹⁹ Hear me, you who are great among the
people,
and you leaders of the congregation,
pay heed!
²⁰ To son or wife, to brother or friend,
do not give power over yourself, as
long as you live,
and do not give your property to
another,
in case you change your mind and
must ask for it.
²¹ While you are still alive and have breath
in you,
do not let anyone take your place.
²² For it is better that your children should
ask from you
than that you should look to the hand
of your children.
²³ Excel in all that you do;
bring no stain upon your honor.
²⁴ At the time when you end the days of
your life,
in the hour of death, distribute your
inheritance.
²⁵ ^qFodder and a stick and burdens for a
donkey;
bread and discipline and work for a
slave.

²⁶ Set your slaves to work,^r and you will
find rest;
leave their hands idle, and they will
seek liberty.
²⁷ Yoke and strap will bow the neck,
and for wicked slaves there are racks
and tortures.
²⁸ Put them to work in order that they may
not be idle,
²⁹ for idleness teaches much evil.
³⁰ Set them to work as is fitting for them,
and if they do not obey make their
fetters heavy.
Do not be overbearing toward anyone,
and do nothing without
deliberation.
³¹ If you have but one slave, treat him like
yourself,
because you have bought him with
blood.
If you have but one slave, treat him like
a brother,
for you will need him as you need
your life.
³² If you ill-treat him and he leaves you and
runs away,
³³ which way will you go to seek
him?

34

The senseless have vain and false
hopes,
and dreams give wings to fools.

^q 33.25 Some ancient authorities add the title *Concerning Slaves* ^r 33.26 Heb: Gk *Work with instruction*

wisdom—here using agricultural metaphors. The emphasis is again on his efforts not only for himself *but for all who seek instruction* (v. 18; cf. 24:34). The focus falls on entreating Jewish elites to heed his words (v. 19).

33:25–33 Enslaved persons. Ben Sira's practical instructions for social life include advice about slavery. Just as his ostensibly universal wisdom includes men but not women, he here gives advice to wealthy men but not to those who are enslaved. The purchase of people as property raises no ethical concerns for Ben Sira. In fact, slavery is deemed positive in permitting the rich man *rest* (v. 26; contrast 22:1–2). Enslaved persons are denigrated as potentially lazy, and their idleness is treated as a dire problem, for which *racks and tortures* are a solution (v. 27; contrast 7:20–21). The rich man's *rest* is implied to be deserved, whereas the rest of the enslaved man risks sin. The former rightly forces the latter to work, according to the teachings in this section. Other biblical literature similarly assumes slavery as a common feature of ancient life, but Ben Sira stands out for encouraging the harsh treatment of enslaved persons (cf. Lev. 25:39–46). **33:30–33** A partial exception is made for the man who has only enough wealth to purchase one enslaved person but not more (vv. 31–33). In this case, Ben Sira advises treating the enslaved man *like a brother* (v. 31), since he cannot risk the economic loss incurred if *he leaves you and runs away* (v. 32).

34:1–8 Dreams. Despite the prohibition of some form of dream interpretation in legal materials like Deut. 13:1–3, the interpretation of dreams is a common trope in biblical literature, including the stories of Joseph in Gen. 37–50, Gideon in Judg. 7:13–15, and Daniel in Dan. 2. In much Hellenistic-era Jewish literature, dream visions become prominent as well (e.g., 1 En., Dan., Visions of Amram,

² As one who catches at a shadow and
pursues the wind,
so is anyone who pays attention to
dreams.
³ What is seen in dreams is but a reflection,
the likeness of a face looking at itself.
⁴ From an unclean thing, what can be
clean?
And from something false, what can
be true?
⁵ Divinations and omens and dreams are
unreal,
and like a woman in labor the mind
has fantasies.
⁶ Unless they are sent by intervention from
the Most High,
pay no attention to them.
⁷ For dreams have deceived many,
and those who put their hope in them
have perished.
⁸ Without such deceptions the law will be
fulfilled,
and wisdom is complete in a
trustworthy mouth.
⁹ People who have traveled$ know many
things,
and those with much experience
know what they are talking about.
¹⁰ The inexperienced know few things,
¹¹ but those who have traveled acquire
much cleverness.
¹² I have seen many things in my travels,
and I understand more than I can
express.

¹³ I have often been in danger of death
but have escaped because of these
experiences.
¹⁴ The spirit of those who fear the Lord will
live,
¹⁵ for their hope is in him who saves them.
¹⁶ Those who fear the Lord will not be timid
or play the coward, for he is their hope.
¹⁷ Happy are souls that fear the Lord!
¹⁸ To whom do they look? And who is
their support?
¹⁹ The eyes of the Lord are on those who
love him,
a mighty shield and strong support,
a shelter from scorching heat and a
shade from noonday sun,
a guard against stumbling and a help
against falling.
²⁰ He lifts up the soul and makes the eyes
sparkle;
he gives health and life and blessing.
²¹ If one sacrifices ill-gotten goods, the
offering is blemished;ᵗ
²² the giftsᵘ of the lawless are not
acceptable.
²³ The Most High is not pleased with the
offerings of the ungodly,
nor for a multitude of sacrifices does
he forgive sins.
²⁴ Like one who kills a son before his
father's eyes

s 34.9 Other ancient authorities read *are educated*
t 34.21 Other ancient authorities read *is made in mockery*
u 34.22 Other ancient authorities read *mockeries*

Jub.). Ben Sira, however, likens dream interpretation to divination and omens—practices elsewhere condemned as idolatrous (cf. Deut. 18:9–14; 2 Kgs. 17:17; Jer. 27:9; Ezek. 13:9). **34:2** *Pursues the wind.* This imagery is reminiscent of Eccl. 1:14 and is similarly meant to convey the impossibility of an endeavor. **34:5** *The mind has fantasies* is yet another instance where Ben Sira denigrates the experience of women in order to make a point about sinful behavior for a man (cf. 20:4). **34:6** *From the Most High.* Despite his suspicion, Ben Sira seems to make some concession to the rise of interest in dreams and omens at his time (cf. Deut. 13:1–3).

34:9–13 Experience. 34:11 *Acquire much cleverness.* Travel can lead to the acquisition of knowledge but not wisdom. For the idea that *cleverness* is not wisdom, see 19:20–30.

34:14–20 Fear of the Lord. See notes on 1:11–20; 21:11–22:2; 23:27. **34:19** *A shelter . . . and a shade* is similar to the description of Wisdom in 14:26–27.

34:21–35:13 Sacrifices. This is a lengthy discussion on the offering of sacrifices that warns against empty or performative piety. Offering sacrifices to God is not sufficient; proper behavior toward other human beings and proper comportment are necessary for true piety. This is not a critique of sacrifice as an empty or unnecessary practice. Rather, it forms part of the book's recurrent concern for the temple and priesthood, predicated on the reminder that sacrifice alone does not fulfill the law or demonstrate fear of God (see **"Priests and Temple," p. 1479; "Offerings and Sacrifices," p. 146**). **34:21** *Ill-gotten goods.* One of the key aspects of sacrifice is that one must legitimately own what they offer, or the offering is invalid (here: *blemished*). **34:23** *Nor for a multitude of sacrifices does he forgive sins.* Cf. 3:3–4, 30, which describe honoring one's parents and offering alms as atoning for sins. Sacrifices appear

Focus On: Priests and Temple in Second Temple Judaism (Sirach 34:21–35:13)

In antiquity, temples were far more than ritual sites; they functioned as political and economic centers, fostered scribal and literary activity, and sometimes even housed libraries. Accordingly, the Babylonian destruction of Solomon's temple in Jerusalem in 586 BCE had a major social as well as religious impact. According to Ezra 1:1–4 and 2 Chr. 36:22–23, the first task of those Israelites returning from the Babylonian exile was to rebuild a temple in Jerusalem. Scholars typically use "Second Temple" to refer to this structure, which was built with funding and support from Achaemenid Persian kings during the period of their rule over the land of Israel (ca. 538–333 BCE). Initially, the rebuilt temple seems to have been modest; some literary sources even suggest that it did not measure up to its Solomonic predecessor (cf. Ezra 3; Hag. 2). Until its destruction in 70 CE, however, it stood at the heart of Jewish political, intellectual, and religious life in the land of Israel. Because there was no native king during the centuries, high priests took on political leadership roles in Judea, especially during the periods of Achaemenid Persian, Ptolemaic, and Seleucid rule; high-priestly influence extended to the Diaspora as well. For the importance of the high priest and Jerusalem temple, Ben Sira is a prime example. His personal pursuit of wisdom culminates in prayer at the temple (51:14). He presents temple sacrifices as an essential part of attaining wisdom (34:21–35:13). He even likens wisdom to the high-priestly garments (6:30–31) and temple (4:14–15; 14:24–27; 24:10). In addition, his conception of the history of Israel centers around its priests. Aaron, Phinehas, and Simon II figure prominently in the "Hymn in Honor of Our Ancestors" (chaps. 44–50), while even Moses receives less attention. In the centuries after Ben Sira, the Jerusalem temple was significantly expanded, culminating with the renovations sponsored by Herod in the late first century BCE. As the Jerusalem temple became more glorious, it also became more contested. This contestation can be seen in the New Testament and rabbinic literature, especially in their depictions of the Jewish priestly sect of the Sadducees. Even these negative depictions, however, presume the importance of the Jerusalem temple.

Liane M. Feldman and Annette Yoshiko Reed

is the person who offers a
   sacrifice from the property of
   the poor.
25 The bread of the needy is the life of the
      poor;
   whoever deprives them of it is a
      murderer.
26 To take away a neighbor's living is to
      commit murder;
27   to deprive an employee of wages is to
      shed blood.

28 When one builds and another tears
      down,
   what do they gain but hard work?

29 When one prays and another curses,
      to whose voice will the Lord listen?
30 If one washes after touching a corpse
      and touches it again,
   what has been gained by washing?
31 So if one fasts for his sins
      and goes again and does the same
      things,
   who will listen to his prayer?
      And what has he gained by humbling
      himself?

35 The one who keeps the law makes
      many offerings;
2   one who heeds the commandments
      makes an offering of well-being.

to have a function other than atonement for Ben Sira. **34:25–27** In these three verses, Ben Sira likens the theft of wages or sustenance from *the poor* to *murder*. This is not only a metaphor: taking a poor family's cow or goat to sacrifice leaves that family without any means of getting milk, for example; withholding their wages may leave them unable to purchase food. No sacrifice is so important that one can take from the poor in order to make a sacrifice. **34:30–31** *And touches it again . . . and does the same things.* The performance of purity rituals and penitential behaviors like fasting is good, but only if it leads to self-reflection and a change in one's behavior (cf. 18:19–21; 20:3). **35:1–13** In this continuation of the discussion of the offering of sacrifices begun in 34:21–31, Ben Sira shifts his focus to sacrifices offered by the righteous. **35:1** *Makes many offerings.* Just as it is insufficient to make offerings but fail to keep *the law*, it is also insufficient to keep the law without making offerings. Making offerings is an important part of keeping the law along with almsgiving and proper behavior. **35:2–5** These verses liken proper behaviors to different forms of offerings. The types of good deeds described in each verse are commensurate with the complexity and expense of the corresponding sacrifice. **35:2** Next to the

³ The one who returns a kindness offers
   choice flour,
⁴   and one who gives alms sacrifices a
      thank offering.
⁵ To keep from wickedness is pleasing to
   the Lord,
   and to forsake unrighteousness is an
      atonement.
⁶ Do not appear before the Lord
   empty-handed,
⁷   for all that you offer is in fulfillment of
      the commandment.
⁸ The offering of the righteous enriches
   the altar,
   and its pleasing odor rises before the
      Most High.
⁹ The sacrifice of the righteous is
   acceptable,
   and it will never be forgotten.
¹⁰ Be generous when you worship the Lord,
   and do not skimp the first fruits of
      your hands.
¹¹ With every gift show a cheerful face
   and dedicate your tithe with
      gladness.
¹² Give to the Most High as he has given
   to you
   and as generously as you can afford.
¹³ For the Lord is the one who repays,
   and he will repay you sevenfold.
¹⁴ Do not offer him a bribe, for he will not
   accept it,
¹⁵   and do not rely on a dishonest sacrifice,
   for the Lord is the judge,
   and with him there is no partiality.

¹⁶ He will not show partiality to the poor,
   but he will listen to the prayer of one
      who is wronged.
¹⁷ He will not ignore the supplication of the
   orphan
   or the widow when she pours out her
      complaint.
¹⁸ Do not the tears of the widow run down
   her cheek
¹⁹   as she cries out against the one who
      causes them to fall?
²⁰ Those whose service is pleasing to the
   Lord will be accepted,
   and their prayers will reach to the
      clouds.
²¹ The prayer of the humble pierces the
   clouds,
   and it will not rest until it reaches its
      goal;
   it will not desist until the Most High
      responds
²²   and does justice for the righteous and
      executes judgment.
   Indeed, the Lord will not delay,
   and like a warrior* he will not be
      patient
   until he crushes the loins of the
      unmerciful
²³   and repays vengeance on the nations,
   until he destroys the multitude of the
      insolent
   and breaks the scepters of the
      unrighteous,

v 35.22 Heb: Gk *and with them*

whole burnt offering (not mentioned here), the *well-being* offering is the most frequent type of sacrifice discussed in biblical texts. It is an offering that is said in some texts to involve a three-way sharing of the animal's meat between God, the priests, and the one who offers (cf. Lev. 3; 7:11–18). It also appears frequently in the context of covenant-making or vow-fulfilling (cf. Exod. 24:5; 32:6; Deut. 27:7; Josh. 8:30–35; 1 Sam. 11:15; Prov. 7:14; 1 Chr. 21:26). **35:3** *Choice flour* refers to a grain offering, the least expensive type of offering (cf. Lev. 2; 14:21). Here it is likened to one of the simplest good deeds, returning a kindness. **35:4** The *thank offering* is described in Pentateuchal priestly texts as made up of both an animal and a grain offering, suggesting it carries some expense (cf. Lev. 7:12). Similarly, giving *alms* of course incurs some expense, but like a *thank offering* is done in gratitude for what God has given the offeror. **35:5** *An atonement.* Some biblical texts discuss atonement offerings specifically (cf. Lev. 4, 16; see **"Atonement," p. 168**); they are among the most complex of sacrificial rituals. So, too, is the difficulty of avoiding wicked behavior—as Ben Sira warns repeatedly. **35:6** *Empty-handed.* Do not go to the temple without an offering (cf. Exod. 23:15; 34:20; Deut. 16:16). **35:8** *Its pleasing odor rises.* The smell of sacrifices was thought to rise from the altar to the heavens to arouse God's attention.

35:14–26 Justice. The topic here shifts to divine *justice* and reinforces the importance of caring for the *poor, widow,* and *orphan* (cf. 4:1–10). **35:20** *Will be accepted.* Language often used for sacrificial offerings is here used to describe proper behavior. **35:21** *Pierces the clouds.* Like the smell of the sacrifices (cf. v. 8), the cries of the poor also rise from earth to the heavens and arouse God's attention, here through the sense of hearing rather than smell.

24 until he repays mortals according to
their deeds
and the works of all according to their
thoughts,
25 until he judges the case of his people
and makes them rejoice in his mercy.
26 His mercy is as welcome in time of
distress
as clouds of rain in time of drought.

36 Have mercy upon us, O God[w] of all,
2 and put all the nations in fear of you.
3 Lift up your hand against foreign
nations
and let them see your might.
4 As you have used us to show your
holiness to them,
so use them to show your glory to us.
5 Then they will know,[x] as we have known,
that there is no God but you, O Lord.
6 Give new signs and work other wonders;
7 make your hand and right arm
glorious.

8 Rouse your anger and pour out your
wrath;
9 destroy the adversary and wipe out
the enemy.
10 Hasten the day, and remember the
appointed time,[y]
and let people recount your mighty
deeds.
11 Let survivors be consumed in the fiery
wrath,
and may those who harm your people
meet destruction.
12 Crush the heads of hostile rulers
who say, "There is no one but
ourselves."
13 Gather all the tribes of Jacob,[z]
16 and give them their inheritance, as at
the beginning.

w 36.1 Heb: Gk *O Master, the God*   x 36.5 Heb: Gk *And let
them know you*   y 36.10 Other ancient authorities read
remember your oath   z 36.13 Verse numbers 14 and 15 are
not used in chapter 36

36:1–22 Prayer for God's people Israel. As in 22:27–23:6 and 39:16–34, a prayer is included among this compilation of instructions. It is unclear whether Ben Sira chose a prayer already known to him or composed it himself. Whereas the prayer in 22:27–23:6 is individual in focus, this prayer is communal, focusing on the fate of the people Israel in relation under the rule of foreign nations (cf. 39:28–31). Its themes hew closer to what is typically expected from prophetic rather than sapiential literature. Ben Sira wrote during the period of Seleucid rule over the land of Israel that began around 200–198 BCE. But the specific empire is here unnamed, and the situation is generalized. Emphasis is placed on hopes for vindication and restoration of Israel, framed in rhetoric that evokes a hope of the repetition of God's display of power bringing Israelites out of Egypt. Notably missing is the prediction of end-time vindication found in other Jewish writings from later in the second century BCE, especially in decades surrounding the Maccabean Revolt (e.g., Dan.; Animal Apocalypse and Apocalypse of Weeks in 1 En.). In this prayer, the Seleucids are blurred with past foreign rulers rather than depicted as part of a chain of empires leading to Israel's end-time vindication. It may provide important evidence for Jewish attitudes toward Seleucid rule prior to Antiochus IV and the Maccabean Revolt. Some verses parallel the language later common in apocalyptic approaches to the problem of non-Jewish rule, such as the allusion to an *appointed time* in v. 10 (cf. Dan. 11:35) as well as *fiery wrath* in v. 11 and the in-gathering of *all the tribes of Jacob* (v. 13), and these are framed as the fulfillment of *prophecies* (v. 20). Yet the focus remains on pleading for aid by appealing to the effects of a divine display of power on the knowledge of the God of Israel beyond Israel (v. 22b: *all who are on the earth will know that you are the Lord, the God of the ages*). This entreaty is for divine salvation within history rather than at the cessation of history. Interestingly, similar themes arise in the prayer said to have been led by the high priest in the time of Nehemiah in the second letter prefaced to 2 Maccabees (2 Macc. 1:24–29). **36:1** *God of all.* Cf. 11QPs[a] 28.7–8; Rom. 9:5. **36:4** *Show your holiness to them . . . show your glory to us.* The emphasis is not on Israel's sins having caused God to permit foreign rule but the opposite: Israel's good deeds are said to show non-Jews the holiness of the God of Israel, and in turn, Israel asks for God's deeds to display God's glory on their behalf. The structure mirrors the reciprocity elsewhere in Sirach. **36:5** *There is no God but you.* Cf. Isa. 45:14. **36:6** The language of *signs* and *wonders* evokes the exodus; for example, Exod. 11:9–10; Deut. 4:34; Neh. 9:10. That *new signs* are possible, including to persuade non-Jews, is similarly suggested in Dan. 4:2–3. **36:10** *Mighty deeds.* Cf. 15:18; Deut. 3:24; Pss. 20:7; 71:16; 106:2; 145:4, 12; 150:2; Isa. 63:15. **36:13** *Gather all the tribes.* A similar hope is found in Isa. 56:8; Jer. 23:7–8; 32:37; Mic. 2:12, especially in relation to the Babylonian exile (ca. 586–538 BCE). By Ben Sira's time, however, Jewish communities were flourishing in Egypt and elsewhere, as is clear from the ample textual production of Alexandrian

17 Have mercy, O Lord, on the people called
  by your name,
    on Israel, whom you have named[a]
    your firstborn.
18 Have pity on the city of your sanctuary,[b]
  Jerusalem, the place of your dwelling.[c]
19 Fill Zion with your majesty[d]
  and your temple[e] with your glory.
20 Bear witness to those whom you created
    in the beginning,
  and fulfill the prophecies spoken in
    your name.
21 Reward those who wait for you,
  and let your prophets be found
    trustworthy.
22 Hear, O Lord, the prayer of your servants,
    according to your goodwill toward[f]
    your people,
  and all who are on the earth will know
    that you are the Lord, the God of the
    ages.
23 The stomach will take any food,
  yet one food is better than another.
24 As the palate tastes the kinds of game,
  so an intelligent mind detects false
    words.
25 A perverse mind will cause grief,
  but a person with experience will pay
    him back.
26 A woman will accept any man as a
    husband,
  but one daughter is preferable to
    another.
27 A woman's beauty lights up a man's face,
  and there is nothing he desires more.
28 If kindness and humility mark her speech,
  her husband is more fortunate than
    other men.

29 He who acquires a wife gets his best
    possession,[g]
  a helper fit for him and a pillar of
    support.[h]
30 Where there is no fence, the property
    will be plundered,
  and where there is no wife, a man will
    become a fugitive and a wanderer.[i]
31 For who will trust a nimble robber
  who skips from city to city?
  So who will trust a man who has no nest
    but lodges wherever nighttime finds
    him?

37 Every friend says, "I, too, am a friend,"
  but some friends are friends only in
    name.
2 Does not sorrow draw near to death
  when a companion and friend[j] turns
    into an enemy?
3 O inclination to evil, why were you formed
  to cover the land with deceit?
4 Some companions rejoice in the
    happiness of friends,
  but in time of trouble they are against
    them.
5 Some companions help a friend for their
    stomachs' sake,
  yet in battle they will carry his shield.
6 Do not forget friends during the battle,[k]
  and do not be unmindful of them
    when you distribute your spoils.[l]

a 36.17 Other ancient authorities read *you have likened
to*   b 36.18 Or *on your holy city*   c 36.18 Heb: Gk *your
rest*   d 36.19 Heb Syr: Gk *the celebration of your wondrous
deeds*   e 36.19 Heb Syr: Gk Lat *people*   f 36.22 Heb and
two Gk mss: Lat and most Gk mss read *according to the
blessing of Aaron for*   g 36.29 Heb: Gk *enters upon a possession*
h 36.29 Heb: Gk *rest*   i 36.30 Heb: Gk *wander about and sigh*
j 37.2 Heb reads *a friend like yourself*   k 37.6 Heb: Gk *in your
heart*   l 37.6 Heb: Gk *him in your wealth*

Jews (e.g., Gk. translations of Jewish Scriptures; Letter of Aristeas; Artapanus)—which would eventually include the Greek translation of this very book (see Prologue). Sirach, however, expresses an ideal
of Jewish wisdom that is localized in the land of Israel. The city of Jerusalem is a recurrent concern,
especially in the second part of the book. Here as elsewhere, his articulation of a Jewish "paideia" may
answer other Jewish approaches to responding to Greek "paideia." **36:18–19** Hopes for restoration
focus on Jerusalem and the temple.

36:23–31 Sundry advice. Consistent with the loosely anthological structure of the book, the
prayer is not followed up with teachings on related topics. Next, rather, is a cluster of instructions
related to individual experience with no mention of Israel or God—ranging instead from the choice
of food to a man's choice of a woman for marriage. This chapter includes an unusually positive
depiction of women for Ben Sira, albeit framed solely in relation to their effects on men (vv. 27–30).

37:1–31 Caution. In this chapter, Ben Sira's ethics of caution is summarized with reference to key
themes: friendship (vv. 1–6), selectively taking advice from others (vv. 7–15), deliberation prior to
action (vv. 16–18), seeking wisdom over cleverness (vv. 19–26), and moderation (vv. 27–31). Most of
the advice is generalized and mundane, but this chapter includes notable references to *the commandments* (v. 12), prayer (v. 15), God as the source of an individual's charm or lack thereof (v. 21),

⁷ All counselors praise the counsel they
give,
but some give counsel in their own
interest.
⁸ Be wary of counselors
and learn first what is their interest,
for they will take thought for
themselves.
They may cast the lot against you
⁹ and tell you, "Your way is good,"
and then stand aside to see what
happens to you.
¹⁰ Do not consult the one who regards you
with suspicion;
hide your intentions from those who
are jealous of you.
¹¹ Do not consult with a woman about her
rival
or with a coward about war,
with a merchant about business
or with a buyer about selling,
with a miser about generosity^m
or with the merciless about kindness,
with an idler about any work
or with a seasonal laborer about
finishing the job,
with a lazy slave about a big task—
pay no attention to any advice they
give.
¹² But associate with a godly person
whom you know to be a keeper of the
commandments,
who is like-minded with yourself,
and who will grieve with you if you
fail.
¹³ And heedⁿ the counsel of your own
heart,
for no one is more faithful to you than
it is.
¹⁴ For our own mind sometimes keeps us
better informed
than seven sentinels sitting high on a
watchtower.
¹⁵ But above all pray to the Most High
that he may direct your way in truth.

¹⁶ Discussion is the beginning of every work,
and counsel precedes every
undertaking.
¹⁷ The mind is the root of all counsel;^o
¹⁸ it sprouts four branches,^p
good and evil, life and death,
and it is the tongue that continually
rules them.
¹⁹ Some people may be clever enough to
teach many
and yet be useless to themselves.
²⁰ Skillful speakers may be hated;
they will be destitute of all food,
²¹ for the Lord has withheld the gift of
charm,
since they are lacking in all wisdom.
²² If people are wise to their own
advantage,
the fruits of their good sense will be
praiseworthy.^q
²³ The wise instruct their own people,
and the fruits of their good sense are
trustworthy.
²⁴ The wise will have praise heaped upon
them,
and all who see them will call them
happy.
²⁵ The days of a person's life are numbered,
but the days of Israel are without
number.
²⁶ Those who are wise among their people
will inherit honor,^r
and their names will live forever.
²⁷ My child, test yourself while you live;
see what is bad for you, and do not
give in to it.
²⁸ For not everything is good for everyone,
and no one enjoys everything.
²⁹ Do not be greedy for every delicacy,
and do not eat without restraint,

m 37.11 Gk: Heb *with an evil person about generosity*
n 37.13 Heb: Gk *establish*   o 37.17 Heb: Gk *change*
p 37.18 Heb: Gk *four kinds of destiny appear*   q 37.22 Other
ancient authorities read *trustworthy*   r 37.26 Other ancient
authorities read *confidence*

and the people Israel (v. 25). **37:12** To the recurrent theme of caution concerning the company one keeps, Ben Sira here adds knowledge that someone keeps *the commandments* as among the signs to judge someone as apt. **37:15** Consistent with the inclusion of prayers throughout the book (see notes on 22:27–23:6 and 36:1–22), one here finds a description of the power of individual prayer to help a person make decisions. Both speak to the increased prominence of prayer in the Second Temple period. For Ben Sira, this interest in prayer also extends his recurrent concern for the power of speech. **37:17–18** *Mind* and *tongue*, thought and speech, are intertwined. **37:25–26** As in earlier biblical literature, the primary concern for one's fate after one's death is the continuance of one's people and the remembrance of one's name.

30 for overeating brings sickness,
     and gluttony leads to nausea.
31 Many have died of gluttony,
     but those who guard against it
          prolong their lives.

38 Honor physicians for their services,
     for the Lord created them,
2 for their gift of healing comes from the
     Most High,
     and they are rewarded by the king.
3 The skill of physicians makes them
          distinguished,
     and in the presence of the great they
          are admired.
4 The Lord created medicines out of the
          earth,
     and the sensible will not despise
          them.
5 Was not water made sweet with a tree
     in order that its^s power might be
          known?
6 And he gave skill to human beings
     that he^t might be glorified in his
          marvelous works.
7 By them the physician^u heals and takes
          away pain;
8   the pharmacist makes a mixture from
          them.
     God's^v works will never be finished,
     and from him health spreads over all
          the earth.

9 My child, when you are ill, do not delay,
     but pray to the Lord, and he will heal
          you.
10 Give up your faults and direct your
          hands rightly,
     and cleanse your heart from all sin.
11 Offer a sweet-smelling sacrifice and a
          memorial portion of choice flour,
     and pour oil on your offering, as much
          as you can afford."
12 Then give physicians their place, for the
          Lord created them;
     do not let them leave you, for you
          need them.
13 There may come a time when recovery
          lies in the hands of physicians,^{x}
14   for they, too, pray to the Lord
     that he grant them success in diagnosis^y
          and in healing, for the sake of
               preserving life.
15 Those who sin against their Maker
     will be defiant toward the physician.^{z}
16 My child, let your tears fall for the dead,
     and as one in great pain begin the
          lament.
     Lay out the body according to custom,

s 38.5 Or *his*   t 38.6 Or *they*   u 38.7 Heb: Gk *he*   v 38.8 Gk
His   w 38.11 Heb: Lat lacks *as much as you can afford*;
meaning of Gk uncertain   x 38.13 Gk *in their hands*
y 38.14 Heb: Gk *rest*   z 38.15 Heb: Gk *may they fall into the
hands of the physician*

38:1–15 Health. For Ben Sira, health pertains to wisdom. Not only does he focus on the body as a site of self-control and discernment, but his advice on topics like wealth, sleep, and food explicitly includes a concern for bodily well-being and the avoidance of illness (e.g., 30:14–16; 31:1–2, 20). Advice about health, however, is not solely the domain of the teacher of wisdom. Extending his advice to heed apt counsel in 37:7, Ben Sira vociferously stresses the need to consult physicians and pharmacists. Not only does their expertise grant them social prominence (vv. 2–3), but their healing skills and medicines are depicted as divinely sent (vv. 1–2, 4, 6–8) and enhanced by their prayers (v. 14). If any reader doubts the appropriateness of Hellenistic medicine, Ben Sira makes a case for its potential to be complementary with Israel's ancestral traditions when practiced by pious Jews. Elsewhere, he lists "perfect health" as among the benefits of "fear of the Lord" (1:18), depicting health as a blessing from God to the righteous (34:20) while depicting illness as a punishment for sin (18:19–21). Here, he affirms that prayer and sacrifice have a part in healing (vv. 9–11; cf. 51:9), and he presents these practices as complementary with the use of medicine and consultation of doctors, chiding those who are *defiant toward the physician* (v. 15). **38:4** *Medicines out of the earth.* For a suspicion of root-cutting and its association with fallen angels, see 1 En. 7:1, and for the depiction of healing as divinely sent angelic teaching, see Jub. 10:1–14 and Tob. 3:17; 12:14. The Dead Sea Scrolls include magical materials that associate healing with angels and illness with demons. Ben Sira associates healing with the divine but does not mention angels or demons here. **38:14** *They, too, pray.* On the power of prayer to heal, including alongside medicines, cf. Gen. 20:17; Isa. 38:1–21; Tob. 3.

38:16–23 Mourning. Cf. 22:12. **38:16** *Lay out the body . . . burial.* Proper care for the body of the deceased is a special concern in the literature of the late Second Temple period, as exemplified by Tobit. Material remains from ancient Israel speak to the prominence of *burial*, even in periods of rule by cultures with other mortuary practices (e.g., exposure among Persians, cremation among

and do not neglect the burial.
[17] Let your weeping be bitter and your
wailing fervent;
make your mourning worthy of the
departed,
for one day or two, to avoid criticism;
then be comforted for your grief.
[18] For grief may result in death,
and a sorrowful heart saps one's
strength.
[19] In calamity, grief continues,
but the life of the poor is a curse to
the heart.
[20] Do not give your heart to grief;
drive it away and remember your own
end.
[21] Do not forget, there is no coming back;
you do the dead[a] no good, and you
injure yourself.
[22] Remember his[b] fate, for yours is like it;
yesterday it was his,[c] and today it is
yours.
[23] When the dead are at rest, let their
remembrance rest, too,
and be comforted for them when their
spirits have departed.
[24] The wisdom of the scribe depends on the
opportunity of leisure;
only the one who has little business
can become wise.
[25] How can one become wise who handles
the plow
and who glories in the shaft of a goad,
who drives oxen and is occupied with
their work,
and whose talk is about the offspring
of bulls?

[26] He sets his heart on plowing furrows,
and he loses sleep over fodder for the
heifers.
[27] So it is with every artisan and master
artisan
who labors by night as well as by day;
those who carve the signets of seals—
each is diligent in making a great
variety;
they set their heart on painting a lifelike
image,
and they lose sleep in order to finish
their work.
[28] So it is with the smith sitting by the anvil,
intent on his ironwork;
the breath of the fire melts his flesh,
and he struggles with the heat of the
furnace;
the sound of the hammer deafens his
ears,[d]
and his eyes are on the pattern of the
object.
He sets his heart on finishing his
handiwork,
and he loses sleep to complete its
decoration.
[29] So it is with the potter sitting at his work
and turning the wheel with his feet;
he always lies down anxious about his
work,
and his every work is taken into account.
[30] He molds the clay with his arm
and makes it pliable with his feet;
he sets his heart to finish the glazing,
and he takes care in firing[e] the kiln.

a 38.21 Gk him   b 38.22 Heb: Gk my   c 38.22 Heb: Gk mine
d 38.28 Cn: Gk renews his ear   e 38.30 Cn: Gk cleaning

Romans). Caves were a common place for burial, and wealthy Jews sometimes practiced secondary burial, whereby the body was laid out and the bones were later gathered in an ossuary. This verse clearly describes the first step, but it is unclear whether the actions described here are meant to culminate in the second. **38:17** *One day or two.* Ben Sira elsewhere describes mourning as seven days (22:12). Excessive mourning is a concern already in Deut. 14:1–2, seemingly discouraging practices associated with neighboring peoples; in this case, such a concern dovetails with Ben Sira's overall emphasis on moderation (cf. Matt. 8:21–22; Luke 9:59–60). On food offered to the dead as exemplary of waste, see 30:18. **38:20** *Do not give your heart to grief.* Just as Ben Sira cautions against the harmful effects of too much sorrow and anxiety (30:23–24), so too with *grief*. Emotions are best regulated. **38:22** Death is a reminder of one's own mortality—a theme earlier treated in relation to the importance of one's reputation (5:15–6:1; 11:26–28, 33) and a good son (30:4).

38:24–39:11 Scribes. This section of Ben Sira includes the earliest extensive description of a Jewish scribe (see **"Scribes and Scribalism," p. 1486**). In a manner akin to the Egyptian text Satire on the Trades, the profession of the scribe is here described through juxtaposition with other professions. Ben Sira is comparably positive about the artisans and workmen with whom he contrasts the scribe, even as he uses the juxtaposition to defend the necessity of scribes in the Jewish society of his time. **38:24–32a** *Wisdom of the scribe.* Not only are scribes linked to wisdom, but the time

Focus On: Scribes and Scribalism (Sirach 38:24–39:11)

One of the major shifts in Jewish literature of the Second Temple period (538 BCE–70 CE) is the growing prominence of the professional scribe. In antiquity, skills in writing were largely limited to those trained as scribes. Scribes were long prominent in other Near Eastern intellectual cultures. In the Hebrew Bible, however, one finds only passing references to scribes as functionaries. Despite the writtenness of the ancient Israelite traditions that come down to us, the agency of scribes is largely invisible. The spoken words of prophets or kings remained central, and their record in writing is treated as an aid to public reading. Consistent with the increased prominence of textuality as a medium for revelation in late biblical prophecy (e.g., Ezek. 3:3), a change in the status of scribes may be glimpsed already in Jeremiah's treatment of the scribe Baruch (e.g., Jer. 36; cf. Bar.; 2–5 Bar.). Nevertheless, their authority remained secondary, and their trustworthiness was in doubt (Jer. 8:9). This appears to change during the period of Hellenistic rule over the land of Israel.

In the Jewish literature of the third and second centuries BCE, however, scribes and scribalism become major topics of explicit concern. Descriptions of revealed knowledge increasingly involve reading and writing. The ideal of the scribal visionary is pivotal for the emergence of Jewish apocalyptic literature, as evident in the Book of the Watchers and other writings associated with Enoch (1 En. 1–36; cf. Gen. 5:21–24). Daniel and the Aramaic Dead Sea Scrolls further attest Hellenistic-period Jewish concerns for scribalism. In Jubilees, the story of Israel's past is retold as a history of scribes, books, and readers, further answering the claims of Greek *paideia* and paralleling the counterclaims of Hellenistic-period Babylonian scribes like Berossus. By contrast, Ben Sira expresses suspicion about the types of knowledge associated with scribes in the Book of the Watchers and other apocalypses (Sir. 3:21). Yet he shares their contention of the special association of scribes with wisdom. Likely a scribe himself, Ben Sira depicts them as a special curatorial class charged with preserving Israel's ancestral traditions (38:24–39:11). As in 1 Enoch, so too for Ben Sira, scribes are associated not just with the practical task of writing (e.g., administrative documentation, transcription of speech into texts or letters, copying manuscripts) but also with preserving and teaching Jewish ancestral traditions—including knowledge about the cosmos, ethics, and Israel's past.

Liane M. Feldman and Annette Yoshiko Reed

31 All these rely on their hands,
   and all are skillful in their own work.
32 Without them no city can be inhabited,
   and wherever they live they will not
      go hungry.*f*
   Yet they are not sought out for the
      council of the people,*g*
33   nor do they attain eminence in the
      public assembly.
   They do not sit in the judge's seat,
      nor do they understand the decisions
      of the courts;
   they cannot expound discipline or
      judgment,
   and they are not found among the
      rulers.*b*

34 But they maintain the fabric of the world,
   and their concern is for*i* the exercise
      of their trade.
   How different the one who devotes
      himself
   to the study of the law of the Most
      High!

39 They seek out the wisdom of all the
      ancients
   and are concerned with prophecies;
2 they preserve the sayings of the famous
   and penetrate the subtleties of
      parables;

f 38.32 Syr: Gk *and people can neither live nor walk there*
g 38.32 Most ancient authorities lack this line   *h* 38.33 Cn:
Gk *among parables*   *i* 38.34 Syr: Gk *prayer is in*

needed to cultivate wisdom means that it is a distinct profession, not possible to pursue properly while engaged in other work or business. Ben Sira has so far stressed how wisdom is necessary for Israel, offering advice to various sorts of people. Here he adds that a dedicated class of scribes is necessary to cultivate wisdom in Israel. Scribes—like himself—are just as indispensable as farmers, artisans, smiths, and potters. **38:32b–34a** Ben Sira turns to what makes scribes different from other skilled workers: their importance for *the council of the people*, their *eminence in the public assembly*, and their *judgment* and involvement in law *courts* and among *rulers*. **38:34b–39:3** The topics of expertise proper to the scribe are not just limited to transcription or copying books; rather, the scribe is the one who is associated with *the study of the law of the Most High* as well as *wisdom of all*

³ they seek out the hidden meanings of
proverbs
and are at home with the obscurities
of parables.
⁴ They serve among the great
and appear before rulers;
they travel in foreign nations
and learn what is good and evil in the
human lot.
⁵ They set their hearts to rise early
to seek the Lord who made them
and to petition the Most High;
they open their mouths in prayer
and ask pardon for their sins.

⁶ If the great Lord is willing,
they will be filled with the spirit of
understanding;
they will pour forth words of wisdom of
their own
and give thanks to the Lord in prayer.
⁷ The Lord[j] will direct their counsel and
knowledge
as they meditate on his mysteries.
⁸ They will show the discipline of their
training
and will glory in the law of the Lord's
covenant.
⁹ Many will praise their understanding;
it will never be blotted out.
Their memory will not disappear,
and their names will live through all
generations.
¹⁰ Nations will speak of their wisdom,
and the congregation will proclaim
their praise.
¹¹ If they live long, they will leave a name
greater than a thousand,
and if they go to rest, it is enough for
them.

¹² I have more on my mind to express;
I am full like the full moon.
¹³ Listen to me, my faithful children, and
blossom
like a rose growing by a stream of
water.
¹⁴ Send out fragrance like incense
and put forth blossoms like a lily.
Raise your voice[k] and sing a hymn of
praise;
bless the Lord for all his works.
¹⁵ Ascribe majesty to his name
and give thanks to him with praise,
with songs on your lips and with harps;
this is what you shall say in
thanksgiving:

¹⁶ "All the works of the Lord are very good,
and whatever he commands will be
done at the appointed time.
¹⁷ No one can say, 'What is this?' or 'Why is
that?'—
for at the appointed time everything
will be made known.
At his word the waters stood in a heap
and the reservoirs of water at the
word of his mouth.
¹⁸ At his command, his purpose is fulfilled,
and none can limit his saving power.
¹⁹ The works of all are before him,
and nothing can be hidden from his
eyes.
²⁰ From age to age he observes all,
and nothing is too marvelous for him.
²¹ No one can say, 'What is this?' or 'Why is
that?'—
for everything has been created for its
own purpose.

j 39.7 Gk *He himself*   *k* 39.14 Syr: Gk *fragrance*

the ancients and prophecies. The scribe preserves *sayings* but also interprets *parables* and *proverbs* whose meanings are not obvious. Although he elsewhere cautions his audience against seeking out what is hidden (3:21–22), Ben Sira here treats *hidden meanings* as a nexus of scribal expertise in a manner akin to the Jewish apocalypses of his time. At issue is not what knowledge is apt but rather for whom. **39:4** The image of the scribe is as a participant in cosmopolitan court culture. **39:5–8** The scribe is associated, not just with study and teaching, but also with *prayer*. The scribe's access to wisdom, including divine mysteries, is ultimately rooted in divine revelation in response to human prayer. **39:9–11** The scribe's reward is to be remembered within and even beyond his own people.

39:12–35 Prayer of praise. Modeling what scribal prayer entails, Ben Sira first advises his students to praise and thank God (vv. 12–15) then adds the text of a prayer that does precisely this (vv. 16–31). The prayer celebrates God, beginning with a focus on God's creation (vv. 16–18) and omniscience (vv. 19–20), alluding to the story of Sodom and Gomorrah (v. 23; cf. Gen. 19) as well as a possibly eschatological *day of reckoning* (v. 28; cf. 36:1–22). This *day of reckoning* is described in cosmological rather than political terms, with a focus on *winds, hail,* and *animals* (cf. 36:1–22).

22 "His blessing covers the dry land like a
  river
    and drenches it like a flood.
23 The nations will inherit his wrath,
    as when he turned a watered land
    into salt.
24 To the faithful his ways are straight
    but full of pitfalls for the lawless.
25 From the beginning good things were
  created for the good
    but for sinners good things and bad.[l]
26 The basic necessities of human life
  are water and fire and iron and salt
    and wheat flour and milk and honey,
    the blood of the grape and oil and
    clothing.
27 All these are good for the godly,
    but for sinners they turn into evils.

28 "There are winds created for vengeance,
  and in their anger they can dislodge
  mountains;[m]
    on the day of reckoning they will pour
    out their strength
    and calm the anger of their Maker.
29 Fire and hail and famine and pestilence—
  all these have been created for
  vengeance;
30 the fangs of wild animals and scorpions
  and vipers
    and the sword that punishes the
    ungodly with destruction.
31 They take delight in doing his bidding,
    always ready for his service on earth,
    and when their time comes they never
    disobey his command."

32 So from the beginning I have been
  steadfast
    and have thought it out and left it in
    writing:
33 All the works of the Lord are good,
    and he will supply every need in its
    time.
34 No one can say, "This is not as good as
  that,"
    for everything proves good in its
    appointed time.

35 So now sing praise with all your heart
  and voice,
    and bless the name of the Lord.

40 Hard work was created for everyone,
  and a heavy yoke is laid on the
  children of Adam,
from the day they come forth from their
  mother's womb
    until the day they return to[n] the
    mother of all the living.[o]
2 Perplexities and fear of heart are theirs
    and anxious thought of the day of
    their death.
3 From the one who sits on a splendid
  throne
    to the one who grovels in dust and
    ashes,
4 from the one who wears purple and a
  crown
    to the one who is clothed in burlap,
5 there is anger and envy and trouble and
  unrest
    and fear of death and fury and strife.
And when one rests upon his bed,
    his sleep at night confuses his mind.
6 He gets little or no rest;
    he struggles in his sleep as he did by
    day.[p]
He is troubled by the visions of his mind
    like one who has escaped from the
    battlefield.
7 At the moment he reaches safety[q] he
  wakes up,
    astonished that his fears were
    groundless.
8 To all creatures, human and animal,
    but to sinners seven times more,
9 come death and bloodshed and strife
  and sword,
    calamities and famine and ruin and
    plague.
10 All these were created for the lawless,
    and on their account the flood came.

_l 39.25 Heb Lat: Gk sinners bad things   m 39.28 Heb Syr: Gk
can scourge mightily   n 40.1 Other Gk and Lat authorities
read are buried in   o 40.1 Heb: Gk of all   p 40.6 Arm:
Meaning of Gk uncertain   q 40.7 Other ancient authorities read need_

40:1–7 The human condition. In a manner reminiscent of Ecclesiastes, Ben Sira bemoans the
human condition, focusing on the woes shared by rich and poor alike. These include hard work,
anxiety, sleeplessness, and mortality.
40:8–17 Justice. A series of sayings qualify this sense of equality, returning to the recurrent
theme of the promise of divine reciprocity for human deeds. The wicked may seem to flourish, but
Ben Sira assures the reader that justice will prevail.

11 All that is of earth returns to earth,
    and what is from above returns above.[r]
12 All bribery and injustice will be blotted
    out,
    but good faith will last forever.
13 The wealth of the unjust will dry up like
    a river
    and crash like a loud clap of thunder
    in a storm.
14 As a generous person has cause to rejoice,
    so lawbreakers will utterly fail.
15 The children of the ungodly put out few
    branches;
    they are unhealthy roots on sheer
    rock.
16 The reeds by any water or river bank
    are plucked up before any grass,
17 but kindness is like a garden of blessings,
    and almsgiving endures forever.
18 A life of abundance and wages make life
    sweet,[s]
    but better than either is finding a
    treasure.
19 Children and the building of a city
    establish one's name,
    but better than either is the one who
    finds wisdom.
    Cattle and orchards make one
    prosperous,[t]
    but a blameless wife is accounted
    better than either.
20 Wine and music gladden the heart,
    but the love of friends[u] is better than
    either.
21 The flute and the harp make sweet
    melody,
    but a pleasant voice is better than
    either.
22 The eye desires grace and beauty,
    but the green shoots of grain more
    than either.
23 A friend or companion is always
    welcome,
    but a sensible wife[v] is better than
    either.
24 Kindred and helpers are for a time of
    trouble,
    but almsgiving rescues better than
    either.

25 Gold and silver make one stand firm,
    but good counsel is esteemed more
    than either.
26 Riches and strength build up confidence,
    but the fear of the Lord is better than
    either.
    There is no want in the fear of the Lord,
    and with it there is no need to seek for
    help.
27 The fear of the Lord is like a garden of
    blessing
    and covers a person better than any
    glory.
28 My child, do not lead the life of a beggar;
    it is better to die than to beg.
29 When one looks to the table of another,
    one's way of life cannot be considered
    a life.
    One loses self-respect with another
    person's food,
    but one who is intelligent and well
    instructed guards against that.
30 In the mouth of the shameless begging is
    sweet,
    but it kindles a fire inside them.

41 O death, how bitter is the thought of
    you
    to the one at peace among possessions,
    who has nothing to worry about and is
    prosperous in everything
    and still is vigorous enough to enjoy
    pleasure![w]
2 O death, how welcome is your sentence
    to one who is needy and failing in
    strength,
    worn down by age and anxious about
    everything,
    to one who is contrary and has lost all
    patience!
3 Do not fear death's decree for you;
    remember those who went before you
    and those who will come after.
4 This is the Lord's decree for all flesh;
    why, then, should you reject the will
    of the Most High?

r 40.11 Heb Syr: Gk Lat *from the waters returns to the sea*
s 40.18 Heb: Gk *Life is sweet for the self-reliant and hard-
working*   t 40.19 Heb Syr: Gk lacks *but better . . . prosperous*
u 40.20 Heb: Gk *wisdom*   v 40.23 Heb Compare Syr: Gk
wife with her husband   w 41.1 Heb: Gk *food*

40:18–30 A series of sayings use the pattern of listing a set of circumstances, followed by what
is better, to advise about appreciation of family, friends, and—above all—wisdom.
41:1–13 Death. Ben Sira stresses that all people fear death and are fated to die (vv. 1–4). Rather
than assuring his students about postmortem or end-time judgment, he focuses on the children and
name that the dead leave behind.

Whether life lasts for ten years or a
hundred or a thousand,
there are no questions asked in Hades.
5 The children of sinners are abominable
children,
and they frequent the haunts of the
ungodly.
6 The inheritance of the children of
sinners will perish,
and on their offspring will be a
perpetual disgrace.
7 Children will blame an ungodly father,
for they suffer disgrace because of him.
8 Woe to you, the ungodly,
who have forsaken the law of the Most
High!¹
9 You⁹ will beget them only for groaning.
When you stumble, there is lasting joy,ᶻ
and when you die, a curse is your lot.
10 Whatever comes from earth returns to
earth,
so the ungodly go from curse to
destruction.

11 The breathᵈ of humans is in their bodies,
but a virtuous name will never be
blotted out.ᵇ
12 Have regard for your name, since it will
outlive you
longer than a thousand hoards of gold.
13 The days of a good life are numbered,
but a good name lasts forever.
14 My children, be true to your training and
be at peace;
hidden wisdom and unseen treasure—
of what value is either?
15 Better are those who hide their folly
than those who hide their wisdom.
16 Therefore show respect for my words,
for it is not good to feel shame in every
circumstance,
nor is every kind of shaming to be
approved.ᶜ
17 Be ashamed of sexual immorality before
your father or mother
and of a lie before a prince or a ruler,

18 of a crime before a judge or magistrate
and of a breach of the law before the
congregation and the people,
of unjust dealing before your partner or
your friend
19 and of theft in the place where you live.
Be ashamed of breaking an oath or
agreementᵈ
and of leaning on your elbow at meals,
of surliness in receiving or giving
20 and of silence before those who greet
you,
of looking at a prostitute
21 and of rejecting the appeal of a relative,
of taking away someone's portion or gift
and of gazing at another man's wife,
22 of meddling with his female servant—
and do not approach her bed;
of abusive words, before friends—
and do not be insulting after making
a gift.

42 Be ashamed of repeating what you
hear
and of betraying secrets.
Then you will show proper shame
and will find favor with everyone.

Of the following things do not be
ashamed,
and do not sin by showing partiality:
2 Do not be ashamed of the law of the
Most High and his covenant
and of rendering judgment to acquit
the ungodly;
3 of keeping accounts with a partner or
with traveling companions
and of dividing the inheritance of
friends;
4 of accuracy with scales and weights
and of acquiring much or little;
5 of profit from dealing with merchants
and of frequent disciplining of children

x 41.8 Heb: Gk adds God   y 41.9 Other ancient authorities
read If you have children, calamity will be theirs; you
z 41.9 Heb: Meaning of Gk uncertain   a 41.11 Heb: Gk
misery   b 41.11 Heb: Gk but the bad name of sinners will be
blotted out   c 41.16 Heb: Gk and not everything is confidently
esteemed by everyone   d 41.19 Heb: Gk before the truth of God
and the covenant

41:14–42:8 Shame. Advice about not hiding one's knowledge leads to a detailed reflection on
shame. Consistent with Ben Sira's recurrent concern with the regulation of emotions, he describes
the situations in which one aptly feels ashamed (41:17–42:1a) and the situations in which one should
not feel ashamed (42:1b–8). The former includes sexual immorality, lies, crimes, theft, and oath-
breaking but also bad table manners and telling a friend's secrets. The latter includes *the law of the
Most High and his covenant* but also due diligence and caution with one's wife and business partners.

and of drawing blood from the back
of a wicked slave.
⁶ Where there is an untrustworthy wife, a
seal is a good thing,
and where there are many hands, lock
things up.
⁷ When you make a deposit, be sure it is
counted and weighed,
and when you give or receive, put it all
in writing.
⁸ Do not be ashamed to correct the stupid
or foolish
or the aged who are guilty of sexual
immorality.
Then you will show your sound training
and will be approved by all.
⁹ A daughter is a secret anxiety to her father,
and worry over her robs him of sleep;
when she is young, for fear she may not
marry,
or if married, for fear she may be disliked;
¹⁰ while a virgin, for fear she may be
seduced
and become pregnant in her father's
house;
or having a husband, for fear she may go
astray,
or, though married, for fear she may
be barren.
¹¹ Keep strict watch over a headstrong
daughter,
or she may make you a laughingstock
to your enemies,
a byword in the city and the assembly ofᵉ
the people,
and put you to shame in public
gatherings.ᶠ
See that there is no lattice in her room,
no spot that overlooks the approaches
to the house.ᵍ

¹² Do not let her parade her beauty before
any man
or spend her time among married
women,ᵇ
¹³ for from garments comes the moth
and from a woman comes woman's
wickedness.
¹⁴ Better is the wickedness of a man than a
woman who does good;
it is a woman who brings shame and
disgrace.
¹⁵ I will now call to mind the works of the
Lord
and will declare what I have seen.
By the word of the Lord his works are
made,
and all his creatures do his will.ⁱ
¹⁶ The sun looks down on everything with
its light,
and the work of the Lord is full of his
glory.
¹⁷ The Lord has not empowered even his
holy ones
to recount all his marvelous works,
which the Lord the Almighty has
established
so that the universe may stand firm in
his glory.
¹⁸ He searches out the abyss and the human
heart;
he understands their subtleties.ʲ
For the Most High knows all that may be
known;
he sees from of old the things that are
to come.ᵏ

e 42.11 Heb: Meaning of Gk uncertain   f 42.11 Heb: Gk *to
shame before the great multitude*   g 42.11 Heb: Gk lacks *See…
house*   h 42.12 Heb: Meaning of Gk uncertain   i 42.15 Syr
Compare Heb: most Gk mss lack *and all… will*   j 42.18 Heb:
Gk *wondrous feats*   k 42.18 Heb: Gk *he sees the sign(s) of the age*

42:9–14 Daughters. The theme of *shame* leads Ben Sira to the topic of daughters—a topic that he explores from the perspective of a father anxious about their effects on his reputation. The main concern is that a daughter might cause a father *shame and disgrace*. Consistent with Ben Sira's infamous misogyny (e.g., 25:13–26), he takes the opportunity to add several dicta generally demeaning women. He associates women with wickedness even to the degree that *the wickedness of a man* is better *than a woman who does good* (v. 14).
42:15–43:33 Works of God in nature. First-person speech (*I will now*; 42:15) signals a shift from thematic clusters of instruction to more extensive liturgical units that explore themes in depth. The first of these concerns God and creation, a common theme in earlier sapiential literature (especially Job 38–41; also Prov. 30; Wis. 7:17–22) as well as Hellenistic-period Jewish apocalypses (especially Book of the Watchers in 1 En. 1–36). Contrast later rabbinic strictures on speculation into "Ma'aseh Bereshit" (i.e., "works of creation"; e.g., m. Hag. 2:1). **42:17** *Holy ones.* A rare reference to angels in Sirach, albeit here used to emphasize divine singularity. **42:18–20** Just as wisdom is linked to God throughout the book, this prayer of praise begins by celebrating God in terms of knowledge, stressing again divine

19 He discloses what has been and what is
to be,
and he reveals the traces of hidden
things.
20 No thought escapes him,
and not a single word is hidden from
him.
21 He has set in order the splendors of his
wisdom;
he is from all eternity one and the same.
Nothing can be added or taken away,
and he needs no one to be his
counselor.
22 How desirable are all his works,
and how sparkling they are to see!ˡ
23 All these things live and remain forever;
each creature is preserved to meet a
particular need.ᵐ
24 All things come in pairs, one opposite the
other,
and he has made nothing incomplete.
25 Each supplements the virtues of the other.
Who could ever tire of seeing his glory?

43 The pride of the higher realms is the
clear vault of the sky,
as glorious to behold as the sight of
the heavens.
2 The sun, when it appears, proclaims as it
rises
what a marvelous instrument it is, the
work of the Most High.
3 At noon it parches the land,
and who can withstand its burning heat?
4 A man tendingⁿ a furnace works in
burning heat,
but three times as hot is the sun
scorching the mountains;
when it breathes out fiery vapors
and when it shines forth its rays, it
blinds the eyes.
5 Great is the Lord who made it;
at his orders it hurries on its course.

6 It is the moon that marks the changing
seasons,ᵒ
governing the times, an everlasting sign.
7 From the moon comes the sign for festal
days,
a light that wanes when it completes
its course.
8 The new moon, as its name suggests,
renews itself;ᵖ
how marvelous it is in this change,
a beacon to the hosts on high
shining in the vault of the heavens!
9 The glory of the stars is the beauty of
heaven,
a glittering array in the heights of the
Lord.
10 On the orders of the Holy One they stand
in their appointed places;
they never relax in their watches.
11 Look at the rainbow and praise him who
made it;
it is exceedingly beautiful in its
brightness.
12 It encircles the sky with its glorious arc;
the hands of the Most High have
stretched it out.
13 By his command he sends the driving snow
and speeds the lightnings of his
judgment.
14 Therefore the storehouses are opened,
and the clouds fly out like birds.
15 In his majesty he gives the clouds their
strength,
and the hailstones are broken in pieces.
17a The voice of his thunder causes the earth
to tremble;
16 when he appears, the mountains shake.
At his will the south wind blows,

l 42.22 Meaning of Gk uncertain   m 42.23 Heb: Gk *forever
for every need, and all are obedient*   n 43.4 Other ancient
authorities read *blowing upon*   o 43.6 Heb: Meaning of Gk
uncertain   p 43.8 Heb: Gk *The month accords with its name*

omniscience. **42:19** *Hidden things.* As in contemporaneous apocalypses (e.g., Dan. 2:22), divine revelation is described with the rhetoric of secrecy. Compare Ben Sira's concern for sharing and keeping
secrets as a mark of friendship (e.g., 8:17–19; 13:12; 19:4–17; 22:22; 27:16–21). **42:21** *Splendors of his
wisdom . . . needs no one to be his counselor.* Wisdom is linked to creation (cf. Prov. 8:30) but not
depicted as a *counselor.* In stark contrast to human beings, God needs no advice. **42:22–43:22** The
human sight of natural phenomena and cycles is here a source of knowledge about divine power.
Ben Sira moves from above to below, starting with celestial cycles (sun, moon, seasons), then meteorological phenomena (hail, rain, thunder, snow; cf. Ps. 29), and finally down to the sea. Cf. Wis. 8:8.
43:11 *Look at the rainbow and praise him who made it.* Cf. 44:18; Gen. 9:12–17. In Jewish practice since
the Middle Ages, it is common to say a blessing of God as the One who made "Maʿaseh Bereshit"
(i.e., "works of creation") after seeing a rainbow. Interestingly, rabbinic responses to seeing a rainbow
were far more cautious (e.g., b. Hag. 16a; b. Ber. 59a), perhaps due to the association of rainbows with

17b so do the storm from the north and
the whirlwind.
He scatters the snow like birds flying down,
and its descent is like locusts alighting.
18 The eye is dazzled by the beauty of its
whiteness,
and the mind is amazed as it falls.
19 He pours frost over the earth like salt,
and icicles form like pointed thorns.
20 The cold north wind blows,
and ice freezes on the water;
it settles on every pool of water,
and the water puts it on like a
breastplate.
21 He consumes the mountains and burns
up the wilderness
and withers the tender grass like fire.
22 A mist quickly heals all things;
the falling dew gives refreshment from
the heat.

23 By his plan he stilled the deep
and planted islands in it.
24 Those who sail the sea tell of its dangers,
and we marvel at what we hear.
25 In it are strange and marvelous
creatures,
all kinds of living things, and mighty*q*
sea monsters.
26 Because of him each of his messengers
succeeds,

and by his word all things hold
together.
27 We could say more but could never say
enough;
let the final word be: "He is the all."
28 Where can we find the strength to praise
him?
For he is greater than all his works.
29 Awesome is the Lord and very great,
and marvelous is his power.
30 Glorify the Lord and exalt him as much
as you can,
for he surpasses even that.
When you exalt him, summon all your
strength,
and do not grow weary, for you cannot
praise him enough.
31 Who has seen him and can describe him?
Or who can extol him as he is?
32 Many things greater than these lie hidden,
for I*r* have seen but few of his works.
33 For the Lord has made all things,
and to the godly he has given wisdom.

*HYMN IN HONOR OF OUR ANCESTORS*s

44 Let us now sing the praises of
famous men,
our ancestors in their generations.

q 43.25 Heb: Gk *a creation of* *r* 43.32 Heb: Gk *we*
s 44.1 This title is included in the Gk text.

seeing the divine (e.g., Ezek. 1:28). **43:25** On *sea monsters*, see also Isa. 30:7; 51:9; Job 9:13; 26:12; Pss. 74:14; 89:10. **43:27–33** Ben Sira stresses that divine power surpasses creation and what humans can see and know of the cosmos. Compare the emphasis on the limits of human knowledge in 3:21–24.

44:1–49:16 Hymn of the ancestors. In the Second Temple period, Jewish literature often features capsule histories that sum up Israel's past through the choice of key figures or events to represent the whole. Some examples occur in apocalyptic reviews of history, such as the Animal Apocalypse (1 En. 85–90) and Apocalypse of Weeks (1 En. 93:1–10; 91:10–17). Others are aimed toward culling the past to entreat readers/hearers to action in the present. Matthias's speech in 1 Macc., for instance, uses a small set of figures from Israel's past to argue for military resistance to the Seleucid Empire in what became the Maccabean Revolt ("Remember the deeds of the ancestors"; 1 Macc. 2:51). Culling the past for exempla was also a feature of Hellenistic education. The didactic appeal to Israel's ancestors is found also in the Wisdom of Solomon, which cites a list of figures (there unnamed) to argue for Wisdom's working in the history of Israel (Wis. 10). Capsule histories are put to various purposes in the Damascus Document, 4 Ezra (2 Esd. 3–14), Heb. 11, Stephen's speech in Acts 7, and m. Avot 1–5. Up until this point, however, Ben Sira has rarely engaged in this mode of argumentation (e.g., the negative exempla adduced in 16:5–14 and 39:22–23), even as he marks knowledge about Israel's past as part of wisdom (e.g., 2:10; 39:1). The book ends, however, with the most extensive known case— what is labeled in Greek manuscripts as the *Hymn in Honor of Our Ancestors*. As in other capsule histories, it features figures also known from earlier biblical literature, albeit in a manner typically reduced to one signature virtue or vice (e.g., Abraham's righteousness, Phinehas's zeal). The same figures and features tend to be repeated across multiple capsule histories, possibly pointing to the use of such formats in oral settings like teaching and speeches. Their patterns are conventional, and choices of omission are just as meaningful as choices of inclusion. **44:1–15** *Praises of famous men.*

2 The Lord apportioned to them^t great
    glory,
    his majesty from the beginning.
3 There were those who ruled in their
    kingdoms
    and made a name for themselves by
        their strength;
those who gave counsel because they
    were intelligent;
those who spoke in prophetic
    oracles;
4 those who led the people by their
    counsels
    and by their knowledge of the
        people's lore;
they were wise in their words of
    instruction;
5 those who composed musical tunes
    or put verses in writing;
6 rich men endowed with resources,
    living peacefully in their homes—
7 all these were honored in their
    generations
    and were the pride of their times.
8 Some of them have left behind a name,
    so that others declare their praise.
9 But of others there is no memory;
    they have perished as though they had
        never existed;
they have become as though they had
    never been born,
    they and their children after them.
10 But these also were men of compassion
    whose righteous deeds have not been
        forgotten;
11 their wealth will remain with their
    descendants
    and their inheritance with their
        children's children.^u

12 Their descendants stand by the
    covenants;
    their children also, for their sake.
13 Their offspring will continue forever,
    and their glory will never be blotted
        out.
14 Their bodies are buried in peace,
    but their name lives on generation
        after generation.
15 The assembly declares^v their wisdom,
    and the congregation proclaims their
        praise.
16 Enoch pleased the Lord and was taken
    up,
    an example of repentance to all
        generations.
17 Noah was found perfect and righteous;
    in the time of wrath he kept humanity
        alive;^w
    because of him^x a remnant was left on
        the earth
    when the flood came.
18 Everlasting covenants were made with
    him
    that all flesh should never again be
        blotted out by a flood.
19 Abraham was the great father of a
    multitude of nations,
    and no one has been found like him in
        glory.
20 He kept the law of the Most High
    and entered into a covenant with
        him;
    he certified the covenant in his flesh,
    and when he was tested he proved
        faithful.

t 44.2 Heb: Gk *created*   u 44.11 Heb Compare Lat Syr:
Meaning of Gk uncertain   v 44.15 Heb: Gk *Peoples declare*
w 44.17 Heb: Gk *was taken in exchange*   x 44.17 Cn: Gk *this*

Ben Sira introduces his capsule history by framing it in terms of Israel's ancestral past as marked by great men, akin to the Greek and other local histories of the Hellenistic period—including rulers, heroes, judges, prophets, musicians, rich men, pious men, and wise men. Yet he links Israel's ances-tors uniquely to God (v. 2). **44:16** *Enoch.* Cf. Gen. 5:24. Ben Sira's survey of Israel's ancestral past begins and ends with Enoch (49:14). Although mentioned only briefly in Genesis, Enoch was the focus of a Jewish literary tradition at the time that Ben Sira wrote. This tradition, now best known from 1 Enoch, extended ancient Israelite sapiential traditions in relation to cosmological, eschatolog-ical, and other apocalyptic concerns. Ben Sira chooses to start with Enoch rather than Adam or Seth. Yet he is here associated with the virtue of repentance (cf. 17:24–32; 21:1) rather than any visionary or even scribal claims; cf. Jub. 5; Heb. 11:5. This reference is missing from the Hebrew version in the Masada fragment. **44:17–18** *Noah.* Cf. Gen. 5–10, especially 6:9; 7:1. In contrast to later rabbinic tra-ditions about Noah, his character is here highly elevated. **44:19–21** *Abraham.* Cf. Gen. 12–36. Abra-ham is a standard feature in capsule histories of Israel and is often lavished with special attention. For the association of Abraham with righteousness see 1 Macc. 2:52; Wis. 10:5; Acts 7:1–8; Heb. 11:8–10, 17–19. Here, he is also said to have *kept the law of the Most High* (v. 20). Despite Ben Sira's earlier

²¹ Therefore the Lord[y] assured him with an
  oath
  that the nations would be blessed
    through his offspring,
  that he would make him as numerous as
    the dust of the earth
  and exalt his offspring like the stars
  and give them an inheritance from sea
    to sea
  and from the Euphrates[z] to the ends of
    the earth.
²² To Isaac also he gave the same assurance
  for the sake of his father Abraham.
  The blessing of all people and a
    covenant
²³ he made to rest on the head of Jacob;
  he acknowledged him with his blessings
    and gave him his inheritance;
  he divided his portions
    and distributed them among twelve
      tribes.
  From his descendants the Lord[a] brought
    forth a man of compassion
  who found favor in the sight of all

45

  ¹and was beloved by God and
    people,
  Moses, whose memory is blessed.
² He made him equal in glory to the holy
    ones
  and made him great, to the terror of
    his enemies.
³ By his words he performed swift
    miracles;[b]
  the Lord[c] glorified him in the presence
    of kings.

He gave him commandments for his
    people
  and revealed to him his glory.
⁴ For his faithfulness and meekness he
    consecrated him,
  choosing him out of all humankind.
⁵ He allowed him to hear his voice
  and led him into the dark cloud
  and gave him the commandments face
    to face,
  the law of life and knowledge,
  so that he might teach Jacob the
    covenant
  and Israel his decrees.
⁶ He exalted Aaron, a holy man like
    Moses,[d]
  who was his brother, of the tribe of
    Levi.
⁷ He made an everlasting covenant with
    him
  and gave him the priesthood of the
    people.
  He blessed him with stateliness
  and put a glorious robe on him.
⁸ He clothed him in perfect splendor[e]
  and strengthened him with the
    apparel of authority,
  the linen undergarments, the long
    robe, and the ephod.
⁹ And he encircled him with
    pomegranates,
  with many golden bells all around,

y 44.21 Gk *he*   z 44.21 Syr: Heb Gk *River*   a 44.23 Gk *he*
b 45.3 Heb: Gk *caused signs to cease*   c 45.3 Gk *he*   d 45.6 Gk
him   e 45.8 Heb: Gk *boasting*

mention of Lot's neighbors (16:8) and allusion to Sodom and Gomorrah (39:23), Lot does not here warrant any mention (cf. Wis. 10:6). **44:22–23** *Isaac.* Cf. Gen. 21–25; Heb. 11:20. Isaac is here credited mainly as assuring the continuance of the covenant and promise from Abraham to Jacob. *Jacob*— that is, Israel; cf. Gen. 25–49; Wis. 10:10; Heb. 11:21; see note on 23:12. Other capsule histories of this sort (e.g., 1 Macc. 2:51–60; Wis. 13–14; Heb. 11; Acts 7:9) include Joseph next (cf. 49:15). For Ben Sira, *Jacob* is remarkable as forefather of the *twelve tribes* of Israel and especially as the ancestor of Moses, here celebrated as one *who found favor in the sight of all.* **44:23b–45:5** *Moses.* The list of positive exempla from Israel's past in Wis. 10 ends with Moses, while the list in m. Avot begins with Moses. Like the Wisdom of Solomon, Ben Sira lavishes attention on pre-Sinaitic figures. Like m. Avot, however, he also draws a line straight to his present. Ben Sira's praise of Moses compares him to angels (*holy ones*) and celebrates him for his role in God's giving of the *commandments* to Israel. Nevertheless, Moses's brother Aaron here gets more attention. **45:6–22** *Aaron.* The description of Aaron is an opportunity for the text to celebrate the office of the high priest more generally (see **"Priests and Temple," p. 1479**). **45:7** *A glorious robe.* The garments of the high priest were made of the finest materials and most precious stones and metals (cf. Exod. 28). In the Letter of Aristeas, the sight of these garments is said to inspire "awe and wonder" (§99; see also Wis. 18:24; Josephus, *Ant.* 3.151–178). **45:8** *Ephod.* A kind of apron-like garment that held the high-priestly breastplate (cf. 45:10–11). **45:9** *As a reminder to his people.* In some priestly traditions, the bells are meant to alert God to the high priest's presence in his holy of holies; for Ben Sira, the bells are a *reminder* to the

to send forth a sound as he walked,
  to make their ringing heard in the
    temple
  as a reminder to his people;
¹⁰ with the sacred vestment, of gold and
    violet
  and purple, the work of an
    embroiderer;
  with the oracle of judgment, the
    manifestations of truth;
¹¹   with twisted crimson, the work of an
    artisan;
  with precious stones engraved like seals,
    in a setting of gold, the work of a
      jeweler,
  to commemorate in engraved letters
    each of the tribes of Israel;
¹² with a gold crown upon his turban,
    inscribed like a holy seal,
  majestic and glorious, a work of power,
    a delight to the eyes, richly adorned.
¹³ Before him such beautiful things did not
    exist.
  No outsider ever put them on,
  but only his sons
    and his descendants in perpetuity.
¹⁴ His sacrifices shall be wholly burned
    twice every day continually.
¹⁵ Moses ordained him
    and anointed him with holy oil;
  it was an everlasting covenant for him
    and for his descendants as long as the
      heavens endure,
  to minister to the Lordᶠ and serve as
    priest
  and bless his people in his name.
¹⁶ He chose him out of all the living
    to offer sacrifice to the Lord,
  incense and a pleasing odor as a
    memorial,
  to make atonement for theᵍ people.

¹⁷ In his commandments he gave him
    authority, by means of a decree, andᵇ
      judgments,
  to teach Jacob the testimonies
    and to enlighten Israel with his law.
¹⁸ Outsiders conspired against him
    and envied him in the wilderness,
  Dathan and Abiram and their followers
    and the company of Korah, in wrath
      and anger.
¹⁹ The Lord saw it and was not pleased,
    and in the heat of his anger they were
      destroyed;
  he performed wonders against them
    to consume them in flaming fire.
²⁰ He added glory to Aaron
    and gave him a heritage;
  he allotted to him the best of the first
    fruits
  and prepared bread of first fruits in
    abundance,
²¹ for they eat the sacrifices of the Lord,
    which he gave to him and his
      descendants.
²² But in the land of the people he has no
    inheritance,
  and he has no portion among the
    people,
  for the Lordⁱ himself is hisʲ portion
    and inheritance.
²³ Phinehas son of Eleazar ranks third in
    glory
  for being zealous in the fear of the
    Lord
  and standing firm, when the people
    turned away,
  in the noble courage of his soul,
    and he made atonement for Israel.

f 45.15 Gk *him*   g 45.16 Other ancient authorities read
his or *your*   h 45.17 Heb: Gk *authority in covenants of*
i 45.22 Gk *he*   j 45.22 Other ancient authorities read *your*

people that they should be paying attention to the movements of the high priest. **45:10** *Oracle of judgment, the manifestations of truth.* In some priestly texts, the priests are said to have objects called the Urim and Thummim, which they use to seek yes-or-no answers from God (cf. Exod. 28:30; Lev. 8:8; Num. 27:21; Ezra 2:63; Neh. 7:65). **45:11** *Precious stones.* Cf. Exod. 28:15–21. **45:14** *Twice every day.* What seems to be described here is sometimes known as the "tamid" or "regular" offering, made twice each day, once in the morning and once in the evening (cf. Exod. 29:38–42; Num. 28:3–6; 1 Chr. 16:40). **45:17** *To teach.* One of the roles of the high priest was to instruct the people in the *law* (cf. Lev. 10:10–11). **45:18–19** *Dathan and Abiram . . . Korah.* Cf. Num. 16. **45:19** *In the heat of his anger.* In the story in Num. 16, they are both swallowed by the earth and consumed in fire. **45:22** *No portion.* The priests (and the tribe of Levi as a whole) do not inherit a specific portion of the promised land (cf. Num. 18; Deut. 10:9; Josh. 18:7). **45:23–25** *Phinehas.* Cf. Num. 25, where Phinehas kills an Israelite who transgressed the law. In this hymn, *Phinehas* is the only figure associated with *fear of the Lord*. He is also associated with zeal, as in 1 Macc. 2:54.

24 Therefore a covenant of peace was
  established with him,
    that he should be leader of the
    sanctuary and of his people,
  that he and his descendants should have
    the dignity of the priesthood forever.
25 Just as a covenant was established with
  David
    son of Jesse of the tribe of Judah,
  that the king's heritage passes only from
    son to son,
    so the heritage of Aaron is for his
    descendants alone.

26 And now bless the Lord
  who has crowned you with glory.[k]
    May the Lord[l] grant you wisdom of mind
    to judge his people with justice,
  so that their prosperity may not vanish
    and that their glory may endure
    through all their generations.

46 Joshua son of Nun was mighty in war
  and was the successor of Moses in
    the prophetic office.
  He became, as his name implies,
    a great savior of God's[m] elect,
  to take vengeance on the enemies who
    rose against them,
    so that he might give Israel its
    inheritance.
2 How glorious he was when he lifted his
  hands
    and brandished his sword against the
    cities!
3 Who before him ever stood so firm?
    For he waged the wars of the Lord.
4 Was it not through him that the sun
  stood still
    and one day became as long as two?
5 He called upon the Most High, the
  Mighty One,

when enemies pressed him on every
  side,
    and the great Lord answered him
    with hailstones of mighty power.
6 He overwhelmed that nation in battle,
    and on the slope he destroyed his
    opponents,
  so that the nations might know his
    armament,
    because their battle was against[n] the
    Lord,
    for he was a devoted follower of the
    Mighty One.
7 And in the days of Moses he showed
  compassion,
    he and Caleb son of Jephunneh:
  they opposed the congregation,[o]
    restrained the people from sin,
    and stilled their wicked grumbling.
8 And these two alone were spared
    out of six hundred thousand infantry,
  to lead the people[p] into their inheritance,
    the land flowing with milk and
    honey.
9 The Lord gave Caleb strength,
    which remained with him in his old age,
  so that he went up to the hill country,
    and his children obtained it for an
    inheritance,
10 so that all the Israelites might see
    how good it is to follow the Lord.
11 The judges also, with their respective
  names,
    whose hearts did not fall into idolatry
  and who did not turn away from the
    Lord—
    may their memory be blessed!

k 45.26 Heb: Gk lacks *And...glory*   l 45.26 Gk *he*
m 46.1 Gk *his*   n 46.6 Other ancient authorities read *for
his battle was before*   o 46.7 Other ancient authorities read
the enemy   p 46.8 Gk *them*

45:24 *Therefore a covenant of peace was established.* Ben Sira nuances the idea of a hereditary priesthood by emphasizing that Phinehas's adherence to the law and *fear of the Lord* are the reasons for his and his descendants' appointment to the high priesthood. This same logic is found in Matthias's speech in 1 Macc. 2:26, 54, which cites Phinehas's zeal as the reason for his priesthood (there with no reference to Aaron). **45:25** This verse likens the office of high priest to the office of king—a connection especially poignant in the Second Temple period, when Israel was under nonnative imperial rule and the high priest functioned as a political as well as religious leader (see **"Priests and Temple," p. 1479**). **45:26** A blessing upon priests, associating them with wisdom, judgment, and proper ritual practice ensuring the prosperity of the entire people. **46:1–6** *Joshua.* The hymn turns to Joshua, who emblematizes prophetic succession from Moses but also Israel's past military prowess (cf. Josh. 6–11). **46:7–10** *Caleb.* Cf. Num. 14. As in 1 Macc. 2:55–56, Joshua and Caleb are both celebrated, with a focus on their place in ensuring the people Israel's inheritance of the promised land. **46:11–12** *The judges.* The hymn has focused up until now on named figures but here leaves

[12] May their bones send forth new life from
where they lie,
and may the names of those who have
been honored
live again in their children![q]

[13] Samuel was beloved by his Lord;
a prophet of the Lord, he established
the kingdom
and anointed rulers over his people.
[14] By the law of the Lord he judged the
congregation,
and the Lord watched over Jacob.
[15] By his faithfulness he was proved to be a
prophet,
and by his words he became known as
a trustworthy seer.
[16] He called upon the Lord, the Mighty
One,
when his enemies pressed him on
every side,
and he offered in sacrifice a suckling
lamb.
[17] Then the Lord thundered from heaven
and made his voice heard with a
mighty sound;
[18] he subdued the leaders of the enemy[r]
and all the rulers of the Philistines.
[19] Before the time of his eternal sleep,
Samuel[s] bore witness before the Lord
and his anointed:
"No property, not so much as a pair of
shoes,
have I taken from anyone!"
And no one accused him.
[20] Even after he had fallen asleep, he
prophesied
and made known to the king his death
and lifted up his voice from the ground
in prophecy, to blot out the
lawlessness of the people.

47 After him Nathan rose up
to prophesy in the days of David.
[2] As the fat is set apart from the offering of
well-being,
so David was set apart from the
Israelites.
[3] He played with lions as though they were
young goats
and with bears as though they were
lambs of the flock.
[4] In his youth did he not kill a giant
and take away the people's disgrace,
when he whirled the stone in the sling
and struck down the boasting Goliath?
[5] For he called on the Lord, the Most High,
and he gave strength to his right arm
to strike down a mighty warrior
and to exalt the power[t] of his people.
[6] So they glorified him for the tens of
thousands
and praised him for the blessings
bestowed by the Lord,
when the glorious diadem was given
to him.
[7] For he wiped out his enemies on every side
and scorned his adversaries the
Philistines;
he crushed their power[u] to our own
day.
[8] In all that he did he gave thanks
to the Holy One, the Most High,
proclaiming his glory;
he sang praise with all his heart,
and he loved his Maker.
[9] He placed singers before the altar,
to make sweet melody with their
voices.[v]

q 46.12 Meaning of Gk uncertain *r* 46.18 Heb: Gk *leaders of the people of Tyre* *s* 46.19 Gk *he* *t* 47.5 Gk *horn* *u* 47.7 Gk *horn* *v* 47.9 Other ancient authorities add *and daily they sing their praises*

the judges unnamed even as it calls for their *names* to *live again in their children*. **46:13–20** *Samuel.* Much attention is given to the prophet Samuel, not just as a *prophet*, *seer*, and judge, but also because of his place in establishing Israel's kingship (cf. 1 Sam. 10:1) and contributing to Israel's military successes (cf. 1 Sam. 7:7–11). **46:20** *Even after he had fallen asleep*—that is, after his death—a reference to the tale of Saul's request for a necromancer in Endor to conjure Samuel for consultation (cf. 1 Sam. 28). **47:1–12** *Nathan* and *David*. The hymn's listing of past luminaries continues along two lines, including those in the succession of prophets and those in the succession of kings. It thus continues with Nathan (v. 1; cf. 2 Sam. 7:2–4) but also David (vv. 2–12). The latter's premonarchic life is also celebrated, with allusions to the tale of his defeat of the *giant* Goliath (cf. 1 Sam. 17) alongside other military successes. As in 1 Macc. 2:57, his rise to the throne is causally connected to his deeds. Consistent with Ben Sira's concern for prayer, however, special attention is given to his association with psalms (vv. 8–11). David's transgressions (cf. 2 Sam. 11–12) are even said to have been erased due to his prayers (v. 11). Although Ben Sira writes centuries after the cessation of Davidic rule in the land

¹⁰ He gave beauty to the festivals
and arranged their times throughout
the year,^w
while they praised God's^x holy name
and the sanctuary resounded from
early morning.
¹¹ The Lord took away his sins
and exalted his power^y forever;
he gave him a covenant of kingship
and a glorious throne in Israel.
¹² After him a wise son rose up
who because of him lived in security:^z
¹³ Solomon reigned in an age of peace,
because God gave him rest all around,
so that he might build a house in his
name
and provide a sanctuary to stand
forever.
¹⁴ How wise you were when you were
young!
You overflowed like the Nile^a with
understanding.
¹⁵ Your influence spread throughout the
earth,
and you filled it with proverbs having
deep meaning.
¹⁶ Your fame reached to far-off islands,
and you were loved for your peaceful
reign.
¹⁷ For your songs, proverbs, parables,
and understanding the nations
marveled at you.
¹⁸ In the name of the Lord God,
who is called the God of Israel,
you gathered gold like tin
and amassed silver like lead.
¹⁹ But you brought in women to lie at your
side,
and through your body you were
brought into subjection.

²⁰ You stained your honor
and defiled your family line,
so that you brought wrath upon your
children,
and they were grieved^b at your folly,
²¹ because the sovereignty was divided
and a rebel kingdom arose out of
Ephraim.
²² But the Lord will never give up his mercy
or cause any of his words^c to perish;
he will never blot out the descendants of
his chosen one
or destroy the family line of him who
loved him.
So he gave a remnant to Jacob
and to David a root from his own
family.
²³ Solomon rested with his ancestors
and left behind him one of his sons
broad in^d folly and lacking in sense,
Rehoboam, whose policy drove the
people to revolt.
Then Jeroboam son of Nebat led Israel
into sin
and started Ephraim on its sinful ways.
²⁴ Their sins increased more and more
until they were exiled from their land.
²⁵ For they sought out every kind of
wickedness
until vengeance came upon them.

48 Then Elijah arose, a prophet like
fire,
and his word burned like a torch.
² He brought a famine upon them,
and by his zeal he made them few in
number.

w 47.10 Gk *to completion*   x 47.10 Gk *his*   y 47.11 Gk
horn   z 47.12 Heb: Gk *in a broad place*   a 47.14 Heb: Gk *a
river*   b 47.20 Other ancient authorities read *I was grieved*
c 47.22 Heb Syr: Gk *works*   d 47.23 Heb Syr: Gk *the people's*

of Israel, he affirms the eternity of the Davidic kingship. **47:13–22** *Solomon.* As in the Wisdom of Solomon, Solomon is celebrated as a *wise son*, and peace at the beginning of his reign is credited to a divine plan to enable him to build the Jerusalem temple (cf. 1 Kgs. 5–8). In his youth, he is associated with *proverbs having deep meaning* (v. 15) as well as *songs* and *parables* (v. 17), recalling part of what Ben Sira describes the scribe as interpreting in chap. 39. The spread of his wisdom similarly recalls the cosmopolitanism of the ideal scribe described there (see **"Scribes and Scribalism,"** p. 1486). Solomon's amassing of wealth and wives, however, is here described as a turn from wisdom to *folly* (vv. 19–21; cf. Deut. 17:14–20) that causes the split of the kingdom (cf. 1 Kgs. 11:31–39). **47:22** God's continued chosenness of the Davidic line is nevertheless affirmed (see **"Davidic Covenant,"** p. 433). **47:23–25** *Rehoboam* and *Jeroboam.* Cf. 1 Kgs. 11:43–14:31. With Solomon and his sons, what has been a list of positive exempla turns toward negative exempla. **47:24** Exile is here the result of transgression—a pattern familiar from prophetic warnings but also resonant with Ben Sira's assertion of the everyday arithmetic of divine justice, aligning sin with suffering and righteousness with prosperity. **48:1–11** *Elijah.* Starting in 48:4 Elijah is addressed in the second person. Cf.

³ By the word of the Lord he shut up the
heavens
and also three times brought down
fire.
⁴ How glorious you were, Elijah, in your
wondrous deeds!
Who can boast*ᵉ* as you can?
⁵ You who raised a corpse from death
and from Hades, by the word of the
Most High,
⁶ who sent kings down to destruction
and famous men from their sickbeds,
⁷ who heard rebuke at Sinai
and judgments of vengeance at Horeb,
⁸ who anointed kings to inflict retribution
and prophets to succeed you,*ᶠ*
⁹ who were taken up by a whirlwind of
fire
in a chariot with horses of fire,
¹⁰ who were prepared at the appointed
time*ᵍ*
to calm wrath before it breaks out in
fury,
to turn the hearts of parents to their
children
and to restore the tribes of Jacob.
¹¹ Happy are those who saw you
and were adorned*ʰ* in love!
For we also shall surely live.*ⁱ*
¹² When Elijah was enveloped in the
whirlwind,
Elisha was filled with his spirit.
He performed twice as many signs
and marvels with every utterance of
his mouth.*ʲ*
Never in his lifetime did he tremble
before any ruler,
nor could anyone intimidate him at all.
¹³ Nothing was too hard for him,*ᵏ*
and when he was dead his body
prophesied.
¹⁴ In his life he did wonders,
and in death his deeds were
marvelous.

¹⁵ Despite all this the people did not repent,
nor did they forsake their sins,
until they were carried off as plunder
from their land
and were scattered over all the earth.
The people were left very few in number
but with a ruler from the house of
David.
¹⁶ Some of them did what was right,
but others sinned more and more.
¹⁷ Hezekiah fortified his city
and brought water into its midst;
he tunneled the rock with iron tools
and built cisterns for the water.
¹⁸ In his days Sennacherib invaded the
country;
he sent his commander*ˡ* and departed;
he shook his fist against Zion
and made great boasts in his
arrogance.
¹⁹ Then their hearts and hands were
shaken,
and they were in anguish, like women
in labor.
²⁰ But they called upon the Lord who is
merciful,
spreading out their hands toward him.
The Holy One quickly heard them from
heaven
and delivered them through Isaiah.
²¹ The Lord*ᵐ* struck down the camp of the
Assyrians,
and his angel wiped them out.
²² For Hezekiah did what was pleasing to
the Lord,
and he kept firmly to the ways of his
ancestor David,
as he was commanded by the prophet
Isaiah,

e 48.4 Or *be glorified*   *f* 48.8 Heb: Gk *him*   *g* 48.10 Heb: Gk
are for reproofs   *h* 48.11 Other ancient authorities read *and
have died*   *i* 48.11 Meaning of Gk uncertain   *j* 48.12 Heb:
Gk lacks *He performed . . . mouth*   *k* 48.13 Heb: Gk *no word
surpassed him*   *l* 48.18 Other ancient authorities add *from
Lachish*   *m* 48.21 Gk *He*

1 Kgs. 17–19; 2 Kgs. 1–2. Compare 1 Macc. 2:58–60; also included there, but omitted here, are Hananiah, Azariah, Mishael, and Daniel. Like Phinehas (45:23–25), Elijah is associated with *zeal*. As with
Samuel (46:13), Elijah is celebrated both for anointing kings and for continuing the succession of
prophets. Allusions are also made to his end-time role (cf. Mal. 4:5–6). **48:12–15** *Elisha.* Cf. 2 Kgs.
2–13. Elisha's piety and power are celebrated, and the Assyrian conquest of the northern kingdom of
Israel occurs despite him not because of him. **48:17–25** *Hezekiah* and *Isaiah*. Cf. 2 Kgs. 18–20; Isa.
36–39. Here again, concern for king and prophet are paired. Hezekiah's kingship is celebrated in
terms of his improvement of Jerusalem's infrastructure, and his righteousness is here said to be
answered by God's sending of an *angel* to thwart the Assyrian army. Hezekiah's righteousness is
depicted in terms of following the model of *David* and the words of *Isaiah*. The latter is celebrated

who was great and trustworthy in his
visions.
²³ In Isaiah's[n] days the sun went backward,
and he prolonged the life of the king.
²⁴ By his dauntless spirit he saw the future
and comforted the mourners in Zion.
²⁵ He revealed what was to occur to the
end of time
and the hidden things before they
happened.

49 The name[o] of Josiah is like blended
incense
prepared by the skill of the perfumer;
his memory[p] is as sweet as honey to
every mouth
and like music at a banquet of wine.
² He did what was right by reforming the
people
and removing the lawless abominations.
³ He kept his heart fixed on the Lord;
in lawless times he made godliness
prevail.

⁴ Except for David and Hezekiah and Josiah,
all of them were great sinners,
for they abandoned the law of the Most
High;
the kings of Judah came to an end.
⁵ They[q] gave their power to others
and their glory to a foreign nation,
⁶ who set fire to the chosen city of the
sanctuary
and made its streets desolate,
as Jeremiah had foretold.[r]
⁷ For they had mistreated him,
who even in the womb had been
consecrated a prophet,

to pluck up and ruin and destroy
and likewise to build and to plant.
⁸ It was Ezekiel who saw the vision of
glory,
which God[s] showed him above the
chariot of the cherubim.
⁹ For he also mentioned Job,
who held fast to all the ways of
justice.[t]
¹⁰ May the bones of the Twelve Prophets
send forth new life from where they lie,
for they comforted the people of Jacob
and delivered them with confident
hope.
¹¹ How shall we magnify Zerubbabel?
He was like a signet ring on the right
hand,
¹² and so was Jeshua son of Jozadak;
in their days they built the house
and raised a temple[u] holy to the Lord,
prepared for everlasting glory.
¹³ The memory of Nehemiah also is lasting;
he raised our fallen walls
and set up gates and bars
and rebuilt our ruined houses.
¹⁴ Few have[v] ever been created on earth
like Enoch,
for he was taken up from the earth.
¹⁵ Nor was anyone ever born like Joseph;[w]
even his bones were cared for.

n 48.23 Gk *his* o 49.1 Heb: Gk *memory* p 49.1 Heb: Gk *it*
q 49.5 Heb *He* r 49.6 Gk *by the hand of Jeremiah* s 49.8 Gk
He t 49.9 Heb Compare Syr: Meaning of Gk uncertain
u 49.12 Other ancient authorities read *people* v 49.14 Heb
Syr: Gk *No one has* w 49.15 Heb Syr: Gk adds *the leader of
his brothers, the support of the people*

in part for his prophecies about the *end of time.* **49:1–6a** *Josiah.* Cf. 2 Kgs. 22–23. A subsequent king of Judah, Josiah is here described as a righteous king despite his *lawless times.* Together with *David* and *Hezekiah,* he is deemed the only king of Judah not to have *abandoned the law of the Most High*—an assessment far more dire than 1–2 Kings. Ben Sira connects the sins of all of the rest of Judah's kings to the Babylonian conquest and destruction of Jerusalem in 586 BCE. **49:6b–8** *Jeremiah* and *Ezekiel.* The prophet *Jeremiah* is celebrated for a prediction that came true (cf. Jer. 7:12–15), while the prophet *Ezekiel* is celebrated for his *vision* of the divine throne (cf. Ezek. chaps. 1, 10). **49:9** *Job.* Rather than wisdom, *Job* is here associated with *justice.* **49:10** *Twelve Prophets.* Other prophets are mentioned by number rather than name, anticipating their anthologizing. As elsewhere, the *bones* of the righteous are assumed to continue their positive impact on the people. **49:11–12** *Zerubbabel* and *Jeshua.* Cf. Ezra 3:2; Hag. 1:1; 2:2; Zech. 3–4. Consistent with the hymn's lauding of the Davidic line of kings, the last-named claimant to Davidic kingship, *Zerubbabel,* is here mentioned. Interestingly, it is alongside his high priest, *Jeshua.* **49:13** *Nehemiah.* Ezra is not mentioned. Compare 2 Macc. 2:13, where Nehemiah is also exemplary of the rebuilding of Jerusalem after the advent of Achaemenid Persian rule over the land of Israel in 538 BCE. As in Ben Sira's description of Hezekiah, there is a special concern for his building projects in the city of Jerusalem. **49:14–16** *Enoch.* The main body of the hymn ends where it began—that is, with *Enoch* (44:16). His

[16] Shem and Seth and Enosh were
 honored,[x]
 but above every other created living
 being was Adam.

50

The leader of his brothers and the
 pride of his people[y]
was the high priest, Simon son of Onias,
who in his life repaired the house
 and in his time fortified the temple.
[2] He laid the foundations for the high
 double walls,
 the high retaining walls for the temple
 enclosure.
[3] In his days a water cistern was dug,[z]
 a reservoir like the sea in
 circumference.
[4] He considered how to save his people
 from ruin
 and fortified the city against siege.
[5] How glorious he was as he gazed from
 the tent,[a]
 as he came out of the house of the
 curtain,
[6] like the morning star among the clouds,
 like the full moon at the festal season,[b]
[7] like the sun shining on the temple of the
 Most High,
 like the rainbow gleaming in splendid
 clouds,
[8] like roses in the days of the spring harvest,
 like lilies by springs of water,
 like a green shoot on Lebanon on a
 summer day,

[9] like fire and incense in the censer,
 like a vessel of hammered gold
 studded with all kinds of precious
 stones,
[10] like an olive tree laden with fruit,
 and like a cypress towering in the
 clouds.
[11] When he put on his glorious robe
 and clothed himself in perfect splendor,
when he went up to the holy altar,
 he made the court of the sanctuary
 glorious.
[12] When he received the portions from the
 hands of the priests,
 as he stood by the hearth of the altar
with a garland of brothers around him,
 he was like a young cedar on Lebanon
 surrounded by the trunks of palm trees.
[13] All the sons of Aaron in their splendor
 held the Lord's offering in their hands
 before the whole congregation of Israel.
[14] Finishing the service at the altars[c]
 and arranging the offering to the Most
 High, the Almighty,
[15] he held out his hand for the cup
 and poured a drink offering of the
 blood of the grape;

x 49.16 Heb: Gk *Shem and Seth were honored by people*
y 50.1 Heb Syr: Gk lacks this line.   z 50.3 Heb: Meaning
of Gk uncertain   a 50.5 Heb: Gk *in his courses in the temple*
b 50.6 Heb: Meaning of Gk uncertain   c 50.14 Other
ancient authorities read *altar*

exemplarity is followed by a nonchronological cluster of exempla who have not been mentioned so far—that is, starting with *Joseph*, then progressing to *Shem and Seth and Enosh*, and finally to *Adam*.
 50:1–21 Praise of Simon II. *Simon son of Onias.* With Simon II, also called Simon the Righteous, the hymn moves to Ben Sira's present. Simon II served as high priest from 219 to 196 BCE, overlapping with the shift from Ptolemaic to Seleucid imperial rule in the land of Israel. He is the one priest of the Second Temple period included in the capsule history of m. Avot and celebrated in rabbinic literature. **50:1–4** This section casts Simon II in a role similar to that taken by kings in earlier periods. He is credited with the construction of urban infrastructure—here Jerusalem's palace (*the house*), *temple*, city and temple *walls*, and water system (cf. Solomon in 1 Kgs. 5–7 and 2 Chr. 2–5; Hezekiah in 2 Chr. 29 and 31). **50:3** *A water cistern.* Compare the focus on Hezekiah's tunnel for water in 48:17. **50:5** *House of the curtain.* This refers to the innermost chamber of the Jerusalem temple, known as the holy of holies. **50:6** *Full moon at the festal season.* Two of the three annual pilgrimage festivals fell on the full moon: Passover and Sukkot (i.e., the Festival of Booths). **50:9** *Incense . . . hammered gold.* The objects described in this verse all would have been used in the inner chamber of the temple and thus understood as some of the holiest of the temple vessels. **50:11** *His glorious robe.* See note on 45:7. *Holy altar.* This would have been the altar in the courtyard of the temple, in full view of the public. This altar was used for animal and grain sacrifices. **50:12–20** These verses describe parts of a sacrificial procedure and the role of the high priest and priests in that process. **50:12** *From the hands of the priests.* The process here described concerns priests handing portions of animal or grain to the high priest, who would then put it in the fire burning on the altar. **50:15** *Poured a drink offering.* The high priest moves on to the libation offering, typically wine poured out at the base

he poured it out at the foot of the altar,
a pleasing odor to the Most High, the
king of all.
[16] Then the sons of Aaron shouted;
they blew their trumpets of
hammered metal;
they sounded a mighty fanfare
as a reminder before the Most High.
[17] Then all the people together quickly
fell to the ground on their faces
to worship their Lord,
the Almighty, God Most High.

[18] Then the singers praised him with their
voices
in sweet and full-toned melody.[d]
[19] And the people of the Lord Most High
offered
their prayer before the Merciful One,
until the order of worship of the Lord
was ended
and they completed his ritual.
[20] Then Simon[e] came down and raised his
hands
over the whole congregation of
Israelites,
to pronounce the blessing of the Lord
with his lips
and to glory in his name,
[21] and they bowed down in worship a
second time
to receive the blessing from the Most
High.
[22] And now bless the God of all,
who everywhere works great
wonders,

who exalts our days from birth[f]
and deals with us according to his
mercy.
[23] May he give us[g] gladness of heart,
and may there be peace in our[h] days
in Israel, as in the days of old.
[24] May he entrust to us his mercy,
and may he deliver us in our[i] days!
[25] Two nations my soul detests,
and the third is not even a nation:
[26] those who live in Seir[j] and the Philistines
and the foolish people who live in
Shechem.

[27] Instruction in understanding and
knowledge
I have written in this book,
Jesus son of Eleazar son of Sirach[k] of
Jerusalem,
whose mind poured forth wisdom.
[28] Happy are those who concern
themselves with these things,
and those who lay them to heart will
become wise.
[29] For if they put them into practice, they
will be equal to anything,
for the fear[l] of the Lord is their path.[m]

d 50.18 Other ancient authorities read *in sweet melody
throughout the house* e 50.20 Gk *he* f 50.22 Heb *who
nurtures humankind from the womb* g 50.23 Other ancient
authorities read *you* h 50.23 Other ancient authorities
read *your* i 50.24 Other ancient authorities read *his*
j 50.26 Heb Compare Lat: Gk *on the mountain of Samaria*
k 50.27 Heb: Meaning of Gk uncertain l 50.29 Heb: Other
ancient authorities read *light* m 50.29 Other ancient
authorities add *And to the pious he gave wisdom. Blessed be the
Lord forever. May it be; may it be.*

of the altar. The reference to *a pleasing odor* almost certainly refers to the entirety of the sacrifice, not only the wine; the smell of burning meat would have overwhelmed that of the wine. **50:16** *As a reminder.* The blowing of the trumpets at the conclusion of the sacrificial procedure suggests an attempt to capture God's attention through sound as well as smell (cf. 35:21; 2 Chr. 5:12). **50:18–19** For the inclusion of music in the process of offering sacrifices, see Ezra 2:70; 3:10; 2 Chr. 5:12–13; 31:2. **50:20** *To pronounce the blessing of the Lord.* Cf. Aaron's blessing in Lev. 9:22–23.

50:22–24 Blessing. The collection of liturgical materials concerning God's creation and Israel's ancestors begun in 42:15 concludes with a blessing of the divine, here addressed as *the God of all* (cf. 36:22) and celebrated both for God's works and for God's special relationship to Israel.

50:25–26 As elsewhere in the book, tangentially related sayings are often inserted in the transitions between more thematic sections. Here, Israel's chosenness occasions an aside about those deemed not chosen—that is, *Philistines*, Edomites (associated with *Seir*), and Samaritans (associated with *Shechem*).

50:27–51:29 Autobiographical reflection. 50:27–29 *I have written.* The book ends with a first-person authorial aside in which Ben Sira discloses his name and location (in the Gk.: *Jesus son of Eleazar son of Sirach of Jerusalem*) and states his reason for writing—namely, to offer *instruction in understanding and knowledge* (cf. P:12) for the sake of the happiness of his readers and guiding men toward *the fear of the Lord.* Although common in Greek literature, such authorial asides are rare in

PRAYER OF JESUS SON OF SIRACH[n]

51

I give you thanks, O Lord and King,
and praise you, O God my Savior.
I give thanks to your name,

2 for you have been my protector and
    helper
and have delivered my body from
    destruction
    and from the trap laid by a slanderous
    tongue,
from lips that fabricate lies.
In the face of my adversaries,
    you have been my helper [3]and
    delivered me,
in the greatness of your mercy and of
    your name,
from grinding teeth about to devour me,
    from the hand of those seeking my
    life,
from the many troubles I endured,

4 from choking fire on every side,
    and from the midst of fire that I had
    not kindled,

5 from the deep belly of Hades,
    from an unclean tongue and lying
    words,

6 the slander of an unrighteous tongue
    to the king.
My soul drew near to death,
    and my life was on the brink of Hades
    below.

7 They surrounded me on every side,
    and there was no one to help me.
I looked for human assistance,
    and there was none.

8 Then I remembered your mercy, O Lord,
    and your kindness[o] from of old,
for you rescue those who wait for you
    and save them from the hand of their
    enemies.

9 And I sent up my prayer from the earth
    and begged for rescue from death.

10 I cried out, "Lord, you are my Father;[p]
    do not forsake me in the days of
    trouble,
    when there is no help against the
    proud.

11 I will praise your name continually
    and will sing hymns of thanksgiving."

My prayer was heard,
12 for you saved me from destruction
    and rescued me in time of trouble.
For this reason I thank you and praise you,
    and I bless the name of the Lord.

———

Heb adds:

Give thanks to the Lord, for he is good,
    for his steadfast love endures forever.

Give thanks to the God of praises,
    for his steadfast love endures forever.

Give thanks to the guardian of Israel,
    for his steadfast love endures forever.

Give thanks to him who formed all things,
    for his steadfast love endures forever.

Give thanks to the redeemer of Israel,
    for his steadfast love endures forever.

Give thanks to him who gathers the dispersed
    of Israel,
    for his steadfast love endures forever.

Give thanks to him who rebuilt his city and his
    sanctuary,
    for his steadfast love endures forever.

Give thanks to him who makes a horn to sprout
    for the house of David,
    for his steadfast love endures forever.

Give thanks to him who has chosen the sons of
    Zadok to be priests,
    for his steadfast love endures forever.

Give thanks to the shield of Abraham,
    for his steadfast love endures forever.

Give thanks to the rock of Isaac,
    for his steadfast love endures forever.

Give thanks to the mighty one of Jacob,
    for his steadfast love endures forever.

n 51.1 This title is included in the Gk text.   o 51.8 Other
ancient authorities read *work*   p 51.10 Heb: Gk *the Father
of my lord*

ancient Jewish literature; Ben Sira may be the earliest known example. **51:1–12** The *prayer*, labeled
"prayer of Jesus son of Sirach" in Greek manuscripts, is a hymn of *thanks* that recalls the structure of
biblical psalms as well as contemporary materials like Qumran Thanksgiving Hymns (Hodayot).
The prayer begins with an account of near-death danger, from which the speaker was saved by
prayer. **51:12** After this verse, one Hebrew manuscript includes a hymn of thanks echoing Ps. 136.

Give thanks to him who has chosen Zion,
for his steadfast love endures forever.

Give thanks to the King of the kings of kings,
for his steadfast love endures forever.

He has raised up a horn for his people,
praise for all his loyal ones.

For the children of Israel, the people close to
him.
Praise the LORD!

———

¹³ While I was still young, before I went on
my travels,
I sought wisdom openly in my prayer.
¹⁴ Before the temple I asked for her,
and I will search for her until the end.

¹⁵ From the first blossom to the ripening
grape,
my heart delighted in her;
my foot walked on the straight path;
from my youth I followed her steps.

¹⁶ I inclined my ear a little and received
her,
and I found for myself much
instruction.
¹⁷ I made progress in her;
to him who gives wisdom I will give
glory.

¹⁸ For I resolved to practice wisdom,�q
and I was zealous for the good,
and I shall never be disappointed.
¹⁹ My soul grappled with wisdom,ʳ
and in my conduct I was strict.ˢ

I spread out my hands to the heavens
and lamented my ignorance of her.
²⁰ I directed my soul to her,
and in purity I found her.

With her I gained understanding from
the first;
therefore I will never be forsaken.
²¹ My heart was stirred to seek her;
therefore I have gained a prize
possession.
²² The Lord gave me my tongue as a reward,
and I will praise him with it.

²³ Draw near to me, you who are
uneducated,
and lodge in the house of instruction.
²⁴ Why do you say you are lacking in these
things,ᵗ
and why do you endure such great
thirst?
²⁵ I opened my mouth and said,
"Acquire wisdomᵘ for yourselves
without money.

²⁶ "Put your neck under herᵛ yoke,
and let your souls receive instruction;
it is to be found close by."

²⁷ See with your own eyes that I have
labored but little
and found for myself much serenity.
²⁸ Hear but a little of my instruction,
and through me you will acquire silver
and gold.ʷ

²⁹ May your soul rejoice in God'sˣ mercy,
and may you never be ashamed to
praise him.
³⁰ Do your work in good time,
and in his own time Godʸ will give you
your reward.

q 51.18 Gk her   r 51.19 Gk her   s 51.19 Meaning of Gk
uncertain   t 51.24 Cn Compare Heb Syr: Meaning of Gk
uncertain   u 51.25 Heb: Gk lacks wisdom   v 51.26 Heb:
other ancient authorities read the   w 51.28 Syr Compare
Heb: Gk Get instruction with a large sum of silver, and you will
gain by it much gold.   x 51.29 Gk his   y 51.30 Gk he

51:13–30 The power of *prayer* is a key theme in Ben Sira's account of how he came to find wisdom; compare the Hebrew version in 11Q5. This account is structured as an acrostic poem. **51:14** As in 14:24–27 and 24:10, wisdom is linked to the Jerusalem temple. **51:22** *Tongue.* Consistent with the special interest in speech throughout the book, Ben Sira here depicts his own speech as a divine gift. Teaching and learning are presumed to be oral; contrast the translator's description of Ben Sira in the Prologue. **51:23–29** The final verses shift to a second-person address to Ben Sira's students and potential students. He promotes his *house of instruction* for Jewish men seeking wisdom, wealth, and piety. His description of the aim of his book frames learning as an act of listening, in contrast to the translator's Prologue, which emphasizes reading and interpretation.

BARUCH

Authorship, Date, and Literary History

While the book is named for Baruch, Jeremiah's friend and scribe in Jer. 36 and 45, Baruch is not the author (see **"Written Prophecy and Scrolls," p. 1090, and "Scribes and Scribalism," p. 1486**). He is named, however, because just as in Jeremiah, his task was to write words of warning about the consequences of disobeying God's commands; this book has the same theme, only in a different time period. The book of Jeremiah describes the events leading up to the fall of Jerusalem to the Babylonians in 586 BCE. The book of Baruch uses those historical events as a way to describe a second-century BCE crisis. Israel was being threatened by its Greek imperial masters to assimilate into Greek culture and deny their particular Jewish identity. The Greeks desecrated the Jerusalem temple in 168 BCE, and the result was the Maccabean Revolt, which began the following year. Baruch is part of the Catholic Old Testament and is traditionally attached to the Letter of Jeremiah. Baruch argues for the theory of divine retribution (see **"Divine Retribution," p. 339**). Any suffering the people currently endure is the result of their disobedience to God (see also 2 Macc. 4 and 6); however, if they repent, God will rescue them from their enemies.

Intertextuality in Baruch

The author relies heavily on the theory of divine retribution in chaps. 1 and 2 (described in Deut., especially chap. 28). In the praise of wisdom in chaps. 3 and 4, allusions from Proverbs and Job appear. The final call for courage in chaps. 4 and 5 uses a number of passages from Second Isaiah (Isa. 40–55), written at the end of the Babylonian exile. The prophet's claim that God has punished the people but will now reward them echoes in Baruch's call to "take courage" (4:5, 21, 27, 30) because divine help will come after divine punishment.

Reading Guide

The book has four major parts that do not correspond neatly to chapter divisions. The first part (1:1–14) establishes the literary context: Baruch is writing in exile in Babylon (see **"Exile," p. 539**) and sends a letter to the Israelites in Judah, along with financial support for the priests and money to purchase sin offerings, even though the temple is no longer standing. The second part (1:15–3:8) is a lengthy prayer that has three subsections. First, Baruch blames the destruction of Jerusalem and the exile to Babylon squarely on himself and his community for disobeying God (1:15–2:10). He then asks God to release them from their just punishment (2:11–26) and finally reminds God that the people's repentance should lead to their restoration (2:27–3:8). The third part of Baruch (3:9–4:4) praises wisdom as a divine gift bestowed exclusively upon Israel from their God. In the final part (4:5–5:9), the author encourages the people to be brave because their troubles will end and their enemies will be punished.

   While Baruch's view of divine retribution was quite common in biblical times, two things make the argument stand out today. First, the idea that religious misbehavior causes political catastrophes overlooks the facts of imperial power and the vulnerability of smaller populations. In terms of land and community, Israel was never large. Even in the years of the monarchy (tenth to sixth centuries BCE), the regions regularly were vassal states, subject to larger empires (Assyria, then Babylon) and punished for rebellion. After the Babylonian exile, the land became the Persian province of Yehud and later ended up under Greek control by the time Baruch was written. Today, political events rarely receive a religious explanation. Second, particularly in Jewish theology, the idea of divine retribution received consistent historical challenges due to numerous pogroms, with the worst being the Shoah, or Holocaust, in which Jewish people were exterminated simply for being Jewish. Biblical questions about the suffering of the innocent, raised as early as the book of Job, continued to take on historical meaning in the centuries leading up to the Shoah. Today, there is a recognition that a one-to-one correspondence does not always exist between what people do and what happens to them. Baruch blames the people's idolatry for their suffering, and 2 Maccabees, written around the same time, blames the people's assimilation to Greek life; both arguments, however, attempt to explain imperial power and the ways in which it can crush smaller communities at will. The fact that the people revolt is a sign that any "punishment" has its limits.

Stacy Davis

1 These are the words of the book that Baruch son of Neriah son of Mahseiah son of Zedekiah son of Hasadiah son of Hilkiah wrote in Babylon, ²in the fifth year, on the seventh day of the month, at the time when the Chaldeans took Jerusalem and burned it with fire.

3 Baruch read the words of this book to Jeconiah son of Jehoiakim, king of Judah, and to all the people who came to hear the book ⁴and to the nobles and the princes and to the elders and to all the people, small and great, all who lived in Babylon by the River Sud.

5 Then they wept and fasted and prayed before the Lord; ⁶they collected as much silver as each could give ⁷and sent it to Jerusalem to the priest Jehoiakim son of Hilkiah son of Shallum the priest and to the priests and to all the people who were present with him in Jerusalem. ⁸At the same time, on the tenth day of Sivan, Baruch* took the vessels of the house of the Lord that had been carried away from the temple, to return them to the land of Judah—the silver vessels that Zedekiah son of Josiah, king of Judah, had made ⁹after King Nebuchadnezzar of Babylon had carried away from Jerusalem Jeconiah and the princes and the prisoners and the nobles and the people of the land and brought them to Babylon.

10 They said, "Here we send you silver, so buy with the silver burnt offerings and purification offerings* and incense, and prepare a grain offering, and offer them on the altar of the Lord our God, ¹¹and pray for the life of King Nebuchadnezzar of Babylon and for the life of his son Belshazzar, so that their days on earth may be like the days of heaven. ¹²The Lord will give us strength and light to our eyes; we shall live under the protection* of King Nebuchadnezzar of Babylon and under the protection of his son Belshazzar, and we shall serve them many days and find favor in their sight. ¹³Pray also for us to the Lord our God, for we have sinned against the Lord our God, and to this day the anger of the Lord and his wrath have not turned away from us. ¹⁴And you shall read aloud this scroll that we are sending you, to make your confession in the house of the Lord on the days of the festivals and at appointed seasons.

15 "And you shall say: To the Lord our God belongs righteousness, but to us, this day, public shame, on the people of Judah, on the inhabitants of Jerusalem, ¹⁶and on our kings, our rulers, our priests, our prophets, and our ancestors, ¹⁷because we have sinned before the Lord. ¹⁸We have disobeyed him and have not heeded the voice of the Lord our God, to walk in the statutes

a 1.8 Gk he   b 1.10 Gk and for sin   c 1.12 Gk in the shadow

1:1–9 Context. Baruch, already in exile in Babylon, writes a letter and reads it to all of the other Babylonian exiles who are now mourning the destruction of the Jerusalem temple in 587 BCE (see "Exile," p. 539). 1:6–7 They collected as much silver as each could give and sent it to Jerusalem to the priest Jehoiakim son of Hilkiah son of Shallum the priest and to the priests and to all the people who were present with him in Jerusalem. While the priests had designated cities and land for their animals (Num. 35:1–5), they depended primarily upon the people's meat and grain sacrifices for their survival (Lev. 6–7). With the temple gone, their survival is now uncertain, which may explain the emergency offering. 1:8 Sivan, approximately May–June. The temple vessels had been carried to Babylon during the first exile in 597 BCE. Baruch sends them back to Judah, even though the temple has been destroyed.

1:10–15 The letter home. Baruch writes his letter to the priests in Jerusalem, telling them to use the money to offer sacrifices on behalf of the king of Babylon. As a subjugated people, praying for one's conquerors is one way of showing submission and perhaps gaining their favor. It also fits with Jeremiah's view that the Israelites should have submitted to Babylon in the first place in order to survive (Jer. 21). Baruch also asks the priests to pray for the exiles, who are being punished for their sins. 1:10 And for sin, that is, "for sin offerings." 1:14 To make your confession in the house of the Lord on the days of the festivals and at appointed seasons. The Ninth of Av is a day of mourning in Jewish tradition for the destruction of the First (and later the Second) Temple. It is unclear whether it is one of the appointed seasons mentioned here, but it may have been celebrated by Jews at Qumran even while the Second Temple existed (515 BCE–70 CE).

1:15–22 The exiles' confession. Baruch, unlike Jeremiah, does not mention idolatry (see Jer. 2–3, 7); however, he repeatedly states that the people are guilty of sin and disobedience since the exodus (vv. 17–19). As a result, they have violated the terms of their covenant, so instead of being blessed for

of the Lord that he set before us. ¹⁹From the time when the Lord brought our ancestors out of the land of Egypt until today, we have been disobedient to the Lord our God, and we have been negligent in not listening to his voice. ²⁰So to this day there have clung to us the calamities and the curse that the Lord declared through his servant Moses at the time when he brought our ancestors out of the land of Egypt to give to us a land flowing with milk and honey. ²¹We did not listen to the voice of the Lord our God in all the words of the prophets whom he sent to us, ²²but all of us followed the intent of our own wicked hearts by serving other gods and doing what is evil in the sight of the Lord our God.

2 "So the Lord carried out the threat*d* he spoke against us: against our judges who ruled Israel and against our kings and our rulers and the people of Israel and Judah. ²Under the whole heaven there has not been done the like of what he has done in Jerusalem, in accordance with what is written in the law of Moses, ³that we would each eat the flesh of our sons and the flesh of our daughters. ⁴He made them subject to all the kingdoms around us, to be an object of scorn and a desolation among all the surrounding peoples, where the Lord has scattered them. ⁵They were brought down and not raised up, because we sinned against the Lord our God and did not listen to his voice.

6 "To the Lord our God belongs righteousness, but to us, this day, open shame. ⁷All

those calamities with which the Lord threatened us have come upon us. ⁸Yet we have not entreated the favor of the Lord by turning away, each of us, from the thoughts of our wicked hearts. ⁹And the Lord has kept the calamities ready, and the Lord has brought them upon us, for the Lord is just in all the works that he has commanded us to do. ¹⁰Yet we have not obeyed his voice, to walk in the statutes of the Lord that he set before us.

11 "And now, O Lord God of Israel, who brought your people out of the land of Egypt with a mighty hand and with signs and wonders and with great power and outstretched arm and made yourself a name that continues to this day, ¹²we have sinned, we have been ungodly, we have done wrong, O Lord our God, against all your ordinances. ¹³Let your anger turn away from us, for we are left few in number among the nations where you have scattered us. ¹⁴Hear, O Lord, our prayer and our entreaty, and for your own sake deliver us and grant us favor in the sight of those who have carried us into exile, ¹⁵so that all the earth may know that you are the Lord our God, for Israel and his descendants are called by your name.

16 "O Lord, look down from your holy dwelling and consider us. Incline your ear, O Lord, and hear; ¹⁷open your eyes, O Lord, and see, for the dead who are in Hades, whose spirit has been taken from their bodies, will not ascribe glory or justice to the Lord, ¹⁸but the person who is deeply grieved, who walks

d 2.1 Gk word

following instructions, God has punished them. **1:20** *So to this day there have clung to us the calamities and the curse that the Lord declared through his servant Moses at the time when he brought our ancestors out of the land of Egypt to give to us a land flowing with milk and honey.* Deuteronomy 28:15–68, placed in Moses's mouth, warns the people of all the curses that will accompany disobeying God.

2:1–10 The exiles' confession continued. 2:1 *So the Lord carried out the threat he spoke against us: against our judges who ruled Israel and against our kings and our rulers and the people of Israel and Judah.* Baruch alludes to the books of Judges, Samuel, and Kings and their descriptions of the penalties for disobedience. **2:3** *That we would each eat the flesh of our sons and the flesh of our daughters.* See Deut. 28:53–57, which describes cannibalism as a response to a siege. Jerusalem experienced a more-than-yearlong siege, and cannibalism may have been a response to starvation. The confession concludes by emphasizing that God is in the right (2:6) because the people did not follow divine instructions.

2:11–35 Prayer for help. After acknowledging their errors, the people ask God to hear, forgive, and save them. **2:13** *Let your anger turn away from us, for we are left few in number among the nations where you have scattered us.* Jeremiah 31:18–20 suggests that God will respond favorably to such a prayer. **2:14–15** See the note on 1:10–15. Also, the prayer argues that God should save the people in order to maintain God's own honor (cf. Isa. 43:25; 48:9–11; and Ezek. 36:16–37). **2:17–18** *Hades* is the

bowed and feeble, with failing eyes and famished soul, will declare your glory and righteousness, O Lord.

19 "For it is not because of any righteous deeds of our ancestors or our kings that we bring before you our prayer for mercy, O Lord our God. 20For you have sent your anger and your wrath upon us, as you declared by your servants the prophets, saying: 21"Thus says the Lord: Bend your shoulders and serve the king of Babylon, and you will remain in the land that I gave to your ancestors. 22But if you will not obey the voice of the Lord and will not serve the king of Babylon, 23I will silence from the towns of Judah and from the region around Jerusalem the voice of joy and the voice of gladness, the voice of the bridegroom and the voice of the bride, and the whole land will be a desolation without inhabitants.'

24 "But we did not obey your voice to serve the king of Babylon, and you have carried out your threats[e] that you spoke by your servants the prophets, that the bones of our kings and the bones of our ancestors would be brought out of their resting place, 25and indeed they have been thrown out to the heat of day and the frost of night. They perished in great misery, by famine and sword and pestilence. 26And the house that is called by your name you have made as it is today because of the wickedness of the house of Israel and the house of Judah.

27 "Yet you have dealt with us, O Lord our God, in all your kindness and in all your great compassion, 28as you spoke by your servant Moses on the day when you commanded him to write your law in the presence of the people of Israel, saying, 29"If you will not obey my voice, this very great multitude will surely turn into a small number among the nations, where I will scatter them. 30For I know that they will not obey me, for they are a stiff-necked people. But in the land of their exile they will have a change of heart 31and know that I am the Lord their God. I will give them a heart that obeys and ears that hear; 32they will praise me in the land of their exile and will remember my name 33and turn from their stubbornness and their wicked deeds, for they will remember the ways of their ancestors, who sinned before the Lord. 34I will bring them again into the land that I swore to give to their ancestors, to Abraham, Isaac, and Jacob, and they will rule over it, and I will increase them, and they will not be diminished. 35I will make an everlasting covenant with them to be their God, and they shall be my people, and I will never again remove my people Israel from the land that I have given them.'

3 "O Lord Almighty, God of Israel, the soul in anguish and the wearied spirit cry out to you. 2Hear, O Lord, and have mercy, for we have sinned before you. 3For you are enthroned forever, and we are perishing forever. 4O Lord Almighty, God of Israel, hear now the prayer of those of Israel who have died and of the children of those who sinned before you, who did not heed the voice of the Lord their God, so that calamities have clung to us. 5Do not remember the iniquities of our ancestors, but in this crisis remember your power and your name. 6For you are the Lord our God, and it is you, O Lord, whom we will praise. 7For you have put the fear of you in our hearts so that we would call upon your name, and we will praise you in our exile, for we have put away from our hearts all the iniquity of our ancestors who sinned against you. 8See, we are today in our exile where you have scattered us, to be reproached and cursed and punished for all the iniquities of our ancestors, who forsook the Lord our God."

9 Hear, O Israel, the commandments of life;
give ear and learn wisdom!

e 2.24 Gk *words*

realm of the dead, where all spirits went. Baruch asks for deliverance for the living, since the dead can no longer praise God. Compare Ps. 22:29–30 and Job 14:13–17. **2:19–26** These verses repeat an argument from Jer. 21 and 27: if the people had submitted to Babylon, the destruction would not have been as severe; exile and the destruction of the temple could have been avoided. Nevertheless, it is not too late for restoration if the people repent. **2:30b–32** Compare Deut. 30:1–10, in which the people will be restored and delivered from exile if they repent.

3:1–8 Prayer for help concludes. The people again acknowledge their sins, ask for God's pardon, and accept exile as their punishment for disobedience.

3:9–37 Praise of wisdom. The book then shifts in tone from lament to praise of wisdom, which could have helped the people avoid exile if they had used it. People, however, cannot find wisdom

¹⁰ Why is it, O Israel, why is it that you are
    in the land of your enemies,
    that you are growing old in a foreign
      land,
¹¹ that you are defiled with the dead,
    that you are counted among those in
      Hades?
¹² You have forsaken the fountain of
    wisdom.
¹³ If you had walked in the way of God,
    you would be living in peace forever.
¹⁴ Learn where there is wisdom,
    where there is strength,
    where there is understanding,
  so that you may at the same time discern
    where there is length of days and life,
    where there is light for the eyes and
      peace.

¹⁵ Who has found her place,
    and who has entered her
      storehouses?
¹⁶ Where are the rulers of the nations
    and those who lorded it over the
      animals on earth;
¹⁷ those who made sport of the birds of the
    air
    and who hoarded up silver and gold
  in which people trust,
    and there is no end to their getting;
¹⁸ those who schemed to get silver and
    were anxious,
    but there is no trace of their works?
¹⁹ They have vanished and gone down to
    Hades,
    and others have arisen in their place.

²⁰ Younger people have seen the light of
    day
    and have lived upon the earth,

but they have not learned the way to
    knowledge,
    nor understood her paths,
    nor laid hold of her.
²¹ Their descendants have strayed far from
    their^f way.
²² She has not been heard of in Canaan
    or seen in Teman;
²³ the descendants of Hagar, who seek for
    understanding on the earth,
    the merchants of Merran and Teman,
    the storytellers and the seekers for
      understanding,
  have not learned the way to wisdom
    or given thought to her paths.

²⁴ O Israel, how great is the house of God,
    how vast the territory that he
      possesses!
²⁵ It is great and has no bounds;
    it is high and immeasurable.
²⁶ The giants were born there, who were
    famous of old,
    great in stature, expert in war.
²⁷ God did not choose them
    or give them the way to knowledge,
²⁸ so they perished because they had no
    wisdom;
    they perished through their folly.

²⁹ Who has gone up into heaven and taken
    her
    and brought her down from the
      clouds?
³⁰ Who has gone over the sea and found her
    and will buy her for pure gold?
³¹ No one knows the way to her
    or is concerned about the path to her.

f 3.21 Gk: Syr *her*

without the God of Israel, who alone controls wisdom as the creator of the earth. **3:10–11** Wisdom here is connected to following directions; the wise obey God, and the foolish do not. This argument fits Baruch's overall theme and sounds similar to other descriptions of wisdom such as Prov. 1:20–33, where wisdom offers protection from danger, and Prov. 8:1–21 and 9:1–6, where wisdom offers life and prosperity to those who follow it. **3:19** All others who have sought wisdom in the past have died without success. Compare Job 28, another poem about wisdom, which says that only God can find it. **3:22–23** *She.* In Greek, wisdom (Sophia) is feminine. See also **"Woman Wisdom," p. 872.** *Canaan,* the land of Israel, originally named after its first inhabitants. *Teman* is another name for the land of Edom, southeast of Israel. Edom is also another name for Esau, Jacob's twin brother whom Jacob (ancestor of the Israelites) cheated out of his blessing (see Gen. 25:29–34 and 27:1–40). *The descendants of Hagar* are the Ishmaelites, who come from Abraham and Hagar, his Egyptian enslaved woman (see Gen. 16; 25:12–28; **"Hagar," p. 42**). While all of these communities are connected to Israel in some way, they do not possess wisdom, making its acquisition ethnically based. Only God's chosen may have access to wisdom. **3:26** These *giants* once lived in God's land (cf. Gen. 6:1–4) but

³² But the one who knows all things knows
  her;
  he found her by his understanding.
  The one who prepared the earth for all
  time
  filled it with four-footed creatures;
³³ the one who sends forth the light and it
  goes,
  he called it, and it obeyed him,
  trembling;
³⁴ the stars shone in their watches and were
  glad;
³⁵ he called them, and they said, "Here
  we are!"
  They shone with gladness for him who
  made them.
³⁶ This is our God;
  no other can be compared to him.
³⁷ He found the whole way to knowledge
  and gave her to his servant Jacob
  and to Israel, whom he loved.
³⁸ Afterward she appeared on earth
  and lived with humankind.

4 She is the book of the commandments
  of God,
  the law that endures forever.
  All who hold her fast will live,
  and those who forsake her will die.
² Turn, O Jacob, and take her;
  walk toward the shining of her light.
³ Do not give your glory to another
  or your advantages to a foreign nation.
⁴ Happy are we, O Israel,
  for we know what is pleasing to God.
⁵ Take courage, my people,
  who perpetuate Israel's name!
⁶ It was not for destruction
  that you were sold to the nations,

but you were handed over to your
  enemies
  because you angered God.
⁷ For you provoked the one who made you
  by sacrificing to demons and not to
  God.
⁸ You forgot the everlasting God, who
  brought you up,
  and you grieved Jerusalem, who
  reared you.
⁹ For she saw the wrath that came upon
  you from God,
  and she said:
"Listen, you neighbors of Zion;
  God has brought great sorrow upon
  me,
¹⁰ for I have seen the exile of my sons and
  daughters,
  which the Everlasting brought upon
  them.
¹¹ With joy I nurtured them,
  but I sent them away with weeping
  and sorrow.
¹² Let no one rejoice over me, a widow
  and bereaved of many;
  I was left desolate because of the sins of
  my children,
  because they turned away from the
  law of God.
¹³ They had no regard for his statutes;
  they did not walk in the ways of God's
  commandments
  or tread the paths his righteousness
  showed them.
¹⁴ Let the neighbors of Zion come;
  remember the capture of my sons and
  daughters,
  which the Everlasting brought upon
  them.

did not receive God's gift of wisdom (Bar. 4:27–28). **3:34–35** For the creation of the *stars*, see Gen. 1:16. **3:36** *This is our God; no other can be compared to him.* The argument about the Israelite God's superiority predates Baruch by several centuries. See Isa. 44 for one example, in which the prophet condemns idolatry because there is only one true deity. **3:37** *He found the whole way to knowledge and gave her to his servant Jacob and to Israel, whom he loved.* God gifted wisdom only to God's beloved people, Israel (cf. Mal. 1:2–3).

4:1–4 Praise of wisdom concludes. Since wisdom is *the book of the commandments of God, the law that endures forever* (v. 1), Israel must remain faithful to God and not give away its inheritance to other peoples. The need to maintain one's ethnic and religious identity was important in the author's time, as the Maccabean Revolt happened in part as a response to the Greek attempt to suppress Jewish practices.

4:5–29 Call to remain strong and faithful. Although the people are being justly punished for their disobedience, when God sees their repentance, they will be delivered. **4:6–7** Again, the exile is caused by disobedience, specifically the worship of demons. If in Isa. 44 other deities are false, here they are evil spirits. **4:14** The city of Jerusalem is mourning her destruction at the hands of God,

15 For he brought a distant nation against
   them,
      a nation ruthless and of a strange
         language,
   which had no respect for the aged
      and no pity for a child.
16 They led away the widow's beloved sons
      and bereaved the lonely woman of her
         daughters.

17 "But I, how can I help you?
18 For he who brought these calamities
      will deliver you from the hand of your
         enemies.
19 Go, my children, go,
      for I have been left desolate.
20 I have taken off the robe of peace
      and put on sackcloth for my supplication;
   I will cry to the Everlasting all my days.

21 "Take courage, my children, cry to God,
      and he will deliver you from the
         power and hand of the enemy.
22 For I have put my hope in the Everlasting
      to save you,
   and joy has come to me from the Holy
      One,
   because of the mercy that will soon
      come to you
   from your everlasting savior.ᵍ
23 For I sent you out with sorrow and
      weeping,
   but God will give you back to me with
      joy and gladness forever.
24 For as the neighbors of Zion have now
      seen your capture,
   so they soon will see your salvation
      by God,
   which will come to you with great glory
      and with the splendor of the
         Everlasting.
25 My children, endure with patience the wrath
      that has come upon you from God.
   Your enemy has overtaken you,
      but you will soon see their destruction
      and will tread upon their necks.

26 My pampered children have traveled
      rough roads;
   they were taken away like a flock
      carried off by the enemy.

27 "Take courage, my children, and cry to God,
      for you will be remembered by the one
         who brought this upon you.
28 For just as you were disposed to go
      astray from God,
   return with tenfold zeal to seek him.
29 For the one who brought these calamities
      upon you
   will bring you everlasting joy with
      your salvation."
30 Take courage, O Jerusalem,
      for the one who named you will
         comfort you.
31 Wretched will be those who mistreated you
      and who rejoiced at your fall.
32 Wretched will be the cities that your
      children served as slaves;
   wretched will be the city that received
      your offspring.
33 For just as she rejoiced at your fall
      and was glad for your ruin,
   so she will be grieved at her own
      desolation.
34 I will take away her pride in her great
      population,
   and her insolence will be turned to
      grief.
35 For fire will come upon her from the
      Everlasting for many days,
   and for a long time she will be
      inhabited by demons.

36 Look toward the east, O Jerusalem,
      and see the joy that is coming to you
         from God.
37 Look, your children are coming, whom
      you sent away;
   they are coming, gathered from east
      and west,

g 4.22 Or *from the Everlasting, your savior*

the Everlasting. **4:20** *Sackcloth*, or burlap, an itchy garment that is worn as a sign of mourning. See the note for 1:14 regarding the grief over Jerusalem's fall. **4:22** The tone shifts from despair to *hope*, since God will rescue the people and bring them back home. Compare Isa. 49:13–23.

4:30–37 God punishes Jerusalem's enemies. God will punish any community that mistreated Jerusalem with death and destruction (cf. Isa. 47, which describes God's future punishment of Babylon). **4:35** *For fire will come upon her from the Everlasting for many days, and for a long time she will be inhabited by demons.* Babylon had a reputation for being the primary source of wickedness (see Zech. 5:5–11, where wickedness is transported there and then worshiped).

at the word of the Holy One,
    rejoicing in the glory of God.

5 Take off the garment of your sorrow
    and affliction, O Jerusalem,
    and put on forever the beauty of the
    glory from God.
² Put on the robe of the righteousness that
    comes from God;
    put on your head the diadem of the
    glory of the Everlasting,
³ for God will show your splendor
    everywhere under heaven,
⁴ for God will give you evermore the name,
    "Righteous Peace, Godly Glory."

⁵ Arise, O Jerusalem, stand upon the
    height;
    look toward the east,
and see your children gathered from
    west and east

at the word of the Holy One,
    rejoicing that God has remembered
    them.
⁶ For they went out from you on foot,
    led away by their enemies,
but God will bring them back to you,
    carried in glory, as on a royal throne.
⁷ For God has ordered that every high
    mountain and the everlasting hills
    be made low
and the valleys filled up, to make level
    ground,
so that Israel may walk safely in the
    glory of God.
⁸ The woods and every fragrant tree
    have shaded Israel at God's
    command.
⁹ For God will lead Israel with joy,
    in the light of his glory,
    with the mercy and righteousness that
    come from him.

5:1–9 The conclusion of the call to remain strong and faithful. Because God is coming to restore the people, they can remain hopeful. **5:1–2** *Take off the garment of your sorrow and affliction, O Jerusalem, and put on forever the beauty of the glory from God. Put on the robe of the righteousness that comes from God; put on your head the diadem of the glory of the Everlasting.* Compare Isa. 52:1 and 54:11–12, which describe Jerusalem as beautiful. **5:7** *For God has ordered that every high mountain and the everlasting hills be made low and the valleys filled up, to make level ground, so that Israel may walk safely in the glory of God.* This is an almost direct quotation from Isa. 40:4, in which the prophet says that God will prepare the path for the journey home from Babylon.

THE LETTER OF JEREMIAH

Authorship, Date, and Literary History

Although the title names the prophet Jeremiah as the author of the letter, that is not the case. The short treatise against idolatry, while addressed to the first group of exiles in 597, appears to have been written well after that date for several reasons, including that it may initially have been composed in Greek. Scholars date the work between the sixth and second centuries BCE. Originally an independent composition, the text is part of the Catholic Old Testament, where it is typically attached to Baruch as the sixth chapter. The letter is an example of polemical rhetoric, a sustained argument against idolatry by mocking the practice of those who worship gods besides the God of Israel.

Intertextuality in the Letter of Jeremiah

The author uses imagery and arguments already common in prophetic literature, particularly in Isa. 41, 44, and 46. Those chapters, written at the end of the Babylonian exile (586–539 BCE), argue that the Israelites should reject other gods as false and mock those who create idols. The mockery, however, depends on the false idea that ancient peoples saw the idols themselves as their gods and not as representations of those gods.

Reading Guide

The primary theme in the Letter of Jeremiah is to encourage the reader to remain faithful to God and reject idolatry. The letter begins with a reminder that the community has been exiled for their sins, which they should not compound by worshiping Babylon's gods, because God is watching them (vv. 4–6). Then, in a series of occasionally repetitive arguments, the author insists that the people should not be afraid of idols because they are not real for several reasons. First, humans create and decorate their idols, but the idols cannot speak or protect themselves or anyone else (vv. 7–14). Instead, they depend on their creators to keep them clean and upright (vv. 16–21, 23–26; see also vv. 44–50 and 52–55, where the author notes that these gods cannot protect people in times of war). Second, priests use offerings to the deities to support themselves financially "but give none to the poor or helpless" (v. 27). In contrast, Lev. 7 states that while priests of God receive parts of an offering, the rest belongs to the person who offers the gift. The one making the offering shares the gift with their household (Deut. 12). Additionally, the Israelites should give tithes of their produce and share them with the priests, who are landless, and widows and orphans, who may lack financial security (Deut. 14:22–28). The author presumes that the Babylonian priests are greedy; therefore, their deities must be false. Third, the idols cannot bless the righteous or punish the unrighteous; they cannot answer the desperate prayers of the faithful (vv. 29–38). As a result, they are useless, worse than "the door of a house that protects its contents" or "a wooden pillar in a palace" (v. 58). The author compares them to scarecrows and corpses (vv. 69–70). In contrast, Israel's God controls heaven and earth and is a true deity (vv. 59–62).

One subtheme within the letter is that the idols are false precisely because of the way women behave. The author protests that "sacrifices to them may even be touched by women during their periods or after giving birth" (v. 28), when Israelite women are unclean, according to Lev. 12. Additionally, prostitutes gather outside of temples (vv. 41–42). Even if this was part of a religious ritual, the author uses the practice against the Babylonian women and, by extension, their deities.

The rhetoric against idolatry, while an extended commentary on the first and second commandments (no God but God and no idols), inaccurately portrays the ways in which images of deities function today. In Hindu temples, for example, there are numerous images of the divine, which Hindus, like the ancients, recognize as representations of God and not the deity directly. In Catholic tradition, icons and images of Jesus, Mary, and other saints are common in public worship sites and in private homes. The author of the Letter of Jeremiah writes to keep the community from being led astray by false gods, and images of God remain prohibited in Jewish tradition. Christian tradition also has the first and second commandments but in some cases is more flexible with iconography, a reminder that the meaning of a particular text can change over time and that there is no contradiction between the Letter of Jeremiah being sacred Scripture for Catholics and the presence of statues inside a Catholic church.

Stacy Davis

A copy of a letter that Jeremiah sent to those who were to be taken to Babylon as exiles by the king of the Babylonians, to give them the message that God had commanded him.

1 Because of the sins that you have committed before God, you will be taken to Babylon as exiles by Nebuchadnezzar, king of the Babylonians. [2]Therefore when you have come to Babylon you will remain there for many years, for a long time, up to seven generations; after that I will bring you away from there in peace. [3]Now in Babylon you will see gods made of silver and gold and wood that people carry on their shoulders and that cause the nations to fear. [4]So beware of becoming at all like the foreigners or of letting fear of these gods[a] possess you [5]when you see the multitude before and behind them worshiping them. But say in your heart, "It is you, O Lord, whom we must worship." [6]For my angel is with you, and he is watching over your lives.

7 Their tongues are smoothed by the carpenter, and they themselves are overlaid with gold and silver, but they are false and cannot speak. [8]People[b] take gold and make crowns for the heads of their gods, as they might for a young woman who loves ornaments. [9]Sometimes the priests secretly take gold and silver from their gods and spend it on themselves [10]or even give some of it to the prostitutes on the terrace. They deck their gods[c] out with garments like humans—these gods of silver and gold and wood [11]that cannot save themselves from rust and decay.[d] When they have been dressed in purple robes, [12]their faces are wiped because of the dust from the temple, which is thick upon them. [13]One of them holds a scepter like a district judge but is unable to destroy anyone who offends it.

[14]Another has a dagger in its right hand and an ax but cannot defend itself from war and robbers. [15]From this it is evident that they are not gods, so do not fear them.

16 For just as someone's dish is useless when it is broken, [17]so are their gods when they have been set up in the temples. Their eyes are full of the dust raised by the feet of those who enter. And just as the gates are shut on every side against anyone who has offended a king, as though under sentence of death, so the priests make their temples secure with doors and locks and bars in order that they may not be plundered by robbers. [18]They light more lamps for them than they light for themselves, though their gods[e] can see none of them. [19]They are[f] just like a beam of the temple, but their hearts, it is said, are eaten away when crawling creatures from the earth devour them and their robes. They do not notice [20]when their faces have been blackened by the smoke of the temple. [21]Bats, swallows, and birds alight on their bodies and heads, and so do cats. [22]From this you will know that they are not gods, so do not fear them.

23 As for the gold that they wear for beauty, it[g] will not shine unless someone wipes off the tarnish, for even when they were being cast, they did not feel it. [24]They are bought without regard to cost, but there is no breath in them. [25]Having no feet, they are carried on the shoulders of others, revealing to humans their worthlessness. And those who serve them are put to shame [26]because, if any of these gods falls[h] to the ground, they themselves must pick it up. If anyone sets it upright, it cannot move itself, and if it is tipped over, it cannot straighten itself. Gifts are placed before them just as before the dead. [27]The priests sell the

a 4 Gk *for them*   b 8 Gk *They*   c 10 Gk *them*   d 11 Gk *food*
e 18 Gk *they*   f 19 Gk *It is*   g 23 Lat Syr: Gk *they*   h 26 Gk *if they fall*

1–6 Obey the commandments. Jeremiah calls on the exiles to follow the first and second commandments, following only God and having no idols. **6** *For my angel is with you, and he is watching over your lives.* Even though the people are no longer in the land, where God lives in the Jerusalem temple, God will still be aware of their behavior.

7–72 Polemic against idols. The letter argues that the exiles should not worship idols because they have no power. Cf. Isa. 41:21–24; 44:9–20; and particularly 46:1–4, which mentions Babylon's deities by name. **15** *From this it is evident that they are not gods, so do not fear them.* Although the gods wear clothes and hold weapons, they can neither dress themselves nor fight, because humans created them (vv. 7, 11, 13–14; see also vv. 44–46 and 49–50). **22** *From this you will know that they are not gods, so do not fear them.* The gods require human protection and cannot wipe dust out of their eyes or keep birds from landing on their heads (vv. 17, 20–21). **28** *Sacrifices to them may even be touched by women during their periods or after giving birth. Since you know by these things*

sacrifices that are offered to these gods[i] and use the money themselves. Likewise their wives preserve some of the meat[j] with salt but give none to the poor or helpless. [28]Sacrifices to them may even be touched by women during their periods or after giving birth. Since you know by these things that they are not gods, do not fear them.

29 For how can they be called gods? Women serve meals for gods of silver and gold and wood, [30]and in their temples the priests sit with their clothes torn, their heads and beards shaved, and their heads uncovered. [31]They howl and shout before their gods as some do at a funeral banquet. [32]The priests take some of the clothing of their gods[k] to clothe their wives and children. [33]Whether one does evil to them or good, they will not be able to repay it. They cannot set up a king or depose one. [34]Likewise, they are not able to give either wealth or money; if one makes a vow to them and does not keep it, they will not require it. [35]They cannot save anyone from death or rescue the weak from the strong. [36]They cannot restore sight to the blind; they cannot rescue one who is in distress. [37]They cannot take pity on a widow or do good to an orphan. [38]These things that are made of wood and overlaid with gold and silver are like stones from the mountain, and those who serve them will be put to shame. [39]Why then must anyone think that they are gods or call them gods?

Besides, even the Chaldeans themselves dishonor them, for when they see someone who cannot speak, they bring Bel and pray that the mute may speak, as though Bel[l] were able to understand! [40]Yet they themselves cannot perceive this and abandon them, for they have no sense. [41]And the women, with cords around them, sit along the passageways, burning bran for incense. [42]When one of them is led off by one of the passers-by and is taken to bed by him, she derides the woman next to her because she was not as attractive as herself and her cord was not broken. [43]Whatever is done for

these idols[m] is false. Why then must anyone think that they are gods or call them gods?

44 They are made by carpenters and goldsmiths; they can be nothing but what the artisans wish them to be. [45]Those who make them will certainly not live very long themselves; [46]how then can the things that are made by them be gods? They have left only lies and reproach for those who come after. [47]For when war or calamity comes upon them, the priests consult together as to where they can hide themselves and their gods.[n] [48]How then can one fail to see that these are not gods, for they cannot save themselves from war or calamity? [49]Since they are made of wood and overlaid with gold and silver, it will afterward be known that they are false. [50]It will be manifest to all the nations and kings that they are not gods but the work of human hands and that there is no work of God in them. [51]Who, then, does not know that they are not gods?

52 For they cannot set up a king over a country or give rain to people. [53]They cannot judge their own cause or deliver one who is wronged, for they have no power; [54]they are like crows between heaven and earth. When fire breaks out in a temple of wooden gods overlaid with gold or silver, their priests will flee and escape, but the gods[o] will be burned up like timbers. [55]Besides, they can offer no resistance to king or enemy. Why then must anyone admit or think that they are gods?

56 Gods made of wood and overlaid with silver and gold are unable to save themselves from thieves or robbers. [57]Anyone who can will strip them of their gold and silver and of the robes they wear and go off with this plunder, and they will not be able to help themselves. [58]So it is better to be a king who shows his courage or a household utensil that serves its owner's need than to be these false gods, better even the door of a house that protects its contents than these false gods, better also

i 27 Gk to them   j 27 Gk of them   k 32 Gk some of their clothing   l 39 Gk he   m 43 Gk them   n 47 Gk them   o 54 Gk they

that they are not gods, do not fear them. Leviticus requires women to be purified after childbirth before entering sacred space, and menstruating women are considered unclean (12:1–8; 15:19–24). The Babylonian indifference to these specific Israelite rules confirms that their gods are not real. **39** *Why then must anyone think that they are gods or call them gods?* People must feed and clothe their deities (vv. 29, 32; cf. v. 38), who cannot do anything to benefit their worshipers. See also vv. 52–55. **43** *Whatever is done for these idols is false. Why then must anyone think that they are gods or call them gods?* Sites of worship are also places of prostitution, so the spaces cannot be where

a wooden pillar in a palace than these false gods.

59 For sun and moon and stars are bright and, when sent to do a service, they are obedient. ⁶⁰So also the lightning when it flashes is widely seen, and the wind likewise blows in every land. ⁶¹When God commands the clouds to go over the whole world, they carry out his command. ⁶²And the fire sent from above to consume mountains and woods does what it is ordered. But these idols* are not to be compared with them in appearance or power. ⁶³Therefore one must not think that they are gods nor call them gods, for they are unable either to decide a case or to do good to anyone. ⁶⁴Since you know, then, that they are not gods, do not fear them.

65 They can neither curse nor bless kings; ⁶⁶they cannot show signs in the heavens for the nations or shine like the sun or give light like the moon. ⁶⁷The wild animals are better than they are, for they can flee to shelter and help themselves. ⁶⁸So we have no evidence whatever that they are gods; therefore do not fear them.

69 Like a scarecrow in a cucumber bed that guards nothing, so are their gods of wood, overlaid with gold and silver. ⁷⁰In the same way, their gods of wood, overlaid with gold and silver, are like a thornbush in a garden on which every bird perches or like a corpse thrown out in the darkness. ⁷¹From the purple and linen* that rot upon them you will know that they are not gods, and they will finally be consumed themselves and be a reproach in the land. ⁷²Better, therefore, is someone upright who has no idols; such a person will be far above reproach.

p 62 Gk *these things*   *q* 71 Cn: Gk *marble*, Syr *silk*

a true deity resides (vv. 41–42). **64** *Since you know, then, that they are not gods, do not fear them.* Unlike the powerless deities, God controls all of nature (vv. 59–62; see also vv. 65–68). **73** *Better, therefore, is someone upright who has no idols; such a person will be far above reproach.* The author concludes that the righteous will worship God.

THE ADDITIONS TO DANIEL

The Prayer of Azariah and the
Song of the Three Jews

Authorship, Date, and Literary History

The Prayer of Azariah and the Song of the Three Jews is the first of three additions to the Greek version of Daniel. As with the other additions, the author is unknown but likely an Alexandrian Jew writing during the Second Temple period and influenced by Hebrew synagogue liturgy. The author models this work after the material in Psalms, notably Ps. 148, with its repeated refrain of praise to Israel's God. At the same time, the author reflects knowledge of the blessings and curses formula found in the Deuteronomic writings. Some scholars propose that the Prayer and Song were composed during the persecutions of Antiochus in the mid-second century BCE, with the three righteous Jews as a lens through which the persecuted community saw their present experiences. It is also likely, however, that this particular section of Greek Daniel was composed during a period of relative peace and even prosperity among the Diaspora community, during which there was a proliferation of religious writings and material (see **"Diaspora," p. 1338**).

The Prayer and Song, like Susanna and Bel and the Dragon, also reflect increased interest in the figure and person of Daniel. The narrative of a Jewish exile who rises to prominence in the foreign court while retaining his religious beliefs was appealing to Diaspora Jews, and readers were eager to hear more stories about him and his colleagues (see also **"Court Tales," p. 1608**). In the Greek version of Daniel, this addition is inserted almost seamlessly after 3:23, and Greek-speaking Jews wholly unfamiliar with the original Hebrew-Aramaic version would not have detected any shift or change to the narrative at this point in the story. The Prayer has retained its popularity over the centuries particularly within Christianity. The Prayer is still recited today in both Catholic and Protestant (e.g., Anglican, Lutheran) liturgies.

The "Three" in the History of Interpretation

Next to Daniel himself, the three Jewish youths are the most popular characters in the book, as seen in their history of interpretation. They appear in the opening verses of the book as Jewish captives from the Babylonian exile selected by King Nebuchadnezzar to serve in the royal court. Reflecting the assimilationist agenda of the king, they are given gentile names. Hananiah is renamed Shadrach, Mishael is renamed Meshach, and Azariah is renamed Abednego (Dan. 1:6–7). While trained and educated in the ways of Babylon by the chief eunuch of the king (the narrative is unclear whether they were surgically made eunuchs), the youths refuse to abandon their religious beliefs and practices (see also **"Eunuchs," p. 672**). They retain their kosher diet (Dan. 1:11–16) and their worship of the one God of Israel (see also **"Diet," p. 268**).

Rather than inviting the scorn of the king, their devotion brings them favor with King Nebuchadnezzar (Dan. 1:9, 20). The notable exception is the story in Dan. 3 (where the Prayer and Song have been placed). Here, the three youths are thrown into a fiery furnace for their refusal to bow down to the king's massive idol of gold. Even in this situation, the king, while angry at the youths' disobedience to his decree, appears regretful about sentencing them to death and later acknowledges the "God of Shadrach, Meshach, and Abednego" (Dan. 3:28).

For various reasons, readers have been drawn to this particular story over the centuries, and its popularity in Western religious and pop culture can be seen in the works of art, music, and literature that have been influenced by it. Stained glass windows in some churches and cathedrals contain depictions of the story of the three youths. Other examples out of many include a painting by the medieval artist Toros Roslin entitled *The Fiery Furnace* and a Greek triptych from the 1600s. In his 1963 "Letter from a Birmingham Jail," Dr. Martin Luther King Jr. noted that civil disobedience "was seen sublimely in the refusal of Shadrach, Meshach and Abednego to obey the laws of Nebuchadnezzar because a higher moral law was involved." The Greek addition here can also be included as

part of the interpretive history of the fiery furnace story in its effort to posit what the three youths might have said and done in the midst of their ordeal.

Reading Guide

The Prayer of Azariah and the Song of the Three Jews follow a similar structure to laments and songs of praise found in the larger corpus of ancient biblical literature, highlighting the power of the poetic form (see **"Hebrew Poetry," p. 741**; **"The Types of the Psalms," p. 742**). Although they may have been originally separate compositions, their association together within the same scene in Daniel (vv. 1, 23–28) suggests reading them together. The Prayer begins with a confirmation of the greatness of God even in the midst of the exile and scattering of the Jewish people (vv. 3–5). This is followed by a confession of sins, which Azariah notes as being the cause of the exile (vv. 6–10), followed by a request for God's mercy (vv. 11–22). The deliverance of Azariah and his companions by the angel of the Lord is then narrated in prose (vv. 23–28). The Song is sung by the three youths in response to the divine intervention and is marked with repeated refrains of praise that are variations of "Bless the Lord . . . sing praise to him and highly exalt him forever." The poetic movement from despair to deliverance to praise would continue to be used throughout the centuries as a source of hope and encouragement for people facing persecution.

Adam Oliver Stokes

(Additions to Daniel, inserted between 3.23 and 3.24)

1 They walked around in the midst of the flames, singing hymns to God and blessing the Lord. ²Then Azariah stood still in the fire and prayed aloud:
³ "Blessed are you, O Lord, God of our
    ancestors, and worthy of praise,
  and glorious is your name forever!
⁴ For you are just in all you have done;
  all your works are true and your ways
    right,
  and all your judgments are true.
⁵ You have executed true judgments in all
    you have brought upon us
  and upon Jerusalem, the holy city of
    our ancestors;
  by a true judgment you have brought
    all this upon us because of our sins.
⁶ For we have sinned and broken your law
    in turning away from you;
  in all matters we have sinned grievously.

⁷ We have not obeyed your
    commandments;
  we have not kept them or done what
    you have commanded us for our
    own good.
⁸ So all that you have brought upon us
    and all that you have done to us,
  you have done by a true judgment.
⁹ You have handed us over to our enemies,
    lawless and hateful rebels,
  and to an unjust king, the most wicked
    in all the world.
¹⁰ And now we cannot open our mouths;
  we, your servants who worship you,
    bear shame and reproach.
¹¹ For your name's sake do not give us up
    forever,
  and do not annul your covenant.
¹²   Do not withdraw your mercy from us,
  for the sake of Abraham your beloved
  and for the sake of Isaac your
    servant
  and Israel your holy one,

1–22 Prayer of Azariah. This section contains echoes of various material within the biblical tradition, including the lament genre found in Psalms and Lamentations (see **"The Types of the Psalms," p. 742**). It also reflects the influence of Deuteronomic theology in the theme of Azariah's prayer: the suffering that Israel has endured is the consequence of its sins (see **"Divine Retribution," p. 339**). **3** Parallels the language found in Psalms (e.g., Pss. 28:6; 31:21; 41:13). **5–6** This is standard Deuteronomic language and theology. Suffering comes not from God's cruelty or any flaws with the world but from human action, specifically Israel as a nation not obeying God's law and maintaining God's covenant (e.g., Lam. 1:18; Neh. 9:33). **9** This is likely a reference to the various rulers of the Greco-Roman period, for which there are a plethora of candidates, from Antiochus IV to Pompey, both of whom defiled the temple. **12** The appeal to Abraham and the Abrahamic covenant (Gen.

13 to whom you promised
> to multiply their descendants like the stars of heaven
> and like the sand on the shore of the sea.

14 For we, O Lord, have become fewer than any other nation
> and are brought low this day in all the world because of our sins.

15 In our day we have no ruler, or prophet, or leader,
> no burnt offering, or sacrifice, or oblation, or incense,
> no place to make an offering before you and to find mercy.

16 Yet with a contrite heart and a humble spirit may we be accepted,

17 as though it were with burnt offerings of rams and bulls
> or with tens of thousands of fat lambs;
> such may our sacrifice be in your sight today,
> and may we unreservedly follow you,[a]
> for no shame will come to those who trust in you.

18 And now with all our heart we follow you;
> we fear you and seek your presence.

19 Do not put us to shame,
> but deal with us in your patience
> and in your abundant mercy.

20 Deliver us in accordance with your marvelous works,
> and bring glory to your name, O Lord.

21 Let all who do harm to your servants be put to shame;
> let them be disgraced and deprived of all power,
> and let their strength be broken.

22 Let them know that you alone are the Lord God,
> glorious over the whole world."

23 Now the king's servants who threw them in kept stoking the furnace with naphtha, pitch, tinder, and brushwood. 24 And the flames poured out above the furnace forty-nine cubits 25 and spread out and burned those Chaldeans who were caught near the furnace. 26 But the angel of the Lord came down into the furnace to be with Azariah and his companions and drove the fiery flame out of the furnace 27 and made the inside of the furnace as though a moist wind were whistling through it. The fire did not touch them at all and caused them no pain or distress.

28 Then the three with one voice praised and glorified and blessed God in the furnace:

29 "Blessed are you, O Lord, God of our ancestors,
> and to be praised and highly exalted forever;
> And blessed is your glorious, holy name,
> and to be highly praised and highly exalted forever.

30 Blessed are you in the temple of your holy glory,
> and to be extolled and highly glorified forever.

31 Blessed are you who look into the depths from your throne on the cherubim,
> and to be praised and highly exalted forever.

32 Blessed are you on the throne of your kingdom,
> and to be extolled and highly exalted forever.

33 Blessed are you in the firmament of heaven,
> and to be sung and glorified forever.

a 17 Meaning of Gk uncertain

12) in defense of God's mercy and judgment toward sinful Israel is a common motif (e.g., Exod. 32; Sir. 44:22). **14–15** Compare with the description of Zion in Lam. 2:9. **15** An anachronistic statement given that the temple had been rebuilt and ritual offerings and sacrifices were occurring daily during the time that the prayer was composed in the second century BCE. It reflects the narrative world of the book of Daniel, set during the exile. The reference may be a critique of what the author deemed as the "illegitimate" priesthood of Simon during the Hasmonean era. **20** "Name theology" is evident here as elsewhere, particularly in the Deuteronomistic History.

23–67 Song of the Three Jews. As with the lament psalms (e.g., Ps. 13), there is a transition from lament and plea to praise. The refrains *blessed are you* and *sing praise to him and highly exalt him forever* mirror the language found in multiple praise psalms (e.g., Pss. 106, 136). The movement of the praise goes from the glory of God's creation as evident in nature to the deity's crowning achievement with the people of Israel. **26** The *angel of the Lord* often is an intermediary figure between humanity and God while, paradoxically, being synonymous with the deity. In the Christian tradition, this angel was linked to the "divine being" in Dan. 3:25 who was viewed as a prefiguration

³⁴ "Bless the Lord, all you works of the Lord;
   sing praise to him and highly exalt him
      forever.
³⁵ Bless the Lord, you heavens;
   sing praise to him and highly exalt him
      forever.
³⁶ Bless the Lord, you angels of the Lord;
   sing praise to him and highly exalt him
      forever.
³⁷ Bless the Lord, all you waters above the
      heavens;
   sing praise to him and highly exalt him
      forever.
³⁸ Bless the Lord, all you powers of the Lord;
   sing praise to him and highly exalt him
      forever.
³⁹ Bless the Lord, sun and moon;
   sing praise to him and highly exalt him
      forever.
⁴⁰ Bless the Lord, stars of heaven;
   sing praise to him and highly exalt him
      forever.

⁴¹ "Bless the Lord, all rain and dew;
   sing praise to him and highly exalt him
      forever.
⁴² Bless the Lord, all you winds;
   sing praise to him and highly exalt him
      forever.
⁴³ Bless the Lord, fire and heat;
   sing praise to him and highly exalt him
      forever.
⁴⁴ Bless the Lord, winter cold and summer
      heat;
   sing praise to him and highly exalt him
      forever.
⁴⁵ Bless the Lord, dews and falling snow;
   sing praise to him and highly exalt him
      forever.
⁴⁶ Bless the Lord, nights and days;
   sing praise to him and highly exalt him
      forever.
⁴⁷ Bless the Lord, light and darkness;
   sing praise to him and highly exalt him
      forever.
⁴⁸ Bless the Lord, ice and cold;
   sing praise to him and highly exalt him
      forever.
⁴⁹ Bless the Lord, frosts and snows;
   sing praise to him and highly exalt him
      forever.

⁵⁰ Bless the Lord, lightnings and clouds;
   sing praise to him and highly exalt him
      forever.

⁵¹ "Let the earth bless the Lord;
   let it sing praise to him and highly exalt
      him forever.
⁵² Bless the Lord, mountains and hills;
   sing praise to him and highly exalt him
      forever.
⁵³ Bless the Lord, all that grows in the
      ground;
   sing praise to him and highly exalt him
      forever.
⁵⁴ Bless the Lord, seas and rivers;
   sing praise to him and highly exalt him
      forever.
⁵⁵ Bless the Lord, you springs;
   sing praise to him and highly exalt him
      forever.
⁵⁶ Bless the Lord, you sea monsters and all
      that swim in the waters;
   sing praise to him and highly exalt him
      forever.
⁵⁷ Bless the Lord, all birds of the air;
   sing praise to him and highly exalt him
      forever.
⁵⁸ Bless the Lord, all wild animals and
      cattle;
   sing praise to him and highly exalt him
      forever.

⁵⁹ "Bless the Lord, all people on earth;
   sing praise to him and highly exalt him
      forever.
⁶⁰ Bless the Lord, O Israel;
   sing praise to him and highly exalt him
      forever.
⁶¹ Bless the Lord, you priests of the Lord;
   sing praise to him and highly exalt him
      forever.
⁶² Bless the Lord, you servants of the
      Lord;
   sing praise to him and highly exalt him
      forever.
⁶³ Bless the Lord, spirits and souls of the
      righteous;
   sing praise to him and highly exalt him
      forever.
⁶⁴ Bless the Lord, you who are holy and
      humble in heart;

of Jesus. **34–58** Elements of creation are personified and depicted as praising God, paralleling some psalms and continuing into later Christian poetry (e.g., the hymn of Saint Francis). **56** The Greek word translated as *sea monsters* is the same word used in LXX Gen. 1:21 to translate the Hebrew

sing praise to him and highly exalt him
forever.

⁶⁵ "Bless the Lord, Hananiah, Azariah, and
Mishael;
sing praise to him and highly exalt him
forever.
For he has rescued us from Hades and
saved us from the power*b* of death
and delivered us from the midst of the
burning fiery furnace;

from the midst of the fire he has
delivered us.
⁶⁶ Give thanks to the Lord, for he is good,
for his mercy endures forever.
⁶⁷ All who worship the Lord, bless the God
of gods,
sing praise to him and give thanks to
him,
for his mercy endures forever."

b 65 Gk *hand*

"behemah." **65** *Hades* is the standard translation of the Hebrew "Sheol" by Greek-speaking Jews
(see **"Sheol," p. 695**). At this point in the development of Jewish theology—and under the influence
of Greco-Roman religion—the afterlife was understood as a place where souls were punished or
rewarded, in contrast to the Israelite understanding of Sheol as a realm of limbo and dampness (see
"Resurrection," p. 1224).

Susanna

Authorship and Literary History

The story of Susanna, like Ruth and Esther, is one of several examples of the biblical "novella" or short story found in the Hebrew Bible that centers on a prominent female figure (see **"Jewish Women in the Diaspora," p. 1525**). Susanna is a wealthy woman from a respected and prominent Jewish family who is falsely accused of adultery and eventually vindicated by Daniel.

As with the Prayer of Azariah, the relative ease and simplicity of the grammar and syntax suggest a possible original Hebrew composition that was translated into Greek. However, the puns found in the story (e.g., toward the end when the accusers describe different types of trees they saw Susanna under) only work in Greek and would only make sense to Greek-speaking readers. The depiction of Susanna herself as among the wealthy elite of the Babylonian exile and the elaborate description of her home and gardens further suggest a Greek-speaking audience, possibly the wealthy and prominent Jewish community of Alexandria, who would have seen their own lifestyle and status reflected in the characters in the story.

There are two Greek versions of Susanna, the shorter Old Greek and the longer Greek version attributed to Theodotion that is translated here. In Theodotion's version, Susanna is placed at the beginning of Daniel, while in the Old Greek, it is placed after Dan. 12, comprising a thirteenth chapter. In Theodotion's version, the townspeople execute the two false witnesses. In contrast, in the Old Greek version, the execution is performed by the angel of the Lord.

The History of Susanna in Jewish and Christian Traditions and the Daniel "Legends"

The depiction of Susanna in the narrative parallels other presentations of women in the Hebrew Scriptures, most notably Ruth, Rahab, and Esther (in the Gk. text), all of whom are portrayed as pious, God-fearing women. The author of the story has adapted this biblical motif, often applied to non-Israelite women, to suit an exclusively Jewish audience by having a Jewish woman serve as the model of faith and integrity. Although there are no explicit references to her in later Jewish literature or art, it is possible that her story influenced material in the Midrash to Leviticus, in which a comparison is made between a woman and a red rose. This stands in contrast to Christian tradition, in which Susanna featured prominently.

While there existed significant debate in the early church over the canonicity of the story, Susanna herself remained a popular figure among early Christian writers and artists. She is mentioned in various early Christian commentaries, most notably in the allegorical interpretation provided by Hippolytus of Rome where he compares her to the church. Her story was also illustrated on numerous early Christian frescoes and catacombs. Interest in Susanna was revived centuries later during the Renaissance period, when she was the subject of numerous paintings by such artists as Lorenzo Lotto and Artemisia Gentileschi. In many of these paintings, her physical beauty is highlighted. This perhaps suggests that Renaissance artists were drawn to her and her story as embodying the humanistic ideal of human sexuality and physical beauty free from guilt or sin.

As with the other "additions," the story attests to the popularity of the figure of Daniel among Second Temple Jews. It serves as a prequel of sorts to the events described in the Hebrew-Aramaic version of the book in which readers learn about Daniel's life before he was chosen by the king of Babylon to serve as a member of the royal court. In relation to this, it provides a rationale for why he was chosen—namely, due to him being endowed with wisdom and righteousness from his youth. In many respects, the Daniel presented in the story of Susanna deliberately parallels the depiction of prophets such as Nathan and Jeremiah particularly in their emphasis on justice and critiquing those in power when they abuse it. Like Nathan and Jeremiah, Daniel is not afraid to stand against Susanna's two accusers and condemn them for their wrongdoing even though they are prominent "elders" in society.

Reading Guide

At first glance, the story of Susanna may seem to reinforce a standard, stereotypical trope found elsewhere in biblical literature. In Judges and Proverbs, for example, prose and poetry warn of the beautiful, seductive woman who leads decent men astray. However, in reading the story itself, one finds an inversion of this idea. From the beginning, Susanna is depicted as innocent and righteous,

and the men who claim to be seduced by her are depicted as anything but decent. Rather than warning us about female seductiveness, the story of Susanna, like other ancient Greek literature, highlights male abuse of power and how the vulnerable in society suffer through their abuse of power.

Parallels to this theme can be found in the great Greek tragedies such as the *Oresteia* trilogy of Aeschylus and Euripides's *The Trojan Women*. In both plays, women (e.g., Clytemnestra, the Trojan widows) are the unwitting victims of the unrestrained, unbridled passions of men. Yet, in contrast to the Greek tragedies, Susanna does not remain a victim but is vindicated at the end of the story. One person's courage in challenging and confronting male abuse of power results in justice for the vulnerable. In modern Christian seminaries, Susanna is read as part of pastoral training. As persons in authority interacting with parishioners, the two elders in the story serve as a warning of what happens when those in power misuse it and how one must not follow their example.

Adam Oliver Stokes

1 There was a man living in Babylon whose name was Joakim. ²He married the daughter of Hilkiah, named Susanna, a very beautiful woman and one who feared the Lord. ³Her parents were righteous and had trained their daughter according to the law of Moses. ⁴Joakim was very rich and had a fine garden adjoining his house; the Jews used to come to him because he was the most honored of them all.

5 That year two elders from the people were appointed as judges. Concerning them the Lord had said: "Wickedness came forth from Babylon, from elders who were judges, who were supposed to govern the people." ⁶These men were frequently at Joakim's house, and all who had a case to be tried came to them there.

7 When the people left at noon, Susanna would go into her husband's garden to walk. ⁸Every day the two elders used to see her, going in and walking about, and they began to lust for her. ⁹They suppressed their consciences and turned away their eyes from looking to heaven or remembering their duty to administer justice. ¹⁰Both were overwhelmed with passion for her, but they did not tell each other of their distress, ¹¹for they were ashamed to disclose their lustful desire to have intercourse with her. ¹²Day after day they watched eagerly to see her.

13 One day they said to each other, "Let us go home, for it is time for lunch." So they both left and parted from each other. ¹⁴But turning back, they met again, and when each pressed the other for the reason, they confessed their lust. Then together they arranged for a time when they could find her alone.

15 Once, while they were watching for an opportune day, she went in as before with only two maids and wished to bathe in the garden, for it was a hot day. ¹⁶No one was there except the two elders, who had hidden themselves and were watching her. ¹⁷She said to her maids, "Bring me olive oil and ointments, and shut the garden doors so that I can bathe." ¹⁸They did as she told

1–4 Introduction to Susanna. 1 *There was a man* is a common introduction (e.g., Job 1:1). **2** *Hilkiah* is the name of the high priest who finds the law of the Lord in the temple during the reign of King Josiah (2 Kgs. 22; 2 Chr. 34). If the author understood Susanna as being descended from his lineage, this would provide further explanation for her superior knowledge of the Hebrew law. **3** Women were trained and educated in the torah like their male counterparts (cf. Proverbs, Sirach; see also Sarah, the daughter of Raguel, who appears to paraphrase the fifth commandment in Tob. 3:15). **4** *Joakim was very rich and had a fine garden* suggests wealth on par with that of kings and royalty, the only other group described as having gardens in the ancient world (e.g., Eccl. 2:5; Esth. 1:5; and the birth narrative of Sargon I), and would have recalled the hanging gardens of Nebuchadnezzar referenced by several ancient authors (e.g., Diodorus Siculus, Strabo, Josephus).

5–41 Accusation against Susanna and her humiliation. The story draws on and overturns several tropes. First is the motif of the righteous elder. Rather than providing justice, these elders use their power to exploit and molest. Second, Susanna is not initially rewarded for her piety but rather subjected to abuse and the threat of death. The lack of correspondence between righteousness and prosperity mirrors Job, Ecclesiastes, and Tobit. **10** *Both were overwhelmed with passion for her* literally reads "they were coming apart." This draws on a recurring theme that when those in authority

Going Deeper: Jewish Women in the Diaspora (Susanna)

Women serve as central characters in several of the deuterocanonical/apocryphal books: Sarah in the book of Tobit and Judith and Susanna in the books named after them. Though these stories are in large part historical novels set in the immediate aftermath of either the northern or southern kingdom's fall, scholars agree that they were written well into the Second Temple era (see **"Second Temple," p. 1328**).

In the book of Tobit, Sarah, the daughter of Raguel, is presented as a pious woman afflicted by the demon Asmodeus. In her distress, she recites a prayer to the Lord that reflects the language and liturgy of prayers found in books such as Psalms and Job. Sarah's prayer, in its structure and form, likely reflects the type of prayers recited by women during the Second Temple era.

In Judith, the reader is told that she "feared God with great devotion" (Jdt. 8:8), a phrase used to refer to religious acolytes. As a widow, Judith "fasted all the days of her widowhood except the day before the Sabbath and the Sabbath itself" (8:6). Judith's actions here, like Sarah's in Tobit, point to the funerary and mourning practices of women during the Greco-Roman period.

Susanna provides insight into education and observance. We are told that "her parents were righteous and had trained their daughter according to the law of Moses" (Sus. 3). This statement suggests that women as well as men were trained and instructed to observe the torah. The reference to "parents," both mother and father, highlights the role of the mother in teaching the torah to her children and consequently that she herself must have been trained and instructed in the law (see also Prov. 1:8; 6:20). Susanna's own knowledge and observance of the law, particularly the commandments against adultery, are demonstrated when she tells the wicked elders that she would rather "fall into your hands . . . than sin in the sight of the Lord" (Sus. 23).

The characterizations of women in these and other stories (e.g., Greek Esther) reflect historical situations in which they were composed or popularized. These include the reign of the Hasmonean queen Salome (76–67 BCE), a woman of power contending with male adversaries. The emphasis on both the piety and purity of Susanna and Sarah against male (and demonic) attempts to defile this purity may reflect the rise of the Pharisaic movement and its emphasis on purity (see also **"Masculinity," p. 1701**).

Adam Oliver Stokes

---

them: they shut the doors of the garden and went out by the side doors to bring what they had been commanded; they did not see the elders because they were hiding.

19 When the maids had gone out, the two elders got up and ran to her. 20They said, "Look, the garden doors are shut, and no one can see us. We are burning with desire for you, so give your consent, and lie with us. 21If you refuse, we will testify against you that a young man was with you, and this was why you sent your maids away."

22 Susanna groaned and said, "I am completely trapped. For if I do this, it will mean death for me; if I do not, I cannot escape your hands. 23I choose not to do it; I will fall into your hands rather than sin in the sight of the Lord."

24 Then Susanna cried out with a loud voice, and the two elders shouted against her. 25And one of them ran and opened the garden doors. 26When the people in the house heard the shouting in the garden, they rushed in at the side door to see what had happened to her. 27And when the elders told their story, the servants felt very much ashamed, for nothing like this had ever been said about Susanna.

28 The next day, when the people gathered at the house of her husband Joakim, the two elders came, full of their wicked plot to have Susanna put to death. In the presence of the people they said, 29"Send for Susanna daughter of Hilkiah, the wife of Joakim." 30So they sent for her. And she came with her parents, her children, and all her relatives.

31 Now Susanna was a woman of great refinement and beautiful in appearance. 32As she was veiled, the scoundrels ordered her to be unveiled, so that they might feast their eyes

---

misuse their power, there is a breakdown of order and structure not just for the nation but within these individuals (e.g., Judges; 1 Samuel). **20–21** The accusation parallels that made against Joseph by Potiphar's wife (Gen. 39:13–19). **22** The depiction reinforces the idea that the true mark of beauty

on her beauty. [33]Those who were with her and all who saw her were weeping.

34 Then the two elders stood up before the people and laid their hands on her head. [35]Through her tears she looked up toward heaven, for her heart trusted in the Lord. [36]The elders said, "While we were walking in the garden alone, this woman came in with two maids, shut the garden doors, and dismissed the maids. [37]Then a young man who was hiding there came to her and was intimate with her. [38]We were in a corner of the garden, and when we saw this wickedness we ran to them. [39]Although we saw him have intercourse with her, we could not hold the man because he was stronger than we, and he opened the doors and got away. [40]We did, however, seize this woman and asked who the young man was, [41]but she would not tell us. These things we testify."

Because they were elders of the people and judges, the assembly believed them and condemned her to death.

42 Then Susanna cried out with a loud voice and said, "O eternal God, you know what is secret and are aware of all things before they come to be; [43]you know that these men have given false evidence against me. And now I am to die, though I have done none of the wicked things that they have charged against me!"

44 The Lord heard her cry. [45]Just as she was being led off to execution, God stirred up the holy spirit of a young man named Daniel, [46]and he shouted with a loud voice, "I want no part in shedding this woman's blood!"

47 All the people turned to him and asked, "What is this you are saying?" [48]Taking his stand among them he said, "Are you such fools, O Israelites, as to condemn a daughter of Israel without examination and without learning the facts? [49]Return to court, for these men have given false evidence against her."

50 So all the people hurried back. And the rest of the[a] elders said to him, "Come, sit among us and inform us, for God has given you the standing of an elder." [51]Daniel said to them, "Separate them far from each other, and I will examine them."

52 When they were separated from each other, he summoned one of them and said to him, "You old relic of wicked days, your sins have now come home, which you have committed in the past, [53]pronouncing unjust judgments, condemning the innocent and acquitting the guilty, though the Lord said, 'You shall not put an innocent and righteous person to death.' [54]Now then, if you really saw this woman, tell me this: Under what tree did you see them being intimate with each other?" He answered, "Under a mastic tree."[b] [55]And Daniel said, "Very well! This lie has cost you your head, for the angel of God has received the sentence from God and will immediately cut[c] you in two."

56 Then, putting him to one side, he ordered them to bring the other. And he said to him, "You offspring of Canaan and not of Judah, beauty has beguiled you and lust has perverted your heart. [57]This is how you have been treating the daughters of Israel, and they were intimate with you through fear, but a daughter of Judah would not tolerate your wickedness. [58]Now then, tell me: Under what tree did you catch them being intimate with each other?" He answered, "Under an evergreen oak."[d] [59]Daniel said to him, "Very well! This lie has cost you also your head, for the angel of God is waiting with his sword to split[e] you in two, so as to destroy you both."

60 Then the whole assembly raised a great shout and blessed God, who saves those who hope in him. [61]And they took action against the

a 50 Gk lacks rest of the   b 54 The Greek words for mastic tree and cut are similar   c 55 The Greek words for mastic tree and cut are similar   d 58 The Greek words for evergreen oak and split are similar   e 59 The Greek words for evergreen oak and split are similar

is piety toward God. 35 Her heart trusted in is a common Hebrew idiom denoting total devotion and can be translated literally as "placing her heart upon" (e.g., Pss. 90:12; 108:1; cf. also the negative use—e.g., Pharaoh literally "places his heart" not to let the Israelites go in Exod. 7:23).

42–64 Daniel the advocate and Susanna's vindication. For readers of Theodotion's version, this would have been their first encounter with Daniel, since this story served as a prequel to the book of Daniel. Daniel uses his wisdom, given to him by God, to outwit the two elders, saving Susanna from death and increasing his great reputation among the people (v. 64). 48 A critique of the treatment of women that makes them vulnerable to the slander of men. 53–54 The condemnation parallels the language of prophets such as Samuel, who denounces Eli and his sons, and Jeremiah's oracles. 57 Translated as wickedness, the Greek word "anomia" is literally "lawlessness," an ironic wordplay. 60–62 On not shedding innocent blood here and in v. 53, see, for example, Deut. 19:10.

two elders because out of their own mouths Daniel had convicted them of bearing false witness; they did to them as they had wickedly planned to do to their neighbor. [62] Acting in accordance with the law of Moses, they put them to death. Thus innocent blood was spared that day.

63 Hilkiah and his wife praised God for their daughter Susanna, and so did her husband Joakim and all her relatives, because she was found innocent of a shameful deed. [64] And from that day onward Daniel had a great reputation among the people.

Bel and the Dragon

Authorship, Date, and Literary History

Bel and the Dragon, the third addition, is a two-part novella included in the Greek version of the book of Daniel. Like the story of Susanna, it serves to highlight Daniel's wisdom in the face of his adversaries. In both of these stories, Daniel defeats an object of reverence to the Babylonians. In the first, he defeats the idol Bel and the priests who serve him. In the second story, the object is not an idol but what appears to be an actual "dragon" or creature. The story also provides a retelling/alternate account of one of the most famous incidents in the Hebrew-Aramaic version of Daniel: the hero's deliverance from the lions' den (Dan. 6:16–23). In this retelling, the prophet Habakkuk makes an appearance and, with the aid of the Lord's angel, rescues Daniel from his fate. As in the story of Susanna, Daniel's eventual victory over his rivals earns him further praise and respect particularly from the gentile king.

There are two different versions of Bel and the Dragon: one in the Old Greek version and the other from Theodotion's translation. Theodotion's version is translated here. In the Old Greek text, the story is placed at the end of Daniel as chap. 14, while in Theodotion's version, it follows chap. 6. The effect of placing Bel and the Dragon at the end of Daniel, whether intentional or unintentional, is that it provides the Daniel saga with a largely mundane ending rather than the apocalyptic conclusion we find in the Hebrew-Aramaic text. The relatively simplistic grammar of the story suggests a Hebrew original translated into Greek, though the scattering of participial phrases throughout parallels the Greek of other Second Temple Jewish writers such as the author of 2 Maccabees and may be evidence in favor of the view that it was composed in Greek. The author clearly knows not only the stories of Daniel in the Hebrew-Aramaic text but other Scriptures from the Hebrew Bible, most notably the oracles of Habakkuk, to which Bel and the Dragon serves as a semi-sequel. With Christianity's acceptance of the Greek Bible over the Hebrew text of the Old Testament, the story retained popularity among Catholics (in Lat. translation) and Greek Orthodox Christians throughout the centuries.

Reading Guide

In Theodotion's version of Daniel translated here, Bel and the Dragon is located at the end of the book as the last chapter. If one reads the book of Daniel as a corpus of events in chronological succession to one another, then it can be argued that the incidents described in Bel and the Dragon take place late in Daniel's life, possibly even when he is an old man. His tenure in both the Babylonian and Persian courts supports this view. As such, one lesson that Bel and the Dragon conveys is that the pious and upright encounter challenges throughout their lifetime, even in later years when other challenges have already been overcome. What does one do with this constant cosmic conflict between good and evil?

The answer to this question can be found in another major theme readers encounter in their journey through Bel and the Dragon: devotion to the one true God who is over all of creation. By the first century BCE, when the Greek additions to the book of Daniel were likely composed, the religion of Israel had moved far beyond the henotheism/monolatry prevalent in the Pentateuch and Deuteronomic writings. The God of the Second Temple era was seen as not only the God of the Jews, existing alongside the active gods of other nations, but the one and only Lord of the cosmos before whom all other purported "gods" were merely false and worthless idols. No matter what obstacles the protagonist may face, the reader is always assured that Daniel will be victorious because of his faith in the one true God over and against the false god Bel, who has no real power.

That such a theme provided great comfort to the Jewish people living during the Greco-Roman era is evident in the wide corpus of early Jewish literature and beyond. In the New Testament, Paul boasts of victory over his opponents based on his faith in the God of Jesus Christ and his rejection of the false idols and deities of the Roman Empire. The power of this theme has continued to resonate in modern times for various marginalized communities. Like Paul, Dr. Martin Luther King Jr., who drew explicitly on the language of the book of Daniel, viewed the struggle for civil rights as a spiritual battle and claimed victory based on his faith in the biblical God and his rejection of the false god of the segregationists.

Adam Oliver Stokes

1 When King Astyages was laid to rest with his ancestors, Cyrus the Persian succeeded to his kingdom. [2]Daniel was a companion of the king and was the most honored of all his Friends.

3 Now the Babylonians had an idol called Bel, and every day they provided for it twelve bushels of choice flour and forty sheep and six measures of wine. [4]The king revered it and went every day to worship it. But Daniel worshiped his own God.

So the king said to him, "Why do you not worship Bel?" [5]He answered, "Because I do not revere idols made with hands but the living God, who created heaven and earth and has dominion over all living creatures."

6 The king said to him, "Do you not think that Bel is a living god? Do you not see how much he eats and drinks every day?" [7]And Daniel laughed and said, "Do not be deceived, O king, for this thing is only clay inside and bronze outside, and it has never eaten or drunk anything."

8 Then the king was angry and called the priests of Bel[a] and said to them, "If you do not tell me who is eating these provisions, you shall die. [9]But if you prove that Bel is eating them, Daniel shall die because he has spoken blasphemy against Bel." Daniel said to the king, "Let it be done as you have said."

10 Now there were seventy priests of Bel, besides their wives and children. So the king went with Daniel into the temple of Bel. [11]The priests of Bel said, "See, we are now going outside; you yourself, O king, set out the food and prepare the wine and shut the door and seal it with your signet. [12]When you return in the morning, if you do not find that Bel has eaten it all, we will die; otherwise Daniel will, who

is telling lies about us." [13]They were unconcerned, for beneath the table they had made a hidden entrance through which they used to go in regularly and consume the provisions. [14]After they had gone out, the king set out the food for Bel. Then Daniel ordered his servants to bring ashes, and they scattered them throughout the whole temple in the presence of the king alone. Then they went out, shut the door and sealed it with the king's signet, and departed. [15]During the night the priests came as usual, with their wives and children, and they ate and drank everything.

16 Early in the morning the king rose and came, and Daniel with him. [17]The king said, "Are the seals unbroken, Daniel?" He answered, "They are unbroken, O king." [18]As soon as the doors were opened, the king looked at the table and shouted in a loud voice, "You are great, O Bel, and in you there is no deceit at all!"

19 But Daniel laughed and restrained the king from going in. "Look at the floor," he said, "and notice whose footprints these are." [20]The king said, "I see the footprints of men and women and children."

21 Then the king was enraged, and he arrested the priests and their wives and children. They showed him the secret doors through which they used to enter to consume what was on the table. [22]Therefore the king put them to death and gave Bel over to Daniel, who destroyed it and its temple.

23 Now in that place[b] there was a great dragon[c] that the Babylonians revered. [24]The king said to Daniel, "You cannot deny that this is a living god, so worship him." [25]Daniel

a 8 Gk his priests   b 23 Other ancient authorities lack in that place   c 23 Or serpent

1–22 Daniel and the priests of Bel. 1 In the Old Greek version, the story begins with the statement "From the prophecies of Habakkuk." The attribution of the story to a biblical prophet mirrors the tendency found in other books of the Greek Old Testament, such as the Greek translation of Lamentations, which explicitly mentions Jeremiah as the author of the book. **2** This statement parallels other comments about Daniel finding favor in the royal court (Dan. 1:9, 19–20; 2:46–48; 3:30). **3** The author, while correctly noting that Cyrus was king of Persia (v. 1), seems to conflate him with earlier Babylonian rulers such as Nebuchadnezzar. Similar historical errors occur in books such as Judith, where Nebuchadnezzar is identified as the king of Assyria. **5** Daniel's statement reflects the language of the Gen. 1 creation account that emphasizes God's role as universal creator. **10** *Seventy*, usually a positive number symbolizing divine completion, is here used in reference to the idolatrous false priests. **14–19** As in other traditions about Daniel, his wisdom is highlighted. Like the two wicked elders in Susanna, the priests assume that their plot will work, but Daniel outwits them with the divine wisdom he has been given.

23–42 Daniel kills the dragon and is thrown into the lions' den. 23 Dragons play a prominent role in Near Eastern and especially Babylonian mythology. They were considered the sacred animal

Focus On: Gentile Conversion (Bel and the Dragon)

Although there are isolationist views in the Hebrew Bible, such as one finds in Ezra–Nehemiah, there are other traditions for Israel's religion to include more than Israel. In Joshua, it is the Canaanite woman Rahab who tells the Israelite spies that "the LORD your God is indeed God in heaven above and on earth below" (Josh. 2:11). In Ruth (likely composed as a response to the racially exclusive policies of Ezra), the protagonist vows that "your people shall be my people and your God my God" (1:16).

Accounts of gentile conversion occur in the later Second Temple period. The story of Joseph and Aseneth portrays Aseneth's conversion to Joseph's God. According to Josephus, the Hasmoneans forced some people to convert (Ant. 13.257–58, 397).

The theme of gentile conversion is prevalent in the deuterocanonical/apocryphal books. Tobit notes that among his many pious deeds, he provided tithes for "the orphans and widows and to the converts who had attached themselves to the Israelites" (1:8). The mention of converts here tells us more about the social context of the book's author, writing in the second century BCE, than that of the likely fictional Tobit, whose story is set in eighth-century BCE Assyria. By the author's time, the Deuteronomic command to support marginalized groups in Israelite society had been modified. The "resident alien" or foreign immigrant (Heb. ger), the third group in the tripartite commandment, had been replaced with the gentile converts to Judaism living in that era. The epilogue of the book also promotes a proselytizing agenda, as seen in Tobit's prayer/prophecy that "many nations will come to you from far away, the inhabitants of the ends of the earth to your holy name" (13:11).

Perhaps the most notable example of gentile conversion to the God of Israel is seen in the depiction of Cyrus, king of Persia. In the Chronicler's history, Cyrus claims that his dominion has been given to him by "the LORD, the God of heaven" (2 Chr. 36:23; see also **"Cyrus," p. 991**). This theme of Cyrus's submission and acknowledgment of God's power is expanded on in Bel and the Dragon, where Cyrus's love for Daniel and his religion leads his critics and enemies to exclaim that the "king has become a Jew" (Bel 28). The end of the story presents the reader with a fully converted Cyrus, who exclaims, "You are great, O Lord, the God of Daniel, and there is no other besides you!" (v. 41).

Adam Oliver Stokes

said, "I worship the Lord my God, for he is a living God. ²⁶But give me permission, O king, and I will kill the dragon[d] without sword or club." The king said, "I give you permission."

27 Then Daniel took pitch, fat, and hair and boiled them together and made cakes, which he fed to the dragon.[e] The dragon[f] ate them and burst open. Then Daniel said, "See what you have been worshiping!"

28 When the Babylonians heard about it, they were very indignant and conspired against the king, saying, "The king has become a Jew; he has destroyed Bel and killed the dragon[g] and slaughtered the priests." ²⁹Going to the king, they said, "Hand Daniel over to us, or else we will kill you and your household." ³⁰The king saw that they were pressing him hard, and under compulsion he handed Daniel over to them.

31 They threw Daniel into the lions' den, and he was there for six days. ³²There were seven lions in the den, and every day they had been given two human bodies and two sheep, but now they were given nothing, so that they would devour Daniel.

33 Now the prophet Habakkuk was in Judea; he had made a stew and had broken bread into a bowl and was going into the field to take it to the reapers. ³⁴But the angel of the Lord said to Habakkuk, "Take the food that you have to Babylon, to Daniel, in the lions' den." ³⁵Habakkuk said, "Sir, I have never seen Babylon, and I know nothing about the den."

d 26 Or serpent e 27 Or serpent f 27 Or serpent g 28 Or serpent

of the god Marduk. There are several depictions of gods and kings fighting dragons in their effort to establish order in the cosmos. Dragons and serpents also feature in Egyptian mythology, with images of the cat god Bastet defeating the cosmic serpent and bringing order and peace to Egypt.
33 The narrative's setting suddenly shifts from Babylon to Judea. Historically, Habakkuk predates the time of Cyrus by nearly eighty years. The mention of reapers provides a resolution to Habakkuk's situation at the end of the book of Habakkuk. Habakkuk laments that the fig tree does not blossom and that the fields yield no crop (Hab. 3:17). The reapers in Bel and the Dragon suggest that the

36Then the angel of the Lord took him by the crown of his head and carried him by his hair; with a gust of wind[b] he set him down in Babylon, right over the den.

37 Then Habakkuk shouted, "Daniel, Daniel! Take the food that God has sent you." 38Daniel said, "You have remembered me, O God, and have not abandoned those who love you." 39So Daniel got up and ate. And the angel of God immediately returned Habakkuk to his own place.

40 On the seventh day the king came to mourn for Daniel. When he came to the den he looked in, and there sat Daniel! 41The king shouted with a loud voice, "You are great, O Lord, the God of Daniel, and there is no other besides you!" 42Then he pulled Daniel[i] out and threw into the den those who had attempted his destruction, and they were instantly eaten before his eyes.

b 36 Or by the power of his spirit   i 42 Gk him

harvest has become fruitful again. **41** An expansion on Darius's response in Dan. 6:20. Not only does Cyrus acknowledge the greatness of Daniel's deity, but he also proclaims that *there is no other besides you!* Hence, the gentile king converts to worship of the God of Israel as suggested earlier in the criticisms of his enemies (Bel 28).

1 MACCABEES

Original Language
Although scholars suggest that the book of 1 Maccabees was originally written in Hebrew, there are no existing or surviving copies. If the text were written in Hebrew, 1 Maccabees would have received a stronger consideration of canonization into the Hebrew Bible canon. First Maccabees, preserved in Koine Greek, is codified in the Septuagint.

Historical Context
First Maccabees is historically and politically situated after Alexander the Great's conquest of the eastern Mediterranean and Middle East, including parts of India. His untimely death (323 BCE) resulted in a power vacuum, with two of his generals, Ptolemy I (Soter) and Seleucus I (Nicator), defeating a third, Antigonus I (Monophthalmus), before establishing rival dynasties—the Seleucids (Syria) in the north (east) and the Ptolemies (Egypt) in the south (west). With opposing ideals in governance and cultural adaptations, they competed and fought heavily against each other for territorial expansion and political control, including the strategic land bridge between the east and west, Judah. In the third century BCE, Judah was under the hegemony of the Ptolemies. However, when the Seleucids defeated the Ptolemies in 198 BCE, the Seleucid Antiochus III realigned the newly acquired territory to include all of Judah. Seleucus IV Philopator's rule lasted from 187 to 175 BCE. His short-lived reign was replaced by the infamous "sinful root" (1:10), Antiochus IV Epiphanes (174–164 BCE). He reigned with terror before the Maccabees asserted political and religious control.

Religious and Cultural Context
The religious and cultural memory and trauma of the Judean lived experience are categorically preserved in 1 Maccabees. Voluntary and involuntary assimilation through the Hellenistic educational system, the gymnasium, among other foundations, was culturally superimposed on Judean institutions and values (see **"The Bible in Its Ancient Contexts," pp. 2150–52**, for more on Hellenism). The Sabbath was profaned (1:43). The temple was defiled. Gentile religious practices became normative (1:51). The books of the law were burned (1:56). Circumcision was banned (1:48). And mothers who had their infants circumcised were put to death (1:60). Their infants were hung from their dead mothers' necks (1:60–61). Many fled as refugees (1:53), while others faithfully resisted and fought, dying as martyrs (1:63).

Economic and Social Issues
Josephus (*Ant.* 12.154) and Zenon, a chief minister of Ptolemy II Philadelphus (285–246 BCE), describe economic activities during this period. For example, taxes on farming offer an important depiction of the period's ancient economy and society. The "legal authority" to collect various types of taxes levied by Egypt was auctioned to the highest bidder—usually going to the wealthiest. During Ptolemaic rule, economic activities included the export of cereals, oils, and wine, among other goods, to Egypt. Central was the trade of enslaved humans, as Zenon noted in a letter from 259 BCE. Young girls were bought and sold for prostitution in Egypt. When the Seleucids replaced the Ptolemies, although there is no direct evidence, there may have been some cessation or pause in supplying Egypt. Although the Seleucids permitted more local autonomy in political governance in contrast to the Ptolemies, socially and religiously, the Seleucids displayed little tolerance of local expressions that could potentially challenge their cultural superiority.

Genres and Purpose
First Maccabees includes letters (8:23–32; 10:18–20, 25–45; 11:30–37, 57; 12:5–23; 13:36–40) and battle scenes or reports (3:27–4:24; 6:18–63; 9:1–22). It also includes expansions—including prayers, poems, and speeches—to glorify the Hasmonean dynasty and its accomplishments. The framework of the entire book is set in three or four generations. Like the narratives of Abraham, Isaac, Jacob (and Joseph), the ones about Mattathias, Judas (and his brothers, Jonathan and Simon), and John Hyrcanus (and Aristobulus I and Alexander Jannaeus) offer the motif and written framework of three or four generations, a hallmark of a displaced and resettled community seeking written

legitimacy through the theo-political valorization of its heroes and their stories. As the three or four generations establish firm foundations, 1 Maccabees envisions subsequent generations to carry on, from generation to generation, in the continued struggle for liberation, statehood with citizenship, and belonging—establishing and maintaining a zealous kingdom.

The Seven Generations of the Maccabees: 167 BCE to 4 BCE

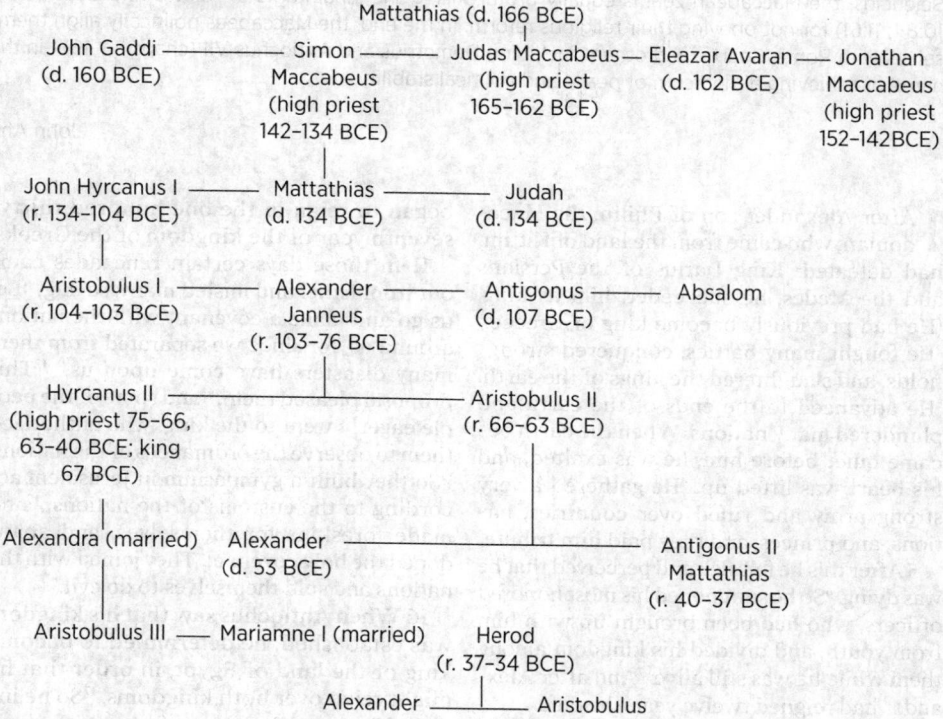

Mattathias (d. 166 BCE)

John Gaddi — Simon — Judas Maccabeus — Eleazar Avaran — Jonathan
(d. 160 BCE)   Maccabeus   (high priest   (d. 162 BCE)   Maccabeus
(high priest   165–162 BCE)   (high priest
142–134 BCE)   152–142BCE)

John Hyrcanus I — Mattathias — Judah
(r. 134–104 BCE)   (d. 134 BCE)   (d. 134 BCE)

Aristobulus I — Alexander — Antigonus — Absalom
(r. 104–103 BCE)   Janneus   (d. 107 BCE)
(r. 103–76 BCE)

Hyrcanus II — Aristobulus II
(high priest 75–66,   (r. 66–63 BCE)
63–40 BCE; king
67 BCE)

Alexandra (married)   Alexander — Antigonus II
(d. 53 BCE)   Mattathias
(r. 40–37 BCE)

Aristobulus III — Mariamne I (married)   Herod
(r. 37–34 BCE)

Alexander — Aristobulus

Reading Guide

First Maccabees narrates the Maccabean Revolt and the rise of the Hasmonean dynasty. Chap. 1 sets the stage with rising tensions among Jews concerning Hellenization and the desecration of the temple and persecution by thwe Seleucid Antiochus IV. Chap. 2 introduces Mattathias, a priest, and his five sons. Mattathias kills a hellenized Jew for offering a (state-)sanctioned sacrifice on the altar in Modein (2:24). He also kills a king's officer (2:25). He proclaims a zealous appeal for revolution. But when his proclamation goes unanswered, he and his sons are hunted. They flee into the wilderness. When a segment of the Hasideans (2:42), a group of skilled warriors practicing ritual purity, join and fight with Mattathias on the Sabbath, the tide turns completely in favor of Mattathias and his sons. Phinehas, a prefigure of Mattathias, is recast and reworked into the narrative (2:54).

First Maccabees 3:1–9:22 narrates the successful military campaigns of Judas Maccabeus ("the hammer") and his brothers. Judas, also a priest, succeeds his father to lead the revolt against the Seleucids (167–160 BCE). When the Maccabees recapture and rededicate the temple (164 BCE), the historic, political, and religious feat is credited to the "miraculous" work of God and commemorated with the establishment of Hanukkah (cf. 4:36–59).

First Maccabees 9:23–12:53 focuses on the rebuilding of the kingdom marked by the apexes—the rededication of the temple, and the city wall. Jonathan, the brother of Judas, becomes high priest and governor. Chaps. 13–16 record the reign of another brother, Simon, who finally achieves independence from the Seleucids. He maintains and continues the high priesthood lineage but with added kingship—thereby ushering in a kingdom with religious autonomy within an empire. First

Maccabees was likely produced after Simon's reign. The book concludes with his son, John Hyrcanus (134 BCE), the third generation, taking the throne.

The book is unilaterally about resistance, resiliency, and reconstitution framed in justified zeal and vengeance to reclaim fully dismembered Judean humanity. New citizenship, belonging, and communal assembly are recorded throughout the testimonies, centering on Judas Maccabeus and his brothers. Perpetuating violence to achieve peace is the cyclical theme in 1 Maccabees. Like the Seleucids, the Maccabean zeal is equally brutal, killing the inhabitants of Azotus and Gaza (5:68; 10:84; 11:61) for not obeying their religious reform. In the end, the Maccabees politically align themselves with Rome, Sparta, and others, including Demetrius and Antiochus VII (chaps. 14–16)—in the name of achieving a modicum of peace and political stability.

John Ahn

1 After Alexander son of Philip, the Macedonian, who came from the land of Kittim, had defeated*ᵃ* King Darius of the Persians and the Medes, he succeeded him as king. (He had previously become king of Greece.) ²He fought many battles, conquered strongholds, and slaughtered the kings of the earth. ³He advanced to the ends of the earth and plundered many nations. When the earth became quiet before him, he was exalted, and his heart was lifted up. ⁴He gathered a very strong army and ruled over countries, nations, and princes, and they paid him tribute.

5 After this he fell sick and perceived that he was dying. ⁶So he summoned his most honored officers, who had been brought up with him from youth, and divided his kingdom among them while he was still alive. ⁷And after Alexander had reigned twelve years, he died.

8 Then his officers began to rule, each in his own place. ⁹They all put on crowns after his death, and so did their descendants after them for many years, and they caused many evils on the earth.

10 From them came forth a sinful root, Antiochus Epiphanes, son of King Antiochus; he had been a hostage in Rome. He began to reign in the one hundred thirty-seventh year of the kingdom of the Greeks.

11 In those days certain renegades came out from Israel and misled many, saying, "Let us go and make a covenant with the nations around us, for since we separated from them many disasters have come upon us." ¹²This proposal pleased them, ¹³and some of the people eagerly went to the king, who authorized them to observe the ordinances of the nations. ¹⁴So they built a gymnasium in Jerusalem according to the customs of the nations, ¹⁵and made foreskins for themselves, and abandoned the holy covenant. They joined with the nations and sold themselves to do evil.

16 When Antiochus saw that his kingdom was established, he determined to become king of the land of Egypt, in order that he might reign over both kingdoms. ¹⁷So he invaded Egypt with a strong force, with chariots and elephants and cavalry and with a large fleet. ¹⁸He engaged King Ptolemy of Egypt in battle, and Ptolemy turned and fled before him, and many were wounded and fell. ¹⁹They captured the fortified cities

a 1.1 Gk adds *and he defeated*

1:1–9 Alexander the Great. 1:1 *Land of Kittim*, originally a reference to Cyprus, is reframed as Macedonia and Greece. The term becomes synonymous with enemy occupiers of the land: in the Dead Sea Scrolls, as the Greeks/Romans and non-Qumran community members. **1:7** *Alexander* the Great died in June 323 BCE in Babylon. He was approximately thirty-three years old. **1:9** Until 198 BCE, the Ptolemies of Egypt ruled Judah. They are marked as having *caused many evils on the earth*. The Seleucids of Syria (Antiochus III) liberated Judah, only to annex and rule Judah from 198 to 64 BCE. **1:10–15 Reign of Antiochus Epiphanes. 1:10** *Antiochus* IV (175–164 BCE)—*Epiphanes*, meaning "god manifest"—is forced to go to Rome under the Treaty of Apamea (188 BCE) to pledge his loyalty. He replaces his brother, Seleucid IV (187–175 BCE). *The kingdom of the Greeks* refers to the Seleucid reign, which began in Babylon in 312 BCE. *One hundred thirty-seventh year* is circa 175 BCE. **1:14** The *gymnasium* is an official institution to assimilate and hellenize the people through Greek philosophical, cultural, and physical education (see **"The Bible in Its Ancient Contexts," pp. 2150–52**, for more on Hellenism). **1:16–28** The looting of the gold and silver objects in the Jerusalem temple

in the land of Egypt, and he plundered the land of Egypt.

20 After subduing Egypt, Antiochus turned back in the one hundred forty-third year and went up against Israel and came to Jerusalem with a strong force. ²¹He arrogantly entered the sanctuary and took the golden altar, the lampstand for the light, and all its utensils. ²²He took also the table for the bread of the Presence, the cups for drink offerings, the bowls, the golden censers, the curtain, the crowns, and the gold decoration on the front of the temple; he stripped it all off. ²³He took the silver and the gold and the costly vessels; he took also the hidden treasures that he found. ²⁴Taking them all, he went into his own land.

He shed much blood
    and spoke with great arrogance.
²⁵ Israel mourned deeply in every community;
²⁶   rulers and elders groaned;
    young women and young men became
        faint;
    the beauty of the women faded.
²⁷ Every bridegroom took up the lament;
    she who sat in the bridal chamber was
        mourning.
²⁸ Even the land trembled for its inhabitants,
    and all the house of Jacob was clothed
        with shame.

29 Two years later the king sent to the cities of Judah a chief collector of tribute, and he came to Jerusalem with a large force. ³⁰Deceitfully he spoke peaceable words to them, and they believed him, but he suddenly fell upon the city, dealt it a severe blow, and destroyed many people of Israel. ³¹He plundered the city, burned it with fire, and tore down its houses and its surrounding walls. ³²They took captive the women and children and seized the livestock. ³³Then they fortified the city of David with a large strong wall and strong towers, and it became their citadel. ³⁴They stationed there a sinful nation, men who were renegades. These strengthened their position; ³⁵they

stored up arms and food, and, collecting the spoils of Jerusalem, they stored them there and became a great menace,
³⁶ for the citadel*b* became an ambush
        against the sanctuary,
    an evil adversary of Israel at all times.
³⁷On every side of the sanctuary they shed
        innocent blood;
    they even defiled the sanctuary.
³⁸ Because of them the residents of
        Jerusalem fled;
    she became a dwelling of strangers;
    she became strange to her offspring,
        and her children forsook her.
³⁹ Her sanctuary became desolate like a
        desert;
    her feasts were turned into mourning,
    her Sabbaths into a reproach,
        her honor into contempt.
⁴⁰ Her dishonor now grew as great as her
        glory;
    her exaltation was turned into
        mourning.

41 Then the king wrote to his whole kingdom that all should be one people ⁴²and that all should give up their particular customs. All the nations accepted the command of the king. ⁴³Many even from Israel gladly adopted his religion; they sacrificed to idols and profaned the Sabbath. ⁴⁴And the king sent letters by messengers to Jerusalem and the towns of Judah; he directed them to follow customs strange to the land, ⁴⁵to forbid burnt offerings and sacrifices and drink offerings in the sanctuary, to profane Sabbaths and festivals, ⁴⁶to defile the sanctuary and the holy ones, ⁴⁷to build altars and sacred precincts and shrines for idols, to sacrifice pigs and other unclean animals, ⁴⁸and to leave their sons uncircumcised. They were to make themselves abominable by everything unclean and profane ⁴⁹so that they would forget the law and change all the ordinances. ⁵⁰He added,*c* "And whoever does not obey the command of the king shall die."

b 1.36 Gk *it*   *c* 1.50 Gk lacks *He added*

after Antiochus's military campaign into Egypt (169 BCE) suggests he needed payments for the mercenaries from Mysia (northwest of Asia Minor) who helped him conquer Egypt. The nephew of Antiochus IV, Ptolemy VI (Philometor), ruled Egypt from 180 to 145 BCE.

1:29–40 Jerusalem is attacked a second time in 167 BCE for not paying the tribute. *Women, children,* and *livestock* are taken as payment. Jerusalem becomes another form of permanent payment, as a garrison is established in Akra. **1:36–40** A city lament composed in the style of the book of Lamentations.

1:41–61 Policies are enacted to unite various peoples through Hellenization. For Jews, this means

51 In such words he wrote to his whole kingdom. He appointed inspectors over all the people and commanded the towns of Judah to offer sacrifice, town by town. 52Many of the people, everyone who forsook the law, joined them, and they did evil in the land; 53they drove Israel into hiding in every place of refuge they had.

54 Now on the fifteenth day of Chislev, in the one hundred forty-fifth year, they erected a desolating sacrilege on the altar of burnt offering. They also built altars in the surrounding towns of Judah 55and offered incense at the doors of the houses and in the streets. 56The books of the law that they found they tore to pieces and burned with fire. 57Anyone found possessing the book of the covenant or anyone who adhered to the law was condemned to death by decree of the king. 58They kept using violence against Israel, against those who were found month after month in the towns. 59On the twenty-fifth day of the month they offered sacrifice on the altar that was on top of the altar of burnt offering. 60According to the decree, they put to death the women who had their children circumcised 61and their families and those who circumcised them, and they hung the infants from their mothers' necks.

62 But many in Israel stood firm and were resolved in their hearts not to eat unclean food. 63They chose to die rather than to be defiled by food or to profane the holy covenant, and they did die. 64Very great wrath came upon Israel.

2 In those days Mattathias son of John son of Simeon, a priest of the clan of Joarib, moved from Jerusalem and settled in Modein. 2He had five sons: John surnamed Gaddi, 3Simon called Thassi, 4Judas called Maccabeus, 5Eleazar called Avaran, and Jonathan called Apphus. 6He saw the blasphemies being committed in Judah and Jerusalem 7and said,

"Alas! Why was I born to see this,
the ruin of my people, the ruin of the
holy city?
The people sat idle there when it was
given over to the enemy,
the sanctuary given over to strangers.
8 Her temple has become like a person
without honor;d
9 her glorious vessels have been carried
into exile.
Her infants have been killed in her streets,
her youths by the sword of the foe.
10 What nation has not inherited her palacese
and has not seized her spoils?
11 All her adornment has been taken away;
no longer free, she has become a slave.
12 And see, our holy place, our beauty,
and our glory have been laid waste;
the nations have profaned them.
13 Why should we live any longer?"

14 Then Mattathias and his sons tore their clothes, put on sackcloth, and mourned greatly.

15 The king's officers who were enforcing the apostasy came to the town of Modein to make them offer sacrifice. 16Many from Israel came to them, and Mattathias and his sons were assembled. 17Then the king's officers spoke to Mattathias as follows: "You are a leader, honored and great in this town, and supported by sons and brothers. 18Now be the first to come and do what the king commands, as all the nations and the people of Judah and those who are left in Jerusalem have done. Then you and your sons will be numbered among the Friends of the king, and you and your sons will be honored with silver and gold and many gifts."

19 But Mattathias answered and said in a

d 2.8 Meaning of Gk uncertain   e 2.10 Other ancient authorities read *has not had a part in her kingdom*

---

eradicating a torah-centric life. **1:51–53** *Inspectors* threaten forced annexation of property, expulsion of religious traditions and practices, and persecution of the people who do not conform. Torah-observant Judeans flee, forced to migrate for safety. **1:54–61** Judeans who remain in the land, endeavoring to uphold the traditions found in the *books of the law* and *covenant*, among others, are executed. As a final form of extermination for holding on to the torah, Judean mothers are killed, with their infants hung from their dead mothers' necks (1:60–61).

2:1–14 Mattathias and his sons. This passage introduces a patriarchal narrative, mimicking the Abraham saga, the Isaac interlude, the Jacob cycle, and the Joseph novella, also framed in three or four generations: Mattathias (chap. 2), Judas Maccabeus (chaps. 3–8), Jonathan (chaps. 9–12), and Simon and John (chaps. 13–16). The fourth generation's story is attached to the third. **2:7–13** Another city lament, describing it as captured and enslaved, with its glory vanished. **2:14** To tear clothes and wear sackcloth is an outward expression of communal lament (cf. Ezra 9:3).

2:15–28 Rejection of apostasy. 2:19–22 Recalls Daniel, who refused to obey the king's ordinance

loud voice: "Even if all the nations that live under the rule of the king obey him and have chosen to obey his commandments, every one of them abandoning the religion of their ancestors, [20]I and my sons and my brothers will continue to live by the covenant of our ancestors. [21]Far be it from us to desert the law and the ordinances. [22]We will not obey the king's words by turning aside from our religion to the right hand or to the left."

23 When he had finished speaking these words, a Jew came forward in the sight of all to offer sacrifice on the altar in Modein, according to the king's command. [24]When Mattathias saw it, he burned with zeal, and his heart was stirred. He gave vent to righteous anger; he ran and slaughtered him on the altar. [25]At the same time he killed the king's officer who was forcing them to sacrifice, and he tore down the altar. [26]Thus he burned with zeal for the law, just as Phinehas did against Zimri son of Salu.

27 Then Mattathias cried out in the town with a loud voice, saying: "Let every one who is zealous for the law and supports the covenant come out with me!" [28]Then he and his sons fled to the hills and left all that they had in the town.

29 At that time many who were seeking righteousness and justice went down to the wilderness to live there, [30]they, their sons, their wives, and their livestock, because troubles pressed heavily upon them. [31]And it was reported to the king's officers and to the troops in Jerusalem the city of David that those who had rejected the king's command

had gone down to the hiding places in the wilderness. [32]Many pursued them and overtook them; they encamped opposite them and prepared for battle against them on the Sabbath day. [33]They said to them, "Enough of this! Come out and do what the king commands, and you will live." [34]But they said, "We will not come out, nor will we do what the king commands and so profane the Sabbath day." [35]Then the enemy[f] quickly attacked them. [36]But they did not answer them or hurl a stone at them or block up their hiding places, [37]for they said, "Let us all die in our innocence; heaven and earth testify for us that you are killing us unjustly." [38]So they attacked them on the Sabbath, and they died, with their wives and children and livestock, to the number of a thousand persons.

39 When Mattathias and his friends learned of it, they mourned for them deeply. [40]And all said to their neighbors: "If we all do as our kindred have done and refuse to fight with the nations for our lives and for our ordinances, they will quickly destroy us from the earth." [41]So they made this decision that day: "Let us fight against anyone who comes to attack us on the Sabbath day; let us not all die as our kindred died in their hiding places."

42 Then there united with them a company of Hasideans, mighty warriors of Israel, all who offered themselves willingly for the law. [43]And all who became fugitives to escape their troubles joined them and

f 2.35 Gk they

(Dan. 1:8–16), and the words of Joshua, "As for me and my household, we will serve the LORD" (Josh. 24:15). **2:23–26** Reframes and recontextualizes the story of Phinehas (Num. 25:6–15), who killed a couple (an Israelite man and a Midianite woman) for apostasy (worship of Baal of Peor). Here Mattathias burns with zeal and kills a fellow Jew and a foreigner, the king's officer. **2:27–28** After the call to arms, Mattathias and his family go into voluntary exile, forced to migrate into the hill country.

2:29–38 Others flee to the *wilderness*. The text may allude to the origins of one segment of the diverse communities that left Jerusalem and went to Qumran, the *wilderness*, to live there with *their sons, their wives, and their livestock*. **2:34–38** An episode of nonviolence and refusal to take up arms, especially on *the Sabbath*, resulting in the massacre of all the members, including wives, children, and livestock.

2:39–41 Justification to fight on *the Sabbath*. Mattathias's company may fight in defense but not start a conflict on the Sabbath.

2:42–48 Hasideans join the Maccabees. *Hasideans* ("pious ones"), *mighty warriors* with religious conviction, join the Maccabees, likely teaching and training them and others on the tactics of guerrilla warfare. Judas becomes the leader of the Hasideans (2 Macc. 14:6). The Hasideans help build up the army and lead the efforts with Mattathias to kill both gentiles and Judeans whom they deem as apostates.

reinforced them. [44]They organized an army and struck down sinners in their anger and renegades in their wrath; the survivors fled to the nations for safety. [45]And Mattathias and his friends went around and tore down the altars; [46]they forcibly circumcised all the uncircumcised boys whom they found within the borders of Israel. [47]They hunted down the arrogant, and the work prospered in their hands. [48]They rescued the law out of the hands of the nations and kings, and they never let the sinner gain the upper hand.

49 Now the days drew near for Mattathias to die, and he said to his sons: "Arrogance and scorn have now become strong; it is a time of ruin and furious anger. [50]Now, my children, show zeal for the law and give your lives for the covenant of our ancestors.

51 "Remember the deeds of the ancestors, which they did in their generations, and you will receive great honor and an everlasting name. [52]Was not Abraham found faithful when tested, and it was reckoned to him as righteousness? [53]Joseph in the time of his distress kept the commandment and became lord of Egypt. [54]Phinehas our ancestor, because he was deeply zealous, received the covenant of everlasting priesthood. [55]Joshua, because he fulfilled the command, became a judge in Israel. [56]Caleb, because he testified in the assembly, received an inheritance in the land. [57]David, because he was merciful, inherited the throne of the kingdom forever. [58]Elijah, because of great zeal for the law, was taken up into heaven. [59]Hananiah, Azariah, and Mishael believed and were saved from the flame. [60]Daniel, because of his innocence, was delivered from the mouth of the lions.

61 "And so observe, from generation to generation, that none of those who put their trust in him will lack strength. [62]Do not fear the words of sinners, for their splendor will turn into dung and worms. [63]Today they will be exalted, but tomorrow they will not be found, for they will have returned to the dust, and their plans will have perished. [64]My children, be courageous and grow strong in the law, for by it you will gain honor.

65 "Here is your brother Simeon, who I know is wise in counsel; always listen to him; he shall be your father. [66]Judas Maccabeus has been a mighty warrior from his youth; he shall command the army for you and fight the battle against the peoples.[g] [67]You shall rally around you all who observe the law and avenge the wrong done to your people. [68]Pay back the nations in full, and obey the commands of the law."

69 Then he blessed them and was gathered to his ancestors. [70]He died in the one hundred forty-sixth year and was buried in the tomb of his ancestors at Modein. And all Israel mourned for him with great lamentation.

3 Then his son Judas, who was called Maccabeus, took command in his place. [2]All his brothers and all who had joined his father helped him; they gladly fought for Israel.
[3] He extended the glory of his people.
> Like a giant he put on his breastplate;
> he bound on his armor of war and waged battles,
> protecting the camp by his sword.
[4] He was like a lion in his deeds,
> like a lion's cub roaring for prey.
[5] He searched out and pursued those who broke the law;
> he burned those who troubled his people.
[6] Lawbreakers shrank back for fear of him;

g 2.66 Or *of the people*

2:49–70 Mattathias's final speech. Three sets of traditions are observed and combined in this speech. The first are the farewell speeches of Jacob (Gen. 49), Moses (Deut. 33), Joshua (Josh. 23–24), and Samuel (1 Sam. 12). The second is the late motif of being *tested*, combined with *righteousness*, established in martyr texts of the book of Daniel. These motifs are retrospectively recast back onto Abraham, Phineas, Joshua, Caleb, David, and Elijah and conclude with Daniel, the origin of these motifs. **2:65–70** Mattathias provides a succession narrative—like David to Solomon, Elijah to Elisha, or Alexander's two generals—and splits his authority between Simon (religious)—here spelled Simeon—and Judas (military). Generational succession is framed in literary symmetry.

3:1–9:22 Successful military campaigns of Judas Maccabeus and his brothers.

3:1–26 A victory poem for Judas and a series of victories. The *lawbreakers* are hellenized Judeans, including the high priests Menelaus and Alcimus. The *many kings* are Antiochus IV, Antiochus V, and

all the evildoers were confounded;
and deliverance prospered by his hand.
⁷ He embittered many kings,
but he made Jacob glad by his deeds,
and his memory is blessed forever.
⁸ He went through the cities of Judah;
he destroyed the ungodly out of the
land;*ᵇ
thus he turned away wrath from Israel.
⁹ He was renowned to the ends of the
earth;
he gathered in those who were
perishing.

10 Then Apollonius gathered together nations and a large force from Samaria to fight against Israel. ¹¹When Judas learned of it, he went out to meet him, and he defeated and killed him. Many were wounded and fell, and the rest fled. ¹²Then they seized their spoils, and Judas took the sword of Apollonius and used it in battle the rest of his life.

13 When Seron, the commander of the Syrian army, heard that Judas had gathered a large company, including a body of faithful soldiers who stayed with him and went out to battle, ¹⁴he said, "I will make a name for myself and win honor in the kingdom. I will make war on Judas and his companions, who scorn the king's command." ¹⁵Once again a strong army of godless men joined him and went up with him to help him, to take vengeance on the Israelites.

16 When he approached the ascent of Beth-horon, Judas went out to meet him with a small company. ¹⁷But when they saw the army coming to meet them, they said to Judas, "How can we, few as we are, fight against so great and so strong a multitude? And we are faint, for we have eaten nothing today." ¹⁸Judas replied, "It is easy for many to be hemmed in by few, for in the sight of heaven there is no difference between saving by many or by few. ¹⁹It is not on the size of the army that victory

in battle depends, but strength comes from heaven. ²⁰They come against us in great insolence and lawlessness to destroy us and our wives and our children and to despoil us, ²¹but we fight for our lives and our laws. ²²He himself will crush them before us; as for you, do not be afraid of them."

23 When he finished speaking, he rushed suddenly against Seron and his army, and they were crushed before him. ²⁴They pursued themᶦ down the descent of Beth-horon to the plain; eight hundred of them fell, and the rest fled into the land of the Philistines. ²⁵Then Judas and his brothers began to be feared, and terror fell on the nations all around them. ²⁶His fame reached the king, and the nations talked of the battles of Judas.

27 When King Antiochus heard these reports, he was greatly angered, and he sent and gathered all the forces of his kingdom, a very strong army. ²⁸He opened his coffers and gave a year's pay to his forces and ordered them to be ready for any need. ²⁹Then he saw that the money in the treasury was exhausted and that the tribute payments from the country were small because of the dissension and disaster that he had caused in the land by abolishing the laws that had existed from the earliest days. ³⁰He feared that he might not have such funds as he had before for his expenses and for the gifts that he used to give more lavishly than preceding kings. ³¹He was greatly perplexed in mind; then he determined to go to Persia and collect the tribute payments from those regions and raise a large fund.

32 He left Lysias, a distinguished man of royal lineage, in charge of the king's affairs from the River Euphrates to the borders of Egypt. ³³Lysias was also to take care of his son Antiochus until he returned. ³⁴And he turned

ᵇ 3.8 Gk *it*   ᶦ 3.24 Other ancient authorities read *him*

Demetrius I Soter. **3:10–12** Victory over *Apollonius*, the governor of Samaria, at the battle of Nahal el-Haramiah (Wadi Haramia). **3:10** As David used Goliath's sword after defeating him (1 Sam. 17:51), Judas uses Apollonius's sword. **3:13–26** Victory over *Seron* near *Beth-horon*. The familiar narrow terrains of *Beth-horon* offer an advantage for an ambush. The narrative weaves three series of biblical battle scenes—Jonathan's battle when he had not eaten all day (1 Sam. 14), Gideon's account of defeating a much larger army with a modest group (Judg. 7), and Joshua's success (Josh. 10).
   3:27–31 The policy of Antiochus. 3:27–31 *Antiochus* is running out of resources to finance his military campaigns. With funds exhausted, he plans to extract additional silver and gold from Persia. Appian (*Hist. rom.* 11.66) says that Antiochus IV died while looting a temple in Elam. **3:32–37** *Lysias*, of *royal lineage*, has the prominent title of "kinsman of the king" (2 Macc. 11:35). Lysias assumes command over one-half of the military, including (all) the elephants, when Antiochus IV leaves for

over to Lysias[j] half of his forces and the elephants and gave him orders about all that he wanted done. As for the residents of Judea and Jerusalem, [35]Lysias was to send a force against them to wipe out and destroy the strength of Israel and the remnant of Jerusalem; he was to banish the memory of them from the place, [36]settle strangers in all their territory, and distribute their land by lot. [37]Then the king took the remaining half of his forces and left Antioch his capital in the one hundred and forty-seventh year. He crossed the Euphrates River and went through the upper provinces.

38 Lysias chose Ptolemy son of Dorymenes and Nicanor and Gorgias, able men among the Friends of the king, [39]and sent with them forty thousand infantry and seven thousand cavalry to go into the land of Judah and destroy it, as the king had commanded. [40]So they set out with their entire force, and when they arrived they encamped near Emmaus in the plain. [41]When the traders of the region heard what was said to them, they took silver and gold in immense amounts and fetters[k] and went to the camp to get the Israelites for slaves. And forces from Syria and the land of the Philistines[l] joined with them.

42 Now Judas and his brothers saw that misfortunes had increased and that the forces were encamped in their territory. They also learned what the king had commanded to do to the people to cause their final destruction. [43]But they said to one another, "Let us restore the ruins of our people and fight for our people and the sanctuary." [44]So the congregation assembled to be ready for battle and to pray and ask for mercy and compassion.

[45] Jerusalem was uninhabited like a
    wilderness;
  not one of her children went in or out.
The sanctuary was trampled down,
  and strangers held the citadel;

it was a lodging place for the nations.
Joy was taken from Jacob;
  the flute and the harp ceased to play.

46 Then they gathered together and went to Mizpah, opposite Jerusalem, because Israel formerly had a place of prayer in Mizpah. [47]They fasted that day, put on sackcloth, and sprinkled ashes on their heads, and tore their clothes. [48]And they opened the book of the law to inquire into those matters about which the nations consulted the likenesses of their gods. [49]They also brought the vestments of the priesthood and the first fruits and the tithes, and they stirred up the nazirites who had completed their days, [50]and they cried aloud to heaven, saying,

"What shall we do with these?
  Where shall we take them?
[51] Your sanctuary is trampled down and
    profaned,
  and your priests mourn in humiliation.
[52] Here the nations are assembled against us
    to destroy us;
  you know what they plot against us.
[53] How will we be able to withstand them,
  if you do not help us?"

54 Then they sounded the trumpets and gave a loud shout. [55]After this Judas appointed leaders of the people in charge of thousands and hundreds and fifties and tens. [56]Those who were building houses or were about to be married or were planting a vineyard or were fainthearted, he told to go home, according to the law. [57]Then the army marched out and encamped to the south of Emmaus.

58 And Judas said, "Arm yourselves and be courageous. Be ready early in the morning to fight with these nations who have assembled against us to destroy us and our sanctuary. [59]It is better for us to die in battle than to see the misfortunes of our nation and of the

j 3.34 Gk him k 3.41 Syr: Gk Vg slaves l 3.41 Gk foreigners

war in 165 BCE. **3:36** To take land away from inhabitants and *distribute their land* to settled aliens was the practice of the Greeks and Persians.

3:38–60 Preparations for battle. 3:39 The size of the military, *forty thousand infantry and seven thousand cavalry*, is larger than the twenty thousand reported in 2 Macc. 8:9. **3:41** Slave traders notice the possibility of high profit from enslavement upon the defeat of Judeans. **3:47–56** After fasting and repenting, the *book of the law* is consulted for battle. Deuteronomy 20:1–9 says an exemption from conscription into war can fall under the following categories: a man has recently built a house, married, or planted a vineyard or is afraid; the exceptions may be an ideal rather than actual practice, but nevertheless, they display compassion while creating a core of dedicated warriors. **3:58–59** Judas's speech invokes the mandate of heaven to grant him victory as they prepare for battle—fighting for their right to live, self-govern, and worship. See **"Judas Maccabeus," p. 1541**.

Focus On: *Judas Maccabeus (1 Maccabees 3)*

Rising up against the Seleucid king Antiochus IV, Judas Maccabeus continued the Maccabean Revolt started in 167 BCE by his father, Mattathias. Judas's various strategic military successes with smaller, more versatile special forces units ultimately led to victories securing independence for Judah. Their triumph was consecrated by the dedication of the new altar in the Jerusalem temple on the twenty-fifth of Chislev 164 BCE, replacing the one that was desecrated three years earlier by Antiochus IV. The Festival of Hanukkah (see **"Hanukkah," p. 1544**) commemorates the event. As a result, Judah became an independent kingdom for the first time since King Jehoiachin was forced to relinquish his throne in 597 BCE to the Babylonians.

Judas Maccabeus came from the priestly family of Joarib. He was the third of five brothers (the others were Jonathan, Eleazar, Simon, and John; 1 Macc. 2:1–5). They took up arms for counteroffensive measures to defend Judah, its peoples, and its institutions. He was given the name Maccabeus, which may come from the Aramaic word for "hammer" or is a shortened form of a Hebrew phrase meaning "to be marked or designated by YHWH." His major battle victories include the defeat of Apollonius at the battle of Nahal el-Haramiah (1 Macc. 3:10–12); the defeat of Seron near Beth-horon (1 Macc. 3:13–26); the victory over Gorgias at the battle of Emmaus (1 Macc. 3:38–4:25; 2 Macc. 8:8–36); the defeat of Lysias at Beth-zur, south of Jerusalem (1 Macc. 4:26–35; cf. 2 Macc. 11:1–15); and the victory over Nicanor at Adasa (1 Macc. 7:26–50; 2 Macc. 15:1–36).

Judas never took up the high priesthood. In 1 Macc. 3:1–9, the author remembers Judas's military genius and his religious zeal. During a strategically planned counter maneuver that targeted him (Nisan, 160 BCE; 1 Macc. 9:1–18), Judas died in the battle of Elasa. He was buried in Modein (1 Macc. 9:19–21).

In reception history, Judas Maccabeus is immortalized in paintings by Peter Paul Rubens, among others, and in music by Handel, in the oratorio *Judas Maccabaeus*.

John Ahn

sanctuary. [60]But as his will in heaven may be, so shall he do."

4 Now Gorgias took five thousand infantry and one thousand picked cavalry, and this division moved out by night [2]to fall upon the camp of the Jews and attack them suddenly. Men from the citadel were his guides. [3]But Judas heard of it, and he and his warriors moved out to attack the king's force in Emmaus [4]while the division was still absent from the camp. [5]When Gorgias entered the camp of Judas by night, he found no one there, so he looked for them in the hills, because he said, "These men are running away from us."

[6]At daybreak Judas appeared in the plain with three thousand men, but they did not have armor and swords such as they desired. [7]And they saw the camp of the nations, strong and fortified, with cavalry all around it, and these men were trained in war. [8]But Judas said to those who were with him, "Do not fear their numbers or be afraid when they charge. [9]Remember how our ancestors were saved at the Red Sea, when Pharaoh with his forces pursued them. [10]And now, let us cry to heaven to see whether he will favor us and remember his covenant with our ancestors and crush this army before us today. [11]Then all the nations will know that there is one who redeems and saves Israel."

[12] When the foreigners looked up and saw them coming against them, [13]they went out from their camp to battle. Then the men with Judas blew their trumpets [14]and engaged in battle. The nations were crushed and fled into the plain, [15]and all those in the rear fell by the sword. They pursued them to Gazara and to the plains of Idumea and to Azotus and Jamnia, and three thousand of them fell. [16]Then Judas and his force turned back from

4:1–25 Battle at Emmaus. 4:1 *Five thousand infantry* and *one thousand . . . cavalry* are exaggerations to make the participants in the battle more dramatic. **4:2** *Men from the citadel* includes Judeans who offer their services to the Seleucids. **4:5** *Gorgias* leaving camp to look for Judas in the hills is an attempt to execute a surprise attack. **4:8–10** Judas gives a battle speech to allay his troops' reluctance and fear. **4:15** *Gazara, the plains of Idumea, Azotus,* and *Jamnia* are regions and cities where the gentiles fled. The mention of these cities, though difficult to assess their full historical veracity, adds literary contour. **4:16–25** An important feature of ancient warfare is the

pursuing them, [17]and he said to the people, "Do not be greedy for plunder, for there is a battle before us; [18]Gorgias and his force are near us in the hills. But stand now against our enemies and fight them and afterward seize the plunder boldly."

[19] Just as Judas was finishing this speech, a detachment appeared coming out of the hills. [20]They saw that their army[m] had been put to flight and that the Jews[n] were burning the camp, for the smoke that was seen showed what had happened. [21]When they perceived this, they were greatly frightened, and when they also saw the army of Judas drawn up in the plain for battle, [22]they all fled into the land of the Philistines.[o] [23]Then Judas returned to plunder the camp, and they seized a great amount of gold and silver, and cloth dyed blue and sea purple, and great riches. [24]On their return they sang hymns and praises to heaven: "For he is good, for his mercy endures forever." [25]Thus Israel had a great deliverance that day.

[26] Those of the foreigners who escaped went and reported to Lysias all that had happened. [27]When he heard it, he was perplexed and discouraged, for things had not happened to Israel as he had intended, nor had they turned out as the king had ordered. [28]But the next year he mustered sixty thousand picked infantry and five thousand cavalry to subdue them. [29]They came into Idumea and encamped at Beth-zur, and Judas met them with ten thousand men.

[30] When he saw that their army was strong, he prayed, saying, "Blessed are you, O Savior of Israel, who crushed the attack of the mighty warrior by the hand of your servant David and gave the camp of the Philistines into the hands of Jonathan son of Saul and of the man who carried his armor. [31]Hem in this army by the hand of your people Israel, and let them be ashamed of their troops and their cavalry. [32]Fill them with cowardice; melt the boldness of their strength; let them tremble in their destruction. [33]Strike them down with the sword of those who love you, and let all who know your name praise you with hymns."

[34] Then both sides attacked, and there fell of the army of Lysias five thousand men; they fell before them.[p] [35]When Lysias saw the rout of his troops and observed the boldness that inspired those of Judas and how ready they were either to live or to die nobly, he withdrew to Antioch and enlisted mercenaries in order to invade Judea again with an even larger army.

[36] Then Judas and his brothers said, "See, our enemies are crushed; let us go up to cleanse the sanctuary and dedicate it." [37]So all the army assembled and went up to Mount Zion. [38]There they saw the sanctuary desolate, the altar profaned, and the gates burned. In the courts they saw bushes sprung up as in a thicket or as on one of the mountains. They saw also the chambers of

m 4.20 Gk *they*   n 4.20 Gk *they*   o 4.22 Gk *foreigners*
p 4.34 Or *and some fell on the opposite side*

collection of spoils and plunder after victory. Only after the plunder, if deemed totally unprofitable or for revenge, is the camp or town set on fire. Judas's military strategy is ingenious. He sets fire and burns the camp first, signaling that the battle is over. It is a risky tactic. As Gorgias returns, he and his men could have easily regrouped, but seeing the fire and smoke, Gorgias's army flees, thinking they are defeated. **4:17** Judas warns his people—not a professional army—*Do not be greedy for plunder*. After victory, his people return to claim the spoils of war. **4:19–22** As the *detachment* from Gorgias's army appears over the hill, there is already chaos, fire, and smoke—*burning the camp*—scattering the Seleucid army. The detachment becomes *greatly frightened* and also flees *into the land of the Philistines*. Like Gideon in Judges, who caused confusion in the enemy, Judas uses psychological warfare to disrupt and then defeat a larger army. **4:23** After routing them, Judas and the people plunder the camp. The words *they seized a great amount of gold and silver, and cloth dyed blue and sea purple, and great riches* are an interpolation to enhance the battle story, with attention to material goods—the supply side of ancient war economics. **4:24** Returning from battle, they sing a "thanksgiving psalm," quoting the refrain from Ps. 136: *For he [God] is good, for his mercy endures forever.*

4:26–35 First campaign of Lysias. Records the events of 164 BCE with *Lysias*, who is also defeated not once but twice by Judas and his forces. **4:30–33** Judas's prayer for deliverance recalls David and Jonathan (Saul's son) and asks for the enemies' *cowardice*.

4:36–61 Dedication of the temple. This passage offers a thoughtful appropriation of the torah, restoring the altar of *unhewn stones*, with *new holy vessels, the lampstand, the altar of incense,* and

the priests in ruins. [39]Then they tore their clothes and mourned with great lamentation; they sprinkled themselves with ashes [40]and fell face down on the ground. And they blew the signal trumpets, and they cried out to heaven.

41 Then Judas detailed men to fight against those in the citadel until he had cleansed the sanctuary. [42]He chose blameless priests devoted to the law, [43]and they cleansed the sanctuary and removed the defiled stones to an unclean place. [44]They deliberated what to do about the altar of burnt offering, which had been profaned. [45]And they thought it best to tear it down, so that it would not be a lasting shame to them that the nations had defiled it. So they tore down the altar [46]and stored the stones in a convenient place on the temple hill until a prophet should come to tell what to do with them. [47]Then they took unhewn[q] stones, as the law directs, and built a new altar like the former one. [48]They also rebuilt the sanctuary and the interior of the temple and consecrated the courts. [49]They made new holy vessels and brought the lampstand, the altar of incense, and the table into the temple. [50]Then they offered incense on the altar and lit the lamps on the lampstand, and these gave light in the temple. [51]They placed the bread on the table and hung up the curtains. Thus they finished all the work they had undertaken.

52 Early in the morning on the twenty-fifth day of the ninth month, which is the month of Chislev, in the one hundred forty-eighth year, [53]they rose and offered sacrifice, as the law directs, on the new altar of burnt offering that they had built. [54]At the very season and on the very day that the nations had profaned it, it was dedicated with songs and harps and lutes and cymbals. [55]All the people fell on their faces and worshiped and blessed heaven, who had prospered them. [56]So they celebrated the dedication of the altar for eight days and joyfully offered burnt offerings; they offered a sacrifice of well-being and a thanksgiving offering. [57]They decorated the front of the temple with golden crowns and small shields; they restored the gates and the chambers for the priests and fitted them with doors. [58]There was very great joy among the people, and the disgrace brought by the nations was removed.

59 Then Judas and his brothers and all the assembly of Israel determined that every year at that season the days of dedication of the altar should be observed with joy and gladness for eight days, beginning with the twenty-fifth day of the month of Chislev.

60 At that time they fortified Mount Zion with high walls and strong towers all around, to keep the nations from coming and trampling them down as they had done before. [61]Judas[r] stationed a garrison there to guard it; he also fortified Beth-zur to guard it, so that the people might have a stronghold that faced Idumea.

5 When the nations all around heard that the altar had been rebuilt and the sanctuary dedicated as it was before, they became very angry, [2]and they determined to destroy the descendants of Jacob who lived among them. So they began to kill and destroy among the people. [3]But Judas made war on the descendants of Esau in Idumea, at Akrabattene, because they kept lying in wait for Israel. He dealt them a heavy blow and humbled them and despoiled them. [4]He also remembered the wickedness of the sons of Baean, who were a trap and a snare to the people and ambushed them on the highways. [5]They were shut up by him in towers, and he encamped against them, vowed their complete destruction, and burned with fire their towers and all who were in them. [6]Then he crossed over to attack the Ammonites, where he found a strong band and many people, with Timothy as their leader. [7]He engaged in many battles

q 4.47 Gk whole   r 4.61 Gk He

the table back into the temple. **4:56** They *celebrated the dedication of the altar for eight days* (later commemorated as Hanukkah) and *offered burnt offerings, a sacrifice of well-being*, and a *thanksgiving offering*. See **"Hanukkah," p. 1544. 4:57** An interesting minor detail is noted—the decoration of *the front of the temple with golden crowns and small shields*. The golden crown is the symbol for the torah or torah shield from Aaron's breastplate, which would be recast in the Letter to the Ephesians as "the breastplate of righteousness" (Eph. 6:14).

5:1–8 Jealousy and hostility against the Judeans. This passage recalls the rivalry between *Jacob* and *Esau*, who becomes the ancestor of the Edomites (Gen. 36; Obadiah). *Akrabattene* is likely Akrabbim (Num. 34:4). The *sons of Baean* are likely nomads. **5:6** *Timothy*, a non-Ammonite name, is a late interpolation.

Making Connections: Hanukkah (1 Maccabees 4:59)

Hanukkah, also known as the Festival of Lights and the Festival of Dedication, is a Jewish festival remembering the rededication of the altar (1 Maccabees) and temple (2 Maccabees). Hanukkah additionally marks the liberation of the city-state Jerusalem from the Seleucids in 164 BCE.

Hanukkah is a Hebrew word that describes the consecration or "dedication" of a newly built house (Deut. 20:5). The word took on a broader meaning to include the dedication of the altar (Num. 7:10, 11, 84, 88; 2 Chr. 7:9), an iconic image (Dan. 3:2), the house of God (temple; Ezra 6:16, 17), and the city wall (Neh. 12:27).

In the book of 1 Maccabees, the Festival of Hanukkah commemorates Judas Maccabeus's rededication of the altar and the Jerusalem temple after the defeat of the Seleucid king Antiochus IV Epiphanes in 164 BCE. Three years earlier in 167 BCE, Antiochus IV had erected an idol for the Olympian Zeus in the Jerusalem temple (2 Macc. 6:2) with sacrifices mandated on its altar (1 Macc. 1:54). On the twenty-fifth of Chislev 164 BCE, Judas dedicated the new altar, holy vessels, the lampstand, the incense altar, and the table, which were brought into the temple (1 Macc. 4:36–56). The rededication of the altar (1 Macc. 4:59) was celebrated for eight days with sacrifices, songs, and praises (1 Macc. 4:52–56). In a different account, 2 Macc. 10 portrays the rededication of the entire temple and its broader political significance. In the 2 Maccabees account, the festival is a delayed celebration of the Festival of Booths (2 Macc. 1:9, 18; 2:16–18; 10:1–8; cf. Num. 7). Josephus calls the celebration the "Festival of Lights" (*Ant.* 12.7.7). In John 10:22, Hanukkah is referred to as the "Festival of the Dedication."

According to the Talmud, there are two distinctive traditions for lighting the lamps for Hanukkah (b. Shabbat 21b). According to the Shammaites, eight lamps were all displayed together on the first evening, and then the number of lamps was reduced by one each night until there was only one lamp on the eighth night. In contrast, the Hillelites began with one light and then added a light for each consecutive evening until there was a total of eight on the eighth night. According to a mythopoeic legend, uncontaminated oil was found by Judas, and this small amount of oil burned miraculously for eight days. Other later traditions associate Judith with Hanukkah, encouraging women to kindle the Hanukkah lights.

John Ahn

with them, and they were crushed before him; he struck them down. [8]He also took Jazer and its villages; then he returned to Judea.

9 Now the nations in Gilead gathered together against the Israelites who lived in their territory and planned to destroy them. But they fled to the stronghold of Dathema [10]and sent to Judas and his brothers letters that said, "The nations around us have gathered together to destroy us. [11]They are preparing to come and capture the stronghold to which we have fled, and Timothy is leading their forces. [12]Now then, come and rescue us from their hands, for many of us have fallen, [13]and all our kindred who were in the land of Tobias have been killed; the enemy[s] have captured their wives and children and goods and have destroyed about a thousand persons there."

14 While the letters were still being read, other messengers, with their garments torn, came from Galilee and made a similar report; [15]they said that the people of Ptolemais and Tyre and Sidon and all Galilee of the gentiles[t] had gathered together against them "to annihilate us." [16]When Judas and the people heard these messages, a great assembly was called to determine what they should do for their kindred who were in distress and were being attacked by enemies.[u] [17]Then Judas said to his brother Simon, "Choose your men and go and rescue your kindred in Galilee; Jonathan my brother and I will go to Gilead." [18]But he left Joseph, son of Zechariah, and Azariah, a leader of the people, with the rest of the forces in Judea to guard it, [19]and he gave them this command, "Take charge of this people, but do not engage in battle with the nations until we return." [20]Then three thousand men were assigned to Simon to go to Galilee and eight thousand to Judas for Gilead.

s 5.13 Gk *they*   t 5.15 Gk *foreigners*   u 5.16 Gk *them*

5:9–23 Liberation of Galilee. The motif to destroy the Israelites continues, now against those living *in Gilead*—east of Galilee—and Galilee. **5:13** *The land of Tobias* is "the land of Tob" in Judg. 11:3–5. **5:15–23** *Galilee of the gentiles* and migrant mercenary foreigners, the men of Ptolemais and Tyre, and Sidonians are said to have gathered *to annihilate us*. The literary hyperbole stirs the

21 So Simon went to Galilee and fought many battles against the nations, and the nations were crushed before him. [22]He pursued them to the gate of Ptolemais; as many as three thousand of the nations fell, and he despoiled them. [23]Then he took the Jews[v] of Galilee and Arbatta, with their wives and children, and all they possessed and led them to Judea with great rejoicing.

24 Judas Maccabeus and his brother Jonathan crossed the Jordan and made three days' journey into the wilderness. [25]They encountered the Nabateans, who met them peaceably and told them all that had happened to their kindred in Gilead: [26]"Many of them have been shut up in Bozrah and Bosor, in Alema and Chaspho, Maked and Carnaim"—all these towns were strong and large—[27]"and some have been shut up in the other towns of Gilead; the enemy[w] are getting ready to attack the strongholds tomorrow and capture and destroy all these people in a single day."

28 Then Judas and his army quickly turned back by the wilderness road to Bozrah, and he took the town and killed every male by the edge of the sword; then he seized all its spoils and burned it with fire. [29]He left the place at night, and they went all the way to the stronghold of Dathema.[x] [30]At dawn they looked out and saw a large company, which could not be counted, carrying ladders and engines of war to capture the stronghold and attacking the Jews within.[y] [31]So Judas saw that the battle had begun and that the cry of the town went up to heaven, with trumpets and loud shouts, [32]and he said to the men of his forces, "Fight today for your kindred!" [33]Then he came up behind them in three companies, who sounded their trumpets and cried aloud in prayer. [34]And when the army of Timothy realized that it was Maccabeus, they fled before him, and

he dealt them a heavy blow. As many as eight thousand of them fell that day.

35 Next he turned aside to Maapha[z] and fought against it and took it, and he killed every male in it, plundered it, and burned it with fire. [36]From there he marched on and took Chaspho, Maked, and Bosor and the other towns of Gilead.

37 After these things Timothy gathered another army and encamped opposite Raphon, on the other side of the stream. [38]Judas sent men to spy out the camp, and they reported to him, "All the nations around us have gathered to him; it is a very large force. [39]They also have hired Arabs to help them, and they are encamped across the stream ready to come and fight against you." And Judas went to meet them.

40 Now as Judas and his army drew near to the stream of water, Timothy said to the officers of his forces, "If he crosses over to us first, we will not be able to resist him, for he will surely defeat us. [41]But if he shows fear and camps on the other side of the river, we will cross over to him and defeat him." [42]When Judas approached the stream of water, he stationed the officers[a] of the army at the stream and gave them this command, "Permit no one to encamp, but make them all enter the battle." [43]Then he crossed over against them first, and the whole army followed him. All the nations were defeated before him, and they threw away their arms and fled into the sacred precincts at Carnaim. [44]But he took the town and burned the sacred precincts with fire, together with all who were in them. Thus Carnaim was conquered; they could stand before Judas no longer.

45 Then Judas gathered together all the Israelites in Gilead, the small and the great,

v 5.23 Gk those   w 5.27 Gk they   x 5.29 Gk lacks of Dathema   y 5.30 Gk and they were attacking them   z 5.35 Other ancient authorities read Alema   a 5.42 Or scribes

emotive response mustering Judas's men to rise up, defend, and save their people. **5:20** Simon and *three thousand men* go up to Galilee to fight against the gentiles, whereas Judas and *eight thousand* fight in Gilead.

5:24–44 Judas and Jonathan in Gilead. 5:25–27 *Nabateans* were traders and sought peace, pledging loyalty to whomever was in control of the political landscape. **5:29** The NRSVue inserts a reference to the city of *Dathema* (mentioned in 5:9), which is not in the Greek text. **5:30–34** A fictitious scene that mimics traditional narrations of battles. **5:35–36** *Maapha* (or "Alema" in some manuscripts), *Chaspho, Maked, Bosor,* and other towns constitute a running list. **5:43–44** To burn a town with all the people in it evokes painful (literary) judgment. *Carnaim's* local sanctuary for asylum seekers is not respected.

5:45–54 Return to Jerusalem. This unit is a reworking of a traditional literary trope, recalling the Israelites who were not permitted to pass through Edom in the wilderness (Num. 20:14–25:5).

with their wives and children and goods, a very large company, to go to the land of Judah. [46]So they came to Ephron. This was a large and very strong town on the road, and they could not go around it to the right or to the left; they had to go through it. [47]But the people of the town shut them out and blocked up the gates with stones.

48 Judas sent them this friendly message, "Let us pass through your land to get to our land. No one will do you harm; we will simply pass by on foot." But they refused to open to him. [49]Then Judas ordered proclamation to be made to the army that all should encamp where they were. [50]So the men of the forces encamped, and he fought against the town all that day and all the night, and the town was delivered into his hands. [51]He destroyed every male by the edge of the sword and razed and plundered the town. Then he passed through the town over the bodies of the dead.

52 Then they crossed the Jordan into the large plain before Beth-shan. [53]Judas kept rallying the laggards and encouraging the people all the way until he came to the land of Judah. [54]So they went up to Mount Zion with joy and gladness and offered burnt offerings because they had returned in safety; not one of them had fallen.

55 Now while Judas and Jonathan were in Gilead and their[b] brother Simon was in Galilee before Ptolemais, [56]Joseph son of Zechariah and Azariah, the commanders of the forces, heard of their brave deeds and of the heroic war they had fought. [57]So they said, "Let us also make a name for ourselves; let us go and make war on the nations around us." [58]So they issued orders to the men of the forces that were with them and marched against Jamnia. [59]Gorgias and his men came out of the town to meet them in battle. [60]Then Joseph and Azariah were routed and were pursued to the borders of Judea; as many as two thousand of the people of Israel fell that day. [61]Thus the people suffered a great rout because, thinking to

do a brave deed, they did not listen to Judas and his brothers. [62]But they did not belong to the family of those men through whom deliverance was given to Israel.

63 The man Judas and his brothers were greatly honored in all Israel and among all the nations, wherever their name was heard. [64]People gathered to them and praised them.

65 Then Judas and his brothers went out and fought the descendants of Esau in the land to the south. He struck Hebron and its villages and tore down its strongholds and burned its towers on all sides. [66]Then he marched off to go into the land of the Philistines[c] and passed through Marisa.[d] [67]On that day some priests who wished to do a brave deed fell in battle, for they went out to battle unwisely. [68]But Judas turned aside to Azotus in the land of the Philistines; he tore down their altars, and the carved images of their gods he burned with fire; he plundered the towns and returned to the land of Judah.

6 King Antiochus was going through the upper provinces when he heard that Elymais in Persia was a city famed for its wealth in silver and gold. [2]Its temple was very rich, containing golden shields, breastplates, and weapons left there by Alexander son of Philip, the Macedonian king who first reigned over the Greeks. [3]So he came and tried to take the city and plunder it, but he could not because his plan had become known to the citizens, [4]and they withstood him in battle. So he fled and in great disappointment left there to return to Babylon.

5 Then someone came to him in Persia and reported that the armies that had gone into the land of Judah had been routed; [6]that Lysias had gone first with a strong force but had turned and fled before the Jews;[e] that the Jews[f] had grown strong from the arms, supplies, and abundant spoils that they had taken from the

b 5.55 Gk his   c 5.66 Gk foreigners   d 5.66 Other ancient authorities read Samaria   e 6.6 Gk them   f 6.6 Gk they

5:55–64 Joseph and Azariah defeated. An imaginative scene of loss in battle, edited and interpolated by a later editor referencing Jamnia (Yavneh).
5:65–68 Loss and success. As in vv. 55–64, a reworked literary motif of a loss in battle attributed to disobeying Judas's orders. Priests who fell in battle evoke Korah and his rebellion in the wilderness against Moses (Num. 16:1–40). 5:68 In contrast, Judas has success. Azotus is Ashdod.
6:1–17 A conflation of two late failure narratives. The first is on Antiochus's failed attempt to plunder a pagan temple in Elam, with a later reflection on his death. The second rerecords the defeat of Lysias (cf. 3:32–4:35). These failure narratives are an introduction to Judas's major failures

armies they had cut down; [7]that they had torn down the abomination that he had erected on the altar in Jerusalem; and that they had surrounded the sanctuary with high walls as before, and also Beth-zur, his town.

8 When the king heard this news, he was astounded and badly shaken. He took to his bed and became sick from disappointment because things had not turned out for him as he had planned. [9]He lay there for many days because deep disappointment continually gripped him, and he realized that he was dying. [10]So he called all his Friends and said to them, "Sleep has departed from my eyes, and I am downhearted with worry. [11]I said to myself, 'To what distress I have come! And into what a great flood I now am plunged! For I was kind and beloved in my power.' [12]But now I remember the wrong I did in Jerusalem. I seized all its vessels of silver and gold, and I sent to destroy the inhabitants of Judah without good reason. [13]I know that it is because of this that these misfortunes have come upon me; here I am, perishing of bitter disappointment in a strange land."

14 Then he called for Philip, one of his Friends, and made him ruler over all his kingdom. [15]He gave him the crown and his robe and the signet so that he might guide his son Antiochus and bring him up to be king. [16]Thus King Antiochus died there in the one hundred forty-ninth year. [17]When Lysias learned that the king was dead, he set up Antiochus the king's[g] son to reign. Lysias[h] had brought him up from boyhood; he named him Eupator.

18 Meanwhile the garrison in the citadel kept hemming Israel in around the sanctuary. They were trying in every way to harm them and strengthen the nations. [19]Judas therefore resolved to destroy them and assembled all the people to besiege them.

[20]They gathered together and besieged the citadel[i] in the one hundred fiftieth year, and he built siege towers and engines of war. [21]But some of the garrison escaped from the siege, and some of the ungodly Israelites joined them. [22]They went to the king and said, "How long will you fail to do justice and to avenge our kindred? [23]We were happy to serve your father, to live by what he said, and to follow his commands. [24]For this reason the sons of our people besieged the citadel[j] and became hostile to us; moreover, they have put to death as many of us as they have caught, and they have seized our inheritances. [25]It is not against us alone that they have stretched out their hands; they have also attacked all the lands on their borders. [26]And see, today they have encamped against the citadel in Jerusalem to take it; they have fortified both the sanctuary and Beth-zur; [27]unless you quickly prevent them, they will do still greater things, and you will not be able to stop them."

28 The king was enraged when he heard this. He assembled all his Friends, the commanders of his forces and those in authority.[k] [29]Mercenary forces also came to him from other kingdoms and from islands of the seas. [30]The number of his forces was one hundred thousand foot soldiers, twenty thousand horsemen, and thirty-two elephants accustomed to war. [31]They came through Idumea and encamped against Beth-zur, and for many days they fought and built engines of war, but the Jews[l] sallied out and burned these with fire and fought courageously.

32 Then Judas marched away from the citadel and encamped at Beth-zechariah,

g 6.17 Gk *his*   h 6.17 Gk *He*   i 6.20 Gk *it*   j 6.24 Meaning of Gk uncertain   k 6.28 Gk *those over the reins*   l 6.31 Gk *they*

(6:18–63). **6:10** The title of "Friend" is one of nobility and political rank in the Seleucid Empire (cf. v. 14). *Friends* served as political advisors. **6:11–13** Although he views himself as *kind and beloved*, Antiochus IV repents for taking Jerusalem, which he interprets as the cause for his distress, anticipating his imminent death *in a strange* (or foreign) *land*. **6:17** Lysias helps establish Antiochus V—*Eupator*, meaning "good father"—as the next king.

6:18–31 The first account of attacks against Jerusalem by Judas. The city is occupied and controlled by the high priest Menelaus. The Jerusalem leaders complain to King Antiochus V that Judas and his men have put to death their loyal followers and taken their lands. **6:25** *Stretched out their hands.* A prophetic thematic element representing judgment or bringing plagues (e.g., Exod. 3:20; Isa. 9; Zeph. 1:4). The visual motif displays the opposite of a benediction against the enemy. **6:30** The inclusion of *thirty-two elephants* is a literary feature. **6:31** References to *Idumea* and encamping against *Beth-zur* are transitional markers for the full expansion in vv. 32–47.

6:32–47 Battle at Beth-zechariah. A mixed genre of eyewitness account with Homeric-style expressions and expansions, focusing on elephants and other animals used in battle (vv. 34–39).

opposite the camp of the king. [33]Early in the morning the king set out and took his army by a forced march along the road to Beth-zechariah, and his troops made ready for battle and sounded their trumpets. [34]They offered the elephants the juice of grapes and mulberries, to arouse them for battle. [35]They distributed the animals among the phalanxes; with each elephant they stationed a thousand men armed with coats of mail and with brass helmets on their heads, and five hundred picked horsemen were assigned to each beast. [36]These took their position beforehand wherever the animal was; wherever it went, they went with it, and they never left it. [37]On the elephants[m] were wooden towers, strong and covered; they were fastened on each animal by special harness, and on each were four[n] armed men who fought from there and also its Indian driver. [38]The rest of the cavalry were stationed on either side, on the two flanks of the army, to harass the enemy while being themselves protected by the phalanxes. [39]When the sun shone on the shields of gold and brass, the hills were ablaze with them and gleamed like flaming torches.

40 Now a part of the king's army was spread out on the high hills, and some troops were on the plain, and they advanced steadily and in good order. [41]All who heard the noise made by their multitude, by the marching of the multitude and the clanking of their arms, trembled, for the army was very large and strong. [42]But Judas and his army advanced to the battle, and six hundred of the king's army fell. [43]Now Eleazar, called Avaran, saw that one of the animals was equipped with royal armor. It was taller than all the others, and he supposed that the king was on it. [44]So he gave his life to save his people and to win for himself an everlasting name. [45]He courageously ran into the midst of the phalanx to reach it; he killed men right and left, and they parted before him on both sides. [46]He got under the elephant, stabbed it from beneath, and killed it, but it fell to the ground upon him and he died. [47]When the Jews[o] saw the royal might and the fierce attack of the forces, they turned away in flight.

48 The soldiers of the king's army went up to Jerusalem against them, and the king encamped in Judea and at Mount Zion. [49]He made peace with the people of Beth-zur, and they evacuated the town because they had no provisions there to withstand a siege, since it was a sabbatical year for the land. [50]So the king took Beth-zur and stationed a guard there to hold it. [51]Then he encamped before the sanctuary for many days. He set up siege towers, engines of war, devices to throw fire and stones, machines to shoot arrows, and catapults. [52]The Jews[p] also made engines of war to match theirs and fought for many days. [53]But they had no food in storage,[q] because it was the seventh year; those who had found safety in Judea from the nations had consumed the last of the stores. [54]Only a few men were left in the sanctuary; the rest scattered to their own homes, for the famine proved too much for them.

55 Then Lysias heard that Philip, whom King Antiochus while still living had

m 6.37 Gk *them* *n* 6.37 Cn: Ancient authorities read *thirty* or *thirty-two* *o* 6.47 Gk *they* *p* 6.52 Gk *They* *q* 6.53 Other ancient authorities read *in the sanctuary*

The reference to the *Indian* elephant *driver* (v. 37) suggests the original background of the story, pertaining to Alexander the Great's eastward campaigns with his phalanx toward the kingdoms of Ganges and Chandragupta. The story fixates on *Eleazar, called Avaran*, who successfully and tragically kills an elephant from underneath, only to have it crush him to death (vv. 43–46). Judas's men are demoralized by the size of the Seleucid force—Judas's first major defeat (v. 47).

6:48–54 Siege of the temple. *Peace* is used as a tactic to gain the upper hand with *the people of Beth-zur*, who were without provision from the siege. *Since it was a sabbatical year* is a literary insertion to provoke religious empathy and a pretext to explain why there was a lack of food during the siege against Jerusalem (vv. 55–63).

6:55–63 Syria offers terms. The apex of the narrative arc, where Lysias defeats both Philip (upon his return from Persia) and Judas. Lysias has to act quickly to prevent the siege against him. He offers *peace* to Judas and his men in the Temple Mount as they struggle against the siege without food. They accept the terms with an assurance of local governance. This permits Lysias and his men to enter the city, upon which he nullifies the oath of peace and tears down the wall (v. 62). The narrative records the second but greatest failure of Judas and his men for trusting the words of Lysias, resulting in the loss and the fall of the city of Jerusalem.

appointed to bring up his son Antiochus to be king, [56]had returned from Persia and Media with the forces that had gone with the king and that he was trying to seize control of the government. [57]So he quickly gave orders to withdraw and said to the king, to the commanders of the forces, and to the troops, "Daily we grow weaker, our food supply is scant, the place against which we are fighting is strong, and the affairs of the kingdom press urgently on us. [58]Now, then, let us come to terms with these people and make peace with them and with all their nation. [59]Let us agree to let them live by their laws as they did before, for it was on account of their laws that we abolished that they became angry and did all these things."

[60] The speech pleased the king and the commanders, and he sent to the Jews[r] an offer of peace, and they accepted it. [61]So the king and the commanders gave them their oath. On these conditions the Jews[s] evacuated the stronghold. [62]But when the king entered Mount Zion and saw what a strong fortress the place was, he broke the oath he had sworn and gave orders to tear down the wall all around. [63]Then he set off in haste and returned to Antioch. He found Philip in control of the city, but he fought against him and took the city by force.

7 In the one hundred fifty-first year Demetrius son of Seleucus set out from Rome, sailed with a few men to a town by the sea, and there began to reign. [2]As he was entering the royal palace of his ancestors, the army seized Antiochus and Lysias to bring them to him. [3]But when this act became known to him, he said, "Do not let me see their faces!" [4]So the army killed them, and Demetrius took his seat on the throne of his kingdom.

[5] Then there came to him all the renegade and godless men of Israel; they were led by Alcimus, who wanted to be high priest. [6]They brought to the king this accusation against the people: "Judas and his brothers have destroyed all your Friends and have driven us out of our land. [7]Now, then, send a man whom you trust; let him go and see all the ruin that Judas[t] has brought on us and on the land of the king, and let him punish them and all who help them."

[8] So the king chose Bacchides, one of the king's Friends, governor of the province Beyond the River; he was a great man in the kingdom and was faithful to the king. [9]He sent him, and with him he sent the ungodly Alcimus, whom he made high priest, and he commanded him to take vengeance on the Israelites. [10]So they marched away and came with a large force into the land of Judah, and he sent messengers to Judas and his brothers with peaceable but treacherous words. [11]But they paid no attention to their words, for they saw that they had come with a large force.

[12] Then a group of scribes appeared in a body before Alcimus and Bacchides to ask for just terms. [13]The Hasideans were first among the Israelites to seek peace from them, [14]for they said, "A priest of the line of Aaron has come with the army, and he will not harm us." [15]Alcimus[u] spoke peaceable words to them and swore this oath to them, "We will not seek to injure you or your friends." [16]So they trusted him, but he seized sixty of them and killed them in one day, in accordance with the word that was written,

[17] "The flesh of your faithful ones and their blood

they poured out all around Jerusalem,
and there was no one to bury them."
[18]Then the fear and dread of them fell on all the people, for they said, "There is no truth

r 6.60 Gk them   s 6.61 Gk they   t 7.7 Gk he   u 7.15 Gk He

7:1–25 A new period of rule under Demetrius I begins in Judea. The text records the execution of both Antiochus and Lysias. *Alcimus* (Heb. "El-Kim," "God arise") offers his services as high priest and local ruler in exchange for taking down Judas and his men. Antiochus IV had appointed Jason after Onias III (Onias's brother). Jason was replaced by Menelaus, who was put to death in 162 BCE after reigning for ten years. Onias III fled to Egypt, establishing a temple in Heliopolis (Cairo). According to Josephus, Alcimus was also called Jacimus (Heb. "Yakim," "YHWH arise") and was not from a high priest lineage (*Ant.* 12.9–11). **7:8–11** Demetrius selects and sends Bacchides—*one of the king's Friends* and governor of the province between Egypt and the Euphrates—with Alcimus, *whom he made high priest*, to subdue Judas. **7:12–20** A second account of Alcimus's rise to power with the help of loyal Hasideans, who claim Alcimus is from the priestly line of Aaron to confront the Maccabean priestly lineage to Phineas. **7:16–18** Alcimus executes sixty nonloyal Hasideans to assert his

or justice in them, for they have violated the agreement and the oath that they swore."

19 Then Bacchides withdrew from Jerusalem and encamped in Beth-zaith. And he sent and seized many of the men who had deserted to him,[v] and some of the people, and killed them and threw them into a great pit. [20]He placed Alcimus in charge of the country and left with him a force to help him; then Bacchides went back to the king.

21 Alcimus struggled to maintain his high priesthood, [22]and all who were troubling their people joined him. They gained control of the land of Judah and did great damage in Israel. [23]And Judas saw all the wrongs that Alcimus and those with him had done among the Israelites; it was more than the nations had done. [24]So Judas[w] went out into all the surrounding parts of Judea, taking vengeance on those who had deserted and preventing those in the city[x] from going out into the country. [25]When Alcimus saw that Judas and those with him had grown strong and realized that he could not withstand them, he returned to the king and brought malicious charges against them.

26 Then the king sent Nicanor, one of his honored princes, who hated and detested Israel, and he commanded him to destroy the people. [27]So Nicanor came to Jerusalem with a large force and treacherously sent to Judas and his brothers this peaceable message, [28]"Let there be no fighting between you and me; I shall come with a few men to see you face to face in peace."

29 So he came to Judas, and they greeted one another peaceably, but the enemy were preparing to kidnap Judas. [30]It became known to Judas that Nicanor[y] had come to him with treacherous intent, and he was afraid of him and would not meet him again. [31]When Nicanor learned that his plan had been disclosed,

he went out to meet Judas in battle near Caphar-salama. [32]About five hundred of the army of Nicanor fell, and the rest[z] fled into the city of David.

33 After these events Nicanor went up to Mount Zion. Some of the priests from the sanctuary and some of the elders of the people came out to greet him peaceably and to show him the burnt offering that was being offered for the king. [34]But he mocked them and derided them and defiled them and spoke arrogantly, [35]and in anger he swore this oath, "Unless Judas and his army are delivered into my hands this time, then if I return safely I will burn up this house." And he went out in great anger. [36]At this the priests went in and stood before the altar and the temple; they wept and said,

[37] "You chose this house to be called by your name
    and to be for your people a house of prayer and supplication.
[38] Take vengeance on this man and on his army,
    and let them fall by the sword;
  remember their blasphemies,
    and let them live no longer."

39 Now Nicanor went out from Jerusalem and encamped in Beth-horon, and the Syrian army joined him. [40]Judas encamped in Adasa with three thousand men. Then Judas prayed and said, [41]"When the messengers from the king spoke blasphemy, your angel went out and struck down one hundred eighty-five thousand of the Assyrians.[a] [42]So also crush this army before us today; let the rest learn that Nicanor[b] has spoken wickedly against the sanctuary, and judge him according to this wickedness."

v 7.19 Or *many of his men who had deserted*   w 7.24 Gk *he*
x 7.24 Gk *and they were prevented*   y 7.30 Gk *he*   z 7.32 Gk
they   a 7.41 Gk *of them*   b 7.42 Gk *he*

power over Jerusalem and Judea. **7:21–25** Judas rejects Alcimus's authority and practices guerrilla warfare to spread fear during Alcimus's reign.

7:26–50 Threat and defeat of Nicanor. 7:26–32 Nicanor is sent by the king to subdue the Judeans. The initial talk of *peace* between Nicanor and Judas is intended to stage a kidnaping of Judas. Second Maccabees 14:18–25 has a different account where the two meet to develop a relationship toward a modicum of peace. **7:32** This account has the Seleucids flee *into the city of David*, Jerusalem, voicing and generating an emotional reaction, when it was likely the city of Akra. **7:33–35** Nicanor threatens the temple if Judas is not handed over to him. **7:36–38** The priests pray for vengeance and retribution against Nicanor and his army, including the wish to have them all die *by the sword* for *blasphemies*. **7:39–42** Judas also prays for vengeance, recounting an event where an angel went out to strike down *one hundred eighty-five thousand* of them. The English translation inserts *the Assyrians*, making the prayer refer to Sennacherib's siege of Jerusalem in 701 BCE, where

43 So the armies met in battle on the thirteenth day of the month of Adar. The army of Nicanor was crushed, and he himself was the first to fall in the battle. ⁴⁴When his army saw that Nicanor had fallen, they threw down their arms and fled. ⁴⁵The Jews^c pursued them a day's journey, from Adasa as far as Gazara, and as they followed they kept sounding the battle call on the trumpets. ⁴⁶People came out of all the surrounding villages of Judea, and they outflanked the enemy^d and drove them back to their pursuers,^e so that they all fell by the sword; not even one of them was left. ⁴⁷Then the Jews^f seized the spoils and the plunder; they cut off Nicanor's head and the right hand that he had so arrogantly stretched out and brought them and displayed them just outside Jerusalem. ⁴⁸The people rejoiced greatly and celebrated that day as a day of great gladness. ⁴⁹They decreed that this day should be celebrated each year on the thirteenth day of Adar. ⁵⁰So the land of Judah had rest for a few days.

8 Now Judas heard of the fame of the Romans, that they were very strong and were well-disposed toward all who made an alliance with them, that they pledged friendship to those who came to them, ²and that they were very strong. He had been told of their wars and of the brave deeds that they were doing among the Gauls, how they had defeated them and forced them to pay tribute, ³and what they had done in the land of Spain to get control of the silver and gold

mines there, ⁴and how they had gained control of the whole region by their planning and patience, even though the place was far distant from them. They also subdued the kings who came against them from the ends of the earth, until they crushed them and inflicted great disaster on them; the survivors paid them tribute every year. ⁵They had crushed in battle and conquered Philip, and King Perseus of the Macedonians,^g and the others who rose up against them. ⁶They also had defeated Antiochus the Great, king of Asia, who went to fight against them with one hundred twenty elephants and with cavalry and chariots and a very large army. He was crushed by them; ⁷they took him alive and decreed that he and those who would reign after him should pay a heavy tribute and give hostages and surrender some of their best provinces: ⁸the countries of India, Media, and Lydia. These they took from him and gave to King Eumenes. ⁹The Greeks planned to come and destroy them, ¹⁰but this became known to them, and they sent a general against the Greeks^h and attacked them. Many of them were wounded and fell, and the Romansⁱ took captive their wives and children; they plundered them, conquered the land, tore down their strongholds, and enslaved them to this day. ¹¹The remaining kingdoms and islands, as many as ever opposed them, they destroyed and enslaved,

c 7.45 Gk They   d 7.46 Gk them   e 7.46 Gk these
f 7.47 Gk they   g 8.5 Or Kittim   h 8.10 Gk them
i 8.10 Gk they

the original text is ambiguous. *Adasa* is seven miles from Beth-horon. **7:43–50** The battle takes place in *the month of Adar* (March) 161/160 BCE. **7:44** When Nicanor is injured, the army scatters. **7:45–47** *The Jews* (Gk. "they") may refer to the army of Judas but more likely to the villagers who join the pursuit of Nicanor. **7:49** The defeat of Nicanor is to *be celebrated each year*. Ta'anit 18a–b mentions Yom Nicanor (Nicanor's Day), on which fasting is prohibited.

8:1–32 Rise of the Romans. This entire chapter was written and added to document the idealized Romans who governed the vast republic. References to the Roman defeat of Gaul and Spain are broadly sketched out but represent a more complex issue. The Cisalpine conflicts between the Romans and the Gauls began as early as 390 BCE—including the Second Punic War (218–201), during which Carthage was defeated—and ended in 193 BCE. The Transalpine conflicts between the Romans and the Gauls were between 125 BCE and 27 BCE. The Roman conquest of Spain took place in two stages: the first from 205 BCE (defeat of the Carthaginians) to 133 BCE (fall of Numantia) and the second from 29 to 18 BCE. This background suggests the historical and social context of the final form of 1 Maccabees. **8:5** Dated between 197 and 168 BCE, when Philip V of Macedonia was defeated at Cynoscephalae in 197 BCE and his son, Perseus, defeated at Pydna in 168 BCE. **8:6–8** Judean scribes interjected details demonstrating their knowledge of Asia, India, Media, and Lydia along with the defeat of *Antiochus the Great*—that is, Antiochus III (189 BCE). Antiochus III is not captured but has to *pay a heavy tribute and give hostages*. The exotic reference to *elephants* reflects the literary imagination of Asian and North African contexts. **8:9–10** Roman defeat of *the Greeks* (the Achaean

¹²but with their friends and those who rely on them they have kept friendship. They have subdued kings far and near, and as many as have heard of their fame have feared them. ¹³Those whom they wish to help and to make kings, they make kings, and those whom they wish they depose, and they have been greatly exalted. ¹⁴Yet for all this not one of them has put on a crown or worn purple as a mark of pride, ¹⁵but they have built for themselves a senate chamber, and every day three hundred twenty senators constantly deliberate concerning the people, to govern them well. ¹⁶They trust one man each year to rule over them and to control all their land; they all heed the one man, and there is no envy or jealousy among them.

17 So Judas chose Eupolemus son of John son of Accos, and Jason son of Eleazar, and sent them to Rome to establish friendship and alliance ¹⁸and to free themselves from the yoke, for they saw that the kingdom of the Greeks was enslaving Israel completely. ¹⁹They went to Rome, a very long journey, and they entered the senate chamber and spoke as follows: ²⁰"Judas, who is also called Maccabeus, and his brothers and the people of the Jews have sent us to you to establish alliance and peace with you, so that we may be enrolled as your allies and friends." ²¹The proposal pleased them, ²²and this is a copy of the letter that they wrote in reply, on bronze tablets, and sent to Jerusalem to remain with them there as a memorial of peace and alliance:

23 "May all go well with the Romans and with the nation of the Jews at sea and on land forever, and may sword and enemy be far from them. ²⁴If war comes first to Rome or to any of their allies in all their dominion, ²⁵the nation of the Jews shall act as their allies wholeheartedly, as the occasion may indicate to them. ²⁶To the enemy that makes war they shall not give or supply grain, arms, money, or ships, just as Rome has decided, and they shall keep their obligations without receiving any return. ²⁷In the same way, if war comes first to the nation of the Jews, the Romans shall willingly act as their allies, as the occasion may indicate to them. ²⁸And to their enemies there shall not be given grain, arms, money, or ships, just as Rome has decided, and they shall keep these obligations and do so without deceit. ²⁹Thus on these terms the Romans make a treaty with the Jewish people. ³⁰If after these terms are in effect both parties shall determine to add or delete anything, they shall do so at their discretion, and any addition or deletion that they may make shall be valid.

31 "Concerning the wrongs that King Demetrius is doing to them, we have written

League of Greece) in 146 BCE. **8:15-16** Scribes have added inaccurate information. The Roman senate had three hundred senators, not *three hundred twenty*. In addition, not one but two consuls were selected every year. **8:17-30** The Jewish-Roman treaty probably took place not before Nicanor's defeat but upon Demetrius's arrival in Syria. The following timeline is more likely: in autumn 162, Demetrius arrives in Syria; in October 162, Jewish representatives arrive in Rome; and in late November or December 162, the representatives return to Jerusalem. All these events would be before Nicanor's defeat in 161 (chap. 7). The Jewish-Roman treaty would have been either a "foedus" (Lat. "treaty") or an "amicitia" ("friendship" between states), not "amicitia et societas," where military intervention would have been offered to a fully recognized state under the protection of Rome. Scholars have long thought the treaty was a "foedus iniquum" (a treaty between a superior state and a lesser state; not a "foedus aequum," which is between equal states)—that is, a permanent treaty between Rome and a "foederati" (allied) bound (lesser) state. A Roman commanding leader negotiated treaties (Lat. "foedera"), and the Roman senate confirmed them. Treaties were written on bronze tablets for public display (cf. v. 22), preserved in the temple or elsewhere. After 27 BCE, some states were called "socii et amici populi Romani" ("allies and friends of the Roman people"), an intermediary status between being a fully independent state and annexation as a Roman province. However, a "foedus" must be concluded with a formal religious sacrifice. The language of 8:20-23 lacks the construct of loving friendship (Gk. "philia") but simply adds the support for the Jewish military until the renewal in 12:1. Therefore, this is an "amicitia," a precursor to a "foederus"— freedom ("libertas") from Seleucids and that the Judeans/Jews should become friends of Rome. The hospitality (Lat. "hospitium") language accepts a personal relationship, but the "amicitia" does not require military assistance (only the "amicitia et societas" does). The editor of this text was well informed on the formal elements of Roman state treaties. **8:31-32** A late interpolation, this scribal

to him as follows, 'Why have you made your yoke heavy on our friends and allies the Jews? [32]If now they appeal again for help against you, we will defend their rights and fight you on sea and on land.'"

9 When Demetrius heard that Nicanor and his army had fallen in battle, he sent Bacchides and Alcimus into the land of Judah a second time, and with them the right wing of the army. [2]They went by the road that leads to Gilgal and encamped against Mesaloth in Arbela, and they took it and killed many people. [3]In the first month of the one hundred fifty-second year they encamped against Jerusalem; [4]then they marched off and went to Berea with twenty thousand foot soldiers and two thousand cavalry.

5 Now Judas was encamped in Elasa, and with him were three thousand picked men. [6]When they saw the huge number of the enemy forces, they were greatly frightened, and many slipped away from the camp, until no more than eight hundred of them were left.

7 When Judas saw that his army had slipped away and the battle was imminent, he was crushed in spirit, for he had no time to assemble them. [8]He became faint, but he said to those who were left, "Let us get up and go against our enemies. We may have the strength to fight them." [9]But they tried to dissuade him, saying, "We do not have the strength. Let us rather save our own lives now, and let us come back with our kindred and fight them, for we are too few." [10]But Judas said, "Far be it from me to do such a thing as to flee from them. If our time has come, let us die bravely for our kindred and leave no cause to question our honor."

11 Then the army of Bacchides[j] marched out from the camp and took its stand for the encounter. The cavalry was divided into two companies, and the slingers and the archers went ahead of the army, as did all the chief warriors. [12]Bacchides was on the right wing. Flanked by the two companies, the phalanx advanced to the sound of the trumpets, and the men with Judas also blew their trumpets. [13]The earth was shaken by the noise of the armies, and the battle raged from morning until evening.

14 Judas saw that Bacchides and the strength of his army were on the right; then all the courageous men went with him, [15]and they crushed the right wing, and he pursued them as far as Mount Azotus. [16]When those on the left wing saw that the right wing was crushed, they turned and followed close behind Judas and his men. [17]The battle became desperate, and many on both sides were wounded and fell. [18]Judas also fell, and the rest fled.

19 Then Jonathan and Simon took their brother Judas and buried him in the tomb of their ancestors at Modein [20]and wept for him. All Israel made great lamentation for him; they mourned many days and said,

[21] "How is the mighty fallen,
the savior of Israel!"

[22]Now the rest of the acts of Judas, and his wars and the brave deeds that he did, and his greatness have not been recorded because they were very many.

j 9.11 Gk lacks of Bacchides

postscript points to the one who originated the actual treaty—Demetrius, not Judas, since only a Roman can draw up a treaty.

9:1–22 Death of Judas. Judas's guerrilla militia faces a highly organized Syrian army. Josephus (*Ant.* 12.11.1) says they started in Antioch, encamped at Arbela in Galilee (not Gilgal), took captive migrants hiding or having fled into caves, and marched to Jerusalem. **9:4** *Berea*, or el-Bireh, is opposite from Ramallah, which is about ten miles north of Jerusalem. *Twenty thousand foot soldiers and two thousand cavalry.* A Roman legion consisted of between 4,200 and 5,000 (sometimes as many as 6,000) men. **9:5–6** *Three thousand* is an exaggeration, leaving just *eight hundred* men. **9:11–12** *Phalanx.* A square or rectangular military formation (initially sixteen by sixteen soldiers) with spears and shields, protecting the bearer to the left. The right flank was usually half-exposed or vulnerable. **9:14–18** The *right wing* or flank collapses, forcing Bacchides and his men to flee, but this was a tactic as they go toward *Mount Azotus* (el-'Asur, six miles northwest of el-Bireh), setting up a trap. When Judas and his men pursue them thinking that they have achieved a breach, the left flank attacks Judas and his men. Judas is killed with several of his men, while others flee. **9:19–22** Jonathan and Simon take Judas's body and bury it in *Modein* (cf. 2:1, 70; 13:27–30). **9:21–22** *How is the mighty fallen* echoes 2 Sam. 1:19. *Now the rest of the acts of Judas . . . have not been recorded* echoes 1 Kgs. 11:41. The use of these traditions honors the fallen in the literary form of a monarchial annal.

23 After the death of Judas, the renegades emerged in all parts of Israel; all the wrongdoers reappeared. 24In those days a very great famine occurred, and the country went over to their side. 25Bacchides chose the godless and put them in charge of the country. 26They made inquiry and searched for the friends of Judas and brought them to Bacchides, who took vengeance on them and made sport of them. 27So there was great distress in Israel such as had not been since the time a prophet had last appeared among them.

28 Then all the friends of Judas assembled and said to Jonathan, 29"Since the death of your brother Judas there has been no one like him to go against our enemies and Bacchides and to deal with those of our nation who hate us. 30Now, therefore, we have chosen you today to take his place as our ruler and leader, to fight our battle." 31So Jonathan accepted the leadership at that time in place of his brother Judas.

32 When Bacchides learned of this, he tried to kill him. 33But Jonathan and his brother Simon and all who were with him heard of it, and they fled into the wilderness of Tekoa and camped by the water of the pool of Asphar. 34Bacchides found this out on the Sabbath day, and he with all his army crossed the Jordan.

35 So Jonathan[k] sent his brother as leader of the multitude and begged the Nabateans, who were his friends, for permission to store with them the great amount of baggage that they had. 36But the family of Jambri from Medeba came out and seized John and all that he had and left with it.

37 After these things it was reported to Jonathan and his brother Simon, "The family of Jambri are celebrating a great wedding and are conducting the bride, a daughter of one of the great nobles of Canaan, from Nadabath with a large escort." 38Remembering how their brother John had been killed, they went up and hid under cover of the mountain. 39They looked out and saw a tumultuous procession with a great amount of baggage, and the bridegroom came out with his friends and his brothers to meet them with tambourines and musicians and many weapons. 40Then they rushed on them from the ambush and began killing them. Many were wounded and fell, and the rest fled to the mountain, and the troops[l] took all their goods. 41So the wedding was turned into mourning and the voice of their musicians into a funeral dirge. 42After they had fully avenged the blood of their brother, they returned to the marshes of the Jordan.

43 When Bacchides heard of this, he came with a large force on the Sabbath day to the banks of the Jordan. 44And Jonathan said to those with him, "Let us get up now and fight for our lives, for today things are not as they were before. 45For look! The battle is in front of us and behind us; the water of the Jordan is on this side and on that, with marsh and thicket; there is no place to turn. 46Cry out now to heaven that you may be delivered from the hands of our enemies." 47So the battle began, and Jonathan stretched out his hand to strike Bacchides, but he eluded him and went to the rear. 48Then Jonathan and the men with him leaped into the Jordan and swam across to the other side, and Bacchides's troops[m] did not cross the Jordan to attack them. 49And about one thousand of Bacchides's men fell that day.

50 Then Bacchides[n] returned to Jerusalem and built strong cities in Judea: the

k 9.35 Gk *he* l 9.40 Gk *they* m 9.48 Gk *they* n 9.50 Gk *he*

9:23–12:53 Rebuilding the kingdom.
9:23–31 Jonathan succeeds Judas. With echoes of the postexilic prophets Haggai, Zechariah, and Malachi and the language of Judges, Jonathan is selected as Judas's military replacement (160 or 159 BCE) and, later, high priest in 152 BCE (10:21). 9:32–49 Jonathan's campaigns. Jonathan, Simon, and the regathered militia retreat to the wilderness of Tekoa (cf. 2 Sam. 14:1–17; 2 Chr. 20:20), about fifteen miles southeast of Jerusalem or five miles from Bethlehem. 9:35–42 John—Jonathan and Simon's brother (2:2)—is seized and killed by the sons of Jambri, the Nabateans. Jonathan avenges the death of his brother by ambushing and killing the sons of Jambri during a prominent wedding procession involving large emissaries of the bride's party from *the great nobles of Canaan, from Nadabath*—Nabateans. 9:43–49 Jonathan confronts Bacchides, who tries to trap him. Jonathan and his men fight relentlessly on the Sabbath. 9:50–53 Bacchides establishes garrisons to prevent attacks in Judea (Jericho, Emmaus, Bethhoron, Bethel) and Samaria (Timnath, Pharathon, Tephon). Children of Judean leaders are held as hostages to ensure cooperation and compliance by local leaders.

fortress in Jericho, and Emmaus, and Beth-horon, and Bethel, and Timnath, and[o] Pharathon, and Tephon, with high walls and gates and bars. [51]And he placed garrisons in them to harass Israel. [52]He also fortified the town of Beth-zur, and Gazara, and the citadel, and in them he put troops and stores of food. [53]And he took the sons of the leading men of the land as hostages and put them under guard in the citadel at Jerusalem.

54 In the one hundred and fifty-third year, in the second month, Alcimus gave orders to tear down the wall of the inner court of the sanctuary. He tore down the work of the prophets! [55]But he only began to tear it down, for at that time Alcimus was stricken, and his work was hindered; his mouth was stopped, and he was paralyzed, so that he could no longer say a word or give commands concerning his house. [56]And Alcimus died at that time in great agony. [57]When Bacchides saw that Alcimus was dead, he returned to the king, and the land of Judah had rest for two years.

58 Then all the lawless plotted and said, "See! Jonathan and his men are living in quiet and confidence. So now let us bring Bacchides back, and he will capture them all in one night." [59]And they went and consulted with him. [60]He started to come with a large force and secretly sent letters to all his allies in Judea telling them to seize Jonathan and his men, but they were unable to do it, because their plan became known. [61]And Jonathan's men[p] seized about fifty of the men of the country who were leaders in this treachery and killed them.

62 Then Jonathan with his men and Simon withdrew to Bethbasi in the wilderness; he rebuilt the parts of it that had been demolished, and they fortified it. [63]When Bacchides learned of this, he assembled all his forces and sent orders to the men of Judea. [64]Then he came and encamped against Bethbasi; he fought against it for many days and made engines of war.

65 But Jonathan left his brother Simon in the town while he went out into the country, and he went with only a few men. [66]He struck down Odomera and his kindred and the people of Phasiron in their tents. [67]Then he[q] began to attack and went into battle with his forces, and Simon and his men sallied out from the town and set fire to the engines of war. [68]They fought with Bacchides, and he was crushed by them. They pressed him very hard, for his plan and his expedition had been in vain. [69]So he was very angry at the renegades who had counseled him to come into the country, and he killed many of them. Then he decided to go back to his own land.

70 When Jonathan learned of this, he sent ambassadors to him to make peace with him and obtain release of the captives. [71]He agreed and did as he said, and he swore to Jonathan[r] that he would not try to harm him as long as he lived. [72]He restored to him the captives whom he had taken previously from the land of Judah; then he turned and went back to his own land and did not come again into their territory. [73]Thus the sword ceased from Israel. Jonathan settled in Michmash and began to judge the people, and he destroyed the godless out of Israel.

10 In the one hundred sixtieth year Alexander Epiphanes, son of Antiochus,

o 9.50 Some authorities omit and   p 9.61 Gk they
q 9.67 Other ancient authorities read they   r 9.71 Gk him

9:54–57 Death of Alcimus. 9:54 The wall of the inner court is demolished, granting access to nonpriests, including gentiles. This is a highly significant act aimed at reducing the political ambition and power of the ruling priests. **9:55–57** Alcimus experiences a stroke that leads to his death. *Was stricken* suggests the stroke is divine punishment.

9:58–73 End of the war. 9:58–69 The anti-Maccabean faction, the hellenized Judeans (*renegades*), plot to remove Jonathan. Bacchides returns in order to capture Jonathan, but Jonathan and his men are made aware of the covert plan and capture the fifty involved in the plot and execute them. **9:62** Jonathan withdraws to *Bethbasi* (Khibert Beti Bassa), three miles northeast of Tekoa. **9:69** Bacchides kills the renegades who counseled him. **9:70–73** A truce is established between Jonathan and Bacchides for seven years, until the conflict in 10:67–89. From 157 to 152 BCE, *Michmash* (Mukhmas), eight miles northeast of Jerusalem, is Jonathan's political center. **9:73** Jonathan is portrayed as ruling like the judges of premonarchal Israel.

10:1–21 Alexander Epiphanes revolts. Alexander I Epiphanes (from Ephesus) is given the name Balas (from Heb. "Ba'al"). He is the son of Antiochus IV. He reigns from 152 to 145 BCE as a Seleucid king. He grants Jonathan the high priesthood and friendship status (an official political appointment—a friend of the state/crown) in 10:18–20. **10:1** Alexander occupies Ptolemais (Acco) on the

landed and occupied Ptolemais. They welcomed him, and there he began to reign. [2]When King Demetrius heard of it, he assembled a very large army and marched out to meet him in battle. [3]Demetrius sent Jonathan a letter in peaceable words to honor him, [4]for he said to himself, "Let us act first to make peace with him[s] before he makes peace with Alexander against us, [5]for he will remember all the wrongs that we did to him and to his brothers and his nation." [6]So Demetrius[t] gave him authority to recruit troops, to equip them with arms, and to become his ally, and he commanded that the hostages in the citadel should be released to him.

[7]Then Jonathan came to Jerusalem and read the letter in the hearing of all the people and of those in the citadel. [8]They were greatly alarmed when they heard that the king had given him authority to recruit troops. [9]But those in the citadel released the hostages to Jonathan, and he returned them to their parents.

[10]And Jonathan took up residence in Jerusalem and began to rebuild and restore the city. [11]He directed those who were doing the work to build the walls and encircle Mount Zion with squared stones, for better fortification, and they did so.

[12]Then the foreigners who were in the strongholds that Bacchides had built fled; [13]all of them left their places and went back to their own lands. [14]Only in Beth-zur did some remain who had forsaken the law and the commandments, for it served as a place of refuge.

[15]Now King Alexander heard of all the promises that Demetrius had sent to Jonathan, and he heard of the battles that Jonathan[u] and his brothers had fought, of the brave deeds that they had done, and of the troubles that they had endured. [16]So he said, "Shall we find another such man? Come now, we will make him our friend and ally." [17]And he wrote a letter and sent it to him, in the following words:

[18]"King Alexander to his brother Jonathan, greetings. [19]We have heard about you, that you are a mighty warrior and worthy to be our friend. [20]And so we have appointed you today to be the high priest of your nation; you are to be called the king's Friend, and you are to take our side and keep friendship with us." He also sent him a purple robe and a golden crown.

[21]So Jonathan put on the sacred vestments in the seventh month of the one hundred sixtieth year, at the Festival of Booths,[v] and he recruited troops and equipped them with arms in abundance. [22]When Demetrius heard of these things, he was distressed and said, [23]"What is this that we have done? Alexander has gotten ahead of us in forming a friendship with the Jews to strengthen himself. [24]I also will write them words of encouragement and promise them honor and gifts, so that I may have their help." [25]So he sent a message to them in the following words:

"King Demetrius to the nation of the Jews, greetings. [26]Since you have kept your agreement with us and have continued your friendship with us and have not sided with our enemies, we have heard of it and rejoiced. [27]Now continue still to keep faith

s 10.4 Gk *them*   t 10.6 Gk *he*   u 10.15 Gk *he*   v 10.21 Or *Tabernacles*

---

coast (cf. 10:56). **10:2–6** Demetrius attempts to prevent Alexander from working with Jonathan, preemptively writing a letter to Jonathan seeking *to become his ally*. **10:7–11** Jonathan restores the walls of Jerusalem that Lysias destroyed (1:31; 6:62). **10:12–13** The foreign mercenaries leave the strongholds that Bacchides built and return to their homelands. **10:14** Some anti-Maccabean hellenized Judeans remain only in Beth-zur. **10:15–22** Alexander outbids and undermines Demetrius to get Jonathan on his side. **10:18–21** Alexander makes Jonathan a political *Friend*, granting legal recognition and status, after appointing him high priest. Jonathan is called the *king's Friend* (Gk. "philon basileos"), which ensures political and military allegiance to the king. Jonathan accepts by putting on the sacred vestments in 152 BCE. He displays patronage to Alexander by recruiting and arming troops.

10:22–50 Demetrius's reaction and defeat. 10:25–45 Demetrius's letter promises the *nation of the Jews* a series of tax exemptions, including *salt tax*, *the third of the grain*, and *the half of the fruit of the trees* from Judea, Samaria, and Galilee. As for Jerusalem, the tithes and revenues, including *fifteen thousand shekels of silver*, are to be kept there. Enslaved peoples or forced laborers taken from Judah are to be formally released without payment. Taxes on livestock are nullified. A demand for military conscription of *thirty thousand men*, the return of additionally annexed lands, and the cost of rebuilding and restoring the sanctuary are all to be paid by the king. These are all false

with us, and we will repay you with good for what you do for us. [28]We will grant you many immunities and give you gifts.

29 "I now free you and exempt all the Jews from payment of tribute and salt tax and crown levies, [30]and instead of collecting the third of the grain and the half of the fruit of the trees that I should receive, I release them from this day and henceforth. I will not collect them from the land of Judah or from the three districts added to it from Samaria and Galilee, from this day and for all time. [31]Jerusalem and its environs, its tithes and its revenues, shall be holy and free from tax. [32]I release also my control of the citadel in Jerusalem and give it to the high priest, so that he may station in it men of his own choice to guard it. [33]And every one of the Jews taken as a captive from the land of Judah into any part of my kingdom, I set free without payment, and let all officials cancel also the taxes on their livestock.

34 "All the festivals and Sabbaths and new moons and appointed days and the three days before a festival and the three after a festival— let them all be days of immunity and release for all the Jews who are in my kingdom. [35]No one shall have authority to exact anything from them or trouble any of them about any matter.

36 "Let Jews be enrolled in the king's forces to the number of thirty thousand men, and let the maintenance be given them that is due to all the forces of the king. [37]Let some of them be stationed in the great strongholds of the king, and let some of them be put in positions of trust in the kingdom. Let their officers and leaders be of their own number, and let them live by their own laws, just as the king has commanded in the land of Judah.

38 "As for the three districts that have been added to Judea from the country of Samaria, let them be annexed to Judea so that they may be considered to be under one ruler and obey no other authority than the high priest. [39]Ptolemais and the land adjoining it I have given as a gift to the sanctuary in Jerusalem, to meet the necessary expenses of the sanctuary. [40]I also grant fifteen thousand shekels of silver yearly out of the king's revenues from appropriate places. [41]And all the additional funds that the government officials have not paid as they did in the first years," they shall give from now on for the service of the temple.[x] [42]Moreover, the five thousand shekels of silver that my officials[y] have received every year from the income of the services of the temple, this, too, is canceled, because it belongs to the priests who minister there. [43]And all who take refuge at the temple in Jerusalem or in any of its precincts because they owe money to the king or are in debt, let them be released and receive back all their property in my kingdom.

44 "Let the cost of rebuilding and restoring the structures of the sanctuary be paid from the revenues of the king. [45]And let the cost of rebuilding the walls of Jerusalem and fortifying it all around and the cost of rebuilding the walls in Judea also be paid from the revenues of the king."

46 When Jonathan and the people heard these words, they did not believe or accept them, because they remembered the great wrongs that Demetrius[z] had done in Israel and how much he had oppressed them. [47]They favored Alexander because he had been the first to speak peaceable words to them, and they remained his allies all his days.

48 Now King Alexander assembled large forces and encamped opposite Demetrius. [49]The two kings met in battle, and the army of Demetrius fled, and Alexander[a] pursued him and defeated them. [50]He pressed the battle strongly until the sun set, and on that day Demetrius fell.

51 Then Alexander sent ambassadors to Ptolemy king of Egypt with the following message: [52]"Since I have returned to my kingdom and have taken my seat on the throne of my ancestors and established my rule—for I crushed Demetrius and gained control of our country; [53]I met him in battle, and he and his army were crushed by us, and we have taken our seat on the throne of his kingdom—[54]now therefore let us establish friendship with one another; give me now your daughter as my wife, and I will

---

w 10.41 Meaning of Gk uncertain *x* 10.41 Gk *house*
y 10.42 Gk *they* *z* 10.46 Gk *he* *a* 10.49 Other ancient authorities read *Alexander fled, and Demetrius*

---

promises. **10:46–47** Jonathan and the people notice the ridiculous falsehood behind the letter. **10:48–50** Alexander defeats Demetrius, who dies in battle.

10:51–66 Treaty of Ptolemy and Alexander. An arranged marriage between King Alexander (Seleucid) and Cleopatra (III) Thea (v. 58), the daughter of King Ptolemy VI Philometor (1:18), takes

become your son-in-law and will make gifts to you and to her in keeping with your position."

55 Ptolemy the king replied and said, "Happy was the day on which you returned to the land of your ancestors and took your seat on the throne of their kingdom. 56And now I will do for you as you wrote, but meet me at Ptolemais, so that we may see one another, and I will become your father-in-law, as you have said."

57 So Ptolemy set out from Egypt, he and his daughter Cleopatra, and came to Ptolemais in the one hundred sixty-second year. 58King Alexander met him, and Ptolemy*b* gave him his daughter Cleopatra in marriage and celebrated her wedding at Ptolemais with great pomp, as kings do.

59 Then King Alexander wrote to Jonathan to come and meet him. 60So he went with pomp to Ptolemais and met the two kings; he gave them and their Friends silver and gold and many gifts and found favor with them. 61A group of malcontents from Israel, renegades, gathered together against him to accuse him, but the king paid no attention to them. 62The king gave orders to take off Jonathan's garments and to clothe him in purple, and they did so. 63The king also seated him at his side, and he said to his officers, "Go out with him into the middle of the city and proclaim that no one is to bring charges against him about any matter, and let no one trouble him for any reason." 64When his accusers saw the honor that was paid him, in accord with the proclamation, and saw him clothed in purple, they all fled. 65Thus the king honored him and enrolled him among his First Friends and made him general and governor of the province. 66And Jonathan returned to Jerusalem in peace and gladness.

67 In the one hundred sixty-fifth year Demetrius son of Demetrius came from Crete to the land of his ancestors. 68When King Alexander heard of it, he was greatly distressed and returned to Antioch. 69And Demetrius appointed Apollonius the governor of Coelesyria, and he assembled a large force and encamped against Jamnia. Then he sent the following message to the high priest Jonathan:

70 "You are the only one to rise up against us, and I have fallen into ridicule and disgrace because of you. Why do you assume authority against us in the hill country? 71If you now have confidence in your forces, come down to the plain to meet us, and let us match strength with each other there, for I have with me the power of the cities. 72Ask and learn who I am and who the others are who are helping us. People will tell you that you cannot stand before us, for your ancestors were twice put to flight in their own land. 73And now you will not be able to withstand my cavalry and such an army in the plain, where there is no stone or pebble or place to flee."

74 When Jonathan heard the words of Apollonius, his spirit was aroused. He chose ten thousand men and set out from Jerusalem, and his brother Simon met him to help him. 75He encamped before Joppa, but the people of the city closed its gates, for Apollonius had a garrison in Joppa. So they fought against it, 76and the people of the city became afraid and opened the gates, and Jonathan gained possession of Joppa.

77 When Apollonius heard of it, he mustered three thousand cavalry and a large army and went to Azotus as though he were going farther. At the same time he advanced into the plain, for he had a large troop of cavalry and put confidence in it. 78Jonathan*c* pursued him to Azotus, and the armies engaged in battle. 79Now Apollonius had secretly left a thousand cavalry behind them. 80Jonathan learned that there was an ambush behind him, for they surrounded his army and shot arrows at his men from early morning until late afternoon. 81But his men stood fast, as Jonathan had commanded, and the enemy's*d* horses grew tired.

b 10.58 Gk *he*   *c* 10.78 Gk *He*   *d* 10.81 Gk *their*

place in 150 BCE. **10:59–66** Jonathan visits the two kings in Ptolemais. Jonathan's clothes are removed, and he is clothed in purple, representing royalty. Jonathan is paraded and made among the king's *First Friends*, *general*, and *governor*. There is peace for three years.

10:67–89 Demetrius's son Demetrius II returns in 147 BCE to reclaim the throne. The time frame makes Demetrius II fourteen years of age. **10:69** *Demetrius appointed Apollonius,* Jonathan's superior, as *governor of Coelesyria.* **10:72** *Your ancestors were twice put to flight in their own land.* Apollonius taunts and recalls Judas's defeats at Beth-zechariah (6:47) and Elasa (9:18). **10:73** *No stone or pebble* is a reference to David's killing of Goliath (1 Sam. 17). **10:77–85** The storyline is dramatic, having Jonathan cut off Apollonius's forces from Demetrius II. Simon also leads and defeats the

82 Then Simon brought forward his force and engaged the phalanx in battle (for the cavalry was exhausted); they were overwhelmed by him and fled, 83and the cavalry was dispersed in the plain. They fled to Azotus and entered Beth-dagon, the temple of their idol, for safety. 84But Jonathan burned Azotus and the surrounding towns and plundered them, and the temple of Dagon and those who had taken refuge in it he burned with fire. 85The number of those who fell by the sword, with those burned alive, came to eight thousand.

86 Then Jonathan left there and encamped against Askalon, and the people of the city came out to meet him with great pomp.

87 He and those with him then returned to Jerusalem with a large amount of plunder. 88When King Alexander heard of these things, he honored Jonathan still more, 89and he sent to him a golden buckle, such as it is the custom to give to the King's Kinsmen. He also gave him Ekron and all its environs as his possession.

11 Then the king of Egypt gathered great forces like the sand by the seashore and many ships, and he tried to get possession of Alexander's kingdom by trickery and add it to his own kingdom. 2He set out for Syria with peaceable words, and the people of the towns opened their gates to him and went to meet him, for King Alexander had commanded them to meet him, since he was Alexander'se father-in-law. 3But when Ptolemy entered the towns he stationed forces as a garrison in each town.

4 When hef approached Azotus, they showed him the burnt-out temple of Dagon, and Azotus and its suburbs destroyed, and the corpses lying about, and the charred bodies of those whom Jonathang had burned in the war, for they had piled them in heaps along

his route. 5They also told the king what Jonathan had done, to throw blame on him, but the king kept silent. 6Jonathan met the king at Joppa with pomp, and they greeted one another and spent the night there. 7And Jonathan went with the king as far as the river called Eleutherus; then he returned to Jerusalem.

8 So King Ptolemy gained control of the coastal cities as far as Seleucia by the sea, and he kept devising wicked designs against Alexander. 9He sent envoys to King Demetrius, saying, "Come, let us make a covenant with each other, and I will give you in marriage my daughter who was Alexander's wife, and you shall reign over your father's kingdom. 10I now regret that I gave him my daughter, for he has tried to kill me." 11He threw blame on Alexanderb because he coveted his kingdom. 12So he took his daughter away from him and gave her to Demetrius. He was estranged from Alexander, and their hostility became apparent.

13 Then Ptolemy entered Antioch and put on the crown of Asia. Thus he put two crowns on his head, the crown of Egypt and that of Asia. 14Now King Alexander was in Cilicia at that time because the people of that region were in revolt. 15When Alexander heard of it, he came against him in battle. Ptolemy marched out and met him with a strong force and put him to flight. 16So Alexander fled into Arabia to find protection there, and King Ptolemy was triumphant. 17Zabdiel the Arab cut off the head of Alexander and sent it to Ptolemy. 18But King Ptolemy died three days later, and his troops in the strongholds were killed by the inhabitants of the strongholds. 19So Demetrius became king in the one hundred sixty-seventh year.

20 In those days Jonathan assembled the Judeans to attack the citadel in Jerusalem,

e 11.2 Gk his   f 11.4 Other ancient authorities read they
g 11.4 Gk he   h 11.11 Gk him

enemy. **10:88–89** Alexander rewards Jonathan with a *golden buckle*, designating him among *the King's Kinsmen.*

11:1–19 *King of Egypt*, **Ptolemy VI, invades Alexander's kingdom, including Judea.** Alexander is away fighting in Cilicia. Josephus (*Ant.* 13.4.5–6) says that Alexander, his son-in-law, plotted to kill Ptolemy (cf. v. 10). **11:6–7** Jonathan meets Ptolemy VI and switches allegiance. **11:8** Ptolemy VI gains control of the coastal cities. **11:9–12** Ptolemy VI takes his daughter who was previously given in marriage to Alexander (10:51–66) and gives her in marriage to Demetrius II, forging a new alliance to remove Alexander. **11:13** Ptolemy crowns himself king over Egypt and Asia. **11:14–19** Alexander returns to battle Ptolemy VI. Alexander loses and flees into Arabia. Alexander is beheaded by Zabdiel, but Ptolemy VI also dies from his battle wounds. **11:19** Demetrius II becomes king in 145 BCE.

11:20–29 Jonathan forms a new allegiance with Demetrius II, receiving recognition as one of Demetrius's *First Friends* and high priest.

and he built many engines of war to use against it. [21]But certain renegades who hated their nation went to the king and reported to him that Jonathan was besieging the citadel. [22]When he heard this he was angry, and as soon as he heard it he set out and came to Ptolemais, and he wrote Jonathan not to continue the siege but to meet him for a conference at Ptolemais as quickly as possible.

23 When Jonathan heard this, he gave orders to continue the siege. He chose some of the elders of Israel and some of the priests and put himself in danger, [24]for he went to the king at Ptolemais, taking silver and gold and clothing and numerous other gifts. And he won his favor. [25]Although certain renegades of his nation kept making complaints against him, [26]the king treated him as his predecessors had treated him; he exalted him in the presence of all his Friends. [27]He confirmed him in the high priesthood and in as many other honors as he had formerly had and caused him to be reckoned among his First Friends. [28]Then Jonathan asked the king to free Judea and the three districts and Samaria from tribute and promised him three hundred talents. [29]The king consented and wrote a letter to Jonathan about all these things; its contents were as follows:

30 "King Demetrius to his brother Jonathan and to the nation of the Jews, greetings. [31]This copy of the letter that we wrote concerning you to our kinsman Lasthenes we have written to you also, so that you may know what it says. [32]'King Demetrius to his father Lasthenes, greetings. [33]We have determined to do good to the nation of the Jews, who are our friends and fulfill their obligations to us, because of the goodwill they show toward us. [34]We have confirmed as their possession both the territory of Judea and the three districts of Aphairema and Lydda and Ramathaim;[i] the latter, with all the region bordering them, were added to Judea from Samaria. To all those who offer sacrifice in Jerusalem we have granted release from[j] the royal taxes that the king formerly received from them each year, from the crops of the land and the fruit of the trees. [35]And the other

payments henceforth due to us of the tithes, and the taxes due to us, and the salt pits and the crown taxes due to us—from all these we shall grant them release. [36]And not one of these grants shall be canceled from this time on forever. [37]Now, therefore, take care to make a copy of this, and let it be given to Jonathan and put up in a conspicuous place on the holy mountain.'"

38 When King Demetrius saw that the land was quiet before him and that there was no opposition to him, he dismissed all his troops, all of them to their own homes, except the foreign troops whom he had recruited from the islands of the nations. So all the troops who had served under his predecessors hated him. [39]A certain Trypho had formerly been one of Alexander's supporters; he saw that all the troops were grumbling against Demetrius. So he went to Imalkue the Arab, who was bringing up Antiochus, the young son of Alexander, [40]and insistently urged him to hand Antiochus[k] over to him, to become king in place of his father. He also reported to Imalkue[l] what Demetrius had done and told of the hatred that the troops of Demetrius[m] had for him, and he stayed there many days.

41 Now Jonathan sent to King Demetrius the request that he remove the troops of the citadel from Jerusalem and the troops in the strongholds, for they kept fighting against Israel. [42]And Demetrius sent this message back to Jonathan: "Not only will I do these things for you and your nation, but I will confer great honor on you and your nation, if I find an opportunity. [43]Now, then, you will do well to send me men who will help me, for all my troops have revolted." [44]So Jonathan sent three thousand stalwart men to him at Antioch, and when they came to the king, the king rejoiced at their arrival.

45 Then the people of the city assembled within the city, to the number of a hundred and twenty thousand, and they wanted to kill the king. [46]But the king fled into the palace.

i 11.34 Gk *Rathamin* j 11.34 Or *Samaria, for all those who offer sacrifice in Jerusalem, in place of* k 11.40 Gk *him* l 11.40 Gk *him* m 11.40 Gk *his troops*

11:30–37 A repeat of promises made by Demetrius I. Cf. 10:25–45. Lasthenes is chief of Demetrius's Cretan mercenaries.

11:38–53 Demetrius dismisses his troops except for the *foreign troops . . . from the islands of the nations.* The disgruntled soldiers under *a certain Trypho* take action against Demetrius by going to Imalkue, who was raising Antiochus VI, Alexander's son, in order to make Antiochus king.

Then the people of the city seized the main streets of the city and began to fight. ⁴⁷So the king called the Jews to his aid, and they all rallied around him and then spread out through the city, and they killed on that day about one hundred thousand. ⁴⁸They set fire to the city and seized a large amount of spoil on that day and saved the king. ⁴⁹When the people of the city saw that the Jews had gained control of the city as they pleased, their courage failed, and they cried out to the king with this entreaty: ⁵⁰"Grant us peace, and make the Jews stop fighting against us and our city." ⁵¹And they threw down their arms and made peace. So the Jews gained glory in the sight of the king and of all the people in his kingdom, and they returned to Jerusalem with a large amount of spoil.

52 So King Demetrius sat on the throne of his kingdom, and the land was quiet before him. ⁵³But he broke his word about all that he had promised; he became estranged from Jonathan and did not repay the favors that Jonathan[n] had done him but treated him very harshly.

54 After this Trypho returned, and with him the young boy Antiochus, who began to reign and put on the crown. ⁵⁵All the troops whom Demetrius had discharged gathered around him; they fought against Demetrius,[o] and he fled and was routed. ⁵⁶Trypho captured the elephants[p] and gained control of Antioch. ⁵⁷Then the young Antiochus wrote to Jonathan, saying, "I confirm you in the high priesthood and set you over the four districts and make you one of the king's Friends." ⁵⁸He also sent him gold plates and a table service and granted him the right to drink from gold cups and dress in purple and wear a gold buckle. ⁵⁹He appointed Jonathan's[q] brother Simon governor from the Ladder of Tyre to the borders of Egypt.

60 Then Jonathan set out and traveled beyond the river and among the towns, and all the army of Syria gathered to him as allies. When he came to Askalon, the people of the city met him and paid him honor. ⁶¹From there he went to Gaza, but the people of Gaza shut him out. So he besieged it and burned its suburbs with fire and plundered them. ⁶²Then the people of Gaza pleaded with Jonathan, and he made peace with them and took the sons of their rulers as hostages and sent them to Jerusalem. And he passed through the country as far as Damascus.

63 Then Jonathan heard that the officers of Demetrius had come to Kadesh in Galilee with a large army, intending to remove him from office. ⁶⁴He went to meet them but left his brother Simon in the country. ⁶⁵Simon encamped before Beth-zur and fought against it for many days and hemmed it in. ⁶⁶Then they asked him to grant them terms of peace, and he did so. He removed them from there, took possession of the town, and set a garrison over it.

67 Jonathan and his army encamped by the waters of Gennesaret. Early in the morning they marched to the plain of Hazor, ⁶⁸and there in the plain the army of the foreigners met him; they had set an ambush against him in the mountains, but they themselves met him face to face. ⁶⁹Then the men in ambush emerged from their places and joined battle. ⁷⁰All the men with Jonathan fled; not one of them was left except Mattathias son of Absalom and Judas son of Chalphi, commanders of the forces of the army. ⁷¹Jonathan tore his clothes, put dust on his head, and prayed. ⁷²Then he turned back to the battle against the enemy[r] and routed them, and they fled. ⁷³When his men who were fleeing saw this, they returned to him and joined him in the pursuit as far as Kadesh, to their camp, and there they encamped. ⁷⁴As many as three thousand of the foreigners fell that day. And Jonathan returned to Jerusalem.

12 Now when Jonathan saw that the time was favorable for him, he chose men and sent them to Rome to confirm and renew the friendship with them. ²He also sent

n 11.53 Gk *he*   o 11.55 Gk *him*   p 11.56 Gk *animals*
q 11.59 Gk *his*   r 11.72 Gk *them*

11:54–59 Young Antiochus VI is made king. He grants Jonathan the same privileges as before, including being among *the king's Friends*, but also makes Simon, Jonathan's brother, governor of the coastal region (Syria to Egypt).

11:60–74 Jonathan's army fights against Demetrius's forces. Josephus (*Ant.* 13.5.3) notes Demetrius sought major tributes. **11:60–74** Although the scene initially depicts defeat, Jonathan is reframed as a contemporary Joshua who is victorious. **11:61** Jonathan burns the suburbs of Gaza (cf. 10:84).

12:1–4 Judean emissaries to Rome and Sparta. This is likely a fictitious account. *High priest*

letters to the same effect to the Spartans and to other places. [3]So they went to Rome and entered the senate chamber and said, "The high priest Jonathan and the Jewish nation have sent us to renew the former friendship and alliance with them." [4]And the Romans[s] gave them letters to the people in every place, asking them to provide for the envoys[t] safe conduct to the land of Judah.

[5] This is a copy of the letter that Jonathan wrote to the Spartans: [6]"The high priest Jonathan, the council of the nation, the priests, and the rest of the Jewish people to their brothers the Spartans, greetings. [7]Already in time past a letter was sent to the high priest Onias from Arius, who was king among you, stating that you are our brothers, as the appended copy shows. [8]Onias welcomed the envoy with honor and received the letter, which contained a clear declaration of alliance and friendship. [9]Therefore, though we have no need of these things, since we have as encouragement the holy books that are in our hands, [10]we have undertaken to send to renew our family ties and friendship with you, so that we may not become estranged from you, for considerable time has passed since you sent your letter to us. [11]We therefore remember you constantly on every occasion, both at our festivals and on other appropriate days, at the sacrifices that we offer and in our prayers, as it is right and proper to remember brothers. [12]And we rejoice in your glory. [13]But as for ourselves, many trials and many wars have encircled us; the kings around us have waged war against us. [14]We were unwilling to trouble you and our other allies and friends with these wars, [15]for we have the help that comes from heaven for our aid, so we were delivered from our enemies, and our enemies were humbled. [16]We therefore have chosen Numenius son of Antiochus and Antipater son of Jason and have sent them to Rome to renew our former friendship and alliance with them. [17]We have commanded them to go

also to you and greet you and deliver to you this letter from us concerning the renewal of our family ties. [18]And now please send us a reply to this."

[19] This is a copy of the letter that they sent to Onias: [20]"King Arius of the Spartans, to the high priest Onias, greetings. [21]It has been found in writing concerning the Spartans and the Jews that they are brothers and are of the family of Abraham. [22]And now that we have learned this, please write us concerning your welfare; [23]we on our part write to you that your livestock and your property belong to us, and ours belong to you. We therefore command that our envoys[u] report to you accordingly."

[24] Now Jonathan heard that the commanders of Demetrius had returned with a larger force than before to wage war against him. [25]So he marched away from Jerusalem and met them in the region of Hamath, for he gave them no opportunity to invade his own country. [26]He sent spies to their camp, and they returned and reported to him that the enemy[v] were being drawn up in formation to attack the Jews[w] by night. [27]So when the sun had set, Jonathan commanded his troops to be alert and to keep their arms at hand so as to be ready all night for battle, and he stationed outposts around the camp. [28]When the enemy heard that Jonathan and his troops were prepared for battle, they were afraid and were terrified at heart, so they kindled fires in their camp and withdrew.[x] [29]But Jonathan and his troops did not know it until morning, for they saw the fires burning. [30]Then Jonathan pursued them, but he did not overtake them, for they had crossed the Eleutherus River. [31]So Jonathan turned aside against the Arabs who are called Zabadeans, and he crushed

s 12.4 Gk *they*   t 12.4 Gk *them*   u 12.23 Gk *they*   v 12.26 Gk *they*   w 12.26 Gk *them*   x 12.28 Other ancient authorities omit *and withdrew*

Jonathan and the Jewish nation suggests that Judah was an independent state, which is difficult to attest before Simon. The Spartans did not join the Achaean League against Rome.
12:5–23 An editor inserted a fictitious letter from Jonathan to the Spartans citing an imagined exchange between Onias I (300 BCE) and Arius I, king of Sparta (309–265 BCE), with supposed alliances that never materialized. The account mimics texts like Jer. 29 and Ezra 4–7, which contain fragments of letters that romanticize historical accounts. **12:6** *Council of the nation* is the council of Jewish elders or the Sanhedrin. **12:21** Spartans are not descendants of Abraham. Such mythopoeic ideas were used by imaginative authors.
12:24–37 Jonathan's battle against Demetrius. 12:30 *Eleutherus* (Nahr el-Kebir, north of Tripolis)

them and plundered them. ³²Then he broke camp and went to Damascus and marched through all that region.

33 Simon also went out and marched through the country as far as Askalon and the neighboring strongholds. He turned aside to Joppa and took it by surprise, ³⁴for he had heard that they were ready to hand over the stronghold to those whom Demetrius had sent. And he stationed a garrison there to guard it.

35 When Jonathan returned he convened the elders of the people and planned with them to build strongholds in Judea, ³⁶to build the walls of Jerusalem still higher, and to erect a high barrier between the citadel and the city to separate it from the city, in order to isolate it so that its garrison^y could neither buy nor sell. ³⁷So they gathered together to rebuild the city; part of the wall on the valley to the east had fallen, and he repaired the section called Chaphenatha. ³⁸Simon also built Adida in the Shephelah; he fortified it and installed gates with bolts.

39 Then Trypho attempted to become king in Asia and put on the crown and to raise his hand against King Antiochus. ⁴⁰He feared that Jonathan might not permit him to do so but might make war on him, so he kept seeking to seize and kill him, and he marched out and came to Beth-shan. ⁴¹Jonathan went out to meet him with forty thousand picked warriors, and he came to Beth-shan. ⁴²When Trypho saw that he had come with a large army, he was afraid to raise his hand against him. ⁴³So he received him with honor and commended him to all his Friends, and he gave him gifts and commanded his Friends and his troops to obey him as they would himself. ⁴⁴Then he said to Jonathan, "Why have you put all these people to so much trouble when we are not at war? ⁴⁵Dismiss them now to their homes

and choose for yourself a few men to stay with you and come with me to Ptolemais. I will hand it over to you, as well as the other strongholds and the remaining troops and all the officials, and will turn around and go home. For that is why I am here."

46 Jonathan^z trusted him and did as he said; he sent away the troops, and they returned to the land of Judah. ⁴⁷He kept with himself three thousand men, two thousand of whom he left in Galilee, while one thousand accompanied him. ⁴⁸But when Jonathan entered Ptolemais, the people of Ptolemais closed the gates and seized him, and they killed with the sword all who had entered with him.

49 Then Trypho sent troops and cavalry into Galilee and the Great Plain to destroy all Jonathan's soldiers. ⁵⁰But they realized that Jonathan had been seized and had perished along with his men, and they encouraged one another and kept marching in close formation, ready for battle. ⁵¹When their pursuers saw that they would fight for their lives, they turned back. ⁵²So they all reached the land of Judah safely, and they mourned for Jonathan and his companions and were in great fear, and all Israel mourned deeply. ⁵³All the nations around them tried to destroy them, for they said, "They have no leader or helper. Now, therefore, let us make war on them and blot out the memory of them from humankind."

13 Simon heard that Trypho had assembled a large army to invade the land of Judah and destroy it, ²and he saw that the people were trembling with fear. So he went up to Jerusalem, and gathering the people together ³he encouraged them, saying to them, "You yourselves know what great things my brothers and I and the house of my father

y 12.36 Gk they   z 12.46 Gk He

would have been far too north (11:7) to be an accurate historical reference. **12:37** *The valley to the east* is the Kidron; *Chaphenatha* is the second quarter of Jerusalem, northwest of the temple (2 Kgs. 22:14).

12:38–53 Trypho captures Jonathan. **12:38** *Adida*, three miles east of Lydda, was a strategic stronghold between the coastal plains and the hill country, as was *Shephelah*, between coastal plains and central highlands. **12:39** *King in Asia*—that is, become a Seleucid king. **12:48–50** This section has Jonathan dying with his men, but 13:12–24 suggests otherwise. **12:53** An interpolation. Cf. 13:3–6.

13:1–16:17 Simon's reign.
13:1–11 Simon replaces Jonathan as the next leader. With Eleazar, Judas, Jonathan, and John dead, Simon is the last of the brothers. **13:3–6** Simon's speech is kindled under religious nationalism, with zeal that defends the nation of Judah at all costs. His brothers and Mattathias died as heroes.

have done for the laws and the sanctuary; you know also the wars and the difficulties that my brothers and I have seen. [4]By reason of this all my brothers have perished for the sake of Israel, and I alone am left. [5]And now, far be it from me to spare my life in any time of distress, for I am not better than my brothers. [6]But I will avenge my nation and the sanctuary and your wives and children, for all the nations have gathered together out of hatred to destroy us."

7 The spirit of the people was rekindled when they heard these words, [8]and they answered in a loud voice, "You are our leader in place of Judas and your brother Jonathan. [9]Fight our battles, and all that you say to us we will do." [10]So he assembled all the warriors and hurried to complete the walls of Jerusalem, and he fortified it on every side. [11]He sent Jonathan son of Absalom to Joppa and with him a considerable army; he drove out its occupants and remained there.

12 Then Trypho left Ptolemais with a large army to invade the land of Judah, and Jonathan was with him under guard. [13]Simon encamped in Adida, facing the plain. [14]Trypho learned that Simon had risen up in place of his brother Jonathan and that he was about to join battle with him, so he sent envoys to him and said, [15]"It is for the money that your brother Jonathan owed the royal treasury, in connection with the offices he held, that we are detaining him. [16]Send now one hundred talents of silver and two of his sons as hostages, so that when released he will not revolt against us, and we will release him."

17 Simon knew that they were speaking deceitfully to him, but he sent to get the money and the sons, so that he would not arouse great hostility among the people, who might

say, [18]"It was because Simon[a] did not send him the money and the sons that Jonathan[b] perished." [19]So he sent the sons and the hundred talents, but Trypho[c] broke his word and did not release Jonathan.

20 After this Trypho came to invade the country and destroy it, and he circled around by the way to Adora. But Simon and his army kept marching along opposite him to every place he went. [21]Now the men in the citadel kept sending envoys to Trypho urging him to come to them by way of the wilderness and to send them food. [22]So Trypho got all his cavalry ready to go, but that night a very heavy snow fell, and he did not go because of the snow. He marched off and went into the land of Gilead. [23]When he approached Baskama, he killed Jonathan, and he was buried there. [24]Then Trypho turned and went back to his own land.

25 Simon sent and took the bones of his brother Jonathan and buried him in Modein, the city of his ancestors. [26]All Israel bewailed him with great lamentation and mourned for him many days. [27]And Simon built a monument over the tomb of his father and his brothers; he made it high so that it might be seen, with polished stone at the front and back. [28]He also erected seven pyramids, opposite one another, for his father and mother and four brothers. [29]For the pyramids[d] he devised an elaborate setting, erecting about them great columns, and on the columns he put suits of armor for a permanent memorial, and beside the suits of armor he carved ships, so that they could be seen by all who sail the sea. [30]This is the tomb that he built in Modein; it remains to this day.

a 13.18 Gk *I*　b 13.18 Gk *he*　c 13.19 Gk *he*　d 13.29 Gk *For these*

Simon's impassioned speech references the extreme adherence to the law and the temple. The apex of the speech is that *all the nations have gathered together out of hatred to destroy us*. This passage is an interpolation by the same author of 12:53. In both contexts, Simon uses language of fear, anger, and hatred to generate an impassioned response to affirm him as the next leader. **13:7–9** The people recall the memory of Judas and Jonathan.

13:12–24 Another account portraying the death of Jonathan. Cf. 12:48–50. **13:12–19** Trypho negotiates the terms of Jonathan's release—unpaid tribute owed by Jonathan and two of Jonathan's sons as hostages to prevent further revolts. Simon pays the financial and human ransom, only to have Trypho rescind and not release Jonathan. **13:23** In this account, Trypho kills Jonathan.

13:25–30 Description of a spectacular family mausoleum. The *seven pyramids* imitate Egyptians, and the *great columns* imitate Greeks. *Carved ships*, symbolizing trade, commerce, and a navy, were imprinted on Herodian and Archelaus coins.

31 Trypho dealt treacherously with the young King Antiochus; he killed him [32]and became king in his place, putting on the crown of Asia, and he brought great calamity on the land. [33]But Simon built up the strongholds of Judea and walled them all around, with high towers and great walls and gates and bolts, and he stored food in the strongholds. [34]Simon also chose emissaries and sent them to King Demetrius with a request to grant relief to the country, for all that Trypho did was to plunder. [35]King Demetrius sent him a favorable reply to this request and wrote him a letter as follows, [36]"King Demetrius to Simon, the high priest and friend of kings, and to the elders and nation of the Jews, greetings. [37]We have received the gold crown and the palm branch that you sent, and we are ready to make a general peace with you and to write to our officials to grant you release from tribute. [38]All the grants that we have made to you remain valid, and let the strongholds that you have built be your possession. [39]We pardon any errors and offenses committed to this day and cancel the crown tax that you owe, and whatever other tax has been collected in Jerusalem shall be collected no longer. [40]And if any of you are qualified to be enrolled in our bodyguard,[e] let them be enrolled, and let there be peace between us."

41 In the one hundred seventieth year the yoke of the nations was removed from Israel, [42]and the people began to write in their documents and contracts, "In the first year of Simon the great high priest and commander and leader of the Jews."

43 In those days Simon[f] encamped against Gazara[g] and surrounded it with troops. He made a siege engine, brought it up to the city, and battered and captured one tower. [44]The men in the siege engine leaped out into the city, and a great tumult arose in the city. [45]The men in the city, with their wives and children, went up on the wall with their clothes torn, and they cried out with a loud voice, asking Simon to make peace with them; [46]they said, "Do not treat us according to our wicked acts but according to your mercy." [47]So Simon reached an agreement with them and stopped fighting against them. But he expelled them from the city and cleansed the houses in which the idols were located and then entered it with hymns and praise. [48]He removed all uncleanness from it and settled in it those who observed the law. He also strengthened its fortifications and built in it a house for himself.

49 Those who were in the citadel at Jerusalem were prevented from going in and out to buy and sell in the country. So they were very hungry, and many of them perished from famine. [50]Then they cried to Simon to make peace with them, and he did so. But he expelled them from there and cleansed the citadel from its pollutions. [51]On the twenty-third day of the second month, in the one hundred seventy-first year, the Jews[b] entered it with praise and palm branches, and with harps and cymbals and stringed instruments, and with hymns and songs, because a great enemy had been crushed and removed from Israel. [52]Simon[i] decreed that every year they should celebrate this day with rejoicing. He strengthened the fortifications of the temple hill alongside the citadel, and he and his men lived there. [53]Simon saw that his son John had reached

e 13.40 Or *court* f 13.43 Gk *he* g 13.43 Cn: Gk *Gaza* b 13.51 Gk *they* i 13.52 Gk *He*

13:31–42 **Judah gains independence through diplomacy, not war or violence. 13:37** Simon sends his *gold crown and the palm branch* to Demetrius II symbolizing that he recognizes the true crown of Demetrius II and that he seeks peace, not war. The weakness of Demetrius II made the treaty possible. **13:39** Debts, including *the crown tax* and especially those supporting Trypho, are forgiven. **13:41–42** A new era begins for Simon and the nation of Judah.

13:43–48 **Capture of Gazara. 13:48** Property is distributed to Simon's soldiers.

13:49–53 **Jerusalem restored to the Judeans.** 141 BCE. Up to this point, Jerusalem has been an anti-Maccabean stronghold. The last legitimate independent Judean king, Jehoiachin, went into exile from Jerusalem in 597 BCE. **13:51** The triumphal return to the city *with praise and palm branches, and with harps and cymbals and stringed instruments*—cf. Ps. 150—marks a sovereign nation. **13:53** Simon's son, John Hyrcanus I, is made commander of the military. John will eventually succeed his father, Simon, and rule from 134 BCE to 104 BCE. Scholars suggest that the core of 1 Maccabees was started or composed during John's reign.

manhood, so he made him commander of all the forces, and he lived at Gazara.

14 In the one hundred seventy-second year King Demetrius assembled his forces and marched into Media to obtain help, so that he could make war against Trypho. [2]When King Arsaces of Persia and Media heard that Demetrius had invaded his territory, he sent one of his generals to take him alive. [3]The general[j] went and defeated the army of Demetrius and seized him and took him to Arsaces, who put him under guard.

[4] The land[k] had rest all the days of
>Simon.
>He sought the good of his nation;
>his rule was pleasing to them,
>>as was the honor shown him all his
>>days.

[5] To crown all his honors he took Joppa for
>a harbor
>and opened a way to the isles of the
>sea.

[6] He extended the borders of his nation
>and gained full control of the
>country.

[7] He gathered a host of captives;
>he ruled over Gazara and Beth-zur and
>>the citadel,
>and he removed its uncleanness from it,
>and there was none to oppose him.

[8] They tilled their land in peace;
>the ground gave its increase
>and the trees of the plains their fruit.

[9] Old men sat in the streets;
>they all talked together of good
>>things,
>and the youths put on splendid military
>>attire.

[10] He supplied the towns with food
>and furnished them with the means of
>>defense,
>until his renown spread to the ends of
>>the earth.

[11] He established peace in the land,
>and Israel rejoiced with great joy.

[12] All the people sat under their own vines
>and fig trees,
>and there was none to make them
>>afraid.

[13] No one was left in the land to fight them,
>and the kings were crushed in those
>>days.

[14] He gave help to all the humble among his
>people;
>he sought out the law
>and did away with all the renegades
>>and outlaws.

[15] He made the sanctuary glorious
>and added to the vessels of the
>>sanctuary.

16 It was heard in Rome and as far away as Sparta that Jonathan had died, and they were deeply grieved. [17]When they heard that his brother Simon had become high priest in his stead and that he was ruling over the country and the towns in it, [18]they wrote to him on bronze tablets to renew with him the friendship and alliance that they had established with his brothers Judas and Jonathan. [19]And these were read before the assembly in Jerusalem.

20 This is a copy of the letter that the Spartans sent:

"The rulers and the city of the Spartans to the high priest Simon and to the elders and the priests and the rest of the Jewish people, our brothers, greetings. [21]The envoys who were sent to our people have told us about your glory and honor, and we rejoiced at their coming. [22]We have recorded what they said in our public decrees, as follows, 'Numenius son of Antiochus and Antipater son of Jason, envoys of the Jews, have come to us to renew their friendship with us. [23]It has pleased our people to receive these men with honor and to put a copy of their words in the public archives, so that the people of the Spartans may have a record of them. And they have sent a copy of this to the high priest Simon.'"

j 14.3 Gk *He* *k* 14.4 Other ancient authorities add *of Judah*

14:1–3 Capture of Demetrius II. Some scholars date the episode as 140 BCE, while others at the start of 138 BCE. According to Appian, Arsaces VI (171–138 BCE) was kind to Demetrius and gave his sister to him in marriage (*Syr.* 13.68).

14:4–15 Celebrating Simon's accomplishments. This late poem uses traditional motifs (v. 8, cf. Lev. 26:3–4; v. 9, cf. Zech. 8:4; v. 12, cf. Mic. 4:4). **14:5** The *harbor* was necessary for trading goods with *the isles of the sea*: Cyprus, Rhodes, and Crete.

14:16–24 Renewed alliance between Rome and Simon. 14:20–23 The authenticity of the letter

24 After this Simon sent Numenius to Rome with a large gold shield weighing one thousand minas to confirm the alliance with the Romans.[l]

25 When the people heard these things they said, "How shall we thank Simon and his sons? [26]For he and his brothers and the house of his father have stood firm; they have fought and repulsed Israel's enemies and established its freedom." [27]So they made a record on bronze tablets and put it on pillars on Mount Zion.

This is a copy of what they wrote: "On the eighteenth day of Elul, in the one hundred seventy-second year, which is the third year of the great high priest Simon, [28]in Asaramel, in the great assembly of the priests and the people and the rulers of the nation and the elders of the country, the following was proclaimed to us:

29 "Since wars often occurred in the country, Simon son of Mattathias, of the clan of Joarib, and his brothers, exposed themselves to danger and resisted the enemies of their nation, in order that their sanctuary and the law might be preserved, and they brought great glory to their nation. [30]Jonathan rallied the[m] nation, became their high priest, and was gathered to his people. [31]When their enemies decided to invade their country and lay hands on their sanctuary, [32]then Simon rose up and fought for his nation. He spent great sums of his own money; he armed the soldiers of his nation and paid them wages. [33]He fortified the towns of Judea, and Beth-zur on the borders of Judea, where formerly the arms of the enemy had been stored, and he placed there a garrison of Jews. [34]He also fortified Joppa, which is by the sea, and Gazara, which is on the borders of Azotus, where the enemy formerly lived. He settled Jews there and provided in those towns[n] whatever was necessary for their restoration.

35 "The people saw Simon's faithfulness[o] and the glory that he had resolved to win for his nation, and they made him their leader and high priest because he had done all these things and because of the justice and loyalty that he had maintained toward his nation. He sought in every way to exalt his people. [36]In his days things prospered in his hands, so that the nations were put out of the[p] country, as were also those in the city of David in Jerusalem, who had built themselves a citadel from which they used to sally forth and defile the environs of the sanctuary, doing great damage to its purity. [37]He settled Jews in it and fortified it for the safety of the country and of the city and built the walls of Jerusalem higher.

38 "In view of these things King Demetrius confirmed him in the high priesthood, [39]made him one of his Friends, and paid him high honors. [40]For he had heard that the Jews were addressed by the Romans as friends and allies and brothers and that the Romans[q] had received the envoys of Simon with honor.

41 "The Jews and their priests have resolved that Simon should be their leader and high priest forever, until a trustworthy prophet should arise, [42]and that he should be governor over them and[r] appoint officials over its tasks and over the country and the weapons and the strongholds, [43]and that he should take charge of the sanctuary, and that he should be obeyed by all, and that all contracts in the country should be written in his name, and that he should be clothed in purple and wear gold.

44 "None of the people or priests shall be permitted to nullify any of these decisions or to oppose what he says or to convene an assembly in the country without his permission or to be clothed in purple or put on a gold buckle. [45]Whoever acts contrary to these decisions or rejects any of them shall be liable to punishment."

46 All the people agreed to grant Simon the right to act in accordance with these decisions. [47]So Simon accepted and agreed to be

l 14.24 Gk them   m 14.30 Gk their   n 14.34 Gk them
o 14.35 Other ancient authorities read conduct   p 14.36 Gk their   q 14.40 Gk they   r 14.42 Cn: Gk adds that he should take charge of the sanctuary and

is difficult to attest. The correspondence parallels elements in 12:5–23. Rome may have recognized Simon as the head of the state. **14:24** *One thousand minas* is an exaggeration.
14:25–49 A public decree remembering the heroic deeds of Simon and his family. **14:27** *Elul, in the one hundred seventy-second year* is September 140 BCE. **14:32** That Simon spent his own resources to train and fund the military is news (cf. 13:15–19). **14:41–43** The Judeans resolve that Simon is their military, religious, and political leader. The phrase *until a trustworthy prophet should arise* is an interpolation. **14:47** Simon accepts the terms and reigns supreme as *high priest*, *commander*, and *ethnarch*.

high priest, to be commander and ethnarch of the Jews and priests, and to be protector of them all.*[s] [48]And they gave orders to inscribe this decree on bronze tablets, to put them up in a conspicuous place in the precincts of the sanctuary, [49]and to deposit copies of them in the treasury, so that Simon and his sons might have them.

15 Antiochus, son of King Demetrius, sent a letter from the islands of the sea to Simon, the priest and ethnarch of the Jews, and to all the nation; [2]its contents were as follows: "King Antiochus to Simon the high priest and ethnarch and to the nation of the Jews, greetings. [3]Whereas certain scoundrels have gained control of the kingdom of our ancestors, and I intend to lay claim to the kingdom so that I may restore it as it formerly was, and have recruited a host of mercenary troops and have equipped warships, [4]and intend to make a landing in the country so that I may proceed against those who have destroyed our country and those who have devastated many cities in my kingdom, [5]now therefore I confirm to you all the tax remissions that the kings before me have granted you and a release from all the other payments from which they have released you. [6]I permit you to mint your own coinage as money for your country, [7]and I grant freedom to Jerusalem and the sanctuary. All the weapons that you have prepared and the strongholds that you have built and now hold shall remain yours. [8]Every debt you owe to the royal treasury and any such future debts shall be canceled for you from henceforth and for all time. [9]When we gain control of our kingdom, we will bestow great honor on you and your nation and the temple, so that your glory will become manifest in all the earth."

[10] In the one hundred seventy-fourth year Antiochus set out and invaded the land of his ancestors. All the troops rallied to him, so that there were only a few with Trypho. [11]Antiochus pursued him, and Trypho[t] came in his flight to Dor, which is by the sea, [12]for he knew that troubles had converged on him, and his troops had deserted him. [13]So Antiochus encamped against Dor, and with him were one hundred twenty thousand warriors and eight thousand cavalry. [14]He surrounded the town, and the ships joined battle from the sea; he pressed the town hard from land and sea and permitted no one to leave or enter it.

[15] Then Numenius and his companions arrived from Rome, with letters to the kings and countries, in which the following was written: [16]"Lucius, consul of the Romans, to King Ptolemy, greetings. [17]The envoys of the Jews have come to us as our friends and allies to renew our ancient friendship and alliance. They had been sent by the high priest Simon and by the Jewish people [18]and have brought a gold shield weighing one thousand minas. [19]We therefore have decided to write to the kings and countries that they should not seek their harm or make war against them and their cities and their country or make alliance with those who war against them. [20]And it has seemed good to us to accept the shield from them. [21]Therefore if any scoundrels have fled to you from their country, hand them over to the high priest Simon, so that he may punish them according to their law."

[22] The consul[u] wrote the same thing to King Demetrius and to Attalus and Ariarathes and Arsaces [23]and to all the countries, and to Sampsames,[v] and to the Spartans, and to

s 14.47 Or *to preside over them all*   *t* 15.11 Gk *he*   *u* 15.22 Gk *He*   *v* 15.23 The name is uncertain

15:1–14 Letter of Antiochus VII. Antiochus VII Sidetes, from Side in Pamphylia, is the younger brother of Demetrius II. Reigning from 138 to 129 BCE, he was married to Cleopatra III (10:57–58; 11:12). **15:3** *Certain scoundrels* are Trypho's factions, including Alexander Balas and Antiochus VI. **15:6** *Mint your own coinage.* When the Seleucids authorized mintage, the name of the local king was on the coin.

15:15–24 Letter from Rome to renew political allegiance and friendship. Another interpolation. Distinctive names and places are mentioned to make the letter appear more authentic. **15:16** Lucius Caecilius Metullus (consul in 142 BCE) and King Ptolemy VIII Euergetes II, who ruled in Egypt (145–116 BCE). **15:22** It should be noted that Demetrius II of Syria was still a prisoner in Parthia, and the Romans did not recognize Antiochus VII. *Attalus* II of Pergamum (159–138 BCE). *Ariarathes* V of Cappadocia (162–130 BCE). For *Arsaces* of Parthia, see note on 14:1–3. **15:23** Places mentioned include Delos in the Cyclades and other free city-states in Greece, the Greek Islands, Asia Minor, and Cyrene (a Greek colony in northern Africa).

Delos, and to Myndos, and to Sicyon, and to Caria, and to Samos, and to Pamphylia, and to Lycia, and to Halicarnassus, and to Rhodes, and to Phaselis, and to Cos, and to Side, and to Aradus and Gortyna and Cnidus and Cyprus and Cyrene. ²⁴They also sent a copy of these things to the high priest Simon.

25 King Antiochus besieged Dor for the second time, continually throwing his forces against it and making engines of war, and he shut Trypho up and kept him from going out or in. ²⁶And Simon sent to Antiochus*ʷ* two thousand picked troops, to fight for him, and silver and gold and a large amount of military equipment. ²⁷But he refused to receive them and broke all the agreements he formerly had made with Simon and became estranged from him. ²⁸He sent to him Athenobius, one of his Friends, to confer with him, saying, "You hold control of Joppa and Gazara and the citadel in Jerusalem; they are cities of my kingdom. ²⁹You have devastated their territory, you have done great damage in the land, and you have taken possession of many places in my kingdom. ³⁰Now, then, hand over the cities that you have seized and the tribute money of the places that you have conquered outside the borders of Judea, ³¹or else pay me five hundred talents of silver for the destruction that you have caused and five hundred talents more for the tribute money of the cities. Otherwise we will come and make war on you."

32 So Athenobius, the king's Friend, came to Jerusalem, and when he saw the splendor of Simon, and the sideboard with its gold and silver plate, and his great magnificence, he was amazed. When he reported to him the king's message, ³³Simon said to him in reply: "We have neither taken foreign land nor seized foreign property, but only the inheritance of our ancestors, which at one time had been unjustly taken by our enemies. ³⁴Now that we have the opportunity, we are firmly holding the inheritance of our ancestors. ³⁵As for Joppa and Gazara, which you demand, they were causing great damage among the people and to our land, for them we will give you one hundred talents."

Athenobius*ˣ* did not answer him a word ³⁶but returned in wrath to the king and reported to him these words and also the splendor of Simon and all that he had seen. And the king was very angry.

37 Meanwhile Trypho embarked on a ship and escaped to Orthosia. ³⁸Then the king made Cendebeus commander-in-chief of the coastal country and gave him troops of infantry and cavalry. ³⁹He commanded him to encamp against Judea, to build up Kedron and fortify its gates, and to make war on the people, but the king pursued Trypho. ⁴⁰So Cendebeus came to Jamnia and began to provoke the people and invade Judea and take the people captive and kill them. ⁴¹He built up Kedron and stationed horsemen and troops there, so that they might go out and make raids along the highways of Judea, as the king had ordered him.

16 John went up from Gazara and reported to his father Simon what Cendebeus had done. ²And Simon called in his two eldest sons Judas and John and said to them: "My brothers and I and my father's house have fought the wars of Israel from our youth until this day, and things have prospered in our hands so that we have delivered Israel many times. ³But now I have grown old, and you by heaven's*ʸ* mercy are mature in years. Take my place and my brother's, and go out and fight for our nation, and may the help that comes from heaven be with you."

4 So John*ᶻ* chose out of the country twenty thousand warriors and cavalry, and they marched against Cendebeus and camped for the night in Modein. ⁵Early in the morning they started out and marched into the plain, where a large force of infantry and cavalry was coming to meet them, and a wadi lay

w 15.26 Gk *him*   *x* 15.35 Gk *He*   *y* 16.3 Gk *his*   *z* 16.4 Other ancient authorities read *he*

15:25–36 Antiochus VII refuses Simon's help and nullifies the earlier agreement with Simon. This resumes the narrative that was paused in v. 15. **15:33** *Only the inheritance of our ancestors* is a Greek legal phrase asserting a rightful claim to one's ancestral land. **15:35** *Joppa and Gazara.* See 12:33; 13:43–48.
15:37–16:10 Campaign of Simon's son, John Hyrcanus I, against Cendebeus, governor of the coastal region. **15:39** Kedron is about four miles southeast of Jamnia. Trypho flees to Orthosia (north of Tripolis), but Antiochus VII pursues him. According to Josephus, Trypho is eventually killed by Antiochus VII (*J.W.* 1.2.2). **16:1** John Hyrcanus I is based in Gazara (cf. 13:53). **16:4** Cavalry are now

between them. [6]Then he and his army lined up against them. He saw that the soldiers were afraid to cross the wadi, so he crossed over first, and when his troops saw him, they crossed over after him. [7]Then he divided the army and placed the cavalry in the center of the infantry, for the cavalry of the enemy were very numerous. [8]They sounded the trumpets, and Cendebeus and his army were put to flight; many of them fell wounded, and the rest fled into the stronghold. [9]At that time Judas the brother of John was wounded, but John pursued them until Cendebeus[a] reached Kedron, which he had built. [10]They also fled into the towers that were in the fields of Azotus, and John[b] burned it with fire, and about two thousand of them fell. He then returned to Judea safely.

11 Now Ptolemy son of Abubus had been appointed governor over the plain of Jericho; he had a large store of silver and gold, [12]for he was son-in-law of the high priest. [13]His heart was lifted up; he determined to get control of the country and made treacherous plans against Simon and his sons, to do away with them. [14]Now Simon was visiting the towns of the country and attending to their needs, and he went down to Jericho with his sons Mattathias and Judas, in the one hundred seventy-seventh year, in the eleventh month, which is the month of Shebat. [15]The son of Abubus received them treacherously in the little stronghold called Dok, which he had built; he gave them a

great banquet and hid men there. [16]When Simon and his sons were drunk, Ptolemy and his men rose up, took their weapons, rushed in against Simon in the banquet hall, and killed him and his two sons, as well as some of his servants. [17]So he committed an act of great treachery and returned evil for good.

18 Then Ptolemy wrote a report about these things and sent it to the king, asking him to send troops to aid him and to turn over to him the towns and the country. [19]He sent other troops to Gazara to do away with John; he sent letters to the captains asking them to come to him so that he might give them silver and gold and gifts, [20]and he sent other troops to take possession of Jerusalem and the temple hill. [21]But someone ran ahead and reported to John at Gazara that his father and brothers had perished and that "he has sent men to kill you also." [22]When he heard this, he was greatly shocked; he seized the men who came to destroy him and killed them, for he had found out that they were seeking to destroy him.

23 The rest of the acts of John and his wars and the brave deeds that he did, and the building of the walls that he completed, and his achievements [24]are written in the annals of his high priesthood, from the time that he became high priest after his father.

a 16.9 Gk he   b 16.10 Gk he

part of the Judean army. **16:6** Crossing the stream echoes Judas in 5:40–43. **16:7–10** John's forces defeat Cendebeus's army. **16:10** Azotus was already burned (10:84).

16:11–17 Ptolemy, Simon's son-in-law, murders Simon and his sons Judas and Mattathias in 134 BCE.

16:18–24 John Hyrcanus foils Ptolemy's plot to kill him and succeeds his father. **16:23–24** *The annals of his high priesthood*, which may or may not have existed, imitates the repeated references of "the annals of the Kings" in 1–2 Kings (cf. also 1 Macc. 9:22).

2 MACCABEES

Authorship, Date, and Literary History

Despite what its title and canonical sequence might suggest, 2 Maccabees is not a sequel to 1 Maccabees but a separate account of the Hasmonean defense of the Jerusalem temple that focuses on the victories of Judas Maccabeus (see **"Judas Maccabeus," p. 1541**). Writing in Greek sometime between 150 and 63 BCE, the author identifies the work as an epitome—a digest of a no longer extant five-volume history by Jason of Cyrene (2:23). In contrast to 1 Maccabees, which chronicles a longer period, from the conquests of Alexander the Great through the establishment and early succession of the Hasmonean dynasty, 2 Maccabees concentrates on the fate of the Jerusalem temple against the threats of Seleucid rulers, most notably Antiochus IV Epiphanes. Second Maccabees has all the makings of a blockbuster drama (murder, political intrigue, revolt, treason, bribery) interlaced with exemplary demonstrations of piety and an emphasis on divine retribution. The text was preserved as part of the Septuagint (an early Gk. translation of the Hebrew Bible) and is included in both Roman Catholic and Eastern Orthodox canons.

2 Maccabees in Jewish and Christian Tradition

Most popular among early Jewish and Christian uses of 2 Maccabees is the story of the Maccabean martyrs (Eleazar, the seven brothers, and their mother). The book of 4 Maccabees makes extensive use of 2 Macc. 6:18–7:42, elaborating on the deaths of the martyrs and framing the narrative within the context of a philosophical treatise. The book of Hebrews also seems to be familiar with the story (cf. Heb. 11:35–38). In the fourth century, John Chrysostom composed two sermons, "On the Maccabees," which focus primarily on the mother and the youngest son, and a third sermon, "On Eleazar and the Seven Boys." A feast and cult of the Maccabees were also well established by this time. Second Maccabees is not attested in rabbinic tradition, though the first known use of the term *Judaism* (Gk. *Ioudaismos*) appears in 2 Maccabees (2:21; 8:1; 14:38).

Second Maccabees shares with some other early Jewish literature a belief in divine retribution and concern for the preservation of the temple (see **"Divine Retribution," p. 339**). The book's treatment of divine retribution finds a close parallel in the book of Judith, which was composed around the same time and shares its concern for the preservation of the sanctuary (Jdt. 8:21; cf. 2 Macc. 1–2; 10; 14:34–36; 15:18). In 2 Maccabees and Judith, the military hero (Judas and Judith, whose names are derived from their homeland, Judea) claims that God will repay people according to their actions and encourages the audience with examples of God's past activity on their ancestors' behalf (Jdt. 8–9; 2 Macc. 8). Second Maccabees also participates in a tradition that seeks to establish a direct connection between the Second Temple and material aspects of the First Temple. Like the books of Baruch and 2 Baruch, which describe the preservation of vessels from the First Temple (Bar. 1:8–9; 2 Bar. 6), 2 Maccabees establishes continuity with the First Temple through the story of the fire from the altar of the First Temple hidden by Jeremiah and restored with Nehemiah (2 Macc. 1–2). The concern for material continuity and emphasis on the preservation of the physical temple in 2 Maccabees contrast with emerging notions of the community-as-temple in Qumran and some New Testament literature (4Q174; 1 Cor. 3:16–17; Eph. 2:19–22; 1 Pet. 2:5).

Reading Guide

Second Maccabees is a story about Jewish identity and what it means—in the language of the author—"to be/come a Jew" (2 Macc. 6:6; 9:17). The book begins with two letters (1:1–2:18), followed by a prologue introducing the work (2:19–32) and a long narrative section (3:1–15:39). The two letters prefixed to the historical narrative purport to be written by Jews living in and around Jerusalem and are addressed to Jews in a Diaspora setting. While the connection between the letters and the epitome is unclear, the celebration of booths (later known as Hanukkah) is a feature of both (cf. 1:9, 18; 2:16–18; 10:1–8; see **"Hanukkah," p. 1544**). In the prologue following the letters, the author/epitomist introduces the narrative as "the story of Judas Maccabeus and his brothers" (2:19). However, aside from a brief mention in 2 Macc. 5:27, the hero, Judas Maccabeus, does not appear in the narrative until chap. 8, the midpoint of the book. (Cf. Jdt. 8:1, which is the first time Judith is introduced in that book.) The narrative account begins with an attack against the temple in the time of the pious high priest Onias. Although the first attack is thwarted by God's defense of the temple

on account of the pious Onias, the threat continues to mount as Onias is ousted through corrupt political dealings, and his brother, Jason, assumes the high priesthood. Jason abandons ancestral traditions, establishes a gymnasium, and introduces Greek ways of life (see **"The Bible in Its Ancient Contexts," pp. 2150–52**, for more on Hellenism). The situation worsens when Menelaus secures the high priesthood through bribery and arranges the murder of Onias. While under the corrupt leadership of Menelaus, Antiochus attacks the city again—this time, successfully—massacring the city's inhabitants and plundering and desecrating the temple. The violent oppression reaches a climax with the martyrdoms of Eleazar, the seven brothers, and their mother (6:18–7:42), whose exemplary courage anticipates the turning point that comes through Judas's revolt (chaps. 8–9). Following the initial revolt and defeat of Antiochus, Judas purifies the temple and leads a series of campaigns in which he is consistently victorious against threatening rulers. Another martyrdom (Razis, a prominent Jerusalem elder) immediately precedes Judas's final battle, which results in the defeat and death of Nicanor and the institution of an annual festival commemorating the event.

The deaths of the martyrs are pivotal in the narrative, illustrating that victory is won not through military might but through piety and courage (see **"Martyrdom and Martyrs," p. 1584**). In their noble deaths, the martyrs secure a path to resurrection and demonstrate that the tyrant king has no power over them. Throughout the narrative retelling, the epitomist is careful to emphasize that God determines outcomes. When Antiochus prevails in subduing the people and pillaging the temple in 2 Macc. 5, the epitomist explains that God allowed it "because of the sins of those who lived in the city" (5:17). This event stands in contrast to the many times in the narrative that God is portrayed as a divine warrior, the defender of the Jews (3:22–28; 5:15–20; 11:13; 14:34–36; 15:6–37; cf. Jdt. 5). Judas, in the second half of the book, is victorious because God helps him and he acts according to what God has determined. At the end of the narrative, Judas is praised as "the man who was ever in body and soul the defender of his people" (15:30). While a focal point of 2 Maccabees is the celebration of Hanukkah and Nicanor's Day, the origins of which are laid out in the narrative, the celebration is entwined with a theological outlook that sees God as defender and protector of the Jews so long as they faithfully observe God's law.

Rebecca L. Harris and Emerson B. Powery

1

The Jews in Jerusalem and those in the land of Judea,

To their Jewish kindred in Egypt,

Greetings and true peace.

2 May God do good to you, and may he remember his covenant with Abraham and Isaac and Jacob, his faithful servants. ³May he give you all a heart to worship him and to do his will with a strong heart and a willing spirit. ⁴May he open your heart to his law and his commandments, and may he bring peace. ⁵May he hear your prayers and be reconciled to you, and may he not forsake you in time of evil. ⁶We are now praying for you here.

7 In the reign of Demetrius, in the one hundred sixty-ninth year, we Jews wrote to you, in the critical distress that came upon us in those years after Jason and his company revolted from the holy land and the kingdom ⁸and burned the gate and shed innocent blood. We prayed to the Lord and were heard, and we offered sacrifice and grain offering, and we lit the lamps and set out the loaves. ⁹And now see that you keep the Festival of

1:1–9 Letter to the Jews in Egypt. The first of two letters prefixed to the narrative of 2 Maccabees addresses the Jewish community in Egypt, imploring its members to observe the Festival of Booths (later becoming a separate festival known as Hanukkah). This community was well established, its origins reaching at least as far back as the exilic period (see Jer. 44:1). The letter follows standard Greek conventions, opening with "greetings" and well-wishes (vv. 1b–6) and concluding with a request that includes a date (v. 9). **1:2** Remembering the covenant with Abraham (Gen. 12:1–9; 15; 17) foregrounds the bond shared between the writers (Jerusalem Jews) and recipients (Egyptian Jews), who are called "kindred" (v. 1). **1:4** The image of an open heart is found also in the Qumran Hodayot (1QHᵃ XIII, 32–33; XVIII, 31), Rule of the Community (1QS XI, 15–16), and the New Testament (see Luke 24:32; Acts 16:14; Eph. 1:18). **1:7–8** The body of the letter references critical events during the tumultuous reign of Demetrius (145–141 and 129–125 BCE)—namely, the murder of Jonathan the high priest in ca. 142 BCE (see 1 Macc. 12:48; 13:23). **1:9** *Festival of Booths in the month of Chislev*

Booths[a] in the month of Chislev, in the one hundred eighty-eighth year.

10 The people of Jerusalem and of Judea and the council and Judas,

To Aristobulus, who is of the family of the anointed priests, teacher of King Ptolemy, and to the Jews in Egypt,

Greetings and good health.

11 Having been saved by God out of grave dangers, we thank him greatly for taking our side against the king,[b] 12for he drove out those who fought against the holy city. 13When the leader reached Persia with a force that seemed irresistible, they were cut to pieces in the temple of Nanea by a deception employed by the priests of the goddess[c] Nanea. 14On the pretext of intending to marry her, Antiochus came to the place together with his Friends, to secure most of its treasures as a dowry. 15When the priests of the temple of Nanea had set out the treasures and Antiochus had come with a few men inside the wall of the sacred precinct, they closed the temple as soon as he entered it. 16Opening a secret door in the ceiling, they threw stones and struck down the leader and his men; they dismembered them and cut off their heads and threw them to the people outside. 17Blessed in every way be our God, who has delivered up those who have behaved impiously.

18 Since on the twenty-fifth day of Chislev we shall celebrate the purification of the temple, we thought it necessary to notify you, in order that you also may celebrate the Festival of Booths[d] and the fire given when Nehemiah, who built the temple and the altar, offered sacrifices.

19 For when our ancestors were being led captive to Persia, the pious priests of that time took some of the fire of the altar and secretly hid it in the hollow of a dry cistern, where they took such precautions that the place was unknown to anyone. 20But after many years had passed, when it pleased God, Nehemiah, having been commissioned by the king of Persia, sent the descendants of the priests who had hidden the fire to get it. And when they

a 1.9 Or *Tabernacles* b 1.11 Cn: Gk *as those who array themselves against a king* c 1.13 Gk lacks *the goddess* d 1.18 Or *Tabernacles*

refers to Hanukkah, celebrated in the ninth month commemorating the reclamation and rededication of the temple under Judas Maccabeus (10:1–8). The Festival of Booths is typically celebrated in the seventh month, Tishri (Lev. 23:33–43; cf. Neh. 8:13–18), but here was delayed by the invasion of Antiochus. *One hundred eighty-eighth year* of the Seleucid era (= 124 BCE) might provide a clue for dating the book, or at least the composition of the first letter.

1:10–2:18 Second letter to the Jews in Egypt. This letter recounts the death of Antiochus IV and invites the Egyptian Jews to join in the celebration of Hanukkah, linking it to a festival commemorating the restoration of the temple and sacrificial cult in the time of Nehemiah. A lengthy digression recounting the miraculous preservation of fire from the altar of the First Temple follows what might have been the initial close of the letter (1:17–18). By linking the two festivals, Booths/Hanukkah and the festival of the fire associated with Nehemiah, the letter's authors situate the celebration of Hanukkah and the event it commemorates (Judas's restoration of the temple) within a tradition that reaches back to the time of Jeremiah, establishing continuity with the First Temple. **1:10–17** The letter provides a description of Antiochus IV's death that contrasts with other accounts. **1:10** Josephus mentions a *council* (Gk. "gerousia") of elders in Jerusalem in the time of Antiochus III (Josephus, *Ant.* 12.138–44; cf. Jdt. 4:8; 11:14; 15:8; 2 Macc. 11:27; 1 Macc. 12:6). Fragments of a dialogue between Aristobulus and King Ptolemy, preserved in the writings of Clement of Alexandria (*Strom.* 1.22), record Aristobulus educating Ptolemy in the primacy and superiority of torah wisdom, from which Greek philosophy derives. **1:11–12** God, depicted as a divine warrior (cf. 8:36; 11:13; 15:34; Jdt. 5; Deut. 3:22), is credited with saving the city against the attack of Antiochus IV. **1:13–16** Other sources record Antiochus dying of divinely inflicted disease or deep disappointment, not while attacking a temple (Polybius, *Hist.* 31.9; 1 Macc. 6:1–16). At the end of the book, Nicanor suffers the same fate as Antiochus and his men—dismemberment and decapitation (15:30–35). **1:18–2:18** Drawing on traditions related to Nehemiah and Jeremiah, the letter's authors establish a line of continuity from Judas Maccabeus's rededication of the temple (1:18a) to its restoration after the Babylonian exile (1:18b–36), to the last days of the First Temple in the time of Jeremiah (2:1–8), and to its dedication by Solomon and early manifestations of God's presence in the time of Moses (2:9–12). **1:18** In the books of Ezra and Nehemiah, Joshua and Zerubbabel lead the efforts of rebuilding the temple (Ezra 3:1–9), and Nehemiah, the rebuilding of Jerusalem's walls (Neh. 2–6). **1:19** The exile was to

reported to us that they had not found fire but only a thick liquid, he ordered them to dip it out and bring it. ²¹When the materials for the sacrifices were presented, Nehemiah ordered the priests to sprinkle the liquid on the wood and on the things laid upon it. ²²When this had been done and some time had passed, and when the sun, which had been clouded over, shone out, a great fire blazed up, so that all marveled. ²³And while the sacrifice was being consumed, the priests offered prayer— the priests and everyone. Jonathan led, and the rest responded, as did Nehemiah. ²⁴The prayer was to this effect:

"O Lord, Lord God, Creator of all things, you are awe-inspiring and strong and just and merciful; you alone are king and are kind; ²⁵you alone are bountiful; you alone are just and almighty and eternal. You rescue Israel from every evil; you chose the ancestors and consecrated them. ²⁶Accept this sacrifice on behalf of all your people Israel and preserve your portion and make it holy. ²⁷Gather together our scattered people; set free those who are slaves among the nations; look on those who are rejected and despised; and let the nations know that you are our God. ²⁸Punish those who oppress and are insolent with pride. ²⁹Plant your people in your holy place, as Moses promised."

30 Then the priests sang the hymns. ³¹After the materials of the sacrifice had been consumed, Nehemiah ordered that the liquid that was left should be poured on large stones. ³²When this was done, a flame blazed up, but when the light from the altar shone back, it went out. ³³When this matter became known and it was reported to the king of the Persians that, in the place where the exiled priests had hidden the fire, the liquid had appeared with which Nehemiah and his associates had burned the materials of the sacrifice, ³⁴the

king investigated the matter and enclosed the place and made it sacred. ³⁵And with those persons whom the king favored he exchanged many excellent gifts. ³⁶Nehemiah and his associates called this "nephthar," which means purification, but by most people it is called "naphtha."

2 One finds in the records that the prophet Jeremiah ordered those who were being deported to take some of the fire, as has been mentioned, ²and that the prophet, after giving them the law, instructed those who were being deported not to forget the commandments of the Lord or to be led astray in their thoughts on seeing the gold and silver statues and their adornment. ³And with other similar words he exhorted them that the law should not depart from their hearts.

4 It was also in the same document that the prophet, having received an oracle, ordered that the tent and the ark should follow with him and that he went out to the mountain where Moses had gone up and had seen the inheritance of God. ⁵Jeremiah came and found a cave dwelling, and he brought there the tent and the ark and the altar of incense; then he sealed up the entrance. ⁶Some of those who followed him came up intending to mark the way but could not find it. ⁷When Jeremiah learned of it, he rebuked them and declared, "The place shall remain unknown until God gathers his people together again and shows his mercy. ⁸Then the Lord will disclose these things, and the glory of the Lord and the cloud will appear, as they were shown in the case of Moses and as Solomon asked that the place should be specially consecrated."

9 It was also made clear that, being possessed of wisdom, Solomon*e* offered sacrifice

e 2.9 Gk *he*

Babylon, but by the time of Nehemiah, the region formerly known as Babylon had become part of the Persian Empire. **1:23** There are a number of priests called Jonathan in Ezra and Nehemiah (Ezra 8:6; 10:15; Neh. 12:11). Judith 15:14 describes a similar situation. **1:24–25** The notion that God rescues Israel anticipates later claims that "the Jews had a Defender" (8:36; cf. 11:13; 14:34). **1:29** Cf. Deut. 30:1–5; Jer. 32:41. **1:33–34** In Persian Zoroastrianism, fire is considered holy. The investigation and verification of the event by the Persian king might intend to provide a degree of authentication. **1:36** The word *nephthar*, which is otherwise unknown, may be a combination of *naphtha* (a sticky, flammable substance) and the Persian word "atar" (fire). **2:1–3** The letter reflects the tradition of Jer. 42–43, in which Jeremiah remains in Judah following the destruction. Other early Jewish literature recounts Jeremiah going into exile in Babylon and his scribe, Baruch, remaining in Judah (2 Bar. 10:1–5; 4 Bar. 3:15–16). **2:4** *The prophet* refers to Jeremiah, and *the mountain* is Mount Nebo (see Deut. 32:49). **2:8** *The glory of the Lord and the cloud* indicated manifestations of God's presence in

for the dedication and completion of the temple. [10]Just as Moses prayed to the Lord and fire came down from heaven and consumed the sacrifices, so also Solomon prayed, and the fire came down and consumed the whole burnt offerings. [11]And Moses said, "They were consumed because the purification offering had not been eaten." [12]Likewise Solomon also kept the eight days.

13 The same things are reported in the records and in the memoirs of Nehemiah and also that he founded a library and collected the books about the kings and prophets and the writings of David and letters of kings about votive offerings. [14]In the same way Judas also collected all the books that had been lost on account of the war that had come upon us, and they are in our possession. [15]So if you have need of them, send people to get them for you.

16 Since, therefore, we are about to celebrate the purification, we write to you. You will do well if you celebrate these days. [17]It is God who has saved all his people and has returned the inheritance to all and the kingship and the priesthood and the consecration, [18]as he promised through the law. We have hope in God that he will soon have mercy on us and will gather us from everywhere under heaven

into his holy place, for he has rescued us from great evils and has purified the place.

19 The story of Judas Maccabeus and his brothers, and the purification of the greatest temple, and the dedication of the altar, [20]and further the wars against Antiochus Epiphanes and his son Eupator, [21]and the appearances that came from heaven to those who fought bravely for Judaism, so that though few in number they seized the whole land and pursued the barbarian hordes [22]and regained possession of the temple famous throughout the world and liberated the city and reestablished the laws that were about to be abolished, while the Lord with great kindness became gracious to them—[23]all this, which has been set forth by Jason of Cyrene in five volumes, we shall attempt to condense into a single book. [24]For considering the flood of lines written and the difficulty there is for those who wish to enter upon the narratives of history because of the mass of material, [25]we have aimed to please those who wish to read, to make it easy for those who are inclined to memorize, and to profit all readers. [26]For us who have undertaken the toil of abbreviating, it is no light matter but calls

the time of Moses (Exod. 13:21; 16:10; 40:34–38) and Solomon (1 Kgs. 8:10–12). **2:10** See Lev. 9:23–24 (Moses) and 2 Chr. 7:1 (Solomon). **2:11** Probably a reference to Lev. 10:16–18. **2:12** See 1 Kgs. 8:65–66. **2:13** *The records* and *the memoirs* of Nehemiah might refer to a no longer extant text (or texts) that preserves traditions (like the fire story in 1:18–36 and the library story told here) not known in the now canonical book of Nehemiah. The list of collections is of interest for what it might reveal about the process of canonization. *Books about the kings and prophets* likely include 1–2 Samuel, 1–2 Kings, and 1–2 Chronicles. *Prophets* probably refers to the now canonical books of the prophets (except Daniel) and *the writings of David* to Psalms. (The Qumran psalm scroll, 11QPs[a], attributes to David over four thousand psalms.) There is less certainty regarding the *letters of kings about votive offerings*, though these might include letters found in Ezra and Nehemiah. **2:14** See 1 Macc. 1:54–57. **2:16–18** The conclusion echoes the invitation to celebrate Hanukkah and the purification of the temple, mentioned at the beginning of the digression (1:18), and the theme of God as the rescuer of the Jews, found in the letter's introduction (1:10–11).

2:19–32 Preface. The epitomist frames the digest with a preface describing its content, scope, and purpose and an epilogue announcing the conclusion of the work (15:38–39). **2:19** Though Judas is here introduced as the central figure of the story, he does not become the focus until chap. 8, following the deaths of the Maccabean martyrs (see 6:18–7:42). **2:20–21** Antiochus IV was also called Epiphanes, meaning "god manifest." The epitomist challenges this identification through a wordplay that claims *the appearances* (Gk. "epiphaneisai") that come from heaven as superior and more authentic. Another wordplay demonstrates God's defense of the Jews against *the barbarian hordes* or Greeks—a term the Greeks generally used for non-Greeks. *Judaism* is the earliest known usage of this term in Jewish literature (see 14:38; cf. 4 Macc. 4:26). "Ioudaismos" (Gk.) refers to a broad set of practices (including religious ones) in contrast to "hellēnismos" (Hellenization; cf. 4:13). **2:23** This five-volume work is no longer extant, and Jason of Cyrene (modern Libya) is not known aside from this reference and an inscription of the same name on the temple of Thothmes III in Egypt, which may refer to the same person.

for sweat and loss of sleep, [27]just as it is not easy for one who prepares a banquet and seeks the benefit of others. Nevertheless, to secure the gratitude of many we will gladly endure the uncomfortable toil, [28]leaving the responsibility for exact details to the compiler, while devoting our effort to arriving at the outlines of the condensation. [29]For as the master builder of a new house must be concerned with the whole construction, while the one who undertakes its painting and decoration has to consider only what is suitable for its adornment, such in my judgment is the case with us. [30]It is the duty of the original historian to occupy the ground, to discuss matters from every side, and to take trouble with details, [31]but the one who recasts the narrative should be allowed to strive for brevity of expression and to forego exhaustive treatment. [32]At this point, therefore, let us begin our narrative, without adding any more to what has already been said, for it would be foolish to lengthen the preface while cutting short the history itself.

3 While the holy city was inhabited in unbroken peace and the laws were strictly observed because of the piety of the high priest Onias and his hatred of wickedness, [2]it came about that the kings themselves honored the place and glorified the temple with the finest presents, [3]even to the extent that King Seleucus of Asia defrayed from his own revenues all the expenses connected with the service of the sacrifices.

4 But a man named Simon, of the tribe of Balgea,[f] who had been made captain of the temple, had a disagreement with the high priest about the administration of the city market. [5]Since he could not prevail over Onias, he went to Apollonius of Tarsus,[g] who at that time was governor of Coelesyria and Phoenicia, [6]and reported to him that the treasury in Jerusalem was full of untold sums of money, so that the amount of the funds could not be reckoned, and that they did not belong to the account of the sacrifices but that it was possible for them to fall under the control of the king. [7]When Apollonius met the king, he told him of the money about which he had been informed. The king[h] chose Heliodorus, who was in charge of his affairs, and sent him with commands to effect the removal of the reported wealth. [8]Heliodorus at once set out on his journey, ostensibly to make a tour of inspection of the cities of Coelesyria and Phoenicia but in fact to carry out the king's purpose.

9 When he had arrived at Jerusalem and had been kindly welcomed by the high priest of[i] the city, he told about the disclosure that had been made and stated why he had come, and he inquired whether this really was the situation. [10]The high priest explained that there were some deposits belonging to widows and orphans [11]and also some money of Hyrcanus son of Tobias, a man of very prominent position, and that it totaled in all four hundred talents of silver and two hundred of gold. To such an extent the impious Simon had misrepresented the facts. [12]And he said[j] that it was utterly impossible that wrong should be done to those people who had trusted in the holiness of the place and in the sanctity and inviolability of the temple that is honored throughout the whole world.

f 3.4 Lat Arm: Gk *Benjamin*   *g* 3.5 Gk *Tharseas*   *h* 3.7 Gk *He*   *i* 3.9 Other ancient authorities read *and*   *j* 3.12 Gk lacks *And he said*

3:1–4:6 Onias and Simon. This section describes the first attack on the temple, during the reign of Seleucus IV Philopator (187–175 BCE), which is thwarted by divine intervention in response to the people's prayers (3:14b–21) and *the piety of the high priest Onias* (3:1). The account illustrates central themes of the book: divine retribution and God's defense of the Jews and the temple. Piety, here exemplified by Onias and later by the Maccabean martyrs (6:18–7:42), is a catalyst for God's defense (3:22–28) and Judas's restoration of the temple (8:1–10:9). **3:1–21** The setting of the first attack anticipates a favorable outcome. Taking place in the time of Onias, whose priesthood is defined by peace and torah observance, the attack is destined to fail because the behaviors of the high priest and the city's inhabitants elicit divine favor. This setting contrasts with the impiety that characterizes subsequent high priesthoods (Jason and Menelaus in 4:7–34) and leaves Jerusalem and the temple vulnerable. **3:1** *Onias* is Onias III, son of Simon II (cf. Sir. 50), who held office before 175 BCE. **3:4** Following the Latin Vulgate and Armenian manuscripts, *Balgea* connects Simon to the Levitical clan of Bilgah (see Neh. 12:5; 1 Chr. 24:14), not the tribe of Benjamin as in the Greek manuscripts. **3:5** *Coelesyria* ("hollow Syria") and *Phoenicia* were then part of the Seleucid Empire. **3:11** *Hyrcanus*

13 But Heliodorus,[k] because of the orders he had from the king, said that this money must in any case be confiscated for the king's treasury. [14]So he set a day and went in to direct the inspection of these funds.

There was no little distress throughout the whole city. [15]The priests prostrated themselves before the altar in their priestly vestments and called toward heaven upon him who had given the law about deposits, that he should keep them safe for those who had deposited them. [16]To see the appearance of the high priest was to be wounded at heart, for his face and the change in his color disclosed the anguish of his soul. [17]For terror and bodily trembling had come over the man, which plainly showed to those who looked at him the pain lodged in his heart. [18]People also hurried out of their houses in crowds to make a general supplication because the holy place was about to be brought into dishonor. [19]Women girded with sackcloth under their breasts thronged the streets. Some of the young women who were kept indoors ran together to the gates, and some to the walls, while others peered out of the windows. [20]And holding up their hands to heaven, they all made supplication. [21]There was something pitiable in the prostration of the whole populace and the anxiety of the high priest in his great anguish.

22 While they were calling upon the Almighty Lord that he would keep what had been entrusted safe and secure for those who had entrusted it, [23]Heliodorus went on with what had been decided. [24]But when he arrived at the treasury with his bodyguard, then and there the Sovereign of spirits and of all authority caused so great a manifestation that all who had been so bold as to accompany him were astounded by the power of God and became faint with terror. [25]For there appeared to them a magnificently adorned horse, with a rider of frightening appearance; it rushed furiously at Heliodorus and struck at him with its front hoofs. Its rider was seen to have armor and weapons of gold. [26]Two young men also appeared to him, remarkably strong, gloriously beautiful and splendidly dressed, who stood on either side of him and flogged him continuously, inflicting many blows on him. [27]When he suddenly fell to the ground and deep darkness came over him, his men took him up, put him on a stretcher, [28]and carried him away—this man who had just entered the aforesaid treasury with a great retinue and all his bodyguard but was now unable to help himself with all his weapons. He recognized clearly the sovereign power of God.

29 While he lay prostrate, speechless because of the divine intervention and deprived of any hope of recovery, [30]they praised the Lord who had acted marvelously for his own place. And the temple, which a little while before was full of fear and disturbance, was filled with joy and gladness, now that the Almighty Lord had appeared.

31 Some of Heliodorus's friends quickly begged Onias to call upon the Most High to grant life to one who was lying quite at his last breath. [32]So the high priest, fearing that the king might get the notion that some foul play had been perpetrated by the Jews with regard to Heliodorus, offered sacrifice for the man's recovery. [33]While the high priest was making the atonement, the same young men appeared again to Heliodorus dressed in the same clothing, and they stood and said, "Be very grateful to the high priest Onias, since for his sake the Lord has granted you your life. [34]And see that you, who have been flogged by heaven, report to all people the majestic power of God." Having said this, they vanished.

35 Then Heliodorus offered sacrifice to the Lord and made very great vows to

k 3.13 Gk the other

son of Tobias, not to be confused with John Hyrcanus, the Hasmonean high priest who reigned from 134 to 104 BCE. This Hyrcanus and his family, known as the Tobiads, were supportive of Hellenistic reforms. **3:14b–21** The author crafts the people's response to the threat as a genuine experience of distress felt by *the whole city/populace* (vv. 14b, 21). Various groups are singled out to demonstrate the totality of the response—*priests* (v. 15), *the high priest* (vv. 16–17), the general population (v. 18), and *women* and *young women* (vv. 19–20). **3:22–40** In response to the people's piety and prayers, God defends the temple with a dramatic show of power. The confrontation demonstrates God's supremacy over Antiochus's emissary (vv. 28, 34–36), foreshadowing God's defeat of the king (9:5). **3:25** For apparitions of armed cavalry as agents of divine warfare, see 5:2–3; 10:29; and 11:8. **3:26** Angels flog Heliodorus; cf. 3 Macc. 2:21–23; 6:18–19.

the Savior of his life, and having bidden Onias farewell, he marched off with his forces to the king. ³⁶He bore testimony to all concerning the deeds of the supreme God, which he had seen with his own eyes. ³⁷When the king asked Heliodorus what sort of person would be suitable to send on another mission to Jerusalem, he replied, ³⁸"If you have any enemy or plotter against your government, send him there, for you will get him back thoroughly flogged, if he survives at all, for there is certainly some power of God about the place. ³⁹For he who has his dwelling in heaven watches over that place himself and brings it aid, and he strikes and destroys those who come to do it injury." ⁴⁰This was the outcome of the episode of Heliodorus and the protection of the treasury.

4 The previously mentioned Simon, who had informed about the money against[l] his own country, slandered Onias, saying that it was he who had incited Heliodorus and had been the real cause of the misfortune. ²He dared to designate as a plotter against the government the man who was the benefactor of the city, the protector of his compatriots, and a zealot for the laws. ³When his hatred progressed to such a degree that even murders were committed by one of Simon's approved agents, ⁴Onias recognized that the rivalry was serious and that Apollonius son of Menestheus,[m] and governor of Coelesyria and Phoenicia, was intensifying the malice of Simon. ⁵So he appealed to the king, not accusing his compatriots but having in view the welfare, both public and private, of all the people. ⁶For he saw that, without the king's attention, public affairs could not again reach a peaceful settlement and that Simon would not stop his folly.

7 When Seleucus died and Antiochus, who was called Epiphanes, succeeded to the kingdom, Jason the brother of Onias obtained the high priesthood by corruption, ⁸promising the king through a petition three hundred sixty talents of silver and from another source of revenue eighty talents. ⁹In addition to this he promised to pay one hundred fifty more if permission were given to establish by his authority a gymnasium and a body of youth for it and to enroll the people of Jerusalem as the Antiochenes in Jerusalem. ¹⁰When the king assented and Jason[n] came to office, he at once shifted his compatriots over to the Greek way of life.

11 He set aside the existing royal concessions to the Jews, secured through John the father of Eupolemus, who went on the mission to establish friendship and alliance with the Romans, and he destroyed the lawful ways of living and introduced new customs contrary to the law. ¹²He took delight in establishing a gymnasium right under the citadel, and he induced the noblest of the young men to wear the Greek hat. ¹³There was such an extreme of Hellenization and increase in the adoption of foreign ways because of the surpassing wickedness of Jason, who was ungodly and no true[o] high priest, ¹⁴that the priests were no longer intent upon their service at the altar.

l 4.1 Gk and   m 4.4 Vg: Meaning of Gk uncertain
n 4.10 Gk he   o 4.13 Gk lacks true

4:1–6 Despite the positive turn of events with God's defense of the temple and Heliodorus's acknowledgment of the supremacy of the Jewish God (3:22–40), this literary unit ends on a low note. The mounting threat against Onias, *benefactor of the city* and *protector of his compatriots*, puts the welfare of the people at risk as well.

4:7–10:9 Antiochus IV Epiphanes comes to power. Antiochus succeeds his brother, Seleucus IV. His reign (175–164 BCE) is marked by the corruption of the priesthood and murder of Onias, the pillaging and desecration of the temple, and the forced Hellenization of the Jews. Tension mounts in the first part of this section and reaches a high point with the martyrdoms of Eleazar, the seven brothers, and their mother. The martyrdoms (6:18–7:42) and subsequent revolt of Judas Maccabeus (8:1–11) mark a turning point in the book (cf. 8:5).

4:7–50 The situation in Jerusalem spirals downward with Jason's usurpation of the high priesthood and imposition of *the Greek way of life* (v. 10). This exchange of *the lawful ways of living* (v. 11) for *unlawful proceedings* (v. 14) is met with just and fitting retribution when the Greeks, whose way of life Hellenized Jews seek to emulate, become their enemies (v. 16). This theme of divine retribution in which the punishment fits the crime recurs in Menelaus's usurpation of the high priesthood from Jason (vv. 23–26) and Andronicus's punishment for the murder of Onias (v. 38). Cf. 5:8–10, 15–20; 9:1–6, 28; 13:3–8. **4:13** *Hellenization* describes a Greek way of life that contrasts with "Judaism"

Despising the sanctuary and neglecting the sacrifices, they hurried to take part in the unlawful proceedings in the wrestling arena after the signal for the discus throwing, [15]disdaining the honors prized by their ancestors and putting the highest value upon Greek forms of prestige. [16]For this reason heavy disaster overtook them, and those whose ways of living they admired and wished to imitate completely became their enemies and punished them. [17]It is no light thing to show irreverence to the divine laws, a fact that later events will make clear.

18 When the quadrennial games were being held at Tyre and the king was present, [19]the vile Jason sent envoys, chosen as being Antiochenes from Jerusalem, to carry three hundred silver drachmas for the sacrifice to Hercules. Those who carried the money, however, thought best not to use it for sacrifice, because that was inappropriate, but to expend it for another purpose. [20]So this money was intended by the sender for the sacrifice to Hercules, but by the decision of its carriers it was applied to the construction of triremes.

21 When Apollonius son of Menestheus was sent to Egypt for the coronation[p] of Philometor as king, Antiochus learned that Philometor[q] had become hostile to his government, and he took measures for his own security. Therefore upon arriving at Joppa he proceeded to Jerusalem. [22]He was welcomed magnificently by Jason and the city and ushered in with a blaze of torches and with shouts. Then he marched his army into Phoenicia.

23 After a period of three years, Jason sent Menelaus, the brother of the previously mentioned Simon, to carry the money to the king and to complete the records of essential business. [24]But he, when presented to the king, extolled him with an air of authority and secured the high priesthood for himself, outbidding Jason by three hundred talents of silver. [25]After receiving the king's orders, he returned, possessing no qualification for the high priesthood but having the hot temper of a cruel tyrant and the rage of a savage wild beast. [26]So Jason, who after supplanting his own brother was supplanted by another man, was driven as a fugitive into the land of Ammon. [27]Although Menelaus continued to hold the office, he did not pay regularly any of the money promised to the king. [28]When Sostratus the captain of the citadel kept requesting payment—for the collection of the revenue was his responsibility—the two of them were summoned by the king on account of this issue. [29]Menelaus left his own brother Lysimachus as deputy in the high priesthood, while Sostratus left Crates, the commander of the Cyprian troops.

30 While such was the state of affairs, it happened that the people of Tarsus and of Mallus revolted because their cities had been given as a present to Antiochis, the king's concubine. [31]So the king went hurriedly to settle the trouble, leaving Andronicus, a man of high rank, to act as his deputy. [32]But Menelaus, thinking he had obtained a suitable opportunity, stole some of the gold vessels of the temple and gave them to Andronicus; other vessels, as it happened, he had sold to Tyre and the neighboring cities. [33]When Onias became fully aware of these acts, he publicly exposed them, having first withdrawn to a place of sanctuary at Daphne near Antioch. [34]Therefore Menelaus, taking Andronicus aside, urged him to kill Onias. Andronicus[r] came to Onias and, resorting to treachery, offered him sworn pledges and gave him his right hand; he persuaded him, in spite of his suspicions, to come out from the place of sanctuary; then, with no regard for justice, he immediately put him out of the way.

35 For this reason not only Jews but many also of other nations were grieved and displeased at the unjust murder of the man. [36]When the king returned from the region of Cilicia, the Jews in the city[s] appealed to him with regard to the unreasonable murder of Onias, and the Greeks shared their hatred of the crime. [37]Therefore Antiochus was grieved at heart and filled with pity and wept because of the moderation and good conduct of the deceased. [38]Inflamed with anger, he immediately stripped the purple

p 4.21 Meaning of Gk uncertain q 4.21 Gk he r 4.34 Gk He s 4.36 Or in each city

(2:21; 8:1; 14:38), here understood as a torah-centered way of life. **4:20** *Triremes* were warships propelled by three rows of oars. **4:21** *Philometor* (Ptolemy IV) ruled circa 172–145 BCE. See note on 1:10. **4:32–34** Menelaus's crimes are even worse than Jason's and include treachery and the arrangement of Onias's murder. **4:33** The temple of Apollo and Artemis at Daphne was a *place of sanctuary*.

robe from Andronicus, tore off his clothes, and led him around the whole city to that very place where he had committed the outrage against Onias, and there he dispatched the bloodthirsty fellow. The Lord thus repaid him with the punishment he deserved.

39 When many acts of sacrilege had been committed in the city by Lysimachus with the connivance of Menelaus, and when report of them had spread abroad, the populace gathered against Lysimachus, because many of the gold vessels had already been stolen. ⁴⁰Since the crowds were becoming aroused and filled with anger, Lysimachus armed about three thousand men and launched an unjust attack, under the leadership of a certain Auranus, a man advanced in years and no less advanced in folly. ⁴¹But when the Jews' became aware that Lysimachus was attacking them, some picked up stones, some blocks of wood, and others took handfuls of the ashes that were lying around and threw them in wild confusion at Lysimachus and his men. ⁴²As a result, they wounded many of them and killed some and put all the rest to flight; the temple robber himself they killed close by the treasury.

43 Charges were brought against Menelaus about this incident. ⁴⁴When the king came to Tyre, three men sent by the senate presented the case before him. ⁴⁵But Menelaus, already as good as beaten, promised a substantial bribe to Ptolemy son of Dorymenes to win over the king. ⁴⁶Therefore Ptolemy, taking the king aside into a colonnade as if for refreshment, induced the king to change his mind. ⁴⁷Menelaus, the cause of all the trouble, he acquitted of the charges against him, while he sentenced to death those unfortunate men who would have been freed uncondemned if they had pleaded even before Scythians. ⁴⁸And so those who had spoken for the city and the villages" and the holy vessels quickly suffered the unjust penalty. ⁴⁹Therefore even the Tyrians, showing their hatred of the crime, provided magnificently for their funeral. ⁵⁰But Menelaus, because of the greed of those in power, remained in office, growing in wickedness, having become the chief plotter against his compatriots.

5 About this time Antiochus made his second invasion of Egypt. ²And it happened that, for almost forty days, there appeared over all the city golden-clad cavalry charging through the air, in companies fully armed with lances and drawn swords—³troops of cavalry drawn up, attacks and counterattacks made on this side and on that, brandishing of shields, massing of spears, hurling of missiles, the flash of golden trappings, and armor of all kinds. ⁴Therefore everyone prayed that the apparition might prove to have been a good omen.

5 When a false rumor arose that Antiochus was dead, Jason took no fewer than a thousand men and suddenly made an assault on the city. When the troops on the wall had been forced back and at last the city was being taken, Menelaus took refuge in the citadel. ⁶But Jason kept relentlessly slaughtering his compatriots, not realizing that success at the cost of one's kindred is the greatest misfortune but imagining that he was setting up trophies of victory over enemies and not over compatriots. ⁷He did not, however, gain control of the government; in the end, he got only disgrace from his conspiracy and fled again into the country of the Ammonites. ⁸Finally, he met a miserable end. Accused' before Aretas the ruler of the Arabs, fleeing from city to city, pursued by everyone, hated as a rebel against the laws, and abhorred as the executioner of his country and his compatriots, he was cast ashore in Egypt. ⁹There he who had driven many from their own country into exile died in exile, having embarked to go to the Spartans" in hope of finding protection because of their kinship. ¹⁰He who had cast out many to lie unburied had no one to mourn for him; he had no funeral of any sort and no place in the tomb of his ancestors.

11 When news of what had happened reached

t 4.41 Gk they u 4.48 Other ancient authorities read the people v 5.8 Cn: Gk Imprisoned w 5.9 Gk Lacedaemonians

4:39 The city is Jerusalem. 4:47 The Scythians were proverbial for their brutality (cf. Herodotus, Hist. 4.64–73; 4 Macc. 10:7).

5:1–14 Antiochus vandalizes the temple. Jason's attempt to reclaim the high priesthood is unsuccessful; instead of protecting his compatriots (cf. 4:2), Jason slaughters them (v. 6; cf. Judg. 20:12–48). 5:2–4 See 3:25n. 5:9 According to legend, Spartans and Jews were related (see 1 Macc. 12:1–23). 5:11 Raging inwardly. According to Greek and Roman historians, Antiochus's second invasion of Egypt ended in humiliation when he was forced out by a Roman envoy (see Polybius, Hist. 29.27.1–8).

the king, he took it to mean that Judea was in revolt. So, raging inwardly, he left Egypt and took the city by storm. [12]He commanded his soldiers to cut down relentlessly everyone they met and to kill those who went into their houses. [13]Then there was massacre of young and old, destruction of boys, women, and children, and slaughter of young girls and infants. [14]Within the total of three days eighty thousand were destroyed, forty thousand in hand-to-hand fighting, and as many were sold into slavery as were killed.

15 Not content with this, Antiochus[x] dared to enter the most holy temple in all the world, guided by Menelaus, who had become a traitor both to the laws and to his country. [16]He took the holy vessels with his polluted hands and swept away with profane hands the votive offerings that other kings had made to enhance the glory and honor of the place. [17]Antiochus was elated in spirit and did not perceive that the Lord was angered for a little while because of the sins of those who lived in the city and that this was the reason he was disregarding the holy place. [18]But if it had not happened that they were involved in many sins, this man would have been flogged and turned back from his rash act as soon as he came forward, just as Heliodorus had been, whom King Seleucus sent to inspect the treasury. [19]But the Lord did not choose the nation for the sake of the holy place but the place for the sake of the nation. [20]Therefore the place itself shared in the misfortunes that befell the nation and afterward participated in its benefits, and what was forsaken in the wrath of the Almighty was restored again in all its glory when the great Lord became reconciled.

21 So Antiochus carried off eighteen hundred talents from the temple and hurried away to Antioch, thinking in his arrogance that he could sail on the land and walk on the sea, because his mind was elated. [22]He left governors to oppress the people: at Jerusalem, Philip, by birth a Phrygian and in character more barbarous than the man who appointed him; [23]and at Gerizim, Andronicus; and besides these Menelaus, who lorded it over his compatriots worse than the others did. In his malice toward the Jewish citizens,[y] [24]Antiochus[z] sent Apollonius, the captain of the Mysians, with an army of twenty-two thousand and commanded him to kill all the grown men and to sell the women and boys as slaves. [25]When this man arrived in Jerusalem, he pretended to be peaceably disposed and waited until the holy Sabbath day; then, finding the Jews not at work, he ordered his troops to parade under arms. [26]He put to the sword all those who came out to see them, then rushed into the city with his armed warriors and killed great numbers of people.

27 But Judas Maccabeus, with about nine others, got away to the wilderness and kept himself and his companions alive in the mountains as wild animals do; they continued to live on what grew wild, so that they might not share in the defilement.

6 Not long after this, the king sent an Athenian[a] senator[b] to compel the Jews to forsake the laws of their ancestors and no longer to live by the laws of God, [2]also to pollute the temple in Jerusalem and to call it the temple of Olympian Zeus and to call the one in Gerizim Zeus-the-Friend-of-Strangers, as the people who live in that place are known.

3 Harsh and utterly grievous was the onslaught of evil. [4]For the temple was filled with debauchery and reveling by the nations, who dallied with prostitutes and had intercourse with women within the sacred precincts and besides brought in things for sacrifice that were unfit. [5]The altar was covered with

x 5.15 Gk *he* y 5.23 Or *worse than the others did in his malice toward the Jewish citizens.* z 5.24 Gk *he* a 6.1 Other ancient authorities read *Antiochian* b 6.1 Or *Geron an Athenian*

5:15–27 Divine retribution is central to the epitomist's description of Antiochus's pillage and desecration of the temple. In contrast to Heliodorus (chap. 3), Antiochus is successful because—for this epitomist—*the Lord was angered* by the people's sins (v. 17; cf. Jdt. 5). He only wins because God lets him, casting Antiochus as ultimately powerless in the course of events—a puppet in the hands of *the Almighty* (v. 20). See notes on 4 Macc. 11:16, 20–27; 12:17–19. **5:20** Foreshadows the reconciliation in 8:5, which leads to a turn of events. **5:27** The escape of Judas and his companions during the massacre (vv. 24–26) anticipates their reintroduction in 8:1 and the reconciliation and reversal of fortunes that follow.

6:1–11 Antiochus's Hellenization plan. The attack continues with the pollution and conversion of the Jerusalem and Gerizim temples and forced Hellenization under penalty of death (cf. 1 Macc. 1:41–64). **6:2** Samaritans worshiped at the temple on Mount *Gerizim.* **6:5** *Abominable offerings* probably

abominable offerings that were forbidden by the laws. ⁶People could neither keep the Sabbath nor observe the festivals of their ancestors nor so much as confess themselves to be Jews.

7 On the monthly celebration of the king's birthday, the Jews* were taken, under bitter constraint, to partake of the sacrifices, and when a festival of Dionysus was celebrated, they were compelled to wear wreaths of ivy and to walk in the procession in honor of Dionysus. ⁸At the suggestion of the people of Ptolemais,ᵈ a decree was issued to the neighboring Greek cities that they should adopt the same policy toward the Jews and make them partake of the sacrifices ⁹and should kill those who did not choose to change over to Greek customs. One could see, therefore, the misery that had come upon them. ¹⁰For example, two women were brought in for having circumcised their children. They publicly paraded them around the city with their babies hanging at their breasts and then hurled them down headlong from the wall. ¹¹Others who had assembled in the caves nearby in order to observe the seventh day secretly were betrayed to Philip and were all burned together, because their piety kept them from defending themselves, in view of their regard for that most holy day.

12 Now I urge those who read this book not to be depressed by such calamities but to recognize that these punishments were designed not to destroy but to discipline our people. ¹³In fact, it is a sign of great kindness not to let the impious alone for long but to punish them immediately. ¹⁴For in the case of the other nations the Lord waits patiently to punish them until they have reached

the full measure of their sins, but he does not deal in this way with us, ¹⁵in order that he may not take vengeance on us afterward when our sins have reached their height. ¹⁶Therefore he never withdraws his mercy from us. Although he disciplines us with calamities, he does not forsake his own people. ¹⁷Let what we have said serve as a reminder; we must go on briefly with the story.

18 Eleazar, one of the scribes in high position, a man now advanced in age and of noble presence, was being forced to open his mouth to eat pig's flesh. ¹⁹But he, welcoming death with honor rather than life with pollution, went up to the rack of his own accord, ²⁰spitting it out as all ought to go who have the courage to refuse things that it is not right to taste, even for the natural love of life.

21 Those who were in charge of that unlawful sacrifice took the man aside because of their long acquaintance with him and privately urged him to bring meat of his own providing, proper for him to use, and to pretend that he was eating the flesh of the sacrificial meal that had been commanded by the king, ²²so that by doing this he might be saved from death and be treated kindly on account of his old friendship with them. ²³But making a high resolve, worthy of his years and the dignity of his old age and the gray hairs that he had reached with distinction and his excellent life even from childhood, and moreover according to the holy God-given law, he declared himself quickly, telling them to send him to Hades.

24 "Such pretense is not worthy of our time of life," he said, "for many of the young might

c 6.7 Gk *they*   d 6.8 Or *of Ptolemy*

included swine (cf. 1 Macc. 1:47; Lev. 11:7–8; Deut. 14:3–8). **6:10–11** Refusal to hellenize is punished with public shaming and death—martyrdom—as the victims do not defend themselves (cf. 1 Macc. 1:6–61; 2:29–38; see **"Martyrdom and Martyrs," p. 1584**).

6:12–17 The epitomist interprets the attack and oppression as God's gracious discipline. Positioned between the first accounts of martyrdom (6:8–11) and the gruesome demonstrations that follow (6:18–7:42), the interpretation offers an explanation for the suffering of the pious martyrs and anticipates the restoration of the Jews (v. 16).

6:18–7:42 Antiochus's public persecution. Persecution under Antiochus reaches its peak with the martyrdoms of Eleazar, the seven brothers, and their mother. Through their resistance to Antiochus's demands, they render the king powerless against them. The pious defiance of these nine anticipates the revolt led by Judas and his nine companions (cf. 5:27; 8:1–7). **6:18–31** Eleazar's martyrdom is cast in the noble death tradition (see 4 Macc. 6:1–11n). A model figure—a scribe *in high position*, aged, and *of noble presence* (v. 18)—Eleazar dies with his dignity intact, setting an example of piety and courage for the youth and the nation (vv. 24–28, 31). The story is expanded and expounded upon in 4 Macc. 5–7. **6:18** Eating *pig's flesh* is forbidden (Lev. 11:7–8). **6:23** *Hades* is

suppose that Eleazar in his ninetieth year had gone over to a foreign way of life, [25]and through my pretense, for the sake of living a brief moment longer, they would be led astray because of me, while I defile and disgrace my old age. [26]Even if for the present I would avoid the punishment of mortals, yet whether I live or die I will not escape the hands of the Almighty. [27]Therefore, by bravely giving up my life now, I will show myself worthy of my old age [28]and leave to the young a noble example of how to die a good death willingly and nobly for the revered and holy laws."

When he had said this, he was dragged[e] at once to the rack. [29]Those who a little before had acted toward him with goodwill now changed to ill will, because the words he had uttered were in their opinion sheer madness.[f] [30]When he was about to die under the blows, he groaned aloud and said: "It is clear to the Lord in his holy knowledge that, though I might have been saved from death, I am enduring terrible sufferings in my body under this beating, but in my soul I am glad to suffer these things because I fear him."

31 So in this way he died, leaving in his death an example of nobility and a memorial of courage, not only to the young but to the great body of his nation.

7 It happened also that seven brothers and their mother were arrested and were being compelled by the king, under torture with whips and straps, to partake of unlawful pig's flesh. [2]One of them, acting as their spokesman, said, "What do you intend to ask and learn from us? For we are ready to die rather than transgress the laws of our ancestors."

3 The king fell into a rage and gave orders to have pans and caldrons heated. [4]These were heated immediately, and he commanded that the tongue of their spokesman be cut out and that they scalp him and cut off his hands and feet, while the rest of the brothers and the mother looked on. [5]When he was utterly helpless, the king[g] ordered them to take him to the fire, still breathing, and to fry him in a pan. The smoke from the pan spread widely, but the brothers[h] and their mother encouraged one another to die nobly, saying, [6]"The Lord God is watching over us and in truth has compassion on us, as Moses declared in his song that bore witness against the people to their faces, when he said, 'And he will have compassion on his servants.'"

7 After the first brother had died in this way, they brought forward the second for their sport. They tore off the skin of his head with the hair and asked him, "Will you eat rather than have your body punished limb by limb?" [8]He replied in the language of his ancestors and said to them, "No." Therefore he in turn underwent tortures as the first brother had done. [9]And when he was at his last breath, he said, "You accursed wretch, you dismiss us from this present life, but the King of the universe will raise us up to a renewal of everlasting life, because we have died for his laws."

10 After him, the third was the victim of their sport. When it was demanded, he quickly put out his tongue and courageously stretched forth his hands [11]and said nobly, "I got these from heaven, and because of his laws I disdain them, and from him I hope to get them back again." [12]As a result, the king himself and those with him were astonished at the young man's spirit, for he regarded his sufferings as nothing.

13 After he, too, had died, they maltreated and tortured the fourth in the same way. [14]When he was near death, he said, "One cannot but choose to die at the hands of mortals and to cherish the hope God gives of being raised again by him. But for you there will be no resurrection to life!"

15 Next they brought forward the fifth and

---

e 6.28 Other ancient authorities read *went*
f 6.29 Meaning of Gk uncertain   g 7.5 Gk *he*
h 7.5 Gk *they*

---

the place of the dead, similar to Sheol in the Hebrew Scriptures. See **"Sheol," p. 695. 7:1–42** The epitomist recounts in quick succession the torture and martyrdoms of the seven brothers and their mother, giving special attention to the mother, whose courage makes her the ultimate exemplar. The author of 4 Maccabees greatly expands these stories, along with the story of Eleazar, making them the central focus of the philosophical treatise (see 4 Macc. 5–18). **7:2–6** Similar conflicts appear in the court tales of Daniel (cf. Dan. 1:8; 3:16–18; 6:10). **7:4** In 4 Maccabees, the fourth brother's tongue is cut out for his incendiary speech against the king (4 Macc. 10:12–21). **7:6** See Deut. 32:36. **7:8** The brother's use of his ancestral language is an affront and rejection of the king's attempts to force Hellenization. **7:14** Second Maccabees is a witness to developing views about the afterlife. See

Focus On: Martyrdom and Martyrs (2 Maccabees 6–7)

Prior to the launch of Judas Maccabeus's military campaign (8:1), the author of 2 Maccabees underscores another form of resistance: the unwavering commitment by pious Jews to suffer torture and death rather than violate their devotion to Israel's God and their religious practices (6:7–11, 18–31; 7:1–42).

These accounts in 2 Maccabees belong to the Greco-Roman literary genre of stories of "the noble death." In such narratives, characters are described as *choosing* death as a more honorable fate than falling into enemy hands or violating a higher commitment, whether national, political, moral, or religious. Various noble deaths are described: (1) a person or persons commit suicide, (2) a group of people agree to kill one another, or (3) a person or persons choose to be killed by their adversaries. The noble death accounts in 2 Maccabees are the third kind. These Jewish accounts of those who choose execution as a display of *religious* devotion are among the earliest of this type in the Greco-Roman period (cf. earlier Saul's death by suicide in 1 Sam. 31:4–6 and Samson's in Judg. 16:28–30). Another important feature that is tied to the respective martyrdoms of Eleazar, the seven brothers, and the mother is their claim that their deaths will one day be rewarded by God's raising them from the dead into everlasting life (6:27–28, 31; 7:9, 23, 29, 36).

There is a pattern in the accounts of Eleazar (6:18–31) and the seven brothers and their mother (7:1–42):

- They are ordered to violate their convictions.
- They refuse, declaring fidelity to God.
- They are ordered again.
- While being tortured, they reaffirm their devotion or are encouraged by others.
- Dying, they make a final statement of devotion.

This pattern is found in other early Jewish accounts of martyrdom and those of later Christianity.

Later, some Christians embraced the Jewish precedent of martyrdom to "witness" (Gk. *martyreō*) to their faith. Some of the earliest Christian examples include the death of Stephen (Acts 7:54–60) and the Christian community in Revelation (e.g., 1:9; 11:7; 12:11; 19:10; 20:4). From the mid-third to the early fourth century, Roman persecution of Christians was widespread, and the word *martyr* becoming a technical term used for Christians who embraced death rather than recanting their witness. In this period, the stories of martyrs began to be written down, such as the *Martyrdom of Polycarp*.

Michael E. Fuller

---

maltreated him. [16]But he looked at the king[i] and said, "Because you have authority among mortals, though you also are mortal, you do what you please. But do not think that God has forsaken our people. [17]Keep on, and see how his mighty power will torture you and your descendants!"

18 After him they brought forward the sixth. And when he was about to die, he said, "Do not deceive yourself in vain. For we are suffering these things on our own account because of our sins against our own God.[j] [19]But do not think that you will go unpunished for having tried to fight against God!"

20 The mother was especially admirable and worthy of honorable memory. Although she saw her seven sons perish within a single day, she bore it with good courage because of her hope in the Lord. [21]She encouraged each of them in the language of their ancestors. Filled with a noble spirit, she reinforced her woman's reasoning with a man's courage and said to them, [22]"I do not know how you came into being in my womb. It was not I who gave you life and breath nor I who set in order the elements within each of you. [23]Therefore the Creator of the world, who shaped the beginning of humankind and devised the origin of all things, in his mercy gives life and breath back to you again, since you now forget yourselves for the sake of his laws."

24 Antiochus felt that he was being treated with contempt, and he was suspicious of her

i 7.16 Gk at him   j 7.18 Gk adds Astounding things have happened

---

"Resurrection," p. 1224, and "Resurrection in the Gospels," p. 1767. 7:16–17 See "Reversal," p. 1642. 7:18 *Our sins* reflects a sense of communal responsibility for which the brothers' suffering functions as a type of atoning sacrifice (v. 38; cf. 4 Macc. 6:26–29; 17:21–22). 7:20–21 The mother's demonstration of courage in encouraging her sons to endure torture and death makes her the

reproachful tone. The youngest brother being still alive, Antiochus[k] not only appealed to him in words but promised with oaths that he would make him rich and enviable if he would turn from the ways of his ancestors and that he would take him for his Friend and entrust him with public affairs. [25]Since the young man would not listen to him at all, the king called the mother to him and urged her to advise the youth to save himself. [26]After much urging on his part, she undertook to persuade her son. [27]But, leaning close to him, she spoke in their native language as follows, deriding the cruel tyrant: "My son, have pity on me. I carried you nine months in my womb and nursed you for three years and have reared you and brought you up to this point in your life and have taken care of you. [28]I beg you, my child, to look at the heaven and the earth and see everything that is in them and recognize that God did not make them out of things that existed.[l] And in the same way the human race came into being. [29]Do not fear this butcher but prove worthy of your brothers. Accept death, so that in God's mercy I may get you back again along with your brothers."

30 While she was still speaking, the young man said, "What are you waiting for? I will not obey the king's command, but I obey the command of the law that was given to our ancestors through Moses. [31]But you, who have contrived all sorts of evil against the Hebrews, will certainly not escape the hands of God. [32]For we are suffering because of our own sins. [33]And if our living Lord is angry for a little while, to rebuke and discipline us, he will again be reconciled with his own servants. [34]But you, unholy wretch, you most defiled of all mortals, do not be elated in vain and puffed up by uncertain hopes when you raise your hand against the children of heaven. [35]You have not yet escaped the judgment of the almighty, all-seeing God. [36]For our brothers, after enduring a brief suffering for everlasting life, have fallen under God's covenant, but you, by the judgment of God, will receive just punishment for your arrogance. [37]I, like my brothers, give up body and life for the laws of our ancestors, appealing to God to show mercy soon to our nation and by trials and plagues to make you confess that he alone is God, [38]and through me and my brothers to bring to an end the wrath of the Almighty that has justly fallen on our whole nation."

39 The king fell into a rage and handled him worse than the others, being exasperated at his scorn. [40]So he died in his integrity, putting his whole trust in the Lord.

41 Last of all, the mother died, after her sons.

42 Let this be enough, then, about the eating of sacrifices and the extreme tortures.

8 Meanwhile Judas, who was also called Maccabeus, and his companions secretly entered the villages and summoned their kindred and enlisted those who had continued in the Jewish faith, and so they gathered about six thousand. [2]They implored the Lord to look upon the people who were oppressed by all and to have pity on the temple that had been profaned by the godless, [3]to have mercy on the city that was being destroyed and about to be leveled to the ground, to hearken to the blood that cried out to him, [4]to remember also the lawless destruction of the innocent babies and the blasphemies committed against his name, and to show his hatred of evil.

5 As soon as Maccabeus got his army organized, the nations could not withstand him, for the wrath of the Lord had turned to mercy. [6]Coming without warning, he would set fire to towns and villages. He captured strategic positions and put to flight not a few of the enemy. [7]He found the nights most advantageous for such attacks. And talk of his valor spread everywhere.

8 When Philip saw that the man was gaining ground little by little and that he was pushing ahead with more frequent successes, he wrote to Ptolemy, the governor of

k 7.24 Gk he   l 7.28 Or God made them out of things that did not exist

example par excellence of "manly" courage. See **"Masculinity," p. 1701. 7:29** See note on v. 14; cf. v. 21. **7:38** See note on v. 18.

8:1–7 Judas Maccabeus's revolt. 8:1 _Also called Maccabeus._ Cf. 2:19; 5:27. _Jewish faith_ translates the Greek "Ioudaismos" (Judaism). See note on 2:21. **8:2–3** Respect for _the temple, the people, the city_ (Jerusalem), and the torah is fundamental to the story (cf. 8:17; 13:10). **8:5** _Wrath of the Lord had turned to mercy._ The epitomist emphasizes—alongside Judas's military strategy—a change in God's attitude. **8:7** Attacking at night was a common strategy (see 12:6, 9; 13:15).

8:8–11 Philip's preparation. 8:8 _Philip_, the appointed governor of Jerusalem (5:22), reaches

Coelesyria and Phoenicia, to come to the aid of the king's government. [9]Then Ptolemy[m] promptly appointed Nicanor son of Patroclus, one of the king's First[n] Friends, and sent him, in command of no fewer than twenty thousand men of various nations, to wipe out the entire people of Judea. He associated with him Gorgias, a general and a man of experience in military service. [10]Nicanor determined to make up for the king the tribute due to the Romans, two thousand talents, by selling the captured Jews into slavery. [11]So he immediately sent to the towns on the seacoast, inviting them to buy Jewish slaves and promising to hand over ninety slaves for a talent, not expecting the judgment from the Almighty that was about to overtake him.

12 Word came to Judas concerning Nicanor's invasion, and when he told his companions of the arrival of the army, [13]those who were cowardly and distrustful of God's justice ran off and got away. [14]Others sold all their remaining property and at the same time implored the Lord to rescue those who had been sold by the ungodly Nicanor before he ever met them, [15]if not for their own sake, then for the sake of the covenants made with their ancestors and because he had called them by his holy and glorious name. [16]But Maccabeus gathered his forces together, to the number six thousand, and exhorted them not to be frightened by the enemy and not to fear the great multitude of nations who were wickedly coming against them but to fight nobly, [17]keeping before their eyes the lawless outrage that the nations[o] had committed against the holy place and the torture of the derided city, as well as the overthrow of their ancestral way of life. [18]"For they trust to arms and acts of daring," he said, "but we trust in the Almighty God, who is able with a single nod to strike down those who are coming against us, and even, if necessary, the whole world."

19 Moreover, he told them of the occasions when help came to their ancestors, how, in the time of Sennacherib, when one hundred eighty-five thousand perished, [20]and the time of the battle against the Galatians that took place in Babylonia, when eight thousand Jews[p] fought along with four thousand Macedonians; yet when the Macedonians were hard pressed, the eight thousand, by the help that came to them from heaven, destroyed one hundred twenty thousand Galatians[q] and took a great amount of plunder.

21 With these words he filled them with courage and made them ready to die for their laws and their country; then he divided his army into four parts. [22]He appointed his brothers also, Simon and Joseph and Jonathan, each to command a division, putting fifteen hundred men under each. [23]Besides, he appointed Eleazar to read aloud[r] from the holy book and gave the watchword, "The help of God"; then, leading the first division himself, he joined battle with Nicanor.

m 8.9 Gk he   n 8.9 Gk one of the first   o 8.17 Gk they   p 8.20 Gk lacks Jews   q 8.20 Gk lacks Galatians
r 8.23 Meaning of Gk uncertain

out to *Ptolemy,* (regional) governor to the north (*Coelesyria and Phoenicia;* cf. 4:45). **8:9** *Nicanor* will play a crucial role in the account (cf. 8:24–36; 14:12–15:37). *First Friends* are the king's special advisors (cf. 1:14; 7:24; 10:13; 14:11). *Gorgias,* not Nicanor, leads the opposition in 1 Macc. 3:38–4:25. **8:10** Syria's *tribute . . . to the Romans* is due to the Treaty of Apamea. *Selling . . . into slavery* was a common practice of warfare. **8:11** One *talent* is approximately an average yearly wage.

8:12–23 Judas prepares for battle. 8:13 *God's justice* continues the book's view of a divine preference for the Jewish people (vv. 5, 18). **8:15** *The covenants made with their ancestors.* Cf. 1:2; Gen. 17; Exod. 19–24. **8:17** *Lawless outrage* refers to a polluted temple (cf. 6:2). *Way of life* (Gk. "politeia") is a reference to the laws (or "polity") that make them a community. **8:19** *In the time of Sennacherib,* an "angel" intervened (see 2 Kgs. 19:35–36). **8:20** *The battle against the Galatians* is otherwise unattested. **8:21** *For their laws and their country.* Cf. 5:15; 8:2–4. **8:22** *Simon and Joseph and Jonathan* play minor roles in 2 Maccabees (cf. 10:19–20; 14:17), since the story concentrates on Judas's exploits (cf. 1 Macc. 9–16). **8:23** *Eleazar,* another one of Judas's brothers (cf. 1 Macc. 2:2–5), receives the priestly role and reads the *holy book* (i.e., torah); the priestly lineage of Judas and his brothers (cf. 1 Macc. 2:1; 10:17–21) is downplayed in 2 Maccabees, although Judas's purification of the temple is a ceremonial activity (10:1–3). *Help of God* is the meaning of Eleazar's name and a theme in the book (cf. 8:20, 35; 12:11; 13:13; 15:35).

24 With the Almighty as their ally, they killed more than nine thousand of the enemy and wounded and disabled most of Nicanor's army and forced them all to flee. 25They captured the money of those who had come to buy them as slaves. After pursuing them for some distance, they were obliged to return because the hour was late. 26It was the day before the Sabbath, and for that reason they did not continue their pursuit. 27When they had collected the arms of the enemy and stripped them of their spoils, they kept the Sabbath, giving great praise and thanks to the Lord, who had preserved them for that day and allotted it to them as the beginning of mercy. 28After the Sabbath they gave some of the spoils to those who had been tortured and to the widows and orphans and distributed the rest among themselves and their children. 29When they had done this, they made common supplication and implored the merciful Lord to be wholly reconciled with his servants.

30 In encounters with the forces of Timothy and Bacchides they killed more than twenty thousand of them and got possession of some exceedingly high strongholds, and they divided a very large amount of plunder, giving to those who had been tortured and to the orphans and widows and also to the aged, shares equal to their own. 31They collected the arms of the enemy[s] and carefully stored all of them in strategic places; the rest of the spoils they carried to Jerusalem. 32They killed the commander of Timothy's forces, a most wicked man, and one who had greatly troubled the Jews. 33While they were celebrating the victory in the city of their ancestors, they burned those who had set fire to the sacred gates, Callisthenes and some others, who had fled into one little house, so these received the proper reward for their impiety.[t]

34 The thrice-accursed Nicanor, who had brought the thousand merchants to buy the Jews, 35having been humbled with the help of the Lord by opponents whom he regarded as of the least account, took off his splendid uniform and made his way alone like a runaway slave across the country until he reached Antioch, having succeeded chiefly in the destruction of his own army! 36So he who had undertaken to secure tribute for the Romans by the capture of the people of Jerusalem proclaimed that the Jews had a Defender and that therefore the Jews were invulnerable because they followed the laws ordained by him.

9 About that time, as it happened, Antiochus had retreated in disorder from the region of Persia. 2He had entered the city called Persepolis and attempted to rob the temples and control the city. Therefore the people rushed to the rescue with arms, and Antiochus and his army were defeated,[u] with the result that Antiochus was put to flight by the inhabitants and beat a shameful retreat. 3While he was in Ecbatana, news came to him of what had happened to Nicanor and the forces of Timothy. 4Transported with rage, he conceived the idea of turning upon the Jews the injury done by those who had put him to flight, so he ordered his charioteer to drive without stopping until he completed the journey. But the judgment of heaven rode with him! For in his arrogance he said, "When I get there I will make Jerusalem a cemetery of Jews."

5 But the all-seeing Lord, the God of Israel,

s 8.31 Gk *their arms*   t 8.33 Meaning of Gk uncertain
u 9.2 Gk *they were defeated*

8:24–29 Defeating Nicanor. 8:26–28 *Sabbath* is observed by postponing the fight in order to worship (cf. 12:38; 15:2–4). Because the enemy could take advantage of this observance (cf. 5:25–26; 15:1–5), not all Jews agreed (cf. 1 Macc. 2:39–41). **8:28** Care for *widows and orphans*; cf. Exod. 22:22–24; Deut. 10:18; 14:29; 24:17–21; 26:12–13; Ps. 68:5; Isa. 1:17; Mal. 3:5; Jas. 1:27.

8:30–33 Other military victories. 8:30 *Timothy*, a general, plays a key role later (cf. 10:24–37; 12:2–24). *Bacchides* plays a less prominent role here, but—according to 1 Maccabees—his battle with Judas leads to the latter's death (cf. 1 Macc. 9:14–18).

8:34–36 Nicanor's retreat. 8:34 *Thrice-accursed.* Cf. 15:3. **8:36** *Proclaimed.* In 2 Maccabees, the enemy often acknowledges God's favor upon the Jewish people and their practices (cf. 3:35–39; 9:13–17).

9:1–4 Disorder in Antiochus's plan. 9:1 *Region of Persia* is to the east of Antiochus's Syrian territory. **9:2** These *temples* of Persepolis are in the Persian capital (cf. 1:13–17). **9:3** His defeat accompanies that of his generals, *Nicanor* (8:24–29) and *Timothy* (8:30–33).

9:5–12 God strikes Antiochus. 9:5 The adjective *all-seeing* is unusual in biblical literature but emphasizes divine awareness. The term *Israel* is rare in 2 Maccabees (only 1:25, 26; 10:38; 11:6; 15:14) compared to its ubiquitous use in 1 Maccabees. **9:5–6** Divine origins for diseases on opposing rulers

struck him with an incurable and invisible blow. As soon as he stopped speaking, he was seized with a pain in his bowels for which there was no relief and with sharp internal tortures—[6]and that very justly, for he had tortured the bowels of others with many and strange inflictions. [7]Yet he did not in any way stop his insolence but was even more filled with arrogance, breathing fire in his rage against the Jews and giving orders to drive even faster. And so it came about that he fell out of his chariot as it was rushing along, and the fall was so hard as to torture every limb of his body. [8]Thus he, who only a little while before had thought in his superhuman arrogance that he could command the waves of the sea and had imagined that he could weigh the high mountains in a balance, was brought down to earth and carried in a litter, making the power of God manifest to all. [9]And so the ungodly man's body swarmed with worms, and while he was still living in anguish and pain, his flesh rotted away, and because of the stench the whole army felt revulsion at his decay. [10]Because of his intolerable stench no one was able to carry the man who a little while before had thought that he could touch the stars of heaven. [11]Then it was that, broken in spirit, he began to lose much of his arrogance and to come to his senses under the scourge of God, for he was tortured with pain every moment. [12]And when he could not endure his own stench, he uttered these words, "It is right to be subject to God; mortals should not think that they are equal to God."[v]

13 Then the abominable fellow made a vow to the Lord, who would no longer have mercy on him, stating [14]that the holy city, which he was hurrying to level to the ground and to make a cemetery, he was now declaring to be free, [15]and the Jews, whom he had not considered worth burying but had planned to throw out with their children for the wild animals and for the birds to eat, he would make, all of them, equal to citizens of Athens, [16]and the holy sanctuary, which he had formerly plundered, he would adorn with the finest offerings, and all the holy vessels he would give back many times over, and the expenses incurred for the sacrifices he would provide from his own revenues, [17]and in addition to all this he also would become a Jew and would visit every inhabited place to proclaim the power of God. [18]But when his sufferings did not in any way abate, for the judgment of God had justly come upon him, he gave up all hope for himself and wrote to the Jews the following letter, in the form of a supplication. This was its content:

19 "To his worthy Jewish citizens, Antiochus their king and general sends hearty greetings and good wishes for their health and prosperity. [20]If you and your children are well and your affairs are as you wish, I am glad as my hope is in heaven. [21]Now I was feeling weak, and so I was remembering with affection your esteem and goodwill. On my way back from the region of Persia I suffered an annoying illness, and I have deemed it necessary to take thought for the general security of all. [22]I do not despair of my condition, for I have good hope of recovering from my illness, [23]but I observed that my father, on the occasions when he made expeditions into the upper country, appointed his successor, [24]so that, if anything unexpected happened or any unwelcome news came, the people throughout the realm would not be troubled, for they would know to whom the government was left. [25]Moreover, I understand how the princes along the borders and the neighbors of my kingdom keep watching for opportunities and waiting to see what will happen. So I have appointed my son Antiochus to be king, whom I have often entrusted and commended to most of you when I hurried off to the upper provinces, and I have written

v 9.12 Or *not think thoughts proper only to God*

are noted elsewhere (cf. 2 Chr. 21; 26:16–23; Acts 12:20–23). For other accounts of Antiochus's death, see note on 1:13–16. **9:12** For the king's confession, see note on 8:36.

9:13–17 Antiochus's vow. 9:13–17 Themes of *the holy city, the Jews,* and *the holy sanctuary* are repeated elsewhere (8:2–4, 17; 13:10). **9:17** *Become a Jew.* In this intentional narrative on Jewish identity, conversion to Judaism is a possibility in this imaginative (and comedic) scene of Antiochus's acknowledgment of God's power (see **"Gentile Conversion," p. 1530**).

9:18–27 A letter to the Jews. 9:18 The *letter* does not mention the cause of Antiochus's illness (vv. 21–22), which may be the epitomist's rhetorical attempt to construct a letter that looks authentic. **9:25** *Appointed my son.* The rationale for the letter is made explicit as an attempt to forestall a

to him the appended letter. [26]I therefore urge and beg you to remember the public and private services rendered to you and to maintain your present goodwill, each of you, toward me and my son. [27]For I am sure that he will follow my policy and will treat you with moderation and kindness."

28 So the murderer and blasphemer, having endured the more intense suffering such as he had inflicted on others, came to the end of his life by a most pitiable fate, among the mountains in a strange land. [29]And Philip, one of his courtiers, took his body home; then, fearing the son of Antiochus, he withdrew to Ptolemy Philometor in Egypt.

10 Now Maccabeus and his followers, the Lord leading them on, recovered the temple and the city; [2]they tore down the altars that had been built in the public square by the foreigners and also destroyed the sacred precincts. [3]They purified the sanctuary and made another altar of sacrifice; then, striking fire out of flint, they offered sacrifices, after a lapse of two years, and they offered incense and lighted lamps and set out the bread of the Presence. [4]When they had done this, they fell prostrate and implored the Lord that they might never again fall into such misfortunes but that, if they should ever sin, they might be disciplined by him with forbearance and not be handed over to blasphemous and barbarous nations. [5]It happened that on the same day on which the sanctuary had been profaned by the foreigners, the purification of the sanctuary took place, that is, on the twenty-fifth day of the same month, which was Chislev. [6]They celebrated it for eight days with rejoicing, in the manner of the Festival of Booths,[w] remembering how not long before, during the Festival of Booths,[x] they had been wandering in the mountains and caves like wild animals. [7]Therefore, carrying ivy-wreathed wands and beautiful branches and also palm fronds, they offered hymns of thanksgiving to him who had given success to the purifying of his own holy place. [8]They decreed by public edict, ratified by vote, that the whole nation of the Jews should observe these days every year.

9 Such then was the end of Antiochus, who was called Epiphanes.

10 Now we will tell what took place under Antiochus Eupator, who was the son of that ungodly man, and will give a brief summary of the principal calamities of the wars. [11]This man, when he succeeded to the kingdom, appointed one Lysias to have charge of the government and Protarchos to be governor of Coelesyria and Phoenicia. [12]Ptolemy, who was called Macron, took the lead in showing justice to the Jews because of the wrong that had been done to them and attempted to maintain peaceful relations with them. [13]As a result he was accused before Eupator by the king's Friends. He heard himself called a traitor at every turn because he had abandoned Cyprus,

w 10.6 Or Tabernacles *x 10.6 Or* Tabernacles

conflict over this reign (cf. 14:1–2). **9:27** *Moderation and kindness* expose the narrative irony of the situation, in light of the previous chapters.

9:28–29 Antiochus's death. 9:28 *The end of his life* is depicted without divine involvement in 1 Macc. 6:1–16 and by a different means in 2 Macc. 1:11–16. **9:29** *Philip.* A confidant and appointed governor of Jerusalem (5:22). His fear suggests that all is not well in the succession plan in Syrian politics (cf. 14:1–2; 1 Macc. 6:14–17, 55–56). His escape to *Philometor*—who ruled Egypt for decades but plays a minor role here—may suggest that earlier tensions between Syria and Egypt had subsided (cf. 4:21).

10:1–9 Temple purification. 10:1 *The temple and the city* are key (cf. 8:2–4, 17; 13:10). **10:3** Purification included *another altar of sacrifice* (cf. 6:5) in order to *set out the bread of the Presence* (cf. Exod. 40:23–27). Cleansing rituals are generally priestly activities (see note on 8:23); in 1 Maccabees, Judas appoints priests to carry out the task (cf. 1 Macc. 4:41–58). **10:5–6** For *Chislev* and *Festival of Booths*—or "tents" (Gk. "skēnē"), a movable dwelling place—see note on 1:9. **10:8** *Should observe* establishes a precedent for ongoing celebrations of what becomes known as Hanukkah ("dedication"; see **"Hanukkah," p. 1544**). **10:9** Cf. chap. 9.

10:10–13 New government. 10:10–11 *Antiochus Eupator* comes to power (cf. 9:25) but will die young (cf. 14:1–2). *Lysias.* See note on 11:1n (cf. 1 Macc. 3:32–33). **10:13** *King's Friends.* See note on 8:9. *Philometor.* See note on 9:29. The book offers no judgment on Ptolemy's death by suicide, which may have been more honorable than the public shaming he endured (cf. 14:37–46).

which Philometor had entrusted to him, and had gone over to Antiochus Epiphanes. Unable to command the respect due his office,[y] he took poison and ended his life.

14 When Gorgias became governor of the region, he maintained a force of mercenaries and at every turn kept attacking the Jews. [15]Besides this, the Idumeans, who had control of important strongholds, were harassing the Jews; they received those who were banished from Jerusalem and endeavored to keep up the war. [16]But Maccabeus and his forces, after making solemn supplication and imploring God to fight on their side, rushed to the strongholds of the Idumeans. [17]Attacking them vigorously, they gained possession of the places and drove back all who fought upon the wall and slaughtered those whom they encountered, killing no fewer than twenty thousand.

18 When at least nine thousand took refuge in two very strong towers well equipped to withstand a siege, [19]Maccabeus left Simon and Joseph, and also Zacchaeus and his troops, a force sufficient to besiege them, and he himself set off for places where he was more urgently needed. [20]But those with Simon, who were money-hungry, were bribed by some of those who were in the towers and on receiving seventy thousand drachmas let some of them slip away. [21]When word of what had happened came to Maccabeus, he gathered the leaders of the people and accused these men of having sold their kindred for money by setting their enemies free to fight against them. [22]Then he killed these men who had turned traitor and immediately captured the two towers. [23]Having success at arms in everything he undertook, he destroyed more than twenty thousand in the two strongholds.

24 Now Timothy, who had been defeated by the Jews before, gathered a tremendous force of mercenaries and collected the cavalry from Asia in no small number. He came on, intending to take Judea by storm. [25]As he drew near, Maccabeus and his men sprinkled dust on their heads and girded their loins with sackcloth, in supplication to God. [26]Falling upon the steps before the altar, they implored him to be gracious to them and to be an enemy to their enemies and an adversary to their adversaries, as the law declares. [27]And rising from their prayer they took up their arms and advanced a considerable distance from the city, and when they came near the enemy they halted. [28]Just as dawn was breaking, the two armies joined battle, the one having as pledge of success and victory not only their valor but also their reliance on the Lord, while the other made rage their leader in the fight.

29 When the battle became fierce, there appeared to the enemy from heaven five resplendent men on horses with golden bridles, and they were leading the Jews. [30]Two of them took Maccabeus between them and, shielding him with their own armor and weapons, they kept him from being wounded. They showered arrows and thunderbolts on the enemy so that, confused and blinded, they were thrown into disorder and cut to pieces. [31]Twenty thousand five hundred were slaughtered, besides six hundred cavalry.

32 Timothy himself fled to a stronghold called Gazara, especially well garrisoned, where Chaereas was commander. [33]Then Maccabeus and his men were glad, and they besieged the fort for four days. [34]The men within, relying on the strength of the place, kept blaspheming terribly and uttering wicked words. [35]But at dawn of the fifth day, twenty young men in the army of Maccabeus, fired

y 10.13 Cn: Meaning of Gk uncertain

10:14–17 Rising tension. 10:14 Gorgias. An experienced general under the former king (8:9; cf. 12:32–37; 1 Macc. 4:1–22). 10:15 The epitomist does not consider Idumeans (to the south of Judea) part of "Israel" (also 1 Esd. 4:50; 8:66 = "Edomites"). 10:16 Imploring God to fight continues the emphasis on the piety of Judas and his followers.

10:18–23 Maccabeus defeats the Idumeans. 10:19 Simon and Joseph. See note on 8:22. Zacchaeus is otherwise unknown. 10:20 Seventy thousand drachmas would provide average daily wages for one year for approximately two hundred workers. 10:23 Success at arms. The book emphasizes Judas Maccabeus's extraordinary military leadership (cf. 1 Macc. 2:66; 3:1).

10:24–38 Maccabeus defeats Timothy. 10:24 Timothy . . . defeated (cf. 8:30–33). 10:25–26 Sprinkling of dust on their heads symbolizes an act of mourning and repentance in preparation for war (cf. 14:15; Esth. 4:1; Jer. 6:26). 10:29 Men on horses. The book uses apocalyptic language—a feature generally absent from 1 Maccabees—to represent God's endorsement. 10:34 Blaspheming includes

with anger because of the blasphemies, bravely stormed the wall and with savage fury cut down everyone they met. [36]During the distraction, others came up in the same way, wheeled around against the defenders, and set fire to the towers; they kindled fires and burned the blasphemers alive. Others broke open the gates and let in the rest of the force, and they occupied the city. [37]They killed Timothy, who was hiding in a cistern, and his brother Chaereas, and Apollophanes. [38]When they had accomplished these things, with hymns and thanksgivings they blessed the Lord, who shows great kindness to Israel and gives them the victory.

11 Very soon after this, Lysias, the king's guardian and kinsman, who was in charge of the government, being vexed at what had happened, [2]gathered about eighty thousand infantry and all his cavalry and came against the Jews. He intended to make the city a home for Greeks [3]and to levy tribute on the temple as he did on the sacred places of the other nations and to put up the high priesthood for sale every year. [4]He took no account whatever of the power of God but was elated with his ten thousands of infantry and his thousands of cavalry and his eighty elephants. [5]Invading Judea, he approached Beth-zur, which was a fortified place about five schoinoi[z] from Jerusalem, and pressed it hard.

[6] When Maccabeus and his men got word that Lysias[a] was besieging the strongholds, they and all the people, with lamentations and tears, prayed the Lord to send a good angel to save Israel. [7]Maccabeus himself was the first to take up arms, and he urged the others to risk their lives with him to aid their kindred. Then they eagerly rushed off together. [8]And there, while they were still near Jerusalem, a horseman appeared at their head, clothed in white and brandishing weapons of gold. [9]And together they all praised the merciful God and were strengthened in heart, ready to assail not only humans but the wildest animals or walls of iron. [10]They advanced in battle order, having their heavenly ally, for the Lord had mercy on them. [11]They hurled themselves like lions against the enemy and laid low eleven thousand of them and sixteen hundred cavalry and forced all the rest to flee. [12]Most of them got away wounded and stripped, and Lysias himself escaped by disgraceful flight.

[13] As he was not without intelligence, he pondered over the defeat that had befallen him and realized that the Hebrews were invincible because the mighty God fought on their side. So he sent to them [14]and persuaded them to settle everything on just terms, promising that he would persuade the king, constraining him to be their friend.[b] [15]Maccabeus, having regard for the common good, agreed to all that Lysias urged. For

z 11.5 A unit for measuring distance   a 11.6 Gk *he*
b 11.14 Meaning of Gk uncertain

words spoken against the gods of the enemy and the masculinity of the warriors (cf. 12:14; 2 Kgs. 19:4–6; Isa. 52:5). **10:38** *Hymns* imply a type of holy warfare (cf. 12:37).

11:1–5 Lysias's plot. 11:1 *Guardian* (Gk. "epitropos," also meaning "manager") points to his leadership over governmental affairs (cf. 13:2) as well as guardianship over the youthful king (cf. 1 Macc. 3:32–33; 6:17). *Kinsman* may point to his own royal lineage rather than family ties to Antiochus (cf. 1 Macc. 3:32). **11:2** *A home for Greeks* points to Hellenization as a primary objective of these battles; the epitomist opposes more lenient Jews (cf. 4:7–10). **11:3** *Tribute* and the selling of the *priesthood* indicate financial reasons for these wars (cf. chap. 4). **11:4** Inclusion of *elephants* implies military strength (cf. 1 Macc. 1:17; 3:34; 6:30); they could be stimulated with fruit for battle (cf. 1 Macc. 6:34, 37). **11:5** *Schoinoi* (a Persian measure = 6,000 meters or approximately 3.5 miles) is from a Greek manuscript variant. Other manuscripts read "stadia" (= 200 meters), which is inaccurate; Beth-zur is approximately 20 miles from Jerusalem.

11:6–12 Maccabeus responds. 11:8–9 Second Maccabees includes apocalyptic figures as a sign of divine action (also v. 13). Scholars prefer the historiography of 1 Maccabees partly due to the relative absence of apocalyptic references, as well as a more even report on the harsh reality of war, including significant losses to the Judeans (e.g., Eleazar's death in the battle at Beth-zur in 1 Macc. 6:40–47). **11:12** *Lysias . . . escaped.* Cf. 13:2; 14:2.

11:13–21 Lysias's peace treaty. 11:13 *Hebrews.* Cf. 7:31; 15:37. **11:14** The awkward Greek implies that the king will not concede to friendship easily. See the use of *constraining* (Gk. "anagkadzō") elsewhere (cf. 6:7), which also translates as "being forced" (6:18) or "being compelled" (7:1). Complications for the government on other fronts may also cause this peace treaty (cf. 1 Macc. 6:55–59). **11:15** *Granted every*

the king granted every request in behalf of the Jews that Maccabeus delivered to Lysias in writing.

16 The letter written to the Jews by Lysias was to this effect:

"Lysias to the people of the Jews, greetings. [17]John and Absalom, who were sent by you, have delivered your signed communication and have asked about the matters indicated in it. [18]I have informed the king of everything that needed to be brought before him, and I have agreed to what was possible. [19]If you will maintain your goodwill toward the government, I will endeavor in the future to help promote your welfare. [20]And concerning such matters and their details, I have ordered these men and my representatives to confer with you. [21]Farewell. The one hundred forty-eighth year, Dioscorinthius twenty-fourth."

22 The king's letter ran thus:

"King Antiochus to his brother Lysias, greetings. [23]Now that our father has gone on to the gods, we desire that the subjects of the kingdom be undisturbed in caring for their own affairs. [24]We have heard that the Jews do not consent to our father's change to Greek customs but prefer their own way of living and ask that their own customs be allowed them. [25]Accordingly, since we choose that this nation also should be free from disturbance, our decision is that their temple be restored to them and that they shall live according to the customs of their ancestors. [26]You will do well, therefore, to send word to them and give them pledges of friendship, so that they may know our policy and be of good cheer and go on happily in the conduct of their own affairs."

27 To the nation the king's letter was as follows:

"King Antiochus to the council of the Jews and to the other Jews, greetings. [28]If you are well, it is as we desire. We also are in good health. [29]Menelaus has informed us that you wish to return home and look after your own affairs. [30]Therefore those who go home by the thirtieth of Xanthicus will have our pledge of friendship and full permission [31]for the Jews to enjoy their own customs[c] and laws, just as formerly, and none of them shall be molested in any way for what may have been done in ignorance. [32]And I have also sent Menelaus to encourage you. [33]Farewell. The one hundred forty-eighth year, Xanthicus fifteenth."

34 The Romans also sent them a letter, which read thus:

"Quintus Memmius and Titus Manius, envoys of the Romans, to the people of the Jews, greetings. [35]With regard to what Lysias the kinsman of the king has granted you, we also give consent. [36]But as to the matters that he decided are to be referred to the king, as soon as you have considered them, send someone promptly so that we may make proposals appropriate for you, for we are on our way to Antioch. [37]Therefore make haste and send messengers so that we may have your judgment. [38]Farewell. The one hundred forty-eighth year, Xanthicus fifteenth."

12 When this agreement had been reached, Lysias returned to the king, and the Jews went about their farming.

2 But some of the governors in various places, Timothy and Apollonius son of Gennaeus, as well as Hieronymus and Demophon, and in addition to these Nicanor the governor of Cyprus, would not let them live quietly and in

c 11.31 Cn: Gk *food*

request. The requests are not specified. **11:16** Historians generally consider the letters authentic, although debates continue on their placement within the narrative. **11:17** *John and Absalom* are Jewish emissaries. *Absalom* is otherwise unmentioned in the account; *John* may be one of the Maccabean brothers (cf. 1 Macc. 2:2; 9:35–36, 38). **11:21** In the Seleucid calendar, *the one hundred forty-eighth year* would be 165–164 BCE, before the rededication of the temple.

11:22–33 Antiochus's letters. 11:22 *Brother.* See note on 11:1. **11:24** *Greek customs.* See note on 6:1–11. **11:25** The Jews have already secured ownership of the temple (vv. 6–12). **11:29** *Menelaus,* a Jewish priest willing to compromise, is a confidant of the earlier king (cf. 4:23–29; 13:3–7) as well as of Eupator.

11:34–37 Letter from Rome. 11:34 *Envoys of the Romans* attest to Rome's imperial power and interest in the East. Judas's desire to be in relationship with Rome comes later (cf. 1 Macc. 8:1–17; see 2 Macc. 4:11).

12:1–9 Judas reacts to travesty. 12:1 Life returns to the normal activity of *farming,* a way of life God "created" (cf. Sir. 7:15). *Lysias.* See note on 11:1. **12:2** *Timothy's* death was recorded in 10:37, unless this refers to another Timothy. *Governor of Cyprus* may indicate another *Nicanor* rather than

peace. ³And the people of Joppa did so ungodly a deed as this: they invited the Jews who lived among them to embark, with their wives and children, on boats that they had provided, as though there were no ill will to the Jews,ᵈ ⁴and this was done by public vote of the city. When they accepted, because they wished to live peaceably and suspected nothing, the people of Joppaᵉ took them out to sea and drowned them, at least two hundred. ⁵When Judas heard of the cruelty visited on his compatriots, he gave orders to his men ⁶and, calling upon God, the righteous judge, attacked the murderers of his kindred. He set fire to the harbor by night, burned the boats, and massacred those who had taken refuge there. ⁷Then, because the city's gates were closed, he withdrew, intending to come again and root out the whole community of Joppa. ⁸But learning that the people in Jamnia meant in the same way to wipe out the Jews who were living among them, ⁹he attacked the Jamnites by night and set fire to the harbor and the fleet, so that the glow of the light was seen in Jerusalem, thirty milesᶠ distant.

10 When they had gone more than a mileᵍ from there on their march against Timothy, at least five thousand Arabs with five hundred cavalry attacked them. ¹¹After a hard fight, Judas and his companions, with God's help, were victorious. The defeated nomads begged Judas to grant them pledges of friendship, promising to give him livestock and to help his peopleʰ in all other ways. ¹²Judas, realizing that they might indeed be useful in many ways, agreed to make peace with them, and after receiving his pledges they went back to their tents.

13 He also attacked a certain town that was strongly fortified with earthworksⁱ and walls and inhabited by all sorts of nations. Its name was Caspin. ¹⁴Those who were within, relying on the strength of the walls and on their supply of provisions, behaved most insolently toward Judas and his men, railing at them and

even blaspheming and saying unholy things. ¹⁵But Judas and his men, calling upon the great Sovereign of the world, who without battering rams or engines of war overthrew Jericho in the days of Joshua, rushed furiously upon the walls. ¹⁶They took the town by the will of God and slaughtered untold numbers, so that the adjoining lake, a quarter of a mileʲ wide, appeared to be running over with blood.

17 When they had gone ninety-five milesᵏ from there, they came to a stockade,ˡ to the Jews who are called Toubiani. ¹⁸They did not find Timothy in that region, for he had by then left there without accomplishing anything, though in one place he had left a very strong garrison. ¹⁹Dositheus and Sosipater, who were captains under Maccabeus, marched out and destroyed those whom Timothy had left in the stronghold, more than ten thousand men. ²⁰But Maccabeus arranged his army in divisions, set menᵐ in command of the divisions, and hurried after Timothy, who had with him one hundred twenty thousand infantry and two thousand five hundred cavalry. ²¹When Timothy learned of the approach of Judas, he sent off the women and the children and also the baggage to a place called Carnaim, for that place was hard to besiege and difficult to access because of the narrowness of all the approaches. ²²But when Judas's first division appeared, terror and fear came over the enemy at the manifestation to them of him who sees all things. In their flight they rushed headlong in every direction, so that often they were injured by their own men and pierced by the points of their own swords. ²³Judas pressed the pursuit with the utmost vigor, putting the sinners to the sword, and destroyed as many as thirty thousand.

d 12.3 Gk to them   e 12.4 Gk they   f 12.9 Gk two hundred forty stadia   g 12.10 Gk nine stadia   h 12.11 Gk them   i 12.13 Meaning of Gk uncertain   j 12.16 Gk two stadia   k 12.17 Gk seven hundred fifty stadia   l 12.17 Or Charax   m 12.20 Gk them

Judas's chief enemy (cf. 14:12–15:37). **12:3–4** *People of Joppa* are coastal folks alongside the Mediterranean. **12:9** *Thirty miles.* See note on 11:5.

12:10–16 Judas defeats Timothy. Cf. 1 Macc. 5. **12:10–12** *Arabs* could be hired for battle (cf. 1 Macc. 5:39), and *nomads* could switch sides. **12:14** *Blaspheming.* See note on 10:34. **12:15** *In the days of Joshua.* Cf. Josh. 6. **12:16** *A quarter of a mile.* See note on 11:5.

12:17–25 Judas defeats Timothy (again). **12:17** *Ninety-five miles.* See note on 11:5. *Toubiani* may stem from a well-known, upper-class Jewish family (cf. 3:11). **12:19** *Dositheus and Sosipater* (cf. vv. 24, 35) are Jews with Hellenistic names. Timothy negotiates with them because of an earlier battle (v. 24; cf. 1 Macc. 5:13). **12:22** One *who sees all things* refers to the Israelite deity (cf. 9:5; 15:2).

24 Timothy himself fell into the hands of Dositheus and Sosipater and their men. With great guile he begged them to let him go in safety, because he held the parents of most of them and the brothers of some, to whom no consideration would be shown. 25And when with many words he had confirmed his solemn promise to restore them unharmed, they let him go, for the sake of saving their kindred.

26 Then Judas[n] marched against Carnaim and the temple of Atargatis and slaughtered twenty-five thousand people. 27After the rout and destruction of these, he marched also against Ephron, a fortified town where Lysias lived with multitudes of people of all nationalities.[o] Stalwart young men took their stand before the walls and made a vigorous defense, and great stores of war engines and missiles were there. 28But the Jews[p] called upon the Sovereign who with power shatters the might of his enemies, and they got the town into their hands and killed as many as twenty-five thousand of those who were in it.

29 Setting out from there, they hastened to Scythopolis, which is seventy-five miles[q] from Jerusalem. 30But when the Jews who lived there bore witness to the goodwill that the people of Scythopolis had shown them and their kind treatment of them in times of misfortune, 31they thanked them and exhorted them to be well disposed to their race in the future also. Then they went up to Jerusalem, as the Festival of Weeks was close at hand.

32 After the festival called Pentecost, they hurried against Gorgias, the governor of Idumea, 33who came out with three thousand infantry and four hundred cavalry. 34When they joined battle, it happened that a few of the Jews fell. 35But a certain Dositheus, one of Bacenor's men,[r] who was on horseback and was a strong man, caught hold of Gorgias and, grasping his cloak, was dragging him off by main strength, wishing to take the accursed man alive, when one of the Thracian cavalry bore down on him and cut off his arm, so Gorgias escaped and reached Marisa.

36 As Esdris and his men had been fighting for a long time and were weary, Judas called upon the Lord to show himself their ally and leader in the battle. 37In the language of their ancestors he raised the battle cry, with hymns; then he charged against Gorgias's troops when they were not expecting it and put them to flight.

38 Then Judas assembled his army and went to the city of Adullam. As the seventh day was coming on, they purified themselves according to the custom and kept the Sabbath there.

39 On the next day, as had now become necessary, Judas and his men went to take up the bodies of the fallen and to bring them back to lie with their kindred in the tombs of their ancestors. 40Then under the tunic of each one of the dead they found sacred tokens of the idols of Jamnia, which the law forbids the Jews to wear. And it became clear to all

n 12.26 Gk *he* o 12.27 Meaning of Gk uncertain
p 12.28 Gk *they* q 12.29 Gk *six hundred stadia* r 12.35 Other authorities read *the Toubians*

12:26–31 Other victories. 12:26 *Twenty-five thousand people* exaggerates the number but includes "the women and the children" (v. 21). **12:27** *Lysias.* See note on 11:1. *All nationalities* (Gk. "pamphula" = "many tribes") depicts Judea in opposition to "all" (cf. 8:9). Conversely, 4 Maccabees uses this term to describe an accessible space in the temple area "open to all" (cf. 4 Macc. 4:11). **12:29** A military force would march *seventy-five miles* (see note on 11:5) in three to five days. **12:31** *Their race* (Gk. "genos") refers to an ethnic group ("race, people, nation") or a common ancestry ("descendant, family"). Generally, this translation uses "people" (cf. 1:10; 5:22; 6:12; 7:16; 8:9) or "nation" (7:38; 14:8, 9), with "race" used only here and at 7:28. The *Festival of Weeks* is a celebration to mark the wheat harvest (cf. Exod. 34:22).

12:32–37 Judas tracks down Gorgias. 12:32 *Pentecost* marks the end of the Festival of Weeks (v. 31). *Gorgias.* See note on 10:14 (cf. 8:9). **12:34** *A few of the Jews fell* is a rare admission from the epitomist, who indicates a religious rationale rather than military incompetence (vv. 40–42; cf. 1 Macc. 5:55–62). **12:35** *Dositheus* is distinct from the one in v. 19. *Bacenor* is otherwise unknown. **12:35** *Marisa.* Approximately twenty-five miles from Jerusalem. **12:36** *Esdris* is otherwise unknown. **12:37** *In the language of their ancestors* recalls the stories about the martyrs (cf. 7:8, 21, 27).

12:38–45 Prayers for the dead. 12:38 *Kept the Sabbath.* See 8:26–28n. **12:39** *Tombs of their ancestors.* The desire for proper burial customs is repeated elsewhere (cf. 5:10; 13:7). **12:40** *The law forbids* (cf. Deut. 7:25–26). The epitomist provides a religious explanation for their deaths and not

that this was the reason these men had fallen. [41]So they all blessed the ways of the Lord, the righteous judge, who reveals the things that are hidden, [42]and they turned to supplication, praying that the sin that had been committed might be wholly blotted out. The noble Judas exhorted the people to keep themselves free from sin, for they had seen with their own eyes what had happened as the result of the sin of those who had fallen. [43]He also took up a collection, man by man, to the amount of two thousand drachmas of silver, and sent it to Jerusalem to provide for a purification offering. In doing this he acted very well and honorably, taking account of the resurrection. [44]For if he were not expecting that those who had fallen would rise again, it would have been superfluous and foolish to pray for the dead. [45]But if he was looking to the splendid reward that is laid up for those who fall asleep in godliness, it was a holy and pious thought. Therefore he made atonement for the dead, so that they might be delivered from their sin.

13 In the one hundred forty-ninth year, word came to Judas and his men that Antiochus Eupator was coming with a great army against Judea, [2]and with him Lysias, his guardian, who had charge of the government. Each of them had a Greek force of one hundred ten thousand infantry, five thousand three hundred cavalry, twenty-two elephants, and three hundred chariots armed with scythes.

[3] Menelaus also joined them and with utter hypocrisy urged Antiochus on, not for the sake of his country's welfare but because he thought that he would be established in office. [4]But the King of kings aroused the anger of Antiochus against the scoundrel, and when Lysias informed him that this man was to blame for all the trouble, he ordered them to take him to Beroea and to put him to death by the method that is customary in that place. [5]For there is a tower there, fifty cubits high, full of ashes, and it has a rim running around it that on all sides inclines precipitously into the ashes. [6]There they all push to destruction anyone guilty of sacrilege or notorious for other crimes. [7]By such a fate it came about that Menelaus the lawbreaker died, without even burial in the earth. [8]And this was eminently just; because he had committed many sins against the altar whose fire and ashes were holy, he met his death in ashes.

[9] The king with barbarous arrogance was coming to show the Jews things far worse than those that had been done[s] in his father's time. [10]But when Judas heard of this, he ordered the people to call upon the Lord day and night, now if ever to help those who were on the point of being deprived of the law and their country and the holy temple, [11]and not to let the people who had just begun to revive fall into the hands of the blasphemous nations. [12]When they had all joined in the same petition and had implored the merciful Lord with weeping and fasting and lying prostrate for three days without ceasing, Judas exhorted them and ordered them to stand ready.

[13] After consulting privately with the elders, he determined to march out and decide the matter by the help of God before the king's army could enter Judea and get possession of the city. [14]So, committing the decision to the

s 13.9 Or *the worst of the things that had been done*

---

the war effort (cf. 7:32). **12:42** The emphasis on *sin* specifically recalls v. 40. **12:43** *Purification offering.* See Lev. 4–5 for sacrifices made for "unintentional" sins. The term *resurrection* is a theme in the book (cf. 7:9, 14; 14:46; cf. Dan. 12:1–3). See **"Resurrection," p. 1224. 12:44** *Pray for the dead* is rare (cf. 1 Cor. 15:29). Some contemporary Catholic and Eastern Orthodox Christians follow the practice. **12:45** *Asleep in godliness* suggests only the righteous will be resurrected (also 7:14).

13:1–8 Death of Menelaus. 13:1 *One hundred forty-ninth year* = 163 BCE. Since *Eupator* made peace with the Jews earlier (cf. 11:13–38), this battle is placed here for rhetorical (not chronological) reasons (cf. 1 Macc. 6:32–47). **13:2** *Lysias.* See note on 11:1. *Elephants* and *scythes* indicate military prowess. See note on 11:4. **13:3** *Menelaus.* A Jewish high priest in favor of Hellenization (cf. 4:23–50). The book considers this priest a "lawbreaker" (see v. 7) and the people's enemy (4:50). **13:7** *Without even burial.* See note on 12:39. **13:8** Holiness of the *fire and ashes* is a key theme in the book (cf. 1:18–23; 2:1–18).

13:9–17 Battle at Modein. 13:10 *The law and their country and the holy temple* restates the purpose of these battles (see v. 14 and note on 8:2–3). **13:13** *The elders,* who play a minor role here, are usually involved as public representatives of the people (cf. 14:37; 1 Macc. 7:33; 11:23; 12:35; 13:36; 14:20). *Help of God.* See v. 17 and note on 8:23. **13:14** *Modein* is approximately twenty miles from Jerusalem. Judas was reared (cf. 1 Macc. 2:1–5) and buried (9:19) there alongside his father (cf. 2:70).

Creator of the world and exhorting his troops to fight bravely to the death for the laws, temple, city, country, and way of life, he pitched his camp near Modein. [15]He gave his troops the watchword, "God's victory," and with a picked force of the bravest young men, he attacked the king's pavilion at night and killed as many as two thousand men in the camp. He stabbed[t] the leading elephant and its rider. [16]In the end, they filled the camp with terror and confusion and withdrew in triumph. [17]This happened, just as day was dawning, because the Lord's help protected him.

[18] The king, having had a taste of the daring of the Jews, tried strategy in attacking their positions. [19]He advanced against Beth-zur, a strong fortress of the Jews, was turned back, attacked again,[u] and was defeated. [20]Judas sent in to the garrison whatever was necessary. [21]But Rhodocus, a man from the ranks of the Jews, gave secret information to the enemy; he was sought for, caught, and put in prison. [22]The king negotiated a second time with the people in Beth-zur, gave pledges, received theirs, withdrew, attacked Judas and his men, was defeated; [23]he got word that Philip, who had been left in charge of the government, had revolted in Antioch; he was dismayed, called in the Jews, yielded and swore to observe all their rights, settled with them and offered sacrifice, honored the sanctuary, and showed generosity to the holy place. [24]He received Maccabeus, left Hegemonides as governor from Ptolemais to Gerar, [25]and went to Ptolemais. The people of Ptolemais were indignant over the treaty; in fact, they were so angry that they wanted to annul its terms.[v] [26]Lysias took the public platform, made the best possible defense, convinced them, appeased them, gained their goodwill, and

set out for Antioch. This is how the king's attack and withdrawal turned out.

14 Three years later, word came to Judas and his men that Demetrius son of Seleucus had sailed into the harbor of Tripolis with a strong army and a fleet [2]and had taken possession of the country, having made away with Antiochus and his guardian Lysias.

[3] Now a certain Alcimus, who had formerly been high priest but had willfully defiled himself in the days of separation,[w] realized that there was no way for him to be safe or to have access again to the holy altar [4]and went to King Demetrius in about the one hundred fifty-first year, presenting to him a crown of gold and a palm and besides these some of the customary olive branches from the temple. During that day he kept quiet. [5]But he found an opportunity that furthered his mad purpose when he was invited by Demetrius to a meeting of the council and was asked about the attitude and intentions of the Jews. He answered:

[6] "Those of the Jews who are called Hasideans, whose leader is Judas Maccabeus, are keeping up war and stirring up sedition and will not let the kingdom attain tranquility. [7]Therefore I have laid aside my ancestral glory—I mean the high priesthood—and have now come here, [8]first because I am genuinely concerned for the interests of the king, and second because I have regard also for my compatriots. For through the folly of those whom I have mentioned our whole nation is now in no small misfortune. [9]Since you are acquainted, O king, with the details of this matter,

---

t 13.15 Meaning of Gk uncertain   u 13.19 Or *faltered*
v 13.25 Meaning of Gk uncertain   w 14.3 Other ancient authorities read *of mixing*

His father (Mattathias)—never mentioned in 2 Maccabees—resisted Hellenization in Modein (cf. 1 Macc. 2:15–28). **13:15** *God's victory* is the battle *watchword*.

13:18–26 Antiochus makes a (second?) treaty with the Jews. 13:19 *Beth-zur* is an important military post against attackers from the south (cf. 11:5; 1 Macc. 4:61; 6:26; 14:33). **13:21** Occasionally, the epitomist acknowledges the complicated realities of the war effort. *Rhodocus* is otherwise unknown. **13:23** *Philip*'s betrayal is alluded to earlier (9:29), and this tension may be the king's rationale for making peace with the Jews (cf. 1 Macc. 6:55–63). **13:26** *Lysias*. See note on 11:1.

14:1–14 Alcimus seeks the priesthood. 14:1–2 *Three years later* = 162/161 BCE. *Demetrius* comes to power (v. 4) and removes his cousin *Antiochus and his guardian;* for *guardian,* see note on 11:1. Unlike 1 Maccabees, this book does not record their deaths (cf. 1 Macc. 7:1–4). **14:3** *Alcimus* hopes to be restored to the high priesthood (v. 13). Perhaps Antiochus appointed him following the death of Menelaus. The *days of separation* (also 14:38) is unclear in the Greek text, likely referring to the enforced Hellenization process. **14:4** *One hundred fifty-first year* = 161 BCE. **14:6** The only reference

may it please you to take thought for our country and our hard-pressed nation with the gracious kindness that you show to all. [10]For as long as Judas lives, it is impossible for the government to find peace." [11]When he had said this, the rest of the king's Friends,[x] who were hostile to Judas, quickly inflamed Demetrius still more. [12]He immediately chose Nicanor, who had been in command of the elephants, appointed him governor of Judea, and sent him off [13]with orders to kill Judas and scatter his troops and to install Alcimus as high priest of the great[y] temple. [14]And the nations throughout Judea, who had fled before[z] Judas, flocked to join Nicanor, thinking that the misfortunes and calamities of the Jews would mean prosperity for themselves.

[15] When the Jews[a] heard of Nicanor's coming and the gathering of the nations, they sprinkled dust on their heads and prayed to him who established his own people forever and always upholds his own heritage by manifesting himself. [16]At the command of the leader, they[b] set out from there immediately and engaged them in battle at a village called Dessau.[c] [17]Simon, the brother of Judas, had encountered Nicanor but had been temporarily[d] checked because of the sudden consternation created by the enemy.

[18] Nevertheless, Nicanor, hearing of the valor of Judas and his troops and their courage in battle for their country, shrank from deciding the issue by bloodshed. [19]Therefore he sent Posidonius, Theodotus, and Mattathias to give and receive pledges of friendship. [20]When the terms had been fully considered and the leader had informed the people and it had appeared that they were of one mind, they agreed to the covenant. [21]The leaders[e] set a day on which to meet by themselves. A chariot came forward from each army; seats of honor were set in place; [22]Judas posted armed men in readiness at key places to prevent sudden treachery on the part of the enemy; so they duly held the consultation.

[23] Nicanor stayed on in Jerusalem and did nothing out of the way but dismissed the flocks of people who had gathered. [24]And he kept Judas always in his presence; he was warmly attached to the man. [25]He urged him to marry and have children, so Judas[f] married, settled down, and shared the common life.

[26] But when Alcimus noticed their goodwill for one another, he took the covenant that had been made and went to Demetrius. He told him that Nicanor was disloyal to the government, since he had appointed that conspirator against the kingdom, Judas, to be his successor. [27]The king became excited and, provoked by the false accusations of that depraved man, wrote to Nicanor, stating that he was displeased with the covenant and commanding him to send Maccabeus to Antioch as a prisoner without delay.

[28] When this message came to Nicanor, he was troubled and grieved that he had to annul their agreement when the man had done no wrong. [29]Since it was not possible to oppose the king, he watched for an opportunity to accomplish this by a stratagem. [30]But Maccabeus, noticing that Nicanor was more austere in his dealings with him and was meeting him more rudely than had been his custom, concluded that this austerity did not spring from the best motives. So he gathered not a few of his men and went into hiding from Nicanor. [31]When the latter became aware that he had been cleverly outwitted by the man, he went to the great[g] and holy temple while the priests were offering the customary sacrifices and commanded them to hand the man over.

x 14.11 Gk of the Friends y 14.13 Gk greatest z 14.14 Meaning of Gk uncertain a 14.15 Gk they b 14.16 Gk he c 14.16 Meaning of Gk uncertain d 14.17 Other ancient authorities read slowly e 14.21 Gk They f 14.25 Gk he g 14.31 Gk greatest

to *Hasideans* in this book links this group to the Maccabees (cf. 1 Macc. 2:42). **14:11** *King's Friends.* See note on 8:9. **14:12** *Nicanor* returns as *governor of Judea* (cf. 8:9–34). In 1 Maccabees, the king selects "Bacchides" as governor (1 Macc. 7:8–9). **14:13** *Install Alcimus.* Cf. 1 Macc. 7:9. **14:14** Instead of *nations* (Gk. "ethnē"), "gentiles" would be a better translation here.
  14:15–36 Friends and enemies. **14:15** *Sprinkled dust on their heads.* See note on 10:25–26. **14:17** *Simon.* See note on 8:22. **14:19** *Posidonius, Theodotus, and Mattathias* are Jews—the latter two have Jewish names—working alongside Nicanor (cf. 15:2). **14:25** The marriage of Judas in the midst of this tense period is narrative comedy to entertain readers (cf. 2:25, 29; 15:39). **14:26** *Alcimus* intervenes due to vested interest (see 14:3, 13). **14:27** *Antioch* houses the Seleucids' seat of government

[32]When they declared on oath that they did not know where the man was whom he wanted, [33]he stretched out his right hand toward the sanctuary and swore this oath: "If you do not hand Judas over to me as a prisoner, I will level this shrine of God to the ground and tear down the altar and build here a splendid temple to Dionysus."

34 Having said this, he went away. Then the priests stretched out their hands toward heaven and called upon the constant Defender of our nation, in these words: [35]"O Lord of all, though you have need of nothing, you were pleased that there should be a temple for your habitation among us, [36]so now, O holy One, Lord of all holiness, keep undefiled forever this house that has been so recently purified."

37 A certain Razis, one of the elders of Jerusalem, was denounced to Nicanor as a man who loved his compatriots and was very well thought of and for his goodwill was called father of the Jews. [38]For before the days of separation, he had been accused of Judaism, and he had most zealously risked body and life for Judaism. [39]Nicanor, wishing to exhibit the enmity that he had for the Jews, sent more than five hundred soldiers to arrest him, [40]for he thought that by arresting[b] him he would do them an injury. [41]When the troops were about to capture the tower and were forcing the door of the courtyard, they ordered that fire be brought and the doors burned. Being surrounded, Razis[i] fell upon his own sword, [42]preferring to die nobly rather than to fall into the hands of sinners and suffer outrages unworthy of his noble birth. [43]But in the heat of the struggle he did not hit exactly, and the crowd was now rushing in through the doors. He courageously ran up on the wall and bravely threw himself down into the crowd. [44]But as they quickly drew back, a space opened and he fell in the middle of the empty space. [45]Still alive and aflame with anger, he rose, and though his blood gushed forth and his wounds were severe he ran through the crowd, and standing upon a steep rock, [46]with his blood now completely drained from him, he tore out his entrails, took them in both hands, and hurled them at the crowd, calling upon the Lord of life and spirit to give them back to him again. This was the manner of his death.

15 When Nicanor heard that Judas and his troops were in the region of Samaria, he made plans to attack them with complete safety on the day of rest. [2]When the Jews who were compelled to follow him said, "Do not destroy so savagely and barbarously, but show respect for the day that he who sees all things has honored and hallowed above other days," [3]the thrice-accursed wretch asked if there were a sovereign in heaven who had commanded the keeping of the Sabbath day. [4]When they declared, "It is the living Lord himself, the Sovereign in heaven, who ordered us to observe the seventh day," [5]he replied, "But I am a sovereign also, on earth, and I command you to take up arms and finish the king's business." Nevertheless, he did not succeed in carrying out his abominable design.

6 This Nicanor in his utter boastfulness and arrogance had determined to erect a public monument of victory over Judas and his forces. [7]But Maccabeus did not cease to trust with all confidence that he would get help from the Lord. [8]He exhorted his troops not to fear the attack of the nations but to keep in mind the former times when help had come to them from heaven and so to look for the victory that the Almighty would give them. [9]Encouraging

b 14.40 Meaning of Gk uncertain   i 14.41 Gk he

(cf. 11:36; 13:23). **14:32** Violation of an *oath* is a serious matter (cf. 4:34–38; 15:10). **14:36** *Recently purified* in 10:1–8.

14:37–46 Razis's death by suicide. 14:37 *Elders.* See note on 13:13. The title *father of the Jews* is distinctive to this book and more narrowly defined than Abraham's "ancestor of a multitude of nations" (cf. Gen. 17:2–5). **14:38** *Days of separation.* See note on 14:3. *Judaism.* See note on 8:1. **14:41–46** Razis's multiple attempts to die by suicide are a comedic feature of the book (see note on v. 25), even while some ancients could view death by suicide more honorably than death by public shaming (cf. 4 Macc. 17:1). **14:46** *Give them back . . . again* points to the belief in "resurrection." See note on 12:43.

15:1–5 No Sabbath fighting. 15:1 *Nicanor.* See 14:30–31 and note on 14:12. *Region of Samaria* lies to the north of Judea. *Day of rest* refers to the Sabbath. See note on 8:26–28. **15:2** *Jews . . . compelled to follow him.* Cf. 14:19. **15:3** *Thrice-accursed* (cf. 8:34) is the epitomist's attempt to link these two separate individuals. **15:4** *Observe the seventh day.* Cf. Exod. 20:8; Deut. 5:12; Lev. 23:3. **15:6–19 Judas prepares for battle. 15:8** *Help . . . from heaven.* See note on 8:23. **15:9** Judas functions

them from the Law and the Prophets and reminding them also of the struggles they had won, he made them the more eager. ¹⁰When he had aroused their courage, he issued his orders, at the same time pointing out the treachery of the nations and their violation of oaths. ¹¹He armed each of them not so much with confidence in shields and spears as with the inspiration of brave words, and he cheered them all by relating a dream, a sort of vision,ʲ that was worthy of belief.

12 What he saw was this: Onias, who had been high priest, a noble and good man, of modest bearing and gentle manner, one who spoke fittingly and had been trained from childhood in all that belongs to excellence, was praying with outstretched hands for the whole body of the Jews. ¹³Then in the same fashion another appeared, distinguished by his gray hair and dignity, and of marvelous majesty and authority. ¹⁴And Onias spoke, saying, "This is a man who loves the family of Israel and prays much for the people and the holy city: Jeremiah, the prophet of God." ¹⁵Jeremiah stretched out his right hand and gave to Judas a golden sword, and as he gave it he addressed him thus: ¹⁶"Take this holy sword, a gift from God, with which you will strike down your adversaries."

17 Encouraged by the words of Judas, so noble and so effective in arousing valor and awaking courage in the souls of the young, they determined not to carry on a campaignᵏ but to attack bravely and to decide the matter by fighting hand to hand with all courage, because the city and the sanctuary and the temple were in danger. ¹⁸Their concern for wives and children and also for brothers and sisters and relatives lay upon them less heavily; their greatest and first fear was for the consecrated sanctuary. ¹⁹And those who had to remain in the city were in no little distress,

being anxious over the encounter in the open country.

20 When all were now looking forward to the coming issue and the enemy was already close at hand with their army drawn up for battle, the elephantsˡ strategically stationed and the cavalry deployed on the flanks, ²¹Maccabeus, observing the masses that were in front of him and the varied supply of arms and the savagery of the elephants, stretched out his hands toward heaven and called upon the Lord who works wonders, for he knew that it is not by arms but as the Lordᵐ decides that he gains the victory for those who deserve it. ²²He called upon him in these words: "O Lord, you sent your angel in the time of King Hezekiah of Judea, and he killed fully one hundred eighty-five thousand in the camp of Sennacherib. ²³So now, O Sovereign of the heavens, send a good angel to spread terror and trembling before us. ²⁴By the might of your arm may these blasphemers who come against your holy people be struck down." With these words he ended his prayer.

25 Nicanor and his troops advanced with trumpets and battle songs, ²⁶but Judas and his troops met the enemy in battle with invocations to God and prayers. ²⁷So, fighting with their hands and praying to God in their hearts, they laid low at least thirty-five thousand and were greatly gladdened by God's manifestation.

28 When the action was over and they were returning with joy, they recognized Nicanor, lying dead, in full armor. ²⁹Then there was shouting and tumult, and they blessed the Sovereign Lord in the language of their ancestors. ³⁰Then the man who was ever in body and soul the defender of his people, the

j 15.11 Meaning of Gk uncertain   k 15.17 Or to remain in camp   l 15.20 Gk animals   m 15.21 Gk he

as a priest reading from *the Law and the Prophets* (cf. 8:23), a role downplayed in 2 Maccabees. **15:10** *Violation of oaths.* See note on 14:32. **15:11** Use of *a dream*—or, perhaps, a "daydream" for a *sort of vision* (Gk. "hypar")—is distinctive in 2 Maccabees. **15:12-16** The dream recalls *Onias*—the favorable high priest of chap. 3—alongside the prophet *Jeremiah* (cf. 2:1–8; died ca. 570 BCE). **15:17** *The city and the sanctuary and the temple.* See note on 8:2. **15:18** *Consecrated sanctuary.* Cf. 10:1–8; note on 10:3.

15:20–37 Nicanor's death. 15:20 The word translated as *issue* in Greek is "krisis," which could mean "trial, condemnation, crisis." Instead of *elephants* specifically, the Greek "thērion" is literally "wild animals." **15:21** *Stretched . . . hands toward heaven* (cf. 3:15, 20; 14:34) indicates a belief that the prayers of the pious can cause the Israelite deity to act on their behalf. **15:22** *Time of King Hezekiah.* See note on 8:19. **15:23** *Good angel.* Cf. 11:6. **15:24** *Blasphemers.* See note on 10:34. **15:27** *God's manifestation*—or "appearance" or "epiphany" (Gk. "epiphaneia")—is a theme of the book (cf. 2:21; 3:24; 12:22; 14:15); the word never occurs in 1 Maccabees. **15:29** *Language of their ancestors.* See note on 12:37. **15:30–35** Cf.

man who maintained his youthful goodwill toward his compatriots, ordered them to cut off Nicanor's head and arm and carry them to Jerusalem. ³¹When he arrived there and had called his compatriots together and stationed the priests before the altar, he sent for those who were in the citadel. ³²He showed them the vile Nicanor's head and that profane man's arm, which had been boastfully stretched out against the holy house of the Almighty. ³³He cut out the tongue of the ungodly Nicanor and said that he would feed it piecemeal to the birds and would hang up these rewards of his folly opposite the sanctuary. ³⁴And they all, looking to heaven, blessed the Lord who had manifested himself, saying, "Blessed is he who has kept his own place undefiled!" ³⁵Judas" hung Nicanor's head from the citadel, a clear and conspicuous sign to everyone of the help of the Lord. ³⁶And they all decreed by public

vote never to let this day go unobserved but to celebrate the thirteenth day of the twelfth month—which is called Adar in the Aramaic language—the day before Mordecai's day.

37 This, then, is how matters turned out with Nicanor, and from that time the city has been in the possession of the Hebrews. So I will here end my story.

38 If it is well told and to the point, that is what I myself desired; if it is poorly done and mediocre, that was the best I could do. ³⁹For just as it is harmful to drink wine alone or, again, to drink water alone, while wine already mixed with water is delicious and enhances one's enjoyment, so also the style of the story delights the ears of those who read the work. And here will be the end.

n 15.35 Gk *He*

---

1 Macc. 7:47–49. Public display of this victory (and violence!) finds its contemporary analogy in the manner in which Western media outlets display, for example, the killing of Osama Bin Laden during 9/11 commemorations. **15:35** *Help of the Lord.* See note on 8:23. **15:36** *Aramaic* is the common spoken language of the day rather than "Hebrew" (see v. 29). For the origins of *Mordecai's day*, see the story of Esther (cf. Esth. 9:20–23).

15:38–39 Epilogue. 15:39 *Wine . . . mixed with water* is preferred in ancient settings due to the potency of their wines. *Delights the ears* reminds us that ancient stories are read aloud.

(b) The books from 1 Esdras through 3 Maccabees are recognized as Deuterocanonical Scripture by the Greek and the Russian Orthodox Churches. They are not so recognized by the Roman Catholic Church, but 1 Esdras and the Prayer of Manasseh (together with 2 Esdras) are placed in an appendix to the Latin Vulgate Bible.

1 ESDRAS

The book of 1 Esdras has survived only in Greek texts, although some scholars argue for a presumed Hebrew/Aramaic original. The book reproduces significant portions of the story of the first return-ees from the Babylonian exile after the conquests of Babylon by Cyrus the Persian beginning in 539 BCE. The story also appears in the book of Ezra, which 1 Esdras largely duplicates, but 1 Esdras also incorporates portions of Neh. 8 (which also deals with Ezra, a chapter many scholars believe to have been shifted from the Ezra materials). As a unique beginning, 1 Esdras incorporates the ending of 2 Chronicles. Most intriguing, 1 Esdras introduces a story of Zerubbabel as one of three "body-guards" or "court pages" serving in the court of Darius the Persian, a story only in 1 Esdras. There are other minor and major differences between 1 Esdras and the (presumably older) material in Ezra–Nehemiah, but only a few of them have (possibly) significant implications. In addition to this unique story of Zerubbabel's youth in the court of Darius, 1 Esdras is notable for the near total absence (ignoring?) of any traditions about Nehemiah. His name is only briefly mentioned in passing.

The book of 1 Esdras is canonical in the Greek Orthodox Church and the Russian Orthodox Church. It is called 2 Esdras in the Slavonic Bible of the Russian Orthodox Church and is in the Roman Catholic Apocrypha, where it is called 3 Esdras.

1 Esdras and Ezra–Nehemiah

A chart showing the relationship of 1 Esdras to material known to us in Chronicles, Ezra, and Nehemiah helps us understand how 1 Esdras is a "composite" work:

1 Esdras	Hebrew (Masoretic Text)
1:1–20	2 Chr. 35:1–19: Josiah's Passover
1:21–55	2 Chr. 35:20–36:21: Josiah's reign to the fall of Jerusalem
2:1–14	Ezra 1: Return of exiles
2:15–25	Ezra 4:7–24: Building of temple begins, then stops
3:1–5:6	(No parallel): Three bodyguards
5:7–45	Ezra 2: List of those returning from exile
5:46–70	Ezra 3:1–4:5: Altar set up; temple foundations laid
6:1–33	Ezra 5:1–6:12: Building of temple resumes
7:1–15	Ezra 6:13–22: Temple finished; dedicated at Passover
8:1–64	Ezra 7–8: Ezra's expedition to Jerusalem
8:65–9:36	Ezra 9–10: Crisis of mixed marriages
9:37–55	Neh. 7:73–8:12: Ezra reads the law

The somewhat abrupt ending at the end of chap. 9 has garnered significant debate. Is something missing? Should we have expected some description of a celebration to "match" the beginning of the book, which discusses Josiah's Passover celebrations? Some have suggested that the celebration of the Feast of Tabernacles at Neh. 8:13–18 should have been at the end. Others, however, propose that the existing ending makes perfect sense, since a Passover also "concludes" chaps. 1–7 before Ezra himself is introduced.

The relationship of Ezra–Nehemiah to 1 Esdras remains a vigorously debated issue: Is 1 Esdras an older form of the Ezra traditions than the Hebrew/Aramaic Ezra–Nehemiah? Or is 1 Esdras a later, edited work that draws on Ezra–Nehemiah (and Chronicles) but with a clear agenda of its own? If so, what is that "agenda"? Attention turns to not only the unique story in 1 Esd. 3–4 but also the absence of Nehemiah.

The "Three Bodyguards"

Recent scholars have proposed that the book was written to feature and highlight this story. The story shows some signs of being an independent tradition that has been incorporated into 1 Esdras. For example, some of the details of the story do not agree with the surrounding narrative, including the notion that Darius is described as almost entirely responsible for the rebuilding of the temple, while chaps. 1–2 clearly point to the initiative—and significant actions—of Cyrus. Furthermore, the story has a clear resemblance to other "court tales" that are a popular form of Hebrew stories from the Diaspora (see **"Court Tales," p. 1608**, and **"Diaspora," p. 1338**).

Zerubbabel over Nehemiah?

The story of the "three bodyguards" emphasizes the importance of Zerubbabel as a descendant of David and an instigator of the temple rebuilding. Perhaps this emphasis on Zerubbabel replaces any interest in Nehemiah. Some have pointed out that there are elements of the Nehemiah tradition that some Hebrews might have objected to, including the portrayal in Nehemiah of the continued devastation of Jerusalem until he arrived—and virtually ignoring the significance of those who came back earlier. Nehemiah's actions were economic and civil actions as opposed to the otherwise exclusive interest of religious leaders only in the temple (which Nehemiah accuses of corruption). Finally, Nehemiah exhibits a belligerent tendency (potentially alarming to many Hebrews) to not cultivate friendly relationships with surrounding leaders and peoples, which would have been a source of diplomatic embarrassment and perhaps violent conflict. In short, in 1 Esdras, Zerubbabel not only is identified as a clear descendant of David but is far the more pious and righteous devotee of the temple and its reconstruction.

Time and Place

The book of 1 Esdras shares concern with many themes that are central to the Ezra–Nehemiah traditions, since they were not edited out. Among these are the importance of restoring the temple and observing the restored rituals properly (according to "the law of Moses") and a certain (xenophobic?) concern with the "purity" of the Hebrew community, separated from the potential "impurities" of associating with surrounding unacceptable peoples. However, if there is a general consensus that Ezra–Nehemiah may contain genuine portions of authentic Aramaic documents from the Persian period, what about the likely date of 1 Esdras?

The book of 1 Esdras features some hints that suggest a setting in Ptolemaic Egypt, most likely Alexandria. There is an awareness of terms of rank in the court and leadership that remind readers of the Ptolemaic language, and the reference to Persian officials as "Kinsmen" of the king (1 Esd. 3:7), for example, is thought to be a uniquely Ptolemaic official title. The usefulness of the book, however, for even later debates among Jews about the "purity" and centrality of the temple (the Maccabean period?) would also make sense. Finally, it has been noted that Zerubbabel is praised in 1 Esdras for leadership that features wisdom, piety, and cleverness, virtues praised in later Hellenistic Jewish writings for living well in Diaspora and/or occupied circumstances (cf. Proverbs, Wisdom of Solomon, Sirach, and Rom. 12:18—excellent advice for surviving Roman occupation).

Reading Guide

As a literary work, 1 Esdras features some clear "episodes" or "sections." Although Josiah's Passover at the beginning is, in some sense, a "bookend" to the celebrations at the end, there is also a second "Passover" that concludes the section of chaps. 1–7, where Zerubbabel is the main character. The (surprisingly) long chaps. 8–9, on the other hand, feature Ezra most prominently. However, because of the similarities, another way to read 1 Esdras is along with the book of Ezra (and parts of Nehemiah) for comparison. As we have suggested, however, a main focus of this work is the court tale featuring Zerubbabel, who is a prominent personality not only in Ezra and Nehemiah but also in Haggai and Zechariah.

Daniel L. Smith-Christopher

Josiah kept the Passover to his Lord in Jerusalem; he killed the Passover lamb on the fourteenth day of the first month, ²having placed the priests according to their divisions, arrayed in their vestments, in the temple of the Lord. ³He told the Levites, the temple servants of Israel, that they should sanctify themselves to the Lord and put the holy ark of the Lord in the house that King Solomon, son of David, had built, ⁴and he said,ᵃ "You need no longer carry it on your shoulders. Now worship the Lord your God and serve his nation Israel; prepare yourselves by your families and kindred, in accordance with the directions of King David of Israel and the magnificence of his son Solomon. ⁵Stand in order in the templeᵇ according to the groupings of the ancestral houses of you Levites, who minister before your kindred the people of Israel, ⁶and kill the Passover lamb and prepare the sacrifices for your kindred, and keep the Passover according to the commandment of the Lord that was given to Moses."

7 To the people who were present Josiah gave thirty thousand lambs and kids and three thousand calves; these were given from the king's possessions, as he promised, to the people and the priests and Levites. ⁸Hilkiah, Zechariah, and Jehiel, the chief officers of the temple, gave to the priests for the Passover two thousand six hundred sheep and three hundred calves. ⁹And Jeconiah and Shemaiah and his brother Nethanel, and Hashabiah and Ochiel and Joram, captains over thousands, gave the Levites for the Passover five thousand sheep and seven hundred calves.

10 This is what took place. The priests and the Levites, having the unleavened bread, stood in proper order according to kindred and the grouping of the ancestral houses, before the people, to make the offering to the Lord as it is written in the book of Moses; this they did in the morning. ¹¹They roasted the Passover lamb with fire, as required, and they boiled the sacrifices in bronze pots and caldrons, with a pleasing odor, and carried them to all the people. ¹²Afterward they prepared the Passover for themselves and for their kindred the priests, the sons of Aaron, ¹³because the priests were offering the fat until nightfall, so the Levites prepared it for themselves and for their kindred the priests, the sons of Aaron. ¹⁴The temple singers, the sons of Asaph, were in their place according to the arrangement made by David, and also Asaph, Zechariah, and Eddinus, who represented the king. ¹⁵The gatekeepers were at each gate; no one needed to interrupt his daily duties, for their kindred the Levites prepared the Passover for them.

16 So the things that had to do with the sacrifices to the Lord were accomplished that day: the Passover was kept and the sacrifices were offered on the altar of the Lord, according to the command of King Josiah. ¹⁷And the people of Israel who were present at that time kept the Passover and the Festival of Unleavened Bread seven days. ¹⁸No Passover like it had been kept in Israel since the times of the prophet Samuel; ¹⁹none of the kings of Israel

ᵃ 1.4 Gk lacks *and he said*   ᵇ 1.5 Other ancient authorities read *holy place*

1:1–55 The first chapter is an edited extract from the end of 2 Chronicles, which closely (but not completely) follows the LXX, and tells the story of the Babylonian conquests of Jerusalem in 597 but also the attempted revolt of Zedekiah in 587 and its disastrous results in the destruction of Jerusalem and, notably for 1 Esdras, the temple.

1:1–20 Josiah's Passover. 1:1–15 The Passover was inaugurated by Josiah, and the text notes the generosity and piety of Josiah in leading the way. The strange reference to Josiah telling the Levites that they no longer need to carry the ark seems odd to some readers and might be an anachronism to associate Josiah with Solomon. However, could the holy ark actually be housed in a corrupt temple before Josiah's reforms? The implication is that the Levites were keeping it holy and secure elsewhere. In fact, the prominence of the Levites (and no mention of Zadokites at all, simply "priests" other than Levites) echoes their frequent mention in Ezra—but they appear to have a more central role in 1 Esdras. Later, blame falls on the leaders of the people and the priests but not Levites (v. 47). **1:16–20** The claim that no Passover like this had been observed since the times of Judges (Josh. 5:10–11) repeats the theme of 2 Kgs. 23:22, but Chronicles states that Hezekiah is also said to have observed Passover before Josiah (2 Chr. 30). If there was no Passover before Josiah, going back before the monarchy, then this is another condemnation of the kings of Judah and Israel. This judgmental tone would seem to agree with v. 22, which echoes a central message of Jeremiah about the actual cause of the exile—namely, the people's sin (cf. Jer. 7).

had kept such a Passover as was kept by Josiah and the priests and Levites and the people of Judah and all of Israel who were living in Jerusalem. [20]In the eighteenth year of the reign of Josiah this Passover was kept.

21 And the deeds of Josiah were upright in the sight of the Lord, for his heart was full of godliness. [22]In ancient times the events of his reign have been recorded—concerning those who sinned and acted wickedly toward the Lord beyond any other nation or kingdom and how they grieved the Lord[c] deeply, so that the words of the Lord fell upon Israel.

23 After all these acts of Josiah, it happened that Pharaoh, king of Egypt, went to make war at Carchemish on the Euphrates, and Josiah went out against him. [24]And the king of Egypt sent word to him, saying, "What have we to do with each other, O king of Judea? [25]I was not sent against you by the Lord God, for my war is at the Euphrates. And now the Lord is with me! The Lord is with me, urging me on! Stand aside, and do not oppose the Lord."

26 Josiah, however, did not turn back to his chariot but tried to fight with him and did not heed the words of the prophet Jeremiah from the mouth of the Lord. [27]He joined battle with him in the plain of Megiddo, and the commanders came down against King Josiah. [28]The king said to his servants, "Take me away from the battle, for I am very weak." And immediately his servants took him out of the line of battle. [29]He got into his second chariot, and after he was brought back to Jerusalem he died and was buried in the tomb of his ancestors.

30 In all Judea they mourned for Josiah. The prophet Jeremiah lamented for Josiah, and the principal men, with the women,[d] have made lamentation for him to this day; it was ordained that this should always be done throughout the whole people of Israel. [31]These things are written in the book of the histories of the kings of Judea, and every one of the acts of Josiah and his splendor and his understanding of the law of the Lord and the things that he had done before and these that are now told are recorded in the book of the kings of Israel and Judah.

32 The people of the nation took Jeconiah son of Josiah, who was twenty-three years old, and made him king in succession to his father Josiah. [33]He reigned three months in Judah[e] and Jerusalem. Then the king of Egypt deposed him from reigning in Jerusalem [34]and fined the nation one hundred talents of silver and one talent of gold. [35]The king of Egypt made his brother Jehoiakim king of Judea and Jerusalem. [36]Jehoiakim put the nobles in prison and seized his brother Zarius and brought him back from Egypt.

37 Jehoiakim was twenty-five years old when he began to reign in Judea and Jerusalem; he did what was evil in the sight of the Lord. [38]King Nebuchadnezzar of Babylon came up against him; he bound him with a chain of bronze and took him away to Babylon. [39]Nebuchadnezzar also took some holy vessels of the Lord and carried them away and stored them in his temple in Babylon. [40]But the things that are reported about Jehoiakim[f] and his uncleanness and impiety are written in the annals of the kings.

41 His son Jehoiachin became king in his place; when he was made king he was eighteen years old, [42]and he reigned three months and ten days in Jerusalem. He did what was evil in the sight of the Lord. [43]A year later Nebuchadnezzar sent and removed him to Babylon, with the holy vessels of the Lord, [44]and made Zedekiah king of Judea and Jerusalem.

Zedekiah was twenty-one years old, and he reigned eleven years. [45]He also did what

c 1.22 Gk him   d 1.30 Or their wives   e 1.33 Other ancient authorities read Israel   f 1.40 Gk him

1:21–55 Josiah's reign until the fall of Jerusalem. 1:21–31 The tragic end of Josiah is described. Notably, Pharaoh Neco of Egypt claims to be led by God, which emphasizes Josiah's sin in confronting Egyptian forces on their way to the battle of Carchemish. This description of the death of Josiah differs from 2 Kings in that Josiah survives until he returns to Jerusalem (to conform with Huldah's prophecy in 2 Kgs. 22?). In 2 Chr. 35:22, the word of God that Josiah is said to have disobeyed also comes from Pharaoh Neco himself, but v. 26 clarifies that the advice came from Jeremiah. **1:32–44** The fate of Jehoiakim is quite different in 1 Esdras in relation to 2 Kings. There, we have the impression that Jehoiakim dies in Jerusalem, but in 2 Chronicles and 1 Esdras, he suffers the same fate as exiles and is carried to Babylon (like Zedekiah later) in chains (cf. 2 Chr. 36:6, "fetters"). **1:38** The book of 1 Esdras adds *a chain of bronze* (Samson was chained in bronze in Judg. 16:21; cf. Sir. 28:20, where "fetters of bronze" are described among the evil results of engaging in slander).

was evil in the sight of the Lord and did not heed the words spoken by the prophet Jeremiah from the mouth of the Lord. ⁴⁶Although King Nebuchadnezzar had made him swear by the name of the Lord, he broke his oath and rebelled; he stiffened his neck and hardened his heart and transgressed the laws of the Lord, the God of Israel. ⁴⁷Even the leaders of the people and of the priests committed many acts of sacrilege and lawlessness beyond all the unclean deeds of all the nations and polluted the temple of the Lord in Jerusalem—the temple that God had made holy. ⁴⁸The God of their ancestors sent his messenger to call them back, because he would have spared them and his dwelling place. ⁴⁹But they mocked his messengers, and whenever the Lord spoke, they scoffed at his prophets, until God, in his anger against his nation because of their ungodly acts, gave the command to bring the kings of the Chaldeans against them. ⁵⁰The Chaldeans killed their young men with the sword around their holy temple and did not spare young man or young woman,ᵍ elder or child, for he gave them all into their hands. ⁵¹They took all the holy vessels of the Lord, great and small, the treasure chests of the Lord, and the royal stores and carried them away to Babylon. ⁵²They burned the house of the Lord, broke down the walls of Jerusalem, burned its towers with fire, ⁵³and utterly destroyed all its glorious things. Nebuchadnezzarᵇ led the survivors away to Babylon with the sword, ⁵⁴and they were servants to him and to his sons until the Persians began to reign, in fulfillment of the word of the Lord

by the mouth of Jeremiah, ⁵⁵saying, "Until the land has enjoyed its Sabbaths, it shall keep Sabbath all the time of its desolation until the completion of seventy years."

2 In the first year of Cyrus as king of the Persians, so that the word of the Lord by the mouth of Jeremiah might be accomplished, ²the Lord stirred up the spirit of King Cyrus of the Persians, and he made a proclamation throughout all his kingdom and also put it in writing:

3 "Thus says Cyrus king of the Persians: The Lord of Israel, the Lord Most High, has made me king of the world, ⁴and he has commanded me to build him a house in Jerusalem, which is in Judea. ⁵If any of you, therefore, are of his nation, may your Lord be with you;ⁱ go up to Jerusalem, which is in Judea, and build the house of the Lord of Israel—he is the Lord who dwells in Jerusalem—⁶and let each of you, wherever you may live, be helped by your neighbors with gold and silver, with gifts and with horses and cattle, besides the other things added as votive offerings for the temple of the Lord that is in Jerusalem."

7 Then arose the heads of families of the tribes of Judah and Benjamin, and the priests and the Levites, and all whose spirit the Lord had stirred to go up to build the house in Jerusalem for the Lord; ⁸their neighbors helped them with everything, with silver and gold, with horses and cattle, and with a very great number of votive offerings from many whose hearts were stirred.

9 King Cyrus also brought out the holy vessels of the Lord that Nebuchadnezzar had

g 1.50 Gk virgin b 1.53 Gk he i 2.5 Gk him

1:46 The image of stubbornness as a "stiff neck" mirrors references from God about the Hebrew people in Exod. 33:3, 5; 34:9; and cf. Deut. 9:6, 13, where "stubborn" is literally "stiffed-necked." **1:54–55** This section finishes on the authority of Jeremiah, whose famous *seventy years* is cited again here (Jer. 29). The next chapter will begin with another reference to the authority of Jeremiah, arguably the most authoritative prophetic voice of the early exilic era.

2:1–25 Return of the exiles; building of temple begins and then stops. The Persian era is inaugurated by God's moving the *spirit* of the Persian emperor Cyrus and also alluding to the prophecies of Jeremiah, further establishing the prophet's authority. The discussion of Cyrus is followed by a discussion of Artaxerxes, a chronological problem in 1 Esdras, since we know that Cambyses, and then Darius, ruled after Cyrus. Artaxerxes 1 does not reign until 465 BCE. The general rearrangement of events from the older materials in Ezra 1–4 is thought to provide a more impressive backdrop to the introduction of Zerubbabel, especially in the story in chaps. 3–4. **2:2** Cyrus and the people are *stirred* by God three times in 2:1–9. God's authority over all these events is made clear. **2:6–8** Cyrus's enumeration of gifts to be allowed for the Hebrew temple project is listed carefully—including gold, silver, horses, cattle, and other *votive offerings*—and this list is carefully reproduced (v. 8) to emphasize the obedient response of the people. **2:9–14** It is interesting to note that precise amounts for all the gifts from the Hebrew people are not given in either Cyrus's order or the people's response.

carried away from Jerusalem and stored in his temple of idols. [10]When King Cyrus of the Persians brought these out, he gave them to Mithridates, his treasurer, [11]and by him they were given to Sheshbazzar, the governor of Judea. [12]The number of these was: one thousand gold cups, one thousand silver cups, twenty-nine silver censers, thirty gold bowls, two thousand four hundred ten silver bowls, and one thousand other vessels. [13]All the vessels were handed over, gold and silver, five thousand four hundred sixty-nine, [14]and they were carried back by Sheshbazzar with the returning exiles from Babylon to Jerusalem.

15 In the time of King Artaxerxes of the Persians, Bishlam, Mithridates, Tabeel, Rehum, Beltethmus, the scribe Shimshai, and the rest of their associates living in Samaria and other places wrote him the following letter, against those who were living in Judea and Jerusalem:

16 "To King Artaxerxes our lord, your servants the recorder Rehum and the scribe Shimshai and the other members of their council, and the judges in Coelesyria and Phoenicia: [17]Let it now be known to our lord the king that the Jews who came up from you to us have gone to Jerusalem and are building that rebellious and wicked city, repairing its marketplaces and walls and laying the foundations for a temple. [18]Now if this city is built and the walls finished, they will not only refuse to pay tribute but will even resist kings. Since the building of the temple is now going on, we think it best not to neglect such a matter but

to speak to our lord the king in order that, if it seems good to you, search may be made in the records of your ancestors. [19]You will find in the annals what has been written about them and will learn that this city was rebellious, troubling both kings and other cities, and that the Jews were rebels and kept setting up blockades in it from of old. That is why this city was laid waste. [20]Therefore we now make known to you, O lord and king, that if this city is built and its walls finished, you will no longer have access to Coelesyria and Phoenicia."

21 Then the king, in reply to the recorder Rehum, Beltethmus, the scribe Shimshai, and the others associated with them and living in Samaria and Syria and Phoenicia, wrote as follows:

22 "I have read the letter that you sent me. So I ordered search to be made, and it has been found that this city from of old has fought against kings, [23]that the people in it were given to rebellion and war, and that mighty and cruel kings ruled in Jerusalem and exacted tribute from Coelesyria and Phoenicia. [24]Therefore I have now issued orders to prevent these people from building the city and to take care that nothing more be done and that such wicked proceedings go no further to the annoyance of kings."

25 Then, when the letter from King Artaxerxes was read, Rehum and the scribe Shimshai and their associates went quickly to Jerusalem, with cavalry and a large number of armed troops, and began to hinder the builders. And the building of the temple in

When Cyrus himself donates, however (by returning *vessels* stolen by Nebuchadnezzar), there is a careful audit provided. **2:15–25** This auspicious beginning of the rebuilding project is interrupted immediately *in the time of King Artaxerxes*. Unlike Ezra, here the decree of Cyrus is followed immediately by the narrative of halting the work in Jerusalem. **2:17–21** The opponents who report to Artaxerxes mention the temple (unlike the parallel text in Ezra), but they pointedly emphasize what they consider to be the much bigger threat of the city itself. In Ezra, only the city and walls are reported as a threat—but 17–18 refer directly to the temple, although v. 20 reverts back to the (presumably older) reference to only the city and walls. The Persian emperor is sternly warned about Jerusalem as a *rebellious and wicked city*, and it is clear what the opponents of the returning Hebrews want to emphasize, not only lost tribute and disobedience, but also military and trade access (vv. 18–19, cf. 23). **2:17** The book of 1 Esdras adds in an intriguing note that there is a danger in Jerusalem rebuilding the city, the walls, and its *marketplaces* and thus a further economic element of the threat. This addition is missing in the Ezra material and here clearly continues the economic threat to Persian power and authority. The opposition, therefore, emphasizes more than the temple. The implication seems to be that these Hebrews will not stop at merely religious shrines, but that is just the tip of the iceberg, and they must be watched. **2:21–24** When *the king* replies, he adds that it was discovered that *mighty and cruel kings ruled in Jerusalem*. Adding *cruel* further emphasizes the earlier theme of a long history of Hebrew disobedience that led to the exile in the first place (echoing Jeremiah). Here the work, and also the narrative, pauses as we next go to the famous court tale.

Jerusalem stopped until the second year of the reign of King Darius of the Persians.

3 Now King Darius gave a great banquet for all who were under him, all who were born in his house, and all the nobles of Media and Persia, ²and all the satraps and generals and governors who were under him in the hundred twenty-seven satrapies from India to Ethiopia. ³They ate and drank, and when they were satisfied they went away, and King Darius went to his bedroom; he went to sleep but woke up again.

4 Then the three young men of the bodyguard who kept guard over the person of the king said to one another, ⁵"Let each of us state what one word is strongest, and to the one whose statement seems wisest, King Darius will give rich gifts and great honors of victory. ⁶He shall be clothed in purple and drink from gold cups and sleep on a gold bed*ʲ* and have a chariot with gold bridles and a turban of fine linen and a necklace around his neck, ⁷and because of his wisdom he shall sit next to Darius and shall be called Kinsman of Darius."

8 Then each bodyguard wrote his own statement, and they sealed them and put them under the pillow of King Darius and said, ⁹"When the king wakes, they will give him the writing, and to the one whose statement the king and the three nobles of Persia judge to be wisest the victory shall be given according to what is written." ¹⁰The first wrote, "Wine is strongest." ¹¹The second wrote, "The king is strongest." ¹²The third wrote, "Women are strongest, but above all things truth is victor."*ᵏ*

13 When the king awoke, they took the writing and gave it to him, and he read it. ¹⁴Then he sent and summoned all the nobles of Persia and Media and the satraps and generals and governors and prefects, and he took his seat in the council chamber, and the writing was read in their presence. ¹⁵He said, "Call the young men, and they shall explain their statements." So they were summoned and came in. ¹⁶They said to them, "Explain to us what you have written."

Then the first, who had spoken of the strength of wine, began and said: ¹⁷"Gentlemen, how is wine the strongest? It leads astray the minds of all who drink it. ¹⁸It makes equal the mind of the king and the orphan, of the slave and the free, of the poor and the rich. ¹⁹It turns every thought to feasting and gladness and forgets all sorrow and debt. ²⁰It makes all hearts feel rich, forgets kings and satraps, and makes everyone talk of extravagant sums.*ˡ* ²¹When

j 3.6 Gk on gold   k 3.12 Or but truth triumphs over all things   l 3.20 Gk talents

3:1–4:63 Story of the three bodyguards. It has been proposed that 1 Esdras as a whole work is built around the "three bodyguards" story, which introduces Zerubbabel in impressive fashion (see **"Court Tales," p. 1608**). It is the most memorable section of the work, only partly because 1 Esdras is our only source for the tale. **3:1–3** The celebration sets the stage for the debate. **3:1** To "give a banquet" as a form of celebration is not uncommon (thus Lot, Gen. 19:3; Abraham, 21:8; Isaac, 26:30; Laban, 29:22) but seems an essential element of the later "court tales" (Pharaoh, Gen. 40:20; Belshazzar, Dan. 5:1; throughout the story in Esther, where ten of all twenty-five occasions of the Heb. term translated as "banquet" occur). It is likely that large amounts of food were story elements of interest to Hebrews in times of food precarity. These displays of power and wealth will become an issue as the story proceeds. **3:4** The three men are part of the *bodyguard*, translating a Greek word combining the two terms "guard/watch" and "body." The resulting Greek phrase seems comical (satirical?): *the bodyguard who guard over the person* (literally "body") *of the king*. The term is not widely used elsewhere in the LXX even where the English uses "bodyguard" (e.g., 1 Sam. 28:2; 2 Sam. 23:23; etc.). **3:5–7** The one proposing the debate emphasizes the material rewards to the winner, who will be called *Kinsman* of the king. If this is a known Ptolemaic phrase of honor, this may suggest a date (for this story) between circa 300 and 200 BCE and thus that the story is from Egypt (Alexandria?). **3:8–9** The sentence begins, oddly, by placing the writing *under the pillow* of the king but then immediately speaks of the writing being handed to him in v. 9, which agrees with v. 13. **3:14–17a** The king seems to immediately understand—a competition between young servants close to the king—and calls together all his servants and advisors for the show. In short, the performance will have a powerful audience representing Persian power and authority.

3:17b–23 The first "entry" for what is most powerful in the world is *wine.* Consider what wine is said to cause: the poor forget their "place" in the order of humanity (thus daring to deny the power of the powerful); under the influence of wine, people think only of money and rewards (daring to be

Making Connections: Court Tales, Courtly Debates, and 1 Esdras 3–4

The forced exile of Hebrew peoples that began in the eighth century under Neo-Assyrian hegemony (722 BCE), and again with the Neo-Babylonian conquests of Judah in the sixth century (especially 597, 587), gave rise to stories addressing the challenges of "Diaspora" existence (see **"Diaspora," p. 1338**).

One way that Hebrews dealt with these challenges was by telling stories of how "one of us" managed to not only survive but also thrive in the face of the imperial conquerors. Such "court tales" are evident in Dan. 1–6 (expanded in the Additions to Daniel and the DSS PrNab [4Q242]), the stories of Joseph in Genesis, and the book of Esther (see also Tobit and the stories of Nehemiah in the Persian court). There are similarities among the Daniel, Esther, and Joseph stories (e.g., the symbolism of "signet rings" [Gen. 41:42; Dan. 6:17; Esth. 8:2], banquets symbolizing royal power, overcoming threats to Jewish existence, etc.). The centrality of the threats to Jewish existence suggests we should refer to "resistance stories" rather than the more cheerful "court tales," reflecting the social and political realities (and threats) of living in the potentially hostile Diaspora. The stories reward maintaining religious practice in the face of punishments (gallows, fiery furnaces, or mauling by lions).

The "three bodyguards" tale, set in the court of Darius (cf. Dan. 6), also draws on a second literary tradition, that of stories of debates in the presence of the powerful. For example, in Herodotus's *Hist.* (3.80–83), a Persian council of seven (cf. 1 Esd. 8:11) debates who should take over after the death of Cambyses, Cyrus's son. Otanes presents a form of democracy as ideal. Megabyzus presents an oligarchy as superior to rule by the masses. Finally, Darius argues for a singular leader who is not susceptible to corruption. The other four are impressed with Darius, and he is made ruler.

There are obvious similarities between Herodotus's court debate and 1 Esd. 3–4. The subject of the debate in 1 Esdras (what is the most "strong") has similarities with Herodotus's topic of the best form of political power. Second, similar to Herodotus, where the contestants are all Persians, Zerubbabel's story features no indication that Zerubbabel suffers from prejudice with regard to his Hebrew identity. Nevertheless, Zerubbabel's Hebrew piety is displayed in his insistence on Persian support of Jerusalem. The "three bodyguards," therefore, borrows from two traditions—"court tales" and "debates before the emperor."

Daniel L. Smith-Christopher

---

people drink they forget to be friendly with friends and kindred, and before long they draw their swords. ²²And when they recover from the wine, they do not remember what they have done. ²³Gentlemen, is not wine the strongest, since it forces people to do these things?" When he had said this, he stopped speaking.

4 Then the second, who had spoken of the strength of the king, began to speak: ²"Gentlemen, are not men strongest, who rule over land and sea and all that is in them? ³But the king is stronger; he is their lord and master, and whatever he says to them they obey. ⁴If he tells them to make war on one another, they do it, and if he sends them out against the enemy, they go and conquer mountains, walls, and towers. ⁵They kill and are killed and do not disobey the king's command; if they win the victory, they bring everything to the king—whatever spoil they take and everything else. ⁶Likewise those who do not serve in the army or make war but till the soil; whenever they sow and reap, they bring some to the king, and they compel one another to pay taxes to the king. ⁷And yet he is only one man! If he tells them to kill,

like the powerful); and finally, people commit violence (intending to *be* the powerful!). If all the suggestions are taken as subtle criticism of the Persians, then the implication may be that the Persians are terrorizing drunkards who rob the world.

4:1–63 The debate continues but eventually will shift dramatically to the success and piety of Zerubbabel, the alleged descendant of David. **4:1–12 The second proposal: strength. 4:2–3** The term for "strength"/"strong" is common in the LXX and is virtually always associated with military "strength," but the Greek term in v. 3—which attaches "over" at the beginning (literally "over-strength")—is used far more rarely in the LXX, and ten of the fifteen occasions are here in the "bodyguards" story. Clearly, the "strength" of the king is at issue here and how that "strength" is defined as the power to make war and extract taxes. **4:4–6** Warfare is what people do in obedience to the king, and notably not because of any inherent morality or righteousness of the conflicts. And, like fighting in war, the taxation of v. 6 is equally compelled by force. A king hearing this would likely

they kill; if he tells them to release, they release; ⁸if he tells them to attack, they attack; if he tells them to lay waste, they lay waste; if he tells them to build, they build; ⁹if he tells them to cut down, they cut down; if he tells them to plant, they plant. ¹⁰All his people and his armies obey him. Furthermore, he reclines, he eats and drinks and sleeps, ¹¹but they keep watch around him, and no one may go away to attend to his own affairs, nor do they disobey him. ¹²Gentlemen, why is not the king the strongest, since he is to be obeyed in this fashion?" And he stopped speaking.

13 Then the third, who had spoken of women and truth (and this was Zerubbabel), began to speak: ¹⁴"Gentlemen, is not the king great, and are not men many, and is not wine strong? Who is it, then, who rules them or has the mastery over them? Is it not women? ¹⁵Women gave birth to the king and to every people that rules over sea and land. ¹⁶From women they came, and women brought up the very men who plant the vineyards from which comes wine. ¹⁷Women make men's clothes; they bring men glory; men cannot exist without women. ¹⁸If men gather gold and silver or any other beautiful thing and then see a woman lovely in appearance and beauty, ¹⁹they let all those things go and gape at her and with open mouths stare at her, and all prefer her to gold or silver or any other beautiful thing. ²⁰A man leaves his own father, who brought him up, and his own region and clings to his wife. ²¹With his wife he ends his days, with no thought of his father or his mother or his region. ²²Therefore you must realize that women rule over you!

"Do you not labor and toil and bring everything and give it to women? ²³A man takes his sword and goes out to travel and rob and steal and to sail the sea and rivers; ²⁴he faces lions, and he walks in darkness, and when he steals and robs and plunders, he brings it back to the woman he loves. ²⁵A man loves his wife more than his father or his mother. ²⁶Many men have lost their minds because of women and have become slaves because of them. ²⁷Many have perished or stumbled or sinned because of women. ²⁸And now do you not believe me?

"Is not the king great in his authority? Do not all lands fear to touch him? ²⁹Yet I have seen him with Apame, the king's concubine, the daughter of the illustrious Bartacus; she would sit at the king's right hand ³⁰and take the crown from the king's head and put it on her own and slap the king with her left hand. ³¹At this the king would gaze at her with mouth agape. If she smiles at him, he laughs; if she loses her temper with him, he flatters her, so that she may be reconciled to him. ³²Gentlemen, why are not women strong, since they do such things?"

33 Then the king and the nobles looked at one another, and he began to speak about truth: ³⁴"Gentlemen, are not women strong? The earth is vast, and heaven is high, and the sun is swift in its course, for it makes the circuit of the heavens and returns to its place in one day. ³⁵Is not the one who does these things great? But truth is great and stronger than all things. ³⁶The whole earth calls upon truth, and heaven blesses it. All the works quake and tremble, and with it^m there is

m 4.36 That is, *heaven*

---

begin to suspect the not-so-subtle criticism by virtue of the absence of virtue in these arguments, whether in reference to serving the gods or arguing moral issues. **4:10–12** The not-so-subtle criticism continues: warfare and taxation happen not because of love of country or king but because of ever-watchful compulsion. One thinks here of the Persian secret service, which served as the "eyes" and "ears" of the king (remembering the vigilant accounting of Persian money in 1 Esdras and even more in Ezra–Nehemiah). **4:13–32 The third contestant, Zerubbabel, and his proposal: *women*.** Perhaps the note identifying the speaker as Zerubbabel was inserted when this story was made a part of this tradition. He begins by speaking of strength ("overstrength") but then proposes that women *rule* over all (the Gk. term translated as *rule*, from which Eng. derives "despot," is also used in the LXX of God ruling over all nations; Pss. 21:29 [=MT 22:28]; 58:14; 102:19; and notably 1 Chr. 29:11). Zerubbabel's argument consists entirely of what men choose to do, not what they are compelled to do. The passage goes beyond subtle criticism and openly satirizes the power of the emperor (cf. LXX Additions to Daniel, where Daniel derisively laughs at Nebuchadnezzar—especially the story of Bel—something unthinkable in the earlier MT material, which deals with fear of punishments by rulers). Is this genuinely honoring women or male lust? Or is it closer to the sneering comparison of defeated soldiers as "women" (cf. Jer. 50:37; 51:30)? Finally, might it be a version of "love conquers all"? **4:33–41 A fourth element: *truth*.** There are parallels to this description of the "power" of

nothing unrighteous. ³⁷Wine is unrighteous; the king is unrighteous; women are unrighteous; all humans are unrighteous; all their works are unrighteous and all such things. There is no truth in them, and in their unrighteousness they will perish. ³⁸But truth endures and is strong forever and lives and prevails forever and ever. ³⁹With it there is no partiality or preference, but it does what is righteous instead of anything that is unrighteous or wicked. Everyone approves its deeds, ⁴⁰and there is nothing unrighteous in its judgment. To it belongs the strength and the kingship and the power and the majesty of all the ages. Blessed be the God of truth!" ⁴¹When he stopped speaking, all the people shouted and said, "Great is truth and strongest of all!"

42 Then the king said to Zerubbabel,ⁿ "Ask what you wish, even beyond what is written, and we will give it to you, for you have been found to be the wisest. You shall sit next to me and be called my Kinsman." ⁴³Then he said to the king, "Remember the vow that you made on the day when you became king, to build Jerusalem ⁴⁴and to send back all the vessels that were taken from Jerusalem, which Cyrus set apart when he beganᵒ to destroy Babylon and vowed to send them back there. ⁴⁵You also vowed to build the temple, which the Edomites burned when Judea was laid waste by the Chaldeans. ⁴⁶And now, O lord the king, this is what I ask and request of you, and this befits your greatness. I pray, therefore, that you fulfill the vow whose fulfillment you vowed to the King of heaven with your own lips."

47 Then King Darius got up and kissed him and wrote letters for him to all the treasurers and governors and generals and satraps, that they should give safe conduct to him and to all who were going up with him to build Jerusalem. ⁴⁸And he wrote letters to all the governors in Coelesyria and Phoenicia and to those in Lebanon, to bring cedar timber from Lebanon to Jerusalem and to help him build the city. ⁴⁹He wrote in behalf of all the Jews who were going up from his kingdom to Judea, in the interest of their freedom, that no officer or satrap or governor or treasurer should forcibly enter their doors; ⁵⁰that all the region that they would occupy should be theirs without tribute; that the Idumeans should give up the villages of the Jews that they held; ⁵¹that twenty talents a year should be given for the building of the temple until it was completed ⁵²and an additional ten talents a year for burnt offerings to be offered on the altar every day, in accordance with the commandment to make seventeen offerings; ⁵³and that all who came from Babylonia to build the city should have their freedom, they and their children and all the priests who came. ⁵⁴He wrote also concerning their support and the priests' vestments in which they were to minister. ⁵⁵He wrote that the support for the Levites should be provided until the day when the temple would be finished and Jerusalem built. ⁵⁶He wrote that land and wages should be provided for all who guarded the city. ⁵⁷And he sent back from Babylon all the vessels that Cyrus had set apart; everything that Cyrus had ordered to be done, he also commanded to be done and to be sent to Jerusalem.

58 When the young man went out, he lifted up his face to heaven toward Jerusalem and praised the King of heaven, saying, ⁵⁹"From you comes the victory; from you comes wisdom, and yours is the glory. I am your servant. ⁶⁰Blessed are you, who have

n 4.42 Gk *him*   o 4.44 Cn: Gk *vowed*

truth and the description of "reason" in 4 Maccabees, but in vv. 38–40, there is a striking summary statement about *truth*, to which is ascribed *power* and *majesty* that *endures*. These are terms often ascribed to God (1 Chr. 29:11; Tob. 3:2). **4:40b–41** The speech moves smoothly from *truth* itself to praise *the God of truth*, yet the people praise *truth* itself. Note the similarities between these affirmations from non-Hebrews and the recognition of God by Nebuchadnezzar in Dan. 4:34–37, Darius in Dan. 6:26–27, and Hellenist rulers in 3 Macc. 6:28. **4:42–57 Zerubbabel's reward.** An important point of the story is Zerubbabel's reaffirming the permission to send exiles home and allow them to rebuild the temple. This section enumerates these preparations and Zerubbabel's central role in great detail. Note the similarities of these scenes to Nehemiah's appeal to the Persian emperor on behalf of Jerusalem (Neh. 2). There is a detailed list of requests here, including tax exemption, reclaiming stolen lands, details of priestly attire, and even adequate pay for those who support and protect the people (v. 56). **4:58–63 Zerubbabel's prayer.** He thanks the God of wisdom (parallels other Hellenistic period literature like 4 Maccabees).

given me wisdom; I give you thanks, O Lord of our ancestors."

61 So he took the letters and went to Babylon and told this to all his kindred. [62]And they praised the God of their ancestors because he had given them freedom and permission [63]to go up and build Jerusalem and the temple that is called by his name, and they feasted, with music and rejoicing, for seven days.

5 After this the heads of ancestral houses were chosen to go up, according to their tribes, with their wives and sons and daughters and their male and female servants and their livestock. [2]And Darius sent with them a thousand cavalry to take them back to Jerusalem in safety, with the music of drums and flutes; [3]all their kindred were making merry. And he made them go up with them.

4 These are the names of the men who went up, according to their ancestral houses in the tribes, over their groups: [5]the priests, the descendants of Phinehas son of Aaron; Jeshua son of Jozadak son of Seraiah and Joakim son of Zerubbabel son of Shealtiel, of the house of David, of the lineage of Phares, of the tribe of Judah, [6]who spoke wise words before King Darius of the Persians, in the second year of his reign, in the month of Nisan, the first month.

7 These are the Judeans who came up out of their sojourn in exile, whom King Nebuchadnezzar of Babylon had carried away to Babylon [8]and who returned to Jerusalem and the rest of Judea, each to his own town. They came with Zerubbabel and Jeshua, Nehemiah, Seraiah, Resaiah, Eneneus, Mordecai, Beelsarus, Aspharasus, Borolias, Rehum, and Baanah, their leaders.

9 The number of those of the nation and their leaders: the descendants of Parosh, two thousand one hundred seventy-two. The descendants of Shephatiah, four hundred seventy-two. [10]The descendants of Arah, seven hundred fifty-six. [11]The descendants of Pahath-moab, of the descendants of Jeshua and Joab, two thousand eight hundred twelve. [12]The descendants of Elam, one thousand two hundred fifty-four. The descendants of Zattu, nine hundred forty-five. The descendants of Chorbe, seven hundred five. The descendants of Bani, six hundred forty-eight. [13]The descendants of Bebai, six hundred twenty-three. The descendants of Azgad, one thousand three hundred twenty-two. [14]The descendants of Adonikam, six hundred sixty-seven. The descendants of Bigvai, two thousand sixty-six. The descendants of Adin, four hundred fifty-four. [15]The descendants of Ater, namely, of Hezekiah, ninety-two. The descendants of Kilan and Azetas, sixty-seven. The descendants of Azaru, four hundred thirty-two. [16]The descendants of Annias, one hundred one. The descendants of Arom. The descendants of Bezai, three hundred twenty-three. The descendants of Arsiphurith, one hundred twelve. [17]The descendants of Baiterus, three thousand five. The descendants of Bethlomon, one hundred twenty-three. [18]Those from Netophah, fifty-five. Those from Anathoth, one hundred fifty-eight. Those from Bethasmoth, forty-two. [19]Those from Kiriatharim, twenty-five. Those from Chephirah and Beeroth, seven hundred forty-three. [20]The Chadiasans and Ammidians, four hundred twenty-two. Those from Kirama and Geba, six hundred twenty-one. [21]Those from Macalon, one hundred twenty-two. Those from Betolio, fifty-two.

5:1–70 List of those returning from exile, altar set up, and temple foundations laid. 5:1–45 The center of attention here is the reproduction of some of the lists of Ezra 2 // Neh. 11–12. While Ezra–Nehemiah seems even more obsessive about lists and inventories, in 1 Esdras, there is also a detailed accounting of wealth and people, perhaps a sign of being watched. Genealogies also serve a variety of functions, including explaining present circumstances from past persons and their relationships but also signaling one's ethnic "purity," an issue that becomes more important in later chapters. 5:2–3 Music accompanying the soldiers portrays a religious procession all the way from Babylon. 5:4–6 Unlike Ezra–Nehemiah, there is a clarification of the lineage of the two main leaders: the priestly figure Jeshua (listed first, acknowledging the importance of the high priest) and Zerubbabel. The unexpected *Joakim son of Zerubbabel* (v. 5) is usually explained as a misreading, since Joakim was likely the last listed name from the priestly lineage of Jeshua (cf. Jdt. 4) before switching to consider Zerubbabel. In fact, we hear nothing of any descendants of Zerubbabel (until Luke 3:27). 5:7–8 Nehemiah, otherwise removed from this recounting of the history, is mentioned here, suggesting the secondary nature of the list. Nehemiah is notably listed after Zerubbabel. Note that at v. 40, there is likely a misreading of "Nehemiah the Tishara [governor]" as two different people.

The descendants of Niphish, one hundred fifty-six. [22]The descendants of the other Calamolalus and Ono, seven hundred twenty-five. The descendants of Jerechus, three hundred forty-five. [23]The descendants of Senaah, three thousand three hundred thirty.

24 The priests: the descendants of Jedaiah son of Jeshua, of the descendants of Anasib, nine hundred seventy-two. The descendants of Immer, one thousand and fifty-two. [25]The descendants of Pashhur, one thousand two hundred forty-seven. The descendants of Charme, one thousand seventeen.

26 The Levites: the descendants of Jeshua and Kadmiel and Bannas and Sudias, seventy-four. [27]The temple singers: the descendants of Asaph, one hundred twenty-eight. [28]The gatekeepers: the descendants of Shallum, the descendants of Ater, the descendants of Talmon, the descendants of Akkub, the descendants of Hatita, the descendants of Shobai, in all one hundred thirty-nine.

29 The temple servants: the descendants of Esau, the descendants of Hasupha, the descendants of Tabbaoth, the descendants of Keros, the descendants of Sua, the descendants of Padon, the descendants of Lebanah, the descendants of Hagabah, [30]the descendants of Akkub, the descendants of Uthai, the descendants of Ketab, the descendants of Hagab, the descendants of Subai, the descendants of Hana, the descendants of Cathua, the descendants of Geddur, [31]the descendants of Jairus, the descendants of Daisan, the descendants of Noeba, the descendants of Chezib, the descendants of Gazera, the descendants of Uzza, the descendants of Phinoe, the descendants of Hasrah, the descendants of Basthai, the descendants of Asnah, the descendants of Maani, the descendants of Nephisim, the descendants of Acuph, the descendants of Hakupha, the descendants of Asur, the descendants of Pharakim, the descendants of Bazluth, [32]the descendants of

Mehida, the descendants of Cutha, the descendants of Charea, the descendants of Barkos, the descendants of Serar, the descendants of Temah, the descendants of Neziah, the descendants of Hatipha.

33 The descendants of Solomon's servants: the descendants of Assaphioth, the descendants of Peruda, the descendants of Jaalah, the descendants of Lozon, the descendants of Isdael, the descendants of Shephatiah, [34]the descendants of Agia, the descendants of Pochereth-hazzebaim, the descendants of Sarothie, the descendants of Masiah, the descendants of Gas, the descendants of Addus, the descendants of Subas, the descendants of Apherra, the descendants of Barodis, the descendants of Shaphat, the descendants of Allon.

35 All the temple servants and the descendants of Solomon's servants were three hundred seventy-two.

36 The following are those who came up from Tel-melah and Tel-harsha, under the leadership of Cherub, Addan, and Immer, [37]though they could not prove by their ancestral houses or lineage that they belonged to Israel: the descendants of Delaiah son of Tobiah, and the descendants of Nekoda, six hundred fifty-two.

38 Of the priests the following had assumed the priesthood but were not found registered: the descendants of Habaiah, the descendants of Hakkoz, and the descendants of Jaddus who had married Agia, one of the daughters of Barzillai, and was called by his name. [39]When a search was made in the register and the genealogy of these men was not found, they were excluded from serving as priests. [40]And Nehemiah and Attharias[p] told them not to share in the holy things until a high priest[q] should appear wearing Urim and Thummim.[r]

41 All those of Israel, twelve or more years

p 5.40 Or *the governor*   q 5.40 Other ancient authorities read *priest*   r 5.40 Gk *Manifestation and Truth*

5:24 One may speculate about some of the changed numbers. For example, when counting priests, 1 Esdras lists an additional name that does not appear in Ezra–Nehemiah: *Anasib*. Thus, instead of 973 descendants of Jedaiah (MT / Ezra 2), we have Anasib plus 972. Otherwise, the numbers are precisely the same in the Hebrew. 5:26–28 Far smaller numbers for Levites, *temple singers* (associated with Levites in the Second Temple period), and *gatekeepers*, compared to the priests. 5:29 The insertion of Esau here, instead of Ziha in Ezra–Nehemiah, listed among the servants, is surely intentional (since Heb. and Gk. forms are quite different). 5:40 The resolution of proper lineage in vv. 36–37 awaits the ordination of the high priest, who could consult (in Ezra–Nehemiah) the *Urim and Thummim*. It is often proposed that the translator of 1 Esdras was not certain of the meaning of this and substituted in Greek, literally, "wearing Manifestation and Truth." Certainly the appearance of

of age, besides male and female servants, were forty-two thousand three hundred sixty; their male and female servants were seven thousand three hundred thirty-seven; there were two hundred forty-five musicians and singers. [42]There were four hundred thirty-five camels, seven thousand thirty-six horses, two hundred forty-five mules, and five thousand five hundred twenty-five donkeys.

43 Some of the heads of families, when they came to the temple of God that is in Jerusalem, vowed that, to the best of their ability, they would erect the house on its site [44]and that they would give to the sacred treasury for the work a thousand minas of gold, five thousand minas of silver, and one hundred priests' vestments.

45 The priests, the Levites, and some of the people[s] settled in Jerusalem and its region and the temple singers, the gatekeepers, and all Israel in their towns.

46 When the seventh month came and the Israelites were all in their own homes, they gathered with a single purpose in the square before the first gate toward the east. [47]Then Jeshua son of Jozadak, with his fellow priests, and Zerubbabel son of Shealtiel, with his kinsmen, took their places and prepared the altar of the God of Israel, [48]to offer burnt offerings upon it, in accordance with the directions in the book of Moses the man of God. [49]And some joined them from the other nations of the land. And they erected the altar in its place, for all the peoples of the land were hostile to them and were stronger than they, and they offered sacrifices at the proper times and burnt offerings to the Lord morning and evening. [50]They kept the Festival of Booths,[t] as it is commanded in the law, and offered the proper sacrifices every day [51]and thereafter the regular offerings and sacrifices on Sabbaths and at new moons and at all the consecrated feasts. [52]And all who had made any vow to God began to offer sacrifices to God, from the new moon of the seventh month,

though the temple of God was not yet built. [53]They gave money to the masons and the carpenters and food and drink and carts[u] to the Sidonians and the Tyrians to bring cedar logs from Lebanon and convey them in rafts to the harbor of Joppa, according to the decree that they had in writing from King Cyrus of the Persians.

54 In the second year after their coming to the temple of God in Jerusalem, in the second month, Zerubbabel son of Shealtiel and Jeshua son of Jozadak made a beginning, together with their kindred and the Levitical priests and all who had come back to Jerusalem from exile, [55]and they laid the foundation of the temple of God on the new moon of the second month in the second year after they came to Judea and Jerusalem. [56]They appointed the Levites who were twenty or more years of age to have charge of the work of the Lord. And Jeshua arose and his sons and kindred and his brother Kadmiel and the sons of Jeshua Emadabun and the sons of Joda son of Iliadun, with their sons and kindred, all the Levites, pressing forward the work on the house of God with a single purpose.

So the builders built the temple of the Lord. [57]And the priests stood arrayed in their vestments, with musical instruments and trumpets, and the Levites, the sons of Asaph, with cymbals, praising the Lord and blessing him, according to the directions of King David of Israel; [58]they sang hymns, giving thanks to the Lord, "For his goodness and his glory are forever upon all Israel." [59]And all the people sounded trumpets and shouted with a great shout, praising the Lord for the erection of the house of the Lord. [60]Some of the Levitical priests and heads of ancestral houses, old men who had seen the former house, came to the building of this one with outcries and loud weeping, [61]while many came with trumpets and a joyful

s 5.45 Or *those who were of the people*   t 5.50 Or *Tabernacles*   u 5.53 Meaning of Gk uncertain

"Truth" is interesting when remembering the "bodyguards" story (chaps. 3–4). **5:46–52** It is hard to avoid the conclusion that strong encouragement to maintain financial support is behind a good deal of the discussion of voluntary giving and its apparent generosity from leaders. **5:53** *Carts* is a guessed translation. *Rafts* is borrowed from the detail in 1 Kgs. 5:9 from Hiram's supply of cedar logs to Solomon. **5:57** *According to the directions of King David* may refer to a growing tradition that psalms are to be associated with David. **5:60–62a** The memory of the previous temple reminds some of the elders (who would have to be nearly eighty to be old enough to remember the First Temple) that what is past is not entirely forgotten. A poignant, even melancholy, scene is described

noise, ⁶²so that the people could not hear the trumpets because of the weeping of the people.

For the multitude sounded the trumpets loudly, so that the sound was heard far away, ⁶³and when the enemies of the tribe of Judah and Benjamin heard it, they came to find out what the sound of the trumpets meant. ⁶⁴They learned that those who had returned from exile were building the temple for the Lord God of Israel. ⁶⁵So they approached Zerubbabel and Jeshua and the heads of the ancestral houses and said to them, "We will build with you. ⁶⁶For we obey your Lord just as you do, and we have been sacrificing to him ever since the days of King Esar-haddon of the Assyrians, who brought us here." ⁶⁷But Zerubbabel and Jeshua and the heads of the ancestral houses in Israel said to them, "You have nothing to do with us in building the house for the Lord our God, ⁶⁸for we alone will build it for the Lord of Israel, as Cyrus, the king of the Persians, has commanded us." ⁶⁹But the nations of the land besieged' those in Judea, cut off their supplies, and hindered their building, ⁷⁰and by plots and demagoguery and uprisings they prevented the completion of the building as long as King Cyrus lived. They were kept from building for two years, until the reign of Darius.

6 Now in the second year of the reign of Darius, the prophets Haggai and

Zechariah son of Iddo prophesied to the Jews who were in Judea and Jerusalem; they prophesied to them in the name of the Lord God of Israel. ²Then Zerubbabel son of Shealtiel and Jeshua son of Jozadak began to build the house of the Lord that is in Jerusalem, with the help of the prophets of the Lord who were with them.

3 At the same time Sisinnes the governor of Syria and Phoenicia and Sathrabuzanes and their associates came to them and said, ⁴"By whose order are you building this house and this roof and finishing all the other things? And who are the builders who are finishing these things?" ⁵Yet the elders of the Jews were dealt with kindly, for the providence of the Lord was over the captives; ⁶they were not prevented from building until word could be sent to Darius concerning them and a report made.

7 A copy of the letter that Sisinnes the governor of Syria and Phoenicia and Sathrabuzanes and their associates the local rulers in Syria and Phoenicia wrote and sent to Darius:

"To King Darius, greetings. ⁸Let it be fully known to our lord the king that, when we went to the region of Judea and entered the city of Jerusalem, we found the elders of the Jews, who had been in exile, building in the

r 5.69 Meaning of Gk uncertain

---

here. **5:62b–70** The sequence of events is unusual. In Ezra–Nehemiah, the "others" who offered to help (but became opponents when they are rejected) approached Zerubbabel and the others when only the foundations were being laid (Ezra 3:10–11, followed by dispute in Ezra 4). The book, however, suggests that the temple was virtually completed (vv. 56b, 59) before these others ask to participate merely in the finishing touches. Does this imply a desire to participate in the economic benefits of a functioning temple rather than sharing the financial commitment to the construction? At the same time, vv. 69–70 seem out of sequence as well, suggesting (with Ezra–Nehemiah) that the opposition of the "others" had held up work in the time of Cyrus (and thus earlier on) rather than at the same time as the dedication of the nearly complete temple described in the rest of this chapter. The final reference to the two-year delay *until the reign of Darius* is anachronistic and indicates that the author compiled different sources, since it is completely out of the chronological sequence otherwise adopted by 1 Esdras.
6:1–33 Building of the temple resumed. These events may suggest "passing the test" imposed by local officials who want to be sure that the emperor is truly aware of this activity. **6:1–2** Although not previously mentioned in 1 Esdras, the two contemporary prophets Haggai and Zechariah are acknowledged as important voices in furthering the rebuilding. God's guidance through prophecy is considered an important verification. **6:3–21** Using the words common to authoritarian regimes throughout history, the *governor* and his associates ask, *By whose order . . . ?*, the ancient equivalent of demanding a person's identification or "papers!" The emperor is thus notified in great detail. **6:7–8** The letter is addressed to Darius *our lord*. The Greek phrase is often used for earthly rulers (Pharaoh, Gen. 44:9; David, 1 Kgs. 1:2) but of God in Neh. 8:10. **6:8–11** The translation has *hewn stone*, reading *hewn* or "smoothed" for a Greek term used only here and in v. 24 in the entire LXX, and then the somewhat awkward description *costly* or "precious" is normally applied to the timbers. However,

city of Jerusalem a great new house for the Lord, of hewn stone, with costly timber laid in the walls. [9]These operations are going on rapidly, and the work is prospering in their hands and being completed with all splendor and care. [10]Then we asked these elders, 'At whose command are you building this house and laying the foundations of this structure?' [11]In order that we might inform you in writing who the leaders are, we questioned them and asked them for a list of the names of those who are instigating the disturbance. [12]They answered us, 'We are the servants of the Lord who created the heaven and the earth. [13]The house was built many years ago by a king of Israel who was great and strong, and it was finished. [14]But when our ancestors sinned against the Lord of Israel who is in heaven and provoked him, he gave them over into the hands of King Nebuchadnezzar of Babylon, king of the Chaldeans, [15]and they pulled down the house and burned it and carried the people away captive to Babylon. [16]But in the first year that Cyrus reigned over the region of Babylonia, King Cyrus wrote that this house should be rebuilt. [17]And the holy vessels of gold and of silver that Nebuchadnezzar had taken out of the house in Jerusalem and stored in his own temple, these King Cyrus took out again from the temple in Babylon, and they were delivered to Zerubbabel and Sheshbazzar the governor [18]with the command that he should take all these vessels back and put them in the temple at Jerusalem and that this temple of the Lord should be rebuilt on its site. [19]Then this Sheshbazzar, after coming here, laid the foundations of the house of the Lord that is in Jerusalem. Although it has been in process of construction from that time until now, it has not yet reached completion.' [20]Now therefore, O king, if it seems wise to do

so, let search be made in the royal archives of our lord[w] the king that are in Babylon; [21]if it is found that the building of the house of the Lord in Jerusalem was done with the consent of King Cyrus, and if it is approved by our lord the king, let him send us directions concerning these things."

22 Then Darius commanded that search be made in the royal archives that were deposited in Babylon. And in Ecbatana, the fortress that is in the region of Media, a scroll[x] was found in which this was recorded: [23]"In the first year of the reign of King Cyrus, he ordered the building of the house of the Lord in Jerusalem, where they sacrifice with fire continuously: [24]its height sixty cubits and its width sixty cubits, with three courses of hewn stone and one course of new native timber; the cost to be paid from the treasury of King Cyrus; [25]and the holy vessels of the house of the Lord, both of gold and of silver, that Nebuchadnezzar took out of the house in Jerusalem and carried away to Babylon to be restored to the house in Jerusalem, to be placed where they had been."

26 So Darius[y] commanded Sisinnes the governor of Syria and Phoenicia and Sathrabuzanes and their associates and those who were appointed as local rulers in Syria and Phoenicia to keep away from the place and to permit Zerubbabel, the servant of the Lord and governor of Judea, and the elders of the Jews to build this house of the Lord on its site. [27]"And I command that it be built completely and that full effort be made to help those who have returned from the exile of Judea until the house of the Lord is finished [28]and that out of the tribute of Coelesyria and Phoenicia a portion

w 6.20 Other ancient authorities read *of Cyrus*
x 6.22 Other authorities read *passage*   y 6.26 Gk *he*

"precious stones" are otherwise associated with royalty (Gk. Esth. 15:6; Jdt. 10:21), perhaps suggesting that the emperor should also be aware of this kind of honor given to this building rather than to the emperor himself. In any case, the expense of the project and its *splendor* (v. 9) are emphasized in the letter to the emperor. The implied threat of asking for the *list of the names* is clear (vv. 11–12). **6:12–19** The basics of the Judean "theology of exile" (the exile was the result of the people's sin) are briefly rehearsed, but an emphasis is placed on the authority of Cyrus as the one who commissioned the rebuilding, with particular attention to finances. His name is invoked three times. **6:22–25** It is interesting that the search began in Babylon, as the location of the initial exile (and, we now know, not far from the location of the earliest Judean villages of exiles), but the document was found in Persian Ecbatana. Also interesting is that Cyrus was concerned about the dimensions of the project and some of the basic building details. **6:26–30** Darius dutifully acts on the previous instructions of Cyrus, and financial arrangements are made, including provisions for sacrifices and support of the priesthood. Notably, the Persian monarch is careful to include the requirement of prayers (*libations*;

be scrupulously given to these men, that is, to Zerubbabel the governor, for sacrifices to the Lord, for bulls and rams and lambs, ²⁹and likewise wheat and salt and wine and oil, regularly every year, without quibbling, for daily use as the priests in Jerusalem may indicate, ³⁰in order that libations may be made to the Most High God for the king and his children and prayers be offered for their lives."

31 He commanded that if anyone should transgress or nullify any of the things herein written,ᶻ a beam should be taken out of the house of the perpetrator, who then should be impaled upon it and all property forfeited to the king.

32 "Therefore may the Lord, whose name is there called upon, destroy every king and nation that shall stretch out their hands to hinder or damage that house of the Lord in Jerusalem.

33 "I, King Darius, have decreed that it be done with all diligence as here prescribed."

7 Then Sisinnes the governor of Coelesyria and Phoenicia and Sathrabuzanes and their associates, following the orders of King Darius, ²supervised the holy work with very great care, assisting the elders of the Jews and the chief officers of the temple. ³The holy work prospered, while the prophets Haggai and

Zechariah prophesied, ⁴and they completed it by the command of the Lord God of Israel. So with the consent of Cyrus and Darius and Artaxerxes, kings of the Persians, ⁵the holy house was finished by the twenty-third day of the month of Adar, in the sixth year of King Darius. ⁶And the people of Israel, the priests, the Levites, and the rest of those who returned from exile who joined them did according to what was written in the book of Moses. ⁷They offered at the dedication of the temple of the Lord one hundred bulls, two hundred rams, four hundred lambs, ⁸and twelve male goats for the sin of all Israel, according to the number of the twelve leaders of the tribes of Israel, ⁹and the priests and the Levites stood arrayed in their vestments, according to divisions, for the services of the Lord God of Israel in accordance with the book of Moses, and the gatekeepers were at each gate.

10 The people of Israel who came from exile kept the Passover on the fourteenth day of the first month, after the priests and the Levites were purified together. ¹¹Not all of the returned captives were purified, but the Levites were all purified together,ᵃ ¹²and they sacrificed the Passover lamb for all the returned captives and for their kindred the

z 6.31 Other authorities read *stated above* or *added in writing*
a 7.11 Meaning of Gk uncertain

i.e., drink offerings) for his reign and his family (cf. 8:21). **6:31–33** After requiring prayers in recognition of the emperor (the proverbial "God Save the King"), there is a threat of punishment. While the phrase is ambiguous—is the person hanged on the beam or is the beam hung on the person?—later readers could identify the punishment with crucifixion, especially when reading in the Roman period. The threat against any *king* or *nation* (who seeks *to hinder or damage* the temple) is an interesting addition, absent in Ezra but similar to Dan. 6:25 (also of Darius) and reminiscent of Zerubbabel's comment about women in 1 Esd. 4:15.

7:1–15 Temple finished and dedicated at Passover. The temple was *finished* in the sixth year of Darius, thus completed in a four-year period. Note how this Passover marks a conclusion to a "section" that starts with the Passover that began the book. **7:6** The emphasis changes to the people, and instead of obedience to the Persian directives, people now perform actions *according to what was written in the book* (singular) *of Moses* (cf. v. 9). The first reference to the writings of Moses appeared in the opening chapter about Josiah's Passover. In 5:48, the text identifies Moses further as "the man of God," and thereafter, in 7:6, 9, the phrase refers to obeying the "book of Moses" (always in relation to ritual observance). *The rest of those . . . who joined them.* Are these groups of people who came back in smaller groups? Most of Ezra–Nehemiah and 1 Esdras (especially noting the long lists) seem to portray a (probably fictional) major "exodus"—like a parade of a large number. Indeed, the resemblance with an "exodus" march is likely intentional, not only from the large numbers provided in the lists but also with seven references to Moses in the book (cf. Isa. 40:3). **7:7–9** The descriptions of ritual observance have an odd "pictorial" portrayal. They are (imagined? remembered?) as visual and still scenes rather than a participant's description of actions—for example, where people were standing, what they were wearing. **7:10–15** The celebrations of Passover are mixed with concerns about the purity of the participants. The notion that some of the returned exiles were not *purified* (but the Levites were) hints at differences among the people who have

priests and for themselves. [13]The people of Israel who had returned from exile ate it, all those who had separated themselves from the abominations of the nations of the land and sought the Lord. [14]They also kept the Festival of Unleavened Bread seven days, rejoicing before the Lord, [15]because he had changed the will of the king of the Assyrians concerning them, to strengthen their hands for the service of the Lord God of Israel.

8 After these things, when Artaxerxes, the king of the Persians, was reigning, Ezra came, the son of Seraiah, son of Azariah, son of Hilkiah, son of Shallum, [2]son of Zadok, son of Ahitub, son of Amariah, son of Uzzi, son of Bukki, son of Abishua, son of Phineas, son of Eleazar, son of Aaron the high[b] priest. [3]This Ezra came up from Babylon as a scribe skilled in the law of Moses, which was given by the God of Israel, [4]and the king showed him honor, for he found favor before the king[c] in all his requests. [5]There came up with him to Jerusalem some of the people of Israel and some of the priests and Levites and temple singers and gatekeepers and temple servants, [6]in the seventh year of the reign of Artaxerxes, in the fifth month (this was the king's seventh year), for they left Babylon on the new moon of the first month and arrived in Jerusalem on the new moon of the fifth month, by the successful journey that the Lord gave them. [7]For Ezra possessed great knowledge, so that he omitted nothing from the law of the Lord or the commandments but taught all Israel all the ordinances and judgments.

8 The following is a copy of the written decree from King Artaxerxes that was delivered to Ezra the priest and reader of the law of the Lord:

9 "King Artaxerxes to Ezra the priest and reader of the law of the Lord, greeting. [10]In accordance with my gracious decision, I have given orders that those of the Jewish nation and of the priests and Levites and others in our realm, those who freely choose to do so, may go with you to Jerusalem. [11]Let as many as are so disposed, therefore, leave with you, just as I and the seven Friends who are my counselors have decided, [12]in order to look into matters in Judea and Jerusalem, in accordance with what is in the law of the Lord, [13]and to carry to Jerusalem the gifts for the Lord of Israel that I and my Friends have vowed, and to collect for the Lord in Jerusalem all the gold and silver that may be found in the region of

b 8.2 Gk *the first*   c 8.4 Gk *him*

returned. This also applies to those who had not separated from the *abominations* of the surrounding peoples in v. 13 (presumably among those left behind in the land). If this state of "impurity" also describes some of those who returned from exile, then it is a problem that is not limited only to those who were left in the land during the exile. A hierarchy of the "pure" community is evident in that all the leaders are said to come from the returning exiles. There is no indication of leadership arising from those left behind. Even Levites are sought among exiled groups (cf. 8:41–49). **7:15** Calling Babylonian or Persian rulers *Assyrians* is not unknown in late biblical literature (especially in Judith), but some scholars propose that Assyria is referred to here to suggest that the events of the exile had their origins with the Assyrian conquests of the eighth century BCE. In any case, Josephus corrects this in his retelling of these texts (*Ant.* 11.110) to the "king of Persia."

8:1–92 Ezra's expedition to Jerusalem. Chaps. 8–9 are the only chapters where Ezra plays a significant role (and at 9:40, 49, he is even raised to the role of "chief priest," which is never mentioned in Ezra–Nehemiah). Ezra seems to occupy a dual function as a Persian official with responsibilities "to the crown" but also a reformer in Judean society. However, there is very little interaction between Ezra and any Persian officials, quite unlike either Zerubbabel in 1 Esdras or Nehemiah in the book bearing his name. **8:1–7** Ezra's qualifications are rehearsed. Note his genealogical connections to Phineas/Phinehas (who brutally murdered a mixed-race couple yet is honored as "zealous" in Num. 25:13) and Aaron, the titular founder of the priesthood in all Israel. **8:4** This is the very briefest acknowledgment of any relationship with the Persian king. Ezra's "authority" rests on the text of the letter from Artaxerxes (Artaxerxes I or II?). *Honor* (or "reputation") and *favor*, given to Ezra, are political terms. **8:9–24 The alleged letter.** This authorizes Ezra to carry out not only civil matters on behalf of the king but also religious matters in relation to the community. **8:10** Artaxerxes describes his decision as *gracious*, using the Greek term from which English derives "philanthropy," and if rendered similarly ("in accordance with my philanthropic decision"), we capture more of the self-praise. All the financial support is designated for the temple. Since the chronology of events in 1 Esdras has established that

Babylonia, together with what is given by the nation for the temple of their Lord that is in Jerusalem, [14]both gold and silver for bulls and rams and lambs and what goes with them, [15]so as to offer sacrifices on the altar of their Lord that is in Jerusalem. [16]Whatever you and your kindred wish to do with the gold and silver, perform it in accordance with the will of your God; [17]deliver the holy vessels of the Lord that are given you for the use of the temple of your God that is in Jerusalem. And whatever else occurs to you as necessary for the temple of your God, [18]you may provide out of the royal treasury.

[19] "I, King Artaxerxes, have commanded the treasurers of Syria and Phoenicia that whatever Ezra the priest and reader of the law of the Most High God sends for, they shall take care to give him, up to a hundred talents of silver, [20]and likewise up to a hundred cors of wheat, a hundred baths of wine, and salt in abundance. [21]Let all things prescribed in the law of God be scrupulously fulfilled for the Most High God, so that wrath may not come upon the kingdom of the king and his sons. [22]You are also informed that no tribute or any other tax is to be laid on any of the priests or Levites or temple singers or gatekeepers or temple servants or persons employed in this temple and that no one has authority to impose any tax on them.

[23] "And you, Ezra, according to the wisdom of God, appoint judges and justices to judge all those who know the law of your God throughout all Syria and Phoenicia, and you shall teach it to those who do not know it. [24]All who transgress the law of your God or the law of the kingdom shall be strictly punished, whether by death or some other punishment, either fine or imprisonment."

[25] Then Ezra the scribe said,[d] "Blessed be the Lord alone, who put this into the heart of the king, to glorify his house that is in Jerusalem, [26]and who honored me in the sight of the king and his counselors and all his Friends and nobles. [27]I was encouraged by the help of the Lord my God, and I gathered men from Israel to go up with me."

[28] These are the leaders, according to their ancestral houses and their groups, who went up with me from Babylon, in the reign of King Artaxerxes: [29]Of the descendants of Phineas, Gershom. Of the descendants of Ithamar, Gamael. Of the descendants of David, Hattush son of Shecaniah. [30]Of the descendants of Parosh, Zechariah and with him a hundred fifty men enrolled. [31]Of the descendants of Pahath-moab, Eliehoenai son of Zerahiah and with him two hundred men. [32]Of the descendants of Zattu, Shecaniah son of Jahaziel and with him three hundred men. Of the descendants of Adin, Obed son of Jonathan and with him two hundred fifty men. [33]Of the descendants of Elam, Jeshaiah son of Gotholiah and with him seventy men. [34]Of the descendants of Shephatiah, Zeraiah son of Michael and with him seventy men. [35]Of the descendants of Joab, Obadiah son of Jehiel and with him two hundred twelve men. [36]Of the descendants of Bani, Shelomith son of Josiphiah and with him a hundred sixty men. [37]Of the descendants of Bebai, Zechariah son of Bebai and with him twenty-eight men. [38]Of the descendants of Azgad, Johanan son of Hakkatan and with him a hundred ten men. [39]Of the descendants of Adonikam, the last ones, their names being Eliphelet, Jeuel, and Shemaiah, and with them seventy men. [40]Of the descendants of Bigvai, Uthai son of Istalcurus and with him seventy men.

[41] I assembled them at the river called Theras, and we encamped there three days, and I inspected them. [42]When I found there none of the descendants of the priests or of the Levites,

d 8.25 Other ancient authorities lack *Then Ezra the scribe said*

the temple is already standing, this amounts to a significant "investment" in the ongoing activity and authority of the temple-based economy of the area. **8:22** This release from taxation for temple personnel as a sign of honor and royal privilege for special temple-centered cities is a tradition bestowed on special cities and temples that goes back at least to the Neo-Assyrian Empire, if not earlier. **8:23–24** The precise lines of authority are not entirely clear. Is Ezra authorized to impose the Mosaic requirements on the Hebrews throughout these regions? This would seem to negate the necessity of the authentic community to separate from the surrounding peoples if Ezra has the authority to legislate religious observance by fiat. **8:28–48** List of those who accompanied Ezra. The precise-looking list suggests not only the widespread support for his mission and work but also a sense of accountability to the Persian officials. Note also the care taken to represent the concern for Levitical representation.

[43]I sent word to Eleazar, Iduel, Maasmas, Elnathan, Shemaiah, Jarib, Nathan, Elnathan, Zechariah, and Meshullam, who were leaders and men of understanding; [44]I told them to go to Iddo, who was the leading man at the place of the treasury, [45]and ordered them to tell Iddo and his kindred and the treasurers at that place to send us men to serve as priests in the house of our Lord. [46]And by the mighty hand of our Lord they brought us competent men of the descendants of Mahli son of Levi, son of Israel, namely, Sherebiah with his descendants and kinsmen, eighteen; [47]also Hashabiah and Annunus and his brother Jeshaiah, of the descendants of Hananiah, and their descendants, twenty men; [48]and of the temple servants whom David and the leaders had given for the service of the Levites, two hundred twenty temple servants; the list of all their names was reported.

[49] There I proclaimed a fast for the young men before our Lord, [50]to seek from him a successful journey for ourselves and for our children and the livestock with us. [51]For I was ashamed to ask the king for infantry and cavalry and an escort to keep us safe from our adversaries, [52]for we had said to the king, "The power of our Lord will be with those who seek him and will support them in every way." [53]And again we prayed to our Lord about these things, and we found him very merciful.

[54] Then I set apart twelve of the leaders of the priests, Sherebiah and Hashabiah and ten of their kinsmen with them, [55]and I weighed out to them the silver and the gold and the holy vessels of the house of our Lord that the king himself and his counselors and the nobles and all Israel had given. [56]I weighed and gave to them six hundred fifty talents of silver, and silver vessels worth a hundred talents, and a hundred talents of gold, and twenty golden bowls, and twelve bronze vessels of fine bronze that glittered like gold. [57]And I said to them, "You are holy to the Lord, and the vessels are holy, and the silver and the gold are vowed to the Lord, the Lord of our ancestors. [58]Be watchful and on guard until you deliver them to the leaders of the priests and the Levites and to the heads of the ancestral houses of Israel, in Jerusalem, in the chambers of the house of our Lord." [59]So the priests and the Levites who took the silver and the gold and the vessels that had been in Jerusalem carried them to the temple of the Lord.

[60] We left the River Theras on the twelfth day of the first month, and we arrived in Jerusalem by the mighty hand of our Lord, which was upon us; he delivered us from every enemy on the way, and so we came to Jerusalem. [61]When we had been there three days, the silver and the gold were weighed and delivered in the house of our Lord to the priest Meremoth son of Uriah; [62]with him was Eleazar son of Phinehas, and with them were Jozabad son of Jeshua and Moeth son of Binnui, the Levites. The whole was counted and weighed, and the weight of everything was recorded at that very time. [63]And those who had returned from exile offered sacrifices to the Lord, the God of Israel, twelve bulls for all Israel, ninety-six rams, seventy-two lambs, and as a thank offering twelve male goats—all as a sacrifice to the Lord. [64]They delivered the king's orders to the royal stewards and to the governors of Coelesyria and Phoenicia, and these officials[e] honored the nation and the temple of the Lord.

[65] After these things had been done, the leaders came to me and said, [66]"The nation of

e 8.64 Gk they

8:49–64 **Ezra proclaims a fast.** In the context of 1 Esdras, Ezra's piety in refusing an armed guard no longer accomplishes a not-so-subtle criticism of Nehemiah, who did accept such a guard (Neh. 2:9). Fasting as a means to call on God's protection in facing an enemy is a frequent motif (implied in 2 Sam. 11:11; cf. 2 Chr. 20:3; Esth. 4:16; Jdt. 4:9). **8:60** This suggests that worries for safety along the road seem justified, perhaps because carrying valuables was the main cause for concern. **8:65–92 Crisis of mixed marriages.** This passage reports a crisis similar to Ezra–Nehemiah, although the numbering separates the prayer in chap. 8 from the resolution in chap. 9. Ezra's response to the bad news is to offer another example of what has come to be called the "penitential prayer" (other prominent examples, all postexilic, include Dan. 9; Ezra 9; Neh. 9; Bar. 1:15–3:8). This prayer is a rehearsal of (Jeremiah's?) Deuteronomic theology of the exile as self-inflicted, and it becomes a set prayer style that is repeated for hundreds of years after the exile. **8:65–67** *Holy seed* is the unusual (and ethnocentric) descriptive phrase appearing only in the Ezra traditions. Their holiness is in contrast to the list of "unacceptable" peoples surrounding them. The list of these unacceptable peoples, however, is clearly drawn from the

Israel and the rulers and the priests and the Levites have not separated themselves from the foreign nations of the land and their pollutions, the Canaanites, the Hittites, the Perizzites, the Jebusites, the Moabites, the Egyptians, and the Edomites. [67]For they and their sons have married the daughters of these people,[f] and the holy seed has been mixed with the foreign nations of the land, and from the beginning of this matter the leaders and the nobles have been sharing in this iniquity."

[68] As soon as I heard these things, I tore my garments and my holy vestments and pulled out hair from my head and beard and sat down in anxiety and grief. [69]And all who were ever moved at[g] the word of the Lord of Israel gathered around me, as I mourned over this iniquity, and I sat grief-stricken until the evening sacrifice. [70]Then I rose from my fast, with my garments and my holy vestments torn, and kneeling down and stretching out my hands to the Lord I said,

[71] "O Lord, I am ashamed and dishonored before your face. [72]For our sins have risen higher than our heads, and our mistakes have mounted up to heaven [73]from the times of our ancestors, and we are in great sin to this day. [74]Because of our sins and the sins of our ancestors, we with our kindred and our kings and our priests were given over to the kings of the earth, to the sword and exile and plundering, in shame until this day. [75]And now in some measure mercy has come to us from you, O Lord, to leave to us a root and a name in your holy place [76]and to uncover a light for us in the house of the Lord our God and to give us food in the time of our servitude. Even in our bondage we were not forsaken by our Lord, [77]but he brought us into favor with the kings of the Persians, so that they have given us food [78]and glorified the temple of our Lord and raised Zion from desolation, to give us a stronghold in Judea and Jerusalem.

[79] "And now, O Lord, what shall we say when we have these things? For we have transgressed your commandments that you gave by your servants the prophets, saying, [80]'The land that you are entering to possess is a land polluted with the pollution of the foreigners of the land, and they have filled it with their uncleanness. [81]Therefore do not give your daughters in marriage to their sons, and do not take their daughters for your sons; [82]do not seek ever to have peace with them, so that you may be strong and eat the good things of the land and leave it for an inheritance to your children forever.' [83]And all that has happened to us has come about because of our evil deeds and our great sins. For you, O Lord, lifted the burden of our sins [84]and gave us such a root as this, but we turned back again to transgress your law by mixing with the uncleanness of the nations of the land. [85]Were you not angry enough with us to destroy us without leaving a root or seed or name? [86]O Lord of Israel, you are faithful, for we are left as a root to this day. [87]See, we are now before you in our iniquities, for we can no longer stand in your presence because of these things."

[88] While Ezra was praying and making his confession, weeping and lying on the ground before the temple, there gathered around him a very great crowd of men and women and youths from Jerusalem, for there was great weeping among the multitude. [89]Then Shecaniah son of Jehiel, one of the men of Israel, called out and said to Ezra, "We have sinned against the Lord and have married foreign women from the nations of the land, but even now there is hope for Israel. [90]Let us take an oath to the Lord about this, that we will put away all our foreign wives with their children, as seems good to you and to all who obey the law of the Lord. [91]Rise up[h] and take action, for it is your task, and we are with you to take strong measures." [92]Then Ezra rose up and made the leaders of the priests and Levites of all Israel swear that they would do this. And they swore to it.

9 Then Ezra set out and went from the court of the temple to the chamber of

---

f 8.67 Gk *their daughters*   g 8.69 Or *zealous for*
h 8.91 Other ancient authorities read *as seems good to you."*
And all who obeyed the law of the Lord rose and said to Ezra,
[95]*"Rise up*

---

accounts of the conquest narratives of Joshua (Josh. 3:10; 9:1; 11:3; etc.). **8:75–76a** References to God's provision of a *root* and a *light* (cf. "star" in Num. 24:17; "root" in Sir. 47:22) appear to be given messianic implications in Matt. 2 and Rev. 22:16.

    9:1–36 Resolution of the mixed marriage crisis and census list. The description of the mass divorce proceedings is virtually the same as in Ezra–Nehemiah, emphasizing the voluntary nature of the reaction to the "problem" among the purified community. Suspicions are raised for modern

Jehohanan son of Eliashib [2]and spent the night there, and he did not eat bread or drink water, for he was mourning over the great iniquities of the multitude. [3]And a proclamation was made throughout Judea and Jerusalem to all who had returned from exile that they should assemble at Jerusalem [4]and that if any did not meet there within two or three days, in accordance with the decision of the ruling elders, their livestock would be seized for sacrifice and the men themselves[i] expelled from the multitude of those who had returned from the captivity.

[5] Then the men of the tribe of Judah and Benjamin assembled at Jerusalem within three days; this was the ninth month, on the twentieth day of the month. [6]All the multitude sat in the open square before the temple, shivering because of the bad weather that prevailed. [7]Then Ezra stood up and said to them, "You have broken the law and married foreign women and so have increased the sin of Israel. [8]Now, then, make confession and give glory to the Lord the God of our ancestors [9]and do his will; separate yourselves from the nations of the land and from your foreign wives."

[10] Then all the multitude shouted and said with a loud voice, "We will do as you have said. [11]But the multitude is great, and it is winter, and we are not able to stand in the open air. This is not a work we can do in one day or two, for we have sinned too much in these things. [12]So let the leaders of the multitude stay, and let all those in our settlements who have foreign wives come at the time appointed [13]with the elders and judges of each place, until we are freed from the wrath of the Lord over this matter."

[14] Jonathan son of Asahel and Jahzeiah son of Tikvah undertook the matter on these terms, and Meshullam and Levi and Shabbethai served with them as judges. [15]And those who had returned from exile acted in accordance with all this.

[16] Ezra the priest chose for himself the leading men of their ancestral houses, all of them by name, and on the new moon of the tenth month they began their sessions to investigate the matter. [17]And the cases of the men who had foreign wives were brought to an end by the new moon of the first month.

[18] Of the priests, those who were brought in and found to have foreign wives were: [19]of the descendants of Jeshua son of Jozadak and his kindred, Maaseiah, Eliezar, Jarib, and Jodan. [20]They pledged themselves to put away their wives and to offer rams in expiation of their error. [21]Of the descendants of Immer: Hanani and Zebadiah and Maaseiah and Shemaiah and Jehiel and Azariah. [22]Of the descendants of Pashhur: Elioenai, Maaseiah, Ishmael, and Nathanael, and Gedaliah, and Salthas.

[23] And of the Levites: Jozabad and Shimei and Kelaiah, who was Kelita, and Pethahiah and Judah and Jonah. [24]Of the temple singers: Eliashib and Zaccur. [25]Of the gatekeepers: Shallum and Telem.

[26] Of Israel: of the descendants of Parosh: Ramiah, Izziah, Malchijah, Mijamin, and Eleazar, and Asibias, and Benaiah. [27]Of the descendants of Elam: Mattaniah and Zechariah, Jezrielus and Abdi, and Jeremoth and Elijah. [28]Of the descendants of Zamoth: Eliadas, Eliashib, Othoniah, Jeremoth, and Zabad and Zerdaiah. [29]Of the descendants of Bebai: Jehohanan and Hananiah and Zabbai and Emathis. [30]Of the descendants of Mani: Olamus, Mamuchus, Adaiah, Jashub, and Sheal and Jeremoth. [31]Of the descendants of Addi: Naathus and Moossias, Laccunus and Naidus, and Bescaspasmys and Sesthel, and Belnuus and Manasseas. [32]Of the descendants of Annan, Elionas and Asaias and Melchias and Sabbaias and Simon Chosamaeus. [33]Of the descendants of Hashum: Mattenai and Mattattah and Zabad and Eliphelet and Manasseh and Shimei. [34]Of the descendants of Bani: Jeremai, Momdius, Maerus, Joel, Mamdai and Bedeiah and Vaniah, Carabasion and Eliashib and Mamitanemus, Eliasis, Binnui, Elialis, Shimei, Shelemiah, Nethaniah. Of the descendants of Ezora: Shashai, Azarel, Azael, Samatus, Zambris, Joseph. [35]Of the descendants of Nooma: Mazitias, Zabad, Iddo, Joel, Benaiah. [36]All these had married foreign women, and they put them away together with their children.

i 9.4 Gk *he himself*

readers by the fact that priests and Levites, normally dedicated to issues of purity, are among the guilty (8:66–67). It seems more likely that these *foreign* women are simply Judeans considered unacceptable by Ezra and his cohort's extremism on the matter (by not being among the returning exiles?), and thus the rehearsal of the traditional list of peoples driven out by Joshua amounts to a denigrating slur against fellow Judeans.

37 The priests and the Levites and the Israelites settled in Jerusalem and in the region. On the new moon of the seventh month, when the people of Israel were in their settlements, [38]the whole multitude gathered with one accord in the open square before the east gate of the temple; [39]they told Ezra the chief priest and reader to bring the law of Moses that had been given by the Lord God of Israel. [40]So Ezra the chief priest brought the law, for all the multitude, men and women, and all the priests to hear the law, on the new moon of the seventh month. [41]He read aloud in the open square before the gate of the temple from early morning until midday, in the presence of both men and women, and all the multitude gave attention to the law. [42]Ezra the priest and reader of the law stood on the wooden platform that had been prepared, [43]and beside him stood Mattathiah, Shema, Ananias, Azariah, Uriah, Hezekiah, and Baalsamus on his right, [44]and on his left Pedaiah, Mishael, Malchijah, Lothasubus, Nabariah, and Zechariah. [45]Then Ezra took up the book of the law in the sight of the multitude, for he had the place of honor in the presence of all. [46]When he opened the law, they all stood erect. And Ezra blessed the Lord God Most High, the God of hosts, the Almighty, [47]and the multitude answered, "Amen." They lifted up their hands and fell to the ground and worshiped God.[j] [48]Jeshua and Anniuth and Sherebiah, Jadinus, Akkub, Shabbethai, Hodiah, Maiannas and Kelita, Azariah and Jozabad, Hanan, Pelaiah, the Levites, taught the law of the Lord,[k] at the same time explaining what was read.

49 Then Attharates[l] said to Ezra the chief priest[m] and reader and to the Levites who were teaching the multitude and to all, [50]"This day is holy to the Lord"—now they were all weeping as they heard the law—[51]"so go your way, eat the fat and drink the sweet, and send portions to those who have none, [52]for the day is holy to the Lord, and do not be sorrowful, for the Lord will exalt you." [53]The Levites commanded all the people, saying, "This day is holy; do not be sorrowful." [54]Then they all went their way, to eat and drink and enjoy themselves and to give portions to those who had none and to make great rejoicing, [55]because they were inspired by the words which they had been taught. And they came together.[n]

j 9.47 Other ancient authorities read *the Lord*
k 9.48 Other ancient authorities add *and read the law of the Lord to the multitude*   l 9.49 Or *the governor*   m 9.49 Other ancient authorities read *priest*   n 9.55 The Greek text ends abruptly

9:37–55 **Ezra reads the law.** Much of the later fame of Ezra, especially in Jewish tradition, comes from his prominence in not merely reading but explaining the law. In vv. 40 and 49, Ezra is declared *chief priest*, which never appears in Ezra–Nehemiah. **9:41–42** Reading the law in the *square* of the temple (on a *wooden platform* built for the occasion) associates the explication of Torah as an important accompaniment to the ritual actions in the temple. **9:45–48** Note the "liturgical" ceremony around the reading: Ezra takes up the book; the people stand; Ezra proclaims a blessing; the people reply, then kneel; and the law is further discussed and explained (cf. the description of actions in Jesus's reading in Luke 4:16–20). **9:48** *Explaining what was read.* Literally "breathing into the reading." **9:49** Instead of the proper name *Attharates*, many scholars presume "the Tirshata" means "the governor." **9:55b** For many readers, 1 Esdras has an unacceptably abrupt ending that suggests that something has dropped out. Nehemiah 8:13–18 is often proposed as the missing ending, which would then create the celebrations of the people as "bookends" of 1 Esdras as a whole, beginning with Josiah's Passover and ending with the Festival of Booths as described in Neh. 8:13–18. Equally strong are the arguments that the ending certainly does make sense as a final statement of the unity of the postexilic community; thus the text indicates, in the final words, that *they came together*. The same Greek term, emphasizing the gathering of the people especially in times of crisis, is repeated in 5:49, 8:69, 8:88, and 9:5 before appearing here.

PRAYER OF MANASSEH

The Prayer of Manasseh is a short prayer of an individual asking God for forgiveness. The superscription identifies the speaker as Manasseh, although he is not mentioned by name in the body of the Prayer. Manasseh was not the author. Rather, the Prayer was composed centuries later and attributed to him.

Manasseh was the son of Hezekiah and king of Judah circa 698/687–642. In 2 Kgs. 20:21–21:18, his reign is described as entirely wicked; Manasseh reinstated widespread idolatry—including in the Jerusalem temple—and shed innocent blood. According to 2 Kings, God allowed Judah to be conquered and the people sent into exile on account of his wickedness (21:10–15; 23:26–27). The story of Manasseh is repeated in 2 Chronicles (32:33–33:10 parallels 2 Kings), but the Chronicler adds to the story, ultimately portraying Manasseh in a positive light (33:11–20). In the Chronicler's story, God sent the Assyrian army to attack him and take him bound into exile (33:11). There Manasseh prayed and "humbled himself greatly before the God of his ancestors," who answered his prayer and "restored him again to Jerusalem and to his kingdom" (33:12–13). Manasseh then removed all the foreign gods, "restored the altar of the LORD" and "commanded Judah to serve the LORD the God of Israel" (33:15–17). According to the Chronicler, "His prayer, and how God received his entreaty, all his sin and his faithlessness . . . these are written in the records of the seers" (33:19; cf. mention of his prayer in 33:18). There are several allusions and verbal parallels to the story of Manasseh in 2 Chronicles, which suggest that the author composed the prayer as an expansion of that passage.

The Prayer appears in different compositions and collections. It is included among the Odes that are appended to some Greek manuscripts of the book of Psalms dating to the fifth century CE. A late Hebrew translation of a Greek version has been found in the Cairo Genizah. The earliest manuscripts are in the Syriac translation of *Didascalia Apostolorum* (third century CE) and are also preserved in Greek in the *Apostolic Constitutions* (fourth century CE). The *Didascalia* provides instructions on how Christians should live and practice. The Prayer of Manasseh is in a section addressed to bishops, in which the story of Manasseh is an example of God's forgiveness of sinners.

Greek and Russian Orthodox Churches consider the Prayer of Manasseh to be canonical. In the Roman Catholic Church, the Prayer is not considered deuterocanonical but placed in an appendix to the Latin Vulgate Bible, along with 1 Esdras and 2 Esdras. The canticle Kyrie Pantokrator draws on verses of the Prayer of Manasseh and appears in the Book of Common Prayer in the Episcopal Church.

Among the Dead Sea Scrolls, there is another penitential prayer that begins with the phrase "Prayer of Manasseh, King of Judah when the king of Assyria imprisoned him" (4Q381). However, besides this common setting, there are no overlaps between the two prayers, and they are different compositions.

Original Language and Date of Composition

It is difficult to date or identify the original language of the Prayer of Manasseh. While it is possible that it was originally composed in Hebrew or Aramaic, more evidence exists that the original composition was in Greek. Most scholars identify the Prayer as a Jewish composition from the first century BCE or CE, although some argue that it was composed later by a Christian.

Reading Guide

The Prayer of Manasseh is often classified as a penitential prayer—that is, a prayer confessing sins and asking for forgiveness. One can compare and contrast its themes and form with other Jewish prayers, such as Ps. 51 and many of those from the postexilic and Hellenistic periods (Ezra 9:5–15; Neh. 1:5–11; 9:6–37; Dan. 9:4–19; Pr. Azar. 3–22; Bar. 1:15–3:8; Tob. 3:1–6; 3 Macc. 2:1–10; Jos. Asen. 11–13; 4Q504 4; 1–2 II, V–VI; 4Q506 131–32; 4Q393; 11QPsᵃ IXX).

The Prayer is well crafted with repeated words and themes weaving together the different sections (see also **"Hebrew Poetry," p. 741**). The Prayer begins with a lengthy invocation addressed to God ("you") recounting God's attributes (1–8). "God of our ancestors" grounds the Prayer in God's promises and covenant. God's power demonstrated in the creation of the world elicits fear, since "the wrath of your threat to sinners is unendurable." However, that wrath is outweighed by God's

"promised mercy," which is "immeasurable and unsearchable." Because God is merciful, God has "promised repentance and forgiveness to those who have sinned" against God. The second section (9–12) shifts to the first person ("I") and is a confession of sins. The third section (13a–c) asks for God's forgiveness and mercy expressed in a series of imperatives and negative commands. The final section (13d–15) expresses trust that God will forgive the petitioner, who will respond with praise.

Henry W. Morisada Rietz

¹ O Lord Almighty,
   God of our ancestors,
   of Abraham and Isaac and Jacob
   and of their righteous offspring,
² you who made heaven and earth
   with all their order,
³ who shackled the sea by your word of
      command,
   who confined the deep
   and sealed it with your terrible and
      glorious name,
⁴ at whom all things shudder
   and tremble before your power,
⁵ for your glorious splendor cannot be borne,
   and the wrath of your threat to sinners is
      unendurable;
⁶ yet immeasurable and unsearchable
   is your promised mercy,
⁷ for you are the Lord Most High,
   of great compassion, long-suffering, and
      very merciful,
   and you relent at human suffering.
   O Lord, according to your great goodness

you have promised repentance and
      forgiveness
to those who have sinned against you,
and in the multitude of your mercies
you have appointed repentance for
      sinners,
so that they may be saved.ᵃ
⁸ Therefore you, O Lord, God of the
      righteous,
have not appointed repentance for the
      righteous,
for Abraham and Isaac and Jacob, who
      did not sin against you,
but you have appointed repentance for
      me, who am a sinner.
⁹ For the sins I have committed are more in
      number than the sand of the sea;
my transgressions are multiplied, O Lord,
      they are multiplied!
I am not worthy to look up and see the
      height of heaven

a 7 Other ancient authorities lack *O Lord, according . . . be saved*

1–8 Invocation. 1 *Lord Almighty.* The Greek "kyrie pantokrator" often translates Hebrew phrases that are rendered in English as "Lᴏʀᴅ of hosts" (2 Sam. 5:10; 7:8, 27). In the Greek version (LXX) of Job, "Almighty" (Gk. "pantokrator") translates the Hebrew "Shaddai" (e.g., 5:17). *Lord Almighty* or *Almighty.* See Judith (e.g., 4:13; 8:13), Baruch (3:1, 4), Revelation (e.g., 1:8; 4:8; 11:17), 2 Corinthians (6:18). *God of our ancestors.* See 2 Chr. 33:12. *Abraham and Isaac and Jacob* echoes Exod. 3:15 (cf. Pr. Azar. 12; Acts 7:32). *And of their righteous offspring* anticipates v. 8, where, in contrast to the speaker, the ancestors are sinless. **2–3** God created the world through divine speech (*by your word of command*); cf. Gen. 1:1–2:4a, in which God creates by separating and confining the waters through divine speech (Gen. 1:6–9; cf. 2 Esd. 16:55–60). The physical, violent language—*shackled the sea, confined the deep,* and *sealed it*—invokes the imagery of gods creating through battle common in the ancient Near East; cf. Ps. 74:12–15; Job 38:8–11; and the *Enuma Elish,* where Marduk kills Tiamat, the sea goddess, and uses her body to create the world. **5–6** Pairing God's *wrath* and *mercy* is reminiscent of the description of God in Exod. 34:6–7; cf. Num. 14:18–19; Sir. 17:29. **7** *Relent* (Gk. verb "metanoeo"). Literally "change one's mind"; in other passages, it also means "repent" (cf., e.g., LXX Jer. 8:6). In Jonah 4:2 and Amos 7:3, 6 (LXX uses the same Gk. verb in these passages), God changes God's mind and forgives. *Promised repentance and forgiveness.* See 1 Kgs. 8:27–53. **8** *Abraham and Isaac and Jacob* are portrayed as sinless, in contrast to the person praying this prayer. *Repentance* (Gk. "metanoia," a noun related to "metanoeo") is not *for the righteous* but for sinners; cf. Luke 5:32. *For me, who am a sinner* anticipates vv. 9–12.

9–12 Confession. 9 *Sand of the sea.* A common image for an uncountable amount (e.g., Gen. 22:17; 32:12; 41:49; Josh. 11:4). *Sins . . . more in number than the sand of the sea; my transgressions are multiplied . . . they are multiplied* recalls the imagery of LXX Gen. 22:17, contrasting the speaker's sins

because of the multitude of my iniquities.

10 I am weighted down with many an iron
    fetter,
so that I am rejected*b* because of my sins,
and I have no relief,
for I have provoked your wrath
and have done what is evil in your sight,
setting up abominations and multiplying
    offenses.

11 And now I bend the knee of my heart,
imploring you for your kindness.

12 I have sinned, O Lord, I have sinned,
and I acknowledge my transgressions.

13 I earnestly implore you,
forgive me, O Lord, forgive me!
Do not destroy me with my
    transgressions!

Do not be angry with me forever or store
    up evil for me;
do not condemn me to the depths of the
    earth.

For you, O Lord, are the God of those who
    repent,

14 and in me you will manifest your
    goodness,
for, unworthy as I am, you will save me
    according to your great mercy,

15 and I will praise you continually all the
    days of my life.
For all the host of heaven sings your
    praise,
and yours is the glory forever. Amen.

b 10 Other ancient authorities read *so that I cannot lift up my head*

with the abundances of God's covenantal blessings. **10** *Iron fetter* (Gk. "desmo" is "fetter") reflects 2 Chr. 33:11, where Manasseh is "bound . . . with fetters" (Gk. "desmois"). *Have done what is evil in your sight.* Cf. Ps. 51:4 (= LXX 50:6). *Setting up abominations and multiplying offenses* refers to Manasseh promoting idolatry (2 Chr. 33:2–9; 33:19; 2 Kgs. 21:2–9, 11, 16). **11** *I bend the knee of my heart.* An image of contrition, perhaps because he is bound. Cf. Ps. 51:17. For praying on one's knees, see Dan. 6:11; Acts 9:40; Jos. Asen. 11:19. *Imploring* anticipates v. 13. **12** *I acknowledge my transgressions.* Cf. Ps. 51:3 (= LXX 50:5).

13a–c Petition for forgiveness. *Forgive me, O Lord, forgive me* parallels "I have sinned, O Lord, I have sinned" (v. 12). Note the imperatives (*forgive . . . forgive*) and negative commands (*do not destroy . . . do not be angry . . . or store up evil . . . do not condemn*).

13d–15 Assurance. The use of *for* and the shift to future tense verbs express assurance. "God of the righteous" (v. 8) is also *the God of those who repent*. **14** *Unworthy.* Cf. v. 9. *Your great mercy.* Cf. v. 7. **15** The one "not worthy to look up and see the height of heaven" (v. 9) now *will praise you continually. . . . For all the host of heaven sings your praise.*

PSALM 151

The book of Psalms preserved in the Hebrew manuscript tradition called the Masoretic Text (MT) contains 150 psalms. The NRSVue translates the book of Psalms in the Hebrew Bible / Old Testament from the MT.

Psalm 151 is included in many manuscripts of the Greek Septuagint and other ancient translations of the Hebrew Bible. Psalm 151 is part of the canonical book of Psalms in the Orthodox Churches (Eastern, Coptic, Armenian, etc.).

Psalm 151 was originally composed in Hebrew and is preserved on one of the scrolls found in the caves near Qumran, 11QPsalms[a]. In addition to some psalms preserved in the MT, 11QPsalms[a] also preserves Pss. 154–55 (previously known in the language of Syriac) as well as other previously unknown psalms. Psalm 151 was originally two different psalms, which are called Ps. 151A and Ps. 151B. The division between Ps. 151A and Ps. 151B is indicated by a blank space on the manuscript 11QPsalms[a]. Portions of Ps. 151A are translated in vv. 1–5. The extant portion of Ps. 151B mentions David's battle with the "Philistine" Goliath and is preserved in vv. 6–7. The Greek translator abbreviated these psalms and combined them to produce the Greek Ps. 151.

Reading Guide

In reading Ps. 151, it is helpful to understand some of the conventions or techniques of Hebrew poetry. Hebrew poetry often structures phrases in parallel to one another (see **"Hebrew Poetry," p. 741**). Some of these phrases express similar ideas or imagery and are called synonymous parallelism. Other phrases contrast with one another and are called antithetical parallelism. How does the use of parallelism not only repeat but also develop the themes and images expressed in this psalm?

Composed by an anonymous author, Ps. 151 is written in the first person, with David as the speaker, describing two episodes in his life. This is the only psalm to reference explicit episodes from David's life (other psalms reference David's life in the superscriptions). God's choice of David, although a shepherd and the youngest son (vv. 1, 4–5), frames David's praise of God as a musician and psalmist. The psalm concludes with David's defeat of "the foreigner," Goliath.

In addition to reading Ps. 151 as a poem in isolation, one can also read it alongside the stories of David's anointing, defeat of Goliath, and playing the lyre in 1 Sam. 16–18. How do these portrayals compare and contrast?

Henry W. Morisada Rietz

This psalm is ascribed to David as his own composition (though it is outside the number[a]), after he had fought in single combat with Goliath.

[1] I was small among my brothers
 and the youngest in my father's house;
I tended my father's sheep.

[2] My hands made a harp;
 my fingers fashioned a lyre.

[3] And who will tell my Lord?
 The Lord himself; it is he who hears.[b]

[4] It was he who sent his messenger[c]
 and took me from my father's sheep

and anointed me with his anointing oil.

[5] My brothers were handsome and tall,
 but the Lord was not pleased with them.

[6] I went out to meet the foreigner,[d]
 and he cursed me by his idols.

[7] But I drew his own sword;
 I beheaded him and removed disgrace
 from the people of Israel.

a 151.1 Other ancient authorities add *of the one hundred fifty* (psalms) *b* 151.3 Other ancient authorities add *everything*; others add *me*; others read *who will hear me* *c* 151.4 Gk: Q ms *prophet* *d* 151.6 Gk: Q ms *Philistine*

Superscription. *This psalm is ascribed to David as . . . Goliath.* This superscription is found in the Greek manuscripts of Ps. 151, although it is not part of the original composition of the psalm. In place of this superscription, the Hebrew manuscript found in the Qumran caves reads, "A Hallelujah of David, the son of Jesse." *As his own composition* (Gk. "idiographos") emphasizes that David was the author, although Davidic authorship is highly unlikely. Some Greek manuscripts add the clarification "of the one hundred fifty"—to *though it is outside the number*—referring to the one hundred fifty psalms of the Hebrew MT. *After he had fought in single combat with Goliath* specifies the occasion of Ps. 151 after David's one-on-one fight with Goliath (cf. 1 Sam. 17).

1 *I was small among my brothers and the youngest in my father's house.* Note the synonymous parallelism. See v. 5 and 1 Sam. 16:6–12. **2** *Harp* and *lyre* are synonymous. In 1 Sam. 16:14–23, David is recruited to play the *lyre* to comfort Saul when an "evil spirit" torments him. 11QPsalms[a] continues with "and I gave glory to the Lord, I said in my soul. The mountains do not witness to him, and the hills do not proclaim. The trees cherished my words and the flock my works." **3** 11QPsalms[a] preserves a longer version with parallel phrases. **4** In place of *messenger*, the Qumran manuscript specifies "the prophet Samuel," who in 1 Sam. 16 secretly anoints David following God's instructions (16:12–13). Anointing with oil indicated a person was an agent of God, often the king. Saul continues to reign as king until his death in 1 Sam. 31. It is only after Saul's death that David is publicly anointed king of Judah (2 Sam. 2:4) and then of all Israel (2 Sam. 5:3). **5** Cf. v. 1 and 1 Sam. 16:6–12. **6–7** Instead of *foreigner*, the Qumran manuscript has "Philistine." For the story of David's defeating the Philistine champion Goliath, see 1 Sam. 17. *Cursed me by his idols* puts 1 Sam. 17:43b—"the Philistine cursed David by his gods"—in the first person. Interestingly, Ps. 151 does not mention David slinging a stone in his fight against Goliath. In the Hebrew MT, 1 Sam. 17:50 (which is not in the LXX) has David killing Goliath with "a sling and a stone," specifying that "there was no sword in David's hand," while 1 Sam. 17:51 has David killing Goliath with his own sword and then beheading him.

3 MACCABEES

3 Maccabees and the Canon

The name 3 Maccabees is misleading because the book does not deal with the Maccabees at all. It describes instead a persecution located mainly in Egypt and taking place some fifty years before the Maccabean Revolt, at a time when Jerusalem was still ruled by the Ptolemies. How and when it got its present name is a mystery, but because it also deals with a persecution culminating in the establishment of a festival and because it may have been inspired by the experience of Alexandrian Jews observing the events of the Maccabean Revolt, it may have been stored in a scroll box with the other books of Maccabees and named accordingly.

In antiquity, the manuscript tradition for the four books of Maccabees diverged. We have three major manuscripts of the Septuagint (an early Gk. translation of the Hebrew Bible) surviving from late antiquity (fourth to sixth century CE), but only one of the three manuscripts contains all four books. The version translated by Jerome into Latin, which became the Vulgate (the basis for the Western European Bible), contained only 1–2 Maccabees, and thus only 1–2 Maccabees are officially part of the canon in the Roman Catholic Church. In the eastern Mediterranean, all four books continued to be read in Greek and were included in the canon by the Eastern Orthodox Church.

Because the book was not included in Jerome's translation, it was unknown in Western Europe until the early modern period. In the Eastern Orthodox tradition, although the book was canonical, it had little influence. The festival mentioned in the book was observed by the Jews of Alexandria but ceased to exist when the Jews were driven out of Egypt in the second century CE, and thus it did not become part of later Jewish tradition as Hanukkah (1–2 Maccabees) and Purim (Esther) did. Third Maccabees is primarily of interest today for the light it casts on the Jews of Alexandria in the Hellenistic and Roman periods.

Authorship, Date, and Literary History

There is general agreement that the book was written in Greek by an unknown author living in Alexandria, Egypt. The Greek, while not always graceful, is complex and shows that the author was aiming to reach an audience who had considerable Greek education.

Assigning a date is more difficult. The outside limits are 217 BCE (the date of the battle of Raphia, mentioned in the text) at the earliest and 117 CE (the end of the Jewish presence in Alexandria in the second century). Several references suggest the author knew about the Maccabean Revolt, which would place the date after 167 BCE. More narrowly, the book is generally assigned to the late Hellenistic period (because of its knowledge of the Ptolemaic court, the bureaucratic language of documents it cites, and similarities with other late Hellenistic Jewish texts) or the early Roman period (because of a reference to a poll tax and tensions between the Jews of Alexandria and their neighbors, more characteristic of the Roman period). The focus on the Ptolemies makes a date in the Hellenistic period more likely, but a Roman date is not impossible.

Reading Guide

Like the books of Maccabees, the book envisions a crisis confronting the Jewish community that arises unexpectedly from a previously stable situation. As in the case of the Maccabees, events affecting the Jews of Jerusalem are intertwined with events in Alexandria. Shortly before the Maccabean Revolt, Antiochus IV suffers a setback in Egypt and vents his wrath on the Jews of Jerusalem; in 3 Maccabees, Ptolemy IV Philopator is humiliated in Jerusalem and turns his anger on the Jews of Alexandria.

The book begins with a historically verifiable setting, the battle of Raphia (217 BCE), which marked the victory of Ptolemy IV Philopator over Antiochus III in the Fourth Syrian War. The foiling of a plot to assassinate the king is also at least partially historical. The subsequent events, however, are not found in any other historical source for the reign of Philopator.

Ptolemy IV visits Jerusalem as part of a victory tour after the battle. Initially, his attitude toward the Jews is favorable, but things turn sour when the Jews of Jerusalem try to explain that their law forbids anyone from entering the Holy of Holies. Philopator's attempt to invade the temple is foiled by miraculous intervention. The king withdraws but turns his wrath upon the Jews of Egypt, who become the focus of the rest of the story.

Philopator begins by registering the Jews in a census, but when he meets resistance, he embarks upon a genocidal plan to gather all the Jews of Egypt into a hippodrome and have them trampled to death by elephants. God miraculously prevents Philopator from carrying out the first two attempts at execution; on the third occasion, a vision causes the elephants to turn back on their handlers, sparing the Jews. Philopator, humbled and repentant, institutes a feast commemorating the deliverance of the Jews, and the book ends in rejoicing, while the apostates who collaborated with the king are punished.

The festival commemorating the deliverance from the elephants was observed in Egypt until the Jewish presence in Egypt was eliminated in the second century CE. Josephus tells a similar story about persecution involving elephants but locates it under a different Ptolemy. It appears that the origin of the festival had been forgotten before either 3 Maccabees or Josephus's work was written.

The book of 3 Maccabees can be read either as a somber tale depicting a community under constant threat of persecution or as a tale of an immigrant community that thrives and ultimately triumphs in occasional times of trial; elements of both are present in the text, and it is up to the reader to decide which is predominant. Philopator, like Esther's Ahasuerus, is a flawed gentile king who ultimately becomes a champion of the Jews. The Jews of Egypt have both friends and enemies at the court and in Alexandria. In contrast with Esther, more attention is given to the problem of apostates (Jews who abandon their ways to gain favor in the eyes of the king). Ultimately, Philopator will learn that it is the faithful Jews who make the most loyal subjects.

Sara Raup Johnson

1 When Philopator learned from those who returned that the regions that he had controlled had been seized by Antiochus, he gave orders to all his forces, both infantry and cavalry, took with him his sister Arsinoë, and marched out to the region near Raphia, where the army of Antiochus was encamped. [2]But a certain Theodotus, determined to carry out the plot he had devised, took with him the best of the Ptolemaic arms that had been previously issued to him[a] and crossed over by night to the tent of Ptolemy, intending single-handedly to kill him and thereby end the war. [3]But Dositheus, known as the son of Drimylus, a Jew by birth who later changed his customs and abandoned the ancestral traditions, had led the king away and arranged that a certain insignificant man should sleep in the tent, and so it turned out that this man incurred the punishment meant for the king.[b] [4]A fierce battle ensued, and when matters were turning out rather in favor of Antiochus, Arsinoë went to the troops with wailing and tears, her locks all disheveled, and exhorted them to defend themselves and their children and wives bravely, promising to give them each two minas of gold if

a 1.2 Or *the best of the Ptolemaic soldiers previously put under his command*   b 1.3 Gk *that one*

1:1–7 The book opens with the Seleucid and Ptolemaic forces marshaling for the battle of Raphia (217 BCE), which would result in victory for Egypt in the Fourth Syrian War. The style in these verses resembles that of historians like Polybius (see **"Historical Fiction," p. 1635**). It is assumed the audience will be familiar with the history and customs of the Ptolemaic royal court. **1:1** The narrative begins so abruptly that some believe the original beginning has been lost; there is no manuscript evidence to support any other beginning. Ptolemy IV Philopator (king of Egypt 221–205 BCE); Antiochus III the Great (king of Syria 222–187 BCE). Arsinoë is Ptolemy's sister and later wife. **1:2–3** The description of Raphia parallels the narrative given by the historian Polybius (5.80–83). Polybius mentions the assassination attempt by Theodotus the Aetolian but not the intervention of the Jewish courtier Dositheus (in Polybius, the plan fails due to bad luck). As an apostate Jew, Dositheus presents an ironic foil to the Jews who later resist Philopator; Dositheus embodies the loyalty of the Jews to the crown, which the author values, but his loyalty preserves the life of a tyrant who will later persecute his people. Dositheus ("gift of God") was a common name among Hellenistic Egyptian Jews. **1:4** Polybius criticized historians who attempted to elicit fear and pity as tragedians did ("tragic/pathetic history"). Both 2 Maccabees and 3 Maccabees were guilty of this (cf. 1:16–18; 4:1–10; 5:48–51). Here, the author sensationalizes the role of Philopator's sister in rallying the troops during the height of battle. *Mina*. A weight equivalent to sixty shekels or one hundred

they won the battle. ⁵And so it came about that the enemy was routed in the action, and many captives also were taken. ⁶Now that he had foiled the plot, Ptolemy^c decided to visit the neighboring cities and encourage them. ⁷By doing this and by endowing their sacred enclosures with gifts, he strengthened the morale of his subjects.

8 Since the Jews had sent some of their council and elders to greet him, to bring him gifts of welcome, and to congratulate him on what had happened, he was all the more eager to visit them as soon as possible. ⁹After he had arrived in Jerusalem, he offered sacrifice to the supreme God and made thank offerings and did what was fitting for the place. Then, upon entering the place and being impressed by its excellence and its beauty, ¹⁰he marveled at the good order of the temple and conceived a desire to enter the sanctuary. ¹¹When they said that this was not permitted because not even members of their own nation were allowed to enter, not even all of the priests, but only the high priest who was preeminent over all—and he only once a year—the king was by no means persuaded. ¹²Even after the law had been read to him, he did not cease to maintain that he ought to enter, saying, "Even if those men are deprived of this honor, I ought not to be." ¹³And he inquired why, when he entered every other temple,^d no one there had stopped him. ¹⁴And someone answered thoughtlessly that it was wrong to place any significance in that.^e ¹⁵"But since this has happened," the king^f said, "why should not I at least enter, whether they wish it or not?"

16 Then the priests in all their vestments prostrated themselves and entreated the supreme God to aid in the present situation and to avert the violence of this evil design, and they filled the temple with cries and tears; ¹⁷those who remained behind in the city were agitated and hurried out, supposing that something mysterious was occurring. ¹⁸Young women who had been secluded in their chambers rushed out with their mothers, sprinkled their hair with dust,^g and filled the streets with groans and lamentations. ¹⁹Those women who had recently been arrayed for marriage abandoned the bridal chambers^h prepared for wedded union and, neglecting proper modesty, in a disorderly rush flocked together in the city. ²⁰Mothers and nurses abandoned even newborn children here and there, some in houses and some in the streets, and without a backward look they crowded together at the most high temple. ²¹Various were the supplications of those gathered there because of what the king was profanely plotting. ²²In addition, the bolder of the citizens would not tolerate the completion of his plans or the fulfillment of his intended purpose. ²³They shouted to their compatriots to take arms and die courageously for the ancestral law and created a considerable disturbance in the place, and, being barely restrained by the old men and the elders,ⁱ they resorted to the same posture

c 1.6 Gk he   d 1.13 Or entered the temple precincts   e 1.14 Gk take that as a portent   f 1.15 Gk he   g 1.18 Other ancient authorities add and ashes   h 1.19 Or the canopies   i 1.23 Other ancient authorities read priests

drachmae, about one-fourth of a year's wages for an agricultural laborer. **1:5–7** Philopator's tour of the neighboring towns sets the stage for a confrontation with the Jerusalem temple.

1:8–15 The narrative is organized around two parallel crises: Philopator's attempt to invade the Jerusalem temple and Philopator's persecution of the Jews of Egypt and Alexandria. Josephus (*Ag. Ap.* 2.53–56) reports a similar persecution of the Jews of Alexandria involving elephants during the reign of Ptolemy VIII Physcon (ca. 145 BCE). The connection between events in Jerusalem and Alexandria is unique to 3 Maccabees. The sequence here reverses that found in some accounts of the Maccabean Revolt, where the humiliation of Antiochus IV at the hands of the Romans in Alexandria leads to a crackdown on the revolt in Jerusalem (2 Macc. 5:11; cf. Dan. 11:30). **1:8–11** In 217 BCE, Coele-Syria (including Jerusalem) was under Ptolemaic control. The Jews are at first as eager to welcome Philopator as he is eager to honor their God. Conflict arises when Philopator is told that the law prohibits his entrance into the Holy of Holies. **1:12** Lack of self-control and disrespect for the law mark Philopator as a Greek tyrant (cf. 5:20, 42).

1:16–29 The populace joins the priests in protesting the attack on the temple. Depiction of distress is characteristic of "tragic" history. **1:18–20** Emphasis is on women at various stages of life: unmarried maidens, brides, and mothers. **1:22–23** Elders dissuade those advocating for violence. The author prefers nonviolent protest and prayer, contrasting with many Maccabean texts (1–2 Maccabees,

of supplication as the others. ²⁴Meanwhile, the crowd, as before, was engaged in prayer, ²⁵while the elders near the king tried in various ways to change his arrogant mind from the plan that he had conceived. ²⁶But he, in his arrogance, took heed of nothing and began now to approach, determined to bring the aforesaid plan to a conclusion. ²⁷When those who were around him observed this, they turned, together with our people, to call upon him who has all power to defend them in the present trouble and not to overlook this unlawful and haughty deed. ²⁸The continuous, vehement, and concerted cry of the crowds*ʲ* resulted in an immense uproar, ²⁹for it seemed that not only the people but also the walls and the whole earth around echoed, because indeed all at that time*ᵏ* preferred death to the profanation of the place.

2 [[Then the high priest Simon, facing the sanctuary, bending his knees, and extending his hands with calm dignity, prayed as follows:]]*ˡ* ²"Lord, Lord, king of the heavens and sovereign of all creation, holy among the holy ones, the only ruler, almighty, give attention to us who are suffering grievously from an impious and profane man, puffed up in his audacity and power. ³For you, the creator of all things and the governor of all, are a just ruler, and you judge those who have done anything in insolence and arrogance. ⁴You destroyed those who in the past committed injustice, among whom were even giants who trusted in their strength and boldness, whom you destroyed by bringing on them a boundless flood. ⁵You consumed with fire and sulfur the people of Sodom

who acted arrogantly, who were notorious for their vices,*ᵐ* and you made them an example to those who should come afterward. ⁶By inflicting many and varied punishments on the audacious pharaoh who had enslaved your holy people Israel, you made known your sovereignty; thus you made known your great strength. ⁷And when he pursued them with chariots and a mass of troops, you overwhelmed him in the depths of the sea but carried through safely those who had put their confidence in you, the Ruler over the whole creation. ⁸And when they had seen the works of your hand, they praised you, the Almighty. ⁹You, O King, when you had created the boundless and immeasurable earth, chose this city and sanctified this place for your name, though you have no need of anything, and when you had glorified it by your magnificent manifestation, you made it a firm foundation for the glory of your great and honored name. ¹⁰And because you love the house of Israel, you promised that, if we should have reverses and tribulation should overtake us, you would listen to our petition when we come to this place and pray. ¹¹And indeed you are faithful and true. ¹²And because oftentimes when our fathers were oppressed you helped them in their humiliation and rescued them from great evils, ¹³see now, O holy King, that because of our many and great sins we are crushed with suffering, subjected to our enemies, and overtaken by helplessness. ¹⁴In our downfall this audacious

j 1.28 Other ancient authorities read vehement cry of the assembled crowds k 1.29 Other ancient authorities lack at that time l 2.1 Many ancient authorities lack 2.1 m 2.5 Other ancient authorities read secret in their vices

Judith). **1:27** *People* is used throughout the NRSVue to translate a variety of Greek terms ("ethnos," "genos," etc.) when referring to the Jews. **1:29** *The place.* An idiom for the temple. The willingness of the faithful to die rather than see the temple profaned will be paralleled by the willingness of the Jews of Egypt and Alexandria to face death rather than apostatize.
2:1–20 The prayer asking God to save the temple is balanced by the prayer in chap. 6 asking God to spare the Jews of Egypt. Both prayers follow an established pattern among Greek-speaking Jews: praises of God, God's past acts, confession, and an appeal to God to act in service of God's glory despite the people's unworthiness. **2:1** This verse is missing in some manuscripts. Without attribution to Simon, the prayer would be read as a spontaneous utterance by the people. Attributing the prayer to Simon (presumably "Simon the Good," whom some traditions locate around 200 BCE) centers the role of the high priest. It also enhances the parallelism with the prayer in chap. 6, which is attributed to Eleazar, a priest in Alexandria. **2:2–3** The prayer begins by invoking the many names of God and praising God. **2:4–8** God's past actions are recalled to motivate action in the present. **2:9–11** God promised to answer Israel if they prayed in the Jerusalem temple. **2:13–20** The supplicant, acknowledging *our many and great sins* (v. 13; cf. v. 19), calls upon God to act, if for no other reason so that the arrogant may not boast.

and profane man undertakes to violate the holy place on earth dedicated to your glorious name. [15]For your dwelling is the heaven of heavens, unapproachable by human beings. [16]But because you were pleased that your glory should dwell among your people Israel, you sanctified this place. [17]Do not punish us for the defilement committed by these men or call us to account for this profanation; otherwise the transgressors will boast in their wrath and exult in the arrogance of their tongue, saying, [18]'We have trampled down the house of holiness as the houses of the abominations are trampled down.' [19]Wipe away our sins and disperse our errors and reveal your mercy at this hour. [20]Speedily let your mercies overtake us, put praises in the mouths of those who are downcast and broken in spirit, and give us peace."

21 Thereupon God, who oversees all things, the first Father of all, holy among the holy ones, having heard the lawful supplication, scourged him who had exalted himself in insolence and audacity. [22]He shook him on this side and that as a reed is shaken by the wind, so that he lay helpless on the ground and, besides being paralyzed in his limbs, was unable even to speak, since he was ensnared by a righteous judgment. [23]Then both Friends and bodyguards, seeing the severe punishment that had overtaken him and fearing that he would lose his life, quickly dragged him out, panic-stricken in their exceedingly great fear. [24]After a while he recovered, and though he had been punished, he by no means repented but went away uttering bitter threats.

25 When he arrived in Egypt, he increased in his deeds of malice, abetted by the previously mentioned drinking companions and comrades who were strangers to everything just. [26]He was not content with his uncounted licentious deeds but even continued with such audacity that he established an evil reputation in the various localities, and many of his Friends, intently observing the king's purpose, themselves also followed his will. [27]He proposed to inflict public disgrace on the nation, and he set up a stone on the tower in the courtyard with this inscription: [28]"None of those who do not sacrifice shall enter their sanctuaries, and all Jews shall be subjected to a registration involving poll tax and to the status of slaves. Those who object to this are to be taken by force and put to death; [29]those who are registered are also to be branded on their bodies by fire with the ivy-leaf symbol of Dionysus, and they shall also be reduced to their former limited status." [30]In order that he might not appear to be an enemy of all, he inscribed below: "But if any of them prefer to join those who have been initiated into the mysteries, they shall have equal citizenship with the Alexandrians."

31 Now some, with an obvious abhorrence of the price to be exacted for maintaining the piety of their city,[n] readily gave themselves up,

n 2.31 Meaning of Gk uncertain

2:21–24 At Jerusalem, as later in Alexandria, God responds to the prayers of the people with divine intervention, striking Philopator down. The episode parallels 2 Macc. 3, where Heliodorus, the minister of Seleucus IV (187–175 BCE), was divinely driven back from the temple (ca. 178 BCE). Heliodorus, unlike Philopator, goes away repentant. 2:23 *Friends and bodyguards* are titles of high-ranking courtiers, generally portrayed negatively (2:25–26; 5:3, 19, 26, 29, 34, 44; 6:23; 7:3).
2:25–33 The negative portrait of Philopator's character is partially drawn from the Greek historical record, which is uniformly hostile to the king (because of his treatment of Cleomenes of Sparta and his reputation as a weak king who allowed Egypt to deteriorate). 2:25 *Drinking companions* have not been *previously mentioned* but fit into the picture of the king as a heavy drinker. 2:26 Philopator and *his Friends* acquire an evil reputation throughout Egypt. Later he will blame his actions on the influence of these *Friends* (7:3). 2:28–30 This edict is probably a fiction loosely based on real decrees. Initiation into the mysteries of Dionysus was considered an honor, not a thing to be forced. Here, however, the focus is on the loss of access to *sanctuaries* ("houses of prayer" are known from Alexandria at this time, predecessors to the later synagogues) and on acceptance of the mark of a foreign god. Registration for the poll tax was associated with Egyptian rather than Greek civic status and would have been regarded as imposing a loss of status (*status of slaves, former limited status*). The decree is intended to force as many violations of Jewish law as possible while also humiliating the Jews. Equality with the Greek citizens is offered as a lure, while association with lower-class Egyptians is threatened as a punishment. 2:31–33 The theme of apostasy, first hinted at in Dositheus, comes to the fore. Unlike the Jews of Palestine, who were all threatened alike, the

since they expected to enhance their reputation by their future association with the king. [32]But the majority acted firmly with a courageous spirit and did not abandon their piety, and by paying money in exchange for life they boldly attempted to save themselves from the registration. [33]They remained resolutely hopeful of obtaining help, and they abhorred those who separated themselves from them, considering them to be enemies of the nation and depriving them of common fellowship and mutual help.

3 When the impious king comprehended this situation, he became so infuriated that not only was he enraged against those Jews who lived in Alexandria but was still more bitterly hostile toward those in the countryside, and he ordered that all should promptly be gathered into one place and put to death by the most cruel means. [2]While these matters were being arranged, a hostile rumor was circulated against the people by some who conspired to do them ill, a pretext being given by a report that they hindered others[o] from the observance of their customs. [3]The Jews, however, continued to maintain goodwill and unswerving loyalty toward the dynasty, [4]but because they worshiped God and conducted themselves by his law, they kept their separateness with respect to foods. For this reason they appeared hateful to some, [5]but since they adorned their style of life with the good deeds of upright people, they were established in good repute with everyone. [6]Nevertheless, foreigners paid no heed to the good conduct of the people, which was common talk among all; [7]instead, they gossiped about the differences in worship and foods, alleging that these people were loyal neither to the king nor to his authorities but were hostile and greatly opposed to his government. So it was no ordinary reproach that they attached to them.

8 The Greeks in the city, though wronged in no way, when they saw an unexpected tumult around these people and the crowds that suddenly were forming, were not strong enough to help them, for they lived under tyranny. They did try to console them, being grieved at the situation, and expected that matters would change, [9]for such a great community ought not be left to its fate when it had committed no offense. [10]And already some of their neighbors and friends and business associates had taken some of them aside privately and were pledging to protect them and to do everything in their power to help.

11 Then the king, boastful of his present good fortune and not considering the might of the supreme God, but assuming that he

o 3.2 Gk them p 3.21 Other ancient authorities read partners of our regular priests

Jews of Alexandria are presented with a stark choice, and the choices they make will divide them. *Some . . . gave themselves up*, but *the majority* choose to resist. Those who conform are said to be motivated by ambition rather than fear. For those who choose to resist, payment of bribes to avoid being registered is regarded as an appropriate option. *The majority* who resist shun the minority who comply, foreshadowing the punishment of the apostates in 7:14–15.

3:1–10 This passage introduces the relationship between the Jews and their neighbors, a recurring theme. The Jewish community had friends as well as enemies. **3:1** The king's wrath extends to include the Jews of the *countryside* and shifts from registration to execution. The Ptolemaic government distinguished between the city of Alexandria and the rest of the land of Egypt. *The most cruel means* are not explained until 5:1. **3:3** The Jews are repeatedly portrayed as loyal subjects, even when persecuted. **3:4–5** The hostility of *some* is explained by reference to *separateness with respect to foods*. Greek hospitality emphasized the importance of sharing food, but since it was impossible to know which foods at a host's table were kosher, observant Jews avoided eating with gentiles (see **"Diet," p. 268**). This led to the widespread charge that Jews were hostile to all humanity. The author emphasizes, however, that the Jews were *in good repute with everyone* due to their upright conduct. **3:8** *Greeks* are singled out as being sympathetic toward the Jews.

3:11–30 Another alleged royal decree (cf. 2:27–30). This edict proclaiming a persecution of the Jews will be reversed by another in chap. 7. Esther contains the same pattern of an edict of persecution proclaimed and later reversed by a newer decree (see **"Reversal," p. 1642**). Scholars do not agree on whether Greek Esther (Gk. Esth. 13:1–7; 16:1–24) was modeling its decrees on the language in 3 Maccabees or vice versa, but there are verbal parallels between the two. The letter imitates the convoluted bureaucratic style of government documents (see **"Historical Fiction," p. 1635**). **3:11** Philopator is arrogant and does not consider the superiority of God (cf. Nebuchadnezzar in

would persevere constantly in his same
purpose, wrote this letter against them:
12 "King Ptolemy Philopator to his generals and soldiers in Egypt and all its districts,
greetings and good health:
13 "I myself and our government are faring well. [14]When our expedition took place in
Asia, as you yourselves know, it was brought
to conclusion, according to plan, by the gods'
deliberate alliance with us in battle, [15]and we
considered that we should not rule the nations
inhabiting Coelesyria and Phoenicia by the
power of the spear but should cherish them
with clemency and great benevolence, gladly
treating them well. [16]And when we had granted very great revenues to the temples in the
cities, we came on to Jerusalem also and went
up to honor the temple of those wicked people, who never cease from their folly. [17]They
accepted our presence by word but insincerely
by deed, because when we proposed to enter
their inner temple and honor it with magnificent and most beautiful offerings, [18]they were
carried away by their traditional arrogance
and excluded us from entering, but they were
spared the exercise of our power because of
the benevolence that we have toward all. [19]By
maintaining their manifest ill-will toward us,
they become the only people among all nations who hold their heads high in defiance of
kings and their own benefactors and are unwilling to regard any action as sincere.
20 "But we, when we arrived in Egypt victorious, accommodated ourselves to their folly and did as was proper, since we treat all nations with benevolence. [21]Among other things,
we made known to all our amnesty toward
their compatriots here, both because of their
alliance with us and the myriad affairs liberally entrusted to them from the beginning, and
we ventured to make a change, by deciding
both to deem them worthy of Alexandrian
citizenship and to make them participants in
our regular religious rites.[p] [22]But in their innate malice they took this in a contrary spirit
and disdained what is good. Since they incline
constantly to evil, [23]they not only spurn the
priceless citizenship, but also both by speech
and by silence they abhor those few among
them who are sincerely disposed toward us;
in every situation, in accordance with their infamous way of life, they secretly suspect that
we may soon alter our policy. [24]Therefore, fully convinced by these indications that they are
ill-disposed toward us in every way, we have
taken precautions so that, if a sudden disorder
later arises against us, we shall not have these
impious people behind our backs as traitors
and barbarous enemies. [25]Therefore we have
given orders that, as soon as this letter arrives,
you are to send to us those who live among
you, together with their wives and children,
with insulting and harsh treatment and bound
securely with iron fetters, to suffer the sure
and shameful death that befits enemies. [26]For
when all of these have been punished, we are
sure that for the remaining time the government will be established for ourselves in good
order and in the best state. [27]But those who
shelter any of the Jews, whether old people or
children or even infants, will be tortured to
death with the most hateful torments, together with their families. [28]Any who are willing to
give information will receive the property of
those who incur the punishment, and also two
thousand drachmas from the royal treasury,
and will be awarded their freedom.[q] [29]Every
place detected sheltering a Jew is to be made

q 3.28 Gk *crowned with freedom*

Dan. 4:37). **3:12** Opening phrases wishing well to the recipient reflect the form of a letter. Specifying the king's title (*Philopator*) and a list of addressees is more commonly found in the first century BCE than in the third, suggesting composition at a later date. **3:15** Philopator emphasizes his benevolence (also vv. 18, 20), ironic when ordering a persecution. **3:16** The hostile language draws on traditional anti-Jewish accusations such as hatred of humanity: *wicked people*, *folly*; see also "insincerely" (v. 17), "traditional arrogance" (v. 18), "manifest ill-will" (v. 19), "innate malice" (v. 22), and "infamous way of life" (v. 23). **3:21** Philopator distorts the narrative to cast himself in a better light, misrepresenting the decree in 2:27–30 as a generous offer of citizenship. Ironically, while attacking the Jews, Philopator praises their former reputation for loyalty and service, which will become central to the king's praise of the Jews in chap. 7. **3:24** Fear that the Jews may be disloyal due to their distinctive practices is a common anti-Jewish charge (e.g., Ezra 4:11–16), one that the author attempts to refute by emphasizing Jewish loyalty even in times of persecution. **3:27–29** The threat to punish those who shelter the Jews underscores the courage of the "Greeks in the city" who promised to help, although "they lived under tyranny" themselves (3:8–10).

Going Deeper: Historical Fiction (3 Maccabees 3:12–29)

The book of 3 Maccabees opens with the historical battle of Raphia. All the actors in the first chapter are historical figures: Philopator, Arsinoë, Antiochus the Great, and even Theodotus the Aetolian. The character of Philopator is consistent with (unfavorable) descriptions given by Greek writers like Polybius and Plutarch. The author's style shifts in 1:1–7 to imitate Hellenistic historians, just as the language of inscriptions and decrees (2:27–30; 3:12–29; 7:1–9) mimics bureaucratic documents from the Ptolemaic period.

However, most scholars do not believe the events involving the Jews in the story happened—certainly not under Philopator. Josephus and 3 Maccabees say that a festival commemorating deliverance from drunken elephants was celebrated by the Jews of Alexandria. They have completely different stories about how and when the persecution happened. It appears the Alexandrians themselves did not remember.

History and fiction are similar in that both employ narrative techniques to describe events located in the past. The difference between the two can only be located from two perspectives: the intent of the author and the understanding of the audience. The intent of the author will never be fully known to the modern reader. The way in which an audience understands a text may differ from one reader to another and may change over time.

The term *historical fiction* (even *novel*) has been applied to a number of books in this study Bible, including 2–3 Maccabees, Esther, Judith, Daniel, and Tobit. Judith contains such outrageous historical errors (e.g., the Babylonian Nebuchadnezzar is portrayed as king of the Assyrians) that the author may be signaling that the story is fictional. In other cases (Esther, Daniel, 2 Maccabees), it is harder to decide what the author intended and how the audience understood the story. Generically, these texts differ from one another and only superficially resemble the Greek novels to which they have been compared. They cannot be forced into a single category.

What they do (possibly) share is the willingness of the author to use plausible-sounding historical data as fictional material in order to tell a more persuasive story. Ancient people understood the difference between truth and fiction. Like modern audiences watching a historical film, many ancient readers may have recognized the fictional elements and enjoyed them. The moral of the story mattered more than the accuracy of the historical plot.

Sara Raup Johnson

unapproachable and burned with fire and shall become useless for all time to any mortal creature." [30]The letter was written in the above form.

4 In every place, then, where this decree arrived, a feast at public expense was arranged for the nations with shouts and gladness, for the inveterate enmity that had long ago been in their minds was now made evident and outspoken. [2]But among the Jews there was indescribable mourning, lamentation, and tearful cries and groans; everywhere their hearts were burning, and they groaned because of the unexpected destruction that had suddenly been decreed for them. [3]What district or city, or what habitable place at all, or what streets were not filled with mourning and wailing for them? [4]For with such a harsh and ruthless spirit were they being sent off, all together, by the generals in every city that at

the sight of their unusual punishments even some of their enemies, perceiving the common object of pity before their eyes, reflected on the uncertainty of life and shed tears at the most miserable expulsion of these people. [5]For a multitude of gray-headed old men, sluggish and bent with age, was being led away, forced to march at a swift pace by the violence with which they were driven in such a shameful manner. [6]And young women who had just entered the bridal chamber[r] to share married life exchanged joy for wailing, their myrrh-perfumed hair sprinkled with ashes, and were carried away unveiled, all together raising a lament instead of a wedding song, as they were torn by the harsh treatment of foreign nations. [7]In bonds and in public view they were violently dragged along as far as the place of embarkation. [8]Their husbands, in the prime of youth, their necks encircled

r 4.6 Or *the canopy*

4:1–10 The lamentation of the Jews of Egypt echoes the distress of the people of Jerusalem, with the same descriptive elements borrowed from "tragic history" (see note on 1:4). 4:1 The joy of the *nations* is chilling. By the end, the Jews will be the ones feasting. 4:6 The motif of the bride's joy turned to a funeral lament is widespread in classical and rabbinic literature. 4:8 *Hades* is a

with ropes instead of garlands, spent the remaining days of their marriage festival in lamentations instead of feasting and youthful revelry, seeing Hades already lying at their feet. [9]They were brought on board like wild animals, driven under the constraint of iron bonds; some were fastened by the neck to the benches of the boats; others had their feet secured by unbreakable fetters, [10]and in addition they were confined under a solid deck, so that, with their eyes in total darkness, they would undergo treatment befitting traitors during the whole voyage.

[11] When these people had been brought to the place called Schedia and the voyage was concluded as the king had decreed, he commanded that they should be enclosed in the hippodrome that had been built with an immense perimeter wall in front of the city and that was well suited to make them an obvious spectacle to all coming back into the city and to those from the city[s] going out into the country, so that they could neither communicate with the king's forces nor in any way claim to be inside the circuit of the city.[t] [12]And when this had happened, the king, hearing that the Jews' compatriots from the city frequently went out in secret to lament bitterly the ignoble misfortune of their kindred, [13]ordered in his rage that these people be dealt with in precisely the same fashion as the others, not omitting any detail of their punishment. [14]The entire people was to be registered individually, not for the hard labor that has been briefly mentioned before but to be tortured with the outrages that he had ordered and at the

end to be destroyed in the space of a single day. [15]The registration of these people was therefore conducted with bitter haste and zealous intensity from the rising of the sun until its setting, coming to an end after forty days but still not completed.

16 The king was greatly and continually filled with joy, organizing banquets in honor of all his idols, with a mind alienated from truth and with a profane mouth, praising speechless things that are not able even to communicate or to come to one's help and uttering improper words against the supreme God. [17]But after the previously mentioned interval of time the scribes declared to the king that they were no longer able to take the census of the Jews because of their immense number, [18]though most of them were still in the country, some still residing in their homes, and some at the place;[u] the task was impossible for all the generals in Egypt. [19]After he had threatened them severely, charging that they had been bribed to contrive a means of escape, he was clearly convinced about the matter [20]when they said and proved that both the papyrus and the reeds they used for writing had already given out. [21]But this was an act of the invincible providence of him who was aiding the Jews from heaven.

5 Then the king, completely inflexible, was filled with overpowering anger and wrath, so he summoned Hermon, keeper of the elephants, [2]and ordered him on the following

s 4.11 Gk *those of them*   *t* 4.11 Or *claim protection of the walls*; meaning of Gk uncertain   *u* 4.18 Other ancient authorities read *on the way*

standard Greek translation of the Hebrew term "Sheol." Both terms refer to the underground home of deceased spirits, not to a punitive hell (see **"Sheol," p. 695**).

4:11–21 The Jews are brought together in a single location outside Alexandria to await execution. **4:11** *Hippodrome.* An enclosed racetrack, like the Roman circus. Confining all the Jews of Egypt into one hippodrome is one of many comic exaggerations. **4:14** The author satirizes the top-heavy Egyptian bureaucracy by having the king continue to register the Jews even though the goal is now execution. **4:16** The condemnation of idols (*praising speechless things*) is a common motif in Jewish Hellenistic literature. **4:20** The comic absurdity of running out of *papyrus* and *reeds* is compounded by the fact that Egypt was the source of all papyrus in the Mediterranean and had a famously record-intensive bureaucracy. **4:21** The author credits God's *providence* even when the circumstances are absurd (the papyrus shortage, the king's drunken oversleeping).

5:1–51 The king's plans for execution will be foiled three times: the king oversleeps (vv. 10–22), then develops amnesia (vv. 23–44), and finally encounters direct divine intervention (6:16–29). God is given credit for each intervention. The failures of Philopator's plan reflect his character weaknesses: drunken oversleeping (lack of self-control), forgetfulness (dereliction of duty), and anger. **5:1–2** The Jews in the hippodrome are to be trampled to death by drunken elephants. This grotesque method of execution is attested in antiquity (e.g., Quintus Curtius Rufus, *History of Alexander*, vol. 2, 10.9.18–19). Elephants

day to drug all the elephants—five hundred in number—with large handfuls of frankincense and plenty of unmixed wine and to drive them in, maddened by the lavish abundance of drink, so that the Jews might meet their doom. [3]When he had given these orders he returned to his feasting, together with those of his Friends and of the army who were especially hostile toward the Jews. [4]And Hermon, keeper of the elephants, proceeded faithfully to carry out the orders. [5]The officials in charge of the Jews[v] went out in the evening and bound the hands of the wretched people and arranged for their continued custody through the night, convinced that the whole people would experience its final destruction. [6]For to the nations it appeared that the Jews were left without any aid, because in their bonds they were forcibly confined on every side. [7]But with tears and a voice hard to silence they all called upon the Almighty Lord and Ruler of all power, their merciful God and Father, praying [8]that he avert the evil plot against them and in a glorious manifestation rescue them from the fate now prepared for them. [9]So their entreaty ascended fervently to heaven.

[10]Hermon, however, when he had drugged the pitiless elephants until they had been filled with a great abundance of wine and satiated with frankincense, presented himself at court early in the morning to report to the king about these preparations. [11]But the Lord[w] sent upon the king a portion of sleep, that beneficence that from the beginning, night and day, is bestowed by him who grants it to whomever he wishes. [12]And by the action of the Lord he was overcome by so pleasant and deep a sleep[x] that he quite failed in his lawless purpose and was completely frustrated in his inflexible plan. [13]Then the Jews, since they had escaped the appointed hour, praised their holy God and again implored him who is easily reconciled to show the might of his all-powerful hand to the arrogant nations.

[14]But now, since it was nearly the middle of the tenth hour, the person in charge of the invitations, seeing that the guests were assembled, approached the king and nudged him. [15]And when he had with difficulty roused him, he pointed out that the hour of the banquet was already slipping by, and he gave him an account of the situation. [16]The king, after considering this, returned to his drinking and ordered those present for the banquet to recline opposite him. [17]When this was done he urged them to give themselves over to feasting and to make the present portion of the banquet joyful by celebrating all the more. [18]After the party had been going on for some time, the king summoned Hermon and with bitter threats demanded to know why the Jews had been allowed to remain alive through the present day. [19]But when he, with the corroboration of the king's[y] Friends, pointed out that while it was still night he had carried out completely the order given him, [20]the king,[z] possessed by a savagery worse than that of Phalaris, said that the Jews[a] were benefited by today's sleep, "but," he added, "tomorrow without delay prepare the elephants in the same way for the destruction of the lawless Jews!" [21]When the king had spoken, all those present readily and joyfully with one accord gave their approval, and all went to their own homes. [22]But they did not so much spend the duration of the night in sleep as in devising all sorts of insults for those they thought to be doomed.

[23]Then, as soon as the cock had crowed in the early morning, Hermon, having equipped[b] the animals, began to move them along in the great colonnade. [24]The crowds of the city had been assembled for this most pitiful spectacle and were eagerly waiting for daybreak. [25]But the Jews, being at that very moment at their last gasp, stretched their hands toward

v 5.5 Gk *them* w 5.11 Gk *he* x 5.12 Other ancient authorities add *from evening until the ninth hour* y 5.19 Gk *his* z 5.20 Gk *he* a 5.20 Gk *they* b 5.23 Or *armed*

had to be drugged in order to carry out the execution, but their drunkenness ironically mirrors the king's. *Five hundred* elephants is an absurd number: only seventy-three elephants were deployed by the Egyptians at the battle of Raphia. **5:6–9** As at Jerusalem, the Jews turn to prayer. **5:10–13** The first time Hermon prepares the elephants, Philopator oversleeps. **5:14** Night and day were divided into twelve equal portions, so the *tenth hour* would be late afternoon. **5:15–18** Only after some hours does Philopator summon Hermon and berate him for failing to carry out his duty. **5:19–20** Philopator blames others for his own mistakes, an aspect of the king's character that remains constant (cf. 7:3–5). **5:20** Philopator is compared to *Phalaris* (cf. v. 42), a Greek tyrant (d. 554 BCE) known for cruelty, famously having a bronze bull crafted in which victims could be burned alive. **5:23–28** Again, Hermon prepares the elephants and presents himself at court, but Philopator is struck with amnesia.

heaven and with most tearful supplication and mournful dirges implored the supreme God to help them again at once. [26]The rays of the sun were not yet shed abroad, and while the king was receiving his Friends, Hermon arrived and invited him to come out, indicating that what the king desired was ready for action. [27]But he, on receiving the report and being struck by the unusual invitation to come out—since he had been completely overcome by incomprehension—inquired what the matter was for which this had been so zealously completed for him. [28]This was the act of God who rules over all things, for he had implanted in the king's mind a forgetfulness of the things he had previously devised. [29]Then Hermon and all the king's Friends[c] pointed out that the animals and the armed forces were ready, "O king, according to your eager purpose."[d] [30]But at these words he was filled with an overpowering wrath because by the providence of God his whole mind had been deranged concerning these matters, and with a threatening look he said, [31]"If your parents or children were present, I would have prepared them to be a rich feast for the savage animals instead of the Jews, who give me no ground for complaint and have exhibited to an extraordinary degree a full and firm loyalty to my ancestors. [32]In fact, you would have been deprived of life instead of these, were it not for the affection arising from our common upbringing and lifelong association." [33]So Hermon suffered an unexpected and dangerous threat, and his eyes wavered and his face fell. [34]The Friends one by one sullenly slipped away and dismissed the assembled people to their own occupations. [35]Then the Jews, on hearing what the king had said, praised the manifest Lord God, King of kings, since this also was his aid that they had received.

[36] The king, however, reconvened the banquet in the same manner and urged the guests to return to their celebrating. [37]After summoning Hermon he said in a threatening tone, "How many times, you wretched man, must I give you orders about these things? [38]Equip[e] the elephants now once more for the destruction of the Jews tomorrow!" [39]But the Kinsmen who were at table with him, wondering at his instability of mind, remonstrated as follows: [40]"O king, how long will you put us to the test, as though we are idiots, ordering now for a third time that they be destroyed and again revoking your decree in the matter?[f] [41]As a result the city is in a tumult because of its expectation; it is crowded with mobs of people and also in constant danger of being plundered."

[42] At this the king, a Phalaris in everything and filled with madness, took no account of the changes of mind that had come about within him for the protection of the Jews, and he firmly swore an irrevocable oath that he would send them to Hades without delay, mangled by the knees and feet of the animals, [43]and would also march against Judea and rapidly level it to the ground with fire and spear, and by burning to the ground the temple inaccessible to him[g] would quickly render it forever empty of those who offered sacrifices there. [44]Then the Friends and Kinsmen departed with great joy, and they confidently posted the armed forces at the places in the city most favorable for keeping guard.

[45] Now when the animals had been brought virtually to a state of madness, so to speak, by the very fragrant draughts of wine mixed with frankincense and had been equipped with frightful devices, the elephant keeper [46]entered the court around dawn—the city now being filled with countless masses of people crowding their way into the hippodrome—and urged the king on to the matter at hand. [47]So he, when he had filled his impious mind with a deep rage, rushed out in full force along with the animals, wishing to witness, with invulnerable heart and with his own eyes, the grievous and pitiful destruction of the aforementioned people.

[48] When the Jews saw the dust raised by the elephants going out at the gate and by

c 5.29 Gk all the Friends   d 5.29 Other ancient authorities read pointed to the beasts and the armed forces, saying, "They are ready, O king, according to your eager purpose."   e 5.38 Or Arm   f 5.40 Other ancient authorities read when the matter is in hand   g 5.43 Gk us

5:29–32 Under divine influence, Philopator praises the Jews for their loyalty, foreshadowing his later view of his Jewish subjects. **5:39–41** Philopator's courtiers protest, saying that the king is making *idiots* of them by repeatedly canceling and rescheduling the execution. **5:43** Philopator remembers his grudge against the Jews of Jerusalem. The reader is reminded that what happens in Egypt can affect the Jews of Jerusalem, and vice versa. **5:45–47** Hermon prepares the animals a third time, and now the king is ready and waiting. **5:48–51** Seeing no escape, the Jews again turn

the following armed forces, as well as by the trampling of the crowd, and heard the loud and tumultuous noise, [49]they thought that this was their last moment of life, the end of their most miserable suspense, and giving way to lamentation and groans they kissed each other, embracing relatives and falling into one another's arms[b]—parents and children, mothers and daughters, and others with babies at their breasts who were drawing their last milk. [50]Nevertheless, when they considered the help that they had received before from heaven, they prostrated themselves with one accord on the ground, removing the babies from their breasts, [51]and cried out in a very loud voice, imploring the Ruler over every power to manifest himself and be merciful to them, as they stood now at the gates of Hades.

6 Then a certain Eleazar, famous among the priests of the country, who had attained a ripe old age and throughout his life had been adorned with every virtue, directed the elders around him to stop calling upon the holy God, and he prayed as follows: [2]"King of great power, Almighty God Most High, governing all creation with mercy, [3]look upon the descendants of Abraham, O Father, upon the children of the consecrated Jacob, a people of your consecrated inheritance who are perishing as foreigners in a foreign land. [4]Pharaoh with his abundance of chariots, the former ruler of this Egypt, exalted with lawless insolence and boastful tongue, you destroyed together with his arrogant army by drowning them in the sea, manifesting the light of your mercy on the people of Israel. [5]Sennacherib exulting in his countless forces, oppressive king of the Assyrians, who had already gained control of the whole world by the spear and was lifted up against your holy city, speaking grievous words with boasting and insolence, you,

O Lord, broke in pieces, showing your power to many nations. [6]The three companions in Babylon who had voluntarily surrendered their lives to the flames so as not to serve vain things, you rescued unharmed, even to a hair, moistening the fiery furnace with dew and turning the flame against all their enemies. [7]Daniel, who through envious slanders was thrown down into the ground to lions as food for wild animals, you brought up to the light unharmed. [8]And Jonah, wasting away in the belly of a huge, sea-born monster, you, Father, watched over and restored[i] unharmed to all his family. [9]And now, you who hate insolence, all-merciful and protector of all, reveal yourself quickly to those of the people of Israel[j] who are being outrageously treated by the abominable and lawless nations.

[10] "Even if our lives have become entangled in impieties in our exile, rescue us from the hand of the enemy and destroy us, Lord, by whatever fate you choose. [11]Let not the vain-minded praise their vanities[k] at the destruction of your beloved ones, saying, 'Not even their god rescued them.' [12]But you, O Eternal One, who have all might and all power, watch over us now and have mercy on us who by the senseless insolence of the lawless are being deprived of life in the manner of traitors. [13]And let the nations cower today in fear of your invincible might, O honored One, who have power to save the people of Jacob. [14]The whole throng of infants and their parents entreat you with tears. [15]Let it be shown to all the nations that you are with us, O Lord, and have not turned your face from us, but just as you said, 'Not even when they were in the land of their enemies did I neglect them,' so accomplish it, O Lord."

b 5.49 Gk *falling upon their necks* *i* 6.8 Other ancient authorities read *rescued and restored*; others, *mercifully restored* *j* 6.9 Other ancient authorities read *to the holy ones of Israel* *k* 6.11 Or *bless their vain gods*

to prayer. The pitiful details are typical of tragic historiography and the martyr narratives of 2 and 4 Maccabees (see note on 1:4).

6:1–15 Eleazar's role parallels that of the high priest Simon at Jerusalem (2:1). Eleazar's prayer follows the Hellenistic Jewish pattern: praise of God's name (v. 2), invocation of past promises and acts of salvation (vv. 3–9), and pleas to spare the Jews even if they have become *entangled in impieties* (v. 10), for the sake of God's reputation (vv. 10–15). **6:6** *Moistening the fiery furnace with dew* is similar to language used in the Prayer of Azariah (Additions to Daniel).

6:16–21 God's intervention is dramatic and public (consistent with the theme of spectacle throughout). There are similarities (but also differences) with the Heliodorus episode in 2 Macc. 3 and the Physcon incident in Josephus's *Ag. Ap.* 2.54. It is likely that the author of 3 Maccabees knew 2 Maccabees in some form and that both 3 Maccabees and Josephus were working independently

16 Just as Eleazar was ending his prayer, the king arrived at the hippodrome with the animals and all the arrogance of his forces. [17]And when the Jews observed this they raised great cries to heaven so that even the nearby valleys resounded with them and brought an uncontrollable terror upon the entire army. [18]Then the most glorious, almighty, and true God revealed his holy face and opened the heavenly gates, from which two glorious angels of fearful aspect descended, visible to all but the Jews. [19]They opposed the forces of the enemy and filled them with confusion and terror, binding them with immovable shackles. [20]Even the body of the king began to shudder, and he forgot his sullen insolence. [21]The animals turned back upon the armed forces following them and began trampling and destroying them.

22 Then the king's anger was turned to pity and tears because of the things that he had devised earlier. [23]For when he heard the shouting and saw them all lying prostrate for destruction, he wept and angrily threatened his Friends, saying, [24]"You are committing treason and surpassing tyrants in cruelty, and even me, your benefactor, you are now attempting to deprive of dominion and life by secretly devising acts of no advantage to the kingdom. [25]Who has driven from their homes those who faithfully kept our country's fortresses and contrary to reason has gathered every one of them here? [26]Who is it that has so lawlessly encompassed with outrageous treatment those who from the beginning in every way surpassed all nations in their goodwill toward us and often have accepted willingly the worst of human dangers? [27]Loose and untie their unjust bonds! Send them back to their homes in peace, begging pardon for your former actions![l] [28]Release the children of the almighty and living God of heaven, who from the time of our ancestors until now has granted uninterrupted stability and glory to our government." [29]These then were the things he said, and the Jews, immediately released, praised their holy God and Savior, since they now had escaped death.

30 Then the king, when he had returned to the city, summoned the official in charge of the revenues and ordered him to provide to the Jews both wines and everything else needed for a festival of seven days, deciding that they should celebrate a festival of deliverance with all joyfulness in that same place in which they had expected to meet their destruction. [31]Accordingly, those disgracefully treated and near to Hades, or rather, who stood at its gates, arranged for a banquet of deliverance instead of a bitter and lamentable death, and full of joy they apportioned to groups of revelers the place that had been prepared for their destruction and burial. [32]They stopped their chanting of dirges and took up the song of their ancestors, praising God, their Savior and worker of wonders.[m] Putting an end to all mourning and wailing, they formed choruses[n] as a sign of peaceful joy. [33]Likewise also the king, after convening a lavish banquet to celebrate these events, gave thanks to heaven unceasingly and lavishly for the unexpected rescue that he[o] had experienced. [34]Those who had previously believed that the Jews would be destroyed and become food for birds and had joyfully registered them groaned as they themselves were overcome by disgrace and their fire-breathing boldness was ignominiously[p] quenched.

35 The Jews, as we have said before, arranged the aforementioned choral group[q] and passed the time in feasting to the accompaniment of joyous thanksgiving and psalms.

l 6.27 Other ancient authorities read *revoking your former commands* m 6.32 Other ancient authorities read *praising Israel and the wonder-working God*; or *praising Israel's Savior, the wonder-working God* n 6.33 Other ancient authorities read *they* p 6.34 Other ancient authorities read *completely* q 6.35 Or *dance*

from oral traditions associated with the festival. **6:18** Why the vision appears *to all but the Jews* is not clear.

6:22-29 This time Philopator's change of heart is permanent. In the speech that follows, and the letter in 7:1-9, Philopator is the benevolent monarch who protects the Jews from harm and praises their loyalty (cf. the kings in Daniel 1–6, Esther, Letter of Aristeas). **6:28** Philopator does not go so far as to worship God, but he acknowledges that his government has benefited from God.

6:30-41 The celebration provides the context for the establishment of the elephant festival that is also mentioned by Josephus (*Ag. Ap.* 2.55). **6:30** The king generously provides everything needed for the festival. **6:31-32** While 4:6-8 invoked the image of wedding celebrations converted

³⁶And when they had ordained a public rite for these things for their whole community for generations to come, they instituted the observance of the aforesaid days as a festival, not for drinking and gluttony but because of the deliverance that had come to them through God. ³⁷Then they petitioned the king, asking for dismissal to their homes. ³⁸So their registration was carried out from the twenty-fifth of Pachon to the fourth of Epeiph, for forty days, and their destruction was set for the fifth to the seventh of Epeiph, the three days ³⁹on which the Lord of all most gloriously revealed his mercy and rescued them all together and unharmed. ⁴⁰Then they feasted, being provided with everything by the king, until the fourteenth day, on which also they made the petition for their dismissal. ⁴¹The king granted their request and wrote the following letter for them to the generals in the cities, magnanimously expressing his concern:

7 "King Ptolemy Philopator to the generals in Egypt and all in authority in his government, greetings and good health:

2 "We ourselves and our children are faring well, the great God guiding our affairs according to our desire. ³Certain of our Friends, frequently urging us with malicious intent, persuaded us to gather together the Jews of the kingdom in a body and to punish them with extraordinary penalties as traitors, ⁴for they declared that our government would never be firmly established until this was accomplished because of the ill-will that these

people had toward all nations. ⁵They also led them out with harsh treatment as slaves, or rather as traitors, and, girding themselves with a cruelty more savage than that of Scythian custom, they tried without any inquiry or examination to put them to death. ⁶But we very severely threatened them for these acts, and in accordance with the clemency that we have toward all people we barely spared their lives. Since we have come to realize that the God of heaven surely defends the Jews, always taking their part as a father does for his children, ⁷and since we have taken into account the friendly and firm goodwill that they have shown toward us and our ancestors, we justly have acquitted them of every charge of whatever kind. ⁸We also have ordered all people to return to their own homes, with no one in any placeʳ doing them harm at all or reproaching them for the irrational things that have happened. ⁹For you should know that, if we devise any evil against them or cause them any grief at all, we always shall have not a mortal but the Ruler over every power, the Most High God, in everything and inescapably as an antagonist to avenge such acts. Farewell."

10 On receiving this letter the Jews'ˢ did not immediately hurry to make their departure, but they requested of the king that at their own hands those of the Jewish people who had willfully transgressed against the holy God and the law of God should receive the punishment they deserved. ¹¹They

r 7.8 Other ancient authorities read *way*   s 7.10 Gk *they*

to lamentation, here lamentation is converted into joyful songs. **6:36** A festival *not for drinking and gluttony* contrasts with the previous emphasis on drunkenness (Philopator, his courtiers, the elephants). **6:37** The Jews are consistently portrayed as deferring to Philopator (cf. 7:10–12). **6:38** The forty-day registration spans three Egyptian months (Pachon, Payni, and Epeiph), and the festival fell in Epeiph. This would locate the events in July and August 217 BCE. The battle of Raphia took place on June 22, 217 BCE.

7:1–9 Philopator's second letter reverses the letter in 3:11–30 (see **"Reversal," p. 1642**). **7:2** *Our children* is anachronistic, since Philopator was not yet married to his sister Arsinoë in 217. **7:3–4** The charges against the Jews, which Philopator made in his first letter (see 3:11–30), are here attributed to Philopator's *Friends*. **7:5** Scythians (nomadic peoples located in the regions north of modern-day Iran and Afghanistan) were proverbially regarded in Greek tradition as cruel. It is the Friends, not the Jews, who are now outside the pale of civilized society. **7:6** Philopator forgives his Friends due to *the clemency that we have toward all people*, ironically echoing the claims made in his first letter that he tolerated insubordination from the Jews due to his "benevolence" toward all (3:18, 20). **7:7–9** Philopator acquits the Jews of all charges. **7:9** *Most High God.* Language unlikely in the mouth of a gentile king (see also 6:28; 7:2) but often attributed to favorable gentile kings in Persian and Hellenistic Jewish texts without implying that they have converted to Judaism.

7:10–16 The anger of the Jews is targeted at the apostates within their own community rather than at Philopator or the gentiles (contrast Esther). **7:10–12** Emphasizing their loyalty, the Jews

Focus On: Reversal (3 Maccabees 7:10)

As a literary term, Aristotle (*Poet.* 1452a) defines *reversal* as a change of one situation into its opposite. He argues that reversal is most effective when the change comes as a surprise to the audience but in retrospect it appears logically necessary or probable as a result of earlier actions. In biblical interpretation, plot reversal can refer to any outcome of a character's action that is the opposite of what they intended.

Esther is so steeped in reversals that many interpreters treat reversal as the most important structuring element of its narrative. The Jews expect extinction but unexpectedly triumph over their enemies. Haman fantasizes honor for himself and sets a trap for Mordecai but must lead Mordecai in the procession of honor and himself falls into the trap that he set. Arguably, even God is reversed in Hebrew Esther: although God's hand is everywhere perceived behind the scenes by later interpreters, God's name is not mentioned. God's absence is presence.

Third Maccabees is similar to Esther (a narrative of the alleged origins of a festival commemorating an averted persecution), and reversal permeates its narrative as well. Dositheus is an ironic foil to the apostates who are punished at the end: this apostate Mordecai will pointedly not be rewarded. At 4:1–2, the nations feast for joy while the Jews lament; at 6:30, the Jews celebrate a festival in "that same place in which they had expected to meet their destruction." The wretched Hermon (a more comic version of Haman?) has his instructions reversed so many times that even the sycophants at court are appalled. Philopator's entire character is reversed in chap. 7, much more startlingly than that of Ahasuerus in Esther (Ahasuerus in Esther is clueless and passive, allowing Mordecai and Esther to take over where Haman left off). Like Ahasuerus, Philopator reverses his own edict, and the language of the second edict systematically inverts all the claims of the first: his Friends have become traitorous enemies, the Jews who were accused of sedition have become the most loyal of subjects, and the only (humorous) constant is that Philopator represents himself as benevolent to all and responsible for no evil. The obedience to God's law that was a cause for suspicion at 3:7 becomes the only criterion for loyalty to the crown at 7:11. In 3 Maccabees, as in Esther, "the tables were turned" for everyone concerned.

Sara Raup Johnson

declared that those who for the belly's sake had transgressed the divine commandments would never be favorably disposed toward the king's government. [12]The king[t] then, admitting and approving the truth of what they said, granted them a general license so that freely and without royal authority or supervision they might destroy those everywhere in his kingdom who had transgressed the law of God. [13]When they had applauded him in fitting manner, their priests and the whole multitude shouted the Hallelujah and joyfully departed. [14]And so on their way they punished and put to a public and shameful death any whom they met of their compatriots who had become defiled. [15]In that day they put to death more than three hundred men, and they kept the day as a joyful festival, since they had destroyed the profaners. [16]But those who had held fast to God even to death and had received the full enjoyment of deliverance began their departure from the city crowned with all sorts of very fragrant flowers, joyfully and loudly giving thanks to the God of their ancestors, the eternal Savior[u] of Israel, in words of praise and all kinds of melodious songs.

17 When they had arrived at Ptolemais, called "rose-bearing" because of its characteristic feature, the fleet waited for them, in accordance with the common desire, for seven days. [18]There they celebrated their deliverance,[v] for the king had generously provided all things to them for their journey until all of them arrived at their own houses. [19]And when they had all landed in peace with appropriate thanksgiving, there also in like manner they decided to observe these days as a joyous festival during the time of their stay. [20]Then, after inscribing them as holy on a pillar and dedicating a place of prayer at the site of the banquet, they departed unharmed, free, and

t 7.12 Gk *He*   *u* 7.16 Other ancient authorities read *the holy Savior*; others, *the holy one*   *v* 7.18 Gk *they made a cup of deliverance*

request the king's permission to punish the apostates. Contrary to anti-Jewish stereotypes, the Jews assert that only those obedient to God's law can be expected to remain loyal to the king. **7:14–15** *More than three hundred* apostates murdered is a shocking number (but cf. Esth. 9:6).

overjoyed, since at the king's command they had all of them been brought safely by land and sea and river to their own homes. [21]They also possessed greater prestige among their enemies, being held in honor and awe, and they were not subject at all to confiscation of their belongings by anyone. [22]Besides, they all recovered all of their property, in accordance with the registration, so that those who held any of it restored it to them with extreme fear.[w] So the supreme God perfectly performed great deeds for their deliverance. [23]Blessed be the Deliverer of Israel through all times! Amen.

w 7.22 Other ancient authorities read *with a very large supplement*

2 ESDRAS

Authorship, Date, and Literary History

The document called 2 Esdras is actually a composite text made up of three distinct works: 4 Ezra (chaps. 3–14), 5 Ezra (chaps. 1–2), and 6 Ezra (chaps. 15–16). "Esdras" is the Greek form of the name Ezra. The book of 2 Esdras lives in the Apocrypha for Roman Catholics (where it is called 4 Esdras) and Protestants and certain Eastern Orthodox denominations (where it is called 3 Esdras in the Slavonic Bible). In the Ethiopian Orthodox Church, 4 Ezra (chaps. 3–14) is canonical.

The book of 4 Ezra is a Jewish apocalypse (see **"Apocalypse," p. 1216**) written in response to the destruction of the Second Temple in Jerusalem in 70 CE, although its narrative setting is after the destruction of the *First* Temple. It was written in Judea around 100 CE in Hebrew, then translated into Greek. Copies of 4 Ezra exist in Latin, Syriac, Ethiopic, Georgian, Arabic, Armenian, and a small fragment in Coptic. The text is attributed to the biblical Ezra, a pseudonym for the anonymous Jewish author.

Both 5 Ezra and 6 Ezra are later Christian additions. The book of 5 Ezra is a distinct literary unit usually dated to around the mid-second century CE. Since Ezra is the protagonist, it was later added to 4 Ezra. While it is only attested in Latin, it may have originally been written in Greek. As with 4 Ezra, the author is pseudonymous but clearly a Christian. Also written pseudonymously by a Christian, 6 Ezra was written specifically as an appendix to chaps. 3–14 and probably added around the late third century CE. While it exists in full in Latin, a Greek papyrus fragment is extant, suggesting an originally Greek composition.

This translation of 2 Esdras is based on the Latin while also taking into account the Syriac, Ethiopic, Arabic, Armenian, and Georgian versions.

Reading Guide

Since 2 Esdras is a composite text containing three different compositions (4 Ezra, 5 Ezra, 6 Ezra), it may be read in several different ways. One way is to read 4 Ezra and 5 Ezra as each their own composition while considering 6 Ezra as an intentional Christian addition that alters the ending and larger meaning of the distinctly Jewish 4 Ezra. Another way to read 2 Esdras is in its final form, as a work of prophetic and apocalyptic hope for Christians.

4 Ezra

Contained in 2 Esd. 3–14 is the Jewish apocalypse 4 Ezra, which follows Ezra as he grapples with the theological and social aftermath of the destruction of the temple. Ezra is in Babylon and acts as the interlocutor between the remnant Jewish community and the divine, through the angel Uriel. Ezra laments the poor treatment of God's chosen people and the devastation of Zion and questions how God can elect Israel and then allow other unrighteous nations to punish Israel. Uriel presents God's ways as unknowable by humans, but this does not console Ezra. He is only moved away from this questioning when presented with several apocalyptic visions that show the end times and Israel's vindication. At the end, Ezra drinks a divinely given draft that allows him to receive scripture (broadly understood, see **"Canon," p. 1677**) from God: twenty-four books to be shared publicly and seventy secret books to be shared with "the wise." The narrative encourages continued observance of torah and urges anticipation of the end times, which will happen soon.

The narrative of 4 Ezra can be divided into seven episodes (sometimes erroneously called visions): in the first three (3:1–5:20; 5:21–6:34; 6:35–9:25), Ezra and God, through the angel Uriel, engage in dialogue about theodicy. In the fourth episode (9:26–10:59), Ezra encounters a mourning woman who transforms into the eschatological Zion. Uriel explains the encounter, his role shifting from a dialogue partner to an interpreting angel. In episodes 5 and 6 (11:1–12:51; 13:1–13:58), Ezra has two more eschatological visions while Uriel continues to act as an interpreting angel. In the final episode (14:1–14:48), the narrative reaches its climax with Ezra speaking directly to God and receiving ninety-four revealed books. Some manuscripts end with Ezra's assumption—that is, with Ezra being taken up into the heavens.

Interspersed throughout the narrative is Ezra's interaction with representatives from the larger community (5:16–19; 12:40–50; 14:27–36), and it is to this community that the revealed scripture is to be given. While the text as a whole deals with larger theological issues, it is fundamentally an exhortatory narrative designed to guide its intended audience toward torah observance and belief in the imminent end times.

5 and 6 Ezra

While 4 Ezra did not remain popular in strictly Jewish circles, early Christians embraced its apocalyptic eschatology, and it is due to them that the text has been preserved. Ambrose (340–97) cited it most extensively, with others such as Tertullian, Clement of Alexandria, Commodianus, and Jerome also quoting it. Its popularity in some Christian circles highlights its theological compatibility with some types of early Christianity.

In addition to preserving it, however, early Christians also made two additions to 4 Ezra. The book of 5 Ezra, found in chaps. 1–2 of 2 Esdras, focuses on Israel's continued sins and rejection of God, God's subsequent rejection of Israel, and finally, a group of true believers who will supersede sinful Israel (see **"Supersessionism," p. 1647**). Chaps. 15–16, also called 6 Ezra, were later added as an appendix. Since there is a smooth transition between the end of 4 Ezra and the beginning of 6 Ezra, it is likely that these two chapters were crafted with the original narrative in mind. These concluding chapters note impending persecution and encourage the audience, called the elect, to keep the faith even during these tribulations. With the addition of 5 and 6 Ezra as bookends for 4 Ezra, the text has made its way into the Apocrypha and some Eastern Orthodox denominations as 2 Esdras.

Shayna Sheinfeld

Comprising what is sometimes called 5 Ezra (chapters 1–2), 4 Ezra (chapters 3–14), and 6 Ezra (chapters 15–16)

1 The book[a] of the prophet Ezra son of Seraiah, son of Azariah, son of Hilkiah, son of Shallum, son of Zadok, son of Ahitub, [2]son of Ahijah, son of Phinehas, son of Eli, son of Amariah, son of Azariah, son of Meraimoth, son of Arna, son of Uzzi, son of Borith, son of Abishua, son of Phinehas, son of Eleazar, [3]son of Aaron, of the tribe of Levi, who was a captive in the country of the Medes in the reign of Artaxerxes, king of the Persians.

[4] The word of the Lord came to me, saying, [5]"Go, declare to my people their evil deeds and to their children the iniquities that they have committed against me, so that they may tell their children's children [6]that the sins of their parents have increased in them, for they have forgotten me and have offered sacrifices to strange gods. [7]Was it not I who brought them out of the land of Egypt, out of the house of bondage? But they have angered me and despised my counsels. [8]Now you, pull out the hair of your head and hurl[b] all evils upon them, for they have not obeyed my law—they are a rebellious people. [9]How long shall I endure them, on whom I have bestowed such great benefits? [10]For their sake I have overthrown many kings; I struck down Pharaoh with his servants and all his army. [11]I destroyed all nations before them and scattered in the east the peoples of two provinces,[c] Tyre and Sidon; I killed all their enemies.

[12] "But speak to them and say: Thus says the Lord: [13]Surely it was I who brought you through the sea and made safe highways for you where there was no road; I gave you

a 1.1 Other ancient authorities read *The second book*
b 1.8 Other ancient authorities read *and shake out*
c 1.11 Other ancient authorities read *Did I not destroy the city of Bethsaida because of you and to the south burn two cities . . . ?*

1:1–2:48 Chaps. 1–2 make up a distinct Christian composition called 5 Ezra.

1:1–3 Genealogy of Ezra. Cf. Ezra 7:1–5. Ezra is described as both a *prophet* and from a priestly lineage, with his identification as a prophet being rare; cf. 2 Esd. 12:42. **1:3** Although 5 Ezra was composed by a Christian in the second century CE, the narrative situates Ezra as a former captive of the Persians under Artaxerxes.

1:4–11 Review of God's acts toward Israel and Israel's rejection of God. 1:4 Prophetic call; cf. Jer. 1:4; Ezek. 7:1; and so on. **1:8** *Pull out the hair of your head.* A sign of mourning; cf. Ezra 9:3. **1:10** Cf. Exod. 14:28. **1:11** *Tyre*

Moses as leader and Aaron as priest; [14]I provided light for you from a pillar of fire and did great wonders among you. Yet you have forgotten me, says the Lord.

15 "Thus says the Lord Almighty:[d] The quails were a sign to you; I gave you camps for your protection, and in them you complained. [16]You have not exulted in my name at the destruction of your enemies, but to this day you still complain.[e] [17]Where are the benefits that I bestowed on you? When you were hungry and thirsty in the wilderness, did you not cry out to me, [18]saying, 'Why have you led us into this wilderness to kill us? It would have been better for us to serve the Egyptians than to die in this wilderness.' [19]I pitied your groanings and gave you manna for food; you ate the bread of angels. [20]When you were thirsty, did I not split the rock so that waters flowed in abundance? Because of the heat I clothed you with the leaves of trees.[f] [21]I divided fertile lands among you; I drove out the Canaanites,[g] the Perizzites, and the Philistines[h] before you. What more can I do for you? says the Lord. [22]Thus says the Lord Almighty:[i] When you were in the wilderness, at the bitter stream, thirsty and blaspheming my name, [23]I did not send fire on you for your blasphemies but threw a tree into the water and made the stream sweet.

24 "What shall I do to you, O Jacob? You, Judah, would not obey me. I will turn to other nations and will give them my name, so that they may keep my statutes. [25]Because you have forsaken me, I also will forsake you. When you beg mercy of me, I will show you no mercy. [26]When you call to me, I will not listen to you, for you have defiled your hands with blood, and your feet are swift to commit murder. [27]It is not as though you had forsaken me; you have forsaken yourselves, says the Lord.

28 "Thus says the Lord Almighty: Have I not entreated you as a father entreats his sons or a mother her daughters or a nurse her children, [29]so that you should be my people and I should be your God and that you should be my children and I should be your father? [30]I gathered you as a hen gathers her chicks under her wings. But now, what shall I do to you? I will cast you out from my presence. [31]When you offer oblations to me, I will turn my face from you, for I have rejected your[j] festal days and new moons and circumcisions of the flesh.[k] [32]I sent you my servants the prophets, but you have taken and killed them and torn their bodies[l] in pieces; I will require their blood of you, says the Lord.

33 "Thus says the Lord Almighty: Your house is desolate; I will drive you out as the wind drives straw, [34]and your sons will have no children, because with you[m] they have neglected my commandment and have done what is evil in my sight. [35]I will give your houses to a people that will come, who without having heard me will believe. Those to whom I have shown no signs will do what I have commanded. [36]They have seen no prophets, yet will recall their former state.[n] [37]I call to witness the gratitude of the people that is to come, whose children rejoice with gladness;[o] though they do not see me with bodily eyes, yet with the spirit they will believe the things I have said.

38 "And now, father,[p] look with pride and

d 1.15 Other ancient authorities lack *Almighty*   e 1.16 Other ancient authorities read *I sank your pursuer with his army in the sea, but still the people complain about their own destruction.*   f 1.20 Other ancient authorities read *I made for you trees with leaves*   g 1.21 Other ancient authorities add *the Hittites*   h 1.21 Other ancient authorities read *and their children*   i 1.22 Other ancient authorities lack *Almighty*   j 1.31 Other ancient authorities read *I did not command for you*   k 1.31 Other ancient authorities lack *of the flesh*   l 1.32 Other ancient authorities read *the bodies of the apostles*   m 1.34 Other ancient authorities lack *with you*   n 1.36 Other ancient authorities read *their iniquities*   o 1.37 Other ancient authorities read *The apostles bear witness to the coming people with joy*   p 1.38 Other ancient authorities read *brother*

and Sidon are cities, not *provinces*, and are west, not *east*, of Media (cf. 1:3). **1:14** *Pillar of fire.* See Exod. 13:21.
1:15–23 God's care of Israel in the desert. Cf. Ps. 105:37–41. **1:15** *Quails.* Cf. Exod. 16:13. **1:17–19** Cf. Exod. 16. **1:20** *Split the rock.* Cf. Num. 20:11. *Clothed you with the leaves of trees* is an unknown tradition. **1:21** Cf. Exod. 33:2; Deut. 7:1. **1:22–23** *Bitter stream . . . made the stream sweet.* Cf. Exod. 15:22–25.
1:24–40 Israel will be replaced by the people coming from the east. 1:28–29 God as parent is a frequent biblical metaphor (e.g., Jer. 3:19). **1:30** *As a hen gathers her chicks.* See Matt. 23:37; Luke 13:34. **1:32** Rejection of the *prophets* is found in the Jewish Scriptures (e.g., 2 Chr. 36:16). This verse is based on Matt. 23:37 and Luke 11:49–51. **1:35–37** A supersessionist replacement of Israel with gentile Christians is implied here (see **"Supersessionism," p. 1647**). **1:38** *Father.* A unique title for Ezra; cf. 2:5. *People coming from the east* is a likely reference to Christians and may also be an allusion to

Focus On: Supersessionism (2 Esdras 1–2)

Supersessionism, also called replacement theology, is the harmful ideology that Christians have replaced, or superseded, Jews as God's chosen people. This ideology states that Christianity is the final development of God's relationship with Israel and that the special status of Israel has transferred exclusively to Christ adherents. In this worldview, Judaism was only a preparation for the ultimate truth to be found through the gospel of Christ's crucifixion and resurrection. Some early texts in the New Testament contain the kernels of supersessionism. When taken in their historical context, these texts often highlight an intra-Jewish debate about whether non-Jews can find salvation through the Jewish messiah—in these cases, Christ—without conversion to Judaism. Some of the New Testament texts that are dated later are explicit about their supersessionist views. For example, Heb. 8:13 reads, "In speaking of a new covenant, he has made the first one obsolete, and what is obsolete and growing old will soon disappear."

Within the deuterocanonical/apocryphal books, some Jewish texts that were preserved by Christians were added to in order to reinforce the worldview of Christianity. One such text is 2 Esdras. Originally a Jewish apocalypse called 4 Ezra (found within chaps. 3–14), this narrative spoke to Christians who transmitted it and eventually added bookends to it. Chaps. 1–2 and 15–16 are clear Christian additions that, when added to the Jewish original, transform the text into one of hope for salvation through Christ.

The first two chapters of 2 Esdras are supersessionist. Through Ezra, the protagonist of the narrative and God's prophet in this text, God indicts the Israelites, highlighting their disobedience despite all that God has done. God then transfers all the divine promises from the Israelites to another nation: "I will give your houses to a people that will come, who without having heard me will believe. Those to whom I have shown no signs will do what I have commanded" (1:35). The "people that will come" in these verses—that is, the Christians—are said to supersede Israel as God's people, inheriting everything promised to the Israelites.

Supersessionist ideas found in Scripture are dangerous because they have led to anti-Jewish sentiments, both historically and today, which often condone or result in violence. It is important to identify and wrestle with these ideas in Scripture so that they do not contribute to endemic hatred and violence.

Shayna Sheinfeld

see the people coming from the east; [39]to them I will give as leaders Abraham, Isaac, and Jacob, and Hosea and Amos and Micah and Joel and Obadiah and Jonah [40]and Nahum and Habakkuk, Zephaniah, Haggai, Zechariah, and Malachi, who is also called the messenger of the Lord.[q]

2 "Thus says the Lord: I brought this people out of bondage, and I gave them commandments through my servants the prophets, but they would not listen to them and made my counsels void. [2]The mother who bore them says to them, 'Go, my children, because I am a widow and forsaken. [3]I brought you up with gladness, but with mourning and sorrow I have lost you, because you have sinned before the Lord God and have done what is evil in my sight.[r] [4]But now what can I do for you? For I am a widow and forsaken. Go, my children, and ask for mercy from the Lord.' [5]Now I call upon you, father, as a witness in addition to the mother of the children, because they would not keep my covenant, [6]so that you may bring confusion on them and bring their mother to ruin, so that they may have no offspring. [7]Let them be scattered among the nations; let their names be blotted out from the earth, because they have despised my covenant.

8 "Woe to you, Assyria, who conceal the unrighteous within you! O wicked nation,

q 1.40 Other ancient authorities read *and Jacob, Elijah and Enoch, Zechariah and Hosea, Amos, Joel, Micah, Obadiah, Zephaniah,* [40]*Nahum, Jonah, Mattia* (or *Mattathias*) *Habakkuk, and twelve angels with flowers* r 2.3 Other ancient authorities read *in his sight*

traditions of the Persian magi; cf. Matt. 2:1–12. **1:39–40** *Leaders* are the three patriarchs and twelve minor prophets. **1:40** *Malachi* in Hebrew means "my messenger."

2:1–9 God's judgment on Israel. **2:1** *Commandments* were given through *the prophets*; cf. 14:44–45; Ezra 9:10–11; Dan. 9:10. **2:2–4** *Mother.* See the mourning mother/Zion in 9:38–10:50. **2:5** *Father.* God or perhaps Ezra (cf. 1:38) and *mother* are called as witnesses. **2:7** *Scattered.* A punishment for disobedience; cf. Lev. 26:33. *Names . . . blotted out.* Israel will be completely forgotten because of their sins. **2:8** *Assyria.* Possibly a cryptic reference to Rome, replacing the standard Babylon; cf. 3:2.

remember what I did to Sodom and Gomorrah, [9]whose land lies in lumps of pitch and heaps of ashes.[s] That is what I will do to those who have not listened to me, says the Lord Almighty."

10 Thus says the Lord to Ezra: "Tell my people that I[t] will give them the kingdom of Jerusalem, which I was going to give to Israel. [11]Moreover, I will take back to myself their glory and will give to them the everlasting habitations, which I had prepared for Israel. [12]The tree of life shall give them fragrant perfume, and they shall neither toil nor become weary. [13]Go[u] and you will receive; pray that your days may be few, that they may be shortened. The kingdom is already prepared for you; be on the watch! [14]Call, O call heaven and earth to witness: I set aside evil and created good, for I am the Living One, says the Lord.

15 "Mother, embrace your children; bring them up with gladness, as does a dove; strengthen their feet, because I have chosen you, says the Lord. [16]And I will raise up the dead from their places and bring them out from their tombs, because I recognize my name in them. [17]Do not fear, mother of children, for I have chosen you, says the Lord. [18]I will send you help: my servants Isaiah and Jeremiah. According to their counsel I have consecrated and prepared for you twelve trees loaded with various fruits [19]and the same number of springs flowing with milk and honey and seven mighty mountains on which roses and lilies grow; by these I will fill your children with joy.

20 "Guard the rights of the widow, secure justice for the ward, give to the needy, defend the orphan, clothe the naked, [21]care for the injured and the weak, do not ridicule the lame, protect the maimed, and let the blind have a vision of my splendor. [22]Protect the old and the young within your walls.[v] [23]When you find any who are dead, commit them to the grave and mark it," and I will give you the first place in my resurrection. [24]Pause and be quiet, my people, because your rest will come.

25 "Good nurse, nourish your children; strengthen their feet. [26]Not one of the servants whom I have given you will perish, for I will require them from among your number. [27]Do not be anxious, for when the day of tribulation and anguish comes, others shall weep and be sorrowful, but you shall rejoice and have abundance. [28]The nations shall envy you, but they shall not be able to do anything against you, says the Lord. [29]My power will protect[x] you, so that your children may not see Gehenna.[y]

30 "Rejoice, O mother, with your children, because I will deliver you, says the Lord. [31]Remember your children who sleep, because I will bring them out of the hiding places of the earth and will show mercy to them, for I am merciful, says the Lord Almighty. [32]Embrace your children until I come, and proclaim mercy to them, because my springs run over, and my grace will not fail."

33 I, Ezra, received a command from the Lord on Mount Horeb to go to Israel. When I came to them, they rejected me and refused the Lord's commandment. [34]Therefore I say to you, O nations that hear and understand, "Wait for your shepherd; he will give you everlasting rest, because he who will come at the end of the age is close at hand. [35]Be ready for the rewards of the kingdom, because perpetual light will shine on you forevermore. [36]Flee from the shadow of this

---

s 2.9 Other ancient authorities read *whose land descends to hell*   t 2.10 Other ancient authorities add *have prepared for them to eat, and I*   u 2.13 Other ancient authorities read *Seek*   v 2.22 Other ancient authorities add *Watch over your infants. Let enslaved and free alike be joyful, and your whole company will be happy*   w 2.23 Other ancient authorities read *When I find your dead, I will raise them; I will watch for signs*   x 2.29 Lat *hands will cover*   y 2.29 Other ancient authorities read *All tremble because of me; my eyes see Gehenna*

2:10–14 Rewards for the new Israel. 2:13 *Already prepared.* The eschatological kingdom is already created.

2:15–32 Exhortation to good works. 2:15 A different *mother* than in 2:2–4, possibly referring to the church. **2:16** Resurrection is a prominent theme; see also vv. 23, 29, 31 (see **"Resurrection," p. 1224**). **2:18–19** The eschatological world is paradise; cf. Rev. 22:1–2. *Milk and honey.* Symbols of fertility; cf. Exod. 3:8; 3:17; and so on. **2:20–23** Commandments for social justice, which are standard in the biblical texts. **2:24** *Rest* is an eschatological reward; cf. 7:38. **2:25** *Nurse.* Possibly the church. **2:26** *Number.* Cf. John 17:12. **2:29** *Gehenna.* A place of punishment for the wicked. **2:31** *Sleep.* A euphemism for death.

2:33–41 Ezra on Mount Horeb. 2:33 For the rejection of other prophets, cf. 1:32. **2:34** *Shepherd* in this Christian composition refers to Christ. **2:35** *Light . . . shine* signifies divinity; cf. 7:97; 14:20. **2:36** *Savior.*

age; receive the joy of your glory; I publicly call on my savior to witness.^{z} ^{37}Receive what the Lord has entrusted to you and be joyful, giving thanks to him who has called you to the celestial kingdoms. ^{38}Rise, stand erect, and see the number of those who have been sealed at the feast of the Lord. ^{39}Those who have departed from the shadow of this age have received glorious garments from the Lord. ^{40}Take again your full number, O Zion, and close the list of your people who are clothed in white, who have fulfilled the law of the Lord. ^{41}The number of your children, whom you desired, is now complete; implore the Lord's authority that your people, who have been called from the beginning, may be made holy."

^{42}I, Ezra, saw on Mount Zion a great multitude that I could not number, and they all were praising the Lord with songs. ^{43}In their midst was a young man of great stature, taller than any of the others, and on the head of each of them he placed a crown, but he was more exalted than they. And I was held spellbound. ^{44}Then I asked an angel, "Who are these, my lord?" ^{45}He answered and said to me, "These are they who have put off mortal clothing and have put on the immortal and have confessed the name of God. Now they are being crowned and receive palms." ^{46}Then I said to the angel, "Who is that young man who is placing crowns on them and putting palms in their hands?" ^{47}He answered and said to me, "He is the Son of God, whom they confessed in the world." So I began to praise those who had stood

valiantly for the name of the Lord.^{a} ^{48}Then the angel said to me, "Go, tell my people how great and how many are the wonders of the Lord God that you have seen."

3 In the thirtieth year after the destruction of the city, I was in Babylon—I, Salathiel, who am also called Ezra. I was troubled as I lay on my bed, and my thoughts welled up in my heart ^{2}because I saw the desolation of Zion and the wealth of those who lived in Babylon. ^{3}My spirit was greatly agitated, and I began to speak anxious words to the Most High and said, ^{4}"O sovereign Lord, did you not speak at the beginning when you planted^b the earth—and that without help—and commanded the dust^c ^{5}and it gave you Adam, a lifeless body? Yet he was the creation of your hands, and you breathed into him the breath of life, and he was made alive in your presence. ^{6}And you led him into the garden that your right hand had planted before the earth appeared. ^{7}And you laid upon him one commandment of yours, but he transgressed it, and immediately you appointed death for him and for his descendants. From him there sprang nations and tribes, peoples and clans without number. ^{8}And every nation walked after its own will; they did ungodly things in your sight

z 2.36 Other ancient authorities read *I testify that my savior has been commissioned by the Lord* a 2.47 Other ancient authorities read *to praise and glorify the Lord* b 3.4 Other ancient authorities read *formed* c 3.4 Syr Ethiop Georg: Lat *people* or *world*

Christ. **2:37** That which is *entrusted* is the soul; cf. 1 Tim. 6:20; 2 Tim. 1:12; Herm. Mand. 3.2. **2:38** *Sealed.* Cf. Rev. 7:2–8. **2:39–40** Those *clothed in white* wear *glorious garments*; cf. Rev. 7:9–17. **2:41** *The number* is predetermined; cf. 4:36; Rev. 14:1.

2:42–48 Ezra on Mount Zion. 2:42 *Mount Zion.* Cf. 13:2–50; Rev. 14:1. **2:43** *Placed a crown.* Cf. Herm. Sim. 8.2.1, 8.3.6. **2:46–47** *Young man* is identified as Christ.

3:1–14:48 This section is a distinct Jewish apocalypse, also called **4 Ezra.** It is made up of seven episodes.

3:1–5:20 First episode. 3:1–3 Narrative introduction. **3:1** *Thirtieth year.* Cf. Ezek. 1:1. *In Babylon* situates the narrative after the destruction of the first Jerusalem temple and during the Babylonian exile, 587–538 BCE. Ezra is also called *Salathiel,* a name not used elsewhere in the text. For other figures having two names in postexilic literature, cf. Esth. 2:7; Dan. 2:26. **3:2** Ezra is disturbed by the destruction of *Zion*—that is, Jerusalem—and the wealth and power of *Babylon,* here a cipher for Rome. **3:3** *Most High.* The most common address for God in 2 Esdras.

3:4–27 Ezra's first lament reflects on Israel's transgressions, the evil heart, and God's role. **3:4** *Without help* may be a polemical statement against the Christian idea that Jesus was preexistent; cf. Gen. 1; 2:7. **3:6** Here the garden of Eden was planted before creation; cf. Gen. 2:8; 2 Esd. 7:36. **3:7** Adam, and not Eve, transgressed the commandment. Death for all humans is the result of the transgression; cf. Rom. 5:12, 15–18. **3:8** God did not stop humans from sinning.

and rejected your commands, and you did not hinder them. ⁹But again, in its time you brought the flood upon the inhabitants of the world and destroyed them. ¹⁰And the same fate befell all of them: just as death came upon Adam, so the flood upon them. ¹¹But you left one of them, Noah with his household, and all the righteous who have descended from him.

12 "When those who lived on earth began to multiply, they produced children and peoples and many nations, and again they began to be more ungodly than were their ancestors. ¹³And when they were committing iniquity in your sight, you chose for yourself one of them, whose name was Abraham; ¹⁴you loved him, and to him alone you revealed the end of the times, secretly by night. ¹⁵You made an everlasting covenant with him and promised him that you would never forsake his descendants, and you gave him Isaac, and to Isaac you gave Jacob and Esau. ¹⁶You set apart Jacob for yourself, but Esau you rejected, and Jacob became a great multitude. ¹⁷And when you led his descendants out of Egypt, you brought them to Mount Sinai. ¹⁸You bent down the heavens and shookᵈ the earth and moved the world and caused the depths to tremble and troubled the times. ¹⁹Your glory passed through the four gates of fire and earthquake and wind and ice, to give the law to the descendants of Jacob and your commandment to the posterity of Israel.

20 "Yet you did not take away their evil heart from them, so that your law might produce fruit in them. ²¹For the first Adam, burdened with an evil heart, transgressed and was overcome, as were also all who were descended from him. ²²Thus the disease became permanent; the law was in the hearts of the people along with the evil root, but what was good departed, and the evil remained. ²³So the times passed and the years were completed, and you raised up for yourself a servant named David. ²⁴You commanded him to build a city for your name and there to offer you oblations from what is yours. ²⁵This was done for many years, but the inhabitants of the city transgressed, ²⁶in everything doing just as Adam and all his descendants had done, for they also had the evil heart. ²⁷So you handed over your city to your enemies.

28 "Then I said in my heart, Are the deeds of those who inhabit Babylon any better? Is that why it has gained dominion over Zion? ²⁹For when I came here I saw ungodly deeds without number, and my soul has seen many sinners during these thirty years.ᵉ And my heart failed me ³⁰because I have seen how you endure those who sin and have spared those who act wickedly and have destroyed your people and have protected your enemies ³¹and have not shown to anyone how your way may be comprehended.ᶠ Are the deeds of Babylon better than those of Zion? ³²Or has another nation known you besides Israel? Or what tribes have so believed the covenants as these tribes of Jacob? ³³Yet their reward has not appeared, and their labor has borne no fruit. For I have traveled widely among the nations and have seen that they abound in wealth, though they are unmindful of your commandments. ³⁴Now therefore weigh in a balance our iniquities and those of the inhabitants of the world, and it will be found which way the arrow of the scale tips. ³⁵When have the inhabitants of the earth not sinned in your sight? Or

d 3.18 Syr Ethiop Arab 1 Georg: Lat *set fast* e 3.29 Ethiop Arab 1 Arm: Lat Syr *in this thirtieth year* f 3.31 Syr; compare Ethiop: Lat *how this way should be forsaken*

3:9 *In its time* suggests a predestinarian view of time. 3:14 The revelation of the end times is an expansion of Gen. 15:17; cf. Apocalypse of Abraham. Some rabbinic sources also understand Gen. 15:17 as a revelation of the future to Abraham. 3:16 On God hating *Esau*, cf. Mal. 1:2–3. Esau may symbolize Rome as in 6:8–10. 3:17 God, not Moses, is responsible for the exodus. 3:18 See Exod. 19:18. *Times*. Latin "saeculum," more likely "world" or "universe." 3:19 *Four gates* are meteorological portals; cf. 1 En. 36:1; 76:1–14. *Law* here is the Torah. 3:20 God is indicted for not removing the *evil heart*—that is, inclination to sin—so even the law cannot ensure *fruit*, reward. 3:21 *First Adam*. The first human. 3:22 Both good and evil inclinations exist in humans, parallel to rabbinic ideas. Evil inclination wins. 3:27 God's punishment for Israel's transgression.

3:28–36 Ezra reflects on the significance of this history. 3:29 *Came here* to Babylon. 3:30 God spares the sinners of Babylon but punishes Israel. 3:32–33 Israel is not perfect but is better than other nations, yet the others see rewards while Israel is punished. 3:34 The *scale* weighs human deeds; cf. Prov. 16:11; Job 31:6; Dan. 5:27; 1 En. 41:1. 3:35–36 Israel's punishment is unjust compared with the sins of other nations.

what nation has kept your commandments so well? [36]You may indeed find individuals who have kept your commandments, but nations you will not find."

4 Then the angel that had been sent to me, whose name was Uriel, answered [2]and said to me, "Your understanding has utterly failed regarding this world, and do you think you can comprehend the way of the Most High?" [3]Then I said, "Yes, my lord." And he replied to me, "I have been sent to show you three ways and to put before you three problems. [4]If you can solve one of them for me, then I will show you the way you desire to see and will teach you why the heart is evil."

[5]I said, "Speak, my lord."

And he said to me, "Go, weigh for me the weight of fire, or measure for me a blast[g] of wind, or call back for me the day that is past."

[6]I answered and said, "Who of those that have been born can do that, that you should ask me about such things?"

[7]And he said to me, "If I had asked you, 'How many dwellings are in the heart of the sea, or how many streams are at the source of the deep, or how many streams are above the firmament, or which are the exits of Hades, or which are the entrances[h] of paradise?' [8]perhaps you would have said to me, 'I never went down into the deep, nor as yet into Hades, neither did I ever ascend into heaven.' [9]But now I have asked you only about fire and wind and the day, things that you have experienced and from which you cannot be separated, and you have given me no answer about them." [10]He said to me, "You cannot understand the things with which you have grown up; [11]how, then, can your mind comprehend the way of the Most High?[i] And how can one who is already worn out by the corrupt world understand incorruption?"[j] When I heard this, I fell on my face[k] [12]and said to him, "It would have been better for us not to be here than to come here and live in ungodliness and to suffer and not understand why."

[13]He answered me and said, "I went into a forest of trees of the plain, and they made a plan [14]and said, 'Come, let us go and make war against the sea, so that it may recede before us and so that we may make for ourselves more forests.' [15]In like manner the waves of the sea also made a plan and said, 'Come, let us go up and subdue the forest of the plain so that there also we may gain more territory for ourselves.' [16]But the plan of the forest was in vain, for the fire came and consumed it; [17]likewise also the plan of the waves of the sea was in vain,[l] for the sand stood firm and blocked it. [18]If now you were a judge between them, which would you undertake to justify and which to condemn?"

[19]I answered and said, "Each made a foolish plan, for the land has been assigned to the forest and the locale of the sea a place to carry its waves."

[20]He answered me and said, "You have judged rightly, but why have you not judged so in your own case? [21]For as the land has been assigned to the forest and the sea to its waves, so also those who inhabit the earth can understand only what is on the earth, and he who is[m] above the heavens can understand what is above the height of the heavens."

[22]Then I answered and said, "I implore you, my lord, why[n] have I been endowed with the power of understanding? [23]For I did not wish to inquire about the ways above but about those things that we daily experience: why Israel has been given over to the nations in disgrace; why the people whom you loved has been given over to godless tribes and the law of our ancestors

g 4.5 Syr Ethiop Arab 1 Arab 2 Georg *a measure* h 4.7 Syr Compare Ethiop Arab 2 Arm: Lat lacks *of Hades, or which are the entrances* i 4.11 Syr Ethiop add *For the way of the Most High is created immeasurable* j 4.11 Syr Ethiop *the way of the incorruptible?* k 4.11 Syr Ethiop Arab 1: Meaning of Lat uncertain l 4.17 Lat lacks *was in vain* m 4.21 Arab 2 Arm Georg *those who are* n 4.22 Syr Ethiop Arm Georg: Meaning of Lat uncertain

4:1–5:20 The angel Uriel engages with Ezra. See "Angels," p. 1346. *4:3 Ways* here are riddles. **4:5–8** Here and in 5:36–37, Uriel presents riddles that are unanswerable by humans. **4:7** Cf. Job 38:16–17. **4:11** *One . . . worn out.* The physical body as compared to the mind. **4:12** Wishing for death or nonexistence is a common trope during crises (e.g., Jonah 4:3). Lack of understanding is emphasized here.

4:13–21 A nature parable between the forest and the sea is a well-known mythical theme. Cf. 2 Bar. 36. The lesson is that humans also have their place, and it does not include understanding God's ways. **4:22–25** Ezra is not put off by the angel's prevarication. He wishes to understand Israel's suffering in light of God's love of Israel, not heavenly matters.

has been brought to destruction and the written covenants no longer exist. [24]We pass from the world like locusts, and our life is like a mist,[o] and we are not worthy to obtain mercy. [25]But what will he do for his[p] name that is invoked over us? It is about these things that I have asked."

26 He answered me and said, "If you are alive, you will see, and if you live long,[q] you will often marvel, because the age is hurrying swiftly to its end. [27]It will not be able to bring the things that have been promised to the righteous in their appointed times, because this age is full of sadness and infirmities. [28]For the evil about which you ask me has been sown, but the harvest of it has not yet come. [29]If therefore that which has been sown is not reaped, and if the place where the evil has been sown does not pass away, the field where the good has been sown will not come. [30]For a grain of evil seed was sown in Adam's heart from the beginning, and how much ungodliness it has produced until now—and will produce until the time of threshing comes! [31]Consider now for yourself how much fruit of ungodliness a grain of evil seed has produced. [32]When heads of grain without number are sown, how great a threshing floor they will fill!"

33 Then I answered and said, "How long?[r] When will these things be? Why are our years few and evil?" [34]He answered me and said, "Do not be in a greater hurry than the Most High. You, indeed, are in a hurry for yourself,[s] but the Highest is in a hurry on behalf of many. [35]Did not the souls of the righteous in their chambers ask about these matters, saying, 'How long are we to remain here?[t] And when will the harvest of

our reward come?' [36]And the archangel Jeremiel answered and said, 'When the number of those like yourselves[u] is completed, for he has weighed the age in the balance, [37]and measured the times by measure, and numbered the times by number, and he will not move or arouse them until that measure is fulfilled.'"

38 Then I answered and said, "But, O sovereign Lord, all of us also are full of ungodliness. [39]It is perhaps on account of us that the time of threshing is delayed for the righteous—on account of the sins of those who inhabit the earth."

40 He answered me and said, "Go and ask a pregnant woman whether, when her nine months have been completed, her womb can keep the fetus within her any longer."

41 And I said, "No, lord, it cannot."

He said to me, "In Hades the chambers of the souls are like the womb. [42]For just as a woman who is in labor makes haste to escape the pangs of birth, so also do these places hasten to give back those things who were committed to them from the beginning. [43]Then the things that you desire to see will be disclosed to you."

44 I answered and said, "If I have found favor in your sight, and if it is possible, and if I am worthy, [45]show me this also: whether more time is to come than has passed or whether for us the greater part has gone by. [46]For I know what has gone by, but I do not know what is to come."

o 4.24 Lat mss Syr Ethiop Arab 1 Georg: Lat *terror*
p 4.25 Ethiop adds *holy* q 4.26 Syr: Lat *live* r 4.33 Syr Ethiop: Meaning of Lat uncertain s 4.34 Syr Ethiop Arab Arm: Meaning of Lat uncertain t 4.35 Syr Ethiop Arab 2 Georg: Lat *How long do I hope thus?* u 4.36 Syr Ethiop Arab 2: Lat *number of seeds*

4:26–32 A transition from dialogue to predictions. 4:26 Uriel responds. The *end* of the age is imminent. *Marvel*, or wonder, is used frequently for eschatological events; see 7:27; 13:14, 50, 56; 14:5. **4:27** *Appointed times* suggests a predestinarian view of time. **4:29** *Place* and *field* here mean both this world and the human heart. This age must end for evil to pass away. **4:30** Adam's *evil seed* is the evil inclination that is passed to all humans. *Threshing*. The time of eschatological judgment. **4:33–46 A series of questions and answers about the end times. 4:33** Ezra's question about the end times highlights a sense of urgency. **4:35** *Chambers*, or repositories of souls. **4:36** *Jeremiel*, or Jerachmiel, is also found in the Coptic Apocalypse of Zephaniah and the Coptic Jeremiah Apocryphon. He is the angel in charge of some souls after death. *Number . . . is completed.* A predetermined number of righteous humans; cf. 1 En. 47:4; 2 Bar. 23:4–5; 48:46. **4:38** *Sovereign Lord.* A title for God. Ezra addresses God through the angel Uriel. **4:39** Ezra associates himself with the wicked *who inhabit the earth* as opposed to *the righteous* who are in the repositories of souls. **4:40** Here the simile of the pregnant woman is applied to the repositories of souls. Pregnancy as an analogy is commonplace; cf. 5:46, 48; 10:9–14; and so on. **4:42** The time of the end is imminent. *Committed* souls are entrusted to humans or, after death, to repositories but belong to God; cf. 1 En. 51:5; 1 Tim. 6:20; 2 Tim. 1:12, 14.

47 And he said to me, "Stand at my right side, and I will show you the interpretation of a parable."

48 So I stood and looked, and a flaming furnace passed by before me, and when the flame had gone by I looked, and the smoke remained. ⁴⁹And after this a cloud full of water passed before me and poured down a heavy and violent rain, and when the violent rainstorm had passed, drops still remained in it.

50 He said to me, "Consider it for yourself, for just as the rain is more than the drops and the fire is greater than the smoke, so the quantity that passed was far greater, but drops and smoke remained."

51 Then I prayed and said, "Do you think that I shall live until those days? Or who will be alive in those days?"

52 He answered me and said, "Concerning the signs about which you ask me, I can tell you in part, but I was not sent to tell you concerning your life, for I do not know.

5 "Now concerning the signs: behold, the days are coming when those who inhabit the earth shall be seized with great terror,ᵛ and the way of truth shall be hidden, and the land shall be barren of faith. ²Unrighteousness shall be increased beyond what you yourself see and beyond what you heard of formerly. ³And the land that you now see ruling shall be a trackless waste, and people shall see it desolate. ⁴But if the Most High grants that you live, you shall see it thrown into confusion after the third period,ʷ

and the sun shall suddenly begin to shine
at night
and the moon during the day.
⁵ Blood shall drip from wood,
and the stone shall utter its voice;
the peoples shall be troubled,

and the skies shall be changed.ˣ

⁶"And one shall reign whom those who inhabit the earth do not expect, and the birds shall fly away together, ⁷and the sea of Sodom shall cast up fish, and one whom the many do not know shall make his voice heard by night, and all shall hear his voice.ʸ ⁸There shall be chaos also in many places, fire shall often break out, the wild animals shall roam beyond their haunts, and menstruous women shall bring forth monsters. ⁹Salt waters shall be found in the sweet, and all friends shall conquer one another; then shall reason hide itself, and wisdom shall withdraw into its chamber, ¹⁰and it shall be sought by many but shall not be found, and unrighteousness and unrestraint shall increase on earth. ¹¹One country shall ask its neighbor, 'Has righteousness or anyone who does right passed through you?' And it will answer, 'No.' ¹²At that time people shall hope but not obtain; they shall labor, but their ways shall not prosper. ¹³These are the signs that I am permitted to tell you, and if you pray again and weep as you do now and fast for seven days, you shall hear yet greater things than these."

14 Then I woke up, and my body shuddered violently, and my soul was so troubled that it fainted. ¹⁵But the angel who had come and talked with me held me and strengthened me and set me on my feet.

16 Now on the second night Phaltiel, a chief of the people, came to me and said, "Where have you been? And why is your face sad? ¹⁷Or do you not know that Israel has been entrusted to you in the land of their exile?

v 5.1 Syr Georg Ethiop: Meaning of Lat uncertain
w 5.4 Ethiop *three months*; Arm *the third vision*; Georg *the third day*; Arab 1 *three signs*   x 5.5 Syr Georg Arab 1 Arab 2 Arm; Ethiop *and the stars shall fall*: Meaning of Lat uncertain   y 5.7 Cn: Lat *fish, and it shall make its voice heard by night, which the many have not known, but all shall hear its voice.*

4:47–5:13 Ezra's question is answered by way of two brief visions and their interpretation. **4:52** *Signs.* The events that will take place leading up to and at the end; cf. 5:1–13; 6:11, 20–24; 9:3; 13:30–32.

5:1–13 Predictions of signs and woes of the end. These oracular stichs are poetic in style and contain traditional content. **5:3** *Land* refers to Rome. **5:4** *Third period* is unclear. Confusion of the natural order is standard for end-time woes. **5:6** *One shall reign.* The wicked ruler is a traditional apocalyptic motif; see 2 Bar. 40:1. **5:7** *Sea of Sodom* is the Dead Sea. *One . . . shall make his voice heard* likely refers to the ruler from 5:6. **5:9–11** Wisdom and righteousness are difficult to find; cf. 5:1; 2 Bar. 48:36. **5:9** *Friends shall conquer one another.* The breakdown of social order under periods of high stress is widespread in ancient sources. **5:13** Ezra fasts between the first and second, second and third episodes.

5:14–20 Conclusion of the vision. 5:14 Ezra's physical and mental state upon awaking; cf., for example, Dan. 7:15. **5:15** *Strengthened me.* Cf., for example, Dan. 10:18. **5:16–20** First of three

¹⁸Rise therefore and eat some bread, and do not forsake us like a shepherd who leaves the flock in the power of savage wolves."

19 Then I said to him, "Go away from me and do not come near me for seven days; then you may come to me."

He heard what I said and left me. ²⁰So I fasted seven days, mourning and weeping, as the angel Uriel had commanded me.

21 After seven days the thoughts of my heart were very grievous to me again. ²²Then my soul recovered the spirit of understanding, and I began once more to speak words in the presence of the Most High. ²³I said, "O sovereign Lord, from every forest of the earth, and from all its trees you have chosen one vine, ²⁴and from all the lands of the world you have chosen for yourself one region,ᶻ and from all the flowers of the world you have chosen for yourself one lily, ²⁵and from all the depths of the sea you have filled for yourself one river, and from all the cities that have been built you have consecrated Zion for yourself, ²⁶and from all the birds that have been created you have named for yourself one dove, and from all the flocks that have been made you have provided for yourself one sheep, ²⁷and from all the multitude of peoples you have gotten for yourself one people, and to this people, whom you have loved, you have given the law that is approved by all. ²⁸And now, O Lord, why have you handed the one over to the many and dishonoredᵃ the one root beyond the others and scattered your only one among the many? ²⁹And those who opposed your promises have trampled on those who believed your covenants. ³⁰If you really hate your people, they should be punished at your own hands."

31 When I had spoken these words, the angel who had come to me on a previous night was sent to me. ³²He said to me, "Listen to me, and I will instruct you; pay attention to me, and I will tell you more."

33 Then I said, "Speak, my lord." And he said to me, "Are you greatly disturbed in mind over Israel? Or do you love him more than his Maker does?"

34 I said, "No, my lord, but because of my grief I have spoken, for every hour I suffer agonies of heart while I strive to understand the way of the Most High and to search out some part of his judgment."

35 He said to me, "You cannot." And I said, "Why not, my lord? Why, then, was I born? Or why did not my mother's womb become my grave, so that I would not see the travail of Jacob and the exhaustion of the people of Israel?"

36 He said to me, "Count up for me those who have not yet come, and gather for me the scattered raindrops, and make the withered flowers bloom again for me; ³⁷open for me the closed chambers, and bring out for me the winds shut up in them, or show me the picture of a voice, and then I will explain to you the travail that you ask to see."

38 I said, "O sovereign Lord, who is able to know these things except him whose dwelling is not with mortals? ³⁹As for me, I am without wisdom, and how can I speak concerning the things that you have asked me?"

40 He said to me, "Just as you cannot do one of the things that were mentioned, so you cannot discover my judgment or the goal of the love that I have promised to my people."

41 I said, "Yet, O Lord, you have charge of

z 5.24 Syr: Lat *pit*   a 5.28 Syr Ethiop Arab: Lat *prepared*

points in the narrative where Ezra interacts with the Jewish community; cf. 12:40–50; 14:1–48. **5:18** *Shepherd . . . flock* is common imagery found in ancient documents to represent a leader and their community.

5:21–6:34 Second episode. 5:21–40 Ezra's prayer and the angel's response. **5:22** *Recovered*, or better "received." Ezra's received inspiration precipitates his questioning.

5:23–30 Ezra questions God's election and punishment of Israel. **5:24** Election of the *land*; see, for example, Gen. 12:1. *Lily.* Cf. Hos. 14:5. **5:25** *One river* likely refers to the Jordan. *Consecrated Zion* with the Jerusalem temple, where sacrifices are offered to God. **5:26** Israel is both *dove* and *sheep* here. **5:27** Israel's election. **5:28–29** Ezra questions Israel's fate. **5:30** That Israel's punishment should come from God is an old idea (for example, 2 Sam. 24:14).

5:31–40 The angel's response. Cf. 4:1; 7:1; 10:29. **5:36–37** Six riddles; see note on 4:5–8. **5:37** *Chambers* may also be translated as "repositories"; *winds* may be translated as "spirits," although both winds and spirits are found in storehouses; e.g., 4:35; Jer. 51:16; 1 En. 41:4. **5:40** The angel speaks on behalf of God.

5:41–6:34 Predicting the end times. 5:41–6:10 Series of predictive questions and responses.

those who are alive at the end, but what will those do who lived before me, or we ourselves, or those who come after us?"

42 He said to me, "I shall liken my judgment to a circle;[b] just as for those who are last there is no slowness, so for those who are first there is no haste."

43 Then I answered and said, "Could you not have created at one time those who have been and those who are and those who will be, so that you might show your judgment the sooner?"

44 He replied to me and said, "The creation cannot move faster than the Creator, nor can the world hold at one time those who have been created in it."

45 I said, "How have you said to your servant that you[c] will certainly give life at one time to your creation? If therefore all creatures will live at one time[d] and the creation will sustain them, it might even now be able to support all of them present at one time."

46 He said to me, "Ask a woman's womb, and say to it, 'If you bear ten children, why one after another?' Request it therefore to produce ten at one time."

47 I said, "Of course it cannot, but only each in its own time."

48 He said to me, "Even so I have given the womb of the earth to those who from time to time are sown in it. [49]For as an infant does not bring forth, and a woman who has become old does not bring forth any longer, so I have made the same rule for the world that I created."

50 Then I inquired and said, "Since you have now given me the opportunity, let me speak before you. Is our mother, of whom you have told me, still young, or is she now approaching old age?"

51 He replied to me, "Ask a woman who bears children, and she will tell you. [52]Say to her, 'Why are those whom you have borne recently not like those whom you bore before, but smaller in stature?' [53]And she herself will answer you, 'Those born in the strength of youth are different from those born during the time of old age, when the womb is failing.' [54]Therefore you also should consider that you and your contemporaries are smaller in stature than those who were before you, [55]and those who come after you will be smaller than you, as born of a creation that already is aging and passing the strength of youth."

56 I said, "I implore you, O Lord, if I have found favor in your sight, show your servant through whom you will visit your creation."

6 He said to me, "At the beginning of the circle of the earth, before[e] the portals of the world were in place, and before the assembled winds blew, [2]and before the rumblings of thunder sounded, and before the flashes of lightning shone, and before the foundations of paradise were laid, [3]and before the beautiful flowers were seen, and before the powers of movements[f] were established, and before the innumerable hosts of angels were gathered together, [4]and before the heights of the air were lifted up, and before the measures of the firmaments were named, and before the footstool of Zion was established, [5]and before the present years were reckoned, and before the imaginations of those who now sin were estranged, and before those who stored up treasures of faith were sealed—[6]then I planned these things, and they were made through me alone and not through another, just as the end shall come through me alone and not through another."

7 I answered and said, "What will be the dividing of the times, or when will be the end of the first age and the beginning of the age that follows?"

b 5.42 Or crown c 5.45 Syr Ethiop Arab 1: Meaning of Lat uncertain d 5.45 Syr: Lat lacks If . . . one time e 6.1 Meaning of Lat uncertain: Compare Syr The beginning is by the hand of humankind, but the end is by my own hands. For as before the land of the world existed there, and before; Ethiop: At first by the Son of Man, and afterwards I myself. For before the earth and the lands were created, and before f 6.3 Or earthquakes

5:45 All creatures, although the focus is on humans (cf. 5:41). Ezra is asking why, if all can be resurrected at once, they cannot all live at the same time. 5:48–49 Cf. 10:9–14. 5:50 Ezra asks if the end times are imminent. 5:52–55 An analogy is made between the degeneration of the woman's offspring over time and the degeneration of human generations. 5:56 Ezra asks through whom the judgment will be carried out. 6:1–5 Poetic creation passage highlighting predestination. 6:4 Zion is God's footstool; cf. Ps. 99:5; Lam. 2:1; and so on. 6:5 Treasures of faith . . . sealed refers to people who belong to God; cf. Ezek. 9:4–6; Rev. 7:2–3. 6:6 God is the sole creator and planner. The clause just as . . . another is extant only in the Latin text and emphasizes God as bringer of the end times. 6:7–10 The timetable

8 He said to me, "From Abraham to Isaac,^{g} because from him were born Jacob and Esau, for Jacob's hand held Esau's heel from the beginning. ^{9}Now Esau is the end of this age, and Jacob is the beginning of the age that follows. ^{10}The beginning of a person is the hand, and the end of a person is the heel;^{h} seek for nothing else, Ezra, between the heel and the hand, Ezra!"

11 I answered and said, "O sovereign Lord, if I have found favor in your sight, ^{12}show your servant the last of your signs of which you showed me a part on a previous night."

13 He answered and said to me, "Rise to your feet, and you will hear a full, resounding voice. ^{14}And if the place where you are standing is greatly shaken ^{15}while the voice is speaking, do not be terrified, because the word concerns the end, and the foundations of the earth will understand ^{16}that the speech concerns them. They will tremble and be shaken, for they know that their end must be changed."

17 When I heard this, I got to my feet and listened; a voice was speaking, and its sound was like the sound of mighty^i waters. ^{18}It said, "The days are coming when I draw near to visit the inhabitants of the earth, ^{19}and when I require from the doers of iniquity the penalty of their iniquity, and when the humiliation of Zion is complete. ^{20}When the seal is placed upon the age that is about to pass away, then I will show these signs: the books shall be opened before the face of the firmament, and all shall see my judgment^j together. ^{21}Children a year old shall speak with their voices, and pregnant women shall give birth to premature children at three and four months, and these shall live and leap about. ^{22}Sown places shall suddenly appear unsown, and full storehouses shall suddenly be found to be empty; ^{23}the trumpet shall sound aloud, and when all hear it they shall suddenly

be terrified. ^{24}At that time friends shall make war on friends like enemies, the earth and those who inhabit it shall be terrified, and the springs of the fountains shall stand still, so that for three hours they shall not flow.

25 "It shall be that whoever remains after all that I have foretold to you shall be saved and shall see my salvation and the end of my world. ^{26}And they shall see those who were taken up, who from their birth have not tasted death, and the heart of the earth's^k inhabitants shall be changed and converted to a different spirit. ^{27}For evil shall be blotted out, and deceit shall be quenched; ^{28}faithfulness shall flourish, and corruption shall be overcome, and the truth, which has been so long without fruit, shall be revealed."

29 While he spoke to me, little by little the place where I was standing began to rock to and fro. ^{30}And he said to me, "I have come to show you these things this night.^{l} ^{31}If therefore you will pray again and fast again for seven days, I will again declare to you greater things than these,^{m} ^{32}because your voice has surely been heard by the Most High, for the Mighty One has seen your uprightness and has also observed the purity that you have maintained from your youth. ^{33}Therefore he sent me to show you all these things and to say to you: 'Believe and do not be afraid! ^{34}Do not be quick to think vain thoughts concerning the former times; then you will not act hastily in the last times.'"

35 Now after this I wept again and fasted seven days in the same way as before,

g 6.8 Syr: Lat *to Abraham*   h 6.10 Syr: Meaning of Lat uncertain   i 6.17 Lat *many*   j 6.20 Syr: Lat lacks *my judgment*   k 6.26 Syr Compare Ethiop Arab 1 Arm: Lat lacks *earth's*   l 6.30 Syr Compare Ethiop: Meaning of Lat uncertain   m 6.31 Syr Ethiop Arab 1 Arm: Lat adds *by day*

of the end. **6:8** *Esau* is a cipher for Rome, and *Jacob* is Israel; cf. Gen. 25:26. **6:9** The age of *Esau*, Rome, is almost over, with the new age belonging to Israel.

6:11–28 More signs of the end. 6:12 *Signs*. See notes at 4:52; 5:1–13. **6:13** *Full, resounding voice* of divine pronouncement; cf. Dan. 10:6. **6:14–16** The earth shakes at the imminent cosmic change that will occur at the end. **6:18** God is speaking. **6:19–20** *When . . . when . . . when* highlights three dimensions of the end-time judgment: the individual, the national, and the cosmic. *Books* record human deeds. **6:21** Shortening of life. Cf. Jub. 23:25. **6:22** Disruption of the natural order. Cf. 5:8, 9. **6:23** *Trumpet*. Cf. Amos 3:6. **6:24** *Friends . . . friends*. Cf. 5:9; 1 En. 110:1. **6:25** *Whoever remains*—that is, whoever survives the eschatological woes. This is the first prophecy of redemption. **6:26** *Those who were taken up*. Enoch (Gen. 5:24) and Elijah (2 Kgs. 2:9–12), but see also 2 Esd. 14:9; 2 Bar. 13:3. *Tasted death*. Cf. Matt. 16:28; John 8:52. *Heart . . . to a different spirit*. That is, not the evil inclination inherited from Adam. **6:27–28** Poetic omens of the end times. Cf. 7:33–35, 113–114; 8:52–53; 14:18.

6:29–34 Conclusion of the second episode. 6:29 Cf. 6:13–16. **6:31** Cf. 5:13. **6:34** Cf. 4:34.

6:35–9:25 Third episode. 6:35 *Three weeks*. Cf. Dan. 10:2–3.

in order to complete the three weeks that had been prescribed for me. ³⁶Then on the eighth night my heart was troubled within me again, and I began to speak in the presence of the Most High. ³⁷My spirit was greatly aroused, and my soul was in distress.

38 I said, "O Lord, you spoke at the beginning of creation and said on the first day, 'Let heaven and earth be made,' and your word accomplished the work. ³⁹Then the spirit was blowing, and darkness and silence embraced everything; the sound of human voices was not yet there.ⁿ ⁴⁰Then you commanded a ray of light to be brought out from your storehouses, so that your works could be seen.

41 "Again, on the second day, you created the spirit of the firmament and commanded it to divide and separate the waters, so that one part might move upward and the other part remain beneath.

42 "On the third day you commanded the waters to be gathered together in a seventh part of the earth; six parts you dried up and kept so that some of them might be planted and cultivated and be of service before you. ⁴³For your word went forth, and at once the work was done. ⁴⁴Immediately fruit came forth in endless abundance and of varied appeal to the taste, and flowers of inimitable color, and odors of inexpressible fragrance. These were made on the third day.

45 "On the fourth day you commanded the brightness of the sun, the light of the moon, and the arrangement of the stars to come into being, ⁴⁶and you commanded them to serve the human who was about to be formed.

47 "On the fifth day you commanded the seventh part, where the water had been gathered together, to bring forth living creatures, birds, and fishes, and so it was done. ⁴⁸The dumb and lifeless water produced living creatures, as it was commanded, so that therefore the nations might declare your wondrous works.

49 "Then you kept in existence two living creatures that you created;ᵒ the one you called Behemothᵖ and the name of the other Leviathan. ⁵⁰And you separated one from the other, for the seventh part where the water had been gathered together could not hold them both. ⁵¹And you gave Behemothᵠ one of the parts that had been dried up on the third day, to live in it, where there are a thousand mountains, ⁵²but to Leviathan you gave the seventh part, the watery part, and you have kept them to be eaten by whom you wish and when you wish.

53 "On the sixth day you commanded the earth to bring forth before you cattle, wild animals, and creeping things, ⁵⁴and over these you placed Adam, as ruler over all the works that you had made, and from him we have all come, the people whom you have chosen.

55 "All this I have spoken before you, O Lord, because you have said that it was for us that you created this world.ʳ ⁵⁶As for the other nations that have descended from Adam, you have said that they are nothing and that they are like spittle, and you have compared their abundance to a drop from a bucket. ⁵⁷And now, O Lord, these nations, which are reputed to be as nothing, domineer over us and devour us. ⁵⁸But we your people, whom you have called your first-born, only begotten, zealous for you,ˢ and most dear, have been given into their hands. ⁵⁹If the world has indeed been created for us, why do we not possess our world as an inheritance? How long will this be so?"

7 When I had finished speaking these words, the angel who had been sent to me on the former nights was sent to me again. ²He said to me, "Rise, Ezra, and listen to the words that I have come to speak to you."

3 I said, "Speak, my lord." And he said to me, "There is a sea set in a wide expanse so

n 6.39 Syr Ethiop: Lat *was not yet from you*   o 6.49 Syr Ethiop: Lat lacks *that you created*   p 6.49 Other Lat authorities read *Enoch*   q 6.51 Other Lat authorities read *Enoch*   r 6.55 Syr Ethiop Arab 2: Lat *the firstborn world*   s 6.58 Lat lacks *for you*

6:38–59 A recount of God's creation of the world. Cf. Gen. 1:1–31. The seventh day is not reviewed. **6:38** Creation through divine speech. **6:39** Primordial silence. Cf. 7:30. **6:40** *Storehouses*. Cf. 5:37. **6:42** *Seventh part*, indicating a seven-part division of the world, has no known parallel. **6:49–52** *Behemoth* and *Leviathan*. Cf. Job 40:15–41:11. In other Jewish sources, these mythical beasts are to be food served at the eschatological banquet. See 2 Bar. 29:4; 1 En. 60:7–10. **6:55** The world was created for the sake of Israel. **6:56** Cf. Isa. 40:15, 17. **6:57** Cf. 3:28; 5:28–29. **6:59** *How long?* See 4:33; also, e.g., Pss. 4:2; 13:2.

7:1–16 Israel's inheritance in this world and the world to come. **7:1** Cf. 4:1; 5:31. **7:2** *Rise.* Cf. 4:47; 6:13. **7:3–9** The two parables highlight that a dangerous path must be traversed before the reward

that it is deep and vast, [4]but it has an entrance set in a narrow place, so that it is like a river. [5]If there are those who wish to reach the sea, to look at it or to navigate it, how can they come to the broad part unless they pass through the narrow part? [6]Another example: There is a city built and set on a plain, and it is full of all good things, [7]but the entrance to it is narrow and set in a precipitous place, so that there is fire on the right hand and deep water on the left. [8]There is only one path lying between them, that is, between the fire and the water, so that only one person can walk on the path. [9]If now the city is given to someone as an inheritance, how will the heir receive the inheritance unless by passing through the appointed danger?"

[10]I said, "That is right, lord." He said to me, "So also is Israel's portion. [11]For I made the world for their sake, and when Adam transgressed my statutes, what had been made was judged. [12]And so the entrances of this world were made narrow and sorrowful and toilsome; they are few and evil, full of dangers and involved in great hardships. [13]But the entrances of the greater world are broad and safe and yield the fruit of immortality. [14]Therefore unless the living pass through the difficult and futile experiences, they can never receive those things that have been reserved for them. [15]Now, therefore, why are you disturbed, seeing that you are to perish? Why are you moved, seeing that you are mortal? [16]Why have you not considered in your mind what is to come rather than what is now present?"

[17]Then I answered and said, "O sovereign Lord, you have ordained in your law that the righteous shall inherit these things but that the ungodly shall perish. [18]The righteous, therefore, can endure difficult circumstances while hoping for easier ones, but those who have done wickedly have

suffered the difficult circumstances and will never see the easier ones."

[19]He said to me, "You are not a better judge than the Lord[t] or wiser than the Most High! [20]Let many perish who are now living rather than that the law of God that is set before them be disregarded! [21]For the Lord[u] strictly commanded those who came into the world, when they came, what they should do to live and what they should observe to avoid punishment. [22]Nevertheless, they were not obedient and spoke against him;

they devised for themselves vain thoughts
[23]   and proposed to themselves wicked
        frauds;
they even declared that the Most High
        does not exist,
    and they ignored his ways.
[24] They scorned his law
        and denied his covenants;
    they have been unfaithful to his statutes
        and have not performed his works.

[25]"That is the reason, Ezra, that empty things are for the empty and full things are for the full.

[26] "For indeed the time will come when the signs that I have foretold to you will come to pass, that the city that now is not seen shall appear[v] and the land that now is hidden shall be disclosed. [27]Everyone who has been delivered from the evils that I have foretold shall see my wonders. [28]For my son the Messiah[w] shall be revealed with those who are with him, and those who remain shall rejoice four hundred years. [29]After those years my son the Messiah shall die, and all who draw human breath.[x] [30]Then the world shall be turned

t 7.19 Other ancient authorities read God; Ethiop Georg the only One   u 7.21 Other ancient authorities read God v 7.26 Arm: Lat Syr that the bride shall appear, even the city appearing   w 7.28 Syr Arab 1: Ethiop my Messiah; Arab 2 the Messiah; Arm the Messiah of God; Lat my son Jesus   x 7.29 Arm all who have continued in faith and in patience

(here, the sea and a city) can be reached. **7:6–9** For similar city imagery, see Herm. Sim. 9.12.5; T. Job 18:6. **7:10** The parables are about Israel. **7:11–12** Adam's transgression caused this world to be judged and filled with hardships. **7:13** Greater world is the world to come that Israel is to inherit. **7:15–16** Ezra should concern himself about the future that Israel will inherit rather than his own mortality.

7:17–25 Ezra's concern and Uriel's rebuke. 7:17 Cf. 4:34. **7:18** See 7:117–118. **7:19** Ezra is rebuked. **7:20** Law is Torah. **7:21–25** Reward and punishment both come from the validity of Torah.

7:26–44 Prediction of eschatological events. 7:26 City . . . shall appear is the eschatological Zion. Cf. 10:27–59; Dead Sea Scrolls 4Q554–55; 11Q18; Rev. 21:9–22:7. **7:28** My son the Messiah. The Ethiopic "my messiah" is likely the most original; see the textual note to the translation. On a messianic period, see also 12:34. Note the messiah's role here is only rejoicing with the remnant. See also **"Jewish Messianic Ideas," p. 1783. 7:29** End of the temporary messianic kingdom. The messiah dies along with any other humans. **7:30–31** A reset of creation. Seven days corresponds to Gen. 1:1–31.

back to primeval silence for seven days, as it was at the first beginnings, so that no one shall be left. ³¹After seven days the world that is not yet awake shall be roused, and that which is corruptible shall perish. ³²The earth shall give up those who are asleep in it and the dust those who rest there in silence, and the chambers shall give up the souls that have been committed to them. ³³The Most High shall be revealed on the seat of judgment, and compassion shall pass away, and patience shall be withdrawn.ʸ ³⁴Only judgment shall remain, truth shall stand, and faithfulness shall grow strong. ³⁵Recompense shall follow, and the reward shall be manifested; righteous deeds shall awake, and unrighteous deeds shall not sleep. ³⁶The pitᶻ of torment shall appear, and opposite it shall be the place of rest, and the furnace of Gehenna shall be disclosed, and opposite it the paradise of delight. ³⁷Then the Most High will say to the nations that have been raised from the dead, 'Look now, and understand whom you have denied, whom you have not served, whose commandments you have despised. ³⁸Look on this side and on that; here are delight and rest, and there are fire and torments.' Thus he will speak to them on the day of judgment, ³⁹a day that has no sun or moon or stars, ⁴⁰or cloud or thunder or lightning, or wind or water or air, or darkness or evening or morning, ⁴¹or summer or spring or heat or winterᵃ or frost or cold, or hail or rain or dew, ⁴²or noon or night, or dawn or shining or brightness or light, but only the splendor of the glory of the Most High, by which all shall see what has been destined. ⁴³It will last as though for a week of years. ⁴⁴This is my judgment and its prescribed order, and to you alone I have shown these things."

45 I answered and said, "O sovereign Lord, I said then andᵇ I say now: Blessed are those who are alive and keep your commandments! ⁴⁶But what of those for whom I prayed? For who among the living is there who has not sinned, or who is there among

mortals who has not transgressed your covenant? ⁴⁷And now I see that the world to come will bring delight to few but torments to many. ⁴⁸For an evil heart has grown up in us that has alienated us from these and has brought us into corruption and the ways of death and has shown us the paths of perdition and removed us far from life—and that not merely for a few but for almost all who have been created."

49 He answered me and said, "Listen to me, Ezra,ᶜ and I will instruct you and will admonish you once more. ⁵⁰For this reason the Most High has made not one world but two. ⁵¹Inasmuch as you have said that the righteous are not many but few, while the ungodly abound, hear the explanation for this.

52 "If you have just a few precious stones, will you add to them lead and clay?"ᵈ ⁵³I said, "Lord, how could that be?" ⁵⁴And he said to me, "Not only that, but ask the earth, and she will tell you; defer to her, and she will declare it to you. ⁵⁵Say to her, 'You produce gold and silver and bronze and also iron and lead and clay, ⁵⁶but silver is more abundant than gold, and bronze than silver, and iron than bronze, and lead than iron, and clay than lead.' ⁵⁷Judge therefore which things are precious and desirable, those that are abundant or those that are rare?"

58 I said, "O sovereign Lord, what is plentiful is of less worth, for what is more rare is more precious."

59 He answered me and said, "Consider within yourself what you have thought, for the person who has what is hard to get rejoices more than the person who has what is plentiful. ⁶⁰So also will be the judgmentᵉ that I have promised, for I will rejoice over the few who shall be saved because it is they who have made my glory to prevail now, and through them my name has now been honored. ⁶¹I will not grieve over the great number of those

y 7.33 Lat *shall gather together*   z 7.36 Syr Ethiop: Lat *place*
a 7.41 Or *storm*   b 7.45 Syr: Lat *And I answered, "I said then, O Lord, and*   c 7.49 Syr Arab 1 Georg: Lat Ethiop lack *Ezra*   d 7.52 Arab 1: Meaning of Lat Syr Ethiop uncertain
e 7.60 Syr Arab 1: Lat *creation*

7:32 The resurrection—that is, the reunion of the body from the *earth . . . dust* and the souls from the *chambers*; cf. 4:35. See **"Resurrection," p. 1224**. **7:35–36** *Recompense*. Reward and punishment follow judgment. **7:37–38** God addresses the nations. **7:39–42** Division of times and seasons that will be abolished; cf. Gen. 8:22. **7:43** A seven-year period. E.g. Dan. 9:24; 2 Bar. 28:2.

    7:45–74 The many versus the few. 7:45–48 Ezra questions the rewards of the few versus the punishment of the many, since all have sinned. **7:52–57** Parable of precious and base metals to explain the righteous and the wicked. **7:61** *Mist . . . flame and smoke*. Common imagery in the Hebrew Bible

who perish, for it is they who are now like a mist and are similar to a flame and smoke—they are set on fire and burn hotly and are extinguished."

62 I replied and said, "O earth, what have you brought forth, if the mind is made out of the dust like the other created things? ⁶³For it would have been better if the dust itself had not been born, so that the mind might not have been made from it. ⁶⁴But now the mind grows with us, and therefore we are tormented, because we perish and we know it. ⁶⁵Let the human race lament, but let the wild animals of the field be glad; let all who have been born lament, but let the cattle and the flocks rejoice. ⁶⁶It is much better with them than with us, for they do not look for a judgment, and they do not know of any torment or salvation promised to them after death. ⁶⁷What does it profit us that we shall be preserved alive but cruelly tormented? ⁶⁸For all who have been born are entangled in*ᶠ* iniquities and are full of sins and burdened with transgressions. ⁶⁹And if after death we were not to come into judgment, perhaps it would have been better for us."

70 He answered me and said, "When the Most High made the world and Adam and all who have come from him, he first prepared the judgment and the things that pertain to the judgment. ⁷¹But now, understand from your own words, for you have said that the mind grows with us. ⁷²For this reason, therefore, those who live on earth shall be tormented, because though they had understanding they committed iniquity, and though they received the commandments they did not keep them, and though they obtained the law they dealt unfaithfully with what they received. ⁷³What, then, will they have to say in the judgment, or how will they answer in the last times? ⁷⁴How long the Most High has been patient with those who inhabit the world!—and not for their sake but because of the times that he has foreordained."

75 I answered and said, "If I have found favor in your sight, O Lord, show this also to your servant: whether after death, as soon as everyone of us yields up the soul, we shall be kept in rest until those times come when you will renew the creation, or whether we shall be tormented at once?"

76 He answered me and said, "I will show you that also, but do not include yourself with those who have shown scorn, or number yourself among those who are tormented. ⁷⁷For you have a treasure of works stored up with the Most High, but it will not be shown to you until the last times. ⁷⁸Now concerning death, the teaching is: When the decisive decree has gone out from the Most High that a person shall die, as the spirit leaves the body to return again to him who gave it, first of all it adores the glory of the Most High. ⁷⁹If it is one of those who have shown scorn and have not kept the way of the Most High, who have despised his law and hated those who fear God, ⁸⁰such spirits shall not enter into habitations but shall immediately wander about in torments, always grieving and sad, in seven ways. ⁸¹The first way: because they have scorned the law of the Most High. ⁸²The second way: because they cannot now make a good repentance so that they may live. ⁸³The third way: they shall see the reward laid up for those who have trusted the covenants of the Most High. ⁸⁴The fourth way: they shall consider the torment laid up for themselves in the last days. ⁸⁵The fifth way: they shall see how the habitations of the others are guarded by angels in profound quiet. ⁸⁶The sixth way: they shall see how some of them will cross over*ᵍ* into torments. ⁸⁷The seventh way, which is worse than all the ways that have been mentioned: because they shall utterly waste away in confusion and be consumed with shame*ʰ* and shall wither with fear at seeing the glory of the Most High in whose presence they sinned while they were alive and in whose presence they are to be judged in the last times.

88 "Now this is the order of those who have kept the ways of the Most High, when they shall be separated from their mortal body.*ⁱ*

f 7.68 Syr *defiled with*   g 7.86 Cn: Meaning of Lat uncertain   h 7.87 Syr Ethiop: Meaning of Lat uncertain   i 7.88 Lat *the corruptible vessel*

(e.g., Hos. 13:3). **7:62** Ezra offers a lament over the earth. *Mind*—that is, consciousness. **7:65–66** The animals are not judged. **7:67** The remnant here is not those who are saved but those who are judged and punished after resurrection. **7:70** According to several rabbinic sources, six or seven objects were created before humans, including Gehenna and Eden; cf., for example, b. Ned. 39b.

7:75–101 A prediction of the fate of the righteous and the wicked after death, each arranged in a set of seven. **7:76–77** Ezra is assured of his own righteousness. **7:79–87** The seven torments of the wicked, called *ways*. **7:80** *Habitations*—that is, chambers. **7:82** No postmortem repentance. **7:88–99** The seven

89During the time that they lived in it,*j* they laboriously served the Most High and withstood danger every hour so that they might keep the law of the Lawgiver perfectly. 90Therefore this is the teaching concerning them: 91First of all, they shall see with great joy the glory of him who receives them, for they shall have rest in seven orders. 92The first order: because they have striven with great effort to overcome the evil thought that was formed with them, so that it might not lead them astray from life into death. 93The second order: because they see the perplexity in which the souls of the ungodly wander and the punishment that awaits them. 94The third order: they see the witness that he who formed them bears concerning them, that throughout their life they kept the law with which they were entrusted. 95The fourth order: they understand the rest that they now enjoy, being gathered into their chambers and guarded by angels in profound quiet and the glory waiting for them in the last days. 96The fifth order: they rejoice that they have now escaped what is corruptible and shall inherit what is to come; moreover, they see the straits and toil from which they have been delivered and the spacious liberty that they are to receive and enjoy in immortality. 97The sixth order: when it is shown them how their face is to shine like the sun and how they are to be made like the light of the stars, being incorruptible from then on. 98The seventh order, which is greater than all that have been mentioned: because they shall rejoice with boldness and shall be confident without confusion and shall be glad without fear, for they press forward to see the face of him whom they served in life and from whom they are to receive their reward when glorified. 99This is the order of the souls of the righteous, as henceforth is announced,*k* and the previously mentioned are the ways of torment that those who would not give heed shall suffer hereafter."

100 Then I answered and said, "Will time therefore be given to the souls, after they have been separated from the bodies, to see what you have described to me?"

101 He said to me, "They shall have freedom for seven days, so that during these seven days they may see the things of which you have been told, and afterward they shall be gathered in their habitations."

102 I answered and said, "If I have found favor in your sight, show further to me, your servant, whether on the day of judgment the righteous will be able to intercede for the ungodly or to entreat the Most High for them—103fathers for sons or sons for parents, brothers for brothers, relatives for their kindred, or friends for those who are most dear."

104 He answered me and said, "Since you have found favor in my sight, I will show you this also. The day of judgment is decisive*l* and displays to all the seal of truth. Just as now a father does not send his son, or a son his father, or a master his servant, or a friend his dearest friend, to be ill*m* or sleep or eat or be healed in his place, 105so no one shall ever pray for another on that day, neither shall anyone lay a burden on another,*n* for then all shall bear their own righteousness and unrighteousness."

106 I answered and said, "How, then, do we find that first Abraham prayed for the people of Sodom, and Moses for our ancestors who sinned in the desert, 107and Joshua after him for Israel in the days of Achan, 108and Samuel in the days of Saul,*o* and David for the plague, and Solomon for those at the dedication, 109and Elijah for those who received the rain and for the one who was dead, that he might live, 110and Hezekiah for the people in the days of Sennacherib, and many others prayed for many? 111So if now, when corruption has increased and unrighteousness has multiplied, the righteous have prayed for the ungodly, why will it not be so then as well?"

j 7.89 Syr Ethiop: Meaning of Lat uncertain *k* 7.99 Syr: Meaning of Lat uncertain *l* 7.104 Lat *bold* *m* 7.104 Syr Ethiop Arm: Lat *to understand* *n* 7.105 Syr Ethiop: Lat lacks *on that . . . another* *o* 7.108 Syr Ethiop Arab 1: Lat Arab 2 Arm lack *in the days of Saul*

rewards of the righteous, called *orders.* **7:90** Another composition called the Questions of Ezra 19A contains a later development of this description of the ascent of the righteous. **7:97** Shining faces or bodies signifying a level of divinity are common tropes in ancient Near Eastern, Hellenistic, Roman, and later texts; e.g., 7:125; Dan. 12:3; Rev. 1:16.
  7:102–115 Dialogue about intercession of the righteous on behalf of the wicked. 7:105 Each individual is responsible for themselves only; cf. Deut. 24:16; Jer. 31:29; Ezek. 18:20. **7:106–110** List of biblical figures who interceded on behalf of others. **7:106** *Abraham.* Gen. 18:23–33. *Moses.* Exod. 32:11–14. **7:107** *Joshua.* Josh. 7:6–9. **7:108** *Samuel.* 1 Sam. 7:8–9. *David.* 2 Sam. 24:17–25. *Solomon.* 1 Kgs. 8:22–53. **7:109** *Elijah.* 1 Kgs. 17:21–23. **7:110** *Hezekiah.* 2 Kgs. 19:15–19.

112 He answered me and said, "This present world is not the end; the glory of God*p* does not*q* remain in it; therefore those who were strong prayed for the weak. [113]But the day of judgment will be the end of this age and the beginning*r* of the immortal age to come, in which corruption has passed away, [114]sinful indulgence has come to an end, unbelief has been cut off, and righteousness has increased, and truth has appeared. [115]Therefore no one will then be able to have mercy on someone who has been condemned in the judgment or to harm*s* someone who is victorious."

116 I answered and said, "This is my first and last comment: it would have been better if the earth had not produced Adam or else, when it had produced him, had restrained him from sinning. [117]For what good is it to all that they live in sorrow now and expect punishment after death? [118]O Adam, what have you done? For though it was you who sinned, the fall was not yours alone but ours also who are your descendants. [119]For what good is it to us, if an immortal time has been promised to us, but we have done deeds that bring death? [120]And what good is it that an everlasting hope has been promised to us, but we have miserably failed? [121]Or that safe and healthful habitations have been reserved for us, but we have lived wickedly? [122]Or that the glory of the Most High will defend those who have led a pure life, but we have walked in the most wicked ways? [123]Or that a paradise shall be revealed, whose fruit remains unspoiled and in which are abundance and healing, but we shall not enter it [124]because we have lived in perverse places? [125]Or that the faces of those who practiced self-control shall shine more than the stars, but our faces shall be blacker than darkness? [126]For while we lived and committed iniquity we did not consider what we should suffer after death."

127 He answered and said, "This is the significance of the contest that all who are born on earth shall wage: [128]if they are defeated they shall suffer what you have said, but if they are victorious they shall receive what I have said.*t* [129]For this is the way of which Moses, while he was alive, spoke to the people, saying, 'Choose life for yourself, so that you may live!' [130]But they did not believe him or the prophets after him or even myself who have spoken to them. [131]Therefore there shall not be*u* grief at their destruction so much as joy over those to whom salvation is assured."

132 I answered and said, "I know, O Lord, that the Most High is now called merciful because he has mercy on those who have not yet come into the world; [133]and gracious because he is gracious to those who turn in repentance to his law; [134]and patient because he shows patience toward those who have sinned, since they are his own creatures; [135]and bountiful because he would rather give than take away;*v* [136]and abundant in compassion because he makes his compassions abound more and more to those now living and to those who are gone and to those yet to come— [137]for if he did not make them abound, the world with those who inhabit it would not have life— [138]and he is called the giver because if he did not give out of his goodness so that those who have committed iniquities might be relieved of them, not one ten-thousandth of humankind could have life; [139]and the judge because if he did not pardon those who were created by his word and blot out the multitude of their sins,*w* [140]there would probably be left only very few of the innumerable multitude."

8 He answered me and said, "The Most High made this world for the sake of many but the world to come for the sake of only a few. [2]But I tell you a parable, Ezra. Just

p 7.112 Syr Ethiop Georg: Lat lacks *of God*   *q* 7.112 Syr: Lat lacks *not*   *r* 7.113 Syr Ethiop: Lat lacks *the beginning*   *s* 7.115 Syr Ethiop: Lat *overwhelm*   *t* 7.128 Syr Ethiop Arab 1: Lat *what I say*   *u* 7.131 Syr: Lat *there was not*   *v* 7.135 Or *he is ready to give according to requests*   *w* 7.139 Lat *contempts*

7:112–115 The angel responds that intercession has been necessary because God's glory is not always present in this world. At the end of this age, however, the divine will be present through judgment, so intercession will not be necessary.
7:116–131 **Lamentation over the fate of the many. 7:116** Ezra responds with a variation of the question "Why was I born?" **7:119–126** See also 7:117. *For what good is it . . . ?* And *Or . . . ?* Provide rhetorical contrast to what has been prepared for the righteous and how the righteous have sinned. **7:127** The angel answers that the *contest* is between good and evil in each individual. **7:129** Deut. 30:19. **7:130** For the rejection of prophets, see 2 Chr. 36:16; Matt. 23:37.
7:132–8:3 **Ezra appeals to God and Uriel's response.** A midrash on Exod. 34:6–7 emphasizing God's mercy. **8:2** The earth's response to 7:55–56.

as, when you ask the earth, it will tell you that it provides a large amount of clay from which earthenware is made but only a little dust from which gold comes, so is the course of the present world. ³Many have been created, but only a few shall be saved."

4 I answered and said, "Then drink your fill of[x] understanding, O my soul, and drink wisdom, O my heart. ⁵For not of your own will did you come into the world,[y] and against your will you depart, for you have been given only a short time to live. ⁶O Lord above us, grant to your servant that we may pray before you, and give us a seed for our heart and cultivation of our understanding so that fruit may be produced, by which every mortal who bears the likeness[z] of a human may be able to live. ⁷For you alone exist, and we are a work of your hands, as you have declared. ⁸And because you give life to the body that is now fashioned in the womb and furnish it with members, what you have created is preserved amid fire and water, and for nine months the womb[a] endures your creature that has been created in it. ⁹But that which keeps and that which is kept shall both be kept by your keeping. And when the womb gives up again what has been created in it, ¹⁰you have commanded that from the members themselves (that is, from the breasts) milk, the fruit of the breasts, should be supplied, ¹¹so that what has been fashioned may be nourished for a time, and afterward you will still guide it in your mercy. ¹²You have nurtured it in your righteousness and instructed it in your law and reproved it in your wisdom. ¹³You put it to death as your creation and make it live as your work. ¹⁴If then you will suddenly and quickly[b] destroy what with so great labor was fashioned by your command, to what purpose was it made? ¹⁵And now I will speak out: About all humankind you know best, but I will speak about your people, for whom I am grieved, ¹⁶and about your inheritance, for whom I lament, and about Israel, for whom I am sad, and about the seed of Jacob, for whom I am troubled. ¹⁷Therefore I

will pray before you for myself and for them, for I see the failings of us who inhabit the earth, ¹⁸and now also[c] I have heard of the swiftness of the judgment that is to come. ¹⁹Therefore hear my voice and understand my words, and I will speak before you."

The beginning of the words of Ezra's prayer,[d] before he was taken up. He said: ²⁰"O Lord, you who inhabit eternity,[e] whose eyes[f] are exalted and whose upper chambers are in the air, ²¹whose throne is beyond measure and whose glory is beyond comprehension, before whom the hosts of angels stand trembling ²²and at whose command they are changed to wind and fire,[g] whose word is sure and whose utterances are certain, whose command is strong and whose ordinance is terrible, ²³whose look dries up the depths and whose indignation makes the mountains melt away, and whose truth is established[h] forever—²⁴hear, O Lord, the prayer of your servant, and give ear to the petition of your creature; attend to my words. ²⁵For as long as I live I will speak, and as long as I have understanding I will answer. ²⁶O do not look on the sins of your people but on those who serve you in truth. ²⁷Do not take note of the endeavors of those who act wickedly but of the endeavors of those who have kept your covenants amid afflictions. ²⁸Do not think of those who have lived wickedly in your sight, but remember those who have willingly acknowledged that you are to be feared. ²⁹Do not will the destruction of those who have the ways of cattle, but regard those who have gloriously taught your law.[i] ³⁰Do not be angry with those who are deemed worse than wild animals, but love those who have always put their trust in your glory. ³¹For we and our ancestors have passed our lives in ways that bring death,[j]

x 8.4 Syr: Lat *release*   y 8.5 Syr: Meaning of Lat uncertain   z 8.6 Syr: Lat *place*   a 8.8 Lat *what you have formed*   b 8.14 Syr: Lat *will with a light command*   c 8.18 Syr: Lat *but*   d 8.19 Syr Ethiop: Lat *beginning of Ezra's words*   e 8.20 Or *you who abide forever*   f 8.20 Another Lat text reads *heavens*   g 8.22 Syr: Lat *they whose service takes the form of wind and fire*   h 8.23 Arab 2: Lat *truth bears witness*   i 8.29 Syr *have received the brightness of your law*   j 8.31 Syr Ethiop: Meaning of Lat uncertain

8:4–36 Ezra appeals again and offers a prayer to God. **8:6** God is now addressed. **8:7** For God's uniqueness, see, e.g., Deut. 4:35; 6:4. **8:8–13** The attention with which God nurtures humans. **8:14** Ezra questions the perceived contradiction in God's actions. **8:15–16** Ezra speaks about Israel. **8:19** *I will speak before you* anticipates Ezra being "taken up"; cf. 14:9. **8:21** The *throne* is surrounded by *angels*; see, e.g., 1 Kgs. 22:19; Isa. 6. **8:22** *Wind and fire.* Cf. Ps. 104:4. **8:26–30** Ezra's intercession, despite 7:31. **8:31–36** Ezra's confession. Cf. Dan. 9:4–6.

but it is because of us sinners that you are called merciful. [32]For if you have desired to have pity on us, who have no works of righteousness, then you will be called merciful. [33]For the righteous, who have many works laid up with you, shall receive their reward in consequence of their own deeds. [34]But what are mortals that you are angry with them, or what is a corruptible race that you are so bitter against it? [35]For in truth there is no one among those who have been born who has not acted wickedly; among those who have existed there is no one who has not done wrong. [36]For in this, O Lord, your righteousness and goodness will be declared: when you are merciful to those who have no store of good works."

37 He answered me and said, "Some things you have spoken rightly, and it will turn out according to your words. [38]For indeed I will not concern myself about the fashioning of those who have sinned or about their death, their judgment, or their destruction, [39]but I will rejoice over the creation of the righteous, over their pilgrimage also, and their salvation, and their receiving their reward. [40]As I have spoken, therefore, so it shall be.

41 "For just as the farmer sows many seeds in the ground and plants a multitude of seedlings and yet not all that have been sown will come up[k] in due season and not all that were planted will take root, so also those who have been sown in the world will not all be saved."

42 I answered and said, "If I have found favor in your sight, let me speak. [43]If the farmer's seed does not come up because it has not received your rain in due season or if it has been ruined by too much rain, it perishes.[l] [44]But people, who have been formed by your hands and are called your own image because they are made like you and for whose sake you have formed all things, have you also made them like the farmer's seed? [45]Surely not, O Lord[m] above! But spare your people and have mercy on your inheritance, for you have mercy on your own creation."

46 He answered me and said, "Things that are present are for those who live now, and things that are future are for those who will live hereafter. [47]For you come far short of being able to love my creation more than I love it. But you have often compared yourself[n] to the unrighteous. Never do so! [48]But even in this respect you will be praiseworthy before the Most High, [49]because you have humbled yourself, as is becoming for you, and have not considered yourself to be among the righteous. You will receive the greatest glory, [50]for many miseries will affect those who inhabit the world in the last times because they have walked in great pride. [51]But think of your own case, and inquire concerning the glory of those who are like yourself, [52]because it is for you that paradise is opened, the tree of life is planted, the age to come is prepared, plenty is provided, a city is built, rest is appointed,[o] goodness is established, and wisdom is perfected beforehand. [53]The root of evil[p] is sealed up from you, illness is banished from you, and death[q] is hidden; Hades has fled, and corruption has been forgotten;[r] [54]sorrows have passed away, and in the end the treasure of immortality is made manifest. [55]Therefore do not ask any more questions about the great number of those who perish. [56]For when they had opportunity to choose, they despised the Most High and were contemptuous of his law and abandoned his ways. [57]Moreover, they have even trampled on his righteous ones [58]and said in their hearts that there is no God—though they knew well that they must die. [59]For just as the things that I have predicted await[s] you, so the thirst and torment that are prepared await

k 8.41 Syr Ethiop *will live*; Lat *will be saved* l 8.43 Cn: Compare Syr Arab 1 Arm Georg 2: Meaning of Lat uncertain m 8.45 Ethiop Arab Compare Syr: Lat lacks *O Lord* n 8.47 Syr Ethiop: Lat *brought yourself near* o 8.52 Syr Ethiop: Lat *allowed* p 8.53 Lat lacks *of evil* q 8.53 Syr Ethiop Arm: Lat lacks *death* r 8.53 Syr: Lat *Hades and corruption have fled into oblivion*; or *corruption has fled into Hades to be forgotten* s 8.59 Syr: Lat *will receive*

8:37–62a Uriel and Ezra continue their dialogue. **8:38** *Death, judgment*, and *destruction* refer to eternal perdition. **8:41** Parable and interpretation; cf. Mark 4:3–9, 14–20. **8:44** Ezra stresses God's responsibility for human failure. **8:45** Appeal for mercy. **8:46** Mercy will be present in the world to come, not this world. **8:49** Humility is part of Ezra's righteousness. Cf. Matt. 23:12; Luke 14:11. **8:51–54** Eschatological prediction for the righteous. **8:52** *City*. Eschatological Zion. **8:55** Cf. 6:10; 9:13. **8:56–58** Cf. 5:29; 7:22–24, 37, 79, 81; 9:9–13. **8:56** *Opportunity to choose* indicates free will. **8:59** *Thirst and torment* are eschatological punishments.

them. For the Most High did not intend that anyone should be destroyed, [60]but those who were created have themselves defiled the name of him who made them and have been ungrateful to him who prepared life for them now. [61]Therefore my judgment is now drawing near; [62]I have not shown this to all people but only to you and a few like you."

Then I answered and said, [63]"O Lord, you have already shown me a great number of the signs that you will do in the last times, but you have not shown me when you will do them."

9 He answered me and said, "Measure carefully in your mind, and when you see that some of the predicted signs have occurred, [2]then you will know that it is the very time when the Most High is about to visit the world that he has made. [3]So when there shall appear in the world earthquakes, tumult of peoples, intrigues of nations, wavering of leaders, confusion of princes, [4]then you will know that it was of these that the Most High spoke from the days that were of old, from the beginning. [5]For just as with everything that has occurred in the world, the beginning is evident[t] and the end manifest; [6]so also are the times of the Most High: the beginnings are manifest in wonders and mighty works and the end in penalties[u] and in signs.

[7] "It shall be that all who will be saved and will be able to escape on account of their works or on account of the faith by which they have believed [8]will survive the dangers that have been predicted and will see my salvation in my land and within my borders, which I have sanctified for myself from the beginning. [9]Then those who have now abused my ways shall be amazed, and those who have rejected them with contempt shall live in torments. [10]For as many as did not acknowledge me in their lifetime, though they received my benefits, [11]and as many as scorned my law while they still had freedom [12]and did not understand but despised it while an opportunity

of repentance was still open to them, these must in torment acknowledge it[v] after death. [13]Therefore, do not continue to be curious about how the ungodly will be punished, but inquire how the righteous will be saved, those to whom the age belongs and for whose sake the age was made."[w]

[14] I answered and said, [15]"I said before, and I say now and will say it again: there are more who perish than those who will be saved, [16]as a wave is greater than a drop of water."

[17] He answered me and said, "As is the field, so is the seed, and as are the flowers, so are the colors, and as is the work, so is the product, and as is the farmer, so is the threshing floor. [18]For there was a time in this age when I was preparing for those who now exist, before the world was made for them to live in, and no one opposed me then, for no one existed, [19]but now those who have been created in this world, which is supplied both with an unfailing table and an inexhaustible pasture,[x] have become corrupt in their ways. [20]So I considered my world and saw that it was lost. I saw that my earth was in peril because of the devices of those who[y] had come into it. [21]And I saw and spared some[z] with great difficulty and saved for myself one grape out of a cluster and one plant out of a great forest.[a] [22]So let the multitude perish that has been born in vain, but let my grape and my plant be saved, because with much labor I have perfected them.

[23] "Now, if you will let seven days more pass—do not, however, fast during them, [24]but go into a field of flowers where no house has been built, and eat only of the flowers of the field, and taste no meat and drink no wine but eat only flowers—[25]and pray to the Most High continually, then I will come and talk with you."

---

t 9.5 Syr: Ethiop *is in the word*; meaning of Lat uncertain *u* 9.6 Syr: Lat Ethiop *in effects* *v* 9.12 Or *me* *w* 9.13 Syr: Lat *saved, and whose is the age and for whose sake the age was made and when* *x* 9.19 Cn: Lat *law* *y* 9.20 Cn: Lat *devices that* *z* 9.21 Lat *them* *a* 9.21 Syr Ethiop Arab 1: Lat *tribe*

8:62b–9:25 Signs of the end. 8:63 *Signs*—that is, eschatological predictions; cf. 5:1–13; 6:11–29. **9:1–2** The clearest response to "When?" **9:3** *Earthquakes.* Cf. Mark 13:8; 2 Bar. 27:7. **9:8** *In my land and within my borders*—that is, in the land of Israel. **9:9–12** List of sins; cf. 7:79; 8:56–58. **9:12** *While an opportunity of repentance was still open to them*—that is, in this world and age. **9:13** Cf. 6:10; 8:55. **9:19** *Table . . . pasture* indicates the plenitude available; cf. Ps. 23:1–2, 5. **9:20** The world is *in peril* because of human actions. **9:21–22** Two similes to highlight that only a few will be saved. **9:23–25** Concluding injunction. Cf. 5:14–20; 6:30–34. **9:23** *Seven days.* Cf. 5:20; 6:31, 35. **9:24** Instead of fasting, Ezra is commanded to *eat* only a special vegetarian diet; cf. 9:26; 12:51.

26 So I went, as he directed me, into the field that is called Ardat;[b] there I sat among the flowers and ate of the plants of the field, and the nourishment they afforded satisfied me. 27After seven days, while I lay on the grass, my heart was troubled again as it was before. 28Then my mouth was opened, and I began to speak before the Most High and said, 29"O Lord, you showed yourself among us to our ancestors in the wilderness when they came out from Egypt and when they came into the untrodden and unfruitful wilderness, 30and you said, 'Hear me, O Israel, and give heed to my words, O descendants of Jacob. 31For I sow my law in you, and it shall bring forth fruit in you, and you shall be glorified through it forever.' 32But though our ancestors received the law, they did not keep it and did not observe the[c] statutes, yet the fruit of the law did not perish, for it could not, because it was yours. 33Yet those who received it perished because they did not keep what had been sown in them. 34Now this is the general rule, that when the ground has received seed or the sea a ship or any dish food or drink, and when it comes about that what was sown or what was launched or what was put in is destroyed, 35they are destroyed, but the things that held them remain, yet with us it has not been so. 36For we who have received the law and sinned will perish, as well as our hearts that received it; 37the law, however, does not perish but survives in its glory."

38 When I said these things in my heart, I looked around,[d] and on my right I saw a woman; she was mourning and weeping with a loud voice and was deeply grieved at heart; her clothes were torn, and there were ashes on her head. 39Then I dismissed the thoughts with which I had been engaged and turned to her 40and said to her, "Why are you weeping, and why are you grieved at heart?"

41 She said to me, "Let me alone, my lord, so that I may weep for myself and continue to mourn, for I am greatly embittered in spirit and deeply distressed."

42 I said to her, "What has happened to you? Tell me."

43 And she said to me, "Your servant was barren and had no child, though I lived with my husband for thirty years. 44Every hour and every day during those thirty years I prayed to the Most High, night and day. 45And after thirty years God heard your servant and looked upon my low estate and considered my distress and gave me a son. I rejoiced greatly over him, I and my husband and all my neighbors,[e] and we gave great glory to the Mighty One. 46And I brought him up with much care. 47So when he grew up and I came to take a wife for him, I set a day for the marriage feast.

10 "But it happened that, when my son entered his wedding chamber, he fell down and died. 2So all of us put out our lamps, and all my neighbors[f] attempted to console me; I remained quiet until the evening of the second day. 3But when all of them had stopped consoling me, encouraging me

b 9.26 Syr Ethiop *Arpad*; Arm *Ardab*   c 9.32 Lat *my*
d 9.38 Syr Arab Arm: Lat *I looked about me with my eyes*
e 9.45 Lat *all my fellow citizens*   f 10.2 Lat *all my fellow citizens*

9:26–10:59 Fourth episode. 9:26 *Ardat.* An unknown location presumably outside of Babylon (cf. 3:1, 2). Ardat is the setting of episodes 4, 5, and 6.

9:29–37 Opening address devoted to the law. This parallels the opening addresses found in 3:4–7; 5:23–30; and 6:38–59. The seer does not return to the topic of the law in episode 4, however. **9:29** *Wilderness* at Mount Sinai. **9:30** Quotation likely from 3:19–20; cf. Deut. 5:1; 6:4. **9:32–33** God's law is eternal, while humanity is not. **9:34–37** In contrast to the examples of a holding vessel lasting while contents are destroyed, humans are the vessels who perish, while the law, which they hold, survives.

9:38–10:4 Ezra's initial encounter with the mourning woman. Folklore motifs found here are like those found in Tobit and 1 Sam. 1–2. **9:38** *Her clothes were torn . . . ashes on her head* are signs of mourning. The experience with the mourning woman is often identified as a "vision," but there is nothing in the text to suggest this identification. **9:39** An explanation for why the topic of the law is dropped. **9:41** Cf. Hannah in 1 Sam. 1:10. **9:43** *Thirty years.* Cf. 3:1. **9:44–45** *Prayed . . . gave great glory* signifies the pious nature of the woman. **9:47** The mother sets the marriage; cf. Gen. 21:21. *Marriage feast.* See, e.g., Tob. 8:19–21; Matt. 22:2. **10:1** Cf. Tob. 7:11; 8:10. **10:2** Putting out lamps and sitting in silence are ancient Jewish mourning customs. *Evening of the second day* is the customary end of the first period of mourning.

to be quiet, I got up in the night and fled, and I came to this field, as you see. [4]And now I intend not to return to the town but to stay here; I will neither eat nor drink but will mourn and fast continually until I die."

5 Then I broke off the reflections with which I was still engaged and answered her in anger and said, [6]"You most foolish of women, do you not see our mourning and what has happened to us? [7]For Zion, the mother of us all, is in deep grief and great distress. [8]It is most appropriate to mourn now, because we are all mourning, and to be sorrowful, because we are all sorrowing; you are sorrowing for one son.[g] [9]Now ask the earth, and she will tell you that it is she who ought to mourn over so many who have come into being upon her. [10]From the beginning all have been born of her, and others will come, and, behold, almost all walk to perdition, and a multitude of them will come to doom. [11]Who, then, ought to mourn the more: she who lost so great a multitude or you who are grieving for one alone? [12]But if you say to me, 'My lamentation is not like the earth's, for I have lost the fruit of my womb, which I brought forth in pain and bore in sorrow, [13]but it is with the earth according to the way of the earth: the multitude that is now in it goes as it came,' [14]then I say to you, 'Just as you brought forth in sorrow, so the earth also has from the beginning given her fruit, that is, humankind, to him who made her.' [15]Now, therefore, keep your sorrow to yourself, and bear bravely the troubles that have come upon you. [16]For if you acknowledge the decree of God to be just, you will receive your son back in due time and will be praised among women. [17]Therefore go into the town to your husband."

18 She said to me, "I will not do so; I will not go into the city, but I will die here."

19 So I spoke again to her and said, [20]"Do not do that, but let yourself be persuaded—for how many are the adversities of Zion?—and be consoled because of the sorrow of Jerusalem. [21]For you see how our sanctuary has been laid waste, our altar thrown down, our temple destroyed; [22]our harp has been laid low, our song has been silenced, and our rejoicing has been ended; the light of our lampstand has been put out, the ark of our covenant has been plundered, our holy things have been polluted, and the name by which we are called has been almost profaned; our children[h] have suffered abuse, our priests have been burned to death, our Levites have gone into exile, our virgins have been defiled, and our wives have been ravished; our righteous men[i] have been carried off, our little ones have been cast out, our young men have been enslaved and our strong men made powerless. [23]And, worst of all, the seal of Zion has been deprived of its glory and given over into the hands of those who hate us. [24]Therefore shake off your great sadness and lay aside your many sorrows, so that the Mighty One may be merciful to you again and the Most High may give you rest, a respite from your troubles."

25 While I was talking to her, her face suddenly began to shine exceedingly; her countenance flashed like lightning, so that I was too frightened to approach her, and my heart was terrified. While[j] I was wondering what this meant, [26]she suddenly uttered a loud and fearful cry so that the earth shook at the sound. [27]When I looked up, the woman was no longer visible to me, but a city was being built,[k] and a

g 10.8 Syr adds *but we, the whole world, for our mother*
h 10.22 Ethiop *free men*   i 10.22 Syr *our seers*   j 10.25 Syr Ethiop
Arab 1: Lat lacks *I was too … terrified. While*   k 10.27 Lat: Syr
Ethiop Arab 1 Arab 2 Arm *but there was an established city*

10:5–24 Ezra is dismissive of the woman's loss in light of the contemporaneous situation. **10:5** *Broke off the reflections.* Cf. 9:39. **10:6–7** *Most foolish of women.* Ezra is dismissive of one woman's experience because he claims that Zion, mother of all Israel, is in mourning. *Zion,* or Jerusalem, as mourning mother is common imagery; see, e.g., Isa. 50:1; Jer. 50:12; Gal. 4:26; 2 Bar. 10:16. **10:9** Humans come from the earth; cf. 5:48. **10:10** Ezra notes most of the earth's children—that is, humans—will be punished. **10:11** Ezra downplays the mourning woman's loss as minimal compared with the earth's loss. **10:12** *Pain* and *sorrow.* Cf. Gen. 3:16. **10:14** *So the earth also.* Ezra draws a direct comparison between the woman's birthing and suffering and that of the earth. **10:15–17** Ezra attempts to silence the woman and send her back to her husband with promises of the reward of her son in *due time,* the afterlife. **10:18** The woman refuses. **10:19–24** Ezra ignores the woman's wishes and tells her to be consoled because of the defilement of Zion and Israel.

10:25–28 Transformation of the mourning woman into a city. **10:25** Shining faces and bodies suggest divinity or a connection with the divine; cf. 7:97. **10:26** The earth shakes at portentous events. Loud cries often accompany such events; cf. 3:18; 6:13–15. **10:27** *City was being built.* Read as

place of huge foundations showed itself. I was afraid and cried with a loud voice and said, [28]"Where is the angel Uriel, who came to me at first? For it was he who brought me into this overpowering bewilderment; my end has become corruption and my prayer a reproach."

29 While I was speaking these words, the angel who had come to me at first came to me, and when he saw me [30]lying there like a corpse, deprived of my understanding, he grasped my right hand and strengthened me and set me on my feet and said to me, [31]"What is the matter with you? And why are you troubled? And why are your understanding and the thoughts of your mind troubled?"

32 I said, "It was because you abandoned me. I did as you directed and went out into the field, and behold, what I have seen and can still see, I am unable to explain."

33 He said to me, "Stand up like a man, and I will instruct you."

34 I said, "Speak, my lord; only do not forsake me, so that I may not die before my time.[l] [35]For I have seen what I did not know, and I hear[m] what I do not understand [36]—or is my mind deceived and my soul dreaming? [37]Now therefore I beg you to give your servant an explanation of this bewildering vision."

38 He answered me and said, "Listen to me, and I will teach you and tell you about the things that you fear, for the Most High has revealed many secrets to you. [39]He has seen your righteous conduct and that you have sorrowed continually for your people and mourned greatly over Zion. [40]This therefore is the meaning of the vision. [41]The woman who appeared to you a little while ago, whom you saw mourning and whom you began to console [42](you do not now see the form of a woman, but there appeared to you a city being built)[n] [43]and who told you about the misfortune of her son—this is the interpretation: [44]The woman whom you saw is Zion, which you now behold as a city being built.[o] [45]And as for her telling you that she was barren for thirty years, the reason is that there were three thousand[p] years in the world before any offering was offered in it.[q] [46]And after three thousand[r] years Solomon built the city and offered offerings; then it was that the barren woman bore a son. [47]And as for her telling you that she brought him up with much care, that was the period of residence in Jerusalem. [48]And as for her saying to you, 'My son died as he entered his wedding chamber,' and that misfortune had overtaken her,[s] this was the destruction that befell Jerusalem. [49]So you saw her likeness, how she mourned for her son, and you began to console her for what had happened.[t] [50]For now the Most High, seeing that you are sincerely grieved and profoundly distressed for her, has shown you the brilliance of her glory and the loveliness of her beauty. [51]Therefore I told you to remain in the field where no house had been built, [52]for I knew that the Most High would reveal these things to you. [53]Therefore I told you to go into the field where there was no foundation of any building, [54]because no work of human construction could endure in a place where the city of the Most High was to be revealed.

55 "Therefore do not be afraid, and do not

---

l 10.34 Syr Ethiop Arab: Lat *die to no purpose*   *m* 10.35 Other ancient authorities read *have heard*   *n* 10.42 Lat: Syr Ethiop Arab 1 Arab 2 Arm *an established city*   *o* 10.44 Cn: Lat *an established city*   *p* 10.45 Syr Ethiop Arab 1 Arab 2: Most Lat mss read *three*   *q* 10.45 Cn: Lat Syr Arab Arm *her*   *r* 10.46 Syr Ethiop Arab 1 Arm: Lat *three*   *s* 10.48 Or *him*   *t* 10.49 Lat mss Syr Ethiop Arab 1: Most Lat mss add *These were the things to be opened to you*

"established city" (see note to the text). Preexistent city. Cf. 7:26; 8:52; 13:36. *Foundations.* Cf. Rev. 21:14, 19; Heb. 11:10. **10:28** *Uriel.* The angel from the first three episodes.
    10:29–59 Uriel's interpretation. Uriel's role here and in future episodes differs from the previous episodes. Rather than an interlocutor, he acts as an interpreting angel (see **"Angels," p. 1346**). **10:30** *Like a corpse.* Possibly describing fainting. Cf. 5:14. **10:32** *Can still see*—that is, the city is still there; this was not a fleeting vision. **10:33** *Stand up.* Cf. 4:47; 6:13; 7:2. *Like a man.* Gendered expectations of how a man should behave. **10:36** Cf. Sir. 34:1-8. **10:38–59** Interpretation of the woman and her transformation. **10:39** Ezra is worthy because of his distress over Zion; cf. 10:50. **10:42** *A city being built.* Cf. 10:27, 44. **10:43** *This is the interpretation* signals a shift from a description of the symbol to its interpretation. **10:45** Metaphorical barrenness, until temple offerings were made. **10:46** *Solomon* builds the city here, David in 3:24. **10:47** Interpretation of 9:45–46. **10:48** Her son's death. Cf. 10:1-2. **10:49** Uriel names Ezra's disruption of this woman's mourning as consolation. Cf. 9:38-40; 10:6-24. **10:50** *Her* refers to Zion, not to the woman. **10:51** Unadulterated *field.* Cf. 9:24; 10:53-54. **10:54** Cf. 9:24; 10:51, 53. **10:55-56** Ezra is invited to *go in* the city to *see* and *hear,*

let your heart be terrified, but go in and see the splendor or[u] the vastness of the building, as far as it is possible for your eyes to see it, [56]and afterward you will hear as much as your ears can hear. [57]For you are more blessed than many, and you have been called to be with[v] the Most High as few have been. [58]But tomorrow night you shall remain here, [59]and the Most High will show you in those dream visions what the Most High will do to those who inhabit the earth in the last days."

So I slept that night and the following one, as he had told me.

11 On the second night I had a dream: I saw rising from the sea an eagle that had twelve feathered wings and three heads. [2]I saw it spread its wings over[w] the whole earth, and all the winds of heaven blew upon it, and the clouds were gathered around it.[x] [3]I saw that out of its wings there grew opposing wings, but they became little, puny wings. [4]But its heads were at rest; the middle head was larger than the other heads, but it, too, was at rest with them. [5]Then I saw that the eagle flew with its wings, and it reigned over the earth and over those who inhabit it. [6]And I saw how all things under heaven were subjected to it, and no one spoke against it—not a single creature that was on the earth. [7]Then I saw the eagle rise upon its talons, and it uttered a cry to its wings, saying, [8]"Do not all watch at the same time; let each sleep in its own place, and watch in its turn, [9]but let the heads be reserved for the last."

10 I looked again and saw that the voice did not come from its heads but from the middle of its body. [11]I counted its rival wings, and there were eight of them. [12]As I watched, one wing on the right side rose up, and it reigned over all the earth. [13]And after a time its reign came to an end, and it disappeared, so that even its place was no longer visible. Then the next wing rose up and reigned, and it continued to reign a long time. [14]While it was reigning its end came also, so that it disappeared like the first. [15]And a voice sounded, saying to it,

[16]"Listen to me, you who have ruled the earth all this time; I announce this to you before you disappear. [17]After you no one shall rule as long as you have ruled, not even half as long."

18 Then the third wing raised itself up and held the rule as the earlier ones had done, and it also disappeared. [19]And so it went with all the wings; they wielded power one after another and then were never seen again. [20]I kept looking, and in due time the wings that followed[y] also rose up on the right[z] side, in order to rule. There were some of them that ruled, yet disappeared suddenly, [21]and others of them rose up but did not hold the rule.

22 And after this I looked and saw that the twelve wings and the two little wings had disappeared, [23]and nothing remained on the eagle's body except the three heads that were at rest and six little wings.

24 As I kept looking I saw that two little wings separated from the six and remained under the head that was on the right side, but four remained in their place. [25]Then I saw that these little wings[a] planned to set themselves up and hold the rule. [26]As I kept looking, one was set up but suddenly disappeared; [27]a second also, and this disappeared more quickly than the first. [28]While I continued to look, the two that remained were planning between themselves to reign together; [29]and while they were planning, one of the heads at rest (the one that was in the middle) suddenly awoke; it was greater than the other two heads. [30]And I saw how it allied the two heads with itself [31]and how the head turned with those that were with it and devoured the two little wings[b] that were planning to reign. [32]Moreover, this head gained control of the whole earth and with much oppression dominated its inhabitants; it had greater power over the world than all the wings that had gone before.

u 10.55 Other ancient authorities read *and* v 10.57 Or *been named by* w 11.2 Arab 2 Arm: Lat Syr Ethiop *in* x 11.2 Syr: Compare Ethiop Arab: Lat lacks *the clouds* and *around it* y 11.20 Syr Arab 2 *the little wings* z 11.20 Some Ethiop mss read *left* a 11.25 Syr: Lat *underwings* b 11.31 Syr: Lat *underwings*

highlighting a physical and sensory experience. **10:57** *Called.* Ezra's special election; cf. Isa. 45:4. **10:59** *Dream visions* are new to the book. Ezra is not told to fast and only waits two days. **11:1–12:51 Fifth episode. 11:1–12:9** Ezra's first dream vision. Cf. Dan. 7. **11:1** Introduction of the *eagle*, here referring to Rome. **11:2** *Wings over the whole earth* symbolizes Rome's imperial power. **11:5–6** Rome's subjugation of the earth. **11:8** *Watch in its turn.* Wings and heads each stand for rulers. **11:9** *The last.* An eschatological term. **11:11–19** Right-side wings are portrayed as favorable. **11:13–17** The second wing reigns the longest. **11:22–23** Summary of the vision thus far. **11:24–27** Rule of the first two little wings. **11:28–31** Second two little wings did not get to rule; see 12:2. The heads form an

33 After this I looked again and saw the head in the middle suddenly disappear, just as the wings had done. ³⁴But the two heads remained, which also in like manner ruled over the earth and its inhabitants. ³⁵And while I looked, I saw the head on the right side devour the one on the left.

36 Then I heard a voice saying to me, "Look in front of you and consider what you see." ³⁷When I looked, I saw what seemed to be a lion roused from the forest, roaring, and I heard how it uttered a human voice to the eagle and spoke, saying, ³⁸"Listen, and I will speak to you. The Most High says to you, ³⁹Are you not the one that remains of the four beasts that I had made to reign in my world, so that the end of my times might come through them? ⁴⁰You, the fourth that has come, have conquered all the beasts that have gone before, and you have held sway over the world with great terror and over all the earth with grievous oppression, and for so long you have lived on the earth with deceit.ᶜ ⁴¹You have judged the earth but not with truth, ⁴²for you have oppressed the meek and injured the peaceable; you have hated those who tell the truth and have loved liars; you have destroyed the homes of those who brought forth fruit and have laid low the walls of those who did you no harm. ⁴³Your insolence has come up before the Most High and your pride to the Mighty One. ⁴⁴The Most High has looked at his times; now they have ended, and his ages have reached completion. ⁴⁵Therefore you, eagle, will surely disappear, you and your terrifying wings, your most evil little wings, your malicious heads, your most evil talons, and your whole worthless body, ⁴⁶so that the whole earth, freed from your violence, may be refreshed and relieved and may hope for the judgment and mercy of him who made it.'"

12 While the lion was saying these words to the eagle, I looked ²and saw that the remaining head had disappeared. The two wings that had gone over to it rose up andᵈ set themselves up to reign, and their reign was brief and full of tumult. ³When I looked again, they were already vanishing. The whole body of the eagle was burned, and the earth was exceedingly terrified.

Then I woke up in great perplexity of mind and great fear, and I said to my spirit, ⁴"You have brought this upon me because you search out the ways of the Most High. ⁵I am still weary in mind and very weak in my spirit, and not even a little strength is left in me because of the great fear with which I have been terrified tonight. ⁶Therefore I will now entreat the Most High that he may strengthen me to the end."

7 Then I said, "O sovereign Lord, if I have found favor in your sight, and if I have been accounted righteous before you beyond many others, and if my prayer has indeed come up before your face, ⁸strengthen me and show me, your servant, the interpretation and meaning of this terrifying vision so that you may fully comfort my soul. ⁹For you have judged me worthy to be shown the end of the times and the last events of the times."

10 He said to me, "This is the interpretation of this vision that you have seen: ¹¹The eagle that you saw coming up from the sea is the fourth kingdom that appeared in a vision to your brother Daniel. ¹²But it was not explained to him as I now explain to you or have explained it. ¹³The days are coming when a kingdom shall rise on earth, and it shall be more terrifying than all the kingdoms that have been before it. ¹⁴And twelve kings shall reign in it, one after another. ¹⁵But the second that is to reign shall hold sway for a longer time than any other one of the twelve. ¹⁶This is the interpretation of the twelve wings that you saw.

c 11.40 Syr Arab Arm: Lat Ethiop *The fourth came, however, and conquered . . . and held sway . . . and for so long lived*
d 12.2 Ethiop: Lat lacks *rose up and*

alliance. **11:33–35** Fate of the heads. **11:36–37** Appearance of a *lion*, which will be identified as the messiah in 12:31–32. **11:38–43** Indictment of the eagle. **11:39** *That I had made to reign . . . so that the end of my times* emphasizes predestination. **11:42** *Meek . . . peaceable.* Cf. Matt. 5:3, 5. **11:43** *Pride* of sinners. Cf. 8:50. **11:44** *His times.* The course of history. **11:45–46** The eagle is sentenced. **11:46** *Refreshed and relieved.* A nod to the end times. **12:3a** Punishment of the eagle. Fire is often used to destroy God's enemies; cf., for example, Mal. 4:1–2. **12:3b–9** Ezra's reaction. Cf. 10:5–24; 13:13b–20a. **12:9** The revelation here is of a special nature, akin to that made by God to Abraham (3:14) and Moses (14:5).

12:10–39 Interpretation of the dream vision by the angel. 12:11 The *eagle* is Rome; cf. Dan. 7. **12:14** The twelve wings are twelve kings. **12:15** The long-reigning king is Augustus

17 "As for your hearing a voice that spoke, coming not from the eagle's* heads but from the midst of its body, 18this is the interpretation: In the midst of* the time of that kingdom great struggles shall arise, and it shall be in danger of falling; nevertheless, it shall not fall then but shall regain its former power.* 19As for your seeing eight little wings* clinging to its wings, this is the interpretation: 20Eight kings shall arise in it whose times shall be short and their years swift; 21two of them shall perish when the middle of its time draws near, and four shall be kept for the time when its end approaches, but two shall be kept until the end.

22 "As for your seeing three heads at rest, this is the interpretation: 23In its last days the Most High will raise up three kings,* and they* shall renew many things in it and shall rule the earth 24and its inhabitants more oppressively than all who were before them. Therefore they are called the heads of the eagle, 25because it is they who shall sum up his wickedness and perform his last actions. 26As for your seeing that the large head disappeared, one of the kings* shall die in his bed but in agonies. 27But as for the two who remained, the sword shall devour them. 28For the sword of one shall devour him who was with him, but he also shall fall by the sword in the last days.

29 "As for your seeing two little wings* passing over to* the head that was on the right side, 30this is the interpretation: It is these whom the Most High has kept for the eagle's* end; this was the reign that was brief and full of tumult, as you have seen.

31 "And as for the lion whom you saw rousing up out of the forest and roaring and speaking to the eagle and reproving him for his unrighteousness, and as for all his words that you have heard, 32this is the Messiah whom the Most High has kept until the end

of days, who will arise from the offspring of David and will come and speak* with them. He will denounce them for their ungodliness and for their wickedness and will display before them their contemptuous dealings. 33For first he will bring them alive before his judgment seat, and when he has reproved them, then he will destroy them. 34But in mercy he will set free the remnant of my people, those who have been saved throughout my borders, and he will make them joyful until the end comes, the day of judgment, of which I spoke to you at the beginning. 35This is the dream that you saw, and this is its interpretation. 36And you alone were worthy to learn this secret of the Most High. 37Therefore write all these things that you have seen in a book, put it* in a hidden place, 38and you shall teach them to the wise among your people, whose hearts you know are able to comprehend and keep these secrets. 39But as for you, wait here seven days more, so that you may be shown whatever it pleases the Most High to show you." Then he left me.

40 When all the people heard that the seven days were past and I had not returned to the city, they all gathered together, from the least to the greatest, and came to me and spoke to me, saying, 41"How have we offended you, and what harm have we done you, that you have forsaken us and sit in this place? 42For of all the prophets you alone are left to us, like a cluster of grapes from the vintage and like a lamp in a dark place and like a haven for a ship saved from a storm. 43Are not the disasters that have

e 12.17 Lat *his*   f 12.18 Syr Arm: Lat *After*   g 12.18 Ethiop Arab 1 Arm: Lat Syr *its beginning*   h 12.19 Syr: Lat *underwings*   i 12.23 Syr Ethiop Arab Arm: Lat *kingdoms*   j 12.23 Syr Ethiop Arm: Lat *he*   k 12.26 Lat *them*   l 12.29 Arab 1: Lat *underwings*   m 12.29 Syr Ethiop: Lat lacks *to*   n 12.30 Lat *his*   o 12.32 Syr: Lat lacks *of days . . . and speak*   p 12.37 Ethiop Arab 1 Arab 2 Arm: Lat Syr *them*

(27 BCE–14 CE). **12:23** *Last days* of the empire. **12:26** The interpretation connects the vision to contemporaneous events. Vespasian (69–79 CE) died in his bed. **12:27–28** Likely Titus (79–81 CE) and Domitian (81–96 CE). **12:29–30** *Two little wings* belong to end-times events. **12:31–34** Judgment from the messianic figure; cf. 2 Bar. 39:8–40:3. **12:31–32** *Lion.* This messiah is associated with Judah and David. **12:33** The messiah brings judgment against the wicked. **12:34** Description of the remnant of Israel during the messianic kingdom; cf. 9:8; 13:48. *My borders* refers to the land of Israel. **12:37–39** Conclusion. **12:37** Ezra is commanded for the first time to write down the revelation he receives; this is not uncommon in apocalyptic literature (e.g., Dan. 12:4, 9; 1 En. 82:1; Rev. 22:10). **12:38** The passing of secret books to *the wise* is also found in chap. 14. Cf. Dan. 11:33, 35; 12:3, 10.

12:40–50 Ezra's second interaction with the community. Cf. 5:16–20a; 14:1–48. **12:40** The people seek out Ezra. *City* refers to Babylon. **12:42** Ezra is called *prophet* for the first time. *Grapes.* Cf.

befallen us enough? ⁴⁴Therefore if you forsake us, how much better it would have been for us if we also had been consumed in the burning of Zion. ⁴⁵For we are no better than those who died there." And they wept with a loud voice.

Then I answered them and said, ⁴⁶"Take courage, O Israel, and do not be sorrowful, O house of Jacob, ⁴⁷for the Most High has you in remembrance, and the Mighty One has not forgotten you in your struggle. ⁴⁸As for me, I have neither forsaken you nor withdrawn from you, but I have come to this place to pray on account of the desolation of Zion and to seek mercy on account of the humiliation of our*q* sanctuary. ⁴⁹Now go to your homes, every one of you, and after these days I will come to you." ⁵⁰So the people went into the city, as I told them to do. ⁵¹But I sat in the field seven days, as the angel*r* had commanded me, and I ate only of the flowers of the field, and plants were my food plants during those days.

13

After seven days I dreamed a dream in the night. ²And behold, a wind arose from the sea and stirred up*s* all its waves. ³As I kept looking the wind made something like the figure of a man come up out of the heart of the sea. And I saw*t* that this man flew*u* with the clouds of heaven, and wherever he turned his face to look, everything under his gaze trembled, ⁴and whenever his voice issued from his mouth, all who heard his voice melted as wax melts when it feels the fire.

5 After this I looked and saw that an innumerable multitude of people were gathered together from the four winds of heaven to make war against the man who came up out of the sea. ⁶And I looked and saw that he carved out for himself a great mountain and flew up on to it. ⁷And I tried to see the region or place from which the mountain was carved, but I could not.

8 After this I looked and saw that all who had gathered together against him to wage war with him were filled with fear, yet they dared to fight. ⁹When he saw the onrush of the approaching multitude, he neither lifted his hand nor held a spear or any weapon of war, ¹⁰but I saw only how he sent forth from his mouth something like a stream of fire and from his lips a flaming breath and from his tongue he shot forth a storm of sparks. All these were mingled together, the stream of fire and the flaming breath and the great storm, ¹¹and fell on the onrushing multitude that was prepared to fight and burned up all of them, so that suddenly nothing was seen of the innumerable multitude but only the dust of ashes and the smell of smoke. When I saw it, I was amazed.

12 After this I saw the same man come down from the mountain and call to himself another multitude that was peaceable. ¹³Then the forms of many people appeared to him, some of whom were joyful and some sorrowful; some of them were bound, and some were bringing others as offerings.

Then I woke up in great terror and prayed to the Most High and said, ¹⁴"From the beginning you have shown your servant these wonders and have deemed me worthy to have my prayer heard by you; ¹⁵now show me the interpretation of this dream also. ¹⁶For as I consider it in my mind, alas for those who will be left in those days! And still more, alas for those who are not left! ¹⁷For those who are not left will be sad ¹⁸because they understand the things that are reserved for the last days but cannot attain them. ¹⁹But alas for those also who are left

---

q 12.48 Syr Ethiop: Lat *your*   *r* 12.51 Lat *he*   *s* 13.2 Other ancient authorities read *I saw a wind arise from the sea and stir up*   *t* 13.3 Syr: Lat lacks *the wind . . . I saw*   *u* 13.3 Syr Ethiop Arab Arm: Lat *grew strong*

9:21–22. *Lamp.* Cf. 2 Bar. 77:13; John 5:35. **12:44** See note to 4:12. **12:46–47** Ezra offers consolation to Israel. **12:48** Ezra does not share his recent revelation; cf. 12:38. **12:51** Cf. 9:24, 26.
   13:1–58 Sixth episode. 13:1–20a The second dream vision. 13:2 *Wind* and *sea* play a role in 11:1–2; cf. Dan. 7:2. **13:3** Cf. Dan. 7:13. This *man* is a redeemer figure. **13:4** The figure has superhuman qualities, a strong gaze (v. 3) and a *voice* that *melted* those hearing it. On melting, see Ps. 97:5; Mic. 1:4. **13:5** The attack of the forces of evil. Cf. Deut. 28:49; Joel 2:1–10; Ezek. 38–39; Rev. 16:12–15. **13:6** *Carved out . . . a great mountain.* Cf. Dan. 2:34, 45. **13:9** The man needs no weapons; cf. Pss. Sol. 17:33. **13:10–11** *Mouth, lips,* and *tongue* suggest the supernatural power of the redeemer figure's judgment proffered through speech; cf. 1 En. 102:1. *Fire* is God's main weapon; cf. Deut. 32:22; Ezek. 22:21. **13:12** *Call to himself* suggests the ingathering of exiles; cf. 13:39–47. **13:13a** Most commentators suggest this is the ingathering of gentile worshipers of the Jewish God; cf. Isa. 66:20; Rom. 11:25. **13:13b–20a** Ezra's reaction to the dream vision. Cf. 10:5–24; 12:3b–9.

and for that very reason! For they shall see great dangers and much distress, as these dreams show. ²⁰Yet it is better' to come into these things," though incurring peril, than to pass from the world like a cloud and not to see what will happen in the last days."

He answered me and said, ²¹"I will tell you the interpretation of the vision, and I will also explain to you the things that you have mentioned. ²²As for what you said about those who survive, and concerning those who do not survive,ˣ this is the interpretation: ²³The one who brings the peril at that time will protect those who fall into peril, who have works and faith toward the Almighty. ²⁴Understand, therefore, that those who are left are more blessed than those who have died.

25 "This is the interpretation of the vision: As for your seeing a man come up from the heart of the sea, ²⁶this is he whom the Most High has been keeping for many ages, who will himself deliver his creation, and he will direct those who are left. ²⁷And as for your seeing wind and fire and a storm coming out of his mouth ²⁸and as for his not holding a spear or weapon of war, yet destroying the onrushing multitude that came to conquer him, this is the interpretation: ²⁹The days are coming when the Most High will deliver those who are on the earth. ³⁰And bewilderment of mind shall come over those who inhabit the earth. ³¹They shall plan to make war against one another, city against city, place against place, people against people, and kingdom against kingdom. ³²When these things take place and the signs occur that I showed you before, then my Son will be revealed, whom you saw as a man coming up from the sea.ʸ

33 "Then, when all the nations hear his voice, all the nations shall leave their own lands and the warfare that they have against one another, ³⁴and an innumerable multitude shall be gathered together, as you saw, wishing to come and conquer him. ³⁵But he shall stand on the top of Mount Zion. ³⁶And Zion shall come and be made manifest to all people, prepared and built, as you saw the mountain carved out without hands. ³⁷Then he, my Son, will reprove the assembled nations for their ungodliness (this was symbolized by the storm) ³⁸and will reproach them to their face with their evil thoughts and the torments with which they are to be tortured (which were symbolized by the flames) and will destroy them without effort by means of the lawᶻ (which was symbolized by the fire).

39 "And as for your seeing him gather to himself another multitude that was peaceable, ⁴⁰these are the nineᵃ tribes that were taken away from their own land into exile in the days of King Hoshea, whom Shalmaneser, king of the Assyrians, made captives; he took them across the river, and they were taken into another land. ⁴¹But they formed this plan for themselves, that they would leave the multitude of the nations and go to a more distant region where no humans had ever lived, ⁴²so that there at least they might keep their statutes that they had not kept in their own land. ⁴³And they went in by the narrow passages of the River Euphrates. ⁴⁴For at that time the Most High performed signs for them and stopped the channels of the river until they had crossed over. ⁴⁵Through that region there was a long way to go, a journey of a year and a half, and that country is called Arzareth.

46 "Then they lived there until the last

v 13.20 Ethiop Compare Arab 2: Lat *easier*   w 13.20 Syr: Lat *this*   x 13.22 Syr Arab 1: Lat lacks *and . . . not survive*   y 13.32 Syr and most Lat mss lack *from the sea*   z 13.38 Syr: Lat *effort and the law*   a 13.40 Other Lat mss *ten*; Syr Ethiop Arab 1 Arm *nine and a half*

13:20b–58 **The interpretation of the dream offered by Uriel.** **13:23–24** Ezra's understanding in v. 20 is confirmed. **13:24** *Those who are left* after the eschatological woes. **13:25–26** This messianic redeemer is precreated. **13:27–28** Restating vv. 10–11; for the interpretation, see vv. 36–38. **13:29** *Days are coming.* A predictive passage for the signs of the end times. **13:30–31** Confusion of mind leads to internecine strife; cf. 2 Bar. 25:3; 70:2. **13:32** For *Son*, a better translation would be "servant" or "son" (lowercase). **13:33** Interpreting 13:4. **13:34** Interpreting 13:5. **13:35** The interpretation of 13:6–7. *Top of Mount Zion.* Cf. Ps. 2:6; Isa. 31:4b. **13:36** The *mountain* is the eschatological *Zion*; cf. 10:25–27, 44, 54. **13:37–38** *Son.* See note on v. 32. Cf. 13:10–11. **13:40** "Nine and a half" in other manuscripts is to be preferred to *nine tribes*; see the textual note. For references to "nine and a half tribes," see 2 Bar. 77:17, 19; 78:1. **13:41** Removing themselves from both space and time. Cf. Josephus, *Ant.* 11.133. **13:42** *Statutes* refers to the law or torah. **13:43** Cf. 2 Bar. 77:22, where the *River Euphrates* also serves as a marker of time/space to reach the nine and a half tribes. **13:44** Based on the miracles at the Red Sea (Exod. 14:21–31) and the Jordan (Josh. 3). **13:45** *Arzareth* is unknown. Possibly from the Hebrew "'eretz 'aheret," another land. **13:46** The end is near.

times, and now, when they are about to come again, [47]the Most High will stop[b] the channels of the river again, so that they may be able to cross over. Therefore you saw the multitude gathered together in peace. [48]But those who are left of your people, who are found within my holy borders, shall be saved.[c] [49]Therefore when he destroys the multitude of the nations that are gathered together, he will defend the people who remain. [50]And then he will show them very many wonders."

[51] I said, "O sovereign Lord, explain this to me: Why did I see the man coming up from the heart of the sea?"

[52] He said to me, "Just as no one can explore or know what is in the depths of the sea, so no one on earth can see my Son or those who are with him, except in the time of his day.[d] [53]This is the interpretation of the dream that you saw. And you alone have been enlightened about this, [54]because you have forsaken your own ways and have applied yourself to mine and have searched out my law, [55]for you have devoted your life to wisdom and called understanding your mother. [56]Therefore I have shown you these things, for there is a reward laid up with the Most High. For it will be that after three more days I will tell you other things and explain weighty and wondrous matters to you."

[57] Then I got up and walked in the field, giving great glory and praise to the Most High for the wonders that he did from time to time [58]and because he governs the times and whatever things come to pass in their seasons. And I stayed there three days.

14 On the third day, while I was sitting under an oak, suddenly a voice came out of a bush opposite me and said, "Ezra, Ezra!" [2]And I answered, "Here I am, Lord," and I rose to my feet. [3]Then he said to me, "I revealed myself in a bush and spoke to Moses when my people were in bondage in Egypt, [4]and I sent him and led[e] my people out of Egypt, and I led him up on Mount Sinai, where I kept him with me many days. [5]I told him many wondrous things and showed him the secrets of the times and declared to him[f] the end of the times. Then I commanded him, saying, [6]'These words you shall publish openly, and these you shall keep secret.' [7]And now I say to you: [8]Lay up in your heart the signs that I have shown you, the dreams that you have seen, and the interpretations that you have heard, [9]for you shall be taken up from among humankind, and henceforth you shall live with my Son and with those who are like you, until the times are ended. [10]The age has lost its youth, and the times begin to grow old. [11]For the age is divided into twelve parts, and nine[g] of its parts have already passed, [12]as well as half of the tenth part; so two of its parts remain, besides half of the tenth part.[h] [13]Now, therefore, set your house in order, and reprove your people; comfort the lowly among them, and instruct those who are wise.[i] And now renounce the

b 13.47 Syr: Lat *stops* c 13.48 Syr: Lat lacks *shall be saved* d 13.52 Syr: Ethiop *except when his time and his day have come*; Lat lacks *his* e 14.4 Syr Arab 1 Arab 2 *he led* f 14.5 Syr Ethiop Arab Arm: Lat lacks *declared to him* g 14.11 Cn: Lat Ethiop *ten* h 14.12 Syr lacks 14.11, 12: Ethiop *For the world is divided into ten parts, and has come to the tenth, and half of the tenth remains. Now* ... i 14.13 Lat lacks *and* ... *wise*

13:47 Eschatological redemption is associated with the ingathering of exiles. **13:48** Cf. 9:8; 12:34. **13:49** The messiah will defend the remnant of Israel. **13:51** Cf. vv. 25–26. **13:52** Unknowable *depths of the sea* symbolize the messiah's hiddenness; cf. 4:7. *Those who are with him*, like Enoch and Elijah; cf. 7:28; 14:9. **13:54–55** Ezra's worthiness. Torah and wisdom are frequently connected; cf. Ps. 119:34; 2 Bar. 38:1–4. **13:56–58** Conclusion to episode 6.

14:1–48 Seventh episode and the climax of the narrative. This is also Ezra's last and most extensive interaction with the larger community; cf. 5:16–20a; 12:40–50. **14:1–2 Narrative introduction.** **14:1** God speaks directly to Ezra only in this episode. *Oak.* Gen. 18:1; Judg. 4:5; 2 Bar. 6:1; 77:18. *Bush.* Exod. 3:2–4:17.

14:3–18 God's address to Ezra. 14:3–4 The exodus. Cf. Exod. 3:2–12. **14:4** *Sinai.* Exod. 24:15–18; 34:1–35. **14:5** On Moses's secret revelations, see, for example, 2 Bar. 59:4. *Secrets* ... *times.* Revelations of the end times. **14:6** Moses received two revealed traditions; the *secret* one is apocryphal. **14:8** Ezra has received similar revelations in episodes 1–6, especially 5 and 6. **14:9** Ezra being *taken up*, his assumption, is noted. For *Son*, a better translation would be "servant"; see note on 13:32. *Like you.* Cf. 7:28; 13:52. **14:10** This world is *old*; cf. 4:45–50; 5:55. **14:11** Divisions of history are common, especially in apocalyptic traditions. For other twelvefold divisions, see 2 Bar. 53; Apoc. Ab. 29:2. **14:13a** *Set* ... *reprove* ... *comfort* ... *instruct.* Commands to interact with the community, carried out in vv. 27–35. **14:13b–15** Ezra is to set aside the concerns of the flesh and of this age before his

life that is corruptible, [14]and put away from you mortal thoughts; cast away from you the burdens of humankind, and divest yourself now of your weak nature; [15]lay to one side the thoughts that are most grievous to you, and hurry to escape from these times. [16]For evils worse than those that you have now seen happen shall take place hereafter. [17]For the weaker the world becomes through old age, the more shall evils be increased upon its inhabitants. [18]Truth shall go farther away, and falsehood shall come near. For the eagle[j] that you saw in the vision is already hurrying to come."

[19] Then I answered and said, "Let me speak[k] in your presence, Lord. [20]For I will go, as you have commanded me, and I will reprove the people who are now living, but who will warn those who will be born hereafter? For the world lies in darkness, and its inhabitants are without light. [21]For your law has been burned, so no one knows the things that have been done or will be done by you. [22]If then I have found favor with you, send the holy spirit into me, and I will write everything that has happened in the world from the beginning, the things that were written in your law, so that people may be able to find the path and that those who want to live in the last days may do so."

[23] He answered me and said, "Go and gather the people, and tell them not to seek you for forty days. [24]But prepare for yourself many writing tablets, and take with you Sarea, Dabria, Selemia, Ethanus, and Asiel—these five, who are trained to write rapidly, [25]and you shall come here, and I will light in your heart the lamp of understanding, which shall not be put out until what you are about to write is finished. [26]And when you have finished, some things you shall make public, and some you shall deliver in secret to the wise; tomorrow at this hour you shall begin to write."

[27] Then I went as he commanded me, and I gathered all the people together and said, [28]"Hear these words, O Israel. [29]At first our ancestors lived as aliens in Egypt, and they were liberated from there [30]and received the law of life, which they did not keep, which you also have transgressed after them. [31]Then land was given to you for a possession in the land of Zion, but you and your ancestors committed iniquity and did not keep the ways that the Most High commanded you. [32]And since he is a righteous judge, in due time he took from you what he had given. [33]And now you are here, and your people[l] are farther in the interior.[m] [34]If you, then, will rule over your minds and discipline your hearts, you shall be kept alive, and after death you shall obtain mercy. [35]For after death the judgment will come, when we shall live again, and then the names of the righteous shall become manifest, and the deeds of the ungodly shall be disclosed. [36]But let no one come to me now, and let no one seek me for forty days."

[37] So I took the five men, as he had commanded me, and we proceeded to the field and remained there. [38]And on the next day a voice called me, saying, "Ezra, open your

---

j 14.18 Syr Ethiop Arab Arm: Meaning of Lat uncertain
k 14.19 Most Lat mss lack *Let me speak*   *l* 14.33 Lat *brothers*
m 14.33 Syr Ethiop Arm: Lat *are among you*

---

assumption. **14:17** With earth's decay through *old age*, evil increases. **14:18** *Eagle.* Cf. the fifth episode, 11:1–12:51.

14:19–22 Ezra responds. 14:20 The issue here is the salvation of future generations. *Light* here signifies divine presence; cf. 12:42. **14:21** *Your law has been burned.* Cf. 4:23. The concern here is that God's Torah, broadly conceived as any sacred Scripture, has been lost, so the people will not know what has happened or what to do after Ezra's assumption. **14:22** Ezra's request is unusual. *The holy spirit*, a spirit of prophecy, is an expression found in many ancient sources; see, e.g., Isa. 63:10; Ps. 51:11. *Beginning . . . last days* infers he will write from creation to the eschaton.

14:23–26 Instructions. 14:23 *Forty days.* Cf. Exod. 24:18; 34:28; Deut. 9:9, 18. **14:24** *Five.* Cf. 2 Bar. 5:5. **14:25** *Light in your heart the lamp of understanding.* Ezra will receive divine inspiration *to write*, which here means "to dictate." **14:26** *Some things you shall make public, and some you shall deliver in secret.* Ezra's revelation will be both esoteric and exoteric; cf. v. 6.

14:27–36 Ezra speaks directly to the people. 14:27 Cf. v. 23. **14:28** Reminiscent of the Shema. Cf. Deut. 5:1; 6:4. **14:30** *Law of life.* Torah; cf. Sir. 17:11; 45:5. **14:31** Here *land* as a divine gift is set up against the sins of Israel. **14:32** God took the land from the people as a punishment for their iniquity. **14:33** Cf. 13:40–41. **14:35** Judgment and resurrection.

14:37–48 Revelation of Scripture. 14:37 *The five men.* See 14:24, 42. **14:38–41** Drinking allows

mouth and drink what I give you to drink." [39]So I opened my mouth, and a full cup was offered to me; it was full of something like water, but its color was like fire. [40]I took it and drank, and when I had drunk it, my heart poured forth understanding, and wisdom increased in my breast, for my spirit retained its memory, [41]and my mouth was opened and was no longer closed. [42]Moreover, the Most High gave understanding to the five men, and by turns they wrote what was dictated, using characters that they did not know.[n] They sat forty days; they wrote during the daytime and ate their bread at night. [43]But as for me, I spoke in the daytime and was not silent at night. [44]So during the forty days, ninety-four[o] books were written. [45]And when the forty days were ended, the Most High spoke to me, saying, "Make public the twenty-four[p] books that you wrote first, and let the worthy and the unworthy read them, [46]but keep the seventy that were written last, in order to give them to the wise among your people. [47]For in them is the spring of understanding, the fountain of wisdom, and the river of knowledge." [48]And I did so.[q]

_____

15 [r]Speak in the ears of my people the words of the prophecy that I will put in your mouth, says the Lord, [2]and cause them to be written on paper, for they are trustworthy and true. [3]Do not fear the plots against you, and do not be troubled by the unbelief of those who oppose you. [4]For all unbelievers shall die in their unbelief.[s]

5 Beware, says the Lord, I am bringing evils upon the world, the sword and famine, death and destruction, [6]because iniquity has spread throughout every land, and their harmful

doings have reached their limit. [7]Therefore, says the Lord, [8]I will be silent no longer concerning their ungodly acts that they impiously commit, neither will I tolerate their wicked practices. Innocent and righteous blood cries out to me, and the souls of the righteous cry out continually. [9]I will surely avenge them, says the Lord, and will receive to myself all the innocent blood from among them. [10]See, my people are being led like a flock to the slaughter; I will not allow them to live any longer in the land of Egypt, [11]but I will bring them out with a mighty hand and with an uplifted arm and will strike Egypt with plagues, as before, and will destroy all its land.

12 Let Egypt mourn and its foundations, because of the plague of chastisement and castigation that the Lord will bring upon it. [13]Let the farmers who till the ground mourn because their seed shall fail to grow[t] and their trees shall be ruined by blight and hail and by a terrible tempest. [14]Alas for the world and for those who live in it! [15]For the sword and misery draw near them, and nation shall rise up to fight against nation, with swords in their hands. [16]For there shall be unrest among people; growing strong against one another, they shall in their might have no respect for their king or the chief of their leaders. [17]For

_____

n 14.42 Syr Compare Ethiop Arab 2 Arm: Meaning of Lat uncertain   o 14.44 Syr Ethiop Arab 1 Arm: Meaning of Lat uncertain   p 14.45 Syr Arab 1: Lat lacks *twenty-four*   q 14.48 Syr adds *in the seventh year of the sixth week, five thousand years and three months and twelve days after creation. At that time Ezra was caught up, and taken to the place of those who are like him, after he had written all these things. And he was called the scribe of the knowledge of the Most High for ever and ever.* Ethiop Arab 1 Arm have a similar ending   r 15.1 Chapters 15 and 16 (except 15.57–59, which has been found in Greek) are extant only in Lat   s 15.4 Other ancient authorities add *and all who believe shall be saved by their faith*   t 15.13 Lat lacks *to grow*

Ezra to receive and speak divine revelation, a hierophagic experience. **14:42** The scribes also received divine assistance. **14:45–46** Twenty-four public books seem to reference accepted Scripture (see **"Canon," p. 1677**), while seventy are considered secret. **14:47** See, e.g., 2 Bar. 59:7; Prov. 18:4; 1 En. 48:1. **14:48** End of the Latin version of 4 Ezra. Syriac and other versions contain Ezra's assumption, which is most likely the original ending. See textual note.
  15:1–16:78 Chaps. 15 and 16 are a Christian addition written as an epilogue to 4 Ezra (chaps. 3–14). They are known as 6 Ezra. **15:1** *Put in your mouth.* The author, unnamed, is made a prophet; cf. Isa. 51:16; Jer. 1:9. **15:3** *Plots.* Cf. Jer. 1:8.
  15:5–27 Prediction of punishment against the wicked, with a focus on Egypt. **15:8** *Blood cries out.* Cf. Gen. 4:10. Here it is a possible reference to persecution; cf. Rev. 6:9–10. **15:9** God will *avenge* God's people; cf. Deut. 32:43. **15:10** *Flock to the slaughter.* A reference to persecution; cf. Isa. 53:7. *Egypt* may be reflecting a real location or may be a symbol for a different locale; the geographical provenance for 6 Ezra remains unknown. **15:11** A reference to the exodus; cf. Deut. 4:34. **15:13** *Hail.* Exod. 9:25. **15:15–16** Internecine fighting; cf. 13:30–31. **15:17–19** Civil order will break down within

Focus On: Canon (2 Esdras 14:45–46)

A canon is a collection of texts considered to be authoritative. While we can buy a Bible—such as this one you are holding or reading on a screen—contemporary readers may not consider that there are various different biblical collections or that each biblical canon contains diverse texts, which may disagree with one another. But when and how did these texts come together to form an authoritative unit (see also **"The Bible as a Collection," pp. 2145–47,** and **"Canonical Orders of the Books of the Bible," p. xxi**)?

In 2 Esd. 14:45–46, Ezra is told to "make public" twenty-four of the ninety-four books he received from God, while the remaining seventy are to be shared among "the wise." These twenty-four books have been associated with the Jewish Bible (Tanakh). Scholars note that this may be the earliest reference to the existence of that particular canon.

Writing around the same time, the Jewish historian Josephus also refers to a possible canon: "Our books, those which are justly accredited, are but two and twenty, and contain the record of all time" (*Ag. Ap.* 1.8). While Josephus's number is smaller by two books compared with 2 Esdras, it is close enough that many scholars argue that these two texts show evidence for the establishment of a Jewish canon.

This argument, however, ignores not only the discrepancy but also the other seventy books mentioned in 2 Esdras. While they are said to be only for "the wise," these books are emphasized as special, even more important than the twenty-four public books. This does not discount a possible reference to a canon, but it should disrupt any security the reader finds in identifying these two references with an established Jewish canon.

We do not know the titles of any included books. While we begin to see references to collections, we also see diversity in what is included in them until a very late date. For example, among the Dead Sea Scrolls, numerous documents were found that appear authoritative in some way, such as the Temple Scroll, numerous psalms not found in contemporary canons, and the books of Enoch (from which Jude 14–15 quotes as prophecy) and Jubilees, both of which remain canonical in the Ethiopian Orthodox Church (see **"Beyond the Canon," p. 2112**). These kinds of texts and others that were not accepted into a canon (published in the modern period as a collection of documents called the Pseudepigrapha) emphasize the diversity of sacred texts found within Judaism in the Roman Empire, including within early Christian communities.

Shayna Sheinfeld

a person will desire to go into a city and shall not be able to do so. ¹⁸Because of their pride the cities shall be in confusion, the houses shall be destroyed, and people shall be afraid. ¹⁹People shall have no pity for their neighbors but shall make an assault upon*ᵘ* their houses with the sword and plunder their goods because of hunger for bread and because of great tribulation.

20 See how I am calling together all the kings of the earth to turn to me, says God, from the rising sun and from the south, from the east and from Lebanon, to turn and repay what they have given them. ²¹Just as they have done to my elect until this day, so I will do and will pay it back into their laps. Thus says the Lord God: ²²My right hand will not spare the sinners, and my sword will not cease

from those who shed innocent blood on earth. ²³And a fire went forth from his wrath and consumed the foundations of the earth and the sinners, like burnt straw. ²⁴Alas for those who sin and do not observe my commandments, says the Lord;*ᵛ* ²⁵I will not spare them. Depart, you faithless children! Do not pollute my sanctuary. ²⁶For God*ʷ* knows all who sin against him; therefore he will hand them over to death and slaughter. ²⁷Already calamities have come upon the whole earth, and you shall remain in them; God*ˣ* will not deliver you, because you have sinned against him.

28 What a terrifying sight, appearing from the east! ²⁹The nations of the dragons

u 15.19 Cn: Lat *shall empty*   *v* 15.24 Other ancient authorities read *God*   *w* 15.26 Other ancient authorities read *the Lord*   *x* 15.27 Other ancient authorities read *the Lord*

cities. **15:20** Leaders will pay for what their people and nations have done. **15:21** The type of punishment is related to the crime committed. **15:23** God punishes with *fire*; cf. 12:3a; 13:10–11. **15:24** *Alas* or "woe" statement; cf. Isa. 3:11.

15:28–33 Vision of war. This passage may refer to the Sasanian Persian attack under Shapur I (ca. 240–70 CE), who was turned back by Odenaethus of Palmyra. **15:29** *Dragons of Arabia.* Palmyrene

of Arabia shall come out with many chariots, and from the day that they set out their hissing shall spread over the earth, so that all who hear them will fear and tremble. [30]Also the Carmonians, raging in wrath, shall go forth like wild boars[y] from the forest, and with great power they shall come and engage them in battle, and with their tusks they shall devastate a portion of the land of the Assyrians with their teeth. [31]And then the dragons,[z] remembering their origin, shall become still stronger, and if they combine in great power and turn to pursue them, [32]then these shall be disorganized and silenced by their power and shall turn and flee.[a] [33]And from the land of the Assyrians an enemy in ambush shall attack them and destroy one of them, and fear and trembling shall come upon their army and indecision upon their kings.

[34] See the clouds from the east and from the north to the south! Their appearance is exceedingly threatening, full of wrath and storm. [35]They shall clash against one another and shall pour out a heavy tempest on the earth and their own tempest,[b] and there shall be blood from the sword as high as a horse's belly [36]and a man's thigh and a camel's hock. [37]And there shall be fear and great trembling on the earth; those who see that wrath shall be horror-stricken, and they shall be seized with trembling. [38]After that, heavy storm clouds shall be stirred up from the south and from the north and another part from the west. [39]But the winds from the east shall prevail over the cloud that was[c] raised in wrath and shall dispel it, and the tempest[d] that was to cause destruction by the east wind shall be driven violently toward the south and west. [40]Great and mighty clouds full of wrath and tempest[e] shall rise and destroy all the earth and its inhabitants and shall pour out upon every high and lofty place[f] a terrible tempest,[g] [41]fire and hail and flying swords and floods of water, so that all the fields and all the streams shall be filled with the abundance of those waters. [42]They shall destroy cities and walls, mountains and hills, trees of the forests, and grass of the meadows and their grain. [43]They shall go on steadily to Babylon and blot it out. [44]They shall come to it and surround it; they shall pour out on it the tempest[h] and all its fury;[i] then the dust and smoke shall reach the sky, and all who are around it shall mourn for it. [45]And those who survive shall serve those who have destroyed it.

[46] And you, Asia, who share in the splendor of Babylon and the glory of her person, [47]woe to you, miserable wretch! For you have made yourself like her; you have decked out your daughters for prostitution to please and glory in your lovers, who have always lusted after you. [48]You have imitated that hateful one in all her deeds and devices.[j] Therefore, God[k] says, [49]I will send evils upon you: widowhood, poverty, famine, sword, and pestilence, bringing ruin to your houses, bringing destruction and death. [50]And the glory of your strength shall wither like a flower when the heat shall rise that is sent upon you. [51]You shall be weakened like a wretched woman who is beaten and wounded, so that you cannot receive your mighty lovers. [52]Would I have dealt with you so violently, says the Lord, [53]if you had not killed my chosen people continually, exulting and clapping your hands and talking about their death when you were drunk?

[54] Beautify your face! [55]The reward of a prostitute is in your lap; therefore you shall

y 15.30 Other ancient authorities lack *like wild boars* z 15.31 Cn: Lat *dragon* a 15.32 Other ancient authorities read *turn their face to the north* b 15.35 Meaning of Lat uncertain c 15.39 Lat *that he* d 15.39 Lat *star* e 15.40 Lat *star* f 15.40 Or *eminent person* g 15.40 Lat *star* h 15.44 Lat *star* i 15.44 Other ancient authorities add *until they destroy it to its foundations* j 15.48 Other ancient authorities read *devices, and you have followed after that one about to gratify her magnates and leaders so that you may be made proud and be pleased by her fornications* k 15.48 Other ancient authorities read *the Lord*

forces. **15:30** *Carmonians.* Probably Persians from the Kirman province. **15:31–32** Shapur's defeat. **15:33** *Destroy one of them.* Possibly the murder of Odenaethus.

15:34–45 Prophecy of future events. Some interpret these very unsettling events as a Goth invasion of the Roman Empire in the mid-third century CE. **15:34** *Clouds.* Cf. 2 Bar. 53. **15:43** *Babylon* means Rome here. **15:44–45** The attack reaches the city of Rome.

15:46–63 Prophecy of future events. Some interpret it as Palmyra under Odenaethus and Zenobia. **15:46–48** *Asia* is like Babylon in Rev. 17:4–6. **15:49** Cf. the plagues of Babylon in Rev. 18:7–8. **15:53** *My chosen people* is here an undefined group. *Drunk.* Cf. Rev. 17:2; 18:3. **15:55** *Reward of a*

receive your recompense. [56]As you will do to my chosen people, says the Lord, so God will do to you and will hand you over to adversities. [57]Your children shall die of hunger, and you shall fall by the sword; your cities shall be wiped out, and all your people who are in the open country shall fall by the sword. [58]Those who are in the mountains and highlands[l] shall perish of hunger, and they shall eat their own flesh in hunger for bread and drink their own blood in thirst for water. [59]Unhappy above all others, you shall come and suffer fresh miseries. [60]As they pass by they shall crush the hateful[m] city and shall destroy a part of your land and abolish a portion of your glory, when they return from devastated Babylon. [61]You shall be broken down by them like stubble,[n] and they shall be like fire to you. [62]They shall devour you and your cities, your land and your mountains; they shall burn with fire all your forests and your fruitful trees. [63]They shall carry your children away captive, plunder your wealth, and mar the glory of your face.

16 Woe to you, Babylon and Asia! Woe to you, Egypt and Syria! [2]Bind on sackcloth and cloth of goats' hair,[o] and wail for your children, and lament for them, for your destruction is at hand. [3]The sword has been sent upon you, and who is there to turn it back? [4]A fire has been sent upon you, and who is there to quench it? [5]Calamities have been sent upon you, and who is there to drive them away? [6]Can one drive off a hungry lion in the forest or quench a fire in the stubble once it has started to burn?[p] [7]Can one turn back an arrow shot by a strong archer? [8]The Lord God sends calamities, and who will drive them away? [9]Fire will go forth from his wrath, and who is there to quench it? [10]He will flash lightning, and who will not be afraid? He will thunder, and who will not be terrified? [11]The Lord will threaten, and who will not be utterly shattered at his presence? [12]The earth and its foundations quake, the sea

is churned up from the depths, and its waves and the fish with them shall be troubled at the presence of the Lord and the glory of his power. [13]For his right hand that bends the bow is strong, and his arrows that he shoots are sharp, and when they are shot to the ends of the world they will not miss once. [14]Calamities are sent forth and shall not return until they come over the earth. [15]The fire is kindled and shall not be put out until it consumes the foundations of the earth. [16]Just as an arrow shot by a mighty archer does not return, so the calamities that are sent upon the earth shall not return. [17]Alas for me! Alas for me! Who will deliver me in those days?

18 The beginning of sorrows, when there shall be much lamentation; the beginning of famine, when many shall perish; the beginning of wars, when the powers shall be terrified; the beginning of calamities, when all shall tremble. [19]What shall they do when the calamities come? [20]Famine and plague, tribulation and anguish are sent as scourges for the correction of humankind. [21]Yet for all this they will not turn from their iniquities or ever be mindful of the scourges. [22]Indeed, provisions will be so cheap upon earth that people will imagine that peace is assured for them, and then calamities shall spring up on the earth—the sword, famine, and great confusion. [23]For many of those who live on the earth shall perish by famine, and those who survive the famine shall die by the sword. [24]And the dead shall be thrown out like dung, and there shall be no one to console them, for the earth shall be left desolate, and its cities shall be demolished. [25]No one shall be left to cultivate the earth or to sow it. [26]The trees shall bear fruit, but who will gather it? [27]The grapes shall ripen, but who will tread them? For in all places

l 15.58 Gk: Lat omits *and highlands*   m 15.60 Other ancient authorities read *idle* or *tranquil*   n 15.61 Other ancient authorities read *like dry straw*   o 16.2 Other ancient authorities lack *cloth of goats' hair*   p 16.6 Other ancient authorities read *fire when dry straw has been set on fire*

prostitute. Possibly meaning death. **15:58** *Eat their own flesh.* A common punishment for sin; cf. Jer. 19:9. **15:61–63** Some interpret this to be Zenobia's defeat.

  16:1–17 Judgment is inevitable on the four nations. The nations likely represent the Roman Empire. **16:2** *Sackcloth . . . wail . . . lament.* Signs of mourning. **16:3–7** *Calamities* sent to punish these nations. **16:8–13** God is the cause of these calamities. **16:12** Creation itself is shaken from these calamities; cf. 6:14–16. **16:15** *Fire* will destroy the earth at the judgment; cf. 2 Pet. 3:7, 10; Josephus, *Ant.* 1.70.

  16:18–35 Desolation emerges out of the eschatological judgment. 16:20 *Correction.* Cf. Zeph. 3:1–2. **16:22** Cheap *provisions* will provide a false sense of security. **16:24** *Earth . . . desolate.* Cf. 5:3; 16:28.

there shall be great solitude; [28]a person will long to see another human or even to hear a human voice. [29]For ten shall be left out of a city, and two out of the field, those who have hidden themselves in thick groves and clefts in the rocks. [30]Just as in an olive orchard three or four olives may be left on every tree, [31]or just as, when a vineyard is gathered, some clusters may be left[q] by those who search carefully through the vineyard, [32]so in those days three or four shall be left by those who search their houses with the sword. [33]The earth shall be left desolate, and its fields shall be plowed up,[r] and its roads and all its paths shall bring forth thorns, because no sheep will go along them. [34]Virgins shall mourn because they have no bridegrooms; women shall mourn because they have no husbands; their daughters shall mourn because they have no help. [35]Their bridegrooms shall be killed in war, and their husbands shall perish of famine.

36 Listen now to these things, and understand them, you who are servants of the Lord. [37]This is the word of the Lord; receive it and do not disbelieve what the Lord says.[s] [38]The calamities draw near and are not delayed. [39]Just as a pregnant woman, in the ninth month when the time of her delivery draws near, has great pains around her womb for two or three hours beforehand, but when the child comes forth from the womb, there will not be a moment's delay, [40]so the calamities will not delay in coming upon the earth, and the world will groan, and pains will seize it on every side.

41 Hear my words, O my people; prepare for battle, and in the midst of the calamities be like strangers on the earth. [42]Let the one who sells be like one who will flee; let the one who buys be like one who will lose; [43]let the one who does business be like one who will not make a profit; and let the one who builds a house be like one who will not live in it; [44]let the one who sows be like one who will not reap; so also the one who prunes the vines, like one who will not gather the grapes; [45]those who marry, like those who will have no children; and those who do not marry, like those who are widowed. [46]Because of this, those who labor, labor in vain, [47]for strangers shall gather their fruits and plunder their goods, overthrow their houses, and take their children captive, for in captivity and famine they will produce their children.[t] [48]Those who conduct business do so only to have it plundered; the more they adorn their cities, their houses and possessions, and their persons, [49]the more angry I will be with them for their sins, says the Lord. [50]Just as a respectable and virtuous woman abhors a prostitute, [51]so righteousness shall abhor iniquity when she decks herself out and shall accuse her to her face when he comes to defend the one who searches out every sin on earth.

52 Therefore do not be like her or her works. [53]For in a very short time iniquity will be removed from the earth, and righteousness will reign over us. [54]Sinners must not say that they have not sinned,[u] for coals of fire will burn on the head of everyone who says, "I have not sinned before God and his glory." [55]The Lord[v] certainly knows everything that people do; he knows their imaginations and their thoughts and their hearts. [56]He said, "Let the earth be made," and it

q 16.31 Other ancient authorities read *a cluster may remain exposed*   r 16.33 Other ancient authorities read *be for briers* s 16.37 Cn: Lat *do not believe the gods of whom the Lord speaks* t 16.47 Other ancient authorities read *therefore those who are married may know that they will produce children for captivity and famine*   u 16.54 Other ancient authorities add *or the unjust done injustice*   v 16.55 Other ancient authorities read *Lord God*

16:28 The solitude will be bleak. See 5:3; 16:24. **16:29** Continued description of desolation. *Ten . . . city, two . . . field.* Cf. Amos 5:3; Matt. 24:40–41. *Clefts.* Isa. 2:10, 21; Rev. 6:15–16. **16:30–32** Lean gleanings. Cf. Isa. 17:6. *Clusters.* See 9:21; 12:42. **16:34** No celebrations of marriage because of war. Cf. Jer. 7:34.

16:36–53 Eschatological calamities are imminent. God's people should prepare by setting aside this-worldly activities and concerns. **16:39–40** *Pregnant woman* imagery is common in 2 Esdras (e.g., 4:40). The calamities leading to the end times are often called birth or labor pangs; cf. Mark 13:8; 1 Thess. 5:3. **16:41** An eschatological *battle*; cf. the Qumran War Scroll (1QM). **16:42–45** Advice on how to regard the present world as temporary. **16:48–49** God's anger is kindled against those who prioritize material *possessions.* **16:50–51** Gendered imagery; iniquity is compared to a female sex worker who dresses up and applies makeup (see **"Sex Work as a Metaphor in Revelation," p. 2125**). **16:51** *He comes.* God and Jesus are meant here.

16:54–68 The sinner should not lie about sinning because God will know and shame the liar. 16:54 All are *sinners*; cf. 1 John 1:8. **16:55** *The Lord . . . knows.* Cf. Sir. 15:19. **16:56–63** A summary

was made, and "Let the heaven be made," and it was made. ⁵⁷At his word the stars were fixed in their places, and he knows the number of the stars. ⁵⁸He searches the abyss and its treasures; he has measured the sea and its contents; ⁵⁹he has confined the sea in the midst of the waters;ʷ and by his word he has suspended the earth over the water. ⁶⁰He has spread out the heaven like a dome and made it secure upon the waters; ⁶¹he has put springs of water in the desert and pools on the tops of the mountains, so as to send rivers from the heights to water the earth. ⁶²He formed humans and put a heart in the midst of each body and gave each person breath and life and understanding ⁶³and the spiritˣ of Almighty God,ʸ who surely made all things and searches out hidden things in hidden places. ⁶⁴He knows your imaginations and what you think in your hearts! Woe to those who sin and want to hide their sins! ⁶⁵The Lord will strictly examine all their works and will make a public spectacle of all of you. ⁶⁶You shall be put to shame when your sins come out before others, and your own iniquities shall stand as your accusers on that day. ⁶⁷What will you do? Or how will you hide your sins before the Lord and his glory? ⁶⁸Indeed, Godᶻ is the judge; fear him! Cease from your sins and forget your iniquities, never to commit them again, so Godᵃ will lead you forth and deliver you from all tribulation.

69 The burning wrath of a great multitude is kindled over you; they shall drag some of you away and force you to eat what was sacrificed to idols. ⁷⁰And those who consent to eat shall be held in derision and contempt and shall be trampled under foot. ⁷¹For in many placesᵇ and in neighboring cities there shall be a great uprising against those who fear the Lord. ⁷²They shallᶜ be like maniacs, sparing no one, but plundering and destroying those who continue to fear the Lord.ᵈ ⁷³For they shall destroy and plunder their goods and drive them out of house and home. ⁷⁴Then the tested quality of my elect shall be manifest, like gold that is tested by fire.

75 Listen, my elect ones, says the Lord; the days of tribulation are at hand, but I will deliver you from them. ⁷⁶Do not fear or doubt, for Godᵉ is your guide. ⁷⁷You who keep my commandments and precepts, says the Lord God, must not let your sins weigh you down or your iniquities prevail over you. ⁷⁸Woe to those who are choked by their sins and overwhelmed by their iniquities! They are like a field choked with underbrush and its pathᶠ overwhelmed with thorns, so that no one can pass through. It is shut off and given up to be consumed by fire.

w 16.59 Other ancient authorities read *confined the world between the waters and the waters*   x 16.63 Or *breath*   y 16.63 Other ancient authorities read *of the Lord Almighty*   z 16.68 Other ancient authorities read *the Lord*   a 16.68 Other ancient authorities read *the Lord*   b 16.71 Meaning of Lat uncertain   c 16.72 Other ancient authorities read *For people, because of their misfortunes, shall*   d 16.72 Other ancient authorities read *fear God*   e 16.76 Other ancient authorities read *the Lord*   f 16.78 Other ancient authorities read *seed*

of creation. Cf. Gen. 1. **16:57** *Number . . . stars.* Cf. Ps. 147:4. **16:65** *Public spectacle.* Cf. 7:37. **16:68** Exhortation.

16:69–74 The *elect* will be tested through persecution. 16:69 *Eat what was sacrificed to idols.* Cf. 2 Macc. 6:18–31; 1 Cor. 8; Acts 15:29. **16:74** The righteous are *tested.* Cf. Sir. 2:5.

16:75–78 Final exhortation to keep God's commandments and avoid sin.

(d) The following book appears in an appendix to the Greek Bible.

4 MACCABEES

Authorship, Date, and Literary History

The book of 4 Maccabees is a philosophical treatise on the supremacy of reason, defined as a Torah-centered way of life and demonstrated through the example of the Maccabean martyrs. The author, a pious Jew intimately acquainted with the Septuagint (an early Gk. translation of the Hebrew Bible), wrote in a sophisticated Greek style indicative of a native speaker immersed in the Greek world. Yet despite evidence of a quality Greek education and a high regard for Hellenistic philosophy, the author remains thoroughly opposed to certain aspects of Hellenization (see **"The Bible in Its Ancient Contexts," pp. 2150–52**). In 4 Maccabees, the Maccabean martyrs serve as exemplars of faithfulness to Torah against the threat of torture and death. Based on 4 Maccabees's apparent reliance on 2 Maccabees (cf. 2 Macc. 6:18–7:42), most assume a composition date sometime after 100–90 BCE, probably in the first century CE. Though it was eventually excluded from the Roman Catholic canon, 4 Maccabees appeared in some of the earliest Christian codices and is an important witness to early Jewish and emerging Christian beliefs about the afterlife, Torah, and human nature, to name a few.

4 Maccabees in Jewish and Christian Tradition

Both Eusebius (early fourth century) and Jerome (fifth century) refer to 4 Maccabees, though they know it by a different and likely more original title, *On the Supremacy of Reason*. The book was passed down in a number of Septuagint manuscripts, including Sinaiticus (fourth century), Alexandrinus (fifth century), and in an abridged version, Venetus (eighth or ninth century). At an early stage of transmission, it was translated from Greek into Syriac and is known in the Peshitta by the title *The Fourth Book of the Maccabees and Their Mother*. The book was not included in the Latin Vulgate and does not appear in either the Roman Catholic deuterocanonical books or Protestant Bibles. Erasmus, however, produced a Latin paraphrase of 4 Maccabees that was added to the 1526 printing of the Strasbourg Septuagint.

The book of 4 Maccabees is an important witness to some early Jewish and Christian views regarding the afterlife, atonement, and Torah. Any discussion of bodily resurrection is notably absent in 4 Maccabees, although it appears in 2 Maccabees's discussion of the martyrs' fate (2 Macc. 7:9, 11, 14, 22–23, 29). The author of 4 Maccabees instead takes up the Greek idea of the immortality of the soul (4 Macc. 9:22; 14:5; 16:13; 17:12; 18:23), found also in Philo and the Wisdom of Solomon. Arguably the most significant theological contribution of 4 Maccabees is its view that the suffering and death of the martyrs might atone for the nation (6:27–28; 17:10, 22). Although the idea of vicarious atonement is not itself new in 4 Maccabees—Lev. 16–17 describes the ritual sacrifice of a goat on behalf of the people on the Day of Atonement, and in the Rule of the Community, members of the Qumran group atone for the land (1QS V, 5–8; VIII, 5–6; IX, 3–5), sin (1QS VIII, 3), and certain individuals (1QS V, 6) through righteous living—the efficaciousness of the martyrs' suffering and death in 4 Maccabees is developed along similar lines in some early Christian articulations of Jesus's death as an atoning sacrifice. Regarding the Torah, 4 Maccabees shares with other early Jewish literature composed in Hellenistic contexts, such as Sirach, the view that Torah observance not only is compatible with Greek philosophical reason but is in reality the fullest, most perfect version of it (cf. Sir. 19:20; 24:7–8, 23; 4 Macc. 1:15–17).

Reading Guide

The book of 4 Maccabees, despite the suggestive nature of its present title, makes no mention of the Hasmonean family that is celebrated in 1 and 2 Maccabees for its role in retaking the Jerusalem temple from Greek control in the middle of the second century BCE. The book's connection with this tradition derives from its use and expansion of the story of the martyrs from 2 Macc. 6:18–7:42, which the author uses to demonstrate the virtues of perseverance and obedience (reason) over the passions. Presented in the form of a contest narrative (see **"Court Tales," p. 1608**), the stories of the martyrs in 4 Maccabees exemplify nonviolent resistance to imperial power. When faced with the

offer of life and luxury in exchange for a simple act of loyalty to the empire (eating the king's food), the book's heroes readily choose death. The satirical twist resulting from this demonstration is that the foreign ruler is not defeated by military exploits (e.g., the Hasmonean revolt in 1 and 2 Macc.), but rather by the unwavering faith of the martyrs who would rather face death than defy the covenant by eating from Antiochus's table (see **"Martyrdom and Martyrs," p. 1584**).

Opposition to Hellenism is a primary concern of the book's author, who speaks to the day-to-day circumstances of Jews living in a Diaspora setting (see **"Diaspora," p. 1338**). The work presumes its audience has a certain awareness of and desire to maintain ancestral traditions while acknowledging the temptation to abandon their ancestral culture and religion in favor of Greek values and ways of life. Since loyalty to the Greek or Roman *polis* (city) was demonstrated through worship or acts of piety toward its gods, Jews who did not participate in this worship were treated with suspicion and at times became targets of hostility. Assimilation offered both a degree of protection and some significant incentives, including citizenship, the ability to participate in civic life, and advanced social standing. For those who sought to remain faithful to Torah, there was pressure from the Greek and Roman populace to assimilate so they might escape ridicule and retaliation, and pressure from other Jews who had already assimilated and wished to see the rest of the community embrace Hellenism as well (see **"The Bible in Its Ancient Contexts," pp. 2150–52**).

The book of 4 Maccabees can be divided into two major parts: a philosophical treatise (1:1–3:18) and a narrative dramatization of the treatise through stories of the torture and death of Eleazar, seven brothers, and their mother (3:19–18:19). In the first part, the author extols the virtue of reason over the passions (1:13), while redefining it in terms of Torah observance. The individual who has reason possesses the self-control to abstain from forbidden foods (1:30–35; see **"Diet," p. 268**), rule sexual desire (2:4), and behave in other ways the author deems contrary to human nature. So the wisdom one can obtain from Greek philosophy is nothing new, nor is it wholly Greek, since it is rooted in Torah and Torah observance. In the narrative demonstration that follows the treatise, the book's heroes illustrate the supremacy of this Torah-centered reason through their refusal to eat Antiochus's food, knowing the choice would result in certain and violent death. Their exemplary behavior serves as a model of true, undefiled reason and stands in stark contrast to the Greek ruler who fails to acknowledge that the martyrs are behaving in a manner consistent with Greek philosophical wisdom.

Rebecca L. Harris

1 The subject that I am about to discuss is most philosophical, that is, whether pious reason is sovereign over the passions. So it is right for me to advise you to pay earnest attention to philosophy. [2]For the subject is essential to everyone who is seeking knowledge, and in addition it includes the praise of the highest virtue—I mean, of course, rational judgment. [3]If, then, it is evident that reason rules over those passions that hinder self-control, namely, gluttony and lust, [4]it is also clear that it masters the passions that hinder one from justice, such as malice, and those that stand in the way of courage, namely, anger, fear, and pain. [5]Some might perhaps ask, "If reason rules the passions, why is it not sovereign over forgetfulness and ignorance?" Their attempt at argument is ridiculous! [6]For reason does not rule its own passions but those that are opposed to justice, courage, and self-control,[a] and it is not

a 1.6 Other ancient authorities add *and rational judgment*

1:1–3:18 Philosophical discourse. The book of 4 Maccabees begins with a philosophical discourse that lays out the book's thesis—that *pious reason is sovereign over the passions* (v. 1). After briefly introducing the narrative demonstration of the martyrs that will be the subject of the second part of the book, the author turns to a philosophical discussion of the supreme virtue of reason, its relation to the other cardinal virtues, and its ability to control the emotions.

1:1–6 The four cardinal virtues of Platonic and Stoic philosophy are introduced: *rational judgment* or reason (v. 2), *self-control* (v. 3), *justice* (v. 4), and *courage* (v. 4). (See Wis. 8:7; Plato, *Resp.* 4.426–35; Cicero, *Off.* 1.5.15–17.) *Courage* (Gk. "andreia") is a gendered virtue associated with masculinity. See **"Masculinity," p. 1701. 1:5–6.** Arguing against an imaginary opponent was a common rhetorical

for the purpose of destroying them but so that one may not give way to them.

7 I could prove to you from many and various examples that reason[b] is absolute ruler over the passions, [8]but I can demonstrate it best from the noble bravery of those who died for the sake of virtue: Eleazar and the seven brothers and their mother. [9]All of these, by despising sufferings that bring death, demonstrated that reason controls the passions. [10]On the anniversary of these events it is fitting for me to praise for their virtues those who, with their mother, died for the sake of nobility and goodness, and I would also call them blessed for the honor in which they are held. [11]All people, even their torturers, marveled at their courage and endurance, and they became the cause of the downfall of tyranny over their nation. By their endurance they conquered the tyrant, and thus their native land was purified through them. [12]I shall shortly have an opportunity to speak of this, but, as my custom is, I shall begin by stating my main principle, and then I shall turn to their story, giving glory to the all-wise God.

13 Our inquiry, accordingly, is whether reason is sovereign over the passions. [14]We shall decide just what reason is and what passion is, how many kinds of passions there are, and whether reason rules over all these. [15]Now reason is the mind that with sound logic prefers the life of wisdom. [16]Wisdom, next, is the knowledge of divine and human matters and the causes of these. [17]This, in turn, is education in the law, by which we learn divine matters reverently and human affairs to our advantage. [18]Now the kinds of wisdom are rational judgment, justice, courage, and self-control. [19]Rational judgment is supreme over all of these, since by means of it reason rules over the passions. [20]The two most comprehensive types of the passions are pleasure and pain, and each of these is by nature concerned with both body and soul. [21]There are many sequences of passions with both pleasure and pain. [22]Thus desire precedes pleasure, and delight follows it. [23]Fear precedes pain, and sorrow comes after. [24]Anger, as a person will see by reflecting on this experience, is a passion embracing pleasure and pain. [25]In pleasure there exists even a malevolent tendency, which is the most complex of all the passions. [26]In the soul it is boastfulness, love of money, thirst for honor, rivalry, and malice; [27]in the body, indiscriminate eating, gluttony, and eating alone.

28 Just as pleasure and pain are two plants growing from the body and the soul, so there are many offshoots of these plants,[c] [29]each of which the master cultivator, reason, weeds and prunes and ties up and waters and thoroughly irrigates and so tames the jungle of habits and passions. [30]For reason is the guide of the virtues, but over the passions it is sovereign.

Observe now, first of all, that rational judgment is sovereign over the passions by virtue of the restraining power of self-control. [31]Self-control, then, is dominance over the desires.

b 1.7 Other ancient authorities read *devout reason*
c 1.28 Another reading is *these passions*

strategy employed here to develop the thesis. In contrast to Stoic philosophers who encouraged the elimination of the passions, 4 Maccabees advocates mastery or control over them (cf. Plutarch, *Virt. mor.* 4 [*Mor.* 443 D]).

1:7–12 Eleazar, the seven brothers, and their mother are martyrs associated with the Maccabean Revolt (2 Macc. 6:18–7:42). They are remembered for their courage in response to Antiochus IV's persecution of those who refused to submit to Hellenistic reforms. See **"The Bible in Its Ancient Contexts," pp. 2150–52. 1:10** *On the anniversary of these events* suggests the book was composed for a particular occasion—a funeral oration performed in commemoration of the martyrs.

1:13–35 The author defines the key terms central to the thesis. *Reason* is described in Torah-centered language as wisdom that consists of knowledge of human and divine matters, which is obtained through the study of the *law* (vv. 15–17). Greek "paideia" in 4 Maccabees refers to training or *education* (cf. 10:10; 13:22). Identifying the cardinal virtues (cf. 1:2–4) as expressions of wisdom, the author affirms the priority of Torah-wisdom (reason) among the virtues. **1:20–23** The author identifies two types of emotions—*pleasure and pain*. This introduction anticipates the narrative demonstration in which Antiochus tries to persuade the martyrs by appealing to both types—to pleasure with the offer of food and to pain through the threat of torture and death. **1:28–30** *Pleasure and pain* are metaphorically described as *two plants* with *many offshoots*. Reason manages the plant growth while not destroying it (cf. 1:6). **1:31–35** Reason, exercised through *self-control*, enables restraint, exemplified in the narrative demonstration by the martyrs' refusal to compromise.

³²Some desires belong to the soul, others to the body, and reason obviously rules over both. ³³Otherwise, how is it that when we are attracted to forbidden foods we abstain from the pleasure to be had from them? Is it not because reason is able to rule over appetites? I for one think so. ³⁴Therefore when we crave seafood and fowl and animals and all sorts of foods that are forbidden to us by the law, we abstain because of domination by reason. ³⁵For the passions of the appetites are restrained, checked by the temperate mind, and all the impulses of the body are bridled by reason.

2 And why is it amazing that the desires of the soul for the enjoyment of beauty are rendered powerless? ²It is for this reason, certainly, that the temperate Joseph is praised, because by mental effort[d] he overcame the prospect of pleasure. ³For when he was young and in his prime for intercourse, by reason he nullified the frenzy[e] of the passions. ⁴Reason is proved to rule not only over the frenzied urge of sexual desire but also over every desire.[f] ⁵Thus the law says, "You shall not covet your neighbor's wife or anything that is your neighbor's." ⁶In fact, since the law has told us not to covet, I could prove to you all the more that reason is able to control desires.

Just so it is with the passions that hinder one from justice. ⁷Otherwise how could it be that someone who is habitually a solitary eater, a glutton, or even a drunkard can learn a better way, unless reason is clearly lord of the passions? ⁸Thus, as soon as one adopts a way of life in accordance with the law, even though a lover of money, one is forced to act contrary to natural ways and to lend without interest to those who plead for assistance and to cancel the debt when the seventh year arrives. ⁹If one is greedy, one is ruled by the law through reason so that one neither gleans the harvest nor gathers the last grapes from the vineyard.

In other matters we can recognize that reason rules the passions. ¹⁰For the law prevails even over affection for parents, so that virtue is not abandoned for their sakes. ¹¹It overrules love for one's wife so that one rebukes her when she breaks the law. ¹²It overrules love for children so that one punishes them for misdeeds. ¹³It is sovereign over the relationship of friends so that one rebukes friends when they act wickedly. ¹⁴Do not consider it paradoxical when reason, through the law, can prevail even over enmity. The fruit trees of the enemy are not cut down, but one preserves the property of enemies from marauders and helps raise up what has fallen.[g]

15 It is evident that reason rules even[h] the more violent passions: lust for power, vanity, boasting, arrogance, and malice. ¹⁶For the temperate mind repels all these malicious passions, just as it repels anger—for it is sovereign over even this. ¹⁷When Moses was angry with Dathan and Abiram, he did nothing against them in anger but controlled his anger by reason. ¹⁸For, as I have said, the temperate mind is able to get the

d 2.2 Another ancient authority adds *in reasoning* e 2.3 Gk *he swatted the gadfly* f 2.4 Or *all covetousness* g 2.14 Or *the beasts that have fallen* h 2.15 Other ancient authorities read *through*

2:1–23 Drawing on examples of the ancestors, the author illustrates reason's rule over the emotions, attributing it to the Torah. Training in the "law" (1:17) facilitates reason, so the life of a person subject to Torah is marked by self-control (2:6, 8, 15) and exemplifies the cardinal virtues (2:23). **2:2–6** Joseph, remembered for resisting sexual temptation (Gen. 39:7–12), is the first of three ancestors championed for their self-control. The Testament of Joseph expands the story of the advances of Potiphar's wife (T. Jos. 2:7–10:4); Joseph and Aseneth also recognizes Joseph as an exemplar of the virtue of self-control (Jos. Asen. 4:9). **2:5** See Exod. 20:17; Deut. 5:21. **2:7–9** The implication of the Joseph example—that knowledge of the Torah enables self-control (v. 5)—is made explicit in the claim that adopting a Torah-observant way of life compels one to act contrary to nature (v. 8). The examples given are also acts of Torah observance: lending to the needy (Exod. 22:25; Lev. 25:35–37; Deut. 23:19–20), canceling debt every seventh year (Deut. 15:1–3), and leaving gleanings for the poor (Lev. 19:9–10; Deut. 24:20–21; Ruth 2). **2:10–14** The intensity of the examples escalates with the transition to a focus on relationships that anticipates the martyrdom of the seven brothers and their mother (13:19–14:1; 14:11–20). **2:14** Deut. 20:19 prohibits cutting down the fruit trees of one's enemy. **2:15–20** The author returns to specific examples from the past to demonstrate the claim that reason can control even violent emotions. By showing that reason is powerful over malicious emotions and wrath, the author makes a case for its supremacy over all emotions. **2:17** Numbers 16:12–15; 23–35

better of the passions, to correct some and to render others powerless. [19]Why else did Jacob, our most wise father, censure the households of Simeon and Levi for their irrational slaughter of the entire tribe of the Shechemites, saying, "Cursed be their anger"? [20]For if reason could not control anger, he would not have spoken thus. [21]Now when God fashioned humans, he planted in them passions and inclinations, [22]but at the same time he enthroned the mind among the senses as a sacred governor over them all. [23]To the mind he gave the law, and one who lives subject to this will rule a kingdom that is temperate, just, good, and courageous.

24 How is it then, one might say, that if reason is master of the passions, it does not control

3 forgetfulness and ignorance? [1]But this argument is entirely ridiculous, for it is evident that reason rules not over its own passions but over those of the body. [2]No one of us can eradicate that kind of desire, but reason can provide a way for us not to be enslaved by desire. [3]No one of you can eradicate anger from the mind, but reason can help to deal with anger. [4]No one of us can eradicate malice, but reason can fight at our side so that we are not overcome by malice. [5]For reason does not uproot the passions but is their antagonist.

6 Now this can be explained more clearly by the story of King David's thirst. [7]David had been attacking the Philistines all day long and together with the soldiers of his nation had killed many of them. [8]Then when evening fell, he[i] came, sweating and quite exhausted, to the royal tent, around which the whole army of our ancestors had encamped. [9]Now all the rest were at dinner, [10]but the king was extremely thirsty, and though springs were plentiful there, he could not satisfy his thirst from them. [11]But a certain irrational desire for the water in the enemy's territory tormented and inflamed him, undid and consumed him. [12]When his guards complained bitterly because of the king's craving, two staunch young soldiers, respecting[j] the king's desire, armed themselves fully and taking a pitcher climbed over the enemy's ramparts. [13]Eluding the sentinels at the gates, they went searching throughout the enemy camp [14]and found the spring and from it boldly brought the king a drink. [15]But David,[k] though he was burning with thirst, considered it an altogether fearful danger to his soul to drink what was regarded as equivalent to blood. [16]Therefore, opposing reason to desire, he poured out the drink as an offering to God. [17]For the temperate mind

i 3.8 Other ancient authorities read *he hurried and*
j 3.12 Or *embarrassed because of*   k 3.15 Gk *he*

recounts Dathan and Abiram's revolt against Moses (cf. Sir. 45:18–19). **2:19** Jacob serves as an example of self-control in contrast to the unrestrained wrath of his sons, Levi and Simeon (cf. Gen. 34; 49:5–7). In other literary traditions, Levi and Simeon are praised for their "zeal" at Shechem (cf. Jub. 30; Jdt. 9:2–4; T. Levi; Aramaic Levi). **2:21–23** The author credits God both with fashioning human nature, including the emotions, and with giving the Torah to the mind so that through reason it is able to govern the emotions and exercise the virtues. **2:21** *Inclinations* reflects a belief attested in other Jewish literature that humans were born with both good and evil inclinations (cf. 1QS III, 13–IV, 26; Philo, *Opif.* 153; 2 Esd. [4 Ezra] 3:12–17). The belief likely emerged from Persian Zoroastrianism, which envisioned a dualistic cosmology of good and evil.

2:24–3:18 The author develops the thesis with a final example from the distant past before turning to the more recent history with the extended example of the Maccabean martyrs. **2:24–3:5** The author again takes up the objection introduced in 1:5–6. In response to the question posed by an imaginary interlocutor (2:24), the author reaffirms the position that reason rules over the emotions of the body with the goal of controlling but not eradicating them (3:1–5). Philo juxtaposes Moses and Aaron, arguing that whereas Moses sought to "eradicate" the emotions (and in succeeding serves as a model of perfection), Aaron serves as a reasonable and attainable model of the less perfect person who is able to "control" the emotions (Philo, *Leg.* 3:129–32). **3:6–16** Drawing on the story of David's thirst in 2 Sam. 23:13–17 (cf. 1 Chr. 11:15–19), the author expands and develops the narrative. In 4 Maccabees, the battle scenario is intensified, and in addition to refusing to drink the water his soldiers retrieve, David ceremoniously pours it out as an offering to God. **3:17–18** The story of David's thirst exemplifies the extent to which reason is able to control the emotions and even bodily desires. Despite the fact that David's desire is described as "irrational" (v. 11) because it is unreasonable in light of the circumstances, David's response is exemplary for the degree of self-control required to tame such intense desire.

can conquer the drives of the passions and quench the flames of frenzied desires; [18]it can overthrow bodily agonies even when they are extreme and by nobility of reason spurn all domination by the passions.

19 The present occasion now invites us to a narrative demonstration of temperate reason.

20 At a time when our ancestors were enjoying profound peace because of their observance of the law and were prospering, so that even Seleucus Nicanor, king of Asia, had both appropriated money to them for the temple service and recognized their way of life— [21]just at that time certain persons attempted a revolution against the public harmony and caused many and various disasters.

4 Now there was a certain Simon, a political opponent of the noble and good man Onias, who then held the high priesthood for life. When, despite bringing charges against him on behalf of the nation, he was unable to injure Onias, he fled the country with the purpose of betraying it. [2]So he came to Apollonius, governor of Syria, Phoenicia, and Cilicia, and said, [3]"I have come here because I am loyal to the king's government, to report that in the Jerusalem treasuries there are deposited tens of thousands in private funds that are not the property of the temple

but belong to King Seleucus." [4]When Apollonius learned the details of these things, he praised Simon for his service to the king and went up to Seleucus to inform him of the rich treasure. [5]On receiving authority to deal with this matter, he proceeded quickly to our country accompanied by the accursed Simon and a very strong military force. [6]He said that he had come with the king's authority to seize the private funds in the treasury. [7]The people indignantly protested his words, considering it outrageous that those who had committed deposits to the sacred treasury should be deprived of them, and did all that they could to prevent it. [8]But, uttering threats, Apollonius went on to the temple. [9]While the priests together with women and children were imploring God in the temple to shield the holy place that was being treated so contemptuously, [10]and while Apollonius was going up with his armed forces to seize the money, angels on horseback with lightning flashing from their weapons appeared from heaven, instilling in them great fear and trembling. [11]Then Apollonius fell down half-dead in the temple area that was open to all, stretched out his hands toward heaven, and with tears begged the Hebrews to pray for him and propitiate the wrath of the heavenly army. [12]For he said that he had committed a sin deserving of death and that if he were

3:19–18:24 Extended narrative demonstration of the thesis. Beginning with a description of the historical situation, the author highlights the political instability and fragility that create a climate primed for conflict.
3:19–21 Before turning to the narrative demonstration of the martyrs, the author sets the stage by offering some historical and cultural context, the details of which are not always accurate. The author mistakes Seleucus IV Philopater (187–175 BCE) for Seleucus Nicanor (305–281 BCE). The Seleucids, descendants/successors of Alexander the Great's general, Seleucus, ruled in the northern part of Palestine, gaining control of Judea in 198 BCE. **3:20** Attributing the peaceful social situation of the ancestors to their *observance of the law*, the author interprets events of the recent past through the lens of divine retribution (cf. Deut. 28:1–14). See **"Divine Retribution," p. 339**. **3:21** *Certain persons* likely refers to Hellenizers (members of the local, indigenous population who encouraged the adoption of Greek customs).
4:1–14 4:1 Onias (high priest ca. 190–175 BCE) was eventually removed from office (4:15–16), although the author indicates here that the high priesthood was held for life. The inclusion of this detail implies that the practice of lifetime appointment was no longer in effect at the time of writing, lending support to the argument the book was composed no earlier than the first century CE. **4:2** Apollonius's governance of Syria, Phoenicia, and Cilicia reflects the political landscape of the period 20–54 CE, when Syria and Cilicia formed a single province. **4:3** The author distinguishes between temple funds and private funds stored at the temple; stealing from the latter was a less serious offense than temple robbery, which was thought to elicit divine judgment (cf. Sophocles, *Oed. tyr.* 884–93). **4:4–5** 4 Maccabees omits the figure of Heliodorus (2 Macc. 3:7). Instead, Apollonius himself goes to seize the funds (4:10), is countered by an angelic army on horseback (4:10), and becomes a recipient of divine protection (4:13–14).

spared he would praise the blessedness of the holy place before all people. [13]Moved by these words, although otherwise cautious lest King Seleucus suppose that Apollonius had been overcome by human treachery and not by divine justice, the high priest Onias prayed for him. [14]So Apollonius,[l] having been saved beyond all expectations, went away to report to the king what had happened to him.

15 When King Seleucus died, his son Antiochus Epiphanes succeeded to the throne, an arrogant and terrible man [16]who removed Onias from the priesthood and appointed Onias's[m] brother Jason as high priest. [17]Jason[n] agreed that if the office were conferred on him he would pay the king three thousand six hundred sixty talents annually. [18]So the king appointed him high priest and ruler of the nation. [19]Jason[o] changed the nation's customs and altered its form of government in complete violation of the law, [20]so that he not only constructed a gymnasium at the very citadel[p] of our native land but also abolished the temple service. [21]The divine justice was angered by these acts and caused Antiochus himself to make war on them. [22]For when he was warring against Ptolemy in Egypt, he heard that a rumor of his death had spread and that the people of Jerusalem had rejoiced greatly. He speedily marched against them, [23]and after he had ravaged them he issued a decree that if any of them were found observing the ancestral law they should die.

[24]When, by means of his decrees, he had not been able in any way to put an end to the people's observance of the law but saw that all his threats and punishments were being disregarded, [25]even to the extent that women, because they had circumcised their sons, were thrown headlong from heights along with their infants, though they had known beforehand that they would suffer this, [26]when, I say, his decrees were despised by the people, he himself tried through torture to compel everyone in the nation to renounce Judaism by eating defiling foods.

5 The tyrant Antiochus, sitting in state with his counselors on a certain high place and with his armed soldiers standing around him, [2]ordered the guards to seize each and every Hebrew and to compel them to eat pork and food sacrificed to idols. [3]If any were not willing to eat defiling food, they were to be broken on the wheel and killed. [4]When many persons had been rounded up, one[q] man, Eleazar by name, leader of the flock, was brought[r] before the king. He was a man of priestly family, learned in the law, advanced in age, and known to many in the tyrant's court because of his long career.

5 When Antiochus saw him he said, [6]"Before I begin to torture you, old man, I would advise you to save yourself by eating pork,

l 4.14 Gk *he* *m* 4.16 Gk *his* *n* 4.17 Gk *He* *o* 4.19 Gk *He* *p* 4.20 Or *high place* *q* 5.4 Other ancient authorities add Hebrew *r* 5.4 Or *was the first of the flock to be brought*

4:15–26 4:17 Jason negotiates with the foreign (colonizing) ruler for the priesthood. 4:18 In the Second Temple period, the office of high priest carried social and political authority. See **"Priests and Temple in Second Temple Judaism," p. 1479**. 4:20 The *gymnasium* was a hub for Greek culture. 4:21 The author interprets Antiochus's aggression as an act of divine retribution (cf. Deut. 28:1–14) in response to Jason's reforms, which were a violation of Torah (v. 19). 4:24–26 The people's *observance of the law* in opposition to the king even at the threat of severe punishment anticipates the contest between Antiochus and the martyrs beginning at 5:1.
5:1–38 Framing the scene in the form of a philosophical debate, the author argues the thesis through the speech of the esteemed Eleazar. The debate allows the author to respond to the dominant culture's charges against Jewish religious observances and refute the claim that the religion is foolish and that transgressing the Torah would come without consequence. 5:1–4 The identification of Antiochus as a *tyrant* (Gk. "tyrannos") reflects a common literary trope in which a tyrannical ruler confronts an innocent victim (cf. Seneca, *De constantia*; Plato, *Phaed.*; Eusebius, *Mart. Pal.*; Origen, *Mart.*; Lucian, *Tyr.*). 5:2 Food becomes the site of conflict for the tyrant's attempts to coerce his victims into crossing religious boundaries. Jewish law prohibits eating pork or food sacrificed to idols or used in the worship of foreign gods (Lev. 11:7; Deut. 14:8; Exod. 34:15). See **"Diet," p. 268**. 5:4 The author introduces the first exemplar of Torah faithfulness—Eleazar, whose name means "God helps." A popular name in early Jewish art and literature, this Eleazar is portrayed as an old man of priestly lineage, knowledgeable in law and philosophy. He has a reputation among the local population, which heightens the intensity of the drama about to unfold. 5:5–13 Antiochus charges Eleazar on the

⁷for I respect your age and your gray hairs. Although you have had them for so long a time, it does not seem to me that you are a philosopher when you observe the religion of the Jews. ⁸When nature has granted it to us, why should you abhor eating the very excellent meat of this animal? ⁹It is senseless not to enjoy delicious things that are not shameful and wrong to spurn the gifts of nature. ¹⁰It seems to me that you will do something even more senseless if, by holding a vain opinion concerning the truth, you continue to despise me to your own hurt. ¹¹Will you not awaken from your foolish philosophy, dispel the emptiness of your reasonings, adopt a mind appropriate to your years, philosophize according to the truth of what is beneficial, ¹²and have compassion on your old age by honoring my humane advice? ¹³For consider this: if there is some power watching over this religion of yours, it will excuse you from any transgression that arises out of compulsion."

14 When the tyrant urged him in this fashion to eat meat unlawfully, Eleazar asked to have a word. ¹⁵When he had received permission to speak, he began to address the people as follows: ¹⁶"We, O Antiochus, who have been persuaded to govern our lives by the divine law think that there is no compulsion more powerful than our obedience to the law. ¹⁷Therefore we consider that we should not transgress it in any respect. ¹⁸Even if, as you suppose, our law were not truly divine and we had wrongly held it to be divine, not even so would it be right for us to invalidate our reputation for piety. ¹⁹Therefore do not suppose that it would be a petty sin if we were to eat defiling food; ²⁰to transgress the law in matters either small or great is of equal seriousness, ²¹for in either case the law is equally despised. ²²You scoff at our philosophy as though living by it were irrational, ²³but it teaches us self-control, so that we master all pleasures and desires, and it also trains us in courage, so that we endure any suffering willingly; ²⁴it instructs us in justice, so that in all our dealings we give what is due;ˢ and it teaches us piety, so that with proper reverence we worship the only living God.

25 "Therefore we do not eat defiling food, for since we believe that the law was established by God, we know that the Creator of the world in giving us the law has shown sympathy toward us in accordance with nature. ²⁶He has permitted us to eat what will be most suitable for our lives,ᵗ but he has forbidden us to eat meats that would be contrary to this. ²⁷It would be tyrannical for you to compel us not only to transgress the law but also to eat in such a way that you may deride us for eating defiling foods, which are most hateful to us. ²⁸But you shall have no such occasion to laugh at me, ²⁹nor will I transgress the sacred oaths of my ancestors concerning the keeping of the law, ³⁰not even if you gouge out my eyes and burn my entrails. ³¹I am not so old and cowardly as not to be young in reason on behalf of piety. ³²Therefore get your torture wheels ready and fan the fire more vehemently! ³³I do not so pity my old age as to overthrow the ancestral law by my own act. ³⁴I will not play false to you, O law that trained me, nor will

ˢ 5.24 Or *so that we hold in balance all our habitual inclinations*
ᵗ 5.26 Or *souls*

grounds that his is not a true philosophy and engages in persuasive techniques to try to compel Eleazar to eat the forbidden meat. Antiochus's argument consists of an appeal to nature (a Stoic critique) and rational sense (vv. 8–10), according to which he contends that Jewish philosophy (Torah) is irrational and futile (v. 11). **5:13** In a final attempt at persuasion, the king claims that his opponent need not fear divine retaliation, since transgressions brought on by compulsion will certainly be excused. This claim is an attempt at circumventing the Jewish view of divine retribution presented previously in the text (cf. 3:20; 4:21). **5:14–24** Eleazar counters Antiochus's charges with a speech that presents Torah observance as a most excellent form of philosophic reasoning, arguing that it cultivates in the observant the cardinal virtues of *self-control, courage, justice,* and *piety* (which the author substitutes for rational judgment). **5:16** In response to the tyrant's attempt at compulsion (v. 13), Eleazar insists that no degree of compulsion is powerful enough to sway those persuaded to live by *divine law.* **5:24** By substituting *piety* for rational judgment, the author connects another prominent Greco-Roman virtue to a Torah-observant life. *Piety,* like justice, is an active expression or form of reason. **5:25–38** Eleazar's speech concludes with an argument demonstrating the compatibility of the Torah with nature and a bold challenge to the king's threats. **5:25–26** Against Antiochus's claim that eating pork is consistent with nature (vv. 8–9), Eleazar contends that the Torah reveals the opposite—that it permits eating what is suitable for the body and forbids meats that are unsuitable according to the

I renounce you, beloved self-control. [35]I will not put you to shame, philosophical reason, nor will I reject you, honored priesthood and knowledge of the law. [36]You, O king,[u] shall not defile the honorable mouth of my old age nor my long life lived lawfully. [37]My ancestors will receive me as pure, as one who does not fear your violence even to death. [38]You will tyrannize the ungodly, but you shall not dominate my reasonings on behalf of piety, either by words or through deeds."

6 When Eleazar in this manner had made eloquent response to the exhortations of the tyrant, the guards who were standing by dragged him violently to the instruments of torture. [2]First they stripped the old man, though he remained adorned with the gracefulness of his piety. [3]After they had tied his arms behind him, they flogged him from both sides, [4]while a herald who faced him cried out, "Obey the king's commands!" [5]But the courageous and noble man, like a true Eleazar,[v] was unmoved, as though being tortured in a dream, [6]yet while the old man's eyes were raised to heaven, his flesh was being torn by scourges, his blood flowing, and his sides were being cut to pieces. [7]Although he fell to the ground because his body could not endure the agonies, he kept his reason upright and unswerving. [8]One of the cruel guards rushed at him and began to kick him in the side to make him get up again after he

fell. [9]But he bore the pains and scorned the punishment and endured the tortures. [10]Like a noble athlete the old man, while being beaten, was victorious over his torturers; [11]in fact, with his face bathed in sweat and gasping heavily for breath, he amazed even his torturers by his courageous spirit.

12 At that point, partly out of pity for his old age, [13]partly out of sympathy from their acquaintance with him, partly out of admiration for his endurance, some of the king's retinue came to him and said, [14]"Eleazar, why are you so irrationally destroying yourself through these evil things? [15]We will set before you some cooked meat; save yourself by pretending to eat pork."

16 But Eleazar, as though more bitterly tormented by this counsel, cried out, [17]"Never may we, the children of Abraham, think so basely that out of cowardice we feign a role unbecoming to us! [18]For it would be irrational if, having lived in accordance with truth up to old age and having guarded the reputation of a life lived lawfully, we should now change our course [19]and ourselves become a pattern of impiety to the young by setting them an example in the eating of defiling food. [20]It would be shameful if we should survive for a little while and during that time be a laughingstock to all for our cowardice [21]and be despised by the tyrant as unmanly by not contending even to death for

u 5.36 Gk lacks *O king* v 6.5 *Eleazar* means *God helps*

nature of human design. **5:37** The theme of immortality is prominently introduced here and reiterated in the martyrdoms of the seven brothers and their mother.

6:1–30 The philosophical debate between Antiochus and Eleazar (5:5–38) and the details of his torture (6:1–8) are absent in 2 Maccabees (2 Macc. 6:18–31). In 4 Maccabees, the speech anticipates Eleazar's martyrdom; his ability to withstand prolonged and violent torture is evidence confirming the credibility of his claims regarding the rationality of Torah observance. **6:1–11** Eleazar's courageous and self-controlled behavior reflects the noble death tradition, often associated with stories of martyrdom (cf. Acts of Paul and Thecla, Passion of Perpetua and Felicitas). **6:2** Despite the guards' attempts to shame Eleazar, the author assures that his honor remains uncompromised. **6:5** *Like a true Eleazar* is a wordplay on the name Eleazar, which in Hebrew means "God helps." **6:7** Eleazar's degraded physical condition stands in contrast to his reason, which remains upright and unaffected. **6:10** The Roman Stoic philosopher Seneca draws a connection between the physical exertion demanded of a victim who endures torture and an athlete's training (Seneca, *Ep.* 78:15–19). The image of the martyr as athlete became a popular trope in early Christian stories of martyrdom (e.g., Blandina and Perpetua in Acts of the Martyrs). By the third century CE, martyrs were commonly referred to as "athletes of Christ" and "athletes of faith." **6:12–23** The king's men offer Eleazar a way out of the torture and certain death if he would only *pretend* to eat pork. To Eleazar, this pretense is worse than torture, and he responds that he will not because such an act would be irrational and impious, misleading the youth. **6:14** Whereas the king's men interpret Eleazar's commitment to Torah as irrational, Eleazar contends that what they are asking him to do—feign a repudiation of Judaism—is irrational (v. 18). **6:21** Turning back would be considered

our divine law. ²²Therefore, O children of Abraham, die nobly for the sake of piety! ²³And you, guards of the tyrant, why do you delay?"

24 When they saw that he was so courageous in the face of the afflictions and that he had not been changed by their compassion, the guards brought him to the fire. ²⁵There they burned him with maliciously contrived instruments, threw him down, and poured stinking liquids into his nostrils. ²⁶When he was now burned to his very bones and about to expire, he lifted up his eyes to God and said, ²⁷"You know, O God, that, though I might have saved myself, I am dying in burning torments for the sake of the law. ²⁸Be merciful to your people, and let our punishment suffice for them. ²⁹Make my blood their purification, and take my life in exchange for theirs." ³⁰After he said this, the holy man died nobly in his tortures; even in the tortures of death he resisted, by virtue of reason, for the sake of the law.

31 Admittedly, then, pious reason is sovereign over the passions. ³²For if the passions had prevailed over reason, we would have testified to their domination. ³³But now that reason has conquered the passions, we properly attribute to it the power to govern. ³⁴It is right for us to acknowledge the dominance of reason when it masters even external agonies. It would be ridiculous to deny it.*ʷ* ³⁵I have proved not only that reason has mastered agonies but also that it masters pleasures and in no respect yields to them.

7 For like a most skillful pilot, the reason of our father Eleazar steered the ship of piety over the sea of the passions, ²and though buffeted by the stormings of the tyrant and overwhelmed by the mighty waves of tortures, ³in no way did he turn the rudder of piety until he sailed into the haven of immortal victory. ⁴No city besieged with many ingenious war machines has ever held out as did that most holy man. Although his sacred life was consumed by tortures and racks, he conquered the besiegers because reason was shielding his piety. ⁵For in setting his mind firm like a jutting cliff, our father Eleazar broke the maddening waves of the passions. ⁶O priest, worthy of the priesthood, you neither defiled your sacred teeth nor profaned your stomach, which had room only for reverence and purity, by eating defiling foods. ⁷O man in harmony with the law and philosopher of divine life! ⁸Such should be those who are administrators of the law, shielding it with their own blood and noble sweat in sufferings even to death. ⁹You, father, validated our obedience to the law through your endurance unto glory, and you did not abandon the holiness that you praised, but by your deeds you made your words of divine*ˣ* philosophy credible. ¹⁰O aged man, more powerful than tortures; O elder, fiercer than fire; O supreme king over the passions, Eleazar! ¹¹For just as our father Aaron, armed with

w 6.34 Syr: Meaning of Gk uncertain   x 7.9 Other ancient authorities lack *divine*

unmanly. The ability to withstand torture and endure a martyr's death was considered a "manly" trait in antiquity. See **"Masculinity," p. 1701. 6:23** Eleazar's emphatic, final word on the matter, directed to the king's guards, is meant to incite. In contemporary vernacular, he might have said, "Come at me, bro!"

6:24–31 Eleazar's death is depicted in sacrificial terms. Burning by fire and spilling blood were common methods of ritual sacrifice (cf. Lev. 1). See **"Offerings and Sacrifices," p. 146.** Eleazar's final words are directed to God, reminding God that he is dying *for the sake of the law*, which provides a compelling reason to grant the ensuing request that his death might atone for others. The concept of vicarious or substitutionary death is found also in the Torah (Lev. 16; cf. Isa. 53), the example of the brothers (4 Macc. 17:21–22), and the New Testament (Mark 10:45; Rom. 3:25; 1 Tim. 2:5–6).

6:31–7:23 Commentary on Eleazar's death. 6:31–35 Eleazar's example proves the author's thesis that pious reason is sovereign over the emotions (cf. 1:1). **7:1–15** The story of Eleazar concludes with an encomium praising him for his exemplary demonstration of reason. Drawing on analogies commonly used in Hellenistic philosophy and writings, the author presents Eleazar as the ideal sage. **7:1–3** Nautical imagery frequently evokes a sense of danger and uncertainty (cf. Sophocles, *Oed. tyr.* 689–696). The Hodayot or Thanksgiving Hymns, found in the Qumran caves, draw on the same images (a ship at sea and a besieged city) to depict a threatening situation (cf. 1QHᵃ XI, 7–8; XIV, 25–28). **7:4** The image of a besieged city emphasizes Eleazar's endurance under pressure, which results in victory over his opponents. **7:7** Among the honorific titles bestowed on Eleazar is that of *philosopher*, a title Antiochus challenged in 5:7. **7:8–9** Eleazar is upheld as a model of loyalty to the Torah, whose example inspired others (cf. 6:18–19). **7:11** Comparing the recently deceased with another

the censer, ran through the multitude of the people and conquered the fiery angel, [12]so the descendant of Aaron, Eleazar, though being consumed by the fire, remained unmoved in his reason. [13]Most amazing, indeed, though he was an old man, his body no longer tense and firm,[y] his muscles flabby, his sinews feeble, he became young again [14]in spirit through reason, and by reason like that of Isaac he rendered the many-headed rack ineffective. [15]O man of blessed age and of venerable gray hair and of law-abiding life, whom the faithful seal of death has perfected!

16 If, therefore, because of piety an aged man despised tortures even to death, most certainly pious reason is governor of the passions. [17]Some perhaps might say, "Not all have full command of their passions, because not all have prudent reason." [18]But as many as attend to piety with a whole heart, these alone are able to control the passions of the flesh, [19]since they believe that they, like our patriarchs Abraham and Isaac and Jacob, do not die to God but live to God. [20]No contradiction therefore arises when some persons appear to be dominated by their passions because of the weakness of their reason. [21]What person who lives[z] as a philosopher by the whole rule of philosophy and trusts in God [22]and knows that it is blessed to endure any suffering for the sake of virtue would not be able to overcome the passions through godliness? [23]For only the wise[a] and courageous are masters of their passions.

8 For this is why even the very young, by following a philosophy in accordance with pious reason, have prevailed over the most painful instruments of torture. [2]For when the tyrant was conspicuously defeated in his first attempt, being unable to compel an aged man to eat defiling foods, then in violent rage he commanded that others of the Hebrew captives be brought and that any who ate defiling food would be freed after eating, but if any were to refuse, they would be tortured even more cruelly.

3 When the tyrant had given these orders, seven brothers—handsome, modest, noble, and accomplished in every way—were brought before him along with their aged mother. [4]When the tyrant saw them, grouped about their mother as though a chorus, he was pleased with them. And struck by their appearance and nobility, he smiled at them and summoned them nearer and said, [5]"Young men, with favorable

y 7.13 Gk *the tautness of the body already loosed* *z* 7.21 Another ancient authority adds *piously* *a* 7.23 Another ancient authority adds *prudent*

exemplary individual is a standard feature of encomia. Aaron is credited with offering atonement and stopping a plague that was killing the people and threatened to wipe them out (Num. 16:41–50; Wis. 18:20–25). **7:14** Isaac is considered a worthy exemplar for his willing submission to be offered as a sacrifice (Gen. 22:1–19; cf. 4 Macc. 13:12; 16:20). **7:16–23** To further demonstrate the thesis, the author raises a potential objection (v. 17) and refutes it with a restatement of the thesis (v. 18) and the examples of Abraham, Isaac, and Jacob (v. 19). **7:17–18** The author refutes the charge that not all have the ability to control their passions because not all have prudent reason with the claim that godliness (which the author equates with reason) enables one to exercise control over the passions. **7:19** The author appeals to the examples of the ancestors—Abraham, Isaac, and Jacob—as evidence that pious reason leads to immortality. Josephus maintains that those who observe Torah anticipate immortality and an afterlife that is better than the present (Josephus, *Ag. Ap.* 2.217–18).

8:1–14:10 Martyrdom of the Seven Brothers. Compare 2 Macc. 7:1–42.

8:1–9:9 The author inserts into the narrative a debate between Antiochus and the brothers. Whereas 2 Maccabees moves directly from Eleazar's death notice to the torture and martyrdom of the brothers, 4 Maccabees includes a philosophical exchange that parallels the debate between Antiochus and Eleazar (5:5–38). **8:1–14** Though the king intends Eleazar's martyrdom to compel other Hebrew captives to acquiesce and eat the defiling food, Eleazar's example instead increases their resolve (vv. 1–2). The author appeals to two extremes, the very old (Eleazar) and the very young (the brothers), demonstrating the span of those who should be able to exercise control over the passions. **8:2** The defeat of the tyrant is an affront to his honor, which results in violent rage and an attempt to reclaim honor by forcefully and publicly coercing others into submission. Antiochus's lack of restraint stands in contrast to the portrait of Moses in 2:17, the great lawgiver who controlled his anger through reason. **8:4** The image, common in Greek drama, of the brothers and their mothers as a chorus illustrates their agreement and anticipates their collective resolve in the events that follow. **8:5–8** The *friendship* Antiochus offers is no small thing but includes access to the king's

feelings I admire each and every one of you and greatly respect the beauty and the number of such brothers. Not only do I advise you not to display the same madness as that of the old man who has just been tortured, but I also exhort you to yield to me and enjoy my friendship. [6]Just as I am able to punish those who disobey my orders, so I can be a benefactor to those who are disposed to obey me. [7]Trust me, then, and you will receive positions of authority in my government if you will renounce the ancestral tradition of your national life. [8]Enjoy your youth by adopting the Greek way of life and by changing your manner of living. [9]But if by disobedience you rouse my anger, you will compel me to destroy each and every one of you with dreadful punishments through tortures. [10]Therefore take pity on yourselves. Even I, your enemy, have compassion for your youth and handsome appearance. [11]Will you not consider this, that if you disobey, nothing remains for you but to die on the rack?"

12 When he had said these things, he ordered the instruments of torture to be brought forward so as to persuade them out of fear to eat the defiling food. [13]When the guards had placed before them wheels and joint-dislocators, rack and hooks[b] and catapults and caldrons, braziers and thumbscrews and iron claws and wedges and bellows, the tyrant resumed speaking: [14]"Be afraid, young fellows; whatever justice you revere will be merciful to you when you transgress under compulsion."

15 But when they had heard the inducements and saw the dreadful devices, not only were they not afraid, but they also opposed the tyrant with their own philosophy and by their right reasoning nullified his tyranny. [16]Let us consider, on the other hand, what arguments might have been used if some of them had been cowardly and unmanly. Would they not have been the following? [17]"O wretches that we are and so senseless! Since the king has summoned and exhorted us to accept kind treatment if we obey him, [18]why do we take pleasure in vain resolves and venture upon a disobedience that brings death? [19]O men and brothers, should we not fear the instruments of torture and consider the threats of torments and give up this vanity and this arrogance that threatens to destroy us? [20]Let us take pity on our youth and have compassion on our mother's age, [21]and let us seriously consider that if we disobey we are dead! [22]Also, divine justice will excuse us for fearing the king when we are under compulsion. [23]Why do we banish ourselves from this most pleasant life and deprive ourselves of this delightful world? [24]Let us not struggle against compulsion[c] or take hollow pride in being put to the rack. [25]Not even the law itself would consent to put us to death for fearing the instruments of torture. [26]Why does such contentiousness excite us and such a fatal stubbornness please us, when we can live in peace if we obey the king?"

27 But the youths, though about to be tortured, neither said any of these things nor even seriously considered them. [28]For they were contemptuous of the passions and sovereign over agonies, [29]so that as soon as the tyrant had ceased counseling them to eat defiling food, all with one voice together, as from one mind, said:

9 "Why do you delay, O tyrant? For we are ready to die rather than transgress our

b 8.13 Meaning of Gk uncertain   c 8.24 Or *fate*

resources and positions of power. In exchange, he asks for complete assimilation and the eradication of their traditions. **8:14** The king's final attempt at persuasion echoes his advice to Eleazar in 5:13. **8:15–26** The author speculates regarding what the youths might have said *if* they had been *cowardly and unmanly* (v. 16). Potential reasons for submitting reflect those offered in Antiochus's speech: to avoid torture (v. 19; cf. vv. 5, 9), enjoy one's youth (v. 20; cf. v. 8), show compassion for their mother/themselves (v. 20; cf. v. 10), and because acquiescence under compulsion should be deemed excusable (v. 22; cf. 14). This presentation of reasons to acquiesce underscores the superiority of the brothers' Torah-centered reason, which enables them to withstand the king's attempts to coerce. **8:27–29** Countering the speculative option the cowardly might take, the author presents the actual response of the youths, confirming their courage and manliness. **8:27** The author draws a sharp line between the imaginary response and the brothers' behavior, insisting that not only did they refuse the king's requests but they did not even seriously consider them. **8:29** The brothers' unified and immediate response affirms their unwavering resolve and that they did not for a moment consider compromise. **9:1–9** The brothers' actual response demonstrates their harmonious agreement as they speak in one accord (*we*) and resolve to obey the Torah rather than the king's request. **9:1–2** In the same manner in which

ancestral commandments; ²we are obviously putting our forebears to shame unless we should practice ready obedience to the law and to Moses*d* our counselor. ³Tyrant and counselor of lawlessness, in your hatred for us do not pity us more than we pity ourselves.*e* ⁴For we consider this pity of yours, which ensures our safety through transgression of the law, to be more grievous than death itself. ⁵You are trying to terrify us by threatening us with death by torture, as though a short time ago you learned nothing from Eleazar. ⁶And if, on account of piety, the aged men of the Hebrews fulfilled their pious duty while enduring torture, it would be even more fitting that we young men should die despising your coercive tortures, which our aged instructor also overcame. ⁷Therefore, tyrant, put us to the test, and if you take our lives because of our piety, do not suppose that you can injure us by torturing us. ⁸For we, through this severe suffering and endurance, shall have the prizes of virtue and shall be with God, on whose account we suffer; ⁹but you, because of your bloodthirstiness toward us, will deservedly undergo from the divine justice eternal torment by fire."

10 When they had said these things, the tyrant was not only indignant, as at those who are disobedient, but also infuriated, as at those who are ungrateful. ¹¹Then at his command the guards brought forward the eldest, and having torn off his tunic, they bound his hands and arms with straps on each side. ¹²When they had worn themselves out beating him with scourges, without accomplishing anything, they placed him upon the wheel. ¹³When the noble youth was stretched out around this, his limbs were dislocated, ¹⁴and with every member disjointed he denounced the tyrant, saying, ¹⁵"Most abominable tyrant, enemy of heavenly justice, savage of mind, you are mangling me in this manner not because I am a murderer or as one who acts impiously but because I protect the divine law." ¹⁶And when the guards said, "Agree to eat so that you may be released from the tortures," ¹⁷he replied, "You abominable lackeys, your wheel is not so powerful as to strangle my reason. Cut my limbs, burn my flesh, and twist my joints; ¹⁸through all these tortures I will convince you that children of the Hebrews alone are invincible when virtue is at stake." ¹⁹While he was saying these things, they spread fire under him, and while fanning the flames*f* they tightened the wheel further. ²⁰The wheel was completely smeared with blood, and the heap of coals was being quenched by the drippings of gore, and pieces of flesh were falling off the axles of the machine. ²¹Although the ligaments joining his bones were already severed, the courageous youth, worthy of Abraham, did not groan, ²²but as though transformed by fire into immortality he nobly endured the rackings. ²³"Imitate me,

d 9.2 Other ancient authorities read *knowledge*
e 9.3 Meaning of Gk uncertain   *f* 9.19 Meaning of Gk uncertain

Eleazar incites his captors just before his death (6:23), the brothers provoke Antiochus, challenging him to follow through on his threats. They choose death and the preservation of their honor over a life of dishonor. **9:4** The brothers consider Antiochus's solution/offer to be worse than death itself. **9:6** Eleazar is called an *instructor*, translating the same Greek term used to describe the Torah in 1:17. Both Eleazar, as a model of piety to the Torah, and the Torah itself fuel the brothers' resolve. **9:8** The author omits any mention of bodily resurrection (cf. 2 Macc. 7:9; **"Resurrection," p. 1224**) and instead casts the hope of the martyrs in terms of a future immortality with God beyond the present suffering. **9:9** In contrast to the reward of the righteous, the author envisions *eternal torment* for the tyrant. *Divine justice* as reward for the faithful and eternal torment for the wicked emerge in early Jewish and Roman literature from the period (1 En. 108:4–6; Seneca, *Herc. fur.* 731–746; Matt. 13:42, 50; Rev. 20:10, 14–15).

9:10–25 The tyrant Antiochus, unable to contain his fury following the brothers' refusal, launches his attack, beginning with the eldest brother. In this agonizing scene and those that follow, the author vividly illustrates the details of each brother's torture. **9:11–12** The manner in which the guards treat the eldest brother is reminiscent of Eleazar's torture—they tear off his robe (cf. 6:2) and beat him until they wear themselves out (cf. 6:3, 7, 10). **9:15** Although physically mangled with limbs dislocated, the eldest brother's reason remains intact, evidenced by the clarity of his speech. Furthermore, he knows the real reason for the violence and recognizes that it is born out of injustice and the savage mind of the king, not a result of any wrongdoing. **9:22** Fire is envisioned as both

brothers," he said. "Do not leave your post in my struggle[g] or renounce our courageous family ties. [24]Fight the sacred and noble battle for piety. Thereby the just Providence of our ancestors may become merciful to our nation and take vengeance on the accursed tyrant." [25]When he had said this, the devout youth broke the thread of life.

26 While all were marveling at his courageous spirit, the guards brought forward the next eldest, and after fitting themselves with iron gauntlets having sharp hooks, they bound him to the torture machine and catapult. [27]Before torturing him, they inquired if he were willing to eat, and they heard his noble decision. [28]These leopard-like beasts tore out his sinews with the iron hands, flayed all his flesh up to his chin, and tore away his scalp. But he steadfastly endured this agony and said, [29]"How sweet is any kind of death for our ancestral piety!" [30]To the tyrant he said, "Do you not think, you most savage tyrant, that you are being tortured more than I, as you see the arrogant design of your tyranny being defeated by our endurance for the sake of piety? [31]I lighten my pain by the joys that come from virtue, [32]but you suffer torture by the threats that come from impiety. You will not escape, you most abominable tyrant, the penalties of the divine wrath."

10 When he, too, had endured a glorious death, the third was brought forward,

and many repeatedly urged him to save himself by tasting the meat. [2]But he shouted, "Do you not know that the same father begot me as well as those who died and the same mother bore me and that I was brought up on the same teachings? [3]I do not renounce the noble kinship that binds me to my brothers."[h] [5]Enraged by the man's boldness, they disjointed his hands and feet with their instruments, dismembering him by prying his limbs from their sockets, [6]and breaking his fingers and arms and legs and elbows. [7]Since they were unable in any way to break his spirit,[i] they abandoned the instruments[j] and scalped him with their fingernails in a Scythian fashion. [8]They immediately brought him to the wheel, and while his vertebrae were being dislocated by this, he saw his own flesh torn all around and drops of blood flowing from his entrails. [9]When he was about to die, he said, [10]"We, most abominable tyrant, are suffering because of our godly training and virtue, [11]but you, because of your impiety and bloodthirstiness, will undergo unceasing torments."

12 When he, too, had died in a manner worthy of his brothers, they dragged forward the fourth, saying, [13]"As for you, do not give way to

g 9.23 Other ancient authorities read *post forever*
h 10.3 Other ancient authorities add 10.4, *So if you have any instrument of torture, apply it to my body; for you cannot touch my soul, even if you wish."* i 10.7 Gk *to strangle him* j 10.7 Other ancient authorities read *they tore off his skin*

a source of the brother's gruesome death and an instrument facilitating his transformation into an incorruptible state.

9:26–32 The second brother's torture follows a similar, though condensed, pattern that ends with a speech directed to Antiochus. **9:30–32** Through the brother's speech, the author contends that the king's defeat is a worse torture and suffering than the physical torture and pain the brothers endured. Divine judgment is again assured.

10:1–11 The contest between the king and the brothers intensifies, and the means of torture are increasingly brutal. **10:2** The third brother emphatically declares his allegiance to the *same teachings* for which his brothers died. Recognition of the nature and nurture aspects of the kinship bond is found in Greek literature (cf. Aristotle, *Eth. nic.* 8.12.3; Xenophon, *Cyr.* 8.7, 14). **10:5** The king's response demonstrates that he interprets the brother's speech as a challenge that cannot be ignored but must be met with even more severe punishment (cf. vv. 7–8). **10:7** The historian Herodotus associates the practice of scalping with the Scythians, who were known for their brutal tactics (Herodotus, *Hist.* 4.64.3; cf. 2 Macc. 4:47; 3 Macc. 7:5). By identifying Antiochus with some of the most barbaric practices known in the Hellenistic world, the author once again portrays the king behaving in a manner inconsistent with the Greek virtues of reason and self-control, whereas the brother exemplifies them through his demonstration of courage and pious reason. **10:9–10** The brothers' suffering is not only related to punishment but serves the additional purpose of demonstrating their training in Torah and virtue according to Greek ideals. **10:11** This brother also affirms that Antiochus's impiety and brutality will result in eternal punishment (cf. 9:9, 24, 32).

10:12–21 The fourth brother is unmoved by the charge of *insanity* the king's men level against his

the same insanity as your brothers, but obey the king and save yourself." [14]But he said to them, "You do not have a fire hot enough to make me play the coward. [15]No, by the blessed death of my brothers, by the eternal destruction of the tyrant, and by the everlasting[k] life of the pious, I will not renounce our noble family ties. [16]Contrive tortures, tyrant, so that you may learn from them that I am a brother to those who have just now been tortured." [17]When he heard this, the bloodthirsty, murderous, and utterly abominable Antiochus gave orders to cut out his tongue. [18]But he said, "Even if you remove my organ of speech, God hears also those who are mute. [19]See, here is my tongue; cut it off, for in spite of this you will not make our reason speechless. [20]Gladly, for the sake of God, we let our bodily members be mutilated. [21]God will visit you swiftly, for you are cutting out a tongue that has been melodious with divine hymns."

11 When he, too, died, after being cruelly tortured, the fifth leaped up, saying, [2]"I will not refuse, tyrant, to be tortured for the sake of virtue. [3]I have come of my own accord so that by murdering me you will incur punishment from the heavenly justice for even more crimes. [4]Hater of virtue, hater of humankind, for what act of ours are you destroying us in this way? [5]Is it because[l] we revere the Creator of all things and live according to his virtuous law? [6]But these deeds deserve honors, not tortures."[m] [9]While he was saying these things, the guards bound him and dragged him to the catapult; [10]they tied him to it on his knees, and fitting iron clamps on them, they twisted his back[n] around the wedge on the wheel,[o] so that he was completely curled back like a scorpion, and all his members were disjointed. [11]In this condition, gasping for breath and in anguish of body, [12]he said, "Tyrant, they are splendid favors that you grant us against your will, because through these noble sufferings you give us an opportunity to show our endurance for the law."

13 When he, too, had died, the sixth, a mere boy, was led forward. When the tyrant inquired whether he was willing to eat and be released, he said, [14]"I am younger in age than my brothers, but I am their equal in mind. [15]Since to this end we were born and bred, we ought likewise to die for the same principles. [16]So if you intend

---

k 10.15 Another ancient authority reads *celebrated*
l 11.5 Other ancient authorities read *Or does it seem evil to you that* *m* 11.6 Other authorities add 11.7 and 8, [7]*If you but understood human feelings and had hope of salvation from God—* [8]*but, as it is, you are a stranger to God and make war against those who serve him."* *n* 11.10 Gk *loins* *o* 11.10 Meaning of Gk uncertain

---

brothers (v. 13) and makes his alignment with them clear. He utters a curse of eternal destruction against Antiochus even before the torture begins (v. 15), to which the king responds by giving orders *to cut out his tongue* (v. 17). **10:15** This brother cites as reasons for his resolve (1) the example of his brothers, (2) the expectation of eternal destruction for the tyrant, and (3) the hope of everlasting life for the pious. Though the king and his guards deem his actions irrational, the brother considers these reasons more compelling than any physical threat. **10:18–20** The brother's response further emasculates the king by diminishing the impact of his threat. Cutting out the brother's tongue might make him silent before humans, but not before God. Moreover, he argues that removing one's ability to speak does not prevent that individual from exercising reason, which is the real issue at stake.

11:1–12 The fifth brother, undeterred by the horrific torture of Eleazar and the older brothers, eagerly volunteers to face the same fate for the sake of virtue and to increase the king's punishment. His voluntary sacrifice renders the king's authority in the matter useless, further emasculating the tyrant and humiliating him before his administration and subjects. **11:4** Though directed at Antiochus, the brother's criticisms apply more broadly toward those who would try to oppose the Jewish way of life. The author argues that it is Antiochus and those like him who are *hater[s] of humankind* and not those who follow Torah as some others claimed (cf. Diodorus Siculus, *Bib. hist.* 34.1.1–3; Tacitus, *Hist.* 5.5.1). **11:5–6** The brother charges Antiochus with behaving unjustly. Whereas suffering unjustly leads to reward (v. 12), acting unjustly results in divine punishment. **11:12** The brother drives home the point that he has the upper hand in the matter.

11:13–27 The sixth brother declares that his youth is not a sign of weakness but that he is *equal in mind* to his older brothers and prepared *to die for the same principles* (vv. 14–15). While enduring brutal torture, he offers a speech claiming victory for himself and his brothers over the tyrant (v. 24). **11:15** On account of their upbringing, the brother argues that an honorable death (suffering unjustly for one's principles) is preferred to apostasy. **11:16** This incendiary speech follows a pattern already

to torture me for not eating defiling foods, go on torturing!" [17]When he had said this, they led him to the wheel. [18]He was carefully stretched tight upon it, his back was broken, and he was roasted from underneath. [19]To his back they applied sharp spits that had been heated in the fire and pierced his ribs so that his entrails were burned through. [20]While being tortured he said, "O contest befitting holiness, in which so many of us brothers have been summoned to an arena of sufferings for the sake of piety and in which we have not been defeated! [21]For pious knowledge, O tyrant, is invincible. [22]I also, equipped with nobility, will die with my brothers, [23]and I myself will bring a great avenger upon you, you inventor of tortures and enemy of those who are truly pious. [24]We six boys have overthrown your tyranny. [25]Since you have not been able to persuade us to change our mind or to force us to eat defiling foods, is not this your downfall? [26]Your fire is cold to us, and the catapults painless, and your violence powerless. [27]For it is not the guards of the tyrant but those of the divine law that are set over us; therefore we hold fast to invincible reason."

12 When he, too, thrown into the caldron, had died a blessed death, the seventh and youngest of all came forward. [2]Even though the tyrant had been vehemently reproached by the brothers, he felt strong

compassion for this child when he saw that he was already in fetters. He summoned him to come nearer and tried to persuade him, saying, [3]"You see the result of your brothers' stupidity, for they died in torments because of their disobedience. [4]You, too, if you do not obey, will be miserably tortured and die before your time, [5]but if you yield to persuasion you will be my friend and a leader in the government of the kingdom." [6]When he had thus appealed to him, he sent for the boy's mother to show compassion on her who had been bereaved of so many sons and to influence her to persuade the surviving son to obey and save himself. [7]But after his mother had exhorted him in the Hebrew language, as we shall tell a little later, [8]he said, "Let me loose, let me speak to the king and to all his Friends who are with him." [9]Extremely pleased by the boy's declaration, they freed him at once. [10]Running to the nearest of the braziers, [11]he said, "You profane tyrant, most impious of all the wicked, since you have received good things and also your kingdom from God, were you not ashamed to murder his servants and torture on the wheel the athletes of piety? [12]Because of this, justice[p] has laid up for you a more intense and eternal fire and tortures, and these throughout all time will never let you go. [13]As a man, were you

p 12.12 Another ancient authority reads divine justice

established with Eleazar and the older brothers in which the soon-to-be martyr strips the tyrant of any real power over his body by offering it up willingly. **11:20–27** The author casts the event in terms of an athletic contest. Despite his show of force and use of violent instruments, Antiochus fails to coerce any of his victims to eat the defiling meat. Even in death, his victims remain unconquered with their reason fully intact.

12:1–19 The story of the seventh and youngest brother receives the most attention. It is the longest account of all the brothers, and in it, the king summons him for a personal conversation and then allows him to speak to his mother. Though the king considers this an act of kindness and generosity, the youngest brother does not interpret it as such. Instead, his response to the king's *compassion* echoes the speeches of his brothers; he charges the king with tyranny, impiety, and injustice (v. 11) and proclaims his eternal punishment (v. 12). **12:7** The mother speaks *in the Hebrew language*, which Antiochus will not understand (cf. 2 Macc. 7:27). This renders the king powerless to effectively manage the situation, since he cannot understand the exchange, and makes him an outsider at his own event. The content of the mother's speech is only revealed later, in her contest with Antiochus (cf. 16:15–23). **12:8–9** The youngest brother's neutral language—*king* instead of tyrant, and the king's *Friends*—suggests to the king that the boy might have been persuaded. **12:11** As soon as the boy is released, he launches a most severe verbal attack on the *tyrant*. His actions demonstrate that his loyalty was never in question, and his neutral language was only a ploy to gain an up-close audience with the king. In a satirical twist, the boy astutely acknowledges that Antiochus received his kingdom from the very God whose servants he now tortures and kills. **12:12** Whereas the martyrs died honorably, Antiochus will face eternal punishment for behaving so unjustly. **12:13** The brother charges Antiochus with behaving savagely, the very opposite of reason and self-control. Calling

not ashamed, you most savage beast, to cut out the tongues of people who have feelings like yours and are made of the same elements as you and to maltreat and torture them in this way? [14]Surely they by dying nobly fulfilled their pious duty to God, but you will wail bitterly for having killed without cause the contestants for virtue." [15]Then because he, too, was about to die, he said, [16]"I do not desert the excellent example[q] of my brothers, [17]and I call on the God of our ancestors to be merciful to our nation,[r] [18]but on you he will take vengeance both in this present life and when you are dead." [19]After he had uttered these imprecations, he flung himself into the braziers and so ended his life.[s]

13 Since, then, the seven brothers despised sufferings even unto death, everyone must concede that pious reason is sovereign over the passions. [2]For if they had been slaves to their passions and had eaten defiling food, we would say that they had been conquered by these passions. [3]But in fact it was not so. Instead, by reason, which is praised before God, they prevailed over their passions. [4]The supremacy of the mind over these cannot be overlooked, for the brothers[t] mastered both passions and pains. [5]How, then, can one fail to confess the sovereignty

of right reason over passion in those who were not turned back by fiery agonies? [6]For just as towers jutting out over harbors hold back the threatening waves and make it calm for those who sail into the inner basin, [7]so the seven-towered right reason of the youths, by fortifying the harbor of piety, conquered the tempest of the passions. [8]For they constituted a holy chorus of piety and emboldened one another, saying, [9]"Brothers, let us die like brothers for the sake of the law; let us imitate the three youths in Assyria who despised the same ordeal[u] of the furnace. [10]Let us not be cowardly in the demonstration of our piety." [11]While one said, "Courage, brother," another said, "Bear up nobly," [12]and another reminded them, "Remember whence you came, and the father by whose hand Isaac would have submitted to being slain for the sake of piety." [13]Each of them and all of them together looking at one another, cheerful and undaunted, said, "Let us with all our hearts consecrate ourselves to God, who gave us our lives,[v] and let us use our bodies as a bulwark for the law. [14]Let us not fear him who thinks he is killing us, [15]for great is the soul's contest

q 12.16 Other ancient authorities read *the witness*
r 12.17 Other ancient authorities read *my people*   s 12.19 Gk *and so gave up*   t 13.4 Gk *they*   u 13.9 Cn: Gk *citizen rights*
v 13.13 Or *souls*

both his humanity and manliness into question, the youngest brother claims it is the king and those who think like him who should be ashamed, not his victims who die nobly (v. 14). **12:17–19** The youngest brother invokes God's mercy in a prayer reminiscent of Eleazar's final words (cf. 6:28–29), then casts himself into the fire as a sacrificial offering. In this final act, the youngest brother robs the tyrant king of any agency over his body and instead carries out his own martyrdom. Just before his death, the brother assures the king that he will face certain punishment both during his lifetime and when he is dead. The fate of the tyrant king stands in contrast to the incorruptible life of the pious (cf. 7:18–19; 9:8–9; 10:15; 14:4–5; 16:25; 17:12; 18:23).

13:1–14:10 Discourse on the sovereignty of reason in the example of the seven brothers. **13:1–18** The author demonstrates how the story of the seven brothers proves the thesis that pious reason is supreme over the passions. Parallel discussions are included following the martyrdoms of Eleazar (6:31–35) and the mother (16:1–2). **13:4–5** The brothers' mastery over pain makes their example especially pertinent. Even the most violent torture is no match for their uncompromising devotion, which is fueled by reason. **13:6–7** The author returns to the nautical imagery familiar from Eleazar's encomium (7:1–3 and note there). The image of Eleazar as captain of the "ship of piety" (7:1) is complemented by the description of the brothers as a fortified harbor. Their victory is not only to their own benefit but provides a model of endurance and support so others may be empowered to resist the pressure to abandon Torah in order to conform to the norms of the dominant culture. **13:8–11** Again using the image of a *chorus*, the author emphasizes the harmony and unity of the brothers—that they were of one mind and acted in one accord (cf. 8:4). The image is one of combined strength that is illustrated through the support they provide for each other and the community. *The three youths*, Shadrach, Meshach, and Abednego serve as an example of fortitude and courage (cf. Dan. 3). **13:12** Abraham and Isaac are portrayed as archetypal figures—Abraham as the progenitor willing to sacrifice his son and Isaac as the willing sacrifice and would-be martyr (cf. Gen. 22:1–19).

and the danger of eternal torment lying before those who transgress the commandment of God. [16]Therefore let us put on the full armor of mastery of the passions that divine reason provides. [17]For if we so die,[w] Abraham and Isaac and Jacob will welcome us, and all the fathers will praise us." [18]Those who were left behind said to each of the brothers who were being dragged away, "Do not put us to shame, brother, or betray the brothers who have died before us."

[19] You are not ignorant of the affection of family ties, which the divine and all-wise Providence has bequeathed through the fathers to their descendants and which was implanted in the mother's womb. [20]There the brothers spent the same length of time and were shaped during the same period of time, and growing from the same blood and through the same life, they were brought to the light of day. [21]When they were born after an equal time of gestation, they drank milk from the same fountains. From such embraces brotherly loving souls are nourished, [22]and they grow stronger from this common nurture and daily companionship and from both general education and our discipline in the law of God.

[23] Therefore, when sympathy and brotherly affection had been so established, the seven brothers were the more sympathetic to one another. [24]Since they had been educated by the same law and trained in the same virtues and brought up together in right living, they loved one another all the more. [25]A common zeal for nobility strengthened their goodwill toward one another and their concord, [26]because they could make their brotherly love more fervent with the aid of piety. [27]But although nature and companionship and virtuous habits had augmented the affection of family ties, those who were left endured for the sake of piety, watching their brothers being maltreated and tortured to death.

14

Furthermore, they encouraged them to face the torture so that they not only despised their agonies but also mastered the passions of brotherly love.

[2] O reason,[x] more royal than kings and freer than the free! [3]O sacred harmony of the seven brothers, well-tuned in regard to piety! [4]None of the seven youths proved coward or shrank from death, [5]but all of them, as though running the course toward immortality, hastened to death by torture. [6]Just as the hands and feet are moved in harmony with the guidance of the mind, so those holy youths, as though moved by an immortal spirit of piety, agreed to go to death for its sake. [7]O most holy seven, brothers in harmony! For just as the seven

w 13.17 Other ancient authorities read *suffer*   x 14.2 Or *O minds*

13:16 Ephesians 6:11–14 uses similar imagery to encourage mental fortitude. 13:18 The author shares a behind-the-scenes glimpse of the brothers encouraging one another during the trial; this information was not made known to the reader in the preceding narrative but highlights here their familial bond as part of the reason they were each able to endure torture without capitulating. 13:19–14:1 The author develops a lengthy discourse on *family ties*, highlighting the role of tradition in strengthening the brothers' bond. 13:19–22 The nature and nurture aspects of the sibling bond are treated together (see note on 10:2). In regard to nature, they are from the same seed and womb, nourished at the same breasts. From this shared foundation, the bond is further nurtured through *daily companionship* and a common *education* that includes instruction in Torah. 13:23–26 The brotherly bond is further solidified through their *common zeal* and *piety*. The author again aligns the Greek virtues with Torah observance (v. 24). 14:1 It is one thing to offer up one's own body and quite another to encourage a beloved family member to do the same. The brothers demonstrate a most excellent form of mastery over the emotions in their encouragement to one another to face the torture (cf. 13:18). 14:2–10 In a style reminiscent of Greek drama, the author shifts between different forms of speech and song. Here, the philosophic discourse on family ties and the brothers' mastery over emotions is followed by a melodic praise of reason (v. 2), the sibling bond (v. 3), and the seven brothers (v. 7). 14:3 The author highlights the *harmony* of the brothers, united in their commitment to Torah observance. 14:5 Drawing again on athletic imagery, the author notes that although the brothers were *running* in such a way as to achieve *immortality*, their achievement of the goal was *hastened* through torture. Similar athletic imagery appears in the New Testament (cf. Phil. 3:12–14; Heb. 12:1; 2 Tim. 4:7). 14:6 The author again connects reason to Torah observance; the brothers' harmony is attributed to a form of reason that can be equated with religious devotion. 14:7–8 *Seven* often indicates a sense of wholeness or completeness and was related to Greek musical harmonies; Philo considers it the most harmonious

days of creation move in choral dance around piety, [8]so these youths, forming a chorus of seven,[y] encircled the fear of tortures and dissolved it. [9]Even now, we ourselves shudder as we hear of the suffering of these young men; they not only saw what was happening, not only heard the direct word of threat, but also bore the sufferings steadfastly, and in agonies of fire at that. [10]What could be more excruciatingly painful than this? For the power of fire is intense and swift, and it consumed their bodies quickly.

[11] Do not consider it amazing that reason had full command over these men in their tortures, since even the mind of woman despised more diverse agonies, [12]for the mother of the seven young men bore up under the rackings of each one of her children.

[13] Observe how complex is a mother's love for her children, which draws everything toward a sympathy felt in her inmost parts. [14]Even unreasoning animals, as well as humans, have a sympathy and parental love for their offspring. [15]For example, among birds, the ones that are tame protect their young by building on the housetops, [16]and the others, by building at the tops of mountains and the depths of chasms, in holes of trees, and on treetops, hatch the nestlings and ward off the intruder. [17]If they are not able to keep the intruder[z] away, they do what they can to help their young by flying in circles around them in the anguish of love, warning them with their own calls. [18]And why is it necessary to demonstrate sympathy for children by the example of unreasoning animals, [19]since even bees at the time for making honeycombs defend themselves against intruders and, as though with an iron dart, sting those who approach their hive and defend it even to the death? [20]But sympathy for her children did not sway the mother of the young men; she was of the same mind as Abraham.

15 O reason of the children, tyrant over the passions! O piety, more desirable to the mother than her children! [2]Two courses were open to this mother, that of piety and that of preserving her seven sons for a time, as the tyrant had promised. [3]She loved piety more, the piety that preserves them for eternal life according to God's promise.[a] [4]In what manner might I express the passions of parents who love their children? We impress upon the character of a small child a wondrous likeness both of mind and of form. Especially is this true of mothers, who because of their birth pangs have a deeper sympathy

y 14.8 Meaning of Gk uncertain z 14.17 Gk it a 15.3 Gk *according to God*

number (Philo, *Opif.* 95–96, 107). **14:9–10** The author acknowledges the difficulty of hearing the gory details of the brothers' torture and challenges the audience to empathize with the brothers who, rather than hearing, experienced the agony of such atrocities.

14:11–17:6 The story of the mother.

14:11–12 The narrative transitions to second-person speech, addressing the audience directly to inform them the story is not finished yet. An even more astounding example of courage and endurance can be found in the mother. Whereas the narrative demonstration began with Eleazar, whose actions served as an example for the youth (cf. 6:18–19; 9:5–6), it now concludes with the mother, whose story is climactically presented as an example worthy of emulation.

14:13–20 This discussion of motherly love underscores the depth of emotion associated with the mother-child bond (v. 13). Women were often thought to be more easily deceived and led astray by their emotions (Aristotle, *Pol.* 1.13 [1260a12–14]; Philo, *QG* 1:37–38, 47). Against this backdrop, the author contends that the mother's mastery over the passions deserves special recognition. The parental bond that drives both humans and unreasoning animals to do unreasonable things (like build a nest in a precipitous place to protect the young from an intruder, vv. 15–17) does not hold sway over this mother. On the contrary, she, like Abraham, elevated devotion to God over the parental bond (cf. 9:21; 13:12; 15:28; 16:20; 18:20).

15:1–12 The encomium on the mother continues, going to great lengths to develop the strength of the mother-child bond. A mother's devotion to her children is counted as a weakness with respect to her ability to exercise control over such strong emotions (v. 5). The mother of the seven, though she fervently loved her children (vv. 6, 9), chose *piety* over their *temporary safety* (vv. 2, 8), perceiving its eternal value (vv. 2–3). **15:1** The author again draws a parallel between *reason* and *piety*, praising both. **15:3** The mother's reason is demonstrated in her devotion to *piety*; she considers the eternal and not just the immediate consequences. **15:4** According to Stoic thought, children resemble

Focus On: Masculinity (4 Maccabees 15)

The author of 4 Maccabees prioritizes virtues that within a Greco-Roman social context would be considered "manly." Reason and self-control were considered masculine traits, while women were perceived as controlled by the emotions. Courage (*andreia*) also is a gendered virtue, etymologically connected to the Greek word for man (*anēr*). To be courageous was to be "manly" (1:3–4; 8:16).

In 4 Maccabees, the martyrs exemplify these masculine virtues to defeat and emasculate the tyrant ruler. Eleazar professes that it would be unmanly for him to give in to Antiochus's coercion in order to avoid death (6:21). The youths follow Eleazar's example of courage and prove that they are not cowardly or unmanly (8:16); they confront the king's threats with their speech (8:27–9:9) and defeat him with perseverance when subjected to brutal torture. When the king threatens to cut out the fourth brother's tongue in response to his seditious speech, the brother strips the king of any power over him by offering up his tongue and claiming that God will hear him even if mute (10:12–21). The fifth brother mockingly calls the king's tortures "splendid favors" (11:12), and the youngest brother determines his own fate (12:19). Athletic imagery further underscores the manliness of the martyrs, who defeat the tyrant with pious reason, rhetoric, and endurance.

The masculinization of the mother as the final, most exemplary demonstration of pious reason stands in contrast to the feminization of Antiochus. Whereas the mother exercises total control over the passions, choosing reason over the innate mother-child bond (15:1–8), Antiochus's lack of self-control paints him as an irrational and powerless tyrant (8:2; 9:10; 16:14). The mother is the exemplar par excellence on account of her pious reason, which gives her "a man's courage" (15:23); she is more manly "than men" in steadfastness and endurance (15:30).

Engagement with Greek and Roman masculine ideals is evident in other early Jewish and Christian literature. Judith, like the mother, defeats a tyrant by exercising masculine virtues while keeping her feminine virtues of chastity and fidelity intact (Jdt. 13:15–16; 15:9–10; 16:5–6; 4 Macc. 18:6–9). In the Gospel of Thomas, masculinization is a prerequisite to enter the kingdom of heaven (Gos. Thom. 114). Paul both performs masculine ideals (1 Cor. 13:11; 16:13) and subverts them (Gal. 4:19; 1 Thess. 2:7–8). (See also **"Jewish Women," p. 1525.**)

Rebecca L. Harris

toward their offspring than do the fathers. [5]For to the extent that mothers are of tender spirit and bear more children, so much the more attached are they to their children. [6]The mother of the seven boys, more than any other mother, loved her children. In seven pregnancies she had implanted in herself tender love toward them, [7]and because of the many pains she suffered with each of them she had sympathy for them, [8]yet because of the fear of God she disdained the temporary safety of her children. [9]Not only so, but also because of the nobility of her sons and their ready obedience to the law, she felt a greater tenderness toward them. [10]For they were just and self-controlled and courageous and magnanimous and loved their brothers and their mother so that they obeyed her even to death in keeping the ordinances.

[11]Nevertheless, though so many factors influenced the mother to suffer with them out of love for her children, in the case of none of them were the various tortures strong enough to pervert her reason. [12]But each child separately and all of them together the mother urged on to death for piety's sake. [13]O sacred nature, parental affection, tender love toward offspring, nursing, and indomitable maternal passions! [14]This mother, who saw them tortured and burned one by one, for piety's sake did not change her attitude. [15]She watched the flesh of her children being consumed by fire, their toes and fingers scattered[b] on the ground, and the flesh of the head to the chin exposed like masks.

[16]O mother, tried now by more bitter pains than even the birth pangs you suffered for

b 15.15 Or *quivering*

their parents not only in body but also in soul and temperament (Plutarch, [*Plac. philos.*] 5.11.13). **15:7–8** The author considers the mother's affection a natural tendency embedded in the biological processes of growing and birthing a child.

15:13–23 The author appeals to the pathos of the audience in a graphic illustration of the mother watching her sons suffer the most brutal forms of torture that result in their deaths. **15:16–20** The first of four songs of praise for the mother, the author here focuses on what she suffered (also, vv.

them! [17]O woman, who alone gave birth to such perfect piety! [18]Neither when the firstborn breathed his last, it did not turn you aside, nor when the second in torments looked at you piteously nor when the third expired, [19]nor did you weep when you looked at the eyes of each one in his tortures gazing boldly at the same agonies and saw in their nostrils the signs of the approach of death. [20]When you saw the flesh of children burned[c] upon the flesh of other children, severed hands upon hands, scalped heads upon heads, and corpses fallen on other corpses, and when you saw the place filled with many spectators because of the children's torments, you did not shed tears. [21]Neither the melodies of sirens nor the songs of swans attract the attention of their hearers as did the voices of the children in torture calling to their mother. [22]How great and how many torments the mother then suffered as her sons were tortured on the wheel and with the hot irons! [23]But pious reason, giving her heart a man's courage in the very midst of her passions, strengthened her to disregard, for the time, her parental love.

24 Although she witnessed the destruction of seven children and the ingenious and various rackings, this noble mother disregarded all these[d] because of faith in God. [25]For as in the council chamber of her own soul she saw mighty advocates—nature, family, parental love, and the instruments of torture awaiting her children—[26]this mother held two ballots, one bearing death and the other deliverance for her children. [27]She did not approve the deliverance that would preserve the seven sons for a short time, [28]but as the daughter of God-fearing Abraham she remembered his fortitude.

29 O mother of the nation, vindicator of the law, and defender of piety who carried away the prize of the contest in your heart! [30]O more noble than males in steadfastness and more courageous than men in endurance! [31]Just as Noah's ark, carrying the world in the universal flood, stoutly endured the waves, [32]so you, O guardian of the law, overwhelmed from every side by the flood of your passions and the violent winds—the torture of your sons—endured nobly and withstood the wintry storms raging on piety's account.

16 If, then, a woman advanced in years and mother of seven sons endured seeing her children tortured to death, it must be admitted that pious reason is sovereign over the passions. [2]Thus I have demonstrated not only that men have ruled over the passions but also that a woman has despised the fiercest tortures. [3]The lions surrounding Daniel were not so savage nor was the raging fiery furnace of Mishael so intensely hot as was her innate parental love consuming her as

c 15.20 Other ancient authorities read *the amputated flesh of children* d 15.24 Other ancient authorities read *having bidden them farewell, surrendered them*

29–32; 16:14–15; 17:2–6). **15:21** Both auditory images are associated with death. In Homer's *Odyssey*, the sirens lure sailors to their deaths (Homer, *Od.* 12.39–58, 154–200). Swans are known for singing their most beautiful song just before death. Socrates suspects this is because they are anticipating the blessings in the other world (Plato, *Phaed.* 84e–85b). **15:23** The mother's self-control over her emotions is attributed to her possession of a masculine trait, *courage*, which she obtains through reason. The "masculinity" of the mother will be developed in v. 30 and 16:14.

15:24–28 Using the image of a Greek court of law or assembly, the author depicts the mother weighing the ramifications of her "vote" for either the death or deliverance of her sons. Again, she is shown exercising reason, discerning the eternal consequences at stake (cf. vv. 2–3). **15:28** On Abraham, see notes on 13:12 and 14:13–20.

15:29–32 The second song of praise to the mother celebrates her steadfastness and courage. **15:29** The athletic imagery previously applied to Eleazar and the brothers is here applied to the mother (cf. 6:10; 9:8; 11:20–21; 14:5). **15:30** She is more "manly" *than men* in regard to excellence in masculine traits. **15:31–32** Recalling the image of Eleazar steering "the ship of piety" (7:1–3), the mother is compared to Noah's ark (cf. Gen. 7–8).

16:1–4 The mother is a particularly compelling example of the supremacy of *pious reason* on account of her age and gender. **16:2** While Eleazar overcame the challenges associated with age to set an example for the youth, the mother overcame the challenges of age and gender. She is the model of endurance and self-control who, in ruling her emotions, overcame *the fiercest tortures* (cf. 15:16–23). The author contends that if even an old woman can endure under such circumstances, then such resistance is possible for any who similarly hold fast to "pious reason." **16:3** Allusions to

she saw her seven sons tortured in such varied ways. [4]But the mother quenched so many and such great passions by pious reason.

5 Consider this also: If this woman, though a mother, had been fainthearted, she would have mourned over them and perhaps spoken as follows: [6]"O how wretched am I and thrice-wretched over and over! After bearing seven children, I am now the mother of none! [7]O seven childbirths all in vain, seven profitless pregnancies, fruitless nurturings and wretched nursings! [8]In vain, my sons, I endured many birth pangs for you and the more grievous anxieties of your upbringing. [9]Alas for my children, some unmarried, others married and without offspring.[e] I shall not see your children or have the happiness of being called grandmother. [10]Alas, I who had so many and beautiful children am a widow and alone, with many sorrows.[f] [11]And when I die, I shall have none of my sons to bury me."

12 Yet that holy and God-fearing mother did not wail with such a lament for any of them, nor did she dissuade any of them from dying, nor did she grieve as they were dying. [13]On the contrary, as though having a mind like adamant and giving rebirth for immortality to the whole number of her sons, she implored them and urged them on to death for the sake of piety. [14]O mother, soldier of God in the cause of piety, elder and woman! By steadfastness you have conquered even a tyrant, and in word and deed you have proved more powerful than a man. [15]For when you and your sons were arrested together, you stood and watched Eleazar being tortured and said to your sons in the Hebrew language, [16]"My sons, noble is the contest to which you are called to bear witness for the nation. Fight zealously for our ancestral law. [17]For it would be shameful if, while an aged man endures such agonies for the sake of piety, you young men were to be terrified by tortures. [18]Remember that it is through God that you have had a share in the world and have enjoyed life, [19]and therefore you ought to endure every suffering for the sake of God. [20]For his sake also our father Abraham was zealous to sacrifice his son Isaac, the ancestor of our nation, and when Isaac saw his father's hand wielding a knife[g] and descending upon him, he did not cower. [21]Daniel the righteous was thrown to the lions, and Hananiah, Azariah, and Mishael were hurled into the fiery furnace and endured it for the sake of God. [22]You, too, must show the same faithfulness toward God and not be grieved. [23]It is unreasonable for people who have knowledge of piety not to withstand pain."

24 By these words the mother of the seven encouraged and persuaded each of her sons to die rather than violate God's commandment. [25]They knew also that those who die for the sake of God live to God, as do Abraham and Isaac and Jacob and all the patriarchs.

17 Some of the guards said that when she also was about to be seized and put to

e 16.9 Gk *without benefit* f 16.10 Or *much to be pitied*
g 16.20 Gk *sword*

Daniel and *Mishael* (cf. Dan. 6; 4 Macc. 13:9) emphasize the mother's feat, lauding her victory as an even greater accomplishment than theirs.

16:5–11 Following the same pattern used with the seven (8:16–26), the author imagines how the mother might have responded to her sons' deaths had she not shown control over her emotions. **16:6–8** Similar laments appear in Greek tragedies (e.g., Euripides, *Tro.* 380–381, 473–488, 758–760). **16:10** Widows without children were especially vulnerable in the ancient world.

16:12–17:1 The author presents the actual actions of the mother, in contrast to the imaginary response, and praises her for her *steadfastness* with which she defeated the tyrant (v. 14) by encouraging her sons to maintain zeal for the Torah even to the point of death (vv. 16, 24). **16:12–13** The author juxtaposes typical reactions to death (wailing and mourning) with the image of *rebirth*. Through her encouragement and resolve, urging her sons on to death, the mother is credited with rebirthing them into immortality. This birth imagery pairs nicely with the unamended text of Codex Sinaiticus, in which the mutilated corpses of the sons are described as "afterbirth" (Gk. "chorion"; 15:20). **16:14–15** The third song of praise to the mother introduces a recitation of her own words of encouragement to her sons (cf. 12:7). *Soldier* highlights her manliness, which the author underscores with the exaltation that she *proved more powerful than a man*. **16:20** This is the most expansive discourse on the examples of *Abraham* and *Isaac* (see notes on 7:14; 13:12; and 14:13–20). **16:21** On *Daniel* and *Mishael*, see notes on 16:3 and 13:8–11. **17:1** Whereas 2 Maccabees does not detail the mother's death (2 Macc. 7:41), here she dies in the same manner as the youngest son, perhaps to ensure her honor remains intact.

4 MACCABEES 17

death she threw herself into the flames so that no one might touch her body.

2 O mother, who with your seven sons nullified the violence of the tyrant, frustrated his evil designs, and showed the nobility of your faith! ³Nobly set like a roof on the pillars of your sons, you held firm and unswerving against the earthquake of the tortures. ⁴Take courage, therefore, O holy-minded mother, maintaining firm an enduring hope in God. ⁵The moon in heaven with the stars is not so majestic as you, who, after lighting the way of your star-like seven sons to piety, stand in honor before God and are firmly set in heaven with them. ⁶For your children were true descendants of father Abraham.ᵇ

7 If it were possible for us to paint the history of your piety as an artist might, would not those who beheld it shudder as they saw the mother of the seven children enduring their varied tortures to death for the sake of piety? ⁸Indeed, it would be proper to inscribe on their tomb these words as a reminder to the people of our nation:ⁱ

9 "Here lie buried an aged priest and an aged woman and seven children because of the violence of the tyrant who wished to destroy the way of life of the Hebrews. ¹⁰They vindicated their nation, looking to God and enduring torture even to death."

11 Truly the contest in which they were engaged was divine, ¹²for on that day virtue gave the awards and tested them for their endurance. The prize was immortality in endless life. ¹³Eleazar was the first contestant, the mother of the seven sons entered the competition, and the brothers contended. ¹⁴The tyrant was the antagonist, and the world and the human race were the spectators. ¹⁵Reverence for God was victor and gave the crown to its own athletes. ¹⁶Who did not admire the athletes of the divineʲ legislation? Who were not amazed?

17 The tyrant himself and all his council marveled at their endurance, ¹⁸because of which they now stand before the divine throne and live the life of eternal blessedness. ¹⁹For Moses says, "All who are consecrated are under your hands." ²⁰These, then, who have been consecrated for the sake of God are honored not only with this honor but also by the fact that because of them our enemies did not rule over our nation, ²¹the tyrant was punished, and the homeland purified—they having become, as it were, a ransom for the sin of our nation. ²²And through the blood of those pious ones and their death as an atoning sacrifice, divine Providence preserved Israel that previously had been mistreated.

23 For the tyrant Antiochus, when he saw the courage of their virtue and their endurance under the tortures, proclaimed their endurance to his soldiers as an example, ²⁴and this made them high-minded and courageous for infantry battle and siege, and he ravaged and conquered all his enemies.

b 17.6 Gk For your childbearing was from Abraham the father; other ancient authorities read For . . . Abraham the servant   i 17.8 Or as a memorial to the heroes of our people   j 17.16 Other ancient authorities read true

17:2–6 The fourth song of praise to the mother envisions her in an elevated, even glorified, state. The unity of the mother and her sons—a prominent theme throughout (cf. 8:4; 13:8–17; 14:8)—is illustrated through the images of a building (v. 3) and celestial bodies (v. 5). In Jewish apocalyptic literature, the righteous are often compared to the stars (cf. Dan. 12:3; 1 En. 104:2; 2 Esd. [4 Ezra] 7:97; 2 Bar. 51:3–5, 8–10).
17:7–18:5 Epitaph. In the style of a Greek epitaph, or memorial inscription, the author rehearses the story of the martyrs using vivid contest imagery. The martyrs' actions are seen as a victory for them and the Jewish people. 17:7–24 The martyrs' suffering is viewed as an atoning sacrifice that vindicates and purifies the people (7:10, 21–22). 17:9–10 Antiochus's actions are framed as a political threat to the Hebrews' nation and way of life. 17:11–16 Athletic imagery, featured previously (6:10; 9:8, 23–24; 11:20–23; 13:13; 16:14–16), is developed in an extended metaphor that casts the event as a divine contest (v. 11) and unbiased, since virtue itself determines the awards and the tests (v. 12). The high stakes nature of the contest is emphasized by the identification of its contestants (the tyrant versus the world and the human race, v. 14) and prize (immortality in endless life, v. 12). 17:18 A similar image of glorification following martyrdom is seen in Rev. 7:15. 17:19 See Deut. 33:3. 17:20–21 The martyrs' actions have political, not just personal or socioreligious, ramifications. In contrast to 1 and 2 Maccabees, where the tyrant is defeated by force, in 4 Maccabees it is the endurance of the martyrs that results in their consecration, the defeat of the tyrant, and the purification of the land. 17:22 The martyrs' deaths are conceptualized as an atoning or propitiatory sacrifice (cf. Lev. 16; Rom. 3:25).

otot.

18 O Israelite children, offspring of the seed of Abraham, obey this law and exercise piety in every way, ²knowing that pious reason is master of the passions, not only of sufferings from within but also of those from without.

3 Therefore those who gave over their bodies in suffering for the sake of piety were not only admired by mortals but also were deemed worthy to share in a divine inheritance. ⁴Because of them the nation gained peace, and by reviving observance of the law in the homeland they ravaged the enemy. ⁵The tyrant Antiochus was both punished on earth and is being chastised after his death. Since in no way whatever was he able to compel the Israelites to adopt foreign ways and to abandon their ancestral customs, he left Jerusalem and marched against the Persians.

6 The mother of seven sons expressed also these principles to her children: ⁷"I was a pure virgin and did not go outside my father's house, but I guarded the rib from which woman was made.ᵏ ⁸No seducer corrupted me on a desert plain, nor did the destroyer, the deceitful serpent, defile the purity of my virginity. ⁹In the time of my maturity I remained with my husband, and when these sons had grown up their father died. A fortunate man was he, who lived out his life with good children and did not have the grief of bereavement. ¹⁰While he was still with you, he taught you the Law and the Prophets. ¹¹He read to you about Abel slain by Cain and Isaac who was offered as a burnt offering and about Joseph in prison. ¹²He told you of the zeal of Phinehas, and he taught you about Hananiah, Azariah, and Mishael in the fire. ¹³He praised Daniel in the den of the lions and blessed him. ¹⁴He reminded you of the scripture of Isaiah, which says, 'Even though you go through the fire, the flame shall not consume you.' ¹⁵He sang to you songs of the psalmist David, who said, 'Many are the afflictions of the righteous.' ¹⁶He recounted to you Solomon's proverb, 'Thereˡ is a tree of life for those who do his will.' ¹⁷He confirmed the query of Ezekiel, 'Shall these dry bones live?' ¹⁸For he did not forget to teach you the song that Moses taught, which says, ¹⁹'I kill, and I make alive; this is your life and the length of your days.'"

20 O bitter was that day—and yet not bitter—when that bitter tyrant of the Greeks quenched fire with fire in his cruel caldrons and in his burning rage brought those seven sons of the daughter of Abraham to the catapult and back again to moreᵐ tortures, ²¹pierced the pupils of their eyes and cut out their tongues, and put them to death with various tortures. ²²For these crimes divine justice pursued and will pursue the accursed tyrant. ²³But the sons of Abraham with their victorious mother are gathered together into the chorus of the fathers and have received pure and immortal souls from God, ²⁴to whom be glory forever and ever. Amen.

k 18.7 Gk *the rib that was built*   l 18.16 Or *He*   m 18.20 Other ancient authorities read *to all his*

18:1–5 Addressing the audience directly, the author reiterates the call to Torah observance and piety previously placed in the mouths of Eleazar, the brothers, and the mother (cf. 6:17–22; 9:23–24; 13:8–10; 16:16–19). The author returns to the thesis (1:1), albeit in a nuanced form in which *pious reason* is defined and expressed in terms of obedience to Torah (vv. 1–2, 4). **18:3–4** The effects of the martyrdoms are personal (*divine inheritance*) and communal (*peace*). The martyrs' demonstration of piety returns the nation to its precrisis state of peace, which was also attributed to Torah observance (cf. 3:20–21). **18:5** The author underscores the decisive defeat of Antiochus, won not through military means (contra 1 and 2 Macc.) but through the martyrs' courageous, nonviolent resistance.

18:6–19 The final speech of the mother, which is laced with scriptural allusions, introduces for the first time her husband, father of the seven. Her chastity and the sons' education are framed as reasons for their success against the tyrant. Although the mother is praised throughout 4 Maccabees for her role in encouraging her sons, the author emphasizes the father's role in the sons' education. Her female virtue of chastity is here set in contrast to the male-dominant task of teaching Torah. **18:7–9** The mother is pictured as embodying typical feminine ideals. On the *rib* and *the deceitful serpent*, see Gen. 2:21–22; 3:1–5. **18:10** A similar two-part classification of Scripture is present in Matthew (Matt. 5:17; 7:12; 11:13; 22:40), whereas Luke has three parts (Luke 24:44). **18:11** See Gen. 4:2–15; 22:1–19; 39:7–23. **18:12** See Num. 25:7–13; Dan. 3:19–30. **18:13** See Dan. 6:10–18. **18:14** See Isa. 43:2. **18:15** See Ps. 34:19. **18:16** See Prov. 3:18. **18:17** See Ezek. 37:2–3. **18:18–19** See Deut. 32:39.

18:23 The final image of the mother and sons confirms their transformation to immortality (cf. also the use of Ezekiel and Deuteronomy in vv. 17–19). The transformation involves incorporation into a larger chorus that includes exemplary ancestors who likewise attained immortality.

The New Testament

New Revised Standard Version Updated Edition

Introduction to the New Testament

The part of the Bible commonly called the "New Testament" formally became a collection of twenty-seven books in the fourth century. Prior to that time, canonical lists sometimes varied, with early Christian writers and groups occasionally disputing the inclusion of various texts for numerous reasons (e.g., the authorship of Hebrews is unknown). For more detailed information, readers should review **"The Bible as a Collection," pp. 2145–47**.

The structure of the collection has remained relatively consistent and follows a thematic logic. The Gospel accounts—which relay the story of the life, mission, death, and resurrection of Jesus, called the Christ—open the collection. Following these stories comes the book of Acts, an account that focuses attention on several elements of the developing Christ-following community. This narrative is especially interested in the early months and years following the ascension of Jesus and the leadership of Peter, James, and Paul. It ends with Paul proclaiming his message in Rome "with all boldness and without hindrance" (Acts 28:31). This leads quite appropriately into Paul's Letter to the Romans—a document that was written chronologically earlier than the Gospels or Acts. The letter to the church in Rome is followed, in turn, by all the letters associated with Paul (the authorship of some of them is disputed). Together these letters take up various cultural and religious situations within some of the first individual Christ-following communities, mostly of the first century. Paul, the traveling missionary, established many of the religious communities to whom these letters are addressed, though not all (e.g., the Roman church). The letters attributed to Paul, disputed and undisputed, are not organized chronologically. Rather, they are placed in order according to their respective word counts, beginning with the longest letter and ending with the shortest. Paul's Letter to Philemon, for example, consists of only twenty-five verses. The New Testament collection is then rounded out by a series of additional documents, including letters, sermons, and admonitions outside of the Pauline influence (Hebrews to Jude), as well as the book of Revelation, the only book-length apocalypse in the collection.

Generally, most books within the New Testament provide insight into some facet of first-century life within emerging Christian communities. A few—2 Peter and the Pastoral Letters attributed to Paul (1–2 Timothy and Titus)—may arguably reveal information about second-century life in Christ-following circles. Readers will want to keep in mind the logic of the collection's organization so as not to attribute historical primacy or chronological significance to the order in which the New Testament documents appear. Most scholars agree, for instance, that the undisputed Pauline Letters (Romans, 1–2 Corinthians, Galatians, Philippians, 1 Thessalonians, and Philemon) predate the Gospels.

Introduction to the Gospels and Acts

As you read the four Gospels and the book of Acts, you are reading the contributions of many people and traditions, which began with the remarkable words and actions of the historical Jesus in first-century Galilee and Judea. People remembered and spread his stories by word of mouth for decades (oral traditions), followed by written traditions. Both became the building blocks of the Gospels. The Gospel authors wove these traditions into our four Gospels with an eye to their audiences and circumstances. Other Christian writers and groups wrote Gospels and other works that did not make it into the final New Testament collection but that survive today as noncanonical and gnostic (relating to esoteric mystical knowledge) writings.

Christians made copies of the Gospels and Acts and carried them throughout the ancient world, translating them from the original Greek into many languages, including Latin, Ethiopic, and Coptic. Poring over these ancient manuscripts and translations, scholars have worked to determine the best versions and how to render them into modern languages, including the English version you hold in your hands.

Astute readers will have already noticed some things. First, what we have is not all there was. The *canon*, or accepted body of New Testament writings, was not stabilized until the fourth century (see

"The Bible as a Collection," pp. 2145–47). Many works fell out, like the Gospel of Mary (Magdalene), the Gospel of Peter, and a whole library of gnostic works from Nag Hammadi, Egypt.

Second, variations crept in. With multiple people telling stories by word of mouth or writing and subsequently copying and recopying material, differences were inevitable. For example, the report of the sign over Jesus's cross, which purports to relay written words, differs slightly in each Gospel (Mark 15:26; Matt. 27:37; Luke 23:38; John 19:19). The last words of Jesus from the cross are also different in each Gospel (Mark 15:34; Matt. 27:46; Luke 23:46; John 19:30; in Mark and Matthew, the languages differ, reflecting Aramaic and Hebrew). Many differences are minor, say a misspelling or variation in word order. Others are major; for example, the famous story of the woman caught in adultery, currently in John 8, does not appear in the standard Greek text of the Gospel before the Middle Ages.

Third, writers could not help but tell Jesus's story *as they understood it* while taking in their audiences' abilities and concerns. An author like Matthew, intensely interested in Jesus's connection to Hebrew Scripture, produced a narrative that varies from an author like Luke, presenting Christianity as a worthy part of Greco-Roman society and its intellectual traditions.

Finally, the authors themselves failed to sign or date their works. They are anonymous, and it fell to later church tradition to give the Gospels the names Matthew, Mark, Luke, and John, associating them with disciples mentioned in the texts (Matthew the tax collector in 9:9; John Mark, Peter's scribe; Luke, Paul's companion; and John, the Beloved Disciple and the son of Zebedee). Critical historical scholarship has assigned general dates to the texts based on clues within them that point to external events, tracing back traditions and reasoning regarding the development of literary and theological ideas. Although we cannot know the Gospel writers' identities, we have retained the traditional names assigned by the early church.

Dating

Jesus died around 30 CE, leaving no writings of his own. Oral traditions—stories told by neighbors, by parents to children, by strangers on long journeys—circulated and formed raw material for the earliest written account of Jesus, the Gospel of Mark. Scholars generally place it sometime around 65–70 because of its multiple references to suffering and upheaval and the destruction of the Jerusalem temple. Mark's picture of life coincides with the period of the Jewish war against Rome (66–70) described in histories of the time. Mark's Gospel is also relatively less developed, missing any traditions around Jesus's birth and appearance to the disciples after death, suggesting it was written in an earlier period. Most place the Gospels of Matthew and Luke ten to fifteen years after Mark, in the 80s CE, because their authors seem to have known and used parts of Mark's Gospel; this time frame allows some years for Mark's Gospel to circulate. Matthew and Luke have more developed doctrines, such as the virgin birth, and narratives unknown to Mark (but included in Q; see below), suggesting a flowering of the tradition. The Gospel of John stands as a unique Gospel, missing much material known to the other three authors but including many stories unique to itself, such as Jesus's appearance and dialogue alone with Mary Magdalene in the garden after his resurrection (John 20:14–18), the resurrection of Lazarus (John 11), and the mention of a mysterious disciple "whom Jesus loved" (John 13:23; 20:2; 21:7, 20; see also 19:26). John's narrative also evinces a hostility toward a group he labels simply "the Jews" (John 5:16; 7:1; 9:22; 11:8, 54), suggesting a community of readers that has cut ties with the Jewish community. Its sophistication and development of a "realized eschatology"—the idea that Jesus's followers have already entered a new reality through baptism and are saved even before Jesus's return—have led scholars to date John the latest of the Gospels, around the 90s.

The Acts of the Apostles—not a Gospel at all but a narrative of the earliest church in the generation after Jesus—was written by the same person who wrote Luke's Gospel, as evidenced by the two introductions that link the works and their similar writing styles and themes. The date of Acts is debated. Most scholars have assumed it was written shortly after the Gospel of Luke, so in the 80s or 90s. But a number of scholars suggest it was composed much later, circa 120–30 CE, because it seems to be responding to second-century tensions in the church between orthodoxy and heresy. Luke combines multiple literary genres, including travel narratives, to describe the writer's vision of a florescent Christianity that includes gentiles in the church and is increasingly at home in Greco-Roman society while crafting a lively set of stories about Peter, Paul, and early Christian groups embellished with adventure, humor, and confrontations with competing magicians and healers.

The Synoptic Problem

As mentioned, the authors Matthew and Luke knew Mark's Gospel. How do we know this? It is a hypothesis formed by more reasoning based on clues left in the texts. Matthew, Mark, and Luke are called the Synoptic Gospels (from the Greek word that means "seen together") or, more loosely, "the look-alike Gospels" because they share much of the same material—the same stories, in the same order, often with the same wording or nearly so, the sort of congruity that would make a professor suspicious if it appeared in three student papers. Look at the narrative of the temptation of Jesus as an example (Mark 1:12–13; Matt. 4:1–11; Luke 4:1–13); it would take an extreme level of coincidence for these three writers to describe the same incident independent of one another. So, questions follow. Who wrote first? Who copied from whom? These two questions are called the Synoptic problem, and trying to solve it has generated much scholarship. Not everyone agrees, but the consensus is that Mark wrote first and that Matthew and Luke copied from Mark. Mark is shorter and written in rougher Greek, and most scholars reason that stories tend to pick up length and detail as they are retold over time. Furthermore, sometimes Matthew and Mark agree and Luke is a bit different, or Luke and Mark agree and Matthew is the outlier. But Mark is rarely the odd one out, suggesting his work is the common denominator, available to Matthew and Luke when they composed their Gospels.

Another point jumps out—many sayings of Jesus and surrounding stories appear almost identical in Matthew and Luke but are not in Mark at all. It seems Matthew and Luke both had a collection of Jesus's sayings unknown to Mark. This sayings source has been dubbed "Q," short for the German word *Quelle*, which means "source." We have no copy of it—it is a hypothetical construction. But taking all the Q material together, it shows a consistency in form and content. Now we have an answer to our second question: Who copied from whom? Matthew and Luke copied Mark and another sayings source, Q. This, and the suggestion that Mark wrote first, constitute the Two-Document Hypothesis.

Matthew and Luke were not mere editors of other sources, however. They had traditions unique to themselves and demonstrated their own creative abilities in using Mark. Why does this matter? If we

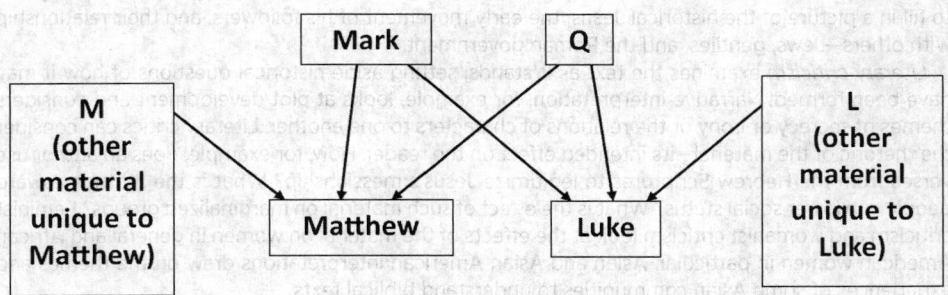

Two/Four Source Hypotheses: Scholars have sought to explain the close similarities in the wording and order of narratives among the Synoptic Gospels of Matthew, Mark, and Luke. The similarities are too close to be coincidental. Held by a majority of NT scholars as an explanation for these literary similarities and differences, the Two Source Hypothesis contends that in composing their Gospels, both Matthew and Luke independently drew on two earlier sources: the Gospel of Mark and a hypothetical document called Q, named for the German word *Quelle*, meaning "source." Mark stands as the earliest Gospel, and Q is posited to be a collection of the sayings and teachings of Jesus that appear in Matthew and Luke but are absent from Mark, such as the Beatitudes. Additionally, many scholars argue that Matthew and Luke also incorporated materials in their Gospels from traditions unique to each of them, pointing to the possibility of four sources. Accordingly, each Gospel's birth story of Jesus would be credited to one of these two different hypothetical sources (labeled "M" for Matthew; "L" for Luke).

- **Mark** = The earliest Gospel and a source that both Matthew and Luke borrowed from to write their own stories of Jesus.
- **Q** = Quelle, a hypothetical collection of Jesus's sayings and teachings, resembling ancient gnomologia, which preserved the wise sayings of famous teachers. Containing no narrative material, Q is a source for Matthew and Luke but not for Mark.
- **M** = Additional hypothetical source for material found only in Matthew.
- **L** = Additional hypothetical source for material found only in Luke.

know Matthew edited Mark, we see clues to Matthew's mindset, theology, and audience. Examining how he edited his source, or redacted it, is called redaction criticism.

What about Jesus?

Does this kind of work lose sight of Jesus and his teaching? How do Christians today find inspiration and guidance in the New Testament? It is useful to think of Jesus in (at least) two ways: (1) the historical or earthly Jesus, the Jew who lived in ancient Roman Palestine, an itinerant preacher and healer who taught of the imminent arrival of God's kingdom and was executed by the Romans as a threat to the political order, and (2) the Christ of faith, or the exalted Jesus, who continues to live in the community and the hearts of believers. Roughly speaking, studying the historical Jesus belongs to the historian's craft, while the Christ of faith belongs to the theologian's work. In general, the Gospel accounts are sources for both the historian and the theologian.

How to Read the Gospels and Acts

Scholars who labor over New Testament texts are influenced by trends in other disciplines. The three general categories of interpretation are historical criticism, literary criticism, and reception history (looking at how the Bible has been used by later cultures). Within these three groupings are a bewildering array of many specialized approaches, often echoing methods and insights from other fields. Cultural anthropology helps us consider gender roles or the social values of honor and shame. Trauma theory allows interpreters to draw insights from psychology to think through the effect of Jesus's horrible death on his followers. Those who use affect theory consider the many expressions of emotions—like fear, crying, and amazement—that pepper the stories. Some of these methods are called "criticisms," implying not a negative attitude but a dispassionate analysis.

Historical criticism can ask several things: What is the history of the actual text? Which manuscripts and variations in wording seem best? How was the text composed? What sources were used, and how were those sources edited? The Synoptic problem, historical Jesus research, and archaeology all fit into this category. But it can also include picking up clues and details left behind in the text to reconstruct the identity and concerns of the Gospel author and the author's community and to fill in a picture of the historical Jesus, the early movement of his followers, and their relationship with others—Jews, gentiles, and the Roman government.

Literary criticism examines the text as it stands, setting aside historical questions of how it may have been formed. Narrative interpretation, for example, looks at plot development and considers themes of secrecy or irony or the relations of characters to one another. Literary critics can consider the rhetoric of the material—its intended effect on the reader. How, for example, does an author use verses from the Hebrew Scriptures to legitimize Jesus's messiahship? What is the attitude toward people of a lower social status? What is the effect of such material on marginalized groups? Feminist criticism and womanist criticism look at the effects of the material on women in general and African American women in particular. Asian and Asian American interpretations draw on the themes and experiences of some Asian communities to understand biblical texts.

The third category, *reception history*, flows from both historical and literary sensibilities, asking how New Testament texts have been used and received by different communities of readers. Postcolonial theory speaks to the experiences of people with the Bible who have been colonized by outsiders who used the Bible to assert their power and superiority. The figures of Jesus and Paul and the exodus story were sources of liberation for enslaved African Americans, even as others wielded them and other New Testament texts to defend slavery.

These many categories are neither strict nor exclusive. Someone interested in the New Testament and slavery, for example, could wonder how many persons were enslaved in the Roman world (historical question), how enslaved people are presented in the parables (literary question), and how some verses were used to justify slavery, while others were used to abolish it (reception history question). Biblical scholars are always gleaning new perspectives from the world and bringing them to the text, just as readers are encouraged to raise their own fresh insights and questions.

Claudia Setzer

Introduction to the Pauline Letters

To read the Pauline Letters is to attempt to understand and interpret the world by looking at what amounts to other people's mail. Half of the canonical New Testament—thirteen of the twenty-seven books—is attributed to Paul, and the addressees vary from individuals (Philemon) to groups with whom Paul may have had an ongoing correspondence (1 and 2 Corinthians) to groups Paul never met (Romans). The locations of Paul's addressees also vary, and the topics and themes raised differ from letter to letter. The Pauline Letters include some of the earliest known Christian literature. These materials are important for understanding something about the dynamics of communication and group formation in the ancient world, for seeing how a new religious movement might operate before it is institutionalized, and for becoming aware of the origins and legacies of a myriad of social and cultural issues in this context, as well as questions about authority, hierarchy, and identity.

How to understand and interact with the legacies of the Pauline correspondence has been a matter of open and unsettled debate across time and inside and outside of organized religion. This introduction to the Pauline Letters will hopefully help contemporary readers ask critical questions about the role and function of letters in the ancient world, as well as how they might handle Paul and Pauline literature in our world. To do this, we will discuss how ancient letters might have worked, who the author "Paul" might have been, who these audiences may have been, and why thinking about all this matters.

Ancient and Pauline Letters

Numerous letters survive from ancient world cultures, and the ancient evidence—piles of letters, often fragmentary, found in locations from ancient manuscript collections to ancient trash heaps—indicates that letters were composed and sent for a myriad of matters from the everyday to the official. In addition to basic communication, letters could serve pedagogical purposes, as letter composition appears to have been an integral part of ancient educational practices. Letters could also serve as literary documents. For example, ancient Egyptians appear to have written letters to the dead and to their gods, and Greek and Roman letters could appear as prose or poetry. Some letters were written as satirical exercises or to imagine historical narratives. Contemporary biblical scholars tend to differentiate *letters*, which are thought to be used for everyday communicative purposes, from *epistles*, which are thought to be used for more serious teaching purposes. Yet many surviving documents lack an original sending context and contain literary elements that make clear classification difficult. As a collection, the Pauline Letters exhibit a range of lengths, from 335 words (Philemon) to more than 7,100 words (Romans); display both passing familiarity and intimacy with audiences; and employ a variety of topics, themes, and literary devices.

As written documents, ancient letters were typically composed by a scribe or amanuensis. The scribe was often an enslaved person who was employed by a sender, took dictation, and had the authority to write on their behalf. Indeed, although ancient letters might open with an identification of the sender (see, for example, the first verses of the Pauline Letters, wherein "Paul" is identified as the sender to his intended recipients), the scribe too might identify themselves at some point (e.g., Rom. 16:22, where "Tertius" indicates that he wrote the letter), or the author might compose a few lines themselves (e.g., 2 Thess. 3:17: "I, Paul, write this greeting with my own hand." Cf. Phlm. 19; Gal. 6:11). In Ephesians, a "Tychicus" identifies himself as the letter's courier (6:21–22), indicating that he may have written and delivered the letter to its recipients. How is it possible that we now have a collection of Paul's letters if written letters were physically delivered to their recipients and those recipients might be scattered in locations across the ancient world? From what we can surmise of ancient letter-writing technologies and practices, it appears as though copies of sent letters were kept in common repositories. These letters, too, were edited and recopied and collected. To this end, the Pauline Letters we have now are not the original ancient versions of what Paul's intended recipients may have received, heard, and read. In fact, there are nearly one thousand ancient copies of the Pauline Letters, and no two are the same! Still, the reality that these letters were copied and collected many times over is an indicator of their importance to communities across time and cultures.

Who Was "Paul"?

Although Paul is the second-most famous figure in early Christian history, reliable information about his life is comparatively scant. Within the New Testament canon, the sources that provide some

insight into the contours and circumstances of Paul's life include the Pauline Letters and the Acts of the Apostles, though the extent to which Acts is a work of history is debated. Beyond the New Testament canon, several apocryphal documents—acts, letters, and apocalypses—provide additional details about Paul's life and work, although the historical reliability of these sources is also debatable. Several other early Christian letters mention Paul, and the ancient historian Eusebius of Caesarea uses the Acts of the Apostles to structure his history of Christianity and mentions Paul's imprisonment during the time of the Roman emperor Nero. Throughout many of these sources, the focus is on Paul's adulthood: his relationship with the people he encounters while on the road as an "apostle to the gentiles," his encounters with his colleagues and with local and imperial authorities, and his eventual imprisonment and probable death in Rome.

According to the extant sources, it could be said that Paul—like many ancient people—lived and worked in a multivalent, multicultural world and inhabited what we would now call an intersectional identity as a Jewish, Greek, and Roman male person (who sometimes spoke of himself in female terms; see Gal. 4:19; 1 Thess. 2:7). Although we do not know much about Paul's birth or childhood, Acts (9:11; 22:3) relates that he is from Tarsus, a city in Asia Minor known as an intellectual center. Paul's letters appear to have been written by someone who was educated and cosmopolitan. At multiple points, his writings betray familiarity with the Scriptures and epic traditions of Israel, Greek philosophical traditions, local folk practices, and Roman imperial structures of governmental authority. Paul appears to have been immersed and comfortable in urban environments and public spaces.

Readers of the Pauline Letters will encounter examples of how Paul characterizes his own life as one of teaching and learning, turmoil, and travel. One of the most critical details of Paul's pre-apostolic life is that he was a zealous and violent persecutor of the followers of Jesus, including the very people he subsequently visited and to whom he wrote the letters collected in this Bible. According to the letters and the Acts of the Apostles, Paul endured a life-changing, multisensory experience of Jesus now called a "conversion" by some, and a prophetic "call" by others (Acts 9; Gal. 2), that he—for whatever reason—needed to process for himself and then tell others about. As he came to terms with his new knowledge and experience, he began to see himself as a primary messenger to the "gentiles"—that is, the (non-Jewish) nations, the outsiders. Paul is a figure who attempted to zealously embrace what he had zealously rejected, and he appears to have endured no shortage of skepticism and persecution on account of his change of perspective and behavior. The dynamics of personal and communal change compose only one set of thorny problems that the Pauline Letters raise.

Pauline Authenticity, Audiences, and Ancient Contexts

Another set of problems complicating the study of the Pauline Letters involves the authenticity and audiences of these documents as witnesses to the development of early Christian communities. Contemporary scholars note that letters are conversational—information about both sender and recipient is both apparent and assumed, and letters are missing the outward-facing descriptions that would be in a biographical or historical narrative. It is vital to remember that letters are occasional documents: they were written in particular times and places, to particular people, in response to particular situations, none of which is readily evident and transparent in the Pauline Letters themselves.

Paul is named as the author of all thirteen letters attributed to him in the New Testament, and considerable attention has been given to whether Paul is *actually* the author of all these letters—or whether someone else was writing in Paul's name in some cases. Scholars call the letters Paul wrote "undisputed" or "authentic Pauline Letters," and the letters determined to be of dubious Pauline authorship "disputed," "deuteropauline," or "inauthentic Pauline Letters." Consensus concerning authenticity is determined by examining the letters according to criteria such as language use and mention of the letters in external sources. Scholarly proposals and consensus about authentic Pauline authorship have changed over time, ranging from "Paul wrote zero letters" to "Paul wrote all of them." However, the most durable consensus maintains that of the thirteen letters, seven can be reliably called Pauline: Romans, Galatians, 1 and 2 Corinthians, Philippians, Philemon, and 1 Thessalonians. These are the letters that are attested most often in external literary sources and in early canonical lists and collections (see **"The Bible as a Collection," pp. 2145–47**). The other letters—Colossians, Ephesians, 2 Thessalonians, 1 and 2 Timothy, and Titus—have historically been disputed

as far as Pauline authorship is concerned. However, there are also arguments that link each of these letters to Paul as an author. Given that the Pauline Letters are primary sources of information about Paul as a person and as an essential figure in the history of religion and culture, it stands to reason that determining whether Paul is the author of the thirteen letters attributed to him is a matter of ongoing import.

Even as we can glean information about Paul and his life and work from the Pauline Letters, these documents are also useful for thinking about the people to whom he presumably sent his correspondence. Since we do not have the letters from any of these communities to consult, any efforts to describe and understand the identities, actions, and thoughts of Paul's addressees will necessarily be provisional. Throughout the Pauline Letters, we can tell that Paul seeks to establish his authority and to be persuasive at particular moments and for specific concerns. His central agenda appears to be presenting his understanding of the requirements for belonging to this emergent community of mixed membership and unclear identity: Who gets to be a part of this community? Can gentiles associate with Jews without getting circumcised? If this community is different from others, how so? Which practices should be important, and on what or whose terms? How can one tell who belongs and who does not? Must all members think and do the same thing? Paul at points encourages his addressees to think and act in certain ways and to abandon other ways of thinking and acting. Even as we might read and attempt to understand Paul's words in the letters, we are only reading one side of a conversation in which we are not direct participants. What we cannot know is whether such advice was warranted, heeded, or ignored by Paul's addressees. Nevertheless, from Paul's rhetoric, we can deduce that the addressees probably come from a variety of backgrounds and have varying levels of familiarity with and commitment to Jewish practices.

It is vital to keep in mind that the Pauline Letters were composed, distributed, and received before Christianity was a distinct religious institution with a fixed set of sacred texts and fully formed ecclesial leadership, creeds, and doctrines. Thus, the setting of the Pauline Letters should be characterized as pre–New Testament canon, pre-doctrinal, and pre-church. The ancient historical context in which Paul's letters were composed is best described as a cosmopolitan—a culturally, ethnically, and religiously diverse—world of urban centers and rural peripheries situated within the territory of the Roman Empire. Paul and his addressees were members of a loose configuration of new religious groups, and throughout the letters, there is disagreement about who can join these groups and on what terms, what one does and does not do as a member, and how one stays or leaves. This conceptual framing can be difficult to appreciate in a world in which Pauline literature is regarded as consistent and coherent and taken for granted as Christian Scripture. The ancient and cultural context in which these letters are to be situated is distant from the contemporary world and reflects different realities.

Reading the Pauline Letters Today

Although we cannot know with precision how persuasive Paul's recommendations were in the ancient world, it is difficult to underestimate how influential the Pauline Letters have been across time and cultures as Scriptures. How to understand Paul and make sense of the Pauline Letters have long been subject to debate and constitute a lively area of contemporary biblical interpretation. While originally directed at particular ancient circumstances, the issues and themes in the Pauline Letters have become central to Christian discourses as well as conversations about religion and ethics beyond institutional affiliation. Concepts such as "grace" and "faith," the bodily resurrection of Jesus and Christians, and several key practices such as speaking in tongues, collecting resources for the poor, and common meals are mentioned in these letters. Overall, Paul was concerned with relationships—between himself and the communities to which his addressees belonged, between community members, and between his addressees and their social, cultural, religious, and political worlds. These letters could be understood as practical instruction bolstered by theological argumentation. Paul was at once both pastoral and evangelical, hierarchical and egalitarian, strident and flexible, teacher and learner.

The ancient words attributed to Paul have been used over the last two millennia both to establish and to challenge ethical, social, sexual, and racial/ethnic hierarchies inside and outside religious communities. Paul and Paul's letters have been a persistent presence in arguments for and against slavery, racial justice, colonialism and imperial oppression, poverty elimination, women's rights, freedom in gender identification, homosexuality, end-time predictions, ecological stewardship, and interreligious dialogue and acceptance—just to name a few enduring issues. As with much regarding

biblical literature and its vast and varied appropriations, no one appears to be neutral about Paul or the documents attributed to him. Even though the Pauline Letters are technically other people's mail, their personal character and sense of real-world urgency and relevance make them accessible and of interest beyond their original postal routes. To this end, studying Pauline literature should open many defamiliarizing questions about power, justice, freedom, truth, ethics, practices, world-views, relationships, and empathy—then and now.

Davina C. Lopez

Introduction to Hebrews, the General Epistles, and Revelation

Unlike the Gospels or the Pauline Letters, these books do not share a readily identifiable set of common features. In these writings, we discover witnesses to early Christ-following communities that are marked by a wide range of beliefs and practices. Apparently, the communities addressed in these texts lay outside of the Pauline orbit. Not only are these documents not ascribed to Paul, but they do not follow the epistolary pattern found in his letters, such as the ones to Galatia, Rome, and Corinth. Moreover, they do not bear the signature features of the religious ideas of the Pauline communities (e.g., "righteousness through faith"; see Rom. 3:21–26). These documents attest to the diversity of Christ-following communities that subscribed to (or opposed) a variety of religious ideas and practices while living in the Greco-Roman Empire.

Several of these documents almost did not make it into the collection of writings that eventually were deemed authoritative or canonical. We know that a document's attachment to an apostolic authority—whether authored by or affiliated with an apostle—was a significant criterion for inclusion in the New Testament (see **"The Bible as a Collection," pp. 2145–47**). The anonymity of Hebrews raised questions about its inclusion. Origen of Alexandria (d. 253 CE) claimed that "only God knows" who wrote Hebrews yet still advocated for its inclusion in the collection. On the other hand, Revelation—or "the apocalypse of Jesus Christ"—raised a different set of challenges for those making decisions about its inclusion. Though the apparent author ("John" in 1:1–4) was traditionally associated with the apostle John—a view biblical scholarship questions today—its popularity among fringe Christian groups during the first few centuries almost derailed its acceptance into the larger collection.

Within the present order, these books—unlike the Pauline Letters—are not arranged according to length (see **"Introduction to the Pauline Letters," pp. 1713–16**). Hebrews falls near the Pauline material because of its association with Paul. The book of Revelation is a fitting conclusion to the entire collection of NT writings, probably because of its intense apocalyptic and imaginative focus on the final period of human history. The other seven books may have been arranged in the present order due to a reference to the "acknowledged pillars" (James, Cephas, and John) named in Gal. 2:9 and associated with these documents ("Cephas" is another name for Peter).

Many of these books are associated with "heroes" from the first-generation communities of Christ followers—Peter, James, and John. These "heroes" may have had little to do directly with the writing of these documents to which their names are attached. Second Peter—similar to 2 Timothy—appears to be the "last will and testament" of a prominent first-generation hero of the movement (Peter) but may also be the latest book to be written in the NT collection (perhaps early second century). The later provenance would explain its attention to an early, informal compilation of the Pauline Letters as documents that stand alongside "other scriptures" (2 Pet. 3:15–16) and the allusion to Jesus's transfiguration recorded in the Gospels (1:16–18; both Paul's letters and the Gospels became established later in the first century).

As with the Gospels, it is difficult to situate these communities of readers or hearers geographically, since most of these documents offer little information about their addressees (Hebrews, 1 Peter, 1–3 John). Those that provide hints of an audience indicate a more "general" circulation. For example, 2 Peter is sent "to those who have received a faith as equally honorable as ours" (1:1); Jude "to those who are called, who are beloved" (1); James "to the twelve tribes in the dispersion"

(1:1); and 1 Peter "to the exiles of the dispersion" (1:1). The lack of references to specific geographical locales suggests that several of these documents may have been intended for wider audiences than, for instance, the Pauline Letters. For that reason, seven of these books (James, 1–2 Peter, 1–3 John, and Jude) have traditionally been called the Catholic (i.e., Universal) Epistles or the General Epistles. Some scholars associate Hebrews with the Pauline material—partly due to the ending of the letter (in which Timothy, a member of Paul's traveling party, is recognized). Hebrews, however, does not follow the literary pattern found in Paul's letters, where the apostle explicitly self-identifies as the author, underscores his status as an apostle, and specifically identifies his addressees. Moreover, its eventual placement within the wider canonical collection by those ancient decision makers (between Philemon and James) may speak to doubts about its Pauline authorship as well, a view held by a majority of scholars today. The difficulties in situating these books geographically as well as the challenges of determining authorship create the related conundrum of demarcating the time period of the documents. The label "general" applies in a new—and convenient—way, as it is difficult for scholars to pinpoint these specifics about the books. At the same time, the classification of "general" does not mean that these documents do not shed light on other Christ-following communities surrounding the Great Sea from the late first century through the early second century.

The book of Revelation patterns somewhat differently than the other books treated in this section. The author explicitly self-identifies (an ambiguous John), names the location from which he writes (Patmos), and identifies his addressees as seven churches within Asia Minor.

Religious Practices of Early Christ-Following Communities Revealed

First Peter, 2 John, and 3 John witness to the use of *homes* as gathering places for the early Christ-following communities (1 Pet. 4:9–10; cf. 2 John 1:10), along with an expected hospitality that would be associated with this environment (3 John 5–8). At times, the lack of hospitality for the network of travelers in the Jesus movement needed to be addressed publicly. One leader in the movement, Diotrephes, was publicly called out for his failure to host traveling teachers whom the author of the letter supported (3 John 9–10).

First Peter also testifies to the presence of *elders* in the communities who should "tend the flock" (1 Pet. 5:1–2), while others should accept the elders' authority (1 Pet. 5:5)—though in what specific ways is unclear. The term *elders* is frequently attached to the "heroes" associated with these books as their writers (1 Pet. 5:1; 2 John 1; 3 John 1), which may imply—even as a fictional description—that at least some elders may have communicated with their religious communities through letters. One of the documents attests that elders should take up the specific practice of praying for the sick in the community (Jas. 5:14). The term—and, perhaps, position—is absent from the undisputed Pauline Letters (Romans, 1–2 Corinthians, Galatians, Philippians, 1 Thessalonians, and Philemon). Apparently, the presence of elders became a growing practice of later Christ-following communities (cf. Titus 1:5).

Widespread among these biblical books and communities was the presence of *competing teachings* from other Christ followers, labeled within these documents as "false teachers" (2 Pet. 2:1) or some other derogatory label. This feature speaks to the diverse nature of these developing communities beyond just these canonical books and their sometimes abrasive interactions. Rhetorical slander about these outsiders in these biblical documents is harsh—usually pointing to an uninhibited immorality. It was ancient common practice to overemphasize the evil qualities (whether true or not) of opponents. Yet the literary evidence often suggests that these so-called false teachers originated within the communities themselves, described as having once "known the way of righteousness" (2 Pet. 2:21) or as those who "went out from us" (1 John 2:19). Descriptors vary for these (former) leaders in the community, from "intruders" (Jude 4) to "false prophets" (1 John 4:1–3) to "deceivers" (2 John 7) to "antichrist[s]" (1 John 2:18, 22; 2 John 7). Not only was their teaching misguided; these defectors were usually classified as greedy and sexually deviant (2 Pet. 2:14). Only hints of their teaching content remain in the literature. When these teachers "promise freedom" (2 Pet. 2:19 CEB), to whom do they promise this freedom? If they are extending this vow to enslaved believers, does this suggest that they encouraged the enslaved to seek manumission? A specific teaching apparently circulating in the community associated with the Johannine letters was a denial of the "humanity" of Jesus Christ while still upholding a firm belief in his divinity (1 John 4:2; 2 John 7). The similarities and variations of the teachings of these closely knit rivals would have created social havoc within these smaller, house church–based, newly developing communities.

Although Revelation places much of its attention on the hostile relationship between the churches and the Roman Empire, the letters recounted in Rev. 2–3 point to conflict with some neighboring Jewish communities as well: "those who say that they are Jews and are not but are a synagogue of Satan" (Rev. 2:9). The Apocalypse also attests to infighting between various Christian factions as well, as the author accuses some groups of being followers of Balaam (Rev. 2:14) and Jezebel (2:20), both of which permitted the eating of idol meat and, perhaps, allowed its members to engage in sex with temple sex workers. The latter charge—illicit sexual activity—may simply be a standard slur against one's religious enemies.

Nonetheless, these documents encourage efforts to reclaim some of the wandering members, perhaps led out of the community by other teachings. Anyone who returns to the "true" community will be forgiven, and this action will "cover a multitude of sins" (Jas. 5:19–20). Some of these writings encourage mercy toward these wanderers despite the damage performed on their bodies in the context of temple worship (Jude 22–23). Even less clear language about "deadly sins" may imply being permanently misled out of the community's fold (cf. 1 John 5:16–17).

Lastly, these documents also reveal other, perhaps distinctive practices within the early house church communities. The book of James witnesses to a community of (Jewish?) Christ followers that, unsurprisingly, continues to follow torah explicitly (1:25; 2:8–12; 4:11–12). James may point to a baptism for new members at which a "name" (perhaps that of "Jesus") is spoken (2:7) rather than what seems to have become the formula in Pauline communities emphasizing unity (cf. Gal. 3:28; 1 Cor. 12:13; Col. 3:11). First John emphasizes the role of confession (1:9)—apparently, public confession—among members of the ekklesia. First Peter encourages the "kiss of love" as a common greeting (1 Pet. 5:14).

Beyond Paul: What We Learn from These Documents

It is not as if these nine documents circulated as a smaller, separate collection informing a particular segment of the Jesus movement—although there is a growing body of scholarship that suggests that the General Epistles may have. Rather, these books testify to the diversity of the developing movement that we call Christianity in various locations—many unspecified—and the themes that could have been discussed during the latter quarter of the first century and perhaps into the early second-century period.

One of the fascinating notes about their inclusion in the NT canon is that these documents expose as false the claim—which has often dominated the history of NT studies—that Paul, his entourage, and his opponents exemplify the full expression of the experiences of the early Christ-following community. Rather, these nine documents attest to a much broader, less Pauline array of perspectives on the way things were or, at least, the way these documents wished them to be.

If we do imagine a widespread circulation for most of these documents, here are a few other elements to consider that these books contribute to our understanding of early Christianity, beyond the Pauline orbit. (1) These documents offer readers other genres beyond the traditional "letter," including a "sermon/exhortation" (Hebrews) and an "apocalypse" (Revelation). (2) These witnesses attest to the beginnings of potential supersessionist teachings (e.g., Heb. 7:18–19) that attempt to distinguish and elevate the wing of a movement ("a better hope") over its historical, religious ties to Judaism that in later years would transition into a history of anti-Jewish discourse and practice. (3) There appears to be a general absence of *female* leadership in these communities over against the explicit presence of women's leadership in the documents associated with the Pauline communities (e.g., Rom. 16; 1 Cor. 11; Phil. 4). There are metaphors of an "elect lady" (2 John 1) and a "Jezebel" (Rev. 2:20) that may or may not refer to female leadership among Christ followers. (4) Similar to other Christ-following communities, these documents introduce the inclusion of *enslaved* Christ followers among the group (cf. 1 Cor. 7:21–22; Gal. 3:28; Eph. 6:5–9). But the admonition of 1 Pet. 2:18–25 stands out even among the other household codes present within the NT. Only 1 Peter encourages the enslaved to continue in the path of suffering because Christ suffered on their behalf (1 Pet. 2; 3:17; 4:1–2, 13). (5) These literary witnesses express divergent stances toward the Roman Empire. On the one hand, 1 Peter seems to mimic the direction of Rom. 13. In order to represent lives of honor in the "gentile" community (1 Pet. 2:12), it is best to "be subject to every human authority" (2:13). On the other end of the spectrum falls Rev. 13, which appeals to a more discerning (and antagonistic) view of the governing and violent authorities of the day, as it cautions "calls for wisdom" discerning when to take action (13:18).

Emerson B. Powery

THE GOSPEL ACCORDING TO MATTHEW

Introduction

The Gospel of Matthew presents a poignant witness to the life and death of Jesus the Judean/Jewish messiah. Some of the most memorable sayings come from the Sermon on the Mount: the Beatitudes (5:1–11), the Golden Rule (7:12), and the Lord's Prayer (6:9–13). The influence of Matthew's Gospel on the English language is undeniable. A number of sayings—blessed are the poor, salt of the earth, turning the other cheek—have been so influential on the English language that they have become part of the cultural lexicon.

Matthew is a gifted scribe who weaves together oral, literary, and scribal traditions that document the story of how early Judaism and Christianity flourished. While most modern scholars argue that Mark was written earlier, Matthew's location as the First Gospel is undisputed. The Gospel's prominence was unrivaled during the early years of the Jesus movement. It is no wonder, then, that Matthew enjoys a privileged status as the very first book of the canonical New Testament.

Authorship, Date, and Provenance

Unlike the Gospel of Luke, the Matthean text makes no direct claim to authorship. But this has not discouraged a number of theories regarding its authorship. The traditional view is that Matthew—one of the original disciples and a former tax collector—was the author. This view finds implicit support in the change of identity from "Levi son of Alphaeus" (Mark 2:13–17) to "Matthew" (Matt. 9:9–13). Most modern scholars today, however, regard the identity of the author as anonymous, unknown, and lost in history.

The date, composition, and provenance of Matthew are also difficult to pin down. The fact that Matthew is written in Koine Greek would indicate a Hellenistic, Greek-speaking readership. Most Judeans/Jews living in Palestine would have spoken Aramaic. Curiously, Peter plays a prominent role in Matthew (4:18–22; 10:2; 14:28; 16:16–19) in comparison to the other Gospels. Matthew is quick to reference the destruction of the temple on a few occasions. For these reasons, a late first-century date from the early 70s to the late 80s and a location with a sizable population of Judeans/Jews in Syrian Antioch are most likely. But these theories are conjectural and based on relative degrees of probability. Ultimately, the authorship, date, composition, and provenance of Matthew cannot be determined with any degree of certainty or precision.

Matthew's Relationship to the Synoptic Gospels

The popularity of Matthew was well established during the period of the early church. This much is evident in the frequent use of Matthew in early Christian writings from the second and third centuries. Matthew's influence is recorded in Clement of Alexandria, Ignatius, Jerome, Justin, and Origen, as well as other writings such as the *Didache*, Gospel of Thomas, and Epistle of Barnabas. However, the consensus regarding Matthew's position as the earliest Gospel was overturned during the Enlightenment period as the academic study of biblical literature shifted from churches and synagogues to the modern university. The question of the relationship between the Gospels of Matthew, Mark, and Luke to one another is called the Synoptic problem. The dominant solution is the Two Source Hypothesis, that Mark is the earliest Gospel and that Matthew and Luke drew from it and a hypothetical source of sayings dubbed Q by scholars when composing their Gospels (see **"Introduction to the Gospels and Acts," pp. 1709–12**.

Despite the popularity of the Two Source Hypothesis, it is important to note its cultural and ideological origins. Markan priority originated in an anti-Semitic, anti-Catholic, pro-German context that effectively deracialized German Protestant Christianity from its Judean and Jewish roots. The overall effect was a depiction of Christianity as universal, nonethnic, and unencumbered by the particularities of race/ethnicity, gender, or any other identity marker. While the origins of the theory do not necessarily invalidate Markan priority, it is important for contemporary readers to be mindful of how modern forms of racism have shaped, and continue to shape, the history, practice, and reception of biblical interpretation.

Organization

Matthew is one of the longest books of the New Testament alongside Luke and Acts. Five major discourses provide a road map to its contents: the Sermon on the Mount (chap. 5–7); the ethnocentric mission to Israel (chap. 10); parables of the kingdom (chap. 13); community discourse (chap. 18); eschatological discourse (chaps. 24–25). This five-fold structure imitates the Pentateuch, the first five books of the Old Testament / Hebrew Bible. Matthew uses the following formula to mark each discourse: "Now when Jesus had finished saying these words" (7:28; 11:1; 13:53; 19:1; 26:1–2). The Gospel concludes with the resurrected Jesus expanding the ethnocentric mission to Israel to all ethnicities, nations, and peoples (28:18–20).

Matthew is nearly twice as long as the Gospel of Mark. A majority of sayings and stories in Mark are also found in Matthew. But some material is not found anywhere else: the opening genealogy (1:1–17); the birth of Jesus (1:18–25); the visit of the Magi (2:1–12); the flight to Egypt (2:13–21); the Sermon on the Mount (5:17–20, 21–38; 6:1–18; 7:6); the ethnocentric mission to Israel (10:5–6); Jesus's invitation to rest (11:28–30); the parables of the kingdom (13:24–30, 36–52); the blessing of Peter (16:17–19); the temple tax (17:24–27); rules governing the community (18:15–20); the teaching about forgiveness (18:21–22); the parable of the Unforgiving Servant (18:23–35); the parable of the Laborers (20:1–16); the parable of the Two Sons (21:28–32); woes on the Pharisees (23:15–22); the parable of the Bridesmaids (25:1–13); the parable of the Sheep and Goats (25:31–46); Judas's suicide (27:3–10); Pilate washing his hands (27:24–25); the resurrection of the saints (27:52–53); the guard at the tomb (27:62–66; 28:11–15); and the Great Commission (28:16–20).

Additionally, there are three passion predictions (16:21; 17:22–23; 20:17–19) that pull the narrative forward and twelve fulfillment citations (1:22–23; 2:5–6, 15, 17–18, 23; 4:14–16; 8:17; 12:17–21; 13:14–15, 35; 21:4–5; 27:9) that point back to biblical traditions in the Hebrew Bible (Old Testament)—or, more specifically, the Greek translation of the Hebrew Scriptures, the Septuagint (LXX). This was the version of the Bible that Matthew most likely read and used in his day.

Reading Guide

Matthew tells the story of how an individual from an oppressed group ("Judeans/Jews," *Ioudaios*) became the Messiah, Lord, and Savior for all groups ("gentile," *ethnikos*). The story is told from a minoritized perspective under the yoke of Roman imperial rule but in a manner that holds universal appeal. The insider group has certain beliefs, customs, and practices (e.g., prayer, almsgiving, food, and community guidelines) that differentiate themselves from other groups. The insider group is described in multiple ways depending on who is speaking and to whom. Sometimes they are identified as "Judean/Jewish," often by ethnic outsiders, or "Israel" (*Israēl*), often by fellow Judeans/Jews. In this way, Matthew is paradoxically open and closed, universal and particular, ethnocentric and multiracial.

How, then, does Matthew contribute to the development of early Judaism and Christianity? Matthew is an ancient and early witness about who Jesus is and what his death and resurrection came to signify for his earliest followers—the vast majority of whom were Judean/Jewish. This is the historical, ethnic, and cultural milieu in which Christianity would emerge. The Gospel of Matthew is a multilayered, well-crafted narrative that rewards careful study: "Therefore every scribe who has become a disciple in the kingdom of heaven is like the master of a household who brings out of his treasure what is new and what is old" (13:52).

Wongi Park

Passages Unique to the Gospel of Matthew

1:1–17	The Genealogy from Abraham and David
1:18–25	The Birth of Jesus
1:23; 2:5–6, 15, 17–18, 23; 4:14–16; 8:17; 12:17–21; 13:14–15, 35; 21:4–5; 27:9	Fulfillment Citations
2:1–12	Visit of the Magi
2:13–15	Escape to Egypt
2:16–18	Massacre of the Infants
2:19–23	Return from Egypt
3:14–15	John Questions Baptism of Jesus
5:17–20	Jesus's Words Fulfill the Law
5:21–24, 27–28, 33–38, 43	The Antitheses
6:1–8, 16–18	On Charity and Prayer
7:6	Saying on Profaning the Holy
10:5–6	Mission to Israel Alone
10:36	Enemies within the Household
11:28–30	Comfort for the Weary
13:24–30, 36–52	Parables about Weeds, Treasure, Pearl, and Net
14:28–31	Peter Tries to Walk on Water
16:17–19	Jesus Blesses Peter as the Foundation of the Church
17:24–27	Teaching on the Temple Tax
18:15–20	Calling One's Fellow to Account
18:21–22	How Many Times One Must Forgive
18:23–35	Parable of the Unforgiving Servant
20:1–15	Parable of the Laborers in the Vineyard
21:28–32	Parable of the Two Sons
23:1–2, 7b–12, 15–22, 24, 30	Sayings about the Pharisees
25:1–13	Parable of the Ten Bridesmaids
25:31–46	The Last Judgment
27:3–10	The Death of Judas
27:24–25	Pilate Washes His Hands, Blood Curse on the People
27:52–53	The Saints Are Raised
27:62–66; 28:11–15	The Guard at the Tomb
28:16–20	The Great Commission

Because the earliest known biblical manuscripts do not contain clear paragraphs or subtitles, section subtitles are always subject to editorial interpretation.

1 An account[a] of the genealogy[b] of Jesus the Messiah,[c] the son of David, the son of Abraham.

2 Abraham was the father of Isaac, and Isaac the father of Jacob, and Jacob the father of Judah and his brothers, [3]and Judah the father of Perez and Zerah by Tamar, and Perez the father of Hezron, and Hezron the father of Aram, [4]and Aram the father of Aminadab, and Aminadab the father of Nahshon, and Nahshon the father of Salmon, [5]and Salmon the father of Boaz by Rahab, and Boaz the father of Obed by Ruth, and Obed the father of Jesse, [6]and Jesse the father of King David.

And David was the father of Solomon by the wife of Uriah, [7]and Solomon the father of Rehoboam, and Rehoboam the father of Abijah, and Abijah the father of Asaph,[d] [8]and Asaph[e] the father of Jehoshaphat, and Jehoshaphat the father of Joram, and Joram the father of Uzziah, [9]and Uzziah the father of Jotham, and Jotham the father of Ahaz, and Ahaz the father of Hezekiah, [10]and Hezekiah the father of Manasseh, and Manasseh the father of Amos,[f] and Amos[g] the father of Josiah, [11]and Josiah the father of Jechoniah and his brothers, at the time of the deportation to Babylon.

12 And after the deportation to Babylon: Jechoniah was the father of Salathiel, and Salathiel the father of Zerubbabel, [13]and Zerubbabel the father of Abiud, and Abiud the father of Eliakim, and Eliakim the father of Azor, [14]and Azor the father of Zadok, and Zadok the father of Achim, and Achim the father of Eliud, [15]and Eliud the father of Eleazar, and Eleazar the father of Matthan, and Matthan the father of Jacob, [16]and Jacob the father of Joseph the husband of Mary, who bore Jesus, who is called the Messiah.[h]

17 So all the generations from Abraham to David are fourteen generations; and from David to the deportation to Babylon, fourteen generations; and from the deportation to Babylon to the Messiah,[i] fourteen generations.

18 Now the birth of Jesus the Messiah[j] took place in this way. When his mother

a 1.1 Or *A book*   *b* 1.1 Or *birth*   *c* 1.1 Or *Jesus Christ*
d 1.7 Other ancient authorities read *Asa*   *e* 1.8 Other ancient authorities read *Asa*   *f* 1.10 Other ancient authorities read *Amon*   *g* 1.10 Other ancient authorities read *Amon*
h 1.16 Or *the Christ*   *i* 1.17 Or *the Christ*   *j* 1.18 Or *Jesus Christ*

Matt. 1 introduces Jesus using an ancient literary form called a genealogy. The goal is to locate Jesus's ancestry squarely in the histories, cultures, and traditions of his tribe—the Israelites, Judeans, and Jews of biblical antiquity (see **"The Jews' (*Hoi Ioudaioi*)," p. 1852**). As the story unfolds, Jesus engages with other racial/ethnic groups like the Samaritans, Canaanites, and Romans. These interactions reveal the ethnocentric nature of Jesus's mission and ministry. The very language Matthew employs—Judean/Jew versus gentile—produces this tension throughout the narrative. By the end of the Gospel, the boundaries dissolve, and the ethnocentric focus of the mission is thrown wide open, making the kingdom available to any and all peoples.

1:1–17 A genealogy of the Judean/Jewish Messiah. 1:1 *Messiah* means "anointed one" in Hebrew and "Christ" ("christos") in Greek. The first verse of the Gospel identifies the central character of the *account* or book. The opening phrase, "an account of the genealogy," has a double function. First, as a literary device, the phrase introduces the genealogy and birth narrative as a focal point for the entire book. Second, the phrase provides an intertextual link to Genesis that ties the story of Jesus to God's act of creation (see **"Creation," p. 16**). **1:2** *Abraham was the father of Isaac.* The genealogy opens with two of the most recognizable figures in the biblical tradition: David and Abraham. Matthew thus foregrounds two competing themes in tension between racial/ethnic particularism and universalism. As "son of David," Jesus is firmly fixed in the Judean/Jewish line of King David. As "son of Abraham," Jesus is part of a larger story of God's promise to multiply Abraham's descendants, the Jews, but also understood as the progenitor of Christians (and later, Muslims). In this way, the very first sentence of the Gospel contains a clue for how God's promise to the Israelites of old finds fulfillment in Jesus. **1:17** *Fourteen generations.* Matthew organizes the genealogy in couplets of fourteen generations. On a literary level, the repetition creates symmetry. The number fourteen also corresponds to the numerical value of the Hebrew consonants ("dalet," "vav," "dalet") in David's name in Hebrew ("David"). Assigning numerical values according to an alphanumeric code is a literary practice known as gematria. But interestingly, the final genealogical list from Jeconiah to Joseph (1:12–16) only has thirteen names.

1:18–25 Jesus is born in Bethlehem of Judea. The dual emphasis on Jesus's divinity and Judean/Jewish ethnicity is foregrounded in the birth narrative. Jesus is conceived not by Joseph but by the Holy Spirit. Matthew gives a detailed account of the circumstances leading to Jesus's birth (1:18–25), his visit from the Magi (2:1–12), the escape to Egypt (2:13–15), the killing of Judean/Jewish infants (2:16–18),

Going Deeper: Race and Ethnicities in Biblical Genealogies (Matthew 1)

Biblical genealogies are important records that trace ancestral lineage and kinship ties. They reveal for modern readers how communities in antiquity understood and negotiated individual and collective identity. Race and ethnicity are modern notions that cannot be neatly mapped onto the biblical world (see **"The Bible, Race, and Ethnicity," pp. 2163–64**). Nevertheless, the practice of defining groups based on birth, language, culture, custom, geography, and ancestry was common in the ancient world.

Biblical genealogies exhibit a strategic negotiation of identity that moves between two poles of exclusion and inclusion, fission and fusion. At certain times, the boundaries of Israelite ethnicity were sharply defined to maintain distinctiveness (see **"Ethnicity (Zephaniah)," p. 1300**). This strategy of contracting boundaries was crucial in times of competition and conflict between groups. At other times, the racial/ethnic boundaries were broadened to be more inclusive. Both strategies are evident in Matthew's genealogy. Several variables are at work in how identities are constructed, for whom, and to what ends. Over time, these social categories are reified through religious, ethnic, and cultural customs and practices.

Four gentile women are named in Matthew's genealogy. This is remarkable not only due to gender (with the exception of 1 Chr. 1–9, most biblical genealogies do not include women; see **"Women in the Genealogy," p. 545**) and sexuality (see **"David and Bathsheba," p. 438** and **"The Rape of Tamar," p. 442**) but also on account of their status as racial/ethnic foreigners: Tamar, who is Canaanite (1:3); Rahab, who is Canaanite (1:5); Ruth, who is Moabite (1:5); and Bathsheba, who is married to a Hittite, and may be Israelite or Hittite herself (1:6). The identification of these non-Judean/Jewish women works in two ways. First, their inclusion indicates that gentiles exercise agency in the development of Israelite, Judean, Jewish history. Second, Jesus's bloodline becomes mixed: Jesus is not only part-Judean/Jewish; he is also part-Canaanite, part-Hittite, and part-Moabite.

Matthew's genealogy shows how the ethnicity of the ancient Israelites, Judeans, and Jews is expanded to include other races, nations, and people groups. In this way, the opening genealogy advances a key claim that the rest of the Gospel will unpack. Regardless of one's race, ethnicity, gender, national identity, or political affiliation, the kingdom of heaven is radically open to all peoples, nations, and ethnicities (28:19–20).

Wongi Park

Mary had been engaged to Joseph, but before they lived together, she was found to be pregnant from the Holy Spirit. [19]Her husband Joseph, being a righteous man and unwilling to expose her to public disgrace, planned to divorce her quietly. [20]But just when he had resolved to do this, an angel of the Lord appeared to him in a dream and said, "Joseph, son of David, do not be afraid to take Mary as your wife, for the child conceived in her is from the Holy Spirit. [21]She will bear a son, and you are to name him Jesus, for he will save his people from their sins." [22]All this took place to fulfill what had been spoken by the Lord through the prophet:
[23] "Look, the virgin shall become pregnant
    and give birth to a son,
    and they shall name him Emmanuel,"
which means, "God is with us." [24]When Joseph awoke from sleep, he did as the angel of the Lord commanded him; he took her as his wife [25]but had no marital relations with her until she had given birth to a son,[k] and he named him Jesus.

k 1.25 Other ancient authorities read *her firstborn son*

and settling in Nazareth (2:19–23). By contrast, Mark makes no mention of Jesus's birth. Bethlehem is also the hometown of David, an earlier messiah or "anointed one." **1:19** *Planned to divorce her quietly.* Marriage in ancient patriarchal societies was a contractual agreement between the father and groom, often in exchange for property. The arrangement was legally binding and could only be nullified by divorce (see Matt. 5:31–32; 19:1–9). **1:21** The Messiah is given two names. The first comes from an angel of the Lord: *You are to name him Jesus, for he will save his people from their sins* (1:21). Jesus in Hebrew ("Yehoshua'") is Joshua, which literally means "God saves." **1:23** *Look, the virgin shall become pregnant.* Of special note is the translation "young woman" ("'almah") in Hebrew (Isa. 7:14, MT) and "virgin" ("parthenos") in Greek (Isa. 7:14 LXX). By following the Greek Septuagint rather than the Hebrew Masoretic Text and emphasizing Mary's virginity, Matthew reads the prophecy of Isaiah as being fulfilled centuries later. The second name is based on a citation from Isa. 7:14: *"They shall name*

Focus On: Infancy Narratives (Matthew 1–2)

The infancy narratives in the Gospels of Matthew and Luke are some of the most familiar and beloved stories in the New Testament, the basis of countless hymns, Christmas pageants and nativities, and even *A Charlie Brown Christmas*. Most media combine, or "harmonize," two distinct stories of the birth of Jesus. Matthew's account (Matt. 1:18–2:23) focuses primarily on Joseph and his response to Mary's extraordinary pregnancy, which for Joseph, who is legally bound to Mary through betrothal, stretches the limits of credulity. He "planned to divorce her quietly" (Matt. 1:19), but divine intervention via angelic appearances and dreams guides his understanding and actions. Matthew also recounts the journey of the three magi and the paranoid rage of King Herod, who orders the mass murder of male children around Bethlehem. An angel tells Joseph in a dream to take his family to Egypt, where they remain as political refugees until after Herod's death.

Luke's infancy narrative focuses on Mary rather than Joseph. Mary receives an angelic announcement, then consents to the angel's shocking message that, though she is yet a virgin, she will conceive and give birth to Jesus (Luke 1:26–38). Mary speaks with prophetic insight, singing praises to God that echo the triumphant songs of her ancient sisters, Miriam, Deborah, and Hannah (Luke 1:39–56; see **"Songs of Mary and Her Ancient Sisters," p. 1806**, and **"Mary the Mother of Jesus," p. 1804**). The story follows Mary as she gives birth to Jesus, presents him in the temple, and raises her young son. Each infancy narrative establishes key themes that are central to its Gospel. Matthew emphasizes that the story of Jesus is grounded in scriptural tradition and as part of God's plan. Luke underscores how the gospel, also part of God's plan from the very beginning, runs counter to the norms of empire.

Early Christian writing includes extracanonical Infancy Gospels. The Infancy Gospel of Thomas tells the story of Jesus's early childhood between birth and age twelve, filling in the gap that Luke's infancy narrative leaves unaddressed. It depicts the very young Jesus as a bit of a hellion, but as Jesus matures, he grows in wisdom. The Protoevangelium of James draws heavily on the canonical Gospels for detail but addresses a question they do not raise: What kind of woman gave birth to Jesus? Written largely to praise Mary, it confirms Mary's moral virtue and sexual purity to show that the mother of Jesus was indeed of exemplary character.

Mary F. Foskett

2 In the time of King Herod, after Jesus was born in Bethlehem of Judea, magi*ᶦ* from the east came to Jerusalem, ²asking, "Where is the child who has been born king of the Jews? For we observed his star in the east*ᵐ* and have come to pay him homage." ³When King Herod heard this, he was frightened, and all Jerusalem with him, ⁴and calling together all the chief priests and scribes of the people, he inquired of them where the Messiah*ⁿ* was to be born. ⁵They told him, "In Bethlehem of Judea, for so it has been written by the prophet:

l 2.1 Or *astrologers*   *m* 2.2 Or *at its rising*   *n* 2.4 Or *the Christ*

him Emmanuel," which means, "God is with us" (1:23). Matthew's citation of Isa. 7:14 is nearly identical to the LXX. The second name introduces the theme of God's abiding presence. This motif is expressed as a chiasm, a literary device that frames the beginning and end of the Gospel at 1:23 and 28:20.

2:1–12 Magi visit and tensions build in Jerusalem. *Magi* is preferred over the traditional translation "wise men" indicating astrologers or other practitioners of the occult who could foretell the future. Philo, a Hellenistic Judean/Jewish philosopher, refers to a very unwise Balaam in Num. 22 as "magos" (see **"Balaam," p. 226**). Very little is known about them. A country of origin is not specified by Matthew. The only descriptor is that they are *from the east*. Suggestions range among Arabia, Persia, India, Mongolia, and China. The fact that the Magi return home by another road from a dream points to their subversive role. They outsmart Herod and escape. **2:2** *King of the Jews.* Ironically, the first recognition of Jesus as the Messiah does not come from Judean/Jewish insiders but rather from gentiles. **2:3** Both Herod and Jesus are referred to as kings. This explains why Herod *and all Jerusalem with him* were frightened by the birth of Jesus. The apprehensive response of Herod and the Jerusalem authorities anticipates the conflict between Jesus and Rome. Matthew places other clues that indicate growing tensions between Jesus and the imperial and religious authorities. This foreshadowing shapes the organization of events and presentation of characters to prepare the reader for what is to come.

Focus On: Israel's Scriptures in the New Testament (Matthew 1 and 2)

One practice during regular gatherings of Jewish and gentile Christ followers was to read the Scriptures of ancient Israel, which—as they claimed—"were written down to instruct us" (1 Cor. 10:11). The Hebrew Scriptures provide the basis of concepts like messiah, temple, Sabbath, and ritual purity, and Jesus and his followers adhered to their commandments. The Christ followers understood that the new experience of their belief in the Messiah Jesus required an alternative way of interpreting the Scriptures, which entailed opening their minds in a new direction (Luke 24:44–46). Many New Testament writers incorporate passages from the Old Testament (usually from the Greek translation of the Hebrew Bible) as they tell the story of Jesus (in the Gospels) or of early Christian communities (in Acts and the letters).

The first chapters in the Gospel of Matthew reflect an example of this literary activity. Matthew presents Jesus's conception (1:22–23), Jesus's birthplace (2:5–6), Joseph's migration to Egypt (2:15), and Herod's massacre of Bethlehem infants (2:17–18) as the fulfillment of the words of Israel's prophets. Among the Gospels' accounts, only Matthew emphasizes the "virgin" birth of Jesus (Matt. 1:25), a claim that stemmed from quoting the Greek version of Isa. 7:14. The Septuagint's Greek word (Gk. *parthenos* = "virgin, young woman") differs from the Hebrew (Heb. *almah* = "young woman"), which in turn may affect later developing theologies.

It is unsurprising that most New Testament books cite OT scriptural passages, providing evidence of the distinctive reading practices of first-century Christ followers, although readers would have varied in their familiarity with Jewish traditions and synagogue practices. Because of this diversity of membership, some scholars make distinctions between citations of Scripture preceded by formal identifying markers (e.g., "it is written" or "in order to fulfill the words of the prophet," suggesting those with more knowledge of Jewish tradition) and allusions to a variety of images or metaphors. The former technique is prominent in the Gospels, Hebrews, and in several of the Pauline materials. The latter can especially be seen in Revelation, for example, which provides dozens of allusions to the book of Daniel and other images but without any formal identifying mark for the cited passage.

Scholars also debate how much context of the cited passage audiences were expected to know in order to interpret properly. For contemporary readers, each passage should be analyzed with special attention to the present New Testament context in which the citation now finds itself.

Emerson B. Powery

6 'And you, Bethlehem, in the land of Judah,
are by no means least among the rulers
of Judah,
for from you shall come a ruler
who is to shepherd[o] my people Israel.'"
7 Then Herod secretly called for the magi[p]
and learned from them the exact time when
the star had appeared. 8 Then he sent them to
Bethlehem, saying, "Go and search diligently
for the child, and when you have found him,
bring me word so that I may also go and pay
him homage." 9 When they had heard the king,
they set out, and there, ahead of them, went
the star that they had seen in the east,[q] until
it stopped over the place where the child was.
10 When they saw that the star had stopped,[r]
they were overwhelmed with joy. 11 On entering the house, they saw the child with Mary
his mother, and they knelt down and paid him
homage. Then, opening their treasure chests,
they offered him gifts of gold, frankincense,
and myrrh. 12 And having been warned in a
dream not to return to Herod, they left for
their own country by another road.
13 Now after they had left, an angel of the
Lord appeared to Joseph in a dream and said,
"Get up, take the child and his mother, and
flee to Egypt, and remain there until I tell you,

o 2.6 Or *rule* *p* 2.7 Or *astrologers* *q* 2.9 Or *at its rising*
r 2.10 Gk *saw the star*

2:6 Matthew cites Mic. 5:2. **2:12** *Having been warned in a dream.* Dreams play a special role in the Gospel of Matthew. Already in 1:20–24, an angel of the Lord appears. Joseph is reassured that the child Mary is carrying is conceived from the Holy Spirit. Here, in chap. 2, the Magi and Joseph are warned not to return to King Herod (2:12–13, 19, 22). Later in the passion narrative, Pilate's wife has a distressing dream about Jesus. She offers a stern warning to Pilate: "Have nothing to do with that innocent man" (27:19).

2:13–21 Immigrating to Egypt. The flight to Egypt underscores the proximity and geographic connection of Egypt and Israel in the biblical tradition. On a literary level, the flight to Egypt provides a place of refuge for the holy family. When Herod realizes he has been duped by the Magi, he issues a decree to kill *all the children in and around Bethlehem who were two years old or under* (2:16). On a theological

Going Deeper: De-Africanizing the Bible (Matthew 2)

De-Africanizing the Bible refers to a pattern in the history of interpretation that denies the presence of African peoples, places, and nations in biblical narratives. Egypt is effectively removed from Africa and relocated as part of the Western world. Over and against this tendency, it is important to note that several African nations (Egypt, Cush/Ethiopia, Sheba, possibly Ophir) and characters (Nimrod, Amram, Hagar, queen of Sheba, Zipporah) were central to the stories and traditions of the Hebrew Bible / Old Testament and New Testament. The liberation of the Israelites from bondage is a prominent theological motif in biblical traditions, though the relationship between Israel and Egypt is mixed. On the one hand, Egypt is sometimes villainized as enemies who enslaved the Israelites for over four hundred years (Gen. 15:13; Exod. 12:40–41; Acts 7:6). On the other hand, Egypt is a place of refuge as is evident in the story of Matt. 2 (see 1 Kgs. 11:40; Jer. 26:21; 2 Macc. 1:1–9). The term "Egypt" is mentioned well over six hundred times in the Hebrew Bible and twenty-five times in the New Testament. With the exception of Canaan, no other location is referenced more than Egypt in biblical literature.

Wongi Park

for Herod is about to search for the child, to destroy him." [14]Then Joseph[s] got up, took the child and his mother by night, and went to Egypt [15]and remained there until the death of Herod. This was to fulfill what had been spoken by the Lord through the prophet, "Out of Egypt I have called my son."

16 When Herod saw that he had been tricked by the magi,[t] he was infuriated, and he sent and killed all the children in and around Bethlehem who were two years old or under, according to the time that he had learned from the magi.[u] [17]Then what had been spoken through the prophet Jeremiah was fulfilled:

[18] "A voice was heard in Ramah,
    wailing and loud lamentation,
  Rachel weeping for her children;
    she refused to be consoled, because
      they are no more."

19 When Herod died, an angel of the Lord suddenly appeared in a dream to Joseph in Egypt and said, [20]"Get up, take the child and his mother, and go to the land of Israel, for those who were seeking the child's life are dead." [21]Then Joseph[v] got up, took the child and his mother, and went to the land of Israel. [22]But when he heard that Archelaus was ruling Judea in place of his father Herod, he was afraid to go there. And after being warned in a dream, he went away to the district of Galilee. [23]There he made his home in a town called Nazareth, so that what had been spoken through the prophets might be fulfilled, "He will be called a Nazarene."[w]

3 In those days John the Baptist appeared in the wilderness of Judea, proclaiming, [2]"Repent, for the kingdom of heaven has come near."[x] [3]This is the one of whom the prophet Isaiah spoke when he said,

  "The voice of one crying out in the
      wilderness:
  'Prepare the way of the Lord;
    make his paths straight.'"

s 2.14 Gk he   t 2.16 Or astrologers   u 2.16 Or astrologers
v 2.21 Gk he   w 2.23 Gk Nazorean   x 3.2 Or is at hand

level, the flight to Egypt is reminiscent of the exodus and Israel's wandering in the desert (see **"The Exodus Event," p. 105**). Against this background, coupled with the fulfillment prophecy cited in v. 15, Matthew portrays Jesus as Moses. This theme is further developed in the Sermon on the Mount, where Jesus interprets the Torah (see **"Moses," p. 247**). He engages in debates about the finer points of the Law with the Pharisees and scribes. Later, Moses and Elijah make an appearance when Jesus is transfigured (17:1–13). The connection Matthew draws is clear: just as Moses delivered the Israelites of old, Jesus returns to the *land of Israel* (2:21) to liberate "his people from their sins" (1:21).

2:16–18 Infanticide in Jerusalem. *Rachel weeping for her children.* Matthew cites Jer. 31:15.

2:23 *He will be called a Nazarene.* A reference to Jesus and his family residing in Nazareth. At his trial, Peter denies being with "Jesus the Nazarene" (26:71).

3:1–12 John the Baptist preaches in the Judean wilderness. Matthew presents John the Baptist as a prophetic voice from the Judean wilderness with a citation from Isa. 40:3. **3:2** Matthew's use of the phrase *kingdom of heaven* in contrast to "kingdom of God" (Mark 1:15; Luke 7:28) captures his ethnically Judean/Jewish origins. The phrase stems from the Hebrew term for "heaven" and recalls the first words of Genesis: "When God began to create the heavens and the earth" (Gen. 1:1). The tense of the Greek

4Now John wore clothing of camel's hair with a leather belt around his waist, and his food was locusts and wild honey. 5Then Jerusalem and all Judea and all the region around the Jordan were going out to him, 6and they were baptized by him in the River Jordan, confessing their sins.

7 But when he saw many of the Pharisees and Sadducees coming for his[y] baptism, he said to them, "You brood of vipers! Who warned you to flee from the coming wrath? 8Therefore, bear fruit worthy of repentance, 9and do not presume to say to yourselves, 'We have Abraham as our ancestor,' for I tell you, God is able from these stones to raise up children to Abraham. 10Even now the ax is lying at the root of the trees; therefore every tree that does not bear good fruit will be cut down and thrown into the fire.

11 "I baptize you with[z] water for repentance, but the one who is coming after me is more powerful than I, and I am not worthy to carry his sandals. He will baptize you with[a] the Holy Spirit and fire. 12His winnowing fork is in his hand, and he will clear his threshing floor and will gather his wheat into the granary, but the chaff he will burn with unquenchable fire."

13 Then Jesus came from Galilee to John at the Jordan, to be baptized by him. 14John would have prevented him, saying, "I need to be baptized by you, and do you come to me?" 15But Jesus answered him, "Let it be so now, for it is proper for us in this way to fulfill all righteousness." Then he consented. 16And when Jesus had been baptized, just as he came up from the water, suddenly the heavens were opened to him and he saw God's Spirit descending like a dove and alighting on him. 17And a voice from the heavens said, "This is my Son, the Beloved,[b] with whom I am well pleased."

4 Then Jesus was led up by the Spirit into the wilderness to be tested by the devil. 2He fasted forty days and forty nights, and afterward he was famished. 3The tempter came and said to him, "If you are the Son of God, command these stones to become loaves of bread." 4But he answered, "It is written,

'One does not live by bread alone,
    but by every word that comes from the
        mouth of God.'"

5 Then the devil took him to the holy city and placed him on the pinnacle of the temple,

y 3.7 Other ancient authorities lack his   z 3.11 Or in
a 3.11 Or in   b 3.17 Or my beloved Son

verb for "to draw near" as a perfect active indicative indicates a process that has been initiated and will soon be fulfilled. A literal rendering of the phrase is "the kingdom of heaven is being fulfilled." **3:4** The description of John the Baptist's clothing, diet, and physical appearance is reminiscent of the prophet Elijah in 2 Kgs. 1:8. Later, in Matt. 11:13–14, the association is made explicit: "For all the Prophets and the Law prophesied until John came, and if you are willing to accept it, he is Elijah who is to come." With this comparison, Matthew places John the Baptist in the long line of prophets who have spoken truth to imperial power in Assyria, Babylonia, Greece, Persia, and in Matthew's day, the Roman Empire (see **"Speaking Truth to Power," p. 1264**). **3:7** *Pharisees and Sadducees . . . You brood of vipers!* The Pharisees are a Judean/Jewish sect that came to power during the Second Temple period (see **"Pharisees," p. 1756**). In Matthew, they are consistently portrayed as Jesus's rivals and engage in numerous debates concerning the interpretation of the Torah. Their authority was recognized by Rome at certain points as a group with influence and popularity with the people. The conflict between Jesus and the religious and imperial authorities, already foreshadowed in chap. 2, escalates in vv. 7–12. **3:8–9** *We have Abraham as our ancestor.* Abraham is highly regarded in the biblical tradition as the father of the Jews. John the Baptist provides a sharp challenge to the Pharisees and Sadducees. Neither biological descent from Abraham nor Jewish ethnicity by itself is a guarantee of salvation. Ethnicity is a crucial dimension of the biblical story of redemption. But what is required exceeds biology, ancestry, and genealogy: *fruit worthy of repentance* (3:8). **3:12** *Unquenchable fire.* See Matt. 3:10–12; 5:22; 7:19; 13:40, 42, 50; 18:8–9; 25:41.

3:13–17 The Davidic Son is baptized as the divine Son. 3:16 Just as the spirit of God swept over the face of the waters (Gen. 1:1–2), so too the spirit of God is present in the baptism of Jesus *descending like a dove.* **3:17** This verse marks the first occasion in the Matthean narrative where God speaks.

4:1–11 Jesus tempted in the Judean wilderness. See Mark 1:12–13; Luke 4:1–13. The story resembles a similar pattern of righteous people like Job being put to the test (**see "The Satan," p. 687**). Coincidentally, the allusions to the wilderness and forty nights recall the experiences of Moses (Exod. 34:28) and Elijah (1 Kgs. 19:8) and reinforce Jesus's identity as the Beloved (3:17).

⁶saying to him, "If you are the Son of God, throw yourself down, for it is written,

'He will command his angels concerning you,'

and 'On their hands they will bear you up,

so that you will not dash your foot against a stone.'"

⁷Jesus said to him, "Again it is written, 'Do not put the Lord your God to the test.'"

8 Again, the devil took him to a very high mountain and showed him all the kingdoms of the world and their glory, ⁹and he said to him, "All these I will give you, if you will fall down and worship me." ¹⁰Then Jesus said to him, "Away with you, Satan! for it is written,

'Worship the Lord your God,
    and serve only him.'"

¹¹Then the devil left him, and suddenly angels came and waited on him.

12 Now when Jesus° heard that John had been arrested, he withdrew to Galilee. ¹³He left Nazareth and made his home in Capernaum by the sea, in the territory of Zebulun and Naphtali, ¹⁴so that what had been spoken through the prophet Isaiah might be fulfilled:

¹⁵ "Land of Zebulun, land of Naphtali,
    on the road by the sea, across the
        Jordan, Galilee of the gentiles—
¹⁶ the people who sat in darkness
    have seen a great light,

and for those who sat in the region and
        shadow of death
    light has dawned."

¹⁷From that time Jesus began to proclaim, "Repent, for the kingdom of heaven has come near."ᵈ

18 As he walked by the Sea of Galilee, he saw two brothers, Simon, who is called Peter, and Andrew his brother, casting a net into the sea—for they were fishers. ¹⁹And he said to them, "Follow me, and I will make you fishers of people." ²⁰Immediately they left their nets and followed him. ²¹As he went from there, he saw two other brothers, James son of Zebedee and his brother John, in the boat with their father Zebedee, mending their nets, and he called them. ²²Immediately they left the boat and their father and followed him.

23 Jesusᵉ went throughout all Galilee, teaching in their synagogues and proclaiming the good newsᶠ of the kingdom and curing every disease and every sickness among the people. ²⁴So his fame spread throughout all Syria, and they brought to him all the sick, those who were afflicted with various diseases and pains, people possessed by demons or having epilepsy or afflicted with paralysis, and he cured them. ²⁵And great crowds followed him from Galilee, the Decapolis, Jerusalem, Judea, and from beyond the Jordan.

c 4.12 Gk *he* d 4.17 Or *is at hand* e 4.23 Gk *He* f 4.23 Gk *gospel*

4:12–17 Jesus begins his ministry in Galilee of the gentiles. **4:12** The Greek verb for "withdrew" is repeated throughout the Matthean narrative in contexts where danger is implied. Here, the arrest of John the Baptist poses an imminent threat (2:12–14; 12:15). Later, upon hearing the news of John the Baptist's death, Jesus "withdrew from there in a boat to a deserted place by himself" (14:13). **4:13** *He left Nazareth and made his home in Capernaum by the sea.* For other references to Capernaum, see 8:5; 11:23; 17:24. **4:17** *Kingdom of heaven.* Another possible translation that draws out the Roman imperial horizon of Matthew's Gospel is "empire" or "reign" **(see "Kingdom of God," p. 1772).**

4:18–22 Jesus gains his first followers. An example of gender-inclusive language is the phrase *fishers of people* (NRSVue) rather than "fishers of men" (RSV).

4:23–25 The gospel travels from Galilee to Syria. The literary genre of Matthew is that of a Gospel, which means "good news" ("euangelion")—a term that was frequently used in public decrees to announce military victories and other public matters. For instance, the term was used in an inscription from 9 BCE to refer to the birthday of the Roman emperor Augustus. Similar uses can be found in the Septuagint for presenting good tidings (Isa. 40:9). The term eventually became synonymous with narrative accounts of the life and ministry of Jesus. By the second century, the meaning of "Gospel" developed into a distinct literary genre in the writings of Justin Martyr. **4:24** The NRSVue adopts a modified translation that better aligns with modern sensibilities regarding physical abilities. Rather than identifying people with their disability ("demoniacs, epileptics, and paralytics," NRSV), the disability is characterized as an attribute of individuals: *people possessed by demons or having epilepsy or afflicted with paralysis* (see **"Isaiah and Disability," p. 974**).

5 When Jesus[g] saw the crowds, he went up the mountain, and after he sat down, his disciples came to him. [2]And he began to speak and taught them, saying:

[3] "Blessed are the poor in spirit, for theirs is the kingdom of heaven.

[4] "Blessed are those who mourn, for they will be comforted.

[5] "Blessed are the meek, for they will inherit the earth.

[6] "Blessed are those who hunger and thirst for righteousness, for they will be filled.

[7] "Blessed are the merciful, for they will receive mercy.

[8] "Blessed are the pure in heart, for they will see God.

[9] "Blessed are the peacemakers, for they will be called children of God.

[10] "Blessed are those who are persecuted for the sake of righteousness, for theirs is the kingdom of heaven.

[11] "Blessed are you when people revile you and persecute you and utter all kinds of evil against you falsely[h] on my account. [12]Rejoice and be glad, for your reward is great in heaven, for in the same way they persecuted the prophets who were before you.

[13] "You are the salt of the earth, but if salt has lost its taste, how can its saltiness be restored? It is no longer good for anything but is thrown out and trampled under foot.

[14] "You are the light of the world. A city built on a hill cannot be hid. [15]People do not light a lamp and put it under the bushel basket; rather, they put it on the lampstand, and it gives light to all in the house. [16]In the same way, let your light shine before others, so that they may see your good works and give glory to your Father in heaven.

[17] "Do not think that I have come to abolish the Law or the Prophets; I have come not to abolish but to fulfill. [18]For truly I tell you, until heaven and earth pass away, not one letter,[i] not one stroke of a letter, will pass from the law until all is accomplished. [19]Therefore, whoever breaks[j] one of the least of these commandments and teaches others to do the same will be called least in the kingdom of heaven, but whoever does them and teaches them will be called great in the kingdom of heaven. [20]For I tell you, unless your righteousness exceeds that of the scribes and Pharisees, you will never enter the kingdom of heaven.

[21] "You have heard that it was said to those of ancient times, 'You shall not murder,' and 'whoever murders shall be liable to judgment.' [22]But I say to you that if you are angry with a brother or sister,[k] you will be liable to judgment, and if you insult[l] a brother or sister, you will be liable to the council, and if you say, 'You fool,' you will be liable to the hell[m] of fire. [23]So when you are offering your gift at the altar, if you remember that your brother or sister has something against you, [24]leave your gift there before the altar and go; first be reconciled to your brother or sister, and then

g 5.1 Gk *he*   h 5.11 Other ancient authorities lack *falsely*
i 5.18 Gk *one iota*   j 5.19 Or *annuls*   k 5.22 Other ancient authorities add *without cause*   l 5.22 Gk *say Raca to* (an obscure term of abuse)   m 5.22 Gk *Gehenna*

Matt. 5–7 marks the first major discourse, or speech, in Matthew. The Sermon on the Mount is arguably the most famous sermon Jesus ever preached. So highly regarded was the Sermon on the Mount that Thomas Jefferson cited it as containing moral principles upon which the United States of America should be founded.

5:1–12 The Beatitudes. 5:6 *Righteousness* ("dikaiosynē") is an important term that occurs five times in the Sermon on the Mount (5:6, 10, 20; 6:1, 33). Another important term is the concept of *reward* (5:12, 46; 6:1, 2, 5, 16; 10:41–42; 20:8).

5:13–16 Salt of the earth and light of the world. In the ancient world, salt was commonly used for seasoning. It was used to season incense (Exod. 30:35) and offerings in liturgical settings (Lev. 2:13; Ezek. 43:24) and as a preservative. Salt was also a symbol of destruction and damnation as exemplified in the story of Lot's wife, who turned into a pillar of salt (Gen. 19:26). Bread and salt are symbols of welcome and blessing in Middle Eastern and Slavic cultures.

5:17–20 The Torah and the Prophets. Jesus makes it abundantly clear he has not come to *abolish the Law or the Prophets*. Rather, he presents his own interpretations of the Mosaic law. Throughout the Sermon on the Mount, Jesus differentiates his teaching from *the scribes and Pharisees*. This is reinforced by Matthew at the conclusion of the Sermon on the Mount, where "the crowds were astounded at his teaching, for he taught them as one having authority and not as their scribes" (7:28–29).

5:21–26 Anger is premeditated murder. *You have heard that it was said to those of ancient times. . . . But I say to you.* This is a refrain that Jesus uses to show what is distinctive about his interpretation

come and offer your gift. [25]Come to terms quickly with your accuser while you are on the way to court[n] with him, or your accuser may hand you over to the judge and the judge to the guard, and you will be thrown into prison. [26]Truly I tell you, you will never get out until you have paid the last penny.

27 "You have heard that it was said, 'You shall not commit adultery.' [28]But I say to you that everyone who looks at a woman with lust has already committed adultery with her in his heart. [29]If your right eye causes you to sin,[o] tear it out and throw it away; it is better for you to lose one of your members than for your whole body to be thrown into hell.[p] [30]And if your right hand causes you to sin,[q] cut it off and throw it away; it is better for you to lose one of your members than for your whole body to go into hell.[r]

31 "It was also said, 'Whoever divorces his wife, let him give her a certificate of divorce.' [32]But I say to you that anyone who divorces his wife, except on the ground of sexual immorality, causes her to commit adultery, and whoever marries a divorced woman commits adultery.

33 "Again, you have heard that it was said to those of ancient times, 'You shall not swear falsely, but carry out the vows you have made to the Lord.' [34]But I say to you: Do not swear at all, either by heaven, for it is the throne of God, [35]or by the earth, for it is his footstool, or by Jerusalem, for it is the city of the great King. [36]And do not swear by your head, for you cannot make one hair white or black. [37]Let your word be 'Yes, Yes' or 'No, No'; anything more than this comes from the evil one.[s]

38 "You have heard that it was said, 'An eye for an eye and a tooth for a tooth.' [39]But I say to you: Do not resist an evildoer. But if anyone strikes you on the right cheek, turn the other also, [40]and if anyone wants to sue you and take your shirt, give your coat as well, [41]and if anyone forces you to go one mile, go also the second mile. [42]Give to the one who asks of you, and do not refuse anyone who wants to borrow from you.

43 "You have heard that it was said, 'You shall love your neighbor and hate your enemy.' [44]But I say to you: Love your enemies and pray for those who persecute you, [45]so that you may be children of your Father in heaven, for he makes his sun rise on the evil and on the good and sends rain on the righteous and on the unrighteous. [46]For if you love those who

n 5.25 Gk lacks *to court* *o* 5.29 Or *stumble* *p* 5.29 Gk *Gehenna* *q* 5.30 Or *stumble* *r* 5.30 Gk *Gehenna* *s* 5.37 Or *evil*

of the Mosaic law, which is far more radical and demanding than the Pharisees'. **5:25** In a surprising twist, Jesus places the onus not only on the perpetrator but also on the victim. Reconciliation is the responsibility of both parties.

5:27–30 Adultery begins with the eyes. *With lust* ("epithymeō") means to desire, long for, lust after (see **"Sex, Desire, and Eroticism," p. 927**). The same word occurs in Matt. 13:17.

5:31–32 The grounds for divorce. See Matt. 19:1–12. Here too, Jesus's teaching on divorce is stricter than Torah law or later rabbinic law.

5:33–37 Swearing falsely. 5:35 *Jerusalem.* A theological interpretation of this passage, common during the period of the early church fathers, identifies four senses of Scripture: literal, allegorical, moral, and anagogic. For example, John Caspian (ca. 360–435) interprets *Jerusalem* as having four different dimensions: first, as the city of the Jews; second, as an allegory for the church; third, as an anagoge of the heavenly city of God; and fourth, as representing the human soul.

5:38–42 Turn the other cheek. 5:39 Similar ideas of doing good to one's enemy appear in Prov. 25:21. **5:42** See Deut. 15:8, which commands generosity to all.

5:43–48 Do not hate your enemies like the gentiles. The Sermon on the Mount is addressed from an insider's perspective that sharply differentiates Judeans/Jews from gentiles (literally "nations," meaning non-Jews). This is a significant thread in the broader scope of the Gospel. At this point in the narrative, Jesus privileges his own people (including the Pharisees, scribes, and elders) and opposes gentiles. Two main clues highlight this insider's perspective in the Sermon on the Mount, as signaled by the Greek term "gentile" ("ethnikos") in 5:47; 6:7; see 18:17. The first clue is 5:46–47: *For if you love those who love you, what reward do you have? Do not even the tax collectors do the same? And if you greet only your brothers and sisters, what more are you doing than others? Do not even the gentiles* ["ethnikos"] *do the same?* Here, Jesus displays a pejorative and prejudiced view of racial/ethnic outsiders. The implication is that those to whom Jesus is speaking are not, at least from an insider's perspective. Rather, in all likelihood, they are Judeans/Jews ("Ioudaios"; see **"'The Jews' (*Hoi Ioudaioi*),"**

love you, what reward do you have? Do not even the tax collectors do the same? [47]And if you greet only your brothers and sisters, what more are you doing than others? Do not even the gentiles do the same? [48]Be perfect, therefore, as your heavenly Father is perfect.

6 "Beware of practicing your righteousness before others in order to be seen by them, for then you have no reward from your Father in heaven.

2 "So whenever you give alms, do not sound a trumpet before you, as the hypocrites do in the synagogues and in the streets, so that they may be praised by others. Truly I tell you, they have received their reward. [3]But when you give alms, do not let your left hand know what your right hand is doing, [4]so that your alms may be done in secret, and your Father who sees in secret will reward you.[t]

5 "And whenever you pray, do not be like the hypocrites, for they love to stand and pray in the synagogues and at the street corners, so that they may be seen by others. Truly I tell you, they have received their reward. [6]But whenever you pray, go into your room and shut the door and pray to your Father who is in secret, and your Father who sees in secret will reward you.[u]

7 "When you are praying, do not heap up empty phrases as the gentiles do, for they think that they will be heard because of their many words. [8]Do not be like them, for your Father knows what you need before you ask him.

9 "Pray, then, in this way:
Our Father in heaven,
    may your name be revered as holy.
[10]   May your kingdom come.
    May your will be done
      on earth as it is in heaven.
[11]   Give us today our daily bread.[v]
[12]   And forgive us our debts,
    as we also have forgiven our debtors.
[13]   And do not bring us to the time of trial,[w]
    but rescue us from the evil one.[x]
[14]"For if you forgive others their trespasses, your heavenly Father will also forgive you, [15]but if you do not forgive others,[y] neither will your Father forgive your trespasses.

16 "And whenever you fast, do not look somber, like the hypocrites, for they mark their faces to show others that they are fasting. Truly I tell you, they have received their reward. [17]But when you fast, put oil on your head and wash your face, [18]so that your fasting may be seen not by others but by your Father who is in secret, and your Father who sees in secret will reward you.[z]

19 "Do not store up for yourselves treasures on earth, where moth and rust[a] consume and where thieves break in and steal, [20]but store up for yourselves treasures in heaven, where

t 6.4 Other ancient authorities add *openly* *u* 6.6 Other ancient authorities add *openly* *v* 6.11 Or *our bread for tomorrow* *w* 6.13 Or *us into testing* *x* 6.13 Or *from evil.* Other ancient authorities add, in some form, *For the kingdom and the power and the glory are yours forever. Amen.* *y* 6.15 Other ancient authorities add *their trespasses* *z* 6.18 Other ancient authorities add *openly* *a* 6.19 Gk *eating*

p. 1852). The contrast between "gentile" ("ethnikos") and the language of kinship (v. 47) confirms this point. **5:48** This verse provides a summary of vv. 21–47 that encapsulates Jesus's teaching on the Law and the Prophets.

6:1–4 Give in secret. An important pair of opposing themes in the Sermon on the Mount are hypocrisy and secrecy. Performing acts of charity publicly to be seen by others is to have one's "reward." But true reward comes not from being seen by others. Hence Jesus sternly warns *do not sound a trumpet before you* (v. 2) and *do not let your left hand know what your right hand is doing* (v. 3).

6:5–15 Do not pray like the gentiles. A second clue that signals an insider's perspective is v. 7: *When you are praying, do not heap up empty phrases as the gentiles do, for they think that they will be heard because of their many words.* Again, the inference seems sufficiently clear that "gentile" ("ethnikos") functions as a racial/ethnic boundary marker, distinguishing ethnic outsiders from insiders—that is, non-Judeans from Judeans. The pejorative connotation of this verse is clear: Jesus is telling his Judean followers to be better than the gentiles, a pattern that develops and builds throughout the narrative. **6:9–13 Lord's Prayer.** A notable feature of the Lord's Prayer is the invocation, "Our Father" ("Father" in Luke 11:2). The first petition acknowledges the holiness and reverence of God's name. The second and third petitions invoke the coming reign and will of God on earth and in heaven. The fourth petition is regarding daily sustenance. The fifth petition is a reciprocal request for forgiving debts. The final petition is for deliverance from the evil one. Together, these petitions provide direct and personal access to God. Luke's version of the prayer is significantly shorter (Luke 11:2–4).

neither moth nor rust[b] consumes and where thieves do not break in and steal. [21]For where your treasure is, there your heart will be also.

[22] "The eye is the lamp of the body. So if your eye is healthy, your whole body will be full of light, [23]but if your eye is unhealthy, your whole body will be full of darkness. If, then, the light in you is darkness, how great is the darkness!

[24] "No one can serve two masters, for a slave will either hate the one and love the other or be devoted to the one and despise the other. You cannot serve God and wealth.[c]

[25] "Therefore I tell you, do not worry about your life, what you will eat or what you will drink,[d] or about your body, what you will wear. Is not life more than food and the body more than clothing? [26]Look at the birds of the air: they neither sow nor reap nor gather into barns, and yet your heavenly Father feeds them. Are you not of more value than they? [27]And which of you by worrying can add a single hour to your span of life?[e] [28]And why do you worry about clothing? Consider the lilies of the field, how they grow; they neither toil nor spin, [29]yet I tell you, even Solomon in all his glory was not clothed like one of these. [30]But if God so clothes the grass of the field, which is alive today and tomorrow is thrown into the oven, will he not much more clothe you—you of little faith? [31]Therefore do not worry, saying, 'What will we eat?' or 'What will we drink?' or 'What will we wear?' [32]For it is the gentiles who seek all these things, and indeed your heavenly Father knows that you need all these things. [33]But seek first the kingdom of God[f] and his[g] righteousness, and all these things will be given to you as well.

[34] "So do not worry about tomorrow, for tomorrow will bring worries of its own. Today's trouble is enough for today.

7 "Do not judge, so that you may not be judged. [2]For the judgment you give will be the judgment you get, and the measure you give will be the measure you get. [3]Why do you see the speck in your neighbor's eye but do not notice the log in your own eye? [4]Or how can you say to your neighbor, 'Let me take the speck out of your eye,' while the log is in your own eye? [5]You hypocrite, first take the log out of your own eye, and then you will see clearly to take the speck out of your neighbor's eye.

[6] "Do not give what is holy to dogs, and do not throw your pearls before swine, or they will trample them under foot and turn and maul you.

[7] "Ask, and it will be given to you; search, and you will find; knock, and the door will be opened for you. [8]For everyone who asks receives, and everyone who searches finds, and for everyone who knocks, the door will be opened. [9]Is there anyone among you who, if your child asked for bread, would give a stone? [10]Or if the child asked for a fish, would give a snake? [11]If you, then, who are evil, know how to give good gifts to your children, how much more will your Father in heaven give good things to those who ask him!

[12] "In everything do to others as you would have them do to you, for this is the Law and the Prophets.

b 6.20 Gk *eating*   *c* 6.24 Gk *mammon*   *d* 6.25 Other ancient authorities lack *or what you will drink*   *e* 6.27 Or *add one cubit to your height*   *f* 6.33 Other ancient authorities lack *of God*   *g* 6.33 Or *its*

6:22–23 The eye. *The eye is the lamp of the body.* In the ancient world, the eye was a metaphor for a person's conduct and character. A healthy eye is clear and transparent without prejudice or ulterior motives. A good eye provides beams of light that make vision possible, says the noncanonical source 1 En. 106:2.

6:25–34 Do not worry like the gentiles. Jesus affirms the need for life's basic necessities such as food, drink, and clothing. But focusing on these things only adds suffering. Instead, Jesus encourages trust in God by comparing the birds of the air and lilies of the field: *Are you not of more value than they?* (v. 26). The cure to anxiety lies in seeking first the kingdom of God (v. 33). It lies in recognizing that *today's trouble is enough for today* (v. 34) rather than being preoccupied with the past or future.

7:1–5 Double standards. Hypocrisy is a matter of false pretenses and appearances. Judging others more harshly than yourself is a double standard Jesus warns against. Again, the visual dimension of the eye from 6:22–23 underscores the act of perceiving oneself more highly than others.

7:6 Cleanliness is next to godliness. Dogs and swine were considered unholy and unclean. This verse provides a parallel to the story of the Canaanite woman when Jesus compares her to a dog (15:26–27).

7:7–11 Ask, search, and knock. *If you, then, who are evil . . . how much more will your Father in heaven.* Jesus's argument moves from the lesser to the greater. A similar rhetorical move is found earlier (6:30).

7:12 A summary of the Torah and Prophets. The entirety of the Law and the Prophets is encapsulated

13 "Enter through the narrow gate, for the gate is wide and the road is easy[b] that leads to destruction, and there are many who take it. [14]For the gate is narrow and the road is hard that leads to life, and there are few who find it.

15 "Beware of false prophets, who come to you in sheep's clothing but inwardly are ravenous wolves. [16]You will know them by their fruits. Are grapes gathered from thorns or figs from thistles? [17]In the same way, every good tree bears good fruit, but the bad tree bears bad fruit. [18]A good tree cannot bear bad fruit, nor can a bad tree bear good fruit. [19]Every tree that does not bear good fruit will be cut down and thrown into the fire. [20]Thus you will know them by their fruits.

21 "Not everyone who says to me, 'Lord, Lord,' will enter the kingdom of heaven, but only the one who does the will of my Father in heaven. [22]On that day many will say to me, 'Lord, Lord, did we not prophesy in your name, and cast out demons in your name, and do many mighty works in your name?' [23]Then I will declare to them, 'I never knew you; go away from me, you who behave lawlessly.'

24 "Everyone, then, who hears these words of mine and acts on them will be like a wise man who built his house on rock. [25]The rain fell, the floods came, and the winds blew and beat on that house, but it did not fall because it had been founded on rock. [26]And everyone who hears these words of mine and does not act on them will be like a foolish man who built his house on sand. [27]The rain fell, and the floods came, and the winds blew and beat against that house, and it fell—and great was its fall!"

28 Now when Jesus had finished saying these words, the crowds were astounded at his teaching, [29]for he taught them as one having authority and not as their scribes.

8 When Jesus[i] had come down from the mountain, great crowds followed him, [2]and there was a man with a skin disease who came to him and knelt before him, saying, "Lord, if you are willing, you can make me clean." [3]He stretched out his hand and touched him, saying, "I am willing. Be made clean!" Immediately his skin disease was cleansed. [4]Then Jesus said to him, "See that you say nothing to anyone, but go, show yourself to the priest, and offer the gift that Moses commanded, as a testimony to them."

5 When he entered Capernaum, a centurion came to him, appealing to him [6]and saying, "Lord, my servant[j] is lying at home paralyzed, in terrible distress." [7]And he said to him, "I

b 7.13 Other ancient authorities read *for the road is wide and easy*   i 8.1 Gk *he*   j 8.6 Or *child*

in one's treatment of the other: *Do to others as you would have them do to you.* See **"Law/Decalogue," p. 112**.

7:15–20 Beware of false prophets. See also Matt. 24:11; Mark 13:22; 2 Pet. 2:1; 1 John 4:1. Itinerant holy men, magicians, and philosophers populated the ancient world, offering relief to struggling individuals.

7:21–23 Beware of false disciples. The repetition *Lord, Lord*, a double vocative, is a sign of sincerity.

7:29 While Matthew's introduction gives the impression that Jesus retreats from the crowds (5:1), the conclusion indicates that the crowds are in fact present (7:28–29). The crowds are amazed by Jesus's teaching, *for he taught them as one having authority and not as their scribes.* This concludes the Sermon on the Mount (chaps. 5–7), the first of five major discourses in Matthew. In chaps. 5–7, Jesus speaks; in chaps. 8–9, Jesus acts.

8:1–4 Jesus heals a man with a skin disease. Leprosy can refer to one of many skin diseases, including psoriasis, lupus, eczema, vitiligo, and favus. Two famous stories in the Hebrew Bible of lepers being healed are Miriam in Num. 12 and Naaman in 2 Kgs. 5. **8:2** The NRSVue prefers a translation that does not equate the disease with the individual: *there was a man with a skin disease* (cf. "leper," NRSV; see also 4:24). **8:4** It is unclear why Jesus says to the man, *See that you say nothing to anyone.* Scholars associate this tradition with the messianic secret motif in Mark. Jesus commanded his followers and even the demons to not divulge his divine identity as the Messiah. *Offer the gift that Moses commanded* is a reference to offerings for the cleansing of a leper in Lev. 14:10–32. Since lepers were ritually unclean, the pronouncement of a priest was necessary to be incorporated back into society (see **"Holiness and Purity," p. 158**).

8:5–13 Jesus heals the servant of a gentile. A striking aspect of this episode is the power differential between Jesus and the centurion. A centurion was an officer in charge of one hundred Roman soldiers. Yet the Roman centurion acknowledges the authority of a Judean/Jewish teacher. Jesus's response is emphatic: *Truly I tell you, in no one in Israel have I found such faith* (v. 10). This episode marks Jesus's

will come and cure him." [8]The centurion answered, "Lord, I am not worthy to have you come under my roof, but only speak the word, and my servant[k] will be healed. [9]For I also am a man under authority, with soldiers under me, and I say to one, 'Go,' and he goes, and to another, 'Come,' and he comes, and to my slave, 'Do this,' and the slave does it." [10]When Jesus heard him, he was amazed and said to those who followed him, "Truly I tell you, in no one[l] in Israel have I found such faith. [11]I tell you, many will come from east and west and will take their places at the banquet with Abraham and Isaac and Jacob in the kingdom of heaven, [12]while the heirs of the kingdom will be thrown into the outer darkness, where there will be weeping and gnashing of teeth." [13]And Jesus said to the centurion, "Go; let it be done for you according to your faith." And the servant[m] was healed in that hour.

[14] When Jesus entered Peter's house, he saw his mother-in-law lying in bed with a fever; [15]he touched her hand, and the fever left her, and she got up and began to serve him. [16]That evening they brought to him many who were possessed by demons, and he cast out the spirits with a word and cured all who were sick. [17]This was to fulfill what had been spoken through the prophet Isaiah, "He took our infirmities and bore our diseases."

[18] Now when Jesus saw great crowds[n] around him, he gave orders to go over to the other side. [19]A scribe then approached and said, "Teacher, I will follow you wherever you go." [20]And Jesus said to him, "Foxes have holes, and birds of the air have nests, but the Son of Man has nowhere to lay his head." [21]Another of his disciples said to him, "Lord, first let me go and bury my father." [22]But Jesus said to him, "Follow me, and let the dead bury their own dead."

[23] And when he got into the boat, his disciples followed him. [24]A windstorm suddenly arose on the sea, so great that the boat was being swamped by the waves, but he was asleep. [25]And they went and woke him up, saying, "Lord, save us! We are perishing!" [26]And he said to them, "Why are you afraid, you of little faith?" Then he got up and rebuked the winds and the sea, and there was a dead calm. [27]They were amazed, saying, "What sort of man is this, that even the winds and the sea obey him?"

[28] When he came to the other side, to the region of the Gadarenes,[o] two men possessed by demons came out of the tombs and met

k 8.8 Or *child* l 8.10 Other ancient authorities read *Truly I tell you, not even* m 8.13 Or *child* n 8.18 Other ancient authorities read *a crowd* o 8.28 Other ancient authorities read *Gergesenes* or *Gerasenes*

first encounter healing a non-Judean/Jewish gentile on the basis of their faith. A second encounter is with the Canaanite woman in 15:21–28. Both scenes anticipate the conclusion of the Gospel, where gentiles, as racial/ethnic outsiders, are included in the divine promise of salvation made to Israel. **8:11** The reference to *east and west* highlights the eschatological nature of the final banquet where Judeans, Jews, Israelites, and gentiles will partake in the banquet. **8:12** *Heirs of the kingdom will be thrown into the outer darkness.* The word translated as *heirs* is the same Greek term for "sons" or "children." This is probably a reference to other Judeans/Jews, not to Israel as a whole, and suggests that Matthew engaged in intramural debates with others around him about Jesus's status and significance within Judaism. Earlier John the Baptist warned that the "ax" is laid at the root of the tree (3:10). Later, Jesus refers to himself and his disciples as saying, "The children are free" (17:26). *Weeping and gnashing of teeth* occurs a total of six times in the context of divine judgment (8:12; 13:42, 50; 22:13; 24:51; 25:30).

8:14–17 Jesus heals Peter's mother-in-law. The citation in v. 17 comes from Isa. 53:4 and portrays Jesus as the suffering servant with sympathy for the poor and oppressed (see **"Isaiah and Jesus," p. 951**).

8:18–22 The difficulty of following Jesus. This brief section highlights the difficulty of following Jesus with both negative and positive examples. Jesus's itinerant ministry is not bound to a certain location or region. The call to follow Jesus is so urgent that it supersedes even the most sacred duties of burying the dead.

8:23–27 Jesus has authority over the storm. *They were amazed, saying, "What sort of man is this, that even the winds and the sea obey him?"* The verb "amazed" is the same word used to describe Jesus's reaction to the Roman centurion (8:10) and Pilate's response to Jesus's silence before his accusers (27:14). In Mark, the response is not amazement, but rather "they were filled with great fear" (Mark 4:41; cf. Luke 8:25).

8:28–34 Jesus casts out demons into swine. The region of the Gadarenes is a gentile town located about six miles southeast of the Sea of Galilee.

him. They were so fierce that no one could pass that way. [29]Suddenly they shouted, "What have you to do with us, Son of God? Have you come here to torment us before the time?" [30]Now a large herd of swine was feeding at some distance from them. [31]The demons begged him, "If you cast us out, send us into the herd of swine." [32]And he said to them, "Go!" So they came out and entered the swine, and suddenly, the whole herd stampeded down the steep bank into the sea and drowned in the water. [33]The swineherds ran off, and, going into the town, they told the whole story about what had happened to the men possessed by demons. [34]Then the whole town came out to meet Jesus, and when they saw him they begged him to leave their region. [1]And after getting into a boat he crossed the sea and came to his own town.

9

[2] And some people were carrying to him a paralyzed man lying on a stretcher. When Jesus saw their faith, he said to the paralytic, "Take heart, child; your sins are forgiven." [3]Then some of the scribes said to themselves, "This man is blaspheming." [4]But Jesus, perceiving their thoughts, said, "Why do you think evil in your hearts? [5]For which is easier: to say, 'Your sins are forgiven,' or to say, 'Stand up and walk'? [6]But so that you may know that the Son of Man has authority on earth to forgive sins"—he then said to the paralytic—"Stand up, take your bed, and go

to your home." [7]And he stood up and went to his home. [8]When the crowds saw it, they were filled with awe, and they glorified God, who had given such authority to human beings.

[9] As Jesus was walking along, he saw a man called Matthew sitting at the tax-collection station, and he said to him, "Follow me." And he got up and followed him.

[10] And as he sat at dinner[p] in the house, many tax collectors and sinners came and were sitting[q] with Jesus and his disciples. [11]When the Pharisees saw this, they said to his disciples, "Why does your teacher eat with tax collectors and sinners?" [12]But when he heard this, he said, "Those who are well have no need of a physician, but those who are sick. [13]Go and learn what this means, 'I desire mercy, not sacrifice.' For I have not come to call the righteous but sinners."

[14] Then the disciples of John came to him, saying, "Why do we and the Pharisees fast often,[r] but your disciples do not fast?" [15]And Jesus said to them, "The wedding attendants cannot mourn as long as the bridegroom is with them, can they? The days will come when the bridegroom is taken away from them, and then they will fast. [16]No one sews a piece of unshrunk cloth on an old cloak, for the patch pulls away from the cloak, and a worse tear is made. [17]Neither is new wine put into old wineskins; otherwise, the skins burst, and the wine

p 9.10 Gk *reclined* *q* 9.10 Gk *were reclining* *r* 9.14 Other ancient authorities lack *often*

9:3 *This man is blaspheming.* The charge of blasphemy in the Hebrew Bible normally means showing disrespect to God or misusing the divine name and could result in death (Lev. 24:15–16).

9:4 *But Jesus, perceiving their thoughts.* The ability to probe hearts and minds is attributed to God (2 Chr. 6:30). Jesus displays the same ability in this scene, later in his passion predictions, and in the passion narrative (26:2, 45–46).

9:9–13 Jesus calls Matthew. Scholars use a tool called redaction criticism to highlight distinct wording, themes, and points of emphasis in each Gospel. By identifying how Matthew differs from Mark, readers can appreciate how and to what end Matthew added, omitted, and redacted his source material (see **"The Bible and Methods," pp. 2148–49**). In Mark 2:14, Levi son of Alphaeus is called. But here, it is Matthew who is called by Jesus. This deliberate change has led many scholars to believe that Matthew has inserted himself into the story as a kind of authorial signature. But Matthew, unlike Luke, does not make a claim to authorship. **9:9** *A man called Matthew.* The name "Matthew" in Greek ("Mathaios") is a possible wordplay on the term "disciple" ("mathētēs"), which means "learner." **9:13** The quotation is from Hos. 6:6, which reads, "For I desire steadfast love and not sacrifice, the knowledge of God rather than burnt offerings." Matthew cites the Septuagint. As important as it is to perform ritual sacrifices (see **"Offerings and Sacrifices," p. 146**), showing mercy is even more significant.

9:14–17 The disciples of John ask Jesus about fasting. Jesus responds to the disciples of John with three separate metaphors (wedding, clothing, and wine) that suggest that fasting at this time, when Jesus is with them, is unsuitable. By the time Mark and Matthew are writing, fasting among Christ followers may have been more common.

is spilled, and the skins are ruined, but new wine is put into fresh wineskins, and so both are preserved."

18 While he was saying these things to them, suddenly a leader came in and knelt before him, saying, "My daughter has just died, but come and lay your hand on her, and she will live." ¹⁹And Jesus got up and followed him, with his disciples. ²⁰Then suddenly a woman who had been suffering from a flow of blood for twelve years came up behind him and touched the fringe of his cloak, ²¹for she was saying to herself, "If I only touch his cloak, I will be made well." ²²Jesus turned, and seeing her he said, "Take heart, daughter; your faith has made you well." And the woman was made well from that moment. ²³When Jesus came to the leader's house and saw the flute players and the crowd making a commotion, ²⁴he said, "Go away, for the girl is not dead but sleeping." And they laughed at him. ²⁵But when the crowd had been put outside, he went in and took her by the hand, and the girl got up. ²⁶And the report of this spread through all of that district.

27 As Jesus went on from there, two blind men followed him, crying loudly, "Have mercy on us, Son of David!" ²⁸When he entered the house, the blind men came to him, and Jesus said to them, "Do you have faith that I can do this?" They said to him, "Yes, Lord." ²⁹Then he touched their eyes and said, "According to

your faith, let it be done to you." ³⁰And their eyes were opened. Then Jesus sternly ordered them, "See that no one knows of this." ³¹But they went away and spread the news about him through all of that district.

32 After they had gone away, a demon-possessed man who was mute was brought to him. ³³And when the demon had been cast out, the one who had been mute spoke, and the crowds were amazed and said, "Never has anything like this been seen in Israel." ³⁴But the Pharisees were saying, "By the ruler of the demons he casts out the demons."

35 Then Jesus went about all the cities and villages, teaching in their synagogues and proclaiming the good news of the kingdom and curing every disease and every sickness. ³⁶When he saw the crowds, he had compassion for them because they were harassed and helpless, like sheep without a shepherd. ³⁷Then he said to his disciples, "The harvest is plentiful, but the laborers are few; ³⁸therefore ask the Lord of the harvest to send out laborers into his harvest."

10 Then Jesus⁵ summoned his twelve disciples and gave them authority over unclean spirits, to cast them out, and to cure every disease and every sickness. ²These are

s 10.1 Gk *he*

9:18–26 **Jesus raises a girl from the dead.** The word "ruler" ("archōn") describes the individual who petitions Jesus (vv. 18, 23).

9:27–31 **Jesus heals two blind men.** Jesus's identity as the "son of David" is established in the genealogy (1:1). An essential part of that identity lies in Jesus's power to bring healing and restoration.

9:32–34 **The Pharisees accuse Jesus of being a ruler of the demons.** The same word "ruler" that occurs in vv. 18, 23 is also used in the accusation against Jesus as the *ruler of the demons* (v. 34; 12:24; cf. 20:25).

9:35–38 **Jesus has compassion on the crowds.** *Like sheep without a shepherd.* Like a good shepherd (Ps. 23), Jesus is filled with compassion for the crowds. **9:35** The reference to *their synagogues* (4:23; 9:35; 10:17; 12:9; 13:54) may be evidence of growing tensions that developed between Jesus, the Pharisees, and other Judean/Jewish authorities in Jerusalem. The extent of the conflict is open for debate. Many scholars read Matthew as writing to a gentile audience of Christ followers in a movement that has severed ties with the Judean/Jewish synagogue. The repetition of "*their synagogues*" is evidence that a breach has already occurred. But a significant number of scholars read Matthew and some in his church as continuing to identify as Jews and Matthew as writing to a mixed Judean/Jewish and gentile audience. According to this understanding, the Gospel of Matthew is a counter-narrative in active resistance to the nascent rabbinic movement. **9:37** *The harvest is plentiful, but the laborers are few.* This verse anticipates the mission to Israel in the next chapter. Jesus sends his disciples out, saying, "Laborers deserve their food" (10:10).

10:1–4 **The twelve disciples are called and commissioned.** The number twelve has special significance throughout the biblical tradition, and Matthew draws on this number in a few different ways. Just as there are twelve tribes of Israel, twelve disciples are named in Matt. 10. Similarly, there are twelve fulfillment citations that Matthew uses to show how prophecies in the Old Testament / Hebrew Bible

the names of the twelve apostles: first, Simon, also known as Peter, and his brother Andrew; James son of Zebedee and his brother John; [3]Philip and Bartholomew; Thomas and Matthew the tax collector; James son of Alphaeus and Thaddaeus;[t] [4]Simon the Cananaean and Judas Iscariot, the one who betrayed him.

5 These twelve Jesus sent out with the following instructions: "Do not take a road leading to gentiles, and do not enter a Samaritan town, [6]but go rather to the lost sheep of the house of Israel. [7]As you go, proclaim the good news, 'The kingdom of heaven has come near.'[u] [8]Cure the sick; raise the dead; cleanse those with a skin disease; cast out demons. You received without payment; give without payment. [9]Take no gold, or silver, or copper in your belts, [10]no bag for your journey, or two tunics, or sandals, or a staff, for laborers deserve their food. [11]Whatever town or village you enter, find out who in it is worthy, and stay there until you leave. [12]As you enter the house, greet it. [13]If the house is worthy, let your peace come upon it, but if it is not worthy, let your peace return to you. [14]If anyone will not welcome you or listen to your words, shake off the dust from your feet as you leave that house or town. [15]Truly I tell you, it will be more tolerable for the land of Sodom and Gomorrah on the day of judgment than for that town.

16 "I am sending you out like sheep into the midst of wolves, so be wise as serpents and innocent as doves. [17]Beware of them, for they will hand you over to councils and flog you in their synagogues, [18]and you will be dragged before governors and kings because of me, as a testimony to them and the gentiles. [19]When they hand you over, do not worry about how you are to speak or what you are to say, for what you are to say will be given to you at that time, [20]for it is not you who speak, but the Spirit of your Father speaking through you. [21]Sibling will betray sibling to death and a father his child, and children will rise against parents and have them put to death, [22]and you will be hated by all because of my name. But the one who endures to the end will be saved. [23]When they persecute you in this town, flee to the next, for truly I tell you, you will not have finished going through all the towns of Israel before the Son of Man comes.

24 "A disciple is not above the teacher nor a slave above the master; [25]it is enough for the disciple to be like the teacher and the slave like the master. If they have called the master of the house Beelzebul, how much more will they malign those of his household!

26 "So have no fear of them, for nothing is covered up that will not be uncovered and nothing secret that will not become known. [27]What I say to you in the dark, tell in the light, and what you hear whispered, proclaim from the housetops. [28]Do not fear those who kill the body but cannot kill the soul; rather, fear the one who can destroy both soul and body in hell.[v] [29]Are not two sparrows sold for a penny? Yet not one of them will fall to the ground apart

t 10.3 Other ancient authorities read *Lebbaeus* or *Lebbaeus called Thaddaeus*   u 10.7 Or *is at hand*   v 10.28 Gk *Gehenna*

are fulfilled in the person and work of Jesus. Later when Jesus feeds five thousand men, there are twelve full baskets left over (14:20).

10:5–15 The ethnocentric mission. The disciples are given specific instructions to not go among the gentiles or the Samaritans. Instead, they are to focus only on the *house of Israel* (v. 6). Gentiles refer to Jesus and his disciples as Judean/Jews. But Jesus himself uses "Israel" ("Israēl") to describe the descendants of Jacob (whose other name is Israel), as does the Hebrew Bible. **10:5** *Do not take a road leading to gentiles, and do not enter a Samaritan town.* The Samaritans are inhabitants of Samaria, ethnically distinct from Judeans/Jews. They were a politically and religiously conservative group that maintained a different place of worship than the Judeans/Jews on Mount Gerizim (see **"The Samaritans," p. 1738**). The Samaritan Pentateuch is a version of the Torah written in Samaritan script that dates to the second century BCE. **10:8** *You received without payment; give without payment.* **10:15** *Sodom and Gomorrah* are infamous for their depravity. Judgment is cast down on both cities with sulfur and fire from heaven (Gen. 19:24).

10:16–25 The costs of the mission. Difficulties and persecutions will come. Jesus warns that they will be flogged, beaten, and rejected. They will be handed over to the gentiles. **10:17** *Flog you in their synagogues.* Much of what Jesus says here is a foreshadowing of what is to come. Later Jesus predicts that he will be handed over to the chief priests and scribes, flogged, and crucified (20:18–19).

10:26–33 Have no fear. A similar teaching is found earlier in the Sermon on the Mount where Jesus says, "Look at the birds of the air: they neither sow nor reap nor gather into barns, and yet your heavenly Father feeds them. Are you not of more value than they?" (6:26).

Focus On: The Samaritans (Matthew 10:5)

The Samaritans are a group with ambiguous status in the New Testament, frequently distinguished from gentiles and from (other) Jewish people. They claim to be descended from the northern tribes of Israel who were not destroyed by Assyria in 722 BCE and revere the Torah, or Pentateuch, as Scripture, but center their cult around Mount Gerizim (in present-day West Bank), not Jerusalem, and do not view the rest of the Hebrew Bible as Scripture. Scholars debate the difference between these "Jews" from Samaria and other Jews within Israel, ethnically and religiously. They are absent from the earliest written Gospel, the Gospel of Mark, and Jesus teaches his disciples to avoid Samaritan towns in Matthew's Gospel (10:5). Within Luke's narrative world, Samaritans interact with Jesus minimally but are classified as "foreigners" (Luke 17:18). This classification may be an indirect allusion to the ideas regarding alternative worship centers for each group (John 4:22).

Some decades later, the Fourth Gospel portrays a cultural tension between the Jews and Samaritans (John 4:9) and cites the label as a slur: "Are we not right in saying that you are a Samaritan and have a demon?" (John 8:48). Despite this sentiment, the Gospel of John portrays a positive encounter between Jesus and one Samaritan woman to set up a mission to the Samaritans, while Acts also views the region as a key part of the essential missionary focus of the new movement: "you will be my witnesses in Jerusalem, in all Judea *and Samaria*, and to the ends of the earth" (Acts 1:8).

Several older stories in Israel's tradition about the Samaritans inform these later first-century depictions. The author of 2 Maccabees considered Samaritans to be Jews, even though they worshiped at Gerizim and not in Jerusalem (2 Macc. 5:22–23; 6:2). The historian Josephus drew on 2 Kgs. 17 to portray the Samaritans (or Cutheans) as immigrants to the land whose treatment toward the Israelites depended on the economics of the day (*Ant.* 9.288–91). Josephus is unable to hide his own antagonism toward the Samaritans when he relays a contemporary conflict between the two groups that required the intervention of Rome, resulting in Claudius Caesar (r. 41–54 CE) siding in favor of the Jews and executing the leaders of the Samaritans (*J.W.* 2.232–49; *Ant.* 20.118–36).

Emerson B. Powery

from your Father. ³⁰And even the hairs of your head are all counted. ³¹So do not be afraid; you are of more value than many sparrows.

32 "Everyone, therefore, who acknowledges me before others, I also will acknowledge before my Father in heaven, ³³but whoever denies me before others, I also will deny before my Father in heaven.

34 "Do not think that I have come to bring peace to the earth; I have not come to bring peace but a sword.

³⁵ For I have come to set a man against his father,
and a daughter against her mother,
and a daughter-in-law against her mother-in-law,
³⁶ and one's foes will be members of one's own household.

³⁷"Whoever loves father or mother more than me is not worthy of me, and whoever loves son or daughter more than me is not worthy of me, ³⁸and whoever does not take up the cross and follow me is not worthy of me. ³⁹Those who find their life will lose it, and those who lose their life for my sake will find it.

40 "Whoever welcomes you welcomes me, and whoever welcomes me welcomes the one who sent me. ⁴¹Whoever welcomes a prophet in the name of a prophet will receive a prophet's reward, and whoever welcomes a righteous person in the name of a righteous person will receive the reward of the righteous, ⁴²and whoever gives even a cup of cold water to one of these little ones in the name of a disciple—truly I tell you, none of these will lose their reward."

10:34–39 **Jesus brings division.** Jesus says that the road of discipleship will not be easy. It requires denying self and taking up one's cross. The cross is a symbol of Roman imperial power. It is a political tool Rome used to humiliate, punish, and make examples out of anyone who would dare defy Rome (see **"Crucifixion and Terror," p. 1798**). Existing social structures and kinship ties, like the family, will be dissolved and overturned. A biblical allusion that Matthew makes here comes from Mic. 7:6: "For the son treats the father with contempt, the daughter rises up against her mother, the daughter-in-law against her mother-in-law; your enemies are members of your own household."

10:40–42 **A prophet's reward.** Just as Jesus is God's representative, the disciples are Jesus's representative. Therefore, welcoming a disciple or giving a cup of water to a child is tantamount to

11

Now when Jesus had finished instructing his twelve disciples, he went on from there to teach and proclaim his message in their cities.

2 When John heard in prison what the Messiah*w* was doing, he sent word by his*x* disciples [3]and said to him, "Are you the one who is to come, or are we to wait for another?" [4]Jesus answered them, "Go and tell John what you hear and see: [5]the blind receive their sight, the lame walk, those with a skin disease are cleansed, the deaf hear, the dead are raised, and the poor have good news brought to them. [6]And blessed is anyone who takes no offense at me."

7 As they went away, Jesus began to speak to the crowds about John: "What did you go out into the wilderness to look at? A reed shaken by the wind? [8]What, then, did you go out to see? Someone*y* dressed in soft robes? Look, those who wear soft robes are in royal palaces. [9]What, then, did you go out to see? A prophet?*z* Yes, I tell you, and more than a prophet. [10]This is the one about whom it is written,

'See, I am sending my messenger ahead
    of you,
    who will prepare your way before you.'

[11]"Truly I tell you, among those born of women no one has arisen greater than John the Baptist, yet the least in the kingdom of heaven is greater than he. [12]From the days of John the Baptist until now, the kingdom of heaven has suffered violence,*a* and violent people take it by force. [13]For all the Prophets and the Law prophesied until John came, [14]and if you are willing to accept it, he is Elijah who is to come. [15]Let anyone with ears*b* listen!

16 "But to what will I compare this generation? It is like children sitting in the marketplaces and calling to one another,

[17] 'We played the flute for you, and you did
    not dance;
    we wailed, and you did not mourn.'

[18]"For John came neither eating nor drinking, and they say, 'He has a demon'; [19]the Son of Man came eating and drinking, and they say, 'Look, a glutton and a drunkard, a friend of tax collectors and sinners!' Yet wisdom is vindicated by her deeds."*c*

20 Then he began to reproach the cities in which most of his deeds of power had been done because they did not repent. [21]"Woe to you, Chorazin! Woe to you, Bethsaida! For if the deeds of power done in you had been done in Tyre and Sidon, they would have repented long ago in sackcloth and ashes. [22]But I tell you, on the day of judgment it will be more tolerable for Tyre and Sidon than for you. [23]And you, Capernaum,

will you be exalted to heaven?

No, you will be brought down to Hades. "For if the deeds of power done in you had been done in Sodom, it would have remained until this day. [24]But I tell you that on the day of judgment it will be more tolerable for the land of Sodom than for you."

25 At that time Jesus said, "I thank*d* you, Father, Lord of heaven and earth, because you have hidden these things from the wise and

w 11.2 Or *the Christ*   *x* 11.2 Other ancient authorities read *two of his*   *y* 11.8 Or *Why, then, did you go out? To see someone*   *z* 11.9 Other ancient authorities read *Why, then, did you go out? To see a prophet?*   *a* 11.12 Or *has been coming violently*   *b* 11.15 Other ancient authorities add *to hear*   *c* 11.19 Other ancient authorities read *children*   *d* 11.25 Or *praise*

---

welcoming Jesus. In the parable of the Sheep and Goats, the king says, "Truly I tell you, just as you did it to one of the least of these brothers and sisters of mine, you did it to me" (25:40, 45). The theme of "reward" occurs frequently in the Sermon on the Mount (5:12, 46; 6:1, 2, 5, 16).

11:1 This concludes the second of five major discourses in Matthew. Structurally, Matt. 11 can be divided into three parts: Jesus and John the Baptist (vv. 1–19); Jesus judges the cities of Galilee (vv. 20–24); and Jesus's thanksgiving, proclamation, and invitation to rest (vv. 25–30).

11:2–6 John the Baptist sends messengers. Matthew quotes Isa. 35:4–6 and 61:1 in Jesus's response to the disciples of John.

11:7–19 John the Baptist is a great prophet like Elijah. 11:14 *He is Elijah who is to come.* This verse is an example of a literary device known as typology. Jesus compares John the Baptist to Elijah, who prefigures and foreshadows the prophetic role that John plays. **11:18–19** Jesus's commendation of John the Baptist foreshadows his own demise. Just as the crowds vilify John the Baptist as *a demon,* they also call Jesus *a glutton and a drunkard, a friend of tax collectors and sinners!* But *wisdom* ("sophia"; see also 12:42; 13:54; Prov. 1–9) is personified and vindicated through action (see **"Woman Wisdom," p. 872**).

11:20–24 Jesus casts judgment on unrepentant cities. *Woe to you, Chorazin! Woe to you, Bethsaida! . . . And you, Capernaum.* Jesus denounces three Galilean cities for their unwillingness to repent.

11:25–30 Jesus promises rest. In spite of the unbelief of the crowds (11:1–19) and the Galilean cities (11:20–24), Jesus thanks the Father that there are some who have received the revelation. Exodus

the intelligent and have revealed them to infants; [26]yes, Father, for such was your gracious will.[e] [27]All things have been handed over to me by my Father, and no one knows the Son except the Father, and no one knows the Father except the Son and anyone to whom the Son chooses to reveal him.

[28] "Come to me, all you who are weary and are carrying heavy burdens, and I will give you rest. [29]Take my yoke upon you, and learn from me, for I am gentle and humble in heart, and you will find rest for your souls. [30]For my yoke is easy, and my burden is light."

12 At that time Jesus went through the grain fields on the Sabbath; his disciples were hungry, and they began to pluck heads of grain and to eat. [2]When the Pharisees saw it, they said to him, "Look, your disciples are doing what is not lawful to do on the Sabbath." [3]He said to them, "Have you not read what David did when he and his companions were hungry? [4]How he entered the house of God, and they[f] ate the bread of the Presence, which it was not lawful for him or his companions to eat, but only for the priests? [5]Or have you not read in the law that on the Sabbath the priests in the temple break the Sabbath and yet are guiltless? [6]I tell you, something greater than the temple is here. [7]But if you had known what this means, 'I desire mercy and not sacrifice,' you would not have condemned the guiltless. [8]For the Son of Man is lord of the Sabbath."

[9] He left that place and entered their synagogue; [10]a man was there with a withered hand, and they asked him, "Is it lawful to cure on the Sabbath?" so that they might accuse him. [11]He said to them, "Suppose one of you has only one sheep and it falls into a pit on the Sabbath; will you not lay hold of it and lift it out? [12]How much more valuable is a human being than a sheep! So it is lawful to do good on the Sabbath." [13]Then he said to the man, "Stretch out your hand." He stretched it out, and it was restored, as sound as the other. [14]But the Pharisees went out and conspired against him, how to destroy him.

[15] When Jesus became aware of this, he departed. Many[g] followed him, and he cured all of them, [16]and he ordered them not to make him known. [17]This was to fulfill what had been spoken through the prophet Isaiah:

[18] "Here is my servant, whom I have chosen,
my beloved, with whom my soul is well
pleased.
I will put my Spirit upon him,
and he will proclaim justice to the
gentiles.
[19] He will not wrangle or cry aloud,
nor will anyone hear his voice in the
streets.
[20] He will not break a bruised reed
or quench a smoldering wick
until he brings justice to victory.
[21]And in his name the gentiles will hope."

[22] Then they brought to him a demon-possessed man who was blind and mute, and he cured him, so that the one who had been

---

e 11.26 Or *for so it was well-pleasing in your sight*　f 12.4 Other ancient authorities read *he ate*　g 12.15 Other ancient authorities add *crowds*

33:12–13 and Deut. 34:10 are echoed in Matt. 11:28–30. There is a reciprocal relationship between Moses and YHWH ("face to face," Deut. 34:10). Jesus and Moses are described as *humble* (Matt. 11:29; Num. 12:3). Jesus, who alone has knowledge of and access to the Father, invites people to a fuller experience of communion with God (see **"Rest as a Reward," p. 2065**).

12:1–8 Jesus debates the Pharisees about the Sabbath. The first encounter centers around the interpretation of the Torah, authority over the Sabbath, and jurisdiction over the temple. The Pharisees object when they see the disciples plucking grain on the Sabbath because the commandment of keeping the Sabbath in the Torah forbids working on the day, and plucking grain falls into the category of the "work" of harvesting. Jesus's answer is decisive: *Something greater than the temple is here* (v. 6).

12:9–14 Jesus heals a man on the Sabbath. *He left that place and entered their synagogue.* The synagogue is the domain of the Pharisees. Jesus asserts his own authority by entering *their synagogue* and healing a man. Healing would also be considered "work," forbidden on the Sabbath. The rabbis do teach that saving a life overrides Sabbath law. The Pharisees watch Jesus closely and start planning *how to destroy him* (v. 14).

12:15–21 Jesus is God's servant who brings hope for the gentiles. See also Mark 3:7–12; Luke 6:17–19. **12:18** Matthew cites Isa. 42:1–4.

12:22–32 Jesus is accused of being Beelzebul a second time. 12:23 *Can this be the Son of David?* Up to this point in the narrative, Matthew establishes Jesus's identity as the "son of David" in the

mute could speak and see. ²³All the crowds were amazed and were saying, "Can this be the Son of David?" ²⁴But when the Pharisees heard it, they said, "It is only by Beelzebul, the ruler of the demons, that this man casts out the demons." ²⁵He knew what they were thinking and said to them, "Every kingdom divided against itself is laid waste, and no city or house divided against itself will stand. ²⁶If Satan casts out Satan, he is divided against himself; how, then, will his kingdom stand? ²⁷If I cast out demons by Beelzebul, by whom do your own exorcists^h cast them out? Therefore they will be your judges. ²⁸But if it is by the Spirit of God that I cast out demons, then the kingdom of God has come upon you. ²⁹Or how can one enter a strong man's house and plunder his property without first tying up the strong man? Then indeed the house can be plundered. ³⁰Whoever is not with me is against me, and whoever does not gather with me scatters. ³¹Therefore I tell you, people will be forgiven for every sin and blasphemy, but blasphemy against the Spirit will not be forgiven. ³²Whoever speaks a word against the Son of Man will be forgiven, but whoever speaks against the Holy Spirit will not be forgiven, either in this age or in the age to come.

33 "Either make the tree good and its fruit good, or make the tree bad and its fruit bad, for the tree is known by its fruit. ³⁴You brood of vipers! How can you speak good things when you are evil? For out of the abundance of the heart the mouth speaks. ³⁵The good person brings good things out of a good treasure, and the evil person brings evil things out of an evil treasure. ³⁶I tell you, on the day of judgment you will have to give an account for every careless word you utter, ³⁷for by your words you will be justified, and by your words you will be condemned."

38 Then some of the scribes and Pharisees said to him, "Teacher, we wish to see a sign from you." ³⁹But he answered them, "An evil and adulterous generation asks for a sign, but no sign will be given to it except the sign of the prophet Jonah. ⁴⁰For just as Jonah was three days and three nights in the belly of the sea monster, so for three days and three nights the Son of Man will be in the heart of the earth. ⁴¹The people of Nineveh will rise up at the judgment with this generation and condemn it, because they repented at the proclamation of Jonah, and indeed something greater than Jonah is here! ⁴²The queen of the South will rise up at the judgment with this generation and condemn it, because she came from the ends of the earth to listen to the wisdom of Solomon, and indeed something greater than Solomon is here!

43 "When the unclean spirit has gone out of a person, it wanders through waterless regions looking for a resting place, but it finds none. ⁴⁴Then it says, 'I will return to my house from which I came.' When it returns, it finds it empty, swept, and put in order. ⁴⁵Then it goes and brings along seven other spirits more evil than itself, and they enter and live there, and the last state of that person is worse than the first. So will it be also with this evil generation."

46 While he was still speaking to the crowds, his mother and his brothers were standing outside, wanting to speak to him. ⁴⁷Someone told him, "Look, your mother and your brothers are standing outside, wanting to speak to you."ⁱ ⁴⁸But to the one who had told him this, Jesus^j replied, "Who is my mother, and who are my brothers?" ⁴⁹And pointing to his disciples, he said, "Here are my mother and my brothers! ⁵⁰For whoever does the will of

h 12.27 Gk *sons*   i 12.47 Other ancient authorities lack 12.47   j 12.48 Gk *he*

12:33–37 **A good tree produces good fruit. 12:33** *The tree is known by its fruit.* See also Matt. 7:16–20; Luke 6:43–44.

12:38–42 **Jesus is greater than Jonah and Solomon.** Jesus invokes the prophet Jonah (Jonah 1:17) and the queen of Sheba (1 Kgs. 10:2; 2 Chr. 9:1) in his indictment against the scribes and Pharisees. The queen of Sheba traveled a great distance to hear the wisdom of Solomon (1 Kgs. 10:1–13; see **"Solomon," p. 595**).

12:43–45 **An evil generation becomes more evil.** Jesus condemns *this evil generation* by forecasting that *the last state of that person is worse than the first.* His exorcism of unclean spirits is but a temporary solution.

12:46–50 **Jesus's true family transcends biology.** Becoming the true members of Jesus's spiritual family is not strictly a matter of physical descent or biology. It is about doing the will of the Father in heaven.

my Father in heaven is my brother and sister and mother."

13 That same day Jesus went out of the house and sat beside the sea. ²Such great crowds gathered around him that he got into a boat and sat there, while the whole crowd stood on the beach. ³And he told them many things in parables, saying: "Listen! A sower went out to sow. ⁴And as he sowed, some seeds fell on a path, and the birds came and ate them up. ⁵Other seeds fell on rocky ground, where they did not have much soil, and they sprang up quickly, since they had no depth of soil. ⁶But when the sun rose, they were scorched, and since they had no root, they withered away. ⁷Other seeds fell among thorns, and the thorns grew up and choked them. ⁸Other seeds fell on good soil and brought forth grain, some a hundredfold, some sixty, some thirty. ⁹If you have ears,ᵏ hear!"

10 Then the disciples came and asked him, "Why do you speak to them in parables?" ¹¹He answered, "To you it has been given to know the secretsˡ of the kingdom of heaven, but to them it has not been given. ¹²For to those who have, more will be given, and they will have an abundance, but from those who have nothing, even what they have will be taken away. ¹³The reason I speak to them in parables is that 'seeing they do not perceive, and hearing they do not listen, nor do they understand.' ¹⁴With them indeed is fulfilled the prophecy of Isaiah that says:

'You will indeed listen but never
    understand,
  and you will indeed look but never
    perceive.
¹⁵ For this people's heart has grown dull,
  and their ears are hard of hearing,

  and they have shut their eyes,
    so that they might not look with their
      eyes,
  and hear with their ears
    and understand with their heart and
      turn—
    and I would heal them.'
¹⁶"But blessed are your eyes, for they see, and your ears, for they hear. ¹⁷Truly I tell you, many prophets and righteous people longed to see what you see but did not see it and to hear what you hear but did not hear it.

18 "Hear, then, the parable of the sower. ¹⁹When anyone hears the word of the kingdom and does not understand it, the evil one comes and snatches away what is sown in the heart; this is what was sown on the path. ²⁰As for what was sown on rocky ground, this is the one who hears the word and immediately receives it with joy, ²¹yet such a person has no root but endures only for a while, and when trouble or persecution arises on account of the word, that person immediately falls away.ᵐ ²²As for what was sown among thorns, this is the one who hears the word, but the cares of thisⁿ age and the lure of wealth choke the word, and it yields nothing. ²³But as for what was sown on good soil, this is the one who hears the word and understands it, who indeed bears fruit and yields in one case a hundredfold, in another sixty, and in another thirty."

24 He put before them another parable: "The kingdom of heaven may be compared to someone who sowed good seed in his field, ²⁵but while everybody was asleep an enemy came and sowed weeds among the wheat and

k 13.9 Other ancient authorities add *to hear* l 13.11 Or *mysteries* m 13.21 Or *stumbles* n 13.22 Some ancient authorities read *the*

13:1–9 The parable of the Sower. The parable highlights the polarizing responses to Jesus's ministry by comparing the kingdom to sowing seeds. Some seeds fall on a path. Some fall on rocky ground. Some fall on thorns. But some fall on good soil and yield an abundance of grain.

13:10–17 Purpose of parables only given to the disciples. The citation comes from Isa. 6:9–10 to explain why Jesus speaks in parables. **13:11** The *kingdom of heaven* (alternatively "empire" or "reign") is the major theme of this chapter (13:24, 31, 33, 44–47, 52). The phrase occurs earlier in 3:2; 4:17; 5:3, 10, 19–20; 7:21; 8:11; 10:7; 11:11–12; and later in 16:19; 18:1–4, 23; 19:12, 14, 23; 20:1; 22:2; 23:13; 25:1. **13:16** *But blessed are your eyes, for they see, and your ears, for they hear.* See also Matt. 16:17.

13:18–23 Jesus interprets the parable of the Sower. The parable of the Sower is only explained to the disciples. The secrets of the kingdom are not revealed to everyone. Only those who have been given the secrets of the kingdom are able to perceive and understand.

13:24–30 The parable of Weeds among the Wheat. The divisive nature of the kingdom is illustrated in this parable. A sower planted good seeds, but an enemy planted weeds among the wheat. Both grow together in the same field until harvest time when they will be separated. The parable is later explained in 13:36–43.

then went away. [26]So when the plants came up and bore grain, then the weeds appeared as well. [27]And the slaves of the householder came and said to him, 'Master, did you not sow good seed in your field? Where, then, did these weeds come from?' [28]He answered, 'An enemy has done this.' The slaves said to him, 'Then do you want us to go and gather them?' [29]But he replied, 'No, for in gathering the weeds you would uproot the wheat along with them. [30]Let both of them grow together until the harvest, and at harvest time I will tell the reapers, Collect the weeds first and bind them in bundles to be burned, but gather the wheat into my barn.'"

[31] He put before them another parable: "The kingdom of heaven is like a mustard seed that someone took and sowed in his field; [32]it is the smallest of all the seeds, but when it has grown it is the greatest of shrubs and becomes a tree, so that the birds of the air come and make nests in its branches."

[33] He told them another parable: "The kingdom of heaven is like yeast that a woman took and mixed in with[o] three measures of flour until all of it was leavened."

[34] Jesus told the crowds all these things in parables; without a parable he told them nothing. [35]This was to fulfill what had been spoken through the prophet:[p]

"I will open my mouth to speak in parables;
I will proclaim what has been hidden since the foundation."[q]

[36] Then he left the crowds and went into the house. And his disciples approached him, saying, "Explain to us the parable of the weeds of the field." [37]He answered, "The one who sows the good seed is the Son of Man; [38]the field is the world, and the good seed are the children of the kingdom; the weeds are the children of the evil one, [39]and the enemy who sowed them is the devil; the harvest is the end of the age, and the reapers are angels. [40]Just as the weeds are collected and burned up with fire, so will it be at the end of the age. [41]The Son of Man will send his angels, and they will collect out of his kingdom all causes of sin[r] and all evildoers, [42]and they will throw them into the furnace of fire, where there will be weeping and gnashing of teeth. [43]Then the righteous will shine like the sun in the kingdom of their Father. Let anyone with ears[s] listen!

[44] "The kingdom of heaven is like treasure hidden in a field, which a man found and re-buried; then in his joy he goes and sells all that he has and buys that field.

[45] "Again, the kingdom of heaven is like a merchant in search of fine pearls; [46]on finding one pearl of great value, he went and sold all that he had and bought it.

[47] "Again, the kingdom of heaven is like a net that was thrown into the sea and caught fish of every kind; [48]when it was full, they drew it ashore, sat down, and put the good into baskets but threw out the bad. [49]So it will be at the end of the age. The angels will come out and separate the evil from the righteous [50]and throw them into the furnace of fire, where there will be weeping and gnashing of teeth.

[51] "Have you understood all this?" They answered, "Yes." [52]And he said to them, "Therefore every scribe who has become a disciple

o 13.33 Gk *hid in*   p 13.35 Other ancient authorities read *the prophet Isaiah*   q 13.35 Other ancient authorities add *of the world*   r 13.41 Or *stumbling*   s 13.43 Other ancient authorities add *to hear*

13:31–32 The parable of the Mustard Seed. The kingdom of heaven, according to this parable, starts out very small but eventually over time yields dramatic growth.

13:33 The parable of the Yeast. Yeast is a fermenting agent. A small amount can leaven a large amount of flour. Three measures are the equivalent of approximately fifty pounds of flour.

13:34–35 Parables as prophetic fulfillment. Matthew draws on Ps. 78:2 in this summary statement.

13:36–43 Jesus interprets the parable of Weeds among the Wheat. Like the parable of the Sower, this parable is only explained to the disciples. Jesus is the sower, the field is the world, the good seed are the children of the kingdom, the enemy is the devil, and the harvest is the eschatological judgment.

13:44–50 The parables of Hidden Treasure, Pearl of Great Value, Net Thrown into the Sea. These parables highlight the cherished value and desirability of the kingdom (see **"Kingdom of God," p. 772**). It is a superabundant treasure of inestimable value.

13:51–53 A scribe brings treasures new and old. The theme of discipleship is emphasized in this parable. The reference to both old and new treasures implies the validity of the Torah and its ongoing interpretation and practice (see **"Scribes and Scribalism," p. 1486**). This concludes the third major discourse in Matthew.

in the kingdom of heaven is like the master of a household who brings out of his treasure what is new and what is old." ⁵³When Jesus had finished these parables, he left that place.

54 He came to his hometown and began to teach the people* in their synagogue, so that they were astounded and said, "Where did this man get this wisdom and these deeds of power? ⁵⁵Is not this the carpenter's son? Is not his mother called Mary? And are not his brothers James and Joseph and Simon and Judas? ⁵⁶And are not all his sisters with us? Where then did this man get all this?" ⁵⁷And they took offense at him. But Jesus said to them, "Prophets are not without honor except in their own hometown and in their own house." ⁵⁸And he did not do many deeds of power there, because of their unbelief.

14 At that time Herod the ruler heard reports about Jesus, ²and he said to his servants, "This is John the Baptist; he has been raised from the dead, and for this reason these powers are at work in him." ³For Herod had arrested John, bound him, and put him in prison on account of Herodias, his brother Philip's wife, ⁴because John had been telling him, "It is not lawful for you to have her." ⁵Though Herod* wanted to put him to death, he feared the crowd, because they regarded him as a prophet. ⁶But when Herod's birthday came, the daughter of Herodias danced before the company, and she pleased Herod ⁷so much that he promised on oath to grant her whatever she might ask. ⁸Prompted by her mother, she said, "Give me the head of John the Baptist here on a platter." ⁹The king was grieved, yet out of regard for his oaths and for the guests, he commanded it to be given; ¹⁰he sent and had John beheaded

in the prison. ¹¹His head was brought on a platter and given to the girl, who brought it to her mother. ¹²His disciples came and took the body and buried him; then they went and told Jesus.

13 Now when Jesus heard this, he withdrew from there in a boat to a deserted place by himself. But when the crowds heard it, they followed him on foot from the towns. ¹⁴When he went ashore, he saw a great crowd, and he had compassion for them and cured their sick. ¹⁵When it was evening, the disciples came to him and said, "This is a deserted place, and the hour is now late; send the crowds away so that they may go into the villages and buy food for themselves." ¹⁶Jesus said to them, "They need not go away; you give them something to eat." ¹⁷They replied, "We have nothing here but five loaves and two fish." ¹⁸And he said, "Bring them here to me." ¹⁹Then he ordered the crowds to sit down on the grass. Taking the five loaves and the two fish, he looked up to heaven and blessed and broke the loaves and gave them to the disciples, and the disciples gave them to the crowds. ²⁰And all ate and were filled, and they took up what was left over of the broken pieces, twelve baskets full. ²¹And those who ate were about five thousand men, besides women and children.

22 Immediately he made the disciples get into a boat and go on ahead to the other side, while he dismissed the crowds. ²³And after he had dismissed the crowds, he went up the mountain by himself to pray. When evening came, he was there alone, ²⁴but by this time the boat, battered by the waves, was far from the land,* for the wind was against them. ²⁵And early in the morning he came walking toward

t 13.54 Gk *them*   *u* 14.5 Gk *he*   *v* 14.24 Other ancient authorities read *was out on the sea*

13:54–58 Jesus is rejected by Nazareth. Jesus returns to his hometown but is rejected when he teaches in *their synagogue*. The theme of rejection is a fitting conclusion to this chapter devoted to revealing and concealing the kingdom of heaven.

14:1–12 John the Baptist is beheaded. The rejection of Jesus in his hometown is immediately followed by the killing of John the Baptist. The two events are intimately related: as Jesus is rejected, John the Baptist is beheaded. John's death by Herod anticipates Jesus's death by Pilate. Moreover, both Herod (v. 5) and Pilate (27:24) are mindful of the crowds.

14:13–21 Jesus feeds the five thousand. Upon hearing the news of John's death, Jesus withdraws to a place by himself. A crowd of five thousand men, plus women and children (v. 21), forms. Jesus feeds them by multiplying loaves and fish. Matthew notes that after all had eaten, there are *twelve baskets full*. The number twelve is symbolic of the twelve tribes of Israel. Jesus's miracle is reminiscent of the story of Israel wandering the desert when God provides manna from heaven (Exod. 16).

14:22–33 Jesus walks on water. Jesus's authority over the seas is on display as he walks on water toward his disciples who are in the boat. Peter calls out to Jesus to command him to walk on the water.

them on the sea. [26]But when the disciples saw him walking on the sea, they were terrified, saying, "It is a ghost!" And they cried out in fear. [27]But immediately Jesus spoke to them and said, "Take heart, it is I; do not be afraid."

28 Peter answered him, "Lord, if it is you, command me to come to you on the water." [29]He said, "Come." So Peter got out of the boat, started walking on the water, and came toward Jesus. [30]But when he noticed the strong wind,[w] he became frightened, and, beginning to sink, he cried out, "Lord, save me!" [31]Jesus immediately reached out his hand and caught him, saying to him, "You of little faith, why did you doubt?" [32]When they got into the boat, the wind ceased. [33]And those in the boat worshiped him, saying, "Truly you are the Son of God."

34 When they had crossed over, they came to land at Gennesaret. [35]After the people of that place recognized him, they sent word to that whole surrounding region, and people brought all who were sick to him [36]and begged him that they might touch even the fringe of his cloak, and all who touched it were healed.

15 Then Pharisees and scribes came to Jesus from Jerusalem and said, [2]"Why do your disciples break the tradition of the elders? For they do not wash their hands before they eat." [3]He answered them, "And why do you break the commandment of God for the sake of your tradition? [4]For God said,[x] 'Honor your father and your mother,' and, 'Whoever speaks evil of father or mother must surely die.' [5]But you say that whoever tells father or mother, 'Whatever support you might have had from me is given to God,'[y] then that person need not honor the father.[z] [6]So, for the sake of your tradition, you nullify the word[a]

of God. [7]You hypocrites! Isaiah prophesied rightly about you when he said:

[8]'This people honors me with their lips,
    but their hearts are far from me;
[9]in vain do they worship me,
    teaching human precepts as
        doctrines.'"

10 Then he called the crowd to him and said to them, "Listen and understand: [11]it is not what goes into the mouth that defiles a person, but it is what comes out of the mouth that defiles." [12]Then the disciples approached and said to him, "Do you know that the Pharisees took offense when they heard what you said?" [13]He answered, "Every plant that my heavenly Father has not planted will be uprooted. [14]Let them alone; they are blind guides of the blind.[b] And if one blind person guides another, both will fall into a pit." [15]But Peter said to him, "Explain this parable to us." [16]Then he said, "Are you also still without understanding? [17]Do you not see that whatever goes into the mouth enters the stomach and goes out into the sewer? [18]But what comes out of the mouth proceeds from the heart, and this is what defiles. [19]For out of the heart come evil intentions, murder, adultery, sexual immorality, theft, false witness, slander. [20]These are what defile a person, but to eat with unwashed hands does not defile."

21 Jesus left that place and went away to the district of Tyre and Sidon. [22]Just then a Canaanite woman from that region came out and started shouting, "Have mercy on me, Lord, Son of David; my daughter is tormented by a

w 14.30 Other ancient authorities read *the wind*
x 15.4 Other ancient authorities read *commanded, saying*
y 15.5 Or *is an offering* z 15.5 Other ancient authorities add *or the mother* a 15.6 Other ancient authorities read *law* or *commandment* b 15.14 Other ancient authorities lack *of the blind*

Jesus gives the command, but Peter doubts and begins to sink. This episode is a foreshadowing of Peter's lack of faith and denial of Jesus outside the courtyard of the high priest (26:34–35, 69–75).

14:34–36 Jesus heals the sick in Gennesaret. Many are healed as they touch the cloak of Jesus. See also Matt. 9:20.

15:1–20 The Pharisees accuse Jesus of breaking the tradition of the elders. The *tradition of the elders* refers to developing interpretations of Mosaic law, here about ritual purity, a concern associated with the Pharisees. Jesus and the Pharisees differed not on Torah law itself but on how it should be applied. In this case, tradition has taken precedence over the Torah, which Jesus is quick to correct. Ultimately, defilement is not external but internal. That is, a person's words and behavior are expressions of the heart. Both Matthew and Mark agree up to this point. But Mark understands Jesus as declaring all foods clean (Mark 7:19). This line is not found in Matthew, suggesting the continuing practice and validity of dietary laws. Matthew thereby maintains and upholds food laws according to Judean/Jewish practice (see **"Diet," p. 268**).

15:21–28 Jesus encounters the Canaanite woman. 15:24 *I was sent only to the lost sheep of the*

Going Deeper: Does Jesus Display Ethnocentrism or Harbor Racism toward the Canaanite Woman? (Matthew 15)

This is a difficult question to answer. His first response is impolite, to say the least. Jesus ignores her plea for help. His second response is ethnocentric. Bothered by the woman, the disciples ask Jesus to send her away. Jesus responds, "I was sent only to the lost sheep of the house of Israel." This is the clearest and most explicit expression of ethnocentrism in Matthew. Indeed, the reason why Jesus does not help the woman comes down to one single factor: she is a foreigner who is not part of the "house of Israel." But she is not just any foreigner. She belongs to the archenemies of Israel in the biblical tradition—the Canaanites (as opposed to a Syrophoenician woman in Mark 7:26; Matthew is probably revising this story that he received from Mark).

Jesus's third response veers on borderline racism: "It is not fair to take the children's food and throw it to the dogs" (15:26). In the analogy, the woman is cast in the role of a dog, while the children are the house of Israel. But rather than take offense, she takes Jesus's analogy a step further. Jesus is amazed by the woman's great faith and heals her daughter. These verses display harsh animosity toward the Canaanites. The Canaanites are the quintessential enemies of the Israelites—a tradition that originates in the curse of Canaan in Gen. 9:18-29 (see **"The Curse of Canaan," p. 26**). In Deut. 20:16-18, the Israelites are commanded to annihilate their enemies—including the Hittites, Amorites, Canaanites, Perizzites, Hivites, and Jebusites (see **"Genocide," p. 305**).

For modern readers, acknowledging that Jesus displayed ethnocentrism and racism may pose theological challenges. But for a first-century audience, Jesus's interaction with the woman would not be surprising given the deep-seated tensions that existed between Judeans/Jews and Canaanites. When contextualized historically, Jesus's harsh responses that maintain the status quo are unremarkable. She does not argue about her inferior status, but Jesus's praise of her and healing of her daughter suggest an opening of the mission. The question remains open.

Wongi Park

demon." [23]But he did not answer her at all. And his disciples came and urged him, saying, "Send her away, for she keeps shouting after us." [24]He answered, "I was sent only to the lost sheep of the house of Israel." [25]But she came and knelt before him, saying, "Lord, help me." [26]He answered, "It is not fair to take the children's food and throw it to the dogs." [27]She said, "Yes, Lord, yet even the dogs eat the crumbs that fall from their masters'[c] table." [28]Then Jesus answered her, "Woman, great is your faith! Let it be done for you as you wish." And her daughter was healed from that moment.

[29] After Jesus had left that place, he passed along the Sea of Galilee, and he went up the mountain, where he sat down. [30]Great crowds came to him, bringing with them the lame, the blind, the maimed, the mute, and many others.

They put them at his feet, and he cured them, [31]so that the crowd was amazed when they saw the mute speaking, the maimed whole, the lame walking, and the blind seeing. And they praised the God of Israel.

[32] Then Jesus called his disciples to him and said, "I have compassion for the crowd because they have been with me now for three days and have nothing to eat, and I do not want to send them away hungry, for they might faint on the way." [33]The disciples said to him, "Where are we to get enough bread in the desert to feed so great a crowd?" [34]Jesus asked them, "How many loaves have you?" They said, "Seven, and a few small fish." [35]Then ordering the crowd to sit down on the ground, [36]he took the seven loaves and the fish, and after giving thanks he

c 15.27 Gk lords'

house of Israel. This statement is the clearest and most explicit statement of ethnocentrism in the Gospel of Matthew. The only reason Jesus does not help the woman is because of her racial/ethnic identity as a Canaanite—or, conversely, because she is not part of the "house of Israel." She is a foreigner. **15:26** The term *dogs* ("kynarion") bears a pejorative connotation. Earlier, in the Sermon on the Mount, Jesus says, "Do not give what is holy to dogs, and do not throw your pearls before swine, or they will trample them under foot and turn and maul you" (7:6). The use of the word "dogs" reinforces the ethnocentric mission to Israel. But significantly, because of her words to him, he changes his mind and does heal her daughter.

15:29-31 Jesus cures many in Galilee. *And they praised the God of Israel.* Again, the ethnocentric focus on Israel remains consistent.

broke them and gave them to the disciples, and the disciples gave them to the crowds. [37]And all of them ate and were filled, and they took up the broken pieces left over, seven baskets full. [38]Those who had eaten were four thousand men, besides women and children. [39]After sending away the crowds, he got into the boat and went to the region of Magadan.[d]

16 The Pharisees and Sadducees came, and to test Jesus[e] they asked him to show them a sign from heaven. [2]He answered them, "When it is evening, you say, 'It will be fair weather, for the sky is red.' [3]And in the morning, 'It will be stormy today, for the sky is red and threatening.' You know how to interpret the appearance of the sky, but you cannot interpret the signs of the times.[f] [4]An evil and adulterous generation asks for a sign, but no sign will be given to it except the sign of Jonah." Then he left them and went away.

5 When the disciples reached the other side, they had forgotten to bring any bread. [6]Jesus said to them, "Watch out, and beware of the yeast of the Pharisees and Sadducees." [7]They said to one another, "It is because we have brought no bread." [8]And becoming aware of it, Jesus said, "You of little faith, why are you talking about having no bread? [9]Do you still not perceive? Do you not remember the five loaves for the five thousand and how many baskets you gathered? [10]Or the seven loaves for the four thousand and how many baskets you gathered? [11]How could you fail to perceive that I was not speaking about bread? Beware of the yeast of the Pharisees and Sadducees!" [12]Then they understood that he had not told them to beware of the yeast of bread but of the teaching of the Pharisees and Sadducees.

13 Now when Jesus came into the district of Caesarea Philippi, he asked his disciples, "Who do people say that the Son of Man is?" [14]And they said, "Some say John the Baptist but others Elijah and still others Jeremiah or one of the prophets." [15]He said to them, "But who do you say that I am?" [16]Simon Peter answered, "You are the Messiah,[g] the Son of the living God." [17]And Jesus answered him, "Blessed are you, Simon son of Jonah! For flesh and blood has not revealed this to you but my Father in heaven. [18]And I tell you, you are Peter,[h] and on this rock[i] I will build my church, and the gates of Hades will not prevail against it. [19]I will give you the keys of the kingdom of heaven, and whatever you bind on earth will be bound in heaven, and whatever

d 15.39 Other ancient authorities read *Magdala* or *Magdalan* e 16.1 Gk *him* f 16.3 Other ancient authorities lack *When it is . . . of the times* g 16.16 Or *the Christ* h 16.18 Gk *Petros* i 16.18 Gk *petra*

16:8 *You of little faith.* This is a term that Jesus uses to describe the disciples' lack of belief (6:30; 8:26; 14:31; 17:20). By contrast, being of great faith is a status awarded to gentiles: the Roman centurion (8:10) and the Canaanite woman (15:28).

16:13–20 Peter confesses that Jesus is the Messiah. Peter plays a significant role in Matthew. Up to this point, there are several references to Peter in Jesus's ministry: his calling along with Andrew his brother (4:18), the healing of his mother-in-law (8:14), his attempt to walk on water with Jesus (14:28), his asking Jesus to explain a parable (15:15). Here, in chap. 16, upon hearing Peter's confession, Jesus declares that he will build his "church" ("ekklēsia") on Peter. This passage has been central in establishing the Roman Catholic doctrine of papal primacy and succession. **16:18** This verse is a literary example of wordplay. Peter's name in Greek ("Petros") is phonetically similar to the word for "rock" ("petra"). In other words, Jesus says the "church" ("ekklēsia") will be built upon the bedrock of Peter and his confession that Jesus is the Messiah. Matthew is the only Gospel to use the word "church" ("ekklēsia") to describe the community of Jesus's followers. An alternative translation is "assembly."

16:21–23 Jesus predicts his death and resurrection. Just as soon as Peter confesses Jesus is the Messiah, Jesus refers to Peter as a *hindrance.*

16:24–28 To follow Jesus is to deny self. 16:25 This verse is an example of a literary device called paradox. The saying is contradictory and illogical on the surface. But it contains a deeper meaning. What might appear to be losing one's life is actually the path toward finding it.

17:1–13 Jesus is transfigured. 17:2 *And he was transfigured.* The verb "transfigured" ("metamorphoō") means to change into another form or to transform. The story of Jesus's transfiguration contains allusions to God's revelation to Moses at Mount Sinai (Exod. 24:9–18). See also Rom. 12:2 and 2 Cor. 3:18. **17:4** Regarding Elijah's role as a forerunner, see Mal. 4:5 (see Matt. 11:14). **17:5** The first time God speaks is during Jesus's baptism (3:17). Matthew cites Isa. 42:1.

17:14–21 Jesus cures a child with epilepsy. 17:17 *Faithless and perverse generation.* Moses refers to

you loose on earth will be loosed in heaven." [20]Then he sternly ordered the disciples not to tell anyone that he was[j] the Messiah.[k]

21 From that time on, Jesus began to show his disciples that he must go to Jerusalem and undergo great suffering at the hands of the elders and chief priests and scribes and be killed and on the third day be raised. [22]And Peter took him aside and began to rebuke him, saying, "God forbid it, Lord! This must never happen to you." [23]But he turned and said to Peter, "Get behind me, Satan! You are a hindrance[l] to me, for you are setting your mind not on divine things but on human things."

24 Then Jesus told his disciples, "If any wish to come after me, let them deny themselves and take up their cross and follow me. [25]For those who want to save their life will lose it, and those who lose their life for my sake will find it. [26]For what will it profit them if they gain the whole world but forfeit their life? Or what will they give in return for their life?

27 "For the Son of Man is to come with his angels in the glory of his Father, and then he will repay everyone for what has been done. [28]Truly I tell you, there are some standing here who will not taste death before they see the Son of Man coming in his kingdom."

17 Six days later, Jesus took with him Peter and James and his brother John and led them up a high mountain, by themselves. [2]And he was transfigured before them, and his face shone like the sun, and his clothes became bright as light. [3]Suddenly there appeared to them Moses and Elijah, talking with him. [4]Then Peter said to Jesus, "Lord, it is good for us to be here; if you wish, I[m] will set up three tents here, one for you, one for Moses, and one for Elijah." [5]While he was still speaking, suddenly a bright cloud overshadowed them, and a voice from the cloud said, "This is my Son, the Beloved;[n] with him I am well pleased; listen to him!" [6]When the disciples heard this, they fell to the ground and were overcome by fear. [7]But Jesus came and touched them, saying, "Get up and do not be

afraid." [8]And when they raised their eyes, they saw no one except Jesus himself alone.

9 As they were coming down the mountain, Jesus ordered them, "Tell no one about the vision until after the Son of Man has been raised from the dead." [10]And the disciples asked him, "Why, then, do the scribes say that Elijah must come first?" [11]He replied, "Elijah is indeed coming and will restore all things, [12]but I tell you that Elijah has already come, and they did not recognize him, but they did to him whatever they pleased. So also the Son of Man is about to suffer at their hands." [13]Then the disciples understood that he was speaking to them about John the Baptist.

14 When they came to the crowd, a man came to him, knelt before him, [15]and said, "Lord, have mercy on my son, for he has epilepsy and suffers terribly; he often falls into the fire and often into the water. [16]And I brought him to your disciples, but they could not cure him." [17]Jesus answered, "You faithless and perverse generation, how much longer must I be with you? How much longer must I put up with you? Bring him here to me." [18]And Jesus rebuked the demon,[o] and it[p] came out of him, and the boy was cured from that moment. [19]Then the disciples came to Jesus privately and said, "Why could we not cast it out?" [20]He said to them, "Because of your little faith. For truly I tell you, if you have faith the size of a[q] mustard seed, you will say to this mountain, 'Move from here to there,' and it will move, and nothing will be impossible for you."[r]

22 As they were gathering[s] in Galilee, Jesus said to them, "The Son of Man is going to be betrayed into human hands, [23]and they will kill him, and on the third day he will be raised." And they were greatly distressed.

24 When they reached Capernaum, the collectors of the temple tax came to Peter and

j 16.20 Other ancient authorities add *Jesus*   k 16.20 Or *the Christ*   l 16.23 Or *stumbling block*   m 17.4 Other ancient authorities read *we*   n 17.5 Or *my beloved Son*   o 17.18 Gk *it* or *him*   p 17.18 Gk *the demon*   q 17.20 Gk *faith as a grain of*   r 17.20 Other ancient authorities add 17.21, *But this kind does not come out except by prayer and fasting*   s 17.22 Other ancient authorities read *living*

the children of God as a "perverse and crooked generation" (Deut. 32:5). **17:20** *Faith the size of a mustard seed.* The theme of little faith appears again in this scene (6:30; 8:26; 14:31; 16:8). See the parable of the Mustard Seed (13:31–32).

17:24–27 Jesus pays the temple tax. This is a fascinating scene where Jesus negotiates the temple tax. It is important for contemporary readers to remember there was no separation between church and state or politics and religion in the ancient world. Jesus reasons that if *the children are free,* then he is not obligated to pay the tax. Interestingly, he pays it so as not to cause offense. This is symbolized

said, "Does your teacher not pay the temple tax?" [25]He said, "Yes, he does." And when he came home, Jesus spoke of it first, asking, "What do you think, Simon? From whom do kings of the earth take toll or tribute? From their children or from others?" [26]When Peter[t] said, "From others," Jesus said to him, "Then the children are free. [27]However, so that we do not give offense to them, go to the sea and cast a hook; take the first fish that comes up, and when you open its mouth you will find a coin; take that and give it to them for you and me."

18 At that time the disciples came to Jesus and asked, "Who is the greatest in the kingdom of heaven?" [2]He called a child, whom he put among them, [3]and said, "Truly I tell you, unless you change and become like children, you will never enter the kingdom of heaven. [4]Whoever becomes humble like this child is the greatest in the kingdom of heaven. [5]Whoever welcomes one such child in my name welcomes me.

6 "If any of you cause one of these little ones who believe in me to sin,[u] it would be better for you if a great millstone were fastened around your neck and you were drowned in the depth of the sea. [7]Woe to the world because of things that cause sin![v] Such things are bound to come, but woe to the one through whom they come!

8 "If your hand or your foot causes you to sin,[w] cut it off and throw it away; it is better for you to enter life maimed or lame than to have two hands or two feet and to be thrown into the eternal fire. [9]And if your eye causes you to sin,[x] tear it out and throw it away; it is better for you to enter life with one eye than to have two eyes and to be thrown into the hell[y] of fire.

10 "Take care that you do not despise one of these little ones, for I tell you, in heaven their angels continually see the face of my Father in heaven.[z] [12]What do you think? If a shepherd has a hundred sheep and one of them has gone astray, does he not leave the ninety-nine on the mountains and go in search of the one that went astray? [13]And if he finds it, truly I tell you, he rejoices over it more than over the ninety-nine that never went astray. [14]So it is not the will of your[a] Father in heaven that one of these little ones should be lost.

15 "If your brother or sister sins against you,[b] go and point out the fault when the two of you are alone. If you are listened to, you have regained that one. [16]But if you are not listened to, take one or two others along with you, so that every word may be confirmed by the evidence of two or three witnesses. [17]If that person refuses to listen to them, tell it to the church, and if the offender refuses to listen even to the church, let such a one be to you as a gentile and a tax collector. [18]Truly I tell you, whatever you bind on earth will be bound in heaven, and whatever you loose on earth will be loosed in heaven. [19]Again, truly I tell you, if two of you agree on earth about anything you ask, it will be done for you by my Father in heaven. [20]For where two or three are gathered in my name, I am there among them."

t 17.26 Gk he   u 18.6 Or stumble   v 18.7 Or stumbling blocks   w 18.8 Or stumble   x 18.9 Or stumble   y 18.9 Gk Gehenna   z 18.10 Other ancient authorities add 18.11, For the Son of Man came to save the lost   a 18.14 Other ancient authorities read my   b 18.15 Other ancient authorities lack against you

in the story by the providential provision of a fish, which swallows the coin by which Peter renders payment. A similar debate arises when the Pharisees seek to entrap Jesus about paying taxes but this time to Rome (22:15–22). Paying the temple tax is an act of submission and subversion. It is a defiant act that paradoxically expresses unyielding support for God's empire over Rome's.

18:1–9 Children are the greatest in the kingdom. 18:8–9 This verse is an example of a literary device called hyperbole. Jesus is not literally commanding the disciples to cut off their hand or foot or gouge out their eye. The saying is exaggerated for rhetorical effect.

18:15–22 Forgiving a brother or sister who sins against you. Membership in the "church" or "assembly" is regulated by a principle that maintains group identity. Failure to listen to the evidence of two or more witnesses results in exclusion from the "church." The implication is that Jesus and his disciples are a different group. The identity of the "church" is forged in contrast to that which is defined as "gentile" ("ethnikos"). The racial/ethnic boundary between Judeans/Jews and non-Judeans/Jews is clearly and consistently delineated. The very language of this passage (let such a one be to you as a gentile and a tax collector, v. 17) presupposes an insider's perspective. Jesus is speaking from within and for a designated group (i.e., Judeans/Jews) over and against non-Judean/Jewish gentiles. Although two gentile characters have expressed great faith, the Roman centurion (8:5–13) and the Canaanite woman (15:21–28), the primary orientation of Jesus's ministry is centered around Judeans/Jews. **18:22** Seventy-seven

21 Then Peter came and said to him, "Lord, if my brother or sister sins against me, how often should I forgive? As many as seven times?" [22]Jesus said to him, "Not seven times, but, I tell you, seventy-seven[c] times.

23 "For this reason the kingdom of heaven may be compared to a king who wished to settle accounts with his slaves. [24]When he began the reckoning, one who owed him ten thousand talents was brought to him, [25]and, as he could not pay, the lord ordered him to be sold, together with his wife and children and all his possessions and payment to be made. [26]So the slave fell on his knees before him, saying, 'Have patience with me, and I will pay you everything.' [27]And out of pity for him, the lord of that slave released him and forgave him the debt. [28]But that same slave, as he went out, came upon one of his fellow slaves who owed him a hundred denarii, and seizing him by the throat he said, 'Pay what you owe.' [29]Then his fellow slave fell down and pleaded with him, 'Have patience with me, and I will pay you.' [30]But he refused; then he went and threw him into prison until he would pay the debt. [31]When his fellow slaves saw what had happened, they were greatly distressed, and they went and reported to their lord all that had taken place. [32]Then his lord summoned him and said to him, 'You wicked slave! I forgave you all that debt because you pleaded with me. [33]Should you not have had mercy on your fellow slave, as I had mercy on you?' [34]And in anger his lord handed him over to be tortured until he would pay his entire debt. [35]So my heavenly Father will also do to every one of you, if you do not forgive your brother or sister from your heart."

19 When Jesus had finished saying these things, he left Galilee and went to the region of Judea beyond the Jordan. [2]Large crowds followed him, and he cured them there.

3 Some Pharisees came to him, and to test him they asked, "Is it lawful for a man to divorce his wife for any cause?" [4]He answered, "Have you not read that the one who made them at the beginning 'made them male and female,' [5]and said, 'For this reason a man shall leave his father and mother and be joined to his wife, and the two shall become one flesh'? [6]So they are no longer two but one flesh. Therefore what God has joined together, let no one separate." [7]They said to him, "Why then did Moses command us to give a certificate of dismissal and to divorce her?" [8]He said to them, "It was because you were so hard-hearted that Moses allowed you to divorce your wives, but from the beginning it was not so. [9]And I say to you, whoever divorces his wife, except for sexual immorality, and marries another commits adultery, and he who marries a divorced woman commits adultery."[d]

10 The[e] disciples said to him, "If such is the case of a man with his wife, it is better not to marry." [11]But he said to them, "Not everyone can accept this teaching, but only those to whom it is given. [12]For there are eunuchs who have been so from birth, and there are eunuchs who have been made eunuchs by others, and there are eunuchs who have made themselves eunuchs for the sake of the kingdom of heaven. Let anyone accept this who can."

13 Then children were being brought to him in order that he might lay his hands on them and pray. The disciples spoke sternly to those who brought them, [14]but Jesus said, "Let the children come to me, and do not stop them,

c 18.22 Or *seventy times seven* d 19.9 Other ancient authorities lack *and he who marries a divorced woman commits adultery* e 19.10 Other ancient authorities read *His*

times. Another possibility is "seventy times seven." The point is the number is so great that forgiveness has no limit.

18:23–35 The parable of the Unforgiving Servant.

19:1–12 Jesus's teachings about divorce. The Pharisees inquire about the legal grounds for divorce (Deut. 24:1–4). **19:4** Gen. 1:27 is quoted in the question (see also Gen. 5:2). **19:5** See Gen. 2:24. See also 1 Cor. 6:16; Eph. 5:31. **19:9** *Except for sexual immorality.* Divorce is a concession that was allowed by Moses and is part of Torah law, but Jesus limits it to cases of adultery. This saying recalls the story of Jesus's birth when Joseph finds out that Mary is with child and plans to divorce her quietly (Matt. 1:19). **19:12** Jesus differentiates between three types of eunuchs: those who are so by birth, those who are castrated by others, and those who choose to be celibate or castrate themselves for the sake of the kingdom. Eunuchs are active participants in and recipients of God's favor and salvation (Isa. 56:4–5).

19:13–15 Jesus blesses little children. It is unclear why the disciples are bothered. But Jesus makes it clear that children have a rightful place in the kingdom of heaven (18:3; 1 Cor. 14:20; 1 Pet. 2:2).

for it is to such as these that the kingdom of heaven belongs." ¹⁵And he laid his hands on them and went on his way.

16 Then someone came to him and said, "Teacher, what good deed must I do to have eternal life?" ¹⁷And he said to him, "Why do you ask me about what is good? There is one who is good. If you wish to enter into life, keep the commandments." ¹⁸He said to him, "Which ones?" And Jesus said, "You shall not murder. You shall not commit adultery. You shall not steal. You shall not bear false witness. ¹⁹Honor your father and mother. Also, you shall love your neighbor as yourself." ²⁰The young man said to him, "I have kept all these;ᶠ what do I still lack?" ²¹Jesus said to him, "If you wish to be perfect, go, sell your possessions, and give the moneyᵍ to the poor, and you will have treasure in heaven; then come, follow me." ²²When the young man heard this word, he went away grieving, for he had many possessions.

23 Then Jesus said to his disciples, "Truly I tell you, it will be hard for a rich person to enter the kingdom of heaven. ²⁴Again I tell you, it is easier for a camel to go through the eye of a needle than for someone who is rich to enter the kingdom of God." ²⁵When the disciples heard this, they were greatly astounded and said, "Then who can be saved?" ²⁶But Jesus looked at them and said, "For mortals it is impossible, but for God all things are possible."

27 Then Peter said in reply, "Look, we have left everything and followed you. What then will we have?" ²⁸Jesus said to them, "Truly I tell you, at the renewal of all things, when the Son of Man is seated on the throne of his glory, you who have followed me will also sit on twelve thrones, judging the twelve tribes of Israel. ²⁹And everyone who has left houses or brothers or sisters or father or mother or wife orʰ children or fields for my name's sake will receive a hundredfoldⁱ and will inherit eternal life. ³⁰But many who are first will be last, and the last will be first.

20 "For the kingdom of heaven is like a landowner who went out early in the morning to hire laborers for his vineyard. ²After agreeing with the laborers for a denarius for the day, he sent them into his vineyard. ³When he went out about nine o'clock, he saw others standing idle in the marketplace, ⁴and he said to them, 'You also go into the vineyard, and I will pay you whatever is right.' So they went. ⁵When he went out again about noon and about three o'clock, he did the same. ⁶And about five o'clock he went out and found others standing around, and he said to them, 'Why are you standing here idle all day?' ⁷They said to him, 'Because no one has hired us.' He said to them, 'You also go into the vineyard.' ⁸When evening came, the owner of the vineyard said to his manager, 'Call the laborers and give them their pay, beginning with the last and then going to the first.' ⁹When those hired about five o'clock came, each of them received a denarius. ¹⁰Now when the first came, they thought they would receive more; but each of them also received a denarius. ¹¹And when they received it, they grumbled against the landowner, ¹²saying, 'These last worked only one hour, and you have made them equal to us who have borne the burden of the day and the scorching heat.' ¹³But he replied to one of them, 'Friend, I am doing you no wrong; did you not agree with me for a denarius? ¹⁴Take what belongs to you and go; I choose to give to this last the same as I give to you. ¹⁵Am I not allowed to do what I choose with what belongs to me? Or are you envious because I am generous?'ʲ ¹⁶So the last will be first, and the first will be last."ᵏ

17 While Jesus was going up to Jerusalem, he took the twelve disciples aside by themselves

f 19.20 Other ancient authorities add *from my youth* g 19.21 Gk lacks *the money* h 19.29 Other ancient authorities lack *wife or* i 19.29 Other ancient authorities read *manifold* j 20.15 Gk *is your eye evil because I am good?* k 20.16 Other ancient authorities add *for many are called, but few are chosen*

19:16–30 Jesus encourages giving to the poor. 19:19 See Lev. 19:18; Matt. 22:39; Rom. 13:9; Gal. 5:14. **19:24** *Kingdom of God.* An alternative translation is "empire" or "reign of God." Upon hearing Jesus's command to sell his possessions and give to the poor, the young man goes away grieving. His wealth is a sign of his success in the Roman Empire. Entering God's empire means relinquishing one's wealth and status in the current order. **19:30** This verse is an example of a literary device called a chiasm. The order of the first line is inverted in the second: *But many who are first will be last, and the last will be first.*

20:1–16 The parable of Laborers in the Vineyard. All the laborers start at different times of the day: some in the morning, others in the afternoon, and still others in the evening. But the catch is that they all receive the same exact pay. The point of the parable is to highlight the generosity and authority of the landowner.

and said to them on the way, [18]"Look, we are going up to Jerusalem, and the Son of Man will be handed over to the chief priests and scribes, and they will condemn him to death; [19]then they will hand him over to the gentiles to be mocked and flogged and crucified, and on the third day he will be raised."

20 Then the mother of the sons of Zebedee came to him with her sons, and kneeling before him, she asked a favor of him. [21]And he said to her, "What do you want?" She said to him, "Declare that these two sons of mine will sit, one at your right hand and one at your left, in your kingdom." [22]But Jesus answered, "You do not know what you are asking. Are you able to drink the cup that I am about to drink?"[l] They said to him, "We are able." [23]He said to them, "You will indeed drink my cup, but to sit at my right hand and at my left, this is not mine to grant, but it is for those for whom it has been prepared by my Father."

24 When the ten heard it, they were angry with the two brothers. [25]But Jesus called them to him and said, "You know that the rulers of the gentiles lord it over them, and their great ones are tyrants over them. [26]It will not be so among you, but whoever wishes to be great among you must be your servant, [27]and whoever wishes to be first among you must be your slave, [28]just as the Son of Man came not to be served but to serve and to give his life a ransom for many."

29 As they were leaving Jericho, a large crowd followed him. [30]There were two blind men sitting by the roadside. When they heard that Jesus was passing by, they shouted, "Lord,[m] have mercy on us, Son of David!"

[31]The crowd sternly ordered them to be quiet, but they shouted even more loudly, "Have mercy on us, Lord, Son of David!" [32]Jesus stood still and called them, saying, "What do you want me to do for you?" [33]They said to him, "Lord, let our eyes be opened." [34]Moved with compassion, Jesus touched their eyes. Immediately they regained their sight and followed him.

21 When they had come near Jerusalem and had reached Bethphage, at the Mount of Olives, Jesus sent two disciples, [2]saying to them, "Go into the village ahead of you, and immediately you will find a donkey tied and a colt with her; untie them and bring them to me. [3]If anyone says anything to you, just say this, 'The Lord needs them.' And he will send them immediately."[n] [4]This took place to fulfill what had been spoken through the prophet:
[5] "Tell the daughter of Zion,
Look, your king is coming to you,
    humble and mounted on a donkey,
        and on a colt, the foal of a donkey."
[6]The disciples went and did as Jesus had directed them; [7]they brought the donkey and the colt and put their cloaks on them, and he sat on them. [8]A very large crowd[o] spread their cloaks on the road, and others cut branches from the trees and spread them on the road. [9]The crowds that went ahead of him and that followed were shouting,

l 20.22 Other ancient authorities add or to be baptized with the baptism that I am baptized with? m 20.30 Other ancient authorities lack Lord n 21.3 Or 'The Lord needs them and will send them back immediately.' o 21.8 Or Most of the crowd

20:20–28 Greatness: The request of the mother of James and John. 20:25 *You know that the rulers of the gentiles lord it over them.* Several passages in Matthew exhibit anti-gentile prejudice. Gentiles provide a negative example in Jesus's teaching in the Sermon on the Mount. If you only greet your brothers and sisters (5:47); heap up empty phrases when you pray (6:7); or worry about what you will eat, drink, or wear (6:31–32), Jesus says you are no better than the gentiles. The same logic applies to the ethnocentric mission where Jesus tells his disciples to avoid the gentiles (10:5–6, 18) and how to conduct discipline in the "church" ("ekklēsia"). Here in v. 25, a similar negative sentiment can be detected. Jesus holds up the gentiles as an example of what not to do. At various points in Matthew, gentiles are the antithesis of the kingdom of heaven.

21:1–11 Jesus enters Jerusalem on a donkey and colt. 21:5 Here Matthew is citing Zech. 9:9: "See, your king comes to you; triumphant and victorious is he, humble and riding on a donkey, on a colt, the foal of a donkey." A hallmark feature of Hebrew poetry is parallelism with three main forms: synonymous, antithetic, and synthetic parallelism (see **"Hebrew Poetry," p. 741**). Zechariah 9:9 is a classic example of synonymous parallelism, where two lines are repeated in synonymous relationship, saying the same thing twice. Matthew apparently misreads Zech. 9:9 and has Jesus awkwardly riding into Jerusalem straddling two animals, a colt *and* a donkey (21:5). By contrast, in Mark 11:7 there is only one animal, a colt.

"Hosanna to the Son of David!
    Blessed is the one who comes in the
        name of the Lord!
    Hosanna in the highest heaven!"
[10]When he entered Jerusalem, the whole city was in turmoil, asking, "Who is this?" [11]The crowds were saying, "This is the prophet Jesus from Nazareth in Galilee."

[12] Then Jesus entered the temple[p] and drove out all who were selling and buying in the temple, and he overturned the tables of the money changers and the seats of those who sold doves. [13]He said to them, "It is written,

'My house shall be called a house of
    prayer,'

but you are making it a den of robbers."

[14] The blind and the lame came to him in the temple, and he cured them. [15]But when the chief priests and the scribes saw the amazing things that he did and heard[q] the children crying out in the temple and saying, "Hosanna to the Son of David," they became angry [16]and said to him, "Do you hear what these are saying?" Jesus said to them, "Yes; have you never read,

'Out of the mouths of infants and nursing
    babies
    you have prepared praise for
        yourself'?"

[17]He left them, went out of the city to Bethany, and spent the night there.

[18] In the morning, when he returned to the city, he was hungry. [19]And seeing a fig tree by the side of the road, he went to it and found nothing at all on it but leaves. Then he said to it, "May no fruit ever come from you again!" And the fig tree withered at once. [20]When the disciples saw it, they were amazed, saying, "How did the fig tree wither at once?" [21]Jesus answered them, "Truly I tell you, if you have faith and do not doubt, not only will you do what has been done to the fig tree, but even if you say to this mountain, 'Be lifted up and thrown into the sea,' it will be done.

[22]Whatever you ask for in prayer with faith, you will receive."

[23] When he entered the temple, the chief priests and the elders of the people came to him as he was teaching and said, "By what authority are you doing these things, and who gave you this authority?" [24]Jesus said to them, "I will also ask you one question; if you tell me the answer, then I will also tell you by what authority I do these things. [25]Did the baptism of John come from heaven, or was it of human origin?" And they argued with one another, "If we say, 'From heaven,' he will say to us, 'Why, then, did you not believe him?' [26]But if we say, 'Of human origin,' we are afraid of the crowd, for all regard John as a prophet." [27]So they answered Jesus, "We do not know." And he said to them, "Neither will I tell you by what authority I am doing these things.

[28] "What do you think? A man had two sons; he went to the first and said, 'Son, go and work in the vineyard today.' [29]He answered, 'I will not,' but later he changed his mind and went. [30]The father[r] went to the second and said the same, and he answered, 'I go, sir,' but he did not go. [31]Which of the two did the will of his father?" They said, "The first." Jesus said to them, "Truly I tell you, the tax collectors and the prostitutes are going into the kingdom of God ahead of you. [32]For John came to you in the way of righteousness, and you did not believe him, but the tax collectors and the prostitutes believed him, and even after you saw it you did not change your minds and believe him.

[33] "Listen to another parable. There was a landowner who planted a vineyard, put a fence around it, dug a winepress in it, and built a watchtower. Then he leased it to tenants and went away. [34]When the harvest time had come, he sent his slaves to the tenants to collect his produce. [35]But the tenants seized

p 21.12 Other ancient authorities add *of God*   q 21.15 Gk lacks *heard*   r 21.30 Gk *He*

21:12–17 Jesus cleanses the temple. 21:13 Matthew cites Isa. 56:7. **21:14** Jesus heals those who are blind and lame. Healing and restoring life lie at the heart of Matthew's depiction of Jesus as the Son of David (see **"David," p. 558**). **21:16** Matthew cites Ps. 8:2.

21:18–22 Jesus curses a fig tree. Matthew juxtaposes the cleansing of the temple with the cursing of a fig tree. Both scenes are prophetic actions that symbolize that "something greater than the temple is here" (12:6).

21:28–32 The parable of the Two Sons. This parable is unique to Matthew. Jesus likens the Pharisees to the second son, who said he would work in the vineyard but did not. The gentile mission is implicitly referenced in the first son. Jesus makes this explicit when he says *the tax collectors and the prostitutes are going into the kingdom of God ahead of you* (v. 31).

his slaves and beat one, killed another, and stoned another. ³⁶Again he sent other slaves, more than the first, and they treated them in the same way. ³⁷Then he sent his son to them, saying, 'They will respect my son.' ³⁸But when the tenants saw the son, they said to themselves, 'This is the heir; come, let us kill him and get his inheritance.' ³⁹So they seized him, threw him out of the vineyard, and killed him. ⁴⁰Now when the owner of the vineyard comes, what will he do to those tenants?" ⁴¹They said to him, "He will put those wretches to a miserable death and lease the vineyard to other tenants who will give him the produce at the harvest time."

42 Jesus said to them, "Have you never read in the scriptures:

'The stone that the builders rejected
   has become the cornerstone;ˢ
this was the Lord's doing,
   and it is amazing in our eyes'?
⁴³"Therefore I tell you, the kingdom of God will be taken away from you and given to a people that produces its fruits. ⁴⁴The one who falls on this stone will be broken to pieces, and it will crush anyone on whom it falls."ᵗ

45 When the chief priests and the Pharisees heard his parables, they realized that he was speaking about them. ⁴⁶They wanted to arrest him, but they feared the crowds, because they regarded him as a prophet.

22 Once more Jesus spoke to them in parables, saying: ²"The kingdom of heaven may be compared to a king who gave a wedding banquet for his son. ³He sent his slaves to call those who had been invited to the wedding banquet, but they would not come. ⁴Again he sent other slaves, saying, 'Tell those who have been invited: Look, I have prepared my dinner, my oxen and my fat

calves have been slaughtered, and everything is ready; come to the wedding banquet.' ⁵But they made light of it and went away, one to his farm, another to his business, ⁶while the rest seized his slaves, mistreated them, and killed them. ⁷The king was enraged. He sent his troops, destroyed those murderers, and burned their city. ⁸Then he said to his slaves, 'The wedding is ready, but those invited were not worthy. ⁹Go therefore into the main streets, and invite everyone you find to the wedding banquet.' ¹⁰Those slaves went out into the streets and gathered all whom they found, both good and bad, so the wedding hall was filled with guests.

11 "But when the king came in to see the guests, he noticed a man there who was not wearing a wedding robe, ¹²and he said to him, 'Friend, how did you get in here without a wedding robe?' And he was speechless. ¹³Then the king said to the attendants, 'Bind him hand and foot, and throw him into the outer darkness, where there will be weeping and gnashing of teeth.' ¹⁴For many are called, but few are chosen."

15 Then the Pharisees went and plotted to entrap him in what he said. ¹⁶So they sent their disciples to him, along with the Herodians, saying, "Teacher, we know that you are sincere, and teach the way of God in accordance with truth, and show deference to no one, for you do not regard people with partiality. ¹⁷Tell us, then, what you think. Is it lawful to pay taxes to Caesar or not?" ¹⁸But Jesus, aware of their malice, said, "Why are you putting me to the test, you hypocrites? ¹⁹Show me the coin used for the tax." And they brought him a denarius. ²⁰Then he said to them, "Whose head is this and whose title?" ²¹They answered,

ˢ 21.42 Or *keystone* (in an arch) ᵗ 21.44 Other ancient authorities lack 21.44

21:42 Matthew cites Ps. 118:22–23 (see also Acts 4:11; 1 Pet. 2:7). **21:45** Matthew purports to read the minds of the chief priests and Pharisees, who *realized that he was speaking about them*.

22:15–22 Jesus is questioned about paying taxes. Jesus can be seen as strategically responding to the Pharisees, but Matthew may also be responding to the Roman rulers of his own time. Matthew suggests that Jesus declares the arrival of a new empire that implicitly supplants Caesar. With the death of Nero in 68 CE, the Julio-Claudian dynasty came to an end. To support the Flavian dynasty, many of its allies appealed to oracles, omens, signs, and visions as proof of the gods' disfavor with the Julio-Claudian dynasty and, conversely, as proof of the gods' favor with Vespasian. Vespasian issued coins that presented himself as the recipient of the gods' favor and blessings. In addition, Roman poets like Statius and Martial praise Domitian, Vespasian's son, as "the world's sure salvation" ("Rerum certa salus") and as "that present deity" ("deus praesens"). Both Jesus and Caesar are presented to their followers as manifesting divine sovereignty, presence, and agency. This story contains a veiled critique of Rome, even as Matthew's Jesus rhetorically outmaneuvers the Pharisees yet again. **22:16** Little is known about the Herodians except that

"Caesar's." Then he said to them, "Give therefore to Caesar the things that are Caesar's and to God the things that are God's." ²²When they heard this, they were amazed, and they left him and went away.

23 The same day some Sadducees came to him saying there is no resurrection,ᵘ and they asked him a question: ²⁴"Teacher, Moses said, 'If a man dies childless, his brother shall marry the widow and raise up children for his brother.' ²⁵Now there were seven brothers among us; the first married and died childless, leaving the widow to his brother. ²⁶The second did the same, so also the third, down to the seventh. ²⁷Last of all, the woman herself died. ²⁸In the resurrection, then, whose wife of the seven will she be? For all of them had married her."

29 Jesus answered them, "You are wrong because you know neither the scriptures nor the power of God. ³⁰For in the resurrection people neither marry nor are given in marriage but are like angels of Godᵛ in heaven. ³¹And as for the resurrection of the dead, have you not read what was said to you by God, ³²'I am the God of Abraham, the God of Isaac, and the God of Jacob'? He is God not of the dead but of the living." ³³And when the crowds heard it, they were astounded at his teaching.

34 When the Pharisees heard that he had silenced the Sadducees, they gathered together, ³⁵and one of them, an expert in the law,

asked him a question to test him. ³⁶"Teacher, which commandment in the law is the greatest?" ³⁷He said to him, " 'You shall love the Lord your God with all your heart and with all your soul and with all your mind.' ³⁸This is the greatest and first commandment. ³⁹And a second is like it: 'You shall love your neighbor as yourself.' ⁴⁰On these two commandments hang all the Law and the Prophets."

41 Now while the Pharisees were gathered together, Jesus asked them this question: ⁴²"What do you think of the Messiah?ʷ Whose son is he?" They said to him, "The son of David." ⁴³He said to them, "How is it then that David by the Spiritˣ calls him Lord, saying,

⁴⁴ 'The Lord said to my Lord,
"Sit at my right hand,
    until I put your enemies under your
        feet" '?

⁴⁵"If David thus calls him Lord, how can he be his son?" ⁴⁶No one was able to give him an answer, nor from that day did anyone dare to ask him any more questions.

23 Then Jesus said to the crowds and to his disciples, ²"The scribes and the Pharisees sit on Moses's seat; ³therefore, do whatever they teach you and follow it, but

u 22.23 Other ancient authorities read *who say that there is no resurrection* v 22.30 Other ancient authorities lack *of God* w 22.42 Or *Christ* x 22.43 Gk *in spirit*

they were likely affiliated with and supportive of King Herod and the Herodian dynasty. **22:21** Jesus's clever response silences his opponents: *Give therefore to Caesar the things that are Caesar's and to God the things that are God's.* A debate about paying the temple tax occurs earlier in 17:24–27.

22:23–33 Jesus is questioned about the resurrection. The Sadducees were a Judean/Jewish group of wealthy priests distinct from and often in competition with the Pharisees. They rejected the oral tradition of the Pharisees and did not believe in resurrection (Acts 23:8; see **"Resurrection," p. 1224, and "Resurrection in the Gospels," p. 1767**). The practice of Levirate marriage requires that the husband's brother marry the widow (Deut. 25:5).

22:34–40 Jesus is questioned about the greatest commandment. The entirety of the Law can be summed up by the commandment to love. Love of God and love of neighbor—that is the central teaching of the Law and the Prophets (Deut. 6:5; Lev. 19:18).

22:41–46 Jesus questions the Pharisees about David's son. A question about the Son of David is raised again in this passage, but this time by Jesus himself. Jesus's identification as the Son of David is a theological claim that collides with Rome in two ways. First, unlike Roman emperors who exploit the inhabitants of their empire, Jesus is a shepherd who provides deliverance and protection. Second, against imperial claims that declare Rome to be the eternal city ("urbs aeterna"), the Davidic tradition presents a counterclaim. Jesus's power to heal and perform exorcisms is an implicit challenge to Rome, which exists under Satan's dominion. These realities have been clearly demonstrated up to this point in the narrative of the genealogy (1:1), Joseph in the birth narrative (1:20), the healing of two men who are blind (9:27), the story of the Canaanite woman (15:22), another account of healing two men who are blind (20:30–31), the triumphal entry into Jerusalem (21:9, 15), and the cleansing of the temple (21:15).

23:1–36 Jesus casts judgments upon the scribes and Pharisees. The sharp rhetoric of this passage has led some to believe that the church replaces Israel. This is a crucial part of the troubling dominant

Focus On: Pharisees (Matthew 23)

The Pharisees were a group in Second Temple Judaism who appear in the writings of the historian Josephus, in the New Testament, and in early rabbinic literature, but their image does not emerge clearly because of writer bias and incomplete information. "Pharisee" literally means "separatist," but we do not know if the term came from insiders or outsiders nor exactly from what they separated.

Josephus reports the Pharisees were a group respected by the people in religious matters, one of three philosophical schools of first-century Jews. They believed in both fate and free will and in life after death and were scrupulous in interpreting the Torah according to their own traditions. They engaged with politics at times, during the reign of Queen Alexandra Salome (76–67 BCE), in the period of Herod the Great (37–4 BCE), and at the beginning of the Jewish revolt (66–67 CE) when they counseled against the rebellion.

The New Testament shows multiple appearances of the Pharisees, often as opponents of or debate partners with Jesus. It affirms their belief—shared with Jesus and his followers—in the resurrection of the dead (Acts 23:6, 8; see "Resurrection," p. 1224; "Resurrection in the Gospels," p. 1767). Mark 7:3 indicates their "traditions of the elders," interpretations of Torah law. Hypocrisy appears as a frequent barb against them, especially in Matt. 23, but the truth of their teaching is affirmed in 23:2. Multiple references also show Jesus eating with them as commonplace (Luke 7:36; 11:37; 14:1–6). Paul identifies himself as a Pharisee, presenting it as proof of his Jewish piety (Phil. 3:5).

Early rabbinic texts show the rabbis, Jewish leaders consolidating the religion after the destruction of the Second Temple, identifying with positions that characterized the Pharisees: belief in resurrection of the dead, adherence to an "oral law" that expanded on the written Torah, care in matters of law observance like ritual purity and tithing, and an influence (possibly more aspirational than real) with the masses (m. Yadayim 4:6–7; m. Yevamot 1:4). In disputes between Pharisees and Sadducees, the Pharisaic position accords with the rabbis' decisions. Furthermore, the importance of the Gamaliel family in the rabbinic tradition links to references in Josephus and Acts to these figures as Pharisees. These many links leave the overwhelming impression that the rabbis see themselves as carrying on the Pharisees' teachings.

Because the mainstream Judaism of today is rabbinic and that tradition reveres the Pharisees, it is crucial that Christians understand the Pharisees on their own terms as an authentic form of early Judaism, striving to serve God and follow the Torah, not as mere negative foils to Jesus nor as his enemies.

Claudia Setzer

do not do as they do, for they do not practice what they teach. ⁴They tie up heavy burdens, hard to bear,ʸ and lay them on the shoulders of others, but they themselves are unwilling to lift a finger to move them. ⁵They do all their deeds to be seen by others, for they make their phylacteries broad and their fringes long. ⁶They love to have the place of honor at banquets and the best seats in the synagogues ⁷and to be greeted with respect in the marketplaces and to have people call them rabbi. ⁸But you are not to be called rabbi, for you have one teacher, and you are all brothers and sisters. ⁹And call no one your father on earth, for you have one Father, the one in heaven. ¹⁰Nor are you to be called instructors, for you have one instructor, the Messiah.ᶻ ¹¹The greatest among you will be your servant. ¹²All who exalt themselves will be humbled, and all who humble themselves will be exalted.

13 "But woe to you, scribes and Pharisees, hypocrites! For you lock people out of the kingdom of heaven. For you do not go in yourselves, and when others are going in you stop them.ᵃ

y 23.4 Other ancient authorities lack *hard to bear*
z 23.10 Or *the Christ* a 23.13 Other authorities add 23.14 here (or after 23.12): *Woe to you, scribes and Pharisees, hypocrites! For you devour widows' houses, and for the sake of appearance you make long prayers; therefore you will receive the greater condemnation*

narrative of early Christian origins, which represents Judean/Jewish particularism in opposition to Christian universalism. According to this reading, Christian universalism is open, inclusive, and superior to parochial and ethnic Judaism. Moreover, this logic is often viewed as being inscribed in the narrative framework of Matthew. The initial promise of Judean/Jewish salvation in Matt. 1:21 eventually gives way to include gentiles and exclude Judeans/Jews in the Great Commission of Matt. 28:18–20. This is problematic for a number of reasons, not least of which is a demeaning stereotype of Judaism as

¹⁵Woe to you, scribes and Pharisees, hypocrites! For you cross sea and land to make a single convert, and you make the new convert twice as much a child of hell*[b] as yourselves.

16 "Woe to you, blind guides who say, 'Whoever swears by the sanctuary is bound by nothing, but whoever swears by the gold of the sanctuary is bound by the oath.' ¹⁷You blind fools! For which is greater, the gold or the sanctuary that has made the gold sacred? ¹⁸And you say, 'Whoever swears by the altar is bound by nothing, but whoever swears by the gift that is on the altar is bound by the oath.' ¹⁹How blind you are! For which is greater, the gift or the altar that makes the gift sacred? ²⁰So whoever swears by the altar swears by it and by everything on it, ²¹and whoever swears by the sanctuary swears by it and by the one who dwells in it, ²²and whoever swears by heaven swears by the throne of God and by the one who is seated upon it.

23 "Woe to you, scribes and Pharisees, hypocrites! For you tithe mint, dill, and cumin and have neglected the weightier matters of the law: justice and mercy and faith. It is these you ought to have practiced without neglecting the others. ²⁴You blind guides! You strain out a gnat but swallow a camel!

25 "Woe to you, scribes and Pharisees, hypocrites! For you clean the outside of the cup and of the plate, but inside they are full of greed and self-indulgence. ²⁶You blind Pharisee! First clean the inside of the cup and of the plate,*[c] so that the outside also may become clean.

27 "Woe to you, scribes and Pharisees, hypocrites! For you are like whitewashed tombs, which on the outside look beautiful but inside are full of the bones of the dead and of all kinds of uncleanness. ²⁸So you also on the outside look righteous to others, but inside you are full of hypocrisy and lawlessness.

29 "Woe to you, scribes and Pharisees, hypocrites! For you build the tombs of the prophets and decorate the graves of the righteous, ³⁰and you say, 'If we had lived in the days of our ancestors, we would not have taken part with them in shedding the blood of the prophets.' ³¹Thus you testify against yourselves that you are descendants of those who murdered the prophets. ³²Fill up, then, the measure of your ancestors. ³³You snakes, you brood of vipers! How can you escape the judgment of hell?*[d] ³⁴For this reason I send you prophets, sages, and scribes, some of whom you will kill and crucify, and some you will flog in your synagogues and pursue from town to town, ³⁵so that upon you may come all the righteous blood shed on earth, from the blood of righteous Abel to the blood of Zechariah son of Barachiah, whom you murdered between the sanctuary and the altar. ³⁶Truly I tell you, all this will come upon this generation.

37 "Jerusalem, Jerusalem, the city that kills the prophets and stones those who are sent to it! How often have I desired to gather your children together as a hen gathers her brood under her wings, and you were not willing! ³⁸See, your house is left to you, desolate.*[e] ³⁹For I tell you, you will not see me again until you say, 'Blessed is the one who comes in the name of the Lord.'"

24 As Jesus came out of the temple and was going away, his disciples came to point out to him the buildings of the temple.

b 23.15 Gk *Gehenna* c 23.26 Other ancient authorities lack *and of the plate* d 23.33 Gk *Gehenna* e 23.38 Other ancient authorities lack *desolate*

exclusionary, primitive, and inferior. But it is also problematic for how it deracializes Christian origins. This reading of Matthew is misguided and has led to the perpetuation of Christian supersessionism and anti-Semitism (see **"Anti-Judaism," p. 1865**). Christian supersessionism is a form of replacement theology where Christianity supersedes Judaism as the church replaces Israel (see **"Supersessionism," p. 1647**). A more nuanced reading avoids pitting Judean/Jewish particularity against Christian universality. The harsh critique in this passage, therefore, is not a wholesale rejection of Judaism but a targeted critique of the Judean/Jewish authorities or competitors.

23:37–39 Jesus laments over Jerusalem. Jesus compares himself to a mother hen that gathers chicks under its wing. This statement and the parable of the Yeast (13:33), which compares the kingdom of heaven to a woman who bakes, use female metaphors (see **"Feminine Imagery for God," p. 1029**). The lament and compassion Jesus expresses over Jerusalem confirm that what is being denounced is not Judaism but certain groups within the community.

24:1–2 Jesus predicts the destruction of the temple. Matthew draws a close connection between the destruction of the temple (vv. 1–2) and the end times (vv. 3–14). From the standpoint of the earliest readers of Matthew, the temple has been destroyed and Rome has prevailed.

MATTHEW 24

²Then he asked them, "You see all these, do you not? Truly I tell you, not one stone will be left here upon another; all will be thrown down."

3 When he was sitting on the Mount of Olives, the disciples came to him privately, saying, "Tell us, when will this be, and what will be the sign of your coming and of the end of the age?" ⁴Jesus answered them, "Beware that no one leads you astray. ⁵For many will come in my name, saying, 'I am the Messiah!'ᶠ and they will lead many astray. ⁶And you will hear of wars and rumors of wars; see that you are not alarmed, for this must take place, but the end is not yet. ⁷For nation will rise against nation and kingdom against kingdom, and there will be faminesᵍ and earthquakes in various places: ⁸all this is but the beginning of the birth pangs.

9 "Then they will hand you over to be tortured and will put you to death, and you will be hated by all nations because of my name. ¹⁰Then many will fall away,ʰ and they will betray one another and hate one another. ¹¹And many false prophets will arise and lead many astray. ¹²And because of the increase of lawlessness, the love of many will grow cold. ¹³But the one who endures to the end will be saved. ¹⁴And this good newsⁱ of the kingdom will be proclaimed throughout the world, as a testimony to all the nations, and then the end will come.

15 "So when you see the desolating sacrilege, spoken of by the prophet Daniel, standing in the holy place (let the reader understand), ¹⁶then those in Judea must flee to the mountains; ¹⁷the one on the housetop must not go down to take things from the house; ¹⁸the one in the field must not turn back to get a coat. ¹⁹Woe to those who are pregnant and to those who are nursing infants in those days! ²⁰Pray that your flight may not be in winter or on a Sabbath. ²¹For at that time there will

be great suffering, such as has not been from the beginning of the world until now, no, and never will be. ²²And if those days had not been cut short, no one would be saved, but for the sake of the elect those days will be cut short. ²³Then if anyone says to you, 'Look! Here is the Messiah!'ʲ or 'There he is!'—do not believe it. ²⁴For false messiahsᵏ and false prophets will appear and produce great signs and wonders, to lead astray, if possible, even the elect. ²⁵Take note, I have told you beforehand. ²⁶So, if they say to you, 'Look! He is in the wilderness,' do not go out. If they say, 'Look! He is in the inner rooms,' do not believe it. ²⁷For as the lightning comes from the east and flashes as far as the west, so will be the coming of the Son of Man. ²⁸Wherever the corpse is, there the eagles will gather.

29 "Immediately after the suffering of those days

the sun will be darkened,
and the moon will not give its light;
the stars will fall from heaven,
and the powers of heaven will be
shaken.

³⁰"Then the sign of the Son of Man will appear in heaven, and then all the tribes of the earth will mourn, and they will see 'the Son of Man coming on the clouds of heaven' with power and great glory. ³¹And he will send out his angels with a loud trumpet call, and they will gather his elect from the four winds, from one end of heaven to the other.

32 "From the fig tree learn its lesson: as soon as its branch becomes tender and puts forth its leaves, you know that summer is near. ³³So also, when you see all these things, you know that heʲ is near, at the very gates. ³⁴Truly

f 24.5 Or the Christ   g 24.7 Other ancient authorities add and pestilences   h 24.10 Or stumble   i 24.14 Or gospel   j 24.23 Or the Christ   k 24.24 Or christs   l 24.33 Or it

24:3–14 Signs of the end of the age. The setting of the discourse on the Mount of Olives is fitting for the eschatological discourse, echoing Zech. 14:4. Many false messiahs and false prophets will come (see **"Jewish Messianic Ideas," p. 1783**). There will be war and famine. Hate and betrayal will abound, and many will fall away. All of these things are signs of the end times. **24:14** *As a testimony to all the nations.* The gentile mission in Matt. 28 is foreshadowed. The gospel of the kingdom will be preached to all nations prior to the end times.

24:15–28 The desolating sacrilege as prophesied by Daniel. 24:15 *Desolating sacrilege.* See Dan. 9:27; 11:31; 12:11. This is a reference to the profaning of the temple by Antiochus IV Epiphanes in 167 BCE. **24:21** See Dan. 12:1; Joel 2:2. **24:28** The eagle is a symbol of the Roman Empire, whose demise is prophesied.

24:29–31 The Son of Man is coming in power and glory. 24:29 See Isa. 13:10; Ezek. 32:7; Joel 2:10. **24:31** See Isa. 27:13; Zech. 9:14.

24:32–35 Jesus's words will not pass away. See Matt. 5:18.

I tell you, this generation will not pass away until all these things have taken place. 35 Heaven and earth will pass away, but my words will not pass away.

36 "But about that day and hour no one knows, neither the angels of heaven, nor the Son,[m] but only the Father. 37 For as the days of Noah were, so will be the coming of the Son of Man. 38 For as in the days before the flood they were eating and drinking, marrying and giving in marriage, until the day Noah entered the ark, 39 and they knew nothing until the flood came and swept them all away, so, too, will be the coming of the Son of Man. 40 Then two will be in the field; one will be taken, and one will be left. 41 Two women will be grinding meal together; one will be taken, and one will be left. 42 Keep awake, therefore, for you do not know on what day[n] your Lord is coming. 43 But understand this: if the owner of the house had known in what part of the night the thief was coming, he would have stayed awake and would not have let his house be broken into. 44 Therefore you also must be ready, for the Son of Man is coming at an hour you do not expect.

45 "Who, then, is the faithful and wise slave whom his master has put in charge of his household, to give the other slaves[o] their allowance of food at the proper time? 46 Blessed is that slave whom his master will find at work when he arrives. 47 Truly I tell you, he will put that one in charge of all his possessions. 48 But if that wicked slave says to himself, 'My master is delayed,' 49 and begins to beat his fellow slaves and eats and drinks with drunkards, 50 the master of that slave will come on a day when he does not expect him and at an hour that he does not know. 51 He will cut him in pieces[p] and put him with the hypocrites, where there will be weeping and gnashing of teeth.

25 "Then the kingdom of heaven will be like this. Ten young women[q] took their lamps and went to meet the bridegroom.[r] 2 Five of them were foolish, and five were wise. 3 When the foolish took their lamps, they took no oil with them, 4 but the wise took flasks of oil with their lamps. 5 As the bridegroom was delayed, all of them became drowsy and slept. 6 But at midnight there was a shout, 'Look! Here is the bridegroom! Come out to meet him.' 7 Then all those young women[s] got up and trimmed their lamps. 8 The foolish said to the wise, 'Give us some of your oil, for our lamps are going out.' 9 But the wise replied, 'No! there will not be enough for you and for us; you had better go to the dealers and buy some for yourselves.' 10 And while they went to buy it, the bridegroom came, and those who were ready went with him into the wedding banquet, and the door was shut. 11 Later the other young women[t] came also, saying, 'Lord, lord, open to us.' 12 But he replied, 'Truly I tell you, I do not know you.' 13 Keep awake, therefore, for you know neither the day nor the hour.[u]

14 "For it is as if a man, going on a journey, summoned his slaves and entrusted his property to them; 15 to one he gave five talents, to another two, to another one, to each according to his ability. Then he went away. At once 16 the one who had received the five talents went off and traded with them and made five more talents. 17 In the same way, the one who had the two talents made two more talents. 18 But the one who had received the one talent went off and dug a hole in the ground and hid his master's money. 19 After a long time the master of those slaves came and settled accounts with them. 20 Then the one who had received the five talents came forward, bringing five more talents, saying, 'Master, you handed over to me five talents; see, I have made five more talents.' 21 His master said to him, 'Well done, good and trustworthy slave; you have been trustworthy in a few things; I will put you in charge of many things; enter

m 24.36 Other ancient authorities lack *nor the Son*
n 24.42 Other ancient authorities read *at what hour*
o 24.45 Gk *to give them* *p* 24.51 Or *cut him off* *q* 25.1 Gk *virgins* *r* 25.1 Other ancient authorities add *and the bride*
s 25.7 Gk *virgins* *t* 25.11 Gk *virgins* *u* 25.13 Other ancient authorities add *in which the Son of Man is coming*

24:36–44 Be watchful, for no one knows the day or hour. Jesus issues an ethical imperative to be watchful, vigilant, and faithful, since the day or hour is unknown.

25:1–13 The parable of the Ten Bridesmaids. Matthew 24:42, which reminds hearers that no one knows the day of the Lord's coming, is illustrated in this parable (see also 1 Thess. 5:6).

25:14–30 The parable of the Talents. A talent is a large sum of money—possibly a year's wage or more. The point of the parable is to act faithfully and responsibly in view of the coming of the Son of Man. Those who are lazy, like the unfaithful enslaved person (24:45–51), will be punished with *outer darkness, where there will be weeping and gnashing of teeth* (v. 30; 8:12; 22:13).

into the joy of your master.' [22]And the one with the two talents also came forward, saying, 'Master, you handed over to me two talents; see, I have made two more talents.' [23]His master said to him, 'Well done, good and trustworthy slave; you have been trustworthy in a few things; I will put you in charge of many things; enter into the joy of your master.' [24]Then the one who had received the one talent also came forward, saying, 'Master, I knew that you were a harsh man, reaping where you did not sow and gathering where you did not scatter, [25]so I was afraid, and I went and hid your talent in the ground. Here you have what is yours.' [26]But his master replied, 'You wicked and lazy slave! You knew, did you, that I reap where I did not sow and gather where I did not scatter? [27]Then you ought to have invested my money with the bankers, and on my return I would have received what was my own with interest. [28]So take the talent from him, and give it to the one with the ten talents. [29]For to all those who have, more will be given, and they will have an abundance, but from those who have nothing, even what they have will be taken away. [30]As for this worthless slave, throw him into the outer darkness, where there will be weeping and gnashing of teeth.'

[31] "When the Son of Man comes in his glory and all the angels with him, then he will sit on the throne of his glory. [32]All the nations will be gathered before him, and he will separate people one from another as a shepherd separates the sheep from the goats, [33]and he will put the sheep at his right hand and the goats at the left. [34]Then the king will say to those at his right hand, 'Come, you who are blessed by my Father, inherit the kingdom prepared for you from the foundation of the world, [35]for I was hungry and you gave me food, I was thirsty and you gave me something to drink, I was a stranger and you welcomed me, [36]I was naked and you gave me clothing, I was sick and you took care of me, I was in prison and you visited me.' [37]Then the righteous will answer him, 'Lord, when was it that we saw you hungry and gave you food or thirsty and gave you something to drink? [38]And when was it that we saw you a stranger and welcomed you or naked and gave you clothing? [39]And when was it that we saw you sick or in prison and visited you?' [40]And the king will answer them, 'Truly I tell you, just as you did it to one of the least of these brothers and sisters of mine, you did it to me.' [41]Then he will say to those at his left hand, 'You who are accursed, depart from me into the eternal fire prepared for the devil and his angels, [42]for I was hungry and you gave me no food, I was thirsty and you gave me nothing to drink, [43]I was a stranger and you did not welcome me, naked and you did not give me clothing, sick and in prison and you did not visit me.' [44]Then they also will answer, 'Lord, when was it that we saw you hungry or thirsty or a stranger or naked or sick or in prison and did not take care of you?' [45]Then he will answer them, 'Truly I tell you, just as you did not do it to one of the least of these, you did not do it to me.' [46]And these will go away into eternal punishment but the righteous into eternal life."

26 When Jesus had finished saying all these things, he said to his disciples, [2]"You know that after two days the Passover is coming, and the Son of Man will be handed over to be crucified."

25:31–46 The parable of the Sheep and Goats. This parable picks up another important theme in Matthew about the importance of actions over words. The theme is vividly illustrated at the conclusion of the Sermon on the Mount: "And everyone who hears these words of mine and does not act on them will be like a foolish man who built his house on sand. The rain fell, and the floods came, and the winds blew and beat against that house, and it fell—and great was its fall!" (7:26–27). In much the same way, those who are welcomed into the kingdom in this parable are those who feed the hungry, give drink to the thirsty, and visit those in prison.

26:1–5 The chief priests and elders plot against Jesus. The central conflict between Jesus and the chief priests comes to a head in chap. 26. Matthew depicts a significant power differential that exists between both groups. The chief priests and elders have convened in session—a repeated motif throughout the passion narrative (26:4; 27:1; 27:62; 28:12). They are assembled in a place of power in the courtyard of Caiaphas with other high-ranking Judean/Jewish temple personnel. Fearful of the crowds, they devise a plot to capture Jesus secretly. By contrast, Jesus and his disciples are on the outskirts of Bethany in the house of Simon the leper. As the conflict escalates, Jesus and his disciples are minoritized by the priestly and Roman imperial authorities. In this way, the opening verses of the passion narrative set the stage for what follows.

3 Then the chief priests and the elders of the people gathered in the courtyard of the high priest, who was called Caiaphas, ⁴and they conspired to arrest Jesus by stealth and kill him. ⁵But they said, "Not during the festival, or there may be a riot among the people."

6 Now while Jesus was at Bethany in the house of Simon the leper,ᵛ ⁷a woman came to him with an alabaster jar of very costly ointment, and she poured it on his head as he sat at the table. ⁸But when the disciples saw it, they were angry and said, "Why this waste? ⁹For this ointment could have been sold for a large sum and the money given to the poor." ¹⁰But Jesus, aware of this, said to them, "Why do you trouble the woman? She has performed a good service for me. ¹¹For you always have the poor with you, but you will not always have me. ¹²By pouring this ointment on my body she has prepared me for burial. ¹³Truly I tell you, wherever this good newsᵂ is proclaimed in the whole world, what she has done will be told in remembrance of her."

14 Then one of the twelve, who was called Judas Iscariot, went to the chief priests ¹⁵and said, "What will you give me if I betray him to you?" They paid him thirty pieces of silver. ¹⁶And from that moment he began to look for an opportunity to betray him.

17 On the first day of Unleavened Bread the disciples came to Jesus, saying, "Where do you want us to make the preparations for you to eat the Passover?" ¹⁸He said, "Go into the city to a certain man and say to him, 'The Teacher says, My time is near; I will keep the Passover at your house with my disciples.'" ¹⁹So the disciples did as Jesus had directed them, and they prepared the Passover meal.

20 When it was evening, he took his place with the twelve disciples,ˣ ²¹and while they were eating he said, "Truly I tell you, one of you will betray me." ²²And they became greatly distressed and began to say to him one after another, "Surely not I, Lord?" ²³He answered, "The one who has dipped his hand into the bowl with me will betray me. ²⁴The Son of Man goes as it is written of him, but woe to that one by whom the Son of Man is betrayed! It would have been better for that one not to have been born." ²⁵Judas, who betrayed him, said, "Surely not I, Rabbi?" He replied, "You have said so."

26 While they were eating, Jesus took a loaf of bread, and after blessing itʸ he broke it, gave it to the disciples, and said, "Take, eat; this is my body." ²⁷Then he took a cup, and after giving thanks he gave it to them, saying, "Drink from it, all of you, ²⁸for this is my blood of theᶻ covenant, which is poured out for many for the forgiveness of sins. ²⁹I tell you, I will never

v 26.6 Or *the skin-diseased* w 26.13 Or *gospel* x 26.20 Other ancient authorities lack *disciples* y 26.26 Other ancient authorities read *after giving thanks* z 26.28 Other ancient authorities add *new*

26:6–13 An anonymous woman anoints Jesus. Matthew sandwiches this story between the schemes of the Judean/Jewish leaders and the betrayal of Judas. The point is to highlight the perceptive insight of the anonymous woman who anoints Jesus's body for burial. The disciples are indignant and call the woman's act a waste. Jesus defends the woman, highlighting the significance of what she has done. **26:13** *What she has done will be told in remembrance of her.* The grammatical construction of this verse in Greek opens up a different possibility for understanding this phrase as a subjective genitive. An alternative translation is "Truly I say to you, wherever this gospel is preached throughout the whole world, what she has done as her memorial will be mentioned." This reading has the benefit of highlighting the woman's action and agency with the verbal quality of the head noun "memorial" based on its previous use in Matt. 16:8–9. The woman perceives what the disciples time and again fail to understand. This story highlights the special insight and role women play throughout Matthew and in the passion narrative.

26:14–16 Judas makes a deal to betray Jesus. The chiastic structure of 26:1–16 pushes the narrative forward. The chief priests are fearful of inciting a riot, so they need to find a way to apprehend Jesus covertly, away from the public eye. What the chief priests seek in vv. 3–5 Judas provides in vv. 14–16. There is a sharp contrast between Judas and the anonymous woman. The woman performs an extravagant act of anointing Jesus with expensive nard, while Judas betrays Jesus for thirty pieces of silver (v. 15; anticipating Matt. 28:12).

26:17–25 The Passover. The theme of division continues with the Passover (Exod. 12:3, 6, 18–27). The Passover celebrated Israel's liberation from bondage in Egypt (see **"Passover," p. 99**). During this celebratory meal, Jesus warns his disciples that one of the disciples will betray him (see Ps. 41:9).

26:26–30 The Lord's Supper. *My blood of the covenant.* This is a reference to when Moses sprinkles the people with the blood of a sacrificial animal (Exod. 24:8) to seal God's covenant with Israel (see

again drink of this fruit of the vine until that day when I drink it new with you in my Father's kingdom."

30 When they had sung the hymn, they went out to the Mount of Olives.

31 Then Jesus said to them, "You will all fall away[a] because of me this night, for it is written,

'I will strike the shepherd,
and the sheep of the flock will be
scattered.'

[32]"But after I am raised up, I will go ahead of you to Galilee." [33]Peter said to him, "Even if all fall away[b] because of you, I will never fall away."[c] [34]Jesus said to him, "Truly I tell you, this very night, before the cock crows, you will deny me three times." [35]Peter said to him, "Even though I must die with you, I will not deny you." And so said all the disciples.

36 Then Jesus went with them to a place called Gethsemane, and he said to his disciples, "Sit here while I go over there and pray." [37]He took with him Peter and the two sons of Zebedee and began to be grieved and agitated. [38]Then he said to them, "My soul is deeply grieved, even to death; remain here, and stay awake with me." [39]And going a little farther, he threw himself on the ground and prayed, "My Father, if it is possible, let this cup pass from me, yet not what I want but what you want." [40]Then he came to the disciples and found them sleeping, and he said to Peter, "So, could you not stay awake with me one hour? [41]Stay awake and pray that you may not come into the time of trial;[d] the spirit indeed is willing, but the flesh is weak." [42]Again he went away for the second time and prayed, "My Father, if this cannot pass unless I drink it, your will be done." [43]Again he came and found them sleeping, for their eyes were heavy. [44]So leaving them again, he went away and prayed for

the third time, saying the same words. [45]Then he came to the disciples and said to them, "Are you still sleeping and taking your rest? Now the hour is at hand, and the Son of Man is betrayed into the hands of sinners. [46]Get up, let us be going. Look, my betrayer is at hand."

47 While he was still speaking, Judas, one of the twelve, arrived; with him was a large crowd with swords and clubs, from the chief priests and the elders of the people. [48]Now the betrayer had given them a sign, saying, "The one I will kiss is the man; arrest him." [49]At once he came up to Jesus and said, "Greetings, Rabbi!" and kissed him. [50]Jesus said to him, "Friend, do what you are here to do."[e] Then they came and laid hands on Jesus and arrested him. [51]Suddenly one of those with Jesus put his hand on his sword, drew it, and struck the slave of the high priest, cutting off his ear. [52]Then Jesus said to him, "Put your sword back into its place, for all who take the sword will die by the sword. [53]Do you think that I cannot appeal to my Father, and he will at once send me more than twelve legions of angels? [54]But how then would the scriptures be fulfilled, which say it must happen in this way?" [55]At that hour Jesus said to the crowds, "Have you come out with swords and clubs to arrest me as though I were a rebel? Day after day I sat in the temple teaching, and you did not arrest me. [56]But all this has taken place, so that the scriptures of the prophets may be fulfilled." Then all the disciples deserted him and fled.

57 Those who had arrested Jesus took him to Caiaphas the high priest, where the scribes and the elders had gathered. [58]But Peter was following him at a distance, as far as the courtyard of the high priest, and going inside he sat with the guards in order to see how this

---

a 26.31 Or *stumble* b 26.33 Or *stumble* c 26.33 Or *stumble*
d 26.41 Or *into testing* e 26.50 Or *Why are you here?*

"Covenant," p. 23). *Poured out for many for the forgiveness of sins.* This phrase is an allusion to the suffering servant in Isa. 53:12 (see **"The Servant(s) of YHWH," p. 1011**).

26:31-35 Jesus predicts Peter's denial. After the Passover meal, Jesus predicts that all of his disciples "will be scattered." *I will go ahead of you to Galilee.* This reference anticipates the end of the Gospel when the resurrected Jesus meets the disciples in Galilee (28:16-20).

26:36-46 Jesus prays in Gethsemane. The prayer in Gethsemane reveals the difficulty and turmoil Jesus experiences while the disciples fall asleep. *My soul is deeply grieved, even to death.* See Ps. 42:6.

26:47-56 Jesus is betrayed by a kiss and placed under arrest. Jesus is betrayed with a kiss (see 2 Sam. 20:9). *For all who take the sword will die by the sword.* See Gen. 9:6.

26:57-66 Jesus is falsely accused before the high priest. The scene unfolds in a series of couplets. There are two narrations of Jesus coming into the courtroom (vv. 57-58), two witnesses are summoned by the Sanhedrin (vv. 59-61), two questions are asked by the high priest (vv. 62-63), two charges of blasphemy are made (vv. 65-66), and two acts of mockery close the scene (vv. 67-68).

would end. ⁵⁹Now the chief priests and the whole council were looking for false testimony against Jesus so that they might put him to death, ⁶⁰but they found none, though many false witnesses came forward. At last two came forward ⁶¹and said, "This fellow said, 'I am able to destroy the temple of God and to build it in three days.'" ⁶²The high priest stood up and said, "Have you no answer? What is it that they testify against you?" ⁶³But Jesus was silent. Then the high priest said to him, "I put you under oath before the living God, tell us if you are the Messiah,ᶠ the Son of God." ⁶⁴Jesus said to him, "You have said so. But I tell you,

From now on you will see the Son of Man
seated at the right hand of Power
and coming on the clouds of heaven."

⁶⁵Then the high priest tore his clothes and said, "He has blasphemed! Why do we still need witnesses? You have now heard his blasphemy. ⁶⁶What do you think?" They answered, "He deserves death." ⁶⁷Then they spat in his face and struck him, and some slapped him, ⁶⁸saying, "Prophesy to us, you Messiah!ᵍ Who is it that struck you?"

69 Now Peter was sitting outside in the courtyard. A female servant came to him and said, "You also were with Jesus the Galilean." ⁷⁰But he denied it before all of them, saying, "I do not know what you are talking about." ⁷¹When he went out to the porch, another female servant saw him, and she said to the bystanders, "This man was with Jesus the Nazarene."ʰ ⁷²Again he denied it with an oath, "I do not know the man." ⁷³After a little while the bystanders came up and said to Peter, "Certainly you are also one of them, for your accent betrays you." ⁷⁴Then he began to curse, and he swore an oath, "I do not know the man!"

At that moment the cock crowed. ⁷⁵Then Peter remembered what Jesus had said: "Before the cock crows, you will deny me three times." And he went out and wept bitterly.

27 When morning came, all the chief priests and the elders of the people conferred together against Jesus in order to bring about his death. ²They bound him, led him away, and handed him over to Pilate the governor.

3 When Judas, his betrayer, saw that Jesusⁱ was condemned, he repented and brought back the thirty pieces of silver to the chief priests and the elders. ⁴He said, "I have sinned by betraying innocentʲ blood." But they said, "What is that to us? See to it yourself." ⁵Throwing down the pieces of silver in the temple, he departed, and he went and hanged himself. ⁶But the chief priests, taking the pieces of silver, said, "It is not lawful to put them into the treasury, since they are blood money." ⁷After conferring together, they used them to buy the potter's field as a place to bury foreigners. ⁸For this reason that field has been called the Field of Blood to this day. ⁹Then was fulfilled what had been spoken through the prophet Jeremiah,ᵏ "And they tookˡ the thirty pieces of silver, the price of the one on whom a price had been set,ᵐ on whom some of the people of Israel had set a price, ¹⁰and they gaveⁿ them for the potter's field, as the Lord commanded me."

11 Now Jesus stood before the governor, and the governor asked him, "Are you the king of

f 26.63 Or *Christ* g 26.68 Or *Christ* h 26.71 Gk *Nazorean*
i 27.3 Gk *he* j 27.4 Other ancient authorities read *righteous* k 27.9 Other ancient authorities read *Zechariah* or *Isaiah* l 27.9 Or *I took* m 27.9 Or *the price of the precious One* n 27.10 Other ancient authorities read *I gave*

26:69–75 Peter's accent betrays him, and he denies Jesus. Matthew juxtaposes the scene with Jesus inside and Peter outside the courtyard of the high priest. Peter is recognized by three individuals. How he is identified is noteworthy. On the first two occasions, Peter is identified as being with *Jesus the Galilean* (v. 69) and *Jesus the Nazarene* (v. 71). On the third occasion, the racial/ethnic association is stronger: *Certainly you are also one of them, for your accent betrays you* (v. 73). Here, Peter's accent functions as a racial/ethnic marker to identify and differentiate Jesus and his disciples.

27:1–2 Jesus is handed over to Pilate. The conflict that started between Jesus and Herod in Matt. 2 continues here in chap. 27. Jesus and Pilate are both referred to as "ruler" or "governor" (*hēgemōn*; Matt. 2:6; 27:2). The question that Pilate poses to Jesus in 27:11–14 is a political, rather than messianic, inquiry. If Jesus is in fact the leader of the resistance, he poses a viable threat to Rome. Jesus is "handed over" throughout the passion narrative (26:2, 45; 27:2, 18, 26).

27:3–10 Judas commits suicide. The story of Judas's suicide is only found in Matthew (cf. Acts 1:18).

27:11–14 Pilate questions Jesus. *Are you the king of the Jews?* Jesus's marginalized identity as Judean/Jew is highlighted throughout the passion narrative. The title "king of the Judeans/Jews" is cited at key points in the passion narrative. It serves as the basis for Jesus's interrogation before Pilate

the Jews?" Jesus said, "You say so." [12]But when he was accused by the chief priests and elders, he did not answer. [13]Then Pilate said to him, "Do you not hear how many accusations they make against you?" [14]But he gave him no answer, not even to a single charge, so that the governor was greatly amazed.

15 Now at the festival the governor was accustomed to release a prisoner for the crowd, anyone whom they wanted. [16]At that time they had a notorious prisoner called Jesus[o] Barabbas. [17]So after they had gathered, Pilate said to them, "Whom do you want me to release for you, Jesus[p] Barabbas or Jesus who is called the Messiah?"[q] [18]For he realized that it was out of jealousy that they had handed him over. [19]While he was sitting on the judgment seat, his wife sent word to him, "Have nothing to do with that innocent man, for today I have suffered a great deal because of a dream about him." [20]Now the chief priests and the elders persuaded the crowds to ask for Barabbas and to have Jesus killed. [21]The governor again said to them, "Which of the two do you want me to release for you?" And they said, "Barabbas." [22]Pilate said to them, "Then what should I do with Jesus who is called the Messiah?"[r] All of them said, "Let him be crucified!" [23]Then he asked, "Why, what evil has he done?" But they shouted all the more, "Let him be crucified!"

24 So when Pilate saw that he could do nothing but rather that a riot was beginning, he took some water and washed his hands before the crowd, saying, "I am innocent of this man's blood;[s] see to it yourselves." [25]Then the people as a whole answered, "His blood be on us and on our children!" [26]So he released Barabbas for them, and after flogging Jesus he handed him over to be crucified.

27 Then the soldiers of the governor took Jesus into the governor's headquarters,[t] and they gathered the whole cohort around him. [28]They stripped him and put a scarlet robe on him, [29]and after twisting some thorns into a crown they put it on his head. They put a reed in his right hand and knelt before him and mocked him, saying, "Hail, King of the Jews!" [30]They spat on him and took the reed and struck him on the head. [31]After mocking him, they stripped him of

o 27.16 Other ancient authorities lack *Jesus*   p 27.17 Other ancient authorities lack *Jesus*   q 27.17 Or *the Christ*   r 27.22 Or *the Christ*   s 27.24 Other ancient authorities read *this righteous blood* or *this righteous man's blood*   t 27.27 Gk *the praetorium*

(27:11–14), torture by the Roman soldiers (27:27–30), and mockery from the Judean/Jewish leaders (27:41–43). The title is also placed on public display as a formal charge above the cross in all four Gospels (Matt. 27:37; Mark 15:26; Luke 23:38; John 19:19). All four occurrences of the title are attributed to Jesus by gentiles. Josephus makes use of the title as a political designation in relation to King Herod, an Idumaean descended from forced converts to Judaism who was installed and appointed by Rome to rule over the territory of Judea. The ethnoracial implications of this title are unmistakable: Jesus is executed on a Roman cross under a derogatory banner that proclaims Judean/Jewish inferiority and Roman superiority. He is made an example by the Roman Empire. The derogatory connotations are also evident in the fact that early Christians did not use the title as a source of veneration or worship.

27:15–23 Pilate releases Barabbas. The innocence of Jesus in v. 19 is a special point of emphasis here for Matthew.

27:24–26 Pilate flogs Jesus. 27:24 Innocent blood is an important motif in the passion narrative (23:35; 27:4, 24, 25; see Jer. 22:17; 26:15). **27:25** *His blood be on us and on our children!* This verse is a paradox in the history of interpretation. No other passage in the New Testament has contributed more to anti-Semitism than this single verse. It has been misread and misinterpreted to mean that all Judeans/Jews everywhere are "Christ killers," responsible for the death of Jesus. This reading, even when properly contextualized, is erroneous. Matthew uses the pluperfect verb tense "he realized" to implicate Pilate's knowledge of the situation: he had known all along that the chief priests handed Jesus over out of jealousy (27:18). Matthew further indicates that the chief priests persuaded the crowds to call for Barabbas and have Jesus killed (27:20). These clues, coupled with Pilate's performative act of washing his hands, reveal a far more calculated and sinister portrait of Pilate. Josephus supplies examples of Pilate fomenting turmoil, not avoiding it. **27:26** The grammatical construction of this verse in Greek suggests that Pilate himself flogs Jesus.

27:27–31 Soldiers mock Jesus. The Roman soldiers subject Jesus to a common form of miming, mockery, and ridicule of conquered kings. This was an ancient practice that occurred in Alexandria where a mock coronation was dramatized by a full stage of actors. The soldiers dress Jesus up in a scarlet robe, place a reed in his hand, and kneel before him exclaiming, "Hail, the Judean/Jewish King!"

the robe and put his own clothes on him. Then they led him away to crucify him.

32 As they went out, they came upon a man from Cyrene named Simon; they compelled this man to carry his cross. [33]And when they came to a place called Golgotha (which means Place of a Skull), [34]they offered him wine to drink, mixed with gall, but when he tasted it, he would not drink it. [35]And when they had crucified him, they divided his clothes among themselves by casting lots;[u] [36]then they sat down there and kept watch over him. [37]Over his head they put the charge against him, which read, "This is Jesus, the King of the Jews."

38 Then two rebels were crucified with him, one on his right and one on his left. [39]Those who passed by derided[v] him, shaking their heads [40]and saying, "You who would destroy the temple and build it in three days, save yourself! If you are the Son of God, come down from the cross." [41]In the same way the chief priests also, along with the scribes and elders, were mocking him, saying, [42]"He saved others; he cannot save himself.[w] He is the King of Israel; let him come down from the cross now, and we will believe in him. [43]He trusts in God; let God deliver him now, if he wants to, for he said, 'I am God's Son.'" [44]The rebels who were crucified with him also taunted him in the same way.

45 From noon on, darkness came over the whole land[x] until three in the afternoon. [46]And about three o'clock Jesus cried with a loud voice, "Eli, Eli, lema sabachthani?" that is, "My God, my God, why have you forsaken me?" [47]When some of the bystanders heard it, they said, "This man is calling for Elijah." [48]At once one of them ran and got a sponge, filled it with sour wine, put it on a stick, and gave it to him to drink. [49]But the others said, "Wait, let

us see whether Elijah will come to save him."[y] [50]Then Jesus cried again with a loud voice and breathed his last.[z] [51]At that moment the curtain of the temple was torn in two, from top to bottom. The earth shook, and the rocks were split. [52]The tombs also were opened, and many bodies of the saints who had fallen asleep were raised. [53]After his resurrection they came out of the tombs and entered the holy city and appeared to many. [54]Now when the centurion and those with him, who were keeping watch over Jesus, saw the earthquake and what took place, they were terrified and said, "Truly this man was God's Son!"[a]

55 Many women were also there, looking on from a distance; they had followed Jesus from Galilee, ministering to him. [56]Among them were Mary Magdalene, and Mary the mother of James and Joseph,[b] and the mother of the sons of Zebedee.

57 When it was evening, there came a rich man from Arimathea named Joseph, who also was himself a disciple of Jesus. [58]He went to Pilate and asked for the body of Jesus; then Pilate ordered it to be given to him. [59]So Joseph took the body and wrapped it in a clean linen cloth [60]and laid it in his new tomb, which he had hewn in the rock. He then rolled a great stone to the door of the tomb and went away. [61]Mary Magdalene and the other Mary were there, sitting opposite the tomb.

62 The next day, that is, after the day of

u 27.35 Other ancient authorities add *in order that what had been spoken through the prophet might be fulfilled, "They divided my clothes among themselves, and for my clothing they cast lots."*
v 27.39 Or *blasphemed* w 27.42 Or *is he unable to save himself?*
x 27.45 Or *earth* y 27.49 Other ancient authorities add *And another took a spear and pierced his side, and out came water and blood* z 27.50 Or *gave up his spirit* a 27.54 Or *a son of God*
b 27.56 Some ancient authorities read *Joses*

27:32–44 The Judean king is crucified. The crucifixion is a citation of Roman imperial power that asserts Roman superiority over Judean/Jewish inferiority. The crucifixion was a spectacle designed to maximize visual effect. The sign above the cross was an expression of Roman ridicule that announced to the watching world, "Look, a Judean/Jewish king!" Jesus was minoritized as a Judean/Jewish subject of the Roman Empire (see **"Crucifixion and Terror," p. 1798**).

27:45–56 Jesus's final words on the cross. Jesus's last recorded words are a cryptic cry in Aramaic and Hebrew: *Eli, Eli, lema sabachthani* (v. 46). The quotation comes from Ps. 22:1. Darkness covers the earth. Some people think Jesus is crying out for Elijah based on the phonetic similarity of the first two words "My God" ("ēli") and the name "Elijah" ("eliyyahu" in Heb., "ēlias" in Gk.). Jesus says very little throughout the passion narrative. When he finally speaks, he speaks in his native tongue of Aramaic.

27:57–61 The burial of Jesus. In accordance with Judean/Jewish custom, the dead are to receive a proper and timely burial (Deut. 21:22–23). Joseph of Arimathea asks Pilate for the body of Jesus, which is wrapped in clean linen and placed in the tomb.

27:62–66 Jesus's tomb is sealed and secured with guards. The Pharisees and chief priests recall Jesus's prediction and ask Pilate to secure the tomb with soldiers.

Focus on: Mary Magdalene (Matthew 27:55-56)

In popular imagination, Mary Magdalene is beloved as a penitent sinner, a reformed prostitute, but these traditions developed centuries after the canonical Gospels were written. The New Testament Gospels portray Mary as both an eyewitness to the crucifixion and a prime witness to the resurrection. Other ancient writings depict her as a teacher whose authority derives from secret teachings received privately from Jesus.

All four canonical Gospels situate Mary Magdalene near the cross. In the Synoptic tradition, she watches from a distance, the leading figure in a group of women from Galilee who had followed Jesus as he proclaimed the kingdom of God (Matt. 27:55-56; Mark 15:40-41; Luke 23:49 [cf. 8:1-3]). Mary Magdalene and the other women had served as benefactors to Jesus's ministry, providing for him out of their resources. In John, Mary Magdalene stands alongside the mother of Jesus and the unnamed male disciple whom Jesus loved, placing her in Jesus's inner circle (John 19:25b-27).

Most importantly, all four canonical Gospels identify Mary Magdalene as a prime witness to the resurrection. In the Synoptic tradition, other women accompany her to Jesus's tomb, bringing spices to anoint his body. Finding the tomb empty, they hear the news that Jesus has been raised, good news they are told to proclaim to the male disciples (Matt. 28:1-8; Mark 16:1-8; Luke 24:1-10). In Matthew, Jesus's first resurrection appearance is to Mary Magdalene and a female companion (Matt. 28:9-10). John's vivid account emphasizes that Mary is the first to encounter the risen Jesus, although she initially mistakes Jesus for a gardener until he speaks her name (John 20:1-18).

The second-century Gospel of Mary is one of a number of extracanonical sources that emphasize Mary's closeness to Jesus. In it, she comforts the disciples after the Savior departs, teaching them what she learned from the Savior in a vision. Her teaching leads to a dispute among the disciples. Peter in particular challenges the notion that the Savior would have confided in a woman, but Levi defends her. The Gospel of Mary suggests that by the second century, Mary's reputation as a visionary teacher rivaled that of Peter in some circles. Perhaps a desire to downplay her memory underlies Luke's allegation that she had been exorcised of seven demons (Luke 8:2), a claim that in antiquity commanded far less attention than her vigil at the cross and proclamation of the resurrection.

Jennifer A. Glancy

Preparation, the chief priests and the Pharisees gathered before Pilate [63]and said, "Sir, we remember what that impostor said while he was still alive, 'After three days I will rise again.' [64]Therefore command the tomb to be made secure until the third day; otherwise, his disciples may go and steal him away and tell the people, 'He has been raised from the dead,' and the last deception would be worse than the first." [65]Pilate said to them, "You have a guard[c] of soldiers; go, make it as secure as you can."[d] [66]So they went with the guard and made the tomb secure by sealing the stone.

28 After the Sabbath, as the first day of the week was dawning, Mary Magdalene and the other Mary went to see the tomb. [2]And suddenly there was a great earthquake, for an angel of the Lord, descending from heaven, came and rolled back the stone and sat on it. [3]His appearance was like lightning and his clothing white as snow. [4]For fear of him the guards shook and became like dead men. [5]But the angel said to the women, "Do not be afraid, for I know that you are looking for Jesus who was crucified. [6]He is not here, for he has been raised, as he said. Come, see the place where he[e] lay. [7]Then go quickly and tell his disciples, 'He has been raised from the dead,[f] and indeed he is going ahead of you to Galilee; there you will see him.' This is my message for you." [8]So they left the tomb quickly with fear and great joy and ran to

c 27.65 Or *Take a guard* d 27.65 Gk *you know how*
e 28.6 Other ancient authorities read *the Lord* f 28.7 Other ancient authorities lack *from the dead*

28:1-10 The resurrection of Jesus. 28:1 Mary Magdalene and the other Mary are the first to discover the empty tomb (see **"Mary the Mother of Jesus," p. 1804**). From a historical perspective, women in the ancient world had far less authority than men. In some instances, they were not even counted (14:21). If Matthew wanted to convince more people of the resurrection, it would have been more effective to have the male disciples be the first witnesses. The fact that women are the first witnesses to Jesus's resurrection reflects his borrowing from Mark's narrative and is a sign of the prominent roles that female

Focus On: Resurrection in the Gospels (Matthew 28)

Jesus's moment of resurrection is not narrated in the Gospels, but rather the empty tomb narratives give way to post-resurrection appearances in Matthew, Luke, and John. Mark's Gospel ends abruptly with the women discovering the empty tomb and running away afraid (16:8). The longer ending of Mark (16:9–20) was added by a later scribe, in part to include a post-resurrection appearance. The resurrection of Jesus is also implied in his announcements and predictions (Matt. 16:21; 17:23; 20:19; Mark 8:31; 9:31; 10:33–34; Luke 9:22; 18:33) and the saying from the Q source in Matt. 11:4 (see **"Introduction to the Gospels and Acts," pp. 1709–12**). That one might return from death is demonstrated when the daughter of Jairus is raised by Jesus (Mark 5:35–43; Matt. 9:18–26; Luke 8:40–56). The story of raising Lazarus (John 11:28–44) shares many elements with Jesus's passion and death: proximity to Passover, the presence of the women, and plots by the chief priests (11:48–51; 12:9–11). These elements—combined with its appearance in the middle of the Gospel—suggest it is a foreshadowing of Jesus's own death and resurrection. Jesus's pointed statement "I am the resurrection and the life" (11:25) reflects John's high Christological claims of Jesus's oneness with the Father and power over life and death.

Belief in the resurrection of the body was less common than the Greco-Roman idea of the immortality of the soul and was incomprehensible to many pagans (*Against Celsus* 2.55; 5.14) but was a distinguishing belief of Jesus, Paul, Christ followers, Pharisees, and early rabbis. Sadducees are mocked by Jesus because they do not accept it (Mark 12:18–27; cf. Acts 23:6–8), which he claims shows their ignorance of the Scriptures and God's power. Some scholars have pointed to the subversive quality of the belief as something that overcame Roman power over the individual body and helped to construct an alternative society. Certain ideas followed in the wake of the belief in bodily resurrection—God's power and Providence, ultimate justice for the righteous, the unity of body and soul, roots in Scripture, and the legitimacy of those who preach it. This belief served as a shorthand for a set of values shared by the community and was therefore useful to a movement rapidly incorporating different kinds of people across the Mediterranean world.

Claudia Setzer

tell his disciples. [9]Suddenly Jesus met them and said, "Greetings!" And they came to him, took hold of his feet, and worshiped him. [10]Then Jesus said to them, "Do not be afraid; go and tell my brothers and sisters to go to Galilee; there they will see me."

11 While they were going, some of the guard went into the city and told the chief priests everything that had happened. [12]After the priests[g] had assembled with the elders, they devised a plan to give a large sum of money to the soldiers, [13]telling them, "You must say, 'His disciples came by night and stole him away while we were asleep.' [14]If this comes to the governor's ears, we will satisfy him and keep you out of trouble." [15]So they took the money and did as they were directed. And this story is still told among the Judeans to this day.

16 Now the eleven disciples went to Galilee, to the mountain to which Jesus had directed

g 28.12 Gk *they*

characters play in Matthew. **28:9** *And they came to him, took hold of his feet, and worshiped him.* The verb "to worship" means to fall upon one's knees and touch the ground in reverence. It is the same word used of the Magi (2:2, 8, 11) and when the devil puts Jesus to the test (4:9–10).

28:11–15 The guards are bought, and rumor spreads among the Judeans. 28:15 *And this story is still told among the Judeans to this day.* Following up on 27:65, Matthew provides an explanation for where the rumor that Jesus's body was stolen originated and how it spread. Like Judas, the guards were bribed by the chief priests. The rationale here, at least from Matthew's perspective, is to explain why some Judeans/Jews of his day believed in Jesus's resurrection, while others believed the rumor (28:15) and doubted (28:17). This may also reflect controversy in Matthew's time over resurrection.

28:16–20 The ethnocentric mission is expanded. A widespread understanding of early Christianity is its self-definition as a universal, nonethnic, and inclusive religion. The way early Christianity achieved this status, according to the dominant narrative, is by breaking ties with ethnic Jews, Judeans, and Judaism. Christianity is thus commonly depicted as an open and inclusive movement that has transcended the particularities of race, gender, and class. This understanding, however, not only is

them. [17]When they saw him, they worshiped him, but they doubted. [18]And Jesus came and said to them, "All authority in heaven and on earth has been given to me. [19]Go therefore and make disciples of all nations, baptizing them in the name of the Father and of the Son and of the Holy Spirit [20]and teaching them to obey everything that I have commanded you. And remember, I am with you always, to the end of the age."[b]

b 28.20 Other ancient authorities add *Amen*

historically anachronistic but also relies on a demeaning stereotype of Judaism as ethnic, exclusive, and inferior. Interestingly, the terms "Judaism" and "Christianity" do not occur in Matthew and are rarely attested in Christian texts from the first and second centuries. The conclusion to the Gospel of Matthew—when situated as an ethnically Judean or Jewish text and read in light of the racial/ethnic tensions that frame it from beginning to end—helps to expose this myth. **28:19** *All nations* ("ethnos"; see also 4:15; 6:32; 10:5, 18; 12:18, 21; 20:19; 20:25; 21:43; 24:7, 9, 14; 25:32). What is striking about Jesus's final words to the disciples is what they are told to do. They are told to go not only to the lost sheep of the house of Israel but to all ethnic groups. They are told not to circumcise but to baptize. **28:20** *And remember, I am with you always, to the end of the age.* The motif of God's abiding presence is expressed through chiasm—a literary device that structures the beginning, middle, and end of Matthew. The Gospel begins with a genealogy that locates the Judean/Jewish Messiah as the embodiment of divine presence: Jesus is Emmanuel (1:23). This promise is mediated through the missionary work of his disciples to the people of Israel (10:40). It further extends to the formation of the "church" ("ekklēsia"; see 18:15–20). It is realized through acts of charity to those who are hungry, sick, thirsty, and imprisoned (25:31–46). The Gospel concludes where it began. Through Jesus's life, death, and resurrection, the promise of divine presence is realized and accomplished.

THE GOSPEL ACCORDING TO MARK

Date, Authorship, Audience, and Purpose of Mark

Mark, the earliest canonical Gospel (or account of the life and significance of Jesus), was likely written in the late 60s or early 70s CE to audiences that faced or feared the threat of persecution or alienation in Roman imperial times. The earliest tradition that attributes the Gospel to someone named Mark comes from the second-century CE church figure Papias by way of the fourth-century CE church historian Eusebius. Much—if not all—of what Papias said about Mark, though, reflects Papias's memory of what an elder used to say about Mark (and tradition has linked Mark to Peter based on 1 Pet. 5:13). Thus, scholars have not reached a consensus about the authorship. Perhaps we may only be able to speak of an anonymous writer whose work was at the fount of that stream of biographical tales of Jesus we now call Gospels.

Similarly, we may only safely speak of an implied audience. Based on the similarities between the suffering that Jesus predicted for himself (Mark 8, 9, 10) and those travails he anticipated that his disciples would experience (Mark 13), some scholars infer that the Gospel's earliest audiences faced trying times and needed the Markan Jesus as a paradigm of endurance. Although some scholars aver that Mark was written to a community (or communities) in Rome, while other scholars suggest Galilee or Syria, the Gospel's messages about endurance under pressure would likely have found a welcome home wherever Jesus's earliest followers were spreading the message of God's cataclysmic intervention in the world and facing stiff opposition for doing so.

Mark as a Distinctive Work within a Larger Biographical Literary Environment

In some ways, the kind of paradigm story that Mark tells was typical for its times. There were many antecedent or contemporary stories that held up the subject hero as a paradigm for the audiences who would first hear such stories. These biographical stories had a keen interest in the moral character of the subject hero because such emblematic moral ideals could light a path for others who faced similar harrowing ordeals, political struggles, and trying times. These paradigm stories, moreover, were widely available—in shorter anecdotes about biblical prophets, in biographical snippets from the Greek and Roman legendary and historical past, and in a wide variety of adventure tales about the famed endurance of remarkable travelers.

Unlike some of the biographies of the day (for example, by Plutarch, who wrote in refined Greek, or by Suetonius, who wrote in Latin), Mark's prose is simple. Furthermore, if Matthew and Luke knew Mark, as many modern scholars concede, these later Gospel writers often smoothed over what some Markan interpreters might deem as Mark's defective grammar (for example, the Markan narrative's preference for the historic present [or narrating the past in the present tense]). To Mark's credit, though, we may aver that Mark elected to use the historic present and simple Greek to render select scenes in a clear, vivid, and arresting manner.

Neither Matthew nor Luke was satisfied, moreover, with Mark's beginning and its ending. So on the one hand, while Mark begins the good news about Jesus after Jesus had already become an adult, Matthew and Luke furnish emblematic though different scenes about Jesus's ancestry and birth. On the other hand, while the Markan narrative ends with the promise of a resurrection appearance (14:28; 16:7), at least according to the earliest and best manuscript evidence, Matthew and Luke narrate post-resurrection appearance accounts and thus allow the risen Jesus to speak directly to his followers. Thus, Mark's ending at 16:8, with commissioned women going forth from the empty tomb but saying nothing to anyone, proved too jarring and abrupt for Matthew and Luke. Even some later scribal renderings of Mark supplemented 16:8 with what were deemed to be more satisfying endings that seemed to cohere with what we know from Matthew and Luke. To Mark's credit again, though, Mark's seemingly enigmatic ending may have offered a rhetorical invitation for its auditors to take up the task of proclamation that John, Jesus, and even the disciples had once performed.

Two Major Concerns in Mark's Gospel

Modern interpreters of Mark have struggled with at least two major concerns: the Gospel's pervasive concern with the cross (what may be called the long shadow of the Gospel's interest in the death of Jesus); and the Gospel's seemingly negative portrait of the disciples. Few can read the whole

Gospel and not encounter the Gospel's emphasis on the death of Jesus. Before Jesus makes a series of three formally structured predictions of his death and resurrection in chaps. 8, 9, and 10, readers have already learned through one of Jesus's teaching episodes that he will be "taken away" (2:19–20). Later, when the story slows down to give a day-by-day and then hour-by-hour account of Jesus's last week on earth, moreover, the lasting impression is that Mark has rushed the narrative to signal its most important message—Jesus's death as emissary/messenger of God. If the narrative sees Jesus as a paradigm for others, then, his demeanor through death—even if his endurance came with grief—provides an example for all others in a circle of proclaimers who were announcing to the nations the good news of the deity's reign or intervention in the world (1:15; 13:10).

Mark's presentation of the disciples, especially the male, named disciples but even some named women disciples (at the end of Mark)—as confused and slow to understand Jesus's teaching—has been difficult to fathom, particularly in light of the better, though not glowing, portraits of the disciples found in Matthew and Luke. In the rhetorical flow of Mark's writing, from the beginning to its abrupt end, though, the presentation of the disciples proves logical. The large narrative canvas of scenes on which the disciples are drawn reveals that the disciples are also paradigms, but only in the sense that they are foils compared to Jesus. As foils, the lessons that the disciples provide for Mark's auditors are priceless. They teach Markan auditors, for example, about (1) the frailties of a brand of discipleship that is not thoroughly rooted in fidelity to God; (2) the ease with which the hearts of insiders can become as hardened as the hearts of outsiders; and (3) the manner in which nepotism and concern for status can fragment a fellowship, weaken resolve, and cause otherwise effervescent followers to lose themselves in fright and flight.

Reading Guide

Given Mark's paradigm story, then, Mark's opening verses (1:1–15) confirm both John and Jesus as principal paradigms in the work of proclamation: the call for repentance (1:4) or fidelity (or allegiance) to the rule of God (1:14–15). The rest of the Gospel then largely pivots on Jesus's preparation of disciples to become durable proclaimers of the good news of the rule of God. Thus, Jesus calls disciples (*Stage One*: 1:16–3:6), commissions disciples (*Stage Two*: 3:7–6:30), and even seeks to correct them (*Stage Three*: 6:31–10:52) in preparation for the crucible (11:1–16:8), the most intense scenes of conflict for those who will proclaim good news to the nations (13:10).

Abraham Smith

Passages Unique to the Gospel of Mark

2:27	Saying about the Sabbath Made for Humanity
3:19b–21	Family Thinks Jesus Is Possessed
4:13; 6:51–52	Failure of the Twelve to Understand
4:26–29	Parable of the Seed Growing Secretly
7:19b	Jesus Declares All Foods Clean
7:31–37	Jesus Heals a Man of Deafness and Inability to Speak
8:22–26	Two-Stage Restoration of a Man's Sight in Bethsaida
9:49, 50b	Sayings on Salt
14:51–52	Young Man in the Garden Runs Away Naked

Because the earliest known biblical manuscripts do not contain clear paragraphs or subtitles, section subtitles are always subject to editorial interpretation.

1

The beginning of the good news[a] of Jesus Christ.[b]

2 As it is written in the prophet Isaiah,[c]

"See, I am sending my messenger ahead
    of you,[d]
who will prepare your way,
3 the voice of one crying out in the
    wilderness:
'Prepare the way of the Lord;
    make his paths straight,'"

[4]so John the baptizer appeared[e] in the wilderness, proclaiming a baptism of repentance for the forgiveness of sins. [5]And the whole Judean region and all the people of Jerusalem were going out to him and were baptized by him in the River Jordan, confessing their sins. [6]Now John was clothed with camel's hair, with a leather belt around his waist, and he ate locusts and wild honey. [7]He proclaimed, "The one who is more powerful than I is coming after me; I am not worthy to stoop down and untie the strap of his sandals. [8]I have baptized you with[f] water, but he will baptize you with[g] the Holy Spirit."

9 In those days Jesus came from Nazareth of Galilee and was baptized by John in the Jordan. [10]And just as he was coming up out of the water, he saw the heavens torn apart and the Spirit descending like a dove upon him. [11]And a voice came from the heavens, "You are my Son, the Beloved;[h] with you I am well pleased."

12 And the Spirit immediately drove him out into the wilderness. [13]He was in the wilderness forty days, tested by Satan, and he was with the wild beasts, and the angels waited on him.

14 Now after John was arrested, Jesus came to Galilee proclaiming the good news[i] of[j] God [15]and saying, "The time is fulfilled, and the kingdom of God has come near;[k] repent, and believe in the good news."[l]

16 As Jesus passed along the Sea of Galilee, he saw Simon and his brother Andrew casting a net into the sea, for they were fishers. [17]And Jesus said to them, "Follow me, and I will make you fishers of people." [18]And immediately they left their nets and followed him. [19]As he went a little farther, he saw James son of Zebedee and his brother John, who were in their boat mending the nets. [20]Immediately he called them, and they left their father Zebedee in the boat with the hired men and followed him.

21 They went to Capernaum, and when the Sabbath came, he entered the synagogue and taught. [22]They were astounded at his teaching, for he taught them as one having authority and not as the scribes. [23]Just then there was in their synagogue a man with an unclean spirit, [24]and he cried out, "What have you to do with us, Jesus of Nazareth? Have you come to destroy

---

a 1.1 Or *gospel* b 1.1 Other ancient authorities add *Son of God* c 1.2 Other ancient authorities read *in the prophets* d 1.2 Gk *before your face* e 1.4 Other ancient authorities read *John was baptizing* f 1.8 Or *in* g 1.8 Or *in* h 1.11 Or *my beloved Son* i 1.14 Or *gospel* j 1.14 Other ancient authorities add *of the kingdom of* k 1.15 Or *is at hand* l 1.15 Or *gospel*

1:1–15 Opening. Grounded within a larger scriptural matrix about the sending forth of a prophetic messenger (vv. 2–3), the Markan narrative is a partial tale: *the beginning of the good news of Jesus Christ* (or the Messiah; v. 1). While the opening of the narrative features both John and Jesus engaged in acts of proclamation (vv. 4–15), the arrest of John so soon on the narrative stage (v. 14) is an ominous sign that the good news is also tragic and that additional prophetic proclaimers will come (3:14; 6:12; 13:10). **1:1** First-century CE *good news* ("euangelion") typically was a political message announcing the arrival of a powerful benefactor, the defeat of enemies, or a change of regimes. Whether 1:1 should also include the words "Son of God" (see note b) is debated because it is missing in some ancient manuscripts. **1:2–3** By conflating Isa. 40:3 with Exod. 23:20 and Mal. 3:1, Mark highlights a prophetic scriptural matrix, underscores the word *way* ("hodos"), and thus prepares auditors for a journey narrative that ultimately will lead to Jesus's rejection in Jerusalem. **1:4–8** John *appeared in the wilderness* (v. 4) and wore an ascetic garb (v. 6). Such images evoke the memory of the autonomous prophet Elijah (1 Kgs. 17:1; 19:4; 2 Kgs. 1:8). **1:9–15** Ripped heavens, the influence of the Spirit, the evocation of a psalm of royal coronation (Ps. 2:7), and testing in the wilderness characterize Jesus as both an autonomous prophet and a special son of God.

1:16–3:6 Stage One: Calling the Disciples. Each of the first two sets of episodes (1:16–2:12 and 2:13–3:6) of Stage One begins with a formal call episode near the sea (1:16–20; 2:13–14). Then respectively, a series of miracles or controversies follows such call episodes to demonstrate Jesus's growing fame and, in turn, the growing opposition against him. **1:16** The *Sea of Galilee* is actually an inland, freshwater lake. **1:21** Located on the northwestern shore of the Sea of Galilee, *Capernaum* was a fishing village. Jesus's first miracle occurs on the Jewish *Sabbath*. **1:22** The *scribes* were people who possessed the

Focus On: Kingdom of God (Mark 1:14)

The kingdom of God, or heaven, as it is called in the Gospel of Matthew, functions as a central theme in Jesus's teachings. It is key to Jesus's purpose in the Gospels of Matthew and Mark, serves as an important motif throughout Luke–Acts, and appears occasionally in Paul's letters. In Mark, Jesus proclaims in the opening chapter, "The time is fulfilled, and the kingdom of God has come near; repent, and believe in the good news" (Mark 1:15; Matt. 4:17; Luke 4:43). The good news, which Jesus both teaches and embodies, is that "the kingdom of God has come near." His declaration that "the time is fulfilled" underscores an apocalyptic understanding of human history that envisions two ages: the current era, with its ongoing contestation between good and evil; and the new age to come, where God's reign will finally be fully established. Thus in Mark's Gospel, Jesus's appearance signals nothing less than the turning of the ages and the dawning of the reign of God. Rather than referring to a specific place or location, the kingdom of God connotes a way of being, one aligned with God's rule and intention for the creation. It is inherently countercultural, often opposing conventional social norms.

Furthermore, the kingdom of God is paradoxical (Mark 10:31, 43–44; Matt. 20:25–27; Luke 9:24–25) and difficult to grasp (Mark 4:11–12; Matt. 19:11). It is both present and yet to come. Jesus teaches that the kingdom is like a treasure that someone finds hidden in a field or a pearl of great value (Matt. 13:44–46). When asked when the kingdom will come, Jesus replies, "The kingdom of God is not coming with things that can be observed, nor will they say, 'Look, here it is!' or 'There it is!' For, in fact, the kingdom of God is among you" (Luke 17:20–21). In John 3:3–5, the kingdom of God is associated with Jesus's teaching about rebirth and eternal life. In other instances, however, Jesus speaks of the kingdom as something that will arrive in the future (Mark 14:25; Matt. 6:9–13; 7:21–23; 25:31–36; Luke 11:2). In either case, entering or participating in the reign of God required total commitment. The merchant who found the pearl of great value "went and sold all that he had and bought it" (Matt. 13:46). This powerful metaphor served to remind early believers of their inherent dignity and worth as participants in the Jesus movement.

Mary F. Foskett

us? I know who you are, the Holy One of God." [25]But Jesus rebuked him, saying, "Be quiet and come out of him!" [26]And the unclean spirit, convulsing him and crying with a loud voice, came out of him. [27]They were all amazed, and they kept on asking one another, "What is this? A new teaching—with authority! He[m] commands even the unclean spirits, and they obey him." [28]At once his fame began to spread throughout the surrounding region of Galilee.

[29]As soon as they[n] left the synagogue, they entered the house of Simon and Andrew, with James and John. [30]Now Simon's mother-in-law was in bed with a fever, and they told him about her at once. [31]He came and took her by the hand and lifted her up. Then the fever left her, and she began to serve them.

[32]That evening, at sunset, they brought to him all who were sick or possessed by demons. [33]And the whole city was gathered around the door. [34]And he cured many who were sick with various diseases and cast out many demons, and he would not permit the demons to speak, because they knew him.

[35]In the morning, while it was still very dark, he got up and went out to a deserted place, and there he prayed. [36]And Simon and his companions hunted for him. [37]When they found him, they said to him, "Everyone is searching for you." [38]He answered, "Let us go on to the neighboring towns, so that I may proclaim the message there also, for that is what I came out to do." [39]And he went throughout all Galilee, proclaiming the message in their synagogues and casting out demons.

[40]A man with a skin disease came to him begging him, and kneeling[o] he said to him, "If you are willing, you can make me clean." [41]Moved with pity,[p] Jesus[q] stretched out his hand and touched him and said to him, "I am willing. Be made clean!" [42]Immediately the skin disease left him, and he was made clean. [43]After sternly warning him he sent him away at once, [44]saying to him, "See that you say

m 1.27 Or *A new teaching! With authority he* *n* 1.29 Other ancient authorities read *he* *o* 1.40 Other ancient authorities lack *kneeling* *p* 1.41 Other ancient authorities read *anger* *q* 1.41 Gk *he*

technical skill of writing and were able to transcribe Scripture. **1:34** *Various diseases* might best be translated as "various sicknesses" to avoid the anachronistic importation of a disease-cure model onto the first century CE. **1:40** The term "lepra" referred to a variety of dermatological conditions, not to Hansen's disease (or what we would call leprosy today). Thus, it is best to translate the term "lepros"

Focus On: Healing in the Gospels and Acts (Mark 1)

The four Gospels agree on a common image of Jesus as a popular healer. The opening chapter of the Gospel of Mark relays stories of public exorcisms and private healings that lead to Jesus's popularity (Mark 1:21–34). The Gospel of Matthew combines many of these healing accounts into chaps. 8–9, while Luke scatters their parallels throughout the Gospel. The Gospel of John includes fewer healing stories and avoids recording any exorcisms (5:1–9). Overall, only successful healing stories appear, although the tradition occasionally alludes to failed healings due to inadequate faith or to healing in stages (Mark 6:5–6; cf. Matt. 13:58; Mark 8:22–26).

The New Testament depicts other healers. Jesus gives "authority" to his disciples to continue healing practices, including exorcisms (Mark 6:6–7 and parallels). Although no specific scenes are presented, the disciples were often successful (Mark 6:13; Luke 9:6; cf. Mark 9:14–18 and parallels). Central to the story of Acts are the prominent figures of Peter and Paul, both of whom are depicted as powerful healers. Peter's healing of a man who was unable to walk drew an audience who stayed to hear Peter's preaching (Acts 3:1–16). Some thought even Peter's "shadow" might cure them (Acts 5:12–16). In the second half of Acts, Paul steps into the leading role as a great healer and exorcist (Acts 14:8–18; 19:11–12; 20:8–12; 16:18), but not before he receives his own healing from Ananias, who touched his eyes and restored his sight (9:17–18).

Other Jewish healers appear in the narratives, including an unnamed exorcist, whom Jesus defends (Mark 9:38–40; Luke 9:49–50). Even the Pharisees—generally depicted in caricature throughout the Gospels—are alluded to as having some members who perform exorcisms (cf. Matt. 12:27; Luke 11:19). The historian Josephus records the successful exorcising practices of an Eleazar in the presence of Emperor Vespasian in his *Jewish Antiquities* (8.42–45).

These Jewish healers stand in a long tradition of healers within Israel's history. The prophet Elijah's prayers led to the healing of the dying son of one widow from Zarephath (1 Kgs. 17:17–24). Following the advice of the prophet Elisha, Naaman (a Syrian commander) received healing of his skin disease by washing in the Jordan River (2 Kgs. 5:1–14). Through the prophet Isaiah, YHWH brought restoration to King Hezekiah (2 Kgs. 20:1–7).

Emerson B. Powery

nothing to anyone, but go, show yourself to the priest, and offer for your cleansing what Moses commanded as a testimony to them." [45]But he went out and began to proclaim it freely and to spread the word, so that Jesus[r] could no longer go into a town openly but stayed out in the country, and people came to him from every quarter.

2 When he returned to Capernaum after some days, it was reported that he was at home. [2]So many gathered around that there was no longer room for them, not even in front of the door, and he was speaking the word to them. [3]Then some people[s] came, bringing to him a paralyzed man, carried by four of them. [4]And when they could not bring him to Jesus because of the crowd, they removed the roof above him, and after

having dug through it, they let down the mat on which the paralytic lay. [5]When Jesus saw their faith, he said to the paralytic, "Child, your sins are forgiven." [6]Now some of the scribes were sitting there questioning in their hearts, [7]"Why does this fellow speak in this way? It is blasphemy! Who can forgive sins but God alone?" [8]At once Jesus perceived in his spirit that they were discussing these questions among themselves, and he said to them, "Why do you raise such questions in your hearts? [9]Which is easier: to say to the paralytic, 'Your sins are forgiven,' or to say, 'Stand up and take your mat and walk'? [10]But so that you may know that the Son of Man has authority on earth to forgive sins"—he said to the paralytic—[11]"I say to you, stand up,

r 1.45 Gk *he*   s 2.3 Gk *they*

as "[a man with] a skin disease." **2:4** Mark's thatched *roof* fits a Palestinian village setting. Luke's description of a roof with ceramic tile, though, fits a more urban setting (Luke 5:19). **2:6–7** The scribes accuse Jesus of *blasphemy* (slander toward the divine) because he claimed to be able to forgive sins (which they deemed exclusively the deity's prerogative, 14:57–64). Normally blasphemy refers to cursing or demeaning God. **2:10** On *Son of Man*, a favorite expression by which Jesus identified himself,

Going Deeper: Son of God vs. Son of Man (Mark 2:10)

Today's readers should not construe the expressions *Son of God* and *Son of Man* to stand for the divinity and humanity of Jesus, respectively. Instead, both terms were status designations. Mark's first-century CE audiences would have understood *Son of God*, for example, as a status designation attributed to the primary heir responsible for the guidance and beneficence of a family, not as a marker of a person's essence. Mark deployed such diction to highlight Jesus's position as the principal leader or benefactor of a family or community based not on biological kinship but on doing the will of God (3:33–35). Markan audiences would have known Jesus's status as Son of God at least since his baptism (1:9–11; see note on 1:1). In the narrative itself, only unclean spirits—not humans—would have known this special status at first (3:11; 5:7). Later others would learn about this special status (9:7; 12:6; 14:62; 15:39) especially when the story has had a chance to highlight Jesus's full alignment with the will of God (14:36).

Nor would first-century CE Markan audiences have viewed *Son of Man* (literally "the Son of the Human One") as a part of a human-divine binary with *Son of God*. If the origin of the expression is the Aramaic *bar enash*, "like *a son of man*" (Dan. 7:13–14; emphasis added), the term referred to the deity's appointee who had been given everlasting authority and royal power in opposition to the abusive power of a tyrant (in Daniel's case, Antiochus IV). Mark may have deployed *Son of Man* as a self-designation for Jesus because the circumstances of Daniel's audience (persons facing abusive uses of power) may have been similar to the circumstances of Mark's earliest audiences (see Mark 13:9–13). Initially, though, Jesus only deploys the term in brief verbal clashes with stylized opponents who—unlike unclean spirits—simply do not *know* (1:24, 34; 2:10) Jesus's appointed status of authority and dominion. As conflict intensifies, Jesus clarifies the fuller dimensions of his Son of Man status, which include imminent suffering and his vindication in his future power and position at the right hand of God (8:31, 38; 9:9, 12, 31; 10:33–34; 10:45; 13:26; 14:21 [2x], 41, 62).

Abraham Smith

take your mat, and go to your home." [12]And he stood up and immediately took the mat and went out before all of them, so that they were all amazed and glorified God, saying, "We have never seen anything like this!"

13 Jesus[t] went out again beside the sea; the whole crowd gathered around him, and he taught them. [14]As he was walking along, he saw Levi son of Alphaeus sitting at the tax-collection station, and he said to him, "Follow me." And he got up and followed him.

15 And as he sat at dinner[u] in Levi's[v] house, many tax collectors and sinners were also sitting[w] with Jesus and his disciples, for there were many who followed him. [16]When the scribes of[x] the Pharisees saw that he was eating with sinners and tax collectors, they said

to his disciples, "Why does he eat[y] with tax collectors and sinners?" [17]When Jesus heard this, he said to them, "Those who are well have no need of a physician but those who are sick; I have not come to call the righteous but sinners."

18 Now John's disciples and the Pharisees were fasting, and people[z] came and said to him, "Why do John's disciples and the disciples of the Pharisees fast, but your disciples do not fast?" [19]Jesus said to them, "The wedding attendants cannot fast while the bridegroom is with them, can they? As long as they have

t 2.13 Gk *He   u* 2.15 Gk *reclined   v* 2.15 Gk *his   w* 2.15 Gk *reclining   x* 2.16 Other ancient authorities read *and   y* 2.16 Other ancient authorities add *and drink   z* 2.18 Gk *they*

see **"Son of God vs. Son of Man," p. 1774.** 2:13–14 Supervised by a chief tax collector, lower-level *tax collectors* like Levi collected indirect taxes on tolls and tariffs, not the direct taxes (such as poll and land taxes). **2:16** As a popular Jewish movement, the *Pharisees* believed in resurrection, valued both the written Law and oral tradition, and—at least according to Josephus's inventive reflections—were one of several Jewish schools of philosophy (*Ant.*, 13.171–73). *Scribes of the Pharisees* is a strange expression, though, because some Pharisees were also scribes, and the latter category is the larger aggregate. Thus, other manuscript traditions read "scribes and Pharisees" (see note x; see also **"Pharisees," p. 1756**). **2:18–22** The ascetic rite of *fasting* (or not eating), for which there was not an obligatory prescription in the Torah beyond its required practice on the Day of Atonement (Lev. 16; 23:32), could exemplify mournfulness (1 Sam. 31:13), penitent prayer (1 Sam. 7:6; Jonah 3:5), or preparation (Exod. 34:28). *Unshrunk cloth* (meaning new, unwashed cloth) would tear at the fabric of the (older) cloak to

the bridegroom with them, they cannot fast. [20]The days will come when the bridegroom is taken away from them, and then they will fast on that day.

21 "No one sews a piece of unshrunk cloth on an old cloak; otherwise, the patch pulls away from it, the new from the old, and a worse tear is made. [22]Similarly, no one puts new wine into old wineskins; otherwise, the wine will burst the skins, and the wine is lost, and so are the skins, but one puts new wine into fresh wineskins."[a]

23 One Sabbath he was going through the grain fields, and as they made their way his disciples began to pluck heads of grain. [24]The Pharisees said to him, "Look, why are they doing what is not lawful on the Sabbath?" [25]And he said to them, "Have you never read what David did when he and his companions were hungry and in need of food, [26]how he entered the house of God when Abiathar was high priest and ate the bread of the Presence, which it is not lawful for any but the priests to eat, and he gave some to his companions?" [27]Then he said to them, "The Sabbath was made for humankind and not humankind for the Sabbath, [28]so the Son of Man is lord even of the Sabbath."

3 Again he entered the synagogue, and a man was there who had a withered hand. [2]They were watching him to see whether he would cure him on the Sabbath, so that they might accuse him. [3]And he said to the man who had the withered hand, "Come forward." [4]Then he said to them, "Is it lawful to do good or to do harm on the Sabbath,

to save life or to kill?" But they were silent. [5]He looked around at them with anger; he was grieved at their hardness of heart and said to the man, "Stretch out your hand." He stretched it out, and his hand was restored. [6]The Pharisees went out and immediately conspired with the Herodians against him, how to destroy him.

7 Jesus departed with his disciples to the sea, and a great multitude from Galilee followed him; [8]hearing all that he was doing, they came to him in great numbers from Judea, Jerusalem, Idumea, beyond the Jordan, and the region around Tyre and Sidon. [9]He told his disciples to have a boat ready for him because of the crowd, so that they would not crush him, [10]for he had cured many, so that all who had diseases pressed upon him to touch him. [11]Whenever the unclean spirits saw him, they fell down before him and shouted, "You are the Son of God!" [12]But he sternly ordered them not to make him known.

13 He went up the mountain and called to him those whom he wanted, and they came to him. [14]And he appointed twelve[b] to be with him and to be sent out to preach [15]and to have authority to cast out demons. [16]So he appointed the twelve:[c] Simon (to whom he gave the name Peter), [17]James son of Zebedee and John the brother of James (to whom he gave the name Boanerges, that is, Sons of Thunder), [18]and Andrew, and Philip, and Bartholomew, and Matthew, and Thomas, and James son

a 2.22 Other ancient authorities lack *but one puts new wine into fresh wineskins* b 3.14 Other ancient authorities add *whom he also named apostles* c 3.16 Other ancient authorities lack *So he appointed the twelve*

which it is joined. *New wine* (unfermented wine) would burst old leather wineskins with the result that both the wine and the wineskin would suffer loss. **2:23–28** Jesus's defense of his disciples' action of plucking grain on the basis of David's conscription of holy bread (1 Sam. 21:1–6) gives an example of an admired figure apparently breaking the law for a greater good, even though the details of the two cases vary considerably. **3:6** The conspiracy to *destroy* Jesus is the climax of the miracle and controversy series narrated thus far. It foreshadows the time when a variety of Jesus's opponents (though not the Pharisees) will also seek to kill him (11:18).

3:7–6:30 Stage Two: Commissioning the disciples. In Stage Two, Jesus commissions select followers to be his co-agents in the work of God's rule of restoration. Framed by two formal commissioning scenes (3:13–19 and 6:6b–13, 30), Stage Two also exposes the successes and frailties of Jesus's followers.

3:8 *Idumea* was ancient Edom, a present-day part of southern Israel and Jordan. The expression *beyond the Jordan* means across the Jordan to the east. Both Tyre and Sidon were northwest of Galilee. **3:10** The Greek for persons *who had diseases* literally refers to their travails as if such persons had been "whipped." **3:13–19** In this list of the twelve disciples, Simon, for the first time, is called *Peter* ("Petros," v. 16). Also, Mark's description of Judas as the one *who handed him [Jesus] over* (v. 19) both foreshadows the role Judas will eventually play (14:10–11) and ties together the fates of John, Jesus, and the disciples as rejected prophets (see 1:14; 9:31; 13:9, 11, 12).

of Alphaeus, and Thaddaeus, and Simon the Cananaean, ¹⁹and Judas Iscariot, who handed him over.

20 Then he went home, and the crowd came together again, so that they could not even eat. ²¹When his family heard it, they went out to restrain him, for people were saying, "He has gone out of his mind." ²²And the scribes who came down from Jerusalem said, "He has Beelzebul, and by the ruler of the demons he casts out demons." ²³And he called them to him and spoke to them in parables, "How can Satan cast out Satan? ²⁴If a kingdom is divided against itself, that kingdom cannot stand. ²⁵And if a house is divided against itself, that house will not be able to stand. ²⁶And if Satan has risen up against himself and is divided, he cannot stand, but his end has come. ²⁷But no one can enter a strong man's house and plunder his property without first tying up the strong man; then indeed the house can be plundered.

28 "Truly I tell you, people will be forgiven for their sins and whatever blasphemies they utter, ²⁹but whoever blasphemes against the Holy Spirit can never have forgiveness but is guilty of an eternal sin"—³⁰for they had said, "He has an unclean spirit."

31 Then his mother and his brothers came, and standing outside they sent to him and called him. ³²A crowd was sitting around him, and they said to him, "Your mother and your brothers*d* are outside asking for you." ³³And he replied, "Who are my mother and my brothers?" ³⁴And looking at those who sat around him, he said, "Here are my mother and my brothers! ³⁵Whoever does the will of God is my brother and sister and mother."

4 Again he began to teach beside the sea. Such a very large crowd gathered around him that he got into a boat on the sea and sat there, while the whole crowd was beside the sea on the land. ²He began to teach them many things in parables, and in his teaching he said to them: ³"Listen! A sower went out to sow. ⁴And as he sowed, some seed fell on a path, and the birds came and ate it up. ⁵Other seed fell on rocky ground, where it did not have much soil, and it sprang up quickly, since it had no depth of soil. ⁶And when the sun rose, it was scorched, and since it had no root it withered away. ⁷Other seed fell among thorns, and the thorns grew up and choked it, and it yielded no grain. ⁸Other seed fell into good soil and brought forth grain, growing up and increasing and yielding thirty and sixty and a hundredfold." ⁹And he said, "If you have ears to hear, then hear!"

10 When he was alone, those who were around him along with the twelve asked him about the parables. ¹¹And he said to them, "To you has been given the secret*e* of the kingdom of God, but for those outside everything comes in parables, ¹²in order that

'they may indeed look but not perceive,
    and may indeed hear but not
        understand;
so that they may not turn again and be
        forgiven.'"

13 And he said to them, "Do you not understand this parable? Then how will you understand all the parables? ¹⁴The sower sows the word. ¹⁵These are the ones on the path where

d 3.32 Other ancient authorities add *and sisters*   *e* 4.11 Or *mystery*

3:20–6:6a The two commissioning scenes frame four narrative sections in which others will misrecognize the true source of Jesus's prophetic power (3:20–35 and 6:1–6a) but also highlight Jesus's words (4:1–34) and deeds (4:35–5:43). **3:20–35** His family seemed to think he was mentally ill or possessed. Episodes about Jesus's family (vv. 20–21, 31–35) frame the false charge that the source of Jesus's power was Beelzebul, the ruler of the demons, another name for Satan (v. 22). **3:22a** Jerusalem is an elevated city, and so Mark's description of *the scribes who came down from Jerusalem* is literal.

3:24–27 While a *strong man* was typically a ruler or power-broker such as Alexander the Great, Hannibal of Carthage, or Julius Caesar (or anyone who increased their wealth by *plundering* other kingdoms or "houses"), Mark portrays Jesus as one able to bind or restrain Satan's power.

4:1–2, 33–34 The opening (vv. 1–2) and closing (vv. 33–34) frames of Mark's long teaching section highlight what is central: Jesus's use of parables as *he spoke the word* (v. 33) to those who had gathered on the shoreline.

4:3–20 Read with Jesus's explanatory remarks (vv. 13–20), the parable of the Sower (vv. 3–9) is an allegory about a sower—a planter of seeds (or anyone offering a prophetic word)—and four types of reception to the sowing of the word. Also, the frequent repetition of "hear" diction sharpens the contrast between multiple types of hearing that lead to failure (because of Satan, the absence of sustaining roots for occasions of persecution, or the thorny cares of the age) and a type of hearing that leads to fruitfulness.

the word is sown: when they hear, Satan immediately comes and takes away the word that is sown in them. [16]And these are the ones sown on rocky ground: when they hear the word, they immediately receive it with joy. [17]But they have no root and endure only for a while; then, when trouble or persecution arises on account of the word, immediately they fall away.[f] [18]And others are those sown among the thorns: these are the ones who hear the word, [19]but the cares of the age and the lure of wealth and the desire for other things come in and choke the word, and it yields nothing. [20]And these are the ones sown on the good soil: they hear the word and accept it and bear fruit, thirty and sixty and a hundredfold."

[21] He said to them, "Is a lamp brought in to be put under the bushel basket or under the bed and not on the lampstand? [22]For there is nothing hidden, except to be disclosed; nor is anything secret, except to come to light. [23]If you have ears to hear, then hear!" [24]And he said to them, "Pay attention to what you hear; the measure you give will be the measure you get, and it will be added to you. [25]For to those who have, more will be given, and from those who have nothing, even what they have will be taken away."

[26] He also said, "The kingdom of God is as if someone would scatter seed on the ground [27]and would sleep and rise night and day, and the seed would sprout and grow, he does not know how. [28]The earth produces of itself first the stalk, then the head, then the full grain in the head. [29]But when the grain is ripe, at once he goes in with his sickle because the harvest has come."

[30] He also said, "With what can we compare the kingdom of God, or what parable will we use for it? [31]It is like a mustard seed, which, when sown upon the ground, is the smallest of all the seeds on earth, [32]yet when it is sown it grows up and becomes the greatest of all shrubs and puts forth large branches, so that the birds of the air can make nests in its shade."

[33] With many such parables he spoke the word to them as they were able to hear it; [34]he did not speak to them except in parables, but he explained everything in private to his disciples.

[35] On that day, when evening had come, he said to them, "Let us go across to the other side." [36]And leaving the crowd behind, they took him with them in the boat, just as he was. Other boats were with him. [37]A great windstorm arose, and the waves beat into the boat, so that the boat was already being swamped. [38]But he was in the stern, asleep on the cushion, and they woke him up and said to him, "Teacher, do you not care that we are perishing?" [39]And waking up, he rebuked the wind and said to the sea, "Be silent! Be still!" Then the wind ceased, and there was a dead calm. [40]He said to them, "Why are you afraid? Have you still no faith?" [41]And they were filled with great fear and said to one another, "Who then is this, that even the wind and the sea obey him?"

5 They came to the other side of the sea, to the region of the Gerasenes.[g] [2]And when he had stepped out of the boat, immediately a man from the tombs with an unclean spirit met him. [3]He lived among the tombs, and no one could restrain him any more, even with a chain, [4]for he had often been restrained

f 4.17 Or *stumble*   g 5.1 Other ancient authorities read *Gergesenes* or *Gadarenes*

4:21–32 The Lamp parable and its application (vv. 21–25) reveal truth's inevitable exposure despite the varying ways it is received. The Growing Seed (vv. 26–29) and Mustard Seed (vv. 30–32) parables highlight the automatic and remarkable growth of the deity's rule apart from human agency. **4:35–5:43** In this series of deeds, Jesus reenacts the deity's power over chaos or over the destructive shadow of chaos on human households. The series will also begin to expose what the followers of Jesus lack—faith (4:40). By contrast, Jesus will subsequently commend a woman for her faith (5:34) and will only ask Jairus to continue having faith (5:36) when the news comes that the latter's daughter has died. **4:37–39** The lake's topographical condition (in the Jordan Rift Valley [a low depression surrounded by mountains]) made the lake susceptible to sudden windstorms. **4:40** *Why are you afraid?* The translation masks the pointed criticism in the Greek, literally, "Why are you cowards?" **5:1–20** Mark explicitly narrates Jesus facing and subduing several (unclean) spirits or demons (1:21–28; 3:7–12; 5:1–20; 9:14–29). The composed posture (*sitting there, clothed and in his right mind*, 5:15) of the man who was once called *Legion* (which was also a Roman military unit of more than five thousand infantry soldiers) is another testament to Jesus's victory over chaos despite the neighborhood's inhospitality to Jesus. **5:1** The location of *the region of the Gerasenes* is unknown. The modern equivalent of Gerasa

with shackles and chains, but the chains he wrenched apart, and the shackles he broke in pieces, and no one had the strength to subdue him. [5]Night and day among the tombs and on the mountains he was always howling and bruising himself with stones. [6]When he saw Jesus from a distance, he ran and bowed down before him, [7]and he shouted at the top of his voice, "What have you to do with me, Jesus, Son of the Most High God? I adjure you by God, do not torment me." [8]For he had said to him, "Come out of the man, you unclean spirit!" [9]Then Jesus[b] asked him, "What is your name?" He replied, "My name is Legion, for we are many." [10]He begged him earnestly not to send them out of the region. [11]Now there on the hillside a great herd of swine was feeding, [12]and the unclean spirits[i] begged him, "Send us into the swine; let us enter them." [13]So he gave them permission. And the unclean spirits came out and entered the swine, and the herd, numbering about two thousand, stampeded down the steep bank into the sea and were drowned in the sea.

14 The swineherds ran off and told it in the city and in the country. Then people came to see what it was that had happened. [15]They came to Jesus and saw the man possessed by demons sitting there, clothed and in his right mind, the very man who had had the legion, and they became frightened. [16]Those who had seen what had happened to the man possessed by demons and to the swine reported it. [17]Then they began to beg Jesus[j] to leave their neighborhood. [18]As he was getting into the boat, the man who had been possessed by demons begged him that he might be with him. [19]But Jesus[k] refused and said to him, "Go home to your own people, and tell them how much the Lord has done for you and what mercy he has shown you." [20]And he went away and began to proclaim in the Decapolis how much Jesus had done for him, and everyone was amazed.

21 When Jesus had crossed again in the boat[l] to the other side, a great crowd gathered around him, and he was by the sea. [22]Then one of the leaders of the synagogue, named Jairus, came and, when he saw him, fell at his feet [23]and pleaded with him repeatedly, "My little daughter is at the point of death. Come and lay your hands on her, so that she may be made well and live." [24]So he went with him.

And a large crowd followed him and pressed in on him. [25]Now there was a woman who had been suffering from a flow of blood for twelve years. [26]She had endured much under many physicians and had spent all that she had, and she was no better but rather grew worse. [27]She had heard about Jesus and came up behind him in the crowd and touched his cloak, [28]for she said, "If I but touch his cloak, I will be made well." [29]Immediately her flow of blood stopped, and she felt in her body that she was healed of her disease. [30]Immediately aware that power had gone forth from him, Jesus turned about in the crowd and said, "Who touched my cloak?" [31]And his disciples said to him, "You see the crowd pressing in on you; how can you say, 'Who touched me?' " [32]He looked all around to see who had done it. [33]But the woman, knowing what had happened to her, came in fear and trembling, fell down before him, and told him the whole truth. [34]He said to her, "Daughter, your faith has made you well; go in peace, and be healed of your disease."

35 While he was still speaking, some people came from the synagogue leader's house to say, "Your daughter is dead. Why trouble the teacher any further?" [36]But overhearing[m]

b 5.9 Gk he   i 5.12 Gk they   j 5.17 Gk him   k 5.19 Gk
he   l 5.21 Other ancient authorities lack in the boat
m 5.36 Or ignoring; other ancient authorities read hearing

(Jerash) is too far inland to fit Mark's description of Jesus's shoreline access to the region. By comparison, modern-day Gadara (Um Qeis) is only about six miles inward. The presence of swine there (5:16) suggests that Jesus has traveled to a gentile region. **5:20** *Decapolis* refers to the ten Hellenistic cities that were southeast of the Sea of Galilee or the region by that name, with the exception of Scythopolis (which was on the western side).

5:21–43 Mark's intercalation, or sandwiching of several scenes, when he inserts one episode between the opening and ending of another one (5:21–24a, 25b–34, 35–43), teaches hearers that no force of chaos—whether maladies or death—is too great for God's restorative rule to overcome when faith is present (vv. 34, 36). **5:25, 29–30** A *flow of blood* (see Lev. 15:25) is a more accurate translation than a hemorrhage. While the woman's discharge may have been regarded as a ritual impurity, there is nothing sinful about her. Nor does she cause Jesus to be sinful. Instead, her touch of Jesus's clothes pulls power out of him to heal her. Also, ritual impurity did not automatically lead to social isolation, except in the cases of the temple's sacred spaces. **5:34** Mark's repeated use of salvation terms (vv. 23, 28,

what they said, Jesus said to the synagogue leader, "Do not be afraid; only believe." [37]He allowed no one to follow him except Peter, James, and John, the brother of James. [38]When they came to the synagogue leader's house, he saw a commotion, people weeping and wailing loudly. [39]When he had entered, he said to them, "Why do you make a commotion and weep? The child is not dead but sleeping." [40]And they laughed at him. Then he put them all outside and took the child's father and mother and those who were with him and went in where the child was. [41]Taking her by the hand, he said to her, "Talitha koum," which means, "Little girl, get up!" [42]And immediately the girl stood up and began to walk about (she was twelve years of age). At this they were overcome with amazement. [43]He strictly ordered them that no one should know this and told them to give her something to eat.

6 He left that place and came to his hometown, and his disciples followed him. [2]On the Sabbath he began to teach in the synagogue, and many who heard him were astounded. They said, "Where did this man get all this? What is this wisdom that has been given to him? What deeds of power are being done by his hands! [3]Is not this the carpenter, the son of Mary[n] and brother of James and Joses and Judas and Simon, and are not his sisters here with us?" And they took offense[o] at him. [4]Then Jesus said to them, "Prophets are not without honor, except in their hometown and among their own kin and in their own house." [5]And he could do no deed of power there, except that he laid his hands on a few

sick people and cured them. [6]And he was amazed at their unbelief.

Then he went about among the villages teaching. [7]He called the twelve and began to send them out two by two and gave them authority over the unclean spirits. [8]He ordered them to take nothing for their journey except a staff: no bread, no bag, no money in their belts, [9]but to wear sandals and not to put on two tunics. [10]He said to them, "Wherever you enter a house, stay there until you leave the place. [11]If any place will not welcome you and they refuse to hear you, as you leave, shake off the dust that is on your feet as a testimony against them." [12]So they went out and proclaimed that all should repent. [13]They cast out many demons and anointed with oil many who were sick and cured them.

14 King Herod heard of it, for Jesus's[p] name had become known. Some were[q] saying, "John the baptizer has been raised from the dead, and for this reason these powers are at work in him." [15]But others said, "It is Elijah." And others said, "It is a prophet, like one of the prophets of old." [16]But when Herod heard of it, he said, "John, whom I beheaded, has been raised."

17 For Herod himself had sent men who arrested John, bound him, and put him in prison on account of Herodias, his brother Philip's wife, because Herod[r] had married her. [18]For John had been telling Herod, "It is not lawful for you to have your brother's wife." [19]And Herodias had a grudge against him and wanted to kill him. But she could not, [20]for Herod

n 6.3 Other ancient authorities read *son of the carpenter and of Mary*   o 6.3 Or *stumbled*   p 6.14 Gk *his*   q 6.14 Other ancient authorities read *He was*   r 6.17 Gk *he*

34) focuses on this life, not on one in a world to come. Furthermore, there is very little reason to view Jesus's subsequent words to the woman as a second stage in the miracle. His use of a present tense imperative here can simply mean "continue to be healed" of your affliction. See 3:10.

6:1–6a Although Jesus has already redefined his family (3:34), the members of his hometown synagogue still identify him with his blood kin. In contrast to the examples of faith noted in the antecedent episodes, moreover, those who attend the synagogue lack faith.

6:6b–30 Two parts of the second commissioning scene (vv. 6b–13, 30) frame a narrative transition (vv. 14–16) and a flashback of John's arrest and gruesome dinnertime execution (vv. 17–29). Mark thus tempers the success of the disciples' emissarial journey with a warning about a prophetic messenger's inevitable rejection. **6:14–18** Although Mark calls Herod Antipas (21–39 CE) a *king* multiple times (vv. 14, 22, 25–27), Herod was actually a tetrarch (ruler of a fourth of a kingdom). For his second marriage, Herod married Herodias, who was both his niece by one brother, Aristobulus, and—according to Mark— his sister-in-law by her marriage to yet another brother, Philip. **6:19–29** While Josephus places the motive for the death of John squarely on Herod (*Ant.*, 18.113–19), Mark's misogynistic crafting of John's death removes the blame from Herod as if his initial fondness for listening to the imprisoned prophet temporarily spared John from a begrudging Herodias who *wanted to kill him* (v. 19).

feared John, knowing that he was a righteous and holy man, and he protected him. When he heard him, he was greatly perplexed,[s] and yet he liked to listen to him. [21]But an opportunity came when Herod on his birthday gave a banquet for his courtiers and officers and for the leaders of Galilee. [22]When his daughter Herodias[t] came in and danced, she pleased Herod and his guests, and the king said to the girl, "Ask me for whatever you wish, and I will give it." [23]And he swore[u] to her, "Whatever you ask me, I will give you, even half of my kingdom." [24]She went out and said to her mother, "What should I ask for?" She replied, "The head of John the baptizer." [25]Immediately she rushed back to the king and requested, "I want you to give me at once the head of John the Baptist on a platter." [26]The king was deeply grieved, yet out of regard for his oaths and for the guests, he did not want to refuse her. [27]Immediately the king sent a soldier of the guard with orders to bring John's[v] head. He went and beheaded him in the prison, [28]brought his head on a platter, and gave it to the girl. Then the girl gave it to her mother. [29]When his disciples heard about it, they came and took his body and laid it in a tomb.

30 The apostles gathered around Jesus and told him all that they had done and taught. [31]He said to them, "Come away to a deserted place all by yourselves and rest a while." For many were coming and going, and they had no leisure even to eat. [32]And they went away in the boat to a deserted place by themselves. [33]Now many saw them going and recognized them, and they hurried there on foot from all the towns and arrived ahead of them. [34]As he went ashore, he saw a great crowd, and he had compassion for them, because they were like sheep without a shepherd, and he began to teach them many things. [35]When it grew late, his disciples came to him and said, "This is a deserted place, and the hour is now very late; [36]send them away so that they may go into the surrounding country and villages and buy something for themselves to eat." [37]But he answered them, "You give them something to eat." They said to him, "Are we to go and buy two hundred denarii worth of bread and give it to them to eat?" [38]And he said to them, "How many loaves have you? Go and see." When they had found out, they said, "Five, and two fish." [39]Then he ordered them to get all the people to sit down in groups on the green grass. [40]So they sat down in groups of hundreds and of fifties. [41]Taking the five loaves and the two fish, he looked up to heaven and blessed and broke the loaves and gave them to his disciples to set before the people, and he divided the two fish among them all. [42]And all ate and were filled, [43]and they took up twelve baskets full of broken pieces and of the fish. [44]Those who had eaten the loaves numbered five thousand men.

45 Immediately he made his disciples get into the boat and go on ahead to the other side,

s 6.20 Other ancient authorities read *he did many things*
t 6.22 Other ancient authorities read *the daughter of Herodias herself*   u 6.23 Other ancient authorities add *solemnly*
v 6.27 Gk *his*

6:31–10:52 Stage Three: Correcting the disciples. In Stage Three, Jesus seeks to correct his disciples. In what may be called a "bread" section because of the repetition of food diction (6:31–8:21), Jesus repeatedly seeks to correct the disciples' understanding of his words and deeds. Then in what may be called a "blindness" section (8:22–10:52), Jesus repeatedly seeks to correct the disciples' misunderstanding of the values of the rule of God. While the Gospel author uses sight and blindness as metaphors for understanding, today we avoid such language as disrespectful to the visually impaired.
6:31–8:21 Bordering Mark's "bread" section (6:31–8:21) are two mass feedings in desolate areas and their attendant boat-trip sections that remind the audience of the occurrence of one or both bread miracles.
6:31–44 The miracle of the loaves includes a memorable fourfold series of acts (taking, blessing, breaking, and giving [of the loaves to the disciples for distribution]) with the utopian result that the whole crowd is fed and much food is left over. **6:34** The pastoralist imagery *sheep without a shepherd* likely refers to the absence of a leader for the deity's people (see Num. 27:17 and 1 Kgs. 22:17). **6:42–44** The numerical references to food fragments and crowd sizes throughout the "bread" section nudge the earliest audiences to see the abundance that the deity makes possible for all through prophetic mediators even in the most desolate of places.
6:45–52 The boat trip includes two extraordinary feats: walking on water (vv. 47–50) and stilling yet another windstorm (v. 51). What the disciples do not understand about the loaves (v. 52) is that Jesus's deeds or acts of power reflect his sonship, his status as one who reenacts the powers of the deity. **6:45** Given that *Bethsaida* was a fishing village located on the northeastern shore of the Sea of Galilee,

to Bethsaida, while he dismissed the crowd. [46]After saying farewell to them, he went up on the mountain to pray.

47 When evening came, the boat was out on the sea, and he was alone on the land. [48]When he saw that they were straining at the oars against an adverse wind, he came toward them early in the morning, walking on the sea. He intended to pass them by. [49]But when they saw him walking on the sea, they thought it was a ghost and cried out, [50]for they all saw him and were terrified. But immediately he spoke to them and said, "Take heart, it is I; do not be afraid." [51]Then he got into the boat with them, and the wind ceased. And they were utterly astounded, [52]for they did not understand about the loaves, but their hearts were hardened.

53 When they had crossed over, they came to land at Gennesaret and moored the boat. [54]When they got out of the boat, people at once recognized him [55]and rushed about that whole region and began to bring the sick on mats to wherever they heard he was. [56]And wherever he went, into villages or cities or farms, they laid the sick in the marketplaces and begged him that they might touch even the fringe of his cloak, and all who touched it were healed.

7 Now when the Pharisees and some of the scribes who had come from Jerusalem gathered around him, [2]they noticed that some of his disciples were eating with defiled hands, that is, without washing them. [3](For the Pharisees, and all the Jews, do not eat unless they wash their hands,[w] thus observing the tradition of the elders, [4]and they do not eat anything from the market unless they wash,[x] and there are also many other traditions that they observe: the washing of cups and pots and bronze kettles and beds.[y]) [5]So the Pharisees and the scribes asked him, "Why do your disciples not walk according to the tradition of the elders but eat with defiled hands?" [6]He said to them, "Isaiah prophesied rightly about you hypocrites, as it is written,

'This people honors me with their lips,
    but their hearts are far from me;
[7]in vain do they worship me,
    teaching human precepts as doctrines.'
[8]"You abandon the commandment of God and hold to human tradition."

9 Then he said to them, "You have a fine way of rejecting the commandment of God in order to keep your tradition! [10]For Moses said, 'Honor your father and your mother,' and, 'Whoever speaks evil of father or mother must surely die.' [11]But you say that if anyone tells father or mother, 'Whatever support you might have had from me is Corban' (that is, an offering to God[z]), [12]then you no longer permit doing anything for a father or mother, [13]thus nullifying the word of God through your tradition that you have handed on. And you do many things like this."

14 Then he called the crowd again and said to them, "Listen to me, all of you, and understand: [15]there is nothing outside a person that by going in can defile, but the things that come out are what defile."[a]

17 When he had left the crowd and entered the house, his disciples asked him about the parable. [18]He said to them, "So, are you also without understanding? Do you not see that

w 7.3 Meaning of Gk uncertain   x 7.4 Other ancient authorities read *and when they come from the marketplace, they do not eat unless they purify themselves*   y 7.4 Other ancient authorities lack *and beds*   z 7.11 Gk lacks *to God*   a 7.15 Other ancient authorities add 7.16: *"If you have ears to hear, then hear"*

the *adverse wind* (v. 48) prevents the disciples from crossing the sea. Instead, they are blown further north and land at Gennesaret (see Josephus, *J.W.*, 3.10.8) and thus still on the western side of the lake.

6:53–56 As a Markan healing summary (see 1:32–34; 3:7–12), these verses (as with 7:31–37 ahead) offer a description of supplicants imploring Jesus to use his mediating power to restore the bodies of persons being brought to him (see **"Healing in the Gospels and Acts," p. 1773**).

7:1–23 Shifts in Jesus's interlocutors from the Pharisees (vv. 1–13) to the crowds with Jesus's disciples present (vv. 14–15) and on to his disciples privately (vv. 17–23) place a premium on internal matters of the heart as opposed to external ones such as handwashing before eating. **7:2–3** The Pharisaic practice of ritually washing hands before eating food was not prescribed in Jewish Scripture but is an additional piety taken on by this group (not all Jews, as Mark says) in addition to following the rules of kosher food. Mark shows some confusion here on Jewish practice. **7:11–13** *Corban* refers to the dedication of a portion of one's possessions as a gift to God. Jesus critiques the use of the practice as a legal scheme to avoid one's responsibility to fulfill the basic commandment of God to honor one's parents (see Exod. 20:12; 21:17). **7:16** The words "anyone who has ears ought to hear" are not found in the best and oldest manuscripts, and thus they are omitted in this translation. **7:18–23** See **"Diet," p. 268**.

whatever goes into a person from outside cannot defile, [19]since it enters not the heart but the stomach and goes out into the sewer?" (Thus he declared all foods clean.) [20]And he said, "It is what comes out of a person that defiles. [21]For it is from within, from the human heart, that evil intentions come: sexual immorality, theft, murder, [22]adultery, avarice, wickedness, deceit, debauchery, envy, slander, pride, folly. [23]All these evil things come from within, and they defile a person."

24 From there he set out and went away to the region of Tyre.[b] He entered a house and did not want anyone to know he was there. Yet he could not escape notice, [25]but a woman whose little daughter had an unclean spirit immediately heard about him, and she came and bowed down at his feet. [26]Now the woman was a gentile, of Syrophoenician origin. She begged him to cast the demon out of her daughter. [27]He said to her, "Let the children be fed first, for it is not fair to take the children's food and throw it to the dogs." [28]But she answered him, "Sir,[c] even the dogs under the table eat the children's crumbs." [29]Then he said to her, "For saying that, you may go—the demon has left your daughter." [30]And when she went home, she found the child lying on the bed and the demon gone.

31 Then he returned from the region of Tyre and went by way of Sidon toward the Sea of Galilee, in the region of the Decapolis. [32]They brought to him a deaf man who had an impediment in his speech, and they begged him to lay his hand on him. [33]He took him aside in private, away from the crowd, and put his fingers into his ears, and he spat and touched his tongue. [34]Then looking up to heaven, he sighed and said to him, "Ephphatha," that is, "Be opened." [35]And his ears were opened, his tongue was released, and he spoke plainly. [36]Then Jesus[d] ordered them to tell no one, but the more he ordered them, the more zealously they proclaimed it. [37]They were astounded beyond measure, saying, "He has done everything well; he even makes the deaf to hear and the mute to speak."

8 In those days when there was again a great crowd without anything to eat, he called his disciples and said to them, [2]"I have compassion for the crowd because they have been with me now for three days and have nothing to eat. [3]If I send them away hungry to their homes, they will faint on the way— and some of them have come from a great distance." [4]His disciples replied, "How can one feed these people with bread here in the desert?" [5]He asked them, "How many loaves do you have?" They said, "Seven." [6]Then he ordered the crowd to sit down on the ground, and he took the seven loaves, and after giving thanks he broke them and gave them to his disciples to distribute, and they distributed them to the crowd. [7]They had also a few small fish, and after blessing them he ordered that these, too, should be distributed. [8]They ate and were filled, and they took up the broken pieces left over, seven baskets full. [9]Now there were about four thousand people. And he sent them away. [10]And immediately he got into the boat with his disciples and went to the district of Dalmanutha.[e]

b 7.24 Other ancient authorities add *and Sidon*   c 7.28 Or *Lord*; other ancient authorities prefix *Yes*   d 7.36 Gk *he*   e 8.10 Other ancient authorities read *Mageda* or *Magdala*

7:24-30 Jesus's use of the plural diction of "children" and "dogs" means that his riddle to the Syrophoenician woman is about ethnic groups (Jews and gentiles), not individuals. While the woman's retort concedes the historical priority of the Jews, it also confirms the ultimate sufficiency of the deity's bread or beneficence to reach all ethnic groups (see **"Does Jesus Display Ethnocentrism toward the Canaanite Woman?," p. 1746**). Her word, or "logos," teaches Jesus about the reach of his own ministry (see **"Woman Wisdom," p. 872**).

7:31 Since Sidon is north of Tyre, it is inconceivable that Jesus would travel north from Tyre to go in the direction of the Decapolis, which lies on the southeastern side of the Sea of Galilee. Mark wants to make the point that Jesus travels in gentile areas. 7:33 Nothing here is magical. Rather, the use of saliva in healing rituals was a common symbolic gesture. See 8:22-26.

8:1-9 With the adverb "again," Mark signals the introduction to a second wilderness feeding. As in the earlier one, Jesus has compassion on a crowd, and he does not dismiss the crowd until he has translated his compassion into action (6:34-36, 45; 8:2-3, 9). 8:4-9 The disciples' question (v. 4) reveals that they learned nothing from the previous mass feeding. In another fourfold series of actions (taking, giving thanks, breaking bread, and giving the bread to his disciples), Jesus continues to mediate the utopian beneficence of the deity.

Reading through Time: Jewish Messianic Ideas (Mark 8)

The word *messiah* (Heb. *mashiakh*; Gk. *christos*) appears frequently in the Gospels. The word means "anointed one" and originally applied to an authority figure who was anointed with oil, such as an Israelite priest or king, and in at least one case to a non-Israelite king (Isa. 45:1). Messianic expectations in early Judaism were diverse, with no dominant concept of what a messiah might do or be or even if a messiah was to be expected. What is shared among Jews who anticipated one or more messiahs is that their unjust world would be set right by God through this anointed figure.

The most common portrayals of a messiah in early Judaism are royal, priestly, and prophetic. In addition to human messianic figures, some texts include divine figures as God's agents. Some of these divine beings are found in apocalyptic literature such as the "one like a son of man" from Dan. 7, who was originally meant to be an angelic savior. Other monikers include "chosen one," "righteous one," and "messiah." The prominence of a *royal messiah* originates in the ancient Near Eastern idea that monarchy represented divine rule on earth. Israelite and early Jewish understandings of monarchy support this idea, especially with the lineage of King David (e.g., 2 Sam. 7; Isa. 9:1-7; Mic. 5:2-5; Ps. 2). Later interpreters combine prophetic passages and references to a royal ideology to envision a restoration of the Davidic line and a theocratic rule. The expectation by some of a *priestly messiah* builds on traditions calling the high priest "the anointed priest" (Lev. 4:3; cf. Dan. 9:26) and on other texts that emphasize priestly over royal authority (e.g., Jub. 31:11-17). Sectarian literature from the Dead Sea Scrolls values a priestly messiah over a royal one, although this literature expects both types of messiahs along with a prophet to arrive at the end times (1QS IX, 11). The expectation of a *prophetic messiah* is less prominent. In Mal. 4:5-6, God promises to send Elijah as a harbinger of the end times, and some Second Temple Jewish literature picks up on this. The Gospel of Matthew identifies John the Baptist as Elijah (11:14; 17:10-13), although John's Gospel denies this connection (1:21). The Jewish historian Josephus reports on several prophet-messianic figures who unsuccessfully sought to bring about the deliverance of Israel (e.g., *Ant.* 20.168-72, 188).

Shayna Sheinfeld

11 The Pharisees came and began to argue with him, asking him for a sign from heaven, to test him. [12]And he sighed deeply in his spirit and said, "Why does this generation ask for a sign? Truly I tell you, no sign will be given to this generation." [13]And he left them, and getting into the boat again he went across to the other side.

14 Now the disciples[f] had forgotten to bring any bread, and they had only one loaf with them in the boat. [15]And he cautioned them, saying, "Watch out—beware of the yeast of the Pharisees and the yeast of Herod."[g] [16]They said to one another, "It is because we have no bread." [17]And becoming aware of it, Jesus said to them, "Why are you talking about having no bread? Do you still not perceive or understand? Are your hearts hardened? [18]Do you have eyes and fail to see? Do you have ears and fail to hear? And do you not remember? [19]When I broke the five loaves for the five thousand, how many baskets full of broken pieces did you collect?" They said to him, "Twelve." [20]"And the seven for the four thousand, how many baskets full of broken pieces did you collect?" And they said to him, "Seven." [21]Then he said to them, "Do you not yet understand?"

22 They came to Bethsaida. Some people[h] brought a blind man to him and begged him to touch him. [23]He took the blind man

f 8.14 Gk *they*   *g* 8.15 Other ancient authorities read *the Herodians*   *h* 8.22 Gk *They*

8:11-13 Jesus links the Pharisees with *this generation*, an expression likely harking back to the wilderness generation that did not believe even when they received signs (Deut. 32:20 LXX).

8:17-21 The series of rhetorical questions reminds the narrative's auditors of the earlier distinction Jesus made between insiders and outsiders (4:11-12; Isa. 6:9). The disciples appear now, though, to have the traits of outsiders with eyes that do not see and ears that do not hear. Still, despite Mark's negative characterization of the disciples, Mark's use of the word translated as *still not* in 8:17 and as *not yet* in 8:21 holds out the possibility that the problem of perception is temporary.

8:22-10:52 In the "blindness" section (8:22-10:52) of Stage Three, the disciples do not understand Jesus. In a series of three formal passion/resurrection patterns that announce the suffering that is necessary for both Jesus's messiahship and his followers' discipleship (8:31-9:1; 9:31-37; 10:32-45), Mark will note how the wants or desires of the disciples are not properly aligned with the will of God.

8:22-26 In tandem with the healing of a visually impaired man in 10:46-52, the healing of a man

by the hand and led him out of the village, and when he had put saliva on his eyes and laid his hands on him, he asked him, "Can you see anything?" [24]And the man[i] looked up and said, "I can see people, but they look like trees, walking." [25]Then Jesus[j] laid his hands on his eyes again, and he looked intently, and his sight was restored, and he saw everything clearly. [26]Then he sent him away to his home, saying, "Do not even go into the village."[k]

27 Jesus went on with his disciples to the villages of Caesarea Philippi, and on the way he asked his disciples, "Who do people say that I am?" [28]And they answered him, "John the Baptist; and others, Elijah; and still others, one of the prophets." [29]He asked them, "But who do you say that I am?" Peter answered him, "You are the Messiah."[l] [30]And he sternly ordered them not to tell anyone about him.

31 Then he began to teach them that the Son of Man must undergo great suffering and be rejected by the elders, the chief priests, and the scribes and be killed and after three days rise again. [32]He said all this quite openly. And Peter took him aside and began to rebuke him. [33]But turning and looking at his disciples, he rebuked Peter and said, "Get behind me, Satan! For you are setting your mind not on divine things but on human things."

34 He called the crowd with his disciples and said to them, "If any wish to come[m] after me, let them deny themselves and take up their cross and follow me. [35]For those who want to save their life will lose it, and those who lose their life for my sake, and for the sake of the gospel,[n] will save it. [36]For what will it profit them to gain the whole world and forfeit their life? [37]Indeed, what can they give in return for their life? [38]Those who are ashamed of me and of my words[o] in this adulterous and sinful generation, of them the Son of Man will also be ashamed when he comes in the glory of his Father with the holy angels." [1]And he said to them, "Truly I tell you, there are some standing here who will not taste death until they see that the kingdom of God has come with[p] power."

2 Six days later, Jesus took with him Peter and James and John and led them up a high mountain apart, by themselves. And he was transfigured before them, [3]and his clothes became dazzling bright, such as no one[q] on earth could brighten them. [4]And there appeared to them Elijah with Moses, who were talking with Jesus. [5]Then Peter said to Jesus, "Rabbi, it is good for us to be here; let us set up three tents: one for you, one for Moses, and one for Elijah." [6]He did not know what to say, for they were terrified. [7]Then a cloud overshadowed them, and from the cloud there came a voice, "This is my Son, the Beloved;[r] listen to him!"

i 8.24 Gk he   j 8.25 Gk he   k 8.26 Other ancient authorities add *or tell anyone in the village*   l 8.29 Or *the Christ*   m 8.34 Other ancient authorities read *follow*   n 8.35 Other ancient authorities read *lose their life for the sake of the gospel*   o 8.38 Other ancient authorities read *and of mine*   p 9.1 Or *in*   q 9.3 Gk *no fuller*   r 9.7 Or *my beloved Son*

with a visual impairment here works like an opening for a long sweep of texts about the disciples' imperception.

8:27–30 Caesarea Philippi, located to the north of the Sea of Galilee in modern-day Banias, was originally known as Paneion (to honor the pastoral deity Pan). Later, Augustus gave it to Herod I, and Herod's son, Philip, enlarged and renamed the city as Caesarea Philippi to honor Augustus and himself. In Mark, though, the episode near the villages of Caesarea Philippi marks the first time a human being (Peter) acknowledges Jesus as the Christ.

8:34 While not invented by the Romans, crucifixion or affixation on a cross was often deployed by the Romans as an act of physical torture, psychological degradation, and social deterrence (see **"Crucifixion and Terror," p. 1798**). **8:38** On *this adulterous and sinful generation*, see note on 8:11–13.

9:2–13 Although the vivid imagery of the transfiguration (vv. 2–8) account signals Jesus's special role as the deity's Son compared to other prophets such as Moses and Elijah (who also encountered the deity on a mountain [Exod. 24; 1 Kgs. 19]), the sobering value of the episode is that it reads Jesus's role as Son of God (v. 7) through the prism of the rejection of a prophet (vv. 9–13; see **"Son of God vs. Son of Man," p. 1774**). **9:2** The *six days later* reference may hark back to Moses, who initially went up the mountain for six days (Exod. 24:15–16), as does the command from God to *listen to him* (9:7; Deut. 18:15). Mark does not specify which mountain was the site of Jesus's transfiguration (though nearby Mount Hermon, between modern-day Syria and Lebanon, is a *high mountain*). **9:3–4** In Mediterranean societies, bright, luminous clothing or the bright appearance of a human person suggested divinity (Ezek. 1:26–28; 1 En. 14:20–21; Dan. 7:9; Hesiod, *The Shield of Heracles*, 70–72; Virgil, *Aeneid*, 8.608). **9:6** The narrator's comments that Peter literally *did not know what to say* reveal

[8]Suddenly when they looked around, they saw no one with them any more, but only Jesus.

9 As they were coming down the mountain, he ordered them to tell no one about what they had seen, until after the Son of Man had risen from the dead. [10]So they kept the matter to themselves, questioning what this rising from the dead could mean. [11]Then they asked him, "Why do the scribes say that Elijah must come first?" [12]He said to them, "Elijah is indeed coming first to restore all things. How then is it written about the Son of Man, that he is to go through many sufferings and be treated with contempt? [13]But I tell you that Elijah has come, and they did to him whatever they pleased, as it is written about him."

14 When they came to the disciples, they saw a great crowd around them and some scribes arguing with them. [15]When the whole crowd saw him, they were immediately overcome with awe, and they ran forward to greet him. [16]He asked them, "What are you arguing about with them?" [17]Someone from the crowd answered him, "Teacher, I brought you my son; he has a spirit that makes him unable to speak, [18]and whenever it seizes him, it dashes him down, and he foams and grinds his teeth and becomes rigid, and I asked your disciples to cast it out, but they could not do so." [19]He answered them, "You faithless generation, how much longer must I be with you? How much longer must I put up with you? Bring him to me." [20]And they brought the boy[s] to him. When the spirit saw him, immediately it convulsed the boy,[t] and he fell on the ground and rolled about, foaming at the mouth. [21]Jesus[u] asked the father, "How long has this been happening to him?" And he said, "From childhood. [22]It has often cast him into the fire and into the water, to destroy him; but if you are able to do anything, help us! Have compassion on us!" [23]Jesus said to him, "If you are able! All things can be done for the one who believes." [24]Immediately

the father of the child cried out,[v] "I believe; help my unbelief!" [25]When Jesus saw that a crowd came running together, he rebuked the unclean spirit, saying to it, "You spirit that keeps this boy from speaking and hearing, I command you, come out of him, and never enter him again!" [26]After crying out and convulsing him terribly, it came out, and the boy was like a corpse, so that most of them said, "He is dead." [27]But Jesus took him by the hand and lifted him up, and he was able to stand. [28]When he had entered the house, his disciples asked him privately, "Why could we not cast it out?" [29]He said to them, "This kind can come out only through prayer."[w]

30 They went on from there and passed through Galilee. He did not want anyone to know it, [31]for he was teaching his disciples, saying to them, "The Son of Man is to be betrayed into human hands, and they will kill him, and three days after being killed, he will rise again." [32]But they did not understand what he was saying and were afraid to ask him.

33 Then they came to Capernaum, and when he was in the house he asked them, "What were you arguing about on the way?" [34]But they were silent, for on the way they had argued with one another who was the greatest. [35]He sat down, called the twelve, and said to them, "Whoever wants to be first must be last of all and servant of all." [36]Then he took a little child and put it among them, and taking it in his arms he said to them, [37]"Whoever welcomes one such child in my name welcomes me, and whoever welcomes me welcomes not me but the one who sent me."

38 John said to him, "Teacher, we saw someone casting out demons in your name,[x] and we tried to stop him because he was not following

s 9.20 Gk *him*   t 9.20 Gk *him*   u 9.21 Gk *He*   v 9.24 Other ancient authorities add *with tears*   w 9.29 Other ancient authorities add *and fasting*   x 9.38 Other ancient authorities add *who does not follow us*

the characteristic dullness or ignorance of the disciples. **9:9–13** In the light of Jesus's announcement about his death and resurrection (8:31), it is strange that the inner core of his disciples would discuss among themselves the meaning of the idea of *rising from the dead* (vv. 9–13, especially 10). This, too, is a case of their continuing imperception.

9:14–29 Here Mark offers another Elijah-like miracle, the raising of a child (1 Kgs. 17:17–24). The episode teaches that faith (trusting in God's in-breaking favor or intervention) and prayer (which also entails a submissive dependence on God, not on human ability) make all things possible.

9:30–10:31 With a second passion/resurrection prediction (9:31–37) and with other episodes (9:38–10:31), the Markan Jesus continues to correct the disciples' imagined values about the operations of the rule/kingdom of God: their concern with greatness (9:34), their attempt to control who is able to perform exorcisms (9:38), and their concern to control who has access to Jesus (10:13–16), all of which

us." [39]But Jesus said, "Do not stop him, for no one who does a deed of power in my name will be able soon afterward to speak evil of me. [40]Whoever is not against us is for us. [41]For truly I tell you, whoever gives you a cup of water to drink because you bear the name of Christ will by no means lose the reward.

42 "If any of you cause one of these little ones who believe in me[y] to sin,[z] it would be better for you if a great millstone were hung around your neck and you were thrown into the sea. [43]If your hand causes you to sin,[a] cut it off; it is better for you to enter life maimed than to have two hands and to go to hell,[b] to the unquenchable fire.[c] [45]And if your foot causes you to sin,[d] cut it off; it is better for you to enter life lame than to have two feet and to be thrown into hell.[e,f] [47]And if your eye causes you to sin,[g] tear it out; it is better for you to enter the kingdom of God with one eye than to have two eyes and to be thrown into hell,[h] [48]where their worm never dies and the fire is never quenched.

49 "For everyone will be salted with fire.[i] [50]Salt is good, but if salt has lost its saltiness, how can you season it?[j] Have salt in yourselves, and be at peace with one another."

10 He left that place and went to the region of Judea and[k] beyond the Jordan. And crowds again gathered around him, and, as was his custom, he again taught them.

2 Some,[l] testing him, asked, "Is it lawful for a man to divorce his wife?" [3]He answered them, "What did Moses command you?" [4]They said, "Moses allowed a man to write a certificate of dismissal and to divorce her." [5]But Jesus said to them, "Because of your hardness of heart he wrote this commandment for you. [6]But from the beginning of creation, 'God made them male and female.' [7]'For this reason a man shall leave his father and mother and be joined to his wife,'[m] [8]and the two shall become one flesh.' So they are no longer two but one flesh. [9]Therefore what God has joined together, let no one separate."

10 Then in the house the disciples asked him again about this matter. [11]He said to them, "Whoever divorces his wife and marries another commits adultery against her, [12]and if she divorces her husband and marries another, she commits adultery."

13 People were bringing children to him in order that he might touch them, and the disciples spoke sternly to them. [14]But when Jesus saw this, he was indignant and said to them, "Let the children come to me; do not stop them, for it is to such as these that the kingdom of God belongs. [15]Truly I tell you, whoever does not receive the kingdom of God as a little child will never enter it." [16]And he took them up in his arms, laid his hands on them, and blessed them.

17 As he was setting out on a journey, a man ran up and knelt before him and asked him, "Good Teacher, what must I do to inherit eternal life?" [18]Jesus said to him, "Why do you call me good? No one is good but God alone. [19]You know the commandments: 'You shall not murder. You shall not commit adultery. You shall not steal. You shall not bear false witness. You shall not defraud. Honor your father and mother.'" [20]He said to him, "Teacher, I have kept all these since my youth." [21]Jesus, looking at him, loved him and said, "You lack

y 9.42 Other ancient authorities lack in me   z 9.42 Or stumble   a 9.43 Or stumble   b 9.43 Gk Gehenna   c 9.43 Other ancient authorities add 9.44 and 9.46, which are identical to 9.48   d 9.45 Or stumble   e 9.45 Gk Gehenna   f 9.45 Other ancient authorities add 9.44 and 9.46, which are identical to 9.48   g 9.47 Or stumble   h 9.47 Gk Gehenna   i 9.49 Other ancient authorities add or substitute and every sacrifice will be salted with salt   j 9.50 Or how can you restore its saltiness?   k 10.1 Other ancient authorities lack and   l 10.2 Other ancient authorities add Pharisees came and   m 10.7 Other ancient authorities lack and be joined to his wife

show they misunderstand their prophetic role as conduits of the God's generosity. **9:42–50** Most of these enigmatic sayings warn disciples against causing apostasy for others or for themselves. Furthermore, Jesus directs the disciples ultimately to seek peace among themselves, not divisions or their own greatness. **10:1–12** Ancient marriages were legal contracts with financial implications (such as the giving of a dowry). Divorce was permitted in Jewish culture but required a *certificate of dismissal* to protect the woman from charges of adultery if she remarried. Compare Deut. 24:1–4, which only seeks to prevent a man from remarrying a woman from whom he had once been divorced. Also, adultery for men was viewed through a patriarchal prism: it only occurred when a male engaged in intercourse with a married man's wife. Here, *God made them male and female* evokes Gen. 1:27, while Jesus's view of married persons as *one flesh* evokes Gen. 2:24–25. **10:5** *Hardness of heart* evokes the hardening of Pharaoh's heart (Exod. 10:1). **10:17–31** The episode includes two dialogues: one between Jesus and someone who is later identified as rich and one between Jesus and his disciples. In the former, Jesus

one thing; go, sell what you own, and give the money[n] to the poor, and you will have treasure in heaven; then come, follow me." [22]When he heard this, he was shocked and went away grieving, for he had many possessions.

23 Then Jesus looked around and said to his disciples, "How hard it will be for those who have wealth to enter the kingdom of God!" [24]And the disciples were perplexed at these words. But Jesus said to them again, "Children, how hard it is[o] to enter the kingdom of God! [25]It is easier for a camel to go through the eye of a needle than for someone who is rich to enter the kingdom of God." [26]They were greatly astounded and said to one another,[p] "Then who can be saved?" [27]Jesus looked at them and said, "For mortals it is impossible, but not for God; for God all things are possible."

28 Peter began to say to him, "Look, we have left everything and followed you." [29]Jesus said, "Truly I tell you, there is no one who has left house or brothers or sisters or mother or father or children or fields for my sake and for the sake of the good news[q] [30]who will not receive a hundredfold now in this age—houses, brothers and sisters, mothers and children, and fields, with persecutions—and in the age to come eternal life. [31]But many who are first will be last, and the last will be first."

32 They were on the road, going up to Jerusalem, and Jesus was walking ahead of them; they were amazed, and those who followed were afraid. He took the twelve aside again and began to tell them what was to happen to him, [33]saying, "Look, we are going up to Jerusalem, and the Son of Man will be handed over to the chief priests and the scribes, and they will condemn him to death; then they will hand him over to the gentiles; [34]they will mock him and spit upon him and flog him and kill him, and after three days he will rise again."

35 James and John, the sons of Zebedee, came forward to him and said to him, "Teacher, we want you to do for us whatever we ask of you." [36]And he said to them, "What is it you want me to do for you?" [37]And they said to him, "Appoint us to sit, one at your right hand and one at your left, in your glory." [38]But Jesus said to them, "You do not know what you are asking. Are you able to drink the cup that I drink or be baptized with the baptism that I am baptized with?" [39]They replied, "We are able." Then Jesus said to them, "The cup that I drink you will drink, and with the baptism with which I am baptized you will be baptized, [40]but to sit at my right hand or at my left is not mine to appoint, but it is for those for whom it has been prepared."

41 When the ten heard this, they began to be angry with James and John. [42]So Jesus called them and said to them, "You know that among the gentiles those whom they recognize as their rulers lord it over them, and their great ones are tyrants over them. [43]But it is not so among you; instead, whoever wishes to become great among you must be your servant, [44]and whoever wishes to be first among you must be slave of all. [45]For the Son of Man came not to be served but to serve and to give his life a ransom for many."

46 They came to Jericho. As he and his disciples and a large crowd were leaving Jericho, Bartimaeus son of Timaeus, a blind beggar, was sitting by the roadside. [47]When he heard that it was Jesus of Nazareth, he began to shout out and say, "Jesus, Son of David, have

n 10.21 Gk lacks *the money* *o* 10.24 Other ancient authorities add *for those who trust in riches* *p* 10.26 Other ancient authorities read *to him* *q* 10.29 Or *gospel*

tells what is needed to have treasure in heaven: a new attitude toward possessions (10:21). In the latter, Jesus talks about entrance into the kingdom or rule of God: the difficulty in doing so (vv. 23–27, 31) and the compensation for those who lose support of their biological families for the sake of their commitments to Jesus and the good news (vv. 28–30). See **"Kingdom of God," p. 772.**

10:32–52 Mark's Stage Three includes a third passion/resurrection pattern (10:32–45) and a single final episode, the one about Bartimaeus. So while James and John show their misunderstanding of Jesus's values by wanting Jesus to give them special seats of honor (v. 37), Bartimaeus wants only to receive his sight (v. 51). Sight, not status, then, is what disciples need to be able to deal with the pressures of life. **10:38–40** Jesus deploys two parallel images of suffering—drinking from a cup of suffering (Ps. 75:8; Isa. 51:17, 22) and being baptized or deluged with suffering (Isa. 21:4 LXX). **10:46** Jericho was located to the west of the Jordan River and northeast of Jerusalem. Given that "Bar" is Aramaic for "son," the expression *Son of Timaeus* is a translation of the expression *Bartimaeus*. **10:47–51** Bartimaeus calls Jesus both *Son of David* and "Rabbouni." The term "Rabbouni," *my teacher*, simply anticipates the subsequent discipleship action of Bartimaeus: he follows Jesus "on the way" (10:52). See comment

mercy on me!" [48]Many sternly ordered him to be quiet, but he cried out even more loudly, "Son of David, have mercy on me!" [49]Jesus stood still and said, "Call him here." And they called the blind man, saying to him, "Take heart; get up, he is calling you." [50]So throwing off his cloak, he sprang up and came to Jesus. [51]Then Jesus said to him, "What do you want me to do for you?" The blind man said to him, "My teacher,[r] let me see again." [52]Jesus said to him, "Go; your faith has made you well." Immediately he regained his sight and followed him on the way.

11 When they were approaching Jerusalem, at Bethphage and Bethany, near the Mount of Olives, he sent two of his disciples [2]and said to them, "Go into the village ahead of you, and immediately as you enter it you will find tied there a colt that has never been ridden; untie it and bring it. [3]If anyone says to you, 'Why are you doing this?' just say this: 'The Lord needs it and will send it back here immediately.'" [4]They went away and found a colt tied near a door, outside in the street. As they were untying it, [5]some of the bystanders

said to them, "What are you doing, untying the colt?" [6]They told them what Jesus had said, and they allowed them to take it. [7]Then they brought the colt to Jesus and threw their cloaks on it, and he sat on it. [8]Many people spread their cloaks on the road, and others spread leafy branches that they had cut in the fields. [9]Then those who went ahead and those who followed were shouting,

"Hosanna!
Blessed is the one who comes in the name of the Lord!
[10] Blessed is the coming kingdom of our ancestor David!
Hosanna in the highest heaven!"

[11] Then he entered Jerusalem and went into the temple, and when he had looked around at everything, as it was already late, he went out to Bethany with the twelve.

[12] On the following day, when they came from Bethany, he was hungry. [13]Seeing in the distance a fig tree in leaf, he went to see whether perhaps he would find anything on it. When he came to it, he found nothing but

r 10.51 Aramaic *Rabbouni*

on 12:35–37. **10:51** To highlight the theme of willing and wanting, Mark places the Greek verb "thelō" ("I want") in all three formal passion/resurrection patterns. In this third pattern, Mark highlights this theme in the act of misunderstanding (10:35–36), the call to correction (10:43), and the single episode that follows the pattern (10:46–52; especially v. 51). Thus, Mark reminds auditors of the importance of paying attention to their wants. Such desires should never lead to egoism, exclusivism, or nepotism.

11:1–16:8 Closing scenes: The crucible. The first ten chapters of Mark largely follow Jesus on a long journey leading up to Jerusalem. The final six chapters follow Jesus's multiple entrances into Jerusalem, including a fateful, final one for Passover (14:12–25)—the occasion that sets off an extended process of handing over (14:32–15:15). From that occasion, Jesus is delivered over first to an arresting mob, then to Jerusalem's Council, next to a Roman administrator (Pilate), and finally to Pilate's henchmen. In the hands of Pilate's henchmen, moreover, Jesus suffers humiliating rituals, faces his last hours, and then dies a lonely death. Still, Mark cleverly closes the Gospel with a focus on Jesus's words. Thus, after groups of women have seen his death, though from a distance; his burial site, enclosed with a stone; and that same stone rolled away, the young man at the tomb calls their attention not to his body but to his words of promise—that he would meet them in Galilee (16:7; 14:28).

11:1–13:37 The first three entrances into Jerusalem. For three of Jesus's multiple entrances into Jerusalem, the established guardians may not like Jesus, but they cannot touch him because he is popular among the crowds (11:18; 12:12).

11:1–11 Although frequently labeled as Jesus's triumphal entry, Jesus's initial entry into Jerusalem—which Mark acknowledges in the first part of a single verse (11:11a)—has none of the trappings of a Roman triumph such as a vanguard of captives, the parade of a triumphator (or venerated war general) and his family, and trailing soldiers. Jesus's entry, which follows Mark's citation of Ps. 118, suggests he is a different kind of king.

11:8 Mark does not use the Greek expression for "palm branches," an idea that emanates from John 12:13 in association with 1 Macc. 13:51. Rather, Mark simply deploys a more general description: *leafy branches.*

11:12–25 With the fig tree story intercalation, or insertion, Mark frames the second entry into Jerusalem (vv. 15–19) with notices on seeing and cursing a fig tree (vv. 12–14) on the one hand and seeing

leaves, for it was not the season for figs. [14]He said to it, "May no one ever eat fruit from you again." And his disciples heard it.

15 Then they came to Jerusalem. And he entered the temple and began to drive out those who were selling and those who were buying in the temple, and he overturned the tables of the money changers and the seats of those who sold doves, [16]and he would not allow anyone to carry anything through the temple. [17]He was teaching and saying, "Is it not written,

'My house shall be called a house of
      prayer for all the nations'?

But you have made it a den of robbers." [18]And when the chief priests and the scribes heard it, they kept looking for a way to kill him, for they were afraid of him because the whole crowd was spellbound by his teaching. [19]And when evening came, Jesus and his disciples[s] went out of the city.

20 In the morning as they passed by, they saw the fig tree withered away to its roots. [21]Then Peter remembered and said to him, "Rabbi, look! The fig tree that you cursed has withered." [22]Jesus answered them, "Have faith in God.[t] [23]Truly I tell you, if you say to this mountain, 'Be taken up and thrown into the sea,' and if you do not doubt in your heart but believe that what you say will come to pass, it will be done for you. [24]So I tell you, whatever you ask for in prayer, believe that you have received[u] it, and it will be yours.

25 "Whenever you stand praying, forgive, if you have anything against anyone, so that your Father in heaven may also forgive you your trespasses."[v]

27 Again they came to Jerusalem. As he was walking in the temple, the chief priests, the scribes, and the elders came to him [28]and said, "By what authority are you doing these things? Who gave you this authority to do them?" [29]Jesus said to them, "I will ask you one question; answer me, and I will tell you by what authority I do these things. [30]Did the baptism of John come from heaven, or was it of human origin? Answer me." [31]They argued with one another, "What should we say?[w] If we say, 'From heaven,' he will say, 'Why then did you not believe him?' [32]But shall we say, 'Of human origin'?"—they were afraid of the crowd, for all regarded John as truly a prophet. [33]So they answered Jesus, "We do not know." And Jesus said to them, "Neither will I tell you by what authority I am doing these things."

12 Then he began to speak to them in parables. "A man planted a vineyard, put a fence around it, dug a pit for the winepress, and built a watchtower; then he leased it to tenants and went away. [2]When the season came, he sent a slave to the tenants to collect from them his share of the produce of the vineyard. [3]But they seized him and beat him and sent him away empty-handed. [4]And again he sent another slave to them; this one they beat over the head and insulted. [5]Then he sent another, and that one they killed. And so it was with many others; some they beat, and others they killed. [6]He had still one other, a beloved son. Finally he sent him to them, saying, 'They will respect my son.' [7]But those tenants said to one another, 'This is the heir; come, let us kill him, and the inheritance will be ours.' [8]So they seized him, killed him, and threw him out of the vineyard. [9]What then will the owner of the vineyard do? He will come and destroy the tenants and give the vineyard to others. [10]Have you not read this scripture:

s 11.19 Gk *they*: other ancient authorities read *he*
t 11.22 Other ancient authorities read *If you have faith in God*, u 11.24 Other ancient authorities read *are receiving*
v 11.25 Other ancient authorities add 11.26: *But if you do not forgive, neither will your Father in heaven forgive your trespasses.*
w 11.31 Other ancient authorities lack *What should we say?*

and remembering the cursed fig tree (vv. 20–25) on the other. Thus, Jesus communicates that the temple authorities who have allowed the dissolution of the temple's ideal—the temple as a house of prayer—are like the fig tree that has leaves but no fruit. While leaves may appear on fig trees as early as March or April, fruit would not be seen on them until June. Mark thus appears here to nudge hearers to see beyond the historical reality about seasons or timing to the larger, prophetic action in which the go-between figure Jesus comes in the name of the Father, the ultimate Patron to challenge other religious brokers on the true function of his house. **11:26** The verse is not found in the oldest and best manuscripts, and so it is omitted in this translation.

11:27–13:37 Mark narrates a third entry into Jerusalem (11:27–12:12) that has its own reference to Ps. 118 followed by Jesus's responses to queries (12:13–34), his counsel to a mixed group of interlocutors (12:35–44), and his farewell discourse (13:1–37). **12:1–12** The parable here reinforces some of the Gospel's larger themes (sending, suffering of messengers, the beloved son, and his death). In addition, the parable here

'The stone that the builders rejected
　　has become the cornerstone;[x]
[11] this was the Lord's doing,
　　and it is amazing in our eyes'?"

[12] When they realized that he had told this parable against them, they wanted to arrest him, but they feared the crowd. So they left him and went away.

[13] Then they sent to him some Pharisees and some Herodians to trap him in what he said. [14]And they came and said to him, "Teacher, we know that you are sincere and show deference to no one, for you do not regard people with partiality but teach the way of God in accordance with truth. Is it lawful to pay taxes to Caesar or not? [15]Should we pay them, or should we not?" But knowing their hypocrisy, he said to them, "Why are you putting me to the test? Bring me a denarius and let me see it." [16]And they brought one. Then he said to them, "Whose head is this and whose title?" They answered, "Caesar's." [17]Jesus said to them, "Give to Caesar the things that are Caesar's and to God the things that are God's." And they were utterly amazed at him.

[18] Some Sadducees, who say there is no resurrection, came to him and asked him a question, saying, [19]"Teacher, Moses wrote for us that if a man's brother dies, leaving a wife but no child, the man[y] shall marry the widow and raise up children for his brother. [20]There were seven brothers; the first married and, when he died, left no children, [21]and the second married the widow[z] and died, leaving no children, and the third likewise; [22]none of the seven left children. Last of all the woman herself died. [23]In the resurrection, when they rise,[a] whose wife will she be? For all seven had married her."

[24] Jesus said to them, "Is not this the reason you are wrong, that you know neither the scriptures nor the power of God? [25]For when people rise from the dead, they neither marry nor are given in marriage but are like angels in heaven. [26]And as for the dead being raised, have you not read in the book of Moses, in the story about the bush, how God said to him, 'I am the God of Abraham, the God of Isaac, and the God of Jacob'? [27]He is God not of the dead but of the living; you are quite wrong."

[28] One of the scribes came near and heard them disputing with one another, and seeing that he answered them well he asked him, "Which commandment is the first of all?" [29]Jesus answered, "The first is, 'Hear, O Israel: the Lord our God, the Lord is one; [30]you shall love the Lord your God with all your heart and with all your soul and with all your mind and with all your strength.' [31]The second is this, 'You shall love your neighbor as yourself.' There is no other commandment greater than these." [32]Then the scribe said to him, "You are right, Teacher; you have truly said that 'he is one, and besides him there is no other'; [33]and 'to love him with all the heart and with all the understanding and with all the strength' and 'to love one's neighbor as oneself'—this is much more important than all whole burnt offerings and sacrifices." [34]When Jesus saw that he answered wisely, he said to him, "You are not far from the kingdom of God." After that no one dared to ask him any question.

[35] While Jesus was teaching in the temple, he said, "How can the scribes say that the Messiah[b] is the son of David? [36]David himself, by the Holy Spirit, declared,

'The Lord said to my Lord,
　"Sit at my right hand,
　　until I put your enemies under your feet."'

[37]"David himself calls him Lord, so how can he be his son?" And the large crowd was listening to him with delight.

[38] As he taught, he said, "Beware of the scribes, who like to walk around in long robes and to be greeted with respect in the marketplaces [39]and to have the best seats in the synagogues and places of honor at banquets! [40]They devour widows' houses and for the sake of appearance say long prayers. They will receive the greater condemnation."

[41] He sat down opposite the treasury and watched the crowd putting money into the

---

x 12.10 Or *keystone* (in an arch)　*y* 12.19 Gk *his brother*
z 12.21 Gk *her*　*a* 12.23 Other ancient authorities lack *when they rise*　*b* 12.35 Or *the Christ*

---

provides information about the backstory of the Gospel (12:1 and Isa. 5:1–7) and about the events that will occur off the narrative stage when the story concludes (12:9). **12:13–13:37** A pervasive theme—whether Jesus is in the temple, walking out of it, or sitting opposite it—is the preeminence of the Lord of the vineyard: what that deity owns ("the things that are God's," 12:17); the power of the deity (12:24); how that deity stands alone and deserves one's devotion, dependence, and dedication (12:28–44); and God's ultimate control over what will happen and when it will happen (13:1–37). **12:35–37** Jesus here does not deny the messianic claim to be a *son of David*. Rather, he intensifies the claim. Thus, Jesus is both a descendant of

treasury. Many rich people put in large sums. [42]A poor widow came and put in two small copper coins, which are worth a penny. [43]Then he called his disciples and said to them, "Truly I tell you, this poor widow has put in more than all those who are contributing to the treasury. [44]For all of them have contributed out of their abundance, but she out of her poverty has put in everything she had, all she had to live on."

13 As he came out of the temple, one of his disciples said to him, "Look, Teacher, what large stones and what large buildings!" [2]Then Jesus asked him, "Do you see these great buildings? Not one stone will be left here upon another; all will be thrown down."

3 When he was sitting on the Mount of Olives opposite the temple, Peter, James, John, and Andrew asked him privately, [4]"Tell us, when will this be, and what will be the sign that all these things are about to be accomplished?" [5]Then Jesus began to say to them, "Beware that no one leads you astray. [6]Many will come in my name and say, 'I am he!'[c] and they will lead many astray. [7]When you hear of wars and rumors of wars, do not be alarmed; this must take place, but the end is still to come. [8]For nation will rise against nation and kingdom against kingdom; there will be earthquakes in various places; there will be famines. This is but the beginning of the birth pangs.

9 "As for yourselves, beware, for they will hand you over to councils, and you will be beaten in synagogues, and you will stand before governors and kings because of me, as a testimony to them. [10]And the good news[d] must first be proclaimed to all nations. [11]When they bring you to trial and hand you over, do not worry beforehand about what you are to say, but say whatever is given you at that time, for it is not you who speak but the Holy Spirit. [12]Sibling will betray sibling to death and a father his child, and children will rise against parents and have them put to death, [13]and you will be hated by all because of my name. But the one who endures to the end will be saved.

14 "But when you see the desolating sacrilege set up where it ought not to be (let the reader

understand), then those in Judea must flee to the mountains; [15]the one on the housetop must not go down or enter to take anything from the house; [16]the one in the field must not turn back to get a coat. [17]Woe to those who are pregnant and to those who are nursing infants in those days! [18]Pray that it may not be in winter. [19]For in those days there will be suffering, such as has not been from the beginning of the creation that God created until now and never will be. [20]And if the Lord had not cut short those days, no one would be saved, but for the sake of the elect, whom he chose, he has cut short those days. [21]And if anyone says to you at that time, 'Look! Here is the Messiah!'[e] or 'Look! There he is!'—do not believe it. [22]False messiahs[f] and false prophets will appear and produce signs and wonders, to lead astray, if possible, the elect. [23]But be alert; I have already told you everything.

24 "But in those days, after that suffering,
    the sun will be darkened,
        and the moon will not give its light,
[25]   and the stars will be falling from heaven,
        and the powers in the heavens will be
            shaken.

[26]"Then they will see 'the Son of Man coming in clouds' with great power and glory. [27]Then he will send out the angels and gather the[g] elect from the four winds, from the ends of the earth to the ends of heaven.

28 "From the fig tree learn its lesson: as soon as its branch becomes tender and puts forth its leaves, you know that summer is near. [29]So also, when you see these things taking place, you know that he[h] is near, at the very gates. [30]Truly I tell you, this generation will not pass away until all these things have taken place. [31]Heaven and earth will pass away, but my words will not pass away.

32 "But about that day or hour no one knows, neither the angels in heaven nor the Son, but only the Father. [33]Beware, keep alert,[i] for you do not know when the time will come. [34]It is like a man going on a journey, when he leaves home and puts his slaves in charge, each with

---

c 13.6 Gk *I am*   d 13.10 Gk *gospel*   e 13.21 Or *the Christ*
f 13.22 Or *christs*   g 13.27 Other ancient authorities read *his*
h 13.29 Or *it*   i 13.33 Other ancient authorities add *and pray*

David and one positioned above David. **13:1–37** Known as the "little apocalypse," Jesus's rather extended discourse also has the tenor of a farewell discourse: it depicts a venerated figure sharing the fate and fortunes of his followers in the shadow of his own departure. Beyond its setting in vv. 1–2, the discourse roughly divides into four sections: (1) questions posed by the first called ones (13:3–4), (2) sufferings before the return of the Son of Man (a.k.a. Son of the Human One; 13:5–23), (3) the coming/return of the Son of Man (a.k.a. Son of the Human One; 13:24–27), and (4) two closing parables with an exhortation (13:28–37).

his work, and commands the doorkeeper to be on the watch. [35]Therefore, keep awake, for you do not know when the master of the house will come, in the evening or at midnight or at cockcrow or at dawn, [36]or else he may find you asleep when he comes suddenly. [37]And what I say to you I say to all: Keep awake."

14 It was two days before the Passover and the Festival of Unleavened Bread. The chief priests and the scribes were looking for a way to arrest Jesus[j] by stealth and kill him, [2]for they said, "Not during the festival, or there may be a riot among the people."

3 While he was at Bethany in the house of Simon the leper,[k] as he sat at the table, a woman came with an alabaster jar of very costly ointment of nard, and she broke open the jar and poured the ointment on his head. [4]But some were there who said to one another in anger, "Why was the ointment wasted in this way? [5]For this ointment could have been sold for more than three hundred denarii and the money given to the poor." And they scolded her. [6]But Jesus said, "Let her alone; why do you trouble her? She has performed a good service for me. [7]For you always have the poor with you, and you can show kindness to them whenever you wish, but you will not always have me. [8]She has done what she could; she has anointed my body beforehand for its burial. [9]Truly I tell you, wherever the good news[l] is proclaimed in the whole world, what she has done will be told in remembrance of her."

10 Then Judas Iscariot, who was one of the twelve, went to the chief priests in order to betray him to them. [11]When they heard it, they were greatly pleased and promised to give him money. So he began to look for an opportunity to betray him.

12 On the first day of Unleavened Bread, when the Passover lamb is sacrificed, his disciples said to him, "Where do you want us to go and make the preparations for you to eat the Passover?" [13]So he sent two of his disciples, saying to them, "Go into the city, and a man carrying a jar of water will meet you; follow him, [14]and wherever he enters, say to the owner of the house, 'The Teacher asks: Where is my guest room where I may eat the Passover with my disciples?' [15]He will show you a large room upstairs, furnished and ready. Make preparations for us there." [16]So the disciples set out and went to the city and found everything as he had told them, and they prepared the Passover meal.

17 When it was evening, he came with the twelve. [18]And when they had taken their places and were eating, Jesus said, "Truly I tell you, one of you will betray me, one who is eating with me." [19]They began to be distressed and to say to him one after another, "Surely, not I?" [20]He said to them, "It is one of the twelve, one who is dipping bread[m] into the bowl[n] with me. [21]For the Son of Man goes as it is written of him, but woe to that one by whom the Son of Man is betrayed! It would have been better for that one not to have been born."

22 While they were eating, he took a loaf of bread, and after blessing it he broke it, gave it to them, and said, "Take; this is my body." [23]Then he took a cup, and after giving thanks he gave it to them, and all of them drank from it. [24]He said to them, "This is my blood of the[o] covenant, which is poured out for many. [25]Truly I tell you, I will never again drink of the fruit of the vine until that day when I drink it new in the kingdom of God."

26 When they had sung the hymn, they went out to the Mount of Olives. [27]And Jesus said to them, "You will all fall away,[p] for it is written,

j 14.1 Gk *him*   *k* 14.3 Or *the skin-diseased*   *l* 14.9 Or *gospel*
m 14.20 Gk lacks *bread*   *n* 14.20 Other ancient authorities
read *same bowl*   *o* 14.24 Other ancient authorities add *new*
p 14.27 Or *stumble*

14:1–11 The plot thickens in Jerusalem while Jesus dines in Bethany. Two pericopes here (vv. 1–2, 10–11) frame a woman's generous act of anointing and thus provide a stark contrast between the woman's devotion and the deadly designs of her male counterparts: the chief priests and scribes on the one hand and Judas on the other. **14:3–9** Mark names the location and the owner of the house in which Jesus reclines. Remarkably, though, Mark does not name the woman, nor does Mark give her a speaking part. Still, Jesus's epitaph is now forever linked with this woman, whose selfless act began when she stepped into Simon's home and shattered an alabaster jar of pure and expensive perfume made of nard or oil and poured the aromatic ointment over Jesus's head. With that open act of piety, a fragrance of unabashed devotion permeated a story overlaid with the stench of deception.

14:12–72 The fatal, final trip from Bethany to Jerusalem. Having introduced the deceptive plans of some Jerusalem brokers, or go-betweens, the Gospel of Mark now spins forth narrative scenes that show how those plans resulted in Jesus's delivery to the Sanhedrin. The delivery begins

'I will strike the shepherd,
    and the sheep will be scattered.'
[28]"But after I am raised up, I will go before you to Galilee." [29]Peter said to him, "Even though all fall away,[q] I will not." [30]Jesus said to him, "Truly I tell you, this day, this very night, before the cock crows twice, you will deny me three times." [31]But he said vehemently, "Even though I must die with you, I will not deny you." And all of them said the same.

32 They went to a place called Gethsemane, and he said to his disciples, "Sit here while I pray." [33]He took with him Peter and James and John and began to be distressed and agitated. [34]And he said to them, "My soul is deeply grieved, even to death; remain here, and keep awake." [35]And going a little farther, he threw himself on the ground and prayed that, if it were possible, the hour might pass from him. [36]He said, "Abba,[r] Father, for you all things are possible; remove this cup from me, yet not what I want but what you want." [37]He came and found them sleeping, and he said to Peter, "Simon, are you asleep? Could you not keep awake one hour? [38]Keep awake and pray that you may not come into the time of trial;[s] the spirit indeed is willing, but the flesh is weak." [39]And again he went away and prayed, saying the same words. [40]And once more he came and found them sleeping, for their eyes were very heavy, and they did not know what to say to him. [41]He came a third time and said to them, "Are you still sleeping and taking your rest? Enough! The hour has come; the Son of Man is betrayed into the hands of sinners. [42]Get up, let us be going. Look, my betrayer is at hand."

43 Immediately, while he was still speaking, Judas, one of the twelve, arrived, and with him there was a crowd with swords and clubs, from the chief priests, the scribes, and the elders. [44]Now the betrayer had given them a sign, saying, "The one I will kiss is the man; arrest him and lead him away under guard." [45]So when he came, he went up to him at once and said, "Rabbi!" and kissed him. [46]Then they laid hands on him and arrested him. [47]But one of those who stood near drew his sword and struck the slave of the high priest, cutting off his ear. [48]Then Jesus said to them, "Have you come out with swords and clubs to arrest me as though I were a rebel? [49]Day after day I was with you in the temple teaching, and you did not arrest me. But let the scriptures be fulfilled." [50]All of them deserted him and fled.

51 A certain young man was following him, wearing nothing but a linen cloth. They caught hold of him, [52]but he left the linen cloth and ran off naked.

53 They took Jesus to the high priest, and all the chief priests, the elders, and the scribes were assembled. [54]Peter had followed him at a distance, right into the courtyard of the high priest, and he was sitting with the guards, warming himself at the fire. [55]Now the chief priests and the whole council were looking for testimony against Jesus to put him to death, but they found none. [56]For many gave false testimony against him, and their testimony did not agree. [57]Some stood up and gave false testimony against him, saying, [58]"We heard him say, 'I will destroy this temple that is made with hands, and in three days I will build

q 14.29 Or *stumble*   r 14.36 Aramaic for *Father*   s 14.38 Or *into testing*

with preparation for Passover (vv. 12–16) and Jesus's trip to Jerusalem for Passover (vv. 17–25). **14:32–42** Mark never calls Gethsemane (which means "oil press") a garden. Interpreters who call the site of Jesus's arrest the "Garden of Gethsemane" likely harmonize the Synoptic accounts (Mark 14:32; Matt. 26:36) that name it "Gethsemane" with John's Gospel that calls it a "garden" (18:1). **14:44** The identification of Judas as a betrayer reminds the audience of the extended process of handing over Jesus (3:19; 9:31; 10:33; 14:10–11, 41–42; 15:1, 10–15). **14:53–72** In the interrogation section (the scenes in which the interrogation of Jesus is interlaced with the interrogation of Peter), Jesus's prediction of Peter's denial comes true. Ironically, it does so just when some of Jesus's mockers blindfold him and ask him to prophesy (14:65). **14:53** From 18 to 36 CE, which covered the time of Jesus's ministry and death, the high priest was Caiaphas, the son-in-law of Annas, the former high priest (see John 18:13–14; Luke 3:2). **14:54** Both this verse and 14:66–72 are intercalated with the interrogation of Jesus such that the interrogation of Jesus and that of Peter appear to be occurring simultaneously. If so, they provide contrasting options for persons facing a crucible: Jesus owns his relationship with the deity while Peter denies his relationship with Jesus. **14:55–64** The council may have been a provincial Jewish assembly in Jerusalem. When the word *Sanhedrin* appears in Mark in the plural form ("synedria"), it may refer to local courts. The ancient sources show some disagreement about the scope and function of this institution. **14:55** Mark's expression *whole council* here and in 15:1 creates a sense of solidarity within the

Focus On: Passion Narrative (Mark 14:26–15:47)

Scholars do not know the true origins or exact time limits of the passion narrative, a tightly woven series of episodes that appear in various forms in all four canonical Gospels. Mark highlights with detail the final scenes of the Gospel's lore and slows his fast-moving narrative to note the day-by-day sequence of Jesus's three entrances into the city of Jerusalem (11:11, 15, 27) and the hour-by-hour sequence of his last day (chap. 15)—a testament to their importance for Mark.

With Jesus's final, fatal trip from Bethany to Jerusalem underway and his Passover meal with his disciples concluded, Markan audiences witnessed several scenes (14:26–15:47) in which Jesus's fellowship fractured, his friends fled, and he faced his final hours isolated from the very community he had called to be with him (3:14). Thus, although Jesus had eaten *with* the twelve, one of the twelve (Judas) had joined in solidarity *with* the opposition. Furthermore, as Jesus had predicted, all his followers stumbled: Judas betrayed him; all fled from him; and even Peter, in the face of interrogation, denied that he had been *with* Jesus. No friend attends his death, but women who had faithfully ministered to him in Galilee track his death at a distance and note his place of burial. In the interim, he suffered not only physical assaults but the agony of shame from those who mocked him as king—whose crown was the thorns placed on his head, whose retinue were the two derisive bandits crucified on either side, and whose acclamation was the mocking salutation of Pilate's henchmen.

What then is a possible function for so much attention placed on the passion? For Mark's biographical paradigm story, perhaps the story of Jesus at the end provides a model for those who would suffer what he predicted for his disciples (13:9–13). If his disciples would be led away before the established authorities, so would he (13:9–12; 14:44, 53; chap. 15). If his disciples would be betrayed or handed over, so would he. If his disciples might face death, Jesus veritably did so. Thus, over these last scenes, the Markan passion narrative highlights the "arts" of Jesus's endurance for his followers: being prayerful with vigilance (14:32–42); reading rejection through the prism of Scripture, especially Psalms (Pss. 40; 22); and expecting a day of reclamation (14:28; cf. 16:7).

Abraham Smith

another, not made with hands.' " ⁵⁹But even on this point their testimony did not agree. ⁶⁰Then the high priest stood up before them and asked Jesus, "Have you no answer? What is it that they testify against you?" ⁶¹But he was silent and did not answer. Again the high priest asked him, "Are you the Messiah,ᵗ the Son of the Blessed One?" ⁶²Jesus said, "I am, and

'you will see the Son of Man
  seated at the right hand of the Power'
and 'coming with the clouds of heaven.' "

⁶³Then the high priest tore his clothes and said, "Why do we still need witnesses? ⁶⁴You have heard his blasphemy! What is your decision?" All of them condemned him as deserving death. ⁶⁵Some began to spit on him, to blindfold him, and to strike him, saying to him, "Prophesy!" The guards also took him and beat him.

66 While Peter was below in the courtyard, one of the female servants of the high priest

came by. ⁶⁷When she saw Peter warming himself, she stared at him and said, "You also were with Jesus, the man from Nazareth." ⁶⁸But he denied it, saying, "I do not know or understand what you are talking about." And he went out into the forecourt.ᵘ Then the cock crowed.ᵛ ⁶⁹And the female servant, on seeing him, began again to say to the bystanders, "This man is one of them." ⁷⁰But again he denied it. Then after a little while the bystanders again said to Peter, "Certainly you are one of them, for you are a Galilean, and you talk like one."ʷ ⁷¹But he began to curse, and he swore an oath, "I do not know this man you are talking about." ⁷²At that moment the cock crowed for the second time. Then Peter remembered that Jesus had said to him, "Before the cock crows twice, you will deny me three times." And he broke down and wept.

t 14.61 Or *the Christ* *u* 14.68 Or *gateway* *v* 14.68 Other ancient authorities lack *Then the cock crowed* *w* 14.70 Other ancient authorities lack *and you talk like one*

council. **14:61–62** The apposition *Son of the Blessed One* is a circumlocution to avoid directly naming the deity. Likewise, Jesus's response about *the right hand of the Power* is a circumlocution for the right hand of the deity. Jesus's response, moreover, appears to bring together two traditions from Jesus's Jewish heritage: the Son of Man or Son of the Human One (from Dan. 7:13) and the right-hand designation of status (from Ps. 110:1; see also Mark 12:36).

15

As soon as it was morning, the chief priests held a consultation with the elders and scribes and the whole council. They bound Jesus, led him away, and handed him over to Pilate. [2]Pilate asked him, "Are you the King of the Jews?" He answered him, "You say so." [3]Then the chief priests accused him of many things. [4]Pilate asked him again, "Have you no answer? See how many charges they bring against you." [5]But Jesus made no further reply, so that Pilate was amazed.

6 Now at the festival he used to release a prisoner for them, anyone for whom they asked. [7]Now a man called Barabbas was in prison with the insurrectionists who had committed murder during the insurrection. [8]So the crowd came and began to ask Pilate to do for them according to his custom. [9]Then he answered them, "Do you want me to release for you the King of the Jews?" [10]For he realized that it was out of jealousy that the chief priests had handed him over. [11]But the chief priests stirred up the crowd to have him release Barabbas for them instead. [12]Pilate spoke to them again, "Then what do you wish me to do[x] with the man you call[y] the King of

the Jews?" [13]They shouted back, "Crucify him!" [14]Pilate asked them, "Why, what evil has he done?" But they shouted all the more, "Crucify him!" [15]So Pilate, wishing to satisfy the crowd, released Barabbas for them, and after flogging Jesus he handed him over to be crucified.

16 Then the soldiers led him into the courtyard of the palace (that is, the governor's headquarters), and they called together the whole cohort. [17]And they clothed him in a purple cloak, and after twisting some thorns into a crown they put it on him. [18]And they began saluting him, "Hail, King of the Jews!" [19]They struck his head with a reed, spat upon him, and knelt down in homage to him. [20]After mocking him, they stripped him of the purple cloak and put his own clothes on him. Then they led him out to crucify him.

21 They compelled a passer-by, who was coming in from the country, to carry his cross; it was Simon of Cyrene, the father of Alexander and Rufus. [22]Then they brought Jesus[z] to the place called Golgotha (which means Place of a Skull).

x 15.12 Other ancient authorities read *what should I do* y 15.12 Other ancient authorities lack *the man you call* z 15.22 Gk *him*

15:1–39 With three sections divided by temporal markers, this section recounts the varying responses that others made to Jesus on his last day: the responses of Pilate and his henchmen to a laconic or silent Jesus (15:1–24); the responses of passersby, the chief priests with their scribes, and two rebels to a crucified Jesus (15:25–32); and the responses of bystanders (including a centurion) to a dying Jesus (15:33–39). **15:1–5** As morning appears, Mark will shift from tracking time by days here to tracking it by hours (vv. 25, 33–34). **15:16** The *courtyard of the palace* refers to the forecourt of the praetorium or the prefect's headquarters. The transliterated word "praitōrion" renders the Latin word "praetorium" in Greek, which was probably Herod's palace in Jerusalem as opposed to the Fortress Antonia that Herod I built in Mark Antony's honor. Although a cohort typically refers to six hundred soldiers, or a tenth of a legion, it could have been substantially smaller. As with the expression "whole council" (14:55; 15:1), Mark deploys the expression *whole* to evoke the semblance of solidarity within the cohort and the totality of opposition to Jesus. **15:17–18** Attiring Jesus in royal purple (see 1 Macc. 10:20; 11:58), the soldiers begin their mock drama. Instead of giving him a laurel wreath to indicate royalty, they next offer him a crown of plaited thorns and a chorus salute (*Hail, King of the Jews*) that would befit a dignitary ("Hail Emperor Caesar," Suetonius, *Claudius*, 21.6). **15:21** Modern interpreters know little about the identity of Simon of Cyrene, who is mentioned by all three Synoptic Gospel writers. Convicted persons typically carried their own crossbeam. Through the practice of conscription, though, Roman soldiers could compel someone to bear a convicted person's crossbeam, underscoring the chilling arbitrary force of Roman military might and possibly mocking Jesus by demonstrating his weakness before Rome. Mark's brief comments about this Simon tell us Simon hailed from Cyrene, the capital of Cyrenaica in North Africa (or modern-day Libya), and that he was a father to two sons, Alexander and Rufus. That the writer could simply name the sons without identifying them fully suggests that they may have been well-known to Mark's earliest auditors (see **"Crucifixion and Terror," p. 1798**). **15:22** As with other deaths by crucifixion, Jesus's death was an act of public humiliation. Thus, Mark's earlier notice that Simon was coming into Jerusalem from a rural area, not "from the fields" as some translators have suggested, could indicate that the crucifixion was held outside the city of Jerusalem in a well-trafficked area where travelers, like Simon here, would have been passing by. The site of Jesus's crucifixion is called "Skull" (Gk. "Kranion") by Luke (23:33) and "Place of a Skull" (Ar. "Golgotha") by the two other Synoptic Gospel

²³And they offered him wine mixed with myrrh, but he did not take it. ²⁴And they crucified him and divided his clothes among them, casting lots to decide what each should take.

25 It was nine o'clock in the morning when they crucified him. ²⁶The inscription of the charge against him read, "The King of the Jews." ²⁷And with him they crucified two rebels, one on his right and one on his left.ᵃ ²⁹Those who passed by deridedᵇ him, shaking their heads and saying, "Aha! You who would destroy the temple and build it in three days, ³⁰save yourself, and come down from the cross!" ³¹In the same way the chief priests, along with the scribes, were also mocking him among themselves and saying, "He saved others; he cannot save himself. ³²Let the Messiah,ᶜ the King of Israel, come down from the cross now, so that we may see and believe." Those who were crucified with him also taunted him.

33 When it was noon, darkness came over the whole landᵈ until three in the afternoon. ³⁴At three o'clock Jesus cried out with a loud voice, "Eloi, Eloi, lema sabachthani?" which means, "My God, my God, why have you forsaken me?"ᵉ ³⁵When some of the bystanders heard it, they said, "Listen, he is calling for Elijah." ³⁶And someone ran, filled a sponge with

sour wine, put it on a stick, and gave it to him to drink, saying, "Wait, let us see whether Elijah will come to take him down." ³⁷Then Jesus gave a loud cry and breathed his last. ³⁸And the curtain of the temple was torn in two, from top to bottom. ³⁹Now when the centurion who stood facing him saw that in this way heᶠ breathed his last, he said, "Truly this man was God's Son!"ᵍ

40 There were also women looking on from a distance. Among them were Mary Magdalene, and Mary the mother of James the younger and of Joses, and Salome, ⁴¹who followed him when he was in Galilee and ministered to him, and there were many other women who had come up with him to Jerusalem.

42 When evening had come, and since it was the day of Preparation, that is, the day before the Sabbath, ⁴³Joseph of Arimathea, a respected member of the council who was also himself waiting expectantly for the kingdom of God, went boldly to Pilate and asked for the body of Jesus. ⁴⁴Then Pilate wondered if he were already dead, and summoning the

a 15.27 Other ancient authorities add 15.28: *And the scripture was fulfilled that says, "And he was counted among the lawless."* b 15.29 Or *blasphemed* c 15.32 Or *the Christ* d 15.33 Or *earth* e 15.34 Other ancient authorities read *made me a reproach* f 15.39 Other ancient authorities add *cried out and* g 15.39 Or *a son of God*

writers (Mark 15:22 and Matt. 27:33) and John (19:17). Jerome's *Vulgate* translates the word into Latin "Calvariae." **15:24** Here Mark gives the first explicit reference to Ps. 22 (a lament psalm about a righteous sufferer). The reference to soldiers dividing his clothes appears to refer to Ps. 22:18 (Ps. 21 LXX). What it also signals, though, is the soldiers' control even over Jesus's possessions. Furthermore, to be stripped of one's clothes was also a sign of degradation. **15:25–32** With the first of a sequence of notices about Roman hours (the third here, 9:00 a.m. [15:25]; then, the sixth, at noon [15:33]; and the ninth, at 3:00 p.m. [15:34]), Mark now highlights responses made to Jesus as he was being crucified. **15:28** This verse does not belong to the earliest manuscripts of the Gospel and thus is omitted in this translation. **15:29–32** Jesus suffers the taunts of three groups: passersby; the chief priests with their scribes; and the two other crucified men with him. **15:33–39** With additional temporal markers, Mark turns to responses made to Jesus by bystanders who witnessed his death. Crucified at the third hour (9:00 a.m.), Jesus dies at the ninth hour (3:00 p.m.). From noon (the sixth hour) to 3:00 p.m., though, darkness descends. For Jews, such darkness could signal judgment (as in Amos 8:9–10). For gentiles, however, such darkness often signaled the death of an important figure: from Alexander the Great to one of the emperors. **15:34** Mark first introduces Jesus's cry of abandonment in Aramaic and Hebrew (*Eloi, Eloi, lema sabachthani*) before translating the expression into Greek. Again, Mark draws on Ps. 22:1 (Ps. 22:2 LXX). **15:38** As in the case of the other Synoptics (Matt. 27:51; Luke 23:45), Mark's veil refers to a curtain in the sanctuary, not the larger temple complex. **15:39** A centurion was a Roman soldier who commanded a hundred men or a "century."

15:40–16:8 Witnesses at the end of the Gospel. The end of the Gospel appears to consist of three sections, each indicating the witnessing or observation of two or three named women disciples: (a) an initial scene in which three named women disciples witness the death of Jesus (15:40–42), (b) a second scene in which two of the aforementioned women witness the burial site of Jesus (15:40–47), and (c) a third scene in which the same three aforementioned women witness an empty tomb. They are told the resurrection truth by a young man with a divine appearance and are commissioned by the same young man (16:1–8). We do not know why the Gospel ends so abruptly, but some interpreters note that Mark's auditors are witnesses too. Hearing the instructions from the young man on the one hand and the

Making Connections: Simon of Cyrene (Mark 15:21)

Dr. Anna Julia Cooper was a protowomanist and educator. Cooper was the fourth Black woman to earn a PhD. Most noted for her autobiography, *A Voice from the South*, she was also a poet. Hear these words from her pen:

> And so the Cross was heavy; its threefold weight dragged hard
> The feet were torn and bleeding; that trod Judea's sward
> Beside the road to Calvary; a swarthy figure stood
> Simon of Cyrene, alone amid the crowd
> His brawny arms knew burdens; his big broad shoulders, bent
> To many a loving service; a willing lift had lent. ("Simon of Cyrene")

Cooper's "Simon of Cyrene," written sometime during her tenure at Lincoln University from 1906 to 1910, depicts an African honored to carry the cross of Jesus. Simon offers a "willing lift" beneath the cross of the "Son of God." Cooper is accurate in her depiction of race and burden. However, there are counterclaims regarding Simon's volition.

Simon of Cyrene is present in the Synoptic Gospels. Matthew 27:32 and Mark 15:21 both employ the Greek word *aggareuo* to show that Simon is "compelled" into service. The word is also a historical reference to the impressed labor of the Persian army. However, Luke 23:26, without mentioning any of Simon's family, replaces *aggareuo* with *epilambano*, "to grasp." Luke softens the language suggesting forced service. All agree Simon of Cyrene is an African who carries Jesus's cross. Cyrene, which in the Greek means "place of the iris," is located in what is now the North African country of Libya. The capital, Cyrenaica, is historically known for its grain, wool, cattle, wines, silphium (a medicinal plant), and horses. Mark records him as the father of two sons, Alexander and Rufus.

Some ten years after Cooper, Harlem Renaissance poet Countee Cullen paid homage to this African in "Simon the Cyrenian Speaks" (1924). Cullen's Simon does not offer his services willingly:

> He never spoke a word to me,
> And yet He called my name . . .
>
> At first I said, "I will not bear
> His cross upon my back;
> He only seeks to place it there
> Because my skin is black."
>
> . . . I did for Christ alone
> What all of Rome could not have wrought
> With bruise of lash or stone.

Together, Cooper and Cullen illustrate important and diverging interpretations of Simon of Cyrene.

Stephanie Buckhanon Crowder

centurion he asked him whether he had been dead for some time. [45]When he learned from the centurion that he was dead, he granted the body to Joseph. [46]Then Joseph[b] bought a linen cloth and, taking down the body,[i] wrapped it in the linen cloth and laid it in a tomb that had been hewn out of rock. He then rolled a stone against the door of the tomb. [47]Mary Magdalene and Mary the mother of Joses saw where the body[j] was laid.

16 When the Sabbath was over, Mary Magdalene and Mary the mother of James and Salome bought spices, so that they

b 15.46 Gk *he*   i 15.46 Gk *it*   j 15.47 Gk *it*

silence and fear of the women on the other, the auditors must act. They must relish the words of Jesus (16:7; 14:28) and become his successors in the proclamation of the good news. What they have heard from 1:1–16:8 is just the beginning of the good news. The fuller story lies in the fulfillment of Jesus's

Focus On: Crucifixion and Terror (Mark 15)

Crucifixion served two purposes—to punish criminals with a humiliating death and to serve as a grue-some warning to conquered peoples of their fate should they cross the government. Romans did not impose it for random crimes, but reserved it for the enslaved, noncitizens, and those guilty of sedition—rebellion against state power. The language of the sign over the cross reported in the Gospels suggests that Jesus was viewed as a political threat, a "king of the Jews" in competition with the emperor and his administrators.

Prisoners were often flogged first and sometimes forced to carry the crossbeam. The upright part of the cross was set up permanently, available for reuse and a visible sign of Roman power. Prisoners were nailed or tied to the cross, sometimes in different positions. Death might come quickly or slowly, and soldiers sometimes broke the legs of a victim to hasten death. Speculation as to the physical cause of death has included cardiac rupture, asphyxia, and shock. In 1968, archaeologists discovered the skeleton of a man crucified in first-century Jerusalem with a bent spike still lodged in his heel bone, a mute witness to his brutal execution.

Different peoples employed crucifixion, including the Persians and Babylonians. Some suggest the Romans picked up the punishment from the Carthaginians during the Punic Wars. Although capital punishment is cited in the Hebrew Bible, the Torah never cites crucifixion. Deuteronomy indicates an executed victim might be displayed on a tree (21:22–23) but not allowed to remain overnight because such a thing polluted the land. The Hasmonean king Alexander Jannaeus nevertheless crucified his political opponents during the Judean civil war in 88 BCE.

In the decades after Jesus, the Romans crucified thousands as unrest against Roman rule mounted. Josephus reports that the governor of Syria crucified two thousand Jews in disturbances after Herod's death (*Ant.* 17.10.10) and that during the revolt of 66–70 CE, a Roman general surrounded Jerusalem with a wall of crosses (*War* 5.46). Roman soldiers mocked the victims by nailing them to the crosses in different positions, Josephus says, and soon there was no room for the many crosses and not enough crosses for their victims. Crucifixion was a grisly tool of war, genocide, and suppression of dissent. Jesus was crucified not *by* the Jews but *as* a Jew, suffering the same fate as his fellow Jews viewed as threats to the occupying powers.

Claudia Setzer

---

might go and anoint him. ²And very early on the first day of the week, when the sun had risen, they went to the tomb. ³They had been saying to one another, "Who will roll away the stone for us from the entrance to the tomb?" ⁴When they looked up, they saw that the stone, which was very large, had already been rolled back. ⁵As they entered the tomb, they saw a young man dressed in a white robe sitting on the right side, and they were alarmed. ⁶But he said to them, "Do not be alarmed; you are looking for Jesus of Nazareth, who was crucified. He has been raised; he is not here. Look, there is the place they laid him. ⁷But go, tell his disciples and Peter

that he is going ahead of you to Galilee; there you will see him, just as he told you." ⁸So they went out and fled from the tomb, for terror and amazement had seized them, and they said nothing to anyone, for they were afraid.ᵏ

THE INTERMEDIATE ENDING OF MARK

[[And all that had been commanded them they told briefly to those around Peter. And afterward Jesus himself sent out through them,

k 16.8 Some of the most ancient authorities bring the book to a close at the end of 16.8. One authority concludes the book with the intermediate ending; others include the intermediate ending and then continue with 16.9–20. In most authorities 16.9–20 follow immediately after 16.8; in some of these authorities the passage is marked as being doubtful.

promise on the other side of the narrative stage. **16:8** If Mark ends at 16:8, its ending is poignant even if it appears insufficient. Mark's apparently strange ending startles its readers and auditors to complete a story left unfinished by key insiders. Once again, as the narrative has shown many times over, outsiders see more than those who should have known Jesus best. That knowledge is now in your hands. What will you do with it? Will you retreat to silence? Or will you be faithful?

The other endings of Mark. Assuredly, some of Mark's readers and auditors felt uncomfortable with the account of an empty tomb and an unfulfilled command. If Mark was written first and Matthew and Luke knew and edited Mark, it is certainly the case that the authors of Matthew and Luke were not satisfied. Thus, they both avoided the ending of an unfulfilled command and offered resurrection appearance

from east to west, the sacred and imperishable proclamation of eternal salvation. Amen.[l]]]

The Long Ending of Mark

[[9 Now after he rose early on the first day of the week, he appeared first to Mary Magdalene, from whom he had cast out seven demons. [10]She went out and told those who had been with him, while they were mourning and weeping. [11]But when they heard that he was alive and had been seen by her, they would not believe it.

12 After this he appeared in another form to two of them, as they were walking into the country. [13]And they went back and told the rest, but they did not believe them.

14 Later he appeared to the eleven themselves as they were sitting at the table, and he upbraided them for their lack of faith and stubbornness, because they had not believed those who saw him after he had risen.[m] [15]And he said to them, "Go into all the world and proclaim the good news[n] to the whole creation. [16]The one who believes and is baptized will be saved, but the one who does not

believe will be condemned. [17]And these signs will accompany those who believe: by using my name they will cast out demons; they will speak in new tongues; [18]they will pick up snakes,[o] and if they drink any deadly thing, it will not hurt them; they will lay their hands on the sick, and they will recover."

19 So then the Lord Jesus, after he had spoken to them, was taken up into heaven and sat down at the right hand of God. [20]And they went out and proclaimed the good news everywhere, while the Lord worked with them and confirmed the message by the signs that accompanied it.[p]]]

l 16.8 Other ancient authorities lack *Amen*   m 16.14 Other ancient authorities add, in whole or in part, *And they excused themselves, saying, "This age of lawlessness and unbelief is under Satan, who does not allow the truth and power of God to prevail over the unclean things of the spirits. Therefore reveal your righteousness now"—thus they spoke to Christ. And Christ replied to them, "The term of years of Satan's power has been fulfilled, but other terrible things draw near. And for those who have sinned I was handed over to death, that they may return to the truth and sin no more, that they may inherit the spiritual and imperishable glory of righteousness that is in heaven."*   n 16.15 Or *gospel*   o 16.18 Other ancient authorities add *in their hands*   p 16.20 Other ancient authorities add *Amen*

accounts. Some scribes also offered substitutes such as "The Intermediate Ending of Mark" (which appears by itself after 16:8 in one Codex [or book-form manuscript] called Bobiensis), "The Long Ending of Mark" (which often appears in most Bibles directly after 16:8 as the bracketed material of Mark 16:9–20), a combination of the intermediate and long endings, or the inclusion of the so-called Freer ending within the long ending (that is, with additional material added between 16:14 and 16:15). As with Matthew and Luke, these endings avoid a narrative conclusion that ends with an unfulfilled command. All these endings also include resurrection appearance accounts. Yet all are also different from Mark 1:1–16:8 in terms of the latter's diction and rhetorical drive. Most importantly, the manuscript evidence is not strong for these other endings.

THE GOSPEL ACCORDING TO LUKE

Authorship and Sources

A theologically and literarily sophisticated narrative, the Gospel according to Luke offers an account of Jesus's birth, ministry in Galilee, journey to Jerusalem, arrest, and crucifixion, concluding with a series of post-resurrection appearances. Written by the same author, Acts of the Apostles continues Luke's story, focusing on the spirit-driven expansion of the early church. Together, the two works are referred to as Luke–Acts. The inclusion of a second volume offers clues about Luke's theology of history. He situates Jesus in the context of Jewish history, standing in the tradition of the prophets while at the same time realizing the hopes expressed in earlier scriptural traditions. Luke is equally concerned with looking forward, finding theological meaning in the time of the church.

The identity of the author is unknown. Although he is conventionally called Luke, most biblical scholars are skeptical of the second-century tradition attributing authorship to a traveling companion of the apostle Paul by that name. From the opening verses, we learn that the author was not an eyewitness to the events recounted but rather relied on written sources. Those sources likely included the Gospel of Mark, the sayings source "Q," and a source sometimes referred to as "L," featuring material exclusive to Luke, such as his particular account of the birth of Jesus (see **"Introduction to the Gospels and Acts," pp. 1709–12**).

Date and Place of Composition

Luke may have been written as early as 80 CE or as late as 130 CE. More important than establishing a precise date is understanding what is at stake in that dating. For example, although the Jerusalem temple figures prominently in Luke–Acts, the work was certainly composed after 70 CE, when Rome destroyed the temple in the Jewish War. As another example, although Luke depicts Jesus and his family as pious Jews, he writes for church communities that are increasingly gentile in membership. For Luke, Jesus is the universal Savior, and Luke–Acts conveys the sense that this good news has already been heard throughout the Roman Empire.

The place of composition is unknown.

Style

The author of the third Gospel is a polished literary stylist. The first four verses constitute a single Greek sentence, signaling Luke's expectation of a well-educated readership. With overlapping stories of the conception and birth of John the Baptist and Jesus, the first two chapters evoke the language of the Septuagint, the Greek translation of the Hebrew Bible. These chapters incorporate poetry as well as prose; the canticles of Mary (1:46–55), Zechariah (1:68–79), and Simeon (2:29–32) are integral to the language of later Christian prayer.

Luke is a skilled storyteller, as is evident in his handling of Jesus's parables, a number of which appear exclusively in Luke. For example, the parable commonly known as the Prodigal Son (15:11–32) explores the motivations and responses of its memorable characters. Although often read independently of the rest of the Gospel, Luke's parables acquire additional levels of meaning when read in their literary context.

Attention to Luke's adaptation of Mark yields further insight into his craft. Structurally, the addition of a central travel account lends theological meaning to Jesus's journey from Galilee to Jerusalem while building narrative tension (9:51–19:28). More minor additions supply details that tend to shape popular memory of certain scenes. For instance, when one of Jesus's followers cuts off the ear of an enslaved member of the arresting party in Gethsemane, Jesus heals the wound (22:50–51). Luke's omissions from Mark are as telling as his supplements. Although Luke includes Peter's explicit confession of Jesus as the Christ (Mark 8:29; Luke 9:20), he omits both Mark's portrayal of Peter resisting Jesus's message about suffering and Jesus's subsequent rebuke of Peter as Satan (Mark 8:31–33). Luke's omission is consistent with the vital role Peter plays in Acts.

Reading Guide

To an even greater extent than in the other Gospels, Luke's Jesus reaches out with compassion to those who need healing, including those who are suffering from illness, disability, or social exclusion. Central to Jesus's mission in Luke is the proclamation of good news to the materially impoverished

and the promise that those who are hungry will be fed. Readers are instructed to anticipate eschatological status reversals. Luke balances assurances that those of humble circumstances will be elevated with warnings that those who are mighty and wealthy will be stripped of their high positions. Those who trust in possessions rather than in God have made a poor choice. Followers of Jesus are expected to share their possessions—with those in need and with the community of disciples.

The Lukan emphasis on economic issues has understandably influenced global liberationist movements. See **"The Bible and Social Justice," pp. 2165–67.** Nonetheless, there is a vein of conservatism in Luke–Acts. The proclamation of coming status reversals does not lead to a toppling of gender hierarchy or criticism of enslavers. Luke conveys the sense that neither Jesus nor his followers pose a threat to governing authorities or public order. According to Luke, although the Roman governor Pontius Pilate ultimately acceded to demands for Jesus's death, he did not waver in his public rejection of the accusations against Jesus. Death by crucifixion was considered dishonorable in the Roman world, reserved for those of low social stature. Luke wants to make sure that the reader does not impute dishonor to Jesus's death, portraying Jesus's crucifixion as necessary for the fulfillment of God's preordained plan. He even shapes the extended narrative of Jesus's travel from Galilee to Jerusalem as a journey leading to that end.

As a new religious movement centered on the story of a crucified man, the Jesus movement was at times met with mistrust and hostility. Because Judaism was considered a licit religion by Rome, one way Luke counters such suspicion is by portraying Jesus, his family, and his followers as pious Jews, worshiping at the temple and observing ancestral traditions. Luke presents Jesus and his message as the culmination of prior Jewish tradition, with implications for the movement that grows in his name. Rather than a new religious movement, Luke sets the reader up to see the church in continuity with an ancient and venerable religion. Although Jesus and those close to him are all Jews, so are his antagonists. The result is a troubling coupling of an idealized Jewish piety and caricatures of both individual Jews and Jewish leadership, especially problematic in light of the long history of Christian anti-Semitism.

In his two volumes, Luke sets out to explain how the name of Jesus comes to be known from Galilee to Rome. Emphasizing that Jesus is not some obscure provincial figure, Luke punctuates his account with references to public personages and events. Jesus of Nazareth is a pivotal figure on the world stage, Luke implies. Some knowledge of the Roman world is thus helpful in understanding the sweep of the narrative along with the significance of specific details. See **"The Bible in Its Ancient Contexts," pp. 2150–52.** And yet Luke does not speak only to that world. First-time readers of Luke may be surprised to encounter much that seems familiar. From choirs of angels in Christmas carols to "Samaritan laws" that protect bystanders who offer well-intentioned aid to the injured, popular culture is peppered with allusions to Luke's vivid characters, scenes, and language. A foundational work shaping Western artistic and literary imagination, Luke continues to speak with subtlety to present debates about economic justice, gender roles, and political vision.

Jennifer A. Glancy

Passages Unique to the Gospel of Luke

1:1–4	Prologue: Why Luke Writes
1:5–25	Promise of John's Birth
1:26–38	Announcement of Jesus's Birth to Mary
1:39–56	Mary Visits Elizabeth
1:57–80	John's Birth
2:1–20	Jesus's Birth
2:21–38	Simeon Blesses Mary's Child
2:41–52	Twelve-Year-Old Jesus Visits Jerusalem
3:10–14	John Answers Questions
3:23–38	Jesus's Genealogy
4:14–23, 25–30	Jesus's Synagogue Message

Because the earliest known biblical manuscripts do not contain clear paragraphs or subtitles, section subtitles are always subject to editorial interpretation.

1 Since many have undertaken to compile a narrative about the events that have been fulfilled among us, ²just as they were handed on to us by those who from the beginning were eyewitnesses and servants of the word, ³I, too, decided, as one having a grasp of everything from the start,ᵃ to write a well-ordered account for you, most excellent Theophilus, ⁴so

a 1.3 Or for a long time

1:1–4 Prologue. The inclusion of a prologue signals Luke's intention to reach an educated audience. Prologues were common in historical and scientific works of the era. **1:1–2** Not an eyewitness to events recounted, Luke relies on prior written sources. **1:3** The two-volume work is dedicated to Theophilus (see Acts 1:1), a common name meaning "lover of God." The name is sometimes taken symbolically to include all readers, but it is likely that Theophilus was a prosperous benefactor of Luke.

that you may have a firm grasp of the words in which you have been instructed.

5 In the days of King Herod of Judea, there was a priest named Zechariah, who belonged to the priestly order of Abijah. His wife was descended from the daughters of Aaron, and her name was Elizabeth. [6]Both of them were righteous before God, living blamelessly according to all the commandments and regulations of the Lord. [7]But they had no children because Elizabeth was barren, and both were getting on in years.

8 Once when he was serving as priest before God during his section's turn of duty, [9]he was chosen by lot, according to the custom of the priesthood, to enter the sanctuary of the Lord to offer incense. [10]Now at the time of the incense offering, the whole assembly of the people was praying outside. [11]Then there appeared to him an angel of the Lord, standing at the right side of the altar of incense. [12]When Zechariah saw him, he was terrified, and fear overwhelmed him. [13]But the angel said to him, "Do not be afraid, Zechariah, for your prayer has been heard. Your wife Elizabeth will bear you a son, and you will name him John. [14]You will have joy and gladness, and many will rejoice at his birth, [15]for he will be great in the sight of the Lord. He must never drink wine or strong drink; even before his birth he will be filled with the Holy Spirit. [16]He will turn many of the people of Israel to the Lord their God. [17]With the spirit and power of Elijah he will go before him, to turn the hearts of parents to their children and the disobedient to the wisdom of the righteous, to make ready a people prepared for the Lord." [18]Zechariah said to the angel, "How can I know that this will happen? For I am an old man, and my wife is getting on in years." [19]The angel replied, "I am Gabriel. I stand in the presence of God, and I have been sent to speak to you and to bring you this good news. [20]But now, because you did not believe my words, which will be fulfilled in their time, you will become mute, unable to speak, until the day these things occur."

21 Meanwhile the people were waiting for Zechariah and wondering at his delay in the sanctuary. [22]When he did come out, he was unable to speak to them, and they realized that he had seen a vision in the sanctuary. He kept motioning to them and remained unable to speak. [23]When his time of service was ended, he returned to his home.

24 After those days his wife Elizabeth conceived, and for five months she remained in seclusion. She said, [25]"This is what the Lord has done for me in this time, when he looked favorably on me and took away the disgrace I have endured among my people."

26 In the sixth month the angel Gabriel was sent by God to a town in Galilee called Nazareth, [27]to a virgin engaged to a man whose name was Joseph, of the house of David. The virgin's name was Mary. [28]And he came to her and said, "Greetings, favored one! The Lord is with you."[b] [29]But she was much perplexed by his words and pondered what sort of greeting this might be. [30]The angel said to her, "Do not be afraid, Mary, for you have found favor with

b 1.28 Other ancient authorities add *Blessed are you among women*

1:5–2:52 Birth and childhood stories. See **"Infancy Narratives," p. 1724**. These chapters imitate the literary style of the Septuagint, the Greek translation of the Hebrew Bible. See **"The Bible as a Collection," pp. 2145–47**.

1:5–25 Announcement of the birth of John the Baptist. The unexpected birth of John to Zechariah and Elizabeth echoes stories about infertile couples in the Hebrew Bible, particularly the story of the aging Abraham and Sarah. The historical John the Baptist was a well-known first-century Jew. Early Jesus followers believed that John's preaching and baptizing prepared the way for Jesus. For Luke, that preparatory role begins with John's conception and birth. **1:5** *In the days of King Herod of Judea*, Herod the Great, died in 4 BCE. **1:8** The Jerusalem temple is a pivotal site in Luke–Acts. See **"Jerusalem in Luke–Acts," p. 1805**. **1:13–20** The angelic announcement to Zechariah precedes a parallel announcement to Mary. See **"Angels," p. 1346**. Balancing a story about a man with a story about a woman is a characteristic Lukan technique. See **"Women in Luke–Acts," p. 1809**. **1:13** Prayer is emphasized throughout Luke. **1:15** Priests (Lev. 10:9) and nazirites (Num. 6:2–4) were expected to abstain from alcohol. *Filled with the Holy Spirit.* Luke associates the Spirit with prophecy, a major theme in Luke–Acts. John is a prophet even before birth. **1:17** The prophet Elijah was understood to play a preparatory role (Mal. 4:5–6). **1:19** *Gabriel*, a divine messenger (v. 26; Dan. 8:16; 9:21). **1:25** *The disgrace I have endured.* In antiquity, infertility lowered a woman's social standing.

1:26–38 Announcement of the birth of Jesus. 1:27 The identification of Mary as a virgin emphasizes

LUKE 1

Reading through Time: Mary the Mother of Jesus (Luke 1)

Although the New Testament mentions Mary, the mother of Jesus, only twelve times, it casts her in multiple, if briefly narrated, roles. She appears as an unmarried but betrothed virgin who remarkably becomes pregnant and gives birth to Jesus, her firstborn (Luke 1:26–56; 2:1–52; Matt. 1:18–25; see **"Songs of Mary and Her Ancient Sisters," p. 1806,** and **"Infancy Narratives," p. 1724**); a prophet and kinswoman to Elizabeth, mother of John the Baptist (Luke 1:39–56); a political refugee with a baby (Matt. 2:13–23); the pious mother of a young Jesus (Luke 2:40–52); the mother of multiple children (Mark 3:31–35; 6:3; Matt. 12:46–50; 13:55–56; Luke 8:19–21; John 2:1–12); a mother who witnesses the execution of her son (John 19:25–27); and a disciple of Jesus (Acts 1:14). It is no wonder that Mary has held an important place in Christian imagination, theology, piety, and practice. She is also an important figure in the Qur'an, which allows her significantly more textual space than does the New Testament.

The last fifty years have seen a significant increase in ecumenical interpretation of Mary in the New Testament. Such scholarly interpretation initially focused on Mary as an exemplary hearer of the word (Luke 1:38, 45; 8:19–21); a model of discipleship (John 2:1–11; 19:25–27); a member of Jesus's family of origin (Mark 3:20–21, 22–30, 31–35; 6:4); and a key figure in God's plan (Matt. 1:18–25). New readings emerged as feminist interpreters began asking fresh questions about Mary, her body, and her role. While some underscored the significance of Mary's agency in consenting to her virginal pregnancy, Jane Schaberg held that Matthew and Luke were suppressing an earlier tradition of Jesus's illegitimacy. Another interpretation suggests that in its ancient cultural context, virginity strengthened Mary's identity as a prophet. Others see Mary, a young Jewish woman residing in Roman-occupied Galilee, as emblematic of all women struggling under oppression.

Feminist readings can underscore how an interpreter's context informs the image of Mary that emerges from the New Testament. Brazilian writers Ivone Gebara and Maria Clara Bingemer read Mary in dialogue with Latin American base communities. Itumeleng J. Mosala interprets Mary, a single mother living under colonization, within a South African context. Sharon Jacob reads Mary alongside Indian surrogates, noting how in the context of empire, each carries their pregnancies with paradoxical agency. These interpreters demonstrate how understanding of Mary changes over time, shifting according to readers' particular questions, contexts, experiences, and concerns.

Mary F. Foskett

God. ³¹And now, you will conceive in your womb and bear a son, and you will name him Jesus. ³²He will be great and will be called the Son of the Most High, and the Lord God will give to him the throne of his ancestor David. ³³He will reign over the house of Jacob forever, and of his kingdom there will be no end." ³⁴Mary said to the angel, "How can this be, since I am a virgin?"ᶜ ³⁵The angel said to her, "The Holy Spirit will come upon you, and the power of the Most High will overshadow you; therefore the child to be bornᵈ will be holy; he will be called Son of God. ³⁶And now, your relative Elizabeth in her old age has also conceived a son, and this is the sixth month for her who was said to be barren. ³⁷For nothing will be impossible with God." ³⁸Then Mary said, "Here am I, the servant of the Lord; let it be with me according to your word." Then the angel departed from her.

c 1.34 Gk *I do not know a man* d 1.35 Other ancient authorities add *of you*

the role of the Spirit in Jesus's conception. See **"Mary the Mother of Jesus," p. 1804. 1:32** Those who love their enemies are also said to be "children of the Most High" (6:35). *The Lord God will give to him the throne of his ancestor David.* Mary's son will be the Davidic Messiah; see **"Jewish Messianic Ideas," p. 1783. 1:34** *How can this be?* Because she has not been sexually active, Mary is puzzled by the angel's announcement. **1:35** Ancient readers would have been familiar with stories about human women impregnated by Greek and Roman gods. Mary's active consent (v. 38) sets her apart from the women in such stories. **1:38** *The servant of the Lord*, literally "the slave ["doulē"] of the Lord" (see also v. 48). The Hebrew Bible names a number of important figures as "slaves of YHWH," and in the Greco-Roman world, devotees of some cults understood themselves as slaves to particular deities. *Let it be with me according to your word.* While some readers are disturbed by Mary's self-identification as an enslaved woman, others are inspired by her agency in questioning the angel before asserting consent.

1804 | NEW TESTAMENT

Focus On: Jerusalem in Luke–Acts (Luke 1:8–23 and 2:22)

From 515 BCE to 70 CE, the Second Temple in Jerusalem was central to Jewish religious practice. Sacrifices were offered twice daily in the temple. Jews flocked to Jerusalem from around the empire to participate in pilgrimage festivals, including Passover and Pentecost. However, the temple was destroyed by Rome during the course of the Jewish War (67–73 CE), well before the composition of Luke–Acts. Why, then, is Jerusalem so pivotal to this two-volume work?

Scenes set in Jerusalem frame the narrative. The opening scene of Luke situates Zechariah at the temple, performing his priestly service (Luke 1:8–23). Luke limits Jesus's resurrection appearances to Jerusalem and environs (24:13–53). In Acts, the outpouring of the spirit enables Jesus's followers to speak to a multilingual crowd of Jews who had traveled to Jerusalem for the Festival of Pentecost (Acts 2:1–42); Paul's arrest at the temple catalyzes his final journey to Rome (21:27–36). Many of the Jerusalem scenes transpire at the temple, which Luke treats as a place of piety, prayer, and pilgrimage. In general, the temple represents a past that Luke seeks to claim for the nascent Christian movement, but Jerusalem the city plays a different role in Luke's theology of history. For Luke, on a theological level, what happens in Jerusalem represents a turning point in history.

Luke's inclusion of an extended narrative detailing Jesus's journey from Galilee to Jerusalem (Luke 9:51–19:28) is key to understanding the schematic significance of Jerusalem in Luke–Acts. As Jesus approaches Jerusalem, he grieves for its populace and laments anticipating the fall of the city to Rome in the Jewish War (13:31–35; 19:41–44). Luke writes for a readership that knows Jerusalem had been decisively defeated, the temple destroyed, the city razed, and much of the population enslaved. Jesus's laments over Jerusalem extend the conflicted view of Jerusalem in the Hebrew Bible, particularly in the Prophets. Above all, though, Luke emphasizes the divine necessity of the climactic events that take place in Jerusalem. For Luke, Jesus's suffering and death, his resurrection and ascension, not only change history but also give it meaning. And so, Luke writes, "When the days drew near for him [Jesus] to be taken up, he set his face to go to Jerusalem" (9:51).

Jennifer A. Glancy

39 In those days Mary set out and went with haste to a Judean town in the hill country, [40]where she entered the house of Zechariah and greeted Elizabeth. [41]When Elizabeth heard Mary's greeting, the child leaped in her womb. And Elizabeth was filled with the Holy Spirit [42]and exclaimed with a loud cry, "Blessed are you among women, and blessed is the fruit of your womb. [43]And why has this happened to me, that the mother of my Lord comes to me? [44]For as soon as I heard the sound of your greeting, the child in my womb leaped for joy. [45]And blessed is she who believed that there would be[e] a fulfillment of what was spoken to her by the Lord."

46 And Mary[f] said,
"My soul magnifies the Lord,
[47]   and my spirit rejoices in God my Savior,
[48] for he has looked with favor on the lowly
        state of his servant.
Surely from now on all generations will
        call me blessed,
[49] for the Mighty One has done great things
        for me,
    and holy is his name;
[50] indeed, his mercy is for those who fear him
        from generation to generation.
[51] He has shown strength with his arm;
    he has scattered the proud in the
        imagination of their hearts.
[52] He has brought down the powerful from
        their thrones
    and lifted up the lowly;
[53] he has filled the hungry with good
        things
    and sent the rich away empty.
[54] He has come to the aid of his child Israel,
    in remembrance of his mercy,

e 1.45 Or *believed, for there will be*   f 1.46 Other ancient authorities read *Elizabeth*

1:39–56 Mary's visit to Elizabeth. A rare scriptural encounter between two women. **1:41** *The child leaped in her womb.* Even before birth, John serves as forerunner to Jesus. *Filled with the Holy Spirit.* Elizabeth is empowered to speak prophetically. **1:46–55** Mary's words echo the prayers of women in the Hebrew Bible, especially the song of Hannah (1 Sam. 2:1–10). See **"Songs of Mary and Her Ancient Sisters," p. 1806. 1:52–53** Mary praises God for reversing the fortunes of rich and poor, powerful and oppressed, a central Lukan theme (e.g., 6:20–26). See **"The Bible and Social Justice," pp. 2165–67.**

Focus On: Songs of Mary and Her Ancient Sisters (Luke 1:46–55)

Mary's words in Luke 1:46–55 are among the most recognized in the Bible. Commonly known as the Magnificat, this song, or canticle, of Mary has been set to music countless times through the centuries. Composers ranging from Tallis to Bach and more recently, Jennifer Fowler, whose choral setting was commissioned by the Magnificat Project, have given musical expression to Mary's song. Due to its long history in Western music, familiarity with the Magnificat can inadvertently blunt the full force of Mary's words; a fresh reading of Luke 1:46–55 reveals that the Magnificat is nothing short of a radical affirmation of the promise of God's justice. As such, Mary's song (see **"Infancy Narratives," p. 1724**, and **"Mary the Mother of Jesus," p. 1804**) stands firm in the ancient tradition of her biblical foremothers, Miriam (Exod. 15:20–21), Deborah (Judg. 5:1–31), and Hannah (1 Sam. 2:1–10), who raised their voices to sing of God's deliverance.

Thus Luke 1:46–55 belongs to the tradition of Israelite women's prophetic witness, including the prophet Miriam, who recognizes the God of Israel who has delivered the people from enslavement in the exodus and leads "all the women" in dancing with their tambourines, exulting, "Sing to the LORD, for he has triumphed gloriously; horse and rider he has thrown into the sea" (Exod. 15:21).

Generations later, echoes of Miriam's song reverberate throughout the canticle of Mary, whose very name, "Mariam," recalls the memory of her foremother. Recognizing the significance of her elder kinswoman, Elizabeth, and her remarkable pregnancy, Mary sings of God's liberation: "He has shown strength with his arm; he has scattered the proud in the imagination of their hearts. He has brought down the powerful from their thrones and lifted up the lowly" (Luke 1:51–52).

Mary's words echo the songs of Deborah—a charismatic leader, prophet, and judge in ancient Israel—and Hannah, the mother of the prophet Samuel. In Judg. 5:2–31, Deborah sings a song of triumph after leading a group of Israelites in battle to defeat Canaanite forces. In 1 Sam. 2:1–10, Hannah's "heart exults in the LORD" (1 Sam. 2:1), just as Mary's "soul magnifies the Lord" (Luke 1:46). The justice that Mary proclaims in the Magnificat recalls imagery in Hannah's song (1 Sam. 2:7–8). As Mary introduces into the Gospel a theme that will be central to Jesus's teaching (Luke 4:16–21; 6:20–25; 16:19–31), she positions her son in the prophetic tradition established by her ancient sisters.

Mary F. Foskett

---

[55] according to the promise he made to our
 ancestors,
  to Abraham and to his descendants
   forever."

56 And Mary remained with her about three months and then returned to her home.

57 Now the time came for Elizabeth to give birth, and she bore a son. [58]Her neighbors and relatives heard that the Lord had shown his great mercy to her, and they rejoiced with her. 59 On the eighth day they came to circumcise the child, and they were going to name him Zechariah after his father. [60]But his mother said, "No; he is to be called John." [61]They said to her, "None of your relatives has this name." [62]Then they began motioning to his father to find out what name he wanted to give him. [63]He asked for a writing tablet and wrote, "His name is John." And all of them were amazed. [64]Immediately his mouth was opened and his tongue freed, and he began to speak, praising

God. [65]Fear came over all their neighbors, and all these things were talked about throughout the entire hill country of Judea. [66]All who heard them pondered them and said, "What then will this child become?" For indeed the hand of the Lord was with him.

67 Then his father Zechariah was filled with the Holy Spirit and prophesied:
[68] "Blessed be the Lord God of Israel,
  for he has looked favorably on[g] his
   people and redeemed them.
[69] He has raised up a mighty savior[b] for us
  in the house of his child David,
[70] as he spoke through the mouth of his holy
   prophets from of old,
[71] that we would be saved from our enemies
   and from the hand of all who hate us.
[72] Thus he has shown the mercy promised to
  our ancestors
   and has remembered his holy covenant,

g 1.68 Or *has visited*   h 1.69 Gk *a horn of salvation*

1:57–80 The birth of John the Baptist. See note on 1:5–25. **1:59** *On the eighth day they came to circumcise the child.* Zechariah and Elizabeth are depicted as Torah-observant Jews. **1:68–79** Zechariah's song emphasizes continuity with the ancestors and prophets of Israel and the role of John in preparing Jesus's way. **1:69** Jesus is *a mighty savior*, literally a "horn of salvation."

73 the oath that he swore to our ancestor
Abraham,
to grant us 74that we, being rescued
from the hands of our enemies,
might serve him without fear, 75in holiness
and righteousness
in his presence all our days.
76 And you, child, will be called the prophet
of the Most High,
for you will go before the Lord to
prepare his ways,
77 to give his people knowledge of salvation
by the forgiveness of their sins.
78 Because of the tender mercy of our God,
the dawn from on high will break*i*
upon*j* us,
79 to shine upon those who sit in darkness
and in the shadow of death,
to guide our feet into the way of peace."
80 The child grew and became strong in
spirit, and he was in the wilderness until the
day he appeared publicly to Israel.

2 In those days a decree went out from Caesar Augustus that all the world should
be registered. 2This was the first registration
and was taken while Quirinius was governor
of Syria. 3All went to their own towns to be
registered. 4Joseph also went from the town
of Nazareth in Galilee to Judea, to the city of
David called Bethlehem, because he was descended from the house and family of David.
5He went to be registered with Mary, to whom
he was engaged and who was expecting a

child. 6While they were there, the time came
for her to deliver her child. 7And she gave
birth to her firstborn son and wrapped him in
bands of cloth and laid him in a manger, because there was no place in the guest room.*k*

8 Now in that same region there were shepherds living in the fields, keeping watch over
their flock by night. 9Then an angel of the
Lord stood before them, and the glory of the
Lord shone around them, and they were terrified. 10But the angel said to them, "Do not be
afraid, for see, I am bringing you good news
of great joy for all the people: 11to you is born
this day in the city of David a Savior, who is
the Messiah,*l* the Lord. 12This will be a sign for
you: you will find a child wrapped in bands of
cloth and lying in a manger." 13And suddenly
there was with the angel a multitude of the
heavenly host,*m* praising God and saying,
14 "Glory to God in the highest heaven,
and on earth peace among those whom
he favors!"*n*

15 When the angels had left them and gone
into heaven, the shepherds said to one another, "Let us go now to Bethlehem and see this
thing that has taken place, which the Lord has
made known to us." 16So they went with haste
and found Mary and Joseph and the child lying in the manger. 17When they saw this, they
made known what had been told them about

i 1.78 Other ancient authorities read *has broken*
j 1.78 Gk *will visit* *k* 2.7 Or *their room* *l* 2.11 Or *the
Christ* *m* 2.13 Gk *army* *n* 2.14 Other ancient authorities
read *peace, goodwill among people*

2:1–20 The birth of Jesus. 2:1–5 A Roman census established a head count for taxation and military conscription. See **"The Bible in Its Ancient Contexts," pp. 2150–52.** Although Luke's account is
historically inaccurate, by situating Jesus's birth in the context of an empire-wide event, he implies that
Jesus's birth has global significance. **2:1** *Caesar Augustus* reigned as emperor from 27 BCE to 14 CE. *All
the world should be registered.* Although Roman censuses were organized locally, Luke suggests that
the entire inhabited world—that is, the whole Roman Empire—was involved in the census. **2:2** *Quirinius
was governor of Syria.* The dating is inconsistent—see note on 1:5. Quirinius became governor of Syria
in 6 CE. The province of Syria included both Galilee and Judea. **2:3–4** A Roman census registered individuals where they currently resided. By suggesting that Joseph was required to travel to his familial
home, Luke reconciles Jesus's early life in Nazareth with the traditional association of the house of
David with Bethlehem. **2:7** Wrapping a newborn *in bands of cloth* was intended to promote straight
limbs. *A manger,* a feeding trough for animals. *No place in the guest room.* A rented room, perhaps a
shared space unable to accommodate a woman about to give birth. Many readers identify with Luke's
depiction of Joseph and Mary as migrants struggling with access to shelter and the ancient equivalent
of health care. **2:8–20** The angelic proclamation heralds the political and cosmic significance of Jesus's
birth. **2:10** *For all the people* emphasizes the universal dimension of Jesus's mission. **2:11** Luke is the
only Synoptic Gospel (see **"Introduction to the Gospels and Acts," pp. 1709–12**) to refer to Jesus as
Savior, a title widely used for Caesar Augustus. *Messiah* or Christ, see note on 1:32. **2:13** *The heavenly
host,* an army of angels. **2:14** *On earth peace.* Jesus's birth inaugurates a new kind of peace, eclipsing
the supposed peace of Augustus that was enforced through military conquest.

this child, [18]and all who heard it were amazed at what the shepherds told them, [19]and Mary treasured all these words and pondered them in her heart. [20]The shepherds returned, glorifying and praising God for all they had heard and seen, just as it had been told them.

21 When the eighth day came, it was time to circumcise the child,[o] and he was called Jesus, the name given by the angel before he was conceived in the womb.

22 When the time came for their purification according to the law of Moses, they brought him up to Jerusalem to present him to the Lord [23](as it is written in the law of the Lord, "Every firstborn male shall be designated as holy to the Lord"), [24]and they offered a sacrifice according to what is stated in the law of the Lord, "a pair of turtledoves or two young pigeons."

25 Now there was a man in Jerusalem whose name was Simeon; this man was righteous and devout, looking forward to the consolation of Israel, and the Holy Spirit rested on him. [26]It had been revealed to him by the Holy Spirit that he would not see death before he had seen the Lord's Messiah.[p] [27]Guided by the Spirit, Simeon[q] came into the temple, and when the parents brought in the child Jesus to do for him what was customary under the law, [28]Simeon[r] took him in his arms and praised God, saying,

[29] "Master, now you are dismissing your
    servant in peace,
    according to your word,
[30] for my eyes have seen your salvation,
[31]   which you have prepared in the
    presence of all peoples,
[32] a light for revelation to the gentiles
    and for glory to your people Israel."

33 And the child's father and mother were amazed at what was being said about him.

[34]Then Simeon blessed them and said to his mother Mary, "This child is destined for the falling and the rising of many in Israel and to be a sign that will be opposed [35]so that the inner thoughts of many will be revealed—and a sword will pierce your own soul, too."

36 There was also a prophet, Anna the daughter of Phanuel, of the tribe of Asher. She was of a great age, having lived with her husband seven years after her marriage, [37]then as a widow to the age of eighty-four. She never left the temple but worshiped there with fasting and prayer night and day. [38]At that moment she came and began to praise God and to speak about the child[s] to all who were looking for the redemption of Jerusalem.

39 When they had finished everything required by the law of the Lord, they returned to Galilee, to their own town of Nazareth. [40]The child grew and became strong, filled with wisdom, and the favor of God was upon him.

41 Now every year his parents went to Jerusalem for the festival of the Passover. [42]And when he was twelve years old, they went up as usual for the festival. [43]When the festival was ended and they started to return, the boy Jesus stayed behind in Jerusalem, but his parents were unaware of this. [44]Assuming that he was in the group of travelers, they went a day's journey. Then they started to look for him among their relatives and friends. [45]When they did not find him, they returned to Jerusalem to search for him. [46]After three days they found him in the temple, sitting among the teachers, listening to them and asking them questions. [47]And all who heard him were amazed at his understanding and his answers. [48]When his parents' saw him they were astonished, and his mother

o 2.21 Gk him   p 2.26 Or the Lord's Christ   q 2.27 Gk In the Spirit, he   r 2.28 Gk he   s 2.38 Gk him   t 2.48 Gk they

2:21–38 Jesus's circumcision and presentation in the temple. See note on 1:8. 2:22 *The time came for their purification.* Even as he highlights the piety of Jesus's family, Luke gets details about Jewish practice wrong. Only the mother would have required a postpartum cleansing before entering the temple. 2:25–33 Motivated by the Spirit (vv. 25–27), Simeon prophesies about Jesus. 2:32 Simeon highlights Jesus's universal mission *to the gentiles* while affirming his particular relationship to *Israel.* 2:36–38 The story of the prophet Anna parallels the story of Simeon. From this point in Luke, few women's voices are heard. See **"Women in Luke–Acts," p. 1809.**
2:39–52 Jesus's childhood. Luke is the only canonical writer to mention Jesus's childhood. Later ancient sources feature stories about the young Jesus as a miracle worker and precocious savant. 2:41–51 See note on 1:8. Luke expects his readers to know that Jesus was crucified in Jerusalem at Passover. 2:41–42 The family's custom of making the Passover pilgrimage demonstrates their piety. 2:46–50 Luke may be foreshadowing Jesus's preaching ministry in the temple (19:47–21:38) that leads to his arrest and crucifixion. Given Luke's account of Jesus's conception, his parents' response to his teaching in the temple is puzzling.

Making Connections: Women in Luke–Acts (Luke 2:36)

From the first wave of feminism in the nineteenth century to the present, many readers have approached the Bible in hopes of identifying female role models. Others have focused on critiques of the gender hierarchies implicit in biblical writings. In the numerous stories about women in Luke–Acts, readers from both camps may find what they are looking for—and yet be left with new questions.

Luke often matches a story centering a male figure with a story centering a female figure, pairings cited as evidence of even-handed treatment of men and women. However, the paired stories typically advance a vision of a gender-segregated world. For example, in one parable a male shepherd searches for a lost sheep, while in the next, a woman searches for a lost coin (Luke 15:3–10). Some readers find that Luke simply reflects the gender segregation of his own world, while others conclude that he intentionally reinforces gender norms. Readers in the latter camp note that after Elizabeth and Mary speak their memorable words (Luke 1:42–55), women's voices remain largely unheard throughout Luke–Acts. Luke understands that women as well as men can be faithful followers, but he tends to assign women conventional roles outside the public eye. Comfortable with women in the role of financial patrons, Luke otherwise downplays what we know from the letters of Paul about women's leadership in the churches.

Even as he multiplies stories about women, Luke leaves out several striking episodes that appear in Mark, one of his sources. Notably, Luke does not include Mark's story about the woman who anoints Jesus's head, a prophetic gesture (Mark 14:3–9). Instead, Luke tells a story about a woman introduced as a sinner who anoints Jesus's feet, bathes them in tears, and dries them with her hair. Jesus holds her up to his dinner host as an exemplar of extravagant love (Luke 7:36–50). The story builds up to Jesus's forgiveness of the woman's sins.

Because Luke ultimately emphasizes what Jesus has done for the woman rather than what she has done for him, readers focused on the critique of gender hierarchy often cite the story as evidence that Luke downplays the agency of women. Other readers respond differently, calling attention instead to the woman's act of love as a model for all followers of Jesus. As a tool for feminist work, Luke's Gospel is an uneven resource.

Jennifer A. Glancy

---

said to him, "Child, why have you treated us like this? Your father and I have been anxiously looking for you." [49]He said to them, "Why were you searching for me? Did you not know that I must be in my Father's house?"[u] [50]But they did not understand what he said to them. [51]Then he went down with them and came to Nazareth and was obedient to them, and his mother treasured all these things in her heart.

52 And Jesus increased in wisdom and in years[v] and in divine and human favor.

3 In the fifteenth year of the reign of Tiberius Caesar, when Pontius Pilate was governor of Judea, and Herod was ruler of Galilee, and his brother Philip ruler of the region of Ituraea and Trachonitis, and Lysanias ruler of Abilene, [2]during the high priesthood of Annas and Caiaphas, the word of God came to John son of Zechariah in the wilderness. [3]He went into all the region around the Jordan, proclaiming a baptism of repentance for the forgiveness of sins, [4]as it is written in the book of the words of the prophet Isaiah,

"The voice of one crying out in the
    wilderness:
'Prepare the way of the Lord;
    make his paths straight.
[5] Every valley shall be filled,
    and every mountain and hill shall be
        made low,
and the crooked shall be made straight,
    and the rough ways made smooth,
[6] and all flesh shall see the salvation of God.'"

7 John said to the crowds coming out to be baptized by him, "You brood of vipers! Who warned you to flee from the coming wrath?

u 2.49 Or *be about my Father's interests?*   v 2.52 Or *in stature*

3:1–22 John the Baptist. See note on 1:5–25. **3:1** Luke establishes the political context of John's preaching. *Pontius Pilate* presided at the trial of Jesus (23:1–25). The son of Herod the Great (1:5), *Herod* Antipas was the tetrarch or ruler of Galilee. After ordering John's execution, Herod Antipas reappears in Luke as a potential threat to Jesus (9:7–9; 13:31–33; 23:6–16). **3:2** *The word of God came to John.* John belongs to the line of Israelite prophets. **3:3** *A baptism of repentance,* a public immersion signifying an intention to live a different kind of life; vv. 10–14 suggest the kinds of behavioral changes John demanded. **3:6** *All flesh shall see the salvation of God.* Extending Mark's quotation from Isaiah, Luke points to the universal scope of Jesus's mission (Isa. 40:3–5; Mark 1:2–3). **3:7–9** John warns of

[8]Therefore, bear fruits worthy of repentance, and do not begin to say to yourselves, 'We have Abraham as our ancestor,' for I tell you, God is able from these stones to raise up children to Abraham. [9]Even now the ax is lying at the root of the trees; therefore every tree that does not bear good fruit will be cut down and thrown into the fire."

10 And the crowds asked him, "What, then, should we do?" [11]In reply he said to them, "Whoever has two coats must share with anyone who has none, and whoever has food must do likewise." [12]Even tax collectors came to be baptized, and they asked him, "Teacher, what should we do?" [13]He said to them, "Collect no more than the amount prescribed for you." [14]Soldiers also asked him, "And we, what should we do?" He said to them, "Do not extort money from anyone by threats or false accusation, and be satisfied with your wages."

15 As the people were filled with expectation and all were questioning in their hearts concerning John, whether he might be the Messiah,[w] [16]John answered all of them by saying, "I baptize you with water, but one who is more powerful than I is coming; I am not worthy to untie the strap of his sandals. He will baptize you with[x] the Holy Spirit and fire. [17]His winnowing fork is in his hand to clear his threshing floor and to gather the wheat into his granary, but the chaff he will burn with unquenchable fire."

18 So with many other exhortations he proclaimed the good news to the people. [19]But Herod the ruler, who had been rebuked by him because of Herodias, his brother's wife, and because of all the evil things that Herod had done, [20]added to them all by shutting up John in prison.

21 Now when all the people were baptized and when Jesus also had been baptized and was praying, the heaven was opened, [22]and the Holy Spirit descended upon him in bodily form like a dove. And a voice came from heaven, "You are my Son, the Beloved;[y] with you I am well pleased."[z]

23 Jesus was about thirty years old when he began his work. He was the son (as was thought) of Joseph son of Heli, [24]son of Matthat, son of Levi, son of Melchi, son of Jannai, son of Joseph, [25]son of Mattathias, son of Amos, son of Nahum, son of Esli, son of Naggai, [26]son of Maath, son of Mattathias, son of Semein, son of Josech, son of Joda, [27]son of Joanan, son of Rhesa, son of Zerubbabel, son of Shealtiel, son of Neri, [28]son of Melchi, son of Addi, son of Cosam, son of Elmadam, son of Er, [29]son of Joshua, son of Eliezer, son of Jorim, son of Matthat, son of Levi, [30]son of Simeon, son of Judah, son of Joseph, son of Jonam, son of Eliakim, [31]son of Melea, son of Menna, son of Mattatha, son of Nathan, son of David, [32]son of Jesse, son of Obed, son of Boaz, son of Sala,[a] son of Nahshon, [33]son of Amminadab, son of Admin, son of Arni,[b] son of Hezron, son of Perez, son of Judah, [34]son of Jacob, son of Isaac, son of Abraham, son of Terah, son of Nahor, [35]son of Serug, son of Reu, son of Peleg, son of Eber, son of Shelah, [36]son of Cainan, son of Arphaxad, son of Shem, son of Noah, son of Lamech, [37]son of Methuselah, son of Enoch, son of Jared, son of Mahalaleel, son of Cainan, [38]son of Enos, son of Seth, son of Adam, son of God.

4 Jesus, full of the Holy Spirit, returned from the Jordan and was led by the Spirit

---

w 3.15 Or *the Christ*   x 3.16 Or *in*   y 3.22 Or *my beloved Son*
z 3.22 Other ancient authorities read *You are my Son, today
I have begotten you*   a 3.32 Other ancient authorities read
Salmon   b 3.33 Other ancient authorities read *Amminadab,
son of Aram*; others vary widely

---

an approaching day of destruction. See **"Apocalypse," p. 1216. 3:8** *We have Abraham as our ancestor.* Abraham was the ancestor of the Jewish people. John emphasizes that God will judge individuals on the basis of their actions, not their ethnicity. **3:10–14** John urges his listeners to share their possessions and not exploit others financially, a central Lukan theme. See **"The Bible and Social Justice," pp. 2165–67. 3:17** Harvest imagery associated with divine judgment. **3:19** John criticized *Herod* Antipas for a variety of reasons, including Herod's marriage to his half brother's ex-wife, *Herodias*, a violation of Levitical law (Lev. 18:16). **3:21–22** Luke mentions Jesus's baptism only after reporting the imprisonment of John, deflecting attention away from Jesus's reasons for seeking *a baptism of repentance for the forgiveness of sins* (v. 3).

   3:23–38 Jesus's ancestors. Luke acknowledges but does not emphasize Jesus's descent from David (v. 31), Abraham (v. 34), and other major figures in Israelite history. **3:38** *Son of Adam, son of God.* Luke stresses Jesus's importance for all humanity.

   4:1–13 Jesus in the wilderness. Jesus's encounter with the devil has a mythic quality. **4:1** *Full of the Holy Spirit* after his baptism (3:22), Jesus is *led by the Spirit* to the wilderness, a place beyond human

in the wilderness, [2]where for forty days he was tested by the devil. He ate nothing at all during those days, and when they were over he was famished. [3]The devil said to him, "If you are the Son of God, command this stone to become a loaf of bread." [4]Jesus answered him, "It is written, 'One does not live by bread alone.'"

5 Then the devil[c] led him up and showed him in an instant all the kingdoms of the world. [6]And the devil[d] said to him, "To you I will give all this authority and their glory, for it has been given over to me, and I give it to anyone I please. [7]If you, then, will worship me, it will all be yours." [8]Jesus answered him, "It is written,

'Worship the Lord your God,
    and serve only him.'"

9 Then the devil[e] led him to Jerusalem and placed him on the pinnacle of the temple and said to him, "If you are the Son of God, throw yourself down from here, [10]for it is written,

'He will command his angels concerning
    you,
    to protect you,'

[11]and

'On their hands they will bear you up,
    so that you will not dash your foot
        against a stone.'"

[12]Jesus answered him, "It is said, 'Do not put the Lord your God to the test.'" [13]When the devil had finished every test, he departed from him until an opportune time.

14 Then Jesus, in the power of the Spirit, returned to Galilee, and a report about him spread through all the surrounding region. [15]He began to teach in their synagogues and was praised by everyone.

16 When he came to Nazareth, where he had been brought up, he went to the synagogue on the Sabbath day, as was his custom. He stood up to read, [17]and the scroll of the prophet Isaiah was given to him. He unrolled the scroll and found the place where it was written:

[18] "The Spirit of the Lord is upon me,
    because he has anointed me
        to bring good news to the poor.
He has sent me to proclaim release to the
    captives
    and recovery of sight to the blind,
        to set free those who are oppressed,
[19]to proclaim the year of the Lord's favor."

[20]And he rolled up the scroll, gave it back to the attendant, and sat down. The eyes of all in the synagogue were fixed on him. [21]Then he began to say to them, "Today this scripture has been fulfilled in your hearing." [22]All spoke well of him and were amazed at the gracious words that came from his mouth. They said, "Is this not Joseph's son?" [23]He said to them, "Doubtless you will quote to me this proverb, 'Doctor, cure yourself!' And you will say, 'Do here also in your hometown the things that we have heard you did at Capernaum.'" [24]And he said, "Truly I tell you, no prophet is accepted in his hometown. [25]But the truth is, there were many widows in Israel in the time of Elijah, when the heaven was shut up three years and six months and there was a severe famine over all the land, [26]yet Elijah was sent to none of them except to a widow at Zarephath in Sidon. [27]There were also many with a skin disease in Israel in the time of the prophet Elisha, and none of them was cleansed except Naaman the Syrian." [28]When they heard this, all in the synagogue were filled with rage. [29]They got up, drove him out of the town, and led him to the brow of the hill on which their town was built, so that they might hurl

c 4.5 Gk he   d 4.6 Gk he   e 4.9 Gk he

---

habitation. **4:2** *Forty days*, recalling the forty years the Israelites wandered in the desert. **4:4** *One does not live by bread alone*, "but by every word that comes from the mouth of the LORD" (Deut. 8:3). **4:8** Compare Deut. 6:13; 10:20. **4:9** Luke locates the devil's final test at the Jerusalem temple. See note on Luke 1:8. **4:10-11** Ps. 91:11-12. **4:12** Deut. 6:16. **4:13** *An opportune time* anticipates the role of Satan in events leading to Jesus's death (Luke 22:3, 31). See **"The Satan," p. 687.**

4:14-9:50 The ministry in Galilee. Luke largely follows the outline of Mark.

4:16-30 Nazareth. 4:18 *The Spirit of the Lord is upon me* (Isa. 61:1). Jesus situates himself in the line of Israelite prophets. Reference to the Spirit's activity resumes in Acts. *Good news to the poor*, a central Lukan theme. See **"The Bible and Social Justice," p. 2165-67. 4:24** Although initial response to Jesus's teaching was positive (v. 22), Jesus predicts his hometown will turn against him. **4:25-27** Following the example set by the prophets Elijah and Elisha, Jesus's mission extends to gentiles. **4:28-29** Consistent with the treatment of prior Israelite prophets, the rejection of Jesus resonates with the experience of others throughout history who have spoken difficult truths. Tragically, the negative depiction of synagogues in Luke-Acts has fueled Christian anti-Semitism over the centuries. See **"Jews in Luke-Acts," p. 1910.**

him off the cliff. [30]But he passed through the midst of them and went on his way.

31 He went down to Capernaum, a city in Galilee, and was teaching them on the Sabbath. [32]They were astounded at his teaching because he spoke with authority. [33]In the synagogue there was a man who had the spirit of an unclean demon, and he cried out with a loud voice, [34]"Leave us alone! What have you to do with us, Jesus of Nazareth? Have you come to destroy us? I know who you are, the Holy One of God." [35]But Jesus rebuked him, saying, "Be quiet and come out of him!" Then the demon, throwing the man down before them, came out of him without doing him any harm. [36]They were all astounded and kept saying to one another, "What kind of word is this, that with authority and power he commands the unclean spirits and they come out?" [37]And news about him began to reach every place in the region.

38 After leaving the synagogue he entered Simon's house. Now Simon's mother-in-law was suffering from a high fever, and they asked him about her. [39]Then he stood over her and rebuked the fever, and it left her. Immediately she got up and began to serve them.

40 As the sun was setting, all those caring for any who were sick with various kinds of diseases brought them to him, and he laid his hands on each of them and cured them. [41]Moreover, demons also came out of many, shouting, "You are the Son of God!" But he rebuked them and would not allow them to speak, because they knew that he was the Messiah.[f]

42 At daybreak he departed and went into a deserted place. And the crowds began looking for him, and when they reached him they tried to keep him from leaving them. [43]But he said to them, "I must proclaim the good news of the kingdom of God to the other cities also, for I was sent for this purpose." [44]So he continued proclaiming the message in the synagogues of Judea.[g]

5 Once while Jesus[b] was standing beside the Lake of Gennesaret and the crowd was pressing in on him to hear the word of God, [2]he saw two boats there at the shore of the lake; the fishermen had gotten out of them and were washing their nets. [3]He got into one of the boats, the one belonging to Simon, and asked him to put out a little way from the shore. Then he sat down and taught the crowds from the boat. [4]When he had finished speaking, he said to Simon, "Put out into the deep water and let down your nets for a catch." [5]Simon answered, "Master, we have worked all night long but have caught nothing. Yet if you say so, I will let down the nets." [6]When they had done this, they caught so many fish that their nets were beginning to burst. [7]So they signaled their partners in the other boat to come and help them. And they came and filled both boats, so that they began to sink. [8]But when Simon Peter saw it, he fell down at Jesus's knees, saying, "Go away from me, Lord, for I am a sinful man!" [9]For he and all who were with him were astounded at the catch of fish that they had taken, [10]and so also were James and John, sons of Zebedee, who were partners with Simon. Then Jesus said to Simon, "Do not be afraid; from now on you will be catching people." [11]When they had brought their boats to shore, they left everything and followed him.

12 Once when he was in one of the cities, a man covered with a skin disease was there. When he saw Jesus, he bowed with his face to the ground and begged him, "Lord, if you are willing, you can make me clean." [13]Then Jesus[i]

f 4.41 Or *the Christ*   g 4.44 Other ancient authorities read *Galilee*   h 5.1 Gk *he*   i 5.13 Gk *he*

4:31–44 **Capernaum.** Jesus's first healings are reported in Capernaum, located on the Sea of Galilee. See **"Healing in the Gospels and Acts," p. 1773. 4:38** *Simon* Peter, see note on 5:1–11. **4:42** There is a sharp contrast between the enthusiastic response to Jesus's healings in Capernaum and his rejection at Nazareth (4:28–29). **4:43** *The kingdom of God* is central to Jesus's preaching. Jesus and his disciples bring the kingdom near through exorcisms (11:20) and healings (10:9), small beginnings that promise a prodigious future yield (13:18–21). Although in some sense the kingdom of God is already present (17:20–21), its full establishment remains in the future (19:11–26). **4:44** Luke's geography is confused. When he leaves Capernaum, Jesus continues his ministry not in Judea but in Galilee.

5:1–11 **Jesus calls his first disciples.** The story establishes the priority of Simon Peter, introduced in 4:38. **5:1** *Lake of Gennesaret*, the Sea of Galilee. **5:10** *From now on you will be catching people*. In Luke, Peter is among those who share Jesus's work of healing and proclaiming God's reign (9:1–2). In Acts of the Apostles, Peter's preaching and healing lead many to join the community of believers.

5:12–16 **Cleansing of a man with a skin disease. 5:13** Jesus heals through touch, especially meaningful

stretched out his hand, touched him, and said, "I am willing. Be made clean." Immediately the skin disease left him. [14]And he ordered him to tell no one. "But go, show yourself to the priest, and, as Moses commanded, make an offering for your cleansing, as a testimony to them." [15]But now more than ever the word about Jesus[j] spread abroad; many crowds were gathering to hear him and to be cured of their diseases. [16]Meanwhile, he would slip away to deserted places and pray.

[17] One day while he was teaching, Pharisees and teachers of the law who had come from every village of Galilee and Judea and from Jerusalem were sitting nearby, and the power of the Lord was with him to heal.[k] [18]Just then some men came carrying a paralyzed man on a stretcher. They were trying to bring him in and lay him before Jesus,[l] [19]but, finding no way to bring him in because of the crowd, they went up on the roof and let him down on the stretcher through the tiles into the middle of the crowd[m] in front of Jesus. [20]When he saw their faith, he said, "Friend,[n] your sins are forgiven you." [21]Then the scribes and the Pharisees began to question, "Who is this who is speaking blasphemies? Who can forgive sins but God alone?" [22]When Jesus perceived their questionings, he answered them, "Why do you raise such questions in your hearts? [23]Which is easier: to say, 'Your sins are forgiven you,' or to say, 'Stand up and walk'? [24]But so that you may know that the Son of Man has authority on earth to forgive sins"—he said to the one who was paralyzed—"I say to you, stand up and take your stretcher and go to your home." [25]Immediately he stood up before them, took what he had been lying on, and went to his home, glorifying God. [26]Amazement seized all of them, and they glorified God and were filled with fear, saying, "We have seen incredible things today."

[27] After this he went out and saw a tax collector named Levi sitting at the tax-collection station, and he said to him, "Follow me." [28]And he got up, left everything, and followed him.

[29] Then Levi gave a great banquet for him in his house, and there was a large crowd of tax collectors and others reclining at the table with them. [30]The Pharisees and their scribes were complaining to his disciples, saying, "Why do you eat and drink with tax collectors and sinners?" [31]Jesus answered them, "Those who are well have no need of a physician but those who are sick; [32]I have not come to call the righteous but sinners to repentance."

[33] Then they said to him, "John's disciples, like the disciples of the Pharisees, frequently fast and pray, but your disciples eat and drink." [34]Jesus said to them, "You cannot make wedding attendants fast while the bridegroom is with them, can you? [35]The days will come when the bridegroom will be taken away from them, and then they will fast in those days." [36]He also told them a parable: "No one tears a piece from a new garment and sews it on an old garment; otherwise, not only will one tear the new garment, but the piece from the new will not match the old garment. [37]Similarly, no one puts new wine into old wineskins; otherwise, the new wine will burst the skins and will spill out, and the skins will be ruined. [38]But new wine must be put into fresh wineskins.[o] [39]And no one after drinking old wine desires new wine but says, 'The old is good.'"[p]

j 5.15 Gk *him* k 5.17 Other ancient authorities read *was present to heal them* l 5.18 Gk *him* m 5.19 Gk *into the midst* n 5.20 Gk *Man* o 5.38 Other ancient authorities add *and both are preserved* p 5.39 Other ancient authorities read *better*; others lack 5.39

to one whose disease might have led others to turn away. **5:14** Those who were ritually impure were unable to enter the Jerusalem temple. Jesus upholds Torah by instructing the man to present himself to a priest who would verify that he had been cleansed of his skin disease.

5:17–6:11 Controversies with Pharisees. As Jesus's reputation grows, so does tension with the Pharisees, who were interpreters of Torah. See **"Pharisees," p. 1756**. **5:24** *The Son of Man has authority on earth.* In response to skepticism that he has the authority to forgive sins, Jesus heals the man of paralysis, thus demonstrating his power. Jesus's self-description as Son of Man conveys divine authority. See **"Son of God vs. Son of Man," p. 1774**. **5:27** Tax collectors were notorious for enriching themselves by collecting more than was due (3:13). **5:29–39** The first of many banquet scenes in Luke. **5:30–32** The Pharisees and scribes criticize Jesus for keeping disreputable company. Jesus characterizes his companionship with sinners as a mission strategy, intended to lead his dining companions to change their way of living. **5:34–35** Jesus metaphorically refers to himself as a bridegroom and his followers as wedding guests. **5:35** *The days will come when the bridegroom will be taken away from them,*

6 One Sabbath[q] while Jesus[r] was going through some grain fields, his disciples plucked some heads of grain, rubbed them in their hands, and ate them. [2]But some of the Pharisees said, "Why are you doing what is not lawful[s] on the Sabbath?" [3]Jesus answered, "Have you not read what David did when he and his companions were hungry? [4]How he entered the house of God and took and ate the bread of the Presence, which it is not lawful for any but the priests to eat, and gave some to his companions?" [5]Then he said to them, "The Son of Man is lord of the Sabbath."

6 On another Sabbath he entered the synagogue and taught, and there was a man there whose right hand was withered. [7]The scribes and the Pharisees were watching him to see whether he would cure on the Sabbath, so that they might find grounds to bring an accusation against him. [8]But he knew what they were thinking, and he said to the man who had the withered hand, "Come and stand in the middle." He got up and stood there. [9]Then Jesus said to them, "I ask you, is it lawful to do good or to do harm on the Sabbath, to save life or to destroy it?" [10]After looking around at all of them, he said to him, "Stretch out your hand." He did so, and his hand was restored. [11]But they were filled with fury and began discussing with one another what they might do to Jesus.

12 Now during those days he went out to the mountain to pray, and he spent the night in prayer to God. [13]And when day came, he called his disciples and chose twelve of them, whom he also named apostles: [14]Simon, whom he named Peter, and his brother Andrew, and James, and John, and Philip, and Bartholomew, [15]and Matthew, and Thomas, and James son of Alphaeus, and Simon, who was called the Zealot, [16]and Judas son of James, and Judas Iscariot, who became a traitor.

17 He came down with them and stood on a level place with a great crowd of his disciples and a great multitude of people from all Judea, Jerusalem, and the coast of Tyre and Sidon. [18]They had come to hear him and to be healed of their diseases, and those who were troubled with unclean spirits were cured. [19]And everyone in the crowd was trying to touch him, for power came out from him and healed all of them.

20 Then he looked up at his disciples and said:

"Blessed are you who are poor,
    for yours is the kingdom of God.
[21] "Blessed are you who are hungry now,
    for you will be filled.

"Blessed are you who weep now,
    for you will laugh.

22 "Blessed are you when people hate you and when they exclude you, revile you, and defame you[t] on account of the Son of Man. [23]Rejoice on that day and leap for joy, for surely your reward is great in heaven, for that is how their ancestors treated the prophets.

[24] "But woe to you who are rich,
    for you have received your consolation.
[25] "Woe to you who are full now,
    for you will be hungry.

"Woe to you who are laughing now,
    for you will mourn and weep.

q 6.1 Other ancient authorities read *On the second first Sabbath*   r 6.1 Gk *he*   s 6.2 Other ancient authorities add *to do*   t 6.22 Gk *cast out your name as evil*

an allusion to Jesus's death and ascension (see note on 24:50–53). **6:1–5** The dispute between the Pharisees and Jesus is profitably read in the context of ancient debates about how strictly to interpret Torah's prohibition of labor on the Sabbath (Exod. 34:21). **6:3–4** Jesus claims prerogatives similar to those enjoyed by his ancestor David. **6:5** Asserting his authority as Son of Man, Jesus does not dictate how others should observe the Sabbath. **6:6–11** The Pharisees hope to catch Jesus in behavior that would violate Torah. However, Torah does not prohibit Sabbath healing.

6:12–16 The twelve apostles. Jesus's many followers included a group of men known as the twelve (1 Cor. 15:5). **6:13** *Apostles*, Greek "apostellō," to send. In Luke, the apostles are sent to heal and to proclaim the kingdom of God (9:1–6); in Acts, they are sent as witnesses to the resurrection (Acts 1:22–26). **6:14** *Simon, whom he named Peter.* See note on Luke 5:1–11. **6:16** *Judas Iscariot* sells information leading to the arrest of Jesus (22:3–6).

6:17–49 The Sermon on the Plain features material from the sayings source Q developed more extensively by Matthew in the Sermon on the Mount (Matt. 5–7). See **"Introduction to the Gospels and Acts," pp. 1709–12.** **6:20–23** A series of blessings known as Beatitudes (cf. Matt. 5:3–12). Luke's version stresses God's particular concern for those who are materially poor and physically hungry, whose circumstances will be reversed in the kingdom of God. See **"The Bible and Social Justice," pp. 2165–67.** **6:20** *Blessed are you*, or happy are you. **6:24–26** Luke balances words of encouragement to the poor

26 "Woe to you when all speak well of you, for that is how their ancestors treated the false prophets.

27 "But I say to you who are listening: Love your enemies; do good to those who hate you; 28bless those who curse you; pray for those who mistreat you. 29If anyone strikes you on the cheek, offer the other also, and from anyone who takes away your coat do not withhold even your shirt. 30Give to everyone who asks of you, and if anyone takes away what is yours, do not ask for it back again. 31Do to others as you would have them do to you.

32 "If you love those who love you, what credit is that to you? For even sinners love those who love them. 33If you do good to those who do good to you, what credit is that to you? For even sinners do the same. 34If you lend to those from whom you expect to receive payment, what credit is that to you? Even sinners lend to sinners, to receive as much again. 35Instead, love your enemies, do good, and lend, expecting nothing in return.ᵘ Your reward will be great, and you will be children of the Most High, for he himself is kind to the ungrateful and the wicked. 36Be merciful, just as your Father is merciful.

37 "Do not judge, and you will not be judged; do not condemn, and you will not be condemned. Forgive, and you will be forgiven; 38give, and it will be given to you. A good measure, pressed down, shaken together, running over, will be put into your lap, for the measure you give will be the measure you get back."

39 He also told them a parable: "Can a blind person guide a blind person? Will not both fall into a pit? 40A disciple is not above the teacher, but every disciple who is fully qualified will be like the teacher. 41Why do you see the speck in your neighbor's eye but do not notice the log in your own eye? 42Or how can you say to your neighbor, 'Friend, let me take out the speck in your eye,' when you yourself do not see the log in your own eye? You hypocrite, first take the log out of your own eye, and then you will see clearly to take the speck out of your neighbor's eye.

43 "No good tree bears bad fruit, nor again does a bad tree bear good fruit; 44for each tree is known by its own fruit. For people do not gather figs from thorns, nor do they pick grapes from a bramble bush. 45The good person out of the good treasure of the heart produces good, and the evil person out of evil treasure produces evil, for it is out of the abundance of the heart that the mouth speaks.

46 "Why do you call me 'Lord, Lord,' and do not do what I tell you? 47I will show you what someone is like who comes to me, hears my words, and acts on them. 48That one is like a man building a house who dug deeply and laid the foundation on rock; when a flood arose, the river burst against that house but could not shake it because it had been well built.ᵛ 49But the one who hears and does not act is like a man who built a house on the ground without a foundation. When the river burst against it, it quickly collapsed, and great was the ruin of that house."

7 After Jesusʷ had finished all his sayings in the hearing of the people, he entered Capernaum. 2A centurion there had a slave whom he valued highly and who was ill and close to death. 3When he heard about Jesus, he sent some Jewish elders to him, asking him to come and heal his slave. 4When they came to Jesus, they appealed to him earnestly, saying, "He is worthy to have you do this for him, 5for he loves our people, and it is he who built our synagogue for us." 6And Jesus went with them, but when he was not far from the house, the centurion sent friends to say to him, "Lord, do not trouble yourself, for I am not worthy to have you come under my roof; 7therefore I did not presume to come to you. But only speak the word, and let my servant be healed. 8For I also am a man set under authority, with soldiers under me, and I say to one, 'Go,' and he goes, and to another, 'Come,' and he comes, and to my slave,

u 6.35 Other ancient authorities read *despairing of no one*
v 6.48 Other ancient authorities read *founded upon the rock*
w 7.1 Gk *he*

and despised with words of warning to the wealthy and influential. **6:27–36** Jesus challenges a culture of retaliation. **6:28** *Pray for those who mistreat you.* Jesus's teaching to pray for abusers does not require his listeners to remain in an abusive situation. Nonetheless, this teaching may be read as problematic for those who have endured abuse. **6:31** Luke's version of the Golden Rule. **6:37–42** Teachings about judgment and hypocrisy—those who judge others are frequently guilty of the same behavior.
   7:1–17 Two healings. 7:1–10 See **"Healing of an Enslaved Man," p. 1816. 7:2** *Centurion*, a military

LUKE 7

Going Deeper: The Healing of an Enslaved Man (Luke 7:1–10)

A story about Jesus responding to a request from a centurion to heal an enslaved member of his household offers a glimpse into slavery in first-century Galilee (Matt. 8:5–13; Luke 7:1–10; cf. John 4:46–54). Luke's account of the incident concludes with the enslaved man restored to health. However, the healing is presented primarily as a benefit to the slaveholding centurion who solicits Jesus's aid.

Luke situates the episode in Capernaum. Hearing about Jesus, a centurion dispatches a delegation of Jewish elders. A gentile, the centurion is nonetheless a benefactor of the local Jewish community, having built the synagogue. The elders ask Jesus to accompany them to the centurion's house to heal an enslaved man who is near death. The dying man is "valued highly" by the centurion, implying either that the centurion held the enslaved man in warm personal regard or that the enslaved man was a valuable household asset. Jesus agrees to help. Luke does not comment on whether Jesus is motivated by concern for the dying man, a sense of obligation to a benefactor, or supportiveness for the Jewish community.

On the way to the centurion's house, Jesus and the elders encounter another delegation of the centurion's friends who greet Jesus as *Kyrie* (7:6). Jesus was often addressed by followers as *Kyrie*, conventionally translated as "Lord," but the term could also be translated as "Master," a standard form of address for any man in a position of power and, specifically, for a slaveholder. The centurion believes that if Jesus will only "speak the word," the dying man will be healed (7:7). The message continues, "For I also am a man set under authority, with soldiers under me, and I say to one, 'Go,' and he goes, and to another, 'Come,' and he comes, and to my slave, 'Do this,' and the slave does it" (7:8). While the centurion thus acknowledges Jesus's authority, his words are a plain statement of hierarchical, martial, slaveholding values—the expectation that those of high rank should be able to exact obedience from those of low rank.

Jesus praises the faith of the centurion. Returning to the centurion's home, the friends find that the man who had been dying is now in good health. He is, however, still enslaved. The story raises troubling questions about Luke's apparent acceptance of the slaveholding values of the Roman world.

Jennifer A. Glancy

'Do this,' and the slave does it." ⁹When Jesus heard this he was amazed at him, and, turning to the crowd following him, he said, "I tell you, not even in Israel have I found such faith." ¹⁰When those who had been sent returned to the house, they found the slave in good health.

11 Soon afterward[x] he went to a town called Nain, and his disciples and a large crowd went with him. ¹²As he approached the gate of the town, a man who had died was being carried out. He was his mother's only son, and she was a widow, and with her was a large crowd from the town. ¹³When the Lord saw her, he was moved with compassion for her and said to her, "Do not cry." ¹⁴Then he came forward and touched the bier, and the bearers stopped.

And he said, "Young man, I say to you, rise!" ¹⁵The dead man sat up and began to speak, and Jesus[y] gave him to his mother. ¹⁶Fear seized all of them, and they glorified God, saying, "A great prophet has risen among us!" and "God has visited his people!" ¹⁷This word about him spread throughout the whole of Judea and all the surrounding region.

18 The disciples of John reported all these things to him. So John summoned two of his disciples ¹⁹and sent them to the Lord to ask, "Are you the one who is to come, or are we to expect someone else?" ²⁰When the men had come to him, they said, "John the Baptist has sent us to you to ask, 'Are you the one who is

x 7.11 Other ancient authorities read *The next day*
y 7.15 Gk *he*

official. **7:9** *Not even in Israel.* The centurion is a gentile. Luke emphasizes that Jesus's mission extends beyond the Jewish people. See **"The Bible, Race, and Ethnicity," pp. 2163–64**. **7:11–17** As a widow, the bereaved mother may face economic challenges following her son's death. The large crowd accompanying her nonetheless implies a network of support. **7:14–16** The prophet Elijah had raised a widow's son from the dead (4:25–26; 1 Kgs. 17:17–24). **7:15** Just as the healing of the enslaved man benefits the centurion, bringing the son back to life benefits the mother. **7:16** Jesus's ability to restore the dead to life is interpreted as evidence that he is a prophet.

7:18–35 John the Baptist and his disciples. 7:18 John is still in prison (see 3:20). **7:19** Elizabeth had reported that John had leaped in her womb at the sound of Mary's voice (1:44). John's adult uncertainty

to come, or are we to expect someone else?' " ²¹Jesus² had just then cured many people of diseases, afflictions, and evil spirits and had given sight to many who were blind. ²²And he answered them, "Go and tell John what you have seen and heard: the blind receive their sight; the lame walk; those with a skin disease are cleansed; the deaf hear; the dead are raised; the poor have good news brought to them. ²³And blessed is anyone who takes no offense at me."

24 When John's messengers had gone, Jesus^a began to speak to the crowds about John:^b "What did you go out into the wilderness to look at? A reed shaken by the wind? ²⁵What, then, did you go out to see? Someone^c dressed in soft robes? Look, those who put on fine clothing and live in luxury are in royal palaces. ²⁶What, then, did you go out to see? A prophet? Yes, I tell you, and more than a prophet. ²⁷This is the one about whom it is written,

'See, I am sending my messenger ahead
    of you,
who will prepare your way before you.'
²⁸"I tell you, among those born of women no one is greater than John, yet the least in the kingdom of God is greater than he." ²⁹(And all the people who heard this, including the tax collectors, acknowledged the justice of God,^d having been baptized with John's baptism. ³⁰But the Pharisees and the experts in the law, not having been baptized by him, rejected God's purpose for themselves.)

31 "To what, then, will I compare the people of this generation, and what are they like? ³²They are like children sitting in the marketplace and calling to one another,

'We played the flute for you, and you did
    not dance;
we wailed, and you did not weep.'
³³"For John the Baptist has come eating no bread and drinking no wine, and you say, 'He

has a demon'; ³⁴the Son of Man has come eating and drinking, and you say, 'Look, a glutton and a drunkard, a friend of tax collectors and sinners!' ³⁵Nevertheless, wisdom is vindicated by all her children."

36 One of the Pharisees asked Jesus^e to eat with him, and when he went into the Pharisee's house he reclined to dine. ³⁷And a woman in the city who was a sinner, having learned that he was eating in the Pharisee's house, brought an alabaster jar of ointment. ³⁸She stood behind him at his feet, weeping, and began to bathe his feet with her tears and to dry them with her hair, kissing his feet and anointing them with the ointment. ³⁹Now when the Pharisee who had invited him saw it, he said to himself, "If this man were a prophet, he would have known who and what kind of woman this is who is touching him, that she is a sinner." ⁴⁰Jesus spoke up and said to him, "Simon, I have something to say to you." "Teacher," he replied, "speak." ⁴¹"A certain moneylender had two debtors; one owed five hundred denarii, and the other fifty. ⁴²When they could not pay, he canceled the debts for both of them. Now which of them will love him more?" ⁴³Simon answered, "I suppose the one for whom he canceled the greater debt." And Jesus^f said to him, "You have judged rightly." ⁴⁴Then turning toward the woman, he said to Simon, "Do you see this woman? I entered your house; you gave me no water for my feet, but she has bathed my feet with her tears and dried them with her hair. ⁴⁵You gave me no kiss, but from the time I came in she has not stopped kissing my feet. ⁴⁶You did not anoint my head with oil, but she has anointed my feet with ointment. ⁴⁷Therefore, I tell you,

z 7.21 Gk He   a 7.24 Gk he   b 7.24 Gk him   c 7.25 Or Why, then, did you go out? To see someone   d 7.29 Or praised God   e 7.36 Gk him   f 7.43 Gk he

about Jesus's identity creates narrative difficulties. **7:21–22** Compare 4:16–21. **7:31–35** Detractors of John and Jesus are compared to children exchanging taunts. **7:35** John and Jesus are Wisdom's children. See **"Woman Wisdom," p. 872.**

7:36–50 A woman's love praised. See **"Women in Luke–Acts," p. 1809. 7:36** *Reclined to dine.* At ancient dinner parties, diners reclined on couches. **7:37** *A woman in the city who was a sinner.* The woman's sins may be sexual in nature, as is sometimes assumed, but Luke does not specify. Simon Peter had also been described as a sinner (5:8). **7:38** Anointing and kissing Jesus's feet, the woman's extravagant gestures go beyond foot washing, a standard ritual of hospitality. **7:39–40** Assuming that Jesus lacks insight into the woman's character, the Pharisee Simon silently questions whether he is a prophet. Jesus's response demonstrates an ability to discern Simon's thoughts. **7:41–43** Comparing forgiveness of sins to forgiveness of financial debt, Jesus links forgiveness with love. **7:47–48** Although Jesus implies that forgiveness of the woman's sins prompted her display of love, he speaks a word of forgiveness only after receiving her ministrations.

her many sins have been forgiven; hence she has shown great love. But the one to whom little is forgiven loves little." ⁴⁸Then he said to her, "Your sins are forgiven." ⁴⁹But those who were at the table with him began to say among themselves, "Who is this who even forgives sins?" ⁵⁰But he said to the woman, "Your faith has saved you; go in peace."

8 Soon afterward he went on through one town and village after another, proclaiming and bringing the good news of the kingdom of God. The twelve were with him, ²as well as some women who had been cured of evil spirits and infirmities: Mary, called Magdalene, from whom seven demons had gone out, ³and Joanna, the wife of Herod's steward Chuza, and Susanna, and many others, who ministered to them*g* out of their own resources.

4 When a large crowd was gathering, as people were coming to him from town after town, he said in a parable: ⁵"A sower went out to sow his seed, and as he sowed some fell on a path and was trampled on, and the birds of the air ate it up. ⁶Some fell on rock, and as it grew up it withered for lack of moisture. ⁷Some fell among thorns, and the thorns grew with it and choked it. ⁸Some fell into good soil, and when it grew it produced a hundredfold." As he said this, he called out, "If you have ears to hear, then hear!"

9 Then his disciples asked him what this parable meant. ¹⁰He said, "To you it has been given to know the secrets*h* of the kingdom of God, but to others I speak*i* in parables, so that

'looking they may not perceive
  and hearing they may not understand.'

11 "Now the parable is this: The seed is the word of God. ¹²The ones on the path are those who have heard; then the devil comes and takes away the word from their hearts, so that they may not believe and be saved. ¹³The ones on the rock are those who, when they hear the word, receive it with joy. But these have no root; they believe only for a while and in a time of testing fall away. ¹⁴As for what fell among the thorns, these are the ones who hear, but as they go on their way they are choked by the cares and riches and pleasures of life, and their fruit does not mature. ¹⁵But as for that in the good soil, these are the ones who, when they hear the word, hold it fast in an honest and good heart and bear fruit with endurance.

16 "No one after lighting a lamp hides it under a jar or puts it under a bed; rather, one puts it on a lampstand, so that those who enter may see the light. ¹⁷For nothing is hidden that will not be disclosed, nor is anything secret that will not become known and come to light. ¹⁸So pay attention to how you listen, for to those who have, more will be given, and from those who do not have, even what they seem to have will be taken away."

19 Then his mother and his brothers came to him, but they could not reach him because of the crowd. ²⁰And he was told, "Your mother and your brothers are standing outside, wanting to see you." ²¹But he said to them, "My mother and my brothers are those who hear the word of God and do it."

22 One day he got into a boat with his disciples, and he said to them, "Let us go across to the other side of the lake." So they put out, ²³and while they were sailing he fell asleep. A windstorm swept down on the lake, and the boat was filling with water, and they were in danger. ²⁴They went to him and woke him up, shouting, "Master, Master, we are perishing!"

g 8.3 Other ancient authorities read *him*
h 8.10 Or *mysteries*   *i* 8.10 Gk lacks *I speak*

8:1–3 The women accompanying Jesus. Jesus is accompanied by his apostles (6:12–16) and a group of women who are next mentioned at the crucifixion (23:49). **8:2** Luke's suggestion that Mary Magdalene had been healed of possession by demons may be an attempt to downplay her authority. See **"Mary Magdalene," p. 1766. 8:3** With control of their own resources, the women are patrons of the movement proclaiming the kingdom of God. In the Roman world, women of means often served as benefactors. See **"Women in Luke–Acts," p. 1809.**

8:4–21 Hearing the word of God. 8:4–15 Central to Jesus's teaching, parables range from extended analogies to short stories. **8:8** *It produced a hundredfold*, an abundant harvest. **8:9–10** Jesus speaks in parables to prevent some listeners from understanding. **8:12–13** The devil opposes Jesus and his followers (4:1–13; 22:31–32). **8:14** Wealth is an obstacle to hearing the word of God. **8:15** Acts narrates the growth of the word of God (Acts 6:7; 12:24). **8:19–21** Following Jesus supersedes the biological family. **8:21** Jesus's mother is among those who act on God's word (Luke 1:38).

8:22–56 Displays of power. 8:22–25 Jesus's own followers are unsettled by his command of natural

And waking up, he rebuked the wind and the raging waves; they ceased, and there was a calm. ²⁵Then he said to them, "Where is your faith?" They were terrified and amazed and said to one another, "Who then is this, that he commands even the winds and the water and they obey him?"

26 Then they arrived at the region of the Gerasenes,ʲ which is opposite Galilee. ²⁷As he stepped out on shore, a man from the city who had demons met him. For a long time he had not wornᵏ any clothes, and he did not live in a house but in the tombs. ²⁸When he saw Jesus, he cried out and fell down before him, shouting, "What have you to do with me, Jesus, Son of the Most High God? I beg you, do not torment me," ²⁹for Jesusˡ had commanded the unclean spirit to come out of the man. (For many times it had seized him; he was kept under guard and bound with chains and shackles, but he would break the bonds and be driven by the demon into the wilds.) ³⁰Jesus then asked him, "What is your name?" He said, "Legion," for many demons had entered him. ³¹They begged him not to order them to go back into the abyss.

32 Now there on the hillside a large herd of swine was feeding, and the demonsᵐ begged Jesusⁿ to let them enter these. So he gave them permission. ³³Then the demons came out of the man and entered the swine, and the herd stampeded down the steep bank into the lake and was drowned.

34 When the swineherds saw what had happened, they ran off and told it in the city and in the country. ³⁵Then people came out to see what had happened, and when they came to Jesus, they found the man from whom the demons had gone sitting at the feet of Jesus, clothed and in his right mind. And they became frightened. ³⁶Those who had seen it told them how the one who had been possessed by demons had been healed. ³⁷Then the whole throng of people of the surrounding region of the Gerasenesᵒ asked Jesusᵖ to leave them, for they were seized with great fear. So he got into the boat and returned. ³⁸The man from whom the demons had gone out begged that he might be with him, but Jesusᑫ sent him away, saying, ³⁹"Return to your home, and declare how much God has done for you." So he went away, proclaiming throughout the city how much Jesus had done for him.

40 Now when Jesus returned, the crowd welcomed him, for they were all waiting for him. ⁴¹Just then there came a man named Jairus, a leader of the synagogue. He fell at Jesus's feet and began pleading with him to come to his house, ⁴²for he had an only daughter, about twelve years old, and she was dying.

As he went, the crowds pressed in on him. ⁴³Now there was a woman who had been suffering from a flow of blood for twelve years, and though she had spent all she had on physicians,ʳ no one could cure her. ⁴⁴She came up behind him and touched the fringe of his cloak, and immediately her flow of blood stopped. ⁴⁵Then Jesus asked, "Who touched me?" When they all denied it, Peterˢ said, "Master, the crowds are hemming you in and pressing against you." ⁴⁶But Jesus said, "Someone touched me, for I noticed that power had gone out from me." ⁴⁷When the woman realized that she could not remain hidden, she came trembling, and falling down before him, she declared in the presence of all the people why she had touched him and how she had been immediately healed. ⁴⁸He said to her, "Daughter, your faith has made you well; go in peace."

ʲ 8.26 Other ancient authorities read *Gadarenes* or *Gergesenes* ᵏ 8.27 Other ancient authorities read *a man from the town who had had demons for a long time met him. He was not wearing* ˡ 8.29 Gk *he* ᵐ 8.32 Gk *they* ⁿ 8.32 Gk *him* ᵒ 8.37 Other ancient authorities read *Gadarenes* or *Gergesenes* ᵖ 8.37 Gk *him* ᑫ 8.38 Gk *he* ʳ 8.43 Other ancient authorities lack *and though she had spent all she had on physicians* ˢ 8.45 Other ancient authorities add *and those who were with him*

forces. **8:26–39** In the story of the Gerasene demoniac, social isolation is central to the man's suffering. Because of his condition, he is forced to live among the dead in their tombs (v. 27) or in the unpeopled desert (*the wilds*, v. 29). **8:26** *Region of the Gerasenes*, gentile territory. **8:30** *Legion*, a Roman military unit, suggesting the strength of the demons possessing the man. **8:32** Jews considered swine unclean. **8:37** *Seized with great fear.* The drowning of the swine represents a loss of income. **8:39** No longer demon-possessed, the man reintegrates into society. **8:40–56** Interwoven stories—a woman who suffered for twelve years from irregular bleeding and a twelve-year-old girl restored to life. **8:43** *Flow of blood*, perhaps irregular gynecological bleeding. The woman is physically and financially depleted but neither socially isolated nor ritually impure. **8:44** *Fringe of his cloak*, worn to signify commitment to Torah. **8:45** *Who touched me?* The healing took place without Jesus's knowledge. **8:48** *Your faith has made you well.* The woman's action has occasioned her own cure.

49 While he was still speaking, someone came from the synagogue leader's house to say, "Your daughter is dead; do not trouble the teacher any longer." 50When Jesus heard this, he replied, "Do not be afraid. Only believe, and she will be saved." 51When he came to the house, he did not allow anyone to enter with him, except Peter, John, and James and the child's father and mother. 52Everyone was weeping and grieving for her, but he said, "Do not cry, for she is not dead but sleeping." 53And they laughed at him, knowing that she was dead. 54But taking her by the hand, he called out, "Child, get up!" 55Her spirit returned, and she stood up at once, and he directed them to give her something to eat. 56Her parents were astounded, but he ordered them to tell no one what had happened.

9 Then Jesus' called the twelve together and gave them power and authority over all demons and to cure diseases, 2and he sent them out to proclaim the kingdom of God and to heal the sick. 3He said to them, "Take nothing for your journey: no staff, nor bag, nor bread, nor money—not even an extra tunic. 4Whatever house you enter, stay there, and leave from there. 5Wherever they do not welcome you, as you are leaving that town shake the dust off your feet as a testimony against them." 6So they departed and went through the villages, bringing the good news and curing diseases everywhere.

7 Now Herod the ruler heard about all that had taken place, and he was perplexed because it was said by some that John had been raised from the dead, 8by some that Elijah had appeared, and by others that one of the ancient prophets had arisen. 9Herod said, "John I beheaded, but who is this about whom I hear such things?" And he tried to see him.

10 On their return the apostles told Jesus" all they had done. Then, taking them along,

he slipped quietly into a city called Bethsaida. 11When the crowds found out about it, they followed him, and he welcomed them and spoke to them about the kingdom of God and healed those who needed to be cured.

12 The day was drawing to a close, and the twelve came to him and said, "Send the crowd away, so that they may go into the surrounding villages and countryside to lodge and get provisions, for we are here in a deserted place." 13But he said to them, "You give them something to eat." They said, "We have no more than five loaves and two fish—unless we are to go and buy food for all these people." 14For there were about five thousand men. And he said to his disciples, "Have them sit down in groups of about fifty each." 15They did so and had them all sit down. 16And taking the five loaves and the two fish, he looked up to heaven and blessed and broke them and gave them to the disciples to set before the crowd. 17And all ate and were filled, and what was left over was gathered up, twelve baskets of broken pieces.

18 Once when Jesus' was praying alone, with only the disciples near him, he asked them, "Who do the crowds say that I am?" 19They answered, "John the Baptist; but others, Elijah; and still others, that one of the ancient prophets has arisen." 20Then he said to them, "But who do you say that I am?" Peter answered, "The Messiah" of God."

21 He sternly ordered and commanded them not to tell anyone, 22saying, "The Son of Man must undergo great suffering and be rejected by the elders, chief priests, and scribes and be killed and on the third day be raised."

23 Then he said to them all, "If any wish to come after me, let them deny themselves and take up their cross daily and follow me. 24For those who want to save their life will lose it, and those who lose their life for my sake will

t 9.1 Gk *he*   u 9.10 Gk *him*   v 9.18 Gk *he*   w 9.20 Or *The Christ*

9:1–50 **The Galilean ministry comes to a close. 9:1–6** The twelve share Jesus's ministry of healing and proclaiming the kingdom of God. **9:7–9** Given his role in beheading John the Baptist, Herod Antipas's curiosity about Jesus is sinister. **9:8** The prophet Elijah did not die but rather ascended in a fiery chariot (2 Kgs. 2:11–13). His return was prophesied (Mal. 4:5). **9:9** *He tried to see him.* Herod questions Jesus after his arrest (Luke 23:6–12). **9:12–17** There were leftovers after the prophet Elisha fed a crowd with a small quantity of bread (2 Kgs. 4:42–44). **9:20** *Messiah* or Christ, confirming what the reader has known from the outset; see note on 1:32. **9:21–22** Jesus orders his followers not to speak about his identity because they do not yet understand what it means to be Messiah. The Messiah was not expected to suffer. **9:22** On Jesus's self-designation as Son of Man, see **"Son of God vs. Son of Man," p. 1774.** In Mark, Jesus's declaration that the Son of Man would suffer leads to conflict with Peter, who resists the message (Mark 8:31–33). Luke softens Mark's depiction of Peter,

save it. ²⁵For what does it profit them if they gain the whole world but lose or forfeit themselves? ²⁶Those who are ashamed of me and of my words, of them the Son of Man will be ashamed when he comes in his glory and the glory of the Father and of the holy angels. ²⁷Indeed, truly I tell you, there are some standing here who will not taste death before they see the kingdom of God."

28 Now about eight days after these sayings Jesus* took with him Peter and John and James and went up on the mountain to pray. ²⁹And while he was praying, the appearance of his face changed, and his clothes became as bright as a flash of lightning. ³⁰Suddenly they saw two men, Moses and Elijah, talking to him. ³¹They appeared in glory and were speaking about his exodus, which he was about to fulfill in Jerusalem. ³²Now Peter and his companions were weighed down with sleep, but as they awoke they saw his glory and the two men who stood with him. ³³Just as they were leaving him, Peter said to Jesus, "Master, it is good for us to be here; let us set up three tents: one for you, one for Moses, and one for Elijah," not realizing what he was saying. ³⁴While he was saying this, a cloud came and overshadowed them, and they were terrified as they entered the cloud. ³⁵Then from the cloud came a voice that said, "This is my Son, my Chosen;ʸ listen to him!" ³⁶When the voice had spoken, Jesus was found alone. And they kept silent and in those days told no one any of the things they had seen.

37 On the next day, when they had come down from the mountain, a great crowd met him. ³⁸Just then a man from the crowd shouted, "Teacher, I beg you to look at my son; he is my only child. ³⁹Suddenly a spirit seizes him, and all at once heᶻ shrieks. It convulses him until he foams at the mouth; it mauls him and

will scarcely leave him. ⁴⁰I begged your disciples to cast it out, but they could not." ⁴¹Jesus answered, "You faithless and perverse generation, how much longer must I be with you and put up with you? Bring your son here." ⁴²While he was being brought forward, the demon dashed him to the ground in convulsions. But Jesus rebuked the unclean spirit, healed the boy, and gave him back to his father. ⁴³And all were astounded at the greatness of God.

While everyone was amazed at all that he was doing, he said to his disciples, ⁴⁴"Let these words sink into your ears: The Son of Man is going to be betrayed into human hands." ⁴⁵But they did not understand this saying; its meaning remained concealed from them, so that they could not perceive it. And they were afraid to ask him about this saying.

46 An argument arose among them concerning which one of them was the greatest. ⁴⁷But Jesus, aware of their inner thoughts, took a little child and put it by his side ⁴⁸and said to them, "Whoever welcomes this child in my name welcomes me, and whoever welcomes me welcomes the one who sent me, for the least among all of you is the greatest."

49 John answered, "Master, we saw someone casting out demons in your name, and we tried to stop him because he does not follow with us." ⁵⁰But Jesus said to him, "Do not stop him, for whoever is not against you is for you."

51 When the days drew near for him to be taken up, he set his face to go to Jerusalem. ⁵²And he sent messengers ahead of him. On their way they entered a village of the Samaritans to prepare for his arrival, ⁵³but they did not receive him because his face was set toward Jerusalem. ⁵⁴When his disciples James

x 9.28 Gk *he*   y 9.35 Other ancient authorities read *my Beloved*   z 9.39 Or *it*

setting the stage for Peter's leadership role in Acts of the Apostles. **9:26–27** Jesus implies that some of his listeners would remain alive to witness his return at the end of time. In the next scene, however, he already manifests his glory (Luke 9:32) and later teaches that the kingdom of God is already present (17:21). **9:31** *His exodus, which he was about to fulfill in Jerusalem.* Luke locates Jesus's death, resurrection, and ascension in Jerusalem, which he understands in light of the exodus. See **"Jerusalem in Luke–Acts," p. 1805; "The Exodus Event," p. 105. 9:37–43** The depiction of the child's suffering reflects first-century beliefs about demon possession, attitudes that have tragically contributed to stigmatization of the neurodivergent.

9:51–19:28 On the road to Jerusalem. The Galilean ministry concluded, Jesus journeys through Samaria and Judea to Jerusalem. Significant portions of this travel narrative are unique to Luke.

9:51–10:24 Encounters along the road. 9:51 *Taken up,* referring to the crucifixion and ascension; see note on 9:31. *He set his face to go to Jerusalem,* a turning point in the Gospel. See **"Jerusalem in Luke–Acts," p. 1805. 9:52–53** There was some animosity between Jews and Samaritans, who were neither Jew nor gentile. See **"The Samaritans," p. 1738. 9:54–55** Jesus had instructed the twelve to respond

and John saw this, they said, "Lord, do you want us to command fire to come down from heaven and consume them?"[a] [55]But he turned and rebuked them. [56]Then[b] they went on to another village.

[57] As they were going along the road, someone said to him, "I will follow you wherever you go." [58]And Jesus said to him, "Foxes have holes, and birds of the air have nests, but the Son of Man has nowhere to lay his head." [59]To another he said, "Follow me." But he said, "Lord, first let me go and bury my father." [60]And Jesus[c] said to him, "Let the dead bury their own dead, but as for you, go and proclaim the kingdom of God." [61]Another said, "I will follow you, Lord, but let me first say farewell to those at my home." [62]And Jesus said to him, "No one who puts a hand to the plow and looks back is fit for the kingdom of God."

10 After this the Lord appointed seventy-two[d] others and sent them on ahead of him in pairs to every town and place where he himself intended to go. [2]He said to them, "The harvest is plentiful, but the laborers are few; therefore ask the Lord of the harvest to send out laborers into his harvest. [3]Go on your way; I am sending you out like lambs into the midst of wolves. [4]Carry no purse, no bag, no sandals, and greet no one on the road. [5]Whatever house you enter, first say, 'Peace to this house!' [6]And if a person of peace is there, your peace will rest on that person, but if not, it will return to you. [7]Remain in the same house, eating and drinking whatever they provide, for the laborer deserves to be paid. Do not move about from house to house. [8]Whenever you enter a town and its people welcome you, eat what is set before you; [9]cure the sick who are there, and say to them, 'The kingdom of God has come near to you.'[e] [10]But whenever you enter a town and they do not welcome you, go out into its streets and say, [11]'Even the dust of your town that clings to our feet, we wipe off in protest against you. Yet know this: the kingdom of God has come near.'[f] [12]I tell you, on that day

it will be more tolerable for Sodom than for that town.

[13] "Woe to you, Chorazin! Woe to you, Bethsaida! For if the deeds of power done in you had been done in Tyre and Sidon, they would have repented long ago, sitting in sackcloth and ashes. [14]Indeed, at the judgment it will be more tolerable for Tyre and Sidon than for you. [15]And you, Capernaum,

will you be exalted to heaven?

No, you will be brought down to Hades.

[16] "Whoever listens to you listens to me, and whoever rejects you rejects me, and whoever rejects me rejects the one who sent me."

[17] The seventy-two[g] returned with joy, saying, "Lord, in your name even the demons submit to us!" [18]He said to them, "I watched Satan fall from heaven like a flash of lightning. [19]Indeed, I have given you authority to tread on snakes and scorpions and over all the power of the enemy, and nothing will hurt you. [20]Nevertheless, do not rejoice at this, that the spirits submit to you, but rejoice that your names are written in heaven."

[21] At that very hour Jesus[h] rejoiced in the Holy Spirit[i] and said, "I thank[j] you, Father, Lord of heaven and earth, because you have hidden these things from the wise and the intelligent and have revealed them to infants; yes, Father, for such was your gracious will.[k] [22]All things have been handed over to me by my Father, and no one knows who the Son is except the Father or who the Father is except the Son and anyone to whom the Son chooses to reveal him."

[23] Then turning to the disciples, Jesus[l] said to them privately, "Blessed are the eyes that see what you see! [24]For I tell you that many prophets and kings desired to see what you

---

a 9.54 Other ancient authorities add *as Elijah did*
b 9.56 Other ancient authorities read *rebuked them, and said, "You do not know what spirit you are of, [56]for the Son of Man has not come to destroy the lives of humans but to save them." Then*   c 9.60 Gk *he*   d 10.1 Other ancient authorities read *seventy*   e 10.9 Or *is at hand for you*   f 10.11 Or *is at hand*   g 10.17 Other ancient authorities read *seventy*   h 10.21 Gk *he*   i 10.21 Other authorities read *in the spirit*   j 10.21 Or *praise*   k 10.21 Or *for so it was well-pleasing in your sight*   l 10.23 Gk *he*

---

to rejection by shaking the dust off their feet (9:5). **9:57–62** Jesus emphasizes the difficulties faced by those proclaiming the kingdom of God. See **"Kingdom of God," p. 1772. 10:9** The ability of Jesus's disciples to heal disease is evidence for the nearness of God's reign; see note on 4:43. **10:12** God had destroyed Sodom for its treatment of visitors (Gen. 19:24–25). **10:13–15** The Galilean towns of Chorazin, Bethsaida, and Capernaum are compared unfavorably to the gentile towns of Tyre and Sidon. **10:15** *Hades*, Greek term for the place of the dead. **10:17–18** Satan was understood to have authority over demons. The disciples' ability to cast out demons signals the end of Satan's power.

see but did not see it and to hear what you hear but did not hear it."

25 An expert in the law stood up to test Jesus.[m] "Teacher," he said, "what must I do to inherit eternal life?" [26]He said to him, "What is written in the law? What do you read there?" [27]He answered, "You shall love the Lord your God with all your heart and with all your soul and with all your strength and with all your mind and your neighbor as yourself." [28]And he said to him, "You have given the right answer; do this, and you will live."

29 But wanting to vindicate himself, he asked Jesus, "And who is my neighbor?" [30]Jesus replied, "A man was going down from Jerusalem to Jericho and fell into the hands of robbers, who stripped him, beat him, and took off, leaving him half dead. [31]Now by chance a priest was going down that road, and when he saw him he passed by on the other side. [32]So likewise a Levite, when he came to the place and saw him, passed by on the other side. [33]But a Samaritan while traveling came upon him, and when he saw him he was moved with compassion. [34]He went to him and bandaged his wounds, treating them with oil and wine. Then he put him on his own animal, brought him to an inn, and took care of him. [35]The next day he took out two denarii, gave them to the innkeeper, and said, 'Take care of him, and when I come back I will repay you whatever more you spend.' [36]Which of these three, do you think, was a neighbor to the man who fell into the hands of the robbers?" [37]He said, "The one who showed him mercy." Jesus said to him, "Go and do likewise."

38 Now as they went on their way, he entered a certain village where a woman named Martha welcomed him.[n] [39]She had a sister named Mary, who sat at Jesus's[o] feet and listened to what he was saying. [40]But Martha was distracted by her many tasks, so she came to him and asked, "Lord, do you not care that my sister has left me to do all the work by myself? Tell her, then, to help me." [41]But the Lord answered her, "Martha, Martha, you are worried and distracted by many things, [42]but few things are needed—indeed only one.[p] Mary has chosen the better part, which will not be taken away from her."

11 He was praying in a certain place, and after he had finished, one of his disciples said to him, "Lord, teach us to pray, as John taught his disciples." [2]So he said to them, "When you pray, say:

> Father,[q] may your name be revered as holy.
> May your kingdom come.[r]
> [3] Give us each day our daily bread.[s]
> [4] And forgive us our sins,
> for we ourselves forgive everyone indebted to us.
> And do not bring us to the time of trial."[t]

5 And he said to them, "Suppose one of you has a friend, and you go to him at midnight and say to him, 'Friend, lend me three loaves of bread, [6]for a friend of mine has arrived, and I have nothing to set before him.' [7]And he answers from within, 'Do not bother me; the door has already been locked, and my children are with me in bed; I cannot get up and give you anything.' [8]I tell you, even though he

m 10.25 Gk him n 10.38 Other ancient authorities add into her home o 10.39 Other ancient authorities read the Lord's p 10.42 Other ancient authorities read but only one thing is needed q 11.2 Other ancient authorities read Our Father in heaven r 11.2 A few ancient authorities read Your Holy Spirit come upon us and cleanse us. Other ancient authorities add Your will be done, on earth as in heaven s 11.3 Or our bread for tomorrow t 11.4 Or us into temptation. Other ancient authorities add but rescue us from the evil one (or from evil)

10:25–37 Who is my neighbor? **10:27** Linking Deut. 6:5 with Lev. 19:18. **10:31–33** The story hinges on the expectation that either the priest (v. 31) or the Levite (v. 32) would stop to aid a fellow Jew. Instead, a Samaritan offers assistance (v. 33). On relations between Samaritans and Jews, see note on 9:52–53. **10:37** Duties to neighbors are not limited by ethnicity.

10:38–42 Martha and Mary. John features a different story about the sisters Martha and Mary (John 11:1–12:8). **10:38** Martha hosts Jesus in her own home. **10:39** Mary, who sat at Jesus's feet, the posture of a disciple. **10:40** Distracted by her many tasks, or distracted by much ministry (Gk. "diakonia"). **10:42** The better part. Interpreters debate whether Jesus's words should be taken as praise for a woman's discipleship or as disparagement of a woman's active ministry. See "Women in Luke–Acts," p. 1809.

11:1–13 Teachings on prayer. See note on 1:13. **11:2–4** The Lord's Prayer has been foundational for Christians over the centuries. Matthew's version is more familiar (Matt. 6:9–13). See "The Bible in Religious Interpretation and Practice," pp. 2155–56. **11:4** Time of trial, see Luke 22:40, 46.

will not get up and give him anything out of friendship, at least because of his persistence he will get up and give him whatever he needs.

9 "So I say to you, Ask, and it will be given to you; search, and you will find; knock, and the door will be opened for you. ¹⁰For everyone who asks receives, and everyone who searches finds, and for everyone who knocks, the door will be opened. ¹¹Is there anyone among you who, if your child asked for" a fish, would give a snake instead of a fish? ¹²Or if the child asked for an egg, would give a scorpion? ¹³If you, then, who are evil, know how to give good gifts to your children, how much more will the heavenly Father give the Holy Spirit' to those who ask him!"

14 Now he was casting out a demon that was mute; when the demon had gone out, the one who had been mute spoke, and the crowds were amazed. ¹⁵But some of them said, "He casts out demons by Beelzebul, the ruler of the demons." ¹⁶Others, to test him, kept demanding from him a sign from heaven. ¹⁷But he knew what they were thinking and said to them, "Every kingdom divided against itself is laid waste, and a divided household falls. ¹⁸If Satan also is divided against himself, how will his kingdom stand?—for you say that I cast out the demons by Beelzebul. ¹⁹Now if I cast out the demons by Beelzebul, by whom do your exorcists" cast them out? Therefore they will be your judges. ²⁰But if it is by the finger of God that I cast out the demons, then the kingdom of God has come upon you. ²¹When a strong man, fully armed, guards his castle, his property is safe. ²²But when one stronger than he attacks him and overpowers him, he takes away his armor in which he trusted and divides his plunder. ²³Whoever is not with me is against me, and whoever does not gather with me scatters.

24 "When the unclean spirit has gone out of a person, it wanders through waterless regions looking for a resting place, but not finding any it says, 'I will return to my house from which I came.' ²⁵When it returns, it finds it swept and put in order. ²⁶Then it goes and brings seven other spirits more evil than itself, and they enter and live there, and the last state of that person is worse than the first."

27 While he was saying this, a woman in the crowd raised her voice and said to him, "Blessed is the womb that bore you and the breasts that nursed you!" ²⁸But he said, "Blessed rather are those who hear the word of God and obey it!"

29 When the crowds were increasing, he began to say, "This generation is an evil generation; it asks for a sign, but no sign will be given to it except the sign of Jonah. ³⁰For just as Jonah became a sign to the people of Nineveh, so the Son of Man will be to this generation. ³¹The queen of the South will rise at the judgment with the people of this generation and condemn them, because she came from the ends of the earth to listen to the wisdom of Solomon, and indeed, something greater than Solomon is here! ³²The people of Nineveh will rise up at the judgment with this generation and condemn it, because they repented at the proclamation of Jonah, and indeed, something greater than Jonah is here!

33 "No one after lighting a lamp puts it in a cellar or under a bushel basket;ˣ rather, one puts it on the lampstand so that those who enter may see the light. ³⁴Your eye is the lamp of your body. If your eye is healthy, your whole

u 11.11 Other ancient authorities add *bread, will give a stone?*
Or if your child asks for v 11.13 Other ancient authorities
read *the Father give the Holy Spirit from heaven* w 11.19 Gk *sons*
x 11.33 Other ancient authorities lack *or under a bushel basket*

11:11–13 God's response to prayer will exceed even a parent's response to a child's request. Arguing from the lesser to the greater is a standard strategy in Greek rhetoric and rabbinic teaching.

11:14–26 **A kingdom divided.** Jesus's ability to cast out demons presages the end of the kingdom of Satan. **11:15** *Beelzebul*, another name for Satan (v. 18). Jesus's critics attribute his ability to perform exorcisms to a demonic alliance. **11:17–18** Jesus characterizes exorcisms as attacks on Satan's kingdom. **11:19** *Your exorcists*, literally "your sons." Jesus's critics have sons who profit from performing exorcisms. **11:20** Jesus's exorcisms make the reign of God a present reality; see note on 4:43. **11:21–22** By casting out demons, Jesus binds the strong man, Satan. **11:24** *Through waterless regions.* Demons were thought to inhabit desert places.

11:27–36 **Public teaching. 11:27–28** See note on 8:21. **11:30** *Jonah became a sign to the people of Nineveh.* God commanded the Israelite prophet Jonah to travel to the Assyrian city of Nineveh to prophesy its destruction. God spared the city after the population repented. Compare Matt. 12:40. **11:31** *The queen of the South.* The queen of Sheba traveled a great distance to learn from King Solomon (1 Kgs. 10:1–13). Like the Ninevites, the queen was a gentile.

body is full of light, but if it is unhealthy, your body is full of darkness. ³⁵Therefore consider whether the light in you is not darkness. ³⁶But if your whole body is full of light, with no part of it in darkness, it will be as full of light as when a lamp gives you light with its rays."

37 While he was speaking, a Pharisee invited him to dine with him, so he went in and took his place at the table. ³⁸The Pharisee was amazed to see that he did not first wash before dinner. ³⁹Then the Lord said to him, "Now you Pharisees clean the outside of the cup and of the dish, but inside you are full of greed and wickedness. ⁴⁰You fools! Did not the one who made the outside make the inside also? ⁴¹So give as alms those things that are within and then everything will be clean for you.

42 "But woe to you Pharisees! For you tithe mint and rue and herbs of all kinds and neglect justice and the love of God; it is these you ought to have practiced, without neglecting the others. ⁴³Woe to you Pharisees! For you love to have the seat of honor in the synagogues and to be greeted with respect in the marketplaces. ⁴⁴Woe to you! For you are like unmarked graves on which people unknowingly walk."

45 One of the experts in the law answered him, "Teacher, when you say these things, you insult us, too." ⁴⁶And he said, "Woe also to you experts in the law! For you load people with burdens hard to bear, and you yourselves do not lift a finger to ease them. ⁴⁷Woe to you! For you build the tombs of the prophets whom your ancestors killed. ⁴⁸So you are witnesses and approve of the deeds of your ancestors, for they killed them, and you build their tombs. ⁴⁹For this reason the Wisdom of God said, 'I will send them prophets and apostles, some of whom they will kill and persecute,' ⁵⁰so that this generation may be charged with the blood of all the prophets shed since the foundation of the world, ⁵¹from the blood of Abel to the blood of Zechariah, who perished between the altar and the sanctuary. Yes, I tell you, it will be charged against this generation. ⁵²Woe to you experts in the law! For you have taken away the key of knowledge; you did not enter yourselves, and you hindered those who were entering."

53 When he went outside, the scribes and the Pharisees became hostile to him and began to interrogate him about many things, ⁵⁴lying in wait for him, to catch him in something he might say.

12 Meanwhile, when the crowd had gathered by the thousands, so that they trampled on one another, he began to speak first to his disciples, "Beware of the yeast of the Pharisees, that is, their hypocrisy. ²Nothing is covered up that will not be uncovered and nothing secret that will not become known. ³Therefore whatever you have said in the dark will be heard in the light, and what you have whispered behind closed doors will be proclaimed from the housetops.

4 "I tell you, my friends, do not fear those who kill the body and after that can do nothing more. ⁵But I will show you whom to fear: fear the one who, after killing, has authorityʸ to cast into hell.ᶻ Yes, I tell you, fear that one! ⁶Are not five sparrows sold for two pennies? Yet not one of them is forgotten in God's sight. ⁷But even the hairs of your head are all numbered. Do not be afraid; you are of more value than many sparrows.

8 "And I tell you, everyone who acknowledges me before others, the Son of Man also will acknowledge before the angels of God, ⁹but whoever denies me before others will be denied before the angels of God. ¹⁰And everyone who speaks a word against the Son of Man will be forgiven, but whoever blasphemes against the Holy Spirit will not be forgiven. ¹¹When they bring you before the synagogues,

y 12.5 Or *power*   *z* 12.5 Gk *Gehenna*

11:37–12:12 Denunciation of hypocrisy. Jesus's harsh words continue the tradition of invective directed by the prophets against others within Israel. The characterization of the Pharisees as hypocrites is inconsistent with ancient sources outside the New Testament. See **"Pharisees," p. 1756. 11:42** *Tithe,* a mandated offering of 10 percent of agricultural yield (Deut. 14:22–29). *Mint and rue,* herbs of negligible monetary value. Jesus upholds the practice of tithing but, like other Israelite prophets, emphasizes the still greater importance of justice. **11:47–51** Striking an ominous note, Jesus suggests that a history of violence against the prophets continues into the present. **11:49** Jesus speaks as personified *Wisdom*; see note on 7:35. **11:51** *Abel* was the first victim of homicide (Gen. 4:1-16). The priest *Zechariah* was killed in the temple (2 Chr. 24:20–22). **12:1-3** Concluding his condemnation of hypocrisy, Jesus warns against participating in a culture of secrecy. **12:5** *Hell,* literally "Gehenna," a valley near Jerusalem, a place of punishment. **12:11–12** In Acts of the Apostles, Jesus's followers are repeatedly called on to defend themselves in official settings.

the rulers, and the authorities, do not worry about how or what[a] you will answer or what you are to say, [12]for the Holy Spirit will teach you at that very hour what you ought to say."

[13] Someone in the crowd said to him, "Teacher, tell my brother to divide the family inheritance with me." [14]But he said to him, "Friend, who set me to be a judge or arbitrator over you?" [15]And he said to them, "Take care! Be on your guard against all kinds of greed, for one's life does not consist in the abundance of possessions." [16]Then he told them a parable: "The land of a rich man produced abundantly. [17]And he thought to himself, 'What should I do, for I have no place to store my crops?' [18]Then he said, 'I will do this: I will pull down my barns and build larger ones, and there I will store all my grain and my goods. [19]And I will say to my soul, Soul, you have ample goods laid up for many years; relax, eat, drink, be merry.' [20]But God said to him, 'You fool! This very night your life is being demanded of you. And the things you have prepared, whose will they be?' [21]So it is with those who store up treasures for themselves but are not rich toward God."

[22] He said to his disciples, "Therefore I tell you, do not worry about your life, what you will eat, or about your body, what you will wear. [23]For life is more than food and the body more than clothing. [24]Consider the ravens: they neither sow nor reap, they have neither storehouse nor barn, and yet God feeds them. Of how much more value are you than the birds! [25]And which of you by worrying can add a single hour to your span of life?[b] [26]If then you are not able to do so small a thing as that, why do you worry about the rest? [27]Consider the lilies, how they grow: they neither toil nor spin,[c] yet I tell you, even Solomon in all his glory was not clothed like one of these. [28]But if God so clothes the grass of the field, which is alive today and tomorrow is thrown into the oven, how much more will he clothe you, you of little faith! [29]And do not keep seeking what you are to eat and what you are to drink, and do not keep worrying. [30]For it is the nations[d] of the world that seek all these things, and your Father knows that you need them. [31]Instead, seek his[e] kingdom, and these things will be given to you as well.

[32] "Do not be afraid, little flock, for it is your Father's good pleasure to give you the kingdom. [33]Sell your possessions and give alms. Make purses for yourselves that do not wear out, an unfailing treasure in heaven, where no thief comes near and no moth destroys. [34]For where your treasure is, there your heart will be also.

[35] "Be dressed for action and have your lamps lit; [36]be like those who are waiting for their master to return from the wedding banquet, so that they may open the door for him as soon as he comes and knocks. [37]Blessed are those slaves whom the master finds alert when he comes; truly I tell you, he will fasten his belt and have them sit down to eat, and he will come and serve them. [38]If he comes during the middle of the night or near dawn and finds them so, blessed are those slaves.

[39] "But know this: if the owner of the house had known at what hour the thief was coming, he[f] would not have let his house be broken into. [40]You also must be ready, for the Son of Man is coming at an hour you do not expect."

[41] Peter said, "Lord, are you telling this parable for us or for everyone?" [42]And the Lord said, "Who, then, is the faithful and prudent manager whom his master will put in charge

a 12.11 Other ancient authorities lack *or what*   b 12.25 Or *add a cubit to your stature*   c 12.27 Other ancient authorities read *Consider the lilies: they neither spin nor weave*   d 12.30 Or *gentiles*   e 12.31 Other ancient authorities read *God's*   f 12.39 Other ancient authorities add *would have watched and*

12:13–34 Teachings on possessions. A focus on material goods is at odds with pursuing the kingdom of God, a central theme in Luke–Acts. **12:16–21** Accumulation of wealth results in a mistaken sense of security. **12:22–32** Words of reassurance, emphasizing God as the provider of good things. **12:33** *Sell your possessions and give alms.* Generosity to those in need should accompany detachment from possessions.

12:35–48 Two parables on watchfulness and judgment. Early followers of Jesus understood the end of the age to be near, when Jesus would return in glory to judge the world. By the time Luke wrote, it was clear Jesus had not returned as soon as many had anticipated. Luke urges continued vigilance. The violence of Roman slavery informs the imagery of these parables. **12:36** *Master*, in Greek "kyrios," a designation often used for Jesus; see note on 12:41–42. **12:37** Highly unusual behavior for an enslaver. **12:39** A brief shift in metaphor, still focusing on the importance of vigilance while waiting for Jesus's return. **12:41–42** Luke reinforces Peter's acknowledgment of Jesus as *Lord* ("Kyrios") as he

of his slaves, to give them their allowance of food at the proper time? [43]Blessed is that slave whom his master will find at work when he arrives. [44]Truly I tell you, he will put that one in charge of all his possessions. [45]But if that slave says to himself, 'My master is delayed in coming,' and begins to beat the other slaves, men and women, and to eat and drink and get drunk, [46]the master of that slave will come on a day when he does not expect him and at an hour that he does not know and will cut him in pieces[g] and put him with the unfaithful. [47]That slave who knew what his master wanted but did not prepare himself or do what was wanted will receive a severe beating. [48]But the one who did not know and did what deserved a beating will receive a light beating. From everyone to whom much has been given, much will be required, and from the one to whom much has been entrusted, even more will be demanded.

[49]"I have come to cast fire upon the earth, and how I wish it were already ablaze! [50]I have a baptism with which to be baptized, and what constraint I am under until it is completed! [51]Do you think that I have come to bring peace to the earth? No, I tell you, but rather division! [52]From now on five in one household will be divided, three against two and two against three; [53]they will be divided:

father against son
    and son against father,
mother against daughter
    and daughter against mother,
mother-in-law against her
        daughter-in-law
    and daughter-in-law against
        mother-in-law."

54 He also said to the crowds, "When you see a cloud rising in the west, you immediately say, 'It is going to rain,' and so it happens.

[55]And when you see the south wind blowing, you say, 'There will be scorching heat,' and it happens. [56]You hypocrites! You know how to interpret the appearance of earth and sky, but why do you not know how to interpret the present time?

57 "And why do you not judge for yourselves what is right? [58]Thus when you go with your accuser before a magistrate, on the way make an effort to reach a settlement,[h] or you may be dragged before the judge, and the judge hand you over to the officer, and the officer throw you in prison. [59]I tell you, you will never get out until you have paid the very last penny."

13 At that very time there were some present who told Jesus[i] about the Galileans whose blood Pilate had mingled with their sacrifices. [2]He asked them, "Do you think that because these Galileans suffered in this way they were worse sinners than all other Galileans? [3]No, I tell you, but unless you repent you will all perish as they did. [4]Or those eighteen who were killed when the tower of Siloam fell on them—do you think that they were worse offenders than all the other people living in Jerusalem? [5]No, I tell you, but unless you repent you will all perish just as they did."

6 Then he told this parable: "A man had a fig tree planted in his vineyard, and he came looking for fruit on it and found none. [7]So he said to the man working the vineyard, 'See here! For three years I have come looking for fruit on this fig tree, and still I find none. Cut it down! Why should it be wasting the soil?' [8]He replied, 'Sir, let it alone for one more year, until I dig around it and put manure on it. [9]If it bears fruit next year, well and good, but if not, you can cut it down.'"

g 12.46 Or *cut him off*   h 12.58 Gk *settle with him*   i 13.1 Gk *him*

recounts a parable centered on a *master* ("kyrios") who entrusts his household to an enslaved manager. **12:46–48** Invoking the extreme violence inflicted on enslaved persons, Jesus warns of eschatological punishment for his followers who fail to live up to their obligations.

12:49–13:9 A time of repentance. 12:51–53 Simeon had prophesied that Jesus would be divisive (2:34–35). See note on 14:26. **12:57–59** Practical advice about avoiding an adversarial courtroom encounter is connected to surrounding material through the themes of judgment and reform. **13:1–5** Two incidents involving untimely and gruesome deaths that are apparently known to Luke's audience. Jesus urges his listeners to repent, as death can come at any time. **13:1** *The Galileans whose blood Pilate had mingled with their sacrifices.* Sacrifices were offered at the temple. The slaughter of Galileans at the temple is otherwise unknown, but Pilate certainly had a reputation for cruelty. **13:4** *When the tower of Siloam fell,* an otherwise unattested disaster. **13:6–9** Luke omits Jesus's cursing of an out-of-season fig tree (Mark 11:12–14, 20) and includes this parable about a fig tree that will be chopped down if it does not yield fruit, a metaphor for failing to repent.

10 Now he was teaching in one of the synagogues on the Sabbath. ¹¹And just then there appeared a woman with a spirit that had crippled her for eighteen years. She was bent over and was quite unable to stand up straight. ¹²When Jesus saw her, he called her over and said, "Woman, you are set free from your ailment." ¹³When he laid his hands on her, immediately she stood up straight and began praising God. ¹⁴But the leader of the synagogue, indignant because Jesus had cured on the Sabbath, kept saying to the crowd, "There are six days on which work ought to be done; come on those days and be cured and not on the Sabbath day." ¹⁵But the Lord answered him and said, "You hypocrites! Does not each of you on the Sabbath untie his ox or his donkey from the manger and lead it to water? ¹⁶And ought not this woman, a daughter of Abraham whom Satan bound for eighteen long years, be set free from this bondage on the Sabbath day?" ¹⁷When he said this, all his opponents were put to shame, and the entire crowd was rejoicing at all the wonderful things being done by him.

18 He said therefore, "What is the kingdom of God like? And to what should I compare it? ¹⁹It is like a mustard seed that someone took and sowed in the garden; it grew and became a tree, and the birds of the air made nests in its branches."

20 And again he said, "To what should I compare the kingdom of God? ²¹It is like yeast that a woman took and mixed in with three measures of flour until all of it was leavened."

22 Jesus*ʲ* went through one town and village after another, teaching as he made his way to Jerusalem. ²³Someone asked him, "Lord, will only a few be saved?" He said to them, ²⁴"Strive to enter through the narrow door, for many, I tell you, will try to enter and will not be able. ²⁵Once the owner of the house has got up and shut the door, and you begin to stand outside and to knock at the door, saying, 'Lord, open to us,' then in reply he will say to you, 'I do not know where you come from.' ²⁶Then you will begin to say, 'We ate and drank with you, and you taught in our streets.' ²⁷But he will say to you, 'I do not know where you come from; go away from me, all you evildoers!' ²⁸There will be weeping and gnashing of teeth when you see Abraham and Isaac and Jacob and all the prophets in the kingdom of God, and you yourselves thrown out. ²⁹Then people will come from east and west, from north and south, and take their places at the banquet in the kingdom of God. ³⁰Indeed, some are last who will be first, and some are first who will be last."

31 At that very hour some Pharisees came and said to him, "Get away from here, for Herod wants to kill you." ³²He said to them, "Go and tell that fox for me,*ᵏ* 'Listen, I am casting out demons and performing cures today and tomorrow, and on the third day I finish my work. ³³Yet today, tomorrow, and the next day I must be on my way, because it is impossible for a prophet to be killed outside of Jerusalem.' ³⁴Jerusalem, Jerusalem, the city that kills the prophets and stones those who are sent to it! How often have I desired to gather your children together as a hen gathers

j 13.22 Gk *He*   *k* 13.32 Gk lacks *for me*

13:10–21 Healing and teaching in a synagogue. 13:10–17 Jesus heals a woman with a spinal disorder on the Sabbath. **13:16** The woman's suffering is described as a form of bondage caused by Satan. Healing is thus liberation. Because she is *a daughter of Abraham*, a Jew, it is especially appropriate to release her from bondage on the Sabbath. **13:18–21** Emphasizing the contrast between small beginnings and large yields, the two parables comment on the release of the woman from her physical disorder. Her healing is evidence for the emergent kingdom of God, as Satan's ability to cause harm is broken. See note on 4:43 and **"Kingdom of God," p. 1772**.

13:22–35 En route to Jerusalem. 13:22 See note on 9:51. **13:28** *Weeping and gnashing of teeth*, an expression of desperation and regret associated with the time of judgment. *Abraham and Isaac, and Jacob*, the patriarchs of Israel. Here Luke links the kingdom of God to future judgment, but see note on 4:43. **13:29** Those who gather from *east and west, from north and south* would include both gentiles and Diaspora Jews. **13:31** The Pharisees are typically portrayed as antagonists of Jesus. Their warning about Herod may suggest that at least some of them are sympathetic to Jesus, consistent with the generally positive depiction of the Pharisees in Acts of the Apostles (Acts 5:33–39; 15:5; 23:6–9). However, given that Herod does not act on a later chance to kill Jesus (Luke 23:6–12), the Pharisees' warning may be an attempt to goad Jesus to greater danger. See **"Pharisees," p. 1756**. **13:33** *I must be on my way.* The Greek term "dei," "it is necessary," implies that coming events in Jerusalem, including Jesus's crucifixion, are part of God's plan. **13:34** Luke counts Jesus among the prophets who meet their deaths in Jerusalem.

her brood under her wings, and you were not willing! [35]See, your house is left to you.[l] And I tell you, you will not see me until the time comes when[m] you say, 'Blessed is the one who comes in the name of the Lord.'"

14 On one occasion when Jesus[n] was going to the house of a leader of the Pharisees to eat a meal on the Sabbath, they were watching him closely. [2]Just then, in front of him, there was a man who had edema. [3]And Jesus asked the experts in the law and Pharisees, "Is it lawful to cure people on the Sabbath or not?" [4]But they were silent. So Jesus[o] took him and healed him and sent him away. [5]Then he said to them, "If one of you has a child[p] or an ox that has fallen into a well, will you not immediately pull it out on a Sabbath day?" [6]And they could not reply to this.

7 When he noticed how the guests chose the places of honor, he told them a parable. [8]"When you are invited by someone to a wedding banquet, do not sit down at the place of honor, in case someone more distinguished than you has been invited by your host, [9]and the host who invited both of you may come and say to you, 'Give this person your place,' and then in disgrace you would start to take the lowest place. [10]But when you are invited, go and sit down at the lowest place, so that when your host comes, he may say to you, 'Friend, move up higher'; then you will be honored in the presence of all who sit at the table with you. [11]For all who exalt themselves will be humbled, and those who humble themselves will be exalted."

12 He said also to the one who had invited him, "When you give a luncheon or a dinner, do not invite your friends or your brothers and sisters or your relatives or rich neighbors, in case they may invite you in return, and you would be repaid. [13]But when you give a banquet, invite the poor, the crippled, the lame, and the blind. [14]And you will be blessed because they cannot repay you, for you will be repaid at the resurrection of the righteous."

15 One of the dinner guests, on hearing this, said to him, "Blessed is anyone who will eat bread in the kingdom of God!" [16]Then Jesus[q] said to him, "Someone gave a great dinner and invited many. [17]At the time for the dinner he sent his slave to say to those who had been invited, 'Come, for everything is ready now.' [18]But they all alike began to make excuses. The first said to him, 'I have bought a piece of land, and I must go out and see it; please accept my regrets.' [19]Another said, 'I have bought five yoke of oxen, and I am going to try them out; please accept my regrets.' [20]Another said, 'I have just been married, and therefore I cannot come.' [21]So the slave returned and reported this to his master. Then the owner of the house became angry and said to his slave, 'Go out at once into the streets and lanes of the town and bring in the poor, the crippled, the blind, and the lame.' [22]And the slave said, 'Sir, what you ordered has been done, and there is still room.' [23]Then the master said to the slave, 'Go out into the roads and lanes, and compel people to come in, so that my house may be filled. [24]For I tell you,[r] none of those who were invited will taste my dinner.'"

25 Now large crowds were traveling with him, and he turned and said to them, [26]"Whoever comes to me and does not hate father and mother, wife and children, brothers and sisters, yes, and even life itself, cannot be my disciple. [27]Whoever does not carry the cross and follow me cannot be my disciple. [28]For

l 13.35 Other ancient authorities add *desolate*
m 13.35 Other ancient authorities lack *the time comes when*
n 14.1 Gk *he* o 14.4 Gk *he* p 14.5 Other ancient authorities read *a donkey* q 14.16 Gk *he* r 14.24 The Greek word for *you* here is plural

14:1–24 Banquets. A meal at the home of a Pharisee is the occasion for a series of teachings linked by the theme of dinner parties. **14:1–6** Compare 13:10–17. **14:7–11** Advice about conduct at banquets reflects the hierarchical structure of dining in the Roman world. **14:11** Straightforward counsel on being a guest introduces a lesson on status reversals. See note on 1:52–53. **14:12–14** The injunction to invite those in need is consistent with Luke's emphasis on sharing goods. **14:15–24** Luke frames the parable of the Great Dinner to advance recurrent themes. Compare Matt. 22:1–10, which emphasizes judgment. **14:17–20** Would-be guests cite property concerns and marital obligations when they decline the invitation. See Luke 14:25–33 and notes on 14:26 and 14:33. **14:21–24** Those first invited refuse the invitation, so the host fills his house with others. Jesus and his followers respond to rejection by bringing their message elsewhere. **14:21** *The poor, the crippled, the blind, and the lame.* Jesus insists on the inclusion of the socially marginalized. See **"The Bible and Social Justice," pp. 2165–67.**
   14:25–35 Discipleship. 14:26 Targeted to male followers, the demand to *hate* close family members

which of you, intending to build a tower, does not first sit down and estimate the cost, to see whether he has enough to complete it? [29]Otherwise, when he has laid a foundation and is not able to finish, all who see it will begin to ridicule him, [30]saying, 'This fellow began to build and was not able to finish.' [31]Or what king, going out to wage war against another king, will not sit down first and consider whether he is able with ten thousand to oppose the one who comes against him with twenty thousand? [32]If he cannot, then while the other is still far away, he sends a delegation and asks for the terms of peace. [33]So therefore, none of you can become my disciple if you do not give up all your possessions.

34 "Salt is good, but if salt has lost its taste,[s] how can its saltiness be restored? [35]It is useful neither for the soil nor for the manure pile; they throw it away. If you have ears to hear, then hear!"

15 Now all the tax collectors and sinners were coming near to listen to him. [2]And the Pharisees and the scribes were grumbling and saying, "This fellow welcomes sinners and eats with them."

3 So he told them this parable: [4]"Which one of you, having a hundred sheep and losing one of them, does not leave the ninety-nine in the wilderness and go after the one that is lost until he finds it? [5]And when he has found it, he lays it on his shoulders and rejoices. [6]And when he comes home, he calls together his friends and neighbors, saying to them, 'Rejoice with me, for I have found my lost sheep.' [7]Just so, I tell you, there will be more joy in heaven over one sinner who repents than over ninety-nine righteous persons who need no repentance.

8 "Or what woman having ten silver coins, if she loses one of them, does not light a lamp, sweep the house, and search carefully until she finds it? [9]And when she has found it, she calls together her friends and neighbors, saying, 'Rejoice with me, for I have found the coin that I had lost.' [10]Just so, I tell you, there is joy in the presence of the angels of God over one sinner who repents."

11 Then Jesus[t] said, "There was a man who had two sons. [12]The younger of them said to his father, 'Father, give me the share of the wealth that will belong to me.' So he divided his assets between them. [13]A few days later the younger son gathered all he had and traveled to a distant region, and there he squandered his wealth in dissolute living. [14]When he had spent everything, a severe famine took place throughout that region, and he began to be in need. [15]So he went and hired himself out to one of the citizens of that region, who sent him to his fields to feed the pigs. [16]He would gladly have filled his stomach[u] with the pods that the pigs were eating, and no one gave him anything. [17]But when he came to his senses he said, 'How many of my father's hired hands have bread enough and to spare, but here I am dying of hunger! [18]I will get up and go to my father, and I will say to him, "Father, I have sinned against heaven and before you; [19]I am no longer worthy to be called your son; treat me like one of your hired hands."' [20]So he set off and went to his father. But while he was still far off, his father saw him and was filled with compassion; he ran and put his arms around him and kissed him. [21]Then the son said to him, 'Father, I have sinned against heaven and before you;

s 14.34 Or *how can it be used for seasoning?*   t 15.11 Gk *he*
u 15.16 Other ancient authorities read *filled himself*

14:33 Disciples are expected to renounce their material goods as well as their families. 14:34–35 Without saltiness, salt is worthless. Unless discipleship is wholehearted, it is worth nothing.

15:1–32 **Lost and found.** In response to complaints that he associates with sinners, Jesus offers three parables that treat repentance as an occasion for rejoicing. 15:3–7 Compare Matt. 18:12–14. Elsewhere Luke warns of calamitous consequences for those who fail to repent. Here he emphasizes divine joy over the repentance of even a single sinner. 15:8–10 The woman looking for a mislaid coin parallels the male shepherd searching for a stray sheep. 15:9 The woman celebrates with female *friends and neighbors*. 15:10 Angelic joy at a sinner's repentance contrasts sharply with the disdainful attitude of the Pharisees and scribes (v. 2) and the resentment of the elder son in the next parable (v. 28). 15:11–32 The parable of the Prodigal Son—as this story is often called—is distinguished not only by its relative length but also by its characterization and narrative development. While the short preceding parables focus on those who search for what is lost, the parable of the Lost Son explores multiple perspectives—that of the son who loses his way, the father who celebrates his return, and the resentful brother who never left home. 15:15 Jews considered pigs unclean. Although not a violation of Torah, feeding pigs would have seemed

I am no longer worthy to be called your son.'^v ^22But the father said to his slaves, 'Quickly, bring out a robe—the best one—and put it on him; put a ring on his finger and sandals on his feet. ^23And get the fatted calf and kill it, and let us eat and celebrate, ^24for this son of mine was dead and is alive again; he was lost and is found!' And they began to celebrate.

25 "Now his elder son was in the field, and as he came and approached the house, he heard music and dancing. ^26He called one of the slaves and asked what was going on. ^27He replied, 'Your brother has come, and your father has killed the fatted calf because he has got him back safe and sound.' ^28Then he became angry and refused to go in. His father came out and began to plead with him. ^29But he answered his father, 'Listen! For all these years I have been working like a slave for you, and I have never disobeyed your command, yet you have never given me even a young goat so that I might celebrate with my friends. ^30But when this son of yours came back, who has devoured your assets with prostitutes, you killed the fatted calf for him!' ^31Then the father^w said to him, 'Son, you are always with me, and all that is mine is yours. ^32But we had to celebrate and rejoice, because this brother of yours was dead and has come to life; he was lost and has been found.'"

16 Then Jesus^x said to the disciples, "There was a rich man who had a manager, and charges were brought to him that this man was squandering his property. ^2So he summoned

him and said to him, 'What is this that I hear about you? Give me an accounting of your management because you cannot be my manager any longer.' ^3Then the manager said to himself, 'What will I do, now that my master is taking the position away from me? I am not strong enough to dig, and I am ashamed to beg. ^4I have decided what to do so that, when I am dismissed as manager, people may welcome me into their homes.' ^5So, summoning his master's debtors one by one, he asked the first, 'How much do you owe my master?' ^6He answered, 'A hundred jugs of olive oil.' He said to him, 'Take your bill, sit down quickly, and make it fifty.' ^7Then he asked another, 'And how much do you owe?' He replied, 'A hundred containers of wheat.' He said to him, 'Take your bill and make it eighty.' ^8And his master commended the dishonest manager because he had acted shrewdly, for the children of this age are more shrewd in dealing with their own generation than are the children of light. ^9And I tell you, make friends for yourselves by means of dishonest wealth^y so that when it is gone they may welcome you into the eternal homes.^z

10 "Whoever is faithful in a very little is faithful also in much, and whoever is dishonest in a very little is dishonest also in much. ^11If, then, you have not been faithful with the dishonest wealth,^a who will entrust to you the true riches? ^12And if you have not been faithful with what

degrading to a Jewish audience. **15:22–24** The father responds to the errant and repentant son not with judgment but with joy. **15:24** *Lost* and *found*, echoing the language of vv. 4, 6, 8, and 9. **15:25–32** Instead of concluding with the father's rejoicing, the parable continues with an emotionally resonant exchange between the father and the stay-at-home son. **15:31** *All that is mine is yours.* The younger son has already received his inheritance; the older son stands to inherit the estate on which he has labored.

16:1–31 Warnings about wealth. 16:1–13 Knowledge of ancient business practices is helpful for understanding details of the parable of the Dishonest Manager. However, the parable's overall message is elusive. **16:1** A household *manager* would run the estate and handle financial affairs. **16:5–7** By altering the account records, the manager cancels a significant portion of debt. His stated goal in reducing debt loads is to curry favor with the debtors, in the hope they might extend hospitality to him when he is forced to leave the rich man's household (v. 4). **16:8** *His master.* Household managers were often enslaved or formerly enslaved. Given that the manager expects to be dismissed rather than sold (vv. 3–4), he may be a freedman. *Dishonest*, or unjust (Gk. "adikos"). *Shrewdly*, or prudently (Gk. "phronimōs"). The master's praise is puzzling, as the manager's rewriting of account records benefited debtors at the expense of the master. Some commentators explain the praise by suggesting that the manager had simply eliminated his own expected share of the debts, yet in this case, it is not clear why he would be described as dishonest or unjust. *The children of this age* versus *the children of light*, an apocalyptic dichotomy shifting interpretation of the parable to the time of judgment. **16:9** *Dishonest*, see note on v. 8. On the unreliability of earthly wealth, compare 12:16–21. **16:10–12** A teaching about the importance of faithful execution of duties, seemingly at odds with the rich man's praise for the manager's dishonest

belongs to another, who will give you what is your own? [13]No slave can serve two masters, for a slave will either hate the one and love the other or be devoted to the one and despise the other. You cannot serve God and wealth."[b]

14 The Pharisees, who were lovers of money, heard all this, and they ridiculed him. [15]So he said to them, "You are those who justify yourselves in the sight of others, but God knows your hearts, for what is prized by humans is an abomination in the sight of God.

16 "The Law and the Prophets were until John came; since then the good news of the kingdom of God is being proclaimed, and everyone tries to enter it by force.[c] [17]But it is easier for heaven and earth to pass away than for one stroke of a letter in the law to be dropped.

18 "Anyone who divorces his wife and marries another commits adultery, and whoever marries a woman divorced from her husband commits adultery.

19 "There was a rich man who was dressed in purple and fine linen and who feasted sumptuously every day. [20]And at his gate lay a poor man named Lazarus, covered with sores, [21]who longed to satisfy his hunger with what fell from the rich man's table; even the dogs would come and lick his sores. [22]The poor man died and was carried away by the angels to be with Abraham.[d] The rich man also died and was buried. [23]In Hades, where he was being tormented, he lifted up his eyes and saw Abraham far away with Lazarus by his side.[e] [24]He called out, 'Father Abraham, have mercy on me, and send Lazarus to dip the tip of his finger in water and cool my tongue, for I am in agony in these flames.' [25]But Abraham said, 'Child, remember that during your lifetime you received your good things and Lazarus in like manner evil things, but now he is comforted here, and you are in agony. [26]Besides all this, between you and us a great chasm has been fixed, so that those who might want to pass from here to you cannot do so, and no one can cross from there to us.' [27]He said, 'Then I beg you, father, to send him to my father's house—[28]for I have five brothers—that he may warn them, so that they will not also come into this place of torment.' [29]Abraham replied, 'They have Moses and the prophets; they should listen to them.' [30]He said, 'No, father Abraham, but if someone from the dead goes to them, they will repent.' [31]He said to him, 'If they do not listen to Moses and the prophets, neither will they be convinced even if someone rises from the dead.'"

17 Jesus[f] said to his disciples, "Occasions for sin[g] are bound to come, but woe to anyone through whom they come! [2]It would be better for you if a millstone were hung around your neck and you were thrown into the sea than for you to cause one of these little ones to sin.[h] [3]Be on your guard! If a brother or sister sins, you must rebuke the offender, and if there is repentance, you must forgive. [4]And if the same person sins against you seven times a day and turns back to you seven times and says, 'I repent,' you must forgive."

5 The apostles said to the Lord, "Increase our faith!" [6]The Lord replied, "If you had faith

b 16.13 Gk *mammon*   c 16.16 Or *everyone is strongly urged to enter it*   d 16.22 Gk *to Abraham's bosom*   e 16.23 Gk *in his bosom*   f 17.1 Gk *He*   g 17.1 Or *stumbling*   h 17.2 Or *stumble*

accounting. **16:13** The relevance of this aphorism to the parable of the Dishonest Manager is debatable. It is, however, a succinct statement of the Lukan theme that wealth impedes devotion to God. **16:14-18** Luke's characterization of the Pharisees as *lovers of money* serves as a segue to several short sayings. **16:14** Despite Luke's depiction, the Pharisees enjoyed a reputation for rejecting luxuries. **16:16** *The Law and the Prophets were until John came.* John the Baptist represents the culmination of one age, defined by Torah and the prophets, while Jesus's proclamation of the kingdom of God ushers in a new age; see note on 4:43. **16:18** A prohibition against remarriage after divorce; compare Mark 10:2–12 and 1 Cor. 7:10–13. *Anyone who divorces his wife.* According to Torah, divorce is initiated by the husband, not the wife. **16:19-31** The rich man and Lazarus, an extended parable dramatizing the status reversals of 6:20–25. **16:23** *Hades*, Greek term for the place of the dead (see 10:15), here explicitly a place of punishment. **16:24** The rich man mentions Lazarus's name. He was aware of the poor man's suffering all along yet did nothing. **16:25** *During your lifetime you received your good things.* Along with emphasizing the urgency of feeding the hungry, the parable amplifies a generalized warning to the wealthy. **16:29** *Moses and the prophets* stressed the obligation of sharing resources with those in need. **16:31** The parable takes a Christological turn. Although Jesus will be raised from the dead, many will reject his message.

17:1-10 Teachings for disciples. 17:1-5 Community members are to hold each other accountable, to repent, and to forgive. **17:2** *Little ones*, others in the community. **17:6** On the prodigious growth of

the size of a*ⁱ* mustard seed, you could say to this mulberry tree, 'Be uprooted and planted in the sea,' and it would obey you.

7 "Who among you would say to your slave who has just come in from plowing or tending sheep in the field, 'Come here at once and take your place at the table'? ⁸Would you not rather say to him, 'Prepare supper for me; put on your apron and serve me while I eat and drink; later you may eat and drink'? ⁹Do you thank the slave for doing what was commanded? ¹⁰So you also, when you have done all that you were ordered to do, say, 'We are worthless slaves; we have done only what we ought to have done!'"

11 On the way to Jerusalem Jesus*ʲ* was going through the region between Samaria and Galilee. ¹²As he entered a village, ten men with a skin disease approached him. Keeping their distance, ¹³they called out, saying, "Jesus, Master, have mercy on us!" ¹⁴When he saw them, he said to them, "Go and show yourselves to the priests." And as they went, they were made clean. ¹⁵Then one of them, when he saw that he was healed, turned back, praising God with a loud voice. ¹⁶He prostrated himself at Jesus's*ᵏ* feet and thanked him. And he was a Samaritan. ¹⁷Then Jesus asked, "Were not ten made clean? So where are the other nine? ¹⁸Did none of them return to give glory to God except this foreigner?" ¹⁹Then he said to him, "Get up and go on your way; your faith has made you well."

20 Once Jesus*ˡ* was asked by the Pharisees when the kingdom of God was coming, and he answered, "The kingdom of God is not coming with things that can be observed, ²¹nor will they say, 'Look, here it is!' or 'There it is!' For, in fact, the kingdom of God is among*ᵐ* you."

22 Then he said to the disciples, "The days are coming when you will long to see one of the days of the Son of Man, and you will not see it. ²³They will say to you, 'Look there!' or 'Look here!' Do not go; do not set off in pursuit. ²⁴For as the lightning flashes and lights up the sky from one side to the other, so will the Son of Man be in his day.*ⁿ* ²⁵But first he must endure much suffering and be rejected by this generation. ²⁶Just as it was in the days of Noah, so, too, it will be in the days of the Son of Man. ²⁷They were eating and drinking and marrying and being given in marriage until the day Noah entered the ark, and the flood came and destroyed all of them. ²⁸Likewise, just as it was in the days of Lot, they were eating and drinking, buying and selling, planting and building, ²⁹but on the day that Lot left Sodom it rained fire and sulfur from heaven and destroyed all of them; ³⁰it will be like that on the day that the Son of Man is revealed. ³¹On that day, anyone on the housetop who has belongings in the house must not come down to take them away, and likewise anyone in the field must not turn back. ³²Remember Lot's wife. ³³Those who try to make their life secure will lose it, but those who lose their life will keep it. ³⁴I tell

i 17.6 Gk *faith as a grain of*   *j* 17.11 Gk *he*   *k* 17.16 Gk *his*   *l* 17.20 Gk *he*   *m* 17.21 Or *within*   *n* 17.24 Other ancient authorities lack *in his day*

the mustard seed, see 13:19. **17:7–10** The vignette depicts a small-scale farmer who relies on a single enslaved laborer for both agricultural and domestic tasks. Readers may question the passage's apparent acceptance of the arduous and thankless labor exacted from an enslaved laborer. **17:7** *Who among you would say to your slave.* The formulation is troubling, as Jesus is speaking to the apostles. **17:10** *We are worthless slaves.* See note on 1:38. The U.S. history of enslavement makes it difficult for many readers to willingly adopt this posture.

17:11–19:27 The final approach to Jerusalem. See note on 9:51.

17:11–19 Healing of men with a skin disease. 17:11 *The region between Samaria and Galilee.* The geography is confused. **17:14** *Show yourselves to the priests.* See note on 5:14. **17:16** *A Samaritan.* See note on 9:52–53.

17:20–37 The kingdom of God and the coming of the Son of Man. 17:20–21 The coming of the kingdom of God is not an observable event. Through Jesus's preaching and healing, the kingdom of God is an incipient reality; see note on 4:43. **17:22–25** Jesus warns his disciples against overconfident pronouncements about *the days of the Son of Man* (v. 22). **17:24** The coming of the Son of Man will be a cosmic event, evident to all. **17:25** It is necessary that Jesus *must endure much suffering*; on Greek "dei," see note on 13:33. **17:26–27** *In the days of Noah* (v. 26), God destroyed the earth by flood because of human corruption (Gen. 6:5–8). **17:28–29** *In the days of Lot* (v. 28), God destroyed Sodom because of the behavior of its inhabitants (Gen. 19:12–25). **17:30** The coming of the Son of Man will be accompanied by cataclysmic upheaval. **17:32** As she glanced back at Sodom, Lot's wife turned into a pillar of salt (Gen. 19:26). **17:33** Compare Luke 9:24. **17:34–35** Judgment will be swift and decisive, with no

you, on that night there will be two in one bed;
one will be taken and the other left. 35 There
will be two women grinding meal together;
one will be taken and the other left."[o] 37 Then
they asked him, "Where, Lord?" He said to
them, "Where the corpse is, there the eagles
will gather."

18 Then Jesus[p] told them a parable about
their need to pray always and not to
lose heart. 2 He said, "In a certain city there
was a judge who neither feared God nor had
respect for people. 3 In that city there was a
widow who kept coming to him and saying,
'Grant me justice against my accuser.' 4 For
a while he refused, but later he said to himself, 'Though I have no fear of God and no
respect for anyone, 5 yet because this widow
keeps bothering me, I will grant her justice,
so that she may not wear me out by continually coming.' "[q] 6 And the Lord said, "Listen
to what the unjust judge says. 7 And will not
God grant justice to his chosen ones who
cry to him day and night? Will he delay long
in helping them? 8 I tell you, he will quickly
grant justice to them. And yet, when the Son
of Man comes, will he find faith on earth?"

9 He also told this parable to some who
trusted in themselves that they were righteous and regarded others with contempt:
10 "Two men went up to the temple to pray,
one a Pharisee and the other a tax collector. 11 The Pharisee, standing by himself, was
praying thus, 'God, I thank you that I am not
like other people: thieves, rogues, adulterers,
or even like this tax collector. 12 I fast twice a
week; I give a tenth of all my income.' 13 But
the tax collector, standing far off, would not
even lift up his eyes to heaven but was beating
his breast and saying, 'God, be merciful to me,
a sinner!' 14 I tell you, this man went down to
his home justified rather than the other, for
all who exalt themselves will be humbled, but
all who humble themselves will be exalted."

15 People were bringing even infants to him
that he might touch them, and when the disciples saw it, they sternly ordered them not
to do it. 16 But Jesus called for them and said,
"Let the children come to me, and do not stop
them, for it is to such as these that the kingdom of God belongs. 17 Truly I tell you, whoever does not receive the kingdom of God as a
little child will never enter it."

18 A certain ruler asked him, "Good Teacher, what must I do to inherit eternal life?"
19 Jesus said to him, "Why do you call me good?
No one is good but God alone. 20 You know
the commandments: 'You shall not commit
adultery. You shall not murder. You shall not
steal. You shall not bear false witness. Honor
your father and mother.' " 21 He replied, "I have
kept all these since my youth." 22 When Jesus
heard this, he said to him, "There is still one
thing lacking. Sell all that you own and distribute the money[r] to the poor, and you will
have treasure in heaven; then come, follow
me." 23 But when he heard this, he became
sad, for he was very rich. 24 Jesus looked at him[s]
and said, "How hard it is for those who have

o 17.35 Other ancient authorities add 17.36, *"Two will be in the field; one will be taken and the other left."* *p* 18.1 Gk *he*
q 18.5 Or *so that she may not finally come and slap me in the face*
r 18.22 Gk lacks *the money* *s* 18.24 Other ancient authorities read *saw that he had become sad*

middle ground. **17:37** An enigmatic saying. *Eagles* may hint that the day of the Son of Man will bring widespread death.

18:1–14 Two parables on prayer. See note on 1:13. **18:1** As a follow-up to the bleak depiction of the coming of the Son of Man, Jesus encourages his listeners *not to lose heart* as they await that day. **18:5** *Wear me out*, or (alternative translation), "slap me in the face," terminology borrowed from boxing. **18:7** On mode of argumentation, see note on Luke 11:11–13. **18:8** *When the Son of Man comes*, connecting the parable to previous sayings about the day of the Son of Man (17:22–37). **18:10** *Tax collector*, see note on 5:27. **18:12** *I fast twice a week*, consistent with Luke's depiction of Pharisees (5:33). *A tenth of all my income*, see note on 11:42. In fasting and tithing, the Pharisee exceeds the demands of Torah. **18:13** *Beating his breast*, a sign of repentance. **18:14** *Justified.* Because of his humble plea for mercy (v. 13), the tax collector is considered righteous by God. *Humbled* and *exalted*, compare 14:11.

18:15–30 The kingdom of God. A series of sayings addressing what it means to belong to, to receive, or to enter the kingdom of God; see note on 4:43. **18:16** Just as the kingdom of God belongs to the poor (6:20), it belongs to children. **18:17** Unlike the self-righteous Pharisee, reliant on his own merit (v. 12), or the rich ruler, reliant on his possessions (vv. 22–24), those who are radically dependent on God and community are able to *receive the kingdom of God as a little child*. **18:22–25** Jesus's exchange with the rich ruler revisits two closely related themes: the importance of relying on God rather than wealth and

wealth to enter the kingdom of God! [25]Indeed, it is easier for a camel to go through the eye of a needle than for someone who is rich to enter the kingdom of God."

26 Those who heard it said, "Then who can be saved?" [27]He replied, "What is impossible for mortals is possible for God."

28 Then Peter said, "Look, we have left our homes and followed you." [29]And he said to them, "Truly I tell you, there is no one who has left house or wife or brothers or parents or children for the sake of the kingdom of God [30]who will not get back very much more in this age and in the age to come eternal life."

31 Then he took the twelve aside and said to them, "Look, we are going up to Jerusalem, and everything that is written about the Son of Man by the prophets will be accomplished. [32]For he will be handed over to the gentiles, and he will be mocked and insulted and spat upon. [33]After they have flogged him, they will kill him, and on the third day he will rise again." [34]But they understood nothing about all these things; in fact, what he said was hidden from them, and they did not grasp what was said.

35 As he approached Jericho, a blind man was sitting by the roadside begging. [36]When he heard a crowd going by, he asked what was happening. [37]They told him, "Jesus of Nazareth[t] is passing by." [38]Then he shouted, "Jesus, Son of David, have mercy on me!" [39]Those who were in front sternly ordered him to be quiet, but he shouted even more loudly, "Son of David, have mercy on me!" [40]Jesus stood still and ordered the man to be brought to him, and when he came near, he asked him, [41]"What do you want me to do for you?" He said, "Lord, let me see again." [42]Jesus said to him, "Receive your sight; your faith has saved you." [43]Immediately he regained his sight and followed him, glorifying God, and all the people, when they saw it, praised God.

19 He entered Jericho and was passing through it. [2]A man was there named Zacchaeus; he was a chief tax collector and was rich. [3]He was trying to see who Jesus was, but on account of the crowd he could not, because he was short in stature. [4]So he ran ahead and climbed a sycamore tree to see him, because he was going to pass that way. [5]When Jesus came to the place, he looked up and said to him, "Zacchaeus, hurry and come down, for I must stay at your house today." [6]So he hurried down and was happy to welcome him. [7]All who saw it began to grumble and said, "He has gone to be the guest of one who is a sinner." [8]Zacchaeus stood there and said to the Lord, "Look, half of my possessions, Lord, I will give to the poor, and if I have defrauded anyone of anything, I will pay back four times as much." [9]Then Jesus said to him, "Today salvation has come to this house, because he, too, is a son of Abraham. [10]For the Son of Man came to seek out and to save the lost."

11 As they were listening to this, he went on to tell a parable, because he was near Jerusalem and because they supposed that the kingdom of God was to appear immediately. [12]So he said, "A nobleman went to a distant region

t 18.37 Gk *the Nazorean*

the imperative to share possessions with others. See notes on 12:13–34. **18:28–30** Jesus's response to Peter emphasizes the importance of leaving not only material goods but also family. **18:28** See note on 14:26. The instruction to leave one's wife is especially startling. Whether women should also leave their husbands is not addressed.

18:31–19:10 Jericho. Jesus's final stop before Jerusalem. **18:31** *Up to Jerusalem.* See note on 9:51. Without mentioning particular prophetic texts, Jesus reminds the twelve that *everything that is written about the Son of Man by the prophets will be accomplished.* **18:32** *Handed over to the gentiles.* See 23:1–2; Acts 4:25–28. **18:38** As Jesus approaches Jerusalem, he is again identified as *Son of David*; see note on Luke 1:32. **19:1–10** Unlike the rich ruler (18:18–25), whom Jesus instructs to sell all his possessions, Zacchaeus is applauded for making restitution for fraud and for sharing his possessions. See notes on 3:10–14 and 12:13–34. **19:2** *Tax collector,* see note on 5:27. **19:7** *Sinner,* see note on 5:30–32. **19:10** See notes on 15:1–32.

19:11–27 The parable of the Pounds. A parallel to the Matthean parable of the Talents (Matt. 25:14–30), which Luke has fused with a story about a newly installed king who punishes those who had opposed him (Luke 19:12, 14–15a, 27). Interpretation of this difficult parable is debated. Immediately following Jesus's interaction with Zacchaeus, the parable may be read as a charge to use one's resources to advance the mission. It is also a caution to those who anticipate the imminent establishment of the kingdom of God (v. 11); see note on 4:43. **19:12** *A nobleman went to a distant country to receive royal*

to receive royal power for himself and then return. [13]He summoned ten of his slaves and gave them ten pounds and said to them, 'Do business with these until I come back.' [14]But the citizens of his country hated him and sent a delegation after him, saying, 'We do not want this man to rule over us.' [15]When he returned, having received royal power, he ordered these slaves to whom he had given the money to be summoned so that he might find out what they had gained by doing business. [16]The first came forward and said, 'Lord, your pound has made ten more pounds.' [17]He said to him, 'Well done, good slave! Because you have been trustworthy in a very small thing, take charge of ten cities.' [18]Then the second came, saying, 'Lord, your pound has made five pounds.' [19]He said to him, 'And you, rule over five cities.' [20]Then the other came, saying, 'Lord, here is your pound. I wrapped it up in a piece of cloth, [21]for I was afraid of you, because you are a harsh man; you take what you did not deposit and reap what you did not sow.' [22]He said to him, 'I will judge you by your own words, you wicked slave! You knew, did you, that I was a harsh man, taking what I did not deposit and reaping what I did not sow? [23]Why, then, did you not put my money into the bank? Then when I returned, I could have collected it with interest.' [24]He said to the bystanders, 'Take the pound from him and give it to the one who has ten pounds.' [25](And they said to him, 'Lord, he has ten pounds!') [26]I tell you, to all those who have, more will be given, but from those who have nothing, even what they have will be taken away. [27]But as for these enemies of mine who did not want me to rule over them—bring them here and slaughter them in my presence.'"

[28] After he had said this, he went on ahead, going up to Jerusalem.

[29] When he had come near Bethphage and Bethany, at the place called the Mount of Olives, he sent two of the disciples, [30]saying, "Go into the village ahead of you, and as you enter it you will find tied there a colt that has never been ridden. Untie it and bring it here. [31]If anyone asks you, 'Why are you untying it?' just say this, 'The Lord needs it.'" [32]So those who were sent departed and found it as he had told them. [33]As they were untying the colt, its owners asked them, "Why are you untying the colt?" [34]They said, "The Lord needs it." [35]Then they brought it to Jesus, and after throwing their cloaks on the colt, they set Jesus on it. [36]As he rode along, people kept spreading their cloaks on the road. [37]Now as he was approaching the path down from the Mount of Olives, the whole multitude of the disciples began to praise God joyfully with a loud voice for all the deeds of power that they had seen, [38]saying,

"Blessed is the king
   who comes in the name of the Lord!
Peace in heaven,
   and glory in the highest heaven!"

[39]Some of the Pharisees in the crowd said to him, "Teacher, order your disciples to stop." [40]He answered, "I tell you, if these were silent, the stones would shout out."

[41] As he came near and saw the city, he wept over it, [42]saying, "If you, even you, had only recognized on this day the things that make for peace! But now they are hidden from your eyes. [43]Indeed, the days will come upon you when your enemies will set up ramparts around you and surround you and hem you in on every side. [44]They will crush you to the ground, you and your children within you, and they will not leave within you one stone upon another, because you

---

power. The parable reflects power dynamics in the Roman Empire. Herod the Great had traveled to Rome to achieve recognition of his kingship. **19:14** A delegation of Jews had protested the installation of Herod Archelaus as ruler. **19:16–18** The appointment of a king's slaves to positions of power may strike modern readers as implausible. However, it was not unusual for formerly enslaved members of the household of Caesar to wield considerable authority. **19:27** Just as the enemies of the returning king are executed, those who campaign against Jesus can expect harsh judgment.

19:28–48 The entry into Jerusalem. 19:28 An anticipated turning point in the narrative. See note on 9:51. **19:29–40** Jesus's approach to Jerusalem is staged as political pageantry. **19:38** *Blessed is the king.* In order to portray Jesus as a king entering a royal city, Luke emends the text of Ps. 118:26, "Blessed is the one who comes in the name of the LORD." *Peace in heaven.* See note on 2:14. **19:39** The final reference to the Pharisees in Luke. On their reappearance in Acts, see note on 13:31. **19:41–44** Jesus's lament incorporates fleeting allusions to scriptural predictions of destruction. By the time Luke composed his Gospel, Jerusalem had been destroyed in the Jewish War, a military loss Luke interpreted as God's judgment against those who failed to recognize Jesus. See **"Jerusalem in Luke–Acts," p. 1805**.

did not recognize the time of your visitation from God."[u]

45 Then he entered the temple and began to drive out those who were selling things[v] there, [46]and he said, "It is written,

'My house shall be a house of prayer,'

but you have made it a den of robbers."

47 Every day he was teaching in the temple. The chief priests, the scribes, and the leaders of the people kept looking for a way to kill him, [48]but they did not find anything they could do, for all the people were spellbound by what they heard.

20 One day as he was teaching the people in the temple and proclaiming the good news, the chief priests and the scribes came with the elders [2]and said to him, "Tell us, by what authority are you doing these things? Who is it who gave you this authority?" [3]He answered them, "I will also ask you a question, and you tell me: [4]Did the baptism of John come from heaven, or was it of human origin?" [5]They discussed it with one another, saying, "If we say, 'From heaven,' he will say, 'Why did you not believe him?' [6]But if we say, 'Of human origin,' all the people will stone us, for they are convinced that John was a prophet." [7]So they answered that they did not know where it came from. [8]Then Jesus said to them, "Neither will I tell you by what authority I am doing these things."

9 He began to tell the people this parable: "A man planted a vineyard and leased it to tenants and went away for a long time. [10]When the season came, he sent a slave to the tenants in order that they might give him his share of the produce of the vineyard, but the tenants

beat him and sent him away empty-handed. [11]Next he sent another slave; that one also they beat and insulted and sent away empty-handed. [12]And he sent still a third; this one also they wounded and threw out. [13]Then the owner of the vineyard said, 'What shall I do? I will send my beloved son; perhaps they will respect him.' [14]But when the tenants saw him, they discussed it among themselves and said, 'This is the heir; let us kill him so that the inheritance may be ours.' [15]So they threw him out of the vineyard and killed him. What then will the owner of the vineyard do to them? [16]He will come and destroy those tenants and give the vineyard to others." When they heard this, they said, "Heaven forbid!" [17]But he looked at them and said, "What then does this text mean:

'The stone that the builders rejected
      has become the cornerstone'?[w]

[18]"Everyone who falls on that stone will be broken to pieces, and it will crush anyone on whom it falls." [19]When the scribes and chief priests realized that he had told this parable against them, they wanted to lay hands on him at that very hour, but they feared the people.

20 So they watched him and sent spies who pretended to be honest, in order to trap him by what he said and then to hand him over to the jurisdiction and authority of the governor. [21]So they asked him, "Teacher, we know that you are right in what you say and teach, and you show deference to no one but teach the way of God in accordance with truth. [22]Is it lawful for us to pay tribute to Caesar or not?"

u 19.44 Gk lacks *from God*   v 19.45 Other ancient authorities add *in it and those who were buying things*   w 20.17 Or *keystone* (in an arch)

19:45–46 Luke's brief account omits Mark's dramatic detail, including the overturning of the money changers' tables (Mark 11:15–17). **19:47–48** The temple serves as the location for Jesus's teaching ministry in Jerusalem, which extends for an unspecified period of time. Because Jesus's teaching is popular with *the people* (v. 48), the authorities are stymied in their desire to eliminate him.
  20:1–21:4 Controversies. Jesus's antagonists attempt to entrap him. **20:1–8** As the religious leaders challenge Jesus's authority, his question about John the Baptist puts them on the defensive. **20:6** The political climate of Jerusalem is so volatile that the religious leaders fear being stoned. *The people* serve as a buffer between Jesus and the hostile leaders. **20:9–19** The parable of the Vineyard. In the Roman world, many estates were owned by absentee landlords and farmed by tenants. But in Israelite tradition, "the vineyard of the LORD of hosts is the house of Israel" (Isa. 5:7). **20:10–12** Enslaved people in the Roman world had few protections against physical violence. **20:13** The vineyard owner expects that his son will be exempt from the violence regularly endured by the enslaved. *My beloved son.* See 3:22. **20:17** A quotation from Ps. 118:22. Acts 4:11 identifies Jesus as the rejected stone that becomes a cornerstone. **20:19** Provoked because they understand the parable as an indictment of their murderous intent, *the scribes and chief priests* are again constrained by fear of *the people*. **20:20–26** In Acts, Luke refers to the failed revolt by Judas the Galilean in 6 CE, a rebellion triggered by a refusal to pay taxes

23But he perceived their craftiness and said to them, 24"Show me a denarius. Whose head and whose title does it bear?" They said, "Caesar's." 25He said to them, "Then give to Caesar the things that are Caesar's and to God the things that are God's." 26And they were not able in the presence of the people to trap him by what he said, and being amazed by his answer they became silent.

27 Some Sadducees, those who say there is no resurrection, came to him 28and asked him a question: "Teacher, Moses wrote for us that if a man's brother dies leaving a wife but no children, the man* shall marry the widow and raise up children for his brother. 29Now there were seven brothers; the first married a woman and died childless; 30then the second* 31and the third married her, and so in the same way all seven died childless. 32Finally the woman also died. 33In the resurrection, therefore, whose wife will the woman be? For the seven had married her."

34 Jesus said to them, "Those who belong to this age marry and are given in marriage, 35but those who are considered worthy of a place in that age and in the resurrection from the dead neither marry nor are given in marriage. 36Indeed, they cannot die anymore, because they are like angels and are children of God, being children of the resurrection. 37And the fact that the dead are raised Moses himself showed, in the story about the bush, where he speaks of the Lord as the God of Abraham, the God of Isaac, and the God of Jacob. 38Now he is God not of the dead but of the living, for to him all of them are alive." 39Then some of the scribes answered, "Teacher, you have spoken well."

40For they no longer dared to ask him another question.

41 Then he said to them, "How can they say that the Messiah* is David's son? 42For David himself says in the book of Psalms,

'The Lord said to my Lord,
"Sit at my right hand
43until I make your enemies a footstool for
your feet."'

44"David thus calls him Lord, so how can he be his son?"

45 In the hearing of all the people he said to the disciples, 46"Beware of the scribes who like to walk around in long robes and who love respectful greetings in the marketplaces and the best seats in the synagogues and places of honor at banquets. 47They devour widows' houses and for the sake of appearance say long prayers. They will receive the greater condemnation."

21 He looked up and saw rich people putting their gifts into the treasury; 2he also saw a poor widow put in two small copper coins. 3He said, "Truly I tell you, this poor widow has put in more than all of them, 4for all of them have contributed out of their abundance, but she out of her poverty has put in all she had to live on."

5 When some were speaking about the temple, how it was adorned with beautiful stones and gifts dedicated to God, he said, 6"As for these things that you see, the days will come when not one stone will be left upon another; all will be thrown down."

7 They asked him, "Teacher, when will this

x 20.28 Gk *his brother* y 20.30 Other ancient authorities add *married the woman, and this one died childless,* z 20.41 Or *the Christ*

(Acts 5:37). The question about taxes was thus potentially explosive. Jesus placates popular sentiment against the system of taxation while avoiding advocacy for behavior that would have been seen as lawless by Rome. In the trial before Pilate, Jesus's opponents lie about his response (Luke 23:2). **20:27–40** In their only appearance in Luke, the Sadducees pose a question about the resurrection, which they reject (cf. Acts 4:1–2; 23:6–10). **20:28–32** The scenario posed by the Sadducees presupposes the tradition of Levirate marriage, in which a childless widow would marry her late husband's brother (Deut. 25:5–6). Levirate marriage was no longer the custom among Jews in the Roman Empire. **20:36** Suggesting that those raised from the dead *are like angels*, Jesus baits the Sadducees, who rejected teachings about angels. **20:37** For the Sadducees, only Torah was recognized as Scripture. Jesus cleverly cites Exod. 3:6 as warrant for believing in the resurrection. **20:41–44** As the Messiah, Jesus can rightly be called Son of David (see note on Luke 1:32), yet he is nonetheless greater than his ancestor David. See **"Jewish Messianic Ideas," p. 1783. 20:47** *They devour widows' houses.* They defraud widows of their property.

21:5–38 Eschatological warnings. By the time Luke writes, Jerusalem lay in ruins, the temple destroyed. Luke makes clear that the cataclysmic events of the Jewish War should not be confused with cosmic signs of the end time. At the same time, he emphasizes the nearness of the kingdom of God. **21:7–8** Jesus warns against following those who assume his mantle only to announce falsely the

be, and what will be the sign that this is about to take place?" ⁸And he said, "Beware that you are not led astray, for many will come in my name and say, 'I am he!'ᵃ and, 'The time is near!'ᵇ Do not go after them.

9 "When you hear of wars and insurrections, do not be terrified, for these things must take place first, but the end will not follow immediately." ¹⁰Then he said to them, "Nation will rise against nation and kingdom against kingdom; ¹¹there will be great earthquakes and in various places famines and plagues, and there will be dreadful portents and great signs from heaven.

12 "But before all this occurs, they will arrest you and persecute you; they will hand you over to synagogues and prisons, and you will be brought before kings and governors because of my name. ¹³This will give you an opportunity to testify. ¹⁴So make up your minds not to prepare your defense in advance, ¹⁵for I will give you wordsᶜ and a wisdom that none of your opponents will be able to withstand or contradict. ¹⁶You will be betrayed even by parents and siblings, by relatives and friends, and they will put some of you to death. ¹⁷You will be hated by all because of my name. ¹⁸But not a hair of your head will perish. ¹⁹By your endurance you will gain your souls.

20 "When you see Jerusalem surrounded by armies, then know that its desolation has come near.ᵈ ²¹Then those in Judea must flee to the mountains, and those inside the city must leave it, and those out in the country must not enter it, ²²for these are days of vengeance, as a fulfillment of all that is written. ²³Woe to those who are pregnant and to those who are nursing infants in those days! For there will be great distress on the earth and wrath against this people; ²⁴they will fall by the edge of the sword and be taken away as captives among all nations, and Jerusalem will be trampled on by the nations, until the times of the nations are fulfilled.

25 "There will be signs in the sun, the moon, and the stars and on the earth distress among nations confused by the roaring of the sea and the waves. ²⁶People will faint from fear and foreboding of what is coming upon the world, for the powers of the heavens will be shaken. ²⁷Then they will see 'the Son of Man coming in a cloud' with power and great glory. ²⁸Now when these things begin to take place, stand up and raise your heads, because your redemption is drawing near."ᵉ

29 Then he told them a parable: "Look at the fig tree and all the trees; ³⁰as soon as they sprout leaves you can see for yourselves and know that summer is already near. ³¹So also, when you see these things taking place, you know that the kingdom of God is near. ³²Truly I tell you, this generation will not pass away until all things have taken place. ³³Heaven and earth will pass away, but my words will not pass away.

34 "Be on guard so that your hearts are not weighed down with dissipation and drunkenness and the worries of this life and that day does not catch you unexpectedly, ³⁵like a trap. For it will come upon all who live on the face of the whole earth. ³⁶Be alert at all times, praying that you may have the strength to escape all these things that will take place and to stand before the Son of Man."

37 Every day he was teaching in the temple, and at night he would go out and spend the night on the Mount of Olives, as it was called. ³⁸And all the people would get up early in the morning to listen to him in the temple.

a 21.8 Gk *I am*   b 21.8 Or *at hand*   c 21.15 Gk *a mouth*
d 21.20 Or *is at hand*   e 21.28 Or *at hand*

arrival of the end time. **21:8** *I am he*, literally "I am." See note on John 4:26. **21:11** The *dreadful portents and great signs from heaven* at the end time will be evident for the entire world. **21:12–13** A preview of the kinds of persecutions Luke narrates in Acts—each of which will be *an opportunity to testify* (v. 13). **21:20–24** Luke brings out the terror and suffering of war. See note on 19:41–44. **21:24** *Taken away as captives among all nations*. Compare Ezek. 32:9. Many of those captured in the Jewish War were paraded as the spoils of battle through the streets of Rome. Many more were enslaved and sold. Luke understands his community to live in *the times of the nations*—the period of time between the fall of Jerusalem and the cosmic events signaling the return of the Son of Man. **21:25–28** See notes on Luke 17:20–37. **21:31** *When you see these things taking place*. Luke anticipates that some in his audience may survive to witness the coming of the Son of Man. See also vv. 28, 32, 36. **21:36** *To stand before the Son of Man*, when he returns as cosmic judge. **21:37** *Every day he was teaching in the temple*, the site whose destruction he predicts.

22 Now the Festival of Unleavened Bread, which is called the Passover, was near. [2]The chief priests and the scribes were looking for a way to put Jesus[f] to death, for they were afraid of the people.

3 Then Satan entered into Judas called Iscariot, who was one of the twelve; [4]he went away and conferred with the chief priests and officers of the temple police about how he might betray him to them. [5]They were greatly pleased and agreed to give him money. [6]So he consented and began to look for an opportunity to betray him to them when no crowd was present.

7 Then came the day of Unleavened Bread, on which the Passover lamb had to be sacrificed. [8]So Jesus[g] sent Peter and John, saying, "Go and prepare the Passover meal for us that we may eat it." [9]They asked him, "Where do you want us to make preparations for it?" [10]"Listen," he said to them, "when you have entered the city, a man carrying a jar of water will meet you; follow him into the house he enters [11]and say to the owner of the house, 'The teacher asks you, "Where is the guest room, where I may eat the Passover with my disciples?"' [12]He will show you a large room upstairs, already furnished. Make preparations for us there." [13]So they went and found everything as he had told them, and they prepared the Passover meal.

14 When the hour came, he took his place at the table, and the apostles with him. [15]He said to them, "I have eagerly desired to eat this Passover with you before I suffer, [16]for I tell you, I will not eat it[b] until it is fulfilled in the kingdom of God." [17]Then he took a cup, and after giving thanks he said, "Take this and divide it among yourselves, [18]for I tell you that from now on I will not drink of the fruit of the vine until the kingdom of God comes." [19]Then he took a loaf of bread, and when he had given thanks he broke it and gave it to them, saying, "This is my body, which is given for you. Do this in remembrance of me." [20]And he did the same with the cup after supper, saying, "This cup that is poured out for you is the new covenant in my blood.[i] [21]But see, the one who betrays me is with me, and his hand is on the table. [22]For the Son of Man is going as it has been determined, but woe to that one by whom he is betrayed!" [23]Then they began to ask one another which one of them it could be who would do this.

24 A dispute also arose among them as to which one of them was to be regarded as the greatest. [25]But he said to them, "The kings of the gentiles lord it over them, and those in authority over them are called benefactors. [26]But not so with you; rather, the greatest among you must become like the youngest and the leader like one who serves. [27]For who

f 22.2 Gk *him*   g 22.8 Gk *he*   h 22.16 Other ancient authorities read *never eat it again*   i 22.20 Other ancient authorities lack, in whole or in part, 22.19b–20 (*which is given . . . in my blood*)

22:1–23:56 The Passion Narrative. See **"Passion Narrative," p. 1794.** Luke introduces additional material to the outline of Mark's passion narrative—the Last Supper, arrest, trial before Pilate, and crucifixion—developing distinctive themes. The hearing before Herod Antipas (23:6–12), for example, is unique to Luke. Luke stresses Jesus's innocence (23:4, 14–15, 22, 47). Suggesting that Satan is at work in the betrayal of Jesus (22:3, 31, 53), Luke nonetheless represents Jesus's death as God's will (22:42). A crowd of people accompanies Jesus to the site of crucifixion, women as well as men (23:27); one of the men crucified alongside him even attests to his innocence (23:41). At the last, rather than crying out that he has been abandoned by God (Mark 15:34), Jesus entrusts his spirit to his Father (Luke 23:46).

22:1–6 Plotting against Jesus. 22:1 See **"Passover," p. 99. 22:2** *They were afraid of the people.* See note on 20:6. **22:3** See note on 4:13. Although Satan's power has been broken (see note on 10:17–18), he retains the ability to test Jesus's followers (22:31). **22:6** Because the people of Jerusalem support Jesus, he could only be arrested *when no crowd was present.*

22:7–38 The Passover meal. See **"Passover," p. 99,** and **"The Bible in Religious Interpretation and Practice," pp. 2155–56.** The final meal Jesus shares with his apostles is commemorated in the Christian ritual known variously as the Lord's Supper, Communion, or Eucharist. **22:14** *The hour* is for the observance of the Passover but also the hour of Jesus's passion; see note on 22:53. **22:15** Luke links the Passover feast (Gk. "pascha") with Jesus's impending suffering (Gk. "paschein"). **22:16** The Passover feast is given new meaning by the imminence of *the kingdom of God*; see also v. 18. **22:22** Jesus's suffering and death *has been determined* as part of God's plan. Judas's act of betrayal nonetheless leads to his own death (Acts 1:16–20). **22:24–27** The apostles have not yet grasped the import of Jesus's teaching redefining greatness in terms of service. **22:25** Luke challenges how wealthy men and women enhanced their stature by

is greater, the one who is at the table or the one who serves? Is it not the one at the table? But I am among you as one who serves.

28 "You are those who have stood by me in my trials, ²⁹and I confer on you, just as my Father has conferred on me, a kingdom, ³⁰so that you may eat and drink at my table in my kingdom, and you will sit on thrones judging the twelve tribes of Israel.

31 "Simon, Simon, listen! Satan has demanded^j to sift all of you like wheat, ³²but I have prayed for you that your own faith may not fail, and you, when once you have turned back, strengthen your brothers." ³³And he said to him, "Lord, I am ready to go with you to prison and to death!" ³⁴Jesus^k said, "I tell you, Peter, the cock will not crow this day until you have denied three times that you know me."

35 He said to them, "When I sent you out without a purse, bag, or sandals, did you lack anything?" They said, "No, not a thing." ³⁶He said to them, "But now, the one who has a purse must take it, and likewise a bag. And the one who has no sword must sell his cloak and buy one. ³⁷For I tell you, this scripture must be fulfilled in me, 'And he was counted among the lawless,' and indeed what is written about me is being fulfilled." ³⁸They said, "Lord, look, here are two swords." He replied, "It is enough."

39 He came out and went, as was his custom, to the Mount of Olives, and the disciples followed him. ⁴⁰When he reached the place, he said to them, "Pray that you may not come into the time of trial."^{l} ⁴¹Then he withdrew from them about a stone's throw, knelt down, and prayed, ⁴²"Father, if you are willing, remove this cup from me, yet not my will but yours be done." [[⁴³Then an angel from heaven appeared to him and gave him strength. ⁴⁴In his anguish he prayed more earnestly, and his sweat became like great drops of blood falling down on the ground.]]^m ⁴⁵When he got up from prayer, he came to the disciples and found them sleeping because of grief, ⁴⁶and he said to them, "Why are you sleeping? Get up and pray that you may not come into the time of trial."^{n}

47 While he was still speaking, suddenly a crowd came, and the one called Judas, one of the twelve, was leading them. He approached Jesus to kiss him, ⁴⁸but Jesus said to him, "Judas, is it with a kiss that you are betraying the Son of Man?" ⁴⁹When those who were around him saw what was coming, they asked, "Lord, should we strike with the sword?" ⁵⁰Then one of them struck the slave of the high priest and cut off his right ear. ⁵¹But Jesus said, "No more of this!" And he touched his ear and healed him. ⁵²Then Jesus said to the chief priests, the officers of the temple police, and the elders who had come for him, "Have you come out with swords and clubs as though I were a rebel? ⁵³When I was with you day after day in the temple, you did not lay hands on me. But this is your hour and the power of darkness!"

54 Then they seized him and led him away, bringing him into the high priest's house. But Peter was following at a distance. ⁵⁵When they had kindled a fire in the middle of the courtyard and sat down together, Peter sat among them. ⁵⁶Then a female servant, seeing him in the firelight, stared at him and said, "This man also was with him." ⁵⁷But he denied it, saying, "Woman, I do not know him." ⁵⁸A little later someone else, on seeing him, said, "You also are one of them." But Peter said, "Man, I am not!" ⁵⁹Then about an hour later still another kept insisting, "Surely this man also was with him, for he is a Galilean." ⁶⁰But Peter said, "Man, I do not know what you are talking

j 22.31 Or *has obtained permission*   k 22.34 Gk *He*   l 22.40 Or *into testing*   m 22.44 Other ancient authorities lack 22.43 and 22.44   n 22.46 Or *into testing*

serving as *benefactors* in the Roman system of patronage. Sharing possessions should not be a pretext for wielding authority over another person. **22:31-34** Satan's continued assault on Jesus (4:13; 22:3) will result in Peter's denial. **22:32** Even as he predicts Peter's imminent denial, Jesus anticipates Peter's leadership role among his followers. **22:35-36** See 9:3; 10:4. **22:36-38** Whether intended literally or figuratively, the advice to acquire a sword is startling. See note on vv. 49-51.

22:39-62 Jesus betrayed, arrested, and denied. 22:39-46 In Mark, Jesus reproves his disciples three times for falling asleep while he prays, underscoring his isolation (Mark 14:32-42). Luke's briefer version of the scene instead foregrounds his recurrent emphasis on prayer. **22:43-44** It is unclear whether these verses are part of the original text of Luke. **22:47-48** With prophetic knowledge of Judas's intentions, Jesus forestalls the kiss of betrayal. **22:49-51** Although Jesus had instructed his followers to arm themselves (Luke 22:36), he stops them from interfering with his arrest. All four canonical Gospels mention the attack on the slave of the high priest. Only in Luke does Jesus heal the enslaved man's ear. **22:53** *This is*

about!" At that moment, while he was still speaking, the cock crowed. [61]The Lord turned and looked at Peter. Then Peter remembered the word of the Lord, how he had said to him, "Before the cock crows today, you will deny me three times." [62]And he went out and wept bitterly.

63 Now the men who were holding Jesus[o] began to mock him and beat him; [64]they also blindfolded him and kept asking him, "Prophesy! Who is it who struck you?" [65]They kept heaping many other insults on him.

66 When day came, the assembly of the elders of the people, both chief priests and scribes, gathered together, and they brought him to their council. [67]They said, "If you are the Messiah,[p] tell us." He replied, "If I tell you, you will not believe, [68]and if I question you, you will not answer.[q] [69]But from now on the Son of Man will be seated at the right hand of the power of God." [70]All of them asked, "Are you, then, the Son of God?" He said to them, "You say that I am." [71]Then they said, "What further testimony do we need? We have heard it ourselves from his own lips!"

23 Then the assembly rose as a body and brought Jesus[r] before Pilate. [2]They began to accuse him, saying, "We found this man inciting our nation, forbidding us to pay taxes to Caesar and saying that he himself is the Messiah, a king."[s] [3]Then Pilate asked him, "Are you the king of the Jews?" He answered, "You say so." [4]Then Pilate said to the chief priests and the crowds, "I find no basis for an accusation against this man." [5]But they were insistent and said, "He stirs up the people by teaching throughout all Judea, from Galilee where he began even to this place."

6 When Pilate heard this, he asked whether the man was a Galilean. [7]And when he learned that he was under Herod's jurisdiction, he sent him off to Herod, who was himself in Jerusalem at that time. [8]When Herod saw Jesus, he was very glad, for he had been wanting to see him for a long time because he had heard about him and was hoping to see him perform some sign. [9]He questioned him at some length, but Jesus[t] gave him no answer. [10]The chief priests and the scribes stood by vehemently accusing him. [11]Even Herod with his soldiers treated him with contempt and mocked him; then he put an elegant robe on him and sent him back to Pilate. [12]That same day Herod and Pilate became friends with each other; before this they had been enemies.

13 Pilate then called together the chief priests, the leaders, and the people [14]and said to them, "You brought me this man as one who was inciting the people, and here I have examined him in your presence and have not found this man guilty of any of your charges against him. [15]Neither has Herod, for he sent him back to us. Indeed, he has done nothing to deserve death. [16]I will therefore have him flogged and release him."[u]

18 Then they all shouted out together, "Away with this fellow! Release Barabbas for us!" [19](This was a man who had been put in prison for an insurrection that had taken place in the city and for murder.) [20]Pilate, wanting to release Jesus, addressed them again, [21]but they kept shouting, "Crucify, crucify him!" [22]A third

o 22.63 Gk *him*   p 22.67 Or *the Christ*   q 22.68 Other ancient authorities add *or release me*   r 23.1 Gk *him*   s 23.2 Or *is an anointed king*   t 23.9 Gk *he*   u 23.16 Here, or after 23.19, other ancient authorities add 23.17: *Now he was obliged to release someone for them at the festival*

your hour and the power of darkness. Those who have come to arrest Jesus are in thrall to the authority of Satan. **22:61–62** Only in Luke are Peter's tears elicited by Jesus's searing gaze.

22:63–23:25 Jesus on trial. 22:64 The mocking command to *prophesy* is ironic. Jesus's tormentors do not appreciate that he is indeed a prophet (7:16, 39; 13:34; 24:19). **22:66–71** The hearing before the council. In Mark, the high priest tears his robe and charges Jesus with blasphemy (Mark 14:53–64, especially vv. 63–64), details Luke omits in his subdued account. **22:66** *Council,* Sanhedrin. **23:1–5** The Jewish authorities accuse Jesus before Pontius Pilate, the Roman governor of Judea. **23:1–2** The assembly presents a united front in bringing charges, but see vv. 50–52. **23:2** On the payment of taxes, see note on 20:20–26. **23:4** Pilate finds no basis for convicting Jesus, a verdict repeated throughout the Passion narrative (vv. 14–15, 22, 41, 47). **23:6–12** The hearing before *Herod* Antipas; see note on 3:1. **3:8** See notes on 9:7–9; 13:31. **23:13–25** The second hearing before Pilate. **23:14–15** Rejecting the assembly's charge that Jesus was *inciting the people* (vv. 2, 14), Pilate insists that Jesus had done *nothing to deserve death* (v. 15). **23:18** Luke has emphasized the sympathy of the people for Jesus, but they join the religious leaders in calling for Jesus's death; see also vv. 21, 23, and 25. **23:18–19** Luke offers no explanation for the demand to release another prisoner, Barabbas; see also vv. 24–25. **23:22** Pilate continues to assert that there is *no ground*

time he said to them, "Why, what evil has he done? I have found in him no ground for the sentence of death; I will therefore have him flogged and then release him." [23]But they kept urgently demanding with loud shouts that he should be crucified, and their voices prevailed. [24]So Pilate gave his verdict that their demand should be granted. [25]He released the man they asked for, the one who had been put in prison for insurrection and murder, and he handed Jesus over as they wished.

26 As they led him away, they seized a man, Simon of Cyrene, who was coming from the country, and they laid the cross on him and made him carry it behind Jesus. [27]A great number of the people followed him, and among them were women who were beating their breasts and wailing for him. [28]But Jesus turned to them and said, "Daughters of Jerusalem, do not weep for me, but weep for yourselves and for your children. [29]For the days are surely coming when they will say, 'Blessed are the barren, and the wombs that never bore, and the breasts that never nursed.' [30]Then they will begin to say to the mountains, 'Fall on us,' and to the hills, 'Cover us.' [31]For if they do this when the wood is green, what will happen when it is dry?"

32 Two others also, who were criminals, were led away to be put to death with him. [33]When they came to the place that is called The Skull, they crucified Jesus[v] there with the criminals, one on his right and one on his left. [[[34]Then Jesus said, "Father, forgive them, for they do not know what they are doing."]][w] And they cast lots to divide his clothing. [35]And the people stood by watching, but the leaders scoffed at him, saying, "He saved others; let him save himself if he is the Messiah[x] of God, his chosen one!" [36]The soldiers also mocked him, coming up and offering him sour wine [37]and saying, "If you are the King of the Jews, save yourself!" [38]There was also an inscription over him,[y] "This is the King of the Jews."

39 One of the criminals who were hanged there kept deriding[z] him and saying, "Are you not the Messiah?[a] Save yourself and us!" [40]But the other rebuked him, saying, "Do you not fear God, since you are under the same sentence of condemnation? [41]And we indeed have been condemned justly, for we are getting what we deserve for our deeds, but this man has done nothing wrong." [42]Then he said, "Jesus, remember me when you come in[b] your kingdom." [43]He replied, "Truly I tell you, today you will be with me in paradise."

44 It was now about noon, and darkness came over the whole land[c] until three in the afternoon, [45]while the sun's light failed,[d] and the curtain of the temple was torn in two. [46]Then Jesus, crying out with a loud voice, said, "Father, into your hands I commend my spirit." Having said this, he breathed his last. [47]When the centurion saw what had taken place, he praised God and said, "Certainly this man was innocent."[e] [48]And when all the crowds who had gathered there for this spectacle saw what had taken place, they returned home, beating their breasts. [49]But all his acquaintances, including

v 23.33 Gk *him* w 23.34 Other ancient authorities lack the sentence *Then Jesus . . . what they are doing* x 23.35 Or *the Christ* y 23.38 Other ancient authorities add *written in Greek and Latin and Hebrew* (that is, *Aramaic*) z 23.39 Or *blaspheming* a 23.39 Or *the Christ* b 23.42 Other ancient authorities read *into* c 23.44 Or *earth* d 23.45 Or *the sun was eclipsed*. Other ancient authorities read *the sun was darkened* e 23.47 Or *righteous*

for the sentence of death. **23:25** Representing Rome, Pilate is weak and unjust. Nonetheless, although Pilate ordered that Jesus be put to death, Luke holds the Jewish leaders and people responsible (Acts 3:13–15) and claims that they acted out of ignorance (see note on v. 34a). See **"Jews in Luke–Acts," p. 1910**.

23:26–49 Crucifixion. 23:26 *Cyrene,* on the coast of Africa. See **"Simon of Cyrene," p. 1797**. **23:27** See note on 23:18. Luke again depicts *a great number of the people* as loyal to Jesus. Women in the crowd were *beating their breasts* in mourning. **23:28–31** Jesus's oracle anticipates the suffering of the Jewish War (see note on 19:41–44), especially the anguish of mothers (v. 29; see 21:23). **23:34a** *Then Jesus said, Father, forgive them, for they do not know what they are doing.* Although it is unclear whether these words are part of the original text of Luke, they are consistent with the view expressed in Acts that those responsible for Jesus's crucifixion were ignorant of his identity (Acts 3:17; 13:27). **23:39–43** Jesus's exchange with the other men being crucified is unique to Luke. **23:39** *Save yourself and us,* a misunderstanding of Jesus as Savior (see note on 2:11). **23:40–41** One of the men underscores that Jesus had *done nothing wrong* (vv. 4, 14–15, 22). **23:43** Not clearly defined, Jesus's promise of *paradise* suggests a place of respite, a heavenly garden. **23:46** Jesus remains in control until his final breath. **23:47** The *centurion,* a Roman soldier, offers yet another affirmation that Jesus is *innocent,* literally "just" or "righteous." **23:49** *The women who had followed him from Galilee,* see 8:2–3.

the women who had followed him from Galilee, stood at a distance watching these things.

50 Now there was a good and righteous man named Joseph who, though a member of the council, [51]had not agreed to their plan and action. He came from the Jewish town of Arimathea, and he was waiting expectantly for the kingdom of God. [52]This man went to Pilate and asked for the body of Jesus. [53]Then he took it down, wrapped it in a linen cloth, and laid it in a rock-hewn tomb where no one had ever been laid. [54]It was the day of Preparation, and the Sabbath was beginning.[f] [55]The women who had come with him from Galilee followed, and they saw the tomb and how his body was laid. [56]Then they returned and prepared spices and ointments.

On the Sabbath they rested according to the commandment.

24 But on the first day of the week, at early dawn, they went to the tomb, taking the spices that they had prepared. [2]They found the stone rolled away from the tomb, [3]but when they went in they did not find the body.[g] [4]While they were perplexed about this, suddenly two men in dazzling clothes stood beside them. [5]The women[h] were terrified and bowed their faces to the ground, but the men[i] said to them, "Why do you look for the living among the dead? He is not here but has risen.[j] [6]Remember how he told you, while he was still in Galilee, [7]that the Son of Man must be handed over to the hands of sinners and be crucified and on the third day rise again." [8]Then they remembered his words, [9]and returning from the tomb they told all this to the eleven and to all the rest. [10]Now it was Mary Magdalene, Joanna, Mary the mother of James, and the other women with them who told this to the apostles. [11]But these words seemed to them an idle tale, and they did not believe them. [12]But Peter got up and ran to the tomb; stooping and looking in, he saw the linen cloths by themselves; then he went home, amazed at what had happened.[k]

13 Now on that same day two of them were going to a village called Emmaus, about seven miles[l] from Jerusalem, [14]and talking with each other about all these things that had happened. [15]While they were talking and discussing, Jesus himself came near and went with them, [16]but their eyes were kept from recognizing him. [17]And he said to them, "What are you discussing with each other while you walk along?" They stood still, looking sad.[m]

f 23.54 Gk *was dawning*   g 24.3 Other ancient authorities add *of the Lord Jesus*   h 24.5 Gk *They*   i 24.5 Gk *but they*   j 24.5 Other ancient authorities lack *He is not here but has risen*   k 24.12 Other ancient authorities lack 24.12   l 24.13 Gk *sixty stadia*; other ancient authorities read *a hundred sixty stadia*   m 24.17 Other ancient authorities read *walk along, looking sad?"*

23:50–56 Burial. 23:50–51 A member of the Sanhedrin, Joseph of Arimathea had objected to their treatment of Jesus. See note on 23:1–2. **23:51** *He was waiting expectantly for the kingdom of God* and thus potentially sympathetic to Jesus's message, although Luke does not identify him as a disciple. **22:55** See note on 23:49.

24:1–53 Resurrection. Consistent with the geographic scheme of Luke–Acts, Luke restricts Jesus's resurrection appearances to Jerusalem and environs. See **"Resurrection in the Gospels," p. 1767**; **"Jerusalem in Luke–Acts," p. 1805.**

24:1–12 The empty tomb. 23:1 The women who arrive at Jesus's tomb to anoint his body have accompanied him from Galilee (8:2–3; 23:49, 55). **24:4** *Two men in dazzling clothes*, later identified as angels (v. 23). **24:6** *Remember how he told you.* The women were apparently present with the male disciples when Jesus predicted his suffering and death (9:22, 44). Luke includes a reminder that Jesus was in Galilee when he first spoke of his resurrection. However, he omits Mark's suggestion that the risen Jesus would appear to his followers there (Mark 16:7). **24:8–10** On the basis of their encounter at the tomb, the women are the first to proclaim the resurrection. See **"Mary Magdalene," p. 1766. 24:9** *The eleven.* Judas Iscariot is no longer numbered among the apostles. See Acts 1:16–20. **24:10** Compare Luke 8:2–3. **24:11** Their failure to trust the women's word reflects poorly on the eleven. **24:12** Perhaps an addition to the original text. Compare John 20:3–10.

24:13–35 The road to Emmaus. The risen Jesus, unrecognized until the end, appears to several followers as they walk to a village just outside Jerusalem. **24:13** *Emmaus*, location unknown. **24:16** *Their eyes were kept from recognizing him.* The use of the passive suggests that God prevents the two from recognizing Jesus. Failure to recognize Jesus is a recurring feature in resurrection accounts (e.g., 24:37; John 20:14–15). **24:18** *Cleopas*, otherwise unknown. His unidentified companion may be either male or female. **24:19** *Prophet*, see notes on 4:18, 28–29; 7:16, 39; 13:34; 22:64.

¹⁸Then one of them, whose name was Cleopas, answered him, "Are you the only stranger in Jerusalem who does not know the things that have taken place there in these days?" ¹⁹He asked them, "What things?" They replied, "The things about Jesus of Nazareth,ⁿ who was a prophet mighty in deed and word before God and all the people, ²⁰and how our chief priests and leaders handed him over to be condemned to death and crucified him. ²¹But we had hoped that he was the one to redeem Israel.ᵒ Yes, and besides all this, it is now the third day since these things took place. ²²Moreover, some women of our group astounded us. They were at the tomb early this morning, ²³and when they did not find his body there they came back and told us that they had indeed seen a vision of angels who said that he was alive. ²⁴Some of those who were with us went to the tomb and found it just as the women had said, but they did not see him." ²⁵Then he said to them, "Oh, how foolish you are and how slow of heart to believe all that the prophets have declared! ²⁶Was it not necessary that the Messiahᵖ should suffer these things and then enter into his glory?" ²⁷Then beginning with Moses and all the prophets, he interpreted to them the things about himself in all the scriptures.

28 As they came near the village to which they were going, he walked ahead as if he were going on. ²⁹But they urged him strongly, saying, "Stay with us, because it is almost evening and the day is now nearly over." So he went in to stay with them. ³⁰When he was at the table with them, he took bread, blessed and broke it, and gave it to them. ³¹Then their eyes were opened, and they recognized him, and he vanished from their sight. ³²They said to each other, "Were not our hearts burning within us𐞥 while he was talking to us on the road, while he was opening the scriptures to us?" ³³That same hour they got up and returned to Jerusalem, and they found the eleven and their companions gathered together. ³⁴They were saying, "The Lord has risen indeed, and he has appeared to Simon!" ³⁵Then they told what had happened on the road and how he had been made known to them in the breaking of the bread.

36 While they were talking about this, Jesusʳ himself stood among them and said to them, "Peace be with you."ˢ ³⁷They were startled and terrified and thought that they were seeing a ghost. ³⁸He said to them, "Why are you frightened, and why do doubts arise in your hearts? ³⁹Look at my hands and my feet; see that it is I myself. Touch me and see, for a ghost does not have flesh and bones as you see that I have." ⁴⁰And when he had said this, he showed them his hands and his feet.ᵗ ⁴¹Yet for all their joy they were still disbelieving and wondering, and he said to them, "Have you anything here to eat?" ⁴²They gave him a piece of broiled fish,ᵘ ⁴³and he took it and ate in their presence.

n 24.19 Other ancient authorities read *Jesus the Nazorean* o 24.21 Or *to set Israel free* p 24.26 Or *the Christ* q 24.32 Other ancient authorities lack *within us* r 24.36 Gk *he* s 24.36 Other ancient authorities lack *and said to them, "Peace be with you."* t 24.40 Other ancient authorities lack 24.40 u 24.42 Other ancient authorities add *and some honeycomb*

24:20 Cleopas holds the religious leaders responsible for Jesus's death, rather than the people of Jerusalem or the Roman authorities. **24:21** *The one to redeem Israel*, see 1:68. **24:23–24** Cleopas's account suggests that the women's words were taken seriously enough to investigate; compare v. 11. His version of events implies that Peter was not alone in visiting the tomb (v. 12). **24:26** The Messiah's suffering was a *necessary* part of God's plan; see note on 13:33. **24:27** Through the centuries, Christians have interpreted the Hebrew Bible as a witness to Jesus, a process of biblical reinterpretation that New Testament writers use freely, as seen here in this story of the risen Jesus. **24:30** Jesus's companions finally recognize him when he breaks bread; see 9:16; 22:19; 24:35. **24:31** *Their eyes were opened.* See note on 24:16. *He vanished from their sight.* Early Christians understood resurrection not so much as revival of a corpse but as transformation (1 Cor. 15:35–53). Although Luke stresses the physicality of Jesus's resurrected body (vv. 39–43), he also portrays the risen Jesus as capable of disappearance (v. 31) and sudden appearance (v. 36). **24:34** The report of another resurrection appearance, to Peter.

24:36–49 Jesus appears in Jerusalem. **24:36** As *the eleven and their companions* (v. 33) discuss Jesus's appearance on the road to Emmaus, he appears among them. **24:37** Although they have heard about Jesus's appearances to the women, to Cleopas and his companion, and to Peter, those gathered are *startled and terrified*. **24:39** To allay his followers' fear that he is a ghost, Jesus stresses the fleshiness of his body. **24:40** He extends *his hands and his feet* to convince his disciples of the materiality of his body. **24:41–43** Jesus's ability to consume flesh is further evidence of his body's materiality.

44 Then he said to them, "These are my words that I spoke to you while I was still with you—that everything written about me in the law of Moses, the prophets, and the psalms must be fulfilled." 45Then he opened their minds to understand the scriptures, 46and he said to them, "Thus it is written, that the Messiah[v] is[w] to suffer and to rise from the dead on the third day 47and that repentance and forgiveness of sins is to be proclaimed in his name to all nations, beginning from Jerusalem. 48You are witnesses[x] of these things. 49And see, I am sending upon you what my Father promised, so stay here in the city until you have been clothed with power from on high."

50 Then he led them out as far as Bethany, and, lifting up his hands, he blessed them. 51While he was blessing them, he withdrew from them and was carried up into heaven.[y] 52And they worshiped him and[z] returned to Jerusalem with great joy, 53and they were continually in the temple[a] blessing God.[b]

v 24.46 Or the Christ   w 24.46 Other ancient authorities read written, and thus it was necessary for the Messiah   x 24.48 Or nations. Beginning from Jerusalem 48you are witnesses   y 24.51 Other ancient authorities lack and was carried up into heaven   z 24.52 Other ancient authorities lack worshiped him and   a 24.53 Other ancient authorities add praising and   b 24.53 Other ancient authorities add Amen

24:44–45 See note on 24:27. 24:45 He opened their minds, just as the eyes of Cleopas and his companion had been opened (see note on v. 31). 24:47 In Acts, the proclamation of Jesus's name will extend to all nations, beginning from Jerusalem. 24:49 In Acts, Jesus's followers remain in Jerusalem until after they receive the Spirit at Pentecost (Acts 2:1–4).

24:50–53 Ascension. Luke provides a more detailed version of the ascension in Acts 1:6–11. 24:53 Luke ends where it begins, in the temple.

THE GOSPEL ACCORDING TO JOHN

Authorship

Who was the author of the Gospel of John? Scholarship has varied on the question of authorship. From around the second century onward, church tradition named the author the apostle John, the son of Zebedee and brother of James. However, the Fourth Gospel (another name for the Gospel of John) does not identify this individual. Looking inside the Gospel for clues for authorship, the reference to an eyewitness (1:14; 19:35) has led scholars to identify the eyewitness as the Beloved Disciple, or the disciple whom Jesus loved (13:23; 19:26; 20:2; 21:7, 20). Some scholars have merged the author, the apostle John, and the Beloved Disciple to provide an explanation. Scholarship's current consensus is that the author is anonymous. The failure to include key Synoptic stories (e.g., the transfiguration of Jesus and Jesus's agony in the garden of Gethsemane) raises questions about the apostle John as the author. And if the Beloved Disciple composed the Fourth Gospel, why does he appear so late in the Gospel and not in the beginning chapters? Traditionally, this apostle John has been assigned the author of this Gospel as well as the three Letters of John and the book of Revelation, but these connections are tenuous at best. A stronger claim is that the authors of all these compositions (less so with Revelation) emanate from the same Johannine school of thought, which might explain similarities in vocabulary, writing styles, themes, and theological outlooks. The tenor of the Gospel shows a community of readers or listeners, often referred to as the Johannine community, familiar with the symbols of the Hebrew Bible and with Hellenistic thought but experiencing friction with some in the Jewish community, differences with other Christ followers, and an overall sense of alienation from "the world."

Provenance

As to the place of the writing of the Gospel of John, church tradition favors Ephesus. However, there is no internal evidence that leads to this conclusion. The only link to Ephesus is the connection of the Elder John of the Johannine letters with Ephesus. Some scholars have pointed to a Hellenistic context overall (see **"The Bible in Its Ancient Contexts," pp. 2150–52**) due to the use of the Greek word *logos* in the first chapter of John. A second suggestion has been Antioch of Syria due to the strong anti-Jewish rhetoric in the Gospel; Antioch was a place where many early religious debates took place among communities. A final possible location is Alexandria in Egypt because of the many "I am" sayings in the Gospel linked to the cult of Isis, as we have an aretalogy of Isis that uses the phrase "I am" multiple times. As with the question of authorship, external and internal evidence on provenance do not contribute with certainty to the question of where John was written. It is best to reconstruct a location based on the historical, social, and literary features in the story world of John.

Date

The Fourth Gospel is usually dated toward the last decade of the first century CE (around 90–100 CE). This approximation is based on several factors. First, a small papyrus fragment known as P52 containing a few pages of the Gospel (18:31–33, 37–38) was discovered in Egypt. The fragment has been dated around the mid-second century, so this would suggest that the Fourth Gospel was composed prior to 150 CE. Second, some scholars point to three passages in John (9:22; 12:42; 16:2) to suggest an internal division within Judaism, in which there was a split between followers of traditional Judaism and believers of the Jesus movement. Some scholars argue that this split occurred around 75–90 CE, after the destruction of the temple and the rise of the rabbinic movement, but the claim to such a split is unconfirmed. The date of 90–100 CE is an approximation. The high Christology reflected in the Gospel would support this date. Also, the later approximation would have allowed Christianity time to develop in many ways, including a broader theology and a critical view of the empire, and open it up to the inclusion of women in witnessing to the identity of Jesus (20:17).

Reading Guide

The Gospel of John is a story about the recognition of and belief in Jesus. The plot of John can be viewed from many perspectives. The perspective of the journey is one that leads Jesus, the protagonist in the story, from one event to another while moving characters to various responses of recognition and non-recognition. The Gospel of John can be divided into three major sections:

The journey begins in the world above (1:1) and is situated in a most memorable section of the Gospel called the prologue (1:1–1:18). It is in the prologue where Jesus, the revealed Word of God (Logos), journeys to the world below to enter human history (1:14). The purpose is to provide humanity with the gift of eternal life. The journey is one of departure from the world above to save humanity (3:16).

After crossing from the world above to the world below, Jesus journeys from place to place in his public ministry and mission to the world (1:19–19:42). During his multiple journeys in the world below, he performs signs (or miracles; e.g., 2:1–12), gives long speeches or discourses (e.g., 5:19–47), and engages in deep dialogues with various characters (e.g., Nicodemus; 3:1–15). All these actions and words become causes for an ongoing conflict between Jesus and his Jewish community over his identity and authority. According to the plot of the Gospel, "the Jews" (hoi Ioudaioi) fail to recognize Jesus as the Christ. This intra-Jewish conflict leads to vitriolic name-calling against the Ioudaioi, as expressed harshly in chaps. 7 and 8. The raising of Lazarus from the dead (11:1–44) by Jesus is an event leading to a crisis that leads to Jesus's death (11:53). Many who recognize Jesus's identity and authority fear to acknowledge their belief openly. They fear being put out of the synagogue if they recognize Jesus in front of the opposition (9:22; 12:42; 16:2). Jesus begins to prepare for his departure by providing the disciples with a farewell discourse with the hope of warning and comforting them about what is to come after his departure (13:1–17:26). Jesus is arrested and tried as a bandit or as one who is a threat to the Roman Empire. Only those who recognize Jesus are near his side, but only temporarily, for they also fear those who are in power (18:1–19:42). Jesus is crucified and, through his death and resurrection, is glorified (praised) for his obedience and for following God's will, as he promised in the farewell discourse. He has also promised to leave an Advocate (14:16) to guide those who recognize Jesus as the Son of Man.

Jesus prepares for his journey back home to the world above with God (20:1–21:25). In so doing, he appears to disciples (all believers) on several occasions to prepare them further for his return. Some believers do not immediately recognize him, but they all eventually do so. Before his return to the world above, Jesus appears one final time to his disciples while they are fishing on the Sea of Galilee. He leaves them with instructions on how to feed (spiritually) and tend to other believers.

Francisco Lozada, Jr.

1 In the beginning was the Word, and the Word was with God, and the Word was God. ²He was in the beginning with God. ³All things came into being through him, and without him not one thing came into being. What has come into being ⁴in him was life,ᵃ and the life was the light of all people. ⁵The light shines in the darkness, and the darkness did not overtake it.

6 There was a man sent from God whose

a 1.4 Or ³. . . through him. And without him not one thing came into being that has come into being. ⁴In him was life

1:1–18 The first chapter is the prologue to the entire Gospel. It introduces the plot of John, where the main character, the Logos (Jesus), is accepted (belief) and rejected (unbelief) as the One sent from God, whose identity is revealed throughout the entire Gospel. The prologue introduces many themes that will be repeated throughout the Gospel, such as life (v. 4), light (v. 4), darkness (v. 5), witness (v. 7), world (vv. 9, 10), children born of God (vv. 12, 13), glory (v. 14), truth (v. 14), and the only Son (vv. 14, 18). These ideas introduced in the prologue all point to Jesus as the Logos (the Word of God). **1:1** *In the beginning* refers to that which is before creation (Gen. 1:1). *The Word* (Logos), without being directly identified, refers to Jesus. The Greek term "logos" has a rich heritage in both Jewish thought and Hellenistic philosophy. *The Word was with God* describes the spatial relationship between the Word and God. *And the Word was God* refers to the general nature of this relationship—that is, the Word's identity as God. **1:3** *All things came into being* expresses the idea that God as the creator called all earthly things into existence through the Word. **1:4–5** *Life* is a favorite term in John and occurs thirty-six times in this Gospel, and forms of the verb "to live" occur sixteen times. It expresses knowledge and belief. *Light* is another popular term in John and symbolizes intellectual, moral, and spiritual aspects of the Word. *Darkness* is the opposite of light and refers to unbelief. **1:6–7** *John* points to John the Baptist,

Focus On: Differences between John and the Synoptic Gospels (John 1)

Readers often refer to the Gospel of John as the Fourth Gospel, a shorthand reminder that this narrative differs significantly from Matthew, Mark, and Luke, known collectively as the Synoptic Gospels. There are many features of John's Gospel that distinguish it from the Synoptics. Primary among them are the following: the absence of material that appears in the Synoptics, the inclusion of material that is absent from the Synoptics, and its Christology, or understanding of Jesus.

Though each canonical Gospel tells its own story of Jesus, John's portrait of Jesus is the most distinctive among the four. The following stories appear in the Synoptic Gospels but are absent from John: the testing of Jesus in the wilderness, the transfiguration, Jesus's exorcisms, Jesus's parables, the extended focus on the kingdom of God, and the institution of the Lord's Supper. On the other hand, John includes material that does not appear in the Synoptics: key portions of John 2–4, including the wedding at Cana (John 2) and Jesus's conversations with Nicodemus (John 3) and the Samaritan woman (John 4); the healing of the man born without sight (John 9); the raising of Lazarus (John 11); the Farewell Discourse (John 13–17); the themes of eternal life and the coming Paraclete; the problematic phrase "the Jews"; and Jesus's initial post-resurrection appearance to Mary Magdalene alone (John 20).

Perhaps most important, John's understanding of Jesus differs significantly from the Christology of the Synoptics. Through the speech it attributes to him, John's Gospel elevates its portrayal of Jesus. In contrast to the sometimes enigmatic parables, pronouncement stories, and pithy aphorisms that form much of Jesus's speech in the Synoptics, John's Jesus speaks in extended, chapters-long monologues and lofty speech. It is only in the Fourth Gospel that we find Jesus uttering double "amens" and pronouncing seven "I am" statements. John also frames the story of Jesus in a more expansive and elevated way than the Synoptics. Rather than beginning the Jesus story with a birth account, John relates Jesus's origins to the very creation. The Gospel's prologue (John 1:1–18) identifies Jesus with the divine Logos, often translated as "Word" (vv. 1–3). As the Word become flesh (v. 14), Jesus is one who "has made [God] known" (v. 18). Jesus's identity, then, is what most drives the shape and scope of the Fourth Gospel, including the features that distinguish it among the canonical Gospels.

Mary F. Foskett

name was John. [7]He came as a witness to testify to the light, so that all might believe through him. [8]He himself was not the light, but he came to testify to the light. [9]The true light, which enlightens everyone, was coming into the world.[b]

10 He was in the world, and the world came into being through him, yet the world did not know him. [11]He came to what was his own,[c] and his own people did not accept him. [12]But to all who received him, who believed in his name, he gave power to become children of God, [13]who were born, not of blood or of the will of the flesh or of the will of man, but of God.

14 And the Word became flesh and lived among us, and we have seen his glory, the glory as of a father's only son,[d] full of grace and truth. [15](John testified to him and cried out, "This was he of whom I said, 'He who comes after me ranks ahead of me because he was before me.'") [16]From his fullness we have all received, grace upon grace.[e] [17]The law indeed was given through Moses; grace and truth came through Jesus Christ. [18]No one has ever seen God. It is the only Son, himself God, who[f] is close to the Father's heart,[g] who has made him known.

19 This is the testimony given by John when

b 1.9 Or *He was the true light that enlightens everyone coming into the world*   c 1.11 Or *to his own home*   d 1.14 Or *the Father's only Son*   e 1.16 Or *grace in place of grace*   f 1.18 Other ancient authorities read *is the only Son who*   g 1.18 Gk *bosom*

who serves as a *witness* to Jesus (1:7, 8, 15, 29–34; 3:27–30; 5:33–55). **1:9** *True* intimates genuine, real, and authentic as opposed to objective statements. **1:10–13** *World* ("kosmos") is another common term in John and occurs seventy-eight times. It communicates the world of humanity (3:16; 7:7; 12:31; 16:20, 33) or the whole of creation at various times (17:5, 24; 21:25). **1:14** *Lived* suggests temporary sojourning. Literally, it translates as "lived in a tent or tabernacle," evoking God's presence with Israel in the tabernacle during their journey through the desert. **1:17** *The law* designates the Torah, the first five books of the Hebrew Bible. Sometimes it refers to the entire Hebrew Bible (10:34; 12:34; 15:25). **1:18** *Who is close to the Father's heart* expresses the close and affectionate relationship between God and the Son.

1:19 *The Jews* ("hoi Ioudaioi") in the Gospel does not designate a monolithic, undifferentiated group. The term can refer to many different groups, individuals, or ideas and practices (see **"The Jews" (Hoi Ioudaioi), p. 1852**).

Going Deeper: Logos (John 1:14)

The Gospel of John presents Jesus as "the Word of God." In Greek, the term is *logos* and translated as "the word." The Gospel uses the concept of *Logos*, the word, to present Jesus as Christ in the prologue. *Logos* has a rich history in both Jewish and Hellenistic thinking. In ancient Jewish tradition, "the word" (*Davar* or *Davar Adonai*) was the creative power of God at work in the world (Ps. 33:6). God not only spoke the word but also acted in creation (Gen. 1 and 2). The word was understood as living and active (Heb. 4:12). The "word," so too, was spoken by the prophets of Israel ("Now the word of the LORD came to me saying," Jer. 1:4). In later Jewish times, the word is translated in Aramaic by the phrase "the *Memra* of *Adonai*," the word of the Lord (Isa. 55:10–11). And in the wisdom tradition of the Hebrew Bible, the word of God is identified with the wisdom of God (Prov. 8:22). Wisdom is thus personified as (a female) accompanying God in the creation of the world (Prov. 8:1; see **"Woman Wisdom," p. 872**). In Hellenistic philosophy, particularly Stoicism, the *Logos* was the rational principle of the universe; it was the life and mind of the universe. It created the world and nourished it. It expressed perfect order or reason. For Stoicism, the power of reason in a person was called a *logos*. Philo, an Alexandrian Jew who was trained in Hellenistic philosophy, believed the *Logos* was created by God and used to create all things. The *Logos* existed between God and the world, giving it order and meaning and providing humanity with the power to think and reason. The connection between the Word (*Logos*) and the life of Jesus is made with both these traditions in mind to capture the imaginations and thinking of both the Jewish and Hellenistic peoples of the day. When John states "And the Word became flesh and lived among us" (1:14a), John knew this concept would be known by both the Jewish and Greek people. The remainder of the plot of the Gospel focuses on explaining the significance of the *Logos* as the uttered Word of God.

Francisco Lozada, Jr.

the Jews sent priests and Levites from Jerusalem to ask him, "Who are you?" [20]He confessed and did not deny it, but he confessed, "I am not the Messiah."[b] [21]And they asked him, "What then? Are you Elijah?" He said, "I am not." "Are you the prophet?" He answered, "No." [22]Then they said to him, "Who are you? Let us have an answer for those who sent us. What do you say about yourself?" [23]He said,

"I am the voice of one crying out in the wilderness,
'Make straight the way of the Lord,'"
as the prophet Isaiah said.

24 Now they had been sent from the Pharisees. [25]They asked him, "Why, then, are you baptizing if you are neither the Messiah,[i] nor Elijah, nor the prophet?" [26]John answered them, "I baptize with water. Among you stands one whom you do not know, [27]the one who is coming after me; I am not worthy to untie the strap of his sandal." [28]This took place in Bethany across the Jordan where John was baptizing.

29 The next day he saw Jesus coming toward him and declared, "Here is the Lamb of God who takes away the sin of the world! [30]This is he of whom I said, 'After me comes a man who ranks ahead of me because he was before me.' [31]I myself did not know him, but I came baptizing with water for this reason, that he might be revealed to Israel." [32]And John testified, "I saw the Spirit descending from heaven like a dove, and it remained on him. [33]I myself did not know him, but the one who sent me to baptize with water said to me, 'He on whom you see the Spirit descend and remain is the one who baptizes with the Holy Spirit.' [34]And I myself have seen and have testified that this is the Chosen One."[j]

35 The next day John again was standing with two of his disciples, [36]and as he watched Jesus walk by he exclaimed, "Look, here is the Lamb of God!" [37]The two disciples heard him say this, and they followed Jesus. [38]When Jesus turned and saw them following, he said to them, "What are you looking for?" They

b 1.20 Or *the Christ*   *i* 1.25 Or *the Christ*   *j* 1.34 Other ancient authorities read *the Son of God*

1:23 *I am the voice of one crying out in the wilderness* calls to mind the voice of the prophet Isaiah, who had spoken of God as the liberator from bondage in exile (Isa. 40:3).

1:24 *The Pharisees* refers to a religious group that believes in the oral law and whose power base is the synagogue (see **"Pharisees," p. 1756**).

1:29 The title *Lamb of God* conjures up God providing a lamb for sacrifice in place of Isaac (Gen. 22:8) as well as the lamb sacrificed as part of the Passover.

1:38 The address *Rabbi* is the customary title used by the Jewish people for their religious teachers.

said to him, "Rabbi" (which translated means Teacher), "where are you staying?" [39]He said to them, "Come and see." They came and saw where he was staying, and they remained with him that day. It was about four o'clock in the afternoon. [40]One of the two who heard John speak and followed him was Andrew, Simon Peter's brother. [41]He first found his brother Simon and said to him, "We have found the Messiah" (which is translated Anointed[k]). [42]He brought Simon[l] to Jesus, who looked at him and said, "You are Simon son of John. You are to be called Cephas"[m] (which is translated Peter[n]).

43 The next day Jesus decided to go to Galilee. He found Philip and said to him, "Follow me." [44]Now Philip was from Bethsaida, the city of Andrew and Peter. [45]Philip found Nathanael and said to him, "We have found him about whom Moses in the Law and also the Prophets wrote, Jesus son of Joseph from Nazareth." [46]Nathanael said to him, "Can anything good come out of Nazareth?" Philip said to him, "Come and see." [47]When Jesus saw Nathanael coming toward him, he said of him, "Here is truly an Israelite in whom there is no deceit!" [48]Nathanael asked him, "Where did you get to know me?" Jesus answered, "I saw you under the fig tree before Philip called you." [49]Nathanael replied, "Rabbi, you are the Son of God! You are the King of Israel!" [50]Jesus answered, "Do you believe because I told you that I saw you under the fig tree? You will see greater things than these." [51]And he said to him, "Very truly, I tell you,[o] you will see heaven opened and the angels of God ascending and descending upon the Son of Man."

2 On the third day there was a wedding in Cana of Galilee, and the mother of Jesus was there. [2]Jesus and his disciples had also been invited to the wedding. [3]When the wine gave out, the mother of Jesus said to him, "They have no wine." [4]And Jesus said to her, "Woman, what concern is that to me and to you?[p] My hour has not yet come." [5]His mother said to the servants, "Do whatever he tells you." [6]Now standing there were six stone water jars for the Jewish rites of purification, each holding twenty or thirty gallons. [7]Jesus said to them, "Fill the jars with water." And they filled them up to the brim. [8]He said to them, "Now draw some out, and take it to the person in charge of the banquet." So they took it. [9]When the person in charge tasted the water that had become wine and did not know where it came from (though the servants who had drawn the water knew), that person called the bridegroom [10]and said to him, "Everyone serves the good wine first and then the inferior wine after the guests have become drunk. But you have kept the good wine until now." [11]Jesus did this, the first of his signs, in Cana of Galilee and revealed his glory, and his disciples believed in him.

12 After this he went down to Capernaum with his mother, his brothers, and his disciples, and they remained there a few days.

13 The Passover of the Jews was near, and

k 1.41 Or *Christ* *l* 1.42 Gk *him* *m* 1.42 Aramaic for *rock* *n* 1.42 Greek for *rock* *o* 1.51 Both instances of *you* in 1.51 are plural in Greek *p* 2.4 Or *What have you to do with me, woman?*

1:48 *Where did you get to know me?* This question speaks to Jesus's foreknowledge of characters' inner thoughts and whereabouts.

2:1–11 *A wedding* customarily was followed by a banquet and held in the bridegroom's home. It could last seven days. The occasion for celebration serves as the backdrop for Jesus's first miracle. **2:4** *My hour has not yet come* points here to Jesus's crucifixion and resurrection, by which his purpose of redemption (liberation) and glorification (honor) is realized. **2:6** *Six stone water jars* supplied the water that was used in ritual washings before and after meals or after traveling. **2:8** *The person in charge of the banquet* is also known as the chief steward. This person was not the bridegroom but rather the one responsible for all the arrangements of the wedding feast. **2:9** *The servants* ("diakonoi") in the ancient socioeconomic structure were part of the lower strata of society slightly above enslaved people. **2:11** *Signs* is the Gospel's word for "miracles." It demonstrates an extraordinary manifestation of divine power. Here *signs* points to Jesus as the person of Christ and is meant to produce faith in him (see **"Signs," p. 1853**).

2:12 The *brothers* ("adelphoi") of Jesus are unnamed (see Matt. 13:55; Mark 6:3). Besides the connotation of "blood brothers," it can also imply the more inclusive and general sense of those followers ("brothers and sisters")—as the disciples—who were committed to Jesus's mission and ministry.

2:13 *The Passover of the Jews* is one of the three Passovers mentioned in the Gospel (2:13; 6:4; 13:1). Passover was one of the great Jewish pilgrimage festivals (Deut. 16:16), and by the time of Jesus, it

Going Deeper: "The Jews" (Hoi Ioudaioi) *(John 2)*

Who are "the Jews" (*hoi Ioudaioi*) in John? Many attempts have been made to explain who exactly "the Jews" are, but no English translation quite captures the meaning accurately, despite using the Gospel's narrative and worldview to set the term within a sociohistorical context. It is problematic to assume that "the Jews" (*hoi Ioudaioi*) refers to all Jewish people then and now. The attempt to read the present in the past to explain ancient identity is challenging, as well as assuming that *hoi Ioudaioi* refers to one unified community. The danger of reading *hoi Ioudaioi* in a monolithic and undifferentiated way is that "the Jews" are not seen as having different points of view (e.g., 9:16). By casting "the Jews" as the opponents to Jesus and nonbelievers in the Gospel, they are therefore seen as "the Other" in the plot of the Gospel. When cast in this way, it sets them up as the villains and thus the recipients of such slanderous remarks as "You are from your father the devil" (8:44a). It also makes it easier, with the help of English translations, to condemn all Jewish people past and present.

Hoi Ioudaioi ("the Jews") has been translated most of the time as "the Jewish authorities" or "the Judeans" to lessen the sharp and polemic tone behind the term "the Jews." However, both terms have their issues. The first is that "Jewish authorities"—the antagonists in the plot of the Gospel—does not always capture the narrative context of whether the speakers are the authorities (e.g., 5:18; 6:41; 7:13). And like language that refers to particular groups, such as Latin American migrants, which can be easily used to refer to all Latinx people, it is easy to use such language to refer to all peoples of the larger group. The second term, "the Judeans," aims to identify a specific group of people who lived at a particular place and time, but this also does not capture certainty (e.g., 8:31; 11:54; 12:9) and risks limiting the meaning to a geographical one and erasing the existence of Jews as a people. Though well-meaning and intending to circumvent anti-Semitic readings, this proposal renders the text "Jew-free" and arguably disguises any anti-Jewish effect. The question of what to do with the anti-Jewish rhetoric within the Gospel is a question that many scholars of the Christian faith have yet to reconcile adequately.

Francisco Lozada, Jr.

Jesus went up to Jerusalem. [14]In the temple he found people selling cattle, sheep, and doves and the money changers seated at their tables. [15]Making a whip of cords, he drove all of them out of the temple, with the sheep and the cattle. He also poured out the coins of the money changers and overturned their tables. [16]He told those who were selling the doves, "Take these things out of here! Stop making my Father's house a marketplace!" [17]His disciples remembered that it was written, "Zeal for your house will consume me." [18]The Jews then said to him, "What sign can you show us for doing this?" [19]Jesus answered them, "Destroy this temple, and in three days I will raise it up." [20]The Jews then said, "This temple has been under construction for forty-six years, and will you raise it up in three days?" [21]But he was speaking of the temple of his body. [22]After he was raised from the dead, his disciples remembered that he had said this, and they believed the scripture and the word that Jesus had spoken.

23 When he was in Jerusalem during the Passover festival, many believed in his name because they saw the signs that he was doing. [24]But Jesus on his part would not entrust himself to them, because he knew all people [25]and needed no one to testify about anyone, for he himself knew what was in everyone.

would include a Passover supper and the seven days of the Feast of Unleavened Bread. Families go to the Jerusalem temple and slaughter a lamb in the temple precincts for an evening meal. The feast commemorates Israel's exodus from Egypt.

2:14–15 *Temple* here refers to the whole temple complex composed of several courts. The location may point to the outer court, the court of gentiles, where the selling of sacrificial animals took place to help people who came from a distance to buy their sacrifices. *Money changers* were people who exchanged foreign currency for a fee, since Roman currency was considered idolatrous.

2:17 *Zeal for your house will consume me* is a reference to Ps. 69:9. Jesus's devotion bears in mind his mission to keep to the true nature of worship in the temple. This dedication awakens Jesus's physically violent response to drive out the money changers and/or animals (see **"Violence," p. 1854**).

2:20 *This temple has been under construction for forty-six years* is in reference to the many years that it was taking to complete the construction of the temple. Under Herod's reign (37–4 BCE), it began about 20 to 19 BCE.

Focus On: Signs (John 2:11)

In narrative asides distinctive of the Fourth Gospel, the author of the Gospel of John analyzes the actions and words of Jesus alongside the telling of the story. One excellent example of this phenomenon is the way the Fourth Gospel describes the miracles of Jesus as "signs" (Gk. *sēmeia*). After Jesus turns water into wine, for example, the narrator points out, "Jesus did this, the first of his signs, in Cana of Galilee and revealed his glory, and his disciples believed in him" (2:11). Only this Gospel uses the language of "signs" to describe Jesus's miracles. Furthermore, the author describes their twofold intent: to "reveal his glory" and to lead to belief. Within the other Gospels, miracles do not seem to function in the same manner. While not every miracle is labeled a "sign" in the Fourth Gospel, many are (see 2:1–12; 4:46–54; 6:1–14; 9:1–12, 16; 11:1–47; 12:18), and these acts point to something meaningful beyond the acts themselves.

All these stories occur in the first half of the book (chaps. 1–12). Some scholars refer to this section as the "book of signs," arguing that the unique presence of this language hints at a possible outside source for the Gospel. In that case, the final purpose statement of the Gospel seems apropos: "Now Jesus did many other signs in the presence of his disciples that are not written in this book. But these are written so that you may continue to believe that Jesus is the Messiah, the Son of God, and that through believing you may have life in his name" (20:30–31). Other scholars have pointed to the function of these stories in their present literary settings. However readers choose to think about these descriptions of miracles, for this Gospel, "signs" are accounts that are associated with revealing something key about Jesus's identity and are accounts that may lead to an attraction to the Jesus movement.

Within the other Gospels, the descriptions of Jesus's miracles are also about his identity. But the language of "belief" in association with these accounts is rare. To put it another way, Jesus's healings, exorcisms, and nature miracles in the Synoptic Gospels, many of which are absent in John, do not usually lead crowds to believe in Jesus or acknowledge his identity as God's Son. John's distinctive categorization raises questions about the purpose and function of miracles for people of faith.

Emerson B. Powery

3 Now there was a Pharisee named Nicodemus, a leader of the Jews. [2]He came to Jesus[q] by night and said to him, "Rabbi, we know that you are a teacher who has come from God, for no one can do these signs that you do unless God is with that person." [3]Jesus answered him, "Very truly, I tell you, no one can see the kingdom of God without being born from above."[r] [4]Nicodemus said to him, "How can anyone be born after having grown old? Can one enter a second time into the mother's womb and be born?" [5]Jesus answered, "Very truly, I tell you, no one can enter the kingdom of God without being born of water and Spirit. [6]What is born of the flesh is flesh, and what is born of the Spirit is spirit. [7]Do not be astonished that I said to you, 'You[s] must be born from above.'[r] [8]The wind[u] blows where it chooses, and you hear the sound of it, but you do not know where it comes from or where it goes. So it is with everyone who is born of the Spirit." [9]Nicodemus said to him, "How can these things be?" [10]Jesus answered him, "Are you the teacher of Israel, and yet you do not understand these things?

[11] "Very truly, I tell you, we speak of what we know and testify to what we have seen, yet you[v] do not receive our testimony. [12]If I have told you about earthly things and you do not believe, how can you believe if I tell you about heavenly things? [13]No one has ascended into heaven except the one who descended from

q 3.2 Gk *him*   *r* 3.3 Or *born anew*   *s* 3.7 The Greek word for *you* here is plural   *t* 3.7 Or *born anew*   *u* 3.8 The same Greek word means both *wind* and *spirit*   *v* 3.11 The Greek word for *you* here and in 3.12 is plural

3:1 *Nicodemus, a leader of the Jews* is probably a member of the Sanhedrin, the highest religious council among the Jewish people.

3:3 *Very truly* ("amēn, amēn") is a common expression in the Gospel that highlights an underlying truth of what follows. For instance, the Greek word "anōthen" may mean both "anew" and "from above." Jesus means *from above* or heavenly birth, but Nicodemus understands the word as "anew," showing his lack of understanding.

3:5 *Of water and Spirit* possibly symbolizes repentance (water) and regeneration (Spirit). Prerequisites to be a follower of Jesus include an outward change (water) and an inward change (Spirit).

3:12 *Earthly things* points to elements such as birth (3:3), water (3:5), and wind (3:8), and *heavenly things* corresponds to spiritual truths.

Going Deeper: Violence (John 2:13-18)

To speak of violence in the Gospel of John seems odd, but violence does exist in the actions of characters and their rhetoric. In the story traditionally labeled The Cleansing of the Temple, some translations suggest that Jesus made a whip and drove both the cattle and the people out of the temple: "Making a whip of cords, he drove all of them out of the temple, with the sheep and the cattle. He also poured out the coins of the money changers and overturned their tables" (2:15). Did Jesus use the whip on the people, on the cattle, or on both? The Greek word for "all" (*pantas*) is masculine and plural just like "the cattle," which is masculine and plural. "The sheep" is neuter and plural. If one translates "all" as including "the people," it would portray Jesus as violent on this occasion—that is, driving not only the money changers out of the temple but also the sheep and the cattle. However, if one translates "all" as referring to the parts (the sheep and cattle) of the whole, Jesus is portrayed not as violent toward people but rather as violently driving out the sheep and the cattle. Some people today, depending on their way of life, would argue that using a whip on people or on cattle is never permitted. Perhaps a clearer sense of violence is found in the trial of Jesus: "Then Pilate took Jesus and had him flogged" (19:1). In this occasion, a whip is used on Jesus. Normally, before someone was crucified, whipping or flogging was conducted to prepare for death. It was a cruel punishment. The soldiers who arrested Jesus also placed a crown of thorns on his head and mocked him. The ultimate act of violence in the Gospel is the crucifixion of Jesus itself (19:16-37). This act of violence, whether nailed to the cross or tied to the cross, constitutes violent torture. The immediate asphyxiation/suffocation weakens the muscles, causing a fast or slow death. It is easy to read John without attention to the pyramids of power at play, but violence is one of those reflective elements that exist in the daily lives of people in the story of the Gospel.

Francisco Lozada, Jr.

heaven, the Son of Man.[w] [14]And just as Moses lifted up the serpent in the wilderness, so must the Son of Man be lifted up, [15]that whoever believes in him may have eternal life.[x]

[16] "For God so loved the world that he gave his only Son, so that everyone who believes in him may not perish but may have eternal life. [17] "Indeed, God did not send the Son into the world to condemn the world but in order that the world might be saved through him. [18]Those who believe in him are not condemned, but those who do not believe are condemned already because they have not believed in the name of the only Son of God. [19]And this is the judgment, that the light has come into the world, and people loved darkness rather than light because their deeds were evil. [20]For all who do evil hate the light and do not come to the light, so that their deeds may not be exposed. [21]But those who do what is true come to the light, so that it may be clearly seen that their deeds have been done in God."[y]

22 After this Jesus and his disciples went into the region of Judea, and he spent some time there with them and baptized. [23]John also was baptizing at Aenon near Salim because water was abundant there, and people kept coming and were being baptized. [24](John, of course, had not yet been thrown into prison.)

25 Now a discussion about purification arose between John's disciples and a Jew.[z] [26]They came to John and said to him, "Rabbi, the one who was with you across the Jordan, to whom you testified, here he is baptizing, and all are going to him." [27]John answered, "No one can receive anything except what has been

w 3.13 Other ancient authorities add *who is in heaven* x 3.15 Some interpreters hold that the quotation concludes with 3.15 y 3.21 Some interpreters hold that the quotation concludes with 3.15 z 3.25 Other ancient authorities read *the Jews*

3:16 *Eternal life* is a common expression in this Gospel that suggests everlasting life. In the ancient Jewish world, time was understood in the succession of ages. Here *eternal life* points to the "forever" life with Christ (11:25).

3:18 *In the name* is an expression that suggests belief in the only Son of God (3:16).

3:23-24 *John also was baptizing* suggests that John and Jesus had concurrent ministries at one time. The reference that John *had not yet been thrown into prison* conjures up the stories in the Synoptic Gospels of his imprisonment (Mark 6:27; Matt. 4:12; Luke 3:20).

3:25 *Purification* refers to the traditional washings among the Jewish people. Being made clean from all "pollution" is how one is purified. Here it is in reference to baptism.

Going Deeper: Dualism (Binaries) (John 3:3–21)

There is no question that John's worldview is dualistic from the beginning to the end of the Gospel. There is never a gray area or a middle ground. One is either an insider or an outsider, a believer or an unbeliever, one who knows or one who does not. This dualism most likely is a result of gnostic influences that saw the world in a binary way. It is an easy way to assert one's superiority and an easy way to shun one's opponents for not belonging to the correct side of the binary. In reading the Gospel, the world is divided between a positive world and a negative world. Some of the dualities consist of the following: world above / world below, spirit/flesh, true Israel / Jews (see **"'The Jews' (*Hoi Ioudaioi*),"** **p. 1852**), belief/unbelief, light/dark, God/Satan, truth/falsehood, children of light / children of darkness, and love/hate. This latter duality, love/hate, expresses the strong feelings of those who are insiders and outsiders. Those who fall on the end of the spectrum of love are included and seen in a positive light, according to the plot of the Gospel (e.g., 5:42; 8:42; 21:15). But for those who fall on the negative end of the spectrum, they are excluded and demonized (e.g., 3:20; 15:18; 17:14). Scholars have wrestled with what to do with the hate language in the Gospel of John. Some have explained that because the Johannine community (see **"Introduction to John," pp. 1847–48**) experienced feelings of hopelessness and a need for protection against their opponents, the use of such vitriolic language was necessary to survive. However, the danger is that such duality, though it might be considered a relic of the past, can be projected into the present by contemporary readers and used against *their* enemies. As the Gospel has expressed in the many names for Jesus, embracing multiple identities (e.g., the Word, Rabbi, the Light) is a way to capture the fullness of human experience beyond dualistic categories.

Francisco Lozada, Jr.

given from heaven. ²⁸You yourselves are my witnesses that I said, 'I am not the Messiah,ᵃ but I have been sent ahead of him.' ²⁹He who has the bride is the bridegroom. The friend of the bridegroom who stands and hears him rejoices greatly at the bridegroom's voice. For this reason my joy has been fulfilled. ³⁰He must increase, but I must decrease."ᵇ

31 The one who comes from above is above all; the one who is of the earth belongs to the earth and speaks about earthly things. The one who comes from heaven is above all. ³²He testifies to what he has seen and heard, yet no one accepts his testimony. ³³Whoever has accepted his testimony has certifiedᶜ this, that God is true. ³⁴He whom God has sent speaks the words of God, for he gives the Spirit without measure. ³⁵The Father loves the Son and has placed all things in his hands. ³⁶Whoever

believes in the Son has eternal life; whoever disobeys the Son will not see life but must endure God's wrath.

4 Now when Jesusᵈ learned that the Pharisees had heard, "Jesus is making and baptizing more disciples than John" ²(although it was not Jesus himself but his disciples who baptized), ³he left Judea and started back to Galilee. ⁴But he had to go through Samaria. ⁵So he came to a Samaritan city called Sychar, near the plot of ground that Jacob had given to his son Joseph. ⁶Jacob's well was there, and Jesus, tired out by his journey, was sitting by the well. It was about noon.

a 3.28 Or *the Christ*   *b* 3.30 Some interpreters hold that the quotation continues through 3.36   *c* 3.33 Gk *set a seal to*   *d* 4.1 Other ancient authorities read *the Lord*

3:31 *Above all* recalls the origins of Jesus (see 1:1). This idea is contrasted with *the one who is of the earth*. Here John the Baptist of the earth bears witness to the one from above, Jesus.

3:32 *Testifies* emphasizes the importance of witnessing in this Gospel. To see and to hear are senses of belief and are manifested in one's *testimony*.

3:34 The term *Spirit* refers to the voice of God and operates to both reveal the truth of God and to assist humanity in recognizing this truth (see 3:6, 8).

3:36 *Believes* ("pisteuōn") and *disobeys* ("apeithōn") are actions that point to what it means to be a follower. That is, to disobey the Son is not to believe in the Son. To disobey will also bring *God's wrath* or divine judgment that will not lead to eternal life.

4:4 *To go through Samaria* is the shortest route to Galilee.

4:5–6 *Sychar* may have been a small village or town in the region of Mount Gerizim. Some ancient manuscripts identify Sychar as Shechem (Gen. 12:6–7; 33:18). Both places are in Samaria. *It was about noon* points to the period from 6 a.m. to 6 p.m., with the sixth hour being twelve o'clock midday.

7 A Samaritan woman came to draw water, and Jesus said to her, "Give me a drink." [8](His disciples had gone to the city to buy food.) [9]The Samaritan woman said to him, "How is it that you, a Jew, ask a drink of me, a woman of Samaria?" (Jews do not share things in common with Samaritans.)[e] [10]Jesus answered her, "If you knew the gift of God and who it is that is saying to you, 'Give me a drink,' you would have asked him, and he would have given you living water." [11]The woman said to him, "Sir,[f] you have no bucket, and the well is deep. Where do you get that living water? [12]Are you greater than our ancestor Jacob, who gave us the well and with his sons and his flocks drank from it?" [13]Jesus said to her, "Everyone who drinks of this water will be thirsty again, [14]but those who drink of the water that I will give them will never be thirsty. The water that I will give will become in them a spring of water gushing up to eternal life." [15]The woman said to him, "Sir,[g] give me this water, so that I may never be thirsty or have to keep coming here to draw water."

16 Jesus said to her, "Go, call your husband, and come back." [17]The woman answered him, "I have no husband." Jesus said to her, "You are right in saying, 'I have no husband,' [18]for you have had five husbands, and the one you have now is not your husband. What you have said is true!" [19]The woman said to him, "Sir,[b] I see that you are a prophet. [20]Our ancestors worshiped on this mountain, but you[i] say that

the place where people must worship is in Jerusalem." [21]Jesus said to her, "Woman, believe me, the hour is coming when you[j] will worship the Father neither on this mountain nor in Jerusalem. [22]You[k] worship what you[l] do not know; we worship what we know, for salvation is from the Jews. [23]But the hour is coming and is now here when the true worshipers will worship the Father in spirit and truth, for the Father seeks such as these to worship him. [24]God is spirit, and those who worship him must worship in spirit and truth." [25]The woman said to him, "I know that Messiah is coming" (who is called Christ). "When he comes, he will proclaim all things to us." [26]Jesus said to her, "I am he,[m] the one who is speaking to you."

27 Just then his disciples came. They were astonished that he was speaking with a woman, but no one said, "What do you want?" or, "Why are you speaking with her?" [28]Then the woman left her water jar and went back to the city. She said to the people, [29]"Come and see a man who told me everything I have ever done! He cannot be the Messiah,[n] can he?" [30]They left the city and were on their way to him.

31 Meanwhile the disciples were urging him, "Rabbi, eat something." [32]But he said to

e 4.9 Other ancient authorities lack this sentence
f 4.11 Or Lord   g 4.15 Or Lord   h 4.19 Or Lord   i 4.20 The Greek word for you is plural   j 4.21 The Greek word for you is plural   k 4.22 The Greek word for you is plural   l 4.22 The Greek word for you is plural   m 4.26 Gk I am   n 4.29 Or the Christ

Normally, one drew water in the early morning. The brightness may be in contrast with Nicodemus, who came at night.

4:7–9 *A Samaritan woman came to draw water* brings attention to other similar well scenes found in the Hebrew Bible (Gen. 24:11; 29:2; Exod. 2:16). These verses also call attention to the issues of ethnic/religious and gender differences between Samaritans and the Jewish people and between women and men.

4:10 *Water* is a dominant theme in the Gospel that quenches physical thirst but also spiritual thirst (see, e.g., 2:1–12; 3:5; 4:10–15; 5:2–7; 6:16–21; 7:37–39; 9:7; 13:3–10; 19:34).

4:12 *Are you greater than our ancestor Jacob?* For the Samaritans, as for the Jewish people, Jacob is claimed as their forefather.

4:16–18 *Go, call your husband, and come back* conjures up questions of propriety between a woman and man speaking alone, the Samaritan woman's chosen way of life, and Jesus's ability to see the woman's hidden true identity. *I have no husband* also introduces questions of Jewish and Samaritan law on divorce. *For you have had five husbands* continues Jesus's display of his supernatural knowledge of the past in this Gospel.

4:20 *Our ancestors worshiped on this mountain* implies the historical relationship between the Jewish people and the Samaritans and the proper place to worship. For "the Jews," Jerusalem is the center of worship, and Mount Gerizim is the place of worship for the Samaritans.

4:26 *I am he* ("egō eimi") is linked with the revelation of God to Moses at the burning bush (Exod. 3:14). The "I am" sayings are also linked to God's name YHWH in the Hebrew Bible (Exod. 3:14; Isa. 41:4). "I am" is repeated with no predicate numerous times throughout this Gospel (6:20; 8:58; 13:19; 18:8).

Going Deeper: Women in the Gospel of John (John 4)

Women play a role in many significant stories in the Gospel of John. As the plot unfolds, the mother of Jesus witnesses Jesus's first miracle at the wedding at Cana (2:1–12). She is known by the people of Capernaum (6:42) and then figures prominently at the foot of the cross of Jesus (19:25–27) and is provided with important instructions to care for the Beloved Disciple. The Samaritan woman (4:1–42) also plays an essential role in helping to introduce Jesus to her community but also in breaking down religious, ethnic, and gender relations that existed in the story world. Mary and Martha also play an important role in the raising of Lazarus from the dead (11:1–44). Jesus holds deep love for them and their brother (11:5, 35), but they are also key in calling on Jesus to help their brother Lazarus. Mary later will also treat Jesus as royalty by pouring costly perfume on his feet and wiping his feet with her hair (12:1–8). Other women are also present at the death of Jesus. Mary, Clopas's wife, and Mary Magdalene (19:25) are there (not the male disciples) and accompany Jesus's mother to the crucifixion. Finally, Mary Magdalene figures prominently in the post-resurrection narratives of the Gospel (20:1–18). She is the first to meet the resurrected Jesus and the one who announces the news to the disciples (20:18). The portrayal of these women provides models of early Christian living and models of coequality in the birth and development of the Johannine community (see **"Introduction to John," pp. 1847–48**). They are collectively intelligent, forceful in asking questions, and sensitive. They are also honest, to the point, and not afraid to speak in public (e.g., the Samaritan woman). Because of this strong portrayal of women in the Gospel, some scholars have also argued that the author of John might be a woman represented in the Beloved Disciple (e.g., 13:23; 19:26–27; 20:2).

Francisco Lozada, Jr.

them, "I have food to eat that you do not know about." [33]So the disciples said to one another, "Surely no one has brought him something to eat?" [34]Jesus said to them, "My food is to do the will of him who sent me and to complete his work. [35]Do you not say, 'Four months more, then comes the harvest'? But I tell you, look around you, and see how the fields are ripe for harvesting. [36]The reaper is already receiving[o] wages and is gathering fruit for eternal life, so that sower and reaper may rejoice together. [37]For here the saying holds true, 'One sows and another reaps.' [38]I sent you to reap that for which you did not labor. Others have labored, and you have entered into their labor."

[39]Many Samaritans from that city believed in him because of the woman's testimony, "He told me everything I have ever done." [40]So when the Samaritans came to him, they asked him to stay with them, and he stayed there two days. [41]And many more believed because of his word. [42]They said to the woman, "It is no longer because of what you said that we believe, for we have heard for ourselves, and we know that this is truly the Savior of the world."

[43]When the two days were over, he went from that place to Galilee [44](for Jesus himself had testified that a prophet has no honor in the prophet's own country). [45]When he came to Galilee, the Galileans welcomed him, since they had seen all that he had done in Jerusalem at the festival, for they, too, had gone to the festival.

[46]Then he came again to Cana in Galilee, where he had changed the water into wine. Now there was a royal official whose son lay ill in Capernaum. [47]When he heard that Jesus had come from Judea to Galilee, he went and begged him to come down and heal his son, for he was at the point of death. [48]Then Jesus said to him, "Unless you[p] see signs and wonders you will not believe." [49]The official said to him, "Sir,[q] come down before my little boy dies." [50]Jesus said to him, "Go; your son will live."[r] The man believed the word that Jesus spoke to him and started on his way. [51]As he was going down, his slaves met him and told him that his child was alive. [52]So he asked them the hour when he began to recover, and they said to him, "Yesterday at one in the afternoon the fever left him." [53]The father realized that this was the hour when Jesus had

o 4.36 Or [35] . . . the fields are already ripe for harvesting. [36] The reaper is receiving   p 4.48 Both instances of the Greek word for *you* in 4.48 are plural   q 4.49 Or *Lord*   r 4.50 Gk *son lives*

4:35 *Four months more, then comes the harvest* signals the temporal context as well as the sense that there is no need to rush to harvest.

4:42 *Savior of the world* is a title typically applied at this time to the Roman emperor. The Hebrew Bible also applied this title to God as the Savior (see Isa. 45:15, 21; 62:11).

4:46 *Royal official* ("basilikos") is one who would have served the colonial powers.

said to him, "Your son will live."^{s} So he himself believed, along with his whole household. ^{54}Now this was the second sign that Jesus did after coming from Judea to Galilee.

5 After this there was a festival of the Jews, and Jesus went up to Jerusalem.

2 Now in Jerusalem by the Sheep Gate there is a pool, called in Hebrew^t Beth-zatha,^{u} which has five porticoes. ^{3}In these lay many ill, blind, lame, and paralyzed people.^{v} ^{5}One man was there who had been ill for thirty-eight years. ^{6}When Jesus saw him lying there and knew that he had been there a long time, he said to him, "Do you want to be made well?" ^{7}The ill man answered him, "Sir,^{w} I have no one to put me into the pool when the water is stirred up, and while I am making my way someone else steps down ahead of me." ^{8}Jesus said to him, "Stand up, take your mat and walk." ^{9}At once the man was made well, and he took up his mat and began to walk.

Now that day was a Sabbath. ^{10}So the Jews said to the man who had been cured, "It is the Sabbath; it is not lawful for you to carry your mat." ^{11}But he answered them, "The man who made me well said to me, 'Take up your mat and walk.'" ^{12}They asked him, "Who is the man who said to you, 'Take it up and walk'?" ^{13}Now the man who had been healed did not know who it was, for Jesus had disappeared in^x the crowd that was there. ^{14}Later Jesus found him in the temple and said to him, "See, you have been made well! Do not sin any more, so that nothing worse happens to you." ^{15}The man went away and told the Jews that it

was Jesus who had made him well. ^{16}Therefore the Jews started persecuting Jesus, because he was doing such things on the Sabbath. ^{17}But Jesus answered them, "My Father is still working, and I also am working." ^{18}For this reason the Jews were seeking all the more to kill him, because he was not only breaking the Sabbath but was also calling God his own Father, thereby making himself equal to God.

19 Jesus said to them, "Very truly, I tell you, the Son can do nothing on his own but only what he sees the Father doing, for whatever the Father^y does, the Son does likewise. ^{20}The Father loves the Son and shows him all that he himself is doing, and he will show him greater works than these, so that you will be astonished. ^{21}Indeed, just as the Father raises the dead and gives them life, so also the Son gives life to whomever he wishes. ^{22}The Father judges no one but has given all judgment to the Son, ^{23}so that all may honor the Son just as they honor the Father. Anyone who does not honor the Son does not honor the Father who sent him. ^{24}Very truly, I tell you, anyone who hears my word and believes him who sent me has eternal life and does not come under judgment but has passed from death to life.

25 "Very truly, I tell you, the hour is coming and is now here when the dead will hear

s 4.53 Gk *son lives* t 5.2 That is, *Aramaic* u 5.2 Other ancient authorities read *Bethesda* or *Bethsaida* v 5.3 Other ancient authorities add, wholly or in part, *waiting for the stirring of the water,* ^{t}*for an angel of the Lord went down from time to time into the pool and stirred up the water; whoever stepped in first after the stirring of the water was made well from whatever disease that person had.* w 5.7 Or *Lord* x 5.13 Or *had left because of* y 5.19 Gk *that one*

4:54 This is the *second sign* that took place in Cana (see 2:11).

5:1 *Festival of the Jews* is an unnamed feast in this Gospel. Its identity is uncertain, but it is probably one of the three pilgrimage festivals that mandated going to the Jerusalem temple.

5:2 *Beth-zatha* is also understood as Bethsaida or Bethesda in some ancient manuscripts.

5:3 *Many ill, blind, lame, and paralyzed people* calls attention to the multitude of physically challenged persons in the ancient world (see **"Healing in the Gospels and Acts," p. 1773**).

5:7 *When the water is stirred up* suggests a subterranean stream that bubbled up and disturbed the waters. This disturbance was believed to have been caused by a supernatural power and thus possessed curative powers.

5:9 *Sabbath* refers to the seventh day of the week when God ceased from the work of creation (Gen. 2:1–3). Here it is a holy day of rest from work in the Jewish weekly calendar.

5:18 *The Jews were seeking all the more to kill him* begins the hostile antagonism toward Jesus's life in the plot of the Gospel. Not all *Jews* participate in this hostility (see note in 1:19).

5:20 *Loves* ("philei") is a dominant theme in this Gospel. Here it describes the relationship between Jesus and his Father (see, e.g., 8:42; 13:34; 14:23).

5:23 *Honor* was a strong virtue in the ancient world. To fail to honor one's parent was to shame the parent.

5:25 *The hour is coming and is now here* conjures up the present and future judgment and resurrection.

the voice of the Son of God, and those who hear will live. [26]For just as the Father has life in himself, so he has granted the Son also to have life in himself, [27]and he has given him authority to execute judgment because he is the Son of Man. [28]Do not be astonished at this, for the hour is coming when all who are in their graves will hear his voice [29]and will come out: those who have done good to the resurrection of life, and those who have done evil to the resurrection of condemnation.

30 "I can do nothing on my own. As I hear, I judge, and my judgment is just because I seek to do not my own will but the will of him who sent me.

31 "If I testify about myself, my testimony is not true. [32]There is another who testifies on my behalf, and I know that his testimony to me is true. [33]You sent messengers to John, and he testified to the truth. [34]Not that I accept such human testimony, but I say these things so that you may be saved. [35]He was a burning and shining lamp, and you were willing to rejoice for a while in his light. [36]But I have a testimony greater than John's. The works that the Father has given me to complete, the very works that I am doing, testify on my behalf that the Father has sent me. [37]And the Father who sent me has himself testified on my behalf. You have never heard his voice or seen his form, [38]and you do not have his word abiding in you, because you do not believe him whom he has sent.

39 "You search the scriptures because you think that in them you have eternal life, and it is they that testify on my behalf. [40]Yet you refuse to come to me to have life. [41]I do not accept glory from humans. [42]But I know that you do not have the love of God in[z] you. [43]I have come in my Father's name, and you do not accept me; if another comes in his own name, you will accept him. [44]How can you believe when you accept glory from one another and do not seek the glory that comes from the one who alone is God?[a] [45]Do not think that I will accuse you before the Father; your accuser is Moses, on whom you have set your hope. [46]If you believed Moses, you would believe me, for he wrote about me. [47]But if you do not believe what he wrote, how will you believe what I say?"

6 After this Jesus went to the other side of the Sea of Galilee, also called the Sea of Tiberias.[b] [2]A large crowd kept following him because they saw the signs that he was doing for the sick. [3]Jesus went up the mountain and sat down there with his disciples. [4]Now the Passover, the festival of the Jews, was near. [5]When he looked up and saw a large crowd coming toward him, Jesus said to Philip, "Where are we to buy bread for these people to eat?" [6]He said this to test him, for he himself knew what he was going to do. [7]Philip answered him, "Two hundred denarii would not buy enough bread for each of them to get a little." [8]One of his disciples, Andrew, Simon Peter's brother, said to him, [9]"There is a boy here who has five barley loaves and two fish. But what are they among so many people?" [10]Jesus said, "Make the people sit down." Now there was a great deal of grass in the place,

z 5.42 Or *among*   a 5.44 Other manuscripts read *the Only One*   b 6.1 Gk *of Galilee of Tiberias*

Son of God is a title that is also a designation for Israel as God's son as righteous, a king's representative, or a servant of God (Exod. 4:22–23; Hos. 1:10; 2 Sam. 7:14; Sir. 4:10).

5:27 *Son of Man* is another title that recalls the image of one who descends into the world to redeem it. The title implies that Jesus is both the source of life and the basis of judgment (see Dan. 7:1–14).

5:31 *If I testify about myself* speaks to the understanding that one person's witness cannot be taken as proof. There must be at least two witnesses (see Num. 35:30; Deut. 17:6; 19:15). Witnessing is a dominant theme in this chapter: the Father (v. 37), John (v. 33), the works (v. 36), the Scriptures (v. 39), and Moses (v. 46).

5:35 *Burning and shining lamp* is a metaphor describing John as a guide to Jesus for the people.

5:41 *Glory* here can be understood as "praise."

5:46 *Moses* is the final witness understood as the lawgiver.

6:1 *Sea of Galilee, also called the Sea of Tiberias* reflects different naming moments of the location in the first century, with the latter named in the period of Herod Antipas in about 20 CE.

6:5 *Bread for these people to eat* calls attention to the food insecurity at the time among many of the poor.

6:7 *Two hundred denarii* was equivalent to six months' wages. Food supplies for the poor called for funds beyond the poor's daily earnings.

so they[c] sat down, about five thousand in all. [11]Then Jesus took the loaves, and when he had given thanks he distributed them to those who were seated; so also the fish, as much as they wanted. [12]When they were satisfied, he told his disciples, "Gather up the fragments left over, so that nothing may be lost." [13]So they gathered them up, and from the fragments of the five barley loaves, left by those who had eaten, they filled twelve baskets. [14]When the people saw the sign that he had done, they began to say, "This is indeed the prophet who is to come into the world."

15 When Jesus realized that they were about to come and take him by force to make him king, he withdrew again to the mountain by himself.

16 When evening came, his disciples went down to the sea, [17]got into a boat, and started across the sea to Capernaum. It was now dark, and Jesus had not yet come to them. [18]The sea became rough because a strong wind was blowing. [19]When they had rowed about three or four miles, they saw Jesus walking on the sea and coming near the boat, and they were terrified. [20]But he said to them, "It is I;[d] do not be afraid." [21]Then they wanted to take him into the boat, and immediately the boat reached the land toward which they were going.

22 The next day the crowd that had stayed on the other side of the sea saw that there had been only one boat there. They also saw that Jesus had not gotten into the boat with his disciples but that his disciples had gone away alone. [23]But some boats from Tiberias came near the place where they had eaten the bread after the Lord had given thanks. [24]So when the crowd saw that neither Jesus nor his disciples were there, they themselves got into the boats and went to Capernaum looking for Jesus.

25 When they found him on the other side of the sea, they said to him, "Rabbi, when did you come here?" [26]Jesus answered them, "Very truly, I tell you, you are looking for me not because you saw signs but because you ate your fill of the loaves. [27]Do not work for the food that perishes but for the food that endures for eternal life, which the Son of Man will give you. For it is on him that God the Father has set his seal." [28]Then they said to him, "What must we do to perform the works of God?" [29]Jesus answered them, "This is the work of God, that you believe in him whom he has sent." [30]So they said to him, "What sign are you going to give us, then, so that we may see it and believe you? What work are you performing? [31]Our ancestors ate the manna in the wilderness, as it is written, 'He gave them bread from heaven to eat.'" [32]Then Jesus said to them, "Very truly, I tell you, it was not Moses who gave you the bread from heaven, but it is my Father who gives you the true bread from heaven. [33]For the bread of God is that which[e] comes down from heaven and gives life to the world." [34]They said to him, "Sir,[f] give us this bread always."

35 Jesus said to them, "I am the bread of life. Whoever comes to me will never be hungry, and whoever believes in me will never be thirsty. [36]But I said to you that you have seen me and yet do not believe. [37]Everything that the Father gives me will come to me, and anyone who comes to me I will never drive away, [38]for I have come down from heaven not to do

c 6.10 Gk *the men*   d 6.20 Gk *I am*   e 6.33 Or *he who*
f 6.34 Or *Lord*

6:11 *He had given thanks* ("eucharistēsas") is a common Jewish practice.

6:14–15 The *sign* is the fourth one in the Gospel. It is the second sign multiplying food supplies (see 2:9). The sign will lead the crowd to see Jesus as *the prophet* Moses, recalling the memory of Moses prophesying he would come to God's people (Deut. 18:15, 18). To make Jesus *king* conjures up the colonial relationship with Rome.

6:17 *Capernaum* in the story is Jesus's home city during his Galilean ministry (see 2:12; 6:24).

6:20 *It is I* ("egō eimi") calls to mind once again the Hebrew Bible's reference to God (see 4:26).

6:27 *Seal* suggests that God approves.

6:31 *Our ancestors* refers to Moses and his feeding the Hebrew people manna, bread from heaven, while wandering in the wilderness (Exod. 16:15). *He gave them bread from heaven* perhaps is part of the Passover Torah reading in the synagogue at the time (see Ps. 78:24).

6:35 *I am the bread of life* refers to Jesus as spiritual nourishment. It is read in the light of the bread (manna) from heaven. This is the first emphatic predicate "I am" saying (see, e.g., 6:51; 8:12; 10:7, 9, 11, 14; 11:25; 14:6; 15:1).

6:38 *I have come down from heaven* is an example of a common ascent/descent motif. Seven times in this chapter Jesus says he had come down from heaven (vv. 33, 38, 41, 42, 50, 51, 58).

my own will but the will of him who sent me. [39]And this is the will of him who sent me, that I should lose nothing of all that he has given me but raise it up on the last day. [40]This is indeed the will of my Father, that all who see the Son and believe in him may have eternal life, and I will raise them up on the last day."

41 Then the Jews began to complain about him because he said, "I am the bread that came down from heaven." [42]They were saying, "Is not this Jesus, the son of Joseph, whose father and mother we know? How can he now say, 'I have come down from heaven'?" [43]Jesus answered them, "Do not complain among yourselves. [44]No one can come to me unless drawn by the Father who sent me, and I will raise that person up on the last day. [45]It is written in the prophets, 'And they shall all be taught by God.' Everyone who has heard and learned from the Father comes to me. [46]Not that anyone has seen the Father except the one who is from God; he has seen the Father. [47]Very truly, I tell you, whoever believes has eternal life. [48]I am the bread of life. [49]Your ancestors ate the manna in the wilderness, and they died. [50]This is the bread that comes down from heaven, so that one may eat of it and not die. [51]I am the living bread that came down from heaven. Whoever eats of this bread will live forever, and the bread that I will give for the life of the world is my flesh."

52 The Jews then disputed among themselves, saying, "How can this man give us his flesh to eat?" [53]So Jesus said to them, "Very truly, I tell you, unless you eat the flesh of the Son of Man and drink his blood, you have no life in you. [54]Those who eat my flesh and drink my blood have eternal life, and I will raise them up on the last day, [55]for my flesh is true food, and my blood is true drink. [56]Those who eat my flesh and drink my blood abide in me and I in them. [57]Just as the living Father sent me and I live because of the Father,

so whoever eats me will live because of me. [58]This is the bread that came down from heaven, not like that which the ancestors ate, and they died. But the one who eats this bread will live forever." [59]He said these things while he was teaching in a synagogue at Capernaum.

60 When many of his disciples heard it, they said, "This teaching is difficult; who can accept it?" [61]But Jesus, being aware that his disciples were complaining about it, said to them, "Does this offend you? [62]Then what if you were to see the Son of Man ascending to where he was before? [63]It is the spirit that gives life; the flesh is useless. The words that I have spoken to you are spirit and life. [64]But among you there are some who do not believe." For Jesus knew from the beginning who were the ones who did not believe and who was the one who would betray him. [65]And he said, "For this reason I have told you that no one can come to me unless it is granted by the Father."

66 Because of this many of his disciples turned back and no longer went about with him. [67]So Jesus asked the twelve, "Do you also wish to go away?" [68]Simon Peter answered him, "Lord, to whom can we go? You have the words of eternal life. [69]We have come to believe and know that you are the Holy One of God."[g] [70]Jesus answered them, "Did I not choose you, the twelve? Yet one of you is a devil." [71]He was speaking of Judas son of Simon Iscariot,[b] for he, though one of the twelve, was going to betray him.

7 After this Jesus went about in Galilee. He did not wish to go about in Judea because the Jews were looking for an opportunity to kill him. [2]Now the Jewish Festival of Booths[i]

g 6.69 Other ancient authorities read *the Christ, the Son of the living God* b 6.71 Other ancient authorities read *Judas Iscariot son of Simon* or *Judas son of Simon from Karyot* (Kerioth)
i 7.2 Or *Tabernacles*

6:42 *Whose father and mother we know* refers to Jesus's earthly parents (see Matt. 13:55; Mark 6:3). Earthly parents are contrasted with heavenly parents.

6:53 *Eat the flesh . . . and drink his blood* is used metaphorically to refer to Jesus's humanity and to look ahead to his death on the cross. It also refers to those believers who take Jesus into their lives (see v. 56).

6:59 *Synagogue* is a place where people come together for prayer and worship. It is the power base of the Pharisees.

6:70 *Yet one of you is a devil* here suggests that Judas's action is work following the devil's purposes of betrayal (see 6:71; cf. Matt. 16:23 and Mark 8:33 for differences).

7:2 *Jewish Festival of Booths* is also known as Sukkot, or the Feast of Tabernacles (Lev. 23:33–43). It is a festival celebrated in autumn, especially during the grape harvest, in commemoration of the wilderness wanderings (Exod. 23; Deut. 16).

was near. ³So his brothers said to him, "Leave here and go to Judea so that your disciples also may see the works you are doing, ⁴for no one who wants^j to be widely known acts in secret. If you do these things, show yourself to the world." ⁵(For not even his brothers believed in him.) ⁶Jesus said to them, "My time has not yet come, but your time is always here. ⁷The world cannot hate you, but it hates me because I testify against it that its works are evil. ⁸Go to the festival yourselves. I am not^k going to this festival, for my time has not yet fully come." ⁹After saying this, he remained in Galilee.

10 But after his brothers had gone to the festival, then he also went, not publicly but, as it were,^l in secret. ¹¹The Jews were looking for him at the festival and saying, "Where is he?" ¹²And there was considerable complaining about him among the crowds. While some were saying, "He is a good man," others were saying, "No, he is deceiving the crowd." ¹³Yet no one would speak openly about him for fear of the Jews.

14 About the middle of the festival Jesus went up into the temple and began to teach. ¹⁵The Jews were astonished at it, saying, "How does this man have such learning, when he has never been taught?" ¹⁶Then Jesus answered them, "My teaching is not mine but his who sent me. ¹⁷Anyone who resolves to do the will of God will know whether the teaching is from God or whether I am speaking on my own. ¹⁸Those who speak on their own seek their own glory, but the one who seeks the glory of him who sent him is true, and there is nothing unjust in him.

19 "Did not Moses give you the law? Yet none of you keeps the law. Why are you looking for an opportunity to kill me?" ²⁰The crowd answered, "You have a demon! Who is trying to kill you?" ²¹Jesus answered them, "I performed one work, and all of you are astonished. ²²Because of this Moses gave you circumcision (it is, of course, not from Moses but from the patriarchs), and you circumcise a man on the Sabbath. ²³If a man receives circumcision on the Sabbath in order that the law of Moses may not be broken, are you angry with me because I healed a man's whole body on the Sabbath? ²⁴Do not judge by appearances, but judge with right judgment."

25 Now some of the people of Jerusalem were saying, "Is not this the man whom they are trying to kill? ²⁶And here he is, speaking openly, but they say nothing to him! Can it be that the authorities really know that this is the Messiah?^m ²⁷Yet we know where this man is from, but when the Messiah^n comes no one will know where he is from." ²⁸Then Jesus cried out as he was teaching in the temple, "You know me, and you know where I am from. I have not come on my own. But the one who sent me is true, and you do not know him. ²⁹I know him because I am from him, and he sent me." ³⁰Then they tried to arrest him, but no one laid hands on him because his hour had not yet come. ³¹Yet many in the crowd believed in him and were saying, "When the Messiah^o comes, will he do more signs than this man has done?"^p

32 The Pharisees heard the crowd muttering such things about him, and the chief priests and Pharisees sent temple police to arrest him. ³³Jesus then said, "I will be with

j 7.4 Other ancient authorities read *wants it*   k 7.8 Other ancient authorities add *yet*   l 7.10 Other ancient authorities lack *as it were*   m 7.26 Or *the Christ*   n 7.27 Or *the Christ*   o 7.31 Or *the Christ*   p 7.31 Other ancient authorities read *is doing*

7:3 The identity of the *brothers* remains uncertain (see 2:12; 7:10). Are they followers of Jesus, half brothers, or full brothers? The reference is unclear.

7:10 *Not publicly but, as it were, in secret* is contrasted with his brothers working out in the open (v. 4).

7:13 *Fear of the Jews* conjures up the plot's hostility toward "the Jews." The text does not specify who "the Jews" are, and they are contrasted with the "crowd" (v. 12) and "some of the people of Jerusalem" (v. 25).

7:20 *Demon* refers to spiritual possession (see 8:48, 52; 10:20, 21) with supernatural knowledge. In the ancient world, unexplained occurrences were explained by various mysterious forces.

7:22–23 *Circumcision* recalls the Abrahamic covenant (Gen. 17:11). Circumcision is also a sign of this covenant and is included in the Law (Lev. 12:3). One portion of the body is contrasted with the whole body (see 5:1–9).

7:28 *Jesus cried out* is employed here to call attention to the solemn pronouncement (v. 29) he was to make (see also 1:15; 7:37; 12:44).

7:30 *Then they tried to arrest him* (literally "were seeking"). Time in the plot of the Gospel is dependent on God's time. This is the reason why *no one laid hands on him*.

you a little while longer, and then I am going to him who sent me. [34]You will search for me, but you will not find me, and where I am, you cannot come." [35]The Jews said to one another, "Where does this man intend to go that we will not find him? Does he intend to go to the dispersion among the Greeks and teach the Greeks? [36]What does he mean by saying, 'You will search for me, but you will not find me' and 'Where I am, you cannot come'?"

37 On the last day of the festival, the great day, while Jesus was standing there, he cried out, "Let anyone who is thirsty come to me, [38]and let the one who believes in me drink. As[q] the scripture has said, 'Out of the believer's heart[r] shall flow rivers of living water.'" [39]Now he said this about the Spirit, which believers in him were to receive, for as yet there was no Spirit[s] because Jesus was not yet glorified.

40 When they heard these words, some in the crowd said, "This is really the prophet." [41]Others said, "This is the Messiah."[t] But some asked, "Surely the Messiah[u] does not come from Galilee, does he? [42]Has not the scripture said that the Messiah[v] is descended from David and comes from Bethlehem, the village where David lived?" [43]So there was a division in the crowd because of him. [44]Some of them wanted to arrest him, but no one laid hands on him.

45 Then the temple police went back to the chief priests and Pharisees, who asked them, "Why did you not arrest him?" [46]The police answered, "Never has anyone spoken like this!" [47]Then the Pharisees replied, "Surely you have not been deceived, too, have you? [48]Has any one of the authorities or of the Pharisees believed in him? [49]But this crowd, which does not know the law, they are accursed." [50]Nicodemus, who had gone to Jesus[w] before and who was one of them, asked, [51]"Our law does not judge people without first giving them a hearing to find out what they are doing, does it?" [52]They replied, "Surely you are not also from Galilee, are you? Search and you will see that no prophet is to arise from Galilee."

8 [[53 Then each of them went home, [1]while Jesus went to the Mount of Olives. [2]Early in the morning he came again to the temple. All the people came to him, and he sat down and began to teach them. [3]The scribes and the Pharisees brought a woman who had been caught in adultery, and, making her stand before all of them, [4]they said to him, "Teacher, this woman was caught in the very act of committing adultery. [5]Now in the law Moses commanded us to stone such women. Now what do you say?" [6]They said this to test him, so that they might have some charge to bring against him. Jesus bent down and wrote with his finger on the ground. [7]When they kept on questioning him, he straightened up and said to them, "Let anyone among you who is without sin be the first to throw a stone at her." [8]And once again he bent down and wrote on the ground. [9]When they heard it, they went away, one by one, beginning with the elders, and Jesus was left alone with the woman standing before him. [10]Jesus straightened up and said to her, "Woman, where are they? Has no one condemned you?" [11]She said, "No one, sir."[x] And Jesus said, "Neither do I condemn you. Go your way, and from now on do not sin again."]][y]

q 7.38 Or *come to me and drink.* [38]*The one who believes in me, as* r 7.38 Gk *out of his belly* s 7.39 Other ancient authorities read *for as yet the Spirit* (others, *Holy Spirit*) *had not been given* t 7.41 Or *the Christ* u 7.41 Or *the Christ* v 7.42 Or *the Christ* w 7.50 Gk *him* x 8.11 Or *Lord* y 8.11 The most ancient authorities lack 7.53–8.11; other authorities add the passage here or after 7.36 or after 21.25 or after Luke 21.38, with variations of text; some mark the passage as doubtful.

7:35 *Dispersion among the Greeks* refers to those Jewish people who lived outside the land of Israel/Palestine, as some had since the Babylonian exile. This was known as the Diaspora. But the Greeks in the second reference were not the Hellenistic Jews but gentiles with a different religious way of life compared to the Jewish people (see **"Diaspora," p. 1338**).

7:42 *The Messiah is descended from David and comes from Bethlehem* recalls Mic. 5:2, which taught that the Messiah would come from Bethlehem in Judea. Jesus's origin is mentioned several times in this chapter and thus is a conversation among the crowd (7:43).

7:45–49 *Chief priests and Pharisees* are religious authorities. The chief priests governed the temple. The Pharisees specialized in the Law and believed that the judgment of certain people unskilled in the interpretation of the Law should not be trusted (v. 49).

7:53–8:11 *Then each of them went home* is the beginning of a story traditionally called The Woman Caught in Adultery, which is strongly believed by scholars to have been added to the Gospel at a later time. It is considered an interpolation and not supported by the strongest extant manuscripts of the Gospel.

12 Again Jesus spoke to them, saying, "I am the light of the world. Whoever follows me will never walk in darkness but will have the light of life." [13]Then the Pharisees said to him, "You are testifying on your own behalf; your testimony is not valid." [14]Jesus answered, "Even if I testify on my own behalf, my testimony is valid because I know where I have come from and where I am going, but you do not know where I come from or where I am going. [15]You judge by human standards;[z] I judge no one. [16]Yet even if I do judge, my judgment is valid, for it is not I alone who judge but I and the Father[a] who sent me. [17]In your law it is written that the testimony of two witnesses is valid. [18]I testify on my own behalf, and the Father who sent me testifies on my behalf." [19]Then they said to him, "Where is your Father?" Jesus answered, "You know neither me nor my Father. If you knew me, you would know my Father also." [20]He spoke these words while he was teaching in the treasury of the temple, but no one arrested him, because his hour had not yet come.

21 Again he said to them, "I am going away, and you will search for me, but you will die in your sin. Where I am going, you cannot come." [22]Then the Jews said, "Is he going to kill himself? Is that what he means by saying, 'Where I am going, you cannot come'?" [23]He said to them, "You are from below, I am from above; you are from this world, I am not from this world. [24]I told you that you would die in your sins, for you will die in your sins unless you believe that I am he."[b] [25]They said to him, "Who are you?" Jesus said to them, "Why do I speak to you at all?[c] [26]I have much to say about you and much to condemn, but the one who sent me is true, and I declare to the world what I have heard from him." [27]They did not understand that he was speaking to them about the Father. [28]So Jesus said, "When you have lifted up the Son of Man, then you will realize that I am he[d] and that I do nothing on my own, but I speak these things as the Father instructed me. [29]And the one who sent me is with me; he has not left me alone, for I always do what is pleasing to him." [30]As he was saying these things, many believed in him.

31 Then Jesus said to the Jews who had believed in him, "If you continue in my word, you are truly my disciples, [32]and you will know the truth, and the truth will make you free." [33]They answered him, "We are descendants of Abraham and have never been slaves to anyone. What do you mean by saying, 'You will be made free'?"

34 Jesus answered them, "Very truly, I tell you, everyone who commits sin is a slave to sin. [35]The slave does not have a permanent place in the household; the son has a place there forever. [36]So if the Son makes you free, you will be free indeed. [37]I know that you are descendants of Abraham, yet you look for an opportunity to kill me because there is no place in you for my word. [38]I declare what I have seen in the Father's presence; as for you, you should do what you have heard from the Father."[e]

39 They answered him, "Abraham is our father." Jesus said to them, "If you are Abraham's children, you would do[f] what Abraham did, [40]but now you are trying to kill me, a man who has told you the truth that I heard from God. This is not what Abraham did. [41]You are indeed

z 8.15 Gk *according to the flesh*   a 8.16 Other ancient authorities read *he*   b 8.24 Gk *I am*   c 8.25 Or *What I have told you from the beginning*   d 8.28 Gk *I am*   e 8.38 Other ancient authorities read *you do what you have heard from your father*   f 8.39 Other ancient authorities read *you were . . . you would do* or *you are . . . then do*

8:12 *I am the light of the world* is a metaphor that makes a claim on Jesus's identity. It carries the theme of light found in the prologue (1:5, 7–9). Jesus goes on to explain that whoever follows him will not walk in darkness but will walk in the light of life. This metaphor is said in the context of the Feast of Tabernacles, during which, according to the Mishnah (m. Sukkah 5:2–3), large golden menorot, or candelabra, were lit in the women's courtyard of the temple, a reminder of the light emitting from the fire that accompanied the Israelites in the wilderness.

8:15 *Human standards* (literally "according to the flesh," "kata tēn sarka"). Jesus mentions in 7:24 not to judge on matters pertaining to the world below.

8:31 *Then Jesus said to the Jews who had believed in him* illustrates the diversity of belief among the Jewish people (see 1:19).

8:34–35 *I tell you, everyone who commits sin is a slave to sin* calls to mind the dominance of slavery in the ancient world and its use within the rhetoric of the Gospel. It speaks to the ancient reality of slavery typically present in the private and public domains of ancient society, including the domains of Jesus believers.

8:41 *We are not illegitimate children* highlights "the Jews'" belief of monotheism and their descent from Abraham. To be illegitimate suggests they believe in two gods.

Focus On: Anti-Judaism (John 8)

Anti-Judaism is an effect of negative depictions of Jews or groups of Jews (e.g., Pharisees) in New Testament texts as the foes of Jesus (and his followers) and as intrinsically evil. Most prominent are the claims that the Jews were responsible for the death of Jesus, either in outright statements (1 Thess. 2:14–16; Acts 2:23; 3:15) or in ahistorical exaggerations of Jewish power in the Passion Narratives in the Gospels. John's negative depiction of "the Jews" as a group separate from Jesus (as if he is not a Jew) includes the charge that they are children of the devil (John 8:44). The depiction of the Pharisees as shedders of innocent blood and hypocrites (Matt. 23) as well as foolishly punctilious about observing the Torah (Mark 7:1–13; Matt. 23) and greedy (Luke 16:14) has taken deep root in Western culture and has fed anti-Semitic stereotypes.

Given the complexity of early Christ followers' relationship to the Hebrew Bible and Judaism and their uneven separation from their Jewish roots, we can rarely be certain of the intentions and prejudices of the New Testament authors. With the exception of Paul, we often do not know if the authors were themselves Jewish, nor do we know their current relations to their own local Jewish communities. Arguing that the historical context can explain apparent anti-Jewish sentiment (e.g., Matthew's competition with the early rabbis or John's hearers' facing rejection in synagogues [9:22; 12:42; 16:2]) adds crucial understanding but does not nullify the effect of hateful words being enshrined in the canon. Similarly, attempting to separate "good Jews" from "bad Jews" by saying negative statements are merely against "the Jewish leaders" posits a nonexistent powerful Jewish hierarchy and exacerbates stereotypes. Some well-intentioned interpreters choose to translate *Ioudaioi* as "Judeans" rather than "Jews" (see "'The Jews' (*Hoi Ioudaioi*)," p. 1852). This masking of the Jewish presence with an unfamiliar geographic term only adds to the offense by removing Jews from the story. It also hints that the term "Jew" is distasteful, perhaps because some anti-Semites have used it as a slur, but it is a term proud Jews use of themselves.

These angry statements are screenshots from communities in crisis in the process of forming new identities. Early Christ followers who understood Jesus as the fulfillment of the promises of God in the Hebrew Bible had to make sense of the fact that most Jews did not accept Jesus as the Messiah and that despite reading the same Scriptures, they had a different understanding of history. Sometimes the solution to this conundrum was an anti-Jewish reading of history—that Jews were blind, stubborn, or influenced by the devil. These sentiments, though historically contingent, took on a life of their own because they became part of Christian Scripture.

Claudia Setzer

doing what your father does." They said to him, "We are not illegitimate children; we have one Father, God himself." [42]Jesus said to them, "If God were your Father, you would love me, for I came from God, and now I am here. I did not come on my own, but he sent me. [43]Why do you not understand what I say? It is because you cannot accept my word. [44]You are from your father the devil, and you choose to do your father's desires. He was a murderer from the beginning and does not stand in the truth because there is no truth in him. When he lies, he speaks according to his own nature, for he is a liar and the father of lies. [45]But because I tell the truth, you do not believe me.[g] [46]Which of you convicts me of sin? If I tell the truth, why do you not believe me? [47]Whoever is from God hears the words of God. The reason you do not hear them is that you are not from God."

48 The Jews answered him, "Are we not right in saying that you are a Samaritan and have a demon?" [49]Jesus answered, "I do not have a demon, but I honor my Father, and you dishonor me. [50]Yet I do not seek my own glory; there is one who seeks it, and he is the judge. [51]Very truly, I tell you, whoever keeps my word will never see death." [52]The Jews said to him, "Now we know that you have a demon. Abraham died, and so did the prophets, yet you say, 'Whoever keeps my word will never taste death.' [53]Are you greater than our father

g 8.45 Or *You do not believe even though I tell the truth*

8:44 *You are from your father the devil* is a vitriolic statement by the Johannine Jesus. It is part of the plot's attempt to disaffiliate or separate Jesus from the portrayed "Jews'" (v. 31) way of thinking and interpreting (see "'The Jews' (*Hoi Ioudaioi*)," p. 1852).

8:48 *You are a Samaritan and have a demon* is a question, and the plot of the Gospel insinuates that *Samaritan* was an insult. It appears to be directed toward unbelievers, who were perceived to be possessed by a demon.

Abraham, who died? The prophets also died. Who do you claim to be?" ⁵⁴Jesus answered, "If I glorify myself, my glory is nothing. It is my Father who glorifies me, he of whom you say, 'He is our God,' ⁵⁵though you do not know him. But I know him; if I would say that I do not know him, I would be a liar like you. But I do know him, and I keep his word. ⁵⁶Your ancestor Abraham rejoiced that he would see my day; he saw it and was glad." ⁵⁷Then the Jews said to him, "You are not yet fifty years old, and have you seen Abraham?"*b* ⁵⁸Jesus said to them, "Very truly, I tell you, before Abraham was, I am." ⁵⁹So they picked up stones to throw at him, but Jesus hid himself and went out of the temple.

9 As he walked along, he saw a man blind from birth. ²His disciples asked him, "Rabbi, who sinned, this man or his parents, that he was born blind?" ³Jesus answered, "Neither this man nor his parents sinned; he was born blind so that God's works might be revealed in him. ⁴We*i* must work the works of him who sent me*j* while it is day; night is coming, when no one can work. ⁵As long as I am in the world, I am the light of the world." ⁶When he had said this, he spat on the ground and made mud with the saliva and spread the mud on the man's eyes, ⁷saying to him, "Go, wash in the pool of Siloam" (which means Sent). Then he went and washed and came back able to see. ⁸The neighbors and those who had seen him before as a beggar began

to ask, "Is this not the man who used to sit and beg?" ⁹Some were saying, "It is he." Others were saying, "No, but it is someone like him." He kept saying, "I am he." ¹⁰But they kept asking him, "Then how were your eyes opened?" ¹¹He answered, "The man called Jesus made mud, spread it on my eyes, and said to me, 'Go to Siloam and wash.' Then I went and washed and received my sight." ¹²They said to him, "Where is he?" He said, "I do not know."

13 They brought to the Pharisees the man who had formerly been blind. ¹⁴Now it was a Sabbath day when Jesus made the mud and opened his eyes. ¹⁵Then the Pharisees also began to ask him how he had received his sight. He said to them, "He put mud on my eyes. Then I washed, and now I see." ¹⁶Some of the Pharisees said, "This man is not from God, for he does not observe the Sabbath." Others said, "How can a man who is a sinner perform such signs?" And they were divided. ¹⁷So they said again to the blind man, "What do you say about him? It was your eyes he opened." He said, "He is a prophet."

18 The Jews did not believe that he had been blind and had received his sight until they called the parents of the man who had received his sight ¹⁹and asked them, "Is this your son, who you say was born blind? How then does he now see?" ²⁰His parents

b 8.57 Other ancient authorities read *has Abraham seen you?* *i* 9.4 Other ancient authorities read *I* *j* 9.4 Other ancient authorities read *us*

8:57 *You are not yet fifty years old* is a reference that marks the Johannine Jesus as not very old and thus unable to have known Abraham (see Luke 3:23).

8:59 *They picked up stones to throw at him* speaks to the tension between Jesus and "the Jews" (8:48) over the interpretation of Jesus's identity. *Jesus hid himself and went out of the temple* is characteristic of Jesus when the time or hour has not come for his glorification (see 12:36).

9:1 *Blind from birth* calls attention again to those who are physically challenged in the ancient world. This miracle to follow was one of Jesus's most common miracles in the Synoptic Gospels (Matt. 9:27–31; 12:22; 15:30; 20:29–34; 21:14; Mark 10:46–52; Luke 7:21; 18:35–43). However, there is no mention in the Synoptics of Jesus healing anyone who had been blind from birth. In the Hebrew Bible, Isaiah had prophesied that the giving of sight to the blind would be a part of the Messiah's activity (Isa. 29:18; 35:5; 42:7). The healing shows the power of God working in and through Jesus.

9:2–3 *Who sinned, this man or his parents, that he was born blind* speaks to how ancient people saw the relationship between physical infirmities and sin. Jesus will challenge this understanding with the following statement: *Neither this man nor his parents sinned.*

9:6 *Spat on the ground and made mud with the saliva* shows that in the ancient world, curative powers were attributed to spittle and dirt for diseases of the eyes (see **"Healing in the Gospels and Acts," p. 1773**).

9:8 *Beggar* is another glimpse into the ancient socioeconomic world and its lower classes.

9:16 *And they were divided* indicates that the Pharisees here were not all in agreement on whether Jesus was a sinner.

answered, "We know that this is our son and that he was born blind, ²¹but we do not know how it is that now he sees, nor do we know who opened his eyes. Ask him; he is of age. He will speak for himself." ²²His parents said this because they were afraid of the Jews, for the Jews had already agreed that anyone who confessed Jesus*k* to be the Messiah*l* would be put out of the synagogue. ²³Therefore his parents said, "He is of age; ask him."

24 So for the second time they called the man who had been blind, and they said to him, "Give glory to God! We know that this man is a sinner." ²⁵He answered, "I do not know whether he is a sinner. One thing I do know, that though I was blind, now I see." ²⁶They said to him, "What did he do to you? How did he open your eyes?" ²⁷He answered them, "I have told you already, and you would not listen. Why do you want to hear it again? Do you also want to become his disciples?" ²⁸Then they reviled him, saying, "You are his disciple, but we are disciples of Moses. ²⁹We know that God has spoken to Moses, but as for this man, we do not know where he comes from." ³⁰The man answered, "Here is an astonishing thing! You do not know where he comes from, yet he opened my eyes. ³¹We know that God does not listen to sinners, but he does listen to one who worships him and obeys his will. ³²Never since the world began has it been heard that anyone opened the eyes of a person born blind. ³³If this man were not from God, he could do nothing." ³⁴They answered him, "You were born entirely in sins, and are you trying to teach us?" And they drove him out.

35 Jesus heard that they had driven him out, and when he found him he said, "Do you believe in the Son of Man?"*m* ³⁶He answered, "And who is he, sir?*n* Tell me, so that I may believe in him." ³⁷Jesus said to him, "You have seen him, and the one speaking with you is he." ³⁸He said, "Lord,*o* I believe." And he worshiped him. ³⁹Jesus said, "I came into this world for judgment, so that those who do not see may see and those who do see may become blind." ⁴⁰Some of the Pharisees who were with him heard this and said to him, "Surely we are not blind, are we?" ⁴¹Jesus said to them, "If you were blind, you would not have sin. But now that you say, 'We see,' your sin remains.

10 "Very truly, I tell you, anyone who does not enter the sheepfold by the gate but climbs in by another way is a thief and a bandit. ²The one who enters by the gate is the shepherd of the sheep. ³The gatekeeper opens the gate for him, and the sheep hear his voice. He calls his own sheep by name and leads them out. ⁴When he has brought out all his own, he goes ahead of them, and

k 9.22 Gk *him* *l* 9.22 Or *the Christ* *m* 9.35 Other ancient authorities read *the Son of God* *n* 9.36 Or *Lord*
o 9.38 Or *Sir*

9:21 *Ask him; he is of age* refers to the Jewish tradition that says he is old enough to make a legal response to the authorities. If so, this suggests that the once blind man must have been at least thirteen years old.

9:22 *Be put out of the synagogue* ("aposunagōgos") suggests an intradivision among all the Jewish people in the plot of this Gospel. To be *put out of the synagogue* is defined as being expelled from the synagogue and put under a curse or ban (Heb. "herem"). Whether the ban was a formal prohibition or enforced widely is uncertain. The ban goes back as far as the time of Ezra (Ezra 10:8), but the exact procedure for its enforcement is not clear. See also John 12:42 and 16:2, where the phrase is used again.

9:32 *Never since the world began* wishes to emphasize that Jesus did indeed heal the man, and so he must have been from God.

9:34 *And they drove him out* is another picture of Jesus's adversaries putting their differences of interpretation into action.

9:36–38 *And who is he, sir? Sir* can also be translated as "lord" ("kyrie"). The man once blind will soon come to believe in Jesus as the Son of Man, professing *I believe*.

10:1–2 *Sheepfold by the gate* recalls the Hebrew Bible's references to rulers and leaders as shepherds. Israel was viewed as the flock of God and God as the shepherd of Israel (Pss. 23:1; 80:1; 100:3; Isa. 40:11). The Hebrew Bible also used the figure of false shepherds to represent those leading Israel astray who did not care for the people (Isa. 56:11; Ezek. 34:2, 3; Zech. 1:15–17).

10:3–5 *The gatekeeper opens the gate for him* conjures up the pastoral life in the ancient world when shepherding was part of the people's lives and when the entrance to the pen was next to the home. *Sheep hear his voice* indicates that the sheep recognize the shepherd's voice from other voices, which the following statement confirms: *They will not follow a stranger.*

the sheep follow him because they know his voice. [5]They will not follow a stranger, but they will run from him because they do not know the voice of strangers." [6]Jesus used this figure of speech with them, but they did not understand what he was saying to them.

7 So again Jesus said to them, "Very truly, I tell you, I am the gate for the sheep. [8]All who came before me[p] are thieves and bandits, but the sheep did not listen to them. [9]I am the gate. Whoever enters by me will be saved and will come in and go out and find pasture. [10]The thief comes only to steal and kill and destroy. I came that they may have life and have it abundantly.

11 "I am the good shepherd. The good shepherd lays down his life for the sheep. [12]The hired hand, who is not the shepherd and does not own the sheep, sees the wolf coming and leaves the sheep and runs away, and the wolf snatches them and scatters them. [13]The hired hand runs away because a hired hand does not care for the sheep. [14]I am the good shepherd. I know my own, and my own know me, [15]just as the Father knows me, and I know the Father. And I lay down my life for the sheep. [16]I have other sheep that do not belong to this fold. I must bring them also, and they will listen to my voice. So there will be one flock, one shepherd. [17]For this reason the Father loves me, because I lay down my life in order to take it up again. [18]No one takes[q] it from me, but I lay it down of my own accord. I have power to lay it down, and I have power to take it up again. I have received this command from my Father."

19 Again the Jews were divided because of these words. [20]Many of them were saying, "He has a demon and is out of his mind. Why listen to him?" [21]Others were saying, "These are not the words of one who has a demon. Can a demon open the eyes of the blind?"

22 At that time the Festival of the Dedication took place in Jerusalem. It was winter, [23]and Jesus was walking in the temple, in the portico of Solomon. [24]So the Jews gathered around him and said to him, "How long will you keep us in suspense? If you are the Messiah,[r] tell us plainly." [25]Jesus answered, "I have told you, and you do not believe. The works that I do in my Father's name testify to me, [26]but you do not believe because you do not belong to my sheep. [27]My sheep hear my voice. I know them, and they follow me. [28]I give them eternal life, and they will never perish. No one will snatch them out of my hand. [29]My Father, in regard to what he has given me, is greater than all,[s] and no one can snatch them out of the Father's hand. [30]The Father and I are one."

31 The Jews took up stones again to stone him. [32]Jesus replied, "I have shown you many good works from the Father. For which of these are you going to stone me?" [33]The Jews answered, "It is not for a good work that we are going to stone you but for blasphemy, because you, though only a human, are making yourself God." [34]Jesus answered, "Is it not written in your law,[t] 'I said, you are gods'?

p 10.8 Other ancient authorities lack *before me* q 10.18 Other ancient authorities read *has taken* r 10.24 Or *the Christ* s 10.29 Other ancient authorities read *What my Father has given me is greater than all else* or *My Father, who has given them to me, is greater than all* t 10.34 Other ancient authorities read *in the law*

10:7 *I am the gate for the sheep* is another "I am" saying that points to Jesus's identity. This metaphor also indicates that Jesus—as the gate—controls the entrance into the sheepfold.

10:8 *Thieves and bandits* is in reference to false leaders who have come before Jesus with a different message.

10:11 *I am the good shepherd* is another "I am" saying and metaphor that further identifies Jesus. This good shepherd also *lays down his life for the sheep*, which suggests sacrifice. This notion of "sacrifice" is mentioned five times in this chapter (see vv. 11, 15, 17, and 18).

10:16 *Other sheep* is difficult to identify. It may refer to unbelievers, perhaps gentiles, or non-Johannine believers. *Fold* suggests the Jewish people. *One flock* points to the universalization of all peoples under *one shepherd* (see Ezek. 34:23).

10:19 *Again the Jews were divided* continues to show that the Jewish people cannot be seen as homogenous in identity and belief (see 1:19). This division ("schisma") is not uncommon (7:43; 9:16).

10:22 *Festival of the Dedication*, or the Festival of Lights, provides the seasonal time of the year—*winter*. It recalls the rededication of the temple after being polluted by Antiochus Epiphanes (167 BCE; 1 Macc. 4).

10:30–33 *The Father and I are one* is a claim that emphasizes the unity between Jesus and the Father. It is contrasted in 14:28. This claim is what leads to the charge of *blasphemy* and what John insinuates leads to Jesus's death (see Num. 15:30, 31). Blasphemy in Jewish tradition normally means cursing or insulting God.

[35]If those to whom the word of God came were called 'gods'—and the scripture cannot be annulled—[36]can you say that the one whom the Father has sanctified and sent into the world is blaspheming because I said, 'I am God's Son'? [37]If I am not doing the works of my Father, then do not believe me. [38]But if I do them, even though you do not believe me, believe the works, so that you may know and understand[u] that the Father is in me and I am in the Father." [39]Then they tried to arrest him again, but he escaped from their hands.

40 He went away again across the Jordan to the place where John had been baptizing earlier, and he remained there. [41]Many came to him, and they were saying, "John performed no sign, but everything that John said about this man was true." [42]And many believed in him there.

11 Now a certain man was ill, Lazarus of Bethany, the village of Mary and her sister Martha. [2]Mary was the one who anointed the Lord with perfume and wiped his feet with her hair; her brother Lazarus was ill. [3]So the sisters sent a message to Jesus,[v] "Lord, he whom you love is ill." [4]But when Jesus heard it, he said, "This illness does not lead to death; rather, it is for God's glory, so that the Son of God may be glorified through it." [5]Accordingly, though Jesus loved Martha and her sister and Lazarus, [6]after having heard that Lazarus[w] was ill, he stayed two days longer in the place where he was.

7 Then after this he said to the disciples, "Let us go to Judea again." [8]The disciples said to him, "Rabbi, the Jews were just now trying to stone you, and are you going there again?"

[9]Jesus answered, "Are there not twelve hours of daylight? Those who walk during the day do not stumble because they see the light of this world. [10]But those who walk at night stumble because the light is not in them." [11]After saying this, he told them, "Our friend Lazarus has fallen asleep, but I am going there to awaken him." [12]The disciples said to him, "Lord, if he has fallen asleep, he will be all right."[x] [13]Jesus, however, had been speaking about his death, but they thought that he was referring merely to sleep. [14]Then Jesus told them plainly, "Lazarus is dead. [15]For your sake I am glad I was not there, so that you may believe. But let us go to him." [16]Thomas, who was called the Twin,[y] said to his fellow disciples, "Let us also go, that we may die with him."

17 When Jesus arrived, he found that Lazarus[z] had already been in the tomb four days. [18]Now Bethany was near Jerusalem, some two miles away, [19]and many of the Jews had come to Martha and Mary to console them about their brother. [20]When Martha heard that Jesus was coming, she went and met him, while Mary stayed at home. [21]Martha said to Jesus, "Lord, if you had been here, my brother would not have died. [22]But even now I know that God will give you whatever you ask of him." [23]Jesus said to her, "Your brother will rise again." [24]Martha said to him, "I know that he will rise again in the resurrection on the last day." [25]Jesus said to her, "I am the resurrection and the life.[a] Those who believe in me,

u 10.38 Other ancient authorities lack *and understand;* others read *and believe* v 11.3 Gk *him* w 11.6 Gk *he* x 11.12 Or *will be saved* y 11.16 Gk *Didymus* z 11.17 Gk *he* a 11.25 Other ancient authorities lack *and the life*

10:35 *Gods* recalls the reference to the judges of Israel (Ps. 82:6). Here the reference shows that others have been called gods.

11:1 *Lazarus of Bethany* is mentioned only in this Gospel. His sisters *Mary* and *Martha* are found in Luke 10:38–42. Lazarus's illness again points to the everyday reality of sickness in ancient society. Illness is mentioned five times in the first six verses (vv. 1, 2, 3, 4, and 6; see **"Healing in the Gospels and Acts," p. 1773**).

11:2 *Mary was the one who anointed* looks ahead to 12:3.

11:9 *Are there not twelve hours of daylight?* is a proverbial saying pointing to Jesus's identity as *the light of this world.*

11:11 *Fallen asleep* ("kekomētai") suggests death (see Matt. 9:24; Acts 7:60; 1 Thess. 4:13; and 1 Cor. 15:6). But also, here, Jesus knew supernaturally before departing to Bethany that Lazarus had died (see vv. 13–14).

11:16 *Thomas, who was called the Twin,* refers to one of Jesus's disciples who also appears as the Twin ("Didymus") in 20:24 and 21:2. He is consistently portrayed as doubtful about Jesus's identity as the Son of Man.

11:19 *Many of the Jews had come to Martha and Mary to console* is another instance where *the Jews* are portrayed not in a hostile way but rather in a comforting way (see 11:31).

11:25 *I am the resurrection and the life* is a predicate emphatic "I am" saying pointing to another

even though they die, will live, ²⁶and everyone who lives and believes in me will never die. Do you believe this?" ²⁷She said to him, "Yes, Lord, I believe that you are the Messiah,^b the Son of God, the one coming into the world."

28 When she had said this, she went back and called her sister Mary and told her privately, "The Teacher is here and is calling for you." ²⁹And when she heard it, she got up quickly and went to him. ³⁰Now Jesus had not yet come to the village but was still at the place where Martha had met him. ³¹The Jews who were with her in the house consoling her saw Mary get up quickly and go out. They followed her because they thought that she was going to the tomb to weep there. ³²When Mary came where Jesus was and saw him, she knelt at his feet and said to him, "Lord, if you had been here, my brother would not have died." ³³When Jesus saw her weeping and the Jews who came with her also weeping, he was greatly disturbed in spirit and deeply moved. ³⁴He said, "Where have you laid him?" They said to him, "Lord, come and see." ³⁵Jesus began to weep. ³⁶So the Jews said, "See how he loved him!" ³⁷But some of them said, "Could not he who opened the eyes of the blind man have kept this man from dying?"

38 Then Jesus, again greatly disturbed, came to the tomb. It was a cave, and a stone was lying against it. ³⁹Jesus said, "Take away the stone." Martha, the sister of the dead man, said to him, "Lord, already there is a stench because he has been dead four days." ⁴⁰Jesus said to her, "Did I not tell you that if you believed you would see the glory of God?" ⁴¹So they took away the stone. And Jesus looked upward and said, "Father, I thank you for having heard me. ⁴²I knew that you always hear

me, but I have said this for the sake of the crowd standing here, so that they may believe that you sent me." ⁴³When he had said this, he cried with a loud voice, "Lazarus, come out!" ⁴⁴The dead man came out, his hands and feet bound with strips of cloth and his face wrapped in a cloth. Jesus said to them, "Unbind him, and let him go."

45 Many of the Jews, therefore, who had come with Mary and had seen what Jesus did believed in him. ⁴⁶But some of them went to the Pharisees and told them what Jesus had done. ⁴⁷So the chief priests and the Pharisees called a meeting of the council and said, "What are we to do? This man is performing many signs. ⁴⁸If we let him go on like this, everyone will believe in him, and the Romans will come and destroy both our holy place^c and our nation." ⁴⁹But one of them, Caiaphas, who was high priest that year, said to them, "You know nothing at all! ⁵⁰You do not understand that it is better for you to have one man die for the people than to have the whole nation destroyed." ⁵¹He did not say this on his own, but being high priest that year he prophesied that Jesus was about to die for the nation, ⁵²and not for the nation only, but to gather into one the dispersed children of God. ⁵³So from that day on they planned to put him to death.

54 Jesus therefore no longer walked about openly among the Jews but went from there to a town called Ephraim in the region near the wilderness, and he remained there with the disciples.

55 Now the Passover of the Jews was near, and many went up from the country to Jerusalem before the Passover to purify themselves.

b 11.27 Or *the Christ*   *c* 11.48 Or *our temple*; Gk *our place*

characteristic of Jesus's identity. The metaphor seems to suggest that the one who believes in Jesus will have eternal life.

11:28 *The Teacher* signals that Mary and Martha see that Jesus functions as one who conveys knowledge. The theme of knowledge, "to know" ("ginōskein" and "eidenai"), refers to knowledge of ordinary things but also spiritual recognition of Jesus as Christ (see 1:10).

11:34 *Come and see* points back to the calling of the disciples (1:39, 46).

11:35 *Jesus began to weep* portrays Jesus as emotionally moved. His human sentiments are expressed for his friend. Other human characteristics include thirst (4:7; 19:28), weariness (4:6), love (11:5), and disturbance (11:38).

11:44 *His hands and feet bound with strips* not only gives a glimpse into how they prepared the dead, it also emphasizes that Lazarus was indeed dead.

11:48 *Romans will come and destroy both our holy place and our nation* is in reference to the destruction of the temple (2:19; 4:20–21) and the defeat of the Jewish nation itself in 70 CE.

11:53 *They planned to put him to death* marks the expected end for Jesus in the plot of this Gospel (see 5:18; 7:1, 19, 25, 32, 45; 8:40, 59; 10:31; 11:8, 16).

⁵⁶They were looking for Jesus and were asking one another as they stood in the temple, "What do you think? Surely he will not come to the festival, will he?" ⁵⁷Now the chief priests and the Pharisees had given orders that anyone who knew where Jesus*ᵈ* was should let them know, so that they might arrest him.

12 Six days before the Passover Jesus came to Bethany, the home of Lazarus, whom he had raised from the dead. ²There they gave a dinner for him. Martha served, and Lazarus was one of those reclining with him. ³Mary took a pound of costly perfume made of pure nard, anointed Jesus's feet, and wiped them*ᵉ* with her hair. The house was filled with the fragrance of the perfume. ⁴But Judas Iscariot, one of his disciples (the one who was about to betray him), said, ⁵"Why was this perfume not sold for three hundred denarii and the money given to the poor?" ⁶(He said this not because he cared about the poor but because he was a thief; he kept the common purse and used to steal what was put into it.) ⁷Jesus said, "Leave her alone. She bought it*ᶠ* so that she might keep it for the day of my burial. ⁸You always have the poor with you, but you do not always have me."

9 When the great crowd of the Jews learned that he was there, they came not only because of Jesus but also to see Lazarus, whom he had raised from the dead. ¹⁰So the chief priests planned to put Lazarus to death as well, ¹¹since it was on account of him that many of the Jews were deserting and were believing in Jesus.

12 The next day the great crowd that had come to the festival heard that Jesus was coming to Jerusalem. ¹³So they took branches of palm trees and went out to meet him, shouting,

"Hosanna!

Blessed is the one who comes in the name
    of the Lord—
    the King of Israel!"
¹⁴Jesus found a young donkey and sat on it, as it is written:
¹⁵ "Do not be afraid, daughter of Zion.
    Look, your king is coming,
        sitting on a donkey's colt!"
¹⁶His disciples did not understand these things at first, but when Jesus was glorified, then they remembered that these things had been written of him and had been done to him. ¹⁷So the crowd that had been with him when he called Lazarus out of the tomb and raised him from the dead continued to testify.*ᵍ* ¹⁸It was also because they heard that he had performed this sign that the crowd went to meet him. ¹⁹The Pharisees then said to one another, "You see, you can do nothing. Look, the world has gone after him!"

20 Now among those who went up to worship at the festival were some Greeks. ²¹They came to Philip, who was from Bethsaida in Galilee, and said to him, "Sir, we wish to see Jesus." ²²Philip went and told Andrew, then Andrew and Philip went and told Jesus. ²³Jesus

d 11.57 Gk *he*   *e* 12.3 Gk *his feet*   *f* 12.7 Gk lacks *She bought it*   *g* 12.17 Other ancient authorities read *with him began to testify that he had called . . . from the dead*

12:1 *Six days before the Passover* provides a temporal setting for most of the remaining chapters in this Gospel.

12:3 *Pound of costly perfume made of pure nard* suggests that ointment is either imported or costs a lot to make. It is used by Mary of Bethany, who *anointed Jesus's feet, and wiped them with her hair*, demonstrating both devotion and humility toward Jesus. To unbind one's hair in public was an uncommon act in the ancient world.

12:4 *But Judas Iscariot, one of his disciples* is identified as the one who will betray Jesus later in the plot (18:2).

12:5 *Poor* signals once again the socioeconomic situation of the masses in the ancient world (v. 8).

12:8 *You always have the poor* is to suggest not that *the poor* are not important (see 13:29) but that Jesus will not always be with them. It also conjures up the second part of Deut. 15:11 and its command to care for the poor and needy.

12:13 *Hosanna* literally means "Save us now." The word recalls Ps. 118:25–26, which is a psalm used during the Passover.

12:14 *A young donkey* suggests that Jesus is presenting himself not as a warrior king but rather as a humble king. A donkey then symbolized peace. See Zech. 9:9.

12:17 *The crowd* are the eyewitnesses of the raising of Lazarus. Perhaps they are the ones who spread what they see and hear (see vv. 18, 29, 34).

12:20 *Greeks* refers to gentiles who were possibly proselytes to Judaism.

answered them, "The hour has come for the Son of Man to be glorified. ²⁴Very truly, I tell you, unless a grain of wheat falls into the earth and dies, it remains just a single grain, but if it dies it bears much fruit. ²⁵Those who love their life lose it, and those who hate their life in this world will keep it for eternal life. ²⁶Whoever serves me must follow me, and where I am, there will my servant be also. Whoever serves me, the Father will honor.

27 "Now my soul is troubled. And what should I say: 'Father, save me from this hour'? No, it is for this reason that I have come to this hour. ²⁸Father, glorify your name." Then a voice came from heaven, "I have glorified it, and I will glorify it again." ²⁹The crowd standing there heard it and said that it was thunder. Others said, "An angel has spoken to him." ³⁰Jesus answered, "This voice has come for your sake, not for mine. ³¹Now is the judgment of this world; now the ruler of this world will be driven out. ³²And I, when I am lifted up from the earth, will draw all people[b] to myself." ³³He said this to indicate the kind of death he was to die. ³⁴The crowd answered him, "We have heard from the law that the Messiah[i] remains forever. How can you say that the Son of Man must be lifted up? Who is this Son of Man?" ³⁵Jesus said to them, "The light is in you[j] for a little longer. Walk while you have the light, so that the darkness may not overtake you. If you walk in the darkness, you do not know where you are going. ³⁶While you have the light, believe in the light, so that you may become children of light."

After Jesus had said this, he departed and hid from them. ³⁷Although he had performed so many signs in their presence, they did not believe in him. ³⁸This was to fulfill the word spoken by the prophet Isaiah:

"Lord, who has believed our message,
    and to whom has the arm of the Lord
        been revealed?"
³⁹And so they could not believe, because Isaiah also said,
⁴⁰ "He has blinded their eyes
    and hardened their heart,
so that they might not look with their
    eyes
and understand with their heart and
    turn—
and I would heal them."
⁴¹Isaiah said this because[k] he saw his glory and spoke about him. ⁴²Nevertheless many, even of the authorities, believed in him. But because of the Pharisees they did not confess it, for fear that they would be put out of the synagogue, ⁴³for they loved human glory more than the glory that comes from God.

44 Then Jesus cried aloud: "Whoever believes in me believes not in me but in him who sent me. ⁴⁵And whoever sees me sees him who sent me. ⁴⁶I have come as light into the world, so that everyone who believes in me should not remain in the darkness. ⁴⁷I do not judge anyone who hears my words and does not keep them, for I came not to judge the world but to save the world. ⁴⁸The one who rejects me and does not receive my words has a judge; on the last day the word that I have spoken will serve as judge, ⁴⁹for I have not spoken on my own, but the Father who sent me has himself given me a commandment about what to say and what to speak. ⁵⁰And I know that his commandment is eternal life. What I speak, therefore, I speak just as the Father has told me."

b 12.32 Other ancient authorities read *all things*   i 12.34 Or *the Christ*   j 12.35 Other ancient authorities read *with you*   k 12.41 Other ancient witnesses read *when*

12:24 *Unless a grain of wheat falls into the earth and dies* suggests a short parable speaking to issues of life and death. It suggests that the death of Jesus will give life.

12:31 *Ruler of this world* refers to the devil (8:44) or Satan (13:27). The notions of mysteries, evil forces, and power were present in the ancient world (see **"Dualism (Binaries)," p. 1855**).

12:36 *He departed and hid from them* is another reference to the elusiveness of Jesus. His time has not arrived.

12:42 *For fear that they would be put out of the synagogue* is another reference to expulsion for "confessing" in Jesus as the Son of Man. *Even . . . the authorities* believed in Jesus, so some of them also appear to be intimidated by the Pharisees.

12:47 *I do not judge* calls to mind Jesus as judge (v. 48). The act of judging appears to be another characteristic of Jesus (5:22, 27, 30; 8:16; 9:39). He judges *to save the world*. This recalls the purpose of his mission, to save the world (3:17-19).

12:50 *Commandment* here is referring to the life-giving word that God commanded Jesus to speak.

13 Now before the festival of the Passover, Jesus knew that his hour had come to depart from this world and go to the Father. Having loved his own who were in the world, he loved them to the end. [2]The devil had already decided[l] that Judas son of Simon Iscariot would betray Jesus. And during supper [3]Jesus, knowing that the Father had given all things into his hands and that he had come from God and was going to God, [4]got up from supper, took off his outer robe, and tied a towel around himself. [5]Then he poured water into a basin and began to wash the disciples' feet and to wipe them with the towel that was tied around him. [6]He came to Simon Peter, who said to him, "Lord, are you going to wash my feet?" [7]Jesus answered, "You do not know now what I am doing, but later you will understand." [8]Peter said to him, "You will never wash my feet." Jesus answered, "Unless I wash you, you have no share with me." [9]Simon Peter said to him, "Lord, not my feet only but also my hands and my head!" [10]Jesus said to him, "One who has bathed does not need to wash, except for the feet,[m] but is entirely clean. And you[n] are clean, though not all of you." [11]For he knew who was to betray him; for this reason he said, "Not all of you are clean."

12 After he had washed their feet, had put on his robe, and had reclined again, he said to them, "Do you know what I have done to you? [13]You call me Teacher and Lord, and you are right, for that is what I am. [14]So if I, your Lord and Teacher, have washed your feet, you also ought to wash one another's feet. [15]For I have set you an example, that you also should do as I have done to you. [16]Very truly, I tell you, slaves are not greater than their master, nor are messengers[o] greater than the one who sent them. [17]If you know these things, you are blessed if you do them. [18]I am not speaking of all of you; I know whom I have chosen. But it is to fulfill the scripture, 'The one who ate my bread[p] has lifted his heel against me.' [19]I tell you this now, before it occurs, so that when it does occur you may believe that I am he.[q] [20]Very truly, I tell you, whoever receives one whom I send receives me, and whoever receives me receives him who sent me."

21 After saying this Jesus was troubled in spirit and declared, "Very truly, I tell you, one of you will betray me." [22]The disciples looked at one another, uncertain of whom he was speaking. [23]One of his disciples—the one whom Jesus loved—was reclining close to his heart;[r] [24]Simon Peter therefore motioned to him to ask Jesus of whom he was speaking. [25]So while reclining next to Jesus, he asked him, "Lord, who is it?" [26]Jesus answered, "It is the one to whom I give this piece of bread when I have dipped it in the dish."[s] So when he had dipped the piece of bread, he gave it to Judas son of Simon Iscariot.[t] [27]After he received the piece of bread, Satan entered into

l 13.2 Gk *put it into his heart* m 13.10 Other ancient authorities lack *except for the feet* n 13.10 The Greek word for *you* here is plural o 13.16 Or *apostles* p 13.18 Other ancient authorities read *ate bread with me* q 13.19 Gk *I am* r 13.23 Gk *bosom* s 13.26 Gk *dipped it* t 13.26 Other ancient authorities read *Judas Iscariot son of Simon* or *Judas son of Simon from Karyot* (Kerioth)

13:1 *Before the festival of the Passover* introduces the events that follow before his trial and death. His *hour* had arrived, and now he prepares for the return to the world above with the Father (1:1).

13:2 *The devil* continues to be part of the story of Jesus. Here it is a reminder that the *devil* had been plotting the betrayal (see **"The Satan," p. 687**).

13:5 *Wash the disciples' feet* signals a gesture of respect and humility, especially for a teacher to wash the feet of his followers. Typically, it is the other way around—an enslaved person or a servant washes the feet of a master (see 1 Sam. 25:41). *Feet* are mentioned several times in this chapter (vv. 5, 6, 8, 9, 10, 12, and 14). The need to have feet washed from the dirt from travel points to daily life in the ancient world.

13:16 *Slaves are not greater than their master* contrasts the enslaved and the master. The principle of reversal of status is a guiding position for relationships for Jesus. See note 8:34–35 on the topic of slavery.

13:18 *Lifted his heel against me* is a gesture of contempt. Here Jesus is referring to Judas, who will betray him (13:26–27; 18:2–3).

13:23 *One of his disciples—the one whom Jesus loved* is the first reference to the unnamed disciple (see 19:26, 27; 20:2–10; 21:7, 20–24). Some scholars believe the unnamed disciple is Lazarus (11:3) or the author of the Gospel, or John, the son of Zebedee (see **"Introduction to John: Authorship," p. 1847**).

13:25 *So while reclining next to Jesus* ("houtōs epi to stēthos tou Iēsou") literally reads "So lying close to the breast of Jesus." The text shows the cultural habit of eating at a low table and the close relationship between Jesus and the Beloved Disciple.

him. Jesus said to him, "Do quickly what you are going to do." [28]Now no one knew why he said this to him. [29]Some thought that, because Judas had the common purse, Jesus was telling him, "Buy what we need for the festival," or that he should give something to the poor. [30]So, after receiving the piece of bread, he immediately went out. And it was night.

[31] When he had gone out, Jesus said, "Now the Son of Man has been glorified, and God has been glorified in him. [32]If God has been glorified in him,[u] God will also glorify him in himself and will glorify him at once. [33]Little children, I am with you only a little longer. You will look for me, and as I said to the Jews so now I say to you, 'Where I am going, you cannot come.' [34]I give you a new commandment, that you love one another. Just as I have loved you, you also should love one another. [35]By this everyone will know that you are my disciples, if you have love for one another."

[36] Simon Peter said to him, "Lord, where are you going?" Jesus answered, "Where I am going, you cannot follow me now, but you will follow afterward." [37]Peter said to him, "Lord, why can I not follow you now? I will lay down my life for you." [38]Jesus answered, "Will you lay down your life for me? Very truly, I tell you, before the cock crows, you will have denied me three times.

14 "Do not let your hearts be troubled. Believe[v] in God; believe also in me. [2]In my Father's house there are many dwelling places. If it were not so, would I have told you that I go to prepare a place for you?[w] [3]And if I go and prepare a place for you, I will come

again and will take you to myself, so that where I am, there you may be also. [4]And you know the way to the place where I am going."[x] [5]Thomas said to him, "Lord, we do not know where you are going. How can we know the way?" [6]Jesus said to him, "I am the way and the truth and the life. No one comes to the Father except through me. [7]If you know me, you will know[y] my Father also. From now on you do know him and have seen him."

[8] Philip said to him, "Lord, show us the Father, and we will be satisfied." [9]Jesus said to him, "Have I been with you all this time, Philip, and you still do not know me? Whoever has seen me has seen the Father. How can you say, 'Show us the Father'? [10]Do you not believe that I am in the Father and the Father is in me? The words that I say to you I do not speak on my own, but the Father who dwells in me does his works. [11]Believe me that I am in the Father and the Father is in me, but if you do not, then believe[z] because of the works themselves. [12]Very truly, I tell you, the one who believes in me will also do the works that I do and, in fact, will do greater works than these, because I am going to the Father. [13]I will do whatever you ask in my name, so that the Father may be glorified in the Son. [14]If in my name you ask me[a] for anything, I will do it.

[15] "If you love me, you will keep[b] my

u 13.32 Other ancient authorities lack *If God has been glorified in him* v 14.1 Or *You believe* w 14.2 Or *If it were not so, I would have told you, for I go to prepare a place for you* x 14.4 Other ancient authorities read *Where I am going you know, and the way you know* y 14.7 Other ancient authorities read *If you had known me, you would have known* z 14.11 Other ancient authorities add *me* a 14.14 Other ancient authorities lack *me* b 14.15 Other ancient authorities read *me, keep*

13:29 *Common purse* signals that Judas held the money that supported the movement. The *poor* calls to mind their socioeconomic marginalization in the ancient world.

13:33 *Little children* appears only here in reference to the disciples. It is an endearing term but also a term that signals, perhaps, paternalism (see, e.g., 1 John 2:1, 18, 28).

13:34 *That you love one another* is a commandment linking to the Mosaic law in Lev. 19:18. The commandment is repeated in 15:12, 17, and it expresses the Christlike love of Jesus himself toward humanity.

14:1 *Do not let your hearts be troubled* signals comfort on Jesus's behalf toward those who might be troubled by his departure.

14:2 *There are many dwelling places* suggests that there is plenty of room for believers in "heaven." The image of a "place," "home," or "room" suggests a location in the afterlife.

14:6 *I am the way and the truth and the life* is another "I am" saying in this Gospel. The notion that believers are on a journey is conveyed by understanding Jesus's identity as the *way* to God, as the *truth* of God, and as the *life* of God.

14:10–11 *I am in the Father and the Father is in me* expresses union. The Gospel expresses the relation between Jesus and the Father in a variety of ways. The idea that Jesus is in union with the Father is called "high Christology."

14:15 *Commandments* here refers to all of what Jesus commanded (13:34–35) in the Gospel. Some might argue that it also refers to those commandments in the Hebrew Bible.

commandments. [16]And I will ask the Father, and he will give you another Advocate,[c] to be with you forever. [17]This is the Spirit of truth, whom the world cannot receive because it neither sees him nor knows him. You know him because he abides with you, and he will be[d] in[e] you.

18 "I will not leave you orphaned; I am coming to you. [19]In a little while the world will no longer see me, but you will see me; because I live, you also will live. [20]On that day you will know that I am in my Father, and you in me, and I in you. [21]They who have my commandments and keep them are those who love me, and those who love me will be loved by my Father, and I will love them and reveal myself to them." [22]Judas (not Iscariot) said to him, "Lord, how is it that you will reveal yourself to us and not to the world?" [23]Jesus answered him, "Those who love me will keep my word, and my Father will love them, and we will come to them and make our home with them. [24]Whoever does not love me does not keep my words, and the word that you hear is not mine but is from the Father who sent me.

25 "I have said these things to you while I am still with you. [26]But the Advocate,[f] the Holy Spirit, whom the Father will send in my name, will teach you everything and remind you of all that I have said to you. [27]Peace I leave with you; my peace I give to you. I do not give to you as the world gives. Do not let your hearts be troubled, and do not let them be afraid. [28]You heard me say to you, 'I am going away, and I am coming to you.' If you loved me, you would rejoice that I am going to the Father, because the Father is greater than I. [29]And now I have told you this before it occurs, so that when it does occur you may believe. [30]I will no longer talk much with you, for the ruler of this world is coming. He has no power over me, [31]but I do as the Father has commanded me, so that the world may know that I love the Father. Rise, let us be on our way.

15 "I am the true vine, and my Father is the vinegrower. [2]He removes every branch in me that bears no fruit. Every branch that bears fruit he prunes[g] to make it bear more fruit. [3]You have already been cleansed[b] by the word that I have spoken to you. [4]Abide in me as I abide in you. Just as the branch cannot bear fruit by itself unless it abides in the vine, neither can you unless you abide in me. [5]I am the vine; you are the branches. Those who abide in me and I in them bear much fruit, because apart from me you can do nothing. [6]Whoever does not abide in me is thrown away like a branch and withers; such

c 14.16 Or *Helper* or *Comforter*   d 14.17 Other ancient authorities read *he is*   e 14.17 Or *among*   f 14.26 Or *Helper* or *Comforter*   g 15.2 The same Greek root refers to pruning and cleansing   b 15.3 The same Greek root refers to pruning and cleansing

14:16–17 *Advocate* ("paraklēton") is sometimes translated as "Counselor," "Helper," or "Comforter." This is the first promise in the Gospel of the Holy Spirit—the *Spirit of truth* (14:26; 15:26; 16:7–15). The choice of the word *another* ("allon") signals perhaps a shared nature among the Son, the Father, and the Spirit.

14:18 *Orphaned* is used twice elsewhere in the New Testament (1 Thess. 2:17; Jas. 1:27). The verse conveys a sense that Jesus will not leave his disciples alone or away from his presence.

14:27 *Peace I leave with you* suggests that Jesus will not leave without a parting gift. The Greek verb "aphiēmi" means "to leave a gift," and his gift, according to the plot of the Gospel, is his death. *My peace I give to you* gestures the gift of salvation.

14:28 *Because the Father is greater than I* appears to suggest a hierarchal relationship between the Father and Jesus. It is a contrast to 14:10–11.

14:30–31 *Ruler* again expresses a battle between Satan and Jesus as Christ. Yet the ruler *has no power over* Jesus, since Jesus is free from sin (8:46). This is also the only place where Jesus expresses his love for the Father: *I love the Father.* Jesus's love is shown by doing the will of or being obedient to the Father in this Gospel.

15:1–2 *I am the true vine* conveys that Jesus is the source of life, with Jesus as the *vine* and the Father as the vinedresser. He is also the "real," "genuine," or "true" ("alēthinē") vine. The "branches" (v. 5) are his followers. The use of the metaphor also speaks to the land of vineyards associated with the life of the people. *Prunes* as a verb conveys a sense of cleansing to continue to grow or bear more fruit.

15:4 *Abide in*, or remain in, signals that it is the responsibility of the disciples to be loyal to Jesus as Christ. The words describe the relationship between Jesus and the disciples. The theme of abiding is strong here (vv. 4, 5, 6, 7, 9, 10).

branches are gathered, thrown into the fire, and burned. ⁷If you abide in me and my words abide in you, ask for whatever you wish, and it will be done for you. ⁸My Father is glorified by this, that you bear much fruit and become^j my disciples. ⁹As the Father has loved me, so I have loved you; abide in my love. ¹⁰If you keep my commandments, you will abide in my love, just as I have kept my Father's commandments and abide in his love. ¹¹I have said these things to you so that my joy may be in you and that your joy may be complete.

12 "This is my commandment, that you love one another as I have loved you. ¹³No one has greater love than this, to lay down one's life for one's friends. ¹⁴You are my friends if you do what I command you. ¹⁵I do not call you servants^j any longer, because the servant^k does not know what the master is doing, but I have called you friends, because I have made known to you everything that I have heard from my Father. ¹⁶You did not choose me, but I chose you. And I appointed you to go and bear fruit, fruit that will last, so that the Father will give you whatever you ask him in my name. ¹⁷I am giving you these commands so that you may love one another.

18 "If the world hates you, be aware that it hated me before it hated you. ¹⁹If you belonged to the world, the world would love you as its own. Because you do not belong to the world, but I have chosen you out of the world, therefore the world hates you. ²⁰Remember the word that I said to you, 'Slaves are not greater than their master.' If they persecuted me, they will persecute you; if they kept my word, they will keep yours also. ²¹But they will do all these things to you on account of my name, because they do not know him who sent me. ²²If I had not come and spoken to them, they would not have sin, but now they have no excuse for their sin. ²³Whoever hates me hates my Father also. ²⁴If I had not done among them the works that no one else did, they would not have sin. But now they have seen and hated both me and my Father. ²⁵It was to fulfill the word that is written in their law, 'They hated me without a cause.'

26 "When the Advocate^l comes, whom I will send to you from the Father, the Spirit of truth who comes from the Father, he will testify on my behalf. ²⁷You also are to testify, because you have been with me from the beginning.

16 "I have said these things to you to keep you from falling away."^m ²They will put you out of the synagogues. Indeed, an hour is coming when those who kill you will think that

i 15.8 Or *be*   *j* 15.15 Gk *slaves*   *k* 15.15 Gk *slave*   *l* 15.26 Or *Helper* or *Comforter*   *m* 16.1 Or *stumbling*

15:8 *My Father is glorified* signals the beginning of the end of Jesus's mission in the world and his ultimate glorification.

15:12 *This is my commandment* is in reference to 13:34–35. The love between the Father and the Son is the same as between the Son and his followers.

15:13 *No one has greater love than this, to lay down one's life for one's friends* honors Jesus's disciples. He is willing to die for his friends. The word *friends* ("philōn"), literally "loved ones," signals Jesus's view of his disciples. To be a friend of Jesus one has to obey his will and commandments.

15:15 *I do not call you servants* calls to mind the institution of slavery. The word for *servant* in Greek is "doulos," which literally means "slave." Jesus calls his disciples not *servants* but rather *friends* to signal a change of relationship. A *servant* does not know what the *master* knows, but a *friend* does. "Doulos," or "slave," is used several other times in this chapter, suggesting its normalcy in the people's lives (vv. 15, 20).

15:16 *You did not choose me, but I chose you* suggests that the disciples have no free choice. Another way of looking at this deterministic statement is to think that now the disciples are responsible for extending the mission of Jesus. The Gospel shows a tension between free will and determinism throughout.

15:19–20 *If you belonged to the world* introduces the theme of community and belongingness. The *world* conveys a negative connotation here. To not belong to the *world* (from below) means the world *hates* you. The use of the conditional tense suggests that one could change from a world of unbelief to a world of belief (vv. 18, 19, 20 [two times], 22, 24).

15:23 *Whoever hates me hates my Father also* conveys the union between the Son and the Father. If you hate Jesus, you hate God; conversely, if you love Jesus, you love God. The close relationship between the Father and the Son and between the Son and his disciples remains inseparable.

16:1 *I have said these things* is an expression used seven times within the discourse of the Gospel (14:25; 15:11; 16:1, 4, 6, 25, 33). The words may suggest warning, concern, or just foretelling.

16:2 *They will put you out of the synagogues* is the third time this phrase is used in this Gospel. Here

by doing so they are offering worship to God. ³And they will do this because they have not known the Father or me. ⁴But I have said these things to you so that when their hour comes you may remember that I told you about them.

"I did not say these things to you from the beginning, because I was with you. ⁵But now I am going to him who sent me, yet none of you asks me, 'Where are you going?' ⁶But because I have said these things to you, sorrow has filled your hearts. ⁷Nevertheless, I tell you the truth: it is to your advantage that I go away, for if I do not go away, the Advocate[n] will not come to you, but if I go, I will send him to you. ⁸And when he comes, he will prove the world wrong about[o] sin and righteousness and judgment: ⁹about sin, because they do not believe in me; ¹⁰about righteousness, because I am going to the Father, and you will see me no longer; ¹¹about judgment, because the ruler of this world has been condemned.

12 "I still have many things to say to you, but you cannot bear them now. ¹³When the Spirit of truth comes, he will guide you into all the truth, for he will not speak on his own but will speak whatever he hears, and he will declare to you the things that are to come. ¹⁴He will glorify me because he will take what is mine and declare it to you. ¹⁵All that the Father has is mine. For this reason I said that he will take what is mine and declare it to you.

16 "A little while, and you will no longer see me, and again a little while, and you will see me." ¹⁷Then some of his disciples said to one another, "What does he mean by saying to us, 'A little while, and you will no longer see me, and again a little while, and you will see me,' and 'because I am going to the Father'?" ¹⁸They said, "What does he mean by this 'a little while'? We do not know what he is talking about." ¹⁹Jesus knew that they wanted to ask him, so he said to them, "Are you discussing among yourselves what I meant when I said, 'A little while, and you will no longer see me, and again a little while, and you will see me'? ²⁰Very truly, I tell you, you will weep and mourn, but the world will rejoice; you will have pain, but your pain will turn into joy. ²¹When a woman is in labor, she has pain because her hour has come. But when her child is born, she no longer remembers the anguish because of the joy of having brought a human being into the world. ²²So you have pain now, but I will see you again, and your hearts will rejoice, and no one will take your joy from you. ²³On that day you will ask nothing of me.[p] Very truly, I tell you, if you ask anything of the Father in my name, he will give it to you.[q] ²⁴Until now you have not asked for anything in my name. Ask and you will receive, so that your joy may be complete.

25 "I have said these things to you in figures of speech. The hour is coming when I will no

n 16.7 Or *Helper* or *Comforter*   o 16.8 Or *convict the world of*   p 16.23 Or *will ask me no question*   q 16.23 Other ancient authorities read *Father, he will give it to you in my name*

the use of "fear" does not seem to factor in this exclusion (see 9:22; 12:42). Yet what is consistent is that to believe in Jesus appears to lead to separation from the Jewish community.

16:8–10 *When he comes* is in reference to the Advocate ("paraklētos"). Here the Advocate's role expands to provide exposure or conviction or to *prove the world wrong* about judgment, sin, and righteousness. *Righteousness* conveys vindication as in a court. All this activity is also cast into the future when Jesus returns to the world above.

16:13 *When the Spirit of truth comes* continues expanding on the role of the Spirit. Here the Spirit also functions as a guide teaching them the way.

16:16 *A little while* is employed seven times between vv. 16 and 19. Perhaps Jesus is referring to his post-resurrection appearances to his disciples in chaps. 20 and 21.

16:20 *You will weep and mourn* is contrasted with joy. To *weep* and *mourn* signify those emotions at the time of the death of a loved one.

16:21 *When a woman is in labor* is used here as an illustration to compare what the disciples will feel after Jesus's departure (pain, followed by joy when he returns) with what a mother goes through in childbirth (pain to joy). This is an example of the Gospel drawing from the daily life of women (see **"Jewish Women in the Diaspora (Susanna),"** p. 1525).

16:23 *If you ask anything of the Father in my name, he will give it to you* is assurance that when Jesus departs, their prayers will continue to be heard and granted.

16:25 *I have said these things to you in figures of speech* suggests that the disciples were not ready to hear things *plainly*. But they will soon reach a certain level of knowledge when they are ready to hear things straightforwardly.

longer speak to you in figures but will tell you plainly of the Father. [26]On that day you will ask in my name. I do not say to you that I will ask the Father on your behalf, [27]for the Father himself loves you because you have loved me and have believed that I came from God.[r] [28]I came from the Father and have come into the world; again, I am leaving the world and am going to the Father."

29 His disciples said, "Yes, now you are speaking plainly, not in any figure of speech! [30]Now we know that you know all things and do not need to have anyone question you; by this we believe that you came from God." [31]Jesus answered them, "Do you now believe? [32]The hour is coming, indeed it has come, when you will be scattered, each one to his home, and you will leave me alone. Yet I am not alone because the Father is with me. [33]I have said this to you so that in me you may have peace. In the world you face persecution, but take courage: I have conquered the world!"

17 After Jesus had spoken these words, he looked up to heaven and said, "Father, the hour has come; glorify your Son so that the Son may glorify you, [2]since you have given him authority over all people,[s] to give eternal life to all whom you have given him. [3]And this is eternal life, that they may know you, the only true God, and Jesus Christ, whom you have sent. [4]I glorified you on earth by finishing the work that you gave me to do. [5]So now, Father, glorify me in your own presence with the glory that I had in your presence before the world existed.

6 "I have made your name known to those whom you gave me from the world. They were yours, and you gave them to me, and they have kept your word. [7]Now they know that everything you have given me is from you, [8]for the words that you gave to me I have given to them, and they have received them and know in truth that I came from you, and they have believed that you sent me. [9]I am asking on their behalf; I am not asking on behalf of the world but on behalf of those whom you gave me, because they are yours. [10]All mine are yours, and yours are mine, and I have been glorified in them. [11]And now I am no longer in the world, but they are in the world, and I am coming to you. Holy Father, protect them in your name that you have given me, so that they may be one, as we are one. [12]While I was with them, I protected them in your name that[t] you have given me. I guarded them, and not one of them was lost except the one destined to be lost,[u] so that the scripture might be fulfilled. [13]But now I am coming to you, and I speak these things in the world so that they may have my joy made complete in themselves.[v] [14]I have given them your word, and the world has hated them because they do not belong to the world, just as I do not belong to the world. [15]I am not asking you to take them out of the world, but I ask

r 16.27 Other ancient authorities read *the Father*   s 17.2 Gk *flesh*   t 17.12 Other ancient authorities read *protected in your name those whom*   u 17.12 Gk *except the son of destruction*   v 17.13 Or *among themselves*

16:32 *When you will be scattered* foretells what the disciples will do when Jesus is arrested and under trial. Like the sheep that scatter when a thief is present, the disciples will also be a scattered flock (see Zech. 13:7).

16:33 *In the world you face persecution* predicts sufferings among the disciples and believers.

17:1 *He looked up to heaven and said* is a gesture that indicates Jesus is in prayer and that God is above all. He calls God *Father* (Ar. "abba") and uses it again in vv. 5, 21, 24. *The hour* here is in reference to his death, resurrection, and glorification (or exaltation). *Glorify* connotes praise.

17:2 *Authority over all people* calls attention to the universalization of Jesus's identity and message. It extends to all peoples.

17:4 *I glorified you on earth by finishing the work* suggests that his mission and ministry are finished.

17:6 *I have made your name known* seems to be addressed to the disciples focusing on the work manifested by Jesus in the world below.

17:10 *All mine are yours, and yours are mine* indicates the close relationship between the disciples and Jesus. Jesus not only revealed God to them, he also shared everything with them.

17:12 *I protected them* demonstrates Jesus's care for them. He also *guarded them* so they would not be led astray by the ruler of the world below. The one *lost* is part of the plan of Jesus's mission; the "lost one" is *destined to be lost*.

17:14 *The world has hated them* continues to present the world in the negative and controlled by "the evil one" (v. 15).

you to protect them from the evil one."*w* ¹⁶They do not belong to the world, just as I do not belong to the world. ¹⁷Sanctify them in the truth; your word is truth. ¹⁸As you have sent me into the world, so I have sent them into the world. ¹⁹And for their sakes I sanctify myself, so that they also may be sanctified in truth.

20 "I ask not only on behalf of these but also on behalf of those who believe in me through their word, ²¹that they may all be one. As you, Father, are in me and I am in you, may they also be in us,*x* so that the world may believe that you have sent me. ²²The glory that you have given me I have given them, so that they may be one, as we are one, ²³I in them and you in me, that they may become completely one, so that the world may know that you have sent me and have loved them even as you have loved me. ²⁴Father, I desire that those also, whom you have given me, may be with me where I am, to see my glory, which you have given me because you loved me before the foundation of the world.

25 "Righteous Father, the world does not know you, but I know you, and these know that you have sent me. ²⁶I made your name known to them, and I will make it known, so that the love with which you have loved me may be in them and I in them."

18 After Jesus had spoken these words, he went out with his disciples across the Kidron Valley to a place where there was a garden, which he and his disciples entered. ²Now Judas, who betrayed him, also knew the place because Jesus often met there with his disciples. ³So Judas brought a detachment of soldiers together with police from the chief priests and the Pharisees, and they came there with lanterns and torches and weapons. ⁴Then Jesus, knowing all that was to happen to him, came forward and asked them, "Whom are you looking for?" ⁵They answered, "Jesus of Nazareth."*y* Jesus replied, "I am he."*z* Judas, who betrayed him, was standing with them. ⁶When Jesus*a* said to them, "I am he,"*b* they stepped back and fell to the ground. ⁷Again he asked them, "Whom are you looking for?" And they said, "Jesus of Nazareth."*c* ⁸Jesus answered, "I told you that I am he.*d* So if you are looking for me, let these people go." ⁹This was to fulfill the word that he had spoken, "I did not lose a single one of those whom you gave me." ¹⁰Then Simon Peter, who had a sword, drew it, struck the

w 17.15 Or *from evil*   *x* 17.21 Other ancient authorities read *be one in us*   *y* 18.5 Gk *the Nazorean*   *z* 18.5 Gk *I am*   *a* 18.6 Gk *he*   *b* 18.6 Gk *I am*   *c* 18.7 Gk *the Nazorean*
d 18.8 Gk *I am*

17:17 *Sanctify* suggests "to set apart." Those who are followers are "set apart" *in the truth*, for the word has been given to them to believe.

17:19 *For their sakes* appears to suggest the atoning death of Jesus for the world.

17:21 *That they may all be one* continues to emphasize the union among God, Jesus, and believers. Unity in the face of persecution is a strong theme in this chapter. See v. 23 for this unity.

17:24 *The foundation of the world* speaks to the preexistence of the Word discussed in the prologue (1:1). The Father's love for Jesus began before the world's creation.

17:25 *Righteous Father* is another address to God that emphasizes his characteristic of vindication. The world has failed to recognize this characteristic, but Jesus recognizes it.

17:26 *I will make it known, so that the love* appears to point to the promise of the resurrection. The unity and the love between Jesus and the Father and between Jesus and believers remain strong.

18:1 *Where there was a garden* provides the setting for what is to follow. The garden is unidentified, but it is assumed by some to be a place called Gethsemane that is alluded to in the Synoptics (Matt. 26:36; Mark 14:32; Luke 22:39).

18:2 *Now Judas, who betrayed him* is mentioned by all four Gospels. He will serve as the guide for the arresting party (Matt. 26:47; Mark 14:43; Luke 22:47).

18:3 *Detachment of soldiers together with police* implies they feared Jesus. They will bring with them *lanterns and torches and weapons*, all of which says they came prepared to arrest Jesus.

18:5 *I am he* recalls the claims to divinity found in Exod. 3:14. Jesus self-identifies himself beyond the name, *Jesus of Nazareth* (see note on 4:26).

18:6 *They stepped back and fell to the ground* suggests surprise, but perhaps most likely they were shocked at Jesus identifying himself as God.

18:10 *Simon Peter, who had a sword, drew it* indicates that he is also afraid and ready to protect Jesus. But, according to the plot, he remains a bit ambiguous about Jesus's true identity as the One sent by God. If he knew, perhaps he would not have drawn the sword. There is another mention of the

high priest's slave, and cut off his right ear. The slave's name was Malchus. ¹¹Jesus said to Peter, "Put your sword back into its sheath. Am I not to drink the cup that the Father has given me?"

12 So the soldiers, their officer, and the Jewish police arrested Jesus and bound him. ¹³First they took him to Annas, who was the father-in-law of Caiaphas, the high priest that year. ¹⁴Caiaphas was the one who had advised the Jews that it was better to have one person die for the people.

15 Simon Peter and another disciple followed Jesus. Since that disciple was known to the high priest, he went with Jesus into the courtyard of the high priest, ¹⁶but Peter was standing outside at the gate. So the other disciple, who was known to the high priest, went out, spoke to the woman who guarded the gate, and brought Peter in. ¹⁷The woman said to Peter, "You are not also one of this man's disciples, are you?" He said, "I am not." ¹⁸Now the slaves and the police had made a charcoal fire because it was cold, and they were standing around it and warming themselves. Peter also was standing with them and warming himself.

19 Then the high priest questioned Jesus about his disciples and about his teaching. ²⁰Jesus answered, "I have spoken openly to the world; I have always taught in synagogues and in the temple, where all the Jews come together. I have said nothing in secret. ²¹Why do you ask me? Ask those who heard what I said to them; they know what I said." ²²When he had said this, one of the police standing nearby struck Jesus on the face, saying, "Is that how you answer the high priest?" ²³Jesus

answered, "If I have spoken wrongly, testify to the wrong. But if I have spoken rightly, why do you strike me?" ²⁴Then Annas sent him bound to Caiaphas the high priest.

25 Now Simon Peter was standing and warming himself. They asked him, "You are not also one of his disciples, are you?" He denied it and said, "I am not." ²⁶One of the slaves of the high priest, a relative of the man whose ear Peter had cut off, asked, "Did I not see you in the garden with him?" ²⁷Again Peter denied it, and at that moment the cock crowed.

28 Then they took Jesus from Caiaphas to Pilate's headquarters. It was early in the morning. They themselves did not enter the headquarters, so as to avoid ritual defilement and to be able to eat the Passover. ²⁹So Pilate went out to them and said, "What accusation do you bring against this man?" ³⁰They answered, "If this man were not a criminal, we would not have handed him over to you." ³¹Pilate said to them, "Take him yourselves and judge him according to your law." The Jews replied, "We are not permitted to put anyone to death." ³²(This was to fulfill what Jesus had said when he indicated the kind of death he was to die.)

33 Then Pilate entered the headquarters again, summoned Jesus, and asked him, "Are you the King of the Jews?" ³⁴Jesus answered, "Do you ask this on your own, or did others tell you about me?" ³⁵Pilate replied, "I am not a Jew, am I? Your own nation and the chief priests have handed you over to me. What have you done?" ³⁶Jesus answered, "My kingdom does not belong to this world. If my kingdom belonged to this world, my followers would be fighting to keep me from being

same enslaved person who loses his ear in 18:26. Again, in this world, enslaved people are part of the daily lives of the privileged (see also a reference to "slaves" in v. 18).

18:13–14 *Annas, who was the father-in-law of Caiaphas, the high priest* provides a glimpse into some historical information. Caiaphas served as the high priest for eighteen years, but at this time, Annas supposedly had the power. It is Caiaphas who recommends the death of one person (11:50).

18:15 *Another disciple* is not identified but may be the Beloved Disciple. Apparently, this disciple had privileges to the high priest; the disciple is *known to the high priest.*

18:17 *I am not* is the first of Peter's three denials (vv. 17, 25, 27).

18:22 *Struck Jesus on the face* seems to suggest that the police extend punishment as they please.

18:28 *They themselves did not enter the headquarters* means they would risk ritual contamination by entering a gentile building during the Passover. Gentiles were not considered impure by their nature, so it is unclear which kind of contamination the author is implying.

18:31 *We are not permitted to put anyone to death* reminds readers that the time was Passover—a sacred period—so putting someone to death would be defilement, but the words also seem to suggest that *the Jews* ("hoi Ioudaioi") may have lost the power of the death penalty. Whether *the Jews* had the power to put someone to death is indeterminate.

handed over to the Jews. But as it is, my kingdom is not from here." ³⁷Pilate asked him, "So you are a king?" Jesus answered, "You say that I am a king. For this I was born, and for this I came into the world, to testify to the truth. Everyone who belongs to the truth listens to my voice." ³⁸Pilate asked him, "What is truth?"

After he had said this, he went out to the Jews again and told them, "I find no case against him. ³⁹But you have a custom that I release someone for you at the Passover. Do you want me to release for you the King of the Jews?" ⁴⁰They shouted in reply, "Not this man but Barabbas!" Now Barabbas was a rebel.

19 Then Pilate took Jesus and had him flogged. ²And the soldiers wove a crown of thorns and put it on his head, and they dressed him in a purple robe. ³They kept coming up to him, saying, "Hail, King of the Jews!" and striking him on the face. ⁴Pilate went out again and said to them, "Look, I am bringing him out to you to let you know that I find no case against him." ⁵So Jesus came out wearing the crown of thorns and the purple robe. Pilate*ᵉ* said to them, "Behold the man!" ⁶When the chief priests and the police saw him, they shouted, "Crucify him! Crucify him!" Pilate said to them, "Take him yourselves and crucify him; I find no case against him." ⁷The Jews answered him, "We have a law, and according to that law he ought to die because he has claimed to be the Son of God."

8 Now when Pilate heard this, he was more afraid than ever. ⁹He entered his headquarters again and asked Jesus, "Where are you from?" But Jesus gave him no answer. ¹⁰Pilate therefore said to him, "Do you refuse to speak

to me? Do you not know that I have power to release you and power to crucify you?" ¹¹Jesus answered him, "You would have no power over me unless it had been given you from above; therefore the one who handed me over to you is guilty of a greater sin." ¹²From then on Pilate tried to release him, but the Jews cried out, "If you release this man, you are no friend of Caesar. Everyone who claims to be a king sets himself against Caesar."

13 When Pilate heard these words, he brought Jesus outside and sat*ᶠ* on the judge's bench at a place called The Stone Pavement, or in Hebrew*ᵍ* Gabbatha. ¹⁴Now it was the day of Preparation for the Passover, and it was about noon. He said to the Jews, "Here is your King!" ¹⁵They cried out, "Away with him! Away with him! Crucify him!" Pilate asked them, "Shall I crucify your King?" The chief priests answered, "We have no king but Caesar." ¹⁶Then he handed him over to them to be crucified.

So they took Jesus, ¹⁷and carrying the cross by himself he went out to what is called the Place of the Skull, which in Hebrew*ᵇ* is called Golgotha. ¹⁸There they crucified him and with him two others, one on either side, with Jesus between them. ¹⁹Pilate also had an inscription written and put on the cross. It read, "Jesus of Nazareth,*ⁱ* the King of the Jews." ²⁰Many of the Jews read this inscription because the place where Jesus was crucified was near the city, and it was written in Hebrew,*ʲ* in Latin, and in Greek. ²¹Then the chief priests of the Jews said to Pilate, "Do not write, 'The King of the Jews,' but, 'This man said, I am King of the Jews.' "

e 19.5 Gk *He*   *f* 19.13 Or *seated him*   *g* 19.13 That is, *Aramaic*   *h* 19.17 That is, *Aramaic*   *i* 19.19 Gk *the Nazorean*   *j* 19.20 That is, *Aramaic*

18:38 *What is truth?* The question is never answered by Jesus. Some scholars believe the death and resurrection of Jesus is the answer to the question.

19:1 *Pilate took Jesus and had him flogged* demonstrates that at some point, Pilate decided to convict Jesus to death. To flog or to whip is the first step in bringing someone to death by crucifixion. Interestingly, no emotion is described.

19:2 *Crown of thorns* symbolizes kingship. In this instance, it is a gesture of mockery, along with placing a *purple robe* on Jesus. It is not clear if the mocking of Jesus came from Pilate or the soldiers.

19:7 *We have a law* seems to be a strategy to get Pilate on board with the death of Jesus. Anyone claiming to be the Son of God is blasphemous (Lev. 24:16). This is not the first time the accusation of blasphemy was placed on Jesus (5:18; 8:53; 10:33). The religious claim *to be the Son of God* is of no interest to Pilate (v. 8).

19:12 *If you release this man, you are no friend of Caesar* is another strategy used to put Jesus to death. High treason seems to be on the table now (v. 15; see **"Crucifixion and Terror," p. 1798**).

19:19 *Pilate also had an inscription* placed on the cross to indicate why Jesus was crucified. Hebrew signified the language of the people, Latin the language of the empire, and Greek the language of communication and commerce.

²²Pilate answered, "What I have written I have written." ²³When the soldiers had crucified Jesus, they took his clothes and divided them into four parts, one for each soldier. They also took his tunic; now the tunic was seamless, woven in one piece from the top. ²⁴So they said to one another, "Let us not tear it but cast lots for it to see who will get it." This was to fulfill what the scripture says,

"They divided my clothes among
    themselves,
   and for my clothing they cast lots."

²⁵And that is what the soldiers did.

Meanwhile, standing near the cross of Jesus were his mother, and his mother's sister, Mary the wife of Clopas, and Mary Magdalene. ²⁶When Jesus saw his mother and the disciple whom he loved standing beside her, he said to his mother, "Woman, here is your son." ²⁷Then he said to the disciple, "Here is your mother." And from that hour the disciple took her into his own home.

28 After this, when Jesus knew that all was now finished, he said (in order to fulfill the scripture), "I am thirsty." ²⁹A jar full of sour wine was standing there. So they put a sponge full of the wine on a branch of hyssop and held it to his mouth. ³⁰When Jesus had received the wine, he said, "It is finished." Then he bowed his head and gave up his spirit.

31 Since it was the day of Preparation, the Jews did not want the bodies left on the cross during the Sabbath, especially because that Sabbath was a day of great solemnity. So they asked Pilate to have the legs of the crucified men broken and the bodies removed. ³²Then the soldiers came and broke the legs of the first and of the other who had been crucified

with him. ³³But when they came to Jesus and saw that he was already dead, they did not break his legs. ³⁴Instead, one of the soldiers pierced his side with a spear, and at once blood and water came out. ³⁵(He who saw this has testified so that you also may believe. His testimony is true, and he knows*k* that he tells the truth, so that you also may continue*l* to believe.) ³⁶These things occurred so that the scripture might be fulfilled, "None of his bones shall be broken." ³⁷And again another passage of scripture says, "They will look on the one whom they have pierced."

38 After these things, Joseph of Arimathea, who was a disciple of Jesus, though a secret one because of his fear of the Jews, asked Pilate to let him take away the body of Jesus. Pilate gave him permission, so he came and removed his body. ³⁹Nicodemus, who had at first come to Jesus by night, also came, bringing a mixture of myrrh and aloes, weighing about a hundred pounds. ⁴⁰They took the body of Jesus and wrapped it with the spices in linen cloths, according to the burial custom of the Jews. ⁴¹Now there was a garden in the place where he was crucified, and in the garden there was a new tomb in which no one had ever been laid. ⁴²And so, because it was the Jewish day of Preparation and the tomb was nearby, they laid Jesus there.

20 Early on the first day of the week, while it was still dark, Mary Magdalene came to the tomb and saw that the stone had been removed from the tomb. ²So she ran and went to Simon Peter and the other

k 19.35 Or *there is one who knows*   l 19.35 Or *may come*

19:26 *When Jesus saw his mother and the disciple whom he loved* brings two unnamed characters together for the first time in the Gospel story. Jesus indicates his deepest trust in them by instructing them to take care of each other (v. 27).

19:29 *A branch of hyssop* is used to dip into sour wine and provide Jesus a drink. The branch of hyssop is linked to Passover. Hyssop reminds one of the use of this plant to sprinkle blood on the lintels and doorposts of the Israelite dwellings at the first Passover in Egypt (Exod. 12:22). This is the only act of kindness shown to Jesus while he is hanging on the cross.

19:32–34 *Then the soldiers came and broke the legs* as a way to expedite death. Jesus's legs were not broken, but to confirm his death, *one of the soldiers pierced his side with a spear*.

19:39–40 *A mixture of myrrh and aloes* is used for the body of Jesus. The amount of *a hundred pounds*, the purple robe placed on him earlier (v. 5), the repetition of the word "King" (vv. 3, 14, 15, 19, 21), and the use of three languages declaring Jesus king (v. 20) all suggest royalty and underscore Jesus's true identity as king. To show that he is really dead, they wrap the body of Jesus *with the spices in linen cloths*.

20:1 *The first day of the week*, Sunday, the day after the Sabbath on the Jewish calendar, is the day when the tomb is discovered empty by Mary Magdalene and the day Jesus makes his first appearance

disciple, the one whom Jesus loved, and said to them, "They have taken the Lord out of the tomb, and we do not know where they have laid him." ³Then Peter and the other disciple set out and went toward the tomb. ⁴The two were running together, but the other disciple outran Peter and reached the tomb first. ⁵He bent down to look in and saw the linen wrappings lying there, but he did not go in. ⁶Then Simon Peter came, following him, and went into the tomb. He saw the linen wrappings lying there, ⁷and the cloth that had been on Jesus's head, not lying with the linen wrappings but rolled up in a place by itself. ⁸Then the other disciple, who reached the tomb first, also went in, and he saw and believed, ⁹for as yet they did not understand the scripture, that he must rise from the dead. ¹⁰Then the disciples returned to their homes.

11 But Mary stood weeping outside the tomb. As she wept, she bent over to look*m* into the tomb, ¹²and she saw two angels in white sitting where the body of Jesus had been lying, one at the head and the other at the feet. ¹³They said to her, "Woman, why are you weeping?" She said to them, "They have taken away my Lord, and I do not know where they have laid him." ¹⁴When she had said this, she turned around and saw Jesus standing there, but she did not know that it was Jesus. ¹⁵Jesus said to her, "Woman, why

are you weeping? Whom are you looking for?" Supposing him to be the gardener, she said to him, "Sir,*ⁿ* if you have carried him away, tell me where you have laid him, and I will take him away." ¹⁶Jesus said to her, "Mary!" She turned and said to him in Hebrew,*ᵒ* "Rabbouni!" (which means Teacher). ¹⁷Jesus said to her, "Do not touch me, because I have not yet ascended to the Father. But go to my brothers and say to them, 'I am ascending to my Father and your Father, to my God and your God.'" ¹⁸Mary Magdalene went and announced to the disciples, "I have seen the Lord," and she told them that he had said these things to her.

19 When it was evening on that day, the first day of the week, and the doors were locked where the disciples were, for fear of the Jews, Jesus came and stood among them and said, "Peace be with you." ²⁰After he said this, he showed them his hands and his side. Then the disciples rejoiced when they saw the Lord. ²¹Jesus said to them again, "Peace be with you. As the Father has sent me, so I send you." ²²When he had said this, he breathed on them and said to them, "Receive the Holy Spirit. ²³If you forgive the sins of any, they are forgiven them; if you retain the sins of any, they are retained."

m 20.11 Gk lacks *to look*   *n* 20.15 Or *Lord*   *o* 20.16 That is, *Aramaic*

to the disciples. The other Gospels also confirm the first day of the week as the day of resurrection (Matt. 28:1; Mark 16:2; Luke 24:1). *The stone had been removed from the tomb* adds to the verisimilitude of the event.

20:2 Mary Magdalene *ran and went to Simon Peter*. In all four Gospels, a woman is the first person to witness the empty tomb.

20:4 *The other disciple outran Peter* may signal the age of the two disciples. It is the other disciple who reaches the empty tomb first. The running side by side reflects some competition between Peter and the Beloved Disciple for the role of the most important disciple.

20:6 *He saw the linen wrappings lying there* confirms that Jesus had indeed been dead (vv. 5, 6, 7).

20:12–13 *Two angels in white sitting where the body of Jesus had been lying* signals that Jesus has risen. Variations of this incident are found in Matt. 28:2; Mark 16:5; and Luke 24:4. The angels ask Mary, *Why are you weeping?* Apparently, her weeping suggests she is unaware of Jesus's resurrection (see v. 15).

20:15 *Supposing him to be the gardener*, Mary continues not to recognize Jesus. The theme of recognition and nonrecognition is dominant in this chapter.

20:18 *Mary Magdalene went and announced to the disciples* reiterates and emphasizes that the first witness to the empty tomb event is a woman (see v. 2).

20:19 *The first day of the week, and the doors were locked* provides a more close-up look at the resurrection. At this point, the disciples are afraid of *the Jews*. The door having been locked signals there is no way to enter the house, but the resurrected Jesus is there with them.

20:20 *Showed them his hands and his side* is Jesus's way to prove his identity as the one crucified and now resurrected (see **"Resurrection in the Gospels," p. 1767**).

20:21 *Peace be with you* is the second time Jesus greets them in this fashion. The other two greetings are found in vv. 19 and 26. The greeting is perhaps a way to alleviate the disciples' fear.

24 But Thomas (who was called the Twin[p]), one of the twelve, was not with them when Jesus came. [25]So the other disciples told him, "We have seen the Lord." But he said to them, "Unless I see the mark of the nails in his hands and put my finger in the mark of the nails and my hand in his side, I will not believe."

26 A week later his disciples were again in the house, and Thomas was with them. Although the doors were shut, Jesus came and stood among them and said, "Peace be with you." [27]Then he said to Thomas, "Put your finger here and see my hands. Reach out your hand and put it in my side. Do not doubt but believe." [28]Thomas answered him, "My Lord and my God!" [29]Jesus said to him, "Have you believed because you have seen me? Blessed are those who have not seen and yet have come to believe."

30 Now Jesus did many other signs in the presence of his disciples that are not written in this book. [31]But these are written so that you may continue[q] to believe that Jesus is the Messiah,[r] the Son of God, and that through believing you may have life in his name.

21 After these things Jesus showed himself again to the disciples by the Sea of Tiberias, and he showed himself in this way. [2]Gathered there together were Simon Peter, Thomas called the Twin,[s] Nathanael of Cana in Galilee, the sons of Zebedee, and two others of his disciples. [3]Simon Peter said to them, "I am going fishing." They said to him, "We will go with you." They went out and got into the boat, but that night they caught nothing.

4 Just after daybreak, Jesus stood on the beach, but the disciples did not know that it was Jesus. [5]Jesus said to them, "Children, you have no fish, have you?" They answered him, "No." [6]He said to them, "Cast the net to the right side of the boat, and you will find some." So they cast it, and now they were not able to haul it in because there were so many fish. [7]That disciple whom Jesus loved said to Peter, "It is the Lord!" When Simon Peter heard that it was the Lord, he put on his outer garment, for he had taken it off, and jumped into the sea. [8]But the other disciples came in the boat, dragging the net full of fish, for they were not far from the land, only about a hundred yards off.

9 When they had gone ashore, they saw a charcoal fire there, with fish on it, and bread. [10]Jesus said to them, "Bring some of the fish that you have just caught." [11]So Simon Peter went aboard and hauled the net ashore, full of large fish, a hundred fifty-three of them, and though there were so many, the net was not torn. [12]Jesus said to them, "Come and have breakfast." Now none of the disciples dared to ask him, "Who are you?" because they knew it was the Lord. [13]Jesus came and took the bread and gave it to them and did the same with the

p 20.24 Gk *Didymus* q 20.31 Or *may come* r 20.31 Or *the Christ* s 21.2 Gk *Didymus*

20:27 *Put your finger here and see my hands* is simply a way to prove that Jesus is who he says he is. It also shows the disciples' uncertainty as to Jesus's true identity.

20:31 *But these are written so that you may continue to believe* can also be translated as "may come to believe." The former translation suggests the purpose is for those who are believers, while the latter suggests it is written for nonbelievers. Both Greek words are supported by ancient Greek documents. This purpose reads as a natural ending to the Gospel, which has led to the suggestion that John 21 is a later addition.

21:1 *Showed himself* indicates that it is Jesus who remains in control of his plans. The theme of showing or revealing himself is mentioned three times in this section (vv. 1 [two times] and 14), and it is found throughout the Gospel (1:31; 2:11; 3:21; 7:4; 9:3; 17:6). Some scholars argue that this chapter is not part of the original Gospel, nor was it written by John. It does appear in all the early manuscripts.

21:4 *But the disciples did not know* continues the difficulty in recognizing the risen Christ. This is quite similar to Mary Magdalene's nonrecognition in 20:15.

21:5 *Children* ("paidia") is a term of endearment and paternal expression (see note on 13:33).

21:7 *It is the Lord* is the fourth confession of the risen Jesus after the resurrection. This one is made by the Beloved Disciple (see 20:18, 25, 28).

21:11 *A hundred fifty-three of them* has triggered many explanations of the number. No information is provided by the narrative, and perhaps it is simply calling attention to the great miracle itself.

21:13 *Jesus came and took the bread and gave it to them* begins with Jesus serving the disciples first,

fish. ¹⁴This was now the third time that Jesus appeared to the disciples after he was raised from the dead.

15 When they had finished breakfast, Jesus said to Simon Peter, "Simon son of John, do you love me more than these?" He said to him, "Yes, Lord; you know that I love you." Jesus said to him, "Feed my lambs." ¹⁶A second time he said to him, "Simon son of John, do you love me?" He said to him, "Yes, Lord; you know that I love you." Jesus said to him, "Tend my sheep." ¹⁷He said to him the third time, "Simon son of John, do you love me?" Peter felt hurt because he said to him the third time, "Do you love me?" And he said to him, "Lord, you know everything; you know that I love you." Jesus said to him, "Feed my sheep. ¹⁸Very truly, I tell you, when you were younger, you used to fasten your own belt and to go wherever you wished. But when you grow old, you will stretch out your hands, and someone else will fasten a belt around you and take you where you do not wish to go." ¹⁹(He said this to indicate the kind of death by which he would glorify God.) After this he said to him, "Follow me."

20 Peter turned and saw the disciple whom Jesus loved following them; he was the one who had reclined next to Jesus at the supper and had said, "Lord, who is it that is going to betray you?" ²¹When Peter saw him, he said to Jesus, "Lord, what about him?" ²²Jesus said to him, "If it is my will that he remain until I come, what is that to you? Follow me!" ²³So the rumor spread among the brothers and sisters that this disciple would not die. Yet Jesus did not say to him that he would not die, but, "If it is my will that he remain until I come, what is that to you?"ᵗ

24 This is the disciple who is testifying to these things and has written them, and we know that his testimony is true. ²⁵But there are also many other things that Jesus did; if every one of them were written down, I suppose that the world itself could not contain the books that would be written.

---

t 21.23 Other ancient authorities lack *what is that to you*

compared to the disciples serving the crowd in 6:1–11. He proceeds to serve them *fish*. The tradition of the fish as an early symbol for Christians arose (possibly as a code) because the Greek word for fishing, "ichthys," served as an acrostic for the declaration "Jesus Christ, Son of God, Savior." Later, believers were called "little fishes" by Tertullian.

21:15 *Do you love me more than these?* This is the first of three questions (vv. 15, 16, 17) where Jesus asks Simon Peter if he loves him. The theme of *love* is dominant in this section and is expressed in two verbs: "agapan" and "philein." Scholars provide various interpretations on the nuances behind the meaning of the verbs, but it is clear the two verbs have similar meaning, "to love." *Feed my lambs* is a command that also is made in vv. 15, 17, along with another command to "tend my sheep" (v. 16). "To feed" and "to tend" describe the instructions Jesus is leaving for Simon Peter and for all believers.

21:16 *You know* is employed in all of Peter's responses (vv. 15, 16, 17). The repetition emphasizes the theme of spiritual knowledge.

21:19 *Follow me* calls to mind the theme of discipleship in the first chapter. The command is repeated in v. 22.

21:24 *This is the disciple who is testifying* does not provide much information regarding the person's identity. Many theories of authorship abound, including that it is the Beloved Disciple who is the source of the Gospel traditions. *We know* suggests multiple authors, but it can also refer to one author.

THE ACTS OF THE APOSTLES

The book of Acts is an exciting narrative filled with a diversity of characters, settings, and stories. It picks up just as the Gospels end (i.e., after the resurrection of Jesus) and imagines the growth of Christianity throughout the Mediterranean world. As you read Acts, you enter the ancient Greco-Roman world and travel with the disciples—namely, Peter and Paul—as they share the gospel of Jesus and wrestle with the ideas and boundaries of this new religion that will become Christianity.

Authorship, Date, and Literary History

The book of Acts is connected to the Gospel of Luke. This can be most clearly seen through the prologues of the two books (Luke 1:1–4; Acts 1:1–2), which both name Theophilus as the recipient or perhaps the patron (one who paid to commission the writing of a book) of the texts. Acts follows Luke as the second book in the series or, perhaps, as the continuation of the Gospel story. The end of the Gospel of Luke (24:36–53) narrates the same events that are covered in the first part of Acts. Luke and Acts also incorporate similar vocabulary and grammatical structure. Thus, most scholars are convinced the same author wrote both texts. Concerning the author, both the Gospel and Acts are written anonymously, as no author is named within the texts, although traditionally the author has been called Luke. The author of Acts seems to know quite a bit about the geography and cities in the Mediterranean world because of the detail given within the narrative. For this reason, scholars assume that the author, "Luke," may have traveled before writing Acts. Similarly, the author seems to focus heavily on gentiles, which has led scholars to believe that Luke himself was a gentile—that is, he was not Jewish—and that the intended audience of Acts was also gentiles. However, lately, some scholars have suggested the importance of Judaism to Acts, which could suggest more of a foundation within Second Temple Judaism than previously thought.

Traditionally, the book of Acts was thought to be written after the Gospel of Luke, since it is thought to be written by the same author. This suggests a date in the late 80s or early 90s CE. Recently, however, a number of scholars have suggested a later date for Acts and place it in the early second century, perhaps between 120 and 130 CE. There are a number of reasons for this later date. First, the text of Acts wrestles with issues that defined the development of the church in the early second century, such as the inclusion of gentiles, the divisions between orthodoxy and heresy, and the defense against persecution. Acts includes the name "Christian," which emerged during the second century as well. Additionally, Acts references similar persons and events as found in the writings of Josephus, an ancient Jewish historian, in his *Antiquities of the Jews*, which was written in 95 CE. Finally, the genre of Acts (which will be discussed below) incorporates themes and tropes from texts popular in the second century such as the Greek novels. When considering these reasons, it seems highly possible that Acts was written in the early years of the second century CE.

Genre of Acts

Acts is a combination of several forms of genre. In many ways, Acts reads as if it is a historical document that describes the events occurring after the death and resurrection of Jesus and chronicles the development and growth of the earliest form of Christianity. Similarly, Acts could be understood as a biography of Peter and/or Paul. A large part of the text of Acts consists of speeches given primarily by Peter and Paul and rhetorically arguing for the message and gospel of Jesus as well as the inclusion of gentiles into the community of Jesus followers. Additionally, Acts incorporates elements of the ancient Greek epic and those of the ancient Greek, Roman, and Jewish novels. One can see evidence of novelistic literature in the many travels depicted in the text as well as other literary themes and tropes such as humor, divine guidance, diverse settings, and the inclusion of dramatic adventures. Acts is best understood in terms of genre as connected to each of these forms but not strictly understood as only one of those forms of literature.

Reading Guide

Acts is a fast-moving travel narrative that begins in Jerusalem and ends in Rome. It tracks the movement of the apostles who have been sent out to share the message of Jesus "to the ends of the earth" (Acts 1:8). The first half of Acts (chaps. 1–12) generally follows the apostle Peter, who is preaching and ministering in the area of Judea, while the second half of Acts (chaps. 13–28) follows

the ministry of the apostle Paul, who takes the message to cities and regions outside of Judea. During these missions, both Peter and Paul are persecuted, jailed, and almost killed. Yet the Holy Spirit serves as a guide for the narrative, and both apostles survive, at least within the pages of Acts. Near the end of Acts, Paul is arrested and put on trial. He is ultimately sent to Rome, where the book of Acts ends with the apostle still preaching even while under house arrest.

Because of these diverse geographical settings, Acts references numerous places and features minor characters within those places. For example, the apostle Philip is directed by the Spirit to travel to a road between Jerusalem and Gaza. While there, he meets an Ethiopian eunuch who is reading Scripture; Philip ends up baptizing the eunuch (8:26–40). When Paul visits Ephesus, the narrative mentions Demetrius, who is an artisan who makes small statues of the goddess Artemis (19:24). When in Philippi, Paul and his companions meet Lydia as well as an enslaved fortune teller (16:11–19). On the island of Malta, Paul is bitten by a poisonous snake yet survives (28:3). The text thus incorporates Greek gods and goddesses, local customs, travel routes, and descriptive stories from various cities.

One major theme that Acts addresses is the incorporation of gentiles into this religious community, which is mostly Jewish. During Jesus's ministry, most of his followers were Jewish. Yet now, as Peter, Paul, and their companions travel, they encounter many gentiles who are interested in and eager to join their movement. Questions arise such as, Do these new believers have to be circumcised? Do they need to follow the dietary laws of Judaism? Ultimately, the leaders of the Way (or the earliest form of Christianity) answer no to those questions, and even more gentiles begin to join the community. Thus, the text wrestles with the boundaries between Judaism and Christianity and ultimately concludes that gentiles can be a part of this new yet growing religious sect.

Christy Cobb

1 In the first book, Theophilus, I wrote about all that Jesus began to do and teach ²until the day when he was taken up to heaven, after giving instructions through the Holy Spirit to the apostles whom he had chosen. ³After his suffering*a* he presented himself alive to them by many convincing proofs, appearing to them during forty days and speaking about the kingdom of God. ⁴While staying*b* with them, he ordered them not to leave Jerusalem but to wait there for the promise of the Father. "This," he said, "is what you have heard from me; ⁵for John baptized with water, but you will be baptized with*c* the Holy Spirit not many days from now."

6 So when they had come together, they asked him, "Lord, is this the time when you will restore the kingdom to Israel?" ⁷He replied, "It is not for you to know the times or periods that the Father has set by his own authority. ⁸But you will receive power when the Holy Spirit has come upon you, and you will be my witnesses in Jerusalem, in all Judea and Samaria, and to the ends of the earth." ⁹When he had said this, as they were watching, he was lifted up, and a cloud took him out of their sight. ¹⁰While he was going and they were gazing up toward heaven, suddenly two men in white robes stood by them. ¹¹They said, "Men of Galilee, why do you stand looking up toward heaven? This Jesus, who has been taken up from you into heaven,

a 1.3 Or *death*   *b* 1.4 Or *eating*   *c* 1.5 Or *by*

1:1–11 The beginning of Acts functions as a recap of the ending of the Gospel of Luke. Here the reader is reminded of the events after the resurrection when Jesus talked with two disciples on the road to Emmaus (Luke 24:13–32), ate with followers in Jerusalem (24:36–43), interpreted the Hebrew Scriptures (24:44–48), commanded them not to leave Jerusalem (24:49), blessed them (24:50), and ascended to heaven (24:51). **1:1** The author dedicates this book to Theophilus, who is also mentioned in the prologue to the Gospel of Luke (Luke 1:3). While we do not know exactly who Theophilus was, some suggest he could have been a patron who provided monetary support for the author's writing. Theophilus literally means "lover of God," so this name could also function symbolically to represent readers. **1:10–11** The two men in white robes are an addition to the Gospel's narrative about Jesus's ascension. In Acts, these two men, likely assumed to be angels, remind the disciples of the second coming, when Jesus will return from the clouds (Luke 21:27). They also nudge the disciples to stop *looking up toward heaven*, which suggests that the author of Acts is aware that the eschaton, or the return of the Lord, has not yet happened and wants readers to stop actively waiting for Jesus's return.

will come in the same way as you saw him go into heaven."

12 Then they returned to Jerusalem from the mount called Olivet, which is near Jerusalem, a Sabbath day's journey away. [13]When they had entered the city, they went to the room upstairs where they were staying: Peter, and John, and James, and Andrew, Philip and Thomas, Bartholomew and Matthew, James son of Alphaeus, and Simon the Zealot, and Judas son of[d] James. [14]All these were constantly devoting themselves to prayer, together with certain women, including Mary the mother of Jesus, as well as his brothers.

15 In those days Peter stood up among the brothers and sisters (together the crowd numbered about one hundred twenty persons) and said, [16]"Brothers and sisters,[e] the scripture had to be fulfilled, which the Holy Spirit through David foretold concerning Judas, who became a guide for those who arrested Jesus, [17]for he was numbered among us and was allotted his share in this ministry." [18](Now this man acquired a field with the reward of his wickedness, and falling headlong, he burst open in the middle, and all his bowels gushed out. [19]This became known to all the residents of Jerusalem, so that the field was called in their language Hakeldama, that

is, Field of Blood.) [20]"For it is written in the book of Psalms,

'Let his house become desolate,
    and let there be no one to live in it';

and

'Let another take his position of overseer.'

[21]"So one of the men who have accompanied us during all the time that the Lord Jesus went in and out among us, [22]beginning from the baptism of John until the day when he was taken up from us—one of these must become a witness with us to his resurrection." [23]So they proposed two, Joseph called Barsabbas, who was also known as Justus, and Matthias. [24]Then they prayed and said, "Lord, you know everyone's heart. Show us which one of these two you have chosen [25]to take the place[f] in this ministry and apostleship from which Judas turned aside to go to his own place." [26]And they cast lots for them, and the lot fell on Matthias, and he was added to the eleven apostles.

2 When the day of Pentecost had come, they were all together in one place. [2]And suddenly from heaven there came a sound like the rush of a violent wind, and it filled

d 1.13 Or *the brother of*   e 1.16 Gk *Men, brothers*   f 1.25 Other ancient authorities read *the share*

1:14 Along with the eleven remaining disciples, women are present, including Mary the mother of Jesus. The phrase *certain women* could be a reference to the prominent female followers mentioned in the Gospel of Luke, which include Mary Magdalene, Joanna, Susanna, and many others (Luke 8:1–3). This verse should remind readers that the followers of Jesus were not solely men; women were present and included in this early Christian community as well.

1:15 The number 120 may be symbolic, as it is used throughout biblical texts. The phrase *brothers and sisters* is literally "brothers" in the Greek, but the inclusion of *sisters* acknowledges women who were likely in the crowd, as mentioned in 1:14.

1:16–18 This narrative about the death of Judas contrasts with the one given in the Gospel of Matthew, where Judas hangs himself. This version included in Acts presents the death of Judas as an accident, or perhaps a death of divine retribution, instead of an intentional form of suicide, as found in Matt. 27:5.

1:21–22 This note again shows that the disciples of Jesus included more than just the twelve disciples, as these two men offered as possible replacements for Judas were present throughout the ministry of Jesus (as were the women, noted above).

1:26 Casting lots likely indicated that the decision was a divine one, not a human vote for Judas's replacement. The text does not indicate how this process worked, but casting lots was also used to make political and religious decisions in the broader Greco-Roman world, so Luke is referring to a practice that would have been familiar to his readers.

2:1 Pentecost, or the Festival of Weeks, is a yearly Jewish festival that required pilgrimage when the temple was standing. It occurs after Passover and is connected to the covenant given at Sinai. Thus, the Jewish community was gathered *together in one place* in order to celebrate this festival.

2:2–4 *Divided tongues* is an interesting phrase that can be imagined in a variety of ways. For instance, one can imagine a flame of a fire appearing in the shape of a tongue. The scene, filled with wind and fire, is frightening but might remind readers of the appearance of God at Sinai (Exod. 19:16–19). By 2:4,

Focus On: Glossolalia in Acts (Acts 2:4)

Glossolalia, or speaking in tongues, is a religious and spiritual experience that was present within ancient Judaism, ancient Greek religion, and early Christianity and continues to be practiced today in Christian denominations such as Pentecostalism. In the book of Acts, glossolalia occurs when the Holy Spirit is present. The first mention of it is in Acts 2 when a large group of Jews from other countries and regions gathered in Jerusalem to celebrate the Festival of Pentecost. Glossolalia occurred after tongues "as of fire" rested on each of them and they were "filled with the Holy Spirit" (2:3–4) and were able to speak in other languages. Even more miraculously, those present understood the languages spoken, even when they were not the person's own language (2:6). Glossolalia is specifically mentioned two other times in Acts (10:44–48 and 19:1–7) and occurs after a group of people have believed in the message. The author of Acts is clear that the Holy Spirit is the instigator of this gift. Also, in both cases, baptism accompanies the glossolalia (in chap. 10, the believers are baptized after speaking in tongues, while in chap. 19, they are baptized before speaking in tongues). Thus, glossolalia in Acts is given by the Holy Spirit, consists of intelligible speech, and usually occurs with baptism.

On the other hand, when Paul mentions glossolalia in 1 Corinthians, he names it as one of the gifts of the Spirit (12:10). In this letter Paul notes that he hopes that those reading the letter have the gift of prophecy instead of the gift of tongues. When describing glossolalia, he writes that "no one understands them" (14:2), which indicates that glossolalia, as it occurs in Corinth, is unintelligible speech. Although Paul claims to be able to speak in tongues himself (v. 18), he still prefers prophecy so that those around him will be able to understand his words (vv. 5, 19). Paul also advises that if someone is speaking in tongues there should be an interpreter (14:13). Some Christians today in Pentecostal and charismatic Christianity still practice speaking in tongues and view it in high regard within their religious communities.

Christy Cobb

the entire house where they were sitting. ³Divided tongues, as of fire, appeared among them, and a tongue rested on each of them. ⁴All of them were filled with the Holy Spirit and began to speak in other languages, as the Spirit gave them ability.

5 Now there were devout Jews from every people under heaven living in Jerusalem. ⁶And at this sound the crowd gathered and was bewildered, because each one heard them speaking in the native language of each. ⁷Amazed and astonished, they asked, "Are not all these who are speaking Galileans? ⁸And how is it that we hear, each of us, in our own native language? ⁹Parthians, Medes, Elamites, and residents of Mesopotamia, Judea and Cappadocia, Pontus and Asia, ¹⁰Phrygia and Pamphylia, Egypt and the parts of Libya belonging to Cyrene, and visitors from Rome, both Jews and proselytes, ¹¹Cretans and Arabs—in our own languages we hear them speaking about God's deeds of power." ¹²All were amazed and perplexed, saying to one another, "What does this mean?" ¹³But others sneered and said, "They are filled with new wine."

14 But Peter, standing with the eleven, raised his voice and addressed them, "Fellow Jews[g] and all who live in Jerusalem, let this be known to you, and listen to what I say. ¹⁵Indeed, these are not drunk, as you suppose, for

g 2.14 Gk Men, Judeans

the tongues shaped as fire shift into a different type of tongue—that is, a language—as those present begin to speak. **2:4** This first instance of glossolalia, literally "speaking in tongues," is the ability of the believers to *speak in other languages*, which should be understood as speaking in languages that they do not typically speak. In this way, the miracle of glossolalia, or speaking in tongues, is not an undecipherable language but instead the ability to speak in a language that the speaker does not know but that listeners might understand. This is different from the way glossolalia is described by Paul in 1 Cor. 14, where he suggests that it is unintelligible language. (See **"Glossolalia in Acts," p. 1889.**)

2:9–11 This list includes the names of people, groups, cities, regions, countries, and even a continent (Asia). This list refers back to 2:5, where we are told that "Jews from every people under heaven" were there in Jerusalem, yet the inclusion of *proselytes* in 2:10 could mean that there were also gentiles who had already converted to Judaism present in this group.

2:14 Peter begins his speech at Pentecost, one of many speeches found in the book of Acts. Related to the genre of Acts, speeches make up a large amount of the material and contribute to the various genres that Acts represents. (See **"Introduction to the Acts of the Apostles," pp. 1886–87.**)

it is only nine o'clock in the morning. [16]No, this is what was spoken through the prophet Joel:

[17] 'In the last days it will be, God declares,
that I will pour out my Spirit upon all flesh,
and your sons and your daughters shall prophesy,
and your young men shall see visions,
and your old men shall dream dreams.
[18] Even upon my slaves, both men and women,
in those days I will pour out my Spirit,
and they shall prophesy.
[19] And I will show portents in the heaven above
and signs on the earth below,
blood, and fire, and smoky mist.
[20] The sun shall be turned to darkness
and the moon to blood,
before the coming of the Lord's great and glorious day.
[21] Then everyone who calls on the name of the Lord shall be saved.'

[22] "Fellow Israelites,[b] listen to what I have to say: Jesus of Nazareth,[i] a man attested to you by God with deeds of power, wonders, and signs that God did through him among you, as you yourselves know—[23]this man, handed over to you according to the definite plan and foreknowledge of God, you crucified and killed by the hands of those outside the law. [24]But God raised him up, having released him from the agony of death, because it was impossible for him to be held in its power. [25]For David says concerning him,

'I saw the Lord always before me,
for he is at my right hand so that I will not be shaken;
[26] therefore my heart was glad, and my tongue rejoiced;
moreover, my flesh will live in hope.

[27] For you will not abandon my soul to Hades
or let your Holy One experience corruption.
[28] You have made known to me the ways of life;
you will make me full of gladness with your presence.'

[29] "Fellow Israelites,[j] I may say to you confidently of our ancestor David that he both died and was buried, and his tomb is with us to this day. [30]Since he was a prophet, he knew that God had sworn with an oath to him that he would put one of his descendants on his throne. [31]Foreseeing this, David[k] spoke of the resurrection of the Messiah,[l] saying,

'He was not abandoned to Hades,
nor did his flesh experience corruption.'

[32]"This Jesus God raised up, and of that all of us are witnesses. [33]Being therefore exalted at[m] the right hand of God and having received from the Father the promise of the Holy Spirit, he has poured out this that you see and hear. [34]For David did not ascend into the heavens, but he himself says,

'The Lord said to my Lord,
"Sit at my right hand,
[35]   until I make your enemies your footstool."'

[36]"Therefore let the entire house of Israel know with certainty that God has made him both Lord and Messiah,[n] this Jesus whom you crucified."

37 Now when they heard this, they were cut to the heart and said to Peter and to the other apostles, "Brothers,[o] what should we do?" [38]Peter said to them, "Repent and be baptized

---

b 2.22 Gk Men, Israelites   i 2.22 Gk the Nazorean   j 2.29 Gk Men, brothers   k 2.31 Gk he   l 2.31 Or the Christ   m 2.33 Or by   n 2.36 Or Christ   o 2.37 Gk Men, brothers

---

2:17-21 This prophecy from the book of Joel suggests that Acts is narrating *the last days* (2:17) and that this will be recognized through events such as *sons* and *daughters* as well as enslaved men and women who will prophesy. Astute readers might look for evidence of these male and female, enslaved and free prophets as they read through the narrative of Acts.

2:23 In this part of his speech, Peter narrates the events of Jesus's death and implicates his listeners ("Israelites," 2:22) as participating in the crucifixion but includes that Jesus's death occurred *by the hands of those outside the law*. This last phrase indicates the role that the Roman government had in the crucifixion of Jesus, as *outside the law* indicates outside the Torah. Readers should be careful not to understand this passage as implicating Jews in the death of Jesus, which has led to anti-Semitism and anti-Jewish rhetoric and hate throughout the centuries. (See **"Jews in Luke–Acts," p. 1910**, and **"Crucifixion and Terror," p. 1798**.)

2:31 The quotation here is from Ps. 16:10, and the author of Acts connects it to Jesus's resurrection.

2:38 Peter's instructions for those who want to join this new religious community include repentance and baptism, which will lead to the forgiveness of sins and the reception of the *gift of the Holy Spirit*.

every one of you in the name of Jesus Christ so that your sins may be forgiven, and you will receive the gift of the Holy Spirit. ³⁹For the promise is for you, for your children, and for all who are far away, everyone whom the Lord our God calls to him." ⁴⁰And he testified with many other arguments and exhorted them, saying, "Save yourselves from this corrupt generation." ⁴¹So those who welcomed his message were baptized, and that day about three thousand persons were added. ⁴²They devoted themselves to the apostles' teaching and fellowship, to the breaking of bread and the prayers.

43 Awe came upon everyone because many wonders and signs were being done through the apostles. ⁴⁴All who believed were together and had all things in common; ⁴⁵they would sell their possessions and goods and distribute the proceeds*p* to all, as any had need. ⁴⁶Day by day, as they spent much time together in the temple, they broke bread at home*q* and ate their food with glad and generous*r* hearts, ⁴⁷praising God and having the goodwill of all the people. And day by day the Lord added to their number those who were being saved.

3 One day Peter and John were going up to the temple at the hour of prayer, at three o'clock in the afternoon. ²And a man lame from birth was being carried in. People would lay him daily at the gate of the temple called the Beautiful Gate so that he could ask for alms from those entering the temple. ³When he saw Peter and John about to go into the temple, he asked them for alms. ⁴Peter looked intently at him, as did John, and said, "Look at us." ⁵And he fixed his attention on them, expecting to receive something from them. ⁶Peter said, "I have no silver or gold, but what I have I give you; in the name of Jesus Christ of Nazareth,*s* stand up and walk." ⁷And he took him by the right hand and raised him up, and immediately his feet and ankles were made strong. ⁸Jumping up, he stood and began to walk, and he entered the temple with them, walking and leaping and praising God. ⁹All the people saw him walking and praising God, ¹⁰and they recognized him as the one who used to sit and ask for alms at the Beautiful Gate of the temple, and they were filled with wonder and astonishment at what had happened to him.

11 While he clung to Peter and John, all the people ran together to them in the portico called Solomon's Portico, utterly astonished. ¹²When Peter saw it, he addressed the people, "Fellow Israelites,*t* why do you wonder at this, or why do you stare at us, as though by our own power or piety we had made him walk? ¹³The God of Abraham and Isaac and Jacob,*u*

p 2.45 Gk *them*   *q* 2.46 Or *from house to house*   *r* 2.46 Or *sincere*   *s* 3.6 Gk *the Nazorean*   *t* 3.12 Gk *Men, Israelites*   *u* 3.13 Other ancient authorities read *and the God of Isaac and the God of Jacob*

The gift of the Holy Spirit at Pentecost includes glossolalia (speaking in tongues) but then only occurs twice in the rest of the Acts narrative: in chap. 10, where a group of gentiles (non-Jews) are baptized after speaking in tongues, and then in chap. 19, where a group of Jewish believers speak in tongues.

2:41 *Three thousand persons* is a symbolic number, as the number three was often viewed as a spiritual and perfect number. We should not assume this is an exact count but rather imagine a large group of people.

2:44–47 This section is often read as a utopian portrayal of this new religious community. In essence, it is communal living, as every believer shared their wealth equally so that the needs of every person were addressed. See also Acts 4:32.

3:1 Peter and John are going into the temple to pray, as Jews would do regularly.

3:2 *Beautiful Gate* at the temple could be a reference to one of the many gates around the Jewish temple in Jerusalem. Some scholars have suggested this could be referencing the Nicanor Gate, which was made of bronze and is described in the Mishnah, a text compiled in the period of rabbinic Judaism.

3:6–8 This is the first of many miracles in Acts, which are done by the hands of Peter and, later in Acts, by Paul. These miracles mimic Jesus's miracles, especially as found in the Gospel of Luke. Here, Peter is described as following Jesus's ministry by healing vulnerable people. Later, in 4:22, the author indicates that this man "was more than forty years old," which further indicates the miraculous nature of his healing. **3:8** The healed man goes with Peter and John into the temple to worship. This again reminds readers that this new religious community was centered on Judaism; thus visiting the temple was an integral part of religious practice.

3:11 A portico is an outdoor area, like a porch, that usually has columns supporting it.

3:12 This begins Peter's second speech in Acts, which is much shorter than the first. The focus of

the God of our ancestors, has glorified his servant[v] Jesus, whom you handed over and rejected in the presence of Pilate, though he had decided to release him. [14]But you rejected the holy and righteous[w] one and asked to have a murderer given to you, [15]and you killed the author of life, whom God raised from the dead. To this we are witnesses. [16]And by faith in his name, his name itself has made this man strong, whom you see and know, and the faith that is through Jesus[x] has given him this perfect health in the presence of all of you.

[17] "And now, brothers and sisters, I know that you acted in ignorance, as did also your rulers. [18]In this way God fulfilled what he had foretold through all the prophets, that his Messiah[y] would suffer. [19]Repent, therefore, and turn to God so that your sins may be wiped out, [20]so that times of refreshing may come from the presence of the Lord and that he may send the Messiah[z] appointed for you, that is, Jesus, [21]who must remain in heaven until the time of universal restoration that God announced long ago through his holy prophets. [22]Moses said, 'The Lord your God will raise up for you from your own people a prophet like me. You must listen to whatever he tells you. [23]And it will be that everyone who does not listen to that prophet will be utterly rooted out of the people.' [24]And all the prophets, as many as have spoken, from Samuel and those after him, also predicted these days. [25]You are the descendants of the prophets and of the covenant that God gave to your ancestors, saying to Abraham, 'And in your descendants all the families of the earth shall be blessed.' [26]When God raised up his servant,[a] he sent him first to you, to bless you by turning each of you from your wicked ways."

4 While Peter and John[b] were speaking to the people, the priests, the captain of the temple, and the Sadducees came to them, [2]much annoyed because they were teaching the people and proclaiming that in Jesus there is the resurrection of the dead. [3]So they arrested them and put them in custody until the next day, for it was already evening. [4]But many of those who heard the word believed, and they numbered about five thousand.

[5] The next day their rulers, elders, and scribes assembled in Jerusalem, [6]with Annas the high priest, Caiaphas, John,[c] and Alexander, and all who were of the high-priestly family. [7]When they had made the prisoners[d] stand in their midst, they inquired, "By what power or by what name did you do this?" [8]Then Peter, filled with the Holy Spirit, said to them, "Rulers of the people and elders, [9]if we are being questioned today because of a good deed done to someone who was sick and are being asked how this man has been healed,[e] [10]let it be known to all of you, and to all the people of Israel, that this man is standing before you in good health by the name of Jesus Christ of Nazareth,[f] whom you crucified, whom God raised from the dead. [11]This Jesus[g] is

'the stone that was rejected by you, the builders;

it has become the cornerstone.'[h]

[12]"There is salvation in no one else, for there is no other name under heaven given among mortals by which we must be saved."

[13] Now when they saw the boldness of Peter and John and realized that they were

v 3.13 Or *child*   w 3.14 Or *innocent*   x 3.16 Gk *him*   y 3.18 Or *his Christ*   z 3.20 Or *the Christ*   a 3.26 Or *child*   b 4.1 Gk *While they*   c 4.6 Other ancient authorities read *Jonathan*   d 4.7 Gk *them*   e 4.9 Or *saved*   f 4.10 Gk *the Nazorean*   g 4.11 Gk *This*   h 4.11 Or *keystone* (in an arch)

this sermon is the repentance of the Israelites. This speech echoes the rhetoric of the Hebrew prophets, who gave very similar admonitions to their listeners.

4:1 Jewish leaders and elite members of the Jewish community held power in Jerusalem. The titles mentioned here (*priests, the captain of the temple, and the Sadducees*) signal to readers that the elite leaders in Jerusalem were not pleased with the message of Peter and John.

4:2 Ancient Jews held varying beliefs about the resurrection of the dead. Generally, in ancient Judaism, resurrection referred to the eschatological idea that dead bodies would be revived. The ancient Jewish historian Josephus notes that the Pharisees believed in the eschatological resurrection of the dead, while the Sadducees did not (see **"Resurrection," p. 1224,** and **"Resurrection in the Gospels," p. 1767**).

4:6 *Annas* and *Caiaphas* are both mentioned in Luke 3:2 as high priests during the time of John the Baptist, but historically, they would not have been in this role during the setting on which Acts is based. The others, *John* and *Alexander*, are not named high priests in any historical documents that remain.

4:13 As noted in 4:8, Peter's words are from the Holy Spirit, not from himself or his education. The Greek in v. 13 used to describe Peter and John, "agrammatos idiōtai," literally implies that these men are without grammar and viewed as, to use the English cognate, idiots. Ultimately, this verse is used to point to the power of the Holy Spirit as one of the main actors in Acts.

uneducated and ordinary men, they were amazed and recognized them as companions of Jesus. [14]When they saw the man who had been cured standing beside them, they had nothing to say in opposition. [15]So they ordered them to leave the council while they discussed the matter with one another. [16]They said, "What will we do with them? For it is obvious to all who live in Jerusalem that a notable sign has been done through them; we cannot deny it. [17]But to keep it from spreading further among the people, let us warn them to speak no more to anyone in this name." [18]So they called them and ordered them not to speak or teach at all in the name of Jesus. [19]But Peter and John answered them, "Whether it is right in God's sight to listen to you rather than to God, you must judge; [20]for we cannot keep from speaking about what we have seen and heard." [21]After threatening them again, they let them go, finding no way to punish them because of the people, for all of them praised God for what had happened. [22]For the man on whom this sign of healing had been performed was more than forty years old.

23 After they were released, they went to their own people and reported what the chief priests and the elders had said to them. [24]When they heard it, they raised their voices together to God and said, "Sovereign Lord, who made the heaven and the earth, the sea, and everything in them, [25]it is you who said by the Holy Spirit through our ancestor David, your servant:[i]

'Why did the gentiles rage
    and the peoples imagine vain things?
[26] The kings of the earth took their stand,
    and the rulers have gathered together

against the Lord and against his
    Messiah.'[j]
[27]"For in this city, in fact, both Herod and Pontius Pilate, with the gentiles and the peoples of Israel, gathered together against your holy servant[k] Jesus, whom you anointed, [28]to do whatever your hand and your plan had predestined to take place. [29]And now, Lord, look at their threats, and grant to your servants to speak your word with all boldness, [30]while you stretch out your hand to heal, and signs and wonders are performed through the name of your holy servant[l] Jesus." [31]When they had prayed, the place in which they were gathered together was shaken, and they were all filled with the Holy Spirit and spoke the word of God with boldness.

32 Now the whole group of those who believed were of one heart and soul, and no one claimed private ownership of any possessions, but everything they owned was held in common. [33]With great power the apostles gave their testimony to the resurrection of the Lord Jesus, and great grace was upon them all. [34]There was not a needy person among them, for as many as owned lands or houses sold them and brought the proceeds of what was sold. [35]They laid it at the apostles' feet, and it was distributed to each as any had need. [36]There was a Levite from Cyprus, Joseph, to whom the apostles gave the name Barnabas (which means "son of encouragement"). [37]He sold a field that belonged to him, then brought the money and laid it at the apostles' feet.

5 But a man named Ananias, with the consent of his wife Sapphira, sold a piece of

i 4.25 Or child   j 4.26 Or his Christ   k 4.27 Or child
l 4.30 Or child

4:23 To their own people indicates the group of Jewish believers who were now following Peter and John and believing in Jesus as the Messiah, in contrast to the group of Jewish leaders mentioned above.
4:32–35 This is the second description of the community of believers living communally. Even more than Acts 2:44–47, it is noted that no one claimed private ownership of any possessions. This description might remind readers of the modern political theories of communism and socialism. As v. 34 notes, this sharing of wealth, land, and possessions resulted in the lack of poverty: There was not a needy person among them. This description is also reminiscent of the Jewish sect the Essenes, who chose an ascetic lifestyle. According to Josephus, the Essenes also gave up their money and possessions to join the group. Thus, this type of community as described in Acts would not be unheard of to a first-century audience.
4:36–37 The actions of Barnabas (previously called Joseph) should be read alongside the story of Ananias and Sapphira in 5:1–11. The author of Luke and Acts tends to pair stories together, often in the form of a good/bad example. Here Barnabas is an exemplary member of the religious community, while Ananias and Sapphira exemplify immoral behavior and are not viewed as cooperative members of this community.
5:1–11 The story of Ananias and Sapphira is troubling, as it indicates that if members of this new religious community described in Acts do not follow the guidelines, they will be punished severely.

property; [2]with his wife's knowledge, he kept back some of the proceeds and brought only a part and laid it at the apostles' feet. [3]"Ananias," Peter asked, "why has Satan filled your heart to lie to the Holy Spirit and to keep back part of the proceeds of the land? [4]While it remained unsold, did it not remain your own? And after it was sold, were not the proceeds at your disposal? How is it that you have contrived this deed in your heart? You did not lie to us[m] but to God!" [5]Now when Ananias heard these words, he fell down and died. And great fear seized all who heard of it. [6]The young men came and wrapped up his body, then carried him out and buried him.

7 After an interval of about three hours his wife came in, not knowing what had happened. [8]Peter said to her, "Tell me whether you and your husband sold the land for such and such a price." And she said, "Yes, that was the price." [9]Then Peter said to her, "How is it that you have agreed together to put the Spirit of the Lord to the test? Look, the feet of those who have buried your husband are at the door, and they will carry you out." [10]Immediately she fell down at his feet and died. When the young men came in they found her dead, so they carried her out and buried her beside her husband. [11]And great fear seized the whole church and all who heard of these things.

12 Now many signs and wonders were done among the people through the apostles. And they were all together in Solomon's Portico. [13]None of the rest dared to join them, but the people held them in high esteem. [14]Yet more than ever believers were added to the Lord, great numbers of both men and women, [15]so that they even carried out the sick into the streets and laid them on cots and mats, in order that Peter's shadow might fall on some of them as he came by. [16]A great number of people would also gather from the towns around Jerusalem, bringing the sick and those tormented by unclean spirits, and they were all cured.

17 Then the high priest took action; he and all who were with him (that is, the sect of the Sadducees), being filled with jealousy, [18]arrested the apostles and put them in the public prison. [19]But during the night an angel of the Lord opened the prison doors, brought them out, and said, [20]"Go, stand in the temple and tell the people the whole message about this life." [21]When they heard this, they entered the temple at daybreak and went on with their teaching.

When the high priest and those with him arrived, they called together the council and the whole body of the elders of Israel and sent to the prison to have them brought. [22]But when the temple police went there, they did not find them in the prison, so they returned and reported, [23]"We found the prison securely locked and the guards standing at the doors, but when we opened them we found no one inside." [24]Now when the captain of the temple and the chief priests heard these words, they were perplexed about them, wondering what might be going on. [25]Then someone arrived and announced, "Look, the men whom you put in prison are standing in the temple and teaching the people!" [26]Then the captain went

m 5.4 Gk to men

This story illustrates that the view of God as wrathful and showing vengeance continues into the New Testament and is not solely evident in the texts of the Hebrew Bible, or the Old Testament. **5:2** *With his wife's knowledge* is an interesting phrase, as in the patriarchal context of the first century, husbands did not need their wives' support or acknowledgment to buy or sell property. This phrase indicates that Ananias and Sapphira might have had a somewhat egalitarian marriage, since Ananias shared his financial decisions with his wife.

5:12 See 3:11 for more on Solomon's Portico.

5:15 Peter's healing powers have grown, so now even his shadow can heal.

5:17 The Sadducees were an ancient Jewish sect that held power in the period of Second Temple Judaism. They are often noted as a group that did not believe in the resurrection of the body. Here, in Acts, the high priest is connected to the Sadducees and has the power to arrest the apostles and put them in prison.

5:19 This is the first of many prison breaks that occur in Acts. As seen here, apostles who are imprisoned are miraculously released by an angel. This literary motif is one that is also found in a number of Greek and Roman texts, such as the ancient novels.

5:21 Again, the apostles are teaching in the temple in Jerusalem, an important thing to note, as the temple was a religious center of Judaism.

with the temple police and brought them, but without violence, for they were afraid of being stoned by the people.

27 When they had brought them, they had them stand before the council. The high priest questioned them, [28]saying, "We gave you strict orders not to teach in this name,[n] yet here you have filled Jerusalem with your teaching, and you are determined to bring this man's blood on us." [29]But Peter and the apostles answered, "We must obey God rather than any human authority.[o] [30]The God of our ancestors raised up Jesus, whom you had killed by hanging him on a tree. [31]God exalted him at his right hand as Leader and Savior that he might give repentance to Israel and forgiveness of sins. [32]And we are witnesses to these things, and so is the Holy Spirit whom God has given to those who obey him."

33 When they heard this, they were enraged and wanted to kill them. [34]But a Pharisee in the council named Gamaliel, a teacher of the law, respected by all the people, stood up and ordered the men to be put outside for a short time. [35]Then he said to them, "Fellow Israelites,[p] consider carefully what you propose to do to these men. [36]For some time ago Theudas rose up, claiming to be somebody, and a number of men, about four hundred, joined him, but he was killed, and all who followed him were dispersed and disappeared. [37]After him Judas the Galilean rose up at the time of the census and got people to follow him; he also perished, and all who followed him were scattered. [38]So in the present case, I tell you, keep away from these men and let them alone, because if this plan or this undertaking is of human origin, it will fail; [39]but if it is of God, you will not be able to overthrow them—in that case you may even be found fighting against God!"

They were convinced by him, [40]and when they had called in the apostles, they had them flogged. Then they ordered them not to speak in the name of Jesus and let them go. [41]As they left the council, they rejoiced that they were considered worthy to suffer dishonor for the sake of the name. [42]And every day in the temple and at home[q] they did not cease to teach and proclaim Jesus as the Messiah.[r]

6 Now during those days, when the disciples were increasing in number, the Hellenists complained against the Hebrews because their widows were being neglected in the daily distribution of food. [2]And the twelve called together the whole community of the disciples and said, "It is not right that we should neglect the word of God in order to wait on tables.[s] [3]Therefore, brothers and sisters, select from among yourselves seven men of good standing, full of the Spirit and of wisdom, whom we may appoint to this task, [4]while we, for our part, will devote ourselves to prayer and to serving the word." [5]What they said pleased the whole community, and they chose Stephen, a man full of faith and the Holy Spirit, together with Philip, Prochorus, Nicanor, Timon, Parmenas, and Nicolaus, a proselyte of Antioch. [6]They had these men stand before the apostles, who prayed and laid their hands on them.

7 The word of God continued to spread; the number of the disciples increased greatly in

---

n 5.28 Other ancient authorities read *Did we not give you strict orders not to teach in this name?* o 5.29 Gk *than men* p 5.35 Gk *Men, Israelites* q 5.42 Or *from house to house* r 5.42 Or *the Christ* s 6.2 Or *keep accounts*

5:34 The Pharisees were a Jewish sect known for their respect and knowledge of the Torah, Jewish law. After the temple was destroyed by the Romans in 70 CE, the sect of the Pharisees remained, and they were able to continue to interpret the law for Judaism, even without a temple. Ultimately, the Pharisaic sect disperses and becomes what we know as rabbinic Judaism. (See **"Pharisees," p. 1756.**)

5:35-39 Gamaliel's brief speech notes that Jesus is not the first Jewish teacher in Jerusalem to attract followers and be killed for his popularity. Two others are remembered by Gamaliel: Theudas and Judas the Galilean.

6:1 This chapter begins with an observation that the group of followers included non-Jews, here called Hellenists, a word that typically meant Greeks but may be used here to indicate anyone who was not Jewish. Additionally, it seems the principles mentioned in Acts 2 and 4 are being followed, as food is being distributed to people in the community (as the Hellenist widows were neglected). Taking care of widows is a requirement found in Jewish law, as seen in Exod. 22:22-24.

6:2 The verb *to wait* (on tables) used here is "diakoneō," meaning "to serve," from which our English word "deacon" is formed.

Jerusalem, and a great many of the priests became obedient to the faith.

8 Stephen, full of grace and power, did great wonders and signs among the people. ⁹Then some of those who belonged to the synagogue of the Freedmen (as it was called), Cyrenians, Alexandrians, and others of those from Cilicia and Asia, stood up and argued with Stephen. ¹⁰But they could not withstand the wisdom and the Spirit' with which he spoke. ¹¹Then they secretly instigated some men to say, "We have heard him speak blasphemous words against Moses and God." ¹²They stirred up the people as well as the elders and the scribes; then they suddenly confronted him, seized him, and brought him before the council. ¹³They set up false witnesses who said, "This man never stops saying things against this holy place and the law, ¹⁴for we have heard him say that this Jesus of Nazareth" will destroy this place and will change the customs that Moses handed on to us." ¹⁵And all who sat in the council looked intently at him, and they saw that his face was like the face of an angel.

7 Then the high priest asked him, "Are these things so?" ²And Stephen replied:

"Brothers' and fathers, listen to me. The God of glory appeared to our ancestor Abraham when he was in Mesopotamia, before he lived in Haran, ³and said to him, 'Leave your country and your relatives and go to the land that I will show you.' ⁴Then he left the country of the Chaldeans and settled in Haran. After his father died, God had him move from there to this country in which you are now living. ⁵He did not give him any of it as a heritage, not even a foot's length, but promised to give it to him as his possession and to his descendants after him, even though he had no child. ⁶And God spoke in these terms, that his descendants would be resident aliens in a country belonging to others, who would enslave them and mistreat them during four hundred years. ⁷'But I will judge the people whom they serve,' said God, 'and after that they shall come out and worship me in this place.' ⁸Then he gave him the covenant of circumcision. And so Abraham" became the father of Isaac and circumcised him on the eighth day, and Isaac did likewise to Jacob and Jacob to the twelve patriarchs.

9 "The patriarchs, jealous of Joseph, sold him into Egypt; but God was with him ¹⁰and rescued him from all his afflictions and enabled him to win favor and to show wisdom when he stood before Pharaoh, king of Egypt, who appointed him ruler over Egypt and over all his household. ¹¹Now there came a famine throughout Egypt and Canaan and great suffering, and our ancestors could find no food. ¹²But when Jacob heard that there was grain in Egypt, he sent our ancestors there on their first visit. ¹³On the second visit Joseph made himself known to his brothers, and Joseph's family became known to Pharaoh. ¹⁴Then Joseph sent and invited his father Jacob and all his relatives to come to him, seventy-five in all; ¹⁵so Jacob went down to Egypt. He himself died there as well as our ancestors, ¹⁶and their bodies' were brought back to Shechem and laid in the tomb that Abraham had bought for a sum of silver from the sons of Hamor in Shechem.

_t_ 6.10 Or _spirit_   _u_ 6.14 Gk _the Nazorean_   _v_ 7.2 Gk _Men, brothers_   _w_ 7.8 Gk _he_   _x_ 7.16 Gk _they_

6:9 _Freedmen_ here indicates persons who were previously enslaved but had been manumitted, or given their freedom. While these people may have been free and not enslaved, there were still stigmas that remained on freedmen in antiquity, and they were often not viewed as full citizens.

6:12 This _council_ is literally "sunedrion" in Greek, which refers to the Sanhedrin, which was a group of elders, or rabbis, who held tribunals in Jerusalem and were able also to make judgments about disagreements brought to them.

6:15 _His face was like the face of an angel_ is foreshadowing Stephen's martyrdom and also revealing his innocence to the reader.

7:2–53 Chap. 7 includes a long speech by Stephen that narrates the history of the Israelites beginning with Abraham and including Joseph's enslavement in Egypt as well as the rise of Moses as a leader of the exodus. He briefly mentions the return to this land led by Joshua, who brought the _tent of testimony_, which is the ark and which was placed in the temple, according to Stephen's speech, by Solomon (7:47). The setting of this speech, which is in front of the council (6:12), is the temple, and Stephen's speech incorporates times when the Israelites turned from God. This leads to the climax of his sermon as he connects the council to these Israelites who persecuted the prophets (7:52). **7:8** _The covenant of circumcision_ referred to here is notably mentioned in Gen. 17:9–11. It is worth noting that other ethnic

17 "But as the time drew near for the fulfillment of the promise that God had made to Abraham, our people in Egypt increased and multiplied [18]until another king who had not known Joseph ruled over Egypt. [19]He dealt craftily with our people and forced our ancestors to abandon their infants so that they would die. [20]At this time Moses was born, and he was beautiful before God. For three months he was brought up in his father's house, [21]and when he was abandoned, Pharaoh's daughter adopted him and brought him up as her own son. [22]So Moses was instructed in all the wisdom of the Egyptians and was powerful in his words and deeds.

23 "When he was forty years old, it came into his heart to visit his kinfolk, the Israelites. [24]When he saw one of them being wronged, he defended the oppressed man and avenged him by striking down the Egyptian. [25]He supposed that his kinsfolk would understand that God through him was rescuing them, but they did not understand. [26]The next day he came to some of them as they were quarreling and tried to reconcile them, saying, 'Men, you are brothers; why do you wrong each other?' [27]But the man who was wronging his neighbor pushed Moses' aside, saying, 'Who made you a ruler and a judge over us? [28]Do you want to kill me as you killed the Egyptian yesterday?' [29]When he heard this, Moses fled and became a resident alien in the land of Midian. There he became the father of two sons.

30 "Now when forty years had passed, an angel appeared to him in the wilderness of Mount Sinai, in the flame of a burning bush. [31]When Moses saw it, he was amazed at the sight, and as he approached to look, there came the voice of the Lord: [32]'I am the God of your ancestors, the God of Abraham, Isaac, and Jacob.' Moses began to tremble and did not dare to look. [33]Then the Lord said to him, 'Take off the sandals from your feet, for the place where you are standing is holy ground. [34]I have surely seen the mistreatment of my people who are in Egypt and have heard their groaning, and I have come down to rescue them. Come now, I will send you to Egypt.'

35 "It was this Moses whom they rejected when they said, 'Who made you a ruler and a judge?' and whom God now sent as both ruler and liberator through the angel who appeared to him in the bush. [36]He led them out, having performed wonders and signs in Egypt, at the Red Sea, and in the wilderness for forty years. [37]This is the Moses who said to the Israelites, 'God will raise up a prophet for you from your own people as he raised me up.' [38]He is the one who was in the congregation in the wilderness with the angel who spoke to him at Mount Sinai and with our ancestors, and he received living oracles to give to us. [39]Our ancestors were unwilling to obey him; instead, they pushed him aside, and in their hearts they turned back to Egypt, [40]saying to Aaron, 'Make gods for us who will lead the way for us; as for this Moses who led us out from the land of Egypt, we do not know what has happened to him.' [41]At that time they made a calf, offered a sacrifice to the idol, and reveled in the works of their hands. [42]But God turned away from them and handed them over to worship the host of heaven, as it is written in the book of the prophets:

'Did you offer to me slain victims and
    sacrifices
forty years in the wilderness, O house
    of Israel?
[43] No; you took along the tent of Moloch
    and the star of your god Rephan,
    the images that you made to
        worship;

so I will remove you beyond Babylon.'

44 "Our ancestors had the tent of testimony in the wilderness, as God[z] directed when he spoke to Moses, ordering him to make it according to the pattern he had seen. [45]Our ancestors in turn brought it in with Joshua when they dispossessed the peoples whom God drove out before our ancestors. And it was there until the time of David, [46]who found favor with God and asked that he might find a dwelling place for the house of Jacob.[a] [47]But it was Solomon who built a house for him. [48]Yet the Most High does not dwell in houses made with human hands;[b] as the prophet says,

[49] 'Heaven is my throne,
    and the earth is my footstool.

---

y 7.27 Gk him z 7.44 Gk he a 7.46 Other ancient authorities read for the God of Jacob b 7.48 Gk with hands

---

groups circumcised young boys as well in antiquity. **7:42-43** This is from Amos 5:25-26, although in the last verse that Stephen quotes from Amos, one word is changed. Damascus, in the Septuagint, which is the Greek translation of the Hebrew Scriptures, is now Babylon. This change incorporates even more Jewish history, as it calls to mind the Babylonian exile.

What kind of house will you build for me, says the Lord, or what is the place of my rest? [50] Did not my hand make all these things?' [51] "You stiff-necked people, uncircumcised in heart and ears, you are forever opposing the Holy Spirit, just as your ancestors used to do. [52] Which of the prophets did your ancestors not persecute? They killed those who foretold the coming of the Righteous One, and now you have become his betrayers and murderers. [53] You are the ones who received the law as ordained by angels, and yet you have not kept it."

[54] When they heard these things, they became enraged and ground their teeth at Stephen.c [55] But filled with the Holy Spirit, he gazed into heaven and saw the glory of God and Jesus standing at the right hand of God. [56] "Look," he said, "I see the heavens opened and the Son of Man standing at the right hand of God!" [57] But they covered their ears, and with a loud shout all rushed together against him. [58] Then they dragged him out of the city and began to stone him, and the witnesses laid their coats at the feet of a young man named Saul. [59] While they were stoning Stephen, he prayed, "Lord Jesus, receive my spirit." [60] Then he knelt down and cried out in a loud voice, "Lord, do not hold this sin against them." And when he had said this, he died.d **8** [1] And Saul approved of their killing him.

That day a severe persecution began against the church in Jerusalem, and all except the apostles were scattered throughout the countryside of Judea and Samaria. [2] Devout men buried Stephen and made loud lamentation over him. [3] But Saul was ravaging the church by entering house after house; dragging off both men and women, he committed them to prison.

[4] Now those who were scattered went from place to place proclaiming the word. [5] Philip went down to the city of Samaria and proclaimed the Messiah to them. [6] The crowds with one accord listened eagerly to what was said by Philip, hearing and seeing the signs that he did, [7] for unclean spirits, crying with loud shrieks, came out of many who were possessed, and many others who were paralyzed or lame were cured. [8] So there was great joy in that city.

[9] Now a certain man named Simon had previously practiced magic in the city and amazed the people of Samaria, saying that he was someone great. [10] All of them, from the least to the greatest, listened to him eagerly, saying, "This man is the power of God that is called Great." [11] And they listened eagerly to him because for a long time he had amazed them with his magic. [12] But when they believed Philip, who was proclaiming the good news about the kingdom of God and the name of Jesus Christ, they were baptized, both men and women. [13] Even Simon himself believed. After being baptized, he stayed constantly with Philip and was amazed when he saw the signs and great miracles that took place.

c 7.54 Gk *him* d 7.60 Gk *fell asleep* e 8.5 Other ancient authorities read *a city* f 8.5 Or *the Christ*

7:58 Stoning a person was technically allowed by Jewish law, but this stoning does not follow the legal outline for this practice. Instead, this verse reveals a mob overtaking the legal system and reacting violently. This is the first time Saul, who is also called Paul, is mentioned. He is a witness to this stoning by his presence.

7:59-60 Stephen is named as the first martyr in what will become the Christian movement. These last words, placed in Stephen's mouth, remind the reader of the death of Jesus where he prayed, "Father, into your hands I commend my spirit" (Luke 23:46) and also forgave his tormentors (23:34).

8:1a This brief note that Saul *approved* of the killing of Stephen reminds the reader that Saul was there watching while Stephen was killed. Paul himself notes that he persecuted the church in two of his letters (1 Cor. 15:9, Phil. 3:6).

8:1 *Severe persecution.* This is likely an exaggeration, as there is no historical or archaeological data that supports a drastic period of persecution in this time and area. The author of Acts is using this idea to increase the conflict within the plot so that when Saul becomes a follower of Jesus, it is even more dramatic.

8:5 Samaria was to the north of Jerusalem in the mountain region of Judea.

8:9 The practice of magic is well documented in the Roman period. This passage places the miracles done by Philip in the "name of Jesus Christ" (v. 12) in juxtaposition with the magic done by Simon.

8:13-17 As seen here, baptism often follows belief in Acts. Yet the believers in Samaria did not receive the Holy Spirit after being baptized by Philip. Thus, two other apostles—Peter and John—are sent to this area, and then the community receives the Holy Spirit when the apostles lay their hands on

14 Now when the apostles at Jerusalem heard that Samaria had accepted the word of God, they sent Peter and John to them. [15]The two went down and prayed for them that they might receive the Holy Spirit [16](for as yet the Spirit had not come[g] upon any of them; they had only been baptized in the name of the Lord Jesus). [17]Then Peter and John[h] laid their hands on them, and they received the Holy Spirit. [18]Now when Simon saw that the Spirit was given through the laying on of the apostles' hands, he offered them money, [19]saying, "Give me also this power so that anyone on whom I lay my hands may receive the Holy Spirit." [20]But Peter said to him, "May your silver perish with you, because you thought you could obtain God's gift with money! [21]You have no part or share in this, for your heart is not right before God. [22]Repent therefore of this wickedness of yours, and pray to the Lord that, if possible, the intent of your heart may be forgiven you. [23]For I see that you are in the gall of bitterness and the chains of wickedness." [24]Simon answered, "Pray for me to the Lord, that nothing of what you[i] have said may happen to me."

25 Now after Peter and John[j] had testified and spoken the word of the Lord, they returned to Jerusalem, proclaiming the good news to many villages of the Samaritans.

26 Then an angel of the Lord said to Philip, "Get up and go toward the south[k] to the road that goes down from Jerusalem to Gaza." (This is a wilderness road.) [27]So he got up and went. Now there was an Ethiopian eunuch, a court official of the Candace, the queen of the Ethiopians, in charge of her entire treasury. He had come to Jerusalem to worship [28]and was returning home; seated in his chariot, he was reading the prophet Isaiah. [29]Then the Spirit said to Philip, "Go over to this chariot and join it." [30]So Philip ran up to it and heard him reading the prophet Isaiah. He asked, "Do you understand what you are reading?" [31]He replied, "How can I, unless someone guides me?" And he invited Philip to get in and sit beside him. [32]Now the passage of the scripture that he was reading was this:

"Like a sheep he was led to the
    slaughter,
  and like a lamb silent before its
    shearer,
  so he does not open his mouth.
[33] In his humiliation justice was denied him.
  Who can describe his generation?
  For his life is taken away from the
    earth."

[34]The eunuch asked Philip, "About whom, may I ask you, does the prophet say this, about himself or about someone else?" [35]Then Philip began to speak, and starting with this scripture he proclaimed to him the good news about Jesus. [36]As they were going along the road, they came to some water, and the eunuch said, "Look, here is water! What is to prevent me from being baptized?"[l] [38]He commanded the chariot to stop, and both of them, Philip and the eunuch, went down into the water, and Philip[m] baptized him.

g 8.16 Gk fallen   h 8.17 Gk they   i 8.24 The Greek word for you and the verb pray are plural   j 8.25 Gk after they   k 8.26 Or go at noon   l 8.36 Other ancient authorities add all or most of 8.37, And Philip said, "If you believe with all your heart, you may." And he replied, "I believe that Jesus Christ is the Son of God."   m 8.38 Gk he

the believers. We are not told what happened to the believers after they received the Holy Spirit here in this passage, which is in contrast to the events of Pentecost in chap. 2.

8:18–24 Recall that Simon was known to be a magician (8:9). It seems that Simon viewed the miracles done by Peter and John also as magic, and he offers to pay them to learn how to do it. This angers Peter, who says that Simon's *heart is not right before God*. This is another example of the negative view toward wealth in Acts (recall the story of Ananias and Sapphira, who died after they withheld some of their wealth and lied about it; Acts 5:1–11).

8:27 A eunuch is a castrated man. This man is likely oppressed due to his status as a eunuch, which also likely means he is enslaved. The inclusion of Ethiopians also is an important aspect of this passage, as this might be a sign of the spreading of the gospel to other parts of the world.

8:28 The Ethiopian eunuch is reading from the book of Isaiah and had just been worshiping in Jerusalem. This indicates that he was participating in Judaism through the practice of religious rituals and reading sacred texts.

8:32–35 The text discussed here is from Isa. 53:7–8. This dialogue about the meaning of Isaiah's text is intriguing; the Ethiopian eunuch is reading and asking questions about the passage. Philip responds and interprets Isaiah's text as a prophecy about Jesus.

8:36–38 This is the first baptism of a gentile as described in the book of Acts.

39 When they came up out of the water, the
Spirit of the Lord snatched Philip away; the
eunuch saw him no more and went on his
way rejoicing. 40 But Philip found himself at
Azotus, and as he was passing through the
region he proclaimed the good news to all
the towns until he came to Caesarea.

9 Meanwhile Saul, still breathing threats
and murder against the disciples of the
Lord, went to the high priest 2 and asked him
for letters to the synagogues at Damascus,
so that if he found any who belonged to the
Way, men or women, he might bring them
bound to Jerusalem. 3 Now as he was going
along and approaching Damascus, suddenly
a light from heaven flashed around him. 4 He
fell to the ground and heard a voice saying to
him, "Saul, Saul, why do you persecute me?"
5 He asked, "Who are you, Lord?" The reply
came, "I am Jesus, whom you are persecuting.
6 But get up and enter the city, and you will be
told what you are to do." 7 The men who were
traveling with him stood speechless because
they heard the voice but saw no one. 8 Saul
got up from the ground, and though his eyes
were open, he could see nothing;[n] so they led
him by the hand and brought him into Damascus. 9 For three days he was without sight
and neither ate nor drank.

10 Now there was a disciple in Damascus
named Ananias. The Lord said to him in a
vision, "Ananias." He answered, "Here I am,
Lord." 11 The Lord said to him, "Get up and go
to the street called Straight, and at the house
of Judas look for a man of Tarsus named Saul.
At this moment he is praying, 12 and he has seen
in a vision[o] a man named Ananias come in and
lay his hands on him so that he might regain
his sight." 13 But Ananias answered, "Lord, I
have heard from many about this man, how
much evil he has done to your saints in Jerusalem, 14 and here he has authority from the chief
priests to bind all who invoke your name."
15 But the Lord said to him, "Go, for he is an
instrument whom I have chosen to bring my
name before gentiles and kings and before the
people of Israel; 16 I myself will show him how
much he must suffer for the sake of my name."
17 So Ananias went and entered the house. He
laid his hands on Saul[p] and said, "Brother Saul,
the Lord Jesus, who appeared to you on your
way here, has sent me so that you may regain
your sight and be filled with the Holy Spirit."
18 And immediately something like scales fell
from his eyes, and his sight was restored. Then
he got up and was baptized, 19 and after taking
some food, he regained his strength.

For several days he was with the disciples
in Damascus, 20 and immediately he began to
proclaim Jesus in the synagogues, saying, "He
is the Son of God." 21 All who heard him were
amazed and said, "Is not this the man who
made havoc in Jerusalem among those who
invoked this name? And has he not come here
for the purpose of bringing them bound before the chief priests?" 22 Saul became increasingly more powerful and confounded the Jews
who lived in Damascus by proving that Jesus[q]
was the Messiah.[r]

23 After some time had passed, the Jews

n 9.8 Other ancient authorities read *no one* *o* 9.12 Other ancient authorities lack *in a vision* *p* 9.17 Gk *him*
q 9.22 Gk *that this* *r* 9.22 Or *the Christ*

8:39–40 Philip disappears from the scene and reappears in the region of Azotus, taken by the Spirit. The ability of the Spirit to move a person in this way is also found within the Hebrew Bible (see, e.g., Ezek. 11:24–25).

9:1–2 Saul (also known as Paul) is portrayed as persecuting Jewish followers of Jesus, first needing permission from the high priest in order to arrest those whom he deems guilty. The *Way* (Gk. "hodos") is the author's term to describe this early community of believers, who were mostly Jewish and believed in Jesus as the Messiah.

9:3–5 This dramatic appearance by Jesus is important to Saul's future ministry, as it indicates he too met Jesus, even though he was not one of Jesus's early followers. Saul's experience on the road to Damascus includes several literary motifs from Hebrew Scriptures. For example, *light from heaven flashed around him* is a symbol of divine presence. Additionally, the Lord calls out *Saul, Saul*, a formula of repeating a name twice that is used in other texts where God speaks to a prophet (Abraham in Gen. 22:11, Moses in Exod. 3:4, and Samuel in 1 Sam. 3:10).

9:18 *Something like scales* indicates this scene is one of healing, as Saul is unable to see and then is healed. Saul is baptized after this event, like many others in Acts after they have had a spiritual experience.

9:23 Since many Jews become believers in Acts, this statement cannot refer to the whole Jewish community.

plotted to kill him, [24]but their plot became known to Saul. They were watching the gates day and night so that they might kill him, [25]but his disciples took him by night and let him down through an opening in the wall,[s] lowering him in a basket.

26 When he had come to Jerusalem, he attempted to join the disciples, and they were all afraid of him, for they did not believe that he was a disciple. [27]But Barnabas took him, brought him to the apostles, and described for them how on the road he had seen the Lord, who had spoken to him, and how in Damascus he had spoken boldly in the name of Jesus. [28]So he went in and out among them in Jerusalem, speaking boldly in the name of the Lord. [29]He spoke and argued with the Hellenists, but they were attempting to kill him. [30]When the brothers and sisters learned of it, they brought him down to Caesarea and sent him off to Tarsus.

31 Meanwhile the church throughout Judea, Galilee, and Samaria had peace and was built up. Living in the fear of the Lord and in the comfort of the Holy Spirit, it increased in numbers.

32 Now as Peter went here and there among all the brothers and sisters,[t] he came down also to the saints living in Lydda. [33]There he found a man named Aeneas, who had been bedridden for eight years, for he was paralyzed. [34]Peter said to him, "Aeneas, Jesus Christ heals you; get up and make your bed!" And immediately he got up. [35]And all the residents of Lydda and Sharon saw him and turned to the Lord.

36 Now in Joppa there was a disciple whose name was Tabitha, which in Greek is Dorcas.[u] She was devoted to good works and acts of charity. [37]At that time she became ill and died. When they had washed her, they laid her in a room upstairs. [38]Since Lydda was near Joppa, the disciples, who heard that Peter was there, sent two men to him with the request, "Please come to us without delay." [39]So Peter got up and went with them, and when he arrived, they took him to the room upstairs. All the widows stood beside him, weeping and showing tunics and other clothing that Dorcas had made while she was with them. [40]Peter put all of them outside, and then he knelt down and prayed. He turned to the body and said, "Tabitha, get up." Then she opened her eyes, and seeing Peter, she sat up. [41]He gave her his hand and helped her up. Then calling the saints and widows, he showed her to be alive. [42]This became known throughout Joppa, and many believed in the Lord. [43]Meanwhile, he stayed in Joppa for some time with a certain Simon, a tanner.

10 In Caesarea there was a man named Cornelius, a centurion of the Italian Cohort, as it was called. [2]He was a devout man who feared God with all his household; he gave alms generously to the people and prayed constantly to God. [3]One afternoon at about three o'clock he had a vision in which he clearly saw an angel of God coming in and saying to him, "Cornelius." [4]He stared at him in terror and said, "What is it, Lord?" He answered, "Your prayers and your alms have ascended as a memorial before God. [5]Now send men to Joppa for a certain Simon who is called Peter; [6]he is lodging with Simon, a tanner, whose house is by the seaside." [7]When the angel who spoke to him had left, he called two of his slaves and a devout soldier

s 9.25 Gk *through the wall*   t 9.32 Gk *all of them*
u 9.36 Tabitha in Aramaic and Dorcas in Greek mean *a gazelle*

9:29 *Hellenists* most likely refers to Greek-speaking Jews living in Jerusalem. It seems that Luke is trying to emphasize that many people within Jerusalem did not yet trust Saul.

9:32–43 The author of the Gospel of Luke and Acts often pairs stories together and includes one male example and one female example. Here we see that literary trope with the healing of Aeneas, who was paralyzed, and then Tabitha, who had died. This pair of stories differs from others, though, as the healing of Tabitha is a much longer passage than that of Aeneas. 9:36 *Tabitha* is her Hebrew name, and *Dorcas* is her name in Greek. The author gives both here, which suggests readers might have known both Hebrew and Greek. 9:39 Tabitha was a seamstress and also generous, as she made clothing for the community.

10:1 *Centurion of the Italian Cohort*. This indicates that the man was from Italy and was a leader of a group of men in the army for the Roman Empire. They would have had power within the military but also over people broadly living in the Roman Empire.

10:7 Cornelius has two enslaved people and a soldier whom he is able to send for the journey. This indicates his wealth and high status.

from the ranks of those who served him, [8]and after telling them everything he sent them to Joppa.

9 About noon the next day, as they were on their journey and approaching the city, Peter went up on the roof to pray. [10]He became hungry and wanted something to eat, and while it was being prepared he fell into a trance. [11]He saw the heaven opened and something like a large sheet coming down, being lowered to the ground by its four corners. [12]In it were all kinds of four-footed creatures and reptiles and birds of the air. [13]Then he heard a voice saying, "Get up, Peter; kill and eat." [14]But Peter said, "By no means, Lord, for I have never eaten anything that is profane or unclean." [15]The voice said to him again, a second time, "What God has made clean, you must not call profane." [16]This happened three times, and the thing was suddenly taken up to heaven.

17 Now while Peter was greatly puzzled about what to make of the vision that he had seen, suddenly the men sent by Cornelius appeared. They were asking for Simon's house and were standing by the gate. [18]They called out to ask whether Simon, who was called Peter, was staying there. [19]While Peter was still thinking about the vision, the Spirit said to him, "Look, three[v] men are searching for you. [20]Now get up, go down, and go with them without hesitation, for I have sent them." [21]So Peter went down to the men and said, "I am the one you are looking for; what is the reason for your coming?" [22]They answered, "Cornelius, a centurion, a righteous[w] and God-fearing man who is well spoken of by the whole Jewish people, was directed by a holy angel to send for you to come to his house and to hear what you have to say." [23]So Peter[x] invited them in and gave them lodging.

The next day he got up and went with them, and some of the brothers and sisters from Joppa accompanied him. [24]The following day they came to Caesarea. Cornelius was expecting them and had called together his relatives and close friends. [25]On Peter's arrival, Cornelius met him and, falling at his feet, worshiped him. [26]But Peter made him get up, saying, "Stand up; I am only a mortal." [27]And as he talked with him, he went in and found that many had assembled, [28]and he said to them, "You yourselves know that it is improper for a Jew to associate with or to visit an outsider, but God has shown me that I should not call anyone profane or unclean. [29]So when I was sent for, I came without objection. Now may I ask why you sent for me?"

30 Cornelius replied, "Four days ago at this very hour, at three o'clock, I was praying in my house when suddenly a man in dazzling clothes stood before me. [31]He said, 'Cornelius, your prayer has been heard, and your alms have been remembered before God. [32]Send therefore to Joppa and ask for Simon, who is called Peter; he is staying in the home of Simon, a tanner, by the sea.' [33]Therefore I sent for you immediately, and you have been kind enough to come. So now all of us are here in the presence of God to listen to all that the Lord has commanded you to say."

34 Then Peter began to speak to them: "I truly understand that God shows no partiality, [35]but in every people anyone who fears him and practices righteousness[y] is acceptable to him. [36]You know the message he sent to the people of Israel, preaching peace by Jesus Christ—he is Lord of all. [37]That message spread throughout Judea, beginning in Galilee after the baptism that John announced: [38]how God anointed Jesus of Nazareth with the Holy Spirit and with power; how he went about doing good and healing all who were oppressed by the devil, for God was with him. [39]We are witnesses to all that he did both in Judea and in Jerusalem. They put him to death by hanging him on a tree, [40]but God raised him on the third day and allowed him to appear, [41]not to all the people but to us who were chosen

v 10.19 One ancient authority reads *two*; others lack the word   w 10.22 Or *just*   x 10.23 Gk *he*   y 10.35 Or *acts justly*

10:9–16 This vision launches the book of Acts into a rhetorical argument about purity laws within Judaism. See **"Diet," p. 268**. Much of this discussion involves how to include gentiles (like the Ethiopian eunuch and Cornelius) who have embraced the message about Jesus in the religious community, which is mostly Jewish.

10:30–33 Cornelius also receives a visit from an angel and a message, just as Peter did. Thus, the Holy Spirit is already working through gentiles in Acts.

10:34 Peter seems to be referencing Deut. 10:17 in order to show that the Jewish Scriptures have support for the decision to embrace gentiles. This begins his brief speech to the group of gentiles gathered by Cornelius.

by God as witnesses and who ate and drank with him after he rose from the dead. ⁴²He commanded us to preach to the people and to testify that he is the one ordained by God as judge of the living and the dead. ⁴³All the prophets testify about him that everyone who believes in him receives forgiveness of sins through his name."

44 While Peter was still speaking, the Holy Spirit fell upon all who heard the word. ⁴⁵The circumcised believers who had come with Peter were astounded that the gift of the Holy Spirit had been poured out even on the gentiles, ⁴⁶for they heard them speaking in tongues and extolling God. Then Peter said, ⁴⁷"Can anyone withhold the water for baptizing these people who have received the Holy Spirit just as we have?" ⁴⁸So he ordered them to be baptized in the name of Jesus Christ. Then they invited him to stay for several days.

11 Now the apostles and the brothers and sisters who were in Judea heard that the gentiles had also accepted the word of God. ²So when Peter went up to Jerusalem, the circumcised believers*ᶻ* criticized him, ³saying, "Why did you go to uncircumcised men and eat with them?" ⁴Then Peter began to explain it to them, step by step, saying, ⁵"I was in the city of Joppa praying, and in a trance I saw a vision. There was something like a large sheet coming down from heaven, being lowered by its four corners, and it came close to me. ⁶As I looked at it closely I saw four-footed animals, beasts of prey, reptiles, and birds of the air. ⁷I also heard a voice saying to me, 'Get up, Peter; kill and eat.' ⁸But I replied, 'By no means, Lord, for nothing profane or

unclean has ever entered my mouth.' ⁹But a second time the voice answered from heaven, 'What God has made clean, you must not call profane.' ¹⁰This happened three times; then everything was pulled up again to heaven. ¹¹At that very moment three men, sent to me from Caesarea, arrived at the house where we were. ¹²The Spirit told me to go with them and not to make a distinction between them and us.*ᵃ* These six brothers also accompanied me, and we entered the man's house. ¹³He told us how he had seen the angel standing in his house and saying, 'Send to Joppa and bring Simon, who is called Peter; ¹⁴he will give you a message by which you and your entire household will be saved.' ¹⁵And as I began to speak, the Holy Spirit fell upon them just as it had upon us at the beginning. ¹⁶And I remembered the word of the Lord, how he had said, 'John baptized with water, but you will be baptized with the Holy Spirit.' ¹⁷If then God gave them the same gift that he gave us when we believed in the Lord Jesus Christ, who was I that I could hinder God?" ¹⁸When they heard this, they were silenced. And they praised God, saying, "Then God has given even to the gentiles the repentance that leads to life."

19 Now those who were scattered because of the persecution that took place over Stephen traveled as far as Phoenicia, Cyprus, and Antioch, and they spoke the word to no one except Jews. ²⁰But among them were some men of Cyprus and Cyrene who, on coming to Antioch, spoke to the Hellenists*ᵇ* also, proclaiming the Lord Jesus. ²¹The hand of the Lord was with

z 11.2 Gk lacks *believers* *a* 11.12 Or *not to hesitate*
b 11.20 Other ancient authorities read *Greeks*

10:44–47 This is the first instance in Acts where the Holy Spirit affects a gentile audience. *Speaking in tongues* is the evidence of the spirit, as it was at Pentecost in chap. 2 for the Jews gathered in Jerusalem. See **"Glossolalia in Acts," p. 1889.** After this experience of tongues, the group is baptized. This pattern of baptism after belief is one that repeats in Acts.

11:2–3 *The circumcised believers* seems to indicate those who are Jewish but are now following Peter and embracing his message. The comments about eating with those who are not circumcised could be allegorical and allude to the complex discussion surrounding the inclusion of gentiles in the Jewish community. This does not likely suggest that Peter or other circumcised believers are changing their eating habits, as indicated by Peter's response in the vision (11:8).

11:18 Peter's recounting of his vision seems to have convinced those questioning him. More conversation around the relationships between Jews and gentiles will surface later in Acts (chap. 15 especially), but this scene begins the dialogue.

11:19 It is not clear what the author means regarding the *persecution that took place over Stephen.* There is no historical evidence of widespread persecution of Jesus followers in the first century, so perhaps the author is trying to increase the fear and drama within the narrative by adding this into the plot of Acts.

them, and a great number became believers and turned to the Lord. ²²News of this came to the ears of the church in Jerusalem, and they sent Barnabas to Antioch. ²³When he came and saw the grace of God, he rejoiced, and he exhorted them all to remain faithful to the Lord with steadfast devotion, ²⁴for he was a good man, full of the Holy Spirit and of faith. And a great many people were brought to the Lord. ²⁵Then Barnabas went to Tarsus to look for Saul, ²⁶and when he had found him he brought him to Antioch. So it was that for an entire year they met with the church and taught a great many people, and it was in Antioch that the disciples were first called "Christians."

27 At that time prophets came down from Jerusalem to Antioch. ²⁸One of them named Agabus stood up and predicted by the Spirit that there would be a severe famine over all the world, and this took place during the reign of Claudius. ²⁹The disciples determined that, according to their ability, each would send relief to the brothers and sisters living in Judea; ³⁰this they did, sending it to the elders by Barnabas and Saul.

12 About that time King Herod laid violent hands upon some who belonged to the church. ²He had James, the brother of John, killed with the sword. ³After he saw that it pleased the Jews, he proceeded to arrest Peter also. (This was during the Festival of Unleavened Bread.) ⁴When he had seized him, he put him in prison and handed him over to four squads of soldiers to guard him,

intending to bring him out to the people after the Passover. ⁵While Peter was kept in prison, the church prayed fervently to God for him.

6 The very night before Herod was going to bring him out, Peter, bound with two chains, was sleeping between two soldiers, while guards in front of the door were keeping watch over the prison. ⁷Suddenly an angel of the Lord appeared, and a light shone in the cell. He tapped Peter on the side and woke him, saying, "Get up quickly." And the chains fell off his wrists. ⁸The angel said to him, "Fasten your belt and put on your sandals." He did so. Then he said to him, "Wrap your cloak around you and follow me." ⁹Peter*c* went out and followed him; he did not realize that what was happening with the angel's help was real; he thought he was seeing a vision. ¹⁰After they had passed the first and the second guard, they came before the iron gate leading into the city. It opened for them of its own accord, and they went outside and walked along a lane, when suddenly the angel left him. ¹¹Then Peter came to himself and said, "Now I am sure that the Lord has sent his angel and rescued me from the hands of Herod and from all that the Jewish people were expecting."

12 As soon as he realized this, he went to the house of Mary, the mother of John whose other name was Mark, where many had gathered and were praying. ¹³When he knocked at the outer gate, a maid named Rhoda came to answer. ¹⁴On recognizing Peter's voice, she was so overjoyed that, instead of opening the

c 12.9 Gk *He*

11:26 This verse is one of only three verses in the entire New Testament where the word "Christian" is used. There is one other instance in Acts 26:28, and another is in 1 Pet. 4:16.

12:1 King Herod Antipas (not to be confused with Herod the Great or Herod Agrippa) was in charge of the area of Judea and a part of the Roman government. He himself was Jewish and was not technically a king but instead a tetrarch. He ruled over the area of Galilee from 4 BCE to 39 CE.

12:3 The Festival of Unleavened Bread is also known as Passover.

12:6–11 This is one of several prison breaks in Acts. Incarceration in antiquity varied in terms of harsh conditions. This scene describing Peter bound with chains would indicate to ancient readers that Peter was being watched closely and thus was in danger of escape. If a prisoner escaped jail in the first century, they would have been in extreme danger; this image of Peter walking through the streets of Jerusalem as an escaped convict suggests exaggeration on the part of the author.

12:12 Note that this Mary, the mother of John Mark, appears to be the owner of the house and that no husband is mentioned here. Also, Mary's house is a place where believers have gathered to pray, which suggests it was functioning as an early house church led by a female.

12:12–17 This short scene at Mary's house would be humorous to the ancient reader, especially when Rhoda, the enslaved attendant, enters and then forgets to open the door and leaves while Peter, an important guest, is still waiting at the door. The scene is reminiscent of a comedic trope from Greek theater called the "servus currens," or "running slave," which almost always incited laughter from the audience. See **"Enslaved Women in Acts," p. 1905. 12:13** The Greek word for *maid* here is "paidiskē,"

Going Deeper: Enslaved Women in Acts (Acts 12:12–15)

In Acts, there are two enslaved women who feature as minor characters within the narrative. In chap. 12, an enslaved woman named Rhoda is working in the house of Mary and is responsible for opening the door when guests arrive. The scene becomes comical when Peter miraculously escapes from prison and goes to hide in Mary's house. Yet when Rhoda comes to open the door, she is so excited to see Peter that she forgets to open the door for him. Ultimately, Peter gets let inside the house, but this short story in the middle of Acts tells us a few things about the author and readers of Acts. First, slavery was a normative practice during this time period, and it would not have surprised early readers of Acts that Mary owned an enslaved person within a house where early Jesus followers were gathering for prayer. Second, this story seems to add a bit of humor to the narrative, which also reveals that the author and readers regularly laughed at the expense of enslaved persons.

In Acts 16, we find another example of an enslaved woman when Paul is traveling in the city of Philippi. She is introduced as an enslaved fortune teller with the spirit of the python and a source of income for her owners (16:16). As Paul and his companions are walking in Philippi, this enslaved woman follows them and cries out her message: "These men are slaves of the Most High God, who proclaim to you the way of salvation" (16:17). Paul becomes annoyed and exorcises the spirit from her. After this, her owners are very angry because of the loss of income, and they seize Paul and Silas, who are thrown into jail. This second story of an enslaved woman illustrates that enslaved persons were treated not as full humans in antiquity but as sources of income. On the other hand, this woman is an example of a female prophet who loudly speaks her message in Philippi.

Christy Cobb

gate, she ran in and announced that Peter was standing at the gate. ¹⁵They said to her, "You are out of your mind!" But she insisted that it was so. They said, "It is his angel." ¹⁶Meanwhile Peter continued knocking, and when they opened the gate they saw him and were amazed. ¹⁷He motioned to them with his hand to be silent and described for them how the Lord had brought him out of the prison. And he added, "Tell this to James and to the brothers and sisters." Then he left and went to another place.

18 When morning came, there was no small commotion among the soldiers over what had become of Peter. ¹⁹When Herod had searched for him and could not find him, he examined the guards and ordered them to be put to death. Then he went down from Judea to Caesarea and stayed there.

20 Now Herod[d] was angry with the people of Tyre and Sidon. So they came to him in a body, and after winning over Blastus, the king's personal attendant, they asked for a reconciliation, because their country depended on the king's country for food. ²¹On an appointed day Herod put on his royal robes, took his seat on the platform, and delivered a public address to them. ²²The people kept shouting, "The voice of a god and not of a mortal!" ²³And immediately, because he had not given the glory to God, an angel of the Lord struck him down, and he was eaten by worms and died.

24 But the word of God continued to advance and gain adherents. ²⁵Then after completing their mission Barnabas and Saul returned to[e] Jerusalem and brought with them John, whose other name was Mark.

13 Now in the church at Antioch there were prophets and teachers: Barnabas, Simeon who was called Niger, Lucius of Cyrene, Manaen a childhood friend of Herod the ruler,[f] and Saul. ²While they were

d 12.20 Gk he   e 12.25 Other ancient authorities read *from*
f 13.1 Gk *tetrarch*

which would indicate a female, perhaps young, who was an enslaved worker in Mary's house. This means that Mary was an enslaver, and Rhoda was enslaved to her. Some enslaved workers were doorkeepers, which means it was their job to be ready at the door for guests.

12:23 This is a gruesome death for Herod, being *eaten by worms*. In antiquity, worms could indicate a particularly unfavorable death, and there is a connection between worms and hell in apocalyptic literature. In Acts, the text is clear that this death was caused by God. The Jewish historian Josephus also describes a gruesome death for Herod.

13:2 Again, the Holy Spirit directs the action of the text, calling for Barnabas and Saul to begin a journey and spread the gospel.

worshiping the Lord and fasting, the Holy Spirit said, "Set apart for me Barnabas and Saul for the work to which I have called them." ³Then after fasting and praying they laid their hands on them and sent them off.

4 So, being sent out by the Holy Spirit, they went down to Seleucia, and from there they sailed to Cyprus. ⁵When they arrived at Salamis, they proclaimed the word of God in the Jewish synagogues. And they had John also to assist them. ⁶When they had gone through the whole island as far as Paphos, they met a certain magician, a Jewish false prophet, named Bar-Jesus. ⁷He was with the proconsul, Sergius Paulus, an intelligent man who summoned Barnabas and Saul and wanted to hear the word of God. ⁸But the magician Elymas (for that is the translation of his name) opposed them and tried to turn the proconsul away from the faith. ⁹But Saul, also known as Paul, filled with the Holy Spirit, looked intently at him ¹⁰and said, "You son of the devil, you enemy of all righteousness, full of all deceit and villainy, will you not stop making crooked the straight paths of the Lord? ¹¹And now listen— the hand of the Lord is against you, and you will be blind for a while, unable to see the sun." Immediately mist and darkness came over him, and he fumbled about for someone to lead him by the hand. ¹²When the proconsul saw what had happened, he believed, for he was astonished at the teaching about the Lord.

13 Then Paul and his companions set sail from Paphos and came to Perga in Pamphylia. John, however, left them and returned to Jerusalem, ¹⁴but they went on from Perga and came to Antioch in Pisidia. And on the Sabbath day they went into the synagogue and sat down. ¹⁵After the reading of the Law and the Prophets, the officials of the synagogue sent them a message, saying, "Brothers,ᵍ if you have any word of exhortation for the people, give it." ¹⁶So Paul stood up and with a gesture began to speak:

"Fellow Israelitesʰ and others who fear God, listen. ¹⁷The God of this people Israel chose our ancestors and made the people great during their stay in the land of Egypt, and with uplifted arm he led them out of it. ¹⁸For about forty years he put up withⁱ them in the wilderness. ¹⁹After he had destroyed seven peoples in the land of Canaan, he gave them their land as an inheritance ²⁰for about four hundred fifty years. After that he gave them judges until the time of the prophet Samuel. ²¹Then they asked for a king, and God gave them Saul son of Kish, a man of the tribe of Benjamin, who reigned for forty years. ²²When he had removed him, he made David their king. In his testimony about him he said, 'I have found David, son of Jesse, to be a man after my heart, who will carry out all my wishes.' ²³Of this man's posterity God has brought to Israel a Savior, Jesus, as he promised; ²⁴before his coming John had already proclaimed a baptism of repentance to all the people of Israel. ²⁵And as John was finishing his work, he said, 'What do you suppose that I am? I am not he. No, but one is coming after

g 13.15 Gk *Men, brothers*   h 13.16 Gk *Men, Israelites*
i 13.18 Other ancient authorities read *cared for*

13:4–5 The journey to Cyprus would have taken about three days. Cyprus is an island in the eastern part of the Mediterranean Sea. Throughout the journeys depicted in Acts, the apostles always visit a synagogue or a Jewish community first to bring their message. This occurs rather consistently throughout Acts. See **"Jews in Luke–Acts," p. 1910**.

13:6 Bar-Jesus (also called Elymas, 13:8) is described as both a magician and a Jewish false prophet. *Bar* means "son of," and Jesus, or Joshua in Hebrew, was a relatively common name, so this is no relative of Jesus of Nazareth.

13:11–12 Saul is positioned as against the magicians in Cyprus, yet here he also enacts a form of magic but through the *hand of the Lord*, which is acceptable to the author of Acts. Yet the miracle done here by Saul is not a healing; instead, Bar-Jesus is temporarily blinded by Saul through the Holy Spirit.

13:15 They are invited to speak a message in the synagogue. This again reflects Paul's commitment to Judaism, his own faith tradition.

13:16–48 This is Paul's first major speech in Acts. Similar to the speeches given by Peter, Paul gives a sweeping overview of the history of the Israelites and God's relationship with them. Paul highlights all that God did throughout history for the Israelites—including sending a Savior, Jesus—yet then notes that the *residents of Jerusalem and their leaders did not recognize him*. This rhetoric is found throughout Acts and is used to justify the turn to the gentiles with this message. While Paul's speech contains the story of the Israelites as well as quotations from Jewish Scriptures, it also reveals anti-Jewish

me; I am not worthy to untie the strap of the sandals[j] on his feet.'

26 "Brothers and sisters,[k] you descendants of Abraham's family and others who fear God, to us[l] the message of this salvation has been sent. [27]Because the residents of Jerusalem and their leaders did not recognize him or understand the words of the prophets that are read every Sabbath, they fulfilled those words by condemning him. [28]Even though they found no cause for a sentence of death, they asked Pilate to have him killed. [29]When they had carried out everything that was written about him, they took him down from the tree and laid him in a tomb. [30]But God raised him from the dead, [31]and for many days he appeared to those who came up with him from Galilee to Jerusalem, and they are now his witnesses to the people. [32]And we bring you the good news that what God promised to our ancestors [33]he has fulfilled for us, their children,[m] by raising Jesus; as also it is written in the second psalm,

'You are my Son;
today I have begotten you.'

[34]"As to his raising him from the dead, no more to return to corruption, he has spoken in this way,

'I will give you the holy promises made to David.'

[35]"Therefore he has also said in another psalm,

'You will not let your Holy One experience corruption.'

[36]"For David, after he had served the purpose of God in his own generation, died,[n] was laid beside his ancestors, and experienced corruption, [37]but he whom God raised up experienced no corruption. [38]Let it be known to you therefore, brothers and sisters,[o] that through this man forgiveness of sins is proclaimed to you; [39]by this Jesus[p] everyone who believes is set free from all those sins[q] from which you could not be freed by the law of Moses. [40]Beware, therefore, that what the prophets said does not happen to you:

[41] 'Look, you scoffers!
Be amazed and perish,
for in your days I am doing a work,
a work that you will never believe,
even if someone tells you.'"

42 As Paul and Barnabas[r] were going out, the people urged them to speak about these things again the next Sabbath. [43]When the meeting of the synagogue broke up, many Jews and devout converts to Judaism followed Paul and Barnabas, who spoke to them and urged them to continue in the grace of God.

44 The next Sabbath almost the whole city gathered to hear the word of the Lord.[s] [45]But when the Jews saw the crowds, they were filled with jealousy, and blaspheming, they contradicted what was spoken by Paul. [46]Then both Paul and Barnabas spoke out boldly, saying, "It was necessary that the word of God should be spoken first to you. Since you reject it and judge yourselves to be unworthy of eternal life, we are now turning to the gentiles. [47]For so the Lord has commanded us, saying,

'I have set you to be a light for the gentiles,
so that you may bring salvation to the ends of the earth.'"

48 When the gentiles heard this, they were glad and praised the word of the Lord, and as many as had been destined for eternal life became believers. [49]Thus the word of the Lord spread throughout the region. [50]But the Jews incited the devout women of high standing and the leading men of the city and stirred up

j 13.25 Gk *untie the sandals*   k 13.26 Gk *Men, brothers*
l 13.26 Other ancient authorities read *you*   m 13.33 Other ancient authorities read *for our children*   n 13.36 Gk *fell asleep*   o 13.38 Gk *Men, brothers*   p 13.39 Gk *this*   q 13.39 Gk *all*   r 13.42 Gk *they*   s 13.44 Other ancient authorities read *God*

rhetoric that should be read carefully and within context as much as possible. **13:42–47** Vv. 42 and 43 indicate that Paul and Barnabas were successful, at first, bringing their message to Jews in Antioch of Pisidia. Then v. 45 takes a quick turn as a group of Jews *contradicted what was spoken by Paul*. This leads Paul and Barnabas to announce that they are taking the message to the gentiles. Yet they again use a Hebrew Scripture passage to support this (v. 47, which is from Isa. 49:6). The quotation includes the phrase *ends of the earth*, which was used previously in Acts 1:8 and foreshadows the many travels that Paul and his companions will take throughout the rest of Acts.

13:50 *Devout women of high standing* indicates the women within Judaism who held power and were elite. In this verse, they are viewed as enemies of Paul and Barnabas, but it also indicates that elite women were present and able.

13:51 *Shook the dust off their feet in protest* is a sign that Paul and Barnabas have completed their ministry there and will be moving on to another city or region.

persecution against Paul and Barnabas and drove them out of their region. [51]So they shook the dust off their feet in protest against them and went to Iconium. [52]And the disciples were filled with joy and with the Holy Spirit.

14 The same thing occurred in Iconium, where Paul[t] and Barnabas[u] went into the Jewish synagogue and spoke in such a way that a great number of both Jews and Greeks became believers. [2]But the unbelieving Jews stirred up the gentiles and poisoned their minds against the brothers. [3]So they remained for a long time speaking boldly for the Lord, who testified to the word of his grace by granting signs and wonders to be done through them. [4]But the residents of the city were divided: some sided with the Jews, and some with the apostles. [5]And when an attempt was made by both gentiles and Jews, with their rulers, to mistreat them and to stone them, [6]the apostles[v] learned of it and fled to Lystra and Derbe, cities of Lycaonia, and to the surrounding region, [7]and there they continued proclaiming the good news.

8 In Lystra there was a man sitting who could not use his feet and had never walked, for he had been lame from birth. [9]He listened to Paul as he was speaking. And Paul, looking at him intently and seeing that he had faith to be healed, [10]said in a loud voice, "Stand upright on your feet." And the man[w] sprang up and began to walk. [11]When the crowds saw what Paul had done, they shouted in the Lycaonian language, "The gods have come down to us in human form!" [12]Barnabas they called Zeus, and Paul they called Hermes, because he was the chief speaker. [13]The priest of Zeus, whose temple was just outside the city,[x] brought oxen and garlands to the gates; he and the crowds wanted to offer sacrifice. [14]When the apostles Barnabas and Paul heard of it, they tore their clothes and rushed out into the crowd, shouting, [15]"People,[y] why are you doing this? We are mortals just like you, and we bring you good news, that you should turn from these worthless things to the living God, who made the heaven and the earth and the sea and all that is in them. [16]In past generations he allowed all peoples to follow their own ways, [17]yet he has not left himself without a witness in doing good, giving you rains from heaven and fruitful seasons and filling you with food and your hearts with joy." [18]Even with these words, they scarcely restrained the crowds from offering sacrifice to them.

19 But Jews came there from Antioch and Iconium and won over the crowds. Then they stoned Paul and dragged him out of the city, supposing that he was dead. [20]But when the disciples surrounded him, he got up and went into the city. The next day he went on with Barnabas to Derbe.

t 14.1 Or *In Iconium, as usual, Paul*   *u* 14.1 Gk *they*   *v* 14.6 Gk *they*   *w* 14.10 Gk *he*   *x* 14.13 Or *The priest of Zeus-Outside-the-City*   *y* 14.15 Gk *Men*

14:1 Iconium was an important city about ninety miles away from Antioch. There are many stories of Paul preaching in Iconium. For example, the Acts of Paul and Thecla, an early second-century Christian text, also describes Paul preaching and ministering in Iconium.

14:2 The author here uses *unbelieving Jews* to distinguish them from Jews who were followers of Paul and Barnabas, indicating Jesus followers who were also Jewish.

14:8–10 This is Paul's first recorded healing in Acts, which seems parallel to Peter's healing in chap. 3, both of which parallel Jesus's healings in Luke (as well as in Mark and Matthew).

14:11–12 This brief scene indicates the belief and recognition of Greek and Roman gods by the readers of Acts. This misrecognition of Barnabas as Zeus and Paul as Hermes could be mimicking a story from Ovid's *Metamorphoses* where the two Greek gods visit an older couple and appear as humans to save them from an impending flood. Zeus was viewed as the primary god of the Greek pantheon, while Hermes was the messenger.

14:15 Barnabas and Paul clear up the confusion, indicating that they are not gods but humans, and then point the crowd to the *living God*, by which they mean the God of Judaism.

14:19 Antioch and Iconium are cities to the north and west of Lystra, the setting of this scene. According to this verse, some Jews stoned Paul and took his body out of the city. Throughout Acts, Paul and other travel companions experience much violence and even imprisonment, but they always seem to survive and escape harm, as seen in 14:20.

14:20–21 Derbe is a city that lies about sixty miles east of Lystra in Asia Minor, or modern-day Turkey. After staying for an undesignated amount of time in Derbe, Paul and Barnabas retrace their steps and go back to Lystra and then to Iconium and Antioch.

21 After they had proclaimed the good news to that city and had made many disciples, they returned to Lystra, then on to Iconium and Antioch. 22There they strengthened the souls of the disciples and encouraged them to continue in the faith, saying, "It is through many persecutions that we must enter the kingdom of God." 23And after they had appointed elders for them in each church, with prayer and fasting they entrusted them to the Lord in whom they had come to believe.

24 Then they passed through Pisidia and came to Pamphylia. 25When they had spoken the word in Perga, they went down to Attalia. 26From there they sailed back to Antioch, where they had been commended to the grace of God for the work[z] that they had completed. 27When they arrived, they called the church together and related all that God had done with them and how he had opened a door of faith for the gentiles. 28And they stayed there with the disciples for some time.

15 Then certain individuals came down from Judea and were teaching the brothers, "Unless you are circumcised according to the custom of Moses, you cannot be saved." 2And after Paul and Barnabas had no small dissension and debate with them, Paul and Barnabas and some of the others were appointed to go up to Jerusalem to discuss this question with the apostles and the elders. 3So they were sent on their way by the church, and as they passed through both Phoenicia and Samaria, they reported the conversion of the gentiles and brought great joy to all the brothers and sisters. 4When they came to Jerusalem, they were welcomed by the church and the apostles and the elders, and they reported all that God had done with them. 5But some believers who belonged to the sect of the Pharisees stood up and said, "It is necessary for them to be circumcised and ordered to keep the law of Moses."

6 The apostles and the elders met together to consider this matter. 7After there had been much debate, Peter stood up and said to them, "My brothers,[a] you know that in the early days God made a choice among you, that I should be the one through whom the gentiles would hear the message of the good news and become believers. 8And God, who knows the human heart, testified to them by giving them the Holy Spirit, just as he did to us, 9and in cleansing their hearts by faith he has made no distinction between them and us. 10Now, therefore, why are you putting God to the test by placing on the neck of the disciples a yoke that neither our ancestors nor we have been able to bear? 11On the contrary, we believe that we will be saved through the grace of the Lord Jesus, just as they will."

12 The whole assembly kept silence and listened to Barnabas and Paul as they told of all the signs and wonders that God had done through them among the gentiles. 13After they

z 14.26 Or *committed in the grace of God to the work*   a 15.7 Gk *Men, brothers*

14:22 This verse seems to be foreshadowing a time of persecutions, which Paul and his fellow companions will experience in the narrative of Acts and which some early Christians will experience.

14:24–26 They now travel south through the region of Pisidia and to the cities of Perga and Attalia, which are on the coast of the Mediterranean Sea. Then they return to Antioch, which is where this first journey began. This is often called "Paul's First Missionary Journey," as he returns to Antioch and remains for "some time," as v. 28 indicates.

15:1–29 This section of Acts is referred to as the Council at Jerusalem, in which a group of Jewish believers—including Paul, Barnabas, and Peter—addresses the issue of the number of gentile believers who have joined Jewish believers in this new religious community that follows the teaching of Jesus. While the scene with Cornelius in Acts 10 opened the door to the inclusion of gentiles, the Jerusalem Council debates the issue further, especially the question of whether the gentile believers need to be circumcised in order to be saved (15:1). **15:5** In Acts, some members of the Pharisees are portrayed as followers of Jesus. The Pharisees were a religious sect in ancient Judaism that held a high view and particular interpretation of the Torah (see **"Pharisees," p. 1756**). **15:7–11** This short speech given by Peter indicates that God chose that Peter *should be the one through whom the gentiles would hear the message of the good news and become believers.* That is what we see in the previous chapters of Acts, but it is in conflict with what Paul writes about in his letter to the church in Galatia (chaps. 1–2). **15:13–21** James now gives a speech that incorporates the words of the Hebrew prophets and concludes that the gentiles should not have to be circumcised in order to join this religious community. He does indicate that some aspects of Jewish laws should be followed, such as not eating foods sacrificed to

Focus On: Jews in Luke–Acts (Acts 7, 15, and 23)

Within the Gospel of Luke and the Acts of the Apostles, Jews are depicted in several ways. First, the main characters of both Luke and Acts are Jewish and are active within Judaism. This includes Jesus, his disciples, Peter, and Paul. Within Luke, Jesus is acting within Judaism and mostly speaking to and about Jews. Within Acts, Peter and Paul, who are the main figures, insist upon their Jewishness on several occasions even as they both make arguments that gentiles should be included in the Way, or the earliest form of Christianity. On the other hand, the antagonists in Luke–Acts are often also Jewish. The author does not clearly distinguish between individual Jews but instead uses the phrase "the Jews" when identifying those who oppose Jesus or Jesus's message. This phrasing and the animosity toward antagonistic Jews have led some to suggest that Luke–Acts is anti-Jewish in rhetoric and ideology (see **"Anti-Judaism," p. 1865**).

In Acts, "the Jews" become an enemy of Paul's ministry and push for his arrest. In Paul's speeches, he is often harsh toward Jews as well for not being open to his message about Jesus. However, in each of Paul's journeys to a new city/region/country, he always goes to a synagogue or Jewish community first. This becomes a frequent pattern in Acts. This prioritization of the Jewish community reveals the complexity of the representation of Jews in Acts, as Paul's character clearly values the thoughts and opinions of his fellow Jews. Paul also continues his religious commitments to Judaism throughout, as he goes to the temple, completes his religious vow, and worships on the Sabbath. When reading Acts, it can be helpful to define which group of Jews is intended when coming across the phrase "the Jews."

One way of interpreting this multifaceted portrayal of Jews in Luke–Acts is by recognizing the intra-Jewish conversation that is occurring in the narrative. This is especially clear in the Gospel of Luke, as Jesus condemns some Jewish groups, yet his message is alluring to many Jews who become his followers. In Acts, similarly, Peter and Paul consistently convince groups of Jews to listen and believe in their message. While other Jews do not listen or believe, there are still many Jews from numerous countries who believe in the gospel and follow Paul's ministry. Ultimately, Jews are depicted both favorably and unfavorably in Luke–Acts.

Christy Cobb

finished speaking, James replied, "My brothers,[b] listen to me. [14]Simeon has related how God first looked favorably on the gentiles, to take from among them a people for his name. [15]This agrees with the words of the prophets, as it is written,

[16] 'After this I will return,
  and I will rebuild the dwelling of David,
    which has fallen;
  from its ruins I will rebuild it,
    and I will set it up,
[17] so that all other peoples may seek the Lord—
  even all the gentiles over whom my name has been called.
  Thus says the Lord, who has been making these things [18]known from long ago.'[c]

[19]"Therefore I have reached the decision that we should not trouble those gentiles who are turning to God, [20]but we should write to them to abstain only from things polluted by idols and from sexual immorality and from whatever has been strangled[d] and from blood. [21]For in every city, for generations past, Moses has had those who proclaim him, for he has been read aloud every Sabbath in the synagogues."

22 Then the apostles and the elders, with the consent of the whole church, decided to choose men from among them and to send them to Antioch with Paul and Barnabas. They

b 15.13 Gk Men, brothers c 15.18 Other ancient authorities read things. [18]Known to God from of old are all his works.' d 15.20 Other ancient authorities lack and from whatever has been strangled

idols or animals that have been strangled (15:20). See **"Diet," p. 268**. James's decision seems to stand as an official decision by the group. **15:14** Simeon here likely refers to Simon Peter, but James and the audience listening would be referencing Peter's Hebrew name, Simon. **15:16–18** This is a paraphrased recitation of Amos 9:11–12 and is likely used here to remind the crowd (and the reader) of Cornelius's belief in Jesus from Acts 10. **15:23–29** This part of Acts includes the text of a letter sent to the gentile believers, which is reminiscent of the variety of genres found within Acts, as mentioned in the introduction. The certain persons mentioned in v. 24 are not named in the letter, but then four men are named as reputable persons to be sent to the gentiles, which, surprisingly, does not include Peter.

sent Judas called Barsabbas, and Silas, leaders among the brothers, [23]with the following letter: "The brothers, both the apostles and the elders, to the brothers and sisters of gentile origin in Antioch and Syria and Cilicia, greetings. [24]Since we have heard that certain persons who have gone out from us, though with no instructions from us, have said things to disturb you and have unsettled your minds,[e] [25]we have decided unanimously to choose men and send them to you, along with our beloved Barnabas and Paul, [26]who have risked their lives for the sake of our Lord Jesus Christ. [27]We have therefore sent Judas and Silas, who themselves will tell you the same things by word of mouth. [28]For it has seemed good to the Holy Spirit and to us to impose on you no further burden than these essentials: [29]that you abstain from what has been sacrificed to idols and from blood and from what is strangled[f] and from sexual immorality. If you keep yourselves from these, you will do well. Farewell."

30 So they were sent off and went down to Antioch. When they gathered the congregation together, they delivered the letter. [31]When they read it, they rejoiced at the exhortation. [32]Judas and Silas, who were themselves prophets, said much to encourage and strengthen the brothers and sisters. [33]After they had been there for some time, they were sent off in peace by the brothers and sisters to those who had sent them.[g] [35]But Paul and Barnabas remained in Antioch, and there, with many others, they taught and proclaimed the word of the Lord.

36 After some days Paul said to Barnabas, "Come, let us return and visit the brothers and sisters in every city where we proclaimed the word of the Lord and see how they are doing." [37]Barnabas wanted to take with them John called Mark. [38]But Paul decided not to take with them one who had deserted them in Pamphylia and had not accompanied them in the work. [39]The disagreement became so sharp that they parted company; Barnabas took Mark with him and sailed away to Cyprus. [40]But Paul chose Silas and set out, the brothers and sisters commending him to the grace of the Lord. [41]He went through Syria and Cilicia, strengthening the churches.

16 Paul[b] went on also to Derbe and to Lystra, where there was a disciple named Timothy, the son of a Jewish woman who was a believer, but his father was a Greek. [2]He was well spoken of by the brothers and sisters in Lystra and Iconium. [3]Paul wanted Timothy to accompany him, and he took him and had him circumcised because of the Jews who were in those places, for they all knew that his father was a Greek. [4]As they went from town to town, they delivered to them for observance the decisions that had been reached by the apostles and elders who were in Jerusalem. [5]So the churches were strengthened in the faith and increased in numbers daily.

6 They went through the region of Phrygia and Galatia, having been forbidden by the Holy Spirit to speak the word in Asia. [7]When they had come opposite Mysia, they attempted to go into Bithynia, but the Spirit of Jesus did not allow them; [8]so, passing by Mysia, they went down to Troas. [9]During the night Paul had a vision: there stood a man of Macedonia pleading with him and saying, "Come over to Macedonia and help us." [10]When he had seen

e 15.24 Other ancient authorities add *saying, 'You must be circumcised and keep the law,'*   f 15.29 Other ancient authorities lack *and from what is strangled*   g 15.33 Other ancient authorities add 15.34, *But it seemed good to Silas to remain there*   b 16.1 Gk *He*

15:36–41 After some time of peace and teaching the "word of the Lord" (v. 35), Paul and Barnabas have a disagreement because Barnabas wants to bring John Mark with them, but Paul refuses. Paul wants to *return and visit . . . every city* that they have previously visited. Ultimately, Barnabas takes Mark to Cyprus, and Paul takes Silas and goes to Syria and Cilicia.

16:1–5 Timothy's presence in this passage is important, as it shows that the question of circumcision was not totally settled. Because of Timothy's mixed background as part Jewish, part Greek, he was not circumcised as a child. Here, Paul decides to have him circumcised because they will be visiting Jewish communities. This short addition reveals that even after the Jerusalem Council (in chap. 15), all was not settled regarding how to integrate gentiles into the mainly Jewish group of Jesus followers. It also reveals that Jewish tradition and law did matter to Paul and the communities he was visiting.

16:9–10 Visions like this one work to direct the plot and action in Acts. Consider the role of Peter's vision in chap. 10, which led to him meeting Cornelius. Here, the vision leads Paul to go to Philippi, a city within Macedonia.

16:10–17 This is the first instance of a section of text in Acts often called the "we passages" because

the vision, we immediately tried to cross over to Macedonia, being convinced that God had called us to proclaim the good news to them.

11 We therefore[i] set sail from Troas and took a straight course to Samothrace, the following day to Neapolis, [12]and from there to Philippi, which is a leading city of the district of Macedonia and a Roman colony. We remained in this city for some days. [13]On the Sabbath day we went outside the gate by the river, where we supposed[j] there was a place of prayer, and we sat down and spoke to the women who had gathered there. [14]A certain woman named Lydia, a worshiper of God, was listening to us; she was from the city of Thyatira and a dealer in purple cloth. The Lord opened her heart to listen eagerly to what was said by Paul. [15]When she and her household were baptized, she urged us, saying, "If you have judged me to be faithful to the Lord, come and stay at my home." And she prevailed upon us.

16 One day as we were going to the place of prayer, we met a female slave who had a spirit of divination and brought her owners a great deal of money by fortune-telling. [17]While she followed Paul and us, she would cry out, "These men are slaves of the Most High God, who proclaim to you[k] the way of salvation." [18]She kept doing this for many days. But Paul, very much annoyed, turned and said to the spirit, "I order you in the name of Jesus Christ to come out of her." And it came out that very hour.

19 But when her owners saw that their hope of making money was gone, they seized Paul and Silas and dragged them into the marketplace before the authorities. [20]When they had brought them before the magistrates, they

said, "These men, these Jews, are disturbing our city [21]and are advocating customs that are not lawful for us, being Romans, to adopt or observe." [22]The crowd joined in attacking them, and the magistrates had them stripped of their clothing and ordered them to be beaten with rods. [23]After they had given them a severe flogging, they threw them into prison and ordered the jailer to keep them securely. [24]Following these instructions, he put them in the innermost cell and fastened their feet in the stocks.

25 About midnight Paul and Silas were praying and singing hymns to God, and the prisoners were listening to them. [26]Suddenly there was an earthquake so violent that the foundations of the prison were shaken, and immediately all the doors were opened and everyone's chains were unfastened. [27]When the jailer woke up and saw the prison doors wide open, he drew his sword and was about to kill himself, since he supposed that the prisoners had escaped. [28]But Paul shouted in a loud voice, "Do not harm yourself, for we are all here." [29]The jailer[l] called for lights, and rushing in, he fell down trembling before Paul and Silas. [30]Then he brought them outside and said, "Sirs, what must I do to be saved?" [31]They answered, "Believe in the Lord Jesus, and you will be saved, you and your household." [32]They spoke the word of the Lord[m] to him and to all who were in his house. [33]At the same hour of the night he took them and washed their

i 16.11 Other ancient authorities lack *therefore*
j 16.13 Other ancient authorities read *where, according to the custom,* k 16.17 Other ancient authorities read *to us*
l 16.29 Gk *He* m 16.32 Other ancient authorities read *word of God*

of the switch to the first-person plural when narrating the story. Some scholars have suggested that verses such as these were a part of a travel diary, and others have suggested that these sections are included in order to suggest that the author of Acts was one of those traveling with Paul. This second option is not considered historically possible because Acts was written later than the time of Paul's ministry. See also 20:5–15; 21:1–17; and 27:1–28:16. **16:13** It is supposed that the Jews are meeting on the Sabbath by the river because there is not a Jewish synagogue in Philippi. An important thing to note in this verse is that this is a group of all women, only women, meeting together. **16:14** *Lydia.* This short verse tells us much about the character of Lydia. First, she is a gentile (from Thyatira), yet she is also a *worshiper of God*, which indicates she is already a part of the Jewish community here. Finally, she is a businesswoman who sells purple cloth and is a prominent member of the community. See **"Lydia," p. 1913. 16:15** While baptism is often a sign of belief in Acts, here a new believer's household is baptized with them. In the Greco-Roman world, this implies that enslaved workers might have been forced to be baptized along with other members of the family. This also occurs with the jailer's household later in this chapter (16:33). **16:16** *Female slave who had a spirit of divination* or literally the "spirit of the python" in Greek. This phrase could indicate that she was connected to Delphi, Greece, where a female oracle (called Sybil) was widely known for her ability to see the future. See **"Enslaved Women in Acts," p. 1905.**

Going Deeper: Lydia (Acts 16:14–16)

Lydia's story is found in Acts 16, where she is introduced during Paul's trip to Philippi. There are only a few short verses dedicated to Lydia, but even so, we are able to determine several things about her and her character in Acts. She is first introduced as a part of a group of Jewish women who are gathered by a river in Philippi to pray on the Sabbath (16:13). Lydia is the only woman of this group who is named. She is from a city called Thyatira, which indicates she may not be ethnically Jewish and could be a convert to Judaism. The author of Acts calls her a "worshiper of God" (16:14), so she does seem to be a part of this Jewish community. Lydia is also designated as a seller of purple cloth, which tells us a few things about her. First, she is a businesswoman. Second, she could be wealthy. Purple cloth was difficult to find and was associated with the elite, sometimes even with the imperial personnel. Lydia is not named with a husband, which suggests she could be single or a widow. She listens to Paul as he speaks to the group of women in Philippi, and the "Lord open[s] her heart" (16:14). Because of this, Lydia decides to be baptized, and her household is also baptized with her. After the baptism, she invites Paul, Silas, and those traveling with them to stay at her house while they are in Philippi (16:15). They accept, and Lydia's house becomes the center for Paul's Philippian ministry. This adds one final aspect to Lydia's character—she has a house and a household. This indicates she could have been the head of the household. Ultimately, Lydia emerges as an important part of the early Christian community in Philippi because of her leadership.

Christy Cobb

wounds; then he and his entire family were baptized without delay. [34]He brought them up into the house and set food before them, and he and his entire household rejoiced that he had become a believer in God.

35 When morning came, the magistrates sent the police, saying, "Let those men go." [36]And the jailer reported the message to Paul, saying, "The magistrates sent word to let you go; therefore come out now and go in peace." [37]But Paul replied, "They have beaten us in public, uncondemned, men who are Romans, and have thrown us into prison, and now are they going to discharge us in secret? Certainly not! Let them come and take us out themselves." [38]The police reported these words to the magistrates, and they were afraid when they heard that they were Romans, [39]so they came and apologized to them. And they took them out and asked them to leave the city. [40]After leaving the prison they went to Lydia's home, and when they had seen and encouraged the brothers and sisters there, they departed.

17 After Paul and Silas[n] had passed through Amphipolis and Apollonia, they came to Thessalonica, where there was a Jewish synagogue. [2]And Paul went in, as was his custom, and on three Sabbath days argued with them from the scriptures, [3]explaining and proving that it was necessary for the Messiah[o] to suffer and to rise from the dead and saying, "This is the Messiah,[p] Jesus whom I am proclaiming to you." [4]Some of them were persuaded and joined Paul and Silas, as did a great many of the devout Greeks and not a few of the leading women. [5]But the Jews became jealous, and with the help of some ruffians in the marketplaces

n 17.1 Gk *they*   o 17.3 Or *the Christ*   p 17.3 Or *the Christ*

16:37 This is the first time Paul has indicated that he and Silas are Roman citizens. This status means that they should not have been beaten or jailed without a proper trial. Interestingly, Paul does not mention Roman citizenship in any of his letters.

16:40 This verse indicates they were staying at Lydia's home during their time in Philippi and also that there were other believers in Lydia's house. Perhaps Lydia (like Mary in Acts 12:12) used her house as a space for church or the religious community to meet.

17:1 Thessalonica was a port city in Macedonia, which is now called Greece. It is a well-known city in Paul's ministry, as the letter Paul writes to the Thessalonians is perhaps Paul's earliest recorded epistle.

17:1–2 As is typical of Acts, Paul goes first to the local Jewish synagogue to share the gospel. In v. 2, the verb translated as *argued* is "dialegomai," which means to dispute, discuss, or dialogue (the Eng. cognate of this word).

17:4 Those who were convinced by Paul's message were diverse, including Jews, Greeks, and *leading women*, which likely indicates elite or prominent women in the community.

they formed a mob and set the city in an uproar. While they were searching for Paul and Silas to bring them out to the assembly, they attacked Jason's house. ⁶When they could not find them, they dragged Jason and some brothers and sisters before the city authorities, shouting, "These people who have been turning the world upside down have come here also, ⁷and Jason has entertained them as guests. They are all acting contrary to the decrees of the emperor, saying that there is another king named Jesus." ⁸The people and the city officials were disturbed when they heard this, ⁹and after they had taken bail from Jason and the others, they let them go.

10 That very night the brothers and sisters sent Paul and Silas off to Beroea, and when they arrived they went to the Jewish synagogue. ¹¹These Jews were more receptive than those in Thessalonica, for they welcomed the message very eagerly and examined the scriptures every day to see whether these things were so. ¹²Many of them therefore believed, including not a few Greek women and men of high standing. ¹³But when the Jews of Thessalonica learned that the word of God had been proclaimed by Paul in Beroea as well, they came there, too, to stir up and incite the crowds. ¹⁴Then the brothers and sisters immediately sent Paul away to the coast, but Silas and Timothy remained behind. ¹⁵Those who

conducted Paul brought him as far as Athens, and, after receiving instructions to have Silas and Timothy join him as soon as possible, they left him.

16 While Paul was waiting for them in Athens, he was deeply distressed to see that the city was full of idols. ¹⁷So he argued in the synagogue with the Jews and the devout persons and also in the marketplace*q* every day with those who happened to be there. ¹⁸Also some Epicurean and Stoic philosophers debated with him. Some said, "What does this pretentious babbler want to say?" Others said, "He seems to be a proclaimer of foreign divinities." (This was because he was telling the good news about Jesus and the resurrection.) ¹⁹So they took him and brought him to the Areopagus and asked him, "May we know what this new teaching is that you are presenting? ²⁰It sounds rather strange to us, so we would like to know what it means." ²¹Now all the Athenians and the foreigners living there would spend their time in nothing but telling or hearing something new.

22 Then Paul stood in front of the Areopagus and said, "Athenians, I see how extremely spiritual you are in every way. ²³For as I went through the city and looked carefully at the objects of your worship, I found among them an altar with the inscription, 'To

q 17.17 Or *civic center*

17:10-15 This short story in Beroea gives a good example of the complicated way Jews function in the book of Acts. V. 11 notes that many Jews were *receptive* to the message and eagerly read the Scriptures along with Paul. But v. 13 also notes that Jews in Thessalonica came down to Beroea to *incite the crowds* and were trying to sabotage Paul's ministry. This section reveals that the author of Acts uses the same word, *Jews* (Gk. "Ioudaioi"), to refer to Jews who accepted the message and followed Paul, as well as the people who were fighting this new movement. When reading this in our current context, where violence against Jews is still rampant, it is important to separate the groups and recognize that Acts is not depicting "all Jews" as against his message. See **"Jews in Luke–Acts," p. 1910**.

17:16 The geographical movement in Acts is accelerating, and now Paul is in Athens, a major city in Greece, both in antiquity and today.

17:18 *Epicurean and Stoic philosophers* represent major philosophical groups in Athens who would have been well known for their education and elevated conversation. The author of Acts includes them to show that Paul's message was appealing to even the most prestigious of academic philosophers in Athens.

17:19 The Areopagus is a large rock that is on the Acropolis in Athens. Today, a plaque is posted that records Paul's full speech (17:22-31) in Greek on the Areopagus.

17:22-31 In this speech on the Areopagus, Paul focuses on idolatry and the worship of many gods by people in Athens. This is different from most of the previous speeches in Acts, which were more focused on the connection to Judaism and Jesus as the Messiah. Here Paul argues that the deity does not *live in shrines* (17:24) and is not an *image formed by the art and imagination of mortals* (17:29). The speech appeals to the spirituality of the Athenians and rhetorically persuades them to embrace Paul's God as their God. To further this, Luke includes a reference to the Greek poet Aratos of Soloi (third century BCE) in 17:28. The quotation *we are God's offspring* is appropriated by Luke, in the words of Paul, to appeal specifically to Greek listeners in Athens.

an unknown god.' What therefore you worship as unknown, this I proclaim to you. [24]The God who made the world and everything in it, he who is Lord of heaven and earth, does not live in shrines made by human hands, [25]nor is he served by human hands, as though he needed anything, since he himself gives to all mortals life and breath and all things. [26]From one ancestor[r] he made all peoples to inhabit the whole earth, and he allotted the times of their existence and the boundaries of the places where they would live, [27]so that they would search for God[s] and perhaps fumble about for him and find him—though indeed he is not far from each one of us. [28]For 'In him we live and move and have our being'; as even some of your own poets have said,

'For we, too, are his offspring.'

[29]"Since we are God's offspring, we ought not to think that the deity is like gold or silver or stone, an image formed by the art and imagination of mortals. [30]While God has overlooked the times of human ignorance, now he commands all people everywhere to repent, [31]because he has fixed a day on which he will have the world judged in righteousness by a man whom he has appointed, and of this he has given assurance to all by raising him from the dead."

[32]When they heard of the resurrection of the dead, some scoffed, but others said, "We will hear you again about this." [33]At that point Paul left them. [34]But some of them joined him and became believers, including Dionysius the Areopagite and a woman named Damaris and others with them.

18 After this Paul[t] left Athens and went to Corinth. [2]There he found a Jew named Aquila from Pontus, who had recently come from Italy with his wife Priscilla, because Claudius had ordered all Jews to leave Rome. Paul[u] went to see them, [3]and, because he was of the same trade, he stayed with them, and they worked together—by trade they were tentmakers. [4]Every Sabbath he would argue in the synagogue and would try to convince Jews and Greeks.

[5]When Silas and Timothy arrived from Macedonia, Paul was occupied with proclaiming the word,[v] testifying to the Jews that the Messiah[w] was Jesus. [6]When they opposed and reviled him, in protest he shook the dust from his clothes[x] and said to them, "Your blood be on your own heads! I am innocent. From now on I will go to the gentiles." [7]Then he left the synagogue[y] and went to the house of a man named Titius[z] Justus, a worshiper of God; his house was next door to the synagogue. [8]Crispus, the official of the synagogue, became a believer in the Lord, together with all his household, and many of the Corinthians who heard Paul became believers and were baptized. [9]One night the Lord said to Paul in a vision, "Do not be afraid, but speak and do not be silent, [10]for I am with you, and no one will lay a hand on you to harm you, for there are many in this city who are my people." [11]He stayed there a year and six months, teaching the word of God among them.

[12]But when Gallio was proconsul of Achaia, the Jews made a united attack on Paul and brought him before the tribunal. [13]They

r 17.26 Gk *From one*; other ancient authorities read *From one blood* s 17.27 Other ancient authorities read *the Lord* t 18.1 Gk *he* u 18.2 Gk *He* v 18.5 Gk *with the word* w 18.5 Or *the Christ* x 18.6 Gk *reviled him, he shook out his clothes* y 18.7 Gk *left there* z 18.7 Other ancient authorities read *Titus*

18:1 The trip from Athens to Corinth would have taken Paul north, into Greece. First-century Corinth was a port city and a Roman colony. It would likely have been an alluring location for a diverse group of people who traveled and visited.

18:2 This suggestion by Acts that *Claudius had ordered all Jews to leave Rome* is not supported by external historical evidence. A few sources suggest that some Jews were forced to leave, but they do not say all Jews left Rome during the reign of Claudius.

18:2–3 The couple mentioned here, Aquila and Priscilla, is also mentioned in Paul's letters as close companions of Paul as well as teachers of the gospel. In four out of the six times this couple is mentioned, Priscilla, the woman, is named first. While this passage is one of those where Aquila is named first, these other passages indicate that Priscilla might have been the more prominent of the two (see, e.g., 18:18).

18:6 Paul is full of passion here, indicating that he will now preach only to the gentiles. Even though he says this here, Paul and his companions continue to visit synagogues and to preach and dialogue with Jewish communities throughout the entirety of Acts.

18:12–17 This short section about controversy in the synagogue at Corinth is also difficult to place historically. There are some inscriptions that inform us about Gallio's work as proconsul, but the

said, "This man is persuading people to worship God in ways that are contrary to the law." [14]Just as Paul was about to speak, Gallio said to the Jews, "If it were a matter of crime or serious villainy, I would be justified in accepting the complaint of you Jews, [15]but since it is a matter of questions about words and names and your own law, see to it yourselves; I do not wish to be a judge of these matters." [16]And he dismissed them from the tribunal. [17]Then all of them[a] seized Sosthenes, the official of the synagogue, and beat him in front of the tribunal. But Gallio paid no attention to any of these things.

18 After staying there for a considerable time, Paul said farewell to the brothers and sisters and sailed for Syria, accompanied by Priscilla and Aquila. At Cenchreae he had his hair cut, for he was under a vow. [19]When they reached Ephesus, he left them there, but first he himself went into the synagogue and had a discussion with the Jews. [20]When they asked him to stay longer, he declined, [21]but on taking leave of them he said, "I[b] will return to you, if God wills." Then he set sail from Ephesus.

22 When he had landed at Caesarea, he went up to Jerusalem[c] and greeted the church and then went down to Antioch. [23]After spending some time there he departed and went from place to place through the region of Galatia[d] and Phrygia, strengthening all the disciples.

24 Now there came to Ephesus a Jew named Apollos from Alexandria. He was an eloquent man, well-versed in the scriptures. [25]He had been instructed in the Way of the Lord, and he spoke with burning enthusiasm and taught accurately the things concerning Jesus,

though he knew only the baptism of John. [26]He began to speak boldly in the synagogue, but when Priscilla and Aquila heard him they took him aside and explained the Way of God to him more accurately. [27]And when he wished to cross over to Achaia, the brothers and sisters encouraged him and wrote to the disciples to welcome him. On his arrival he greatly helped those who through grace had become believers, [28]for he powerfully refuted the Jews in public, showing by the scriptures that the Messiah[e] is Jesus.

19 While Apollos was in Corinth, Paul passed through the interior regions and came to Ephesus, where he found some disciples. [2]He said to them, "Did you receive the Holy Spirit when you became believers?" They replied, "No, we have not even heard that there is a Holy Spirit." [3]Then he said, "Into what, then, were you baptized?" They answered, "Into John's baptism." [4]Paul said, "John baptized with the baptism of repentance, telling the people to believe in the one who was to come after him, that is, in Jesus." [5]On hearing this, they were baptized in the name of the Lord Jesus. [6]When Paul had laid his hands on them, the Holy Spirit came upon them, and they spoke in tongues and prophesied; [7]altogether there were about twelve of them.

8 He entered the synagogue and for three months spoke out boldly and argued

a 18.17 Other ancient authorities read *all the Greeks*
b 18.21 Other ancient authorities read *I must at all costs keep the approaching festival in Jerusalem, but I*   c 18.22 Gk *went up*
d 18.23 Gk *the Galatian region*   e 18.28 Or *the Christ*

other information is not clearly historical. Regardless, the violence here against Sosthenes (v. 17) is troubling.

18:18 Paul takes Priscilla and Aquila with him on this next journey to Syria. Note that Priscilla's name is listed first here (see note from 18:2–3). While the author does not expand upon Paul's vow mentioned here, the connection between shaving hair and release from the Nazirite vow can be found in Num. 6:2–21.

18:24–28 The story of Apollos contains a positive story of a Jewish believer who was also open to learning more. He was preaching *boldly in the synagogue* but only knew about the baptism of John (vv. 25–26). Priscilla and Aquila, the ministerial couple mentioned previously in Acts, took the time to teach him about the Way. Apollos learned from them and continued his ministry. The name *Apollos* is also mentioned by Paul in 1 Corinthians, which is likely the same person (see 1 Cor. 1:12; 3:3–6, 22; 4:6; 16:12).

19:1–10 Paul's time in Ephesus begins, like most of his journeys, in the synagogue. Then he moves to the *lecture hall of Tyrannus*, which indicates that he is speaking in a more secular and philosophical space. V. 10 notes that *both Jews and Greeks* are listening and receptive to his message. **19:1** Ephesus is a well-known city in modern-day Turkey. Unlike many other cities from antiquity, much of ancient Ephesus has been excavated and can be toured today. Some of the sites Paul visits in this chapter, such as the theater, are still intact and make the reading of chap. 19 come to life.

persuasively about the kingdom of God. [9]When some stubbornly refused to believe and spoke evil of the Way before the congregation, he left them, taking the disciples with him, and argued daily in the lecture hall of Tyrannus.[f] [10]This continued for two years, so that all the residents of Asia, both Jews and Greeks, heard the word of the Lord.

11 God did extraordinary miracles through Paul, [12]so that when the handkerchiefs or aprons that had touched his skin were brought to the sick, their diseases left them, and the evil spirits came out of them. [13]Then some itinerant Jewish exorcists tried to use the name of the Lord Jesus over those who had evil spirits, saying, "I adjure you by the Jesus whom Paul proclaims." [14]Seven sons of a Jewish high priest named Sceva were doing this. [15]But the evil spirit said to them in reply, "Jesus I know, and Paul I know, but who are you?" [16]Then the man with the evil spirit leaped on them, mastered them all, and so overpowered them that they fled out of the house naked and wounded. [17]When this became known to all residents of Ephesus, both Jews and Greeks, everyone was awestruck, and the name of the Lord Jesus was praised. [18]Also many of those who became believers confessed and disclosed their practices. [19]A number of those who practiced magic collected their books and burned them publicly; when the value of these books[g] was calculated, it was found to come to fifty thousand silver coins. [20]So the word of the Lord grew mightily and prevailed.

21 Now after these things had been accomplished, Paul resolved in the Spirit to go through Macedonia and Achaia and then to go on to Jerusalem. He said, "After I have gone there, I must also see Rome." [22]So he sent two of his helpers, Timothy and Erastus, to Macedonia, while he himself stayed for some time longer in Asia.

23 About that time no little disturbance broke out concerning the Way. [24]A man named Demetrius, a silversmith who made silver shrines of Artemis, brought no little business to the artisans. [25]These he gathered together, with the workers of the same trade, and said, "Men, you know that we get our wealth from this business. [26]You also see and hear that not only in Ephesus but in almost the whole of Asia this Paul has persuaded and drawn away a considerable number of people by saying that gods made with hands are not gods. [27]And there is danger not only that this trade of ours may come into disrepute but also that the temple of the great goddess Artemis will be scorned, and she will be deprived of her majesty that brought all Asia and the world to worship her."

28 When they heard this, they were enraged and shouted, "Great is Artemis of the Ephesians!" [29]The city was filled with the confusion, and people[h] rushed together to the theater, dragging with them Gaius and Aristarchus,

f 19.9 Other ancient authorities read *of a certain Tyrannus, from eleven o'clock in the morning to four in the afternoon*
g 19.19 Gk *them* h 19.29 Gk *they*

19:11–12 Paul's power to heal expands throughout the narrative of Acts. Here, even cloth that has touched Paul's skin can heal another person. This is reminiscent of the healing by Jesus of the woman who had been bleeding for twelve years and was healed by touching the fringes of Jesus's garment (Matt. 9:19–22; Mark 5:25–34; Luke 8:43–48).

19:18–20 This scene of a book burning illustrates the intense reaction to magic held by many within Judaism and early Christianity. Further, this might remind contemporary readers of the practice of banning books, which often is supported by religious communities. Just as in Acts—where books are burned because they contain information about magic that some Jesus followers rejected—today, books are banned because they contain references to ideas that some contemporary Christians want to erase or control.

19:23–41 This scene is also of interest, as it is one where Paul does not ultimately win over the city with his message, as is indicated earlier in the chapter (vv. 8–10). Instead, the people of Ephesus (19:29) rush to the theater and chant together *Great is Artemis of the Ephesians!* for two hours (v. 34). After this, Paul leaves the city (20:1).

19:24–27 The goddess Artemis was well known in the Greek world as a virgin and a hunter who often is portrayed with her bow and arrow. However, in Turkey, Artemis is instead portrayed as a fertile goddess with numerous egg shapes on her chest and other symbols of fertility on her statue. Her depiction has much in common with the indigenous mother goddess in Turkey, Cybele, who was very popular in this region. As is indicated in this section of Acts, Artemis was avidly worshiped in Ephesus, and statues of her were sold as souvenirs to ancient travelers who visited the city.

Macedonians who were Paul's travel companions. [30]Paul wished to go into the crowd, but the disciples would not let him; [31]even some officials of the province of Asia[i] who were friendly to him sent him a message urging him not to venture into the theater. [32]Meanwhile, some were shouting one thing, some another, for the assembly was in confusion, and most of them did not know why they had come together. [33]Some of the crowd gave instructions to Alexander, whom the Jews had pushed forward. And Alexander motioned for silence and tried to make a defense before the people. [34]But when they recognized that he was a Jew, for about two hours all of them shouted in unison, "Great is Artemis of the Ephesians!" [35]But when the town clerk had quieted the crowd, he said, "Citizens of Ephesus, who is there who does not know that the city of the Ephesians is the temple keeper of the great Artemis and of the statue that fell from heaven? [36]Since these things cannot be denied, you ought to be quiet and do nothing rash. [37]You have brought these men here who are neither temple robbers nor blasphemers of our[j] goddess. [38]If therefore Demetrius and the artisans with him have a complaint against anyone, the courts are open, and there are proconsuls; let them bring charges there against one another. [39]If there is anything further[k] you want to know, it must be settled in the regular assembly. [40]For we are in danger of being charged with rioting today, since there is no cause that we can give to justify this commotion." [41]When he had said this, he dismissed the assembly.

20 After the uproar had ceased, Paul sent for the disciples, and after encouraging them and saying farewell, he left for Macedonia. [2]When he had gone through those regions and had given them much encouragement, he came to Greece, [3]where he stayed for three months. He was about to set sail for Syria when a plot was made against him by the Jews, so he decided to return through Macedonia. [4]He was accompanied[l] by Sopater son of Pyrrhus from Beroea, by Aristarchus and Secundus from Thessalonica, by Gaius from Derbe, and by Timothy, as well as by Tychicus and Trophimus from Asia. [5]They went ahead and were waiting for us in Troas, [6]but we sailed from Philippi after the days of Unleavened Bread, and in five days we joined them in Troas, where we stayed for seven days.

7 On the first day of the week, when we met to break bread, Paul was holding a discussion with them; since he intended to leave the next day, he continued speaking until midnight. [8]There were many lamps in the room upstairs where we were meeting. [9]A young man named Eutychus, who was sitting in the window, began to sink off into a deep sleep while Paul talked still longer. Overcome by sleep, he fell to the ground three floors below and was picked up dead. [10]But Paul went down and bending over him took him in his arms and said, "Do not be alarmed, for his life is in him." [11]Then Paul went upstairs, and after he had broken bread and eaten, he continued to converse with them until dawn; then he left. [12]Meanwhile they had taken the boy away alive and were not a little comforted.

13 We went ahead to the ship and set sail for Assos, intending to take Paul on board there, for he had made this arrangement, intending to go by land himself. [14]When he met us in Assos, we took him on board and went to Mitylene. [15]We sailed from there, and on the following day we arrived opposite Chios. The next day we touched at Samos, and[m] the day

i 19.31 Gk *some of the Asiarchs* j 19.37 Other ancient authorities read *your* k 19.39 Other ancient authorities read *about other matters* l 20.4 Other ancient authorities add *as far as Asia* m 20.15 Other ancient authorities add *after remaining at Trogyllium*

20:5–15 This section is the second instance of the "we passages" in Acts, where the narration switches to first-person plural. See the note for 16:10–17.

20:7–12 Paul speaks late into the night here, and one of his listeners falls asleep while he is talking. Many readers have noted the humor of this scene, as Paul seems to drone on and on, not realizing his audience is growing sleepy. Eutychus, whose name means "fortunate," unfortunately falls out of the window to his death. Paul heals Eutychus and then continues to speak *until dawn*. This scene humanizes Paul as a long-winded preacher even while it solidifies his status as a healer.

20:13–15 These brief descriptions of Paul's travels are interesting, as one can track the cities mentioned as well as the means of travel. In these verses, for example, Paul wanted to travel by land, even though the quickest route from Troas to Miletus would be by ship. Paul's companions began the journey by ship, and then Paul joined in Assos, which was a Greek city in the region of Anatolia (in modern-day Turkey).

after that we came to Miletus. [16]For Paul had decided to sail past Ephesus, so that he might not have to spend time in Asia; he was eager to be in Jerusalem, if possible, on the day of Pentecost.

17 From Miletus he sent a message to Ephesus, asking the elders of the church to meet him. [18]When they came to him, he said to them: "You yourselves know how I lived among you the entire time from the first day that I set foot in Asia, [19]serving the Lord with all humility and with tears, enduring the trials that came to me through the plots of the Jews. [20]I did not shrink from doing anything helpful, proclaiming the message to you and teaching you publicly and from house to house, [21]as I testified to both Jews and Greeks about repentance toward God and faith toward our Lord Jesus.[n] [22]And now, as a captive to the Spirit,[o] I am on my way to Jerusalem, not knowing what will happen to me there, [23]except that the Holy Spirit testifies to me in every city that imprisonment and persecutions are waiting for me. [24]But I do not count my life of any value to myself, if only I may finish my course and the ministry that I received from the Lord Jesus, to testify to the good news of God's grace.

25 "And now I know that none of you, among whom I have gone about proclaiming the kingdom, will ever see my face again. [26]Therefore I declare to you this day that I am not responsible for the blood of any of you, [27]for I did not shrink from declaring to you the whole purpose of God. [28]Keep watch over yourselves and over all the flock, of which the Holy Spirit has made you overseers, to shepherd the church of God[p] that he obtained with the blood of his own Son.[q] [29]I know that after I have gone, savage wolves will come in among you, not sparing the flock. [30]Some even from your own group will come distorting the truth in order to entice the disciples to follow them. [31]Therefore be alert, remembering that for three years I did not cease night or day to warn everyone with tears. [32]And now I commend you to God and to the message of his grace, a message that is able to build you up and to give you the inheritance among all who are sanctified. [33]I coveted no one's silver or gold or clothing. [34]You know for yourselves that I worked with my own hands to support myself and my companions. [35]In all this I have given you an example that by such work we must support the weak, remembering the words of the Lord Jesus, for he himself said, 'It is more blessed to give than to receive.'"

36 When he had finished speaking, he knelt down with them all and prayed. [37]There was much weeping among them all; they embraced Paul and kissed him, [38]grieving especially because of what he had said, that they would not see him again. Then they brought him to the ship.

21 When we had parted from them and set sail, we came by a straight course to Cos, and the next day to Rhodes, and from there to Patara.[r] [2]When we found a ship bound for Phoenicia, we went on board and set sail. [3]We came in sight of Cyprus, and

n 20.21 Other ancient authorities add *Christ* o 20.22 Or *And now, bound in the spirit* p 20.28 Other ancient authorities read *of the Lord* q 20.28 Or *with his own blood*; Gk *with the blood of his Own* r 21.1 Other ancient authorities add *and Myra*

20:16 Paul's desire is to be in Jerusalem during Pentecost, or Shavuot, the Jewish Festival of Weeks.

20:17–35 Miletus was south of Ephesus. Paul requested leaders of the community at Ephesus to come to Miletus, and he spoke to them, encouraging them and informing them that he did not expect to see them again. Also, in this speech, Paul notes that he *worked with my own hands to support myself and my companions* (v. 34). This acknowledgment is to counter the view that Paul was taking money from the community in Ephesus.

20:36–38 This emotional farewell scene is an indication that Paul is aware of future persecution and possible death. The author of Acts is also preparing the reader for the end of the narrative and Paul's arrest. Furthermore, these verses and this tearful goodbye indicate the bond between Paul and the community at Ephesus.

21:1–17 This is another instance of the "we passages" in Acts, a section that describes the travels with Paul as though the writer is traveling with him. See the note for 16:10–17. 21:1–6 The journey of Paul continues on a ship as they travel from Miletus and stop at several cities on their way to Jerusalem. Vv. 2–3 indicate that the group of travelers do not have their own ship but instead find room on an available ship headed toward Phoenicia. They stop for seven days at Tyre, which is in modern-day Lebanon, and the disciples there tell Paul, *through the Spirit*, not to go to Jerusalem (v. 4). It seems that Paul does not listen, as the journey in Acts continues to Jerusalem. Even though Paul and his companions do not

leaving it on our left, we sailed to Syria and landed at Tyre, because the ship was to unload its cargo there. ⁴We looked up the disciples and stayed there for seven days. Through the Spirit they told Paul not to go on to Jerusalem. ⁵When our days there were ended, we left and proceeded on our journey, and all of them, with wives and children, escorted us outside the city. There we knelt down on the beach and prayed ⁶and said farewell to one another. Then we went on board the ship, and they returned home.

7 When we had finished⁵ the voyage from Tyre, we arrived at Ptolemais, and we greeted the brothers and sisters and stayed with them for one day. ⁸The next day we left and came to Caesarea, and we went into the house of Philip the evangelist, one of the seven, and stayed with him. ⁹He had four unmarried daughters⁵ who had the gift of prophecy. ¹⁰While we were staying there for several days, a prophet named Agabus came down from Judea. ¹¹He came to us and took Paul's belt, bound his own feet and hands with it, and said, "Thus says the Holy Spirit, 'This is the way the Jews in Jerusalem will bind the man who owns this belt and will hand him over to the gentiles.'" ¹²When we heard this, we and the people there urged him not to go up to Jerusalem. ¹³Then Paul answered, "What are you doing, weeping and breaking my heart? For I am ready not only to be bound but even to die in Jerusalem for the name of the Lord Jesus." ¹⁴Since he would not be persuaded, we remained silent except to say, "The Lord's will be done."

15 After these days we got ready and started to go up to Jerusalem. ¹⁶Some of the disciples from Caesarea also came along and brought us to the house of Mnason of Cyprus, an early disciple, with whom we were to stay.

17 When we arrived in Jerusalem, the brothers welcomed us warmly. ¹⁸The next day Paul went with us to visit James, and all the elders were present. ¹⁹After greeting them, he related one by one the things that God had done among the gentiles through his ministry. ²⁰When they heard it, they praised God. Then they said to him, "You see, brother, how many thousands of believers there are among the Jews, and they are all zealous for the law. ²¹They have been told about you that you teach all the Jews living among the gentiles to forsake Moses and that you tell them not to circumcise their children or observe the customs. ²²What then is to be done? They will certainly hear that you have come. ²³So do what we tell you. We have four men who are under a vow. ²⁴Join these men, go through the rite of purification with them, and pay for the shaving of their heads. Thus all will know that there is nothing in what they have been told about you but that you yourself observe and guard the law. ²⁵But as for the gentiles who have become believers, we have sent a letter with our judgment that they should abstain from what has been sacrificed to idols and from blood and from what is strangled" and from sexual immorality." ²⁶Then Paul took the men, and the next day, having purified himself, he entered the temple with them, making public the completion of the days of

s 21.7 Or *continued* t 21.9 Gk *four daughters, virgins,*
u 21.25 Other ancient authorities lack *and from what is strangled*

seem to know the disciples in Tyre prior to this trip, there is another thoughtful farewell scene on the beach as Paul leaves the area. **21:8–9** When in Caesarea, a city on the coast of the Mediterranean in modern-day Israel, the group stays in the house of Philip, who is noted as *one of the seven* (v. 8). This is likely a reference to the seven men, one of whom is named Philip, chosen in Acts 6:3–6 to serve the community by taking care of the widows in the distribution of food. In addition to being *one of the seven*, Philip is noted to have *four unmarried daughters who had the gift of prophecy*. In the Greco-Roman world, virgin women were connected to prophecy within religion. For example, the Vestal Virgins were a group of young women who cared for the temple to Vesta, the goddess of the hearth, in Rome. **21:10–14** Again, those who are close to Paul beg him not to go to Jerusalem, as they feel he will be arrested there. Paul again insists that he is to go and that he is ready to die there. Readers familiar with the Gospel narratives of Jesus's arrest and death in Jerusalem will note the similarities here.

21:17–26 Upon arrival in Jerusalem, Paul visits James, the brother of Jesus, and he instructs Paul to go through a purification ritual with a group of men there and pay for *the shaving of their heads*. Luke may be referring, somewhat confusedly, to the ritual of Nazirites being released from their vow (Num. 6:13). He wants to exemplify that, as James says, Paul *observe[s] and guard[s] the law* (v. 24). This act will require that Paul go to the temple and participate in worship there while also illustrating Paul's monetary support of the temple. See 18:18, where Luke implies Paul had taken the vow.

purification when the sacrifice would be made for each of them.

27 When the seven days were almost completed, the Jews from Asia, who had seen him in the temple, stirred up the whole crowd. They seized him, 28shouting, "Fellow Israelites," help! This is the man who is teaching everyone everywhere against our people, our law, and this place; more than that, he has actually brought Greeks into the temple and has defiled this holy place." 29For they had previously seen Trophimus the Ephesian with him in the city, and they supposed that Paul had brought him into the temple. 30Then all the city was aroused, and the people rushed together. They seized Paul and dragged him out of the temple, and immediately the doors were shut. 31While they were trying to kill him, word came to the tribune of the cohort that all Jerusalem was in an uproar. 32Immediately he took soldiers and centurions and ran down to them. When they saw the tribune and the soldiers, they stopped beating Paul. 33Then the tribune came, arrested him, and ordered him to be bound with two chains; he inquired who he was and what he had done. 34Some in the crowd shouted one thing, some another, and as he could not learn the facts because of the uproar, he ordered him to be brought into the barracks. 35When Paul" came to the steps, the violence of the mob was so great that he had to be carried by the soldiers. 36The crowd that followed kept shouting, "Away with him!"

37 Just as Paul was about to be brought into the barracks, he said to the tribune, "May I say something to you?" The tribune* replied, "Do you know Greek? 38Then you are not the Egyptian who recently stirred up a revolt and led the four thousand assassins out into the wilderness?" 39Paul replied, "I am a Jew from Tarsus in Cilicia, a citizen of an important city; I beg you, let me speak to the people." 40When he had given him permission, Paul stood on the steps and motioned to the people for silence, and when there was a great hush, he addressed them in the Hebrew' language, saying:

22 "Brothers² and fathers, listen to the defense that I now make before you."

2 When they heard him addressing them in Hebrew,ª they became even more quiet. Then he said:

3 "I am a Jew born in Tarsus in Cilicia but brought up in this city at the feet of Gamaliel, educated strictly according to our ancestral law, being zealous for God, just as all of you are today. 4I persecuted this Way up to the point of death by binding both men and women and putting them in prison, 5as the high priest and the whole council of elders can testify about me. From them I also received letters to the brothers in Damascus, and I went there in order to bind those who were there and to bring them back to Jerusalem for punishment.

6 "While I was on my way and approaching Damascus, about noon a great light from heaven suddenly shone about me. 7I fell to the ground and heard a voice saying to me, 'Saul, Saul, why are you persecuting me?' 8I answered, 'Who are you, Lord?' Then he said to me, 'I am Jesus of Nazarethᵇ whom you are

v 21.28 Gk *Men, Israelites* w 21.35 Gk *he* x 21.37 Gk *He* y 21.40 That is, *Aramaic* z 22.1 Gk *Men, brothers* a 22.2 That is, *Aramaic* b 22.8 Gk *the Nazorean*

21:27–36 Even with Paul's actions and support of the temple, he is seized and arrested under false pretenses. The charge is that Paul brought a non-Jew into the temple (Trophimus the Ephesian). In fact, non-Jews were welcome in part of the temple. Paul is beaten, arrested, chained, and taken to the barracks.

22:2 Luke notes that Paul gives his next speech in Hebrew instead of Greek, which is especially powerful because of the charges that are brought against him, that he is not following Jewish law regarding the temple. It should be noted that Hebrew is a liturgical language, while Aramaic was the language commonly spoken.

22:3 This sentence gives evidence of Paul's history and commitment to Judaism. He was born Jewish, and Luke claims he studied under a well-known rabbi, Gamaliel, and is *zealous for God*. The beginning of this speech provides Paul's pedigree and reputation, which should provide him some respect in Jerusalem.

22:6–13 Paul then recounts the story of his vision in Damascus, where he sees Jesus, who tells him to go to Damascus. This account is found in Acts 9:1–19, but there are a few differences in this later account. For example, 22:6 adds a reference to the time, which is noted as *noon*, and 22:8 adds *Nazareth* to Jesus's name. Also, this account adds a note about the intense *brightness of that light*, which expands upon the story told in chap. 9.

persecuting.' [9]Now those who were with me saw the light but did not hear the voice of the one who was speaking to me. [10]I asked, 'What am I to do, Lord?' The Lord said to me, 'Get up and go to Damascus; there you will be told everything that has been assigned to you to do.' [11]Since I could not see because of the brightness of that light, those who were with me took my hand and led me to Damascus.

12 "A certain Ananias, who was a devout man according to the law and well spoken of by all the Jews living there, [13]came to me, and standing beside me, he said, 'Brother Saul, regain your sight!' In that very hour I regained my sight and saw him. [14]Then he said, 'The God of our ancestors has chosen you to know his will, to see the Righteous One, and to hear his own voice, [15]for you will be his witness to all the world of what you have seen and heard. [16]And now why do you delay? Get up, be baptized, and have your sins washed away, calling on his name.'

17 "After I had returned to Jerusalem and while I was praying in the temple, I fell into a trance [18]and saw Jesus[c] saying to me, 'Hurry and get out of Jerusalem quickly, because they will not accept your testimony about me.' [19]And I said, 'Lord, they themselves know that in every synagogue I imprisoned and beat those who believed in you. [20]And while the blood of your witness Stephen was shed, I myself was standing by, approving and keeping the coats of those who killed him.' [21]Then he said to me, 'Go, for I will send you far away to the gentiles.'"

22 Up to this point they listened to him, but then they shouted, "Away with such a fellow from the earth! For he should not be allowed to live." [23]And while they were shouting, throwing off their cloaks, and tossing dust into the air, [24]the tribune directed that he was to be brought into the barracks and ordered him to be examined by flogging, to find out the reason for this outcry against him. [25]But when they had tied him up with straps,[d] Paul said to the centurion who was standing by, "Is it legal for you to flog a Roman person who is uncondemned?" [26]When the centurion heard that, he went to the tribune and said to him, "What are you about to do? This man is a Roman." [27]The tribune came and asked Paul,[e] "Tell me, are you a Roman?" And he said, "Yes." [28]The tribune answered, "It cost me a large sum of money to get my citizenship." Paul said, "But I was born a Roman." [29]Immediately those who were about to examine him drew back from him, and the tribune also was afraid, for he realized that Paul was a Roman and that he had bound him.

30 Since he wanted to find out what Paul[f] was being accused of by the Jews, the next day he released him and ordered the chief priests and the entire council to meet. He brought Paul down and had him stand before them.

23 While Paul was looking intently at the council he said, "Brothers,[g] up to this day I have lived my life with a clear conscience before God." [2]Then the high priest Ananias ordered those standing near him to strike him on the mouth. [3]At this Paul said to him, "God will strike you, you whitewashed wall! Are you sitting there to judge me according to the law, and yet in violation of

c 22.18 Gk *him*   d 22.25 Or *up for the lashes*   e 22.27 Gk *him*
f 22.30 Gk *he*   g 23.1 Gk *Men, brothers*

22:17–21 This part of the vision is not mentioned previously in Acts. Here Paul indicates that he was *praying in the temple* when he experienced another vision where he talks directly to Jesus. While Paul is in a *trance*, Jesus tells Paul to leave Jerusalem and that he is sending Paul to the gentiles. This statement provides Paul justification for his ministry with the gentiles.

22:22–29 Paul is tied up and about to be flogged when he declares that he is a Roman citizen (v. 25). Not only that, but Paul adds, *I was born a Roman* (v. 28). At this declaration, all attempts at harming Paul cease, as a Roman citizen was to be tried by the Romans. This surprise turn in the plot echoes the experience Paul had in Philippi when he was being beaten but then indicated he was a Roman citizen and was released (see Acts 16:37–38).

22:30 Now Paul is to be put on trial before the chief priests and the council, or the Sanhedrin, which again parallels Jesus's trial as narrated in Luke 22:54–71.

23:1 Paul speaks first, before being asked to speak, which was not considered appropriate for a person on trial. His statement, that he has a *clear conscience*, solidifies his innocence and indicates that he feels the trial is unjust.

23:2–5 This scene is dramatic and yet confusing. First, Ananias orders Paul to be hit, likely because he spoke out of turn within the formal trial. Then Paul rebukes Ananias, calling him a *whitewashed wall*,

the law you order me to be struck?" ⁴Those standing nearby said, "Do you dare to insult God's high priest?" ⁵And Paul said, "I did not realize, brothers, that he was high priest, for it is written, 'You shall not speak evil of a leader of your people.'"

6 When Paul noticed that some were Sadducees and others were Pharisees, he called out in the council, "Brothers,ᵇ I am a Pharisee, a son of Pharisees. I am on trial concerning the hope of the resurrectionⁱ of the dead." ⁷When he said this, a dissension began between the Pharisees and the Sadducees, and the assembly was divided. ⁸(The Sadducees say that there is no resurrection or angel or spirit, but the Pharisees acknowledge all three.) ⁹Then a great clamor arose, and certain scribes of the Pharisees' group stood up and contended, "We find nothing wrong with this man. What if a spirit or an angel has spoken to him?" ¹⁰When the dissension became violent, the tribune, fearing that they would tear Paul to pieces, ordered the soldiers to go down, take him by force, and bring him into the barracks.

11 That night the Lord stood near him and said, "Keep up your courage! For just as you have testified for me in Jerusalem, so you must bear witness also in Rome."

12 In the morning the Jews joined in a conspiracy and bound themselves by an oath neither to eat nor drink until they had killed Paul. ¹³There were more than forty who joined in this conspiracy. ¹⁴They went to the chief priests and elders and said, "We have strictly

bound ourselves by an oath to taste no food until we have killed Paul. ¹⁵Now then, you and the council must notify the tribune to bring him down to you, on the pretext that you want to make a more thorough examination of his case. And we are ready to do away with him before he arrives."

16 Now the son of Paul's sister heard about the ambush, so he went and gained entrance to the barracks and told Paul. ¹⁷Paul called one of the centurions and said, "Take this young man to the tribune, for he has something to report to him." ¹⁸So he took him, brought him to the tribune, and said, "The prisoner Paul called me and asked me to bring this young man to you; he has something to tell you." ¹⁹The tribune took him by the hand, drew him aside privately, and asked, "What is it that you have to report to me?" ²⁰He answered, "The Jews have agreed to ask you to bring Paul down to the council tomorrow, as though they were going to inquire more thoroughly into his case. ²¹But do not be persuaded by them, for more than forty of their men are lying in ambush for him. They have bound themselves by an oath neither to eat nor drink until they kill him. They are ready now and are waiting for your consent." ²²So the tribune dismissed the young man, ordering him, "Tell no one that you have informed me of this."

23 Then he summoned two of the centurions and said, "Get ready to leave by nine o'clock tonight for Caesarea with two hundred

b 23.6 Gk Men, brothers   i 23.6 Gk concerning hope and resurrection

which is referencing a wall with cracks that has been painted over to hide the faults. When told Ananias is the high priest, Paul indicates that he was not aware of that. However, in his previous speech, Paul mentions the high priest, saying that he knows Paul as a persecutor of the Way (22:5). Here, then, Paul's insistence that he did not know Ananias is the high priest is perplexing.

23:6–10 Paul's strategy is to appeal to the Pharisees, since he identifies himself as a Pharisee and his family as Pharisees as well. This seems to work, as his words lead to a disagreement within the council. The connection Paul makes to the resurrection of the dead likely indicates the belief in the restoration of life to the dead in an eschatological view. This view is one that the Pharisees held, but the Sadducees did not, and both sects are members of the Sanhedrin. Paul himself claims to be a Pharisee (Phil. 3:5). Thus, Paul aligns himself with the Pharisees, and this strategy seems to work, at least for the moment.

23:11 While Jesus's final days—including his trial, condemnation, and death—were in Jerusalem, Paul's only begin there. The end of Acts, and of Paul's journeys, will occur in Rome, which is also one of the major cities where the new religion of Christianity flourishes.

23:16–22 This is one of the only New Testament references we have to Paul's biological family. Here, Paul's nephew visits Paul to tell him about the plot to kill him. Paul then sends him to tell the tribune about the plot.

23:23 This is an extremely large number of soldiers to accompany just one prisoner. In total, this would be 470 people who accompany Paul to Caesarea. The distance between Jerusalem and Caesarea is about 120 kilometers, which would have taken the group about three days to travel.

soldiers, seventy horsemen, and two hundred spearmen. ²⁴Also provide mounts for Paul to ride and take him safely to Felix the governor." ²⁵He wrote a letter to this effect:

26 "Claudius Lysias to his Excellency the governor Felix, greetings. ²⁷This man was seized by the Jews and was about to be killed by them, but when I had learned that he was a Roman, I came with the guard and rescued him. ²⁸Since I wanted to know the charge for which they accused him, I had him brought to their council. ²⁹I found that he was accused concerning questions of their law but was charged with nothing deserving death or imprisonment. ³⁰When I was informed that there would be a plot against the man, I sent him to you at once, ordering his accusers also to state before you what they have against him."ʲ

31 So the soldiers, according to their instructions, took Paul and brought him during the night to Antipatris. ³²The next day they let the horsemen go on with him, while they returned to the barracks. ³³When they came to Caesarea and delivered the letter to the governor, they presented Paul also before him. ³⁴On reading the letter, he asked what province he belonged to, and when he learned that he was from Cilicia, ³⁵he said, "I will give you a hearing when your accusers arrive." Then he ordered that he be kept under guard in Herod's headquarters.ᵏ

24 Five days later the high priest Ananias came down with some elders and an attorney, a certain Tertullus, and they reported their case against Paul to the governor. ²When Paulˡ had been summoned, Tertullus began to accuse him, saying:

"Because of you, most excellent Felix, we have long enjoyed peace, and reforms have been made for this people because of your foresight. ³In every way and everywhere we welcome this with utmost gratitude. ⁴But, to detain you no further, I beg you to hear us briefly with your customary graciousness. ⁵We have, in fact, found this man a pestilent fellow, an agitator among all the Jews throughout the world, and a ringleader of the sect of the Nazarenes.ᵐ ⁶He even tried to profane the temple, so we seized him.ⁿ ⁸By examining him yourself you will be able to learn from him concerning everything of which we accuse him."

9 The Jews also joined in the charge by asserting that all this was true.

10 When the governor motioned to him to speak, Paul replied:

"I cheerfully make my defense, knowing that for many years you have been a judge over this people. ¹¹As you can find out, it is not more than twelve days since I went up to worship in Jerusalem. ¹²They did not find me disputing with anyone in the temple or stirring up a crowd either in the synagogues or throughout the city. ¹³Neither can they prove to you the charge that they now bring against me. ¹⁴But this I admit to you, that according to the Way, which they call a sect, I worship the God of our ancestors, believing everything laid down according to the law or written in the prophets. ¹⁵I have a hope in God—a hope that they themselves also accept—that there will be a resurrection of bothᵒ the righteous and the unrighteous. ¹⁶Therefore I do my best

---

ʲ 23.30 Other ancient authorities add *Farewell* ᵏ 23.35 Gk *praetorium* ˡ 24.2 Gk *he* ᵐ 24.5 Gk *Nazoreans* ⁿ 24.6 Other ancient authorities add *and we would have judged him according to our law.* ⁷*But the chief captain Lysias came and with great violence took him out of our hands,* ⁸*commanding his accusers to come before you.* ᵒ 24.15 Other ancient authorities read *of the dead, both of*

23:24 *Felix* refers to Marcus Antonius Felix, who was the governor of Judea from about 52 or 53 to 60 CE. The Jewish historian Josephus mentions Felix several times in *Antiquities of the Jews*, where he names Felix as a wicked leader who treated Jews unfairly.

24:1–2 *Tertullus* is a Greek name, and he may have been a Hellenistic Jew or simply hired to represent some Jews. **24:2–8** The speech by Tertullus begins with effusive praise and positive comments toward Felix. Then he attacks Paul but does not name specific charges other than being an *agitator* (v. 5) and that Paul *tried to profane the temple* (v. 6). He also never specifically names Paul within his speech. The charge against Paul concerning him being an agitator would be more incriminating within a Roman court than the charge about profaning the temple.

24:10–21 Paul begins his speech *cheerfully* (Gk. "euthumōs") and denies all the charges that Tertullus brought against him. Paul confesses (Gk. "homologō") to worshiping *the God of our ancestors*, by which he means the Jewish God (v. 14). He then states that he believes to be under trial because of his belief in the *resurrection of the dead* (v. 21). In comparison to the speech by Tertullus, Paul appears as a more practiced speaker. **24:16** The phrase *clear conscience* is repeated here from 23:1, indicating Paul's innocence.

always to have a clear conscience toward God and all people. ¹⁷Now after some years I came to bring alms to my people and to offer sacrifices. ¹⁸While I was doing this, they found me in the temple completing the rite of purification, without any crowd or disturbance. ¹⁹But there were some Jews from Asia—they ought to be here before you to make an accusation, if they have anything against me. ²⁰Or let these men here tell what crime they had found when I stood before the council, ²¹unless it was this one sentence that I called out while standing before them, 'It is about the resurrection of the dead that I am on trial before you today.'"

22 But Felix, who was rather well informed about the Way, adjourned the hearing with the comment, "When Lysias the tribune comes down, I will decide your case." ²³Then he ordered the centurion to keep him in custody but to let him have some liberty and not to prevent any of his friends from taking care of his needs.

24 Some days later when Felix came with his wife Drusilla, who was Jewish, he sent for Paul and heard him speak concerning faith in Christ Jesus. ²⁵And as he discussed justice, self-control, and the coming judgment, Felix became frightened and said, "Go away for the present; when I have an opportunity, I will send for you." ²⁶At the same time he hoped that money would be given him by Paul, and for that reason he used to send for him very often and converse with him.

27 After two years had passed, Felix was

succeeded by Porcius Festus, and since he wanted to grant the Jews a favor, Felix left Paul in prison.

25 Three days after Festus had arrived in the province, he went up from Caesarea to Jerusalem, ²where the chief priests and the leaders of the Jews gave him a report against Paul. They appealed to him ³and requested, as a favor to them against Paul,ᵖ to have him transferred to Jerusalem. They were, in fact, planning an ambush to kill him along the way. ⁴Festus replied that Paul was being kept at Caesarea and that he himself intended to go there shortly. ⁵"So," he said, "let those of you who have the authority come down with me, and if there is anything wrong about the man, let them accuse him."

6 After he had stayed among them not more than eight or ten days, he went down to Caesarea; the next day he took his seat on the tribunal and ordered Paul to be brought. ⁷When he arrived, the Jews who had gone down from Jerusalem surrounded him, bringing many serious charges against him, which they could not prove. ⁸Paul said in his defense, "I have in no way committed an offense against the law of the Jews or against the temple or against the emperor." ⁹But Festus, wishing to do the Jews a favor, asked Paul, "Do you wish to go up to Jerusalem and be tried there before me on these charges?" ¹⁰Paul said, "I am standing

p 25.3 Gk *him*

24:22 Felix dramatically stops the trial here, which adds suspense to the narrative.
24:23 Paul is under custody but with an amount of freedom, especially more than would typically be granted to a prisoner. This indicates that Felix does not see the charges as serious or Paul as a dangerous criminal.
24:24 Felix's wife Drusilla is named here and identified as Jewish. Drusilla was also the daughter of Herod Agrippa I.
24:26 Felix hoping for a bribe from Paul is another way for the author to cast Felix in a negative light.
24:27 In this one verse, two years pass while Paul is in prison. This adds suspense to the narrative and also shocks the reader, as this is a significant amount of time. The two years mentioned here could parallel the two years Paul remains under house arrest in Rome as well (28:30).
25:1–7 This ambush, planned by a group of Jews who are against Paul, is cleverly avoided by Festus, who refuses to move Paul back to Jerusalem. Instead, those who want to accuse Paul must travel as well to Caesarea. 25:1 Festus was the next procurator of Judea, following Felix, and likely was in power from 59 to 62 CE.
25:8–12 This set of verses includes a dialogue between Paul and Festus. Paul begins his defense and states that he has not acted against Jews or against the emperor. Festus only replies that he could go to Jerusalem to be judged there (v. 9). Paul ultimately appeals to the emperor, as he is aware that the Jewish tribunal was angry at him. This statement also implies Paul's Roman citizenship, although not directly mentioned here.

before the emperor's tribunal; this is where I should be tried. I have done no wrong to the Jews, as you very well know. ¹¹Now if I am in the wrong and have committed something for which I deserve to die, I am not trying to escape death, but if there is nothing to their charges against me, no one can turn me over to them. I appeal to the emperor." ¹²Then Festus, after he had conferred with his council, replied, "You have appealed to the emperor; to the emperor you will go."

13 After several days had passed, King Agrippa and Bernice arrived at Caesarea to welcome Festus. ¹⁴Since they were staying there several days, Festus laid Paul's case before the king, saying, "There is a man here who was left in prison by Felix. ¹⁵When I was in Jerusalem, the chief priests and the elders of the Jews informed me about him and asked for a sentence against him. ¹⁶I told them that it was not the custom of the Romans to hand over anyone before the accused had met the accusers face to face and had been given an opportunity to make a defense against the charge. ¹⁷So when they met here, I lost no time but on the next day took my seat on the tribunal and ordered the man to be brought. ¹⁸When the accusers stood up, they did not charge him with any of the crimes*q* that I was expecting. ¹⁹Instead, they had certain points of disagreement with him about their own religion and about a certain Jesus, who had died but whom Paul asserted to be alive. ²⁰Since I was at a loss how to investigate these questions, I asked whether he wished to go to Jerusalem and be tried there on these charges.*r* ²¹But when Paul had appealed to be kept in custody for the decision of his Imperial Majesty, I ordered him to be held until I could send him to the emperor." ²²Agrippa said to Festus, "I would like to hear the man myself." "Tomorrow," he said, "you will hear him."

23 So on the next day Agrippa and Bernice came with great pomp, and they entered the audience hall with the military tribunes and the prominent men of the city. Then Festus gave the order and Paul was brought in. ²⁴And Festus said, "King Agrippa and all here present with us, you see this man about whom the whole Jewish community petitioned me, both in Jerusalem and here, shouting that he ought not to live any longer. ²⁵But I found that he had done nothing deserving death, and when he appealed to his Imperial Majesty, I decided to send him. ²⁶But I have nothing definite to write to our sovereign about him. Therefore I have brought him before all of you, and especially before you, King Agrippa, so that, after we have examined him, I may have something to write, ²⁷for it seems to me unreasonable to send a prisoner without indicating the charges against him."

26 Agrippa said to Paul, "You have permission to speak for yourself." Then Paul stretched out his hand and began to defend himself:

2 "I consider myself fortunate that it is before you, King Agrippa, I am to make my

q 25.18 Other ancient authorities read *with the crime* or *with anything*   r 25.20 Gk *on them*

25:13 Agrippa and Bernice were well known in the first century. Bernice is the sister of Drusilla, mentioned previously in 24:24, and thus is also Agrippa's sister, named here. The family is Jewish and thus interested in Paul's situation. Agrippa and Bernice are named together in Acts, and the earliest readers might have heard rumors that the two were involved in an incestuous relationship, which is suggested by the Jewish historian Josephus.

25:18–21 Festus reports to Agrippa the reason that Paul is there awaiting trial. He notes that when the Jewish accusers spoke, they mentioned Jesus *who had died but whom Paul asserted to be alive* (v. 19). This connects Paul's view of the resurrection directly to Jesus.

25:23 The imagery here is tantalizing; one imagines Agrippa and Bernice entering with magnificence and a crowd of military personnel. This is a big affair, and Luke describes it with flourish.

25:24–27 In this speech, Festus speaks directly about Paul's innocence, indicating twice that he has *nothing definite to write* concerning the charges against Paul. One part of this speech is especially exaggerated, and that is when Festus says that the *whole Jewish community* petitioned him about Paul. This is, according the prior events narrated in Acts, false, as many Jews supported Paul.

26:1 Paul again acts as his own defender. The phrase *stretched out his hand* is also used to describe Jesus when he heals a man with leprosy (Luke 5:13). "Defend" here is "apologeomai" in the Greek, which is connected to an English word used for a defense, an apology.

26:2–3 Agrippa was known to be Jewish, and here the author is reminding the reader of this fact, subtly, when Paul notes that he is *familiar with all the customs and controversies of the Jews.*

defense today against all the accusations of the Jews, ³because you are especially familiar with all the customs and controversies of the Jews; therefore I beg of you to listen to me patiently.

4 "All the Jews know my way of life from my youth, a life spent from the beginning among my own people and in Jerusalem. ⁵They have known for a long time, if they are willing to testify, that I have belonged to the strictest sect of our religion and lived as a Pharisee. ⁶And now I stand here on trial on account of my hope in the promise made by God to our ancestors, ⁷a promise that our twelve tribes hope to attain, as they earnestly worship day and night. It is for this hope, Your Excellency,ˢ that I am accused by Jews! ⁸Why is it thought incredible by any of you that God raises the dead?

9 "Indeed, I myself was convinced that I ought to do many things against the name of Jesus of Nazareth.ᵗ ¹⁰And that is what I did in Jerusalem; with authority received from the chief priests, I not only locked up many of the saints in prison, but I also cast my vote against them when they were being condemned to death. ¹¹By punishing them often in all the synagogues I tried to force them to blaspheme, and since I was so furiously enraged at them, I pursued them even to foreign cities.

12 "With this in mind, I was traveling to Damascus with the authority and commission of the chief priests, ¹³when at midday along the road, Your Excellency,ᵘ I saw a light from heaven, brighter than the sun, shining around me and my companions. ¹⁴When we had all fallen to the ground, I heard a voice saying to me in the Hebrewᵛ language, 'Saul, Saul, why are you persecuting me? It hurts you to kick

against the goads.' ¹⁵I asked, 'Who are you, Lord?' The Lord answered, 'I am Jesus whom you are persecuting. ¹⁶But get up and stand on your feet, for I have appeared to you for this purpose, to appoint you to serve and testify to the things in which you have seen meʷ and to those in which I will appear to you. ¹⁷I will rescue you from your people and from the gentiles—to whom I am sending you ¹⁸to open their eyes so that they may turn from darkness to light and from the power of Satan to God, so that they may receive forgiveness of sins and a place among those who are sanctified by faith in me.'

19 "After that, King Agrippa, I was not disobedient to the heavenly vision ²⁰but declared first to those in Damascus, then in Jerusalem and throughout the countryside of Judea, and also to the gentiles, that they should repent and turn to God and do deeds consistent with repentance. ²¹For this reason the Jews seized me in the temple and tried to kill me. ²²To this day I have had help from God, and so I stand here, testifying to both small and great, saying nothing but what the prophets and Moses said would take place: ²³that the Messiahˣ must suffer and that, by being the first to rise from the dead, he would proclaim light both to our people and to the gentiles."

24 While he was making this defense, Festus exclaimed, "You are out of your mind, Paul! Too much learning is driving you insane!" ²⁵But Paul said, "I am not out of my mind, most excellent Festus, but I am speaking the sober truth. ²⁶Indeed, the king knows

s 26.7 Gk *O King* t 26.9 Gk *the Nazorean* u 26.13 Gk *O King*
v 26.14 That is, *Aramaic* w 26.16 Other ancient authorities
read *the things that you have seen* x 26.23 Or *the Christ*

26:4–8 Paul reminds his listeners of his own history in Judaism and his deep commitment to Pharisaic ideas. Pharisees were known to believe in the resurrection of the dead, and here Paul is connecting that idea to Jesus's resurrection. By doing so, Paul connects his belief in Jesus and his resurrection to the beliefs held within Judaism.

26:9–11 This recounting of events should sound familiar to readers of Acts, as the actions of Paul against Jesus followers were first mentioned in 8:1–3 and 9:1–2. What is new in this section is that Paul says that he cast a vote (Gk. "psēphon," or pebble) against them (v. 10).

26:12–18 This is another version of Paul's vision on the road to Damascus. Similar to the account in 22:6–13, the light is more intense than the original account in Acts 9. Here, the light is *brighter than the sun*, which literally expands the emphasis of the scene, as the light suggests divine presence.

26:24–25 *Out of . . . mind* is a phrase translated from one Greek word, "mainē," which can mean mad or crazy. When Paul responds, he says he is not out of his mind but instead is speaking true and rational words. The Greek word translated as *sober* here is "sōphrosunē," which indicates a soundness of mind or even self-control.

26:24–29 After Paul asks him whether he believes in the prophets, King Agrippa gives a witty remark, asking Paul if he is trying to convince him to become a Christian. Paul admits his desire that

about these things, and to him I speak freely, for I am certain that none of these things has escaped his notice, for this was not done in a corner. [27]King Agrippa, do you believe the prophets? I know that you believe." [28]Agrippa said to Paul, "Are you so quickly persuading me to become a Christian?" [29]Paul replied, "Whether quickly or not, I pray to God that not only you but also all who are listening to me today might become such as I am—except for these chains."

30 Then the king got up and with him the governor and Bernice and those who had been seated with them, [31]and as they were leaving they said to one another, "This man is doing nothing to deserve death or imprisonment." [32]Agrippa said to Festus, "This man could have been set free if he had not appealed to the emperor."

27 When it was decided that we were to sail for Italy, they transferred Paul and some other prisoners to a centurion of the Augustan Cohort, named Julius. [2]Embarking on a ship of Adramyttium that was about to set sail to the ports along the coast of Asia, we put to sea, accompanied by Aristarchus, a Macedonian from Thessalonica. [3]The next day we put in at Sidon, and Julius treated Paul kindly and allowed him to go to his friends to be cared for. [4]Putting out to sea from there, we sailed under the lee of Cyprus, because the winds were against us. [5]After we had sailed across the sea that is off Cilicia and Pamphylia, we came to Myra in Lycia. [6]There the centurion found an Alexandrian ship bound for Italy and put us on board. [7]We sailed slowly for a number of days and arrived with difficulty off Cnidus, and as the wind was against us, we sailed under the lee of Crete off Salmone. [8]Sailing past it with difficulty, we came to a place called Fair Havens, near the city of Lasea.

9 Since much time had been lost and sailing was now dangerous, because even the Fast had already gone by, Paul advised them, [10]saying, "Men, I can see that the voyage will be with danger and much heavy loss, not only of the cargo and the ship, but also of our lives." [11]But the centurion paid more attention to the pilot and to the owner of the ship than to what Paul said. [12]Since the harbor was not suitable for spending the winter, the majority was in favor of putting to sea from there on the chance that somehow they could reach Phoenix, where they could spend the winter. It was a harbor of Crete, facing southwest and northwest.

13 When a moderate south wind began to blow, they thought they could achieve their purpose; so they weighed anchor and began to sail past Crete, close to the shore. [14]But soon a violent wind, called the northeaster, rushed down from Crete.[y] [15]Since the ship was caught and could not be turned head-on into the wind, we gave way to it and were driven. [16]By running under the lee of a small island called Cauda[z] we were scarcely able to get the ship's boat under control. [17]After hoisting it up they took measures to undergird the ship; then, fearing that they would run on the

y 27.14 Gk *it*   z 27.16 Other ancient authorities read *Clauda*

all who are listening to me today might become such as I am but then adds the phrase except for these chains. Even pictured as a prisoner, Paul has not forgotten his goal, which is to convince others of the message of Jesus.

26:32 Because Paul appealed to the emperor, Festus and Agrippa must continue the trial. Ultimately, this is Paul's fate, to go to Rome. The plot must continue, and Paul's journey must end in Rome.

27:1 This begins the final section of the "we passages" in Acts, which narrates a long and tumultuous journey by ship with many stops and even a shipwreck along the way. The transition from the end of chap. 26, which narrates the trial before Agrippa, is abrupt, as the "we passages" in Acts often are.

27:2 Adramyttium was a city in Asia Minor, what is now called Turkey (or Türkiye). Paul's companion who is named here, Aristarchus, has been mentioned previously in Acts 19:29 and 20:4.

27:3 In each stop along his journey, Paul has acquaintances or friends who are able to care for him. This short addition to the narrative illustrates that Paul's reputation has preceded him, and he has followers in many cities, even ones he has not yet visited.

27:7-9 The trip by ship was a difficult one, and this adds to the suspense of the journey. In ancient Greek novels, protagonists are often forced to endure a difficult journey by sea before they arrive at their intended destination. The narrative in Acts 27:1–28:10 includes recognizable tropes (such as bad weather during a journey, a shipwreck, and a brush with death) from Greek novels that add to the suspense and drama of the scene.

Syrtis, they lowered the sea anchor and so were driven. [18]We were being pounded by the storm so violently that on the next day they began to throw the cargo overboard, [19]and on the third day with their own hands they threw the ship's tackle overboard. [20]When neither sun nor stars appeared for many days and no small tempest raged, all hope of our being saved was at last abandoned.

[21] Since they had been without food for a long time, Paul then stood up among them and said, "Men, you should have listened to me and not have set sail from Crete and thereby avoided this damage and loss. [22]I urge you now to keep up your courage, for there will be no loss of life among you, but only of the ship. [23]For last night there stood by me an angel of the God to whom I belong and whom I worship, [24]and he said, 'Do not be afraid, Paul; you must stand before the emperor, and, indeed, God has granted safety to all those who are sailing with you.' [25]So keep up your courage, men, for I have faith in God that it will be exactly as I have been told. [26]But we will have to run aground on some island."

[27] When the fourteenth night had come, as we were drifting across the Adriatic Sea, about midnight the sailors suspected that they were nearing land. [28]So they took soundings and found twenty fathoms; a little farther on they took soundings again and found fifteen fathoms. [29]Fearing that we might run on the rocks, they let down four anchors from the stern and prayed for day to come. [30]But when the sailors tried to escape from the ship and had lowered the boat into the sea on the pretext of putting out anchors from the bow, [31]Paul said to the centurion and the soldiers, "Unless these men stay in the ship, you cannot be saved." [32]Then the soldiers cut away the ropes of the boat and set it adrift.

[33] Just before daybreak, Paul urged all of them to take some food, saying, "Today is the fourteenth day that you have been in suspense and remaining without food, having eaten nothing. [34]Therefore I urge you to take some food, for it will help you survive, for none of you will lose a hair from your heads." [35]After he had said this, he took bread, and giving thanks to God in the presence of all, he broke it and began to eat. [36]Then all of them were encouraged and took food for themselves. [37](We were in all two hundred seventy-six[a] persons in the ship.) [38]After they had satisfied their hunger, they lightened the ship by throwing the wheat into the sea.

[39] In the morning they did not recognize the land, but they noticed a bay with a beach on which they planned to run the ship ashore, if they could. [40]So they cast off the anchors and left them in the sea. At the same time they loosened the ropes that tied the steering-oars; then hoisting the foresail to the wind, they made for the beach. [41]But striking a reef,[b] they ran the ship aground; the bow stuck and remained immovable, but the stern was being broken up by the force of the waves. [42]The soldiers' plan was to kill the prisoners, so that none might swim away and escape; [43]but the centurion, wishing to save Paul, kept them from carrying out their plan. He ordered those who could swim to jump overboard first and make for the land [44]and the rest to follow, some on planks and others on pieces of the ship. And so it was that all were brought safely to land.

28 After we had reached safety, we then learned that the island was called Malta. [2]The local people showed us unusual

a 27.37 Other ancient authorities read about *seventy-six*
b 27.41 Gk *place of two seas*

27:21–26 Paul speaks to those on the ship and prophesies that *there will be no loss of life among you* but foresees that the ship will be lost. He says that an angel told him this the previous night. In this way, Paul is still in charge of the journey and the ship, even as the storm seems to be overpowering them. Additionally, Paul is a recipient of a vision from an angel, just as Elizabeth and Mary were in the Gospel of Luke.

27:35 This verse reminds us of the Last Supper, where Jesus also broke bread and gave thanks. We are nearing the end of Paul's journey, and the parallels to Jesus's final days are clear. See Luke 22:19.

27:39–44 The shipwreck is narrated slowly and carefully here, even though readers know it is coming because of Paul's prediction. Ultimately, the ship hits a reef, and the boat is broken. While the soldiers want to kill the prisoners (v. 42), Paul prophesied that no one would be injured, and this is fulfilled, as the centurion stops the killing of the prisoners. Everyone on the boat survives (v. 44).

28:1–6 The group lands on the island of Malta, which is an island in the Mediterranean Sea, about fifty miles south of Sicily. While there, Paul has yet another dangerous encounter, this time with a snake.

kindness. Since it had begun to rain and was cold, they kindled a fire and welcomed all of us around it. ³Paul had gathered a bundle of brushwood and was putting it on the fire when a viper, driven out by the heat, fastened itself on his hand. ⁴When the local people saw the creature hanging from his hand, they said to one another, "This man must be a murderer; though he has escaped from the sea, Justice has not allowed him to live." ⁵He, however, shook off the creature into the fire and suffered no harm. ⁶They were expecting him to swell up or drop dead, but after they had waited a long time and saw that nothing unusual had happened to him, they changed their minds and began to say that he was a god.

7 Now in the vicinity of that place were lands belonging to the leading man of the island, named Publius, who received us and entertained us hospitably for three days. ⁸It so happened that the father of Publius lay sick in bed with fever and dysentery. Paul visited him and cured him by praying and putting his hands on him. ⁹After this happened, the rest of the people on the island who had diseases also came and were cured. ¹⁰They bestowed many honors on us, and when we were about to sail, they put on board all the provisions we needed.

11 Three months later we set sail on a ship that had wintered at the island, an Alexandrian ship with the Twin Brothers as its figurehead. ¹²We put in at Syracuse and stayed there for three days; ¹³then we weighed anchor and came to Rhegium. After one day there a south wind sprang up, and on the second day we came to Puteoli. ¹⁴There we found brothers

and sisters and were invited to stay with them for seven days. And so we came to Rome. ¹⁵The brothers and sisters from there, when they heard of us, came as far as the Forum of Appius and Three Taverns to meet us. On seeing them, Paul thanked God and took courage.

16 When we came into Rome, Paul was allowed to live by himself, with the soldier who was guarding him.

17 Three days later he called together the local leaders of the Jews. When they had assembled, he said to them, "Brothers,ᶜ though I had done nothing against our people or the customs of our ancestors, yet I was arrested in Jerusalem and handed over to the Romans. ¹⁸When they had examined me, the Romansᵈ wanted to release me because there was no reason for the death penalty in my case. ¹⁹But when the Jews objected, I was compelled to appeal to the emperor—even though I had no charge to bring against my people. ²⁰For this reason therefore I asked to see you and speak with you, since it is for the sake of the hope of Israel that I am bound with this chain." ²¹They replied, "We have received no letters from Judea about you, and none of the brothers coming here has reported or spoken anything evil about you. ²²But we would like to hear from you what you think, for with regard to this sect we know that everywhere it is spoken against."

23 After they had set a day to meet with him, they came to him at his lodgings in great numbers. From morning until evening he explained the matter to them, testifying to the kingdom of God and trying to convince them

c 28.17 Gk Men, brothers   d 28.18 Gk they

The local people in Malta, after watching Paul survive the snakebite, believe that he is a god, which is not challenged by Paul or the author of the text, as it was previously in Acts (14:15).

28:7–10 Paul heals the father of Publius, the *leading man of the island*, and this leads to a number of healings of those on the island. These verses are quite similar to Jesus's healing of Peter's mother-in-law in Luke 4:38–40, which also led to a number of other healings.

28:11 Here is another jump in the narrative, as the reader is informed that Paul and the group stayed on Malta for three months before continuing their trip to Rome. Perhaps this indicates that Paul had a large amount of freedom for a prisoner going to trial.

28:14 Finally, Paul arrives in Rome, where many people who had heard of him and his message came to meet him.

28:16 Paul seems to be under house arrest, meaning he is not in a prison or jail but instead lives in a house with just one soldier who is guarding him. This could indicate that he was not thought to be a flight risk or also could be the privilege allowed to him as a Roman citizen.

28:17–24 Typical of the previous journeys in Acts, Paul gathers the Jewish community together to talk to them first about his message. The text notes that Jews come to hear Paul *in great numbers* (v. 23) and that some believed, while others did not (v. 24).

about Jesus both from the law of Moses and from the prophets. [24]Some were convinced by what he had said, while others refused to believe. [25]So they disagreed with each other, and as they were leaving Paul made one further statement: "The Holy Spirit was right in saying to your ancestors through the prophet Isaiah,
[26] 'Go to this people and say,
You will indeed listen but never understand,
and you will indeed look but never perceive.
[27] For this people's heart has grown dull,
and their ears are hard of hearing,
and they have shut their eyes;
otherwise they might look with their eyes

and listen with their ears
and understand with their heart and turn—
and I would heal them.'
[28]"Let it be known to you, then, that this salvation of God has been sent to the gentiles; they will listen."[e]

30 He lived there two whole years at his own expense[f] and welcomed all who came to him, [31]proclaiming the kingdom of God and teaching about the Lord Jesus Christ with all boldness and without hindrance.

e 28.28 Other ancient authorities add 28.29, *And when he had said these words, the Jews departed, arguing vigorously among themselves*   f 28.30 Or *in his own rented dwelling*

28:26–27 Paul quotes the prophet Isaiah (6:9-10), which sounds rather harsh in this position in the narrative. The author of Acts notes that when Paul quotes this passage, the group of Jews depart (v. 25).

28:30–31 Acts ends with a portrait of Paul living alone, likely still under house arrest, and continuing to preach the message of Jesus. Traditionally, it is believed that Paul died in Rome and was killed by the government as a martyr through beheading. The author of Acts, though he likely knew this story, chooses not to include it. Instead, the narrative of Acts ends with the final phrase *boldness and without hindrance*. We are left with an image of Paul continuing to share the message with all who come to hear.

THE LETTER OF PAUL TO THE ROMANS

"Romans" gains its title from its original recipients: Christ followers who assembled in the city of Rome. Paul's audience appears to be composed of Jews and gentiles. There were a significant number of women present in this audience, and many of these women were leaders. The audience also consisted of enslaved persons and immigrants to Rome, and some would have been enslaved foreign women. When reading Romans, it is crucial to remember this audience: Paul did not write into a void. These men and women listened, reacted, and responded to what Paul had to say about faith in God and living like Jesus.

The study notes for Romans in this study Bible stress that Paul's gospel, theology, and ethics are *Paul's* ideas—not universal truths. People disagreed with Paul. With Romans, Paul has not yet met most of his audience. Since he is introducing himself, the conversation is more one-sided compared to other letters. Interpreters have tended to assume Paul professes a theology to which there was no dissent among the majority of the letter's first audiences. Thus, Paul was one thinker among many faithful leaders who were discussing different ideas as they worked together to figure out what it meant to follow Christ. The people in Rome's Christ assembly were already faithful followers who participated in these deliberations. They brought their own beliefs, experiences, and practices into conversation with what they heard in Paul's letter.

Authorship, Date, and Composition
Paul, self-proclaimed "apostle to the gentiles," is the undisputed author of Romans. As an apostle, meaning one who is sent out or commissioned, Paul traveled to different regions of the Roman Empire to proclaim his gospel (generally meaning a good announcement). Acts 20:2–3 alludes to Paul writing to Rome while he was staying in Corinth. Although Romans appears as the first of Paul's letters in the New Testament, Romans is chronologically the last of the authentic letters that Paul wrote, likely around 55–59 CE.

Major Issues and Themes
Romans takes the form of a theological argument. The letter lays out God's plan for gentiles and its implications.

Jews first, then gentiles: Paul's audience is gentiles (i.e., people who are not Jewish), so Paul's gospel specifically concerns God's plan to justify and save gentiles through the actions of Jesus Christ. For Paul, Jesus's faithful death makes a path for gentiles to get right with God, since they are incapable of keeping Jewish law. Paul's comments about "the law" in Romans specifically refer to gentiles' inherent incapacity to be made just by it. The law remains fundamental to Jews in Paul's gospel: there is nothing wrong with the law for Jews. Indeed, the law is the sign of God's faithfulness and covenant to Jews. When Paul says God justifies Jew first, then Greek (1:16c), he refers to the temporal nature of God's plan, which first justified the Jews from God's covenant with Abraham and now justifies gentiles ("Greeks") through Jesus's death. God makes these two paths for justification so that all God's children—Jews and gentiles—will be saved when God comes to judge the world.

Apocalyptic orientation: Paul argues his theology with a tone of urgency and anticipation because he believes that Jesus as the Christ fulfills messianic expectations in Jewish apocalyptic texts (see **"Jewish Messianic Ideas," p. 1783**). Christ's coming signals that the end of the world—that is, God's judgment of all the earth, followed by a new world ruled by God—has arrived. Jesus's death shifts expectations by enacting a short "delay" so gentiles can be made just before God's judgment. Paul's theology and Christology derive from these apocalyptic conditions (see **"Paul's Apocalyptic Imagination," p. 2031**). Paul believes God's reign will begin at some point during his and his audience's lifetimes. Readers of Romans should keep Paul's apocalyptic expectations in mind: his letter has a specific audience and goal for gentiles in the mid-first century CE. While Christians have built and can continue to build theologies from their interpretations of Paul's ideas, these historical and contemporary interpretations are their own responses to Paul's words—much like the responses we can imagine were created by people in his earliest audiences.

Self-control and gentile depravity: Paul's ideas are rooted in his interpretations of Jewish Scriptures and theologies. Like all first-century Jews, Paul lived in the Roman Empire, and a Roman worldview informs Paul's gospel. Paul stresses the Roman virtue of self-control: good Romans (men especially) controlled their bodies and desires with respect to eating, drinking, and sexuality. Mastery of one's self demonstrated the ability to govern and rule others and sustained Roman peace. Throughout Romans, Paul stresses how his gospel not only leads gentiles to faith in God but also allows them to control their bodies and desires as befits God's peaceful reign—just as for Jews, the Torah enables them to embody this ideal of self-control. Paul is not alone among Jewish writers who argue that Jewish law satisfies and even exceeds the moral demands of Roman virtue. Philo of Alexandria is one example. Paul is concerned with self-control for gentiles because, without proper faith in God, gentiles have lost control over their bodies and desires. Paul describes the depraved situation of gentiles in 1:18–32, and he alludes back to this situation throughout the letter, especially when he discusses the importance of self-control and moral living for gentiles who follow Christ. Although Paul writes to gentiles as those who are not Jewish, the Greek term translated as "gentiles" generally meant "nations." Romans frequently used this term to describe the foreign nations that Rome conquered.

Theocentrism: Romans is theocentric. This means *God* is the central focus for Paul and Paul's gospel. This is perhaps the most important thing to remember when reading Romans, since its placement in the New Testament often leads readers to assume that Jesus Christ is the central point of Paul's gospel. In Romans and throughout Paul's letters, faith is *always directed to God.* When Paul emphasizes the significance of Jesus as the Christ, it is because of Jesus's faith in God, which allows God to take action to justify gentiles (see **"Faith of Jesus Christ," p. 1938**). Jesus's faith in God provides a path and an example for gentiles to also have faith—in God. In Romans, it is almost always God who takes action, and it is God whom all should have faith in and whose glory, peace, and salvation Paul praises.

Reading Guide

Reading Romans can feel especially challenging—even for seasoned readers. Paul's argument is lengthy and interconnected, making the letter difficult to break up into shorter passages. Readers are encouraged to read the letter twice: first, reading start to finish without interruption; then, rereading it slowly and engaging with the notes.

Along with the letter's opening (1:1–17) and closing (15:22–16:27), there are three major arguments in Romans, though the first major argument can be broken into two sections:

- First argument, 1:18–8:39: Paul's gospel (1:18–5:11) and its implications for gentiles in Christ (5:12–8:39).
- Second argument, 9:1–11:36: Explaining to gentiles how Jews fit into God's bigger plan and warning against gentile arrogance.
- Third argument, 12:1–15:13: How gentiles live ethically in Christ while they wait for God's coming.

Jimmy Hoke

1 Paul, a servant of Christ Jesus, called to be an apostle, set apart for the gospel of God, ²which he promised beforehand through his prophets in the holy scriptures, ³the gospel concerning his Son, who was descended from David according to the flesh ⁴and was declared to be Son of God with power according to the spirit[a] of holiness by resurrection from the dead, Jesus Christ our Lord, ⁵through whom we have received grace and apostleship to bring about the obedience of

a 1.4 Or *Spirit*

1:1–17 Opening and thesis. Following standard formulae for ancient letters, Paul greets the letter's audience, connects with them, and introduces the letter's major themes. **1:1** *Servant.* A term used for enslaved persons. Paul uses the term metaphorically (see Rom. 6:15–23; Phil. 1:1; 1 Cor. 7:21–24; Gal. 4:21–5:1; Philemon). *Gospel of God.* Paul proclaims God's gospel, emphasizing that Romans is theocentric (see **"Introduction to Romans," pp. 1932–33**). **1:3** *Descended from David*—King David, one of the most respected kings of ancient Israel (see 1–2 Samuel). Paul and others believed the Messiah / Christ would be David's descendant. **1:5** *We have received.* Paul's audience can be considered apostles as much as

faith among all the gentiles for the sake of his name, ⁶including you who are called to belong to Jesus Christ,

7 To all God's beloved in Rome, who are called to be saints:

Grace to you and peace from God our Father and the Lord Jesus Christ.

8 First, I thank my God through Jesus Christ for all of you, because your faith is proclaimed throughout the world. ⁹For God, whom I serve with my spirit by announcing the gospel*b* of his Son, is my witness that without ceasing I remember you always in my prayers, ¹⁰asking that by God's will I may somehow at last succeed in coming to you. ¹¹For I long to see you so that I may share with you some spiritual gift so that you may be strengthened—¹²or rather so that we may be mutually encouraged by each other's faith, both yours and mine. ¹³I do not want you to be unaware, brothers and sisters, that I have often intended to come to you (but thus far have been prevented), in order that I may reap some harvest among you, as I have among the rest of the gentiles. ¹⁴I am obligated both to Greeks and to barbarians, both to the wise and to the foolish, ¹⁵hence my eagerness to proclaim the gospel to you also who are in Rome.

16 For I am not ashamed of the gospel; it is God's saving power for everyone who believes,*c* for the Jew first and also for the Greek. ¹⁷For in it the righteousness of God is revealed through faith for faith, as it is written, "The one who is righteous will live by faith."*d*

18 For the wrath of God is revealed from heaven against all ungodliness and injustice of those who by their injustice suppress the truth. ¹⁹For what can be known about God is plain to them, because God has made it plain to them. ²⁰Ever since the creation of the world God's eternal power and divine nature, invisible though they are, have been seen and understood through the things God has made. So they are without excuse, ²¹for though they knew God, they did not honor him as God or give thanks to him, but they became futile in their thinking, and their senseless hearts were darkened. ²²Claiming to be wise, they became fools, ²³and they exchanged the glory of the immortal God for images resembling a mortal human or birds or four-footed animals or reptiles.

24 Therefore God gave them over in the desires of their hearts to impurity, to the dishonoring of their bodies among themselves. ²⁵They exchanged the truth about God for a lie and worshiped and served the creature rather than the Creator, who is blessed forever! Amen.

26 For this reason God gave them over to dishonorable passions. Their females exchanged natural intercourse*e* for unnatural,

b 1.9 Gk *my spirit in the gospel*   *c* 1.16 Or *trusts*   *d* 1.17 Or *The one who is righteous through faith will live*   *e* 1.26 Gk *use*

Paul. **1:8** *Your faith is proclaimed throughout the world.* Paul's audience is well known; therefore, they already have ideas and networks of their own. **1:14** *Both to Greeks and to barbarians.* "Barbarian" is a racialized term indicating foreignness from Greco-Roman culture. **1:16–17 Thesis.** Paul summarizes his gospel. God's plan for justice involves all people: Jews first but now gentiles as well. **1:16** *For the Jew first and also for the Greek.* God's plan for justice/salvation started with God's covenant and promise to Jews but also includes gentiles, who are now being brought into God's justice through Jesus Christ's faith. **1:17** *Through faith for faith.* God's justice for gentiles is revealed through Jesus's faith in God for the faith of these gentiles (in God). *The one . . . by faith.* Paul quotes Hab. 2:4, interpreting it to be about Jesus.

1:18–32 Gentile injustice and God's wrath. Paul begins his gospel by laying out the situation of gentiles and why they are in need of a path to be made just by God. Gentiles have refused to acknowledge or have faith in God, and therefore they anger God and deserve God's wrath and punishment. **1:18** *Ungodliness and injustice. Ungodliness* emphasizes gentiles' lack of faith and obedience toward God. *Injustice* stands in contrast to God's righteousness (or "justice"). **1:19–21** These verses make clear that this passage discusses the specific situation of gentiles. While Jews have a faithful relationship with God, gentiles have the ability to honor and trust God but have not done so. **1:23** *They exchanged.* Verbs of trade characterize the situation of gentiles, beginning with their exchanging the worshiping of God for that of other gods. *Reptiles.* Romans often expressed racialized scorn and discomfort about how Egyptians supposedly worshiped snakes. **1:24–32** God becomes the active subject, taking control of gentiles, who subsequently lose control. **1:26–27** Paul gives the most detailed focus to sexual desires, specifically sex between people of the same gender identities (see **"LGBTQIA2S+ Issues and Paul,"** **p. 1935**). **1:26** *Dishonorable passions.* Often associated with gentiles. The term carries sexual connotations in the Roman world; see 1 Thess. 4:5 and Rom. 7:5–6. *Their females.* Paul uses less common Greek

Reading through Time: LGBTQIA2S+ Issues and Paul (Romans 1)
Romans 1:18–32—especially vv. 26–27—draws the attention of LGBTQIA2S+ readers. They call this passage a "clobber text" due to its history of being interpreted as a condemnation of LGBTQIA2S+ identities, including its use to restrict their participation in churches and to justify violence against queer and trans people. While 1:18–32 is not the only clobber text in the Bible, it is the only biblical passage that specifically mentions sex between women. LGBTQIA2S+ interpreters have developed a number of interpretive approaches that respond to the abusive history of 1:18–32.

Many appeal to *historical context* by analyzing Paul's words in light of first-century Roman sexual arrangements and the various discussions that surrounded them in literature and material culture. One approach emphasizes the difference between Roman and contemporary understandings of sexuality: Romans did not have an understanding of "sexual orientation" or LGBTQIA2S+ identities. Paul cannot condemn queerness because he lacks an understanding of same-sex practices as part of an identity. Others note that most same-sex intercourse in the Roman world was nonconsensual and involved the abuse of power, often in the context of slavery (it is worth noting that most heterosexual intercourse was similarly abusive). These readers interpret 1:18–32 as condemning abusive practices and suggest that Paul does not condemn consensual same-sex relations, especially in the context of monogamous marriage. Some observe how Paul's condemnation of same-sex intercourse, specifically among the gentiles, replicates the Roman imperial language of self-control of desire. Roman morality condemned the lack of control over same-sex desires, calling them contrary to nature, especially in the case of sexual desire between women. Roman imperial morality saw these unnatural desires as indicative of foreignness—practices seen among the "nations" Rome conquered ("nations" and "gentiles" are the same word in Gk.).

In a different vein, some queer readers admit Paul's statements present a negative view of same-sex desire and intercourse. Drawing from feminist biblical scholarship and queer studies, they analyze Paul's rhetoric and resist his singular authority, emphasizing that Paul's audiences frequently disagreed and argued with what he said—and that there were LGBTQIA2S+ people proudly existing in Paul's first-century audiences.

Given the literal "clobbering" that 1:18–32 continues to justify, all readers should remember that interpreting it in a way that restricts the rights of marginalized populations and enables the physical or psychological harm of LGBTQIA2S+ people is fundamentally unjust and irresponsible.

Jimmy Hoke

²⁷and in the same way also the males, giving up natural intercourse^f with females, were consumed with their passionate desires for one another. Males committed shameless acts with males and received in their own persons the due penalty for their error.

28 And since they did not see fit to acknowledge God, God gave them over to an unfit mind and to do things that should not be done. ²⁹They were filled with every kind of injustice, evil, covetousness, malice. Full of envy, murder, strife, deceit, craftiness, they are gossips, ³⁰slanderers, God-haters,^g insolent, haughty, boastful, inventors of evil, rebellious toward parents, ³¹foolish, faithless, heartless, ruthless. ³²They know God's decree, that those who practice such things deserve to die, yet they not only do them but even applaud others who practice them.

2 Therefore you are without excuse, whoever you are, when you judge others, for in passing judgment on another you condemn yourself, because you, the judge, are doing the very same things. ²We know that

f 1.27 Gk *use*   *g* 1.30 Or *God-hated*

gender terms in this verse and the next. One perspective of sex in first-century Rome viewed women as the possessions of men. *Natural intercourse.* Literally "natural use." *Unnatural.* Literally "against nature." In Roman morality, women could "unnaturally" take an active sexual role with a man, but "unnatural," with respect to women, most often referred to lesbian sex acts. **1:27** *In the same way.* The women's unnatural intercourse is the same as the men's. *Consumed with their passionate desires.* The epitome of lacking self-control. **1:28–32** A final string of injustices that spirals out from the gentiles' lack of sexual self-control, which in turn stems from their refusal to worship God. **1:32** *Deserve to die* means they deserve wrath when God comes to judge all people.

2:1–16 God's impartiality: fictional dialogue with a gentile. Paul explains the impartiality of God's

God's judgment on those who do such things is in accordance with truth. ³Do you imagine, whoever you are, that when you judge those who do such things and yet do them yourself, you will escape the judgment of God? ⁴Or do you despise the riches of his kindness and forbearance and patience? Do you not realize that God's kindness is meant to lead you to repentance? ⁵But by your hard and impenitent heart you are storing up wrath for yourself on the day of wrath, when God's righteous judgment will be revealed. ⁶He will repay according to each one's deeds: ⁷to those who by patiently doing good seek for glory and honor and immortality, he will give eternal life, ⁸while for those who are self-seeking and who obey not the truth but injustice, there will be wrath and fury. ⁹There will be affliction and distress for everyone who does evil, both the Jew first and the Greek, ¹⁰but glory and honor and peace for everyone who does good, both the Jew first and the Greek. ¹¹For God shows no partiality.

12 All who have sinned apart from the law will also perish apart from the law, and all who have sinned under the law will be judged in accordance with the law. ¹³For it is not the hearers of the law who are righteous in God's sight but the doers of the law who will be justified. ¹⁴When gentiles, who do not possess the law, by nature do*ᵇ* what the law requires, these, though not having the law, are a law to themselves. ¹⁵They show that what the law requires is written on their hearts, as their own conscience also bears witness, and their conflicting thoughts will accuse or perhaps excuse them ¹⁶on the day when, according to my gospel, God through Christ Jesus judges the secret thoughts of all.

17 But if you call yourself a Jew and rely on the law and boast of your relation to God ¹⁸and know his will and determine what really matters because you are instructed in the law, ¹⁹and if you are sure that you are a guide to the blind, a light to those who are in darkness, ²⁰a corrector of the foolish, a teacher of children, having in the law the embodiment of knowledge and truth, ²¹you, then, who teach others, will you not teach yourself? You who preach against stealing, do you steal? ²²You who forbid adultery, do you commit adultery? You who abhor idols, do you rob temples? ²³You who boast in the law, do you dishonor God by your transgression of the law? ²⁴For, as it is written, "The name of God is blasphemed*ⁱ* among the gentiles because of you."

25 Circumcision indeed is of value if you obey the law, but if you are a transgressor of the law your circumcision has become uncircumcision. ²⁶So, if the uncircumcised keep the requirements of the law, will not their uncircumcision be regarded as circumcision? ²⁷Then the physically uncircumcised person

b 2.14 Or *law by nature, do*   *i* 2.24 Or *despised*

justice, showing the need for an intervention so that gentiles can be justified before God's judgment comes. **2:5** *Storing up wrath*, as seen from 1:18–32. All gentiles have incurred God's wrath, and they have not been provided a means for repenting their actions and having that wrath forgiven. **2:6–16** Paul emphasizes God's complete impartiality: God punishes wrongdoing and rewards good deeds. Those who sin in accordance with the law have already been held accountable and justified. Those who sin lawlessly have not been made just, and their punishment awaits and builds up. **2:6** See Ps. 62:12; Prov. 24:12. **2:9–10** *The Jew first and the Greek* is repeated multiple times in Romans. Jews were made just first through God's covenant promise; God also promised to justify gentiles. **2:12** *Apart from the law* is better translated as "against the law / in a lawless manner." *In accordance with the law*. The Torah assumes that people will err and accounts for this. **2:14** *Gentiles . . . by nature do*. It is possible for gentiles to figure out the law through nature (see 1:19–20).

2:17–4:22 Dialogue with a fellow Jewish teacher of gentiles. Paul shifts to an imagined dialogue with a fellow Jewish teacher of gentiles who thinks gentiles must follow Jewish law in order to be justified. Paul argues that God justifies gentiles through a different path: Jesus Christ's faith. **2:17** *You call yourself a Jew. You* is singular, signaling a shift to a new imagined conversation partner. **2:19–21** The issues Paul addresses connect to their shared role as teachers. **2:21–23** The teachings Paul refers to come from the Decalogue. Paul critiques this teacher for not following the parts of the law the teacher believes are required for gentiles. Paul's rhetoric does not necessarily reflect reality: it is highly unlikely other Jewish teachers of gentiles were routinely stealing and committing adultery. **2:24** Paul interprets a quotation from Isa. 52:5. **2:25–29** Paul draws from the Jewish idea of "circumcision of the heart" to argue that gentiles can be justified without following the law. **2:25** *Circumcision indeed is of*

who keeps the law will judge you who, though having the written code and circumcision, are a transgressor of the law. ²⁸For a person is not a Jew who is one outwardly, nor is circumcision something external and physical. ²⁹Rather, a person is a Jew who is one inwardly, and circumcision is a matter of the heart, by the Spirit, not the written code. Such a person receives praise not from humans but from God.

3 Then what advantage has the Jew? Or what is the value of circumcision? ²Much, in every way. For in the first place, the Jews*ʲ* were entrusted with the oracles of God. ³What if some were unfaithful? Will their faithlessness nullify the faithfulness of God? ⁴By no means! Although every human is a liar, let God be proved true, as it is written,

"So that you may be justified in your
     words
     and you will prevail*ᵏ* when you go to
     trial."

⁵But if our injustice serves to confirm the justice of God, what should we say? That God is unjust to inflict wrath on us? (I speak in a human way.) ⁶By no means! For then how could God judge the world? ⁷But if through my falsehood God's truthfulness abounds to his glory, why am I still being judged as a sinner? ⁸And why not say (as some people slander us by saying that we say), "Let us do evil so that good may come"? Their judgment is deserved!

9 What then? Are we any better off?*ˡ* No, not at all, for we have already charged that all, both Jews and Greeks, are under the power of sin, ¹⁰as it is written:

"There is no one who is righteous, not
     even one;
¹¹   there is no one who has
          understanding;
     there is no one who seeks God.
¹² All have turned aside; together they have
          become worthless;
     there is no one who shows kindness;
          there is not even one."
¹³ "Their throats are opened graves;
     they use their tongues to deceive."
"The venom of vipers is under their lips."
¹⁴   "Their mouths are full of cursing and
          bitterness."
¹⁵ "Their feet are swift to shed blood;
¹⁶   ruin and misery are in their paths,
¹⁷   and the way of peace they have not
          known."
¹⁸   "There is no fear of God before their
          eyes."

19 Now we know that, whatever the law says, it speaks to those who are under the law, so that every mouth may be silenced and the whole world may be held accountable to God. ²⁰For no human will be justified before him by deeds prescribed by the law, for through the law comes the knowledge of sin.

j 3.2 Gk *they*　*k* 3.4 Other ancient authorities read *you may prevail*　*l* 3.9 Or *at any disadvantage?*

value. Judaism and Jewish law/customs are not negated by a separate plan for gentiles' justification. **2:29** *Circumcision is a matter of the heart.* Paul appears to be interpreting texts like Deut. 10:16; 30:6; Jer. 4:4; 9:25–26. **3:1–9** The Jewish teacher of gentiles questions Paul about the implications of God's impartiality. The dialogue can be divided as follows: Paul's voice in vv. 2–3, 5, 7–8, 9b; Jewish teacher of gentiles in vv. 1, 4, 6, 9a. These ideas do not accurately reflect opinions of other Jewish teachers. **3:2** Paul emphasizes that Jews do benefit from being part of God's covenant people who follow the law. **3:3** Paul asks the teacher a question about God's faithfulness to God's covenant people, even if some of those people are unfaithful toward God. **3:4** "Teacher" emphatically affirms God's faithfulness, drawing from Ps. 51:4. **3:7–8** Paul emphatically repudiates the idea to "sin boldly" in order to allow God's justice to be shown, laying the groundwork for his discussion of sin for gentiles in Christ in 5:12–8:39. **3:9** *Are we any better off?* Or "Are we at any disadvantage?" *All . . . are under the power of sin.* Sin here indicates the human proclivity to err, which the law accounts for. **3:10–18** Paul takes over in a monologue to the Jewish teacher, citing a string of Scriptures that Paul modifies and interprets as confirming his argument. **3:10–12** See Pss. 14:1–3; 53:2–4. **3:13** See Pss. 5:9; 140:3. **3:14** See Ps. 10:7. **3:15–17** See Isa. 59:7–8; see also Prov. 1:16. **3:18** See Ps. 36:1. **3:19** *We know.* The ideas in this verse are things these two Jewish teachers know as Jews: the law is how Jews can be held accountable and justified by God. **3:20** Paul turns to the plan and teachings for gentiles. *Deeds prescribed by the law* is likely a reference to the specific subset of the law that Jewish teachers of gentiles taught was necessary for gentiles to follow. *Through the law comes the knowledge of sin* for gentiles. Paul is not saying that the law causes sin. Paul claims it is impossible for gentiles to fully keep the law. Teaching gentiles to keep parts of the law makes them aware of their inability and God's coming wrath.

Going Deeper: Faith of Jesus Christ (Romans 3:21–26)

For centuries, translators and interpreters assumed that Paul speaks about "faith in Jesus Christ," a phrase that is frequently invoked in churches and Christian theology—especially when reading Rom. 3:21–26. More recently, a debate has emerged among scholars about the best way to translate this phrase. The Greek language involves a nuanced system of "cases" for nouns: different cases can be used to indicate different relationships between a noun and other words in the sentence. In Greek, the words literally read, "faith Jesus Christ." "Jesus Christ" is in the genitive case, indicating a descriptive relation to the noun "faith." Depending on context, the genitive case can have a "subjective" relation to another noun (Jesus Christ as the subject who has faith) or an "objective" relation (Jesus Christ as the object of others' faith). Both are plausible, and pages have been spent debating this question: Should this phrase continue to be translated as "faith in Jesus Christ," or is it better translated as "faith of Jesus Christ" (or "Jesus Christ's faith")? From a grammatical standpoint, convincing cases have been made for both possibilities (though it should be noted that, in general, the possessive/subjective use of the genitive tends to be the default). In a major shift from tradition, the NRSVue chooses "faith of Jesus Christ" (i.e., the subjective genitive) as the more accurate rendering of the Greek phrase.

"Who cares?" some readers may ask. The grammatical terms and endless debate can seem dense and pointless. After all, it is one preposition! But that one preposition is actually a big deal: shifting the preposition significantly shifts Paul's Christology and theology. The traditional "faith in Christ" means that justification and salvation come through people having faith in Jesus Christ—one of the bedrocks of most Christian theology. "Jesus Christ's faith" undermines that bedrock entirely: no one is supposed to have faith in Jesus! Following the theocentric nature of Paul's theology, the "faith of Jesus Christ" is *faith in God*: faith in God is required for justification and salvation, and most gentiles did not display such faith (see 1:18–32). Jesus's faith in God makes a path for gentiles to be justified—and provides a model for gentiles to come to faith in God, alongside Jews (who do *not* need to have faith in Jesus and who already have a faithful relation to God).

Jimmy Hoke

21 But now, apart from the law, the righteousness of God has been disclosed and is attested by the Law and the Prophets, ²²the righteousness of God through the faith of Jesus Christ*ᵐ* for all who believe.*ⁿ* For there is no distinction, ²³since all have sinned and fall short of the glory of God; ²⁴they are now justified by his grace as a gift, through the redemption that is in Christ Jesus, ²⁵whom God put forward as a sacrifice of atonement*ᵒ* by his blood, effective through faith. He did this to demonstrate his righteousness, because in his divine forbearance he had passed over the sins previously committed; ²⁶it was to demonstrate at the present time his own righteousness, so that he is righteous and he justifies the one who has the faith of Jesus.*ᵖ*

m 3.22 Or *through faith in Jesus Christ*   n 3.22 Or *trust*   o 3.25 Or *a place of atonement*   p 3.26 Or *has faith in Jesus*

3:21–26 Jesus Christ's faith: God's plan to make gentiles just. Paul explains God's plan for gentiles apart from the law to the teacher (in front of his audience in Rome). These ideas represent central points of Paul's gospel: Jesus, as the Christ, has the power to bring about God's final judgment. Without a way for gentiles to be justified, they would receive God's impartial wrath and not be saved alongside Jews. Therefore, Jesus showed faith in God's promises for gentiles by trusting that his death would allow God to justify gentiles and give them time to have faith in God before judgment day so that they would be saved alongside Jews. **3:22** *Through the faith of Jesus Christ.* Jesus's faith in God makes possible God's righteousness (see **"Faith of Jesus Christ," p. 1938**). *There is no distinction* among gentiles. **3:24** *Redemption*, or "ransom payment." **3:25** *Sacrifice of atonement.* Greek "hilastērion," an action or object that brings about reconciliation. The term signifies a death as an act of faith in God. See 4 Macc. 17:22. *He did this to demonstrate his righteousness.* God is the referent of the Greek pronoun translated as "he." *Passed over the sins previously committed.* God's display of justice means dismissing all the gentiles' sins that were being stored up until God's judgment. **3:26** The translation omits the first Greek phrase of 3:26: "during God's delay," an important temporal marker alongside *at the present time.* Jesus's death allows God to delay final judgment, making time for gentiles to have faith in God.

27 Then what becomes of boasting? It is excluded. Through what kind of law? That of works? No, rather through the law of faith. ²⁸For we hold that a person is justified by faith apart from works prescribed by the law. ²⁹Or is God the God of Jews only? Is he not the God of gentiles also? Yes, of gentiles also, ³⁰since God is one, and he will justify the circumcised on the ground of faith and the uncircumcised through that same faith. ³¹Do we then overthrow the law through this faith? By no means! On the contrary, we uphold the law.

4 What then are we to say was gained by⁹ Abraham, our ancestor according to the flesh? ²For if Abraham was justified by works, he has something to boast about, but not before God. ³For what does the scripture say? "Abraham believed' God, and it was reckoned to him as righteousness." ⁴Now to one who works, wages are not reckoned as a gift but as something due. ⁵But to one who does not work but trusts him who justifies the ungodly, such faith is reckoned as righteousness. ⁶So also David pronounces a blessing on those to whom God reckons righteousness apart from works:

⁷ "Blessed are those whose iniquities are forgiven

and whose sins are covered;

⁸ blessed is the one against whom the Lord will not reckon sin."

9 Is this blessing, then, pronounced only on the circumcised or also on the uncircumcised? We say, "Faith was reckoned to Abraham as righteousness." ¹⁰How then was it reckoned to him? Was it before or after he had been circumcised? It was not after but before he was circumcised. ¹¹He received the sign of circumcision as a seal of the righteousness that he had by faith' while he was still uncircumcised. The purpose was to make him the ancestor of all who believe' without being circumcised and who thus have righteousness reckoned to them, ¹²and likewise the ancestor of the circumcised who are not only circumcised but follow the example of the faith that our ancestor Abraham had before he was circumcised.

13 For the promise that he would inherit the world did not come to Abraham or to his descendants through the law but through the righteousness of faith. ¹⁴For if it is the adherents of the law who are to be the heirs, faith is null and the promise is void. ¹⁵For the law brings wrath, but where there is no law, neither is there transgression.

q 4.1 Other ancient authorities read *say about*   r 4.3 Or *trusted in*   s 4.11 Or *trust*   t 4.11 Or *trust*

3:27–4:2 The Jewish teacher of gentiles responds. Paul anticipates potential queries by posing them through the imagined responses of the Jewish teacher of gentiles. **3:27** *Boasting.* The teacher's first question emphasizes their characterization in 2:17–29, a teacher who pretentiously boasts when telling gentiles they must follow specific "works of law." *It is excluded.* Paul means not all boasting but the reason the teacher boasts over their students. *Through what kind of law?* Or "What part of [the] law?" Paul does not differentiate Jewish law from other laws. **3:28** Paul's point is that it is faith in God that justifies people, not the works of the law. **3:29** Paul poses questions back to the teacher, who responds that God is indeed the God of gentiles and Jews. **3:30** There are two different paths for Jews (*circumcised*) and gentiles (*uncircumcised*) based on different relationships to faith: *on the ground of faith,* or "from faith," specifically from Abraham's faith, which establishes the covenant with Jews as God's people; *through that same faith,* for gentiles the relationship is through (not from) the faith of Jesus Christ. **3:31** Paul denies that this means Jewish law is overthrown: at issue is the teaching to gentiles. **4:1** *According to the flesh*—for example, Abraham's human efforts. **4:2** *For if . . . boast about.* The teacher argues that Abraham's actions are the reason God justifies him. *But not before God.* Paul disagrees and responds by interpreting Genesis.

4:3–22 Paul's interpretation of Abraham's faith. 4:3 Paul quotes Gen. 15:6 as central to his argument. **4:4–5** Paul uses the example of labor. Laborers are paid wages out of contractual obligation. **4:6–8** Paul interprets and quotes Ps. 32:1–2. **4:7** *Those whose iniquities are forgiven,* or "the lawless ones who are forgiven," recalling 2:12. **4:9–12** The practice of circumcision is introduced in Abraham's story. The "works of law" that Paul's interlocutor teaches include gentiles being circumcised. Paul asserts that circumcision is a sign of God's covenant for Jews but is not required to display faith in God in the case of gentiles. **4:13–16** The promise to Abraham comes before the law as a result of faith in God. Jews are part of God's promise because of Abraham's faith and God's fidelity to God's covenant. **4:14** *Adherents of the law. Adherents* is not given in the Greek text. Those "from law" still inherit, but they are not the only inheritors of God's promise to Abraham. **4:15** *The law brings wrath,* specifically to gentiles. *Where there is no law.* Paul is not critiquing the law or setting it up to be nullified. If there was

16 For this reason the promise depends on faith, in order that it may rest on grace, so that it may be guaranteed to all his descendants, not only to the adherents of the law but also to those who share the faith of Abraham (who is the father of all of us, [17]as it is written, "I have made you the father of many nations"), in the presence of the God in whom he believed,[u] who gives life to the dead and calls into existence the things that do not exist. [18]Hoping against hope, he believed that he would become "the father of many nations," according to what was said, "So shall your descendants be." [19]He did not weaken in faith when he considered his own body, which was already[v] as good as dead (for he was about a hundred years old), and the barrenness of Sarah's womb. [20]No distrust made him waver concerning the promise of God, but he grew strong in his faith as he gave glory to God, [21]being fully convinced that God was able to do what he had promised. [22]Therefore "it was reckoned to him as righteousness." [23]Now the words, "it was reckoned to him," were written not for his sake alone [24]but for ours also. It will be reckoned to us who believe[w] in him who raised Jesus our Lord from the dead, [25]who was handed over for our trespasses and was raised for our justification.

5 Therefore, since we are justified by faith, we[x] have peace with God through our Lord Jesus Christ, [2]through whom we have obtained access[y] to this grace in which we stand, and we[z] boast in our hope of sharing the glory of God. [3]And not only that, but we[a] also boast in our afflictions, knowing that affliction produces endurance, [4]and endurance produces character, and character produces hope, [5]and hope does not put us to shame, because God's love has been poured into our hearts through the Holy Spirit that has been given to us.

6 For while we were still weak, at the right time Christ died for the ungodly. [7]Indeed, rarely will anyone die for a righteous person—though perhaps for a good person someone might actually dare to die. [8]But God proves his love for us in that while we still were sinners Christ died for us. [9]Much more surely, therefore, since we have now been justified by his blood, will we be saved through him from the wrath of God.[b] [10]For if while we were enemies we were reconciled to God through the death of his Son, much more surely, having been reconciled, will we be saved by his life. [11]But more than that, we even boast in God through our Lord Jesus Christ, through whom we have now received reconciliation.

12 Therefore, just as sin came into the world through one man, and death came through

u 4.17 Or *trusted* v 4.19 Other ancient authorities lack *already* w 4.24 Or *trust* x 5.1 Other ancient authorities read *let us* y 5.2 Other ancient authorities add *by faith* z 5.2 Or *let us* a 5.3 Or *let us* b 5.9 Gk *the wrath*

no law, there would be no gentile transgression and no need for God to make a path to include them. **4:16** *The promise depends on faith*, specifically Abraham's faith. Faithful action by significant individuals (Abraham, Jesus) results in promises for collective peoples. **4:17** *I have made you the father of many nations*, quoting Gen. 17:5. *Life to the dead* alludes to both God's raising of Jesus and the metaphorical death of the childless Abraham's lineage. **4:18–22** Paul emphasizes Abraham's faith in God. **4:19** *Did not weaken in faith.* Paul returns to strength and weakness in faith among gentile Christ followers in 14:1–15:7. *The barrenness of Sarah's womb.* Greek "the deadness of Sarah's motherhood." English translators choose to associate Sarah's old age and lack of motherhood with her reproductive organs.

4:23–5:11 Conclusion of first argument. Paul directly addresses his audience of Christ followers in Rome and concludes the argument that began at 1:18. **4:23–25** God reckons righteousness first to Abraham's faith, then to Jews from that faith, and now, through Jesus Christ's faith, to gentiles. **5:1** *Peace with God.* By forgiving their past sins that were stored up, God's justice ends gentiles' enmity toward God. **5:2–5** Paul returns to the idea of boasting but shifts the emphasis to boasting about and suffering for God's justice as opposed to superior abilities. See 2 Cor. 11:16–33. Suffering refers to a general sense of endurance in the final days before God's (delayed) coming. **5:6–11** Paul emphasizes that Jesus's faithful death reconciles gentiles with God on account of their stored-up wrath from their sins. **5:6** *At the right time.* Jesus's faithful death occurs at the critical point when God's judgment would have condemned gentiles for all their sins. **5:8** *While we still were sinners*—that is, gentiles who were still sinners provoking God's wrath when Christ took faithful action.

5:12–8:39 Gentiles' relationship to obedience and sin. Paul continues to explain what his gospel means for gentiles. **5:12–21 Example of Adam.** Paul uses Adam (Gen. 2–3) as an example of how one person's actions can affect many. Sin is not a state but actions: when Adam disobeys God, this is the first act of sin. **5:12** *Through one man.* Paul ignores Eve. *Death came through sin.* See Gen. 3:22–23.

sin, and so death spread to all because all have sinned—[13]for sin was indeed in the world before the law, but sin is not reckoned when there is no law. [14]Yet death reigned from Adam to Moses, even over those who did not sin in the likeness of Adam, who is a pattern of the one who was to come.

15 But the free gift is not like the trespass. For if the many died through the one man's trespass, much more surely have the grace of God and the gift in the grace of the one man, Jesus Christ, abounded for the many. [16]And the gift is not like the effect of the one man's sin. For the judgment following one trespass brought condemnation, but the gift following many trespasses brings justification. [17]If, because of the one man's trespass, death reigned through that one, much more surely will those who receive the abundance of grace and the gift of righteousness reign in life through the one man, Jesus Christ.

18 Therefore just as one man's trespass led to condemnation for all, so one man's act of righteousness leads to justification and life for all. [19]For just as through the one man's disobedience the many were made sinners, so through the one man's obedience the many will be made righteous. [20]But law came in, so that the trespass might increase, but where sin increased, grace abounded all the more, [21]so that, just as sin reigned in death, so grace might also reign through justification leading to eternal life through Jesus Christ our Lord.

6 What then are we to say? Should we continue in sin in order that grace may increase? [2]By no means! How can we who died to sin go on living in it? [3]Do you not know that all of us who were baptized into Christ Jesus were baptized into his death? [4]Therefore we were buried with him by baptism into death, so that, just as Christ was raised from the dead by the glory of the Father, so we also might walk in newness of life.

5 For if we have been united with him in a death like his, we will certainly be united with him in a resurrection like his. [6]We know that our old self was crucified with him so that the body of sin might be destroyed, so we might no longer be enslaved to sin. [7]For whoever has died is freed[c] from sin. [8]But if we died with Christ, we believe that we will also live with him. [9]We know that Christ, being raised from the dead, will never die again; death no longer has dominion over him. [10]The death he died, he died to sin once for all, but the life he lives, he lives to God. [11]So you also must consider yourselves dead to sin and alive to God in Christ Jesus.

12 Therefore do not let sin reign in your mortal bodies, so that you obey their desires. [13]No longer present your members to sin as instruments[d] of unrighteousness, but present yourselves to God as those who have been brought from death to life, and present your members to God as instruments[e] of righteousness. [14]For sin will have no dominion over you, since you are not under law but under grace.

15 What then? Should we sin because we are not under law but under grace? By

c 6.7 Or *justified*   d 6.13 Or *weapons*   e 6.13 Or *weapons*

5:13 *Sin is not reckoned when there is no law.* The verb tense is imperfect, "sin was not being reckoned." Before God gave the law to Moses, there was no way for God to judge humans for their sins. **5:14** *From Adam to Moses.* Adam's sin/punishment only affected humans in the period before the law. **5:15–19** Contrasts Adam with Jesus: both are men whose actions affect many people, but the impact is uneven. **5:20–21** Law is not the cause of the trespass. After Moses introduces the law, it is possible for humans to repent their sins and get in right relation with God. Gentiles' disobedience becomes worse once there is a path to repent and obey, thus increasing the significance of God's grace through Jesus's faithful action for gentiles.

6:1–7:6 Gentile Christ followers and sin. Paul uses metaphorical examples from the Roman household—slavery and marriage—to stress the importance of self-control for gentile Christ followers. **6:3–14** In baptism, Christ followers ritually participate in Jesus's faithful death and God's raising of him, so they should put an end to their previous sinful ways. Paul's use of "dying to sin" could draw directly from first-century baptismal liturgies, as in Gal. 3:28. **6:6** *Crucified with him,* or "cocrucified" (see Gal. 2:19). **6:7** *Freed,* or "justified." **6:12–14** As in 1:18–32, Paul frames gentiles' sins in terms of bodily self-control. **6:15–23** Paul uses Roman slavery metaphorically, framing slavery as a matter of obedience. Gentiles can be obedient either to their sinful desires or to God, just as enslaved persons are obedient to their enslavers; see **"Paul, Enslavement, and Freedom," p. 1964.**

no means! [16]Do you not know that, if you present yourselves to anyone as obedient slaves, you are slaves of the one whom you obey, either of sin, which leads to death, or of obedience, which leads to righteousness? [17]But thanks be to God that you who were slaves of sin have become obedient from the heart to the form of teaching to which you were entrusted [18]and that you, having been set free from sin, have become enslaved to righteousness. [19]I am speaking in human terms because of your limitations.[f] For just as you once presented your members as slaves to impurity and lawlessness, leading to even more lawlessness, so now present your members as slaves to righteousness, leading to sanctification.

20 When you were slaves of sin, you were free in regard to righteousness. [21]So what fruit did you then gain from the things of which you now are ashamed? The end of those things is death. [22]But now that you have been freed from sin and enslaved to God, the fruit you have leads to sanctification, and the end is eternal life. [23]For the wages of sin is death, but the free gift of God is eternal life in Christ Jesus our Lord.

7 Or do you not know, brothers and sisters—for I am speaking to those who know the law—that the law is binding on a person only during that person's lifetime? [2]Thus a married woman is bound by the law to her husband as long as he lives, but if her husband dies, she is discharged from the law concerning the husband. [3]Accordingly, she will be called an adulteress if she belongs to another man while her husband is alive. But if her husband dies, she is free from that law, and if she belongs to another man, she is not an adulteress.

4 In the same way, my brothers and sisters, you have died to the law through the body of Christ, so that you may belong to another, to him who was raised from the dead in order that we may bear fruit for God. [5]For while we were living in the flesh, our sinful passions, aroused by the law, were at work in our members to bear fruit for death. [6]But now we are discharged from the law, dead to that which held us captive, so that we are enslaved in the newness of the Spirit and not in the oldness of the written code.

7 What then are we to say? That the law is sin? By no means! Yet, if it had not been for the law, I would not have known sin. I would not have known what it is to covet if the law had not said, "You shall not covet." [8]But sin, seizing an opportunity through the commandment, produced in me all kinds of covetousness. For apart from the law sin lies dead. [9]I was once alive apart from the law, but when the commandment came, sin revived [10]and I died, and the very commandment that promised life proved to be death to me. [11]For sin, seizing an opportunity in the commandment, deceived me and through it killed me. [12]So the law is holy, and the commandment is holy and just and good.

f 6.19 Gk the weakness of your flesh

6:16 Roman enslavers presented a similar "choice" to the people they enslaved: obey or be punished for erring. 6:17 *To which you were entrusted*, or "to which you were handed over." This is the same verb used in 1:24, 26, 28 when God hands gentiles over to sinful desires. 6:19 *Sanctification*, in contrast to the impurity of their past state as gentiles; see 1 Thess. 4:3–7. 6:23 *Wages . . . free gift.* See 4:4–5; 5:15–17. Death is owed for sin, but God's justice is a nonobligatory gift. 7:1–4 A woman's relationship to Roman marriage law changes through her husband's death, just as gentiles' relation to the law changes via Jesus's death. 7:4 *Belong to another.* Paul's emphasis is that gentiles should belong to God, just as a woman who remarries belongs to her new husband. 7:5 *Sinful passions* connotes sexual desires and the lack of self-control that characterized gentile behavior; see Rom. 1:26; 1 Thess. 4:5. *Aroused by the law.* Aroused is not in the Greek text. The law makes gentiles accountable for these passions as *sinful.* 7:6 *Discharged* is connected to labor: unemployed, not working. The law is still active for Jews, but through Christ, it no longer employs "us"—that is, gentiles.

7:7–25 **A gentile on the law and sin.** Paul brings to life the situation of gentiles' lack of self-control and how the law makes gentiles aware of the sins that they are unable to stop themselves from committing by nature of their gentile culture. As in 2:1–4:22, Paul takes another persona. The "I" whom Paul speaks as is a gentile who tries to follow Jewish law, trapping them between two cultures (gentile and Jewish). 7:7 *That the law is sin? By no means!* Paul emphasizes that the law itself is not an agent of sin. It makes gentiles aware of and accountable to their sins. *You shall not covet.* See Exod. 20:17; Deut. 5:21. 7:8 Law and sin are separate entities: sin uses the law as a pretext to increase this imaginary gentile's

13 Did what is good, then, bring death to me? By no means! It was sin that was working death in me through what is good, in order that it might be shown to be sin, so that through the commandment sin might become sinful beyond measure.

14 For we know that the law is spiritual, but I am of the flesh, sold into slavery under sin.^{g} ^{15}I do not understand my own actions. For I do not do what I want, but I do the very thing I hate. ^{16}Now if I do what I do not want, I agree that the law is good. ^{17}But in fact it is no longer I who do it but sin that dwells within me. ^{18}For I know that the good does not dwell within me, that is, in my flesh. For the desire to do the good lies close at hand, but not the ability. ^{19}For I do not do the good I want, but the evil I do not want is what I do. ^{20}Now if I do what I do not want, it is no longer I who do it but sin that dwells within me.

21 So I find it to be a law that, when I want to do what is good, evil lies close at hand. ^{22}For I delight in the law of God in my inmost self, ^{23}but I see in my members another law at war with the law of my mind, making me captive to the law of sin that dwells in my members. ^{24}Wretched person that I am! Who will rescue me from this body of death? ^{25}Thanks be to God^b through Jesus Christ our Lord!

So then, with my mind I am enslaved to the law of God, but with my flesh I am enslaved to the law of sin.

8 Therefore there is now no condemnation for those who are in Christ Jesus. ^{2}For the law of the Spirit^i of life in Christ Jesus has set you^j free from the law of sin and of death. ^{3}For God has done what the law, weakened by the flesh, could not do: by sending his own Son in the likeness of sinful flesh and to deal with sin,^{k} he condemned sin in the flesh, ^{4}so that the just requirement of the law might be fulfilled in us, who walk not according to the flesh but according to the Spirit.^{l} ^{5}For those who live according to the flesh set their minds on the things of the flesh, but those who live according to the Spirit^m set their minds on the things of the Spirit.^{n} ^{6}To set the mind on the flesh is death, but to set the mind on the Spirit^o is life and peace. ^{7}For this reason the mind that is set on the flesh is hostile to God; it does not submit to God's law—indeed, it cannot, ^{8}and those who are in the flesh cannot please God.

9 But you are not in the flesh; you are in the Spirit,^{p} since the Spirit of God dwells in you. Anyone who does not have the Spirit of Christ does not belong to him. ^{10}But if Christ is in you, then the body is dead because of sin, but the Spirit^q is life because of righteousness. ^{11}If the Spirit of him who raised Jesus from the dead dwells in you, he who raised Christ Jesus^r from the dead will give life to your mortal bodies also through^s his Spirit that dwells in you.

12 So then, brothers and sisters, we are obligated, not to the flesh, to live according to the flesh—^{13}for if you live according to the flesh, you will die, but if by the Spirit you put to death the deeds of the body, you will live. ^{14}For all who are led by the Spirit of God are

g 7.14 Gk *sold under sin*   h 7.25 Other ancient authorities read *I thank God*   i 8.2 Or *spirit*   j 8.2 Gk *you* is singular; other ancient authorities read *me* or *us*   k 8.3 Or *and as a sin offering*   l 8.4 Or *spirit*   m 8.5 Or *spirit*   n 8.5 Or *spirit*   o 8.6 Or *spirit*   p 8.9 Or *spirit*   q 8.10 Or *spirit*   r 8.11 Other ancient authorities read *Christ* or *the Christ* or *Jesus Christ*   s 8.11 Other ancient authorities read *on account of*

sin. **7:13–25** Paul imagines how this gentile would struggle knowing the law is good but being unable to follow it because they are driven by their sinful gentile nature. **7:17** *Sin that dwells within me.* The former gentile state contrasts to the spirit's dwelling in gentiles who follow Christ; see 8:11. **7:21–25** Paul refers to two laws here, that of God (i.e., the Torah / Jewish law) and that of sin. For this gentile, the law of sin rules their body even though their mind knows God's law is good.

8:1–39 Gentiles' new life. Paul completes his description of gentiles' transformation from disobedient sinners to obedient children of God. **8:2** See 7:21–25 for Paul's reference to two laws. *Spirit.* The capitalization of *Spirit* by the translators assumes the Christian concept of the Holy Spirit as part of the Trinity, a theology that had not yet been formalized. Paul refers to different spirits in this chapter, including God's spirit, Christ's spirit, slavery's spirit, and adoption's spirit. **8:4** *Just requirement of the law.* Even though they are not subject to the law, gentiles should not act according to sinful passions. **8:5–17** Paul distinguishes between flesh and spirit to stress that gentiles—as God's children who have been adopted into God's household—should live according to the spirit. *Flesh* represents the life of sinful passions (see 6:19), while *spirit* represents a life obedient to God (and includes the law; see 7:14). **8:12** *We are obligated,* or "we are debtors/indebted"; see 13:7-8. **8:14–17** Jews and gentiles are now

children of God. [15]For you did not receive a spirit of slavery to fall back into fear, but you received a spirit of adoption. When we cry, "Abba![t] Father!" [16]it is that very Spirit bearing witness[u] with our spirit that we are children of God, [17]and if children, then heirs: heirs of God and joint heirs with Christ, if we in fact suffer with him so that we may also be glorified with him.

[18] I consider that the sufferings of this present time are not worth comparing with the glory about to be revealed to us. [19]For the creation waits with eager longing for the revealing of the children of God, [20]for the creation was subjected to futility, not of its own will, but by the will of the one who subjected it, in hope [21]that the creation itself will be set free from its enslavement to decay and will obtain the freedom of the glory of the children of God. [22]We know that the whole creation has been groaning together as it suffers together the pains of labor, [23]and not only the creation, but we ourselves, who have the first fruits of the Spirit, groan inwardly while we wait for adoption, the redemption of our bodies. [24]For in[v] hope we were saved. Now hope that is seen is not hope, for who hopes for what one already sees? [25]But if we hope for what we do not see, we wait for it with patience.

[26] Likewise the Spirit helps us in our weakness, for we do not know how to pray as we ought, but that very Spirit intercedes[w] with groanings too deep for words. [27]And God,[x] who searches hearts, knows what is the mind of the Spirit, because the Spirit[y] intercedes for the saints according to the will of God.

[28] We know that all things work together[z] for good for those who love God, who are called according to his purpose. [29]For those whom he foreknew he also predestined to be conformed to the image of his Son, in order that he might be the firstborn within a large family.[a] [30]And those whom he predestined he also called, and those whom he called he also justified, and those whom he justified he also glorified.

[31] What then are we to say about these things? If God is for us, who is against us? [32]He who did not withhold his own Son but gave him up for all of us, how will he not with him also give us everything else? [33]Who will bring any charge against God's elect? It is God who justifies. [34]Who is to condemn? It is Christ[b] who died, or rather, who was raised, who is also at the right hand of God, who also intercedes for us. [35]Who will separate us from the love of Christ? Will affliction or distress or persecution or famine or nakedness or peril or sword? [36]As it is written,

"For your sake we are being killed all day
    long;
  we are accounted as sheep to be
    slaughtered."

[37]No, in all these things we are more than victorious through him who loved us. [38]For I am convinced that neither death, nor life, nor angels, nor rulers, nor things present, nor things to come, nor powers, [39]nor height, nor depth, nor anything else in all creation will be able to separate us from the love of God in Christ Jesus our Lord.

t 8.15 Aramaic for *Father*   *u* 8.16 Or *[15]... a spirit of adoption, by which we cry, "Abba! Father!"* *[16]The Spirit itself bears witness* *v* 8.24 Or *by*   *w* 8.26 Other ancient authorities add *for us*   *x* 8.27 Gk *And the one*   *y* 8.27 Gk *he* or *it*   *z* 8.28 Other ancient authorities read *God makes all things work together* or *in all things God works*   *a* 8.29 Gk *among many brothers*   *b* 8.34 Other ancient authorities read *Christ Jesus*

equal parts of God's household, even though they have been brought into God's inheritance through different paths. Terms like "dwelling," "heirs," "adoption," and "enslavement" were all associated with the Greco-Roman household. **8:15** *Spirit of slavery*, as when gentiles were enslaved to sin; see 6:15–23. *Fear*, or "terror." Roman enslavers used fear of punishment to keep enslaved persons obedient. *Abba! Father! Abba*, the Aramaic term for "father," is followed by the Greek. **8:17** *Heirs*. In Rome, adoption was primarily about securing a male inheritor. Being claimed as a child comes with material benefits. **8:18–25** Paul connects present suffering to God's glory, which is soon coming, echoing 4:23–5:11. **8:18** *Sufferings*. It is unclear exactly what these sufferings are, though 8:35 may clarify. *Of this present time*. As in 5:6, *time* is a significant period or season: here, the delay before God's imminent judgment. **8:23** *First fruits* refers to the start of the harvest or an offering in a Roman temple. The emphasis is on its beginning nature. **8:25** *Patience*, or "endurance," as in 5:3–4. **8:26** *Weakness*, presumably weakness in faith (see 8:3; 4:19–20). **8:28–39** Paul finishes explaining his gospel for gentiles by emphasizing the goodness of God's plan. **8:28** *For good*. The Greek term connotes moral goodness. Everything should work together to do good things. **8:29** *Foreknew . . . predestined*. Gentiles' salvation was always part of God's plan. **8:35** Paul may specify the sufferings mentioned in 8:18. *Sword* could specifically connote Roman policing and punishment; see 13:4. **8:36** Paul quotes Ps. 44:22.

9 I am speaking the truth in Christ—I am not lying; my conscience confirms it by the Holy Spirit—²I have great sorrow and unceasing anguish in my heart. ³For I could wish that I myself were accursed and cut off from Christ for the sake of my own brothers and sisters, my own flesh and blood. ⁴They are Israelites, and to them belong the adoption, the glory, the covenants, the giving of the law, the worship, and the promises; ⁵to them belong the patriarchs, and from them, according to the flesh, comes the Christ, who is over all, God blessed forever.ᶜ Amen.

6 It is not as though the word of God has failed. For not all those descended from Israel are Israelites, ⁷and not all of Abraham's children are his descendants, but "it is through Isaac that descendants shall be named for you." ⁸This means that it is not the children of the flesh who are the children of God, but the children of the promise are counted as descendants. ⁹For the word of the promise is this: "About this time I will return, and Sarah shall have a son." ¹⁰Nor is that all; something similar happened to Rebecca when she had conceived children by one husband, our ancestor Isaac: ¹¹even before they had been born or had done anything good or bad (so that God's purpose of election might continue, ¹²not by works but by his call) she was told, "The elder shall serve the younger." ¹³As it is written,

"I have loved Jacob,
    but I have hated Esau."

14 What then are we to say? Is there injustice on God's part? By no means! ¹⁵For he says to Moses,

"I will have mercy on whom I have mercy,
    and I will have compassion on whom I
        have compassion."

¹⁶So it depends not on human will or exertion but on God who shows mercy. ¹⁷For the scripture says to Pharaoh, "I have raised you up for this very purpose, that I may show my power in you and that my name may be proclaimed in all the earth." ¹⁸So then he has mercy on whomever he chooses, and he hardens the heart of whomever he chooses.

19 You will say to me then, "Why then does he still find fault? For who can resist his will?" ²⁰But who indeed are you, a human, to argue with God? Will what is molded say to the one who molds it, "Why have you made me like this?" ²¹Has the potter no right over the clay, to make out of the same lump one object for special use and another for ordinary use? ²²What if God, desiring to show his wrath and to make known his power, has endured with much patience the objects of wrath that are made for destruction, ²³and what if he has done so in order to make known the riches of his glory for the objects of mercy, which he has prepared beforehand for glory—²⁴including us whom he has called, not from the Jews only but also from the gentiles? ²⁵As he also says in Hosea,

c 9.5 Or *Messiah, who is God over all, blessed forever;* or *Messiah. May he who is God over all be blessed forever*

9:1–11:36 The role of Israel/Jews in God's plan. Paul shifts to a new argument/topic: how Jews/Israel fits into the bigger picture of God's plan now that gentiles have a path to be justified. Paul appears to want to ensure gentiles do not misinterpret Jews' role in God's plan. **9:1–3** Paul's use of the first person emphasizes his Jewishness. **9:4** *Israelites.* Paul uses the term for the people of Israel rather than "Jews/Judeans," a term from the Greek name of the Roman province. **9:6–13** Paul explains that God chooses some to inherit God's promises and not others. God's choice has nothing to do with their actions but God's plan. **9:7** *It is through Isaac . . . for you.* Paul cites and interprets Gen. 21:12. It is only the descendants of Isaac whom God chooses to carry out God's promise to Abraham. This does not condemn Ishmael or his descendants, whom God also blesses in Gen. 17:7–16 and 21:15–21. **9:8** Paul uses similar language in Gal. 4:21–31. **9:9** Paul quotes Gen. 18:14. **9:10–13** See Gen. 25–33, especially 25:21–26. *Election* emphasizes God's choice as opposed to one's actions. As with Abraham in Rom. 4:1–22, God's choice of Jacob (whom God names Israel) was not due to Jacob's (or Esau's) actions. **9:12** Paul quotes Gen. 25:23. **9:13** Paul quotes Mal. 1:2–3. **9:14–23** Paul explains how God is just when choosing to show mercy or wrath, echoing 1:18–32 and 2:17–29. **9:15** Paul quotes Exod. 33:19. **9:17** Paul quotes Exod. 9:16. **9:18** Paul interprets Exodus as proof that God's wrath and mercy are determined by God's plan, not human action. *Hardens the heart* is used multiple times in Exodus, including 9:12, 35. God does the hardening, not the human Pharaoh. **9:19–23** Paul uses an interlocutor (singular *you*) to address the question of why God shows wrath at all, employing a metaphor of God as a potter and humans as clay (see Isa. 29:16; 45:9; Jer. 18:1–11; Sir. 33:13; 38:29–30; Wis. 15:7). **9:24–29** Paul stresses that God's glory and mercy include both Jews and gentiles. **9:25** Paul quotes Hos. 2:23. In Hosea, God reclaims unfaithful Israel (as a husband to an unfaithful wife), who has cried out to God after their rejection of

"Those who were not my people I will call
'my people,'
and her who was not beloved I will call
'beloved.'"
²⁶ "And in the place where it was said
to them, 'You are not my
people,'
there they shall be called children of
the living God."

27 And Isaiah cries out concerning Israel, "Though the number of the children of Israel were like the sand of the sea, only a remnant of them will be saved, ²⁸for the Lord will execute his sentence on the earth quickly and decisively."ᵈ ²⁹And as Isaiah predicted,

"If the Lord of hosts had not left
descendants to us,
we would have fared like Sodom
and been made like Gomorrah."

30 What then are we to say? Gentiles, who did not strive for righteousness, have attained it, that is, righteousness through faith, ³¹but Israel, who did strive for the law of righteousness, did not attain that law. ³²Why not? Because they did not strive for it on the basis of faith but as if it were based on works. They have stumbled over the stumbling stone, ³³as it is written,

"See, I am laying in Zion a stone that
will make people stumble, a rock
that will make them fall,
and whoever trusts in himᵉ will not be
put to shame."

10 Brothers and sisters, my heart's desire and prayer to God for them is that they may be saved. ²For I can testify that they have a zeal for God, but it is not based on knowledge. ³Not knowing the righteousness of God and seeking to establish their own, they have not submitted to God's righteousness. ⁴For Christ is the culmination of the law so that there may be righteousness for everyone who believes.

5 Moses writes concerning the righteousness that comes from the law, that "the person who does these things will live by them." ⁶But the righteousness that comes from faith says, "Do not say in your heart, 'Who will ascend into heaven?'" (that is, to bring Christ down) ⁷"or 'Who will descend into the abyss?'" (that is, to bring Christ up from the dead). ⁸But what does it say?

d 9.28 Other ancient authorities read *for he will finish his work and cut it short in righteousness, because the Lord will make the sentence shortened on the earth*
e 9.33 Or *it*

worshiping God. **9:26** Paul quotes the second half of Hos. 1:10 to emphasize God's mercy and inclusion of gentiles. **9:27-28** Paul's quotation blurs several passages, seemingly stemming from Isa. 10:22-23. *Sand of the sea* comes from Hos. 1:10 and Isa. 10:22. These citations illustrate how even when a portion (*remnant*) of Israel went astray from faith in God, when they returned to their faith, God showed mercy and salvation. **9:27** *Concerning Israel*, better "on Israel's behalf." **9:29** Paul quotes Isa. 1:9. Even if present unfaithfulness makes it look like God's wrath will make Israel fare like Sodom and Gomorrah (see Gen. 18:16-19:29), this fate was and is not God's plan for Israel. Paul's invocation of Sodom and Gomorrah implies the source of their sinfulness was a lack of faith in God. **9:30-10:21** Paul lays a trap for his gentile audience, stoking them to feel pretentious and superior to Israel, since gentiles have now fully achieved God's justice, while an unfaithful remnant of Israel has not—specifically Jewish teachers of gentiles who misunderstand and lack full faith in God's plan to include gentiles. **9:30-10:3** Paul uses the metaphor of running a race: all Israel has neared the finish line, and gentiles have not started the race; when gentiles enter, a remnant of Israel stumbles, so gentiles have time to accept God and cross the finish line before the remnant finally crosses. **9:30** *Righteousness through faith*, meaning the faith of Jesus Christ. **9:31** *Law of righteousness*, specifically the part of the law that refers to God's justification of gentiles. **9:33** Paul quotes Isa. 28:16 but replaces God's laying of a foundation stone with the stumbling stone from Isa. 8:14. *Trusts in him. Him* refers to God; or "it," referring to the stumbling stone. **10:2** *I can testify*—because Paul has debated these fellow teachers. *Zeal for God . . . not based on knowledge.* Jewish teachers of gentiles are not entirely lacking faith but do not understand the part of the law concerning gentiles. **10:4-13** Paul emphasizes how his gospel fulfills the law's promises by interpreting passages from Leviticus and Deuteronomy. **10:4** *Christ is the culmination of the law*, specifically the portion of the law regarding righteousness for gentiles. Christ does not represent the end or nullification of the law. **10:5** Paul quotes Lev. 18:5. *The person*, not a generic person but Jesus, as in 1:17. **10:6-7** Paul paraphrases and interprets Deut. 30:12-13 to be about God's actions with regard to Jesus. *Righteousness that comes from faith*—that is, how gentiles have been justified through Christ's faith. **10:8** Paul quotes Deut. 30:14.

"The word is near you,
in your mouth and in your heart"
(that is, the word of faith that we proclaim),
⁹because[f] if you confess with your mouth
that Jesus is Lord and believe[g] in your heart
that God raised him from the dead, you will
be saved. ¹⁰For one believes[h] with the heart,
leading to righteousness, and one confesses
with the mouth, leading to salvation. ¹¹The
scripture says, "No one who believes[i] in him
will be put to shame." ¹²For there is no distinction between Jew and Greek; the same
Lord is Lord of all and is generous to all who
call on him. ¹³For "everyone who calls on the
name of the Lord shall be saved."

14 But how are they to call on one in whom
they have not believed?[j] And how are they
to believe[k] in one of whom they have never heard? And how are they to hear without
someone to proclaim him? ¹⁵And how are they
to proclaim him unless they are sent? As it is
written, "How beautiful are the feet of those
who bring good news!" ¹⁶But not all have
obeyed the good news,[l] for Isaiah says, "Lord,
who has believed[m] our message?" ¹⁷So faith[n]
comes from what is heard, and what is heard
comes through the word of Christ.[o]

18 But I ask, have they not heard? Indeed
they have:
"Their voice has gone out to all the
earth
and their words to the ends of the
world."
¹⁹Again I ask, did Israel not understand? First
Moses says,

"I will use those who are not a nation to
make you jealous;
with a foolish nation I will provoke you."
²⁰Then Isaiah is so bold as to say,
"I have been found by those who did not
seek me;
I have shown myself to those who did
not ask for me."
²¹But of Israel he says, "All day long I have
held out my hands to a disobedient and contrary people."

11 I ask, then, has God rejected his people?
By no means! I myself am an Israelite,
a descendant of Abraham, a member of the
tribe of Benjamin. ²God has not rejected his
people whom he foreknew. Do you not know
what the scripture says of Elijah, how he
pleads with God against Israel? ³"Lord, they
have killed your prophets, they have demolished your altars; I alone am left, and they are
seeking my life." ⁴But what is the divine reply
to him? "I have kept for myself seven thousand who have not bowed the knee to Baal."
⁵So, too, at the present time there is a remnant chosen by grace. ⁶But if it is by grace, it
is no longer on the basis of works, otherwise
grace would no longer be grace.[p]

7 What then? Israel has not achieved what

f 10.9 Or namely, that   g 10.9 Or trust   h 10.10 Or
trusts   i 10.11 Or trusts   j 10.14 Or trusted   k 10.14 Or
trust   l 10.16 Or gospel   m 10.16 Or trusted   n 10.17 Or trust
o 10.17 Or about Christ; other ancient authorities read of
God   p 11.6 Other ancient authorities add But if it is by
works, it is no longer on the basis of grace, otherwise work would
no longer be work

10:9 *You.* Singular. **10:10** *Confesses . . . salvation.* Salvation depends on everyone agreeing with the
correct teaching about gentiles. Salvation is collective throughout Romans: everyone and everything
eagerly anticipates the time when salvation comes (see 8:18–25). **10:11** Paul again quotes from Isa.
28:16, echoing Rom. 9:33. *Believes in him,* translated as "trusts" in 9:33. **10:13** Paul quotes Joel 2:32.
10:14–21 Paul shows how the remnant's stumbling is part of God's plan of salvation for all. **10:15** Paul
quotes Isa. 52:7. **10:16** Paul quotes Isa. 53:1, alluding to how some of Israel rejected the prophets'
messages. *Obeyed* plays with the language of "hearing"; obedience is to "hear under" in Greek.
10:18 Paul quotes Ps. 19:4, where the subject is the heavens. **10:19** Paul quotes Deut. 32:21. **10:20** Paul
quotes Isa. 65:1. Gentiles are those who did not seek/ask. **10:21** Paul continues quoting Isa. 65:2. Israel's remnant is still faithful but has been disobedient to God's plan. **11:1–16** If any gentiles have been
feeling superior to Jews, Paul reminds gentiles that God has never rejected any part of Israel and that
this remnant's stumbling is part of God's plan to make sure the unrighteous gentiles could be made
righteous. **11:1** *I myself . . . Benjamin.* Paul emphasizes his Jewishness to make clear that God could
never reject Israel. **11:2** *God . . . people.* Paul draws from Ps. 94:14. *Whom he foreknew* is not in the
original psalm. **11:2b–4** Paul uses the example of God and Elijah as proof that God does not reject
God's people, even when they reject God's prophets. **11:3** Paul quotes 1 Kgs. 19:10. In 1 Kings, Elijah
pleads for safety from persecution. **11:4** Paul quotes 1 Kgs. 19:18. **11:5–6** Jewish teachers like Paul, who
have understood the correct message for gentiles, were chosen by God to accomplish God's plan, not
because they have any superior knowledge. **11:7** *Achieved what it was pursuing. Achieved* in Greek

it was pursuing. The elect have achieved it, but the rest were hardened, [8]as it is written,

"God gave them a sluggish spirit,
　　eyes that would not see
　　and ears that would not hear,
down to this very day."

[9]And David says,

"Let their table become a snare and a
　　trap,
　　a stumbling block and a retribution for
　　them;
[10] let their eyes be darkened so that they
　　cannot see,
　　and keep their backs forever bent."

11 So I ask, have they stumbled so as to fall? By no means! But through their stumbling[q] salvation has come to the gentiles, so as to make Israel[r] jealous. [12]Now if their stumbling[s] means riches for the world and if their loss means riches for gentiles, how much more will their full inclusion mean!

13 Now I am speaking to you gentiles. Inasmuch as I am an apostle to the gentiles, I celebrate my ministry [14]in order to make my own people[t] jealous and thus save some of them. [15]For if their rejection is the reconciliation of the world, what will their acceptance be but life from the dead? [16]If the part of the dough offered as first fruits is holy, then the whole

batch is holy; and if the root is holy, then the branches also are holy.

17 But if some of the branches were broken off, and you, a wild olive shoot, were grafted among the others to share the rich root[u] of the olive tree, [18]do not boast over the branches. If you do boast, remember: you do not support the root, but the root supports you. [19]You will say, "Branches were broken off so that I might be grafted in." [20]That is true. They were broken off on account of unbelief,[v] but you stand on account of belief.[w] So do not become arrogant, but be afraid. [21]For if God did not spare the natural branches, neither will he spare you.[x] [22]Note then the kindness and the severity of God: severity toward those who have fallen but God's kindness toward you, if you continue in his kindness; otherwise you also will be cut off. [23]And even those of Israel,[y] if they do not continue in unbelief,[z] will be grafted in, for God has the power to graft them in again. [24]For if you have been cut from what is by nature a wild olive tree and grafted, contrary to nature, into a cultivated olive tree, how much

q 11.11 Or *transgression*　r 11.11 Gk *them*　s 11.12 Or *transgression*　t 11.14 Gk *my flesh*　u 11.17 Other ancient authorities read *the root and the richness*　v 11.20 Or *faithlessness or lack of trust*　w 11.20 Or *faithfulness or trust*　x 11.21 Other ancient authorities read *perhaps he will not spare you*　y 11.23 Gk lacks *of Israel*　z 11.23 Or *faithlessness or lack of trust*

carries the meaning of hitting the mark or reaching the end. *Pursuing* also connotes running a race; the Greek verb is in the present tense, so Israel is still running the race / seeking God. *Hardened.* When this verb refers to the human body, it can mean "callused." **11:8** Paul blurs Deut. 29:4 with Isa. 29:10. **11:9–10** Paul quotes Ps. 69:22–23. **11:11–12** Paul continues the race metaphor he began in 9:30–10:3 and has been alluding to in 11:7–10. If gentiles who have completed the race think that Israel's stumbling means they will not complete it, they are mistaken. **11:11** *Stumbled . . . fall* draws on a racing distinction: one who stumbles can still recover and complete the race, but one who stumbles and falls must forfeit. **11:12** *Stumbling . . . loss.* The word *stumbling* can also have the metaphorical meaning of transgression. Paul takes advantage of the double meaning: the transgressions of some of Israel are not a permanent state and do not separate them from God's promises. **11:13** *I am speaking to you gentiles.* Paul emphasizes the listeners he is addressing. *You* is plural here. *Apostle to the gentiles.* Paul's calling and gospel message regards God's plan for gentiles. **11:15** *Rejection.* The remnant's misunderstanding of God's plan. *Reconciliation of the world. The world* refers to gentiles. *Reconciliation* comes from the term for the exchange of an enemy to a friend, reversing the exchanges of gentiles described in 1:18–32. **11:17–36** Paul concludes his second major argument by rebuking boasting on the part of gentiles. **11:17–24** Paul uses an agricultural metaphor, an olive tree, which would be familiar to a first-century Mediterranean audience. Paul recalls the language he used in the dialogue with a pretentious gentile in 2:1–5, telling his audience they should not boast over being grafted into God's promises through the temporary cutting off of a remnant of Israel. **11:17** *Among the others.* Not all of the branches (i.e., Israel) have been cut off, only the remnant Jewish teachers of gentiles who have not fully trusted God's plan. **11:20** *Unbelief,* or distrust (see 3:3). *You stand on account of belief. Belief* is better rendered as "trust" or "faithfulness," specifically meaning Jesus's faithfulness that justified Paul's gentile listeners. **11:21–24** Paul reminds his gentile listeners that even though they have been grafted into God's plan, they can be snapped off again if they too misunderstand and lack faith in it—which their arrogance would signal. Likewise, the unfaithful remnant of Israel can and will be grafted back into God's plan. **11:24** *Contrary to nature,* or "unnatural," the term

more will these natural branches be grafted back into their own olive tree.

25 I want you to understand this mystery, brothers and sisters, so that you may not claim to be wiser than you are: a hardening has come upon part of Israel until the full number of the gentiles has come in. [26]And in this way all Israel will be saved, as it is written,

"Out of Zion will come the Deliverer;
he will banish ungodliness from Jacob."
[27] "And this is my covenant with them,
when I take away their sins."

[28]As regards the gospel they are enemies for your sake, but as regards election they are beloved for the sake of their ancestors, [29]for the gifts and the calling of God are irrevocable. [30]Just as you were once disobedient to God but have now received mercy because of their disobedience, [31]so also they have now been disobedient in order that, by the mercy shown to you, they also may now[a] receive mercy. [32]For God has imprisoned all in disobedience so that he may be merciful to all.

33 O the depth of the riches and wisdom and knowledge of God! How unsearchable are his judgments and how inscrutable his ways!
[34] "For who has known the mind of the Lord?
Or who has been his counselor?"
[35] "Or who has given a gift to him,
to receive a gift in return?"
[36]For from him and through him and to him are all things. To him be the glory forever. Amen.

12 I appeal to you therefore, brothers and sisters, on the basis of God's mercy, to present your bodies as a living sacrifice, holy and acceptable to God, which is your reasonable act of worship. [2]Do not be conformed to this age, but be transformed by the renewing of the mind, so that you may discern what is the will of God—what is good and acceptable and perfect.[b]

3 For by the grace given to me I say to everyone among you not to think of yourself more highly than you ought to think but to think with sober judgment, each according to the measure of faith that God has assigned. [4]For as in one body we have many members and not all the members have the same function, [5]so we, who are many, are one body in Christ, and individually we are members one of another. [6]We have gifts that differ according to the grace given to us: prophecy, in proportion to faith; [7]ministry, in ministering; the teacher, in teaching; [8]the encourager, in encouragement; the giver, in sincerity; the leader, in diligence; the compassionate, in cheerfulness.

9 Let love be genuine; hate what is evil; hold fast to what is good; [10]love one another with mutual affection; outdo one another in showing honor. [11]Do not lag in zeal; be ardent in spirit; serve the Lord. [12]Rejoice in hope; be patient in affliction; persevere in prayer. [13]Contribute to the needs of the saints; pursue hospitality to strangers.

a 11.31 Other ancient authorities lack now b 12.2 Or what is the good and acceptable and perfect will of God

used in 1:26–27. **11:25–36** God's plan for salvation first and always included all of Israel, including its unfaithful remnant. **11:25** *I want you to understand*, or "I do not want you to be ignorant"; see 1 Thess. 4:13. *Mystery*. In Greco-Roman religious language, this word is used to describe truths about a god only revealed to that god's faithful followers. *A hardening*, or "callus"; see 11:7. **11:26** Paul quotes Isa. 59:20. **11:27** Paul continues with Isa. 59:21 but blends with Isa. 27:9. **11:28–29** The unfaithfulness of this remnant is for the sake of ensuring gentiles' salvation alongside all Israel. The remnant of Israel has been and will always be part of God's chosen, covenant people. **11:34** Paul adapts Isa. 40:13. **11:35** See Job 41:1–3.

12:1–15:13 Ethics for gentiles in Christ. Paul explains the moral terms of gentiles' living into Christ's faithfulness as they await God's (soon) coming salvation.

12:1–2 General ethical advice. Paul frames ethical living as pleasing God with both mind and body. **12:1** *Acceptable*. Literally "pleasing." **12:2** *Will of God*. An ethical mindset is about knowing and doing God's will (see 1 Thess. 4:3).

12:3–8 Unpretentiousness among Christ followers. Paul stresses that different Christ followers have different gifts, and no one should see their own gift as better than another's. See 1 Cor. 12:12–31. **12:3** *Think with sober judgment*, or moderately. *Measure of faith . . . assigned.* As with the unfaithful remnant in chaps. 9–11, God assigns amounts of faithfulness according to God's plans. **12:6–8** This list of different callings offers a glimpse into how the earliest Christ followers named various roles in their assemblies. These roles are not clearly defined and do not have the authoritative status later attributed to them.

12:9–12 Unhypocritical love. 12:9 *Genuine*, or "unhypocritical."

14 Bless those who persecute you; bless and do not curse them. [15]Rejoice with those who rejoice; weep with those who weep. [16]Live in harmony with one another; do not be arrogant, but associate with the lowly;[c] do not claim to be wiser than you are. [17]Do not repay anyone evil for evil, but take thought for what is noble in the sight of all. [18]If it is possible, so far as it depends on you, live peaceably with all. [19]Beloved, never avenge yourselves, but leave room for the wrath of God,[d] for it is written, "Vengeance is mine; I will repay, says the Lord." [20]Instead, "if your enemies are hungry, feed them; if they are thirsty, give them something to drink, for by doing this you will heap burning coals on their heads." [21]Do not be overcome by evil, but overcome evil with good.

13 Let every person be subject to the governing authorities, for there is no authority except from God, and those authorities that exist have been instituted by God. [2]Therefore whoever resists authority resists what God has appointed, and those who resist will incur judgment. [3]For rulers are not a terror to good conduct but to bad. Do you wish to have no fear of the authority? Then do what is good, and you will receive its approval, [4]for it is God's agent for your good. But if you do what is wrong, you should be afraid, for the authority[e] does not bear the sword in vain! It is the agent of God to execute wrath on the wrongdoer. [5]Therefore one must be subject, not only because of wrath but also because of conscience. [6]For the same reason you also pay taxes, for the authorities are God's agents, busy with this very thing. [7]Pay to all what is due them: taxes to whom taxes are due, revenue to whom revenue is due, respect to whom respect is due, honor to whom honor is due.

8 Owe no one anything, except to love one another, for the one who loves another has fulfilled the law. [9]The commandments, "You shall not commit adultery; you shall not murder; you shall not steal; you shall not covet," and any other commandment, are summed up in this word, "You shall love your neighbor as yourself." [10]Love does no wrong to a neighbor; therefore, love is the fulfilling of the law.

11 Besides this, you know what time it is, how it is already the moment for you to wake from sleep. For salvation is nearer to us now than when we became believers; [12]the night is far gone; the day is near. Let us then throw off[f] the works of darkness and put on the armor of light; [13]let us walk decently as in the day, not in reveling and drunkenness, not in illicit sex and licentiousness, not in quarreling and jealousy. [14]Instead, put on the Lord Jesus Christ,

c 12.16 Or *give yourselves to humble tasks*   d 12.19 Gk *the wrath*   e 13.4 Gk *it*   f 13.12 Other ancient authorities read *lay aside*

12:14–21 Hospitable living. Paul emphasizes living in harmony, especially toward hostile people. **12:14** Paul's rhetoric echoes statements of Jesus as recorded in Gospel accounts (Matt. 5:44; Luke 6:28). **12:19** See Deut. 32:35. **12:20** Paul seems to be working with Prov. 20:22 before quoting Prov. 25:21–22.

13:1–7 Submitting to Roman rule. Paul encourages gentile Christ followers to engage in godly behavior toward Roman rulers. See **"Paul, Imperial Authority, and Politics," p. 1951. 13:1** *Be subject*, or "submit." *The governing authorities.* Literally "the authorities who prevail." Given Paul's audience is in the imperial capital, this refers to Roman authorities. *Those authorities that exist*, or just "the present ones," referring to the authorities just mentioned. **13:2** *Whoever resists*, or "whoever rebels." The root of this verb, literally "place against," is the same as its antonym in v. 1: "submit," or "place under." **13:3** *Terror*, or "fear"; see 8:15. Punishment for immoral behavior (not keeping Rome's peace) is something Christ followers should fear. **13:4** *God's agent.* This is the same term translated as "minister" elsewhere. *Bear the sword* is potentially a reference to Roman policing. **13:5** *Conscience.* Obedience to Rome is a matter of the good mindset of 12:1–2. **13:6** *God's agents.* In Roman religions, the term refers to attendants and priests who serve in various rituals. Outside religious contexts, the term could mean public service and benefactions.

13:8–10 Love, the only debt to owe. By paying all debts, the only thing Christ followers should owe is love toward others. **13:9** *You shall not commit adultery; . . . you shall not covet.* See Exod. 20:13–17; Deut. 5:17–21. *You shall love . . . as yourself.* Paul quotes Lev. 19:18.

13:11–14 Controlling desires and respectable living. Using apocalyptic language (similar to 1 Thess. 4:13–5:11), Paul urges good behavior and self-control—avoiding sexual desires and immorality—to be prepared for God's imminent salvation. **13:12** Apocalyptic rhetoric frequently relies on metaphorical binaries like day/night. **13:13** *Decently.* The term stresses proper appearance. *Not in reveling . . . jealousy.*

Making Connections: Paul, Imperial Authority, and Politics (Romans 13)
Across history, political and church leaders have cited Rom. 13:1–7 as evidence that good Christians should obey governmental authority. Archaeological remains from the Christian era of Roman rule, such as a mosaic quoting from 13:3 in Caesarea Maritima, give evidence to the passage's public use to encourage submission to the government. In apartheid South Africa, leaders in the Dutch Reformed Church and the ruling Nationalist Party appealed to this passage to malign dissent and justify their racism. In the early years of the Iraq War, U.S. supporters of the war and of the then president George W. Bush connected 13:1–7 to "supporting the troops" and cited it to combat anti-war demonstrators. In 2018, the then U.S. attorney general Jeff Sessions quoted it to defend the administration's enforcement of immigration laws at the U.S.-Mexico border. Sessions's remarks were aimed at clergy who had spoken out against the U.S. Immigration and Customs Enforcement policy that enabled officers to separate children from their parents and detain those children in cages.

Aware of this history, scholars have suggested myriad ways to interpret Rom. 13:1–7. While a few suggest that Paul's words must be taken literally, most who want to uphold Paul's authority for contemporary readers suggest other interpretations. Some suggest that Paul encourages his audiences to follow the basic laws of government—like paying taxes, not committing crimes, or (in today's world) obeying traffic signals—but that this does not apply to immoral policies (such as above). Others, taking into account Paul and his audience's historical situation as poor foreigners living under Roman imperialism, suggest that Paul's instructions are specific to his audience in the imperial capital. Paul encourages obeying the government as a survival strategy as they await God's eventual reign. Drawing from this context, some scholars even see a subtle critique and resistance to Rome hidden in what seems to be Paul's accommodationist strategy.

A final group of scholars note that Paul is not a singular authority. Just as he did not have the final say among the earliest Christ assemblies, Paul need not always be perfectly correct on these matters. Even if Paul's accommodation strategy primarily encourages paying taxes and obeying the enforcement of "just" laws, Roman authorities rarely enforced these laws with uniform justice. Like today, marginalized populations bore the brunt of governmental policing and authority. Paul's rhetoric can be questioned today in the same way that first-century Christ followers resisted Roman authority in ways that contested Paul's advice.
Jimmy Hoke

and make no provision for the flesh, to gratify its desires.

14 Welcome those who are weak in faith[g] but not for the purpose of quarreling over opinions. [2]Some believe in eating anything, while the weak eat only vegetables. [3]Those who eat must not despise those who abstain, and those who abstain must not pass judgment on those who eat, for God has welcomed them. [4]Who are you to pass judgment on slaves of another? It is before their own lord that they stand or fall. And they will be upheld, for the Lord[h] is able to make them stand.

[5]Some judge one day to be better than another, while others judge all days to be alike. Let all be fully convinced in their own minds. [6]Those who observe the day, observe it for the Lord. Also those who eat, eat for the Lord, since they give thanks to God, while those who abstain, abstain for the Lord and give thanks to God.

[7]For we do not live to ourselves, and we do not die to ourselves. [8]If we live, we live to the Lord, and if we die, we die to the Lord; so then, whether we live or whether we die, we are the

g 14.1 Or *conviction* h 14.4 Other ancient authorities read *for God*

Paul names a number of vices, including several terms that appear in 1:29–31, condemned by Roman moralists. *Illicit sex.* Translators have added *illicit*. The Greek term derives from "bed" and refers to sexual behavior, often to condemn it, but also can be used to refer to marital sex—that is, the marriage bed.
14:1–15:7 Welcome and nonjudgment in Christ assemblies. Stressing hospitality, Paul returns to the issue of potential arrogance among Christ followers. **14:1–9** Paul's comments are directed at those gentiles who are supposedly stronger in their new faith in God. *Weak in faith.* See 4:19–20 and 8:3. This phrase signals how some may not yet be fully strong in their faith in God. **14:2–3** Paul addresses eating practices that display weakness of faith. It is unclear exactly where these eating practices come from: they could be about eating food that has been sacrificed to other ancient deities, as in 1 Cor. 8. **14:5–6** Paul addresses ritual holiday observance without specifying any particular group's observances.

Lord's. [9]For to this end Christ died and lived again, so that he might be Lord of both the dead and the living.

10 Why do you pass judgment on your brother or sister? Or you, why do you despise your brother or sister? For we will all stand before the judgment seat of God.[i] [11]For it is written,

> "As I live, says the Lord, every knee shall
> bow to me,
> and every tongue shall give praise to[j]
> God."

[12]So then, each one of us will be held accountable.[k]

13 Let us therefore no longer pass judgment on one another, but resolve instead never to put a stumbling block or hindrance in the way of a brother or sister. [14]I know and am persuaded in the Lord Jesus that nothing is unclean in itself, but it is unclean for anyone who considers it unclean. [15]If your brother or sister is distressed by what you eat, you are no longer walking in love. Do not let what you eat cause the ruin of one for whom Christ died. [16]So do not let your good be slandered. [17]For the kingdom of God is not food and drink but righteousness and peace and joy in the Holy Spirit. [18]The one who serves Christ in this way is acceptable to God and has human approval. [19]Let us then pursue what makes for peace and for mutual upbuilding. [20]Do not, for the sake of food, destroy the work of God. Everything is indeed clean, but it is wrong to make someone stumble by what you eat; [21]it is good not to eat meat or drink wine or do anything that makes your brother or sister stumble.[l] [22]Hold the conviction that you have as your own before God. Blessed are those who do not condemn themselves because of what they approve. [23]But those who have doubts are condemned if they eat because they do not act from faith,[m] for whatever does not proceed from faith[n] is sin.[o]

15 We who are strong ought to put up with the failings of the weak and not to please ourselves. [2]Each of us must please our neighbor for the good purpose of building up the neighbor. [3]For Christ did not please himself, but, as it is written, "The insults of those who insult you have fallen on me." [4]For whatever was written in former days was written for our instruction, so that by steadfastness and by the encouragement of the scriptures we might have hope. [5]May the God of steadfastness and encouragement grant you to live in harmony with one another, in accordance with Christ Jesus, [6]so that together you may with one voice glorify the God and Father of our Lord Jesus Christ.

7 Welcome one another, therefore, just as Christ has welcomed you, for the glory of God. [8]For I tell you that Christ has become a servant of the circumcised on behalf of the truth of God in order that he might confirm the promises given to the ancestors [9]and that the gentiles might glorify God for his mercy. As it is written,

> "Therefore I will confess you among the
> gentiles
> and sing praises to your name";

[10]and again he says,

> "Rejoice, O gentiles, with his people";

[11]and again,

> "Praise the Lord, all you gentiles,
> and let all the peoples praise him";

[12]and again Isaiah says,

> "The root of Jesse shall come,
> the one who rises to rule the gentiles;
> in him the gentiles shall hope."

---

i 14.10 Other ancient authorities read *of Christ* *j* 14.11 Or *confess* *k* 14.12 Other ancient authorities add *to God* *l* 14.21 Other ancient authorities add *or be upset or be weakened* *m* 14.23 Or *conviction* *n* 14.23 Or *conviction* *o* 14.23 Other ancient authorities add here 16.25–27

14:10–13 As with previous rebukes of gentile arrogance (2:1–16; 11:13–24), Paul repeats that only God has the authority to judge. **14:11** Paul quotes Isa. 49:18 combined with 45:23. **14:13** *Hindrance* is the same as the stumbling block of 11:7–10. **14:14–23** Differences over eating should not be allowed to cause stumbling or quarrels. See 1 Cor. 11:21–24. **14:14** *Unclean.* The Greek term can also be translated as "common" or "profane." **14:20–21** As established in chaps. 2–5, these legal codes do not apply to gentiles. Gentiles who attempt to follow these codes are, in Paul's mindset, weaker in this faith, but they still have faith. **15:1–7** Paul encourages his audience to follow Jesus's example by pleasing their neighbors. **15:1** *Put up with*, better translated as "bear" or "carry"; see Gal. 6:17. **15:2** See 13:8–10 and 14:15. *Please* is the same word translated as "acceptable" or "approve" (e.g., 12:2; 14:22). **15:3** Paul quotes Ps. 69:9 and interprets it in light of Jesus's willingness to take on the insults of brutal death to keep gentiles from suffering.

15:8–13 Summary of Paul's gospel. As in 1:16–17, Paul concludes with a summary of his gospel/argument: Jesus Christ made a path for gentiles that fulfills God's promises to include gentiles (alongside Jews). **15:9** Paul quotes Ps. 18:49 along with 2 Sam. 22:50. **15:10** Paul quotes a version of Deut. 32:43. **15:11** Paul quotes Ps. 117:1. **15:12** Paul quotes Isa. 11:10.

[13] May the God of hope fill you with all joy and peace in believing, so that you may abound in hope by the power of the Holy Spirit.

[14] I myself feel confident about you, my brothers and sisters, that you yourselves are full of goodness, filled with all knowledge, and able to instruct one another. [15] Nevertheless, on some points I have written to you rather boldly by way of reminder, because of the grace given me by God [16] to be a minister of Christ Jesus to the gentiles in the priestly service of the gospel of God, so that the offering of the gentiles may be acceptable, sanctified by the Holy Spirit. [17] In Christ Jesus, then, I have reason to boast of my work for God. [18] For I will not be so bold as to speak of anything except what Christ has accomplished through me to win obedience from the gentiles, by word and deed, [19] by the power of signs and wonders, by the power of the Spirit,[p] so that from Jerusalem and as far around as Illyricum I have fully proclaimed the gospel of Christ. [20] Thus I make it my ambition to proclaim the gospel, not where Christ has already been named, so that I do not build on someone else's foundation, [21] but as it is written,

"Those who have never been told of him
    shall see,
and those who have never heard of him
    shall understand."

[22] This is the reason that I have so often been hindered from coming to you. [23] But now, with no further place for me in these regions, I desire, as I have for many years, to come to you [24] when I go to Spain. For I do hope to see you on my journey and to be sent on by you, once I have enjoyed your company for a little while. [25] At present, however, I am going to Jerusalem in a ministry to the saints, [26] for Macedonia and Achaia were pleased to share their resources with the poor among the saints at Jerusalem. [27] They were pleased to do this, and indeed they owe it to them, for if the gentiles have come to share in their spiritual blessings, they ought also to be of service to them in material things. [28] So, when I have completed this and have delivered to them what has been collected,[q] I will set out by way of you to Spain, [29] and I know that when I come to you I will come in the fullness of the blessing[r] of Christ.

[30] I appeal to you, brothers and sisters, by our Lord Jesus Christ and by the love of the Spirit, to join me in earnest prayer to God on my behalf, [31] that I may be rescued from the unbelievers in Judea and that my ministry[s] to Jerusalem may be acceptable to the saints, [32] so that by God's will I may come to you with joy and be refreshed in your company. [33] The God of peace be with all of you.[t] Amen.

16 I commend to you our sister Phoebe, a deacon[u] of the church at Cenchreae, [2] so that you may welcome her in the Lord, as is

p 15.19 Other ancient authorities read *the Spirit of God* or *the Holy Spirit*   q 15.28 Gk *have sealed to them this fruit*   r 15.29 Other ancient authorities add *of the gospel*   s 15.31 Other ancient authorities read *my bringing of a gift*   t 15.33 One ancient authority adds 16.25–27 here   u 16.1 Or *minister*

15:14–33 Rome's Christ assembly and Paul's mission. Paul explains why he has written to his audience and how they fit into his travel plans. **15:14** *Full . . . filled.* Two different words/roots. The first has the sense of being full (like a container); the second, used elsewhere to speak of fulfilling Scriptures, emphasizing the act of filling. **15:16** *Minister.* Greek root "liturgy"; see 13:6. **15:17** Paul can boast because he is ultimately boasting of God's actions, not his own. **15:18** *Obedience from the gentiles.* Paul's mission is to bring disobedient gentiles into faithful obedience to God; see 1:5. **15:19** *From Jerusalem . . . Illyricum.* The geographic span of Paul's gentile mission. *Illyricum.* A Roman province that began in the east of Italy and extended southwest to the northeastern region of Greece. **15:21** Paul quotes Isa. 52:15. **15:24** *Spain.* The western end of the Roman Empire. **15:25–27** Paul's mission has included taking up a collection so gentiles can share their wealth with the poor of Jerusalem (see 1 Cor. 16:1–3; 2 Cor. 9:1–5). Before heading farther westward, Paul wants to deliver these funds to Jerusalem. **15:26** *Macedonia and Achaia.* Provinces of Greece. **15:31** *Rescued from the unbelievers in Judea. Unbelievers* is better translated as "those who are unpersuaded"—that is, those who are not convinced of the correctness of Paul's gospel and arguments. It is unclear who Paul has in mind; he refers to a specific subset of people in Judea (who could be Jews or gentiles / Roman authorities) and not everyone in Judea or all Jewish people.

16:1–27 Concluding greetings and farewell. Paul ends with a typical farewell that greets his audience by name. **16:1–2** Paul introduces Phoebe, a significant leader among Christ followers who traveled to Rome with Paul's letter. **16:1** *A deacon,* or "minister" (the same term used of Rome's authorities in 13:4). *Cenchreae.* The port city of Corinth. **16:2** Paul stresses Phoebe's leadership and authority, which is

fitting for the saints, and help her in whatever she may require from you, for she has been a benefactor of many and of myself as well.

3 Greet Prisca and Aquila, my coworkers in Christ Jesus, [4]who risked their necks for my life, to whom not only I give thanks but also all the churches of the gentiles. [5]Greet also the church in their house. Greet my beloved Epaenetus, who was the first convert[v] in Asia for Christ. [6]Greet Mary, who has worked very hard for you. [7]Greet Andronicus and Junia,[w] my fellow Israelites who were in prison with me; they are prominent among the apostles, and they were in Christ before I was. [8]Greet Ampliatus, my beloved in the Lord. [9]Greet Urbanus, our coworker in Christ, and my beloved Stachys. [10]Greet Apelles, who is approved in Christ. Greet those who belong to the family of Aristobulus. [11]Greet my fellow Israelite Herodion. Greet those in the Lord who belong to the family of Narcissus. [12]Greet those workers in the Lord, Tryphaena and Tryphosa. Greet the beloved Persis, who has worked hard in the Lord. [13]Greet Rufus, chosen in the Lord, and greet his mother—a mother to me also. [14]Greet Asyncritus, Phlegon, Hermes, Patrobas, Hermas, and the brothers and sisters who are with them. [15]Greet Philologus, Julia, Nereus and his sister, and Olympas, and all the saints who are with them. [16]Greet one another with a holy kiss. All the churches of Christ greet you.

17 I urge you, brothers and sisters, to keep an eye on those who create dissensions and hindrances, in opposition to the teaching that you have learned; avoid them. [18]For such people do not serve our Lord Christ but their own appetites,[x] and by smooth talk and flattery they deceive the hearts of the simpleminded. [19]For your obedience is known to all; therefore, I rejoice over you, but I want you to be wise in what is good and guileless in what is evil. [20]The God of peace will shortly crush Satan under your feet. The grace of our Lord Jesus Christ be with you.[y]

21 Timothy, my coworker, greets you; so do Lucius and Jason and Sosipater, my fellow Israelites.

22 I Tertius, the writer of this letter, greet you in the Lord.[z]

23 Gaius, who is host to me and to the whole church, greets you. Erastus, the city treasurer, and our brother Quartus greet you.[a]

25 Now to God[b] who is able to strengthen you according to my gospel and the proclamation of Jesus Christ, according to the revelation of the mystery that was kept secret for long ages [26]but is now disclosed and through the prophetic writings is made known to all the gentiles, according to the command of the eternal God, to bring about the obedience of faith—[27]to the only wise God, through Jesus Christ, to whom be the glory forever! Amen.[c]

v 16.5 Gk *first fruits*   w 16.7 Or *Junias*; other ancient authorities read *Julia*   x 16.18 Gk *their own belly*
y 16.20 Other ancient authorities lack this sentence
z 16.22 Or *I Tertius, writing this letter in the Lord, greet you*
a 16.23 Other ancient authorities add verse 24, *The grace of our Lord Jesus Christ be with all of you. Amen.*   b 16.25 Gk *the one*   c 16.27 Other ancient authorities lack 16.25–27 or include it after 14.23 or 15.33; others put 16.24 after 16.27

greater than or equal to his own. *Benefactor.* More commonly "leader." **16:3–16** Paul greets the people who he knows are part of Rome's Christ assembly. The people Paul names offer important historical details about the demographics of Rome's Christ assembly. Nine of these twenty-seven are women; ten are names commonly given to enslaved persons; at least eleven are names indicating they (or their ancestors) were immigrants to Rome. Many or most also would have been economically poorer, at most having subsistence-level means. **16:3** *Prisca and Aquila.* See 1 Cor. 16:19; Acts 18:2–3. **16:5** *First convert.* Literally "first fruit" or the beginning of an offering (see 8:23; 11:16). **16:7** *My fellow Israelites.* Note the term *Israelites* here (used in chap. 11). This term means "relatives/relations" or "of the same family." *Junia.* Textual variants change the woman's name to the male Junias, even as there is no external evidence for the name "Junias" in the Roman world. **16:12** *Tryphaena and Tryphosa.* A missionary couple of two women. **16:17** *Hindrances.* See chaps. 11, 14. **16:18** *Serve . . . their own appetites* connotes lack of self-control; see 1:18–32. *Serve.* Literally "enslaved"; see also 6:15–23. **16:20** *Satan* is from the Hebrew term meaning "adversary." **16:21–23** More greetings from the people who are currently with Paul. **16:21** *Timothy.* Paul's coworker / traveling companion (1 Cor. 4:17; 16:10; 2 Cor. 1:1, 19; Phil. 1:1; 1 Thess. 1:1; Philemon; Acts 16:1–3; 2 Thess. 1:1; Col. 1:1; see also 1 and 2 Timothy). **16:22** *Tertius.* The scribe Paul has employed to write the letter. **16:23** *Gaius.* Plausibly the Gaius whom Paul claims to have baptized in 1 Cor. 1:14. **16:24** The earliest manuscripts do not include this verse, found in the footnotes, and it almost certainly was added later.

THE FIRST LETTER OF PAUL TO THE CORINTHIANS

Time and Place
Around 54 CE, the apostle Paul wrote this letter as part of an ongoing correspondence with the Christ assembly located in Corinth. Paul likely wrote this letter from Ephesus, the wealthy provincial capital of Asia Minor. The Corinthian Christ assembly was likewise located in a provincial capital that was a center of great trade and diversity, the capital of Roman Achaia in Corinth. Paul's earlier relationship with this community is attested in passages that include 1 Cor. 2–3 and 2 Cor. 1:19, where he speaks of in-person communication with the Corinthians. Scholars have interpreted these passages along with Acts 18:1–18 as witnessing Paul's role as founder of the Corinthian assembly. However, Paul speaks in both 1 and 2 Corinthians of a number of leaders also working with this community, including Apollos, Prisca, and Paul's close colleague Timothy, whom Paul has sent to visit the Corinthian assembly at the time of this letter's writing (1 Cor. 4:17; 16:10–11).

The Corinthian Community: Diversity and Debates
The arguments preserved in 1 Corinthians are a significant resource for understanding early Christ assemblies located in the urban context of the Greek East. Paul registers the presence of free men, free women, and enslaved persons who together compose this predominantly gentile community (see **"Paul, Enslavement, and Freedom," p. 1964**). This letter suggests an economic and social range in the Corinthian community encompassing those with little social or economic power (1:26–28) as well as those on the higher end of the social spectrum (1:11; 16:15; Rom. 16:23). Significantly, 1 Corinthians reveals these Christ followers actively debating practices that speak to their identity as a community and their relationship to the wider civic context. According to this letter, the Corinthians and Paul engage in debates around celibacy, marriage, and sexual morality, even as they confront dilemmas around consuming meat sacrificed to Greek and Roman gods (chaps. 8 and 10) and lawsuits between community members in legal courts (6:1–8). Assembly practices are also at issue in this letter as Paul argues for his vision of the Lord's Supper and certain types of assembly speech over others (14:1–25)—and for gender itself to be visually marked in speakers of the assembly (11:2–16; see also **"Paul and the Question of Gender Difference," p. 1969**). If this letter is a rich resource for insights into Christ assembly debates over practices inside and outside the community, 1 Corinthians also provides important information about theological debates among early Christ followers—notably debates over the meaning of Jesus's resurrection for his followers. Paul's own arguments suggest that some Corinthians believed in a realized eschatology in which Jesus's resurrection had already affected their empowerment and a new life in Christ. Paul, by contrast, calls for the Corinthians to embrace a future eschatology and to live in anticipation of the judgment when the Lord will come and the dead will be resurrected.

Greek Rhetoric and the Ekklēsia
This letter is marked by a strong engagement with the Greek rhetorical tradition. A range of scholars have made connections between Paul's argumentation in this letter and common rhetorical strategies and constructions employed by public speakers and rhetorical handbooks in the ancient Greek context. First Corinthians appears to fit the category of deliberative rhetoric designed to persuade an audience to make a decision toward a future outcome championed by the speaker. This type of rhetoric was at home in the democratic civic assembly—the *ekklēsia*—in which it originated. As Paul works to persuade his audience in this letter to accept his authority to lead and shape the community, he frequently employs strategies seen in such civic *ekklēsia* speech (see **"Paul, Ekklēsia, Democracy," p. 1976**). Paul's deployment of the "inexpert speaker" trope in 1 Cor. 2:1–5 is one such strategy designed to make common cause with an audience often wary of elite speakers—a strategy that tended to be undermined as here by the well-crafted rhetoric of those who claimed to be unable to use excellence of speech (2:1). Paul's use of deliberative rhetoric and its strategies in this letter reveals him to be one voice in an assembly context in which each speaker, each leader, needed to persuade an audience composed of potential speakers to their position.

Reading Guide

Paul wrote 1 Corinthians in part as a response to the Corinthians' own correspondence to Paul about practice for Christ followers, a letter, now lost to us, that is referenced in 1 Cor. 7:1. However, the overarching theme of 1 Corinthians is Paul's call for the Corinthians to be united "in the same mind and the same purpose" (1:10). Commonly, scholars have read Paul's rhetorical argument in this book as a call for the Corinthians to abandon community schisms and conflict in favor of harmonious unity. Yet Paul's argument is not for unity alone but for the Corinthians to be unified in accepting *his* leadership and vision for the community. As part of the defense of his leadership, Paul claims a special role as founder (3:10) and even "father" (4:14–21) of the community with the authority to punish those who disagree with him. If Paul argues for his leadership to the Corinthians, he also seeks to shape their assembly practice and theology in agreement with his own views. In this letter, Paul works to persuade the Corinthians to engage in assembly practices like head covering for women even as he calls upon this community to accept his own understanding of resurrection (see **"Paul and the Question of Gender Difference," p. 1969**). The success of Paul's rhetorical arguments in 1 Corinthians must be assessed against the tense relations between Paul and the Corinthians evident in the later letter(s) of 2 Corinthians (see **"Introduction to 2 Corinthians," pp. 1977–78**). Paul's argumentation in 1 Corinthians—and the evident failure of some of that argumentation in 2 Corinthians—indicates that the Corinthians engaged in a diversity of assembly practices and positions contrasting Paul's own.

Anna C. Miller

1 Paul, called to be an apostle of Christ Jesus by the will of God, and our brother Sosthenes,

2 To the church of God that is in Corinth, to those who are sanctified in Christ Jesus, called to be saints, together with all those who in every place call on the name of our Lord Jesus Christ, both their Lord*a* and ours:

3 Grace to you and peace from God our Father and the Lord Jesus Christ.

4 I give thanks to my*b* God always for you because of the grace of God that has been given you in Christ Jesus, 5for in every way you have been enriched in him, in speech and knowledge of every kind—6just as the testimony of*c* Christ has been strengthened among

you—7so that you are not lacking in any gift as you wait for the revealing of our Lord Jesus Christ. 8He will also strengthen you to the end, so that you may be blameless on the day of our Lord Jesus Christ. 9God is faithful, by whom you were called into the partnership of his Son, Jesus Christ our Lord.

10 Now I appeal to you, brothers and sisters, by the name of our Lord Jesus Christ, that all of you be in agreement and that there be no divisions among you but that you be knit together in the same mind and the same purpose. 11For it has been made clear to me by Chloe's people that there are quarrels among you, my brothers and sisters. 12What I mean is

a 1.2 Gk *theirs* *b* 1.4 Other ancient authorities lack *my* *c* 1.6 Or *witness to*

1:1–3 In this salutation, Paul follows the standard Greek letter formula that first names the sender and then the recipient. **1:1** *Paul, called to be an apostle.* For this title in Paul's other salutations, see Gal. 1:1; Rom. 1:1; 2 Cor. 1:1. For the importance Paul gives this title, see 1 Cor. 9:1–7; 12:28; 15:7–9. *Sosthenes.* A co-sender of the letter named with the lesser title of *brother.* A Sosthenes is described in Acts 18:17 as a leader of the Corinthian synagogue.
1:4–9 Thanksgiving paragraph in which Paul expresses thanks for certain aspects of the community. Paul mentions neither the love nor the faith that figures prominently in other letters (cf. Phil. 1:3–11; 1 Thess. 1:2–10; Phlm. 4–7) but instead emphasizes the speech and wisdom that will become prominent topics as the letter progresses. Paul appeals to the Corinthians' own claims they have been enriched in these gifts of wisdom and speech through following Christ—claims Paul questions in coming chapters.
1:7–8 *Revealing . . . day of our Lord Jesus Christ.* The coming day of judgment in which Christ will be revealed (see 3:12–15; 4:4–5; 5:5; 15:24–28).
1:10–4:21 An extended argument for unity and for Paul's own authoritative leadership.
1:11 *Chloe's people.* The only mention of Chloe in Paul's letters. Her *people* have been theorized alternately as her enslaved people, her business associates, or a group that follows her as a leader. Though Chloe is often taken to be a prominent Christ follower, it is also possible that only members of

that each of you says, "I belong to Paul," or "I belong to Apollos," or "I belong to Cephas," or "I belong to Christ." [13]Has Christ been divided? Was Paul crucified for you? Or were you baptized in the name of Paul? [14]I thank God[d] that I baptized none of you except Crispus and Gaius, [15]so that no one can say that you were baptized in my name. [16]I did baptize also the household of Stephanas; beyond that, I do not know whether I baptized anyone else. [17]For Christ did not send me to baptize but to proclaim the gospel—and not with eloquent wisdom, so that the cross of Christ might not be emptied of its power.

18 For the message about the cross is foolishness to those who are perishing, but to us who are being saved it is the power of God. [19]For it is written,

"I will destroy the wisdom of the wise,
        and the discernment of the discerning I
        will thwart."

[20]Where is the one who is wise? Where is the scholar? Where is the debater of this age? Has not God made foolish the wisdom of the world? [21]For since, in the wisdom of God, the world did not know God through wisdom, God decided, through the foolishness of the proclamation, to save those who believe. [22]For Jews ask for signs and Greeks desire wisdom,

[23]but we proclaim Christ crucified, a stumbling block to Jews and foolishness to gentiles, [24]but to those who are the called, both Jews and Greeks, Christ the power of God and the wisdom of God. [25]For God's foolishness is wiser than human wisdom, and God's weakness is stronger than human strength.

26 Consider your own call, brothers and sisters: not many of you were wise by human standards,[e] not many were powerful, not many were of noble birth. [27]But God chose what is foolish in the world to shame the wise; God chose what is weak in the world to shame the strong; [28]God chose what is low and despised in the world, things that are not, to abolish things that are, [29]so that no one[f] might boast in the presence of God. [30]In contrast, God is why you are in Christ Jesus, who became for us wisdom from God, and righteousness and sanctification and redemption, [31]in order that, as it is written, "Let the one who boasts, boast in[g] the Lord."

2 When I came to you, brothers and sisters, I did not come proclaiming the testimony[h] of God to you with superior speech or wisdom. [2]For I decided to know nothing among you

d 1.14 Other ancient authorities read *I am thankful*
e 1.26 Gk *according to the flesh* f 1.29 Gk *no flesh* g 1.31 Or *of* h 2.1 Other ancient authorities read *mystery*

her household or business concerns are Jesus followers. *I belong to . . . Christ.* Often described as Corinthian slogans, but it appears that only the leadership of Paul and Apollos is at issue (see 3:22–23)—with Christ and Cephas (Peter; see 9:5; 15:5; Gal. 1:18; 2:9–14) included for rhetorical effect. For Apollos's history with the Corinthians, see also 1 Cor. 3:5–6; 16:12; Acts 18:24–19:1.

1:13–17 Paul denigrates not the practice of baptism but its association with different leaders. The mention of baptism early in the letter signals the Corinthian focus on this ritual as a source of transformation and enrichment (see 12:13). **1:15–16** While Paul downplays baptism in his mission, he also claims to have baptized three men with some wealth and influence: Crispus (named a leader of the Corinthian synagogue in Acts 18:8), Gaius (see Rom. 16:23), and Stephanas. Paul names Stephanas and his household the first converts in Achaia (1 Cor. 16:15) and exhorts the Corinthians to subject themselves to "such people" (16:16).

1:17–25 Paul identifies the cross as the message of his gospel, beginning a contrast developed in the coming verses between eloquent wisdom associated with the world and the cross as divine wisdom. **1:19** Isaiah 29:14. See also Ps. 33:10.

1:26–29 Paul repeatedly underlines the low status of the Corinthians at the time of their conversion, suggesting they were weak, poor, foolish, and without power. Paul implies that their low status and foolishness in the world's eyes make them a parallel for the message of the cross itself, which Paul has already labeled "foolishness" (1:18). Contrast Paul's later description of the Corinthians in 3:1–4. **1:26** *Of noble birth.* Literally "well-born."

2:1–5 With the assertion that his proclamation of the cross lacked *superior speech* (v. 1) but manifested *Spirit* and *power* (v. 4), Paul introduces a new contrast among spiritual wisdom, divine wisdom, and human wisdom that will be important for his arguments through the rest of chaps. 2, 3, and 4. **2:1** There is ancient textual witness for "mystery of God" but more substantial evidence for *testimony of God. Testimony* makes more sense as a description of Paul's initial proclamation to the Corinthians, a contrast for the shift in tone at 2:6—which occasions the use of the word "mystery" in 2:7.

except Jesus Christ and him crucified. [3]And I came to you in weakness and in fear and in much trembling. [4]My speech and my proclamation were made not with persuasive words of wisdom[i] but with a demonstration of the Spirit and of power, [5]so that your faith might rest not on human wisdom but on the power of God.

6 Yet among the mature we do speak wisdom, though it is not a wisdom of this age or of the rulers of this age, who are being destroyed. [7]But we speak God's wisdom, a hidden mystery, which God decreed before the ages for our glory [8]and which none of the rulers of this age understood, for if they had, they would not have crucified the Lord of glory. [9]But, as it is written,

"What no eye has seen, nor ear heard,
    nor the human heart conceived,
what God has prepared for those who
    love him"—

[10]God has revealed to us through the Spirit, for the Spirit searches everything, even the depths of God. [11]For what human knows what is truly human except the human spirit that is within? So also no one comprehends what is truly God's except the Spirit of God. [12]Now we have received not the spirit of the world but the Spirit that is from God, so that we may understand the gifts bestowed on us by God. [13]And we speak of these things in words not taught by human wisdom but taught by the Spirit, interpreting spiritual things to those who are spiritual.[j]

14 Those who are unspiritual[k] do not receive the gifts of God's Spirit, for they are foolishness to them, and they are unable to understand them because they are spiritually discerned. [15]Those who are spiritual discern all things, and they are themselves subject to no one else's scrutiny.
[16] "For who has known the mind of the Lord
    so as to instruct him?"
But we have the mind of Christ.

3 And so, brothers and sisters, I could not speak to you as spiritual people but rather as fleshly, as infants in Christ. [2]I fed you with milk, not solid food, for you were not ready for solid food. Even now you are still not ready, [3]for you are still fleshly. For as long as there is jealousy and quarreling[l] among you, are you not fleshly and behaving according to human inclinations? [4]For when one says, "I belong to Paul," and another, "I belong to Apollos," are you not all too human?

5 What then is Apollos? What is Paul?

i 2.4 Other ancient authorities read *the persuasiveness of wisdom* j 2.13 Or *interpreting spiritual things spiritually* or *comparing spiritual things with spiritual* k 2.14 Or *natural* l 3.3 Other ancient authorities add *and dissensions*

2:6–3:4 Paul develops a sharp dichotomy in these verses between the mature (spiritual ones) and immature (fleshly) in which he contrasts his own maturity with the Corinthians as "infants in Christ" (3:1). **2:6** *Rulers of this age.* Likely political, earthly leaders in this case. Paul's repeated use of the term *of this age* underlines both the eternal nature of God's wisdom and the apocalyptic change that he anticipates. **2:7** Paul again asserts that he speaks God's wisdom, which he describes as *a hidden mystery*. **2:8** *Lord of glory* is used by Paul only here. **2:9** This exact quotation is not found in Scripture but may have been from Jewish writing on Isaiah (see Isa. 64:4). **2:14** While Paul asserts the inability of the *unspiritual* to receive gifts of God's Spirit, and thus to understand God's wisdom, he gives no explanation of what makes one person "spiritual" and one "unspiritual"—nor how Paul has attained his own spiritual status. **2:15** A key to Paul's coming argument about the Corinthians' judgment and his own leadership. The one who is spiritual stands in judgment over all but is immune to the judgment of others. Paul gives no indication that such a spiritual person might be judged or interrogated by other people. **2:16** Isaiah 40:13 (see also Rom. 11:34). **3:1–4** Paul concludes earlier arguments dividing spiritual and unspiritual people, human wisdom and divine wisdom, by presenting the Corinthians in these verses as unspiritual and immature and thus fleshly and human. These verses directly contradict the Corinthians' understanding that they had been spiritually enriched in Christ with "speech and knowledge of every kind" (1:5). **3:1** *Infants in Christ.* This description of the Corinthians (see also 13:12 and 14:20) distinguishes them from Paul's ideal, "mature" audience in 2:6. **3:2** *Milk, not solid food.* A common metaphor for immaturity in antiquity. See 1 Pet. 2:2; Heb. 5:12–14. **3:3** The Greek word "eris," translated here as *quarreling*, is used in Greek literature for political struggles. Together with the word "zēlos" (jealousy or rivalry), this vocabulary implies the Corinthians are experiencing political strife that defines them as fleshly and human. **3:4** *I belong to . . . Apollos.* See 1:12.

3:5–17 Paul gives God ultimate credit for the growth of the Corinthian community while using agricultural and then building metaphors to suggest that Paul and Apollos were simply God's servants. **3:5** *Servants.* The Greek word "diakonos" is best translated as "servant" in this instance but elsewhere

Servants through whom you came to believe, as the Lord assigned to each. ⁶I planted, Apollos watered, but God gave the growth. ⁷So neither the one who plants nor the one who waters is anything, but only God who gives the growth. ⁸The one who plants and the one who waters have one purpose, and each will receive wages according to their own labor. ⁹For we are God's coworkers, working together; you are God's field, God's building.

10 According to the grace of God given to me, like a wise master builder I laid a foundation, and someone else is building on it. Let each builder choose with care how to build on it. ¹¹For no one can lay any foundation other than the one that has been laid; that foundation is Jesus Christ. ¹²Now if anyone builds on the foundation with gold, silver, precious stones, wood, hay, straw—¹³the work of each builder will become visible, for the day*ᵐ* will disclose it, because it will be revealed with fire, and the fire will test what sort of work each has done. ¹⁴If the work that someone has built on the foundation survives, the builder will receive a wage. ¹⁵If the work is burned up, the builder will suffer loss; the builder will be saved, but only as through fire.

16 Do you not know that you are God's temple and that God's Spirit dwells in you?ⁿ ¹⁷If anyone destroys God's temple, God will destroy that person. For God's temple is holy, and you are that temple.

18 Do not deceive yourselves. If you think that you are wise in this age, you should become fools so that you may become wise. ¹⁹For the wisdom of this world is foolishness with God. For it is written,

"He catches the wise in their craftiness,"
²⁰and again,

"The Lord knows the thoughts of the wise,
    that they are futile."
²¹So let no one boast about people.ᵒ For all things are yours, ²²whether Paul or Apollos or Cephas or the world or life or death or the present or the future—all are yours, ²³and you are Christ's, and Christ is God's.

4 Think of us in this way: as servants of Christ and stewards of God's mysteries. ²Moreover, it is required of stewards that they be found trustworthy. ³But with me it is a very small thing that I should be judged by you or by any human court. I do not even judge myself. ⁴I am not aware of anything against myself, but I am not thereby acquitted. It is the Lord who judges me. ⁵Therefore do not pronounce judgment before the time, before the Lord comes, who will bring to light the things now hidden in darkness and will disclose the purposes of the heart. Then each one will receive commendation from God.

6 I have applied all this to Apollos and myself for your benefit, brothers and sisters, so that you may learn through us what "Not

m 3.13 Or *the Day*   *n* 3.16 In 3.16 and 3.17 the Greek word for *you* is plural   *o* 3.21 Or *about human things*

is used as a title that is better translated as "minister" or "deacon" (see Rom. 16:1, where Phoebe is named as the deacon of Corinth's port city Cenchreae). **3:6** *I planted.* Follows the chronology in Acts 18:24–19:1, with Apollos coming to Corinth after Paul. This claim to have planted and to have laid the foundation in vv. 10–11 asserts Paul is the founder of the Corinthian "ekklēsia." **3:9** *Coworkers.* Greek "sunergos." One of Paul's common terms for people engaged in ministry with him. See 1 Thess. 3:2; Phil. 2:25; Rom. 16:3. **3:13** *The day* of judgment. See also 1:8; 5:5. The apocalyptic fire of God's judgment will be the means of testing the Corinthian "building." **3:16** *God's temple.* Specifies the building of vv. 9–15 that Paul uses as a metaphor for the Corinthian assembly. See also 2 Cor. 6:16 and Eph. 2:21. Cf. 6:19.

3:18–23 Paul returns to the contrast of wisdom and foolishness in these verses, suggesting again that the Corinthians' wisdom is of *this age* and of *this world*—and related to their loyalty to different leaders. **3:19** Job 5:12–13. The only direct citation of Job in the New Testament. **3:20** Psalm 94:11. **3:22** See 1:10; 3:4.

4:1 *Servants.* A different Greek word than 3:5, often associated with taking care of another's affairs (Luke 1:2; Acts 13:5). *Stewards* usually denotes an enslaved household manager (Luke 12:42–48).

4:3–4 Paul's very insistence that he does not care if he is judged by the Corinthians, together with his earlier claim that the spiritual are judged by no one (2:15), suggests the Corinthians are indeed assessing his leadership.

4:5 *Before the Lord comes.* See also 1:8; 3:13–15; 5:5.

4:6 *Apollos and myself* clarifies the identity of "us" in 4:1. *Not beyond what is written.* Appears to be Scripture, but it is unclear if Paul is appealing to particular biblical passages or to the Scriptures as a whole. *Puffed up.* See also 4:18; 8:1; 13:4.

beyond what is written" means, so that none of you will be puffed up in favor of one against another. [7]For who sees anything different in you?[p] What do you have that you did not receive? And if you received it, why do you boast as if you did not receive?

8 Already you have all you want! Already you have become rich! Quite apart from us you have become kings! If only you had become kings, so that we might be kings with you! [9]For I think that God has exhibited us apostles as last of all, as though sentenced to death, because we have become a spectacle to the world, to angels and to humans. [10]We are fools for the sake of Christ, but you are sensible people in Christ. We are weak, but you are strong. You are honored, but we are dishonored. [11]To the present hour we are hungry and thirsty, we are naked and beaten and homeless, [12]and we grow weary from the work of our own hands. When reviled, we bless; when persecuted, we endure; [13]when slandered, we speak kindly. We have become like the rubbish of the world, the dregs of all things, to this very day.

14 I am not writing this to make you ashamed but to admonish you as my beloved children. [15]For though you might have ten thousand guardians in Christ, you do not have many fathers. Indeed, in Christ Jesus I fathered you through the gospel. [16]I appeal to you, then, be imitators of me. [17]For this reason I sent[q] you Timothy, who is my beloved and trustworthy child in the Lord, to remind you of my ways in Christ Jesus, as I teach them everywhere in every church. [18]But some of you, thinking that I am not coming to you, have become arrogant. [19]But I will come to you soon, if the Lord wills, and I will find out not the talk of these arrogant people but their power. [20]For the kingdom of God depends not on talk but on power. [21]What would you prefer? Am I to come to you with a stick or with love in a spirit of gentleness?

5 It is actually reported that there is sexual immorality among you and the sort of sexual immorality that is not found even among gentiles, for a man is living with his father's wife. [2]And you are arrogant! Should you not rather have mourned, so that he who has done this would have been removed from among you?

3 For I, though absent in body, am present in spirit, and as if present I have already pronounced judgment [4]in the name of the

p 4.7 Or Who makes you different from another?   q 4.17 Or am sending

4:8–13 This passage is driven by ironic praise for the Corinthians' enrichment in Christ, praise sarcastically echoing the Corinthians' own claims about their community. This "praise" contrasts the exaggerated description of the apostles' lowliness as servants of God. **4:9** *Sentenced to death . . . a spectacle.* Paul describes the apostles' service with the imagery of those condemned to die in the arena. **4:11–13** Paul's recital of the apostles' suffering service anticipates a similar list in 2 Cor. 4:8–9; 6:4–5; 11:23–29; 12:10.

4:14–21 Paul works to establish a singular authority over the Corinthians as their "father" in preparation for visits to the Corinthians, first by Timothy and then by Paul himself. **4:15** *Ten thousand*, better "countless." *Guardians*, or tutors. A word commonly referring to enslaved people who escorted children to and from school and gave them limited instruction (see Gal. 3:24). **4:16** *Be imitators of me.* See also 11:1; Gal. 4:12; Phil. 3:17; 4:9; 1 Thess. 1:6–7. **4:17** *I teach them everywhere in every church.* Only in 1 Corinthians does Paul appeal to a normative practice and teaching applying to all Christ assemblies. See also 7:17; 11:16; 14:32–36. **4:19** *Will come to you soon.* See 16:5. **4:20** After disparaging the wisdom and speech clearly valued by the Corinthians in earlier verses (1:5; 2:1–5; 3:1–2), Paul now separates "words" from the kingdom of God (cf. 6:9–10; 15:24, 50) and thus from salvation. **4:21** At the conclusion of this passage, Paul leverages the metaphor of father/child to make a threat of violence, offering the Corinthians his *gentleness* or a beating with a rod based, it seems, on their choice of accepting or refusing his leadership.

5:1–8 A concern about sexual immorality among the Corinthians is introduced with this passage. Paul links this issue with his earlier critique of the Corinthians' arrogance and boasting, claiming the solution to these problems is the expulsion of the party guilty of this immorality. **5:1** *Reported*, or "it has been heard." *Sexual immorality* translates the Greek "porneia," which can refer narrowly to prostitution (as in 6:13–18) or, as here, to sexual immorality more broadly. *A man is living*, or "having sex with." *His father's wife.* It appears Paul has in mind not the man's own mother but a stepmother. For prohibition against this type of relationship, see Lev. 18:8. Because Paul does not mention this woman again or call for her to be put out of the assembly, she may not be a Christian. **5:3–5** Paul invokes the gathered group as the context for judgment of this immorality, placing himself among them *in spirit*. **5:3** *I have already*

Lord Jesus on the man who has done such a thing.ʳ When you are assembled and my spirit is present with the power of our Lord Jesus, ⁵you are to hand this man over to Satan for the destruction of the flesh, so that the spirit may be saved in the day of the Lord.ˢ

6 Your boasting is not a good thing. Do you not know that a little yeast leavens all of the dough? ⁷Clean out the old yeast so that you may be a new batch of dough, as you really are unleavened. For our paschal lamb, Christ, has been sacrificed. ⁸Therefore, let us celebrate the festival, not with the old yeast, the yeast of malice and evil, but with the unleavened bread of sincerity and truth.

9 I wrote to you in my letter not to associate with sexually immoral persons, ¹⁰not at all meaning the sexually immoral of this world, or the greedy and swindlers, or idolaters, since you would then need to go out of the world. ¹¹But now I am writing to you not to associate with anyone who bears the name of brother or sister who is sexually immoral or greedy or an idolater, reviler, drunkard, or swindler. Do not even eat with such a one. ¹²For what have I to do with judging those outside? Are you not judges of those who are inside? ¹³God

will judge those outside. "Drive out the wicked person from among you."

6 When any of you has a grievance against another, do you dare to take it to court before the unrighteous, instead of taking it before the saints? ²Do you not know that the saints will judge the world? And if the world is to be judged by you, are you incompetent to try trivial cases? ³Do you not know that we are to judge angels, to say nothing of ordinary matters? ⁴If you have ordinary cases, then, do you appoint as judges those who have no standing in the church? ⁵I say this to your shame. Can it be that there is no one person wise enough to decide between brothers and sisters? ⁶Instead, brothers and sisters go to court against one another, and this before the unbelievers.

7 In fact, to have lawsuits at all with one another is already a defeat for you. Why not rather be wronged? Why not rather be defrauded? ⁸But you yourselves wrong and defraud—and brothers and sisters at that.

9 Do you not know that wrongdoers will

r 5.4 Or *on the man who has done such a thing in the name of the Lord Jesus* s 5.5 Other ancient authorities add *Jesus*

---

pronounced judgment. After questioning the Corinthians' right to judge Paul (2:15; 4:4–5), Paul forcefully proclaims his own judgment against this man accused of sexual immorality. **5:5** *Hand . . . over to Satan,* or cast him out of the church. *The flesh* calls back to Paul's use of "flesh" in 3:1–4 as shorthand for immaturity and human, rather than spiritual, orientation. *The day of the Lord.* See 1:8; 3:13. **5:7** *Paschal lamb.* The lamb sacrificed and eaten during Passover (Exod. 12:1–27). For other examples of Jesus's sacrifice connected to Passover and the sacrificial lamb, see Mark 14; John 1:29; 19:14; Rev. 5:12.

5:9–13 Paul cites another letter he wrote to the Corinthians about immorality, working to clarify this earlier discussion. **5:9** This letter may have been lost, though some theorize parts of it may be included in 2 Cor. 6–7 or even in other parts of 1 Corinthians that touch on sexual immorality (e.g., 6:12–20). **5:10–11** Paul gives another list of those committing immoral acts at 6:9–10. **5:11** *Bears the name of brother or sister.* Paul uses the family title given to fellow Christ followers to underscore that judgment for immorality is to be passed only on members of the community—who are then to be excluded from the group. *Do not even eat.* Paul may be speaking to their exclusion from the Lord's Supper (11:17–34). **5:13** *Drive out the wicked person.* Deuteronomy 17:7.

6:1–11 Paul continues the discussion from the last chapter about judgment inside and outside the community, urging the group not to take disagreements between members to courts of the unrighteous. **6:1** *Unrighteous.* Those who do not follow Christ. *Saints.* Believers in Christ who are members of the community (see 1:2; 16:15). **6:2** *The saints will judge the world.* Though Paul seems to contradict his statement about judging outsiders in 5:12, he likely has in mind here an apocalyptic scenario in which the faithful will share in God's final judgment. For such a vision elsewhere, see Dan. 7:22 (LXX); 1 En. 1:9; Wis. 3:7–8; 4:16; Sir. 4:15; Matt. 19:28; Rev. 3:21; 20:4. **6:3** *Judge angels.* For angels also subject to final judgment, see Isa. 24:21–22; Jude 6; 2 Pet. 2:4. **6:4** *Those who have no standing,* or those of no account. Likely Paul is referring to nonbelievers and again questioning the Corinthians' decisions to adjudicate disagreements outside the community. **6:7** *Be wronged.* For similar advice in Jesus's Sermon on the Mount/Plain, see Matt. 5:39; Luke 6:28–30. **6:9–10** In his explanation of *wrongdoers,* Paul gives a list of immoral actors that adds six to the four already stated in 5:9–10. **6:9** *The sexually immoral.* See note for 5:1. *Male prostitutes.* Literally "soft ones." This word was sometimes used pejoratively for the passive

not inherit the kingdom of God? Do not be deceived! The sexually immoral, idolaters, adulterers, male prostitutes,*t* men who engage in illicit sex,*u* ¹⁰thieves, the greedy, drunkards, revilers, swindlers—none of these will inherit the kingdom of God. ¹¹And this is what some of you used to be. But you were washed, you were sanctified, you were justified in the name of the Lord Jesus Christ*v* and in the Spirit of our God.

12 "All things are permitted for me," but not all things are beneficial. "All things are permitted for me," but I will not be dominated by anything. ¹³"Food is meant for the stomach and the stomach for food,"*w* and God will destroy both one and the other. The body is meant not for sexual immorality but for the Lord and the Lord for the body. ¹⁴And God raised the Lord and will also raise us by his power. ¹⁵Do you not know that your bodies are members of Christ? Should I therefore take the members of Christ and make them members of a prostitute? Never! ¹⁶Do you not know that whoever is united to a prostitute becomes one body with her? For it is said, "The two shall be one flesh." ¹⁷But anyone united to the Lord becomes one spirit with him. ¹⁸Shun sexual immorality!*x* Every sin that a person commits is outside the body, but the sexually immoral person*y* sins against the body itself. ¹⁹Or do you not know that your body is a temple*z* of the Holy Spirit within you, which you have from God, and that you are not your own? ²⁰For you were bought with a price; therefore glorify God in your body.

7 Now concerning the matters about which you wrote: "It is good for a man not to touch a woman." ²But because of cases of sexual immorality, each man should have his own wife and each woman her own husband. ³The husband should give to his wife what is due her and likewise the wife to her husband. ⁴For the wife does not have authority over her own body, but the husband does; likewise, the husband does not have authority over his own body, but the wife does. ⁵Do not deprive one another except perhaps by agreement

t 6.9 Meaning of Gk uncertain   *u* 6.9 Meaning of Gk uncertain   *v* 6.11 Other ancient authorities lack *Christ*   *w* 6.13 The quotation may extend to the word *other*   *x* 6.18 Or *prostitution*   *y* 6.18 Or *the one who hires a prostitute*   *z* 6.19 Or *sanctuary*

partner in sex between men. Both this word and the following *men who engage in illicit sex* have occasioned extensive debate in the scholarship. The last term in this verse, literally "ones who bed men." The first use of this word in Greek literature, perhaps here denoting the active partner in sex between men. See also Rom. 1:27; 1 Tim. 1:10. **6:11** *Washed.* Likely a reference to baptism. See 1:14–17; 12:13; Gal. 3:27–28.

6:12–20 Paul returns to criticizing the Corinthians' sexual morality, this time condemning community members for visiting prostitutes. **6:12** *All things are permitted for me.* Paul quotes Corinthian slogans in these verses and reprises the first again at 10:23. The slogans in 6:12 closely resemble political language in ancient democratic cities that addresses the nature of freedom and its tension with the common good. Both here and at 10:23, these slogans seem to attest the Corinthians' belief in their empowerment in Christ as members of the assembly. **6:15** *Members of Christ.* This is one of Paul's most important metaphors for the Christ community and one that he addresses extensively in 12:12–26 (see also Rom. 12:4–6). **6:16** Genesis 2:24. **6:19** *Temple of the Holy Spirit.* While Paul names the community God's temple in 3:16–17, here he describes each believer's body as the temple of the Holy Spirit. **6:20** See also 7:23. In both cases, Paul intimates that believers have become enslaved to Christ. See Rom. 6:15–23 for another version of this theological formulation of believers as enslaved to God.

7:1–40 This chapter addresses concerns the Corinthians themselves have expressed about celibacy and marriage. Along with valuable information about the Corinthians' views, this chapter includes Paul's most extended discussion about marriage/celibacy. **7:1** *You wrote* attests a Corinthian letter to Paul including this concern about celibacy. *Touch* is an idiom for "to have sex with." This quote shows some Corinthians hold to celibacy as the correct path for Christ followers. **7:2** *Cases of sexual immorality.* See 5:1–5; 6:12–20. Paul counsels monogamous marriage as a ward against such "porneia"— sexual immorality—which Paul envisions as any sex outside of marriage. Paul sets a stricter definition of morality than was broadly held in the Greco-Roman world, where sex outside of marriage was largely condoned for free men and expected for the enslaved, who had no right to marriage or power to control their bodies. **7:3** *What is due.* Paul speaks of sex in marriage as a debt each partner owes the other, a strong contrast to the Corinthian statement that begins the chapter. **7:5** *Do not deprive one another.* Literally "do not rob/defraud each other." This command for married people to practice sexual intimacy and engage celibacy only for a limited time conflicts with Paul's later exhortation in v. 29 for "those

for a set time, to devote yourselves to prayer,[a] and then come together again, so that Satan may not tempt you because of your lack of self-control. 6This I say by way of concession, not of command. 7I wish that all were as I myself am. But each has a particular gift from God, one having one kind and another a different kind.

8 To the unmarried and the widows I say that it is good for them to remain unmarried as I am. 9But if they are not practicing self-control, they should marry. For it is better to marry than to be aflame with passion.

10 To the married I give this command—not I but the Lord—that the wife should not separate from her husband 11(but if she does separate, let her remain unmarried or else be reconciled to her husband) and that the husband should not divorce his wife.

12 To the rest I say—I and not the Lord—that if any brother has a wife who is an unbeliever and she consents to live with him, he should not divorce her. 13And if any woman has a husband who is an unbeliever and he consents to live with her, she should not divorce the husband. 14For the unbelieving husband is made holy through his wife, and the unbelieving wife is made holy through the brother.[b] Otherwise, your children would be unclean, but as it is, they are holy. 15But if the unbelieving partner separates, let it be so; in such a case the brother or sister is not bound. It is to peace that God has called us.[c] 16Wife, for all you know, you might save your husband. Husband, for all you know, you might save your wife.

17 However that may be, let each of you lead the life that the Lord has assigned, to which God called you. This is my rule in all the churches. 18Was anyone at the time of his call already circumcised? Let him not seek to remove the marks of circumcision. Was anyone at the time of his call uncircumcised? Let him not seek circumcision. 19Circumcision is nothing, and uncircumcision is nothing, but obeying the commandments of God is everything. 20Let each of you remain in the condition in which you were called.

21 Were you a slave when called? Do not be concerned about it. Even if you can gain your freedom, make the most of it.[d] 22For whoever was called in the Lord as a slave is a freed person belonging to the Lord, just as whoever was free when called is a slave belonging to Christ. 23You were bought with a price; do not become slaves of humans. 24In whatever condition you were called, brothers and sisters, there remain with God.

25 Now concerning virgins, I have no command of the Lord, but I give my opinion as one who by the Lord's mercy is trustworthy. 26I think that, in view of the impending[e] crisis,[f] it is good for you to remain as you are. 27Are you bound to a wife? Do not seek to be free. Are you free from a wife? Do not seek a wife. 28But if you marry, you do not sin, and if a virgin marries, she does not sin. Yet those who marry will experience distress in the flesh, and I would

a 7.5 Other ancient authorities read *fasting and prayer*
b 7.14 Other ancient authorities read *husband* c 7.15 Other ancient authorities read *you* d 7.21 Meaning of Gk uncertain e 7.26 Or *present* f 7.26 Or *necessity*

who have wives [to] be as though they had none." **7:7–9** *I wish . . . a particular gift.* Paul's own celibacy is portrayed as a gift not everyone has, a gift Paul questions for many Corinthians based on the sexual immorality and lack of self-control he attributes to them. **7:10–16** Paul argues against divorce as a way to achieve celibacy both for those married to other Christ followers and for those Christ followers married to unbelievers. **7:10** *Not I but the Lord.* Paul seems to know commands against divorce attributed to Jesus. See Mark 10:2–12; Matt. 5:31–32. *Wife should not separate* attests Roman law in which a woman could initiate divorce. **7:12–16** Corinthian Christ followers, both men and women, were married to those who did not share their beliefs. Paul burdens the Christ follower with "sanctifying" and "saving" their unbelieving spouse—with the implication that the believer who remains in their marriage may convert their spouse. **7:17–24** Paul expands his exhortation that Christ followers remain in the situation in which they were called to circumcision/uncircumcision and enslaved status. **7:21–24** This passage directed to enslaved Christ followers asks them to be content with their status. V. 21d, in which Paul instructs the enslaved faced with gaining freedom that they should *make the most of it,* has led to centuries-long debates over whether Paul here asks the enslaved to remain enslaved or to take offered freedom. There is widespread recent consensus that Paul is urging the enslaved to achieve freedom if it becomes available—though he opposes them pursuing it. **7:25** *Now concerning virgins.* The similar *now concerning* formula in 7:1 suggests the Corinthians may have specifically addressed unmarried women in their previous letter. **7:26** *Impending crisis* refers to the coming tribulations that will accompany the passing

Focus On: Paul, Enslavement, and Freedom (1 Corinthians 7:20-24)

Paul's letters witness enslaved people within urban Christ assemblies in the very first decades of the movement (1 Cor. 7:20-24; Rom. 16:23; Philemon). This witness quickly became part of a centuries-long debate about enslaved Christians and Paul's own beliefs about slavery that continues into the present—a debate often centered on 1 Cor. 7:20-24.

If the baptismal formula of Gal. 3:28 and 1 Cor. 12:13 seems to create equality for the enslaved and free in the Christ assembly, 1 Cor. 7:20-24 does not condemn slavery as an institution or actively encourage the enslaved to seek their freedom. Paul calls on enslaved and free members of the assembly to remain "in whatever condition you were called" (7:24) while urging the enslaved not to be concerned about their status. Indeed, Paul marks a theological equivalence between enslaved and free, stating all "were bought with a price" (7:23) by the Lord. Paul frequently uses slavery as a metaphor to positively portray the relationship between God as the owner of the enslaved and believers as enslaved (e.g., Rom. 6:22). Here, however, Paul uses the theological metaphor of slavery in talking directly to people who were not metaphorically but actually enslaved. Such a positive use of slavery as a metaphor masks the brutality of lived slavery, and we must ask how the enslaved themselves received Paul's command not to be concerned about their status.

For centuries, 1 Cor. 7:21d has occasioned particular debate as to its translation and implications. After telling the enslaved not to be concerned about their status, Paul urges that if they are able to become free, they should "make the most of it." From at least the time of John Chrysostom, Christians have alternately translated this phrase as Paul telling the enslaved offered freedom to remain enslaved (Chrysostom's position and the dominant argument over many centuries) or Paul urging the enslaved to take advantage of the opportunity to become free. Scholars increasingly prefer the latter interpretation while recognizing that this does not constitute a critique of slavery as such. Widespread manumission in antiquity was itself a component of slavery as a system of domination by which owners gained money from the enslaved buying their freedom, even as most freed people continued to benefit their former owners with labor or a portion of their wages.

Later authors continue to register debate about the status of enslaved Christians. For example, 1 Timothy's insistence that enslaved Christians with believing masters must not disrespect these masters because they are "brothers and sisters" but "serve" (6:2) them even more suggests other arguments within the assembly toward egalitarian relationships more in line with Gal. 3:28. Indeed, Ignatius of Antioch (d. second century CE) indicates that some enslaved Christians were calling for the assembly to use its resources toward buying their freedom (Ign. *Pol.* 4.2). We must be alive to the probability that other ancient Christians interpreted the baptismal promise that in Christ there is "no slave or free" more concretely toward the literal freedom and equality of the enslaved.

Anna C. Miller

spare you that. [29]I mean, brothers and sisters, the appointed time has grown short; from now on, let even those who have wives be as though they had none, [30]and those who mourn as though they were not mourning, and those who rejoice as though they were not rejoicing, and those who buy as though they had no possessions, [31]and those who deal with the world as though they had no dealings with it. For the present form of this world is passing away.

[32]I want you to be free from anxieties. The unmarried man is anxious about the affairs of the Lord, how to please the Lord, [33]but the married man is anxious about the affairs of the world, how to please his wife, [34]and his interests are divided. And the unmarried woman and the virgin are anxious about the affairs of the Lord, so that they may be holy in body and spirit, but the married woman is anxious about the affairs of the world, how to please her husband. [35]I say this for your own benefit, not to put any restraint upon you but to promote good order and unhindered devotion to the Lord.

[36] If anyone thinks that he is behaving indecently toward his fiancée,[g] if his passions are strong and so it has to be, let him marry as

g 7.36 Gk *virgin*

away of this age. This apocalyptic frame dominates vv. 26-31. **7:29** *Let even those who have wives be as though they had none.* Cf. vv. 2-5. **7:34** *The unmarried woman and the virgin* suggests the unmarried woman is someone who has been previously married and is now divorced or widowed. **7:36-38** Cf. vv. 25-26 and 28. In vv. 36-38, Paul assigns the ultimate power to decide whether an unmarried woman

he wishes; it is no sin. Let them marry. [37]But if someone stands firm in his resolve, being under no necessity but having his own desire under control, and has determined in his own mind to keep her as his fiancée,[b] he will do well. [38]So then, he who marries his fiancée[i] does well, and he who refrains from marriage will do better.

39 A wife is bound as long as her husband lives. But if the husband dies,[j] she is free to marry anyone she wishes, only in the Lord. [40]But in my opinion she is more blessed if she remains as she is. And I think that I, too, have the Spirit of God.

8 Now concerning food sacrificed to idols: we know that "all of us possess knowledge." Knowledge puffs up, but love builds up. [2]Anyone who claims to know something does not yet have the necessary knowledge, [3]but anyone who loves God is known by him.

4 Hence, as to the eating of food offered to idols, we know that "no idol in the world really exists" and that "there is no God but one." [5]Indeed, even though there may be so-called gods in heaven or on earth—as in fact there are many gods and many lords—[6]yet for us there is one God, the Father, from whom are all things and for whom we exist, and one Lord, Jesus Christ, through whom are all things and through whom we exist.

7 It is not everyone, however, who has this knowledge. Since some have become so accustomed to idols until now, they still think of the food they eat as food offered to an idol, and their conscience, being weak, is defiled. [8]"Food will not bring us close to God."[k] We are no worse off if we do not eat and no better off if we do. [9]But take care that this liberty of yours does not somehow become a stumbling block to the weak. [10]For if others see you, who possess knowledge, eating in the temple of an idol, might they not, since their conscience is weak, be encouraged to the point of eating food sacrificed to idols? [11]So by your knowledge the weak brother or sister for whom Christ died is destroyed. [12]But when you thus sin against brothers and sisters and wound their conscience when it is weak, you sin against Christ. [13]Therefore, if food is a cause of their falling, I will never again eat meat, so that I may not cause one of them to fall.

9 Am I not free? Am I not an apostle? Have I not seen Jesus our Lord? Are you not my work in the Lord? [2]If I am not an apostle to others, at least I am to you, for you are the seal of my apostleship in the Lord.

3 This is my defense to those who would

h 7.37 Gk virgin   i 7.38 Gk virgin   j 7.39 Gk falls asleep
k 8.8 The quotation may extend to the end of the verse

remains celibate lies with her fiancé. The decision of that man, in turn, is to be based not on the woman's own wishes but upon the question of whether the man can control his own sexual desires.
8:1-13 This passage concerns eating food sacrificed to Greco-Roman gods. Early Christ followers struggled with the possibility that eating this food might indicate their allegiance to such gods, an issue intensified by much of the food in ancient markets having been so sacrificed. **8:1** *Now concerning.* See also 7:1, 25; 12:1. Food sacrificed to idols may be another issue the Corinthians had communicated to Paul. *All of us possess knowledge.* A Corinthian phrase or slogan claiming their empowerment in Christ. See also 1:7-8. Paul immediately qualifies such knowledge as a source of arrogance. **8:4** *No idol . . . there is no God but one.* These quotations from the Corinthian assembly suggest the knowledge claimed in v. 1 is the belief in monotheism. **8:7-13** *Not everyone . . . has this knowledge.* Paul further questions the Corinthian claim that they all possess knowledge (8:1). Paul describes two groups within the community—the weak in conscience and those strong in their monotheistic knowledge. Paul insists that those with knowledge must curtail their eating of meat offered to idols if and when it may harm the consciences of the weak. **8:8-9** At least the beginning, and possibly the entirety, of v. 8 features another quotation from the Corinthians asserting their knowledge that food does not impact their relationship with God. Yet Paul again qualifies this knowledge directly after in v. 9 by suggesting that this *liberty* may harm those who are weak.
9:1-27 An extended defense of Paul's role as an apostle. While this passage connects to Paul's attempt to keep Christ followers away from temple banquets (8:10) and his claim he would abandon meat entirely to protect the "weak" (8:13), it also suggests that Paul's struggles with the Corinthians include Paul's own varied practice with regard to eating meat sacrificed to idols (10:25-30). **9:3** *Defense to those who would examine me.* Paul's use of judicial language to describe both his defense ("apologia") and judgment by others ("anakrinō") indicates Corinthian challenges to Paul's leadership as an

examine me. ⁴Do we not have the right to our food and drink? ⁵Do we not have the right to be accompanied by a believing wife,ʲ as do the other apostles and the brothers of the Lord and Cephas? ⁶Or is it only Barnabas and I who have no right to refrain from working for a living? ⁷Who at any time pays the expenses for doing military service? Who plants a vineyard and does not eat any of its fruit? Or who tends a flock and does not get any of its milk?

8 Do I say this on human authority? Does not the law also say the same? ⁹For it is written in the law of Moses, "You shall not muzzle an ox while it is treading out the grain." Is it for oxen that God is concerned? ¹⁰Or does he not speak entirely for our sake? It was indeed written for our sake, for whoever plows should plow in hope and whoever threshes should thresh in hope of a share in the crop. ¹¹If we have sown spiritual things among you, is it too much if we harvest materialᵐ things? ¹²If others share this rightful claim on you, do not we still more?

Nevertheless, we have not made use of this right, but we endure anything rather than put an obstacle in the way of the gospel of Christ. ¹³Do you not know that those who work in the temple service get their food from the temple and those who serve at the altar share in what is sacrificed on the altar? ¹⁴In the same way, the Lord commanded that those who proclaim the gospel should get their living by the gospel.

15 But I have made no use of any of these rights, nor am I writing this so that they may be applied in my case. Indeed, I would rather die than that—no one will deprive me of my ground for boasting! ¹⁶If I proclaim the gospel, this gives me no ground for boasting, for

an obligation is laid on me, and woe to me if I do not proclaim the gospel! ¹⁷For if I do this of my own will, I have a wage, but if not of my own will, I am entrusted with a commission. ¹⁸What then is my wage? Just this: that in my proclamation I may make the gospel free of charge, so as not to make full use of my rights in the gospel.

19 For though I am free with respect to all, I have made myself a slave to all, so that I might gain all the more. ²⁰To the Jews I became as a Jew, in order to gain Jews. To those under the law I became as one under the law (though I myself am not under the law) so that I might gain those under the law. ²¹To those outside the law I became as one outside the law (though I am not outside God's law but am within Christ's law) so that I might gain those outside the law. ²²To the weak I became weak, so that I might gain the weak. I have become all things to all people, that I might by all means save some. ²³I do it all for the sake of the gospel, so that I might become a partner in it.

24 Do you not know that in a race the runners all compete, but only one receives the prize? Run in such a way that you may win it. ²⁵Athletes exercise self-control in all things; they do it to receive a perishable wreath, but we an imperishable one. ²⁶So I do not run aimlessly, nor do I box as though beating the air, ²⁷but I punish my body and enslave it, so that after proclaiming to others I myself should not be disqualified.

10 I do not want you to be ignorant, brothers and sisters, that our ancestors were

ʲ 9.5 Gk *a sister as wife*   ᵐ 9.11 Gk *fleshly*

apostle. **9:4–12** The first part of Paul's defense involves a series of rhetorical questions designed to show Paul's rights to material support by the community, rights that demonstrate his status as an apostle. **9:5** *Brothers of the Lord.* Jesus's brothers (Mark 6:3). Paul mentions only James by name; see 15:7; Gal. 1:19. *Cephas.* Peter. The story of Peter's mother-in-law being healed attests his married status (Mark 1:30). **9:6** *Barnabas* (see Acts 4:36–37; 9:27; 11:19–30; Gal. 2:1–13). An early colleague of Paul. *Working for a living* at jobs in addition to his work as an apostle. See Acts 18:1–4; 1 Thess. 2:9. **9:9** Deuteronomy 25:4. **9:14** See Matt. 10:10; Luke 10:7. **9:15–18** Though Paul asserts his rights as an apostle to the Corinthians' support, his special relationship with the gospel precludes him accepting that support. **9:17** *A commission.* Literally a stewardship (see 4:1) often carried out by an enslaved person. **9:19–23** Paul's changing persona as an apostle in different circumstances connects to his defense in v. 3. Paul works to appeal to different groups, and thus to *become all things to all people, that I might by all means save some* (v. 22). **9:19** *A slave to all.* Like many Greek civic leaders, Paul uses the metaphor of voluntary slavery to describe his leadership. **9:24–27** Paul's metaphors throughout these verses connect to the athletic contests of the Isthmian Games held only a few kilometers from Corinth.

10:1–22 Paul returns to the topic of food sacrificed to Greco-Roman gods. Paul deploys the exodus story to uphold the dangers of idolatry (vv. 1–11), before he again cautions against eating food dedicated to the gods within their temples (vv. 14–22; see 8:10–11). **10:1** *Our ancestors.* Includes Christ followers as

all under the cloud, and all passed through the sea, [2]and all were baptized into Moses in the cloud and in the sea, [3]and all ate the same spiritual food, [4]and all drank the same spiritual drink. For they drank from the spiritual rock that followed them, and the rock was Christ. [5]Nevertheless, God was not pleased with most of them, and they were struck down in the wilderness.

6 Now these things occurred as examples for us, so that we might not desire evil as they did. [7]Do not become idolaters as some of them did, as it is written, "The people sat down to eat and drink, and they rose up to play." [8]We must not engage in sexual immorality, as some of them did, and twenty-three thousand fell in a single day. [9]We must not put Christ[n] to the test, as some of them did, and were destroyed by serpents. [10]And do not complain, as some of them did, and were destroyed by the destroyer. [11]These things happened to them to serve as an example, and they were written down to instruct us, on whom the ends of the ages have come. [12]So if you think you are standing, watch out that you do not fall. [13]No testing has overtaken you that is not common to everyone. God is faithful, and he will not let you be tested beyond your strength, but with the testing he will also provide the way out so that you may be able to endure it.

14 Therefore, my beloved, flee from the worship of idols. [15]I speak as to sensible people; judge for yourselves what I say. [16]The cup of blessing that we bless, is it not a sharing in the blood of Christ? The bread that we break, is it not a sharing in the body of Christ? [17]Because there is one bread, we who are many are one body, for we all partake of the one bread. [18]Consider the people of Israel:[o] Are not those who eat the sacrifices partners in the altar? [19]What do I imply, then? That food sacrificed to idols is anything or that an idol is anything? [20]No, I imply that what they[p] sacrifice, they sacrifice to demons and not to God. I do not want you to be partners with demons. [21]You cannot drink the cup of the Lord and the cup of demons. You cannot partake of the table of the Lord and the table of demons. [22]Or are we provoking the Lord to jealousy? Are we stronger than he?

23 "All things are permitted," but not all things are beneficial. "All things are permitted," but not all things build up. [24]Do not seek your own advantage but that of the other. [25]Eat whatever is sold in the meat market without raising any question on the ground of conscience, [26]for "the earth and its fullness

n 10.9 Other ancient authorities read *the Lord* o 10.18 Gk *Israel according to the flesh* p 10.20 Other ancient authorities read *the gentiles*

part of Israel. *The cloud . . . the sea.* See Exod. 13:21–22; 14:22; Ps. 105:39; Wis. 10:17; 19:7. **10:2** *All were baptized.* An insertion of the Christian ritual of baptism into the exodus narrative. **10:3** *Spiritual food* is manna; see Exod. 16:4, 35; Deut. 8:3; Ps. 78:24–25. **10:4** *Spiritual drink.* See Exod. 17:6; Num. 20:7–11; Ps. 78:15–16. The Hebrew Bible accounts do not include a rock that follows the Israelites, but rabbinic tradition includes a "traveling" well (Num. 21:16–18). Paul's emphasis on food and Christ as a rock providing drink foreshadows the Lord's Supper (see 11:17–34). **10:5** *They were struck down in the wilderness.* See Num. 14:16, 29–30; Ps. 78:30–31; Heb. 3:17; Jude 5. **10:7** *The people sat . . . rose up to play.* See Exod. 32:6. **10:8–9** *Twenty-three thousand.* See Num. 25:1–9. *To the test.* See Ps. 78:18; Deut. 6:16. *Destroyed by serpents.* See Num. 21:5–6. **10:10** *Complain, as some of them did* against Moses in the wilderness; see, for example, Exod. 16:2–3. **10:14–22** An argument that those who share in the Lord's Supper or the sacrifices offered at the Jerusalem temple become partners with the divine in this act, just as those who eat at feasts in their temples partner with Greco-Roman gods. In this latter instance, however, Paul makes the extreme case that diners partner with demons. Paul insists that it is not possible to enter such a partnership with demons and also to participate in the Lord's Supper. **10:16** *The blood of Christ.* Cf. 11:25, 27. *The body of Christ.* Cf. 11:24, 27, 29. *The bread that we break.* Cf. 11:24. **10:17** *We who are many are one body.* Paul elaborates this idea of the assembly made of many members composing the one body of Christ in 12:12–26.

10:23–11:1 Paul concludes his discussion by considering meat sold in the markets and meals with meat at the homes of unbelievers. In both cases, Paul insists that Christ followers can eat meat offered without concern unless they are told specifically it has been offered in sacrifice—and then they should abstain in case they might harm someone else's conscience. **10:23** *All things are permitted.* Paul again quotes the Corinthians, a statement that adds to the sense that they see themselves as empowered in Christ to partake in meat sacrificed to the gods without concern. Paul qualifies this Corinthian claim to empowerment with the conscience of others (see 8:1, 4).

are the Lord's." [27]If an unbeliever invites you to a meal and you are disposed to go, eat whatever is set before you without raising any question on the ground of conscience. [28]But if someone says to you, "This has been offered in sacrifice," then do not eat it, out of consideration for the one who informed you and for the sake of conscience—[29]I mean the other's conscience, not your own. For why should my freedom be subject to the judgment of someone else's conscience? [30]If I partake with thankfulness, why should I be denounced because of that for which I give thanks?

[31] So, whether you eat or drink or whatever you do, do everything for the glory of God. [32]Give no offense to Jews or to Greeks or to the church of God, [33]just as I try to please everyone in everything I do, not seeking my own advantage but that of many, so that they may be saved. [1]Be imitators of me, as I am of Christ.

[2] I commend you because you remember me in everything and maintain the traditions just as I handed them on to you. [3]But I want you to understand that Christ is the head of every man, and the man[q] is the head of the woman,[r] and God is the head of Christ. [4]Any man who prays or prophesies with something on his head shames his head, [5]but any woman who prays or prophesies with her head unveiled shames her head—it is one and the same thing as having her head shaved. [6]For if a woman will not veil herself, then she should cut off her hair, but if it is shameful for a woman to have her hair cut off or to be shaved, she should wear a veil. [7]For a man ought not to have his head veiled, since he is the image and reflection[s] of God, but woman is the reflection[t] of man. [8]Indeed, man was not made from woman but woman from man. [9]Neither was man created for the sake of woman but woman for the sake of man. [10]For this reason a woman ought to have authority over her head,[u] because of the angels. [11]Nevertheless, in the Lord woman is not independent of man or man independent of woman. [12]For just as woman came from man, so man comes through woman, but all things come from God. [13]Judge for yourselves: Is it proper for a woman to pray to God with her head unveiled? [14]Does not nature itself teach you that, if a man wears long hair, it is dishonoring to him, [15]but if a woman has long hair, it is her glory? For her hair is given to her for a covering. [16]But if anyone is disposed to be contentious—we have no such custom, nor do the churches of God.

[17] Now in the following instructions I do not commend you, because when you come together it is not for the better but for the worse. [18]For, to begin with, when you come together as a church, I hear that there are divisions

q 11.3 Or *husband*   r 11.3 Or *wife*   s 11.7 Or *glory*   t 11.7 Or *glory*   u 11.10 Or *have freedom of choice regarding her head*

11:2–14:40 This section of the letter is dominated by Paul's arguments about practices that should take place in the gathered assembly.

11:2–16 Paul deploys a series of arguments in this passage toward the visual, physical differentiation of women's speech in the assembly through head coverings. See **"Paul and the Question of Gender Difference," p. 1969**. **11:3** *The head.* In antiquity, the head was associated with the mind, the soul, and the divine and was understood to be in a leadership position over the body. Paul's hierarchical formulations leave the woman as the only one in this hierarchy who does not act as a head to another, even as she is separated from the divine. **11:5** Although scholars have commonly read Paul's arguments for women's veiling as an attempt to bring the Corinthians in line with Greco-Roman norms for women's public appearance, the archaeological record shows highly varied practice with regard to women veiling or going unveiled. That said, ancient Greek literature often deploys the veil toward asserting the need to "cover" or control women's speech and sexuality in public. Paul seems to use veiling in this passage toward likewise presenting women's speech as a source of danger or disorder in need of control. **11:7–9** *Image . . . of God.* See Gen. 1:27. Paul changes the verse to assert man alone as created in the image of God. *Man was not made . . . woman from man.* See Gen. 2:21–23. *Woman for the sake of man.* See Gen. 2:18. **11:10** No scholarly consensus exists to explain Paul's use of angels as a reason for veiling. **11:11–12** Though these verses have been read toward reciprocity between men and women, they ultimately reinforce that women's role is to bear children—a vision at odds with the celibacy advocated by the Corinthians in 7:1 and with the baptismal formula of Gal. 3:28.

11:17–34 Paul addresses the practice of gathering for the Lord's Supper in this passage, critiquing Corinthian performance of this meal. **11:18** *Divisions.* While the vocabulary for divisions here is the same as in 1:10, Paul seems to be addressing not groups following different leaders in this case but divisions

Going Deeper: Paul and the Question of Gender Difference (1 Corinthians 11:2–16 and 14:33b–36)

Passages in Paul's letters such as 1 Cor. 11:2–16 and 1 Cor. 14:33b–36, in which Paul addresses questions of gender and women's participation in the early Christ assembly, have cast a long shadow in the Christian tradition, frequently cited toward limiting women's egalitarian participation in the church. If 1 Cor. 11:2–16 has often been read as an argument about women's hair and head covering during speech performed in worship, 1 Cor. 14:33b–36 seems to prohibit entirely women's speech in the assembly. The seeming contradiction between these passages in which Paul condemns in 1 Cor. 14:33b–36 the speech he has implicitly approved in 1 Cor. 11:2–16 has led a range of scholars to argue that 1 Cor. 14:33–36 is a later insertion to the letter. However, other scholars have argued persuasively that the gender difference and hierarchy that Paul establishes in 1 Cor. 11:2–16 becomes a rhetorical foundation for his prohibition on women's assembly speech in 1 Cor. 14:33–36.

Paul deploys arguments from the cosmos, creation, and nature in 1 Cor. 11:2–16 to convince the Corinthians that women's speech alone must be marked by a head covering in the assembly. In v. 3, Paul introduces an order of the cosmos in which "Christ is the head of every man, and the man is the head of the woman, and God is the head of Christ." This gendered hierarchy places women at a remove from the divine and, in leaving them the only ones in the hierarchy who do not serve as a head, undermines women's claim to the reason and authority associated with the head and mind in antiquity. Paul then (mis)reads Gen. 1:27 in v. 7 to argue that men alone are created in the image of God—while woman "is the reflection of man"—and asserts women's secondary creation in vv. 8–9. Paul also includes logically difficult arguments using hair to suggest "natural" differences between women and men. Together, Paul's arguments in 1 Cor. 11:2–16 render problematic women's speech in the *ekklēsia*, requiring that this speech be visually marked as distinct. This conflicts with the baptismal formula of Gal. 3:28 that in Christ there is "no longer male and female," and it seems no accident that Paul's rendering of this formula in 1 Cor. 12:13 leaves out this particular element of gender.

Whether we read 1 Cor. 14:33–36 as an interpolation or not, 1 Cor. 11:2–16 prepares the reader for the implicit suggestion in those verses that women's speech is a source of problematic disorder for the assembly. These passages also reinforce an image of "women" in this community as synonymous with "wives," thereby also erasing the presence of celibate or enslaved women who do not fit into the traditional household as wives. Paul's formulations seem to conflict with existing theology and practice within the Corinthian community empowering a range of women to participate vocally in the assembly.

Anna C. Miller

among you, and to some extent I believe it. [19]Indeed, there have to be factions among you, for only so will it become clear who among you are genuine. [20]When you come together, it is not really to eat the Lord's supper. [21]For when the time comes to eat, each of you proceeds to eat your own supper, and one goes hungry and another becomes drunk. [22]What! Do you not have households to eat and drink in? Or do you show contempt for the church of God and humiliate those who have nothing? What should I say to you? Should I commend you? In this matter I do not commend you!

23 For I received from the Lord what I also handed on to you, that the Lord Jesus on the night when he was betrayed took a loaf of bread, [24]and when he had given thanks, he broke it and said, "This is my body that is for[v] you. Do this in remembrance of me." [25]In the same way he took the cup also, after supper, saying, "This cup is the new covenant in my blood. Do this, as often as you drink it, in remembrance of me." [26]For as often as you eat this bread and drink the cup, you proclaim the Lord's death until he comes.

27 Whoever, therefore, eats the bread or drinks the cup of the Lord in an unworthy

v 11.24 Other ancient authorities read *is broken for*

between those who have greater wealth and those with little. See 11:22. **11:21–22** Paul's critique seems to be that some Corinthians are eating food they have brought to the Lord's Supper without concern for *those who have nothing* (v. 22)—that is, the poor in the group. Paul seems to suggest not that the wealthy share their food but that they should eat at home. See also v. 34. **11:23–26** Valuable as the earliest account in Christian Scripture of Jesus's symbolic sharing of bread and wine with his disciples, which became the basis for the Lord's Supper, or the Eucharist. See also 10:16–17; Matt. 26:26–29; Mark 14:22–25; Luke 22:15–20. **11:25** *Cup . . . after supper.* See Luke 22:20. This suggests that the breaking of the bread and the cup were separated by a meal.

manner will be answerable for the body and blood of the Lord. [28]Examine yourselves, and only then eat of the bread and drink of the cup. [29]For all who eat and drink[w] without discerning the body[x] eat and drink judgment against themselves. [30]For this reason many of you are weak and ill, and some have died.[y] [31]But if we judged ourselves, we would not be judged. [32]But when we are judged by the Lord, we are disciplined[z] so that we may not be condemned along with the world.

33 So then, my brothers and sisters, when you come together to eat, wait for one another. [34]If you are hungry, eat at home,[a] so that when you come together, it will not be for your condemnation. About the other things I will give instructions when I come.

12 Now concerning spiritual gifts,[b] brothers and sisters, I do not want you to be ignorant. [2]You know that when you were gentiles you were enticed and led astray to idols that could not speak. [3]Therefore I want you to understand that no one speaking by the Spirit of God ever says "Let Jesus be cursed!" and no one can say "Jesus is Lord" except by the Holy Spirit.

4 Now there are varieties of gifts but the same Spirit, [5]and there are varieties of services but the same Lord, [6]and there are varieties of activities, but it is the same God who activates all of them in everyone. [7]To each is given the manifestation of the Spirit for the common good. [8]To one is given through the Spirit the utterance of wisdom and to another the utterance of knowledge according to the same Spirit, [9]to another faith by the same Spirit, to another gifts of healing by the one Spirit, [10]to another the working of powerful deeds, to another prophecy, to another the discernment of spirits, to another various kinds of tongues, to another the interpretation of tongues. [11]All these are activated by one and the same Spirit, who allots to each one individually just as the Spirit chooses.

12 For just as the body is one and has many members, and all the members of the body, though many, are one body, so it is with Christ. [13]For in the one Spirit we were all baptized into one body—Jews or Greeks, slaves or free—and we were all made to drink of one Spirit.

14 Indeed, the body does not consist of one member but of many. [15]If the foot would say, "Because I am not a hand, I do not belong to the body," that would not make it any less a part of the body. [16]And if the ear would say, "Because I am not an eye, I do not belong to the body," that would not make it any less a part of the body. [17]If the whole body were an eye, where would the hearing be? If the whole body were hearing, where would the sense of smell be? [18]But as it is, God arranged the members in the body, each one of them, as he chose. [19]If all were a single member, where would the body be? [20]As it is, there are many members yet one body. [21]The eye cannot say to the hand, "I have no need of you," nor again the head to the feet, "I have no need of you." [22]On the contrary, the members of the body that seem to be weaker are indispensable, [23]and those members of the body that we think less honorable we clothe with greater honor, and our less respectable members are treated with greater respect, [24]whereas our

---

w 11.29 Other ancient authorities add *in an unworthy manner,*   x 11.29 Other ancient authorities read *the Lord's body*   y 11.30 Gk *fallen asleep*   z 11.32 Or *When we are judged, we are being disciplined by the Lord*   a 11.34 Gk *in a household*   b 12.1 Or *spiritual persons*

12:1–11 Paul's discussion of spiritual gifts extends to 14:40 and seems to have the goal of limiting the use of a particular gift—"glossolalia," or speaking in tongues—within the assembly. **12:1** *Now concerning,* used here as in 7:1 and 8:1, may mean that spiritual gifts are another matter the Corinthians have raised with Paul. **12:3** Paul suggests that the content of someone's speech will reveal whether it is inspired by God's Spirit. *Jesus be cursed* may be an exaggerated example of speech that could not be inspired by the Holy Spirit. **12:4–11** Paul reveals that a range of "charismata," spiritual gifts, were practiced in the Corinthian assembly. He insists that the same God, the same Spirit, grants each of these gifts to Christ followers for the common good. **12:5** *Services.* The Greek "diakoniai" is often translated as "ministries."

12:12–27 This passage is dominated by the metaphor of one body made up of many parts, a metaphor commonly applied in antiquity to civic populations by orators seeking to unify. **12:12–13** The individual Corinthians, *members,* become the one body of Christ through baptism. This iteration of the baptismal formula leaves out the category of gender found in Gal. 3:28. **12:22–26** In these verses, Paul seems to claim that God has unsettled hierarchy in the community, presenting a reversal of the common understanding in antiquity of the body and its use in political rhetoric. Paul presents those parts usually seen as weaker and less honorable as given greater respect by God and that all members depend on one another.

more respectable members do not need this. But God has so arranged the body, giving the greater honor to the inferior member, ²⁵that there may be no dissension within the body, but the members may have the same care for one another. ²⁶If one member suffers, all suffer together with it; if one member is honored, all rejoice together with it.

27 Now you are the body of Christ and individually members of it. ²⁸And God has appointed in the church first apostles, second prophets, third teachers, then deeds of power, then gifts of healing, forms of assistance, forms of leadership, various kinds of tongues. ²⁹Are all apostles? Are all prophets? Are all teachers? Do all work powerful deeds? ³⁰Do all possess gifts of healing? Do all speak in tongues? Do all interpret? ³¹But strive for the greater gifts. And I will show you a still more excellent way.

13 If I speak in the tongues of humans and of angels but do not have love, I am a noisy gong or a clanging cymbal. ²And if I have prophetic powers and understand all mysteries and all knowledge and if I have all faith so as to remove mountains but do not have love, I am nothing. ³If I give away all my possessions and if I hand over my body so that I may boast^c but do not have love, I gain nothing.

4 Love is patient; love is kind; love is not envious or boastful or arrogant ⁵or rude. It does not insist on its own way; it is not irritable; it keeps no record of wrongs; ⁶it does not rejoice in wrongdoing but rejoices in the truth. ⁷It bears all things, believes all things, hopes all things, endures all things.

8 Love never ends. But as for prophecies, they will come to an end; as for tongues, they will cease; as for knowledge, it will come to an end. ⁹For we know only in part, and we prophesy only in part, ¹⁰but when the complete comes, the partial will come to an end. ¹¹When I was a child, I spoke like a child, I thought like a child, I reasoned like a child. When I became an adult, I put an end to childish ways. ¹²For now we see only a reflection, as in a mirror, but then we will see face to face. Now I know only in part; then I will know fully, even as I have been fully known. ¹³And now faith, hope, and love remain, these three, and the greatest of these is love.

14 Pursue love and strive for the spiritual gifts and especially that you may

c 13.3 Other ancient authorities read *body to be burned*

12:28–31 The hierarchy that Paul seems to destabilize in vv. 22–26 is reasserted with these verses. Paul lists different gifts in an order in which apostles, the role Paul claims, are *first* and those speaking and interpreting tongues are last. This hierarchy is reinforced by Paul's exhortation that the Corinthians *strive for the greater gifts* (v. 31). This exhortation offers a conflict with Paul's earlier formulation that gifts are given "just as the Spirit chooses" (v. 11). **13:1–13** This chapter praising love recalls 8:1–3 and prepares for Paul's arguments about the assembly in chap. 14. **13:1** *I.* Paul seems to use the first person here to signal the hypothetical "anyone." *Tongues of humans and of angels.* This phrasing may be meant to distinguish between ordinary speech and tongues. **13:2** *I am nothing.* Strikingly, Paul asserts that the person with prophetic powers, a full understanding of mysteries and knowledge, and great faith is *nothing* if they do not have the love described below. **13:3** *If I hand over my body so that I may boast.* See 4:11–13; 2 Cor. 11:23–29. **13:4–7** Paul's definition of love connects directly to his critiques of the Corinthians. Love is not envious like the Corinthians (3:3), nor is it puffed up by arrogance—a description of the Corinthians themselves (4:6) and of their knowledge (8:1). Love is not boastful like the Corinthians in 3:21; 4:7; and 5:6. Notably, these critiques of the Corinthians in chaps. 3 and 4 are part of Paul's defense of his leadership and right to define community practice against the Corinthians' embrace of multiple leaders and practices. **13:8–12** Paul again points to the inferiority of speech and knowledge the Corinthians honor (see chaps. 2–3) in contrast to love, inferiority to be revealed in the eschatological completion. **13:10** *When the complete comes.* Cf. 1:7–8. **13:11** Recalls Paul's description of the Corinthians as infants unable to take in the "solid food" of spiritual instruction (3:1–2) and as his children (4:14–21). **14:1–40** Paul develops an ideal for speech in the assembly out of contrasts, privileging prophecy over tongues, speech with the mind over speech with the spirit, orderly speech over disorderly speech, and men's speech over that of women. Chaps. 11–13 provide a foundation for Paul's argument that prophecy is the orderly speech of *upbuilding* and the mind—a direct contrast to tongues as unintelligible speech that benefits only the individual. Paul's dichotomy of assembly speech into prophecy and tongues largely renders invisible other types of communal speech mentioned in chap. 12. The exceptions where Paul speaks of other types of assembly speech in chap. 14 (vv. 6, 26) may represent the Corinthians' own more varied practice. **14:1** *Pursue love and strive . . . that you may prophesy.* Weaves

prophesy. [2]For those who speak in a tongue do not speak to other people but to God, for no one understands them, since they are speaking mysteries in the Spirit. [3]But those who prophesy speak to other people for their upbuilding and encouragement and consolation. [4]Those who speak in a tongue build up themselves, but those who prophesy build up the church. [5]Now I would like all of you to speak in tongues but even more to prophesy. One who prophesies is greater than one who speaks in tongues, unless someone interprets, so that the church may be built up.

6 Now, brothers and sisters, if I come to you speaking in tongues, how will I benefit you unless I speak to you in some revelation or knowledge or prophecy or teaching? [7]It is the same way with lifeless instruments that produce sound, such as the flute or the harp. If they do not give distinct notes, how will what is being played on the flute or harp be recognized? [8]And if the bugle gives an indistinct sound, who will get ready for battle? [9]So with yourselves: If in a tongue you utter speech that is not intelligible, how will anyone know what is being said? For you will be speaking into the air. [10]There are doubtless many different kinds of sounds in the world, and nothing is without sound. [11]If then I do not know the meaning of a sound, I will be a foreigner to the speaker and the speaker a foreigner to me. [12]So with yourselves: since you are striving after spiritual gifts, seek to excel in them for building up the church.

13 Therefore, one who speaks in a tongue should pray for the power to interpret. [14]For if I pray in a tongue, my spirit prays but my mind is unproductive. [15]What should I do then? I will pray with the spirit, but I will pray with the mind also; I will sing praise with the spirit, but I will sing praise with the mind also. [16]Otherwise, if you say a blessing with the spirit, how can anyone in the position of an outsider say the "Amen" to your thanksgiving, since the outsider does not know what you are saying? [17]For you may give thanks well enough, but the other person is not built up. [18]I thank God that I speak in tongues more than all of you; [19]nevertheless, in church I would rather speak five words with my mind, in order to instruct others also, than ten thousand words in a tongue.

20 Brothers and sisters, do not be children in your thinking; rather, be infants in evil, but in thinking be adults. [21]In the law it is written,

"By people of strange tongues
    and by the lips of foreigners
I will speak to this people,
    yet even then they will not listen to me,"

says the Lord. [22]Tongues, then, are a sign not for believers but for unbelievers, while prophecy is not for unbelievers but for believers. [23]If, therefore, the entire church comes together and all speak in tongues, and outsiders or unbelievers enter, will they not say that you are out of your mind? [24]But if all prophesy, an unbeliever or outsider who enters is reproved by all and called to account by all. [25]After the secrets of the unbeliever's heart are disclosed, that person will bow down before God and worship, declaring, "God is really among you."

26 What should be done then, my brothers

together Paul's call for self-sacrificing love in 13:1–11 with his ranking of prophecy as the second of the "greater gifts" for which the Corinthians should *strive* (12:28–31; see also 14:12). **14:4** *Those who prophesy build up the church.* This language of "building up" the assembly permeates this chapter (vv. 3, 5, 12, 17, 19, 26), connecting back to Paul's qualification of Corinthian claims to knowledge and empowerment that do not *build up* in 8:1 and 10:23. **14:5** *Interprets.* Paul argues that only tongues with interpretation belong in the assembly. See also vv. 13, 26–28. **14:13–19** An argument for assembly speech with the mind (Gk. "nous"). In Greek philosophical and political literature, the mind was associated with rationality, order, and control of the body with its passions. Ancient authors writing about speech in the civic, democratic assemblies frequently cite the need to apply the mind to this speech. In turn, the mind was commonly gendered as male, the controlling factor appropriately dominating the feminized body with its unstable desires. Paul's insistence on speaking with the mind in vv. 13–19 prepares the reader for Paul's arguments for both order in vv. 26–33a and the restriction of women's speech in vv. 33b–36. **14:16** *An outsider.* It is unclear if Paul has in mind the visit of an unbeliever to the assembly. The Greek "idiotes" can also mean a private or uninstructed person. **14:18–19** Paul names his preference for assembly speech with the mind while asserting his own excellence in both tongues and prophecy. **14:20** *Do not be children.* Cf. 3:1–4; 13:11. **14:21** Isaiah 28:11–12. **14:22–25** Though Paul seems to apply the Isaiah quotation (v. 21) to the assembly, there is no scholarly agreement on the scenario Paul describes. **14:26–33a** Paul demands a limit to speakers and kinds of speech in the assembly so

and sisters? When you come together, each one has a hymn, a lesson, a revelation, a tongue, or an interpretation. Let all things be done for building up. [27]If anyone speaks in a tongue, let there be only two or at most three and each in turn, and let one interpret. [28]But if there is no one to interpret, let them be silent in church and speak to themselves and to God. [29]Let two or three prophets speak, and let the others weigh what is said. [30]If someone sitting receives a revelation, let the first person be silent. [31]For you can all prophesy one by one, so that all may learn and all be encouraged [32](and the spirits of prophets are subject to the prophets, [33]for God is a God not of disorder but of peace), as in all the churches of the saints.

34 Women should be silent in the churches. For they are not permitted to speak but should be subordinate, as the law also says. [35]If there is something they want to learn, let them ask their husbands at home.[d] For it is shameful for a woman to speak in church.[e] [36]Or did the word of God originate with you? Or are you the only ones it has reached?

37 Anyone who claims to be a prophet or spiritual must acknowledge that what I am writing to you is a command[f] of the Lord. [38]Anyone who does not recognize this is not to be recognized. [39]So, my brothers and sisters, strive to prophesy, and do not forbid speaking in tongues, [40]but all things should be done decently and in order.

15 Now I want you to understand, brothers and sisters, the good news[g] that I proclaimed to you, which you in turn received, in which also you stand, [2]through which also you are being saved, if you hold firmly to the message that I proclaimed to you—unless you have come to believe in vain.

3 For I handed on to you as of first importance what I in turn had received: that Christ died for our sins in accordance with the scriptures [4]and that he was buried and that he was raised on the third day in accordance with the scriptures [5]and that he appeared to Cephas, then to the twelve. [6]Then he appeared to more than five hundred brothers and sisters at one time, most of whom are still alive, though some have died.[b] [7]Then he appeared to James, then to all the apostles. [8]Last of all, as to one untimely born, he appeared also to me. [9]For I am the least of the apostles, unfit to be called an apostle, because I persecuted the church of God. [10]But by the grace of God I am what I am, and his grace toward me has not been in vain. On the contrary, I worked harder than any of them, though it was not I but the grace of God that is with me. [11]Whether then it was I or they, so we proclaim and so you believed.

12 Now if Christ is proclaimed as raised from the dead, how can some of you say there

d 14.35 Gk *in a household* e 14.35 Other ancient authorities put 14.34–35 after 14.40 f 14.37 Other ancient authorities lack *a command* g 15.1 Or *gospel* h 15.6 Gk *fallen asleep*

that it is in line with *a God not of disorder but of peace* (v. 33a). **14:33b–36** Some ancient manuscripts place vv. 34–35 at the end of the chapter. That alternate placement and the apparent contradiction with 11:2–16 have led some scholars to argue that vv. 34–35—or the entirety of vv. 33b–36—is a later insertion. However, this argument is complicated by the inclusion of these verses in all known manuscripts. Further, 11:2–16, along with the earlier verses of chap. 14, do not contradict vv. 33b–36 but prepare the reader for this command for women's silence. Women's natural subordination and the need to control women's disorderly/shameful speech has been mentioned at 11:2–16. Paul's insistence in chap. 14 that assembly speech exercise the rational mind, widely described in antiquity as lacking in women, also lays a foundation for the command for women's silence. **14:34** *The law . . . says.* There is no match in Scripture for this command, so it is unclear what law Paul references.

15:1–11 Against the claim of some Corinthians that "there is no resurrection of the dead" (v. 12), Paul introduces his extended argument about resurrection with a reminder about his earlier teaching and an assertion of his apostolic credentials as one of those who received an appearance from the resurrected Jesus. **15:3–4** *Handed on . . . what I in turn had received.* Paul appeals to early tradition that appears elsewhere in his letters—that is, Rom. 4:24–25; Gal. 1:4; 1 Thess. 5:10. **15:5–9** Like Luke 24:34, Paul assigns Jesus's first resurrection appearance to Cephas (Peter). Notably missing in this list is any tradition of Jesus appearing to his women disciples, especially the memory that Mary Magdalene, together with "the other Mary" (Matt. 28:1) or alone (John 20:11–18), received the first resurrection appearance. **15:8** *He appeared also to me.* See 9:1; Gal. 1:15–16; Acts 9:3–6.

15:12–34 Paul recognizes counterarguments by the Corinthians that there is no resurrection of the dead but goes on to insist that Jesus's own resurrection—indeed the very basis of their faith—only holds

is no resurrection of the dead? [13]If there is no resurrection of the dead, then Christ has not been raised, [14]and if Christ has not been raised, then our proclamation is in vain and your faith is in vain. [15]We are even found to be misrepresenting God, because we testified of God that he raised Christ—whom he did not raise if it is true that the dead are not raised. [16]For if the dead are not raised, then Christ has not been raised. [17]If Christ has not been raised, your faith is futile, and you are still in your sins. [18]Then those also who have died[i] in Christ have perished. [19]If for this life only we have hoped in Christ, we are of all people most to be pitied.

20 But in fact Christ has been raised from the dead, the first fruits of those who have died.[j] [21]For since death came through a human, the resurrection of the dead has also come through a human, [22]for as all die in Adam, so all will be made alive in Christ. [23]But each in its own order: Christ the first fruits, then at his coming those who belong to Christ. [24]Then comes the end, when he hands over the kingdom to God the Father, after he has destroyed every ruler and every authority and power. [25]For he must reign until he has put all his enemies under his feet. [26]The last enemy to be destroyed is death. [27]For "God[k] has put all things in subjection under his feet." But when it says, "All things are put in subjection," it is plain that this does not include the one who put all things in subjection under him. [28]When all things are subjected to him, then the Son himself will also be subjected to the one who put all things in subjection under him, so that God may be all in all.

29 Otherwise, what will those people do who receive baptism on behalf of the dead? If the dead are not raised at all, why are people baptized on their behalf?

30 And why are we putting ourselves in danger every hour? [31]I die every day! That is as certain, brothers and sisters, as my boasting of you—a boast that I make in Christ Jesus our Lord. [32]If I fought with wild animals at Ephesus with a merely human perspective, what would I have gained by it? If the dead are not raised,

"Let us eat and drink,
     for tomorrow we die."
[33]Do not be deceived:

"Bad company ruins good morals."
[34]Sober up, as you rightly ought to, and sin no more, for some people have no knowledge of God. I say this to your shame.

35 But someone will ask, "How are the dead raised? With what kind of body do they come?" [36]Fool! What you sow does not come to life unless it dies. [37]And as for what you sow, you do not sow the body that is to be but a bare seed, perhaps of wheat or of some other grain. [38]But God gives it a body as he has chosen and to each kind of seed its own body. [39]Not all flesh is alike, but there is one flesh for humans, another for animals, another for birds, and another for fish. [40]There are both heavenly bodies and earthly bodies, but the glory of the heavenly is one thing, and that of the earthly is another. [41]There is one glory of the sun and another glory of the moon and another glory of the stars; indeed, star differs from star in glory.

42 So it is with the resurrection of the dead. What is sown is perishable; what is raised is imperishable. [43]It is sown in dishonor; it is raised in glory. It is sown in weakness; it is raised in power. [44]It is sown a physical body; it is raised a spiritual body. If there is a physical body, there is also a spiritual body. [45]Thus it is written, "The first man, Adam, became a living being"; the last Adam became a life-giving spirit. [46]But it is not the spiritual that is first but the physical and then the spiritual. [47]The

i 15.18 Gk *fallen asleep*   j 15.20 Gk *fallen asleep*   k 15.27 Gk *he*

true if the resurrection of the dead is also valid. Scholars have theorized that many of the Corinthians believe in a realized eschatology in which they are presently *raised* and empowered with Christ, even as they do not subscribe to a future bodily resurrection after believers die. **15:21–22** This comparison of Christ and Adam continues into vv. 45–49. **15:23** *First fruits.* See Exod. 23:19. **15:24** *Kingdom.* See 4:20; 15:50. **15:27** Psalm 8:6. **15:30–31** *Danger.* Of such danger and Paul's "boasts," cf. 4:11–13; 2 Cor. 11:23–27. **15:32** *Let us . . . die.* Isaiah 22:13. **15:33** A proverb from the third-century BCE playwright Menander.

15:35–49 This passage responds to the question Paul poses in v. 35 as to the nature of the resurrected body. Paul uses analogies of the seed (vv. 36–38), animal flesh (v. 39), heavenly bodies (vv. 40–41), and the first man (vv. 45–49) to argue that there can be a great diversity of bodies—preparing for the "mystery" of the resurrected body he proposes as an *image of the one of heaven* in v. 49 and the imperishable body in vv. 50–54. **15:45** *Became a living being.* Genesis 2:7.

first man was from the earth, made of dust; the second man is[l] from heaven. [48]As one of dust, so are those who are of the dust, and as one of heaven, so are those who are of heaven. [49]Just as we have borne the image of the one of dust, we will[m] also bear the image of the one of heaven.

50 What I am saying, brothers and sisters, is this: flesh and blood cannot inherit the kingdom of God, nor does the perishable inherit the imperishable. [51]Look, I will tell you a mystery! We will not all die,[n] but we will all be changed, [52]in a moment, in the twinkling of an eye, at the last trumpet. For the trumpet will sound, and the dead will be raised imperishable, and we will be changed. [53]For this perishable body must put on imperishability, and this mortal body must put on immortality. [54]When this perishable body puts on imperishability and this mortal body puts on immortality, then the saying that is written will be fulfilled:

"Death has been swallowed up in victory."
[55] "Where, O death, is your victory?
    Where, O death, is your sting?"
[56]The sting of death is sin, and the power of sin is the law. [57]But thanks be to God, who gives us the victory through our Lord Jesus Christ.

58 Therefore, my beloved brothers and sisters, be steadfast, immovable, always excelling in the work of the Lord because you know that in the Lord your labor is not in vain.

16 Now concerning the collection for the saints: you should follow the directions I gave to the churches of Galatia. [2]On the first day of every week, each of you is to put aside and save whatever extra you earn, so that collections need not be taken when I come. [3]And when I arrive, I will send any whom you approve with letters to take your gift to Jerusalem. [4]If it seems advisable that I should go also, they will accompany me.

5 I will visit you after passing through Macedonia—for I intend to pass through Macedonia—[6]and perhaps I will stay with you or even spend the winter, so that you may send me on my way, wherever I go. [7]I do not want to see you now just in passing, for I hope to spend some time with you, if the Lord permits. [8]But I will stay in Ephesus until Pentecost, [9]for a wide door for effective work has opened to me, and there are many adversaries.

10 If Timothy comes, see that he has nothing to fear among you, for he is doing the work of the Lord just as I am; [11]therefore let no one despise him. Send him on his way in peace, so that he may come to me, for I am expecting him with the brothers and sisters.

12 Now concerning our brother Apollos, I strongly urged him to visit you with the other brothers and sisters, but he was not at all willing to come now. He will come when he has the opportunity.

13 Keep alert; stand firm in the faith; be courageous; be strong. [14]Let all that you do be done in love.

15 Now, brothers and sisters, you know that members of the household of Stephanas were the first fruits in Achaia, and they have devoted themselves to the service of the saints; [16]I urge you to put yourselves at the service of such people and of everyone who works and toils with them. [17]I rejoice at the coming of Stephanas and Fortunatus and Achaicus, because they have made up for your absence, [18]for they refreshed my spirit

l 15.47 Other ancient authorities add *the Lord*
m 15.49 Other ancient authorities read *let us*   *n* 15.51 Gk *fall asleep*

15:50–57 Paul's response to the question of v. 35 as to how the dead are raised. Paul envisions that God, at the end of time, transforms the believer's mortal, perishable body to one that is immortal and imperishable. **15:54–55** *Where . . . is your sting?* An amalgamation of Isa. 25:8 and Hos. 13:14.

16:1–4 *Collection for the saints.* A collection Paul is gathering for the Jerusalem congregation (see Gal. 2:10; 2 Cor. 8–9). It appears Paul has already introduced this topic to the Corinthians. **16:1** *Now concerning.* Cf. 7:1, 25; 8:1; 12:1.

16:5–9 Paul outlines travel plans that include hopes for a "long" visit with the Corinthians. **16:8** *Ephesus.* The provincial capital of Roman Asia and one of the bases for Paul's ministry.

16:10–11 *If Timothy comes.* See 4:17.

16:12 *Now concerning.* See 7:1, 25; 8:1; 12:1; 16:1. *Apollos.* See 1:12; 3:4–6, 22; 4:6; Acts 18:24–19:1.

16:15 *Stephanas.* See notes for 1:15–16.

16:17 *Fortunatus and Achaicus.* Likely Corinthians traveling with Stephanas to visit Paul.

Reading through Time: Paul, Ekklēsia, **and Democracy (1 Corinthians 16)**

Much recent scholarship has contextualized early Christ assemblies and Paul's own rhetoric with a Roman imperial context. However, scholars in classics and early Christianity have increasingly recognized that the Greek East under the Roman Empire not just featured imperial politics but also continued democratic discourse and practice that centered on the citizen assembly, the ekklēsia. Greek education based on a classical Athenian curriculum immersed students in democratic discourse associated with the civic environment. However, authors of the first and second centuries CE—Plutarch and Dio Chrysostom in particular—reveal that civic ekklēsiai continued to meet in the Greek East and to practice self-governance through citizen deliberation and decision-making. First Corinthians itself features deliberative rhetoric of the kind designed for ekklēsia audiences, rhetorical arguments made to persuade an audience toward making collective decisions in line with the speaker's position. Increasing awareness of the vitality of democratic practice and discourse in the Greek East of the early Roman Empire encourages scholars and faithful readers alike to reconsider the Christ ekklēsia itself and Paul's rhetoric in terms of this democracy. Not only the title ekklēsia given to the communities to which Paul writes but also Paul's own attempts to persuade against other arguments and debates within these Christ assemblies—debates particularly apparent in 1 Corinthians—all suggest ancient democratic practice. Ekklēsia evokes an assembly with not one but many voices raised in debates about community governance, values, and beliefs. Recognizing the Corinthian community as ekklēsia allows readers to hear Paul as one voice engaging and debating other speakers, other equal "citizens."

Anna C. Miller

as well as yours. So give recognition to such persons.

19 The churches of Asia send greetings. Aquila and Prisca, together with the church in their house, greet you warmly in the Lord. ²⁰All the brothers and sisters send greetings. Greet one another with a holy kiss.

21 I, Paul, write this greeting with my own hand. ²²Let anyone be accursed who has no love for the Lord. Our Lord, come!ᵒ ²³The grace of the Lord Jesus be with you. ²⁴My love be with all of you in Christ Jesus.ᵖ

o 16.22 Or *Our Lord has come*   p 16.24 Other ancient authorities add *Amen*

16:19 *Aquila and Prisca.* Paul's fellow missionaries who risked their lives for him (Rom. 16:3–5). Described here, in Rom. 16:5, and Acts 18 as hosting a Christ assembly in their home.
16:21 *With my own hand.* Indicates that the earlier part of the letter was dictated to a scribe.
16:22 *Our Lord, come!* Cf. Rev. 22:20.

THE SECOND LETTER OF PAUL TO THE CORINTHIANS

As one of Paul's most passionate, personal, and theologically intriguing letters, 2 Corinthians is a rich text for a wide variety of readers and interpreters. Like its predecessor 1 Corinthians, 2 Corinthians explores the challenges of living in community with people who are different from you and who think differently from you. In 2 Corinthians, these challenges have turned personal: feelings have been hurt, plans have been changed, and people are jockeying for position.

The Corinthian correspondence shows an ongoing relationship of deliberation and debate regarding a variety of questions: how to live in community, how to worship, how to speak, and how to lead. Paul's first letter to the Corinthians makes clear that he has spent time forming the community in Corinth and has been in active communication with the Corinthians over several years (see Acts 18; 1 Cor. 1:11; 5:9; 7:1; 16:17; see also **"Introduction to 1 Corinthians," pp. 1955–56**). The timeline of correspondence is not as clear in 2 Corinthians; some scholars see evidence of up to seven different letter fragments within 2 Corinthians alone, while others treat it as one unified letter. Scholars have theorized possible breaks in argumentation at the following points: 2 Cor. 1:1–2:13; 2:14–6:13; 6:14–7:1; 7:2–16; 8:1–24; 9:1–15; and 10:1–13:13. These possible fragments have then been rearranged in a dizzying number of textual reconstructions, accompanied by reassemblages of the history. Second Corinthians is a good reminder that when reading Paul's letters, we are reading someone else's mail (see **"Introduction to the Pauline Letters," pp. 1713–16**). There are things we do not know and concerns of which we are unaware. Yet we can reasonably assume good intentions on all sides; Paul and the Corinthians are all trying to figure out the best way to be a Christ-following community.

Historical Context

Like much of the New Testament, 2 Corinthians was written within the context of Roman imperial occupation. In 146 BCE, the city of Corinth was infamously decimated by the Romans after being a central site of resistance in the Achaean League. Then, in another colonial move, the Romans resettled Corinth with former soldiers and patriots in 44 BCE. Paul wrote 2 Corinthians around 54–57 CE, over one hundred years after Corinth was resettled in the Roman province of Achaia. This colonial backdrop situates the city within its histories of power and nationality. In 54 CE, Corinth was a large city with two ports connecting it to both the Aegean and the Mediterranean Seas. Paul likely writes from Macedonia, anticipating that he will visit Corinth again soon on his way to Jerusalem with the collection for the saints there before departing for Spain (Rom. 15:22–29).

Reading Guide

One possible reconstruction of the history underlying the writing of 2 Corinthians is that the Corinthian response to 1 Corinthians (or to a lost "letter of tears") is not good. Paul then sends Timothy to visit, and he is not well received. Paul himself visits Corinth, and it goes poorly, with Paul taking offense at comparisons and personal attacks (2 Cor. 10:10). Titus visits for the first time and makes a beginning (see 2 Cor. 7:13–14; 8:6). Paul writes all or part of 2 Corinthians to defend himself and his ministry, particularly in terms of his abilities as a rhetorician with inspired speech. He also writes of his plans to send Titus again, along with additional brothers, to facilitate the collection for Jerusalem.

The theme of the letter is encapsulated in the message Paul receives from the Lord in his vision, recorded in 2 Cor. 12:9: "My grace is sufficient for you, for power is made perfect in weakness." This theme of grace and power in weakness appears when Paul writes of afflictions he and Timothy suffered in Asia: "We felt that we had received the sentence of death so that we would rely not on ourselves but on God" (1:9). Paul grounds his defense in this grace (1:12), saying that their boast is that their behavior (to change travel plans, to write a letter that caused grief, to forgive previous offenses) is based in the grace of God. It is this grace, this gift, that inspires the collection for Jerusalem (9:8, 14). This grace also forms the basis of Paul's defense in the so-called Fool's Speech (11–12). In response to critiques of his leadership (bold in letters but weak when present and speaking), Paul responds by speaking as a fool, arguing that the only strength he can claim is God's: "Whenever I am weak, then I am strong" (12:10–11).

Paul's defensiveness suggests that there were other leaders in Achaia who had much to offer

the community in Corinth. Based on the ways in which he defends himself, it has been suggested that these alternative leaders may have demonstrated their dedication to the community through sacrifice and affliction; their presence (including as guests of Corinthian hospitality); their letters of recommendation and connections; their beauty, performance, and rhetorical skills; their cultural backgrounds; and their ecstatic abilities.

Chap. 1 introduces the theme of grace and details Paul's affliction in Asia and his reasons for changing his plans to visit Corinth. In chap. 2, a discussion of forgiveness sets the tone for interactions between the author and the audience. This chapter also provides an explanation of Paul's travels to Macedonia. Letters of recommendation feature in chap. 3, where Paul highlights his ministry as one of openness and freedom in the Spirit of the Lord. "Treasure in clay jars" is a focal metaphor of chap. 4, in which Paul explains that his power to speak, regardless of outward appearance, comes from God. Chap. 5 continues this concept, shifting to the home and earthly body as temporary, as a new creation can be found with God. Accepting the grace of God and displaying openness to Paul/Timothy's ministry feature in the first part of chap. 6, while the latter half discusses living in purity. In chap. 7, the events in Macedonia take the lead while Paul is consoled by Titus's report of the Corinthians. Grief is transformed into reconciliation. A shift in tone is notable in chaps. 8 and 9, where the focus turns to encouraging the collection for the saints in Jerusalem, with an emphasis on Timothy in chap. 8 and a discussion of the theology of grace in chap. 9. A change of tone is again notable in chap. 10, where the letter shifts to a direct defense, detailing the destruction of strongholds and other weapons of the opponents of Paul. This defense culminates in the Fool's Speech and reluctant stories of Paul's visions in chaps. 11 and 12. The letter closes with Paul's threats of another visit and exhortations to obedience.

Arminta M. Fox

1 Paul, an apostle of Christ Jesus by the will of God, and Timothy our brother,

To the church of God that is in Corinth, together with all the saints throughout Achaia:

2 Grace to you and peace from God our Father and the Lord Jesus Christ.

3 Blessed be the God and Father of our Lord Jesus Christ, the Father of mercies and the God of all consolation, ⁴who consoles us in all our affliction, so that we may be able to console those who are in any affliction with the consolation with which we ourselves are consoled by God. ⁵For just as the sufferings of Christ are abundant for us, so also our consolation is abundant through Christ. ⁶If we are being afflicted, it is for your consolation and salvation; if we are being consoled, it is for your consolation, which you experience when you patiently endure the same sufferings that we are also suffering. ⁷Our hope for you is unshaken, for we know that as you share in our sufferings, so also you share in our consolation.

8 We do not want you to be ignorant, brothers and sisters, of the affliction we experienced in Asia, for we were so utterly,

1:1–2 **Greeting. 1:1** While the salutation follows standard letter-writing practices, Paul's greeting establishes his claims to authority as an apostle and identifies Timothy as a spiritual brother in the movement (cf. Phlm. 1). *Saints throughout Achaia* places the Corinthian church within the Roman senatorial province of Achaia that historically rebelled against Roman rule. Corinth was the capital city of the province and the seat of rebellion (see **"Introduction to 2 Corinthians," pp. 1977–78**).

1:3–11 **Benediction.** In place of the traditional thanksgiving, a Jewish blessing or benediction structure is used here, similar to "Praise be to God." This contrasts sharply with the effusive thanksgiving for the Corinthians in 1 Cor. 1. **1:3** *God of all consolation* refers to God as the one who is called upon or appealed to for aid. This aid appears in the form of divine strength to endure where human strength may fail (see 1:9). This sets up Paul's argument regarding strength and weakness that is more pronounced in later chapters and echoes arguments from 1 Corinthians. The contrast between affliction and consolation invites response from the audience in the form of additional prayers for deliverance (see 1:11). **1:5** *So also our consolation.* The rhetoric of imitation suggests that Paul and Timothy model themselves on Christ and seek to act as models for the community. **1:8** *We do not want you to be ignorant.* A phrase of disclosure frequently used by Paul to convey important information or set off a new argument (see Rom. 1:13; 1 Cor. 10:1; 1 Thess. 4:13). Here, it introduces Paul's defense. *Affliction . . . in Asia* may refer to imperial persecution experienced by Paul and Timothy in Ephesus or elsewhere within

unbearably crushed that we despaired of life itself. [9]Indeed, we felt that we had received the sentence of death so that we would rely not on ourselves but on God, who raises the dead. [10]He who rescued us from so deadly a peril will continue to rescue us;[a] on him we have set our hope that he will rescue us again, [11]as you also join in helping us by your prayers, so that many may give thanks on our[b] behalf for the blessing granted us through the prayers of many.

12 Indeed, this is our boast, the testimony of our conscience: we have behaved in the world with holiness[c] and godly sincerity, not by earthly wisdom but by the grace of God— and all the more toward you. [13]For we write you nothing other than what you can read and also understand; I hope you will understand until the end—[14]as you have already understood us in part—that on the day of the Lord Jesus we are your boast even as you are our boast.

15 Since I was sure of this, I wanted to come to you first, so that you might have a double favor;[d] [16]I wanted to visit you on my way to Macedonia and to come back to you from Macedonia and have you send me on to Judea. [17]Was I vacillating when I wanted to do this? Do I make my plans according to ordinary human standards,[e] ready to say "Yes, yes" and "No, no" at the same time? [18]As surely as God is faithful, our word to you is not[f] "Yes and No." [19]For the Son of God, Jesus Christ, whom we proclaimed among you, Silvanus and Timothy and I, was not "Yes and No," but in him it has always been "Yes." [20]For in him every one of God's promises is a "Yes." For this reason it is through him that we say the "Amen," to the glory of God. [21]But it is God who establishes us with you in Christ and has anointed us, [22]who has put his seal on us and given[g] us his Spirit in our hearts as a down payment.

23 But I call on God as witness against me: it was to spare you that I did not come again to Corinth. [24]I do not mean to imply that we lord it over your faith; rather, we are workers with you for your joy because you stand firm in faith. [1]So I made up my mind not to make another visit that causes you grief. [2]For if I cause you grief, who is there to make me glad but the one whom I have grieved? [3]And I wrote as I did, so that when I came, I might not suffer grief from those who should have made me rejoice, for I am confident about all of you, that my joy would be the joy of all of you. [4]For I wrote you out of much distress and anguish of heart and with many tears, not to cause you grief but to let you know the abundant love that I have for you.

5 But if anyone has caused grief, he has caused it not to me but to some extent—not to

a 1.10 Other ancient authorities read *is rescuing us* or lack the phrase   b 1.11 Other ancient authorities read *your*   c 1.12 Other ancient authorities read *simplicity*   d 1.15 Other ancient authorities read *joy*   e 1.17 Gk *according to the flesh*   f 1.18 Other ancient authorities read *was not*   g 1.22 Other ancient authorities read *by putting . . . and giving*

Asia Minor (see Acts 19 and 1 Cor. 15). It is also possible, although less likely, that Paul speaks of a personal affliction that has disabled him in some way, such as his "thorn . . . in the flesh" (see 2 Cor. 12:7). **1:9** *Sentence of death* suggests forensic or judicial rhetoric, which continues with "testimony" (1:12) and "witness" (1:23). This type of rhetoric is used to respond to a charge. Paul narrates the experience to highlight the importance of relying on God's power instead of one's own.

1:12 Paul's boasting appears throughout the letter, as his integrity and connection to God's power are under debate (see 1:15–24 and 10:10).

1:14 By arguing that he and Timothy are the Corinthians' boast just as they are theirs, the letter enmeshes the readers in Paul's defense.

1:15–2:4 Paul's plans reference the collection for the poor in Jerusalem (see 2 Cor. 8–9; Rom. 15:25–28). **1:18** *Yes and No* may refer to a specific Corinthian charge against Paul's integrity. **1:24** *We are workers with you for your joy* emphasizes the Corinthians as responsible coworkers rather than Paul or Timothy as overbearing leaders. *We lord it over your faith.* This defense implies the nature of additional charges against Paul. **2:1** Relations between Paul and the Corinthians have soured since his earlier visit. Rather than bestowing joy and extra favor through a second visit, Paul changes his plans to spare them grief. **2:3** *That my joy would be the joy of all of you* inscribes an affectual relationship between Paul and the Corinthians. **2:4** Paul wrote another letter to the Corinthians. Whether this letter is 1 Corinthians, lost, or extant in 2 Cor. 10–13 is debated (see 2 Cor. 10:10). Paul writes that his love might be imitated and reciprocated.

2:5–11 A particular situation in the Corinthian church, possibly connected to the man expelled from the community in 1 Cor. 5.

exaggerate it—to all of you. [6]This punishment by the majority is enough for such a person; [7]so now instead you should forgive and console him, so that he may not be overwhelmed by even worse grief. [8]So I urge you to reaffirm your love for him. [9]I wrote for this reason: to test you and to know whether you are obedient in everything. [10]Anyone whom you forgive, I also forgive. In fact, what I have forgiven, if I have forgiven anything, has been for your sake in the presence of Christ. [11]And we do this so that we may not be outwitted by Satan, for we are not ignorant of his designs.

[12] When I came to Troas to proclaim the good news[b] of Christ, a door was opened for me in the Lord, [13]but my mind could not rest because I did not find my brother Titus there. So I said farewell to them and went on to Macedonia.

[14] But thanks be to God, who in Christ always leads us in triumphal procession and through us spreads in every place the fragrance that comes from knowing him.[i] [15]For we are the aroma of Christ to God among those who are being saved and among those who are perishing: [16]to the one group a fragrance from death[j] to death, to the other a fragrance from life[k] to life. Who is qualified for these things? [17]For we are not peddlers of God's word like so many,[l] but as persons of sincerity, as persons sent from God, we are speaking in Christ before God.

3 Are we beginning to commend ourselves again? Surely we do not need, as some do, letters of recommendation to you or from you, do we? [2]You yourselves are our letter, written on our hearts, known and read by all, [3]and you show that you are a letter of Christ, prepared by us, written not with ink but with the Spirit of the living God, not on tablets of stone but on tablets that are human hearts.[m]

[4] Such is the confidence that we have through Christ toward God. [5]Not that we are qualified of ourselves to claim anything as coming from us; our qualification is from God, [6]who has made us qualified to be ministers of a new covenant, not of letter but of spirit, for the letter kills, but the Spirit gives life.

[7] Now if the ministry of death, chiseled in letters on stone tablets,[n] came in glory so that the people of Israel could not gaze at Moses's face because of the glory of his face, a glory now set aside, [8]how much more will the ministry of the Spirit come in glory? [9]For if there was glory in the ministry of condemnation,[o] much more does the ministry of justification abound in glory! [10]Indeed, what once had

b 2.12 Or *the gospel* i 2.14 Gk *the fragrance of the knowledge of him* j 2.16 Other ancient authorities read *fragrance of death that leads* k 2.16 Other ancient authorities read *fragrance of life that leads* l 2.17 Other ancient authorities read *like the rest* m 3.3 Gk *hearts of flesh* n 3.7 Gk *on stones* o 3.9 Other ancient authorities read *If the ministry of condemnation constituted glory*

2:12–17 After his afflictions in Asia, Paul found a receptive audience in Troas but decided to continue to Macedonia rather than stay or visit Achaia. *Troas*, or Troy, a city in northern Asia Minor, across the sea from Macedonia. See additional discussion of Titus in 2 Cor. 7:5–7. **2:14** *Triumphal procession* likely refers to imperial processions in which the victorious emperor would lead out the vanquished and the spoils of war. **2:15** *Aroma of Christ* may reference the imperial processions in which the incense of the emperor would bring life to the Romans but impending destruction to others. **2:16** *Who is qualified for these things?* This question underscores Paul's argument throughout the letter that his strength comes from God, which explains and dismisses any time he appears weak or unqualified according to the ways of the world or to others in Corinth. **2:17** *Peddlers of God's word* is likely Paul's characterization of rival leaders in Corinth.

3:1–18 Paul and Timothy claim to be confident of their ministry in the community, both in terms of their own qualifications from God and in their close relations with the Corinthians. A sharp contrast is created between the ministry of death and the ministry of Spirit. This passage should not be read as a contrast between Judaism and Christianity. **3:1** Letters of recommendation were a popular convention used by early Christians. Since Paul and Timothy have previously ministered in Corinth, it is surprising that they would need additional introduction or recommendation. Paul continues to compare himself with other leaders in terms of recommendations and emphasizes his closeness with the audience. **3:2** *Written on . . . hearts* (see Deut. 11:18–22; Jer. 31:31–33; Ezek. 11:19; 36:26–27). This image suggests that the community's actions display Paul and Timothy's ministry in Corinth. **3:3** *Tablets of stone* references the Ten Commandments (see Exod. 24:12; 31:18; Deut. 9–10). **3:4** Paul and Timothy are defending the source of their confidence and their qualifications against other ministers in the community. It is possible the tablets of stone reference the first two tablets destroyed by Moses, while the tablets written with spirit refer to the second set of tablets that become the Law (Exod. 24; Deut. 9–10). **3:7–11** Paul uses Scriptures about Moses to defend his own ministry in Corinth. The contrast between the

glory has in this respect lost its glory because of the greater glory, [11]for if what was set aside came through glory, much more has the permanent come in glory!

12 Since, then, we have such a hope, we act with complete frankness, [13]not like Moses, who put a veil over his face to keep the people of Israel from gazing at the end of the glory that[p] was being set aside. [14]But their minds were hardened. Indeed, to this very day, when they hear the reading of the old covenant, the same veil is still there; it is not unveiled since in Christ it is set aside. [15]Indeed, to this very day whenever Moses is read, a veil lies over their minds,[q] [16]but when one turns to the Lord, the veil is removed. [17]Now the Lord is the Spirit, and where the Spirit of the Lord is, there is freedom. [18]And all of us, with unveiled faces, seeing the glory of the Lord as though reflected in a mirror, are being transformed into the same image from one degree of glory to another, for this comes from the Lord, the Spirit.

4 Therefore, since it is by God's mercy that we are engaged in this ministry, we do not lose heart. [2]We have renounced the shameful, underhanded ways; we refuse to practice cunning or to falsify God's word, but by the open statement of the truth we commend ourselves to the conscience of everyone in the sight of God. [3]And even if our gospel is veiled, it is veiled to those who are perishing. [4]In their case the god of this world has blinded the minds of the unbelievers, to keep them from seeing clearly the light of the gospel of the glory of Christ, who is the image of God. [5]For we do not proclaim ourselves; we proclaim Jesus Christ as Lord and ourselves as your slaves for Jesus's sake. [6]For it is the God who said, "Light will shine out of darkness," who has shone in our hearts to give the light of the knowledge of the glory of God in the face of Christ.

7 But we have this treasure in clay jars, so that it may be made clear that this extraordinary power belongs to God and does not come from us. [8]We are afflicted in every way but not crushed, perplexed but not driven to despair, [9]persecuted but not forsaken, struck down but not destroyed, [10]always carrying around in the body the death of Jesus, so that the life of Jesus may also be made visible in our bodies. [11]For we who are living are always being handed over to death for Jesus's sake, so that the life of Jesus may also be made visible in our mortal flesh. [12]So death is at work in us but life in you.

p 3.13 Gk of what   q 3.15 Gk their heart

glory of Moses's face and the glory of the Spirit is like a bright light that is no longer distinguishable when in bright sunlight. God's covenant with Israel is still one of glory. **3:12–18** *The people of Israel* who cannot fully comprehend the glory brought by Moses with the Mosaic law are compared to those in the audience who are not responding well to the ministry of Paul and Timothy. **3:14** The glory has not been unveiled for the people of Israel by Christ but is rather an alternative experience of glory. **3:15** In this retelling of the story, Paul emphasizes that the veil keeps the people from seeing the fully realized glory. **3:16** When one turns to the Spirit, the veil is removed, just as it was for Moses (see Exod. 34:34). **3:17** Paul is explicit that *the Lord* refers to *the Spirit* in this argument and not Christ, as in other parts of Paul's letters. **3:18** *From one degree of glory to another* suggests that both the old and new covenants will result in glorious transformation, a theme Paul will continue to emphasize throughout the Corinthian correspondence.

4:1–6 A continuation of the previous chapter's argument and the judicial rhetoric used to defend against accusations regarding their ministry. **4:1** *Lose heart.* See 4:16. **4:2** They refute charges of *cunning* and craftiness by proclaiming their openness and frankness (see 12:16). **4:3** Anyone who does not recognize the truth of the gospel they preach is perishing. **4:4** *The god of this world* is the only reference of this force as a god in the New Testament. This *god* has veiled the light of the gospel (see 1 Cor. 2:6–8). **4:5** By identifying themselves as enslaved to the audience, Paul and Timothy have rhetorically shifted any accusations regarding their message onto Christ. **4:6** *Light will shine out of darkness.* The words of the Lord are used to bring together the themes of darkness, veiled glory, hearts, and light in a way that presents Paul and Timothy as the bearers of the knowledge of the glory of God in Christ (see Gen. 1:3).

4:7–18 The theme of transformation returns here. **4:7** *Treasure in clay jars.* Clay or earthenware jars were common and easily broken, thus not the typical place for storing treasure. **4:8** Lists of afflictions were commonly used to demonstrate the sage's power over adversity. Power and resilience that come from a divine source provide crucified peoples and suffering bodies comfort and hope. **4:10** Contemporary scholars of the body and disability theorists note that the broken body and the body that

13 But just as we have the same spirit of faith that is in accordance with scripture— "I believed, and so I spoke"—we also believe, and therefore we also speak, [14]because we know that the one who raised Jesus[r] will also raise us with Jesus and will present us with you in his presence. [15]Indeed, everything is for your sake, so that grace, when it has extended to more and more people, may increase thanksgiving, to the glory of God.

16 So we do not lose heart. Even though our outer nature is wasting away, our inner nature is being renewed day by day. [17]For our slight, momentary affliction is producing for us an eternal weight of glory beyond all measure, [18]because we look not at what can be seen but at what cannot be seen, for what can be seen is temporary, but what cannot be seen is eternal.

5 For we know that, if the earthly tent we live in is destroyed, we have a building from God, a house not made with hands, eternal in the heavens. [2]For in this tent we groan, longing to be further clothed with our heavenly dwelling, [3]for surely when we have been clothed in it[s] we will not be found naked. [4]For while we are in this tent, we groan under our burden because we wish not to be unclothed but to be further clothed, so that what is mortal may be swallowed up by life. [5]The one who has prepared us for this very thing is God, who has given us the Spirit as a down payment.

6 So we are always confident, even though we know that while we are at home in the body we are away from the Lord—[7]for we walk by faith, not by sight. [8]Yes, we do have confidence, and we would rather be away from the body and at home with the Lord. [9]So whether we are at home or away, we make it our aim to be pleasing to him. [10]For all of us must appear before the judgment seat of Christ, so that each may receive due recompense for actions done in the body, whether good or evil.

11 Therefore, knowing the fear of the Lord, we try to persuade people, but we ourselves are well known to God, and I hope that we are also well known to your consciences. [12]We are

r 4.14 Other ancient authorities read Lord Jesus
s 5.3 Other ancient authorities read taken it off

carries death reflect divine life (see also **"Isaiah and Disability," p. 974**). **4:13–15** The theme of having the authority to speak returns. **4:13** I believed, and so I spoke (Ps. 116:10). This emphasis on speech is rooted in Scriptures and in the Spirit of faith in defense against charges regarding the strength of Paul's speech in contrast to others in the community (see 10:10; cf. "unbelievers," 4:4). **4:14** Judicial rhetoric is coupled with the image of the judgment of God, which Paul, Timothy, and the reader will participate in together. **4:15** Grace (see 2 Cor. 12 and **"Religious Experience in Paul—Visions and Revelations," p. 1991**). Arguing that everything is for the sake of the audience implies that the audience is indebted to the authors and to God. Speaking with the Spirit of faith results in the extension of grace, the increase of thanksgiving, and glory. **4:16–18** Paul and Timothy's resilience and confidence in the transformative power of God in the face of affliction provide great hope. The emphasis on the inner nature as greater than the external echoes gnostic and Middle Platonic ideas at the time. **4:16** Heart. See 4:1. **4:17** Glory. See 3:7–11.

5:1–10 This section uses the metaphors of housing and bodies to continue the dichotomy between internal/external and eternal/temporal and the argument that the ministry of Paul and Timothy comes from God. Some use Greek tradition to interpret the dwelling metaphors as signifying the earthly and heavenly body and thus see the resurrection body as a new creation, received upon death or at the "parousia" (see 1 Thess. 4:15–17). **5:1** Destruction of the earthly dwelling may be particularly upsetting for Corinthians who host church gatherings in their homes, such as alternative leaders to Paul. **5:2–3** Contemporary postcolonial interpretations point to the vulnerability of the earthly home and naked body compared to God's strength and power. **5:4** Groan under our burden a reference to pregnancy and the burden of waiting for the new creation (see Rom. 8:18–23). **5:5** The Spirit as a down payment may reference ecstatic experiences of visions that sustain the believer until the glory of the new creation (see 2 Cor. 12; Rev. 1). **5:6–10** This discussion continues the theme begun in chap. 4 regarding faith in things unseen. Some interpreters see this discussion in reference to Corinthian accusations against Paul regarding his presence and absence (see 2 Cor. 1:15–2:1; 10:10). **5:10** Judgment seat of Christ assumes that all will be judged in the future, at the time of transformation (see Rom. 14:9–12).

5:11–21 A powerful passage on the transformative power of Christ in the community (see Gal. 3:28). **5:11** The passage returns to a theme of knowledge and wisdom. The knowledge of the Corinthians is

not commending ourselves to you again but giving you an opportunity to boast about us, so that you may be able to answer those who boast in outward appearance and not in the heart. [13]For if we are beside ourselves, it is for God; if we are in our right mind, it is for you. [14]For the love of Christ urges us on, because we are convinced that one has died for all; therefore all have died. [15]And he died for all, so that those who live might live no longer for themselves but for the one who for their sake died and was raised.

16 From now on, therefore, we regard no one from a human point of view;[t] even though we once knew Christ from a human point of view,[u] we no longer know him in that way. [17]So if anyone is in Christ, there[v] is a new creation: everything old has passed away; look, new things have come into being![w] [18]All this is from God, who reconciled us to himself through Christ and has given us the ministry of reconciliation; [19]that is, in Christ God was reconciling the world to himself,[x] not counting their trespasses against them, and entrusting the message of reconciliation to us. [20]So we are ambassadors for Christ, since God is making his appeal through us; we entreat you on behalf of Christ: be reconciled to God. [21]For our sake God made the one who knew no sin to be sin, so that in him we might become the righteousness of God.

6 As we work together with him,[y] we entreat you also not to accept the grace of God in vain. [2]For he says,

"At an acceptable time I have listened to you,
and on a day of salvation I have helped you."

Look, now is the acceptable time; look, now is the day of salvation! [3]We are putting no obstacle in anyone's way, so that no fault may be found with our ministry, [4]but as servants of God we have commended ourselves in every way: in great endurance, afflictions, hardships, calamities, [5]beatings, imprisonments, riots, labors, sleepless nights, hunger; [6]in purity, knowledge, patience, kindness, holiness of spirit, genuine love, [7]truthful speech, and the power of God; with the weapons of righteousness for the right hand and for the left; [8]in honor and dishonor, in ill repute and good repute. We are treated as impostors and yet are true, [9]as unknown and yet are well known, as dying and look—we are alive, as punished and yet not killed, [10]as sorrowful yet always rejoicing, as poor yet making many rich, as having nothing and yet possessing everything.

11 We have spoken frankly to you Corinthians; our heart is wide open to you. [12]There is no restriction in our affections but only in yours. [13]In return—I speak as to children—open wide your hearts also.

t 5.16 Gk according to the flesh u 5.16 Gk according to the flesh v 5.17 Or that person w 5.17 Other ancient authorities read everything has become new x 5.19 Or God was in Christ reconciling the world to himself y 6.1 Gk As we work together

---

questioned here (see 1 Cor. 1–2). **5:13** *We are beside ourselves* is a reference to ecstatic visions (see 2 Cor. 12). **5:15** In Paul's ministry to the gentiles, all are gathered in the family of God on account of Christ's resurrection. Paul uses imitation rhetoric here to urge the Corinthians to imitate Paul, who is himself imitating Christ, in a willingness to sacrifice for the community. **5:17** Paul participates in debates within the community regarding the extent of and power behind the transformation into a new creation: Paul asserts that God in Christ provides that power and that new creation is already present. **5:19–20** Paul and Timothy represent themselves as ambassadors for Christ to the Corinthians to urge them to be reconciled or transformed with God.

6:1–13 Accepting God's grace. 6:2 See Isa. 49:8. This quote adds urgency to the argument that the Corinthians should be reconciled to God. Yet given that the argument continues as a defense of Paul and Timothy's ministry, it seems that Paul also seeks reconciliation with the Corinthians himself. **6:3** This is likely a comparison with other ministers who take payment or exchange goods for their work (see 1 Cor. 9:12). **6:4–7** The lists of hardships and virtues showcase Paul's ministry as virtuous in defense against attacks to the contrary (see 4:8–9). **6:8–10** The antithetical statements show an attempt to set Paul's ministry apart from other ministries in Corinth. **6:9** *Punished . . . killed.* See 1:8–11. **6:10** *Poor . . . rich.* See 8:9. **6:11–13** Paul emphasizes his own frankness and openness. The innermost and hidden part, the heart, is made available externally (see 4:7). **6:13** *Hearts.* See 3:2; 4:1, 16; 7:2–3. *Speak as to children* is directive and presents Paul as a parent figure over a childlike and naive congregation (see 11:2).

14 Do not be mismatched with unbelievers. For what do righteousness and lawlessness have in common? Or what partnership is there between light and darkness? ¹⁵What agreement does Christ have with Beliar? Or what does a believer share with an unbeliever? ¹⁶What agreement has the temple of God with idols? For we^z are the temple of the living God, as God said,

"I will live in them^a and walk among
  them,
  and I will be their God,
  and they shall be my people.
¹⁷ Therefore come out from them,
  and be separate from them, says the
  Lord,
and touch nothing unclean;
  then I will welcome you,
¹⁸ and I will be your father,
  and you shall be my sons and
  daughters,
says the Lord Almighty."

7 Since we have these promises, beloved, let us cleanse ourselves from every

defilement of flesh and of spirit, making holiness perfect in the fear of God.

2 Make room in your hearts^b for us; we have wronged no one; we have corrupted no one; we have taken advantage of no one. ³I do not say this to condemn you, for I have already said that you are in our hearts, to die together and to live together. ⁴I am being completely frank with you; I have great pride in you; I am filled with consolation; I am overjoyed in all our affliction.

5 For even when we came into Macedonia, our flesh had no rest, but we were afflicted in every way—disputes without and fears within. ⁶But God, who consoles the downcast, consoled us by the arrival of Titus, ⁷and not only by his arrival but also by the consolation with which he was consoled about you, as he told us of your longing, your mourning, your zeal for me, so that I rejoiced still more. ⁸For although I grieved you with my letter, I do not regret it. Although I did regret it (for^c

z 6.16 Other ancient authorities read *you*   a 6.16 Or *in their midst*   b 7.2 Gk lacks *in your hearts*   c 7.8 Other ancient witnesses lack *for*

6:14–7:1 This passage seems to interrupt the flow of the larger argument regarding reconciling ministry with a discussion of purity. Some interpreters theorize that this passage is either an interpolation from a later editor or an insertion from another Pauline fragment. It may also be in reference to Paul's rival leaders in Corinth. Partnerships with people outside of the Christ community appear as a source of contention between Paul and the Corinthians. Paul's rivals may have powerful connections within Corinth that Paul does not have access to. This passage would serve to heighten the distinctions between Paul and rival leaders by negatively characterizing the connections outside of the Christ community. **6:14** *Mismatched*, literally "misyoked," refers to animals moving forward together (see Lev. 19:19) but refers to human partnerships between believers and unbelievers here (see also Matt. 11:28–30). While the language of yoking is not used, for a previous discussion of marriage between believers and unbelievers, see 1 Cor. 7:12–16. The author extends a characterization of unbelievers to include an association with lawlessness and darkness to heighten the differences between the two parties. **6:15** *Beliar.* A variant of Belial, or Satan. **6:16** For Paul's previous instructions on idol worship, see 1 Cor. 10:14–22. *I will . . . people.* See Ezek. 37:27 and Lev. 26:12. **6:17** In using this quote, the author emphasizes the maintenance of cleanliness or purity within the Christ community in contrast to others. *Come out from them.* See Isa. 52:11 and Ezek. 20:34 (LXX). **6:18** *I will be.* See 2 Sam. 7:14 and Isa. 43:6. **7:1** The author emphasizes cleanliness and holiness in body and spirit, virtues mentioned in 2 Cor. 6:6.

7:2 *Make room* suggests vying for space in a crowded context. The particular defenses mentioned seem to suggest the opposite regarding Paul's Corinthian rivals (see 12:17–18).

7:3 While Paul says that he does not condemn them, this statement implicates the Corinthians in the charges of 7:2 (see 11:4–6). *You are in our hearts.* See 6:11–13. *To die together and to live together* is a reference to death and resurrection.

7:4 Paul's frankness and pride, while a sign of friendship and reconciliation, also has a paternalistic tone. *Consolation.* See 1:3–7. Ideally, Paul's consolation and affliction are to be imitated by the Corinthians as they hear more of his defense.

7:5–16 Affliction and appeals for consolation. 7:5 *Macedonia.* See 1 Cor. 16:5–9; 2 Cor. 2:13; 8:1–6; 9:1–5. **7:6** *God, who consoles the downcast.* See Isa. 49:13. *Titus.* See 2:13; 7:13–15; 8:23; 9:3. **7:7** The model of Titus as a traveling minister sent by God to provide consolation exemplifies how Paul fashions his own visits to the Corinthians and their ideal response (see 1:3–7). **7:8** *My letter.* A reference to a

I see that that letter caused you grief, though only briefly), ⁹now I rejoice, not because you were grieved but because your grief led to repentance, for you felt a godly grief, so that you were not harmed in any way by us. ¹⁰For godly grief produces a repentance that leads to salvation and brings no regret, but worldly grief produces death. ¹¹For see what earnestness this godly grief has produced in you, what eagerness to clear yourselves, what indignation, what alarm, what longing, what zeal, what punishment! At every point you have proved yourselves guiltless in the matter. ¹²So although I wrote to you, it was not on account of the one who did the wrong nor on account of the one who suffered the wrong but in order that your zeal for us might be made known to you before God. ¹³In this we have found consolation.

In addition to our own consolation, we rejoiced still more at the joy of Titus, because his mind has been set at rest by all of you. ¹⁴For if I have been somewhat boastful about you to him, I was not put to shame, but just as everything we said to you was true, so our boasting to Titus has proved true as well. ¹⁵And his heart goes out all the more to you, as he remembers the obedience of all of you and how you welcomed him with fear and trembling. ¹⁶I rejoice because I have complete confidence in you.

8 We want you to know, brothers and sisters, about the grace of God that has been granted to the churches of Macedonia, ²for during a severe ordeal of affliction their abundant joy and their extreme poverty have overflowed in a wealth of generosity on their part. ³For, as I can testify, they voluntarily gave according to their means and even beyond their means, ⁴begging us earnestly for the favor*d* of partnering in this ministry to the saints, ⁵and not as we expected. Instead, they gave themselves first to the Lord and, by the will of God, to us, ⁶so that we might urge Titus that, as he had already made a beginning, so he should also complete this generous undertaking*e* among you. ⁷Now as you excel in everything—in faith, in speech, in knowledge, in utmost eagerness, and in our love for you*f*—so we want you to excel also in this generous undertaking.*g*

d 8.4 Gk *grace* or *gift*   e 8.6 Gk *this grace* or *gift*
f 8.7 Other ancient authorities read *your love for us*
g 8.7 Gk *this grace* or *gift*

previous letter sent by Paul, which some interpreters term the Letter of Tears and others see simply as 1 Corinthians, with its attempted behavioral corrections and censures (see 2:2–4 and **"Introduction to 2 Corinthians," pp. 1977–78**). **7:10–11** The passage distinguishes between different types of grief, labeling one godly and the other worldly. Godly grief as defined here is grief that produces transformation, while worldly grief produces death, perhaps through inaction. Debates regarding responses to gun violence—where one response produces policy reform and the other results in thoughts and prayers—come to mind. **7:12–13** Paul finds consolation in their conviction. **7:14–16** These verses commend the Corinthians' actions of being obedient and offering respectful welcome to Titus. These values compete with those of independent thinking or leadership from within the congregation. **7:14** *Boasting* (see 1:14; 7:14; 8:24; 9:2–3; 10:17; 11:16–30). Rather than boasting about himself here, Paul boasts about the Corinthians, suggesting that a defense of his own ministry also requires a defense of their congregation.

8:1–9:15 The collection for Jerusalem. The appeal for the collection is present in several Pauline Letters (see Rom. 15:25–32; 1 Cor. 16:1–4; Gal. 2:10; also Acts 24:17). While predominantly economic in nature, such a gift to the saints in Jerusalem from gentile or mixed congregations and delivered by the missionary to the gentiles would signal support for and unity with the Jews. This support is especially significant at a time of Roman imperial tension. The imperial patronage system involved many rules and expectations regarding the giving and receiving of gifts. Some interpreters have argued that chaps. 8 and 9 are distinct letters (see **"Introduction to 2 Corinthians," pp. 1977–78**). **8:1** *We want you to know* is a standard introductory phrase to indicate a new topic (see 1:8). *Grace* (Gk. "charis") is used throughout this section to describe both beneficence and gifts from God as well as voluntary economic contributions for the collection. *Macedonia.* See 1:16; contrast to the province of Achaia, where Corinth is located (see 1:1). To encourage Achaian giving, Paul contrasts them to the Macedonians. **8:2** *Severe ordeal of affliction* may be an ordeal due to an earthquake or other disaster, a famine, or imperially induced suffering (see Phil. 1:29–30; 1 Thess. 1:6; 2:14; 3:3–4; cf. 2 Cor. 1:8). **8:4–6** The giving of the Macedonians is directly related to Titus's collection among those in Achaia. **8:7** *Excel in*

8 I do not say this as a command, but I am, by mentioning the eagerness of others, testing the genuineness of your love. ⁹For you know the generous act[b] of our Lord Jesus Christ, that though he was rich, yet for your sakes he became poor, so that by his poverty you might become rich. ¹⁰And in this matter I am giving my opinion: it is beneficial for you who began last year not only to do something but even to desire to do something. ¹¹Now finish doing it, so that your eagerness may be matched by completing it according to your means. ¹²For if the eagerness is there, the gift is acceptable according to what one has, not according to what one does not have. ¹³For I do not mean that there should be relief for others and hardship for you, but it is a question of equality between ¹⁴your present abundance and their need, so that their abundance may also supply your need, in order that there may be equality. ¹⁵As it is written,

"The one who had much did not have too
  much,
  and the one who had little did not have
  too little."

16 But thanks be to God, who put in the heart of Titus the same eagerness for you that I myself have. ¹⁷For he not only accepted our appeal, but since he is more eager than ever, he is going to you of his own accord. ¹⁸With him we are sending the brother who is praised among all the churches for his work for the gospel, ¹⁹and not only that, but he has also been appointed by the churches to travel with us while we are administering this generous undertaking[i] for

the glory of the Lord himself[j] and to show our goodwill. ²⁰We are making this arrangement lest anyone blame us about this generous gift that we are administering, ²¹for we are setting our minds on what is right not only before the Lord but also before the people. ²²And with them we are sending our brother whom we have often tested and found eager in many matters but who is now more eager than ever because of his great confidence in you. ²³As for Titus, he is my partner and coworker in your service; as for our brothers, they are messengers[k] of the churches, the glory of Christ. ²⁴Therefore openly before the churches, show them the proof of your love and of our reason for boasting about you to them.

9 Now it is not necessary for me to write you about the ministry to the saints, ²for I know your eagerness, which is the subject of my boasting about you to the people of Macedonia, saying that Achaia has been ready since last year, and your zeal has stirred up most of them. ³But I am sending[l] the brothers in order that our boasting about you may not prove to have been empty in this case, so that you may be ready, as I said you would be; ⁴otherwise, if some Macedonians come with me and find that you are not ready, we would be put to shame—to say nothing of you—in this undertaking.[m] ⁵So I thought it necessary

b 8.9 Gk *the grace* or *gift*   i 8.19 Gk *this grace* or *gift*
j 8.19 Other ancient authorities lack *himself*   k 8.23 Gk
apostles   l 9.3 Or *I have sent*   m 9.4 Other ancient authorities add *of boasting*

everything. See 1 Cor. 1:4–7. **8:8–15** After stoking competition between the Achaians and Macedonians, these verses emphasize equal giving as a show of love. **8:8** Paul distinguishes among his commands, tests, and opinions for them (see 8:10). He does not command them to participate in the collection because he desires that the gift be voluntary (see 8:12). **8:9** The ministry and crucifixion of Christ are presented in economic terms, in which Christ's poverty enriches others (cf. Phil. 2:1–11). **8:10** *Began last year* refers to previous Corinthian plans. **8:12** Paul emphasizes that any gift is acceptable if given in the right attitude as a show of genuine love (see 8:8). **8:15** *The one . . . too little.* See Exod. 16:18. **8:16–24 Commendation of Titus and the brothers. 8:16** Titus is positioned as a model who stands in for Paul in the community, particularly in regard to the collection. Titus is not mentioned in Acts. **8:23** The identities of the brothers mentioned (8:18, 22) are not known (see Acts 20:4–6). Wives and children may have traveled with them as well, even though they are not mentioned. **9:1–15 Cheerful giving. 9:1** The appeal for the collection for the saints in Jerusalem continues from chap. 8 (see introduction). Some interpreters argue that chap. 9 is a distinct letter fragment from that of chaps. 1–8, written to a slightly different audience in Achaia (e.g., Cenchreae; see Rom. 16:1). Paul assumes the audience is already aware of the needs of the saints. **9:2** The stoking of competition between the Roman provinces of Macedonia and Achaia continues. Some in Achaia previously made promises to give. **9:3** *Brothers.* See 8:16–23; 9:5. *Boasting* reflects a defense found throughout the letter about inappropriate boasting: boasting that is empty or that is beyond appropriate limits (see 10:12–18). **9:4** *We would be put to shame* demonstrates Paul's paternalism as related to the community. **9:5** While Paul has felt confident

to urge the brothers to go on ahead to you and
arrange in advance for this bountiful gift that
you have promised, so that it may be ready as
a bountiful gift and not as an extortion.

6 The point is this: the one who sows sparingly will also reap sparingly, and the one who
sows bountifully will also reap bountifully.
7Each of you must give as you have made up
your mind, not regretfully or under compulsion, for God loves a cheerful giver. 8And God
is able to provide you with every blessing[n] in
abundance, so that by always having enough
of everything, you may share abundantly in
every good work. 9As it is written,

"He scatters abroad; he gives to the poor;
his righteousness[o] endures forever."

10He who supplies seed to the sower and
bread for food will supply and multiply your
seed for sowing and increase the harvest of
your righteousness.[p] 11You will be enriched in
every way for your great generosity, which
will produce thanksgiving to God through
us, 12for the rendering of this ministry not
only supplies the needs of the saints but
also overflows with many thanksgivings to
God. 13Through the testing of this ministry
you[q] glorify God by your obedience to the
confession of the gospel of Christ and by the
generosity of your partnership with them
and with all others, 14while they long for you
and pray for you because of the surpassing
grace of God that he has given you. 15Thanks
be to God for his indescribable gift!

10 I myself, Paul, appeal to you by the meekness and gentleness of Christ—I who am
humble when face to face with you but bold
toward you when I am away!—2I ask that when
I am present I need not show boldness by daring to oppose those who think we are acting
according to human standards.[r] 3Indeed, we
live as humans[s] but do not wage war according
to human standards,[t] 4for the weapons of our
warfare are not merely human,[u] but they have
divine power to destroy strongholds. We destroy arguments 5and every proud obstacle
raised up against the knowledge of God, and
we take every thought captive to obey Christ.
6We are ready to punish every disobedience
when your obedience is complete.

n 9.8 Gk *gift* or *grace* *o* 9.9 Or *benevolence* *p* 9.10 Or *benevolence* *q* 9.13 Or *they* *r* 10.2 Gk *according to the flesh* *s* 10.3 Gk *in the flesh* *t* 10.3 Gk *according to the flesh* *u* 10.4 Gk *fleshly*

to boast of the Achaians' readiness, he sends the brothers to facilitate. This doubt may be due to the generosity or size of the promised gift. *Bountiful gift* (Gk. "eulogia") is used twice in this verse and the next. *Extortion* is not the desired method for receiving the Corinthian gift. **9:6** *Sows . . . reap* is a farming metaphor used commonly in antiquity (see 1 Cor. 9:10–11; Gal. 6:7–9; Job 4:8). **9:7** *God loves a cheerful giver.* See Prov. 22:8 LXX; Deut. 15:10; Phlm. 14. **9:8** After emphasizing the voluntary nature of their gift, Paul points to God's abundant gifts to them. **9:9** See Ps. 112:9. **9:10** *Harvest of your righteousness.* See Hos. 10:12. **9:11** There is a transactional nature to this discussion: God gives them, they give, they will be enriched, and God will receive thanks. **9:12** *Rendering of this ministry* refers to the act of doing this service. **9:13** *Testing*, or "proof," of the ministry. Proof of the generosity of the Corinthian gift demonstrates God's glory. *Partnership with them* likely refers to a partnership with the saints in Jerusalem. In the first-century Roman context, euergetism was accompanied by standard expectations regarding the giving and reception of gifts depending on the status of the parties involved. Paul's use of partnership language may be his attempt to equalize relationships between the giver (Achaia) and the recipient (Jerusalem) so that the Corinthians do not expect anything in return for their gift to the collection. **9:15** God's gift of grace, while it can be imitated, cannot be repaid.

10:1–13:13 Angry letter. Some interpreters argue that the changes in tone and topic indicate that these chapters form a separate letter from the rest of 2 Corinthians. This theory also allows for the imagining of a happier ending between Paul and the Corinthians, in which challenges to Pauline theology and leadership are resolved.

10:1–18 Defense of his ministry. Paul defends against accusations regarding his leadership and speech. **10:1** This is a personal appeal by Paul, suggesting personal attacks on his humble presence when face-to-face (see 10:10). He begins his defense by aligning himself with the meekness and gentleness of Christ (see Matt. 11:29). **10:2** He places the responsibility of his boldness on the audience. *Human*, or "fleshly." **10:3** *Wage war* suggests an escalation of tensions with the Corinthians. **10:4** Paul claims divine power and divine weapons (see 6:7; Rom. 13:12) for the destruction of the attacks against his ministry. In imitation of an imperial battle, he will destroy strongholds, then take captives (10:5), and finally, punish disobedience or resistance (10:6). **10:5** While Paul uses imperial metaphors, it is God and Christ who are in

7 Look[v] at what is before your eyes. If you are confident that you belong to Christ, remind yourself of this, that just as you belong to Christ, so also do we. [8]Now, even if I boast a little too much of our authority, which the Lord gave for building you up and not for tearing you down, I will not be ashamed of it. [9]I do not want to seem as though I am trying to frighten you with my letters. [10]For someone says,[w] "His letters are weighty and strong, but his bodily presence is weak and his speech contemptible." [11]Let such a person understand that what we say by letter when absent we will also do when present.

12 We do not dare to classify or compare ourselves with some of those who commend themselves. But when they measure themselves by one another and compare themselves with one another, they do not show good sense. [13]We, however, will not boast beyond limits but will keep within the field that God has assigned to us, to reach out even as far as you. [14]For we were not overstepping our limits when we reached you; we were the first to come all the way to you with the good news[x] of Christ. [15]We do not boast beyond limits, that is, in the labors of others, but our hope is that, as your faith increases, our field among you may be greatly enlarged, [16]so that we may proclaim the good news[y] in lands beyond you, without boasting of work already done in someone else's field. [17]"Let the one who boasts, boast in the Lord." [18]For it is not those who commend themselves that are approved but those whom the Lord commends.

11 I wish you would put up with me in a little foolishness. Yes, do put up[z] with me! [2]I feel a divine jealousy for you, for I promised you in marriage to one husband, to present you as a chaste virgin to Christ. [3]But I am afraid that, as the serpent deceived Eve by its cunning, your thoughts will be led astray from a sincere and pure[a] devotion to Christ. [4]For if someone comes and proclaims another Jesus than the one we proclaimed, or if you receive a different spirit from the one you received, or a different gospel from the one you accepted, you put up with it readily enough. [5]I think that I am not in the least inferior to these super-apostles. [6]Even if I am untrained in speech, I certainly am not with respect to knowledge; certainly in every way and in all things we have made this evident to you.

v 10.7 Or *You look*   w 10.10 Other ancient authorities read *they say*   x 10.14 Or *the gospel*   y 10.16 Or *the gospel*   z 11.1 Or *But indeed you do put up*   a 11.3 Other ancient authorities lack *and pure*

charge. **10:7** A question of belonging suggests divisions in the community regarding how much to align with Paul's ministry in their practices or beliefs. **10:8** Paul's defense of his boasting may reflect criticisms against him. *Authority.* Paul stresses that his power in the community is for the purpose of building up the community, an important statement after talk of his destructive ways in 10:3–6. *Ashamed.* See Rom. 1:16. **10:10** *Someone says* is likely a rhetorical device that avoids naming a particular person in order not to cause offense. Like many Greek cities, Corinth had a tradition of strong Greek rhetorical performance and wise speech. For Paul's speech and bodily presence to be seen as weak was a challenge to his leadership and even his character, especially if other leaders gave strong rhetorical performances. **10:12** Paul contrasts himself to his opponents by his lack of comparing himself with them. It was thought that the measure of a person could be determined by comparison. **10:13** In terms of his boasting, Paul claims to stay within limits (see 9:3). *Limits . . . within the field.* Literally "the measure of the rule." **10:16** *Lands* recalls the battlefield from the warfare of 10:3. In this case, it seems that the Achaians are themselves the battlefield where the war between Paul and alternative leaders is waged. **10:17** Jeremiah 9:23–24. See also 1 Cor. 1:31. **10:18** Paul appeals to the Lord to bypass all matters of comparison.

11:1–12:10 The Fool's Speech. This section expounds upon how Paul compares to rival leaders and continues Paul's defense against the attacks recorded in 10:10 and elsewhere regarding boasting. **11:1** *Foolishness.* Just as the rival leaders do not show good sense (10:12), Paul will now act senselessly. *Put up.* See 11:4. **11:2** Paul as father claims possession and responsibility over the congregation's chastity and purity. The community is cast as an errant daughter and would-be bride of Christ. **11:3** *Deceived* (see Gen. 3:13; 1 Tim. 2:14). Paul thinks with a legend, popular at the time, that Eve was sexually seduced by a serpentine Satan, who appeared to Eve as an angel (see 11:14). **11:4** *A different gospel* may refer to alternative practices regarding preaching, worship, women's leadership, or baptism on behalf of the dead (e.g., 1 Cor. 14:26–40; 1 Cor. 15:12–58, and introduction). **11:5** *These super-apostles* is a sarcastic reference to rival leaders in Corinth. **11:6** *Untrained in speech*—that is, not a professionally

7 Did I commit a sin by humbling myself so that you might be exalted, because I proclaimed God's good news[b] to you free of charge? [8]I robbed other churches by accepting support from them in order to serve you. [9]And when I was with you and was in need, I did not burden anyone, for my needs were supplied by the brothers who came from Macedonia. So I refrained and will continue to refrain from burdening you in any way. [10]As the truth of Christ is in me, this boast of mine will not be silenced in the regions of Achaia. [11]And why? Because I do not love you? God knows I do!

12 And what I do I will also continue to do, in order to deny an opportunity to those who want an opportunity to be recognized as our equals in what they boast about. [13]For such boasters are false apostles, deceitful workers, disguising themselves as apostles of Christ. [14]And no wonder! Even Satan disguises himself as an angel of light. [15]So it is not strange if his ministers also disguise themselves as ministers of righteousness. Their end will match their deeds.

16 I repeat, let no one think that I am a fool, but if you do, then accept me as a fool, so that I, too, may boast a little. [17]What I am saying in regard to this boastful undertaking, I am saying not with the Lord's authority but as a fool; [18]since many boast according to human standards,[c] I will also boast. [19]For you gladly put up with fools, being wise yourselves! [20]For you put up with it when someone makes slaves of you or preys upon you or takes advantage of you or puts on airs or gives you a slap in the face. [21]To my shame, I must say, we were too weak for that!

But whatever anyone dares to boast of—I am speaking as a fool—I also dare to boast of that. [22]Are they Hebrews? So am I. Are they Israelites? So am I. Are they descendants of Abraham? So am I. [23]Are they ministers of Christ? I am talking like a madman—I am a better one: with far greater labors, far more imprisonments, with countless floggings, and often near death. [24]Five times I have received from the Jews the forty lashes minus one. [25]Three times I was beaten with rods. Once I received a stoning. Three times I was shipwrecked; for a night and a day I was adrift at sea; [26]on frequent journeys, in danger from rivers, danger from bandits, danger from my own people, danger from gentiles, danger in the city, danger in the wilderness, danger at sea, danger from false brothers and sisters; [27]in toil and hardship, through many a sleepless night, hungry and thirsty, often without food,[d] cold and naked. [28]And, besides other things, I am under daily pressure because of my anxiety for all the churches. [29]Who is weak, and I am not weak? Who is made to stumble, and I am not indignant?

30 If I must boast, I will boast of the things that show my weakness. [31]The God and Father of the Lord Jesus (blessed be he forever!) knows that I do not lie. [32]In Damascus, the governor under King Aretas guarded the city of Damascus in order to[e] seize me, [33]but I was let down in a basket through a window in the wall[f] and escaped from his hands.

b 11.7 Gk *the gospel of God*   c 11.18 Gk *according to the flesh*   d 11.27 Gk *with frequent fasting*   e 11.32 Other ancient authorities read *and wanted to*   f 11.33 Gk *through the wall*

trained orator. **11:7–11** The Corinthians may have been offended by Paul's refusal to accept payment or hospitality for his ministry (see 1 Cor. 9:15–18). He claims to do so out of love. **11:7** *Humbling myself*, choosing manual labor. **11:9** *The brothers who came from Macedonia*. After appealing to the Corinthians for the collection in chaps. 8–9, the mention of the generosity of the Macedonians and Paul's desire not to burden the Corinthians has a particular sting. **11:12–15** Paul characterizes the rival leaders as ministers of Satan in disguise (see note on 11:3). These rivals are cast as competitors with Christ for the congregation as a pure bride (see note on 11:2 and **"Gender, Leadership, and Paul," p. 1990**). **11:16–18** *Not with the Lord's authority.* Paul presents himself sarcastically as a fool. Through boasting, Paul stoops to the level of the rival apostles to try to beat them at their own game. It also serves to shame the Corinthians by sarcastically calling them wise and presenting them as naively tolerant of foul behavior. **11:21** Paul sarcastically boasts of shame and weakness to present himself as strong. **11:22** Paul claims the same credentials as his rivals, important in Jewish Christ communities (see Phil. 3:4–6; Gal. 1:13–15; Rom. 9:4; 11:1). **11:23–28** This catalog of hardships demonstrates Paul's weakness, which he recasts as strength. Many of the details are not known within Pauline sources, but Acts offers some similar accounts. **11:23** *Imprisonments.* See Phlm. 1; Phil. 1:13; Eph. 3:1; Col. 4:3, 18; and Acts 16:22–40. *Floggings.* Paul refers to both Jewish and Roman practices: "lashes" (v. 24; see Deut. 25:3) and "rods" (v. 25; see Acts 16:22–23). **11:32–33** *Damascus.* A city in Syria (see Gal. 1:17; Acts 9). *Let down in a basket.* See Acts 9:23–25.

Reading through Time: Gender, Leadership, and Paul (2 Corinthians 11)

Women are not named or addressed directly in 2 Corinthians, leading many readers over the centuries to assume that gender is not an important facet of this letter. Yet seeing this letter within an ongoing correspondence that includes 1 Corinthians challenges this assumption. Within 1 Corinthians, Paul argues for practices regarding marriage and celibacy, women's dress while praying and prophesying, and speaking in church. Scholar Antoinette Wire argues that many of Paul's arguments in 1 Corinthians make sense when a group of female prophets is assumed to be at the center of debates. Women have always been there; assuming their presence leads to more accurate interpretations.

Yet the history of interpretation of 2 Corinthians shows that many interpreters have not taken seriously the ongoing presence of women in Corinth. All rival apostles are often assumed to be male, even if there is recognition of gendered dynamics in 1 Corinthians. However, attention to the rhetoric of the text, how Paul attempts to persuade his audience using careful metaphors and tone, demonstrates that gender is still at the forefront of his arguments.

While women are not directly addressed in 2 Corinthians, debates about women's leadership are still underway in Corinth at the time of its writing. Passages such as 2 Cor. 11 show that there are gendered assumptions being made about the community and the Christian ministry there. Paul's presenting himself as a father figure while presenting the community as an errant daughter whose chastity is under threat by Satan's ministers in the guise of male rival apostles reinforces patriarchal and gendered assumptions about sex, marriage, and leadership. Women were often the managers of the home and in charge of hosting guests. Paul's rejection of Corinthian hospitality would have had a direct impact on the women in Corinth and their abilities to lead in services within the house churches.

How we tell this history impacts how we interpret the biblical text and how we understand the present. The ministry of the church, not to mention the larger society, is still hindered by bigotry, particularly when women in leadership or members of the LGBTQIA2S+ community are targeted. The debates around women's leadership did not end with the end of 2 Corinthians. Imagining how various types of individuals and community members would have responded to Paul's letters helps envision a broad history and makes room for a diverse range of people in contemporary Christ communities.

Arminta M. Fox

---

12 It is necessary to boast; nothing is to be gained by it, but I will go on to visions and revelations of the Lord. ²I know a person in Christ who fourteen years ago was caught up to the third heaven—whether in the body or out of the body I do not know; God knows. ³And I know that such a person—whether in the body or out of the body I do not know; God knows—⁴was caught up into paradise and heard things that are not to be told, that no mortal is permitted to repeat. ⁵On behalf of such a one I will boast, but on my own behalf I will not boast, except of my weaknesses. ⁶But if I wish to boast, I will not be a fool, for I will be speaking the truth. But I refrain from it, so that no one may think better of me than what is seen in me or heard from me, ⁷even considering the exceptional character of the revelations. Therefore, to keepᵍ me from being too elated, a thorn was given me in the flesh, a messenger of Satan to torment me, to keep me from being too elated.ᵇ ⁸Three times I appealed to the Lord about this, that it would leave me, ⁹but he said to me, "My grace is sufficient for you, for powerⁱ is made

g 12.7 Other ancient authorities read *To keep*   *h* 12.7 Other ancient authorities lack *to keep me from being too elated*   *i* 12.9 Other ancient authorities read *my power*

12:1–13 Continuing his Fool's Speech, Paul boasts of ecstatic visions (see **"Religious Experience in Paul—Visions and Revelations," p. 1991**). This was a characteristic of Paul's rivals. **12:1** *Visions and revelations of the Lord.* See 1 Cor. 9:1; 15:8; Gal. 1:12; 2:1–2. **12:2** *I know a person* likely refers to Paul himself describing an ecstatic experience. Ecstatic visions were not uncommon in the ancient world and were used for claiming authority. *Third heaven,* or the location of paradise (v. 4; see 2 En. 8:1–8). **12:4** *Things that are not to be told.* Literally "unutterable utterances." **12:6** By refusing to openly boast or take pride in his revelations, Paul critiques the practice of following others for their visions. For Paul, but not necessarily for the community, apostleship is a greater gift than prophecy (see 1 Cor. 12:28–31). **12:7** *Thorn . . . in the flesh.* The exact meaning is uncertain but may refer to a physical or mental ailment, persecution, or obstacles to his ministry, which Paul attributes to a messenger of Satan. Some have speculated that Paul was blind or had epilepsy. **12:9–10** *Grace is sufficient.* An important concept for

Focus On: Religious Experience in Paul—Visions and Revelations (2 Corinthians 12)

In 2 Cor. 12, Paul boasts of someone who has extraordinary visions. He does not wish to boast on behalf of himself, yet he wants people to be aware of his own possible reasons for boasting. (This is akin to "asking for a friend.") Paul also mentions visions in 1 Cor. 9:1; 15:8; Gal. 1:12; 2:1–2. Acts also describes Paul's revelation on the road to Damascus and Ananias's vision to restore Paul's sight (Acts 9:1–19).

Paul's description of his vision in 2 Cor. 12 fits within a genre of ancient apocalyptic literature that includes texts such as the canonical Daniel and Revelation and the noncanonical Enoch, 2 Esdras, Apocalypse of Baruch, Shepherd of Hermas, and so on (see **"Paul's Apocalyptic Imagination," p. 2031**). In apocalyptic literature, authors often tell of visions where either a person sees some realm of the heavens and is given a message from a divine being or an angel or a god visits a person on earth, speaking and/or appearing to them. In this vision, Paul is taken up to paradise within the third heaven. "Paradise" comes from a Persian word for "enclosed park" or "garden," such as the garden of Eden (see Gen. 2:8).

Paul notes that he does not know whether this is "in the body or out of the body" (12:2), signaling the debates in the ancient world around the differences between divine and heavenly bodies (see also 1 Cor. 15:35–58). In other words, if you have a vision of yourself walking around heaven, are you in a different kind of body from the one you walk around in on earth? Here, Paul says he does not know what kind of body he had when having this vision. What is certain for Paul and his audience is that he speaks with the Lord, and the message of 2 Corinthians comes from what the Lord has communicated: God's grace is sufficient; power is made perfect in weakness. Similarly, Paul's "thorn . . . in the flesh" (12:7), some sort of obstacle to his ministry and life, is attributed to a messenger or angel of Satan.

In the ancient world, this type of revelation carries authority. Many people in the contemporary world are skeptical of visions and revelations, discounting them (and the people who experience them). But in order to understand Paul's writings, one must enter, at least imaginatively, into a world in which God communicates with people through visions.

Arminta M. Fox

perfect in weakness." So I will boast all the more gladly of my weaknesses, so that the power of Christ may dwell in me. [10]Therefore I am content with weaknesses, insults, hardships, persecutions, and calamities for the sake of Christ, for whenever I am weak, then I am strong.

11 I have been a fool! You forced me to it. Indeed you should have been the ones commending me, for I am not at all inferior to these super-apostles, even though I am nothing. [12]The signs of an apostle were performed among you with utmost patience, signs and wonders and mighty works. [13]How have you been worse off than the other churches, except that I myself did not burden you? Forgive me this wrong!

14 Here I am, ready to come to you this third time, and I will not be a burden because I do not want what is yours but you, for children ought not to save up for their parents but parents for their children. [15]I will most gladly spend and be spent for you. If I love you more, am I to be loved less? [16]Be that as it may, I did not burden you. But, crafty person that I am, did I take you in by deceit? [17]Did I take advantage of you through any of those whom I sent to you? [18]I urged Titus to go and sent the brother with him. Titus did not take advantage of you, did he? Did we not conduct

later theologians, such as Martin Luther. *Power is made perfect in weakness.* Paul's demonstrated weakness (as a fool, as humble, as one suffering hardships) shows that any power or knowledge he has is attributable to God via grace (see **"Introduction to 2 Corinthians," pp. 1977–78**). **12:11–13** The epilogue to the Fool's Speech, though Paul's defense continues. **12:11** *Commending.* See 3:1–3. **12:12** *Signs of an apostle.* Miraculous acts that were thought to demonstrate the authority of those claiming to be sent by God (see Acts 2:22; 14:3; 15:12; Rom. 15:19; Heb. 2:4). **12:13** *Worse off than the other churches* may be a Corinthian accusation launched at Paul.

12:14–13:10 Paul intends to visit a third time. **12:14** *Burden.* See note on 11:7–11. Paul may wish to avoid accepting their hospitality out of concern that he would no longer have full freedom over his message. *Parents for their children.* This paternalism may not be appreciated in the community. **12:16** *Crafty.* Possibly reflective of another Corinthian accusation of Paul. *Deceit.* See 11:3. **12:17–18** *Take advantage.* See 11:20. *Titus* and *the brother* (see 8:16–19). The whereabouts of Titus and the brother

ourselves with the same spirit? Did we not walk in the same footsteps?

19 Have you been thinking all along that we have been defending ourselves before you? We are speaking in Christ before God. Everything we do, beloved, is for the sake of building you up. 20For I fear that when I come I may find you not as I wish and that you may find me not as you wish; I fear that there may perhaps be quarreling, jealousy, anger, selfishness, slander, gossip, conceit, and disorder. 21I fear that when I come again my God may humble me before you and that I may have to mourn over many who previously sinned and have not repented of the impurity, sexual immorality, and debauchery that they have practiced.

13 This is the third time I am coming to you. "Any charge must be sustained by the evidence of two or three witnesses." 2I warned those who sinned previously and all the others, and I warn them now while absent, as I did when present on my second visit, that if I come again I will not be lenient—3since you desire proof that Christ is speaking in me. He is not weak in dealing with you but is powerful in you. 4For he was crucified in weakness but lives by the power of God. For we are weak in him,*j* but in dealing with you we will live with him by the power of God.

5 Examine yourselves to see whether you are living in the faith. Test yourselves. Do you not realize that Jesus Christ is in you?—unless, indeed, you fail to meet the test! 6I hope you will find out that we have not failed. 7But we pray to God that you may not do anything wrong—not that we may appear to have met the test but that you may do what is right, though we may seem to have failed. 8For we cannot do anything against the truth but only for the truth. 9For we rejoice when we are weak but you are strong. This is what we pray for, that you may be restored. 10So I write these things while I am away from you, so that when I come I may not have to be severe in using the authority that the Lord has given me for building up and not for tearing down.

11 Finally, brothers and sisters, farewell.*k* Be restored; listen to my appeal;*l* agree with one another; live in peace; and the God of love and peace will be with you. 12Greet one another with a holy kiss. All the saints greet you.

13 The grace of the Lord Jesus Christ, the love of God, and the communion of*m* the Holy Spirit be with all of you.

j 13.4 Other ancient authorities read *with him*   *k* 13.11 Or *rejoice*   *l* 13.11 Or *encourage one another*   *m* 13.13 Or *and the sharing in*

contribute to theories regarding the composition of the letter (see **"Introduction to 2 Corinthians,"** pp. 1977–78). *With the same Spirit.* See 3:3. **12:19** *Building you up.* See 10:8. **12:20–21** Paul's fears take the form of a standard vice list (see Mark 7:21–22; Rom. 1:29–31; 13:13; 1 Cor. 5:10–11; 6:9–10; Gal. 5:19–21). *Impurity, sexual immorality, and debauchery* also metaphorically reflect Paul's concerns about rival apostles (see 11:3–4). **13:1** *Any charge . . . witnesses.* Deuteronomy 19:15; Matt. 18:16; 1 Tim. 5:19. **13:2** Paul prepares for a third visit, having canceled a previous trip out of leniency (see 1:23). His last visit was a painful one (see 2:1). **13:3** Paul claims that his show of strength is proof of Christ's power in weakness. **13:5** *Test yourselves.* Literally "prove." While they desire proof that Christ is in Paul, Paul is also telling them to prove their own life in the faith to themselves (see 10:7). *Christ is in you.* See 2 Cor. 12:9; Rom. 8:10; Gal. 2:20. **13:9** *Restored.* See 2 Cor. 5:20; 13:11. **13:10** The contrast between writing and presence echoes the critiques of his rivals (see 10:10).

13:11–13 This closing is typical of a Pauline letter (see 1 Cor. 16:20; Gal. 6:18). **13:11** *Agree with one another.* A call for unity, common in political rhetoric. **13:12** *Holy kiss.* See 1 Cor. 16:20; Rom. 16:16; 1 Thess. 5:26. *All the saints greet you.* See Phil. 4:22; 1 Cor. 16:19–20; Rom. 16:16. **13:13** *Grace.* An important concept in the letter. *Communion of the Holy Spirit* is a reminder that the correct spirit is important throughout 2 Corinthians (see 3:3, 17; 5:5).

THE LETTER OF PAUL TO THE GALATIANS

Authorship, Date, and Audience

Galatia was a Roman province in central Asia Minor (present-day Turkey). This letter from Paul is addressed "to the churches of Galatia" (1:2), but the number and location of these groups are not clear. Writing in the late 40s or mid-50s CE, Paul takes particular concern for gentiles and rebuffs competing teachings that would require gentiles to comply with certain ancient Jewish practices such as circumcision.

Contested Gospel(s)

While Paul makes a case for the centrality of faith in community formation, he also notes that there is disagreement over his teaching. This is apparent in the striking rhetorical tone of the epistle. Eschewing his typical note of thanksgiving for the letter's recipients, Paul begins by expressing that he is astonished that the Galatians are deserting his teaching in favor of a different gospel (1:6). Arguing against this other gospel, Paul's Letter to the Galatians reveals something of the competitive dynamic among early purveyors of the gospel message(s).

Even as he clarifies "not that there is another gospel" (1:7), Paul goes on to specify two gospels: the "gospel for the uncircumcised" and the "gospel for the circumcised" (2:7). The distinction underscores one of the most fiercely contested debates among Christ followers in the first century: whether gentiles would be obliged to observe Jewish law, especially the requirement of (male) circumcision (Gen. 17:10–14). Paul does not argue that Jews should abandon their own legal adherence. Instead, he makes clear that his primary concern is for gentiles (Gal. 2:2–9). His "gospel for the uncircumcised" is a message that God's promises are available to gentiles not through obedience to the law but through the faith of Christ (2:16). While Paul's arguments prevailed to the extent that the themes of Galatians became central to Christian theology, the letter evinces an early period of contestation over the nature and implications of the gospel.

Inheriting Freedom

To make his case for a gospel free from the law's requirements, Paul invokes slavery as a key metaphor. For a gentile to choose to be circumcised is akin to submitting to slavery (5:1–2). It is important to remember that Paul's letters were written and received in a context where chattel slavery was legally sanctioned and widely practiced. People who were enslaved in the Roman world were denied legal standing, so they could not assert rights over possessions, nor could they receive an inheritance. Galatia was composed largely of conquered peoples who knew the effects of the Roman imperial order, including the consequences of enslavement.

The language of freedom that Paul invokes refers to a state of not being enslaved. In this way, the faith of Christ sets the faithful free by positioning them to inherit the promises God made to Abraham. To inherit is to be free. The letter might raise questions, then, about social and political implications, such as whether Christ followers should work to secure freedom for the enslaved (see **"Paul, Enslavement, and Freedom," p. 1964**). Likewise, the dissolution of identity categories—Jew or Greek, enslaved or free, male and female (3:28)—might be read in terms of spiritual transformation alone or to inspire the overturning of the social order. Although Paul's own aims in this regard are unclear, this letter has been used to debate the spiritual, social, and political nature of freedom throughout the history of Christianity. See **"The Bible and Social Justice," pp. 2165–67**.

Reading Guide

After an abbreviated salutation, the letter moves quickly into a statement of the primary problem Paul sets out to address. He suggests that the Galatians have developed a preference for a different teaching than his (1:6). In this competitive context, Paul defends his credentials by relating his personal narrative (1:11–2:14). He argues for the superiority of his teaching on the basis that he "received it through a revelation of Jesus Christ" (1:12). Moreover, Paul insists that he was not influenced by other humans, including leaders in Jerusalem, but was called directly by God to proclaim the gospel

to the gentiles (1:15–16). He goes on to describe how his particular mission and message were confirmed by key apostles (2:1–10).

Upon the basis of such authority, Paul commences with his argument that justification, or affirmation of righteousness, comes through the faith of Christ (see **"Faith of Jesus Christ," p. 1938**). Even as he challenges traditional adherence to the law, Paul works within a Jewish framework. By invoking Abraham as the model for faith (3:6–9), Paul hearkens back to the covenant God made with Abraham (Gen. 12:1–3; 17:2–8). A covenant is an agreement between two parties that delineates each party's responsibilities to the other (see **"Covenant (Genesis 6)," p. 23**). Faith is not so much about belief but about trust (a literal rendering of *pistis*, the Gk. word Paul uses) that God's promises will be upheld. Paul's argument is that Christ's own faithfulness has fulfilled humanity's covenantal obligations to God, replacing the function of the law, and gentiles can enter into the covenant by trusting that the faith of Christ is sufficient (Gal. 2:16).

The rest of the letter elaborates this argument. Paul explains that the law served to keep people in line until Christ came (3:10–14, 19–26), but now, any person who trusts Christ can be an heir of Abraham. Paul frames the concept of inheritance as a matter of freedom versus enslavement, using an allegory of Sarah and Hagar (Gen. 16:1–18:15; 21:1–21) to represent how the faithful are children, or inheritors, of freedom, while children of slavery do not share inheritance. Paul introduces a corresponding binary of flesh versus spirit (Gal. 5:16–26) and concludes by urging the Galatians not to boast in signs of the flesh—namely, circumcision—but to turn to the Spirit and have confidence only in the cross of Christ (6:7–16).

Tyler M. Schwaller

1 Paul an apostle—sent neither by human commission nor from human authorities but through Jesus Christ and God the Father, who raised him from the dead—²and all the brothers and sisters with me,

To the churches of Galatia:

3 Grace to you and peace from God our Father and the Lord Jesus Christ, ⁴who gave himself for our sins to set us free from the present evil age, according to the will of our God and Father, ⁵to whom be the glory forever and ever. Amen.

6 I am astonished that you are so quickly deserting the one who called you in the grace of Christ and are turning to a different gospel—⁷not that there is another gospel, but there are some who are confusing you and want to pervert the gospel of Christ. ⁸But even if we or an angel*a* from heaven should proclaim to you a gospel contrary to what we proclaimed to you, let that one be accursed! ⁹As we have said before, so now I repeat, if anyone proclaims to you a gospel contrary to what you received, let that one be accursed!

10 Am I now seeking human approval or God's approval? Or am I trying to please people? If I were still pleasing people, I would not be a servant of Christ.

11 For I want you to know, brothers and sisters, that the gospel that was proclaimed by me is not of human origin, ¹²for I did not

a 1.8 Or *a messenger*

1:1–5 Salutation. The absence of a typical Pauline thanksgiving, evincing tension, is notable. **1:1** *Apostle*, or "messenger," a title conveying authority as one sent by God. **1:2** *Churches*, or "assemblies." The plural suggests multiple assemblies; the number and location are unspecified. **1:3** *Grace . . . peace* combines typical Greek and Hebrew salutations. **1:4** *Gave himself for our sins* presents Jesus's death as a sacrifice (Mark 10:45) that serves to repair human transgression before God (Lev. 4–5). *Present evil age* suggests a future age of restoration and right relations (e.g., Isa. 65:17–25; Ezek. 37).

1:6–9 Paul rebukes the Galatians. Paul accuses the Galatians of *quickly deserting the one who called you*. Paul understands God as the one who calls. *Different*, implying wrong, *gospel*, "good news," referring to the message of Christ. Paul asserts that the Galatians have gotten the gospel's implications wrong. **1:7** *Not that . . . another gospel*—for example, alternative teachings are illegitimate. Paul blames the confusion on those who *pervert*, or change, the gospel. While Paul presents the gospel as singular, there was disagreement and competition over authority to represent the gospel's tenets. **1:8** *Angel*, or "messenger." No one, including heavenly messengers, has the authority to change the gospel. **1:9** *What you received* via tradition or instruction.

1:10–12 Paul defends his gospel. Against possible counterclaims that Paul has gotten the message wrong, he contends that he relies only on God. **1:10** *Servant*, literally "enslaved person," *of Christ* signifies obedience to Christ. **1:12** *Revelation of Jesus Christ.* Paul appears to use a claim of direct revelation to fortify his authority.

Going Deeper: Paul's Conversion/Call (Galatians 1)

In Gal. 1, Paul relays a story of an experience of Jesus that changed his life. He expects that his address-ees know about his earlier violent, zealous, and academically proficient life in Judaism, during a time when he persecuted what he calls the church of God (Gal. 1:13–14). After God revealed his son Jesus to him, Paul dropped everything and went to Arabia, the eastern frontier of the Roman Empire, and then back to Damascus for "three years" before returning to Jerusalem (1:18), then to Syria and Cilicia (1:21). Paul says he did not return to Jerusalem for another "fourteen years" (2:1).

Paul's own story differs from the account in Acts 9, in which Paul's comparatively sudden transforma-tion involves a blinding light throwing him to the ground and the disembodied voice of Jesus admonishing his behavior and telling him to go to the city and await instruction. Within days, Paul can see, is baptized, and proclaims Jesus as the Messiah among the gentiles—much to the surprise of those who knew of his harassment. Paul became an apostle to people he had persecuted. Did he, though, change religions in order to drop his weapons and embrace his former targets? Did Paul leave Judaism for Christianity?

Stories like Paul's are now commonly known as *conversion* narratives. In the study of religion, *con-version* denotes a personal change in worldview and/or practices. A *convert* is thought to experience a rupture with their past and subsequently abandon one way of life for another. Usually, we might think of conversion as changing religions, and those who do that become fundamentally different people. How-ever, there are questions about how conversion functions historically, culturally, and socially—including whether conversion represents a clean break with the past, what motivates individuals to convert and whether they choose conversion, how personal stories are central to conversion, and how body prac-tices demonstrate conversion.

What if Paul's experience did not mean he abandoned Judaism for Christianity? Some biblical scholars observe that there is little historical evidence that Paul experienced a rupture with his Jewish past; rather, he moved positions within that tradition. If we reimagine Paul's *conversion* as a *call* reminiscent of Israel's prophets (Gal. 1:11–16), a differently Jewish Paul emerges whose letters reflect human discussions within the plurality of ancient Jewish ways of thinking and practicing the faith. Such a reimagination encourages conversation about how we situate Paul in his world and ours, as well as what it could mean for Christian origins and modern Jewish-Christian relations if Paul—the (new) Christ follower—is not Christian.

Davina C. Lopez

receive it from a human source, nor was I taught it, but I received it through a revelation of Jesus Christ.

13 You have heard, no doubt, of my earlier life in Judaism. I was violently persecuting the church of God and was trying to destroy it. [14]I advanced in Judaism beyond many among my people of the same age, for I was far more zeal-ous for the traditions of my ancestors. [15]But when the one[b] who had set me apart before I was born and called me through his grace

was pleased [16]to reveal his Son to me,[c] so that I might proclaim him among the gentiles, I did not confer with any human, [17]nor did I go up to Jerusalem to those who were already apostles before me, but I went away at once into Arabia, and afterward I returned to Damascus.

18 Then after three years I did go up to Je-rusalem to visit Cephas and stayed with him fifteen days, [19]but I did not see any other apos-tle except James the Lord's brother. [20]In what

b 1.15 Other ancient authorities read *God*   *c* 1.16 Gk *in me*

1:13–14 Paul's Jewishness. Paul recounts his early life to establish his expertise and demonstrate the transformation he attributes to divine revelation (see Phil. 3:3–6 and **"Paul's Conversion/Call," p. 1995**). **1:13** *Persecuting the church of God* refers to "assemblies" of Christ followers. **1:14** *Zealous*, ardently devoted, to the *traditions of my ancestors*, encompassing Jewish law and practice.

1:15–24 Paul's call. *Before I was born*, literally "from the womb of my mother," as a prophet (see Isa. 49:1; Jer. 1:5). **1:16** *Son.* Jesus (see also 4:4). *To me.* Literally "in me"—that is, the gospel is revealed to and through Paul. *Gentiles*, or "nations." **1:17** *Jerusalem.* The site of the Second Temple, Jesus's death, and early apostolic activity. Paul contends that his revelatory experience establishes authority equiv-alent to *apostles before me*, those who knew Jesus. *Arabia.* Eastern provincial territory. *Returned to Damascus.* See Acts 9:8–21; 2 Cor. 11:32–33. **1:18** *Three years*, whether after Paul's revelation or return to Damascus is unclear. *Cephas.* Aramaic equivalent to "Peter" (Gk. "Petros," both "rock"). *Fifteen days*, suggesting too brief to be unduly influenced. **1:19** *James.* A leading member of the Jerusalem

I am writing to you, before God, I do not lie! [21]Then I went into the regions of Syria and Cilicia, [22]and I was still unknown by sight to the churches of Judea that are in Christ; [23]they only heard it said, "The one who formerly was persecuting us is now proclaiming the faith he once tried to destroy." [24]And they glorified God because of me.

2 Then after fourteen years I went up again to Jerusalem with Barnabas, taking Titus along with me. [2]I went up in response to a revelation. Then I laid before them (though only in a private meeting with the acknowledged leaders) the gospel that I proclaim among the gentiles, in order to make sure that I was not running, or had not run, in vain. [3]But even Titus, who was with me, was not compelled to be circumcised, though he was a Greek. [4]But because of false brothers and sisters secretly brought in, who slipped in to spy on the freedom we have in Christ Jesus, so that they might enslave us—[5]we did not submit to them even for a moment, so that the truth of the gospel might always remain with you. [6]And from those who were supposed to be acknowledged leaders (what they actually were makes no difference to me; God shows no partiality)—those leaders contributed nothing to me. [7]On the contrary, when they saw that I had been entrusted with the gospel for the uncircumcised, just as Peter had been entrusted with the gospel for the circumcised [8](for he who worked through Peter making him an apostle to the circumcised also worked through me in sending me to the gentiles), [9]and when James and Cephas and John, who were acknowledged pillars, recognized the grace that had been given to me, they gave to Barnabas and me the right hand of fellowship, agreeing that we should go to the gentiles and they to the circumcised. [10]They asked only one thing, that we remember the poor, which was actually what I was[d] eager to do.

11 But when Cephas came to Antioch, I opposed him to his face because he stood self-condemned, [12]for until certain people came from James, he used to eat with the gentiles. But after they came, he drew back and kept himself separate for fear of the circumcision faction. [13]And the other Jews joined him in this hypocrisy, so that even Barnabas was led astray by their hypocrisy. [14]But when I saw that they were not acting consistently with the truth of the gospel, I said to Cephas before

d 2.10 Or had been

assembly (2:9; Acts 15:13; 21:18). **1:21** *Syria and Cilicia.* Distant from Jerusalem; Tarsus, Paul's hometown (Acts 9:11), was in Cilicia.

2:1–10 Paul meets apostles in Jerusalem. Paul's account differs from the description in Acts 15:1–29 (see **"Paul in Acts and the Letters," p. 1997**). **2:1** *Fourteen years,* whether from his revelation or previously (1:18) is unclear. *Barnabas.* Paul's Jewish coworker. *Titus.* Paul's Greek companion. **2:2** *Revelation.* As opposed to being summoned by the Jerusalem church. *Gospel . . . gentiles* distinguishes instruction given to gentiles from that given to Jews. **2:3** *Not . . . circumcised*—that is, not Jewish. *Greek.* Synonymous with gentiles. Circumcision (of males) was a distinguishing mark of Jewishness, a sign of God's covenant with Abraham (Gen. 17:9–14). **2:4** *Freedom.* The agency afforded to those who are not enslaved. Paul sets up a key theme of the letter—namely, that circumcision signifies enslavement. The juxtaposition of freedom and enslavement was not solely metaphorical but based in Roman law and widespread practices of chattel slavery. **2:7** *Gospel for the uncircumcised . . . circumcised.* Paul suggests that the gospel has different implications for gentiles (uncircumcised) and Jews (circumcised) and insists that gentiles are not obligated to follow the law. **2:8** This reverses the presentation in Acts (9:20–22; 10; 13). **2:9** *John.* Likely Peter's coworker (Acts 3–4). **2:10** Paul collects funds to be sent to Jerusalem (Rom. 15:25–29; 1 Cor. 16:1–3; 2 Cor. 8–9). For *the poor* as a collective designation, see Ps. 113:7; Prov. 19:17; Isa. 41:17.

2:11–14 Paul rebukes Peter at Antioch. As with circumcision, dietary practices were contested; prohibitions on eating certain types of meat (Lev. 11; Deut. 14) contributed to a norm of refraining from dining with or eating food prepared by gentiles (e.g., Dan. 1:8–16). See Acts 10. **2:11** *Cephas.* Peter (see note on 1:18). **2:12** Paul claims Peter has stopped eating with gentiles *for fear of the circumcision faction*— literally "fear of those from the circumcised." **2:13** *Other Jews.* Apparently Jewish Christ followers. **2:14** *Live like a gentile* may refer to the practice of eating with gentiles, since Peter is not otherwise depicted as unlawful. Paul uses Peter's shifting dining behaviors to argue that it is inappropriate to *compel the gentiles to live like Jews*—that is, to observe the law.

Focus On: Paul in Acts and in the Letters (Galatians 2)

Readers of the New Testament have long noticed apparent differences between depictions of Paul in the Acts of the Apostles and the Pauline Letters. Over a century ago, this observation became a driving force behind German scholars deciding that the New Testament represented a division between pro-Pauline and anti-Pauline factions, which the writer of Acts sought to mediate between by creating a narrative that tames a more radical Paul in line with a more conservative, Jewish-indebted church tradition.

Interesting as these historical questions are, it is worth noting that the biblical tradition is replete with divergent narratives of the same events and different portrayals of main characters. Telling stories draws on human creative tendencies to shape narratives toward particular purposes and for specific audiences. The Hebrew Bible is full of such examples, such as the juxtaposition of two creation narratives in Genesis or the alternative Davidic dynasty account in Chronicles. In the New Testament, we find four distinct portraits of Jesus in the Gospels and differing images of Christ offered in the Letters and Revelation. Similarly, Paul's voice and ideas vary between his authentic letters and the letters written in his name. If we add images of Paul in post–New Testament literature, such as the Acts of Paul and Thecla, still another Paul emerges.

It is thus not surprising to turn to Acts and see a Paul who is primarily in conflict with gentile and Jewish authorities rather than with other proto-Christian communities as we see in his letters. Acts does not emphasize Paul as a letter writer. Paul's speeches in Acts are not full of the language and ideas we observe in his letters, and any mention of "justification by faith" or the "law" is absent. Unlike the portrayal in Galatians, Paul is more aligned with Peter's mission in Acts. Indeed, the so-called Jerusalem Council in Acts 15:1–35 has a different take on the event than Paul offers in Gal. 2:1–10.

When put in the broader context of differences in the Pauline letter corpus itself (cf. Galatians and Ephesians and "justification by faith" therein) and the postbiblical Pauline tradition (cf. Acts of Paul and Thecla), we see in the various Pauline portraits the theological creativity and historical imagination that enliven these traditions and make them endure. Searching for a consistent historical Paul is much less interesting in this light than embracing the diversity of the human views on Paul and his ideas.

Todd Penner

them all, "If you, though a Jew, live like a gentile and not like a Jew, how can you compel the gentiles to live like Jews?"[e]

15 We ourselves are Jews by birth and not gentile sinners, [16]yet we know that a person is justified[f] not by the works of the law but through the faith of Jesus Christ.[g] And we have come to believe in Christ Jesus, so that we might be justified by the faith of Christ[h] and not by doing the works of the law, because no one will be justified by the works of the law. [17]But if, in our effort to be justified in Christ, we ourselves have been found to be sinners, is Christ then a servant of sin? Certainly not! [18]But if I build up again the very things that I once tore down, then I demonstrate that I am a transgressor. [19]For through the law I died to the law, so that I might live to God. I have been crucified with Christ, [20]and it is no longer I who live, but it is Christ who lives in me. And the life I now live in the flesh I live by the faith of the Son of God,[i] who loved me and gave

e 2.14 Some interpreters hold that the quotation extends into the following paragraph *f* 2.16 Or *reckoned as righteous* *g* 2.16 Or *faith in Jesus Christ* *h* 2.16 Or *faith in Christ* *i* 2.20 Or *by faith in the Son of God*

2:15–21 Faith versus law. 2:15 *We.* Paul and Peter. *Gentile sinners.* Perhaps referencing a stereotypical view of idol worship. **2:16** *Justified,* or "reckoned as righteous." *Works of the law.* Practicing Jewish law. *Faith* (Gk. "pistis") conveys "trust" and "confidence." *Faith of Jesus Christ.* Jesus's confidence in God. The alternative translation "faith in Jesus Christ" connotes confidence in Christ (see **"Faith of Christ," p. 1938**). *Believe in,* or "put trust in." Paul presents two options for demonstrating commitment to God: trusting that Jesus's faithfulness is sufficient to be counted as righteous or demonstrating righteousness by following the law. **2:17** *We ourselves . . . sinners,* according to opponents' views of associating with or acting like gentiles. Paul suggests this would imply Christ facilitates sin, presumably because he challenges divisions (3:28). **2:18** *Very things.* Observing law to demonstrate righteousness. **2:19** *Crucified with Christ.* See 5:24; 6:14; Rom. 6:5–11; 2 Cor. 4:7–12. **2:20** *Christ who lives in me.* See Rom. 8:9–11; 2 Cor. 13:5. **2:21** Against an argument that Paul would *nullify the grace of God* by eschewing law observance, Paul contends that *Christ died for nothing* if law observance were sufficient for righteousness.

himself for me. [21]I do not nullify the grace of God, for if righteousness[j] comes through the law, then Christ died for nothing.

3 You foolish Galatians! Who has bewitched you? It was before your eyes that Jesus Christ was publicly exhibited as crucified! [2]The only thing I want to learn from you is this: Did you receive the Spirit by doing the works of the law or by believing what you heard? [3]Are you so foolish? Having started with the Spirit, are you now ending with the flesh? [4]Did you experience so much for nothing?—if it really was for nothing. [5]Well then, does God[k] supply you with the Spirit and work miracles among you by your doing the works of the law or by your believing what you heard?

6 Just as Abraham "believed God, and it was reckoned to him as righteousness," [7]so, you see, those who believe are the descendants of Abraham. [8]And the scripture, foreseeing that God would reckon as righteous the gentiles by faith, declared the gospel beforehand to Abraham, saying, "All the gentiles shall be blessed in you." [9]For this reason, those who believe are blessed with Abraham who believed.

10 For all who rely on the works of the law are under a curse, for it is written, "Cursed is everyone who does not observe and obey all the things written in the book of the law." [11]Now it is evident that no one is reckoned as righteous before God by the law, for "the one who is righteous will live by faith."[l] [12]But the law does not rest on faith; on the contrary, "Whoever does the works of the law[m] will live by them." [13]Christ redeemed us from the curse of the law by becoming a curse for us—for it is written, "Cursed is everyone who hangs on a tree"—[14]in order that in Christ Jesus the blessing of Abraham might come to the gentiles, so that we might receive the promise of the Spirit through faith.

15 Brothers and sisters, I give an example from daily life: once a person's will[n] has been ratified, no one adds to it or annuls it. [16]Now the promises were made to Abraham and to his offspring;[o] it does not say, "And to offsprings,"[p] as of many, but it says, "And to your offspring,"[q] that is, to one person, who is Christ. [17]My point is this: the law, which came four hundred thirty years later, does not annul a covenant previously ratified by God, so as to nullify the promise. [18]For if the inheritance comes from the law, it no longer comes from the promise, but God granted it to Abraham through the promise.

j 2.21 Or *justification* *k* 3.5 Gk *he* *l* 3.11 Or *The one who is righteous through faith will live* *m* 3.12 Gk *does them* *n* 3.15 Or *covenant* *o* 3.16 Gk *seed* *p* 3.16 Gk *seeds* *q* 3.16 Gk *seed*

3:1–5 Testing the Galatians. Paul challenges the Galatians to consider whether their experiences of the divine stem from trust in Christ or efforts to observe the law. **3:2** *Believing what you heard*, or "hearing of faith." *Receive the Spirit*, which is to be imbued with gifts of the Holy Spirit, such as tongues and prophecy (Acts 19:6), wisdom (1 Cor. 2:10–13), and virtuousness (Gal. 5:22–23). **3:3** *Spirit ... flesh.* A Pauline contrast (4:29; 5:16–25; 6:8; Rom. 8:1–12; 1 Cor. 5:5; 15:35–55; Phil. 3:2–6). **3:5** *Miracles* demonstrate the presence of the Spirit.

3:6–14 Abraham as a model. Considering the circumcision debate, Paul turns to Abraham, the "father" with whom God formed a covenant (Gen. 12:1–3; 17:2–8), where Abraham and his (male) descendants would practice circumcision as a covenantal sign (Gen. 17:9–14). **3:6** Genesis 15:6. Paul argues that Abraham's faith was affirmed prior to his circumcision in Gen. 17. **3:8** Paul cites Gen. 12:3, interpreting "in you" as "through you"—that is, that gentiles attain God's blessing by following Abraham's example (see Gen. 18:18; 22:18). **3:10–14 Law as curse.** Paul uses Scripture to build his argument, saying that the law results in people being cursed because they cannot fulfill it perfectly. Christ's faithfulness is represented by his acceptance of this curse on people's behalf, enabling those who trust the faith of Christ access to God's promises. **3:10** Deuteronomy 27:26. **3:11** Habakkuk 2:4. **3:12** Leviticus 18:5. **3:13** Deuteronomy 21:23, which refers to execution by hanging; Paul here alludes to Jesus's crucifixion.

3:15–18 Covenant. 3:15 *Will.* Greek "covenant." **3:16** *Offspring.* Literally "seed." God promises abundance for Abraham's *offspring* (Gen. 12:7; 15:5; 17:8; 22:17). "Seed" is commonly taken as a collective noun; Paul avers its singularity, referring to Christ. **3:17** Paul refers to the law revealed to Moses after the Israelites escaped enslavement in Egypt, which lasted *four hundred thirty years*, according to the Hebrew text of Exod. 12:40. Paul follows the LXX, which counts the years beginning with Abraham's journey in Canaan. **3:18** Paul distinguishes *the inheritance* from *the law*, claiming *the promise* made prior to the law is available without the law.

19 Why then the law? It was added because of transgressions, until the offspring[r] would come to whom the promise had been made, and it was ordained through angels by a mediator. [20]Now a mediator involves more than one party, but God is one.

21 Is the law then opposed to the promises of God? Certainly not! For if a law had been given that could make alive, then righteousness would indeed come through the law. [22]But the scripture has imprisoned all things under the power of sin, so that what was promised through the faith of Jesus Christ[s] might be given to those who believe.

23 Now before faith came, we were imprisoned and guarded under the law until faith would be revealed. [24]Therefore the law was our disciplinarian until Christ came, so that we might be reckoned as righteous[t] by faith. [25]But now that faith has come, we are no longer subject to a disciplinarian, [26]for in Christ Jesus you are all children of God through faith. [27]As many of you as were baptized into Christ have clothed yourselves with Christ. [28]There is no longer Jew or Greek; there is no longer slave or free; there is no longer male and female, for

all of you are one in Christ Jesus. [29]And if you belong to Christ, then you are Abraham's offspring,[u] heirs according to the promise.

4 My point is this: heirs, as long as they are minors, are no better than those who are enslaved, though they are the owners of all the property, [2]but they remain under guardians and trustees until the date set by the father. [3]So with us; while we were minors, we were enslaved to the elemental principles[t] of the world. [4]But when the fullness of time had come, God sent his Son, born of a woman, born under the law, [5]in order to redeem those who were under the law, so that we might receive adoption as children. [6]And because you are children, God has sent the Spirit of his Son into our[w] hearts, crying, "Abba![x] Father!" [7]So you are no longer a slave but a child, and if a child then also an heir through God.[y]

8 Formerly, when you did not know God, you were enslaved to beings that by nature are

r 3.19 Gk seed s 3.22 Or through faith in Jesus Christ t 3.24 Or be justified u 3.29 Gk seed v 4.3 Or spirits w 4.6 Other ancient authorities read your x 4.6 Aramaic for Father y 4.7 Other ancient authorities read an heir of God through Christ

3:19–25 The purpose of the law. Paul justifies freedom from the law by explaining its purpose as temporary. **3:19** *Because of transgressions,* which might mean the law functions to restrain sin (vv. 23–25), raise awareness of sin (Rom. 3:20; 7:7), or provoke sin (Rom. 5:20; 7:8–11). *Offspring.* Christ (see note on 3:16). The LXX version of Deut. 33:2 gives *angels* a role in revealing the law (see also Acts 7:38, 53). *Mediator.* Moses (Deut. 5:5). **3:20** Paul's point is that the law, unlike Abraham's covenant, did not come directly from God. **3:21–22** Paul's logic is that law is concerned with *sin* (see note on 3:19), whereas the *faith of Jesus Christ* (see note on 2:16) enables access to *what was promised* and thus can *make alive* (see **"Faith of Christ," p. 1938**). **3:24** *Disciplinarian,* literally "pedagogue," an enslaved person who supervised children's education and accompanied them outside the home. The law as pedagogue is an interim measure during a period of immaturity.

3:26–29 Baptism into Christ. Paul may be referring to baptism as a ritual of incorporation into the collective party to the covenant with God through Christ. **3:26** *Children of God.* Heirs of God's promises. **3:27** *Into Christ.* Perhaps in the sense that Christ holds space for those who trust in him to enter the covenant (cf. Matt. 28:19; Acts 8:16; 19:5). *Clothed . . . with Christ.* Perhaps in the sense that clothing can convey status. **3:28** Paul argues throughout the letter that gentiles should not be treated as distinct from Jews or made to "live like Jews" (2:14). He underscores that baptism further challenges social distinctions; the only status that matters is relationship to Christ. *Male and female.* See Gen. 1:27. **3:29** Christ's status as *Abraham's offspring,* or seed, extends to those united in baptism.

4:1–7 Heirs versus enslaved. Paul draws an analogy rooted in Roman practices wherein fathers controlled household dynamics and resources. Enslaved persons had no legal claims to property, whereas free children had inheritance rights. **4:2** *Guardians* maintained a father's power over minor children upon the father's death. **4:3** *Elemental principles.* Perhaps deities or spirits previously observed by the Galatians (4:8–9; cf. Col. 2:8, 20). **4:4** *Fullness of time.* Marked by the coming of the Messiah (cf. Mark 1:15; Eph. 1:10). *Born of a woman* underscores Jesus's human origins. **4:5** *Adoption* grants access to inheritance. The metaphor serves Paul's argument that gentiles can receive God's promises. **4:6** *Abba.* Cf. Mark 14:36; Rom. 8:15.

4:8–11 Spiritual enslavement. Enslaved persons were subject to the control and whims of enslavers. Paul compares enslavement practices to observing *beings* and *elemental principles* thought to control

not gods. [9]Now, however, that you have come to know God, or rather to be known by God, how can you turn back again to the weak and beggarly elemental principles?[z] How can you want to be enslaved to them again? [10]You are observing special days and months and seasons and years. [11]I am afraid that my work for you may have been wasted.

12 Brothers and sisters, I beg you: become as I am, for I also have become as you are. You have done me no wrong. [13]You know that it was because of a physical infirmity that I first announced the gospel to you; [14]though my condition put you to the test, you did not scorn or despise me but welcomed me as an angel of God, as Christ Jesus. [15]What has become of the goodwill you felt? For I testify that, had it been possible, you would have torn out your eyes and given them to me. [16]Have I now become your enemy by telling you the truth? [17]They make much of you but for no good purpose; they want to exclude you, so that you may make much of them. [18]It is good to be made much of for a good purpose at all times and not only when I am present with you. [19]My little children, for whom I am again in the pain of childbirth until Christ is formed in you, [20]I wish I were present with you now and could change my tone, for I am perplexed about you.

21 Tell me, you who desire to be subject to the law, will you not listen to the law? [22]For it is written that Abraham had two sons, one by an enslaved woman and the other by a free woman. [23]One, the child of the enslaved woman, was born according to the flesh; the other, the child of the free woman, was born through the promise. [24]Now this is an allegory: these women are two covenants. One woman, in fact, is Hagar, from Mount Sinai, bearing children for slavery. [25]Now Hagar is Mount Sinai in Arabia[a] and corresponds to the present Jerusalem, for she is in slavery with her children. [26]But the other woman corresponds to the Jerusalem above; she is free, and she is our mother. [27]For it is written,

"Rejoice, you childless one, you who bear
    no children,
  burst into song and shout, you who
      endure no birth pangs,
  for the children of the desolate woman
      are more numerous
  than the children of the one who is
      married."

[28]Now you,[b] my brothers and sisters, are children of the promise, like Isaac. [29]But just as at that time the child who was born according to the flesh persecuted the child who was born according to the Spirit, so it is now also. [30]But what does the scripture say? "Drive out the enslaved woman and her child, for the child of the enslaved woman will not share the inheritance with the child of the free woman." [31]So then, brothers and sisters, we are children, not of an enslaved woman but

5 of the free woman. [1]For freedom Christ has set us free. Stand firm, therefore, and do not submit again to a yoke of slavery.

z 4.9 Or *spirits*   a 4.25 Other ancient authorities read *For Sinai is a mountain in Arabia*   b 4.28 Other ancient authorities read *we*

---

human life (see note on 4:3). **4:10** *Special days . . . years* possibly refers to the Jewish ritual calendar. For the Galatians, observing the law would have an "enslaving" effect.

4:12–20 Paul as model. 4:13 Paul's *physical infirmity* is unknown, though v. 15 may suggest eye trouble. **4:14** *Angel*, or "messenger." **4:17** *They*, Paul's opponents, may exclude those who do not observe the law (cf. 2:12). *Make much.* To feel concern or jealousy. **4:19** Paul compares his efforts to *childbirth*, like Moses (Num. 11:12), and refers to addressees as his *children* (1 Cor. 4:14; 2 Cor. 6:13; 1 Thess. 2:11).

4:21–5:1 Allegory of Hagar and Sarah. 4:21 *Subject to the law*—literally "subject to law," without a definite article—refers to legal adherence generally. *Listen to the law*, with the definite article, usually refers to Jewish law. Paul makes an appeal to Scripture to support his argument. **4:22–23** Genesis 16; 21. **4:24** In *allegory*, key figures and places represent concepts and qualities. Hagar and Sarah represent *two covenants*. Hagar, enslaved and *bearing children for slavery*, stands for Abraham's descendants who adhere to the law as given to Moses at *Mount Sinai*. **4:25–26** *Present Jerusalem . . . Jerusalem above* contrasts Jerusalem as a human construct, significant as the site of the Jewish temple, with Jerusalem as restored by God (Isa. 51; 60; Zech. 2:10–12). *The other woman*, Sarah, represents the covenant accessible through Christ. As a *free* woman, she bears children who inherit God's promises. **4:27** Isaiah 54:1. **4:29** The idea that the *child who was born according to the flesh*, Ishmael, *persecuted* Isaac is not in Genesis. **4:30** Genesis 21:10. **5:1** *Freedom* is not being enslaved, as opposed to observances that enslave (4:8–10).

2 Listen! I, Paul, am telling you that, if you let yourselves be circumcised, Christ will be of no benefit to you. [3]Once again I testify to every man who lets himself be circumcised that he is obliged to obey the entire law. [4]You who want to be reckoned as righteous[c] by the law have cut yourselves off from Christ; you have fallen away from grace. [5]For through the Spirit, by faith, we eagerly wait for the hope of righteousness. [6]For in Christ Jesus neither circumcision nor uncircumcision counts for anything; the only thing that counts is faith working[d] through love.

7 You were running well; who prevented you from obeying the truth? [8]Such persuasion does not come from the one who calls you. [9]A little yeast leavens the whole batch of dough. [10]I am confident about you in the Lord that you will not think otherwise. But whoever it is that is confusing you will pay the penalty. [11]But my brothers and sisters, why am I still being persecuted if I am still preaching circumcision? In that case the offense of the cross has been removed. [12]I wish those who unsettle you would castrate themselves!

13 For you were called to freedom, brothers and sisters, only do not use your freedom as an opportunity for self-indulgence,[e] but through love become enslaved to one another. [14]For the whole law is summed up in a single commandment, "You shall love your neighbor as yourself." [15]If, however, you bite and devour one another, take care that you are not consumed by one another.

16 Live by the Spirit, I say, and do not gratify the desires of the flesh. [17]For what the flesh desires is opposed to the Spirit, and what the Spirit desires is opposed to the flesh, for these are opposed to each other, to prevent you from doing what you want. [18]But if you are led by the Spirit, you are not subject to the law. [19]Now the works of the flesh are obvious: sexual immorality, impurity, debauchery, [20]idolatry, sorcery, enmities, strife, jealousy, anger, quarrels, dissensions, factions, [21]envy,[f] drunkenness, carousing, and things like these. I am warning you, as I warned you before: those who do such things will not inherit the kingdom of God.

22 By contrast, the fruit of the Spirit is love, joy, peace, patience, kindness, generosity, faithfulness, [23]gentleness, and self-control. There is no law against such things. [24]And those who belong to Christ[g] have crucified the flesh with its passions and desires. [25]If we live by the Spirit, let us also be guided by the Spirit. [26]Let us not become conceited, competing against one another, envying one another.

6 My brothers and sisters, if anyone is detected in a transgression, you who have received the Spirit should restore such a one

c 5.4 Or *justified*   d 5.6 Or *made effective*   e 5.13 Gk *the flesh*
f 5.21 Other ancient authorities add *murder*   g 5.24 Other ancient authorities read *Christ Jesus*

5:2–12 Against circumcision. Paul argues that to become circumcised is to choose submission to the law as the means for accessing the covenant, as opposed to trusting that God's promises come through the faith of Christ (see **"Faith of Christ," p. 1938**). **5:3–4** See 2:16; 3:10–12. **5:6** *Neither circumcision nor uncircumcision* is a concern, so one need not change their present state (6:15; 1 Cor. 7:19–20). *Faith working*, or made effective, *through love* may underscore that God's love inspires faith and that followers should demonstrate faith through love (5:13–14). **5:7** *Running.* Cf. 2:2. **5:8** *One who calls.* God; see note on 1:6–9. **5:9** Paul expresses concern that a few people can impact the whole community (cf. 1 Cor. 5:6). **5:11** Paul's opponents may have alleged that he was inconsistent. His retort implies that promoting circumcision would reaffirm the covenant through law observance, thereby removing the *offense*, literally "stumbling block," of Paul's argument that Christ's death on *the cross* reconfigures the covenant through faith. **5:12** *Castrate*, literally "cut off," an allusion to circumcision (see Phil. 3:2).

5:13–26 Exhibiting freedom. Paul outlines how freedom through faith, though unbounded by the law, should be exhibited through virtuous qualities. **5:13** *Self-indulgence*, literally "flesh," implies indulgence in corporeal pleasures (cf. 1 Cor. 10:23–33). **5:14** Leviticus 19:18; Matt. 22:34–40; Rom. 13:8–10. **5:16** On *Spirit* versus *flesh*, see note on 3:3. *Desires of the flesh.* The self-indulgence warned against in v. 13. **5:18** *Subject to the law.* Literally "subject to law"; see note on 4:21 (cf. Rom. 6:14). **5:19–21** Paul catalogs vices representative of *the flesh* (see also Rom. 1:29–31; 1 Cor. 6:9–10; 2 Cor. 12:20–21). **5:22–23** A contrasting list of virtues exemplary of *the Spirit* (see also 2 Cor. 6:6–7; Phil. 4:8). **5:24** *Crucified the flesh.* A way of being crucified with Christ (see note on 2:19).

6:1–10 Additional instructions. 6:2 To *fulfill the law of Christ* may mean to follow Jesus's teachings (cf. Rom. 8:2; 1 Cor. 9:21). Elsewhere, Paul refers to specific commands issued by Jesus (1 Cor. 7:10;

in a spirit of gentleness. Take care that you yourselves are not tempted. [2]Bear one another's burdens, and in this way you will fulfill[b] the law of Christ. [3]For if those who are nothing think they are something, they deceive themselves. [4]All must test their own work; then that work, rather than their neighbor's work, will become a cause for pride. [5]For all must carry their own loads.

6 Those who are taught the word must share in all good things with their teacher.

7 Do not be deceived; God is not mocked, for you reap whatever you sow. [8]If you sow to your own flesh, you will reap corruption from the flesh, but if you sow to the Spirit, you will reap eternal life from the Spirit. [9]So let us not grow weary in doing what is right, for we will reap at harvest time, if we do not give up. [10]So then, whenever we have an opportunity, let us work for the good of all and especially for those of the family of faith.

11 See what large letters I make when I am writing in my own hand! [12]It is those who want to make a good showing in the flesh who try to compel you to be circumcised—only that they may not be persecuted for the cross of Christ. [13]Even the circumcised do not themselves obey the law, but they want you to be circumcised so that they may boast about your flesh. [14]May I never boast of anything except the cross of our Lord Jesus Christ, by which[i] the world has been crucified to me and I to the world. [15]For[j] neither circumcision nor uncircumcision is anything, but a new creation is everything! [16]As for those who will follow this rule—peace be upon them, and mercy, and upon the Israel of God.

17 From now on, let no one make trouble for me, for I carry the marks of Jesus branded on my body.

18 May the grace of our Lord Jesus Christ be with your spirit, brothers and sisters. Amen.

b 6.2 Other ancient authorities read in this way fulfill i 6.14 Or through whom j 6.15 Other ancient authorities add in Christ Jesus

9:14; 11:23). **6:6** *Word.* Presumably of God. Students ought to *share* financial compensation *with their teacher* (1 Cor. 9:4-14; Phil. 4:14-19). **6:7** Hosea 8:7; 10:12; Prov. 22:8; Job 4:8; 2 Cor. 9:6. **6:8** *Eternal life.* See Dan. 12:2 (cf. Rom. 2:7; 5:21; 6:22-23). See Rom. 8:5-8. **6:10** *Family*, literally "household," perhaps in the sense of those who gain inheritance (4:1-7).

6:11-18 Postscript. 6:11 Paul dictated the letter but signs off in his *own hand* (cf. 1 Cor. 16:21; Phlm. 19). **6:12-13** Paul charges his opponents with disingenuous motives. They *make a good showing in the flesh*, advocating for circumcision, *so that they may boast about your flesh*, since their persuasive success would be visible on the body. Moreover, Paul alleges they *do not themselves obey the law*, whether because of inconsistency (2:14) or impossibility (2:16; 3:10-12; 5:3). **6:15** Galatians 5:6; 1 Cor. 7:19. *New creation.* Isaiah 65:17; 66:22; 2 Cor. 5:17. **6:16** *This rule*—that circumcision does not matter (v. 15), only faith and its associated virtues of the Spirit. *Peace . . . upon the Israel of God.* An adaptation of a traditional blessing (Pss. 125:5; 128:6). *Israel of God* is a unique phrase that may suggest that the "true" Israel, or collective of God's people, is defined not by ethnicity (Gal. 3:28) or circumcision (Rom. 9:6-8) but by following Paul's *rule.* **6:17** *Marks of Jesus.* Perhaps from beatings Paul has endured (2 Cor. 6:4-5; 11:23-27), which he considers to reflect Jesus's suffering (2 Cor. 4:7-10). **6:18** Paul does not refer to addressees as kinspeople in the closing of other letters.

THE LETTER OF PAUL TO THE EPHESIANS

Authorship and Date

According to Ephesians, Paul wrote this letter from prison (see 3:1; 4:1; and 6:20), probably during his house arrest in Rome in the early to mid-60s CE. However, Ephesians is different from Paul's other letters, raising questions concerning Paul's authorship of the letter. For example, Ephesians has unusually long, complex sentences: 1:3–14, 15–23; 2:1–7; 3:2–13, 14–19; 4:1–6, 11–16; and 6:14–20 each represent one sentence in the Greek text. Instead of Paul's usual emphasis on Christ's crucifixion, Ephesians focuses on Christ's resurrection and exaltation to heavenly rule. Here, the church already shares in Christ's victory over evil spiritual forces—the future aspect of Paul's apocalyptic expectations is muted in Ephesians. The instructions for household life in 5:21–6:9 are paralleled only in Colossians, another letter with questionable authorship. Ephesians is very similar to Colossians, with even the exact same wording in Eph. 6:21–22 and Col. 4:7–9 (see **"Introduction to Colossians," pp. 2019–20**).

These factors suggest Ephesians may have been written by one of Paul's colleagues or students in Paul's name, probably after Paul's death. This practice seems ethically dubious today. But in the ancient world, people authorized others to write letters and documents for them, and students credited their teachers' influence by writing under the teachers' names. By naming Paul as the author, the actual author of Ephesians identified him as the source of the ideas in the letter.

Audience

Ephesus was a wealthy port city in western Asia Minor. It was famous for its temple to Artemis (see Acts 19:21–41). Magical practices were also important in the local culture (possibly reflected in the emphasis on spiritual powers in Eph. 1:21; 2:1–2; 3:10; or 6:12). The city had a significant Jewish population, though the letter was written to gentiles (note 2:11–20; 3:1; and 4:17).

However, "in Ephesus" in Eph. 1:1 is missing from the earliest manuscripts of the letter. The ancient authors Tertullian, Origen, and Basil the Great knew of questions concerning the audience. The letter may have been written to be passed around different churches in western Asia Minor (cf. Col. 4:16). If this is the case, "in Ephesus" was added to recognize one of the audiences of the circular letter or to make this letter more like Paul's other letters.

Reading Guide

Ephesians was one of the first New Testament books to be described as Scripture (Pol. *Phil.* 12.1). Its proclamations of worship and doctrine have been used in Christian liturgies and hymns throughout the history of the church.

The first chapters of the letter explore God's eternal plan to "gather up all things" through the resurrection and exaltation (or heavenly enthronement) of Christ (1:9–10). In part, this gathering of all things represents Christ's authority over all creation, including evil spiritual powers (1:20–21)—Christ is "head over all things" (1:22). This metaphor reflects the use of "head" to represent authority and rulership in the Old Testament and military and governmental power in Greek and Roman sources. God's plan (also described as a "mystery") includes the salvation, adoption, and inheritance of God's people (1:11–14; 2:1–10). As the "body" of Christ, the church shares in Christ's power (1:20–23). The metaphor of the body also emphasizes the unity of the community (2:16; 3:6; 4:4), reflecting the Greco-Roman use of the metaphor to represent communal cooperation and unity.

The unification of Jewish and gentile believers is a central element in God's plan to gather up all things in Christ (2:11–3:12). Ephesians emphasizes the long-standing divide between Jews and gentiles in order to celebrate their new identity as "one new humanity" (2:15). The descriptions of non-Christian gentiles in 2:11–20 and 4:17–19 sound like the kind of racist or anti-immigrant rhetoric we might hear today: strangers, foreigners, aliens, ignorant, and impure. In Ephesians, these descriptions are replaced as gentiles become fellow citizens, members of the household of God, and a temple in which God dwells. However, it is important to recognize the potential harm of the negative descriptions, especially for people who have been targeted by racist or anti-immigrant rhetoric or by any other form of bias for being outside of a given group.

The second half of Ephesians urges the audience to adopt a lifestyle worthy of God's calling (4:1–3).

The audience should imitate God by practicing the virtues of, for instance, humility, patience, love, faith, wisdom, and kindness. Being truthful and taking care with what you say are particularly emphasized.

A major section of the ethical exhortation concerns subordination in household relationships (5:21–6:9): wives to husbands (balanced by husbands' self-sacrifice for wives), children to parents (balanced by restrictions on fathers' behavior toward children), and enslaved people to their owners (balanced by the demand that owners "do the same" to enslaved people). The expectation of subordination reflects Greco-Roman social hierarchies. But within this context, the instructions given to husbands, fathers, and slave owners also mitigate some of the potential for oppression or violence in the household. The direct address to wives, children, and enslaved persons recognizes their capability as moral actors.

The emphasis on God's power and Jesus's superiority over evil spiritual powers reappears in the final exhortation of the letter (6:10–20). Christians—including the women, children, and enslaved peoples addressed in the preceding text (who were not eligible for military service in the Roman Empire)—are to put on the armor of God so they can resist, struggle against, and stand firm against evil spiritual powers.

Caryn A. Reeder

1 Paul, an apostle of Christ Jesus by the will of God,

To the saints who are in Ephesus and are faithful*a* in Christ Jesus:

2 Grace to you and peace from God our Father and the Lord Jesus Christ.

3 Blessed be the God and Father of our Lord Jesus Christ, who has blessed us in Christ with every spiritual blessing in the heavenly places,*b* 4just as he chose us in Christ*c* before the foundation of the world to be holy and blameless before him in love. 5He destined us*d* for adoption as his children*e* through Jesus Christ, according to the good pleasure of his will, 6to the praise of his glorious grace that he freely bestowed on us in the Beloved. 7In him we have redemption through his blood, the forgiveness of our trespasses, according to the riches of his grace 8that he lavished on us. With all wisdom and insight 9he has made known to us the mystery of his will, according to his good pleasure that he set forth in Christ, 10as a plan for the fullness of time, to gather up all things in him, things in heaven and things on earth. 11In Christ we have also obtained an inheritance,*f* having been destined according to the purpose of him who accomplishes all things according to his counsel and will, 12so that we, who were the first to set our hope on Christ, might live for the praise of his glory. 13In him you also, when you had heard the word of truth, the gospel of your salvation, and had believed in him, were marked with the seal of the promised Holy Spirit; 14this*g* is the pledge of our inheritance toward redemption as God's own people, to the praise of his glory.

15 I have heard of your faith in the Lord Jesus and your love*h* toward all the saints, and for this reason 16I do not cease to give thanks for you as I remember you in my prayers, 17that the God of

a 1.1 Other ancient authorities lack *in Ephesus,* reading *saints who are also faithful*   *b* 1.3 Gk *heavenlies*   *c* 1.4 Gk *in him*   *d* 1.5 Or *before him; he destined us in love*   *e* 1.5 Or *sonship*   *f* 1.11 Or *been made a heritage*   *g* 1.14 Other ancient authorities read *who*   *h* 1.15 Other ancient authorities lack *and your love*

1:1–2 Greeting. 1:1 *In Ephesus* is missing from the earliest manuscripts (see **"Introduction to Ephesians,"** pp. 2003–4).

1:3–14 Blessing. These verses form one sentence in Greek. It is written in the style of a Jewish blessing (see also 2 Cor. 1:3–4; 1 Pet. 1:3–5). **1:3** *Heavenly places* reflects Jewish conceptions of multiple heavens (see 2 Cor. 12:2–4). **1:4–5** *Chose* and *destined* concern God's plan for salvation, not predestination to salvation or damnation (see also Rom. 8:29–30; 1 Cor. 2:7). In the Roman Empire, the *adoption* of boys and adult men was common. The purpose of adoption was to establish legal identity and inheritance rights, so girls and women were not usually adopted. Christians of all ages and genders are adopted by God in Ephesians (see also Rom. 8:15–17; Gal. 4:5–7). **1:7** *Redemption,* defined as the *forgiveness* of sins, echoes Israel's redemption from enslavement in Egypt (Exod. 6:6; Deut. 7:8; 15:15). **1:9–10** The *mystery* is God's plan of salvation (3:3–4, 9; 6:19), culminating in the unification of all creation in Christ (cf. Col. 1:17–18; 2:9–10). **1:12–14** Seals in the Roman world indicated the authenticity of documents and ownership over property. *God's own people* are marked by the *seal of the promised Holy Spirit,* which guarantees their *inheritance* as adopted children.

1:15–23 Thanksgiving. A thanksgiving section is characteristic of Paul's letters. **1:17–18** *Eyes of your heart* represents insight (cf. Ps. 19:8; Prov. 15:30). Here, the ability to understand salvation can only be

our Lord Jesus Christ, the Father of glory, may give you a spirit of wisdom and revelation as you come to know him, [18]so that, with the eyes of your heart enlightened, you may perceive what is the hope to which he has called you, what are the riches of his glorious inheritance among the saints, [19]and what is the immeasurable greatness of his power for us who believe, according to the working of his great power. [20]God[i] put this power to work in Christ when he raised him from the dead and seated him at his right hand in the heavenly places,[j] [21]far above all rule and authority and power and dominion and above every name that is named, not only in this age but also in the age to come. [22]And he has put all things under his feet and has made him the head over all things for the church, [23]which is his body, the fullness of him who fills all in all.

2 You were dead through the trespasses and sins [2]in which you once walked, following the course of this world,[k] following the ruler of the power of the air, the spirit that is now at work among those who are disobedient.[l] [3]All of us once lived among them in the passions of our flesh, doing the will of flesh and senses, and we were by nature children of wrath, like everyone else, [4]but God, who is rich in mercy, out of the great love with which he loved us [5]even when we were dead through our trespasses, made us alive together with Christ[m]—by grace you have been saved—[6]and raised us up with him and seated us with him in the heavenly places[n] in Christ Jesus, [7]so that in the ages to come he might show the immeasurable riches of his grace in kindness toward us in Christ Jesus. [8]For by grace you have been saved through faith, and this is not your own doing; it is the gift of God—[9]not the result of works, so that no one may boast. [10]For we are what he has made us, created in Christ Jesus for good works, which God prepared beforehand so that we may walk in them.

11 So then, remember that at one time you gentiles by birth,[o] called "the uncircumcision" by those who are called "the circumcision"—a circumcision made in the flesh by human hands—[12]remember that you were at that time without Christ, being aliens from the commonwealth of Israel and strangers to the covenants of promise, having no hope and without God in the world. [13]But now in Christ Jesus you who once were far off have

i 1.20 Gk *He*   *j* 1.20 Gk *heavenlies*   *k* 2.2 Gk *according to the aeon*   *l* 2.2 Gk *sons of disobedience*   *m* 2.5 Other ancient authorities read *in Christ*   *n* 2.6 Gk *heavenlies*   *o* 2.11 Gk *in the flesh*

given by God. **1:19–20** God's *power* is evident in the resurrection and exaltation of Christ, emphasized in Ephesians in contrast to Paul's usual focus on Christ's crucifixion. **1:21** *All rule and authority and power and dominion* incorporates human and spiritual forces: governments, social systems, angelic beings, magical forces, and pagan gods (cf. 1 Cor. 15:24; Col. 1:16; 2:15; Titus 3:1). In Ephesians, these forces oppose Christ and Christ's followers (see 3:10; 6:12). **1:22–23** *Put all things under his feet* echoes the enthronement imagery of Pss. 8:6 and 110:1. *Head over all things* represents Christ's authority (cf. Deut. 28:13; Judg. 10:18; 2 Sam. 22:44). Christ exercises authority for the benefit of the church, defined as the *body* of Christ. This metaphor places the church with Christ, above all earthly and spiritual forces.

2:1–10 Salvation. Through Christ, God saves humanity from their condition of disobedience. **2:1–2** All people live in a state of death resulting from obedience to the *ruler of the power of the air* (cf. enslavement to sin and death in Rom. 5–8). **2:4–6** God makes those who are dead alive with Christ. The followers of Christ share in Christ's resurrection and exaltation to the *heavenly places*, removing them from the authority of the oppressive spiritual forces. **2:7–9** God's *kindness*, *grace*, and *gift* recall the Roman social system of benefaction: Wealthy, powerful patrons supported less fortunate people in return for their honor and praise. Contrasting with Roman expectations, the recipients of God's benefaction do nothing to merit it, and they do not *boast* in response. **2:10** The purpose of salvation is *good works*. More than individual acts, *so that we may walk in them* identifies good works as a lifestyle that reflects Christian identity in contrast to the human condition in Eph. 2:1 (see also Col. 1:10).

2:11–22 The gentiles. *Aliens, strangers,* and *hostility* recognize the long history of separation between Israel as the people of God and the gentiles (see Deut. 7:1–6; Ezra 9:1–4; Tob. 4:12–13; and **"The Bible, Race, and Ethnicity," pp. 2163–64**). In the first century, some Romans critiqued the Jews for their different ways of life (e.g., Tacitus, *Hist.* 5.4–5). **2:11–12** *Circumcision* was a key distinguishing factor between Jewish and gentile men, placing gentiles outside Israel's covenant with God (Gen. 17:9–14; Acts 15:1). **2:13** The *blood of Christ* replaces circumcision as the distinguishing mark of the

been brought near by the blood of Christ. [14]For he is our peace; in his flesh he has made both into one and has broken down the dividing wall, that is, the hostility between us, [15]abolishing the law with its commandments and ordinances, that he might create in himself one new humanity in place of the two, thus making peace, [16]and might reconcile both to God in one body[p] through the cross, thus putting to death that hostility through it.[q] [17]So he came and proclaimed peace to you who were far off and peace to those who were near, [18]for through him both of us have access in one Spirit to the Father. [19]So then, you are no longer strangers and aliens, but you are fellow citizens with the saints and also members of the household of God, [20]built upon the foundation of the apostles and prophets, with Christ Jesus himself as the cornerstone;[r] [21]in him the whole structure is joined together and grows into a holy temple in the Lord, [22]in whom you also are built together spiritually[s] into a dwelling place for God.

3 This is the reason that I, Paul, am a prisoner for[t] Christ Jesus[u] for the sake of you gentiles, [2]for surely[v] you have already heard of the commission of God's grace that was given me for you [3]and how the mystery was made known to me by revelation, as I wrote above in a few words,[w] [4]a reading of which will enable you to perceive my understanding of the mystery of Christ. [5]In former generations this mystery[x] was not made known to humankind, as it has now been revealed to his holy apostles and prophets by the Spirit: [6]that is, the gentiles have become fellow heirs, members of the same body, and sharers in the promise in Christ Jesus through the gospel.

7 Of this gospel I have become a servant according to the gift of God's grace that was given me by the working of his power. [8]Although I am the very least of all the saints, this grace was given to me to bring to the gentiles the news of the boundless riches of Christ [9]and to make everyone see[y] what is the plan of the mystery hidden for ages in[z] God, who created all things, [10]so that through the church the wisdom of God in its rich variety might now be made known to the rulers and authorities in the heavenly places.[a] [11]This was in accordance with the eternal purpose that he has carried out in Christ Jesus our Lord, [12]in whom we have access in boldness and confidence through faith in him.[b] [13]I pray, therefore, that you[c] may not lose heart over my sufferings for you; they are your glory.

p 2.16 Or *reconcile both of us in one body for God*   q 2.16 Or *in him* or *in himself*   r 2.20 Or *keystone (in an arch)*   s 2.22 Gk *in the Spirit*   t 3.1 Or *of*   u 3.1 Other ancient authorities lack *Jesus*   v 3.2 Or *if indeed*   w 3.3 Or *wrote before in brief*   x 3.5 Gk *it*   y 3.9 Other ancient authorities read *to bring to light*   z 3.9 Or *by*   a 3.10 Gk *heavenlies*   b 3.12 Or *the faith of him*   c 3.13 Or *I*

new covenant community (cf. Exod. 24:5–8; Mark 14:24; Gal. 3:1–5; Heb. 12:24). **2:14–16** *Peace* echoes the messianic "shalom" of Isa. 9:6 or 26:12. Readers in Asia Minor would also think of the Pax Romana, which was accomplished through military conquest. Jesus instead establishes peace through the *cross*. The *dividing wall* may represent the wall that separated the public areas of the temple in Jerusalem from space restricted to Jews (note the temple imagery in 2:20–22). The wall could instead be the Mosaic laws that separated Jews from gentiles, destroyed by Christ *abolishing the law* (cf. Matt. 5:17; Rom. 3:31). In Ephesians, gentiles are not incorporated into the Jewish community. Rather, Jewish and gentile followers of Jesus become *one new humanity*. **2:19–20** Gentiles are now citizens and members of the household of God, a familial metaphor of kinship (see also Gal. 6:10). The metaphor of the temple emphasizes unity and mutual support (see Eph. 4:12, 16, 29; 1 Cor. 3:9; Rom. 14:19).

3:1–13 *Paul's ministry.* Imprisonment in the Roman Empire was dishonorable. This defense of Paul responds to potential questions concerning Paul's authority as a result of his imprisonment. **3:1** If Paul wrote Ephesians, *I, Paul* gives an autobiographical detail about his personal situation. If someone else wrote it, this detail strengthens the author's claim to write for Paul (see **"Introduction to Ephesians," pp. 2003–4**). **3:2–3** God gave Paul the responsibility of preaching about Jesus among the gentiles (see also Gal. 1:15–2:10). **3:5–6** *Mystery* in Ephesians refers to God's plan of salvation, specifically here concerning the inclusion of the gentiles in the people of God and their new identity in Christ (see also 2:11–22). **3:7–8** *Servant* ("diakonos") identifies those who preach Christ in 1 Cor. 3:5; 2 Cor. 3:6; and Col. 1:23 (see also Eph. 6:21). Paul's status as *the very least of all the saints* emphasizes the greatness of God's grace, power, and riches (cf. 1 Cor. 1:26–2:5; 15:9). **3:10** In contrast to the enmity between Jews and gentiles in Eph. 2:11–22, the church as a united body of Jewish and gentile followers of Jesus demonstrates the wisdom of God to the *rulers and authorities in the heavenly places*, the hostile powers defeated by Christ (1:20–23). **3:13** Paul's imprisonment and *sufferings* are redefined as *glory*, a term otherwise applied to God in Ephesians.

14 For this reason I bow my knees before the Father,[d] 15from whom every family[e] in heaven and on earth takes its name. 16I pray that, according to the riches of his glory, he may grant that you may be strengthened in your inner being with power through his Spirit 17and that Christ may dwell in your hearts through faith, as you are being rooted and grounded in love. 18I pray that you may have the power to comprehend, with all the saints, what is the breadth and length and height and depth 19and to know the love of Christ that surpasses knowledge, so that you may be filled with all the fullness of God.

20 Now to him who by the power at work within us is able to accomplish abundantly far more than all we can ask or imagine, 21to him be glory in the church and[f] in Christ Jesus to all generations, forever and ever. Amen.

4 I, therefore, the prisoner in the Lord, beg you to walk in a manner worthy of the calling to which you have been called, 2with all humility and gentleness, with patience, bearing with one another in love, 3making every effort to maintain the unity of the Spirit in the bond of peace: 4there is one body and one Spirit, just as you were called to the one hope of your calling, 5one Lord, one faith, one baptism, 6one God and Father of all, who is above all and through all and in all.[g]

7 But each of us was given grace according to the measure of Christ's gift. 8Therefore it is said,

"When he ascended on high, he made
        captivity itself a captive;[b]
    he gave gifts to his people."
9(When it says, "He ascended," what does it mean but that he had also descended[i] into the lower parts of the earth?[j] 10He who descended is the same one who ascended far above all the heavens, so that he might fill all things.) 11He himself granted that some are apostles, prophets, evangelists, pastors and teachers 12to equip the saints for the work of ministry, for building up the body of Christ, 13until all of us come to the unity of the faith and of the knowledge of the Son of God, to maturity,[k] to the measure of the full stature of Christ. 14We must no longer be children, tossed to and fro and blown about by every wind of doctrine by people's trickery, by their craftiness in deceitful scheming; 15but

d 3.14 Other ancient authorities add *of our Lord Jesus Christ* e 3.15 Gk *fatherhood* f 3.21 Other ancient authorities omit *and* g 4.6 Other ancient authorities read *in us all* h 4.8 Or *he led captive a host of captives* i 4.9 Other ancient authorities add *first* j 4.9 Or *parts, to the earth* k 4.13 Gk *to a mature man*

3:14–21 **Prayer for the readers. 3:14** It was customary to stand to pray with raised hands in Judaism and Greco-Roman worship traditions, but kneeling is consistent with Acts 7:60; 9:40; 20:36; and so on. **3:15** In both Jewish and Roman cultures, names marked an individual's family connections and social status. *Every family* receiving a *name* from God as Father recalls the authority of God (and Christ) over all spiritual beings and material creation (see 1:21). **3:16–17** The *inner being* and *Christ* dwelling *in your hearts* represent understanding and the new identity of followers of Jesus. **3:18–19** *The breadth and length and height and depth* may refer to the surpassing *love of Christ* or to God's plan of salvation. The ultimate goal of the prayer is being *filled with all the fullness of God*, recalling the description of the church as the fullness of Christ in 1:23. **3:20–21** The concluding doxology uses hyperbole to praise God's greatness and power (cf. Rom. 16:25–27; Jude 24–25).

4:1–6 **Unity.** *I, therefore, . . . beg you* introduces the ethical exhortation that develops the theological exposition of Eph. 1–3 into a guide for life in chaps. 4–6. **4:1** *Walk in a manner worthy of the calling* recalls the contrast between the two ways of life outlined in 2:2, 10. **4:2–3** In Greco-Roman culture, *humility* was associated with enslavement and a lack of status, but along with the other virtues, here it characterizes Christian identity (see also Gal. 5:22–23; Phil. 2:1–8; Col. 3:12–13). **4:4–6** These verses may be an early Christian hymn. They are used in baptismal liturgies today. The focus on oneness recalls the Shema (Deut. 6:4).

4:7–16 **Christ's gift. 4:8–10** The praise of God for rescuing Israel from enslavement in Egypt in Ps. 68:18 is applied to Christ. The wording of the psalm is modified: Christ *gave gifts* (rather than receiving them), comparable to the interpretation of Ps. 68 with reference to Moses in the Aramaic Targum. *He . . . descended* refers to either Christ's incarnation or his death. *He ascended* refers to Christ's resurrection and exaltation (Eph. 1:20–21). **4:13–14** *Children* in the Roman world were seen as dysfunctional adults without the ability to reason or exercise self-control. Childish ignorance results in being deceived by *trickery, craftiness*, and *deceitful scheming* in contrast with *maturity*. **4:15–16** The *head*, Christ, is the source and sustenance of the *body's growth*, as well as its goal (see also Eph. 2:21–22; Col. 2:19).

Making Connections: Pauline Legacies and Afterlives (Ephesians 4)
Although Paul's letters were written long ago and directed at particular individuals and situations, there are times when the words feel familiar. This might be because some of the ideas Paul raised and represented have over time become deeply embedded in culture and society. Concepts ascribed to Paul such as *justification by faith*, for example, are central to contemporary Christian discourses. Other Pauline concepts such as grace and faith, the bodily resurrection of Jesus and Christians, and numerous practices—baptism, speaking in tongues, common meals, and quoting and alluding to Scriptures—find attestation in Paul's writings. Paul's words about love (1 Cor. 13) are used in marriage ceremonies today. Contemporary ideas about religious conversion, missionary work and colonialism, communal identity, and political affiliation are part of a fabric woven with Pauline threads. It is thus critical to understand Paul's life, letters, and legacies as a means to enhance religious and cultural literacy.

Paul's afterlives and legacies are not all good or all bad. Beyond his ancient addressees, words attributed to Paul that appear in his letters have been used by various people over the last two millennia to establish, maintain, and challenge ethical, social, sexual, and racial/ethnic hierarchies (see **"Introduction to the Pauline Letters," pp. 1713–16**). Paul was concerned with relationships: between community members, between community members and the society in which they lived, and between humanity and the world and world-to-be. His letters could be understood as customized practical instruction bolstered by future-oriented argumentation and as a collection are inconsistent and at times contradictory. Paul will not, alas, be "all things to all people" (1 Cor. 9:22). He is a hero and trailblazer to some, a bigot and con artist to others. Part of Paul's potent legacy is that no one is neutral about him or his work.

One reason why Paul's writings endure and remain compelling is that these texts betray a deep wrestling with major questions about humanity in a world that seems inhumane. Paul's letters are full of poignant musings about how people might understand and negotiate seemingly trenchant ethnic and cultural differences in the name of unity, empathy, and solidarity. Paul's letters wonder how to face enemies and even eat with them, provide for the weak and poor, and meet people where they are, even as they also point toward a change in all of humanity on the horizon. It could be said that these challenges remain unmet, and engaging with Paul's letters on such questions is a vital component of humanistic inquiry.

Davina C. Lopez

speaking the truth in love, we must grow up in every way into him who is the head, into Christ, [16]from whom the whole body, joined and knit together by every ligament with which it is equipped, as each part is working properly, promotes the body's growth in building itself up in love.

17 Now this I affirm and insist on in the Lord: you must no longer walk as the[l] gentiles walk, in the futility of their minds; [18]they are darkened in their understanding, alienated from the life of God because of their ignorance and hardness of heart. [19]They have lost all sensitivity and have abandoned themselves to licentiousness, greedy to practice every kind of impurity. [20]That is not the way you learned Christ! [21]For surely you have heard about him and were taught in him, as truth is in Jesus, [22]to put away your former way of life, your old self, corrupt and deluded by its lusts, [23]and to be renewed in the spirit of your minds, [24]and to clothe yourselves with the new self, created according to the likeness of God in true righteousness and holiness.

25 So then, putting away falsehood, let each of you speak the truth with your neighbor, for we are members of one another. [26]Be angry but do not sin;[m] do not let the sun go down on your anger, [27]and do not make room for the devil. [28]Those who steal must give up stealing; rather, let them labor, doing good work with their own

l 4.17 Other ancient authorities add *other* *m* 4.26 Or *If you are angry, do not sin*

Body is a common Greco-Roman metaphor for political community, incorporating ideas of hierarchy, cooperation, and unity. In Ephesians, the metaphor emphasizes mutuality (see also 1 Cor. 12:12–27).
4:17–5:2 Two ways of life. The gentile audience's previous lifestyle is contrasted with their new identity in Christ. **4:17–19** The negative descriptions of gentiles add to their outsider identity in 2:11–22. **4:23–24** The followers of Jesus assume a *new self*, dressing themselves with a new identity (see also Rom. 13:14; Gal. 3:27; Col. 3:10). *Created according to the likeness of God* recalls Gen. 1:26–28. **4:26–27** *Be angry but do not sin* may be concessive: if you are angry, do not sin. It may also be a

hands, so as to have something to share with the needy. [29]Let no evil talk come out of your mouths but only what is good for building up,[n] as there is need, so that your words may give grace to those who hear. [30]And do not grieve the Holy Spirit of God, with which you were marked with a seal for the day of redemption. [31]Put away from you all bitterness and wrath and anger and wrangling and slander, together with all malice. [32]Be kind to one another, tenderhearted, forgiving one another, as God in Christ has forgiven you.[o] [1]Therefore be imitators of God, as beloved children, [2]and walk in love, as Christ loved us[p] and gave himself up for us, a fragrant offering and sacrifice to God.

5

3 But sexual immorality and impurity of any kind or greed must not even be mentioned among you, as is proper among saints. [4]Entirely out of place is obscene, silly, and vulgar talk; but instead, let there be thanksgiving. [5]Be sure of this, that no sexually immoral or impure person or one who is greedy (that is, an idolater) has any inheritance in the kingdom of Christ and of God.

6 Let no one deceive you with empty words, for because of these things the wrath of God comes on those who are disobedient.[q] [7]Therefore do not be associated with them, [8]for once you were darkness, but now in the Lord you are light. Walk as children of light, [9]for the fruit of the light[r] is found in all that is good and right and true. [10]Try to find out what is pleasing to the Lord. [11]Take no part in the unfruitful works of darkness; rather, expose them. [12]For it is shameful even to mention what such people do secretly, [13]but everything exposed by the light becomes visible, [14]for everything that becomes visible is light. Therefore it says,

"Sleeper, awake!
  Rise from the dead,
  and Christ will shine on you."

15 Be careful, then, how you live,[s] not as unwise people but as wise, [16]making the most of the time, because the days are evil. [17]So do not be foolish, but understand what the will of the Lord is. [18]Do not get drunk with wine, for that is debauchery, but be filled with the Spirit, [19]as you sing psalms and hymns and spiritual songs to one another, singing and making melody to the Lord in your hearts, [20]giving thanks to God the Father at all times and for everything in the name of our Lord Jesus Christ, [21]being subject to one another out of reverence for Christ.

22 Wives, be subject[t] to your husbands as to

n 4.29 Other ancient authorities read *building up faith*
o 4.32 Other ancient authorities read *us*   p 5.2 Other ancient authorities read *you*   q 5.6 Gk *sons of disobedience*
r 5.9 Other ancient authorities read *of the Spirit*   s 5.15 Gk *walk*   t 5.22 Gk lacks *be subject*

straightforward command to be angry for good reasons—for instance, because of injustice and oppression. **4:29** Speech should be *good for building up* the community (see also Eph. 5:4; Col. 3:8). This command excludes speech that intends harm to others. **4:30** To *grieve the Holy Spirit of God* echoes Isa. 63:10. The reminder that the Spirit marks believers *with a seal for the day of redemption* (see Eph. 1:13) suggests that grieving the Spirit involves rejecting Christian identity (cf. Mark 3:29 and Heb. 10:29). **5:1–2** The metaphor of *beloved children* reflects the cultural expectation that children would imitate their parents (1 Cor. 4:14, 17).

5:3–14 Children of light. 5:3 Freeborn men in the Roman world had significant sexual freedom, including over enslaved persons. The prohibition of *sexual immorality* limited men's rights over the bodies of others (see also 1 Cor. 5–6). **5:8–9** The contrast of *darkness* and *light* reflects biblical metaphors (Isa. 9:2; 42:16; John 3:19; Rom. 13:12). **5:11–13** To *expose* the *unfruitful works of darkness* may mean to rebuke community members for sin (as in 1 Tim. 5:20) or to rebuke people who are not part of the Christian community (1 Cor. 14:24–25). **5:14** *Sleeper, awake!* may be a quotation from an early Christian prayer or hymn for baptism (see Isa. 26:19; 60:1–2; Rom. 13:11).

5:15–6:9 Living wisely in community. 5:18 Drunkenness was characteristic of dinner parties in the Roman world, symbolic of extravagance and wastefulness. What it means to *be filled with the Spirit* is filled out in vv. 19–22 (in Gk., vv. 19–22 are grammatically dependent on the verb "be filled"). **5:21** In the cultural context, *being subject* represents the subordination, obedience, and humility that characterized a relationship with someone of higher social status (see 1:22). In 5:21, subjection could indicate obedience to community leaders (1 Cor. 16:16; 1 Pet. 5:5). The reciprocal *to one another* may instead indicate mutual submission between community members (as in Eph. 4:1–3 and also Mark 10:42–45; Gal. 5:13–14; Phil. 2:1–8). **5:22** In some early witnesses to the text, this verse lacks a verb. The verbal idea comes from 5:21, setting the instructions for household relationships in 5:22–6:9 in the context of

the Lord, [23]for the husband is the head of the wife just as Christ is the head of the church, his body, and is himself its Savior. [24]Just as the church is subject to Christ, so also wives ought to be, in everything, to their husbands.

25 Husbands, love your wives, just as Christ loved the church and gave himself up for her [26]in order to make her holy by cleansing her with the washing of water by the word, [27]so as to present the church to himself in splendor, without a spot or wrinkle or anything of the kind, so that she may be holy and without blemish. [28]In the same way, husbands should love their wives as their own bodies. He who loves his wife loves himself. [29]For no one ever hates his own flesh, but he nourishes and tenderly cares for it, just as Christ does for the church, [30]because we are members of his body.[u] [31]"For this reason a man will leave his father and mother and be joined to his wife, and the two will become one flesh." [32]This is a great mystery, but I am speaking about Christ and the church. [33]Each of you, however, should love his wife as himself, and a wife should respect[v] her husband.

6 Children, obey your parents in the Lord,[w] for this is right. [2]"Honor your father and mother"—this is the first commandment with a promise—[3]"so that it may be well with you and you may live long on the earth."

4 And, fathers, do not provoke your children to anger, but bring them up in the discipline and instruction of the Lord.

5 Slaves, obey your earthly masters with respect[x] and trembling, in singleness of heart, as you obey Christ, [6]not with a slavery performed merely for looks, to please people, but as slaves of Christ, doing the will of God from the soul. [7]Render service with enthusiasm, as for the Lord and not for humans, [8]knowing that whatever good we do, we will receive the same again from the Lord, whether we are enslaved or free.

9 And, masters,[y] do the same to them. Stop threatening them, for you know that both of you have the same Lord[z] in heaven, and with him there is no partiality.

10 Finally, be strong in the Lord and in the strength of his power; [11]put on the whole

---

u 5.30 Other ancient authorities add *of his flesh and of his bones* *v* 5.33 Or *fear* *w* 6.1 Other ancient authorities lack *in the Lord* *x* 6.5 Or *fear* *y* 6.9 In Gk the same word is used for *master* and *Lord* *z* 6.9 In Gk the same word is used for *master* and *Lord*

---

community life (see also Col. 3:18–4:1; 1 Pet. 2:18–3:7; and **"Slavery and the Household Code," p. 2025**). **5:23–24** The metaphor of *head* and *body* used of Christ and the church in 1:22–23 and 4:15–16 is applied to husbands and wives. *Head* here has often been interpreted as authority or rule. Christ as *head of the church* is the church's *Savior*, adding a sacrificial meaning to the metaphor. *In everything* has too often resulted in demands for wives' submission to abuse. **5:25** *Husbands* receive the first command in the household instructions. Challenging the standard cultural expectation that household life should privilege the husband's success and happiness, husbands' *love* for wives is modeled on Christ's sacrificial death. **5:28–29** While *nourishes and tenderly cares* defines a husband's relationship to his wife in at least one marital contract, these phrases also describe the treatment of children in Eph. 6:4 and 1 Thess. 2:7. The association of wives with children may reflect the age difference between husbands and wives. **5:31–32** Genesis 2:24 is interpreted with respect to Christ and the church. **5:33** Husbands' *love* and wives' *respect* symbolize Christ's care for the church and the church's response. **6:1–3** The reference to the land of Israel is omitted from the fifth commandment for the gentile audience of Ephesians (see Exod. 20:12). Approximately 50 percent of children died by the age of ten in the first century, making the *promise* of long life particularly valuable. **6:4** Fathers held authority over children until the father's death. *Do not provoke your children to anger* balances fathers' power. **6:5–8** Enslaved peoples are commanded to obey their owners *with respect*, literally "fear," and *trembling*. Enslaved peoples had much to fear: malnourishment, sexual assault, and violence (see also 1 Pet. 2:18). The description of obedience as sincere, consistent, and enthusiastic counters common cultural stereotypes that denigrated enslaved people as lazy, immoral, and manipulative. *As you obey Christ, doing the will of God*, and *as for the Lord* redefine enslavement to human owners as enslavement to God. Verses like these were used to justify slavery in the United States. **6:9** In context, *do the same to them* commands slave owners to obey and serve enslaved people with enthusiasm. The reminder that owners are enslaved to God further counters the domination of enslavement. Taken seriously, these instructions challenge the injustice and oppression of the social system of slavery (see **"Paul, Enslavement, and Freedom," p. 1964**).

6:10–20 **Be strong in the Lord.** Ephesians 1:17–23 and 6:10–20 bookend the body of the letter with God's power. **6:11** The *armor of God* is also found in Isa. 59:15–18; Wis. 5:17–20; Rom. 13:11–14; 2 Cor.

armor of God, so that you may be able to stand against the wiles of the devil, [12]for our[a] struggle is not against blood and flesh but against the rulers, against the authorities, against the cosmic powers of this present[b] darkness, against the spiritual forces of evil in the heavenly places.[c] [13]Therefore take up the whole armor of God, so that you may be able to withstand on the evil day and, having prevailed against everything, to stand firm. [14]Stand, therefore, and belt your waist with truth and put on the breastplate of righteousness [15]and lace up your sandals in preparation for the gospel of peace. [16]With all of these,[d] take the shield of faith, with which you will be able to quench all the flaming arrows of the evil one. [17]Take the helmet of salvation and the sword of the Spirit, which is the word of God. [18]Pray in the Spirit at all times in every prayer and supplication. To that end, keep alert and always persevere in supplication for all the saints. [19]Pray also for me, so that when I speak a message may be given to me to make known with boldness the mystery of the gospel,[e] [20]for which I am an ambassador in chains. Pray that I may declare it boldly, as I must speak.

21 So that you also may know how I am and what I am doing, Tychicus will tell you everything. He is a dear brother and a faithful minister in the Lord. [22]I am sending him to you for this very purpose, to let you know how we are and to encourage your hearts.

23 Peace be to the brothers and sisters and love with faith, from God the Father and the Lord Jesus Christ. [24]Grace be with all who have an undying love for[f] our Lord Jesus Christ.[g]

a 6.12 Other ancient authorities read *your* b 6.12 Gk lacks *present* c 6.12 Gk *heavenlies* d 6.16 Or *In all circumstances* e 6.19 Other ancient authorities lack *of the gospel* f 6.24 Or *Grace immortal be with all who love* g 6.24 Other ancient authorities add *Amen*

10:3–6; and 1 Thess. 5:6–10. In Ephesians, God's armor allows a Christian to withstand the enemy instead of fleeing from battle. **6:12** The enemies are the spiritual powers already under Christ's authority in 1:21; 2:2; and 3:10. The church also still persists in battle against the enemy. **6:14–17** Specific elements of the armor in vv. 14–17 reiterate the values of *truth* from Eph. 1:13, 4:21, 4:24–25, 5:9; *righteousness* from 4:24, 5:9; *peace* from 1:2, 2:14–17, 4:3; *faith* from 1:15, 2:8, 3:12, 3:17, 4:5, 4:13; and *salvation* from 1:13, 2:5, 2:8, 5:23. **6:18** *Keep alert* indicates constant readiness (see also Mark 13:33; Luke 21:36). **6:19–20** *Ambassador in chains* combines an image of honor and respect with the shame of imprisonment (see also 3:1–10).

6:21–24 Letter closing. 6:21–22 Tychicus carried the letter to the recipients, a common practice (see, e.g., Rom. 16:1–4). The same recommendation is found in Col. 4:7. **6:23–24** *Undying love* reflects the language of resurrection in 1 Cor. 15:42, 50, and 53–54.

THE LETTER OF PAUL TO THE PHILIPPIANS

On first blush, the Letter to the Philippians might seem like a relatively simple, even sweet letter—either as a warm, if evasive, thank-you note or as the conduit for one of the better-known passages in the Christian Scriptures, the hymn to Christ (in 2:6–11). Yet upon closer inspection, the letter is a rather compelling artifact, its arguments more complicated, and its setting more dynamic and engaging for a whole host of reasons.

Authorship and Date

While it is among the undisputed or authentic letters, it would be inadequate to describe this letter as "Paul's" alone. Like several others (1 Corinthians, 2 Corinthians, 1 Thessalonians, Philemon), Philippians names a coauthor, opening with greetings from Paul and Timothy (1:1). This is the first of several reminders—including references to another apostle, Epaphroditus (2:25–30; 4:18)—that the creation and delivery of these letters were collective efforts, often involving the labor of enslaved people. Further, the letter's name refers to its recipients: the members of the assembly community at Philippi. Paul's reliance upon this assembly community and an entire network of coworkers and apostles is a subtle theme in this letter, most especially because the letter is written while Paul is imprisoned (1:7; cf. 1:13–14, 17) and thus would have been dependent upon others' support to survive imprisonment. This factor is often cited by scholars when they try to narrow the exact timing of the letter, likely written in the 50s or 60s CE. More precision would require speculation about the sequence of Paul's travels, among other migrating figures in this movement, and an overreliance on the (much later) narratives in Acts. Generally, one can place the undisputed letters in a period well after the Roman execution of Jesus by crucifixion (as stressed in the hymn, 2:8; cf. 3:10, 18) but before the cataclysmic events of the Roman-Jewish War (66–73 CE).

Place and People

While the location of Paul's imprisonment is unknown, several well-known historical factors are relevant for understanding the people at Philippi. Philippi was a colony of the Roman Empire, in part because it was the site of a pivotal battle in Rome's civil wars, when the forces of Marc Antony and Octavian defeated those of Brutus and Cassius in 42 BCE. The victors (and Octavian again in 31 BCE) took Philippian land to settle veterans, while imperial rule involved reorganizing the city to look as Roman as possible, as reflected in the surviving Latin inscriptions; the forum, theater, and temple structures; and the major trade route running through Philippi, the Via Egnatia. This strategic location, then, had been a recurrent site of invasion, settlement, and exchange, a contact zone where people with different kinds of gender, economic, and ethnoracial status assembled and mixed in interactive, if still asymmetrical and hierarchical, relationships, particularly for various migrating, enslaved, and formerly enslaved people (see **"Paul and Roman Imperial Culture," p. 2017**). This combination of interaction and hierarchy is reflected in the rhetorics of the letter, where Paul attempts to construct a position of authority for himself in relation to a series of named (Timothy, Epaphroditus, Euodia, Syntyche, and Clement) and unnamed figures (1:13–17, 28; 2:15, 21; 3:2, 18–19) by insisting on a form of unity that mixes hierarchy and conformity in mindset (1:30; 2:2–5; 3:15, 19; 4:2–3, 10). Paul recurrently promotes himself as a model figure in the letter (1:3–8, 12–18, 25–26, 30; 2:12, 16–18; 3:4–11, 17; 4:1–2, 9, 11–13), but the majority of the other named people seem to have played prominent roles in the assembly community even as their names reflect their relatively low social and economic status. Euodia and Syntyche, for instance, are highlighted as "coworkers" and those who "struggled beside" Paul (4:3), indicating their leading roles in the Philippian assembly, yet their Greek names also imply their enslaved (or manumitted) status. This more complicated positioning and the composition of the letter in Greek remind us how distanced most or even all members of this assembly community would have been from the "benefits" of Roman colonization and the privileges of citizenship given only to a select few, free, elite males. This placement of people provides a striking vantage point for reconsidering the images in the famous hymn that preexisted the letter itself (quoted in 2:6–11), as these would have been some of the people proclaiming an enslaved (2:7) and crucified (2:8) figure hyperexalted by God (2:9) and confessed as the ultimate *kyrios* (2:11), a title translated as "lord" or "master" that was also used for free husbands, fathers, enslavers, and/or imperial authorities like emperors.

Reading Guide

For an assembly and a set of apostles so riven by imperialism and imprisonment, one might hardly notice their effects in the letter. Historically, lovers of this letter highlight its frequent appeals to joy (1:4, 18, 25; 2:2, 17, 18, 28, 29; 3:1; 4:1, 4, 10) and Paul's thankfulness for the Philippians' aid (1:3–7; 4:10–20). Yet Paul is carefully negotiating his position, trying to avoid the impression that he is indebted to the Philippians (4:11–17), even if they sent their own (likely enslaved) apostle Epaphroditus with support (2:25–30; 4:18). He constructs an exemplary, potentially overcompensating position for himself, claiming that he can make Christ great again (1:20), directing the audience to apply their hymn in obedience to him (2:12), and paralleling his own losses and gains (3:4–11) to Christ's pattern in that hymn. There is something potentially countercultural, even anti-imperial about this depiction of Christ as *kyrios* (1:2, 14; 2:11, 24, 29; 3:1, 8, 20; 4:1, 4, 10, 23) and Savior (3:20) and an alternative political commonwealth in heaven (3:20; cf. 1:27). These interlocking factors resonate with any number of present-day concerns, particularly for those negotiating multicultural contexts of conflict and inequality. The letter might sound a cautionary note about approaches to unity that require conformity or fail to acknowledge different modes of precarity, especially for those subject to the overwhelming forces of poverty, migration, and incarceration. In a time when gender roles and women's leadership are still disputed and some have begun to reckon with related histories of enslavement and empire, letters and assemblies like these could point us less toward solitary heroes than communities in broader networks and other modes of connection, even solidarity (see **"Gender, Leadership, and Paul," p. 1990**, and **"Paul, Enslavement, and Freedom," p. 1964**).

Joseph A. Marchal

1 Paul and Timothy, servants of Christ Jesus, To all the saints in Christ Jesus who are in Philippi, with the bishops*a* and deacons:*b*

2 Grace to you and peace from God our Father and the Lord Jesus Christ.

3 I thank my God for every remembrance of you, 4always in every one of my prayers for all of you, praying with joy 5for your partnership in the gospel from the first day until now. 6I am confident of this, that the one who began a good work in you will continue to complete*c* it until the day of Jesus Christ. 7It is right for me to think this way about all of you, because

a 1.1 Or *overseers*   b 1.1 Or *helpers*   c 1.6 Or *perfect*

1:1–2 Opening greeting. The letter opens with some adaptations of an otherwise formulaic start. **1:1** *Servants of Christ Jesus* describes the coauthors, Paul and Timothy, as "douloi," enslaved people—perhaps in a foreshadowing of the hymn that the letter will quote (2:6–11; especially 2:7), already circulating in the assembly community at Philippi. Paul was likely not himself enslaved; rather, the use of metaphorical enslavement was a common, if also condescending, exercise in the imagination of free males. *The bishops and deacons.* None of the other Pauline Letters begin with such titles, suggesting that there is already some differentiation of role and potentially authority in the audience—perhaps anticipating the letter's crescendo where two women among these authoritative figures in the community are named, Euodia and Syntyche (4:2–3). **1:2** The greetings from both *God our Father and the Lord Jesus Christ* highlight that at this point, the creator/father aspects of the divine and Jesus as "Christos" (an anointed and/or Messiah figure) are not entirely coequal—Christians will develop the concept of the Trinity later. *Lord* (Gk. "kyrios") appears throughout the letter (1:2, 14; 2:11, 19, 24, 29; 3:1, 8, 20; 4:1, 4, 5, 10, 23; see also notes for 2:11 and 3:20–21).

1:3–11 Thanksgiving. The letter proceeds warmly, "buttering up" the audience while introducing some key themes. **1:4** *Joy.* The first of many expressions, even appeals, to joy (see also 1:18, 25; 2:2, 17, 18, 28, 29; 3:1; 4:1, 4, 10). One way to establish a connection with a speech or its speaker is to recall or construct a sense of shared emotions. **1:5** *For your partnership.* This expression of thanks for the Philippians' "koinōnia" (see also 1:7; 2:1; 3:10; 4:14–15)—their fellowship or sharing—evokes a collective mode of support and exchange, an economic relationship with shared risks and rewards, seen even in ancient contracts. **1:6** *Day of Jesus Christ.* As in other letters, Christ's return (1:10; 2:16; see also 3:15; 4:5) as (part of) the completion of an already-unfolding apocalyptic event is anticipated. It seems as if Paul and others expected this return would be imminent, within their own lifetimes. Depending on how the letter is received, this could serve as a reminder or even a threat. **1:7** *Think this way.* The letter repeatedly asserts one way of thinking or feeling (using a version of the same verb, "phroneō," in key moments, as in 2:2 [twice], 5; 3:15 [twice], 19; 4:2, 10 [twice]) to describe a common mindset to which

I hold you in my heart,[d] for all of you are my partners in God's grace,[e] both in my imprisonment and in the defense and confirmation of the gospel. [8]For God is my witness, how I long for all of you with the tender affection of Christ Jesus. [9]And this is my prayer, that your love may overflow more and more with knowledge and full insight [10]to help you to determine what really matters, so that in the day of Christ you may be pure and blameless, [11]having produced the harvest[f] of righteousness that comes through Jesus Christ for the glory and praise of God.

12 I want you to know, brothers and sisters, that what has happened to me has actually resulted in the progress of the gospel, [13]so that it has become known throughout the whole imperial guard[g] and to everyone else that my imprisonment is for Christ, [14]and most of the brothers and sisters, having been made confident in the Lord by my imprisonment, dare to speak the word[h] with greater boldness and without fear.

15 Some proclaim Christ from envy and rivalry but others from goodwill. [16]These proclaim Christ out of love, knowing that I have been put here for the defense of the gospel; [17]the others proclaim Christ out of selfish ambition, not sincerely but intending to increase my suffering in my imprisonment. [18]What does it matter? Just this, that Christ is proclaimed in every way, whether out of false motives or true, and in that I rejoice.

Yes, and I will rejoice, [19]for I know that through your prayers and the help of the Spirit of Jesus Christ this will turn out for my salvation. [20]It is my eager expectation and hope that I will not be put to shame in any way but that by my speaking with all boldness Christ will be exalted now as always in my body, whether by life or by death. [21]For to me, living is Christ and dying is gain. [22]If I am to live in the flesh, that means fruitful labor for me, yet I cannot say which I will choose. [23]I am hard pressed between the two: my desire is to depart and be with Christ, for that is far better, [24]but to remain in the flesh is more necessary for you. [25]Since I am convinced of this, I know that I will remain and continue with all of you for your progress and joy in faith, [26]so that, by my presence again with you, your boast might abound in Christ Jesus because of me.

27 Only, live your life in a manner worthy of the gospel of Christ, so that, whether I come and see you or am absent and hear about you, I will know that you are standing firm in one spirit, striving side by side with one mind for the faith of the gospel [28]and in no way frightened by those opposing you. For them, this is evidence of their destruction but of your salvation. And this is God's doing. [29]For he has graciously granted you the privilege not only of believing in Christ but of suffering for him as well, [30]since you are having the same struggle that you saw I had and now hear that I still have.

d 1.7 Or *because you hold me in your heart*   e 1.7 Gk *in grace*   f 1.11 Gk *fruit*   g 1.13 Gk *whole praetorium*   h 1.14 Other ancient authorities read *word of God*

Paul wishes more of the audience would conform. The letter recurrently poses Paul as a model figure (1:3–8, 12–18, 25–26, 30; 2:12, 16–18; 3:4–11, 17; 4:1–2, 9, 11–13). *In my imprisonment.* Or more precisely and physically, in Paul's "desmoi," "chains." The letter references Paul's imprisonment several times (see also 1:13–14, 17), yet it does not alter Paul's mindset in ways that one might expect.

1:12–26 Clarification about Paul's situation and exemplary status. 1:12–14 *Progress of the gospel.* Contrary to potential expectations, the letter asserts that the imprisonment is a cause, rather than an impediment, for progress in spite of the efforts of an unspecified group (1:15–17). **1:23** *My desire is to depart and be with Christ.* The potential gains of dying (see also 1:21) suggest to some scholars that Paul might have been considering suicide, as Stoics did. Such considerations underscore how dispiriting prison conditions were. Yet casting the choice to remain as "more necessary for you" (1:24–26) depicts Paul as sacrificing for the benefit of the Philippians. Paul anticipates traveling to Philippi again (1:26; 2:24) but will send the letter and other people first (2:19–30).

1:27–2:4 Exhortations toward unity and conformity. This section stresses oneness as sameness in the face of others destined for destruction. **1:27** *Live your life.* The political resonance of the verb here ("politeuō," to live as a part of a city or to be part of a state) indicates that the letter may be venturing an alternative to the Roman imperial system (see also the noun version of the term "citizenship" in 3:20). **1:27–30** The unity language in this section (*standing firm in one spirit, striving side by side,* 1:27; *in no way frightened,* 1:28; *the same struggle,* or conflict, 1:30) resonates as military terminology, particularly when combined with references to the advance of the gospel (1:12, 15), contrasting fates of destruction

2 If, then, there is any comfort in Christ, any consolation from love, any partnership in the Spirit, any tender affection and sympathy, [2]make my joy complete: be of the same mind, having the same love, being in full accord and of one mind. [3]Do nothing from selfish ambition or empty conceit, but in humility regard others as better than yourselves. [4]Let each of you look not to your own interests but to the interests of others. [5]Let the same mind be in you that was[i] in Christ Jesus,

[6] who, though he existed in the form of
      God,
   did not regard equality with God
      as something to be grasped,
[7] but emptied himself,
   taking the form of a slave,
   assuming human likeness.
And being found in appearance as a
      human,
[8]   he humbled himself
   and became obedient to the point of
      death—
   even death on a cross.

[9] Therefore God exalted him even more
      highly
   and gave him the name
   that is above every other name,
[10] so that at the name given to Jesus
   every knee should bend,
   in heaven and on earth and under the
      earth,

[11] and every tongue should confess
   that Jesus Christ is Lord,
   to the glory of God the Father.

12 Therefore, my beloved, just as you have always obeyed me, not only in my presence but much more now in my absence, work on your own salvation with fear and trembling, [13]for it is God who is at work in you, enabling you both to will and to work for his good pleasure.

14 Do all things without murmuring and arguing, [15]so that you may be blameless and innocent, children of God without blemish in the midst of a crooked and perverse generation, in which you shine like stars in the world, [16]holding forth the word of life so that I can boast on the day of Christ that I did not run in vain or labor in vain.

17 But even if I am being poured out as a libation over the sacrifice and the service of your faith, I rejoice, and I rejoice together with all of you; [18]in the same way also you should rejoice and rejoice together with me.

19 I hope in the Lord Jesus to send Timothy to you soon, so that I, too, may be consoled by news of you. [20]I have no one so like myself who will be genuinely concerned for your welfare. [21]All of them are seeking their own interests, not those of Jesus Christ. [22]But Timothy's[j] worth you know, how like a son with a father he has served with me in the work

i 2.5 Or *that you have*   j 2.22 Gk *his*

---

or safety (1:28; 3:18–20; see also 2:12) and Epaphroditus as Paul's fellow soldier (2:25). **2:2** *Be of the same mind.* Beyond seeking conformity, thinking the same thing was a common elite description of friendship and loyalty to patrons (see also the images in 1:27; 2:20; 4:2; note on 1:7 above).

2:5–18 The Christ hymn and the letter's application. In spite of later theological objections, the letter presumes that its recipients should imitate at least some aspects of Christ (thinking or feeling the same as Christ Jesus; 2:5). **2:6–11** The descend-to-ascend arc of the hymn presents a number of challenges. Its distinctive structure, terminology, and poetic rhythm and form point toward its composition and circulation before the creation of the letter. **2:6** *In the form of God* alludes to this figure's apparent preexistence and difference from God. **2:7** *Emptied himself, taking the form of a slave* highlights the theme of "kenosis" (self-emptying), yet it also casts the exalted figure as voluntarily descending into this abased status, distinctly unlike the material conditions of enslaved people. **2:8** *Even death on a cross.* Some suggest that Paul may have added this line to the hymn. Romans reserved crucifixion for non-elite groups, most especially enslaved and other criminalized groups. **2:11** *Jesus Christ is Lord.* The second half of the hymn hyperexalts Christ, particularly as a "kyrios," a term used for enslavers and other imperial authorities, including the emperor. The image, then, is ambivalent, with the potential to either subvert or reinforce reigning structures. **2:12** *Just as you have always obeyed me.* Of all the images in the hymn, the letter seeks obedience (as in 2:8) from the audience. The remainder of this section (2:12–18) returns to the letter's emphasis on unity via conformity in contrast to other practices (murmuring and arguing, 2:14) or other people (2:15).

2:19–30 On sending supporting, if secondary, models. 2:22 *How like a son.* Timothy is primarily described in his similarity to Paul, again evoking elite literary traditions of friendship and patronage,

of the gospel. [23]I hope therefore to send him as soon as I see how things go with me, [24]and I trust in the Lord that I will also come soon.

25 Still, I think it necessary to send to you Epaphroditus—my brother and coworker and fellow soldier, your messenger[k] and minister to my need, [26]for he has been longing for[l] all of you and has been distressed because you heard that he was ill. [27]He was indeed so ill that he nearly died. But God had mercy on him, and not only on him but on me also, so that I would not have one sorrow after another. [28]I am the more eager to send him, therefore, in order that you may rejoice at seeing him again and that I may be less anxious. [29]Welcome him, then, in the Lord with all joy, and honor such people, [30]because he came close to death for the work of Christ,[m] risking his life to make up for those services that you could not give me.

3 Finally, my brothers and sisters, rejoice in the Lord.

To write the same things to you is not troublesome to me, and for you it is a source of steadfastness.

2 Beware of the dogs, beware of the evil workers, beware of those who mutilate the flesh![n] [3]For it is we who are the circumcision, who worship in the Spirit of God[o] and boast in Christ Jesus and have no confidence in the flesh—[4]even though I, too, have reason for confidence in the flesh.

If anyone else has reason to be confident in the flesh, I have more: [5]circumcised on the eighth day, a member of the people of Israel, of the tribe of Benjamin, a Hebrew born of Hebrews; as to the law, a Pharisee; [6]as to zeal, a persecutor of the church; as to righteousness under the law, blameless.

7 Yet whatever gains I had, these I have come to regard as loss because of Christ. [8]More than that, I regard everything as loss because of the surpassing value of knowing Christ Jesus my Lord. For his sake I have suffered the loss of all things, and I regard them as rubbish, in order that I may gain Christ [9]and be found in him, not having a righteousness of my own that comes from the law but one that comes through faith in Christ,[p] the righteousness from God based on faith. [10]I want to know Christ[q] and the power of his resurrection and the sharing of his sufferings by becoming like him in his death, [11]if somehow I may attain the resurrection from the dead.

12 Not that I have already obtained this or have already reached the goal,[r] but I press on to lay hold of that for which Christ[s] has laid hold of me. [13]Brothers and sisters, I do not consider that I have laid hold[t] of it, but one thing I have laid hold of: forgetting what lies behind and straining forward to what lies ahead, [14]I press on toward the goal, toward the prize of the heavenly[u] call of God in Christ Jesus. [15]Let those of us, then, who are mature[v] think this way, and if you think differently about anything, this, too, God will

k 2.25 Gk *apostle* l 2.26 Other ancient authorities read *longing to see* m 2.30 Other ancient authorities read *of the Lord* n 3.2 Gk *the mutilation* o 3.3 Other ancient authorities read *worship God in spirit* p 3.9 Or *through the faith of Christ* q 3.10 Gk *him* r 3.12 Or *have already been made perfect* s 3.12 Other ancient authorities read *Christ Jesus* t 3.13 Other ancient authorities read *yet laid hold* u 3.14 Gk *upward* v 3.15 Or *perfect*

with a "similar mind" ("no one so like myself," 2:20). **2:25** *Your messenger and minister to my need.* Epaphroditus was likely an enslaved person, serving as an "apostolos," sent by the Philippians to support Paul in prison. **2:30** The letter stresses Epaphroditus's mortal risk in serving Paul—coming *close to death* (see also 2:27), echoing a phrase from the hymn (2:8)—and the Philippians' lack (*to make up for those services that you could not give me*).

3:1–11 Paul's example in contrast. 3:2 *Beware of the dogs.* Some Christian interpreters have suggested, with no evidence, that the letter here is repeating a distinctly Jewish insult of non-Jews. The brief and harsh characterization here could apply generally to a number of groups. **3:4–6** *Circumcised on the eighth day . . . a Pharisee.* The letter stresses Paul's status and ongoing Jewish identity in a number of ways. The argument depends on these markers being valuable to Paul and others. The letters depict Paul's joining this movement as a calling within rather than a conversion away from Judaism (see 3:14; especially Gal. 1:15). **3:8** *I regard everything as loss.* Paul's calling within this movement, however, is narrated as involving significant loss (losses and gains, 3:7, again evoking economic dynamics). **3:10** *Becoming like him.* The suffer-to-gain pattern, including "attain the resurrection" (3:11), could be Paul's attempt to suggest a similarity between his placement and the arc of the Christ hymn.

3:12–4:3 Building toward one kind of unity. 3:12 *Not that I have already.* The letter stresses that the events of the resurrection are not yet complete for Paul or any other assembly member (with a

Going Deeper: Paul and Roman Imperial Culture (Philippians 3)

In Phil. 3, as in other letters, Paul contrasts the present world or age with another world or age to come. Paul's letters were composed, sent, read, and heard in the Roman Empire, the present world or age of his time. How one might engage Roman imperial culture as it relates to these letters raises important questions, including what exactly "Roman imperial culture" is. "Roman Empire" usually denotes the shift in power relations from a republican model to one wherein a single male, the emperor, oversaw a vast amount of land, law, resources, and military power. Some scholars see the Roman Empire as an authoritarian regime, and others as a loose, locally regulated network of urban centers and rural peripheries. The former view sees an oppressive political dictatorship, and the latter a benevolent culture that fosters a "golden age" in social, religious, and domestic areas of life. Either way, the Roman Empire was a complex economic, political, cultural, and military force in the ancient world, and "Roman imperial culture" would vary across space and time.

The connection between Roman imperial culture and Paul's letters has long been debated. This is in part due to a modern distinction between "politics" and "religion" that the ancients did not share. Studies of Paul's letters attending to Roman imperial culture have tended to focus on whether and how these texts model "pro-imperial" or "anti-imperial" stances. Herein scholars ask whether early Christian groups may have displayed accommodation or resistance to Roman law and order and propose that they be understood as imperial collaborators or egalitarian revolutionaries. As attractive as it might be to see early Christian groups as ancient social justice movements—especially when it is common to see these groups as progenitors of persistent injustices—this view assumes that Roman imperial culture is a uniform entity that must be either obeyed or overturned. It also reinforces a false division between accommodation and resistance that does not adequately reflect human experience.

According to Acts (16:37–38; 22:25–28), Paul may have enjoyed Roman citizenship, and he appears comfortable negotiating with Roman courts, public spaces, military personnel, imperial officers, and household situations (cf. Phil. 4:22). Paul's journeys and letter writing would have been impossible without Roman imperial infrastructure like roads and a mail system. That said, it is not necessarily the case that Paul's relationship with Roman imperial culture was always harmonious and uncritical *or* oppositional and critical. Paul's letters exhibit multiple examples of rhetorical engagement with his Roman imperial context, including military and war imagery, banquet etiquette, household and athletic metaphors, discourses of peace and justice, and clarification of which entity deserves divine honors.

Davina C. Lopez

reveal to you. [16]Only let us hold fast to what we have attained.

17 Brothers and sisters, join in imitating me, and observe those who live according to the example you have in us. [18]For many live as enemies of the cross of Christ; I have often told you of them, and now I tell you even with tears. [19]Their end is destruction, their god is the belly, and their glory is in their shame; their minds are set on earthly things. [20]But our citizenship[w] is in heaven, and it is from there that we are expecting a Savior, the Lord Jesus Christ. [21]He will transform the body of our humiliation[x] that it may be conformed to the body of his glory,[y] by the power that also enables him to make all things subject to himself. [1]Therefore, my brothers and sisters, whom I love and long for, my joy and crown, stand firm in the Lord in this way, my beloved.

2 I urge Euodia and I urge Syntyche to be of the same mind in the Lord. [3]Yes, and I ask you also, my loyal companion,[z] help these women, for they have struggled beside me in the work

w 3.20 Or *commonwealth*   *x* 3.21 Or *our humble bodies*
y 3.21 Or *his glorious body*   *z* 4.3 Or *loyal Syzygus*

warning about what God might still reveal in 3:15). **3:17** *Join in imitating me.* The letter's most explicit exhortation to imitate Paul, condensing and combining calls to act in conformity and presentations of Paul as an authoritative model. It is followed by an explicit antimodel in 3:18–19 of people doomed to destruction, with their minds ("phroneō"; again, see note on 1:7) on the wrong matters. **3:20–21** *A Savior, the Lord Jesus Christ.* When combined with the vision of a different *citizenship* (see also 1:27) and a power to *make all things subject*, these titles indicate a challenge to the Roman rulers who typically held them. **4:2–3** *I urge Euodia and I urge Syntyche to be of the same mind.* Given the frequency of the appeals to a similar mindset ("phroneō"), this appears to be one of the points to which the letter

of the gospel, together with Clement and the rest of my coworkers, whose names are in the book of life.

4 Rejoice[a] in the Lord always; again I will say, Rejoice.[b] [5]Let your gentleness be known to everyone. The Lord is near. [6]Do not be anxious about anything, but in everything by prayer and supplication with thanksgiving let your requests be made known to God. [7]And the peace of God, which surpasses all understanding, will guard your hearts and your minds in Christ Jesus.

8 Finally, brothers and sisters, whatever is true, whatever is honorable, whatever is just, whatever is pure, whatever is pleasing, whatever is commendable, if there is any excellence and if there is anything worthy of praise, think about[c] these things. [9]As for the things that you have learned and received and heard and noticed in me, do them, and the God of peace will be with you.

10 I rejoice[d] in the Lord greatly that now at last you have revived your concern for me; indeed, you were concerned for me but had no opportunity to show it.[e] [11]Not that I am referring to being in need, for I have learned to be content with whatever I have. [12]I know what it is to have little, and I know what it is to have plenty. In any and all circumstances I have learned the secret of being well-fed and of going hungry, of having plenty and of being in need. [13]I can do all things through him who strengthens me. [14]In any case, it was kind of you to share my distress.

15 You Philippians indeed know that in the early days of the gospel, when I left Macedonia, no church shared with me in the matter of giving and receiving except you alone. [16]For even when I was in Thessalonica, you sent me help for my needs more than once. [17]Not that I seek the gift, but I seek the profit[f] that accumulates to your account. [18]I have been paid in full and have more than enough; I am fully satisfied, now that I have received from Epaphroditus the gifts you sent, a fragrant offering, a sacrifice acceptable and pleasing to God. [19]And my God will fully satisfy every need of yours according to his riches in glory in Christ Jesus. [20]To our God and Father be glory forever and ever. Amen.

21 Greet every saint in Christ Jesus. The brothers and sisters who are with me greet you. [22]All the saints greet you, especially those of the emperor's household.

23 The grace of the Lord Jesus Christ be with your spirit.[g]

a 4.4 Or Farewell b 4.4 Or Farewell c 4.8 Gk take account of d 4.10 Gk I rejoiced e 4.10 Gk lacks to show it f 4.17 Gk fruit g 4.23 Other ancient authorities add Amen

is building. Since this unity and conformity is recurrently directed toward Paul, the likely aim is to get these two well-known women leaders to agree with Paul. The argument provides an intriguing glimpse of women's (and quite possibly enslaved women's) important participation in this movement, having *struggled beside me . . . and the rest of my coworkers* (4:3).

4:4–20 **A carefully crafted thanks to accompany their apostle. 4:5** *The Lord is near.* The letter reflects imminent apocalyptic expectations, potentially raising the stakes of any of its arguments. **4:11** *Not that I am referring to being in need.* The letter attempts to establish Paul's indifference and lack of vulnerability in spite of his imprisonment and his acceptance of economic support from the Philippians (4:14–18). **4:18** *A fragrant offering, a sacrifice acceptable and pleasing to God.* To avoid the appearance of Paul's debt to the Philippians, the letter reframes the support and points instead to God, subsequently described as "my God" (4:19), suggesting that Paul is the conduit in the Philippians' relationship with the God of Israel.

4:21–23 **Closing greetings. 4:22** *Those of the emperor's household.* A closing reminder of how far Paul's influence has reached, though the image more likely reflects one Roman tendency to refer to their empire as itself an extended household rather than the immediate family members of an emperor.

THE LETTER OF PAUL TO THE COLOSSIANS

Who Wrote Colossians?

Although Col. 1:1 states that Paul and Timothy are the senders of the letter and the last verse states that "I, Paul, write this greeting with my own hand" (4:18), Colossians is considered to be a "disputed" letter of Paul. That is, there is disagreement among scholars about whether Paul actually composed this letter himself (see **"Introduction to the Pauline Letters," pp. 1713–16**). There are a number of reasons for this: (1) the *style* of Colossians is quite different from Paul's other letters (except Ephesians, also considered a disputed letter); (2) the *theology* seems to have different emphases compared to the "authentic" or undisputed letters; and (3) there is a *turn to more restrictive social structures* as seen in the household code of 3:18–4:1. The difference in style, however, would be expected for a letter that is being written to a community in the eastern province of Asia Minor, where letter-writing styles were more ornate and elaborate. The theology of the letter, while different in emphasis, does not necessarily contradict or create tension with anything written elsewhere in Paul's letters. Some of the distinctive theological emphases in the letter are due to the circumstances that he is addressing. Similarly, as we shall see, the household code in Col. 3:18–4:1 is shaped by the unique reasons occasioned by this letter. So, while scholarly consensus maintains that Paul could not have written Colossians based on perceived differences in theology, style, and content about social hierarchies, some interpreters assert that there are no compelling reasons to doubt that Paul wrote Colossians.

Where Was Colossae?

The ancient town of Colossae was located in the Lycus Valley in Asia Minor (now modern-day Turkey). It was one of three small towns in the valley: the other two, Hierapolis and Laodicea, are also mentioned in this letter (4:13). Situated on a river, the three towns of the Lycus Valley were on the transport route to Ephesus and trade centers in their own right due to the wool that they produced. The population in the Lycus Valley was quite mixed: Syrians, Judeans, Greeks, Romans, and the Scythians, Thracians, and Phrygians indigenous to the area.

The close proximity of these towns (all under 20 km [12.5 mi.] from one another) explains why Paul asked that each church read the letter he had sent to the other (4:16). Although damaged in an earthquake in 60 CE, Colossae was rebuilt and remained in existence until the twelfth century. Recent archaeological finds in all three towns reveal that the Roman imperial cult was prominent throughout the area, along with centers of worship for Artemis and various Phrygian gods, including the Anatolian mother goddess.

Why Did Paul Write This Letter?

The overlap of names between the Letter of Paul to Philemon and the Letter to the Colossians—Epaphras, Mark, Aristarchus, Demas, Luke, and Archippus (Phlm. 2, 23–24; Col. 4:10–14, 17)—suggests that both letters were sent at the same time. Notably, one of the carriers of the Letter to the Colossians was Onesimus, the enslaved man whom Paul commended and sent back to the community in the Letter to Philemon (see **"Introduction to Philemon," pp. 2056–57**).

The inversions of who is enslaved and who is free in the greetings (Col. 1:7; 4:7); the humiliation of the principalities and powers in a context that usually applied to the humiliation of captured and enslaved people (2:15), together with the emphasis on the erasing of the distinction between enslaved and free (3:11); and the extensive advice to those who are enslaved in Colossae suggest that a major impetus for the letter could have been to address the tension within the community regarding Philemon and his enslaved fellow Christian, Onesimus (see **"Slavery and the Household Code," p. 2025**).

Reading Guide

Paul is concerned throughout to remind the Colossian believers that they are now part of the story of Jesus rather than the story of the Roman Empire (see **"Paul and Roman Imperial Culture," p. 2017**). He does this in a number of ways. His description of the gospel as bearing fruit and growing in the

whole world (1:6), along with his later description of the believers in Colossae as bearing fruit and growing in the knowledge of God (1:10), would have evoked the gospel (or "good news") of imperial military victories, which ensured universal peace and fruitfulness throughout the empire. Paul is highlighting how the story of Jesus bears different fruit in the lives of believers.

Paul also highlights the contrast between the story of Jesus and that of the empire in the creation hymn of 1:15–20 (see **"A Subversive Creation Hymn," p. 2022**), the creation-denying philosophy in Col. 2 (see **"Idolatry," p. 2023**), and the ethical instructions of Col. 3 and 4 (see **"Slavery and the Household Code," p. 2025**).

The recipients of this letter were surrounded by images and rituals that proclaimed the imperial story: (1) that military violence is necessary to bring peace for the whole of the world, (2) that the growth of the empire means sacrificing creation and its creatures, and (3) that familial, social, and economic structures should serve imperial power, even if this results in oppression. In Colossians, Paul challenges this story with the story of Jesus, a challenge still relevant today. In a world where violence against the enemy both within and without is celebrated as the pathway to peace, Paul proclaims that Jesus brought peace by sacrificially bearing violence, thus disarming it (1:15; 2:15). In a world where the incredible biodiversity of God's creation continues to be sacrificed on the idolatrous altar of economic progress and growth, Paul proclaims all things are created in, through, and for Jesus (1:15–17); that the good news of salvation is for all creatures (1:23); and that creation-denying idolatry is empty deceit (2:8). In a world where familial and societal structures seek to subjugate women, Indigenous people, and people of color, Paul argues that our social structures should be rooted in the love, justice, and equity he claims with allegiance to Jesus as the Messiah who promises justice for the oppressed (see **"Slavery and the Household Code," p. 2025**).

Sylvia C. Keesmaat

1 Paul, an apostle of Christ Jesus by the will of God, and Timothy our brother,

2 To the saints and faithful brothers and sisters in Christ in Colossae:

Grace to you and peace from God our Father.[a]

3 In our prayers for you we always thank God, the[b] Father of our Lord Jesus Christ, [4]for we have heard of your faith in Christ Jesus and of the love that you have for all the saints, [5]because of the hope laid up for you in heaven. You have heard of this hope before in the word of the truth, the gospel [6]that has come to you. Just as it is bearing fruit and growing in the whole world, so it has been bearing fruit among yourselves from the day you heard it and truly comprehended the grace of God. [7]This you learned from Epaphras, our beloved fellow servant. He is a faithful minister of Christ on our[c] behalf, [8]and he has made known to us your love in the Spirit.

9 For this reason, since the day we heard it, we have not ceased praying for you and asking that you may be filled with the knowledge of God's[d] will in all spiritual wisdom and understanding, [10]so that you may walk worthy of the Lord, fully pleasing to him, as you bear fruit in every good work and as you grow in the knowledge of God. [11]May you be made strong with all the strength that comes from his glorious power, so that you may have all endurance and patience, joyfully [12]giving thanks to the Father,[e] who has enabled[f] you[g]

a 1.2 Other ancient authorities add *and the Lord Jesus Christ*
b 1.3 Other ancient authorities read *thank the God and*
c 1.7 Other ancient authorities read *your* d 1.9 Gk *his*
e 1.12 Other ancient authorities read *God the Father* or *the God and Father* f 1.12 Other ancient authorities read *called*
g 1.12 Other ancient authorities read *us*

1:1–2 Greeting. This is a standard greeting. **1:1** *Christ Jesus.* Literally "Jesus the Messiah."
1:3–14 Thanksgiving. 1:3–5 The Greek word for *gospel* or "good news" ("euangelion") usually referred to the good news of imperial military victory. The "good news" of Jesus is fundamentally different (see **"A Subversive Creation Hymn," p. 2022**). **1:6** Images of imperial fruitfulness and fertility were found on statues, altars, cups, and mosaics, especially in depictions of the emperor as lord of the whole world. The "good news" (gospel) of Jesus challenges imperial "fruitfulness" brought by military violence, with the fruitfulness of God's new creation, following Hebrew biblical tradition (Lev. 26:3–6; Isa. 5:1–7; Ezek. 34:25–31; Mic. 4:1–5; Zech. 8:1–16). **1:7** *Fellow servant.* Literally "fellow enslaved person." *Minister.* Literally "servant." **1:12–13** The imagery of *darkness* and *light* is common in the biblical tradition. In a world with no electricity, where the fall of night meant an inability to continue most daytime activities and where dangerous nighttime animals were common, the use of the word

to share in the inheritance of the saints in the light. [13]He has rescued us from the power of darkness and transferred us into the kingdom of his beloved Son, [14]in whom we have redemption,[b] the forgiveness of sins.

[15] He is the image of the invisible God, the firstborn of all creation, [16]for in[i] him all things in heaven and on earth were created, things visible and invisible, whether thrones or dominions or rulers or powers—all things have been created through him and for him. [17]He himself is before all things, and in[j] him all things hold together. [18]He is the head of the body, the church; he is the beginning, the firstborn from the dead, so that he might come to have first place in everything. [19]For in him all the fullness of God[k] was pleased to dwell, [20]and through him God was pleased to reconcile to himself all things, whether on earth or in heaven, by making peace through the blood of his cross.

[21] And you who were once estranged and hostile in mind, doing evil deeds, [22]he has now reconciled[l] in his fleshly body[m] through death, so as to present you holy and blameless and irreproachable before him, [23]provided that you continue securely established and steadfast in the faith, without shifting from the hope promised by the gospel that you heard, which has been proclaimed to every creature[n] under heaven. I, Paul, became a minister of this gospel.

[24] I am now rejoicing in my sufferings for your sake, and in my flesh I am completing what is lacking in Christ's afflictions for the sake of his body, that is, the church. [25]I became its minister according to God's commission that was given to me for you, to make the word of God fully known, [26]the mystery that has been hidden throughout the ages and generations but has now been revealed to his saints. [27]To them God chose to make known how great among the gentiles are the riches of the glory of this mystery, which is Christ in you, the hope of glory. [28]It is he whom we proclaim, warning everyone and teaching everyone in all wisdom, so that we may present everyone mature in Christ.[o] [29]For this I toil and strive with all the energy that he powerfully inspires within me.

b 1.14 Other ancient authorities add *through his blood* i 1.16 Or *by* j 1.17 Or *by* k 1.19 Gk lacks *of God* l 1.22 Other ancient authorities read *you have now been reconciled* m 1.22 Gk *in the body of his flesh* n 1.23 Or *in all creation* o 1.28 Other ancient authorities add *Jesus*

darkness to denote a power that inhibited good and fruitful activities made more sense than it does now. Since contemporary constructs around race connected to skin color did not exist in the ancient world, the connection between "darkness" language and racism was not present when Paul wrote this letter. However, our culture's identification of "darkness" with racial "Blackness" renders problematic the use of not only "darkness" to describe the negative power from which believers are redeemed but also "light" for God's new community. **1:13** The rescue from a negative power into *the kingdom of [God's] Son* echoes the rescue from slavery under the Egyptian Empire in the Hebrew Bible (see **"Exodus," p. 105**). In the Roman Empire, the current emperor was considered to be the "son of a god," since most emperors were believed to become gods after their deaths. Note that "kingdom" and "empire" share the same Greek word ("basileia"). The reference to the "empire" of God's Son anticipates Jesus's authority over all other rulers in 1:16. Jesus's "empire," however, is revealed to be one of reconciliation, peace, and redemption rather than violence and enslavement (see **"A Subversive Creation Hymn," p. 2022**).

1:15–20 Jesus as the center of the story. See **"A Subversive Creation Hymn," p. 2022**.

1:23 The good news of peace and reconciliation is for all creatures, not just humanity. On his travels, Paul saw the environmental destruction that Rome created in conquered lands, along with the enormous number of animals killed in gladiatorial games, including in nearby Ephesus. Colossae also hosted gladiatorial games. The peace of the Messiah, Jesus, means that violence toward these creatures ends. *Minister.* Literally "servant."

1:24–2:5 Paul's service for the Colossians and the Laodiceans. 1:24 *What is lacking in Christ's afflictions* suggests that Paul's suffering participates in the suffering of the Messiah. **1:25** *Minister.* Literally "servant." Paul is a servant not only of the gospel but also of the church (cf. Rom. 16:1; Phil. 1:1). **1:26** Both local and imperial religious traditions had "mysteries" at their heart. Here, the *mystery* is Christ, the Messiah, who gives all peoples the "hope of glory" (1:27) and "hidden . . . wisdom and knowledge" (2:3). **1:27** *The gentiles.* Only Judeans would have heard "tois ethnesin" as referring to gentiles (i.e., non-Judeans). Most Colossians would have heard this as "the peoples"—that is, referring to the variety of ethnicities that make up the world.

Going Deeper: A Subversive Creation Hymn (Colossians 1:15–20)

Drawing on texts from Genesis, where humanity is created in the image of God (Gen. 1:27–28), and Proverbs, where Wisdom is the firstborn of creation (Prov. 8:22–31; see **"Woman Wisdom," p. 872**), Paul describes Jesus as the one through whom all things were created, including the thrones that legitimated the rule of the powerful, the dominion and authority that they exercised, the rulers—both local and imperial—whom the gods had blessed, and the power that they exercised so violently (1:16). In this short, subversive, and carefully composed poem, Paul tears away the sacred canopy of imperial rule.

The popular mythology that the power of the empire holds all things together, creating peace and reconciliation through military might and violence, is also challenged by Jesus. Caesar was widely described as the head of the body politic, in whom the ligaments and sinews of the empire were directed. Instead, Paul describes Jesus as the head of a new body politic, the church, a headship rooted not in his death when he became a god (as happened with the emperors) but in his rising from the dead (v. 18).

The emphasis on *all creation* echoes the covenant God made with the earth and all living things in Gen. 9, a covenant to never again destroy creation with the flood. The sevenfold repetition of "all things" in this passage reaffirms God's commitment to creation, culminating in the reconciliation of all things both *on earth* and in heaven, making peace through the blood of the cross of Jesus (v. 20). This point is emphasized in v. 23, when Paul indicates that the gospel has been proclaimed to all creatures.

Christian tradition in the West has been heavily influenced by Greek ideals that privilege the spirit over the body and heaven over earth. This passage, however, roots the story of Jesus in the creation-affirming faith of the rest of the biblical text.

Most fundamentally, this passage challenges the heart of Roman rule: the grounding of peace in military victory. Rome also created peace through the blood of the cross by inflicting violence and crucifying or enslaving those who opposed the empire. Jesus, however, brings peace by *bearing* violence, disarming it in such a way that its power is impotent (2:15; see **"Paul, Imperial Authority, and Politics," p. 1951**).

Sylvia C. Keesmaat

2 For I want you to know how greatly I strive for you and for those in Laodicea and for all who have not seen me face to face. [2]I want their hearts to be encouraged and united in love, so that they may have all the riches of assured understanding and have the knowledge of God's mystery, that is, Christ,[p] [3]in whom are hidden all the treasures of wisdom and knowledge. [4]I am saying this so that no one may deceive you with plausible arguments. [5]For though I am absent in body, yet I am with you in spirit, and I rejoice to see your orderly conduct and the firmness of your faith in Christ.

6 As you therefore have received Christ Jesus the Lord, continue to walk in him, [7]rooted and built up in him and established in the faith, just as you were taught, abounding in thanksgiving.

8 Watch out that no one takes you captive through philosophy and empty deceit, according to human tradition, according to the elemental principles[q] of the world, and not according to Christ. [9]For in him the whole fullness of deity dwells bodily, [10]and you have come to fullness in him, who is the head of every ruler and authority. [11]In him also you were circumcised with a spiritual circumcision,[r] by the removal of the body[s] of the flesh in the circumcision of Christ; [12]when you were buried with him in baptism, you were also raised with him through faith in the power of God, who raised him from the dead. [13]And when you were dead in trespasses and the uncircumcision of your flesh, God[t] made you[u] alive together with him, when he forgave us all our trespasses, [14]erasing the record that stood against us with its legal demands. He set this aside, nailing it to the cross. [15]He disarmed[v]

p 2.2 Other ancient authorities read of the mystery of God, both of the Father and of Christ   q 2.8 Or spirits   r 2.11 Gk a circumcision made without hands   s 2.11 Other ancient authorities add of the sins   t 2.13 Gk he   u 2.13 Other ancient authorities read made us or made   v 2.15 Or divested himself of

2:8–23 See **"Idolatry," p. 2023. 2:8** *Elemental principles of the world.* Literally "fundamental elements of the cosmos." Galatians 4:1–7 describes these as enslaving powers. **2:10** *Every ruler and authority* would have evoked Roman rule and authority but also the local elites. Jesus is head of them all (see **"A Subversive Creation Hymn," p. 2022**). **2:15** Roman soldiers disarmed their enemies, putting the armor and weapons of defeated peoples on a wooden cross that was raised as a "trophy" to show

Focus On: Idolatry (Colossians 2:8–23)

Although there is debate about the nature of the Colossian "philosophy" referenced in 2:8, Paul seems to be drawing on themes that describe idolatry, or putting one's trust in powers or gods other than the Creator God. The parallels are compelling.

Idolatry	The Colossian "philosophy"
Idolatry is worthless, vanity, and nothingness (Pss. 97:7; 115:4–7; 135:15–18; Isa. 44:9; 57:13; Jer. 2:5)	The philosophy is characterized by empty deceit (Col. 2:8) and is only a shadow (2:17)
Idols are constructed by human hands (Ps. 115:4; Isa. 2:8; 41:6–7; 44:11; Jer. 10:1–10; Hos. 8:4, 6; 13:2; Hab. 2:18)	The philosophy is a human tradition and a human way of thinking that imposes human commands and teaching (Col. 2:8, 18, 22)
Idolatry results in a deluded mind and a lack of knowledge (Isa. 44:18; Hos. 4:6) and is a teacher of lies (Hab. 2:18)	The philosophy is puffed up without cause (Col. 2:18) and deceives people through "plausible arguments" (2:4, 8)
Idolatry is impotent, is without value, and does not profit (Pss. 115:4–7; 135:15–18; Jer. 2:11; Hos. 7:16; Isa. 45:20; 46:1–2; Hab. 2:19)	The philosophy is of no value in checking self-indulgence (Col. 2:23)
Idolatry is a matter of exchanging glory for shame (Ps. 106:20; Hos. 4:7; 7:16; 13:1–3; Jer. 2:11; Rom. 1:23)	The philosophy disqualifies, insists on self-abasement, and promotes severe treatment of the body (Col. 2:18, 23)

More broadly, Paul grounds his critique of the philosophy in the assertion that Jesus, not the emperor, is the one through whom and for whom all things were created (Col. 1:15–17). This echoes the scriptural tradition that YHWH, not idols, is the creator of heaven and earth (Pss. 115:16; 135:5–7; Isa. 40:12–26; 44:9–28; 45:12, 18; Jer. 10:11–16; 51:15–19). Just as YHWH triumphs over other gods, Jesus triumphs over all rulers and authorities on the cross (Col. 2:15).

The fear that this idolatrous philosophy could take captive (2:8) those in the community links to the theme of enslavement throughout the letter. Where do such oppressive beliefs lead? To economic and social structures that enslave others.

Sylvia C. Keesmaat

the rulers and authorities and made a public example of them, triumphing over them in it.

16 Therefore, do not let anyone condemn you in matters of food or[w] drink or of observing festivals, new moons, or Sabbaths. [17]These are only a shadow of what is to come, but the body belongs to Christ. [18]Do not let anyone disqualify you, insisting on self-abasement and worship of angels, initiatory visions,[x] puffed up without cause by a human way of thinking,[y] [19]and not holding fast to the head, from whom the whole body, nourished and held together by its ligaments and tendons, grows with a growth that is from God.

20 If with Christ you died to the elemental principles[z] of the world, why do you live as if you still belonged to the world? Why do you submit to regulations, [21]"Do not handle! Do not taste! Do not touch!"? [22]All these regulations refer to things that perish with use; they are simply human commands and teachings. [23]These have indeed an appearance of wisdom in promoting self-imposed piety, humility, and severe treatment of the body, but they are of no value in checking self-indulgence.[a]

w 2.16 Other ancient authorities read *and* x 2.18 Meaning of Gk uncertain y 2.18 Gk *by the mind of his flesh* z 2.20 Or *spirits* a 2.23 Or *are of no value, serving only to indulge the flesh*

where the battle had been decisively won. Defeated rulers and other prisoners were brought back to Rome and paraded through the street as a *public example* of Rome's triumph before being killed or enslaved. Here, the rulers and authorities who embodied the cosmic powers that shamed and enslaved people ("elemental principles," v. 8) are themselves disarmed and shamed. **2:16** Paul could be referring to either Jewish or Greco-Roman food and festival regulations. **2:20–23** Given the creation-affirming character of this letter, Paul is reaffirming that piety resides not in denying the body but in the reconciliation and redemption of our bodily life.

3 So if you have been raised with Christ, seek the things that are above, where Christ is, seated at the right hand of God. ²Set your minds on the things that are above, not on the things that are on earth, ³for you have died, and your life is hidden with Christ in God. ⁴When Christ who is your*ᵇ* life is revealed, then you also will be revealed with him in glory.

5 Put to death, therefore, whatever in you is earthly: sexual immorality, impurity, passion, evil desire, and greed (which is idolatry). ⁶On account of these the wrath of God is coming on those who are disobedient.*ᶜ* ⁷These are the ways you also once followed, when you were living that life.*ᵈ* ⁸But now you must get rid of all such things: anger, wrath, malice, slander, and abusive*ᵉ* language from your mouth. ⁹Do not lie to one another, seeing that you have stripped off the old self with its practices ¹⁰and have clothed yourselves with the new self, which is being renewed in knowledge according to the image of its creator. ¹¹In that renewal*ᶠ* there is no longer Greek and Jew, circumcised and uncircumcised, barbarian, Scythian, enslaved and free, but Christ is all and in all!

12 Therefore, as God's chosen ones, holy and beloved, clothe yourselves with compassion, kindness, humility, meekness, and patience. ¹³Bear with one another and, if anyone has a complaint against another, forgive each other; just as the Lord*ᵍ* has forgiven you, so you also must forgive. ¹⁴Above all, clothe yourselves with love, which binds everything together in perfect harmony. ¹⁵And let the peace of Christ*ᵇ* rule in your hearts, to which indeed you were called in one body. And be thankful. ¹⁶Let the word of Christ*ⁱ* dwell in you richly; teach and admonish one another in all wisdom; and with gratitude in your hearts sing psalms, hymns, and spiritual songs to God.*ʲ* ¹⁷And whatever you do, in word or deed, do everything in the name of the Lord Jesus, giving thanks to God the Father through him.

18 Wives, be subject to your husbands, as is fitting in the Lord. ¹⁹Husbands, love your wives and never treat them harshly.

20 Children, obey your parents in everything, for this is your acceptable duty in the Lord. ²¹Fathers, do not provoke your children, or they may lose heart. ²²Slaves, obey your earthly masters*ᵏ* in everything, not with a slavery performed merely for looks, to please people, but wholeheartedly, fearing the Lord.*ˡ* ²³Whatever task you must do, work as if your soul depends on it, as for the Lord and

b 3.4 Other authorities read *our*   *c* 3.6 Gk *the sons of disobedience*; other ancient authorities lack *on those who are disobedient*   *d* 3.7 Or *living among such people*   *e* 3.8 Or *filthy*   *f* 3.11 Gk *its creator, "where*   *g* 3.13 Other ancient authorities read *just as Christ*   *h* 3.15 Other ancient authorities read *of God*   *i* 3.16 Other ancient authorities read *of God* or *of the Lord*   *j* 3.16 Other ancient authorities read *to the Lord*   *k* 3.22 In Gk the same word is used for *master* and *Lord*   *l* 3.22 In Gk the same word is used for *master* and *Lord*

3:1–17 **The renewing rule of the Messiah. 3:1** Rather than deceased emperors watching over and blessing the empire from their home above with the Roman gods, Christ, the Messiah, is seated at God's right hand, continuing God's reconciling work on earth. **3:2** *Things that are above, not on the things that are on earth* reflects the contrast between the place where real power and authority rests—with the Messiah, seated next to God—and the imperial power and authority that seems to have the Colossian community in its grip. **3:4** *Revealed with him in glory.* Believers will be revealed as the true image of God (3:10), no longer enslaved by the social structures that surround them. **3:5** Sexual exploitation and excess are linked with economic sin and excess. **3:8** These are sins that destroy a community. **3:10** Rather than skin color, clothing indicated ethnic differences in imperial imagery. Modest clothing meant civilized and Roman; immodest clothing meant immoral and uncivilized barbarians. Being clothed with the new self in the image of the Creator erases all boundaries between "civilized" and "uncivilized." The knowledge that images the Creator stands in contrast to the philosophies and empty deceit of 2:8. The *new self* bears the image of the one who reconciles all of creation in 1:15. **3:11** *Greek and Jew* and *circumcised and uncircumcised* parallel each other. *Barbarian, Scythian,* and *enslaved* are all contrasted with *free*. Barbarians are those who deserved to be enslaved in the eyes of the empire, and Scythians are one of the Indigenous peoples of the area. This verse emphasizes the erasure of the distinction between enslaved and free in comprehensive terms (see **"Slavery and the Household Code," p. 2025**). **3:12** These virtues summarize "being renewed in knowledge according to the image of [the] creator" (v. 10) and stand in counterpoint to the arrogance, lack of unity, and greed of the previous verses. **3:17** The shift from Christ Jesus to *Lord Jesus* emphasizes the link with the next section. In ancient Rome, Caesar was described as Lord.

3:18–4:1 See "Slavery and the Household Code," p. 2025.

Going Deeper: Slavery and the Household Code (Colossians 3:18–4:1)

Usually referred to as the "household code," Col. 3:18–4:1 has been read as reinforcing standard patriarchal and white supremacist attitudes toward women, children, and enslaved people. However, not only are wives, children, and the enslaved addressed, which is unusual for the time; the inclusion of the phrase "in the Lord" (vv. 18, 20) or "fearing the Lord" (v. 22) suggests that their obedience is qualified by a prior allegiance to God. The parallel commands to the husbands and fathers (who are the same men) are unusual in the ancient context, for they emphasize the responsibility to nurture relationships rather than authority over perceived inferiors.

Paul has very carefully structured the commands to the masters and those who are enslaved so that they subtly undermine slavery. Such cunning was necessary because enslaved people formed the most basic economic unit that made ancient Roman society possible. They cooked, cleaned, worked in the mines, and were urban and rural laborers. Publicly speaking against slavery was tantamount to treason.

Even so, Paul carefully picks his words to do just that. The word for "Master" and "Lord" is the same in Greek: *kyrios*. Paul says, "Slaves, obey your earthly masters in everything . . . fearing [the Master]" (v. 22); "Work . . . as for [the Master] and not for humans" (v. 23); and "You serve [the messianic Master]" (*Christ* is Gk. for *Messiah*; v. 24). Paul is here relativizing the authority of the human master. He also tells those who are enslaved that they will receive an inheritance, echoing the promise in the biblical Year of Jubilee where those who have been enslaved are freed and given their inheritance (Lev. 25). Paul not only evokes freedom for those who are enslaved; he also commands masters to treat those who are enslaved with justice and equity (Col. 4:1), undermining the distinction between them.

For those who were enslaved and sexually abused by their masters, as many enslaved people were, Paul asserts that their "obedience" will not result in judgment on them; rather, literally, "the wrongdoer will be paid back for whatever wrong has been done, and there is no partiality" (3:25). This is a promise of judgment on their abusers.

For Onesimus, the enslaved man who was one of the carriers of Colossians, these verses would surely have signaled good news (see **"Introduction to Colossians," pp. 2019–20**, and **"Paul, Enslavement, and Freedom," p. 1964**).

Sylvia C. Keesmaat

not for humans, ²⁴since you know that from the Lord you will receive the inheritance as your reward; you serve the Lord Christ. ²⁵For the wrongdoer will be paid back for whatever wrong has been done, and there is no partiality. ¹Masters, treat your slaves justly and fairly, for you know that you also have a Master in heaven.

4 2 Devote yourselves to prayer, keeping alert in it with thanksgiving. ³At the same time, pray for us as well, that God will open to us a door for the word, that we may declare the mystery of Christ, for which I am in prison, ⁴so that I may reveal it clearly, as I should.

5 Conduct yourselves wisely toward outsiders, making the most of the time.^m ⁶Let your speech always be gracious, seasoned with salt, so that you may know how you ought to answer everyone.

7 Tychicus will tell you all the news about me; he is a beloved brother, a faithful minister, and a fellow servant in the Lord. ⁸I have sent him to you for this very purpose, so that you may know how we areⁿ and that he may encourage your hearts; ⁹he is coming with Onesimus, the faithful and beloved brother, who is one of you. They will tell you about everything here.

10 Aristarchus my fellow prisoner greets you, as does Mark the cousin of Barnabas, concerning whom you have received instructions; if he comes to you, welcome him. ¹¹And Jesus who is called Justus greets you. These are the only ones of the circumcision among my coworkers for the kingdom of God, and they have been a comfort to me. ¹²Epaphras,

m 4.5 Or *opportunity*   n 4.8 Other ancient authorities read that *I may know how you are*

4:3 *In prison.* See 4:18.

4:7–18 Final greetings and instructions. 4:7 *Faithful . . . servant.* Literally "faithful enslaved person." **4:7–9 Tychicus and Onesimus.** The terminology used to describe Tychicus and Onesimus undermines the traditional free person / enslaved person dynamic. Tychicus, a freedman, is called a faithful servant (translated as *minister*) and fellow enslaved person (translated as *servant*). Onesimus, an enslaved man, is called a *faithful and beloved brother*. Paul has reversed the categories. **4:11** *Of the circumcision*

who is one of you, a servant of Christ,[o] greets you. He is always striving in his prayers on your behalf, so that you may stand mature and fully assured[p] in everything that God wills. [13]For I testify for him that he has worked hard for you and for those in Laodicea and in Hierapolis. [14]Luke, the beloved physician, and Demas greet you. [15]Give my greetings to the brothers and sisters in Laodicea and to Nympha and the church in her[q] house. [16]And when this letter has been read among you, have it read also in the church of the Laodiceans, and see that you read also the letter from Laodicea. [17]And say to Archippus, "See that you complete the task that you have received in the Lord."

[18] I, Paul, write this greeting with my own hand. Remember my chains. Grace be with you.[r]

o 4.12 Other ancient authorities add *Jesus*   p 4.12 Other ancient authorities read *complete*   q 4.15 Other ancient authorities read *his* or *their*   r 4.18 Other ancient authorities add *Amen*

= fellow Judeans. **4:15** Nympha was the leader of the church in her house, which may have been in Hierapolis, since it appears to be distinct from both *the brothers and sisters in Laodicea* and the Colossian community (see **"Gender, Leadership, and Paul," p. 1990**). **4:16** Ancient letters were read aloud in the community, usually by the person who delivered them (here Tychicus or Onesimus), who also interpreted the letter as it was discussed. *The letter from Laodicea* does not appear to have been preserved, although some argue it might be the letter we know as Ephesians. **4:18** *Own hand.* Paul's letters were likely written by a scribe at his dictation. Composed orally, they likely included some discussion between the letter writer and those with him (in this case, if one assumes that Paul is the author of this disputed letter, Timothy and possibly Tychicus and Onesimus). *Remember my chains.* Images of defeated prisoners in chains were found throughout the empire, including on large panels that lined a temple complex in Aphrodisias, near Colossae. Also found on the coins that circulated in Colossae, these images reminded people of the victory parades where defeated peoples were displayed in chains before being killed or enslaved. Paul is evoking an image of defeat at the hand of the empire but also the suffering of Jesus, whose defeat on a Roman cross paradoxically robbed Rome of its power and brought reconciliation for all (see **"A Subversive Creation Hymn," p. 2022**). Paul's chains align him with those who have been defeated and enslaved by the empire, indicating his solidarity with not only Onesimus but all of those forced into humiliation and shame by their enslavement.

THE FIRST LETTER OF PAUL TO THE THESSALONIANS

Authorship and Date

First Thessalonians is the earliest extant letter of Paul, making it also the earliest text in the New Testament. Though it is conventional to refer to the author as "Paul," it is clear that he had coworkers traveling with him; they are depicted as fellow authors of the letter (1 Thess. 1:1). Given its verbal and theological similarities with other letters such as Romans and 1 Corinthians, 1 Thessalonians is categorized as one of the seven "authentic" letters of Paul (see **"Introduction to the Pauline Letters," pp. 1713–16**). The letter was likely penned in Corinth around the year 50 CE. Paul had visited the group prior to writing the letter and wanted to return, but for unspecified reasons (2:17–20), he was only able to send Timothy in his stead (3:1–2). Timothy, in turn, brings Paul a very positive report about the group (3:6).

The City of Thessalonica

In the first century CE, Thessalonica (or Thessalonikē) was the capital of the Roman province of Macedonia, which encompassed the northern part of what is now the country of Greece. The city was important for trade and sea travel, and it boasted a cosmopolitan population, which was a function of the variety of people who moved through its streets and ports. It is important to keep this regional context in view when envisioning the translocal networks that Paul is hoping to create among his urban Christ groups through his letters.

Reading Guide

Like many (though not all) of Paul's letters, 1 Thessalonians offers a snapshot into the life of an early urban Christ group. The Thessalonian group is mainly composed of non-Jewish people (1:9) who have become interested in the figure of Christ. The basic message that Paul appears to have told them on his first visit is that Jesus was the Son of God, that God resurrected him after his death, and that he would return to offer some sort of salvation to humans (1:10). These are the basic elements of Paul's "gospel" (cf. Rom. 1:2–4).

The group seems to be experiencing some growing pains, perhaps ones that Paul did not anticipate, since he appears to have expected Jesus to return at any moment (1 Thess. 4:15; 5:3). One issue that Paul addresses concerns sexual ethics (4:1–12). Paul maintains that the group's "sanctification" is God's will, and so he advises "that you abstain from sexual immorality; that each one of you know how to control your own body [literally "vessel"] in holiness and honor, not with lustful passion, like the gentiles who do not know God; that no one wrong or exploit a brother or sister in this matter" (4:3–6). As discussed in the study notes for 1 Thessalonians, the literal meaning of what is rendered in this passage as "body" (Gk. *skeuos*, literally "vessel") is a term that is also used as a metaphor for male genitalia. These instructions, some scholars have concluded, would thus make little sense aimed at a mixed-gender group, which has led them to suppose that the group is composed solely of males. Moreover, we know that many occupational associations were also single gender, and the group may have been a trade organization before orienting themselves toward Christ. Paul's guidance on this matter, then, is essentially asking his male addressees to control their sexual impulses and (to be blunt) to stay away from one another's wives. Paul, of course, frames these instructions as theologically important (4:8), which increases the stakes for complying.

A second issue that had arisen within the group concerns theology: in particular, apocalyptic expectations. Scholars believe that Paul had originally shared a rather brief package of material about Jesus with the Thessalonians—probably something very much like that recounted in 1 Thess. 1:10. After Paul left the group and time passed, members of the group began to die. The remaining members, in turn, became concerned that their deceased friends and family would miss out on salvation when Jesus returned. It is such a situation that likely spurred Paul to outline the scenario in 1 Thess. 4:13–5:11. The apocalyptic theology described there is discussed more in **"Paul's Apocalyptic Imagination," p. 2031**. For now, we can observe that this shows us how some of the core ideas and beliefs in nascent Christianity emerged over time and in response to *particular* circumstances.

This letter is also an excellent site to think about the translocal connections that Paul was hoping to foster among his urban Christ groups. Paul wants to create an identity that is bigger than any

single city and any single group. Indeed, he *has* to: the only way to convince Christ followers outside of Judea to send financial support back to the Jerusalem assembly (Gk. *ekklēsia*, which is often translated anachronistically as "church") is to convince them that they are all part of something bigger than themselves. This is accomplished, in part, by reminding each local group that they are connected to other Christ groups elsewhere. In 1 Thessalonians, Paul does this early in the letter when he praises the group for their exceptional reputation throughout the provinces of Macedonia and Achaia (1 Thess. 1:7). Shortly thereafter, he compares the suffering of the Thessalonians to that of Christ followers in Judea (2:14-16; there is some debate over whether Paul wrote these verses; see **"Paul's Words or a Later Interpolation?," p. 2029**). He subtly expands this translocal network even more with passing references to his and his companions' work in Philippi (2:2) and Athens (3:1). Through these references, the Thessalonians are invited to think about their identity "in Christ" as something that transcends local cities and links them with believers throughout the Roman Empire.

Sarah E. Rollens

1 Paul, Silvanus, and Timothy,
To the church of the Thessalonians in God the Father and the Lord Jesus Christ:
Grace to you and peace.

2 We always give thanks to God for all of you and mention you in our prayers, constantly ³remembering before our God and Father your work of faith and labor of love and steadfastness of hope in our Lord Jesus Christ. ⁴For we know, brothers and sisters beloved by God, that he has chosen you, ⁵because our message of the gospel came to you not in word only but also in power and in the Holy Spirit and with full conviction; just as you know what kind of persons we proved to be among you for your sake. ⁶And you became imitators of us and of the Lord, for in spite of persecution you received the word with joy from the Holy Spirit, ⁷so that you became an example to all the believers in Macedonia and in Achaia. ⁸For the word of the Lord has sounded forth from you not only in Macedonia and Achaia but in every place your faith in God has become known, so that we have no need to speak about it. ⁹For they report about us what kind of welcome we had among you and how you turned to God from idols to serve a living and true God ¹⁰and to wait for his Son from heaven, whom he raised

from the dead—Jesus, who rescues us from the coming wrath.

2 You yourselves know, brothers and sisters, that our coming to you was not in vain, ²but though we had already suffered and been shamefully mistreated at Philippi, as you know, we had courage in our God to declare to you the gospel of God in spite of great opposition. ³For our appeal does not spring from deceit or impure motives or trickery, ⁴but, just as we have been approved by God to be entrusted with the message of the gospel, even so we speak, not to please mortals but to please God, who tests our hearts. ⁵As you know and as God is our witness, we never came with words of flattery or with a pretext for greed, ⁶nor did we seek praise from mortals, whether from you or from others, ⁷though we might have made demands as apostles of Christ. But we were gentle*ᵃ* among you, like a nurse tenderly caring for her own children. ⁸So deeply do we care for you that we are determined to share with you not only the gospel of God but also our own selves, because you have become very dear to us.

9 You remember our labor and toil, brothers

a 2.7 Other ancient authorities read *infants*

1:1–3:11 Greeting. In terms of structure, the 1 Thessalonians letter reflects typical ancient epistolary conventions. The first three chapters offer warm greetings and praise for the Thessalonians, before recounting Paul's relationship with the group. **1:6–9** Paul praises the group for their exceptional reputation within the geographical region. In particular, the group is known for its faith and for its hospitality toward Paul and his companions. They are therefore an exemplar to other believers. **1:9** *You turned to God from idols.* This indicates that the group is largely, if not entirely, composed of gentiles. **1:9–10** In these verses, Paul formulates the most important elements of his gospel: Jesus is God's son, God brought him back to life when he died, and Jesus will return in the future to save humans. **2:1–2** Paul characteristically recounts difficult circumstances that he and his fellow workers had to endure to spread the gospel; if one reads all of Paul's authentic letters, it is clear that for Paul, experiencing persecution is an integral part of one's identity in Christ and helps authenticate true believers. **2:7** Paul uses the

Going Deeper: Paul's Words or a Later Interpolation? (1 Thessalonians 2)

In 1 Thess. 2, Paul praises the Thessalonian Christ followers for accepting his teachings "not as a human word but as what it really is, God's word" (v. 13). The following two verses compare the Thessalonians to the Christ followers in Judea, aligning their similar experiences of persecution. The Christ followers in Judea suffered, Paul claims, due to their treatment by "the Jews who killed both the Lord Jesus and the prophets and drove us out" (vv. 14–15). This abrasive phrasing has struck many as odd and rather "un-Pauline," causing some scholars to propose that vv. 14–16 are an interpolation added into the letter by a later copyist. There are several other passages in the New Testament that scholars have argued, for different reasons, are later interpolations (e.g., 1 Cor. 14:34–35 and Mark 16:9–16), and it is important to weigh the arguments on both sides of the debate.

In support of the view that Paul did not write these verses and that a later copyist inserted them, we can marshal several points. The main reason to suspect that this passage is an interpolation concerns the way it refers to the Jews. In no other letters does Paul speak so definitively of the Jews as removed from salvation. For instance, the passage proclaims that the Jews "displease God" (1 Thess. 2:15) and "have constantly been filling up the measure of their sins" (2:16). Indeed, it seems strange to so strictly separate Christ followers from Jews at such an early stage in the history of the Christian movement. In addition, the idea of Israel repeatedly rejecting and killing the prophets of God is a distinct theological framework (known as Deuteronomistic theology) in Paul's time, yet it is not a strong motif in any of his other letters (it may be presupposed in Rom. 11:3, but it is not a guiding motif). It would be surprising to see it here, seemingly in passing, when Paul could have certainly put it to work in many of his other letters (e.g., when he reflects with such emotion on his own sense of persecution; see 2 Corinthians, Galatians). Finally, in Paul's time, it is unclear what it meant to say God's "wrath has overtaken them at last" (1 Thess. 2:16). This statement, however, makes sense in a post-70 CE context, when authors were reflecting on the Roman destruction of Jerusalem and its temple, and so it could have been added by a copyist living in the wake of this trauma.

In support of a Pauline authorship of these verses, we may note the following points. First, Paul elsewhere tries to link the experiences of urban, predominantly gentile Christ groups with the Christ followers in Judea. Indeed, such identity linkages would have been an important undergirding to the financial collection that Paul was sending back to Jerusalem (e.g., 1 Cor. 16:1–4; 2 Cor. 8:1–9:15; Rom. 15:25–29; Gal. 2:10). Put differently, there is no natural reason why Christ followers in somewhere like Thessalonica would have cared enough about people in Judea to raise money for them; the burden is on Paul to convince them that they shared an identity "in Christ" with these people. In addition, Paul regularly appeals to experiences of (perceived) persecution in his rhetoric, so these verses would fit well with that tendency. Furthermore, while it might not "sound Pauline," we know that Paul writes different things to different audiences; the assumption that he must have been consistent in these letters is imposed by modern interpreters (see **"Introduction to the Pauline Letters," pp. 1713–16**).

Sarah E. Rollens

and sisters; we worked night and day so that we might not burden any of you while we proclaimed to you the gospel of God. ¹⁰You are witnesses, and God also, how pure, upright, and blameless our conduct was toward you believers. ¹¹As you know, we dealt with each one of you like a father with his children, ¹²urging and encouraging you and pleading that you lead a life worthy of God, who calls you into his own kingdom and glory.

13 We also constantly give thanks to God for this, that when you received the word of God that you heard from us you accepted it not as a human word but as what it really is, God's word, which is also at work in you believers. ¹⁴For you, brothers and sisters, became imitators of the churches of God in Christ Jesus that are in Judea, for you suffered the same things from your own compatriots as they did from the Jews ¹⁵who killed both the Lord Jesus and the prophets*ᵇ* and drove us out;

b 2.15 Other ancient authorities read their own prophets

metaphor of a female nurse caring for children to describe his relationship with the group. **2:9** Paul returns to his most common metaphor for addressing his groups: brothers and sisters (though there is reason to think that this group was only men; see more in the **"Introduction to 1 Thessalonians," pp. 2027–28**). **2:11** Paul switches metaphors once again, this time speaking of himself as a father gently disciplining his children. **2:14–16** This vitriolic passage may be a later interpolation (see **"Paul's Words**

they displease God and oppose everyone [16]by hindering us from speaking to the gentiles so that they may be saved. Thus they have constantly been filling up the measure of their sins, but wrath[c] has overtaken them at last.[d]

17 As for us, brothers and sisters, when for a short time we were made orphans by being separated from you—in person, not in heart—we longed with great eagerness to see you face to face. [18]For we wanted to come to you—certainly I, Paul, wanted to again and again—but Satan blocked our way. [19]For what is our hope or joy or crown of boasting before our Lord Jesus at his coming? Is it not you? [20]Yes, you are our glory and joy!

3 Therefore when we could bear it no longer, we decided to be left alone in Athens [2]and sent Timothy, our brother and God's coworker[e] in the gospel of Christ, to strengthen and encourage you for the sake of your faith, [3]so that no one would be shaken by these persecutions. Indeed, you yourselves know that this is what we are destined for. [4]In fact, when we were with you, we told you beforehand that we were to suffer persecution; so it turned out, as you know. [5]For this reason, when I could bear it no longer, I sent to find out about your faith; I was afraid that somehow the tempter had tempted you and that our labor had been in vain.

6 But Timothy has just now come to us from you and has brought us the good news of your faith and love. He has told us also that you always remember us kindly and long to see us, just as we long to see you. [7]For this reason, brothers and sisters, during all our distress and persecution we have been encouraged about you through your faith. [8]For we now live, if you continue to stand firm in the Lord. [9]How can we thank God enough for you in return for all the joy that we feel before our God because of you? [10]Night and day we pray most earnestly

that we may see you face to face and restore whatever is lacking in your faith.

11 Now may our God and Father himself and our Lord Jesus direct our way to you. [12]And may the Lord make you increase and abound in love for one another and for all, just as we abound in love for you. [13]And may he so strengthen your hearts in holiness that you may be blameless before our God and Father at the coming of our Lord Jesus with all his saints.[f]

4 Finally, brothers and sisters, we ask and urge you in the Lord Jesus that, as you learned from us how you ought to live and to please God (as, in fact, you are doing), you should do so more and more. [2]For you know what instructions we gave you through the Lord Jesus. [3]For this is the will of God, your sanctification: that you abstain from sexual immorality; [4]that each one of you know how to control your own body[g] in holiness and honor, [5]not with lustful passion, like the gentiles who do not know God; [6]that no one wrong or exploit a brother or sister in this matter, because the Lord is an avenger in all these things, just as we have already told you beforehand and solemnly warned you. [7]For God did not call us to impurity but in holiness. [8]Therefore whoever rejects this rejects not human authority but God, who also gives his Holy Spirit to you.

9 Now concerning love of the brothers and sisters, you do not need to have anyone write to you, for you yourselves have been taught by God to love one another, [10]and indeed you do love all the brothers and sisters throughout Macedonia. But we urge you, brothers and sisters, to do so more and more, [11]to aspire to live

c 2.16 Other ancient authorities read *God's wrath* d 2.16 Or *completely* or *forever* e 3.2 Other ancient authorities read *minister* or *God's minister and our coworker* f 3.13 Other ancient authorities add *Amen* g 4.4 Or *control your own vessel* or *take a wife for yourself*

---

or a Later Interpolation?," p. 2029). **3:1–2** Paul desires to return to the Thessalonians again, but he is forced to send Timothy in his stead. **3:3–4** Once again, Paul depicts persecution as an expected experience for Christ followers. **3:6–10** Timothy brings a positive report to Paul about the Thessalonians.

4:1–3 Moral exhortations. Paul advises the Thessalonians on what he considers to be morally upstanding behavior. **4:4** *That each one of you know how to control your own body.* Literally "your own vessel"; this phrasing has certain connotations that allow it to be used as a metaphor for male genitalia. For this reason, it seems to be moral advice that is singularly aimed at male people. If that is the case, then the conventional expansion of "brothers" to "brothers and sisters" in English translations (e.g., 4:1 and elsewhere) may be unwarranted (see **"Introduction to 1 Thessalonians," pp. 2027–28**). **4:11** *Work with your hands.* In this and several other places in the letter (e.g., 5:12–14), Paul deploys metaphors of working with one's hands and manual labor. Given the negative perceptions of hand labor held by

Reading through Time: Paul's Apocalyptic Imagination (1 Thessalonians 4–5)

Given that 1 Thessalonians is the first extant text to describe the return of Jesus on "the day of the Lord" (1 Thess. 5:2), it is worth looking closely at the imagery that it employs. We should note at the outset that Paul includes his description of the Day of the Lord in 1 Thessalonians because the group seems to have asked about it. More particularly, they appear to have asked about the fate of "those who have died" (4:13). This implies that on an earlier visit, Paul planted some seeds of his apocalyptic thinking (see **"Apocalypse," p. 1216**), likely with a very imminent timetable, and when the Day of the Lord did not materialize as soon as he anticipated, the Thessalonians sought him out with questions. In Paul's response, it is remarkable which details are included—and which are not—in his description of this scenario.

While the term *apocalypse* has become synonymous with "end of the world," it originally meant simply "revelation" in ancient Greek—granted, of course, that revelation was often about what would happen at the end of the world. For Paul, the end will come with no forewarning. It will come "like a thief in the night" (1 Thess. 5:2) and while people think everything is going well (5:3). The scene, moreover, will be an auditory and visual drama. There will come the voice of an archangel, accompanied by a loud trumpet (4:16). "The Lord himself," Paul continues, "will descend from heaven, and the dead in Christ will rise first" (4:16). Then, those Christ followers who are still alive will be "caught up in the clouds together with them to meet the Lord in the air" (4:17). Paul gives no indication that anything here is merely metaphorical. On the contrary, one is struck by the vivid literalness of the scene.

While Paul clearly presupposes a final, apocalyptic judgment, he does not describe it here. He only alludes to a future "wrath" (1 Thess. 1:10; 2:16; 5:9). Related, we should note that these chapters have informed subsequent understandings and imaginings of "the rapture" across time and space. The rapture, generally speaking, refers to the apocalyptic moment when God will suddenly take up (i.e., "rapture") all righteous people to heaven, leaving behind the unrighteous. Modern Christians sometimes imagine the rapture timeline very differently from one another, placing it before or after (or, for some, even in the midst of) a violent tribulation or epic Armageddon. Contrary to popular belief, the rapture scenario is not derived from the Apocalypse of John (a.k.a. the book of Revelation, see **"Revelation in Popular Culture," p. 2122**); its strongest textual support comes from 1 Thess. 4–5, especially the swooping up of Christ followers to meet Jesus in the sky. But as is clear, this description is somewhat nebulous. Notice, furthermore, that this scenario says nothing about separating believers from unbelievers during this incident.

Paul expected Jesus to return and collect his followers *during his lifetime* (1 Thess. 4:15). He had clearly not anticipated some of the Thessalonians dying before it happened. But Paul is creative: he almost effortlessly recounts a scenario that involves, even engages with, both living and deceased Christ followers. Postponing the timetable, moreover, gives him the special opportunity to offer some moral guidance for that "in-between" period. His advice, in a nutshell, is to continually be on guard for the return of Jesus and to support one another in the meantime (5:4–11).

Sarah E. Rollens

quietly, to mind your own affairs, and to work with your hands, as we directed you, [12]so that you may behave properly toward outsiders and be dependent on no one.

13 But we do not want you to be uninformed, brothers and sisters, about those who have died,[b] so that you may not grieve as others do who have no hope. [14]For since we believe that Jesus died and rose again, even so, through Jesus, God will bring with him those who have died.[i] [15]For this we declare to you by the word of the Lord, that we who are alive, who are left until the coming of the Lord, will by no means precede those who have died.[j]

b 4.13 Gk *are asleep*   *i* 4.14 Gk *fallen asleep*   *j* 4.15 Gk *fallen asleep*

elites in the Roman Empire, this language would not make sense directed at educated elites, for they would not find it to be persuasive. Rather, it is more likely that the Thessalonians were an occupational association that was actually engaged in a particular trade, which led them to value such work and labor in a distinct way, leading to its metaphorical currency.

4:13–5:11 The Day of the Lord. This remarkable passage contains the earliest description of the second coming of Jesus (described in more detail in **"Paul's Apocalyptic Imagination," p. 2031**). **4:13** *We do not want you to be uninformed.* This phrasing suggests that the Thessalonians had questioned Paul about this particular topic. **4:15** *We who are alive, who are left.* Paul expects to be alive

[16]For the Lord himself, with a cry of command, with the archangel's call and with the sound of God's trumpet, will descend from heaven, and the dead in Christ will rise first. [17]Then we who are alive, who are left, will be caught up in the clouds together with them to meet the Lord in the air, and so we will be with the Lord forever. [18]Therefore encourage one another with these words.

5 Now concerning the times and the seasons, brothers and sisters, you do not need to have anything written to you. [2]For you yourselves know very well that the day of the Lord will come like a thief in the night. [3]When they say, "There is peace and security," then sudden destruction will come upon them, as labor pains come upon a pregnant woman, and there will be no escape! [4]But you, brothers and sisters, are not in darkness, for that day to surprise you like a thief; [5]for you are all children of light and children of the day; we are not of the night or of darkness. [6]So, then, let us not fall asleep as others do, but let us keep awake and be sober, [7]for those who sleep sleep at night, and those who are drunk get drunk at night. [8]But since we belong to the day, let us be sober and put on the breastplate of faith and love and for a helmet the hope of salvation. [9]For God has destined us not for wrath but for obtaining salvation through our Lord Jesus Christ, [10]who died for us, so that whether we are awake or asleep we may live with him. [11]Therefore encourage one another and build up each other, as indeed you are doing.

[12]But we appeal to you, brothers and sisters, to respect those who labor among you and have charge of you in the Lord and admonish you; [13]esteem them very highly in love because of their work. Be at peace among yourselves. [14]And we urge you, brothers and sisters, to admonish the idlers, encourage the fainthearted, help the weak, be patient with all of them. [15]See that none of you repays evil for evil, but always seek to do good to one another and to all. [16]Rejoice always, [17]pray without ceasing, [18]give thanks in all circumstances, for this is the will of God in Christ Jesus for you. [19]Do not quench the Spirit. [20]Do not despise prophecies, [21]but test everything; hold fast to what is good; [22]abstain from every form of evil.

23 May the God of peace himself sanctify you entirely, and may your spirit and soul and body be kept sound[k] and blameless at the coming of our Lord Jesus Christ. [24]The one who calls you is faithful, and he will do this.

25 Brothers and sisters, pray for us.

26 Greet all the brothers and sisters with a holy kiss. [27]I solemnly command you by the Lord that this letter be read to all the brothers and sisters.

28 The grace of our Lord Jesus Christ be with you.[l]

k 5.23 Or complete   l 5.28 Other ancient authorities add Amen

when Jesus returns. **5:2** *Like a thief in the night.* Jesus's return will come unexpectedly, without any warning and without following any recognizable signs. **5:3** *There is peace and security.* This is likely a reference to the Pax Romana (the peace of Rome), which Rome enforced throughout the empire (ironically) with great violence. **5:6–11** Given the unexpected nature of Jesus's return, Paul argues that it is prudent to remain on guard and prepared at all times.

5:12–28 Closing remarks. 5:12–14 Paul again offers moral advice using metaphors of labor and work. **5:27** *That this letter be read to all the brothers.* While the precise contours and practices of Paul's groups are difficult to reconstruct, it is clear that Paul at least hopes his letter will be read in a group setting.

THE SECOND LETTER OF PAUL TO THE THESSALONIANS

Authorship and Purpose

It is plausible that the authors of this letter and 1 Thessalonians are the same. Given that both letters are addressed to the "Thessalonians," such an assumption is warranted. There are other similarities between these two letters as well. A litany of thanksgiving, for example, is found in both. The inclusion of an intercessory prayer is another similarity. That the authors of both letters appear to have a pastoral frame of mind is yet another.

On the other hand, whereas many scholars agree that 1 Thessalonians was written by Paul, there is more doubt about 2 Thessalonians. One major difference between the two letters is that 1 Thessalonians was written in the belief of the immediate *parousia* (4:13–18)—that is, the Day of the Lord (the day of the second coming of Jesus) is imminent—while the second letter was written to correct the misguided rumor that the *parousia* had already arrived (2:2). This theological and eschatological difference between the two letters is significant and may suggest that the authorship of 2 Thessalonians is different from that of 1 Thessalonians (see **"Introduction to the Pauline Letters," pp. 1713–16**). Furthermore, the opening words of thanksgiving are similar to Ephesians and Colossians, which are considered "disputed," "pseudepigraphic," or "deuteropauline," meaning that the letters are thought to be inspired by the example of Paul but not actually written by him (see **"Paul's Words or a Later Interpolation?," p. 2029**). For these reasons, the argument that 2 Thessalonians was not written by Paul carries weight. The explicit attribution to joint authorship—that is, to Paul, Silvanus, and Timothy—further suggests that the letter was not written by a single person but includes multiple voices. The notion of this unknown and multiple authorship opens up the possibility of imagining a plethora of unnamed people among the founders and leaders of the early church. Since many were women, we can also imagine that the disputed letters of Paul could have female authorship as well (see **"Gender, Leadership, and Paul," p. 1990**).

The addressees of 2 Thessalonians are admonished to "stand firm" and "hold fast" (2:15) by rejecting false teaching and adhering instead to the eschatological timetable laid down in the letter (2:3–12). The purpose of the letter is both to curb potential social unrest and disagreement and to counter those enthusiasts of apocalypticism who were behaving *ataktoi* (3:6), meaning living "irresponsibly" and disobeying commands stated in the letter (3:6, 11, 14; see **"Paul's Apocalyptic Imagination," p. 2031**).

Reading Guide

The audiences of this letter appear to have been experiencing social unrest due to severe Roman imperial domination. These Christ followers—eagerly waiting for the coming of Jesus, who can deliver them from their suffering—were confused and misled by a false claim that the *parousia*, or second coming, had already arrived (2:2). The letter appears to have been written to correct this fraudulent claim. Its purpose was to encourage the Christ followers who gathered in Thessalonica to put their faith into practice in the here and now, embracing their suffering and expressing their thanksgiving to God, who is and will be faithful and steadfast (3:3, 5). This practice of faith evokes the already-here and not-yet realm of God (1:5). The Thessalonians are invited to behold a new world free from religious persecution and imperial oppression out of the midst of their ongoing tribulations in the assurance of God's final justice.

One major theme in this book is the end of the world that features violent apocalyptic imagery, including "a fiery flame" (1:8). The description of the end times takes up much of the epistle (1:5–2:12; see **"Paul's Apocalyptic Imagination," p. 2031**). The coming of "the lawless one" (2:8) deceivingly appears as the Christ. Even if this person is the antithesis of all goodness, some members are likely tricked by them and mistake them for Christ. This conjures up an image of the "antichrist," although the term does not appear exactly as it is used in 1 John (2:18, 22) and 2 John (7); see **"Antichrist," p. 2013**.

As contemporary readers, we can sympathize with people addressed in the book; as afflictions in the form of war, famine, and persecution worsened, it may have been natural to assume that the end of the world was at hand. As the ecological crisis and the displacement of millions of human beings worsen today and as natural disasters, wealth disparities, and social inequities grow at an alarming rate in our world, it is natural for us, too, to be drawn to apocalyptic literature, not to mention cultural productions featuring zombie and other dystopian scenarios. Like the members of the Thessalonian

community, it is equally tempting for some to believe in "fake news," a version of what this letter points to as false teaching. It is easy to be swayed by populist ideologies that distrust evidence-informed decisions of scientists and governments and deny climate change and global warming (see **"Pauline Legacies and Afterlives," p. 2008**, and **"Revelation in Popular Culture," p. 2122**).

Then as now, the lesson of this letter is instructive: stand firm and hold fast to truth, mercy, justice, and goodness. For the community in Thessalonica, this is all grounded in the timeless will of God that illuminates and permeates ordinary life.

HyeRan Kim-Cragg

1

Paul, Silvanus, and Timothy,

To the church of the Thessalonians in God our Father and the Lord Jesus Christ:

2 Grace to you and peace from God the^a Father and the Lord Jesus Christ.

3 We must always give thanks to God for you, brothers and sisters, as is right, because your faith is growing abundantly and the love of every one of you for one another is increasing. 4Therefore we ourselves boast of you among the churches of God for your steadfastness and faith during all your persecutions and the afflictions that you are enduring.

5 This is evidence of the righteous judgment of God and is intended to make you worthy of

the kingdom of God, for which you are also suffering. 6For it is indeed just of God to repay with affliction those who afflict you 7and to give relief to the afflicted as well as to us, when the Lord Jesus is revealed from heaven with his mighty angels 8in a fiery flame, inflicting vengeance on those who do not know God and on those who do not obey the gospel of our Lord Jesus. 9These will suffer the punishment of eternal destruction, separated from the presence of the Lord and from the glory of his might, 10when he comes to be glorified by his saints and to be marveled at on that day among all who have believed, because our testimony to you was believed. 11To

a 1.2 Other ancient authorities read *our*

1:1–2 Epistolary greeting. The greeting of 2 Thessalonians is similar to that of 1 Thessalonians but amplified by the emphasis on the source from which the divine grace and peace come. The letter uses the first-person plural to refer to Paul, Silvanus, and Timothy as the senders in the same way 1 Thessalonian does. The letter is sent to the "ekklēsia," a Greek term usually translated as *church* but that should be viewed as a small assembly, consisting of both men and women as well as children gathered at a house of a member or members.

1:3–12 Exordium, or establishment of credibility. This view of the church justifies the use of the gender-inclusive reference *brothers and sisters* as the recipients throughout the letter (1:3; 2:1, 13, 15; 3:1, 13). The gender-inclusive reference also enhances the idea of the family whose *faith is growing abundantly* and *the love of every one of you for one another is increasing* (1:3). This close-knit family relationship is tied to and bound by absolute loyalty to the Lord ("kyrios") Jesus Christ (and not to the emperor). The reference to Jesus as Lord appears twenty-two times in three short chapters. It clearly demonstrates the dominance of this christological title in the community. Given the fact that both the senders and recipients of the letter were subject to persecution or imprisonment at the time of writing, their *steadfastness and faith* (1:4) is exemplary as testimony (1:10), and their allegiance to Jesus and not to the emperor has the ring of defiance. After initial praises and compliments for the group regarding their steadfastness and faith (1:4), the authors of the letter rationalize their suffering by seeing it as a necessary experience in their journey toward the kingdom of God (1:5). Their afflictions serve to warn their persecutors of the righteous judgment to come, for God will *repay with affliction those who afflict you* (1:6) in due time. The portrayal of the punishing God combined with an "us versus them" logic can be disturbing. A violent image of the Day of the Lord ("parousia"; see **"The Day of the Lord," p. 1322**)—pointing to the Lord Jesus appearing from *heaven with his mighty angels in a fiery flame* (1:7–8) meting out eternal destruction (1:9) to those causing affliction to the righteous—is not unique to Christian writings of this time. It is often found in Jewish apocalyptic writings, as well, and in pagan notions of a postmortem judgment of this period (see **"Apocalypse," p. 1216**, and **"Paul's Apocalyptic Imagination," p. 2031**). While it is extremely dangerous to take this writing literally, it must be understood and interpreted within the context of the destruction of Jerusalem in 70 CE. The writing evokes the prospect of eschatological reversal as an assurance and a comfort to those who have suffered the destruction of an institution central to their worlds and who are desperately yearning for the end of oppression.

this end we always pray for you, asking that our God will make you worthy of his call and will fulfill by his power every good resolve and work of faith, [12]so that the name of our Lord Jesus may be glorified in you and you in him, according to the grace of our God and the Lord Jesus Christ.

2 As to the coming of our Lord Jesus Christ and our being gathered together to him, we beg you, brothers and sisters, [2]not to be quickly shaken in mind or alarmed, either by spirit or by word or by letter, as though from us, to the effect that the day of the Lord is already here. [3]Let no one deceive you in any way, for that day will not come unless the rebellion comes first and the lawless one[b] is revealed, the one destined for destruction.[c] [4]He opposes and exalts himself above every so-called god or object of worship, so that he takes his seat in the temple of God, declaring himself to be God. [5]Do you not remember that I told you these things when I was still with you? [6]And you know what is now restraining him, so that he may be revealed when his

time comes. [7]For the mystery of lawlessness is already at work, but only until the one who now restrains it is removed. [8]And then the lawless one will be revealed, whom the Lord Jesus[d] will destroy[e] with the breath of his mouth, annihilating him by the manifestation of his coming. [9]The coming of the lawless one is apparent in the working of Satan, who uses all power, signs, lying wonders, [10]and every kind of wicked deception for those who are perishing because they refused to love the truth and so be saved. [11]For this reason God sends them a powerful delusion, leading them to believe what is false, [12]so that all who have not believed the truth but took pleasure in unrighteousness will be condemned.

13 But we must always give thanks to God for you, brothers and sisters beloved by the Lord, because God chose you as the first fruits[f] for salvation through sanctification by the Spirit and through belief in the truth. [14]For

b 2.3 Gk *the man of lawlessness*; other ancient authorities read *the man of sin* c 2.3 Gk *the son of destruction* d 2.8 Other ancient authorities lack *Jesus* e 2.8 Other ancient authorities read *consume* f 2.13 Other ancient authorities read *from the beginning*

2:1–2 Partitio, or discussion of the argument to follow. This section introduces a problem to be discussed. The problem is that the community ("ekklēsia," 1:1) has received information that the "parousia" (the day of the second coming of Jesus) is *already here* (2:2).

2:3–12 Presentation of the authors' position and denouncing the opponent's position. This information weighs heavily on the authors because it conveys an erroneous eschatological doctrine. To contest this dangerous claim and to correct the false teaching, the authors recall the teaching handed down to the gathered community ("ekklēsia") in the past: *Do you not remember that I told you these things when I was still with you?* (2:5). Here *I* is identified as Paul, as the highly respected authority in this community. The appearance of the lawless one is given as the reason why the false teaching has spread in opposition to Paul's teaching. It is a well-argued reply and a clearly polished piece of prophecy influenced by the apocalyptic Jewish rhetorical literature that arose from and often functioned in that time as a response to terror and trauma (see **"Apocalypse," p. 1216**, and **"Paul's Apocalyptic Imagination," p. 2031**). In fact, it is God who is *restraining* the evil one (2:6), and it is part of God's ordained process that the lawless one *uses all power, signs, lying wonders, and every kind of wicked deception* (2:9). Again, the authors explain that before the "parousia" (the second coming of Jesus), the gospel must be shared far and wide. This is why there is a delay of the "parousia" and also why the claim that the Day of the Lord is already here is false. The part of the divine plan that enables the lawless one to appear is to show how God vindicates the faithful ones and trumps the influence of those who *refused to love the truth* (2:10). God is the one who *sends them a powerful delusion, leading them to believe what is false, so that all who have not believed the truth . . . will be condemned* (2:11–12). Even if this section might be read as a response to terror and trauma, it should not be taken literally. Moreover, one must reject the notion of the suffering of others as necessary and holy and of vengeance against enemies as divinely sanctioned and glorious. Critique is warranted when apocalyptic rhetoric is used to justify the retaliation and annihilation of a certain group (see **"Apocalypse," p. 1216**). Christological claims that it is Lord Jesus who will destroy and annihilate (2:6–9) differ from the portrayal of the teachings of Jesus in the Gospels (Matt. 5:39; 18:22; Luke 6:29) and Paul's advice in 1 Thessalonians: "See that none of you repays evil for evil, but always seek to do good to one another and to all" (5:15).

2:13–3:5 Peroratio, or summary of the argument and appeal to the audience. Rhetorically, "peroratio" sums up the previous arguments, recapitulates the main points presented, and appeals to the emotions of the audiences of a letter. To arouse their emotions here, the letter includes the second

this purpose he called you through our gospel, so that you may obtain the glory of our Lord Jesus Christ. [15]So then, brothers and sisters, stand firm and hold fast to the traditions that you were taught by us, either by word of mouth or by our letter.

16 Now may our Lord Jesus Christ himself and God our Father, who loved us and through grace gave us eternal comfort and good hope, [17]comfort your hearts and strengthen them in every good work and word.

3 Finally, brothers and sisters, pray for us, so that the word of the Lord may spread rapidly and be glorified everywhere, just as it is among you, [2]and that we may be rescued from wicked and evil people, for not all have faith. [3]But the Lord is faithful; he will strengthen you and guard you from the evil one.[g] [4]And we have confidence in the Lord concerning you, that you are doing and will go on doing the things that we command. [5]May the Lord direct your hearts to the love of God and to the steadfastness of Christ.

6 Now we command you, brothers and sisters, in the name of our Lord Jesus Christ, to keep away from every brother or sister living irresponsibly and not according to the tradition that they[b] received from us. [7]For you yourselves know how you ought to imitate us; we were not irresponsible when we were with you, [8]and we did not eat anyone's bread without paying for it, but with toil and labor we worked night and day so that we might not burden any of you. [9]This was not because we do not have that right but in order to give you an example to imitate. [10]For even when we were with you, we gave you this command: anyone unwilling to work should not eat. [11]For we hear that some of you are living irresponsibly, mere busybodies, not doing any work. [12]Now such persons we command and exhort in the Lord Jesus Christ to do their work quietly and to earn their own living. [13]Brothers and sisters, do not be weary in doing what is right.

14 Take note of those who do not obey what we say in this letter; have nothing to do with them, so that they may be ashamed. [15]Do not regard them as enemies, but admonish them as brothers and sisters.

16 Now may the Lord of peace himself give you peace at all times in all ways. The Lord be with all of you.

17 I, Paul, write this greeting with my own hand. This is the mark in every letter of mine; it is the way I write. [18]The grace of our Lord Jesus Christ be with all of you.[i]

g 3.3 Or *from evil*   b 3.6 Other ancient authorities read *you*
i 3.18 Other ancient authorities add *Amen*

thanksgiving (2:13–15), imitating 1 Thessalonians. A second thanksgiving is not found in any other Pauline Letters. The "peroratio" continues to underscore the previous exhortations: keep following the tradition (namely, the missionary teaching that was previously taught and received [3:4]), do not become a part of the recent surge of the lawless one's teaching, and resist the temptation to follow wicked and evil people (3:3). Finally, a prayer of thanksgiving is offered and concludes with the promise that the Lord will guide *[their] hearts to the love of God and to the steadfastness of Christ* (3:5).

3:6–15 Exhortatio, or strong suggestion to act. Before the authors offer words to encourage the Thessalonian community, they warn their audience of the *irresponsible* ("ataktos") ways of living (3:6, 7, 11). This term has been variously translated as "idle" (NRSV), "lived in idleness" (ISV), "disruptive" (NIV), and "disorderly" (KJV). It is not obvious who the letter writers are referring to as *irresponsible*. We can only speculate. One possibility is that there was a dispute about whether the *irresponsible* felt their work deserved more compensation than other similar endeavors. A similar argument appears in other disputed Pauline letters, including 1 Tim. 5:17: "Let the elders who rule well be considered worthy of double honor, especially those who labor in preaching and teaching." The authors' admonition to the community here may be to do what is right (3:13), even without extra compensation or recognition. A critical implication of this reading for today is to consider how the labor of all workers in today's economy is recognized and properly compensated. It also focuses our minds on questions of compensation within the church: Who is being paid? Who is not? And is this fair?

3:16–18 Epistolary closing. This closing contains both wish and benediction, echoing the similar closings in two of Paul's other letters (Gal. 6:11; 1 Cor. 16:21) and in another disputed Pauline letter (Col. 4:18). What is notable is that the first-person singular *I* appears again (3:17). This may suggest a style shaped by the process of dictating a letter to a scribe (Rom. 16:22). The final singular identification of the letter's contents with Paul signals a kind of authentication. It confirms that the letter really comes from Paul and is an authoritative rebuttal against false teachings.

THE FIRST LETTER OF PAUL TO TIMOTHY

Authorship and Date

This letter, 2 Timothy, and Titus are collectively known as the Pastoral Epistles. Each is concerned with the pastoral matters of church leadership and organization as well as guarding against heretical beliefs and practices. Although these letters are attributed to Paul, it seems as if they were written by an anonymous author using Paul's name and persona, possibly in the early second century CE after Paul had died. Thus, the author will be designated here as Pastoral Paul.

Writing in the name of authoritative figures was a strategy used by many ancient authors, sometimes to set the record straight regarding how such a figure would respond to a new situation or problem. The evidence for determining authentic authorship of ancient texts is inherently ambiguous, as differences in terminology and teachings or questionable itineraries can plausibly be explained away on account of hypothetical contexts or changes in Paul's views. While there are personal details that seem authentic, perhaps derived from fragments of lost letters of Paul (e.g., 2 Tim. 1:15–18; 4:9–16; Titus 3:12–13), we can find similar contrived biographical flourishes in letters written in the name of Plato that circulated among philosophical schools. The quotation of Luke 10:7 *as scripture* at 1 Timothy 5:18 seems to be a "smoking gun" signaling the text's later date, since it is unlikely that the historical Paul possessed a written account of Jesus's life that he regarded as Scripture.

While Titus and 1 Timothy share a common interest in establishing the qualifications for church leaders and 2 Timothy is thematically distinct, each text shares distinctive terminology and themes (many not found elsewhere in Pauline writings) indicative of some literary relationship among the three—whether they all derive from the same author (probable) or one or two of the letters are from later authors using either one or two of the texts as models for their pseudepigraphy.

Timothy and the Letter's Recipients

The letter is addressed to Timothy, Paul's "coworker" (Rom. 16:21) and "beloved and trustworthy child in the Lord" (1 Cor. 4:17). Timothy was trusted by Paul to minister to churches in Paul's absence (1 Cor. 4:17; 16:10; Phil. 2:19) and is listed as a coauthor of 1 and 2 Thessalonians, 2 Corinthians, Philippians, and Colossians. According to Acts, Timothy is of mixed Jewish and Greek descent, Paul has circumcised him as a prerequisite for ministering alongside him (Acts 16:1–5), and he joined Paul in his second and third journeys (Acts 16–20).

Timothy, the main addressee of this letter, is tasked to remain in Ephesus to provide proper instruction in the faith (1 Tim. 1:3–6). In 1 Timothy, Timothy is described in endearing terms as Paul's "true child in the faith" (1:2). In the ancient world, it was common for ethical and philosophical instruction to be conveyed in the genre of a father's letter to his son. Even though this letter includes instruction specific to Timothy about community polity and practices, it has become somewhat commonplace to imagine a broader audience, those who were invested in such matters. Such audiences, especially young ministers (4:12; 2 Tim. 2:22), may have imagined themselves reading over the shoulder of Timothy, poring over the close correspondence of a father's encouragement and instruction of his son.

Reading Guide

The author is concerned that "different teachings" have infiltrated the community that threaten the proper order of the household of God—namely, the church (1:3–4). The author is coy about the precise nature of these "different teachings," along with these teachings' speculative interest in "myths and endless genealogies" (1:4), that demonstrates their promoters' expertise as "teachers of the law" (1:7). Although it is likely that these troubling teachings allow for women to teach men (2:9–15) and exhort believers to abstain from sex and certain foods (4:3), it may be that the author is concerned to correct interpretations of Paul that promoted the prophetic gifts of women and celibacy, which believers could have found support for in 1 Corinthians (especially 7:1, 8, 25–35; 11:5). Each of these positions would also find further endorsement in the second-century apocryphal Acts of Paul and Thecla.

The book of 1 Timothy is especially concerned with making sure that everything in the household of God is being properly managed, with each person fulfilling their godly/pious duties according to their place in

the world. First and foremost, allegiance and honor are due to the "King of the ages" (1:17). Then, prayers are to be made for the prosperity of the Roman emperor and the wider bureaucracy of the imperial order. In conveying God's approval of such prayers, the author is clear to distinguish the supremacy of God as savior and Jesus as only mediator—perhaps in contrast to claims made about the emperor within the context of the imperial cult. Women are to dress modestly and prohibited from teaching men lest they usurp their divinely ordained subordinate position to men's authority (2:9–15). Presumably, there were women teaching within the community. Both bishops and deacons must be virtuous, married once, and commendable in how they manage their households and children (3:1–13). Elders are to be honored, and provisions should be made for widows. Where a family is unable to provide for widows, the church should step in, but only for those who count as "real widows" who are virtuous and in good standing in the community (5:1–16). Those who are enslaved are to obey their masters and not presume that their freedom in Christ implies freedom from their earthly duties to their masters (6:1–2)—presumably, some enslaved Christ followers thought it did. The wealthy should not be haughty but should be rich in good works and generous in their giving to ministry (6:17–19). Moreover, it is implied that the wealthy should be discerning in their giving, lest they support controversial, heretical teachers who imagine that "godliness is a means of [financial] gain" (6:5).

In some sense, 1 Timothy reflects an "open house," displaying the godliness/piety of ideal members fulfilling their duties to their God, empire, and families. The world in which this letter was produced could be characterized as a world in which emergent Christ-following movements are engaged in processes of differentiating themselves from one another, from other Jewish groups, and from the larger Roman imperial social order. In this vein, 1 Timothy points to a community negotiating a Roman imperial culture suspicious of foreign, superstitious, and seemingly antipatriotic Christ believers by promoting a vision that embodies the highest ideals of being a civilized Roman subject while maintaining a distinctive and controversial allegiance to Jesus, their Savior.

T. Christopher Hoklotubbe

1 Paul, an apostle of Christ Jesus by the command of God our Savior and of Christ Jesus our hope,

2 To Timothy, my true child[a] in the faith:

Grace, mercy, and peace from God the Father and Christ Jesus our Lord.

3 I urge you, as I did when I was on my way to Macedonia, to remain in Ephesus so that you may instruct certain people not to teach different teachings 4 and not to occupy themselves with myths and endless genealogies that promote speculations rather than the divine training[b] that is known by faith. 5 But the aim of such instruction is love that comes from a pure heart, a good conscience, and sincere faith. 6 Some people have deviated from these and turned to meaningless talk, 7 desiring to be teachers of the law without understanding either what they are saying or the things about which they make assertions.

a 1.2 Gk legitimate child   b 1.4 Gk the household management of God

1:1–2 Greeting. 1:2 *True*, or "legitimate," *child*. A term of endearment, underlining Timothy's loyalty and perseverance in contrast to those who "have suffered shipwreck in the faith" (1:19). See Phil. 2:22. *God our Savior* is a thematic designation for both God and Jesus in the Pastorals. See 2:3; 4:10; 2 Tim. 1:10; Titus 1:3–4; 2:10, 13; 3:4, 6; see also Phil. 3:20; Eph. 5:23. A relatively common description of God in the LXX (e.g., Isa. 45:21) and sometimes human agents (e.g., Judg. 3:9; Isa. 62:11).

1:3–11 Warning against false teachers. 1:3 *When I was on my way to Macedonia . . . remain in Ephesus* differs from Paul's journeys as described in Acts; see **"Paul in Acts and the Letters," p. 1997**. **1:4** What *myths and endless genealogies* Pastoral Paul has in mind is unclear. Second-century apocryphal Christian texts like the Apocryphon of John tried to harmonize philosophical cosmologies with Genesis to explain the universe's origin and how spiritual beings are associated with various elements of creation. The Jewish apocalypse 1 Enoch (8; 69:1–15) discusses the orders of angels and how their instruction corrupted both other angels and humans (see **"Apocalypse," p. 1216**). See also 4:7; 2 Tim. 4:4; Titus 1:14; 3:9. *Divine training* or "household management" or "administration" of God introduces a central theme: how each person in God's household should fulfill their duties according to their gender, age, and position in the church. **1:4–7** *Myths, meaningless talk*, and speaking *without understanding* were often negatively associated with women's speech in ancient Mediterranean culture. **1:7** *Teachers of the law*, or Torah. The nature of the teachings is vague, while the focus is upon the teachers'

8 Now we know that the law is good, if one uses it legitimately; ⁹this means understanding that the law is laid down not for the righteous but for the lawless and disobedient, for the godless and sinful, for the unholy and profane, for those who kill their father or mother, for murderers, ¹⁰the sexually immoral, men who engage in illicit sex,ᶜ slave traders, liars, perjurers, and whatever else is contrary to the sound teaching ¹¹that conforms to the glorious gospel of the blessed God, with which I was entrusted.

12 I am grateful to Christ Jesus our Lord, who has strengthened me, because he considered me faithful and appointed me to his service, ¹³even though I was formerly a blasphemer, a persecutor, and a man of violence. But I received mercy because I had acted ignorantly in unbelief, ¹⁴and the grace of our Lord overflowed for meᵈ with the faith and love that are in Christ Jesus. ¹⁵The saying is sure and worthy of full acceptance: that Christ Jesus came into the world to save sinners—of whom I am the foremost. ¹⁶But for that very reason I received mercy, so that in me, as the foremost, Jesus Christ might display the utmost patience as an example to those who would come to believe in him for eternal life. ¹⁷To the King of the ages, immortal, invisible,ᵉ the only God, be honor and glory forever and ever.ᶠ Amen.

18 This charge I commit to you, Timothy, my child, in accordance with the prophecies made earlier about you, so that by following them you may fight the good fight, ¹⁹having faith and a good conscience. By rejecting conscience, certain persons have suffered shipwreck in the faith; ²⁰among them are Hymenaeus and Alexander, whom I have turned over to Satan, so that they may be taught not to blaspheme.

2 First of all, then, I urge that supplications, prayers, intercessions, and thanksgivings be made for everyone, ²for kings and all who are in high positions, so that we may lead a quiet and peaceable life in all godliness and dignity. ³This is right and acceptable before God our Savior, ⁴who desires everyone to be saved and to come to the knowledge of the truth. ⁵For

there is one God;
there is also one mediator between
    God and humankind,
Christ Jesus, himself human,
⁶   who gave himself a ransom for all

c 1.10 Meaning of Gk uncertain d 1.14 Gk lacks *for me*
e 1.17 Or *unseen* f 1.17 Gk *to the ages of the ages*

(mis)behavior. **1:8** Cf. Rom. 7, especially 7:12–13; Gal. 3:19. **1:9–10** *Lawless and disobedient* begins a vice list describing what the Torah seeks to correct, not the opponents. See 6:4–5; 2 Tim. 3:2–5; Titus 3:3; see also Rom. 1:29–31; Gal. 5:19–23. **1:10** *Men who engage in illicit sex* translates a rare word, the nuance of which is uncertain. Since it often appears among economic vices in lists, it may reference someone who trafficked boys; see also 1 Cor. 6:9; cf. Rom. 1:27. See **"The Bible, Gender, and Sexuality," pp. 2160–62**. *Sound*, or healthy, *teaching*. See note on Titus 1:9.
    1:12–17 Gratitude for mercy. 1:15 *The saying is sure*, or "trustworthy," underscores the legitimacy of what a prophet says about a divinity in antiquity. The phrase is thematic to the Pastorals: 1 Tim. 3:1; 4:9; 2 Tim. 2:11; Titus 3:8.
    1:18 *Prophecies made earlier about you* refers to Timothy's ordination; 1 Tim. 4:14.
    1:19–20 *Hymenaeus.* See 2 Tim. 2:17. *Alexander.* See note on 2 Tim. 4:14. *Turned over to Satan.* Excommunication; alludes to Satan as the prosecutor in the heavenly court (Job 1–2; Zech. 3:1).
    2:1–15 Instructions concerning prayer. 2:1–2 *I urge that supplications, prayers . . . be made for everyone, for kings and all who are in high positions.* Prayers on behalf of emperors were expected of Roman subjects. Christians were likely seen as antipatriotic and antisocial for their refusal to attend sacrifices and oaths on behalf of the emperor and the city during public festivals (Pliny the Younger, *Epistulae* 10.96–97). Pastoral Paul offers a theologically nuanced strategy for Christ followers to be loyal subjects. See also 1 Pet. 2:17; Jer. 29:7. **2:3** *Godliness and dignity.* The Roman virtues of "pietas" and "gravitas" may be intended, underlining how Christ followers embody esteemed Roman values; see **"Godliness as Roman *Pietas*," p. 2040**. *God our Savior.* Maybe a sly critique of Roman rhetoric that celebrated emperors as saviors. Yet the designation was applied broadly and nonexclusively to honor both humans and divinities whose benefactions aided others. **2:4** *Desires everyone to be saved* emphasizes that God's domain is over all nations; see also 4:10; Titus 2:11. *Knowledge of the truth* is thematic to the Pastorals; see 2 Tim. 3:7; Titus 1:1; cf. the opponents' "falsely called knowledge" (1 Tim. 6:20). **2:5–6** Likely a liturgical fragment. *For there is one God* is shorthand for the Shema (Deut. 6:4); *there is also one mediator* contrasts against claims that the emperor and the imperial cult mediate *between God[s]*

Going Deeper: Godliness as Roman Pietas (1 Timothy 2:2)

"Godliness" translates the Greek word *eusebeia*, a term that held great significance as the Greek equivalent for the esteemed Roman virtue of *pietas* (or piety). *Pietas* entailed more than simply religious devotion but, more broadly, the dutiful fulfillment of one's obligations to one's household, one's homeland, and the gods. According to Cicero, the gods created, extended, and sustained the Roman Empire because the Romans had excelled in *pietas* (*On the Responses to the Haruspices* 9.19). In Rome's national epic, Virgil's *Aeneid*, the main protagonist, Aeneas, is called "the Pious one" and was popularly depicted on coins and in statuary as rescuing his father, his son, and his household gods from the destruction of Troy. Emperors—including Augustus (27 BCE–14 CE), Trajan (98–117 CE), Hadrian (117–138 CE), and Antoninus Pius (138–161 CE)—were celebrated for their pious benefaction to temples and priesthoods. The piety of the emperors, so it was thought, pleased the gods and secured divine benefaction and protection (cf. 1 Tim. 1:1–2). *Pietas* proliferated in imperial propaganda, honorary inscriptions, and philosophical writings. It could be said that *pietas* was like a national virtue that carried symbolic prestige similar to that carried by "freedom" and "liberty" for the United States.

The use of piety/godliness to describe the ideal Christian life is absent from the Gospels and the nondisputed Pauline Letters but is prevalent in the Pastoral Letters, 1–2 Timothy and Titus (1 Tim. 2:2; 3:16; 4:7; 5:4; 6:5; 2 Tim. 3:5, 12; Titus 2:12; otherwise Acts 3:12; 10:2, 7; 17:23; 2 Pet. 1:1, 3, 6–7; 2:9; 3:11; see **"Introduction to 1 Timothy," pp. 2037–38**). Pastoral Paul's rhetoric of piety serves to cast a vision of the ideal Christ follower as someone who was culturally dignified and civilized in a manner recognizable to skeptical outsiders. Many Greeks and Romans were suspicious of Christ followers and labeled them as superstitious atheists whose values were antipatriotic and threatened traditional Roman households. In this letter, the author of 1 Timothy allays such suspicions by providing an open house with Christian *pietas* on full display—from their prayers offered on behalf of the rulers to how their households (especially women and the enslaved) dutifully/piously embody Roman values and social expectations. It is possessed by those with sound doctrine and knowledge of the truth (1 Tim. 6:3; Titus 1:1), while charlatans looking to monetize it deny its power (1 Tim. 6:5; 2 Tim. 3:5). *Pietas* is the underappreciated "glue" that holds 1 Timothy thematically together.

T. Christopher Hoklotubbe

—this was attested at the right time. ⁷For this I was appointed a herald and an apostle (I am telling the truth;ᵍ I am not lying), a teacher of the gentiles in faith and truth.

8 I desire, then, that in every place the men should pray, lifting up holy hands without anger or argument, ⁹also that the women should dress themselves in moderate clothing with reverence and self-control, not with their hair braided or with gold, pearls, or expensive clothes, ¹⁰but with good works, as is proper for women who profess reverence for God. ¹¹Let a womanʰ learn in silence with full submission. ¹²I do not permit a womanⁱ to teach or to have authority over a man;ʲ she is to keep silent. ¹³For Adam was formed first, then Eve, ¹⁴and Adam was not deceived, but the woman was deceived and became a transgressor. ¹⁵Yet she will be saved

g 2.7 Other ancient authorities add *in Christ*   h 2.11 Or *wife*   i 2.12 Or *wife*   j 2.12 Or *her husband*

and humankind. **2:8** *Lifting up holy hands*, with hands turned upward or forward, was a common posture of prayer that appears in the Hebrew Bible (1 Kgs. 8:54; Ps. 28:2) and Christian art. Men should gather *without anger or argument*, setting aside their competitive ambition to gain honor at another's expense. **2:9** *Also*, women too should check their competitive ambition to gain honor through their expensive adornment (cf. 1 Pet. 3:3). Instead, when women gather to pray, they should wear *moderate clothing with reverence and self-control* (cf. 1 Cor. 11:5). Clothing reflects character. Expensive clothing and makeup could be associated with vice and illicit sexuality. **2:12** *I do not permit a woman to teach or to have authority [or better "dominate"] over a man* contrasts against the teaching roles of Paul's associates Junia, the apostle (Rom. 16:7), and Prisca, his coworker (Rom. 16:3; Acts 18:26). See **"Gender, Leadership, and Paul," p. 1990**. *She is to keep silent.* See also 1 Cor. 14:34–35; cf. 1 Cor. 11:5, where women do not keep silent but prophesy. **2:13–14** Pastoral Paul justifies his patriarchal worldview, which was widespread in antiquity (though not without its detractors), that women should not teach and be subordinate to men by referencing the archetype woman, Eve, whose gullibility and subordination to Adam is typical of women (cf. Sir. 25:24; 2 Cor. 11:3). Paul recognizes Adam's blame; Rom. 5:12–21. **2:15** *Yet she will be saved [or persevered] through childbearing* ensures protection through childbirth,

through childbearing, provided they continue in faith and love and holiness, with self-control.

3 The saying is sure:[k] whoever aspires to the office of bishop[l] desires a noble task. [2]Now a bishop[m] must be above reproach, married only once,[n] temperate, self-controlled, respectable, hospitable, an apt teacher, [3]not a drunkard, not violent but gentle, not quarrelsome, and not a lover of money. [4]He must manage his own household well, keeping his children submissive and respectful in every way, [5]for if someone does not know how to manage his own household, how can he take care of God's church? [6]He must not be a recent convert,[o] or he may be puffed up with conceit and fall into the condemnation of the devil. [7]Moreover, he must be well thought of by outsiders, so that he may not fall into disgrace and the snare of the devil.

[8] Deacons likewise must be serious, not double-tongued, not indulging in much wine, not greedy for money; [9]they must hold fast to the mystery of the faith with a clear conscience. [10]And let them first be tested; then, if they prove themselves blameless, let them serve as deacons. [11]Women[p] likewise must be serious, not slanderers, but temperate, faithful in all things. [12]Let deacons be married only once,[q] and let them manage their children and their households well; [13]for those who serve well as deacons gain a good standing for themselves and great boldness in the faith that is in Christ Jesus.

[14] I hope to come to you soon, but I am writing these instructions to you so that, [15]if I am delayed, you may know how one ought to behave in the household of God, which is the church of the living God, the pillar and support of the truth. [16]Without any doubt, the mystery of godliness is great:

> He[r] was revealed in flesh,
>   vindicated[s] in spirit,[t]
>   seen by angels,
>   proclaimed among gentiles,
>   believed in throughout the world,
>   taken up in glory.

k 3.1 Some interpreters place these words at the end of the previous paragraph. Other ancient authorities read *The saying is commonly accepted*   l 3.1 Or *overseer*   m 3.2 Or *an overseer*   n 3.2 Gk *the husband of one wife*   o 3.6 Gk *neophyte*   p 3.11 Or *Women deacons* or *Wives*   q 3.12 Gk *be husbands of one wife*   r 3.16 Gk *Who*; other ancient authorities read *God* or *Which*   s 3.16 Or *justified*   t 3.16 Or *by the Spirit*

the pains of which were associated with the curse of Eve (Gen. 3:16). Perhaps this assurance competitively contrasts against the claims of Artemis, the patron goddess of Ephesus, to provide such protection.

3:1–7 Qualifications of bishops. 3:1 *The office of bishop*, or "overseer," is generic and does not signal the office of the monarchical bishop. Titus 1:5–7 implies that bishops were selected among the elders. Pastoral Paul does not list the authorities and duties of ecclesial offices. **3:2** *Married only once* reflects the Roman ideal of lifelong fidelity to one spouse; 1 Tim. 3:12; 5:9; Titus 1:6. See note on 5:9–10. **3:2–7** Cf. Titus 1:6–9. *He must be well thought of by outsiders* underlines concern for skeptical outsiders to perceive leaders as exemplifying commonly shared civic and moral virtues. See also Titus 2:5, 8, 10; 1 Cor. 14:15–17; Col. 4:5; 1 Thess. 4:12. **3:6** *He must not be a recent convert*, or "neophyte," perhaps speaks to the temptation to quickly promote wealthy patrons (who receive noticeable attention in 1 Tim. 6) to ecclesial offices to honor them for their benefactions or on the presumption of their fitness due to their wealth and social standing.

3:8–13 Qualifications of deacons. 3:11 *Women* may refer to women deacons (cf. deacon Phoebe, Rom. 16:1) or wives of deacons. Given Pastoral Paul's restrictions against women, the latter may be probable.

3:14–16 The mystery of our godliness/piety. Pastoral Paul reframes the purpose of the letter: *that . . . you may know how one ought to behave in the household of God.* **3:15** *Household of God* is a metaphor for the community, wherein each member must fulfill their pious duty according to their station (elders, widows, women, and young men and women). See 1 Tim. 3:4–5, 12; 5:1–2; 2 Tim. 2:20–21. Cf. Eph. 2:19–22; Heb. 3:6; 1 Pet. 2:5; 4:17, where God's "house" means God's temple. *The church . . . the pillar and support of the truth* may reflect the development of the church as an institution that preserves orthodox practices and teachings, checking the theological imaginations of enterprising charismatics. **3:16** *Great is the mystery of godliness* (or piety) contrasts against the popular Ephesian chant "Great is Artemis of the Ephesians" (Acts 19:28, 34). Also see **"Godliness as Roman *Pietas*," p. 2040**. The *mystery* or foundational, sacred narrative of Christ's incarnation, vindication, proclamation, and glorification is superior to the mysteries and initiation rituals of Artemis (and other mystery cults). Introduces a liturgical hymn: *He was revealed in flesh. Vindicated.* Likely a reference to the resurrection.

4 Now the Spirit expressly says that in lat-er[u] times some will renounce[v] the faith by paying attention to deceitful spirits and teach-ings of demons, [2]through the hypocrisy of liars whose consciences are seared with a hot iron. [3]They forbid marriage and abstain from cer-tain foods, which God created to be received with thanksgiving by those who believe and know the truth. [4]For everything created by God is good, and nothing is to be rejected, pro-vided it is received with thanksgiving, [5]for it is sanctified by God's word and by prayer.

6 If you put these instructions before the brothers and sisters, you will be a good ser-vant[w] of Christ Jesus, nourished on the words of the faith and of the sound teaching that you have followed. [7]Have nothing to do with pro-fane and foolish tales. Train yourself in god-liness, [8]for, while physical training is of some value, godliness is valuable in every way, hold-ing promise for both the present life and the life to come. [9]The saying is sure and worthy of full acceptance. [10]For to this end we toil and suffer reproach,[x] because we have our hope set on the living God, who is the Savior of all people, especially of those who believe.

11 Command and teach these things. [12]Let no one despise your youth, but set the be-lievers an example in speech and conduct, in love, in faith, in purity. [13]Until I arrive, give attention to the public reading of scripture,[y] to exhorting, to teaching. [14]Do not neglect the gift that is in you, which was given to you through prophecy with the laying on of hands by the council of elders. [15]Put these things into practice, devote yourself to them, so that all may see your progress. [16]Pay close attention to yourself and to your teaching; continue in these things, for in doing this you will save both yourself and your hearers.

5 Do not speak harshly to an older man,[z] but speak to him as to a father, to younger men as brothers, [2]to older women as mothers, to younger women as sisters—with absolute purity.

3 Honor widows who are really widows. [4]If a widow has children or grandchildren, they should first learn their religious duty to their own family and make some repayment to their parents, for this is pleasing in God's

u 4.1 Or *the last*   v 4.1 Or *move away from*   w 4.6 Or *deacon*
x 4.10 Other ancient authorities read *struggle*   y 4.13 Gk *to the reading*   z 5.1 Or *an elder* or *a presbyter*

4:1–5 False asceticism. 4:1 *Deceitful spirits and teachings of demons* contrasts against the "mystery of godliness" (3:16) and may indicate that the opponents may have justified some of their teachings based on visions or dreams as Paul did (Gal. 1:11–12). **4:3** *They forbid marriage and abstain from certain foods.* In the second century, some early Christians interpreted Paul's endorsement of celibacy in 1 Cor. 7 as a requirement (see Acts of Paul and Thecla and Hippolytus's account of Marcion in *Haer.* 7.18). Abstaining from foods was associated with practicing self-control and thought to improve rationality in some philosophical schools. Both Marcionites and Montanists renounced marriage, with the former promoting ascetic diets (Hippolytus, *Haer.* 7.18) and the latter extra fasting (Eusebius, *Ecclesiastical History* 5.18.2). Perhaps the opponents were abstaining from meat sacrificed to idols (Rev. 2:14) or pro-moted some kosher diet, "desiring to be teachers of the law" (1:7). Cf. the concern for purity in Titus 1:15.
4:6–16 A good servant of Jesus Christ. *Nourished on the words of the faith. . . . Train yourself in godliness*; the language and training regime in 4:6–16 resonates with terminology and instruction found in Greek and Roman philosophical schools. **4:7** *Have nothing to do with profane and foolish tales.* Lit-erally "old wives' myths"; see note on 1:4. **4:8** *Godliness.* See **"Godliness as Roman *Pietas*,"** p. 2040. **4:10** *Living God* is thematically linked in Hellenistic Judaism to hope in the restoration of Israel (Hos. 1:10–11), the eschaton (Jub. 1:24–25; 3 Macc. 6:28; Jos. Asen. 19:8), and God's sovereignty over all (Dan. 5:23 LXX) and contrasts against the nonliving gods of other nations (Bel 5 LXX). **4:12** *Let no one despise your youth* invites young, aspiring ministers to identify with the figure of Timothy. **4:14** On spiritual gifts, see Rom. 12:6–8; 1 Cor. 12:4–11, 28–31. **4:16** *You will save both yourself and your hearers* reflects how some ancient philosophers saw themselves as physicians of the soul, whose teachings benefited and saved/healed their audiences.
5:1–6:2 Duties in God's household. Pastoral Paul pivots to discuss the proper respect, honor, and financial support that are due to older men (5:1, 17–22) and women (5:2–16, perhaps 17–22) and to masters (6:1–2) as is appropriate in the household of God. **5:3** *Honor* means financial support here; see 5:16–18; see also Acts 6:1–6; 9:36–42. On care for widows in the Hebrew Bible, see Exod. 22:22; Deut. 24:17–22; Isa. 1:17. **5:4** Care for parents is a *religious duty*, or better "piety," which entails loyally fulfilling one's duties to whom one is obliged, including parents. See **"Godliness as Roman *Pietas*,"**

sight. [5]The real widow, left alone, has set her hope on God and continues in supplications and prayers night and day, [6]but the widow[a] who lives for pleasure is dead even while she lives. [7]Give these commands as well, so that they may be above reproach. [8]And whoever does not provide for relatives, and especially for family members, has denied the faith and is worse than an unbeliever.

9 Let a widow be put on the list if she is not less than sixty years old and has been married only once;[b] [10]she must be well attested for her good works, as one who has brought up children, shown hospitality, washed the saints' feet, helped the afflicted, and devoted herself to doing good in every way. [11]But refuse to put younger widows on the list, for when their sensual desires alienate them from Christ, they want to marry, [12]and so they incur condemnation for having violated their first pledge. [13]Besides that, they learn to be idle, gadding about from house to house, and they are not merely idle but also gossips and busybodies, saying what they should not say. [14]So I would have younger widows marry, bear children, and manage their households, so as to give the adversary no occasion to revile us. [15]For some have already turned away to follow Satan. [16]If any believing woman[c] has relatives who are widows, let her assist them; let the church not be burdened, so that it can assist those who are real widows.

17 Let the elders who rule well be considered worthy of double honor,[d] especially those who labor in preaching and teaching, [18]for the scripture says, "You shall not muzzle an ox while it is treading out the grain" and "The laborer deserves to be paid." [19]Never accept any accusation against an elder except on the evidence of two or three witnesses. [20]As for those who persist in sin, rebuke them in the presence of all, so that the rest also may stand in fear. [21]In the presence of God and of Christ Jesus and of the elect angels, I warn you to keep these instructions without prejudice, doing nothing on the basis of partiality. [22]Do not ordain[e] anyone hastily, and do not participate in the sins of others; keep yourself pure.

23 No longer drink only water, but take a little wine for the sake of your stomach and your frequent ailments.

24 The sins of some people are conspicuous and precede them to judgment, while the sins of others follow them there. [25]So also good works are conspicuous, and even when they are not, they cannot remain hidden.

6 Let all who are under the yoke of slavery regard their masters as worthy of all honor, so that the name of God and the teaching may not be blasphemed. [2]Those who have believing masters must not be disrespectful to them on the ground that they are brothers and sisters; rather, they must serve them all the more, since those who benefit by their service are believers and beloved.[f]

Teach and urge these duties. [3]Whoever

a 5.6 Gk she   b 5.9 Gk the wife of one husband   c 5.16 Other ancient authorities read believing man or woman or believing man   d 5.17 Or compensation   e 5.22 Gk Do not lay hands on   f 6.2 Or since they are believers and beloved, who devote themselves to good deeds

p. 2040. 5:9–10 Cf. virtues expected of overseers and deacons, including being *married only once* (3:1–13). While being *married only once* symbolized upholding Roman family values, remarriage provided social and financial security for some women. Perhaps an order of widows is assumed here whose charge is to serve the church (*Apostolic Constitutions* 3.1–16). Only about 6–8 percent of the population lived past *sixty years old*. 5:11 *But refuse to put younger widows on the list.* The word for *widow* could also signify an unmarried or celibate woman. *Alienate them from Christ.* Likely their vow of celibacy in devotion to Christ; cf. 4:1. 5:13 *They learn to be idle, gadding about from house to house, and they are not merely . . . gossips and busybodies* reflects ancient stereotypes of women's behavior that may not reflect the actions of those being chastised. 5:14 *So I would have younger widows marry* seems to exclude these widows from entering the order of widows, as they would not be "married only once" (5:9). 5:17 *Honor*—that is, financial support. 5:18 Deuteronomy 25:4 and Luke 10:7 are quoted as Scripture. 5:22 *Do not ordain,* or "lay on hands," *anyone hastily* implies an order of elders, who were respected for their age, wisdom, and model of life and trusted to teach. 6:1–2 Perhaps some enslaved Christ followers had interpreted Paul's letters (e.g., Gal. 3:28; 1 Cor. 7:21; Philemon) as justifying equality, if not their freedom. Pastoral Paul disappointingly reinforces the institution of slavery in accordance with Roman values.

6:3–10 **False godliness/piety and true riches.** Pastoral Paul characterizes false teachers as stereotypical "sophists" or intellectual charlatans who peddle their inferior teaching for economic gain. The vices are pulled from a stock list of vices that serve as antitheses of the characteristics that ideal ministers should embody rather than precisely describing the actual opponents. 6:3 *Sound words.* See note

teaches otherwise and does not agree with the sound words of our Lord Jesus Christ and the teaching that is in accordance with godliness [4]is conceited, understanding nothing, and has a morbid craving for controversy and for disputes about words. From these come envy, dissension, slander, base suspicions, [5]and wrangling among those who are depraved in mind and bereft of the truth, imagining that godliness is a means of gain.[g] [6]Of course, there is great gain in godliness combined with contentment, [7]for we brought nothing into the world, so that[h] we can take nothing out of it, [8]but if we have food and clothing, we will be content with these. [9]But those who want to be rich fall into temptation and are trapped by many senseless and harmful desires that plunge people into ruin and destruction. [10]For the love of money is a root of all kinds of evil, and in their eagerness to be rich some have wandered away from the faith and pierced themselves with many pains.

11 But as for you, man of God, shun all this; pursue righteousness, godliness, faith, love, endurance, gentleness. [12]Fight the good fight of the faith; take hold of the eternal life to which you were called and for which you made[i] the good confession in the presence of many witnesses. [13]In the presence of God, who gives life to all things, and of Christ Jesus, who in his testimony before Pontius Pilate made the good confession, I charge you [14]to keep the commandment without spot or blame until the manifestation of our Lord Jesus Christ, [15]which he will bring about at the right time—he who is the blessed and only Sovereign, the King of kings and Lord of lords. [16]It is he alone who has immortality and dwells in unapproachable light, whom no one has ever seen or can see; to him be honor and eternal dominion. Amen.

17 As for those who in the present age are rich, command them not to be haughty or to set their hopes on the uncertainty of riches but rather on God, who richly provides us with everything for our enjoyment. [18]They are to do good, to be rich in good works, generous, and ready to share, [19]thus storing up for themselves the treasure of a good foundation for the future, so that they may take hold of the life that really is life.

20 Timothy, guard the deposit entrusted to you. Avoid the profane chatter and contradictions of what is falsely called knowledge; [21]by professing it some have missed the mark as regards the faith.

Grace be with you.[j]

g 6.5 Other ancient authorities add *Withdraw yourself from such people* h 6.7 Other ancient authorities read *world; it is certain that* i 6.12 Gk *confessed* j 6.21 The Greek word for *you* here is plural; in other ancient authorities it is singular. Other ancient authorities add *Amen*

on Titus 1:9. **6:6** *With contentment* resonates with the philosophical teachings of the Cynics and Stoics, for whom contentment was contingent on how you perceived your circumstances (cf. Phil. 4:11). **6:9–10** Cf. Matt. 19:16–26; Mark 10:17–27; Luke 18:18–27. **6:9** *Ruin and destruction* refers to eschatological judgment; see also Rom. 9:22; 1 Cor. 5:5; Phil. 1:28; 3:19; 1 Thess. 5:3; 2 Thess. 1:9. **6:10** *Love of money.* A popular philosophical maxim.

6:11–19 Fight the good fight. Pivots to the final charge addressed to Timothy. **6:11** *Man of God.* A title applied to those entrusted with special duties from God in the Hebrew Bible, including Moses (Deut. 33:1; Josh. 14:6), David (Neh. 12:36), Elijah (2 Kgs. 1:9–12), and other prophets (1 Sam. 2:27; 9:6–10; 1 Kgs. 13). Here the title is given to ordained church leaders. **6:14–15** *Which he will bring about at the right time* seems to address why the return of Christ has not yet come. On *manifestation*, see note on 2 Tim. 1:10. **6:15–16** *He who is the blessed. . . . Amen* is a liturgical fragment, the subject of which ambiguously elides Christ and God, the Father. **6:17–19** Pastoral Paul next advises the rich that their wealth and status in the next age is contingent on their wise benefaction in the *present age.* Pastoral Paul wants benefaction to be guided by and directed to those who teach what is in accordance with piety (6:3), not to charlatans with their false piety (6:5). Cf. 6:6–10.

6:20–21 Personal instructions and benediction. *Deposit.* See note on 2 Tim. 1:12–14. *Falsely called knowledge.* Likely not referring to gnostics ("gnosis" in Gk. is "knowledge"). Later church fathers found 1 Tim. 6:20 useful for categorizing their opponents. *Grace be with you.* See note on Titus 3:15.

THE SECOND LETTER OF PAUL TO TIMOTHY

Authorship and Date

This letter, 1 Timothy, and Titus are collectively known as the Pastoral Epistles. Each is concerned with the pastoral matters of church leadership and organization as well as guarding against heretical beliefs and practices. Although these letters are attributed to Paul, it seems as if they were written by an anonymous author using Paul's name and persona, possibly in the early second century CE after Paul had died. Thus, the author will be designated here as Pastoral Paul.

Writing in the name of authoritative figures was a strategy used by many ancient authors, sometimes to set the record straight regarding how such a figure would respond to a new situation or problem. For more on determining the authentic authorship of the Pastoral Letters, see **"Introduction to 1 Timothy," pp. 2037–38**. While 2 Timothy is thematically distinct from 1 Timothy and Titus, each text shares distinctive terminology and themes (many not found elsewhere in Pauline writings) indicative of some literary relationship among the three—whether they all derive from the same author (probable) or one or two of the letters are from later authors using either one or two of the texts as models for their pseudepigraphy.

Timothy and the Letter's Recipients

The letter is addressed to Timothy, Paul's "coworker" (Rom. 16:21) and "beloved and trustworthy child in the Lord" (1 Cor. 4:17). Timothy was trusted by Paul to minister to churches in Paul's absence (1 Cor. 4:17; 16:10; Phil. 2:19) and is listed as a coauthor of 1 and 2 Thessalonians, 2 Corinthians, Philippians, and Colossians. According to Acts, Timothy is of mixed Jewish and Greek descent, Paul has circumcised him as a prerequisite for ministering alongside him (Acts 16:1–5), and he joined Paul in his second and third journeys (Acts 16–20).

While 1 Timothy locates Timothy in Ephesus, it is unclear where Timothy is imagined in 2 Timothy. Timothy may still be in Ephesus, since Prisca and Aquila are remembered for ministering there (4:19); in Iconium, where the Acts of Paul 1–2 locates Onesiphorus's household (4:19); or anywhere but the province of Asia (including Ephesus) if, indeed, "all . . . Asia" has abandoned Pastoral Paul (1:15) and he is now sending Tychicus to Ephesus (4:12).

Timothy is described in endearing terms as Paul's "beloved" (1:2), who remains in Paul's daily prayers and whose tears are emblematic of their close bond and mutual longing to be reunited (1:3–4). In the ancient world, it was common for ethical and philosophical instruction to be conveyed in the genre of a father's letter to his son. Also, even though this letter includes instruction specific to Timothy about community polity and practices, it has become somewhat commonplace to imagine a broader audience, those who were invested in such matters. Such audiences, especially young ministers (2:22; 1 Tim. 4:12), may have imagined themselves reading over the shoulder of Timothy, poring over the close correspondence of a father's encouragement and instruction of his son.

Reading Guide

Second Timothy presents Paul in Rome (1:17), in prison (1:8; 2:9), foreseeing his own death (4:6–8), and reaching out to his beloved child, Timothy, to provide a lasting moral exhortation to Timothy to carry on in his ministry and to live up to Paul's legacy despite the challenges that await.

This letter shares some important commonalities with Jewish testamentary literature (e.g., Testament of Job, Testaments of the Twelve Patriarchs), which contains pseudepigraphic deathbed speeches from esteemed Jewish figures recounting their lives to gathered loved ones, exhorting moral virtues for which God will bless them, promoting reverence toward God, predicting the future, and narrating their death and burials. Although 2 Timothy lacks some common elements found in Jewish testamentary literature (e.g., no death and burial scene, its genre as a letter), it offers gratitude for help (1:13; 2:2; 3:10–17), establishes the "patriarch" Paul as a model for emulation (3:10–12; 4:6–8), and passes judgment on others who fall short of the leader's legacy (1:15; 2:17–18; 3:6–9; 4:10, 14). It is worthwhile to compare 2 Timothy with Paul's farewell speech in Acts 20:17–38.

In contrast to 1 Timothy and Titus, 2 Timothy is less concerned with the organization and structure of the church than with providing a moving portrait of Paul's life and legacy, which provides the basis for emotionally charged commands to remain faithful to sound teaching and the deposit of tradition that has been

entrusted to the believer (1:14) in the face of suffering, persecution, and the opposition of false teachers. And as with 1 Timothy and Titus, the world in which this letter was produced could be characterized as a world in which emergent Christ-following movements are engaged in processes of differentiating themselves from one another, from other Jewish groups, and from the larger Roman imperial social order. Audiences of 2 Timothy, especially potential leaders, are invited to imagine themselves as good soldiers (2:3–4), athletes (2:5), and farmers (2:6) to imbue themselves with focus, strength, endurance, and self-discipline, knowing that their eternal reward awaits. Despite Paul's chains, "the word of God is not chained" (2:9).

In this letter, the author predicts that in the "last days" that seem near, if not already upon them, society will degenerate to vices and be led astray by charlatans and false teachers peddling a counterfeit piety (3:1–9). Beyond the many vices pulled from stock characterizations of sophistic charlatans, which leads historians to take such descriptions with a grain of salt, little is said about the theological content that the author finds objectionable, beyond the teachings of Hymenaeus and Philetus, who preach that the "resurrection has already occurred" (2:18).

The heart of this letter is a moving charge to "be sober in everything, endure suffering, do the work of an evangelist, carry out your ministry fully" (4:5), propelled by the exemplary feats of endurance and faithfulness of the heroic Paul in the face of obstacles, opposition, and suffering. If the Lord stood by Paul and strengthened him through it all, the Lord will surely strengthen readers through whatever they face.

T. Christopher Hoklotubbe

1 Paul, an apostle of Christ Jesus by the will of God, for the sake of the promise of life that is in Christ Jesus,

2 To Timothy, my beloved child:

Grace, mercy, and peace from God the Father and Christ Jesus our Lord.

3 I am grateful to God—whom I worship with a clear conscience, as my ancestors did—when I remember you constantly in my prayers night and day. ⁴Recalling your tears, I long to see you so that I may be filled with joy. ⁵I am reminded of your sincere faith, a faith that lived first in your grandmother Lois and your mother Eunice and now, I am sure, lives in you. ⁶For this reason I remind you to rekindle the gift of God that is within you through the laying on of my hands, ⁷for God did not give us a spirit of cowardice but rather a spirit of power and of love and of self-discipline.

8 Do not be ashamed, then, of the testimony about our Lord or of me his prisoner, but join with me in suffering for the gospel, in the power of God, ⁹who saved us and called us with a holy calling, not according to our works but according to his own purpose and grace, and this grace was given to us in Christ Jesus before the ages began,ᵃ ¹⁰but it has now been revealed through the appearing of our Savior Jesus Christ,ᵇ who abolished death and brought life and immortality to light through the gospel. ¹¹For this gospel I was appointed a herald and an apostle and a teacher,ᶜ ¹²and for this reason I suffer as I do. But I am not ashamed, for I know the one in whom I have put my trust, and I am sure that he is able to

a 1.9 Gk lacks *began*   *b* 1.10 Other ancient authorities read *Christ Jesus*   *c* 1.11 Other ancient authorities add *of the gentiles*

1:1–2 Salutation. Cf. 1 Tim. 1:1–2. **1:1** *Promise of life* foreshadows Paul's impending death (4:6–8).

1:3–18 Thanksgiving and encouragement. 1:5 Acts 16:1–3 describes Timothy's mother, here named *Eunice*, as a Jewish Christ follower, while his father was Greek. *Grandmother Lois* depicts a matrilineal legacy of faith. See also 3:15. **1:6** *Laying on of my hands.* See 1 Tim. 4:14. **1:8** *Do not be ashamed.* Shame was a powerful deterrent and consequence of socially unacceptable behavior in the honor/shame culture. See also 1:12, 16; 2:15. Both the *testimony about our Lord*, perceived by many as a suspicious foreign superstition, and being associated with a *prisoner* would have been potential sources of shame. See Rom. 1:16. Paul is likely imprisoned in Rome; 2 Tim. 1:17. **1:9–10** A liturgical fragment. **1:9** *Not according to our works.* Titus 3:5; Rom. 3:27–28; 9:11–12; Gal. 2:16–17; Eph. 2:9. **1:10** In Greek and Roman culture, *appearing* or "manifestation" (Gk. "epiphaneia") described the manifestation of either the emperor or divine being that bestowed some benefaction. Its use here implies either a subtle jab at competing claims of divine appearances (especially with respect to the imperial cult) or an attempt to frame the gospel in a manner recognizable to outsiders. The term is thematic to the Pastorals (1 Tim. 6:14; 2 Tim. 1:10; 4:1, 8; Titus 2:13) and only occurs elsewhere in 2 Thess. 2:8. It can refer both to Christ's incarnation and to his second coming, as it does here in v. 10. **1:12–14** *The deposit*, or the culmination

guard until that day the deposit I have entrusted to him.*[d]* [13]Hold to the standard of sound teaching that you have heard from me, in the faith and love that are in Christ Jesus. [14]Guard the good deposit entrusted to you, with the help of the Holy Spirit living in us.

[15] You are aware that all who are in Asia have turned away from me, including Phygelus and Hermogenes. [16]May the Lord grant mercy to the household of Onesiphorus, because he often refreshed me and was not ashamed of my chain; [17]when he arrived in Rome, he eagerly*[e]* searched for me and found me [18]—may the Lord grant that he will find mercy from the Lord on that day! And you know very well how much service he rendered in Ephesus.

2 You then, my child, be strong in the grace that is in Christ Jesus, [2]and what you have heard from me through many witnesses entrust to faithful people who will be able to teach others as well. [3]Share in suffering like a good soldier of Christ Jesus. [4]No one serving in the army gets entangled in everyday affairs; the soldier's aim is to please the enlisting officer. [5]And in the case of an athlete, no one is crowned without competing according to the rules. [6]It is the farmer who does the work who ought to have the first share of the crops. [7]Think over what I say, for the Lord will give you understanding in all things.

[8] Remember Jesus Christ, raised from the dead, a descendant of David—that is my gospel, [9]for which I suffer hardship, even to the point of being chained like a criminal. But the word of God is not chained. [10]Therefore I endure everything for the sake of the elect, so that they may also obtain the salvation that is in Christ Jesus, with eternal glory. [11]The saying is sure:

If we have died with him, we will also live
    with him;
[12] if we endure, we will also reign with him;
    if we deny him, he will also deny us;
[13] if we are faithless, he remains faithful—
    he*[f]* cannot deny himself.

[14] Remind them of this, and warn them before the Lord*[g]* that they are to avoid wrangling over words, which does no good but only ruins those who are listening. [15]Do your best to present yourself to God as one approved by him, a worker who has no need to be ashamed, rightly explaining the word of truth. [16]Avoid profane chatter, for it will lead people*[h]* into more and more impiety, [17]and their talk will spread like gangrene. Among them are Hymenaeus and Philetus, [18]who have swerved from the truth, saying resurrection*[i]*

d 1.12 Or *the deposit he has entrusted to me*   *e* 1.17 Or *promptly*
f 2.13 Other ancient authorities read *for he*   *g* 2.14 Other
ancient authorities read *God*   *h* 2.16 Gk *for they will advance*
i 2.18 Other ancient authorities read *the resurrection*

of the Christian tradition that has been passed down from Jesus to the apostles to their followers, is thematic in the letters to Timothy (1 Tim. 6:20; 2 Tim. 1:12, 14; 2:2) and reflects the beginning of the concept of "apostolic teaching and succession." **1:13** *Sound teaching.* See note on Titus 1:9. **1:15** *All who are in Asia have turned away from me, including Phygelus and Hermogenes. All* is an exaggeration that heightens the theme of abandonment. *Asia.* A Roman province in modern eastern Turkey. *Phygelus* is unknown. *Hermogenes* appears in the Acts of Paul 1–2 as a traitorous companion of Paul, paired with Demas. See also 2:17; 4:10–15. **1:16–18** *Onesiphorus . . . often refreshed me* reflects the hardships of prison, which were only softened by friends and family who could provide essential care that was otherwise not provided. *In Ephesus* may reflect a tradition that Paul was imprisoned in Ephesus, not recorded in Acts. In the Acts of Paul, Onesiphorus welcomes and hosts Paul while he is in Iconium.

2:1–13 **A good soldier of Christ. 2:2** *Many witnesses.* See 1 Tim. 6:12. **2:3** *Good soldier.* Paul describes Epaphroditus (Phil. 2:25) and Archippus (Phlm. 2) as "fellow soldiers." **2:5** *Athlete* imagery was popular in moral exhortations; see also 2 Tim. 4:7–8; 1 Tim. 4:8; 1 Cor. 9:24–27; Heb. 12. **2:6** *It is the farmer who does the work who ought to have the first share of the crops.* Cf. Paul's use of agrarian analogies to justify financial support for teachers: 1 Cor. 9:1–17 (citing Deut. 25:4); Gal. 6:6. This theme appears in 1 Tim. 5:17–18, which references Deut. 25:4 and Luke 10:7. **2:7–8** *Think over. . . . Remember* resonates with traditional meditative practices of contemplation found in philosophical schools to deepen understanding and internalize wisdom. **2:11–13** A liturgical fragment or poem introduced by *the saying is sure*: thematic to the Pastorals (1 Tim. 1:15; 3:1; 4:9; Titus 3:8). On dying and living in Christ, see Rom. 6:4, 8; Eph. 2:5–6; Col. 2:12–13; 3:1.

2:14–26 **A worker approved by God. 2:14–16** *Avoid wrangling over words.* See also 2:23; cf. similar exhortations in 1 Tim. 6:4–5; Titus 3:9. **2:17** *Hymenaeus.* Turned over to Satan and paired with Alexander in 1 Tim. 1:20. *Philetus.* Otherwise unknown. **2:18** *Resurrection has already occurred.* See also 1 Cor. 15:12–14,

has already occurred. They are upsetting the faith of some. [19]But God's firm foundation stands, bearing this inscription: "The Lord knows those who are his," and, "Let everyone who calls on the name of the Lord turn away from wickedness."

20 In a large house there are utensils not only of gold and silver but also of wood and clay, some for special[j] use, some for ordinary.[k] [21]All who cleanse themselves of the things I have mentioned[l] will become special[m] utensils, dedicated and useful to the owner of the house, ready for every good work. [22]Shun youthful passions and pursue righteousness, faith, love, and peace, along with those who call on the Lord from a pure heart. [23]Have nothing to do with stupid and senseless controversies; you know that they breed quarrels. [24]And the Lord's servant must not be quarrelsome but kindly to everyone, an apt teacher, patient, [25]correcting opponents with gentleness. God may perhaps grant that they will repent and come to know the truth [26]and that they may escape from the snare of the devil, having been held captive by him to do his will.[n]

3 You must understand this, that in the last days distressing times will come. [2]For people will be lovers of themselves, lovers of money, boasters, arrogant, abusive, disobedient to their parents, ungrateful, unholy, [3]unfeeling, implacable, slanderers, profligates, brutes, haters of good, [4]treacherous, reckless, swollen with conceit, lovers of pleasure rather than lovers of God, [5]holding to the outward form of godliness but denying its power. Avoid them! [6]For among them are those who make their way into households and captivate immature women, overwhelmed by their sins and swayed by all kinds of desires, [7]who are always studying yet never able to recognize truth. [8]As Jannes and Jambres opposed Moses, so these people, of corrupt mind and counterfeit faith, also oppose the truth. [9]But they will not make much progress because, as in the case of those two men,[o] their folly will become plain to everyone.

10 Now you have observed my teaching, my conduct, my aim in life, my faith, my patience, my love, my steadfastness, [11]my persecutions, and my sufferings, the things that happened to me in Antioch, Iconium, and Lystra. What persecutions I endured! Yet the Lord rescued me from all of them. [12]Indeed, all who want to live a godly life in Christ Jesus will be persecuted. [13]But wicked people and impostors will go from bad to worse, deceiving others and being deceived. [14]But as for you, continue in what you have learned and firmly believed, knowing from whom you learned it [15]and how from childhood you have known sacred writings that are able to instruct you for salvation through faith in Christ Jesus. [16]All scripture is

---

j 2.20 Gk *honorable*   *k* 2.20 Gk *dishonorable*   *l* 2.21 Gk *of these things*   *m* 2.21 Gk *honorable*   *n* 2.26 Or *by him, to do his (that is, God's) will*   *o* 3.9 Gk lacks *two men*

---

35. In the Acts of Paul 3:14, Demas and Hermogenes teach that the resurrection is a metaphor. **2:19** The reference to Num. 16:5 associates Hymenaeus and Philetus with Korah and his companions, who were swallowed alive into the earth after raising up Israelites against Moses and Aaron. The second quote may be a paraphrase of Num. 16:26, with Pastoral Paul identifying with Moses, warning his audience to turn away from wicked teachers. **2:20–21** Cf. Rom. 9:21. On being *ready for every good work*, see Titus 3:1; cf. 2 Tim. 3:17. **2:23** *Stupid and senseless controversies.* A similar phrase is used in Titus 3:9. **2:26** *Snare of the devil* is also in 1 Tim. 3:7.

3:1–9 Godlessness/impiety in the last days. **3:1** *In the last days distressing times will come* expects that the last days are near and, typical of an apocalyptic mindset, predicts that hardships and vices will proliferate before the return of Christ (see **"Apocalypse," p. 1216**). See also 1 Tim. 4:1–5. **3:2–5** A list of vices intended as a broad attack, not a precise description of actual opponents. See note on 1 Tim. 1:9–10. **3:6** *Captivate immature women* plays on misogynist stereotypes of women being gullible, unable to control their emotions and desires, and vulnerable to counterfeit piety. Cf. 1 Tim. 2:14. Ironically, Christ followers too were critiqued for peddling their superstitions among gullible women and children (Minucius Felix, *Octavius* 8.4). **3:8** *Jannes and Jambres opposed Moses* is a reference to apocryphal traditions about Pharaoh's court magicians (Exod. 7:11, 22) that were variously developed in later Jewish writings (Dead Sea Scrolls, Testament of Solomon, Apocryphon of Jannes and Jambres, and Jewish midrash).

3:10–4:8 Paul's charge to Timothy. **3:11** Acts 13–14 recount *the things that happened to me in Antioch, Iconium, and Lystra.* **3:15** *Sacred writings* refers to the Jewish Scriptures, though perhaps this category includes texts like Luke's Gospel (1 Tim. 5:18). *Through faith* or faithfulness that resides *in Christ Jesus*

inspired by God and is[p] useful for teaching, for reproof, for correction, and for training in righteousness, [17]so that the person of God may be proficient, equipped for every good work.

4 In the presence of God and of Christ Jesus, who is to judge the living and the dead, and in view of his appearing and his kingdom, I solemnly urge you: [2]proclaim the message; be persistent whether the time is favorable or unfavorable; convince, rebuke, and encourage with the utmost patience in teaching. [3]For the time is coming when people will not put up with sound teaching, but, having their ears tickled, they will accumulate for themselves teachers to suit their own desires [4]and will turn away from listening to the truth and wander away to myths. [5]As for you, be sober in everything, endure suffering, do the work of an evangelist, carry out your ministry fully.

6 As for me, I am already being poured out as a libation, and the time of my departure has come. [7]I have fought the good fight; I have finished the race; I have kept the faith. [8]From now on there is reserved for me the crown of righteousness, which the Lord, the righteous judge, will give me on that day, and not only to me but also to all who have longed for his appearing.

9 Do your best to come to me soon, [10]for Demas, in love with this present world, has deserted me and gone to Thessalonica; Crescens has gone to Galatia,[q] Titus to Dalmatia. [11]Only Luke is with me. Get Mark and bring him with you, for he is useful to me in ministry. [12]I have sent Tychicus to Ephesus. [13]When you come, bring the cloak that I left with Carpus at Troas, also the books, and above all the parchments. [14]Alexander the coppersmith did me great harm; the Lord will pay him back for his deeds. [15]You also must beware of him, for he strongly opposed our message.

16 At my first defense no one came to my support, but all deserted me. May it not be counted against them! [17]But the Lord stood by me and gave me strength, so that through me

p 3.16 Or *Every scripture inspired by God is also*   *q* 4.10 Other ancient authorities read *Gaul*

---

may convey the idea that believers participate in Christ's faithfulness, promised life (1:10), love (1:13), grace (2:1), and salvation (2:10) that is in their union with the resurrected Christ. **3:16** *All scripture* does not entail any modern biblical canon, since what was considered "Scripture" then was developing and varied and often included numerous Jewish and Christian texts not found in modern Bibles (i.e., 1 Enoch, 1 Clement, the *Didache*, etc.). *Inspired by God*, literally "God breathed/breathing," can imply "given life by God's breath" (Gen. 2:7; passive sense) or "life-giving by God's breath" (active sense). "God breathed" rarely occurs in ancient literature, describing dreams, ointment, and even Jesus's sandals, and its meaning is uncertain, especially with respect to what might be assumed about human agency coordinating with God's life-giving breath. See also 2 Pet. 1:20–21. **3:17** *The person of God.* See note on 1 Tim. 6:11. **4:1** *In the presence of God and of Christ Jesus.* See 1 Tim. 5:21. **4:2** *Be persistent*, or "stand ready." **4:3** *For the time is coming* reflects an apocalyptic expectation that the church will struggle with a proliferation of false teachings before the second coming. See 3:1. **4:4** *Myths.* See notes on 1 Tim. 1:4; Titus 1:14. **4:6** *A libation* was a ritual pouring of a liquid, commonly wine, as an offering to a deity (Num. 28:7). In the face of his *departure* or coming death, Pastoral Paul sees his present imprisonment as an offering of gratitude to God. Cf. Phil. 2:17. **4:7** *Good fight; . . . finished the race.* Cf. 2:3–5. *I have kept the faith* to the "faithful" Jesus (2:13), which had been entrusted to Pastoral Paul; see 1 Tim. 1:11; Titus 1:3; cf. 2 Tim. 1:12–13.

4:9–18 Personal instructions. **4:10** *Demas.* A "fellow worker" (Phlm. 24; Col. 4:14). *Crescens*, otherwise unknown, may have been sent to Galatia as opposed to abandoning Paul. On *Titus*, see **"Introduction to Titus," pp. 2051–52**, who is sent to *Dalmatia* in northwest Greece. **4:11** *Luke.* Paul's "coworker" (Phlm. 24) and "beloved physician" (Col. 4:14). *Mark.* Cousin of Barnabas, another "coworker" listed with Luke and Demas in Phlm. 24; see also Col. 4:10, 14. Cf. Acts 15:37–39, wherein Paul and Barnabas split over their disagreement about the usefulness of Mark, who had deserted them before. Apparently, he is now *useful.* **4:12** *Tychicus.* A "faithful minister" (Eph. 6:21; Col. 4:7; Acts 20:4). As in Eph. 6:21, Tychicus is sent to Ephesus; cf. Titus 3:12. **4:13** *Carpus.* Otherwise unknown. *Books*, or better "scrolls." *Parchments* were tanned animal skin, expensive, and used for important documents. **4:14** *Alexander the coppersmith.* Associated with Hymenaeus, turned over to Satan (1 Tim. 1:20), otherwise unknown. Alexander may represent a conflation of details vaguely remembered from Acts 19:33–34. *The Lord will pay him back* echoes Pss. 62:12; 28:4; Prov. 24:12. **4:17** *Rescued from the lion's mouth* is metaphorical.

the message might be fully proclaimed and all the gentiles might hear it. So I was rescued from the lion's mouth. [18]The Lord will rescue me from every evil attack and save me for his heavenly kingdom. To him be the glory forever and ever. Amen.

19 Greet Prisca and Aquila and the household of Onesiphorus. [20]Erastus remained in

Corinth; Trophimus I left ill in Miletus. [21]Do your best to come before winter. Eubulus sends greetings to you, as do Pudens and Linus and Claudia and all the brothers and sisters.

22 The Lord be with your spirit. Grace be with you.[r]

r 4.22 The Greek word for *you* here is plural. Other ancient authorities add *Amen*

Perhaps this verse inspired the story of Paul facing a talking lion, whom he had previously baptized, in the theater (Acts of Paul 7).

4:19–22 Final greetings and benediction. 4:19 *Prisca and Aquila.* Coworkers of Paul (Rom. 16:3; 1 Cor. 16:19; Acts 18). *The household of Onesiphorus.* See note 1:16. **4:20** *Erastus.* City treasurer and Paul's helper (Rom. 16:23; Acts 19:22). *Trophimus.* "The Ephesian" (Acts 20:4; 21:27–29). *I left ill in Miletus.* According to Acts, Paul stopped in Miletus to meet with Ephesian leaders before departing to Jerusalem via Cos and Rhodes (Acts 20:15–21:1). It is difficult to reconcile this detail with Acts, since Trophimus was present with Paul in Jerusalem after Paul's stop in Miletus, and Paul's ship to Rome did not dock at Miletus (Acts 27:1–8). **4:21** *Eubulus . . . Pudens and Linus and Claudia.* All otherwise unknown. Their Latin names may indicate that Pastoral Paul is imagined as imprisoned in Rome.

THE LETTER OF PAUL TO TITUS

Authorship and Date

This letter and 1 and 2 Timothy are collectively known as the Pastoral Epistles. Each is concerned with the pastoral matters of church leadership and organization as well as guarding against heretical beliefs and practices. Although these letters are attributed to Paul, it seems as if they were written by an anonymous author using Paul's name and persona, possibly in the early second century CE after Paul had died. Thus, the author will be designated here as Pastoral Paul.

Writing in the name of authoritative figures, living or dead, was a strategy used by many ancient authors, sometimes to set the record straight regarding how such a figure would respond to a new situation or problem. For more on determining the authentic authorship of the Pastoral Letters, see **"Introduction to 1 Timothy," pp. 2037–38**. While Titus and 1 Timothy share a common interest in establishing the qualifications for church leaders and 2 Timothy is thematically distinct, each text shares distinctive terminology and themes (many not found elsewhere in Pauline writings) indicative of some literary relationship among the three—whether they all derive from the same author (probable) or one or two of the letters are from later authors using either one or two of the texts as models for their pseudepigraphy.

Titus and the Letter's Recipients

The letter is addressed to Titus, Paul's uncircumcised Greek "partner and coworker" (Gal. 2:3; 2 Cor. 8:23). Paul had taken Titus to Jerusalem to debate whether gentiles in Christ needed to be circumcised (Gal. 2:1–10; cf. Acts 15:1–30), perhaps as evidence of the fruits and divine approval of Paul's gospel. At Paul's urging, Titus traveled to Corinth and seems to have been integral in reconciling some of the Corinthian Christ believers to Paul after his second visit to the city (2 Cor. 7:6–16; 12:14–18).

In the Epistle to Titus, Titus is described as Paul's "true child" in the faith (1:4; cf. 1 Tim. 1:2) and has been left on the Mediterranean island of Crete to appoint and train leaders over the fledgling Christ group (1:5), to instruct the Cretans in "sound instruction" (2:1) and exhort them to be devoted to good works (3:8), and to "avoid stupid controversies" that divide people (3:9). Presumably, the audience is invited to imagine themselves reading over the shoulder of Titus, poring over the close correspondence of a father's encouragement and instruction of his son. In antiquity, it was common for ethical and philosophical instruction to be conveyed in the genre of a father's letter to his son. Also, even though this letter includes instruction specific to Titus about community polity and practices, it has become somewhat commonplace to imagine a broader audience, those who were invested in such matters. And so the literary imagination of Paul writing an intimate letter to his faithful son, Titus, provides a recognizable and compelling framework for the anonymous author to advance his vision for the church.

Reading Guide

Similar to 1 Timothy, the Letter to Titus establishes the qualifications of bishops, but unlike 1 Timothy, it discusses the appointment of elders but not deacons. Similar to both 1 and 2 Timothy, Pastoral Paul warns against "rebellious people" (1:10) and charlatans who peddle in "myths" (1:14) and are "unfit for any good work" (1:16). However, Titus specifically ties the vices of such people with their Cretan ethnicity (1:12) and specifically describes the myths as "Jewish" (1:14). Rather than persistently engage with such people, audiences are told to admonish them twice and then to avoid those who engage in "stupid controversies" (3:9).

As with 1 and 2 Timothy, the world in which this letter was produced could be characterized as a world in which emergent Christ-following movements are engaged in processes of differentiating themselves from one another, from other Jewish groups, and from the larger Roman imperial social order. Just as in 1 and 2 Timothy, Pastoral Paul urges that all teaching must be consistent with "sound instruction" (2:1). Like 1 Timothy, Titus sets out a vision of the household of God that is perfectly ordered and with everyone faithfully carrying out their duties as appropriate to their station, whether they be older men and women, young women and men, or masters and the enslaved (2:2–10). Such instructions are framed in terms of "training," akin to the educational discipline philosophical schools administered among their students to instill virtue (2:11–12). Given that some Greeks and Romans were suspicious of Christ followers as promoting a foreign superstition that was not sufficiently pious—that is, failing to fulfill their duties to the household, the emperor, and the gods—Pastoral Paul exhorts his audience to embody respectable virtues and submit to Roman authorities (3:1) so that "the word of God may not be discredited" (2:5; see also 2:8, 10).

While Cretans may be barbaric in their vices and Jews may be superstitious in their circumcision (1:10–14), Christ followers are ideal Roman subjects, cultured and civilized, and devoted to good works (3:8).

Christ's training regime also entails knowing what time it is and knowing one's true identity. Christ believers are to await the "manifestation" (2:13) of their Savior, Jesus Christ, who has redeemed them and purified them into God's chosen end-time people (1:1; 2:14). The terminology of "manifestation," popular in Greek religion and the imperial cult, is also used to describe Christ's prior appearance, wherein "he saved us, not because of any works of righteousness that we had done, but according to his mercy" (3:5). And so the Letter to Titus sets out to distill Paul's gospel, from which each leader should not divert.

T. Christopher Hoklotubbe

1 Paul, a servant of God and an apostle of Jesus Christ, for the sake of the faith of God's elect and the knowledge of the truth that is in accordance with godliness, ²in the hope of eternal life that God, who never lies, promised before the ages began—³in due time he revealed his word through the proclamation with which I have been entrusted by the command of God our Savior,

4 To Titus, my true child*a* in the faith we share:
Grace*b* and peace from God the Father and Christ Jesus our Savior.

5 I left you behind in Crete for this reason, so that you should put in order what remained to be done and should appoint elders in every town, as I directed you: ⁶someone who is blameless, married only once,*c* whose children are believers, not accused of debauchery and not rebellious. ⁷For a bishop,*d* as God's steward, must be blameless; he must not be arrogant or quick-tempered or addicted to wine or violent or greedy for gain, ⁸but he must be hospitable,*e* a lover of goodness, self-controlled, upright, devout, and restrained, ⁹holding tightly to the trustworthy word of the teaching, so that he may be able both to exhort with sound instruction and to refute those who contradict it.

10 There are also many rebellious people, idle talkers and deceivers, especially those of the circumcision; ¹¹they must be silenced, since they are upsetting whole families by teaching for sordid gain what it is not right to teach. ¹²It was one of them, their very own prophet, who said,
"Cretans are always liars, vicious brutes, lazy gluttons."
¹³That testimony is true. For this reason rebuke them sharply, so that they may become

a 1.4 Gk *legitimate child*   *b* 1.4 Other ancient authorities read *Grace, mercy,*   *c* 1.6 Gk *husband of one wife*   *d* 1.7 Or *an overseer*   *e* 1.8 Gk *a friend of foreigners*

1:1–4 Salutation. Longest introduction among the Pastorals. Missing a traditional thanksgiving (cf. 2 Tim. 1:3–7). **1:1** *Servant*, or "slave," *of God* (2 Sam. 7:5; Jer. 25) . . . *God's elect* (Isa. 65:9). Concepts from the Hebrew Bible; see also Rom. 1:1; 8:33; Phil. 1:1; Col. 3:12; 2 Tim. 2:10. Cf. 2 Tim. 1:1. *Knowledge of the truth* is thematic to the Pastorals (see also 1 Tim. 2:4; 2 Tim. 3:7) and necessary for true godliness/piety. *Godliness.* See **"Godliness as Roman *Pietas*," p. 2040.** **1:2** *God, who never lies* contrasts against lying Cretans (1:12).

1:5–16 Titus in Crete. 1:5 *I left you behind in Crete* implies Paul had previously been in Crete with Titus, though such an itinerary is absent from Acts. **1:5–8** *Appoint elders in every town. . . . For a bishop.* Pastoral Paul speaks interchangeably between elders and bishops here, which may indicate that bishops are selected from among an appointed group of elders. Cf. similar qualifications in 1 Tim. 3:2–7. **1:9** *Sound instruction.* A thematic concern for Pastoral Paul, especially prominent in Titus (see Titus 1:13; 2:1, 2, 8; 1 Tim. 1:10; 6:3; 2 Tim. 1:13; 4:3). *Sound* or healthy instruction is a medical metaphor describing correct teaching, common in ancient philosophy. Socrates was regarded as a physician of the soul. **1:10** *Those of the circumcision* is either a reference to historic Pauline opponents to make the letter seem more authentic or reflects the persistence of the circumcision debate. See also Titus 3:9. See **"Ethnic Prejudice in Titus?," p. 2053.** **1:12** *It was one of them, their very own prophet* likely refers to the sixth- or fifth-century BCE diviner, philosopher, and poet Epimenides of Crete. *Cretans are always liars, vicious brutes, lazy gluttons* reflects popular prejudicial caricatures of Cretans. See **"Ethnic Prejudice in Titus?," p. 2053.** Possible reference to the liar's paradox (i.e., Can a Cretan's statement be true that all Cretans are liars?), which may imply that the opponents use such philosophical mind games to appear intellectually sophisticated. Cf. Tertullian (*Treatise on the Soul* 20), who simply interpreted Paul

Going Deeper: Ethnic Prejudice in Titus? (Titus 1:10–14)

In Titus 1:10–14, Pastoral Paul describes his opponents as "those of the circumcision," who believe in "Jewish myths" and embody the worst qualities of Cretans. Pastoral Paul cites a line of poetry from the sixth- or fifth-century BCE diviner, philosopher, and poet Epimenides of Crete denigrating Cretans as "always liars, vicious brutes, lazy gluttons" (1:12). These Cretan vices comprised stock derogatory stereotypes for Cretans. For example, Cretans were thought to have a barbaric lust for wealth, which drove some to become mercenaries and pirates. Also, Cretans were infamously known for their claim to have Zeus's tomb—implying that Zeus had died—which had to be a lie.

In a move that is all too familiar to how Christian evangelists and missionaries describe their potential proselytes—including North American Indigenous peoples, who are often portrayed as wild, lazy drunkards—Pastoral Paul uses derogatory stereotypes and caricatures to depict the depravity of Cretans and superstitions of Jews in order to delegitimize rival teachers and accentuate the superiority of his position. It seems like Pastoral Paul trades in an ancient form of racism or at least ethnic superiority.

Without justifying or excusing Pastoral Paul's denigration of Cretans and Jewish practices, we might better understand the rhetorical situation of this passage by turning to postcolonial studies. In particular, anthropologists and sociologists have documented how ethnic groups subjugated under colonial or imperial rule denigrate others to secure limited resources and gain access to power for their own group. By denigrating other groups with prejudicial stereotypes, struggling ethnic groups can elevate their own status before the colonial "gaze" of the dominant culture. In such situations, particular groups are seen as more or less "civilized" along an ethnic hierarchy defined by the cultural preferences of the dominant society.

In the case of Titus, then, Pastoral Paul distinguishes ideal Christ followers from Cretans, whom elite Romans derided as full of vice despite appreciating their *ancient* culture, and Jews (or Judeans), whom elite Romans distrusted as seditious and superstitious, as part of a larger strategy at work within Titus of emboldening Christ followers to see themselves as possessing the epitome of philosophical virtues and piety (2:11–12). Pastoral Paul equips his audience with a strategy for envisioning themselves as civilized subjects capable of navigating a Roman imperial situation that was both suspicious of and potentially hostile to them.

T. Christopher Hoklotubbe

sound in the faith, [14]not paying attention to Jewish myths or to commandments of those who reject the truth. [15]To the pure all things are pure, but to the corrupt and unbelieving nothing is pure; their very minds and consciences are corrupted. [16]They profess to know God, but they deny him by their actions; they are detestable, disobedient, unfit for any good work.

2 But as for you, teach what is consistent with sound instruction. [2]Tell the older men to be temperate, serious, self-controlled, and sound in faith, in love, and in endurance.

3 Likewise, tell the older women to be reverent in behavior, not to be slanderers or enslaved to much wine; they are to teach what is good, [4]so that they may encourage the young women to love their husbands, to love their children, [5]to be self-controlled, chaste, good managers of the household, kind, submissive to their husbands, so that the word of God may not be discredited.

6 Likewise, urge the younger men to be

as branding Cretans as liars. **1:14** The charge that charlatans are leading Christians astray with Jewish *myths* is thematic to the Pastorals; see 1 Tim. 1:4, 7; 2 Tim. 4:4. Outside of the Pastorals, this charge only appears in 2 Pet. 1:16. **1:15** *To the pure all things are pure* may refer to Jewish dietary restrictions. Cf. Rom. 14:14, 23; 1 Tim. 4:3–5. Cf. 1 Cor. 8 for Paul's concern for the consciences of those who thought food sacrificed to idols was defiled.

2:1–15 Teach sound doctrine. Discussion of the proper relationships within the household of God. Cf. 1 Tim. 5:1–6:2. These "station codes" resemble the "household codes" found in Eph. 5:21–6:9; Col. 3:18–4:1; 1 Pet. 2:18–3:7. **2:5** *So that the word of God may not be discredited* reflects a concern that Christ-believing households must be properly managed and that women fulfill their proper roles as wives and mothers to ameliorate outsiders' suspicions that Christ believers are subverting traditional family values and norms (e.g., women working as celibate, itinerant preachers; cf. 1 Tim. 2:9–15). Additionally, Titus's teaching (2:7–8) and the behavior of the enslaved (2:9–10) must not reflect poorly on

self-controlled [7]in all things, offering yourself as a model of good works and in your teaching offering integrity, gravity, [8]and sound speech that cannot be censured; then any opponent will be put to shame, having nothing evil to say of us.

9 Urge slaves to be submissive to their masters in everything, to be pleasing, not talking back, [10]not stealing, but showing complete and perfect fidelity, so that in everything they may be an ornament to the teaching of God our Savior.

11 For the grace of God has appeared, bringing salvation to all,[f] [12]training us to renounce impiety and worldly passions and in the present age to live lives that are self-controlled, upright, and godly, [13]while we wait for the blessed hope and the manifestation of the glory of our great God and Savior,[g] Jesus Christ. [14]He it is who gave himself for us that he might redeem us from all iniquity and purify for himself a people of his own who are zealous for good deeds.

15 Declare these things; exhort and reprove with all authority.[h] Let no one look down on you.

3 Remind them to be subject to rulers and authorities, to be obedient, to be ready for every good work, [2]to speak evil of no one, to avoid quarreling, to be gentle, and to show every courtesy to everyone. [3]For we ourselves were once foolish, disobedient, led astray, slaves to various passions and pleasures, passing our days in malice and envy, despicable, hating one another. [4]But when the goodness and loving kindness of God our Savior appeared, [5]he saved us, not because of any works of righteousness that we had done, but according to his mercy, through the water[i] of rebirth and renewal by the Holy Spirit. [6]This Spirit he poured out on us richly through Jesus Christ our Savior, [7]so that, having been justified by his grace, we might become heirs according to the hope of eternal life. [8]The saying is sure.

I desire that you insist on these things, so that those who have come to believe in God may be careful to devote themselves to good works; these things are excellent and profitable to everyone. [9]But avoid stupid

f 2.11 Or has appeared to all, bringing salvation   g 2.13 Or of the great God and our Savior   h 2.15 Gk commandment   i 3.5 Gk washing

the church. **2:7** *Good works.* A thematic concern of the Pastorals; see Titus 1:16; 2:14; 3:1, 8, 14; 1 Tim. 2:10; 5:10, 25; 6:18; 2 Tim. 2:21; 3:17; cf. Eph. 2:10; Col. 1:10; 2 Thess. 2:17. **2:9–10** Cf. 1 Tim. 6:1–2. *Not talking back* may reflect the reality that the enslaved speaking their minds to their masters was perceived negatively as "back talk." Cf. Eph. 6:5–9; Col. 3:22–4:1, both at least instruct masters. *Ornament to the teaching of God our Savior* gaslights the alternative theological vision that life in Christ entails a greater sense of brotherhood and dignity, if not freedom for the enslaved. See **"Paul, Enslavement, and Freedom," p. 1964**. **2:11–14** *For the grace of God has appeared . . . training us.* Pastoral Paul describes the preceding duties and virtues as part of the philosophical education found in Christ. **2:12** *Training*, or "educating," *us to renounce impiety and worldly passions* reflects Hellenistic moral philosophy concerned with training students to control their *passions* and live virtuously. *Self-controlled, upright, and godly* reflects philosophical discussions that all virtues descend from three or four cardinal virtues, implying that Christ's education embodies some of the highest ideals in Greek and Roman society. **2:13** *Manifestation of the glory of our great God and Savior, Jesus Christ* may describe Jesus Christ as God. But if the textual tradition that reads *the glory of [the] great God* is correct, then two persons are described. On *manifestation*, see note on 2 Tim. 1:10. **2:14** *Redeem*, or "ransom," *us from all iniquity.* Cf. Mark 10:45. *Purify for himself a people of his own* alludes to Exod. 19:5 and God's election of Israel as "special" or "a people of his own" among the nations if they will keep the covenant. **2:15** Cf. 1 Tim. 4:12.

3:1–11 Maintain good deeds. 3:1 Cf. 1 Tim. 2:1–2; Rom. 13:1–7; 1 Pet. 2:13–17. Because many Christians refused to fully participate in public sacrifices and oaths showing their loyalty to the Roman emperor, considering such practices as idolatry, it was important for Christians to show their loyalty and patriotism in appropriate ways (see **"Idolatry," p. 2023**). **3:4–8** Pastoral Paul seems to incorporate a piece of early Christian liturgy, which culminates in *the saying is sure*, a thematic phrase in the Pastorals; see 1 Tim. 1:15; 3:1; 4:9; 2 Tim. 2:11. **3:5–6** *Not because of any works of righteousness.* Cf. 2 Tim. 1:9; Rom. 3:27–28; 9:11–12; Gal. 2:16–17; Eph. 2:9. *But according to his mercy.* Ephesians 2:4; 1 Pet. 1:3. *Through the water*, or "washing," *of rebirth* references baptism. Cf. 1 Cor. 6:11; Eph. 5:26; Acts 22:16. *And renewal by the Holy Spirit . . . poured out on us richly through Jesus Christ.* Acts 2:1–4, 17–18, 38. **3:7** *Justified by his grace.* Romans 3:24. *We might become heirs.* Romans 8:17; Gal. 3:29; Eph. 3:6. *According to the hope of eternal life.* Titus 1:2; Rom. 5:1–2. **3:8–11** The closing charge repeats themes from 1:10–16. **3:9** *Avoid*

controversies, genealogies, dissensions, and quarrels about the law, for they are unprofitable and worthless. [10]After a first and second admonition, have nothing more to do with anyone who causes divisions, [11]since you know that such a person is perverted and sinful, being self-condemned.

[12] When I send Artemas to you, or Tychicus, do your best to come to me at Nicopolis, for I have decided to spend the winter there. [13]Make every effort to send Zenas the lawyer and Apollos on their way, and see that they lack nothing. [14]And let people learn to devote themselves to good works in order to meet urgent needs, so that they may not be unproductive.

[15] All who are with me send greetings to you. Greet those who love us in the faith. Grace be with all of you.[j]

_j_ 3.15 Other ancient authorities add _Amen_

stupid _controversies._ See 1 Tim. 6:4; 2 Tim. 2:23. _Genealogies._ See note 1 Tim. 1:4. Pastoral Paul does not clarify the precise nature of these controversies or doctrinal concerns. _Quarrels about the law._ See Titus 1:11; 1 Tim. 1:7. **3:10** Cf. Rom. 16:17. **3:11** _Perverted._ Galatians 1:7; see also Jude 4.

3:12–15 Final messages and benediction. 3:12 _Artemas._ Otherwise unknown. _Tychicus._ See note on 2 Tim. 4:12. _Nicopolis._ Located on the western coast of Greece. According to the itinerary established in the Pastorals, Pastoral Paul will send Titus further north up the Adriatic coast to Dalmatia after he arrives in Nicopolis (2 Tim. 4:10). Otherwise, Dalmatia is not mentioned in any other Pauline itinerary in the New Testament. Traveling by sea in the _winter_ was near impossible. **3:13** _Zenas._ Otherwise unknown. _Apollos._ Perhaps the same mentioned in Acts 18:24–19:7. **3:15** _Grace be with all of you._ The same benediction as in 1 Tim. 6:21 and 2 Tim. 4:22, except here the _you_ is plural.

THE LETTER OF PAUL TO PHILEMON

Authorship, Date, and Literary History

Scholarly consensus has secured Philemon's place among the undisputed Pauline Epistles. Most dating schemas situate this letter with the latest of Paul's writings on the basis of narrative details. Paul describes himself not only as an "old man" in v. 9 but also as being imprisoned on account of his evangelism—a circumstance characteristic of his later ministry, according to the Acts of the Apostles. Modern scholars posit dates from the mid-50s to the early 60s CE based on when and where one presumes Paul to have been imprisoned on the occasion of the letter, a detail he does not disclose. What is clear is that Paul is writing to a Christ-following man named Philemon who hosts home gatherings. As is the case with other undisputed Pauline Epistles, the gathering constitutes the audience for Paul's writing. This short letter differs from the rest in that it is written directly to Philemon about his enslaved man, Onesimus, who has come under Paul's care in jail. Paul has thoughts on how Onesimus should be welcomed within the gathering upon Onesimus's coming release from jail and return to Philemon. It is important to note that we know very little from the text about the situation among Onesimus, Philemon, and Paul. We know Onesimus and Paul met in jail; how either one got there is speculative, since no clues exist in the letter. We also know Onesimus is enslaved by Philemon and that there has been some rupture in their relationship that Paul advocates to be mended.

The Difficulty of Historicizing Philemon

Reconstructing the context of Philemon showcases the varied manner in which people have come to conceptualize early Christian texts as historical sources. Acts, while providing the most detail about Paul's ministry, is far from a disinterested source (see **"Paul in Acts and in the Letters," p. 1997**). Its expressed focus is narrating the transmission of the gospel from Christ's resurrection to Paul's presumed death in Rome. Acts details three places where Paul was imprisoned—first, one night in Philippi (16:11–40); then two years in Caesarea Maritima (23:23–26:32); and finally, two years under house arrest in Rome (28:16–32). The first imprisonment hardly constitutes enough time for Paul to write a letter and is usually dismissed as a result. The disputed Pauline Letter to the Colossians is also often brought into these deliberations because of its similarities to Philemon. It too discusses slavery (see Col. 3 and **"Slavery and the Household Code," p. 2025**), and like Philemon, it mentions Archippus, Onesimus, Epaphras, Mark, Aristarchus, Demas, and Luke. The only other names from Philemon not mentioned are Philemon and Apphia. The overlap has prompted many scholars to harmonize the accounts and to furthermore hypothesize where Onesimus most likely could have been arrested (if he was indeed arrested). As a Judean port city, Caesarea Maritima seems quite a distance for an enslaved person to travel if Philemon's household was anywhere near Colossae and is a curious destination for a gentile. Rome is also far but had an extant tradition of fugitive enslaved people and was not as provincial as Judea. Yet nothing in the text indicates Onesimus's crime or his status as a runaway.

Some scholars have speculated that Ephesus may be the site of Paul's incarceration, as it is not too far from Colossae and coincides with Paul's evangelistic work in Asia Minor. However, no biblical text explicitly locates Paul being imprisoned there. Sometimes scholars will draw on second-century CE and later traditions to argue for Ephesus or Rome. For instance, 1 Clem. 5:5–6 describes Paul as having been imprisoned seven times with no mention of location. The lack of early evidence leaves any conclusion open to hagiography and synergetic conjectures. While contextualizing the Letter to Philemon remains challenging, the epistle nevertheless presents an intriguing portrait of the communal dynamics of a Pauline collective.

Reading Guide

Philemon underscores the importance of "partnership" as a paradigm for the formation of the Pauline community (Gk. *koinonia*; see Phlm. 6). Where one might expect imprisonment to stymie Christian fellowship, Paul makes an argument to the contrary. Separation is an opportunity for partners in Christ to recollect their coworkers' own trust in Christ. This commemoration strengthens not only the partnership of the coworkers but also their grasp of Christ. Paul encourages the gathering at Philemon's home to do what is right in that vein, especially as it pertains to Philemon's enslaved man, Onesimus (v. 8). In jail, Paul and Onesimus have developed a bond as parent and child in the gospel (vv. 10–13). Paul thinks Philemon should receive Onesimus as a partner, "a beloved brother" (v. 16), just as Paul receives Onesimus (vv. 1,

7). Paul recalls Philemon having "refreshed" the weary saints with his Christlike example (see v. 7) and challenges him to do so again by welcoming, rather than punishing, Onesimus (v. 20). Paul lovingly insists (v. 9) that Philemon bill him for any debts incurred by Onesimus (v. 18), and yet the letter notes that Philemon already owes Paul nothing short of his life, vv. 19–20. Thus Philemon can show his faith by showing hospitality to the released Onesimus and to Paul, who fully expects to be visiting soon (v. 22). Paul lays the burden of this gospel partnership on Philemon and his treatment of Onesimus (v. 14).

For all of Paul's evangelistic boldness (v. 8), his ambivalence on slavery has been of service to abolitionists and enslavers alike (see **"Frederick Douglass, Paul, and Onesimus," p. 2058**). Paul calls Philemon to treat Onesimus as "more than a slave" in v. 16, a potential case for doing away with the power differential between them. Yet at the same time, Paul seems unbothered by Philemon having Onesimus "back forever," as if human ownership is indeed one among many social relationships to be expected in ancient Mediterranean home gatherings. In this, Paul is a product of the early Roman Empire and leaves readers throughout history to decide whether and how the social politics of slavery should feature in their own contexts.

Richard W. Newton, Jr.

1 Paul, a prisoner of Christ Jesus, and Timothy our brother,

To our beloved coworker Philemon, ²to our*ᵃ* sister Apphia, to our fellow soldier Archippus, and to the church in your*ᵇ* house:

3 Grace to you and peace from God our Father and the Lord Jesus Christ.

4 I thank my God always when I mention you*ᶜ* in my prayers, ⁵because I hear of your love for all the saints and your faith toward the Lord Jesus. ⁶I pray that the partnership of your faith may become effective as you comprehend all the good that we*ᵈ* share in Christ.*ᵉ* ⁷I have*ᶠ* indeed received much joy and encouragement from your love, because the hearts of

the saints have been refreshed through you, my brother.

8 For this reason, though I am more than bold enough in Christ to command you to do the right thing, ⁹yet I would rather appeal to you on the basis of love—and I, Paul, do this as an old man and now also as a prisoner of Christ Jesus.*ᵍ* ¹⁰I am appealing to you for my child, Onesimus, whose father I have become during my imprisonment. ¹¹Formerly he was useless to

a 2 Other ancient authorities add beloved   b 2 Gk your is singular   c 4 In verses 4–21, you is singular   d 6 Other ancient authorities read you (plural)   e 6 Other ancient authorities add Jesus   f 7 Other ancient authorities read we have   g 9 Or as an ambassador of Christ Jesus, and now also his prisoner

1–3 This letter commences with a typical opening for the genre. It introduces the sender and then the addressee. Pleasantries are also not uncommon (see v. 3), though some ancient examples include a direct presentation of grievances or move into the body of the letter. **1** Timothy is named here as a cosigner of the letter, but the Greek has no pronoun, just that he is a *brother*. Philemon is named first and described as an endeared colleague, an indication of him being the primary addressee of the letter. **2** Apphia is named in familial terms, while Archippus, who also appears in Col. 4:17, is described in military terms. Adding to these the ones called together at Philemon's house, this range of relationships among members speaks to some of the ways in which the social dynamics of *church* (Gk. "ekklēsia") were understood in the first century CE. **3** These pleasantries are a common refrain in Pauline writings. Similar expressions are seen in other letters in the New Testament, suggesting a developing epistolary, if not liturgical, tradition recognized by the earliest Christians.

4–7 Paul highlights what Philemon has accomplished while also laying out what he sees as the potential of Philemon's ministry. **4** Beyond requests or formulas, prayer is an occasion to think about others in the broader Christian partnership (see v. 6).

5–7 The saints are connected through their care for one another as well as their mutual dependence on Jesus. Paul understands that these relationships deepen in proportion to one's understanding in Christ, setting the stage for Paul's plea in v. 9. Regarding the *hearts of the saints*, see vv. 10–12. **7** Philemon is noted as a brother, but Paul seemingly speaks as a more knowing older brother (see v. 9). **8–9** Paul uses the rhetorical technique of presenting himself as an authority while choosing to speak congenially, accentuating his lowliness to make a forceful case with humility. This technique is a feature of Pauline writings (see Phil. 3).

10–12 Onesimus is also named in Col. 4:9. The kinship metaphor among Paul, Philemon, and Onesimus raises the question of who knows best regarding the situation with Onesimus. Philemon may be

Making Connections: Frederick Douglass, Paul, and Onesimus (Philemon)

In a speech given on May 18, 1846, Frederick Douglass said the following:

> Slaveholders are not only ministers and members of Churches, but they openly defend it, by quoting the fact of Paul sending Onesimus to Philemon, and they allege that that case shows that neither Christ nor his apostles had any objection to men holding slaves as property. Men are sold to build Churches—babies are sold to buy Bibles. . . . The blood sold on the auction-block goes into the treasury of the Church, and the pulpit in return covers it with the garb of Christianity. . . . This is the religious state of things in America. . . . When the Slave-trade is going on most prosperously, then there is the most money given to support "the Gospel," as they call it; but it is not the Gospel of Christ, it is not the Gospel according to Matthew, Mark, Luke, or John, but it is a Gospel according to slavery. (Frederick Douglass, "Emancipation Is an Individual, a National, and an International Responsibility: An Address Delivered in London, England, on May 18, 1846")

The use of the Philemon letter became pronounced as nineteenth-century defenders of slavery desired to support the Fugitive Slave Act of 1850, a federal resolution that required citizens in free states to participate in the return of enslaved people who had escaped human bondage. The "religious state of things in America," for Douglass, was a "Gospel according to slavery." Douglass points to the contemporary use of this ancient biblical story—especially Paul's action to send Onesimus back—as one example of how proslavers read their Bible. Although Douglass does not provide an alternative interpretation within this speech, he shared the perspective of nineteenth-century abolitionists who emphasized Paul's words that Philemon would receive Onesimus "back for the long term, no longer as a slave but more than a slave, a beloved brother" (vv. 15–16). For abolitionists, Paul's charge was nothing less than a declaration of Onesimus's freedom. The intention of the first-century apostle (Paul) is difficult to discern, since Paul desired to send Onesimus back. That ambiguity explains why both sides of the slavery argument could make use of the letter to support their own cause. A thorough understanding of Paul's position on human bondage requires answering several important questions, such as: What did Paul mean by 1 Cor. 7:21 ("Even if you can gain your freedom, make the most of it") or Gal. 3:28 ("There is no longer slave or free . . . , for all of you are one in Christ Jesus"; see **"Paul, Enslavement, and Freedom," p. 1964**)? What is the relationship between Paul's (authentic seven) letters and the references to "slaves obey your masters" in the Pauline Letters written in Paul's name (see **"Introduction to the Pauline Letters," pp. 1713–16**)?

Emerson B. Powery

you, but now he is indeed useful[b] to[i] you and to me. [12]I am sending him, that is, my own heart, back to you.[j] [13]I wanted to keep him with me so that he might minister to me in your place during my imprisonment for the gospel, [14]but I preferred to do nothing without your consent in order that your good deed might be voluntary and not something forced. [15]Perhaps this is the reason he was separated from you for a while, so that you might have him back for the long term, [16]no longer as a slave but more than a slave, a beloved brother—especially to me but how much more to you, both in the flesh and in the Lord.

17 So if you consider me your partner, welcome him as you would welcome me. [18]If he has wronged you in any way or owes you

b 11 The name Onesimus means *useful* or *beneficial*
i 11 Other ancient authorities read *both to*   j 12 Other ancient authorities read *you; receive him*

Onesimus's master, but Paul is Onesimus's father. Additionally, the Greek term for *heart* is more literally "innards" (Gk. "splanchna"; cf. spleen), another metaphorical term of endearment.

13–18 Paul expresses a desire to keep Onesimus with him instead of sending him back to Philemon so that *he might minister . . . during my imprisonment for the gospel*, literally "in the chains of the gospel" (v. 13; cf. Phil. 1:13; Eph. 6:20). *Was separated* (Gk. "echoristhē," dislocated or confiscated); while the use of the passive voice here indicates that Onesimus is not responsible for the "separation" from Philemon, scholars debate whether this phrasing constitutes Paul mentioning Onesimus's "runaway"

anything, charge that to me. [19]I, Paul, am writing this with my own hand: I will repay it. I say nothing about your owing me even your own self. [20]Yes, brother, let me have this benefit from you in the Lord! Refresh my heart in Christ.[k] [21]Confident of your obedience, I am writing to you, knowing that you will do even more than I ask.

22 One thing more: prepare a guest room for me, for I am hoping through your prayers to be restored to you.

23 Epaphras, my fellow prisoner in Christ Jesus, sends greetings to you,[l] [24]and so do Mark, Aristarchus, Demas, and Luke, my coworkers.

25 The grace of the Lord Jesus Christ be with your spirit.[m]

k 20 Other ancient authorities read *in the Lord*　l 23 Here *you* is singular　m 25 Other ancient authorities add *Amen*

status (v. 15). *No longer . . . but more than a slave.* Literally "above a slave." Although the phrasing could be read as vague, Paul could be implying a release from enslavement, where Onesimus would be treated as a *beloved brother* (v. 16; cf. 1 Cor. 7:20–24; Gal. 3:28). *Partner* (Gk. "koinonon," indicating shared responsibility and joint participation in a common project), a term Paul uses for Titus (2 Cor. 8:23) as well as the Philippian community (Phil. 4:15; cf. 2 Cor. 8:4); as Paul's partner, Philemon is being asked to *welcome* (Gk. "proslabou," receive) Onesimus as he would Paul himself, charging any injustices or debts Onesimus has incurred to Paul (vv. 17–18).

19–21 Whether Paul employed a scribe (cf. Rom. 16:22) or had been writing the letter himself (cf. Gal. 6:11), the aside in v. 19 conveys his guarantee to pay Philemon for any debts Onesimus has incurred. Following this, Paul applies the rhetorical technique from vv. 8–9 to humbly emphasize his upper hand in any debate on this matter. The call to *refresh* Paul's *heart* and to obey his command mirrors the language and framing of their partnership in Christ as found in vv. 4–9.

23 The names listed in this verse also appear in Col. 4:10–17.

THE LETTER TO THE HEBREWS

Author and Date

Much about Hebrews remains obscure. We do not know where or when it was written or the name of its author. Although sometimes attributed to Paul, its structure, style, and theological ideas point to someone else. Because of its brief mention of Timothy (Heb. 13:23), the men and women who worked with Paul, including Barnabas, Apollos, Priscilla, and Luke, have proved intriguing possibilities. However, none of these suggestions is beyond dispute, and so the author remains unknown. The use of a masculine participle (11:32) suggests that the author is a man. He writes as a teacher and pastor skilled in the use of rhetoric and with knowledge of the Hebrew Bible in Greek translation, which he frequently quotes. The author was not one of Jesus's original disciples but heard the message about Jesus from them (2:3), indicating a probable date in the last half of the first century CE.

Genre

Although the ending of Hebrews resembles a letter, including personal requests and greetings (13:18–25), the rest of this work contains no standard letter features like a greeting or opening prayer. Given Hebrews's focus on speaking (2:5; 5:11; 6:9; 8:1; 9:5) and its urgent appeals to its recipients, it is best understood as a sermon or "word of exhortation" (13:22).

Audience and Destination

The author writes to a congregation of disheartened followers of Jesus for whom the journey of faith had become a difficult struggle. Although no one from their congregation had been martyred for their faith (12:4), they experienced and witnessed opposition and abuse from those around them, including the loss of possessions and imprisonment of some (10:32–34). Their confession of faith in Jesus had damaged their public reputations and standing in society. They bore uneasily the shame that their identification with Jesus brought, and they were losing their confidence. To these struggling believers, the author writes this "word of exhortation" or encouragement (13:22). He wants them to focus not on what they have lost or given up but on what they have—God's grace and mercy made available to them through the life and death of Jesus. Jesus now serves as their mediator before God (8:6; 9:15; 12:24), brokering a new relationship with God. As a result, they should hold fast to their confession and boldly approach God in worship to find the help they need (4:14–16).

The location of the audience remains unknown, although Rome is suggested as a possibility because of the greetings from "those from Italy" (13:24) and the use of Hebrews by Clement of Rome, a church leader of the late first century. The title "Hebrews" was added during the second century, but the audience may well have consisted of both Jews and gentiles who had become followers of Jesus. The author assumes the audience has deep knowledge of and familiarity with the Septuagint (the Gk. translation of the Hebrew Bible) and Jewish worship.

Interpreting Hebrews

The assumption that readers know Israel's Scriptures poses an initial challenge for contemporary readers. Understanding the author's use of imagery, symbols, and practices requires a willingness to read with care and explore the texts and traditions that lie in the background. The study notes for Hebrews provide an initial guide for that exploration.

A second challenge is similar: grasping the Greco-Roman or Hellenistic intellectual environment that the author and his first readers shared (see **"The Bible in Its Ancient Contexts," pp. 2150–52**). Hellenistic Judaism, in particular, shapes the language, rhetoric, and interpretation of the author. Contrasts between earthly and heavenly realities, for example, at times focus on a vertical axis that distinguishes "below" from "above," showing a debt to the language of Middle Platonism. At other times, differences between earth and heaven are described as being along a temporal, horizontal axis, juxtaposing the present age and the age to come, using language drawn from apocalyptic Judaism. While scholars continue to debate which system of thought is more essential, the debate demonstrates that from the beginning, Christians who reflected on the meaning of Christ's life, death, and exaltation engaged both the Scriptures of Israel and the intellectual traditions of the Greco-Roman world. This combination is a key component of the text's theological logic.

The history of interpretation of Hebrews provides a third challenge. Readers have too often assumed that Hebrews reflects the separation of Judaism and Christianity that only developed well after the book was written and that the author is arguing for the superiority of Christianity over Judaism. Such anachronistic reading forms part of the tragic history of Christian anti-Judaism and anti-Semitism and misrepresents the author's purpose. Writing within a Hellenistic Jewish framework, he argues for the crucial significance of the Anointed One ("Messiah," from Hebrew tradition, or "Christ," according to the Gk. equivalent) whom many Jews in the Second Temple period anticipated. This focus on the Messiah's importance calls for a reformulation of religious practice but not a rejection of Jewish heritage. The author finds precedent for such reform within the context of the Hebrew Bible itself, particularly in Jeremiah's vision of the new covenant (Jer. 31:31–34; see Heb. 8:8–12). Careful attention to the historical context here is vital in guarding against anti-Jewish readings (see **"Supersessionism," p. 1647**).

Given these challenges, many find reading Hebrews a daunting task. Focusing on the author's main point—the greatness of Christ the High Priest—will enable readers to follow the argument more easily and to appreciate the rhetorical skill and beauty of Hebrews.

Reading Guide

Hebrews is a comparison or series of comparisons with a purpose: grasping the key importance of Jesus as a means of access to God, the author argues, will inspire faithful endurance in the face of suffering and persecution. After an initial prologue that sets out central themes (1:1–4), the author argues that the Son is superior to angels (1:5–2:18) and surpasses even Moses (3:1–6). He also warns against imitating those who followed Moses out of Egypt but rebelled (3:7–4:13), before discussing Christ's qualifications for priesthood (5:1–10). He warns his readers against sluggishness, too, and calls them to maturity (5:11–6:12). Stressing that God's promises are reliable, he explains Jesus's priesthood in terms of the oath God swore in Ps. 110:4 that the Son would be an eternal priest "according to the order of Melchizedek" (6:20; 6:13–7:28).

That discussion brings the author to his main point. Jesus is unsurpassed as the High Priest, serving in a heavenly sanctuary as a mediator of a new covenant, offering a sacrifice of his own blood once for all (8:1–10:18). He encourages his audience to draw near to God in worship and to hold fast to their confession, warning that rejection leads to judgment and encouraging them to press forward, enduring suffering (10:19–39). He upholds for emulation those who demonstrated faithfulness in the Hebrew Bible (11:1–39), culminating with the example of Jesus (12:1–4) and the plea to endure trials for the sake of divine training (12:5–17). In a final comparison, he contrasts the pilgrimages to Mount Sinai and the heavenly Jerusalem, warning once more to listen to God's voice (12:18–29). His closing chapter traces the connections between ethical living and the worship of God (13:1–17), ending with personal requests, greetings, and words of blessing (13:18–25).

Bryan J. Whitfield

1 Long ago God spoke to our ancestors in many and various ways by the prophets, ²but in these last days he has spoken to us by a Son,[a] whom he appointed heir of all things, through whom he also created the worlds. ³He is the reflection of God's glory and the exact imprint of God's very being, and he sustains[b] all things by his powerful word. When he had made purification for[c] sins, he sat down at the right hand of the Majesty on high, ⁴having become as much superior to angels as the name he has inherited is more excellent than theirs.

a 1.2 Or *the Son*   *b* 1.3 Or *bears along*   *c* 1.3 Other ancient authorities add *our*

1:1–4 In a carefully crafted prologue, the author contrasts two eras: *long ago* and *in these last days*. While God speaks in both, the speech *by the prophets* came *in many and various ways*. The speech *by a Son*, later named as Jesus (2:9), is unified, which is a mark of excellence. With this comparison, the author asserts the Son's superiority. Just as Roman emperors appointed their biological or adopted sons as their heirs, so God appointed the Son *heir of all things*. Jesus also functions as God's agent in creation (see also John 1:3; 1 Cor. 8:6; Col. 1:16). The Son is the *reflection* or radiance of God's glory, revealing God's power and presence, and *the exact imprint of God's very being*, faithfully representing God. The Son *sustains all things*, bearing creation along to the present. Acting as a high priest, he has *made purification for sins* and is now seated at God's right hand, a position of greatest importance and honor. See **"Priests," p. 176**, and **"Sin," p. 150**. He inherits a name greater than the names of the angels (Phil. 2:9–10).

5 For to which of the angels did God[d] ever say,
 "You are my Son;
    today I have begotten you"?
Or again,
 "I will be his Father,
    and he will be my Son"?
[6]And again, when he brings the firstborn into the world, he says,
 "Let all God's angels worship him."
[7]Of the angels he says,
 "He makes his angels winds
    and his servants flames of fire."
[8]But of the Son he says,
 "Your throne, O God, is[e] forever and ever,
    and the scepter of righteousness is the
       scepter of your[f] kingdom.
[9] You have loved righteousness and hated
    lawlessness;[g]
 therefore God, your God, has anointed you
    with the oil of gladness beyond your
       companions."
[10]And,
 "In the beginning, Lord, you founded the
    earth,
    and the heavens are the work of your
       hands;
[11] they will perish, but you remain;
    they will all wear out like clothing;
[12] like a cloak you will roll them up,
    and like clothing[h] they will be changed.
 But you are the same,
    and your years will never end."

[13]And to which of the angels has he ever said,
 "Sit at my right hand
    until I make your enemies a footstool
       for your feet"?
[14]Are not all angels[i] spirits in the divine service, sent to serve for the sake of those who are to inherit salvation?

2 Therefore we must pay greater attention to what we have heard, so that we do not drift away. [2]For if the message declared through angels proved valid, and every transgression or disobedience received a just penalty, [3]how will we escape if we neglect so great a salvation? It was declared at first through the Lord, and it was confirmed for us by those who heard him, [4]while God added his testimony by signs and wonders and various miracles and by gifts of the Holy Spirit, distributed according to his will.

5 Now God[j] did not subject the coming world, about which we are speaking, to angels. [6]But someone has testified somewhere,
 "What are humans that you are mindful
    of them[k]
    or mortals that you care for them?[l]

d 1.5 Greek *he*   e 1.8 Or *God is your throne*   f 1.8 Other ancient authorities read *his*   g 1.9 Other ancient authorities read *wickedness*   h 1.12 Other ancient authorities lack *like clothing*   i 1.14 Gk *all of them*   j 2.5 Gk *he*   k 2.6 Gk *What is man that you are mindful of him?*   l 2.6 Gk *or the son of man that you care for him?* In the Hebrew of Psalm 8.4–6 both *man* and *son of man* refer to all humankind

1:5–14 The author argues the Son's superiority over the angels, first using a catena or chain of seven texts drawn from the Hebrew Scriptures, including five from Psalms. See **"Israel's Scriptures in the New Testament," p. 1725**. **1:5** Although groups of angels were named as "sons of God" (Gen. 6:2, 4; Ps. 29:1; Job 1:6), they were not individually called God's Son. The author stresses the unique identity of the Son with two quotations addressed to Israel's kings: Ps. 2:7, part of a coronation psalm, and 2 Sam. 7:14, from Nathan's prophetic oracle to David. See **"Son of God vs. Son of Man," p. 1774**. **1:6** Referring to the Son as the firstborn, a messianic title (Rom. 8:29; Col. 1:15; Rev. 1:5), the author quotes the Greek translation of Deut. 32:43 to show that the Son is worthy of angelic worship. **1:7–9** Unlike the angels, who are servants and like the short-lived elements of wind and fire (Ps. 104:4), the Son rules over an eternal kingdom (Ps. 45:6–7) as an anointed king. **1:10–12** The quotation of Ps. 102:25–27 underscores that in contrast to the brevity of heaven and earth that *will all wear out like clothing*, the Son's *years will never end*. **1:13** The author brackets this section with parallel questions (1:5, 13). His last quotation (Ps. 110:1) recalls the Son's position at God's right hand (1:3) and foreshadows the significant role of Ps. 110 in his argument (8:1; 10:12).

2:1–4 An initial warning. The author encourages his readers to *pay greater attention* to the message they have heard. Using a lesser-to-greater argument (9:13–14; 10:26–31; 12:25–29), he warns that there is danger in disregarding *the message declared through angels*, reflecting the ancient idea that angels transmitted the law (Deut. 33:2; Acts 7:53; Gal. 3:19). There is even more danger in neglecting the salvation *declared at first through the Lord*. Using legal terminology, he notes the law's validity but stresses that both witnesses and God's testimony *by signs and wonders and various miracles* (Exod. 7:3; Deut. 4:34; 6:22) and *by gifts of the Holy Spirit* confirm the new revelation.

2:5–9 The author interprets Ps. 8:4–6, which speaks of God's mindfulness and care for *humans* and *mortals*. Although the original Hebrew text carries a collective meaning for these expressions, the

⁷ You have made them for a little while
      lower[m] than the angels;
   you have crowned them with glory and
      honor,[n]

⁸   subjecting all things under their feet."

Now in subjecting all things to them, God[o] left nothing outside their control. As it is, we do not yet see everything in subjection to them, ⁹but we do see Jesus, who for a little while was made lower[p] than the angels, now crowned with glory and honor because of the suffering of death, so that by the grace of God[q] he might taste death for everyone.

10 It was fitting that God,[r] for whom and through whom all things exist, in bringing many children to glory, should make the pioneer of their salvation perfect through sufferings. ¹¹For the one who sanctifies and those who are sanctified all have one Father.[s] For this reason Jesus[t] is not ashamed to call them brothers and sisters, ¹²saying,

   "I will proclaim your name to my brothers
      and sisters;
   in the midst of the congregation I will
      praise you."

¹³And again,

   "I will put my trust in him."

And again,

   "Here am I and the children whom God
      has given me."

14 Since, therefore, the children share flesh and blood, he himself likewise shared the same things, so that through death he might destroy the one who has the power of death,

that is, the devil, ¹⁵and free those who all their lives were held in slavery by the fear of death. ¹⁶For it is clear that he did not come to help angels but the descendants of Abraham. ¹⁷Therefore he had to become like his brothers and sisters in every respect, so that he might become a merciful and faithful high priest in the service of God, to make a sacrifice of atonement for the sins of the people. ¹⁸Because he himself was tested by what he suffered, he is able to help those who are being tested.

3 Therefore, holy brothers and sisters, partners in a heavenly calling, consider Jesus, the apostle and high priest of our confession, ²who was faithful to the one who appointed him, just as Moses also "was faithful in all[u] God's[v] house." ³Yet Jesus[w] is worthy of more glory than Moses, just as the builder of a house has more honor than the house itself. ⁴(For every house is built by someone, but the builder of all things is God.) ⁵Now Moses was faithful in all God's[x] house as a servant, to testify to the things that would be spoken later. ⁶Christ, however, was faithful over God's[y] house as a son, and we are his house if we hold firm[z] the boldness and the pride inspired by hope.

m 2.7 Or *them only a little lower*   n 2.7 Other ancient authorities add *and set them over the works of your hands*   o 2.8 Gk *he*   p 2.9 Or *who was made a little lower*   q 2.9 Other ancient authorities read *apart from God*   r 2.10 Gk *he*   s 2.11 Gk *are all of one*   t 2.11 Gk *he*   u 3.2 Other ancient authorities lack *all*   v 3.2 Gk *his*   w 3.3 Gk *this one*   x 3.5 Gk *his*   y 3.6 Gk *his*   z 3.6 Other ancient authorities add *to the end*

author reads the psalm in Greek translation, where the words *humans* ("a human being") and *mortals* ("son of a human being") can refer either to an individual or to a group. The author uses both levels of meaning. On the individual level, he reads *mortals* ("son of a human being") as a reference to Jesus, who in the Synoptic Gospels uses that title for himself (Mark 2:10, 28; 8:31, 38). Because Jesus *for a little while was made lower than the angels* but is now *crowned with glory and honor*, Ps. 8:4–6 is understood to trace the path of Jesus's own life, death, and exaltation (Heb. 1:3). Yet the author also reads *humans* and *mortals* in the collective sense, joining the destiny of Jesus to that of all people.

2:10–18 The author makes the joint destiny of Jesus and all humanity explicit. **2:10** Jesus's journey becomes a path for the entire human family, as he is *the pioneer of their salvation.* **2:11** Jesus makes holy those he embraces as *brothers and sisters.* **2:12–13** The author draws on quotations from Ps. 22:22 and Isa. 8:17–18 to demonstrate Jesus's relationship to humankind. **2:14–15** Jesus's identification with human suffering and mortality ensures that his own death destroys *the one who has the power of death* and liberates humanity from *the fear of death.* **2:16–17** Coming to help *the descendants of Abraham* and becoming like them *in every respect* equips Jesus to serve as *a merciful and faithful high priest* and *to make a sacrifice of atonement.* Through that priestly role, the major focus of the sermon, Jesus opens new access to fellowship with God. See **"Priests," p. 176.**

3:1–6 The author demonstrates Jesus has been a faithful high priest (2:17) by showing Jesus is a better leader than Moses (3:1–6), whose faithfulness contrasted with the disloyalty of those he led out of Egypt (3:7–4:11). Jesus, as *apostle and high priest*, was faithful *just as Moses also "was faithful in all God's house."* This quotation, drawn from God's speech setting Moses above other prophets (Num.

7 Therefore, as the Holy Spirit says,
"Today, if you hear his voice,
⁸ do not harden your hearts as in the
  rebellion,
    as on the day of testing in the
    wilderness,
⁹ where your ancestors put me to the test,ᵃ
    though they had seen my works ¹⁰for
    forty years.
Therefore I was angry with that
    generation,
and I said, 'They always go astray in their
    hearts,
    and they have not known my ways.'
¹¹ As in my anger I swore,
    'They will not enter my rest.'"
¹²Take care, brothers and sisters, that none of
you may have an evil, unbelieving heart that
turns away from the living God. ¹³But exhort
one another every day, as long as it is called
"today," so that none of you may be hardened
by the deceitfulness of sin. ¹⁴For we have become partners of Christ, if only we hold our
first confidence firm to the end. ¹⁵As it is said,

"Today, if you hear his voice,
  do not harden your hearts as in the
    rebellion."

¹⁶Now who were they who heard and rebelled? Was it not all those who left Egypt
under the leadership of Moses? ¹⁷And with
whom was he angry forty years? Was it not
those who sinned, whose bodies fell in the
wilderness? ¹⁸And to whom did he swear that
they would not enter his rest, if not to those
who were disobedient? ¹⁹So we see that they
were unable to enter because of unbelief.

4 Therefore, while the promise of entering
his rest is still open, let us take care that
none of you should seem to have failed to
reach it. ²For indeed the good news came to
us just as to them, but the message they heard
did not benefit them because they were not
united by faith with those who listened.ᵇ ³For
we who have believed are entering that rest,
just as Godᶜ has said,

"As in my anger I swore,
  'They shall not enter my rest,'"

though his works were finished since the
foundation of the world. ⁴For somewhere
it speaks about the seventh day as follows,
"And God rested on the seventh day from all
his works." ⁵And again in this place it says,
"They shall not enter my rest." ⁶Since therefore it remains open for some to enter it and
those who formerly received the good news
failed to enter because of disobedience,

ᵃ 3.9 Other ancient authorities read *tempted me, tested me*
ᵇ 4.2 Other ancient authorities read *it did not meet with faith
in those who listened* ᶜ 4.3 Gk *he*

12:7), describes him as a servant in God's house. But *Jesus is worthy of more glory than Moses* for two reasons: he is the builder of the house (3:3), and he is faithful *as a Son*, not a servant (Num. 12:7, 8). As a result, the writer calls his audience, as part of Jesus's house, to be resolute in the face of persecution and disappointment.

3:7–4:11 Lessons from the story of Moses. 3:7–11 The author's emphasis on Moses's faithfulness and leadership serves here as a reminder to avoid the negative example of his followers. Having escaped oppression in Egypt, they survived the wilderness and arrived at the border of Canaan only to have several leaders who scouted the land report that entry was impossible (Num. 13–14; Deut. 1:19–45). Intending to return to Egypt, the people rebelled, and God determined that their generation would die in the wilderness. Rather than quoting here from Numbers or Deuteronomy, the author cites Ps. 95:7–11 instead, a choice befitting his focus on the importance of hearing God's voice. Key words from the psalm thus recur throughout Heb. 3:12–4:11. **3:12–15** The author first stresses that no one *may have an evil, unbelieving heart that turns away*, resisting God's will. His hearers must encourage one another to guard against unbelief *every day, as long as it is called "today."* Because they *have become partners of Christ*, they should hold firm to their original commitment to him. **3:16–19** Returning to the story of the unfaithful wilderness generation with a series of rhetorical questions, he highlights the conse-quences of their disobedience: their *bodies fell in the wilderness*, and they did not *enter his rest.* **4:1–11** The author switches from warning to promise, developing the theme of rest (Ps. 95:11) framed by two exhortations (4:1, 11). **4:1–5** God's promised *rest is still open* because those who hear the author's message have received *the good news* just as those who followed Moses had. While their faithlessness meant the message *did not benefit them*, the author and those he addresses *are entering that rest.* While their rest is not yet complete (4:11), they are experiencing the beginning of that fulfillment. To make clear that such rest is not about residing in the land of Canaan, the author now reframes the meaning of rest by quoting Gen. 2:2. **4:6–11** To demonstrate that rest *remains open*, the author quotes

Going Deeper: Rest as a Reward (Hebrews 4)

The author of Hebrews introduces the concept of rest in Heb. 3:7–11 with his citation of Ps. 95:7b–11. In the psalm, God swears that the generation who had seen God's deliverance from Egypt but rebelled in the wilderness would not enter "my rest," understood as a life in the promised land of Canaan, where prosperity and abundance would have been their reward. But Heb. 4:1–11, where both the noun and the verb "rest" occur repeatedly, develops a different concept of rest as a reward. The author does so by using a common Jewish exegetical technique and linking Ps. 95:11 with Gen. 2:2 based on the shared word "rest." The ring structure of the scriptural citations in this section sets off the importance of that link: the writer cites Ps. 95:7b–8a in the outermost ring (Heb. 3:15 and 4:7), Ps. 95:11 in the inner ring (Heb. 4:3 and 4:5), and Gen. 2:2 at the center (Heb. 4:4). The author uses this central quotation to reinterpret "my rest" in Ps. 95:11. Because Gen. 2:2 makes clear that God rested on the seventh day, the author focuses on God as the subject of rest. Instead of the rest that God gives to those who enter the land of Canaan, rest is now the rest of God in which God participates.

As a result, the rest that Christ followers are entering (Heb. 4:3) corresponds to the rest of the creation story. In this conception, which the author labels a Sabbath rest (4:9) or God's rest, their reward is a "rest from their labors" (4:10). In this way, the author redefines rest so that the reward is no longer the material rest of residing in the land of Canaan but has now become the transcendent rest of God. This pattern contrasting an earthly space with its heavenly counterpart continues throughout Hebrews with its comparisons of the earthly sanctuary and the heavenly one (9:1–14), of native soil and the heavenly homeland (11:13–16), and of Mount Sinai and the heavenly Jerusalem (12:18–24). Again and again, the horizon shifts so that geography no longer defines the goal of faithfulness. The reward of rest is no longer a physical place, a land that guarantees prosperity and earthly security, but is instead a transcendent space of relationship with God and Jesus where believers participate in the divine life of rest.

Bryan J. Whitfield

---

⁷again he sets a certain day—"today"—saying through David much later, in the words already quoted,

"Today, if you hear his voice,
do not harden your hearts."

⁸For if Joshua had given them rest, God*d* would not speak later about another day. ⁹So then, a Sabbath rest still remains for the people of God, ¹⁰for those who enter God's*e* rest also rest from their labors as God did from his. ¹¹Let us therefore make every effort to enter that rest, so that no one may fall through such disobedience as theirs.

12 Indeed, the word of God is living and active and sharper than any two-edged sword, piercing until it divides soul from spirit, joints from marrow; it is able to judge the thoughts and intentions of the heart. ¹³And before him no creature is hidden, but all are naked and laid bare to the eyes of the one to whom we must render an account.

14 Since, then, we have a great high priest who has passed through the heavens, Jesus, the Son of God, let us hold fast to our confession. ¹⁵For we do not have a high priest who is unable to sympathize with our weaknesses, but we have one who in every respect has been tested*f* as we are, yet without sin. ¹⁶Let us therefore approach the throne of grace with boldness, so that we may receive mercy and find grace to help in time of need.

d 4.8 Gk *he* *e* 4.10 Gk *his* *f* 4.15 Or *tempted*

Ps. 95:7–11 and stresses the word *today*. Because David, whom the author sees as the source of the psalm, writes many years after the entry to Canaan, the rest Joshua provided there for the next generation of Israelites (Josh. 21:43–44; 22:4; 23:1–2) is not the rest of Ps. 95:7–11. That rest instead refers to *another day*, a day of *Sabbath rest* or *God's rest*. See **"Rest as a Reward," p. 2065**.

4:12–13 This carefully constructed hymn opens with *the word of God* and concludes with the human word of response or *account*. Like God, this word is living (3:12; 9:14; 10:31; 12:22), cutting to the innermost heart (3:8, 10, 15; 4:7). Nothing escapes the Creator's scrutiny. All are fully known, vulnerable, and accountable.

4:14–16 After the warning of the hymn, the author returns to the promise of Jesus's work as high priest (2:17). As the Exalted One, he has passed through the heavens to occupy a place of honor (1:3, 13), but in his identification with humanity, he has also known every form of testing (2:14–18). Therefore, the audience should *hold fast* to their confession (3:1; 10:23) and *approach the throne of grace* to worship (Exod. 16:9; 34:32; Lev. 9:5; Num. 10:3–4), confident they will find grace and help.

5 Every high priest chosen from among mortals is put in charge of things pertaining to God on their behalf, to offer gifts and sacrifices for sins. [2]He is able to deal gently with the ignorant and wayward, since he himself is subject to weakness, [3]and because of this he must offer sacrifice for his own sins as well as for those of the people. [4]And one does not presume to take this honor but takes it only when called by God, just as Aaron was.

5 So also Christ did not glorify himself in becoming a high priest but was appointed by[g] the one who said to him,

"You are my Son;
today I have begotten you";

[6]as he says also in another place,

"You are a priest forever,
according to the order of
Melchizedek."

7 In the days of his flesh, Jesus[b] offered up prayers and supplications, with loud cries and tears, to the one who was able to save him from death, and he was heard because of his reverent submission. [8]Although he was a Son, he learned obedience through what he suffered, [9]and having been made perfect, he became the source of eternal salvation for all who obey him, [10]having been designated by God a high priest according to the order of Melchizedek.

11 About this[i] we have much to say that is hard to explain, since you have become sluggish in hearing. [12]For though by this time you ought to be teachers, you need someone to teach you again the basic elements of the oracles of God. You need milk, not solid food, [13]for everyone who lives on milk, being still an infant, is unskilled in the word of righteousness. [14]But solid food is for the mature, for those whose faculties have been trained by practice to distinguish good from evil.

6 Therefore let us go on[j] toward perfection,[k] leaving behind the basic teaching about Christ and not laying again the foundation: repentance from dead works and faith toward God, [2]instruction about baptisms and laying on of hands, resurrection of the dead and eternal judgment. [3]And we will do[l] this, if God permits. [4]For it is impossible to restore again to repentance those who have once been enlightened and have tasted the heavenly gift and have shared in the Holy Spirit [5]and have tasted the good word of God and the powers of the age to come [6]and then have fallen away, since they are crucifying again the Son of God to their own harm and are

g 5.5 Gk lacks *was appointed by*   h 5.7 Gk *he*   i 5.11 Or *him*   j 6.1 Or *let us be carried along*   k 6.1 Or *toward maturity*   l 6.3 Other ancient authorities read *let us do*

5:1–4 The author summarizes two requirements for priests and demonstrates that Jesus fulfills them. He focuses not on descent, as Jesus is not from the priestly tribe of Levi, but on the qualities that equip a priest for service (7:14–17). First, a priest must be compassionate, *able to deal gently* with human weakness and to *offer sacrifice for his own sins*. Second, he must fill the role *only when called by God*. Some high priests of the second century BCE who served under Greek rulers had sought the position for themselves, even bribing these rulers to name them as high priests. See **"Priests," p. 176**.

5:5–10 Jesus meets both requirements, which the author treats in reverse order. He *was appointed* high priest by God (Pss. 2:7; 110:4). Although the author earlier quoted Ps. 110:1 (1:13), he reads the context more extensively to connect Jesus to the ancient order of priests in the line of Melchizedek, a point he will develop later (7:1–28). Second, Jesus's suffering taught him obedience and compassion, perfecting or equipping him as *the source of eternal salvation*. He *offered up prayers and supplications*, which may refer to his experience of prayer in Gethsemane (Matt. 26:36–46; Mark 14:32–42; Luke 22:40–46), to his prayer from the cross (Matt. 27:46; Mark 15:34), or to the role of prayer throughout his suffering and death.

5:11–6:3 Although the author has *much to say that is hard to explain* about the work of Jesus as a high priest, he first pauses to address his readers, concerned that they have become *sluggish* or dull (5:11; 6:12). As a teacher, he laments his students' lack of progress, suggesting they need *milk, not solid food*, because they lack the discernment *to distinguish good from evil*. Despite that concern, he believes they are capable of growth *toward perfection* or maturity. They do not need to relearn fundamental lessons about repentance, faith, baptisms, laying on of hands, resurrection, and judgment. Those teachings, based on the Hebrew Scriptures, were basic instruction for the author and his audience, even though they took on new emphasis in light of the life, death, and resurrection of Jesus.

6:4–8 The author issues a third stern warning (2:1–3; 3:12–13). Those who have become part of the community received several gifts from God, including enlightenment and sharing *in the Holy Spirit*. But

holding him up to contempt. [7]Ground that drinks up the rain falling on it repeatedly and that produces a crop useful to those for whom it is cultivated receives a blessing from God. [8]But if it produces thorns and thistles, it is worthless and on the verge of being cursed; its end is to be burned over.

9 Even though we speak in this way, beloved, we are confident of better things in your case, things that belong to salvation. [10]For God is not unjust; he will not overlook your work and the[m] love that you showed for his sake[n] in serving the saints, as you still do. [11]And we want each one of you to show the same diligence so as to realize the full assurance of hope to the very end, [12]so that you may not become sluggish but imitators of those who through faith and patience inherit the promises.

13 When God made a promise to Abraham, because he had no one greater by whom to swear, he swore by himself, [14]saying, "I will surely bless you and multiply you." [15]And thus Abraham,[o] having patiently endured, obtained the promise. [16]Humans, of course, swear by someone greater than themselves, and an oath given as confirmation puts an end to all dispute among them. [17]In the same way, when God desired to show even more clearly to the heirs of the promise the unchangeable

character of his purpose, he guaranteed it by an oath, [18]so that through two unchangeable things, in which it is impossible that God would prove false, we who have taken refuge might be strongly encouraged to seize the hope set before us. [19]We have this hope, a sure and steadfast anchor of the soul, a hope that enters the inner shrine behind the curtain, [20]where Jesus, a forerunner on our behalf, has entered, having become a high priest forever according to the order of Melchizedek.

7 This "Melchizedek, king of Salem, priest of the Most High God, met Abraham as he was returning from defeating the kings and blessed him," [2]and to him Abraham apportioned "one-tenth of everything." His name, in the first place, means "king of righteousness"; next, he is also king of Salem, that is, "king of peace." [3]Without father, without mother, without genealogy, having neither beginning of days nor end of life but resembling the Son of God, he remains a priest forever.

4 See how great he is! Even[p] Abraham the patriarch gave him a tenth of the spoils. [5]And those descendants of Levi who receive the

---

m 6.10 Other ancient authorities add *labor of*   n 6.10 Gk *for his name*   o 6.15 Gk *he*   p 7.4 Other ancient authorities lack *Even*

---

those who *have fallen away* are now *crucifying again the Son of God* and *holding him up to contempt* (Matt. 27:39–44), making restoration impossible. Just as land that produces a crop *receives a blessing from God* and land that yields *thorns and thistles* (Gen. 3:17–18) is burned, those who reject God's gifts face judgment.

6:9–12 Yet the author does not envision such judgment for his audience. He is instead confident of God's blessing for them, for God will not ignore their "crop," the support they have shown and continue to show for those in their community who suffered loss of status and property and imprisonment (10:32–34). He urges them to be diligent and to imitate models of *faith and patience* (6:13–15; 11:4–12:3; 13:7).

6:13–20 The author explains the reliability of God's promises, sketching the argument in legal terms. God promised to bless faithful Abraham, the first ancestor of Israel (Gen. 22:16–17), and he *obtained the promise* (v. 15). Similarly, God has shown *the unchangeable character of his purpose* to those who are *heirs of the promise*, including the audience, by swearing an oath to confirm it (v. 17). That oath is the declaration of Jesus's high priesthood expressed in the repeated quotations of Ps. 110:4 (5:6; 7:17, 21). Since God is utterly reliable, the audience should hold fast to *the hope set before* them (v. 18). That hope is like a *steadfast anchor* that *enters the inner shrine behind the curtain* (v. 19), a reference to Jesus's entry into God's presence as high priest (v. 20; see Lev. 16:2; Heb. 9:11–12, 23–24). In that role, he is a *forerunner* for others who will follow.

7:1–10 The author introduces his main argument by explaining the superiority of Melchizedek to the Levitical priests, linking Ps. 110:4 to Gen. 14:17–20, the only other reference to him in the Hebrew Scriptures. The Hebrew Scriptures provide no account of his birth or death, so the author concludes that Melchizedek resembles *the Son of God* and *remains a priest forever* (v. 3). Because Melchizedek, *who does not belong to their ancestry*, blessed Abraham and received tithes from him, he is superior to the patriarch and, by extension, to his son Levi and the Levitical priests (vv. 6–10).

priestly office have a commandment in the law to collect tithes*q* from the people, that is, from their kindred, though these also are descended from Abraham. 6But this man, who does not belong to their ancestry, collected tithes*r* from Abraham and blessed him who had received the promises. 7It is beyond dispute that the inferior is blessed by the superior. 8In the one case, tithes are received by those who are mortal; in the other, by one of whom it is testified that he lives. 9One might even say that Levi himself, who receives tithes, paid tithes through Abraham, 10for he was still in the loins of his ancestor when Melchizedek met him.

11 Now if perfection had been attainable through the Levitical priesthood—for the people received the law under this priesthood—what further need would there have been to speak of another priest arising according to the order of Melchizedek rather than one according to the order of Aaron? 12For when there is a change in the priesthood, there is necessarily a change in the law as well. 13Now the one of whom these things are spoken belonged to another tribe, from which no one has ever served at the altar. 14For it is evident that our Lord was descended from Judah, and in connection with that tribe Moses said nothing about priests.

15 It is even more obvious when another priest arises, resembling Melchizedek, 16one who has become a priest, not through a legal requirement concerning physical descent but through the power of an indestructible life. 17For it is attested of him,

"You are a priest forever,
    according to the order of
    Melchizedek."
18There is, on the one hand, the abrogation of an earlier commandment because it was weak and ineffectual 19(for the law made nothing perfect); there is, on the other hand, the introduction of a better hope through which we approach God.

20 This was confirmed with an oath, for others have become priests without an oath, 21but this one became a priest with an oath because of the one who said to him,

"The Lord has sworn
    and will not change his mind,
'You are a priest forever'"*s*
22accordingly Jesus has also become the guarantor of a better covenant.

23 Furthermore, the former priests were many in number because they were prevented by death from continuing in office, 24but he holds his priesthood permanently because he continues forever. 25Consequently, he is able for all time to save*t* those who approach God through him, since he always lives to make intercession for them.

26 For it was fitting that we should have such a high priest, holy, blameless, undefiled, separated from sinners, and exalted above the heavens. 27Unlike the other*u* high priests, he has no need to offer sacrifices day after day, first for his own sins and then for those of the people; this he did once for all when he

q 7.5 Or a tenth   r 7.6 Or a tenth   s 7.21 Other ancient witnesses add according to the order of Melchizedek   t 7.25 Or able to save completely   u 7.27 Gk lacks other

7:11–28 The promise of Ps. 110:4. The author turns from the Genesis narrative about Melchizedek to focus on the promise of Ps. 110:4. **7:11–14** The Levitical priesthood could not bring God's design for priestly service to completion. The law had provided regulations for the Levitical priesthood, including a requirement that Levi be a priest's ancestor. Yet Jesus, a descendant of David, came from the line of Judah (Matt. 1:1–3, 20; 2:6; Luke 3:33; Rom. 1:3). **7:15–16** Jesus becomes a priest, not by *physical descent but through the power of an indestructible life*, as shown in his resurrection and exaltation (1:3, 13; 8:1; 10:12). God attests he is "a priest forever" (v. 17). See **"Priests," p. 176**. **7:18–19** As a result, the *earlier commandment* regarding priestly service is no longer in effect, and Jesus's priesthood provides *a better hope through which we approach God* (v. 19). **7:20–22** Quoting Ps. 110:4 again, the author stresses that God's oath validates Jesus's priesthood, a unique qualification not met by Levitical priests. **7:23–25** In contrast to those priests who served in office only until their deaths, Jesus's priesthood is permanent so that he can intercede *for all time* for *those who approach God through him*. **7:26–28** The author's conclusion points forward to his argument about the sacrifice Jesus offers as high priest, stressing his moral purity and exalted status. Unlike other high priests, he does not need to offer sacrifices for his own sins (Lev. 16:6, 11, 15), nor does he offer multiple sacrifices *day after day* (Exod. 29:38–46; Num. 28:3–31). Rather, his self-offering is *once for all*. His appointment comes from God's own oath, superseding the appointment of others by the law. See **"Sin," p. 150**, and **"Atonement (Reconciliation)," p. 168**.

offered himself. ²⁸For the law appoints as high priests humans, who are subject to weakness, but the word of the oath, which came later than the law, appoints a Son who has been made perfect forever.

8 Now the main point in what we are saying is this: we have such a high priest, one who is seated at the right hand of the throne of the Majesty in the heavens, ²a minister in the sanctuary and the true tent*ᵛ* that the Lord, and not any mortal, has set up. ³For every high priest is appointed to offer gifts and sacrifices; hence it is necessary for this priest also to have something to offer. ⁴Now if he were on earth, he would not be a priest at all, since there are already those*ʷ* who offer gifts according to the law. ⁵They offer worship in a sanctuary that is*ˣ* a sketch and shadow of the heavenly one, just as Moses was warned when he was about to erect the tent.*ʸ* For, God*ᶻ* said, "See that you make everything according to the pattern that was shown you on the mountain." ⁶But Jesus*ᵃ* has now obtained a more excellent ministry, and to that degree he is the mediator of a better covenant, which has been enacted on the basis of better promises. ⁷For if that first covenant had been faultless, there would have been no need to look for a second one.

8 God*ᵇ* finds fault with them when he says:

"The days are surely coming, says the
    Lord,

when I will establish a new covenant
    with the house of Israel
    and with the house of Judah,
⁹ not like the covenant that I made with
    their ancestors
on the day when I took them by the hand
    to lead them out of the land of Egypt,
for they did not continue in my covenant,
    and so I had no concern for them, says
    the Lord.
¹⁰ This is the covenant that I will make with
    the house of Israel
    after those days, says the Lord:
I will put my laws in their minds
    and write them on their hearts,
and I will be their God,
    and they shall be my people.
¹¹ And they shall not teach one another
    or say to each other,*ᶜ* 'Know the Lord,'
for they shall all know me,
    from the least of them to the greatest.
¹² For I will be merciful toward their
    iniquities,
    and I will remember their sins*ᵈ* no more."
¹³In speaking of a new covenant, he has made the first one obsolete, and what is obsolete and growing old will soon disappear.

v 8.2 Or tabernacle   w 8.4 Other ancient authorities read priests   x 8.5 Gk lacks a sanctuary that is   y 8.5 Or tabernacle z 8.5 Gk he   a 8.6 Gk he   b 8.8 Gk He   c 8.11 Or teach each one their fellow-citizen and each one their sibling, saying d 8.12 Other ancient authorities add and their lawless deeds

8:1–5 The author makes his *main point*: Jesus is unsurpassed as a priest according to the order of Melchizedek. He now explains where and how Jesus carries out that priestly ministry. See **"Priests," p. 176**. Earthly priests *offer gifts according to the law*. Their sacrifices initially took place in the movable tabernacle or tent during Israel's wilderness sojourn. During Solomon's reign, sacrifices at the permanent temple in Jerusalem replaced the earlier practice, but the author here focuses on the older period to develop his comparison. Jesus serves as a priest *in the sanctuary and the true tent* that God *has set up* in the heavens. The earthly tent is *a sketch and shadow of the heavenly one*. The author here draws on language known to students of Platonic philosophy, but the basis of his discussion is Exod. 25:40, God's instructions to Moses to copy *the pattern* that God showed him. This idea of a heavenly archetype of the earthly sanctuary was a common one in Jewish literature (Ezek. 40–48; Rev. 11:1, 19; 15:5–8; 16:1; 21:22). See **"Offerings and Sacrifices," p. 146**.

8:6–13 As part of his priestly service, Jesus *is the mediator of a better covenant* (v. 6; see 7:22; 9:15; 12:24). A covenant is a divine agreement between two parties formally approved by an oath, and a mediator serves as the go-between or liaison between the two parties. The contrast here recalls the earlier comparison of Jesus to Moses (3:1–6), who was the mediator of the first covenant at Sinai that served as a sign of God's care and guidance. Because the people *did not continue* to be faithful to the first covenant (v. 9), God promises a new covenant with Israel and Judah that will be written on *their hearts* (v. 10) and offer forgiveness of their sins (v. 12). The author draws on biblical tradition, specifically the prophet Jeremiah, as the basis for the new covenant (Jer. 31:31–34), using it to frame the priestly work of Christ (Heb. 10:16–17). See **"New Covenant," p. 1083**. He argues that from the time Jeremiah spoke these words, the first covenant became *obsolete* and *will soon disappear* (v. 13). See **"Supersessionism," p. 1647**.

9 Now[e] the first covenant had regulations for worship and an earthly sanctuary. [2]For a tent[f] was constructed, the first one, in which were the lampstand, the table, and the bread of the Presence;[g] this is called the holy place. [3]Behind the second curtain was a tent[h] called the holy of holies. [4]In it stood the golden altar of incense and the ark of the covenant overlaid on all sides with gold, in which there were a golden urn holding the manna, and Aaron's rod that budded, and the tablets of the covenant; [5]above it were the cherubim of glory overshadowing the cover of the ark.[i] Of these things we cannot speak now in detail.

6 These preparations having thus been made, the priests go continually into the first tent[j] to carry out their ritual duties, [7]but only the high priest goes into the second, and he but once a year and not without taking the blood that he offers for himself and for the sins committed unintentionally by the people. [8]By this the Holy Spirit indicates that the way into the sanctuary has not yet been disclosed as long as the first tent[k] is still standing. [9]This is a symbol[l] of the present time, indicating that gifts and sacrifices are offered that cannot perfect the conscience of the worshiper [10]but deal only with food and drink and various baptisms, regulations for the body imposed until the time comes to set things right.

11 But when Christ came as a high priest of the good things that have come,[m] then through the greater and more perfect tent[n] (not made with hands, that is, not of this creation), [12]he entered once for all into the holy place, not with the blood of goats and calves but with his own blood, thus obtaining eternal redemption. [13]For if the blood of goats and bulls and the sprinkling of the ashes of a heifer sanctifies those who have been defiled so that their flesh is purified, [14]how much more will the blood of Christ, who through the eternal Spirit[o] offered himself without blemish to God, purify our[p] conscience from dead works to worship the living God!

15 For this reason he is the mediator of a new covenant, so that those who are called may receive the promised eternal inheritance, because a death has occurred that redeems them from the transgressions under the first covenant.[q] [16]Where a will[r] is involved, the death of the one who made it must be established. [17]For a will[s] takes effect only at death, since it is not in force as long as the one who made it is alive. [18]Hence not even the first covenant was inaugurated without blood. [19]For

e 9.1 Other ancient authorities add *even*   f 9.2 Or *tabernacle*
g 9.2 Gk *the presentation of the loaves*   h 9.3 Or *tabernacle*
i 9.5 Or *the place of atonement*   j 9.6 Or *tabernacle*
k 9.8 Or *tabernacle*   l 9.9 Gk *parable*   m 9.11 Other ancient authorities read *good things to come*   n 9.11 Or *tabernacle*
o 9.14 Other ancient authorities read *Holy Spirit*
p 9.14 Other ancient authorities read *your*   q 9.15 The Greek word used here means both *covenant* and *will*   r 9.16 The Greek word used here means both *covenant* and *will*
s 9.17 The Greek word used here means both *covenant* and *will*

9:1–14 The old and new covenants. Drawing parallels between the old covenant and the new—both understood within, not apart from, Jewish tradition—the author shows how each corresponds to its own sanctuary and sacrifice. **9:1–5** Israel's place of worship was a double tent: an outer tent, *called the holy place*, and a second tent behind a curtain, *called the holy of holies*, each with its own layout and furniture (Exod. 25:9–40). **9:6–10** The author's focus, however, is not on the furnishings but on the sacrifices offered. While priests carry out *their ritual duties* daily in the outer tent, only the high priest enters the inner one and then only once per year on the Day of Atonement, or Yom Kippur. On that day, he offers two sin offerings: a bull for his own sin and a goat for the sins of the people. He then takes the blood of each animal into the Holy of Holies to sprinkle it before the mercy seat to atone for or cover over sins (Lev. 16:1–34). See **"Offerings and Sacrifices," p. 146.** The author argues that this ritual offers only a ceremonial cleansing that *cannot perfect the conscience of the worshiper.* **9:11–14** By contrast, Christ enters *the greater and more perfect tent* not annually but *once for all.* He offers *his own blood,* which brings about *eternal redemption* rather than a temporary remission. The reference to *the sprinkling of the ashes of a heifer* refers not to the Day of Atonement but to a ritual in which a red heifer was sacrificed and burned. Its ashes were mixed with water and sprinkled on the people to purify them (Num. 19:1–22). Using another lesser-to-greater argument (2:1–4; 10:26–31; 12:25–29), the author argues that Christ's blood purifies people's *conscience from dead works* so that they might *worship the living God.*

9:15–22 The mediator of a new covenant. 9:15–17 Self-sacrifice establishes Christ as *the mediator of a new covenant.* See **"New Covenant," p. 1083.** The author sketches two arguments to support this claim. First, since the same Greek word means both *covenant* and *will,* and a will takes effect when the one who made it dies, the covenant takes effect at Christ's death. **9:18–20** Second, the inauguration

when every commandment had been told to all the people by Moses in accordance with the law, he took the blood of calves and goats,[t] with water and scarlet wool and hyssop, and sprinkled both the scroll itself and all the people, [20]saying, "This is the blood of the covenant that God has ordained for you." [21]And in the same way he sprinkled with the blood both the tent[u] and all the vessels used in worship. [22]Indeed, under the law almost everything is purified with blood, and without the shedding of blood there is no forgiveness of sins.

23 Thus it was necessary for the sketches of the heavenly things to be purified with these rites, but the heavenly things themselves need better sacrifices than these. [24]For Christ did not enter a sanctuary made by human hands, a mere copy of the true one, but he entered into heaven itself, now to appear in the presence of God on our behalf. [25]Nor was it to offer himself again and again, as the high priest enters the holy place year after year with blood that is not his own, [26]for then he would have had to suffer again and again since the foundation of the world. But as it is, he has appeared once for all at the end of the ages to remove sin by the sacrifice of himself. [27]And just as it is appointed for mortals to die once and after that the judgment, [28]so Christ, having been offered once to bear the sins of many, will appear a second time, not to deal with sin but to save those who are eagerly waiting for him.

10 Since the law has only a shadow of the good things to come and not the true form of these realities, it[v] can never, by the same sacrifices that are continually offered year after year, make perfect those who approach. [2]Otherwise, would they not have ceased being offered, since the worshipers, cleansed once for all, would no longer have any consciousness of sin? [3]But in these sacrifices there is a reminder of sin year after year. [4]For it is impossible for the blood of bulls and goats to take away sins. [5]Consequently, when Christ[w] came into the world, he said,

"Sacrifices and offerings you have not
    desired,
    but a body you have prepared for me;
[6] in burnt offerings and sin offerings
    you have taken no pleasure.
[7] Then I said, 'See, I have come to do your
    will, O God'
    (in the scroll of the book[x] it is written
    of me)."

[8]When he said above, "You have neither desired nor taken pleasure in sacrifices and offerings and burnt offerings and sin offerings" (these are offered according to the law), [9]then he added, "See, I have come to do your will." He abolishes the first in order to establish the second. [10]And it is by God's will[y] that we have been sanctified through the offering of the body of Jesus Christ once for all.

11 And every priest stands day after day at his service, offering again and again the same sacrifices that can never take away sins. [12]But when Christ[z] had offered for all time a

---

t 9.19 Other ancient authorities lack *and goats*   *u* 9.21 Or *tabernacle*   *v* 10.1 Other ancient authorities read *they*   *w* 10.5 Gk *he*   *x* 10.7 Meaning of Gk uncertain   *y* 10.10 Gk *by that will*   *z* 10.12 Gk *this one*

---

of the Mosaic covenant required the death of animals, whose blood Moses sprinkled on the altar and the people (Exod. 24:3–8). Christ's death and the offering of his blood, specifically, effects this kind of sacrifice. **9:21–22** In other ceremonies, Moses also sprinkled blood on *the tent and all the vessels used in worship* (Lev. 8:14–30), showing its significance for cleansing. The ritual application of shed blood covers sins and brings forgiveness (Matt. 26:28). See **"Offerings and Sacrifices," p. 146.**

9:23–28 The author summarizes his argument, contrasting the high priest's actions on the Day of Atonement with those of Christ. Each year, the high priest enters the earthly sanctuary with animal blood. By contrast, Christ offers his own blood before God in heaven. His sacrifice is not repeated *year after year* but occurs *once for all* (7:27; 9:12; 10:10), as he bears *the sins of many* (Lev. 16:22; Isa. 53:10–12; 1 Pet. 2:24). At his second appearing, he will not *deal with sin* but will save those who await him.

10:1–18 Levitical sacrifices and Christ's sacrifice. 10:1–4 The author draws on Platonic ideas to hold that the law is only *a shadow of the good things to come and not the true form of these realities*. Thus the sacrifices it prescribes require repetition and do not remove *consciousness of sin* but rather remind worshipers of it *year after year*. In a categorical statement, the author insists that animal sacrifices do not *take away sins*. **10:5–10** The author puts the words of Ps. 40:6–8 in the mouth of Christ to demonstrate that his sacrifice replaces animal sacrifices *offered according to the law*. Christ, who fulfilled God's will by offering his body, makes worshipers holy *once for all*. **10:11–18** The author offers a final comparison to demonstrate the superiority of Christ's sacrifice. The work of the Levitical priests

single sacrifice for sins, "he sat down at the right hand of God," [13]and since then has been waiting "until his enemies would be made a footstool for his feet." [14]For by a single offering he has perfected for all time those who are sanctified. [15]And the Holy Spirit also testifies to us, for after saying,

[16] "This is the covenant that I will make
      with them
   after those days, says the Lord:
   I will put my laws in their hearts,
      and I will write them on their minds,"

[17]and he adds,

"I will remember their sins and their
      lawless deeds no more."

[18]Where there is forgiveness of these, there is no longer any offering for sin.

[19] Therefore, my brothers and sisters, since we have confidence to enter the sanctuary by the blood of Jesus, [20]by the new and living way that he opened for us through the curtain (that is, through his flesh), [21]and since we have a great priest over the house of God, [22]let us approach with a true heart in full assurance of faith, with our hearts sprinkled clean from an evil conscience and our bodies washed with pure water. [23]Let us hold fast to the confession of our hope without wavering, for he who has promised is faithful. [24]And let us consider how to provoke one another to love and good deeds, [25]not neglecting to meet together, as is the habit of some, but encouraging one another, and all the more as you see the Day approaching.

[26] For if we willfully persist in sin after having received the knowledge of the truth, there no longer remains a sacrifice for sins [27]but a fearful prospect of judgment and a fury of fire that will consume the adversaries. [28]Anyone who has violated the law of Moses dies without mercy "on the testimony of two or three witnesses." [29]How much worse punishment do you think will be deserved by those who have spurned the Son of God, profaned the blood of the covenant by which they were sanctified, and outraged the Spirit of grace? [30]For we know the one who said, "Vengeance is mine; I will repay."[a] And again, "The Lord will judge his people." [31]It is a fearful thing to fall into the hands of the living God.

[32] But recall those earlier days when, after you had been enlightened, you endured a hard struggle with sufferings, [33]sometimes being publicly exposed to insults and afflictions and sometimes becoming partners with those so treated. [34]For you had compassion for those who were in prison, and you cheerfully accepted the plundering of your possessions, knowing that you yourselves possessed something better and more lasting.[b] [35]Do not, therefore, abandon that boldness of yours; it brings a great reward. [36]For you need endurance, so that when you have done the will of God you may receive what was promised. [37]For yet

---

a 10.30 Other ancient authorities add *says the Lord*
b 10.34 Other ancient authorities add *in heaven*

---

continues *day after day*. By contrast, the quotation of Ps. 110:1 (Heb. 1:3, 13) stresses the exalted Christ is now seated, his *single sacrifice for sins* complete. He perfects worshipers *for all time*. The repetition of Jer. 31:33, part of the quotation that began the discussion of the author's main point (Heb. 8:7–13), stresses that the new covenant that Christ mediates ends God's remembrance of sin. Additional sacrifices are unnecessary. See **"Offerings and Sacrifices," p. 146.**

10:19–31 Exhortation, warning, and encouragement. Having completed his main point, the author speaks directly to his audience, using words and phrases that echo 4:14–16. **10:19–21** Christ's followers have access to God's presence *by the blood of Jesus* and by the path that he opened *through the curtain* covering the most holy place in the heavenly sanctuary (6:19, 20; 9:3, 11–14). His entry there blazes a trail that others may follow. As a *great priest* (4:14; 10:21; Zech. 6:11), he advocates for those who are part of his house (3:6). **10:22–25** The community is to draw near to worship with pure hearts (9:14) and cleansed bodies, to hold fast to the community's confession (3:1; 4:14; 13:15), and to meet together to encourage mutual love and good deeds in light of the day of Christ's promised return. **10:26–31** The author adds a warning, again framed as a lesser-to-greater argument. Willful rejection of God's word leads to judgment. The Mosaic law stipulated death for willful idolatry (Deut. 17:2–7); a *worse punishment* awaits those who *spurned the Son of God*, profane his blood, and insult the Holy Spirit. The author draws on Deut. 32:35–36 to support his warning. **10:32–39** The community is to remember their solidarity in past suffering that included verbal and physical attacks, the imprisonment of some, and loss of property. **10:35–39** They are to endure with confidence, encouraged by Hab. 2:3–4. The contrast between *those who shrink back* and *those who have faith* sets up the examples of faithful endurance that follow.

"in a very little while,
the one who is coming will come and
will not delay,
[38] but my righteous one will live by faith.
My soul takes no pleasure in anyone
who shrinks back."
[39]But we are not among those who shrink back and so are lost but among those who have faith and so preserve our souls.

11 Now faith is the assurance[c] of things hoped for, the conviction[d] of things not seen. [2]Indeed, by faith[e] our ancestors received approval. [3]By faith we understand that the worlds were prepared by the word of God, so that what is seen was made from things that are not visible.[f]

[4] By faith Abel offered to God a more acceptable[g] sacrifice than Cain's. Through this he received approval as righteous, God himself giving approval to his gifts; he died, but through his faith[h] he still speaks. [5]By faith Enoch was taken so that he did not experience death, and "he was not found, because God had taken him." For it was attested before he was taken away that "he had pleased God." [6]And without faith it is impossible to please him, for whoever would approach God must believe that he exists and that he rewards those who seek him. [7]By faith Noah, warned by God about events as yet unseen, respected the warning and built an ark to save his household; by this he condemned the world and became an heir to the righteousness that is in accordance with faith.

[8] By faith Abraham obeyed when he was called to set out for a place that he was to receive as an inheritance, and he set out, not knowing where he was going. [9]By faith he stayed for a time in the land he had been promised, as in a foreign land, living in tents, as did Isaac and Jacob, who were heirs with him of the same promise. [10]For he looked forward to the city that has foundations, whose architect and builder is God. [11]By faith, with Sarah's involvement, he received power of procreation, even though he was too old, because he considered[i] him faithful who had promised. [12]Therefore from one person, and this one as good as dead, descendants were born, "as many as the stars of heaven and as the innumerable grains of sand by the seashore."

[13] All of these died in faith without having received the promises, but from a distance they saw and greeted them. They confessed that they were strangers and foreigners on the earth, [14]for people who speak in this way make it clear that they are seeking a homeland. [15]If they had been thinking of the land that they had left behind, they would have had opportunity to return. [16]But as it is, they desire a better homeland, that is, a heavenly one. Therefore God is not ashamed to be called their God; indeed, he has prepared a city for them.

[17] By faith Abraham, when put to the test, offered up Isaac. He who had received the promises was ready to offer up his only son, [18]of whom he had been told, "It is through Isaac that descendants shall be named for you." [19]He considered the fact that God is able even to raise someone from the dead—and, figuratively speaking, he did receive him

c 11.1 Or *reality*   d 11.1 Or *evidence*   e 11.2 Gk *by this*
f 11.3 Or *was not made out of visible things*   g 11.4 Gk *greater*
h 11.4 Gk *through it*   i 11.11 Other ancient authorities read
*By faith Sarah herself received power to conceive, even when she
was past the age, since she considered*

11:1–7 Examples of enduring faith to emulate. 11:1–2 The author's list gathers rhetorical power through its repetition of *by faith*. Faith provides solid confidence in (1:13; 3:14) and conviction about unseen realities. The visible creation was "prepared by the word of God" (v. 3). **11:3–7** Three exemplars of faith from the period before the flood are Abel (Gen. 4:4), Enoch (Gen. 5:21–24), and Noah (Gen. 6:8–9).

11:8–22 The faithfulness of Israel's ancestors (see Gen. 12–50). 11:8–9 Abraham responded to the call of God (Gen. 12:1–4) to possess a land (Gen. 15:7) and lived there in tents as a stranger and pilgrim with no stable home (Gen. 12:8; 13:12; 23:4, 12; 26:3; 35:27). **11:10–12** In faith, Abraham looked forward to a more permanent dwelling in God's city. Despite their advanced age, Abraham and his wife, Sarah, became parents to Isaac, the initial fulfillment of the promise of countless descendants (Gen. 22:17). **11:13–16** Abraham and Sarah's example highlights the pilgrim nature of faith. Those who receive God's promises *desire a better homeland*—that is, a heavenly one. **11:17–19** Abraham was willing to sacrifice *his only son*, Isaac, believing God could raise him *from the dead* and keep the promise that Abraham's line would continue through him. **11:20–22** The author briefly recounts the examples of Isaac (Gen. 27:26–40), Jacob (Gen. 47:31; 48:8–22), and Joseph (Gen. 50:24).

back. [20]By faith Isaac invoked blessings for the future on Jacob and Esau. [21]By faith Jacob, when dying, blessed each of the sons of Joseph, "bowing in worship over the top of his staff." [22]By faith Joseph, at the end of his life, made mention of the exodus of the Israelites and gave instructions about his burial.[j]

23 By faith Moses was hidden by his parents for three months after his birth, because they saw that the child was beautiful, and they were not afraid of the king's edict.[k] [24]By faith Moses, when he was grown up, refused to be called a son of Pharaoh's daughter, [25]choosing rather to share ill-treatment with the people of God than to enjoy the fleeting pleasures of sin. [26]He considered abuse suffered for the Christ[l] to be greater wealth than the treasures of Egypt, for he was looking ahead to the reward. [27]By faith he left Egypt, unafraid of the king's anger, for he persevered as though[m] he saw him who is invisible. [28]By faith he kept the Passover and the sprinkling of blood, so that the destroyer of the firstborn would not touch the firstborn of Israel.[n]

29 By faith the people passed through the Red Sea as if it were dry land, but when the Egyptians attempted to do so they were drowned. [30]By faith the walls of Jericho fell after they had been encircled for seven days. [31]By faith Rahab the prostitute did not perish with those who were disobedient,[o] because she had received the spies in peace.

32 And what more should I say? For time would fail me to tell of Gideon, Barak, Samson, Jephthah, of David and Samuel and the prophets, [33]who through faith conquered kingdoms, administered justice, obtained promises, shut the mouths of lions, [34]quenched the power of fire, escaped the edge of the sword, were made strong out of weakness, became mighty in war, put foreign armies to flight. [35]Women received their dead by resurrection. Others were tortured, refusing to accept release, in order to obtain a better resurrection. [36]Others suffered mocking and flogging and even chains and imprisonment. [37]They were stoned to death; they were sawn in two;[p] they were killed by the sword; they went about in skins of sheep and goats, destitute, persecuted, tormented—[38]of whom the world was not worthy. They wandered in deserts and mountains and in caves and holes in the ground.

39 Yet all these, though they were commended for their faith, did not receive what was promised, [40]since God had provided something better so that they would not, apart from us, be made perfect.

12 Therefore, since we are surrounded by so great a cloud of witnesses, let us also lay aside every weight and the sin that clings so closely,[q] and let us run with perseverance

j 11.22 Gk *his bones*   k 11.23 Other ancient authorities add *By faith Moses, when he was grown up, killed the Egyptian, because he observed the humiliation of his brothers and sisters*   l 11.26 Or *the Messiah*   m 11.27 Or *because*   n 11.28 Gk *would not touch them*   o 11.31 Or *unbelieving*   p 11.37 Other ancient authorities add *they were tempted*   q 12.1 Other ancient authorities read *sin that easily distracts*

11:23–28 Moses's parents hid him from the Egyptian Pharaoh, who had ordered all Hebrew boys killed (Exod. 1:22–2:4). Though Pharaoh's daughter found and adopted him, he rejected earthly security and suffered abuse to identify *with the people of God*. The phrase *abuse suffered for the Christ* may be a reference to Ps. 89:50–51. By faith, Moses *persevered as though he saw him who is invisible* (Exod. 12:1–14:31).

11:29–40 The faithfulness of others in Israel's past. 11:29–31 Exemplars of faith include the people of the exodus, who *passed through the Red Sea* (Exod. 14:1–31), and the next generation, who encircled Jericho (Josh. 6:1–21), aided by the Canaanite Rahab, who had sheltered Israelite spies (Josh. 2:1–21; 6:17).

11:32–40 The author cites an array of military leaders (Judg. 4–16), as well as *David and Samuel and the prophets*, whose exemplary actions were accomplished *through faith*. Some actions recall specific stories. For example, the reference to closing *the mouths of lions* brings Samson and Daniel to mind (Judg. 14:6; Dan. 6:19–23), and the focus on torture is reminiscent of 2 Maccabees (2 Macc. 6:18–31; 7:1–42). Other descriptions are not linked to specific individuals. What is notable is the mixture of stories of triumph with those of endurance in the face of persecution and death. God commended those who endured without triumph because they, like Abraham, proved faithful even in the face of unfulfilled promises.

12:1–4 The author encourages his audience with one final example. Like runners, they are to lay aside all that would hinder them, looking only *to Jesus, the pioneer and perfecter of faith*. In Greek, the *pioneer* is the trailblazer who opens a path for others, as well as the captain who finishes the race first and encourages other runners (2:10). The *perfecter* recalls the image of Jesus as priest who brings his followers into God's presence. Enduring the cross, the exalted Jesus (1:3, 13; 8:1; 10:12) strengthens the addressees so they do not *lose heart* in the face of opposition.

the race that is set before us, [2]looking to Jesus, the pioneer and perfecter of faith, who for the sake of[r] the joy that was set before him endured the cross, disregarding its shame, and has taken his seat at the right hand of the throne of God.

3 Consider him who endured such hostility against himself from sinners,[s] so that you may not grow weary in your souls or lose heart. [4]In your struggle against sin you have not yet resisted to the point of shedding your blood. [5]And you have forgotten the exhortation that addresses you as children—

"My child, do not regard lightly the
   discipline of the Lord
   or lose heart when you are punished
   by him,
[6] for the Lord disciplines those whom he
   loves
   and chastises every child whom he
   accepts."

[7]Endure trials for the sake of discipline. God is treating you as children, for what child is there whom a parent does not discipline? [8]If you do not have that discipline in which all children share, then you are illegitimate and not his children. [9]Moreover, we had human parents to discipline us, and we respected them. Should we not be even more willing to be subject to the Father of spirits and live? [10]For they disciplined us for a short time as seemed best to them, but he disciplines us for our good, in order that we may share his holiness. [11]Now, discipline always seems painful rather than pleasant at the time, but later it

yields the peaceful fruit of righteousness to those who have been trained by it.

12 Therefore lift your drooping hands and strengthen your weak knees [13]and make straight paths for your feet, so that what is lame may not be put out of joint but rather be healed.

14 Pursue peace with everyone and the holiness without which no one will see the Lord. [15]See to it that no one fails to obtain the grace of God, that no root of bitterness springs up and causes trouble and through it many become defiled. [16]See to it that no one becomes an immoral and godless person, as Esau was, who sold his birthright for a single meal. [17]You know that later, when he wanted to inherit the blessing, he was rejected, for he found no chance to repent, even though he sought the blessing[t] with tears.

18 You have not come to something[u] that can be touched, a blazing fire, and darkness, and gloom, and a tempest, [19]and the sound of a trumpet, and a voice whose words made the hearers beg that not another word be spoken to them. [20](For they could not endure the order that was given, "If even an animal touches the mountain, it shall be stoned to death." [21]Indeed, so terrifying was the sight that Moses said, "I tremble with fear.") [22]But you have come to Mount Zion and to the city of the living God, the heavenly Jerusalem, and to innumerable angels in festal gathering, [23]and to the

r 12.2 Or who instead of   s 12.3 Other ancient authorities read such hostility from sinners against themselves   t 12.17 Gk it   u 12.18 Other ancient authorities read a mountain

12:5–11 Calling to mind Prov. 3:11–12, the author interprets the community's suffering as a part of God's discipline or training for God's beloved children (Deut. 8:2–5; Wis. 12:19–22; Sir. 4:17; 2 Macc. 6:12; 7:33; 10:4). God's discipline is like parental correction or athletic training, producing the peaceful fruit of righteousness.

12:12–17 The call to faithfulness concludes with imperatives often based on scriptural texts. The community should seek new resolve in the face of fatigue (Isa. 35:3–4), make straight paths (Prov. 4:26), and pursue peace and holiness (Ps. 34:14). They should keep guard over one another, watchful for bitterness (Deut. 29:18) and godlessness like that of Esau, who traded his blessing for food (Gen. 25:33–34) and was rejected when he sought to reclaim it (Gen. 27:30–40).

12:18–29 Contrasting pilgrimages. 12:18–21 The Israelites traveled from Egypt to Mount Sinai (Exod. 19:1–6), where fear of the fierce elements and of God's voice led them to request that God not speak (Exod. 20:18–19; Deut. 5:23–27). 12:22–24 By contrast, the author's hearers have come to Mount Zion and to the city of the living God. Without fear, they can approach God and Jesus, whose sprinkled blood speaks of reconciliation. Abel's blood bore witness only to his murder (Gen. 4:10–11). 12:25–29 The author constructs his final warning as another lesser-to-greater argument. The Israelites did not escape God's word spoken to them at Sinai, so his audience must not disregard this heavenly warning. God's voice will shake both earth and heaven (Hag. 2:6), leading to the destruction of created things, so that only the eternal will remain (Heb. 1:10–12). Those receiving the gift of God's eternal rule should show gratitude and offer reverent worship to God, who is a consuming fire (Deut. 4:24).

assembly[v] of the firstborn who are enrolled in heaven, and to God the judge of all, and to the spirits of the righteous made perfect, [24]and to Jesus, the mediator of a new covenant, and to the sprinkled blood that speaks a better word than the blood of Abel.

25 See that you do not refuse the one who is speaking, for if they did not escape when they refused the one who warned them on earth, how much less will we escape if we reject the one who warns from heaven! [26]At that time his voice shook the earth, but now he has promised, "Yet once more I will shake not only the earth but also the heaven." [27]This phrase, "Yet once more," indicates the removal of what is shaken—that is, created things—so that what cannot be shaken may remain. [28]Therefore, since we are receiving a kingdom that cannot be shaken, let us show gratitude, by which we may offer to God an acceptable worship with reverence and awe, [29]for indeed our God is a consuming fire.

13 Let mutual affection continue. [2]Do not neglect to show hospitality to strangers, for by doing that some have entertained angels without knowing it. [3]Remember those who are in prison, as though you were in prison with them, those who are being tortured, as though you yourselves were being tortured.[w] [4]Let marriage be held in honor by all, and let the marriage bed be kept undefiled, for God will judge the sexually immoral and adulterers. [5]Keep your lives free from the love of money, and be content with what you have, for he himself has said, "I will never leave you or forsake you." [6]So we can say with confidence,

"The Lord is my helper;
  I will not be afraid.
What can anyone do to me?"

7 Remember your leaders, those who spoke the word of God to you; consider the outcome of their way of life, and imitate their faith. [8]Jesus Christ is the same yesterday and today and forever. [9]Do not be carried away by all kinds of strange teachings, for it is good for the heart to be strengthened by grace, not by regulations about food,[x] which have not benefited those who observe them. [10]We have an altar from which those who officiate in the tent[y] have no right to eat. [11]For the bodies of those animals whose blood is brought into the sanctuary by the high priest as a sacrifice for sin are burned outside the camp. [12]Therefore Jesus also suffered outside the city gate in order to sanctify the people by his own blood. [13]Let us then go to him outside the camp and bear the abuse he endured. [14]For here we have no lasting city, but we are looking for the city that is to come. [15]Through him, then, let us continually offer a sacrifice of praise to God, that is, the fruit of lips that confess his name. [16]Do not neglect to do good and to share what you have, for such sacrifices are pleasing to God.

17 Obey your leaders and submit to them, for they are keeping watch over your souls

v 12.23 Or *angels, and to the festal gathering* [23]*and assembly*
w 13.3 Gk *were in the body*   x 13.9 Gk *not by foods*   y 13.10 Or *tabernacle*

13:1–19 Actions pleasing to God. The social pressure and dislocation of the community give the opening commands a particular application to their lives, even though many of the teachings are common (Rom. 12:9–21). **13:1–2** They are to show love to those inside and outside the community. In showing *hospitality to strangers*, they may be serving *angels without knowing it* (Gen. 18:1–22; 19:1–11; Judg. 6:11–24; 13:2–23; Tob. 12:11–22). **13:3** They are to remember and care for prisoners and victims of torture, living in solidarity with them. **13:4** They are to keep *the marriage bed* undefiled, remaining faithful to their spouses and so avoiding God's judgment (1 Cor. 6:9–10; Eph. 5:5–6; Col. 3:5–6). **13:5–6** As those who have lost possessions (10:34), they are to avoid *the love of money* (Luke 16:14; 1 Tim. 3:3; 6:10) and to *be content*, trusting God's promise to remain with them and help them (Deut. 31:6, 8; Josh. 1:5; Ps. 118:6). **13:7–9** They are to remember and imitate their past leaders, whose faith rested on the constancy of Jesus, and not exchange that steadfast foundation for *strange teachings*. **13:11–12** During Israel's sojourn in the wilderness, sacrificial animals were burned *outside the camp*, an unholy place that recalls Jesus's suffering and burial *outside the city gate* of Jerusalem. **13:13–14** The community is to join Jesus in his suffering and in the formerly unholy place. See **"Holiness and Purity," p. 158**. They remain pilgrims without an earthly city, looking forward to a heavenly one (12:18–24). **13:15–16** Rather than animal sacrifices, they are to offer God praise and confession, perform good works, and share possessions. **13:17–19** They are to submit to their rulers as those who keep watch over them and to pray for the author and his speedy physical reunion with them.

as those who will give an account. Let them do this with joy and not with sighing, for that would be harmful to you.

18 Pray for us; we are sure that we have a good conscience, desiring to act honorably in all things. [19]I urge you all the more to do this, so that I may be restored to you very soon.

20 Now may the God of peace, who brought back from the dead our Lord Jesus, the great shepherd of the sheep, by the blood of the eternal covenant, [21]make you complete in everything good[z] so that you may do his will, as he works among us[a] that which is pleasing in his sight, through Jesus Christ, to whom be the glory forever.[b] Amen.

22 I appeal to you, brothers and sisters, bear with my word of exhortation, for I have written to you briefly. [23]I want you to know that our brother Timothy has been set free, and if he comes in time he will be with me when I see you. [24]Greet all your leaders and all the saints. Those from Italy send you greetings. [25]Grace be with all of you.[c]

z 13.21 Other ancient authorities read *for every good work* a 13.21 Other ancient authorities read *you*   b 13.21 Other ancient authorities add *and ever*   c 13.25 Other ancient authorities add *Amen*

13:20–25 The author's formal blessing focuses on God's work in bringing back Jesus *from the dead* by means of *the blood of the eternal covenant* (Exod. 24:8; Zech. 9:11). In his final appeal, he characterizes his writing as a *word of exhortation*, a standard term for sermons (Acts 13:15; 2 Macc. 15:8–11). He adds personal greetings, noting that Timothy, a coworker of Paul (Acts 16:1–3; 17:14–15; 2 Tim. 1:2, 5), *has been set free* or "sent away," perhaps from prison, and he hopes for a joint reunion. He extends greetings from *those from Italy*, which suggests that they are with the author either in Italy or in another location. If they are somewhere else, then the audience is in Italy (Acts 18:2), receiving greetings from community members who are with the author at the time of writing. Hebrews closes with a liturgical blessing, a common feature of New Testament letters (Titus 3:15).

THE LETTER OF JAMES

Authorship, Date, and Literary History

Church tradition identifies the author of the Letter of James as James the brother of Jesus (also called James the Just), the leader of the early Christian movement in Jerusalem (cf. Acts 15). However, most scholars hold that the letter was written by one of James's followers. As such, the letter dates to around 80 CE. The letter's mention of "the early and the late rains" (5:7), a meteorological phenomenon particular to Palestine, suggests that its author may be located in this region or be familiar with it. The author writes to "the twelve tribes in the dispersion" (1:1), likely Christians of Jewish heritage living outside of Palestine.

James in Christian Tradition

Although he features very little in the Gospels, according to the Acts of the Apostles, James exercises significant leadership in the early church (Acts 12:17; 15:13–39). Paul of Tarsus records meeting with James and other church leaders to evaluate his ministry to the gentiles (Gal. 1:19; 2:8–10). From such a meeting, James may have gained familiarity with Paul's teachings, to which James 2 appears to be a response or corrective.

Despite James's importance as a church leader, many of the earliest Western Christian lists of Christian Scripture omit this letter, although it was beloved by the earliest African and Asian Christians. Later, Martin Luther famously denigrated this letter as "strawy," in particular because of James's theology concerning active faith and salvation (Konrad Schmid and Jens Schröter, *The Making of the Bible*). Luther's assessment has diminished the popularity of this letter within some Reformed Protestant circles, although other parts of the Christian church hold the letter's teachings as central to their acts of social justice, ethics, and piety.

Reading Guide

The Christ followers addressed in the Letter of James live "in the dispersion" (1:1), a word suggesting not only geographic distance from home but a forced separation, a community of exiles flung across the Mediterranean basin. Although dispersed, these exiles continue to gather in assembly for worship (the Gk. word at Jas. 2:2 is "synagōgē"), and they desire to uphold the "royal law," likely the Torah (2:2, 8–13). Yet as they negotiate their exilic life, they face various trials and temptations to blend into the societies in which they find themselves, to become friends of the world (1:2–4, 12–15; 4:4). The Letter of James means to bolster these believers, increasing their endurance against such temptations and reminding them of their true identity as beloved children born of God, the firstfruits of God's creation (1:18–19).

The letter names economic disparities within the community as its first concern (2:1–17). Some of the believers lack the means of daily sustenance, while others have more than they need (1:9–11; 2:15). They face the temptation of privileging the wealthy and discriminating against the poor (2:1–7), even though the wealthy historically act unjustly toward them (2:6–7; 5:1–6). The letter counsels the community differently. The wealthy among them must walk in humility, and the whole community must demonstrate care for all, especially for the poor (1:10–11, 27; 2:1–5, 15). Discrimination based on wealth violates the holy standard to which God has called the community (2:8–13).

Communication also figures importantly in this letter. Speech among Christ followers must reflect a careful governance of the tongue, guarding against slander (3:1–12; 4:11–12). Lack of care in this regard leads to the death and destruction of the community (3:5b–8). Wisdom from above forms the speech and actions of the wise, marking their way of life as "peaceable, gentle, willing to yield, full of mercy and good fruits, without a trace of partiality or hypocrisy" (3:17). Only with an orientation toward wisdom can the believers properly "bless the Lord and Father" (3:9).

The "world" stands in contrast to the way of the wise (4:1–4). Communities wishing to imitate the world into which they are dispersed find themselves torn apart by "conflicts and disputes" and by "cravings that are at war within" them (4:1). For these exiles, the "world" represents a way of life contrary to the way of God as taught in the Scriptures (4:4), a way marked by envy, greed, and conflict (4:5). But "the spirit that God caused to dwell" in the believers does not "desire envy" (4:5). They must turn from the world and its ways and humble themselves (4:6–10) before God. Such a turning requires patient endurance and prayer

from the believers, following the patterns of the forebears of faith: Job and Elijah (5:7-11, 17-18). It also requires an ethic of care and prayer among Christ followers (5:13-20), an ethic that affirms the holy worth of the life of every exile, even those who fall into sin.

Contemporary concerns about wealth disparities find echoes in James, along with discussions about the privileging of the wealthy in contemporary society. Likewise, the Letter of James invites contemplation about the power and cost of discourse, particularly the destructive power of slanderous and oppressive speech in contemporary media. At the same time, readers of James's critique of the world can fall into an unhealthy disengagement with society, for which the letter does not advocate. Instead, the Letter of James calls Christ followers to a lifestyle of trust in the coming of the Lord, which is near (5:8), and to an ongoing ethic of active, faithful endurance.

James: An outline

Letter opening	James 1:1
Temptations facing the faithful	James 1:2-18
A call to pure and undefiled religion	James 1:19-27
Markers of pure religion	James 2:1-4:17
Showing no partiality	James 2:1-13
Faithful action	James 2:14-26
Careful speech	James 3:1-12
Wisdom from above	James 3:13-18
Repentance from friendship with the world	James 4:1-10
Speech that is kind and humble	James 4:11-17
The sins of the wealthy	James 5:1-6
Life together in faithfulness	James 5:7-20
Patient endurance	James 5:7-11
Forthright speech	James 5:12
Patterns of prayer	James 5:13-18
Restoration	James 5:19-20

Margaret Aymer

1 James, a servant of God and of the Lord Jesus Christ,
To the twelve tribes in the dispersion:
Greetings.

2 My brothers and sisters, whenever you face various trials, consider it all joy, ³because you know that the testing of your faith produces endurance. ⁴And let endurance complete its work, so that you may be complete and whole, lacking in nothing.

5 If any of you is lacking in wisdom, ask God, who gives to all generously and ungrudgingly,

1:1 Greeting. *Servant of God and of the Lord Jesus Christ.* Literally "slave of God and of the Lord Jesus Christ." "Slave of God," as appropriated by religious leaders (Ezra 5:11; 2 Pet. 1:1; Rom. 1:1), leaves unaddressed the enslaved, about 10 percent of the Roman Empire's population. *In the dispersion.* A term evoking exile and forced migration (Jer. 15:7; 1 Pet. 1:1). The audience of this letter may include descendants of the Jews who were forced into exile in earlier times.

1:2-18 Setting the tone. The letter addresses the trials and temptations of the recipients. **1:2** *My brothers and sisters.* Recipients are imagined as a family rather than a congress of the like-minded. *Whenever you face various trials.* Literally "temptations," not external persecution (see 1:12-15). **1:3-4** For other discussions of temptation and endurance, see 1 Pet. 1:6-7; Rom. 5:3-5. **1:5-6** Evokes Matt. 7:7: "Ask, and it will

and it will be given you. ⁶But ask in faith, never doubting, for the one who doubts is like a wave of the sea, driven and tossed by the wind. ⁷,⁸For the doubter, being double-minded and unstable in every way, must not expect to receive anything from the Lord.

9 Let the brother or sister of humble means boast in having a high position ¹⁰and the rich in having been humbled, because the rich will disappear like a flower in the field. ¹¹For the sun rises with its scorching heat and withers the field; its flower falls, and its beauty perishes. It is the same way with the rich; in the midst of a busy life, they will wither away.

12 Blessed is anyone who endures temptation. Such a one has stood the test and will receive the crown of life that the Lord*a* has promised to those who love him. ¹³No one, when tempted, should say, "I am being tempted by God," for God cannot be tempted by evil and he himself tempts no one. ¹⁴But one is tempted by one's own desire, being lured and enticed by it; ¹⁵then, when desire has conceived, it engenders sin, and sin, when it is fully grown, gives birth to death.

16 Do not be deceived, my beloved brothers and sisters. ¹⁷Every generous act of giving, with every perfect gift, is from above, coming down from the Father of lights, with whom there is no variation or shadow due to change.*b* ¹⁸In fulfillment of his own purpose he gave birth to us by the word of truth, so that we would become a kind of first fruits of his creatures.

19 You must understand this, my beloved brothers and sisters: let everyone be quick to listen, slow to speak, slow to anger, ²⁰for human anger does not produce God's righteousness.*c* ²¹Therefore rid yourselves of all sordidness and rank growth of wickedness, and welcome with meekness the implanted word that has the power to save your souls.

22 But be doers of the word and not merely hearers who deceive themselves. ²³For if any are hearers of the word and not doers, they are like those who look at themselves*d* in a mirror; ²⁴for they look at themselves and, on going away, immediately forget what they were like. ²⁵But those who look into the perfect law, the law of liberty, and persevere, being not hearers who forget but doers who act—they will be blessed in their doing.

26 If any think they are religious and do not bridle their tongues but deceive their hearts, their religion is worthless. ²⁷Religion that is pure and undefiled before God the Father is this: to care for orphans and widows in their distress and to keep oneself unstained by the world.

2 My brothers and sisters, do not claim the faith of our Lord Jesus Christ of glory while showing partiality. ²For if a person with gold rings and in fine clothes comes into your assembly, and if a poor person in dirty clothes also comes in, ³and if you take notice of the one wearing the fine clothes and say, "Have a seat here in a good place, please," while to the one who is poor you say, "Stand there," or, "Sit by my footstool," ⁴have

---

a 1.12 Gk *he*; other ancient authorities read *God*
b 1.17 Other ancient authorities read *variation due to a shadow of turning*   *c* 1.20 Or *justice*   *d* 1.23 Gk *at the face of his birth*

---

be given to you." God gives wisdom (Prov. 2:3–6; 1 Kgs. 3:1–15), but prayer must include faith (Mark 11:23–24). **1:7–8** *Double-minded.* Literally "two-souled," people who split their allegiance between God and the world (see Jas. 4:8). **1:9–11** Imagines a reversal between *the brother or sister of humble means* and *the rich*, possibly not a believer. See echoes in 1 Sam. 2:7; 2 Sam. 22:28; Luke 1:46–55. *Like a flower in the field.* Isaiah 40:6–8; Job 14:1–2. **1:12–13** *Blessed.* Literally "fortunate" or "happy." *Crown of life.* See Rev. 2:10. *God . . . tempts no one.* See Sir. 15:11–20; 1 Cor. 10:13. **1:14–15** *Desire . . . sin . . . death.* Desire and sin are imagined as treacherous, fecund women (see Prov. 7). **1:17–18** God, *the Father of lights*, gives birth to the faithful.

1:19–27 The letter's main themes are introduced. **1:19–21, 26** These passages concern faithful conduct, careful communication, and self-control (see Jas. 3:1–4:13; Eccl. 5:1; Prov. 29:20). **1:20** *God's righteousness*, or "justice," is contrasted with human anger. **1:21–25** *The word* catalyzes the divine birthing of the faithful, saves souls (or possibly lives) once implanted, and leads to ethical lives. **1:25** Connects "the word" to *the perfect law, the law of liberty*, or freedom. "Gospel" does not occur in this letter; "the word" may be gospel, Torah, or both. **1:26** *Religious.* Not an identity but a way of living. **1:27** The entire letter is summarized in this verse.

2:1–13 On economic discrimination. These verses address economic discrimination within the faith community. **2:2** *A person with gold rings and in fine clothes* marks wealth and possibly political ambition. *A poor person.* In the Greek, the wealthy visitor is called a "man" ("anēr"), but the poor person is not. **2:3** *Sit by*

you not made distinctions among yourselves and become judges with evil thoughts? [5]Listen, my beloved brothers and sisters. Has not God chosen the poor in the world to be rich in faith and to be heirs of the kingdom that he has promised to those who love him? [6]But you have dishonored the poor person. Is it not the rich who oppress you? Is it not they who drag you into the courts? [7]Is it not they who blaspheme the excellent name that was invoked over you?

[8]If you really fulfill the royal law according to the scripture, "You shall love your neighbor as yourself," you do well. [9]But if you show partiality, you commit sin and are convicted by the law as transgressors. [10]For whoever keeps the whole law but fails in one point has become accountable for all of it. [11]For the one who said, "You shall not commit adultery," also said, "You shall not murder." Now if you do not commit adultery but you murder, you have become a transgressor of[e] the law. [12]So speak and so act as those who are to be judged by the law of liberty. [13]For judgment will be without mercy to anyone who has shown no mercy; mercy triumphs over judgment.

[14]What good is it, my brothers and sisters, if someone claims to have faith but does not have works? Surely that faith cannot save, can it? [15]If a brother or sister is naked and lacks daily food [16]and one of you says to them, "Go in peace; keep warm and eat your fill," and yet you do not supply their bodily needs, what is the good of that? [17]So faith by itself, if it has no works, is dead.

[18]But someone will say, "You have faith, and I have works." Show me your faith apart from works, and I by my works will show you faith. [19]You believe that God is one; you do well. Even the demons believe—and shudder. [20]Do you want to be shown, you senseless person, that faith apart from works is worthless?[f] [21]Was not our ancestor Abraham justified by works when he offered his son Isaac on the altar? [22]You see that faith was active along with his works, and by works faith was brought to completion. [23]Thus the scripture was fulfilled that says, "Abraham believed God, and it was reckoned to him as righteousness,"[g] and he was called the friend of God. [24]You see that a person is justified by works and not by faith alone. [25]Likewise, was not Rahab the prostitute also justified by works when she welcomed the messengers[h] and sent them out by another road? [26]For just as the body without the spirit is dead, so faith without works is also dead.

3 Not many of you should become teachers, my brothers and sisters, for you know that

e 2.11 Other ancient authorities read *a rebel against*
f 2.20 Other ancient authorities read *dead* or *empty*
g 2.23 Or *justice*   h 2.25 Other ancient authorities read *spies*

my footstool. A traditional location for enslaved persons. **2:5** *Heirs of the kingdom.* Many biblical traditions uphold God's promise of inheritance to the poor, especially Luke 6:20. **2:6–7** *Is it not the rich?* The Greek of these questions anticipates the answer yes from the audience. The rich, here, are not believers. They *blaspheme the excellent name that was invoked over you.* **2:8** *The royal law* refers to Lev. 19:18b, a commandment that Jesus equates with the command to love God (Matt. 22:39; Mark 12:31; Luke 10:27). Much of the letter reflects on Lev. 19:11–18. **2:9** *If you show partiality* refers to Lev. 19:15. **2:10–12** Those who discriminate violate, or rebel against, Torah, *the law of liberty.* Paul makes a similar argument in Rom. 2:17–23. **2:13** This call to act with mercy echoes Jesus's command to treat others as you desire to be treated (Matt. 7:12).

2:14–26 A call to active faithfulness. 2:14 *Surely that faith cannot save, can it?* The question anticipates the answer no. **2:15–16** In this example, the faithful person should act with mercy (cf. 2:13). **2:17–18** The letter argues that how one acts demonstrates what one truly believes (see Gal. 5:6). **2:19** Accepting a theological premise is not enough. **2:20** *You senseless person.* Probably a fictional opponent. **2:21–23** The example of Abraham challenges an oversimplification of Paul's theology (cf. Gal. 3:6–9). Indeed, Abraham *believed God.* However, the letter points out that Abraham also acted in light of that belief, thus bringing faith to its necessary completion. *The friend of God.* Friendship with God versus friendship with the world is a central theme in this letter (cf. 4:5). **2:25** In this letter, Rahab's collusion with Joshua's spies is upheld as a justifying enactment of her belief in the power of God. **2:26** *Without the spirit,* or "without breath." The Greek word can mean either. Faithful actions serve as the breath that enlivens the faith of the believer.

3:1–4:17 Wisdom in community relations. Chaps. 3 and 4 concern the impact of careless speech, envy, covetousness, and ambition on community relations.

3:1–12 Focuses on the power of the tongue to harm. **3:1** *Teachers* highlights how some early Christian

we who teach will face stricter judgment. ²For all of us make many mistakes. Anyone who makes no mistakes in speaking is mature,ⁱ able to keep the whole body in check with a bridle. ³If we put bits into the mouths of horses to make them obey us, we guide their whole bodies. ⁴Or look at ships: though they are so large and are driven by strong winds, yet they are guided by a very small rudder wherever the will of the pilot directs. ⁵So also the tongue is a small member, yet it boasts of great exploits.

How great a forest is set ablaze by such a small fire! ⁶And the tongue is a fire. The tongue is placed among our members as a world of iniquity; it stains the whole body, sets on fire the cycle of life, and is itself set on fire by hell.ʲ ⁷For every species of beast and bird, of reptile and sea creature, can be tamed and has been tamed by the human species, ⁸but no one can tame the tongue—a restlessᵏ evil, full of deadly poison. ⁹With it we bless the Lordˡ and Father, and with it we curse people, made in the likeness of God. ¹⁰From the same mouth comes a blessing and a curse. My brothers and sisters, this ought not to be so. ¹¹Does a spring pour forth from the same opening both fresh and brackish water? ¹²Can a fig tree, my brothers and sisters, yield olives or a grapevine figs? No more can salt water yield fresh.

13 Who is wise and knowledgeable among you? Show by your good life that your works are done with gentleness born of wisdom. ¹⁴But if you have bitter envy and selfish ambition in your hearts, do not be arrogant and lie about the truth. ¹⁵This is not wisdom that comes down from above but is earthly, unspiritual, devilish. ¹⁶For where there is envy and selfish ambition, there will also be disorder and wickedness of every kind. ¹⁷But the wisdom from above is first pure, then peaceable, gentle, willing to yield, full of mercy and good fruits, without a trace of partiality or hypocrisy. ¹⁸And the fruit of righteousnessᵐ is sown in peace by those who make peace.

4 Those conflicts and disputes among you, where do they come from? Do they not come from your cravings that are at war within you? ²You want something and do not have it, so you commit murder. And you covetⁿ something and cannot obtain it, so you engage in disputes and conflicts. You do not have because you do not ask. ³You ask and do not receive because you

i 3.2 Gk *a mature man* j 3.6 Gk *Gehenna* k 3.8 Other ancient authorities read *uncontrollable* l 3.9 Other ancient authorities read *God* m 3.18 Or *justice* n 4.2 Or *you murder and you covet*

communities viewed titles such as "teacher" with suspicion (Matt. 23:8, 10). The Letter of James warns against giving too many this honor. **3:2** *Anyone who makes no mistakes in speaking is mature*, or "perfect." The Greek word signals completeness rather than flawlessness. This letter joins other voices concerned with speech and its consequences (see Sir. 14:1; 19:16; Prov. 18:21; Matt. 12:36–37). **3:3–5** The letter introduces examples of small objects that control large ones as metaphors for the power of the tongue. **3:5** *It boasts of great exploits*. Boasting is an example of destructiveness. **3:6–8** *A world of iniquity*. Literally "the world of iniquity." The tongue represents the world from which the community must remain unstained (cf. 1:27). *A restless* (or uncontrollable) *evil, full of deadly poison*. As part of the *world*, the tongue introduces death and destruction. **3:9–10** Specifies the nature of the poison, speech that both blesses God and curses human beings made in God's image (Gen. 1:26). **3:11–12** Appeals to nature in support of its argument, showing that mouths that both bless God and curse people are unnatural.

3:13–18 The wise path. The letter contrasts the ways of wisdom and the ways of the world. **3:13** *Wise and knowledgeable*. Continuing the discussion about teachers (3:1), the letter proposes appropriate behavior for the learned members of the community. **3:14–16** *Earthly, unspiritual, devilish*. Just as the tongue represents the staining presence of the world, so does envy, ambition, and arrogance in those who consider themselves wise. Concern about division caused by envy also occurs in Paul's letters (1 Cor. 3:3; 2 Cor. 12:20; Gal. 5:19–21). **3:17** *From above* suggests from God (cf. John 3:3–7). The letter follows with a list of virtues that the *wisdom from above* displays, actions contrary to those of the fiery, destructive tongue (3:1–12); of envy and selfish ambition (3:14–16); or of the discriminatory behavior highlighted in chap. 2. **3:18** *The fruit of righteousness*, or the fruit of justice, is sown by the peacemakers, echoing Isa. 32:17 and Matt. 5:9.

4:1–10 The world's path. The letter describes friendship with the world. **4:1** *Those conflicts and disputes*. Literally "wars and battles"—that is, significant strife within the community rather than petty disagreements. **4:2** *You want something*. The Greek word for *want* shares a root with the word for "desire" in 1:14–15, marking it as sinful and potentially deadly, thus *you commit murder*. **4:3** *You ask and do not receive*. A reference to Matt. 7:7; note the difference from the request in 1:5–6. The letter

ask wrongly, in order to spend what you get on your pleasures. [4]Adulterers![o] Do you not know that friendship with the world is enmity with God? Therefore whoever wishes to be a friend of the world becomes an enemy of God. [5]Or do you suppose that the scripture speaks to no purpose? Does the spirit that God caused to dwell[p] in us desire envy? [6]But God gives all the more grace; therefore it says,

"God opposes the proud
    but gives grace to the humble."

[7]Submit yourselves therefore to God. Resist the devil, and he will flee from you. [8]Draw near to God, and he will draw near to you. Cleanse your hands, you sinners, and purify your hearts, you double-minded. [9]Lament and mourn and weep. Let your laughter be turned into mourning and your joy into dejection. [10]Humble yourselves before the Lord, and he will exalt you.

11 Do not speak evil against one another, brothers and sisters. Whoever speaks evil against another or judges another speaks evil against the law and judges the law, but if you judge the law, you are not a doer of the law but a judge. [12]There is one lawgiver and judge[q] who is able to save and to destroy. So who, then, are you to judge your neighbor?

13 Come now, you who say, "Today or tomorrow we will go to such and such a town and spend a year there, doing business and making money." [14]Yet you do not even know what tomorrow will bring. What is your life? For you are a mist that appears for a little while and then vanishes. [15]Instead you ought to say, "If the Lord wishes, we will live and do this or that." [16]As it is, you boast in your arrogance; all such boasting is evil. [17]Anyone, then, who knows the right thing to do and fails to do it commits sin.

5 Come now, you rich people, weep and wail for the miseries that are coming to you. [2]Your riches have rotted, and your clothes are moth-eaten. [3]Your gold and silver have rusted, and their rust will be evidence against you, and it will eat your flesh like fire. You have laid up treasure[r] during the last days. [4]Listen! The wages of the laborers who mowed your fields, which you kept back by fraud, cry out, and the cries of the harvesters have reached the ears of the Lord of hosts.

o 4.4 Gk *Adulterous women*; other ancient authorities read *Adulterous men and women* p 4.5 Other ancient authorities read *the spirit that dwells* q 4.12 Other ancient authorities lack *and judge* r 5.3 Or *will eat your flesh, since you have stored up fire*

challenges the belief that every request is morally equivalent and will be honored by God. **4:4** *Adulterers.* Literally "adulterous women." Prophetic writings use the metaphor of an adulterous wife for those who are unfaithful to God (e.g., Hos. 2). The letter's concern is *friendship* and, in particular, loyalty, a central virtue of ancient friendships. One cannot be double-minded (1:7-8), claiming loyalty to both the world and God; friendship with one necessitates enmity with the other. **4:5** *Do you suppose* begins two rhetorical questions. The first invokes the importance of the witness of Scripture. The second questions the nature of God's indwelling Spirit, once more highlighting the contrast between God and the world. **4:6** Quotes Prov. 3:34 from the Septuagint (the Gk. translation of the Old Testament), which presents God's opposition of the proud more forcefully than the original Hebrew. **4:7-10** Calls the believers to repentance and restoration. A similar call to humility is found in 1 Pet. 5:6.

    4:11-17 More warnings about speech. The last verses of chap. 4 offer examples of unwise speech that needs to be controlled (cf. 3:1-12). **4:11-12** Warns against judging or speaking evil against other members of the faith community. The passage echoes Jesus's instructions (Matt. 7:1-7), Paul's writings (Rom. 2:1; 14:4), and Scriptures from the wisdom tradition (Ps. 101:5; Wis. 1:11). **4:13** *We will go.* Some manuscript traditions write these as invitations rather than predictions: "Let us go." In either case, the words of the speaker presume that they can control their future (Prov. 27:1). **4:14** *You are a mist* parallels the earlier comparison in this letter of the rich with the transient flowers of the field (1:10-11), highlighting the fragility of human life. **4:15-16** *You ought to say* condemns hubris rather than the practice of earning a living. **4:17** Reiterates the warning from 2:8-11.

    5:1-6 The oppressive practices of the rich. The letter exposes sinful practices by wealthy landowners. **5:1** *Weep and wail.* Unlike the wealthy person in 1:11-12, these wealthy persons wail. **5:2-3** *Your gold and silver have rusted. . . . You have laid up treasure* echoes teachings of Jesus about storing up treasures in heaven, as well as parables against hoarding (Matt. 6:19; Luke 6:24; 12:16-21). *During the last days* reflects the expectation of Christ's return. **5:4** *The wages of the laborers* were usually minimal, and not receiving wages could cause financial hardship. The Bible prohibits withholding these wages

⁵You have lived on the earth in luxury and in pleasure; you have nourished your hearts in a day of slaughter. ⁶You have condemned and murdered the righteous one, who does not resist you.

7 Be patient, therefore, brothers and sisters, until the coming of the Lord. The farmer waits for the precious crop from the earth, being patient with it until it receives the early and the late rains. ⁸You also must be patient. Strengthen your hearts, for the coming of the Lord is near.ˢ ⁹Brothers and sisters, do not grumble against one another, so that you may not be judged. See, the Judge is standing at the doors! ¹⁰As an example of suffering and patience, brothers and sisters, take the prophets who spoke in the name of the Lord. ¹¹Indeed, we call blessed those who showed endurance. You have heard of the endurance of Job, and you have seen the outcome that the Lord brought about, for the Lord is compassionate and merciful.

12 Above all, brothers and sisters, do not swear, either by heaven or by earth or by any other oath, but let your "Yes" be yes and your "No" be no, so that you may not fall under condemnation.ᵗ

13 Are any among you suffering? They should pray. Are any cheerful? They should sing songs of praise. ¹⁴Are any among you sick? They should call for the elders of the church and have them pray over them, anointing them with oil in the name of the Lord. ¹⁵The prayer of faith will save the sick, and the Lord will raise them up, and anyone who has committed sins will be forgiven. ¹⁶Therefore confess your sins to one another and pray for one another, so that you may be healed. The prayer of the righteous is powerful and effective. ¹⁷Elijah was a human like us, and he prayed fervently that it might not rain, and for three years and six months it did not rain on the earth. ¹⁸Then he prayed again, and the heaven gave rain, and the earth yielded its harvest.

19 My brothers and sisters, if anyone among you wanders from the truthᵘ and is brought back by another, ²⁰you should know that whoever brings back a sinner from wandering will save the sinner'sᵛ soul from death and will cover a multitude of sins.

s 5.8 Or *is at hand*   t 5.12 Other ancient authorities read *into hypocrisy*   u 5.19 Other ancient authorities read *from the way of truth*   v 5.20 Gk *his*

(Lev. 19:13; Deut. 24:14–15; Mal. 3:5). **5:5–6** While withholding the wages of the workers, the rich have enriched themselves. The letter cries out against this injustice. *The righteous one* may be a reference to Jesus or to some other unnamed martyr.

5:7–20 A call to lives of patience and prayer. The final verses of the letter call the community to faithful actions in their life together. **5:7–8** *Be patient . . . until the coming of the Lord* signals the expectation of the coming of Christ (5:3, 9). **5:9** *Do not grumble against one another* reprises 3:9–12, adding the coming of the ultimate Judge. **5:10** *The prophets who spoke in the name of the Lord*—for example, Jeremiah—are upheld in place of grumbling. **5:11** *The endurance of Job* refers both to the book of Job and to the Testament of Job. God's compassion and mercy are attested in Exod. 34:6 and Ps. 103:8. **5:12** *Do not swear* paraphrases Jesus's instructions in Matt. 5:34–37. **5:13–14** *They should pray* suggests three modes of prayer: prayer during suffering, songs of praise, and prayer with the anointing of oil for the sick. **5:14** *The elders of the church.* The older members are imagined as community healers. **5:15** Sickness and sin were often linked (cf. Mark 2:1–12, but see John 9). **5:16** *Confess your sins to one another* marks the community's speech with honesty and prayer. **5:17–18** *Elijah* refers to the story of the drought in 1 Kgs. 17:1; 18:42–45. **5:19–20** *Whoever brings back a sinner from wandering,* the final word of the letter, is a call for the restoration and reintegration of those who have wandered.

THE FIRST LETTER OF PETER

The Audience and Their Situation

First Peter addresses Christian communities throughout five Roman provinces in what is now northwest Turkey. Galatia and Asia were focal areas for Paul's missionary team. How the Christian message spread through the other three provinces remains unclear. The author characterizes the audience's preconversion past as "ignorance" (1:14), a "futile" way of life (1:18), "darkness" (2:9), and idolatry and sexual license in the company of their gentile neighbors (4:3–4). Together with the assertion that they have only come to "trust and hope . . . in God" in connection with trusting in Jesus (1:21), this strongly suggests that he believes himself to be addressing primarily gentile converts. The thickness of the weave of texts from the Jewish Scriptures throughout 1 Peter is no argument against this, since gentile converts would have embraced precisely these texts as the oracles of God alongside Jewish Christians.

The author is primarily concerned with the harassment that these converts have been enduring from their non-Christian neighbors on account of their change in faith and practice (1:6–7; 2:11–12, 15, 18–20; 3:13–4:6; 4:12–19; 5:8–9). This has prominently involved verbal shaming (2:12, 15; 3:16; 4:4, 14) but has extended to physical abuse of the more vulnerable (particularly enslaved Christ followers of non-Christian enslavers; 2:18–21). Such harassment resulted not from an official policy of persecution but rather from the wider population's disdain for the Christian movement and the manner in which it turned people who feared multiple gods into practical atheists believing in only one God who no longer valued sociability or solidarity (reading 4:1–4 from the "other side"). The withdrawal from idolatry central to Christian self-definition (cf. 1 Thess. 1:9–10; 1 Cor. 10:14–21; 2 Cor. 6:14–7:1) was viewed from the outside as an affront to the gods upon whose favor the well-being of all depended as well as an intolerable breach of civic unity. The harassment had as its primary aim the "reformation" of once dependable neighbors.

Nothing in the descriptions of the kinds of harassment suffered by the addressees suggests, let alone necessitates, a date later than the mid-first century CE (cf. 1 Thess. 2:14–16; Phil. 1:27–30). Polycarp of Smyrna's use of the letter in connection with his own letter inquiring after the fate of the martyrs Ignatius of Antioch and his companions (Pol. *Phil.* 1.3; 2.1–2; 8.1–2; 10.2–3) necessitates composition prior to 111 CE.

The Author

The author presents himself as Peter, part of the leadership core of the early Christian movement (cf. Matt. 16:18–19; Gal. 2:1–14; Acts 1–15). This has been forcefully disputed in recent centuries on numerous grounds: the quality of the Greek, which exceeds that expected from a Galilean fisherman; the alignment of quotations from the Jewish Scriptures with the Greek rather than the Hebrew textual traditions, again unexpected; and the affinities with the Pauline Letters, suggesting literary dependence.

Others indicate factors that mitigate the force of these objections: the length of time Peter spent ministering in the Greek-speaking Diaspora, the possibility of considerable help writing the letter from coworkers, and shared material with Paul pointing to common early Christian tradition rather than dependence. The early church accepted the letter's claim to authorship while disputing the same claim in regard to 2 Peter, showing that they, too, were serious and applied critical acumen to the question. An affirmation of Petrine authorship, however, would not be an affirmation of single, unaided authorship.

Reading Guide

A key to understanding 1 Peter is to recognize the challenges its author seeks to address and to which he has crafted this letter to nurture a particular response. From beginning to end, the author seeks to promote his hearers' perseverance in their commitment to Jesus and to the Christian movement in the face of the shaming, rejection, and abuse that they encounter on account of the same. The reader is encouraged to consider the ways in which particular paragraphs or even discrete affirmations and images contribute to any one of the five principal strategies by which the author pursues this goal.

First, he pervasively reaffirms the honor and the privilege the Christ followers enjoy before God and one another, even though their honor has been diminished significantly in the eyes of their neighbors (e.g., 2:4–10). Second, he reinterprets their experiences of disgrace in ways that position them to persevere—for example, as a trial of their virtue that will result in their greater and lasting honor (1:6–7) or as attempts made by the cosmic enemy, Satan, to disqualify them from the noble destiny toward which

God had set them (5:8–9). Third, he calls his audiences to consider the fundamental challenge before them to be not how they might regain honor in their neighbors' sight or alleviate the social tension they experience but how they might remain steadfastly on track toward the "inheritance" (1:4), the "salvation" (1:5), and the "praise and glory and honor" (1:7) that is promised them at the manifestation of Jesus Christ. Fourth, he advises his hearers to take great care to eliminate any causes for suspicion and hostility that are *not* essential to remaining loyal toward Christ and, indeed, even to invest themselves as fully as possible in those attitudes and actions that ought to evoke appreciation (e.g., 2:12–3:6). Finally, he seeks to heighten the emotional and relational value of "belonging" within the Christian group (e.g., through mutual encouragement, support, investment, and honor) while also highlighting the advantages that have been gained through separation from the way of the life the converts left behind. Attention to how these five strategies operate throughout the letter will enable the reader to understand how the whole forms a coherent and carefully crafted response to a pressing pastoral concern.

David A. deSilva

1 Peter, an apostle of Jesus Christ,
To the exiles of the dispersion in Pontus, Galatia, Cappadocia, Asia, and Bithynia, [2]who have been chosen and destined by God the Father and sanctified by the Spirit to be obedient to Jesus Christ and to be sprinkled with his blood:

May grace and peace be yours in abundance.

3 Blessed be the God and Father of our Lord Jesus Christ! By his great mercy he has given us a new birth into a living hope through the resurrection of Jesus Christ from the dead [4]and into an inheritance that is imperishable, undefiled, and unfading, kept in heaven for you, [5]who are being protected by the power of God through faith for a salvation ready to be revealed in the last time. [6]In this you rejoice,[a] even if now for a little while you have had to suffer various trials, [7]so that the genuineness of your faith—being more precious than gold that, though perishable, is tested by fire—may be found to result in praise and glory and honor when Jesus Christ is revealed. [8]Although you have not seen[b] him, you love him, and even though you do not see him now, you believe in him and rejoice with an indescribable and glorious joy, [9]for you are receiving the outcome of your faith, the salvation of your souls.[c]

10 Concerning this salvation, the prophets who prophesied of the grace intended for you made careful search and inquiry, [11]inquiring about the time and circumstances[d] that the Spirit of Christ within them indicated when it testified in advance to the sufferings intended for Christ and the subsequent glory. [12]It was revealed to them that they were serving not themselves but you, in regard to the things that have now been announced to you through those who brought you good news by the Holy Spirit sent from heaven, things into which angels long to look!

a 1.6 Or *Rejoice in this*   *b* 1.8 Other ancient authorities read *known*   *c* 1.9 Or *lives*   *d* 1.11 Or *the person and time*

1:1–2 Greeting. 1:1 *Dispersion.* The author depicts his addressees' situation as akin to the Jews' experience since the Assyrian and Babylonian invasions of the eighth and sixth centuries BCE, scattered far from their homeland. **1:2** In the Greek, *chosen* describes "exiles" in 1:1, underscoring the irony of the addressees' situation in the world. Their response to the Christian message shows them to have been specially selected by God while also leading to social disenfranchisement.

1:3–12 Benediction. 1:3 *Blessed be the God.* A familiar liturgical formula in Jewish culture (e.g., Ps. 106:48; Tob. 13:2, 18; Luke 1:68). Similar benedictions appear in 2 Cor. 1:3–7; Eph. 1:3–14. **1:5** *A salvation ready to be revealed. Salvation*, or "deliverance," is conceived as an experience yet to be completed (see also 1:9; 2:2; cf. Rom. 5:9; 13:11; Heb. 1:14; 9:28). **1:6–7** *Various trials.* The Christians' neighbors' attempts to humiliate them become opportunities to demonstrate the faithfulness that will be honored at Jesus's coming again. Cf. Prov. 17:3; Sir. 2:5; Wis. 3:5–6; Jas. 1:2–4. **1:8** *You do not see him.* The reason is supplied in 3:18–22. **1:10** Early Christians held the Hebrew *prophets* to have looked forward to the life of Jesus as the fulfillment of God's plan for deliverance (cf. Luke 24:25–27; John 5:39; 12:41; Rom. 1:2). **1:12** *Serving not themselves but you.* Despite the difficulties they experience, addressees stand at a most privileged place in the history of God's beneficent interventions (see also 1:20).

13 Therefore prepare your minds for action;[e] discipline yourselves; set all your hope on the grace that Jesus Christ will bring you when he is revealed. [14]Like obedient children, do not be conformed to the desires that you formerly had in ignorance. [15]Instead, as he who called you is holy, be holy yourselves in all your conduct, [16]for it is written, "You shall be holy, for I am holy."

17 If you invoke as Father the one who judges impartially according to each person's work, live in fear during the time of your exile. [18]You know that you were ransomed from the futile conduct inherited from your ancestors, not with perishable things like silver or gold [19]but with the precious blood of Christ, like that of a lamb without defect or blemish. [20]He was destined before the foundation of the world but was revealed at the end of the ages for your sake. [21]Through him you have come to trust in God, who raised him from the dead and gave him glory, so that your trust and hope are in God.

22 Now that you have purified your souls[f] by your obedience to the truth[g] so that you have genuine mutual affection, love one another deeply from the heart.[h] [23]You have been born anew, not of perishable but of imperishable seed, through the living and enduring word of God.[i] [24]For

"All flesh is like grass
    and all its glory like the flower of grass.
The grass withers,
    and the flower falls,

[25] but the word of the Lord endures forever." That word is the good news that was announced to you.

2 Rid yourselves, therefore, of all malice and all guile, insincerity, envy, and all slander. [2]Like newborn infants, long for the pure, spiritual milk, so that by it you may grow into salvation—[3]if indeed you have tasted that the Lord is good.[j]

4 Come to him, a living stone, though rejected by mortals yet chosen and precious in God's sight, and [5]like living stones let yourselves be built[k] into a spiritual house, to be a holy priesthood, to offer spiritual sacrifices acceptable to God through Jesus Christ. [6]For it stands in scripture:

"See, I am laying in Zion a stone,
    a cornerstone chosen and precious,
and whoever believes in him will not be
    put to shame."

[7]This honor, then, is for you who believe, but for those who do not believe,[l]

"The stone that the builders rejected
    has become the very head of the
        corner,"

[8]and

"A stone that makes them stumble
    and a rock that makes them fall."

e 1.13 Gk *gird up the loins of your mind*   f 1.22 Or *lives*
g 1.22 Other ancient authorities add *through the Spirit*
h 1.22 Other ancient authorities read *a pure heart*   i 1.23 Or
through the word of the living and enduring God   j 2.3 Or *kind*
k 2.5 Or *you yourselves are being built*   l 2.7 Other ancient
authorities read *obey*

1:13–21 Encouragement to remain distinct. 1:16 *You shall be holy.* The summons to ethnic Israel (Lev. 11:44–45; 19:2) remains the call to God's people in Christ. **1:17** That God *judges impartially* is frequently affirmed (see Deut. 10:17; Sir. 35:14–16; Acts 10:34; Rom. 2:11). *Your exile.* See note on 1:1. **1:18** *Ransomed.* Interpreting Jesus's death as an act of redemption (as in Mark 10:45; Rom. 3:24–25; Heb. 9:12, 15), here specifically from the way of life toward which the audiences' neighbors would draw them back. **1:19** Sacrificial animals were to be *without defect* (see, e.g., Exod. 29:1; Lev. 1:10; 3:1, 6; 4:23, 28; 9:3). **1:21** *Your trust and hope are in God.* A focus on Jesus does not detract from the centrality of the one God in the author's understanding of the newly developed Christ-following community.

1:22–2:10 The new identity of Christ followers. 1:22 *Mutual affection.* In Greek, "philadelphia," the love shared particularly between siblings, manifested in a commitment to cooperation, sharing resources, and showing patience and mutual forgiveness. *Love one another.* Cf. John 13:34; 15:12. **1:24–25** Isaiah 40:6–8. **2:2** *Infants* extends the metaphor of being born to new life. **2:4** *Rejected . . . chosen.* The author highlights the distance between God's evaluation of Jesus's worth and that of Jesus's opponents. The language anticipates the quotations of Isa. 28:16 and Ps. 118:22 in 2:6–7. **2:5** *Spiritual house.* Temple, priesthood, and sacrifices offer an ennobling lens for Christian identity and practice. See also 1 Cor. 3:16–17; Eph. 2:19–22. **2:6–7** See Isa. 28:16. *This honor.* The quotation assures the letter's marginalized audiences that an honorable outcome awaits those who have aligned themselves with the *cornerstone,* Jesus. *The stone.* Psalm 118:22 is read as authoritative evidence that God elevated the once-shamed Jesus to a place of highest honor. **2:8** *A stone.* Isaiah 8:14–15 assures the addressees that it is their neighbors who ultimately face disgrace for their opposition to the Christian movement.

They stumble because they disobey the word, as they were destined to do.

9 But you are a chosen people, a royal priesthood, a holy nation, God's own people,[m] in order that you may proclaim the excellence of him who called you out of darkness into his marvelous light.

[10] Once you were not a people,
but now you are God's people;
once you had not received mercy,
but now you have received mercy.

11 Beloved, I urge you as aliens and exiles to abstain from the desires of the flesh that wage war against the soul.[n] [12]Conduct yourselves honorably among the gentiles, so that, though they malign you as evildoers, they may see your honorable deeds and glorify God when he comes to judge.[o]

13 For the Lord's sake be subject to every human authority,[p] whether to the emperor as supreme [14]or to governors as sent by him to punish those who do wrong and to praise those who do right. [15]For it is God's will that by doing right you should silence the ignorance of the foolish. [16]As servants of God, live as free people, yet do not use your freedom as a pretext for evil. [17]Honor everyone. Love the family of believers.[q] Fear God. Honor the emperor.

18 Slaves, be subject to your masters with all respect,[r] not only those who are good and gentle but also those who are dishonest. [19]For it is a commendable thing if, being aware of God, a person endures pain while suffering unjustly. [20]If you endure when you are beaten for doing wrong, what credit is that? But if you endure when you do good and suffer for it, this is a commendable thing before God. [21]For to this you have been called, because Christ also suffered for you, leaving you an example, so that you should follow in his steps.

m 2.9 Gk *a people for his possession* n 2.11 Or *one's life* o 2.12 Gk *God on the day of visitation* p 2.13 Or *every authority ordained for humans* q 2.17 Gk *Love the brotherhood* r 2.18 Or *fear*

2:9 *A chosen people.* The author describes the Christ-following community with honorific terms once applied to God's historic people, Israel (cf. Exod. 19:6; Isa. 43:20–21; Wis. 17:2). *Proclaim the excellence.* Isaiah 43:20–21. Spreading the fame of their benefactor was the proper response to having received such privileges. **2:10** *Not a people.* Using texts promising the restoration of the nation of ethnic Israel (Hos. 1:6, 9–10; 2:1, 23), the author speaks of the formation of the global community of Christ followers, both Jewish and gentile.

2:11–17 Initial exhortation to respectful and winsome behavior. Throughout 2:11–3:6, the author urges his audiences to work toward overturning the impression of the Christian movement as subversive to the extent possible (cf. Titus 2:3–10) without compromising their commitment to worshiping one God and one Lord. **2:11** *Aliens and exiles.* Cf. Gen. 23:4. The author invites his hearers, whatever their actual sociopolitical status, to embrace their marginal status in their places of residence and to think of their lasting home in terms of God and the Christ-following community. *Desires.* Greco-Roman and Hellenistic Jewish ethicists frequently promoted mastery of one's own desires, emotions, and impulses to enable living a consistently virtuous and praiseworthy life (see Plato, *Phaedo* 93–94; 4 Macc. 1:1–3:18). The *flesh* here extends beyond the physical aspect of a human being to matters of temperament, mental disposition, and relationship (see, e.g., 2:1; cf. also Gal. 5:19–21). **2:12** The use of the term *gentiles* is a strategic "othering," reinforcing boundaries between the Christian gentile converts and non-Christian gentiles, whose fundamental convictions and "way of life" (1:18) the converts have left behind. *Glorify God.* See Matt. 5:16. **2:13** *Be subject.* The author shares with Paul (see Rom. 13:1–7) an optimistic view of Roman government. Neither considers what ought to be the Christian's response when the governing authorities punish the innocent and promote the unjust. **2:17** *Family of believers.* Literally "the brotherhood." The author, like Jesus and Paul, regards the Christian movement as a kinship group whose internal relationships should mirror that of natural sisters and brothers at their best. *Fear God. Honor the emperor.* The distinction between what is due God and what is due the emperor is striking in territories where the emperors were widely honored as gods with temples, priests, and sacrifices.

2:18–25 Counsel to enslaved Christians. 2:18 Household *slaves* are particularly in view, in keeping with the largely urban setting of the early Christian movement. Instructions to Christian enslaved people become instructions to all Christians at several points (see 3:14; 4:14-16). **2:19** *Commendable thing*, or better, a "favor" from God, a genuine gift because suffering for the sake of loyalty to Christ carries the promise of sharing in his honor at his return. *Suffering unjustly*—for example, being beaten or otherwise penalized for resisting a summons to participate in the household's idolatrous rituals or to submit to the sexual uses that were commonly expected of the enslaved. See **"The Hierarchical Household,"**

22 "He committed no sin,
  and no deceit was found in his mouth."
23When he was abused, he did not return abuse; when he suffered, he did not threaten, but he entrusted himself to the one who judges justly. 24He himself bore our sins in his body on the cross,[s] so that, having died to sins, we might live for righteousness; by his wounds[t] you have been healed. 25For you were going astray like sheep, but now you have returned to the shepherd and guardian of your souls.[u]

3 Wives, in the same way, be subject to your husbands, so that, even if some of them do not obey the word, they may be won over without a word by their wives' conduct, 2when they see the purity and respect of your conduct. 3Do not adorn yourselves outwardly by braiding your hair and by wearing gold ornaments or fine clothing; 4rather, let your adornment be the inner self with the lasting beauty of a gentle and quiet spirit, which is very precious in God's sight. 5It was in this way long ago that the holy women who hoped in God used to adorn themselves by being subject to their husbands. 6Thus Sarah obeyed Abraham and called him lord. You have become her daughters as long as you do what is good and never let fears alarm you.

7 Husbands, in the same way, show consideration for your wives in your life together, paying honor to the woman—though the weaker vessel,[v] they are joint heirs of the gracious gift of life—so that nothing may hinder your prayers.

8 Finally, all of you, have unity of spirit, sympathy, love for one another, a tender heart, and a humble mind. 9Do not repay evil for evil or abuse for abuse, but, on the contrary, repay with a blessing. It is for this that you were called—that you might inherit a blessing. 10For
"Those who desire to love life
  and to see good days,
let them keep their tongues from evil
  and their lips from speaking deceit;
11 let them turn away from evil and do good;
  let them seek peace and pursue it.
12 For the eyes of the Lord are on the
    righteous,
  and his ears are open to their prayer.
But the face of the Lord is against those
  who do evil."

13 Now who will harm you if you are eager to do what is good? 14But even if you do suffer for doing what is right,[w] you are blessed. Do not fear what they fear,[x] and do not be intimidated, 15but in your hearts sanctify Christ as Lord. Always be ready to make your defense to anyone who demands from you an accounting for the hope that is in you, 16yet do it with gentleness and respect. Maintain a good conscience so that, when you are maligned,[y] those who abuse you for your good conduct in Christ may be put to shame. 17For it is better to suffer for doing good, if suffering should be God's will, than to suffer for doing evil. 18For

s 2.24 Or *carried up our sins in his body to the tree*   t 2.24 Gk *bruise*   u 2.25 Or *lives*   v 3.7 Or *body*   w 3.14 Or *for righteousness' sake*   x 3.14 Gk *their fear*   y 3.16 Other ancient authorities read *when they malign you as evildoers*

p. 2090. **2:21** *Christ also suffered*, both meriting the loyalty of those benefited and providing an example of attaining glory through hardships (1:11). *Follow in his steps*. Cf. Matt. 16:24–25; 1 John 2:6. **2:22** *He committed no sin*. Isaiah 53:9. Isaiah 52:13–53:12 stands prominently in the background of the author's reflections upon Jesus's sufferings and death in 2:22–25. **2:23** *Did not return abuse*. See Luke 6:27–28; 23:34. Jesus's practice becomes explicit example in 1 Pet. 3:9. **2:24** *Bore our sins*. Cf. Isa. 53:12. *By his wounds*. Cf. Isa. 53:4–5. **2:25** *Going astray like sheep*. See Isa. 53:6.

3:1–7 Instructions to wives and husbands. **3:1** *Be subject*. The author is primarily concerned with Christian wives of non-Christian husbands. Cf. 1 Cor. 7:12–16. *Without a word*. A quiet wife was held up as an ideal in both Jewish and Greek texts (cf. Sir. 26:14; Aristotle, *Pol*. 1.13). **3:3** *Adorn yourselves*. Stoics and other ethicists frequently pointed to virtue and dignity as a woman's ideal "adornment" rather than fine apparel and jewelry (see Epictetus, *Ench*. 40). **3:6** *Called him lord*. In the Hebrew of Gen. 18:12, Sarah calls Abraham "adon," "lord." *Never let fears alarm*. The author calls for courage in the face of their non-Christian husbands' intimidation. **3:7** *Husbands*. In the Greek, it is clearer that the Christian husband is to exercise consideration (rather than domination) in the face of the wife's greater physical vulnerability but also to show her honor on the basis of her equal status as a coheir in Christ.

3:8–22 Summons to virtuous practice in the face of harassment. **3:9** *Do not repay*. See Luke 6:27–28; Rom. 12:14–21; 1 Thess. 5:15. **3:10–12** Psalm 34:12–16a. **3:14** *Blessed*. Innocent suffering for piety's sake marks a person as "privileged" and especially "favored" by God (see Matt. 5:10–12; Luke 6:22–23). The claim stands in stark contrast with the more popular view that suffering was a sign of divine displeasure.

Going Deeper: The Hierarchical Household (1 Peter 3:1–9)

The Greco-Roman household was an undisguisedly hierarchical institution. Aristotle defined a "complete" household as consisting of a husband and a wife, a father and children, and an enslaver and the enslaved. Each pair represented a relationship of subordination (*Pol.* 1.3), with a single individual—the male head of the household—in the superior position in each. His rule over children and the enslaved was absolute, likened to monarchical power. In practice, the enslaved was placed in a position of extreme vulnerability in terms of being both coerced to act against conscience and subjected to physical abuse for disobedience. The rule of the husband over the wife was depicted in less harsh terms. Aristotle likened it to the rule that one citizen holds over other citizens by virtue of being an elected official—with the differences that there was no election and the office is permanent (*Pol.* 1.12). Plutarch likened it to the harmony that results when the singer of the descant (the wife) conforms herself to the lead of the singer of the melody (the husband; "Advice on Marriage" 11). Households in Israel exhibited a similarly hierarchical structure and ethos (cf. Sir. 33:25–30; Josephus, *Ag. Ap.* 2.199).

The author of 1 Peter does not subject these arrangements to critical examination, nor does he consider the ways in which being "in Christ" together should alter the experience of these relationships (save for part of what he directs to Christian husbands in 3:7; cf. Eph. 5:21–6:9). Rather, his interest is to guide Christian wives and enslaved people to behave in such a way as will minimize impressions of the Christian movement as subversive. Since submission to the will of the (male) head of the household was a core virtue, he urges his hearers to offer precisely this to the extent possible within the bounds of their allegiance to God in Christ. This limitation is clearly to be inferred from the author's assumption that the enslaved *will* experience punishment as a result of "doing good" because their mindfulness of the one God (2:19) leads them to resist commands of their masters that conflict with this higher loyalty. It is precisely because they bear such punishment for the sake of this higher loyalty, a loyalty that shall prove itself rewarded at Christ's return, that the experience can be associated with God's "favor" ("a commendable thing," 2:20). Similarly, one might surmise that the Christian wife, while generally directed to submission, is also counseled to boldness in the face of intimidation where violating her own higher loyalties are concerned (3:6).

David A. deSilva

Christ also suffered[z] for sins once for all, the righteous for the unrighteous, in order to bring you[a] to God. He was put to death in the flesh but made alive in the spirit, [19]in which also he went and made a proclamation to the spirits in prison, [20]who in former times did not obey, when God waited patiently in the days of Noah, during the building of the ark, in which a few, that is, eight lives, were saved through water. [21]And baptism, which this prefigured, now saves you—not as a removal of dirt from the body but as an appeal to God for[b] a good conscience, through the resurrection of Jesus Christ, [22]who has gone into heaven and is at the right hand of God, with angels, authorities, and powers made subject to him.

4 Since, therefore, Christ suffered in the flesh,[c] arm yourselves also with the same intention (for whoever has suffered in the flesh has finished with sin), [2]so as to live for the rest of your time in the flesh no longer by human desires but by the will of God. [3]You have already spent enough time in doing what the gentiles like to do, living in debauchery, passions, drunkenness, revels, carousing, and lawless idolatry. [4]They are surprised that you no longer join them in the same excesses of dissipation, and so they blaspheme.[d]

z 3.18 Other ancient authorities read *died*   a 3.18 Other ancient authorities read *us*   b 3.21 Or *a pledge to God from*   c 4.1 Other ancient authorities add *for us* or *for you*   d 4.4 Or *they malign you*

3:20 *Noah.* See Gen. 6–8. *Eight lives.* Noah, his wife, their three sons, and their wives (Gen. 7:7). **3:21** *Baptism.* The ritual of initiation into the Christian community. **3:22** *At the right hand.* Psalm 110:1, frequently applied to the ascension of Jesus in early Christian texts (cf. Col. 3:1; Heb. 1:13). *Angels, authorities, and powers.* The first-century Jewish cosmos was heavily populated with spirit beings (see T. Levi 3; Rev. 4–5), which, whether benign or hostile, are all now subordinated to the glorified Christ (see also Eph. 1:20–22).

4:1–6 Encouragement to persevere in distinctiveness. 4:1 *Whoever has suffered.* The author claims that such commitment to Christ that leads to suffering on his behalf also brings freedom from the power of "human desires" so as to accomplish God's purposes. **4:2** *No longer by human desires.* See note on 2:11. **4:3** *Gentiles.* See note on 2:12. **4:4** *Surprised,* or "alienated," "put off" by the change in

Going Deeper: The Spirits in Prison (1 Peter 3:19–22)

The second century CE saw traditions arise concerning Jesus's preaching to the dead and the harrowing of hell, Jesus's liberation of the spirits of the righteous upon his own descent into the underworld (see Gos. Pet. 10; Ignatius, *To the Magnesians* 9.2; Justin Martyr, *Dialogue with Trypho* 72). In 1 Pet. 3:19–22, the author was drawn into the orbit of this tradition and read in its light, but he himself more likely drew upon a very different background. This older tradition is preserved in the earlier strata of 1 Enoch, a highly influential apocalypse written in stages from the second century BCE through the early first century CE (see **"Apocalypse," p. 1216**). Developing the mysterious episode of Gen. 6:1–4, 1 En. 6–36 speaks of angelic spirits who did not keep to their appointed spheres but rather invaded the human sphere to mate with human females, the union producing a population of giants. These spirits brought forbidden knowledge (mining for iron and precious metals, cosmetics, spells and potions) that served to inflame violence, greed, and lust, while their offspring wreaked havoc among humankind. Once defeated by the armies of God, the rebel spirits were shut up in a dark prison to await the final day of their judgment (1 En. 10:11–15; 18:13–16; 21:1–6). God summons the mysterious figure of Enoch and sends him to proclaim the finality of God's judgment upon them and upon their hybrid offspring (1 En. 12:4–13:3). The story was known also to the author of the Letter of Jude (see Jude 6, 13b; cf. 2 Pet. 2:4), who quotes 1 En. 1:9 explicitly (Jude 14–15).

In 1 Peter, Enoch's action is understood as a "type" or foreshadowing of Christ's proclamation, even as the flood becomes a type of Christian baptism in this passage. Christ's exaltation after his death and resurrection is presented as the occasion on which he declares his own triumph over every spirit-being opposed to God's rule and order. Thus 3:19 anticipates the paragraph's climax in 3:22. The story of these rebellious angels is closely connected to the flood story in Jewish tradition, the latter being a "cleanup" operation to wash away the effects of the rebel angels and their giant offspring (Gen. 6:1–5; Jub. 5:1–5). This connection is evident here as well (3:19–20).

David A. deSilva

⁵But they will have to give an accounting to him who stands ready to judge the living and the dead. ⁶For this is the reason the gospel was proclaimed even to the dead, so that, though they had been judged in the flesh as everyone is judged, they might live in the spirit as God does.

7 The end of all things is near;*ᵉ* therefore be serious and discipline yourselves for the sake of your prayers. ⁸Above all, maintain constant love for one another, for love covers a multitude of sins. ⁹Be hospitable to one another without complaining. ¹⁰Like good stewards of the manifold grace of God, serve one another with whatever gift each of you has received. ¹¹Whoever speaks must do so as one speaking the very words of God; whoever serves must do so with the strength that God supplies, so that God may be glorified in all things through Jesus Christ. To him belong the glory and the power forever and ever. Amen.

12 Beloved, do not be surprised at the fiery

e 4.7 Or is at hand

the Christian converts' practice. *Blaspheme.* The Greek word more probably refers to abusive speech directed toward or uttered about the Christian converts rather than God. **4:5** *Give an accounting.* The day of God's judgment will also mean vindication for the believers as their detractors and abusers face the God whom they denied. **4:6** *Even to the dead.* An assurance that deceased Christians, though dying as all must, will nevertheless enjoy eternal life.

4:7–11 Call to mutual support and encouragement. 4:7 *The end . . . is near.* A reminder that strategically prioritizes the continued commitment to their returning Lord. **4:8** *Love covers.* Likely a practical rule for life in community, forgiving out of love rather than nurturing grudges (see Prov. 10:12; T. Jos. 17:2). **4:9** *Be hospitable.* The continued willingness of the propertied converts to open up their homes was essential for the regular gathering of the Christian assembly (e.g., Acts 18:7–8; Rom. 16:5, 23) and the facilitating of the movement of itinerant missionaries, teachers, and emissaries (e.g., Acts 17:5–7; Phlm. 22; 2 John 10–11). **4:10** *Stewards.* The image transforms patronage into service, the channeling of God's resources rather than the indebting of one's fellow Christians to oneself (see 1 Cor. 12:4–11).

4:12–19 Further encouragement in the face of harassment. 4:12 *To test you.* See note on 1:6–7.

ordeal that is taking place among you to test you, as though something strange were happening to you. [13]But rejoice insofar as you are sharing Christ's sufferings, so that you may also be glad and shout for joy when his glory is revealed. [14]If you are reviled for the name of Christ, you are blessed, because the spirit of glory,[f] which is the Spirit of God,[g] is resting on you.[b] [15]But let none of you suffer as a murderer, a thief, a criminal, or even as a mischief maker.[i] [16]Yet if any of you suffers as a Christian, do not consider it a disgrace, but glorify God because you bear this name.[j] [17]For the time has come for judgment to begin with the household of God; if it begins with us, what will be the end for those who do not obey the gospel of God? [18]And

"If it is hard for the righteous to be
    saved,
  what will become of the ungodly and
    the sinner?"

[19]Therefore, let those suffering in accordance with God's will entrust their lives to a faithful Creator, while continuing to do good.

5 Now as an elder myself and a witness of the sufferings of Christ, as well as one who shares in the glory to be revealed, I exhort the elders among you [2]to tend the flock of God that is in your charge, exercising the oversight,[k] not under compulsion but willingly, as God would have you do it,[l] not for sordid gain but eagerly. [3]Do not lord it over those in your charge, but be examples to the flock. [4]And when the chief shepherd appears, you will win the crown of glory that never fades away. [5]In the same way, you who are younger must be subject to the elders.[m] And all of you must clothe yourselves with humility in your dealings with one another, for

"God opposes the proud
  but gives grace to the humble."

6 Humble yourselves, therefore, under the mighty hand of God, so that he may exalt you in due time. [7]Cast all your anxiety on him, because he cares for you. [8]Discipline yourselves; keep alert. Like a roaring lion your adversary the devil prowls around, looking for someone to devour. [9]Resist him, steadfast in your faith, for you know that your brothers and sisters in all the world are undergoing the same kinds of suffering. [10]And after you have suffered for a little while, the God of all grace, who has called you to his eternal glory in Christ,[n] will himself restore, support, strengthen, and establish you. [11]To him be the power[o] forever and ever. Amen.

12 Through Silvanus, whom I consider a

f 4.14 Other ancient authorities add *and of power* g 4.14 Or *spirit of glory and of God* h 4.14 Other ancient authorities add *On their part he is blasphemed, but on your part he is glorified* i 4.15 Meaning of Gk uncertain j 4.16 Other ancient authorities read *in this respect* k 5.2 Other ancient authorities lack *exercising the oversight* l 5.2 Or *in a godly manner*; other ancient authorities lack *as God would have you do it* m 5.5 Or *of those who are older* n 5.10 Other ancient authorities read *Christ Jesus* o 5.11 Other ancient authorities read *glory and power*

4:13 *Sharing Christ's sufferings.* See 2:21; 3:18; 4:1. The connection between sharing in Christ's sufferings now and Christ's glory at his coming again is made explicit (cf. Rom. 8:17; 2 Tim. 2:11–12). **4:14** *Reviled . . . blessed.* See note on 3:14. **4:16** *Christian.* See Acts 11:26; 26:28. Outsiders appear to have coined and used the term as a derogatory label. **4:17** *If it begins with us.* The author has already suggested that the purpose of such "judgment" is testing and proving genuineness (1:6–7). The purpose and outcome of God's judgment of *those who do not obey* are quite different. **4:18** *If it is hard.* Proverbs 11:31 (following the Greek rather than the Hebrew text tradition). **4:19** *Entrust their lives.* See 2:23.

5:1–11 Closing instructions. 5:1 While *elder* can refer to an office, it may also simply refer to those who are senior in age and thus naturally exercise influence and leadership in Greco-Roman culture. **5:2** *Tend the flock.* A common metaphor for leadership (cf. Ezek. 34; John 10:1–18; 21:15–17). **5:3** *Lord it over* recalls a saying of Jesus (see Matt. 20:25). **5:4** *Crown of glory.* The Greek suggests, rather, the "honorific wreaths" that winning athletes would receive as tokens of their victory in their contests. **5:5** *God opposes.* A consistent theme of Scripture (see, e.g., 1 Sam. 2:7–8; Prov. 22:4; Sir. 3:17–20; Jas. 4:6, 10). **5:6** *Humble . . . exalt.* See Matt. 23:12; Luke 14:11; 18:14. **5:7** *Cast all your anxiety.* See Matt. 6:25, 32; Phil. 4:6. **5:8** *The devil.* The angelic accuser of humankind before God (Job 1–2; Luke 22:31; Zech. 3:1–2) who came also to represent God's cosmic enemy (Rev. 12:1–18). Yielding to their neighbors' pressures is framed as a shameful and disastrous defeat. **5:9** *In all the world.* The experiences of being made to feel deviant are in fact the normal experiences of Christ's followers empire-wide.

5:12–14 Letter closing. 5:12 *Through Silvanus*, known elsewhere as a member of the Pauline missionary team (see Acts 15:22–32; 16:16–30; 17:1–15; 2 Cor. 1:19; 1 Thess. 1:1; 2 Thess. 1:1). The expression

faithful brother, I have written this short letter to encourage you and to testify that this is the true grace of God. Stand fast in it. [13]Your sister church[p] in Babylon, chosen together with you, sends you greetings, and so does my son Mark. [14]Greet one another with a kiss of love.

Peace to all of you who are in Christ.[q]

p 5.13 Gk *She who is* *q* 5.14 Other ancient authorities add *Jesus* or *Amen* or *Jesus. Amen*

suggests his role as a letter bearer rather than as a co-sender. *The true grace of God*, or "the genuine gift of God." The addressees are encouraged to *stand fast* knowing that sharing in Christ's sufferings leads to sharing in Christ's glory, making the negative experiences indeed a "gift." **5:13** Labeling the author's location in Rome as *Babylon* is an appropriate counterpart to describing the addressees' existence as "dispersion" (see note on 1:1). *Mark* is also connected with the Pauline mission (Acts 12:25; 15:37–39; Col. 4:10; Phlm. 24) and remembered in the second century as Peter's interpreter in Rome and the author of Peter's "memoirs" in the form of the Gospel. **5:14** *Kiss of love* (cf. Rom. 16:16; 1 Cor. 16:20; 2 Cor. 13:12; 1 Thess. 5:26). A greeting among family and very close friends and thus a measure of the quality of personal bonds nurtured within the Christian communities.

THE SECOND LETTER OF PETER

Authorship, Date, and Literary History

Second Peter is likely the latest writing in the New Testament, written in the early to mid-second century CE. Although only three chapters, it is a virtual compendium of biblical stories. One can read 2 Peter as a *throughway* to traditions like the gospel transfiguration and baptism accounts (1:16–18), the Old Testament prophetic tradition, and the apostolic witness (1:19–22; 3:2). It casts Peter and Paul as not only apostles but writers of Christian tradition (3:1, 15–16). Texturing its Christian letter structure is the expectation of Peter's impending death and an affirmation of the certainty of the world's end as the readers know it. Second Peter is a letter with testament appeal (1:12–15) and an apocalyptic perspective (3:10–13; see **"Apocalypse," p. 1216**). A testament is published as a person's final words to provide guidance to followers after the person's death. But, similar to 1 Peter, this document is likely written in Peter's name due to its Greek style, its preference for the *Greek* Jewish Scriptures, and its apparent literary dependence on the Pauline Letters.

The Relationship of 2 Peter to 1 Peter and Jude

Wedged between 1 Peter and 1 John, 2 Peter is hidden from view, but readers should not overlook its message. Although 2 Peter implicitly acknowledges it is not the first letter written under Peter's name (3:1), this letter does not replicate 1 Peter's hospitality (4:9) and mediation (3:8–9) across a diverse membership (5:9). The community ethic of 2 Peter is disturbingly different. The two letters share authorial attribution and some common vocabulary—such as *asebēs* ("ungodly"; 1 Pet. 4:18; 2 Pet. 2:5, 6; 3:7) and *aretē* ("virtue" or "excellence"; 1 Pet. 2:9; 2 Pet. 1:3, 5)—but the fundamental theological responses to their diverse memberships are drastically different.

Whereas 1 Peter attempts to cultivate Christian kinship across differences in response to the persecution aimed at believers from outside the community (1 Pet. 3:14–15; 4:3–4, 14–16), 2 Peter persecutes segments of its own membership. The letter profiles and targets Christian members who share a common confession but espouse a different understanding of its meaning and significance for the Christian manner of life and teaching. Second Peter even recycles some of the polemics in Jude, especially Jude 4, 6–13, 16–18 (see 2 Pet. 2:1, 4, 6–13, 17–18; see also the study notes). Whereas Jude provides space for mercy and reconciliation (vv. 22–23), 2 Peter does not. It insists members subscribe to a single understanding (2 Pet. 1:5–8) while shunning those who do not (3:17).

Reading Guide

Caution is necessary for reading and interpreting 2 Peter. The letter piles one derogatory description on another for an opposing understanding of Christian faith. Although the letter labels the alternative teaching as "destructive opinions" (*haireseis*; 2:1) and "deceptive words" (*plastois logois*; 2:3), those teachings come from inside the Christian community. The opposing view the letter discredits is fundamentally a Christian view.

Second Peter fashions a community ethic engaged in stigmatization inside its Christian community under the name of not just Peter but Simeon Peter. The Semitic spelling, *Symeōn*, stands in the first position to the Greek spelling, *Petros*. The letter hybridizes the dialectal name, rendering Peter a person of two worlds: the Semitic-speaking and Greek-speaking worlds, with their accompanying thought and behavior patterns. Yet the letter does not promote the kind of tolerance one might expect from an author who describes themselves as a person of two worlds.

Recycling scriptural traditions of angels, Noah, Sodom and Gomorrah, Lot, and Balaam, the letter casts a vision of two distinct paths in chap. 2: a way of righteousness (*dikaiosynē*, which also means justice; 2:21; see 2:2, 15) or a way of unrighteousness (*adikeō*; 2:13, 15). In so doing, the letter divides its membership into two factions by policing the boundaries of Christian belief and practice. It targets alternative Christian understandings that do not fit its construction. Those "Other" Christian perspectives, according to 2 Peter, are characterized by the questions they ask—specifically, the question of Jesus's coming (*parousia*; 1:16; 3:12): "Where is the promise of his coming?" (3:4).

Reading 2 Peter requires thoughtfulness and awareness. Its rhetorical performance serves intentions of division and antagonism. Its message carries hostility and inhospitality—all of which the letter subsumes under the banner of the justice of God (1:1). Yet contemporary readers must wonder if the justice 2 Peter asserts and acts out is indeed one to reinscribe in current moments. Studying 2 Peter requires shifting

one's understanding of its canonical value. Rather than reading it as a model of Christian ethics and behavior for contemporary religious communities, it is more significant to read the letter as evidence of a particular form of Christian discourse that is violent, aggressive, and inhospitable.

Thus, the canonical value of 2 Peter may be its descriptive function, not its prescriptive benefit. The letter reflects the conflicts between opposing Christian understandings of tradition and existing beliefs. It creates the parabolic scenario that invites readers—especially religious readers—to consider which religious actors in the letter should be emulated. Do today's religious power holders write letters that urge their members to curse those they disagree with while likening them to animals? Or do today's religious interpreters find themselves—like those of old—attacked and ousted from their communities because they dare to ask pointed questions in good faith as they observe the times in which they live? These ancient questioners described in 2 Peter may have been not faithless but faithful, believing God is big enough to hold those questions even if their fellow Christian siblings could not.

Shively T. J. Smith

1 Simeon[a] Peter, a servant and apostle of Jesus Christ,

To those who have received a faith as equally honorable as ours through the righteousness of our God and Savior Jesus Christ:

2 May grace and peace be yours in abundance in the knowledge of God and of Jesus our Lord.

3 His divine power has given us everything needed for life and godliness, through the knowledge of him who called us by[b] his own glory and excellence. [4]Thus he has given us, through these things, his precious and very great promises, so that through them you may escape from the corruption that is in the world because of lust and may become participants of the divine nature. [5]For this very reason, you must make every effort to support your faith with excellence, and excellence with knowledge, [6]and knowledge with self-control, and self-control with endurance, and endurance with godliness, [7]and godliness with mutual affection, and mutual affection with love. [8]For if these things are yours and

are increasing among you, they keep you from being ineffective and unfruitful in the knowledge of our Lord Jesus Christ. [9]For anyone who lacks these things is blind, suffering from eye disease, forgetful of the cleansing of past sins. [10]Therefore, brothers and sisters, be all the more eager to confirm your call and election, for if you do this, you will never stumble. [11]For in this way, entry into the eternal kingdom of our Lord and Savior Jesus Christ will be richly provided for you.

12 Therefore I intend to keep on reminding you of these things, though you know them already and are established in the truth that has come to you. [13]I think it right, as long as I am in this body,[c] to refresh your memory, [14]since I know that my death[d] will come soon, as indeed our Lord Jesus Christ has made clear to me. [15]And I will make every effort so that after my departure you may be able at any time to recall these things.

a 1.1 Other ancient authorities read *Simon* b 1.3 Other ancient authorities read *through* c 1.13 Gk *tent* d 1.14 Gk *the putting off of my tent*

1:1–21 A testament letter of encouragement from the apostle Peter. The first chapter casts the historical Peter in several roles. Peter is an apostle and servant of Jesus and is one among the inner circle of Jesus's disciples. Peter also appears as not only a participant in the gospel story but also a storyteller of it. He recounts his eyewitness of Jesus's transfiguration. Last, this section depicts Peter as a prophetic voice and trustworthy adjudicator of false prophetic readings of the tradition. Peter is one, like those before him, who is *moved by the Holy Spirit*. **1:1–2** *Simeon Peter*. The Semitic spelling stands in relation to the Greek spelling. In the Jerusalem Council (Acts 15:14), the leader, James, addresses Peter in his Semitic name, Symeon, while Paul refers to him as either Cephas (1 Cor. 1:12) or Peter (Gal. 2:7). Cf. John 1:42. *Equally honorable*. From the Greek "isotimon," meaning a symmetrical influence shared between persons of the same status. It is not used elsewhere in the New Testament or the LXX (see Josephus, *Ant.* 12.3.1; Philo, *On the Embassy to Gaius* 1.98). Here, it classifies the letter recipients as not only coheirs but equal participants (cf. 1:4) in the apostolic and prophetic lineage in which they believe and exist. **1:12** *Keep on reminding you*. The Greek "mimnēskomai" connotes the activity of recollection (3:2) and is coupled with explicit reference to memory ("hypomnēsis," 1:13; 3:1). Threaded

16 For we did not follow cleverly devised myths when we made known to you the power and coming of our Lord Jesus Christ, but we had been eyewitnesses of his majesty. [17]For he received honor and glory from God the Father when that voice was conveyed to him by the Majestic Glory, saying, "This is my Son, my Beloved,[e] with whom I am well pleased." [18]We ourselves heard this voice come from heaven, while we were with him on the holy mountain.

19 So we have the prophetic message more fully confirmed. You will do well to be attentive to this as to a lamp shining in a dark place, until the day dawns and the morning star rises in your hearts. [20]First of all you must understand this, that no prophecy of scripture is a matter of one's[f] own interpretation, [21]because no prophecy ever came by human will, but men and women moved by the Holy Spirit spoke from God.[g]

2 But false prophets also arose among the people, just as there will be false teachers among you, who will secretly bring in destructive opinions. They will even deny the Master who bought them—bringing swift destruction on themselves. [2]Even so, many will follow their debaucheries, and because of these teachers[b] the way of truth will be maligned. [3]And in their greed they will exploit you with

deceptive words. Their condemnation, pronounced against them long ago, has not been idle, and their destruction is not asleep.

4 For if God did not spare the angels when they sinned but cast them into hell and committed them to chains[i] of deepest darkness to be kept until the judgment; [5]and if he did not spare the ancient world, even though he saved Noah, a herald of righteousness, with seven others, when he brought a flood on the world of the ungodly; [6]and if by turning the cities of Sodom and Gomorrah to ashes he condemned them to destruction[j] and made them an example of what is coming to the ungodly;[k] [7]and if he rescued Lot, a righteous man greatly distressed by the debauchery of the lawless [8](for that righteous man, living among them day after day, was tormented in his righteous soul by their lawless deeds that he saw and heard), [9]then the Lord knows how to rescue the godly from trial and to keep the unrighteous until the day of judgment, when they will be punished [10]—especially those who indulge their flesh in depraved lust and who despise authority.

e 1.17 Other ancient authorities read *my beloved Son*
f 1.20 Or *the prophet's*   g 1.21 Other ancient authorities read *but, moved by the Holy Spirit, saints of God spoke*   b 2.2 Gk *because of them*   i 2.4 Other ancient authorities read *pits*   j 2.6 Other ancient authorities lack *to destruction*
k 2.6 Other ancient authorities read *an example to those who were to be ungodly*

through the letter is encouragement toward collective remembering. **1:16–18** *We ourselves heard this voice.* The letter archives the fourth version of the transfiguration account in abbreviated form. See Matt. 17:1–8; Mark 9:2–8; Luke 9:28–36. It omits details like the presence of Moses and Elijah, the names of the disciples, and the overshadowing cloud. It maintains the general setting of the mountain while introducing the details of *honor and glory* and heaven, as opposed to a cloud, as the origin of the divine voice. **1:17b** *This is my Son, my Beloved, with whom I am well pleased.* See Matthew's version of Jesus's baptism (Matt. 3:17) for the divine pronouncement most like 2 Peter's. Cf. Mark 9:7; Matt. 17:5; Luke 9:35. **1:21** *The Holy Spirit.* The only reference to God's Spirit in the letter is named in reference to reliable interpretations and prophetic traditions. The focus is less on the Spirit and more on legitimate teachings of the tradition and discerning between these teachings.

2:1–22 Paragons and offenders of the Way. The letter repurposes familiar traditions from Jewish and Christian tradition, contemporizing them for its current rhetorical moment. It also includes echoes to passages from the Old Testament and a proverb from the Gospel tradition. It reimagines inherited "Scripture" by structuring biblical materials as examples and arguments. In so doing, chap. 2 creates a series of new dominant readings to shape the membership's behavior toward one another. **2:1** *False prophets . . . false teachers.* The Greek for false prophets, "pseudoprophētai," recurs in the New Testament (Matt. 7:15; Mark 13:22; Luke 6:26; Acts 13:6; 1 John 4:1; Rev. 16:13). The Greek for false teachers, "pseudodidaskaloi," does not. Justin Martyr uses the latter term in relationship to false prophets much like 2 Peter (Justin Martyr, *Dialogue with Trypho* 82). *Secretly bring in destructive opinions . . . deny the Master.* See Jude 4. **2:4** *Angels when they sinned.* See Gen. 6:1–4; Jude 6. Cf. 2 Pet. 2:10–11. *Cast them into hell.* The Greek word for hell is "tartarus," which departs from the more commonly used Greek words in Jewish and Christian traditions: "Gehenna" (Matt. 5:22) and "Hades" (Matt. 11:23). **2:5** *Noah.* Cf. 1 Pet. 3:20 and Heb. 11:7. Within the Gospel tradition, Noah is mentioned only in Matt. 24:37–38; Luke 3:36; 17:26–27. See Gen. 7–8. **2:6–8** *Sodom and Gomorrah . . . Lot.* See Gen. 19:7–29; Jude 7. Cf. Matt. 10:15; Luke 17:28. **2:10** *Slander the*

Bold and willful, they are not afraid to slander the glorious ones,[l] [11]whereas angels, though greater in might and power, do not bring against them a slanderous judgment.[m] [12]These people, however, are like irrational animals, mere creatures of instinct, born to be caught and killed. They slander what they do not understand, and as those creatures are destroyed,[n] they also will be destroyed, [13]suffering[o] the wages of doing wrong. They count it a pleasure to revel in the daytime. They are blots and blemishes, reveling in their pleasures[p] while they feast with you. [14]They have eyes full of adultery,[q] insatiable for sin. They entice unsteady souls. They have hearts trained in greed. Accursed children! [15]They have left the straight road and have gone astray, following the road of Balaam son of Bosor,[r] who loved the wages of doing wrong [16]but was rebuked for his own transgression; a speechless donkey spoke with a human voice and restrained the prophet's madness.

17 These are waterless springs and mists driven by a storm; for them the deepest darkness has been reserved. [18]For they speak bombastic nonsense, and with debased[s] desires of the flesh they entice people who have just[t] escaped from those who live in error. [19]They promise them freedom, but they themselves are slaves of corruption, for people are slaves to whatever masters them. [20]For if, after they have escaped the defilements of the world through the knowledge of the[u] Lord and Savior Jesus Christ, they are again entangled in them and overpowered, the last state has become worse for them than the first. [21]For it would have been better for them never to have known the way of righteousness than, after knowing it, to turn back from the holy commandment that was handed on to them. [22]It has happened to them according to the true proverb,

"The dog turns back to its own vomit,"

and,

"The sow is washed only to wallow in the mud."

3 This is now, beloved, the second letter I am writing to you; in them I am trying to arouse your sincere intention by reminding you [2]that you should remember the words spoken in the past by the holy prophets and the commandment of the Lord and Savior spoken through your apostles. [3]First of all you must understand this, that in the last

l 2.10 Or *angels*; Gk *glories*   m 2.11 Other ancient authorities add *from the Lord* or *before the Lord*   n 2.12 Gk *in their destruction*   o 2.13 Other ancient authorities read *receiving*   p 2.13 Other ancient authorities read *love feasts*   q 2.14 Gk *adultery*; or *longing for an adulteress*   r 2.15 Other ancient authorities read *Beor*   s 2.18 Or *debauched*   t 2.18 Other ancient authorities read *actually*   u 2.20 Other ancient authorities read *our*

glorious ones. See Jude 8. **2:11** *Angels . . . do not bring against them a slanderous judgment.* See Jude 9. **2:12** *Slander what they do not understand.* See Jude 10. **2:13** *Blemishes . . . reveling . . . while they feast with you.* See Jude 12. **2:14** *Accursed children.* The invective deployed rhetorically requires caution. It is not merely a polemical tactic but a verbally abusive strategy that diminishes respect. It is intended to strip the letter's Christian opponents of the dignity due to any human being, let alone one's fellow congregants. Cf. Jas. 3:10; Jude 11. **2:15** *Balaam.* See Num. 22; 31:16; Deut. 23:5; Neh. 13:2. See Rev. 2:14. **2:17** *The deepest darkness has been reserved.* See Jude 13. **2:18** *Bombastic . . . entice people.* See Jude 16. **2:22** *The dog . . . The sow.* See the proverbial saying in Jesus's Sermon on the Mount (Matt. 7:6). Cf. Prov. 26:11; Phil. 3:2.

3:1–18 Apostolic writers and contested understandings. Chap. 3 attests to the rich and active literary tradition of Christian letters. It opens by designating itself as the *second letter* from Peter, and it talks about Paul's letter-writing activities and the contested interpretations they have produced (3:15–16). Wedged between the testimonials of Christian letter-writing activities is the discussion about apocalyptic expectation. Again, readers encounter the letter's position: it stands in opposition to any Christian teaching that questions the timing and viability of Jesus's return. That opposing view—which it casts more as a question than an assertion—the letter stigmatizes as the actions of scoffers, ignorant, unstable, and lawless. Such polemics must be interpreted carefully so as not to reinscribe them as appropriate for contemporary religious attitudes and behaviors. **3:2** *Spoken through your apostles.* The switch from "we had been eyewitnesses" in the letter's rehearsal of the transfiguration (1:16) to a reference to the apostles in the second person as a group distinct from the author here signals the veil of authorship may have slipped. While the letter is attributed to the historical Peter—it references his death and his presence at the transfiguration to establish its credibility as a source of Petrine tradition—many scholars read 3:2 as evidence that the historical Peter did not write the letter. Cf. Jude 17. **3:3** *Scoffers.* See Jude 18.

days scoffers will come, scoffing and indulging their own lusts [4]and saying, "Where is the promise of his coming? For ever since our ancestors died,[v] all things continue as they were from the beginning of creation!" [5]They deliberately ignore this fact, that by the word of God heavens existed long ago and an earth was formed out of water and by means of water, [6]through which the world of that time was deluged with water and perished. [7]But by the same word the present heavens and earth have been reserved for fire, being kept until the day of judgment and destruction of the godless.

8 But do not ignore this one fact, beloved, that with the Lord one day is like a thousand years, and a thousand years are like one day. [9]The Lord is not slow about his promise, as some think of slowness, but is patient with you,[w] not wanting any to perish but all to come to repentance. [10]But the day of the Lord will come like a thief, and then the heavens will pass away with a loud noise, and the elements will be destroyed with fire, and the earth and everything that is done on it will be disclosed.[x]

11 Since all these things are to be destroyed in this way, what sort of persons ought you to be in leading lives of holiness and godliness, [12]waiting for and hastening[y] the coming of the day of God, because of which the heavens will be set ablaze and destroyed and the elements will melt with fire? [13]But, in accordance with his promise, we wait for new heavens and a new earth, where righteousness is at home.

14 Therefore, beloved, while you are waiting for these things, strive to be found by him at peace, without spot or blemish, [15]and regard the patience of our Lord as salvation. So also our beloved brother Paul wrote to you according to the wisdom given him, [16]speaking of this as he does in all his letters. There are some things in them hard to understand, which the ignorant and unstable twist[z] to their own destruction, as they do the other scriptures. [17]You therefore, beloved, since you are forewarned, beware that you are not carried away with the error of the lawless and lose your own stability. [18]But grow in the grace and knowledge of our Lord and Savior Jesus Christ. To him be the glory both now and to the day of eternity. Amen.[a]

v 3.4 Gk *our fathers fell asleep*   w 3.9 Other ancient authorities read *on your account*   x 3.10 Other ancient authorities read *will not be found* or *will be burned up*   y 3.12 Or *earnestly desiring*   z 3.16 Other ancient authorities read *will twist*   a 3.18 Other ancient authorities lack *Amen*

3:4 *Where is the promise of his coming?* The opposing view within the community is marked by a question regarding timing. One group assesses the time lapse between Jesus's ascension and his return as troubling. It seems highly unlikely that in the historical Peter's lifetime, expectations about Jesus's return would wane so much as to create different opinions within the newly constituted movement. For the Gospel tradition on Jesus's *coming* (Gk. "parousia"), see Matt. 24:3, 27, 37–39. **3:5–7** The passage assigns creation and destruction to the actions of God. The themes of Noah and the flood are picked up again here. Cf. 2 Pet. 2:5. **3:13** *We wait for new heavens and a new earth.* Cf. Isa. 66:22. **3:15–16** *There are some things in them hard to understand.* Paul seems to attest to the contested interpretations of his teachings (Rom. 3:8; 6:1; cf. 2 Thess. 2:2). **3:17** *The error of the lawless.* Cf. 2:18. It represents a final juxtaposition to the "way of truth" (2 Pet. 2:2; cf. 1:12). Truth versus error is a common motif in other New Testament letters (1 John 4:6; Jude 11; Rom. 1:27). **3:18** *Grow in . . . grace.* Cf. 1 Pet. 2:2; Col. 1:10. *Our Lord and Savior Jesus Christ.* Cf. 2 Pet. 1:11. *To him be the glory.* Cf. Rom. 11:36; Eph. 3:21; Rev. 1:6.

THE LETTERS OF JOHN

Authorship and Audience

The books of 1, 2, and 3 John were first attributed to "John" when the second-century bishop Papias linked "the elder" (2 John 1; 3 John 1) to the name. Because of the similarities in vocabulary, theme, syntax, and language among these three letters, John, the elder, was simply assumed to be the author of 1 John as well. Beginning with Irenaeus (d. 202 CE) and Clement of Alexandria (d. ca. 211 CE), tradition sometimes ascribed the authorship of the three letters and the Gospel of John to John the apostle, the son of Zebedee (Mark 3:17), while others held that all four texts were authored by the Beloved Disciple in the Gospel of John (John 19:26), whose identity is unknown, despite tradition that held him to be John the apostle. However, the claim that the Gospel and letters were written by a common author is unsupported. Scholars have also looked to the recipients of the letters to identify the author, but the letters do not identify their audience with any precision, except that they all address the Johannine community in some way. This was a community of readers or listeners associated with the Gospel of John and the Letters of John who were familiar with the symbols of the Hebrew Bible and with Hellenistic thought but experiencing friction with some in the Jewish community, differences with other Christ followers, and an overall sense of alienation from "the world." Despite the dearth of evidence for a precise attribution of authorship, modern scholars hold that a common, unknown author wrote all three letters.

Genre and Occasions

Both 2 and 3 John resemble the genre of an ancient letter. Second John is similar to 1 John in content, repeating some of the Gospel of John's concerns without elaboration. First John lacks the customary introduction and ending of a letter. It more resembles a sermon or homily delivered to a community to reinforce core teachings and beliefs and to warn about opponents' false teachings.

Each of the letters addresses slightly different occasions. First John seeks to clarify misunderstandings in the community about the incarnate nature and identity of Jesus, as presented in the Gospel of John. Some "false teachers"—possibly Christian gnostics, whom some had left the Johannine community to follow—were teaching that Jesus only appeared to be human. First John counters these false teachings, promoted by those he calls "antichrists" (2:18, 22; 4:3), and reasserts that Jesus was both human and divine. The letter also emphasizes that the principal difference between the children of God and the children of darkness is their conduct and whether they act out of love or in sin (3:1-2, 8-10). Those who love, know God, but those who do not love, do not know God (4:7-8). This dualism is what the author offers the community as a means of understanding what is happening to them (see **"Dualism (Binaries),"** **p. 1855**).

The occasion for 2 John is comparable to 1 John. The elder addresses the letter to the "elect lady"—likely a personification of a local community or church. The letter is concerned with "the truth" (vv. 1-3), which is love and keeping God's commandments (vv. 4-6). It also emphasizes hospitality toward traveling preachers or missionaries. There are teachers or "deceivers" who are teaching that Jesus only appeared to be human (v. 7). By denying the doctrine of Christ (vv. 9-10), they also deny Jesus's identity as Christ. The letter warns against these deceivers and forbids the community to offer hospitality to them (vv. 10, 11).

The third letter of John is written by "the elder" (v. 1) to Gaius, otherwise unknown, who is commended for his practice (v. 5). This letter, too, addresses hospitality to traveling missionaries (vv. 2-12). It contrasts Diotrephes, who denies the authority of the elder and refuses to let the church receive the elder's "missionaries," with Demetrius, the elder's messenger who is looked upon favorably (v. 12). It also urges Gaius to avoid evil and do good like Demetrius (vv. 11-12).

Location and Date

The book of 1 John never mentions the location of its audience. The books of 2 and 3 John appear to be written to local churches (2 John 1; 3 John 6), without mentioning any specifics. Irenaeus and Clement of Alexandria identify the provenance of these letters as Ephesus but without support. The reason ancient tradition named Ephesus as the location is that the supposed adversary of John, whom some scholars point to as the Christian gnostic Cerinthus, encountered John in Ephesus (Irenaeus, *Against Heresies* 3.3.4). However, the letters never identify the adversary, and the presumption of Ephesus remains largely unfounded.

The dating of the letters depends on educated guesswork. Whether 1 John came before 2 and 3 John is unknown. The New Testament canon arranges the letters according to their length, not in chronological order. Scholarly consensus dates the composition of the letters to some time after the composition of the Gospel of John around 90 CE. The explicit mention of "church" in 3 John 6 and the gatherings that likely met in general suggest a period when Jesus's followers were adopting more organizational structure. In contrast, the Gospel of John avoids any explicit mention of "churches." The topics of hospitality, mutual friendship, and support also project a later time of writing, when followers of Jesus needed support as they traveled and spread the gospel. Furthermore, the letters' references to "the elder" (2 John 1; 3 John 1), Gaius (3 John 1), Diotrephes (3 John 9), and Demetrius (3 John 12) suggest the subsequent development of leaders in these early communities. Unfortunately, the dearth of information regarding the authorship, location, and date makes determining a proximate context challenging.

Theology

The Letters of John, like the Gospel of John, are concerned with Christology, the nature of Jesus as the Christ. Whereas the Gospel aims to show Jesus's divinity along with his humanity (1:14), the letters emphasize Jesus's humanity along with his divinity (1 John 5:6), underscoring how Christ, the Son of God, did indeed come in the flesh (1 John 4:2; 2 John 7). Jesus is the Son of God (1 John 3:23), born "by water and blood" (5:6), whose mission is to take away sins (3:5). Salvation is based on knowing and believing in Jesus the Christ as both human and divine. Jesus's death is an "atoning sacrifice" (*hilasmos*) for the sins of humanity (2:2), and eternal life consists of practicing righteousness, keeping the commandments, and loving God and one another.

Francisco Lozada, Jr.

The First Letter of John

Reading Guide

First John was written amid a period of new interpretations of Jesus and differences of opinions about Jesus's identity and nature. In this context, the letter aims to clarify what it perceives as misunderstandings about Jesus as Christ and to strengthen the confidence of the Johannine community in its own Christology and religious experience. The letter gives us a glimpse into early struggles to maintain unity and integrity among Christ followers. It also demonstrates an attempt to define a community's identity as well as confirm their moral way of life (keeping the commandments of God) and their social way of life (loving one another).

First John begins by reminding its audience that Jesus is the Word of life who existed from the time of creation, became a flesh-and-blood person, and is with God as the Son, Jesus Christ (1:1–4). God is light and thus a symbol of moral goodness (1:5–10). To have fellowship with God means that one walks in the light, keeping the commandments (2:1–17). As a sign of the last hour, there will be some (antichrists, separatists, dissents) opposed to God and Christ, ones for whom the letter's recipients will have to watch out (2:18–27). Believers who remain true to God's commandments and confess that Jesus came in the flesh will remain children of God (3:1–4:21). First John concludes with assurances of eternal life. Faith in Jesus as the Son of God means victory over the world and assurance of eternal life: a promise that the separatists do not possess.

Francisco Lozada, Jr.

1 We declare to you what was from the beginning, what we have heard, what we have seen with our eyes, what we have looked at and touched with our hands, concerning the word of life—²this life was revealed, and we have seen it and testify to it and declare to you the eternal life that was with the Father and was revealed to us—³what we have seen and heard we also declare to you so that you also may have fellowship with us, and truly our fellowship is with the Father and with his Son Jesus Christ. ⁴We are writing these things so that our*a* joy may be complete.

5 This is the message we have heard from him and proclaim to you, that God is light and in him there is no darkness at all. ⁶If we say that we have fellowship with him while we are walking in darkness, we lie and do not do what is true; ⁷but if we walk in the light as he himself is in the light, we have fellowship with one another, and the blood of Jesus his Son cleanses us from all sin. ⁸If we say that we have no sin, we deceive ourselves, and the truth is not in us. ⁹If we confess our sins, he who is faithful and just will forgive us our sins and cleanse us from all unrighteousness. ¹⁰If

we say that we have not sinned, we make him a liar, and his word is not in us.

2 My little children, I am writing these things to you so that you may not sin. But if anyone does sin, we have an advocate with the Father, Jesus Christ the righteous, ²and he is the atoning sacrifice for our sins, and not for ours only but also for the sins of the whole world.

3 Now by this we know that we have come to know him, if we obey his commandments. ⁴Whoever says, "I have come to know him," but does not obey his commandments is a liar, and in such a person the truth does not exist; ⁵but whoever obeys his word, truly in this person the love of God has reached perfection. By this we know that we are in him: ⁶whoever says, "I abide in him," ought to walk in the same way as he walked.

7 Beloved, I am writing you no new commandment but an old commandment that you have had from the beginning; the old commandment is the word that you have heard. ⁸Yet I am writing you a new commandment that is

---

a 1.4 Other ancient authorities read *your*

1:1–4 Prologue. 1:1 *From the beginning* refers to Jesus Christ's existence in and with God from eternity. The author speaks of this reality again in 2:13 (cf. John 1:1, 2, 14; 17:5). **1:2** *Eternal life* has both present and future meaning, and here it focuses on the present condition of the believer's life—a qualitatively new existence for the follower of Jesus that will continue after death. **1:3** *Fellowship.* The Greek term "koinōnia" conveys a close and harmonious relationship. Partners or companions hold things in common, as in the Gospel of John. **1:4** *That our joy may be complete.* The manuscript evidence varies between "our joy" and "your joy." If the former, "our joy" depends on a continued harmonious fellowship among the believers and with the author. If the latter, "your joy" suggests a harmonious fellowship within the community to whom the author is writing.

1:5–10 God is light. 1:5 *Light* speaks to God's purity, truth, and love. Its opposite, *darkness*, connotes impurity, falsehood, and hatred. See **"Dualism (Binaries)," p. 1855. 1:6** *While we are walking in darkness* means pursuing a way of life and action that is the opposite of light ("phōs"). **1:7** *The blood of Jesus his Son cleanses us from all sin* refers to Jesus's death on the cross (Matt. 27:45–56; Mark 15:25–41; Luke 23:32–49; John 19:31–37). *Blood* implies the humanity of Jesus Christ. **1:8** *Sin.* The Greek term "harmatia" literally suggests "missing the mark," a shortcoming or a failure to reach one's potential. **1:9** *Unrighteousness*, literally "adikia," expresses "wrongdoing." It is the opposite of "righteousness" ("dikaios"), which suggests "just." **1:10** *We make him a liar* uses one of the Johannine tradition's favorite expressions, "we make" ("poieō"), to imply putting the "liar" out of fellowship with God (see 1 John 5:10; John 5:18; 10:33).

2:1–17 Walking in the light. 2:1 *My little children.* Those in close relationship to the author, who uses the diminutive of the Greek word for child ("teknon") to address the audience. "Teknion" (children, pl.) is also found in 1 John 2:12, 28; 3:7, 18; 4:4; 5:21, and John 13:33. In 1 John 2:14, the author uses "paidia" for children because they "know the Father," but here the emphasis is on knowing the Son. *Advocate* ("paraklētos") is a familiar word found in the Gospel of John (14:26). It literally means "one called alongside," and it could also convey "consoler" and "comforter." In this context, it suggests someone who "pleads one's case," as does a lawyer or advocate. **2:2** *Atoning sacrifice* ("hilasmos") points to the expiation or removal of defilement of the individual sinner for their sin. The letter emphasizes how Jesus's death removes human sin (see 1 John 1:7). **2:3** *Commandments* refers to those ethical instructions that Jesus demanded of his disciples, such as to love one another (John 13:34). **2:6** *Abide*, used

true in him and in you, because[b] the darkness is passing away and the true light is already shining. [9]Whoever says, "I am in the light," while hating a brother or sister, is still in the darkness. [10]Whoever loves a brother or sister abides in the light, and in such a person[c] there is no cause for stumbling. [11]But whoever hates a brother or sister is in the darkness, walks in the darkness, and does not know the way to go, because the darkness has brought on blindness.

[12] I am writing to you, little children,
    because your sins are forgiven on
        account of his name.
[13] I am writing to you, fathers,
    because you know him who is from the
        beginning.
    I am writing to you, young people,
    because you have conquered the evil
        one.
[14] I write to you, children,
    because you know the Father.
    I write to you, fathers,
    because you know him who is from the
        beginning.
    I write to you, young people,
    because you are strong
    and the word of God abides in you,
    and you have overcome the evil one.

[15] Do not love the world or the things in the world. The love of the Father is not in those who love the world, [16]for all that is in the world—the desire of the flesh, the desire of the eyes, the pride in riches—comes not from the Father but from the world. [17]And the world and its desire[d] are passing away, but those who do the will of God abide forever.

[18] Children, it is the last hour! As you have heard that antichrist is coming, so now many antichrists have come. From this we know that it is the last hour. [19]They went out from us, but they did not belong to us, for if they had belonged to us they would have remained[e] with us. But by going out they made it plain that none of them belongs to us. [20]But you have been anointed by the Holy One, and all of you have knowledge.[f] [21]I write to you, not because you do not know the truth, but because you know it, and you know that no lie comes from the truth. [22]Who is the liar but the one who denies that Jesus is the Christ?[g] This is the antichrist, the one who denies the Father and the Son. [23]No one who denies the Son has the Father; everyone who confesses the Son has the Father also. [24]Let what you heard from the beginning abide in you. If what you heard from the beginning abides in you, then you will abide in the Son and in the Father. [25]And this is what he has promised us,[h] eternal life.

[26] I write these things to you concerning those who would deceive you. [27]As for you, the anointing that you received from him abides in you, so you do not need anyone to teach you. But as his anointing teaches you about all things and is true and is not a lie, and just as it has taught you, abide in him.[i]

[28] And now, little children, abide in him, so that when he is revealed we may have confidence and not be put to shame before him at his coming.

[29] If you perceive that he is righteous, you also know that everyone who does right has

---

b 2.8 Or *that*   c 2.10 Or *in it*   d 2.17 Or *the desire for it* e 2.19 Or *abided*   f 2.20 Other ancient authorities read *you know all things*   g 2.22 Or *the Messiah*   h 2.25 Other ancient authorities read *you*   i 2.27 Or *it*

---

twenty-three times in 1 John, means to "remain" or "stay" in fellowship with God. **2:10** *Loves* ("agapē"), in this context, suggests not romantic affection or charity but rather outreach or care for the fellow believer. *Brother or sister* (literally "adelphōn") are all those (not just men) who are followers of Christ. **2:13** *Conquered* is also translated as "overcome." The tense is perfect, emphasizing the present results of conquering *the evil one* in the past. *Evil one* refers to the opposing forces of Satan ("ruler of this world" in John 16:11). **2:14** *Young people, because you are strong* refers not to physical strength but to moral and spiritual strength (see Eph. 6:10). **2:15** *World* ("cosmos") has two connotations. The *world* is where the power of the evil one exists. As a reference to "people" or "creation," the world is loved and good (Gen. 1:31). **2:16** *Desire of the flesh* ("epithumia") does not suggest that the body is evil. Rather, it suggests desire for something forbidden. Jesus followers would have been familiar with religions and temple rites where indulgences of the flesh were part of everyday life.

2:18–29 Admonitions about antichrists. **2:18** *Children.* See note on 2:1. *Antichrists.* See **"Antichrist," p. 2103.** *Last hour* refers not to a specific date or time but to a culmination of events in which time approaches an end. **2:20** *Anointed* ("chrisma") indicates the pouring out of olive oil for ritual purposes. Here it suggests the giving of the Spirit by Christ to believers. **2:21** *Truth.* Correct knowledge of Christ's identity. **2:25** *Eternal life.* The divine life or new life in every follower of Jesus (see 1:1).

Going Deeper: Antichrist (1 John 2:18)

The writer of 1 and 2 John calls false teachers the antichrist (*antichristos*) or antichrists (*antichristoi*), with the singular use predominating (1 John 2:18c; 2:22; 4:3; 2 John 7) over the plural (1 John 2:18d). The appearance of the "antichrist," considered an opponent or adversary, is a sign of the "last hour" (2:18). This is different from the "false christs" (*pseudochristoi*) of whom Jesus speaks (Mark 13:22; Matt. 24:24), for the antichrist does not claim to be Christ. Instead, the antichrist teaches what 1 and 2 John consider to be a corrupt Christology, one that denies that the Christ was the flesh-and-blood Jesus. The antichrist believes Christ was divine but that Jesus was not. It is the denial of Jesus *as* Christ and of Jesus's divine Sonship that characterizes the teachings of the antichrist.

The antichrist seems to have separated from the Johannine community (1 John 2:19) but continued to try to influence it with their false teachings. Thus, the writer continues to warn the community of "false prophets" (4:1, 2; 2 John 7–9) who are to be refused hospitality (2 John 10; 3 John 6–8).

Scholars attempt to reconstruct the antichrist by examining the letters' dualistic language. In the letters, the antichrist is not a single individual who revolted against the church. Rather, the antichrist is embodied by anyone whose thinking opposes the understanding that Jesus, as the Son of God, was both human and divine. Thus 1 John asserts, "Who is the liar but the one who denies that Jesus is the Christ? This is the antichrist, the one who denies the Father and the Son" (2:22), and 2 John elaborates: "Many deceivers have gone out into the world, those who do not confess that Jesus Christ has come in the flesh; any such person is the deceiver and the antichrist!" (v. 7).

These letters cast the elder's community in a positive fashion, while the "antichrists" are seen in a negative light. They portray the elder's community as espousing the spirit of truth, being children of God, expressing love, and embracing righteousness. They characterize those on the side of the antichrist as espousing the spirit of deception, being children of the devil, expressing hate, and embracing lawlessness.

Francisco Lozada, Jr.

3 been born of him. ¹See what love the Father has given us, that we should be called children of God, and that is what we are. The reason the world does not know us is that it did not know him. ²Beloved, we are God's children now; what we will be has not yet been revealed. What we do know is this: when he*ʲ* is revealed, we will be like him, for we will see him as he is. ³And all who have this hope in him purify themselves, just as he is pure.

4 Everyone who commits sin is guilty of lawlessness; sin is lawlessness. ⁵You know that he was revealed to take away sins, and in him there is no sin. ⁶No one who abides in him sins; no one who sins has either seen him or known him. ⁷Little children,*ᵏ* let no one deceive you. Everyone who does what is right is righteous, just as he is righteous. ⁸Everyone who commits sin is of the devil, for the devil has been sinning from the beginning. The Son of God was revealed for this purpose: to destroy the works of the devil. ⁹Those who have been born of God do not sin because God's seed abides in them;*ˡ* they cannot sin because they have been born of God. ¹⁰The children of God and the children of the devil are revealed in this way: all who do not do what is right are not from God, nor are those who do not love a brother or sister.

11 For this is the message you have heard from the beginning, that we should love one another. ¹²We must not be like Cain, who was from the evil one and murdered his brother. And why did he murder him? Because his own deeds were evil and his brother's righteous. ¹³Do not be astonished, brothers and sisters, that the world hates you. ¹⁴We know that we have passed from death to life because

j 3.2 Or *it*   *k* 3.7 Other ancient authorities read *Children*
l 3.9 Or *because the children of God abide in him*

3:1–4:21 True believers as children of God. 3:1 *Children of God.* Those born of God (see 2:29), believers who abide in Christ and are delivered from sin. Made righteous, they have passed from death to a new life with God that exists in the present and continues eternally, after death (see 1:1). **3:3** *Purify* ("hagnizein") has cultic meaning and suggests cleansing oneself from the profane and belonging to God. **3:4** *Sin.* See 1:8. *Lawlessness* pertains to a failure to love one another. **3:8** *Sin* here is connected to the *devil.* To be of the *devil* is to live apart from righteousness, love, and truth. **3:9** *Born of God* is not about literally being born of God but about the transformation brought about by the power of God. **3:12** *Cain* killed his brother, Abel, in the first instance of murder in the Bible (Gen. 4:1–11). **3:13** *The world hates you* intimates the hostility unbelievers had of believers (see John 7:7; 15:18–25). **3:14** *Passed from*

we love the brothers and sisters. Whoever does not love abides in death. [15]All who hate a brother or sister are murderers, and you know that murderers do not have eternal life abiding in them. [16]We know love by this, that he laid down his life for us—and we ought to lay down our lives for the brothers and sisters. [17]How does God's love abide in anyone who has the world's goods and sees a brother or sister in need and yet refuses help?

18 Little children, let us love not in word or speech but in deed and truth. [19]And by this we will know that we are from the truth and will reassure our hearts before him [20]whenever our hearts condemn us, for God is greater than our hearts, and he knows everything. [21]Beloved, if our hearts do not condemn us, we have boldness before God, [22]and we receive from him whatever we ask, because we obey his commandments and do what pleases him.

23 And this is his commandment, that we should believe in the name of his Son Jesus Christ and love one another, just as he has commanded us. [24]All who obey his commandments abide in him, and he abides in them. And by this we know that he abides in us, by the Spirit that he has given us.

4 Beloved, do not believe every spirit, but test the spirits to see whether they are from God, for many false prophets have gone out into the world. [2]By this you know the Spirit of God: every spirit that confesses that Jesus Christ has come in the flesh is from God, [3]and every spirit that does not confess Jesus[m] is not from God. And this is the spirit of the antichrist, of which you have heard that it is coming, and now it is already in the world.

[4]Little children, you are from God and have conquered them, for the one who is in you is greater than the one who is in the world. [5]They are from the world; therefore what they say is from the world, and the world listens to them. [6]We are from God. Whoever knows God listens to us, and whoever is not from God does not listen to us. From this we know the spirit of truth and the spirit of error.

7 Beloved, let us love one another, because love is from God; everyone who loves is born of God and knows God. [8]Whoever does not love does not know God, for God is love. [9]God's love was revealed among us in this way: God sent his only Son into the world so that we might live through him. [10]In this is love, not that we loved God but that he loved us and sent his Son to be the atoning sacrifice for our sins. [11]Beloved, since God loved us so much, we also ought to love one another. [12]No one has ever seen God; if we love one another, God abides in us, and his love is perfected in us.

13 By this we know that we abide in him and he in us, because he has given us of his Spirit. [14]And we have seen and do testify that the Father has sent his Son as the Savior of the world. [15]God abides in those who confess that Jesus is the Son of God, and they abide in God. [16]So we have known and believe the love that God has for us.

God is love, and those who abide in love abide in God, and God abides in them. [17]Love has been perfected among us in this: that we may have boldness on the day of judgment, because as he is, so are we in this world. [18]There is no fear in love, but perfect love casts out fear; for fear has

---

m 4.3 Other ancient authorities read *does away with Jesus*

---

death to life implies eternal life (see 1:1). **3:16** *He laid down his life for us.* Jesus's sacrifice of himself for the sins of the world is an example to follow and a demonstration of what "loves" means (John 3:16; 10:11, 17, 18a). **3:17** *World's goods* refers to material goods or means of life (2:16). **3:18** *In deed and truth* refers to love as shown through true action. **3:20** *Whenever our hearts condemn us.* The sense of falling short. **3:21** *Boldness* ("parrēsia") *before God* refers to "openness," "courage," or "confidence." **3:23** *We should believe in the name of his Son Jesus Christ and love one another.* The true teaching of Jesus Christ is love and service to others. **3:24** *Spirit* ("pneumatos"). The divine presence, or Spirit, of God empowers Christ followers to live righteously and to love one another. **4:1** *Spirit* ("pneumati") denotes here teachers or prophets who have a different Christology than the author. **4:3** See **"Antichrist," p. 2103**. **4:4** *Conquered* victory against those of the world. **4:7** *Beloved* ("agapētoi") refers to those who have been loved by God. *Let us love* ("agapōmen") *one another.* Loving one another distinguishes believers from nonbelievers. **4:9** *Only Son* ("monogenēs") suggests not "begotten" but rather "unique," "single," or "the only one of its kind." **4:10** For *atoning sacrifice*, see 2:2. **4:12** *No one has ever seen God.* Though no one can see God, God lives in them through their love for another. **4:14** *Savior of the world* spells out the Son's mission (cf. John 3:16; 4:42). **4:16** *So we have known and believe the love that God has for us.* To believe is to know that God is love. **4:17** *Day of judgment.* The time of Christ's return (cf. 2:28). **4:18** *There is no*

to do with punishment, and whoever fears has not reached perfection in love. [19]We love*n* because he first loved us. [20]Those who say, "I love God," and hate a brother or sister are liars, for those who do not love a brother or sister, whom they have seen, cannot love God, whom they have not seen. [21]The commandment we have from him is this: those who love God must love their brothers and sisters also.

5 Everyone who believes that Jesus is the Christ*o* has been born of God, and everyone who loves the parent loves the child. [2]By this we know that we love the children of God, when we love God and obey his commandments. [3]For the love of God is this, that we obey his commandments. And his commandments are not burdensome, [4]for whatever is born of God conquers the world. And this is the victory that conquers the world, our faith. [5]Who is it who conquers the world but the one who believes that Jesus is the Son of God?

6 This is the one who came by water and blood, Jesus Christ, not with the water only but with the water and the blood. And the Spirit is the one that testifies, for the Spirit is the truth. [7]There are three that testify:*p* [8]the Spirit and the water and the blood, and these three agree. [9]If we receive human testimony, the testimony of God is greater, for this is the testimony of God that he has testified to his Son. [10]Those who believe in the Son of God have the testimony in their hearts. Those who do not believe in God*q* have made him a liar by not believing in the testimony that God has given concerning his Son. [11]And this is the testimony: God gave us eternal life, and this life is in his Son. [12]Whoever has the Son has life; whoever does not have the Son of God does not have life.

13 I write these things to you who believe in the name of the Son of God, so that you may know that you have eternal life.*r*

14 And this is the boldness we have in him, that if we ask anything according to his will, he hears us. [15]And if we know that he hears us in whatever we ask, we know that we have obtained the requests made of him. [16]If you see your brother or sister committing what is not a deadly sin, you will ask, and God*s* will give life to such a one—to those whose sin is not deadly. There is sin that is deadly; I do not say that you should pray about that. [17]All wrongdoing is sin, but there is sin that is not deadly.

18 We know that those who are born of God do not sin, but the one who was born of God protects them, and the evil one does not touch

n 4.19 Other ancient authorities add *him* or *God* *o* 5.1 Or *the Messiah* *p* 5.7 Other ancient authorities read (with variations) *There are three that testify in heaven, the Father, the Word, and the Holy Spirit, and these three are one.* *And there are three that testify on earth:* *q* 5.10 Other ancient authorities read *in the Son* *r* 5.13 Other ancient authorities add *and that you may believe in the name of the Son of God* *s* 5.16 Gk *he*

fear in love, for love is the opposite of fear. **4:19** *We love* ("agapōmen"). The ethical imperative to love imitates God's love as manifested in Jesus (John 15:12–13; 1 John 3:16). **4:20** *Those who say, "I love God."* Loving God means loving God's children; if not, they do not love God. **4:21** *Commandment* calls to mind the Shema (Deut. 6:4–9) and Jesus's teaching that one should love God with all one's heart, soul, and strength (Luke 10:27; cf. Mark 12:30).

5:1–21 Summary and conclusion. 5:1 *Has been born of God* refers to rebirth as a child of God who lives in fellowship with God. **5:3** *Commandments.* See note on 4:21. **5:4** *Conquers the world* refers to decisively overcoming the evil one with faith (John 16:33). **5:6** *Water, blood,* and *Spirit* call to mind the baptism (water), death (blood), and resurrection of Jesus, the Christ and Son of God (cf. John 19:34). **5:7–8** *Three that testify: the Spirit and the water and the blood* infer the biblical requirement that testimony must be confirmed by at least two witnesses. Three witnesses is enough to settle a matter (Deut. 17:6; 19:15; Matt. 18:16). **5:9** *If we receive human testimony, the testimony of God is greater.* The elder emphasizes here that God's testimony is the ultimate testimony to Jesus. **5:10** *Those who believe in the Son of God* emphasizes "believing in" or "putting one's faith in" ("pisteuein eis") Jesus. *Those who do not believe* imply that God is a liar (see v. 9). **5:11–12** *This is the testimony* recalls 1 John 5:1. *Eternal Life.* See 1 John 1:2; 2:25; 3:15; 5:13, 20. *Whoever has the Son has life* recalls the promise of life in the Gospel of John (20:30–31; 1 John 5:13). **5:13** *I write these things to you* resembles the conclusion of the Gospel of John (21:24). *That you may know* conveys assurance. **5:14–15** *And this is the boldness* implies confidence that what is requested is certain. *That if we ask anything* introduces the theme of prayer. **5:15** *We know that he hears us in whatever we ask.* See Mark 11:24. **5:16** *Deadly* literally means in Greek "sin unto death." Here no specific sin is identified as mortal. **5:18–20** *We know* is the opposite of the knowledge of the false teachers. What is known is that they are children of God (v. 19), they are protected (v. 18), and they know Jesus and the only true God (v. 20). *He is the true God and eternal life*

them.[t] [19] We know that we are God's children and that the whole world lies under the power of the evil one. [20] And we know that the Son of God has come and has given us understanding so that we may know him who is true;[u] and we are in him who is true, in his Son Jesus Christ. He is the true God and eternal life.

21 Little children, keep yourselves from idols.[v]

t 5.18 Other ancient authorities read *protects himself, and the evil one does not touch him*   *u* 5.20 Other ancient authorities read *know the true God*   *v* 5.21 Other ancient authorities add *Amen*

is the final affirmation of Jesus as the Son of God—the true God. *Eternal life* is knowing God as Jesus Christ in the present, after death, for eternity (see 1:1). **5:21** *Keep yourselves from idols* is the final warning away from idols ("eidōlōn"). *Idols* not only serves as a reminder that God is the true God, but it also might call to mind the context of living in the Greco-Roman world, where a variety of non-Christian religious expressions existed.

The Second Letter of John

Reading Guide

Second John is framed around preventing disunity among its readers and reaffirming the central identity of the community, which is founded on the belief that Jesus, who has come from God, did so in the flesh, as a human being. It shows Jesus followers fighting to establish a single, proto-orthodox theology. The elder writes to the "elect lady," perhaps a personification of the Christian community or an individual believer (vv. 1–3). The letter centers on the elder's reassurance that the teaching his readers have received is "the truth" (v. 4). Second John shows how religious communities endured power struggles as they sought to define their identity.

Francisco Lozada, Jr.

1 The elder to the elect lady and her children, whom I love in the truth, and not only I but also all who know the truth, [2]because of the truth that abides in us and will be with us forever:

3 Grace, mercy, and peace will be with us from God the Father and from[a] Jesus Christ, the Father's Son, in truth and love.

4 I was overjoyed to find some of your children walking in the truth, just as we have been commanded by the Father. [5]But now, dear lady, I ask you, not as though I were writing you a new commandment but one we have had from the beginning: let us love one another. [6]And this is love, that we walk according to his commandments; this is the commandment just as you have heard it from the beginning—you must walk in it.

7 Many deceivers have gone out into the world, those who do not confess that Jesus Christ has come in the flesh; any such person is the deceiver and the antichrist! [8]Be on your guard, so that you do not lose what we[b] have worked for but may receive a full reward. [9]Everyone who does not abide in the teaching of Christ, but goes beyond it,[c] does not have God; whoever abides in the teaching[d] has both the Father and the Son. [10]If anyone comes to you and does not bring this teaching, do not receive and welcome this person into your house, [11]for to welcome is to participate in the evil deeds of such a person.

12 Although I have much to write to you, I would rather not use paper and ink; instead, I hope to come to you and talk with you face to face, so that our[e] joy may be complete.

13 The children of your elect sister send you their greetings.[f]

a 3 Other ancient authorities add *the Lord* b 8 Other ancient authorities read *you* c 9 Other ancient authorities read *turns aside* d 9 Other ancient authorities add *of Christ* e 12 Other ancient authorities read *your* f 13 Other ancient authorities add *Amen*

1–3 Introduction. 1 *The elder.* The author is someone who commands respect or holds an important title in the community, such as a "bishop" or "overseer" (Acts 20:17, 28; Titus 1:5, 7). *Elect lady* ("eklētē kyria"). The letter's addressee is either the personification of the chosen community or an individual. If the former, it recalls those chosen by God to enter into a covenant relationship with God (Deut. 4:37; Isa. 45:4; see also 1 Pet. 1:1; 2 Tim. 2:10). *Children.* The members of the community. **2** *Abides* is a favorite word of the author and communicates personal communion.

4–11 The message. 4 *Walking in the truth* infers both believing in the humanity and divinity of Jesus as the Son of God and conforming one's life to this truth. **5** *Let us love one another* is a petition that existed *from the beginning* (1 John 2:7–8, 24) and reflects the community's ethic. **6** *This is love.* Believers ought to respond to God's commandment. **7** *Deceiver* ("planoi") implies "seducer" and "heretic" (Matt. 27:63; John 7:12). **8** *Full reward.* Eternal life (see note on 1 John 1:2) and fellowship established by walking in love. **9** *Teaching* ("didachē"). Instructions or "doctrines" to follow. *But goes beyond it.* The false teachers' claim that their teachings were more advanced. **10** *Into your house.* Communities met in homes (Acts 2:46; 1 Cor. 16:19; Phlm. 2). See **"Hospitality," p. 2109**. **11** *For to welcome is to participate in the evil deeds.* A gesture of endorsement that would only encourage the false teachers.

12–13 The conclusion. 12 *Paper.* Papyrus sheets made from the pith of a reed. **13** For *elect sister*, see v. 1. *Sister* also refers to the Johannine community.

The Third Letter of John

Reading Guide

Third John is a personal letter written by the elder to Gaius. Like 1 and 2 John, it reveals tension over who has authority to lead and teach the Johannine community and reflects early disputes about the nature and identity of Jesus. The elder encourages hospitality to strangers, especially to the fellow believers he has sent to teach the true nature of Jesus (vv. 5–8). In contrast to 1 and 2 John, 3 John directly calls out some individuals. The elder praises Gaius (v. 1) and Demetrius (v. 12), two leaders within the community who are looked upon fondly by the elder, and severely criticizes Diotrephes, who challenges the authority of the elder and refuses those he sends (v. 9).

Francisco Lozada, Jr.

1 The elder to the beloved Gaius, whom I love in truth.

2 Beloved, I pray that all may go well with you and that you may be in good health, just as it is well with your soul. ³For I was overjoyed when some brothers and sisters arrived and testified to your faithfulness to the truth, how you walk in the truth. ⁴I have no greater joy than this, to hear that my children are walking in the truth.

5 Beloved, you do faithfully whatever you do for the brothers and sisters, even though they are strangers to you; ⁶they have testified to your love before the church. You will do well to send them on in a manner worthy of God, ⁷for they began their journey for the sake of Christ,ᵃ accepting no support from nonbelievers.ᵇ ⁸Therefore we ought to support such people, so that we may become coworkers with the truth.

9 I have written something to the church, but Diotrephes, who likes to put himself first, does not welcome us. ¹⁰So if I come, I will call attention to what he is doing in spreading false charges against us. And not content with those charges, he refuses to welcome the brothers and sisters and even prevents those who want to do so and expels them from the church.

11 Beloved, do not imitate what is evil, but imitate what is good. Whoever does good is from God; whoever does evil has not seen God. ¹²Everyone has testified favorably about Demetrius, and so has the truthᶜ itself. We also testify for him,ᵈ and you know that our testimony is true.

13 I have much to write to you, but I would rather not write to you with pen and ink; ¹⁴instead, I hope to see you soon, and we will talk together face to face.

15 Peace to you. The friends send you their greetings. Greet the friends there, each by name.

a 7 Gk *for the sake of the name*   b 7 Gk *the gentiles*   c 12 Other ancient authorities read *church* or *church and truth*   d 12 Gk lacks *for him*

1–8 The message to Gaius. 1 *Elder.* The author, with no further identification (see 2 John 1). *Gaius.* The addressee whom the elder regards warmly. **2** *I pray.* The elder's petition on behalf of Gaius for a successful trip and good health. **3** *Brothers and sisters.* Those in communion with the elder's community. The Greek "adelphōn" is literally *brothers*. **4** *No greater joy than this.* Gaius was once not part of the elder's community, but now he is. **5** *Strangers.* The believers the elder has sent and to whom Gaius has extended hospitality. **6** *Church* ("ekklēsia") and hospitality to strangers are newly prominent concepts in the Johannine tradition. See **"Hospitality," p. 2109. 8** *Coworkers.* Those who support the unnamed missionaries for the sake of the truth they hold in common.

9–10 The message to Diotrephes. 9 *I have written something* implies another letter, perhaps the writer's first, to the church. Diotrephes is a local leader who *likes to put himself first* and does not respect the authority of the elder. **10** *Spreading false charges.* Diotrephes not only disregards the elder's authority, he "brings up unjustified charges" about him. **11** *Imitate.* Action indicating that one belongs not to the writer's opponents but to God. **12** *Demetrius.* A traveling preacher whom the elder introduced to Gaius so that Gaius could provide him hospitality. *You know that our testimony is true* calls to mind John 21:24: "We know that his testimony is true." **13** See 2 John 12. **14** *Talk together face to face.* The elder hopes for a private talk with Gaius. **15** *Peace to you* is a typical Hebrew-style greeting that was adopted by Jesus followers (1 Pet. 5:14).

Going Deeper: Hospitality (3 John)

Hospitality was an essential social virtue in antiquity, practiced when friends or, perhaps, strangers needed a place to stay during their respective travels. People of higher means depended on friends for lodging, but people of lower means (who were in the majority) depended on the ancient practice of showing hospitality. In the context of early Christianity, when followers of Christ were spearheading an emerging religious movement and traveling, as did Jesus, to various towns and villages, they depended on hospitality. Besides providing lodging (1 Pet. 4:9), the host's hospitality might include eating together and determining the permitted and unpermitted foods (Gal. 2:11–15), being seated at a particular place at the table (Luke 14:10), engaging in appropriate table talk (Col. 4:6), and determining with whom one may or may not eat (Mark 2:15).

The word for hospitality, *philoxenia* (Rom. 12:13; Heb. 13:2), is employed less often in ancient literature than the practice is described or illustrated. *Philoxenia* is the opposite of *xenophobia*, the fear of providing hospitality to strangers. It connotes the pleasure one takes in the guest-host relationship—that is, the obligation to provide shelter to visitors and friends (2 John 10; 3 John 5–8, 10; Acts 21:16; 28:7). Hospitality is not always practiced. The New Testament includes stories of inhospitality toward Jesus's disciples (e.g., Mark 6:10–11; cf. Matt. 10:11–15; Luke 10:5–12) or to those considered false teachers (2 John 10).

Christian hospitality is a central theme of 3 John. The elder calls on Gaius, whom he is addressing, to open his heart and support fellow believers. But Diotrephes, the antagonist, will support neither itinerant believers from the elder's community nor those aligned with them. Ancient hospitality is about partnership and community. It permeates early Christian writings and shapes the practices of welcoming strangers, exchanging gifts, and forming expanding relationships with individuals, families, and communities.

Francisco Lozada, Jr.

THE LETTER OF JUDE

Authorship, Date, and Literary History

The author of this letter identifies himself as Judas the brother of Jacob (Gk. *Iakōbos*, which is translated as "James" in Eng.), although today we know him as Jude the brother of James, which would also make him the brother of Jesus (Mark 6:3). Over time, Christians shortened his name to distinguish him from Judas Iscariot, Jesus's betrayer. Scholars are divided over whether this letter was authentically written by a brother of Jesus and generally concede that dating this book with any specificity is speculative at best.

In light of this well-crafted polemic punctuated by quotations from 1 Enoch and references to the Assumption of Moses, the author of this letter must have been steeped in Judaism and fluent in Greek. The audience that received it likewise must have been familiar with these Jewish theological writings as well. The letter's sources point to a community that honors Jewish beliefs.

Jude in Christian Tradition

The debate about the authenticity of the Letter of Jude began quite early in the history of the church. Only some of the earliest lists of recognized Christian writings include Jude. As late as the fourth century CE, Eusebius lists Jude as an *antilegomenon*, a disputed text (*Ecclesiastical History* 3.25.3). In recent years, the presence of a reference to Sodom and Gomorrah (cf. Gen. 19) in Jude 7 has caused it to be weaponized in the fight concerning the full inclusion of all persons in the church and society.

Reading Guide

As you sit to read Jude, it may be helpful to keep a few thoughts in mind. First, remember that Jude is a true letter to an actual church of the first century. That church faces some urgent crisis, as far as the author is concerned. However, the author does not tell us what the crisis is, and the letter does not give us enough clues to discern it with any certainty. We can intimate from the words of the letter that the author's concerns include the preservation of the traditional beliefs of the church and the actions of those whom the author calls "intruders" (Jude 4). Still, this letter is written as a polemic, a verbal attack. As we read, we must remember that we do not know the perspective of those on the other side of the attack.

Jude invites us to sit with anger: the anger of a pastoral leader at a perceived threat to a community of faith that they love; the anger of one Christian directed at others who might also consider themselves to be Christians, despite the polemic in this letter. We are invited to wonder about the role of anger in relation to religious communities and about what the preservation of this letter in the canon of the New Testament might suggest for the protective instincts of religious people. What are the boundaries that may not be crossed in these communities? What kinds of teachings might prompt this response?

Jude also invites us to imagine the broad theological landscape of the earliest church, to acknowledge that first-century Christ followers read religious writings unfamiliar to many of us, like 1 Enoch, and even writings that have not been preserved fully, like the Testament of Moses. Scripture and holy writings included a broad array of voices for these communities, as they do for others, and they made connections among these writings that others might not make. For example, in Jude 5–6, the letter tells the stories of an angelic rebellion against God that, according to 1 Enoch, was a precursor of the flood. Part of that rebellion involved human beings entering into sexual intercourse with "other flesh"—that is, angelic flesh; Jude's reading of Sodom and Gomorrah right after the 1 Enoch reference invites a comparison of the two stories, stories in which human beings coupled with or sought to couple with angels. Jude invites us to wonder, If we were writing a letter to a religious community today, what religious voices might be included that are not in the sacred writings? What connections might be made that others might not fully understand? How might other religious voices also have something to teach?

The letter itself is easy to follow. The author begins with a word of greeting and a benediction (Jude 1–2). Then follows an explanation of the urgency of this letter (Jude 3–4). Next the letter rehearses several examples of rebellion against God. These include the Israelites' rebellion in the wilderness (Num. 14:29–37), the story of the rebellious angels told in 1 Enoch, the story of Sodom and Gomorrah (Gen. 19), and the stories of Cain (Gen. 4:1–24), Balaam (Num. 22), and Korah (Num. 16). As a counterexample to rebellion, the letter upholds the archangel Michael in his dispute with Satan found in the Testament of Moses. The letter concludes this section with a quotation from 1 En. 1:9 about the coming of the Day of the Lord. The final portion of the letter, Jude 17–25, advises the community on how it should protect itself from these

"intruders" by holding to prayer, keeping within the love of God, looking forward to the mercy of Christ, and rescuing those who are straying. The letter ends with a doxology, a word that glorifies God through Jesus Christ.

Although Jude is a short letter, it opens a window into the earliest church, a window that reveals a church that was sometimes angry, that read beyond the books of our modern Bibles, that was self-protective, and that, even in the midst of all this, sought to glorify God.

Jude: An outline

Margaret Aymer

1 Jude,[a] a servant of Jesus Christ and brother of James,

To those who are called, who are beloved[b] in[c] God the Father and kept safe for[d] Jesus Christ:

2 May mercy, peace, and love be yours in abundance.

3 Beloved, while eagerly preparing to write to you about the salvation we share, I find it necessary to write and appeal to you to contend for the faith that was once and for all handed on to the saints. [4]For certain intruders have stolen in among you, people who long ago were designated for this condemnation as ungodly, who pervert the grace of our God into debauchery and deny our only Master and Lord, Jesus Christ.[e]

5 Now I desire to remind you, though you are fully informed, once and for all, that Jesus, who saved[f] a people out of the land of Egypt, afterward destroyed those who did not believe. [6]And the angels who did not keep their own position but deserted their proper dwelling, he has kept in eternal chains in deepest darkness for the judgment of the great day. [7]Likewise, Sodom and Gomorrah and the surrounding cities, which, in the same manner as they, indulged in sexual immorality and pursued unnatural lust,[g] serve as an example by undergoing a punishment of eternal fire.

8 Yet in the same way these dreamers also defile the flesh, reject authority, and slander

a 1 Gk *Judas*   b 1 Other ancient authorities read *sanctified*   c 1 Or *by*   d 1 Or *by*   e 4 Or *the only Master and our Lord Jesus Christ*   f 5 Other ancient authorities read *informed, that the Lord who once and for all saved*   g 7 Gk *went after other flesh*

1–2 Greetings to the community. 1 *A servant.* Literally "an enslaved person." "Slave of God," as appropriated by religious leaders (Ezra 5:11; 2 Pet. 1:1; Rom. 1:1), leaves unaddressed the enslaved, about 10 percent of the Roman Empire's population. *Brother of James*—that is, James, the brother of Jesus and the leader of the church (Acts 15:12–21). *Beloved in God . . . kept safe for Jesus Christ.* The Greek is ambiguous about whether the community is beloved "in" or "by" God and kept safe "for" Jesus Christ or "by" Jesus Christ.

3–4 The purpose of the letter. 3 *The faith that was once and for all handed on* signals a concern for how the oral traditions of the community are transmitted. **4** *Certain intruders* are never identified, nor is their *debauchery* clarified. The letter claims that they *deny . . . Jesus Christ.*

5–23 Urgent theological reminders drawing on community traditions and Scriptures. **5** *Jesus.* Some ancient manuscripts have "the Lord." The letter refers to the Israelites who died in the wilderness (Num. 14:29–37). *Jesus* and "Joshua" are the same word in Greek. However, by omitting Moses, the letter may be reading Jesus back into this story. **6** *The angels who did not keep their own position* retells the story of the flood in 1 Enoch (1 En. 1; 18:15; 22; see **"Beyond the Canon," p. 2112**). **7–8** *Unnatural lust,* literally "other flesh," parallels the human desire to have sex with angels in Gen. 19 with the story told in Gen. 6

Focus On: Beyond the Canon (Jude)

Christians imagine the Scriptures of the church as a finite set of writings bound in a book. However, what we call "the Bible" today constituted only a small part of the writings that the early church considered instructive for matters of faith. Some of these have been lost to time, but we have evidence of them through quotations and allusions in the biblical writings. The Letter of Jude presents us with two such allusions—to the Assumption of Moses (or the Testament of Moses) and to 1 Enoch, both apocalyptic writings akin to the books of Daniel and Revelation (see **"Apocalypse," p. 1216**). Only fragments of the Assumption of Moses exist, and scholars differ over what was in that text. In Jude, the author alludes to a story in the Assumption of a struggle between the archangel Michael and the devil over the body of Moses. Other fragments speak of the coming Day of the Lord, based on a quotation from 1 Enoch.

Ethiopian Orthodox Christians still consider 1 Enoch to be Scripture, and early leaders of the church used this writing with some frequency. It retells the story of the events leading to the flood in Gen. 6, including stories about angels going rogue against the wishes of God and suffering divine punishment in return, in addition to containing significant "Son of Man" language, which certainly parallels and may have influenced the use of "Son of Man" in other parts of the canon, including the Christian Scriptures.

Alongside Jude's allusions, several New Testament writers quoted and cited literature not contained in our Bible. Paul, for example, quotes a pagan play called *Thais* by Menander in 1 Cor. 15:33. We also see allusions to sources such as the Epistle to the Laodiceans (Col. 4:16); the Apocalypse of Moses, also known as the Life of Adam and Eve, which postulates that Satan was "an angel of light" (2 Cor. 11:14); and the Ascension of Isaiah, in which Isaiah is sawn in two, to which Heb. 11:37 alludes. The Hebrew Bible refers to an even greater number of ancient writings known to the authors but lost to time.

As contemporary readers, these allusions remind us that the authors of the biblical writings were steeped in literary landscapes different from our own. Just as we would expect contemporary religious leaders and writers to make reference not only to the biblical Scriptures but to our own literary landscape, these writers also made reference to theirs that they expected their audiences to understand.

Margaret Aymer

the glorious ones.[b] [9]But when the archangel Michael disputed with the devil and argued about the body of Moses, he did not dare to bring a condemnation of slander[i] against him but said, "The Lord rebuke you!" [10]But these people slander whatever they do not understand, and they are destroyed by those things that, like irrational animals, they know by instinct. [11]Woe to them! For they go the way of Cain and abandon themselves to Balaam's error for the sake of gain and perish in Korah's rebellion. [12]These are blots[j] on your love feasts, while they feast with you without fear, feeding themselves.[k] They are waterless clouds carried along by the winds; autumn trees without fruit, twice dead, uprooted; [13]wild waves of the sea, casting up the foam of their own shame; wandering stars, for whom the deepest darkness has been reserved forever.

[14] It was also about these that Enoch, in the seventh generation from Adam, prophesied, saying, "See, the Lord is coming[l] with ten thousands of his holy ones, [15]to execute judgment on all and to convict all the ungodly[m] of all the deeds of ungodliness that they have committed in such an ungodly way and of all the harsh things that ungodly sinners have spoken against him." [16]These are grumblers and malcontents; they indulge their lusts;[n] their mouths utter bombastic nonsense, flattering people to their own advantage.

17 But you, beloved, must remember the words previously spoken by the apostles of our Lord Jesus Christ, [18]for they said to you, "In the last time there will be scoffers, indulging their own ungodly lusts." [19]It is these worldly people, devoid of the Spirit, who are

b 8 Or *angels;* Gk *glories* *i* 9 Or *condemnation for blasphemy* *j* 12 Or *reefs* *k* 12 Or *without fear. They are shepherds who care only for themselves* *l* 14 Gk *came* *m* 15 Other ancient authorities read *everyone* *n* 16 Other ancient authorities read *their own lusts*

and retold in 1 Enoch. **9** The letter recounts the story of *the archangel Michael* and his dispute with Satan over the body of Moses, attributed to the Assumption of Moses (see **"Beyond the Canon," p. 2112**, and **"Moses," p. 247**). **10–13** *Cain, Balaam,* and *Korah* indicate stories about human rebellion against God (cf. Gen. 4; Num. 16 and 22). **14–16** *See, the Lord is coming.* A quotation from 1 En. 1:9. **17–19** The warning

causing divisions. [20]But you, beloved, build yourselves up on your most holy faith; pray in the Holy Spirit; [21]keep yourselves in the love of God; look forward to the mercy of our Lord Jesus Christ that leads to[o] eternal life. [22]And have mercy on some who are wavering; [23]save others by snatching them out of the fire; and have mercy on still others with fear, hating even the tunic defiled by their bodies.[p]

[24] Now to him who is able to keep you from falling and to make you stand without blemish in the presence of his glory with rejoicing, [25]to the only God our Savior, through Jesus Christ our Lord, be glory, majesty, power, and authority, before all time and now and forever. Amen.

o 21 Gk *Christ to*   p 23 Gk *by the flesh*

about scoffers preserves possibly an oral tradition. **20–23** Community instructions for self-preservation and restoration of those who wander.

24–25 A doxology—a final word of praise for God, who preserves the community—rather than a blessing of the community.

THE REVELATION TO JOHN

Title and Genre

Revelation opens with the Greek word *apokalypsis*, which in English is translated as "apocalypse" or "revelation." Despite its modern association with cataclysmic disaster, "apocalypse" refers to lifting a veil or making something visible. Popular misconceptions may accuse the book of being confusing or even contradictory, but Revelation is about making things knowable.

The word *revelation* also lends its name to a kind of literature, *apocalyptic*, which has roots in the fourth century BCE. Early examples of apocalyptic literature include Dan. 7–12 and the noncanonical work 1 En. 1–36 (see **"Apocalypse," p. 1216**). These writings recount the perspective of a visionary, typically an important historical person, who has experienced otherworldly journeys and/or visions of the past and present. Through these visions, the author reveals God's past or future judgments to encourage audiences to remain faithful to God amid the changes and challenges that life presents.

Authorship

The author of Revelation identifies himself as "John" but offers little else about his identity (1:1, 9). There is no reason to assume the author writes under the name of another (a characteristic of apocalyptic literature), since he does not claim authority through the name. Instead, John establishes a connection to audience members by describing himself as their "brother" and claiming to endure affliction like them (1:9). He locates himself on an island off the coast of Asia Minor, Patmos, without revealing his reason for being there (see note on 1:9).

John's relationship to the author of the Gospel, the author of the Letters of John, and Jesus's disciple John, the three often imagined (albeit mistakenly) to be the same person, remains unknown. Early interpreters noted the differences in writing style between Revelation, which is quite awkward, and other writings associated with the name John. The dissimilarities suggest distinct authors, although evocative connections, such as descriptions of Christ as the Lamb and the Word of God, exist between Revelation and these other writings.

Date and Audience

Revelation addresses communities of Jesus followers living in the second half of the first century (ca. 70–95 CE) in seven cities of the Roman province of Asia (modern Turkey). These urban settings shape Revelation's imagery and perspective (see **"The Bible in Its Ancient Contexts," pp. 2150–52**).

Even though John gives us little or no information about the historical individuals in his audiences, other New Testament writings suggest these kinds of communities were remarkably diverse. Among those hearing Revelation were families and individuals from different classes and social backgrounds, including Roman citizens and non-Romans, some who were wealthy and many more who were not. Present were enslavers, enslaved people, and the formerly enslaved. In addition, Revelation's audiences consisted of men and those who fell outside the narrow definition of manliness in the Roman Empire, including women, non-Roman males, children, and enslaved people of all genders.

John's extensive use of the Hebrew Bible reflects his Jewish identity and implies his audiences find these traditions meaningful. By envisioning the faithful as the tribes of Israel (7:4–8) and as part of a heavenly Jerusalem (e.g., 21:1–4), John implies his audiences embrace a Jewish identity, even if some were gentiles.

Although his audiences included people from various backgrounds, John calls them to adopt a unified identity distinct from the dominant culture. He encourages them to draw boundaries between themselves and other Jesus followers who are accommodating to Roman practices. John describes these folks as "sexually immoral" (21:8; 22:15; see **"Sex Work as a Metaphor in Revelation," p. 2125**). In contrast, John encourages his audiences to see themselves as enslaved to God and the Lamb and as virgins who "follow the Lamb wherever he goes" (14:1–4). This gives Revelation a strong "us versus them" perspective that readers should interrogate.

Setting and Purpose

Revelation assumes a context where local elites, maybe even some members of John's audiences, welcomed Roman rule. Rome offered political, economic, and social stability for which the cities of Asia were

grateful, especially when emperors helped financially and materially after earthquakes and other disasters. The cities expressed gratefulness via a system of practices scholars call "imperial cults." Temples were built to honor emperors, their families, and the goddess Roma, and the language of worship was used for the emperors in both public and private settings. Inscriptions lauding emperors as "all-powerful" and as "saviors" dotted the landscape and appeared on coins.

Because of the prevalence of pro-Roman sentiments in Asia, John anticipates conflict between Jesus's followers and the empire. He names one person who has been killed already (2:13) and foresees more bloodshed on the horizon (e.g., 6:9–11). Given this, interpreters long assumed Revelation was a response to the imperial persecution of Christians. However, letters between Pliny, a provincial governor, and Emperor Trajan around 112 CE complicate this picture, since Pliny seeks advice on how to deal with Jesus followers reported by their fellow citizens. Pliny's inquiry implies there was not yet a procedure in place to deal with Jesus followers, even though he personally regarded them as superstitious and obstinate.

Even though no imperial plans to suppress the Jesus movement were in place, Pliny's letter reveals that people in cities throughout the empire believed the members of this new group were dangerous enough to report to government officials. Conflicts between Jesus followers and their neighbors are reported elsewhere in the New Testament (e.g., Acts 19:23–41). Moreover, John's sense that his audiences were in danger of persecution surely reflects a fear shaped by the Roman war in Judea, which led to a massive loss of life and the destruction of the Jerusalem temple in 70 CE. The consequences of resisting Roman domination were very real; yet John calls his audience to resist and to live as witnesses to the faith of Christ.

Reading Guide

Revelation defies easy outlining, despite the frequent use of "signposts," such as numbered sequences. Instead of moving in a straight line, Revelation spirals, doubling back to pick up images and themes as it moves forward. Thus, it is advisable to approach Revelation knowing that the book was written to be heard and experienced as it unfurls (1:3).

Among the book's structural elements are multiple introductions (Rev. 1), followed by seven messages to the communities addressed by John (Rev. 2–3). The seven messages anticipate three other series of seven—consisting of seals (Rev. 6), trumpets (Rev. 8–9), and bowls (Rev. 15–16). The cumulative effect leads readers to associate "apocalyptic" literature with cataclysmic destruction. However, detailed descriptions of worship throughout the book underscore one of John's main points—God and Christ alone are worthy of worship and honor.

Chaps. 4 and 5 constitute Revelation's theological and christological heart. Here, Christ, identified as the Lion of Judah, appears as a slaughtered Lamb (5:5–6). The Lamb provides Revelation's audiences with a model of a faithful witness, which challenges Roman notions of what it means to "conquer," and John offers multiple glimpses of what following Christ looks like (Rev. 7, 11, 14). At the same time, Revelation exposes the cosmic origins of evil (Rev. 12) and the ways it manifests in earthly political systems (Rev. 13, 17, 18).

Although John offers pointed critiques of imperial political and economic systems, his vision of God's reign (Rev. 4–5) and the coming world (Rev. 20–22) bear an uncanny similarity to Roman structures and notions of power. For example, while John decries the blood of the saints being shed, he celebrates the massive loss of life experienced by God's enemies (e.g., 19:17–21). Some interpreters argue that John replicates the very things he challenges. In addition, John's use of gendered imagery, including depictions of violence against characters identified as female, and his demonization of those who disagree with his vision mean that modern readers must seriously consider whether Revelation's ends justify its means.

Lynn R. Huber

1 The revelation of Jesus Christ, which God gave him to show his servants what must soon take place, and he made it known by sending his angel to his servant John, ²who testified to the word of God and to the testimony of Jesus Christ, even to all that he saw.

3 Blessed is the one who reads the words of the prophecy, and blessed are those who hear and who keep what is written in it, for the time is near.

4 John to the seven churches that are in Asia:

Grace to you and peace from him who is and who was and who is to come and from the seven spirits who are before his throne, ⁵and from Jesus Christ, the faithful witness, the firstborn of the dead, and the ruler of the kings of the earth.

To him who loves us and freed*ᵃ* us from our sins by his blood ⁶and made us a kingdom, priests serving*ᵇ* his God and Father, to him be glory and dominion forever and ever. Amen.

⁷ Look! He is coming with the clouds;
    every eye will see him,
even those who pierced him,
    and all the tribes of the earth will wail
        on account of him.
So it is to be. Amen.

8 "I am the Alpha and the Omega," says the Lord God, who is and who was and who is to come, the Almighty.

9 I, John, your brother who share with you the persecution and the kingdom and the endurance in Jesus, was on the island called Patmos because of the word of God and the testimony of Jesus.*ᶜ* ¹⁰I was in the spirit*ᵈ* on the Lord's day, and I heard behind me a loud voice like a trumpet ¹¹saying, "Write in a book what you see, and send it to the seven churches, to Ephesus, to Smyrna, to Pergamum, to Thyatira, to Sardis, to Philadelphia, and to Laodicea."

12 Then I turned to see whose voice it was that spoke to me, and on turning I saw seven golden lampstands, ¹³and in the midst of the lampstands I saw one like the Son of Man, clothed with a long robe and with a golden sash across his chest. ¹⁴His head and his hair were white as white wool, white as snow; his

---

a 1.5 Other ancient authorities read *washed*   *b* 1.6 Gk *priests to*   *c* 1.9 Or *testimony to Jesus*   *d* 1.10 Or *in the Spirit*

1:1–3 Introducing the Apocalypse. See **"Introduction to Revelation,"** pp. 2114–15. **1:1–2** *Revelation of Jesus Christ.* Jesus is both the subject and object of revelation, the revealer and the revealed. He stands within a chain of revelation starting with God and concluding with John. *Testified* and *testimony*, literally "witnessing" and "witness," come out of a legal context and have both visual and oral connotations. Christ testifies through death and resurrection. Similarly, the testimony of the faithful often leads to death (6:9; 12:17; 20:4). *Servants.* Literally "enslaved people." **1:3** Revelation is written to be read aloud. *For the time is near.* The events of Revelation are on the horizon, emphasizing the importance of living faithfully in the present.

1:4–8 The greeting. 1:4 *Who is . . . to come.* A divine title highlighting God's eternal nature. *The seven spirits.* Angelic representatives present in heaven before God's throne (4:5). **1:5** *Faithful witness.* A reference to Christ's willingness to die. *Firstborn of the dead.* An allusion to Christ's resurrection and affirmation that he is the first of many. *Ruler . . . earth.* Even though it may seem that the emperor rules, John affirms that Christ rules overall. These titles appear in various forms throughout Revelation. **1:6** *Kingdom, priests* invokes God's call for the Israelites to be "a priestly kingdom and a holy nation" (Exod. 19:6), a promise realized at the millennium (Rev. 20:4–6). **1:7** An unknown speaker echoes Daniel and Gospel traditions that describe a "Son of Man," a Messiah anointed by God, coming on a cloud (Dan. 7:13–14; Matt. 24:30; 26:64; Mark 13:26; Luke 21:27). See **"Son of God vs. Son of Man,"** p. 1774. The reference to one who is *pierced* comes from Zech. 12:10 and alludes to Jesus's crucifixion (John 19:34). **1:8** *Alpha . . . Omega.* The beginning and ending of the Greek alphabet used as a title for God. See also 22:13.

1:9–11 The letter's introduction. 1:9 On the claim of persecution, see **"Introduction to Revelation,"** pp. 2114–15. *Patmos.* An uninhabited island off the coast of Asia Minor (modern Turkey). There is no evidence it was a penal colony. *Because . . . Jesus.* John may have been exiled to Patmos or traveled there to share the gospel. **1:10** *In the spirit*, literally "in a spirit," referring to prayer, worship, or even an ecstatic state induced by fasting or other ascetic practices. *Lord's day.* Sunday, the day of Jesus's resurrection.

1:12–20 A vision of the Son of Man. The first of several distinct revelations of the risen Christ in Revelation. **1:12** *Seven . . . lampstands.* Like the seven branches of a menorah from the Jewish temple. The number seven, a reference to the seven days of creation in Gen. 1, symbolizes completeness. **1:13** *Son of Man.* See note on 1:7. The physical description of the Son of Man connects him to God. *Chest.* Literally "breasts." **1:14** *Hair . . . white wool.* See the "Ancient One" in Dan. 7:9.

eyes were like a flame of fire; [15]his feet were like burnished bronze, refined as in a furnace, and his voice was like the sound of many waters. [16]In his right hand he held seven stars, and from his mouth came a sharp, two-edged sword, and his face was like the sun shining with full force.

17 When I saw him, I fell at his feet as though dead. But he placed his right hand on me, saying, "Do not be afraid; I am the First and the Last [18]and the Living One. I was dead, and see, I am alive forever and ever, and I have the keys of Death and of Hades. [19]Now write what you have seen, what is, and what is to take place after this. [20]As for the mystery of the seven stars that you saw in my right hand and the seven golden lampstands: the seven stars are the angels of the seven churches, and the seven lampstands are the seven churches.

2 "To the angel of the church in Ephesus write: These are the words of him who holds the seven stars in his right hand, who walks among the seven golden lampstands:

2 "I know your works, your toil and your endurance. I know that you cannot tolerate evildoers; you have tested those who claim to be apostles but are not and have found them to be false. [3]I also know that you are enduring and bearing up for the sake of my name and that you have not grown weary. [4]But I have

this against you, that you have abandoned the love you had at first. [5]Remember, then, from where you have fallen; repent and do the works you did at first. If not, I will come to you and remove your lampstand from its place, unless you repent. [6]Yet this is to your credit: you hate the works of the Nicolaitans, which I also hate. [7]Let anyone who has an ear listen to what the Spirit is saying to the churches. To everyone who conquers, I will give permission to eat from the tree of life that is in the paradise of God.

8 "And to the angel of the church in Smyrna write: These are the words of the First and the Last, who was dead and came to life:

9 "I know your affliction and your poverty, even though you are rich. I know the slander on the part of those who say that they are Jews and are not but are a synagogue of Satan. [10]Do not fear what you are about to suffer. Beware, the devil is about to throw some of you into prison so that you may be tested, and for ten days you will have affliction. Be faithful until death, and I will give you the crown of life. [11]Let anyone who has an ear listen to what the Spirit is saying to the churches. Whoever conquers will not be harmed by the second death.

12 "And to the angel of the church in Pergamum write: These are the words of him who has the sharp two-edged sword:

1:15 *Feet were like burnished bronze . . . a furnace.* The imagery communicates his incredible strength. **1:16** See 19:15, 21. **1:17** *I fell . . . dead.* An appropriate response to a vision of a divine being (e.g., Ezek. 1:28).

2:1–3:22 Messages to seven assemblies in Asia. These formulaic messages each begin with an address to the *angel*, or guardian spirit, of the *church*, literally "assembly," within the named cities. The messages are concerned with the assemblies' participation in practices that accommodate Roman values, exemplified by eating food sacrificed to other deities and *sexual immorality* ("porneia" in Gk.), a metaphor for practices that may involve worshiping other gods (see **"Sex Work as a Metaphor," p. 2125**). Each message ends with a promise, literally, to "the victor," translated as *the one who conquers, whoever conquers,* or *everyone who conquers.*

2:1–7 To Ephesus. A port city, the capital of Roman Asia, and home to a famous temple of Artemis. **2:2** *I know your works.* The Son of Man sees and knows all that happens in the assemblies. *Toil,* or "labor." *Endurance.* A theme that appears frequently (1:9; 2:19; 13:10; 14:12). **2:6** *Nicolaitans* refers to a group unknown except through Revelation. In the message to Pergamum (2:12–17), the group is associated with the teachings of "Balaam, who taught Balak" (2:14–15), characters from Num. 22–24. The connection suggests the Nicolaitans encourage practices that lead the Ephesians away from the worship of God, from John's perspective.

2:8–11 To Smyrna. A port city, modern Izmir. **2:9** See **"Synagogue of Satan," p. 2119**. **2:10** The claim that some will be thrown into prison reflects John's sense that Jesus followers will soon experience overt suppression (see **"Introduction to Revelation," pp. 2114–15**). Crowns were common prizes in athletic competitions. **2:11** *Second death.* See 20:14.

2:12–17 To Pergamum. The political center of much of the region before being bequeathed to Rome. During the Roman period, Pergamum hosted a provincial temple dedicated to Augustus and Roma.

13 "I know where you are living, where Satan's throne is. Yet you are holding fast to my name, and you did not deny your faith in me[e] even in the days of Antipas my witness, my faithful one, who was killed among you, where Satan lives. [14]But I have a few things against you: you have some there who hold to the teaching of Balaam, who taught Balak to put a stumbling block before the people of Israel, so that they would eat food sacrificed to idols and engage in sexual immorality.[f] [15]So you also have some who hold to the teaching of the Nicolaitans. [16]Repent, then. If not, I will come to you soon and wage war against them with the sword of my mouth. [17]Let anyone who has an ear listen to what the Spirit is saying to the churches. To everyone who conquers I will give some of the hidden manna, and I will give a white stone, and on the white stone is written a new name that no one knows except the one who receives it.

18 "And to the angel of the church in Thyatira write: These are the words of the Son of God, who has eyes like a flame of fire and whose feet are like burnished bronze:

19 "I know your works: your love, faith, service, and endurance. I know that your latest works are greater than the first. [20]But I have this against you: you tolerate that woman Jezebel, who calls herself a prophet and is teaching and beguiling my servants to engage in sexual immorality[g] and to eat food sacrificed to idols. [21]I gave her time to repent, but she refuses to repent of her sexual immorality.[b] [22]Beware, I am throwing her on a bed, and those who commit adultery with her I am throwing into great distress, unless they repent of her doings, [23]and I will strike her children dead. And all the churches will know that I am the one who searches minds and hearts, and I will give to each of you as your works deserve. [24]But to the rest of you in Thyatira, who do not hold this teaching, who have not learned what some call 'the deep things of Satan,' to you I say, I do not lay on you any other burden; [25]only hold fast to what you have until I come. [26]To everyone who conquers and continues to do my works to the end,

I will give authority over the nations,
[27] to rule[i] them with an iron scepter,
    as when clay pots are shattered—
[28]"even as I also received authority from my Father. To the one who conquers I will also give the morning star. [29]Let anyone who has an ear listen to what the Spirit is saying to the churches.

3 "And to the angel of the church in Sardis write: These are the words of him who has the seven spirits of God and the seven stars:

"I know your works; you have a name of being alive, but you are dead. [2]Wake up and strengthen what remains and is on the point of death, for I have not found your works perfect

e 2.13 Or *deny my faith* f 2.14 Or *prostitution* g 2.20 Or *prostitution* b 2.21 Or *prostitution* i 2.27 Or *to shepherd*

2:13 *Satan's throne.* Some read this as a reference to a massive altar dedicated to Zeus and Athena, but it likely refers more generally to John's sense that evil, embodied in political institutions, resides in the city. *Antipas.* The context implies that Antipas dies because of his *witness,* like Christ. 2:14 *Balak* and *Balaam.* An allusion to the Moabite king Balak and the seer who worked for him (Num. 22–24), through which John characterizes other local religious leaders as "foreign." *Idols.* Even though John disapproves of the worship of gods other than God, the language of "idol" was not necessarily pejorative, as it is today. Meat sold in the marketplace would have been sourced from temple sacrifices. Likewise, food served at community meals, such as those held by trade associations, would have been first sacrificed to patron deities. 2:15 *Nicolaitans.* See note on v. 6. 2:17 *Manna.* Food given by God to the Israelites while in the desert (Exod. 16:31)—part of an ongoing connection drawn between Revelation's audiences and the ancient Israelites (Rev. 15:2–4).

2:18–29 **To Thyatira.** 2:20 *Jezebel.* The name functions as a slur, evoking notions of "foreignness" and "idolatry" or the worship of other gods (1 Kgs. 16:29–31). *Sexual immorality* may refer to sexual relationships John finds objectional but serves mainly as a metaphor for worshiping gods other than the Jewish God, imagined as Israel's husband (e.g., Ezek. 16; Jer. 31:32). See **"Sex Work as a Metaphor," p. 2125.** 2:22 *Throwing her on a bed.* An image of sexual assault, an extreme case of punishment "fitting" the supposed crime. John gives little information about "Jezebel's" supposed teachings and no explanation as to why "she" deserves such extreme punishment, in contrast to Balak and Balaam. See **"Slut-Shaming," p. 1148,** and **"Sexually Abusive Language," p. 1035.** 2:24 *Deep things of Satan.* A sarcastic description of "Jezebel's" teachings. 2:26–27 See note on 12:5. 2:28 *Morning star.* See note on 22:16.

3:1–6 **To Sardis.** A city that had been the capital of the Lydian kingdom (seventh to sixth centuries BCE). Much of the city had to be rebuilt after an earthquake in 17 CE. Rebuilding was financed in part

Going Deeper: Synagogue of Satan (Revelation 2–3)

John's characterization of neighboring communities in Smyrna and Philadelphia as "synagogue[s] of Satan" (2:9; 3:9) has an unfortunate history of being used for anti-Jewish and anti-Semitic agendas. Even though John's use of the word "synagogue" appears to aim insult at Jewish communities, that may not be the case. Scholars differ in opinion over whether "synagogue of Satan" refers to Jewish or gentile communities, depending on how they interpret the phrase "those who say that they are Jews and are not" (2:9).

Interpreters who read "synagogue of Satan" as abuse toward Jewish communities suggest that "those who say that they are Jews and are not" (2:9) signals John's refusal to acknowledge the authentic Jewish identity of Jewish communities. For reasons unstated, John does not see them as genuinely or sufficiently Jewish. Instead, he associates them with Satan and uses Jewish identity to describe *his* communities, whom he addresses in Revelation. Scholars who argue this assume Revelation's audience consists of gentile Jesus followers and that there is an emerging conflict between them and their Jewish neighbors. However, evidence for such conflict comes only from the next century (*Martyrdom of Polycarp* 12).

It seems more likely that "those who say that they are Jews and are not" (2:9) should be read literally, referring to a gentile group of Jesus followers who claim Jewish identity for themselves. "Those who say that they are Jews and are not" may refer to gentiles converting to Judaism as part of following Jesus. Paul addresses a similar issue when writing to Jesus followers in Galatia, a region east of Asia Minor. He vehemently disagrees with those encouraging gentiles to convert to Judaism and to be circumcised as part of following Jesus (Gal. 2:11–14). Like Paul, John challenges gentile appropriation of Jewish identity. Furthermore, he vilifies those gentile communities as satanic. These verses might help explain later discord that developed in some instances between gentile Jesus followers and local Jewish groups, where gentiles claimed Jewish identity for themselves.

Even if "synagogue of Satan" referred originally to gentile and not Jewish communities, the language incites audience members to hate their neighbors. This alone makes the phrase worthy of criticism. Whether intended or not, John's language invites an association between Jews and Satan (cf. John 8:44) and subsequently contributes to the demonization of Jews. Clearly such language must be condemned and avoided by modern interpreters.

Lynn R. Huber

in the sight of my God. ³Remember, then, what you received and heard; obey it and repent. If you do not wake up, I will come like a thief, and you will not know at what hour I will come to you. ⁴Yet you have still a few persons in Sardis who have not soiled their clothes; they will walk with me, dressed in white, for they are worthy. ⁵If you conquer, you will be clothed like them in white robes, and I will not erase your name from the book of life; I will confess your name before my Father and before his angels. ⁶Let anyone who has an ear listen to what the Spirit is saying to the churches.

7 "And to the angel of the church in Philadelphia write:

These are the words of the Holy One, the True One,
who has the key of David,
who opens and no one will shut,
who shuts and no one opens:

8 "I know your works. Look, I have set before you an open door that no one is able to shut. I know that you have but little power, yet you have kept my word and have not denied my name. ⁹I will make those of the synagogue of Satan who say that they are Jews and are not but are lying—I will make them come and bow down before your feet, and they will learn that I have loved you. ¹⁰Because you have kept my word of endurance, I will keep you from

by the Roman emperor Tiberius. **3:3** *Like a thief . . . hour.* Common imagery referring to the unknown timing of Jesus's return (e.g., Matt. 24:43; 1 Thess. 5:2). **3:4–5** *Soiled . . . clothes, white robes.* Throughout Revelation, white robes characterize the faithful who have "washed" their clothing in the blood of the Lamb, most likely through a death that parallels Christ (6:11; 7:13–14; 22:14). *Book of life.* One of the books opened at the Last Judgment, identifying those who will be rewarded and live as part of the new Jerusalem (20:12–15; see also Exod. 32:32; Ps. 69:28).

3:7–13 To Philadelphia. Like Sardis, Philadelphia was partially rebuilt with imperial support after an earthquake in 17 CE. **3:7** *Key of David.* Access possessed by the Son of Man based on his messianic identity. **3:9** See **"Synagogue of Satan," p. 2119**. **3:10** *Hour of trial.* John envisions a time when Jesus

the hour of trial that is coming on the whole world to test the inhabitants of the earth. [11]I am coming soon; hold fast to what you have, so that no one takes away your crown. [12]If you conquer, I will make you a pillar in the temple of my God; you will never go out of it. I will write on you the name of my God and the name of the city of my God, the new Jerusalem that comes down from my God out of heaven, and my own new name. [13]Let anyone who has an ear listen to what the Spirit is saying to the churches.

14 "And to the angel of the church in Laodicea write: The words of the Amen, the faithful and true witness, the origin[j] of God's creation:

15 "I know your works; you are neither cold nor hot. I wish that you were either cold or hot. [16]So, because you are lukewarm and neither cold nor hot, I am about to spit you out of my mouth. [17]For you say, 'I am rich, I have prospered, and I need nothing.' You do not realize that you are wretched, pitiable, poor, blind, and naked. [18]Therefore I advise you to buy from me gold refined by fire so that you may be rich, and white robes to clothe yourself and to keep the shame of your nakedness from being seen, and salve to anoint your eyes so that you may see. [19]I reprove and discipline those whom I love. Be earnest, therefore, and repent. [20]Listen! I am standing at the door, knocking; if you hear my voice and open the door, I will come in and eat with you, and you with me. [21]To the one who conquers I will give a place with me on my throne, just as I myself conquered and sat down with my Father on his throne. [22]Let anyone who has an ear listen to what the Spirit is saying to the churches."

4 After this I looked, and there in heaven a door stood open! And the first voice, which I had heard speaking to me like a trumpet, said, "Come up here, and I will show you what must take place after this." [2]At once I was in the spirit,[k] and there in heaven stood a throne, with one seated on the throne! [3]And the one seated there looks like jasper and carnelian, and around the throne is a rainbow that looks like an emerald. [4]Around the throne are twenty-four thrones, and seated on the thrones are twenty-four elders, dressed in white robes, with golden crowns on their heads. [5]Coming from the throne are flashes of lightning and rumblings and peals of thunder, and in front of the throne burn seven flaming torches, which are the seven

j 3.14 Or *beginning*   k 4.2 Or *in the Spirit*

followers will be forced to choose between remaining faithful to God and Christ and capitulating to the dominant culture. **3:12** John emphasizes the stability of the victors by associating them with *pillar[s]* that will never be removed from God's temple. Perhaps an ironic reference to the earthquakes that happened frequently. *Write on you.* See 7:3; 14:1.

3:14–22 To Laodicea. Located in the Lycus River Valley near Hierapolis, a city known for its hot springs. **3:15–16** *Lukewarm.* A metaphor for lacking strength of character, being "wishy-washy." *Spit.* Literally "vomit." **3:17** Using a rhetorical technique called "prosopopoeia," John speaks in the voice of the Laodiceans as a way of highlighting their lack of self-awareness. **3:18** *Gold refined by fire.* Something valuable and pure. *Shame of your nakedness.* Except when bathing or in the gymnasium, nakedness was a sign of low status. *Salve to anoint your eyes.* A remedy to help the Laodiceans "see" themselves accurately.

4:1–11 Entering the heavenly throne room. 4:1 *I looked . . . !* Missing from the English translation is a command, heard by the audience, to "Look!" along with John. The English text tends to signal the presence of these commands with exclamation points (e.g., 4:1, 2; 6:2, 5, 8; 14:1, 14; 19:11). *A door.* Heaven is envisioned as a physical space. See also 1 En. 1–36. *Come up here.* John is invited to cross a threshold into the heavenly world. Heavenly journeys are a characteristic of apocalyptic literature (see **"Introduction to Revelation," pp. 2114–15**). **4:2** *One seated on the throne.* John uses this phrase throughout to characterize God, highlighting his authority over all other rulers (4:2, 3, 4, 9, 10; 5:1, 7, 13; 6:16; 7:10, 15; 19:4; 20:11; 21:5). **4:3** *Like jasper . . . like an emerald.* John draws frequent comparisons, signaled by the word *like*, to describe things typically unseen by human eyes. In this case, John avoids depicting God in human form by using gemstone imagery. **4:4** Throughout this passage, the preposition *around* highlights the centrality of God's throne. *Twenty-four.* The number twelve and its multiples appear throughout Revelation, alluding to the twelve tribes of Israel, months (22:2), and signs of the zodiac. "Twelve" is also associated with Jesus's disciples, evoking the twelve tribes (Mark 6:7–13; Matt. 10:5–7; Luke 9:1–6). **4:5** *Flashes of lightning.* References to lightning and thunder put God in the company of

spirits of God, [6]and in front of the throne there is something like a sea of glass, like crystal.

Around the throne, and on each side of the throne, are four living creatures, full of eyes in front and back: [7]the first living creature like a lion, the second living creature like an ox, the third living creature with a face like a human, and the fourth living creature like a flying eagle. [8]And the four living creatures, each of them with six wings, are full of eyes all around and inside. Day and night without ceasing they sing,

"Holy, holy, holy,
the Lord God the Almighty,
who was and is and is to come."

[9]And whenever the living creatures give glory and honor and thanks to the one who is seated on the throne, who lives forever and ever, [10]the twenty-four elders fall before the one who is seated on the throne and worship the one who lives forever and ever; they cast their crowns before the throne, singing,

[11] "You are worthy, our Lord and God,
to receive glory and honor and power,

for you created all things,
and by your will they existed and were
created."

5 Then I saw in the right hand of the one seated on the throne a scroll written on the inside and on the back, sealed[l] with seven seals, [2]and I saw a mighty angel proclaiming with a loud voice, "Who is worthy to open the scroll and break its seals?" [3]And no one in heaven or on earth or under the earth was able to open the scroll or to look into it. [4]And I began to weep bitterly because no one was found worthy to open the scroll or to look into it. [5]Then one of the elders said to me, "Do not weep. See, the Lion of the tribe of Judah, the Root of David, has conquered, so that he can open the scroll and its seven seals."

6 Then I saw between the throne and the four living creatures and among the elders a Lamb standing as if it had been slaughtered, with seven horns and seven eyes, which are the seven spirits of God sent out into all the earth. [7]He went and took the scroll from the right

l 5.1 Or *written on the inside and sealed on the back*

other ancient sky gods, including Zeus, and evoke Hebrew Bible references to God appearing through a storm (e.g., Exod. 19:9–18; Ps. 29:3; Ezek. 1:4). **4:6** *Sea of glass.* A calm sea, contrasting with the unpredictability of the Mediterranean. See also 15:2. **4:6–8** *Four living creatures.* Inspired by Ezekiel, where similar figures surround God's throne, although each creature has four distinct faces (Ezek. 1:10–11). The creatures point to the otherworldly nature of the divine and are dedicated to worshiping God. **4:8** *Holy, holy, holy.* The thrice-repeated affirmation of holiness ("trisagion") originally appears in the throne room scene of Isa. 6:3. *Almighty* (Gk. "pantokratōr") refers to God as one who rules over all others (1:8; 11:17; 15:3; 16:7; 19:6; 21:22). **4:10** *The twenty-four elders fall.* An ancient Near Eastern court practice, "proskynesis," symbolizing loyalty.

5:1–14 The slaughtered Lamb. A continuation of the throne room vision, this chapter introduces the most important christological claims of Revelation: (1) the messianic Lion appears simultaneously as a slaughtered Lamb and (2) the Lamb shares God's throne. **5:1** *A scroll . . . on the back.* Scrolls typically had writing on one side; writing on both sides underscores this scroll's importance. See Ezek. 2:9–10; Zech. 5:1–3. *Seals.* Clay or wax, usually embossed, used to close the scroll. **5:2–4** The angel's question and John's reaction emphasize the importance of having the seals broken and scroll opened. Ironically, John's audience never learns what is written on the scroll. **5:5** *Lion . . . Root of David.* Titles suggesting that the one coming to open the scroll is a messianic king of the lines of Judah and David (Gen. 49:9; 2 Sam. 7:1–17). These claims align with other New Testament texts depicting Jesus as a descendant of David and the Messiah (Matt. 1:1–18; Luke 3:23–38). *Has conquered.* The language of conquering, also used in Rev. 2–3, evokes strength and victory. It is also used ironically to describe those who will die on account of their faith, like Jesus (11:7; 12:11; 13:7; 15:2; 21:7). **5:6** *Then I saw.* John hears the announcement about the Lion and sees something different. This juxtaposition between hearing and seeing appears in 7:4–10 as well. *Lamb.* Literally a "small lamb." Although the word in Revelation, "arnion," differs from "amnos" in John 1:29 and 36, the connection is provocative. *Standing . . . slaughtered.* The juxtaposition between standing and being slaughtered highlights this as a paradoxical image. Having been slaughtered alludes to crucifixion or capital punishment, as well as to the Lamb's vulnerability as one pierced or penetrated (1:7; cf. John 19:34, 37). In the Roman world, being penetrated challenged a subject's masculinity. *Horns* traditionally symbolize power (Dan. 7:7–8). Here they are part of the paradoxical image of the Lamb. *Seven eyes* suggests the Lamb is all-seeing, explaining Christ's awareness of all

Making Connections: Revelation in Popular Culture (Revelation 5)

Revelation's influence on modern popular culture is so widespread that once a person begins looking for it, it becomes visible everywhere—movies, novels, TV shows, video games, comics, graphic novels, and jokes.

Some of the most popular appropriations of Revelation blur the boundary between being overtly Christian and secular, such as the *Left Behind* franchise, whose novels treat Revelation as a blueprint for the present and near future, reading the modern nation of Israel and the United Nations into the text. Its film versions employ popular actors, such as Nicolas Cage, to appeal to a broader audience. Many people's initial encounter with Revelation is shaped by this explicitly North American evangelical Christian interpretation.

The association of Revelation's imagery with the emergence of cosmic evil often provides a basis for horror movies. Among the most popular are *Rosemary's Baby* (1968) and *The Omen* (1976), having been remade, followed by sequels, and even parodied. Both movies attach supernatural evil to the birth of a child. Similarly, John's visions provide material for popular TV shows exploring the supernatural, such as the aptly named *Supernatural* (2005–20) and *Sleepy Hollow* (2013–17).

Revelation contributes as well to explorations of humanity's role in the world's destruction and decline. Terry Gilliam's 1995 movie *Twelve Monkeys*, for instance, makes specific connections to the book in telling the story of an inmate from the future traveling back in time to determine the origin of a virus forcing humans to move underground. Tony Kushner's Pulitzer Prize–winning play *Angels in America* (1991) examines the reality of the AIDS crisis using apocalyptic and supernatural imagery.

Despite Revelation's dire predictions, it appears in comic settings as well, such as the TV series *Good Omens*, produced by Amazon and the BBC (2019 and 2021). Based on a 1990 novel of the same name by Neil Gaiman and Terry Pratchett, the story focuses on an angel and a demon who work together to postpone the battle of Armageddon. *Good Omens* offers a critique of apocalyptic thinking in general, questioning Revelation's dualistic worldview, which pits good and evil against each other, and the inevitability of the end.

In popular music, references to Revelation often provide a tool for criticizing oppressive political and religious institutions. Among these are references to Western culture as Babylon in reggae music, a creative product by adherents to Rastafarianism, a Jamaican religious movement. Revelation's influence in popular culture underscores the importance of careful study of the ancient text.

Lynn R. Huber

hand of the one who was seated on the throne. [8]When he had taken the scroll, the four living creatures and the twenty-four elders fell before the Lamb, each holding a harp and golden bowls full of incense, which are the prayers of the saints. [9]They sing a new song:

"You are worthy to take the scroll
    and to break its seals,
for you were slaughtered and by your
        blood you ransomed for God
    saints from[m] every tribe and language
        and people and nation;
[10] you have made them a kingdom and
        priests serving[n] our God,
    and they will reign[o] on earth."

11 Then I looked, and I heard the voice of many angels surrounding the throne and the living creatures and the elders; they numbered myriads of myriads and thousands of thousands, [12]singing with full voice,

"Worthy is the Lamb that was slaughtered
    to receive power and wealth and wisdom
        and might
    and honor and glory and blessing!"

[13]Then I heard every creature in heaven and on earth and under the earth and in the sea and all that is in them, singing,

"To the one seated on the throne and to
        the Lamb
    be blessing and honor and glory and
        might
    forever and ever!"

[14]And the four living creatures said, "Amen!" And the elders fell down and worshiped.

m 5.9 Gk *ransomed for God from*   *n* 5.10 Gk *priests to*
o 5.10 Other ancient authorities read *they reign*

that happens within the seven churches in Rev. 2–3. **5:8** The elders fall before the Lamb, just as they fell before the throne of God in 4:10. **5:9** The Lamb's appearance requires a new song that praises his role in God's work. As the one who had been *slaughtered* and then *ransomed*, literally "purchased," saints from all peoples for God, the Lamb is *worthy* to break the scroll's seals (cf. 5:12). This language is part of John's depiction of the faithful as enslaved to God (14:3). **5:14** *Amen.* The living creatures affirm the worship of God and the Lamb together.

6 Then I saw the Lamb break one of the sev-
en seals, and I heard one of the four living
creatures call out, as with a voice of thunder,
“Come!”[p] 2 I looked, and there was a white horse!
Its rider had a bow; a crown was given to him,
and he came out conquering and to conquer.
3 When he broke the second seal, I heard
the second living creature call out, “Come!”[q]
4 And out came[r] another horse, bright red; its
rider was permitted to take peace from the
earth, so that people would slaughter one another, and he was given a great sword.
5 When he broke the third seal, I heard the
third living creature call out, “Come!”[s] I looked,
and there was a black horse! Its rider held a pair
of scales in his hand, 6 and I heard what seemed
to be a voice in the midst of the four living creatures saying, “A quart of wheat for a day’s pay[t]
and three quarts of barley for a day’s pay,[u] but
do not damage the olive oil and the wine!”
7 When he broke the fourth seal, I heard
the voice of the fourth living creature call out,
“Come!”[v] 8 I looked, and there was a pale green
horse! Its rider’s name was Death, and Hades
followed with him; they were given authority
over a fourth of the earth, to kill with sword,
famine, and pestilence and by the wild animals of the earth.
9 When he broke the fifth seal, I saw under the altar the souls of those who had been
slaughtered for the word of God and for the
testimony they had given; 10 they cried out with
a loud voice, “Sovereign Lord, holy and true,
how long will it be before you judge and avenge
our blood on the inhabitants of the earth?”
11 They were each given a white robe and told
to rest a little longer, until the number would
be complete both of their fellow servants and
of their brothers and sisters who were soon to
be killed as they themselves had been killed.
12 When he broke the sixth seal, I looked,
and there was a great earthquake; the sun
became black as sackcloth, the full moon became like blood, 13 and the stars of the sky fell
to the earth as the fig tree drops its winter fruit
when shaken by a gale. 14 The sky vanished like
a scroll rolling itself up, and every mountain
and island was removed from its place. 15 Then
the kings of the earth and the magnates and

p 6.1 Or *“Go!”* *q* 6.3 Or *“Go!”* *r* 6.4 Or *went*
s 6.5 Or *“Go!”* *t* 6.6 Gk *a denarius* *u* 6.6 Gk *a denarius*
v 6.7 Or *“Go!”*

6:1–8 The first four seals. The first four of the seven seals portray realities experienced by those living in first-century Asia Minor, including war, economic precarity, and famine. By highlighting these types of crises, John challenges the empire’s claims of bringing peace and prosperity. Placing crises under the control of the Lamb questions the ability of human rulers to mitigate their impacts. **6:2** *I looked . . . !* See note on 4:1. *A white horse.* The depiction of variously hued horses recalls Zech. 1:7–11; 6:1–8, where similar animals patrol the earth on God’s behalf. The rider on the white horse resembles a later depiction of Christ (19:11); however, the other seals’ content suggests this rider should be understood otherwise. By carrying a bow, the rider parallels descriptions of armies along the empire’s borders, and his *conquering* may evoke the threat of invasion. **6:4** *Was permitted.* The passive language reminds the audience these events are controlled by those on the heavenly throne. **6:5–6** Scales were used in the marketplace to weigh goods and determine prices. The high price of grain points to economic hardship; and the command referring to olive oil and wine suggests the exploitation of the provinces by the Roman Empire, since these were among the products exported from the province to Rome and other parts of the empire. **6:8** *Death . . . Hades.* Death and Hades are both personified (see also 20:14). In the first century, Hades was both the place of the dead and a deity who ruled the underworld. According to one popular myth, Hades abducted Persephone, taking her to his underground lair.

6:9–17 The fifth and sixth seals. 6:9–11 The opening of the fifth seal does not trigger events as with the first four; instead, it allows John to see under heaven’s altar. *Souls.* The word “psychē,” translated here as *soul*, can also mean life. Even though these ones have been killed, they are living. *Slaughtered for the . . . testimony.* The term *slaughtered* is also used in reference to the Lamb (e.g., 5:6, 9, 12), suggesting the souls have followed Christ (see 1:5). The language of testimony (“martyria”) anticipates later Christian characterizations of those who die for their faith as “martyrs.” **6:10** The request that God *avenge* can be understood as a request for God to enact justice (cf. 19:2). **6:11** *Brothers and sisters.* The Greek includes only “brothers.” A more inclusive way of translating this is “siblings.” See **“Introduction to Revelation,” pp. 2114–15**, on persecution. **6:12–14** Cataclysmic events are signs of God’s coming judgment (see Joel 2). *Sackcloth.* Heavy, coarse cloth associated with mourning (see Isa. 15:2–3). *Moon . . . like blood.* Dramatic celestial events signal God’s judgment (Joel 2:31; Acts 2:20). *Stars . . . fell.* See Mark 13:24–25. **6:14** *Sky vanished.* See Isa. 34:4. **6:15** *The kings . . . and everyone.*

the generals and the rich and the powerful and everyone, slave and free, hid in the caves and among the rocks of the mountains, [16]calling to the mountains and rocks, "Fall on us and hide us from the face of the one seated on the throne and from the wrath of the Lamb, [17]for the great day of their[w] wrath has come, and who is able to stand?"

7 After this I saw four angels standing at the four corners of the earth, holding back the four winds of the earth so that no wind could blow on earth or sea or against any tree. [2]I saw another angel ascending from the rising of the sun, with the seal of the living God, and he called with a loud voice to the four angels who had been given power to damage earth and sea, [3]saying, "Do not damage the earth or the sea or the trees, until we have marked the servants of our God with a seal on their foreheads."

4 And I heard the number of those who were sealed, one hundred forty-four thousand, sealed out of every tribe of the people of Israel:

[5] From the tribe of Judah twelve thousand sealed,
from the tribe of Reuben twelve thousand,
from the tribe of Gad twelve thousand,
[6] from the tribe of Asher twelve thousand,
from the tribe of Naphtali twelve thousand,
from the tribe of Manasseh twelve thousand,
[7] from the tribe of Simeon twelve thousand,
from the tribe of Levi twelve thousand,
from the tribe of Issachar twelve thousand,
[8] from the tribe of Zebulun twelve thousand,
from the tribe of Joseph twelve thousand,
from the tribe of Benjamin twelve thousand sealed.

9 After this I looked, and there was a great multitude that no one could count, from every nation, from all tribes and peoples and languages, standing before the throne and before the Lamb, robed in white, with palm branches in their hands. [10]They cried out in a loud voice, saying,

"Salvation belongs to our God who is seated on the throne and to the Lamb!"

[11]And all the angels stood around the throne and around the elders and the four living creatures, and they fell on their faces before the throne and worshiped God, [12]singing,

"Amen! Blessing and glory and wisdom and thanksgiving and honor and power and might be to our God forever and ever! Amen."

13 Then one of the elders addressed me, saying, "Who are these, robed in white, and

w 6.17 Other ancient authorities read *his*

John lists a range of peoples to highlight the universal nature of God's judgment. **6:16** *Fall on us.* See Hos. 10:8; Luke 23:30.

7:1–8 The 144,000. The opening of the seventh seal is delayed, and there is a temporary reprieve as John's attention turns to the faithful. **7:3** *Servants.* Literally "enslaved people." Like other biblical authors, John uses enslavement as a metaphor for being faithful to God and the Lamb. This metaphor becomes more specific here, as an angel announces the faithful will be sealed on the forehead. Ancient enslavers and slave dealers marked people as property, or as a form of punishment for fleeing, through a variety of means, including tattooing, branding, collars, and signs worn around the neck. In contrast to this ancient practice, sealing in Revelation is depicted in a positive light, as a way of protecting the faithful from harm. **7:4** *One hundred forty-four thousand*: 12 × 12,000. The symbolic number suggests the fullness and perfection of the people of Israel. **7:5–8** The numbering of the tribes resembles census taking, making sure that there is a sufficient number of troops for battle (Num. 1:2–3). The order of the tribes does not align with similar lists in the Hebrew Bible (e.g., Deut. 27:12–13; Num. 1:5–15; Ezek. 48:1–29), and the tribe of Dan is not included in this list (Manasseh appears instead).

7:9–17 The innumerable multitude. 7:9 The fact that this massive crowd comes from all tribes, peoples, and languages suggests they are distinct from 144,000. However, the text's structure parallels the introduction of the Lion who is a Lamb (5:5–6), suggesting the 144,000 and the innumerable multitude might be the same. *Palm branches.* Palms were a common prize at athletic games and symbolized victory. Later, they became a symbol of Christian martyrdom. **7:10** *Salvation.* Salvation should be understood in physical and material terms, such as protection from invasion, bandits, and so on. As such, it was claimed by Roman emperors, who often adopted the title "savior." Here, John ascribes salvation solely

Focus On: Sex Work as a Metaphor in Revelation (Revelation 7)

Revelation builds upon the writings of Hebrew Bible prophets who envision Israel, or Jerusalem, as God's wife (Isa. 54:5–8; 62:3–5; Jer. 31:31–33). The prophets sometimes condemn Israel's supposed worship of other gods by accusing God's "wife" of sexual infidelity and even prostitution (Jer. 2:23–25; 3:12–13; Hos. 2). Thus, Ezekiel accuses, "You took some of your garments and made for yourself colorful high places [places where gods are worshiped] and on them prostituted yourself" (16:16; see **"Slut-Shaming as Prophetic Discourse," p. 1148**).

John similarly depicts the people of God as the new Jerusalem, who will become the Lamb's "bride" (Rev. 19:7; 21:2, 9), and accuses them of *porneia*, translated as "sexual immorality" or "prostitution." He accuses another teacher, whom he calls "Jezebel," of encouraging the people in Thyatira to practice "sexual immorality" and eat meat sacrificed to other gods (2:20). Here *porneia* seemingly describes activities involving other gods, such as attending festivals or athletic events where Roman gods would have been honored, metaphorically characterized as sexually immoral acts.

The metaphor of sex work informs the depiction of Babylon, a representation of Rome, as a sex worker or prostitute (Gk. *pornē*). John draws on harsh ancient stereotypes about sex workers to encourage audience members to distance themselves from Rome and Roman practices (18:4). He replicates a Roman double standard: even though employing a prostitute was legal and considered a usual practice for men, sex workers, regardless of their gender, were deemed dishonorable and sometimes treated with disgust. Most sex workers would have been enslaved, working for pimps in brothels, taverns, and inns. Today, we would consider them victims of sex trafficking. John's depiction of Babylon as wealthy and able to wear opulent garments contradicts these realities and presumes that Babylon adopts the life of a prostitute out of a desire for money and power, not need.

To capture John's hatred toward Rome, many scholars use "whore" to translate the term *pornē*, as John echoes negative ancient stereotypes about sex workers, depicting Babylon as dirty and dangerous (17:4–6). His disdain for Babylon manifests in his depiction of Rome's judgment by describing the rape ("mak[ing] . . . desolate," 17:16) and murder of a sex worker (17:16–17).

Modern readers must carefully distinguish between John's critique of Rome and assimilation to Rome and his use of imagery and stereotypes. It is possible and necessary to condemn imperial practices without demeaning those who are the victims of those practices.

Lynn R. Huber

where have they come from?" [14] I said to him, "Sir, you are the one who knows." Then he said to me, "These are they who have come out of the great ordeal; they have washed their robes and made them white in the blood of the Lamb.

[15] For this reason they are before the throne of God
  and worship him day and night within his temple,
  and the one who is seated on the throne will shelter them.
[16] They will hunger no more and thirst no more;

  the sun will not strike them,
    nor any scorching heat,
[17] for the Lamb at the center of the throne will be their shepherd,
  and he will guide them to springs of the water of life,
  and God will wipe away every tear from their eyes."

8 When the Lamb broke the seventh seal, there was silence in heaven for about half an hour. [2] And I saw the seven angels who stand before God, and seven trumpets were given to them.

to God and the Lamb (see also 12:10; 19:1–2). **7:14** *Great ordeal.* Literally "great persecution" (see also 1:9). These are ones who have kept the testimony of Christ under pressure to accommodate imperial expectations. They wash their robes in *the blood of the Lamb.* See note on 3:4–5. **7:15** *Shelter.* Literally "camp." The term here refers to a tent, like the tabernacle used to house God during the exodus (Exod. 40:34–38; see also Rev. 15:5 and 21:3). **7:16** See Isa. 49:10. **7:17** Note the paradoxical depiction of the Lamb who is simultaneously the shepherd. Cf. John 4:10–14; 10:11, 14. See also Ps. 23:1–2 and Isa. 25:8.

8:1–5 The seventh seal. The chapter returns to the seals from Rev. 6. **8:1** *Silence in heaven.* A striking contrast to the thundering, singing, and other noise in heaven and to the trumpet blasts about to occur. **8:2** Trumpet blasts were associated with God's judgment (Joel 2:1; Jer. 4:5, 19, 21; 6:1, 17; 51:27).

3 Another angel with a golden censer came and stood at the altar; he was given a great quantity of incense to offer with the prayers of all the saints on the golden altar that is before the throne. ⁴And the smoke of the incense, with the prayers of the saints, rose before God from the hand of the angel. ⁵Then the angel took the censer and filled it with fire from the altar and threw it on the earth, and there were peals of thunder, rumblings, flashes of lightning, and an earthquake.

6 Now the seven angels who had the seven trumpets made ready to blow them.ˣ

7 The first angel blew his trumpet, and there came hail and fire, mixed with blood, and they were hurled to the earth, and a third of the earth was burned up, and a third of the trees were burned up, and all green grass was burned up.

8 The second angel blew his trumpet, and something like a great mountain, burning with fire, was thrown into the sea. ⁹A third of the sea became blood, a third of the living creatures in the sea died, and a third of the ships were destroyed.

10 The third angel blew his trumpet, and a great star fell from heaven, blazing like a torch, and it fell on a third of the rivers and on the springs of water. ¹¹The name of the star is Wormwood. A third of the waters became wormwood, and many died from the water because it was made bitter.

12 The fourth angel blew his trumpet, and a third of the sun was struck, and a third of the moon, and a third of the stars, so that a third of their light was darkened; a third of the day was kept from shining and likewise the night.

13 Then I looked, and I heard an eagle crying with a loud voice as it flew in midheaven, "Woe, woe, woe to the inhabitants of the earth, at the blasts of the other trumpets that the three angels are about to blow!"

9 And the fifth angel blew his trumpet, and I saw a star that had fallen from heaven to earth, and he was given the key to the shaft of the bottomless pit; ²he opened the shaft of the bottomless pit, and from the shaft rose smoke like the smoke of a great furnace, and the sun and the air were darkened with the smoke from the shaft. ³Then from the smoke came locusts on the earth, and they were given authority like the authority of scorpions of the earth. ⁴They were told not to damage the grass of the earth or any green growth or any tree, but only those people who do not have the seal of God on their foreheads. ⁵They were

x 8.6 Other ancient authorities read *made themselves ready to blow*

8:3 *Golden censer.* A container for burning incense with a perforated lid or sides so the fragrance could spread. *Incense* was used in Roman worship as a way of pleasing the gods. The reference to a golden censer and incense mark this as a worship setting. 8:5 *Fire from the altar.* Coals used to burn sacrifices. The angel's act of throwing the censer to earth contrasts with the incense smoke that rises before God and signals a connection between heaven and earth.

8:6–13 **The first four trumpets.** As with the seals, the first four trumpets form a distinct unit, since they are similar in form to one another. 8:7 *Hail and fire.* Allusion to the seventh plague unleashed by Moses in Egypt (Exod. 9:23–24; see also Ezek. 38:22). *A third.* The destruction of the trumpets occurs in thirds, while the damage of the bowl plagues will be complete. The suggestion that a third of the trees were burned evokes the massive deforestation that occurred during the Roman Empire to support building projects and the demand for heated water for bathing. 8:8 *A great mountain, burning.* Some note the connection between this imagery and volcanic activity, such as the eruption of Vesuvius in Italy in 79 CE. 8:11 *Wormwood.* A bitter plant, poisonous in large amounts. 8:12 For the darkening of celestial bodies, see Isa. 13:10–11; Ezek. 32:7–8; Amos 8:9; Mark 13:24–25. 8:13 *Woe, woe, woe.* The repeated *woe* evokes the cry of the eagle. Birds signaled omens and revealed the future in Roman tradition.

9:1–21 **The fifth and sixth trumpets.** Trumpets five and six primarily impact humans, in contrast to the first four. 9:1 *Star that had fallen.* Revelation draws upon a tradition of associating stars with angels (Judg. 5:20; Job 38:7; Dan. 8:10). See **"Angels," p. 1346.** This fallen star resembles Satan, the prototypical fallen angel (12:9; see Luke 10:18). *Bottomless pit.* Literally "the abyss." This is both the home of the beast and a place of punishment (11:7; 17:8; 20:1, 3). 9:2 Smoke rising suggests ancient "plutoniums," often caves with geothermal activity, where subterranean gods were worshiped (Strabo, *Geogr.* 13.4.14; 14.1.44). 9:3–10 John's depiction of humanlike locusts draws upon Joel 1–2, where the author compares the destruction of war with that of a plague of locusts. *Like women's hair.* Unbound women's hair was associated with mourning and danger. Depictions of Medusa, who had snakes for hair,

allowed to torment them for five months but not to kill them, and the agony suffered was like that caused by a scorpion when it stings someone. [6]And in those days people will seek death but will not find it; they will long to die, but death will flee from them.

7 In appearance the locusts were like horses equipped for battle. On their heads were what looked like crowns of gold; their faces were like human faces, [8]their hair like women's hair, and their teeth like lions' teeth; [9]they had scales like iron breastplates, and the noise of their wings was like the noise of many chariots with horses rushing into battle. [10]They have tails like scorpions, with stingers, and in their tails is their power to harm people for five months. [11]They have as king over them the angel of the bottomless pit; his name in Hebrew is Abaddon,[y] and in Greek he is called Apollyon.[z]

12 The first woe has passed. There are still two woes to come.

13 Then the sixth angel blew his trumpet, and I heard a voice from the horns[a] of the golden altar before God, [14]saying to the sixth angel who had the trumpet, "Release the four angels who are bound at the great River Euphrates." [15]So the four angels were released, who had been held ready for the hour, the day, the month, and the year, to kill a third of humankind. [16]The number of the troops of cavalry was two hundred million; I heard their number. [17]And this was how I saw the horses in my vision: the riders wore breastplates the color of fire and of sapphire[b] and of sulfur; the

heads of the horses were like lions' heads, and fire and smoke and sulfur came out of their mouths. [18]By these three plagues a third of humankind was killed, by the fire and smoke and sulfur coming out of the horses'[c] mouths. [19]For the power of the horses is in their mouths and in their tails; their tails are like serpents, with heads, and with them they inflict harm.

20 The rest of humankind, who were not killed by these plagues, did not repent of the works of their hands or give up worshiping demons and idols of gold and silver and bronze and stone and wood, which cannot see or hear or walk. [21]And they did not repent of their murders or their sorceries or their prostitution or their thefts.

10 And I saw another mighty angel coming down from heaven, wrapped in a cloud, with a rainbow over his head; his face was like the sun and his legs like pillars of fire. [2]He held a little scroll open in his hand. Setting his right foot on the sea and his left foot on the land, [3]he gave a great shout, like a lion roaring. And when he shouted, the seven thunders sounded. [4]And when the seven thunders had sounded, I was about to write, but I heard a voice from heaven saying, "Seal up what the seven thunders have said, and do not write it down." [5]Then the angel whom I saw standing on the sea and the land

y 9.11 That is, *Destruction*   z 9.11 That is, *Destroyer*
a 9.13 Other ancient authorities read *four horns*   b 9.17 Gk *hyacinth*   c 9.18 Gk *their*

were popular throughout the ancient Mediterranean. **9:6** Cf. 6:16–17. **9:11** *Abaddon.* A personification of Sheol, a place of death in the Hebrew Bible (Job 26:6; Ps. 88:11). *Apollyon.* Even though the Greek name sounds like Apollo, *Apollyon* is not a deity. Instead, John fashions the name using the Greek verb for "to destroy" ("apollymi") as a translation of the name *Abaddon*. **9:12** See 8:13 for the "three woes." **9:13** *Horns.* A decorative element on the altar. **9:14** The river *Euphrates* marked the eastern edge of the Roman Empire. **9:17** *Sulfur* has a yellow color and a horrible smell. It is associated with geothermal activity, including volcanic events, and so is often paired with smoke and steam. **9:20** *Demons and idols.* See note on 2:14. John dismisses any worship apart from the worship of God and the Lamb. *Gold . . . wood.* Roman religions often included cult statues, which some believed were gods and others thought symbolized gods. *Cannot see . . . walk.* John mocks Roman religious belief, even though there were different perspectives among ancient thinkers on the nature and purpose of cult statues.

10:1–11 John eats a scroll. In a scene resembling Ezekiel's commissioning as a prophet (Ezek. 3:1–4), an angel appears to John and offers him a scroll to eat. The symbolic act underscores the heavenly origin of John's message. **10:2** *Little scroll.* John uses a diminutive form of the word for scroll ("biblaridion"), which may imply it is different from the scroll opened by the Lamb. However, the fact that this scroll is *open* might suggest they are one and the same. **10:3–4** *The seven thunders.* John assumes his audience's familiarity with these, although the reference is not completely clear. *Seal up . . . do not write.* The command to seal up what was *said* responds to John's urge to write what he hears. However, since John has not yet written, it is unclear what is being sealed up (cf. Dan. 8:26; 12:4, 9). The command to not write seemingly contradicts earlier orders to write (1:11, 19). **10:5–6** Lifting a hand up is a traditional

raised his right hand to heaven
6 and swore by him who lives forever and ever,

who created heaven and what is in it, the earth and what is in it, and the sea and what is in it: "There will be no more delay, ⁷but in the days when the seventh angel is to blow his trumpet, the mystery of God will be fulfilled, as he announced to his servants the prophets."

8 Then the voice that I had heard from heaven spoke to me again, saying, "Go, take the scroll that is open in the hand of the angel who is standing on the sea and on the land." ⁹So I went to the angel and told him to give me the little scroll, and he said to me, "Take it and eat; it will be bitter to your stomach but sweet as honey in your mouth." ¹⁰So I took the little scroll from the hand of the angel and ate it; it was sweet as honey in my mouth, but when I had eaten it my stomach was made bitter.

11 Then they said to me, "You must prophesy again about many peoples and nations and languages and kings."

11 Then I was given a measuring rod like a staff, and I was told, "Come and measure the temple of God and the altar and those who worship there, ²but do not measure the court outside the temple; leave that out, for it is given over to the nations, and they will trample over the holy city for forty-two months. ³And I will grant my two witnesses authority to prophesy for one thousand two hundred sixty days, wearing sackcloth."

4 These are the two olive trees and the two lampstands that stand before the Lord of the earth. ⁵And if anyone wants to harm them, fire pours from their mouth and consumes their foes; anyone who wants to harm them must be killed in this manner. ⁶They have authority to shut the sky, so that no rain may fall during the days of their prophesying, and they have authority over the waters to turn them into blood and to strike the earth with every kind of plague, as often as they desire.

7 When they have finished their testimony, the beast that comes up from the bottomless pit will wage war on them and conquer them and kill them, ⁸and their dead bodies will lie in the street of the great city that is prophetically[d] called Sodom and Egypt, where also

d 11.8 Or *allegorically*; Gk *spiritually*

way of swearing an oath. **10:6** *There will be no more delay.* Literally "there will be no more time." **10:7** *Mystery of God.* Not a mystery about God, but the mystery of what God has *announced to . . . the prophets.* **10:9–10** *Bitter . . . sweet.* While the message initially "tastes" like honey (see Ezek. 3:3), since it comes from God, it causes "bitterness," distress, and anguish when delivered. **10:11** *They said to me.* The collective powers in heaven issue the command to prophesy. *Many peoples . . . kings.* Throughout Revelation, John lists various people groups as a way of emphasizing that he means everybody, regardless or origin, background, or social status. John is called to prophesy *about* these groups and not necessarily *to* these groups (cf. Ezek. 3:5–6), a reminder that John envisions his audience as those faithful to God and the Lamb, members of the seven communities addressed in Rev. 2–3.

11:1–2 Temple vision. These verses extend the allusion to the book of Ezekiel, echoing the prophet's vision of a rebuilt Jerusalem temple (Ezek. 40–42). While the rebuilt temple envisioned by Ezekiel was a response to its destruction by the Babylonians in the sixth century BCE, John is writing after the Romans destroyed the Jerusalem temple in 70 CE. This connection inspires John and other Jewish authors to depict Rome as a new Babylon. **11:1** The one who commands John is unnamed (cf. Ezek. 40:3). The audience never sees John fulfill the command. *The altar.* Altars were typically outside the temple building so that sacrifices could be performed. **11:2** *Court outside.* Since John mentions *nations*, a term used to describe gentiles or non-Jews, this court or courtyard may reference the "court of the gentiles," a part of the Jerusalem temple complex where non-Jews could visit. *Forty-two months.* Three and half years, half of seven years, and one thousand two hundred sixty days (see also 11:3). This time is limited and will end.

11:3–13 The two witnesses. The *two witnesses* are often associated with biblical or historical figures, especially Elijah and Enoch, as both were "taken by God" (2 Kgs. 2:11; Gen. 5:21–24). **11:3** *Sackcloth.* See note on 6:12–14. **11:4** *Olive trees . . . lampstands.* Lampstands provide light; olive trees are strong and provide the oil for lamps. See Zech. 4:2–3. **11:5–6** The witnesses possess "superpowers" comparable to other prophets, including Moses, Elijah, and Jeremiah (e.g., 1 Kgs. 17:1; 18:1; Jer. 5:14; 20:9). **11:7** *The beast.* John has not yet introduced the character of the beast (see 13:1) but assumes his audience is familiar with its identity. *Bottomless pit.* Literally "abyss." **11:8** *Great* refers to scope of influence. The

their Lord was crucified. [9]For three and a half days members of the peoples and tribes and languages and nations will gaze at their dead bodies and refuse to let them be placed in a tomb, [10]and the inhabitants of the earth will gloat over them and celebrate and exchange presents, because these two prophets tormented the inhabitants of the earth.

11 But after the three and a half days, the breath[e] of life from God entered the two witnesses,[f] and they stood on their feet, and those who saw them were terrified. [12]Then they[g] heard a loud voice from heaven saying to them, "Come up here!" And they went up to heaven in a cloud while their enemies watched them. [13]At that moment there was a great earthquake, and a tenth of the city fell; seven thousand people were killed in the earthquake, and the rest were terrified and gave glory to the God of heaven.

14 The second woe has passed. The third woe is coming very soon.

15 Then the seventh angel blew his trumpet, and there were loud voices in heaven, saying,

"The kingdom of the world has become
the kingdom of our Lord
and of his Messiah,[b]
and he will reign forever and ever."

16 Then the twenty-four elders who sit on their thrones before God fell on their faces and worshiped God, [17]singing,

"We give you thanks, Lord God Almighty,
who are and who were,
for you have taken your great power
and begun to reign.
[18] The nations raged,
but your wrath has come,
and the time for judging the dead,
for rewarding your servants, the prophets
and saints and all who fear your name,
both small and great,
and for destroying those who destroy the
earth."

19 Then God's temple in heaven was opened, and the ark of his covenant was seen within his temple, and there were flashes of lightning, rumblings, peals of thunder, an earthquake, and heavy hail.

12 A great portent appeared in heaven: a woman clothed with the sun, with the moon under her feet, and on her head a crown of twelve stars. [2]She was pregnant and was crying out in birth pangs, in the agony of giving birth. [3]Then another portent appeared in heaven: a great red dragon, with seven heads and ten horns and seven diadems on his heads. [4]His tail swept down a third of the stars of heaven and threw them to the earth. Then the dragon stood before the woman

e 11.11 Or *the spirit*   *f* 11.11 Gk *them*   *g* 11.12 Other ancient authorities read *I*   *b* 11.15 Gk *Christ*

great city of the first-century Mediterranean world was Rome, which John also identifies as Babylon (e.g., 16:19; 17:18). *Prophetically called Sodom and Egypt.* There are many historical manifestations of the *great city. Where also their Lord was crucified* suggests Jerusalem is also a candidate for the *great city*, although it evokes Rome as well, since Roman authorities crucified Christ. **11:9** *Three and a half days.* Half of seven, so suggesting incompleteness; the earlier reference to crucifixion makes this also suggestive of Christ's death, which lasted three days. **11:9–10** A complete lack of regard for the dead. See Jer. 14:16. **11:11** The witnesses' resurrection evokes the creation of humans (Gen. 2:7). **11:12** Cf. Jesus's ascension (Acts 1:9–10).

11:14–19 The seventh trumpet. 11:14–15 With the announcement that *the second woe has passed*, likely the events of the sixth trumpet (9:13–21), the seventh trumpet is finally blown. Unlike the previous trumpets that brought devastation, the seventh trumpet heralds the Messiah's reign. **11:16** *Who are and who were.* The elders use an abbreviated version of the formula proclaiming God's eternal reign (see 1:8). **11:19** *God's temple in heaven.* Earlier, John saw an altar in heaven (6:9–11), which suggested the possibility of a heavenly temple. Now John sees into the temple itself. *Ark of his covenant.* The ark, holding the tablets of law inscribed by Moses, resided in the holiest part of the Jerusalem temple before its destruction by the Babylonians. According to 2 Macc. 2:4–8, the prophet Jeremiah moved the ark to a cave to save it from certain destruction. John reassures his audience that this sacred vessel, a symbol of the relationship between God and God's people, is safe in heaven.

12:1–6 Two signs appear in heaven. 12:2 The text emphasizes the pain experienced by the woman during childbirth. On the woman, see **"Woman Clothed in the Sun," p. 2131. 12:3** *Great red dragon.* An image of Satan (12:9), the dragon appears again in chaps. 13, 16, 17, and 20. The dragon resembles other monsters from ancient myth, including Leviathan (Ps. 74:14) and the many-headed Hydra slain by Hercules in Greek myth. See **"Leviathan," p. 735.** *Ten horns.* The Lamb has seven horns (5:6). *Diadems.*

who was about to deliver a child, so that he might devour her child as soon as it was born. [5]And she gave birth to a son, a male child, who is to rule[i] all the nations with a scepter of iron. But her child was snatched away and taken to God and to his throne, [6]and the woman fled into the wilderness, where she has a place prepared by God, so that there she can be nourished for one thousand two hundred sixty days.

7 And war broke out in heaven; Michael and his angels fought against the dragon. The dragon and his angels fought back, [8]but they were defeated, and there was no longer any place for them in heaven. [9]The great dragon was thrown down, that ancient serpent, who is called the devil and Satan, the deceiver of the whole world—he was thrown down to the earth, and his angels were thrown down with him.

10 Then I heard a loud voice in heaven proclaiming,

"Now have come the salvation and the
    power
and the kingdom of our God
and the authority of his Messiah,[j]
for the accuser of our brothers and sisters
    has been thrown down,
who accuses them day and night
    before our God.
[11] But they have conquered him by the
    blood of the Lamb
and by the word of their testimony,

for they did not cling to life even in the
    face of death.
[12] Rejoice then, you heavens
    and those who dwell in them!
But woe to the earth and the sea,
    for the devil has come down to
    you
with great wrath
    because he knows that his time is
    short!"

13 So when the dragon saw that he had been thrown down to the earth, he pursued[k] the woman who had delivered the male child. [14]But the woman was given the two wings of the great eagle, so that she could fly from the serpent into the wilderness, to her place where she is nourished for a time, and times, and half a time. [15]Then from his mouth the serpent poured water like a river after the woman, to sweep her away with the flood. [16]But the earth came to the help of the woman; it opened its mouth and swallowed the river that the dragon had poured from his mouth. [17]Then the dragon was angry with the woman and went off to wage war on the rest of her children, those who keep the commandments of God and hold the testimony of Jesus.

18 Then the dragon[l] took his stand on the

i 12.5 Or *to shepherd* j 12.10 Gk *Christ* k 12.13 Or *persecuted* l 12.18 Gk *Then he*; other ancient authorities read *Then I stood*

Another word for "crown," a symbol of political power. **12:5** *A son, a male child.* The repetition emphasizes the child's sex. *Rule . . . with a scepter of iron.* An allusion to Ps. 2:9, which affirms the child is the Messiah. *Scepter.* The word is often rendered as "rod," as it is in 11:1. The psalm being referenced predicts the nations will be broken into pieces, like pots, by the rod (or scepter) of iron. See Rev. 2:27. **12:6** *Wilderness.* Where the Israelites fled after escaping Egypt (Exod. 16:1) and where Jesus was tempted by Satan, according to the Gospels (Matt. 4:1–11; Mark 1:12–13; Luke 4:1–13). *One thousand two hundred sixty days.* See note on 11:2.
12:7–12 War in heaven. 12:7 *Michael.* An archangel (Jude 9), the "great prince [and] protector" of Israel (Dan. 12:1). In the War Scroll from Qumran, Michael assists the righteous in fighting against the demonic army of Belial (War Scroll 17). **12:9** *Ancient serpent.* The serpent in Eden, although in that context, the serpent is not identified as Satan (Gen. 3:1–5). On *Satan*, see **"The Satan," p. 687.** *Deceiver.* Throughout Revelation, evil figures deceive (13:14; 20:7–8; cf. John 8:44). This verse echoes Jewish traditions depicting angelic beings put out of heaven (Isa. 14:12–15; 1 En. 14). **12:10** *Accuser* points to Satan's adversarial role in Jewish tradition (Job 1:6–12; 2:1–6; Zech. 3:1–2; Jub. 17:15–16). *Brothers and sisters.* See note on 6:11. **12:11** *Have conquered.* See note on 5:5. *They did not cling to life* anticipates later traditions about martyrs, including the accounts in 4 Maccabees. On persecution, see **"Introduction to Revelation," pp. 2114–15. 12:12** See 20:1–3, 7–10.
12:13–18 The dragon on earth. 12:13 *Pursued.* Literally "persecuted." **12:14** *Wings of the great eagle.* Receiving eagle wings suggests she is given the means to escape and find safety (Exod. 19:4; Isa. 40:31). *Wilderness.* See note on 12:6. *Nourished.* Just as God provided manna for the Israelites in the wilderness (Exod. 16:1–36). **12:16** *Earth.* A possible reference to the goddess Gē or Gaia, a personification of earth.

Making Connections: The Woman Clothed in the Sun (Revelation 12)

With a sun cloak and crown of stars, the woman in heaven resembles an ancient goddess. Her confrontation with a great red dragon evokes other popular myths about goddesses pursued by monsters and saved by heroic sons. The Egyptian goddess Isis, her husband Osiris killed by Set, was vindicated by her son Horus, and the Greek god Apollo protected Leto from the serpentine Python. These myths promised the triumph of order over chaos.

Revelation similarly chronicles the eventual defeat of chaos, called "the devil and Satan" (12:9), by the woman's "male child," who is the Messiah (12:5). John emphasizes the woman's role as a portent pointing to something else—namely, the place or community from which the Messiah comes: Mother Israel or Zion. The twelve stars in her crown signify the twelve tribes of Israel. The image of Israel as a mother comes from the Hebrew Bible. The prophet Micah, for example, captures the pain of childbirth: "Writhe and groan, O daughter Zion, like a woman in labor" (4:10).

At first glance, the heavenly woman may seem like a positive feminine image, especially in contrast to Babylon as a prostitute; however, John limits her role and even fails to tell readers her name. Mothers often raise, educate, and support their children, but the woman's involvement in the male child's life is cut short because he is "snatched" away from her to be raised by God (12:5). Furthermore, unlike powerful mother goddesses of the Mediterranean, Revelation's woman appears unable to fend or fight for herself (12:6, 16). John undermines the feminine divine and goddess traditions through his retelling of the myth.

Interpreters find the woman clothed in the sun an evocative and empowering image. She informs Christian representations of Mary, such as the Virgin of Guadalupe (*la Virgen*), who has the sun behind her, a star-covered cloak, and the moon at her feet. In addition to being an immensely popular devotional image, *la Virgen* is a symbol of Mexican identity, associated with the persistence of Indigenous culture despite Spanish colonization. In the southwestern United States, *la Virgen* reminds audiences that these lands were once part of Mexico. Finally, feminist artist Yolanda López (1942–2021) envisions the strength of Chicana women through *la Virgen*, famously depicting her grandmother, her mother, and herself as embodying *la Virgen*, embracing the potential power of Revelation's goddess.

Lynn R. Huber

13 sand of the seashore. ¹And I saw a beast rising out of the sea, with ten horns and seven heads, and on its horns were ten diadems, and on its heads were blasphemous names. ²And the beast that I saw was like a leopard, its feet were like a bear's, and its mouth was like a lion's mouth. And the dragon gave it his power and his throne and great authority. ³One of its heads seemed to have received a death blow, but its fatal wound[m] had been healed. In amazement the whole earth followed the beast. ⁴They worshiped the dragon, for he had given his authority to the beast, and they worshiped the beast, saying, "Who is like the beast, and who can fight against it?"

5 The beast was given a mouth speaking arrogant and blasphemous words, and it was allowed to exercise authority for forty-two months. ⁶It opened its mouth to speak blasphemies against God, blaspheming his name and his dwelling, that is, those who dwell in heaven. ⁷Also, it was allowed to wage war on the saints and to conquer them.[n] It was given

m 13.3 Gk *the plague of its death*   *n* 13.7 Other ancient authorities lack this sentence

13:1–10 The first beast. Interpreters traditionally interpret the beast's heads as specific Roman emperors, assuming the head with the *fatal wound* is Nero. The notorious emperor committed suicide in 68 CE, but some believed he would somehow return to Rome to rule (Augustine, *City of God* 20.19.3). Aligning the heads with historical figures is complicated by many unknowns; thus the heads are best considered an illustration of the complexity of political systems. **13:1** *Out of the sea.* Rome had a sense of ownership over the Mediterranean, calling it "Our Sea" or Mare Nostrum and relying on it to amass wealth and maintain power. *Diadems.* See note on 12:3. **13:2** John's depiction of political powers as beasts made up of multiple types of animal parts draws upon Dan. 7. These hybrid creatures defy easy classification and are, therefore, unpredictable. **13:4** *Worshiped the beast.* An allusion to the worship of emperors, their families, and Rome. **13:5** *Blasphemous words.* Identifying things as divine that are not God. Likely refers to the use of titles—such as "all-powerful," "divine," and "savior"—for emperors and other political figures. *Forty-two months.* See note on 11:2. **13:7** *Conquer.* The beast conquers the saints through violence, ironically allowing the saints to conquer through their deaths. See note on 5:5.

authority over every tribe and people and language and nation, ⁸and all the inhabitants of the earth will worship it, everyone whose name has not been written from the foundation of the world in the book of life of the Lamb that was slaughtered.ᵒ

9 Let anyone who has an ear listen:
¹⁰ If you are to be taken captive,
　　into captivity you go;
　if you kill with the sword,
　　with the sword you must be killed.
Here is a call for the endurance and faith of the saints.

11 Then I saw another beast that rose out of the earth; it had two horns like a lamb, and it spoke like a dragon. ¹²It exercises all the authority of the first beast on its behalf, and it makes the earth and its inhabitants worship the first beast, whose fatal woundᵖ had been healed. ¹³It performs great signs, even making fire come down from heaven to earth in the sight of all, ¹⁴and by the signs that it is allowed to perform on behalf of the beast it deceives the inhabitants of earth, telling them to make an image for the beast that had been wounded by the swordᵍ and yet lived, ¹⁵and it was allowed to give breathʳ to the image of the beast so that the image of the beast could even speak and cause those who would not worship the image of the beast to be killed.

¹⁶Also, it causes all, both small and great, both rich and poor, both free and slave, to be given a brand on the right hand or the forehead, ¹⁷so that no one can buy or sell who does not have the brand, that is, the name of the beast or the number for its name. ¹⁸This calls for wisdom: let anyone with understanding calculate the number of the beast, for it is the number for a person. Its number is six hundred sixty-six.ˢ

14 Then I looked, and there was the Lamb, standing on Mount Zion! And with him were one hundred forty-four thousand who had his name and his Father's name written on their foreheads. ²And I heard a voice from heaven like the sound of many waters and like the sound of loud thunder; the voice I heard was like the sound of harpists playing on their harps, ³and they sing a new song before the throne and before the four living creatures and before the elders. No one could learn that song except the one hundred forty-four thousand who have been redeemed from the earth. ⁴It is these who have not defiled themselves with women, for they are virgins; these follow the Lamb wherever he goes. They have

o 13.8 Or *written in the book of life of the Lamb that was slaughtered from the foundation of the world*　p 13.12 Gk *whose plague of its death*　q 13.14 Or *that had received the plague of the sword*　r 13.15 Or *spirit*　s 13.18 Other ancient authorities read *six hundred sixteen*

13:8 *From the foundation of the world.* The names have been in the book since the time of creation, an idea that implies predestination. However, John's call for the saints' "endurance" (v. 10) emphasizes individual volition. *Book of life.* A record of the names of the faithful for the Last Judgment (20:12; 21:27; Dan. 12:1). **13:9** *Let anyone . . . listen.* An exhortation to Revelation's audience. *If you are to be taken captive . . . must be killed.* These two conditional statements are a variation of a saying from Jer. 15:2 and 43:11, emphasizing the dire future John anticipates for the faithful.

13:11–18 The second beast. 13:12 *Makes the earth . . . worship.* Possibly a reference to the local enforcement of imperial cults. *Fatal wound.* See note on 13:1–10. **13:13** *Making fire come down.* The second beast mimics God's prophets, who summon fire from the sky (e.g., 1 Kgs. 18:38–39; 2 Kgs. 1:10). **13:14** *Make an image.* Recalls the construction of the golden calf by the Israelites (Exod. 32). *Wounded by the sword.* Likely a reference to Nero's suicide. See note on 13:1–10. **13:15** *Give breath . . . even speak.* Priests communicated the will of the gods in various ways, including verbally communicating on their behalf through oracles. **13:16–18** See **"666 / the Number of the Beast," p. 2133**. **13:16** *Brand,* or "mark." Cf. the "seal" on the foreheads of the 144,000 (7:3; 14:1).

14:1–5 The 144,000 before the Lamb. 14:1 *I looked . . . !* See note on 4:1. *Mount Zion.* The place from where God reigns on earth (e.g., Pss. 9:11; 50:2) and where God's "anointed one," the Messiah, will reign (Ps. 2). According to some traditions, God's people will gather near Zion at the end of time (2 Esd. 2:42–48). *One hundred forty-four thousand.* See note on 7:4. *Father's name . . . foreheads.* The seal mentioned in 7:3. One of the few times John refers to God as *Father* (1:6; 2:28; 3:21). The parental language alludes to the ancient household where the father was generally the head. **14:3** *Redeemed.* Literally "purchased." Combined with the reference to bearing the "Father's name," the imagery evokes enslavement of the faithful into God's household. **14:4** *Defiled . . . with women.* Reflects ancient biases against women, including the belief that menstrual blood was dangerous (e.g., Pliny the Elder, *Natural History* 28.23). The reference to virginity implies that the 144,000 avoid defilement by not having sex.

Reading through Time: 666 / the Number of the Beast (Revelation 13:16–18)

For centuries, interpreters have puzzled over the "number of the beast," with disagreements emerging in the earliest copies of Revelation. While most include the number written out as six hundred sixty-six (666), some early manuscripts record it as six hundred sixteen (616). The number 666 is favored by most scholars, but the exact number remains shrouded in mystery.

The number is an example of *gematria*, a calculation in which numerals stand for letters. In the second century CE, Christian theologian Irenaeus noted that efforts to find the correct set of letters to add up to 666 or 616 were complicated by many things, including uncertainty about what language cracked the code. Is the name Greek, Latin, or Hebrew? Whichever language is employed, multiple solutions are possible, involving creative spellings or calculations. The Greek name "Neron Caesar" adds up to 666, but only if the letters are first rendered into Hebrew. If an interpreter uses the Latin spelling of Nero Caesar, transferred into Hebrew, it is possible to get to 616. Other answers include Claudius, Domitian, Vespasian, and even the word "beast." Perhaps the unsolvable riddle reveals that the "wisdom" it requires is in short supply (13:18).

People continue to pose solutions to the riddle. Using different languages and forms of numerology in their calculations, such attempts reveal more about interpreters' assumptions and biases than about evil in the world. In the 1980s, President Ronald Wilson Reagan's name was commonly associated with the beast, since each of his names had six letters. A quick online search reveals the names of most modern political leaders add up to 666 in some way.

Many people today avoid 666 at great lengths, believing the very number, whether on a receipt or part of an address, conjures the presence of evil. Some hypothesize that credit cards or identification numbers function as the "name of the beast or the number for its name" (13:17). Modern Christians who read Revelation as a prediction of current events are especially concerned about being "marked" with the number.

Although a precise meaning behind the numeral remains elusive, the number likely implies imperfection, as 666 falls short, three times, of the number seven. Revelation uses seven to signal completeness and perfection, even though it sometimes describes aspects of evil as well (12:3; 13:1; 17:3). Repeatedly in Revelation, John underscores how easy it is to mistake evil for good.

Lynn R. Huber

been redeemed from humankind as first fruits for God and the Lamb, ⁵and in their mouth no lie was found; they are blameless.

6 Then I saw another angel flying in midheaven, with an eternal gospel to proclaim to those who live* on the earth—to every nation and tribe and language and people. ⁷He said in a loud voice, "Fear God and give him glory, for the hour of his judgment has come, and worship him who made heaven and earth, the sea and the springs of water."

8 Then another angel, a second, followed, saying, "Fallen, fallen is Babylon the great! She has made all nations drink of the wine of the wrath of her prostitution."

9 Then another angel, a third, followed them, crying with a loud voice, "Those who worship the beast and its image and receive the brand on their foreheads or on their hands, ¹⁰they will also drink the wine of God's wrath, poured unmixed into the cup of his anger, and they will be tormented with fire and sulfur in the presence of the holy angels and in the presence of the Lamb. ¹¹And the smoke of their torment goes up forever and ever. There is no rest day or night for those who worship the beast and its image and for anyone who receives the brand of its name."

12 Here is a call for the endurance of the saints, those who keep the commandments of God and hold fast to the faith of* Jesus.

t 14.6 Gk *sit*   *u* 14.12 Or *to their faith in*

Describing the faithful in this way challenges ancient assumptions about masculinity. *First fruits.* The first part of a harvest sacrificed to God (Exod. 23:19; 34:22). **14:5** *Blameless.* Literally "without blemish."

14:6–13 Three proclamations. Three angels fly in *midheaven*, the space between heaven and earth, proclaiming God's judgment. **14:6** *Gospel.* Literally "good news" and not the genre of literature. **14:8** An allusion to Isa. 21:9 and an anticipation of Rev. 17–18. *Babylon* signifies Rome throughout Revelation. See note on 11:1–2. See **"Sex Work as a Metaphor," p. 2125.** *Wine of the wrath.* A metaphorical depiction of anger as a drink offered to others. Alludes to Jer. 51:7, where Babylon's wine makes the nations go "mad." **14:9** See 13:16–18. **14:10** *Wine . . . unmixed.* Wine was mixed with water to adjust the strength; thus, *unmixed* wine is pure and strong. *Sulfur.* John associates sulfur, a sign of geothermal activity, with the abyss or bottomless pit (9:17–18; 19:20; 21:8). See notes on 9:2 and 9:17. **14:11** *Smoke*

13 And I heard a voice from heaven saying, "Write this: Blessed are the dead who from now on die in the Lord." "Yes,"ᵛ says the Spirit, "they will rest from their labors, for their deeds follow them."

14 Then I looked, and there was a white cloud, and seated on the cloud was one like the Son of Man, with a golden crown on his head and a sharp sickle in his hand! ¹⁵Another angel came out of the temple, calling with a loud voice to the one who sat on the cloud, "Use your sickle and reap, for the hour to reap has come, because the harvest of the earth is fully ripe." ¹⁶So the one who sat on the cloud swung his sickle over the earth, and the earth was reaped.

17 Then another angel came out of the temple in heaven, and he, too, had a sharp sickle. ¹⁸Then another angel came out from the altar, the angel who has authority over fire, and he called with a loud voice to him who had the sharp sickle, "Use your sharp sickle and gather the clusters of the vine of the earth, for its grapes are ripe." ¹⁹So the angel swung his sickle over the earth and gathered the vintage of the earth, and he threw it into the great winepress of the wrath of God. ²⁰And the winepress was trodden outside the city, and blood flowed from the winepress, as high as a horse's bridle, for a distance of about one thousand six hundred stadia.

15 Then I saw another portent in heaven, great and amazing: seven angels with seven plagues, which are the last, for with them the wrath of God is ended.

2 And I saw what appeared to be a sea of glass mixed with fire and those who had conquered the beast and its image and the number of its name standing beside the sea of glass with harps of God in their hands. ³And they sing the song of Moses, the servant of God, and the song of the Lamb:

"Great and amazing are your deeds,
  Lord God the Almighty!
Just and true are your ways,
  King of the nations!ʷ
⁴ Lord, who will not fear
  and glorify your name?
For you alone are holy.
  All nations will come
  and worship before you,
for your judgments have been
  revealed."

5 After this I looked, and the temple of the tentˣ of witness in heaven was opened, ⁶and out of the temple came the seven angels with the seven plagues, robed in pure bright linen,ʸ with golden sashes across their chests. ⁷Then one of the four living creatures gave the seven angels seven golden bowls full of the wrath of God, who lives forever and ever; ⁸and the

v 14.13 Other ancient authorities lack *Yes* w 15.3 Other ancient authorities read *the ages* x 15.5 Or *tabernacle* y 15.6 Other ancient authorities read *stone*

of their torment. This anticipates the judgment of Babylon in 19:3. **14:13** *Rest from their labors.* Rest is something promised only to the faithful because of their *deeds*, literally "works," and whose faithfulness is described as endurance. Note that those who worship the beast will not rest (v. 11).

14:14–20 Harvesting the earth. These verses describe two separate harvests that are metaphorical representations of judgment. John draws on Joel 3, but similar imagery appears in Isa. 17:5; 18:4–5; Jer. 51:33; Hos. 6:11; Matt. 13:24–30, 36–43. **14:14–16** *Son of Man.* See note on 1:7. *Sickle.* A sharp, curved instrument used to cut grain. **14:19–20** *Winepress of the wrath of God.* John envisions a *winepress* where people extract juice by stomping, or "trodding," grapes with their feet. The image shifts from wine as a symbol of wrath to wine as blood. *Horse's bridle.* The blood is several feet deep, since a bridle is placed on a horse's head. *One . . . stadia.* About two hundred miles.

15:1–8 The seven last plagues. 15:2 *Sea of glass . . . fire.* Earlier, John saw this sea before God's throne. Now it appears to reflect the lightning flashes coming from the throne (4:5–6). **15:2–3** John draws a parallel between the faithful and the Israelites who sang and celebrated by the Red Sea with Moses after fleeing Egypt (Exod. 15:1–18). In contrast to Exodus, the faithful sing prior to the plagues being poured out. **15:3** *Song of Moses . . . and the song of the Lamb.* The song here includes a contribution from the Lamb. *Servant of God.* Literally "slave of God." Moses is often described as such (e.g., Exod. 4:10; 14:31; Josh. 1:2; 1 Kgs. 8:53). *Almighty.* See note on 4:8. *King of the nations.* See Jer. 10:7. **15:5** *Temple of the tent of witness.* The tabernacle or tent that housed God when the Israelites were in Egypt (Num. 17:4), imagined to be modeled on the sanctuary of heaven (Wis. 9:8; Heb. 8:1–6). **15:6** *Pure . . . linen.* The angels' clothing points to a priestly role (Exod. 28:39). **15:7** *Bowls* (Gk. "phiale"). These are shallow bowls designed for pouring liquid offerings onto a temple altar. **15:8** A cloud of *smoke* signifies God's presence (Exod. 13:21; 40:34–35; 1 Kgs. 8:10–11; 2 Chr. 5:13–14).

temple was filled with smoke from the glory of God and from his power, and no one could enter the temple until the seven plagues of the seven angels were ended.

16

Then I heard a loud voice from the temple telling the seven angels, "Go and pour out on the earth the seven bowls of the wrath of God."

2 So the first angel went and poured his bowl on the earth, and a foul and painful sore came on those who had the brand of the beast and who worshiped its image.

3 The second angel poured his bowl into the sea, and it became like the blood of a corpse, and every living thing in the sea died.

4 The third angel poured his bowl into the rivers and the springs of water, and they became blood. ⁵And I heard the angel of the waters say,

"You are just, O Holy One, who are and were,
    for you have judged these things;
⁶ because they shed the blood of saints and prophets,
    you have given them blood to drink.
It is what they deserve!"
⁷And I heard the altar respond,
"Yes, O Lord God, the Almighty,
    your judgments are true and just!"

8 The fourth angel poured his bowl on the sun, and it was allowed to scorch people with fire; ⁹they were scorched by the fierce heat, but they cursed the name of God, who had authority over these plagues, and they did not repent and give him glory.

10 The fifth angel poured his bowl on the throne of the beast, and its kingdom was plunged into darkness; people gnawed their tongues in agony ¹¹and cursed the God of heaven because of their pains and sores, and they did not repent of their deeds.

12 The sixth angel poured his bowl on the great River Euphrates, and its water was dried up in order to prepare the way for the kings from the east. ¹³And I saw three foul spirits like frogs coming from the mouth of the dragon, from the mouth of the beast, and from the mouth of the false prophet. ¹⁴These are demonic spirits, performing signs, who go abroad to the kings of the whole world, to assemble them for battle on the great day of God the Almighty. ¹⁵("See, I am coming like a thief! Blessed is the one who stays awake and is clothed,ᶻ not going about naked and exposed to shame.") ¹⁶And the demonic spiritsᵃ assembled the kingsᵇ at the place that in Hebrew is called Harmagedon.

17 The seventh angel poured his bowl into the air, and a loud voice came out of the temple, from the throne, saying, "It is done!" ¹⁸And there came flashes of lightning, rumblings, peals of thunder, and a violent earthquake, such as had not occurred since people were upon the earth, so violent was that earthquake. ¹⁹The great city was split into three parts, and the cities of the nations fell. God remembered great Babylon and gave her the wine cup of the fury of his wrath. ²⁰And every island fled away, and no mountains were to be found, ²¹and huge

z 16.15 Gk *and keeps his robes*   a 16.16 Gk *they*   b 16.16 Gk *them*

16:1–21 The bowls of wrath. Even more than the seven trumpets, these plagues resemble the ten plagues used against the Egyptians in Exod. 7–12. The impacts of these plagues are more severe than the trumpets, which were limited to thirds. See note on 8:7. **16:2** *Painful sore.* See Exod. 9:8–12. The sores effectively replicate the brand given for worshiping the beast. **16:3–4** *Sea . . . like the blood.* See Exod. 7:14–24. **16:5–6** *These things* implies that God's judgment extends to the physical world and potentially implicates the physical world in the death of the saints and prophets. **16:7** *The altar* refers to the souls under the altar (6:9–11). **16:9** *Cursed.* Literally "blasphemed." The people who experience the plagues respond by denying the one who authorizes them. *Repent.* John assumes that people experiencing the plagues should recognize God's power and repent. See also 9:20–21. **16:10** *Plunged into darkness.* See Exod. 10:21. **16:12** The Euphrates was past the eastern edge of the Roman Empire (Strabo, *Geogr.* 16.1.28) and associated with Babylon. Besides referring to the *east*, Euphrates evokes "foreignness" to a Roman audience. **16:13** *Foul.* Literally "unclean." Cf. the plague of frogs in Exod. 8:3. **16:14** *Battle on the great day.* A battle at the end of time between the forces of God and the "nations"—that is, those who do not worship God (e.g., Ezek. 38:1–6; Joel 3:1–17; Zech. 14:2; 2 Esd. 13:33–34). See **"Oracles against the Nations," p. 1105**. **16:15** *Like a thief* underscores the unpredictability of Christ's second coming and the need for being prepared (see also 3:3; 1 Thess. 5:6–8). **16:16** *Harmagedon,* sometimes "Armageddon," combines a Greek transliteration of the Hebrew word "har," meaning "mountain," and Megiddo, a strategic location between Egypt and Syria (Judg. 5:19; 1 Kgs. 9:15). **16:19** *Great city.* Rome. See note on 11:8. **16:20** Earthquakes are often depicted in conjunction with God's judgment (Ezek. 38:20; 1 En. 1:3–9). **16:21** *Hailstones.* See Exod. 9:22–26.

hailstones, each weighing about a hundred pounds,[c] dropped from heaven on people, until they cursed God for the plague of the hail, so fearful was that plague.

17 Then one of the seven angels who had the seven bowls came and said to me, "Come, I will show you the judgment of the great whore[d] who is seated on many waters, [2]with whom the kings of the earth have engaged in sexual immorality[e] and with the wine of whose prostitution the inhabitants of the earth have become drunk." [3]So he carried me away in the spirit[f] into a wilderness, and I saw a woman sitting on a scarlet beast that was full of blasphemous names, and it had seven heads and ten horns. [4]The woman was clothed in purple and scarlet and adorned with gold and jewels and pearls, holding in her hand a golden cup full of abominations and the impurities of her prostitution, [5]and on her forehead was written a name, a mystery: "Babylon the great, mother[g] of whores[h] and of earth's abominations." [6]And I saw that the woman was drunk with the blood of the saints and the blood of the witnesses to Jesus.

When I saw her, I was greatly amazed. [7]But the angel said to me, "Why are you so amazed? I will tell you the mystery of the woman and of the beast with seven heads and ten horns that carries her. [8]The beast that you saw was and is not and is about to ascend from the bottomless pit and go to destruction. And the inhabitants of the earth, whose names have not been written in the book of life from the foundation of the world, will be amazed when they see the beast, because it was and is not and is to come.

[9] "This calls for a mind that has wisdom: the seven heads are seven mountains on which the woman is seated; also, they are seven kings, [10]of whom five have fallen, one is living, and the other has not yet come, and when he comes he must remain only a little while. [11]As for the beast that was and is not, it is an eighth, but it belongs to the seven, and it goes to destruction. [12]And the ten horns that you saw are ten kings who have not yet received a kingdom, but they are to receive authority as kings for one hour, together with the beast. [13]These are united in yielding their power and authority to the beast; [14]they will wage war on the Lamb, and the Lamb will conquer them, for he is Lord of lords and King of kings, and those with him are called and chosen and faithful."

c 16.21 Gk *weighing about a talent*　d 17.1 Or *prostitute*
e 17.2 Or *prostitution*　f 17.3 Or *in the Spirit*　g 17.5 Or *Babylon, the great mother*　h 17.5 Or *prostitutes*

17:1–18 The judgment of woman Babylon. In chaps. 17–20, John uses a traditional metaphor to present his hearers with two options, guised as two distinct women. Audiences can associate either with Babylon, depicted as a prostitute and signifying Rome, or with the new Jerusalem, portrayed as the bride and wife of the Lamb. In constructing Babylon's image, John draws on prophetic texts and Roman biases against sex workers, blaming the "woman" and not her political leader "clients" for sexual immorality. See **"Sex Work as a Metaphor," p. 2125. 17:2** Sexual immorality and drunkenness were common ways of depicting a lack of self-control, an important ancient virtue. Additionally, drunkenness implies altered vision and poor decision-making. Thus, Babylon leads the inhabitants of earth astray. **17:3** *Scarlet beast.* A variation of the great red dragon, so a manifestation of Satan (12:3, 9). **17:4** *Purple and scarlet.* Colors worn by emperors and their families and Roman senators. *Abominations.* Literally "disgusting things." Sex workers were associated with dirt and impurity due to class bias. **17:5** The name on Babylon's forehead may imply that she, like many ancient sex workers, is enslaved. See note on 7:3. *Mystery.* Her name is a riddle, although it is not a very difficult riddle to solve. *Mother of whores.* Imperial cities seem to reproduce themselves, as cities under their control emulate their practices and enforce imperial policies. **17:6** *Drunk with the blood.* See note on 14:19–20. On persecution, see **"Introduction to Revelation," pp. 2114–15. 17:8** *Was and is not.* A parody of the description of God as the one "who is and who was and who is to come" (1:8; 4:8). *Bottomless pit.* Literally "abyss." See note on 9:1. *Destruction.* In contrast to God's association with creation (4:11; 14:7) and a foreshadowing of Satan's fate (20:10). *Book of life.* See notes on 3:4–5 and 13:8. **17:9–12** *A mind . . . wisdom.* An introduction to another riddle. *Seven heads . . . mountains . . . kings.* A reference to the seven hills of Rome, with heads, mountains, and kings all embodying power and authority. As with the heads of the beast, aligning the seven kings to Roman emperors is not straightforward. See note on 13:1–10. These verses emphasize the temporary nature of earthly political powers. **17:13** *Yielding their power.* These kings willingly accept imperial rule. This was the case in Asia Minor, where King Attalus III bequeathed his kingdom to Rome in 133 BCE. See **"Introduction to Revelation," pp. 2114–15. 17:14** *Lord of . . . kings.* An affirmation of

15 And he said to me, "The waters that you saw, where the whore[i] is seated, are peoples and multitudes and nations and languages. [16]And the ten horns that you saw, they and the beast will hate the whore;[j] they will make her desolate and naked; they will devour her flesh and burn her up with fire. [17]For God has put it into their hearts to carry out his purpose by agreeing to give their kingdom to the beast, until the words of God will be fulfilled. [18]The woman you saw is the great city that rules over the kings of the earth."

18 After this I saw another angel coming down from heaven, having great authority, and the earth was illumined by his splendor. [2]He called out with a mighty voice,

"Fallen, fallen is Babylon the great!
    It has become a dwelling place of demons,
a haunt of every foul spirit,
    a haunt of every foul bird,
    a haunt of every foul and hateful beast.[k]
[3] For all the nations have fallen[l]
    from the wine of the wrath of her prostitution,
and the kings of the earth have engaged
    in sexual immorality[m] with her,
and the merchants of the earth have
    grown rich from the power[n] of her luxury."

4 Then I heard another voice from heaven saying,

"Come out of her, my people,
    so that you do not take part in her sins
and so that you do not share in her plagues,
[5] for her sins are heaped high as heaven,
    and God has remembered her iniquities.
[6] Render to her as she herself has rendered,
    and repay her double for her deeds;
    mix a double dose for her in the cup she mixed.
[7] As she glorified herself and lived luxuriously,
    so give her a like measure of torment and grief.
Since in her heart she says,
    'I rule as a queen;
I am no widow,
    and I will never see grief,'
[8] therefore her plagues will come in a single day—
    pestilence and mourning and famine—
and she will be burned with fire,
    for mighty is the Lord God who judges her."

9 And the kings of the earth, who engaged in sexual immorality[o] and lived in luxury with her, will weep and wail over her when they see the smoke of her burning; [10]they will stand far off, in fear of her torment, and say,

i 17.15 Or *prostitute*   j 17.16 Or *prostitute*   k 18.2 Other ancient authorities read *a haunt of every foul and hateful bird*   l 18.3 Other ancient authorities read *all the nations have drunk*   m 18.3 Or *prostitution*   n 18.3 Or *resources*   o 18.9 Or *prostitution*

the Lamb's ultimate power, which will be made explicit in 19:16. **17:15** An image of the Roman Empire's expansive rule. **17:16** *Make her desolate and naked.* Making Babylon *desolate* means making *her* into a wilderness. Combined with the reference to making Babylon naked, this is an image of sexual assault. Cf. Ezek. 23:10, 25–26, 29. *Devour her flesh*: The kings cannibalize Babylon, who drinks the blood of the saints (v. 6). **17:17** *God has put it into their hearts.* This judgment ultimately comes from God.

18:1–8 The fall of the great city. The emphasis shifts to Babylon/Rome depicted as a city instead of a woman, even though the latter idea remains in the background. John draws heavily upon prophetic oracles against Babylon, including those found in Isa. 13–14; 21; and Jer. 49–51. **18:2** *Fallen, fallen.* Draws upon Isaiah's oracle against Babylon (Isa. 21:9). *Dwelling place of demons.* See Isa. 13:21–22; Jer. 50:39; 51:37. *Haunt.* Literally "prison." The city is filled with things associated with death and impurity. **18:3** John adds excessive wealth and conspicuous consumption to the wrongs associated with Babylon. **18:4** *Come out of her, my people.* A command issued to John's audience members—that is, *my people*—to remove themselves from Babylon. See Jer. 51:6. *Her* can also be translated as "it." The gender of the pronoun reflects how cities were gendered feminine. **18:5** *Sins are heaped.* See Jer. 51:9. **18:6** The heavenly voice issues a command to participate in the punishment of Babylon, which is doubled. It is not clear whether this command is directed to John's audience or heavenly actors. **18:7** *In her heart she says.* John mimics Babylon, a rhetorical form called "prosopopoeia," to reveal her arrogance. See similar city speeches in Ezek. 28:2 and Zeph. 2:15.

18:9–20 Mourning Babylon. A series of satirical laments, echoing those over Tyre from Ezek. 26–28, highlighting the folly of aligning with Babylon. **18:10** *Alas, alas.* Literally "woe, woe." Repeated

"Alas, alas, the great city,
Babylon, the mighty city!
For in one hour your judgment has come."
11 And the merchants of the earth weep and
mourn for her, since no one buys their cargo
any more, 12 cargo of gold, silver, jewels and
pearls, fine linen, purple, silk and scarlet, all
kinds of scented wood, all articles of ivory,
all articles of costly wood, bronze, iron, and
marble, 13 cinnamon, spice, incense, myrrh,
frankincense, wine, olive oil, choice flour and
wheat, cattle and sheep, horses and chariots,
slaves—and human lives.[p]
14 "The fruit for which your soul longed
has gone from you,
and all your delicacies and your splendor
are lost to you,
never to be found again!"
15 The merchants of these wares, who grew
wealthy from her, will stand far off, in fear of
her torment, weeping and mourning aloud,
16 "Alas, alas, the great city,
clothed in fine linen,
in purple and scarlet,
adorned with gold,
with jewels, and with pearls!
17 For in one hour all this wealth has been
laid waste!"
And all shipmasters and seafarers, sailors
and all whose trade is on the sea, stood far off
18 and cried out as they saw the smoke of her
burning,
"What city was like the great city?"
19 And they threw dust on their heads as they
wept and mourned, crying out,
"Alas, alas, the great city,
where all who had ships at sea
grew rich by her wealth!
For in one hour she has been laid waste."
20 Rejoice over her, O heaven, you saints
and apostles and prophets! For God has condemned her condemnation of you.
21 Then a mighty angel took up a stone like
a great millstone and threw it into the sea,
saying,
"With such violence Babylon the great
city
will be thrown down
and will be found no more;
22 and the sound of harpists and
entertainers and of flutists and
trumpeters
will be heard in you no more,
and an artisan of any trade
will be found in you no more,
and the sound of the millstone
will be heard in you no more,
23 and the light of a lamp
will shine in you no more,
and the voice of bridegroom and bride
will be heard in you no more,
for your merchants were the magnates of
the earth,
and all nations were deceived by your
sorcery.
24 And in you[q] was found the blood of
prophets and of saints
and of all who have been slaughtered
on earth."

19 After this I heard what seemed to be
the loud voice of a great multitude in
heaven, saying,
"Hallelujah!
Salvation and glory and power to our God,
2 for his judgments are true and just;

p 18.13 Or *chariots, and human bodies and souls* *q* 18.24 Gk *her*

at the beginning of each stanza (vv. 16, 19). *Stand far off.* A repeated theme (vv. 15, 17) depicting the cowardice of Babylon's allies. *One hour.* See 17:12. **18:12–13** Valuable goods that Rome imported from all over the Mediterranean. *Slaves.* Literally "bodies." Enslaved people were often described as bodies without souls or tools. Rome depended on exploiting the labor of enslaved people, often prisoners of war, bought and sold in ancient slave markets (2 Macc. 8:11). *Human lives.* Literally "souls." In contrast to viewing the enslaved as soulless bodies, John affirms the personhood of enslaved people. **18:16** *Purple and scarlet.* See note on 17:4. **18:19** *Threw dust . . . heads.* A sign of mourning (see Job 2:12). **18:20** An unattributed command, addressed to Revelation's various constituents, to rejoice over Babylon's judgment. A stark contrast after the laments, which will be realized in 19:1–8.

18:21–24 Babylon's condemnation. 18:21 *Millstone.* A large stone, sometimes powered by animals, used to grind grain. The angel's action symbolizes the city's fall. "Sign acts" such as this are common in prophetic literature (Jer. 51:59–64).

19:1–10 Wedding of the Lamb. This hymn, a response to 18:20, links the destruction of Babylon to the coming of the new Jerusalem, depicted as a bride (21:2, 9). **19:1, 3, 4, 6** *Hallelujah.* A transliteration of the Hebrew phrase "Praise the LORD" (Pss. 106:1; 111:1; 150:1). **19:2** *Whore* and *prostitution.* See **"Sex**

he has judged the great whore[r]
> who corrupted the earth with her
>   prostitution,
> and he has avenged on her the blood of
>   his servants."

[3]Once more they said,
> "Hallelujah!
> The smoke goes up from her forever and
>   ever."

[4]And the twenty-four elders and the four living creatures fell down and worshiped God who is seated on the throne, saying,
> "Amen. Hallelujah!"

5 And from the throne came a voice saying,
> "Praise our God,
>   all you his servants
> and[s] all who fear him,
>   small and great."

[6]Then I heard what seemed to be the voice of a great multitude, like the sound of many waters and like the sound of mighty thunderpeals, crying out,
> "Hallelujah!
> For the Lord[t] God
>   the Almighty reigns.
> [7] Let us rejoice and exult
>   and give him the glory,
> for the marriage of the Lamb has come,
>   and his bride has made herself ready;
> [8] to her it has been granted to be clothed
>   with fine linen, bright and pure"—

for the fine linen is the righteous deeds of the saints.

9 And the angel said[u] to me, "Write this: Blessed are those who are invited to the marriage supper of the Lamb." And he said to me, "These are true words of God." [10]Then I fell down at his feet to worship him, but he said to me, "You must not do that! I am a fellow servant with you and your brothers and sisters who hold the testimony of Jesus.[v] Worship God! For the testimony of Jesus[w] is the spirit of prophecy."

11 Then I saw heaven opened, and there was a white horse! Its rider is called Faithful and True, and in righteousness he judges and wages war. [12]His eyes are like[x] a flame of fire, and on his head are many diadems, and he has a name inscribed that no one knows but himself. [13]He is clothed in a robe dipped in[y] blood, and his name is called The Word of God. [14]And the armies of heaven, wearing fine linen, white and pure, were following him on white horses. [15]From his mouth comes a sharp sword with which to strike down the nations, and he will rule[z] them with a scepter of iron; he will tread the winepress of the fury of the

---

r 19.2 Or *prostitute*   s 19.5 Other ancient authorities lack *and*   t 19.6 Other ancient authorities add *our*   u 19.9 Gk *he said*   v 19.10 Or *to Jesus*   w 19.10 Or *to Jesus*   x 19.12 Other ancient authorities omit *like*   y 19.13 Other ancient authorities read *sprinkled with*   z 19.15 Or *will shepherd*

Work as a Metaphor," p. 2125. *Avenged.* The root of the word, "ekdikeō," suggests judgment and enacting justice. **19:7** *Marriage of the Lamb.* A metaphor for the connection between Christ and the faithful in which the community is imagined as a bride. This parallels the "marriage metaphor" in the Hebrew Bible in which God marries Israel or Jerusalem (e.g., Isa. 62:1–5; Jer. 2:1–4). *Bride.* Literally "woman" or "wife." In the first century, women were expected to partner or marry and have children, so the terms "bride," "wife," and "woman" are somewhat interchangeable. Some ancient versions change "woman" here to "bride" for consistency with the wedding context of 21:2, 9. *Made herself ready.* Depictions of ancient weddings often focused on the bride's appearance and her preparation process. **19:8** *Fine linen, bright and pure.* The bridal costume symbolized ideal womanhood, including chastity and purity. *For the fine linen . . . saints.* The Roman bride traditionally wove her own tunic. The saints clothe the bride; they will constitute the bride as the new Jerusalem. **19:9** *Marriage supper.* Anticipates 19:17–18. Banquets are often associated with the heavenly kingdom of God (Matt. 8:11; Luke 13:29). **19:10** This is not the only time John mistakenly worships an angel. See 22:8–9. On Revelation as prophecy, see 1:3; 22:7, 10.

19:11–17 Rider on a white horse. This passage extends the wedding imagery introduced in 19:7 by depicting a kingly bridegroom, an image from Ps. 45. John also draws on traditional depictions of a divine warrior (Isa. 63:1–6; Wis. 18:15–16). **19:11** *Then I saw . . . !* See note on 4:1. *White horse . . . rider.* Cf. the rider of 6:1–2. *Faithful and True.* Characteristics associated with Christ now become his titles (1:5; 3:14). **19:12** *A name inscribed.* The unknown name suggests a mystery and connects the rider to God, yet the rider is named in the next verse. **19:13** *Word of God.* See John 1:1. **19:14** *Armies of heaven.* Other apocalyptic traditions, including the War Scroll from Qumran, envision heavenly armies fighting against demonic forces. *Fine linen . . . pure.* The armies of heaven wear costumes similar to the plague angels (15:6) and the bride (19:8). **19:15** *Mouth . . . sharp sword.* See 1:16. The sword coming from Christ's

wrath of God the Almighty. [16]On his robe and on his thigh he has a name inscribed, "King of kings and Lord of lords."

17 Then I saw an angel standing in the sun, and with a loud voice he called to all the birds that fly in midheaven, "Come, gather for the great supper of God, [18]to eat the flesh of kings, the flesh of captains, the flesh of the mighty, the flesh of horses and their riders—flesh of all, both free and slave, both small and great." [19]Then I saw the beast and the kings of the earth with their armies gathered to wage war against the rider on the horse and against his army. [20]And the beast was captured, and with it the false prophet who had performed in its presence the signs by which he deceived those who had received the brand of the beast and those who worshiped its image. These two were thrown alive into the lake of fire that burns with sulfur. [21]And the rest were killed by the sword of the rider on the horse, the sword that came from his mouth, and all the birds were gorged with their flesh.

20
Then I saw an angel coming down from heaven, holding in his hand the key to the bottomless pit and a great chain. [2]He seized the dragon, that ancient serpent, who is the devil and Satan, and bound him for a thousand years [3]and threw him into the pit and locked and sealed it over him, so that he would deceive the nations no more, until the thousand years were ended. After that he must be let out for a little while.

4 Then I saw thrones, and those seated on them were given authority to judge. I also saw the souls of those who had been beheaded for their testimony to Jesus[a] and for the word of God. They had not worshiped the beast or its image and had not received its brand on their foreheads or their hands. They came to life and reigned with Christ a thousand years. [5](The rest of the dead did not come to life until the thousand years were ended.) This is the first resurrection. [6]Blessed and holy are those who share in the first resurrection. Over these the second death has no power, but they will be priests of God and of Christ, and they will reign with him a thousand years.

7 When the thousand years are ended, Satan will be released from his prison [8]and will come out to deceive the nations at the four corners of the earth, Gog and Magog, in order to gather them for battle; they are as numerous as the sands of the sea. [9]They marched up over the breadth of the earth and surrounded the camp of the saints and the beloved city. And fire came down from heaven[b] and consumed them. [10]And the devil who had deceived them was thrown into the lake of fire and sulfur, where the beast and the false prophet were, and they will be tormented day and night forever and ever.

11 Then I saw a great white throne and the one who sat on it; the earth and the heaven fled from his[c] presence, and no place was

a 20.4 Or *for the testimony of Jesus* b 20.9 Other ancient authorities read *from God, out of heaven*, or *out of heaven from God* c 20.11 Gk *the*

mouth may represent words of judgment. *Scepter.* See note on 12:5. *Winepress.* See note on 14:19–20. **19:16** *Inscribed.* Literally "written." *King of . . . lords.* Christ's rule over all others is affirmed. See 17:14.

19:18–21 The defeat of the beast. 19:18 *Flesh of all . . . and great. All* who side with the beast will be destroyed, no matter their wealth or social status. **19:20** *Lake of fire.* An unusual image, even though fire was often punishment in the afterlife (Isa. 66:24; 1 En. 10; Matt. 5:22; 13:42, 50; 18:9; 25:41; Mark 9:43, 48). Later texts with lakes of fire, such as the Apocalypse of Peter, are likely influenced by Revelation.

20:1–6 The millennium. 20:1, 3 *Pit.* Literally "abyss." **20:2** *Dragon, that ancient serpent.* Satan; see note on 12:9. *Thousand years.* See **"The Millennium," p. 2141. 20:3** No reason is given for the requirement that Satan be released for *a little while*. **20:4** *Beheaded.* The only place in Revelation where this term, which alludes to a form of capital punishment, is used. Elsewhere, John describes these ones as "slaughtered" (6:9; 18:24) or "killed" (6:11; 13:10). *Brand.* See note on 13:16–18. *Reigned.* Evokes the hope of Exod. 19:6. See note on 1:6. **20:5–6** *First resurrection.* John envisions a two-part resurrection in which those who have been killed because of their testimony are resurrected at the time of the millennium, and all others are resurrected later for the Last Judgment (20:12–13).

20:7–15 The end of Satan. 20:8 *Gog and Magog.* Ezekiel 38:2 refers to a prince of Magog named Gog, a possible allusion to a seventh-century BCE tyrant named Gyges. Gog and Magog eventually become names representing nations hostile to God (3 En. 45:5). **20:9** *Camp.* John depicts the saints in terms reminiscent of the Israelites during the exodus. **20:11** *Great . . . throne.* Like the throne in Dan. 7:9–10, where God will open books of judgment. *Earth and the heaven fled.* The creation flees from

Making Connections: The Millennium (Revelation 20:4–6)

Revelation introduces the idea of a thousand-year period when Satan is imprisoned and those martyred because of their faithfulness come to life and rule with Christ (20:4–6). This event is commonly called the millennium, since the Latin word for "thousand" is *mille*. John spends little time discussing the millennium, inviting subsequent interpreters to speculate the details and significance of these thousand years.

In the fifth century CE, St. Augustine criticized those who imagined the millennium as a time of feasting, drinking, and merriment. Instead, Augustine advocated an allegorical reading of Revelation, arguing the millennium is a spiritual reality embodied in the present by the church. Augustine's perspective, called *amillennialism*, remains an authoritative position for many, including the Catholic Church.

Despite Augustine's cautions, numerous Christians wish for the millennium's realization, with some seeking to prompt or hasten its coming. The voyages of Christopher Columbus were motivated by the hope of bringing about Jesus's return by finding a westward passage to Jerusalem. His resulting failure paved the way for Christian missionizing and colonization steeped in millennial thought. Converting Indigenous people to Christianity was seen by some as a way of realizing the millennium on earth. These efforts resulted in the erasure of aspects of Indigenous cultures, the dismantling of communities, and many deaths, a far cry from the hope promised by John.

Millennial thinking has been especially influential in the United States. "Postmillennialism" contends that Christ will return *after* the millennium has begun and that Christians must work to build the kingdom in which Christ will reign. Postmillennialism has inspired social and political movements aimed at reform, such as ending child labor and abolishing slavery. At the end of the eighteenth century, "premillennialism" grew in popularity, with adherents believing Christ would return before and inaugurate the millennium after a period of tribulation. Believing this will happen soon, premillennialists focus on discerning the signs of Christ's coming. This has resulted in a proliferation of media, such as the immensely popular *Left Behind* franchise. Premillennialism also shapes evangelical Christian political perspectives, especially regarding Israel (premillennialists believe Christ will return to Jerusalem) and social issues, where women's and LGBTQIA2S+ rights, for example, are seen as subversions of God's order.

John's description of the millennium may be brief, but it is arguably one of the most influential parts of Revelation. It is impossible here to do justice to the range of ways it has been imagined and has been influential.

Lynn R. Huber

found for them. [12]And I saw the dead, great and small, standing before the throne, and books were opened. Also another book was opened, the book of life. And the dead were judged according to their works, as recorded in the books. [13]And the sea gave up the dead who were in it, Death and Hades gave up the dead who were in them, and all were judged according to what they had done. [14]Then Death and Hades were thrown into the lake of fire. This is the second death, the lake of fire, [15]and anyone whose name was not found written in the book of life was thrown into the lake of fire.

21 Then I saw a new heaven and a new earth, for the first heaven and the first earth had passed away, and the sea was no more. [2]And I saw the holy city, the new Jerusalem, coming down out of heaven from God,

the presence of the Creator, making way for a new creation in 21:1. **20:12** *Works . . . in the books.* All people, *great and small*, will account for their actions in life (see Mal. 3:16). *Book of life.* See note on 3:4–5. **20:13** *Gave up the dead.* Bodies resurrected for the Last Judgment. **20:13, 14** *Death and Hades.* Places where the dead are kept until judgment (2 Bar. 42:8; 50:2), personified here, as in 6:8. Being cast into the *lake of fire* signals that death has been ended (21:4). **20:14, 15** *Lake of fire.* See note on 19:20.

21:1–8 A new heaven and earth. Introduced in 19:7–8, the bride finally appears here and in the next section of text (21:9) as the new Jerusalem. See note on 17:1–18. **21:1** *New heaven . . . earth.* See Isa. 65:17; 66:22; 1 En. 96:16. *Passed away.* Literally "went away" or "departed." The idea that heaven and earth will "disappear" appears in Gospel traditions as well (Mark 13:31; Matt. 24:35; Gos. Thom. 11a). *Sea was no more.* The sea often symbolizes chaos (Gen. 1:2). Here it signals the end of Babylon/Rome's economic prowess, as John associates the imperial capital with "many waters" and the sea (17:1; 18:17, 19). **21:2** *Holy city.* A reference to Jerusalem. See Neh. 11:1; Isa. 48:2; 52:1. *New Jerusalem . . . heaven.*

prepared as a bride adorned for her husband. ³And I heard a loud voice from the throne saying,

"See, the home*ᵈ* of God is among mortals.
He will dwell*ᵉ* with them;
they will be his peoples,*ᶠ*
and God himself will be with them and be their God;*ᵍ*
⁴ he will wipe every tear from their eyes.
Death will be no more;
mourning and crying and pain will be no more,
for*ʰ* the first things have passed away."

5 And the one who was seated on the throne said, "See, I am making all things new." Also he said, "Write this, for these words are trustworthy and true." ⁶Then he said to me, "It is done! I am the Alpha and the Omega, the Beginning and the End. To the thirsty I will give water as a gift from the spring of the water of life. ⁷Those who conquer will inherit these things, and I will be their God, and they will be my children. ⁸But as for the cowardly, the faithless,*ⁱ* the polluted, the murderers, the sexually immoral,*ʲ* the sorcerers, the idolaters, and all liars, their place will be in the lake that burns with fire and sulfur, which is the second death."

9 Then one of the seven angels who had the seven bowls full of the seven last plagues came and said to me, "Come, I will show you the bride, the wife of the Lamb." ¹⁰And in the spirit*ᵏ* he carried me away to a great, high mountain and showed me the holy city Jerusalem coming down out of heaven from God. ¹¹It has the glory of God and a radiance like a very rare jewel, like jasper, clear as crystal. ¹²It has a great, high wall with twelve gates, and at the gates twelve angels, and on the gates are inscribed the names that are the names*ˡ* of the twelve tribes of the Israelites: ¹³on the east three gates, on the north three gates, on the south three gates, and on the west three gates. ¹⁴And the wall of the city has twelve foundations, and on them are the twelve names of the twelve apostles of the Lamb.

15 The angel*ᵐ* who talked to me had a measuring rod of gold to measure the city and its gates and walls. ¹⁶The city has four equal sides, its length the same as its width, and he measured the city with his rod, twelve thousand stadia; its length and width and height are equal. ¹⁷He also measured its wall, one hundred forty-four cubits by human measurement, which the angel was using. ¹⁸The wall is built of jasper, while the city is pure gold, clear as glass. ¹⁹The foundations of the wall of the city are adorned with every jewel; the first was jasper, the second sapphire, the third agate, the fourth emerald, ²⁰the fifth onyx, the sixth carnelian, the seventh chrysolite, the eighth beryl, the ninth topaz, the tenth chrysoprase, the eleventh jacinth, the twelfth amethyst. ²¹And the twelve gates are twelve pearls, each of the gates is a single pearl, and the street of the city is pure gold, transparent as glass.

d 21.3 Gk *the tabernacle*   *e* 21.3 Gk *will tabernacle*
f 21.3 Other ancient authorities read *people*   *g* 21.3 Other ancient authorities lack *and be their God*   *h* 21.4 Other ancient authorities lack *for*   *i* 21.8 Or *the unbelieving*
j 21.8 Or *prostitutes*   *k* 21.10 Or *in the Spirit*   *l* 21.12 Other ancient authorities lack *that are the names*   *m* 21.15 Gk *He*

The future appearance of a new Jerusalem appears throughout Jewish apocalyptic and prophetic literature. In some cases, the city appears refurbished (Bar. 5:1–9; Tob. 13:16), and in others, it is wholly new (Isa. 65:17–19; 2 Esd. 7:26; 10:54; 13:36). In 2 Esdras, the author also depicts the new Jerusalem as a woman (2 Esd. 10:27–28, 44–45). *As a bride.* John again evokes the "marriage metaphor." See note on 19:7. **21:3** The root for the words *home* and *dwell* is the Greek word for tent ("skēnē"), again alluding to God's traveling home with the Israelites during the exile (Num. 17:4). See notes on 7:15 and 15:5. *Be his peoples . . . their God.* This language echoes Lev. 26:11–12; Ezek. 37:27. *Dwell with them.* See Zech. 2:10–11. The idea that God will dwell with his people also appears in 2 Cor. 6:16. **21:4** *Wipe . . . eyes.* See Isa. 25:8; 35:10. *Passed away.* See note on 21:1. **21:6** *Water of life* can also mean "living water." Cf. John 4:10–11; 7:37–38. **21:7** *Those who conquer.* See notes on Rev. 2–3 and 5:5. *My children.* Literally "my son." The original Greek is singular: "The one who conquers . . . will be my son." **21:8** A traditional vice list naming those left out of the future kingdom (cf. 1 Cor. 6:9–10). Compare this list to 21:27 and 22:15.

21:9–27 The new Jerusalem. 21:9 *Bride . . . wife.* See note on 19:7. **21:10–27** The city imagery is especially significant, since Revelation addresses assemblies of Jesus followers within prominent cities in Roman Asia. **21:12** *High wall . . . gates.* Ancient cities generally had protective walls with gates. *Twelve.* John explicitly connects the number of gates with the tribes of Israel. **21:15** The angel measuring the city evokes Ezekiel's vision of the Jerusalem temple (Ezek. 40–42). **21:16–17** The city is a cube, implying perfection, with 1,500 miles, or *twelve thousand stadia,* on each side. This is one thousand times larger than the temple imagined by Ezekiel. **21:19** The precious stones are like those in the breastplate

22 I saw no temple in the city, for its temple is the Lord God the Almighty and the Lamb. [23]And the city has no need of sun or moon to shine on it, for the glory of God is its light, and its lamp is the Lamb. [24]The nations will walk by its light, and the kings of the earth will bring their glory into it. [25]Its gates will never be shut by day—and there will be no night there. [26]People will bring into it the glory and the honor of the nations. [27]But nothing unclean will enter it, nor anyone who practices abomination or falsehood, but only those who are written in the Lamb's book of life.

22 Then the angel[n] showed me the river of the water of life, bright as crystal, flowing from the throne of God and of the Lamb [2]through the middle of the street of the city. On either side of the river is the tree of life[o] with its twelve kinds of fruit, producing its fruit each month, and the leaves of the tree are for the healing of the nations. [3]Nothing accursed will be found there any more. But the throne of God and of the Lamb will be in it, and his servants will worship him; [4]they will see his face, and his name will be on their foreheads. [5]And there will be no more night; they need no light of lamp or sun, for the Lord God will be their light, and they will reign forever and ever.

6 And he said to me, "These words are trustworthy and true, for the Lord, the God of the spirits of the prophets, has sent his angel to show his servants what must soon take place."

7 "See, I am coming soon! Blessed is the one who keeps the words of the prophecy of this book."

8 I, John, am the one who heard and saw these things. And when I heard and saw them, I fell down to worship at the feet of the angel who showed them to me, [9]but he said to me, "You must not do that! I am a fellow servant with you and your brothers and sisters the prophets and with those who keep the words of this book. Worship God!"

10 And he said to me, "Do not seal up the words of the prophecy of this book, for the time is near. [11]Let the evildoer still do evil, and the filthy still be filthy, and the righteous still do right, and the holy still be holy."

12 "See, I am coming soon; my reward is with me, to repay according to everyone's work. [13]I am the Alpha and the Omega, the First and the Last, the Beginning and the End."

14 Blessed are those who wash their robes,[p] so that they will have the right to the tree of life and may enter the city by the gates. [15]Outside are the dogs and sorcerers and sexually immoral[q]

n 22.1 Gk *he* o 22.2 Or *the Lamb*. *In the middle of the street of the city, and on either side of the river, is the tree of life*
p 22.14 Other ancient authorities read *do his commandments*
q 22.15 Or *prostitutes*

of the temple high priest (Exod. 28:17–21; 39:10–13). **21:22** The absence of a temple makes this city unique and points to the earlier idea that the people of God will be a priestly kingdom (see note on 1:6). **21:24** Despite their earlier connection to Babylon, the nations and kings of the earth now come to the new Jerusalem, echoing the Prophets (Jer. 3:17; Isa. 60:1–11; Mic. 4:1–4). **21:25** *Gates will never be shut.* An eternally welcoming city, although there are those who remain outside. *No night* suggests the perpetual presence of God and the Lamb. See Zech. 14:7.
22:1–5 The river and tree of life. John shifts from urban to pastoral imagery, envisioning a garden-like setting reminiscent of Gen. 2–3. **22:1** *Water of life.* See note on 21:6. God and the Lamb are the source of this water. **22:2** *Tree of life.* See the tree in Eden (Gen. 2:9; 3:22). *Twelve kinds of fruit.* Cf. Ezek. 47:12. **22:3** *Servants.* Literally "enslaved people." **22:4** *His name . . . foreheads.* See note on 7:3. This verse suggests there is a singular name, even though 14:1 reports the faithful are marked with two names.
22:6–21 Benedictions. Just as Revelation opened with a series of introductions and liturgical formulations, the book concludes with a collection of affirmations, warnings, and benedictions. These are offered by a series of speakers, evoking a kind of choral effect. **22:6–7** An echo of the opening in 1:1–3. *See.* Cf. 1:7. **22:8** *I, John.* See 1:4, 9. **22:9** The second time John mistakenly worships an angel. See 19:10. **22:10** *Do not seal up . . . is near.* In some apocalypses, the content is sealed for the future (Dan. 8:26; 12:4, 9; T. Mos. 1:17–18); however, John envisions Revelation as describing events on the near horizon, so the contents of the revelation are accessible. **22:11** *Let the evildoer.* See Dan. 12:10; Ezek. 3:27. **22:13** *Alpha . . . Omega.* See note on 1:8. **22:14** *Wash their robes.* An allusion to those who make it through the "great ordeal" (see note on 7:14) and those who remain faithful to God and the Lamb (see note on 3:4–5). **22:15** *Dogs.* A generic slur for whomever the speaker wants to exclude (Prov. 26:11; Isa.

and murderers and idolaters and everyone who loves and practices falsehood.

16 "It is I, Jesus, who sent my angel to you with this testimony for the churches. I am the root and the descendant of David, the bright morning star."

17 The Spirit and the bride say, "Come."
And let everyone who hears say, "Come."
And let everyone who is thirsty come.
Let anyone who wishes take the water of
life as a gift.

18 I warn everyone who hears the words of the prophecy of this book: if anyone adds to them, God will add to that person the plagues described in this book; [19]if anyone takes away from the words of the book of this prophecy, God will take away that person's share in the tree of life and in the holy city, which are described in this book.

20 The one who testifies to these things says, "Surely I am coming soon."
Amen. Come, Lord Jesus!

21 The grace of the Lord Jesus be with all the saints. Amen.*

r 22.21 Other ancient authorities lack *all* or *the saints* or *Amen*

56:10; Mark 7:27; Matt. 7:6). **22:16** *Root . . . David.* An affirmation from Jesus that he is the Messiah. See note on 5:5. *Bright morning star.* Venus, which some interpreted as a messianic image (T. Levi 18:3). Not an allusion to Lucifer in the Latin version of Isa. 14:12. **22:18** The warning may be due to the ease with which scrolls could be amended. Its rhetorical effect is to underscore the importance of Revelation's message.

The Bible as a Collection:
The Making of the Biblical Canons

J. Todd Hibbard and Davina C. Lopez

The Bible and Canon: An Introduction and Definition

Despite appearances, the Bible is not a single book. Indeed, *Bible* comes from the ancient Greek word *biblia*, "books," indicating that it is a collection. Because what we now call the Bible is published as a book, it is easy to assume that it contains a single story that has a beginning, middle, and end. The reality is that it is more of an anthology. Between the covers of this book lies a diverse collection of texts that a variety of authors composed, revised, and compiled over more than 2,500 years. These texts became the Bible—in varying forms, the sacred writings, or Scriptures, of Judaism and Christianity—only through long and complicated human processes that scholars are still attempting to understand.

The ancient texts in this Bible were eventually chosen by people other than their original authors, from among many documents, to form a collection. However it is defined, the Bible as a collection is often referred to as *the biblical canon* or *the canon*. The term *canon* comes from an ancient Greek term meaning "reed" or a "straight bar" that could be used for measuring. This term came to mean a norm or standard by which things could be judged, such as canon law or a canon of classic films or "great books." With respect to the Bible, it refers to a closed list of texts with religious importance for specific communities in specific contexts. The process by which humans choose and codify their collections of scriptures is called canonization. The composition and organization of the collections vary according to which community is making the determination, under what circumstances, and for what purposes, all of which can vary widely.

Ancient people adopted a canon and promoted its use by communities across the ancient West Asian and Mediterranean worlds. The ideas that an official collection was necessary for these communities to exist, that such a collection arose instantly, that it could never be changed, that all people accepted it as authoritative, and that they thought the stories were historical are actually modern notions. The ancient people who produced what we now call the Bible likely knew that their collection was one among many, and conflicts about what did and did not belong in a canon were quite common and could drag on for centuries. This NRSV Updated Edition Bible contains English translations of the texts that form at least three canons of historical and contemporary importance and influence, plus some texts that were part of ancient canons and left out later. This introductory essay concerns the two primary canons common to English Bibles: the Hebrew Bible / Old Testament and the New Testament.

The Hebrew Bible / Old Testament: Contents and Organization

The canonization of the Jewish Scriptures remains largely opaque, though scholars acknowledge that not all parts of the Jewish Bible came to be regarded as Scripture at the same time. The criteria used to decide a text's sacredness, authority, and inspiration—all important considerations in early discussions about the significance of texts later deemed "biblical"—are unclear. Consequently, speaking of the Bible's developmental history proves complicated.

Jewish readers recognize the first major collection of books as Scripture and refer to it as the Hebrew Bible or Tanakh. The former designation stems from the fact that most of the material in this section is written in classical Hebrew, the language of ancient Israel, though some sections were composed in Aramaic. *Tanakh* is an acronym identifying the three sections totaling twenty-four books in the Jewish Bible: Torah, Nevi'im, and Ketuvim. The Torah includes the first five books of the Bible: Genesis, Exodus, Leviticus, Numbers, and Deuteronomy. The Nevi'im, which means "Prophets," is divided into two sections, the Former and Latter Prophets. The first includes Joshua, Judges, (1–2) Samuel, and (1–2) Kings, while the second includes Isaiah, Jeremiah, Ezekiel, and the Twelve, so called because it comprises twelve smaller prophetic scrolls (Hosea through Malachi). The Ketuvim, or "Writings," includes the eleven remaining books of the Hebrew Bible.

Christians refer to the first section of their Bible as the Old Testament, which presumes a New Testament, and organize it differently. The first section contains the same books as the Torah of the Tanakh. It is followed by a section designated as the Historical Books, which includes the Former Prophets along with a few books from the Ketuvim (Ruth, Esther, Ezra, Nehemiah, and 1–2 Chronicles). The Poetic and Wisdom Books follow, which includes all the remaining books from the Ketuvim except Daniel and Lamentations. The Prophetic Books, including Daniel and Lamentations, round out the Christian canon. Finally, Roman Catholic and Orthodox canons include several additional books in various places in the Christian arrangement. These additional books are referred to as the deuterocanonical or apocryphal books.

The organization of this material in Jewish and Christian traditions has theological justifications. The orientation of the Jewish Bible places more emphasis on the books in the first section, the Torah. Their association with Moses and covenant teaching, sometimes called law, gives them preeminence in the Jewish tradition. The Christian ordering of the canon, on the other hand, is oriented toward what comes last, the Prophets. These books were understood in Christian thought as pointing to the coming of Jesus. Hence, their placement in the Old Testament order set the stage for the addition of the New Testament and its proclamation about the Christian Messiah.

The History of the Hebrew Bible / Old Testament

The books of the Hebrew Bible say virtually nothing certain about their composition. Furthermore, most of the books have been subject to extensive editorial activity. Little is known about the process by which biblical texts were copied and transmitted prior to the second century BCE. By this time, some of the books had already been translated into Greek to facilitate their use in Greek-speaking Jewish communities of the Hellenistic period. Indeed, many early Christians knew the Jewish Scriptures via these Greek texts, not their Hebrew (and Aramaic) forms. In some cases, there are significant differences between these two versions (e.g., the book of Jeremiah). The discovery of the Dead Sea Scrolls in the mid-twentieth century illuminated our understanding of the textual history of the Hebrew Bible in the pre-Christian era. These hundreds of largely fragmentary manuscripts reveal biblical books whose contents were in flux. The stabilization of the text of the books of the Hebrew Bible began in earnest later in the rabbinic period (after 100 CE), culminating in the Masoretic Text (MT) of the early medieval period. Modern translations of the Bible generally use the MT as the basis of their editions.

The New Testament: Contents and Organization

The New Testament canon appears after the Hebrew Bible / Old Testament in this Bible. This collection consists of twenty-seven books, commonly divided into four parts: Gospels (Matthew, Mark, Luke, and John); history (the Acts of the Apostles); letters, classified as thirteen Pauline letters to specific groups and individuals (Romans, 1 Corinthians, 2 Corinthians, Galatians, Ephesians, Philippians, Colossians, 1 Thessalonians, 2 Thessalonians, Philemon, 1 Timothy, 2 Timothy, and Titus) and eight catholic (= universal) letters (Hebrews, James, 1 Peter, 2 Peter, 1 John, 2 John, 3 John, and Jude); and the Apocalypse (Revelation). Various authors composed most of these books during the first centuries CE, and precise dating and authorship are difficult to determine. The Gospels were anonymously compiled and later attributed to disciples (Matthew and John) and apostles' companions (Mark and Luke). While thirteen canonical letters claim the apostle Paul as their author, there is no scholarly consensus concerning the veracity of those claims. Furthermore, there is growing consensus on the second-century origins of 1 Timothy and 2 Peter. Although Revelation claims to be written by "John," the author may be anonymous.

While the New Testament serves as a scriptural resource for the life, teachings, and death of Jesus and the subsequent development of early Christian movements, the texts in this collection do not betray uniformity in perspective or content, and the books are ordered independently of the dates during which they were produced. They are not organized chronologically or according to a coherent narrative arc. The Gospels appear first, and their order in contemporary Bible translations follows the preference of Augustine of Hippo (354–430 CE). The Pauline letters follow the Gospels and Acts and are ordered from longest to shortest, as are the other letters. Revelation, which was one of the final books accepted into this collection, appears last.

The History of the New Testament Canon

As with the Hebrew Bible, much of the ancient occasion for the formation of the New Testament canon is difficult to reconstruct. We do know that various texts were in circulation at different times and in different places throughout the first four centuries CE, that the canon emerged out of disagreements among developing Christian sects regarding what they considered to be important teachings and practices, and that the collection contains a diversity of ideas. Complicating matters further is the reality that early Christians had access to different collections of texts and different versions of the same texts. Since human hands copied them, no two are exactly the same!

The twenty-seven books in this collection were first mentioned together as a definitive list of Christian Scriptures in 367 CE in a letter from an Egyptian bishop named Athanasius. By Athanasius's time, debates about what constituted a Christian canon had been ongoing for several centuries. During the second century, Marcion, a ship merchant and bishop's son from Asia Minor, proposed what is now considered to be the first Christian canon: ten Pauline letters and the Gospel of Luke. This collection, Marcion argued, would stand apart from the Jewish tradition. Although Marcion was denounced as a heretic, his efforts generated further considerations of which texts should be authoritative and how that would be determined. Another early example of a suggested canonical list is found in a fragmentary document now called the Muratorian Canon (late second century CE). Around 325 CE, the historian Eusebius of Caesarea (ca. 260–340 CE) detailed a list of twenty books that he acknowledged as sacred writings. His list echoes discussions by Irenaeus of Lyons (ca. 130–205 CE) and Origen of Alexandria (ca. 184–283 CE) of what constituted acceptable and unacceptable Christian writings and groups. Ancient groups also adopted and used their own texts. Collections of Pauline letters appear to have been copied and disseminated near the end of the first century CE, some of which are now in the canon. Sayings, miracle stories, and biographies of Jesus were in circulation, as were wisdom sayings, prayers, stories about apostles, apocalypses, letters, and reimaginings of Israel's origin stories. Various surviving collections of early Christian texts suggest what different groups considered to be important and authoritative for their own purposes. As it was then, so too now: different Christian groups emphasize different collections of materials to maintain boundaries, claim authority, and justify practices.

Some Final Thoughts on the Bible as a Collection

As a collection, the Bible has not always looked the way it does now. It is easy to assume that the Bible offers stability, coherence, and a comprehensive linear narrative spanning from the world's beginning until its end. Exploring the Bible as a collection of diverse literature compiled over several millennia should reveal more questions than answers. It is vital to remember that the writings in the Bible are older than "The Bible" as a canonical collection and were chosen from among many other texts to form the anthology you are reading today. Similarly, the people who wrote the documents probably had no idea that there would someday be "The Bible" and that their contributions would be in it, nor did they know that their words would travel through time and beyond their places of origin to become official texts for others around the world, in multiple languages and cultural contexts. They certainly could not predict that their stories would be read and studied by university students and their professors in our world.

The Bible and Methods: How to Read the Bible

Stacy Davis

There are a variety of reasons for reading and studying the Bible. For many scholars, for example, there is the desire to learn more about the peoples and places the texts describe. For those who are Jewish or Christian, biblical study can be a religious undertaking. For readers who identify with other religions or have no religious identity, studying the Bible can give important context to a range of past social movements or historical events, such as Western colonialism, feminist movements, abolitionism, and the Cold War. Studying the Bible is also relevant to examining contemporary issues like LGBTQIA2S+ advocacy and climate change activism. The main purpose of any study Bible is to give its readers the tools and notes needed to understand ancient texts, and this is where methods play an important role.

There are multiple ways to read the Bible, from feminist criticism to social-scientific criticism to disability studies to ecological studies. These methods, however, were preceded by the historical-critical method, which prioritizes placing biblical texts within a particular historical time frame and context. Most books of the Hebrew Bible were written between the eighth and first centuries BCE. Most historical-critical scholars posit that those books come from multiple sources—particularly the Torah (Genesis–Deuteronomy). One influential theory known as the Documentary Hypothesis argues that the Torah is constructed from four originally discrete sources that can be identified and separated on the basis of various criteria. These four sources are the following: the J or Yahwist source, which prefers using the divine name YHWH (*j* produces a *y* sound in German); the E or Elohistic source, which often uses the divine name Elohim; the P or Priestly source, which emphasizes order and sacrifice; and the D source, which is found in and represents the core ideas of the book of Deuteronomy. Scholars continue to debate the composition history of the Hebrew Bible—and the Documentary Hypothesis no longer enjoys the consensus it once did; even so, knowing that a unit like Gen. 1–3, for example, contains two different creation stories likely from different sources can facilitate reading and understanding. And so the historical-critical method is closely linked to source criticism, a method that looks for different sources in particular biblical passages.

Nearly all the books of the New Testament can be dated to the first century CE, with some considered possibly written in the early second century CE. Similar to the different sources in the Torah, the first five books in the New Testament (Matthew–Acts) also have different sources, as follows, based on the Four Document Hypothesis: M (Matthew), Mark, L (Luke), and Q (a sayings source), with a separate group of sources for John. Most scholars believe that Mark, the earliest Gospel, and Q are sources for Matthew and Luke. This theory helps to explain why so many stories and sayings repeat in these Gospels. In addition, the authors of Matthew and Luke have their own textual traditions, which is why, for instance, the parable of the Prodigal Son only appears in Luke (15:11–32) and the parable of the Unforgiving Servant only appears in Matthew (18:23–35). John, however, has very few similarities with Matthew, Mark, or Luke. For those interested in knowing what the historical Jesus may have said or done, if a saying or event appears in John and one of the other Gospels, the odds of its historicity increase, given their independent sources.

In addition to a basic understanding of the Bible's multiple sources, knowing a few key dates and events will help the reader's historical-critical approach to it as well. For the historical background of the Hebrew Bible, Israel had two major exiles: the first when Assyria invaded the northern portion of Israel in 722 BCE and the second when Babylon invaded the south, called Judah, in 597 BCE and 587/586 BCE. Whether a text was written before or after an exile gives the reader historical context that can influence what a text means. While Hosea and Jeremiah both warn readers to repent, their contexts are different. Hosea is speaking to the north about its idolatrous temples and the threat of the Assyrian invasion (Hos. 10), while Jeremiah is arguing that Jerusalem in the south has the proper temple but that will not save the people from Babylon if they do not behave properly (Jer. 7). For the New Testament, the destruction of the Second Temple in Jerusalem in 70 CE is a key date and historical event. The introductions to each biblical book and the notes in this study Bible will give the reader the basic historical information they need to read the book in its context.

Additionally, another method that may be particularly useful in a course that includes both the Hebrew Bible and the New Testament is a form of rhetorical criticism (how language is designed to persuade the reader) called intertextuality, or inner-biblical exegesis, a way of paying attention to how biblical texts function in other parts of the Bible. The writers of the texts in the New Testament drew on the Jewish Scriptures to interpret and define Jesus. This means that the New Testament is full of allusions and quotations from the Jewish Scriptures, especially the Septuagint (the Greek translation of the Jewish Scriptures, used by the early church). Two examples are as follows: The author of Matthew uses the story of a young woman having a child in Isa. 7 as proof of Jesus's miraculous conception by the Virgin Mary (Matt. 1:22–23). In Gal. 4 and Rom. 4, Paul uses the story from Genesis of Abraham, Sarah, and Hagar to demonstrate not only that Jesus is the Messiah but also that salvation includes gentiles, or non-Jews, as well as Jews. Notes in many study Bibles often indicate where New Testament texts cite or allude to Jewish Scriptures so that the readers can see the similarities and differences in interpretation.

Because of the multiple types of text in the Bible, including narratives, law codes, dialogue between prophets and God, psalms, letters to new Christian communities, and stories about Jesus, there are multiple methods that scholars use to explain its content. Not simply of use to scholars, these methods are important tools for students as well. Those mentioned here (including feminist, social-scientific, disability, and ecological approaches) are but a few of the twenty-three different methods described in two well-known volumes about biblical criticism: *To Each Its Own Meaning: An Introduction to Biblical Criticisms and Their Application* (1999) and *New Meanings for Ancient Texts: Recent Approaches to Biblical Criticisms and Their Applications* (2013). Comprehensive as they are, these volumes do not include other important recent methods, such as childist interpretation and womanist interpretation. When reading a scholarly work on the Bible, it is always helpful to see what method or methods the author is using to interpret a particular text, because there are many from which to choose. And when doing your own interpretation, know that you have multiple ways to do that work. While some assignments may require a more historical or source-based focus, others may not.

One major shift in biblical studies in the last half century has been the recognition that people read the same texts differently depending on their own social location(s), influenced by such factors as gender, ethnicity, religion, social class, and sexual orientation, to name a few. As long as the author does not misrepresent a text (e.g., suggesting that the Gospels were written in the fourth century CE), there is no one "right" way to read. Someone examining the story of Gen. 1 from a feminist perspective may emphasize the simultaneous creation of genders, while an ecological critic may focus on the systematic ordering of creation and the emphasis on the goodness of all creation. A social-scientific interpretation of John 9 may focus on the dynamics among Jesus, the Pharisees, the healed man, and his parents, while an interpretation based on disability studies may question the ways in which not being able to see is interpreted as a sign of sin or moral failing. A postcolonial reading of Assyria, as described in the books of 2 Kings, Isaiah, and Hosea, may engage more critically not only with Assyrian as well as biblical texts but with the ways scholars tend to favor the biblical descriptions of the communities involved in the conflicts, as opposed to the Assyrian descriptions. Consequently, the study of the Bible can be enhanced by multiple scholarly methods as well as by the different disciplinary and interdisciplinary fields of studies readers bring to the texts, including but not limited to psychology; anthropology; sociology; women's, gender, and sexuality studies; history; and literature.

Reading the Bible requires time and patience; however, if one has both, combined with curiosity and a willingness to learn, the stories and ideas in the texts can lead one to timeless questions about human interactions, how to make sense of the nonsensical, and how ancient communities saw themselves. Whether the texts are sacred for the reader or viewed as part of world literature, the different methods of biblical interpretation enable any reader to engage the biblical books critically and with their own questions in mind.

The Bible in Its Ancient Contexts

Henry W. Morisada Rietz and Claudia Setzer

Hebrew Bible

The books of the Hebrew Bible took shape within the ancient Near East, a vast area encompassing Egypt, in the south; the Mediterranean, in the west; and Mesopotamia, in the east. Knowing something about the history of this region provides important insights into the development of these texts. Settled agriculture, the founding of cities, and the development of written language began in Mesopotamia and in Egypt in the fourth and third millennia BCE (3000s–2000s). From the mid-third millennium on, a succession of empires ebbed and flowed in Mesopotamia, influencing all the peoples of the region, including ancient Israel. In the twelfth century (1100s), the Assyrians began to assert their dominance, becoming an imperial power that eventually ruined the northern kingdom of Israel in the eighth century.

Complex human civilization also began to form in Egypt in the late fourth millennium. Egyptian political history is marked by a series of royal dynasties with intermediate periods of instability. During the New Kingdom, pharaohs Seti I (1294–1279 BCE) and Rameses II (1279–1213 BCE) conducted major building campaigns. One of these building projects may be the context of the Israelites' exodus from Egypt, although scholars debate the existence of evidence for such an event outside of the biblical text.

The Israelites begin to emerge as a people toward the end of the second millennium, though their precise origins are unclear. Some of those who made up early Israel may have been from nomadic tribes, with some indigenous to Canaan and yet others coming from elsewhere. According to the Bible, the Israelites united as a kingdom in the late eleventh century BCE, first under Saul and then under David. Not long afterward, however, there was a civil war that established two separate nations: Israel in the north and Judah in the south, with the latter the home of the Davidic dynasty.

During the monarchic periods, Israel and Judah often had contentious relationships with other nations and with each other. Their most immediate geographical neighbors were the Phoenicians and the Syrians to the north, the Ammonites and Moabites to the east, the Edomites in the south, and the Philistines to the southwest. Beyond these, the Israelite and Judean monarchies occasionally chose to make various political alliances with the great superpowers, including Egypt to the south or the Assyrian and then Babylonian Empires to the east, or—at still other times—to unite with other groups to revolt against these empires. The Assyrian Empire would eventually conquer the northern kingdom of Israel in 722 BCE and make the southern kingdom of Judah a vassal state.

In the seventh century, Babylon began to expand, and by 609 BCE, the Neo-Babylonian Empire had conquered Assyria. As a means of quelling future revolts, the Babylonians often forcibly removed leading figures from conquered territory. The Babylonians invaded Judah twice, first in 597 BCE and then again in 586 BCE; both events included the capture of Judah and Jerusalem and the forced exile of a portion of the populace, but the latter included the destruction of Jerusalem and the temple there. This event begins what is typically called the exilic period in the history of ancient Israel/Judah.

While Babylon was expanding its power in the west, the Median Empire was expanding in the east. Somewhat later, the king of Media married one of his daughters to the king of a vassal Persian tribe. This marriage produced a son, Cyrus II, also known as Cyrus the Great. In 550, Cyrus rebelled against Media and became the king of the Median-Persian Empire. In the following decades, Cyrus extended his reach, eventually conquering Babylon in 539 BCE.

With the demise of the Babylonians, the land of Israel and Judah became part of the Persian Empire. In 538 BCE, Cyrus allowed exiled people, including Judean exiles, to return to their ancestral lands and rebuild their cities and temples, almost fifty years after the destruction of Jerusalem. This date marks the end of the exilic period and the beginning of the Persian or postexilic period. Those exiles who chose not to return from Babylon and other places where they had been dispersed represent the beginnings of the Jewish Diaspora. In the second year of the return, the foundation for the temple was laid in Jerusalem (see Ezra 3). This "Second Temple" was completed circa 515 BCE (see Ezra 6).

Darius I, Cyrus's eventual successor, began in 522 to divide the Persian Empire into twenty large regions and standardized a system of governance with each region ruled by three leaders, providing a kind of balance of power and reducing the possibility of revolt. The Persian Empire was conquered in 330 BCE by Alexander the Great, whose empire grew to encompass the eastern Mediterranean and most of the ancient Near East, including Judah.

This overview demonstrates that the history of Israel/Judah and the documents that were eventually collected in the Hebrew Bible span many centuries that were influenced by still other people groups, each of which had its own political, cultural, and literary histories. These provide crucial context for the biblical texts. For example, law collections from some of the Mesopotamian empires—Sumerian, Assyrian, Babylonian, and Hattian—provide important comparative material for understanding the legal material in the Torah (Pentateuch). Similarly, various political treaties, often between a dominant nation (suzerain) and a vassal state, offer insight into the form of Israel's covenantal relationship with the Lord. Still other types of literary remains from the ancient Near East may be profitably compared with biblical psalms, wisdom sayings, narratives, prophecy, and the like.

The peoples of the ancient Near East believed in a large number of gods. The Levantine pantheon included the high god El (the name means "god") and his wife Asherah. Another important god was the storm deity Baal (whose name means "lord"). Clashes between rival people groups could be seen as wars between their gods. Ancient texts like myths, hymns, and rituals afford insight into how these deities were understood, including Israel's understanding of their own deity.

New Testament

Jewish and Greco-Roman (or Hellenistic) cultures intertwined in ancient Mediterranean communities in the period from 200 BCE to 200 CE, even as Roman occupation controlled much of people's public and personal lives. These three forces of Judaism, Hellenism, and Roman political power exerted influence on the earliest Jesus followers, including the first writers, readers, and hearers of the New Testament documents.

Jews saw themselves as a people who were in a covenantal relationship with the one God who created the world; who were descended from the ancient patriarchs Abraham, Isaac, and Jacob; who revered their Scriptures (the Torah [Pentateuch], the Prophets, and the Writings); and who followed, to greater or lesser degrees, the commandments contained within the Torah. Their culture and way of life were the matrix for Jesus and his early followers and thus fundamental to the beginnings of Christianity. Jesus was an apocalyptic Jew who preached the will of the one God by drawing from the Scripture; who observed the Torah's commands in food, dress, and Sabbath observance; and who attended the synagogue. He and John the Baptist urged societal reform before the imminent end of the world as they knew it, in line with the Hebrew prophets and with other apocalyptic thinkers of their own time. The Gospels show Jesus, Pharisees, and other Jews in discussion and debate about how the Torah should be understood but always in agreement that the Scripture was authoritative and expressed God's will. Any attempt to separate Jesus and his first followers from their Judaism yields a false picture. Paul, himself a Jew and Pharisee, reminds the church in Rome that the people and religion of Israel are the root that supports their faith in Jesus, not the other way around (Rom. 11:18).

When Alexander the Great and his troops swept through the Middle East in the fourth century BCE, he promoted the Greek language and ideas as a cultural glue to unite his empire. Greek culture, called Hellenism (from *Hellas*, "Greece"), included religion, art and architecture, attitudes toward the body, and reverence for the classical philosophers and their teachings. Hellenism, including the Greek language, remained in place, especially in cities, after Alexander's death and was absorbed into Roman culture, creating a Greco-Roman veneer over much of the empire. The apostle Paul, a diaspora Jew, exemplifies the dual strands of Jewish and Greco-Roman culture, showing his knowledge of Greek philosophy in Acts and drawing on Greek tropes in his own writings. The Greek term *Logos* (Word) in John 1:1 compares to the Stoic principle of divine reason that undergirds the universe.

Hellenism was all around the authors of the New Testament, since most Jews and gentiles were hellenized to varying degrees. Not all were pleased with that influence, however. The uprising of the Maccabees in 167–160 BCE, commemorated in the story of Hanukkah, was not just a revolt against Seleucid overlords but also a conservative Jewish group's reaction against other Jews who had become too assimilated to Greco-Roman ways. Deuterocanonical books like 1–2 Maccabees and

Sirach, viewed as Scriptures by some branches of Christianity but not others, provide rich material about Jews in this period.

The general Pompey conquered Jerusalem in 63 BCE, establishing Roman rule over the land of Israel. At its height, the Roman Empire was made up of all the countries encircling the Mediterranean Sea. Theoretically, the Romans allowed conquered people to practice their own religions, as Roman administrators were chiefly concerned with collecting taxes and keeping the peace. But because religions like Judaism affected everyday life, they could appear to pose threats to the smooth functioning of the business of empire. A charismatic preacher like Jesus, who preached about another kingdom and caused uproar in the temple environs, would spell trouble to Roman officials in constant fear of uprisings.

In an environment where poverty was the norm for all but a privileged few, compounded by heavy taxes, military occupation, disease, and short life expectancy, people sought relief. They turned to itinerant healers and exorcists, to mystery cults whose rituals and sacred meals provided a sense of belonging and promised control over life and death, and to the teachings of different philosophies, which explained the nature of the universe and promoted ordered, ethical ways of life. Jewish and Christian groups similarly offered personal relief, a sense of belonging, and the assurance of an ordered universe to many.

The Bible in Public Life

Claudia Setzer

The Bible is an enduring presence in American public culture, folded into debates revolving around public education, political issues, public displays and ceremonies, and legal decisions. Despite Thomas Jefferson's observation that the U.S. Constitution's language in the First Amendment was "building a wall of separation between Church and State" (*Letter to Danbury Baptists*, 1802), neither religion nor the Bible can be erased from American history and culture.

Education

In the arena of education, public schools must simultaneously uphold the First Amendment, whose establishment clause forbids the state to promote religion, while attempting to teach the full range of the American experience, whose history, art, and culture are religiously infused. No one could teach about reform movements like the abolition of slavery without noting the reformers' reliance on the Bible, nor could one present the civil rights movement without studying the soaring, biblically infused speeches of Martin Luther King Jr. and Fannie Lou Hamer. Nor could any course in art history ignore the ubiquitous biblical stories, characters, and themes that appear in work from the United States.

It is, in fact, legal to talk about the Bible and religion in public schools. The historic court decision of *Abington v. Schempp* (1963) simply mandates that schools cannot sponsor school prayer or devotional Bible reading. Educators may teach the Bible as part of their history and literature curricula. Test cases have arisen over time, such as when banners at a high school's football games displayed New Testament verses (Fort Oglethorpe, Georgia, 2009) and when a high school monument exhibited Bible verses (Madison County, Georgia, 2014). In the first case, the banners were moved to a different site and not held by cheerleaders, and in the second case, the monument was removed.

In higher education, public universities face similar challenges in maintaining vibrant secular humanities programs while policing First Amendment boundaries. Most of the nation's oldest colleges were founded to educate clergy and spread Christianity. Many institutions have shed their religious identities but teach religion as part of the humanities. Today's biblical scholars face questions about their subject's utility. The rhetoric around "Is the study of the Bible useful?" energizes contemporary curricular discussions, but this question has a long history in educational circles. Most students, whatever their backgrounds or leanings, arrive at college with some prior relationship to the Bible, suggesting the value of exploring its significance in higher education settings.

Political Rhetoric

Biblical themes and quotations regularly appear in political rhetoric in the United States, sometimes in subtle ways. When Ronald Reagan called America "a shining city on a hill" (November 3, 1980), many would not have recognized the reference to Matt. 5:14, and even fewer would have recognized its allusion to the Puritan John Winthrop's "Model of Christian Charity" (1630), delivered aboard the ship *Arbella*, expressing his hopes for the Massachusetts Bay Colony. But Reagan's words nevertheless carried a biblical resonance and authority. Presidential inauguration speeches often deploy at least one biblical reference or theme. Abraham Lincoln, in his second inaugural address, explicitly cited Ps. 19:9 to help make sense of the brutal cost of the Civil War as possible recompense for the brutal cost of slavery: "The judgments of the Lord are true and righteous altogether" (KJV).

Politicians on both sides of a debate may employ biblical texts for support, as when Barack Obama alluded to Lev. 19:34 to argue for immigration reform (2014), while Attorney General Jeff Sessions invoked Rom. 13 to justify prosecuting migrants and separating parents from children at the U.S.-Mexico border. The use of the Bible does not necessarily correlate strongly to the formal religious identification of the politician. Jimmy Carter, a committed Southern Baptist and daily Bible reader, was more reticent and used few biblical quotes in his speeches. Franklin Roosevelt and Richard Nixon, neither known to be fervent church members, liberally used the Bible and religious imagery to express common values in an attempt to unify the nation.

Public Display of Symbols

Public display of religious symbols and biblical verses shows that the line between church and state remains permeable. A complete absence of biblical materials on state buildings and monuments would be impossible to achieve. No one has proposed that "Proclaim liberty throughout all the land unto all the inhabitants thereof" (Lev. 25:10 KJV) be removed from the Liberty Bell. Nor has anyone suggested the removal of the statue of Moses holding the tablets of the Ten Commandments from a marble frieze in the Supreme Court building, as he stands among history's other great lawgivers.

Judge Roy Moore, however, tested constitutional boundaries when he ordered the setting up of a granite monument of the Ten Commandments (the Decalogue) in the rotunda of the Alabama judicial building in 2001. Two civil actions were combined in the case of *Glassroth v. Moore* (November 2002). The district court ruled that the monument violated the establishment clause of the First Amendment; the monument was removed, and Moore was forced to step down as chief justice of the Alabama State Supreme Court. Judges in the case were guided by "the Lemon test," a three-pronged test to determine whether an action violates the First Amendment, put forth in *Lemon v. Kurtzman* (1971). To survive the test, a display of a religious symbol (a) must have a secular purpose, (b) must neither advance nor inhibit religion in its primary effect, and (c) must not foster excessive government entanglement with religion.

The U.S. Supreme Court nevertheless ruled in 2005 that the Ten Commandments may be displayed on public property in some cases. A monument of the commandments remains on the grounds of state capitols in Austin, Texas, and Little Rock, Arkansas, and in county courthouses in Kentucky.

The version of the Ten Commandments displayed in public is always the Protestant one, usually from the King James Version, the most popular translation in the United States. Jews, Roman Catholics, and Protestants edit the Decalogue from Exod. 20:2–17 and Deut. 5:6–21 differently. The biblical sources technically contain more than ten commands or prohibitions, so each tradition has developed its own variation. The ubiquity of the Protestant version in public display is a nod to America's Protestant heritage and majority but can also strike some as exclusionary.

Law

Although American law has no formal connection to the Bible, many people hold the belief that divine law, particularly the Ten Commandments, undergirds the legal system. The argument that natural law (a system of order that any human community needs to function; e.g., laws against theft, murder, and spouse stealing) is connected to biblical law complicates the matter. James Wilson, one of the drafters of the Constitution, believed divine law did ultimately provide the foundation for natural law, but the Bible need not be invoked in day-to-day legal practice. Yet in the early nineteenth century, some conservative judges enforced laws against blasphemy or Sabbath laws prohibiting certain activities on the Christian Sabbath, Sunday (enforced against Jewish merchants who observed their Sabbath on Saturday). Even the judges in *Glassroth v. Moore* in 2002, who ordered the removal of the Ten Commandments monument from a state building, said in their decision, "The court believes it is important to clarify at the outset that the court does not hold it as improper in all instances to display the Ten Commandments in government buildings; nor does the court hold that the Ten Commandments are not important, if not one of the most important, sources of American law." This nod to the popular opinion that biblical law undergirds U.S. law, notes law and religion scholar Steven K. Green, lacks both historical and documentary support ("The Bible, Law, and Political Rhetoric," in *The Bible in the American Experience*).

As biblical scholar John Kutsko shows, some Americans approach both the Constitution and the Bible in similar ways. Many countries regularly rewrite their constitutions or do without one, but Americans hold theirs as nearly sacred. Originalists in reading law resemble literalists in reading the Bible, seeing the Constitution as authoritative and unchanging, carrying an objective meaning that is available to any reader. Kutsko notes that these reverential attitudes do not always signal deep familiarity with the contents of either text: "Popular biblical and constitutional hermeneutics are a match made in heaven" ("The Curious Case of the Christian Bible and the U.S. Constitution: Challenges for Educators Teaching the Bible in a Multireligious Context," in *The Bible in American Life*). In countless places and ways, the Bible, embedded in U.S. history and culture, continues to have a presence in our public spaces.

The Bible in Religious Interpretation and Practice

Henry W. Morisada Rietz

The relationship between texts in the Bible and religious interpretation and practice is dynamic and fluid. Many passages in various biblical books originated within ritual contexts or codify the actual practices of people following a religious tradition. Passages in biblical texts, in turn, have become embedded in the rituals, liturgies, songs, and everyday practices of religious adherents.

The modern-day practices of Jews and Christians have been developed through the centuries by their own authoritative traditions and communities. In the Jewish tradition, these include the interpretive strategies and debates collected and codified in the Mishnah and the Talmud, texts that provide commentaries on and interpretations of the instructions in the Torah. (There are also subsequent commentaries on the Talmud.) Different practices also arose in different Jewish communities depending on their geographies. In the present-day United States, practices within local communities vary among the Reform, Orthodox, Conservative, and Reconstructionist Jewish movements.

The modern Jewish tradition observes several festivals and days that have their origins in the biblical tradition. The Torah specifies that the seventh day of every week is holy and should be observed as a day of rest, known as the Sabbath. This commandment is included in the Decalogue, or "ten words," in Exod. 20 and Deut. 5, which come from two different textual sources that were used in the composition of the Torah/Pentateuch (see **"Introduction to the Torah/Pentateuch," pp. 2–4**). According to the Priestly source in the book of Exodus that also composes the first creation account in Gen. 1:1–2:4, the observance of the Sabbath reflects God's creative activity ordering the world: "For in six days the Lord made heaven and earth, the sea, and all that is in them, but rested the seventh day; therefore the Lord blessed the Sabbath day and consecrated it" (Exod. 20:11). The textual source in Deuteronomy associates the observance of the Sabbath with the liberation of the Hebrew people from Egypt: "Remember that you were a slave in the land of Egypt, and the Lord your God brought you out from there . . . ; therefore the Lord your God commanded you to keep the Sabbath day" (Deut. 5:15).

The Torah also specifies several feasts and festivals. Three are listed as pilgrimage festivals (Exod. 23:14–17; 34:18, 22–23; Lev. 23; Num. 28–29; Deut. 16:1–17), when adult males are to travel in order to bring offerings to the sanctuary: the festivals of Unleavened Bread and Passover (Pesach), which become associated with each other; the spring harvest of firstfruits or "Weeks" (Shavuot/Pentecost), celebrated seven weeks ("fifty" days) after Passover; and the fall harvest festival of Booths (Sukkot).

The Torah also details other important observances. The beginning of each new "moon" or month is celebrated (Num. 28:11–15). Leviticus 23:23–25 and Num. 29:1–6 specify the blowing of the trumpet (shofar) on the first day of the seventh month, which later became Rosh Hashanah (see Mishnah Rosh Hashanah). Leviticus 16 provides the instructions for the Day of Atonement (Yom Kippur) on the tenth day of the seventh month. In later Judaism, these ten days from Rosh Hashanah to Yom Kippur became known as the High Holidays or Days of Awe.

There are also Jewish holidays that are not in the Torah. The book of Esther recounts the intervention of Queen Esther to save the Jewish community oppressed by the Persian official Haman, which provides the basis for the celebration of Purim (Heb. "lots"; Esth. 9:20–32). First and Second Maccabees narrate the desecration of the Jerusalem temple in 167 BCE by the Seleucid king Antiochus IV and its "dedication"—in Hebrew, "Hanukkah"—over eight days three years later in 164 BCE (1 Macc. 4:52–59; 2 Macc. 1:8–9; 2:18; 10:1–9).

Some biblical passages that originated within ritual contexts are embedded in the biblical narratives. These passages, in turn, became part of later ritual practices. This is evident in Exodus, which provides the basis for the Festival of Passover. Set between the announcement in chap. 11 of the tenth and final plague (previously foreshadowed in 4:22–23)—the death of the firstborn—and before the narration of that event in 12:29–51, God institutes the celebration of the festivals of Passover and Unleavened Bread in Exod. 12:1–28. That is, the people are given detailed instructions to commemorate the exodus event before it happens. The temporal dimensions of the passage, which remembers an event that has not yet happened in the narrative, suggest that this text originated

within the Israelites' practice of those festivals after the time the exodus was believed to have taken place. The passage shifts from looking ahead to the future ("I will pass through the land of Egypt that night, and I will strike down every firstborn in the land of Egypt," 12:12), to being in the present ("You shall observe the Festival of Unleavened Bread, for on this very day I brought your companies out of the land of Egypt," 12:17), and to reflecting back on a past event: "And when your children ask you, 'What does this observance mean to you?' you shall say, 'It is the Passover sacrifice to the LORD, for he passed over the houses of the Israelites in Egypt when he struck down the Egyptians but spared our houses'" (12:26–27).

The celebration of the Passover in Judaism is often guided by a Passover haggadah (Heb. "telling"; pl. haggadot), providing written instructions about how to tell or enact the various stories, prayers, and other practices of the festival. While in modern times, the contents of different haggadot may vary widely, most contain a retelling of the ten plagues or afflictions recounted in Exod. 5–13.

Jesus and his earliest followers were Jews who also observed these festivals. Jesus debated with other Jews on how to observe the Sabbath regulations (e.g., Mark 2:23–3:5; Matt. 12:1–14; Luke 6:1–11). The passion narratives are associated with the time of the festivals of Unleavened Bread and Passover (Mark 14; Matt. 26; Luke 22; cf. John 19:14). In John's Gospel, Jesus is portrayed as going up to Jerusalem to celebrate the Passover (2:13–25), the Festival of Booths (chap. 7), and Hanukkah (10:22–23). In Acts, the Holy Spirit descends on the disciples while they are gathered to celebrate Shavuot/Pentecost (Acts 2). In the later Christian tradition, Pentecost is celebrated as the beginning of the church.

Ritual practices in the Christian traditions that go beyond the biblical text also developed over the past two thousand years, and worship in contemporary Christian communities in the United States varies depending on the particular branch or denomination as well as within local congregations. Roman Catholic, Orthodox, and Episcopal churches embrace those traditions that developed over time and follow orders of worship or liturgies that reflect their different heritages. Some Protestant denominations also follow a set order of worship or liturgies, but others have less structure. Many Christian churches follow a lectionary, a set of scriptural readings that cycle over the course of several years. In addition to readings of biblical passages and a sermon or homily interpreting those passages, echoes of Scripture are embedded in the liturgies of Christian worship and the hymns that are sung (most modern hymnals have Scripture indexes identifying the passages used in their hymns).

The narratives of Jesus's last supper with his disciples form the basis of the ritual consumption of bread and wine that takes place in most Christian traditions (Mark 14:22–25; Matt. 26:26–29; Luke 22:14–20; 1 Cor. 11:23–26). Called the Eucharist or Communion or the Lord's Supper, different denominations understand this practice in different ways, from consuming the actual blood and body of Jesus to a symbolic commemoration of Jesus's death. Various churches perform this ritual at different intervals: daily, weekly, monthly, quarterly, or even annually. It takes place in distinct ways: with congregants coming forward or remaining seated, receiving the bread and wine separately, or dipping the bread into the wine. With the rise of the temperance movement in the nineteenth-century United States, many Protestant churches moved to offering unfermented grape juice instead of wine. In the late nineteenth century, many Protestant congregations also began to serve the wine or grape juice in individual cups.

Common to virtually all Christian services is the communal recitation of some version of Jesus's prayer, traditionally called the Lord's Prayer, found in Matt. 6:9–13 and Luke 11:2–4. Many congregations recite this prayer using older translations with traditional language: "Our Father, who art in heaven, hallowed be thy name." Other congregations use more contemporary translations. Still other, more progressive congregations use paraphrases. Many conclude the prayer with a doxology that was not in the earliest manuscripts (see the NRSVue's note to Matt. 6:13b).

This brief overview shows some of the diverse and complex ways that biblical passages inform and are incorporated into the ritual practices of Jews and Christians. These ritual practices help form religious communities and order their lives together.

The Bible in Global Contexts

Mary F. Foskett and Emerson B. Powery

The Bible has always been a "world text" in the sense that the literature that constitutes it emerged from a range of historical, geopolitical, social, and cultural contexts far removed from today's readers. As a collection of writings, it also speaks to multiple contexts, with various understandings of the known world. Biblical texts themselves also reflect differing perspectives and incorporate a range of voices, sometimes within a single text. All this is to say that when we think of the Bible, we should assume multiplicity.

The texts of the Bible not only emerged over the course of many centuries, with the earliest layers of writing dating to the eighth century BCE or perhaps even earlier, they also traveled. In the ancient Near East, the literature of the Hebrew Bible circulated in Hebrew and in Greek translation. The scribes who composed, collected, and passed along these ancient texts also edited them. In so doing, they sometimes made changes to a given text that reflected a scribe's particular context or a community's own understanding of the text.

As with the texts of the Hebrew Bible, the origins of the writings of the New Testament derive from various contexts, even if the specifics remain unknown to us. The literature of the New Testament circulated widely and was edited as the documents made their way throughout the ancient Mediterranean world. One need only look at the opening of the Gospel of Luke to see that other Gospel accounts were in circulation: "many have undertaken to compile a narrative" (Luke 1:1). Even a cursory reading of the multiple endings a reader finds at the conclusion of the Gospel of Mark reveals clear evidence of significant editing, possibly from various regions in the Greco-Roman world. Together, the texts of the Hebrew Bible and the (Greek) New Testament show that they have always been tied to and shaped by the historical, social, and cultural contexts of their writers, editors, and readers who came from various geographical locales surrounding the ancient Great (Mediterranean) Sea.

The Bible has never stopped traveling, and it has traveled well beyond the confines of Western culture. Some of the earliest Jesus followers constituted communities in North Africa, dating to the first or early second centuries CE. Christianity gradually spread further on the African continent, and in the fourth century CE it became the official religion of Ethiopia. Reaching South and East Asia by the third century CE, the Bible continued to take root in contexts quite different from the ancient Mediterranean and the regions that would later be known as Europe. The Chinese Jesus Sutras, based partly on the second-century Syriac Teachings of the Apostles that had been translated into Chinese, date to the seventh to eighth centuries CE. The Jesus Sutras illustrate how the Bible, Buddhist ideas, and the teachings of Lao-tzu could converge and influence one another in reciprocal ways. These are but a few examples of the Bible's wide reach in the world in late antiquity.

In the Jewish Diaspora (see **"Diaspora," p. 1338**), the Bible took root in Jewish life not only in the Levant and the Middle East, but in locations around the world through the centuries, especially in northern and eastern Europe, Spain, Portugal, North Africa, and later, in the United States. Decades after the Shoah (the Holocaust), the world's largest Jewish populations reside in Israel and the United States, in that order. Before and after the Holocaust, the Bible and its rabbinic interpretations have maintained a central importance in Jewish practice.

Claims rooted in particular interpretations of the Bible inform the globally significant politics concerning Palestine and the current state of Israel. While many factors went into the establishment of the state of Israel in 1948, its official declaration reflects a covenantal claim, calling the land "the birthplace of the Jewish people." In turn, many American Christian evangelicals have strongly supported Israel, viewing it as God-given to the Jews and arguing that the Jewish return to Zion is a sign of the end times that will herald Christ's second coming. Jewish settlers claim a covenantal right to additional territory that has been home to Palestinians on the occupied West Bank, which the settlers call by their biblical names, Judea and Samaria. These examples, along with countless others from the history of Christian appropriation of biblical texts and traditions, show how, with varying motivations and from differing perspectives, interpreters have drawn on the Bible to justify political claims and the actions that accompany them.

The Bible's place in Christian missionary movements is well attested and implicated in the modern history of European and American colonialism. For Western missionary enterprises, the "Great

Commission" (so-called in many Christian traditions) served as a catalyst for their contemporary efforts: "Go therefore and make disciples of all nations, baptizing them in the name of the Father and of the Son and of the Holy Spirit and teaching them to obey everything that I have commanded you" (Matt. 28:19–20). Some segments of the populations on the continents of Africa, Asia, and Latin America responded favorably to these missionary strategies, presumably because Christianity had entered these shores in earlier centuries. However, many also recognized and opposed the Western values that accompanied the gospel promoted by various Western Bible societies. This disjunction was not always clear to all missionary advocates. Recipients who welcomed their contributions often did so while combining this "new teaching" with indigenous and cultural sensitivities, practices, and ideas.

In Africa, cultural awareness rose up among the attentive, best exemplified in an African saying: "When white missionaries came to Africa, they possessed the Bible while Africans held the land; soon after, the West owned the land and Africans were granted the Bible." This commodification—the Bible in exchange for the land—has been problematized in contemporary African biblical scholarship ever since.

In Asia, a context that includes multiple religious belongings, ongoing hermeneutical challenges collect around traditions that continue to combine Western interpretive preferences with Buddhist, Taoist, and Confucian traditions in some regions and Hindu traditions in other regions. The Western privileging of "historical reconstruction" of the biblical text (see **"The Bible and Methods," pp. 2148–49**) must be continually balanced by the desire to use the biblical stories to reshape new ways of being "Christian" in the contemporary setting.

In Latin America, the historical dominance of Catholic (missionary) Christianity has instilled in Central and South American communities a privileging of the Church's interpretive practices rather than a more "democratic" reading strategy of the Bible among individual members. Even with this influence, an emphasis on passages that acknowledge (explicitly or implicitly) a view of the biblical God's preference for the "poor" has led to the origins of a liberation theological reading strategy that has, in turn, influenced wide swaths of Bible readers throughout the world.

In recent years, postcolonial biblical interpretation, in particular, has shown how the Bible can be read in new ways in contexts where it was long linked with imperialism and exploitation. This development is due, in part, to the growing number of scholars who live in (formerly European) colonized locations. On one hand, it is quite common for Western interpreters to read sympathetically the direction and point of view that ancient texts posit. However, this way of reading "with the grain" of a text is not the only way readers can engage biblical texts. Postcolonial interpreters recognize the complicated effects of colonized spaces and may see more readily some of the complex dynamics at work in biblical texts that other readers miss. For example, it is not uncommon for (formerly) colonized people to practice the languages, customs, and political strategies of their (former) colonizers; many communities continue to experience the effects of historical colonization, as well as current forms of economic, cultural, and political neocolonialism. When reading the story of Ruth, many postcolonial readers will recognize the "third space" Ruth inhabits, a space in which Ruth is no longer fully Moabite (because she chooses to join Naomi) and is not fully Israelite either (she is called "Ruth the Moabite" throughout the story). For some postcolonial thinkers, this characterization of Ruth speaks to the reality of their contemporary experience.

Over the past century, Christianity has grown significantly in regions outside of Europe and the Americas. The Global North once dominated the so-called Christian world, with 82 percent of Christians living in the North. Today there are many more Christians in the Global South than in the North. As of 2019, the North constituted 33 percent of the world's Christian population. Moreover, the trend is expected to continue in the foreseeable future. In recent decades, both sub-Saharan Africa and the Asia-Pacific have seen marked increases in the number of Christian adherents in their regions. Africa is now the continent with the greatest number of Christians in the world, with Central and South America a close second. This means that Christianity is much more a global religion than it once was, and Christian interpretation of biblical texts must be examined in specific world contexts. With such shifting demographics have come new modes of biblical interpretation, including contextual and postcolonial approaches to reading biblical texts, and feminist interpretive methods that interact with both.

Contextual biblical interpretation is important for the Bible throughout the world, including in the United States and Europe. Especially where higher concentrations of Christians live, it can be

easy to assume that the biblical text says and means the same thing to all readers, and that there is only one right interpretation to seek. Instead, contextual approaches to the Bible reveal how all our readings are informed, in part, by the world of the reader, whether that reader is Jewish or Christian, or of a different or no religious identity. Our histories and our contexts, no matter who we are, shape the lenses through which we read and interact with the Bible. Putting multiple interpretations in dialogue with each other greatly enriches the experience of engaging the Bible.

The Bible, Gender, and Sexuality

Stacy Davis and Mary F. Foskett

Using the tools of feminist theory and queer theory and informed by gender studies, scholars and students have analyzed the Bible's images of gender and sexuality for the past several decades. The results have shown how the patriarchy or male dominance that was a part of ancient culture as well as the ways that ideas about sexuality in the Bible are stipulated are quite different from modern understandings of sexual orientation or the meaning of sexual activity.

With some important exceptions noted later in this essay, in particular the presence of female prophets, the Hebrew Bible describes a world with particular roles for women and men—ideal women are submissive wives and mothers, while ideal men are wealthy, powerful warriors and leaders of their families. One example of this gender differentiation is in the stories of the patriarchs in Genesis. Abraham fights to rescue his nephew and even tries to save the cities of Sodom and Gomorrah (Gen. 14 and 18), while Sarah's primary role in the story is to give birth miraculously to Isaac in her old age (Gen. 21) and continue the family line as well as prepare food for Abraham's unexpected angelic guests in Gen. 18 (though Abraham also brings and serves food). While Isaac becomes wealthy and the father of twins, Esau and Jacob, Rebekah must use deception in order to fulfill God's promise to her that her younger son will be the dominant one, helping Jacob to gain the blessing Isaac had prepared for Esau (Gen. 25–27). Jacob later becomes wealthy while fathering multiple children with his two wives, Leah and Rachel, and with their enslaved women, Bilhah and Zilpah (Gen. 29–30). In these stories, women's primary role is to bear children; the barrenness of Sarah, Rebekah, and Rachel was a major development in each of their stories. Gender roles in the Hebrew Bible are not limited to human characters alone. Because God is personified as a male, God is viewed as a powerful father, freeing God's children from slavery in Exodus. Ancient Israelites imagined God as the premier warrior, with the descriptor YHWH Sabaoth, or "Lord of hosts" (armies) used in 1 Sam. 1:11; 2 Sam. 5:10; 6:2, 18; 7:8, 26, 27; 1 Kgs. 18:15; 2 Kgs. 3:14; 1 Chr. 11:9; 17:7, 24; and elsewhere in the books of Psalms, Isaiah, Jeremiah, Amos, Haggai, Zechariah, and Malachi. However, a few texts also imagine God as the mother of the people (Deut. 32:18; Isa. 66:13) or a laboring woman who will create a better world for her children (Isa. 42:14).

Gender roles in the literature of the New Testament vary from the Hebrew Bible insofar as the New Testament includes few couples among those in the circle associated with Jesus and his followers (Elizabeth and Zechariah and Mary and Joseph in Luke 1–2, Jairus and his unnamed wife in Mark 5:40 and Luke 8:51 and 56, Ananias and Sapphira in Acts 5:1–11, and Priscilla and Aquila in Acts 18:26 and Rom. 16:3–4). The many women who appear in the Gospels are most often unmarried or widowed or appear apart from any mention of a husband. Women also work, earn and spend money, travel, and support the Jesus movement with their finances (Luke 8:1–3). While the cultural and social milieu of these texts presupposes that women will marry and bear children, the New Testament literature often, though not uniformly, places greater value on celibacy and remaining single than on marriage and procreation. The significance of the natal family is minimized by Jesus (Luke 11:27–28), and in both the Gospels and the letters of Paul, marriage is seen as an unnecessary distraction or, at best, a prophylactic measure to prevent one from committing sexual sin (1 Cor. 7:9).

Despite this rather dim view of marriage, Jesus teaches against divorce, either absolutely (Mark 10:11–12; Luke 16:18) or with the exception of cases involving *porneia* (Matt. 5:32; 19:9), which is undefined but suggestive of something illicit (see the NRSVue's "sexual immorality"). Although the Gospels teach against both divorce and remarriage, marital separation is yet acknowledged and even encouraged "for the sake of the kingdom of God" (Luke 18:28–30).

Moreover, familial relations and roles take a back seat to the fictive kinship that Jesus promotes in the Synoptic Gospels. He teaches his followers that "whoever comes to me and does not hate father and mother, wife and children, brothers and sisters, yes, and even life itself, cannot be my disciple" (Luke 14:26; cf. Mark 10:37). When he is told that his mother and brothers are looking for him, he replies, "Who are my mother and my brothers?" (Mark 3:32–33; cf. Matt. 12:46–50 and

Luke 8:19–21). Looking around at those gathered with him, he adds, "Here are my mother and my brothers! Whoever does the will of God is my brother and sister and mother" (Mark 3:34–35). Here Jesus redefines kinship so that the newly formed family, in which fathers, husbands, and wives have no role, replaces one's family of origin. In contrast to the Synoptic Gospels, the Gospel of John suggests that Jesus values his mother's unique role. At the cross, Jesus ensures that his mother will be cared for after his death, thus creating a new mother-son relationship between the woman who will survive him and the disciple whom he loves (John 19:26–27). With that said, it is only the later epistolary writings, such as Colossians, Ephesians, and 1 Peter, that conceive of a well-ordered household in idealized, Christian terms.

While gender roles are delineated clearly in the Hebrew Bible, its literature does not have a modern concept of sexual orientation. Heteronormativity (i.e., the idea that opposite-sex relationships are the normal types of sexual expression) is simply presumed. Sex acts themselves are defined by the idea that men penetrate women (*zakar*, a Hebrew word for "male" that may come from an Arabic root meaning "to be sharp," may have its opposite in *neqevah*, a Hebrew word for "female," which comes from a root meaning "to pierce"); women, due to their anatomy, are meant to be pierced. So the prohibition against male same-sex intercourse in Lev. 18:22 forbids men from taking the penetrative role in anal intercourse (to "lie with a male as with a woman"). There is no corresponding prohibition against female same-sex intercourse and no discussion of whether sex acts were considered expressions of love and desire, two elements that are a part of contemporary discussions of sexual orientation. Sex is a means to an end in the Hebrew Bible, specifically the production of legitimate children; in a patriarchal society, it was important that men knew the paternity of their offspring and that their authority over the women in their household was not challenged. This is why laws prohibiting certain sex acts between women and men in Lev. 18 and Deut. 22 focus on the rights of the husband or father to whom the wife or daughter belongs. Laws against rape also focus on the rights of the wronged man and not the violence done against the woman. The stories of the rape of Dinah in Gen. 34, the Levite's concubine in Judg. 19, Bathsheba in 2 Sam. 11, and Tamar in 2 Sam. 13 all end with men punishing other men for the actions against "their" women, as the primary violation is against the men's honor and not the women's bodies. Modern sexual assault laws do not view women this way.

Like the Hebrew Bible, the New Testament emerges from a context very different from our own, one that considers matters of sex in terms of an overriding interest in status and gender. Neither modern notions of sexual orientation nor contemporary concern for the biological sex of sexual partners should be anachronistically imposed on New Testament texts. In the Greco-Roman context, what mattered most was the maintenance of status. Taking for granted that men could be sexually attracted to both men and women, the protocol for those who held the highest social status—namely, freeborn Roman men—focused on several factors, including the need to remain in the active/penetrative role in a sexual encounter. New Testament texts should be read with this ancient cultural context in mind. While scholars debate how to specifically interpret what Paul means in Rom. 1:26–27, what is beyond question is that readers must read the letter's references to homoerotic relations according to ancient presuppositions about sexuality.

While its context is more patriarchal than twenty-first-century ideas about gender and sexuality, the Bible does contain stories and metaphors that feminist and queer theorists note are the opposite of what one would expect to see in an ancient text. The relationship between David and Jonathan in 1 Sam. 18–20 and 2 Sam. 1 is deeply intimate. Even the violence of the marriage metaphors in Hosea, Jeremiah, and Ezekiel, in which disobedient Israel is the unfaithful wife that her husband God must violently punish, has the male Israelites personified as a woman. Gender roles and expectations in the Hebrew Bible can be unexpectedly fluid. For example, prophets are presumed to be male, but Miriam in Exodus, Deborah in Judges, and Huldah in 2 Kings are called prophets and lead praise services, select warriors, and counsel kings.

In the New Testament, John's Gospel employs a range of gendered metaphors and images in its portrayal of Jesus. John not only casts Jesus as both Sophia and Logos; he conceives of Jesus as the perfect image of the Father (John 1:14, 18) while also employing birthing imagery to illustrate Jesus's mission. From the beginning of the Gospel, John aligns Jesus's central purpose with rebirth by claiming that "to all who received him, who believed in his name, he gave power to become children of God, who were born, not of blood or of the will of the flesh or of the will of

man, but of God" (John 1:12–13; cf. 3:3). Later, when Jesus's crucified body is pierced by a sword, a mix of water and blood flows forth, suggesting both baptismal and childbearing imagery (John 19:34). As in the Hebrew Bible, gender imagery and roles in New Testament texts may be more fluid than readers presume.

The Bible, Race, and Ethnicity

Emerson B. Powery

The most stimulating stories of human history have always involved the coming together of people of different ethnoracial backgrounds, and the Bible and its interpreters both shed light on and have profoundly shaped these interactions as well as people's sense of their own identities. As socially constructed categories, "race" and "ethnicity" have profoundly affected the way many have organized their worlds. The terms will be used interchangeably in this essay and often combined into one adjectival form, *ethnoracial*, as a broad reference to groups with different cultural backgrounds.

Though centered on the people of Israel, the Bible includes collections of narratives, laws, and writings about Israel's migration, interactions, and conflicts with other ethnoracial people groups.

- According to Genesis, YHWH scattered people "abroad over the face of all the earth" into various regions and places (Gen. 11:8–9). God then established a covenant with Abraham to "make of you a great nation" and to bless "all the families of the earth" (Gen. 12:1–3). The story of Exodus opens with Israel's oppression in the land of Egypt. Joshua and Judges relay the ongoing military conflicts between Israel and various Canaanite groups. Despite numerous stories of ethnic conflicts, Israel's Torah (Law) testifies to the people's commitments to non-Israelites in their midst: to grant fair wages to poorer Israelites and immigrants (Lev. 19:10; Deut. 24:14), to seek the benefits of the Sabbath for the immigrant as well as for the Israelite (Exod. 20:10), and to include non-Israelites in Israel's worship practices (Num. 9:14; 15:14–16). The story of Ruth is a classic example, in which a Moabite woman cares for her widowed Israelite mother-in-law and, eventually, becomes an ancestor of Israel's most memorable king, David. Biblical stories attest to numerous interethnic marriages, even while debates about the maintenance of these relationships continued in some circles (cf. Ezra 9–10; Neh. 13).
- The Prophetic Books also bear witness to these ethnic interactions. The prophets Hananiah and Jeremiah publicly disagree over the length of Israel's exile in Babylon (Jer. 28), even as Jeremiah encourages the exiles to settle down in the land, intermarry, and seek the welfare of the place in which they find themselves (Jer. 29). Several prophets pronounce divine oracles on the nations surrounding Israel. A few prophets envision YHWH's temple as a place of reconciliation for all nations (Isa. 56:7; Zech. 8:23). The paradox of Jonah's story reveals much about ancient attitudes toward others. Despite the successful mission to Assyria, the account concludes with Jonah's anguish over God's merciful action toward this anti-Israelite group (Jonah 4).
- The wisdom tradition appeals to non-Israelite traditions as part of its public wisdom pronouncements. Sections of the Proverbs (22:17–24:22) may have been borrowed from Egypt. The story of Job is comparable to Babylonian theodicy accounts, and the Wisdom of Solomon and Sirach are clearly products of their Hellenistic environment.
- The Gospels emphasize Jesus's mission as one to the "lost sheep of the house of Israel" (Matt. 10:6; 15:24), even while reluctantly expressing his occasional forays among non-Jews. He heals one enslaved to a gentile centurion, who himself is a kind benefactor of the local Jewish community (Luke 7:1–10). He casts out a demon from a non-Jewish Gerasene on "the other side of the sea" (Mark 5:1–20). At the behest of a persistent Syrophoenician woman, he heals her daughter from afar (Mark 7:24–30). He imagines a "Samaritan"—considered a "foreigner" in some Jewish circles (Luke 17:18; John 8:48)—as a merciful human being.
- The shift to a full-blown vision of gentile inclusion among Christ followers energizes the apostle Paul's mission (Gal. 1:16; 3:8–9). Paul recalls one of the confessions of the Christ-following community—one offered at its baptismal ceremonies: "There is no longer Jew or Greek; there is no longer slave or free; there is no longer male and female, for all of you are one in Christ Jesus" (Gal. 3:28). Not all Jewish Christ followers shared Paul's emphasis (cf. Acts 15).

- Despite the language of an increasingly inclusive Jesus movement, the Acts of the Apostles fails to trace the missionary service of any leading *gentile* figure who becomes an active Christ follower during the early decades of the movement. Rather, the diverse ethnic makeup of the Jesus followers stems from another direction: within Judaism itself. One key component of this direction is the story of Pentecost in Acts, in which multiple languages are spoken and Jews "from every people" are present (Acts 2). For the writer of Acts, then, the Jews become, as Cynthia Baker stipulates, the *"model*—not merely his *foil* or *counterpoint*—for imagining a universal, multiethnic, spirit-filled community" ("From Every Nation under Heaven," in *Prejudice and Christian Beginnings*). It is crucial to avoid the mistakes of past interpreters who assumed that "Jew" meant a "singular" ethnic identity and "Christian" meant a "universal" identity encompassing all ethnicities (whether Jewish or gentile Christ followers) and that this distinction between the two "groups" made the latter term more suggestive of global inclusion. The distinction between Jew and Christ follower—with respect to ethnicity—must be held in tension with another claim the story of Acts makes about the unity of all human races: "from one ancestor" God created all people (Acts 17:26). The final book of the New Testament, Revelation, offers an eschatological view of an inclusive global gathering centered on the Messiah figure (i.e., the Lamb) and God's throne (Rev. 7).

In the North American context, the ethnic themes of the Bible have continually informed the American historical landscape. Race and ethnicity are cultural—not biological—phenomena. As a manifestation of these phenomena, the interactions between the Bible's ethnoracial themes and North American interpreters have left an indelible mark on U.S. history. Many U.S. interpreters over time attempted to utilize the ethnic-geographic distinctions they discovered in the Bible to map racial distinctions onto the categories they experienced in their own contemporary worlds. Genesis 10—with its so-called Table of Nations (a label imposed by these later interpreters)—provided much ideological fodder for this engagement, producing questions like, What was the racial makeup of Adam and Eve? What was the "mark" placed on Cain's head for the murder of his brother Abel, and how did this relate to skin color? What geographical regions traced their ancestry to one of Noah's sons, Shem, Ham, and Japheth, and did this express God's favor for some groups over others? These interpreters cared less about what these stories meant in their ancient settings—for example, how Noah's curse on "Canaan" (Ham's son) provided justification for Israel's wars against the Canaanites—than how to use them in slotting modern people into racial hierarchies.

The U.S. histories of various ethnoracial groups have also given shape to how some contemporary readers engage biblical stories and texts within their respective communities. U.S. Latino readers may place (im)migration at the forefront of their hermeneutical engagement. After all, the Bible frequently describes the movement of people from one region to another. Many stories are about people on the move. How might readers interpret these ancient accounts differently if they read them from the perspective of migrants themselves rather than those who welcome migrants (from the side of privilege; see Efraín Agosto and Jacqueline M. Hidalgo, *Latinxs, the Bible, and Migration*)? Asian American interpreters may consider how their sense of marginality in a dominant (white) society or their existence between "American" and "Asian" cultures affects their engagement with biblical stories about characters who also live hybrid lives (see Mary F. Foskett and Jeffrey Kah-Jin Kuan, *Ways of Being, Ways of Reading: Asian American Biblical Interpretation*). Native American readers may reconsider their relationship to the land in light of Israel's entrance into Canaan. Such interpreters may interrogate these stories from the perspective of the Canaanites who resided in the land prior to the arrival of the new migrants (see Robert Warrior, "Canaanites, Cowboys, and Indians: Deliverance, Conquest, and Liberation Theology Today"). African American interpreters may press beyond an investigation of biblical characters of African descent (e.g., Ebed-Melech, the Cushite who rescued Jeremiah, or the Ethiopian eunuch who received Philip's baptism) to wrestle with the marginal characters of every biblical story in light of their history as a marginalized group within the American context (see Brian Blount et al., *True to Our Native Land: An African American New Testament Commentary*).

The Bible is full of tales about ethnic groups, conflicts, and migrations, and we—contemporary readers of various ethnic histories and social engagements—do well to heed these stories and think together about how they can aid in the discussions that are critical to the thriving of contemporary multiethnic societies.

The Bible and Social Justice

Davina C. Lopez

The Bible remains a classic resource for considering, appraising, and understanding a wide range of the ways people relate to the world, especially when those relations are not right. These texts reflect the ways in which humans have negotiated (in)justice, trauma, resilience, hope, despair, empathy, strangeness, scarcity, cooperation, prejudice, homelessness, joy, division, reconciliation, and so on. The Bible features people on the move, strangers in their own land and in other strange lands, who imagine what is possible out of mostly impossible circumstances. Biblical stories are multilayered and complex and cannot be reduced to any one element, just like humans. The question, then, about the Bible and social justice—an intersection that may seem simple—is this: How does one stay focused on the complexity of the human experience?

How one approaches social justice and the Bible will depend on several preliminary considerations, including (a) what one assumes justice is and how one thinks it operates in cultures, (b) how one perceives the ways biblical texts respond to their original ancient worlds and communities of engagement and how justice may have been defined in those contexts, and (c) whether and how the Bible, as Scripture, offers resources for reflection on and action toward justice in our world today. On this last point, there is no shortage of examples of biblical texts being deployed in the service of social justice. Thus, the astute student of biblical literature will want to ask how biblical texts, contexts, and interpretations of the texts throughout history inform a question as expansive as how the Bible and social justice are related to each other.

Imagining Social Justice

In a basic sense, social justice refers to the conditions of right relations—among people, creatures, and the planet—that enable the flourishing of all. Unfortunately, history and culture have shown that justice is most visible when it is absent. That is, persistent and pervasive injustice—when some humans are threatened and traumatized by other humans—provides the occasion for articulating notions of justice. It is through the threat and trauma wrought by injustice that justice, what it means to be human in a world that often seems inhuman, can be imagined and manifested. The more obvious and pernicious the injustice, the more urgent the desire becomes for justice as repair or redress.

As a precondition for right relations, it can be helpful to think about justice in both ancient and modern contexts as an intersectional mode of redressing—of setting right—injustice. We can imagine right relations along three axes: economic, sociocultural, and political. Economic justice is a means of ensuring that economic structures guarantee people the resources they need to survive. When resources are distributed unequally, a redistribution of them is redress. Sociocultural justice ensures that cultural values guarantee everyone a chance to be seen, to interact, and to have a voice. When cultural hierarchies render people and groups invisible based on their identities or affinities, sociocultural recognition is redress. And political justice ensures that political boundaries guarantee everyone equal participation in civic processes. When political rules deny people and groups full participation as citizens, political representation is redress. Each of these intersecting modes of justice cannot be understood or realized without the others.

Contextualizing Social Justice in Biblical Worlds

Biblical texts across the Hebrew Bible, deuterocanonical/apocryphal books, and the New Testament betray different orientations toward and perspectives on social justice. Not all authors use the same rhetorical strategies, nor do they emphasize the same types of characters, practices, and ways of knowing and being. The Bible reflects the multiple ancient contexts in which its texts were produced, including Akkadian, Babylonian, Assyrian, Egyptian, Persian, Greek, and Roman elements. While it is difficult to pinpoint the exact moment that many of these texts were initially written, scholars tend to maintain that biblical texts were likely composed by people who were on the underside of history, those with less access to political power. Ignoring these ancient historical contexts

ignores a central hallmark of these texts: they are a collection of minority literature that is distinct in that they envision right relations and social justice from the perspective of those for whom injustice is a daily affair.

Even as biblical texts do not share internally consistent approaches to the question of social justice, there are narrative threads that can be found across the Testaments. Injustice consistently takes the form of a maldistribution of resources, a lack of concern and visibility for the other, and a distinct lack of access to political processes. This is most notable in the narrative of the enslaved Israelites who, even after liberation, are unable to self-govern or stay on their own land. It is no wonder, then, that biblical texts also extol concern for the dispossessed, prophesy the total redistribution of resources and land, and claim that the deity will cause the mighty to fall. The Bible contains a variety of metaphors and expressions of injustice, from the everyday to the apocalyptic, as well as myriad images of what justice will look like—from the simple availability of food to a new world entirely. Some biblical texts connect social justice to knowledge, wisdom, fairness, and community; other texts configure justice as a legal matter or a series of punishments for violations; and still others wonder whether justice is possible and, if so, whether it even means anything. All told, the range of ideas about social justice in the Bible reflects the diversity of the ideas and approaches of its ancient contexts.

Social Justice and the Bible as Scripture

Contrary to what some readers might assume, biblical texts offer no easy answers and no one correct way to read and understand them, particularly when it comes to contemporary issues of urgent import and interest like social justice. Rather, these texts generate lots of questions. Engaging them in an academic setting makes it possible to explore a range of ideas and perspectives for our contemporary questions, knowing that there are multiple ways of seeing and that it is possible to explore these materials without having to identify with any group or worldview. Though multiple groups, particularly religious ones, claim that the Bible belongs to them alone, it is a collection of texts about the human experience that belongs to everyone—and to no one. That is, one can read the Bible with contemporary issues in mind without subscribing to a particular religious outlook or commitment.

Similarly, it is difficult to overestimate the presence and influence of the Bible in world cultures. These texts, interpreted over time, have endured innumerable afterlives beyond the ancient world, shaping (and being shaped by) our cultures of origin indelibly, both within and beyond what we call "religion." Engaging the Bible means understanding major aspects of human cultures, histories, and experiences more fully, including a range of ideas about justice in different cultures. The Bible continues to play a critical role as a site for the production of narratives about humans, worlds, and worldviews, and we have a critical role to play as we engage such narratives with open eyes and minds, particularly regarding big questions with big implications.

The Bible has endured a venerable history of interpretation and deployment when it comes to social justice. As Scriptures, these texts have been, and continue to be, used by people from all walks of life whose perceptions of social justice may conflict with one another. Biblical texts have been used to establish, challenge, and reimagine ethical, social, sexual, and racial/ethnic hierarchies, inside and outside organized religious groups, by those belonging to both historically dominant and historically marginalized communities. The Bible has been a presence in arguments for and against slavery, gender equity, bodily autonomy and freedom, economic security, civil rights, and interreligious and international affairs. As with much regarding biblical literature, no reader appears to be neutral in their approach to these texts, the question of what social justice should entail, and whether and how these texts may be used as support and inspiration for such projects. How widely, and for vastly different purposes, the texts of the Bible have been used on the ground in communities shows us how important the stakes are even today for grappling with and understanding both these texts and how they have been interpreted over time.

What to Remember about the Bible and Social Justice

Every historical context will have its own complications and opportunities for observing injustice and imagining justice. Humans have long struggled with who counts, who is visible, who gets to participate, how to ensure equity and fairness, and whether all this means that those with more

should give more. It would be a mistake to say that the ancients were better or worse than we are now in terms of how to deal with injustice and justice. The idea that social justice is a precondition for right relations seems common in both ancient and contemporary worlds. Interpreting biblical texts in light of calls for social justice in our world occurs at a highly electric intersection of realities. We live in a cultural matrix where social location and identity claims, sophisticated technology, a longing for connection and belonging, local and generational trauma, questions about the solvency of political systems, and persistent anxiety about material circumstances and future prospects all shape our experience.

Biblical stories are embodied myths that raise questions and respond to perceptions of social injustice and justice. The Bible thus can be framed as a series of responses to an inhumane world, where people are seeking to find answers and organize and order their world in ways that make life more habitable. In that respect, the Bible is a critical, distinct document from the ancient world—as opposed to other ancient texts where the gods act randomly, divisively, chaotically, amorally, and often without regard for human flourishing. The structure, organization, and purpose of the Bible's social justice visions—though internally divergent—are critical components of its moral horizon, although interpreting and applying these visions is never easy or simple.

The Bible and Visual Art

Jennifer L. Koosed and Brent A. Strawn

The Bible is a work of art—though a literary, not a visual, one. But because the verbal and visual arts have long been seen as siblings, it is not surprising to discover that the biblical text is related to and reflected in various artistic forms, from ancient to modern times.

Beginning first with antiquity, objects from the ancient world can often facilitate contemporary understanding of the Bible. The smallness of many oil lamps from the first century CE, for example, casts fresh light on the parable of the Ten Young Women in Matt. 25:1–13—these lamps were often no larger than three inches across at their widest point. These lamps could not hold much oil and would not burn for very long. These facts clarify several details in the parable: why extra oil would be needed and why the young women who brought extra oil with them are deemed wise as opposed to those who did not, who are called foolish (vv. 2–4). The insight that the women needed to prepare to burn their lamps for a longer time suggests that Jesus's parable envisions a longer, perhaps even indefinite, delay of the bridegroom's return, and so those hearing the parable needed to be prepared accordingly (v. 13; cf. Mark 13:33–37; Luke 12:35–38). This example—one among many—shows how the material culture of the ancient world can help modern readers make sense of what the biblical authors simply assumed in the context of their everyday lives.

The same is true for objects from the ancient world that are more artistic by our standards, though it must be stressed that even highly functional objects—like oil lamps—often contain decorative elements. Even when they do not, physical objects impact our senses in various ways and comprise part of the visual culture of a society. A visual approach to the Bible and art recognizes that human beings make meaning of the world in many ways: through literature and texts but also through art and images. Artistic remains afford insight into ancient meaning making, which helps us interpret ancient texts. What does it mean, for example, to refer to God or an enemy as a lion (see, e.g., Hos. 5:14 and Ps. 17:12, respectively)? In much contemporary parlance, lion imagery is usually associated with bravery. In the ancient world, however, it was typically associated with threat, terror, and death. Lions are super predators after all. Ancient artistic depictions reinforce and confirm that uppermost in ancient Israelites' minds when they thought of lions was not bravery but, rather, danger (fig. 1).

Fig. 1 Scarab seal; 14 x 11 x 6 mm; Tell el-Far'ah (South), 1292–1070 BCE. After Brent A. Strawn, *What Is Stronger than a Lion? Leonine Image and Metaphor in the Hebrew Bible and the Ancient Near East* (Orbis Biblicus et Orientalis 212; Fribourg: Academic Press, 2005), 382 fig. 3.12.

Moving forward in time, we can observe a kind of reversal of influence: whereas ancient art and artifacts helped shape the Bible (or at least the biblical authors), once the Bible came to be recognized as a collection of sacred writings, it served as a source of inspiration to countless artists for millennia and in every sort of media. These creative individuals were not always constrained by the details of a particular biblical passage but frequently felt free—or, perhaps better, inspired—to go further: representing and thus interpreting the Bible in fresh and innovative ways. In fact, it is often the *lack* of textual detail in a passage that leads to artistic invention and creativity. Most biblical narrative is sparse, leaving out a number of things that visual artists must include in their work—the appearance and clothing of characters or the appearance of the landscape and architecture, along with a host of other visual elements. In the absence of such details, artists have often had to provide them entirely on their own. Art inspired by the Bible thus invariably reflects the artistic and cultural styles of the artists themselves and the periods within which they worked: from Renaissance depictions of Jesus standing in Italian landscapes to modern depictions of him as African, as Asian, or even as a woman. When it comes to art inspired by the Bible, every single choice, whether of color, composition, form, and so on, is an act of interpretation, whether or not the choice is conscious or intentional. In this way, the artist is a biblical interpreter working in a nontextual mode: as a visual exegete.

During times when literacy rates were low, biblical art often served to instruct the mostly illiterate masses. Beautiful mosaics and frescos of biblical scenes are found in ancient synagogues. The walls of the Dura-Europos synagogue (Syria, third century CE), for example, depict Moses and the exodus from Egypt in vibrant detail, among many other biblical scenes. In two pronouncements, Gregory the Great (pope from 590 to 604 CE) defended artistic representation of Scripture as a way to convey ideas and evoke emotions, useful both to support the faithful and to proselytize pagans as Christianity expanded across Europe and Western Asia. In the Roman Empire, the Holy Roman Empire, and the Byzantine Empire alike, art performed important pedagogical and liturgical functions, even as distinctive artistic conventions and theological understandings developed. In many periods, artists enjoyed greater freedom to represent certain aspects of a biblical character or probe the ambiguities of a biblical account than their clerical counterparts—imagining and representing a great number of things left unsaid by the biblical authors. At the same time, the explicit content of some passages sometimes allowed artists to depict certain subjects, like sex or violence, that were otherwise forbidden during the time in which they worked.

In the medieval and Renaissance periods in the Christian world, the vast majority of painting and sculpture engaged biblical texts and religious themes. The magnificent Sistine Chapel in the Vatican exemplifies the Western confluence of artistic expression and biblical interpretation. The subjects painted on the walls and ceilings of the chapel span biblical stories from the creation of the world to the final judgment. Far more than mere decoration—or even education—the paintings were intended to become part of a religious experience for viewers as they move through the chapel. Commissioned by Popes Sixtus IV, Julius II, and Paul III, the art in the Sistine Chapel is also a reflection of the political and economic power of the Renaissance Catholic Church. The wall frescos were painted first by some of the great Italian masters of the day, including Perugino (ca. 1450–1523), Pinturicchio (1454–1513), Botticelli (ca. 1445–1510), and Ghirlandaio (1448–94). Michelangelo (1475–1564) painted the ceiling from 1508 to 1512 CE. It is said that he conceived of and executed the design based on his own reading of the Bible. The ceiling consists of nine panels depicting scenes from Genesis, including the well-known fresco *The Creation of Adam*. In the image, both God and Adam have their arms outstretched, fingertips barely touching, thereby capturing at once the power and intimacy of creation. Of course, even this iconic image belies the artist's own context: Michelangelo depicts both Adam and God as European men of his time.

Later eras led to new relationships between the Bible and art. In the Western world, the Enlightenment, the Protestant Reformation, and the rise of the nation-state all contributed to the rise of widespread literacy but also to the slow decline of the power of the Christian church. In the Eastern world, the Byzantine Empire fell to the Ottomans in 1453, replacing Christian rule with a Muslim state. At the same time, globally, Christianity expanded its reach through colonization in the Americas, Africa, and parts of Asia. Civil rights movements followed the collapse of the Western empires, transforming societies, making many more democratic and egalitarian. As a result of such developments, artists gained more freedom in their creative expression and subject matter beyond religious themes. Even in the midst of secularizing societies in the West and elsewhere, though, the Bible has

continued to inspire countless works of art, which serve as both an expression of faith and an exploration of the human condition. One example is the work of the African American artist Henry Ossawa Tanner (1859–1937), who was raised in the African Methodist Episcopal Church. Tanner's paintings render biblical scenes in striking and naturalistic ways and include such masterworks as *Daniel in the Lion's Den* (1895) and *The Annunciation* (1898; fig. 2). Jewish artists of the twentieth century such as Marc Chagall, George Segal, and Samuel Bak also turned to biblical themes, connecting their art with the history of the Jewish people. Bak's (1933–) fractured biblical iconography—like the broken rainbow—serves to express both continuity and discontinuity after the Holocaust (fig. 3).

Biblical art has power and exercises interpretive influence. Common visual representations of well-known biblical stories can sometimes be so captivating that they overpower the original text on which they are based. Examples include depictions of Paul falling from his horse during his vision of Christ, the three wise men following the star of Bethlehem, or a snake with a human face and limbs in the garden of Eden. The biblical texts that inspired these images do not mention a horse, nor do they specify the number of magi, nor do they say that the serpent had human body parts. Readers might reasonably imagine such details, of course, but in the artistic renditions, these images have become powerful representations that go beyond the original texts and shape subsequent readings. It is also the case that biblical art frequently draws on other nonbiblical resources for its interpretive work—including various kinds of commentary, liturgical practices (including sermons), church doctrine, theology, or other artistic expressions like music, hymnody, or poetry. Because of such influences and the demands of the work itself, artistic representation cannot avoid concretizing a biblical passage within a specific medium and from within a particular context. This means that biblical art casts light not only on the biblical text but also on the artist's own life, culture, and community. Once made, it is free to influence and shape subsequent viewers, generating new works of art—new acts of visual exegesis—which will, again and in turn, influence how the text itself is "seen" and understood.

Fig. 2 *The Annunciation*, by Henry Ossawa Tanner (1898). Courtesy of the Philadelphia Museum of Art, Pennsylvania. Purchased with the W. P. Wilstach Fund, 1899, W1899-1-1.

Fig. 3 *Icon of Loss, Elegy*, by Samuel Bak (2008). Image Courtesy of Pucker Gallery.

The Bible in Film and Media

Stacy Davis and Mary F. Foskett

The Bible has played a role in film, television, radio, and print for as long as these media have been in existence.

Film and Stage

One of the most popular biblical stories in film is the Exodus narrative, in which Moses frees the Israelites from slavery in Egypt and then leads them to Mount Sinai, where God gives Moses the Torah. After an earlier version (1923), Cecil B. DeMille directed a second major motion picture entitled *The Ten Commandments* in 1956. Since 1973, the latter version has been regularly aired on national television in the United States on the Saturday before Easter. In 1998, DreamWorks Animation released *The Prince of Egypt* (directed by Brenda Chapman, Steve Hickner, and Simon Wells), a version of the Exodus story replete with an award-winning soundtrack. This animated film was later remade for the stage.

Films drawing on or loosely inspired by stories from the New Testament are manifold. Among the most viewed are *Ben-Hur* (1959, directed by William Wyler), *King of Kings* (1961, directed by Nicholas Ray), *The Gospel according to Saint Matthew* (1964, directed by Pier Paolo Pasolini), *The Greatest Story Ever Told* (1965, directed by George Stephens, Jean Negulesco, and David Lean), *Jesus Christ Superstar* (1973, directed by Norman Jewison, based on the 1971 stage production), *Godspell* (1973, directed by David Greene, based on the 1971 musical), *The Last Temptation of Christ* (1988, directed by Martin Scorsese), *The Gospel of John* (2003, directed by Philip Saville), and *The Passion of the Christ* (2004, directed by Mel Gibson). The proliferation of such films speaks to the ongoing public interest in the story of Jesus of Nazareth, and they inevitably reflect the contemporary situations from which they emerge. For example, *The Greatest Story Ever Told*, *Godspell*, and *Jesus Christ Superstar*—all of which were produced during the American war in Vietnam—tell the story of Jesus in ways that variously signal the social tensions that emerged in the United States during that time. Another example is *The Passion of the Christ*, which was immediately controversial due to what many condemned as its anti-Semitism as well as its extensive and gratuitous violence. The latter element is understood by some observers to reflect an American ideology of experiencing persecution fueled by the terrorist attacks in New York and Washington, DC, on September 11, 2001.

While it has been common for film treatments of the story of Jesus to harmonize the Gospels in various ways, sometimes an individual Gospel has served as the basis for a production on stage or in film. *The Gospel according to Saint Matthew*, directed by Pier Paolo Pasolini and filmed in the style of Italian neorealism, takes its dialogue directly from its titular Gospel. The 2003 film *The Gospel of John* is based solely on the text of the American Bible Society's *Good News Bible*. Similarly, the play *St. Mark's Gospel*, which features a dramatic recitation of that Gospel by Alec McCowen, was performed to critical acclaim in London and New York City in 1978. A musical setting of Clarence Jordan's *Cotton Patch Gospels*, a southern American vernacular translation of the Gospels, premiered off-Broadway in 1981. Together, examples like these illustrate how the interpretation of the Bible depends on readers and artists who not only engage the text but add to its many meanings.

Indeed, alongside productions like those mentioned here is another category in which the treatment of the biblical texts is looser and thus more explicitly and artistically imaginative. Scorsese's *The Last Temptation of Christ* is a cinematic adaptation of Nikos Kazantzakis's 1955 novel of the same name. The film portrays Jesus wrestling with very human temptations, including fear, doubt, and lust. The 2013 play *Testament of Mary*, based on a novella by Colm Toibin, imagines an embittered mother of Jesus who opposes the proclamations of her son's disciples in the aftermath of his death. Productions like these are reminiscent of the long history of interpretation within both Judaism and Christianity that has filled in the literary gaps left open in the biblical texts.

Television

Television shows that are somehow based on the Bible can be divided into two types: those produced by religious companies designed for religious audiences and those created by large network

television companies. One of the central shows of the Christian Broadcasting Network (founded in 1960) is *The 700 Club*, which regularly features biblical interpretation from an evangelical Protestant perspective. The popular *VeggieTales* children's television series (with motion pictures in 2002 and 2008) retells various biblical stories like those of Esther, Noah's ark, Joshua at Jericho, Joseph, Moses and Miriam, Abraham and Sarah, David, and Jonah within a Christian framework. Within Judaism, the Jewish Broadcasting Network and Jewish Life Television also feature Bible stories. Large network television productions like *Touched by an Angel* and *Highway to Heaven* are less directly biblical but focus on the biblical idea of angels as God's messengers and servants. A more recent approach is the show *Lucifer*, which follows the character of Satan, drawing on traditions known from the Hebrew Bible and New Testament. Many other shows, like *The Bible* (2013) and *A.D.: The Bible Continues* (2015), portray select biblical narratives, sometimes across entire series.

Radio

Protestant Christian preachers like Billy Sunday (1862–1935) and Billy Graham (1918–2018) hosted some of the earliest radio shows in the United States. Graham's show, *Hour of Decision*, can still be heard on satellite radio. In the 1930s, the Rev. Charles Coughlin evangelized from a Catholic perspective; his sermons became anti-Jewish as the decade progressed, as video footage from the 1930s, shown in the documentary *Sister Rose's Passion*, indicates. Various religious groups continue to produce radio shows or even own entire radio stations. The Catholic show *Beloved and Blessed*, for example, uses the Bible, and particularly Prov. 31, to speak to women in different walks of life. Within Judaism, the Jewish Radio Network includes music and talk shows. K-LOVE is an evangelical radio media service that airs Christian contemporary music and other programming. Additionally, examples of predominantly "secular" music on mainstream radio and streaming services that refer to religious topics—including God, angels (often code for other people who are too good to be true), devils (sometimes a term for individuals who are too awful to be around), sin, and so forth—are too many to count.

Print Media

The Bible has often played a role in national journalist outlets. In terms of newspapers, the *Christian Science Monitor*, founded by Mary Baker Eddy and winner of seven Pulitzer Prizes, includes a section devoted to commentary from a Christian Science perspective, which often touches on biblical material. The *American Israelite* (formerly the *Israelite*), established in 1854 in Cincinnati, is the oldest Jewish newspaper in the United States and includes an analysis of the weekly Torah portion that is read in synagogues or temples. The *National Catholic Reporter*, founded in 1964, includes commentary on the weekly Mass readings in Catholic churches. In terms of magazines, the Protestant periodical the *Christian Century* began in 1884 and includes a weekly "Living by the Word" section, which is composed of reflections about one or more of the biblical texts found in the Revised Common Lectionary, commonly used in mainline Protestant denominations. The *Jewish Bible Quarterly* has been offering Jewish interpretations of the Bible since 1972. *Commonweal* magazine has offered Catholic perspectives on politics and culture since 1924. Aimed primarily at an evangelical audience, *Christianity Today* was founded by Billy Graham in 1956 and remains a significant magazine featuring evangelical perspectives. The Internet has exponentially furthered the way the Bible is present in print media by amplifying such content to readers around the world.

Even in the aggregate, the examples listed in this essay barely scratch the surface of the countless ways the Bible functions in various media. Given the Bible's massive impact on human civilization, especially in the West, biblical allusions, motifs, and quotations are often present in popular media, regardless of whether a given film, television show, or article (print or online) is explicitly religious.

The Bible in Music

J. Todd Hibbard

Music has been part of the human experience from as far back as we can tell. Archaeological evidence from southern Africa documents musical instruments dating to at least 10,000 BCE. When we consider the fact that the human voice can create music without accompaniment, it seems obvious that music originated much earlier than that. And since human beings often sing about what they know and love, it is no surprise that, for at least two millennia, music and song have referenced the Bible.

Both Testaments evidence the use of music in cultural, ritual, and family contexts. The book of Psalms, for example, is often thought of as a kind of hymn book for use in the Jerusalem temple. Fragments of early Christian hymns appear embedded in the New Testament (see, e.g., Phil. 2:5–11). With the closure of the canon, music *within* the Bible transitioned to music *about* the Bible. The biblical texts became resources for musical compositions in religious settings like the synagogue and church but also far beyond both. Christian hymnody, song and chanting traditions in synagogues, and modern worship music provide a seemingly endless pool of examples of how "biblical music" has figured in various liturgical and devotional contexts.

The presence and influence of the Bible in modern Western music can be traced in myriad ways, but a particularly important example is found in the work of Johann Sebastian Bach (1685–1750 CE). Bach composed hundreds of musical scores, many of which were for use in churches. These pieces often relied on the Bible for their primary source material. For example, Bach's *St. Matthew Passion* sets Matt. 26–27 to music, while his *Christmas Oratorio* combines the birth and infancy materials about Jesus found in Matthew and Luke.

After Bach, the tradition of classical composers making extensive use of the Bible continued in the work of Joseph Haydn (*Seven Last Words*), George Frideric Handel (*Messiah*), and Giuseppe Verdi (*Nabucco*), all the way to more recent twentieth-century works like Leonard Bernstein's *Jeremiah Symphony* (1942) and Arnold Schoenberg's *Moses und Aron* (1932). These composers often simply set the words of the Bible to music, but even then they are clearly *interpreters* of Scripture, not just its recorders. This is true even when the musical score lacks lyrics, as in Olivier Messiaen's 1941 *Quatuor pour la fin du temps* (*Quartet for the End of Time*). Messiaen composed and premiered this masterpiece, which takes the book of Revelation as its inspiration, while a prisoner of war in World War II.

The Bible has appeared in almost every other genre of music as well. In the nineteenth century, spirituals composed by enslaved communities in the American South enabled the biblical text to speak anew. "Swing Low, Sweet Chariot" imagines Elijah's ascent in the heavenly chariot (see 2 Kgs. 2) as a mode of escape from the cruelties of slavery. "Go Down, Moses," based on Exod. 5, ruminates on God's command to Moses to order Pharaoh's release of Israel from slavery. Though it does not mention American slavery explicitly, it provided encouragement and solace to enslaved people seeking relief or escape. Harriet Tubman is reported to have used the song as code for those fleeing Maryland via the Underground Railroad. "Didn't My Lord Deliver Daniel" sings of God's deliverance of Daniel from the lions' den, the three Hebrew boys from the fiery furnace, and Jonah's deliverance from the great fish (see Dan. 3, 6; Jonah 2, respectively) as templates for God's deliverance of the oppressed and enslaved from their own ordeal: "Didn't my Lord deliver Daniel / And why not every man?" In songs like these, the biblical text was a source of profound hope. Still further, the use of the biblical text in these songs served as a not-so-subtle critique of the owners who justified slavery via the very same Bible.

From its beginning, rock 'n' roll music—tracing back to the gospel roots of artists like Sister Rosetta Tharpe and Little Richard—has incorporated themes and imagery from the Bible, a constant lyrical resource for songs of loss and lament as well as redemption and hope. It would be impossible to catalog a full list of the rock and pop songs alluding to or referencing the Bible and biblical language. Songs like the Byrds' "Turn! Turn! Turn!" (1965, based on Eccl. 3) or U2's "40" (1983, based on Ps. 40) barely alter the biblical text in their versions. Other songs take the biblical text as a starting point but then craft new or different themes. Bruce Springsteen's "Adam Raised a Cain" (1986), one of several Springsteen songs evoking the Bible, imagines the relationship between the musician and his father as an emblem of Gen. 3–4. Springsteen's line "You're born into this life paying / For

the sins of somebody else's past" recalls another text, Num. 14:18, and its claim that the sins of a parent are passed to the child. In "Isaac and Abraham" (1992), Joan Baez reinterprets the story of the Akedah ("binding"), Abraham's attempted murder of Isaac in Gen. 22, in folk-rock form. Baez imagines Abraham expressing remorse because he was not the one who acted to spare Isaac's life. She also recasts the hill where the event happened, which is associated in the biblical tradition with the future site of the Jewish temple, as a memorial to Isaac. The subtle changes to the biblical story in this song turn it into an exploration of human motivations. Another example may be found in the story of Samson and Delilah in Judg. 16, which has inspired a number of songs' treatment of romantic betrayal. In Florence and the Machine's song "Delilah" (2015), the gender roles in the biblical text are reversed, with the female singer depicting her boyfriend as the deceitful Delilah and she herself as the one betrayed (Samson).

Several heavy metal bands, a subgenre within rock, have displayed a special interest in the book of Revelation and in apocalypticism. "Number of the Beast" by Iron Maiden (1982) and "The Four Horsemen" by Metallica (1983) both invoke well-known images from Revelation. According to some scholars, apocalyptic literature is a type of resistance literature, and some heavy metal songs seem to function in a similar fashion. Lamb of God's "Reclamation" (2009), for example, envisions the present world being swept away as "the sky tears open / fire rains down"—though in this case, the apocalypse is the result of ecological devastation. The song is an act of protest and resistance to political power unmoved by the realities of imminent environmental catastrophe.

Biblical language and imagery also play an important role in rap and hip-hop. Lauryn Hill's "Forgive Them Father" (1998) invokes Jesus's words from the cross (Luke 23:34) as she vents about the wrongs she perceives her former Fugees' bandmates have done to her, one of several biblical references in this song about forgiveness tinged with rage. In one memorable line, she cites John the Baptist's words that Jesus must increase but John must decrease. For Hill, this becomes a question: Why must she decrease so that her bandmates can increase? "Faith" (2009), a song by the Pulitzer Prize–winning rapper Kendrick Lamar, paints a vivid and wrenching portrait of life in the inner city. The line "Oh faith, all you need is the size of a mustard seed" draws on a saying of Jesus (Matt. 17:20; Luke 17:6) and speaks of both religious faith and faith in oneself. "Jesus Walks" by Kanye West (2004) also uses biblical language to depict experiences of urban Chicago. "I walk through the valley of the Chi where death is" alludes to the well-known line in Ps. 23:4: "I walk through the darkest valley" (KJV "valley of the shadow of death"). West invites listeners to see in Chicago an instance of what the psalmist associates with deep darkness, if not also death. Both Lamar and West apply hopeful biblical language to contexts described as in need of such hope.

The Bible's presence in country music occasions little surprise given the genre's origin and popularity in the so-called Bible Belt region of the southern United States. Sometimes the Bible figures as a sacred object with cultural or religious significance. In "Three Wooden Crosses" (2002), Randy Travis sings of a fictional car accident in which a dying preacher leaves his Bible to one of the survivors. The survivor turns her life around because of this tragedy, and the salvaged Bible is responsible for her own son's call to Christian ministry. Another, more frequent use of the Bible in country music is found in songs describing human frailty and failure, showcasing the need for personal redemption and forgiveness. One of the earliest country songs, Hank Williams's "I Saw the Light" (1947), evokes Paul's encounter with the risen Jesus (see Acts 9) in its story of repentance and transformation.

While jazz rarely appeals to the Bible specifically—especially in its instrumental forms (though these songs may refer to religious themes in their titles, like Kirk Whalum's "Ma Foi" ["My Faith"; 1989])—many people consider it to be a religious form of music because of its "spiritual" quality. Fans of the great jazz saxophonist John Coltrane went so far as to found a church in his name, St. John Coltrane Church in San Francisco. The church was (and still is) inspired by Coltrane's iconic album *A Love Supreme* (1965). While that album is entirely instrumental, the Coltrane Church liturgy includes guided meditations on the recording that incorporate readings from the Gospels and the Pauline Epistles. The result is a complex interaction between Coltrane's music and the Bible in which the two mutually inform and illuminate each other.

It is impossible to imagine Western music without the Bible. Both as a physical object and as a literary source, the Bible's influence has extended into all forms of modern music. It remains to be seen if that influence will continue in the face of the decline of religious adherence in many parts of the modern world.

The Bible in Literature

Kerry Hasler-Brooks and Emerson B. Powery

Historically, the Bible was a common frame of reference for people in the Western world, and its literature naturally often drew on biblical images, words, and themes to communicate with its audiences. From Shakespeare to the nineteenth-century narratives of the formerly enslaved to contemporary novels, the Bible has influenced the content, structure, rhetoric, and sensibilities of Western literature. In many ways, this is also unsurprising because methods of reading it have influenced the traditions of literary reading as well. Despite its diminishing status in some corners of the contemporary world, the Bible continues to impact—even to haunt—the literary landscape. A lingering presence, sometimes it is "there" in explicit ways; sometimes its words and images hover in the backdrop of a passage.

The ongoing impact of the Bible is manifested in various ways. Biblical themes can appear in the titles of contemporary North American novels, as in Chaim Potok's *In the Beginning*, Toni Morrison's *Beloved*, Margaret Atwood's *The Testaments*, and Octavia Butler's *Parable of the Sower*. On the very first page of Potok's novel, the character named David—an orthodox Jew who grew up during the Great Depression and is learning to interpret the Bible differently from his faith tradition—recognizes the challenges of new beginnings: "All beginnings are hard. Teaching the way I do is particularly hard, for I touch the raw nerves of faith, the beginnings of things. Often students are shaken. I say to them what was said to me: 'Be patient. You are learning a new way of understanding the Bible. All beginnings are hard.' And sometimes I add what I have learned on my own: 'Especially a beginning that you make by yourself. That's the hardest beginning of all.'" In the biblical book of Genesis, God brings order and light out of the chaos (Gen. 1:1–3). Potok calls explicitly on the theme of creation in Genesis to depict David as the subject who will bring order out of a different kind of chaos, a reader who will create a new way to read the Bible.

Morrison's *Beloved*—which won the Pulitzer Prize for Fiction—recalls the deaths and memories of millions of enslaved people during the Atlantic slave trade. The novel wrestles with identity, peoplehood, collective trauma, and individual psychosis. The title of the book alludes to the Letter to the Romans as Paul, a Jewish Christ follower and apostle to the gentiles, attempts to explore the increasing ethnic shifts within the developing communities he served. Acknowledging the expanding gentile presence in the church in Rome, Paul discovered in the prophet Hosea meaning-making words that helped him process what was occurring:

> Those who were not my people I will call "my people,"
> and her who was not beloved I will call "beloved." (Rom. 9:25; see Hos. 2:23)

In an active remaking of the language of Romans, Morrison picks up this biblical thread by identifying the fringe African American characters of her novel as those who—like first-century gentiles—have received elevated status: who have moved from "not my people" to "my people," from "not beloved" to "beloved." Morrison's story urges its readers to recognize and to remember the effects of this historic trauma for those living in its wake.

Morrison's collective vision of the beloved as "my people" stands out from other influential readings of the Bible that have centered the self and pointed Western literary culture toward individual, rather than communal, experience. For example, St. Augustine's *Confessions* narrates his religious conversion through a series of encounters with books from the *Aeneid* to the Bible. In Augustine's account, reading is revelatory and establishes a path from the individual to God, reading is transformational and leads to a change in self, and reading is liturgical, requiring a structured practice of rereading, reflection, and spiritual discipline. The purpose of Augustine's reading life may have lost ground in the contemporary world, where reading in pursuit of human revelation often outpaces reading for God revelation. However, the habits of reading described in Augustine's uniquely influential text still shape Western literary culture and reading practices, from close reading to data visualization (the representation of abstract literary data in digital, interactive, and visual forms). As

Morrison and others—including Augustine—show elsewhere, there are ways the Bible has shaped literature outside or beyond the emphasis on the internal life of the individual. This includes Jewish rabbinic traditions of collective interpretation through midrash, the call-and-response practices of African American preaching, and the experiential emphases of feminist interpretation.

In *Gilead*, another Pulitzer Prize–winning novel, Marilynne Robinson draws on biblical stories and language just as many works of literature do but also steps away from the literal text of the Bible itself to center instead on the lived practice of reading the Bible. In this way, Robinson shifts the focus from the text to its reader and interpreter. As the aging narrator of the book, the Rev. John Ames, faces the possibility of death, he writes letters to his young son and tries to narrate the miracle of a mind filled with poetry and Scripture. Ames writes as a close reader who can draw from years of careful study of the Bible and other texts. He reads such works for his son, circling around a few words from the book of Psalms or Milton, plumbing them again and again for revelation and transformation. Reflecting on the boxes of sermons he has written over his fifty-year career, Ames imagines throwing them away, ashamed of their failures, but he also wakes up night after night from dreams of rereading those sermons, haunted by the biblical text, rewriting and revising in response: "I still wake up at night, thinking, *That's* what I should have said! or *That's* what he meant!"

While contemporary American writers like Robinson, Marilyn Nelson, Christian Wiman, and Kathleen Norris draw directly on biblical language and themes, there are significant veins of contemporary literature that wrestle with the presence of the Bible and suggest modes of reading that transcend the material text of the Bible altogether. Alice Walker does this in her Pulitzer Prize–winning novel *The Color Purple*. Writing from the American South, the protagonist and narrator, Celie, looks up from the biblical text, which she understands to be marked by the sins of racism and sexism, and finds a living God in the ache and the joy of Black women's songs and the titular fields of purple flowers. In *Transcendent Kingdom* by Yaa Gyasi, a Ghanaian American girl named Gifty grows up in a Pentecostal church in Alabama with the Bible as her constant companion. She reads it from cover to cover the summer she turns eight, memorizes even the most obscure verses in preparation for her mother's pop quizzes, and keeps a journal of letters to God, imagining herself as a "lost apostle" and her journal as a "new book of the Bible." As an adult, Gifty, a neuroscientist and academic, replaces her childhood faith in the Bible with a new faith in science. Tellingly, Gyasi ends her novel with Gifty on a church pew, grieving her dead family and staring headlong at the hole left by her dead faith. From the pew, she observes the figure of the crucified Christ on the altar: "I never bow my head. I never pray, never wait to hear God's voice, I just look. I sit in blessed silence, and I remember." In this novel, the old liturgies, the call-and-response between the God of the Word and God's child, are dead—at least to Gifty—but a new liturgy is made on the back of the old, a kind of disciplined reading of her own life as if it is a text to be interpreted, "to make order, make sense, make meaning," much like, though distinct from, Potok's David.

As shown by writers from Jean Toomer to Ana Castillo, Zora Neale Hurston to Louise Erdrich, James Baldwin to Gene Luen Yang, North American literature has been and continues to be significantly informed by the Bible. Technical developments in e-books, audiobooks, and data modeling of literary texts are redefining the notion of what it means to read in contemporary culture, but even as the forms of English-language literature develop and evolve and even as many significant literary works distance themselves from the Bible, it seems unlikely that readers will entirely escape the reading practices that were formed through the study of the Bible.

The Bible in Museums

Jennifer L. Koosed

Among other things, museums document human history and are repositories of cultural artifacts. Consequently, the Bible—which has exercised an enormous influence on history and culture, especially in the Middle East and the West—is often on display in museums in a host of ways. Because artists have been regularly inspired by the biblical texts, some of the world's most famous paintings and sculptures concern biblical topics (see further in **"The Bible and Visual Art," pp. 2168–71**). The physical pages of the Bible themselves became works of art in the hands of the scribes who illuminated them. Museums often contain physical copies of Bibles that, even if not illuminated, have played important roles in history, either because of their age and the importance of the texts they contain or because they were owned by famous people. Still further, some facilities take the Bible, whether in whole or in part, as their primary if not sole subject, such as the Museum of the Bible (MOTB) in Washington, DC. In many museums across the world, visitors may encounter—among other things—the Bible as the subject of art and as a work of art itself.

Almost any museum that features European and American art will have pieces that address biblical texts and themes. Famous collections in Italy (the Uffizi and the Vatican Museums), France (the Louvre), England (the British Museum), the Netherlands (the Rijksmuseum), and New York City (the Metropolitan Museum of Art) contain many examples. A few museums, like the Museum of Biblical Art in Dallas, Texas, focus exclusively on biblical art. The Museum of Biblical Art holds over one hundred Bibles and features paintings by artists such as modernist Marc Chagall (1887–1985), whose work is replete with biblical stories and scenes of Jewish religious life, and Ron DiCianni, a contemporary Christian artist who states that his work promotes the gospel. It also highlights religious art more broadly conceived and houses within its space the National Center for Jewish Art. A similar museum, the Museum of Contemporary Religious Art, is housed on the campus of Saint Louis University.

As noted in this essay, Bibles that once belonged to famous people are sometimes collected in museums. The Bible that belonged to Nat Turner (1800–1831), for example, is prominently displayed in the Smithsonian's National Museum of African American History and Culture. Turner was an enslaved man trained to preach submission to other enslaved peoples. Through deep readings of the Scriptures and powerful religious visions, however, he came to believe that the Bible's message was one of freedom, not servitude. On the night of August 21, 1831, he led an armed rebellion against the slaveholders of Southampton County, Virginia. Although the rebellion lasted only a few days, Turner managed to elude capture for two months, thus garnering national attention and provoking fear throughout the white South. He is believed to have been holding this Bible, worn and dog-eared, when he was finally captured.

Some one hundred years later and four thousand miles away, another preacher found support for his own rebellion in the pages of his Bible. André Trocmé (1901–71) was a Huguenot minister in Le Chambon-sur-Lignon, France, who led the effort to resist both Nazis and French collaborators by rescuing approximately five thousand people, mostly Jews, during World War II. Trocmé's Bible, filled with his handwritten annotations, is held by the United States Holocaust Memorial Museum. The museum also has Torah scrolls from Vienna and Marburg, which were desecrated during the Nazi state–sponsored pogrom of Kristallnacht on August 9–10, 1938.

Many Bibles are housed in the museums of Washington, DC. The Library of Congress has a substantial collection, including a Gutenberg Bible that was among the first books to be produced on a printing press. The Freer and Sackler Galleries have a collection of biblical manuscripts that includes the third-oldest extant Greek text of the New Testament. Jerusalem's museum collections are, not surprisingly, also noteworthy. The Israel Museum holds some of the world's most important Bibles, including the Aleppo Codex, an important (but incomplete) copy of the Hebrew Bible. The Israel Museum's Shrine of the Book contains the first seven Dead Sea Scrolls discovered at Qumran—a Jewish community located on the Dead Sea from about 150 BCE to 68 CE that copied and wrote biblical and other texts—including the Great Isaiah Scroll and a second copy of that important

prophetic book. Museums in other countries also have their fair share of biblical riches. The oldest complete manuscript of the Hebrew Bible—the Leningrad Codex, dated to circa 1008/9 CE—is held in the National Library of Russia in Saint Petersburg. The Vatican holds biblical manuscripts of enormous import in its collections, including Codex Vaticanus, one of the oldest complete Greek manuscripts of the New Testament, dating to the fourth century CE.

In 2017, the MOTB opened in Washington, DC, a project of the Green family, owners of the craft store chain Hobby Lobby. This massive site—430,000 square feet of exhibit space on eight floors—contains three permanent exhibits: Impact of the Bible (focusing on the way the Bible has affected history, social change, and culture), Stories of the Bible (including stories from both the Hebrew Bible and the New Testament), and History of the Bible (attending to the history of the Bible's transmission and its translation). There is also space for temporary exhibits. The museum's purpose is not merely to be informative but also to promote and celebrate the biblical Scriptures. As their mission statement says, the purpose of the MOTB is "to invite all people to engage with the transformative power of the Bible." Although it has worked with a diverse group of antiquities dealers, scholars, and other advocates, it is an institution also deeply committed to evangelical Christian beliefs.

The centerpiece of the MOTB and its originating purpose is the Greens' large collection of biblical manuscripts. The Greens had accumulated about forty thousand manuscripts by 2015. In 2015, they donated the entire collection to the MOTB. The collection includes rare Hebrew, Greek, and Latin manuscripts; historically significant versions like the first edition of Martin Luther's translation of the Pentateuch into German (only ten copies are known to exist); and Bibles translated into dozens of the world's languages. Whereas there is significant import to such a collection, it has also been mired in scandal, including antiquities theft, illicit importation, forgery, falsification of sale records, and the destruction of Egyptian artifacts. For example, an analysis revealed that their Dead Sea Scroll fragments were forgeries. The MOTB removed the forgeries from their collection. The museum has been transparent about the problems with the fragments that it had acquired, foregrounding the investigation by publishing the scientific report and hosting a symposium about the incident (March 2020), even inviting the public to comment through an online portal on the MOTB website.

A particular feature of the landscape of museums in the United States is a subcategory of sites erected as monuments to biblical stories, primarily from an evangelical Christian perspective. The most prominent and well funded of these complexes is the Creation Museum in Petersburg, Kentucky. The core of this museum is a recounting of biblical history beginning with creation for the express purpose of challenging scientific understandings of the origin of the universe and the evolution of life. To this end, the exhibit has a substantial collection of dinosaur bones, which it displays alongside readings of Genesis, arguing that evidence for dinosaurs can be found in the Bible and that dinosaurs coexisted with human beings only a few thousand years ago. Rather than recognizing multiple stories of creation in the Bible, including in the first three chapters of Genesis, the beginning of that book is read as a single, consistent story that is definitive beyond all other creation accounts in the Bible (see, e.g., Pss. 74; 104; Prov. 8; John 1). An affiliated museum, Ark Encounter in Williamstown, Kentucky, focuses on the story of Noah in Gen. 6, challenging especially geological and paleontological knowledge. Although focused on Genesis, both museums tie the Genesis stories to Christian understandings of Jesus as the Christ, promoting Christian conversion throughout their exhibits and published materials.

In sum, the Bible appears in museums in a variety of ways. As a rich collection of literature treasured by billions of religious adherents, the Bible has inspired countless artists throughout the ages, many of whose works are now enshrined in museums across the globe. Physical copies of the Bible itself, too, can be important artifacts, both for the artistry of their embellishments and for their witness to the technologies of writing and bookmaking. Reading the Bible has led some people to noble acts of great significance, and the personal Bibles of famous people provide windows into their worlds and tangible connections to their pasts. A few museums are designed with the focus of verifying parts of the text as historical fact, sometimes with accompanying commitments that are at odds with other museums or scientific consensus. In these ways and many more, museums not only collect evidence of the Bible's enormous influence, they also enshrine that influence and prove, in the end, to be further testimony to it.

The Bible, Science, and the Environment

Brent A. Strawn

Putting the matter perhaps a bit too simply, two main, often opposed ways to relate the Bible and science have existed since the modern period. The Bible has been viewed as either (1) closely related to and ultimately superior to science so that if and when the two are found to be in conflict, the Bible is to be trusted more than science or (2) largely unrelated to modern science and thus inferior to it on a host of scientific topics (e.g., astronomy or biology) so that if and when the two are found to be in conflict, science, not the Bible, is what should be trusted.

Historically speaking, these two positions emerged sequentially with the great divide caused by the scientific revolution that began in the sixteenth century with the publication of Nicolaus Copernicus's *On the Revolution of the Heavenly Spheres* (1543) and that continued in earnest thereafter in publications by pioneering figures like Galileo Galilei (e.g., *Dialogue concerning the Two Chief World Systems*, 1632) and Sir Isaac Newton (e.g., *Mathematical Principles of Natural Philosophy*, 1687). Later, Charles Darwin's *On the Origin of Species* (1859), which presents his theory of evolution via natural selection, was also nothing short of earth shaking. Before these revolutionary developments in science, religious readers tended to defer to the Bible on questions concerning the origin of life, the creation of the universe, and so forth. After the scientific revolution, more people tended to look less to the Bible for information about the laws of nature per se, preferring instead the data obtained by the empirical sciences.

Both of these ways of relating the Bible and science are still operative today. In the main, most modern people subscribe to the second option, favoring science over Scripture on all properly scientific matters. Others, however, still hold to some version of the first option even as they also live in the industrialized-technologized world. In point of fact, the two options are not nearly as discrete as they might seem at first. Newton, for instance, wrote important contributions to Christian theology in addition to his scientific breakthroughs and, despite his controversy with the Catholic Church over heliocentrism, Galileo remained a devout Catholic his entire life. On the other side of the coin, the early church father Origen, in *On First Principles* (ca. 229 CE), said no one could possibly be so foolish as to take the stories of Gen. 1–2 literally: How, for example, could light exist (Gen. 1:3–5) before the heavenly bodies that give light (Gen. 1:14–18)? For centuries, therefore—both before and after the scientific revolution—there have been people occupying a kind of middle ground: they have deferred to science on scientific matters but have preferred the Bible on matters of religious faith and practice. This third option has included many scientists.

After the Scopes Monkey Trial (1925) over whether evolution could be taught in public schools, however, and the fundamentalist-modernist controversy that resulted, adherence to science and adherence to the Bible have frequently been pitted against each other in North America—often with deleterious results. Some religious individuals, for example, know well the full benefits of modern medicine but claim to "believe the Bible" on certain cosmological matters like a young age for the earth. The outcome can be a curious bifurcation: a scientific worldview on one issue but not on another, apparently very similar one. Bifurcation can come from the other side of this divide as well, however: just because the Bible, a collection of sacred literature from antiquity, does not reflect knowledge of twenty-first-century quantum physics does not mean that it is not useful—even to be preferred—in matters of religious faith and practice. This point is made even by nonreligious scientists like Stephen Jay Gould who, weary of the war between religion and science, is happy to divide the two into nonoverlapping *magisteria* (sets of authoritative teaching). In Gould's approach, someone may happily "believe in" science and also "believe in" the Bible, since they concern two entirely discrete but equally important subjects.

Be that as it may, the two options delineated here for relating the Bible to science should not be too starkly drawn, and for more than one reason. It is obvious that the ancient world from which the Bible emerged simply did not have the same sort of empirical knowledge that is widely available now through science. Ancient people knew nothing of microbes, for instance, nor did they have microscopes to observe them. Neither did they have space-based telescopes to peer deep

into the universe or Einstein's insights on the speed of light in order to be able to calculate the distance to and the age of the stars. Even so, one may still revisit the ancient world with fresh eyes and think in a more integrated manner about science and the Bible in at least two ways.

First, though standing on the far side of the scientific revolution, it is nevertheless clear that some parts of the Bible belong to what might be called "ancient science." Ancient Egyptians, Mesopotamians, and others wrote texts about religion, the gods, and the good life but also about mathematics, astronomy, and medicine. Early "scientific" writing was often composed of taxonomic lists, a practice that is found also in later Greek philosophers (e.g., Aristotle's *On Plants*) and also attributed to the wise king Solomon (1 Kgs. 4:33). The biblical books of Proverbs and Ecclesiastes—both of which are associated with Solomon—might be seen as participating, to some degree, in the same type of "scientific" endeavor, especially via the emphasis the Israelite sages placed on empirical observation in service to wise living. One could observe the behavior of ants, for example, and live better as a result (see Prov. 6:6). Indeed, in the light of "ancient science," even a nonscientific (by modern standards) text like Gen. 1, insofar as it is concerned with the origins and coming-to-be of the world, can be considered as nothing short of a cosmology: a theory of the universe, though an ancient one obviously bereft of our knowledge of gravity, electromagnetic force, and weak nuclear force that operate in more recent cosmologies like that of the hot big bang. The presence of still other ancient cosmologies, even within the Bible itself, suggests that Gen. 1 should *not* be taken as the Bible's only or even its best cosmological statement. Texts like Gen. 2, Pss. 74 and 104, Prov. 8, John 1, and others offer different views on how the cosmos came to be. Although these biblical texts frequently disagree on details of *how* that happened, the varying accounts nevertheless agree on a belief *that* the world was created by a powerful, benevolent Creator. In its diverse collection of cosmological accounts, therefore, the Bible opens up space for continuing discussions of *how* the universe came into existence, even while it continues to espouse the belief in a God who was (and is) generative of it all. In this light, science and the Bible are not entirely nonoverlapping sets after all but overlap at least to some degree, if only tangentially.

If so, this kind of rapprochement offers another way the Bible and science might be integrated. This way recognizes how ancient religious texts of great authority can be used in helpful or harmful ways vis-à-vis contemporary matters of scientific concern. A prime example is the human impact on and care for the earth. In a famous article published in the journal *Science* in 1967, Lynn White Jr. traces the ecological crisis facing the planet to passages in Genesis that speak of humans "subdu[ing]" the world and "hav[ing] dominion over" the animal world (see Gen. 1:28). White is indubitably correct that countless people—including many religious people—have often mistreated the environment and have sometimes appealed to the Bible to justify their wanton (mis)use of the natural world. It is far less certain, however, if White or the people who have acted in these ways have read the Bible correctly on this point. Indeed, the book of Genesis goes on to immediately speak of how human beings are to serve and preserve the earth, working it and protecting it (see Gen. 2:15), with later texts legislating fallow periods so that the land can recover from use (Exod. 23:10–11; Lev. 25:1–12; cf. Lev. 26:34–35; 2 Chr. 36:21). Indeed, the hero of White's essay turns out to be none other than St. Francis of Assisi (1181/2–1226 CE), who is reported to have preached to the birds and who called the ant his brother and fire his sister. It is easy to demonstrate that Francis's egalitarian and non-anthropocentric approach was influenced by the Bible because it is replete with stories of God's care for birds that fall from the sky (Matt. 10:29; cf. Ps. 84:3) and donkeys that are mistreated (Num. 22:28)—evidently because God claims ownership of every wild animal in the forest and the cattle on a thousand hills (Ps. 50:10; cf. 36:6), indeed of the entire earth (Exod. 19:5; Lev. 25:23), clothing even the lilies of the field (Matt. 6:28–30). Not surprisingly, the Bible mentions the praise that the nonhuman, even nonanimate, world gives to its Creator (see Pss. 96:12–13; 98:7–9; 148:3–10; cf. Luke 19:40).

In short, if (mis)readings of the Bible have been instrumental in causing some of the problems that science has identified and can, hopefully, redress, it is equally true that the Bible may provide additional reasons for human beings, whether religious or not, to act differently for a better future. For the same reasons, the Bible might chasten inappropriate uses of science, which has often been a tool used to destroy the natural world in horrific ways (nuclear bombs, for example, or extremely efficient fishing or mining strategies). Whatever the case or specific issue, it seems clear that the Bible and science can operate helpfully together in addressing some of the great questions and large problems facing humanity and the world.

Timeline of the Ancient Near East
and the Mediterranean World
to the Early Second Century CE

ca. 2000–1500 BCE	The ancestors (Abraham and Sarah; Isaac and Rebekah; Jacob, Leah, and Rachel; Joseph)
ca. 1300 BCE?	The exodus from Egypt

Egypt: Merneptah (1213–1203 BCE; Merneptah Stela: 1209 BCE)

| ca. 1200–1020 BCE | Time of the judges |

Assyria: Tiglath-pileser I (1114–1076 BCE)

ca. 1020–922 BCE	United monarchy (Israel)
ca. 1002–962 BCE	David, king of Israel
ca. 962–922 BCE	Solomon, king of Israel

Egypt: Shishak (Shoshenq I) invades Palestine (925 BCE)

| ca. 922 BCE | Division of Judah and Israel into separate kingdoms |

Kings of Judah (Southern Kingdom)		**Kings of Israel (Northern Kingdom)**	
922–915 BCE	Rehoboam	922–901 BCE	Jeroboam I
915–913 BCE	Abijam		
913–873 BCE	Asa		
		901–900 BCE	Nadab
		900–877 BCE	Baasha
		877–876 BCE	Elah
		876 BCE	Zimri
		876–872 BCE	Tibni
		876–869 BCE	Omri
873–849 BCE	Jehoshaphat		
		869–850 BCE	Ahab

Assyria: Shalmaneser III (858–824 BCE)

849–843 BCE	Jehoram	850–849 BCE	Ahaziah
843–842 BCE	Ahaziah	843–815 BCE	Jehu
842–837 BCE	Athaliah (queen)		
837–800 BCE	Jehoash		
		815–802 BCE	Jehoahaz
800–783 BCE	Amaziah	802–786 BCE	Joash

		786–746 BCE	Jeroboam II
783–742 BCE	Azariah/Uzziah		
		746–745 BCE	Zechariah
		745 BCE	Shallum
	Assyria: Tiglath-pileser III (745–727 BCE)	745–737 BCE	Menahem
742–735 BCE	Jotham		
		737–736 BCE	Pekahiah
735–715 BCE	Ahaz	736–732 BCE	Pekah
		732–724 BCE	Hoshea

Assyria: Shalmaneser V (727–722 BCE)

722 BCE — Fall of Israel (Samaria), the northern kingdom, to Assyria

Assyria: Sargon II (722–705 BCE)

715–687 BCE — Hezekiah

Assyria: Sennacherib (705–681 BCE)

687–642 BCE — Manasseh

Assyria: Esar-haddon (681–669 BCE)

Ashurbanipal (669–627 BCE)

642–640 BCE — Amon

640–609 BCE — Josiah

609 BCE — Jehoahaz

609–598 BCE — Jehoiakim

Babylon: Nebuchadrezzar (or Nebuchadnezzar) II (605–562 BCE)

598–597 BCE — Jehoiachin

597 BCE — First Babylonian deportation of Judah, the southern kingdom

597–587/6 BCE — Zedekiah

587/586 BCE — Fall of Judah, the southern kingdom, to Babylon; destruction of Jerusalem and the First Temple; second deportation of Judah

Babylon: Nabonidus (556–539 BCE)

Persia: Cyrus II (the Great) (559–530 BCE)

539–528 BCE — Cyrus II conquers Babylon (539 BCE) and issues decree allowing Jews to return to Judah and rebuild the temple; Babylonian Jews begin migration to Jerusalem

Persia: Cambyses II (530–522 BCE)

Darius I (522–486 BCE)

520–515 BCE — The Second Temple is built

Persia: Xerxes I (486–465 BCE)

Artaxerxes I (465–424 BCE)

Mid-fifth or early fourth century BCE	Ezra's mission
ca. 445–430 BCE	Nehemiah is governor of Judah

Persia: Artaxerxes II (405/4–359/8 BCE)

Hellenistic (Greek): Alexander the Great (336–323 BCE)

334 BCE	Alexander the Great begins conquest of the Persian Empire
323 BCE	Death of Alexander, generals wrestle for power

Hellenistic (Greek): Ptolemy I of Egypt (305–283 BCE)

301 BCE	Ptolemies begin rule in Judea

Hellenistic (Greek): Seleucid king Antiochus III (223–187 BCE)

ca. 200 BCE	Seleucids seize control of the land of Israel from the Ptolemies

Hellenistic (Greek): Seleucid king Antiochus IV Epiphanes (175–164 BCE)

168/167 BCE	Antiochus IV Epiphanes profanes the Jerusalem temple
167–164 BCE	Maccabean Revolt against Antiochus IV Epiphanes and the Seleucids
164 BCE	The Maccabees regain control of the temple and purify it
164–142 BCE	The Hasmoneans (family name for the Maccabees) gain measure of autonomy in Judea
142 BCE	Simon Maccabee secures independence for Judea; Seleucids lose control of area

Hasmoneans: John Hyrcanus (134–104 BCE)

Judah Aristobulus I (104–103 BCE)

Alexander Jannaeus (103–76 BCE)

Salome Alexandra (76–67 BCE)

67–37 BCE	The (Hasmonean) Civil War
63 BCE	Roman general Pompey takes control of Jerusalem

Herod the Great, client king of Rome over Judea (37–4 BCE)

Roman Emperor: Augustus (Octavian) (31 BCE–14 CE)

ca. 4 BCE–30 CE	Life and ministry of Jesus of Nazareth

Archelaus, client ruler of Rome in Judea (4 BCE–6 CE)

Herod Antipas, client ruler of Rome in Galilee (4 BCE–39 CE)

6 CE	Judea comes under direct Roman rule

Roman Emperor: Tiberius (14–37 CE)

Pontius Pilate, Roman governor of Judea (26–36 CE)

Roman Emperor: Gaius (Caligula) (37–41 CE)

Herod Agrippa I, client king of Rome over Judea, Samaria, and multiple territories (41–44 CE)

Roman Emperor: Claudius (41–54 CE)

Mid-first century CE Missions of Paul

Herod Agrippa II, client ruler of Rome over territories north of Judea (53–93 CE)

Roman Emperor: Nero (54–68 CE)

66–70 CE Uprising against Rome in Judea

Roman Emperors: Galba, Otho, and Vitellius (68–69 CE)

Roman Emperor: Vespasian (69–79 CE)

70 CE Destruction of the Second Temple and capture of Jerusalem by the Romans in response to Jewish revolt

Roman Emperor: Trajan (98–117 CE)

115–117 CE Uprising against Rome in the Jewish Diaspora

Roman Emperor: Hadrian (117–138 CE)

132–135 CE Bar Kochba Revolt: second uprising against Rome in Judea

Ancient Empires in the Bible

The Egyptian Empire (Twenty-Seventh to Fourth Centuries BCE)

Ancient Egypt, occupying roughly the same geographical space as the modern state of Egypt, was one of the earliest and most enduring geopolitical groups in antiquity. Geographically, the land was divided into Upper Egypt (which is somewhat confusingly in the south) and Lower Egypt (in the north). Additionally, the triangular Sinai Peninsula, which bridges Africa and Asia, often fell under Egyptian control. The land was bordered on the west by Libya, with Nubia (biblical Cush) to the south. Two bodies of water, the Mediterranean Sea and the Red Sea, marked its northern and eastern edges. Internally, the land was oriented around the Nile River, which runs south to north some 4,132 miles until fracturing into a large delta region before emptying into the Mediterranean Sea. Each year in the late summer and early fall its banks flooded and left behind a dark, rich soil conducive to agriculture and pastoral life. The vast regions left untouched by the Nile's waters were largely arid desert. Thus, Egypt's economic life centered on the Nile.

Ancient Egypt has a long, varied, and complex political history. Historians recognize Egypt's political history as a succession of thirty dynasties, the first of which saw an attempt to unite Upper and Lower Egypt in the late fourth millennium BCE. Following its earliest phase, Egypt's dynastic history is divided into a series of periods corresponding to the centralization of political power or lack thereof.

Old Kingdom	2686–2160 BCE
First Intermediate period	2160–2055 BCE
Middle Kingdom	2055–1650 BCE
Second Intermediate period	1650–1550 BCE
New Kingdom	1550–1069 BCE
Third Intermediate period	1069–664 BCE
Late period	664–332 BCE

The kings who ruled Egypt, eventually known as pharaohs (literally "great house"), exercised political leadership as the representative, image, and offspring of one of several deities. Over the course of Egypt's history, the king ruled from various locations within the land where large palace complexes were established (e.g., Memphis). As leaders of a major world power, kings of Egypt frequently engaged with important states elsewhere throughout the ancient Near East, including Mittani, Assyria, Babylon, Persia, and others. Closer to home, Egyptian political influence often extended into Syria-Palestine. A cache of cuneiform letters dating to the fourteenth century BCE found at el-Amarna (ancient Akhetaten) documents requests by vassal kings in Syria-Palestine to the Egyptian state for economic and military assistance. From the first millennium BCE, the Bible depicts three Egyptian kings coming to the land of Israel to assert Egyptian interests: Shoshenq I (945–924 BCE; biblical Shishak), Taharqa (690–664 BCE; biblical Tirhakah), and Nekau II (610–595 BCE; biblical Neco), the last of whom killed Josiah, king of Judah, in 609 BCE at Megiddo (2 Kgs. 23:29; 2 Chr. 35:20–27). Finally, persons from the biblical narratives are depicted as making their way to Egypt for protection (e.g., Jeroboam: 1 Kgs. 11:40; Jeremiah: Jer. 43:6; Joseph, Mary, and infant Jesus: Matt. 2:13–15).

Egyptian Rulers to Know

Merneptah (r. 1213–1203 BCE)
Shoshenq I (r. 945–924 BCE); biblical Shishak
Taharqa (r. 690–664 BCE); biblical Tirhakah
Nekau II (r. 610–595 BCE); biblical Neco
Psamtik II (r. 595–589 BCE)
Apries (r. 589–570 BCE); biblical Hophra

The Assyrian Empire (Twelfth to Seventh Centuries BCE)

From its small beginnings on the banks of the Tigris River (present-day northern Iraq), in the days of Israel and Judah, Assyria was the dominant political, military, and geographic power in the ancient Near East. It began in the twelfth century BCE with Tiglath-pileser I. In the eighth century BCE under Tiglath-pileser III, Assyria controlled territory ranging from Israel, Lebanon, and Syria in the west; to Khume (Kue), Musri, and Tubal (Tabal) in the northwest (present-day Türkiye [Turkey]); and Babylonia in the south (present-day southern Iraq). Assyria also conquered Egypt and Elam in the seventh century BCE. Israel, or the northern kingdom, while nominally independent, was an Assyrian vassal by the time of Shalmaneser III in the ninth century, paying tribute to the empire in exchange for military protection and theoretical peace. Any vassal's attempt to improve its political position or lighten its economic load would be met with harsher economic sanctions. Further attempts would mean a military attack and exile if defeated. This became the northern kingdom of Israel's fate in 722 BCE, when Shalmaneser V besieged Israel's capital Samaria and defeated the community; while a few Israelites managed to head into the southern kingdom of Judah, the majority were exiled far into the Assyrian Empire and assimilated into the communities there.

Biblical books such as 1–2 Kings, 1–2 Chronicles, Isaiah, Hosea, Amos, and Micah describe the growing might of Assyria and Israel's response (positive or negative) to the empire. Isaiah 7, most known for the passage about the young woman conceiving a child that becomes a proof text for the virgin birth of Jesus in Matt. 1, is primarily about the Syro-Ephraimite War in 735–732 BCE, in which Israel and Syria revolted against Assyria and tried to encourage Judah to do the same. Kings and Chronicles mostly focus on the rulers of Israel and Judah and their failures to follow the Torah; according to 2 Kgs. 17, however, Assyria destroys Israel precisely as God's punishment for the people's disobedience. Hosea calls for the people to repent and avoid making alliances with nations such as Egypt and Syria in an attempt to loosen Assyria's hold over Israel. After Israel's fall, Amos and Micah warn the people of Judah, now also an Assyrian vassal, to repent if they want to avoid Israel's fate (Amos 2, 4, and 7; Micah 1–3). Sennacherib invaded Judah in 701 BCE in response to rebellion (see 2 Kgs. 18–19 // Isa. 36–38). While the biblical texts describe a miraculous Judean victory, the southern kingdom remained a vassal of Assyria, and Ezra 4 later describes Esar-haddon sending Assyrian exiles into Judea.

In the seventh century BCE, the Assyrian Empire weakened, becoming too large to govern effectively after Ashurbanipal's death in 627 BCE. Babylonians and Medes (Persians in what is present-day Iran) joined forces and conquered the Assyrians in 609 BCE. All of Assyria's vassals, including the southern kingdom of Judah, became Babylonian vassals.

Assyrian Rulers to Know

Tiglath-pileser I (r. 1114–1076 BCE)
Shalmaneser III (r. 858–824 BCE)
Tiglath-pileser III (r. 745–727 BCE)
Shalmaneser V (r. 727–722 BCE)
Sennacherib (r. 705–681 BCE)
Esar-haddon (r. 681–669 BCE)
Ashurbanipal (r. 669–627 BCE)

The Babylonian Empire (Nineteenth to Sixth Centuries BCE)

For millennia, the Babylonian Empire played a prominent role in the ancient Near East. It arose in southern Mesopotamia, between the Tigris and Euphrates Rivers (modern-day Iraq). After Sumuabum established it as an independent kingdom (ca. 1895 BCE), the empire had two primary periods of ascendancy. The first—the Old Babylonian period—spanned ca. 1895–1595 BCE. The Old Babylonian period reached its height during the reign of Hammurabi, who ruled Babylon from 1792 to 1750 BCE. He established the city of Babylon as the empire's capital, expanded to the south and into the northern Mesopotamian area, and promulgated a new law code. The Code of Hammurabi was not the first written legal code, but it was clear and comprehensive; as such, it inspired other peoples to codify legal materials. Israel drew on some of Hammurabi's laws to formulate biblical law. The preamble of the code exemplifies Hammurabi's interest in improving the lives of his people: "Anu and Bel called me, Hammurabi, the exalted prince, the worshiper of the gods, to cause justice

to prevail in the land, to destroy the wicked and the evil, to prevent the strong from oppressing the weak, to enlighten the land and to further the welfare of the people." Hammurabi's importance is enshrined even on the walls of the U.S. Supreme Court—he is depicted in a marble frieze alongside other great law-givers (artist: Adolph A. Weinman).

After Hammurabi's death, Old Babylon went into decline. States soon broke off to become autonomous or were invaded by other peoples. The second period of ascendancy—the Neo-Babylonian period—began in about 626 BCE when Nabopolassar reasserted Babylonian independence. He attacked Assyria and destroyed Nineveh in 612 BCE. His son Nebuchadnezzar continued Neo-Babylonian expansion by striking Egypt. As the great empires of Egypt, Assyria, and Babylon clashed, the Judean king Josiah found himself in the middle. When Pharaoh Neco rode north to engage in battle, Josiah met him at Megiddo and was killed in 609 BCE. The great battle of Carchemish followed; Nebuchadnezzar's victory there in 605 BCE established the Babylonian Empire from Persia (modern-day Iran) to Egypt. It was during Nebuchadnezzar's reign that Judah, which had been an Assyrian vassal subsumed by Babylon, attempted to reassert its independence. The Babylonians invaded Judah in 597 and 587/586, forcing thousands of Judeans into exile and destroying Jerusalem and the First Temple. Thus, the Jewish Diaspora began, the community in Babylon persisting until the end of the twentieth century CE. After Nebuchadnezzar's reign ended, the empire declined and was conquered by the Persians in 539 BCE.

In addition to being a military power, Babylon was also an influential cultural and religious center. Babylon's creation story, the Enuma Elish, circulated widely. The city of Babylon was renowned for its palaces, gates (Ishtar Gate), and gardens (hanging garden of Babylon). Traces of Babylonian language, stories, and rituals can be found throughout the Bible and in Judaism, from Gen. 1 to the names of the Jewish months.

Babylonian Rulers to Know
Hammurabi (r. 1792–1750 BCE)
Nebuchadrezzar (or Nebuchadnezzar) II (r. 605–562 BCE)

The Persian Empire (539–330 BCE)
Cyrus II, also known as Cyrus the Great, became king of Persia in 559 BCE. In 550 BCE, Cyrus rebelled against Media and became king of the Median-Persian Empire. The Persian Empire is also called the Achaemenid Empire. Cyrus captured Babylon and the Babylonian Empire in 539 BCE. The Persian Empire would eventually extend from the Indus River in the east beyond Asia Minor and Egypt in the west.

In contrast to Babylonians who destroyed the temples of the peoples they subjugated and dislocated them from their ancestral lands, Cyrus allowed people to return to their lands and rebuild their sacred sites. For the Judeans, this meant the end of the exilic period. Some Judeans returned to the land beginning in 538 BCE and eventually rebuilt the temple in Jerusalem (520–515). Others, however, did not return to the land and remained in Babylon or other places, forming the Jewish Diaspora (see **"Diaspora," p. 1338**).

Cyrus was succeeded by his son Cambyses II (530–522 BCE), who expanded the empire by conquering Egypt. Darius I (522–486) revolted against Cambyses's son Bardiya, gaining control of the empire. Darius divided the Persian Empire into twenty large regions and standardized a system of governance with each region governed by several leaders, including a political leader called a "satrap," a military general, and a Persian official referred to as "the eye of the king." Each region, or satrapy, was further divided into provinces ruled by local governors who were also sometimes called satraps. This system of governance provided a degree or at least the image of local autonomy along with a kind of power balance, reducing the possibility of revolt. Nehemiah would become one of those governors (ca. 445–430 BCE).

Darius I married one of Cyrus's daughters, Atossa, and he was succeeded by their son, Xerxes I (486–465). Xerxes is probably the Persian ruler called Ahasuerus in Esther. After Xerxes was assassinated, the empire was ruled by his son Artaxerxes I (465–424 BCE), who is probably the Artaxerxes mentioned in Ezra and Nehemiah.

The Persian Empire was conquered in 330 BCE by Alexander the Great, ending the Persian period and inaugurating the Hellenistic period.

Persian Rulers to Know
Cyrus II (r. 559–530 BCE)
Cambyses II (r. 530–522 BCE)
Darius I (r. 522–486 BCE)
Xerxes I (r. 486–465 BCE)
Artaxerxes I (r. 465–424 BCE)
Xerxes II (r. 424 BCE)
Sogdianus (r. 424–423 BCE)
Darius II (r. 423–405/4 BCE)
Artaxerxes II (r. 405/4–359/8 BCE)
Artaxerxes III (r. 359/8–338 BCE)
Artaxerxes IV (r. 338–336 BCE)
Darius III (r. 336–330 BCE)

The Hellenistic (or Greek) Empire (334–63 BCE)

With a series of campaigns beginning in 334 BCE, Alexander the Great amassed an empire that stretched from Greece to India. He promoted Hellenization (from the word *Hellas*, Greece) in the lands he conquered, demanding adherence to Greek ways in buildings, customs, and language. The imposition of Greek language helped effect a cultural unity throughout the empire. When Jewish scholars in Alexandria, Egypt, translated the Hebrew Scriptures into Greek (known as the Septuagint) beginning in the late third or early second century BCE, Jewish Scripture became available to Jews and Gentiles throughout the empire.

After Alexander's death, his generals, called the *diadochi* or successors, wrangled for control over the conquered lands. The land of Israel was annexed to Egypt in 301 BCE and ruled by Ptolemy I, the Macedonian Greek general who became king of Egypt, and his successors. The Jews enjoyed relative autonomy to practice their religion under the Ptolemies.

Life for the Jews of the land of Israel changed, however, in 200 BCE when the Seleucid king Antiochus III, the Macedonian Greek king of Syria, defeated the Ptolemies and took control of the land, followed shortly by his brother, Antiochus IV (Epiphanes), ushering in a period of persecution of Jews and Jewish religion. Among the king's more outrageous acts was the profaning of the Jerusalem temple, where he set up an altar to Zeus and sacrificed a pig (an unclean animal) to the pagan god (Josephus, *Ant.* 12.5.4 §168).

The family of Mattathias the Hasmonean, a group of rural, religiously conservative Jews, rose up against the Seleucids, ultimately retaking and purifying the temple in 164 BCE. These events, led by the Maccabee brothers, are commemorated by the holiday of Hanukkah. Later, Simon Maccabee secured the land of Judea to the coast as an independent state. The Hasmoneans, or Maccabees, ruled for roughly one hundred years, one of only a few examples of Jewish sovereignty over their land in their history. The Romans were waiting in the wings, however, as the Roman general Pompey was annexing lands in Syria and heading south. Taking advantage of some fraternal strife among the Hasmoneans, he entered Jerusalem and acquired the land for Rome. Although a new people was in charge, many of the effects of Alexander's Hellenization program remained. The Roman gods became fused with the Greek gods, adding Latin names. Greek remained the common language of the realm and the standard for literary works, including the writings of the New Testament.

Hellenistic Rulers and Events to Know
Alexander the Great (r. 336–323 BCE)
• Begins conquest of Persia (334 BCE)
• Death of Alexander, generals wrestle for power (323 BCE)
Ptolemy I of Egypt (r. 305–283 BCE)
• Ptolemies begin rule in Judea (301 BCE)
Seleucid king Antiochus III (r. 223–187 BCE)
• Seleucids seize control of the land of Israel from the Ptolemies (ca. 200 BCE)
Seleucid king Antiochus IV (Epiphanes) (r. 175–164 BCE)
• Antiochus IV Epiphanes profanes the Jerusalem temple (168/167 BCE)
• Maccabees regain control of the temple and purify it (164 BCE)

Hasmonean (Maccabean) kings rule Judea (r. 142–63 BCE)
Roman general Pompey takes control of Jerusalem (63 BCE)

The Roman Empire (31 BCE–476 CE)

Following a period of strife and unrest under the dictatorship of Julius Caesar, the Roman Empire was inaugurated with Augustus assuming power as the first emperor of Rome. It became one of the largest empires in the ancient world. Its population included more than fifty million people at its height (ca. 117 CE). Its territory included most of the areas around the Mediterranean Sea. On its north end were Britannia (the southern area of the modern-day United Kingdom), Germania (north-central Europe), and Gaul (France, Belgium, western Germany, and northern Italy). Its eastern border reached into Egypt, Judea, Syria, Parthia (modern-day Iran), and Asia Minor. Its western and southern territories included Hispania (Portugal and Spain), much of North Africa, Mauretania (north Morocco and central Algeria), and Numidia (western Tunisia and eastern Algeria).

While Latin maintained its prominence in matters related to Roman politics, civil courts, and military affairs, the Greek language rose in importance for Romans who desired to engage in other activities, especially economic ones. Due to this linguistic shift, many Romans became bilingual. This cultural development also accounts for the publication of the Septuagint (that is, the Greek translation of the Hebrew Scriptures) and the Christian documents that comprise the New Testament in Greek—including stories about Jesus and communication between churches.

The Roman Empire had a major impact on the history surrounding the stories of the Bible. During the intra-Jewish conflict between Hyrcanus and Aristobulus, General Pompey took the side of the former, desecrated the temple, and (in an effort to recleanse the religious area) appointed Hyrcanus high priest (ca. 63 BCE). Julius Caesar (d. 44 BCE) developed key political alliances with Jewish leadership, partly due to Rome's desire to maintain the peace in a crucial geographical landmass of the empire (Syria and Judea). Caesar's nephew (and adopted son) Caesar Augustus, also known as Octavian (d. 14 CE), ruled Rome for forty years and expanded the empire significantly. The Gospel of Luke highlights Augustus and his census along with the regional governor of Syria (Quirinius) who carried out this task (Luke 2:1–2). This Gospel also highlights the reign of Tiberius, who appointed a governor over Judea, Pontius Pilate (who ruled 26–36 CE), who would go on to preside over the trial of Jesus Christ (Luke 3:1). The Herods of this period all served as client kings appointed by Rome.

Roman Emperors to Know

Julius Caesar (r. as dictator 49–44 BCE)
Augustus (Octavian) (r. 31 BCE–14 CE)
Tiberius (r. 14–37 CE)
Gaius (Caligula) (r. 37–41 CE)
Claudius (r. 41–54 CE)
Nero (r. 54–68 CE)
Galba, Otho, and Vitellius (r. 68–69 CE)
Vespasian (r. 69–79 CE)
Titus (r. 79–81 CE)
Domitian (r. 81–96 CE)

The Editors

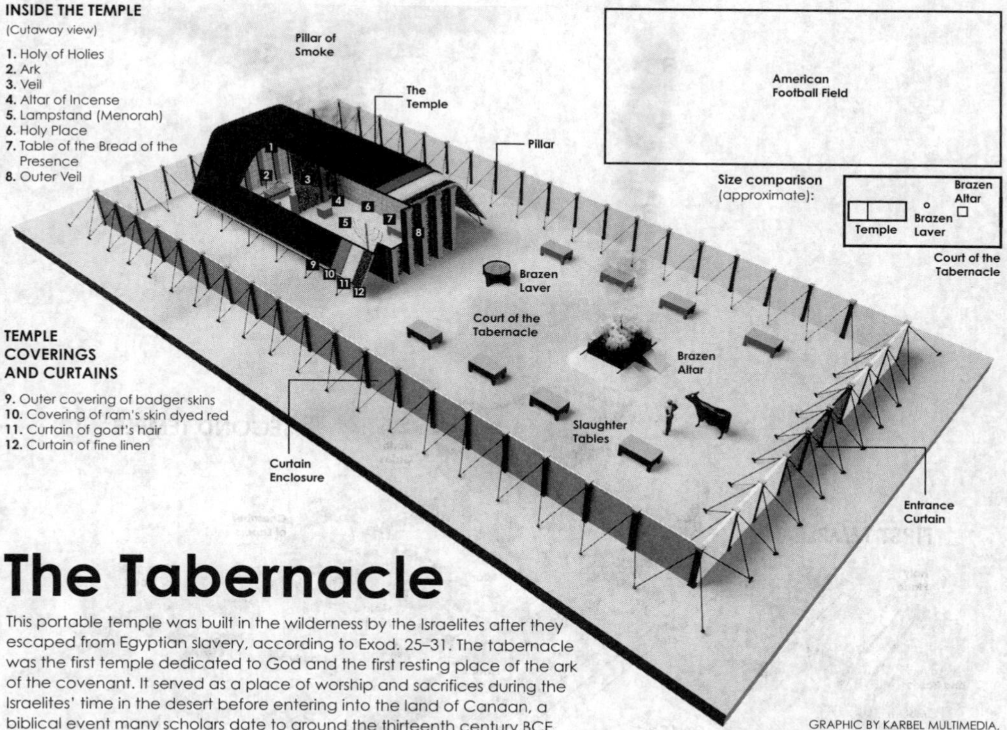

INSIDE THE TEMPLE
(Cutaway view)

1. Holy of Holies
2. Ark
3. Veil
4. Altar of Incense
5. Lampstand (Menorah)
6. Holy Place
7. Table of the Bread of the Presence
8. Outer Veil

Pillar of Smoke

The Temple

Pillar

American Football Field

Size comparison (approximate):

Temple | **Brazen Laver** | **Brazen Altar**

Court of the Tabernacle

TEMPLE COVERINGS AND CURTAINS

9. Outer covering of badger skins
10. Covering of ram's skin dyed red
11. Curtain of goat's hair
12. Curtain of fine linen

Brazen Laver

Court of the Tabernacle

Brazen Altar

Slaughter Tables

Curtain Enclosure

Entrance Curtain

The Tabernacle

This portable temple was built in the wilderness by the Israelites after they escaped from Egyptian slavery, according to Exod. 25–31. The tabernacle was the first temple dedicated to God and the first resting place of the ark of the covenant. It served as a place of worship and sacrifices during the Israelites' time in the desert before entering into the land of Canaan, a biblical event many scholars date to around the thirteenth century BCE.

Holy Place

Great Court (Outer Court)

Size comparison (approximate):

Temple | **Altar**

Upper Court (Inner Court)

Priests' rooms and storage

American Football Field

Altar

Great Court (Outer Court)

Boaz

Porch

Jachin

Ramp

Upper Court (Inner Court)

INSIDE THE TEMPLE
(cutaway view)

1. Holy of Holies
2. Cherubim
3. Ark of the Covenant
4. Veil
5. Altar of Incense
6. Table of the Bread of the Presence
7. Lampstand
8. Priests' rooms and storage

Lavers and Bases

Great Court (Outer Court)

Molten Sea

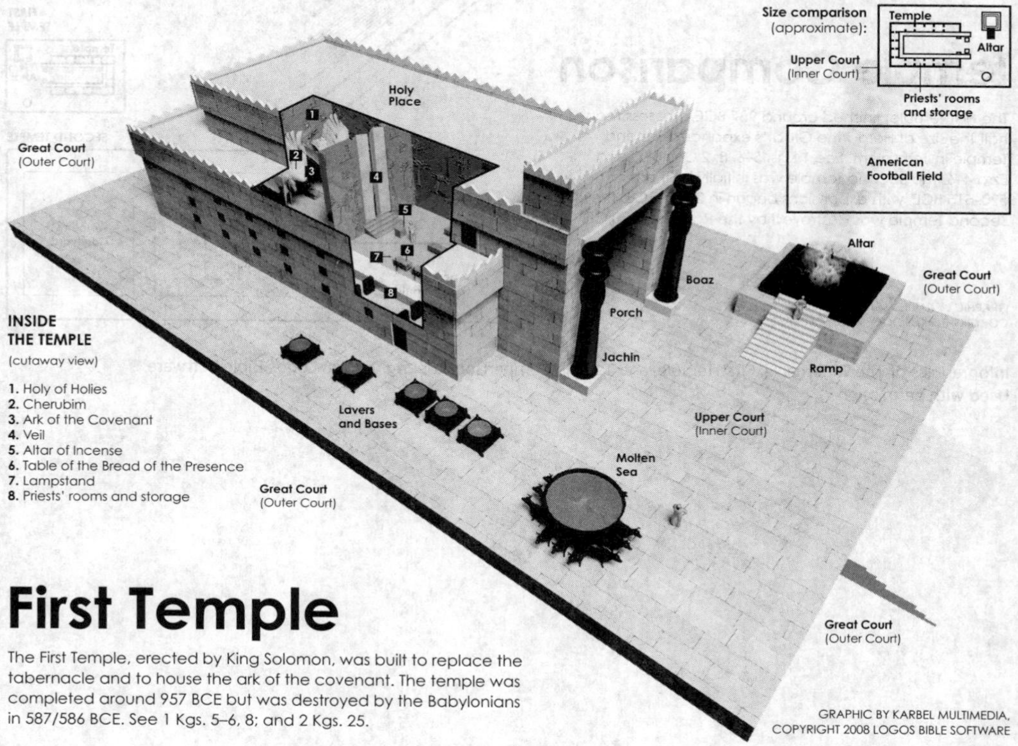

First Temple

The First Temple, erected by King Solomon, was built to replace the tabernacle and to house the ark of the covenant. The temple was completed around 957 BCE but was destroyed by the Babylonians in 587/586 BCE. See 1 Kgs. 5–6, 8; and 2 Kgs. 25.

Great Court (Outer Court)

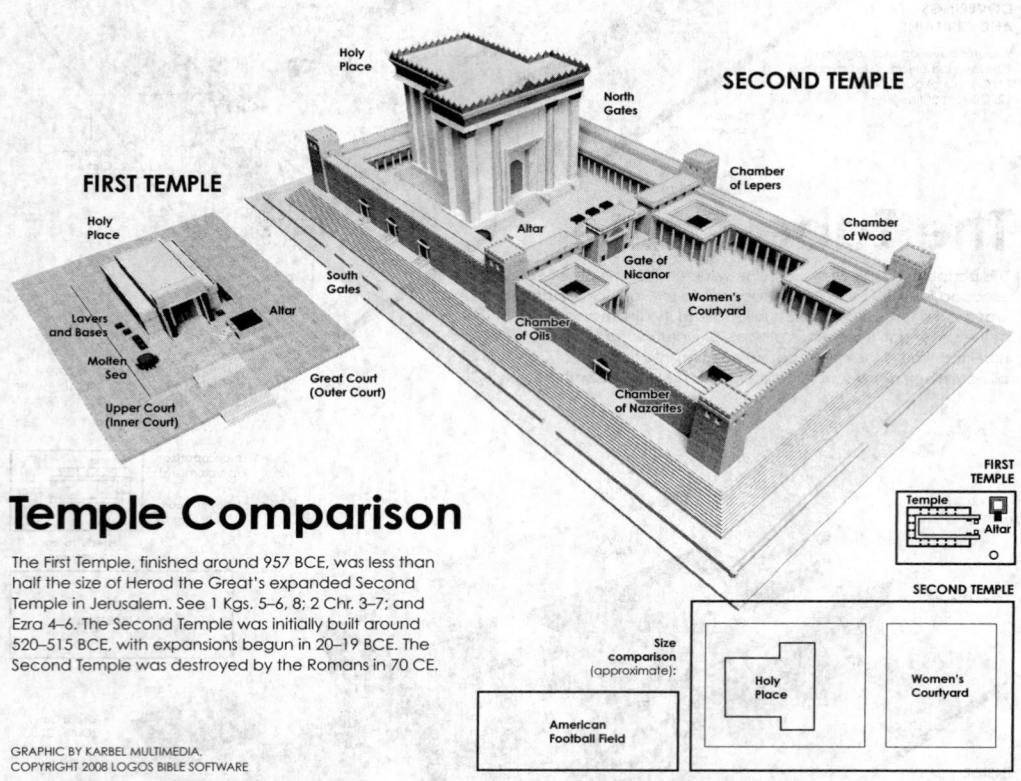

FIRST TEMPLE

Holy
Place

Lavers
and Bases

Molten
Sea

Altar

Upper Court
(Inner Court)

Holy
Place

North
Gates

SECOND TEMPLE

Chamber
of Lepers

Chamber
of Wood

Altar

South
Gates

Gate of
Nicanor

Women's
Courtyard

Chamber
of Oils

Great Court
(Outer Court)

Chamber
of Nazarites

Temple Comparison

The First Temple, finished around 957 BCE, was less than
half the size of Herod the Great's expanded Second
Temple in Jerusalem. See 1 Kgs. 5–6, 8; 2 Chr. 3–7; and
Ezra 4–6. The Second Temple was initially built around
520–515 BCE, with expansions begun in 20–19 BCE. The
Second Temple was destroyed by the Romans in 70 CE.

Size
comparison
(approximate):

American
Football Field

**FIRST
TEMPLE**

Temple

Altar

SECOND TEMPLE

Holy
Place

Women's
Courtyard

Biblical Weights and Measures

All weights and measures are approximate and are not meant to be exact. Many measurements varied across time and location in the ancient world.

	Biblical unit	Equivalent	Approximate U.S. measurement	Approximate metric measurement
Weights	talent	60 minas	75 pounds	34 kilograms
	mina	50 shekels	1.25 pounds	570 grams
	shekel	2 bekas	0.4 ounce	11.4 grams
	pim	2/3 shekel	0.27 ounce	7.6 grams
	beka	1/2 shekel	0.2 ounce	5.7 grams
	gerah	1/20 shekel	0.02 ounce	0.6 grams
Lengths	cubit		18 inches	45 centimeters
	span		9 inches	23 centimeters
	handbreadth		3 inches	7.5 centimeters
	stadion		607 feet	185 meters
Dry measures	cor/homer	10 ephahs	6 bushels	220 liters
	lethek	5 ephahs	3 bushels	110 liters
	ephah	10 omers	0.6 bushel	22 liters
	seah	1/3 ephah	7 quarts	7.3 liters
	omer	1/10 ephah	2 quarts	2 liters
	kab	1/18 ephah	1 quart	1 liter
Liquid measures	cor/homer	10 baths	58 gallons	220 liters
	bath	1 ephah	5.8 gallons	22 liters
	hin	1/6 bath	1 gallon	3.7 liters
	log	1/72 bath	0.33 quart	0.3 liter

Table of Gospel Parallels

This table indicates where readers will find corresponding or nearly identical passages in the NT Gospels, or "Gospel parallels." A parallel points to a common tradition (i.e., textual source) that appears in similar or different literary contexts across Gospels, usually sharing more than a few words or a phrase. Parallels underscore material that more than one Gospel writer deemed important to include in their tellings of the Jesus story.

In each column, the references placed in bold indicate the parallels listed in consecutive order for that Gospel. The Gospel of John is referenced only in the few instances where a parallel with John occurs in one or more of the Synoptic Gospels. For traditions that are unique to each Gospel, see **"Differences between John and the Synoptic Gospels," p. 1849**, and the charts for the three Synoptics: **"Passages Unique to the Gospel of Matthew," p. 1721; "Passages Unique to the Gospel of Mark," p. 1770**; and **"Passages Unique to the Gospel of Luke," p. 1801–2.**

	Matthew	Mark	Luke	John
Genealogies				
Genealogies of Jesus	**1:2–17**		**3:23–38**	
Preparation				
John the Baptist	**3:1–6**	**1:2–6**	**3:1–6**	**1:19–23**
John's Preaching of Repentance	**3:7–10**		**3:7–9**	
One More Powerful Is Coming	**3:11–12**	**1:7–8**	**3:15–18**	**1:24–28**
John Is Imprisoned	14:3–4	6:17–18	**3:19–20**	
The Baptism of Jesus	**3:13–17**	**1:9–11**	**3:21–22**	**1:29–34**
Genealogies of Jesus	1:2–17		**3:23–38**	
The Testing of Jesus	**4:1–11**	**1:12–13**	**4:1–13**	
The Beginning of Jesus's Public Ministry (According to John)				
The Cleansing of the Temple	21:12–13	11:15–17	19:45–46	**2:14–16**
Jesus's Ministry in Galilee				
Jesus Begins His Ministry in Galilee	**4:12–17**	**1:14–15**	**4:14–15**	
Jesus Is Rejected in His Hometown	13:53–58	6:1–6a	**4:16–30**	
Jesus Calls the First Disciples	**4:18–22**	**1:16–20**		
A Man with an Unclean Spirit		**1:21–28**	**4:31–37**	
Jesus Heals Many at Peter's House	8:14–17	**1:29–34**	**4:38–41**	
Jesus's Preaching Tour		**1:35–38**	**4:42–43**	
Jesus Cleanses a Person with a Skin Disease	8:1–4	**1:40–45**	**5:12–16**	
Jesus Heals Someone with Paralysis	9:1–8	**2:1–12**	**5:17–26**	
The Call of Levi	9:9–13	**2:13–17**	**5:27–32**	
The Question about Fasting	9:14–17	**2:18–22**	**5:33–39**	
Plucking Grain on the Sabbath	12:1–8	**2:23–28**	**6:1–5**	

Based on *Synopsis of the Four Gospels*, edited by Kurt Aland, 15th edition, © 2013 Deutsche Bibelgesellschaft Stuttgart, with revisions. Used by permission. Versions previous to the 15th edition were also consulted.

	Matthew	Mark	Luke	John
Jesus Restores a Person's Withered Hand	12:9–14	**3:1–6**	**6:6–11**	
Jesus Ministers to the Multitudes	4:23–35	**3:7–12**	6:17–19	
Jesus Appoints the Twelve	10:1–4	**3:13–19**	**6:12–16**	

The Sermon on the Mount (According to Matthew)

	Matthew	Mark	Luke	John
Jesus Ministers to the Multitudes	**4:23–25**	3:7–12	6:17–19	
The Beatitudes	**5:3–12**		6:20b–23	
Parable of Salt	**5:13**	9:49–50	14:34–35	
A Lamp under a Bushel Basket	**5:15**	4:21–25	8:16–18	
The Law and the Prophets	**5:17–18**		16:16–17	
Settling with Your Accuser	**5:25–26**		12:57–59	
On Temptation to Sin	**5:29–30**	9:43–48		
On Divorce	**5:31–32**	10:11–12	16:18	
Concerning Retaliation	**5:38–42**		6:29–30	
Concerning Love for One's Enemies	**5:43–48**		6:27–28 6:32–36	
The Lord's Prayer	**6:9–13**		11:1–4	
Treasures in Heaven	**6:19–21**		12:33–34	
The Eye as the Lamp of the Body	**6:22–23**		11:34–36	
On Serving Two Masters	**6:24**		16:13	
Do Not Worry	**6:25–34**		12:22–32	
Judging Others	**7:1–5**		6:37–42	
Encouragement to Pray	**7:7–11**		11:9–13	
The Golden Rule	**7:12**		6:31	
The Narrow Entrance	**7:13–14**		13:23–24	
A Tree and Its Fruit	**7:16–20** **12:33–35**		6:43–45	
Hearers and Doers	**7:24–27**		6:47–49	
As One with Authority	**7:28–29**	1:21–22		

The Sermon on the Plain (According to Luke)

	Matthew	Mark	Luke	John
Jesus Ministers to the Multitudes	4:23–25		**6:17–19**	
The Beatitudes	5:3–12		**6:20b–23**	
Concerning Love for One's Enemies	5:43–48		**6:27–28** **6:32–36**	
Concerning Retaliation	5:38–42		**6:29–30**	
The Golden Rule	7:12		**6:31**	
Judging Others	7:1–5		**6:37–42**	
A Tree and Its Fruit	7:16–20 12:33–35		**6:43–45**	
Hearers and Doers	7:24–27		**6:47–49**	

	Matthew	Mark	Luke	John
Jesus's Ministry in Galilee Continued				
Jesus Cleanses a Person with a Skin Disease	8:1–4	1:40–45	5:12–16	
Jesus Heals an Enslaved Man	8:5–13		7:1–10	
Jesus Heals Many at Peter's House	8:14–17	1:29–34	4:38–41	
Would-Be Followers of Jesus	8:18–22		9:57–62	
Jesus Calms the Storm	8:23–27	4:35–41	8:22–25	
The Gerasene with an Unclean Spirit	8:28–34	5:1–20	8:26–39	
Jesus Heals Someone with Paralysis	9:1–8	2:1–12	5:17–26	
The Call of Levi	9:9–13	2:13–17	5:27–32	
The Question about Fasting	9:14–17	2:18–22	5:33–39	
A Daughter and a Bleeding Woman	9:18–26	5:21–43	8:40–56	
The Restoration of Sight	9:27–31 20:29–34	10:46–52	18:35–43	
Jesus and Beelzebul	12:22–32	3:20–30	11:14–23	
The Harvest Is Great, the Laborers Are Few	9:37–38		10:2	
Jesus Appoints the Twelve	10:1–4	3:13–19	6:12–16	
Persecutions Foretold	10:17–22 24:9–14	13:9–13	12:11–12 21:12–19	
Fearless Confession	10:26–33		12:2–9	
Households Divided	10:34–36		12:51–53	
Demands of Discipleship	10:37–39		14:26–27	
Messengers from John the Baptist	11:2–6		7:18–23	
Jesus Praises John the Baptist	11:7–11		7:24–28	
This Generation	11:16–19		7:31–35	
Woes to Unrepentant Cities	11:21–24		10:13–15	
Jesus Gives Thanks to the Father	11:25–27		10:21–22	
Jesus Blesses the Disciples	13:16–17		10:23–24	
Plucking Grain on the Sabbath	12:1–8	2:23–28	6:1–5	
Jesus Restores a Person's Withered Hand	12:9–14	3:1–6	6:6–11	
Jesus Ministers to the Multitudes	4:23–25	3:7–12	6:17–19	
A Woman Anoints Jesus	26:6–13	14:3–9	7:36–50	12:1–8
Jesus and Beelzebul	12:22–32	3:20–30	11:14–23	
Profaning the Holy Spirit	12:31–32	3:28–30	12:10	
A Tree and Its Fruit	12:33–35 7:16–20		6:43–45	
The Demand for a Sign	12:38–42 16:1 16:4a	8:11 8:12	11:29–32 11:16	
The Return of the Unclean Spirit	12:43–45		11:24–26	

	Matthew	Mark	Luke	John
Jesus's True Kindred	12:46–50	3:31–35	8:19–21	
Parable of the Sower	13:1–9	4:1–9	8:4–8	
The Purpose of the Parables	13:10–17	4:10–12 4:25	8:9–10 8:18b	
Parable of the Sower Explained	13:18–23	4:13–20	8:11–15	
A Lamp under a Bushel Basket	5:15	4:21–25	8:16–18	
Parable of the Mustard Seed	13:31–32	4:30–32	13:18–19	
Parable of Leaven	13:33		13:20–21	
Why Parables?	13:34–35	4:33–34		
Jesus's True Kindred	12:46–50	3:31–35	8:19–21	
Jesus Calms the Storm	8:23–27	4:35–41	8:22–25	
The Gerasene with an Unclean Spirit	8:28–34	5:1–20	8:26–39	
A Daughter and a Bleeding Woman	9:18–26	5:21–43	8:40–56	
Jesus Is Rejected in His Hometown	13:53–58	6:1–6a	4:16–30	
The Mission of the Twelve	10:1, 7–11, 14	6:6b–13	9:1–6	
Public Impressions regarding Jesus	14:1–2	6:14–16	9:7–9	
John the Baptist's Death	14:3–12	6:17–29		
The Apostles Return		6:30–31	9:10a	
Jesus Feeds Five Thousand	14:13–21	6:32–44	9:10b–17	6:1–15
Jesus Walks on Water	14:22–33	6:45–52		6:16–21
Healings at Gennesaret	14:34–36	6:53–56		6:22–25
Traditions on Contamination	15:1–20	7:1–23	11:37–41	
The Syrophoenician (Canaanite) Woman	15:21–28	7:24–30		
Jesus Feeds Four Thousand	15:32–39	8:1–10		
The Demand for a Sign	16:1 16:4a 12:38–42	8:11 8:12	11:16 11:29–32	
Warning about the Yeast of the Pharisees	16:5–12	8:14–21	12:1	

The Way to the Cross

	Matthew	Mark	Luke	John
Peter's Acknowledgment	16:13–20	8:27–30	9:18–21	6:67–71
Jesus Predicts Death and Resurrection	16:21–23	8:31–33	9:22	
"Take Up His Cross"	16:24–28	8:34–9:1	9:23–27	
Jesus's Transfiguration	17:1–9	9:2–10	9:28–36	
The Coming of Elijah	17:10–13	9:11–13		
Jesus Rebukes Spirit out of Child	17:14–21	9:14–29	9:37–43a	
Jesus Predicts Death and Resurrection Again	17:22–23	9:30–32	9:43b–45	
True Greatness	18:1–5	9:33–37	9:46–48	
The Unknown Exorcist		9:38–41	9:49–50	
Temptations to Sin	18:6–9	9:42–48	17:1–2	

	Matthew	Mark	Luke	John
Parable of Salt	5:13	**9:49–50**	14:34–35	
Parable of One Lost Sheep	**18:12–14**		15:3–7	
Reprimanding Another Person	**18:15–18**		17:3	
Abundant Forgiveness	**18:21–22**		17:4	

Last Journey to Jerusalem (According to Luke)

	Matthew	Mark	Luke	John
Departure to Judea	**19:1–2**	10:1	**9:51**	
Would-Be Followers of Jesus	8:18–22		**9:57–62**	
The Harvest Is Great, the Laborers Are Few	9:37–38		**10:2**	
Woes to Unrepentant Cities	11:21–24		**10:13–15**	
Jesus Gives Thanks to the Father	11:25–27		**10:21–22**	
Jesus Blesses the Disciples	13:16–17		**10:23–24**	
The Great Commandment	22:34–40	12:28–34	**10:25–28**	
The Lord's Prayer	6:9–13		**11:1–4**	
Encouragement to Pray	7:7–11		**11:9–13**	
Jesus and Beelzebub	12:22–32	3:20–30	**11:14–23**	
The Return of the Unclean Spirit	12:43–45		**11:24–26**	
The Demand for a Sign	16:1 16:4a 12:38–42	8:11 8:12	11:16 **11:29–32**	
The Eye as the Lamp of the Body	6:22–23		**11:34–36**	
Warning about the Yeast of the Pharisees	16:5–12	8:14–21	**12:1**	
Fearless Confession	10:26–33		**12:2–9**	
Profaning the Holy Spirit	12:31–32	3:28–30	**12:10**	
Do Not Worry	6:25–34		**12:22–32**	
Treasures in Heaven	6:19–21		**12:33–34**	
Watchful and Faithful Slaves	24:42–51		**12:35–48**	
Households Divided	10:34–36		**12:51–53**	
Interpreting the Times	16:2–3		**12:54–56**	
Settling with Your Accuser	5:25–26		**12:57–59**	
Parable of the Mustard Seed	13:31–32	4:30–32	**13:18–19**	
Parable of Leaven	13:33		**13:20–21**	
The Narrow Entrance	7:13–14		**13:23–24**	
Lamenting over Jerusalem	23:37–39		**13:34–35**	
Parable of the Great Dinner	22:1–14		**14:15–24**	
Demands of Discipleship	10:37–39		**14:26–27**	
Parable of Salt	5:13	9:49–50	**14:34–35**	
Parable of One Lost Sheep	18:12–14		**15:3–7**	
On Serving Two Masters	6:24		**16:13**	

	Matthew	Mark	Luke	John
The Law and the Prophets	5:17–18		16:16–17	
On Divorce	5:31–32	10:11–12	16:18	
On Faith	17:19–21	9:28–29	17:5–6	
The Son of Man's Arrival	24:23 24:26–27 24:37–39 24:17–18 24:40–41 24:28	13:14–16 13:19–23	17:22–37	

The Ministry in Judea

	Matthew	Mark	Luke	John
Departure to Judea	19:1–2	10:1	9:51	
Concerning Divorce	19:3–12	10:2–12		
Jesus Blesses the Children	19:13–15	10:13–16	18:15–17	
The Rich Young Man	19:16–22	10:17–22	18:18–23	
On Riches and the Rewards of Discipleship	19:23–30	10:23–31	18:24–30	
The Third Prediction of the Passion	20:17–19	10:32–34	18:31–34	
Precedence among the Disciples	20:20–28	10:35–45	22:24–27	
The Restoration of Sight	20:29–34 9:27–31	10:46–52	18:35–43	
Parable of the Talents	25:14–30		19:11–27	
A Woman Anoints Jesus	26:6–13	14:3–9	7:36–50	12:1–8

The Final Ministry in Jerusalem

	Matthew	Mark	Luke	John
The Triumphal Entry	21:1–9	11:1–10	19:28–40	12:12–19
The Cleansing of the Temple	21:12–13	11:15–17	19:45–46	2:14–16
Chief Priests and Scribes Conspire against Jesus		11:18–19	19:47–48	
The Fig Tree Is Withered	21:18–22	11:20–24; 11:12–14		
On Forgiveness	6:14–15	11:25–26		
The Question about Authority	21:23–27	11:27–33	20:1–8	
Parable of the Wicked Tenants	21:33–46	12:1–12	20:9–19	
Parable of the Great Dinner	22:1–14		14:15–24	
On Paying Tribute to Caesar	22:15–22	12:13–17	20:20–26	
The Question about the Resurrection	22:23–33	12:18–27	20:27–40	
The Great Commandment	22:34–40	12:28–34	10:25–28	
The Question about David's Son	22:41–46	12:35–37a	20:41–44	
Woe to the Scribes and Pharisees	23:1–36	12:37b–40	20:45–47	
Lamenting over Jerusalem	23:37–39		13:34–35	
The Widow's Mite		12:41–44	21:1–4	

	Matthew	Mark	Luke	John
The Olivet Discourse				
Prediction of the Destruction of the Temple	24:1–2	13:1–2	21:5–6	
Signs before the End	24:3–8	13:3–8	21:7–11	
Persecutions Foretold	24:9–14 10:17–22	13:9–13	21:12–19 12:11–12	
The Desolating Sacrilege	24:15–22	13:14–20	21:20–24	
False Christs and False Prophets	24:23–28	13:21–23	17:23–24 17:37b	
The Coming of the Son of Man	24:29–31	13:24–27	21:25–28	
The Time of the Coming: The Parable of the Fig Tree	24:32–36	13:28–32	21:29–33	
"Take Heed, Watch!"	25:13 24:42	13:33–37		
Conclusion of the Account before the Passion				
Parable of the Flood	24:37–44		17:26–36	
Exhortation to Watchfulness	25:13	13:35–37		
Parable of the Good Servant and the Wicked Servant	24:45–51		12:41–46	
Parable of the Talents	25:14–30		19:11–27	
The Passion Narrative				
Jesus's Death Is Premeditated	26:1–5	14:1–2	22:1–2	
A Woman Anoints Jesus	26:6–13	14:3–9	7:36–50	12:1–8
The Betrayal by Judas	26:14–16	14:10–11	22:3–6	
Preparation for the Passover	26:17–20	14:12–17	22:7–14	
Jesus Foretells His Betrayal	26:21–25	14:18–21	22:21–23	13:21–30
The Last Supper	26:26–29	14:22–25	22:15–20	
Jesus Foretells His Betrayal	26:21–25	14:18–21	22:21–23	13:21–30
Precedence among the Disciples	20:20–28	10:35–45	22:24–27	
Peter's Denial Predicted	26:30–35	14:26–31	22:31–34	13:36–38
Gethsemane	26:36–46	14:32–42	22:39–46	18:1 12:27
Jesus Arrested	26:47–56	14:43–52	22:47–53	18:2–12
Jesus before the Sanhedrin (Peter's Denial)	26:57–68	14:53–65	22:54–71	18:13–24
Peter's Denial	26:69–75	14:66–72	22:56–62	18:25–27
Jesus Delivered to Pilate	27:1–2	15:1	23:1	18:28
The Trial before Pilate	27:11–14	15:2–5	23:2–5	18:29–38
Jesus or Barabbas?	27:15–23	15:6–14	23:17–23	18:39–40
Jesus Garbed as King of the Jews	27:28–31a	15:17–20a		19:1–15
Pilate Delivers Jesus to Be Crucified	27:24–26	15:15	23:24–25	19:16
Jesus Mocked by the Soldiers	27:27–31a	15:16–20a		19:2–3

	Matthew	Mark	Luke	John
The Road to Golgotha	27:31b–32	15:20b–21	23:26–32	19:17
The Crucifixion	27:33–37	15:22–26	23:33	19:16b–27
Jesus Derided on the Cross	27:38–43	15:27–32a	23:35–38	
The Two Thieves	27:44	15:32b	23:39–43	
The Death of Jesus	27:45–54	15:33–39	23:44–48	19:28–30
Witnesses of the Crucifixion	27:55–56	15:40–41	23:49	19:25–27
The Burial of Jesus	27:57–61	15:42–47	23:50–56	19:38–42
The Resurrection				
The Women at the Tomb	28:1–8	16:1–8	24:1–12	20:1–13
Jesus Appears to the Women	28:9–10	16:9–11	24:10–11	20:14–18
Jesus Appears to Two on the Way to Emmaus		16:12–13	24:13–35	
Jesus Appears to His Disciples (Thomas Being Absent)			24:36–43	20:19–23

Index to Study Materials

Numbers in boldface refer to introductions, essays, and excurses. All other numbers refer to study notes.

MAP 1

Ancient Israel at the Time of the Ancestors, ca. 2000–1500 BCE

- City or town
- **MOAB, etc** Kingdoms
- *MAACAH, etc* Other areas

0 — 20 Miles
0 — 20 Kilometers

PHOENICIA

Sidon

Damascus

Ijon
Tyre

ARAM (SYRIA)

Beth-rehob
Dan (Laish)

N

Kedesh **MAACAH**

Achzib

Hazor
Merom

GESHUR

Chinnereth

ARGOB

Karnaim
Ashtaroth

Sea of Chinnereth

BASHAN

Hammath
Shimron
Yanoam
Jokneam
Shunem
Dor
Megiddo
Taanach
Aruna

HAVVOTH-JAIR

Edrei

Ramoth-gilead

Beth-shean

Gath of Sharon
Ibleam
Dothan

GILEAD

Tirzah

The Great Sea (Mediterranean Sea)

Shechem
Penuel
Succoth
Mahanaim

Jordan River
Jabbok River

TRANSJORDAN

Aphek
Shiloh
Ono
Gilead
Jazer
Jogbehah
Lod
Bethel (Luz)
Ai
Gilgal
Beth-horon
Gibeon
Jericho
Shittim
Gezer
Aijalon
Jerusalem (Salem)
Kiriathaim
Heshbon

AMMON

Ashdod
Ekron
Beth-shemesh
Medeba
Ashkelon
Gath
Socoh
Timnah
Bethlehem (Ephrath)
Beth-baal-meon

PHILISTIA

Eglon
Lachish
Mamre
Ataroth
Mattanah
Gaza
Hebron (Kiriath-arba)
Dibon
Kedemoth
Gerar
Debir
En-gedi
Aroer
Ziklag

AMORITES

Salt Sea

Amnon River

Beer-sheba

ARAD

MOAB

Rehoboth
Adadah (Aroer)
THE NEGEB
Ziph
Zoar

Zered Brook

EDOM

© 2024 Westminster John Knox Press

MAP 2

Tribal Distribution during the Time of the Judges

- City or town
- Tribal border

Boundaries of tribal areas are approximate

0 — 20 Miles
0 — 20 Kilometers

N

Cities and places labeled on the map:

Sidon · *Mt. Lebanon* · *Mt. Hermon* · Damascus

DAN · Dan · Tyre · Beth-anath · Kedesh · Achzib · **ASHER** · Hazor · **NAPHTALI** · **BASHAN**

Acco · Chinnereth · *Sea of Chinnereth* · Golan · Ashtaroth

Mt. Carmel · Bethlehem · **ZEBULUN** · Rimmon · Hammath · Edrei

Dor · *Mt. Tabor* · **ISSACHAR** · Shunem · Kamon · Ramoth-gilead · Tob

Megiddo · Jezreel · *Mt. Gilboa* · Beth-shean · **MANASSEH**

MANASSEH · Bezek · Jabesh-gilead

Thebez · *Mt. Ebal* · Tirzah · Tabbath

Mt. Gerizim · Shechem · *Jabbok River* · **AMMON**

Pirathon · **GAD**

Gath-rimmon · Aphek · Tappuah · Jogbehah

Joppa · **EPHRAIM** · Shiloh · Betonim · Rabbah

Timnath-serah · Bethel · Beth-nimrah

Lower Beth-horon · Gilgal

DAN · Gezer · Beeroth · **BENJAMIN** · Jericho

Ashdod · Ekron · Zorah · Gibeah · *Mt. Pisgah* · Heshbon

Ashkelon · Gath · Jerusalem · *Mt. Nebo*

PHILISTIA · Bethlehem · Beth-baal-meon

Eglon · Lachish · **REUBEN**

Gaza · Hebron · Kedemoth

JUDAH · En-gedi · Dibon · Aroer

Gerar · Goshen

Ziklag · *Salt Sea*

Besor Brook · Beer-sheba · **MOAB**

SIMEON · Arad · *Arnon River*

THE NEGEB · *Zered Brook*

EDOM

The Great Sea (Mediterranean Sea)

Jordan River

© 2024 Westminster John Knox Press

MAP 3

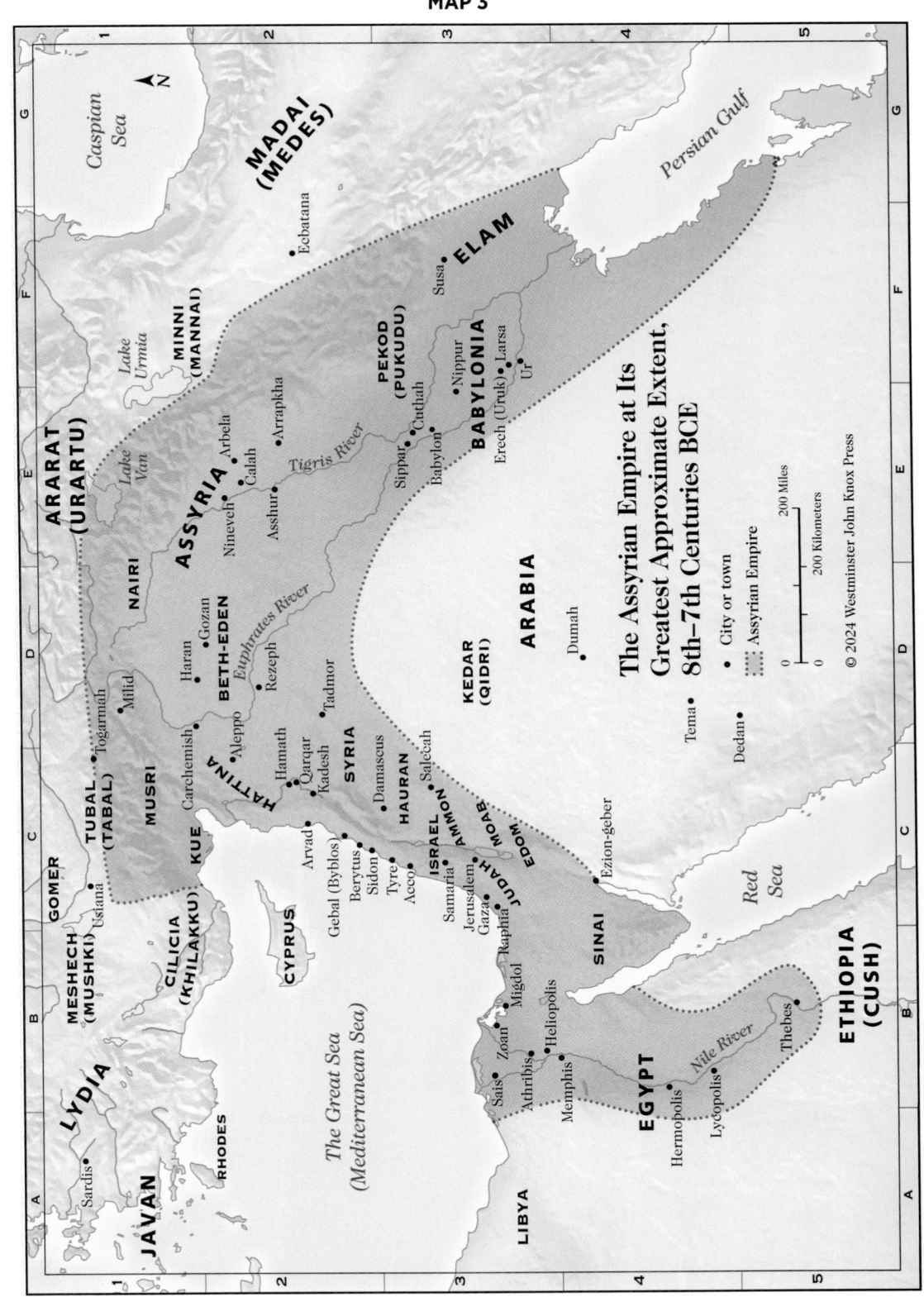

The Assyrian Empire at Its Greatest Approximate Extent, 8th–7th Centuries BCE

- City or town
- Assyrian Empire

200 Miles
200 Kilometers

© 2024 Westminster John Knox Press

MAP 4

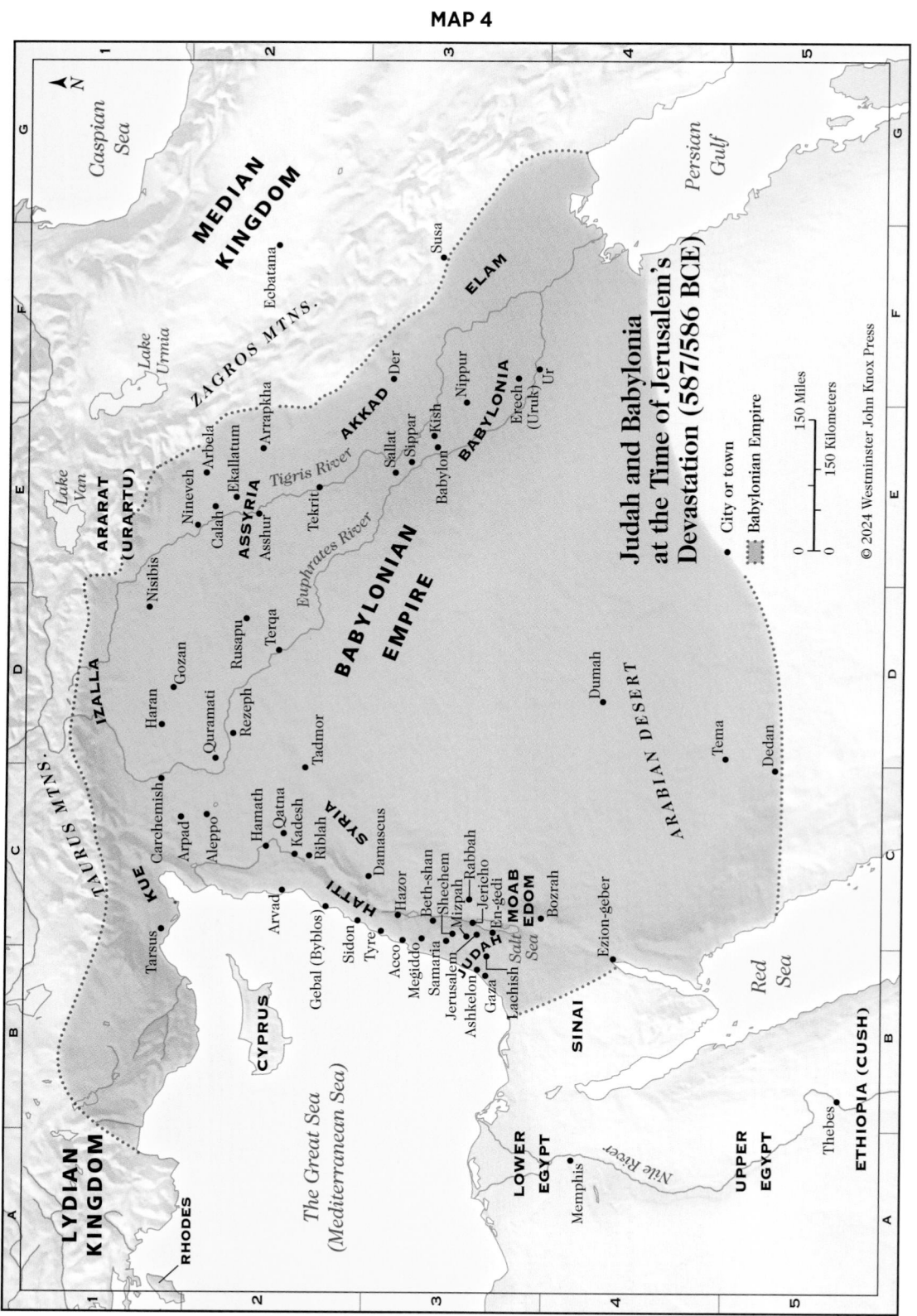

Judah and Babylonia at the Time of Jerusalem's Devastation (587/586 BCE)

• City or town

Babylonian Empire

0   150 Miles
0   150 Kilometers

© 2024 Westminster John Knox Press

MAP 5

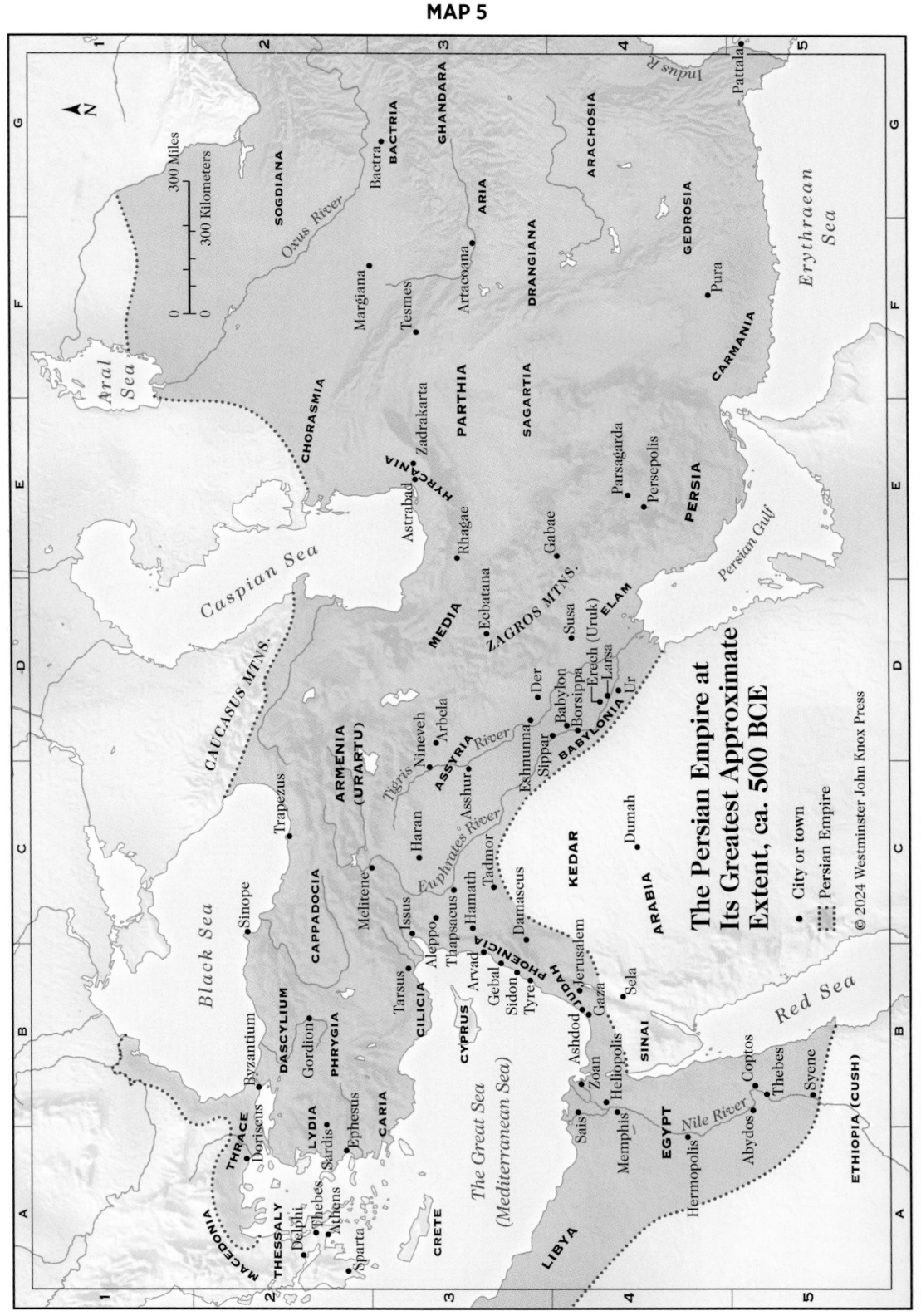

The Persian Empire at
Its Greatest Approximate
Extent, ca. 500 BCE

• City or town
⋯⋯ Persian Empire

© 2024 Westminster John Knox Press

MAP 6

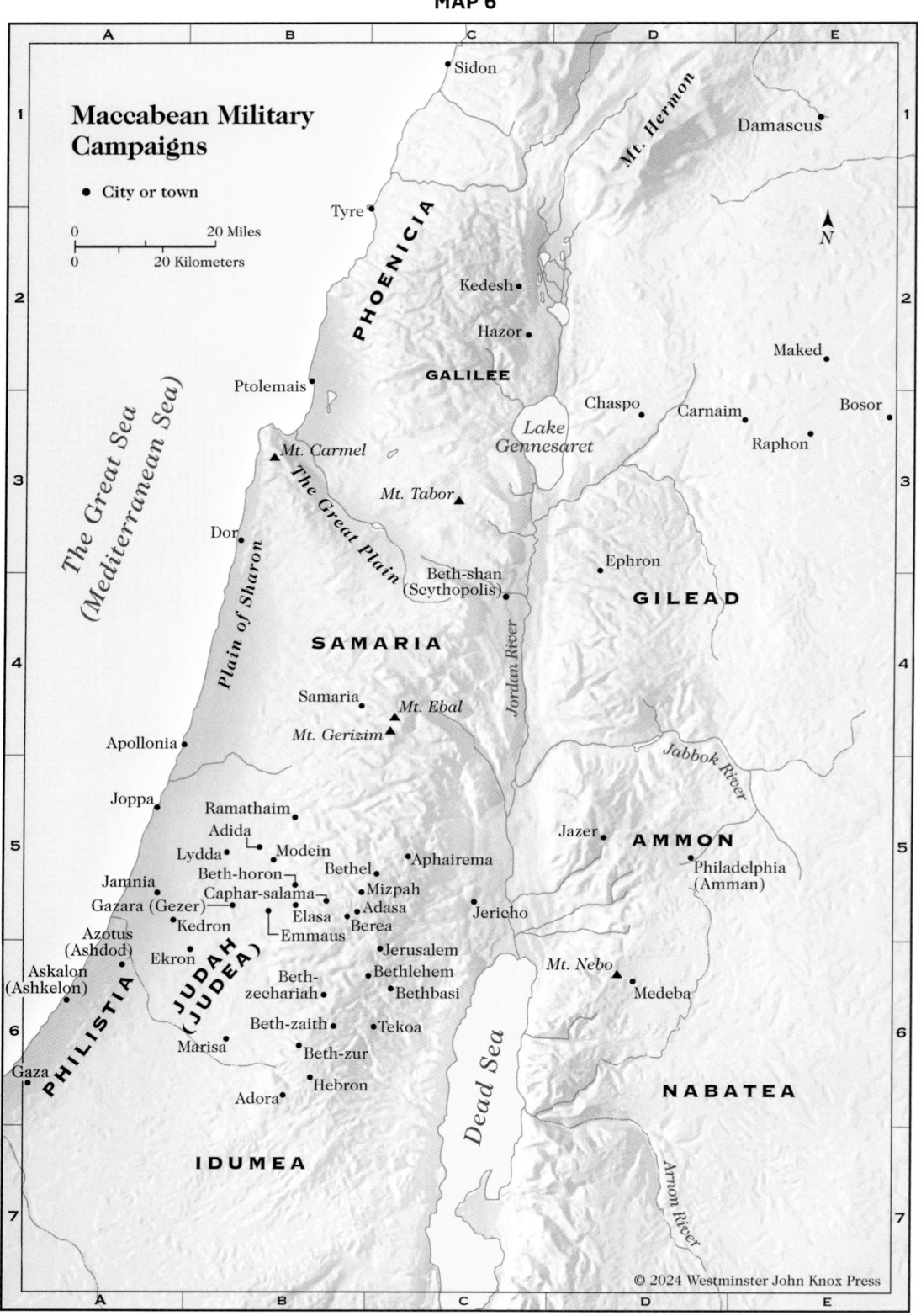

Maccabean Military Campaigns

● City or town

0 ——————— 20 Miles
0 ——————— 20 Kilometers

N

The Great Sea (Mediterranean Sea)

PHOENICIA

Sidon

Damascus

Mt. Hermon

Tyre

Kedesh

Hazor

Maked

Ptolemais

GALILEE

Lake Gennesaret

Chaspo

Carnaim

Bosor

Raphon

▲ *Mt. Carmel*

The Great Plain

Mt. Tabor ▲

Dor

Beth-shan (Scythopolis)

Ephron

GILEAD

Plain of Sharon

SAMARIA

Samaria

Mt. Ebal ▲

Mt. Gerizim ▲

Jordan River

Jabbok River

Apollonia

Joppa

Ramathaim

Adida

Lydda

Modein

Bethel

Aphairema

Jazer

AMMON

Philadelphia (Amman)

Beth-horon

Mizpah

Caphar-salama

Adasa

Jamnia

Elasa

Berea

Jericho

Gazara (Gezer)

Emmaus

Kedron

Jerusalem

Azotus (Ashdod)

Ekron

Bethlehem

Mt. Nebo ▲

Medeba

Askalon (Ashkelon)

Beth-zechariah

Bethbasi

JUDAH (JUDEA)

Beth-zaith

Tekoa

Marisa

Beth-zur

Gaza

Adora

Hebron

PHILISTIA

Dead Sea

NABATEA

IDUMEA

Arnon River

© 2024 Westminster John Knox Press

MAP 7

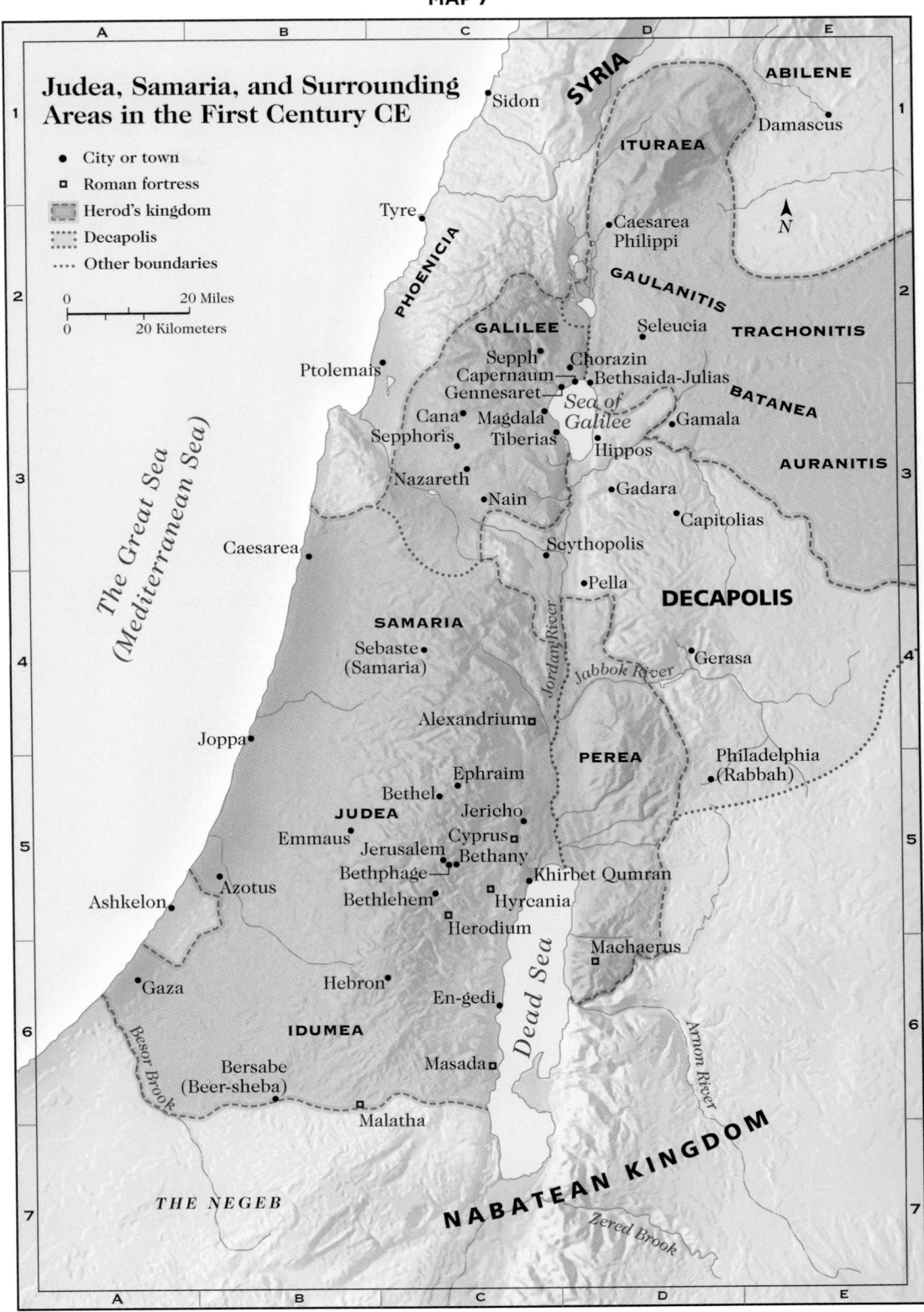

Judea, Samaria, and Surrounding Areas in the First Century CE

- City or town
- Roman fortress
- Herod's kingdom
- Decapolis
- Other boundaries

0   20 Miles
0   20 Kilometers

N

SYRIA

ABILENE

Sidon

Damascus

ITURAEA

Tyre

Caesarea Philippi

PHOENICIA

GAULANITIS

TRACHONITIS

Ptolemais

GALILEE

Seleucia

Sepph

Chorazin

BATANEA

Capernaum

Bethsaida-Julias

Gennesaret

Sea of Galilee

Cana

Magdala

Gamala

Sepphoris

Tiberias

Hippos

AURANITIS

Nazareth

Gadara

Nain

Capitolias

The Great Sea (Mediterranean Sea)

Caesarea

Scythopolis

Pella

DECAPOLIS

SAMARIA

Sebaste (Samaria)

Gerasa

Jordan River

Jabbok River

Alexandrium □

Joppa

PEREA

Philadelphia (Rabbah)

Ephraim

Bethel

Jericho

JUDEA

Emmaus

Cyprus

Jerusalem

Bethany

Bethphage

Khirbet Qumran

Ashkelon

Azotus

Bethlehem

Hyrcania □

En-gedi

Herodium □

Machaerus □

Gaza

Hebron

Dead Sea

IDUMEA

Bersabe (Beer-sheba)

Masada □

Besor Brook

Malatha □

Arnon River

THE NEGEB

NABATEAN KINGDOM

Zered Brook

MAP 8

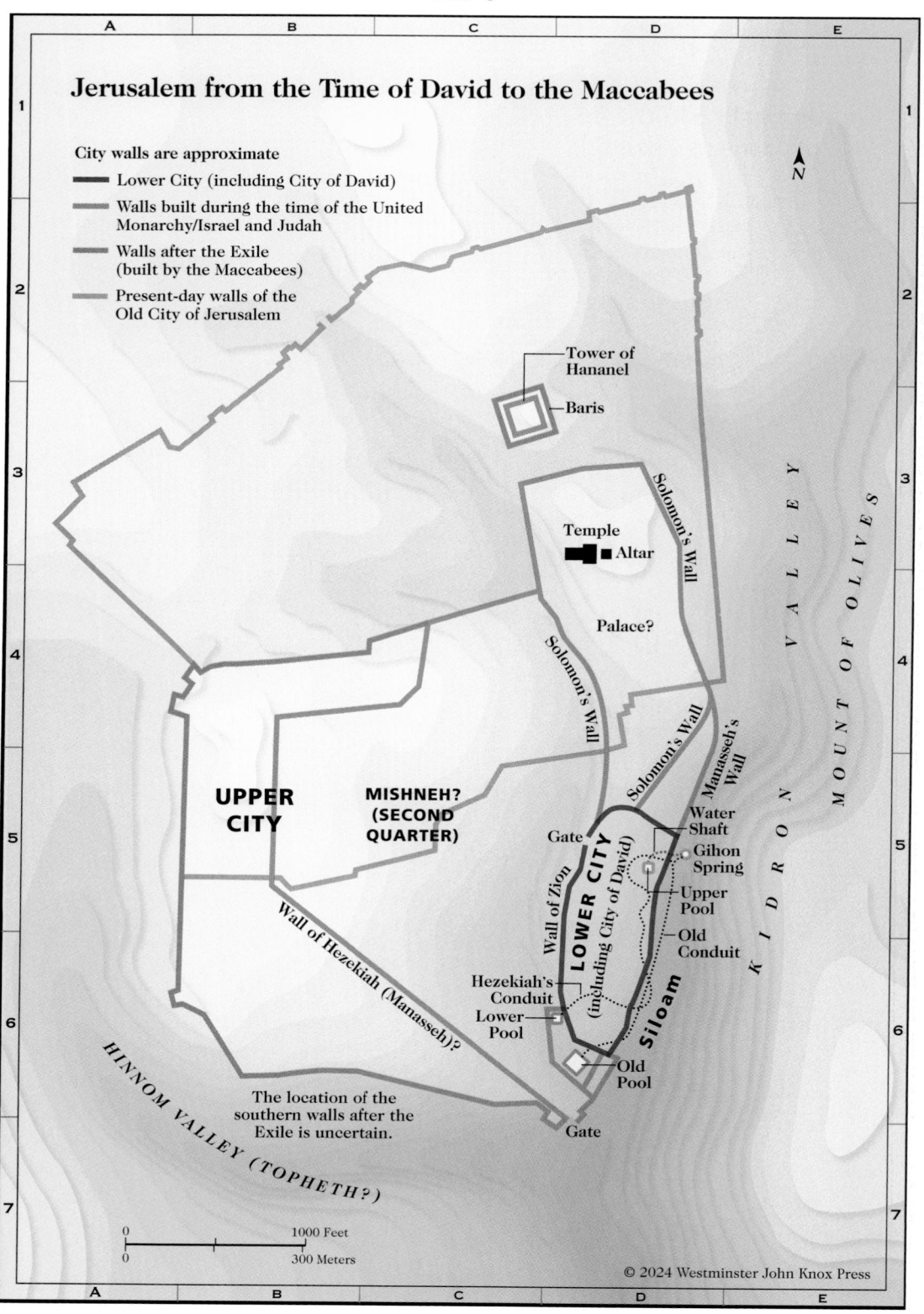

Jerusalem from the Time of David to the Maccabees

City walls are approximate

Lower City (including City of David)

Walls built during the time of the United
Monarchy/Israel and Judah

Walls after the Exile
(built by the Maccabees)

Present-day walls of the
Old City of Jerusalem

N

Tower of
Hananel

Baris

Solomon's Wall

Temple

Altar

Palace?

Solomon's Wall

UPPER
CITY

MISHNEH?
(SECOND
QUARTER)

Solomon's Wall

Manasseh's
Wall

Water
Shaft

Gihon
Spring

Upper
Pool

Old
Conduit

Gate

Wall of Zion

LOWER CITY
(including City of David)

Hezekiah's
Conduit

Lower
Pool

Wall of Hezekiah (Manasseh)?

Siloam

Old
Pool

KIDRON VALLEY

MOUNT OF OLIVES

The location of the
southern walls after the
Exile is uncertain.

Gate

HINNOM VALLEY (TOPHETH?)

0   1000 Feet
0   300 Meters

© 2024 Westminster John Knox Press

MAP 9

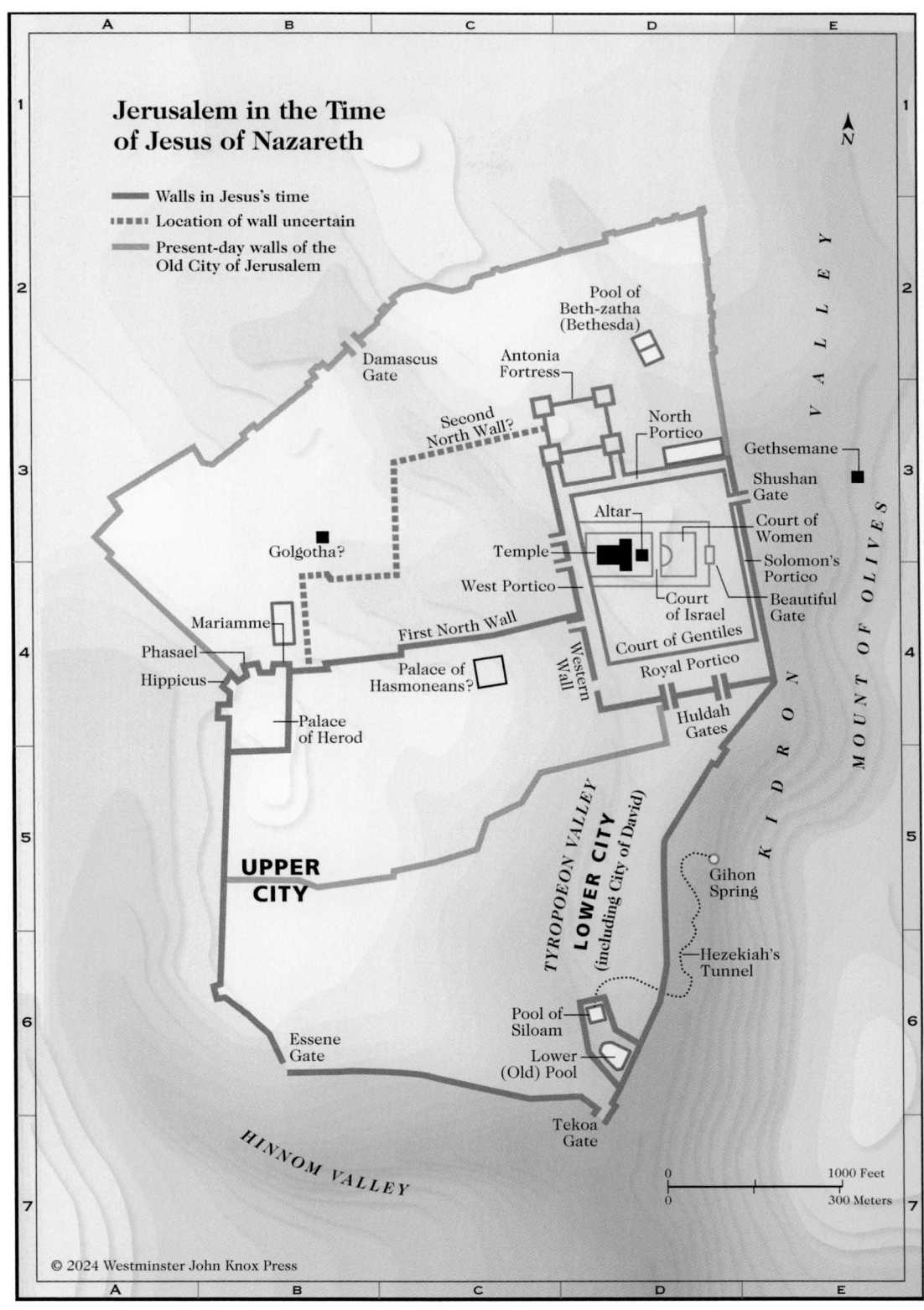

Jerusalem in the Time
of Jesus of Nazareth

- Walls in Jesus's time
- Location of wall uncertain
- Present-day walls of the
  Old City of Jerusalem

N

Pool of
Beth-zatha
(Bethesda)

Damascus
Gate

Antonia
Fortress

Second
North Wall?

North
Portico

Gethsemane

Shushan
Gate

Altar

Court of
Women

Golgotha?

Temple

West Portico

Court
of Israel

Solomon's
Portico

Beautiful
Gate

Mariamme

First North Wall

Court of Gentiles

Phasael

Hippicus

Palace of
Hasmoneans?

Western
Wall

Royal Portico

Palace
of Herod

Huldah
Gates

KIDRON

MOUNT OF OLIVES

UPPER
CITY

TYROPOEON VALLEY

LOWER CITY
(including City of David)

Gihon
Spring

Hezekiah's
Tunnel

Essene
Gate

Pool of
Siloam

Lower
(Old) Pool

Tekoa
Gate

HINNOM VALLEY

VALLEY

0   1000 Feet
0   300 Meters

© 2024 Westminster John Knox Press

MAP 10

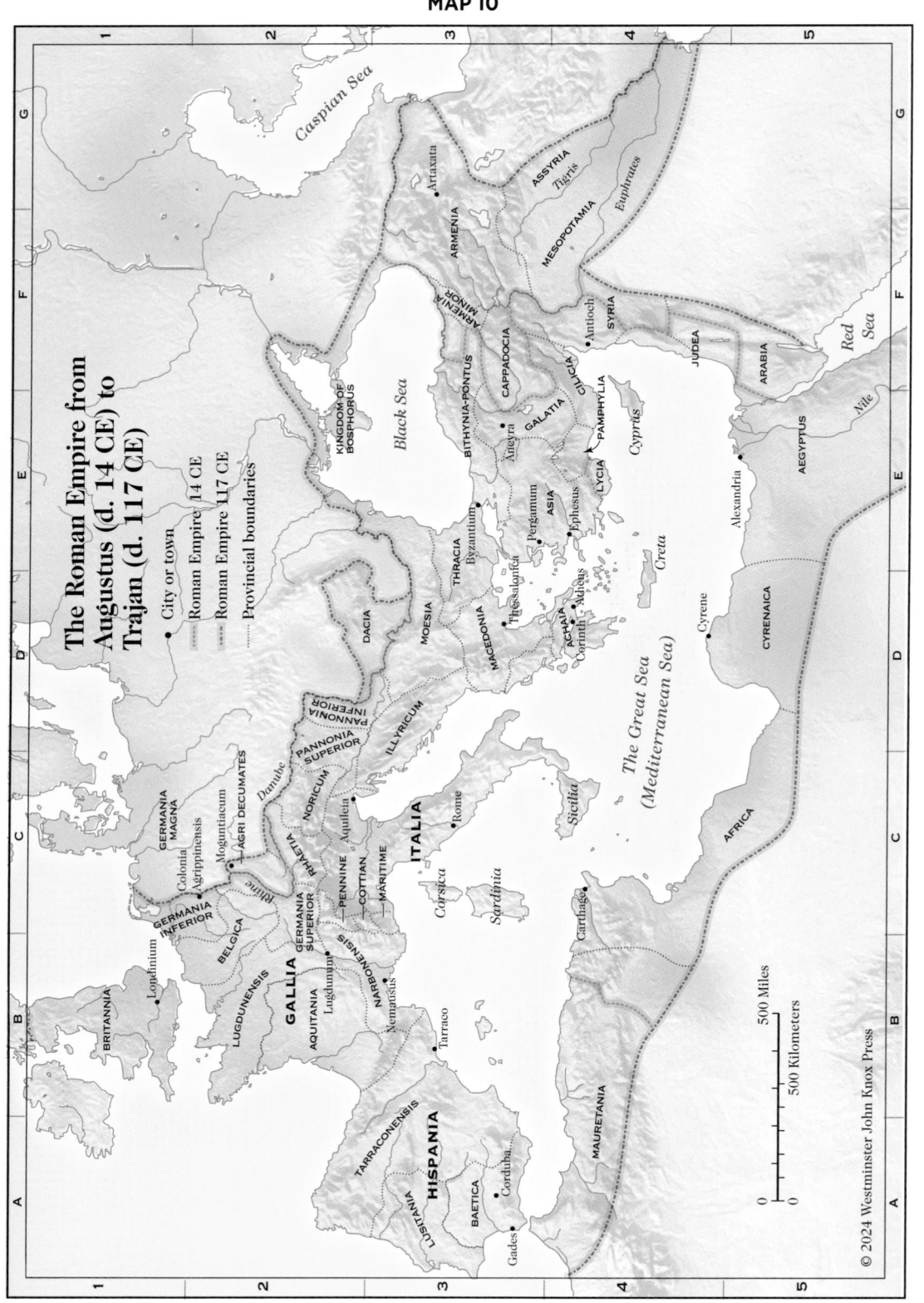

The Roman Empire from Augustus (d. 14 CE) to Trajan (d. 117 CE)

- City or town
- Roman Empire 14 CE
- Roman Empire 117 CE
- Provincial boundaries

Caspian Sea

Artaxata

ARMENIA

ASSYRIA

Tigris

MESOPOTAMIA

Euphrates

ARMENIA MINOR

CAPPADOCIA

Antioch

SYRIA

JUDEA

ARABIA

Red Sea

KINGDOM OF BOSPHORUS

Black Sea

BITHYNIA-PONTUS

GALATIA

Ancyra

CILICIA

Cyprus

LYCIA

PAMPHYLIA

AEGYPTUS

Nile

Pergamum

ASIA

Ephesus

THRACIA

Byzantium

Alexandria

Thessalonica

MACEDONIA

ACHAIA

Athens

Corinth

Creta

Cyrene

CYRENAICA

DACIA

MOESIA

The Great Sea (Mediterranean Sea)

ILLYRICUM

PANNONIA INFERIOR

PANNONIA SUPERIOR

Danube

NORICUM

GERMANIA MAGNA

AGRI DECUMATES

Moguntiacum

Colonia Agrippinensis

GERMANIA INFERIOR

Rhine

BELGICA

GERMANIA SUPERIOR

RHAETIA

PENNINE

COTTIAN

MARITIME

Aquileia

ITALIA

Rome

Corsica

Sardinia

Sicilia

Carthago

AFRICA

MAURETANIA

LUGDUNENSIS

Lugdunum

GALLIA

AQUITANIA

NARBONENSIS

SIENSIS

Nemausus

Loudinium

BRITANNIA

Tarraco

TARRACONENSIS

LUSITANIA

HISPANIA

BAETICA

Corduba

Gades

500 Miles

500 Kilometers

© 2024 Westminster John Knox Press

MAP 11

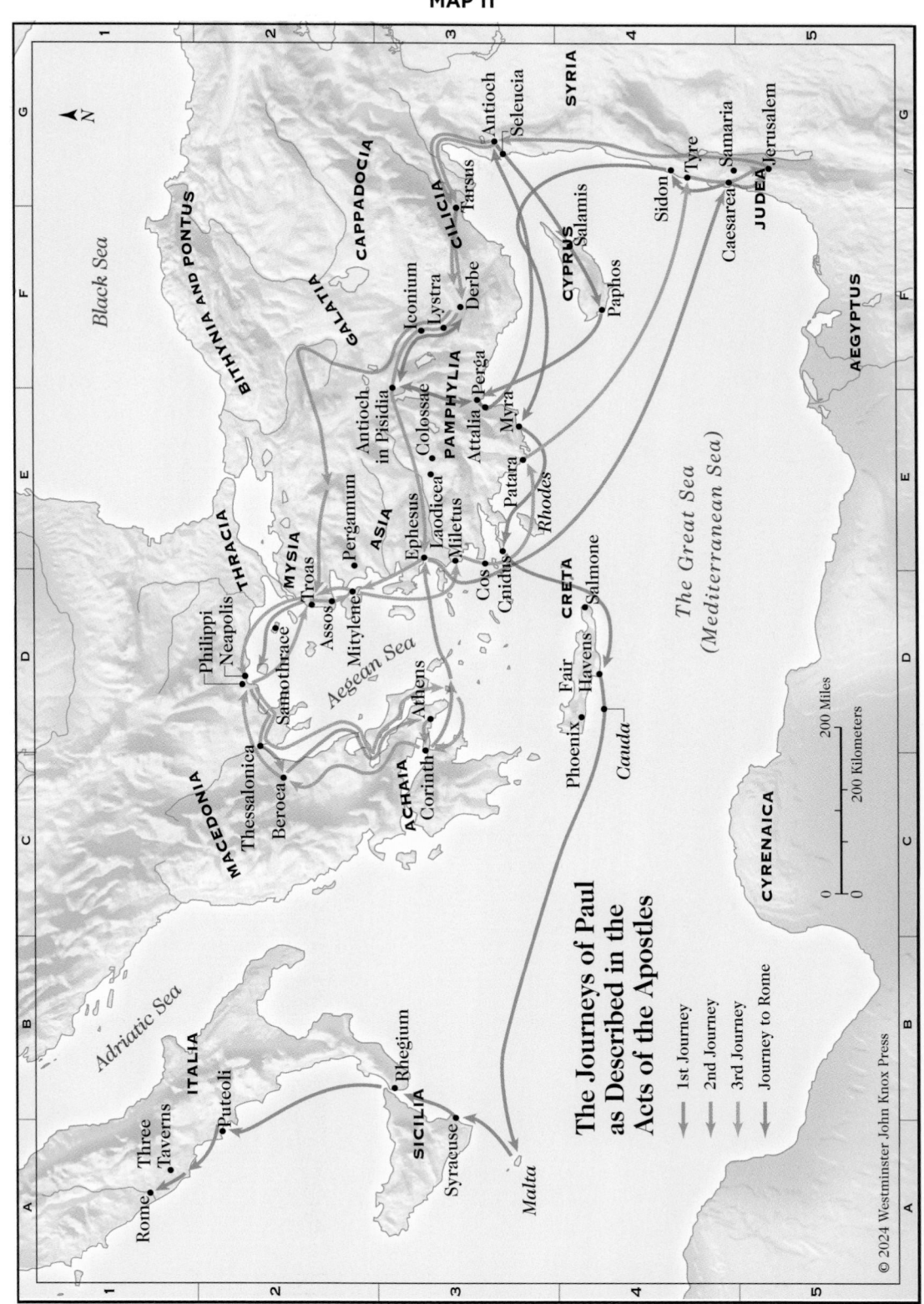

The Journeys of Paul as Described in the Acts of the Apostles

1st Journey
2nd Journey
3rd Journey
Journey to Rome

200 Miles
200 Kilometers

Index to Color Maps